AN

# ANGLO-SAXON DICTIONARY

## SUPPLEMENT

# AN
# ANGLO-SAXON DICTIONARY

## BASED ON THE MANUSCRIPT COLLECTIONS
## OF JOSEPH BOSWORTH

## SUPPLEMENT

BY

## T. NORTHCOTE TOLLER

WITH

## REVISED AND ENLARGED ADDENDA

BY

## ALISTAIR CAMPBELL

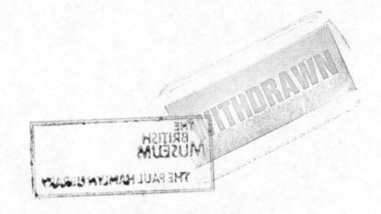
## OXFORD UNIVERSITY PRESS

Oxford University Press, Great Clarendon Street, Oxford OX2 6DP

Oxford New York

Athens Auckland Bangkok Bogotá Buenos Aires Calcutta
Cape Town Chennai Dar es Salaam Delhi Florence Hong Kong Istanbul
Karachi Kuala Lumpur Madrid Melbourne Mexico City Mumbai
Nairobi Paris São Paulo Singapore Taipei Tokyo Toronto Warsaw

and associated companies in
Berlin Ibadan

Oxford is a registered trade mark of Oxford University Press

First edition 1921
Reprinted from sheets of the first edition
1955, 1966, 1972, 1973, 1980, 1992, 1995, 1998

British Library Cataloguing in Publication Data
Data available
ISBN 0-19-863112-X

Printed in Great Britain by
Antony Rowe Ltd,
Chippenham

# PREFACE

A FEW words of explanation from the editor may seem called for in view of the amount of material, especially under the letters A–G, contained in this Supplement. As already mentioned in the Preliminary Notice to Parts I and II of the Dictionary and in the Preface to the Dictionary itself most of the work under A–F was printed before Dr. Bosworth's death; and much of that under G was mistakenly supposed to have been completed for the press. It is not then surprising that considering the advance made during the last fifty years in all that relates to the study of Old English a revisal of the earlier part of the Dictionary should call for large additions or alterations. In the case of the material under the letters from G to the end it is hoped that the need for an apology is less as is certainly the excuse for one.

The thanks of the editor are specially due to Dr. Henry Bradley for very many and very helpful comments and suggestions: to the late Professor A. S. Napier for advance and separate copies of articles connected with lexicography: and to Dr. Max Förster of Leipzig for help of the same kind. He must also acknowledge his obligations to the late Professor Cosijn, at the sale of whose library the Delegates of the Clarendon Press purchased copies of the first and second editions of Bosworth's Dictionary and of Grein's *Sprachschatz*. In these Professor Cosijn had noted passages to illustrate many words; and though the editor had often already made the same note, this was not always the case, and he acknowledges an obligation where it is too late to offer thanks.

*June*, 1921.

**Ælfc. Gr. Zup.** later **Ælfc. Gr. Z.**

**An. Ox.** Anecdota Oxoniensia. Old English Glosses, edited by Arthur S. Napier.

**Archiv.** Archiv für das Studium der neueren Sprachen und Literaturen, herausgegeben von Prof. Dr. Brandl und Prof. Dr. Morf.

**Basil admn.; Norm.** later **Hex.**

**Bd.; Sch.** König Alfreds Übersetzung von Bedas Kirchengeschichte, herausgegeben von Jacob Schipper (Grein's A.S. Prose Library).

**Beiblatt.** Beiblatt zur Anglia.

**Blickl. Gl.** later **Bl. Gl.**

**Blick. Homl.** later **Bl. H.**

**Bl. N.** Napier's notes on Blickling Homilies, Modern Philology, vol. i. no. 2.

**Boutr. Scrd.** later **Scrd.**

**Bt.; Fox** later **Bt.; F.**

**Bt.; S.** King Alfred's Old English Version of Boethius De Consolatione Philosophiae, edited by W. G. Sedgefield, Oxford, 1899.

**Ch. T.** Tyrwhitt's Chaucer.

**Chart. Erl.** later **Cht. E.; Chart. Th.** later **Cht. Th.**

**Chr.; P.** Two of the Saxon Chronicles, ed. by Charles Plummer.

**Chrd.** The Old English version, with the Latin original, of the Enlarged Rule of Chrodegang, edited by Prof. A. S. Napier. E. E. T. S., No. 150, 1916.

**Cht. Crw.** The Crawford Charters, ed. Napier and Stevenson.

**Cod. Dip. B.** later **C. D. B.**

**Cod. Dip. Kmbl.** later **C. D.**

**Coll. Monast. Th.** later **Coll. M.**

**Corp. Gl. ed. Hessels** later **Corp. Gl. H.**

**D. D.** The Dialect Dictionary, compiled by Prof. J. Wright.

**E. H. D. H.** Select English Historical Documents, ed. by F. E. Harmer.

**E. M. Furn.** An English Miscellany, presented to Dr. Furnivall in honour of his seventy-fifth birthday. Oxford, 1901.

**E. W.** The Fifty Earliest English Wills. E. E. T. S., No. 78, 1882.

**Engl. Stud.** later **E. S.**

**Gall.** Vorstudien zu einem altniederdeutschen Wörterbuche, von J. H. Gallée, Leiden, 1903.

**Goetz.** Corpus Glossariorum Latinorum, ed. Georg. Goetz, 7 vols.

**Gr. Dial.** later **Gr. D.** Übersetzung der Dialoge Gregors des Grossen, herausgegeben von Hans Hecht, Leipzig, 1900.

**Grm. D. M. (trans.).** Teutonic Mythology, by Jacob Grimm, translated from the fourth edition by J. S. Stallybrass, 4 vols., 1888.

**Guthl.; Gdwin.** later **Guth.**

**Guth. Gr.** Das angelsächsische Prosa-Leben des hl. Guthlac, herausgegeben von Paul Gonser, Heidelberg, 1909.

**H. R. N.** History of the Holy Rood-tree, edited by Prof. A. S. Napier. E. E. T. S., No. 103, 1894.

**Hamp. Ps.** Hampole's Psalms and Canticles with a Commentary, edited by H. R. Bramley, Oxford, 1884.

**Hexam.; Norm.** later **Hex.**

**Homl. Ass.** later **Hml. A.**

**Homl. Skt.** later **Hml. S.**

**Homl. Th.** later **Hml. Th.**

**Hymn. Surt.** later **Hy. S.**

**Jord.** Die altenglischen Säugetiernamen, von Richard Jordan, Heidelberg, 1903.

**Jud. Grn. Epilog.** See vol. i of Grein's Bibliothek der Angelsächsischen Prosa, pp. 263-5.

**Kl. Nom. Stam.** Nominale Stammbildungslehre der altgermanischen Dialekte, von Friedrich Kluge, Halle, 1886.

**L.; Th.** later **Ll. Th.**

**Lchdm.** later **Lch.**

**Ld. Gl. G.** Das Leidener Glossar. Program des kgl. humanistischen Gymnasiums St. Stephan in Augsburg, verfasst von P. Plazidius Glogger, 1901.

**Ld. Gl. H.** A late eighth-century Latin-Anglo-Saxon Glossary, preserved in the Library of the Leiden Universi edited by J. H. Hessels, Cambridge, 1906.

**Ll. Lbmn.** Die Gesetze der Angelsachsen. Herausgegeben im Auftrage der Savigny-Stiftung von F. Liebermann. 3 vols.

**Lor. H.** The Lorica Hymn, in Bibliothek der Angelsächsischen Prosa, sechster Band.

**Mart. H.** An Old English Martyrology with Introduction and Notes by George Herzfeld. E. E. T. S., No. 116, 1900.

**Midd. Flur.** Altenglisches Flurnamenbuch, von Dr. Heinrich Middendorf, Halle, 1902.

**Mt. Kmbl., Lind., Rush.** later **Mt., L., R.**

**N. E. D.** The Oxford English Dictionary.

**Nap.** Contributions to Old English Lexicography, by Arthur S. Napier, published in the Philological Society's Transactions, 1906.

**Nic. H.** Gospel of Nicodemus in Hone's Apocryphal New Testament.

**Nicod.; Thw.** later **Nic.** quoted by page and line.

**O. Engl. Homl.** later **O. E. Hml.**

**O. L. Ger.** v. Gallée.

**Ors.; Bos., Ors.; Swt.** later **Ors.; B., Ors.; S.**

**Ors.; Th.** King Ælfred's Anglo-Saxon version of the history of Paulus Orosius, ed. by B. Thorpe. Bohn's Antiquarian Library.

**Past.; Swt.** later **Past.**

**Philol. Trans.** Transactions of the Philological Society.

**Pref. [Ælfc.] Thw.** v. Ælfc. Gen. Thw.

**Prehn's Rätsel des Exeterbuches** later **Prehn.**

**Prose Psalter.** The Earliest English Prose Psalter, ed. by Dr. Buelbring. E. E. T. S., No. 97, 1891.

**Prov. Kmbl.** later **Prov. K.**

**Prov. M.** Proverbia Anglo-Saxonica, in Collectanea Anglo-Saxonica, edited by L. C. Müller, Havniae, 1835.

**Ps. Cam.** Der Cambridger Psalter, herausgegeben von Karl Wildhagen, Hamburg, 1910 (Bibliothek der Angelsächsischen Prosa, vii. Band).

**Ps. Cant.** Eadwine's Canterbury Psalter, ed. by F. Harsley. E. E. T. S., No. 92, 1889.

**Ps. Lamb.** later **Ps. L.**

**Ps. L. Lind.** Der Lambeth-Psalter, herausgegeben von U. Lindelöf, Helsingfors, 1909.

**Ps. Rdr.** Der Altenglische Regius-Psalter, herausgegeben von Dr. Fritz Roeder, Halle, 1904.

**Ps. Stev.** or **Surt.** later **Ps. Srt.**

**Ps. V.** The Vespasian Psalter, in Old English Texts, edited by H. Sweet.

**Ps. Vos.** Der Altenglische Junius-Psalter, herausgegeben von Eduard Brenner, Heidelberg, 1909.

**R. Ben. Interl.** later **R. Ben. I.**

**Salm. Kmbl.** later **Sal. K.**

**Solil. H.** King Alfred's Old English Version of St. Augustine's Soliloquies, ed. by H. L. Hargrove, New York, 1902.

**Steinm.** Die althochdeutschen Glossen, Steinmeyer and Sievers, Berlin, 1879-98.

**Swt. Rdr. II.** A Second Anglo-Saxon Reader, archaic and dialectal, by Henry Sweet, Oxford, 1887.

**Te Dm. Lye.** See Anglia, ii. 357.

**Tupper.** The Riddles of the Exeter Book, ed. by Frederic Tupper, 1910.

**Verc. Först.** Der Vercelli-Codex CXVII, von Max Förster, Halle, 1913.

**Vis. Lfc.** An Old English Vision of Leofric, Earl of Mercia, by A. S. Napier. Philological Society's Transactions, 1908.

**Vit. Cuth.** Bede's Latin life of St. Cuthbert.

**Vit. Cuth. poet.** The poetical version of the life.

**Whitman.** The Birds of Old English Literature, by C. H. Whitman. The Journal of Germanic Philology, vol. ii, No. 2, 1898.

**Wulfst.** later **Wlfst.**

In passages cited from the poetry reference is made to Grein's Bibliothek and only the contractions used in his Lexicon are given; e.g. instead of Cd. 43; Th. 56, 21; Gen. 915 only Gen. 915 is given.

# ADDITIONAL CONTRACTIONS

**An. Ox.**  Old English Glosses, edited by Arthur S. Napier, M.A., Ph.D., Oxford, 1900.

**Archiv.**  Archiv für das Studium der neueren Sprachen und Literaturen, begründet von Ludwig Herrig.

**Bd. ; Sch.**  König Alfreds Übersetzung von Bedas Kirchengeschichte, herausgegeben von Jacob Schipper (vol. iv of Grein's Bibliothek der A.S. Prosa).  Quoted by book and chapter, and by page and line.

**Beiblatt.**  Beiblatt zur Anglia.

**Bl. N.**  Notes on the Blickling Homilies in Modern Philology, vol. i, Part II.

**Bt. ; S.**  King Alfred's Old English Version of Boethius De Consolatione Philosophiae, edited by W. G. Sedgefield, Oxford, 1899.

**Cht. Crw.**  The Crawford Collection of Early Charters and Documents now in the Bodleian Library, edited by A. S. Napier and W. H. Stevenson, Oxford, 1895.

**Chr. ; P.**  Two of the Saxon Chronicles, edited by Charles Plummer, M.A., Oxford, 1892.

**D. D.**  The Dialect Dictionary, by Prof. Joseph Wright.

**Gall.**  Vorstudien zu einem altniederdeutschen Wörterbuche, von J. H. Gallée, Leiden, 1903.

**Goetz.**  Corpus Glossariorum Latinorum, ed. Georg. Goetz., Lips., 1888–1901.

**Grm. D. M. (trans.).**  Teutonic Mythology, by Jacob Grimm, translated from the fourth edition by J. S. Stallybrass, 1882.

**H. R. N.**  The Legend of the Cross, from a twelfth-century MS., &c., edited by Prof. A. S. Napier, E. E. T. Soc. Pub., No. 103.

**Kl. Nom. Stam.**  Nominale Stammbildungslehre der altgermanischen Dialecte, von F. Kluge, Halle, 1886.

**Ld. Gl. H.**  A late eighth-century Latin-Anglo-Saxon Glossary, preserved in the library of the Leiden University, edited by J. H. Hessels, Cambridge, 1906.

**Ll. Lbmn.**  Die Gesetze der Angelsachsen, herausgegeben von F. Liebermann, Halle, 1903-.

**Lor. H.**  The Lorica Hymn, in vol. vi of Grein's Bibliothek der Angelsächsischen Prosa.  Quoted by page and line.

**Mart. H.**  An Old English Martyrology, edited by George Herzfeld, Ph.D.  [E. E. T. Soc. Pub., No. 116, 1900.]

**Midd. Flur.**  Altenglisches Flurnamenbuch, von Dr. Heinrich Middendorff, Halle, 1902.

**N. E. D.**  The New English Dictionary, edited by Dr. Murray.

**Nap.**  Contributions to Old English Lexicography, by Prof. A. S. Napier.  [Philological Society's Transactions, 1906.]

**Nic. H.**  The Gospel of Nicodemus in the Apocryphal New Testament, printed for William Hone.  [10th edition, 1872.]

**Prov. M.**  Proverbia Anglosaxonica, in Collectanea Anglosaxonica, edited by L. C. Müller, Havniae, 1835.

**Ps. V.**  The Vespasian Psalter, in O. E. Texts, edited by H. Sweet.

**Solil. H.**  King Alfred's Old English Version of St. Augustine's Soliloquies, edited by H. L. Hargreve, Ph.D. [Yale Studies in English.]  New York, 1902.

**Whitman.**  The Birds of Old English Literature, Journal of Germanic Philology, vol. ii, No. 2, 1898.

# A

**a**; *prep. Omit:* Ps. Th. 18, 8 *belongs to* â.

**â (ô)**; *adv. Ever. Add:* **A. always;** *semper.* **I. in reference to eternity.** (1) *alone:*—Ealle gesceafta woldon â bión; ǽlcere wuhte is gecynde ðæt hit wilnige ðæt hit â sié, Bt. 34, 12; F. 152, 18. (2) *defined by adverbs:*—Â forþ éce, Az. 112. Â forþ heonan, Cri. 582. (3) *emphasized by noun phrases:*—Ǽfre sig Dryhten gebletsod, â worulda woruld, Nic. 19, 24. Â on worlda forþ, Hy. 7, 123. Â tô woruldle forþ, 6, 13. Â tô worulde, â bûtan ende, Sat. 315. Â bûtan ende éce, Cri. 415. Â tô ealdre, Dôm. 29. Â tô feore, Cri. 1678. **II. denoting continuity or continual recurrence in temporary matters:**—Â þenden standeþ woruld, Gen. 915: B. 283. Â fordh *in dies,* Txts. 70, 529. Forþ unwemme â, Cri. 300. Â mid ældum in ǽlce tíd geweorþad, 405. Ús freódôm gief from yfla gehwâm â tô wîdan feore, Hy. 5, 11. Â in wintra worn, Dan. 324. Â ic symles wæs willan þínes georn, An. 64. Ic â and symble cwæþ, Ps. 94, 10. Â on symbel *semper,* Gr. D. 283, 6. On ðâ gerâd ðæt hî gecuron heora kynecyn ââ on ðâ wîshealfa, Chr. Erl. p. 3, 16. Of Angle sê â syððan stôd wêstig, 449; Erl. 13, 16. Ââ after ðâm hit yfelode, 975; Erl. 127, 32. Hê wîslîce rædde oftost â simle, 959; Erl. 119, 26. Wæs â blíðemôd, 1065; Erl. 196, 34. Hî â bærndon swâ hî gefêrdon, 1010; Erl. 144, 1. **II a.** of continuity in space-measurement:—Wæs ðæt land genemnad Nazanleóg â oþ Certices ford, Chr. 508; Erl. 15, 19. **II b.** of continuous increase or decrease (with comparatives):—Sceal him ðanan forð â þe bet belimpan, Wlfst. 39, 11. Ðeós woruld is sorhful and fram dæge tô dæge â swâ leng swâ wyrse, 189, 6. **II c.** of continuous correspondence, *quite (as)* :—Ðâ sendon hié eft Marius angeán Geoweorþan, â swâ lytigne and â swâ brægdenne swâ hê wæs *Marius, qui non minore pene quam ipse praeditus erat astutia,* Ors. 5, 7; S. 228, 32. Þǽr wæs â swâ micel dem swâ on Alexandria wæs. 6, 14; S. 270, 2. **III.** making a condition emphatic:—Nân mâran unrǽde ðone him â behôfode *(anything though always small, though never great)* hys âgenre findincge dôn geþrîstlǽce *nullus quippiam quamuis parum sua propria adinuentione agere presumat,* Angl. xiii. 441, 1081. **B.** *at any time; unquam.* **I.** *in any case, at all:*—Mid mâran unrǽde ðone him â behôfode *(than was at all proper for him),* Chr. 1093; Erl. 229, 3. Gif hê ô wǽre gecnyssed mid mænniscre herenesse, Gr. D. 59, 28. Eá lâ! ðæt ðû â woldest sǽne weorþan, An. 203. Hwæðer siððan â Drihten âmetan wolde wrece be gewyrhtum, Met. 9, 34. **II.** strengthening a negation:—Hié â noldon, Dan. 189. Nô ðæs fela ... ðæt â se rîca rêcan wolde, 596: B. 779. Ne ðǽr hleonaþ oo unsmêþes wiht, Ph. 25. Nô waniaþ ô holtes frætwe, 72: Cri. 313: Gen. 833. **III.** emphasizing a question, *(why) ever:*—Hwî eów â lyste (cf. hwî gê wilnigen, Bt. F. 68, 26), Met. 10, 18. **IV.** *in any degree, any* (with comparatives):—Ne oncnâwð â lengc stôwe *non cognoscet amplius locum,* Ps. L. 102, 16 : An. 1469: H. R. 17, 22. Hwæþer ðû hit â sweotolor ongiton mæge, Bt. 34, 4; F. 138, 16 : 35, 5; F. 166, 23 : 30, 1; F. 108, 28. Â lator Gr. D. 59, 19. Hwî eart ðû ðonne â ðý betera, Bt. 13; F. 38, 9. Wênst ðû ðæt hî â þe deórwyrþran seón, 14, 2; F. 44, 2 : 27, 2; F. 98, 9. [*Goth.* aiw: *O. Sax. O. H. Ger.* êo: *Ger.* je: *Icel.* ǽ, ei (ey).] *v.* âwa.

[*Omit the part within brackets at end of* â.]

**â-** [*O. Sax. O. Frs.* â: *O. H. Ger.* ar- (ir-, ur-): *Goth.* us-] *v.* ǽ-.

**âb.** *v.* ô-web.

**â-bacan** *to bake:*—Nim ǽlces cynnes melo and âbacæ man hlâf, Lch. i. 404, 5. Dæt tô cicle âbacen, 364, 15: Gr. D. 87, 21. Hlâfas on beágwîsan âbacene, 343, 15.

**â-bédan.** *Substitute the following:* **I. to force, wring:**—Ele âbêdan and âwringan of þâm beorgum *ab oliuis exigere oleum torquendo,* Gr. D. 250, 22. **II. to compel:**—Gif ðæt nýd âbǽdeþ *cum exhiberi mysterium ipsa necessitas compellit,* Bd. 1, 27; S. 497, 1. Ne hê on horses hrycg cuman wolde, nemne hwylc nýd mâre âbǽdde *nisi at major necessitas compulisset,* 3, 5; S. 526, 28. Wê beóþ genýdede and âbǽdede, ðæt wê sceolon âgyldan, Gr. D. 350, 10. **III. to demand, require.** (1) where the object is something needed or requisite:—Nâniges fultumes âbǽdeþ (-d, MS.) sió lâr *nullum adjutorium expostulet ratio,* Nar. 2, 2. Gif se geleáfa âbǽdeþ *si fides exigat,* Gr. D. 176, 14 : 333, 19. Ðâ ðe se hring ealles geáres on wurþunge symbeldaga âbǽdde *ea quae totius anni circulus in celebratione dierum festorum poscebat,* Bd. 4, 18; M. 314, 23. Hî ðæt scyp gehlǽsted hæfdon mid ðâm ðingum ðe swâ mycles sîþfætes nýd âbǽdde *quae tanti itineris necessitas poscebat,* 5, 9; S. 623, 18. Hî wǽron gefêdde mid ðæs gecyndes neádþearfnysse âbǽde

(? the passage seems to mean ' that they fed on what nature required for her needs '), Hml. S. 23 b, 130. (2) where the object is something due, a tax, or the like:—Ic him âlýfde alle nédbâde tuêgra sceopa, ðâ ðe âbaedde beóð from ðaem nédbâderum, C. D. i. 114, 20. Ys fîra ǽnig ðâra ðe ... an man âge deáð âbǽde, ǽr se dæg cyme *is there any man whom death can claim before the appointed day comes?* (? the passage seems corrupt), Sal. 478.

**â-bǽran** *to bring out, bring to light:*—Ðæt ðæt dîhle wæs openum wordum sý eall âbǽred *omnia luci verbis reddantur apertis,* Dôm. L. 41. *v.* ǽ-bǽre (-bêre), â-beran.

**abal.** *v.* afol.

**â-bannan.** *Add:*—Âbanie (-banne?) *jussus,* Germ. 391, 55.

**â-barian.** *Add:* **I. to make bare, strip:**—Stôwe rôde âbarude *locum cruce denudatum,* Angl. xiii. 427, 894. **II. to lay bare, expose, disclose:**—Ælfremeda wunda nâ âbarian *(detegere)* and geswutelian, R. Ben. I. 80, 12. Gylt âbarian *delictum denudare,* Scint. 195, 2. For âbaredum (âbored, *in marg.*) *ob detectum, apertum, revelatum,* Hpt. Gl. 474, 78. Âbarude *retectos,* Germ. 393, 64. [*O. H. Ger.* ar-barôn *denudare, prodere.*]

**abbod-hâd.** *Add:*—Ðâ ðe ðæne abbod tô abbodhâde gecuron *qui abbatem ordinant,* R. Ben. 124, 16. Sê ðe tô abbodhâde sceal *qui ordinandus est,* 118, 3.

**abbodisse.** *Add:*—Seó abbodyssa, Lch. iii. 428, 16. Abbodesse, L. In. 23; Th. i. 118, 1. Abbudesse, Chr. 805; Erl. 60, 17.

**abbod-leást, e**; *f. Lack of an abbot:*—Ðæt mynstres þincg ne forwyrþan for abbudleáste *ut non res monasterii abbatis privatione depereant,* C. D. B. i. 155, 37.

**â-beátan.** *Add:*—Ic ðe ðîne teþ of âbeáte, Lch. i. 326, 15.

**âbécêdê** (?); *f. An ABC, alphabet:*—Seó forme âbécêdê on ðâm gerîme ys bûtan pricon, and seó ôðer ys gepricod on ðâ swýðran healfe, and seó þrydde on ðâ wynstran healfe. ... Hêræfter wê wyllaþ tôdǽlan ðâ abecedaria on twâ tôdǽlednyssa, Angl. viii. 332, 42. Wê willaþ ðâ stafas onsundron gewrîðan ðe ðâ êstfullan preóstas on heora getæle habbaþ, and ðærǽfter Ebrêiscra âbécêdê wê willaþ geswutelian, and Grêciscra, and ðæt getæl ðǽra stafena wê þencaþ tô cýðanne, 335, 39.

**â-bedecian; p. ode** *To get by begging. v.* a-beþecian *in Dict.,* and bedecian.

**â-bégendlîc, a-behôfian.** *v.* un-âbígendlîc, â, B. I.

**â-belgan.** *Add:*—Âbealg *exacerbavit, provocavit, adflixit,* Wrt. Voc. ii. 144, 56. Âbulge *offenderet,* 63, 4. Âbolgen *ringescens,* 90, 47. (1) *with dat. or uncertain:*—Ðâ ǽbylignesse gebête ðe heó Gode âbylgð (âbealh, *v.l.*) *iram Dei, quam excitaverit, placare,* L. Ecg. P. ii. 16; Th. ii. 188, 4. Gif ûs hwâ âbylgð, ðonne beó wê sôna yrre, Bl. H. 33, 26. Ðone mon eft lufian ðe him ǽr âbealg, Past. 220, 26. Hwî irsast ðû wiþ ûs? on hwâm âbulgon wê ðê? Bt. 7, 5; F. 24, 1. Gif hê hwâm âbulge, Wlfst. 180, 10: Ors. 6, 11; S. 266, 10. (2) *with acc.:*—Ðý lǽs hê âbelge mid ðǽre suîgean ðone dôm ðæs Sceáweres *ne spectatoris judicium ex silentio offendat,* Past. 93, 5. Forbeád se biscop ðæt hî ne weópon, ðý lǽs [hî] ðâ hâlgan treów þurh heora wôp and teáras âbulgen *monuit sacerdos ut pergeremus fletum ululatumque nostrum sacras arbores dicens offendisse.* Nar. 32, 14. Þâ âne þe him ǽr âbolgen wæs, Ors. 2, 5; S. 80, 17. Âbolgene (-bloncgne *in text*) wêron *indignati sunt,* Mt. L. 26, 8. [*Laym.* abalh; *p.*; abolʒen; *pp.*: *O. Sax.* â-belgan: *O. H. Ger.* ar-belgan.]

**â-beligan.** *v.* â-bilgan.

**â-beódan.** *Add:* (1) *to announce, declare* a message:—Hê word âbeád *he delivered the words of his message,* B. 390. Ðæt hê hyre ǽrende abude ðâm bisceope ðysum wordum, Hml. S. 2, 68. Ðæt ic wiþ ðê sceolde ǽrendsprǽce âbeódan, Rä. 61, 16. Âboden bið *praedicabitur,* Lk. R. 12, 3: 24, 47. (1 a) where the message is given by a clause:—Hê âbeád ðæt ǽgðer ðâra folca ôþrum âgeáfe ealle ðâ men ðe hié gehergead hæfdon, Ors. 4, 6; S. 178, 12. (2) *to announce* what is coming:—Heáhengel hǽlo âbeád Marian, ðæt heó Meotod sceolde cennan, Men. 50: An. 96. Ðæt ðû hellwarum hyht ne âbeóde, An. 695. Se deáþ him tô cymeþ Godes dôm tô âbeódenne, Bl. H. 59, 12. (2 a) *to announce* the coming of a person:—Hǽfde hê seleweard âseted, sundornytte beheóld, eoton weard âbeád *(the guard's special office was to give notice of Grendel's coming),* B. 668. (3) in formulae of greeting, *to bid* farewell, (hǽl âbeódan) *to hail:*—Hê hǽlo âbeád heorðgeneátum *he bade farewell to*

*his comrades*, B. 2418. Hēht hē Elenan hǣl ābeódan *he sent salutation to Elene*, El. 1004. (4) *to announce* what may be accepted, *to offer*:— Nū ic ðē cyst ābeád *lo! I have offered you a choice*, Gen. 1919. Fela gē mē earda āboden habbaþ, Gū. 280. (5) *to announce* what is to be obeyed, *to bid, command*:—Hē up lōcade, swā se ār ābeád, El. 87: Gen. 1362. Ābeád cyning þegnum sīnum, ðæt hié ..., 1869. Ðē ābeódan hēt hē, ðæt ðū ..., Gū. 1348. Engel stefne ābeád, hēt ðæt treów ceorfan, Dan. 510. (6) *to summon, call out*:—Hē fyrde hēt ūt ābeódan, Chr. 1091; Erl. 227, 33. Ābeódende *eliciens* (*igniferas fulminum coruscationes*, Ald. 62), Wrt. Voc. ii. 85, 46. Bið geban micel and āboden þider eal Adames cnósl *omnes homines cogentur adesse*, Dōm. L. 128. [He his ærnde abed (bed, 2nd MS.), Lay. 4423. *O. H. Ger.* arbiotan *exhibere, offerre: Ger.* er-bieten.]

**ā-beofian.** v. ā-bifian.

**ā-beornan** (-bi(e)rnan). *Add:*—Ābyrnð *exardescit*, Ps. L. 38, 4. Hē ābarn (*exarsit*) mid ðȳ bryne wælhreównesse, Gr. D. 162, 22. Ðæt his mōd āburne (*exardesceret*), 337, 33. Āburnon *exarserunt*, Ps. L. 117, 12.

**ā-beówed.** v. ā-bīwan.

**ā-beran.** *Add:* I. with sense of movement, (1) *to bear off, bring, carry*:—Se hwæl hine ābær tō Niniuēa birig, Ǣlfc. T. Grn. 10, 13. Mid ðȳ wē ūre scyp fram ðām ȳþum upp ābæron (*exportaremus*), Bd. 5, 1; S. 614, 11. Ic gaderode mē ... ðā wlitegostan treówo be ðām dǣle ðe ic āberan mihte; ne com ic mid ānre byrðene hām, ðe mē ne lyste ealne ðane wude hām brengan, gif ic hyne ealne āberan mihte, Shrn. 163, 5-11. (1 a) *reflex.*:—Hē ongann tō ðām swȳðe cwacian and mid fōtum tealtian, ðæt hē uneáðe hine sylfne āberan mihte *coepit tremere, seque ipsum nutanti gressu vix posse portare*, Gr. D. 36, 21. (2) *to bring forth*, (a) *to bear* a child:—Ðæt bearn ðe ābær ūrne Hǣlend, Hml. A. 25, 16: Hml. Th. i. 198, 1. (b) *to bring* to light:— Se goldhord ne mæg beón forholen, nū hit swā upp is āboren, Hml. S. 23, 604. II. with sense of rest (metaph.). (1) *to bear with, tolerate*:—Seó cyrice ... swā ābireþ (*portat*) and ældeth, ðæt oft ðæt yfel āberende (*portando*) and yldende beweraþ, Bd. 1, 27; S. 491, 31. (2) *to bear, endure, not to give way under* trial, suffering, &c.:—Hē þā wītu ābær *tormenta ferebat*, Bd. 1, 7; S. 477, 46. Hwæðer sió gecynd ðæs līchoman sié strang, and eáþelíce mæge ðā strangan lǣcedómas āberan, Lch. ii. 84, 13. Se drenc wæs deádbǣre, ðā ðā hē ne mihte lífes tācn āberan (*the vessel containing the liquor had burst when the sign of the cross was made*), Hml. Th. ii. 158, 23. (3) *to bear, be under an obligation for* an imposition, &c.:—Ābere se borh ðæt hē āberan scolde, L. Edg. ii. 6; Th. i. 268, 9. [*Goth.* us-bairan *auferre, proferre, portare: O. H. Ger.* ar-beran *edere, afferre*.]

**ā-bered.** *Add:*—Feónd ābered *hostis callidus*, Scint. 92, 12: 209, 2. Ābered, litig *callidus*, Germ. 390, 41.

**ā-berendlic.** *Add:*—Swilc forgifnes swilce hit for Gode gebeorhlic sȳ, and for weorulde āberendlic, L. Edg. ii. 1; Th. i. 266, 6. Dôm ... for worolde āberendlic, L. Eth. vi. 10; Th. i. 318, 7. v. un-āberendlíc, -e.

**ā-berstan;** *p.* -bærst *To burst forth*:—Se wilm ðæs innoðes ūt ābirst (-biersð, Hat. MS.) and wierð tō sceabbe *fervor intimus usque ad cutis scabiem prorumpit*, Past. 70, 9. Ðonne ābirst (-biersð, Hat. MS.) ðær hwæðhwugu ūt ðæs ðe hē swugian sceolde *difficile est, ut non ad aliquid, quod dicere non debet, erumpat*, 164, 15. Ūt ābærst *eruperit*, up ābærst *emerserit*, Hpt. Gl. 512, 68. Ðā ābærst micel ðunor and līget, Hml. Th. ii. 184, 4. Ðæt āborstene clif (*the detached crag*) hreás ofdūneweard, Gr. D. 12, 9. [*O. H. Ger.* ar-brestan *erumpere*.]

**ā-bet, beþecian, -bicgan.** v. ā, B. IV, -bedecian, -bycgan.

**ā-bīdan.** *Add:* (1) absolute:—Hē fōr intō Loðene and ðær ābād, Chr. 1091; P. 226, 36. Maximus mid firde bād (ābād, *v.l.*) æt Aquileia *Aquileiae Maximus insederat*, Ors. 6, 36; S. 292, 25. Hē forlēt his here ābīdan mid Scottum, Chr. P. p. 5, 6. Nū wolde ic gebētan, gif ic ābīdan mōste (*if I might continue to live*) ... ac ic wāt ðæt ic ne eom wyrðe ðæs fyrstes, Hml. S. 26, 251. (2) with gen.:—Hwæs ābītst ðū?, Hml. S. 24, 23. Hē wederes ābād, Chr. 1094; P. 229, 2. Hī ābiden heora mǣles *they waited for their pay*, 1055; P. 186, 19. (3) case uncertain:—Ābíd dryht *expecta Dominum, sustine Dominum*, Ps. Srt. 26, 14. [*Goth.* us-beidan *expectare: O. H. Ger.* ar-bītan.]

**ā-biddan.** *Add:* I. *to pray*:—Tō mæginþrymme þínum tō ābiddanne (*idoneos*) *ad majestatem tuam exorandum*, Rtl. 87, 31. II. *to pray to, entreat* a person:—Ābiddaþ (biddaþ, *v.l.*) hine, Bt. 42: F. 258, 21. III. *to ask for, entreat*, (1) with acc. of thing:—Seó áwyrgednes ðe eówer yldran ābǣdon sylfe, ... ðā hió cwǣdon ..., H. R. 7, 22. (1 a) where the person *from whom* is given:—Heó ābæd ān hridder hire tō lǣne æt ōðrum wīfe *praestari sibi capisterium petiit*, Gr. D. 96, 33. Hī ābǣdon (*petierunt*) æt ðām Egiptiscon hira fatu, Ex. 12, 35. Ðæm ðe bið māre befæst, from ðæm māre bið ābeden, R. Ben. 14, 4. (1 b) where the person *for whom* is given:—Willtū wit unc ābiddan drincan?, Bd. 5, 3; S. 616, 30. (2) the request given in a clause:—Ðū ābǣde æt mē, ðæt ic ðē write, Guth. 4. 20. IV. *to get by asking*, (1) with acc. of thing:—Hié sendon Hannan, and hē hit ābæd *Annonis oratione meruerunt*, Ors. 4, 7; S. 182, 13. Ðā ābæd heó ān hridder *she borrowed a sieve*, Hml. Th. ii. 154, 15. Hē wênde ðæt

hit sum ōðer man ābiddan wolde oþþe gebicgan (*would get it by asking or by purchase*), Chr. 1044; P. 164, 11. Ðeáh ðe ic georne bǣde, ne mihte ic lȳfnesse ābiddan *porro diligentius obsecrans, nequaquam impetrare potui*, Bd. 5, 6; S. 619, 8. (1 a) the object a clause:—Ðā ābǣdan hȳ uneáðe, ðæt mon gedȳlgode sume hwíle, Wlfst. 100, 7. (1 b) the object an acc. and infin.:—Lucius bæd hine Crīstenne beón and eác ābæd, Bd. 1, 4; S. 475, 25. (2) where the person *from* whom the object (acc. or clause) is obtained is given:—Ðā ābædon hié æt Gode, ðæt hit rínde *ad invocationem nominis Christi vis pluviae effecta est*, Ors. 6, 13; S. 268, 15. Ðæt gē æt ǣnegum godum mehten rēn ābiddan *ut optati imbres superveniant*, 4, 10; S. 194, 26: Bl. H. 187, 19. Hē hæfde of ōþerum þeódum ābeden IIII CM, Ors. 2, 5; S. 80, 5. Gif hē wolde ābiddan æt Gode, ðæt hé mōste his feónde āfyllan, Chr. 626; P. 25, 11: 1093; P. 228, 15. (3) where the person *for* whom is given:—Ðæt oft wǣpen ābæd his mondryhtne *weapon oft it* (a sheath) *got for its lord*, Rä. 56, 12. (4) where the purpose *for* which is given:—Hió hiere tō fultume ābæd Molosorum cyning *prosequente rege Molossorum*, Ors. 3, 11; S. 148, 11. (5) where (2) and (3) are combined:—Monige men him forgifenesse æt ūrum Drihtne ābiddaþ, Bl. H. 65, 8. Ðā Pyhtas heom ābædon wíf æt Scottum, Chr. P. p. 3, 15. (6) with gen. of thing:—Sē ðe sum wundorlíc ðing on Godes naman dōn wile, oððe sē ðe sumes wundres dyslíce æt Gode ābiddan wile, Hml. Th. 170, 30. (7) govt. uncertain:—Gif hwā him ryhtes bidde, and ābiddan ne mæge, L. In. 8; Th. i. 106, 21. [*Goth.* us-bid(j)an *optare: O. Sax.* ā-biddian: *O. H. Ger.* ar-bitan *obsecrare, exposcere: Ger.* er-bitten.] v. un-ābeden *and* ābeden in Dict.

**ā-bifian.** *Add:*—Ðæt hūs ābifode (*contremuit*), Gr. D. 182, 21. Ðonne hē his siðfæt gemunde, ðonne āblācode hē eall and ābifode, Shrn. 52, 2. Ðæt forscildgode wíf eallum limum ābifode, Ap. Th. 26, 17. [*O. H. Ger.* ar-beben *contremere: Ger.* er-beben.]

**ā-bígan** *to deflect, turn away*:—Hē nā ne āfīymde ne ne ābȳgde fram him sylfum ðone ege his módes (*the verbs here seem a mistranslation of divulgavit in the original*), Gr. D. 107, 16. Ne mihton hī ðone stream ābȳgan (*deflectere*), 192, 24. [Add here ā-bēgan in Dict., *and* cf. un-ābígendlic.]

**ā-bilgan** *to offend, exasperate, irritate, provoke*:—Ongan mancyn ābeligan God for sunnandæges weorcum, Wlfst. 213, 11. Ābælgede wērun *indignati sunt*, Mt. R. 26, 8. [*O. H. Ger.* ar-belgen *offendere, laedere*.] v. ā-bǣligan, -bylgan in Dict.

**ā-bindendlic.** v. un-ābindendlic.

**ā-birgan.** *Add to* ā-byrgan (in Dict.): (1) *with gen.*:—Heora ǣlc ābyrige ðæs hāligwæteres, Ll. Th. i. 226, 24. (2) *with acc.*:—Hē ābyrgde ðā forbodenan fictreówes blǣda, Sal. K. 182, 34. v. on-birgan.

**ā-birging, e;** *f. Taste*:—Ābiringe *gustum*, Confess. Pecc. 183, 12.

**ā-bisgian=Ābysegode *exercitos*, Germ. 388, 12. I. *to busy, employ, engage, occupy, exercise*, (1) with acc. of person (or passive) and (a) gen. of occupation:—Ne sceal hē hyne nā ābysgian worldlícra bysgunga *non debet occupari mundanis negotiis*, L. Ecg. P. i. 7; Th. ii. 174, 27. (b) gerundial infin.:—Hē wæs ābysgod wíngeard tō settanne *ad putandam vineam occupatus*, Gr. D. 88, 17. (c) with prepositions (α) mid, *to occupy* a person with something:—Ðonne hié mid ðissum hwílendlicum ðingum hié selfe ābisgiaþ (-bisegiaþ, Hat. MS.) *dum temporali sollicitudini incaute deserviunt*, Past. 138, 7. Mid ðǣm inneran ānum ābisgad (-bisegad, (Hat. MS.) *solis interioribus occupatus*, 126, 15: L. Ecg. P. iii. 9; Th. ii. 198, 23. Ðīn mōd wæs ābisgod mid ðǣre ansíne ðissa leásena gesǣlða *occupato ad imagines visu*, Bt. 22, 2; F. 78, 9. (β) on, *to engage in* something:—Ne ābysga ðū ðín mōd on mislícum ðingum, Bas. 38, 18. Gif ðín willa bið gelóme ābysgod on Godes herungum, 40, 8. Ābysgod on wæccum and on sealmsange *occupatus vigiliis et psalmis*, Bd. 4, 25; S. 600, 40. (γ) ymbe, *to busy, concern* about something:—Ðæt hē hine sylfne ne ābysige ymbe nāne worldlíce ābysgunge (*occupari circa aliqua mundana negotia*), L. Ecg. P. i. 6; Th. ii. 174, 19. Hē wæs ābisgod ymb ðæs folces ðearfe *infirmantium negotiis urgetur*, Past. 103, 1. On smeáunga ābisgod ymb ðā hālgan ǣ *sacrae legis meditationibus intentus*, 169, 1. Ymb Godes þeówdōm ābisgod, Bl. H. 283, 1. Ymb his sáule hǣlo ābysgod *erga sanitatem animae suae occupatus*, Bd. 4, 25; S. 601, 10. Ymbe nāne woroldbysgunge ābysgode *mundano negotio nullo occupati*, L. Ecg. P. i. 8; Th. ii. 198, 22. Ðā hwíle ðe ðā ǣmettan ymbe ðā stēdan ābisgode beóð *dum formicae circa eos occupatae sunt*, Nar. 35, 15. (δ) wiþ, *to employ against*:—Hē wið ðone here ābisgod wæs, Chr. 894; P. 37, 8. (2) with acc. of time, *to employ* time in a pursuit:—Munecas ðe heora cildhād habbaþ ābisgod on cræftigum bócum, Angl. viii. 321, 27. (3) with acc. of place:—Wildeór ābysgiaþ þā stōwe *occupaverunt bestiae loca*, Gr. D. 258, 20. (4) used intransitively, *to engage in*:—Hē on ðǣre mānfullan scilde ābisgode, Ap. Th. 2, 4. II. with the idea of trouble, worry, oppression, *to trouble, worry, embarrass, exercise, harass*, (1) with acc. of person alone:—Gif hī mē ābysgaþ, ðonne ne mæg ic smeágan míne unscylda, Ps. Th. 18, 12. (2) also with prep, (α) mid:—Gif hwā sié ābisgod (-bisegod, Hat. MS.) mid hwelcum scyldum *si praeoccupatus fuerit homo in aliquo delicto*, Past. 158, 10. His mōd bið swíðe iéðegende and swíðe ābisgad mid eorðlicra

monna worðum *valde inter humana verba cor defluit*, 169, 12. Ðeáh
hē mid ðǽre mænigfealdnysse ðǽre synne bysgunge ābysgod sig *licet
multiplicitate negotii peccati suspensus sit*, L. Ecg. P. i. 9; Th. ii. 176, 8.
Hē (*Cicero*) wæs swíþe ābisgod mid ðǽre ylcan sprǽce *he was much
exercised by the same question;* querela vehementer agitata, Bt. 41, 3;
F. 246, 28. Wē beóþ mid mycclum hungre yfelra geþōhta ābisgode,
Bl. H. 19, 15. (β) on:—Wíf ðe ðē on nánum þincgum ne ābysige,
Shrn. 183, 11. Heora mōd wæs ābisgod on ðisse worulde willnunga,
Bt. 41, 3; F. 246, 30. *v. other instances under* ā-bysgian *in Dict.*

ā-bisgung, e; *f.* *Substitute the following for* ā-bysgung *in Dict.* I.
*occupation, employment, business.* v. ā-bisgian, I:—For ðǽre ūterran
ābisgunge . . . for ðǽre ābisgunge ðára ūterra weorca *in exteriorum
occupatione*, Past. 127, 9, 12. Worldlíce ābysgunge *mundana negotia*,
L. Ecg. P. i. 6; Th. ii. 174, 20. II. *trouble, disturbance.*
v. ā-bisgian, II:—Hit is cúð ðætte sió ūterre ābisgung ðissa worold-
ðinga ðæs monnes mōd gedréfð and hine scofett hidres ðædres, oð ðæt
hē āfield of his āgnum willan *constet, quod cor externis occupationum
tumultibus impulsum a semetipso corruat*, Past. 169, 12. Onstyred mid
ðǽre wunde his ābysgegunge, Gr. D. 4, 11.

ā-bítan. *Add:* I. *to lacerate with the teeth, mangle, tear to
pieces,* (a) of animals:—Seó leó ābít ǽrest hire lādteów *primus lacer dente
cruento domitor*, Bt. 25; F. 88, 13. Micel draca ābāt ðone þriddan dǽl
ðæs folces, Shrn. 88, 23. Ðæt flǽsc ðæt wildro ābiton *flesh that is torn
of beasts,* Ex. 22, 31. Hine wulfas ābiton and frǽton, Bl. H. 193. 7:—
Gen. 41, 4. Be hundes slite. Gif hund mon tōslíte oþþe ābíte
(*desubitet aut mordeat*), L. Alf. pol. 23; Th. i. 78, 2. Ðæt hē mehte
Godes þeówas on dōn, ðæt hié diór ābíte *in quo sanctos bestiis objiceret
laniandos*, Ors. 6, 31; S. 286, 12. (b) of a serpent:—Hēt hió ðā
nǽdran dōn tō hiere earme (*Cleopatra . . . serpentis morsu in sinistro
tacta brachio*) . . . ðǽre nǽdran gecynd is ðæt ǽlc uht ðæs ðe hió ābítt
scel his líf on slǽpe geendian, Ors. 5, 13; S. 246, 24–27. II. *to
eat up, devour:*—Se wulf cymð tō ðām sceápum, sume hē ābítt, sume hē
tōstencð, Hml. Th. i. 240, 23. Ābítende (*lupus*) *devorans*, Hpt. Gl.
451, 65. III. *with gen.* = on-bítan, *to taste, partake of:*—God
lýfde Adame, ðæt hē mōste brúcan ealra wæstma, būtan ánes treówes
wæstm hē him forbeád, ðæt hē ðæs nǽfre ne ābite, Wlfst. 9, 8. [þu
starest so þu wille abiten al þat þu miht mid clivre smiten, O. and N. 77.
*O. H. Ger.* ar-pīzan *percutere, occidere.*]

ā-biterian, -bitrian. I. *to grow bitter:*—Ābiteraþ se líchoma
eall, Lch. ii. 10, 15: 106, 22. On ðām magan se mete ābiteraþ, 160, 1.
Ābitriaþ (-biteriaþ, Hat. MS.) ðā blēda *fructus amarescit*, Past. 340,
24. II. *to make bitter, to embitter, exasperate:*—Exasperat .i. *sevit,
provocat vel* ābiterie, Wrt. Voc. ii. 144, 60.

a-bitweónum. *Dele.*

ā-bíwan, -beówan (-býwan, v. *Dict.*), *to rub up, polish, burnish,
scour:*—Ǽren fæt nýþewerd ābýwed, Lch. iii. 292, 10. Ābeówed
*defricatum*, Wrt. Voc. ii. 138, 26.

ā-blācian. *Substitute:* I. *to turn pale* from fear, weakness, &c.:—
Hē dranc ātor, and ne āblācode, Shrn. 32, 24. Ðonne hē his síðfæt
gemunde, ðonne āblācode hē eall and ābisode, 52, 2. I a. *to grow
faint:*—Āblācode *emarcuit, elanguit*, Wrt. Voc. ii. 143, 25: elanguet,
142, 76. Āblācodon *obriguerunt*, Ex. 15, 18 (v. Thw. Hept. p. 30, at
end). II. of material, *to get dull* or *tarnished, lose colour:*—Ðæt
fægere híw ðæs goldes sié āblācod (*pallescit*), Past. 135, 2. [*O. H. Ger.*
ar-bleichēn *obpallescere:* Ger. er-bleichen.]

ā-blācung, e; *f.* *Pallor:*—Āblācungum (ǽ-, An. Ox. 4897, *q.v.*)
*palloribus*, Hpt. Gl. 518, 62.

ā-blǽst; *adj.* I. *inspired:*—Āblǽst *afflatus* (*spiritu*), Hpt. Gl.
466, 8. II. *infuriated, furious:*—Hē hēt geótan týn orcas fulle
eles, ðæt hē wolde ðæt ðæs fýres hǽto ðe reðre wǽre and ðe āblǽstre *that
the heat of the fire might be the more fierce and furious*, Angl. xvii. 113, 16.

ā-blǽwan. *Add:* I. *to breathe* (trans.):—Críst ābleów ðone blíðan
Gāst upon ðā apostolas, Hml. Th. i. 324, 31. Ðæt lēht . . . ðætte ðencum
ðū ābleáwe *illud lumen quod mentibus aspirasti*, Rtl. 2, 15. II.
*to blow away:*—Sume cwǽdon ðæt ðæt heáfod sceolde āblāwan
Herodiaden, swā ðæt heó fērde mid windum geond ealle woruld, Hml.
Th. i. 486, 5. III. *to blow up, swell:*—Ðā mettas ðe āblāwan
monnan mǽgen, Lch. ii. 254, 24. Tācn āblāwenre lifre, 160, 24.
[Crist ableow þana halga gast ofer þa apostolas, O. E. Hml. i. 99.
*O. H. Ger.* ar-blājan *inflare*.]

ā-blāwness, e; *f.* *Upblowing, inflation:*—Wiþ āblāunesse ðæs innoþes, Lch. ii. 170, 21.

ā-blāwung, e; *f.* A *blowing* or *swelling up, inflation:*—Sió āblāwung
on ðǽre lifre, Lch. ii. 204, 17, 23: 206, 1: 248, 5. Sió āþenung ðæs
magan and sió āblāwunge hǽto, 192, 17. Sealf gōd wið swelcre
āblāwunge (*quinsy*), 48, 11. Hē onfindeþ swile and ðæt ðā ōman beóð
inne betýnde þurh ðā āblāwunge, 174, 23.

ā-blegned; *adj.* *Ulcerated:*—Wiþ ūt āblegnedum ōmum, Lch. ii.
10, 5: 98, 25: iii. 42, 25.

ā-blend. *Take with next word.*

ā-blendan. *Add:* (1) literal, (a) where sight is destroyed:—

Āblendeþ *suffundit* (cf. ? oculi suffusio = *cataract*), Wrt. Voc. ii. 121, 47.
Sedechias man āblende, Ælfc. T. 8, 13. Hī hine (*Samson*) āblendon,
Jud. 16, 21. Hēt se cyng āblendan Ælfgār, Chr. 993; P. 127, 29.
Him burston ūt his eágan . . . hē wearð āblend, Hml. S. 19, 129.
Wulfeáh and Ufegeat wǽron āblende, Chr. 1006; P. 136, 10. Sume
wurdon āblǽnde, 1075; P. 212, 8. (b) where sight is impeded:—Gē
tysliaþ eów on Denisc āblendum eágum (*with the hair falling over the
eyes?*), Engl. Stud. viii. 62, 5. (2) fig.:—Gītsung hī āblent, Bt. 36, 6;
F. 130, 34. Lāc āblendaþ (*excoecant*) glǽwne, Ex. 23, 8. Āblændaþ,
L. Alf. 46; Th. i. 54, 18. Hē bið āblend mid unwísdōme, Past. 69, 16.
Āblendað, ðæt is, beswicen, Rtl. 197, 23. Se āblenda Datianus, Hml. S.
14, 128. (3) as a medical term:—Cancer āblendan *to prevent suppuration
in a cancer*, Lch. i. 6, 24: 88, 20. [*Laym., A. R., R. Glouc., Ayenb.,
Piers P.* a-blende[n]: *O. H. Ger.* ar-blenden *obcoecare*.] v. ā-blindan.

ā-blēred *bald, bared of hair. v. passage in Dict. under* tyslian.

ā-blícan. *Add:*—Ic beó gewhītad *vel* āblicen *dealbabor*, Wrt. Voc.
ii. 139, 83: Bl. Gl. [*O. H. Ger.* ar-blīchan *resplendere*.]

ā-blicgan. v. ā-blycgan.

ā-blindan. *Substitute:* p. de To *make blind:*—Hié wurdon sōna
āblinde, Bl. H. 151, 4.

ā-blindian; p. ode To *become blind:*—Se mon āblindode, Shrn. 145,
29. [Gif þet eȝe ablindað, O. E. Hml. i. 109, 8. Ha ablindeð, þ ha
nabbeð sihðe nan, Marh. 15, 23. Heo ablindeð in þe inre eien, A. R.
92. *O. H. Ger.* ar-blindēn: Ger. er-blinden.]

ā-blinn. v. un-āblinn.

ā-blinnan. *Add:*—Ne āblinnaþ *non desistunt*, Wrt. Voc. ii. 59, 51.
Āblinnende *desistens*, āblon *desistit*, 25, 44, 45. Āblunnan *desierant*, 26,
6. (1) of persons, (a) absolute, *to cease, leave off, stop:*—Ic āblinne
*cessam*, i. *desistam*, Wrt. Voc. ii. 131, 5. Tō hwan āblinnest ðū? Bl.
H. 189, 2. Ne āblind *non cessabit*, Kent. Gl. 799: 961. Hē for ðæs
weges earfoðnysse ne āblan, ac feor gewāt, Hml. S. 30, 36. Clypa, ne
āblin ðū, Hml. A. 138, 9. Ǽfre syngiende and nǽfre āblinnende, Nar.
47, 13. (b) with gen.:—Se ðe nǽfre ne āblind ungestæððignesse *cui
carnis petulantia sine cessatione dominatur*, Past. 71, 3. Hē nǽfre
gōdes weorces ne āblon, Bl. H. 227, 6. (c) with an infin.:—Hē beheóld
ðone heorot, and āblan his ǽhtan, Hml. S. 30, 39. (d) with a clause:—
Ne āblinnan wē ðæt wē Gode cwēmon, Bl. H. 47, 10. (e) with a
prep.:—On ðām seofoðan dæge āblan Drihten fram ǽlcum weorce,
Wlfst. 210, 25. Monige men nellaþ āblinnan from heora unrihtum
gestreónum, Bl. H. 25, 5. (2) of things, *to cease, stop, fail, come to an
end:*—Ðæt leóht on nānre tíde ne āblinneþ, Bl. H. 21, 16. Se rēn
āblon, Ors. 4, 10; S. 194, 19. Seó scadu āblann *umbra cessavit*, An.
Ox. 40, 15. On ungyldan ðā nǽfre āblunnon, Chr. 1097; P. 234, 4.
Rēnas ðe ealles geáres ne āblunnon, 1098; P. 234, 30. Āblinnendum
sǽpe *cessante* (*deficiente*) *succo*, Hpt. Gl. 419, 71. Æfter āblunnenre
ēhtnysse, Hml. Th. i. 544, 9. v. un-āblinnende, -āblinnendlíc.

ā-blinnendlíce = *fatigabiliter* in Hpt. Gl. 429, 32:—*Infatigabiliter* .i.
*indefatigabiliter* āblindnendlíce. v. un-āblinnendlíce.

ā-blinnedness, e; *f.* *Cessation:*—Būtan āblinnendnysse *unceasingly*,
Hml. S. 23 b, 98.

a-blīsian. v. ā-blysian.

ā-blissian *to make glad:*—God ne byð nǽfre geblissod (āblissod, *v. l.*)
mid earmra manna cwale *Deus miserorum cruciatu non parcitur*, Gr. D.
335, 14.

ā-bloncgne. v. ā-belgan.

ā-blycgan; p. de; pp. -blyged, -blycged. I. *to get affected by fear, get
dismayed:*—Diriguit, i. *obstipuit, horruit, induruit* āblycde, Wrt. Voc.
ii. 140, 46. Ðā āblicgde Aman unblíþum andwlitan, and ne mihte nā
ācuman ðæs cyninges graman, Hml. A. 100, 265. Hē wearð swíðe
þearle āblycged *vehementer territus*, Gr. D. 133, 3. Ic eom āblicged
*consternor*, Ælfc. Gr. 222, 9. Hē wearð āblicged . . . and forhtmód
wafode . . . hē sæt āblicged, Ælfc. T. 17, 40–4. Hē wearð þurh ðās
bodunge āblicged . . . hí cwǽdon him tō, 'Hwæs ondrǽtst ðū ðē?', Hml.
Th. ii. 342, 16. Hí urnon tō āblicgede, and woldon ðæt fýr mid wætere
ofgeótan, 166, 7. II. *to get affected by wonder, get amazed,
astonished:*—Mid āblicendum eárum *attonitis auribus*, R. Ben. I. 2, 10.
Ðā wearð seó menigu swíðe āblicged, and mid wundrunge cwǽdon,
Hml. Th. i. 314, 16: Hml. A. 116, 447: Hml. S. 3, 120. Wurdon hí
þurh ðæt wundor āblicgede, 5, 89: Hml. Th. i. 386, 35. Ābliccedum
*attonitis*, An. Ox. 3506. v. un-geblycged *in Dict.*

a-blýsgung. *Substitute:* ā-blysung, e; *f.* *Reddening* with shame,
*confusion:*—Tō sceame and tō āblysunge hí sint ūs *nobis rubor confusionis est*, R. Ben. 133, 11.

ā-blysian *to redden* with shame, *to blush, to be ashamed:*—Āblysien
*erubescant*, Bl. Gl. Āblysian, Ps. L. 6, 11: 34, 26. *Add passage
from* a-blīsian *in Dict.*

ā-bolgenness, e; *f.* *Exasperation, irritation:*—Exacerbatio, *irritatio*
ābolgennes, Wrt. Voc. ii. 144, 53.

ā-borgian. *Add:* I. *to be security for* (a) a person. *v. ex. in Dict.*
(b) an agreement:—Bchāte hē and on wedde sylle ðæt . . ., and
āborgian his frýnd ðæt, L. Edm. B. 1; Th. i. 254. 7. Weddige se

brýdguma ðæs, and hit áborgian hís frýnd, 2 ; Th. i. 254, 9.  II. *to borrow :*—Hit gelamp ðæt hire fæder áborgude .xxx. punda æt Godan, Ch. Th. 201, 15.

**á-brácian, -brǽcian** (?) ; *p.* ode To emboss, stamp :—*Celatum* ábrácod, út áþrungen, Wrt. Voc. ii. 14, 22. Ábrectat ( =ábrǽcad?) *celatum*, Txts. 49. 451. [Cf. *O. H. Ger.* ka-práchit *impressa* : ki-práhtia (*ac. pl.*) *celata* : *Ger.* prägen.]

**á-brǽdan, -e** ; *p.* de To fry :—Ábrǽd cicel, Lch. ii. 114, 25.

**á-brǽdan** ; *p.* de To dilate, extend, spread out :—Ábraed múð ðínne *dilata os tuum*, Ps. Srt. 80, 11. Ðeáh ðe seofon middangeardas sýn ealle onefn ábrǽdde, Salm. K. p. 150, 29. Mid ábrǽdedum handum, Hml. S. 23 b, 701. [*Goth.* us-braidjan *expandere.*]

**á-brastlian** to resound, crash :—Áweóx and ábraslude mára swég and hefigra *gravior sonitus excrevit*, Gr. D. 236, 12.

**á-breátan.** *The p. t. here given may be taken as an irregular form (on the model of reduplicating verbs, cf. heóf, p. t. of heófan) belonging to* á-breótan *q. v.*

**á-brecan.** *Add:* I. *trans.* (1) *to break up, break to pieces, destroy the connexion between the parts of* an object :—Hié bánhringas ábrecan þóhton, An. 150. Ðæt his byrne ábrocen wǽre, Fin. 44. Báncofa ábrocen weorðeþ, Vy. 35 : Gú. 1341. Ábrocen land *broken ground* ; *anfractus*, Wrt. Voc. i. 55, 12. Gif sceáp sý ábrocen (*have the skin broken by disease*) . . . geót in ðæt ábrocene sceáp, Lch. iii. 56, 15. Up ábrecende *rumpente* (of a chain), Hpt. Gl. 522, 3. (1 a) *to break down* a wall :—Hié ðone weall ábrǽcon *perfractis muris*, Ors. 3, 9 ; S. 134, 22. Hé hét ábrecan ðone weall, ðeáh ðe hé brád wǽre, Hml. S. 25, 448. (1 b) *to break off, separate forcibly* :—Ðá ábrǽc ðæt mægdeþ ðæt gold of ðǽm godgeldum, Shrn. 106, 3. (1 c) *to destroy* a person :—Ábrocene burhweardas, Exod. 39. (1 d) *to break, violate* :—Heó Godes bebodu ábrǽc, Bl. H. 5, 25. Nis áléfed ðis fæsten tó ábrecan[n]e, Wlfst. 285, 12. Hié frið ábrocen hæfdon *violatores pacis*, Ors. 4, 7 ; S. 182, 9. Hié Godes hæfdon bodscipe ábrocen, Gen. 783. (2) *to take by storm, to storm* a place :—Sé ðe fæste burg ábrycð *expugnator urbium*, Past. 218, 17. Mon his geweorc ábrǽc, Chr. 894 : P. 87, 3. Hí ábrǽcon án geweorc, 893 ; P. 84, 11. Gotan ábrǽcon Rómeburg, 409 ; P. 10, 12 : Bt. 1 ; F. 2, 3. Ær hé helwara burg ábrǽce, Rä. 56, 7. Ábrecan *expugnare*, Ors. 3, 9 ; S. 132, 12 : *capere*, Bd. 3, 16 ; S. 542, 20 : Chr. 921 ; P. 101, 8. Wæs Rómaburh ábrocen fram Gotum *fracta est Roma a Gothis*, Bd. 1, 11 ; S. 480, 12 : Met. 1, 18 : Chr. 1003 ; P. 135, 5.  II. *intrans.* *To break* out, forth, away, &c. :—Hit ábricð út on ídle ofersprǽce, Past. 277, 11. *Erumpunt procedunt* up ábrecaþ, Wrt. Voc. ii. 144, 7. Hé ábrǽc intó ðám búre, Ap. Th. 1, 18. Hannibal ábrǽc mid gefeohte ofer ðá beorgas . . . oþ hé com tó Alpis and ðǽr eác ofer ábrǽc, Ors. 4, 8 ; S. 186, 13–16. Up ábrǽcon *ebulliebant*, Hpt. Gl. 488, 11 : *exundaverunt*, 499, 47. Up ábrýcan *erumperunt*, Kent. Gl. 45. Oð ðæt seó eá eft up ábrece, Lch. iii. 254, 3. Seó fæstnung ne geþafaþ ðæt hí ǽfre út ábrecon, Hml. Th. i. 332, 21. Sé ðe nolde of ðǽre róde ábrecan, sé árás of ðǽre byrgene. Mǽre wundor wæs ðæt hé of deáðe árás, ðonne hé cucu of ðǽre róde ábrǽce, 226, 13–15. [*O. H. Ger.* ar-brechan *effringere, dis-, e-rumpere.* Cf. *Goth.* us-brukan *to be broken off.*]

**á-brecendlic, -brectat, -brédan, -brednes.** v. un-ábrecendlic, á-brácian, -bregdan, -bryrdness.

**á-brégan.** *Add:* —Ðæt níwe wíte ábrégeþ (*terret*) ðæs mannes mód, Gr. D. 135, 19. God heora mód ábrégde, 249, 10. Ábrége *terreat*, Lch. i. 69, 5. Áfyrhted and ábréged *territus*, Gr. D. 222, 15. Swíðe ábréged *vehementer exterritus*, 39, 7. Hié forhte and ábrégde cwǽdon, Bl. H. 85, 9. Wǽron ðá sýnd ábrégede mid ðý egesan, Shrn. 136, 15. [*O. H. Ger.* ar-bruogen *ex-, per-terrere.*]

**á-bregdan, -brédan.** *Add:* I. *trans.* with idea of quick or forcible movement, (1) *to drag, pull, snatch, pluck* :—Se heofon ábrét ðás tunglan underbæc, Angl. vii. 14, 137. Februarius mónð bissextus up ábrét, viii. 307, 29. Hí ðone mete him of ðám múðe ábrúdon, Hml. Th. i. 404, 5. Ðá cwelleras hire cláðas of ábrúdon, Hml. S. 7, 146. Hí hine þanon ábrúdon, 23, 647. Ábregd cniht of ðǽ, Gen. 2914. Ábréd of ðá fiðeru, Lev. 1, 17 : Lch. i. 362, 5. Gif man wǽpn ábregde, L. Th. i. 32, 11. Búton hé ðá wyrte up ábréde, Lch. i. 246, 5. Ðæt seó gitsung his willan ne ábrúde fram láre, Hml. Th. i. 394, 14. Ábrédan *exerere, evaginare*, Wrt. Voc. ii. 144, 75 : Sal. 164. Ábrogden *vulsum*, Wrt. Voc. ii. 93, 55 : Ps. Th. 108, 28. Swelce ðú hæbbe ðá duru ábróden (cf. on-bregdan) *as if you had flung open the door*, Bt. 35, 3 ; F. 160, 5. Ábródenes *retecti*, An. Ox. 52, 4. Ábródenum *subtracto*, Kent. Gl. 996. Áweg ábróden *avulsus*, Wrt. Voc. ii. 74, 4. Ábrogden from ðǽm eorðlican *exempta terrenis*, Bt. 18, 4 ; F. 68, 17. Alexander weard from ðǽm burgwarum in ábróden, Ors. 3, 9 ; S. 134. 14. Of Godes yrre ábrogdene *de ira eruti*, Bd- 2, 1 ; M. 96, 28. Of ðám þeóstrum ábrogdene *exempti tenebris*, 5, 12 ; M. 428, 26. Hé wæs heálíce up ábrogden *ad alta rapitur*, Past. 101, 2. Up ábróden *exhaustum*, Wrt. Voc. ii. 144, 51. Ne sind míne eágan up ábródene (*elati*), R. Ben. 26, 16. (2) *of rapine* :—Swá hwylc swá hwæthugu of círican þurh stale út ábrygdeð (-brédeþ, S. 490, 5) *si quis aliquid de ecclesia furtu abstulerit*, Bd. 1, 27 ; M. 66, 29. Stíþ[líce] ágeán ábrédeþ *violenter*

*auferunt*, An. Ox. 5440.  II. *intrans.* (1) *to make a movement with something* :—Hé ábrægd mid ðý bille, Gen. 2931. (2) *to move one's self quickly, to start* from sleep, *wake with a start* :—Hé fǽringa ábréd *suddenly he woke up*, Guth. 94, 21. [His sweord he ut abræid, Lay. 26553. Adam abraid (*awoke*), Gen. and Ex. 232. Ulixes out of slepe abraid, Gow. iii. 54, 4.]

**á-breótan.** *Add:* Also with *p.* -breút, *pl.* -breóton, and *wk.* -breútte :—Weg synfulra ábreútcð (*exterminabit*), Ps. Srt. 145, 9. Ðone ðe heó on ræste ábreút, B. 1298. Hé ábreútte (*exterminavit*) hié, Ps. Srt. 77, 45 : 79, 14. Hié his heáfdes segl ábreúton mid billes ecge, An. 51. Biað ábreútte *exterminabuntur*, Ps. Srt. 36, 9. Wǽran sweordum ábrotene *in gladio ceciderunt*, Ps. Th. 77, 64.

**á-breóþan.** *Substitute for* all but the two instances from Ælfc. Gr. : I. *intrans.* To degenerate, deteriorate. fall away, fail, (1) of persons, (a) physical :—Oft hyre hleór ábreóðeð *her good looks are lost*, Gn. Ex. 66. (b) moral :—Se deófol sendeð earhscype, swá ðæt se man ábrýð æt ælcere þearfe, Wlfst. 53, 13. Gif hé ábrýð on ðǽre éhtnysse, Hml. Th. i. 250, 21. Se yfela, swá hé oftor on ðǽre fandunge ábrýð, swá hé forcúðra bið, 268, 29. Sume menn . . . ðonne seó hǽte cymð, ðæt is seó costung, ðonne ábreóðað hí (*these in time of temptation fall away*, Lk. 8, 13), ii. 90, 34. Ðæt teóðe werod ábreáð and áwende on yfel, i. 10, 18. Ðá seonde hé ðæt man sceolde ðá scipu tóheáwan ; ac hí ábrudon, ðá ðe hé tó þóhte (*those he looked to failed in their duty*), Chr. 1004 ; P. 135, 30. Hí sume æt ðǽre neóde ábrudon, and fram ðám cynge gecyrdon, 1101 ; P. 237, 6. Ðæt se man ábreóðe on ælcere neóde náhtlíce ǽfre, Wlfst. 59, 12. God ús gescylde, ðæt wé ne ábreóðon on ðǽre fandunge, Hml. Th. i. 268, 11. Ábroþen *degener, ignobilis*, An. Ox. 46, 2. Ábroþen (abroten, MS., *but see* Angl. viii. 450) *vel* dwǽs *vafer vel fatuus vel socors*, Wrt. Voc. i. 18, 62. Apostatan ábroðene, Wlfst. 164, 10 note. (2) of actions, *to fail, come to nought* :—Ábreóðe his angin, By. 242.  II. *trans. and wk.* To destroy :—Ábreóþeð *perdet*, Mt. R. 21, 40. Se cyning ábriódde (*perdidit*) myrðra, 22, 7. [Si lage swið abreað *this law degenerated very much*, O. E. Hml. i. 235, 29.]

**á-breótness, e** ; *f.* Destruction :—Ðára ábreútnissa *exterminia*, Txts. 182, 86.

**á-brítan** ; *p.* te To destroy :—Beóþ ábrýtte *exterminabuntur*, Ps. Spl. C. 36, 9.

**a-broten?.** v. á-breóþan.

**á-broþenness, e** ; *f.* Degeneracy, ignobleness, baseness :—Ignauia, ðæt is ábroðennyss oððe náhtnyss, Wlfst. 58, 17. Ongeán ðæs módes strengðe se deófol forgifð ábroðennysse, 59, 12. v. á-breóþan.

**á-brúcan** ; *p.* -breác To partake of (gen.), eat :—Hé ábreác ðæs forbodenan treówes ǽpples, Angl. xi. 1, 17.

**á-bryrdan.** *Add:* I. *to* instigate, stimulate, incite :—Ic trúwige ðæt sum wurðe ábrird, ðæt hine liste gehíran ðá hálgan láre, Ll. Th. ii. 364, 17. Æfter ðisum wordum wurdon ðá munecas mycclum ábryrde, Hml. S. 6, 344. Hí beóð ábrerde (*divinae dilectionis stimulo*) *compunguntur*, An. Ox. 973.  II. *to make contrite, remorseful* :—Áspiwan synna þurh ábryrde andetnysse, Wlfst. 150, 4. Hí ne synt ábyrde (*compuncti*), Ps. L. 34, 16. Ðám ábryrdum *contritis*, An. Ox. 4122. v. on-bryrdan.

**á-bryrdness, e** ; *f.*  I. *keen feeling, ardour* :—Ábry[r]dnysse (ábrednysse, Hpt. Gl. 434, 56) *amoris*, An. Ox. 1184. Mid his heortan ábryrdnysse *intentione cordis*, R. Ben. 80, 12. Mid sibbe and mid sóðre ábryrdnysse, 106, 1.  II. *compunction, contrition* :—Ábryrdnesse *conpunctionis*, An. Ox. 601 : *penitudinis .i. penitentie*, 1768. v. on-bryrdness.

**a-brytan.** v. á-brítan.

**á-búgan.** *Add:* *to bow, bend, turn*, (1) of motion (lit. and fig.) :—Hé tó eorðan ábeáh, Hml. S. 14, 134. Ðá ábeáh seó módor tó hire bearne, 25, 174. Hwæþer þé of móde ábeáh *has it escaped your memory?*, Gr. D. 40, 24. (1 a) where motion indicates reverence :—Hí on cneówum ábúgað tó his dǽdum bánum, Chr. 979 ; P. 123, 27 : Hy. 7, 10. Hí wurhton fela gedwimera on anlícnessum and ðǽrtó ábugan, Wlfst. 11, 5. Men sceolon ábúgan tó gehálgodre róde, Hml. Th. ii. 306, 21. (2) of action, (a) yielding, submission :—Ðám wé sceolon ábúgan, and hé ne ábýhð ná ús, Hml. A. 8, 211. Nó ðágeác *non cessit*, Wrt. Voc. ii. 61, 26. Ábeah Uhtred eorl tó him, Chr. 1013 ; P. 143, 14. Ealle men him tó ábugon and him áðas swóron, 1086 ; P. 222, 12 : 221, 31. Ðá nolde seó burhwaru ábúgan ac heóldan mid fullan wíge ongeán, 1013 ; P. 143, 27 : Hml. S. 25, 119. Ðæt folc nolde Gode ábúgan *Deo non cesserant*, Ors. 1, 7 ; S. 38, 17 : Hml. S. 25, 170 : Hml. Th. ii. 304, 20 : Wlfst. 197, 9. Hé wiste ðæt se man ábúgan (*yield to temptation*) wolde, Angl. vii. 24, 224. (b) abandonment :—Ðá ðe ábúgað (*declinant*) from bebodum ðínum, Ps. L. 118, 21. (3) of shaping, *to bend, curve* ; fig. *to be humble* :—Heó wæs ábogen *erat inclinata*, Lk. 13, 11. Ábogenre, eádmódre *cernua*, i. *humilis*, An. Ox. 1278. Ábogene *dimissa*, i. *humilia*, Wrt. Voc. ii. 140, 31.

**á-bunden** ; *pp.* (*adj.*) Unimpeded ; *expeditus*, Wrt. Voc. ii. 107, 45 : 29, 53.

á-búrod; pp. (adj.) Deprived of peasants (gebúras):—Ðá wæs hit ierfælæás and mid ǽdnum folce áburód omni pecunia caruit et pauperibus hominibus erat destitutum, Cht. Th. 162, 29.

á-bútan. Dele first passage and add: I. prep. dat. acc. marking (1) position:—Stódon him ábútan swearte gástas, Hml. Th. i. 414, 9. Ðú tǽcst folce gemǽro ábútan ðone munt constitues terminos populo per circuitum, Ex. 19, 12. (2) motion outside:—His scipu wendon út ábúton Legeceastre, Chr. 1000; P. 133, 14. Hé wende ábútan East-Englum in tó Humbran múðan, 1013; P. 143, 13. (3) approximation:—Ábútan feówer hund manna, 1055; P. 186, 6. II. adv. marking (1) position:—Ábútan beringede circumdati, Scint. 103, 11. Gehwár ábútan circumquaque, An. Ox. 3775. (2) motion outside a place:—Hí fóron west ábúton, Chr. 915; P. 99, 11. Com se here eft ábúton in tó Temese, 999; P. 131, 19. (3) motion round an axis or centre:—Gif ðú sumne cláð sceáwast, ne miht ðú hine calne tógædere geseón, ac wenst ábútan (you turn it round), ðæt ðú ealne hine geseó, Hml. Th. i. 286, 25. (4) rotation:—Se consul sceolde beón heora yldost tó ánes geáres fyrste; féng ðonne óþer tó óþres geáres firste tó ðam ylcan anwealde, and eóde swá ábútan be heora gebirdum, Jud. p. 161, 25. v. on-bútan.

á-bycgan. Substitute: To abye. v. N. E. D. I. to buy off, redeem a person:—Drihten ús mid his blóde ábohte of helle hæfnéde, Bl. H. 91, 12. II. to pay for, atone for wrong-doing:—Gif frí man wið fríes mannes wíf geligeð, his wergelde abicge, Ll. Th. i. 10, 7. [Mid here micele fals þ hi ealle abohton, Chr. 1125; P. 255, 16. Þu me smite . . . ah sare þu it salt abuggen, Lay. 8158. Bute ȝif he abugge þe sunne þet he wrouhte, A. R. 306.] III. to perform what was necessary for the discharge of a legal obligation:—Clíroc feówra sum hine clǽnsie, and áne his hand on wiófode; óðre ætstanden að ábycgan, i.e. the principal, with one hand on the altar, made oath; the compurgators stood by and by their oaths redeemed him from the obligation under which, so long as his oath was unsupported, he lay (cf. Ll. Th. i. 180, 17-19), Ll. Th. i. 40, 18. [If byrgan (cf. borg) could be read for bycgan, the function of the compurgators would be made more evident.] Cf. á-ceápian.

á-byffan; p. te To mutter, mumble (v. buff to stammer, D. D. and N. E. D.):—Abyffan muttire, Wrt. Voc. ii. 57, 62. [Wyllam þe rede kyng . . . was of speche hastyf, boffyng, R. Glouc. 414, 14. Cf. bufferes stammerers, Wick. Is. 32, 4.]

a-bylgnes, -bylgþ, -byrgan, -bysgian, -býwan. v. ǽ-bylgnys, -byl(i)gþ(u), á-birgan, -bisgian, -bíwan.

ac. Add:—Nó ðæt án ðæt . . . ac (eác), Bt. 21; F. 74, 18: 5, 3; F. 14, 7. Ah ðeáhhwæðre, Past. 305, 1. Nis ðæt mín miht, ac gif (unless) ðú gelýfest. Ðá cwæð hé tó him: 'Ac tó hwon sweriað git mán?', Guth. 64, 5: 74, 5. Hwæt gelamp ðé nú ðá? ac ðé on ðysse nihte sum untrymnys gelamp?, 80, 16.

ác. Take here the passage given under ǽc and add: dat. ǽc (ác); pl. ǽc. Aac robor, arbor (in the Corpus Glossary this is followed by 'robor, virtus, rubor color est,' ed. Hessels, p. 103: this may suggest an explanation for the earlier gloss aac color, Txts. 53, 535, which is copied in Wrt. Voc. ii. 14, 75), Txts. 93, 1749. Ác, Wrt. Voc. i. 285, 28: quercus vel ilex, 79, 73. Iung ác robur, 32, 28. Tó ðǽre gemearcodan ǽc, Cht. E. 355, 20. On thá radeludan ác; of ðǽre radeludan ǽc, C. D. B. iii. 44, 21. On ðǽ rúgan ǽc; of ðǽre ǽc . . . on ðá wón ác, 319, 5-7. Tó ðǽre mǽran ǽc; of ðǽre ǽc, C. D. iii. 78, 36. On ðá smédan ác; of ðǽre ǽc, 79, 20. On ðá greútan ác; of ðǽre ác, 121, 22. In fíf ácana weg; æfter ðám wege innon ðá líf ǽcc; of ðám ácan, 382, 19. On ðá hálgan ǽc, vi. 233, 32. On eahta ǽc, C. D. B. iii. 667, 32. v. mǽr-ác.

á-cæglod pegged, as if studded with pegs(?):—Ðá cwom sum deór of ðǽm fenne; wæs ðǽm deóre eall se hrycg ácæglod (cf. Angl. iv. 157 where atæglod is read) the back was as if all studded with pegs; the Latin has belua serrato tergo, Nar. 20, 26. [Cf. Cailis nine-pins, Rel. Ant. ii. 224. O. H. Ger. chegel paxillus, clavus.]

á-calan; p. -cól. Substitute: To die of cold:—Wið ðon ðe men ácale ðæt fel of ðám fótum in case the skin die off a man's feet with cold, Lch. ii. 6, 24. [Hungry and akale, Piers P. 18, 392.]

acan. Add:—Ǽced ðæt ofer eall, Lch. iii. 8, 21. Wið ðon ðe mon on heáfod ace, ii. 304, 25.

ác-cærn. Dele.

accent, es; m. Accent:—Bóceras . . . ámearkiaþ heora accentas . . . acutus accentus, ðæt ys gescyrpt accent; baria, ðæt ys hefig accent . . . circumflexus accentus, ðæt ys gebíged accent, Angl. viii. 333, 22-26.

accutian. v. á-cunnian.

ác-cynn. Add:—Wrt. Voc. ii. 49, 54.

ác-drenc. Add:—Ácdrenc cirta, Wrt. Voc. ii. 23, 5: 131, 28.

á-cealdian. Add:—Swá ðæt wearme wlacaþ ǽr hit eallunga ácealdige ita a calore per teporem reditur ad frigus, Past. 447, 6. Hé læg ácealdod on nyþeweardum limum, Hml. Th. i. 534, 10. [Acoaldest, A. R. 404. O. H. Ger. er-kalten.]

á-ceápian. Add: To buy off or out, where a result is obtained by

payment:—Hæþenne here him fram áceápian, C. D. B. iii. 75, 3. Búton hé him wille fǽhðe of áceápian unless he will buy off the feud from himself, Ll. Th. i. 150, 2. On ðá gerád ðæt hine náge nán man of tó áceápienne on the condition that no man is to buy him out of the land he holds, i. e. get it by paying a higher rent, Cht. Th. 151, 14. [Cf. O. H. Ger. er-kaufen redimere.] Cf. á-bycgan.

a-cearfan. Dele.

á-célan. Substitute: v. trans. To cool, make cool (lit. and fig.):—Ácéle ðú wealhát ísen, Lch. ii. 256, 14. Ðæt ic beó ácéled ut refrigerer, Ps. L. 38, 14. Ðæs þearfan ne bið þurst ácéled, Met. 7, 17. [Water akelþ alle þo þet hit drinkeþ, Misc. 30, 9. Þe anguysse akelde hym, R. Glouc. 442, 13. O. H. Ger. er-chuolen refrigerare, satiare.]

á-cennan. Add: I. to produce, &c., (1) where the product is of the same kind as the producer, (a) in reference to men or animals:—Tó ácennene ad propagandam, An. Ox. 1400. Ácennende wæs enixa est, Wrt. Voc. ii. 29, 38. Ácenned cretus, 21, 23. Ðæs ácendan engles mægen, Bl. H. 165, 5. His ácænnedan dohtor, Ap. Th. 24, 19. (b) of things:—Ácennede exorti (flores), An. Ox. 549. (2) where the product is different, (a) of men:—Ácende edidit (opera), An. Ox. 2316. (b) of things:—Ðone cwyld ðe se súðerna wind ácænd, Lch. iii. 276, 7. Wið ðá wunda ðe on ðám men beóð ácenned, i. 158, 12. II. to attribute, assign. v. cennan, II:—Hý betǽhton (ácendon, v l.) and benemdon hyra deófolgyldum ðá neát ðá ðe hý woldon syllan, Mart. 198, 11. [O. H. Ger. er-kennen gignere; agnoscere.] v. eft-, un-ácenned.

á-cennedlic. Add:—Ácennedlica nascentia, R. Ben. I. 70, 16. Ácennedlicum nativa, Wrt. Voc. ii. 59, 75.

á-cennedness. Add:—Gif gé willað ðone fruman sceaft geþencan, and ðone scippend, and siþþan eówer ælces ácennednesse si primordia vestra, auctoremque Deum spectes, Bt. 30, 2; F. 110, 18. v. eft-, frum-ácennedness; á-cenness.

á-cennend, es; m. A parent:—Ácennendum parentibus suis, Rtl. 197, 21.

á-cennedlic; adj. In the glosses:—Ácennendlicum genuina, An. Ox. 1243: nascentibus, 2419.

á-cenness, e; f. Birth, nativity:—Úres Dryhtnes ácenness, Ors. 1, 14; S. 58, 11. Geðence hé ðá ædelu ðǽre æfterran ácennesse, ðæt is on ðǽm fulluhte nobilitatem intimae regenerationis aspiciat, Past. 85, 15. Fram Crístes ácennesse, Chr. P. p. 2, 2. On ðǽm eahteþan dæge æfter his ácennysse, Shrn. 47, 21: 48, 9. v. á-cennedness.

á-cennicge (? cf. for suffix sealticge), an; f. A (female) parent:—Ácennic and hehstald genetricis et virginis, Rtl. 69, 9. Accunic genetricem, 51, 31.

á-ceócian. Add:—Se deófol gefrédde ðone angel Crístes godcundnysse, þurh ðá hé wæs tó deáðe áceócod, Hml. Th. i. 216, 16. [Adam þaroffe bot, and weard þarmide acheked, and þureh þat one snede weard al his ofspring acheked, O. E. Hml. ii. 181, 33. Cf. Icel. kok gullet, koka to gulp.]

á-ceócung rumination. v. preceding word.

á-ceorfan. Add: To cut away, cut down a tree:—Ic of ácorfe abscido, Ælfc. Gr. 172, 2: amputo, 277, 7. Wé scylda mid láre anweg áceorfað, Past. 167, 7. Ácearf abscindet, Ps. Spl. C. 76, 8. Hé his eáre of áceorf (amputavit), Mk. 14. 47. Se engel him ðá cennendan leomu of áceorf, Gr. D. 26, 27. Ðæt hé ealle ðá geþóhtas of his móde ne áceorfe, Past. 139, 26. Ðæt him man heáfod of áceorfe, Bl. H. 189, 33. Gif mon áceorfe án treów, Ll. Th. i. 130, 2. Ácorfan fram ússe heortan unclǽne geþóhtas, Shrn. 47, 23.

á-ceósan. Add: To pick out, select; á-coren; pp. choice, excellent, select, elect:—Hié ácuron endlefan þúsend monna, Ors. 2, 5; S. 78, 24. Ðára monna ðe hé him tó fultume hæfde ácoren (consilii causa legerat), 6, 2; S. 256, 2. Paulus wæs bodigend and ácoren láreów, Hml. A. 149, 148: 182, 43. On ðára ácorenra monna heortan in electorum cordibus, Past. 237, 21: 465, 10. On gódum and ácorenum módum bonis mentibus, Gr. D. 57, 1. Ðú wilt habban ealle fægere ðing and ácorene, Hml. Th. ii. 410, 19. [Aceas he him leorninchnihtes, O. E. Hml. i. 229, 1. O. Sax. á-kiosan: O. H. Ger. er-kiosan eligere.]

a-ceósung, dele. a-cerran. Substitute: á-cirran; ác-hál, dele.

ác-hangra, an; m. An oak wood on a slope:—On áchangran, C. D. v. 179, 28.

ác-holt, es; m. An oak wood:—Tó thám ácholte, C. D. B. iii. 44, 28. Ǽlce geáre fiftig fóðra and án hund of ðæs cinges ácholte, C. D. vi. 243, 13.

á-cígan. Add:—Fram deáþes ðrescwalde wæs ácígende mortis limite revocans, Bd. 5, 6; S. 618, 34. Tó giriord áceigid aron ad coenam vocati sunt, Rtl. 70, 37.

á-cirran; p. de To turn away, turn over, change:—Hú lange ácyrrest ðú (avertis) ansýne ðín fram mé?, Ps. Spl. T. 12, 1. Hé ácyrde convertit, hí ácyrdon averterunt, ácyrrendum avertente, Bl. Gl. Ácer anséne ðíne fram synnum mínum, Ps. L. 50, 11: Ps. Srt. 53, 7: 101, 3. Et nú ðás sídan ðe gehirsted is, and on ðú ða óþre, Shrn. 116, 3. Ácyraþ verte, Kent. Gl. 398. Ne ácerre ne avertaris, Mt. L. 5, 42. Of ácerred evertendam, Lk. p. 10, 4. Hé geseah his hors ácyrred fram his weðenheortnesse (a sua vesania immutatum), Gr. D. 78, 16. Synd calle ðás

eorðlican þing ácerrede, ðæt heó ne syndon swylce heó iu wǽron, Wlfst. 212, 1. [*Add passages from* á-cerran, -cyrran *in Dict.*]

**á-cirredness.** v. onweg-ácirredness.

**á-clǽnsian.** *Add:* I. *to cleanse* an object from impurity:— Hé mid hys worde hreóflan áclǽnsode, Hml. A. 152, 45. Ðá deádan árǽran and áclǽnsian ðá hreóflan, Hml. S. 16, 145. Horwum áfeormad, þearle áclǽnsad *sordibus ablutus*, Dom. L. 157. Mid ælmesdǽdum áclǽnsode, Hml. A. 142, 110. II. *to remove* impurity from an object:—Ðá nebcorn hé of ðám andwlitan áclǽnsað, Lch. i. 348, 26.

**ác-leác** (-leáf ?):—Ácleác *quernum*, Wrt. Voc. i. 285, 71.

**á-cleófan** *to split, cleave:*—iiii. fóðera áclofenas gauolwyda, Cht. Th. 145, 5.

**á-cleopian.** *Add:*—Ic ácliopie *ciebo*, Wrt. Voc. ii. 21, 52. Se gást his naman ácleopode and ámeldode, Gr. D. 200, 23.

**aclian.** *l.* áclian.

**á-clingan;** *p.* -clang; *pp.* -clungen To *wither:*—Áclungne *flaccentia, contracta*, Wrt. Voc. ii. 149, 22.

**ác-melu.** *Add:*—Wið tóðwyrmum, genim ácmela, Lch. ii. 50, 16.

**á-cnáwan** *to know:*—Ðæt hí ácnáwan, ðæt hí sylfe sculon beón gyldende *ut debitores se esse cognoscant*, Gr. D. 335, 21. þurh scere synd ácnáwene *per tonsuram noscuntur*, R. Ben. I. 10, 10. v. oncnáwan.

**á-cnycendlic.** v. un-ácnycendlic.

**á-cnyssan.** *Add:*—Út ácnysed hí synd *expulsi sunt*, P. Spl. 35, 13.

**á-cofrian.** *Add:*—Wunda opene raþe ácofriað (*exalant*), belocene þearle wundiað, Scint. 40, 12. [*Uorto acoueren his heale, A.R. 364. O.H.Ger.* ar-koborôn.]

**acol.** *l.* ácol.

**á-cólian.** *Add:* (1) lit.:—Ðæt se líg in him sylfum ácólode (*refrigesceret*), Gr. D. 48, 10. Seó hǽto ðæs fýres ácólode, Hml. S. 30, 451. Se ofon ácólode sóna, Shrn. 31, 22. Ðú díne fét lǽte in deáðe ácólian, Angl. xii. 508, 15. Gif wund on men ácólod sý, Lch. i. 194, 23. Of ðám swíðe ácólodan magan, oððe of ðám tó swíðe áhátodan, ii. 60, 18. (2) fig.:—Manegra lufu ácólað (*refrigescet*), Mt. 24, 12. Hé mid ealle ácólað (*frigescit*), Past. 447, 10. Ðý lǽs anda ákólige, 150, 1. Ácólige, Lch. iii. 442, 21. Ácólige (*tepescat*) bryne gástes, Hy. S. 26, 32. Ǽr ðæt fýr ðǽre willunge from ðám móde ácólie, Bd. 1, 27; M. 80, 31. Hí lǽtað ácólian ðá innecundan lufan, Past. 139, 8. Weard se sóða geleáfa ácólad, Wlfst. 270, 2. Bið manna lufu ácólod, Hml. Th. ii. 542, 26. Ic Godes þeówdóm ácóledne behreówwsige, C. D. iii. 349, 8.

**ácolmódian.** v. ge-ácolmódian.

**á-costnian;** *p.* ode To *try, prove:*—Ácostnod *exercitatus*, Wrt. Voc. i. 50, 21. Ácos[t]node *probatos*, Angl. xiii. 367, 33.

**á-cræftan.** *Add:*—Ealle ðá neáhþeóda ne mehton áþencean ne ácræftan hú hí ðǽm wífmonnum wiðstondan mehten, Ors. 1, 10; S. 46, 29.

**á-crammian.** *Add:*—Ácrammian (*printed* -crum-) *farcire*, Wrt. Voc. ii. 147, 43.

**á-crimman.** *Substitute:* To *cram, stuff:*—Ácrymman *farcire* (*stomachum*, Ald. 204), Wrt. Voc. ii. 96, 46: 37, 45. Ácrummen *farsa*, 108, 29: 35, 10: *farsa, i. impleta*, 147, 46. Tunnan wǽron ácrummene *cupae farciuntur* (Ald. 48), 82, 41: 34, 24: 37, 13.

**ác-rind.** *Add:*—Lch. ii. 49, 14.

**ác-tán,** es; *m. An oak-twig:*—Áctánas, Lch. ii. 322, 19.

**á-cuman.** *Add:* I. *intrans.* To *come:*—Hé ne mihte búton ðám hrófe ácuman *he could not get outside the house*, Hml. Th. ii. 184, 12. II. *trans.* (1) *to bear, bring:*—Hí þurh deófles lǽre ðá menniscnesse tó deáðe ácóman, Wlfst. 22, 23. (2) *to bear, support* trouble, &c.:—Hwá ácymð *quis sustinebit*, Bl. Gl. Ic ácom *certavi* (*bonum certamen*), An. Ox. 1349. Strang gyld, ðæt man hit uneáðe ácom (mihte ácuman, *v. l.*), Chr. 1040; P. 160, 30. Heó éhtnysse ácom, Hml. S. 7, 3. Hé ælc þing dó and ácume, R. Ben. 113, 10. Hé wítu ácóme, Hml. S. 23, 119. Ðæt hí ðone cyle ácóman, 11, 221. Ácuman (*impetum*) *ferre, perferre*, Kent. Gl. 1014: An. Ox. 7, 314. Ácuman *costnunge, ceáste, módleáste, graman*, Hml. Th. i. 4, 8: Hml. S. 7, 243: 9, 125: Hml. A. 100, 266. Úre ceaster is þearfende and ne mæg díne ædelborennesse ácuman, Ap. Th. 9, 8. Ðæt hé nánum men máre ne beóde ðonne hé ácuman mæge *ut auditoris sui animum ultra vires non trahat*, Past. 459, 7. Ne mæg ic ána ácuman (*sustinere*) eall ðis folc, Num. 11, 14.

**á-cumba.** *Add:*—Ácumb *stuppa*, Germ. 391, 20. Ácumba *putamina*, An. Ox. 3293: s[t]*uppea*, Wrt. Voc. ii. 94, 9. *Naptarum heordena* ácumba, 59, 48. Ácumban *putamine*, An. Ox. 3728. Ácuman *putamina*, 2, 187. Ðá hét se undergeréfa ontendan hí mid ácuman, Hml. S. 4, 333. v. ǽ-cambe.

**á-cumendlic.** *Add:* (1) *tolerable:*—Ðá sárnyssa on ðyssere worulde oððe hí sind leohte and ácumenlice, oððe hí sind wǽre and hrædlíce ðá sáwle út ádrǽfað, Hml. Th. i. 592, 13. Ús is ácumendlicere eówer gebelh ðonne Godes grama, 96, 5. (2) *possible:*—Ácumenlic *possibile*, R. Ben. I. 5, 14. Ealle þing synd ðám geleáffullan ácumendlice *omnia possibilia credenti*, Angl. vii. 30, 280. v. un-ácumendlic.

**á-cumendlicness.** *Add:*—Ácumendlicnys *facultas, i. possibilitas*, An. Ox. 3393.

**á-cunnan** *to accuse:*—Tó ácunnenne *ad excusandum*, Ps. Srt. 140, 4. Ðæt hí ná ne álýsað (*printed* -lýf-) ðá hálgan stówe áne fram heora synnum, ac eác hí beóð ácunnen (*printed* -cum-) ðý swýþor for ðám gylte ðǽre unálýfedlican bælde *quatenus eos sacra loca non liberent, sed etiam culpa temeritatis accuset*, Gr. D. 342, 2. v. oncunnan.

**á-cunnian.** *Add:* (1) *to put to the proof, try, test:*—Se ongebróhta teóna ácunnað (*probat*), húlic gehwilc man byþ, Gr. D. 47, 9. Ácunna mé *proba me*, Ps. Spl. C. 25, 2. Ácunnian *experiri*, Wrt. Voc. ii. 32, 68. Ácunnod (beón), 145, 50. Wæs ácunnad *temtabatur*, Mk. L. 1, 13. Bið ácunned *nititur*, Rtl. 59, 27. Folc byþ ácunnod (*experiretur*): Gr. D. 204, 13. Áfandod and ácunnod *experimentum habens*, 262, 5. Ácunnod on geleáfan, Hml. S. 31, 134. Gif úre crístendóm ne bið ácunnod, 4, 248. Be his regolum ácunnod *tried by its rules*, Lch. iii. 250, 7. (2) *to experience, ascertain by trial:*—Ǽlce dæge wé ácunniað ðæt ðǽre sóþfæstnysse word beóþ gefyllede, Gr. D. 51, 24. Swá hé hit oft ácunnad hæfde, Past. 375. I. (3) *where a test is successfully undergone, to prove:*—Ðá biscopas ácunnodan ðæt hió wǽren clǽne fram ðám synnum, Hml. A. 136, 663. Bið ácunnod *conprobatur*, Wrt. Voc. ii. 23, 41. Ðæt is ácunnod *it is an approved remedy*, Lch. ii. 44, 12. [*Cf. O. H. Ger.* ar-kunnên *experiri*.]

**á-cunnung,** e; *f. Experience, trial*; *experimentum*, Gr. D. 300, 26: 261, 8.

**acúsan;** *p.* te To *accuse:*—Ðæt hié acúste hine, Mt. L. 12, 10.

**á-cwacian;** *p.* ode To *quake, tremble:*—Ácwacode seó eorðe *contremuit terra*, Ps. Th. 17, 7. Eall se líchama ðæs cnihtes ácwacode (*contremuit*), Gr. D. 166, 12.

**á-cwealdness** (-cwelled-), e; *f. Slaughter:*—Sceáp ácwæðlednesse *oves occisionis*, Ps. Spl. T. 43, 25.

**á-cweccan.** *Add:* (1) *trans.:*—Eall ðæs scipes fæt wæs ácweht (*quassatum*), Gr. D. 248, 25. (2) *intrans.* To *quiver:*—Hé hine sylfne hetelíce ðýde, ðæt him on ácwehte, Hml. Th. i. 88, 10.

**á-cwelan.** *Add:*—Hit nǽfre ne ácwið, Bt. 13; F. 38, 29. Sihtríc ácwæl, Chr. 926; P. 107, 20. Ealle fiscas ácwǽlan for ðǽre hǽte, Ors. 5, 4; S. 226, 7. Gif ceorl ácwyle be libbendum wífe, Ll. Th. i. 30, 3. Ðý lǽs hié selfe ácwelen *ne ipsi moriantur*, Past. 371, 11. Ðæt hé þurh hungres scearpnesse ácwǽle, Hml. Th. i. 58, 32. Ðæs hearperes wíf sceolde ácwelan, Bt. 35, 6; F. 168, 4. Ðý lǽs hié selfe ácwelen ðǽr ðǽr hié ðá óðre lácniað, Past. 371, 11. Gif sié sió hond oðcweðen (ácwolon, *v. l.*), Ll. Th. i. 134, 17. Ðá ealdan sculan licgan heápmǽlum hungre ácwolene, Wlfst. 295, 16. Ðá óðre (hors) wǽron hungre ácwolen Chr. 894; P. 87, 25.

**á-cwellan.** *Add:*—Sume hí man hreówlíce ácwealde, Chr. 1036 P. 158, 27. Áqualdun *necabantur*, Txts. 81, 1376. Ácuoeldon (-cweledum, R.) *interficerent*, Jn. L. 12, 10. Sóðfæstne man ne ácwele ðú (*non occides*), Ll. Th. i. 54, 15. Gif ðú mæge, ácwel hine, Bl. H. 243 19. Ácwellað mé ðý deáðe ðe hé sylfa álýfe mé tó ácwyllane, Gr. D. 254, 8. Ðý lǽs hié hié selfe ácwellen *ne moriantur*, Past. 370, 11 Neron wolde hátan his fósterfæder ácwellan, Bt. 29, 2; F. 104, 19 Wilde deór willnaþ óþer tó ácwellenne, 39, 1; F. 212, 3. Tó ácuellanne *interficere*, Jn. L. 8, 37. Ácweald *peremptus*, Wrt. Voc. ii. 145, 20 Ácweald *trucidabatur*, An. Ox. 4869. Domicianus weard ácweald æt hi witena handum, Hml. Th. i. 60, 3. Sié ácwelled *moriatur*, Mt. L. 15, 4 Ácwealde *multate*, Wrt. Voc. ii. 57, 21. [*O. Sax.* á-quellian: *O. H. Ger.* ar-quellen *necare, interficere*.]

**á-cwencan.** *Add:* (1) of flame (lit. or fig.):—O3pryhte, þ á ácweinte *compressit* (*flammantis foci potestatem*), An. Ox. 4125. Ði ðe líg grǽdignysse ácwenton (*extinxerunt*), Scint. 112, 10. Fýr ácwencean, Ors. 4, 10; S. 200, 17. Ácwencan (-cwæncan, *v. l.*), Wlfst. 157 9. Ðá fýr wǽron ádwæscte and ácwencte, Nar. 23, 20. Brynas ácwencte *faculas restinctas*, An. Ox. 4391. (2) of other things:—Gesihða yfele ácwencð (*extinguit*) hungor, Scint. 56, 14. Se crístendóm ne mihte beón þanonford ácwænced nǽfre, Ll. Th. ii. 372, 20.

**á-cwencedlic,** ácweorna. v. un-ácwencedlíc, ácwern.

**á-cweorran.** *Add:*—Ácworren t oferfull *crapulatus*, Ps. L. 77, 65 Bl. Gl. v. mete-cweorra.

**ácwern.** *Add:*—Áqueorna, áquorna, ácurna *scirra*, Txts. 95, 1811 *Dispridulus* (= *aspriolus*) ácuaerna *vel sciron* (= *sciurus*), Hpt. 33, 250, 7 [*Ne oter ne acquerne, beuveyr ne sablyne, Misc.* 70, 358. *Cf. O. H. Ger.* eihhorn *spiriolus: Ger.* eichhorn: *Icel.* íkorni *squirrel.*]

**á-cweþan.** *Add:* (1) *to say, utter, declare:*—Hé ácwæð hine fram his hyldo *he proclaimed him out of his favour*, Gen. 304. Hí hogodon hú hí fácen and unriht ácwǽdon *cogitaverunt et locuti sunt nequitiam* Ps. Th. 72, 6. Hé ne mihte word ácweþan *neque ulla verba edere valebat* Gr. D. 183, 27. Ácueden is *dicitur*, Mt. L. 10, 2: *dictum est*, 5, 21 Ácueden wæs, 21, 4. Ácueðeð bið *dicitur*, Mk. p. 1, 19. Ácuoeðer wǽron *dicta erant*, Lk. L. 2, 18. Ácwoedoni *dicto*, Mt. L. 26, 30 (2) *to respond.* v. on-cweþan:—Wé lǽrað ðæt ænig mæssepreóst án: ne mæssige, ðæt hé næbbe þone þe him ácweðe, Ll. Th. ii. 250, 32

[Hornes aqueðen, Lay. 27444. *Goth.* uskwiþan þata waurd *diffamare sermonem.*]

**á-cwician.** *Add:* I. *intrans.* (1) *to become lively:*—þurh his (*the west wind*) blǽd ácuciað ealle eorðlice blǽda, Lch. iii. 274, 20. Se Crístendóm ácucode, Hml. S. 29, 330. Se ðe on óðrum dagum sleac wǽre tó gódnesse, he sceal on ðisum dagum ácucian on gódum þiggengum, Hml. Th. ii. 100, 23 (= Wlfst. 286, 9). Se seóca mann eft ácwicod *aeger redivivus,* Gr. D. 90, 7. (2) *to come to life:*—Ealle deáde menn mannes bearnes stefne gehýrað, and hí ealle ácuciað, Hml. S. 23, 385. On niht he forþférde, ac on dagunge he eft ácwicode, Bd. 5, 12; S. 627, 13. II. *trans.* *To make lively;* vivificare, Ps. Th. 118, 159. [*O. Sax.* á-quikôt *come to life.* Cf. *O. H. Ger.* arquicchen *recreare, vivificare.*]

**á-cwilman;** *p.* de *To kill:*—Hí hine bysmorlíce ácwylmdon, oftorfedon mid bánum, Chr. 1012; P. 142, 22 note. Selre ús ys ðæt we ús sylfe ofsleán, ðonne hig ús yfelum deáðe ácwylmon, Hml. A. 185, 138. He het Pilatum ðam fúlestan deáðe ácwylman, 190, 257. Titus and Vespasianus hig habbað yfelum deáðe ácwylmede, 191, 293.

**á-cwilmian;** *p.* ode *To suffer:*—Ðá ðá tó helle becumaþ, ne cumaþ hig nǽfre tó reste, ah ðǽr ácwylmiaþ mid sáule on ðám líchaman æfter dómes dæge, Wlfst. 220, 5. Sý he betǽht ðam deófle intó helle grunde and ðǽr ácwylmie, búte geswíce, C. D. iv. 107, 17.

**á-cwínan.** *Add:*—Ácwínan tabescere, Ps. L. 38, 12. v. cwínan.

**á-cwincan.** *Add:* (1) *of fire* (lit. or fig.):—Ðá candela ácwuncon, Hml. S. 35, 314. Ácwunce *delitesceret* (*scintilla*), Angl. xiii. 365, 9. Ðæt leóhtfæt sceolde ácwyncan, Hml. S. 23, 810. (2) *of other things:*—Ic ácwince *fatesco,* Hpt. Gl. 501, 21. Ácwincað *fatescunt,* i. *deficiunt* (*blandimenta*), An. Ox. 2384. Ácwanc *fatescit* (*caligo*), 3298. Á-cwi(n)cende *fatescens* (*umbra*), 4065.

**ác-wudu,** a; *m. An oak wood:*—Betwénan ácwudu and wulleleáh, C. D. vi. 218, 23.

**a-cwylan,** dele. **á-cyrran.** v. á-cirran.

**á-cýþan.** *Add:*—þeáh he ǽr yfel wolde, þonne nyste he hú he hit swá fullíce ácýðde, ǽr he fulne anweald hæfde, Bt. 16, 3; F. 56, 23. Sý on þone synnigan bróðor seó sóðe lufu ácýd and gefæstnod *confirmetur in eo karitas,* R. Ben. 51, 7. [*O. H. Ger.* ar-kunden *demonstrare.* Cf. *Goth.* us-kunþs *manifest.*]

**ád.** *Add:* [*m.* and] *n. A fire for burning the living or the dead:*—Aad *rogus,* Wrt. Voc. i. 39, 52. Ád, 85, 29. Ðæt ád wæs forburnen, Hml. S. 4, 336. Hine (*the Phenix*) ád beceð, Ph. 365. Bán, ádes láfe, 272. Ádes *rogi,* An. Ox. 3519. 'Eówer hrá bryttað lácende líg' ... þá wurdon hié deádes on wénan, ádes, El. 585. Se líg ne móste heora fex forswǽlan on þám áde (*the fiery furnace*), Hml. S. 16, 76. Hí hine tó ðǽm áde beran wyllað, Ors. 1, 1; S. 20, 27. Æt áde ... bánfatu bærnan, Beo. 1114. Ád *pyram,* An. Ox. 2455. Ád hladan, Gen. 2901. Ád unwáclicne, helmum behongen, hildebordum, beorhtum byrnum, Beo. 3138. Het mycel ád ontendan on ymbhwyrfte ðæs mǽdenes, Hml. S. 9, 117. Ád *incendia,* An. Ox. 3951. Áda *flammarum,* i. *rogorum,* 3554. Ontendnessum, ádum *incendiis,* 1432. Ádum *torribus,* i. *caminis,* 4025. [*O. L. Ger.* ēd *pyra.*]

**á-dǽlan.** *Add:*—He hine nǽfre ádǽlde fram þám incundan leóhte *interna nunquam luce destituit,* Gr. D. 274, 26. Ðæt is mycel syn tó geþencenne þe Gode ðæt ǽnig gód sié from him ádǽled, Bt. 34, 3; F. 138, 6. Ðone ðe (*John the Baptist*) swá feor from eallum monnum ádǽlæd wæs, Bl. H. 169, 6. [*O. Sax.* á-délian: *O. H. Ger.* ar-teilen *distinguere, decernere, judicare.*]

**a-deádan.** *Substitute:* **á-deádian;** *p.* ode *To become dead, lose vitality or feeling, become paralysed:*—Ádeádaþ *fatescit,* Wülck. Gl. 408, 6. Gif se líchama næfð mete, þonne forweornað he and ádeádað, Hml. Th. i. 168, 32. Wiþ springe ádeádedum ... Lǽcedómas be ádeádedum líce ... gif ðæt líc tó þon swíþe ádeádige ðæt þær gefelnes on ne sý, Lch. ii. 8, 7-14. Ðætte se milte ðám monnum ádeádige oþþe of sié, 242, 23. Wið ádeádodum magan and tácn ádeádodes magan, 158, 14. Sáwul góde ádeádod, Hml. Th. i. 160, 15. Hire lima ealle wurdon ádeádode, Hml. S. 31, 489.

**a-deáf.** *Dele.*

**á-deáfian.** *Add:*—Gif éaran willen ádeáfian oþþe yfel hlyst sié, Lch. ii. 40, 22.

**á-deáfung,** e; *f. A growing deaf:*—Wið éarena ádeáfunge, Lch. ii. 38, 24: 42, 6.

**adela.** *Add: also* adel, es (?); *m. Filth* (cf. addled); *a filthy place, sewer:*—Ðá swýn hí gecuron for ðǽre fúlnysse senlices adelan, Hml. Th. ii. 380, 8: 472, 7. His líchama læg on þám adelan, Hml. S. 5, 463. Ðæt cweartern weard áfylled mid fúlum adelan, 35, 244. Ic me sylfe on ðám adele forligeres besylede, 23 b, 342. Fýlþe, adelan *sentina,* An. Ox. 566: 1738. Adelan *cloacas,* 3416.

**á-delfan.** *Add:*—Ic út ádelfe *effodio,* Ælfc. Gr. 179, 11. (1) *to dig, dig out a pit:*—He ádylfð ðone pytt *lacum effodit,* Ps. Th. 7, 15. *Also* v. Dict. (2) *to dig up* the ground:—Hí ádulfon gehwylcne dǽl þæs wyrtgeardes þæs þe þǽr ǽr undolfen wæs *cuncta horti illius spatia quae inculta fuerant coluerunt,* Gr. D. 202, 3. Seó eorðe wæs swíðe

heard and he ne mihte heó ádelfan, Hml. S. 23 b, 768. (3) *to dig up a plant:*—Ádelf niþerweardne sláhðorn, Lch. ii. 92, 30: 230, 6. Ádelfe ompran, 78, 1. (4) *to dig out, pick out:*—Up ádelfað *effodiant* (*oculum corvi*), Kent. Gl. 1092. Ǽlcne pocc man sceall áweg ádelfan mid þorne, Lch. ii. 106, 4.

**adeliht.** *Add:*—þǽm adelihtum *cenosis,* Wrt. Voc. ii. 20, 16. Adelihtum, 97, 16. *Cenosas* þá fennigan meras, i. *paludes paludosas vel* adelihtan, fúlan *lutosas, fetidas, immundas,* 130, 68.

**adel-seáþ.** *Add:*—Adelseáþes *cloace,* An. Ox. 4290. Adelseáþe *latibulo,* 4754. Hí behýddon his líchaman on ánum adelseáðe, Hml. S. 5, 458. Adolseáðe, Shrn. 121, 25, 27. Adelseáþa *cloacorum,* An. Ox. 3319.

**á-déman.** *Add:*—Ðæt is seó stów on ðǽre syndon tó ádémanne et tó clǽnsianne monna sáula *ipse est locus in quo examinandae et castigandae sunt animae,* Bd. 5, 12; S. 630, 4. [*O. Sax.* á-dómian *to judge.*]

**á-deorcian.** *Substitute:* *To become dark, become tarnished:*—Sunne áþýstrað and móna ádeorcað, Wlfst. 92, 21. Nú hit (a)deo(rcað) *en tetrica aura est,* An. Ox. 56, 200. Hwý ðis gold ádeorcað (*obscuratum*)? Past. 133, 10.

**á-derian;** *p.* ede *To injure:*—Ðæt fýr hí áderian ne mihte, Gr. D. 219, 19.

**adesa.** *Add:*—Adesa *ascia,* Wrt. Voc. ii. 10, 20. A&sa *dolatorium, ascia,* Hpt. 33, 250, 10. Mid adesan *ascia,* Ps. Th. Spl. L. 76, 6. Eadesan, Ps. Srt. Adosan, Bd. 4, 3; M. 264, 6. He sceal habban æcse, adsan, bil, Angl. ix. 263, 1. [He ber acse and eadusan, Angl. x. 143, 90.]

**ád-fær.** *l.* ád-faru.

**ád-fynig,** es; *n. A damp place where a bonfire was made* (?):—Be eástan pyte tó ðám ealdan ádfini; of ðám finie, C. D. v. 194, 2. v. fynig.

**á-dídan.** *Add to* a-dýdan: (1) *to destroy,* &c.:—Ádýt *mortificat,* Ps. L. fol. 186, 6. Ǽlc man bið fordémed ðe hine sylfne ádýt, Hml. S. 19, 229. Ealle gesceafta ðæt wæter ádýdde, Hml. ii. 60, 11: 122, 17. Hig manega ádýddon (*ad mortes plurimorum*), Num. 21, 6. Se unlybba ne mihte hine ádýdan, Hml. Th. ii. 178, 12: Hml. S. 17, 176: Scrd. 22, 29. Weard se mǽsta dǽl mid hungre ádýd, Hml. Th. i. 404, 11: Hml. S. 17, 33: 4, 428. On ðám inran menn ádýdd, Hml. Th. i. 492, 4. Ðær ðá leahtras ðurh ðá bebodu ádýdde beón, ii. 210, 6: 218, 28. Ðá deádan ðe ðær ádýdde wǽron, Hml. A. 68, 77. Ádýdra *mortificatorum,* Ps. L. 78, 11. (2) *to deaden, make torpid; to mortify:*—Ys ádýdd flǽsc *mortificatur caro,* Scint. 47, 5. Treówa cuciað on lenctenes tíman ðe þurh wyntres cyle wurdon ádýdde, Hml. S. 12, 32. [*O. H. Ger.* ar-tôden *morti tradere, mortificare.*]

**á-dífan** *to render inaudible:*—Se organ ealle ðá býman oferhleóðrað and ealle ðá óðre he ádýfeð, Salm. K. 152, 13.

**á-dihtian.** v. fore-ádihtian.

**á-díl(i)gian.** *Add:* (1) *to destroy,* &c., *obliterate:*—Ic ádýlgie *diruo,* An. Ox. 18 b, 19. Hosp ádílegode *calumpniam explodit,* 1263. Hergung ádíligode Godes cyrican, Chr. 793; P. 57, 2. Hí woldon his gemynd on erðan ádílgian, 979; P. 123, 21. He wolde ðá geleáffullan of heora lande ádýlegian, Hml. S. 25, 543. Ádíligiende *obliterantes,* Wrt. Voc. ii. 62, 49. Ðæt hire mǽgðhád wurde mid hǽmede ádýlegod, Hml. S. 20, 10. (2) *where the process is remedial. to blot out* iniquity, &c.:—Gefelsode oððe ádílegode *expiavit,* Wrt. Voc. ii. 31, 24. Ðæt he ðá synne ádýlogode, Hml. S. 3, 635. Ádílega míne unrihtwísnessa, Bl. H. 87, 28. Ðæt hié mid gebedum ðá scylde ádíligien (*deleant*), Past. 397, 15. Nú man ǽlc yfel mæg mid góðe ádílgian (-dílegian, Hatt. MS.) *cum mala cuncta bonis sequentibus deluantur,* 348, 16. v. *also* a-dylegian *in Dict.*

**á-dimmian.** *Substitute:* *To become dim.* *Add:*—Him ádimmiað ðá eágan, Wlfst. 147, 30. Mid ðǽm gewunan ðára wóna weorca ðæt mód bið ádimmod, Past. 69, 7.

**ádl.** *Add:* [*f.* and] *n.:*—Ádl *morbus,* Wrt. Voc. i. 45, 60. Ne seó ádl ðám deáðe ne forestæpð, ac se sylfa deáð ðǽre ádle yldinge forhradað, Hml. Th. ii. 124, 10. Ádle *tabo,* Wrt. Voc. ii. 82, 55. He læg on ádle, Cht. E. 255, 2. He gehǽlde ðone cnapan fram ðǽre mycelan ádle (hreófan ádle, l. 7) *morbo elephantino,* Gr. D. 157, 1. Ádle and wóle *luem,* Wrt. Voc. ii. 53, 3. He ðæt ádl gestilde, Hml. Th. ii. 150, 11. Ádla *clades,* Wrt. Voc. ii. 19, 33. Ádle *valitudines,* 81, 54. Hefige ádlu, Lch. i. 262, 2. Uncúð ádlo (aiðulo, R.) *plagas,* Mk. L. 3, 10. v. circul-, fefor-, múþ-, þeór-, wæter-, wæterælf-, yfel-ádl.

**ádle.** *Add:*—Hú ðeós ádle scyle ende gesettan? Gú. 995. (Ádle Rä. 44, 4 *might be pl.*)

**ádlian.** *Add:* (1) *to ail,* &c.:—Lange he ádlað and áríst *diu languet et surget,* Lch. iii. 151, 6, 7, 23, 25. He ádlað and he swelt, 26: Scint. 41, 3. Míne eágan ádlodan (*languerunt*), Ps. L. 87, 10. Hǽlwende ádligendum líchaman, Hml. Th. i. 86, 22. (2) *to make ill, cause disease:*—Gást ádliende *spiritus pestilens,* Rtl. 121, 38. v. ge-ádlian.

**ádlig** (*dele* ádlíc *and* addle). *Add:*—Ðý lǽs ðe án ádlig sceáp ealle heorde besmíte, R. Ben. 53, 4. Mín ádlige cneów is yfele gehæfd, Hml. Th. ii. 134, 32. Tácn ádlies magan, Lch. ii. 174, 20. He ðone

his ádligum mǽge on ðone múð begeát, Hml. Th. ii. 150, 10. Gesáwon hí hine ádligne, 24, 28. Middaneard ádligne *mundum languidum*, Hy. S. 34, 24. Lifre ádlige *jecur morbidum*, 29, 23. Wǽron geǽlede fela ádlige menn, Hml. S. 20, 114. Unhálra l ádligra *languentium*, Jn. L. R. 5, 3. Ádligum dǽdum *morbidis actibus*, R. Ben. I. 12, 9. Ádlige *valitudinarios*, An. Ox. 4938. Hí settað heora handa ofer ádlige men and him bið tela, Hml. Th. i. 304, 22. v. fót-ádlig.

**ádlung**, e; f. *Illness, ailment, disease:*—Sóðlíce hé sylf ætbrǽd úre ádlunga, and úre sárnyssa hé sylf ábær *vere languores nostros ipse tulit, et dolores nostros ipse portavit*, Hml. Th. i. 122, 31.

**á-dón.** *Dele* Ælfc. T. 5, 25: Gen. 7, 23: 9, 11, *and add: with words further marking removal*, (1) fram:—Ic ádyde (*abstuli*) hosp fram eówrum cynne, Jos. 5, 9. Ádoo from ðé ðá byrðenne, Past. 225, 11. Uton fácen from úrum heortum ádoon, Bl. H. 95, 27. Ðæt ǽlc stán ne sý fram óþrum ádón, 79, 1. From milcum ádóen *ablactatus*, Bl. Gl. From ádóenre *remota*, Wrt. Voc. ii. 119, 1. (2) of:—Hé ádéð eów of ðisse worulde, Bt. 19; F. 70, 17. Ðú ádydes ðá bearwas of londe, Past. 355, 11. Tó tácne ðæt hé hié of ðeówdóme dyde (ádyde, *v. l.*) *ob detersam servitutem*, Ors. 4, 11; S. 204, 9. Hé ádyde Húnas of Galliam *Gallias a barbaris occupatas liberavit*, 6, 28; S. 278, 8. Gif man bán of ádó, Ll. Th. i. 98, 13. Tó ádóanne of hine *ad deponendum eum*, Mk. L. 15, 36. (3) onweg:—Hé ádyde ðæt heáfod onweg, Bl. H. 183, 24. Onweg ádónum *dempto*, Wrt. Voc. ii. 27, 66. (4) up:—Ðæt hé hine up ádyde *that he should take up the body from the tomb*, Hml. S. 21, 138. Hædde hét his líchoman up ádón and lǽdon tó Wintonceastre (*translatus in Ventam civitatem*), Bd. 3, 7; S. 529, 24. Ðanon (*from hell*) ne byð ǽnig upp ádón, Nar. 50, 24. (5) út. v. út, I. 4:—Út ádyde *excepit*, Wrt. Voc. ii. 32, 33. Hí ðá fýlde ádydon út, Hml. S. 25, 381. Him hét se cyng ðá eágan út ádón, Chr. 1096; P. 232, 22.

**á-drǽdan.** *Add:*—Ic ádrǽde, ðæt . . , Wlfst. 297, 19. Hé him Godes dómes ádrǽd, Hml. A. 196, 35. Hig ádrǽdon him *timuerunt*, Lk. 8, 35. Ðæt hé dómdæg ádrǽdæ, Wlfst. 308, 16. v. on-drǽdan.

**á-drǽfan.** *Add:*—Leáse welan hí sind, for ðan ðe hí ne ádrǽfað úre sáule hafenleáste, Hml. Th. ii. 88, 26. Hé ðone deófol ádrǽfde of ðám preúste, 170, 3: i. 406, 1. Drihten ðá cýpan út ádrǽfde, 410, 35: Chr. 1097; P. 234, 13. Hiene Cynewulf on Andred ádrǽfde, 755; P. 46, 22. Hí ðone cyning ofer sǽ ádrǽfdon, 874; P. 72, 26: 878; P. 74, 26. Ádrǽf *repelle*, Hy. S. 23, 35. Ádrǽfen *detrudere*, An. Ox. 4053. Út ádrǽfende *exterminans*, 4079. Ádrǽfed *explodatur*, 814. Wǽre ádrǽfed *arceretur, pulsetur*, 4886. Út ádrǽfed *eliminatus* i. *expulsus*, 822. Ádrǽfedne *pulsum*, i. *ejectum*, 276. Be him libbendum and of ádrǽfdum, Chr. 1053; P. 184, 13.

**á-dragan;** p. -dróg *To draw out:*—Malcus his swurd ádróh, Hml. A. 180, 356. [Aldolf his sweord adroh, Lay. 16487. Adraweth 3oure suerdes, R. Glouc. 361.]

**á-drencan.** *Add:* (1) where the subject is a person:—Hí man on sǽ ádrencte, Hml. S. 28, 127. Brettas hié bedrífon út on áne eá and monige ádrencton, Chr. 890; P. 82, 14. Hí ádrengton má ðonne ǽnig man wiste tó tellanne, 1087; P. 224, 19. Hí hig sylfe ádrencton, Jud. p. 162, 27. (2) where the subject is the water:—Án sǽflód ðá men ádrencte, Ors. 2, 5; S. 90, 21. Sǽflód ádrencte feala túna, Chr. 1014; P. 145, 29. Ðǽre sǽ wæteru hig ádrencton, Deut. 11, 4. Hé lét flód ádrencan eal, Wlfst. 10, 8. (3) subject uncertain:—Ðǽr wæs ðæs folces mycel ádrenct, Chr. 1066; P. 196, 35. Ádrenced, Exod. 458. Ádreintum *suffocato*, An. Ox. 832.

**á-dreógan.** *Add:* I. to bear off:—Ic ádreóge *digero*, An. Ox. 18 b, 22. I a. with the idea of pain:—Hárnessa ádreóhende *canos* (*suos*) *ducentes* (*ad inferos*), 3368. I b. to bear what is painful, *suffer, endure:*—Ic ádreáh mycel broc, Bl. H. 175, 12. Wylm ádráh *fervorem exegit*, An. Ox. 2512. Ádreógende *laturus* (cf. *laturus, passurus*, 78, 31), ádreág *laturae*, Wrt. Voc. ii. 50, 1, 2. Ðá þrowunga ðe hé ádreág æt ðæm folce, Bl. H. 97, 16. Bysmra ádreógan, 15, 34. I c. to bear with, tolerate:—Ic bidde ðé, ðæt ðú mé geþyldelíce ábere and ádreoge, Gr. D. 267, 17. Ic wundrige hú seó sǽ ádruge míne unrihtlican lustas, Hml. S. 23 b, 385. Ðær beóþ geþyldelíce tó ádreóganne tá yfian men, Gr. D. 108, 33. II. to pass, spend time:—Se mid wiglungum his líf ádríhð, Hml. Th. i. 102, 15. Ná lang líf heo ádrýcd, Lch. iii. 190, 8. Ádreáh *transegit*, i. *percurrit* (*horas*), An. Ox. 1944. Hé þurhwacole niht búton slǽpe ádreáh, Hml. Th. i. 86, 17. Hú sárig ðá twelf mónað ádreáh, 566, 10. Hé ádreáh his líf on dyslicum weorcum, Hml. S. 26, 245. Hí ealne ðone dæg on Godes herungum ádrugon, Hml. Th. ii. 182, 28. Swá stemmǽlum on þám þi wucan ádreógan (*printed* adreosan, *with note 's of unusual shape'; v. An. Ox. 1944 supra*) *sic alternati in eo ebdomadam percurra(n)t*, Angl. xiii. 385, 280. Líf ádreógan *vitam ducere*, Coll. M. 28, 27. Be Maures dihte ádreógan his líf, Hml. S. 6, 221. III. to carry out, perform:—Ádreáh láre gessi *studium*, An. Ox. 2011. Ádrēg *agit*, Germ. 388, 22. Ádrogenum máne *peracto flagitio*, Scint. 236, 2.

**á-dreógendlic** glosses agendus, gerendus:—Seó átreógenlíce *agenda*, R. Ben. I. 37, 12. Lifes ádreógen(d)lices *vite gerende*, Hy. S. 103, 3.

**á-dreósan**, Angl. xiii. 385, 280. v. á-dreógan, II.

**á-drífan.** *Add:* I. to drive, cause to move (with violence):—Heó geseh niman hyre cild, and ádrífan ísene næglas þurh ðá handa, Hml. Th. i. 146, 11. II. to drive off, drive away:—Ic ádrífe *depellar*, Wrt. Voc. ii. 27, 68. Hé ðá herelǽfe tó his lande ádráf, Ælfc. T. 9, 38. Hí ádrifon *abigerant*, An. Ox. 3654. Hié ðone cyning norþ ofer Temese ádrifon, Chr. 823; P. 60, 15. Ádrífende *pellentes*, Wrt. Voc. ii. 92, 63. Ádrifen, bewered wǽre *arceretur*, 3, 52. Ádrifen *elim(in)atus*, 76, 58. Ádrifene *eliminate*, 96, 17. Hǽlde hine Penda ádrífenne, Chr. 658; P. 32, 6. II a. with words further marking removal, (1) áweg:—Hí hine áweg ádrifon, Bl. H. 221, 22: Chr. 1086; P. 222, 3. Is áweg ádrifen *explodatur*, Wrt. Voc. ii. 32, 71. (2) fram:—Ðú mé ádrífest from earde nímum, Gen. Gif gé mé fram ádrýfaþ (*expellitis*), Coll. M. 29, 23. Ðú ús ádrífe fram *repulisti nos*, Ps. Th. 107, 10. Se fugel ádráf ealle ðá óþre fuglas fram ðǽm líchoman, Shrn. 57, 3. Fram ádreofon *abegerunt*, Wrt. Voc. ii. 82, 73. Ádríf hí fram ðé, Bt. 7, 2; F. 18, 9. Hí sýn fram ðínre handa ádrífene *de manu tua expulsa sunt*, Ps. Th. 87, 5. (3) heonon:—Ðá man mæg mid fæstenum heonon ádrífan, Dóm. L. 30, 46. (4) of:—Hé his bróðer ádráf of ðeðle, Chr. 380; P. 11, 10: Sat. 201: Bo. 18. Gif man folan of ádrífe, Ll. Th. i. 72, 1. Ðæt hé ðæt deófol of men ádrífe, Bl. H. 43, 23. Hí woldon heora kynehláford of his cyneríce ádrífan, Chr. 1075; P. 211, 20: Sat. 174. Se frumstól ðe hié of ádrifen wurdon, Gen. 964. (5) út:—Út ádriofan *arcebant*, Wrt. Voc. ii. 9, 28. Ðá heretohan ðe hí ǽr út ádrifon, hí woldan eft út ádrífan for hiora ofermēttum, Bt. 16, 2; F. 50, 11. Yð út feor ádráf on Wendelsǽ wígendra scola, Met. 26, 30. Ðæt Egypti ádrifen Moyses út, Ors. 1, 5; S. 34, 16. Út ádrífende *explodens*, An. Ox. 17, 22. Út ádrifenum *explosis*, út ádrífenre *explosa*, Wrt. Voc. ii. 32, 14, 15. [*Goth.* us-dreiban: *O. H. Ger.* ar-trîban *expellere, repudiare*.]

**á-drifenness**, -drígan. v. onweg-ádrifenness, á-drýgan.

**á-drincan.** *Add:* I. to drink up, quench thirst:—Ic of ádrince *ebibo*, Ælfc. Gr. 275, 9. Hwǽr hié wæteres hæfden þæt hié mehten him þurst of ádrincan, Ors. 2, 5; S. 80, 10. II. to be drowned; of ships, to be sunk:—Manega menn ádrincað on ánum dæge tógædere, ðe on mislicum tídum tó middanearde cómon, Hml. S. 5, 275. Eall ðæt mancynnes elles wæs, eall hit ádranc, Wlfst. 10, 13. On ðǽre sǽ ádranc Pharao, Hml. Th. ii. 200, 17: Chr. 933; P. 107, 4. Heora feala ádruncon, 794; P. 57, 14: Ors. 1, 7; S. 38, 34. Ðeáh ðe hié ǽr eorþe bewrigen hæfde, oððe on wætere ádruncan, Bl. H. 95, 15. Ðǽr wearþ monig mon ofslægen and ádruncen, Chr. 853; P. 66, 2: Ors. 2, 5; S. 82, 27. Heora folces wæs V M ofslagen, and heora scipa xxx gesangen, and iiii and án hund ádruncen . . . and Rómana scipa ix ádruncen, 4, 6; S. 176, 12–14. [Þene put þ hit adronc inne, A. R. 58. In ane watere heo adronken, Lay. 2490. Þat water þer Abren was adrunken, 2497. In þe se adronke he was, R. Glouc. 430. *O. H. Ger.* ar-trinkan to be drowned; ar-trunken crapulatus (a vino): Ger. er-trinken.]

**á-drúgian**, -drúwian. *Add:* I. intrans. To dry up, (1) of material containing moisture (lit. and fig.):—Ádrúgað (*aruit*) heorte mín, Ps. Srt. 101, 5. Wǽstmas ádrúgiaþ, Bl. H. 59, 3. Ádrúgade *exaruit*, Mk. R. 4, 6. Ðá wǽtan hrægel ádrugedon, Bd. 5, 12; S. 631, 25. Míne bán ádrúchedon, Ps. L. 101, 4. Hig ádrúwodon *nestuaverunt*, Mt. 13, 6. Ádrúwodon ðá hláfas swá swá stán, Hml. S. 23 b, 520. Oþ ðæt ðæt dolh ádrúgie, Lch. ii. 208, 24. Ðeáh wé treówu for hrædlíce tó ðǽm weorce dón ne mægen for grénnesse ǽr ðǽm ðe hí ádrúgien *tamen non repente in fabrica ponitur lignum, ut prius vitiosa sigu viridita exsiccetur*, Past. 445, 2. Ðonne lungena wel ádrugode synd, Lch. ii 216, 8. (2) of fluids:—Sǽ ádrúgiaþ, Bl. H. 91, 27. Ádrúwode seó sǽ xxx. míla, Shrn. 150, 21. Seó eá ádrúwode him ætforan, Hml. S. 19 96. Ǽrþan þe ðæt flód mihte beón ádrúwod, Angl. vii. 36, 336. II. trans.:—Ádrúgie *desiccet*, Wrt. Voc. ii. 139, 27. v. un-ádrúgod.

**á-drýgan.** *Add: to dry up* (lit. and fig.). (1) to extract the moisture from material:—Hé ðá miltan ádríged, Lch. i. 334, 24. Gást unrót ádrígd (*exsiccat*) bánu, Scint. 167, 11. Hé ealle ðá costunga o his ágnum líchoman ádrígde *omni illa tentatione carnis caruit*, Gr. D 190, 24. Hit ádríg, Lch. i. 332, 26. Ádríg tó duste, ii. 144, 1. Genim ácmistel and ádríge, 88, 5. Ádríged on réce, 216, 8. Swá swá treówu swíður ádrýgde blóð on eorðan *quo plus in infimis humor excoquitur* Past. 445, 3. (2) to dry up a fluid:—Ðú ádrýgdes (*exsiccasti*) flódas Ps. Srt. 73, 15. Hé ðone Reádan Sǽ ádrígde, Ors. 1, 7; S. 38, 29 Heortes horn hafað mægen ǽlcne wǽtan tó ádrígenne, i. 334, 3 (3) to dry up moisture on material, wipe off:—Hé ðáre hýde ádrígde *abstergit*, Kent. Gl 764. Seó hand ðínre sprǽce ádrígde (*tersit*) fram mé ðone tweón, Gr. D 150, 25. Hé ðǽre hýde giocðan of ádrýgde, Past. 71, 11. Ádrýg horu *absterge sordes*, Hy. S. 23, 3. Ǽlc mon ádrýge of ðerra monna móde ðone wénan be mán ǽlces yfeles, Past. 451, 22. Ðæt hé mæge ádrýggean (-drýgean, Hatt. MS.) (*tergat*) of monna heortan ðæt fúlsié, 74, 21. Hát gefeormian mín blód and ðonon ádrýgan, Bl. H. 183 27. (4) to dry material on which there is moisture, wipe dry:—Se wísdóm ádrígde mínes módes eágan, Bt. 3, 1; F. 4, 27.

á-drysendlic. v. un-ádrysendlic.

á-drysnan; p. ede To extinguish, repress:—Unsmyltnise ádrysnede tempestatem compescens, Mk. p. 3, 6. Ðæt fýr ne bið ádrysned (non extinguitur), Mk. L. 9, 46 : Rtl. 38, 23. v. un-ádrysnende.

á-drysnendlic, adsa. v. un-ádrysnendlic, adesa.

á-dumbian. Add:—On ðám dóme ádumbiað ða ýdelan lyffeteras, Hml. Th. ii. 570, 35. 'Beó ðú dumb' . . . And hé ða ádumbode, i. 202, 7. Wið ðon ðe wíf færunga ádumbige, Lch. iii. 58, 16. Hét hé ðone hund ádumbian, Hml. S. 31, 1133. Se fæder wæs ádumbod, Hml. Th. i. 352, 32. Hí ealle wurdon ádumbode, ii. 486, 11.

á-dún, -dúne (-a). Add : (1) á-dún:—Feall nú ádún, Hml. Th. i. 166, 19 : Hml. S. 11, 108. Hé ofdræd slóh ádún, 23. 718. (2) á-dúne (-a):—Feól hé ádúne, Hml. Th. 1, 316, 29. Hí lédon heora wǽpna ádúne, Hml. S. 29, 171. Clif áscoren rihte ádúne, 31, 316. Heáfod ádúne gewended, Bl. H. 173, 4. Ásend ðeh ádúna (deorsum), Lk. L. 4, 9. Cumað ádúne of heofonum tácn, Wlfst. 137, 12. Hé his gesyhða ádúna on eorðan besette, R. Ben. 31, 8. Úre blód fleóð tó úrum fótum ádúne, Hml. S. 11, 191. Doppettan ádúne tó grunde, Hml. Th. ii. 516, 7. v. of-dúne.

á-dustrian to imprecate (?):—Ða ongann hé ádustriga (ʒustriga, R.) tunc coepit detestari, Mt. L. 26, 74. Cf. ʒustrungæ abominationem, Mt. R. 24, 15.

á-dwǽscan. Add : I. to extinguish fire, light (lit. or fig.):— Ðæt wæter and seó eorþe eallunga ne ádwǽsceþ ðæt fýr, Bt. 33, 4 ; F. 130, 14. Ðǽm gelícost ðe mon drýpe ænne eles dropan on án micel fýr, and þence hit mid ðǽm ádwǽscan ; ðonne is wén, swá micle swíðor swá hé þencð ðæt hé hit ádwǽsce, ðæt hé hit swá micle swíðor ontýdre, Ors. 4, 7 ; S. 182, 25. Sunne wearð ádwǽsced, Cri. 1133. Móna biþ ádwǽsced, Bl. H. 93, 18 : Angl. viii. 315, 38. Ádwǽscedum extirpatis (fomitibus), An. Ox. 1134. II. to put an end to, put down, suppress a practice, doctrine, &c. :—Seó sunne ðá þeostre ádwǽscþ, Bt. 4 ; F. 6, 33. Swá swá wæter ádwǽscð fýr, swá ádwǽscð seó ælmysse synna, Hml. Th. ii. 106, 7. Hié ádwǽscað ðá sibbe, Past. 359, 22. Ðæt hé ðǽra gedwolmanna gedyrstignesse ádwǽsce, Hml. Th. i. 70, 7 : Hml. S. 26, 13. Hé heora goda offrunga ádwǽste, 15, 34. Drýcræft ádwǽscan, 14, 54 : 23, 362 : 37, 13. Bodunge ádwǽscan, Hml. i. 586, 33. III. to put down, suppress, destroy a person:—God ðá hǽðenan ðeóda ætforan heora gesihðum eallunga ádwǽscte, Hml. Th. i. 46, 20. Ic beóde ðæt hé ðæne unrihtwísan tó rihte gebíge gyf hé mæge ; gyf hé ne mæge, ðonne wille ic ðæt hé hine on earde ádwǽsce, oððe út of earde ádrǽfe, Cht. E. 230, 25. Se preóst is ádwǽsced (he was killed by a fall), Hml. Th. ii. 164, 8. Ádwǽsced explodatur i. deleatur (draco), An. Ox. 814. v. un-ádwǽsced.

á-dwǽscedlic, -dwǽscendlic. v. un-ádwǽscedlic, -ádwǽscendlic.

á-dwelian. Dele -dwealde, -dweald, and add : I. intrans. To wander, stray:—Nýtenu hé hét faran áweg tó ðǽre eówode ðe hí of ádwelodon, Hml. Th. ii. 514, 23. Ðá hrægel from hǽlo gife ne ádweledon indumenta a gratia curandi non vacarunt, Bd. 4, 31 ; S. 611, 6. II. trans. (in Dict.) v. next word.

á-dwellan ; p. -dwealde ; pp. -dweald. I. to lead astray, seduce :—Ðá ðe galdorcræftas begangað and mid ðǽm unwære men beswícaþ and ádwellaþ, Bl. H. 61, 24. Hý deófol ádwealde, Wlfst. 11, 8. Ðá beóð ádwealde and þurh deófol beswícene, 5, 7. II. to retard, impede, obstruct, hinder :—Ðæt hé his láre ðurh drýcræft ádwellan sceolde, Hml. Th. ii. 412, 26. [Cf. O. H. Ger. ar-twelan torpere ; ar-twellen to delay (intrans.).]

á-dwínan. Add :—Ðá nigontýne geár gedóð ðæt án dæg mid ðǽre nihte ádwínð, and swylce ic swá cwede tó náhte gewyrð, Angl. viii. 308, 32. Ádwínendan tabida, Txts. 104, 1044.

a-dýdan, -dylegian, -dylf. v. á-dídan, -díligian, -delfan.

á-dysigian ; p. ode To become foolish :—Manna mód syndon earmlíce áþýstrode and ádysgode, Wlfst. 185, 12.

æ. Omit the remarks on this letter.

ǽ. Add : ǽ(w) ; g. d. ac. ǽ, ǽe, ǽwe (g. ǽs in N. Gospels) ; g. pl. ǽa : f. and n. (? in Bd. 4, 5 ; S. 573, 17). I. law, &c. :—Ðis is seó ǽ (lex) ðe Moises foresette, Deut. 4, 44 : Past. 5, 23. Ðætte ænigum folce his ǽgenu ǽ gelícade tó healdenne, Ors. 5, 15 ; S. 250, 19. Ǽew Dryhtnes, Ps. Srt. 18, 8. Ðǽre ǽ (ǽs, L.) láreów, Mt. 22, 35. Ǽwe juris, Wrt. Voc. ii. 45, 18. Ðǽre ealdan ǽwe veteris legis, An. Ox. 40, 20. Ðæt hé of ðǽre ǽwe ne cerre, Past. 175, 5 : 181, 1 : 439, 30. Ace legem, Ps. Srt. 26, 11. Ǽa legum, Germ. 388, 16. Ǽwum cerimoniis, Hpt. xxxiii. 239, 26. II. matrimony:—Se hálga wer ðǽre wíflufan wordum stýrde unryhtre ǽ, Jul. 297. Lufiað eówere wíf on ǽwe . . . and healdað eówere ǽwe, Hml. Th. ii. 322, 26. Wíf ðæt him mid rihtre ǽ (rihtum ǽwe, v. l.) forgifen sí, Bd. 4, 5 ; S. 573, 17. Be ðám ðe ǽwe brecað ðe eo qui adulterat, Ll. Th. ii. 180, 12. Ic lǽrde weras ðæt hí heora ǽwe heóldon, Hml. Th. i. 378, 25 : ii. 222, 18. See also ǽw in Dict., and take ǽ life under this word. v. æfter-, sundor-, tungol-ǽ ; cyric-, mægden-, riht-ǽw.

ǽ-bǽr. Substitute : ǽ-bǽre (-bére) ; adj. Brought to light (of the criminal or the crime where guilt is manifest), notorious, proved :—

Æbǽre (-bére) morð (apertum murdrum, Lat. Vers.), Ll. Th. i. 410, 5. Ábǽre, Wlfst. 274, 24. Se ǽbǽra þeóf (fur probatus, Lat. Vers.), Ll. Th. i. 390, 27. Æbǽra (-bǽra), 268, 22. Æbǽre hórcwénan, 172, 21. Æbǽre manslagan, 324, 11. Æbǽre (-bére) manswícan, Wlfst. 46, 27. Ǽbǽre apostatan, 165, 28. ¶ Æbǽre þeóf occurs in a list of privileges granted to a monastery :—On eallan þingan . . . ðe ðǽr mid rihte tó gebyrað. mid fyrdwíte and fyhtwíte and ǽbǽre þeóf and gridbryce and forsteall and hámsócne, C. D. iv. 222, 23. [All þeʒʒre æbǽre unnþannkess, Orm. 7189. Þu ebure (ebare, 2nd MS.) sot, Lay. 2271. Ðat eber file, C. M. 813. O. Frs. ábere, áubere.] v. á-bǽran. See also ebere morþ in Dict.

ǽ-béc, -ber, -bilignes. v. ǽ-bóc, -bǽre, -byligness. In ǽ-blǽcnys read Lchdm. i.

ǽ-blǽcung. v. á-blǽcung.

ǽ-blǽte (?) ; adj. Livid, pale :—On ǽblǽtan (-blǽcan ? v. ǽ-blǽce) and w[litan] albo vultu, An. Ox. 46, 19. v. blát.

æ-blǽc. Substitute : ǽ-blǽce ; adj. Pallid, pale, livid :—Æblǽce decolor, pallidus, Germ. 392, 69 : pallidus, An. Ox. 1868. On plúm-federum hé lið ac þǽhweðere oft ǽblǽce, E. Stud. viii. 473, 19. Hé wearð geangsumod, and ǽblǽce on nebbe cwæþ, Hml. S. 37, 213. Ðá áxode hé mid ǽblǽcum andwlitan his réðan cwelleras, 129. Be hiora híwe . . . hí beóð ǽblǽce, Lch. ii. 232, 2.

ǽ-bóc book of law :—Æbéc libri juris, Wrt. Voc. ii. 53, 78.

ǽ-bod. Add : A statute : Æbod pragma, Wrt. Voc. i. 20, 34. Æbodas, 35.

ǽ-brece (ǽw-, eáw-) ; adj. Law-breaking. (1) sacrilegious, impious:— Gehýrde gé ðǽra deófla frófor on ðisum eáwbrǽcum ðe úre godas geyrsode ne ondrǽt ? Hml. Th. i. 426, 20. (2) adulterous :—Ðæt se wer gewítnað on ǽwbrǽcum wífe, ðæt wrecð God on ǽwbrǽcum were, 378, 26. Eáwbrǽcum, ii. 322, 18. Be ðám ðe ǽwe brecað oððe ǽwbrǽce (adulteram) habbað, Ll. Th. ii. 180, 12.

ǽ-brec. Dele.

ǽ-breca (ǽw-breca, q. v. in Dict.), an ; m. An adulterer : of a man in orders, one who does not observe celibacy :—Se man ðe his rihtǽwe forlǽt and óðer wíf nimð, hé bið ǽwbreca (adulter), Ll. Th. ii. 184, 22. Ðá ǽwbrecan ðe þurh heálicne hád ciricǽwe underféngan, and syððan ðæt ábrǽcan, 334, 14. Æwbrecan and ðá fúlan forlegenan, Wlfst. 26, 15. v. ǽ-bryce.

ǽ-brecþ, e ; f. Sacrilege :—Þurh ǽbrecþe per sacrilegium, Ps. L. fol. 182 b.

æbreda. v. æfreda.

ǽ-brucol ; adj. Sacrilegious :—Æbrucolon sacrilegis, Germ. 402, 86.

ǽ-bryce (ǽw-bryce, q. v. in Dict.):—Adultery : of a churchman, neglect of celibacy :—Ðá ðe on sinscipe wuniað and heora ǽwe healdað búton ǽwbryce, Hml. A. 21, 178. Ðá ðe ǽwbryce ne wyrceað, 19, 140. Se ðe ofer his ǽwe hǽmð, hé is forlír ðurh his ǽwbryce, Hml. Th. ii. 208, 17. Nis nánum weóiorðþéne álýfed ðæt hé wífian móte . . . nú is þeáh ðǽra calles tó fela ðe ðone ǽwbryce wyrcað, Ll. Th. ii. 334, 17, 22. Scyldað eów wið ǽwbrycas (-brecas, v. l.), Wlfst. 40, 12. Æwbricas, 130, 4.

æbs. Substitute : Æbs, æps, æspe (from confusion with æspe aspen), a fir-tree :—Æps (æbs v. l.) abies, Ælfc. Gr. Z. 14, 11 : 52, 14. Æps abies, Wrt. Voc. i. 80, 24. Etspe ii. 98, 14. Æspe, 4, 10. [From Latin.]

ǽ-bylg ; m. :—Gexfsan ǽbylg Godes to excite God's anger, Gú. 1211.

ǽ-bylga, an ; m. Anger :—Æbylgan indignationem, Ps. L. 77, 49.

ǽ-bylgan, -byligan, -bylian. Add :—Æbylgað exasperant, Ps. Spl. 65, 6. Æbiliaþ, 67, 7. v. ge-ǽbyl(i)gan.

ǽ-byl(i)gness. Add :—Æbylgnis indignatio, Bl. Gl. Of ðám leahtre (weámét) cymð hreám, and ǽbylgnes, Hml. Th. ii. 220, 14. Hé hí mid gedréfedre ǽbilignysse him fram ádráf, 24, 30 : Ap. Th. 4, 10. Racha getácnað ǽbylignysse oððe yrre, Ælfc. Gr. Z. 279, 18. Æbilignysse, 280, 3. Ðæt heó ðá ǽbylignysse gebéte ðe heó Gode ábylgð iram Dei quam excitaverit placare, Ll. Th. ii. 188, 4. v. a-bylgnes in Dict.

ǽ-byl(i)gþ(u) ; f. (but n. in El. 401). Add : (1) anger :—Æbylgðu indignatio, Ps. Srt. 68, 25. In ǽbylgðu in indignatione, 29, 6. Gif hwylce beóð ðǽra ðe hwæt ǽbylhða wið óðre habbað, ðonne sceolan hig ðá forgyfan if there are any of those that have any angry feelings against others, they shall give up those feelings, Ll. Th. ii. 434, 7. (2) what causes anger, offence, injury :—Ðá sendon Rómáne ǽrendracan and bǽdon ðæt him man gebéte ðæt him ðǽr tó ábylgðe (ǽ., v. l.) gedón wæs missi a Romanis legati, ut de illatis quererentur injuriis, Ors. 4, 1 ; S. 154, 11. Nánum syllende ǽnige ǽbyligþe (offensionem). Scint. 116, 14. Wé ðæt ǽbylgð nyton ðe wé gefremedon wið ðec, El. 401. Þeáh wé ǽbylgð wið hine oft gewyrcen, synna wunde, 513. [Cf. O. H. Ger. gi-buluht ira.] v. a-bylgþ in Dict.

ǽc an oak. Dele : the passage belongs to ác, q. v.

ǽ-cambe, -cembe, an ; f. Oakum :—Ecambe s[t]uppa, Txts. 99, 1925. Æcemban s[t]upparum, Wrt. Voc. ii. 82, 15. [O. H. Ger. á-chambi stuppa.]

ǽ-celma. Add :—Ecilma palagra, Txts. 85, 1500. Æcilma, Wrt. Voc. i. 288, 70. Æcelma, ii. 67, 61. Æcelman mulas, An. Ox. 1386.

ǽcelmehte ; adj. Having chilblains :—Ecilmehti palagdrigus, Txts. 85, 1523.

**ǣcen**; *adj. Of oak.* [*In* Lch. iii. 52, 2 *for* ǣcenan *read* (?) ǣrenan.] [*O. H. Ger.* eichīn : *Icel.* eikinn.] v. next word.

**ǣcen** *a wood of oaks*:—Ǣcen *roboretum*, Wrt. Voc. i. 285, 82.

**æcer.** *Add*: I. in a general sense, *field, land*:—Æcer *ager*, Wrt. Voc. i. 53, 53. Si jaceat, jaceat in ungildan ækere, Ll. Th. i. 301, 23. (v. un-gilde.) I a. of arable land:—Gesāwen æcer *vel* land *seges*, Wrt. Voc. i. 53, 55. Se æker, Past. 411, 18. Hē on his æcere eóde, and his sulh on handa hæfde, Ors. 2, 6; S. 88, 8. Se Hǣlend fōr ofer æceras (acras, R.) *abiit Jesus per sata*, Mt. 12, 1. Hiora gemǣnan æceras oþþe gærs, Ll. Th. i. 128, 7. I b. *the crop* raised on the land (cf. *Icel.* akr *crop*):—Ðā đā đæt ān corn feóll, đǣr ārās þicce æcer (*seges*), Gr. D. 240, 3. Ne þolie hē đāra æcra (æcera, *v. l.*), Ll. Th. i. 146, 5. II. a definite quantity of land, *an acre*. The *acer* seems to have been four rods broad, and forty rods long. v. Seebohm, Vill. Comm. s. v. *acre*, and Sax. Engl. i. 96:—Æceras *jugeri*, Wrt. Voc. ii. 46, 5. Twelf æceras mǣde, C. D. vi. 244, 12. xl æcera (cf. quadraginta jugeribus, l. 7), 1, 18. iii. æcera brǣde (v. *passage under* weall-stellung *in Dict.*), Ll. Th. i. 224, 9. v. bydel-, līn-, sulh-æcer, bōc-æceras.

**æcer-ceorl.** *Add*:—Æcerceorl *rusticus*, Wrt. Voc. i. 73, 33. [Cf. *Icel.* akr-karl *a ploughman* or *reaper*.]

**æceren.** v. æcern.

**æcer-geard**, es; *m. An enclosure of arable land* (? = *Icel.* akra-, akrgerđi) or *the fence of a field* (? v. geard):—On đone æcergeard; ā be đǣm gearde, C. D. iii. 458, 24. v. next word.

**æcer-hege**, es; *m. A field-hedge*:—On đone æcerhege; ondlong đæs æcerheges, C. D. iii. 33, 2.

**æcer-mǣlum**; *adv. By acres*:—Đæt land līđ hīdmǣlum and æcermǣlum, C. D. vi. 98, 5.

**æcer-mann.** *Add*:—Æcerman *agricola*, Wrt. Voc. i. 74, 67. [Akerman, Halliw. Dict., *O. H. Ger.* achar-man *arator*: *Icel.* akr-mađr.]

**æcern.** *Add*:—Đis æceren (æcern, *v. l.*) *haec glans*, Ælfc. Gr. Z. 61, 8: 312, 6: *glandix*, Wrt. Voc. i. 289, 29: ii. 41, 27. Heó eteđ hnyte oþþe æceran, Lch. iii. 144, 20.

**æcern-spranca**, an; *m. An acorn-sprout*:—Æcernspranca (æcer-, *v. l.*) ođđe āc *ilex*, Ælfc. Gr. Z. 69, 15.

**æcer-sǣd**, es; *n. Seed for an acre*:—Man sælde đæt æcersǣd hwǣte, đæt is twēgen sēdlǣpas, tō six scillingas, and đæt bærlic, đæt is þrē sēdlǣpas, tō six scillingas, and đæt æcersǣd āten, đæt is feówer sēdlǣpas tō feówer scillingas, Chr. 1124; P. 254, 14-16. vi. æcersǣd . . . tō tióþunge . . . viiii. æcersēd (cf. twā hund æcera sǣd, 26; feórđ healf hund æcere sēd, 21), C. D. B. iii. 367, 30, 31, 27, 28.

**æcer-splott**, es; *m. An acre-plot, an acre*:—Đæs healfes weres bōc and đæs æcersplottes đe đǣrtō līđ (cf. Cum unius jugeris sibi adjacentis portione, 134, 33), C. D. vi. 136, 12.

**æcer-teóþung**, e; *f. Tithe from the produce of arable land*:—Ārīse seó æcerteóđung ā be đām đe seó sulh đone teóđan æcer ǣr geeóde, Wlfst. 310, 24. [Cf. *Icel.* akr-tīund *tithe paid on arable land*.] v. Seebohm, Vill. Comm. pp. 114 sqq.

**æcer-tȳning**, e; *f. Fencing of fields*:—Æcertȳninge .xv. gyrda, C. D. iii. 451, 2.

**æcer-weg**, es; *m. A field-road*:—Andlang æcerweges . . . eft on đone æcerweg, C. D. vi. 137, 17, 22.

**æcer-weorc**, es; *n. Field-work, agricultural labour*:—Fra[m] hys æcerweorce *agresti bonus*, Germ. 391, 60. [*Icel.* akr-verk *field-work, harvest-work*.]

**ǣ-cilma.** v. ǣ-celma.

**ǣ-cnōsle**; *adj. Degenerate*:—Ǣcnōsle *degener, ignobilis, dissimilis parentibus*, ǣcnōslum ādle *degeneri languore*, Wrt. Voc. ii. 138, 30-32: 75. v. ge-ǣcnōslian.

**ǣ-cræftig.** *Add*:—Ǣcræftiga *Pharisaei*, ǣcræftgum *Pharisaeis*, Mt. L. 12, 24, 38.

**ǣd(d)er**, e; *f.* ǣd(d)re, an; *f.* (wæter-ǣdre *occurs once neuter*). *Add to* ǣdre: I. *a channel for fluids*:—Đīn ēdra *thy fountain* (vena), Kent. Gl. 107: 330. Ealle eorđan ǣddre onsprungon ongeán đām heofonlican flōde, Wlfst. 206, 18. Ǣþro *botre* (cf. botrus *fossa, via imbribus excavata*, Migne), Wrt. Voc. i. 287, 28. Ǣddrum *cataractis*, An. Ox. 515. Đæt wæter gewende þurh đā dīglan ǣddran đisse eorþan (*per occultas terrae venas*), Angl. vii. 36, 342. I a. in reference to living things:—Ǣddre *arteria*, Wrt. Voc. i. 64, 63: *vena*, 71, 44. His cræft gecymþ on ǣlcere ǣdre, Bt. 34, 11; F. 152, 2. Blōd lǣtan of đām swīđran earme on đǣre niþeran ǣdre, Lch. ii. 210, 10: 82, 16. Lege on đā ǣdre, 148, 18. Swā swā ǣddran licgeađ on đæs mannes līchaman, iii. 254, 22. On ōđrum mōnþe đā ǣdron beóđ geworden, on lxv and þreó hundræd hī beóđ tōdǣlede, and đæt blōd đonne flōweđ on đā fēt, Nar. 49, 27. Ic eów, ǣddran (*venae*), bidde đæt gē wylspringas ontȳnan tō teárum, Dōm. L. 26. Tōcnāwan be his ǣdrena hrepunge (*by feeling his pulse*) hweđer hē hrađe swulte, Hml. S. 3, 569. Ǣddrum *fibris, venis*, An. Ox. 376: *fibrarum rivulis*, 11, 135. Wiþ đā đe habbađ ætstandene ǣdran, swā đæt đæt blōd ne mæg hys gecyndelican ryne habban, Lch. i. 90, 11. II. *a sinew*:—Tōlǣtenum ǣddrum *laxis fibris*, Hy. S. 102, 22. Đā forcurfon hié him đā twā ǣdran on twā healfa đāra eágena *resectis palpebris*, Ors. 4, 6; S. 178, 23. III. *a rein, kidney*:—Hēđir *renis*, Txts. 93, 1731. Ǣddran *renes*, Wrt. Voc. i. 65, 25. Ǣdran (ēđre, Ps. V.), Ps. Spl. 15, 7. Ēdran, Kent. Gl. 884. Ēdra *renium*, Txts. 410, 27. Wiđ ǣddrena sāre, Lch. i. 190, 7. Ǣdrena, 232, 17. Ǣddran (ēđre, Ps. V.) *renes*, Ps. Spl. C. 7, 10. v. geótend-, lungen-, middel-, wind-ǣd(d)re.

**ǣd[d]er-seax.** *Add*:—*Flebotomum* blōdseax ođđe ǣdderseax. *Græce namque fleps vena, tomum vero incisio nominatur*, Wrt. Voc. ii. 39, 22.

**æd-fæst.** *Dele, and see* æt-fæstan.

**ædre.** *l.* ǣdre: **ǣdre** (= ǣđre? *cpve. of* eāđe) *levius*, Wrt. Voc. ii. 53, 58.

**ǣ-fægred** *disfigured*:—Ǣfæ(g)rede *larbatos* [cf. hreófe *larbatos* (the passage is the same in both glosses), Wrt. Voc. ii. 86, 64; se unfægera *larbata* (*facies*), 95, 68], An. Ox. 4936.

**ǣ-fæst** (ǣw-, eáw-, -fest). *Add*: I. *religious*:—Se ǣwfæsta (*religiosus*) wer Laurentius, Gr. D. 12, 17. Mynstermen and widwan eáwfæstes līfes, Ll. Th. ii. 440, 27. Tō đām ǣwfæstum heápe, Hml. S. 28, 67. Ǣwfæstra manna līc *hominum religiosorum cadavera*, Ll. Th. ii. 160, 24. Mid eáwfæstum monnum, 176, 1. Se weorđscipe đisse worolde is gecierred tō weorđscipe đǣm ǣwfæstum, đæt đā sindon nū weorđoste đe ǣwfæstoste sindon; for đon līcet monig đæt hē ǣwfæsđ lāreów sié, Past. 27, 2-5. Ǣfeste (eáwfæste, *v. l.*) men, R. Ben. 119, 7. II. *married*:—Yfel ǣwbryce biđ đæt ǣwfæst (eáw-, *v. l.*) man mid ǣmtige forlicge, Ll. Th. i. 404, 21. Se apostol āwrāt be eáwfæstum werum: 'Lufiađ, gē weras, eówere wīf on ǣwe,' Hml. Th. ii. 322, 25. Ic manode ǣwfæste wīf, i. 378, 27.

**æ-fæstan**, Wrt. Voc. ii. 44, 72. v. æt-fæstan.

**ǣ-fæsten** (ǣw-). *Add*:—On ǣwfæstenum ic gesyngode, Angl. xi. 102, 66. Ǣfæstenu ic oft āgǣlde, 99, 62: Ll. Th. ii. 144, 23.

**ǣ-fæstlic**; *adj.* I. *legitimate*:—Ǣwfæstlicere *legitime*, An. Ox. 851. II. *religious*:—Hē forgitt đæt hē ǣr ǣfæstlices (-fest-, Cott. MSS.) geđōhte *obliviscitur quidquid religiose cogitavit*, Past. 57, 8.

**ǣ-fæstlīce**; *adv. Religiously*:—Lifde hē ǣfestlīce his līf *religiosam gerens vitam*, Bd. 5, 12; S. 627, 10.

**ǣ-fæstnes** (ǣw-, eáw-, -fest-, -feast-). *Add*:—Ǣfæstnis clǣne *religio munda*, Rtl. 29, 11. Ege Drihtnes ingehȳdes ǣwfæstnyss (*religiositas*), Scint. 65, 9. Aefeastnisse *religionis*, Rtl. 96, 9. Gewītan fram đām bīgange ūre ǣfestnysse, Bd. 1, 7; S. 477, 21. Hī āxode hine hwylcere eáwfæstnysse hē wǣre, Hml. S. 22, 204. Eáwfæstnysse (*regularis*) *discipline*, Hpt. Gl. 403, 16. Mid ǣfæsnesse, R. Ben. 139, 7.

**æf-dæl.** *Substitute*: æf-dæll, -dell, es; *n.*:—Tō æfdæll (-delle, R.), Lk. L. 19, 37. v. of-dæle. Cf. next word.

**æf-dȳne**, es; *m. A descent, declivity*:—Ǣfdȳni (ęsdyni, MS.) *defexum, decliuium* (cf. deuexu[m], declibium, descensum, Corp. Gl. Hessels. 41, 140), Hpt. 33, 250, 3.

**æ-felle**, a-felle. *l.* ǣ-felle.

**ǣfen.** *Add*: ǣfen[n], ēf(e)rn; [*m.* and] *n.* I. *evening*:—Ǣfen *vesperum*, bedtīd *serum*, Wrt. Voc. i. 53, 15. Seó niht hæfđ seofan dǣlas . . ōþer is *uesperum*, đæt is ǣfen, đonne se ǣfensteorra betwux đǣre repsunge æteówađ, Lch. iii. 242, 28: Angl. viii. 319, 28. Đā ēfern (ǣfen, R.) warđ *vespere facto*, Mt. L. 26, 20. Đā hyt ǣfen (ēfern, L.; æt ǣfenne, R.) wæs *cum sero factum esset*, Mt. 27, 57. Ēfrn, Mk. L. 11, 11, 19. Hī ǣton ǣne on dæg, and đæt wæs tō ǣfennes, Bt. 15; F. 48, 9. Ēfernes, Mt. p. 20, 5. Ǣr ǣfenne, Bd. 1, 27; S. 496, 28. On đām ǣfene, Mt. 26, 20. Ođ đæt ǣfen forđ fram dæges orde, El. 139. Metod æfter sceáf ǣfen ǣrest, Gen. 138. II. *eve, the evening preceding a day* (of festival). v. eáster-, mæsse-, mōnan-, sunnan-, Þunresǣfen:—Đām restedæges ǣfene (ēfenne, R.; ēfern, L.) sē đe onlīhte on đām forman restedæge, Mt. 28, 1. Ārwurđiađ đisne ǣfen, and đone freólsdæg đe eów tō merigen becymđ, Hml. Th. ii. 370, 1. In đone hālgan ǣfen Pentecosten, Chr. 626; P. 24, 8. On đone hālgan ǣfen Inuentione sce crucis, 912; P. 96, 30. On twelftan ǣfen, 1053; P. 182, 38. v. gestran-ǣfen.

**ǣfen-dreám.** *Add*:—Se ǣfensang sȳ geendod mid feówer sealma dreáme . . . ealle đā ōþre sȳn tō đām ǣfendreáme gesungene *vespera quattuor psalmorum modulatione canatur* . . . *reliqui omnes in vespera dicendi sunt*, R. Ben. 43, 7-18.

**ǣfen-gebēd.** *l.* -gebed, *and add* Wrt. Voc. i. 28, 30.

**ǣfen-gereord**, e; *f. Substitute*: es; *n. and add*: Used in pl. for a single meal:—Gif hit beó seó tīd ǣfengereordes, ārīsen hȳ sōna swā hȳ heora mete hæbben, and sitten on ānre stōwe *si tempus fuerit prandii mox ut surrexerint a cena sedeant omnes in unum*, R. Ben. 66, 15. Ǣfter his ǣfengereorde *post caenam*, Bd. 3, 11; S. 536, 12: Angl. xiii. 437, 1034. Ūre Dryhten offrode æt his ǣfengereorde, Btwk. 218, 9. Wǣron geworden Drihtnes ǣfengereordu *facta est cena Domini*, Hml. A. 153, 41. Seó gālnes æt hyre ǣfengereordum (*in caena*) sitt, Prud. 40 a. Hē sæt mid him æt đǣm ǣfengereorde, Bl. H. 73, 5: 143, 6. Martha gearwode đām Hǣlende ǣfengereordu, 67, 26. Heora underngereordu and ǣfengereordu hié mengdon tōgædere, 99, 23.

**ǣfen-gereordian.** *l.* -gereordan; *p.* de *To provide with supper*:—Dagum on đām ǣfengereorde synt gebrōþru *diebus quibus cenaturi sunt fratres*, Angl. xiii. 437, 1030. v. next word.

æfen-gereordung, e; f. Supper:—Tô æfengereordunga lambes ad cenam Agni, Hy. S. 82, 3.

æfen-geweorc, es; n. Evening-work:—Sele bollan fulne tô gedrincanne æfter æfengeweorce, Lch. ii. 190, 3.

æfen-gifl. Add:—Gyf wê fæstað and ðæt underngereord tô ðam æfengifle healdað, ðonne ne bið ðæt nân fæsten, ac ... bið ðæt æfengyfel getwifealdad, Ll. Th. ii. 436, 30. Gif hý on twâ mæl etað, sý gehealden ðæs pundmætan hláfes se þridda dæl tô ðam æfengifle, R. Ben. 63, 16. Uton nû brûcan ðisses undernmetes swâ ðâ sculon ðe hiora æfengifl on helle gefeccan sculon prandete tamquam apud inferos coenaturi, Ors. 2, 5; S. 86, 1: Past. 27, 8: 323, 19.

æfen-glôma, an; m. Evening-twilight:—Seó niht hafað seofon tôdǽlednyssa. Crepusculum ys seó forme, ðæt ys æfenglôma, Angl. viii. 319, 27: Lch. iii. 242, 27.

æfen-glommung, e; f. Evening-twilight:—Swâ ðæt oft on middre niht geflit cymeð ðam behealdendum hwæþer hit sî ðe æfenglommung ðe on morgen deágung ita ut medio saepe tempore noctis in quaestionem ueniat intuentibus, utrum crepusculum adhuc permaneat uespertinum, an iam aduenerit matutinum, Bd. S. 473, 31. Æfenglommunge crepusculum, Hy. S. 16, 31.

æfen-hrepsung. v. æfen-repsung.

æfen-lic. Add:—Æfernlicum tîdum vespertinis horis, Rtl. 174, 37.

æfen-lîce; adv. In the evening:—Ârlîce mane, æfenlîce vespere, Rtl. 166, 3.

æfen-lof, es; n. Even-song:—Æfter æfenlofe post uespertinalem laudem, Angl. xiii. 437, 1035.

æfen-mete, es; m. Add:—Æfenmete cena, Wrt. Voc. i. 290, 66: ii. 17, 26. Ðende hiæ æt ðæm æfenmete wêrun coenantibus eis, Mt. R. 26, 26.

æfen-mete; adj. (?) Provided with supper:—ᵹ (= æt?) æfenmeti wêron hiá coenantibus eis, Mt. L. 26, 26. v. preceding word.

æfen-rǽding, e; f. An evening reading; collatio (apud monachos sacrorum librorum lectio quae maxime post coenam coram iis fiebat, Migne):—Ðænne æfenrǽding (collatio) byþ gerǽdd, Angl. xiii. 393, 400. Tácne æfenrǽdincge gestyredum signo collationis moto, 416, 723. Nihtsang æfter æfterrǽdincge (l. æfen-) completorium post collationem, 423, 828.

æfen-repsung, e; f. Eventide, night-fall:—Hê slêp swâ hwær swâ hine seó æfenrepsung gemётte he slept wherever night overtook him, Hml. S. 236, 154. Sunne heó ðâ tô setle âhylde, and ðære æfenrepsunge geneálæhte, 498.

æfen-rima. Dele.

æfen-sang. Add:—Ne sý æfensang geendod bûtan ðam drihtlican gebede, R. Ben. 38, 15. Se æfensang mid antefene sý gecweden, 39, 20. Se æfensang sý geendod mid feówer sealma dreáme, 43, 7. Ðone lofsang (the Magnificat) ðe wê singað on Godes cyrcan æt ælcum æfensange, Hml. Th. i. 202, 26. Sê ðe ... dæghwámlîce his circan gesêcan ne mæge, hê hûru ðinga on ðam sunnandagum ... þider cume tô ... æfensange, Hml. A. 144, 11. Singan æfen oþþe nihtsange cantare vesperum aut completorium, Coll. M. 34, 3. Æfensang vesperam, Angl. xiii. 392, 385: vespertinalem sinaxim, 425, 863: 432, 964. Æfensangas singan vesperas celebrare, 415, 711.

æfen-sceóp, -sprǽc. l. æfen-scop, -sprǽc.

æfen-steorra. Add:—Æfensteorra hesperos, Germ. 394, 329. Ðes æfensteorra hic vesper, Ælfc. Gr. Z. 43, 12. Se fîfta is gehaten Venus, sê is æfensteorra, Scrd. 18, 36. Vesperum, ðæt is æfen, ðonne se æfensteorra æteówað, Lch. iii. 242, 28.

æfen-þênung, -þegnung. Add: I. evening service of the Church:—Æfenðênunge singe ânra gehwilc vespertinum officium canat unusquisque, Angl. xiii. 422, 823. Hý scylon embe ðâ nigoðan tîde heora mæssan gestandan and æfter ðâm heora æfenþênunga, Hml. A. 141, 74. II. serving of food in the evening, supper:—Æfenþênunge cene, R. Ben. I. 71, 1. Hî árîsað fram æfenþênunge (cena), 74, 10. Æfenþênunga gedôure cena facta, Angl. xiii. 437, 1030. Gif hî sceolan on æfen gereordian of ðam sylfan þunde se þridda dæl sý gehealden tô âgifenne on æfenþênungum. R. Ben. I. 71, 3.

æfen-þeówdôm. Add:—Wrt. Voc. i. 28, 30.

æfen-tîd. Add:—Hoc vesperum oððe vespere bið æfentîd, Ælfc. Gr. Z. 43, 12 note. Afeóll (âsâh, v. l.) seó æfentîd ðæs dæges diei tardior hora incubuerat, Gr. D. 83, 15. Hêr wæs Eádweard cyng ofslagen on æfentîde, Chr. 979; P. 123, 6. On æfentîd, Shrn. 116, 8. On ðâ æfentîd, Nar. 29, 21. In æfentîd vespere, Mt. L. 8, 16. On æfrntîd (æfern-, R.) sero, Mk. L. 13, 35. Oþ æfentîd ad vesperum, Bd. 1, 27; S. 496, 34.

æfen-tîma. Add:—On æfentîman ûre Dryhten offrode æt his æfengereorde, Btwk. 218, 9: Hml. S. 15, 58.

æfen-tungel. Dele æfenian, æfenung. v. æfnian, æfnung. æfer, Lch. ii. 22, 7. v. âfor.

æferðe, an; f. A plant-name:—Dolhsealf: âcrind, æferðe ..., Lch. ii. 94, 14. Æferðe niþeweard, 110, 1. Nim æferþan nioþowearde, 142, 23: 340, 3.

æfesa (-e; f.?), an; m. Produce of woods on which swine might be fed:—Mid mæste and mid æuesan ... and ic ann ðæt ðridde swun (?) of æuesan ðæs nêxtan wudes ðe liþ tô kyngesbyrig cum porcorum esca et cum fructibus ... quoque dono tertiam sarcinam iumentariam fructuum qui nascuntur in sylua proxime ad kyngesbyrig sita, C. D. iv. 202, 2–12. [In the Domesday of St. Paul's of the year 1222 (Camden Society, 1858) is this entry: 'Debent dare de singulis animalibus .iij. ob' þ annum si ad pasturam dũi venerint similiter de equis et de singulis porcis .j. ð. þ Garsavese,' p. 51. See also note p. lxviii on garsavese, where another instance of its use is given as well as an instance of a verb avesare (avesabit porcos).] v. æfesn, æfes-weorc.

æfesc. v. efes.

æfesn. Add: Pannage. v. æfesa, and E. Stud. 27, 218: æfesne obscenitas. v. æpsen.

æf-ést. l. æf-est(-æst, -ist), æfst, æfstu; m. f. Add: I. in a bad sense:—Se dierna æfst, Past. 79, 13. Be ðâm is âwriten ðætte ðis fiǽsclice lîf sié æfesð (invidia), 235, 13. For ðæs æfstes scylde per livoris vitium, 237, 1. Æfestes, Wrt. Voc. ii. 50, 12. Mid ðære biteran æfeste, Bl. H. 25, 7. Mid ðâm þyccylum ðære æfæste invidiae, Gr. D. 117, 28: 118, 2. Æfstu, Ps. Th. 69, 4. Hié hié nyllað healdan wið ðæm æfste (livore) ... for ðæs lytegan fióndes æfeste (invidia) deáð becôme ofer eorðan, Past. 233, 17–19. Âweorpan ðone æfst, 25. Hié him æfest tô genâman they became envious of him, Bl. H. 7, 11. Æfeste ânforlǽtan, Gû. 158: Fä. 36. Æfest invidiam, Mt. p. 1, 10. Þurh æfeste (æfst, L.), Mt. R. 27, 18: Mk. R. 15, 10. Nið and æfesta odium et invidiae, Ll. Th. ii. 174, 32. Æfisto invidias, Rtl. 25, 25. II. in a good sense, zeal:—Be gôdum æfste (zelo) ðe munecas habban sceolon, R. Ben. 131, 11. Elnung ł æfista hûses ðînes zelus domus tuae, Jn. R. 2, 17.

æfeste (?); adj. Envious:—Se æfæsta (æfæstiga, v. l.) mæssepreóst, Gr. D. 117, 18. v. æfestian.

æf-éstian, -estigan. Substitute: æf(e)stian. I. to envy:—Hit þweora manna þeáw is ðæt hî æfæstiað ôþra manna gôddǽde mos pravorum est invidere aliis virtutis bonum, Gr. D. 117, 4. II. to grow envious:—Æfestian libescant, Wrt. Voc. ii. 50, 41. v. æf(e)stigian, æf(e)stung, æfeste.

æf(e)stig. Add: I. in a bad sense, envious:—Beón andetta ðæt hê æfestig sý, Bl. H. 65, 4. Ne sý hê æfestig (zelotipus), R. Ben. 121, 13. Æfstig emulus, Wrt. Voc. ii. 143, 46. Se æfæstiga mæssepreóst, Gr. D. 117, 18. Æfestiga, æfstigea, 118, 20. Hwâ mæg beón ungesǽlgra ðonne se æfstiga (-ega, v.l.), Past. 231, 22. Ðæs æfestigan invidi, Hy. S. 16, 3. Ne sýn wê tô æfestige (-æst-, v.l.), Wlfst. 253, 6. Ðâ æfestgan (æfstegan, v.l.) invidi, Past. 229, 11. Æfestigra manna, R. Ben. 92, 12. Ðæm æfstegum invidis, Past. 233, 16. II. in a good sense, zealous (against):—Æfstig wið ôðra monna yfelu contra aliena vitia aemulator, Past. 79, 12.

æf(e)stigian; p. ode. I. with acc. to envy, be envious of:—Hié æfestigeað ôþera monna gôddǽde, Gr. D. 117, 4. Ðâ æfestgodon ðæt sume men, Shrn. 74, 28. Se ealda feónd ongan æfstigian (invidens) ðæs ôðres lufan, Gr. D. 99, 7. II. with prep. to look with envy or ill will on, have envy towards:—Ðes iunga man ne æfestigað on nânum ðingum ðe hê hêr gesihð, Ap. Th. 14, 25. Se âwyrgda gâst æfestgaþ on ðâ ðe hê gesyhþ tô Gode higian, Bl. H. 29, 21. Ðâ geseah hê ðæs sácerdes môd byrnan and æfæstigian wiþ his life, Gr. D. 119, 6. v. ge-æf(e)stigian.

æf(e)stung, e; f. Envy:—Mid þyccylum ðære æfestunge, Gr. D. 117, 28. Æfstunge, 118, 2.

æf(e)s-weorc, es; n. Pasturage:—Æfsweorc sive lǽnes landes bryce fructus, Wrt. Voc. ii. 39, 31. v. æfese, æfesn.

æf-gǽlp, e; f. Superstition:—Efgælþe superstitionis, An. Ox. 8, 186. Æfgælþe superstitione, 8, 176: 3233. Æfgælþa, 4021. Idelum æfgælþum superstitiosa cultura, 3933.

æf-geréfa glosses exactor:—Ðý lǽs se doemere seled ðec ðǽm æf-groefe (exactori) and se æfgroefa (exactor) sendað ðec in carcern, Lk. L. 12, 58.

æf-grynde, es; n. An abyss:—Þine dômas synt swâ deópe swâ swâ æfgrynde judicia tua abyssus multa, Ps. Th. 35, 6. [O. H. Ger. abgrunti, n. abyssus. Cf. Goth. af-grundiþa an abyss.]

æf-gydel (?); adj. Idolatrous, superstitious:—Idelum ł feóndlicum æfgidelum (-gildum?; the ide is not clear; v. Angl. vi. 101: cf. also An. Ox. 3933 (v. æf-gælþ), where the same passage is glossed, and see note there) superstitiosa, Hpt. Gl. 498, 77. [Cf. O. H. Ger. ab-got idolum.]

æf-hende (-hynde); adj. Absent:—Gif hê æfhynde byþ si absens fuerit, Angl. xiii. 387, 316. v. of-hende, ge-hende.

æ-firmþa; f. Offscourings, sweepings, dregs, refuse:—Æfyrm[þa] purgamenta (spurca latrinarum), An. Ox. 3918. Add the quotation in Dict. under æ-fyrmþa. Cf. â-feormian.

æfne ability. v. efne.

æfnian. Add:—Ðâ ðâ se dæg æfnode vesperascente die, Gr. D. 75, 2. Oþ ðæt hit æfnode, Hml. S. 13, 27. Swylce hit æfnige, Lch. iii. 260 7.

Mid ðī ðe hit æfnian wolde, Hml. S. 23, 245. Æfni(g)endum ðām dæge, Gr. D. 253, S.

**æfnung.** *Add:*—On æfenunga, Hml. S. 11, 43. On æfnunge, 153 : Hml. Th. ii. 334, 34 : Lch. iii. 238, 27. Seó sunne gæð on æfnunge under ðyssere eorðan, 240. 14. Æfnunge *crepusculo*, An. Ox. 85.

[æfr-ælc(-ic) *every* :—On æfrice styde *in omnibus omnino locis*, C. D. iv. 209, 20. Æuric ríce man, Chr. 1137; P. 264, 1. v. æfre, III.]

[æfr-ænig *any at all* :—Mid æfrænige þinge, C. D. iv. 209, 24. v. æfre, III.]

**æfre.** *Add:* I. *ever:* semper, (1) of eternity :—Wæs æfre on his ēcum ræde ðæt hē wolde gewyrcan ðás woruld, Hex. 22, 7. Nænig ys sē ðe æfre lybbe, Scint. 215, 2. (2) of continuity or continuous recurrence in time, *at all times, on every occasion* :—Æfri is *deinceps*, An. Ox. 56, 103. Wearð æfre fleám āstiht, and æfre hī æt ende sige āhton, Chr. 998 ; P. 131, 15. Full neáh æfre þe óðer man *very nearly every other man*, 1086; P. 217, 29. Gif wē æfre widsacað deófle, Hml. Th. i. 170, 16. Æfre swā hī neár and neár eódon, Hml. S. 23, 424. II. *ever, at any time, in any case;* unquam :—Ne wearð wæl māre æfer (æfre, *v. l.*) gieta, Chr. 937; P. 109, 24. Ne him līg sceðeð æfre tó ealdre, Ph. 40. Gē wyllað sweltan ær ðan ðe gē æfre his geleáfan widsacon, Hml. Th. ii. 308, 9. Būton heó hit æfre gebēte, Hml. S. 17, 156: An. 1014. III. giving emphasis in what*ever*, (as) *ever*, &c.:—Swā rihtlíce gesēman swā him æfre rihtlícost þūhte, C. D. iii. 292, 32. Eall ðæt æfre beón wæs, Chr. 1048; P. 174, 23. Hwæt ðis æfre beón scyle? Hml. S. 23, 532. Hū hē æfre embe hỹ sceolde, 311. Æfre ðeáh (*any how*) for his hālgena earnunge, hē him ðis geþanc on mōde āsende, 313. Æfre ælc ðæl his cynnes, 348. Æfre ælcne Deniscne cyning ūtlagede hī gecwædon, Chr. 1014; P. 145. 11. Ymbe æfre ælce neóde, Wlsf. 20, 19: Ll. Th. i. 372, 30. Gif æfre ænig (cf. æfr-ænig) man ciricgrið ābrece, 340, 6.

**æf-ræda,** an; *m. Tow. oakum :—Naptarum* heordena, æbreda, ācumba (*for the original here glossed* cf. An. Ox. 1649). Wrt. Voc. ii. 59, 58. *Putamine* of æfredan, ācumban, An. Ox. 3728. *Stamine* æfredan, *putamine* of hniglan, 7, 266. [In this word perhaps *-reda* is for earlier *-ræda*, connected with *ge-ræedan*, which is used of dressing the hair ; in the same way Icel. *greiða* is used, and *ull greiða* = to card or comb wool, so that *æf-reda* might compare with *æ-cambe*.]

**æfric, æfse, æfst.** v. æfr-ælc, æspe, æfest : æfstnung, Hpt. Gl. 436, 32 (æstnung, MS. v. Angl. vi. 99). *l.* costnung, cf. An. Ox. 1260.

**æfs-weorc.** v. æfes-weorc.

**æftan.** *Add: From behind :—*Ælc ōþerne æftan heáwed, Wlsf. 160, 4. [*Goth.* aftana : *Icel.* aptan.] v. wiþ-æftan.

**æftemest.** *Dele* superlative of æftera, *and add :—*Se æftemysta cwyde, Hml. Th. i. 554, 14. From heora ærestan cyninge oþ heora æftemæstan (-mest-, *v. l.*), Ors. 6, 1 ; S. 252, 14. [*Goth.* aftumists.] v. æftera.

**æften (?)** *evening :—*Eftern lōcað *aduesperascit* (the glosser seems to have read *vesper aspicit:* in the Rushworth gloss also the word has been misunderstood, as it is rendered by *ēfern longeð ðū wast,* the last two words apparently suggested by *-scit*), Lk. L. 24, 29. Cf. *Icel.* aptan.

**æften-stemn,** Wrt. Voc. i. 63, 37 *l.* æftera stemn.

**æfter.** *Add: A. prep.* I. with dat. (1) marking position :—Ðā eóde ðæt wíf æfter him, Bt. 35, 6 ; F. 170, 13. (2) marking direction :—Beheald æfter ðē *look behind thee,* Bl. H. 245, 6. (3) marking order, sequence :—Ðæt hē æfter him tó eallum his gestreónum fēnge, Ors. 5, 13 ; S. 244, 23. Stephanus ðone martyrdōm æfter Gode āstealde, Hml. Th. i. 50, 1. (4) marking order in time :—Æfter ðissum gefeohte, Chr. 871 ; P. 72, 5. (5) marking extension, with an object which determines position or direction, *among, through, along* :—Ðā giemmas licggeað tōworpne æfter stræta endum (*in platearum capite*) æfter strætum, Past. 135, 3–4. Wē mōston būian æfter ðām folce, Ps. Th. 28, 8. Faran gind lond swā swā læce æfter untrumra monna hūsum, Past. 59, 23. Hē æfter wudum fōr and on mōrfæstenum, Chr. 878 ; P. 74, 29. Fōron hié æfter ðæm wealda, 894 ; P. 84, 27. Ðā gesāwon wē æfter ðære eá ferian *vidimus hostes per medium amnem praetervehi,* Nar. 11, 18. Hī hine drōgan æfter ðæm stānum on ðære eorðan, Shrn. 74, 31. Andlang ðære rinde oþ ðone helm, and siððan æfter ðām bogum, Bt. 34, 10 ; F. 150, 3. Æftær þiódwege on ðone díc ; æfter díce, C. D. v. 187, 30. (6) with an object to which an action (pursuit, search, inquiry, &c.) is directed :—Hē stōd æfter ūs gewend, and cliopode æfter ūs, Past. 405, 35. Rād séo fird æfter ðæm herige, Chr. 896 ; P. 89, 19. Hē him æfter rād, 878 ; P. 76, 12. Ðæt ðā gódan men niman æfter þeora gódnesse, and for(f)león yfelnesse, 1086 ; P. 221, 24. Ðā sende se cyng æfter Anláfe, 994 ; P.129, 15. Heora wíf him sendon ærendracan æfter, Ors. 1, 10; S. 44, 20. Hē lēt hine faran æfter ðām feó, Hml. Th. ii. 358, 23 : Chr. 997; P.131, 28 : 1048; P. 171, 19. Wē æfter ferscum wætre hié frūnon, Nar. 11, 22. Winnan æfter ríce, Chr. 685; P. 39, 23 : Ors. 6, 28 ; S. 278, 9. His gerēfan nieddon hī æfter gafole (*pressed them for tribute*), 6, 34 ; S. 290, 24 : Bt. 16, 2 ; F. 52, 3. Æghwylc hine þreátode æfter ðām bōcum, Shrn. 123, 29, 32. (7) with an object which serves as example or measure :—Æfter steorwíglunge *juxta constellationem,* An. Ox. 7, 179. Æfter ðære tíde (*secundum tempus*) ðe hē geáxode, Mt. 2, 16. Him eákiað æfter ðæm

mægenum ðā costunga, Past. 163, S : Hml. S. 13, 130. Æfter ðínum willan, Bt. 26, 1 ; F. 90, 23. Lufian wē ūrne Sceppend æfter ūrum gemete, Bl. H. 5, 35. Forgolden æfter his gewyrhtum, 45, 2. Ðes niónaþ is se ýtemesta æfter Lýdenwarum, Angl. viii. 306, S. Se Hælend cwæþ æfter bíspellum heora, Mt. R. 22, 1. Niman gedyld æfter Iobe, Hml. Th. ii. 328, 28. Æfter æþelborennysse oferhýdige *haughty after the manner of noble birth,* 174, 7. Æfter ðon *accordingly,* Bl. H. 81, 27. Hit biþ geornlíc ðæt mon heardlíce gníde ðone hnescestan mealmstān æfter ðæm ðæt (*according as*) hē þence ðone soelestan hwetstān on tō geræceanne, Ors. 4, 13 ; S. 212, 28. II. with acc. (rare except in Northumbrian Glosses) :—Æfter hrædlíce tíde, Ors. 1, 10; S. 44, 28. Æfter óðer healf hund daga, Gen. 8, 3. Æfter ðás *post haec,* Lk. L. R. 10, 1. Ende . . . swýlcne hē æfter worhte, Jud. 65. Hē ðā gesihð lūted æfter, Sal. 402. Æfter tíd *secundum tempus,* Mt. L. 2, 16. III. with instrumental :—Æfter ðýs lífe, Bt. 11, 2 ; F. 36, 1. B. *adv.* (1) of time :—Monncwealm ðe him raðe ðær æfter com, Ors. 2, 6 ; S. 86, 25. Ðisse ādle fruman mon mæg ýþelíce gelácnian . . . , and æfter unéð, Lch. ii. 232, 17. Ðā æfter fēng tó ðām ercebiscopdóme Iustus, Chr. 616; P. 24, 23. (2) of position :—His wíf belāf æfter in ðam castele, Chr. 1076 ; P. 211, 29. (3) of direction, cf. A. 6 :—Ðā fōr Eádweard æfter, Chr. 905; P. 94, 1 : 999; P. 133, 9. Hig æfter ridon, Jos. 2, 7. v. sprecan, VI. ¶.

**æftera.** v. æfterra.

**æfter-æ** ; *f. Second-law, Deuteronomy :—*Seó bōc ðe is genemned . . . on Grēcisc *Deuteronomium* . . . and on Englisc seó æfteræ, Deut. proem.

**æfter-boren.** *Dele* [ = æfter-genga, q. v.], *and add :—*Æfterbora (*l. -cn*) *postumus,* An. Ox. 17, 34.

**æfter-cyning,** es ; *m. A succeeding king :—*Þā æftercyningas *reges posteriores,* Bd. 2, 14; Sch. 173, 20.

**æfter-eala,** an ; *m. l.* æfter-ealo (-a, -u); *n. :* æfter-fæce, *dele.*

**æfterest.** v. æfterra.

**æfter-fyl(i)gan** ; *p. de To follow :—*Ðæt folc nū gyt ðæt tācn æfterfylgeað, Ors. 1, 5 ; S. 34, 22. Ðā ðe æfterfylydon *quae sequebantur,* Mt. L. 21, 9. Mildheortnys ðín æfterfylge (*subsequetur*) mē, Ps. L. 22, 6. Ān scort ræps æfterfylige (*subsequatur*), R. Ben. 34, 13: 60, 4. Æfter ðæm ræpsum æfterfyligan (-fylian, *v. l.*) ōþre syx sealmas, 33, 21. Ðes æfterfiligenda cwyde is egefull, Hml. Th. i. 130, 28. Seó hālgung ðæs æfterfilgendan bisceopes, Chr. 984; P. 124, 3. Æfterfylgendre *prepostero,* Wrt. Voc. ii. 66, 77. Ðās æfterfylgendan (-fylig-, *v. l.*) lāre, Gr. D. 1, 16. Ðā æfterfiligendan yrmða, Hml. Th. i. 408, 18.

**æfter-fylgedness,** e ; *f. A sequel :—*Ne forlæt ðū ðā æfterfylgednysse swā hālwendre gerecednysse, Hml. S. 23 b, 365.

**æfter-fylgend.** *Add :—*Alexandres æfterfylgendas, Ors. 3, 11 ; S. 142, 11. Heora æfterfyligendas *successores eorum,* Bd. 2, 5 ; S. 506, 2. Him sylfum and his æfterfiligendum eallan, Chr. 995 ; P. 128, 39.

**æfter-fylgendlíce** ; *adv. In continuation* or *succession :—*Hié ðus æfterfyligendlíce mid blisse clypiað *subsequuntur gaudentes et dicentes,* R. Ben. 77, 11.

**æfter-fylgendness,** e; *f. Success :—*Æfterfyligendnyssum *successibus,* Hy. S. 11, 8.

**æfter-fylgung,** e; *f. Pursuit :—*Efterfylginc *sectatio,* Kent. Gl. 371. v. gedwild-æfterfylgung.

**æfter-fylian.** v. æfter-fyl(i)gan : **æfter-gān,** *dele* : **æfter-gegeng-edness.** v. æfter-gengness, II.

**æfter-genga.** *Substitute for first quotation :—*Æftergenga *posterus,* Ælfc. Gr. Z. 275, 3, *and add :* I. *one living at a later time;* where those of the same stock are referred to, *a descendant :—*Æftergencgena *posteriorum* (*natorum*), Hpt. Gl. 445, 60. Æftergen(gena) *liberorum,* i. *filiorum,* An. Ox. 584. Æftergengan *nepotibus,* 3370 : *posteris,* Germ. 399, 344: *futuris,* Hpt. Gl. 485, 41. Sume men wæron gió . . . ðā bisnodon hiora æftergengum, Bt. 39, 11 ; F. 230, 3. II. *one coming after in an office, a successor :—*Æftergenga *successor,* i. *subsequenter obtinens locum,* An. Ox. 1996. Eádwine and twēgen his æftergengan, Hml. S. 26, 10. Ðā apostolas . . . eác heora æftergengan, Hml. A. 56, 146. III. *a follower* of a creed, &c.:—Æftergengum *sequipedes, sequaces* (*catolicae fidei*), An. Ox. 1957.

**æfter-gengel,** es ; *m. A successor :—*Nān mín æftergengles (*successores*) . . . mín curs and ealle mín æftergengle, C. D. v. 30, 11, 23. Cf. Mine aððele uoregenglen, Lay. 25082. O. H. Ger. nāh-gengil *a familiar.*]

**æfter-gengness,** e ; *f.* I. *posterity :—*Æftergencnesse *posteritatis,* An. Ox. 849. Æftergengnesse *posteritate,* 2695. Æftergennysse, 3610. Ðæra gesceafta æftergengnyssa, Hml. Th. ii. 206, 10. II. *succession* in an office :—For ðære gewissan æftergencgnysse (-gegengcgednysse, *v. l.*), ðæt is ðæt se sunu sceolde symle fōn tó ðām hāde æfter his fæder geendunge, Hml. S. 10, 219. Mid fæderlíce æftergengnysse *in lineal succession,* 18, 385. III. *inferiority* of position, *occupation of the lowest place :—*Mid æftergencnysse hylde *extremitate contentus,* R. Ben. I. 33, 14.

**æfter-hætu.** *Substitute :* æfter-hæþa (-e ?), an; *m. (f. ?) Parching by heat after wet :—*Mid ungemætre hærfestwætan and æfterhæþan *humor aestatis vel autumni divitis indigesta illecebra,* Ors. 3, 3; S. 102. 7. v. hæþung.

æfter-hýrigean. *l.* æfter-hyr(i)gan, *and add:*—Mē gelamp ðæt ic ðæt gehýrde, ðæt ic æfterhyrgan ne mæg *me audire contingit quod imitari non valeo,* Gr. D. 182, 16.

æfter-ild(o). v. æfter-yldo *in Dict.*

æfter-lic; *adj. Second:*—Ðý æfterlicum hāde *secundi sexus,* Wrt. Voc. ii. 83, 72.

æfterra, æft(e)ra; *cpve.:* æft(e)resta; *spve.* I. where relation of two objects is marked, (1) in time, *latter:*—Se æfterra anweald—se ærra, Bt. 16, 1; F. 50, 12. Wæs heora æftra sýð wyrse ðonne se ærra, Chr. 1001; P. 133, 25. (2) in place, *hinder, lower:*—Ðæt ærre folc and ðæt æfterre *those before and those behind,* Bl. H. 81, 25. Se æftera stemn *puppis,* Wrt. Voc. i. 63, 37. Se æftra stream *aquae inferiores,* Jos. 3, 16. On ðæm æftran teāme *bimus,* Wrt. Voc. ii. 12, 70. I a. giving order of a group in a series, *latter:*—Sý alleluia gecweden mid ðām syx æftrum (*posterioribus*) sealmum, R. Ben. 39, 17. I b. where there are more than two objects the superlative æftresta = last:—Ðreó frigedagas, se æresta . . . se nýhsta . . . se æftresta, Angl. xi. 3, 69. II. where there is juxtaposition, immediate sequence, *next, following:*—On ðæm æfterran geáre ðæs *anno post hunc subsequente,* Ors. 3, 6; S. 108, 15. On ðām æftran geáre þe se arcb wæs gemartyrod, Chr. 1013; P. 143, 9. On ðæm æfteran dæge, Bl. H. 71, 34. Ðýs æftran geáre *sequente anno,* Nar. 30, 11. III. as an ordinal, *second:*—Ærest . . . se æftera . . . se þridda, Chr. 827; P. 60, 27. Sió æfterre tā . . . sió feórðe tā, Ll. Th. i. 90, 20. Hēr endað sió forme bóc and onginð sió æfterre, Ors. 1, 14; S. 58, 12: 1, 7; S. 36, 26. Ðā æðelu ðære æfterran ácennesse (*regenerationis*), Past. 85, 15. Ðæs æfteran sealmes capitul, Ps. Th. 2, arg. On ðære æfteran mīle fram Rōme, Bl. H. 193, 19.

æfter-ræding. v. æfen-ræding.

æfter-ræpe *a crupper:*—Æfterræpe *postela,* Wrt. Voc. i. 23, 15. Mid æfterræpum *postelis,* Hpt. 31, 14, 336. [*O. H. Ger.* after-reifi *postelina.*] Cf. æfter-ráp *in Dict., where add:* [*O. H. Ger.* after-reif *postella*].

æfter-rīdan. *l.* æfter rīdan.

æfter-sang. *Substitute: Matins:*—Se forma tīdsang is ūhtsang mid ðām æftersange ðe ðārtó gebirað, Ll. Th. ii. 376, 6. Tó æftersange *ad matutinas,* Angl. xiii. 396, 449: 402, 528. Æftersanga *symbolnys matutinorum sollempnitas,* R. Ben. I. 43, 2. Æftersangum *matutino,* 46, 13. Æftersangas *matutinas,* Angl. xiii. 428, 904. [*In R. Ben.* I. 45, 17 æftersang *vespera is probably a mistake for* æfensanc.]

æfter-sanglic; *adj. Of matins:*—Lofe hī singon æftersingallice (*l.* sanglice) *laudes psallant matutinales,* Angl. xiii. 398, 476.

æfter-spræc, -sprecan. *l.* æfter-spræc, æfter sprecan. v. sprecan, VI. ¶.

æfter-weard. *Substitute:* I. adj. (1) *later, latter:*—Ver novum foreweard lencten *vel* middeweard lencten, *ver. adultum* æfterweard lencten. *Eodem modo et aestas et autumnus vocantur,* Wrt. Voc. i. 53, 27. (2) *being behind* (?), *absent:*—Ðeáh ðe hē licumlice ðær æfterweard (æfweard, *v. l.*) wære *quamvis corporaliter absens,* Bd. 3, 15; Sch. 264, 6. II. *adv. prep. After:*—Hī urnon ealle him æfterweard, Hml. S. 31, 995. Weorþan æfterweard *to be after, to pursue, follow:*—Iohannes heów ðæt hors mid ðām spuran and weorð him æfterweard . . . and cwæð tó ðām fieóndum, Ælfc. T. 18, 22: Rä. 16, 14. Petrus weard æfterweard *Peter followed,* Hml. Th. i. 374, 6. v. æfte-weard.

æfter-weardness, e; *f. Posterity:*—Æfterweardnesse *posteritatem,* Wrt. Voc. ii. 65, 66.

æfter-wearþ. v. æfter-weard.

æfter-writen; *adj. (ptcpl.) Written later on:*—Ðā ærgenemnedan lǽcedōmas and ðā æfterwritenan, Lch. ii. 186, 12.

æfte-weard. *Dele first quotation, and add:*—On æfteweardum ðǽm sealme *in the latter part of the psalm,* Ps. Th. 38, arg. On æftewyrdne December, and on foreweardan Ianuarie ðām mónþe, Lch. iii. 154, 12. ¶ substantive use:—On æfteweardan ðæs regoles, Hml. S. 3, 150. On æfteweardan ylde heó bið on bedde lange licgende, Lch. iii. 184, 6. *Hand* sceal habban *h* on forewerdan and *d* on æfteweardan, Ælfc. Gr. Z. 292, 3.

æf-þanc, &c. *Add:*—Æfþancan *invidia,* An. Ox. 8, 161: Angl. xiii. 33, 157. Gif hwylc yfeldǽde man þurh ǽnigne æfþancan ōþerne begaleþ, Lch. i. 190, 9. Sē ðe lǽrð sunu his on æfþuncan (*in zelum*) *he that teacheth his son grieveth the enemy* (Ecclus. 30, 3), Scint. 176, 12. Ðā wræc hē his æfþancas on his feóndum, Guth. 14, 4.

æftresta, æf-þunca. v. æfterra, æf-þanc.

æftum; *adv. After:*—Swilce ne wæs oþ þis nū ne æftum ne weorþaþ, Mt. R. 24, 21.

æf-weard. *Add:*—Æfweardum (*absente*) ðam abbode, Gr. D. 35, 32: 64, 11. Sē cwið yfel ðǽm deáfan, sē ðone æfweardan tǽlð *surdo maledicere est absenti derogare,* Past. 453, 2. Hē ðā word ðāra æfweardra swa geara wiste swā ðāra andweardra, Guth. 70, 4: Gr. D. 311, 1. Hē sægde ðā æfweardan þing andweardum mannum *praesentibus absentia nuntiare coepit,* 126, 11: Guth. 86, 9. [*O. H. Ger.* aba-wart *absens.*]

æf-weardness. *Add:*—Hī ofer ðæt swā dōn noldon in ðæs fæder æfweardnysse, ðan hī ongēton ðæt hē him symble wæs ondweard on his gāste, Gr. D. 127, 25. On heora hláfordes æfweardnysse, 29, 2.

æf-wela, an; *m. Decrease of wealth:*—Gyf man mēte þ hē his hūs timbrie þ byð his weaxnes (þ hys gód byþ weaxende, *v. l.*). Gyf him

þince þ his hūs sī tōworpen sum æfwela (ætlǽtnes, *v. l.*) him bið tōweard, Lch. iii. 170, 13.

æf-wirdla, -werdla. *Add:*—Dispendium, i. *damnum, impedimentum, defectio, periculum, detrimentum* æfwerdla, wonung, woni, wana, *vel* hēnþa, Wrt. Voc. ii. 140, 68. Æfwyrdlan *dispendio,* An. Ox. 353: *detrimentum,* i. *contentium,* 452: *jacturam,* Wrt. Voc. ii. 43, 67. Ðæt hē him ðæs befæstan eówdes nänne æfwirdlan (æwyrdlan, *v. l.*) hæbbe *ne detrimenta gregis sibi commissi non patiatur,* R. Ben. 14. 9. Ðæt hī hwylcne æfwyrdlan (æwyrdlan, *v. l.*) geþrowedon heora āgenra sāwla *animarum damna patirentur,* Gr. D. 50, 24. Scipes æfywrdlan *navis jacturam,* 141, 13. Æfwerdlan ārǽfnede *damna pertulit,* 205, 1. Ðā æfwerdlan (æwyrdlan, *v. l.*) selfe hire leoma *ipsa detrimenta membrorum,* 284, 5. Æfwyrdlan, An. Ox. 965: 1864. v. æ-wirdla.

æf-wirth(u)(?); *f. Degradation, disgrace:*—Nyðerunga, æfwyrðe *detrimenta,* R. Ben. I. 16, 6.

æ-fyrmþa. *Dele: washing, ablutions; and see* æ-firmþa.

æg. *l.* æg, *and add:*—Dō æges ðæt hwīte tō, Lch. ii. 20, 12. Genim æges ðæt geoluwe, 22, 19. Æges *geola,* 130, 12. Nō ðonne būtan medmycelne dǽl hlāfes and ān henne æg mid lytle meolc wætere gemengedre hē onfēng, Bd. 3, 23; S. 554, 33. Ðreó ægero, Shrn. 135, 18. Gif hit festendæg sié selle mon fisces and butran and ægera ðæt mon begeotan maege, C. D. i. 293, 11. Genim nigon ægra . . . and nim eall swā fela dropena wīnes swā ðæra ægra beó, Lch. i. 380, 1-5. Sellan ægra tó sūpanne, ii. 220, 7. Genim gebrædde ægru, 100, 11. Gif hē gesihð henne ægru lecgan, iii. 204, 30. Hwæt mǽre ytst ðū? Wyrta and ægra, Coll. M. 34, 27.

æ-gafol (-e?); *adj. Free from tax, rent,* &c.:—Ān hīwissce ægesǽles landæs *hidam liberam,* C. D. v. 137, 23.

ægen. *See other instances under* āgen: ægen-felma; *m.* (not *f.*).

æger-geolu, wes; *n. The yolk of an egg:*—Aegergelu *fitilium,* Txts. 62, 429.

æ-gewrītere. In Kent. Gl. 245 'legum conditores' is rendered by a word which Zupitza reads as *scepttenras.* In Junius' copy of the MS. is given by *ægewriteras.* The *scept* is uncertain, and Zupitza gives *egewritteras* as a more possible reading than that of Junius.

æg-gemang, es; *n. A mixture of eggs:*—Aeggimong *ogastrum* (olgastrum, 46), Wrt. Voc. ii. 115, 44. Æggemang, 63, 38. [Beþe mid aagemoge, Lch. iii. 38, 2.] v. æg-mang.

æg-hwā. *Add:*—Hió gehǽt him æghwæs genóg *abundantiam promittit,* Past. 71, 23: Sch. 94. Sēlre byð æghwām, An. 320: El. 1270: Met. 8, 5. Æghwām, B. 1384: Sat. 363: Met. 8, 38. Fira æghwām, Ps. Th. 134, 3. Ic eom gehéned on æghwām *humiliatus sum usquequaque,* Past. 465, 29. Hēt ic æghwæt swā dōn swā hē ūs bebeād, Nar. 27, 14. Æghwæt gefremman ðæs ðe hié woldan, Bl. H. 137, 1. Hē him æghwæt sealtes beorge, Lch. ii. 130, 8. ¶ æghwæs *in every respect, quite, altogether:*—Æghwæs hē wæs ansund *incolumis inventus est,* Gr. D. 213, 7. Se earm stód ungebígendlic æghwæs þām āgendfreán ungewylde, 254, 38: Th. 44: Jul. 593: Cri. 1421. Æghwæs untǽle, B. 1865. Æghwæs unrīm *quite countless,* 3135. Æghwæs ealne dæg *tota die,* Ps. Th. 55, 4.

æg-hwǽr. *Dele* ā-hwǽr, *and add:* -hwār, -wern. I. local, (1) *in every place,* (a) referring to the whole of space:—God bið ā wesende and æghwǽr ondweard, Bl. H. 19, 26. Æghwār, 23, 21. (b) of limited space:—Oeghuer, -huuēr, ōghuuaer *vulgo, passim,* Txts. 107, 2173. Ægiwern *passim,* An. Ox. 11, 160. Wē forhealdað æghwǽr (-hwār, *v. l.*) Godes gerihta, Wlfst. 157, 14. Hié hergodon æghwǽr þe ðām sǽ, Chr. 918; P. 98, 12: 998; P. 131, 13. Him wæs æghwǽr wā, Sat. 342. Æghwǽr onbūtan *circumquaque,* An. Ox. 2, 251. Æghwǽr on eorþan, Gen. 2705. Geneósian ealra þeóda æghwǽr landes *ad visitandas omnes gentes,* Ps. Th. 58, 5. Æghwǽr eorðan *usquequaque,* Ps. L. 118, 107. [*In Met.* 10. 58 *substitute:*—*the likes of them are everywhere.*] (2) *to every place, in every direction:*—Se wind mæg fēran æghwǽr, Rä. 41, 69. Hié sendon ægwern æfter fultume, Ors. 4, 1; S. 154, 22. II. *in every case:*—Bið andgit æghwǽr sēlest, B. 1059: Gū. 573. III. *in every respect:*—Æghwǽre *usquequaque,* R. Ben. I. 36, 10.

æg-hwæþer. *Add:* I. of two, (1) substantival:—Wæs æghwæþer sāwla full, Bd. 5, 12; S. 627, 39: Cri. 1577: Sal. 108. Æghwæþer ōþerne oftrǽdlice ūt drǽfde, Chr. 887; P. 80, 28. Fæder ðāra æðelinga æghwædres, Rä. 47, 5. Æghwædres . . . worda and weorca, B. 287. Æghwædrum wæs brōga fram ōðrum, 2564. Hæfde æghwǽþre (-hwæþer?, *but for pl. cf.* II. *below*) ende geféred *an end had come to both,* 2844. (b) adjective:—Æghwæþer ende līþ on sǽ, Bd. 1, 25; S. 486, 21. II. of more than two:—Ðrittig manna . . . æghwæþer ðāra wǽron on drohtnunge munuclifes well geléared, Bd. 4, 4; S. 570, 36. ¶ Æghwæþer ge . . . ge (and) *both . . . and:*—Hī æghwæðer ge an farað ge eft cumað, Met. 20, 12. Æghweþer, Bl. H. 125, 8: 215, 13. Forwyrnednesse æghweðer ge on mete, ge on hrægle, ge on æghwy!cum þinge, 219, 29. Wæs ægweder ðæm eádigan were ge seó Godes lufu hāt . . . and him wæs eác manna lufu mycel, 225, 35. v. ægþer.

æg-hwanan. *Add:* I. local, (1) of motion, *from all sides:*—Gegadorode micel folc hit ægþer ge of Cent, ge of Eást-Seaxum, ge æghwonan of ðám nīhstum burgum, Chr. 921; P. 102, 12. Wē beóð

æghwanum cumene, Dóm. L. 120. (2) where action proceeds from all sides and its operation is felt on all sides, *on all sides :*—Mid costungum wē sint æghwonon ūtan behrincgde, Past. 163, 16. Ēghwanon gecnissed, Hml. S. 30, 192. Hē hine æghwanon mid ðǽre rōde tācne gewǽpnode, 23 b, 776. Hī mon æghwanone sēcan sceolde, 23, 236. Nū is æg-hwonon hreám and wōp, nū is heáf æghwonon, nū is æghwonon yfel and slege, and æghwonon ðes middangeard flýhþ from ūs, Bl. H. 115, 15–17. II. fig. *on all sides, in every respect, utterly :*—Ic eom gehēned æghwonane *humiliatus sum usquequaque,* Past. 465, 29. Ne forlǽt ðū mē æghwanan (*usquequaque*), Ps. L. 118, 8. Ic mē ongite æghwonan scyldigne, Bt. 8; F. 24, 12. Ic æghwanane eom ungesǽlig, Hml. S. 30, 205.

**æg-hwider.** *Add: In every direction :*—Hī fērdon æghwider, Chr. 1011; P. 141, 21. Hē æghwider beseah on æghwilce healfe, Hml. S. 23, 503. Dūn mid blóstmium gegyred æghwyder ymbūtan *mons floribus usquequaque vestitus,* Bd. 1, 7; S. 478, 23.

**æg-hwilc.** *Add:* I. as substantive, (1) absolute :—Egsan sceal æghwylc habban, Ps. Th. 75, 9. Æghwylc gecwǽð, B. 987. His brūcan mōt æghwylc on eorðan, Sch. 66. Hē tō æghwylcum sōð sprecende wæs, Bl. H. 223, 29. Fȳr biþ ymbūtan on æghwylcum, þeáh hē uppe seó, Sat. 265: An. 350. (2) with a genitive :—Æghwylc ðāra manna, Bl. H. 37, 3. Hæleða æghwylc, Sat. 194. Gumena æghwilc, Gen. 465. Æghwylc āura heora, Bl. H. 121, 8. Þeóda æghwilc hæfdon . . ., Met. 26, 43. Æghwilc heora tōstencte weorðan sceolden, 29, 88. Æt æghwylcum ānra, Gū. 4. Æghwylcne āura ðāra ðe him bið egesa tō me, Kr. 86. Æghwylc ealra, Ps. Th. 134, 8. Oeghwelce ðinga *omni modo,* Wrt. Voc. ii. 115, 50. Æghwylce þinga, 63, 42. II. as adjective :—Æghwelc man, Bt. 24, 3; F. 84, 11. Æghwylc heáhgerēfa wæs gewita, Bl. H. 177, 14. Æghwylc mennisc leahter, 163, 15. Æghwylces mannes dǽda, 83, 13. Æghwylces mennisces monnes gemet, 163, 35. Būtan ægwylcum leahtre, 4. Tō æghwilcre unríhtnesse, 241, 4. Ælce wīgwǽpna and æghwylce woruldsaca lǽte man stille, Wlfst. 170, 9. ¶ with ān, (1) substantival, cf. I. 2 :—Ðæt ūre æghwylc ān mæg ēce líf geearnian, Wlfst. 283, 21. Æt æghwylcum ānum ðāra, Bl. H. 127, 33. (2) adjectival :—Æghwylcum men gyldan, Bl. H. 123, 33: 125, 7. Æghwylce āne dæge, 91, 29.

**ǽ-gift, e;** *f. Substitute :* **ǽ-gift, es;** *m. or n.; e; f.* (cf. *ǽ-rist for gender*) *A giving up, return, repayment, restoration :*—Sigelm āgef Godan .xxx. punda . . . Ðā ætsōc Goda ðæs feós ǽgiftes (*Goda negavit sibi xxx libras persolutas fuisse*), Cht. Th. 201, 29 : 202, 6. Bǽd Ælfsige ǽgiftes his mannes (*a woman who had been stolen from him*), and hē hine āgef, 206, 30. Ǽgifta *redditus,* An. Ox. 5, 38 : 8, 300. v. ā-gifan.

**æ-gilde;** *adv. l. ǽ-gilde; adj., and add :—Unpaid for,* applied to a slain man for whom *wergild* was not paid :—Gyf þrǽl ðæne þegen āfylle, licge ǽgylde (-gilde, *v. l.*) ealre his mǽgðe; and gyf se þegen ðæne þrǽl ðe hē ǽr āhte afylle, gylde þegengylde, Wlfst. 162, 8.

**æg-lǽc.** *l.* æg-lǽc, -lǽca.

**æg-mang** *a mixture of eggs :*—Aegmang *agastrum,* Wrt. Voc. ii. 99, 55. v. æg-gemang.

**ægnan;** *pl. Awns* (*awn,* with husbandmen, the spire or beard of barley or other bearded grain, Bailey), *chaff, refuse, husks :*—Aegnan *paleae,* Txts. 85, 1526: *quisquiliae,* 91, 1696. [En. graunge vus gardet des arestes (*fro agunes*), Wrt. Voc. i. 155, 1. Hec *arista* a nawn, 233, col. 2. Awene, awne *arista,* Promp. P. 18. Goth. *ahana paleae: Icel.* ögn; *pl.* aguar (-ir) *chaff: O. H. Ger.* agana *arista, migma, festuca.*]

**ægnetrem.** v. trem *in Dict.: ægnian. l.* ægnian, *and substitute :*—v. āgnian.

**æg-scill, e;** *f. An egg-shell :*—Clǽnes huniges āne ægscylle fulle, Lch. iii. 6, 29. iii ægscylla, 14, 22. Twā ægscille fulle, i. 376, 8.

**æg-þer.** *Add:* I. substantival :—Ægþer ðāra ðe com from mē, Bt. 7, 3; F. 20, 5. Hyra ægðer rīxade .xxx. wintra, Chr. 560; P. 19, 2. Wit hǽman sceoldon, and uncer lāþette ægþer oþer, þeáh þe hē hit ōþrum ne tǽle, Shrn. 39, 22. Heora ægðer ōðerne ofslōg, Ors. 2, 3; S. 68, 18. Ðāra folca ægðer on ōðerum micel wæl geslōgan, 3, 1; S. 98, 6. Ægðer heora on ōðer hāwede, Chr. 1003; P. 135, 12. Hē hié ægðres benam ge heora cyninges ge heora anwaldes, Ors. 2, 1; S. 64, 9, 12: Ll. Th. i. 346, 5. Wit willnaþ ðāra ægðres, 2, 1; F. 152, 9. Ægðrum emnneáh, 39, 7; F. 222, 8. Of ægðrum his rīca, Ps. Th. 9, 36. Ðā dyde hē him ægþer tō gewealdon, Ors. 3, 7; S. 112, 25. Hū ne hæfdon wē ǽr gereht ðæt ðā gesǽlþa and sió godcundnes ān wǽre? Sē ðe ðonne ðā gesǽlþa hæfþ, ðonne hæfþ hē ǽgþer; sē ðe ðon(u)e ǽgþer hæfþ, hū ne bið sē ðonne full eádig?, Bt. 34, 5; F. 138, 33. On ægðer þǽra bōca sind feówertig cwyda, Hml. Th. ii. 2, 13. Hwí sceal ic beón bedǽled ægðer mīnra sunena (*utroque filio*), Gen. 27, 45. Ne hafað hió eágena ægðer twēga, Rä. 40, 11. Ðæt hē mehte ǽgþerne gerǽcan, Chr. 894; P. 84, 26. II. adjectival :—Æt ægþrum cirre, Chr. 918; P. 98, 29. Hēt hē ægðer eáge ūt ādōn, 1995; P. 231, 27. III. conjunction, (1) with two clauses :—Ægðer wið East-Engle ge wið Norðhymbre, Chr. 906; P. 94, 22. (2) with more than two :—Ægðer ge eargast, ge wrǽnast, ge ofermōdgast, Ors. 2, 2; S. 66, 28. Ægðer ge ðone cyning, ge his sunu, ge

ealle ðā ðe cynecynnes wǽron, 36: Chr. 897; P. 90, 16. Ægðer be ðǽm sǽriman on Eást-Seaxum, and on Centlande, and on Sūð-Seaxum, and on Hamtūnscīre, 994; P. 129, 7. v. æg-hwæþer.

**æg-wern.** v. æg-hwǽr.

**æ-gylt.** *Dele* a breach of the law, *and add :*—Ǽgylt *excesus,* Wrt. Voc. ii. 107, 79. Ægylt, 30, 7: *excessus, i. culpa, delicta,* 145, 67. v. ā-gyltan.

**æ-gype.** *l.* ǽ-gīpe (?) *without skill or cunning.* Cf. geáp *callidus.*

**æhher.** v. eár.

**æ-híw, es;** *n. Pallor :*—Ǽhíwum *palloribus,* An. Ox. 4897.

**æ-híwe;** *adj.* I. *without colour, pallid :*—Ǽhíwe *decolor, pallidus,* Germ. 392, 69. Oðre hwíle hē bið blǽc and æhíwe, An. Ox. 4897, note. II. *without form, ugly, deformed :*—Ǽhíwe *deformes* (*opifices turpi natura corporis*), An. Ox. 2, 498.

**æ-hlȳp.** *Dele* ǽ *law.*

**æhri(g)e** (?), an; *f. The husk of an ear* (?) :—Aehrian, ægrihan (æhrigan?) *quisquiliae,* Txts. 90, 840. v. æhher.

**æht.** *Add: In Ll. Th. i. 6, 3 the weak form,* ealle ðā æhtan, *occurs, and a form not feminine.* mīnes ágenes æhtes, 194, 16. I. *what is owned, a possession :*—Æht *res,* heánra manna (man, Wrt.) *vel* ceorla (-ic, Wrt.) æhta *peculium,* Wrt. Voc. i. 20, 57, 59. Ǽhta *gadzarum,* An. Ox. 3155. Gif ceorl deóflum gelde, hē sié ealra his æhta (MS. æhtan) scyldig, Ll. Th. i. 40, 5, 6. Selle hē his wǽpn and his æhta his freóndum tō gehealdenne, 60, 8. I a. of landed property :—Ðæt seó æht (*hereditas*) ūre sȳ, Lk. 20, 14. Nǽht elles hire ne sealde būton .vi. yntsan ānre æhte (*possessiunculae*), Gr. D. 222, 26. Hī genāmon of ðæs biscopes æhte (*v. l.* lande) twēgen cnihtas; seó æht (ðæt land, *v. l.*) wæs underþeódod ðǽre foresǽdan ceastre, 80, 7. Gyf ðū ðæs wyrte on ðīnre æhte hafast oððe hyre sǽd on ðīn hūs āhēhst, Lch. i. 308, 12. Ðæt ðæt yrfe on his æhte geboren wǽre, Ll. Th. i. 204, 14. Ic hit āgnian wille tō āgenre æhte, 184, 5. I b. of movables as opposed to land :—Hwǽm ic mīnes landes geunnen hæbbe and ealre mīnre æhte, C. D. iv. 55, 5. Fōe tō londe and tō ǽlre æhte, i. 234, 29. Hwīlum be āre, hwīlum be æhte, Ll. Th. i. 328, 12. Mīnra yldrena ðe mē mín ār of com and mīne æhta, Cht. Th. 529, 1. Fōn ðā nēhstan frȳnd tō ðam lande and tō ðām æhtan, Ll. Th. i. 416, 10: 420, 10. Of lande mid heora æhtum gewīten, i. 38, 2. I c. of cattle :—Gif heora menn sleán ūre æhta, Ll. Th. i. 288, 10. I d. of slaves. Cf. æht-boren :—Gif hwylc man his æht (*servum*) ofslyhð, Ll. Th. ii. 182, 29: 268, 9. II. *possession :*—Hilde gebohte tȳn hīda landes hire on æhte, Bd. 3, 24; S. 557, 2. Gif ðū wēne ðæt hit ðín bócland sȳ, ðæt ðū on eardast, and on āgene æht geseald, Wlfst. 260, 3. v. fær-, on- (?), weorold-æht.

**ā-ēhtan** *to persecute :*—Āoehtad gē bíðon *persequentur,* Lk. L. 21, 12.

**æht-boren;** *adj. Slave-born.* v. æht, I d, *and* þeów-boren :—Nā ðā āne ðe freó synt, ac gyt mā ðe æhtborene (*ex conditione servili*) synt, R. Ben. 138, 20.

**æhte-mann.** *Add: a serf :*—Be manna metsunge. Ānan esne gebyreð tō metsunge . . . Deówan wīfmen. . . . Eallum æhtemannum gebyreð . . ., Ll. Th. i. 436, 25–33. Ðā weard gefullod fæder and sunu mid heora innhýrede and heora æhtemannum, Hml. S. 5, 308. v. æht, I d.

**æhtere.** *l.* eahtere.

**æht-spéd, e;** *f. Wealth, riches :*—Gefylled is eorðe æhtspéde mid ðīnre *impleta est terra possessione tua,* Ps. L. 103, 24.

**æht-spédig.** *Add: having great possessions :*—Sum ríce man and for worlde æhtspédig, Bl. H. 197, 27.

**æ-hwænne.** v. ā-hwænne : **æ-hwǽr** = æg-hwǽr, Ps. Th. 88, 31.

**æl** *an awl.* *Add* v. awel : **æl** *oil. l.* æle.

**æl.** *Add :*—Ǽl *anguila,* Wrt. Voc. ii. 100, 39. Ǽl, ii. 7, 1 : i. 77, 65. Smæl ǽl *anguilla,* 66, 6. Ǽl *muraenula,* 5: 281, 66: ii. 55, 76: 56, 21. Eil, 114, 25. Ǽl *mula, sǽl murenula,* 57, 73–4. Ðonne ðū fisc habban wyle . . . Ǽles tācen is . . . swā swā mon ǽl dēð ðonne hine mon on spite stagan wyle, Tech. ii. 124, 6–11. v. leaxas and hundteóntig ǽla, Ll. Th. i. 146, 20.

**ǽl, e;** *f. Burning :*—Ðāra eágan scīnað swā leóhte swā is ān micel blācern on ǽle (onǽle ? cf. on-ǽl) *their eyes shine as bright as is a great lamp a-light,* Nar. 37, 18.

**æ-lǽrende.** *l.* ǽ-lǽrend.

**ǽ-lǽte;** *adj. Desert, desolate :*—Oð ðæt heora burga weorðan ǽlǽte and weorðan heora eardas swȳðe āwēste *donec desolentur civitates absque habitatore, et domus sine homine, et terra relinquetur deserta,* Wlfst. 47, 21. v. next word.

**ǽ-lǽte, an;** *f.: es; n. A desert :*—Ǽlǽtan (ā-, Wrt.) *deserta, s. vocata quae non seruntur,* Wrt. Voc. ii. 139, 14. Wēstensetlan ðe feor fram mannum gewītað and wēste stōwa and ǽlǽtu lufiaþ, R. Ben. 134, 12. v. preceding word.

**ǽ-lǽte, an;** *f. A divorced woman :*—Ne gewīfige on gehālgodre nunnan ne on ǽlǽtan ǽnig crīsten man, Wlfst. 271, 13: 308, 9: Ll. Th. i. 318, 18. Ǽlǽten, 364, 26. v. *preceding words, and* ā-lǽtan.

**æ-lagol;** *adj. Legislative :*—Ǽlagol *legifer,* Germ. 397, 363.

**ǽlan.** *l.* ǽlan, *and add*: I. *to kindle* light, fire:—Hí fýr ǽlað, Wal. 22. Ne scyle nán mon blácern ǽlan under mittan, Past. 43, 2. Ǽldon *adolent, incendunt,* Germ. 402, 68. II. *to burn up.* v. Ph. 222: 526: Cri. 813 (*in Dict.*). III. *to burn, expose to fire* what is not consumed:—Se deópa seáð giémeð gǽsta, ǽleð hý mid ðý ealdan líge, Cri. 1547. [Se geréfa hét bringen leáden fæt, and hét hit mid wætere áfyllan, and dyde hit ǽlen swýþe hát, Nar. 46, 4.]

**ǽ-láreów,** es; *m. A doctor of the law, a Pharisee:*—Gebed ðæs ǽláruas *oratio pharisaei,* Lk. p. 9, 13. Mið ǽlárua *apud pharisaeum,* p. 7, 10. Ǽláruas *pharisaei,* p. 5, 5. Ðá ǽláruuas, 5, 17. Tó ðæm aeláruum, Jn. 9, 13.

**ǽlaþ, aelbitu.** v. ealaþ, ilfette.

**ǽlc.** *Add*: I. *each.* (1) substantival:—þ ǽlc preósta scrífe, Ll. Th. ii. 258, 9. Ǽlc ðæra ðe ðás míne word gehýrð, Mt. 7, 24. Ǽlces mé þincþ ðæt hé sié wyrþe . . . þone weorþscipe hé forgifþ ǽlcum ðára ðe hine lufað, Bt. 27, 2; F. 96, 29-32. Hira geféra ǽlces ðára ðe wel doo, Past. 75, 12. Unscildig eówres ǽlces blódes, 379, 14. (1 a) *combined with* án:—Nim ðyssa wyrta ǽlcre ánre swá micel swá ðára óþra, Lch. iii. 72, 14. On ǽlcum ánum hí sint ealle, Bt. 33, 3; F. 126, 15. (1 b) *with* óþer, *where there is reciprocal action:*—Bere eówer ǽlc óðres byrðenne, Past. 219, 12. þurh ðæt ðe hí him sylfe ǽlc óþerne forfóre, Chr. 1052; P. 181, 22. Hí þegniað ǽlc óðrum, Met. 25, 12. (2) *adjectival:*—Hwílum on áne healfe, hwílum on ǽlce healfe, Chr. 892; P. 82, 34. (2 a) *combined with* án:—Ǽlc án hagelstán wegeð fíf pund, Wlfst. 228, 6. On ǽlcre ánre talentan wæs lxxx punda, Ors. 4, 6; S. 170, 28. (2 b) *in plural, all:*—Wæs hé ǽlcum witum láþ, Bt. 28; F. 100, 27. On ǽlcum þingum, R. Ben. 15, 20. Se ilca is wendende ǽlce onwaldas, Ors. 2, 1; S. 64, 2. Ǽlce misdǽda ágyldan, Ll. Th. i. 328, 15. Hí forbudon ǽlce wífunga, ii. 374, 35: 286, 30. Ǽlce wígwǽpna lǽte man stille, Wlfst. 170, 8. In *excluding* phrases, *any:*—Búton ǽlcon þegne Crēca lond sēcan, Ors. 4, 1; S. 156, 32. Búton ǽlcre hreówe, 2, 1; S. 64, 7: Past. 37, 2. Búton ǽlcere mēder . . . búton ǽlcum eorðlicum fæder, Hml. Th. ii. 6, 5-7. On ánum báte būtan ǽlcum gerēþrum, Chr. 891; P. 82, 19. Wiðūtan ǽlcon wǽpnon, 1086; P. 220, 28. II a. *combined with* án:—Būtan ǽlcre ānre tale (*printed* arentale), Cht. Th. 563, 16. *See also* ǽfre, III.

**ǽlc-hwega,** -hugu *every:*—Ðæt ic hwelcnehugu (ǽlcne—, Cott. MS.) dǽl gesecge Alexandres dǽda, Ors. 3, 7; S. 110, 13.

**ǽlcor, ǽlcra.** v. elcor, elcra: ǽlecung. v. R. Ben. 14, 7 note.

**ǽled.** *l.* ǽled, *and* deļe [*pp. of* ǽlan.]

**ǽled-fýr.** *l.* ǽled fýr: ǽle-lendisc. v. ele-lendisc.

**ǽle-grǽdig;** *adj. Very greedy, ravenous:*—Gezabel sceolon etan ǽlegrǽdige hundas, Hml. S. 18, 213.

**ǽle-midde,** an; *f. The exact middle;* only in the phrase on *ǽle-middan* = just in the middle:—Seó firmamentum tyrnð symle onbūtan ús. . . . Seó eorðe stent on ǽlemiddan, Lch. iii. 254, 16. Ðǽre sunnan hǽtu wyrcð fíf dǽlas on middanearde. . . . Án ðæra dǽla is on ǽlemiddan, weallende, 260, 20. Wæs óðer treów on ǽlemiddan paradisum, Hex. 24, 17. Agnes stód on ǽlemiddan gesund, Hml. S. 7, 223. Ðá hēngon ðá cempan Críst on ǽlemiddan, and ðá twēgen sceaðan him on twá healfa, Hml. Th. ii. 254, 22.

**ǽ-leng.** *l.* ǽ-lenge, ǽlinge, *and add*:—Mē þincþ ðæt . . . tó ǽlenge (MS. -legge) tó gehýranne, Shrn. 195, 21. On ǽlengum ðingum geðyldige, Past. 41, 16. v. *next two words, and see* elenge, alange *in* N. E. D.

**ǽ-lenge,** ǽlinge *tedium, weariness:*—Ðý lǽs ǽlinge ūt ádrífe selfiicne secg, Met. Einl. 6.

**ǽ-lengness,** ǽlingness, e; *f. Tedium, weariness:*—Ǽlengnes *fastidium,* Wrt. Voc. ii. 146, 46. Ǽlingnysse þolaþ rihtwís *tedium patitur justus,* Scint. 216, 9.

**ǽlepe** *origanum,* Wrt. Voc. i. 68, 28. [*Wülcker prints* ǽlere; *perhaps* ǽlene *should be read: cf. origanum* elene, Lch. iii. 304, col. 1.]

**ǽle-puta;** *m. l.* ǽle-pūte; *f., and add*:—Myne *vel* ǽlepūte *capito,* Wrt. Voc. i. 55, 75.

**ǽ-léten.** Dele. v. ǽ-lǽte.

**ǽle-wealdend** *almighty:*—Ǽlewealdend fæder *cuncti parens,* Germ. 401, 128. [O. Sax. alo-waldand.] v. eall-wealdend.

**Ǽlf,** e; *f. The Elbe:*—Ǽlfe mūða ðǽre ié, Ors. 1, 1; S. 16, 6, 27. [*Icel.* Elfr.]

**ǽlf.** *l.* e; *f., and add*:—Gif men hwilc yfel costung weorþe oþþe ǽlf oþþe nihtgengan, Lch. ii. 344, 16. v. dūn-, land-ǽlf; ilf.

**-ǽlfen.** *Add*: feld-, sǽ-, wæter-ǽlfen: ǽl-fer, n. l. ǽl-faru; f.

**ǽl-físc,** es; *m. An eel:*—Ic geeácnode tó ðǽre ǽrran sylene týn þúsenda ǽlfixa ǽlce geáre ðám munecum, C. D. iii. 61, 5.

**ǽl-fremed** (el-). *Add*: I. *strange, foreign, not belonging to one:*—Næs mid him [god] elfremed (*alienus*), Cant. M. ad fil. 12. Se ælfremeda Herōdes ðæs ríces geweóld, Hml. Th. i. 82, 4. Hē earmlíce geendode on ǽlfremedum earde, Hml. S. 25, 547. On eorðan elfremedre *in terra aliena,* Ps. L. 136, 4. þurh ǽlfremede horwan gefýled *defiled by others' pollution,* Hml. S. 7, 129. Ealle middaneardlice ðing swá swá ǽlfremede forhogigende *cuncta hujus mundi velut aliena spernendo,* Hml. Th. ii. 130, 1. II. *with* fram, *stranger to anything, without a*

*share in, free from:*—Se munuc sceal beón ælfremed fram eorðlicum dǽdum, Hex. 36, 24. Swá freóh fram deáðes sárnysse swá swá ǽlfremed fram líchamlicere gewemmednysse, Hml. Th. i. 76, 15. Culfre is fram geallan biternysse ǽlfremed, 584, 35. Wē wǽron þurh synna ǽlfremede fram Gode; ðá wurde wē eác ǽlfremede fram his englum getealde, 38, 15. Fram ðám ēcan wurðmynte ǽlfremede beón, Hml. A. 21, 169.

**Ǽlfric.** For an account of Ælfric see 'Ælfric, a new study of his life and writings,' by C. L. White (Yale Studies in English)

**ælf-sciéne,** -sciéno; **ælf-scínu.** *Take together under* ǽlf-scíne.

**ælf-siden.** *Add*:—Þeós sealf is gōd wiþ ǽlcre feóndes costunga and ǽlfsidenne, Lch. ii. 334, 18. [Cf. (?) *Icel.* síða *to charm*; seiðr *a charm.*]

**ælf-þone;** *f.?* *Dele* ?: ǽl-fylc. *l.* ǽl-fylce.

**ǽl-hýd(?),** e; *f. An eel-skin:*—Man sceal habban ǽlhýde, ofnrace, mexscofle, Angl. ix. 265, 2.

**ǽ-lic** (ǽw-). *Add*: I. *of law, concerned with law, belonging to law:*—Hē (John) wæs ǽgðer ge ǽlic ge godspellic, Hml. S. 16, 101. Ǽlice *legalia (volumina),* An. Ox. 4949. Tó ðám fíf ǽlicum bōcum, Hml. Th. i. 188, 20: 98, 33: Hml. A. 24, 14. II. *in accordance with law, fixed by law, legal, legitimate:*—Ǽlicere *legitimae,* Hpt. Gl. 411, 69. Oð ðæt hí becōmon tō ǽlicre yldo *until they came of age,* Hml. A. 129, 439. Oð ǽlice yldo, 132, 536. Ǽlice *legitimi,* Angl. xiii. 369, 57. Ǽlicera (-e, MS.) bebóda *praeceptorum legalium,* An. Ox. 1017. Tó ðám ǽlicum onsǽgednyssum, Num. 18, 2. Ǽlice *legalia (scita),* An. Ox. 5144. II a. *with special reference to marriage.* v. ǽ:—Ǽulice hǽmæd *legitimum connubium,* An. Ox. 415. Ǽwlices gegæderscipes *legitime jugalitatis,* 582. Ǽcenned of ǽlicum gesinscype, Bd. 1, 27; S. 495, 22. Tó ǽlicum gyftum, Hml. A. 129, 441.

**ǽ-líce;** *adv. Lawfully, legitimately:*—Ǽlíce lybbende, Hml. A. 24, 12. Ǽwlíce *legitime,* Angl. xiii. 369, 50.

**ǽ-lifne (?);** *adj. Without means of support* (v. lifen), *nourished by others (?):*—Aelisnae *alumnis (alumni ?),* Ep. Gl. 3 d, 38.

**ǽling** *burning. Substitute:*—Lígrǽsc *vel* ǽling *coruscatio,* i. *fulgor, splendor,* Wrt. Voc. ii. 136, 3. Synna ne beóð nǽfre áfeormode for nánes fýres ǽlincge, Hml. Th. ii. 590, 20.

**ǽling** *weariness.* v. ǽ-lenge: **ǽlingness.** v. ǽ-lengness.

**ælmes-bæþ,** es; *n. Washing of the poor done as an act of charity:*—Sceóte man ælmessan . . . hwílum ælmesbæð, hwílum þearfena fótþweál, Wlfst. 171, 2.

**ælmes-dǽd,** e; *f. An alms-deed, a charitable action:*—Ðá ðing ðe God bebeád, ðæt is . . . ælmesdǽda, Hml. Th. ii. 22, 10: 602, 10. Nis nán ðearfa fram ælmesdǽdum áscyred, 106, 8. Hē on ælmesdǽdum áwunode *in eleemosynis permansit,* Bd. 5, 19; S. 636, 28. Gif se mon áhefð his handa tó ælmesdǽdum, Bl. H. 37, 24: H. R. 17, 27: Wlfst. 238, 24. Mid ælmesdǽdum and mid óðrum gódum weorcum, 142, 24. Góde weorc began and ælmesdǽda, 286, 6: Hml. Th. ii. 100, 21.

**ælmes-feoh.** *Add*:—Peter's pence (v. Alms-fee in N. E. D.), Ll. Th. i. 432, 9.

**ælmes-full;** *adj. Liberal with alms, charitable:*—Ælfgár ð se ælmesfulla, Chr. 1021; P. 154, 30. Wē gehýrdan secgan þe ðám ælmesfullan hū góde sáwle hē hæfð, Hml. A. 166, 61. Ælmysfulle *eleemosynis largi,* Ll. Th. ii. 224, 27. [Sein Martin þe bigan on his guwuðe to bien almesful, O. E. Hml. ii. 85, 10. Milde and allmessfull, Orm. 9931.]

**ælmes-gedál,** es; *n. Distribution of alms:*—Bisceopes dægweorc . . . his ælmesgedál, Ll. Th. ii. 314, 22: Wlfst. 171, 3. Ælmesgedál dǽle man gelōme, mete ðám ofhingredum, 74, 2.

**ælmes-georn.** *Add*:—Heó wæs swíðe ælmesgeorn, and ðá ðearfan . . . mid cystigum mōde . . . áfēdde, Hml. Th. i. 60, 14. Ælmysgeorn, Shrn. 98, 4. Sýn wē rúmmóde þearfendum mannum and earmum ælmesgeorne, Bl. H. 109, 15. Ælmesgeorne and árdǽde wið earme men, 131, 2. Mildheorte and ælmesgeorne, 95, 26: Wlfst. 109, 12. [Elmesgeorn nes heo nefre, O. E. Hml. i. 43, 32.]

**ælmes-gifa,** an; *m. An almsgiver:*—Sē ðe wǽre gítsiende óðra manna þinga, weorðe of his ágenan rihte begytenan ælmesgyfa (-gifa, *v. l.*) georne, Wlfst. 72, 4.

**ælmes-gifu,** e; *f. What is given as alms, alms:*—Ðæt ðæt heom góde men tó ælmesgife for Godes lufan sealdon, Wlfst. 159, 20.

**ælmes-hláf,** es; *m. Bread given as alms:*—Willa ic gesellan of ðém ærfe ðe mē God forgef ǽlce gēre CL. hláfa, L. hwítehláfa, CXX. elmes-hláfes, Cht. Th. 474, 26.

**ælmes-leóht,** es; *n. Light brought to church by one keeping a vigil during a fast:*—Ðonne man fæste . . . forlǽte man ǽlce worldbysga, and dæges and nihtes swá man oftost mæge on cirican gewunige, and mid ælmesleóhte wacigan ðár þ, Ll. Th. ii. 288, 1.

**ælmes-lic;** *adj.* I. *of the nature of alms, eleemosynary, charitable:*—Hié hígon geféormien and hígon ús mid heora godcundum gódum swǽ gemynen swǽ ús árlic and him ælmeslic sié, Cht. Th. 476, 34. Swē hit him rehtlicast and elmestlicast wēre, 465, 24. II. *depending upon alms, poor:*—Ælmysli[cum] *paupertino,* An. Ox. 56, 302.

**ælmes-líce;** *adv. Charitably:*—Fōe hē tó thaem londe and hit forgelde and thaet wiorth gedaele sore hiora gástas suae aelmeslíce and suae rehtlíce suae hē him seolfa on his wísdôme geleornie, C. D. i. 234, 34.

**ælmes-mann**, es; *m. An alms-man* (v. N. E. D.), *one supported by alms, a bedesman* or *a beggar*:—Ðeáh se man nime æune stán and lecge on fúl slóh, ðæt se ælmesman mæge mid ðám óðrum fét steppan on ðá clǽnan healfe, Wlfst. 239, 10. On ælmesmannes hiwe, Hml. S. 23, 562. Ðæt gé dæghwámlíce dǽlan ælmessan ... ælmesmannum oððe wydewum, Wlfst. 238, 28: Lch. i. 400, 17. Ðonne wille ic ðæt man nime tó ǽlcan ðissa háma twelf ælmesmen, and gif hwæt hera ǽnigan getíde, sette man ðǽr óperne tó, C. D. B. iii. 75, 38.

**ælmes-riht**, es; *n. A right* or *obligation in reference to alms* (cf. Riht is ðæt man betǽce ... þriddan dǽl (folces ælmessan) ðám þearfum, Ll. Th. ii. 256, 30):—Ǽghwilc ælmesriht ðe man on Godes ést scolde mid rihte georne gelǽstan, ælc man gelitlað oððe forhealdeð, Wlfst. 159, 21. Ðrælriht wǽron generwde and ælmesriht gewanode, 158, 16.

**ælmesse**. *Add*: I. *alms, what is given in charity*:—Wist *vel* ælmesse *stips*, Wrt. Voc. i. 17, 8. Ælmesse *agape*, 33: *eleemosyna vel agape*, 28, 56. Swá swá wæter ádwæscð fýr, swá ádwæscð seó ælmysse synne, Hml. Th. ii. 106, 7. Ne selle mon tó fela ... ðý lǽs him gehreúwe sió ælmesse, Past. 325, 8. Ðé þúhte ǽfre tó lytel úre ælmesse, Wlfst. 241, 3. Ælmæssan *stipis*, Wrt. Voc. ii. 78, 35. Ðæt gé dæghwámlíce dǽlan ælmessan be ðám dǽle ðe ǽlcum men tó onhagige, þeáh hit ne sý bútan feórðan dǽl ánes hláfes, Wlfst. 238, 26. Wé lǽrað ðæt preóstas swá dǽlan folces ælmessan ðæt hig ... folc tó ælmessan gewǽnian. And wé lǽrað ðæt preóstas sealmas singan ðonne hí ðá ælmessan dǽlan, Ll. Th. ii. 256, 7-11. Ic ðás ælmessan gesette on mínem erfelande, Cht. Th. 475, 26. Hwæt sceoldon ðé úre ælmessan? Wlfst. 240, 15. 'Forgyfað, and eów bið forgyfen. Syllað, and eów bið geseald.' Ðás twá ælmessena cynn ús sind tó begánne, Hml. Th. ii. 100, 31. Ðá góde weorc ðára ælmæssena, Gr. D. 320, 25. Geornfull on árfæstum wæstmum ælmesena, Bd. 4, 11; S. 579, 7. Tó ælmessum *ad agapem*, Wrt. Voc. ii. 86, 57. II. *a charitable action*:—þeáh se man ne nime búton ǽnne stán and ðæne gelecge on fúl slóh, ðæt se ælmesman mid óðrum fét stæppan on ðá clǽnan healfe, ðæt him bytð swýþe micel ælmesse, Wlfst. 303, 11. Ic bidde eów þæt (þǽre?) ælmyssan ðæt ic móte ánes þinges áxian, Hml. S. 23, 721. III. *an offering*:—Éghwelc cwicu almes (almus, L.) *omnis victima*, Mk. R. 9, 49. [Perhaps the word shows Celtic influence; cf. Old Irish *almsan*.]

**ælmes-selen**, e; *f. Alms-giving*:—Ðæt hálige gebed and seó hlútre lufu Godes and seó ælmessylen, Wlfst. 146, 4: Dóm. L. 28, 9. Fæsten and wæccan and ælmessylena æfter úrum gemete, Bl. H. 73, 27. Tó ðám weorce ælmæssylena *eleemosynarum operibus*, Gr. D. 329, 13: 321, 24. Hé hit hæfde geearnod mid ælmæsselenum and gódum weorcum, 330, 18. Mid bénum and mid ælmessylenum, Ll. Th. ii. 324, 32.

**ælmes-weorc**, es; *n. Alms-deed, work of charity*:—Ðæt wé úre synna béton mid fæstenum and mid gebedum and mid ælmesweorcum, Bl. H. 25, 17. [To wirrkenn allmeswerrken, Orm. 10118.]

**ælpig**. v. án-lípig.

**æl-syndrig** *quite apart, single*:—Ælsyndrio *singuli*, Lk. R. 2, 3.

**æl-tǽwe**. l. æl-tǽwe, -teáwe, -teówe, -tówe, *and add*:—Ic ongite ðætte æltǽwe anweald nis on nánum woruldríce, Bt. 33, 1; F. 120, 3. Se geleáfa strengra bið ðær ðær hé æltǽwe bið, Hml. Th. i. 250, 20. Hyt is æltǽwe gyf hí mon hreáwe swylgeþ, Lch. i. 344, 16. Hyra (*joy and sorrow*) náðer ne mæg beón æltǽwe bútan óðrum, Prov. K. 71. Se mon ðe his módgeðanc æltówe byþ, Gr. D. 2, 5. Hé hét geáxian sumne æltǽwne drý, Hml. S. 14, 49. Ic ðá égðyrle macige ðe ælteówe beóð, 36, 69. Ðá æltǽwan mód ðára gódra esua *piae subditorum mentes*, Past. 199, 3. Ðeáh hié wieton ðæt hié æltǽwe ne sín *cum de imperfectione reprehenduit*, 7. Hé ne nom náne ware húlice hié wǽron, for ðon hiera wæs má forcúþra ðonne æltǽwra, Ors. 5, 4; S. 224, 23. Hæfde ic ælteówe þénas nǽre ic ðus eáðelíce oferswíðed, Hml. S. 11, 226.

**æl-tǽwlíce**. *Add*:—Ðone mon ðú meaht gelácnian æltǽwlíce, Lch. ii. 348, 16, 22.

**æl-þeód**, &c., **ǽ-manne**, **æmbern**. v. el-þeód, &c., ǽ-men, embren.

**ǽ-melle**; *adj. Insipid*:—Insipidum, *quod saporen non habet, hoc est* unmeagle *sive* ǽmelle, Wrt. Voc. ii. 49, 37. Cf. á-mællad.

**ǽ-melness**. *Add*: I. *want of energy* or *interest, sloth*:—Se sixta heáfodleahtor (*accidia*) is ásolcennys oððe ǽmelnys. Se leahtor déð ðæt ðám men ne lyst nán ðing tó góde gedón, ac gǽð him ásolcen fram ǽlcere dugeðe, Hml. Th. ii. 220, 22. Æmylnys, Hml. S. 1, 107. II. *weariness, tedium, disgust*:—Æmelnes *fastidium*, Wrt. Voc. ii. 146, 46. Ðǽr beóð ealle unrótnyssa, ádl and yrre and ǽmelnys *taedia, tristitiae, indignatio, languor* (Dóm. L. p. 25, 115), Wlfst. 139, 18: Dóm. L. 228. Unrótnes, ǽmelnys *taedia, tristitiae*. Snoffan ǽmylnysse *nausiae tedio*, Angl. xiii. 369, 50. Ænmælnessa *fastidia*, Hpt. 33, 238, 5.

**ǽ-men**. *Add*: ǽ-menne, ǽ-mann (? v. *next word; for declension cf.* ǽ-mód):—Ðá wundrade Alexander hwý hit swá ǽmenne wǽre *vacuam civitatem ratus*, Ors. 3, 9; S. 134, 12. Hié hit ðær swá ǽmenne métton, 2, 4; S. 76, 16.

**ǽ-menne** *solitude*:—'Ðú beþorftest ðæt ðú hæfdest dígele stówe and ǽmanne (-menne?) ǽlces óðres þinges (*ista solitudinem meram desiderant*) and fǽáwa cúðe men.' Ðá cwæt ic: 'Ic nebbe nán ðára ne ðonne ǽmenne ne óðera manna fultum ne dýgela stówe,' Shrn. 165, 8-12.

**ǽmerge**, an; *f.* I. *embers, ashes*:—Se hláf wæs mid ðám glédum and mid ðǽre ǽmyrgan (-yrian, -ergean, *v. ll.*) (*cineribus*) bewrigen, Gr. D. 87, 11. Berèc hý on háte ǽmergean, Lch. iii. 30, 18. II. *fig. dust*:—Ic nán gást ne com ac ǽmerge and axe and eall fláesc, Hml. S. 23 b, 286. [O. H. Ger. cimuria *busta: Icel.* eimyrja; *f. embers.*]

**ǽmet-bed(d)**, es; *n. An ant-hill*:—Genim ǽmetbed mid ealle, ðára ðe hwílum fleogað, beóþ reáde, Lch. ii. 338, 21.

**ǽmete**. l. ǽmet(t)e, *and add*:—Æmette *formica*, Wrt. Voc. i. 78, 65. Æmete *chameleon*, ii. 15, 59. Swá þicce hié áweóllon swá ǽmettan, Nar. 11, 13. Émetan *formicas*, Kent. Gl. 1102. Geseah ic micelne ǽmettena heáp, Hml. A. 204, 315.

**ǽmet-hwíl**. *Add*:—Ðæs restedæges ǽmethwíle (æn-, MS.) *Sabbati otium*, An. Ox. 40, 18.

**ǽmet-hyll**. *Add*:—Past. 191, 25.

**ǽmetta**, ǽmeta, ǽmta. *Add*:—On ǽmettan *in tranquilitate*, Past. 59, 1. Beóð hié swíður on hiera móde geswenced for ðǽm ǽmettan (ǽmtan, Hatt. MS.) *ipsa deterius sua quiete fatigantur*, 126, 24. Swá oft swá hí ǽmtan (ǽmettan, *v. l.*) habbaþ *quotiescumque vacant*, Bd. 4, 25; S. 601, 16: Ll. Th. i. 236, 3. v. un-ǽmetta.

**ǽmetig**, ǽmetig, ǽmtig. *Add*: I. *of space, empty, void, vacant*:—Seó stów ne bið nóht longe ǽmettugu, Shrn. 82, 24. Æmettig, ǽmtig, Bd. 4, 30; Sch. 537, 6. Æmtig innoþ, Scint. 57, 4. Gyt is rýmet ǽmtig, Hml. Th. ii. 376, 9. Ælc beóð ǽmtig (*vacua*) byþ gesewen, Coll. M. 28, 33. Ðæt ǽmtige fæc bufon ðǽre lyfte, Lch. iii. 242, 16. Æne ǽmtige cytan, Hml. S. 33, 170. Æmtige fatu mid wíne áfyllan, Hml. Th. ii. 58, 14. I a. *with gen.*:—Byden ǽlces eles ǽmtig, Gr. D. 160, 10. II. *devoid, void of, free from*:—'Wes ðú hál, geofena ful.' Heó wæs ful cweden, næs ǽmetugu, Bl. H. 5, 5. II a. *with gen.*:—Æmetig gástlicra mægena, Bl. H. 37, 9. Hí widinnan ǽmtige wǽron ðæs gódan ingehýdes, Hml. Th. ii. 570, 7. II b. *with fram*:—Hé wæs ǽmtig fram ðám incundan andgite, Hml. Th. ii. 556, 1. Spræc ǽmtegu fram mægenes byrðene, Gr. D. 151, 1. Ídelne and ǽmtigne fram ðám écum gódnyssum, Hml. Th. i. 204, 11. III. *unoccupied, at leisure, exempt* from:—Ic eom ǽmtig (ǽmptig, *v. l.*) *vacat mihi*, Ælfc. Gr. 206, 13. Martha swanc, and Maria sæt ǽmtig, Hml. Th. ii. 440, 1. Se ǽmettega (ǽmetiga, Hatt. MS.), Past. 190, 18. Ðonne hig bysega nabbon and ǽmtige synd, R. Ben. 84, 19. Swá hié ǽmettegran (ǽmetegran, Hatt. MS.) beóð ðonne óðre men, Past. 190, 14. III a. *with gen.*:—Hié ǽmtige (ǽmtige, Hatt. MS.) beóð ðǽre scíre, Past. 126, 23. Ðá menn ðe ǽmtige beóð ðæs ðæt hié for óðre men swincen, 191, 13. III b. *with fram*:—Fram ðám gewinne ðǽre þénunge ǽmettig (ǽmtig, ǽmetig, *v. ll.*) wæs *a labore et ministerio vacabat*, Bd. 4, 3; Sch. 351, 11. III c. *with tó, free* to do:—Ðǽm ðe ǽmettige (ǽmtig, Hatt. MS.) bið his ágenne willan tó wyrceanne *illi sibimet vacanti*, Past. 190, 24. Hié wilniað ðæt hié bión freó and ǽmettige (ǽmtige, Hatt. MS.) tó gástlicum weorcum, 134, 26. IV. *unmarried* (*vacuus homo*):—Gif hwylc ǽmtig man (*vacuus homo*) gewemme óðres wíf ... And gif hwylc man ðe on his rihtan gesynscipe libbe ǽmtigne man (*vacuam*) gewemme, Ll. Th. ii. 164, 32, 34. Yfel ǽwbryce bið ðæt ǽwfæst man mid ǽmtige (émtige, *v. l.*) forlicge, i. 404, 22. Hí gemengan wið ðá ǽmtegan wífmen (*feminis vacantibus*), Past. 401, 24.

**ǽmet(ti)gian**, ǽmtig(i)an. *Add*: I. *to empty*:—Ic ǽmtige (émtigie, ǽmptig(i)e, *v. ll.*) *vacuo*, Ælfc. Gr. 137, 4. II. *fig.* v. ǽmettig, II:—His spréc wæs ǽmetegod (*vacua*) ðǽre mycelnysse his gódan mægnes, Gr. D. 151, 1. III. *to be at leisure*, v. ǽmettig, III:—Ne on dæge ðú aemtiga (*vaces*), Scint. 31, 8. Aemetgiað *vacate*, Ps. Srt. 45, 11. Hí ǽmtian *vacent*, R. Ben. I. 81, 15. III a. *with dat.* (*in Latin glosses*) *to devote one's self to, take time for*:—Æmta rǽdincge *vaca lectioni*, Scint. 222, 5. Se ðe émtige (*vacet*) ídelnesse, R. Ben. I. 83, 8. Rǽdinge hí ǽmtian, 82, 9, 14. Émtian, 83, 15. III b. *with reflex. pron. and tó*:—Mid ymnum hé hine ǽmetegode tó Gode *studebat hymnis Deo vacare*, Gr. D. 282, 4. Æmtigað eów tó rǽdinge *vacate lectioni*, Ælfc. Gr. 206, 13. Ðá men ðe hié selfe tó ðǽre ciricean wlite ǽmtegian sceoldon, Past. 135, 5. v. ge-, uu-ǽmettgian.

**ǽmettigness**, e; *f. Emptiness; an open space*:—Ádrifen fram ðǽre heortan ǽmtignesse *ab ipso cordis ostio repulsa*, Gr. D. 35, 17.

**ǽ-mirce**; *adj. Excellent, distinguished*; *egregius*, Wrt. Voc. ii. 30, 28.

**ǽ-mód**. *Add*:—Émód *amens*, Wrt. Voc. ii. 100, 15. Æmód, 6, 57. Wǽron ðá synna ealle ádílegode bútan ánre; seó wæs seó mǽste, and heó weard ðá ǽmód, Hml. S. 3, 553. Man sceal lǽwedum mannum secgan be heora andgites mǽðe, swá ðæt hí ne beón ðurh ðá deópnysse ǽmóde, Hml. Th. ii. 446, 8.

**ǽmta**, **ǽmtig**, &c. v. ǽmetta, ǽmettig, &c.

**ǽ-mynde**; *n. Want of care* (?), *neglect*:—Funde ic hwæt eorðe mæg wið andan and wið ǽminde and wið ðá micelan mannes tungan ... beó gé gemindige mínes gódes, Lch. i. 384, 22.

**ǽmyrge**. v. ǽmerge.

**ǽnbrece**. This in the facsimile of the MS. seems to be the form in El. 1029, the passage given in the Dict. under *an-bróce* (q.v.). If *æþelu*

be taken as a noun, the first part of the word might be (?) *æn* (cf. *æn-lic*), and the meaning be *unique* (?).

**æncnetrym** = æn(i)gne trym (?) or ængne trym (?) *a narrow step;* an acc. used adverbially with same force as colloquial *a little bit* (?). The word *pedetemptim* (An. Ox. 7, 221: 8, 165) is glossed by this form in the passage: Qui pedetemptim in pubertatis primordio instrumentis medicinalibus imbuti, Ald. 41, 33. v. trem *in Dict.*

**æne.** *Add:* I. as adverb answering question *how often :—*Ælce dæg æne *semel per diem*, Jos. 6, 3. Oft næs æne, Wlfst. 243, 2: El. 1253. Oftor ðonne æne, Ll. Th. ii. 334, 1. Æne ðrowade Crīst ðurh· hine sylfne, ac dæghwomlīce bið his þrowung geednīwod þurh gerȳnu ðæs hūsles, Hml. Th. ii. 276, 10. Ná æne ac æfre, Hml. S. 1, 141. I a. as multiplier :—Æne seofon beóð seofon, Angl. viii. 304, 28. II. with ordinal force, *a first time :—*Ðá wæs se deófol æne oferswīðed . . . Ðá wæs se deófol óðere sīðe oferswīðed, Hml. Th. i. 168, 35–170, 31. Hī hine swungon æne and óðre sīðe, ii. 302, 9. Æne hē sende and eft, i. 522, 1. III. marking indefinite time, *once, at any time :—*Hweðer ðá ðe ðær beóð æne (*semel*) besæncte, sculon hī ðær beón aa byrnende, Gr. D. 334, 4: 108, 24. Sē ðe æne ðæron befyld, ne wyrð hē næfre ālȳsed, Hml. Th. ii. 352, 29: Hml. S. 23, 375. Gif ðū æne behātest Gode hē wyle ðonne habban ðæt ðū h:m behēte, Hex. 50, 4. IV. of past time, *once, at some former time :—*Ðá ðe æne mid sygefæstum deáðe middangeard oferswīðde, Hml. Th. i. 84, 31. Þurh ðē Freá æne on ðás eorðan ūt sīðade, Cri. 329. Ic ðē æne ábealh, ðá wit Adam eaples þigdon, Sat. 410 (*substitute this for translation in Dict.*). V. at once :—Æne ic fare tō ðē and ādīlgige ðē *semel ascendam in medio tui et delebo te*, Ex. 33, 5. Ðanne samod becumað eall engla werod . . . æne bið geban micel, Dóm. L. 128. v. ænes.

**æned, æn-ége.** v. ened, án-eáge.

**ænes;** *adv. Once.* I. cf. æne, I :—Ænes ic swór *semel juravi*, Ps. L. 88, 36. Gif bescoren man gange him an gestlīðnesse, gefe him man ænes, Ll. Th. i. 38, 13. II. cf. æne, II :—Ðá se bróður ðás word gehȳrde ænes, hē forhtode . . . and óðere nihte hē wæs gemanod mid ðam ylcan wordum, Gr. D. 338, 4.

**ænet-ness.** v. next word.

**ænett, es;** *n. Solitude, retirement :—*Ænettes *solitudinis*, An. Ox. 2383: *anachoreseos*, 3638. Ænyttes, 2, 233. Tō ðære stōwe his leófan ænettes (ánetnysse, ænetnesse, *v. ll.*) *ad locum dilectae solitudinis*, Gr. D. 105, 27. Cf. ánett.

**ænga.** *Substitute: Solitary :—*Hē lifað leódum feor, lōcað geneahhe fram ðam unlædan ængan hláford *he lives far from men, (with) the wretched solitary often are his lord's looks turned*, Sal. 382. v. ánga.

**ængan-cundes;** *adv. In a way that is unique* (?) :—Crīst stód ofer ādle (alde, MS.) ængancundes (*as none other did*), Lch. iii. 36, 25.

**ænge;** *adv.,* Ængle. v. ange, Engle.

**ænig.** *Add:* I. substantival, (1) absolute :—Ic lære ðæt ænig ne āfȳle . . . hine sylfne, ðæt ænig ne healde yrre on his heortan tō lange, ne ænig ðurh worldhoge forsorgie tō swȳðe, Wlfst. 69, 14–16. Ænigum *cuivis, cuilibet*, Wrt. Voc. ii. 137, 66. Næs riht on ðære stōwe ænigne tō ācwellanne, Nar. 30, 2. ¶ gen. pl. combined with ælc to emphasize? cf. ánra gehwilc :—Gefultuma mē ænegra (-e, *v. l.*) ælces fylstes bedæled, Hml. S. 23 b, 441. [*Or ?* áneg = *single, sole; cf. O. Sax.* ēnag: *O. H. Ger.* einag *unicus*.] (2) with gen. :—Ic mē ne ondréd ðæt mē ðæra ænig beswice, Nar. 30. 1. Aenge þinga *quoquo modo*, Wrt. Voc. ii. 118, 60. II. adjectival :—On ænige óðre wīsan *aliter*, Wrt. Voc. ii. 2, 56. Ic ænigra mē weána ne wēnde, B. 932. II a. with qualitative force :—Ne beó ðū ænig manslaga, Wlfst. 66, 17. [*O. Sax.* ēnig: *O. H. Ger.* einīc.]

**æn-īge, ænig-wiht.** v. án-īge, wiht, II a *in Dict.*

**æniht.** *Add:* I. as substantive :—Ne æniht hiá gelædde *ne quid tollerent*, Mk. L. 6, 8. Ne ondueardest ðū æniht (*quicquam*), 14, 60. Æniht of ðæm ðá ðe gesēgon, Lk. L. 9, 36. Ne spildie of ðæm æniht † ōht *non perdidi ex ipsis quemquam*, Jn. L. 18, 9. Ne spræc ic æniht *locutus sum nihil*, 20. Wyrca ænight *facere quicquam*, 5, 30: 9, 33: Lk. L. 20, 40. II. as adjective :—Næfdes ðū mæht wið mec æniht (*ullam*), Jn. L. 19, 11. III. as adverb :—Ne forstondes æniht wīfigæ *non expedit nubere*, Mt. L. 19, 10: Mk. L. 5, 26: Jn. L. 6, 63.

**æn-lic.** *Add:* I. *only, single :—*Aenli *simplex*, Txts. 115, 156. Ðū ðe ænlic eart Godes bearn, Hml. S. 23, 806. Ænlican mīne *unicam meam*, Ps. Spl. 34, 20. Ænlic (*unicus*) and ðearfa ic eom, Ps. Spl. 24, 17. III. *excellent, peerless,* &c. :—Hū beorht, mære, ænlic O *preclara, i. splendida*, An. Ox. 1266. Ænlic *aurea*, 1461: Hy. S. 24, 7. Sum swīðe ænlic wer and foremære *quidam spectabilis vir*, Gr. D. 307, 1. Adrianus wæs geong and ænlic, Shrn. 59, 28. Fæger on ansȳne and ænlic, 88, 13. Ænlica Godes drūt *alma Dei genetrix*, Dóm. L. 290. Ænlicum *claro*, An. Ox. 3082: *preclaram*, 3721. Hī ealle licgað on ænlicum wurðmynte, Hml. S. 29. 333. Tō Antiochia ðære ænlican byrig, 3, 298. On Eferwīc ðære ænlice mynster, 26, 109. Tō ænlicum *aurea (in astra)*, An. Ox. 1438. Hē oft dyde swȳðe ænlice ðincg, Hml. S. 13, 270. Ðá ænlecan heápa· *investes catervas*, Wrt. Voc. ii. 44, 40. Ænlicre (elicire, Wrt.) wæs

*prestare*, 81, 64. Ænlicoste *pulcherrima, i. speciosissima*, An. Ox. 2113. Hē arn tō ánum ylpe ðe ðær ænlicost wæs, Hml. S. 25, 581. [Ungerīm swȳðe ænlices folces, Chr. 1120; P. 249, 20.]

**æn-līce.** *Add :—*Ænlīce gefretewod, Hml. S. 9, 24: 18, 341. Ðá cwæð ðæt folc ðæt hē ænlīce spræc, 18, 111: 36, 79: Hml. A. 103, 44.

**æn-līpe, -līpig, -ness.** v. án-līpe, -līpig, -ness: Æ-not, *l.* æ-note: **æpel-.** v. æppel-: **æpening.** v. æppel-cynn.

**æppel.** *Add: nom. ac. pl.* æp(p)la, ap(p)la, æpplas (*apples of eye*); *gen. pl.* appla, æpplena; *m.:* appla (-u, v. finger-æppel), æppel (? æppel *mala*, Wrt. Vcc. ii. 54, 40) ; *n.* I. *an apple* (in a special and in a general sense as in oak-*apple*) :—Æppel *pomum*, Ælfc. Gr. 31, 4. Æppel *malum*, Kent. Gl. 962. Scoldon hangian reáde apla (*mala punica*). Hwæt is getācnod ðurh ðá reádan apla (appla, l. 13) ? Se æppel bið betogen mid rinde, Past. 95, 3–6. On ðæs æples (*pomi*) gewilnunge, 309, 17. Eaples, Sat. 411. Æppeles seáw, Lch. i. 350, 2. Æples, ii. 132, 11. Æpples, 111, 36, 31. Sing ðæt galdor on ðone æppel, 38, 4. Gebrædedne æppel, sūrne æppel, ii. 132, 14, 15. Of ðám treówe ðe man hāteþ nōrbeám nim æppel . . . hwītne æppel ðe ðonne gyt ne reádige, i. 330, 19–22, 25. Ðá ðá Adam geæt ðone forbodenan æppel, Hml. Th. ii. 240, 21. Liðe æppla (appla, *v. l.*) *mitia poma*, Ælfc. Gr. 274, 13. Gecyrnlede (-u *in margin*) appla *mala granata*, Hpt. Gl. 496, 60: An. Ox. 2, 258. Ðá Affracaniscan æppla *mala punica*, Wrt. Voc. ii. 83, 52. Æpla, Lch. ii. 244, 2. Æpplena *pomorum*, Ps. L. 78, 1. Appla *dactilorum*, An. Ox. 2394. Wið grēne æpla, Lch. ii. 208, 10. v. milisc *in Dict.* II. *an apple-shaped object :—*Æpples *sphaerae*, Wrt. Voc. ii. 32, 44. Cnuca tōsomne ðám gelīce ðe ðū ánne æppel wyrce, Lch. i. 250, 10. II a. *an eye-ball :—*Gif se æppel lef biþ, Bt. 38, 5 ; F. 204, 29. Se óðer æppel wæs geēmtigod, and se óðer hangode gehál æt his hleóre, Hml. S. 21, 280. Beóð ðá æplas hāle . . . sió scearpnes ðæs æples (æpples, Hatt. MS.) . . . Ðurh ðone æpl ðæs eágean, Past. 68, 2, 4, 17. v. cod-, corn-, hunig-, weax-æppel.

**æppel-bære.** *Add :—*Æpelbære *malifer*, Wrt. Voc. ii. 54, 44.

**æppel-berende;** *adj. Apple-bearing :—*Æppilberende *pomiferam*, Rtl. 98, 33.

**æppel-cynn, es;** *n. A kind of apple :—*Selle him etan . . . manigfeald æppelcynn, peran, æpeningas (*medlars*), Lch. ii. 180, 14.

**æppel-cyrnel, es;** *n. Substitute: An apple-pip :—*Æppelcyrnlu *mala granata* (the glosser seems to have read this as = pips of apples, instead of = apples with pips; cf. the more correct gloss in Hpt. Gl. 496, 60 (v. under *æppel*)), Wrt. Voc. ii. 54, 43.

**æppel-fæt, es;** *n. A vessel for carrying apples :—*Æppelfæt (-fæc, MS.) *apoforeta, vasa pomis ferendis apta*, Hpt. 31, 15, 401.

**æppel-sceal.** *l.* -scealu, *and add: The sheath that encloses the pip of an apple :—*Filmenum, æpelscealum ymb ðá cyrnlu *cittis*, Wrt. Voc. ii. 17, 69.

**æppel-treów.** *Add :—*Apoltrē (or = apuldre, q. v. ?) *malum*, Lk. L. 6, 22. Æpeltreówu *granata* (v. æppel), Wrt. Voc. ii. 42, 2.

**æppel-tūn.** *Add :—*Æppeltūn *pomerium*, Wrt. Voc. i. 84, 53· Eappultūn, Ps. Srt. 78, 1. ' Ælc gōd treów . . . and yfel treów . . .' Ne mænde ūre Drihten ðá treówa ðe on æppeltūne weaxað, Hml. Th. ii. 406, 10. On æppeltūne gán anxsumnysse getācnað, Lch. iii. 206, 17. Binnon his æppeltūn *in hortum arboribus consitum*, Hml. A. 100, 269. On orcgearde . . . on æppeltūnum *in hortis*, Past. 381, 14, 16.

**æppel-wīn.** *Add :—*Æppelwīn *idromelum*, Wrt. Voc. ii. 49, 57·

**æps** *a fir-tree*. v. æbs: **æps** *aspen.* v. æsp.

**æpsen;** *adj. Impudent, shameless, foul :—*Æpsin *frontosa*, An. Ox. 7, 301. v. next two words.

**æpsen, æf(e)sn, e ;** *f. Impudence, foulness :—*Ungerīsendre æfesne (ungerysenre æfsna *in marg.*) *indecens obscenitas*, Hpt. Gl. 492, 60: An. Ox. 3674 (where see note).

**æpsenness, e ;** *f. Shame, disgrace :—*Æpsenyss *dedecus*, Scint. 174, 9·

**ær; m.** *l.* ár.

**ær ;** *adj. Add:* [Without positive (*for* ærne mergen *l.* ærnemergen), *but see* ær; *adv.*] :—From æran morgene, Chr. 538; P. 17, note 11. Ðá ðe on æran tīman līfes wæron, Lch. iii. 436, 5. Ðære æran hæle *incolomitati pristinae*, An. Ox. 4354. On ðá æran hæle, 1875. On ærum tīdum, Lch. iii. 432, 21 : 442, 22. On ðam twám ærrum bōcum, Hml. S. pref. 41. Hē bebeád ærest monna *primus statuit*, Ors. 6, 30; S. 284, 8: Shrn. 49, 20. Æt ærestan, Lch. ii. 118, 19. v. ærra.

**ær ;** *adv.* I. positive, (1) *early :—*Swȳþe ær in dagunge *primo diluculo*, Bd. 4, 23; S. 596, 17. Swȳþe ær on morgen, Ps. Th. 45, 5· (2) expressing readiness, quickness, *soon :—*Sweord ær gebræd gūðcyning, B. 2562. Hē wel ær árás . . . Se apostol cwæð tō him : ' For hwon ārise ðū swā hraðe ?, Gr. D. 227, 4· Nȳtenu etað swā ær swā hī hit habbað, Hml. S. 16, 317. Ðū wilt higian ðon ær ðe ðū hine ongitest, Bt. 11, 2 ; F. 34, 8. Ðonne ær ðe hē ðæt gewealdleþer forlæt . . . ðonne forlætaþ hī ðá sibbe, 21; F. 74, 31. II. cpve. (1) *earlier, before :—*Dæge ær *pridie*, Wrt. Voc. ii. 68, 50. Ær *dudum, ante*, An. Ox. 1920 : *jam*, 5483. Ær ðonne hē, B. 1182. Gefyrn ær *jam*, An. Ox. 56, 93. Ær gefyrn, Cri. 63. Ær oððe æfter, 1692. Ær biforan, 468: El. 1132. [*See also* siþ *in Dict.*] ¶ *on* ær *previously, before-hand :—*Drihten ðe on ær wāt eal ðæt tōweard is, Lch. iii. 436, 20:

C

Hml. Th. i. 114, 3 : Chr. 1067 ; P. 201, 26. Hē wolde warnian on ǽr, Gen. 6, 6. Fela þing wiste se hālga wer on ǽr, lange ǽr hī gelumpon, Hml. S. 31, 788. (1 a) making present perfect and preterite pluperfect :—Redic ete ǽr, ne mæg ðē nān man āttre āwyrdan *if you have eaten radish, nobody can injure you by poison*, Lch. ii. 110, 10. Ðæt feoh ðæt hī ǽr lǽfdon *the money they had left* (*when they were spending before*, v.l. 200), Hml. S. 23, 213. Wǽron ðǽre hlǽddre stapas ālēfede on ǽr *the steps of the ladder had been weakened*, 31, 602. (2) marking readiness, *sooner* :—Ic nōht ðon ǽr blon *I stopped none the sooner*, Bd. 5, 6 ; S. 619, 15. Nāhte ðy̆ ǽr, Gr. D. 152, 17. ¶ with correlative conjunction. v. ǽr ; *conj.* (1) *before* :—Hié ǽr fiugon, ǽr hié tōgædere geneálǽcten, Ors. 4, 6 ; S. 170, 24 : Past. 433, 28. Ðæt hē hié forceorfe ǽr, ǽr hié on ðā eágan feallen, 141, 10. Hē wolde on ǽr ðæt godspell āwrītan, ǽr ðām ðe hé gewende him fram, Hml. S. 15, 139. (2) *sooner* :—Manegum men is leófre ðæt hé ǽr swelte, ǽr hē geseó his wíf and his bearn sweltende, Bt. 10 ; F. 28, 39. Ǽr ic mē sylfne ofsleá, ǽr ðon ic sende mīne hond on ðás fǽmnan, Shrn. 130, 26. III. superlative (ǽrest), *first:* —Ðū meaht ǽlcne undeáw on ðǽm men ǽresð be sumum tācnum ongietan . . . ǽr hē hit mid wordum cȳðe, Past. 157, 19. Tō hwilces tīman se steorra him ǽrst æteówode, Hml. Th. i. 78, 18. Ǽst of ānre byrig, ðonne of ōðerre. Ors. 3, 7 ; S. 112, 22. Hē angan tō smeágenne ǽrest þinga hū hē his līf gerihtlǽcan meahte, Lch. iii. 438, 29 : Ll. Th. ii. 316, 11. v. ǽror.

ǽr ; *conj.* *Add:* (1) with indic. (or uncertain) :—Hȳ hié hindan ofrīdan ne meahte, ǽr hié on ðām fæstenne wǽron, Chr. 877 ; P. 74, 18. Hī cwǽdon ðæt Crīst wǽre, ǽr ācenned wæs of Marian, Hml. Th. i. 70, 5. Hit long first wæs ǽr hē ūt wolde faran tō gefeohte, ǽr him mon sǽde ðæt hié wolden faran tō Italiam, Ors. 5, 8 ; S. 232, 4. (2) with subjunctive :—Hē hēt ātimbran ðā burg, ǽr hē ðonan fōre, Chr. 919 ; S. 100, 14. Nānwuht ne byð yfel, ǽr mon wēne ðæt hit yfel seó, Bt. 11, 1 ; F. 32, 30. (3) with the verb to be inferred :—Ðæt se Fæder wǽre ǽr se Sunu, Hml. Th. i. 290, 7. Nān þing næs ǽr hē, Hml. S. 1, 65. Blōdlǽs is tō forgānne fíftȳne nihtum ǽr hlāfmæsse, Lch. ii. 146, 8. Ðā geācsedon ðā consulas ðæt ǽr, ǽr Hannibal, Ors. 4, 10 ; S. 198, 23. Heó cymð ǽr ðā wyrðmyndu, Past. 299, 16. *See* ǽr ; *adv.* II. ¶, III.

ǽr ; *prep.* *Add:* I. with dat. (1) *before a certain time or circumstance* :—Ǽr ðære teóðan tīde, Ll. Th. ii. 436, 7. Ǽr Martines mæssan, Chr. 971 ; P. 119, 22. Ǽr Crīstes gefǽscnesse, P. 4, 22. Ǽr Pendan deáþe, Bd. 3, 21 ; S. 551, 29. Ǽr ðære costunge, Past. 103, 25. Ǽr ðæs monnes hryre, 299, 18. Ǽr anginne, Hml. S. 1, 17. (1 a) *before the proper time.* v. ǽr-ǽt :—Ðæt men ǽr tīman ne gereordige, Hml. S. 16, 316. Ǽr mǽle, Hml. Th. ii. 590, 25. (2) *ago*, cf. for :—Ǽr monigum geárum (*ante annos plures*) be his life wē āwriton, Bd. 4, 28 ; S. 605, 12. Ðæt nū ǽr þrim geárum geworden wæs *quod ante triennium factum est*, 4, 32 ; S. 611, 11. (3) marking priority :—His brōþor ǽr him rīce hæfde, Bd. 3, 14 ; S. 539, 19. Gif hire forðsíð getīmige ǽr him, Wlfst. 304, 23. Hē ǽr worolde rícsode, Past. 33, 13 : Cri. 1346. (4) marking preference (*in the phrase* ǽr ðām (ðan) ðe) :—Sum wíf wolde hire líf forlǽtan, ǽr ðan ðe heó luge, Hml. S. 12, 179. Wolde se cwellere mid him sweltan, ǽr ðan ðe hine slōge, 19, 102. Hī sweltan woldon, ǽr ðan ðe hī wiðsōcon Gode, and heora líf ālēton ǽr ðan ðe heora geleáfan, 19, 102-3. II. with acc. :—God ǽr ealle worulda, Hml. Th. ii. 280, 13 : 596, 28. Wæs hē beforan ǽr þā þreó geár gecrístnod, Bl. H. 215, 36.

**ǽra**, an ; *m. A scraper* (*of brass*) :—Aera, ǽren screop *strigillus*, Wrt. Voc. ii. 121, 41.

**ǽ-reáfe** (-reáfe) ; *adj. Discovered:* —Hī drifon stacan on Wulfstānes feder, and ðet werð ǽreáfe, Cht. Th. 230, 16. v. ā-rāfian.

**ǽr-ǽt**, es ; *m. Eating too soon* [v. ǽr ; *prep.* I. (1 a) ; cf. Ll. Th. ii. 436, 6, 33-38] :—Mīne synna . . . on ǽrǽte and on oferfylle, Angl. xi. 102, 88. Swā hwæt swā wē misdōð . . . on ǽrǽte and on oferdrincæ, xii. 514, 10. Leahtras . . . ðæt is ǽrǽtas and oferdruncennessa, Wlfst. 135, 2. Wið ǽrǽtas, 290, 32.

**ǽr-beþōht** ; *adj. Premeditated:* —Hwæðer ðe gewealdes ðe ungewealdes, hwæðer ðe fǽrlīce ðe þurh ǽrbeþōhte wīsan, Ll. Th. ii. 428, 12.

**ǽrc** *a chest.* v. earc : **ǽrce** *archbishop's pallium.* v. arce *in Dict.*

**ǽrce-biscop.** *Add:*—Arcebiscop *archiepiscopus*, Wrt. Voc. i. 42, 3. Hēr forðfērde Sigerīc arcebisceop, Chr. 994 ; P. 126, 10. Ǽrcebiscepes (erce-, v.l.) burhbryce .xc. scitt., Ll. Th. i. 88, 7. Gif mon beforan ǽrcebiscepe gefeohte, 70, 18. Ic geliornode æt mīnum ǽrcebiscepe, Past. 7, 21 : Chr. 601 ; P. 20, 21. Ercebisc̃, 625 ; P. 24, 5.

**ǽrcebiscop-dōm**, es ; *m. Archiepiscopal dignity, archbishopric:* —Æfter him fēng Mellitus tō arceðdōme (ercebiscopdōme, 23, 27), Chr. 616 ; P. 24, 2.

**ǽrcebiscop-rīce.** v. arcebiscop-rīce *in Dict.*

**ǽrcebiscop-stōl**, es ; *m. Archiepiscopal see:* —Æfter him fēng Mellitus tō arceðstōle, Chr. 616 ; P. 22, 37 : 988 ; P. 125, 16. Hē gesæt his arcebiscopstōl *inthronizatur cathedra archipresulatus sui*, 1048 ; P. 172, 4.

**ǽrce-diácon.** *Add:*—Arcedeácon (-diácon), Gr. D. 186, 21. Ðæs arcedeácnes innoþ, 187, 3. Arcediácones geban, Ll. Th. ii. 290, 24.

Archidiácones, Shrn. 115, 31. Sumne ercediácon, Hml. S. 29, 213. v. erce-diácon *in Dict.*

**ǽrce-hád.** v. erce-hád *in Dict.*

**ǽrce-rīce**, es ; *n. Archbishopric:* —Se cyng sealde Rōtbearde ðæt arcerīce, Chr. 1051 ; P. 170, 31.

**ǽrce-stōl**, es ; *m. Archiepiscopal see:* —Ælfeáh fēng tō ðām ǽrcestōle, Chr. 1006 ; P. 136, 8. Arcestōle, 988 ; P. 125, 24. Wæs Dūnstān æt ðām ercestōle, Hml. S. 21, 458. Hē heóld ðone arcestōl mid mycclan weorðmynte, Chr. 1069 ; P. 204, 11.

**ǽr-dǽd.** *Add:*—Hū micel is ðæt wīte ðe byð for ǽrdǽdum . . . cyninge wile dēman ānra gehwylcum be ǽrdǽdum *quanta malis maneant tormenta . . . adveniet judex mercedem reddere cunctis*, Dōm. L. 93, 96 : Wlfst. 137, 1, 3.

**ǽr-dæg**, II. *Add:*—Se cyning ne gemunde ðára monigra teónena ðe hiora ǽgðer ōþrum on ǽrdagum (*dudum*) gedyde, Ors. 1, 12 ; S. 52, 23. Ðā burg, seó wæs on ǽrdagum heora ieldrena ēðel *urbem, auctorem originis suae*, 4, 5 ; S. 168, 10.

**-ǽre** *-oared*, in cmpds. :—Ǽnne scegð .lxiiii. ǽre, Cht. Crw. 23, 8. [*Icel.* -ǽrr.]

**ǽ-reáfe.** v. ǽ-rǽfe.

**ǽren.** *Add:* I. *brazen:* —Ǽren ceác, Past. 105, 2. Ǽrenu elebyt *lenticula*, Wrt. Vóc. ii. 50, 75. Ǽren byt, i. 25, 17. Aeren screop *strigillus*, ii. 121, 41. Ásleah .iiii. scearpan mid ǽcenan (ǽrenan ?) brande, Lch. iii. 52, 2. Ǽrenne bogan *arcum aeneum*, Ps. Th. 17, 33. Ǽnne ǽrenne oxan, Hml. S. 30, 421. Āne ǽrene anlícnysse, Hml. Th. ii. 166, 2. Ǽrne, Bl. H. 239, 21. Gyldene, sylfrene, ǽrene, cyperene, Ors. 5, 2 ; S. 216, 3. Ðā ǽrenan scyttelas, Bl. H. 85, 7. Ðā ǽrenan, Ps. Srt. 106, 16. II. *sounding* as brass, *tinkling* (?) :—*Tinnulus, a tinniendo dicitur, id est* eran (=ǽren ?), Wrt. Voc. ii. 122, 45. [*O. H. Ger.* erîn.]

**ǽren-byt.** l. ǽren byt. v. ǽren : **ǽrend.** v. ǽrende.

**ǽren-dæg.** l. ǽran dæg. v. ǽr ; *adj.*

**ǽrend-bōc.** *Add:*—Ǽrendbēc *pi(c)tacia* (cf. ǽrendgewritu, An. Ox. 4839), Wrt. Voc. ii. 86, 53.

**ǽrende.** *Add:* I. *a message:* —Mycel wæs ðes ǽrendwreca, and mycel ǽrende brōhte hē, Bl. H. 9, 13. Ðislic ǽrende se pāpa onsende and ðás word cwæð, 205, 22. Hē geswōr ðæt hē ðæt ǽrende ābeódan wolde . . . Æfter hē hit āboden hæfde, hē hié heálsode ðæt hié nānuht ðára ǽrenda ne underfēnge . . . Āsǽdon his geféran hū hé heora ǽrenda ābeád, Ors. 4, 6 ; S. 178, 10-22. Earmra manna ǽrende wrecan (ǽrendo ābeódan, v.l.), Bd. 3, 6 ; Sch. 209, 20. Ǽrende wreccan *legationem volvere*, 2, 9 ; Sch. 146, 25. Se ealdormon geliéfedlíce ðára ǽrenda anfēng, Ors. 3, 1 ; S. 96, 20. Hieówsende for ðām ǽrendum ðe se wítga him sǽde, Ps. Th. 50, arg. Sōna swā se hālga man ðás ǽrendu gehȳrde (*quo audito*), Gr. D. 29, 14. Geatward ðe mid gesceáde cunne answara syllan and ǽrenda underfōn, R. Ben. 126, 16. Ðurh Nōðhelmes ǽrenda and gesægene (cf. hē mē ealle . . . onsende ðurh Nōðhelm, l. 2), Bd. pref. ; S. 472, 8. II. *an errand, a mission:* —Gif hwelc rīce mon on his hlāfordes ǽrende færþ, cymþ ðonne on ælþeódig folc *si quis multiplici consulatu functus in barbaras nationes devenerit*, Bt. 27, 3 ; F. 98, 21. Ðā hwíle ðe hē fōr on heora ǽrende, Chr. 1064 ; P. 192, 6. Fōr Aldred ofer sǽ ðæs kynges ǽrende, 1054 ; P. 185, 24 : 1065 ; P. 193, 11. Medmycel ǽrende wē ðyder habbað, and ūs is þearf ðæt hē þēh gefyllon, Bl. H. 233, 11. Sǽdon ðæt hī hæfdon nyt ǽrende (ǽrend, v.l.) and nytne intingan sumne *haberent aliquid legationis et causae utilis*, Bd. 5, 10 ; Sch. 600, 9.

**ǽrend-fǽst** ; *adj. Bound on an errand:* —Fērde sum ǽrendfæst ridda . . . and lǽdde hit forð mid him ðǽr hē fundode tō, Hml. S. 26, 221.

**ǽrend-gewrit.** *Add:*—Ǽrendgewrit *commonitorium*, Wrt. Voc. ii. 22, 33. Ān ǽrendgewrit of Lǽdene on Englisc āreccean, Past. 3, 15. Sumes gerēfan dohtor hē āhredde fram fefore þurh his ǽrendgewrit, Hml. Th. ii. 512, 9. Ǽrendgewrite *pittacia*, Wrt. Voc. ii. 67, 21. *Pitaciolis*, i. *membranulis* bōcfellum, ǽrendgewritum, An. Ox. 4570.

**ǽrendian.** *Add:* I. *to go on an errand* (*acc.*), *act as emissary or advocate* in a matter :—Se munuc ðe hit ǽrendode *the monk that had been sent on this business*, Gr. D. 29, 28. Gif hwelc forworht monn bitt ūrne hwelcne ðæt wē hine lǽden tō sumum rīcum menn and him geðingien, . . . Gif hē mē cūð ne bið, ic wille him cueðan : 'Ne mæg ic ðæt ǽrendigean (ǽrendian, Cott. MSS.)' *si quis veniat, ut pro se ad intercedendum nos apud potentem quempiam virum, qui nobis est incognitus, ducat, protinus respondemus : 'Ad intercedendum venire non possumus,'* Past. 63, 5. I a. *to go on* an errand to (*tō*) a person :—Ðā sende hē monn tō ðǽm arcebiscope and tō Eádberhte, and him hēht sæcgan ðæt hē wilnade ðæs londes. Ðā se arcebiscop and Eádberht hit wǽrun ǽrndiende tō cyninge *when they were advocating the matter to the king*, Cht. Th. 47, 30. II. *to go on* an errand for a person (*dat.*) to (*tō*) another, *intercede:* —Grīpan on ðā scīre ðæt hē ǽrendige ōðrum monnum tō Gode *apud Deum intercessionis locum pro populo arripere*, Past. 63, 7 : Gen. 665. III. *to go on* a mission for an object (*gen.*), *negotiate* for :—Ðā ǽrenddracan ðe his cwale ǽrendedon (-odon, ǽrnddedon, v.ll.) *those who had been sent to procure his death,*

Bd. 2, 12; Sch. 160, 23. **III a.** with dat. of person for whom :—Se esne ðe ærendað his woroldhláforde wífes *the servant who is sent to procure a wife for his lord,* Past. 143, 1. [He bad heom arndien him to þan´ kingen, Lay. 23315. Ernde me to þi lauerd *funde preces ad dominum,* Kath. 2127.] v. ge-ærendian.

**ærend-raca.** *Add:*—Yldest ærendraca *a responsis,* i. *magister responsorum,* Wrt. Voc. i. 60, 33. Hé ðæs ærendes ærendraca wæs from Alexandre, Ors. 3, 11 ; S. 144, 22. Swifte ærendracan *veltes,* Wrt. Voc. i. 18, 23. Ærendracum *gerulis,* An. Ox. 7, 281. Ærenddracan, Past. 39, 3 : Bd. 2, 12 ; Sch. 160, 22.

**ærend-scip, es;** *n. A small boat, a skiff* :—Ærendscip *scapha,* Wrt. Voc. i. 63, 31.

**ærend-secgan.** *Dele :* ærend-spræc. *l.* -spræc.

**ærendung.** *Substitute :* **I.** *carrying a message, acting as an emissary* :—Gif hwylc bróðor gedyrstlæcð ðæt hé ænige geþeódrædene nime wið ðone ámánsumedan, oððe þurh ænige spræce oðþe þurh æniges óþres mannes ærendunge *(by any other man's carrying a message).* R. Ben. 50, 13. **II.** *a message, an errand* :—Ðæt wæs hræd ærendraca; sé tylode tó secganne hys ærndunge ær ðon ðe hé lyfde, Shrn. 95, 21. [þ we þurh hire erndunge *(intercession, mediation)* nioten iseon hire, Marh. 23, 16 : O. E. Homl. i. 207, 31.]

**ærend-wreca.** *Add :*—Ærendwreca(n) unnytnesse *nugigerulus,* Wrt. Voc. ii. 60, 21. Gabriel wæs ðissa brýdþinga ærendwreca, Bl. H. 3, 19. Érendwrica *legatus,* Txts. 180, 10. Philippes tíd ðæs apostoles and ðæs Godes ærendwrecan, Shrn. 78, 4. Ærendwreocan, 108, 14. Ðá sende hé his ærendwreocan tó Wulfhearde, Cht. Th. 47, 9. Érendwrecan *legati,* Ps. Srt. 67, 32. Ðá kyningas Gode and his ærendwrecum hérsumedon, Past. 3, 6. God sendeþ his engla gástas tó ærendwrecum, Bl. H. 203, 14. v. wrecan, I b *in Dict.*

**ærend-wreccan (?);** *p.* wrehte *To deliver a message* :—Ðá eóde hé in swá swá hé his hláfordes ærende secgan sceolde; and mid ðý hé ðá geswippre múþe lícettende ærend (ærende, *v. l.*) wrehte (ærendwrehte?) *intravit quasi nuntium domini sui referens; et cum simulatam legationem ore astuto volveret,* Bd. 2, 9; Sch. 146, 23.

**ær-gedón.** *Add :*—Dryhten hine ðreáde for his ærgedónum weorcum, Past. 443, 27. Ðá ðe ðá ærgedónan synna wépað, 177, 23.

**ær-gefremed;** *adj. Before-committed* :—Ðá ærgefremedan synna, Ll. Th. ii. 434, 14.

**ær-gelǽred;** *adj. Previously instructed* :—Ærgelǽred *praemonita,* Mt. L. 14, 8.

**ær-genemned.** *Add :*—Ealle ðá ærgenemnedan lǽcedómas, Lch. ii. 186, 11.

**ær-gescod.** *l.* ær gescód, *and see* ge-sceþþan.

**ær-glæd.** *Substitute: Kind from of old?, very kind* :—Eów mihtig God niltse gecýðde ærglade *to you mighty God hath shewn mercy exceeding kind,* Exod. 293. v. next word.

**ær-gód.** *Substitute: Good from of old?, very good.* v. *exs. in Dict.,* and cf. (?) O. Sax. ér-þungan.

**ær-hwílum;** *adv. In earlier times, formerly* :—Ðá micclan welan ðe hig ærhwílon ǽhton, Guth. 14, 23. Oft ic nú miscyrre cúðe spræce, and þeáh uncúðre ærhwílum *(quondam)* fond, Met. 2, 9. Cf. ær-dæg.

**ær-ildo (?);** *f. Former age* :—Æryeldo *antisitus* (but the Latin in Ald. 152, 31 is *ante situm*), Wrt. Voc. ii. 91, 19. Æreldo *anteritus* (has the glosser read *anteritas?*), 5, 52.

**æring.** *Add :*—On æring mane, Mk. L. 13, 35. On æringe *diluculo,* 1, 35.

**ǽ-rist.** *Add:* es; *n.* :—Se drihtenlica ærist *anastasis dominica,* An. Ox. 2753. Seó wunderlíce ærest eallum mannum wæs geopenod, Shrn. p. 6. Ðæt gemǽnelíce ærist, Hml. Th. i. 394, 25. Mínes æristes dæg, 74, 18 : ii. 224, 25. Ðone tóhopan deádra monna æristes (-restes, Hatt. MS.)... Ðá Saducie andsacedon ðære æriste... ðá Fariséos geliéfdon ðære æriste, Past. 364, 4-6. On ðám æriste, Mt. 22, 28-30 : Mk. 12, 23 : Lk. 20, 33 : Hml. Th. i. 394, 32. Æfter ðære æriste, Ps. Th. 47, arg. [O. H. Ger. ur-rist *resurrectio.*] v. eft-ærist.

**ær-leóf;** *adj. Very dear* :—[Æ]rl[e]óf *gratus,* An. Ox. 56, 296.

**ær-líc, -líce.** v. ár-líc, -líce.

**ær-lyft, e;** *f. The air of early morning* :—Sió þicce ærlyft *gravis,* Wrt. Voc. ii. 41, 74.

**ær-morgen.** *Add :*—*Diluculum,* ðæt ys se ærmærien (-mergen, *v. l.*), betweox ðám dægrede and sunnan upgange, Lch. iii. 244, 6. Se ærmerigen wæs fram Adam oð Nóe, Hml. Th. ii. 74, 18. Gewordenum ðám ærmergene *mane facto,* Gr. D. 72, 11. Ærmergene, 201, 25. From ærmorgenne oð heáne undern, R. Ben. 74, 10. From ærmergenne (-morgene, MS. E.), Chr. 538; P. 16, 12. Ærmergen *mane,* Wrt. Voc. ii. 58, 65. On ærmergen, Ps. Th. 5, 3. On ærmorgenum *in matutinis,* Ps. L. 72, 14. v. ærne-mergen, ár-morgen *in Dict.*

**ær-morgenlic** (ár-); *adj. Of the early morning* :—Ármorgenlic *auroram,* Rtl. 182, 37. Ármorgenlicum tídum *matutinis horis,* 124, 15. v. ærne-mergenlic.

**ærn.** *Add:* [older ræn. v. ærn-þegen] :—Gif ealo áwerd sié, genim cleahtran, lege on ðá feówer sceátas ðæs ærnes and ofer ðá duru and

---

under ðone þerxwold and under ðæt ealofæt, Lch. ii. 142, 11. Healde hine mon on óðrum ærne (húse, *v. l.*), Ll. Th. i. 64, 15 : Bl. H. 221, 16. Seó reáde netele ðe þurh ærne in wyxð, Lch. iii. 52, 12. Genim grundeswyligean ðá ðe on ærenu wexeð, 48, 29. v. bæþ-, beód-, geréf-, hálig-, mete-, mót-, sealt-, spræc-, stál-, wæsc-, wíte-ærn; tigel-ærne; earn *in Dict.*

**ærnan.** *Add:* v. ymb-ærnan: ærne. v. tigel-ærne: ǽr-nemd. v. ær-nemned.

**ærne.** *l.* ærne-mergen, -morgen *early morning* :—Clǽnnyss sý swá swá ærnemergen *(diluculum),* Hy. Srt. 16, 27. *Diluculum,* ðæt is se ærnemergen, Lch. iii. 244, 6. Se dæg hæfð þreó tódǽlednyssa.... Seó forme hátte *mane,* ðæt ys ærnemergen,... seó niht hafað seofon tódǽlednyssa... seó seofoðe ys... *diluculum,* ðæt ys ærnemergen, Angl. viii. 319, 21, 34. From ærnemorgen oð undern, R. Ben. 74, 10. Fram ærnemærien oð ofer midne dæg, Hml. S. 3, 341. On ærnemærgen (-merien, *v.l.*), 344. On ærnemergen *primo mane,* Coll. M. 20, 29. On ealne ærnemergen, Chr. 1050; P. 170, 14. On ærnemorgen (ærmergen, -morgen, *v. ll.*) *mane primo,* Bd. 5, 6; Sch. 578, 23.

**ærnemergen-líc;** *adj. Of the early morning* :—Mæssan ærnemergenlíce *missam matutinalem,* Angl. xiii. 384, 277. v. ær-morgenlíc.

**ær-nemned;** *adj. Before-named* :—Se ærnæmda cyning, Ll. Th. i. 36, 8.

**ærning.** *Add:*—'Hwæt ðú mé mycel yfel dést mid ðínre ærninge.' And ic nóht ðon ǽr ðære ærninge blon '*quam magnum vae facis mihi sic equitando.' Et ego nihilominus coeptis institi vetitis,* Bd. 5, 6 ; Sch. 576, 19. Mid swíðe geswenctan horse for ærninge *vehementer equo in cursu fatigato,* Gr. D. 38, 30. v. fær-ærning.

**ærn-þegen, es;** *m. The officer of a house* :—Rendegn *aedituus, templi vel aedis minister,* Txts. 109, 1137.

**ǽror.** *Add:* (1) temporal, *earlier, before* :—Nán mann ǽror nán swylc ne gemunde, Chr. 1032; P. 159, 5. Ǽrer hé hit ærǽrde, 1086; P. 219, 4. Swá swá wé áwriton ǽror, Ælfc. T. Grn. 4, 15. (2) *rather* :—Ðá óðre þrý godspelleras áwriton ǽror be Crístes menniscnysse, Hml. Th. i. 70, 3.

**ǽrra.** *Add:*—Ðære ærran *prioris,* An. Ox. 1675 : Hml. Th. i. 62, 16. Tó ðám ærrum *in pristinum,* An. Ox. 1831 : Hml. Th. i. 68, 19. On ærron dæg *nudiustertius,* Ælfc. Gr. 224, 2. On his ðæt ærre mynster *in primum suum monasterium.* Bd. 5, 19; S. 641, 17. Ðæt (*what*) ærran woroldwitan geræddon, Ll. Th. i. 350, 6.

**ǽrst, ærþe-land, ærpling.** v. ǽr; *adv.* **III,** irþ-land, irþling.

**ær-wacol.** *Add:*—Se apostol ærwacol tó ðære cyrcan com, Hml. Th. i. 74, 20.

**ǽs.** *Add:* (1) *food* :—Áwyrpað his líc fugelum tó æse and hundum tó mete, Hml. S. 37, 235. Næs se here swá strang ðæt on Angelcynne æs him gefetede, Chr. 975; P. 121, 12. (2) *a bait* :—Ðá getímode ðám deófle swá swá ded ðám grǽdigan fisce, ðe gesihð ðæt æs, and ne gesihð ðone angel ðe on ðám æse sticað: bið ðonne grǽdig ðæs æses, and forswylcð ðone angel mid ðám æse, Hml. Th. i. 216, 9-13. Angel *vel* æs ic *(the fisherman)* wyrpe, Coll. M. 23, 11. Fugel, ðonne hé gífre bið, hé gesihð ðæt æs *(escam)* on eorðan, and ðonne for ðǽm luste ðæs metes hé forgiet ðæt grin, Past. 331, 17.

**æsc.** *Add:* **I.** *ash-tree* (v. C. D. vi. 252-3 for the large number of place-names in which *æsc* occurs) :—Æsces sceal mǽst *there must be most of ash,* Lch. ii. 86, 8. **IV.** *a ship* :—Aesc *cerculus,* Wrt. Voc. ii. 103, 56. Æsc *cercylus,* 14, 16. Ðá Deniscan leóde on Norðhymbra lande gelendon mid æscum, Hml. S. 32, 31. v. ceaster-æsc.

**ǽ-scǽre.** *l.* ǽ-scære.

**æscan** *to demand* :—And ðæt ceápgild árise á ofer .xxx. pæng oð healf pund syþþan wé hit æscað, Ll. Th. i. 234, 16.

**ǽ-scapo.** v. ǽ-sceap.

**ǽ-scapo.** *Add:* **I.** *question, inquiry* :—Uton áhsien úrne Drihten... Wé gehýraþ æfter ðisse æscan (-ean, *v.l.*) *(post hanc interrogationem)* Drihten andswariendne, R. Ben. 3, 16. Hé angan tó befrínenne... Hé weard æfter ðysse æscan ontend, Lch. iii. 432, 29. Ðá áxunga ðære æscan tówríðende *interrogationi interrogationem jungens,* Hml. S. 23 b, 495. **II.** as a legal term, *search for stolen cattle* :—Beó sý æsce forð *let the search go on,* Ll. Th. i. 234, 17 : 238, 9. Ðæt man ne forlǽte náne æscan, 232, 18 : 234, 25. Fó sé syþþan tó ðe ðæt land áge and hæbbe him ðá æscan, 352, 17.

**ǽ-sceáda, an;** *m. Bran* :—Healmes láf *stipulae,* ceaf *palea,* æsceáda *migma,* Wrt. Voc. i. 38, 51-3. Æsceádan *furfures, purgamentum farinae,* ii. 152, 4. Cf. á-sceáða.

**ǽ-sceap, es;** *n. What is cut off, a remnant, patch* :—Ðæt æsceapa *commissura,* Lk. L. 5, 36. Æscapo *subsiciva,* Wrt. Voc. i. 287, 34. v. scip *a patch.*

**æsceda.** v. ǽ-sceáda: æsce-geswáp. v. swæpa *in Dict.*

**æscen.** *Substitute: f., m.* or *n. A* (*wooden*) *vessel, pail, bottle* [*v.* ashen; *sb.* in D. D.] :—Æscen *lagena,* Wrt. Voc. i. 25, 8. Arn án wencel mid treówenum æscene (treówene æscne, *v. l.*) *(lignea situla),* Gr. D. 11, 21. Of ðám æscene ðe is óðre namon hrygilebúc gecleopad... and of ðám óðran æscene, Cht. Th. 439, 25, 29. Man sceal habban trogas, æscena, Angl. ix. 264, 15. v. next word.

æscen; *adj. Add :*—Genim grēnne æscenne stæf, Lch. ii. 42, 10.

æscene *vastaretur*, An. Ox. 37, 4 [ = ? æ-scefe; cf. (?) scafan: *O. H. Ger.* ar-scaban *eradere*].

æsc-fealu; *adj. Ashy-coloured :*—Æscfealu *vel* æscgræg *cinereus, deterrimus color,* Wrt. Voc. ii. 131, 14.

æsc-græg; *adj. Ashy-grey.* v. preceding word: æschetung, Hpt. 510, 66. v. ceahhetung.

æsc-man. *Add :*—Andlang streámes æt æscmannes yre (yfre?), C. D. vi. 100, 7. Æscmen *piratici,* Wrt. Voc. ii. 68, 13.

æsc-stéde, -þræc. *l.* æsc-stede, -þracu.

æscstede-rōd, e; *f. A cross marking a battlefield ? :*—Of ðǽre greátan apeidre on æscstederōde, C. D. iii. 135, 22.

æsc-þrote. *Add :*—Aescthrotae *ferula,* Txts. 64. 450. Æscþrote, Wrt. Voc. ii. 38, 78: *furula,* 35, 29: *firula,* i. 67, 80: *ferula,* i. *harundo, virgula vel nomen holeris,* ii. 147, 70. Æscþrotu *annuosa* ( = *anchusa.* v. Lch. ii. 368), i. 30, 52. Niþeweard æscþrotu, Lch. ii. 36, 19.

æ-sellend, es; *m. A law-giver :*—Se mǽra æsyllend Mōyses, Hml. A. 24, 13. Æsellend *legislatorem,* Ps. L. 9, 21. v. æ-syllend *in Dict.*

æ-slítend, es; *m. A law-breaker :*—Æslítendras *praevaricantes,* Ps. L. 118, 119, 158.

æ-smæl *a contraction of the pupil of the eye :*—Wiþ æsmælum ·and wiþ eallum eágna wærce, Lch. ii. 338, 1 : 2, 9 : 36, 16, 19.

æ-smogu; *pl. n. The slough of a snake;* exuviae :—Sceal mon nǽdran æsmogu seóþan on eie, Lch. ii. 236, 4. v. in-smoh.

æspe *aspen. Add :*—Aespe *arbutus,* Txts. 41, 202. Aespe *aespae.* espe *tremulus,* 103, 2048. Æspe, Wrt. Voc. i. 285, 36. Tō ðǽre gemearcodan æfsan, C. D. v. 195, 11.

æspe *abies.* v. æbs.

æsp-hangra, an; *m. An aspen wood :*—On ðonæ æsphangran, C. D. v. 173, 11. v. hangra.

æ-(eá-)spryng, -sprynge; *m. f.* (?): -spring; *n.*        I. *source, fountain, spring :*—Oft æspringe ūt āwealleð . he siðþan tōsceáden wyrð, Met. 5, 12. Wæs se æspring (sió æspryng, Hatt. MS.) sió sōðe lufu, Past. 48, 12. Gif wē ðone biteran wille æt ðæm æsprynge forwyrcean, 307, 1. Ealle ðás gód cumaþ of ðam æsprenge Godes mildheortnesse, Bl. H. 29, 11. Ðā gemētton hi eáspryng (æsprincg), Gr. D. 129, 4. Cūðberihtus ān æspring (eá-, *v. l.*) of drígre eorðan wæs gelǽdende, Bd. 4, 28; Sch. 518, 2. Of æspryngum *de fontibus,* Ps. Srt. 67, 27.        II. *departure, defection.* v. ā-springan, II :—Nǽnig ðæs frōd leofað ðæt his (*the sun's*) mæge æspringe witan, hū geond grund fǽreð goldtorht sunne in ðæt wonne genip under wætra geþring, Sch. 77.

æstel. *l.* æstel; Wrt. Voc. i. 81, 23 : Ælfc. Gr. Z. 31, 9.

æ-swáp. v. swǽpa *in Dict., and* An. Ox. 608 : 4155.

æ-swic; *m. l.* ǣ-swic; *n., dele* [*æ law . . .*] *and add :*—Nēd is cumende æswic (*scandala*): hweþre þonne wā ðǽm menn þe þurh hine æswic (*scandalum*) cymeþ, Mt. R. 18, 7. Æswice, wrōhte *insimulatione,* .i. *acussatione,* An. Ox. 4842. Hē symble ūs ætstandeþ tō æswice *ad decipiendum semper assistat,* Gr. D. 221, 15. In æswic *in scandalum,* Ps. Srt. 105, 36. [*O. H. Ger.* ā-suih *scandalum.*]

ǣ-swica. *l.* -swica, *and add :*—Æswica *desertor, seductor,* Wrt. Voc. ii. 139, 12. Ðæt hē wǽre leás drý and scyldig æswica, Bl. H. 175, 8. Hē ongan hine cīgan æswica (*impostorem*), Gr. D. 200, 13. þára æswicena gástas *apostatas spiritus,* 304, 28.

ǣ-swic[c]; *adj. Apostate :*—Ðā æswiccan gástas *apostatas spiritus,* Gr. D. 304, 28.

ǣ-swice, es; *m. Failure in the keeping of the law :*—þurh lahbrycas and æswicas, Wlfst. 164, 3.

ǣ-swician. *l.* -swician, *and add :* I. *to desert :*—Ic ðe nǽfre ne æswicige, Hml. Th. ii. 246, 2. Ealle gē mē æswiciað, 244, 33.        II. *to be apostate :*—Æswician *apostatare,* Wrt. Voc. ii. 3, 2.        III. *to offend :*—Gif honde þíne æswicaþ ðec . gif eágan ðín æswiceþ ðec, Mt. R. 18, 8, 9. Sē æswicað ōðrum ðe hine on Godes dǽle beswīcð, Hml. Th. i. 514, 18. Gif ðín hand þē æswicige, 516, 4. Ðe lǽs wē hí æswicien, 512, 2. v. ge-æswician.

ǣ-swicness, e; *f. Offence :*—On æswicnesse *in scandalum,* Ps. L. 105, 36.

ǣ-swicung. *l.* -swicung, *and add :* I. *seduction, deceit :*—Ālȳs ūs from deōficum costnungum and fram eallum æswicungum unrihtwīsra wyrhtena, Hml. S. 11, 42.        II. *sedition :*—Folcslite *vel* æswicung *seditio,* Wrt. Voc. i. 21, 30.        III. *offence :*—Æswicung *scandalum,* Ps. L. 48, 14. 'Mannes bearn . . gegaderað of his ríce ealle æswicunga.' On ðām upplican ríce is heálic sib, and ðǽr ne bið nān æswicung gemēt, Hml. Th. i. 562, 24. Wā middangearde for æswicungum . Neód is ðæt æswicunga cumon, i. 514, 33 : 516, 1. Intinga æswicunga (*scandalorum*), R. Ben. I. 115, 4. Æswicunga (*scandala*) hí fēdað, 109, 17. Ne āstyra ðū æswicunga ǽnigum men on life, Hex. 44, 27.

ǣ-swind *inert, sluggish :*—Ésuind, āsolcen *iners,* Wrt. Voc. ii. 111, 27. Æswind, 45, 50. v. ā-swindan.

æt. *Add:* A. *prep. followed by a case.*        I. *with dat.* (1) *temporal. at :*—Æt ðǽm ȳtmestan dæge, Bl. H. 51, 8. Æt þisse ilcan tíde, 91, 14. Æt twām cierrun and æt ðǽm þriddan cierre, Ors. 5, 7 ;

---

S. 228, 28.        (1 a) *where the time is fixed by an occurrence or a condition :*—Æt orwēnum lífe *in extremitate vitae,* Ll. Th. ii. 170, 18. Gif æt þirsa misdǽda hwelcere se hund losige, i. 78, 5. Gif his mon getilað æt ðǽre yfelan wǽtan (*when the evil humour is present*), Lch. ii. 240, 18. Æt ǽnigre neóde, Wlfst. 171, 11. Lofsang æt ðām wundrum singan, Hml. S. 21, 246.        (1 b) *with absolute dat.* (cf. similar use in Gothic and Icelandic) :—Æt þām gewordenan ǽfne, Nic. 10, 36.        (2) *local* (a) *where there is motion to an object :*—Hié hēton Iōhannes æt his mynstre gebrengan, Ors. 6, 10; S. 264, 21 : Bt. 7, 3 ; F. 22, 1. Æt hām gebring, Lch. ii. 292, 25.        (b) *motion from :*—Se sceocca sceall āswǽman æt ūs, . . . and Críst hine ādrǽfð þæt hē ūs derian ne mæge, Hml. S. 17, 203.        (c) *rest* (a) *marking point at which, object by or in contact with which something is placed :*—Hē geseah āne hlǽdre standan æt him . . . æt ðǽm uferran ende Dryhten hlinode, Past. 101, 19. Ðā gesáwon hí ðǽr monige men æt him beón (*adfuisse*), Bd. 3, 11 ; S. 536, 21. Hí gesǽton æt mē (*circa me*), ōþer æt mínum heáfde, ōþer æt mínum fōtum, 5, 13; S. 632, 35. Gegyred myd hǽran æt hyre lȳchaman, Shrn. 149, 20.        ¶ *in place-names :*—On ðǽr estōwe 'ðe is cweden Æt twyfyrde, Bd. 4, 28; S. 606, 5. In loco qui uulgari dictione nuncupatur at Archet, C. D. ii. 213, 33. Kōka ealdormon tōwearp ðā burg æt Hierusalem, Past. 311, 6. (β) *marking person with whom or place at* or *in which a person resides :*—Ðā befeng Ælfsige þone mann æt Wulfstāne, Cht. Th. 206, 23. Leófríc æt (*who lived at*) Hwítcirícean . . . and Godwine æt Worðige, Chr. 1001 ; P. 132, 6, 8. Seó cyrice sceal fēdan þā þe æt hire eardiaþ, Bl. H. 41, 28.        (3) *in various cases* (a) *marking object with which one is occupied :*—Hí æt lāre wǽron, Hml. S. 29, 10. Ic stande æt gebede, Ps. Th. 5, 3. Hē sæt æt þām æfengereordum, Bl. H. 73, 4.        (b) *marking person with whom another is brought into relation :*—Hē hæfde mycele gife æt his hlāforde, Gen. 39, 4. Swā ūs bið æt Gode, ðonne wē wið hine gesyngiað, Past. 425, 4. Hit stent on ūrum dihte hū ūs bið æt Gode gedēmed, Hml. Th. i. 52, 32.        (c) *implying adhesion :*—Ealle ðā men þe æt þǽre lāre wǽron þæt mon Pompeius ofslōg *omnes interfectores Pompeii,* Ors. 5, 12; S. 242, 22. Hē feóll mid eallum ðām englum ðe æt his rǽde wǽron, Hex. 18, 3.        (d) *marking object on which action takes effect :*—Þonne āh se teónd āne swingellan æt him, Ll. Th. i. 132, 9. Wē magon beón nyttran æt him *utilius apud eos proficimus,* Past. 211, 21. Wē habbað gedón swā swā ūs swutelung fram eów com æt ðam þ. Æðelnōðe, Cht. Th. 314, 2. Ðæt his fōt æt stāne oþspurne, Bl. H. 29, 31.        (e) *marking object in respect to which some condition or circumstance is given, in the case of* (a) *of persons :*—Sē ðe scyldunga bǽde æt (*in the case of*) ofslagenum þeófe, Ll. Th. i. 204, 27. Be ordāle æt þām mannum þe oft betihtlede wǽron, 202, 24.        (β) *of things :*—Æt þām feówer tōðum fyrestum, æt gehwylcum, .vi. scillingas, Ll. Th. i. 16, 2, 14, 15 : 18, 17. Ic eom unscyldig æt þǽre tihtlan, 180, 16. Ðæt hē feorh ne gesēce æt openre þȳfðe, 392, 3 : 240, 30. Æt þȳfðe gewita beón, 200, 20. Ealles folces þing byð þe betere æt þām þȳfðum, 238, 20 : 250, 5. Æt eallum slyht and æt ealre þǽre hergunge and æt eallum þām hearmum . . . man eall onweig lǽte, 288, 1. Hwæt tō bōte mihte æt þām fǽrcwealme, 270, 9 : Cht. Th. 265, 10. Ðæt se mæssepreóst æt þām þingum (*in illis rebus*) þone bisceop āspelian mōte, Ll. Th. ii. 176, 33.        (f) *marking source* (a) *at* or *from which something is got :*—Hē geceápade mid his feó æt þǽm consule þæt . . . , Ors. 5, 7; S. 228, 15. Hwæt hæfst ðū æt þām gifum?, Bt. 13; F. 38, 4. Hē hine gebohte æt þām mannum, Gen. 39, 1 : Hml. S. 29, 150.        (β) *at* or *from which something is sought, learnt, known, &c. :*—Leornige gehwā Godes beboda æt wísum lāreówum, Hml. S. 12, 136. Hē undernam lāre æt him, 29, 76. Hí ætgædere gelǽrede wǽron æt Aristotele *sibi apud Aristotelem condiscipulum,* Ors. 3, 9; S. 132, 2. Eówer blōd ic ofgange æt wilddeórum and eác æt þām men, Gen. 9, 5. Ic ne mæg findan æt mē seolfum þæt ic hine geseó, Ors. 5, 12; S. 244, 1.        (g) *where there is contributory payment :*—Æt ǽlcon scīll. penig, Ll. Th. i. 226, 3. Æt heáfde peninc, æt sylh peninc, gesyfledne hláf æt hreócendum heorde, Wlfst. 170, 20.        (h) *with verbs of saving, redeeming, &c., from :*—Ðæt lond æt him ālēsan, Ors. 1, 10; S. 44, 9. Gyf hit man æt ðeófes handa āhret, Ll. Th. i. 226, 4. Hí āhreddon þæt cild æt þām wulfe, Hml. S. 30, 186.        (i) *marking object of which one is deprived :*—Gif hwylc man reáfige ōðerne æt his dehter *si homo quis alterum filia sua spoliaverit,* Ll. Th. ii. 208, 7. Gif man beó æt his ǽhtan berǽfod, i. 286, 16: Gen. 43, 18: Ex. 32, 25. Hē hine berǽdde æt þām ríce, Chr. 887; P. 80, 18.        (j) *marking source from which action proceeds :*—Hē weard ācweald æt his witena handum, Hml. Th. i. 60, 4. Hí wǽron gemartyrode æt þām mānfullan Nero, Hml. S. 29, 117. Heó weard gehǽled æt þām apostole, 36, 264.        II. *with instrumental :*—Æt sume cierre, Past. 131, 12.        III. *with acc., marking limit.* Cf. oþ.        (1) *temporal, until :*—Hē hit nō ne ylde æt nōn, þonne hē tō middes dæges sceolde hām cuman, Gr. D. 206, 22. Seó is nū get æt þysne andweardan dæg mid wuldrum geweorþod, Bl. H. 129, 17. Ríneþ blōdig regn æt æfen, 91, 34 : 93, 3. Eall eorþe bið mid þeóstrum oferþeaht æt þā endlyftan tíd, 93, 6.        (2) *local, unto, up to :*—Hí hine beseancton on þā eá æt his cneówa, Bl. H. 43, 30. Geond ealle corþan gǽþ heora swēg, æt þā ȳtmestan gemǽro heora lār and heora

word, 133, 35. Andlanges ðǽre díc æt ðǽne ellenstyb, C. D. iii. 24, 3.   B. adv. or without following case. (1) where there is motion to an object:—Sē sē ðe swelc ne sié ðǽr nō æt ne cume, Past. 59, 10. Ic eów cleopode tō mē, ac gē mē noldon æt cuman, 247, 21. (2) motion from:—Eówerne gefeán eów nān mon æt ne genimð, Past. 187, 22. Wiþ ðæt beón æt ne fleón, Lch. i. 96, 25. (3) rest:—Mid eallum his geféran ðe ðǽr æt wǽron (qui aderant), Bd. 1, 25; S. 487, 7: Gr. D. 220, 6. Æt wǽron úre brōþru, Bd. 4, 5; S. 572, 12. Ðā men ðe him æt wǽron, 5, 5; S. 618, 6: Hml. S. 30, 144. Mē wǽron æt manige men, Gr. D. 83, 13. Būton ic æt wese (adsim) eów, Coll. M. 28, 21. Ic bidde þæt þū æt sý mínum sangum, Lch. i. 308, 22. Ðǽm brēðer ðe him æt stōd, Shrn. 64, 12: Bl. H. 149, 31. Ðā ðe mē æt sǽton qui mihi adsederant, Bd. 5, 13; S. 623, 12. See also passages in Dictionary under æt-befōn, -beón, -eom, -gebicgan, -gebrengan.

ǽt. Add: I. food:—Ǽt edulium, Wrt. Voc. ii. 29, 5. Hē ǽtes ne gímde, Ælfc. T. Grn. 3, 16. Tō mōse, ǽte ad edulium, i. ad uescendum, An. Ox. 3762. Be ǽte de cibo, Ll. Th. ii. 128, 20. Seó leó bringð his hwelpum hwæt tō etanne; hié gecýðað on ðǽm ǽte . . . , Ors. 3, 11; S. 142, 25. Wurmum tō ǽte, Wlfst. 145, 19. Hē tō micel nimð on ǽte oððe on wǽte, Hml. S. 16, 270. Hē forosceáwian, Hml. Th. ii. 138, 35. þū scealt þā ōþre ǽtas sellan, Lch. ii. 90, 12. See also passages under wǽt. II. eating:—Be ðæs lambes ǽte de agni esu, An. Ox. 40, 29. For æppla and hnuta ǽte from the eating of apples and nuts, Lch. ii. 246, 21. Sē þe hine gelaðode tō ǽte (ad manducandum), Gr. D. 128, 29. Swylce þā gebrocu þæs hláfes þurh þone ǽt (per esum) weóxon, 252, 23. v. ǽr-, flǽsc-, un-ǽt.

ǽta. Add: v. hláf-ǽta.

æt-beran. Add:—To carry off:—Swerie hē þ hē ǽfre ne stele, ne feoh ne ætbere, Ll. Th. i. 332, 21.

æt-berstan. Add: I. of actual motion, (1) absolute:—Hē ætbærst and hē ys geworden nū tō wealdgengan, Ælfc. T. Grn. 18, 5. Se here ætbærst, Chr. 992; P. 127, 17. Uneáþe cwic ætberstende, Coll. M. 27, 3. (2) when person from whom or place from which is given, (a) dat.:—Hē heom ætbærst, Chr. 1052; P. 179, 21. (b) with adv. or prep.:—Sē ætbærst ðanon, Chr. 605; P. 23, 10. Nǽre þ hí on niht ūt ne ætburston of þǽre byrig, 943; P. 111, 17. (3) where direction, road, or manner of escape is given:—His geféran mid fleáme ætburston, Hml. Th. ii. 248, 11. Þā menn up ætberstan intō þǽre byrig, Ll. Th. i. 286, 2. þ hē ne ætburste on wætere, Chr. 1050; P. 167, 34. II. fig. (1) to escape, be free from the power of a person (dat.):—Ic ne mæg þām Almihtigan ætberstan on lífe oþþe on deáðe, Hml. S. 25, 100. (2) to escape, be safe from danger, evil, &c. (a) with dat.:—Ne mæg nán man ætberstan þām gemǽnelican deáðe, Hml. A. 54, 105. Sé þe wile synnum ætberstan, Scrd. 22, 43. (b) with acc.:—Hí ætberstaþ frecnyssa evadunt pericula, Coll. M. 25, 1. (3) of things, to be lost to a person (dat.):—His feoh him ætbyrst, Hml. S. 12, 85: Wlfst. 142, 7. Ne ætberst þām bydele his geswinces edleán, Hml. Th. ii. 534, 16.

æt-bredan; &c. l. æt-bregdan, -brēdan; p. -brægd, -brǽd, pl. -brugdon, -brūdon; pp. -brogden, -brōden, and add: To take away from (with dat. or with preps. of, fram):—Ætbræt detorsit, Germ. 397, 368. I. with idea of deprivation:—God forgeaf ðā ǽhta, and God hí eft ætbræd, Hml. Th. ii. 328, 30. Drihten mancynne ætbræd wuldor, þæt hē him wuldor forgeáfe, i. 578, 15. II. with idea of spoliation:—Ic ætbrēde vel ic forgrīpe diripio, i. rapio, abstraho, eripio, Wrt. Voc. ii. 140, 48. Gif ic þurh unriht fācn ǽnigum men āht ætbræd (abstuli), Ll. Th. ii. 136, 9. Hē ætbræd mē mīne frumcennedan, and nū ōðre sīðe forstæl mīne bletsunga, Gen. 27, 36. Hig calle heora bigleofan ætbrūdon, Jud. 6, 4. Nele hē his ǽhta him ætbrēdan, Hml. Th. ii. 522, 21. Þā wyrta þe hē mid stale gewilnode tō ætbrēdanne, Gr. D. 25, 16. Gif nýten byð ætbrōden (captum ab hostibus), Ex. 22, 10. þā land ðā hǽdenan ætbrodon hæfdon, Hml. S. 30, 307. Æt-brōden direpta, An. Ox. 3647. III. with idea of rescue:—Ic ætbrēde oððe āhredde eripio, Ælfc. Gr. Z. 168, 9. Sē ðe úre fæderas feóndum ætbræd, Hml. S. 19, 153. þām þe hē þám deófle ætbræd, 156. IV. with idea of seduction:—þ hē ūs forðó and ūs Drihtne ætbrēde, Hml. A. 5, 122. þā Gode gebrōhte þe se deófol ætbrēdan wolde, Hml. S. 5, 24. V. with idea of withdrawal, abstention:—Se wīsdóm hine sylfne ætbrēt fram mōdes hīwunge, Hml. Th. ii. 326, 3. Hē hine ætbræd þām flǽsclicum lustum, i. 58, 18. Hí ætbrūdon menn fram flǽsclicum lustum, 576, 23. Hē ætbrēde (subtrahat) his līchaman of mette, R. Ben. I. 85, 5. VI. with idea of withholding, prevention:—Ic ðe ætbrēde mīne rēnas, þæt heó þīnre eorðan ne rīnað, Wlfst. 259, 25. Hē ætbræd þ gefeoht he would not let the battle take place, Hml. S. 31, 126. Ætbrōdenum his dǽle of wīne, R. Ben. I. 77, 14. VII. with idea of destroying, putting an end to:—þ þū ādýlegie synna, þū þe synna ætbrýtst, Hml. S. 3, 544. Sē ðe ætbrýt and ādýlegað middaneardes synna, Hml. Th. ii. 38, 29. Þā blisse ūs ne ætbrēt nān man, Hml. A. 78, 144. Sē þe ætbræt (aufert) gāst ealdra, Ps. L. 75, 13. Sē ðe ætbrūde synna, Hml. Th. ii. 40, 9. God mihte heora geswinc him ætbrēdan, 162, 5. v. æt-brēdendlic in Dict.

æt-bryidan. v. brigdan.

æt-clifian. Add:—Ætfélun (vel ætclofodon in a later hand) adheserunt, Ps. V. 101, 6.

æt-clīðende glosses aderentem, Txts. 181, 64. Cf. cliða.

æt-dēman to give judgement adverse to a claimant (dat.) in respect to what he claims (acc.):—Ðā ætdēmdon him Myrcna witan land būton hē his wer āgulde, Cht. Th. 207, 32. Cf. æt-reccan.

ǽte. Add:—Eft, sealf; ǽtan gecnūa, lege on, Lch. ii. 118, 28. v. self-ǽte. -ǽte. v. micel-, ofer-ǽte.

æt-eáca, an; m. An addition, appendix:—Etheácan appendices, An. Ox. 53, 18.

æt-ealdod; adj. Too aged:—Þonne heó forwerod byð and teámes ætealdod (too old to bear children), Hml. A. 20, 159.

æt-eáwan, æt-eom, æt-eów-, ǽtere, ǽtern, æt-ēw-. v. æt-īwan, æt, æt-īw-, sceáp-ǽtere, ǽtren, æt-īw-.

æt-fæstan. Add: I. to inflict:—Æ(t)fæstan inpingere, Wrt. Voc. ii. 44, 72. II. to commit, entrust, deposit:—Ædfæst depositum, Wrt. Voc. i. 21, 4. II a. to give in marriage:—þā ætfæste hē mē mīne efenþeówene, seó þe wæs ǽr ōðres gemecca, Shrn. 39, 8. Cf. oþ-fæstan.

æt-fæstnian; p. ode To commit, deposit:—Hweðer geleornodest þū þe myd þām eágum þe mid þām ingeþance? þā cwæð ic: Mid ǽgðrum ic hyt geleornode. . . . þā eágan hyt ætfæstnodon mīnum ingeþance, Shrn. 175, 10.

æt-faran; p. -fōr To go away, make off:—Ān fox þone scōh gelæhte and ætfaran (-en, MS.) þōhte, Shrn. 14, 23. Cf. oþ-faran.

æt-feallan. Add: I. lit. to fall, drop from:—Þām cwellere ætfeóll his gold, Hml. S. 12, 216. II. fig. (1) to fall away, (a) diminution:—Ætfealle sió bōt þǽm godfæder swā ilce swā þ wīte þām hláforde dēð, Ll. Th. i. 150, 18. (b) deterioration:—þ geleáfa swā earmlīce ætfeallan sceolde, Hml. S. 23, 373. (c) desertion:—Se lǽweda mōt ōðre sīðe wīfigan, gyf his wīf him ætfylð, Ll. Th. ii. 346, 22. His frýnd him ætfeallað, Hml. S. 12, 85: Wlfst. 142, 6. (2) to befall, come upon:—Hē bið ācōlod and for þon ætfilð him wæterbolla, Lch. ii. 206, 11. Cf. oþ-feallan.

æt-fecgan, -felgan. v. æt-feólan: æt-feohtan, dele I.

æt-feólan. l. æt-feólan, and add: (from -feolhan); p. -fealh, pl. -fulgon, and -fǽlon (as if from -felan). I. to adhere, cleave (lit. and fig.):—Ætfiled adhereat, Ps. Srt. 136, 6. Ætfalh adhesit, 43, 25: 62, 9. Ætfélun (-fulgon, Ps. Spl. C.) adheserunt, 24, 21. Ætfealan (not -feolan as in Dict.), 72, 28. II. fig. of continued action, to stick to, (a) with idea of diligence, be instant in:—Ðæt hē geornlīce ætfealh ðǽre ðēnunge ministerio sedulus insistere, Bd. 3, 19; S. 547, 14. Ðā hē geornlīce his leornunge ætfealh cum lectioni operam dedisset, 4, 23; S. 596, 16. Hié geornlīce heora gebedum ætfulgon, Bl. H. 201, 18. Ætfeolh ðū ðīnum fæstenum jejuniis insiste, Bd. 4, 25; S. 599, 41. Ðearf is þ ic weacenum ætfeóle, S. 601, 3. Ðæt gē ætfeólen ðǽre lāre ut praedicationi servias, Past. 375, 5. (b) with idea of persistence:—Ðā ætfealh se gesīþ geornlīce his bēnum comes obnixius precibus instans, Bd. 5, 4; S. 617, 12. III. to press, impress, (a) lit.:—Writ þām horse on þām heáfde foran Crīstes mǽl and on leoþa gehwilcum þe þū ætfeólan mæge, Lch. ii. 290, 24. (b) fig.:—þā þā him eádmōdlīce ætfeólan his þegnas and lǽrdon hine, þ hē onfénge þ yrfe cum ei discipuli humiliter imminerent, ut possessiones acciperet, Gr. D. 201, 9. Cf. oþ-feólan.

æt-feorrian to take away:—Nā ætfeorra þū non auferas, Scint. 160, 7.

æt-ferian. Add:—Man mid unrihte N. orf ætferede, Ll. Th. i. 180, 1. Cf. oþ-ferian.

æt-fleón. Add: (1) absolute, to escape, flee away:—Ðā ōðre ætflugon, Hml. S. 25, 294: Chr. 1056; P. 186, 31. Hē ofslōh þā þe ætfleón ne mihton, 1068; P. 203, 26. Fleón þe mæg, ac hē ætfleón ne mæg, Ap. Th. 7, 5. (2) to escape from (dat.):—Him nān þing ætfleón ne mæg, Hml. S. 1, 44. Wē rǽdaþ be þǽre león, þ ðā ōðre deór þe mihton hire ætfleón þurh heora fōta swiftnysse, þ hí beóð swā āfyrhte þ hí fleón ne durron, Hml. A. 63, 480. (3) to escape to (tō):—Hē tō scypum ætfleáh, Chr. 1076; P. 211, 28. Ðā ōðre ætflugon tō Philistéa lande, Hml. S. 25, 321. Þéh scip ætfleó tō hwilcre friðbyrig, Ll. Th. i. 286, 1. Cf. oþ-fleón.

æt-fōn. Substitute: To arrest, apprehend, attach stolen or lost property:—Gif man ōðrum mæn feoh forstele, and se āgend hit eft ætfó, Ll. Th. i. 30, 8. Gif feoh man eft æt þām mæn in Cent ætfó, 34, 6. Cf. 160, 8.

æt-foran. Add: I. prep. (1) local, (a) confronting, (a) of persons, before, in the presence of, in the sight of:—Ætforan (ante) þǽre engelican gæderunge, An. Ox. 1749. Wē synd hēr ætforan (coram) þē, Coll. M. 34, 1. Hē wæs Gode gecwēme and gife ætforan him gemētte, Gen. 6, 8: 11. (β) of objects, before, in front of:—His sceatt ætstōd ætforan him, Hml. S. 12, 54. þone fōtscamul ætforan his bedde (æt his reste foran, v.l.), Gr. D. 20, 28. (b) preceding, in front of, at the head of:—Gād ætforan þām folce praecedite populum, Jos. 3, 6. (2) temporal, (a) marking date:—Ætforan scs Andreas mæssan, Chr. 1010; P. 141, 3. (b) marking priority:—Swā wel haldan swā ǽnig kyngc ætforan him betst dyde, Chr. 1066; P. 200, 22. (3) marking precedence, preference:—

Hē geendebyrde þone unspēdigan fiscere ætforan ðām rīcan cāsere, Hml. Th. i. 578, 10. Þ heregyld wæs æfre ætforan ōðrum gyldum þe man geald, Chr. 1052; P. 173, 22. II. *adv. Before, beforehand:—* Wǣron þā wǣlisce men ætforan mid þām cynge, Chr. 1048; P. 174, 9.

**æt-fylgan.** *Add:* . -fylgan:—Him ætfylgedon his þegnas, Gr. D. 201, 9. v. æt-feólan, III b.

**æt-gædere.** *In passage from* Met. 20, 160 *insert* mǣst *after* biþ, *and add:* I. marking association:—Him leófre wǣre þæt hié mid þǣre byrig ætgædere forwurdon þonne hié mon būtan him tōwurpe, Ors. 4. 13; S. 210, 23. Hié ætgædere wǣron on heora gebedstōwe, Bl. H. 133, 18: 24. Lǣt hī beón hēr ætgædere gelēde, Hml. S. 30, 443. Hī ne mihton ealle ætgædere gewunian, Chr. 3, 9. Þā hergas fōron bēgen ætgædere, 894; P. 87, 10: 1014; P. 145, 18. II. marking simultaneous action:—Þe lǣs wē ætgædere ealle forweorðan, Wlfst. 166, 3. Se cyning lȳhte of his horse . . . ðā lyhte se biscop eác somod ætgædere, Bd. 3, 22; S. 553, 34. Būton hē bēgra ætgæddre getilian mæge, P. 457, 15.

**æt-gæderum;** *adv. Together:—*Him ðā eallum ætgæderum sittendum, Lch. iii. 428, 16.

**æt-gære.** v. next word.

**æt-gār.** *Add:* æt- (æte-, ate-) gār; *m.* -gǣre; *n.* (The pl. seems sometimes used to gloss Latin sing.):—Falarica, i. *theca gladii, telae genus* vel *hastae grandis* vel *lancea magna* ætgār, Wrt. Voc. ii. 147, 9: 33, 49. Ætgāre *framea*, 36, 11: *falarica (armatum)*, An. Ox. 8, 312. Ætgāre, Angl. xiii. 29, 46. Aetgaere *ansatae*, Txts. 41, 167. Ætgaeru (-gāru. Sievers, Gram. § 273, ann. 4, takes this to be a *u*-stem) *framea*, 65, 922. Ætgēro (ægtero, MS.) *falarica*, 63, 839. Ategāra *falarica* (v. 8, 312 above), An. Ox. 5023. Ategārum *falarica* (v. Angl. xiii. 29, 46 above), 786. Ategāras *ansatas*, 2, 502. Ætgāras, Wrt. Voc. ii. 3, 68.

**æt-gebicgan, -gebrengan.** *l.* æt gebicgan, gebrengan. v. æt.

**æt-geniman.** *Substitute:* æt-genumen *removed, taken away:—*þā ætgenumenan *erepta*, Wrt. Voc. ii. 95, 30.

**æt-glīdan;** *p.* -glād *To slip away, disappear:—*Ædglide *delitescere!* (cf. *another gloss of the same passage in* An. Ox. 2089: Bemiþe, fordwine; *and* fordwīnan *delitescere.* 2152), An. Ox. 7, 132.

**æt-habban.** *Add:—*Nāmon ðā tō rǣde, þæt him wǣrlícor wǣre, þæt hī sumne dǣl heora landes wurðes æthǣfdon, Hml. Th. i. 316, 24. Æthabban *retinere*, Scint. 57, 7, 8.

**æðan.** *Dele, and see* ā-īþan: **æþan.** v. ge-æþan.

**æt-healdan;** *p.* -heóld *To withhold:—*Þinc fram Drihtne ætheóld (*reseruauit*), Scint. 109, 18.

**æt-hebban;** *p.* -hóf *To remove, withdraw:—*Hē hine æthóf from ōðerra monna gefērrǣdenne, Past. 113, 13.

**æþel.** v. æþele.

**æþel-boren.** *Add:* I. *of gentle birth*, in contrast with **servile** birth:—Ægðer ge æþelboren ge þeówetling, Hml. Th. i. 92, 1. Ne sceal hē þone æþelborenan settan beforan þane þeówborenan *non preponatur ingenuus ex servitio convertenti*, R. Ben. 12, 12. II. in a general sense, *noble:—*Æthelboren *nobilis*, Wrt. Voc. i. 85, 60. Eðelboren, Kent. Gl. 1147. Gif hwylc rīce mon and æþelboren *si quis de nobilibus*, R. Ben. 103, 10. Eádgār . . cincg æþelboren (*egregius*), Angl. xiii. 365, 5. Ealdorman æfter worulde swīðe æþelboren, Hml. S. 30, 3. For worulde æðelboren, Hml. Th. ii. 118, 10. Swȳðe æþelboren on weorulde and rīce, Chr. 654; P. 29, 15. Of æðelborenre mǣgðe, Hml. Th. ii. 118, 6: 174, 6: Hml. S. 8, 41. Æðelborene weras þe wǣron ēstlíce āfēdde, 31, 335. Næs heó swā nū æðelborene men synt mid ofermēttum āfylled, Lch. iii. 428, 31. Gif æðelborenan wīfmen þis gelimpe, Ll. Th. i. 70, 1. ¶ definite form as noun:—Tō gewrīþenne æþelborenan (*nobiles*) heora, Ps. L. 149, 8. III. *inborn, natural.* Cf. æþelu, I:—Æþelborene *ingenitam* (probably a gloss on Ald. 66, 9: Venustatem . . . genuina consparsione *ingenitam*), Wrt. Voc. ii. 47, 45. [O. Sax. aðal-boran.] v. un-æþelboren, *and next word.*

**æþelborenness.** *Add:* I. *nobleness of birth, gentle birth:—*Ne teáh nān æðelborennyss nǣnne man tō wurðscype, būtan hē wīsdóm leornode, Hml. S. 3, 6. Æþelborenysse *stemmatis*, Hy. S. 47, 14. Wǣron hī æfter æþelborennysse oferhȳdige, Hml. Th. ii. 174, 8. Hē wæs æðelboren, ac hē oferstāh his æðelborennysse mid hālgum ðeáwum, 118, 10. II. *nobleness, nobility, dignity:—*'Mycel æðelborennys bið þ man bē Crīstes ðeów' . . . 'næbbe wē nāne æþelborennysse for ðan þe wē forseóð Crīstes ðeówdōm' . . . eówer æðelborennys becymð tō bysmorfullum hæftnēde, Hml. S. 8, 46–51. Æþelborennes *generositas*, Wrt. Voc. ii. 40, 32. Hlāford, ūre ceaster is þearfende and ne mæg þīne æðelborennesse ācuman, Ap. Th. 9, 8: 15, 22. III. *inborn nature:—*Æþelbornesse *indolem*, An. Ox. 4518. v. preceding word.

**æþel-cund.** *Add:—*Manige his cūðra manna ge æþelcunde ge ōðre *multi viri noti ac nobiles*, Gr. D. 22, 15.

**æþel-cyning.** *Add:* [O. Sax. aðal-kuning.]

**æþele.** *Add:* , æþel [cf. O. Sax. eðili, aðal: O. H. Ger. edele, adal]. I. in the following glosses:—Aeðile *generosus*, Wrt. Voc. ii. 109, 58. Þæs æþelan *fausta*, 33, 76. Þā æþelan *emeritos*, 32,

73. II. of persons :—Æþel *gnarus* (*cultor*), An. Ox. 2637. On þǣre stōwe wunode swȳþe æþel wer (sum æðele wer, *v. l.*) *quo in loco vir nobilis manebat*, Gr. D. 61, 30. Sum æþel (æðele, *v. l.*) wer *vir quidam nobilis*, 140, 3. Cwēn . . þeáh hió æðelu sī, Rä. 78, 5. Æþeles *indolis* (indolis *titulus principum*, *adolescentium maxime, honorarius*, Migne), An. Ox. 2869: *indolis*, i. *iuuenis ingenuus*, 2, 114. Mǣran, æþelan *illustris* (*Agathae*), 4362. Þone æþelan geongan *indolem*, Wrt. Voc. ii. 44, 80. Iosue þone æþelan, Jos. 4, 14. Þæs æþelran lāreówes *egregii dogmatiste*, An. Ox. 4362. Þā æðelestan ealdras *nobilissimi principes*, Num. i. 16. III. of things :—Æþele *alu carenum*, Wrt. Voc. ii. 23, 1. Æþele crætt *an excellent medicine*, Lch. ii. 28, 10. Æðele *fortunatum* (*praesagium*), An. Ox. 7, 167. Mid æþelum *celebri* (*fama*), 2421. Hē getimbrade æþele myuster, Shrn. 50, 29. Lēcedōmas micle and eþele, Lch. ii. 160, 8. Æþelum *claris* (*natalibus*), Wrt. Voc. ii. 94, 59. Æþeleste cyn *celeberrimum*, i. *opinatissimum* (*spectaculi*) *genus*, An. Ox. 2082.

**æþelferþing-wyrt,** e; *f. Stitchwort, bird's tongue:—*Æþelferðingwyrt, Lch. ii. 80, 12 : 94, 10 : iii. 28, 22. Æðelferðingcwyrt, 40, 16. Æðelferðingwyrt (*auis lingua*), 24, 1 : 4, 29. Æðelfyrdingwyrt *alfa* (cf. *agrimonia alpha* eathelferthingwyrt ꝥ glofvyrt, Lch. iii. 299, col. 2), Wrt. Voc. i. 32, 10. Nim æþelferþincgwyrte, Lch. i. 180, 26 : 166, 28.

**æþelian.** un-. *l.* an-: **æðel-ic,** -īce. v. æþel-(l)ic, -(l)īce.

**æþeling.** *Add:* I. *a prince* of an English royal house :—Æþelingc *clito* (clitones *universim filii omnes regum apud Anglo-Saxones*, Migne), Wrt. Voc. i. 72, 62. Æðeling, 42, 15. Æþeling *clyton*, ii. 22, 40. Ceadwalla West-Seaxna æþeling (*de regio genere Geuissorum*), Bd. 4, 15; S. 583, 25. Æðelwald (*Edward's cousin*) æðeling and Byrhtsige Beornōðes sunu æðelingas, Chr. 905; P. 94, 12. Hēr ādranc Ædwine æðeling (*son of Edward*), 933; P. 107, 4. Se æðeling Eádmund (*Edmund Ironside*), 1015; P. 146, 13. Se cyng (*Ethelred*) sende Ælfūn ꝥ mid þām æþelinge (-um, *v. l.*) Eádwarde and Ælfrēde ofer sē, 1013; P. 144, 15. Hē gean Ælfrīdæ ðæs cyningæs wīfæ ðæs landæs . . . and ðām yldran æðælingæ, ðæs cyngæs suna and hiræ, . . . ānæs swurdæs, C. D. iii. 127, 25. Wǣron þā æþelingas befæste Egcbrihte cynge . . . wæs se cyng heora fæderan sunu, Eorcenbrihtes, Lch. iii. 424, 11. Þā eðelingas Æðelfrīðes (*K. of Northumbria*) suna, Chr. 617; P. 24, 29. I a. *of English leaders before the conquest of Britain :—*þā sendon Brytwalas tō Anglum and Angelcynnes æðelingas þes ilcan bǣdon, Chr. 443; P. 13, 4. II. *a prince, noble* other than English :—Wilnade sum æðeling tō rīcsianne . . . Falores (*Phalaris*) wæs hāten, Ors. 1, 12; S. 54, 16. Alcibiades se æðeling, Bt. 32, 2; F. 116, 19. Odda (*the emperor's nephew*) wæs Leódulfes sunu æþelinges, Chr. 982; P. 124, 31. Be sumum Rōmāniscum æðelinge se wæs hāten Liberias (*the Latin is :* liberum quendam virum), Bt. 16, 2; F. 52, 19. Twēgen æþelingas *duo regii juvenes*, Ors. 1, 10; S. 44, 24. III. *used of Christ :—*Ācende Maria þone heofoulican æðeling, Hml. Th. i. 356, 9. Þæt se ælmihtiga cyning sceolde besceúfan tō cwale his āncennedan æðeling, ii. 6, 21. [O. H. Ger. ediling *nobilis.*]

**æþeling-hād,** es; *m. Princely condition:—*Sōna swā hē tō his cynedōme gecoren wearþ, wæs swīþe gemundige his behātes þe hē on his æþelincghade Gode behēt, Lch. iii. 438, 5.

**æþel-(l)ic.** *Add:—*þǣre æþelican *inlustris*, Wrt. Voc. ii. 44, 75. [O. H. Ger. adal-līh *insignis, nobilis, inlustris, liber.*]

**æþel-(l)īce.** *Add:—*Æþelíce *eleganter*, Wrt. Voc. ii. 31, 71 : *insigniter*, 44, 83. Hē ðā ciricean æþellíce gefretwode, Shrn. 50, 31. Swā fulfremed þæt nǣnig æþelícor ne sang, 127, 13. [O. H. Ger. adallícho *eleganter, nobiliter.*] v. un-æþellíce.

**æþel-nes.** *Add:—*Seó æþelnes heora gebyrda, Gr. D. 151, 22. Tūddres æþelnes, Bl. H. 115, 10. Beorht mid eorðlicere æðelnysse, Shrn. 151, 18. Þū leórest tō þǣre upplican eþelnesse, 119, 30. v. un-æþelness.

**æþelo.** *Add: f. and in pl. n.* I. *nature,* (a) in respect to other than rational beings :—Nim swā wuda swā wyrt of þǣre stōwe þe his eard and æþelo biþ on tō weaxanne, and sette on uncynde stōwe him, ðonne ne gegrēwþ hit ðǣr nāuht, Bt. 34, 10; F. 148, 26. Hē þǣre sunnan wlite herede æðelo cræftas reahte (cf. hē herede þǣre sunnan gecynd and hiore cræftas and hiore biorhto, Bt. 41, 1; F. 244, 7), Met. 30, 7. Deáde gesceafte ferðgewit of hyra æðelum ǣnig ne cūðen, Cri. 1185. Monige cynn swā wē æðelu ne magon āreccan, Pa. 2. Ic þæs beámes mæg æðelu secgan, Rä. 56, 8. (b) in respect to rational beings :—Him ides æfter æðelum (*in the natural course*) eaforan fēdde, Gen. 1054. II. *condition determined by birth* or *descent :—*þæt is cūð hwanon þām ordfruman æðelu onwōcon; hē wæs āfēded on þysse folcsceare, An. 683. Þā wǣron æðelum Abrahames bearn *by birth they were children of Abraham*, Dan. 193. For cynn æfter cynne; cūðe ǣghwilc mǣgburga riht, eorla æðelo, Exod. 353. II a. *noble condition that comes from birth* or *descent :—*Sceolon gelȳfan eorlas hwæt mīn æðelo sién (*men shall believe my divinity*), An. 735. Cniht þāg swā him cynde wǣron æðelo from yldrum, Gen. 2772 : 1716. Him from Myrgingum æðelu onwōcon, Víd. 5. Geðence hē ðā æðelu (*nobilitatem*) ðǣre æfterran ācennesse . . . Be ðǣm æðelum (*nobilitati*) ðæs gāstes (*the

*nobility that comes from spiritual birth*) Petrus cwæð : Gê sint ácoren kynn Gode and kynelices preósthádes, Past. 85, 14-19. Ic wylle míne æðelo eallum gecýðan, þæt ic wæs on Myrcon miccles cynnes, By. 216. Ælc mon ðe allunga underþeóded biþ unþeáwum forlæt his fruman sceaft and his æþelo, Bt. 30, 2 ; F. 110, 22 : Met. 17, 25. **II b.** *noble birth, nobility :*—Hwý gê eów for æðelum up áhebben, Met. 17, 18. Deáð forsiehð þá æþelo, and þone rícan gelíce and þone heánan forswelgþ, Bt. 30, 1 ; F. 68, 33. Ðæt án ic wát gódes on þá æþelu, þ manigne mon sceamaþ þ hê weorþe wyrsa ðonne his eldran wæron, Bt. 30, 1 ; S. 69, 12. Hê forseah eorðlic æðelu, gemunde hám in heofonum, Gú. 68. **III.** *nobility, excellence :*—þæt Israhêla æðelu môten ofer middangeard rícsian, æcræft eorla, El. 433. Æðelum cræftige *excellently skilful*, 315. **IV.** *nobility* in a concrete, collective sense (?), *noble things :*—Heáhhlioðo horde onféngon and æðelum eác eorðan túdres, Gen. 1440. Flôd áhôf earce from eorðan and þá æðelo mid, 1389. [*O. Sax.* aðali ; *n. noble family : O. H. Ger.* adal, edeli ; *n. prosapia, genus, nobilitas ;* edilî ; *f. generositas : Icel.* aðal ; *n. nature.*]

**æt-híde.** *Dele.*

**æt-hindan.** *Add : prep. with dat. :*—Se kyning fêrde him æthindan, Ælfc. T. 5, 24 : Hml. A. 105, 106.

**æþm.** *Add :*—Æþm *alitus*, Wrt. Voc. i. 287, 71. Aethm, ii. 99, 78. Aethme *vapore*, 123, 14. **I.** *breath* of a living creature :—Ælces fisces sciell bið tô ôðerre gefêged ðæt ðær ne mæg nán æðm út betwuxn *una squama uni conjungitur, et ne spiraculum quidem incedit per eas*, Past. 361, 19. **II.** *hot breath, blast* of fire :—Hê gefrêt þæs fýres æþm, Hml. Th. i. 616, 24. Hî ásprungon up mid ðám fýre . . . and þær slôh út ormæte stenc mid ðám æðmum, ii. 350, 25. **III.** *hot vapour* from liquids :—þ se æþm (*steam from a hot kettle*) ne mæge út, Lch. ii. 338, 18. Drince on þám baþe and ne læte on þone æþm, 78, 24. þá hátan wæter reócað and mycele æþmas (*vapores*) wyrcað, Gr. D. 343, 4. Baþena æþmas *thermarum uapores*, An. Ox. 4778. **IV.** *vapour* of the human body :—Of hômena æþme and stíeme cymð eágna mist, Lch. ii. 26, 26. þá þing þe windigne æþm on men wyrcen, 214, 3.

**æþmian.** *Substitute :* **I.** *to send forth vapour, be heated, be in a ferment :*—þá þe on gewilnunge grædignysse æþmeað *qui desiderio cupiditatis exestuant*, Scint. 112, 11. **II.** *to send forth a smell :*—Æþmmigende *redolentia*, Germ. 391, 202. [*O. H. Ger.* át(o)môn *flare, spirare.*]

**æt-hredan.** *Dele, and v.* æt-bregdan, III.

**æt-hrínan.** *Add :*—Ætrînþ *tangat*, Wrt. Voc. ii. 135, 10. Ethrínð *tetigerit*, Kent. Gl. 167. Æthrîned *adhaerebit*, Lk. L. 16, 13. Æthrán *adhaesit*, 10, 11. Ætrán, 15, 15. Ne ðú ne ethrîn *nec adtingas*, Kent. Gl. 874. (1) with gen. :—Gyf ic hys reáfes æthríne, Mt. 9, 21. Gyf hwylc man hyra æthríneð, Nar. 34, 2. Hyra nán hys ne æthrán *nemo misit in illum manus*, Jn. 7, 30. Heó his hrægeles fnædes æthrán, Hml. A. 182, 49 : 187, 177. þ fýr heora ne æthrán, Hml. S. 30, 454. Ne æthrín ðú mín *noli me tangere*, Jn. 20, 17. (2) with dat. :—Ic næfre ne æthrán hire leomum, Hml. A. 204, 304. Heó nolde were æthrínan, 135, 654. (3) with acc. :—Hê hig æthrán, Mt. 17, 7. Heó æthrán hys reáfes fnæd, 9, 20. (4) case uncertain :—Hê cwæð þæt hê hyre næfre ne æthríne, Hml. A. 135, 660. Ær þon þe hê eorþan æthríne, Bl. H. 165, 19.

**æt-hríne, es ; *m.* *Touch :*—Æthrin[e] *tactus*, Wrt. Voc. i. 42, 55. þ ne worhte nánes mannes æthríne, Gr. D. 87, 24. On æthríne *in tactu*, Angl. xi. 116, 14. Mid hys æthríne hý onweg gewítað *at a touch from it they will go away*, Lch. i. 336, 14. Hnesce on æthríne *soft to the touch*, 108, 1 : 110, 5.

**æþro. v.** æd(d)er.

**æ-þrot, es ; *n.* *Weariness, disgust :*—Æþrot *fastidium*, Wrt. Voc. ii. 146, 45. Æhþrot is *pertesum est*, An. Ox. 11, 166. Fore æþrote *prae tedio*, Ps. Srt. 118, 28. Hî heora tídla singaþ oþ þæs sealmsanges ende bútan æþrote þurhwuniende, R. Ben. 138, 2. Æþrotu *fastidia*, Wrt. Voc. ii. 146, 48. Gelærede æþrotu *docta fastidia* (-*gia*, MS.), 141, 69. **v.** á-þrotsum.

**æ-þryt.** *l.* æ-þryt[t], -]ryte, *and add :*—Náht is lang, náht ys æþryte (*longum*) þ ná on sceortum sý geendud, Scint. 217, 6. Gyf hit ne þúhte æþryt (-þrytt, *v. l.*) tô áwrítenne, Lch. iii. 276, 3. Þý læs ðe hit eów æðryt þince, Hml. Th. i. 88, 32. Þe læs þe hyt beó æþryt geléredum preóstum, Angl. viii. 333, 13. Him ðincð æðryt tô gehýrenne ymbe ðá clænnesse, Hml. Th. ii. 374, 21. Þincð him æþryt þ hê embe þ þence, An. Ox. 4582, note. (*In any but the first of these passages perhaps* æþryt *is a noun ; v. next word, and cf.* æhþrot *is pertesum est*, An. Ox. 11, 166.)

**æ-þryt[t], es ; *n.* **I.** *weariness, disgust :*—Ne durre wê ðás bôc gelengan, ðí læs ðe heó ungemetegod sý and mannum æðryt þurh hire micelnysse ástyrige, Hml. Th. ii. 520, 5. **II.** *wearisomeness, tediousness :*—Ic ðôhte þæt hit wære læsse æðryt tô gehýrenne, gif man ðá áne bôc ræt on ánes geáres ymbryne, and ðá óðre on ðám æftran geáre, Hml. Th. ii. 2, 11.

**æ-þrytness.** *l.* æ-þrytness, *and add :*—Æþrytnesse *tedium*, Hy. S. 133, 28. Æþretnysse, 25, 24. **v.** á-þrytness.

**æ-þryttan ; *p.* -te *To weary :*—Æþrytte *pertensum* (-*taesum*, Ald.) *est*, An. Ox. 4582. Æþyrdte, 4, 83. Ædrette, Hpt. Gl. 512, 42. (*All are glosses on the same passage.*) þæt hí ne beón ðurh ðá langsumnysse æðrytte, Hml. Th. ii. 446, 8.

**æþung. v.** eþung.

**æt-hwá. *Add :*—Sácerdum gebyreþ þ hí gcorne tô rihte æthwám fylstan, Ll. Th. ii. 312, 39. [*O. H. Ger.* ete-wer *aliquis*.]

**æt-hwára (-e) ; *adv.* *Somewhat :*—Æthwáre *aliquan'ulum*, Hpt. Gl. 421, 37. [*O. H. Ger.* ete-wár *alicubi ;* ete-wára *quocumque*.] **v.** hwæthwára.

**æt-hweg ; *adv.* *How :*—Gê magan þe þissum ánum (deófies men) gecnáwan, þá hê ðurh deófol swylcne cræft hæfde ongeán swylce Godes þegnas, . . . æthweg hit bið þonne se deófol cymð, Wlfst. 101, 1.

**æt-hwega. *Add :* -hwigan :*—Æthwega (-hwigan *modice*, R. Ben. I. 92, 16) beteran, R. Ben. 90, 11 : *aliquatenus*, R. Ben. I. 107, 8 : 115, 15 : *aliquantulum*, 95, 8 : An. Ox. 638 : *paulatim*, Angl. xiii. 365, 9. Æthwege *paulisper*, An. Ox. 5390. Hit æthwego ádríg, Lch. i. 332, 26.

**æt-hwôn. *Add :*—Æthwôn *pene*, Mt. p. 1, 13.

**æt-hýde.** *l.* æt-hýdan (?) *to take away the skin :*—Æthýd *eviscerata* (*cf. viscera* beséagen flǽ(s)c, Wrt. Voc. i. 45, 7), Wrt. Voc. ii. 29, 50. Athêd (aeohed, Ep. Gl.), Txts. 59, 768.

**æt-ícan, -ícness. v.** tô-ætícan, ætícness, *and* æt-ýcan, -ýcnes *in Dict.*

**æt-íw(i)an (-eáw-, -eów-, -ēw-, -iéw-, -ýw-. In Ps. L. 16, 15 a distinction between the mutated and not mutated forms seems to be made, the former being transitive (cf. *Goth.* at-augjan *to shew*), the latter intransitive :—Ic beó ætýwed í ætæówie *apparebo :* but this distinction is not generally made). **I.** *trans.* To shew, (1) what may be seen by the eye :—Hwylc tácn ætýwst (-eówes, R., ædeáues, L. *ostendis*) þú ús ?, Jn. 2, 18. Ic ætæówode þone god ðe ðín brôðor wurðoðe him gebundenne, Hml. Th. i. 468, 22. Hê hiene ætíewde (-iéde, Hatt. MS.) æfter ðære æriste, Past. 42, 20. Steorran hié ætíewdon (-êwdon. MS. E.), Chr. 540 : P. 16, 14. Ætýw (-eáw, R., ædeáw, L.) ðe þára sácerda ealdre, Mk. 1, 44. Ædeáua, Lk. L. 5, 14. His wíte þǽm Godes þegne ætêwed wæs, Shrn. 86, 5. Ætýwed (-eówed, R., ædeáwd, L.) on óðrum híwe, Mk. 16, 12. Tácna ætýwde wæron, Bd. 4, 9 ; S. 576, 13. Hê ongiet be sumum ðingum útanne ætíewdum eall ðæt hié innan ðenceað, Past. 155, 10. (2) what is perceived by the mind, *to manifest, reveal :*—Ic ætýwe (ædeáua, L.) hwám hê gelíc is, Lk. 6, 47. Ædeáuades *reuelasti*, Lk. 10, 21. Hî þurh gewrite atîwdon, hwí hí ðær beón ne mihton, Chr. 1070 ; P. 204, 6. Ætýw mé þín good, Ps. Th. 58, 10. Atýwian mid gesceáde, þ hé mid rihte crafede, Chr. 1070 ; P. 206, 12. Mê byð æteáwed (*manifestabitur*) ðín wuldor, Ps. Th. 16, 15. (2 a) where the object is a person :—Ic æteówo (ædeáua, L.) him mec solfne. . . . Ús æteówes í ðú æteówende arð (ædeáuas í ðú eáuande arð, L.) *manifestabo ei me ipsum . . . nobis manifestaturus es*, Jn. R. 14, 21, 22. **II.** *intrans.* To appear, (1) *to be shewn, be seen :*—Ateáuð *aparuit*, Kent. Gl. 1116. Hî ætíewað on openum ýsle, Past. 439, 6. Ætéawde hê him on swefne, Shrn. 70, 13 : Hml. S. 30, 57, 58. Ætýwde (-eáwðe, R., ædeáude, L.), Mt. 17, 3 : (-eáude, R., ædeáwade, L.), 2, 19 : (-cówde, R., aedeáwde, L ), Mk. 16, 9. Ætéowde se steorra, Chr. 892 ; P. 82, 31. Ætéowde (cf. weard ætýwed, MS. A.), 975 ; P. 121, 16 : (cf. was ateówod, MS. F.), 995 ; P. 129, 23. Atéowede, 678 ; P. 38, 28. Ætéowode, Hml. Th. i. 74, 13 : 76, 9. Færlíce ætéowode mín látteów swá swá scínende steorra, ii. 352, 2. Ætêwde, Shrn. 49, 5. Ætíewde *conparuit*, Wrt. Voc. ii. 16, 4. Ús ætíewde (-iéde, Hatt. MS.) se Hálga Gást on culfran anlícnesse, Past. 290, 6. Atíwede, Chr. 1066 ; P. 196, 2. Ætýwde, Bd. 4, 8 ; S. 576, 8. Ðæm biscope æteáwdon fægre fæmnan, Shrn. 63, 16. Hêr atéowden twêgen cometan, Chr. 729 ; P. 45, 1. (2) with complementary adjective :—Eall ðá hrægel swá hwít and swá níwe ætýwdon, swá hé ðý ylcan dæge mid gegearwod wære, Bd. 4, 30 ; S. 608, 41. Cf. oþ-íwan.

**æt-íwedness. *Add :* **I.** *shewing, display :*—On ætýwednysse wundorlíces tácnes *in ostensione admirabilis signi*, Gr. D. 19, 3. Ædeáudnesse (*ostensione*) hondo and fóta, Lk. p. 11, 13. **II.** *revelation, manifestation :*—þurh Godes ætýwednesse hê funde þ heáfod, Shrn. 151, 26. þurh ætéowednyss fram Gode þære gástlican gesihþe, Hml. S. 23 b, 38. **v.** æt-íwness.

**æt-íw(i)endlic ; *adj.* *Demonstrative :*—Iste þes ys æteówiendlic (-eówendlic, -ýwigendlic, *v. ll.*), Ælfc. Gr. Z. 93, 9.

**æt-íwness, e ; *f.* **I.** *shewing, display* of what may be seen or noted :—Seó ætéownes þára wíta ne byþ ná gelíce nyt eallum mannum, Gr. D. 317, 23. In þære ætýwnesse (-eáw-, *v. l.*) wundorlícnes foretácnes, 19, 4. In ætéownysse (-eáwnesse, *v. l.*) þæs ídlan gylpes, 77, 3. **I a.** *shewing* which serves as proof :—Ðerh menigo ðæra táceno ædeáunisse *per multa signorum experimenta*, Jn. p. 2, 1. **II.** *shewing, making known, manifestation* (a) of a circumstance :—Éristes aedeáuinse *resurrectionis manifestatio*, Jn. p. 8, 1. Áríse hine ðió engelica ædeáunise (*revelatione*) ongéton, Lk. p. 11, 8. (b) of a person, *bringing into public notice :*—On dæg ædeáunise (-eównisse, R.) his *in diem ostensionis suae*, Lk. L. 1, 80. ¶ in a special sense *Epiphany :*—Ðone hálgan dæg æt Drihtnes ætýwnesse. . . . On ðone sextan dæg þæs mónðes bið se mæra dæg þone Grécas nemnað epiphania . . . þ is on úre geþeóde Drihtnes ætýwnesse

dæg, Shrn. 48, 9–15. **III.** *shewing, making clear* by explanation, exposition:—Bíspell gesætte breht ædeáwnise *parabolam exponit clara manifestatione,* Mk. p. 3, 4. **III a.** *shewing* by orderly arrangement, *argument* of a book:—Æteáuunis *argumentum,* Jn. p. 1, 1. **IV.** *what is seen, a vision, an apparition:*—Hé wolde witan ymbe þá ætýwnysse þe him æteáwde, and cwæð: Hwæt is þeós gesihð þe mé æteáwde?, Hml. S. 30, 56. Ealle þá ætýwnysse þára áwerigdra gásta onweg gewiton, Guth. 48, 18. v. æt-ýwnys *in Dict.*

æt-íwung *Epiphany:*—Ætýwincge Drihtnes *epiphaniam Domini,* Angl. xiii. 402, 531. v. æt-éwung *in Dict.*

æt-lǽtnes. v. æf-wela, *and* cf. for-lǽt(en)nes (*or* ? æt-lǽdan).

æt-lic; *adj. Eatable, to be eaten:*—Ǽtlicum éstum *edendis dapibus,* Wrt. Voc. ii. 142, 33.

æt-limpan; *p.* -lamp, *pl.* -lumpon *To fall away, be lost:*—Hí ðára sáwla bemǽndon þe tó heofona ríce faran sceoldon, þ hí Gode swá earmlíce ætlumpon, Hml. S. 30, 67. Mycel is mé unbliss mínra dýrlinga miss, þ hí ús swá sǽrlíce mid ealle sýn ætlumpene, 272.

æt-lutian. *Add:* (1) absolute:—Hé on dymhofon ætlutode, Hml. Th. ii. 122, 4. (2) with dat. of person from whom one hides:—Hé ætluðode his éhterum, Hml. S. 19, 21. Ætlutian his feóndum, Jud. 4, 18.

æt-ness, e; *f. Edibility:*—Ætnes edilitas, Wrt. Voc. ii. 142, 37.

æt-níman. *l.* -niman: ǽtran. v. ǽtrian.

æt-reccan; *p.* -re(a)hte *To declare forfeited:*—Swá . . . swá him man ætrehte béc and land ealle þá þe hé áhte *ita quod per judicium judicatus sit perdere omnia quae de rege tenuit,* Cht. Th. 202, 14. Gif cinges geréfena hwylc gyltig biþ . . . hwá is manna tó þám ungescead þæt hé þæm cyninge his áre ætrecce, for þí þe his geréfa forwyrht biþ, Lch. iii. 444, 8. Cf. æt-déman.

ǽtren. *Add:*—Ǽttræn *purulentus,* An. Ox. 4929. Nǽnig ǽtern wyrm, Nar. 28, 6. Ǽterno wǽte, Lch. ii. 16, 13. Ǽtternes *venenosi,* Rtl. 122, 26. Ne ðǽr (*Ireland*) monn ǽnigne ǽtterne (ǽtrene, *v. l.*) wyrm ne gesihþ, Bd. 1, 1; S. 474, 33. Wæs þára wyrma oroð and éþung ǽterne, Nar. 14, 16. Ǽt(r)ene *venefici,* Bl. Gl. Þonne ealle ǽterno þing fieógaþ, Lch. ii. 146, 10. Allo aetterna nétno *omnia venenosa animalia,* Rtl. 145, 16. Ðá wonnan aetrínan *livida toxica,* Wrt. Voc. ii. 112, 69. Ǽnig his ǽtrenra (ǽttrenra, ǽttreua, *v. ll.*) wǽpna, Wlfst. 35, 18. Þára ǽterna wǽtena, Lch. ii. 176, 11. ¶ in the northern Gospels and the Ritual the word is used as substantive or adjective of the viper:—Sió hátterne *vipera,* Rtl. 125, 27. Cynna ǽterna (cynn ǽterne, R.) *genimina uiperarum,* Lk. L. 3, 7. Cynn ǽtterna *progenies uiperarum,* Mt. L. 3, 7: 23, 33. Ǽterna, 12, 34.

ǽtren-ness, e; *f. Poisonousness:*—For þǽre lyfte wylme and ǽternesse, Lch. ii. 146, 16.

ǽtrian, ǽt(t)ran. **I.** *to make poisonous.* Cf. ge-ǽttred. **II.** *to become poisonous or corrupt:*—Ǽttredon *tabescerent,* Angl. xiii. 366, 14.

ǽtrig, ǽttrig; *adj. Poisonous, venomous:*—Eall hit bið ǽtrig (ǽttrig *v. l.*) þ him (*the devil*) of cymð, Hml. S. 17, 127. Ǽttrig *virulentus,* Hpt. Gl. 450, 10. Mid ǽttrigere clufþunge *letali toxa,* 427, 55. Gif hwá mid his fét ofstepð ǽttrig bán snacan oððe nǽddran, Lch. i. 152, 1. Ǽttrige *venenata,* Hpt. Gl. 450, 38. Ǽttrigera (-ia, MS.) *virulentorum,* 423, 41. Stíðran leáfum and eác ǽtrigum, Lch. i. 94, 9. Fram ðám ǽttrigum synnum gehǽlede, Hml. Th. ii. 240, 10. Nǽdre wyle ðá wegfarendan mid hire ǽttrigum tóðum slítan, Wlfst. 192, 23.

æt-sacan. *Add:* **I.** *to deny* a statement, (1) with gen.:—Rihte ðu hyt ongytst, ne mæg ic þæs ætsacan, Shrn. 182, 7. (2) with clause:—Ǽtsace (oð-. *v. l.,* *neget*) sé, sé þe dyrre, þæt þæt angin nǽre gestilled for Gode, Ors. 6, 4; S. 260, 4. **I a.** where the statement is a charge against a person, (1) absolute:—Gif man ætsace, lǽdige hine mid þrý-fealdre láde, Ll. Th. i. 404, 2: ii. 298, 7, 10, 13. (2) with gen.:—Sege ús hwǽr se hord sý þe þú fundest and hine bedyrndest; þý lǽs þe þú his ætsace, hér is se man þe sum þ feoh hæfð on handa, Hml. S. 23, 663. **II.** *to deny* a fact, *not to admit* that something has been done, with gen.:—Ǽtsóc Goda þæs feós ǽgiftes *negavit sibi libras persolutas fuisse,* Cht. Th. 201, 28. Gif mon sié dumb geboren, þ hé ne mǽge his synna ætsacan, Ll. Th. i. 70, 15. **III.** *to deny, refuse permission:*—Nis ǽnig dǽl mínes líchaman þ ic þé ætsacan wille þ þú hine þweá, Hml. A. 157, 147. **IV.** *to deny* a person, *disown,* (1) with gen.:—Ne ætsace ic þín *non te negabo,* Mk. 14, 31. Hé ætsæcð Crístes, Wlfst. 85, 1. Þæt hí Godes ætsacan and deófle tó gebúgan, 97, 3. (2) with acc., Mk. 14, 72: Lk. 22, 34. v. æt-sæcst *in Dict.*

æt-samne. *Add:*—Ǽtsamne sóhton *conquirerunt,* Wrt. Voc. ii. 73, 19. Þá apostoli wǽron ætsamne, Bl. H. 229, 4. Raðe þæs híe wurdon bégen ætsemne (-somne, *v. l.*) ofslagen *cum quo simul continuo interfectus est,* Ors. 6, 22; S. 274, 6. Þæt híe fóron ealle út ætsomne, Chr. 905; P. 94, 4.

æt-slídan. *Add: To slip up, fall:*—Ætslád se hálga wer on ðám grádum swá þæt hé forneán eal weard tócwýsed, Hml. Th. ii. 512, 10. Þá ætslídendan (*printed* -slidan) beheald *labentes respice,* Hy. S. 7, 13.

æt-speornan. *l.* æt-spornan, -spurnan, *and add:* **I.** *trans. To strike against:*—Ǽtspearn *conlidit,* i. *allidit,* Wrt. Voc. ii. 134, 64. Þe lǽs þe ðú æt stáne þínne fót ætspurne, Hml. Th. i. 516, 30. Þæt þú ne þurfe

---

ðínne fót æt stáne ætspurnan, 166, 21. Ætspornan *inpingere,* Wrt. Voc. ii. 85, 15. **II.** *intrans. To strike* against (æt, on), *stumble:*—And (fót ðín) ne etspernð *et pes tuus non impinget,* Kent. Gl. 47. Ic æ:spearn (-sporn, -speorn, *v. ll.*) æt ánum fótsceamole *in scabello suppedaneo impegi,* Gr. D. 22, 22. **II a.** *fig. To be hindered, to be offended:*—Forðon áðreát ðá hieremenn ryhtes lífes, ðonne hié wilniað gǽstlíce libban, þe ðǽm yfelum bisenum ðe sé dǽð ðe him fore beón sceolde; ðonne ætspornað hié and weorðað mid ðǽm áscrencte *unde subjectorum vita torpescit; quia, cum proficere spiritaliter appetit, in exemplo ejus qui sibi praelatus est quasi in obstaculo itineris offendit,* Past. 129, 6. Þára wóhnys ætspearn (bealh, *v. l.*) æt þám regole his rihtinge *quorum tortitudo in norma ejus rectitudinis offendebat,* Gr. D. 104, 15. Heora wóhnys on ðám regole ætspearn, Hml. Th. ii. 158, 11. v. un-ætspornen; oþ-spornan.

·æt-sporning, e; *f. Offence:*—Ætsporningum *offensis,* Angl. xiii. 381, 230.

æt-spyrning, e; *f. Offence:*—Ætspyrningum *offensis,* Hy. S. 142, 6.

æt-standan. *Add:* **I.** where there is or may be movement, (1) of a moving body, *to stop, come to rest:*—Seó sunne cymð tó þám sunnstede and þǽr ætstent, Lch. iii. 250, 24. Swá swá wæter scýt of ðǽre dúne and ætstent on dene, Hml. Th. i. 362, 22. His sceaft ætstód ætforan him (*the shaft got fixed in the ground in front of him*), and þ hors hine bær forð swá þ þ spere him eóde þurh út, Hml. S. 12, 54. Mid þám ðe Drihten hrepode ðá bǽre, ðá ætstódon þá bǽrmenn, Hml. Th. i. 494, 7. Ne beseoh þú underbæc, ne þú ne ætstande náhwár on þisum earde, Gen. 19, 17. Hé hét ðá hundas ætstandan þe urnon, Hml. Th. ii. 514, 24. (2) of a body at rest, *to remain standing:*—Ealle gefeóllan . . bútan Dúnstán ána ætstód uppon ánum beáme, Chr. 978; P. 123, 3. Hí feorr ætstódon *de longe steterunt,* Ps. Spl. 37, 12. **II.** where there is or may be change of condition, (1) *to stop growing, cease to operate:*—Þá weard þ týr gestilled and ætstód sóna, Hml. S. 8, 229. Gif se hlyst ætstande, þ hé ne mæge gehiéran, Ll. Th. i. 92, 23. Corn and wæstmas wǽron ætstandene, Chr. 1075; P. 217, 19 (v. **II** *in Dict.*). (2) *to stop, remain* in a certain state:—Hé ne ætstent l hé ne þurhwunaþ *non subsistet,* Ps. L. 102, 16. Þ hús wearþ forburnen . . . se port ána ætstód asund, Hml. S. 26, 234. Ætstód se streám swá steáp swá munt, Hml. Th. ii. 212, 22. v. oþ-standan.

æt-standend; *m. A bystander, an attendant:*—Seó heofenlíce cwén cwæð tó hire ætstandendum, Hml. Th. i. 450, 31. Hé þone Hǽlend bodode eallum ætstandendum, Hml. S. 29, 255.

æt-standende; *adj.* (*ptcpl.*) *By-standing:*—Þá heortan þára ætstandendra wífa, Gr. D. 284, 21.

æt-stapan. *l.* -steppan.

æt-steall. *Substitute:* æt-steall, es; *m. A station, camp:*—On ætstealles beorh, C. D. iv. 31, 2. Ðú feohtan sóhtest æt ðám ætstealle, Vald. 1, 21. Hé gyrede hine mid gǽstlicum wǽpnum, wong bletsade him tó ætstealle (v. Stephens' *Waldere's Lay,* p. 83), Gú. 150.

æt-strengan; *p. de To deforce, withhold wrongfully:*—Gif hláford gelómlíce his gafoles myngað, and geneátman áheardað and hit þencð tó ætstrengenne, Ll. Th. i. 270, 21.

æt-styntan; *p.* te. **I.** *to blunt:*—Téð hé ætstente *dentes retundat,* Hy. S. 16, 3. **II.** *to make inactive* or *ineffective:*—Hé ætstynte, gedrehte *elideret (favorabile praeconium),* An. Ox. 2779. Mód ætstentan *animum retundi,* Hy. S. 70, 19. [Etstunten þe strencþe of mine swenges, Marh. 15. Þat ufel wes atstunt, Lay. 31903.]

æt-swígan; *p. de To become silent, keep silence* about something:—Be Lazares mægnum wæs ætswíged *de Lazari virtutibus tacetur,* Gr. D. 217, 18. v. oþ-swígan.

æt-swymman. *l.* -swimman; *and see* oþ-swimman.

á-ettan; *p.* te *To eat up, consume:*—Deór áytte hine *ferus depastus est eam,* Ps. L. 79, 14. [Cf. *O. H. Ger.* ezzen *depascere.*]

æt-telg (?) (= (?) ed-telg *what springs again without sowing,* cf. telga; *but see* telg) *flax* (?):—Aettaelg *rediva* (= rediviva (?); possibly glossing Ald. 19, 30 ut sit virginitas purpura, castitas rediviva: cf. An. Ox. 1379 rediviva, i. *linum* flex), Wrt. Voc. ii. 119, 9.

æt-þringan. *Add: To thrust away, deprive of by violence:*—Hé his feorh him ætþrang *ejus animam excussit,* Gr. D. 75, 26. v. oþ-þringan.

ættrig, æt-wǽsend. v. ǽtrig, æt-wesende.

æt-wenían. *Add:*—Þæt hí heora gingran Gode gestrýnan and hí deófle ætwǽnian (-wenian, *v. l.*), Wlfst. 38, 24 : 301, 16.

æt-wesende; *adj.* (*ptcpl.*) *At hand, imminent:*—Ætwesendre *inminente,* Wrt. Voc. ii. 45, 44. Ætweosendre, 110, 67.

æt-windan. *l.* æt-windan; *p.* -wand, *pl.* -wundon; *pp.* -wundea, *and add:* **I.** *to escape* from a person, (1) absolute:—Gif hé ætwinde, Ll. Th. i. 210, 12, 9. (2) with dat.:—Þá ætwand him án preóst *a priest escaped from them,* Hml. S. 19, 19. Án sceáp him ætwunden wæs, Hml. Th. i. 340, 1. **II.** *to escape, evade* what is unpleasant, (1) absolute:—Se þe áfeald earfoðlíce he ætwint (*evadet*), Lch. iii. 150, 2, 4. Ætwand *evasit,* An. Ox. 4392. Þæt hé ætwindan móste *that he migh' escape (unpleasant consequences),* Hml. Th. i. 598, 28. (2) with dat.:—Ðám (*death*) ne ætwint nǽn eorðlic mann, Hml. Th. ii. 232.

22. Hé ðám wítum ætwunde, Hml. S. 23. 118. Ðám ēcum wítum ætwindan, 16, 93 : Hml. A. 34, 251. (3) with acc. :—þá þe middangeard oferswíðdon and his yrmða ætwundon, Hml. Th. i. 84, 32. v. oþ-windan.

**æt-wítan.** *Add : To reproach a person (dat.) with something (acc. or clause)* :—For hwý ætwíte gē eówerre wyrde þ hió nán geweald náh, Bt. 39, 1 ; F. 210, 25. Tó hwam ætwite þú mē þ dū hí forlure ?, 7, 3 ; F. 20, 2. Heó ætwát ðǽm hǽþnum heora dysignesse, Sl:rn. 57, 33. Se hálga wer him ætwát þ þ hē on þám wege dyde *ei vir sanctus hoc quod in via egerat improperavit*, Gr. D. 129, 23. Hē ætwát him sylfum þæt hē ne hreówsode his synna, Ps. Th. 31, arg. þæt hié ætwite *improperasse*, Wrt. Voc. ii. 87, 39 : 47, 9. Ðý lǽs him ætwite (*exprobrarent*) his geþoftan þ hē for ege ðæs deáþes ðá ðing dyde, Bd. 5, 13 ; S. 632, 23. Mē is mín ágen ætwiten swilce ic hit hæbbe forstolen, Hml. S. 23, 599. v. oþ-wítan.

**æt-wrencan** ; *p.* te *To cheat a person out of something, deprive by fraud* :—Lyt monna weorð lange fægen ðæs ðe hē óðerne bewrencð ( æt-wrencð, *v. l.*), Prov. K. 34. [Cf. æt-wrenchen *to twist away, escape,* Marh. 15, 20 : O. and N. 248.]

**æt-ȳc-.** v. æt-íc-.

**ǽ-tynge** ; *adj. Speechless* :—Ǽtinge *elinguis*, An. Ox. 46, 45.

**æt-ȳw-.** v. æt-íw-.

**ǽw.** I. *law.* v. ǽ. II. *a wife.* v. ǽwe, and riht-ǽwe.

**ǽw** *lawful.* l. ǽwe.

**ǽ-wǽde** ; *adj. Stripped of clothes* :—Ǽwǽde *nudatum*, Wrt. Voc. ii. 144, 70.

**ǽwe** ; *f. n.* (? v. Hml. Th. ii. 322, 33 *infra*.) *A married woman* ; in pl. *married people* :—Gif hē cyfesan hæbbe and náne rihtǽwe . . . beó hit cyfes beó hit ǽwe (*uxor*), Ll. Th. ii. 186, 2-5 : 270, 6. Ciric is sácerdes ǽwe ; náh hē mid rihte ǽnige óþre, 334, 24 : 340, 5. Oð þæt hē on rihtre ǽwe gewífige, and hæbbe þá ǽwe and náne óþre þá hwíle þe seó libbe, Wlfst. 304, 21. Úre Drihten forbeád twǽmincge betwux twám ǽwum ðus : 'Swá hwá swá his ǽwe forlǽt and óðer genimð, Hml. Th. 322, 31-3. Hē gehǽlde sum wíf, ānes ealdormannes ǽwe, 150, 3. Forlicgan wið óðres ǽwe oþþe wið gehádode, Ll. Th. i. 404, 22. Se ðám men þes his ǽwe (*uxorem*) forlǽt and be þám wífe (*muliere*) þe hire wer forlǽt, ii. 180, 13, 15. Healde gehwá his ǽwe þá hwíle þe heó libbe, 300, 26. v. riht-ǽwe.

**ǽ-welm.** v. ǽ-wilm: **æ-wên.** l. ǽ-wêne: **ǽwen-bróðor.** l. ǽwen bróðor *germanus*, Wrt. Voc. ii. 41, 11 : **ǽ-werd, -werdla.** v. ǽ-wird, -wirdla.

**ǽwe-weard,** es ; *m. A guardian of the divine law, a priest* :—Wæs swíþe mycel ǽweweard þæs noma wæs Zacharias, Bl. H. 161, 27. [O. H. Ger. ē-, ēo-wart *sacerdos*.]

**ǽ-wilm.** *Add* :—Ðǽre anwilnesse ǽwilm is ofermétta, Past. 307, 2. þ wæter innon þá eorþan cymþ up æt ðam ǽwelme, wyrþ ðonne tó bróce, ðonne tó eá, ðonne andlang eá oþ hit wyrþ eft tó sǽ, Bt. 34, 6 ; F. 140, 19.

**ǽ-wird, -werd** ; *adj. Corrupt* :—Sē bið ǽwerd on his lífe, Lch. iii. 162, 11. v. á-wirde.

**ǽ-wirdla, -werdla, -wyrdla.** *Add* :—Éuuerdlu (ǽwerdlo, R.) *damnatione*, Lk. L. 23, 40. Ǽwyrdlan *jacturam*, Wrt. Voc. ii. 76, 8. Gif hwá wíf gewerde, bête þone ǽwerdlan, Ll. Th. i. 48, 18. Ǽwyrdlan 50, 28 note. Éwyrdlu *detrimentum*, Mt. R. 16, 26. v. æf-wirdla.

**ǽwisc** *dishonour.* v. ǽwisce.

**ǽwisc** ; *adj. Shameless, impudent, foul* :—Hí (*certain women*) syndon ǽwisce on líchoman and unweorðe *sunt publicato corpore et inhonesto*, Nar. 38, 13. v. un-ǽwisc, and ǽwisce.

**ǽwisc-berend,** es ; *m. A name for the middle finger* (cf. in Cotgrave *le doigt sale* the middle finger) ; *impudicus (digitus)*, Wrt. Voc. i. 283, 22. Cf. middel finger *medius* vel *impudicus*, 44, 6.

**ǽwisce** (and ǽwisc?), es ; *n. Dishonour, shame, foulness* :—Ǽwisce *obscenitas*, Angl. xiii. 35, 204 : An. Ox. 8, 193. Ǽwisc, 7, 265. Ǽwys, 4302 : 7, 300. Hē cwæð þæt him tó micel ǽwisce wǽre þæt hē swá emnlíce wrixlæde *he said that it was too much dishonour for them to treat on such an equal footing*, Ors. 4, 6 ; S. 178, 16. On ǽwisce (ǽswice ? cf. 105, 26) *in scandalum*, Ps. Th. 68, 23. Ǽwiscu (*here or under* ǽwisc ; *adj.*?) *ludicra .i. inhonesta* (neu timeat scriptor terrentis *ludicra* linguae, Ald. 214, 19), An. Ox. 21, 6. [*Goth.* aiwiski ; *n. dedecus*.]

**ǽwisc-firen** ; *adj. Guilty of shameless sin* ; def. form used substantively, *a shameless sinner* :—Beó þe swá hǽþenna and cáwisfirina *sit tibi sicut ethnicus et publicanus*, Mt. R. 18, 17. Ǽwisfirine *publicani*, 21, 31. Éwisfirinæ, 32. v. next word.

**ǽwisc-firenend,** es ; *m. One who sins shamelessly* :—Áwiscferinend *publicani*, Wrt. Voc. ii. 72, 36. v. preceding word.

**ǽwisc-líc** ; *adj. Shameful, infamous* :—Tó ǽwisclicum *ad infame*, An. Ox. 4308. Ǽwyslicre, 7, 302.

**ǽwisc-nys.** *Add : Shamelessness, impudence* :—Ǽwyscnes *impudentia*, An. Ox. 4306. Ǽwisnes, *obscenitas*, 4, 69. On ǽwiscnesse

*in propatulo*, Wrt. Voc. ii. 75, 16 : 46, 57. Ǽwiscnessum (ǽswic-?) *opprobrium*, Ps. L. 122, 4.

**ǽwis(c)od** (?) *made public* :—þæt hiæ ne gecûðne ł ēwisade hine dydun *ne manifestum eum facerent*, Mt. R. 12, 16. *For form* cf. ēwis-firinæ *under* ǽwisc-firen, *and for meaning* cf. *the same word and the rendering of* in propatulo *under* ǽwiscness.

**ǽw-líc.** v. ǽ-líc.

**ǽwnian.** v. ge-ǽwnod.

**ǽwnung, e ; *f. Wedlock* :—Ǽwnung *conubium*, An. Ox. 416 : *jugalias*, 1370. Ǽwnunge *jugalitatis*, 440 : 1168. v. ǽwung.

**ǽ-writere.** v. ǽ-gewrítere.

**ǽwul** *for cawel* ? cf. *cawl* in Cornish dialect for a fish-basket.

**ǽwung** (ǽwnung? *q. v.*), e ; *f. Wedlock* :—Ǽwunge *jugalitatis*, An. Ox. 339. (Cf. un-iǽwedan, 5248.)

**ǽ-wyrp.** *Add* : I. *a casting away, what is cast away* :—Ic eom manna hosp and folces ǽwyrp, R. Ben. 29, 13. II. (*an*) *abortion* :—Wíf seó þe tó ǽwyrpe gedó hire geeácnunga *mulier quae utero conceptum excusserit*, Ll. Th. ii. 154, 15. [Cf. *Goth.* us-waurpa *amissio, rejectio*; abortivus : O. H. Ger. á-wèri *abjectio*; abortivus : Icel. ör-verpi *decrepitude*; a *mis-birth*.]

**æx.** *Add* :—Sió æcs áwient of ðǽm hielfe, Past. 165, 25 : 167, 7. 9. Sió æx (æxs, Hatt. MS.). 338, 14. Ex *securis*, Wrt. Voc. i. 84, 61. Treów wyrðe scearpre æxe, Hml. Th. ii. 408, 16. Slóh hine án heora mid ánre æxe ýre, Chr. 1012 ; P. 142, 24. Mon ne gehiúrde æhxe (æxe, Hatt. MS.) hlem, Past. 252, 17. Se ðunor hit ðrysceð mid ðǽre fýrenan æcxe, Salm. K. 148, 6. Hē bær him æcse and adesan on handa, tácnode on ðám þ hē nales tó ídelnysse on þ mynster eóde, Bd. 4, 3 ; S. 567, 26 : Angl. ix. 263, 1. Æxa *bipennes*, An. Ox. 2, 71. Æcssa, 2231. Mid ęcesum *securibus*, Ps. Srt. 73, 5. v. blód-, brád-, brádlást-, hand-, stán-, tapor-æx.

**af, dele : a-fæged.** l. á-fægen *to depict, and for* v. a-fægrian *substitute* v. fág : **a-fægniende, dele :** a-fǽlan. v. á-fillan, á-fýlan.

**á-fǽran.** *Add* :—God áfǽrde (*perterruit*) þone ealdorman, Jud. 4, 15. Sum munuc mē áfǽrde mid guornunge hefiges ǽrendes *gravis nuntii moerore me perculit*, Gr. D. 250, 2. Hē þá men áfǽrde. þæt hié ealle ongeán hiene wǽron feohtende, Ors. 4, 6 ; S. 172, 21. Weard hē áfyrht and áfǽred, Lch. iii. 424. 36. Hwý sceal ic beón áfǽrd ?, Ps. Th. 26, 2. Wǽron sume tó deáðe áfǽrede, St. A. 34, 32.

**á-fæstan** *to fast.* *Add* : *with cognate object* :—Tylege hē þæt hē þis fæsten áfæste, Wlfst. 284, 12. Ǽrþon hyra fæsten sig áfæst *antequam jejunium eorum jejunatum fuerit*, Ll. Th. ii. 158, 25.

**á-fæstan** ; *p.* te *To entrust, let out land to a person* :—Hē áfæste wíngeard ðǽm londbígengum, Mk. R. 12, 1.

**á-fæstnian.** *Add* :—Ic gesēþe vel áfæstnie *confirmo,* i. *astruo.* Wrt. Voc. ii. 133, 29. Áfestnað *affirmat*, Kent. Gl. 805. Áfestniað *definunt*, 847. Ic áfæstnode *fixi*, Wrt. Voc. ii. 149, 3. Ic on gewryte áfæstnode þ ic wǽre þæs deófles, Hml. S. 3, 415. Ðú afesnadest *definisti*, Kent. Gl. 121. Hē þá weorc on gewritum áfæstnode, Ælfc. T. Grn. 5, 45. Áfestnige *transfigat*, Kent. Gl. 217. Áfæstnia *untrymnisse hire muniat infirmitatem suam*, Rtl. 110, 1. His fultum mehte mǽstra ǽlcne heora fíana on hiora feónðum áfæstnian (*configere*), Ors. 6, 36 ; S. 294, 28. Ðá ðeóda sýn áfæstnode (*infixae*) on earfoðum, Ps. Th. 9, 14. Wē sié áfæstnodo *muniamur*, Rtl. 8, 19.

**á-fǽttian** ; *p.* de *To fatten* :—Ele þæs synfullan ne áfǽttaþ (*inpinguet*) heáfod mín, Ps. L. 140, 5.

**á-fandelíc.** v. á-fandodlíce.

**á-fandian.** *Add* : I. *to try, test,* (1) *with gen.* :—God áfandode Abrahames . . . God áfandað þæs mannes, Angl. vii. 50, 486-9. Ne sceole wē ná biddan þæt God úre ne áfandige, Hml. Th. i. 268, 10. (2) *with acc.* :—þus áfandode God his gecorenan, ná swylce hē nyte heora ingehýd, Angl. vii. 52, 500. Iób weard áfandod þurh þone deófol, Ælfc. T. Grn. 10, 44. Beón áfandud *temptari*, Scint. 211, 16. II. *to experience* :—Ús gedafenað þæt wē Godes swingle andwerde and áfandode ondrǽdan, Hml. Th. ii. 124, 6. III *to approve.* v. á-fandod :—Áfanded [is] *comprobatur*, An. Ox. 1141. Bið áfandad (-an, MS.), Kent. Gl. 610. v. un-áfandod.

**á-fandigendlíc.** *Add* :—þeáh þe rihtwísra drohtnung on þisum life áfandigendlic (*probabilis*) sý, Scint. 227, 6.

**á-fandod** ; *adj.* (*ptcpl.*) *Tried, experienced ; approved, excellent.* v. á-fandian, III :—Se Hǽlend wæs áfandod (-on, MS.) wer (*vir approbatus a Deo*), Past. 443, 5. Hē wæs on forhæfednysse weorcum se áfandedesta geworden, Hml. S. 23 b, 24.

**á-fandodlíc** ; *adj. To be approved, laudable* :—Áfadodlíc *reprobabilis* (= áfandodlíc *probabilis*), Kent. Gl. 628. v. next word.

**á-fandodlíce** ; *adv. In a manner to be approved* :—Áfande(d)lícor *probabilius,* i. *laudabilius*, An. Ox. 2295.

**á-fandung, -fandigung.** *Add* : I. *trial, probation* :—Seó gedréfednys wyrcð geðyld, and þæt geðyld áfandunge (*probationem,* v. Scint. 7, 19), and seó áfandung hiht. . . . Seó áfandung eówres geleáfan, Hml. Th. i. 554, 25-31. Áfandung *temptatio*, Scint. 211, 17. II. *trial, experiment, experience* :—Áfandgung (*printed* -fandung) *experientia*, Wülck. Gl. 249,

4. þurh cunnunge and áfandunge witan *per experimentum scire*, Gr. D. 261, 1, 19.

á-faran. *Add*: Hé of ðære wícstówe áfor, Ors. 2, 4; S. 76, 13. Hé þonan áfór . . . and him from áfaran hêt ealla þá burgware, 2, 5; S. 80, 29. Áfór Alexander þonan on Frigam, 3, 9; S. 124, 22. Þæt hié from þæm fæstenne áfóren, 4, 11; S. 206, 17. Siþþan Gallia út of þære byrig áfóran, 2, 8; S. 92, 28. Hié of þæm londe áfóron, Chr. 794; P. 56, 4. Of Eádweardes anwalde áfaran, 918; P. 98, 23. Hé wæs út áfaren on hergaþ, 894; P. 86, 20. Hé wæs áfaren tó ðam castele, 1087; P. 224, 10. Hé inn áfaren wæs, Hml. Th. i. 178, 3. Ðú wære út áfaren of þínes fæder éþele, Bt. 5, 1; F. 8, 29. Ðá Apollonius áfaren wæs, Ap. Th. 5, 12. Þá beóð áfarenne *proficiscuntur*, R. Ben. I. 86, 9.

á-feallan. *Add*: I. of movement, (1) of that which has been standing, (a) involuntary, *to fall down, tumble down*:—Assael hrædlíce áfeóll *Asael protinus occumbit*, Past. 296, 16. Hé mid þý horse áfeóll, Ors. 3, 7; S. 118, 5. Hé áfeóll ofdúneweard, Gr. D. 24, 25. Þá engias þe þanon áfeóllon, Hml. A. 2, 34. Nán mon ne bitt óðerne ðæt hé hine rære, gif hé self nát ðæt hé áfeallen bið, Past. 441, 10. ¶ used figuratively:—Ðæt· hefige mód glít niðor and niðor, oð hit mid ealle áfield . . . hit sceal niedenga áfeallan for ðæm slide, Past. 279, 2-5. Ðætte ðá ðe gestondan ne meahton, gif hí áfeallan scolden, ðæt hí áfeóllen on ðæt hnesce bedd ðæs gesinscipes, 397, 22. (b) voluntary, *to fall* at a person's feet:—Ic for þám ege nyþer on þá eorþan áfeóll, and hé mé up áhóf, Nic. 10, 40: Hml. A. 183, 75. Efne Aman niþer áfeallen tó þære cwéne fótum, 100, 272. (2) of that which has been fixed, *to fall off, out, away*:—Hym of þám andwlytan nyðer áfeóll se cancer, Hml. A. 183, 70. Him ðá hær áfeóllon, Gr. D. 157, 8. Þæm áfeóllan þá eágan of þæm heáfde, Shrn. 93, 37. Se hreófla weard nyðer áfeallen, Hml. A. 192, 320. II. of the approach of night. Cf. night-*fall*:—Mé áfeóll seó æfentíd þæs dæges, Gr. D. 83, 15. III. metaph. (1) of health, *to fall sick*:—Sé þe áfeald earfoðlíce áctwint, Lch. iii. 150, 1. (1 a) of moral failure, *to fall* into sin:—Hí áfellað on hefegum scyldum, Past. 437, 3. Hí áfeallað on micla scylda, 7. (2) *to fall* from power, &c.:—Áscoben áfeóll *inpulsus versatus sum*, Bl. Gl. Ðæt wé ne mægen ástígan on ðá áre ðe hé of áfeóll, Past. 361, 5. (3) of deterioration, *to fall off, away, to sink, decline, decay*:—Sé áfealleþ, sé þe deófol weorþeþ, Bl. H. 31, 1. Ælc þára áfeald þe þé (God) flýgð, Shrn. 166, 24. Láriówas áfeóllun, Cht. Crw. 19, 7. Sió lár áfeallen wæs, Past. 7, 16. Áfeallan of ðære weámódnesse ðe hit ær on áhafen wæs, 297, 19. (4) of destruction, *to fall to the ground, be destroyed*:—Ælc riht áfeoll, Chr. 1100; P. 235, 24.

á-feccan, *dele, and see* á-fón.

á-fédan. *Add*: I. *to feed, nourish, support, maintain*, (1) of a person that provides food, &c.:—Hú áfést (*pascis*) þú hafocas þíne? Hí fédaþ hig sylfe and mé on wintra, Coll. M. 25, 37. Áfédde seó wudewe þone wítegan mid ðám melewe, Hml. S. 18, 65. Gif hé ðá móder ðe hine gebær and áfédde nele árwurðian, Hml. Th. ii. 208, 12. Gestreón þanon ic mé áféde (*pascam*) and mín wíf and mínne sunu, Coll. M. 27, 21. Hé gyrnde landes þ hé mihte hine on áfédan, Chr. 1049; P. 168, 17. Áfoedde *confoti*, Wrt. Voc. ii. 105, 25. (2) of that which produces food:—Hú þis land mihte þone here áfédan, Chr. 1085; P. 216, 1. (3) of material which is food:—Manna wæs geháten se heofonlica mete þe áfédde þæt folc on wéstene, Hml. Th. i. 76, 17. II. *to bring* forth, *produce*, (1) of persons:—Se wífman sé hire cild áfédan ne mæg . . . cweþe þás word: 'Ðis mé tó bóte þære láþan lætbyrde,' Lch. iii. 68, 18. (2) of plants:—Mid eallum missenlicum áféddum blóstmum gefrætwod, Bl. H. 7, 31. III. *to bring up, nurture*:—Þám gelícost þe sum cyning háte sum wíf dón on carcern, and heó cenne cniht, and sé sý ðær áféded oð hé þ twéntigwintre, Wlfst. 3, 1. On mínre scóle áféd and geléred (*innutritus*), B. 3, 1; F. 4, 19. Áféded on his þénunge *nutritus in ejus obsequio*, Gr. D. 56, 23. Áféded and geléred (*nutritus*) fram Anastasie, 48, 21. Seó wæs áféded mid Scé Agnan, Shrn. 57, 32. Hié . . . þe án ánum hiérede wæron áfédde and getýde, Ors. 3, 11; S. 152, 29. Geonge menn gif hí beóð yfle áfédde *si male nutriantur*, Gr. D. 289, 2. IV. *In* Ps. L. 48, 15 áfédan *glosses depascere*:—Deáþ áfédeþ hig *mors depascet eos*.

á-fégan; *p.* To join:—Áfoegedo *sociata*, Rtl. 79, 30. Þte þ bið áfoegid *ut quod jungitur*, 109, 6.

á-féhþ. *Substitute* v. á-fón.

á-feohtan. *Add*: I. trans. *To fight against*:—Áfeht ðú (*expugna*) ðá onfehtendo mé, Rtl. 167, 39. II. intrans. *To fight one's way, make one's way by fighting*:—Þæt sume þurh ealle þá truman út áfuhten, gif hié mehten, Ors. 5, 7; S. 230, 21.

á-feohtendlic, á-feónge. v. un-áfeohtendlic, á-feóung.

á-feormian. *Add*: *to cleanse* an object from impurity (*dat. or prep.* fram, of):—Þú áfeormast fram fúlum synnum þæra heortan, Angl. xiii. 112, 3. Ús fram sennum hí áfeormian (*abluant*), Hy. S. 118, 23. Ús áfeormigende *nos abluendo*, 52, 19. Áfeormod seofonfealdlíce *purgatum septuplum*, Ps. L. 11, 7. Horwum áfeormod *sordibus ablutus*, Dóm. L. 156. Heortan mid ymbsnidenysse áfeormode fram leahtrum,

Hml. Th. i. 98, 14. Ðá áfeormodan fram horwum *expiatos sordibus*, Hy. S. 4, 22. Wyrttruman of ðære rinde wel áfeormadne, Lch. i. 300, 18. II. *to clear off* impurity from an object:—Ælcne gylt áfeorma (*ablue*), Hy. S. 53, 30. Horu þú áfeormige, 23, 21. Þ wé áfeormian (*purgemus*) þ werste, 14, 15. Áfeormudre yfelnysse *expurgata malitia*, An. Ox. 40, 24. Synna þe beóð þurh þæt fýr áfeormode, Hml. Th. ii. 590, 14. v. á-fírman.

á-feormung. *Add*:—Gástlicre áfeormunge (*purgaminis*), Angl. xiii. 387, 312. Wið wífa áfeormunge (*purgationem*), Lch. i. 186, 9. Áfeormunge *mundationem*, Scint. 28, 9.

a-feorran. *l.* á-feorrian; *omit first and last passages, and add*: I. trans. *To remove, take away*:—Bið heó áfeorrod suíðe feor from ðære sóðan heánesse *ab altitudine verae celsitudinis elongatur*, Past. 301, 20. Eardbegengnes mín áfeorrad (*áfirred*, Ps. Srt.) is *incolatus meus prolongatus est*, Ps. L. 119, 5. II. intrans. *To remove, depart*:—God ne áfearra ðú from mé *Deus ne elonges a me*, Ps. Srt. 70, 12. Áfearriað (áfearrad, L.) from mé *discedite a me*, Lk. R. 23, 27. Þte áfirrade *ut discederet*, Mk. L. 5, 17. v. á-firran.

á-feorsian. *Add*: [*a 3rd sing. indic.* áfyrseþ as from á-firsan *occurs*]. I. trans. *To remove* from (*dat. or prep.*):—Ic áfyrsige ðá yfelan deór eów fram, Hml. S. 13, 162. Seó hálgung þe deófla áfyrsað, Ll. Th. i. 360, 32. Áfyrseþ *aufert*, Ps. Spl. 75, 12. Áfyrseþ hé þás earfoðnesse fram ús, Bl. H. 247, 4. Hí áfyrsiað næddran, Hml. Th. i. 304, 20. Þæt hé áfyrsode ðæs deófles éhtnysse him fram, ii. 528, 5. Hé þám mannum hyra líf áfyrsode *istis vitam abstulit*, Gr. D. 162, 7. Áfyrsa hí *expelle eos*, Ps. L. 5, 11. Ne áfyrsa þú fultum fram mé *ne elongaveres auxilium a me*, 21, 20. Ne áfyrsa *ne longe facias*, 39, 12. Áfyrsiað þone yfelan fram eów, Hml. Th. i. 124, 31. Man hí áfirsige of earde, Ll. Th. i. 348, 29. Áfirsie *tollat*, Num. 21, 7. Áfyrsige, Hml. Th. ii. 238, 15. Þ hit þám geleáffullum áfyrsige þære ðrowunge forhtunge, Hml. S. 9, 122. Eardbegengnes mín áfeorsod (*printed* aforfeorsode) is *incolatus meus prolongatus est*, Ps. Spl. 119, 5. Wyrð deófol þanon áfyrsad (-firsod *v. l.*), Wlfst. 36, 4. II. intrans. *To remove, depart*:—Ic áfyrsode fleónde *elongavi fugiens*, Ps. L. 54. 8. v. á-feorrian, -firran.

á-feóung, e; *f. Hate*:—Áfeónge (=? on feónge; cf. feóunga *exosa*, 31, 38, *and* gé beóð on hatunge, Mt. 10, 22) *exosas* (-*us*, Ald.), Wrt. Voc. ii. 79, 82.

áfer. v. áfor: á-fered *delusus*. v. á-sirwan.

á-ferian. *Take the last two passages under next word, and add*:—On weg áferide, an uoeg áueridæ *avehit*, Txts. 43, 246. Siððon þú forð ofer þone bist áferod, Bt. 36, 3; S. 105, 14. Þ ne sý áfered *ut non auferetur*, An. Ox. 11, 56.

aferian; *p.* ode *To perform carrying service* (*averagium.* v. Seebohm, Vill. Comm. s. v., *and* average in N. E. D.) *for a lord* (*Take here the last two passages under* á-ferian in *Dict., and add*):—Se geneát sceal wyrcan swá on lande swá of lande, . . . and rídan and auerian and láde lædan, Cht. E. 377, 3.

á-ferran. v. á-firran: á-fétigan. *l.* afetigan, *and* v. hafetian.

Affrican. v. African: af-god, -nes, *dele*.

á-figen *fried*:—Áfigaen *frixum*, Wrt. Voc. ii. 109, 19. Áfigen, 36, 7.

á-fillan *to cause to fall down* or *off* (v. á-feallan). I. lit.:—Þá áfylde sum cnapa þ fæt *a boy knocked the vessel down*, Hml. S. 31, 1127. Gegrípan þ palmtwig and tó eorþan áfyllan (*to cast it to the earth*), Bl. H. 151, 16. II. metaph. *to cause to cease, put an end to*:—Hé áfylleþ þá inwittfullan word of his tungan *he puts away deceitful words from his tongue*, Bl. H. 55, 16. Áfyl *praecipita*, Ps. Spl. 54, 9. Áfael, Wrt. Voc. ii. 118, 72. Getríówie hé hine be þám wíte and mid þý þ wíte áfelle (-fylle, *v. ll.*) *make the fine not recoverable*, Ll. Th. i. 84, 16. Hæfð hé þ wíte áfylled mid þý ðæ, 136, 3. Áfyldum *effeta* (*voluntate*, Ald. 66, 21), Wrt. Voc. ii. 30, 58. v. á-fælan, -fyllan *in* Dict.

a-fíndan. *l.* á-findan; *p.* -fand, -funde; *pl.* -fundon; *pp.* -funden, *and add*: I. *to find out* as the result of search, enquiry, trial:—Ic áfunde Dauid æfter mínre heortan, Hml. S. 18, 30. Man áfunde mid him swutele tácnu, Hml. A. 95, 116. Ásændon hí inn ænne his byrðena, and sé áfunde his hláford lícgan heáfodleásne, 113, 364. Helena ðá róde áfunde, H. R. 99, 8. Hé hyne áxode hwæt hé áfunde be þám Hælende, St. A. 44, 11. Hé ne mihte on his móde áfindan (*he could not find it in his heart*) þæt hé þone nacodan ne gefréfrode, Hml. Th. ii. 500, 25. Gif ænig mæðen mihte beón áfunden, Hml. A. 94, 72. Ðæra sceápa hláford com hám áfundenum sceápe, Hml. Th. i. 340, 5. II. where knowledge comes without search, etc., (1) *to become* or *be made aware* of something:—Gif man áfindeð his æhte, syððan hé hit gebohte hæfeð, unhál *if a person's cattle turns out, after he has bought it, to be unsound*, Ll. Th. i. 180, 20. Mága gerecednysse hé áfunde *affinium relatione comperit*, An. Ox. 3143. Eóde heó in tó hire berne; þá áfunde heó þ hire sunu hæfde þearfum gedæled þone hwæte, Gr. D. 68, 17. Gif man áfinde þ heora ænig on wóhre gewitnesse wære, Ll. Th. i. 204, 23. Ær hine þá men áfundan *before the men became aware of him*, Chr. 755; P. 49, 1. Hé wæs deófol áfunden *he turned out to be a devil*, Hml. S. 18, 48. (2) *to find out, learn the nature* of something, *experience*:—Swiþa áfinden *mastigias experiamur*, An. Ox. 5369. Ne ðearf ic ðé

secgan hū hefig sorg men beoþ seó gēmen his bearna, for đām đū hit
hafast áfunden be þē selfum, Bt. 31, 1; F. 112, 19.   (3) *to find, discover,
meet with* a person, (a) lit.:—Hī forlēton hine tō ānum treówe gebundenne.   Hē wearđ áfunden fram đām folce þǣr, Hml. A. 107, 158.   (b)
fig.:—Hī blissodon þ hī swilcne foresprecan him áfunden hæfdon, 101,
317.   [*O. H. Ger.* ar-findan *experiri, deprehendere.*]   v. áfunden; on-
findan.

**á-firman** (?) *to clear off :*—Lege þās wyrte tō þām sāre, heó hyt
áfyrmeþ ( = (?) á-feormaþ; *v. l.* áfyrreþ), Lch. i. 280, 2.

**á-firran.**   *Add :*   I. *trans. To remove,* &c., (1) place whence not
given:—Se deáþ hit áfirreþ (-ferred, *v. l.*) ... hē cynđ ... þ hē þ líf
áfyrre (-ferre, *v. l.*), Bt. 8; F. 26, 4-7.   Heó hyt áfyrred, Lch. i. 280, 2 :
284, 8.   Dióblas hē áfirde (*eiciebat*), Mk. L. R. 1, 34.   Hē áfyrde
(*abstulit*) folc his, Ps. Spl. 77, 57.   His strengo mæg bión áfyrred
(-feorred, *v. l.*), Bt. 32, 2 ; F. 116, 31.   Áfirred *exorcizatum*, Rtl. 113. 28.
Áweg áfyrred, Lch. i. 340, 21.   Áfirredum *abjecta*, Rtl. 38, 9.   Áfyr-
redne *evulsam*, Wrt. Voc. ii. 33, 25.   (2) place whence given, (a) by
dative :—Hē him ǽlc geswinc áferþ, Ps. Th. 31, arg.   Þā henna hire
áfyrde ān fox, Gr. D. 69, 27.   Hē þysum mannum heora líf áfyrde, 162, 7.
Hū hē þ rīce đām cyninge áferran mihte, Bt. 1; F. 2, 19.   Đæt hié ne
sién đǣm ingeđonce áfierrede (-firrede, *v. l.*), Past. 139, 5.   (b) preposition :—Ic áfyrre (*auferam*) yfel wilddeór and gewinn fram eów, Lev. 26, 6.
Hē áfierđ fram ūs ǽlc gefeoht, Ps. Th. 45, 8.   Đā áfirrađ (*elongant*) hié
from đē, Ps. Srt. 72, 27.   Þte from ūsig áfirdest (*expelleres*) mæht, Rtl.
23, 38.   God áfyrde þæt unrihtwrigels of heora heortan, Bl. H. 105, 30.
Ne áfyr (*elongaveris*) þū fultum fram mē, Ps. L. 21, 10.   Fācen from
ūrum heortum ádoon and áfyrran, Bl. H. 95, 28.   From ūs đióstro áfirra
(*depellere*), Rtl. 37, 9.   Eft wē sié áfirred from ... *retrahamur a* ...,
17, 15.   Se brýdguma byđ áfyrred (-firred, R.) fram him *auferetur ab
eis sponsus,* Mt. 9, 15 : Bl. H. 67, 36.   II. *intrans. To remove,
depart :*—Áfirres from mē *discedite a me*, Mt. L. 7, 23.   Bidda hine
ongunnan þte hē áfirde (*discederet*) from gimǣrum heora, Mk. R. 5, 17.
[*O. H. Ger.* ar-firren *auferre.*]   v. á-feorrian.

**á-firsian.**   v. á-feorsian.

**á-fleán ;** *p.* -flóh, *pl.* -flógon ; *pp.* -flǣgen *To flay, strip off* the skin :—
Hē him hēt of deádum áfleán þone þwang fram þām hneccan oþ þone
hóh *ejus cutem jam mortui a vertice usque ad calcaneum incidit,* Gr. D.
198, 9.   Hweþer hī findan mihton ǽnig tācen þæs áflǣgenan þwanges
si quod signum de incisione monstrari potuisset, 199, 3.

**á-fleón.**   *Dele* II. *v. trans.* ... ; *fugare, and add :*—Áflīđ *effugiet,*
Kent. Gl. 670.   Se þorn of þām man áfleáh, Guth. 68, 22.   Bearn
áfleóndra (? *printed* áflundra) *filii excussorum,* Ps. Spl. M. 126, 5.   Se
mæssepreóst andswarode þ hē wǣre on niht onweg áflogen *hunc presbyter
fugisse respondit,* Gr. D. 254, 2.   ¶ *In* Rtl. 121, 17 *the form glosses
a transitive verb :*—Tō áfleánn (cf. tō fleánne, 100, 31) allne mæht
fióndes *ad effugandum omnem virtutem inimici.*

**á-fleótan ;** *p.* -fleát, *pl.* -fluton ; *pp.* -floten *To skim :*—Wyl þā wyrta
on þǣre buteran swíđe, áfleót þ fām of clǣne, Lch. ii. 94, 20 : 308, 28.

**a-flían.**   *l.* á-flían.   v. á-flígan : *aflíden elis*, Wrt. Voc. ii. 31, 37.
*l.* á-sliden *elisa.*

**a-fligan.**   *l.* á-flígan, -flían, *and add :*—Ic áflíge *fugo*, Wrt. Voc. ii.
151, 53.   Þā unclǣnan gāstas þū áflígst, Hml. S. 24, 92.   Sibb áflígđ
ungeđwǣrnysse, Hml. Th. i. 606, 6.   Sume menn áflýađ þā áwyrgedan
gāstas fram ofsettum mannum, 344, 28.   Áflýgde *abigit, repellit,* An.
Ox. 50, 41.   Hē áflýgde þā crístenan of Alexandria, Hml. S. 2, 33.   Gē
áflígdon deóflu, Hml. Th. i. 64, 22.   Sē forgeaf ūs đas mihte þæt wē
untrume gehǣlon áflígan, 466, 3.   Þā þýstru áflígean, Gr. D. 171,
2.   Wē sceolan mid rōdetācne þā rēđan áflían, Hml. S. 17, 145.   Áfliged
mon *homo apostata*, Kent. Gl. 141.   Þæt hý mid þǣm ungemete áfligede
ne sýn (*effugentur*), R. Ben. 75, 10.   Áflígde, Wrt. Voc. ii. 142, 66.
Áflēgedo, Rtl. 147, 17.   Áflígedum *profligatis,* An. Ox. 3886.

**á-fliman,** -flýman.   *Add :*   I. where there is conflict, *to put to flight,*
(1) of actual fighting :—Hē hyg áflímde and ofslôh mā þonne .xxx.
gôdra đegna, Chr. 1052 ; P. 179, 11.   Wē mid strǣlum hié scotodon and
hié sôna onweg áflýmdon, Nar. 22, 18.   Hý đǣr áflýmede wurdon,
Chr. 1001 ; P. 132, 22.   (2) *to drive away* what is unpleasant or
hurtful :—Áflýman ealle þā þeóstru þǣre nihte, Gr. D. 171, 2.   Diúl
sē đe áflíemed is (*fugitivus est*) from galle fisces đerh đone hēhengel,
Rtl. 146, 37.   II. of expulsion, banishment.   (1) lit. :—Hié hine
(*Pope Leo*) of his setle áfliémdon, Chr. 797 ; P. 56, 11.   Geūtod, áflýmed
*exiliata,* An. Ox. 4849.   Hine (*Egbert*) hæfde Offa áfliémed .iii. geár of
Angelcynnes lande on Fronclond, Chr. 836 ; P. 62, 22.   Weard áflēmed
ūt (man ūtlagode, MS. D.) Ōsgot Clapa, 1044 ; P. 165, 15.   (2) fig. :—
Áflýman *eliminare* (*verborum tonitrua*), An. Ox. 1963.   Ūt áflýmed
*explosa* (*vesania*), 5012.   Ūt áflēmdum gálfreólsum *abdicatis* (i. ex-
pulsis) *lupercalibus,* 4860.   v. á-flíman *in Dict.*

**a-fliung.**   *l.* á-fíung.

**á-flówan.**   *Add :* *pp.* -flówen (-flógen?) *To flow away :*—Đonne
áflēwđ đæt sār of đǣre wunde mid đý wormse, Past. 259, 1.   Seó
wæterádl ūt áflóweđ, Lch. i. 364, 20.   Þ flǣsc áfulađ and neþer áflóweþ,
Bl. H. 101, 3 : Hml. A. 165, 42.   Ne áflówan *ne effluant,* Kent. Gl. 47.

Eal his mōd biođ áflōwen (áflôgen [*or* ? -flogen *from* -fleón *or* -fleógan],
Hatt. MS.) tō gæglbærnesse *ad lasciviam defluens,* Past. 72, 12.   Genim
eoferes blǣdran mid þām micgan, āhefe upp, and ābíd oþ þ se wǣta
of áflôgen (-flôwen, *v. l.*) sý, Lch. i. 360, 6.

**a-flyge,** *dele.*

**á-flygennes,** e ; *f. Attack :*—Wiđ nǣddrena eardunge and áflygennysse
*to prevent the dwelling near one of snakes and their attack,* Lch. i. 366, 8.
Cf. on-flyge, -geflogen.

**á-flýman.**   v. á-flíman.

**afol.**   *Add :* v. weorold-afol.

**á-fón.**   *Add :*—Hē áfēhđ hī *suscipiet eam*, Ps. Spl. 47, 3.   Áfēcđ
*acceperit,* 48, 16.   Sum wíf wæs áfangen (-foncgen, *v. l.*) of hire mōde
(*mente capta*), Gr. D. 176, 17.   Áfangenre *accepta*, R. Ben. I. 69, 11.

**afor.**   *l.* áfor.   *Dele Goth.* abrs, *and add :*   I. *bitter* to the taste, *acid,
sour :*—Áuur (suur ?) lēc *acerbum cepe,* Germ. 394. 262.   Gedô tō þām
hunige emfela ecedes þæs ne sié swíþe áfor ne swíđe swēte ... and
ne sié on bergnesse tō sweotol þæs ecedes áfre scearpnes, Lch. ii. 224,
17-22.   Ne scearp ne tō áfor (δριμύ) ... þā scearpan áfran þing (τὰ
στύφοντα) sint tō fleónne, 210, 20, 29.   Swēte wín sēl mylt þonne
þ áfre, 196, 25.   Por and cawel eal þā þe sýn áfer, 26, 18.   Swā
hwylce þincg swā syndon áfore ođđe bitere, i. 310, 12.   II. *bitter,*
of complaint, &c. :—Mid biterum (áfrum) heófum *amaris questibus,*
An. Ox. 2828.   III. *severe* in its operation, of a remedy :—Gehwæ-
þeres sceal mon nyttian and miscian, þ þone líchoman hǣle and æfer
mægen hæbbe, Lch. ii. 22, 7.   Gif se maga þæs ne fēle, lege ôþra on-
legena on strengran and áferran, 192, 21.   [*O. H. Ger.* eivar *acerbus,
amarus.*]

**afor-feorsian.**   v. á-feorsian.

**á-forhtian.**   *Add :*   I. (1) *intrans. To become afraid :*—Ic andette
þ ic áforhtade, Hml. A. 204, 302.   Heó þā áforhtode, Hml. S. 30, 347.
(1 a) with cause given :—Hē áforhtode for hire bēne, Gr. D. 17, 23.
Hē þearle áforhtode for þām þe hē geþrístlǣhte dôn tō bysmore swā
mycelum werc, 131, 32.   Þā áforhtade uncer mōd forþan wit wēndan
þ ..., Hml. A. 206, 362.   Wē syndon áforhtigende for þām đe ...,
186, 147.   (2) *trans.* (a) *To become afraid of* something :—Helle áforhtian
*gehennam expavescere,* R. Ben. I. 21, 3.   Deáđ áforhtigende *mortem
pavescens,* Hy. S. 139, 21.   (b) *to be afraid of* doing something :—Ic
áforhtige tō secgenne hwæt mē becom, Hml. A. 206, 357.   II.
*to become amazed at :*—Áforhtiende *obstupescens* (*tanta prodigia*), An.
Ox. 2, 388.

**á-forþ.**   *l.* á forþ: *aforud,* dele.

**á-frēfran,** -frēfrian.   *Add :*—Þes man ūs áfrēfrađ (*consolabitur*), Gen.
5, 29.   Áfroebirdun *lenirent*, Txts. 75, 1210.   Þīn gyrd and þín stæf
mē áfrēfredon, Ps. Th. 22, 5 : Past. 125, 24.   Þēh þe hē þ mōd áfrēfrie
(-frēfre, *v. l.*), Gr. D. 258, 27.   Áfrēfrige, Bl. H. 37, 30.   Þā wolde hē
hié áfrēfran, 131, 29.   Áfrēfriende, Gr. D. 112, 26 : 190, 17.   Áfrefrede,
Bl. H. 25, 21.

**á-fremdan** (-đan), -fremdian ; *p.* -fremde, -fremdede ; *pp.* -fremd (-đ).
fremded (-od).   I. *to alienate, estrange* a person :—Ic wolde þæt
hý þē áfremdedon, Wlfst. 255, 13.   Áfremdæ sind đā synfullan *alienati
sunt peccatores*, Ps. Srt. 57, 4.   II. *to alienate, deprive* a person of
something :—Swā rihtwíslícre gesíhđe áfremdad, Hml. S. 23 b, 676.
[*O. H. Ger.* ar-fremidit *alienatus.*]   v. fremdian.

**á-fremdung,** e ; *f. Alienation :*—In áfremđunge *in alienatione,* Ps. Srt.
ii. p. 190, 29.

**á-freón ;** *p.* de *To free, deliver :*—Áfriá ūsih from yfle, Lk. R. 11, 4.
Uē sié áfriódo *liberemur*, Rtl. 91, 22.

**a-freoðan ;** *p.* ede.   *l.* á-freóþan ; *p.* -freáþ.

**African.**   *Add :*—Geseah ic miccle meniu Affricana, Hml. S. 23 b, 346.

**Africanisc.**   *Add :*—Đā Affricaniscan æppla *mala punica,* Wrt. Voc.
ii. 56, 76.   Affracaniscan, 83, 52.

**afu(h)-lic ;** *adj.* Awkly (v. N. E. D.), *perverse :*—Afulic geflit *perversa
contentio,* Mt. p. 2, 11.   [Cf. *Prompt. Parv.* awke or angry *perversus :
O. Sax.* abuh : *O. H. Ger.* abuh, apuh (-ah, -oh) *perversus, nequam,
improbus :* *Icel.* ǫfugr *turned wrong way.*   v. also awk, awkly ; *adv.,*
awkness *in* N. E. D.]

**a-fúl,** *dele, and see* afu(h)-lic.

**á-fúlian.**   *Add :*—Nama árleásra áfulađ (*putrescit*), Scint. 202, 1.
Þæt oređ stincđ and áfúlađ, Wlfst. 148, 7 : Bl. H. 101, 3.   Þ nǣfre
ne áfúlaþ, þ mid þisse smerenesse gesmered biþ, 73, 22.   Þā áfúlode
hē swā đæt nǣnig mon ne meahte árǣfnan þone stenc, Shrn. 111, 24.
Áfúlie *squalescat, sordescat,* An. Ox. 586.   Áfúliendum líchaman hī forwurdon, Gr. D. 207, 17.   Áfúlud *putrefactus,* Scint. 85, 5.   Weard uncer
wegnyst áfúlod, Hml. A. 205, 352.   Áfúlodan, áfúlat *tabida, putrefacta,*
Txts. 104, 1044.   [*O. H. Ger.* ar-fúlēn *putrescere.*]

**á-funden ;** *adj.* (*ptcpl.*) *Experienced :*—Wer on manegum áfunden
*vir in multis expertus,* Scint. 211, 19 : 212, 1.   v. un-áfunden.

**á-fundennes.**   *Add :*—as a gloss to *adinventio,* Ps. L. 27, 4 : 76, 13 :
experimentum, An. Ox. 82 : 3896 : R. Ben. I. 100, 3.   Ic áfandige
manna heortan, and ǣlcum sylle æfter his ágenre áfundennysse, Hml.
Th. i. 114, 17.   v. on-fundenness.

**á-fýlan.** *Add:*—Ðæt ðæt hé mid hreówsunga geclǽnsode hé eft áfýlde, Past. 421. 9. Þæt ǽnig ne áfýle mid fúlan forligere hine sylfne, Wlfst. 69, 14. **Áfýlan** *polluere*, Germ. 401, 35. On gefeohte handa áfýlan, Hml. Th. ii. 502, 7: Hml. S. 25, 858: 32, 86. Swelce hí hí mid ðǽre hreówsunge tó ðǽm áðweán ðæt hí hí mǽgen eft áfýlan *cum se lacrymis lavant, ut mundi ad sordes redeunt*, Past. 419, 26. Ne lǽt þú mé mín mǽgþhád áfýlan, Hml. A. 172, 68. **Áfýled** mid þý duste eorðlicra dǽda, Gr. D. 4, 34. Þá yfelan sint fulle ǽlces yfeles, hí bióþ áfýlde. Bt. 37, 3; F. 190, 19. Fúle áfýlede hórcwénan, Ll. Th. i. 172, 21. **Áfýledum** *infectis*, An. Ox. 380. v. un-áfýled.

**á-fyllan.** *Add:* I. *to fill* a vessel, space, &c.:—Sé áfylde ealle þá stówe, Hml. Th. ii. 350, 25. Wynsum brǽd þá lyfte áfylde, Hml. S. 27, 111. Áfyl ðá wunde, Lch. ii. 22, 20. Þá hié heora cawelas áfylled hæfdon, Ors. 4, 8; S. 188, 27. **I a.** *with gen.:*—Mon áfielde diófolgielda þá cirican, Ors. 6, 3; S. 258, 7. Áfylled monnes blódes, 76, 32. **I b.** *with prep.* mid:—Ðone sǽ mid scipun and mid his fultume áfyllan, Ors. 2, 5; S. 84, 14. Áfyllan fatu mid wætere, Hml. Th. i. 58, 12. Seó dene wæs áfylled mid manna sáwlum, ii. 350, 9. **II.** *to fill, supply abundantly,* (a) *with gen.:*—Þín heáhsetl is þrymmes áfylled, Wlfst. 254, 18. (b) *with mid:*—Gebytla mid wistum áfyllede and mid ēcum leóhte, Hml. Th. i. 68, 3. Þ folc þæs fægnode áfylde (-fyllede, *v. l.*) mid þám brǽde, Hml. S. 27, 112. [*Goth.* us-fulljan: *O. H. Ger.* ar-fullen *replere* (with gen. or *mit*).]

**á-fyllan** *to fell.* v. á-fillan: **á-fylledlíc, -fyllendlíc, -fyllendlíce.** v. un-áfylledlíc, -áfyllendlíc, -áfyllendlíce: **a-fyran,** dele.

**á-fýran** (*and* á-fýrd, -fýrida). *Add:*—Sindun áfýrde (*eunuchi*) þá ðe swá ákende wērun, and syndun áfýrde þá þe wurdon from monnum, and sindun áfýrde þá þe hié sylfum áfýrdun (*castraverunt*), Mt. R. 19, 12. Áfýred (-id) olbenda *dromidus*, Txts. 57, 707. Ðá áfýrdan *eunuchi*, Past. 407, 33: 409, 1. Áfýrdum *spadonibus*, Wrt. Voc. ii. 84, 76. [*O. H. Ger.* ar-fúren *castrare*.]

**á-fyrhtan.** *Add:*—Þ hí ne áfyrhte þ gewin þæs síþfætes, Bd. 1, 23; S. 486, 1. Hiora rýung þá elpendas meahte áfyrhton, Nar. 21, 26. Wearð hé áfyrht and áǽred, Lch. iii. 424, 36. Áfyrhted, Bl. H. 185, 36. Woeron áfryhtad *periclitabantur*, Lk. L. 8, 23. Áfyrhte *attoniti*, Wrt. Voc. ii. 101, 19. Mon ongitan mehte hú hié áfyrhtede wæron, Ors. 4, 10; S. 194. 10.

**á-fýrida, -fyrran, -fyrsian.** v. á-fýran, -firran, -feorsian.

**á-fyrþan** *to remove:*—Hit áfirþeð (-fyrred, *v. l.*) þá wommas, Lch. i. 294, 2. Cf. forþ, (ge-)forþian.

**á-fýsan.** *Add: to make eager, inspire with longing:*—Þonne hwylcum men gelimpeþ þ his fæder gefærþ, ne mæg þ ná beón þ þá bearn langunga nabban æfter þǽm freóndum. Swá wiste úre heofonlica fæder his þá leófan bearn áfýsed æfter him, Bl. H. 131, 28.

**ag,** dele.

**ága.** *Add:*—Sum mycel ága þæs nama wæs Characterius *possessor quidam Carterius nomine*, Gr. D. 230, 11. [*O. H. Ger.* eigo.]

**á-gǽlan.** Dele II. *v. intrans.* . . . esse, *and add:* I. *to make* gál (*q. v.*), *to profane.* v. tó-gǽlan:—Ne ic ne besmíte ł ágǽle míne gekýðnesse *neque profanabo testamentum meum*, Ps. L. 88, 35. **II.** *to neglect, delay doing:*—Se sláwa ágǽlð and foríelt ðæt weorc ðe him niéððearf wǽre tó wyrceanne *piger necessaria agere negligit*, Past. 283, 25. Ic ágǽlde þæt tó mínre sáwle frætwum belumpe, Angl. xi. 98, 29: 99, 63. Ic ágǽlda (forgýmde *above the line*), xii. 510, 19. Þá gyt ágǽlde hé hyt and hyt him ne sǽde, Shrn. 98, 13. Sé his ferwerne oðða hit ágǽlde, Cht. Th. 476, 2. **III.** *to hinder from doing* something (*gen.*):—Ágǽleþ *inpedit*, Wrt. Voc. ii. 48, 8. Hí þone Godes man his horses bereáfodon and hine his síðes ágǽldon, Gr. D. 15, 17. Gif hé hine ágǽlde Godes þeówdómes *if he hindered himself from doing God's service*, Bl. H. 23, 17. **III a.** *to hinder* by diverting a person's energies, *to pre-occupy:*—Swá eall þ folc wearþ mid him ánum ágǽled, þæt hié þæs wealles náne giéman ne dydon, Ors. 3, 9; S. 134, 20.

**á-gǽledlíce.** v. un-ágǽledlíce.

**á-gǽlwed.** *Add:* [-gǽlwed (?); *but cf.* (?) gealh(-g) *dismayed, troubled* (?):—Hié áfyrhtede wǽron and ágǽlwede *incredibili totius civitatis metu*, Ors. 4. 10; S. 194, 10.

**á-galan.** *Add:*—Þá ðe cunnan galder ágalan, Wlfst. 194, 19. Bióð ágalene *incantantur*, Ps. Srt. 57, 6.

**a-gálan.** l. á-gálian; *p.* ode *To become remiss:*—Ástreccað eówre ágálodan (*remissas*) honda, Past. 65, 18. v. á-gǽlan.

**á-gán.** Dele III, *and add:* I. *to go off, away:*—Ágá, yrming, út of ðysum mæn, Gr. D. 223, 10. Þá hé út ágán wæs *cum ille abiisset*, Gen. 27, 5. Þá hí út ágáne wǽron *cum essent in agro*, al. 2: *cum fuissent egressi*, Num. 12, 4: Mt. 9, 32. Wǽron þá men uppe on londe of ágáne, Chr. 897; P. 90, 26. **II.** *of time, to pass:*—Ic nát hwænne míne dagas ágáne beóð *ignorem diem mortis meae*, Gen. 27, 2. Manige geár syndon ágán, Bl. H. 187, 3. Wē ná ne rímdon þá ágánan dagas, Gr. D. 345. 32. **II a.** *to run out* (of a lease). v. un-ágán in Dict. **III.** *to pass off, lose strength:*—Ágáþ *evanuerit* (v. Mt. 5, 13), Wrt. Voc. ii. 30, 62. Ágǽþ, 72, 2. **IV.** *to come off, come to pass, happen:*—Hit ágǽd eallswá hé spricð *evenerit quod locutus est*, Deut. 13, 2. Þín swefen ágǽd bútan frecednysse . . . þ swefen ágǽd mid gefeán, Lch. iii. 154, 25-6. Ǽfter langre tíde hit ágǽd, 156, 3. Þá sǽde hé hú hit gewurðan scolde, and hit sóna æfter þám ealswá áeóde, Wlfst. 17, 18: 44, 23 [= K. de visione Isaiae in Dict.). **IV a.** with dat. *of person to whom something happens:*—Him áeóde swá se hálga him gewítegode, Hml. Th. ii. 168, 34. Hé on swefne áne gesihðe be him sylfum geseah swá swá him syðdan áeóde, 432, 28. Swá swá hit him sorhlice ágióde, C. D. iv. 56, 27. **V.** *to come out, become known:*—Hé lētt ágán út hú fela hundred hýda wǽron innon þǽre scíre *he made it come out how many hundred hides there were in the shire*, Chr. 1085; P. 216, 18.

**ágan.** Dele II, *and add:* pres. indic. 2 sg. áht (in Lind.), *pl.* ágaþ (in Scint.). I. *of possession:*—Becýp eall þæt þú áhst, Mt. 19, 21. Gē ágað *possidebitis*, Scint. 7, 12. Hí ágað *possident*, 158, 17. Prǽlas ne móton habban þæt hí ágon on ágenan hwílan mid earfeðan gewunnen, Wlfst. 158, 38. Ðæt hé ealne ðisne middangeard áge, Past. 333. 9. Þ yrfewyrdnysse gē ágan (*possideatis*), Scint. 24, 7. Hē þæt weorð nolde ágan (*would not retain in his possession*), ac hit óþrum monnum sealde, Ors. 4, 10; S. 198, 17. Eall þ him wæs leófost tó ágenne, Bl. H. 111, 26. Tó áganne, Met. 21, 19. **I a.** of a husband's relation to his wife. Cf. *Icel.* eiga konu:—Ðám gefarenan brēðer ðe ðæt wíf ǽr áhte, Past. 43, 15. Sē þe him idese ágan wolde, Gen. 2702. **II.** *of accomplishment:*—Gif þet Godes wille seó, þæt heó þ færeld áge, Cht. Th. 481, 12. **III.** *describing a state or condition, to have* need, &c.:—Drihten þæs áh þearfe, Bl. H. 71, 1. Ðǽm ðe lǽssan þearfe áhton, Bt. 38, 7; F. 208, 26. Hí sceande ágon *confundantur*, Ps. Th. 108, 2. **IV.** *of obligation, to have* to do something:—Æt swá miclon swá mín bróðor wát þ ic heom mid rihte tó gyldanne áh, Cht. Th. 561, 31. Þ feoh þe heó mē áh tó gyldenne, 553, 18. Micel is þ sácerd ðá tó dónne, Ll. Th. i. 360, 30. Swilce þēnisce dōn swilce hig ágon tó dōne, Cht. Th. 609, 17. Huu micel áht ðú tó geldanne *quantum debes*?, Lk. L. 16, 5. Án áhte tó geldanne (*debebat*) penninga fíf hund, 7, 41: Mt. L. 18, 24, 28. **V.** *to make possessor of* something?, *endow* with:—Þē ic ágan sceal *I will surely endow thee*, Gen. 2724. Ne meahton freó ne þeówe heora bregoweardas bearnum ágan *neither bond nor free could make their lords possessors of children* (the passage refers to the women afflicted with barrenness), 2747. v. ge-ágan, nágan; blǽd-, bold-, burg-, folc-, mægen-ágende.

**á-gangan.** *Add:* I. *to go off, out:*—Eallum út ágangendum *cunctis egressis*, Bd. 1, 7; Sch. 24, 414. **II.** *to pass* (of time):—Þisse eldo is se mǽsta dǽl ágangen, efne nigon hund wintra and lxxi on þýs geáre, Bl. H. 119, 1. **III.** *to come to pass, happen:*—Þ forebeácno þá þe . . . geweorþan sceoldan, ealle þá syndon ágangen . . . fífe þára syndon ágangen on þisse eldo, Bl. H. 117, 30-36. v. á-gán.

**á-gánian;** *p.* ode *To gape, yawn:*—Hē ágánode *oscitavit*, Gr. D. 216, 17.

**áge.** *Add:* [Icel. eiga *property*.]

**á-geldan** *to requite.* v. á-gildan: **á-geldan** *to punish.* *Add:* [Cf. *O. H. Ger.* rehto ingalte *justa ultione puniti*.]

**á-gelwan.** v. á-gǽlwan.

**ágen.** *Add:* , ǽgen. I. *as adj.:*—Þæt is ágen cræft (*a property*) wætres and eorðan, Met. 20, 122. Ǽnigum folce his ǽgenu ǽ gelícade tó healdenne, Ors. 5, 15; S. 250, 19. Þæs wæteres ágnu cýþ is on eorþan, Bt. 33, 4; F. 130, 14. Þis is mín ágen cýð, Met. 24, 49. Ágen *vel* gecynde sprǽc *idioma, proprietas linguae*, Wrt. Voc. i. 55, 46. Binnan heora ǽgenre hýde, Bt. 14, 2; F. 44, 23. Mid míne ágne mægene, Past. 39, 18. Hié magon ongietan hiera ágen (*gen.*, Hatt. MS.) yfel, 214, 14. Tó tælenne ágenne Godes freónd, Hml. A. 13, 9. His áhgen leóht, Bt. 3, 2; S. 9, 12. Þæt (*what*) hí ágon on ágenan hwílan gewunnen, Wlfst. 158, 38. Gif hē þá Godes wæccor behwyrfð þonne þ hē him tó ágenum teleð, þonne him micele ágenre is þ him ǽfre gelǽst, Ll. Th. i. 272, 12. **I a.** *proper* (name, noun):—Sume synd ágene naman swá swá is Eádgár, sume gemǽnelíce, Ælfc. Gr. 11, 16. On as geendiað ágene naman; Aeneas is ágen nama, 25, 14-16. **II.** *as subst., one's own* (people, land, property, &c.):—Wē brúcað úres ágnes (ǽgnes, Hatt. MS.), Past. 336, 19. Ǽgenes, 339, 2. Þ gē mē geunnon mínes ágenes, Ll. Th. i. 196, 16. Eall hiera ágen ðæt hié synderlíce ðenceað oððe dóð hié wēnað ðæt ðæt sié ðæt betste, Past. 209, 9. Hiora ágen (ǽgen, Hatt. MS.) wē him sellað, meahts úre, 334, 18. Gif ðú ðín ágen myrre, ne wít ðú nit ná Gode, Prov. K. 51: Wlfst. 158, 37. Tó his ágenum hē com *in propria venit*, Jn. 1, 11. Cúþan mon ofslóg, and Ceaulin hwearf tó his ágnum, Chr. 584; P. 20, 4. Hié eft tó hiora ágnum becóman *restituti sunt*, Ors. 4, 3; S. 162, 21. Ðá gewænde seó wydewe hám tó hyre ágenum, Hml. S. 2, 144. v. un-ágen.

**ágend.** *Add:*—Ágend *possessor*, Kent. Gl. 543. Gif man mægðman nēde genimeð, þám ágende .L. scillinga, and ǽrt æt þám ágende sinne willan æt gebicge, Ll. Th. i. 24, 3-4: 42, 21.

**ágend-freá.** *Add:*—Ne eardað nǽnig ágendfreá *nullus possessor inhabitat*, Gr. D. 258, 19. Se earm stód þám ágendfréau ungewylde *the man could not move his own arm*, 254, 38. Cf. ágen-frígea.

**ágend-líce.** *Add:*—As if something belonged to one's self, *imperi-*

*ously:*—Gé ludon suíðe ríclíce and suíðe ágendlíce *vos cum austeritate imperabatis eis et cum potentia,* Past. 145, 5. Cf. ágend-(ágen-)freá.

**ágen-frigea.** *l.* -frígea, *and add:*—Se ágenfrígea (-fríga, *v.l.*), Ll. Th. i. 132, 14: 276, 15. Cf. ágend-freá.

**ágen-líc;** *adj.* **I.** *own;* *proprius:*—Ágenlíces dǽdes *propriae actionis,* Rtl. 49, 32. Æfter ágenlíc mægn *secundum propriam virtutem,* Mt. L. 25, 15. Ðá áganlíco *propria,* p. 15, 5. **II.** *owed, due;* *debitus.* v. ágan, IV:—Ágenlíc(e) hérnise *debitam servitutem,* Rtl. 106, 13. [*Icel.* eigin-ligr.]

**ágen-nama.** *l.* ágen nama, v. ágen, I.

**ágen-ness.** *Substitute:* A *property:*—Seó sunne hæfð ðreó ágennyssa on hire, Hml. Th. i. 282, 8 : ii. 606, 11.

**ágen-slaga.** *Add:* A *suicide:*—Nán sylfcwala, þ is ágenslaga, ne becymð tó Godes ríce, O. E. Hml. i. 296, 14. Ælc ágenslaga on écnysse ðrowað, Hml. S. 19, 230: Hml. Th. ii. 250, 22.

**ágen-spræc.** *l.* ágen spræc, v. ágen, I : **ágenung.** v. ágnung.

**á-geolwian.** *Add:*—Se líchoma ágeolwaþ swá gód geolu seoluc, Lch. ii. 10, 15. Þá téð ágeolwiað, þá þe wǽron hwíte, Wlfst. 148, 6. Micge ágeolwod, Lch. ii. 258, 15. Þá ágeolewedan *crocata,* Wrt. Voc. ii. 137, 12.

**á-geóm(e)rian;** *p.* ode To *mourn, lament:*—Ic ágeómrige, Gr. D. 5, 23. Hé ágeómrode *ingemuit,* 42, 33. Hé ágeómrode for his ágenre scylde, 345, 10.

**á-geótan.** *Add:* **I.** *to pour out* a liquid:—Gif hé (*a priest*) his calic ágýt (*effundat*), Ll. Th. ii. 128, 20. Þ wæter ic niðer ágeát (*effudi*), Nar. 8, 10. Þá fatu þe hé ǽr on ágeát litelne dǽl þæs wǽtan, Gr. D. 59, 13. Ág(e)át *exsicat,* Wrt. Voc. ii. 145, 23. Ágaett *effudit,* Mk. L. 14, 3. Þ wín bið ágotten, 2, 22. Þ wæter binnan þǽre cyrcan wearð ágoten, Gr. D. 26, 195. Þæs eles náht út ágoten beón ne mihte, Gr. D. 160, 2. ¶ *figuratively:*—Hí him betwýnon gemǽnelíce him on águton þá swétan lífes word, 170, 3. **I a.** *to shed* tears, blood:—Swá hwá swá ágít mannes blód, his blód bið ágoten, Gen. 9, 6. Ic ágeát míne teáras, Hml. Th. i. 66, 29. Ofiysted þæt hé his blód águte, Guth. 44, 23. **II.** *to cast, found* (of metal); in pp. *molten* (image):—Cræt of golde ágoten, Hml. Th. ii. 494, 23, 24. Godas ágotene of áre, Hml. S. 7, 132. Ágotene oððe ágrafene, 4, 136. **III.** *to consume, destroy:*—Hé ágeát gylp wera, Exod. 514. Þonne bið se glencg ágoten and se þrym tóbrocen, Wlfst. 263, 8. [*O. H. Ger.* ar-giuzan *effundere.*]

**a-getan** *to destroy. l.* á-gétan, *and* v. á-gítan : **á-giéta.** v. á-gíta.

**á-gifan.** *Add:* **I.** *to give back* what has been taken, *to restore:*—Gif þú wed nime æt þínum nǽhstan, ágif (*reddes*) him his reáf ǽr sunnan setlgange, Ex. 22, 26. Hé háteþ þá eorþan eft ágifan þ heó ǽr onféng, Bl. H. 21, 30. Gode his dǽl ágeofau þe hit þé ǽr sealde, 195, 21. **II.** *to render, pay* what is due:—Ágyfað þám Cásere þá þing þe þæs Cáseres synt, Mt. 22, 21. Þ gé of mínum ágenum góde ágifan þá teóðunga, Ll. Th. i. 194, 6. Gé sceolon ágifan þæt ilce tigolgetel, Ex. 5, 18. Wǽstm ágifan and ágildan, Bl. H. 55, 6. Circsceat mon sceal ágifan, Ll. Th. i. 140, 12. Gif hé hæbbe ealle on fóðre tó ágifanne, 9. **III.** *to give up, abandon:*—Ic hine tó heora sylfra dóme ágeaf, Bl. H. 177, 25. Se ágend þone banan ágefe, Ll. Th. i. 26, 9 : 28, 5. Hé hét þá sceáweras ágifan, Jos. 2, 3. Ágifen *destitutum,* Wrt. Voc. ii. 141, 33. [*Goth.* us-giban : *O. Sax.* a-gebau : *O.H.Ger.* ar-geban *reddere, retribuere.*] v. un-ágifen.

**á-gifan;** *p.* ode To *bestow, grant:*—Ágefaiga (so in MS.) *largiatur,* Rtl. 124, 36.

**a-gift,** *dele, and see* ǽ-gift.

**á-gildan.** *Add:* **I.** *to pay back, repay:*—Hwonon ágelte ðú *unde restituas,* Kent. Gl. 850. Wé eall ágyldan sceolan þ hé ús ǽr sealde, Bl. H. 51, 25. **II.** *to render, pay* what is due (v. riht, VII):—Ic ágylde *dependo,* i. *reddo, persolvam,* Wrt. Voc. ii. 138, 80. Ágilst þú (*reddis*) Drihtene þás þing? Deut. 32, 6. Ic lǽrde þ hié heora gafol águldon, Bl. H. 185, 20. Wǽstm ágildan *to bring forth fruit,* 55, 6. **II a.** of duty or service, *to pay, perform:*—Ic ágeald *reddidi* (*vota mea*), Kent. Gl. 197. Gesceád ágyldan *to render an account,* Hml. Th. i. 274, 3. **III.** *to pay for, make retribution for:*—Hí sculon deúre ágildan eal þæt hí forgímdon, Wlfst. 190, 22. Þá ǽrrau þing ágoldene wǽron, Ors. 5, 15; S. 250, 31. [*Goth.* us-gildan : *O. Sax.* á-geldau.] v. á-gyldan *in Dict.*

**á-gíman;** *p.* de To *regard:*—Þám tímum þe ic hys (*eternal life*) ágýme . . . ne lufige ic nánwiht þisses andweardan lýfes ofer þ, Shrn. 177, 12. Ágémde *curavit,* Lk. p. 5, 19.

**á-gímeleásian.** *Add:* (1) with acc.:—Gif wé hit ágímeleásiaþ, Bl. H. 53, 1 : 57, 19. Hié ágímeleásiað (-gýme-, Cott. MSS.) ðone ymbhogan, Past. 137, 1. (2) with clause:—Gif se hierde ágíémeleásað ðæt hé hiera helpe, 137, 14. Hé ágýmeleásede þ hé heólde his líchaman forhæfdnesse, Gr. D. 241, 17. Ðæt hié ne ágímeleásien ðæt hí hira mód gebríðligen, Past. 215, 6.

**á-ginnan.** *Add:* **I.** *to begin* to do (*infin. or gerund*):—Marcus áginþ wrítan þ godspell, Chr. 47 ; P. 7, 31. Ágann Landfranc atýwian, 1070; P. 206, 12. Ágan se cyng tó smeágenne, 1006 ; P. 137, 19. **II.** *to attempt:*—Gif man beforan æðelinge gefeoht áginneð, Ll. Th. i. 332,

4. Áginne hé hit georne *let him diligently attempt it,* ii. 282, 2. Mæg þeáh bót cuman, wille hit man georne on eornost áginnan, i. 348, 24. Ǽr þám þe hí habban bóte águnnen, 324, 13. **III.** *to act, proceed:*—Ic wið eów stíðlícor áginne ðonne ic tale wið eów habban wylle *I shall proceed too severely against you for me to be willing to have speech with you,* Hml. S. 23, 183. Þá anlícnessa hé gemacode þurh drýcræft þæt hý águnnon swylce hý cwice wǽron *he made the images by magic to act as if they were alive,* Wlfst. 99, 1. v. on-ginnan.

**á-girnan,** -geornan ; *p.* de To *desire, be eager for:*—Hé ágeornde (-gyrnde, *v.l.*) þ hé manigra manna sáwla gelǽdde tó Drihtne *multorum animas ad Deum perducere satagebat,* Gr. D. 205, 19.

**á-gíta,** -giéta. *Add:* a *waster, prodigal:*—Monig bið ágíta (-giéta, Hatt. MS.) his góda and wilnað mid ðý geearnian ðone hlísan ðæt hé sié rúmgiful *saepe se effusio sub appellatione largitatis occultat,* Past. 148, 6. Oððe eft se gilpna and se ágíta for his góda mirringe gilpe and wéne ðæt hé sié cystig and mildheort *aut cum effuse quid perditur largum se glorietur,* 19. v. á-gítan.

**á-gitan.** *Add:* **I.** *to find, get to know* (1) a person:—Wille wé be him áwrítan swá swá wé hine ágeáton *we will write of him as we found him,* Chr. 1086 ; P. 219, 19. (2) a fact:—Gif se abbod his geearnunga swá ágitt *quem si talem esse perspexerit abba,* R. Ben. 110, 3. Swá raðe swá hé ágite þ hit fremian mæge *prout viderit expedire,* 120, 9. Be hwylcum tácne man ágytan nihte hwænne his tócyme tówerd wurde, Wlfst. 88, 22. Áfunden, ágyten *expertus,* An. Ox. 2538. Gif ǽni man ágiten wurðe þ ǽnige hǽðenscipe dreóge *if any one be found to practise heathen rites,* Ll. Th. ii. 296, 27. **I a.** *to find out, get to know of:*—Gyf hé hwæt be óðrum gehýre oððe sylf ágyte, Ll. Th. ii. 316, 19. Gyf wiccean innan þysan earde weorðan ágytene, Wlfst. 309, 23. v. on-gitan. **II.** *to get, take away:*—Hié eágena gesihð ágéton (-gétton?) gára ordum, An. 32. [*O. H. Ger.* ar-gezan *abolere, obliterare.*]

**a-gitan** *to destroy. Substitute:* á-gítan, -giétan, -gétan; *p.* te To *waste, destroy:*—Hwá mín fromcynn ágétte eall of earde, Rä. 80, 8. Sumne sceal gár ágétan, Vy. 16. Hí woldon heafolan gescénan, gárum ágétan, An. 1145. Þǽr læg secg mænig gárum ágéted, Ædelst. 18. v. á-geótan, III, á-gíta.

**a-gitan** *to pour out. Dele.*

**ag-lác,** -lǽca, &c. *l.* ág-lác, -lǽca, &c. [Cf. *Mid. E.* egleche : *O.H.Ger.* aigi-laihi *phalanx.*]

**á-gleddian;** *p.* ode To *smear, stain:*—Ágleddego *labefacare,* Txts. 111, 9. Cf. be-gleddian.

**á-glídan.** *Add: to slip off, away:*—In lust áglád *in luxum labescit,* Wrt. Voc. ii. 86, 16 : 52, 45. Wíte georne þ sió wyrt áweg ne áglíde, Lch. ii. 356, 24.

**ágnere, es;** *m. An owner, possessor:*—Meus mín hæfð vocatiuus ná þæs ágneres (ágneres, áhneres, *v.ll.*), ac ðæs óðres hádes, Ælf. Gr. Z. 110, 19. Ácneres (= ágneras?) *municipes,* An. Ox. 11, 92.

**agnere,** Wrt. Voc. i. 43, 2. v. angnere : **agnes.** v. ang-ness.

**ágnett, es;** *n. Usury, interest:*—Mið águettum *cum usuris,* Lk. L. 19, 23.

**ágnettan;** *p.* te To *appropriate, usurp:*—Ágnette (-aettae, -etae) *usurpavit,* Txts. 107, 2171.

**ágnian.** *Add:* **I.** *to possess:*—Ðá ðe ic áh í ágnigo *quae possideo,* Lk. L. 18, 12. Alle ðá ðe ágnegæð í áh (ǽngað, R.) *omnia quae possidet,* 12, 44. Ágnigeð (-að, R.), 15. Ágnaged (-igað, R.), 11, 21. Ágneges *possidete,* Mt. L. 25, 34. Ágnege (ágan, R.) gold *possidere aurum,* 10, 9. **II.** of legal possession, *to declare one's self the owner of* property, so rendering *teám* (q. v., also *tíman,* II) unnecessary:—Swá hé hit ágnode swá hé hit týmde *whether he declared himself to have been the owner or traced possession to another,* Ll. Th. i. 160, 8. Gif þú ná furðor teám ne cenð ac ágnian wile *if any one does not carry the* teám *further, but declares himself to have been the owner,* i. 290, 19. **III.** *to appropriate* to one's self, *usurp, arrogate:*—Gif hé ðá gód þe ús God tó gemánan sealde him synderlíce ágnað (ǽgnað, Hatt. MS.) *qui commune Dei munus sibi privatum vindicant,* Past. 334, 13. Ðá unwaran þe him ágniað (-at, Hatt. MS.) ðone cræft ðæs láreówdómes þe hí ná ne geleornodon, 24, 13. Tó hwon ágnodest þú þé ánum þæt ic inc bám sealde, Wlfst. 259, 15. Áhni[ende] (áhniend, Hpt. 523, 4) *usurpans,* An. Ox. 5127. v. ge-ágnian ; ágnung.

**á-gnídan;** *p.* -gnád, *pl.* -gnidon To *rub off:*—Sié ágniden *defricabitur,* Wrt. Voc. ii. 26, 12. v. next word.

**á-gniden[n], e; *f.* A *rubbing off:*—Ágnidinne (-ine) *detriturigine,* Txts. 56, 345. Ágnidene *detriturigine,* Wrt. Voc. ii. 139, 45.

**ágniend.** *Add:* v. ágnian, II: **ágniend-líc.** *Add:* v. geágniendlíc.

**ágnung.** *Add:* **I.** *possession, property:*—Áhnung *possessio,* An. Ox. 1321. Ágnungum *proprietatibus,* 879. **II.** *declaration of ownership.* v. ágnian, II:—Wé cwédon sé þe týman scolde þ . . . Swá wé cwédon be þǽre ágnunge þ ylce, Ll. Th. i. 158, 18. **II a.** *proof of ownership:*—Gewrítrǽden *vel* ágnung *cyrographum,* Wrt. Voc. ii. 137, 70. Þá getǽhte man Wynflǽde þ hió móste þ land hyre geáhnian (*prove her ownership of the land*). Ðá gelǽdde hió þ áhnunga, Cht. Th. 289, 1.

ā-gotenness. *Add:*—Ágotenes *suffusio*, Kent. Gl. 904. Mýnes blôdes āgotenys, Shrn. 96, 33. For āgotennysse þines blôdes, Hml. Th. i. 594, 17. Mid teára āgotennysse *cum lacrymarum effusione*, Ll. Th. ii. 136, 20: Lch. iii. 428, 11.

ā-grafan. *Add:* I. *to engrave, emboss, inscribe:*—Se engel āgrôf mid his fingre rôdetācn on ðām stānum, Hml. Th. i. 466, 13. Āgrôf se mon on ǽrenum brede drýcræftæs word, Shrn. 141, 15. Þás race on ānum leádenum tabulan mid stafcn hī āgrôfon, Hml. S. 23, 343. Wǽs his anlícnys on (þām feó) āgrafen, 660. Ágraben *caelatum*, Wrt. Voc. ii. 103, 40. Ágrafen, 14, 6. Ágrafen, āstemped *celatum*, i. *pictum*, 130, 57. Ágrafen ceác *expolita pelvis*, Germ. 403, 16. Hyre āgrafenan beáh, Cht. Th. 533, 32. Ágrafene *anagliva*, Wrt. Voc. ii. 4, 55. Ágrafenum fatum, Hml. A. 92, 16. II. *to grave, carve*; *sculpere:*—Onlícnessa þe fullremedlíce ne beóð āgrafene (*sculpta*), Gr. D. 283, 24. Ágrafene ðurh manna handa, Hml. Th. i. 424, 10. Ágotene odðe āgrafene, Hml. S. 4, 136. [*Goth.* us-graban *to dig out*: *O. H. Ger.* ar-graban *caelare, sculpere.*]

a-grafenlíce, an; *n. Substitute:* ā-grafenlic; *adj. Graven, sculptured.*

ā-grāpian; *p.* ode *To handle, grasp:*—Būton mīn líchama beó on þīnum bendum genyrwod aud fram ðīnum cwellerum on þīnum copsum āgrāpod *unless my body in thy fetters be handled (tormented) by thy executioners*, Hml. S. 8, 121. [*O. H. Ger.* ar-greifôn, *palpare, pertractare.*]

ā-grētan; *p.* te *To attack:*—Ágroette hine se diówl *elisit illum daemonium*, Lk. L. R. 9, 42.

ā-grimetian; *p.* ode: -grimettan; *p.* te *To rage, be furious:*—Se ealda feónd āgrimetede (-grymetode, *v. l.*) and hine gebealh *antiquus hostis infremuit*, Gr. D. 211, 22. Se fæder āgrimette *pater infremuit*, 238, 21.

ā-grīsan. *Add:*—Ondrǽde man dômdæg and for helle āgríse, Wlfst. 75, 6. Ágrýse, 179, 16. v. a-grise *in N. E. D.*

a-grýndan; &c. *l.* ā-gryndan; *p.* de.

agu. *Add:* [Cf. *O. H. Ger.* agalstra, agaza *pica.*]

Agustus. *Add to* II: *gen.* Agustes:—In Agustes mônþe *mense Augusto*, Nar. 6, 8: Lch. i. 70, 7.

ā-gyltan. *Add:* (1) absolute:—Oft āgyltað (*offendunt*) ðā hlāfordas, and ðā menn wuniað on Godes hyldo, Past. 321, 2. Þeáh hwā āgylte, Ll. Th. i. 376, 15: Ors. 6, 11 ; S. 266, 10. Wið ðāra āgyltendra undeáwas *contra delinquentium vitia*, Past. 107, 10. (2) with means or manner of sin given:—Wē āgyltaþ þurh feówer þing (*thought, word, deed, will*), Bl. H. 35, 13. Hwǽr āgylte wē ǽfre on his gegerelan?, 167, 34. (2 a) with acc.:—Þæt (*what*) wē mid gītsigendum eágum āgylton, Hml. Th. i. 68, 26. (3) with object against which sin is done:—Swā swā wē forgyfað ðām þe wið ūs āgyltað, 258, 23. Gif neáhgebúr wið ôðerne āgilte *qui irrogaverit maculam cuilibet civium suorum*, Lev. 24, 19. Hē āgylt hæfde ongeán Godes bebod, Hml. S. 12, 22. (4) combining (2) and (3):—Sume men on lytlum ðingum wið God āgylton, Hml. Th. ii. 396, 34.

ā-gylting, e ; *f. Sin, fault, offence:*—Ágyltinges ūsra ondetnisse *reatus nostri confessio*, Rtl. 18, 9. Forgefnisse synna í āgyltingo *indulgentiam culparum*, 23, 15.

ā-gytan. v. ā-gitan.

ā-habban. *Add:* I. *to restrain:*—Þ hī hī from wífum āhæfden, Bd. 1, 27; S. 496, 5. Þ hī āhabban hī fram swylcum unrihtum, 491, 24. Heó sceolde hī āhabban fram Godes hūses ingange, 493, 15: 489, 17. Fram ingange is tô āhabbanne *ab ingressu abstinendum est*, 495, 20. Hine fram þām sídíæte āhæbbende, Hml. S. 23 b, 161. II. *to support* (cf. *O. H. Ger.* ant-habên *suspendere, sustinere*):—Áhæfd (anhaebd, -hæbd) *suspensus*, Txts. 99, 1947.

ā-haccian; *p.* ode *To peck out:*—Fugelas þára martyra eágan ūt āhaccedon, Hml. S. 23, 78.

ā-hafenness. *Add:* v. up-āhafenness.

ā-hālsian; *p.* ode *To implore:*—Áhālsian *obsecrare*, R. Ben. I. 15, 3.

ā-hangian; *p.* ode *To hang* (intrans.)—Án of ðǽm ðā ðe āhongadon (*pendebant*), Lk. L. 23, 39.

ā-hātan; *p.* -hēt *To call, name:*—Wæs āhēten *dicebatur* (*Barabbas*), Mt. L. 27, 16.

ā-hātian; *p.* ode *To become hot:*—Áhātode heorte mīn *concaluit cor meum*, Ps. L. 38, 4. Sē cymð of þām swíðe ācôlodan magan oþþe of þām tô swíðe āhātodan, Lch. ii. 60, 19. [*O. H. Ger.* ar-heizên *incalescere, exardescere.*]

ā-healdan *to hold:*—Hāl from suǽ hwælc unhǽlo uēre āhaldan *sanus a quocumque languore tenebatur*, Jn. L. 5, 4.

ā-heardian. *Add:* I. physical:—Twǽgen healfa hlāfas ic brôhte . . . ādruwodon hī swā swā stān and āheardodon, Hml. S. 23 b, 520. Seó hýd ne wile āheardian, 35, 162: Lch. ii. 250, 4. Hire wæs āweaxen swā āheardod hýd (*obdurata cutis*) swylce olfendan, Gr. D. 287, 4. Tācn āheardodre lifre, Lch. ii. 204, 4. Gif hwylcum men ǽdran āheardode sýn, i. 196, 5. II. figurative. (1) of persons, (a) *to prove stern, inflexible:*—þām mannum hē sceal dôn synna forgife-

nysse þe hē gesihð þæt beóð onbryrde ðurh Godes gife, and þām hē sceal āheardian þe nāne behreówsunge nabbað heora misdǽda, Hml. Th. i. 234, 4. (b) *to become hard, not to yield:*—Ēstfulle heortan āheardiað on stānes gecynde ongeán costnungum, Hml. Th. ii. 56, 9. (c) *to harden, become impervious to good:*—Ðā ðe suā āheardigað ðæt hī yfel for nānum ege ne forlǽtað *qui sic in iniquitate duruerunt ut neque per flagella corrigantur*, Past. 175, 23. Ðā ðe beóð āheardode on unryhtwīsnesse, 263, 4. Eówre heortan āheardode siondon, H. R. 7, 19. (d) *to become inured:*—Áheardode hǽrescit (*lautomiae liminibus*), An. Ox. 4641. (2) of things, *to be rigid, be insisted upon, not to be relaxed:*—Gif þæs ealdres cwide þurhwunað and his gebod āheardað si *in sua sententia prioris imperium perduraverit*, R. Ben. 128, 17. [*O. H. Ger.* ar-hartên.] v. ā-hirdan, -hyrdan (*not* -hyrdian).

ā-heardung. *Add:*—Áheardung ðæs magan, Lch. ii. 198, 12 : 204, 5. Be ðǽre lifre āheardunge, 200, 19.

ā-heáwan. *Add:*—Se hālga wolde āheáwan ǽnne pínbeám . . . Ðā hǽðenan āheówon þæt treów þæt hit sāh tô ðām hālgan were, Hml. Th. ii. 508, 22–34. Ic him hēt þā honda of āheáwan, Nar. 17, 1. Áheáwen *cesa*, i. *abscisa, occisa*, Wrt. Voc. ii. 131, 2. Áhǽwenum *absciso*, An. Ox. 1552. Of āheáwenum ðý heáfde Pendan *desecto capite*, Bd. 3, 24; S. 557, 15. Ðā ðornas beóð āheáwene, Past. 411, 17.

ā-hebban. *Add:* A. as a strong verb. I. literal, (1) *to raise from a lower to a higher position:*—Heora nǽnig þā bǽre ne āhôf, Bl. H. 153, 3. Þā āhôf Drihten hié up, 157, 21. Áhôf Paulus up his heáfod, 187, 35. Hēt Benedictus eft āhebban þæt elefæt (*pick up the vessel*), Hml. Th. ii. 178, 31. (2) *to place above:*—Wæs se Hālga Gāst āhafen ofer þā leorneras, Bl. H. 135, 3. Ðā níetenu beóð hwæðwugununges from eorðan āhafen (-hæfen, Hatt. MS.), Past. 154, 16. (3) *to lift, carry, remove:*—Hwā āhefeþ hī heonon *quis eos hinc levat ?*, Gr. D. 208, 24. Nis nāuum men cūð hwider hyre líchama āhafen sý, Hml. Th. i. 440, 20. Wæs of rôde āhafen rodera Wealdend, El. 482. (4) *to raise, erect, build:*—Se cāsere hēt āhebban ǽnne wāh, Hml. S. 35, 335. II. figurative, (1) implying attempt, attack :—Gif se mon āhefþ his handa tô ælmesdǽdum, Bl. H. 37, 24. Syððan hē wǽpen āhôf wið hetendum, El. 17. Up āhef (ahefe, Ps. Srt. Spl.) þīne handa *leva manus tuas*, Ps. L. 73, 3. (2) of hostile action or feeling :—Hī gewinn up āhôfon, Chr. 1094; P. 230, 3. Hié wið Godes bearne níð āhôfon, El. 838. Ongan winn up āhebban wið heofnes wealdend *raised war against heaven's ruler*, Gen. 259. (3) *to remove:*—Hē ðām menn undeáдlicnysse onweg āhôf *immortalitatem homini abstulit*, Bd. 1, 27; S. 493, 7. (4) *to bear, support:*—Se maga and se unmaga ne magon nā gelíce byrðene āhebban, Ll. Th. i. 328, 17. Þā þe þā yldo nabbað þ hig þ fæsten āhebban magon, ii. 436, 10. (5) *to uphold:*—Hē bið up āhafen *sublevabitur*, Kent. Gl. 1069. (6) *to give rise to, cause, raise* a laugh :—Ýdelu word þā þe unnytte hleahtor up āhebben, Ll. Th. ii. 416, 35. (7) *to raise to a higher position, to elevate:*—Tô ðý þæt hē wǽre on mǽrlicum cynesetle āhafen, Hml. Th. i. 82, 24. Hē wæs tô his cinestôle āhofen, Chr. 795; P. 57, 19. Hē wæs tô þām swýðe up āhafen swylce hē weólde þæs cynges and ealles Englalandes, 1052; P. 176, 22. Hwī sind gē āhafene ofer Drihtenes folc *cur elevamini super populum Domini ?*, Num. 16, 3. (8) *to give higher worth or value to, to exalt:*—Up āhef hig *extolle eos*, Ps. L. fol. 195 b, 23. Ǽlc man sceal his gôdan dǽda āhebban, gif hē sceal gôd and medeme weorþan, Bl. H. 129, 35. (9) expressing pride, elation, *to exalt* (in a bad sense), *puff up:*—Wālā wā þ ǽnig man sceolde môdigan swā, hine sylf upp āhebban and ofer ealle men tellan, Chr. 1086; P. 221, 20. Ne wæs hē on oferhygd āhafen, Bl. H. 215, 32. Up āhafen *arrogans*, Kent. Gl. 796. Áhofyn, Ps. Spl. C. 130, 1. (10) referring to sound, *to lift the voice, raise* a song :—Hī soug āhebbað, Ph. 540. Þā āhôf Petrus his stefne and wæs cweþende, Bl. H. 145, 16. Þā reordade ríce þeóden, wǽrfæst cyning word āhôf, An. 416. Iudéa cynn wið Godes bearne āhôf hearmcwide, 560. Wē on bence beót āhôfon, By. 213. Weard hreám āhafen, 106. B. as a weak verb. v. a-hefen *in Dict., and cf.* ā-hefednes:—Heó hire heáfod of ðǽre mýsan āhefde, Hml. Th. ii. 184, 4. Þā āhefde Moyses his handa on gebedum, Hml. S. 13, 14, 19. Mid þām mægenþrymme sý āhefed heofon and eorþe, Sch. 89. [*Goth.* us-hafjan: *O. Sax.* ā-hebbian: *O. H. Ger.* ar-heffen *elevare, exaltare.*]

a-hefan. *l.* ā-hebban, *and see preceding word.*

a-hefig. Ahefegum (=an hefegum? Cf. Hē gesceafta gesette on hefe, Hml. Th. ii. 584, 29–32) hefe āsette wēron *gravi mole constiterant*, Kent. Gl. 265.

ā-hefigian. *Add:*—Áhefegiað hira heortan ðā byrðenna ðæs forhwirfdan gewunan *the burdens of perverse custom weigh down* (praegravant) *their hearts*, Past. 67, 16. Áhefigad (-hefgad, R.) *gravatum* (*cor*), Lk. L. 21, 34. Hī beóð āhefegode (*gravati*) mid byrðenne þæs líchaman, Gr. D. 138, 20.

ā-held. v. ā-hildan.

ā-helian *to cover, conceal:*—Áscyledum í āhe(ledum), forheledum *tectis*, Hpt. Gl. 528, 15.

ā-helpan. *Add:*—Wē sié āholpeno *foveamur*, Rtl. 30, 29. Wē sié āholpen *adjuvemur*, 46, 28.

**á-hénan..** v. á-hínan.

**a-heólorian.** *l.* á-heolorian, *and add:*—Áwæh, áheolrede *trutinabit* (áholrede *trutinabat*, Hpt. Gl. 513, 2), An. Ox. 4603. Áhiolorod *librate*, Wrt. Voc. ii. 91, 47 : 52, 30. Áheolrude *trutinatas*, An. Ox. 7, 26.

**á-heordan.** *Add :* (-heóran?) *To guard* (?). [Cf. *Icel.* hirða *to keep safe.*]

**a-hérian** *to hire. l.* á-héran. v. á-hýran.

**a-hérian** *to praise. l.* á-herian, *and add :*—Þte sié áheredo *laudari*, Rtl. 105, 5.

**á-hildan.** *Add :* I. literal, of downward direction, (1) *trans. :*— 'Áhyld hit wærlice' (cf. áhyld þá flaxan *inclina flasconem*, Gr. D. 142, 5) ... Hé áhylde þæt wín wærlice, Hnl. Th. ii. 170, 18–20.. Heó áhylde hire heáfod tó ðære mýsan, 184, 2. Áhældon þ onsíon on eorðo *declinarent vultum in terram*, Lk. L. 24, 5. Næs him nán wên þ se beám áhwár wende búton tó ðám hálgan swá swá hé áhy ld wæs, Hml. Th. ii. 508, 32: Hml. S. 31, 407. Áhyldne *reclinem*, An. Ox. 2127. Áhyldum heáfde *inclinato capite*, R. Ben. I. 36, 2: Hml. Th. ii. 258. 2. (2) *intrans. :*—Sunne tó setle áhylde, Hml. S. 23 b, 498. Ðeós wyrt þ ðæþ leáf nyþer wið þá eorþan áhyldende, Lch. i. 274, 14. II. figurative, (1) *trans.* (a) *to incline, decline :*—Hí (*conjunctions*) áhyldað and gebígað heora swég tó ðám stæfgefége þe him ætforan stent, Ælfc. Gr. Z. 265, 2. Ne ne áhylde *nec inclinat* (*statum cordis*), An. Ox. 7, 307. Hé bið áheld *declinatur* (*a malo*), Kent. Gl. 549. (b) *to cast down, decline :*—Áfyl þ áhyld *praecipita*, Ps. Spl. 54, 9: Bl. Gl. Áheldre *declivi, vel proni, humiliati*, Wrt. Voc. ii. 138, 12. (2) *intrans.* To *incline, decline :*—Ealle hí áhyldon *omnes declinaverunt*, Ps. Spl. 13, 4. Ne áhaeld ðú from ðíowe ðínum *ne declines a servo tuo*, Ps. Srt. 26, 9. v. á-hyldan *in Dict.*, and heald, on-hildan.

**á-hildendlic;** *adj. Ready to incline :*—Sume (*conjunctions*) synd gehátene *inclinativae*, þæt is on Englisc áhyldendlice, Ælfc. Gr. Z. 265, 1.

**á-hiltan;** *p.* te *To make to halt, to cripple a person's movement :*—Þá on hyge þóhtan þæt hí áhyltan mé and mínne gang *qui cogitaverunt supplantare gressus meos*, Ps. Th. 139, 5. [Cf. *O. H. Ger.* ar-helzit, arlemit *debilitatum.*]

**á-hínan** *to accuse :*—Hine gié áhénas *eum accusatis*, Lk. L. R. 23, 14. Ðeh áhénas *te accusant*, Mk. L. R. 15, 4. v. á-hénan *in Dict.*

**á-hirdan** *to harden :*—Nellen gé eówere heortan áhyrdan, R. Ben. 10, 2. Ðæt yfel hiora unrihtwísnesse hié hæfð ðonne git áhirde (-hierde, Hatt. MS.) *quos malitia suae impietatis exasperat*, Past. 362, 20. [Cf. *O. H. Ger.* ar-hartén *indurare.*] v. á-hyrdan *in Dict.*

**á-hirding,** e ; *f. Hardening :*—Áhyrdincg *induratio*, Scint. 232, 19.

**á-hirstan** *to roast, fry :*—Gáte blædre, áhyrste, sele etan, Lch. ii. 88, 25.

**a-hiscean, -hiðan, -hiðend.** v. á-hyscan, -hýþan, -hýþend.

**á-hládan.** *l.* á-hladan, *and add :*—Áhlæt *exhauriet*, Scint. 199, 16.

**á-hlǽnsian** *to grow* or *make lean,* (1) literal :—Heora nebwlite þurh ðá mycclan sorhge áhlǽnsode, Hml. S. 23, 126. (2) figurative :—Gif mid hungre fæstena leahtras líchaman beóð áhlǽnsude (*macerentur*), Scint. 57, 13.

**á-hleápan.** *Add :*—Þ íren forð áhleóp (*prosiliens*) of þam hylfe, Gr. D. 113, 26. Seó mycelnes þæs stánclifes swá áhleóp (*saltum dedit*) þ hit ná gehrán þæs scræfes hrófe, 213, 28. Ðá áhleóp se líchoma up of ðám wætere, Shrn. 143, 27. [*Goth.* us-hlaupan.]

**á-hléfan** (-léfan?, cf. *Icel.* lófi *palm of the hand*) *to pluck out :*—Þte áhloefa *ut evellas*, Rtl. 55, 20.

**á-hleóþrian ;** *p.* ode *To sound, resound :*—Áhleóðrede (*intonuit*) se heofon, Gr. D. 208, 24. Hit áhleóðrode (*insonuit*) swylce eall seó cyrice wǽre onstyred, 236, 13.

**á-hlinian, -hlinnan.** v. á-lynian, -lynnan.

**á-hlocian** [-locian? cf. á-lúcan?] ; *p.* ode *To dig out :*—Áhloca þ erue *eum* (*oculum*, Mt. R.) 5, 29 (*the late southern version has here aholeke: can hloc- in the older form =holc-?* v. holc, *and* holk *in* N. E. D.). Áhloca þ áteóh of þæt, 18, 9. Áhlocadum, ach(l)ocadum *effossis*, Txts. 59, 721.

**á-hlówan** *to low :*—Áhlówan *reboasse*, Wrt. Voc. ii. 77, 60.

**a-hluttrian.** *l.* á-hlút(t)rian, *and add :*—Áwring þá wyrte þurh cláð and áhlúttra swíþe wel, Lch. ii. 36, 14. Áhlútrod wín *defecatum*, Wrt. Voc. i. 290, 59: ii. 26, 23. Áhlúttrad, 138, 22. Þá áhlútredan *elucubrate* (-am, Ald.), 31, 39. Áhlúttredes hunigteáres *defecati nectaris*, Hpt. Gl. 468, 36. [Cf. *O. H. Ger.* ir-liutertiz silber *purgatum.*] v. next word.

**á-hlýt(t)r(i)an** *to make pure :*—Áhlúttra swíþe wel, Lch. ii. 270, 24. Áhlýttre þá buteran, 308, 28. Seáw wel áhlýtred (-ttred, *v.l.*), i. 214, 19. Þý áhlýtrede *elucubrate*, Wrt. Voc. ii. 87, 15. Ðá áhlýtredan *merulenti*, 79, 75 : 56, 69.

**a-hnescian.** *Substitute :* á-hnescian, -hnexian. I. *to become weak :*—An hwý hit gelang wǽre þ Numentie swá raðe áhnescaden, swá hearde swá lié longe wǽron, Ors. 5, 3 ; S. 222, 15. II. *to make weak, weaken, soften :*—Ðá ánrédnesse his heortan áhnescian (-nescian, *v.l.*) *cordis ejus emollire constantiam*, Bd. 1, 7; Sch. 23, 9. His mód áhnexian þurh wíta, Hml. S. 37, 124.

**á-hnigan.** I. *intrans. To sink, fall down :*—Hí áhnigon *occubuerunt*,

---

An. Ox. 3352. II. *trans.* (1) literal, *to bend down :*—Áhnigenum heáfde, Techm. ii. 121, 19. (2) figurative, *to humble :*—Hine seolfne of dúne áhnág *semet ipsum exinanivit*, Rtl. 21, 20. v. on-hnígan.

**a-hnyscan.** v. á-hyscan.

**a-hogod ;** *adj.* (*ptcpl*) *Solicitous :*—Swýþur áhogod be þǽra manna wísan þonne be his sylfes hǽle *de illorum potius quam de sua salute sollicitus*, Gr. D. 277, 15. Cf. ymb-hoga.

**a-holan, -hold, -holede.** *Dele.*

**á-holian.** *Add :* *to hollow out :*—Þ stánclif hwæthwega áholiað *rupem in modico cavate*, Gr. D. 113, 5. Áholad *anaglifa*, Wrt. Voc. ii. 6, 68. Ágrafene ðde áholede, 4, 55. Áholad *exesum*, 144, 76. Wæs beboden Ezechie': ðæt hé scolde ðone alter habban uppan áholodne *ad Ezechielem in itari fieri fossa praecipitur*, Past. 217, 19.

**á-hón.** *Add :* I. *to hang* (trans.), *suspend :*—Gyf mon þás wyrte on mannes swyran áhéhð (-héð, *v.l.*), Lch. i. 280, 10. Man áhéhð (-héð, *v.l.*) mid searwum mycle sweras, Gr. D. 270, 4. Hé áhéng þ dúst on ǽnne post, Hml. S. 26, 226, 233. Hé sǽde þ hé on ðá lyfte áhénge (ic wæs áhónde, *v.l.*) þ mynster *dixit se cellulam in aera suspendisse*, Gr. D. 30, 17. Sié áwegen oððe áhangen *expendatur*, Wrt. Voc. ii. 30, 33. II. *to hang on a gallows or cross :*—Ðonne hine man on gealgan áhéhð *quando appensus fuerit in patibulo*, Deut. 21, 22. Áhéngon *infurcarunt*, áhongen *infurcatus*, Wrt. Voc. ii. 49, 40, 41. Hé hié ðǽr áhón hét, Chr. 897; P. 91, 17. His stíward hét se cyng on róde áhón, 1096; P. 232, 23. Hí hiene hét áhón *in crucem suspendit*, Ors. 4, 4; S. 164, 33. Sié áhóen *crucifigatur*, Mt. L. 27, 22 : Lk. L. 23, 23. [*Goth.* us-háhan.]

**á-hopian** *to trust in* (tó) :—Þonne se móna wexeþ, hé bið gelíc þǽm gódum men þe áhopað (á hopað ?) tó þǽm écean leóhte, Bl. H. 17, 23. v. hopian.

**á-hrécan** *to clear out, spit out :*—Sele þ geagl tó swillanne þ hé þý sél mæge þ yfel út áhrécean, Lch. ii. 24, 13.

**á-hrǽscian** (?) *to shake off :*—Áhrǽsc(s)od þ of áscacen ic eom *excussus sum*, Ps. L. 108, 13. v. á-hrisian, *and cf. Dan.* ruske *to shake.*

**á-hreddan.** *Add :* I. *to rescue, &c. :*—Hié þá herehýþa áhreddon, Chr. 894; P. 85, 20: 917; P. 98, 7. Gener *vel* árede erue, i. *defende*, Wrt. Voc. ii. 144, 6. II. *to rescue from,* (1) with gen. :—Áhrede mé hefiges níðes feónda mínra, Ps. Th. 58, 1. (2) with dat. :—Mennen þe þú áhreddest wælclonimum, Gen. 2127. Hé hí wolcne bewreáh, wrǽðum áhredde *expandit nubem in protectionem eorum*, Ps. Th. 104, 34. Þone wérgan heáp wrǽðum áhreddan, Cri. 16. (3) with prep. (a) æt :—Drihten hý áhret æt þám synfullum *Dominus eruet eos a peccatoribus*, Ps. Th. 36, 39. Gyf hit man æt ðeófes handa áhret, Ll. Th. i. 226, 4. Hí áhreddon þ cild æt þám wulfe, Hml. S. 30, 185. Áhrede míne sáwle æt þám unrihtan wísan *eripe animam meam ab impio*, Ps. Th. 16, 12. Tó læt þ hé þá sáuwle æt þon wiþerweardan áhredde, Bl. H. 43, 24. Hé wæs áhred æt his feóndum, Ps. Th. 4, arg. Þ hé hí áhredde fram deófles anwealde, Hml. Th. i. 334, 7. Hé hí fram frecednyssum áhredde, 574, 20. Þæt wé beón áhredde fram forwyrde, ii. 266, 12. (γ) of :—Betere wé áhreddon ús sylfe of ðissere burhware gehlýde, Hml. S. 23, 202. Ðeófles gewealde áhreddan, Wlfst. 22, 3. Tó áhreddenne Loth of þám fýre, Scrd. 22, 40. (δ) on :—Woruldfeoh ðæs ic on sceotendum áhredde, Gen. 2144. (ε) wiþ (*dat. acc.*) *to save from, protect against :*—Swá God his folc áhredde wið þone cyning . . . swá hé árett his gecorenan wið þone deófol, Hml. Th. ii. 200, 10–14. Godes módor hí áhredde wið heora feóndum, Chr. 994; P. 129, 4. Hé áhredde þ folc wiþ þone hunger, Gen. pref. Thw. 3, 23. Hí his mágas áhredde wið heora réðnysse, Hml. S. 25, 409. Þ hé ús áhredde wið þone feónd, 26, 20. Ic wylle áhreddan míne eowde wið eów, Hml. Th. i. 242, 13. Wið þysne cyning tó áhreddenne (-dd-, *v.l.*) úre leóde, Hml. S. 26, 23. Hí áhredde wurdon wið Pharao, Hml. Th. ii. 266, 20. [*O. H. Ger.* ar-retten *eruere, liberare, defendere.*]

**á-hredding,** e ; *f. Saving, rescue, deliverance :*—Heó bæd God þ hé hire gewissode his folce tó áhreddinge on þǽre frecednysse, Hml. A. 111, 281. Ús tó fullan fultume and tó áhreddingge gyf ús neód byð, Cht. E. 230, 11.

**a-hreófod.** *Substitute :* á-hreófsian ; *p.* ode *To become leprous :*—Hé áhreófode and tóbærst mid wundum, Shrn. 132, 8.

**á-hreósan.** *Add :* I. *to fall down :*—Áhreósað ealle steorran nyðer, Wlfst. 137, 10. On áhriásð *incidat* (= -et), Kent. Gl. 830. Wit unc ondrédon hwonne wit sceoldon seallan of þám olfende and of áhreósan, Hml. A. 202, 228. II. *to be destroyed :*—Áhriósð *corruet*, Kent. Gl. 386 : *concidet*, 1048. v. á-hríran.

**á-hrepian.** *Add :* *to treat :*—Ic hæbbe áhrepod be þám tíðþénungum þe man dón sceall, Btwk. 220, 40.

**á-hréran.** *Add :*—Ðæt áhrérede mód *commotae mentes*, Past. 297, 16.

**á-hríran ;** *p.* de *To cause to fall down, to destroy :*—Áhrýrþ *diruit*, Germ. 389, 87. Áhrý[rde?] *destruxit*, An. Ox. 2263. Áhrýred *dirutus*, i. *erutus*, Wrt. Voc. ii. 140, 57. Up álocene *vel* áhrérede *eruta*, i. *distructa*, 144, 11. v. á-hreósan.

**á-hrisian ;** *p.* ede. I. *to shake :*—Genim bétan, ádelf and áhrise, Lch. ii. 230, 6. Áhyrsod *impulsus*, Ps. L. 117, 13. II. *to excite :*

*arouse :—*Âhrisige hē ôðre tô geornfulnesse gôdra weorca, Past. 461, 16. [*Goth.* us-hrisjan.] v. â-hrysian *in Dict.*

**â-hrydred, -hrysian, âhsian, âht, ahtian.** v. â-rydran, -hrisian, âscian, â-wiht, eahtian.

**â-hûðan.** *In the passage read :* Fŷnd ahudan.

**â-hwâ.** *Add :* â-hwæt *anything :—*Gif âhwæt tô icenne byþ *si quid addendum fuerit,* Angl. xiii. 371, 81 : Germ. 393, 170.

**â-hwǽnan.** *Add : to grieve, afflict :—*Wâ þâm þe wudewan and steópcild oftost âhwǽned (*ut essent viduae praeda eorum, et pupillos diriperent,* Isaiah 10, 2), Wlfst. 48, 2. Þæt hî wydewan and steópcile tô oft ne âhwǽnan, ac georne hŷ gladian, 309, 3 : Ll. Th. i. 326, 25. For ðisum wearð Theodosius þearle âhwǽned, and hē his lîc for ðǽre sârignysesse mid wâcon reáfe scrŷdde . . . God hine nâ lengc âhwǽnede habban nolde, Hml. S. 23, 393, 402. Utan frêfrian âhwǽnede and hyrtan ormôde, Wlfst. 119, 8. [Þe lavedies to me meneþ And wel sore me ahweneþ, O. and N. 1564.]

**â-hwǽnne.** *Substitute :* **â-hwænne** (-hwonne, -hwanne). I. interrogative, *whenever :—*Drihten, âhwænne (*quando*) beheahtst ðû?, Ps. Spl. 34, 20. II. *at any time :—*Ðî lǽs âhwænne gegrîpe *ne quando rapiat,* Ps. Spl. 7, 2. Âhwanne, Ps. L. 2, 12. Gif hit âhwænne (*aliquando*) swâ gelimpð, Ll. Th. ii. 188, 25 : 190, 7 : R. Ben. 99, 21 : 103, 2. Ǽhwænne, R. Ben. I. 2, 1 : 103, 4. III. *at every time, at all times :—*Þâ môdigan unrihtlîce dydon âhwonne (*usquequaque*), Ps. L. 118, 51, 43.

**â-hwǽr.** *l.* -hwer, -wer, *and add :* â-wâr, ô-wer. I. local :—Âhwǽr *usquam,* Germ. 394, 251. Âhwǽr ût of mynstre etan, R. Ben. 79, 17. Âhwǽr elles, Ps. Th. 102, 15. Âhwǽr (ôwer, *v. l.*) elles bûton on helle, Gr. D. 303, 5. Gif hî mihton þone here âhwǽr ûtene betræppen, Chr. 992; P. 127, 13. Ealle his sceattas þe hî mihton âhwâr þær geâxian, 1064; P. 190, 18. Þâ wîsuste menn hé âwâr gecneôw, 995; P. 128, 21. Âhwer *usquam, i. ad ullum locum,* An. Ox. 3780. Ealle þe hé âwer (-hwer, *v. l.*) mêtte, Ors. 114, 3. Nis âhwǽr (âwer, ôwer, *v. ll. nequaquam*) gemêted on bôcum, Bd. 1, 27; Sch. 68, 10. Âwer on neáweste, Bt. 16, 1; F. 50, 3 : El. 33. Ôwer londes, Cri. 1002 : 199. Ôwer feor oððe neáh, B. 2870. Ôwer geféran, Jul. 331. Ôwhwǽr (hôwer, *v. l.*), Bd. 4, 23; S. 595, 3. II. *in any case, in any way, in any point :—*Ne gē âhwǽr (-hwâr, *v. l.*) ne beón, þæs ðe gé bêtan magan, gewitan ǽniges morðres, Wlfst. 40, 6. Deófol gelǽrð þæt ungesǽlig man ne ârige âhwâr, 53, 23 : 166, 33. Heó nele âbûgan fram hyre Drihtne âhwâr, Hml. A. 28, 100 : Hml. S. 16, 93. Gif hé ðé âhwâr geyfelode, þæt ðû scealt forgifan, Hml. Th. i. 54, 25. Âwâr, ii. 100, 33 : i. 484, 7 : 500, 5. Ne gesacu ôhwǽr ecghete eóweð, B. 1737. v. nâ-hwǽr.

**â-hwǽrgen, -hwǽrne.** v. â-hwergen.

**â-hwæper.** *Add :* âþer, ôwþer, âuþer, âþor *Either.* I. *pronoun :—*Ne can þára idesa ôwðer beorna neáwest, Gen. 2466. Ǽr þára folca âþer fluge, Ors. 4, 10; S. 198, 25. Sieððan hé hit mid ðâra âwðrum (âþrum, Cott. MSS.) cŷð, Past. 157, 21. Gif hé auðer ðissa forlǽt, 87, 14. Gif hé ðǽra þénunga âþere dêð, Wlfst. 34, 7. Sē ðe âðor forlǽt, Hml. S. 25, 68. I a. *where the alternatives referred to by the pronoun are given in apposition :—*Gif hé aðor dyde, oðþe ofergimde, oðþe forgeat, oðþe tôbræc ǽnig þing, R. Ben. 71, 15. II. *conjunction :—*þæt nân crîsten man ne môte his ǽlmessan âhwaþer behâtan oððe tô bringan, Wlfst. 303, 14. Be menn þe sealmas singð âwðer oþþe for hine sylfne oððe for ôðerne mann, Ps. Th. 30, arg. Âuðer oððe . . . oððe, Past. 281, 12. Hé forbŷt ǽlcum men aðor tô bycganne oððe tô syllanne, Wlfst. 200, 3. Aðor oþþe on bôclande oþþe on folclande, Ll. Th. i. 160, 11. Aþer oðþe on kycenan, oþþe on hêderne, oþþe on bæcerne, oþþe on wyrtûne, oðþe on ǽnigum ôðerum cræfte, R. Ben. 71, 17. Aþer oððe ettan oððe erian, Ors. 1, 1; S. 18, 25. v. aðor *in Dict.*

**â-hwanon; adv.** I. *from anywhere :—*Ic nolde þ ðû wêndest þ him âhwonon ûtane côme his gôdnes *I would not have you suppose that his goodness came to him from anywhere without,* Bt. 34, 3; F. 136, 23. Ôhwonan, Rä. 36, 8. II. *in any direction :—*Mid þ ic on þâm wealle nǽnige duru ne ǽnig eágþyrl âhwonon (ôhwanon, onhwonan, *v. ll.*) on ǽnige healfe geseón mihte *cum in muro nullam januam vel fenestram alicubi conspicerem,* Bd. 5, 12; Sch. 623, 11. v. nâ-hwanon.

**â-hweorfan.** *Add :—*Se cyning and se biscop sceoldan beón folca hyrdas and hî from eallum unrihtwîsum âhweorfan, Bl. H. 45, 26.

**â-hwerfan.** v. â-hwirfan.

**â-hwergen, -hwǽrne, -wyrn, ô-wern; adv. Anywhere; in any case :—**Gif âhwǽrne (? -hwænne, *v. l.*) wer oððe wîf þás þing âbrecað *si aliquando vir vel mulier has res violaverit,* Ll. Th. ii. 190, 7. Ne hŷrde ic guman âwyrn ǽnigne ǽr ǽfre bringan sêlran lâre, Men. 101. Nǽnige swaþe his ôwwern ætŷwdon *nullum ejus uspiam vestigium apparuerit,* Bd. 4, 23; Sch. 473, 9. v. nâ-hwǽrn, ǽg-wern, *and* â-hwǽrn *in Dict.*

**â-hwettan.** *Add :—*Is mē swîþe earfeðe hiera môd tô âhwettanne *necessarium acumen elicere non possum,* Ors. 4, 13; S. 212, 30. His

---

môd wæs mid þǽm bismre âl.wet *hac contumelia quasi cote ad virtutem usus est,* 6, 30; S. 280, 14.

**â-hwider.** *Substitute : Anywhither, to any place, in any direction :—*Ðâ þâ on ŷtinge âhwyder farað *hi qui in via diriguntur,* R. Ben. 91, 8. Þeah þû wille âhwyder, faran þû ne miht, Hml. S. 23 b, 620. Þæt nân crîsten man ne môte his broces bôte sêcean âhwider bûton tô Crîste sylfum, Wlfst. 303, 15.

**ahwilc ?.** The gloss cited is :—*Terribilis* ahwilc *vel* egeslic *vel* dryslic.

**â-hwilfan;** *p.* ce *To roll over, overturn :—*Seó sǽ slôh tôgædere and âhwylfde Pharaones cratu, Ex. 14, 27. Hî fæsthealde weorcstân upp âhwylfdon, Hml. S. 23, 424. Âlege I âhwelf hig *depone eos,* Ps. L. 58, 12. Hé sǽde swâ oft swâ þæt scip wære ofðûne âl.wylfed, þ hē sǽte ofer þǽre bytman *quoties carabo a superiori þarte deorsum verso ipse carinae ejus supersederat,* Gr. D. 347, 23. [Cf. He hwelfde at þare sepulchre dure enne grete ston, Misc. 51, 513. *Icel.* hvelfa *to turn upside down ; impr. to capsize.* Cf. also O. H. Ger. hwalbôn *volubilis esse.*] v. be-hwylfan; hwealf.

**â-hwirfan;** *p.* de *To turn away, turn over :—*Hié ôðre of hira gedwolan âhwierfað (*convertant*), Past. 403, 22. Âhwersdon *evertere,* Wrt. Voc. ii. 144, 28. Ne âhwyrf þû þîne onsŷne from mē, Bl. H. 83, 11. Hû lange wilt þû âhwyrfan (*avertes*) þînne andwlitan fram mē, Ps. Th. 12, 1. Gedwolan fram Godes eágum âhwyrfan (-hwerfan, -hweorfan, *v. ll.*) *errores a Dei oculis abscondere,* Bd. 5, 13; Sch. 642, 11. Âhwerfede *versa vice,* An. Ox. 592. Âhwerfde *deruta, i. eversa,* Wrt. Voc. ii. 139, 6. v. â-hwerfan, -hwyrfan *in Dict.*

**â-hwistlian;** *p.* ode *To hiss, speak indistinctly :—*Seó tunge âwistlað þe ǽr I ǽfde getinge sprǽce and gerâde, Wlfst. 147, 31.

**â-hwonan, -hwonne, -hwylfan, -hwyrfan.** v. â-hwanon, -hwænne, -hwilfan, -hwirfan : **â-hwylc**, *dele.*

**â-hŷdan.** *Add :—*Hé âhŷded (*abscondit*) mē in getelde his, Ps. Srt. 26, 5. Se Hǽlend âhŷdde hine, Jn. L. 8, 59 : Gr. D. 141, 30 : 194, 14. Hé hine sylfne âhŷdde wið þâ Langbeardan, 293, 15. Âhŷd þâ ælmessan under þæs þearfan sceáte, Wlfst. 257, 18. Sē ðe hine âhŷde from hǽto his, Ps. Srt. 18, 7. Hé wolde hine sylfne âhŷdan fram þâm scuccum, Gr. D. 289, 17. God, ðû hafast monigne hâligne ofer eorðan âhŷded, Shrn. 141, 2.

**â-hyldan, -hyldendlic, -hyltan.** v. â-hildan, -hildendlic, -hiltan.

**â-hŷran, -hŷrian** (q. v. *in Dict.*) *to hire :—*Ic âhŷre *conduco,* Wrt. Voc. i. 20, 61. Âhêran *conducere,* ii. 73, 2 : 17, 49. Se ceorl sē þe hæfð ôðres geoht âhŷrod (-ed, *v. l.*), Ll. Th. i. 140, 8.

**â-hyrdan, -hyrding, -hŷrian, -hyrstan.** v. â-hirdan, -hirding, -hŷran, -hirstan.

**â-hyscan** *to mock :—*Fŷnd ûre âhnyscton (-hyscton? : *subsannaverunt*) ûs, Ps. Spl. 79, 7. Cf. on-hyscan.

**â-hyspan;** *p.* te *To reproach :—*Âhyspton (*exprobrabant*) mē mine feónd, Ps. L. 101, 9.

**â-hŷðan, -hîðan.** *Add :—*Wildeór âhîðende wes hié *ferus depastus est eam,* Ps. Srt. 79, 14.

**â-hŷþend** (-hîþ-), *es; m. A destroyer, ravager :—*Hergiend and âhîðend *grassator,* Wrt. Voc. ii. 40, 38.

**â-îdan;** *p.* de *To dispossess* (? cf. eád), *to turn out, expel :—*Âîdeþ *eliminat,* Wrt. Voc. ii. 29, 23. Âŷdan *eliminare,* An. Ox. 8, 108. Ût âîdan *eliminare,* 7, 109: Angl. xv. 208, 12. [The rarity of the verb (the three last instances are glosses in different MSS. of the same passage in Aldhelm), and the fact that *eliminare* is elsewhere glossed by â-nîdan, â-ŷtan (q. v.) may suggest a doubt as to the genuineness of â-îdan.]

**â-îd(e)l(i)an.** *Add :* I. *to become vain,* (1) *to lose force, worth, &c. :—*Âîdliaþ *exolescunt,* Wrt. Voc. ii. 32, 50. Þe lǽs þe hē innar âîdlode (*inanesceret*), Gr. D. 59, 27. Âŷdlian *tabescere,* Ps. L. 38, 12 þâ geseah se ârleása âîdlian his smeágunge, Hml. S. 4, 399. (2) *to vanish :—*Se âwyrigeda gâst efne swâ smîc beforan his ansŷne âîdlode Guth. 34, 4. II. *to make vain, deprive of force, worth, &c. :—*Âîdlie *obunco,* An. Ox. 18 b, 66. Þæt hē þâ þe mid ofermêttum hŷ sylfe for âht teliaþ âîdele, R. Ben. 191, 3. Ðî hé com þæt hē âîdlige ealle ðâ hǽðengyld, Hml. Th. i. 456, 14. Ðisne geleáfan woldon gedwolmen âîdlian and of Crîstes geladunge mid ealle âdwǽscan, Hml. S 23, 361. Âîdlian *frustrari,* Wrt. Voc. ii. 151, 35. Âîdlad *frusta,* 92 24: *cassata,* 93, 58. Wæs âîdlad *cassaretur,* 20, 37. Hî rǽddon þæ ealle his gesetnyssa âŷdlode wǽron *they decided that all his decree should be annulled,* Hml. Th. i. 60, 5. Ðâ ðe beôð âîdlode on ofer sprǽce *multiloquio vacantes,* Past. 271, 10. Sume synd on dyrnlicar gâlscipe inne âîdlode, Ll. Th. ii. 322, 14. II a. *to deprive o* (*with gen.*) :—Bedǽled and âîdlad ælces gôdes weorces *a bonis actibu funditus exors vacat,* Past. 67, 10. Hé bið innan âîdlad ðǽre ryht wîsnesse *intus veritate vacuatur,* 111, 9.

**â-ildan;** *p.* de *To put off, delay :—*Ic hit âyldan ne mæg *eam declinar nequeo,* Gr. D. 21, 22.

**ain, aina** (*l.* â mâ), *dele.*

**â-irnan** (-yrnan, q. v. *in Dict.*). *Add :—*Âurnenum, âmetenum *emenso i. numerato,* An. Ox. 947 : Wrt. Voc. ii. 29, 34. v. â-rinnan.

**â-îþan;** *p.* de *To lay waste, destroy, devastate :—*Âîðan *abolere,* Wrt

Voc. ii. 5, 7. Hē wolde for wera synnum eall áǽdan þæt on eorðan wæs, Gen. 1280. Áiéðende *exterminans*, Wrt. Voc. ii. 84, 53 : 31, 27. Áíþende *demolitus*, 25, 41. [*O. H. Ger.* ar-óden *vastare, devastare*.]

ál, es ; *n. A fire* :—Ál *incendia*, An. Ox. 4470. Ála *pyrarum*, 4389. v. on-ál ; ál-fæt, -geweorc ; ǽlan.

á-ládian. *Add* :—Áládiendre *apologetico*, Wrt. Voc. ii. 2, 45.

á-lǽccan ; *p.* -lǽhte *To get hold of, catch* :—Se kyng álehte hine betwux his earmes, Chr. 1123 ; P. 251, 9.

á-lǽdan. *Add* : I. *to lead off, carry off* :—Ic of álǽde *abduco*, Ælfc. Gr. Z. 275, 10. (1) of captivity :—Cirus cyning hī ásende eft ongeán tō ludéa lande, þanon þe hī álǽdde wǽron, Ælfc. T. Grn. 8, 37. (2) of removal from difficulty, danger :—Loth God álǽdde þanon, 4, 18 : Bl. H. 67, 19. Hē álǽdde (*eduxit*) mē fram þám pytte yrmða, Ps. Th. 39, 1. Úp álǽdde *explicuit*, Wrt. Voc. ii. 145, 14. Þá þe mid him æðleón mihton hē út álǽdde, Chr. 1072 ; P. 208, 27. Álǽd mē út of þyssum bendum, Bl. H. 87, 33. Gang on ðá ceastre and álǽde hine of ðǽre ceastre, 237, 3. (3) of guidance :—þ dysig ðá earman men gedwelaþ and álǽt of þám rihtan wege, Bt. 32, 3 ; F. 118, 7. Oþ þæt hine mon on gewitte álǽde *until he be brought to exercise his reason* (cf. *to bring a person to reason* : on gewitte gebringan, Hml. Th. i. 458, 11), Gn. Ex. 48. Tō ware álǽd (is) *ad tutelam dirigitur*, An. Ox. 3335. II. *to bear off, carry off* an object :—Swá hwæt swá hī (*two ravens*) mihton gegrípan, hī þæt woldon onweg álǽdan, Guth. 50, 24. Ealle þá scipu þe hié álǽdan ne mehton hié tōbrǽcon, Chr. 896 ; P. 89, 20. Wæs Scē Óswaldes líchoma álǽded of Beardanigge, 906 ; P. 95, 24. His bán wǽron eft álǽded þanon in ðá ceastre Constantinopili, Shrn. 138, 31. Álǽd *translatus, portatus*, An. Ox. 5, 35. [*O. H. Ger.* ar-leiten.]

á-lǽdness. v. onweg-álǽdness.

á-lǽnan ; *p.* de (not ede). *Add* : (1) *to lend, grant the temporary use of* :—Be ðám Engliscum gewritum ðe ic dē álǽnde, Hml. A. 1, 4. Hē wæs úre munuc, wē willað hine habban for þan þe wē hine álǽndon ǽr, Hml. S. 31, 1447. Ðone ylcan (*St. Martin*) þe hī ǽr álǽndon tō ðám biscopdóme of heora burhscíre, Hml. Th. ii. 518, 21. Hē nǽfde þæt feoh him tō álǽnenne, 178, 3. (2) of a lord's grant to a vassal :—Ælcon híredmen his onrid þe hē álǽned hæfde, Cht. Crw. 23, 25. (2 a) of God's grant to men :—Beó se ríca gemyndig þæt hē sceal ealra ðǽra góda þe him God álǽnde ágyldan gesceád, Hml. Th. i. 274, 2 : ii. 102, 1. (3) of land, *to lease* :—Hī ænlǽnað Ælfrēde .XL. hída landes æfter ðǽre lǽna ðe Túnbryht ǽr álǽnde his yldran, C. D. v. 162, 24. Ðæt land eóde eft intō ðǽre stówe ðe hit út álǽned wæs, iv. 267, 6.

á-lǽtan. *Add* : I. of intentional movement :—Hē unwǽrlíce nyðer álǽt (*submittens*) on þ wæter þ fæt, Gr. D. 114, 28. Hī hine on ánre wilian álǽton ofer ðone weall, Hml. Th. i. 388, 9. Hwí wolde þīn hláford þē álǽtan tō mē (*let thee come to me*), Hml. S. 36, 65. II. of deprivation, loss :—Gē hit álǽtað (*you will lose it*), þonne gē lǽst wēnað, Wlfst. 46, 10. Hē þá handa álýse oþþe hig álǽte, Ll. Th. i. 404, 10. III. of abandonment :—Wið ðan ðe se cing ðá onspǽce álǽte *provided the king would abandon the charge*, Cht. Th. 540, 22. IV. of grant, delivery :—Heofonan ríce wæs álǽten þisum gebróðrum for heora nette, Hml. Th. i. 580, 22. IV a. fig. :—Hē wolde hine tō lífe álǽtan (cf. *deliver to death*), ii. 252, 8. V. of release :—Álǽten cempa *emeritus*, Wrt. Voc. i. 18, 15. [*Goth.* us-lētan : *O. Sax.* á-látan : *O. H. Ger.* ar-lázan.] v. next two words.

á-lǽtan *deserta*. v. ǽ-lǽtan.

á-lǽtnes. *Add* : I. loss. v. á-lǽtan, II :—Gif him þince þ his earm sý of áslegen, þ byþ his góda álǽtnes, Lch. iii. 170, 17. II. remission :—Synna álǽtnes, Nar. 47, 12.

Alamanne ; *pl. The Alamanni* :—Gratianus gefeaht wið Alomonne (Alamanne, *v. l.*) þǽm folce and heora fela M ofslóg (*plus quam triginta millia Alamannorum interfecta*), Ors. 6, 34 ; S. 290, 16.

alan. *Dele* II. In the passage there given the glosser seems to have thought that *parent* might be from either of the two verbs *parĕre, parēre*, and has glossed it by *foedað* ꝺ *alað* ꝺ *adéauæð* : the Rushworth gloss has only *foedað* ꝺ *aleð*.

a-langian. l. á langian, and see langian.

á-láþian ; *p.* ode. I. *to be hateful, odious*. v. láþ, I :—Dýpe stencum áláþode *fundus fetoribus horrebat*, An. Ox. 4771 : 2, 383 : 8, 294. II. *to be hostile to, to loathe, hate*. v. láþ, II :—Unclænnessa áláþode (*mens*) *squalores horrescit*, 4456. III. *to make hostile, make threatening* :—Yrmþa gequis áláþode (beótode) *calamitates conspiratio intentabat*, 4958.

á-latian ; *p.* ode *To grow sluggish, dull* :—Álatode *uilesceret*, An. Ox. 7, 131. Cf. the gloss to the same word : *Uilesceret* i. *tardaret vel* latode, Angl. xv. 208, 13.

albe, an ; *f. An alb* :—Albe *alba*, Wrt. Voc. i. 81, 41. Mid gyrdle alban *cingulo albe*, Angl. xiii. 406, 589. Mid alban gescrýdd, 426, 878. Mid alban (*albis*) gescrýdde, 408, 618. Alpan, 403, 543.

ald-. v. eald-.

á-lecgan. *Add* : I. *to lay down, deposit* :—Hié hié selfe álecgeað on eorðan, Past. 157, 9. Hē þá mancessas álegde in his ágene cyste, Gr. D.

---

63, 27. Swá hwæt swá þǽr man on álegde, Bl. H. 127, 1. Men feówer stánas on þǽre ilcan stówe álegdon, 189, 15. Ðeós geofu on heora heortan álegd wes, 137, 4. Álédne *delatum* (*in sarcophago*), Wrt. Voc. ii. 26, 50. II. of the placing of material in construction, *to lay* :—Hēt Maxentius oferbricgian ðá eá mid scipum and syððan ðylian swá swá óðre bricge . . . hē ne gemunde ðǽre leásan bricge þe hē álecgan hēt, Hml. Th. ii. 304, 21-27. III. *to lay aside, put off, away* what is worn or carried :—Ðá álēde ic mínne kynegyrlan, Nar. 18, 1. Heó álegde þ pælmtwig þe heó ǽr onfēng . . . and heó eác álegde hire hrægl, Bl. H. 139, 4-6. Hē his beard álēde, Hml. S. 6, 228. Álege þīne woruldlican gegyrlan, 33, 81. Deóplíc dǽdbót bið þ lǽwede man his wǽpna álecgan, Ll. Th. ii. 280, 17. IV. *to lay aside, discontinue* a practice :—þæt hī ne sceolon for manna ðwyrnysse heora bodunge álecgan, Hml. Th. ii. 232, 15. IV. fig. *to put down*, (1) of persons, *to cast down, overthrow, deprive of power or life* :—Se cǽsere álēde þone Godes feónd, Hml. S. 22, 60. Tóbrýt ðás hǽðenan and álege hī mid swurdum, 25, 273. Álege hig *depone eos*, Ps. Spl. 58, 12. Þeáh ðe þú þone líchaman álecge on deáðe, Hml. S. 36, 382. Álýfed tō álecgenne hís fýnd, 25, 684. Álegd wǽron ðá haldendo *exterriti sunt custodes*, Mt. L. 28, 4. (2) of things, *to suppress, abolish, put an end to* :—Álēde Eádward cyng þ heregyld, Chr. 1052 ; P. 173, 18. Swylc geréfa swylc mǽdsceat nime and óðres ryht þurh þ álecge, Ll. Th. i. 222, 6. Þæt hig his leásunga álecgon, Ælfc. T. Grn. 3, 45. Unþeáwas álecgean, Chr. 1067 ; P. 201, 30. Godes lof, geleáfan, wuldor álecgan, Ælfc. T. Grn. 11, 24 : Hml. S. 16, 200 : 25, 660. Hē ne mihte þ gafol álecgan þe heó gelǽstan sceolde *he could not remit the tax that she had to pay*, 3, 181. Áléded *sedato*, An. Ox. 50, 46. [*Goth.* us-lagjan : *O. H. Ger.* ar-leggen.] v. á-licgan.

a-lefan *to become weak. Substitute* : á-léfian, -léwian ; *p.* ode, ede ; *p.* od, ed *To make weak, sick, to maim, lame, cripple*. I. of living creatures :—Antecríst álēuað and geuntrumað ðá hálan, Hml. Th. i. 4, 22. Hē ealle ðá gehǽlde þe ðá drýmen álēfedon, ii. 472, 16. Ðóð þæt hī ne magon úre tungan gehremman ne ús álēfian, 488, 6. Gif hwá álēfed wǽre oððe limleás, i. 236, 29. þæt þæt álēfed wæs, þæt ic gehǽle, 242, 16. Álēfed *paralysed*, ii. 546, 30. Þæt wanhál wæs and álēwed (álýfed, *v. l.*) *quod debile erat*, R. Ben. 51, 16. Þ wē fæston swá þ úre líchama álēfed ne wurðe *so that our body be not injured*, Hml. S. 13, 104. Wearð his cneów mid heardum geswelle álēfed, Hml. Th. ii. 134, 24. Ðá þe ðurh þæs dracan blǽde álēfode wǽron, 294, 31. Þreó hund geára ylpas libbað, gif hī álēfede ne beóð, Hml. S. 25, 570. Wundru hē worhte on álēfedum mannum, Hml. A. 10, 255. Gegadera ðearfan and álēfede (*pauperes ac debiles, Lk.* 14, 21), Hml. Th. ii. 374, 27. Ðá álēfedan men (*men who had been practised on by wizards*), 486, 19. II. of an inanimate object :—Wǽron þǽre hlǽddre stapas álēfede on ǽr, Hml. S. 31, 602. v. lef.

a-lefan. v. á-lífan.

á-léfedness, e ; *f. Infirmity, lameness, crippledness* :—Wæs sum earm ceorl egeslíce gehoferod and ðearle getíged. . . . Ðám weard geswutelod þ hē sceolde gefeccan æt Swýðunes byrgene his líchaman hǽle and þǽre álēfednysse (*the cure of his crippledness*), Hml. S. 21, 99.

á-léfian. v. a-lefan : á-léned. v. á-linnan : á-lénian, *dele, and see* á-línian.

á-leógan. *Add* : I. *to fail to perform* a promise, pledge, &c., *to be false to* one's promise :—Hī hit eall álugon, ge wed ge áþas, Chr. 947 ; P. 112, 25. Gif hwá geniéd sié tō hláfordsearwe . . . þ is ryhtre tō áleóganne þonne tō gelǽstanne. Gif hē þissa ǽnig áléoge, Ll. Th. i. 60, 3-7. Gif hē þissa ǽnig áléoge, 332, 23. Ðæt man Gode beháte ne áléoge man ǽfre, Wlfst. 71, 6. Deófol wyle gedón þæt wē áleógan þæt þæt wē behétan, 38, 6. I a. with dat. of person to whom promise has been given :—Gif hē álíhð Gode þ hē sylfwylles behǽt, Hml. S. 26, 271. Hī áleógaþ him má þonne hī him gelǽstan *they break more promises to them than they perform*, Bt. 26, 1 ; F. 90, 18. Ðú ús gehéte gebedo and wæccan, and þú hit ús áluge, Wlfst. 240, 17. þæt wē áleógan Gode þæt þæt wē behéton, 301, 8. Gif gē him ne álugen iówra wedd and eówre áþas *si fidem foederis servavissent*, Ors. 3, 8 ; Swt. 122, 13. II. *to do falsely* :—Be ðám ðe hiora gewitnessa beforan bisc áleógað. Gif hwá beforan biscepe his gewitnesse and his wed áléoge, Ll. Th. i. 110, 9-12. Ne gehát ðú nán þing tuwa ; hwæt sceal hit ðē eft gehǽten, búton hit wǽre ǽr álogen (*unless the first time the promise was made falsely*), Prov. K. 21. III. *to lie to* a person (dat.), *deceive* :—Áleáh ꝺ álogen is unrihtwísnys heom *mentita est iniquitas sibi*, Ps. L. 26, 12. Ðú hæfst álogen þám Hálgan Gáste, Hml. Th. i. 316, 27. Álogen *fallitur*, An. Ox. 1734. [*O. H. Ger.* ar-liugan *frustrare*.]

á-león ; *p.* -láh *To lend* :—Álíh *accommoda*, Rtl. 41, 23. v. on-león.

á-leonian, -leopian. v. á-linian, -líþian.

á-leóran, *p.* de *To go away* :—Út áleórde *emigrabit*, Ps. Srt. 51, 7.

aler. *Add* :—Aler (-aer) *alnus*, Txts. 39, 116. Be ðǽre alra ofesce, C. D. iii. 393, 11.

aler-bróc, es ; *m. A brook with alders on the banks* :—In ælrbróc, and seoððan swá alrbróc lígeð, C. D. iii. 393, 17.

**aler-holt.** Add:--Alerholt *alneta*, Wrt. Voc. ii. 99, 68. Alorholt, 6, 45 : i. 285, 41.

**aler-sceaga,** an ; *m. An alder-copse:*--On arlscagan, of alrscagan, C. D. B. iii. 667, 18.

**á-lesan.** Add: *to pick out, select, excerpt:*--þá cwidas þe þú of þisum bócum álése, Shrn. 200, 15. Þá cwidas þe Ælfréd kining álæs of þére béc, 204, 29. Hé geceás and álæs (*eligens*) calle þá óðre lác and on sundron áléde, and þá þe Characterius sende hé áwearp, Gr. D. 230, 24. Monig óþer tácn mæg on þére béc gemétan swá hwylc swá hié rǽdeð, þe wé þás of álǽson (-lésan, *v. l.*) de quo haec excerpsimus, Bd. 4, 10 ; Sch. 400, 21. [O. Sax. á-lesan : O. H. Ger. ar-lesan *eligere*.]

**a-ledran.** *l.* á-léþran, *and* v. á-líþran : **a-létlic,** *dele:* **álette** v. hálettan : á-léwed. v. á-léñan.

**alexandrinisc ;** *adj. Of Alexandria :*--Sum Alexandrinesca *quidam Alexandrinus*, Mt. p. 10, 13. Alexandriniscæ biscob *Alexandriae episcopus*, Mk. p. 2, 2.

**alexandrisc ;** *adj. Of Alexandria :*--Alexandresca cirica *Alexandrinae ecclesiae*, Mt. p. 8, 10.

**ál-fæt, es ;** *n. A vessel that may be placed on the fire* (v. ál), *a cooking-vessel:*--Gif hit (*the ordeal*) wæter sý . . . sí þ álfæt ísen oþþe æren, leáden oþþe lǽmen, Ll. Th. i. 226, 15. Aalfatu *cocula : omnia vasa coquendi sic dicuntur*, Wrt. Voc. ii. 135, 39. v. ól-fæt *in Dict.*

**ál-geweorc.** Add:--Aalgewerc, álgiuu[eo]rc, -giuerc *ign(i)arium*, Txts. 69, 1040. Álgeweorc, Wt. i. 284, 22 : ii. 45, 35.

**á-libban,** -lifian, -leofian. Add: *to have life, not be inanimate:*--Wiðsac ðú þíne godas þe synd stǽnene, and gebide þé tó þínum Scyppende þe sóðlíce áleofað, Hml. S. 8, 110. (2) *to live, not to die of an injury:*--Gif wulf orf tóslíte and hit for þan deád beó . . . gif hit ályfað, Ll. Th. ii. 212, 27. Gif lama weorðe forlǽten, and hé æfter þám þreó niht álibbe, i. 172, 17. (3) *to live a life, pass one's days:*--Hé oserférde and álifde his selfes ylde mid andgite *aetatem suam intellectu transibat*, Gr. D. 338, 23.

**á-licgan.** Add: *to be at an end, come to an end, be brought low:*--Mín wynn álæg *there was an end to my joy*, Ps. Th. 119, 5. Nó hira þrym álæg, An. 3. Ful oft þér wíg ne álæg *rarely did war cease*, Vid. 119. Symbel ne álégon *feasts never failed*, Reim. 5. Álicgan heonan forð þá unlaga *henceforth let there be an end of all bad laws*, Ll. Th. i. 312, 13. Þæt on his dagum sceolde rihtwísnes and wísdóm beón swá swíðe álegen (*be brought so low*), Ps. Th. 11, arg. Þǽr weard heora anweald and heora dóm álegen, Ors. 3, 1 ; S. 96, 34. Wyrþ oft gódes monnes lof álegen (*coarctabitur*), Bt. 18, 3 ; F. 64, 31. [O. H. Ger. ar-liggen *deficere*.] v. á-lecgan.

**á-lífan** (-lýfan, q. v. *in Dict.*). **I.** *to permit:*--Álýfde *concessit*, i. *permisit, concedit*, Wrt. Voc. ii. 136, 9. (1) *to permit* a person (*dat.*) *to do something:*--Þæt hié him ælce geáre gesealden swá fela talentena swá hié him þonne áliéfden *that they should pay them each year as many talents as they might be pleased to fix for them to pay when the time came*, Ors. 4, 10 ; S. 202, 23. Tó álýfenne *permittendi, consentiendi*, Hpt. Gl. 486, 6. Álýfed *licitus*, Ælfc. Gr. Z. 264, 9-10. On álýfedum tíman *oportuno tempore*, Angl. xiii. 373, 117. (2) *to permit* a person *to have or enjoy, to grant:*--Ðonne him God ðone first áléfð *expectanti Domino*, Past. 403, 26. Ic waes beden from þaem bisceope þæti ic him áléfde alle néðbáde tuégra sceopa, C. D. i. 114, 10. Álýfde, 179. Ús þín ríce álýf, Hy. 7, 28. Ðæt mé unne God écean dreámes, líf álýfe, 4, 33. Noldan him þá londleóde þæt fæsten áliéfan, Ors. 5, 11 ; S. 238, 7. Hé wuda and wætres nyttað, þonne him bið wíc álýfed, Gn. Ex. 110. Þæs áléfdan indulte, Wrt. Voc. ii. 84, 6. (3) *to hand over* a person :--Ne álýf þú mé on fyrenfulra fǽcne geðancas *ne tradas me peccatori*, Ps. Th. 139, 8. **II.** *to be permitted:*--Álýft (is áléfed, L. R.) restedagum wel tó dónne hweþer ðe yfele *licet sabbatis bene facere an male?*, Mk. 3, 4. Hwæþer álýft (*licet*) ænegum men his wíf forlǽtan, 10, 2. Þá heofonlican gerýno þá nánegum men ne álýfað tó secganne, Guth. 86, 6. Álýfende *licens*, Ælfc. Gr. Z. 264, 11. [Goth. us-laubjan : O. H. Ger. ar-lauben *permittere*.] v. un-álífed.

**á-lífedlic.** v. á-lýfedlic *in Dict., and add:* v. un-álífedlic.

**á-lífedlíce ;** *adv. Lawfully, allowably :*--Álýfedlíce *licenter*, Ælfc. Gr. Z. 264, 11. Lícað him ðæt hié ðæt unáliéfede dóð áliéfedlíce *libet ut licenter illicita faciant*, Past. 145, 11. Þæt hé his ǽwe healde, and álýfedlíce for folces eácan bearn gestreóne, Hml. Th. ii. 94, 20. Álífedlícur *expedius*, Wrt. Voc. ii. 32, 42.

**á-lífedness,** -lífendlic, -líce. v. un-álífedness, -lífendlic, -líce.

**á-lífian.** v. á-libban.

**á-líhtan** *to alight.* Add: **I.** *to lighten, relieve, alleviate:*--Álíht *leuigat*, Scint. 11, 2. Hé manega þe unrihtlíce fram yflum démum genyþrode wǽron álýhte, Hml. S. 30, 8. Álíhte, gehýþegode *expedita, libera, leuigata*, Germ. 391, 33. **II.** *to alight, descend:*--Zachéus swiðslíce of ðam treówe álíhte, Hml. Th. i. 580, 35.

**á-líman ;** *p. de.* **I.** *to come forth brilliantly:*--Up álýman *emersisse* (the passage is : Illaesa venustate virgines e thermis emersisse leguntur, Ald. 68, 9), Hpt. Gl. 516, 52. (In An. Ox. 4784 the form is *álýmdan*.) In two other glosses *emergere* is rendered by *ámýlan* (? á-lýman):--Up

ámýlde *emergeret* (si Homerus ab inferis emergeret, Ald. 33, 30), An. Ox. 2427. Up ámýlþ *emergat*, Wrt. Voc. ii. 143, 27.) **II.** *to bring forth, shew forth:*--Dægrima rynas up álýmþ *aurora cursus provehit*, Hy. Srt. 16, 33. v. líman.

**á-linian,** -linnan. v. á-lynian, -lynnan.

**á-lísan** (-lýsan, q. v. *in Dict.*). **I.** *to detach, remove:*--Næs wlóh of brægle álýsed ne loc of heáfde, An. 1474. **II.** *to redeem a fault:*--Ðá synna hié mid hira ælmessan áliésað *peccata eleemosynis redimunt*, Past. 327, 14. Ðæt hé heora senna álýsan mæge, Bl. H. 43, 14. **III.** *to release, rescue, redeem, free :*--Ðú álést *liberabis*, Kent. Gl. 883. Áliéset *eximet*, Wrt. Voc. ii. 107, 46. Álýst *evellet*, i. *eruet*, 144, 31. Þá áliésde Eádweard hine mid .xl. pundum, Chr. 918 : P. 98, 15. **III a.** *to release* from something, (1) with a case :--Álýs mé feóndum, Ps. Th. 70, 3. Leahtra álýsed, Dóm. 77. (2) with prep. (*æt, fram, of*) :--Mildheortnyss álýst fram ðám écan deáðe, Hml. Th. ii. 102, 3. Þæt hine God álýsde ǽgðer ge æt his mettrumnesse ge æt his feóndum, Ps. Th. 27, arg. God hine álýsde æt his feóndum . . . hé sceolde álýsed beón ǽgðer ge fram Iudéum ge of ðý deáðe, 29, arg. Se cyng eall Normandig æt him mid feó álísde, Chr. 1096 ; P. 232, 32. Ðæt lond æt him álésan, Ors. 1, 10 ; S. 44, 9. Bióð álésede of *liberabuntur*, Kent. Gl. 355. **III b.** *to make free* in respect to a person or thing (*wiþ, for*):--Nú álýse ic mé sylfne wið God *I will free myself in relation to God*, Hml. S. 17, 75. For leahtrum áles þíne gescęft, Hy. 8, 33. [Goth. us-lausjan: O. Sax. á-lósian : O. H. Ger. ar-lósen.]

**á-lísedness, e ;** *f. Salvation, redemption:*--Þæt mannes álýsednys wurde gebodod, Scrd. 21, 39. Ánes engles geærnung ne genihtsumode tó álýsednysse ealles mancynnes, 17, 37. Álésedness *saluationum*, Ps. L. 27, 8. v. á-lýsednys *in Dict.*

**á-lísend, es ;** *m. A saviour, redeemer:*--Oð þæt se Álýsend com þe ðone ealdan deófol gewylde, Hml. Th. i. 94, 7. Se Áliésend monna cynnes, Past. 129, 17. Álýsend, Bl. H. 65, 30. Middangeardes Álýsend, 87, 9. v. á-lýsend *in Dict.*

**á-lísendlic.** v. un-álísendlic, *and* á-lýsendlic *in Dict.*

**á-lísendness, e ;** *f. Redemption, absolution :*--Þ lác for álýsendnesse his sáwle *pro absolutione ejus animae sacrificium*, Gr. D. 347, 14.

**alisian.** *Dele.*

**á-lísness, e ;** *f.* **I.** *redemption, release* by payment or otherwise :--Þ weorð his álýsnesse (-lés-, *v. l.*) *pretium suae redemtionis*, Bd. 4, 22 ; Sch. 461, 1. On his álýsnesse æt his feóndum, Ps. Th. 31, arg. His álýsnesse of his earfoðum, 22, arg. **II.** as a religious term, *redemption :*--Þére tíde neáléhte úre álésnesse, Bl. H. 77, 14. Tó écre álýsnesse, Bd. 4, 22 ; Sch. 462, 12. Heora álýsnesse of heora scyldum æfter fulluhte, Ps. Th. 22, arg. v. á-lýsness *in Dict.*

**á-líþian,** -leoþian (q. v. *in Dict.*) ; ode To *dismember, separate, take away :*--Ic áhredde oððe út áliðige *eruo*, Ælfc. Gr. Z. 167, 14. Þ unmǽte stánclif onweg áleoðian (-liðian, *v. l.*) *ingens illud saxum levare*, Gr. D. 213, 24. Seó hálige sáwl wæs onlýsed and áleoðod of þám líchaman *sancta illa anima carne soluta est*, 285, 26. Álýsed and geleoðod (álýðod, *v. l.*), 282, 17. Út álocene, up áliþode *euulsum*, i. *abscisum*, An. Ox. 2903.

**á-líþran** *to lather:*--Dó þære ealdre sápan cucler fulne . . . on niht álýþre, Lch. ii. 76, 13. v. á-léþran *in Dict.*

**al(1).** v. eal(1).

**á-loccian.** Add:--Hét hé sum his folc feohtan on þæt fæsten þæt hié mid þǽm þæt folc út áloccoden, Ors. 5, 3 ; S. 222, 3.

**á-locian.** v. á-hlocian.

**alor, alr.** v. aler.

**altar.** Add: , *alter, altare:*--Ðá colu ðæs alteres, Past. 51, 1. Altares, R. Ben. 103, 14. Tó þínum hálgan altare, Ps. Th. 5, 7. Ymb þínne alter, 25, 6. Uppan þone altare, R. Ben. 101, 7, 8. Altras *altaria*, Bl. Gl. [O. H. Ger., O. Sax. altári (-eri) ; *m.*: O. Frs. altáre (-er) ; *m.*: Icel. altari ; *n.* (and *m.*). *From Latin* altare.] v. heáh-altar.

**á-lúcan.** Add:--Up álúcþ *eradicat, extirpat*, Wrt. Voc. ii. 144, 19. Út álúcþ *evellit*, i. *eradicat*, 32. Hé út álúceð (*evellet*) of grýne fót mínne, Ps. Spl. 24, 16 : 51, 5. Hit álúcð þæs mannes mód, Wlfst. 242, 9. Þý lés álúcæ (*eradicetis*) þone hwǽte, Mt. R. 13, 29. Áweg álúcan *discludere*, Wrt. Voc. ii. 27, 51. Of ðám munte álúcan þ hreósonde clif *ruituram rupem ex monte evellere*, Gr. D. 213, 16. Biþ út álocan *excluditur*, i. *ejicitur, extra ponitur*, Wrt. Voc. ii. 146, 23. Út álocena *evellantur*, 32, 71. Up álocene *eruta*, 144, 10. Út álocene *euulsum*, An. Ox. 2903. Út álocen sý *evellatur* (*foenum*), Ps. Spl. 128, 5. Næs þ cedertreów upp álocen (*evulsum*), Gr. D. 191, 8. Upp álocenum þornum *spinis erutis*, 103, 17. Hé wæs álocen (*evulsus est*) of ðére wununge his líchoman, 326, 14. Se wyrtruma of his heortan biþ álocen and onweg ánumen, Bl. H. 55, 9. [O. H. Ger. ar-lúchan *evellere*.]

**á-lútan.** Add: *to bend,* (1) absolute :--Se hálga áleát, Hml. Th. ii. 510, 18. Álotenum heáfde, Hml. S. 35, 303. Ðá nýtenu hé lét gán álotene, Hml. Th. i. 276, 5. (2) where direction is given :--Hé tó ðám cyninge áleát, Lch. ii. 426, 34. Seó cwén áleát tó þæs cyninges fótum, Hml. A. 100, 295 : 110, 247. Hé áleát wið þæs Hælendes, Hml. Th. i. 120, 12 : Num. 22, 31. Hí ealle tó him áluton, Guth. 16, 9. Hé nolde álútan ne lyffettan þám Amane, Hml. A. 97, 194. Hí ealle

ālotene beóð tō þære eorðan weard, Hml. S. 1, 55. Forþ ālotene *cernui*, Hy. S. 5, 29. (3) where purpose is given :—Se þēn tō his bletsunge mid ðām fæte ālcát, Hml. Th. ii. 158, 19. (4) *to make an inclination* with :—Seó leó āleát mid þām heáfde, Hml. S. 30, 417.

**á-lýfan**, &c. *to permit.* v. ā-lífan, &c. : ā-lýfed *weakened.* v. ā-léfan.

**á-lynian**, -lynnan. *Add* :—Ioseph Crīstes līchaman of rōde ālinode, Btwk. 218, 12. Hī þæs þeófes fōt āhlinode (*solvit*) of þām hege þe hē ǣr fæste on clifode, Gr. D. 25, 10. Hī ðæs scræfes locstān ūt ālynedon, Hml. S. 23, 426. Āhlinnað ł āhebbað gatu *attollite portas*, Ps. L. 23, 9. Eall hit wyrð gebunden, būtan gē þā bendas ālynian, Wlfst. 178, 5. Ne mæg nān man of mīnre handa ūt ālinian (*eruere*), Deut. 32, 39. Ūt ālyniende *eiciens*, An. Ox. 4424. Sī dū ūt ālened *eruere*, Kent. Gl. 127. Sī āleoned *euulsam*, An. Ox. 3464. Ūt ālynedum *extirpatis*, 1134 (*and see note*). [*Cf. Goth.* us-luneins *redemptio*.]

**á-lýsan**, &c. v. ā-lísan, &c. : **a-lystan** *l.* ā lystan : **ā-lýþran**. v. ā-līþran.

**ám.** *Add* :—Aam *cautere; cautere, ferrum id est* haam, Txts. 47, 352. *Cautere* i. aam, Wrt. Voc. ii. 129, 78. Hē sceal habban ... amb (= ām ?), Angl. ix. 263, 13.

**á-mællud.** Cf. ǣ-melle.

**á-mǣran; p.** de *To make famous, celebrate* :—Ongan se hlīsa swā myccles mægenes feor and wīde beón āmǣred *coepit tantae virtutis fama longe lateque crebrescere*, Gr. D. 206, 24. [*Goth.* us-mērjan *diffamare*.]

**á-mǣran**, -mǣrian; **p.** de *To exterminate* :—Ne wæs ǣnig cyninga þ mā hiora landa ūt (ūte *v.l.*) āmǣrde and tō gewealde underþeódde *nemo in regibus plures eorum terras, exterminatis indigenis, tributarias fecit*, Bd. 1, 34; Sch. 104, 3. Þā lond bigengan ūt āmǣran (-ian, *v.l.*) *indigenas exterminare*, 4, 16; Sch. 425, 4. Hī hæfdon ūt āmǣrde þā bīgengan, 1, 16; Sch. 44, 10. Cf. ge-mǣre *terminus*.

**a-mǣst.** v. ā-mǣstan.

**á-mǣstan; p.** -mǣste (*not* -mǣstede). *Add* :—Āmest *impinguat*, Kent. Gl. 538. Þū āmǣstest ł þū gefǣtnodest *impinguasti*, Ps. L. 22, 5. Hió biþ āmǣst *impinguabitur*, Past. 381, 3. Āmǣsted *saginatum*, Wrt. Voc. ii. 73, 59. Fuglas oððe āmǣste fugelas *altilia*, 9, 1.

**á-mang.** *Add* :—Sē ðe his calic āgeóte āmang his mæssan (*inter missam suam*), Ll. Th. ii. 218, 17. Gelamp hit āmang þām (*meanwhile*), Hml. S. 23, 136. Āmang þissan, Chr. 1066; P. 197, 32.

**á-mánsod.** *Add* :—Ne ǣnig man gemānan wið āmānsode (-mānsumode, *v.l.*) hæbbe, Wlfst. 71, 3. [*O. E. Hom., Kath., O. and N., R. Glouc.* amansed : *Piers P.* mansed.] v. ā-mānsung.

**á-mánsumian.** *Dele bracket and add* : **I.** *to accurse* :—Heó nolde āgan þæs wælhreówan hærereáf ac āmānsumode, Hml. A. 115, 426. Sī þeós buruh āmānsumod *sit civitas haec anathema*, Jos. 6, 17. **II.** *as an ecclesiastical term, to excommunicate* :—Gif gē ne dōð, ic eów āmānsumige, Hml. Th. ii. 176, 13. Nānum ne sý ālýfed þæt hē ǣnigne brōðra ne āmānsumige, būtan þām ānum þe se abbod þæs anweald sealde, R. Ben. 129, 15. Geþeódrǣdene niman wið þone āmānsumedan, 50, 12. Hiene tō āmānsumianne, Ors. 6, 30; S. 284, 1. [*O. H. Ger.* ar-meinsamōn *excommunicare*.]

**á-mánsumung.** *Dele bracket and add* :—Þone cwyde þære āmānsumunge (-mæn-, *v. l.*), Gr. D. 152, 11. Þære āmānsumunge gemet, R. Ben. 48, 15. Hē āmǣnsumenge (-mānsumunge, *v. l.*) underhnīge, 48, 10. v. next word.

**á-mánsung**, e; **f.** *Excommunication* :—Gif hwylc brōðor for āmānsunge (*si excommunicatus*) gebētan nelle, R. Ben. 52, 5. Beó hē on āmānsumunge (-mānsunge, *v. l.*) *excommunicetur*, 79, 19. [Þe ilke amanzinge . . . 'Guoþ ye acorsede,' Ayenb. 189, 25.]

**á-marian** *to confound.* [*Cf.* (?) *Icel.* merja; *pp.* mariðr *to crush.*] v. next word.

**á-masian; p.** ode *To amaze, stupefy, confound* :—þū āmasost þeóda *obstupefacies gentes*, Cant. Ab. 12. Stent hē heortleás and earh, āmasod and āmarod, mihtleás, āfǣred *pavor percutiet stupidis cunctorum corda querelis*, Dōm. L. 125 : Wlfst. 137, 23.

**ambeht; m.** *Add* :—Weard, ombeht unforht, B. 287. Ic eom Hrōðgāres ār and ombiht, 336. Ðe ambeht ł se ðegn *discipulus ille*, Jn. L. 21, 23. Ðone ilca ambeh[t], 20. Ðāra ambihta *discipulorum*, 20, 30. Ambehtum *discipulis*, 21, 14. Abraham sprǣc tō his ombihtum : 'Rincas mīne,' Gen. 2879. Onbehtum, Cri. 370. [*According to Festus Lat.* ambactus *is of Celtic origin* : 'Ambactus apud Ennium lingua gallica servus appellatur.']

**ambeht; n.** *Dele*: Lat. ambitus, *and add* :—Ic þīn eom scealc ombehte *ego servus tuus*, Ps. Th. 115, 6. In cummenum foreonfoeng dearfscipes in gesendena embichta ðeodōmes is *in venientibus praesumtio temeritatis, in missis obsequium servitutis est*, Mt. p. 8, 2. v. embeht (-iht), ymbeaht.

**ambehtan; p.** te: embeht(i)an (q.v. *in Dict.*); **p.** ode *To minister, serve* :—Sē ðe embehtað, -bihtað(-as) *qui ministrat*, Lk. L. R. 22, 27. Embehtes (-bihtas, R.) ł gehēres *ministrat*, Jn. L. 12, 26. Martha embihtade *ministrabat*, 2. Ne embigto wē ðe *non ministravimus tibi*, Mt. L. 25, 44. Manige cræftigan and eác mā ōþra weorcmanna þe þām onbyhtan (-behtum, *v.l.*) and hýrdon *artifices multos ac plures subministrantes operarios*, Gr. D. 251, 14. Embehtadon *ministrabant*, Lk. L. 8, 3.

---

Embihta mē *ministra mihi*, 17, 8. Cuom hē tō embehtana (*ministrare*) ōðrum, Mt. L. 20, 28. Embehtande *ministrantem*, Jn. p. 6, 16. [*Goth.* andbahtjan : *O. H. Ger.* ambahten *ministrare*.] v. ge-ambehtan.

**ambehtere** (emb-), es; **m.** *A servant* :—Embehtere *ministrator*, Lk. L. 22, 26. [*O. H. Ger.* ambahtāri *minister*.]

**ambeht-híra** (-hēra), an; **m.** *A vassal* :—Eom ic cáðmōd his ombiehthēra, þeów geþyldig, Gū. 571. v. hýra.

**ambeht-hús.** *Add* :—Ambihthūs *officina*, Angl. xiii. 441, 1087. [*O. H. Ger.* ambaht-hūs *officina*.]

**ambeht-mǣcg.** *Add* :—Þīnne āgenne ombihtmǣcg *servum tuum*, Ps. Th. 143, 11.

**ambeht-mann.** *Add* :—Ambehtmonn *minister*, Mt. L. 20, 26. Embehtmonn (-biht-, R.), Mk. L. 10, 43. Ðæs embehtmonnes *ministrantis*, Lk. p. 7, 1. Ðæm embehtmenn (-biht-, R.), Lk. 4, 20. Æmbehtmenn *discipuli*, Jn. L. 20, 25. Ðā embehtmenn *ministri*, Mk. L. R. 14, 65. Hē sǣnde his ambihtmæn (an-, *v. l.*) *suos apparitores misit*, Gr. D. 238, 21. [*O. Sax. O. H. Ger.* ambaht-man.]

**ambeht-ness**, e; **f.** *Service* :—Embihtnisse hē gefe Gode *obsequium se praestare Deo*, Jn. R. 16, 2.

**ambeht-scealc.** *Add* :—Ealle his āgene onbyhtscealcas *omnes servi Domini*, Ps. Th. 133, 1. Ābeúd þeódcyning þegnum sīnum, ombihtscealcum, Gen. 1870.

**ambeht-þegn.** *Add* :—Hine wunade mid ān ombehtþegn, Gū. 973: 1119. Hē sprǣc tō his ombehtþegne, tō his treówum gesīðe, 1268 : 1172. Hē sealde his sweord ombihtþegne, B. 673. Byrlas, ombehtþegnas, An. 1536.

**amber; m. f. n.** *A vessel; a measure. Add* :—Ambaer, ember, omber *situla*, Txts. 96, 923. Ambaer, ombar, amber *urna*, 106, 1076. Amber *bodonicula* (v. stoppa), Wrt. Voc. i. 288, 3 : *amphora*, ii. 73, 62 : 9, 3. Þæs wīnes sý ān ambur (-er, *v.l.*) full, Lch. i. 136, 5. Dō tō wōse amber fulne, ii. 106, 16. Gesamna tū ambru hrýþra micgean and amber fulne holenrinda, Lch. ii. 332, 15. Ambras *cados*, Wrt. Voc. ii. 102, 41 : 13, 8: *lag(uo)enas*, 53, 37. [Add to cognate forms : 'Perhaps originally an adaptation of Lat. *amphora*, assimilated to a Teut. form and meaning,' N. E. D.] v. tīn-ambre; embren.

**ambiht** (-yht). v. ambeht: **ambern.** v. embren.

**am-byr.** *l.* am-byre. *Dele down to 'equal,' and add* cf. byre.

**á-meallian; p.** ode *To become insipid, lose savour* :—Āmealaþ (a t *erased between* l *and* aþ) *euanuerit* (sal, Mt. 5, 13), An. Ox. 61, 4 (see the note). Āmeallud *exinanita* (*faex*), Ps. Spl. C. 74, 8. Cf. ā-mǣllad.

**á-mearcian.** *Add* : **I.** *to give the form or limits of, write out, to describe, define* :—Þā Homērus on hys bōcum āmearcode *Homer gives these particulars in his books*, Lch. i. 168, 17. Wē wyllað þās þing preóstum āmearkian, Angl. viii. 304, 37. Nū wylle wē heom hēr āmearkian eall gewiss ymbe his ryne, 328, 14. Yfen hēr æfter ys āmearcod *the symbol for the hyphen is given afterwards*, 333, 30. Þǣra mōnða naman synd hēr āmearcode, 8. **II.** *to mark out, distinguish by a mark* :—Ælc þǣra stæpa þe wē gestæppað, ealle hī beóð āmētte and āmearcode mid gildenum stafum on heofenum, Wlfst. 302, 28. **III.** *to mark, give a distinguishing form to, denote* :—Tyn hīw habbað þā bōceras mid þām hig tōdǣlað and āmearkiað þ°ra accentas, Angl. viii. 333, 22. Yfen ys þus āmearcod, 31. **III a.** *to mark by a name, to denominate* :—Synt þā feówer tīman āmearcod lengten, sumor, hærfest, and winter, 299, 23. **IV.** *to mark out for an end, to design, destine, assign* :—Mid eallum þām þingum on circulum þe þā þeódwitan þǣrtō āmearcodon, 321, 41. Stōw gecwēme gebrōþrum sī āmearcud (*designetur*), Angl. xiii. 397, 461. Syndan wē nū eft þider āmearcode tō þām gefeán neorxna wanges, Wlfst. 252, 14.

**amel.** *Add* :—Amelas *amulas*, Wrt. Voc. ii. 6, 14.

**á-melcan; pp.** -molcen *To milk* :—Nim gāte meoluc, þonne hió furþum āmolcen sié, Lch. ii. 188, 12. Nīwan āmolcene, 202, 16. [*O. H. Ger.* ar-melchan.]

**á-meldian.** **I.** *to make known* what is secret, *to reveal, disclose* :—Gemyne ðū, mucgwyrt, hwæt ðū āmeldodest, Lch. iii. 30, 28. Ic bidde þē þæt ðū uncre sprǣce on mīnum līfe nānum ne āmeldige, Hml. Th. ii. 146, 36. Se apostol his gesihðe mannum āmeldian ne mōste, 332, 26. Heó ne mōste nā hire cynn āmeldian, Hml. A. 95, 92. Hī (*the seven sleepers*) wurdon ðā (*after their waking*) āmeldode þām burhwarum, Hml. Th. ii. 426, 5. **II.** *to make known* what one desires to conceal, *to expose, disclose* :—Hē āmeldode heora mānlice geþōhtas, Hml. A. 76, 75. Hē him sylf his gylt āmeldian nolde, R. Ben. 72, 2. Weard Melantia ofsceamod, wēnde þ heó wolde hyre weorð āmeldian, Hml. S. 2, 179. Hit weard þurh þā āmeldad þe hē geþōht hæfde þæt hine tō þære dǣde fylstan sceolde *quae res per ministros prodita*, Ors. 4, 5; S. 166, 29. **III.** *to give information that leads to discovery or detection,* (1) *about persons, to denounce, betray, inform against* :—Sume āmeldodon heora crīstenan māgas, Hml. Th. ii. 542, 22. Wē nellað þē āmeldian, Hml. S. 23, 591. Hē hine nolde āmeldian ðām ēhterum, 19, 37. Ūs ne gebyrað

tó ameldigenne ðā scyldigan, Hml. Th. ii. 492, 3. Hē wearð āmeldod fram his āgenum fæder, 500, 6. Hē wearð āmeldod (the lot fell upon him), Jos. 7, 18. Heó wolde geneálǽcan on wærlicum hīwe, þ heó ne wurde āmeldod, Hml. S. 2, 53. Se bróðor þe giltig āmeldod bið ðām abbode þurh óðerne man and nó þurh hine selfne, R. Ben. 71, 13. Wurdon āmeldode seofon hālige men, Hml. S. 23, 119. (2) about things :—Ǽnig þāra þe þ dyrne orf āmeldað any one that gives information about stolen cattle, Ll. Th. i. 276, 33. Heó hyt āmeldode and þus cwæð : 'Hyt is belocen on mȳnre bedcofan,' Hml. A. 189, 241. Scealt þū þīnes unþances þone hord āmeldian, þe þū sylfwilles ǽr noldest cȳðan, Hml. S. 23, 716.

**ā-meltan**; pp. -molten To melt (intrans.) :—þā āmoltenan wecgas, Hml. S. 5, 234.

**ā-merian**. Add :—Hē āmeraþ conflagrat, conburet, concremat, Wrt. Voc. ii. 133, 16 : excudit, Germ. 396, 192. þū āmeredest ūs on fȳres fandunge, R. Ben. 27, 15. Āmearedes, Ps. Srt. 16, 3. Āmere examina, judica vel proba, Wülck. Gl. 230, 9. Hine sylfne symle āmeriende se semper examinans, Gr. D. 107, 14. Beón āmerede and geclǽnsode of synnum, Wlfst. 95, 22. Āmerode, 96, 6. Womma gehwylces geclǽnsod, āmered, El. 1312. Mānes āmerede, Ph. 633.

**ā-metan**. Add : I. to measure (lit. or fig.) :—Ðū ām[et]st adpendes, Wrt. Voc. ii. 6, 21. Āmet metitur, An. Ox. 20. Hē āmæt eorðan mensus est terram, Cant. Ab. 6. Gif gē āgiémeleásiað ðæt gē āmeten eów selfe hwelce gē sién dum vosmetipsos metiri negligitis, Past. 53, 13. Āmetenum emenso, An. Ox. 947. Syndon tredre burge weallum twelf mīla āmetene up tó þǣm heán cnolle, Bl. H. 197, 23. Syndon betwyh þām twām mynstrum þreóttȳne mila āmetenra (-metene, v. l.), Bd. 4, 23 : Sch. 480, 14. Āmetenra demetarum, Wrt. Voc. ii. 28, 18. II. to mete out justice, &c. :—Eów bið āmeten swā swā gē āmǣton, Hml. Th. ii. 322, 4. [Goth. us-mitan : O. H. Ger. ar-mezan emetiri.] v. uu-āmeten.

a-**metan** to paint. l. ā-mētan, and add :—Wæs ðǣr ān myrige dūn mid wyrtum āmét (mons laetus, uariis herbarum floribus depictis, Bd. 1, 7), Hml. S. 19, 108. Seó heofon is mid steorrum āmétt (-mēt, v. l.), Lch. iii. 232, 21 : Angl. viii. 310, 1. Hī beóð āmétte and āmearcode mid gildenum stafum, Wlfst. 302, 27.

**ā-metendlic**; adj. Measurable, limited, brief :—Āmetendlīce ðū āsettest dagas mīne mensurabiles posuisti dies meos; thou hast made my days as an handbreadth, A. V., Ps. L. 38, 6. v. next word.

**ā-metendlíce**; adv. Within measurable limits, compendiously, briefly :—Āmetendlícor compendiosius, Wrt. Voc. ii. 132, 60. v. preceding word.

**ā-metsian**; p. ode To provide food for :—Man him āmetsode, Chr. 1006; P. 137, 27 note.

**ā-midlod** unbridled :—Āmīdludes effrenate, Wrt. Voc. ii. 142, 61.

**amigdal**, es; m. An almond :—Mid amigdales ele, Lch. i. 104, 22 : 132, 9. Syle him etan amigdalas, iii. 134, 23. [Nutes amgdeles, Gen. and Ex. 3840. From Lat. Gk.]

**ā-miltan**; p. te To melt (trans.) :—Lǽt ūs āmyltan þā sylfrenan godas, Hml. S. 5, 233. Drincan āmylte buteran, Lch. ii. 106, 3 : 268, 12. v. un-āmelt.

**ā-mirran**. Add to ā-myrran : I. to lead astray, misguide, (1) in a physical sense :—Se yrðlincg āmyrð his furuh (will not make a straight furrow) gif hē lócað tó lange underbæc, Hml. S. 16, 180. (2) in a moral sense :—Irre oft āmirreð monnes mód, ðæt hē ne mæg ðæt riht tócnāwan, Prov. K. 28. 'Hwī āmyrdest ðū mīnne bróðor mid þīnum drȳcræfte?' 'Ne āmyrde ic hine, ac ic hine āwende fram hǽðenum gylde tó Gode,' Hml. Th. i. 468, 12–15. Hē mid his drȳcræfte ðæs folces geleáfan āmyrde, 372, 3. þā diófla hī āmirdon, þ hié ne cūþan angitan þæt hit Godes wracu wæs, Ors. 4, 4; S. 162, 26. Hī mid heora gedwolsprǽce eall folc āmyrdon, Hml. S. 23, 309. Hwī woldest ðū āmyrran mīn sunu, and tó Crīste gewēman?, 4, 198. Swā hwā swā nylle þ hine ǽnig mon oððe ǽnig ðing mage āmerran quisquis cupit nullis deviis falli, Bt. 35, 1; F. 154, 21. II. to hinder, prevent right course or action, (1) of persons :—Wyrð ðæt mód āmierred from ðǣre incundan hreówe mens ab intentione poenitentiae suspenditur, Past. 415, 36. (2) of acts :—Hē ongan mid hlūdum stefnum tóslītan and āmyrran (interrumpere) þāra bróðra sangas, Gr. D. 324, 23. III. to injure, mar :—Gif oxa wiel oððe wylne āmyrð si servum ancillamque invaserit, Ex. 21, 32. Mē hæfde þiós unrótnes āmerredne þ ic hit hæfde mid ealle forgiten ob injuriae dolorem nuper oblita, Bt. 36, 1; F. 172, 3. IV. to waste, use to no purpose :—Ic nāt hū nyt ic þā hwīle beó þe ic þās word sprece, būtan ðæt ic mīn geswinc āmirre, Ors. 4, 13; S. 212, 27. On ðǣre gǽlinge þe hē þā hwīle āmirð (-mierred, v. l.), Past. 38, 1. V. to destroy, lay waste :—Ðū ofslihst ūs and āmyrst, Hml. S. 25, 131. Gif hwilc wīf hyre cild āmyrð (perdiderit) innan hire, Ll. Th. ii. 182, 24. Hī ǽhta forspillað and eard āmirrað, Wlfst. 312, 1. Se deófol ealle his (Job's) ǽhta āmyrde, Hml. Th. i. 472, 29. Wīngeardas hī fordydon and burga forbærndon and swīðe þet land āmyrdon, Chr. 1073; P. 209, 9. Ne āmyr þū sāwle mīne ne perdas animam meam, Ps. L. 25, 9 : Hml. S. 35, 148. þ folc tó āmierrenne ad populandos agros, Ors. 3, 10; S. 138, 8. Him wæs lǽd tó āmyrrenne his āgenne folgað, Chr. 1048; P. 173,

13. VI. to lose :—Hwīlon befeóll ān sīðe of ðām snǽde intó ānum seáðe. Benedictus wolde gefréfrian ðone wyrhtan ðe þæt tól āmyrde (cf. forlorenum þām īrene ferro perdito, Gr. D. 114, 2 : both passages describe the same incident), Hml. Th. ii. 162, 12. [O. Sax. ā-merrian.]

**a-molsnian**. Substitute: **ā-molsnian** to decay, lose power :—Him (the old man) āmolsniað and ādimmiað þā eágan, Wlfst. 147, 29.

**amer**(?), es; n. A kind of corn, spelt. In C. D. iii. 118, 20 occurs omer-lond, and in iv. 157, 34 omer-mād. Could the omer in either case correspond to O. H. Ger. amer far, ador ? : cf. O. H. Ger. place-names Amar-lant, -feld. Or is the form to be identified with amore? (v. next word).

**amore**. v. omer in Dict.

**ampella**. Substitute: ampelle (-olle, -ulle), an; f. A bottle, flask :—Cróges oþþe ampellan lenticule, Wrt. Voc. ii. 94, 26 : 52, 62. Se wer bletsode ele on ānum fæte þe wē anpolan hātaþ . . . on ānre glæsenan anpollan, Hml. S. 31, 1120, 1124. Gedó on ǽrene ampullan, Lch. ii. 30, 8. Anpullan lecythum, i. ampullam oleariam, An. Ox. 3876. Ampellan oððe elefæt, Wrt. Voc. ii. 52, 76. Gē sceolon habban þreó ampullan gearuwe tó þām þrȳm elum, Ll. Th. ii. 390, 6. [From Latin.]

**ampre**. Add : , ompre :—Amprae (-e), omprae varix, Txts. 106, 1073. Ampre cocilus, 55, 595. Ompre, Wrt. Voc. ii. 15, 37. Ompre varix, i. 289, 41 (in a list of plant-names). Ompre, docce rodinaps, 68, 53. Drenc of ompran, Lch. ii. 106, 18 : 108, 1. Tó sealfe . . . ompran neoþowearde þā þe swimme, 52, 18 : 76, 4. Wiþ wōum mūþe genim ompran, 54, 22. Ādelse ompran, 78, 1. Ampron, 116, 12. [O. H. Ger. ampfra acitura : Ger. ampfer sorrel.] v. fen-, sund-ampre.

**ā-mundian**. Add :—þonne mōte wē ābūgan þām heretogan tó his mannrǽdene, þ hē ūs āmundige, Hml. A. 108, 190. Nū bidde ic ðone bisceop ðæt hē āmundige mīne lāse and ðā þing ðe ic hyre lǽfe, C. D. iii. 305, 12.

**ā-mylp**. v. ā-līman.

**ā-myrdrian**. Add : , -myrþr(i)an :—Ǽr hē Beorn āmyrðrode, Chr. 1049; P. 171, 21.

**án**. Add : I. as numeral, one. (1) cardinal, (a) alone, (α) as adj. :—þes ān blinda man getācnode eall mancynn, Hml. Th. i. 154, 10. Hī forþférdon on ānum mónþe, Chr. 888; P. 82, 4. Āne (-um, v. l.) geáre ǽr his deáþe, 46 ; P. 6, 20 : 885 ; P. 78, 22. Āne sīðe (āne sīða, v. l.) semel, Bd. 4, 5 ; Sch. 377, 12. Man singe ān fīftig sealmas, Ll. Th. i. 222, 19. (β) as subst. a single object :—þises ānes gewilnode Maria, Hml. Th. ii. 440, 15. Gif man ānum wōh beóde, bētan hit ealle, Ll. Th. ii. 316, 16. Ealle geþwǣrlǣhton on þām ānum all agreed on the one point, Hml. S. 1, 35. Āne mā once more, An. 492. Ǽne sīþa semel, Ps. Srt. 61, 12. (b) helping to form larger numbers, (α) by addition :—Ān and twēntig uiginti unum, Ǽlfc. Gr. Z. 281, 16. Gemǽne tó ðām ān and twēntigum hīdum, C. D. v. 319, 20. (β) by subtraction :—Ān lǽs twēntig undeuiginti, Ǽlfc. Gr. Z. 287, 6. Hē wæs þā āna wana .XXX. wintra, Chr. 972 ; P. 119, 8. Mid ceastrum ānes wana þrīttigum, Bd. 1, 1 ; Sch. 9, 10. (2) helping to form ordinals :—Se ān and twēnteogoða uicesimus primus, Ǽlfc. Gr. Z. 283, 7. Se ān and hundnigonteóða, R. Ben. 37, 21. þone ān and twēntigoðan dæg, Ex. 12, 18. II. associated with óþer, án, having more or less of an ordinal force, one, the first :—Tuā bebodu, ān is ðæt wē lufigen God, óðer ðæt wē lufien ūre niehstan, Past. 49, 12. Twā ðing, ān is Scyppend, óðer is gesceaft, Hml. Th. i. 276, 8. Hī urnon ān æfter ānum, ii. 32, 7. Fram ānre tȳde tó óðre, Chr. 999 ; P. 133, 7. Mid ii scipum, þām ānan steórde Harold and þām óðran his bróðor, 1046; P. 168, 10. Twēgen englas, ænne æt þām heáfdon and óðerne æt þām fótum, St. A. 40, 11. Gif man ðā āne bóc rǽt on ānes geáres ymbryne and ðā óðre on ðām æftran geáre, Hml. Th. ii. 2, 12. III. distributive :—Hī heom betweónan ān and ān (one by one) hnappodon, Hml. S. 23, 247. Hē geceápade tó þām senatum, tó ānum and tó ānum, Ors. 5, 7; Swt. 228, 17. Nǽht be ānan oððe twām (by ones or twos), ac swā þiclíce þ hit nān mann āteallan ne mihte, Chr. 1095 ; P. 230, 29. IV. as indefinite article :—Hū mon ænne mon scyndan scyle, Past. 455, 1. V. with numerals used adjectively, a partitive ē inflection :—Āne III dagas syndon syððan ic wæs getogen, Bl. H. 243, 35. Nū for ānum xii nihtum, Gr. D. 79, 11. Embe āne feówer dagas oððe fīfe, R. Ben. 96, 9. V a. with feáwa, (1) feáwa used adjectively :—For ānum feáwum geárum, Ǽlfc. Gr. Z. 3, 12. Hē ābād āne feáwa dagas, Hml. Th. ii. 516, 29 : R. Ben. 96, 10. (2) used substantively, (a) alone :—Ealle būton ānum feáwum, Ǽlfc. Gr. 50, 13. Āne feáwa hē geheóld, Hml. Th. ii. 158, 33. (β) governing a genitive :—Āne feáwa daga, Hml. S. 10, 171. Āne feáwa geára, 12, 121. Āne feáwa gesérena, 23, 733. Sprecan āne feáwa worda, Nic. 5, 40. VI. with much the same force as sum, marking an individual member of a group, one (of) :—Heó eóde mid ānre hire ðignenne, Bd. 3, 11 ; S. 536, 18. From his ānan men ofsceoten, Chr. 1100 ; P. 235, 16. Hē forleás his āne scóh, Shrn. 14, 12. Āxode se cāsere þone ænne preóst (one of the priests), Hml. Th. ii. 310, 15. VII. one, as an in each one, any one. (1) combined with indefinite pronouns to express universality, (a) in agreement :—Ūre ǽghwylc ān, Wlfst. 283, 21. Ǽghwylcum ānum men, Bl. H. 123, 33. Æt ǽghwylcum ānum þāra, 127, 34. On ǽlcum ānum, Bt. 33, 3; F. 126, 15. Andwerd ānum

gehwilcum men, Hml. S. 35, 208. Ánum gehwilcum gelýfedum men, Hml. Th. i. 144, 26. Ánum gehwilcum is hæl gehendre, 602, 21. (b) governed by the pronoun:—Æghwylc ánra heora, Bl. H. 121, 8. Ánra manna gehwylc, 57, 33: 101, 29. Ánra gehwylc þára apostola, 22. Úre ánra gehwylc, 63, 29. ¶ in the following passage *ánra gehwilc* seems treated as a compound :—Ánra gehwilces mannes wíte, Gr. D. 333, 18. (2) to express indefinite generality, (any) one, (some) one (governed by the pronoun in the gen.):—Ðonne ðæt mód bið on monig tódǽled, hit bið on ánes hwǽm (*on any one*) ðe unfæstre, Past. 37, 15. On ðǽm chore beóð manige menn gegadrode ánes hwæt tó singanne, 347, 6. Seldhwonne bið þte manegum monnum ánes hwæt lícige *it seldom happens that any one thing pleases many men*, Bt. 18, 3; F. 64, 30. On heora ánra hwylcum . . . on ðæra ánra hwilcum . . . úre ánra hwelc, 33, 2; F. 124, 23–28: 39, 4; F. 216, 21. VIII. referring to a previous noun :—On Angolcynnes gereorde . . . and Ledenwara, þ án is, þ Leden, . . . þám óðrum gemǽne *Anglorum lingua . . . et Latinorum, quae . . . ceteris est facta communis*, Bd. 1, 1; Sch. 10, 9. Sum bróþor is . . . sě is se án geornfullesta godcundra gewrita, Gr. D. 218, 25. IX. marking singleness, isolation, *sole, alone*:—Ána *solus*, Ælfc. Gr. Z. 91, 5. Ána *solus*, ánes *solius*, 115, 1. (1) marking isolation, want of companions, *alone*:—Hé ána wið ealle þá burgware hiene áwerede, Ors. 3, 9; S. 134, 24. Hé ána sæt *solus residens*, Bt. 2, 9; Sch. 150, 7: Hml. A. 204, 310. Hé hyne ána (áne, L. R. *solus*) gebæd . . . hé wæs ána þǽr, Mt. 14, 23. Ðá gesceafta sindon góde; ac sě ána (*singly*) is betere ðe hí ealle gesceóp, Hml. Th. ii. 440, 15. Hé wæs him ána cnihtleás, Hml. S. 23, 395. Lazarus wæs ána sittende mid Hælende, Bl. H. 67, 36. (1 a) marking relinquishment, abandonment :—Lǽtt án ðæt gefeoht, Past. 227, 10. Þá þá þú hí ána forlǽte, Hml. A. 122, 184. (2) marking separateness, exclusiveness, *alone, only, none but*, (a) with pronouns :—Ic ána ætbærst, Hml. Th. ii. 450, 8. Þú eart ána gecoren in þínum cynne hyre tó hyrde, Hml. A. 131, 517. Hé óðre gehǽlde, and heó ána læg swá, Hml. S. 10, 238. Sě ðe ána is sóð God, Hml. Th. ii. 440, 13. Þurh ðæs ánes mihte ðe ealle ðing gesceóp, Hex. 10, 21: Shrn. 48, 23. Nis ná ðæs ánes ðearf . . . ac is ðearf ðær . . . , Past. 273, 3. Sě ðe for ðǽm ánum gód dēð, 265, 7. Ne sceal hé nó ðæt án dón, 193, 21: St. A. 4, 10. Gif hí mě ǽnne habbað, Hml. Th. ii. 104, 7. Ðá áne þe hié ne forlǽtað, Past. 218, 14. Hí wéndon þ hí ána wǽron gecorene, Hml. S. 10, 176. For monigra monna ðingum, næs for hiera ánra, Past. 41, 22. Búton þám ánum þe áfeóllan, Hml. A. 2, 34. Nis hit þ án þ him ánum þǽm apostolum wǽre geofu seald, Bl. H. 137, 10. Gif gě ðá áne lufiað þe eów lufiað, Hml. Th. ii. 216, 20. ¶ with a possessive instead of a personal pronoun :—Mid þínes ánes geþeahte, Bt. 33, 4; F. 128, 20. (b) with a preceding noun :—Nán gesceaft búton se man ána, Hml. A. 12, 295. His forðfóre begeat seó þingung ána, Gr. D. 54, 1. Bútan Gode ánum, Hml. S. 1, 89. For nánum óðran þinge búton for bearnteame ánum, Hml. A. 20, 161. Wǽron þysses eálondes bígengan Bryttas áne *haec insula Brettones solum incolas habuit*, Bd. 1, 1; Sch. 10, 13. Ðá sáwla ána sceolden underfón, Hml. S. 23, 376. Of Persa ánra anwealde búton hiera wiþerwinnum, Ors. 2, 5; S. 84, 29. Búton þám clǽnum ánum, Hml. A. 42, 462. Þás feówer (*the evangelists*) ána syndon tó underfónne, Hml. S, 15, 222. Synna ána mid him ferigende, Hml. Th. i. 66, 13. Swá þæt gě hlyston þá word ána bútan þám weorcum *auditores tantum*, Ælfc. T. 14, 38. Ðá þing ána þe hí behófedon underfónde, ii. 130, 2. (Cf. this passage in Bede: þá þing ǽn (áne, *v. l.*) þá þe . . . *ea tantum quae*, 1, 26; Sch. 57, 4.) ¶ Ánum *not agreeing with noun* :—Búton synne (-a) ánum, Hml. Th. i. 24, 35: 588, 14. (c) with a following noun :—Seó án sáwul is æðelboren þe þone lufað þe heó fram com *only that soul is noble that loves him from whom she came*, Hml. S. 1, 93. Þæt hús hæfdon hié tó ðǽm ánum tácne geworht, Ors. 3, 5; S. 106, 12. Cwæð þín án word *tantum dic verbo*, Mt. 8, 8. Þá áne men habbaþ Críst on heora heortan, þe geteóde beóþ tó ðon écean lífe, Bl. H. 75, 25. (d) with adverbial or conjunctional use :—Þæt án *dumtaxat, tantummodo*, Ælfc. Gr. Z. 241, 7. Næs hit ná þ án þ þú wǽre . . . , ac eác . . . , Bt. 5, 3; F. 14, 6. Ná þ án his fíind ac eác swilce his frínd, Ap. Th. 7, 12. Andbidiað ánum (*only*) fíf dagas, Hml. A. 108, 186. Þám þe Gode án þeówodon *to those that did nothing but serve God*, 118, 54. Ðá ðá heó áne þás word gehýrde *at the mere hearing of these words*, 121, 157. For án eówre yrfe sceal beón hér *oves tantum vestrae et armenta remaneant*, Ex. 10, 24. Hé for án wénde þ ǽlc hine gecneówe *he had no other thought but that every one knew him*, Hml. S. 23, 573. Him for án þúhte þ . . . , 631. Hit mǽre is for án þonne þreó hund geára *it cannot be less than 300 years*, 701. (3) marking singleness, uniqueness, *one, sole, single* :—Ðú geweorðest án cyning and hláford ealles middangeardes, Nar. 32, 4. Nán þing nys wuniende þe se án wyrhta ne gesceópe, Hml. S. 1, 19. Þ is sió án ræst eallra úrra geswinca, sió án hýþ byþ simle smyltu, þ is seó án friðstów and sió án frófer, Bt. 34, 8; F. 144, 26–29. Ic andette ðá ánan hálgan and ðá apostolican gelaðunge, and án fulluht, Hml. Th. ii. 598, 10–12. X. marking identity, *one (and the same)* :—Hit geweorðeð þ án and þ ilce mód ægþer ge weaxeð and eác wērgað, Gr. D. 204, 22. Se án monn ongitt þ þ hé on óþrum ongit synderlíce, Bt. 41, 5; F. 252, 16. Án miht ys þysse wyrt and þæs

wyrttruman and þæs sǽdes, Lch. i. 290, 2. Hú ne hæfdon wě ǽr gereht þ ðá gesǽlþa and sió godcundnes án wǽre *beatitudo vero est ipsa divinitas*, Bt. 34, 5; F. 138, 32. Ne gedafenað hit nó ðæt wě ealle men on áne wísan lǽren, forðám hié ne sint ealle ánes módes and ánra ðeáwa, Past. 173, 17–18. Críst ðe simle ánes willan wæs and God Fæder *filius hominis cui una semper cum Patre voluntas est*, 307, 8. Hit ne cwylmeþ ánum gemete ealle þá synfullan, Gr. D. 333, 17. Tó singanne ánum wordum and ánre stefne, Past. 347, 7. Ealle hí singað ǽnne lofsang, forðan hí ealle healdaþ ǽnne geleáfan, Hml. Th. i. 214, 9–10. Þá Finnas and þá Beormas sprǽcon neáh án geþeóde, Ors. 1, 1; S. 17, 34. X a. used substantively in phrases expressing agreement:—Geweard him and þám folce ánes, þ hí hine horsian sceoldon, Chr. 1014; P. 145, 17. Cuom micel sciphere on West-Walas, and hié tó ánum gecierdon, and wiþ Ecgbryht winnende wǽron, 835; P. 62, 16. þ hí ánrǽde weorþan and ealle án lufian, Ll. Th. ii. 316, 16. Gif þú hí onscunast, wit cweðaþ þonne án *we shall agree in what we say*, Hml. S. 8, 78. On án gesworene *conjurati*, Wrt. Voc. ii. 20, 22. XI. marking union, indivisibility :—Se ána God on þrynnesse and on ánnysse . . . on ðisne ǽnne God wě sceolon geleáfan, Hml. S. 1, 32–39. Drihten, þú þe wunast on Suna, and Fæder on þě, and þú eart ána mid Hálige Gáste, Bl. H. 141, 15. XII. marking continuity, uninterruptedness :—He nǽfre ne stent stille on ánum *it moves continually without interruption*, Hex. 10, 30. Feówertig daga on án *forty days together*, 2, 15 : Hml. S. 34, 189. v. on, B. I. (4). XIII. marking independence, and having much the same force as *self* (q. v.) :—Ne sceal hé nó ðæt án dón ðæt hé ána wacie, ac hé sceal eác his friénd wreccan. Ne ðynce him nó genóg ðæt hé ána wel libbe, búton eác ðá ðe hé fore beón sceal from ðære slǽwðe his synna átió *non solum ut ipse vigilet, sed etiam ut amicum suscitet. Ei vigilare bene vivendo non sufficit, si non et illum, cui praeest, a peccati torpore disjungat*, Past. 193, 20–23. Heó is ána módor and mǽden *she is in her own person mother and maid*, Hml. A. 33, 221. Eal þis ic mě áne wát *all this I myself know*, 177, 248. Ná þ wě ána (*we without effort on our part*) habbon ús ðone wurðmynt, ac swá man mǽre swincð, swá man máran měde hæfð, 57, 161.

**án-ád.** *l.* ánad (-æd), *and* dele the bracket.

**á-nægled**; *adj.* (*ptcpl.*) Covered with that which is nailed on :—þá wágas wǽron mid gyldnum þelum ánæglede *the walls were covered with golden plates nailed on to them*, Nar. 4, 25.

**an-ædelian.** *Dele* an = un, *and v.* un-æðelian. *Add:* [Cf. *O. H. Ger.* ant-adalen *to degrade*.]: **ana-wyrm.** *Dele the bracket.*

**an-bestingan.** v. be-stingan.

**an-bíd** (-bid?). *Add:*—Hé áhsode hwæt his anbíd wǽre (*quae est expectatio mea?*, 38, 9), Ps. Th. 39, arg. Hit is eldung and anbíd þæs héhstan déman. For þám anbíde . . . , Bt. 38, 3; F. 202, 17. On ðǽm anbíde ðe hé hira fandige *interveniente correptionis articulo*, Past. 153, 15. Ðæt hí ne sién freó on ðǽm anbíde ðæs máran wítes *ut suo interim examine non sit absoluta*, 429, 18. On þǽm anbíde Perdica fór mid firde, Ors. 3, 11; S. 146, 1.

**an-bidian.** *l.* an-bídian (and-), *and add.:* I. *to wait* :—His wíte andbidað on ðære tóweardan worulde *his punishment waits in the world to come*, Hml. S. 16, 305. Andbidað (an-, *v.l.*) se déma, Hml. A. 8, 202. Ic anbidode þæt ic ðe máre folc gestrýnde *I waited that I might gain thee more people*, Hml. Th. i. 74, 29. Hé anbidode on lífe seofon niht, Hml. S. 22, 234. Andbidiað hér, Hml. Th. ii. 60, 24. Anbydie wě, Angl. viii. 322, 35. On plegstówe andbidian, Lch. iii. 206, 16. II. *to wait for* (*gen.*) :—Þín andbidað þæt éce forwyrd *eternal perdition waits for you*, Hml. Th. i. 593, 9. Hé anbidode þæs ealdormannes tócymes, Hml. S. 11, 64. Wě andbidodon ðín, Hml. Th. ii. 172, 22. þ wě anbydion þæs sunnandæges, Angl. viii. 310, 38. Anbidian (and-, *v. l.*) þæs écan ǽristes, Hml. S. 25, 144. Andbidiende þæs écan lífes, Ælfc. T. 19, 45. v. ge-anbidian.

**anbíd-stów.** v. onbíd-stów.

**an-bídung.** *l.* an-bidung (and-), *and add:*—Anbidinc *prestolatio*, Kent. Gl. 374: 886. Hé mě áhredde, fram ælcere anbidunge Iudéisces folces (*de omni expectatione plebis Judaeorum*, Acts 12, 11), Hml. Th. ii. 382, 16. On mínre andbidunge (an-, *v.l.*), R. Ben. 100, 12. Andbidunga *inducias*, i. *moras*, An. Ox. 3396.

**án-bíme**; *adj. Made out of a single trunk* :—Ánbýme scip *trabaria*, Wrt. Voc. i. 56, 28.

**an-bringelle, an-bróce, an-brucol, an-burge.** v. on-bringelle, æn-bręce, on-brucol (*in Dict.*), borh : **an-byrdnys.** *l.* v. ge-anbyrdan.

**án-cenned.** *Add:*—Se cniht wæs áncenned sunu his měder, Hml. Th. i. 492, 5.

**ancleów;** *m. l. n., and add:* , ancleówe; *f.* :—Ancleó *talus*, Wrt. Voc. i. 65, 44. Ang(c)leów (*c* added above the line), Wülck. Gl. 307, 28. Oncleóuue, Wrt. Voc. ii. 122, 7. Under þám ancleówe . . . under þám óþran ancleówe, Lch. ii. 118, 21–23. Under ancleówe, 116, 25. Oþ ancleów *talo tenus*, Wrt. Voc. ii. 87, 67: An. Ox. 8, 381. His loccas hangodon tó ðám ancleówum, Hml. Th. i. 466, 25. Niðer oð ðá andcleówa, Ll. Th. ii. 370, 3. Oð ðá andcleów *talo tenus*, Ælfc. Gr. Z. 273, 4. Oð þá ancleów, Hpt. Gl. 526, 29.

**ancor** *an anchor*. *Add:*—Scipes ancerstreng byð áþenæd on gerihte fram þám scype tó þám ancre . . . se ancer byð gefæstnod on ðǽre eorðan, þeáh þ scip sí úte on ðǽre sǽ, Shrn. 175, 18–22. v. aucra.

**áncor.** *l.* ancor, *transfer the bracket to next word, and add:*—þu sǽdest me mé þ ic óðer tǽhte, óðer eówer ancor, Hml. A. 13, 4. Án hálig ancer genam ǽnne deófol . . . Ðá cwæð se deófol tó ðám ancre, Wlfst. 214, 23–25. v. ancra, *and next word.*

**áncora** (*as if* án-cora, *cf. the O. Sax. and O. H. Ger. forms*), an; *m. A hermit:*—Ðá cóman hí tó sumum aancoran (ancran, *v.l.*), Bd. 2, 2; Sch. 116, 10. v. ancra.

**ancor-bend** *a cable:*—Scip oncerbendum (oncear bendum, MS.) fæst, B. 1918. Cf. ancor-ráp, -streng.

**ancor-líc;** *adj. Of a hermit:*—Ancorlíc setl *onochareis* (l. *anachoresis*), Wrt. Voc. ii. 65, 19.

**ancor-líf** (áncor-). *Add:*—On ancerlífes (ancor-, *v.l.*) drohtnunge *in anchoretica conversatione* . . . tó ancerlífe *ad heremiticam vitam*, Bd. 3, 19; Sch. 283, 1, 3. Áncerlífes, 4, 28; Sch. 518, 14. On áncorlífe, 5, 9; Sch. 596, 7. Hé ancorlíf lǽdde *vitam solitariam duxerit*, 4, 27; Sch. 511, 2: Gr. D. 210, 26: 229, 7.

**ancor-ráp.** *Add:*—Hý gehýdað scipu tó ðám unlonde oncyrrápum, Wal. 14.

**ancor-setl.** *Add:*—Ancersetl *i* el forscip *prora*, Wrt. Voc. i. 48, 12.

**ancor-setl.** *Add:*—Ancersetles *anachoreseos*, An. Ox. 3638. On ancorsetle, Wrt. Voc. ii. 2, 54. On ancersetle and lífe *in anchoretica vita*, Bd. 5, 1; Sch. 549, 3. Wunode sum sácerd on ancersetle . . . Se hálga onette tó ðám ancersetle ðǽr hé ǽr gesæt, Hml. Th. ii. 152, 4, 20. Hé on ancorsetle wunade, Shrn. 71, 9. Hé gesæt ancersetl on Fearne, 72, 19.

**ancor-setla,** an; *m. An anchorite, a hermit:*—Hé him cytan árǽrde on sumere dígelnesse, swylce hé ancersetla eáðe beón mihte, Hml. S. 31, 1070. Ancersetlena drohtnung, Hml. Th. i. 544, 26: 546, 1. [The two following are doubtful:—Ancersetlan *anachoreseos*, Hpt. Gl. 465, 48. Óðer kyn is dan-orseclena (ancorsetlena?) *secundum genus est anachoritarum*, R. Ben. I. 9, 18.]

**áncor-stów** (ancor-). *Add:*—On dýgle ancorstówe (aancor-, *v.l.*), Bd. 5, 12; Sch. 614, 23.

**ancor-streng.** *See* ancor *above:* **ancpælgnysse** (= anwælgnysse), Hpt. Gl. 421, 14. v. on-wealhness *in Dict.*

**ancra** *an anchor.* *Add:*—Hét hé hym gebyndan ánne ancran on his sweoran . . . se ancra wæs big gesæted, Shrn. 150, 19–24: Hml. Th. i. 564, 7, 22. Mid fæstum geþances ancran, Angl. xiii. 367, 34. Hig brúdon úp heora ancran, Chr. 1052; P. 180, 16.

**anc(e)ra** *an anchorite.* *Add:*—Hé wende tó wéstene and wæs ðǽr ancra, Hml. S. 7, 400. Scē Antonius se ancra, Shrn. 50, 14: 59, 17. Scē Gúðláces swyster þæs ancran, 50, 2. Anceran, 71, 3: 72, 19. Paulus and Antonius ðá ǽrostan ancran, Sal. K. 190, 24. Oþer muneca cyn is ancrena, þæt is wéstensetlena, R. Ben. 9, 5.

**án-cyn.** *Add:*—Ánkennan míne ł míne ánlícan *unicam meam*, Ps. L. 21, 21.

**and;** *prep.* In the examples given under II *and* = *an, on.* To the instances given add:—Tóðǽled & (on, Cott. MSS.) tó monigfealda sprǽca, Past. 277, 15. Wé sceolun þrowian weán and wergum, nalles wuldres leóht habban in heofonum, Sat. 42.

**and;** *conj.* *Add:* , end:—Aend suilcae, end suilce *atqueve*, Txts. 42, 98. **I.** introductory to a clause which is not preceded by one with which it can be connected:—Ðá cwæð Eustachius: 'And ne sǽde ic þ wilde deór hí gelǽhton?', Hml. S. 30, 371. **II.** connecting a subordinate clause or phrase with the principal clause, and so superfluous:—Mid þí þe hié gehýrdon þára sácerda ealdormen, and hié cwǽdon hit betweónan, Bl. H. 239, 29. Him þá gyt sprecendum and þá beorht wolcn hig ofersceán, Mt. 17, 5. **III.** connecting coordinate clauses, (1) in which the subject of the second is the object of the first, but is not expressed; *and* may be rendered by a relative:—Gemétte ic sumne man, and (*and he, who*) mé þrý penegas sealde, Hml. S. 23 b, 490. Ic geseah þǽr manige góde, and on Godes þeódscipe heora líf lǽddon, Guth. 70, 23. Ic geseó Godes engel standende ætforan ðé, and wípað ðíne limu, Hml. Th. i. 426, 30. Ðá ábæd his fóstormódor án hridder, and tóbærst on emtwá, ii. 154, 16. (2) where the object of the second is that of the first, but is not expressed:—Hér Æþelburg tówearp Tántún and (þe, þone, *v. ll.*). Íne ǽr timbrede, Chr. 722; P. 42, 23. (3) where *and* = *þæt:*—þá geímode hit ymbe twelf mónað æfter Agathes þrowunge, and Ethna up ábleów, Hml. S. 8, 222. **IV.** in clauses in which comparison is made, *as:*—Gelíce and (*quasi*) mon mǽd máwe, hié wǽron þá burg hergende, Ors. 2, 8; S. 92, 15. Nú sió burg swelc is, gelíce and heó wǽre tó bisene ásteald, 2, 4; S. 74, 24; 1. 52, 11, 29. þ bið gelíc and eágan bót, Ll. Th. i. 94, 21. Ne bið ná gelíc þ man wið swustor gehǽme and hit wǽre feor sibb, 404, 27. Þ cild þá gýtseras lǽton efenscyldig and hit gewittig wǽre, 420, 2. Hé wæs ǽfre efenmihtig and hé gyt is, Wlfst. 16, 7. Ðú gelýfst þínum hláforde bet ðonne ðé selfum, and þínum géferum æmnwel and ðé selfum, Shrn. 196, 24. Críst simle ánes

---

willan wæs and God Fæder *Filio hominis una semper cum Patre voluntas est*, Past. 307, 8.

**anda.** *Add:*—Anda is twyfeald, þæt is yfel and gód. Yfel bið se anda þe andað ongeán gódnysse, and se anda is gód ðe nid lufe andað ongeán yfelnysse, Hml. Th. ii. 54, 22–24. Þá heáfodleahtras sind . . . anda (*invidia*), 592, 6: Wlfst. 245, 14. Andan *livoris*, Wrt. Voc. ii. 50, 16. Onǽled mid ryhtwíslicum andan wið his hiéremonna scylda, Past. 163, 20. For ryhtwísnesse hé sceal habban andan tó hira yfele *contra delinquentium vitia per zelum justitiae erectus*, 75, 13. Þurh his swefn hig hine hatedon and hæfdon andan tó him *haec causa somniorum invidiae et odii fomitem ministravit*, Gen. 37, 8. Forlǽt ðæt ðú næbbe tó óðrcs mannes góde andan, Prov. K. 33. ¶ in the Northern specimens the word means *fear:*—Ondo and fyrhto *tremor et pauor*, Mk. L. R. 16, 8. Ondo *timor*, Lk. L. 1, 12, 65. Ondes *timoris*, Rtl. 120, 5. On onde fiónda *in timore inimicorum*, 78, 30. Búta ondo *sine timore*, Lk. L. R. 1, 74.

**án-dæge.** *Dele last passage, for which see next word.*

**and-ǽges** (-eáges?, -ēges, ? = íeges?); *adv. In the face:*—Nǽnig dorste þ hire andǽges eágum starede *none dared to look her in the face*, B. 1935. [Cf. *Goth.* and-augi *face;* and-augjó *openly.*]

**án-daga.** *Add:*—Hé cwæð þæt hé wolde sylf on ðæm dæge ðe hé gecwæd ðǽr gecuman . . . Hí georne ðæs ándagan cépton. Þá æteówode Benedictus . . . on þǽre nihte þe se ándaga on merigen wæs, Hml. Th. ii. 172, 9–17. Æfter þam fyrste and ándagan þe se heáhengel gecwæd tó Danihele, 14, 18. Tó þám ándagan þe hé him gewissode, Hml. A. 97, 167. Hé hæfð gecweden ándagan, þ hé sceall ácwellan míne mǽgðe, 99, 262. Þ mann sceolde settan swylcne ándagan Gode, þ hé binnan iíf dagum þám folce gehulpe, 108, 211. Nis se man on eorðan þe wite þæne ándagan (*the appointed end of the world*) bútan Gode sylfum, Wlfst. 90, 1. Þá cende hé tém and lét þone forberstan and forbéh þone ándagan, Cht. Th. 206, 29. v. riht-ándaga, *and next word.*

**án-dagian.** *Add:*—Ðá cwæð ic þæt hé wolde cunnigan, and bæd ðone cing ðæt hé hit ándagade (*that he would appoint a day for taking the oath*), and hé swá dyde, and hé gelǽdde ðá tó ðon ándagan ðone áð . . . and wé ridan ðá tó ðon ándagan, Cht. Th. 171, 18–34. [*Icel.* ein-daga *to fix a day for.*]

**and-beorma.** *Dele.*

**and-bícnian;** *p.* ode *To make signs to:*—Hleóðriende andbécniað ciebant, Wrt. Voc. ii. 21, 50.

**and-bida, -bidian.** v. and-bita, an-bidian.

**and-bita.** *Substitute:*—Andbita, beorma *azyma*, Wrt. Voc. ii. 9, 5. Andbida, beorma (v. Mk. 14, 1), 74, 26. [Cf. *O. H. Ger.* int-pizzun *refecerunt:* im-piz *refectio, prandium.*] Cf. on-bítan.

**and-bryrdness.** v. on-bryrdness.

**and-cweþan** (?). *This form seems to be given as an alternative to* wiðercweðan, *as a gloss to* frustrari, contra dicere, Hpt. Gl. 491, 32. [Cf. *Goth.* and-kwiþan: *O. Sax.* ant-queðan: *O. H. Ger.* ant-quedan.] v. and-cwiss, on-cweþan.

**and-cýþness,** e; *f. Experience:*—Hé wilnade þætte eall seó þeód þe hé fore wæs mid þǽre gife ðæs crístnan geleáfan gelǽred wǽre, þæs geleáfan ondcýðnesse (ɔ-, *v.l.*) hé swíðust onféng on sigegefeohtum ellreordra cynna *desiderans totam, cui praeesse coepit, gentem fidei Christianae gratia inbui, cujus experimenta permaxima in expugnandis barbaris ceperat*, Bd. 3, 3; Sch. 199, 5. [Cf. *O. H. Ger.* ant-kundi *expertus*.] Cf. un-andcýþigness.

**and-eáw.** *Dele bracket, and add: ostentatious* (? cf. eáwan, íwan *to shew*, and *Goth.* and-augjó *openly*):—Ælc andeáw *omnis arrogans*, Scint. 151, 17. Andeáwe weras *arrogantes uiri*, 152, 12. Andeáwum *arrogantibus*, 221, 8.

**and-efn.** *Substitute:* **and-ef(e)n** (v. evene *in N. E. D.*), e: *pl.* -ef(e)nu; *f. Measure:*—Neáh andefene *prope modum*, Wrt. Voc. ii. 66, 73. **I.** of persons, *quality, capacity, nature:*—For ðǽre ungelícnesse ðára hiéremonna sculon beón ungelíc ðá word ðæs láreówes, ðæt hé hiene selfne geðeóde tó eallum his hiéremonnum, tó ǽghwelcum be his andefne (-efene, *v.l.*) *pro qualitate audientium formari debet sermo doctorum, ut ad sua singulis congruat*, Past. 175, 4. Dóð gé eówrum monnum ðæt ilce be hira andefne (-efene, *v.l.*), 203, 1. Ælc gesceaft is tó árianne be hire andefne, and symle sió héhste swíþost, Bt. 32, 2; F. 116, 14. Engelum hé gef be heora andefne, and manna sáulum hé gyfð ælcre be hyre andefne swilca gyfa, Shrn. 192, 2–3. Witað ðæt ðæt iów gemetlic sié and íower ondefenu (-efnu, *v.l.*) sién tó witenne *sapere ad sobrietatem*, Past. 95, 1. Ðonne sió úpáhæfenes bið átyht ofer hire andefnu (-efenu, *v.l.*) *dum elatio supra se tenditur*, 301, 19. **II.** of things, *quantity, amount, nature, extent:*—Tóðǽlað hí his feoh on fíf oððe syx, hwýlum on má, swá swá þæs feós andefn bið, Ors. 1, 1; S. 20, 29. Be þǽre andefne heora unrihtwísnesse *secundum multitudinem impietatum eorum*, Ps. Th. 5, 11. Be ðæs gyltes andefne (-efene, *v.l.*), Past. 195, 10: Bl. H. 45, 29: Bt. 38, 7; F. 210, 8. Æfter þæs deóres mihte & efne (= andefne or and cine?), Lch. i. 328, 15. Æfter heora gecarnunga anddyfene *secundum merita*, R. Ben. 13, 7. Ælc hæfð be

þám andefnum þe hé ǽr æfter cornað *each will have according to the extent of his previous efforts*, Shrn. 201, 2. v. land-efn.

**andel-bǽre** (= and-hél-bǽre; cf. Icel. 'and-hæli, *n. monstrosity*; medic. *the heels being in the place of the toes*, andhælis-ligr *absurd*.' Cl. & V. Dict.); *adj. Reversed, inverted*:—Andelbǽrre tíde *tempore prepostero* (id est, vernali non autumnali, Ald. 33, 12), An. Ox. 7, 282: 8, 207. Andelbǽre, 2, 257: 4, 74: Hpt. Gl. 496, 42: Angl. xiii. 35, 218 (all are glosses on the same passage).

**andergilde**:—Ne weorðe ðé nǽfre tó þæs wá ðæt ðú ne wéne betran andergilde, Prov. K. 41. In the passage given under *un-andergilde* (q.v.), *hwæt unandergildes* should render *quod non vilescat;* this would make *andergilde; adj.* = of little value, for which little is paid. Such a force for *ander-* might perhaps be supported by the glosses *andran, andarn* in vanum given in Heyne's Altniederdeutsche Denkmäler. *Andergilde* in the proverb might thus mean *at little cost, without effort* (?), and the proverb be translated : Never let it get so bad with you that you don't hope for something better by things righting themselves.

**andet.** *Add:* [Goth. anda-hait *confession:* O. H. Ger. ant-heiz *professio*.]

**andet-nes.** *Add:*—Ðurh ondetnesse, Past. 367, 6. Wé byddaþ þé þ þú sylle andetnysse Gode, Nic. 10, 28. Mid andetnessum eallra þæra mærða, Hml. S. 25, 505. v. ge-andetness.

**andet(t)a.** *Substitute : The word seems indeclinable and to be used only in the phrase* beón (wesan, weorþan) andetta = *to admit* a charge, liability, &c., (1) with gen.:—Gielde sé þæs sleges andetta sié wer and wíte *let him that admits the slaying* (*acknowledges that he slew the man*) *pay* '*wer*' *and* '*wíte*,' Ll. Th. i. 80, 7. Ic þé eom andetta mínra synna, Angl. xiii. 501, 15. Ic þé eom andetta bóte *I admit to thee my liability to make amends*, 501, 17, 23. Ðonne cuæð se biscop and ðára hína wiotan þet hió hím néren máran ondeta (*that they did not admit to him liability for more*) þonne hit ǽræded wæs on Æðelbaldes dæge, Cht. Th. 70, 25. (2) with a clause:—Swíþe seldon ǽnig man wile beón andetta þ hé æfestig sý, Bl. H. 65, 4. Heó hím tó sprǽcon ymbe þ land, þ hé his hím geúðe; ðá wæs hé ondeta þ hé swá walde *he admitted that he was willing to do so*, Cht. Th. 47, 18. Þú hæbbe forgitan þæt ðú ǽr andætta wére þ þú wisse, Shrn. 191, 26. [O. H. Ger. ant-heiz(z)o ; ih in antheizo uuard.]

**andettan.** *Add:* andet(t)ian:—Heó andette *fatebatur*, Wrt. Voc. ii. 34, 48. **I.** *to confess* what one has done wrong:—Hé andette and cwæð, 'Sóðlíce ic syngode,' Jos. 7, 20. **II.** *to confess, admit the truth* of a charge, unfavourable statement, &c.:—Ic andette þæt hig cómun tó mé *fateor, venerunt ad me*, Jos. 2, 4. **III.** *to confess* a person (v. andettere), *acknowledge excellence in* something:—Ælc ðæra ðe mé andet ætforan mannum, ic andette hine ætforan mínum Fæder, Hml. Th. ii. 558, 27. Ondettigað heofenas wundur ðín, Ps. Srt. 88, 6. **IV.** *to acknowledge acknowledgement* of a benefit to a person, *to give thanks, praise* to:—Þeós Drihtne andette and be him sprǽc, Lk. 2, 38. Ondettigen ðé (*tibi*) folc, ondettien ðé folc, Ps. Srt. 66, 4. Ondette (-ie), 6. Ondittien Dryhtne wundur his bearnum monna *ok that men would praise the Lord for his wonderful works to the children of men*, 106, 31. **V.** *to confess* a purpose, *to promise, vow:*—Wæs hé swá swýþe onbryrded, þæt hé andette Gode, gif hé him ðæs mergendæges geunnan wolde, þæt hé his þeów beón wolde, Guth. 14, 27. [Goth. and-haitan *to confess, profess.*] v. un-andet.

**andettend**, es; *m. A confessor:*—Forgef ondettendum (*or ptcpl.?*) *ignosce confitentibus*, Ps. Srt. ii. p. 203, 37.

**andet(t)ere.** *Add:*—On ðone .V.an dæg þæs mónðes biþ ðæs Godes andetteres tíd Sci Quinti, Shrn. 126, 11. Ondetteres, Rtl. 65, 6. Ondeteres, 49, 4: 88, 40. On ðæra hálgena mæssedagum þe wé hátað *confessores*, þæt sind andeteras. Ðá sind hálige andeteras þe Crístes naman mid sóðum geleáfan andetton bealdlíce betwux gedwolmannum, Hml. Th. ii. 558, 21–24. Þæt hé ús his andetterum ðá æddran geopenige, i. 562, 5. v. andettan, III.

**andet(t)ing.** *Add:*—Ondetung *confessio*, Lk. p. 4, 17.

**and-fang**, es; *m.* **I.** *acceptance:*—Þte hé hæbbe ondfong ðerh Godes milsæ on heofnum, Jn. Skt. p. 188, 10. **II.** in a personal sense. Cf. under-fang:—Andfang(a ?) *appetitorum*, Wrt. Voc. ii. 10, 17. v. and-feng.

**and-fangol** *glosses* susceptor:—Andfangol úre *susceptor noster*, Ps. L. 45, 12.

**and-feax;** *adj. Bald:*—Andfeaxe (-fexe, *v.l.*) weorðaþ ðæra swýðe manega *very many of them shall become bald* (cf. Isaiah 3, 17, 24), Wlfst. 46, 1. [O. H. Ger. ant-fahsiu *crebro capillitio vulsa.*]

**and-feng.** *Substitute for citations :* **I.** assumptio, susceptio, acceptio:—Háda andfeng *personarum acceptio*, R. Ben. 57, 20. Dagas ondfenges (andfenga, W. S.) his *dies assumptionis ejus*, Lk. L. 9, 51. Be cumena andfenge *de hospitibus suscipiendis*, R. Ben. 80, 17. Andfencge, 96, 2: 102, 10. Feówer land hé forgeaf þí þeódigum tó andfencge (*for the entertainment of strangers*), Hml. S. 7, 387. Hé sylf biþ underfangen on heora anfenge, Hml. Th. i. 514, 8. **II.** susceptor:—Drihten andfeng (*susceptor*) is sáwle mínre, Ps. Spl. 53, 4:

90, 2. Andfenge, Ps. L. 45, 8. God seolfa wæs eallum andfeng, Sat. 245. **III.** *sumtus:*—Hé teleð þá andfengas (*sumtus*) þe him behéfe synt, Lk. 14, 28. [O. H. Ger. ant-fang, -fangi *susceptio, acceptio*.] v. on-feng.]

**and-fenga.** *Add:*—Gif þæs ondfengan ellen dohte, Rä. 62, 7.

**and-fenge.** *l. That can be received*, and add : **I.** *acceptable :*—Nán good ne bið andfenge búton mon ǽr ðæt yfel forlǽte, Past. 349, 17. Andfæncge gebed, Hml. S. 4, 280. Mǽden werum þfæncge, Lch. iii. 186, 25. Þín ælmesse sý andfengu, Ps. Th. 19, 3: Gr. D. 327, 23. Ðeós hýrsumnes bið Gode antfenge, R. Ben. 20, 17. Úre gebeda beóð andfenge, 45, 21; Bl. H. 113, 28. Andfænge, Shrn. 74, 2. Eádigra fædra and Gode þfengra, Bd. 4, 17; Sch. 433, 7. Ic beó andfengra mínum cyninge, Hml. Th. i. 594, 12. Byð his dǽdbót Gode andfengre, Wlfst. 155, 14. Anfengre, Ch. Th. 431, 37. Ðá lác beóð Gode ealra andfengeost, Past. 222, 21. **II.** *that can receive :*—Andfenge stówe *conceptacula*, Wrt. Voc. ii. 136, 13. **III.** *that can help*, v. andfenga:—Wæs mé andfencge écere hǽlu (*susceptor salutis meae*), Ps. Th. 88, 23. [O. H. Ger. ant-fengi *acceptus*.] v. on-fenge.

**and-fengend.** *Add:* **I.** *a receiver:*—Gafeles andfen(d)gend *numerarii*, Wrt. Voc. ii. 62, 34. **II.** *a defender;* susceptor:—þú eart mín andfengend *susceptor meus es*, Ps. Th. 41, 10: 45, 10. Anfengend, Ps. L. 17, 3.

**and-fengnes.** *Substitute :*—Ne bið þær háda andfengnes, Wlfst. 253, 21. Andfengnessa *receptacula*, Wrt. Voc. ii. 84, 4. v. on-fengness.

**and-findan.** v. on-findan.

**and-gelóman.** *Add:*—Andgelóman *instrumentis*, Wrt. Voc. ii. 43, 66.

**and-getfull, -getul.** v. and-gitfull, -gitol.

**and-git.** *Add:* **I.** *understanding, intellect :*—Swǽ ðurhfærd his andgiet (-git, Hatt. MS.) ðæt níod his hiéremonna, Past. 154, 11. Se geleáfa ne bið on geárum, ac bið on glǽwum andgitum, Hml. S. 7, 112. **II.** *sense, faculty of perception :*—Hé læg cwydeleás búton andgite, Hml. Th. i. 86, 26. Heora módes andgytu hí fordytton, Hml. S. 23, 379. **III.** *plan, purpose :*—Hí þone Hǽlend bǽdon þ hé tówurpe þæs wælreówan andgyt (*the intention of destroying the city*), Hml. S. 3, 239. **IV.** *sense, purport, meaning :*—Ic nime on sumum þ andgit án, on sumum þá word mid þám andgite *in quibusdam sensum solummodo, in quibusdam verba cum sensu teneo*, Gr. D. 9, 10–12. Wendan hwílum word be worde, hwílum andgit of andgite, Past. 7, 20. Ærendgewrit on þyson andgite gediht *a letter to this effect*, Hml. S. 23, 792. Hé áwrát be sumum ðegene þisum andgite reccende, Hml. Th. ii. 356, 22. Gástlicum angite *allegoriam* . . . heofenlicum angite *anagogen*, An. Ox. 182, 184. Ðæt ys on angite þ . . . *the meaning is that* . . ., Jud. p. 157, 34. Ðæt is on ðrím andgitum tó understandenne *that is to be understood in three senses*, Hml. Th. i. 264, 31.

**and-gite.** *Add:*—Gúðlác on his ondgietan engel sealde þæt him swedraden synna lustas, Gú. 852. Gif þú his ondgitan ǽnige hæbbe, An. 1523.

**andgit-full** (-get-). *Add:*—Þá hé andgitfull wæs *when he had come to years of discretion*, Shrn. 12, 17. Se man déð swylce hé andgytful sý þe lytel can tó geráde, Wlfst. 53, 4. Andgytful *capax*, An. Ox. 3101. þæs antgytfullan *intellectualis*, 897. Oð þ hig tó andgitfullre ylde cumon *usque ad intelligibilem aetatem perveniant*, R. Ben. 116, 12. þá andgytfullan *sensatos, i. prudentes*, Scint. 105, 12. v. un-andgitfull.

**andgitfullíce.** *Add:*—Andgytfullice *liquido, i. clare* ł *perspicue*, An. Ox. 1518. Angytfullíce, 83. Andgytful[líce] *sensatim*, 56, 121. Andgitfullícost, Past. 7, 24.

**andgit-leás.** *Add:* **I.** of human beings, *senseless :*—þú earma andgitleása, Hml. S. 8, 157. Eorðan ymbhwyrft fiht for Gode ongeán þá andgitleásan (*insensatos*), Hml. Th. ii. 540, 5. **II.** of things, *without reason :*—þá treówa þe on æppeltúne wexað, þá þe sind andgitleáse, Hml. Th. ii. 406, 11.

**andgit-leást,** e; *f. Want of understanding, senselessness :*—Hwónlíce fremað þæs mannes líf ðe for andgitleáste ne cann his mód áwendan tó ðám écan lífe, Hml. Th. ii. 442, 9. Be andgytléste, Wlfst. 47, 11. Ongeán þám andgyte þe of Godes gyfe cymð se deófol sǽwð angytléste (-leáste, *v. l.*), 53, 2.

**andgit-lic.** *Add:*—Fæder þæs angitlican leóhtes *pater intelligibilis lucis*, Shrn. 166, 8.

**andgit-líce.** *Add:*—Andgitlíce *liquido*, Wrt. Voc. ii. 75, 19: 52, 25. v. andgitfullíce.

**and-gitol.** *Add:*—Andgetul *capax*, Wrt. Voc. ii. 128, 28. Andgitel *intelligens*, Ps. L. 13, 2. Andgyttol, R. Ben. 25, 15. Tó andgyttolre yldo *ad intelligibilem aetatem*, 117, 12.

**and-heáfdu** (-a); *n. pl. Headlands, the unploughed ground at the end of the furrows where the plough was turned:*—Andlang ðára andheáfda, C. D. v. 298, 7, 9. be ðém andheáfdan, ii. 172, 29: iii. 193, 8: vi. 8, 27, 29 (cf. on ðá heáfda, 36). Ofer ðá mǽd, ðæt swá be ðára andheáfdan, 234, 7. Tó ðám andheáfdan, iii. 279, 17, 18 (cf. andlang heáfda, 26). Be onheáfdan, 464, 19. Oþ ðá andheáfda; of ðám andheáfdum, 408, 28.

and-héfe, and-hladan. v. un-andhéfe, on-hladan.

andian. *Add:*—*to be envious;* in a good sense, *to be zealous, jealous,* (1) absolute:—Sóð lufu nā andað *caritas non emulatur,* Scint. 75, 7. Angað *invidet,* Kent. Gl. 1050. Andigen *liuescant,* An. Ox. 5372. Andigende *invidendo,* Scint. 75, 19. Mē þone ðū andigendne for-bǽre, Hml. Th. ii. 418, 9. Þone andigendan wer, Hex. 46, 18. Andigendra *invidentium,* R. Ben. I. 93, 15. (2) with preps.:—Yfel bið se anda þe andað ongeán gódnysse, and se anda is gód ðe mid lufe andað ongeán yfelnysse . . . þā ðe þus andiað ongeán unriht . . ., Hml. Th. ii. 54, 22–25. Gif hwylc bróþor þyhþ, on þæt hý andiaþ, R. Ben. 139, 26. Ic andede ofer þā unrihtwīsan *zelavi super iniquos,* Ps. Spl. 72, 3. Se niðfulla deófol andode on ðæs munuces lufe, Hml. Th. ii. 156, 8. Hē on his weorcum andode, 500, 6: Hml. S. 31, 35. Hē andodon on hys dǽdum, Hml. A. 66, 29. Ne andgiað on þone welegan, Ps. Th. 48, 16. Ne andige hē on ðām foreðeóndum, Hml. Th. i. 346, 32. Lāðlīce andigan ongeán þā māran, Hml. A. 41, 417. Hē ongann andian on þæs hálgan weres gecneordnyssum *sancti viri studiis coepit aemulari,* Gr. D. 117, 8.

andig. *Add:*—Andig *invidus,* Scint. 76, 6, 18. Ne hē ne beó andig (æfestig, *v. l.*), R. Ben. 120, 13. Andig *zelotypus,* An. Ox. 364. Andiges *invidi,* 2708. Andigum *invido,* Scint. 75, 11.

and-lang; *prep. Add:* (1) with gen.:—Ollonc ðæs gemǽrheges . . . ūp ollonc streámes, C. D. vi. 234, 1, 6. (2) with acc.:—Wrīt ðis andlang ðā earmas, Lch. iii. 38, 29. (3) as adverb:—Wende þē þonne .iii. sunganges, ástrece þonne on andlang, Lch. i. 400, 10.

and-langes; *prep. adv. Along,* (1) prep. with gen.:—Andlanges herpaðes, Cht. Crw. 1, 11 (see note, p. 57). Andlanges wealles, C. D. i. 1, 16. Andlanges ðǽr(e) eá, vi. 217, 5. Andlangas, iii. 172, 29. Ond-longes, 52, 19. Ðanone on andlanges hrycges, vi. 168, 23. Olluncges iii. 35, 3. (2) adv.:—Fram ðǽre wíc tó ðǽre cortan, and swā andlanges tó Sūðsexan, C. D. vi. 217, 7.

andlang-cempa (?), an; *m. A soldier who fights along with others* (?), *who is in line with others:*—Anlangcempa *miles ordinarius* (cf. ordinarius miles qui integro ordine militat, Corp. Gl. H. 87, 266), Wrt. Voc. ii. 59, 13.

and-leán. *Add:*—Heó þolian ne wolde yfel and ondleán, Gen. 2264.

and-leofa, -lífa (an-), an; *m. Sustenance, food:*—Wesaþ þancfulle þon Hǽlende eóweres andleofan, Bl. H. 169, 16. Eal he sealde būton ðone dæghwāmlican andleofan þe hē nēde big lífgean sceolde, 213, 20: Sat. 522. Eów andlifan syllan and eów eówre þearfe forgifan *quae uictui sunt necessaria ministrare,* Bd. 1, 25; Sch. 55, 11. Andleofan, 20. Hē him eallum hēt dōn andlifan genōhne, Ll. Th. ii. 372, 30. v. an-leofa *in Dict.*

and-leofen, es; *n. l.* e; *f.,* but also *gen.* andlifenes, *acc.* ondlifen, *and add:*—Andliofen *expensa,* Wrt. Voc. 30, 5. Andlifen *pulmentum,* 78, 5. Hiera ondliefene (-lifene, *v. l.*) þone dǽl ðe hī him selfum oftióð *ea quae sibi de alimentis subtrahant,* Past. 315, 22. Seó eá mǽst eall genom þæt binnan þǽre byrg wæs þǽra monna ondliefene, Ors. 4, 7; S. 180, 19. Gode þancie hē his dæghwāmlicre ondlyfene, Ll. Th. ii. 420, 7. Þætte ealles þæs andliefenes (-lyf-, *v.l.*) feówer dǽlas beón sceolon *ut omni stipendio quattuor debeant fieri portiones,* Bd. 1, 27; Sch. 62, 4. Feoh him tó andlyfne *money to support him,* Gr. D. 201, 1. Anleofene *edulio,* Hpt. Gl. 429, 72. Mīnre anlifene *victui meo,* Kent. Gl. 1078. Andlifene *cibaria,* 1139. Ealle hyre andlyfene *omnem uictum suum,* Lk. 21, 4: Hml. S. 11, 347. Þigede hē þæs (þās?) andlyfene þe hē big leofode, Guth. 26, 18. Hī him andlifene (-lyfne, *v. l.*) and āre (*debita stipendia*) forgeáfon, Bd. 1, 15; Sch. 41, 12. Hē him ondlifen forgeaf and weoruldþearfe *victum temporalem administravit,* 1, 25; Sch. 55, 20 note. Seó wǽdl þǽra andlyfna *alimentorum indigentia,* Gr. D. 145, 6. Mid þissum andlyfenum bið ǽlc mægen gefēd, Ll. Th. ii. 404, 5.

and-lōman. *Add:* -laman, -luman:—Andluman *utensilia,* Wrt. Voc. i. 83, 27: An. Ox. 4665: 8, 275: Angl. xiii. 36, 249. Andlaman, An. Ox. 7, 318: Hpt. Gl. 514, 26 (the last five are glosses of the same passage). Andluman *vasa,* R. Ben. I. 62, 1. Inorf. andlu[man] *suppellex,* An. Ox. 4664: Hpt. Gl. 514, 25. Hē sceal fela tōla tó tūne tilian and fela andlōmena tó hūsan habban, Angl. ix. 262, 27. Andlamena, 264, 8. Andlumena, Cht. Th. 538, 36. Sylle him man tōl tó his weorce and andlaman tó his hūse, Ll. Th. i. 434, 26.

an-drysenlic, -dryslíce, -drysne. v. on-drysnlic, -dryslíce, -drysne.

and-saca. *Add:*—Borges andsaca (-u?) *inficiatio (-tor?),* Wrt. Voc. ii. 49, 27.

and-sacian. *Add:*—Ðā Saducie andsacedon (ant-, *v.l.*) ðǽre ǽriste æfter deáðe, Past. 362, 5.

and-sacu (?), e; *f. Denial, contradiction:*—Būtan ǽlcre ansæce, Chr. Th. p. 103, note.

and-sǽc; *n. Add:*—Berst se teám swā wel swā hē sylf andsǽc worhte . . . ā bið andsǽc swīðere þonne onsagu, Ll. Th. i. 290, 15–17. Ne beó hē nānes andsæces wyrðe *he shall not be entitled to make denial,* 288, 9. Þone þe tó nānan andsæce ne mæge, 228, 14. 'Ne mæg ic wunian.' . . . Ðā ðā heó his andsæc gehŷrde . . ., Hml. Th. ii. 184, 1. Þū ondsæc dydest, þæt þū on feorwegas fēran ne cūðe, An. 929.

and-sǽte. *Add:* I. of that which is evil:—His forligr Gode and-sǽte wæs, Hml. Th. i. 484, 15: ii. 528, 11: Hex. 54, 19. Ǽlc hīwung

is antsǽte (and-, an-, *v. ll.*) Gode, Hml. S. 12, 246. Cosdrue wæs andsǽte eallum his leódum, H. R. 101, 27. Andsǽte bið þ treów þe ǽfre grēwð on leáfum and nǽfre nænne wæstm ne bringð, Hml. S. 4, 246. Him byð egle and andsǽte se stenc, Hex. 50, 24. Andsǽtne *invisum, odiosum,* An. Ox. 2728. Þ gᵉ andsǽtan wiglunge forlǽtan, Hml. S. 17, 70. Hý synt andsǽte (*abominabiles*) gewordene on heora lustum, R. Ben. 25, 7. Þā ansǽtan *execranda,* An. Ox. 1897. II. of that which is good:—Beóð lāðe and tó andsǽte þā þe God lufiað, Wlfst. 89, 17. [*Goth.* anda-sēts *abominable.*]

and-sliht. [*Take here the passages given under hand-sliht, in which the alliteration seems to require a vowel.*] *A return-stroke.*

and-speornan. *l.* and-spornan, -spurnan, *to strike against:*—Þy lēs ðū andspurne æt stáne þínum fótum *ne forte offendas ad lapidem pedem tuum,* Mt. R. 4, 6. *The verb occurs (and with weak forms) several times in the Northern Gospels, glossing* offendere, scandalizare:—Ond-spyrnað *scandalizat,* Mt. L. 18, 8. Ondspurnað, 9. Ondspyrneð, Jn. L. 6, 61: *offendit,* 11, 9. Ondspyrnað *offendet,* 10. Þte gié ne ondspyrniga *ut non scandalizemini,* 16, 1. Ondspyrnende *scandalizatus,* Mt. L. 11, 6. Ondspurnendra *scandalizantium,* Mk. p. 4, 9. v. ge-andspornan.

and-standan. *Dele.*

and-swarian. *Add:*—Þis leóð him andswarað (*respondebit*) for gewitnysse, Deut. 31, 21. Ondsuorade, Mt. L. 26, 23. Þā andswaredon (-sweoredon, *v. l.*) Scottas him, BJ. 1, 1; Sch. 11, 8. v. and-swerian.

and-swaru. *Add:*—Him andswaru (an-, *v. l.*) ne com, Hml. S. 18, 117. Seó gōde andswaru (ant-, *v. l.*), R. Ben. 55, 8. Hnesce andswore *responsio mollis,* Kent. Gl. 502. Underfōn andswore (*responsum*) R. Ben. I. 112, 6. Ondsuǽre, Jn. L. 1, 22. Ondsuere (-swore, R.), Lk. L. 2, 26. Andswara, rǽdas *consulta,* i. *interrogata,* An. Ox. 2524. Antswara, 8, 130. Ðā bysmrode ic hine mid mínum ondswarum . . . þā wæs hē gefeónde mínra ondswaro, Nar. 18, 13–18. Ondsuearum (-sworum, R.) *responsis,* Lk. L. 2, 47.

and-swerian. *Add:*—Andsweras *respondeas,* R. Ben. I. 3, 1. Andsweraþ *respondit,* Coll. M. 30, 37. Andswyraþ, Cant. Ez. 15. Andswerede, Bl. H. 233, 10. Ondsweorede, Ps. Srt. 101, 24. Andswyra *responde,* Cant. Ez. 14.

and-þrec. v. on-þræc: and-þwǽre, *del.:* and-timber. v. an-timber.

andung, e; *f. Jealousy:*—Tó andunge (*aemulationem*) hine hig tihton, Ps. L. 77, 58.

andustrian, andustrung. v. ā-dustrian.

and-weald. *Add:* also neuter:—Hē hæfde þisne andweald, Hml. Th. ii. 360, 29. Andwealdu *sceptra, potestates,* Hpt. Gl. 414, 15: 424, 57. Andwealda, An. Ox. 2902. Andwealdum *sceptris,* 4046.

and-weard. *Add:* -wurd, -wyrd. I. local:—Hē is ǽghwǽr andweard . . . hē is on ǽlcere stówe, Hml. Th. i. 158, 4. Ic wæs andweard sumum brēðer, Gr. D. 267, 24. Him biþ beforan andweard engla cynn, Bl. H. 83, 11. Swā swā hē hyre andweardre tó sprǽce, Bd. 4, 8; S. 575, 32: 4, 24; S. 597, 30. Þeáh þe wē nū þér andwearde ne sŷn, Bl. H. 129, 29. II. temporal:—Fleón ðis andwearde yfel, Past. 263, 13. III. *active:*—Swā andweard seó wyrt is þ heó þý ylcan dæge þā stānas forbrycð, Lch. i. 212, 14. Andwyrdre, dǽdlicere *practicae,* i. *actualis,* An. Ox. 994: 2506. Andwerdum *practica (vita),* i. *activa,* 3634. Andwurdan *practicam,* 2433. Andwyrd *actualem,* 996. v. un-andweard, and-weardnes.

and-wearde *answered,* and-weardian. v. and-wyrdan, ge-and-weardian.

and-weardlíce. *Add:*—Swā Drihten ondweardlíce (*when present with them*) sprǽc tó his gingrum, Bl. H. 131, 30.

and-weardnes. *Add:* -wurd-, -wyrd-nes. I. local:—Þǽr bið engla andweardnis, Ll. Th. ii. 408, 26. Hié mon tó his andweardnesse hēht gestandan *they were summoned to stand before him,* Bl. H. 173, 10. For þǽre andweardnesse þínes yrres *a vultu irae tuae,* Ps. Th. 37, 3. Se Hǽlend Petrum lǽrde on his andweardnysse (*while present*), Hml. Th. i. 378, 15. On andwerdnysse beón *to be present,* ii. 288, 7. On andwyrdnysse standan, 30, 12. Tó andwerdnesse (-wurdnysse, Hpt. Gl. 477, 21) *ad praesentiam,* An. Ox. 3015. II. temporal:—Þysses dæges hit wē nū on andweardnesse (*at the present time*) weorþiað, Bl. H. 115, 30. Anweardnesse, 211, 15. III. *action, operation:*—Hit is on þæs Hǽlendes andweardnesse hwænne hē hit geendige *in presentia Saluatoris est ipsum determinare,* Wlfst. 243, 25: Angl. viii. 336, 16. v. and-weard.

and-wendlic. v. un-andwendlic.

and-weorc. *Add:*—Andweorc tó wealle *cimentum,* Wrt. Voc. i. 85, 27. Ār bið hlūdre ðonne ǽnig óðer andweorc (ond-, *v. l.*) *aes amplius metallis ceteris sonitum reddit,* Past. 266, 24. Anweorces (-wurces, Hpt. Gl. 441, 21) *materiae,* An. Ox. 1484. Tó þām ic clipige þe eall gesceafte geworhte būtan ǽlcum andweorce, Angl. xii. 511, 18. Gold þe is deórwierðe ofer eal óðer ondweorc *aurum quod metallis ceteris praeeminet,* Past. 132, 14. Gif smið monnes andweorc onfō, Ll. Th. i. 74, 10. Saga mē ðæt andworc ðe Adam wæs of geworht, Sal. K. p. 180, 3. Þā stānas þára andweorca (-werca, *v. l.*) *corpora metallorum,* Gr. D. 270, 9: 321, 13. Geolewum andweorcum *fulvis metallis,* Wülck. Gl. 245, 36. v. an-weorc *in Dict.*

and-wíg, es; *n. Resistance:*—Andwíges heard, Gú. 147.

and-wille (?); *adj. Obstinate:*—Ne sý hē andwille (ann-, an-, *v. ll.*) *non sit obstinatus*, R. Ben. 121, 13.

and-wís. *Add:* v. un-andwís: and-wísnes. *Add:*—Andwísnis *experimentum*, Wrt. Voc. ii. 107, 50 : 29, 57.

and-wist, e; *f. Sustenance:*—Eorþan andwist *the sustenance that earth supplies*, An. 1542. Cf. and-leofen.

and-wlata. *Add:*—Anwlatan *frontis*, Scint. 172, 5 : *formae*, An. Ox. 5169. Lege ofer þā eágan on þone andwlatan, Lch. i. 72, 5. Begeót dæne andwlatan, 200, 10. Anwlatan, 356, 20. [wlata *from earlier* wliota, wlita.] v. next word.

-andwlatod. v. ge-andwlatod.

and-wlita. *Add: I. face, countenance:*—Andwlita ora, Wrt. Voc. ii. 92, 26 : 64, 43 : *vultus*, Wülck. Gl. 156, 19. Anwlita *vel neb facies*, Wrt. Voc. i. 42, 51 : *vultus*, 282, 45. Eówer mód is āwend and eówer andwlita, Hml. Th. i. 62, 32. His andwlita sceán, ii. 518, 11. Wearp seó eorþe hit tó þæs mannes andwleotan, Bl. H. 127, 2 : 223, 35. Ondwleatan *vultu*, Ps. Srt. 37, 4 : 45, 6. Þ hiora nān ōðerne on þone andwlitan ne slóge, Ors. 5, 12; S. 242, 11. Habban glædne andwlitan būtan blācunge and forhtunge, Hml. Th. i. 72, 27. Ondwliotan *vultum*, Ps. Srt. ii. p. 202, 34. Slógon ondwlitto (*faciem*) his, Lk. L. 22, 64. *II. form, appearance:*—Andwlitan *formae*, An. Ox. 8, 325. Đā eágan ongitaþ ðone andwlitan (*formam*) þæs líchoman, Bt. 41, 4; F. 252, 13.

and-wlítan. *Dele.*

and-wlite. *Add:*—Andwlite Drihtnes *vultus Domini*, Ps. L. 33, 17. Þínes andwlites *vultus tui*, 79, 17. Hē geseah beorhtnesse on his andwlite, Hml. S. 24, 138.

andwlite-full *glosses* vultuosus, Germ. 393, 172.

and-wyrdan. *Add:* (-weard-, -ward-, -word- *in North Gospels*):— Ne andwyrtst (-wyrdest, R.) þū nān þing ongēn þā *nihil respondes ad ea?*, Mt. 26, 62. Ondueardest (-wordes, R.), Mk. L. 14, 60. Se smiþ andwyrt (*respondit*), Coll. M. 31, 15. Đonne andwyrt se cyning þām rihtwísan þissum wordum, Wlfst. 288, 24. Onduearded, Mt. L. 25, 45. Onduardas *respondebunt*, 37. Ic ðā sóna eft mē selfum andwyrde and cwæð, Past. 5, 22 : Bt. 5, 3; F. 12, 3. Hē him andwyrde þissara worda, Gr. D. 299, 5. Đā andwearde se Hælend and cwæð, Hml. Th. i. 166, 14. Onduearde (onwyrde, R.), Mt. L. 15, 26. Onduarde, 12, 39. Onduorde, 24, 2. Ondearde, Mk. L. 10, 24. Þ ic þē andwyrdan scyle, Bt. 5, 3; F. 12, 16: Ors. 3, 9; S. 126, 30. Onduearda (-worda, R.), Mk. L. 14, 40. [*O. Sax.* and-wordian: *O. H. Ger.* ant-wurten.] v. ge-andwyrdan.

and-wyrde. *Add:*—Wæs Hannibale þ andwyrde láð, Ors. 4, 10; S. 202, 6 : 5, 3; S. 222, 20. For ðæm andwyrde geegsade, 21. Þ hē nān ryht andwyrde nyte, gif mon ácsaþ, Bt. 35, 1; F. 156, 8. [*Goth.* anda-waurdi: *O. Sax.* and-wordi: *O. H. Ger.* ant-wurti.]

and-wyrding. *Add:*—Fácengecwis oððe andwyrding *conspiratio*, Wrt. Voc. ii. 19, 8. (Cf. ge-anwyrdan *conspiraverant*, 134, 11.)

āne, æne. *Dele, and see* ān, æne.

ān-eága, -ége. *Add:*—Ānége *luscus*, Wrt. Voc. ii. 113, 12 : 71, 2. Āneges *monoptalmi*, 93, 38. Ānége *luscum*, Mk. L. 9, 47. Ānégum *monoptalmis, luscis*, An. Ox. 7, 225. Ænégum, Wrt. Voc. ii. 81, 40 : 56, 73. [*O. H. Ger.* ein-ougi *luscus, monoptalmus*.] v. ān-íge.

āneg, Hml. S. 23 b, 441. v. ænig, I. (1).

ān-éged. *l.* ān-eágede, -égede, *and add:*—Ānégede *luscus vel monoptalmus*, Wrt. Voc. i. 75, 41. Sum bróþor wæs ānégede . . . him weard āgifen his eáge, Hml. S. 33, 321. Ānégedum *monoptalmis*, An. Ox. 2, 142.

ā-neglod, *dele:* ānes, āness, *dele:* ānet-ness. v. ænett.

ānett, e; *f. Solitude:*—Hié þāra geearnunga hiora dígelnesse and ánette bet trūwien *secretum praeponit suum*, Past. 46, 2. v. ænett.

ān-feald. *Add:*—Ānfeald *simplex*, Wrt. Voc. ii. 74, 50. Ānfald *simpla*, 120, 55. *I. as numeral, single, sole:*—Ānfealdre *simplo* (*volumine*), An. Ox. 2376. Tó ānfealdan gewinne *ad singularem pugnam*, R. Ben. i. 10, 2. Náht þæs būton his ānfealdne gegyrelan, Bl. H. 215, 3. On eallum þisum men sēcaþ ānfealde eádignesse (*solam beatitudinem*), Bt. 24, 3; F. 84, 10. Gif mon næbbe būton ānfeald hrægl, Ll. Th. i. 52, 24. *II. simple, not resolvable into components:*—Ānfeald and untódælendlic, þeáh hine dysige men on mænig tódælen, Bt. 33, 1; S. 74, 30: 76, 9: 33, 2; S. 76, 12. *III. simple, unmixed:*—Þeáh hit ūs manigfealdlic ðince, sum gód, sum yfel, hit is þeáh him ānfeald gód, Bt. 39, 6; F. 220, 8. Hit hwílum gewyrþ þ þæm gódum becymþ ānfeald yfel, and þām yfium ānfeald gód, and ōþre hwíle ægþer gemenged, 39, 9; F. 224, 29. Tó tācnunge ānfealdes sáres, 7, 2; F. 18, 21. *IV. simple, without addition or amplification, no more than:*—Se Iōhannes wæs ácenned swā swā ōðre menn beóð and wæs ānfeald man, mære and gedungen (*he was simply a great and illustrious man*), Hml. Th. ii. 36, 29. Þonne wē sceolan habban ānfeald leán þæs þe wē on lífe ær geworhtan, Ll. Th. i. 370, 21: Wlfst. 209, 13: 208, 33. Fela árison mid Críste ðe wærou ānfealde men, ðeáh ðe Críst God sý, Hml. Th. i. 226, 5. *V. simple, plain,*

(1) *of persons:*—Đā bilwitan ānfealdan *simplices*, Past. 237, 14. Mid ðæm bilwitum and mid ðæm ānfealdum *cum simplicibus*, 243, 17. Críst geceás hyrdas and yrðlingas and ānfealde fisceras, Hml. S. 5, 225. (2) *of things:*—Þonne þincþ þām ungelæredum þ eall þ andgit beó belocen on þære ānfealdan gerecednisse, Ælfc. Gen. Thw. 2, 32. *VI. simple, uniform, fixed, invariable:*—Þ is openlíce cūþ þ sió godcunde foreteohhung is ānfeald and unáwendendlic *illud certe manifestum est, immobilem simplicemque gerendarum formam rerum esse providentiam*, Bt. 39, 6; F. 220, 16: 39, 4; F. 216, 30. Æt þæm stillan and æt þæm gestæþþigan and æt þæm ānfealdan Gode *ex divinae mentis stabilitate*, 39, 5; F. 218, 15: 39, 6; F. 220, 25.

ānfealdlíce. *Add: I. in the singular:*—Hē ne cwæþ nā menifealdlíce 'tó ūrum anlícnissum,' ac andfealdlíce 'tó ūre anlícnisse,' Ælfc. Gen. Thw. 3, 17. *II. simply, without reference to or connexion with anything else:*—Gif hí nāne æhta tó sellenne næbben, offrigen hyra bearn ānfealdlíce (*simpliciter*), R. Ben. 105, 9. Mid stilnesse ānfealdlíce (*simpliciter*) hē ingange, 81, 10. *III. simply, without ornament, amplification, &c.:*—Hit is ānfealdlíce gecweden, Hml. Th. ii. 244, 20. Þis godspel is nū ānfealdlíce gesæd, 404, 6. Agathes andwyrde ānfealdlíce, Hml. S. 8, 18.

ānfealdnes. *Add: Simplicity, ingenuousness:*—Biliwitnes and ānfealdnes his weorca *simplicitas actionis*, Past. 243, 13. Đæt hié geícen ðā gód hira ānfealdnesse mid wærscipe *ut simplicitatis bono prudentiam adjungant*, 237, 16. Críst lærde sóðfæstnysse and ānfealdnysse, Wlfst. 55, 10.

an-fealt. v. an-filte: an-féðe, *dele*.

an-filt. *Substitute:* an-filte, es; *n.;* an-fealt, e; *f.;* an-filt; *f. n.* (?) *An anvil*—Onfilti *incuda*, Txts. 69, 1072. Osifelti (on-?) *incus*, 112, 53. Anfilte, An. Ox. 53, 33: Wrt. Voc. i. 34, 56: *cudo*, 286, 77: ii. 16, 72. Anfilt, Ælfc. Gr. Z. 60, 8: 178, 11. Ōmiges anfiltes *scabrae incudis*, An. Ox. 479. Anfealte onsméðre, 11, 67. [*Mid. E.* an-felt, -feld, -veld, -vilt.]

ān-forlǽtan. *Add: I. to let go* (1) *what one holds:*—'Ic bebeóde þ gē hine leng ne beran, ac hine ānforlǽtan.' And hié sóna hine forlētan and hē gefeól, Bl. H. 189, 12. (2) *what one possesses, to lose:*—Ic geþence hwæt ic ānforlēt (*amisi*), and þonne ic geþence hwæt ic forleás (*perdidi*), Gr. D. 5, 9. Hié ne gēmdon hwonne hié þ gestreón eall ānforlǽtan sceoldon, Bl. H. 99, 30. *II. to leave unnoticed, to omit, neglect:*—þā gódan weorc wē ānforlǽtaþ þe wē begān sceoldan, Bl. H. 109, 4. Þ nán dæg ne sý betweoh ānforlǽten (*praetermittatur*), þ on þām ne sý geoffrod seó onsægdnes, Gr. D. 345, 29. *III. to lose as the result of fault:*—Tó náhte nyt ne biþ þ man gódne mete ete . . . gif þ gelimpeþ þ hē hit eft spíwende ānforlǽteþ; swā wē þā gāstlican lāre unwærlíce ne sceolan ānforlǽtan, Bl. H. 57, 5-9. Hē (*Adam*) gemunde þā gefeán þe hē ær ānforlēt (*amiserat*), Gr. D. 261, 5: Wlfst. 2, 10. *IV. to let go what ought to be kept, to forsake, abandon:*—Seó sāwel byþ deádlic þonne heó ānforlēt syngiende þ heó eádiglíce lifige *mortalis quia beate vivere amittit*, Gr. D. 337, 2. Manige men hwæthugu gód begangaþ, and raþe hié hit ānforlǽtaþ, Bl. H. 57, 3. Hē his swostor ānforlēt, Chr. 658; P. 32, 7. *V. to give up what one has a claim to:*—Gif wē ūsse brýde ānforlǽtað *if we give up those who ought to be our wives*, Shrn. 86, 22.

ān-forlǽtness, e; *f. I. loss.* v. ān-forlǽtan, III:—Æt neorxnawanges ānforlǽtnesse, Bl. H. 85, 31. *II. intermission.* Cf. ān-forlǽtan, II:—Būton ānforlǽtnesse *sine intermissione*, Gr. D. 227, 16.

anga, an; *m. A sting:*—Se anga ðære wrænnesse *aculeus libidinis*, Past. 309, 15. v. onga *in Dict.*

ānga. *Dele II, and add:*—Ic wæs mínra yldrena āuuga bearn, Shrn 36, 22. Míne āngan sáwle *unicam meam animam*, Ps. Th. 34, 17. [*Goth.* ainaha: *O. Sax.* ēnag: *O. H. Ger.* einac *unicus.*]

ang-breóst. *Add:*—Wiþ hwóstan and wiþ angbreóste, Lch. ii. 58, 11. Wið angcbreóste, iii. 48, 1.

ange. *Dele all but passage from Orosius, and substitute:* ange (onge, ænge); *adv. Anxiously, painfully, with anxiety:*—Blind sceal his eágna þolian . . . þæt him biþ sār in his móde, onge þonne hē hit āna wāt, Gn. Ex. 42. Þū eart bitere ætfæsted, ænge and yfele, Ps. Th. 136, 8.

angel *a hook. Add:*—Fiscere *piscator*, angel *amus*, Wrt. Voc. i. 73, 42. Hwanon fiscere angcel?, Coll. M. 30, 33. Hū gefēhst þū fixas? Angil ic wyrpe, 23, 11. Se grædiga fisc gesihð þæt æs and ne gesihð ðone angel ðe on ðām æse sticað, Hml. Th. i. 216, 11. Angul *hamum*, Wrt. Voc. ii. 72, 75.

angel *an angel. Add:*—Angel *angelus*, Lk. L. 1, 26: Rtl. 58, 5. Angla *angelos*, Jn. L. 1, 51. v. angel-lic.

Angel-cyning. *Add:*—Eádgāres Angulcynincges, C. D. iii. 49, 28. Ongelcyningum *regibus Anglorum*, Bd. 5, 19; S. 640, 16.

Angel-cynn. *Add:*—þā hālgan þe Angelcynn wurþað, Hml. S. p. 4, 42. On Angolcynnes bócum, ðæt is on *Istoria Anglorum*, Shrn. 137, 6: 59, 12. Mid wópe Angelcynnes monna, 134, 24. Æðelbryht ǽrest fulluht onfēng on Angelcynne, Ll. Th. i. 58, 26. Geond Angelcynn (-kynn, *v. l.*) . . . on Angelcynne (-kynne, *v. l.*) . . . behionan Humbre . . .

begiondan Humbre, Past. 3, 3–16. ¶ where the reference is to North-umbria :—Ongan þæt mægen Angelcynnes rīces tōflōwan, Bd. 4, 26 ; S. 602, 28. Benedict wæs Angelcynnes man, Shrn. 50, 23.

**Angel-cyrice**, an ; *f. The church in England :*—In Ongelcyricean, Bd. 1, 27 ; S. 489, 11 : 492, 2.

**ān-geld.** *l.* ān-gelde, *and see* ān-gilde.

**an-gelíc.** *Add :* [*O. H. Ger.* ana-galih.] v. next word.

**an-gelícness**, e ; *f. A likeness, image :*—Angelícnessum *characteribus*, Wrt. Voc. ii. 85, 83 : 18, 66.

**angel-(l)ic** ; *adj. Angelic :*—Æfter ðære angelica gesihðo *post angeli-cam visionem*, Jn. p. 8, 3.

**Angel-þeód.** *Add :* I. of the continental invaders :—Angelþeód (Ongel-, *v. l.*) wæs gelaðod fram Bryttum *invitata Brittaniam gens Anglorum* . . . Angelþeód and Seaxna wæs gelaðod *Anglorum sive Saxonum gens invitata*, Bd. 1, 15 ; Sch. 40, 1, 15. Bryttas ærest on Angelðeóde sige genāman, 1, 16 ; Sch. 44, 4. II. of the northern English :—Monige Ongelþeóde, Bd. 4, 26 ; Sch. 507, 8. Þ spell þ ic āwrāt be Angelþeóde and Seaxum *historiam gentis Anglorum quam edideram*, pref. ; Sch. 1, 5.

**angel-twicce.** *Add :*, -twecca, -twæcca, -twicca ; *m. :*—Angeltwicce *lumbricus*, An. Ox. 23, 19. Angeltwicca (-twicce, -twiccæ, [-twæcche], *v. ll.*), Ælfc. Gl. Z. 309. Angeltwecca *lacontrapis*, Wrt. Voc. ii. 53, 44. Genim angeltwæccean gehālne, Lch. ii. 44, 14. v. angol-twæcce (*l.* -a) *in Dict.*

**ān-genga.** *Add :*—Ðā tungelwītegan gesāwon nīwne steorran beorhtne, nā on heofenum betwux ōðrum tunglum, ac wæs āngenga betwux heofenum and eorðan, Hml. Th. i. 106, 26. Sum mōdig fearr wearð āngencga and þære heorde drāfe oferhogode, 502, 11. Hwī se fearr āngenga his heorde forsāwe, 17.

**an-geræd.** v. un-geræd.

**ān-geweald.** *Add :* [Cf. *Icel.* ein-vald *sovereignty, monarchy.*]

**ān-gild.** *l.* ān-gilde, *and substitute for the passages from the laws the following :*—Ā sié þ wīte .LX. sciłł. oð þ āngylde ārīse tō .XXX. sciłł. ; siþþan hit tō þām ārīse, þ āngylde, siþþan sié þ wīte .CXX. sciłł., Ll. Th. i. 68, 3–5. Þolie hē his āngyldes (-gildes, *v. l.*), 76, 7. Mana þone byrgean þæs āngyldes ; gif hē næbbe, gyld þū þ āngylde, 116, 11–12. Forgylde hē þ āngylde, and þ wīte swā tō þām āngylde belimpe, 66, 3. Be gehwelces ceápes āngelde (-gilde, wyrðe, *v. l.*), 138, 9. Þ āngylde forgyldan, 260, 7. ¶ *ān-gildes, -gilde* seem used adverbially in the following :—Gylde man þām teónde his ceápgyld ān-gyldes (-gildes, -geldes, *v. ll.*), 268, 19. Gylde hē āngyldes þ hē mid beléd wæs, 354, 15. Forgylde þ yrfe āngylde, 236, 24. Gilde hē āngylde (*or acc.*?), 294, 17. Cf. twi-gylde *in Dict., and next word.*

**ān-gilde** ; *adj. To be compensated for, for which* āngilde (q. v.) *is to be paid :*—Būton hiora hwæðer ær þingode þ hē hit āngilde healdan ne þorfte *unless either of them previously made the condition that he was not to be liable to make compensation for damage done to the material entrusted to him*, Ll. Th. i. 74, 12.

**an-gin.** *Add :* I. *a beginning :*—Angin *origo*, Wrt. Voc. ii. 128, 42. Of anginne *ex integro*, 145, 4. Tō anginne, tō edstaþelungum *ad lumina vitae*, An. Ox. 2214. Tō anginum *ad lumina* (v. Hpt. Gl. 507, 61, which has *limina*), 4342. Seó wyrt gehnæcceþ ðā anginnu (*the beginnings of the disease*) þām wæterseócum, Lch. i. 272, 15. II. *an enterprise, under-taking, attempt :*—Þ angin (*building a fleet*) weard tīdlīce þurhtogen, Ors. 4, 6 ; S. 172, 3. Þ þ angin (*a war*) nære gestilled, 6, 4 ; S. 260, 5. Romulus hiora anginn (*founding Rome*) geunclænsode mid his brōðor slege, 2, 2 ; S. 64, 23. Gif hwylc man ūre angin (*writing Guthlac's life*) and weorc tæle, Guth. 4, 1. III. *persistent effort, enterprise, endeavour, pertinacity :*—Þāra þegna angin . . . þ hié noldon þæs weall-gebreces geswīcan *the pertinacity of the thanes in not desisting from breaking down the wall*, Ors. 3, 9 ; S. 134, 27. Ðæt hē ðā medwīsan tō māran angienne (*ad majora*) gespōne, Past. 205, 17. Hū God þā mæstan ofermētto and þæt mæste angin on swā heánlīce ofermētto (*the extreme perseverance in such contemptible pride?*) geniðerade, Ors. 2, 5 ; S. 84, 11. Anginna *pertinacia*, Kent. Gl. 1170. III a. *practice of a rite, study :*—Næfre nān man ne geþrīstlæce ænigne deófles bigencg tō dōnne, ne on wiccedōme, ne on ænegum īdelum anginne, Hml. A. 143, 123. Forsægenum þām onginnum (*studiis ; v. l.* bigengum) þāra bōc-cræfta, Gr. D. 95, 26. Þ hē forlēte þā ongin þæra bōccræfta *relictis literarum studiis*, 96, 19. IV. *attempt on, attack :*—Ne becume mē fōt † angin ofermōdignesse *non veniat mihi pes superbiae*, Ps. L. 35, 12. Onginnum *inceptis (machinamentorum)*, An. Ox. 4709. V. *gesture, action :*—Angin *gesticulatio*, An. Ox. 2872. Hē færinga feóll tō þære eorðan mid egeslicum anginne, Chr. 1042 ; P. 162, 14. Anginnum *gestibus*, An. Ox. 7, 241 : 8, 180. VI. *action, proceedings, behaviour, treatment :*—Þā hē ðæs cāseres myclan hreówsunga geseah, him þ hreów and his þ sārlice anginn (*his piteous proceedings*), Hml. S. 23, 402. Hē began tō dreccenne mid dyrstigum anginne þā bisceopas *he troubled the bishops by his audacious treatment of them*, 37, 34. His cempan hine gelæhton mid dyrstigum anginne (*treated him with the utmost audacity*), Hml. Th. ii. 252, 24. Hī tīgdon þā fēt tōgædere mid gramlicum anginne, Hml. S.

35, 166. Hī woldon Egeam ācwellan and ālædan ðone apostol of ðām cwearterne. Ðā cwæð Andreas : ‘ Ne āstyrige gē Drihten tō yrsunge mid eówerum anginne,’ Hml. Th. i. 592, 4. Mid þæm þe þā burgware swā geómorlic angin hæfdon *while the citizens were engaged in such melancholy proceedings*, Ors. 4, 5 ; S. 166, 15. [*O. H. Ger.* ana-ginn(i) *initium.*] See also ongin *in Dict.*

**Angle.** *Add :*, Ongle :—Feówer þeóda hine (*Oswald*) underfēngon tō hlāforde, Peohtas and Bryttas, Scottas and Angle, Hml. S. 26, 106. Ongle, Shrn. 113, 33. Of Germania lande Ongla ðeód com on þās Breotone, 77, 38. Augustinus ærest fullwiht brohte on ðās Breotone on Angla þeóde, 87, 3. v. Engle.

**Anglisc**, Onglisc ; *adj. English :*—Ongliscre sprǽce, Hml. S. 16, 33. v. Englisc.

**ang-mōd.** *Add :*—Ne beó hē drēfende ne angmōd (ancg-, *v. l.*) *non sit turbulentus et anxius*, R. Ben. 120, 12. Wurdon heora eágan āfyllede mid teárum and angmōde geómrodon ealle heora heortan, Hml. S. 23, 244.

**ang-mōdness.** *Add :*—Gif seó sāwl slīdan sceal in þā ēcan wīta and mid deóflum drohtnoð habban in angmōdnysse earmra sāwla, Wlfst. 188, 6.

**ang-nægl.** *Substitute :*—*A corn on the foot :*—Wiþ angnægle, Lch. ii. 8, 9 : 80, 21.

**angnere**, es ; *m. The corner of the eye :* — Yrqui beáhhyrne *vel* a(n)gneras ; *volvos dicimus angulos oculorum*, Wrt. Voc. i. 43, 2. v. ongnere *in Dict.*

**ang-ness.** *Add :* I. *of physical pain :*—Hwīlum wyrmas gesēceð þā uferan dǽlas and heortcoþe wyrceað and angnessa and geswōwunga, Lch. ii. 176, 13. II. *in a more general sense :*—Ne bið þær a[n]gnes ne uǽnigu gnornung *non angor, moeror*, Dōm. L. 266. Ealle angnysse and uneáðnysse, Lch. iii. 156, 13. Brōðer on angnyssum (*angustiis*) byð āfandud, Scint. 15, 4.

**angol-twæcce.** *l.* -twæcca, *and see* angel-twicce.

**an-grislic.** *l.* an-grislic, *and add :*—Þær bið angrislic ege and fyrhto, Wlfst. 139, 16. Se angrislica sūðwesterna wind him ongeán stōd, Ap. Th. 11, 4. v. on-grislic *in Dict.*

**ang-seta** ; *m. Add :*—Angseta *pustula*, Wrt. Voc. ii. 68, 51 : *cronculus*, i. 45, 33. Ongseta, ii. 22, 68. *Frunculus, quasi ferunculus, id est* ongseta, *Graece antrax, ab igne*, 39, 16.

**ang-sum.** *Add :*—Hī þæne ancsuman weg geceósað, be þǽm se Hælend cwyð, ‘ Ancsum and neara is se weg þe tō līfe lǽt,’ R. Ben. 20, 9.

**angsume** ; *adv. In trouble, in difficulties :*—þonne þē ealra angsumest byð on þīnum mōde geðenc þū mīn *when you are most troubled in mind, remember me*, Shrn. 15, 18. [*For the construction* cf. ange, *and* Ælfc. Gr. Z. 231, 4.]

**angsumian.** v. ge-angsumian.

**angsumlíce** ; *adv. Painfully :*—Hē egeslīce hweós and angsumlīce siccetunga teáh, Hml. Th. i. 86, 8.

**ang-sumnes.** *Add :* I. *distress of body :*—Hē (*Herod when dying*) mid ormǽtre angsumnysse wæs gecwylmed, Hml. Th. i. 88, 5. Sume hī cuwon heora gescý for ðære micclan angsumnysse ðæs hātan hungres, 404, 6. Mislice angsumnyssa hē forbær, ðā ðā hē næfde ne bigleofan, ne hǽlðe, ne hætera, 330, 13. II. *distress of mind :*—Ne angsumnys ne ænig gnornung *non angor, moeror*, Wlfst. 139, 32. Þæs weges ongin þe tō Crīste lǽt ne mæg beón begunnen būtan sumre ancsumnysse (ang-, *v. l.*) *via salutis non est nisi angusto initio incipienda*, R. Ben. 5, 17. Mid hyra anxsumnysse *anxietate sua*, Scint. 3, 5 : Lch. iii. 200, 4. Anxumnyssum *suspiria, anxietates*, Hpt. Gl. 429, 61. Hē geheald fram ancsumnyssum (*angustiis*) sāwle his, Scint. 79, 5.

**ān-haga.** *Add :*—Wulf sceal on bearowe, earm ānhaga, Gn. C. 19.

**an-hefedness, -hende.** v. on-hefedness, -hende *in Dict.*

**ān-hende.** *Add :*—Ānhendi, -haendi *mancus*, Txts. 76, 626. Ān-hende, Wrt. Voc. i. 75, 44 : ii. 71, 18 : 54, 73. Gōd is þē ānhende tō līfe þonne twā honda hæbbende sīð sended in ēcce fȳr, Mt. R. 18, 8. Blinde, ānhende *caecos, debiles*, 15, 30.

**ān-hīwe** ; *adj. Of one form or colour :*—Ānhīwes *uniformi*, An. Ox. 1046.

**an-horna.** *Add :* [*O. H. Ger.* ein-hurno.]

**ānhund-wintre** ; *adj. A hundred years old :*—Hē āxode hyne hū eald hē wære. Þā andswarode hē : ‘ Āuhundwintre and þrītigwintre,’ Gen. 47, 9.

**ān-hyrne.** *Add :* as noun. *a unicorn* (; as adj., *having one horn*) :—Ānhyrne *monoceros*, Wrt. Voc. ii. 57, 41. Of þām hornum þāra ānhyrna (*unicornuorum*), Ps. Th. 21, 19. Ānhyrnera, Ps. Srt. 21, 22. Ānhyrnra, 28, 6 : 77, 69.

**ān-hyrned.** *Add :*, -hyrnede :—Ānhyrned deór *unicornis*, Wrt. Voc. i. 78, 1 : Ps. L. 77, 69. Ānhyrnede *unicornis*, Bl. Gl. Ānhyrnedra *unicornium*, Ps. L. 28, 4.

**ā-nīdan.** *Add :* I. *without adverb :*—þū ānýdest (*repellis*) gebed mīn, Ps. Spl. 87, 15. Fram ūs wē ānýdaþ, Scint. 210, 5. Þū ānīddest ūs *repulisti nos*, Ps. Spl. 43, 11. Ne anýd þū *ne repellas*, 26. II. *with adverb :*—Ic ūt anýde *elimino, foras ejicio, expello*, Wrt. Voc. ii.

143, 7. Heú út ánýdeþ ðá untrumnysse, Lch. i. 202, 8 : 248, 14. Hé fram him lufa áweg ánýt (*repellit*), Scint. 28, 13. Hí fram him heortan ofermódigra áweg ánýdaþ (*repellunt*), 21, 6. þú út ánýddest (*expulisti*) hí, Ps. Spl. 43, 3. God ánýdde út Adam of ðære myrhðe, Wlfst. 154, 3. Ne út ánýd þú mé fram bebodum ðínum, Ps. Spl. 118, 10. Hí man sceal út of Godes circan ánýdan, Hml. A. 149, 126. Út tó ánýdenne *expellendum*, Scint. 210, 13. Út ánéddum *effossis, evulsis*, Wrt. Voc. ii. 142, 63.

**án-íge.** Add :—Ánígne *luscum*, Wrt. Voc. ii. 73, 38. Áníge þyrsas *cyclopes*, 22, 37. Æníge *luscos*, 92, 62. v. án-eáge.

**á-niman.** Add : I. *to take, accept, retain* :—Gif ic þá word ániman wolde *si ipsa verba tenere voluissem*, Gr. D. 9, 15. II. *to take away, remove* :—þá ánam hé þæt fýr fram manna bearnum, Wlfst. 213, 10 : 221, 32. Ánimað, ánimað hraðe þá réþan wiccan, Hml. S. 7, 209. Ic wille ániman and áteón fram þám þe þás bóc rædaþ þone intingan ælcre tweónge *ut dubitationis occasionem legentibus subtraham*, Gr. D. 9, 5. Ælc tæl sié ánumen (*tollatur*) fram eów, Past. 222, 9. Of his heortan onweg ánumen, Bl. H. 55, 9.

**áninga.** Add :—Is se dæg cumen þ ðú scealt áninga (*certainly*) óðer twéga líf forleósan oððe lange dóm ágan mid eldum, Wald. 14.

**an-íwan.** v. on-íwan : **an-læc.** l. an-léc, *and see* on-léc *in Dict.*

**án-lécan;** *p.* -léhte *To unite* :—Ánléhte *adunaret*, Hpt. Gl. 479, 42. þá ánléhtan *coadunatas, compositas*, 472, 2. v. ge-ánlæcan.

**án-lǽtan;** *Dele* : **an-lǽtan.**

**án-laga;** *adj. Substitute* : *Acting alone* :—Ánlaga *solitare* (the passage in Aldhelm is: Carnalis pudicitiae immunitas . . . *solitaria nequaquam paradisi valvam recludere valeat*, 16, 34), Wrt. Voc. ii. 77, 35. [Icel. ein-lagi; *adj. Acting alone.*]

**anlang cempa.** v. andlang-cempa : **án-lápum.** v. án-lípum.

**an-léc.** l. an-léc, *and see* on-léc *in Dict.*

**án-leger.** l. án-legere, *dele bracket, and for* R. 8 *substitute* Wrt. Voc. i. 50, 43. v. leger *in Dict.*

**an-leofa.** v. and-leofa : **án-lépe, -lépig.** v. án-lípe, -lípig.

**an-líc.** Add :—Ne fiust þú þær náuht anlíces, Bt. 18, 3 ; F. 66, 11. v. on-líc *in Dict.*

**án-líc.** Add : I. *single* :—Ánlic *unica*, An. Ox. 1800. Ánlic anweald *monarchia*, 18 b, 54. II. *of the only church, catholic, orthodox* :—Ánlic *catholica*, An. Ox. 5105. Seó ánlice, 1359. Ánlices *orthodoxae*, Hpt. Gl. 415, 74. Ánlicra *catholicorum*, An. Ox. 172. III. *of singular excellence, beautiful* :—Mid ánlicre *formosa*, Wrt. Voc. ii. 34, 58. v. æn-líc.

**án-líce, an-lícian.** v. on-líce, ge-anlícian *in Dict.*: **án-lícian.** v. ge-ánlícian.

**an-lícnes.** Add : I. *likeness, resemblance* :—Hwí is gecweden ægþer ge anlícnyss (*imago*) ge gelícnyss (*similitudo*)? Seó anlícnyss is tó understandenne on þære écnysse, and seó gelícnyss on hire þeáwum, Angl. vii. 20, 178. Hé gestrínde sunu tó his gelícnesse and anlícnysse, Gen. 5, 3. II. *an example, model, figure,* (in speaking) :—Sió anlícnes wæs gecueden *figurate per habitum sacerdotis dicit*, Past. 95, 11. Siexfealdre anlícnesse *sena paradigmata*, Wrt. Voc. ii. 89, 39. III. *an image, figure* :—Anlícnes *anagrippa*, Wrt. Voc. i. 285, 10 : ii. 8, 30. Anlícnesse *colcri*, An. Ox. 1637. Scm árgeótere, sé mehte dón missenlica anlícnessa, Ors. I, 12 ; S. 54, 20. III a. *an image used for worship, an idol* :—Anlícnyssum *simulacrorum*, An. Ox. 3472. Hiora anlícnessa (*imagines*) hefenisc fýr forbærnde, Ors. 2, 8 ; S. 94, 14. Rachel hæfde þá andlícnyssa (*idola*) forstolen, Gen. 31, 32. Ne wirce gé eów náne andlícnissa (*sculptam similitudinem aut imaginem*) ne wǽpmannes ne nýtenes ne fugeles, Deut. 4, 16. v. and-, on-lícnes *in Dict.*

**án-lípe (æn-)** ; *adj.* I. *single, alone, solitary, by one's self, not combined with anything else* :—Ne wénen hié ðæt hiera fæsten ánlípe (-lépe, Cott. MSS.) heálíc mægen sié, ðý læs hié wénen ðæt hit anlípe micelre geearnunge mægen sié, Past. 315, 9–11. Ænlípe *solitaria*, An. Ox. 1147 : 2, 30. On ðone ánlípan beorh, C. D. ii. 317, 24. ðær ægðer wære unnyt ge mildheortnes ge steór, gif hié ánlípe (-lépe, Cott. MSS.) wæron, búton hí bútú ætsomne sién, Past. 125, 3. II. *of number, single (with one)* :—Wísdóm is án ánlépe cræft ðære sáwle, and ðeáh wé witon ðæt he sié betera ðonne ealle ðá óðre cræftas, Bt. 32, 1 ; F. 116, 3. Nán ánlípe (*ne una quidem*) tó láfe ne wunode, Gr. D. 67, 18. Swæ feáwa hiora wæron ðæt ic furðum ænne ánlépne ne mæg gedéncean, Past. 3, 17. III. *single, distinct from others, individual* :—Ðus hit byð gedón in ánlépra gehwylcre (cf. ánra gehwylc) sáwle *sic in unaquaque anima agitur*, Gr. D. 205, 8. IV. *special (as opposed to general)* :—Ænlípe *specialis*, An. Ox. 7, 386 : 8, 401. V. *single, private, not having office* :—Ðá underðiúddan and ðá ánlépan menn ðe ǽmtige beóð ðæs ðæt hié for óðre menu suíncen . . . Se ǽmetiga and se ánlípa (-lépa, Cott. MSS.), Past. 191, 13–18. [Icel. ein-hleypr *single (man)*] v. án-lépe *in Dict.*

**án-lípig (æn-).** Add : *Single* ; *singulus* :—Ænlípige men *singuli homines*, Ælfc. Gr. 284, 5. I. *single, sole, by one's self, alone* :—Ánlípig aldormon (*one or other alderman acting by himself* : MS. F has *ealdormen*) and cyninges þegnas oft ráde onrídon, Chr. 871 ; P.

72, 14. Hwílum ánlépig, hwílum tógædere gedón, Lch. ii. 62, 6. Ic ænlípigu oþstód, Hml. S. 23 b, 409. Sume ðæs seáwes ænlípiges nyttiað, Lch. ii. 30, 16. Martinus gelácnode mid ænlipium cosse (*with nothing but a kiss* ; or under II *with one single kiss*) ænne hreófiinne mannan, Hml. Th. ii. 512, 5. Oð ðone ánlípigan þorn . . . On ðone ánlípian stán, C. D. iii. 467, 7, 8. Mín swustur lét mé ænlípie (*solam*) þénian, Lk. 10, 40. Ne sculon mæssepreóstas ænlípie bútan óðrum mannum mæssan syngan, Ll. Th. ii. 406, 21. Ðá wuniað twám and þrim ætgædere and hwilon ænlípige, R. Ben. 9, 15. Hí námon him ðá gedwollmenn ænlípige (*heretics only*) tó gemynde, Hml. S. 23, 390. I. *of number, (one) single* :—Læcedóm onsundron ánlípig *a single recipe by itself*, Lch. ii. 12, 7. On ðære ealdan ǽ wæs ánlípig hús Gode tó wurðmynte áræred . . . ealle óðre þeóda fela templa árærdon . . . þæt ánlípige Godes tempel wæs wundorlíce gecræft, Hml. Th. ii. 574, 24–29. For ðám þrim rædingum sý án ánlípig (ænlýpig, *v. l.*) rædincg geræd, R. Ben. 34, 11. Án ǽlpi mónð, Angl. viii. 320, 11. Nán ánlípig (*ne una quidem*) tó láfe ne wunode, Gr. D. 67, 18. III. *single, distinct from others, individual* :—Ðæt ná nán ænlípig ne módige, ðonne mynstres notu manegum bið betǽht *ut dum pluribus committitur unus non superbiat*, R. Ben. 125, 10. Ælcan ænlýpium wæs geseald be ðám ðe hé behófade, 57, 19. Ðus hit byð gedón in ænlípigre gehwylcre sáwle (*in unaquaque anima*), Gr. D. 205, 8. Swilce hí wæron ðám ænlípige góde and wæron syððan for ðám menn ealle swíðe góde *quasi ante essent singula bona, propter hominem autem omnia valde bona*, Angl. vii. 20, 187. Hí ealle mid angsumum móde ænlípige cwædon, Hml. Th. ii. 244, 2. Gehwilce ænlípige on heora burgum be him sylfum cendon, i. 34, 4 : ii. 124, 10. Ðone ic oft ásende tó ænlípigum burgum *I send him to the different towns*, Hml. S. 36, 42. IV. *each* :—Six wæterfatu healdende ænlípige twyfealde gemetu, Hml. Th. ii. 56, 22. Hé getimbrode twelf mynstra, on ðám ænlípium hé gesette twelf munecas, 158, 33. V. *with distributive force* :—Ænlípige munecas geond ænlýpige bed restan, R. Ben. 47, 3. þá underféngon hí ænlípige penegas, An. Th. 74, 15. [Orm. anlepiȝ : A. R. onlepi, elpi : O. E. Hml. enlepi, alpi : Laym. anlæpi, ælpi : Ayenb. onlepi.] v. onelepi *in N. E. D.*

**án-lípum** ; *adv. Singly* :—Ingunnun ánlépum cweþan, Mt. R. 26, 22. v. án-lápum *in Dict.*

**an-lútung (?)** *a wrapper* :—Anlútungum (-lúcungum ?) *involucris*, Germ. 402, 54.

**án-méde,** es ; *n. Unanimity* :—þú eart se man þe mé wære on ánméde *tu vero, homo unanimis*, Ps. Th. 54, 13.

**an-medla.** l. -médla, *and add* :—Hwær beóð þonne his wlencea and his anmedlan? Bl. H. 111, 34. v. on-médla *in Dict., and cf.* an-mód.

**an-méttan (án-?).** v. ge-anméttan.

**an-mitta (and-, on-).** *Dele all but second passage, and add* : *A balance, scale* :—Andmitta (hand-) *exagium*, Txts. 61, 793. Anmitta *statera*, Kent. Gl. 343. Habbaþ rihtne anmittan and emne wǽgan *statera justa et aequa sint pondera*, Lev. 19, 35. On anmittum *in stateris*, Bl. Gl. v. on-mitta *in Dict.*

**an-mód.** Add : In some of the passages perhaps án-mód should be read :—Onmód (an-) *contumax*, Txts. 48, 202. Anmóde, Wrt. Voc. ii. 14, 67. *Contumax,* i. *superbus* anmóda *contemptor*, 135, 23. v. on-mód *in Dict., and cf.* an-medla.

**án-mód.** Add :—þæt werod wæs swá ánmód (cf. Hom. i. 101, 4) swilce him eallum wære án heorte and án sáwul, Hml. Th. i. 326, 25. þú ánmóde *tu unanimis*, Ps. L. 54, 14. Mid ánmóde willan monigra *multorum unanima intentione*, Bd. 5, 6 ; Sch. 575, 12. Mid ánmóðre geþafunge eallra, 4, 17 ; Sch. 430, 5. Moston beón *uniri per concordiam*, Past. 345, 10. Ðá geseah se cyning þæt hí ánmóde wæron, Hml. Th. i. 570, 27. Ánmódde *unanimes*, Ps. Srt. 67, 7. [We ware onmode godes wille to done, Hom. ii. 183, 8.]

**an-módlíce (án-?)** ; *adv.* I. *without hesitation* :—Ðá ástód hé ætforan him, and him anmódlíce tó cwæð, Hml. Th. i. 580, I. Cúðberhtus ðá tó ðám engle anmódlíce cwæð, ii. 134, 31. II. *constantly, persistently, steadfastly* :—Hé clypede anmódlíce tó Gode, Hml. S. 18, 126. 400. v. an-mód.

**án-módlíce.** Add :—Ánmódlíce *concorditer,* i. *unanimiter*, An. Ox. 2595 ; *unanimiter*, Coll. M. 36, 5 : Wlfst. 68, 3 : Ll. Th. i. 36, 11 : Hml. Th. i. 570, 23 : Bl. H. 219, 35 : 139, 20.

**an-módnes.** Add :—*resolution, constancy, steadfastness* :—Gyf him þince þ hé mid gyrdel sió gyrded, ðæt byð anmódnes, Lch. iii. 170, 22.

**án-módnes.** Add :—Sió ánmódnes ryhtes geleáfan *fidei unitas*, Past. 95, 5. Ðá ánmódnesse ðæra ðe ðærtó hlýstað *unitas audientium*, 93, 25. Geornlíce gebinde ge eów tósomne mid ánmódnesse and mid sibbe *sollicite servare unitatem spiritus in vinculo pacis*, 345, 17. Oferswíðed mid ánmódnesse (*unanimitate*) eallra þára witena, Gr. D. 329, 17.

**án-nes.** Dele II, *and add* : I. *unity (as opposed to separation)* :—þá gód ealle on ánnesse bióþ, and sió ánnes bið on écnesse . . . Sió ánnes and sió gódnes án þing sié, Bt. 34, 9 ; F. 146, 23–33. II. *union (as opposed to disagreement)* :—Hú mycel gód is ðær ðær gebróðru beóð on ánnysse *quam bonum habitare fratres in unum*, Hml. S. 5, 394.

Lufige hé ánnysse and bróðorrǽdene betwux mannum, Hml. Th. i. 142, 10. Eal se here him swór ánnesse, þæt hié eal þæt woldon þæt hé wolde, Chr. 921; P. 103, 16.

**án-nihte;** *adj. One day old:*—Ácenned on ánnihtne móna[n], Lch. iii. 160, 18. Ánnihte, 176, 16.

**án-rǽd.** *Add:* , -rǽde. **I.** *of one (and the same) counsel, agreed, in agreement, in harmony,* (1) *of persons:*—Þurcil and hé wǽran ánrǽde, Chr. 1023; P. 157, 30. Ealle hí wǽron ánrǽde æt eallum þám ðingum, Ll. Th. ii. 336, 11. (2) *of things:*—Þ man menn blód ne lǽte ǽr þæm þe se móna and seó sǽ beón ánrǽde, Lch. iii. 154, 2. **II.** *of one (unvarying) counsel, steadfast, constant, resolute:*—Gestæþþig, ánrǽde *constans, stabilis,* Wrt. Voc. ii. 133, 69. (1) *of persons:*—Áfandað God ðæs mannes mód, hwæðer hé ánrǽde sý, Hml. Th. i. 268, 16. Beó ðú ánrǽde and unforht, ii. 480, 3: Guth. 96, 1: Hml. S. 36, 292. Tó þám ánrǽde þæt hé ne áwácad, Wlfst. 97, 6. Wæs þ cild snotor and ánrǽde, Shrn. 127, 12: R. Ben. 108, 21. Ánrǽd *constans,* Kent. Gl. 1153. Hé hine hét þæt hé ne tweóde, ac þæt hé wǽre ánrǽd, Guth. 30, 7. Eádgár se æþela and se ánrǽda cyning, Jud. p. 163, 11. Rihtwísnysse mid ánrǽdum móde symle healdan, Hml. Th. ii. 228, 19: Hml. S. 1, 166. Beóð ánrǽde and habbað sum eornost, Hml. A. 48, 582: Shrn. 59, 26. Hí wǽron swá ánrǽde on geleáfan þæt tintrega hí ne mihte fram Gode gebígan, Hml. Th. ii. 540, 21. Þone ánrǽdestan (*constantissimum*) andettere, Gr. D. 238, 22. Mid ðám ánrǽdystum mannum þe him mid fuhton, Hml. S. 25, 668. (2) *of things:*—Swá ánrǽde seó wyrt ys þ heó þy ylcan dæge þá stánas forbrycð, Lch. i. 212, 14. Habban ánrǽde geðanc and ánrǽdne geleáfan, Wlfst. 32, 17. [*O. H. Ger.* ein-ráti: *Icel.* ein-ráðr.]

**án-rǽdlic;** *adj. Unhesitating, decided:*—Þ wæs ánrǽdlicu eáþmódnes þ heó sylf hié þeówen nemde, Bl. H. 13, 13.

**án-rǽdlíce.** *Add:* **I.** *in reference* (1) *to persons, unanimously,* (2) *to things, uniformly:*—Hý cwǽdon ealle ánrǽdlíce þ hit riht wǽre, Ll. Th. ii. 336, 2. Wið þám þe hí ealle ánrǽdlíce tó him gecyrdon, Chr. 1014; P. 145, 9. Gesetnys ánrǽdlíce (*uniformiter*) gehealden, R. Ben. I. 50, 3. **II.** *of a single act, definitely, decidedly, positively, resolutely, without hesitation or uncertainty:*—Heó cwæd ánrǽdlíce: 'Ne gewurð þæt nǽfre swá,' Hml. A. 128, 401: Ælfc. T. Grn. 17, 37: Hml. S. 18, 247. Drihten andwyrde ánrǽdlíce Petre: 'Þú mé wiðsæcst,' Hml. Th. ii. 246, 3. Ic ánrǽdlíce spræc ná módelíce *I spoke resolutely, not proudly,* Hml. S. 34, 325. Gé habbað gehýred ánrǽdlíce hwæt eów tó dónne is *you have heard definitely what there is for you to do,* Ll. Th. ii. 362, 17. Hí swíðe ánrǽdlíce wið þæs heres wǽron *they were very resolutely making their way towards the Danes,* Chr. 1003; P. 135, 9. **III.** *of continuous action, constantly, persistently, pertinaciously:*—Ánrǽdlíce *pertinaciter, constanter,* An. Ox. 771. Ánrǽdlíce syngian *perseveranter peccare,* Scint. 130, 16. Ánrǽdlíce læran *instanter erudire,* 175, 17: Hml. Th. ii. 324, 33. Þæt hé wiðsace ánrǽdlíce deófles gemánan, Wlfst. 32, 14. Ánrǽdlíce gelýfan, 33, 10: H. R. 101, 30. Swíðe ánrǽdlíce heó ætwát ðæm hǽþnum, Shrn. 57, 33. Þ hé ánrǽdlíce gefulfremige þá gód þe hé beginne, Hml. A. 150, 154. Of þám dæge hí ánrǽdlíce þóhton þ hí hyne ofslógon, 66, 20. [*O. H. Ger.* ein-rátlíhho *constanter.*]

**án-rǽdnes.** *Add:* **I.** *unanimity, concord:*—Bróþerlic ánrǽdnyss *fraterna concordia,* Scint. 13, 4. Þ hí (*bishops*) smeágan ymbe ánrǽdnesse and sóðe gesibsumnesse, Ll. Th. ii. 316, 12. **II.** *of a single act, decision, resolution:*—Heó mid módes ánrǽdnesse áwrát óðer gewrit, Ap. Th. 21, 1. **III.** *of continued action, constancy, perseverance, resolution:*—Ánrǽdnes *perseuerantia, assiduitas,* An. Ox. 1163. *Fortitudo,* þ is strangð oððe ánrǽdnyss, Hml. S. 1, 165. *Instantia* boni *operis,* þ is ánrǽdnyss gódes weorces, 16, 357. Oþer is módignyss, óþer is ánrǽdnyss *pride is one thing, constancy another,* 34, 325. Wacigende on ealre ánrǽdnysse (*instantia*), Scint. 30, 11: An. Ox. 75: *constantia,* 1653. Oferwinnan ásolcennysse mid sóðre ánrǽdnysse, Hml. Th. ii. 222, 23: Hml. A. 20, 155. For heora ánrǽdnisse and heora trýwðe wið God, Ælfc. T. Grn. 1, 2. Hé on gódum gelimpum ne forlǽt his ánrǽdnysse, Wlfst. 51, 23. Ánrǽdnysse *statum* (*cordis*), An. Ox. 4468.

**án-reces.** *Add:* [*Connected with* reccan *as* án-streces *with* streccan?] anrode, Bl. H. 137, 5. l. ánrǽde *or* arode.

**an-sǽc,** -scéát (-sceót), -sceón, -scód. v. and-sacu, on-sceótan, -scógan.

**an-scuta,** Hpt. Gl. 425, 14, *read* ansata. v. An. Ox. 786, *note*.

**án-seld.** Under this word for *dwell in* substitute *turn to*.

**án-setl, es;** *n. A hermitage:*—Hí ánsetles wununge geceósaþ *solitarii sedere desiderant,* R. Ben. 135, 9.

**án-setla, an;** *m. An anchorite, a hermit:*—Þær eardode sum swíþe myccles mægnes wer, sé wæs ánsetla in wéstenne *illic vir quidam solitarius magnae virtutis habitabat,* Gr. D. 306, 1. Þridde cyn muneca is ánsetlena (*anachoritarum*) þe hié sylfe on syndrigum húsum belúcaþ ... Feórþe cyn is þára þe hý under leásum hiwe ánsetlan teliaþ ... ne wyrþ nǽfre fulfremed sé þe on þus níwan anginne ánsetla beón wile ... Nán man ne dear for árwyrðnesse þæs ánsetlan leahtras tǽlan, R. Ben. 134, 22—135, 18. [*O. H. Ger.* ein-sidilo *anachoreta, heremita.*]

**an-sín.** *Add:* **I.** *a face:*—Ansýn *facies,* Wrt. Voc. i. 70, 39. Hine Drihten cúðe of ansíne tó ansíne, Deut. 34, 10. Hié gesáwon ródetácen on his onsiéne, Bl. H. 243, 13. Lǽded fore onsýne éces déman, Cri. 796. Ic míne handa and ansýne (-u, *v. l.*) áðwóh, Hml. S. 23 b, 502. Þanon ic ne wende onsióu míne, El. 349. Ne áhwyrf þú þíne onsýne from mé, Bl. H. 89, 11. Anséna eówere ne beóð gescænde *facies tuae non confundentur,* Ps. L. 33, 6. Gefyll heora ansýna[n] mid teónan, 82, 17. Ansýna, Ps. Th. 81, 2. **I a.** *the surface* of an object:*—On ansýne scræfes *in superficie antri,* An. Ox. 1888. **II.** *sight, visible appearance:*—Næs þæs wyrmes þær onsýn ænig *there was nothing to be seen of the dragon,* B. 2772. Þ hé leng from Crístes onsýne wǽre *that he should be longer without a sight of Christ,* Bl. H. 225, 29. On Drihtnes onsýne wunian *to dwell where God could be seen,* 103, 33. Hé heora ǽrendracan swá unweordlíce forseah þ hé heora self onseón nolde *legatos Romanorum injuriosissime a conspectu suo abstinuit,* Ors. 4, 8; S. 186, 7. Ic mé warnade hyre onsýne, Gú. 1157. **III.** *aspect, look, appearance, shape, form,* (1) *of living creatures:*—On lǽces ansýne (onsíone, *v. l.*) *in medici specie,* Gr. D. 161, 1. In culfran ansýne (*specie*), 169, 8. Onsiéne (*corporis*) habitudine, Wrt. Voc. ii. 86, 24. Hé geseah león ansýne, Guth. 46, 24. Fearres gelícnysse and beran ansýne, 48, 2. Englas gehwyrfde on manna onsýne, Bl. H. 233, 5. Gedyde ic þæt þú onsýn hæfdest mægwlite mé gelícne, Cri. 1383. (2) *of things:*—Seó sǽ þe ǽr gladu onsíene wæs, Met. 5, 11. Seó cyrice is on onsýne útan yfeles heówes, Bl. H. 197, 11. Þá lástas á beóþ on þære ilcan onsýne þe hié on þá eorþan bestapene wǽron, 127, 20. Þá ádle mon mæg ongitan be þám útgange, hwilc sé on onsýne sié, Lch. ii. 276.

**an-speca.** v. on-spreca *in Dict.* : **an-spel.** *For Cot. 56 substitute:*—Conjecturam anspel (cf. *conjectionis* bodunge, 67), Wrt. Voc. ii. 23, 69. **an-sprǽc.** v. on-sprǽc.

**án-sprǽce.** l. -sprǽce *saying the same, unanimous:*—Worhton hý heora gemót and wǽran ealle ánsprǽce *loquebantur simul,* Ps. Th. 40, 7. [Cf. *O. Sax.* én-wordi *unanimous.*]

**án-standende** *alone. Substitute:*—Munuc oððe ánstandende *monachus,* Wrt. Voc. i. 71, 81. Wolde hé ðá ánstandende ancerlíf ádreógan, Hml. Th. ii. 142, 27. Hé (*Adam*) wæs sume hwíle ánstandende, i. 12, 32. Fleáh hé ánstandende tó ánre dúne, 162, 6. Þæt hié (*hermits*) ánstandende (*sola manu*) ongeán deófol winnan magan, R. Ben. 9, 7.

**an-stiga(n),** -stigo. v. stíga, stig *in Dict.*: **an-styllan.** v. on-stillan: **án-sūnd.** l. an-sund: **an-sweóp.** v. swápan *in Dict.*: **an-sýn.** v. an-sín: **an-tállic.** Cf. un-tállíce *in Dict.*

**antef(e)n, es; m.:** e; f. *Add:*—Bútan antefene (-ifene, *v. l.*), R. Ben. 37, 7. Gesungennum antefne, Angl. xiii. 403, 550. Cweþan þæne antefn, 422, 811. Þæt hý ne beginnen náðer ne sealm ne antefene (-efen, *v. l.*), R. Ben. 49, 5. Sealmas and antefenas, 39, 7. Antefnas, Angl. xiii. 401, 518. Sealmas mid antefnan beón gecwedene, 402, 532. Syx sealmas mid þrím antefenum, R. Ben. 33, 13. Mid feówer sealmum geendod mid heora antephanum, 41, 10.

**antefnere, es; m. An anthem-book:*—Antefnas on antefnere (*antiphonario*), Angl. xiii. 405, 571: 409, 634.

**an-þracian,** -pracung, -præc, -præclic, -timber. v. on-þracian, -þracung, -præc, -þræclic, -timber.

**án-tíd.** *Add as an alternative meaning: An appointed hour, time when something is due:*—Ymb ántíd óðres dógores wundenstefna gewaden hæfde þæt þá líðende land gesáwon, i. e. *the boat was in sight of land at the time when it was due to be so.* Cf. án-daga.

**án-waldan.** *Dele.*

**an-weald, &c.** In some of the following instances (e. g. anwald *monarchiam,* Wrt. Voc. ii. 54, 45) perhaps ánweald, &c. should be read, but for the most part the passages may be taken as additions to the onweald, &c. forms, q. v.

**an-weald; m. f. n.:*—Anuuald (-uald, -uualda) *monarchia,* Txts. 76, 622. Anwald *jus,* Wrt. Voc. ii. 49, 19. Hé wile reáfian ðone ðe hié him sealde his anwaldes *jus dantis invadit,* Past. 371, 25. On ælcum ende mínes anwealdes, Ll. Th. i. 274, 2. Hú Assael hine unwærlíce mid anwealde ðreátode *hunc cum Assael vi incautae praecipitationis impeteret,* Past. 295, 14. On þǽm anwalde wǽron Somnite swá bealde Pontius, dux eorum, in tantum abusus est victoriae securitate, Ors. 3, 8; S. 120, 31. Fón tó anwalde *imperium tenere coepere,* 6, 37; S. 294, 33. God hí hǽþenum leódum lét tó anwealde, Jud. pref. Anwald *monarchiam,* Wrt. Voc. ii. 54, 45. Hé hæfþ his fóta anweald, Bt. 36, 4; F. 178, 11. Gynd ealne mínnc anweald, Ll. Th. i. 246, 23. Ofer ealne þæs cynges anweald, 270, 1. Ðreáta ðæt hié wieten ðæt gé sume anwald habbað ofer hié *argue cum omni imperio,* Past. 291, 19. Hé þ anweald (þone anwald, *v. l.*) þæs ríces forlét *regni sceptra reliquit,* Bd. 5, 19; Sch. 653, 1. *Potestates* sind anwealdu, Hml. Th. i. 342, 28: 610, 23. Næs ná má cyninga anwalda bútan þysan þrím rícum, Ors. 1, 5; S. 34, 30. Bist ðú þæs deófles anwealdum betǽht, Hml. Th. ii. 170, 8.

**an-weald; adj. Powerful:*—Hí wuldrodon þá anwaldan and hergendlican þrynysse, Hml. S. 30, 452. v. an-wealdness.

**an-wealda.** *Add:*—Hē wæs swā milde swā him nān onwald (an-wealda, *v. l.*) næs ǽr þēm, Ors. 6, 2 ; S. 254, 22.

**an-wealdend,** es ; *m. A ruler:*—From onwealdendum (*the Latin is* abominationem *which the glosser has misread as* a dominatione?), Ps. Spl. T. 87, 8.

**an-wealdian.** v. ge-anwealdian.

**an-wealdness,** e ; *f. Power, possession:*—Anwealdnesse *possessiones*, Ps. L. 104, 21. On anwealdnesse *in potestatem*, 135, 9. On anwealdnyssum *in potestatibus*, 19, 7.

**an-wealh.** v. on-wealh.

**an-wedd** (and-?), es ; *n. Security for a loan, recognizance:*—Hire fæder āborgude XXX punda æt Godan and betǣht him þæt land þæs feós tó anwedde (*pro vadimonio eidem dedit terram*), Cht. Th. 201, 17.

**an-wíg.** *Add:*—Ānwíges biddan *to challenge to a duel*, Ors. 3, 6 ; S. 108, 10 : Bl. H. 201, 22. Golias clypode bysmor Godes folce, gearu tó ānwíge, Hml. S. 18, 21. Ðā geweard him bām þ hí twēgen tó ānwíge eódon, 27, 53 : Ælfc. T. Grn. 7, 17. Rómāne curon III hund cempena and siex þæt sceolde tó ānwíge gangan wið swā fela Sabína *cum sex et trecenti Fabii speciale sibi adversus Vejentes decerni bellum expetivissent,* Ors. 2, 4 ; S. 72, 16 : 2, 6 ; S. 86, 22. Hē gecwæð ānwíg wið ðone cyning, . . . and heora ægðer óðerne ofslóg, 2, 3 ; S. 68, 16. Hē oft feaht ānwíg *gladiatoriis armis in ludo depugnavit,* 6, 14 ; S. 268, 28. Of ānwígum *congressibus*, Wrt. Voc. ii. 133, 41. [O. H. Ger. ein-wíg, -wígi *singulare certamen, duellum, spectaculum :* Icel. ein-vígi.]

**án-wíg-gearo.** *l.* an wíg gearo : **án-wíglíce.** *Substitute :*—Ānwíglíce seohtende *singulariter congrediens,* Wrt. Voc. ii. 87, 1.

**án-wille.** *Add:*—Ānwille *pertinax*, An. Ox. 2955 : Wrt. Voc. ii. 67, 39 : *rigidus*, 93, 29. Yfele ānwille *male pertinax*, Germ. 388, 14. Swā ānwille þæt him leófre bið þæt hē lybbe ǽfre be his ágenum dihte, Ælfc. T. Grn. 20, 7 : Prov. K. 8. Ānwille *pervicaci*, Germ. 393, 63. Þæt yfel þe yfelum mannum becymð for heora ānwillan yfelnysse, Hml. Th. ii. 538, 24. Ne flýt ðū nā wið ānwilne man, Prov. K. 5. Ānwille *obstinatam*, Wrt. Voc. ii. 63, 2. Þā ānwillan, 82, 66. Ðā fortrūwudan and ðā ānwillan *protervi*, Past. 209, 20. [O. H. Ger. ein-willi *pertinax.* Cf. Icel. ein-vili *self-will.*]

**án-willíce.** *Add:*—Anuuillíce *pertinaciter*, Wrt. Voc. ii. 116, 74. Ānwillíce, An. Ox. 3239.

**án-wilnes.** *Add:* I. *in a bad sense:*—Ānwilnes *obstinatio, pertinacia*, Wrt. Voc. i. 51, 30. Ānwilnysse *contumaciae*, Scint. 104, 7 : *obstinationis*, 122, 10. Ānwilnesse (-wil-, *v. l.*), Past. 47, 16. For nānre ānwilnesse (*pertinacia*), 12. Mid ānwilnesse *procaciter*, R. Ben. 15, 13. Gyt git þurhwuniað on incre ānwilnesse, Bl. H. 187, 33. Hē hit for his ānwylnysse dēd, Hml. S. 12, 6 : 13, 92. Forlǽt þīne ānwylnysse, 8, 114 : Hml. Th. i. 422, 31. II. *in a good sense, persistence:*—Godes ríce wunað on ānwylnysse þæs hālgan geleáfan, Guth. 2, 15.

**án-wintre.** v. ēn-wintre *in Dict.*: **an-wlǣta,** *dele, and see* and-wlata.

**an-wlite,** *dele, and see* un-wlite *in Dict.*

**an-wlóh.** *Add: Not flourishing, like a tree without leaves.* In Dan. 585 the *ríce* is compared with the stump of the tree which for seven years shewed no signs of life, and the statement *swā þín ríce bið anwlóh* expresses the same as *swā þín blǽd líð* in 563. Cf. ge-wló, an epithet which describes a kind of rich growth.

**an-wrigennes.** v. on-wrigennes *in Dict.*: **an-wunigende.** *l.* an wunigende.

**án-wunung,** e ; *f. Solitary dwelling:*—Ōþer cyn is muneca þe feor fram mannum gewítað and wēste stówa and ānwununge lufiaþ (*deserta loca sequi atque habitare perhibentur*), R. Ben. 134, 12.

**án-wyrdan.** v. ge-ānwyrdan : **á-nýdan.** v. á-nídan : **an-ýwan.** v. on-íwan *in Dict.*

**apa.** *Add:*—Apa *phitecus* (=πίθηκος), Txts. 90, 827 : Wrt. Voc. ii. 68, 11 : i. 288, 76 : *simia*, 78, 14. Þā stód þǽr sum man mid ānum apan (*simia*), Gr. D. 62, 15. [O. H. Ger. affo : Icel. api.]

**á-pēcan.** *Add:* Ll. Th. ii. 186, 23.

**á-parian.** *Add:*—Hine mon þǽræt āparade, Cht. Th. 172, 25.

**ap-flód.** *Dele:* á-pínedlíce. v. un-āpínedlíce *in Dict.*

**á-pícan** (?) *to pick out:*—Wilt þū ūt āpytan (-pýcan?) ūre eágan *an oculos nostros vis eruere?*, Num. 16, 14. v. pícan *in Dict.*

**á-pinsian.** *Add:*—Dryhten heorte and nā spēde āpinsað (*pensat*), Scint. 60, 6. Bóceras ǽrest āpinsað wærlicum móde þā naman and heora declinunga, and gýmað hwylce naman geendað on a, Angl. viii. 313, 4. Hit geríst þ wē þisra epacta gerýnu āpinsiun, 300, 48 : 305, 47 : 322, 23. Þæt getæl is tó āpinsianne, þæt hit getācnað, Wlfst. 245, 9. Mid willan sýfernysse bót byð āpinsud (*pensatur*), Scint. 42, 17.

**á-pinsung,** e ; *f. Weighing, estimating:*—Mid rihtwísere tódāles āpinsunge wegendres *justa discretionis lance librantis*, An. Ox. 1757.

**á-plantian.** *Add:*—Þā ðe heora heortan wyrtruman on his lufe āplantodon, Hml. Th. i. 612, 29. Āplanta on dīnre heortan þā sóðan lufe, ii. 410, 1. Hē hæfde āplantod ān fíctreów binnon his wíngearde, 406, 35 : Ps. Th. 1, 3.

**á-plated.** v. platian *in Dict.*

**á-pluccian ;** *p.* ode *To pluck off :*—Ic of āpluccige *excerpo*, Ælfc. Gr. Z. 170, 14.

**apostata.** *Add:*—Sume synd apostatan þe sceoldan wesan Godes cempan, Ll. Th. ii. 322, 15.

**apostol.** *Add:*—Petrus se apostolus, Ors. 6, 4 ; B. 118, 12. Tó ðāra apostla fótum, Ll. Th. ii. 370, 36.

**apostol-(l)ic.** *Add:*—þæs apostolican bebodes, R. Ben. I. 61, 13. Mid þām apostolican werode, Wlfst. 242, 19.

**á-priccan.** v. prician *in Dict.*

**apulder.** For *n.?* substitute *f.*, and add apuldre (-er?), es ; *m. :*—Apuldur, *malus*, Txts. 76, 636. Apuldur, Wrt. Voc. ii. 54, 41. Swētre apuldre rind, Lch. i. 358, 14. Tó ðǽre hāran apoldre, C. D. v. 148, 29. On þone longan apuldre, of þām apuldre, C. D. B. iii. 586, 8. The word occurs not infrequently in charters, v. Cht. Crw. p. 52, and remains in the place-name Appledore. [*Icel.* apaldr ; *m.*] v. worþ-apulder ; apuldre.

**Apulder.** v. preceding word.

**apulder-tún.** *Add:*—Apuldertún *ortus pomorum*, Wrt. Voc. ii. 64, 8. Apeldertún, i. 285, 75.

**apuldre.** *Add:*—Apuldro *malus*, Txts. 76, 636. Apuldre (apeldre, *v. l.*), Ælfc. Gr. Z. 312, 5. Apeldre, An. Ox. 56, 358. Æt þǽre hāran apuldran, Chr. 1066 ; P. 199, 28. On þā apoldran, of þēre apoldran, C. D. B. ii. 79, 6. See other examples in charters, Cht. Crw. p. 53. [O. H. Ger. affultra ; *f. malus.*]

**á-pullian.** *Add:*—Gif þū smyrest hraðe ðā stówe þe þā hǽr beóð of āpullud, ne geþafað seó smyrung þ hý eft wexen, Lch. i. 362, 10.

**á-pyffan ;** *p.* te *To puff out, exhale :*—Āpyft (*printed* -þyft) *exalet, spiret*, Wrt. Voc. ii. 144, 41. Ūt āpyfte *exalavit*, An. Ox. 4931. Ūt āpyfhte, Hpt. Gl. 472, 43.

**á-pyndrian** *to weigh :*—Āpyndrað (*printed* -wyndrað) *trutinabat*, Hpt. Gl. 512, 78. Cf. pundar, pundere, pundern.

**á-pytan.** v. á-pícan.

**ár** ore. *Add:*—Ār *aes*, Wrt. Voc. ii. 8, 53 : *eramentum*, An. Ox. 1371. Groeni ār *aurocalcum*, Wrt. Voc. ii. 101, 36 : 7, 49 : i. 286, 65. Sī þe heofene swilce ār *sit tibi coelum aeneum*, Deut. 28, 23. Hē geworhte ānes fearres anlícnesse of āre *taurum aeneum fecit*, Ors. 1, 12 ; S. 54, 24.

**ár** honour. *Add:* I. *honour :*—Ǣghwylc heáh ār hēr on worulde bið mid frecnessum embeseald, Wlfst. 262, 2. Seó hēhste ār . . ., cyninges þrym, . . . ār and fægernes werum and wífum, 265, 6–9. Seó ār and seó eádignes þæs heán heáhengles tíde, Bl. H. 197, 3. Ne onmun þū mē nānre āre wyrþne, 183, 1. Āre *honore*, Ps. Spl. C. 8, 6. On āre beón *in honore esse*, Ps. Th. 48, 11. For þæs crístendómes āre *from respect for Christianity*, Ors. 2, 8 ; S. 94, 5 : Angl. xii. 510, 1. Wyrþe þū eart þ þū onfó wuldor and āre, Bl. H. 75, 1. Lof secgean þǽra āra and þǽra weorþmenda þe Drihten mancynne forgeaf, 123, 4. Ðætte hió him funden suelce londāre swelce hē mid ārum on beón maehte, C. D. i. 222, 30. II. *mercy, favour, benefit :*—Eów tó nānre āre *of no benefit to you*, Bl. H. 41, 23. Þan hýrēde tó āre and hire sāwle tó reste, Cht. Th. 203, 31. Gif hē næsð ðā āre ðe hē on beón mæge *si hunc manus misericordiae non commendat*, Past. 137, 6. Bidde hē him Godes āre *veniam a Deo petat*, Ll. Th. ii. 136, 35 : Bl. H. 107, 21. Gode þancian þæra āra þe hē be wege hæfdon, Ps. Th. 22, arg. III. *property :*—Gange seó ār unbefiitan intó Sćē Petre, Cht. Th. 148, 4. Þeós ār, 203, 37. Man Eádgife berýpte ǽlcere āre *despoliata sum omnibus terris meis et rebus*, 203, 12. þ hí mōstan beón heora þinga and āre wurðe ðe heom mid unrihte benumen wæs, Chr. 1051 ; P. 181, 34. Þǽre āre brūcan þe him geāhnod wæs, Hml. S. 3, 354. Of þǽre Godes āre (*church property*) þe hē hæfde of manegum hālgum stówum, Chr. 1052 ; P. 182, 14. Hē gerād sóna ealle Sigeferðes āre and Morcares, 1015 ; P. 146, 8 : Ors. 1, 12 ; S. 54, 8. Þ man sceolde cennan his āre *every man was to state the amount of his property (for taxing)*, Hml. Th. i. 30, 5. Hí behwyrfden heora āre on gymstānum, 60, 28. Þā āre þe hē him forgeaf, wícstede weligne, B. 2606. Hí hire āre āgefon *restituit mihi terras meas et omnia mea*, Cht. Th. 203, 23. Þā āre þe hē þǽr āhte, xx hída æt Sendan, x æt Sunnanbyrg, 208, 24. Ic geswutelige on ðisum gewrite hū ic mīne āre and mīne ǽhta geunnen hæbbe, 557, 14. v. land-, un-, weorold-ār.

**ár** an oar. *Add:*—Āra remi, Wrt. Voc. i. 63, 42. Ārena *remorum*, An. Ox. 36.

**Arabisc ;** *adj. Arabian :*—Arabisc man *hic et haec Arabs*, Ælfc. Gr. Z. 65, 12. Hic Fenix, swā hātte ān fugel on Arabiscre ðeóde, 70, 12. [O. H. Ger. Arabisc.]

**á-rēcan.** *Add:* I. *to get at :*—Hē nāhte his fēþes geweald ne furðon ne mihte his mete him ārǣcan, Hml. S. 5, 138 : Hex. 14, 17 : Lch. i. 246, 4. II. *to hold forth :*—Se hopa ārǣhte (*offert*) sweord þǽre eádmódnesse, Prud. 35 a : 37 a. Ārǣc (*pretende*) mildheortnesse þīne ongitendum þē, Ps. L. 35, 11. Ārǣce þīne handa, Bl. H. 153, 9. Þā hēt hē him his seax ārǣcan, Hml. Th. i. 88, 9. Ārǣht *porrectus*, Wrt. Voc. ii. 68, 65.

**á-rǣd ;** *adj. Add: Resolute* (?)—Wyrd bið ful ārǣd, Wand. 5 : Gn. Ex. 193 (?). *With* Bt. 70, 6 cf. Met. 10, 45, *which has* aroda.

a-ræd, Bt. 78, 20, *l.* â-sæd.

â-rédan; *p.* -rêd *and* -rædde; *pp.* -ræden *and* -ræd(ed). *Under* I *dele last passage, under* II *dele last two passages; and add:* I. *to determine, fix:*—Hié þæt fæstnodon mid âþum swâ swâ hê hit âred, Chr. 921; P. 103, 20. Aethelnôth and his wîf âræddan hiora erfe, C. D. i. 234, 26. Ðet hió him nêren mêran ondeta ðon hit âræded wæs on Aeðelbaldes dæge . . . hió môsten mid âðe gecýðan ðet hit suâ wêre âræden on Aeðelbaldes dæge, 279, 2-7. Ne cymst þû on þînne êþel for þon ðîn êþel (? wyrd) hit swâ be þînum heáfde and fôre hafað âræded *vivus in patriam non reverteres, quum fata ita de tuo capite statuerunt*, Nar. 29, 14. II. *to read a riddle:*—Ic ârædde Antiochus rædels, Ap. Th. 24, 12: 5, 2. Hê þ sôð ârædde, 4, 20. Þæt hê him bôcstafas ârædde and ârehte, Dan. 741. Swâ hwilc man swâ mînne rædels riht âræde, Ap. Th. 3, 10. Hê ârædan ne mihte þæs apostoles dêgol, Bl. H. 181, 17. III. *to read* what is written:—Næs þ wel þ þû self âræddest þâ stafas ofer hire byrgene, Ap. Th. 26, 10. Se biscop orationem ofer mê ârædde, Bd. 5, 3; Sch. 566, 4. Þæt yrfegewrit man ârædde beforan eallum Westseaxena witum. Þâ hit âred wæs, Cht. Th. 486, 15-17. Englisc gewrit ârædan, Past. 7, 13, 17. Beforan him hê hêt ârædan þæs kâseres dôm . . . Þâ se dôm âræded wæs, Shrn. 129, 1-4. Þ gewrit âræded wæs, Bl. H. 177, 35. IV. *to prepare:*—Áræddun (-rêddun) *expedierant*, Txts. 61, 784. [*Goth.* ur-rêdan *decernere:* O. H. Ger. ur-râtan *conjicere, prophetizare, argumentari.*] v. rædan *in Dict.*

â-ræfan *to set free, unwrap:*—Áræfdon *expedierunt*, Wrt. Voc. ii. 145, 37. Áræfdan (*printed* ârærdan) *expedierant*, 29, 64. v. â-râfian, æ-ræfe.

a-ræfnan: *l.* â-ræfnan (-ian), *and add:* I. *to bear, endure:*—Eall ic hit âræfnie for þînum ondsene, Bl. H. 241, 33. Gif hit mon geðyldiglîce âræfnþ, Bt. 11, 1; F. 32, 32. Wê eall âræfnaþ, Bl. H. 13, 9. Ic hit âræfnede þ ic eów æteówe hwylcum gemete gê sceolan âræfnan, 237, 12. Þû his dômas on þê sylfum âremdest (*v. l.* geþolodest), Angl. xii. 505, 4. Hû hê âræfnede ðæs cwelres hand, Shrn. 129, 9. Áræfne þû ealle . . . Áræfna þâs tintrego, Bl. H. 237, 8, 13. Brocu âræfnan (-refnian, *v. l.*), Ors. 3, 7; S. 120, 9. Costnunga âræfnan, Hml. S. 33, 116. Swâ þu hâtost mæge âræfnan, Lch. ii. 124, 21: 130, 7. Áræfnian, Hml. Th. ii. 34, 3. Se cyng ne mihte âræfnian his dohtor teâras, Ap. Th. 22, 25. Strengra tô âræfnanne, Wlfst. 207, 24. Syle ûs geðyld tô âræfnigenne, Hml. S. 30, 135. Nâ âræfnigende *non ferentes*, An. Ox. 8, 302. II. *to bear* in mind, *ponder:*—Áræfnaþ *exigit*, Wrt. Voc. ii. 144, 81. Áraebndae *expendisse*, Txts. 58, 353. Áræfnde, Wrt. Voc. ii. 29, 55. Áraefndun *exigebant*, 107, 80. III. *to carry out, practise, perform:*—Ic yfelæs tô fela âræfnde (*v. l.* gefremede), Angl. xii. 510, 20. Hê him rehte hwylce searwa se drý âræfnde, Bl. H. 173, 8. Árefna *exerce*, An. Ox. 46, 42. Se lîchoma geunlustaþ þâ geoguðlustas tô fremmenne, þâ þe him swête wæron tô âræfnenne, Bl. H. 59, 10.

â-ræfned, -ræfnedlic. v. un-âræfned, -âræfnedlic.

â-ræfn(i)endlic; *adj.* *Tolerable, possible:*—Áræfniendlic *possibile*, Wülck. Gl. 250, 4: 251, 22. v. un-âræfnendlic.

â-ræfsan. v. râpsan *in Dict.* â-ræman. *Dele:* DER. up-aræman, ræman: a-ræpsan. v. ræpsan *in Dict.*

â-réran. *Add:* I. of direction, *to raise, lift up:*—Martinus hine upheáh ârærde, Bl. H. 219, 20. Ne ðû up ne ârêr ne ârær *ne erigas (oculos tuos)*, Kent. Gl. 863. Seó rôd bið âræred on ðæt gewrixle þâra tungla, Bl. H. 91, 23. Áræredne *porrectam (turrem)*, Wrt. Voc. ii. 85, 49. II. *to raise* a building, *erect, build:*—Hê ârærð ceastre *castra erigit*, Past. 162, 12. Árærdon construxere, i. *aedificauerunt*, An. Ox. 3420. Sê þe þâra mihta hæbbe ârære cirican Gode tô lofe, Ll. Th. ii. 282, 5. Wurdon fela cyrcan ârærede, Hml. Th. i. 562, 25. III. *to establish, set up:*—Hî ælc gôd ârærdon, Hml. S. 21, 462. Þæt man unriht âlecge and Godes riht ârære, 16, 67. IV. *to raise, cause to grow:*—Þæt hê sylle .XV. swýn tô sticunge, hæbbe sylf þ hê ofer þ ârære, Ll. Th. i. 436, 14. V. *to raise* from torpor, death, &c., *to arouse:*—Árærest *suscitabis*, An. Ox. 2137. Hê ârêrð *refrigerabit*, Kent. Gl. 1062. Hê ârærde *suscitavit*, i. *excitavit*, An. Ox. 1843: 3502. Mîn Drihten ârære ðê (*the dead widow*), Hml. Th. i. 60, 17. Áræran *suscitare*, i. *restaurare*, An. Ox. 2110. VI. *to excite, disturb, break up* a meeting:—Gif hê folcgemôt mid wæpnes brýde ârære, Ll. Th. i. 86, 16. VII. *to raise, increase* price:—Gif wê gyld ârærdon . . . swâ man þ weorð up âræran mihte . . . Gif wê þ ceápgild ârærað, Ll. Th. i. 234, 5, 10. 16. Gif se hlâford him wile þ land âræran tô weorce and tô gafole *if the lord want to raise the rent of the land for him by exacting work as well as payment*, 146, 4. VIII. *to extol:*—Up âhefde, ârærde *extollit*, An. Ox. 2425. Tô ârærenne *attollenda*, i. *extollenda*, 330. [*Goth.* ur-raisjan.]

â-rærend, es; *m.* *One who arouses:*—Árærend môda *excitator mentium*, Hy. S. 18, 31.

â-résan. *Add:*—Þæt folc færlîce ongonn forð ârêsan, Hml. Th. ii. 140, 13. v. forð-âræsan *in Dict.*

â-râfian. *Add:*—Árâfaþ *desolvit*, Wrt. Voc. ii. 139, 33. [? Arubfdxm = aruaedum (= ? ârâuedum) *extirpatis*, Kent. Gl. 1165.] v. â-ræfan; râfian.

â-râsian. *Add:* I. *to try, put to the proof:*—Hê sceolde gecunnian and

ârâsian, hwæþer se Drihtnes wer hæfde wîtedômes gâst *an vir Dei prophetiae spiritum haberet, explorare conatus est*, Gr. D. 130, 29. ¶ â-râsod *tried, experienced:*—Þâs þing þincað þâm ârâsedum clericum unweordlîce, Angl. viii. 312, 43. II. *to find out, detect:*—Hû hê ârâsode þâ hîwunge Totillan *de simulatione Totilae deprehensa*, Gr. D. 130, 13. Ðâ upâhafenesse hê ârâsode and hié getælde *elationem publice feriendo reprehendit*, Past. 39, 21. Hê ârâsode heora deófles cræft, Hml. Th. ii. 472, 15. Se man sê þ ârâsie, Ll. Th. i. 40, 2. Gif hwilc man forstolen þingc hâm tô his cotan bringe and hê ârâsod wurðe, 418, 18. Árâsad *interceptum*, Wrt. Voc. ii. 110, 79. Sê ðonne sê hit ðégellîce dêð and ðeáh wolde ðæt hê wurde ârâsod and siððan for ðý hered *qui in secreto suo bono opere deprehendi ac laudari concupiscit*, Past. 451, 19. þâ drýcræftigan wurdon ârâsode (*deprehensi*), Gr. D. 27, 15: 132, 9. III. *to blame, reprehend:*—Hê nyle hié ârâsian . . . ðæm synfullan menn bið oftogen ðæt hine mon stîðlîce ârâsige . . . ða hié suiðe stîðlîce ârâsigeað and mid ealle ofðrysceað *corripere non praesumit . . . correptionis duritia peccanti subtrahitur . . . hos asperitate rigidae invectionis premunt*, Past. 143, 9, 19: 145, 1.

âr-bléd. *Add:*—Árbled *palmula*, Wrt. Voc. i. 63, 44.

arblast *a cross-bow:*—Mid ânan arblaste ofscoten, Chr. 1079; P. 214, 29. [*From French.*]

arce- (archi-). v. ærce-.

âr-dǽde; *adj.* *Merciful:*—Uton beón ælmesgeorne and ârdæde wið earme men, Bl. H. 131, 2.

âr-dæg. v. weorþung-dæg *in Dict.:* ardlîce. v. arodlîce: are *a court-yard.* *Dele.*

âre *honour.* *The instances given belong to* âr: a-reccan. *l.* â-reccan. â-reccan. *Add:* I. *to stretch out, spread out:*—Álecge hê his swîþran hand him under heáfod âreahte, Lch. ii. 214, 10. II. *to hold out to, to grant.* v. reccan, II:—Árecte (-æ) *concesserim*, Txts. 53, 523 (cf. 106, 1089). Árectæ, Wrt. Voc. ii. 14, 69. III. *to raise, lift up:*—Dryhten âreced (*eregit*) alle gecnysede, Ps. Srt. 144, 14. Hê ârehte (*erexit*) horn haelu, ii. p. 199, 6. Up ârehte sindun *erecti sumus*, 19, 9. Upp ârehte *arrectas*, Wrt. Voc. ii. 10, 3. IV. *to excite, astonish* [cf. *O. H. Ger.* arrachte *exciti*]:—Áreahtum *attonitis (oculis)*, Kent. Gl. 579. Árehtum *attonitis (auditoribus)*, An. Ox. 7, 144: *attonitis (spectatoribus)*, 8, 187. V. *to recount, tell, declare:*—Árecco *eructuabo*, Wrt. Voc. ii. 30, 65. Árecþ *refert*, 142, 39. Árehtun (-an, -on) *expresserunt*, 108, 5: 30, 14: 145, 55: *retulerunt*, i. *narraverunt*, An. Ox. 2910. Þæt hyra nân ne wandode for mînum ege þæt hý þæt folcriht ârehton, Cht. Th. 486, 25. Hwâ is þæt þe eall ðâ yfel þe hî dônde wæron âsecgean mæge oððe âreccean?, Ors. 1, 8; S. 42, 7. Tô âreccganne (-secganne ?) *expediari*, Lk. p. 3, 7. VI. *to explain, expound*—Áreccan *explanare*, Wrt. Voc. ii. 30, 46. Swæ ic hié andgitfullicost âreccean meahte, Past. 7, 24. Dis wê willað hwêne rûmedlîcor âreccean *haec paulo latius replicando disseramus*, 75, 17. Sié âreaht *expolietur*, Wrt. Voc. ii. 31, 69. [*O. H. Ger.* ar-recchen *exprimere, edere, explicare, exponere, digerere.*]

â-reccendlic. v. un-âreccendlic.

â-réceleásian; *p.* ode *To be negligent:*—Ic âréceleásode and tô læt wæs mîne cyrcan tô sêcenne, Angl. xi. 102, 68.

ared. v. arod: a-rêde (*l.* ârede) *cared for.* *Dele.*

a-rêdian. *l.* â-redian, *and add:* I. *to make ready, adapt:*—Hit bið mid ðære liðelican manunga tô ðâm âredod ðæt hit sceal suiðe hrædlîce âfeallan of ðære weâmôdnesse, Past. 297, 18. II. *to carry out, effect, make:*—Eall ðiss âredað se rectore suiðe ryhte *omne hoc a rectore agitur*, Past. 169, 3. Gif hê ceáp âredige *if he make a bargain*, Ll. Th. i. 274, 23. Drihten ûs geunne þæt wê magan his willan âredian, Wlfst. 50, 8. III. *to find out* by experience:—Gif hê swâ âredad bið (cf. *the later (Winteney) version:* Gyf heó swilc âfunde byð) on þære cumlîðnesse þæt hê ne sý wyrðe þære scyrunge *si non fuerit talis qui mereatur proici*, R. Ben. 109, 20. þe læs þe hý unwære wurðan âredode (-reodade, *v. l.*), Wlfst. 79, 16: 273, 18. IV. *to find out* what is appropriate, *to hit upon:*—Futuma mê þ ic simle þone ræd ârædige ðe ðê lîcworðe sî, Shrn. 170, 30: Angl. xii. 512, 32. Bûton hê ðone tîman âredige ðæs læcedómes *nisi cum tempore medicamenta conveniant*, Past. 153, 4. Wê sculon geleornian ðæt wê suiðe wærlîce gecôpe tiid âredigen, and ðonne sió stemn gesceádwîslîce ðone mûð ontýne, and eác ðâ tîd gesceádwîslîce âredigen ðe sió suîge hine betýnan scyle *nobis caute discendum est quatenus os discretum et congruo tempore vox aperiat, et rursum congruo taciturnitas claudat*, 277, 1-3. Áblend þisse þeóde andgyt, þæt hî ræd ne âredian, Wlfst. 47, 21. Hié nabbað ðâ gesceádwîsnesse ðæt hié cunnen ðæs ðinges tîman âredian, Past. 287, 7. Rihtne weig âredian tô þâm êcan hâme, Shrn. 163, 27. Þone circul þâs iunge preóstas ne mihton næfre âredian, for þâm þe ys uneáðe cûð þâm ealdum witum, Angl. viii. 319, 9. Nabbe gê nâ gôdne tîman âredodne, mîn dohtor is nû swîþe bisig, Ap. Th. 20, 5.

â-rencan (?) *to make proud, exalt:*—Swuran on flæslicre ic upp ârengde (= -rencte ?) ofermôdignesse *collum in carnali erexi superbia*, Angl. xi. 117, 32. v. ranc, *and cf.* wlanc, wlencan.

á-rendan; *p. de To tear off:*—Árend þá rinde of þām wyrttruman, Lch. ii. 270, 4.

á-rengde. v. -árencan: árentale. v. ǽlc; II a.

á-reódian. *Add:*—Se ylca bróðor hálwendlíce geþreád him gescea-mode and áreúdode *idem frater salubriter correptus erubuit*, Gr. D. 160, 20.

á-rétan. Dele '*set right*' (*in last two passages* á-rétan = *to comfort*), *and add:*—Hé hæfde his wíf mid him þe hine árétte, þeáh hé his bearna þolode, Hml. S. 30, 204. On þǽm sealme hé wæs cleopiende tó Drihtne, wilnode þæt hé hine árétte, Ps. Th. 27, arg. Be eallum þám þe gebrocode wǽron and eft árétte, 28, arg.

arewe. *Add:*—Gif hwylc man mid arwan (*sagitta*) deór ofsceóte, Ll. Th. ii. 212, 20. Arwan *framea*, An. Ox. 37, 1. Arewan, *gauelucas catapultas*, 4238. [*Icel.* ǫr.]

ár-fæst. *Add:* I. *pious, righteous, honourable:*—Árfæst *pius*, Wrt. Voc. i. 75, 67. Weard Nerua, swíðe árfæst man, tó cásere gecoren, Hml. Th. i. 60, 6. Mid árfæsððes (-fæstes, *v. l.*) ingeðonces láre *pia intentione*, Past. 167, 7. II. *merciful, gracious, clement:*—þæt hé hīwige swylce hé árfæst sȳ, Wlfst. 59, 19. Gif Drihten ús árfæst (*propitius*) bið, Num. 14, 8. þú ǽrfæstosta Hǽlend, Angl. xi. 114, 75.

árfæstlic; *adj.* Pious:—Árfæstlicum oeste *pia devotione*, Rtl. 39, 17.

árfæstlíce; *adv.* I. *piously:*—Árfæstlíce gileſeð *pie credit*, Rtl. 40, 9: 77, 5. Se bisceop stóp tó þǽre cyste and árfæstlíce (árfullíce, *v. l.*) strǽc (*pie violentus*) tóbrǽc þǽre cyste locu, and þǽr genam þá twelf mancosas and hí gedǽlde þám þearfendum mannum, Gr. D. 64, 13. II. *graciously, kindly:*—Árfæstlíce hé mancynne eádmódnysse bisne onstealde, Hml. A. 151, 3.

árfæstnes. *Add:* I. *piety:*—*Pietas* árfæstnys, Angl. xi. 107, 8. Ǽrfastness, Wülck. Gl. 251, 18. II. *mercy, clemency, kindness:*—Ðurh ðā mildheortnesse his árfæsðnesse *per pietatis viscera*, Past. 99, 1. Ðone greádan his árfæstnesse and his frófre hé gebræt *sinum pietatis expandit*, 407, 11: Gr. D. 146, 28. Hé bæd ðone ælmihtigan for his árfæstnysse þ hé þám preóste gemiltsode, Hml. S. 6, 167: 30, 350. Ongeán þǽre árfæstnysse hé syld árleásnysse, þæt hé ne árige his under-þeóddum ne his gelícum, Wlfst. 59, 16.

ár-fæt. *Add:*—Clǽm on árfæt . . . mylte syþþan on ðǽm árfæte, Lch. iii. 16, 24. Dó on árfæt, lǽt standan on þám árfate, ii. 34, 5. Meng on árfæt, 124, 25. [*O. H. Ger.* ér-faz *aeramentum*.]

ar-faran. Dele; *the line cited should read:*—Ge ǽr fara\ð ge eft cumað.

ár-full. *Add:* I. *shewing honour or respect:*—Ǽghwylc man wið óðerne árful sȳ on ǽlcum þǽra góda þe hé him tó áre gecweðan oðþe gedón mæge, Hml. A. 160, 191. Utan beón árfulle fæder and mēder, Wlfst. 119, 3. II. *shewing kindness, mercy, favour:*—God is swíðe árfull and mildheort *Deus pius est*, Gr. D. 335, 15. Ic iów wæs árful geworden and milde, Wlfst. 222, 4. þearfendum mannum árfulle, 257, 3. Hé dyde manegu árfull weorc (*pia opera*), Gr. D. 331, 27.

árfullíce. v. árfæstlíce, II.

ar-gang. v. ears-gang.

argentille, an; *f. Argentil, parsley-pert:*—Argentille *camiculo* (cf. canicula, argentilla, 31, 68), Wrt. Voc. i. 79, 36. Argen[tille] *camicula*, An. Ox. 56, 47. Archentille, 408. [In Lch. iii. 300, col. 2 *camicula* is glossed *argella*.] [From *Lat.* argentilla.]

ár-geweorc. For Cot. 79 *read* Wrt. Voc. ii. 32, 75: ár-glǽd. Dele.

árian. *Add:* I. *to honour,* (1) with dat.:—Ára þínum fæder (árig ðone fæder, L., āre fæder ðīn *honora patrem*, R. Mt. 19, 19), Ll. Th. i. 44, 15. (2) with acc., Bt. 41, 2; F. 246, 19 (in Dict.). II. *to shew mercy, kindness,* with dat. inst. (1) *to do kindness:*—Ára mē and genere mē of deáþes bendum, Bl. H. 89, 22. Ic þe bidde þæt þú mē árige *ut eripias me*, Ps. Th. 39, 15. Ne yld þæt þú mē árie, 21. Drihten him þone þearfan geheóld, þ hé him miltsian sceolde, ðā þára óðerra manna him nán árian ne wolde, Bl. H. 215, 2. Gif wē beóð on hwylcum earfoþum . . . gif hē ús árian and miltsian wile, 51, 30. (2) *to refrain from unkindness, to spare:*—Ne árað *non parcet*, Kent. Gl. 173. Sē ðe áreð *qui parcit*, 468. þá ofslihð se deófol ðe him wiðstandað . . . þá ðe his leásungum gelyfað, þām hē árað, Hml. Th. i. 6, 5. Dū ðínum bearne ne árodest, ii. 62, 8. þ hé ne furþum wiflíce (-um, *v. l.*) hāde árede *ut ne sexui quidem muliebri parceret*, Bd. 2, 20; Sch. 185, 11. Ára nū and mā wæter of þínum mūþe þú ne send, Bl. H. 247, 7. þú nelt árian þǽre stówe *non parces loco illi*, Gen. 18, 24. Miltsian and árian mannum, Hml. Th. i. 68, 25. [*O. Sax. O. H. Ger.* érôn.]

árigend, es; *m. A patron, protector, benefactor:*—Heó wæs wuduwena and steópcilda árigend, Lch. iii. 430, 2: Wlfst. 257, 4.

á-riht. *Add:*—Gif heora hwilc þone rǽdels áriht rǽdde, Ap. Th. 3, 17: 5, 16. Áriht understanden, Wlfst. 155, 3: 33, 5. þ hé hit áriht nǽme, Ll. Th. i. 286, 18. v. riht, III.

á-ríman. *Add:*—Dis ðæt wē nū feám wordum árímdon *haec quae breviter enumerando perstrinximus*, Past. 75, 16. Árím letanias, Lch. i. 400, 10. Hwā is þætte áríman mæge hwæt þǽr moncynnes forweard, Ors. 1, 11; S. 50, 13: Bl. H. 59, 33: 63, 1. Manige óþre þe is lang

tó árímenne, Gr. D. 266, 18. Árímende *enumerans*, Wrt. Voc. ii. 94, 32. [*O. H. Ger.* ar-rímen.]

á-rinnan. *Add:* [*Goth.* ur-rinnan: *O. H. Ger.* ar-rinnan.]

á-rísan. *Add:* I. *to arise,* (1) *to stand up* from sitting or lying:—'Andrea, árís' . . . Andreas þá árás on þæs folces gesihþe, Bl. H. 241, 15. Weard se deáda man cwic and teolode tó arísenne, 219, 19. (2) *to rise* after sleeping:—Hé wel ǽr árás . . . Se apostol cwæð tó him: 'For hwon árise þú swā hraðe?,' Gr. D. 227, 8. Hé hié áwehte and cwæð: 'Arísað,' Bl. H. 235, 20. (2a) *of the sun:*—Seó sunne áríst swíðe ǽr on morgen up, Ps. Th. 18, 5. (3) *to rise* after death:—Árás *emersit* (*tumbis atris*), Wrt. Voc. ii. 93, 18. Drihten hét ealle árísan þe on þām wætere wǽron, Bl. H. 247, 26. Hé geswutelode þæt hé árisen wæs, Hml. Th. i. 222, 9. II. *to arise* with intent to act:—Hwā áríst tó þǽm þæt hé sylle hǽlo?, Ps. Th. 13, 11. Uton wē árísan and ácwellan þá apostolas, Bl. H. 149, 34. II a. of hostile action:—Áríseþ þeód wiþ þeóde, Bl. H. 107, 27. þá gingran árísaþ wiþ þām yldrum, 171, 23. III. *to arise, be produced, come to be,* (a) of physical growth:—Hit gedéþ þ þá swylas eft ne árísað, Lch. i. 356, 2. (b) figurative:—Gif for godbótan feohbót áríseð, Ll. Th. i. 328, 4. Of manegum landum mǽre landriht árist tó cyninges gebanne, 432, 6. Hit áríseþ eówrum sáulum tó hundteóntigfealdre mēde *it will come to be a hundredfold reward for your souls*, Bl. H. 41, 19. Swā hwǽr swā þæt feoh up áríse *wherever such payment has to be made*, Wlfst. 181, 10. Áríse seó æcerteóðung á be ðám ðe seó sulh þone teóðan æcer ǽr geeóde (cf. þ hé his teóðunge á swā seó sulh þone teóðan æcer gegá rihtlíce gelǽste, Ll. Th. i. 342, 12), 310, 24. Gif ús feoh áríse æt úrum gemǽnum sprǽcum, Ll. Th. i. 232, 5. Gif preóst circan miswurðige þe eal his wurðscipe of sceal árísan, ii. 294, 11. IV. *to rise, mount up:*—Oð þ ángylde áríse tó .xxx. scill; siþþan hit tó þām áríse . . ., Ll. Th. i. 68, 3-4. þriefealdlíce hit áríse *it shall increase threefoldly*, 88, 3. [*Goth.* ur-reisan: *O. Sax.* á-rísan: *O. H. Ger.* ar-rísan.]

á-rísende, Bl. H. 225, 17. *l.* rísende. v. rísan *to raven*.

ár-leás. *Add:* I. *dishonourable, shameful:*—Hé swealt mid árleáse deáðe, Shrn. 120, 14. II. *wicked:*—Árleás *impius*, Wrt. Voc. i. 75, 68. Fordón þá rihtwísan mid þām árleásan (*impio*), Gen. 18, 23. Ic and mín folc sind árleáse (*injusti*), Ex. 9, 27. [*O. H. Ger.* ér-lós *impius*.]

árleáslíce. *Add:*—Hé þá hálgan róde genam hām tó his earde árleáslíce dyrstig, Hml. S. 27, 26. Hét hé his ágenne sunu árleáslíce ácwellan, Hml. Th. i. 88, 7: 13.

árleás-nes. *Add:*—Ongeán þǽre árfæstnysse hé syld árleásnysse, Wlfst. 59, 16. Hwilc mān and hwilce árleásnesse se unrihtwísa cásere worhte, Bt. 16, 4; F. 58, 2.

ár-lic; *adj.* Early:—Árlic morgen *aurora*, Rtl. 69, 2. Tíde árlica horam matutinam, 171, 37.

árlíce *honourably. Add:*—Hé him árlíce tó sprǽc, Past. 305, 8. Heó wyllað geunnan healfes þ þȳ árlícor on þǽre stówe beón mæge, Cht. Th. 137, 19. þ hé cume and sí micle árlícor þonne hé ǽr wæs, Shrn. 204, 9.

ár-loc, es; *n. A rowlock:*—Árlocu *columbaria* (columbarium foramen in navi per quod remus in aquam mittitur), Wrt. Voc. i. 63, 41.

ár-morgenlic. v. ǽr-morgenlic.

arod *strenuous, bold. Add:*—Arod *promptus*, Kent. Gl. 821. *Efficax* hwæt, i. *citus, expeditus, astutus, acutus, sollers, peritus* arud, Wrt. Voc. ii. 142, 55. Hé bið suíðe arod and suíðe gereðre on ryhtum weorcum *constanter se in bono opere dirigit*, Past. 306, 15. Arod tó deófles willan, Hml. S. 11, 13. Fús and arod tó þǽre þrowunge *ad passionem promta*, Gr. D. 231, 10. Beó arod and ne ondrǽd þe nó deáþ, Shrn. 119, 26. Tó ðám arod *so bold*, Jud. 275. Arude *strenua* (*luctamina*), An. Ox. 5, 1. þ wíf wæs á siððan þȳ aredra on hire bēne, Shrn. 99, 36.

arodlíce. *Add:*—Hé síðode arodlíce tó ðǽre dúne, Hml. Th. ii. 60, 22. Heó árdlíce fǽrde, Hml. S. 2, 35. Swā hwæt swā þín hand mage wyrcan, wyrce arudlíce (ard-, *v. l.*) (*instanter*), Gr. D. 327, 26. Ongunnon þá wyrhtan ardlíce (*instanter*) biddan heom metes, 251, 18. Hé cwæð swíðe ardlíce *constanter ait*, 254, 4. Hé swíðe ardlíce geteohhode *constanter decrevit*, 255, 33. Aredlícor (*instantius*) sēcan, 258, 24.

arodness, e; *f. Boldness, constancy, resolution:*—Hí in heora arod-nesse (-ed-, *v. l.*) ealle wǽron ácwealde *in sua constantia omnes occisi sunt*, Gr. D. 232, 18. Hié habbað ðā arodnesse (-ud-, *v. l.*) and ðā bieldo ðæt hié magon anweald habban *auctoritatis fortitudine erecti sunt*, Past. 41, 17.

Aro-sǽte(-an) *the name of an English people* (*district*):—Arosǽtna landes is syx hund hýda, C. D. B. i. 414, 26.

ár-sápe. Dele sápe . . . stillare.

ár-þing, es; *n. A thing of value, gift:*—Dā ðe gisendun árðing (*munera*) hiora in gazophilacium, Lk. R. 21, 1. v. þing, I. 1 a. a.

árung. *Add:*—Hié him sendon áne tunecan ongeán, þ hé ealles buton árunge tó Rôme ne com, Ors. 5, 10; S. 234, 24.

ár-wéla. *l.* ár-wela.

ár-weorþ, -wierþe (u, y). *Add:*—Ðú árwurð fæder, R. Ben. 114, 21. Se árwierþa (-wurþa, *v. l.*) wer, Chr. 716; P. 42, 14. Swíðe árwyrðe wer, 1052; P. 173, 17: Bl. H. 209, 15. Þæt árwyrðe weófod, 207, 15. Móder árwyrðe *mater honorificata*, Rtl. 45, 25: *veneranda*, 66, 21. Árweorðra (-wierð-, *v. l.*) monna mód, Past. 128, 25. Hé geceás árwurðe weras *electis viris strenuis*, Ex. 18, 25. Árwyrþran *prestantiorem*, An. Ox. 1112.

árweorþ-full; *adj. Honourable:*—On eallum þeáwum árwurðful, Hml. S. 5, 7. Ic mæg habban árwurðfulle lícðénunge, Hml. Th. i. 86, 33.

ár-weorþian. *Add:*—Árwyrða (-wordig) fæder ðínne, Mk. R. 10, 19. Árweorþian wé Críst, Bl. H. 11, 7. Wé sceoldan hine árwyrþian, 71, 23. Ælcne man mon sceal árweorðian, R. Ben. 16, 20. v. ge-, un-árweorþian.

ár-weorþig. *Dele.*

ár-weorþlic. *Add:*—Árweorðlic *decora*, Ps. L. 146, 1. Árwurðlic *honorabile*, 71, 14. Gif æni þinc árwurðlic (árwyrþlicast) *si quod prestantissimum*, An. Ox. 2012. Árwyrðlicne *venerabilem*, Rtl. 77, 27.

ár-weorþlíce. *Add:*—Sceal mon bi sumum dæle árwierðelíce (-wyrð-, *v. l.*) wandigende suíðe wærlíce stiéran *sub quadam sunt cautela reverentiae parcendo feriendi*, Past. 295, 11. Swá þæt wé on dæge árwurðlíce (*honeste*) faron, Hml. Th. i. 604, 6.

ár-weorþnes. *Add:*—Þú eart úres folces árwurðnyss, Hml. A. 114, 391. Be gebedes árweorðnesse *de reverentia orationis*, R. Ben. 6, 27. Tó árweorðnesse þære hálgan þrynesse, 33, 17. Mid ealre árwurðnisse, Chr. 1012, 2: 1054; P. 143, 2: 1054; P. 184, 20. Ða árwyrðnesse æfestnesse *reverentia religionis*, Past. 132, 15.

ár-wesa *honoured:*—Þá gingran hyra yldran *nonnos* nemnen, þæt is, leóf and árwesa *juniores priores suos nonnos vocent, quod intelligitur paterna reverentia*, R. Ben. 115, 20.

á-ryddan, -(h)rydran, -rytran *to strip:*—Árydid *expilatam*, Txts. 61, 817. Árytrid, 789. Áritrid, 58, 372. Áhrydred, Wrt. Voc. ii. 29, 68. Áþrýd *vel* árydred *expilatam*, i. *conquassatam*, 145, 13. [*Cf. O. H. Ger.* ar-riuten *exstirpare* : *Icel.* ryðja *to clear* ; rjóðr ; *n. A clearing* ; hrjóða *to strip, clear.*] v. hryding.

á-sægdnes, -sædnes *sacrifice, mystery :*—Ásægdnise *mysterium*, Lk. L. 8, 10: p. 4, 9: *hostiam*, 2, 24. Ásægduisum *sacrificiis*, 13, 1. Ásædnessum *holocaustis*, Bl. Gl. v. on-sægednes.

asal, asald. *Add:*—Asald *asinus*, Lk. L. R. 14, 5. Fola asaldes, 19, 30: Jn. L. R. 12, 15. Aseldes, p. 6, 13. Asales byrðen, Mk. L. 9, 42. Assales, Mt. p. 18, 16. Tó asalde *asinae*, Mk. p. 4, 16. On assalde, Rtl. 95, 6. Assald (easald, R.), Lk. L. 13, 15. Assald i sadal (asald, R.) *asellum*, Jn. 12, 14. Ofer asal *super asinam*, Mt. L. 21, 5. Asalda i asales byrðenstán *asinaria*, 18, 6. [From Celtic. Cf. *O. Ir.* asal.]

á-sáwan. *Add: to sow* land:—Ðú þás eorþan áseówe mistlicum sæde, Bt. 33, 4; F. 132, 26. Þá hét he him bringan bere tó sæde and ofer ælcne tíman ða eorðan áseów, Hml. Th. ii. 144, 12. Ásáwen æcer *seges*, Wrt. Voc. i. 80, 47.

á-scafan. v. á-sceafan.

asc-bacen; *adj. Baked in the ashes, on the hearth :*—His gebróðra gegearwodon axbakenne (heorðbæcenne, *v. l.*) hláf (*panem subcinericium*), Gr. D. 86, 30.

asce. *Add:*—Asce *cinis*, Wrt. Voc. i. 284, 16. Æsce, 66, 43. Acse, ii. 16, 61. Seó acxe . . . hundes heáfod gebærned tó acxan, Lch. i. 370, 10-13. Weorðað hig (*apples of Sodom*) tó acxan *fatiscunt in cinerem*, Ors. 1, 3; S. 32, 15. Foxes lungen on hátre æscan gesoden, Lch. i. 340, 4. Heortes horn gebærned . . . nim þæs hornes acxan (axan *v. l.*), 334, 17. Ða asca of fótum *pulverem de pedibus*, Mt. L. 10, 14: Lk. L. R. 9, 5. Gé synd dust and acsan, Guth. 38, 23. Bestreówod nid axum, Hml. Th. ii. 516, 31. v. axe, axse *in Dict.*

á-sceacan. *Add:* I. *to shake off, remove by shaking :*—Ic of ásceace (-scace, *v. l.*) *excutio*, ic on ásceace *incutio*, Ælfc. Gr. Z. 169, 8, 9. Ásceacan *excutere*, ásceacene *excussam, expulsam*, Wrt. Voc. ii. 146, 20, 21. (1) literal :—Hé ásceó hí (*the viper*) in tó fýre, Hml. Th. i. 574, 15. Ásceaccað asca, Lk. L. 9, 5. (2) figurative :—Gif he his fram ásceað yfelu *si sua discusserit mala*, Scint. 164, 2. Hé his sáwle him from ásceóc *animam ejus excuteret*, Gr. D. 136, 2. Ic wolde þ clericas ásceócon fram heora andgites orðance ælce sleacnysse, Angl. viii. 301, 4. Þý læs he þurh þ sár ða lácnunge of him ásceace, Lch. i. 302, 16. Gif ðæs módes forhæfdnes mid ungeðylde ne ascóke (*excuteret*) ða sibbe of ðæm sceáte ðære smyltnesse, Past. 311, 15. Wé sceolon ásceacan ðone sleacan slǽp ús fram, Hml. Th. i. 602, 15. His geoc of heora swuran ásceacan, 212, 10: R. Ben. 98, 14. Hé of þám slǽpe ásceacen wearð, Hml. S. 31, 891. II. *to shake* (trans.) :—Hé wæs hyne ásceacende eal swá earn þonne hé myd hrædum flyhte wyle forð áfleón, Nic. 14, 35.

á-sceádan. *Add:*—Áweg álúcan oððe ásceádan *discludere*, Wrt. Voc. ii. 27, 51. Sý fram ásceádan *excipiatur*, i. *segregatur*, 145, 11. I. *to separate, dissociate*, (1) literal : — Þém áscádendum,

*quia carbones inseparunt scoria de ferro* [*marginal gloss on* cum carbonibus], Bl. Gl. (2) figurative :—Bisceopas áscádað út of cyrican þá þe hý sylfe forgyltan, Wlfst. 104, 10. Hé hine ásceád (*v. l.* -scéd) of ðám woroldríce, Past. 39, 21. Áscádan ðá forhæfdnesse from ðære ánmódnesse, 347, 2. Fram eallum crístendóme beón ásceáden, Ll. Th. ii. 424, 5. Ásceáden (*segregatus*) from synnfullum, Rtl. 90, 34. Ne sié ásceáden from fultumum *non destituatur auxiliis*, 18, 23. II. *to separate, distinguish :*—Gif ic ásceáde mid mearcunge þára namena *si nominum praenotatione distinguo*, Gr. D. 7, 2. Gode þancie hé þte hé hine from nýtenum áscéd, Ll. Th. ii. 420, 8. III. *to make distinct, clear :*—Ásceádan is *declaratur*, Jn. p. 8, 1. [*O. H. Ger.* ar-sceidan *separare, disjungere, designare.*]

á-sceafan, -scafan *to shave off :*—Ádelf niþeweardne sláhðorn, áscaf þá ýtemestan rinde, Lch. ii. 92, 30. Sceafoþan of felle áscafen mid pumice, 100, 14. Áscæfen *obrasum*, Wrt. Voc. ii. 64, 77. [*O. H. Ger.* arscaban *eradere.*]

á-scealian; *pp.* od *To take off the husk :*—Áscealode *enucleata*, Wrt. Voc. ii. 32, 61.

á-sceaman *to be ashamed :*—Ásceamen *erubescant*, Wrt. Voc. ii. 144, 14.

á-sceamelic; *adj. Shameful :*—Tó áscamelicum (*but cf.* áscunelicum, An. Ox. 4016) *ad detestabilem*, Hpt. Gl. 500, 58.

asce-geswáp, á-scelede, -scended, -sceonian, -sceortian. v. swǽpa (*in Dict.*), á-scilian, un-áscended, á-scunian, -scortian.

á-sceótan. *Add:* I. *intrans. To shoot, move rapidly :*—Sió costung út ásciét (-sciéð, *v. l.*) on weorc *tentatio usque ad operationem prosilit*, Past. 71, 7. Án út ásceát of weorode, Ors. 3, 6; S. 108, 10. Se scyttel ásceát of þære fetere, Hml. S. 21, 419. Áscuton þá gástas of ðære niwelnysse, Hml. Th. ii. 350, 32. II. *trans.* (1) of motion, *to shoot a missile* :—Án scytta áscét ána flán, Hml. S. 18, 220. Weard upp áscoten swýðlíce mycelnes þæs stánclifes *ingentis saxi moles erupta est*, Gr. D. 12, 8. (2) of position, *to make prominent, thrust out :*—Se stán wæs ásceoten gecyndelíce of þám munte *saxum naturaliter egrediens*, Gr. D. 49, 7. (3) *to shoot, strike* an object :—Hí cwǽdon þ se lǽce sceolde ásceótan (*lance*) þ geswell ; þá dyde he swá, and þær sáh út wyrms, Hml. S. 20, 63. Ásceótende *eviscerando*, An. Ox. 46, 47. Hine wearþ óþer eáge mid ánre flán út ásceoten *ictu sagittae oculum perdidit*, Ors. 3, 7; S. 112, 15. [*O. H. Ger.* ar-sciozan *germinare.*]

á-sceppan, -sceran. v. á-scippan, -sciran.

áscian. *Add:* I. *absolute :*—Mon sceal sprecan ásciende, Past. 185, 9. II. *with acc. of person addressed, to question, interrogate :*—His rihta dóm áhsað (*interrogat*) manna bearn. Se ylca Drihten áhsað rihtwíse and unrihtwíse, Ps. Th. 10, 5, 6. Hié sculon God áscian, Past. 103, 8. III. *to ask* a person (*dat. acc.*) a question :—Ic ácsige þe hwí latast þú swá lange, Dóm. L. 65. Hé ácsode hiom hwæs tácen þ bión mihte, H. R. 5, 13. IV. *to ask, enquire about,* (1) with gen. :—Ic secge hwæs ic áscian wylle *aperiam propositionem meam*, Ps. Th. 48, 4. Gif þeós cwén þises áxian wylle, H. R. 9, 7. Þ ic móte ánes þinges áxian, Hml. S. 23, 721, 723. (1 a) and with acc. of person asked :—Ic áhsige eów ánre sprǽce, Mt. 21, 24. God ácsað eów þises, Wlfst. 49, 5. Hú hé ondwyrdan sceolde þæs hé hiene áscade *quid sibi tamquam consulenti responderi velit*, Ors. 3, 9; S. 126, 30. Hé sumra wyrta (worda, *v. l.*) ácsode þone wyrtweard *hortulanum quaedam requireret*, Gr. D. 180, 20. Ácsa hine his wísena, Ll. Th. ii. 260, 21. Ne áxa nánne wiccan rǽdes *nec sit qui pythones consulat*, Deut. 18, 11. ' Mót ic þe áhtes ácsian ?' Cwæð hé :—'Ácsa þæs þe þú wille' '*licet aliquid interrogare*.' '*Interroga*,' inquit, '*quod vis*,' Bd. 4, 3; Sch. 358, 1. Se scrift sceal áhsian gehwylces þinges þone þe tó him his þearfe sprycð, Ll. Th. ii. 428, 17. (1 b) and with dat. of person :—Þæs ic hiom áxian wille, H. R. 7, 25. (1 c) and with person governed by prép. :—Áhsa þæs æt þám wífe, Lch. ii. 330, 25. (2) with prep. :—Áhsiað be ealdum dagum, Deut. 4, 32. Suelce hé be óðrum menn sprece and áscie (áxige, *v. l.*), Past. 185, 10. (2 a) and with acc. of person asked :—Tó hwí áxige gé mé be ðám Hǽlende ðus ?, Hml. Th. ii. 300, 7. V. *to ask, demand to be told :*—Ic áxige þone intingan, Hml. S. 10, 135. Iówan ðæt him mon tó áscað, Past. 173, 2. VI. *to ask after, enquire for, search for :*—Syþþan wé hit áscað, Ll. Th. i. 234, 16. Mann ús ofer eall sóhte and ús man georne gehwár áxode, Hml. S. 23, 451. Hé sende tó þám brýdguman and hí áxode þǽr, ac heó þǽr næs, 33, 182. Hé befrán for hwylcum intingan hí hine áxodon, 10, 117. Wé ealle hine áxodan, Ll. Th. i. 234, 12. Hió ongan swíðe giornlíce áxian þá næglas, H. R. 15, 20. Mín hláford ásende mé tó þysum earde tó áxienne wyrhtan, Hml. S. 36, 35. VII. *to learn, find out by enquiry :*—Hí sóna, þá hí þǽr þone hálgan wer áscodon, þóhton þæt hí woldon þǽr þone man gebringan, Guth. 58, 15. v. be-, ge-, of-áscian.

ásciend-lic; *adj. Interrogative :*—An is *interrogativa*, þæt is áxiendlic, Ælfc. Gr. Z. 260, 14. v. áxiend-lic *in Dict.*

á-scildan *to protect :*—Ué sié áscildad *protegamur*, Rtl. 75, 9: 80, 19.

á-scilian. *Perhaps words of different origin have this form. As a gloss to enucleare the verb seems connected with scealu; cf. á-scealian :*

as a gloss to dividere, it seems cognate with Icel. skilja. (1) Áscilian enucleare (the corresponding gloss in An. Ox. 3898 is: enucleare i. manifestare spyrian), Wrt. Voc. ii. 83, 80 : 30, 70. Áscyled enucleata (cf. enucleata, i. investigata gecneátade, An. Ox. 176), 75, 35 : 30, 69. (2) Áscylidre secretae, An. Ox. 5434. Áscilede (-scelede, Hpt. Gl. 438, 49) beóð dirimuntur, i. dividuntur, 1367. Áscyledum tectis (motibus intus agit), 5410 : excipientibus, i. segregantibus, 5448. v. scilian.

á-scímod. v. scímian in Dict.

á-scínan. Add: I. literal:—In þære sceáwunge seó áscán þám útran eágum in illa luce quae exterioribus oculis fulsit, Gr. D. 174. 11 : Bl. H. 249, 1. Ásceán, 145, 12. II. figurative:—His líf áscán, Gr. D. 12, 4. Hié on swíþe manegum godcundum mægenum wuldorlíce áscínon, Bl. H. 161, 20. Ne oncneów ic hweþer in Langbeardum æfre ásceonan ænigra manna líf mid mægnum non in Italia aliquorum vitam virtutibus fulsisse cognovi, Gr. D. 7, 8. [O. H. Ger. ar-scínan resplendere, refulgere.]

á-scippan; p. scóp To create, originate:—Perseus þære þeóde óþerne naman áscóp be him syluum Perseus nomen genti dedit, Ors. 1, 8 ; S. 40, 33. Áscæpen am creata sum, Rtl. 68, 18. [O. H. Ger. ar-scaffan efficere.]

á-scíran (e, y); p. -scær, pl. -scæron ; pp. -scoren To cut off, away:— Gif hé þone beard of áscire (-scyre, v. l.), Ll. Th. i. 84, 8. Wæs án ormæte clif áscoren rihte ádúne, Hml. S. 31, 316. Of áscoren raderetur, An. Ox. 2, 337.

á-scíran; p. de To make clear. (1) lit.:—Biþ se flæschoma áscýred swá glæs, Bl. H. 109, 36. (2) fig.:—þæt hálige godspel ne áscýrde hú hí gefreatwode wæron, Hml. Th. i. 298, 33.

á-scírian. Add:—Ic áscirige separo, Ælfc. Gr. Z. 277, 7. I. to separate, part, remove:—Se sácerd sceolde hine (the leper) fram mannum áscirian, Hml. Th. i. 124, 6. Heora sáwle bióþ áscyrede in helle diópnesse, Wlfst. 219, 10. Áscyrede, ásyndrede sequestrantur, i. segregantur, An. Ox. 1366. Áscyredum remotis, 5389. II. to set apart :— Úre Drihten áscyrede tó láfe þ þ wé eft of áwócon, Angl. xi. 2, 42. Ásceredre peculiaris, An. Ox. 11, 5. þá áscyredan privatam, i. singularem, 361. III. to cut off from association, to hold aloof:—Sé þe hine áscyrede for þyssere scearpnysse fram ús, Hml. S. 11, 167. Se man þe his mód áwent fram eallum þisum bócum, and bið him swá ánwille, þæt him leófre bið, þæt hé lybbe be his ágenum dihte áscired fram þisum, Ælfc. T. Grn. 20, 8. IV. with idea of exclusion, expulsion :—Gítsung and unrihtlice welan ðé áscyriað and ásyndriað fram Gode, Hex. 52, 18. Áscyrige man hig fram þære þenunge abscidantur a ministerio, Ll. Th. ii. 198, 3. Áflýman, áscirian eliminare, i. expoliare, An. Ox. 1963. Ðone áscyrian and ámánsumian fram crístenum mannum, Hml. Th. i. 124, 29. Mæden þe hine ne móste áscyrian fram his clænum lufe, Hml. S. 4, 14. Ne geþafa þú þ ic beó fram ðé áscired, 15, 72. Hé trúwode þæt hé nære áscyred fram martirdóme þæs hálgan weres, Hml. Th. ii. 310, 28. þ hé wurðe ne beó þ hé beó þanon áscyred non talis qui mereatur proici, R. Ben. 108, 22. Beón áscirod and fram áworpen, Hml. S. 23 b, 438. Beón hig áscyrede (abscidantur) fram eallum gehádodum mannum, Ll. Th. ii. 200, 1. Áscirode, Hml. A. 2, 43. V. to cut off, rob :— Ælmyssan þearfan ná áscyra þú elemosinam pauperis ne fraudes, Scint. 157, 5. v. un-áscirod in Dict.

á-scirigendlic. Add: v. un-áscirigendlic.

á-scirpan. Add:—His mód and his ondgit ðæt gecynd áscirpð . . . his ondgit bið áscirped, Past. 69, 8, 13. Áscearptun exacuerunt, Ps. Srt. 63, 4.

á-scirpan (v. sceorp) to dress, make ready; succingere:—Sió wiðerweardnes bið simle untælu and wæru, áscirped mid þære styringe hire ágenre frecennesse adversam fortunam videas sobriam succinctamque et ipsius adversitatis exercitatione prudentem, Bt. 20 ; 5, 47, 27. v. gescerpan in Dict.

á-scirred. l. á-scirped. v. preceding word.

á-scortian to run short, run out, be exhausted:—Æt ðám giftum áscortode wín, Hml. Th. ii. 56, 10.

á-screádian. Add:—þæt hí þá misweaxendan bógas of áscreádian, Hml. Th. ii. 74, 12.

á-screncan. Add: to trip up, cause to stumble:—Hé mid ðære synne ðæt mód áscrencte mentem peccato supplantat, Past. 415, 11. Áscrencte elideret, i. offenderet, áscrencte elisi, Wrt. Voc. ii. 143, 9-12. Áscrencan elisisse, 87, 52 : 31, 41. Ðonne ætspornað hié and weordað mid ðæm áscrencte subjectorum vita quasi in obstaculo itineris offendit, Past. 129, 7. Gif ðá fét weordað áscrencte, eal se líchoma wierð gebíged and ðæt heáfod gecymð on ðære eorðan, 133, 1. Hié weordað áscrencte on ðæm scyfe ðære styringe motionis impulsu praecipites, 215, 12.

á-screopan. l. -screpan, and add: to clear off:—þonne áscrypð hió þ áter áweg, Lch. ii. 144, 17. Áscrep þá greátan rinde of, 270, 17. Áscrepan (-screfan, Erf.) egerere, áscrepen (-aen, Erf., -an, Wrt. Voc. ii. 29, 17) egesta, Txts. 59, 730-1 : Wrt. Voc. ii. 29, 16 : 142, 68.

a-screpan to bear out. Dele, and see preceding word.

á-scrincan to shrivel up. v. un-áscruncen.

á-scrúdnian, -scrútniau; p. ode To examine, investigate :—Áscrúdnige

borhigenda ealle spéde his scrutetur foenerator omnem substantiam eius, Ps. L. 108, 11. þ wé áscrútnion his fare and ápinsiun his síð hwanon hé cóme, Angl. viii. 305, 46. Heora gerýna áscrútnian, 301, 32. Hig habbað áscrútnod Serium and Priscianum, and þurhsmógun Catus cwydas, 321, 28. [Cf. O. H. Ger. ar-scrudilôn scrutari, discutere.]

á-scúfan. Add:—Áscúfið praecipitat, Txts. 89, 1644. Ásceáf on weg explodit, excludit, Wrt. Voc. ii. 29, 72. I. literal, where an object is moved:—Hé hit ásceáf fram his múðe, Hml. Th. ii. 254, 17. Út áscúfen eliminant, An. Ox. 4697. Scipu út áscúfan, Chr. 897 ; P. 91, 13. Hí woldon hine niðer áscúfan (of clife), Hml. Th. ii. 236, 34. Ásceófan, Hml. S. 18, 350. Beseah hé tó þære sceande (Iezebel) up and hét hí ásceófon underbæc, 345. Wæs ic ána út ásceofen, 23 b, 415. Betwux þám leónum ásceofen, Hml. Th. ii. 174, 4. II. figurative, (1) to drive away, repel :—Hig þæne deófol fram heom áscúfað, Angl. viii. 330, 25. Hé þá stræle þára áwerigdra gásta him fram ásceáf, Guth. 44, 1. Áscýfað yfelgiornisse deponentes malitiam, Rtl. 25, 23. þte þú áscúfe (retrudas) from mé ða ungesewenlican næglas, Lch. i. lxxi, 3. Ælc gesceaft onscunað þ þ hire wiþerweard biþ, and tiolaþ þ hit him þ from áscúfe, Bt. 16, 3 ; F. 56, 5. (2) to expel :—Beó út áscofen trudatur, An. Ox. 823. Of his cyneríce áscofen, Hml. Th. i. 488, 16. Hí beóð út áscofan exterminabuntur, Ps. L. 36, 11. Mancynn wearð ásceofen of myrhðe neorxna wanges, Hml. Th. i. 154, 11 : Bl. H. 17, 15. (3) to drive forward, impel, overthrow:—Áscúf praecipita, Ps. L. 54, 10. Áscoben impulsus, Bl. Gl. (4) to give up :—Se cyning þone wítegan him tó handum ásceáf, Hml. Th. i. 570, 28. [O. H. Ger. ar-sciuban alienare.]

áscung. Add:—Hió þóhtan hwæt seó ácsung beón scolde, H. R. 7, 27. Mé sprekendum is óðer áxung (quaestio) on mód becumen, Gr. D. 137, 29. Áxsung (interrogatio) múð þinne geopenige, Scint. 81, 8. Hit is þeáw þære spræce and þære áscunge talis est materia, Bt. 39, 4 ; F. 216, 18. Críst áxode Philippum . . . getácnode hé mid þære áscunge þæs folces nytennysse, Hml. Th. i. 188, 14. Yfele wé dydon mid þissere áxunge, ii. 300, 14. þá áxunga (áhsunge, v. l.) þære áscan tó wríðende interrogationi interrogationem jungens, Hml. S. 23 b, 495. Áxungum, spyrungum adinventionum (-ibus ?), An. Ox. 5214. v. geáscung.

á-scunelic; adj. Detestable:—Tó áscunelicum ad detestabile, An. Ox. 4016.

á-scúnian. l. á-scunian, and add: I. to abhor, detest:—Eal lufian þ hé lufað, and eal áscunian þ hé áscunað, Ll. Th. i. 178, 5. 'þú gesáwe gehwæde mot on þínes bróðor eáge' . . . þæt is on andgite : þú ásceonudest þá læstan gyltas on þíne gingran, R. Ben. 12, 5. Ælc þæra þinga bétan þe hí ealle áscunedon, Chr. 1014 ; P. 145, 7. Wé ásittað þ þá bóceras áscunion þ wé ymbe heora dígolnyssa þus rúmlíce sprecað, Angl. viii. 332, 34. Hwæt hí lufian sceolon and hwæt hí sceolon hatian and ásceonian, Wlfst. 303, 24. On áscunigendre synne in detestabili flagitio, Scint. 137, 7. I a. to express hate or scorn of :— Hí ásceonodon í hyspton (exprobraverunt) sáwle míne, Ps. L. 34, 70. II. to reject because of hate or scorn :—Hé ásceonaþ í áwyrpð (reprobat) smeáunga folca, Ps. L. 32, 10. Beún áscunod and fram áworpen, Hml. S. 23 b, 438 note. Áscunad excusso (cf. excussam, expulsam, 21), Wrt. Voc. ii. 146, 12. v. on-scunian.

á-scuniendlic. Add:—Ásceonigendlic í gehyspendlic abominabilis, Ps. L. 13, 1. Slipor í ásceonigendlic lubricum, 34, 6. Áscuniendlica intestabilis, Germ. 393, 77. þá áscuniendlican inepta, i. abjecta, An. Ox. 1900. v. on-scuniendlic.

á-scylfan to throw down, destroy :—Wíbed áscylfan aram pessumdare, Germ. 393, 49. Cf. scylf.

á-scyndan. Add: to drive away:—Drihten hí ealle mid gebeáte út áscynde, Hml. Th. i. 406, 8.

á-scywung shadowing : v. for-áscywung : á-sealcan. v. á-seolcan, -solcen.

á-seárian. Add:—Sóna áseáriað ðá twigu, Past. 308, 1. Treówa hé deð færlíce blówan and eft raðe áseárian, Wlfst. 196, 2.

á-sécan. Add: I. to seek out, search for:—Ácsa hine his wísena and ásec his dæda, Ll. Th. ii. 260, 21. Ðæt seó sáwel dysi forbúge and wísdóm áséce, Hex. 40, 1. II. to search through, explore :—Hí hæfdon þá burh ealle ásóhte, Chr. 1011 ; P. 142, 2 note. [Goth. ussôkjan: O. H. Ger. ar-suochen expetere, examinare.]

á-sécendlic; adj. To be sought out :—Ásécendlice exquisita, Ps. L. 110, 2.

á-secgan. Add:—Ásægde edidit, Wrt. Voc. ii. 31, 30. Ásaecgan edissere, 106, 80. Ásæcgan effarier, dicere, 142, 42. Ásecgan, 94, 53 : edissere, i. exponere, 29, 6 : effari, i. edicere, An. Ox. 3449. I. absolute, to speak out, utter a word :—Hí ne meahton ásecgan for þæs leóhtes mycelnesse, Bl. H. 145, 14. II. to tell, narrate, (1) with acc. :—Ðæt ic ásecgu (enarrem) all wundur ðín, Ps. Srt. 25, 7. Ðú ásagas (enarras) rehtwísnisse míne, 49, 16. Hié bismra on hié selfe ásædon, Ors. 4, 4 ; S. 164, 5. Se man wandaþ þæt hé þá synna æfre ásecgge, Bl. H. 43, 18. Ásecgan þá lufan, 103, 19. Ðá yfel ásecgan oððe áreccean, Ors. 1, 8 ; S. 42, 7. (2) with prep.—Mé sceal áðreótan

E

ymbe Philopes gewin tó ásecgenne *taedit Pelopes referre certamina*, Ors. 1, 8; S. 42, 13.    [III =on-secgan *tc offer*:—Ásægcas (-sægas, R.) *immolant*, Mk. L. 14, 12.  Âsægde *offerret*, Rtl. 25, 43.-]  [*O. H. Ger.* ar-sagén *edissere.*]

**á-secgendlic.** *Add:*—On cwyde ásecgendlic *dictu affabilis,* Ælfc. Gr. Z. 135, 12.  Nân ásecgendlic fracodlicnysse hîwung, Hml. Skt. 23 b, 382.  v. un-ásecgendlic.

**á-secgendlíce.** v. un-ásecgendlíce : **á-sédan,** -seddan.  v. sédan, un-ásedd.

**á-segendness,** e; *f. An offering*:—Nymþe hé mid ásegendnisseum (*muneribus*) in eóde, Nar. 24, 17.  Cf. on-sægdness.

**á-sellan.** *Add:*—Ásald is mé *data est mihi,* Mt. L. 28, 18.

**á-sencan;** *p.* te *To sink* (trans.):—On âsc(i)ntum (*i* above the line) *summerso,* i. *absorbto,* An. Ox. 829.

**á-sendan.** *Add:*—Ásend swylcne dôm ofer þá cyningas swylcne hig ofer þone Hælend âsendon, St. A. 38, 21-3.  Tô wîte âsend mid unsehte *relegatus,* Wrt. Voc. i. 21, 23.  On wræcsîð âsend, Hml. Th. i. 488, 16.  Âsend *intromittitur,* An. Ox. 5118.  [*Goth.* us-sandjan.]

**á-séngan.** *l.* (?) á-secgan.

**á-seódan** (?) *to disburse* (? cf. seód), *pay*:—Tô áseódenne *expendere,* Wrt. Voc. ii. 108, 2.  (*But see* á-seóþan.)

**á-seolcan;** *p.* -solcen *To become sluggish*:—Ðæt seó tunge ne áseolce ne semetipsam lingua pigre restringat,* Past. 275, 20.  v. á-solcen, -sealcan.

**á-seón** *to look at*:—Nelle ic mýnes Dryhtnes andwlitan áseón, Hml. A. 190, 255.  [*Goth.* us-saihwan *to look at: O. H. Ger.* ar-sehan *respicere.*]

**á-seón** *to strain. Add: pp.* -siwen, -seowen:—Âsîh healfne bollan, Lch. iii. 20, 8, 5.  Genim bollan fulne wînes, gemenge wið þ and âseóhhe, ii. 288, 5.  Âsîende *excolantes,* Mt. R. 23, 24.  Ealo ær þon hit âsiwen sié, Lch. ii. 124, 14.  Huniges âsiwenes, 184, 19.  Áseownes, 26, 11.  Áseowones, 200, 16.

**á-seonod** *deprived of sinews*:—Âsionod *enervata,* Wrt. Voc. ii. 143, 53.

**á-seóþan.** *Add:*—Áseóþan *decoqui,* Germ. 396, 196.    I. *to clear from impurity*:—Âsoden weax *obrisum metallum,* Wrt. Voc. ii. 65, 14.  Âsoden wîn *carenum,* An. Ox. 4, 5.    II. *to clear* impurity from something:—Leahtras âsêð âdl *uitia exquoquit languor,* Scint. 165, 6.  Þæt eall þ se ofen þære costunge of âsude (*excoqueret*), Bd. 4, 9; Sch. 393, 16.    III. *to try, examine*:—Âsude *examinasti, probasti,* Wrt. Voc. ii. 144, 57.  Tô áseódenne *expendere* (see á-seódan *above.  d* sometimes=ð *in this glossary*), Wrt. Voc. ii. 108, 2.  [*O. H. Ger.* ar-siudan *excoquere, examinare;* ar-sotan gold *obrizum.*]

**á-seówan,** -síwan, -seowian *to sew, stitch*:—Mið néthle âsiówid (-síuuid) *pictus acu,* Txts. 87, 1591.  v. un-áseowod.

**á-seðendlic.** v. un-áseðendlic.

**á-settan.** *Add:* I. *to set, put, move* an object to a place:—Ðû on âsets *conseres,* Kent. Gl. 948.  Heó hire fôt âsette, Gen. 8, 9.  Âsete on hâte sunnan, Lch. ii. 252, 9.  Âsette gé þone lîchoman tô þære byrgenne, Bl. H. 147, 31.    Ia. *intrans. To move one's self, transport one's self*:—Hý upp âsetton on ænne sîþ þ hý côman tô Æþelingadene, Chr. 1001; P. 132, 3.  Hié âsettan him (hî, *v. l.*) on ânne sîþ ofer mid horsum mid ealle, 893; P. 84, 3.  Matheum hé gedyde gangan tô þâm eástdæle mid his discipulum and âsetton on þâ dûne þér se apostol wæs, St. A. 14, 14.    II. *of building, to set, place, build*:—Âsette hé þær Godes ciricean oþþe mynster getimbrede, Bl. H. 221, 4.  Wæs seó burh mid þ hreóde âsett and geworht *oppidum ex his arundinibus erat edificatum,* Nar. 10, 14.  Ne ðâ get âsette wéron (-seted, *v. l.*) cyrce, Gr. D. 43, 29.  Ne ðâ get âsette wéron *necdum* (*montes*) *constiterant,* Kent. Gl. 266.    III. *to put in, out of an office, &c.*:—Þâm preóste þe hé of his circan âsette, Ll. Th. ii. 290, 13.  Hé âsette þâ mihtigan of heora setle, Bl. H. 159, 11.    IV. *to lay, impose* punishment, &c.:—Hé þ wîte and þ éce wræc âsette on þone aldor deófla, Bl. H. 83, 23.    V. *to set, propose* a riddle, &c.:—Þû âsettest rædels, Ap. Th. 4, 22.    VI. =on-settan *to oppress*:—Of þâm âsettum mannum (of þâm mannum þe hî geswencton, *v. l.*), Gr. D. 71, 7.  [*Goth.* us-satjan: *O. H. Ger.* ar-sezzen.]

**á-sican;** *p.* -sâc *To sigh*:—Âsîcð *suspirabit,* Scint. 223, 11.  Âsîhð *suspirat,* 28, 17: 158, 4.

**a-sícyd.** *l.* á-sícyd. **á-siftan.** *Add:*—Âsifte þurh sife, Lch. ii. 72, 28.

**á-sîgan.** *Add:*—Þone wâh þe ne âsîhð næfre, Hml. S. 36, 68.  On nôntîde âsîhð seó sunne, Hml. Th. ii. 76, 20.  Sunne âsâh, Lk. 4, 40.  Âsâh seó æfentîd, Gr. D. 83, 15.  Âsige *procumberet,* An. Ox. 1579.  Âsigen tô yfele, Bt. 24, 4; F. 84, 28.

**á-sincan** *to sink down*:—Bufon ðâm wætere ðér þæt îsen âsanc, Hml. Th. ii. 162, 13.  Tôbærst seó eorðe and þ templ âsanc, Hml. S. 4, 378.

**á-singan.** *Add:* I. *to recite* verse:—Hé þý betstan leóðe gegienged him âsong and âgeaf þæt him beboden wæs, Bd. 4, 24; Sch. 485, 22.  Ðâ se wîsdôm and seó gesceádwîsnes þis leóð þus âsungen hæfdon, Bt. 13; F. 36, 30 (and often).    II. *to compose* verse:—Wrât hé bôc and þâ meterfersum âsang and gelærede spræce gesette *scripsit liórum quem versibus exametris et prosa conposuit,* Bd. 5, 15; Sch. 651, 8.  [*Goth.* us-siggwan: *O. H. Ger.* ar-singan *recitare.*]

**á-sirwan** (?) *to delude*:—Âsered (*printed* afered) *delusus,* Wrt. Voc. ii. 71, 57: 26. 29.

**á-sittan.** *Add:* I. *to sit* up:—Hé âcwicode and semninga upp âsæt (*resedit*), Bd. 5, 12; S. 627, 14: 5, 19; S. 640, 27.  Hé næfre ne mihte of his reste ârîsan þ hé upp âsǽte, Gr. D. 281, 18.    II. *to remain sitting;* of a ship, *to be aground*:—Ðâra óþerra scipu âsǽton; þâ wurdon eác swîðe uneðelíce âseten, þreó âsǽton on ðâ healfe þæs deópes ðe ðâ Deniscan scipu âseten wǽron, and þâ óðru eall on óþre healfe, Chr. 897; P. 90, 20–91, 4.    III. *trans. with* ût, *to reduce by siege*:—Holofernus wolde hí ût âsittan and hé heora wæterscipe mid weardmannum besette, Hml. A. 107, 171.    IV. *to be apprehensive, afraid* (with gen. or clause):—Wé âsittað þ þâ bôceras áscunion þ wé þus rûmlíce sprecað, Angl. viii. 332, 34.  Wé ne þurfon þanon nênes hearmes ûs âsittan, Cht. E. 230, 10.  [*Goth.* us-sitan *to sit up.*]

**á-siwen.** v. á-seón *to strain.*

**á-slacian.** *Add:* I. *to slacken, become slack,* (1) physical:—Bið ðæs mannes wæstm gebîged, his swura âslacod, Hml. Th. i. 614, 13.  (2) figurative:—Âsleacað his tunge tô ðære godcundan bodunge, Hml. Th. ii. 442, 25.  Gif wé âsleacað fram gôdum weorcum, 98, 15.  Gif wé âslaciað þæs frîdes and þæs weddes þe wé seald habbað, Ll. Th. i. 238, 21.  Ðý lǽs se anwald âslacige (-slacie, *v. l.*) ðæs recendômes *ne solvantur jura regiminis,* Past. 118, 4.  Ðý lǽs hira lufu âslacige *ne eorum dilectio torpeat,* 143, 9.  Þæt hî ðurh orsorhnesse ne âsleacion, Hml. Th. i. 610, 16.  Hé hæfð tô gôdum weorce gewunad, and lǽt ðæt âslacian, Past. 65, 15.  Gewilnunga lǽtan âslacian, Hml. S. 33, 120.  Âslacad hand *manus remissa,* Kent. Gl. 318.  Âsclacad *dissoluta,* 696.  Âsclǽcadun *dimis(s)is,* Wrt. Voc. ii. 106, 52.  Âslæcadum, 25, 56.    II. *to make slack*:—Âslacudae, âsclacade *hebitavit,* Txts. 66, 491.  Âslacude, Wrt. Voc. ii. 43, 45.  Âslacige (*solet*) *enervare,* 96, 51.  Âsleacod *enervata,* 143, 53.  Âslacod *evacuatum,* 144, 52.  v. next word.

**á-slæccan.** *Add:*—Âslæcte *dissolverat,* Wrt. Voc. ii. 25, 58.  Âscaeltte, 106, 56.

**á-slæcian.** v. á-slacian.

**á-slæwan** *to make slow or dull*:—Âslæwe *obtundo,* An. Ox. 18 b, 65.

**á-slápan.** *Add:*—Lǽcedômas wiþ âslápenum (*paralysed*) lîce, Lch. ii. 12, 17.  þâ âslápenan sina, 282, 8.  [*O. Sax.* â-slâpan.]

**á-sláwian.** *Add:*—Âslâwie *obtorpeo,* An. Ox. 18 b, 64.    I. physical, *to become dull* of hearing:—Ðâ eáran âslâwiað þá þe ær wǽron swifte tô gehýrenne, Wlfst. 148, 1.    II. *of conduct, to become torpid, sluggish, inert*:—Swâ ðeáh hé âslâwað *quamvis torpescat,* Past. 282, 7.  Hé âslâwað *torporem patitur,* 287, 24.  Ðý lǽs hé óðre âwecce mid his wordum and himself âslâwige gôdra weorca *ne in semetipsis torpentes opere alios excitent voce,* Past. 461, 15.  Âslâwien *torpescant,* 415, 10.  Ðæt ðâ îdlan ne âslâwien *ut otiosis non fiat torpor,* 453, 24.

**á-sleán.** *Add:* I. *to strike off, remove by a stroke*:—Him mon âslôg þæt heáfod of, Ors. 6, 34; S. 290, 14.  Hé âslôh of (âslôg *amputavit,* Lind.) ânes þeówan eáre, Mt. 26, 51.  Hé þ heáfod of âslôh, Hml. A. 15, 357.  Hé hêt his heáfod of âsleán, Hml. S. 26, 162.    II. *to strike, make a mark* (*cut*) *by a stroke*:—Âsleah þrý scearpan on, Lch. ii. 104, 7.    III. *to strike with the hand*:—Âslôgon ł ðurscon *caedentes,* Mk. L. 22, 63.    IIIa. *to strike with* a hammer:—Gylden þel âslægen *bratea,* Wrt. Voc. ii. 12, 42.    IV. *of paralysis, to strike, paralyse*:—Lǽcedôm wiþ âslegenum lîce, Lch. ii. 12, 17: 126, 12, 14, 18.    V. *to strike* out a path, *make way*:—Se bryne ðe on ðæm innoðe bið ût âslihð tô ðære hýde, Past. 71, 6.  [*O. H. Ger.* ar-slahan.]

**á-slídan.** *Add:*—Âslâd and gefióll *labat,* Wrt. Voc. ii. 50, 62.    I. literal, *to slip, fall*:—Sceal ðæt heáfod gîman ðæt ðâ fét ne âslîden, Past. 133, 1.  Hé sceolde âslîdan on þâ eá, Gr. D. 319, 13.  His fôt weard âsliden, 320, 9: 81, 25.  Se cniht feóll of ðâm munte . . . hwær se lîchama þæs âslidenan cnihtes mihte beón funden, 212, 29.  Gástas hwîlum on heánnesse upp worpene, hwîlum eft âslidene on grund, Bd. 5, 12; S. 628, 25.    Ia. *to fall, be removed* to an unfavourable place:—Ne lǽt mé âslîdon on þâ firenfullan eardungstôwe, Angl. xii. 503, 5.    II. figurative, (1) *to fall* into sin, *lapse, relapse*:—Þæs mannes môd âslît tô ðære geðafunge, Hml. Th. i. 176, 2.  Wé âslîdað on ðǽm undeáwe, Past. 313, 17.  On lust âslâd *in luxum labescit,* An. Ox. 4651.  Mîn fôt âslâd, Hml. Th. ii. 392, 10.  Þæt ic ne âslîde, Ps. Th. 16, 5.  Gif se man æfter his fulluhte âslîde, Hml. Th. i. 292, 23.  Gif wé hwær âslîdon, 170, 18.  Þâ þe ǽne âslîdan, Hml. S. 31, 740.  Âslidenum *lapsis,* Hy. Srt. 7, 11: relapsis,* An. Ox. 4746: Hml. Th. i. 492, 11.  (2) *to fall, be hurt* or *destroyed*:—Fram deófium forbrôden hé âslât (cf. *occubuit,* Ald. 60, 26), Shrn. 56, 12.  Gif hit þ wære þ þin dohtor on ǽnig lâð âsliden wǽre, Hml. S. 3, 422.  Âsliden and gewǽht *elisa et labefacta,* An. Ox. 4789: Wrt. Voc. ii. 86, 44.  Ealle âslidene *omnes elisos,* Ps. L. 144, 14.

**á-slíding,** e; *f. Slipping*:—Of âslîdinge, Germ. 388, 62.

**á-smeágan.** *Add:* I. *to investigate,* (1) where the object is concrete:—Þâ hî hæfdon þâ burh ealle âsmeáde, Chr. 1011; P. 142, 2.

(2) object abstract :—Ásmeáð *requirit*, Scint. 42, 16. Ásmeáde *exquirit*, i. *investigat*, An. Ox. 2796. Ásmeágian *percunctari*, Angl. xiii. 366, 11. Sé bið on geþance wísast, sé ðe óðerne can raðost ásmeágean, Wlfst. 55, 22. Ásmeáde *exposita* .i. *tractata*, An. Ox. 174 : *trutinatas*, i. *pensatas*, 198. Þá ásmeádan *exquisita*, 324. II. *to find out by investigation, devise* :—Swá hwæt swá ðé is geðúht gyt máre on tintregum ásmeá, Hml. Th. i. 594, 12. Man ne mihte geþencan ne ásmeágan (-smǽgian, *v. l.*) hú man of earde hí gebringon sceolde, Chr. 1006 ; P. 137, 16 (v. p. 295). Ásmeáde *elucubratam*, An. Ox. 5101.

**á-smeágendlic**, Angl. viii. 310, 3. v. Lch. iii. 232, 23 *under* un-ásmeágendlic.

**á-smiþian**. *Add* :—Se fæder hét ásmiðigan of smætum golde hyre an-lýcnysse, Hml. S. 2, 113. Scrín of seolfre ásmiþod, 26, 173. Smicere geworhte, ásmiðode *fabrefactum*, Wrt. Voc. ii. 33, 68.

**á-smorian**. *Add* :—Ne mæg se man eþelíce eþian ac biþ ásmorod, Lch. ii. 46, 11. Mid ðære wilnunge ðisse worlde bið ásmorod (*suffocatum*) ðæt sǽd Godes worda, Past. 67, 22. Ðǽr hine ongeáton Adam and Eua þær hí ásmorede wǽron mid deópum ðeóstrum, Shrn. 68, 13.

**á-smorung**, e ; *f.* *Choking, suffocation* :—Wiþ ásmorunge, Lch. ii. 48, 12.

**á-smúgan** *to investigate* :—Hí synt tó ásmúganne mid scrútniendre scrútnunge, Angl. viii. 302, 35.

**á-snǽsan**. *Add* :—[Þene horn þet he asneseð mide alle þeo þet ha areacheð, A. R. 200.] v. snǽsan *in Dict.*

**á-sníþan**. *Add* : I. *to cut out, off* :—His téþ wǽron swá ásniden ísen *his teeth were as cut iron*, Nar. 43, 15. II. *to cut away, amputate* :—Scealt þú eal þ deáde of ásníþan oþ þ cwice líc, Lch. ii. 82, 27. Lim áceorfan oððe ásníðan of líchoman, 84, 22, 27. III. *to cut corn* :—þ ásnidene gerip, Gr. D. 290, 20. [O. H. Ger. ar-snídan *resecare, excidere*.]

**á-solcen**. *Add* :—Ásolcaen (-æn, -en) *iners*, Txts. 70, 531. Ásolcen *desidiosus*, Angl. xiii. 434, 982. Læt and ásolcen *tardus et tepidus*, 440, 1072. Ásolcen (*remissus*) on weorcum, Scint. 79, 5. Bróðor swá gýmeles and swá ásolcen (*desidiosus*) þæt hé nelle hálige béc smeágan, R. Ben. 75, 4. Ásolcennys déð þæt ðám men ne lyst nán ðing tó góde gedón, ac gǽð him ásolcen fram ǽlcere dugeðe, Hml. Th. ii. 220, 23. Se ásolcena ðeówa *the slothful servant*, 552, 29. For ðæs wintres cyle nolde se ásolcena (*piger*) erigan, Hml. A. 9, 229. Be ðám ásolcenum þe hwónlíce caraðymbe his sáwle ðearfe, Hml. Th. i. 340, 35. Ásolcene *desides*, Hy. Srt. 19, 3 : *desidiosi*, R. Ben. 133, 11. Synd wé swá ásolcene þ wé swincan nellað nán þincg, Hml. S. 28, 132.

**á-solcenlíce**. v. un-ásolcenlíce.

**á-solcennys**. *Add* :—*Accidia* is ásolcennyss oþþe slǽwð on Englisc, Hml. S. 16, 296. Hí ne wandiað tó licgenne on stuntnysse heora ásolcennysse, Hml. Th. ii. 554. 3. Þæt ðú mid þínre hýrsumnesse geswince tó Gode gecyrre þe þú ǽr fram buge mid ásolcennysse (*per desidiam*) ðínre unhýrsumnesse, R. Ben. 1, 5. Náht ásolcennyse (*ignavia*) fúllícor, Scint. 98, 1. Synna on ásolcennyssa, Angl. xi. 102, 83. Ásolcennesse *tepore*, xiii. 38, 319.

**á-spanan**. *Add* :—Be þám men þe wífman fram his hláforde áspaneð (*allicit*) for unrihtum hǽmede, Ll. Th. ii. 180, 24. Sicilie healfe áspónan (-speónnon, *v. l.*) Læcedemonie him on fultum, and healfe Athenienses *Catanenses ab Atheniensibus auxilia poposcunt, at Syracusani auxilium a Lacedaemoniis petunt*, Ors. 2, 7 ; S. 90, 7. Here þǽra wícinga þe hié him tó fultume áspanen hæfdon, Chr. 921 ; P. 102, 19. Wæs hé ásponen (-sponnen, -spannen, *v. ll.*) of Kent fram Willferðe *invitatus de Cantia a Wilfrido*, Bd. 4, 2 ; Sch. 346, 1. ¶ *without object* :—Hé út gewende and him þá tó áspeón þet hé heafde .xx. scipa, Chr. 1009 ; P. 138, 18.

**á-spannan** ; *p.* -speónn *To unbind, unclasp* :—Þá racenteáge þe se Drihtnes wer áspeón (*solverat*) of his fét, Gr. D. 214, 24.

**á-sparian** ; *p. ode* *To spare, keep* :—Se Godes wer nolde þ þǽr wǽre áht tó láfe in þám mynstre, þ ǽnig man cweþan mihte þ hit wǽre þurh unhýrsumnysse ásparod *ne in cella aliquid per inobedientiam remaneret*, Gr. D. 159, 24. [Cf. *Ger.* er-sparen.]

**á-spelian**. *Add* :—Gif hé wrítan ne cunne, bidde óþerne þæt hine áspelige *si non scit litteras, alter ab eo rogatus scribat*, R. Ben. 101, 5. Þ se mæssepreóst æt þám þingum þone bisceop áspelian móte *ut presbytero in illis rebus episcopi munere fungi liceret*, Ll. Th. ii. 176, 34. Sý se hordere áspeled (-ad, *v. l.*) æt þǽre þénunge *cellarius excusetur a coquina*, R. Ben. 59, 2.

**á-spendan**. *Add* : (1) *with a concrete object* :—Hé áspende (*dispersit*) his ðing, Hml. Th. i. 254, 21 : Bl. Gl. Man wíslíce his ǽhta áspende, Hml. S. 16, 327. Áspendre *erogatae* (*stipis*), An. Ox. 1841. (2) *with abstract object* (time, life, talents, &c.) :—Þá ðe mid gýmeleáste heora dagas áspendað, Hml. Th. ii. 78, 8. Hí ðá niht mid hálgum sprǽcum ðurhwacole áspendon, 184, 15. Hí þá andgitu getreówlíce áspendon, 556, 10. Hú þes freólsdæg beó áspend mid lofe, i. 436, 29. (3) *with the object of expenditure also given* :—þeáh ðe ic áspende míne ǽhta on ðearfena bigleofan, Hml. i. 54, 2. Hé þás fíf andgitu áspent on unnyt,

ii. 374, 2 : Hml. S. 12, 135. Hí on heora lustum heora líf áspendað, 17, 240. Áspende hé his feoh on ælmyssum, 14, 14. Hé on swilce weorc áspende his ðing, 31, 68. Þone ofereácan his ǽhta hé áspende on Godes þearfum, Hml. Th. ii. 118, 31. Miccle spéda on his lácum áspendan, 580, 17. Þone máran dǽl his lífes áspendan on his lustum, 574, 8. Áspendan úre spéda on þearfum, Hml. S. 3, 51. Eal ðeós niht sceal beón áspend on ðe mid pínungum, Hml. Th. i. 428, 29.

**á-speoftan** (-spoftan ?, -speáftan ?) ; *p.* -speaft *To spit out* :—Áspeaft (-speoft, R.) *expuit*, Jn. L. 9, 6.

**aspide**. *Add* :—Betwux dracum and aspidum, Hml. Th. i. 486, 35.

**á-spillan** ; *p. de* *To destroy* :—Áspildon *interficerent*, Jn. L. 12, 10.

**á-spinnan** *to spin* :—Áspunnen is *netum est*, Wrt. Voc. ii. 60, 15 : 83, 22.

**á-spíwan**. *Add* :—Ut áspáu *evomuit*, Wrt. Voc. ii. 32, 58. (1) literal :—Se seóca man áspíwð þone yfelan wǽtan onweg, Lch. ii. 60, 22. Se hund wile etan ðæt hé ǽr áspáw, Past. 419, 27 : Hml. Th. ii. 602, 26. Heó þ réðe áttor út áspáw, Hml. S. 2, 138. (1 a) used reflexively :—Hé sceal gán and hyne styrian ǽr ðám ðe hé hyne áspíwe, Lch. i. 316, 18. (2) figurative :—þ man áspíwe þ áttor (*sin*) út, Ll. Th. ii. 278, 22. Áspíwan synna þurh góde láre mid andetnesse, 280, 1 : Wlfst. 150, 4. Úre synna ús fram áspýwan, 103, 19.

**á-sprengan** ; *p. de* *To cause to spring away, send flying* :—Þá spearn hors tó and ásprencde hine ofer bord, Hml. S. 8, 213.

**á-spreótan**. *l.* á-sprútan : á-sprettan. v. á-spryttan : á-sprian, *Dele.*

**á-springan**. *Add* : I. *of motion*, (1) *of water* :—Seó eá up áspryngð néh þǽm clife, Ors. 1, 1 ; S. 12, 29. (2) *of a spark, to be emitted* :—þ ásprunge sùm spearca *forsitan scintilla dissiliit*, Bt. 35, 5 ; F. 164, 2. (3) *of the heavenly bodies, to arise* :—Hwǽr þæs mónan níwnys beó on Martio up ásprungen, Angl. viii. 310, 36 : 323, 6. Up ásprung[n]um *exorto*, An. Ox. 86. (4) *with idea of violence, to rush up, burst forth* :—Ásprang up tó þan swíðe sǽfióð swá nán man ne gemunet þ hit ǽfre ǽror dyde, Chr. 1099 ; P. 235, 5. Ðǽna up of heile geate ásprong *Aetna eruptionibus aestuabat*, Ors. 2, 6 ; S. 88, 31. Ásprong up Eþna fýr *Aetna ignes eructavit*, 5, 2 ; S. 220, 15. Ðǽre sǽ gemengednyssa ungewunelíce gyt ne ásprungan, Hml. Th. i. 602, 12. I a. figurative :—Godes word þe of Gode silfum ásprungon, Wlfst. 190, 14. II. *marking growth, descent, to spring*, (1) *of human beings* :—Án mǽgð ásprang of Seme, Wlfst. 12, 16. Dauid of ðám cynne ásprang, 13, 8. Of ǽðelum cynne heó wæs ásprungon, Chr. 1067 ; P. 202, 19. (2) *of plant-growth* :—Hit út áspringð on leáfum, Bt. 34, 10 ; F. 150, 4. Ǽlcne telgor ǽr þám þe hé upp ásprunge on eorðan (*antequam oriretur in terra*), Gen. 2, 5. (3) *of things, to spring up, come into existence* :—Hé gedyde þ leóht up ásprang, Hml. S. 30, 61. (3 a) *of abstract things* :—Of þissum syx tídum áspringð up bissextus, Angl. viii. 306, 4. Áspringað clǽne geþóhtas on móde, Hml. Th. i. 362, 17. Ásprang micel heófung and sárlic wóp on ðám háme, 434, 14. Seó dyrstignys ásprang, ii. 472, 24. Ásprang gehwǽr mycel gedwyld, Hml. S. 23, 353 : Ll. Th. ii. 372, 12. Mage of ðám þe ne mage nán unhlísa áspringan, 376, 24. Sceal áspringan sacu and clacu, Wlfst. 88, 9. Up ásprungenne *exortam* (*crudelitatem*), An. Ox. 3804. III. *to spread* (intrans.) *out* (of fame, report, &c.) :—Þá ásprang his word wíde geond land, Hml. S. 7, 388 : 10, 75 : 26, 239. Iudan ege ásprang wíde geond land, 25, 322. Of ðám deáde ásprang his nama geond ealne middangeard, Hml. Th. i. 226, 20. Ásprang hire hlísa ofer land and sǽ, Hml. S. 9, 1. His hlísa ásprang tó Syrian lande, 16, 137. IV. *to run out, cease, fail* :—Ne áspringeð him nán gód *non deficient omni bono*, Ps. Th. 33, 10. Eal tungla leóht áspringeþ, Bl. H. 91, 23. In him ásprang and áteorode (*deficeret*) his líchaman mægn, Gr. D. 227, 11. Is swá tó lǽtanne swá þ líflíce mægen ne áspringe, Lch. ii. 254, 13. Ðý lǽs wé áspringa *ne deficiamus*, Rtl. 18, 3. Áspringa *deficere*, 72, 20. Þá swétnesse þú him ne lǽtst nǽfre áspringan, Ps. Th. 30, 21. Mótan ealle weóda wyrtum áspringan *may there be no weeds for the plants*, Lch. iii. 36, 27. Áspringendi *defectura*, Wrt. Voc. ii. 106, 10. Ásprungen *defectus*, 138, 19. Háligdóm is full neáh ásprungen *defecit sanctus*, Ps. Th. 11, 1. [O. H. Ger. ar-springan *oriri, expergiscere, perfluere*.] v. un-áspringende : á-sprungen.

**á-springnes**. v. up-áspringnes.

**á-springung**, e ; *f.* *Failing, defection* :—In áspringunge *in deficiendo*, Ps. Srt. 141, 4.

**á-sprungen** ; *adj.* (*ptcpl.*) *Defunct* :—Is þeáw þ ásprungenra manna líc and ǽwfæstra manna man byreð on ciricean *consuetudo est monachorum et hominum religiosorum cadavera* (cf. monachos vel homines religiosos *defunctos*, 53, 9) *in ecclesiam portare*, Ll. Th. ii. 160, 24. v. á-springan, IV ; á-sprungennes, I.

**á-sprungennes**. *Add:* -sprungnes. I. *failure, decease* :—Seó sáwel þrowað deáð bútan deaþe and ásprungennesse *anima mortem sine morte, defectum sine defectu patitur*, Gr. D. 337, 9. II. *eclipse* :—*Exlypsis*, þ is ðæs sunnan ásprungnis oðþe þǽre mónan, Nar. 28, 10. Ðý geáre ðǽre foresprecenan sunnan ásprungennysse, Bd. 4, 1 ; S. 563, 10. Be þǽre ásprungnisse sunnan and mónan, Nar. 3, 13. v. up-ásprungennes.

ā-sprýtan. *l.* ā-spryttan, *and add:* I. of a plant, *to sprout out, spring up:*—Eall gærs and wyrta ǽr þan þe hig upp āspritton *omnem herbam prius quam germinaret,* Gen. 2, 5. Ðeáh hié up āspryttæn, Past. 67, 23. Þonne beóð up āsprytte synfulle swā swā gærs *cum exorti fuerint peccatores sicut foenum,* Ps. L. 91, 8. II. of a root, seed, *to put forth sprouts, sprout out:*—For ðām þā wyrttruman magon eft ðanon āsprettan (*printed* -spretgan) ne talige ic þē þeáh þ tō nānre scylde, Shrn. 184, 21.

ā-spýlian. *l.* -spylian (*but* -swylian? v. swilian *in Dict.*), *and dele the cognates.*

ā-spyrgeng. *Add:*—Āspyrgengum *adinventionibus,* Wrt. Voc. ii. 87, 34.

ā-spyrian. *Add:* I. *to track, reach by following the track:*—Hwā āspyreð ðæt deófol of geofones holte and hine gebringeð on Crīstes cempena fæðmum, Sal. K. 146, 27. II. *to investigate, examine so as to get knowledge of a subject:*—Se sceáwre þe þis gewrit āspyrað, Angl. viii. 331, 1. Swýðe nearwelīce hē hit lētt ūt āspyrian (of the compilation of Doomsday Book), Chr. 1085; P. 216, 26. Ne magon ðǽre turgan mægnes swiðmódnisse āspyrian, Sal. K. 150, 4. Ðæt nǽre nǽnig manna ðæt mihte ðǽra twēgra tweón āspyrian *that there was no man could settle by his investigations the doubt about the two* (subst. this for trans. in Dict.), Sal. 434. Tō āspyrienne *ob indaganda,* Wrt. Voc. ii. 77, 64. Fore tō āspyrianne, 62, 55. Hyt ys tō āspyrianne hwæt hyt getācnað, Angl. viii. 336, 46: 333, 8. Āspyrigende *indagantes,* Wrt. Voc. ii. 44, 10. III. *to find out:*—Iulius se cāsere þisne bissextum gemētte oððe āspirode, Angl. viii. 306, 40. [*O. H. Ger.* ar-spurien *peragrare.*]

ā-spyr(i)gend, es; m. *An investigator:*—Ūra breósta āspyrgend (*investigator*), Ps. Srt. ii. p. 204, 1.

ā-spyrigendlic. v. un-āspyrigendlic.

ᴀssa. *Dele :* asse, es; *m., and add:*—Assa *asinus vel asina,* Wrt. Voc. i. 78, 7. Healf mann and healf assa *onocentaurus,* 17, 40. On sumon lande assan (eoselas, *v. l.: onagri*) býð ākende, þā habbað swā micle hornas swā oxan, Nar. 34, 15. [Cf. *O. Irish* assan.]

ᴀssen. *Add:*—Hors of stēdan and of assenne *burdo,* Wrt. Voc. i. 17, 24.

Assyrias. *Add:*—Fram Assyria cynge, Ps. Th. 45, arg. Ālýsed æt Assirium, 29, arg. Asirium, 28, arg.

Assyrisc; *adj. Assyrian:*—Assirisce seres, i. *orientalis,* An. Ox. 26, 20.

ast. *l.* āst, e; *f., and add:*—On odene cylne macian ōn and āste and fela ðinga sceal tō tūne, Angl. ix. 262, 3. See *oast* in D. D.

ā-stǽgan; *p. de To ascend, mount up:*—Āstǽgdun on scip *ascendentes in naui,* Mk. R. 6, 32.

a-stǽlan. *l.* ā-stǽlan, *and subst. : To charge, impute:*—þ mē nǽfre deófol on āstǽlan ne mæge þ ic būton andetnese beó mīnra synna *that the devil may never be able to lay to my charge that I am without confession of my sins,* Ll. Th. ii. 264, 15. v. stǽlan.

ā-stǽnan. *Add:*—Āstaenid *stellatus,* Wrt. Voc. ii. 121, 37. Gyrdel āstǽned (*printed* æ-) *baltheus bullifer,* 75, 82. Mid compgimmum āstǽned, Sal. K. 150, 10: Wlfst. 263, 4.

ā-standan. *Add:* I. of position, *to stand:*—Ðe aldormon ðe fore ongaegn āstōd *centurio qui ex adverso stabat,* Mk. L. 15, 39. Arās āstōd *surgens stetit,* Lk. L. 6, 8, 17: 24, 36. Ān āstōd *unus adsistens,* Jn. L. R. 18, 22. II. of motion, *to stand up, arise,* (1) denoting simply change of position :—Se cyning gebīgedum cneówum gebæd . . . Hē āstōd ðā, Hml. Th. ii. 578, 23. Hē bæd ðā weras þæt hī āstōdon and heora sealmas sungon, 96, 35. Hī ealle āstōdon þe ǽr lāgon, Hml. S. 10, 21. Uton āstandan *exsurgamus,* R. Ben. 2, 4. Up āstandan *emersisse,* An. Ox. 4784. (2) implying intention to act :—Ðā āstōdon sume and woldon his lāre oferswīðan, Hml. Th. i. 44, 24. III. *to stand, continue,* (1) *not to be overturned, destroyed :*—Eall þāra āstynt þe on ðē gewunat, Shrn. 166, 25. Seó studu gesund āstōd and āwunode *posta tuta remansit,* Bd. 3, 10; Sch. 234, 16. Ðǽre āstandendan þrynesse, Angl. xi. 97, 8. (2) *to persist, continue to act:*—þ hē on gebedum āstōde and āwunode *quia in orationibus persteterit,* Bd. 3, 12 ; Sch. 245, 4. IV. *to stand, support, endure :*—Swā liðne lǣcedōm swā se týdra līchoma mǣge āstandan, Past. 455, 31. V. *to stand, stop* (intrans.) :—Āstōd ðiú blōdes blōdes *stetit fluxus sanguinis,* Lk. R. L. 8, 44. [Þisne lǣcecræft mann sceal dōn manne þ swýþe spīwaþ gif wullaþ þat hit āstonden, Lch. iii. 132, 16.] [*Goth.* us-standan *to stand up: O. Sax.* ā-standan: *O. H. Ger.* ar-standan *surgere, exsurgere.*]

ā-standendness, e; *f. Continuance, persistence, perseverance:*—On þǽre gebedes āstandendnysse, Hml. S. 23 b, 272.

ā-stellan. *Add: To set up,* (1) *to set* an example:—Æfter þǽre bysne þe God on Adame āstealde, Wlfst. 154, 15. Mid his eádmódnysse āstellan ðā bysne, Hml. Th. ii. 40, 23. (2) of initial action, (a) *to do something first:*—Stephanus ðone martyrdōm æfter Gode āstealde *Stephen was the first to suffer martyrdom after Christ,* Hml. Th. i. 50, 2. Sē þe gōd beginnan þence, hē þæt angin on him sylfum āstelle *let him make a beginning with himself,* Lch. iii. 438, 32. (b) *to found* a place, *institute* an office:—Heó hæfde āsteald mynster, Hml. S. 2, 310. Hū bisceophādas

wurdan ǽrest āstealde, Wlfst. 176, 6. (c) *to establish* a practice, doctrine, &c. :—Hē āstealde ealle gifa and ealle sōðfæstnyssa, Hml. Th. i. 198, 2. Ðā lāre þe hē āstealde, ii. 586, 3 : Hml. S. 25, 704. þæt him beón heora ǽhta eallum gemǽne, swā ðā apostoli hit āstealdon, Hml. Th. i. 318, 10. þis fæsten wæs āsteald, ii. 100, 1. Cumlīðnys wæs āsteald ðurh hālgum heáhfæderum, 386, 16. (3) *to establish, confirm:*—Hē ā his bodunga mid gebysnungum āstealde and eác mid wundrum geglengde, Hml. Th. ii. 148, 27.

ā-stellan (i, y); *p. de To leap, rush, fly off:*—Se þorn, efne swā swā strǣl of bogan āstelleþ, swā hē of þām man āfieáh, Guth. 68, 22. Hē hraþe āstylde (forð ārǣsde, *v. l.*) of his rǣste *ex lecto prosiliit,* Gr. D. 21, 28.

ā-stempan; *p.* ed *To stamp, emboss:*—Āgrafen, āstemped *celatum,* i. *pictum,* Wrt. Voc. ii. 130, 57.

ā-sten. v. stinan (*l.* stenan) *in Dict.*

ā-stencan; *p.* te *To scatter :*—Tō þām þ hī hī mid tintregum āstencton (tōdrifon, *v. l.*) *ut eos per tormenta discuterent,* Gr. D. 42, 33.

ā-steópness. v. ā-stípness.

ā-steóran, -stýran; *p. de To steer, guide, govern:*—Þū āstýrst and wildest æallum þis middangearde, Shrn. 168, 9.

ā-steorfan. *Add:*—Āstorfene *obeuntem,* i. *morientem,* An. Ox. 3661. Swā unclǣne men þ hī āstorfen ǽton, Shrn. 74, 26. [*O. H. Ger.* ar-sterban *mori.*]

ā-stēpan, -stēpness, -stēpedness. v. ā-stípan, -stípness.

ā-stífian. *Add:*—Āstífode *obrigesceret,* āstífedan *obriguerunt,* Wrt. Voc. ii. 63, 62, 65. (1) lit. *to become incapable of motion :*—Hē āstífode and se earm stōd ungebīgendlic, Gr. D. 254, 36. Heora handa āstífedon, Hml. Th. i. 598, 11. þā mūlas āstífodon, Hml. S. 31, 985. Hē āstífod lǣge, Bl. H. 193, 8. Hī stōdon swilce hī āstífode wǽron, Hml. S. 31, 375. Āstífode on stāna gelīcnysse, 1001. (2) fig. *to become incapable of action* from fear, wonder :—Āstífedon (*obriguerunt*) ealle þā búendan, Ps. L. fol. 187 b, 12 (= Ex. 15, 15). þǽr stǽnt āstífad stāne gelīcast eal ārleás heáp *stupet attonito impia turba timore,* Dōm. L. 173.

ā-stígan. *Add:* A. *intrans.* I. *without adv. or prep. that marks upward or downward,* (1) of motion lit. or fig. (a) downward :—Heó stīhð oð þæs heófenes heánesse, and þanon āstīhð, Ps. Th. 18, 6. Crīst on þīnne innoþ āstīgeþ, Bl. H. 5, 14. þā þe on eorðan āstīgað *qui descendunt in terram,* Ps. Th. 21, 27. Tō ðām munte Synay āstāh se Scyppend, Hml. Th. ii. 196, 22. Of heofenum āstāh (*descendit*) mannes Bearn, 386, 2 : Ps. Spl. 7, 17. Þū āstige on helle grund, Bl. H. 87, 14. Of heofenum oþ eorþan āstīgan, Bd. 4, 3; S. 567, 40 : 570, 1. Tō eorþan āstīgan *to land,* Bl. H. 233, 27. Āstīgendum in seáð *descendentibus in lacum,* Ps. Srt. 27, 1. (b) upward :—Nān mann ne āstīhð (*ascendit*) tō heofenum, Hml. Th. ii. 386, 1. Hē āstāh (-stāhg, R.) on þone munt *ascendit in montem,* Mt. 5, 1. 'Āstīgað on mīn scip.' Hē þā āstāg on þ scip mid his discipulum, Bl. H. 233, 23. (c) direction not strongly marked :—Þonne āstīgeþ wolcen from norþdǽle, Bl. H. 91, 32. Storm of ðǽm munte āstāg, 203, 8. Seóð þā bān āne beón lǣfed, āstīge þǽrin gelōmlīce, Lch. i. 340, 26. (2) metaphorical :—Ic lǣrde wlance men þ hié ne āstīgan on ofermēdu, Bl. H. 185, 14. Hē wæs on swā micle ofermētto āstīgen *efferatus superbia,* Ors. 6, 9 ; S. 264, 8. II. *with adv. or prep.* (1) of motion, lit. or fig. (a) downward :—Se Hālga Gāst ofer hié āstāg, Bl. H. 13,328. Āstīh ādūne, Hml. Th. ii. 196, 27. Wē leornedon þ se Drihtnes Gāst ofer hiene āstige on culfran onlīcnesse, Bl. H. 135, 1. þām brōþrum wæs uneáðe niþer tō āstīgenne tō þām wæterseáðe, Gr. D. 112, 17. Of dūne āstīgende (-stīgende, *v. l.*) *condescendendo,* Past. 101, 14. (b) upward :—Āstīh up tō mē, Hml. Th. ii. 196, 29. Āstīg up, Bl. H. 87, 22. þæt hié up āstīgen *emersisse,* Wrt. Voc. ii. 31, 35. (2) of direction :—Se munt āstīhð up ðreó mīla on heánnysse, Hml. Th. ii. 164, 14. Se stīpel sceolde āstīgan upp tō heofenum, Ælfc. T. Grn. 4, 9. (3) of excess :—Ne āstīhð nān getel ofer þæt, Hml. Th. i. 188, 35. B. *trans.* (1) *to descend, go down into :*—þā ðe āstīgað on scipum *qui descendunt mare in navibus,* Ps. Spl. 106, 23. Staþu āstīgan, Lch. iii. 210, 16. (2) *to ascend, mount :*—Ic āstīge mīn scyp *ego ascendo navem,* Coll. M. 26, 31. Wē gelýfað þæt of mancynne swā micel getel āstīge þæt uplice rīce, Hml. Th. i. 344, 13. Āstīgan þæt heofenlice rīce, ii. 82, 9. Scyp āstīgan, Lch. iii. 184, 13. [*Goth.* us-steigan: *O. H. Ger.* ar-stīgan *ascendere.*]

ā-stigenness (-stīgness?). v. up-āstigenness.

ā-stigian; *p.* ode *To ascend, mount,* (1) *intrans. :*—Astigedon in scip *ascendentes in navi,* Mk. L. 6, 32. (2) *trans. :*—Ic āstigie mīn scyp *ascendo navem,* Coll. M. 23, 9.

ā-stihting, e; *f. Instigation:*—Of āstīhtinge *instinctu,* i. *doctrina,* An. Ox. 2707. [So also Hpt. Gl. 469, 65. Napier (v. note) takes the word as an error for *ātihtinge,* but cf. :—Paulus for his līchaman stihtunga (*de carnis suae stimulo*) bæd, Gr. D. 166, 25.]

ā-stingan; *p.* -stang, *pl.* -stungon. I. *to thrust out:*—Heó his swýþran ēge ūt āstang, Nar. 44, 14. Rōmāne his eágan āstungon, Chr. 797; P. 56, 11. II. *to stab :*—Hē hine sylfne mid his swurd of

ástang *he stabbed himself to death with his sword*, Nor. 48, 24. [*Goth.* us-stiggan.]

á-stípan; *p.* te; *pp.* -stíped, -stípt *To bereave* (with gen.) :—Se earma man ástýped (-stǽped, *v. l.*) and bereáfod his suna *miser orbatus*, Gr. D. 75, 27. Se ástýpta (-stēpta, *v. l.*) ceorl *orbatus rusticus*, 165, 19. þām ástýptan (-stēptan, *v. l.*) wífe, 18, 15. Þ ástēpede wíf, 14. Wē wæron ástýpede (-stýpte, *v. l.*) þæs heofenlican ríces, Wlfst. 252, 11. Ástýpte, Bl. H. 107, 4.

á-stípedness, e; *f. Bereavement:*—Hē wæs byrnende for þām heáfe þǽre ásteópnesse (-stēpednesse, *v. l.*) *orbitatis luctu aestuans*, Gr. D. 165, 12.

á-stípness, e; *f. Bereavement:*—Ástēpnessum *orbitationibus* (Aldhelm's Latin is: orbitatis quaestibus), Wrt. Voc. ii. 86, 61. v. preceding word.

á-stirred; *adj. Starred, starry:*—Geseón heofen ástyrredne (*stellatum*), Scint. 180, 3.

á-stíðian. *Add: to become strong, grow up* (cf. ge-stíþian) :— Þ swá wæs oð Eádgár ástíðude *usque ad tempora Eadgari regis*, Cht. Th. 203, 20. v. un-ástíðod.

á-streccan. *Add:* I. *to stretch out, hold out:*—Hí ástræhton heora swuran tō slæge, Hml. S. 28, 71. Leóht ofer þ geteld ástreht stód up tō heofonum (*columna lucis ad caelum usque porrecta*, Bd. 3, 11), Hml. S. 26, 183. Ástrehtne hneccan *erectam cervicem*, Scint. 83, 18. I a. *of time, to extend:*—Seó fífte yld stód ástreht oð þæt Críst sylf com, Ælfc. T. Grn. 8, 31 : 19. 41. II. *to prostrate*, (1) *of a person's posture, lit. or fig.:*—Hē hine ástreahte ofer leomu þæs deádan mannes, Bl. H. 217, 27. Hē hine on gebed ástreahte, 219, 17. Hié sculon licgean ástreahte *debent jacere substrati*, Past. 109, 23. (2) *to lay low:*—Críst oferswíðde hine and ástrehte, Hml. Th. i. 176, 29. Hē ástrehte middangeardes wuldor, 578, 33. Ǽr ðan þe se fǽrlica slege ūs ástrecce, ii. 124, 21.

á-stregdan. *Add: also pp.* -strogden:—Stregd (ástregd, *v. l.*) þis gehálgode wæter ofer þæs mannes líchaman, Gr. D. 82, 17. Ástregde (-strēde, *v. l.*) man þone wǽtan mid háligwætere *liquor aspergatur aqua benedicta*, Ll. Th. ii. 214, 29. Ástrogden *asparsus*, Rtl. 118, 5 : 119, 11 : 122, 22.

á-stregdness ((?), -strogd- (?)), e; *f. sprinkling:*—Ðerh ástr(e)gdnise (v. Skeat's collation) *per assparsionem*, Rtl. 117, 10. v. stregdness, strogdness.

á-strengð. *Add:* , -strenged :—Ástrenged *ductili, i. levi, fusili*, Wrt. Voc. ii. 142, 11. [Cf. astrengdet *productiles malleo*, Grff. vi. 757.]

á-strowennes *glosses* proceritas :—Ástrowenesse *proceritatis, longitudine* (cf. An. Ox. 1558, where Napier reads *ástrofenesse*), Hpt. Gl. 443, 12.

á-stundian. *Substitute: To take upon one's self:*—Eal hē mōt ástundian swá hwæt swá fram his gingrum forgýmeleásod bið *ad ipsum respicit quicquid a discipulis delinquitur*, R. Ben. 61, 7. Būton gē hí ámeldian, gē sceolon heora wíte ástundian, Hml. S. 23, 299.

á-stýfecigan. *Add:*—Hí sint tō manienne ðonne hí lícettað ðæt hí willen ástýfecean ðæt yfel on him selfum, ðæt hí hit ðonne ne dyrren sǽwan on óðrum monnum *admonendi sunt, ut si eradicare mala dissimulant saltem seminare pertimescant*, Past. 427, 18. Hwæðer þín ealde gýtsung eallunga of ðínum mōde ástýfcod wēre, Shrn. 184, 3.

á-styltan. *Add:*—Ástylton *stupebant*, Lk. L. R. 2, 47. Ástyltdon, 4, 32.

á-styntan. I. *to blunt, dull:*—Hí angyt ástyntað *sensum obtundunt*, Scint. 56, 13. Mōd byð ástynt *mens retunditur*, 152, 11. Ástyntid *hebitatus*, Wrt. Voc. ii. 110, 27. Ástynt, 42, 64. II. *to check, stop:*—Ic ástynte *confuto*, Hpt. Gl. 455, 31. Lārcówas [hē] ástynte *magistros confutat, i. vincit*, An. Ox. 2102. þæt hē ástente *elideret, i. offenderet*, Hpt. Gl. 471, 32. Ástyntende arewan *retundens catapultas*, An. Ox. 4235. Cf. æt-styntan.

á-stýran. v. á-stéoran.

á-styrian. *Add:* A. *trans.* I. *to move* a thing from its place :— Hē ástirode his geteld *movens tabernaculum suum*, Gen. 13, 18. Hē ástyrede his fyrdwíc forð tō Jordanen, Jos. 3, 1. Fram ástere *remove*, Kent. Gl. 78. Ne bið ástered *non commovebitur*, 340. Fram ðē ástyred, Hml. S. 15, 72. I a. *to cause a living creature to move itself:*—Ic mē of þǽre stōwe ástyrede, Hml. S. 236, 457. Hí of ðām stedum þá hors ástyrian ne mihton, Gr. D. 15, 6. I b. *with the idea of guidance:*—þū ealle ðā unstillan gesceafta tō þínum willan ástyrast *das cuncta moveri*, Bt. 33, 4 ; F. 128, 9. II. *to stir up,* (1) *to cause motion in* something :—Syle drincan, sōna hyt þone innoð ástyreþ, Lch. i. 226, 17. Ðeós wyrt þone migþan ástyreþ, 278, 8. (2) *to cause emotion in a person :*— þonne þæt mōd se wind strongra geswinca ástyrað, Bt. 12 ; F. 36, 19. Mid wistlunga mon mæg hund ástyrigean *sibilus catulos instigat*, Past. 173, 22. Heródes wearð micclum ástyred, Hml. Th. i. 78, 9. Wæs þis land swíðe ástirad, Chr. 1007 ; P. 222, 27. Wearð se cásere for þǽre wōgunge ástyrod, Hml. S. 7, 301. Wearð þ folc ástyrod on swiðlicum hreáme *they cried out excitedly*, 31, 281. Ástirod ongen eów *adversum vos concitatus*, Deut. 9, 19 : Chr. 1052 ; P. 180, 9. Se cyng wearð wið

hine ástyrod, 1095 ; P. 230, 23. Hē wearð swá swíðe ástirod (*commota fuerunt viscera ejus*), þæt him feóllon teáras, Gen. 43, 30. Wæs hire heorte ástired, Hml. S. 30, 339. Ásterede *concitati*, Kent. Gl. 1013. (3) *to: cause strife, passion*, &c. :—Ne ástyrað þǽra rihtwísra gesihð him nænne ōgan, Hml. Th. i. 334, 8. Hē sace ne ástyrede, 320, 15. Se deófol ástyrode þá ehtnysse, Hml. S. 16, 198. Ðī læs seó bóc ǽðryt þurh hire micelnysse ástyrige, Hml. Th. ii. 520, 5. Wearð ástyred mycel ehtnys, Hml. S. 11, 5. Ástyrod, Ll. Th. ii. 342, 19. B. *intrans. To stir, move one's self:*—Hū se deáda stán oððe þ dumbe treów mæge gehelpan, þonne hí sylfe ne ástyriað of ðǽre stōwe nǽfre, Hml. S. 17, 135. v. un-ástyrod.

á-styrigend, es; *m. One stirring up;* ventilator, Germ. 393, 78.

á-styrigendlic. v. un-ástyrigendlic.

á-styrung, e; *f.* I. *a stirring, removal.* v. á-styrian, I:—Hē ne sealde tō ástyrunge (*commotionem*) míne fēt, Ps. L. 65, 9. II. *stirring up.* v. á-styrian, II. (1):—Wið þæs innoðes ástyrunge, Lch. i. 254, 8 : 272, 17. Wiþ migþan ástyringe, 58, 5, 10.

á-súgan. *Add:*—Ic hēt hié gebindan ðæt hié on niht wǽron from þæm wyrmum ásogone *ut nocte a serpentibus consumerentur*, Nor. 16, 26.

á-sundrian. *Add:*—Þte ne sié ásundrad fultumum *ut non destituatur auxiliis*, Rtl. 8, 11.

á-sundrodlic. v. un-ásundrodlic.

á-súrian. *Add:*—Ásúrige *acescatur*, Wrt. Voc. ii. 97, 27 : 5, 74. Gif men sié maga ásúrod, Lch. ii. 356, 11.

á-swǽman. *Substitute; p.* de. I. *to be grieved, confounded:*—Ic ne áswǽme *non erubescam*, Ps. L. 24, 20. Ic áswǽmde *tabescebam*; I was grieved (A. V.), 118, 158 : 138, 21. Ic ne sý áswǽmed *non erubescam*, 24, 2. Sē þe sceal áswǽman (*or under* II ?) sárigferð, wát his sincgiefan beheldne, Gū. 1326. II. *to wander away* (cf. *Icel.* sveima *to wander about*):—Ðā earman synfullan sceolon sáre áswǽman fram asnýne úres Drihtnes and fram wlite and fram wuldre heofena ríces, Wlfst. 185, 8. v. swǽman *in Dict.*, á-swámian.

á-swǽtan; *p.* te *To break out into a sweat:*—On ðǽm miclan wintres cele þonne hē ymb þæt spræc ðonne áswǽtte hē eall, Shrn. 51, 34.

a-swáp. v. swǽpa *in Dict.*: á-swarcan, -swarcian. *l.* á-swárcan, -swárcian.

á-swárcnian *to be grieved, confounded:*—Ic áswárcnode *tabescebam*, Ps. L. 138, 21.

á-swárnian. *Add:*—Áswárnian hí *erubescant*, Ps. L. 6, 11.

á-swaþian; *p.* ode *To follow out a track, investigate:*—Áswaþode *investigatam*, An. Ox. 5, 11.

á-sweartian. *Add:*—Se mōna mid ealle ásweartað, Lch. iii. 240, 24. Ásweartode seó heofen, 278, 3. Seó sunne ásweartade, Shrn. 67, 17. Ðá læg se king and ásweartode eall mid þǽre sage, Cht. Th. 339, 38. *Fuscatus, i. denigratus, obnubilatus* ásweartad, forsworcen, forþrysmed, Wrt. Voc. ii. 152, 7. Bē ásweartedum líce . . . weorþeð hwílum líc ásweartod, Lch. ii. 82, 1–3.

á-swefecian. *Substitute: To extirpate:*—Ásuefecad *extirpatus*, Wrt. Voc. ii. 77, 32. Áswefecad, 31, 5. Cf. á-stýfecian.

á-swēgan; *p.* de *To resound:*—On áswēgde *intonuit*, Ps. L. 28, 3.

á-swellan. *Add:* þ-sweoll *To swell up:*—Ðonne ásuilt ðæt lim, Past. 73, 10. Þá þe áþindað and áswellað þurh þá wilnunge þæs ídlan gylpes, Gr. D. 40, 4. His andwlita ásweoll, 20, 32. Seó hýd ásweoll, 157, 8. Ásweoll him se líchama, Guth. 68, 8. Ásuollen, ássuollan *tuber, tumor*, Txts. 103, 2071. Gif sié þá ceácan áswollen, Lch. ii. 46, 21 : 48, 27. Bē áswollenre lifre . . . Gif se geswollena mon swá áswollen gebít, 200, 18–23. [O. H. Ger. ar-swellan *intumescere*.]

á-sweltan. *Add:*—Ásualt *diem obiit*, Wrt. Voc. ii. 106, 34. Ásuealt, 25, 48. Hér Heródes áswalt, Chr. 46 ; P. 6, 20. Ásuelte *ocumbat*, Wrt. Voc. ii. 64, 66 : *moriatur*, Jn. R. 11, 50. Ásuelte *expiravit*, Mk. L. 15, 37. Ic wæs áswolten and mín gewit forleás *velut emoriens sensum perdidi*, Bd. 5, 6 ; Sch. 577, 7. Man earmlíce deáþe áswolten, Bl. H. 219, 11.

á-swencan; *p.* te *To afflict, vex, trouble:*—Hē míne arfenuman nǽfre ne áswence, C. D. iv. 107, 18. Ásuoenctes folces *afflicti populi*, Rtl. 42, 31. Uē biðon ásuoencde *affligimur*, 7, 1. Asuoencte, 43, 27. Ðæm ásuoenctum *afflictis*, 9.

á-swengan. *Add:*—Fram áswengde *excussit*, Wrt. Voc. ii. 146, 17. Ðá stánas wǽron áswengde on ðára onsýn þe þǽr onsǽton, Shrn. 81, 3.

á-sweorfan. *The citation may be found also Germ.* 391, 41.

á-sweotole, *Dele:* a-swícian. *l.* á-swician, *and add* v. ge-áswician ; ǽ-swician.

á-swicung *scandal, offence:*—Áswicunga *scandalorum*, R. Ben. I. 44, 10. v. á-swicung.

á-swifan. *Add:*—Ásuáb *exorbitans*, Wrt. Voc. ii. 107, 74. Áswífende *exorbitans*, 83, 7 : 86, 10.

á-swindan. *Add:*—Mōd áswint *mens torpet*, Hy. Srt. 23, 27. Þū gedést þæt hē áswint on his mōde *tabescere fecisti animam ejus*, Ps. Th. 38, 12. Hraðe se líchama áswint, gif him bið oftogen his bigleofa, Hml. Th. i. 266, 3. Áswindeð se níðfulla tō náhtlicum ðingum, Hex. 46, 27. Hý áswindaþ *contabescunt*, Wrt. Voc. ii. 134, 72. Ásuand *hebesceret*,

110, 28. Áswond *enervat*, 107, 23 : *tabuisset*, 122, 3. Áswand *distabuit*, 141, 28 : *enervat*, i. *marcescet*, 143, 50 : *fatescit*, 147, 25. For ðínum feóndum ic áswand on mínum móde (*tabescebam*), Past. 353, 6. Ásundun, *distabuerunt*, Wrt. Voc. ii. 106, 44. Áswundon, 25, 52. Áswindende *torpentem*, i. *languentem*, An. Ox. 597. Áswunden *reses*, 45, 2. Áfúlat and ásuunden *tabida et putrefacta*, Txts. 104, 1044. Hé bið áswunden oninnan him selfum *intus tabescit*, Past. 235, 20. Áswunden *elumbem*, i. *enervem*, Wrt. Voc. ii. 143, 15 : *enervus*, i. *sine virtute*, *emortuus*, 51. þá áswundenan *enervata*, 29, 8. [O. H. Ger. ar-swindan *evanescere*, *tabescere*.]

á-swingan *to scourge* :—Uê sê ásungeno *flagellamur*, Rtl. 42, 11.

á-sworettan. *Add* :—Ic ásworette *suspiro*, Gr. D. 5, 25. Seó ásworeteð (-etteð, *v. l.*), 245, 22. Ásworette *suspiravit*, 16.

a-swunan, *Dele* : á-swundenlíce. v. un-áswundenlíce : á-swýðerian, *Dele*.

á-synderlic ; *adj. Remote* :—On ásynderlicum hulce *in remoto tugurio*, An. Ox. 2514.

á-syndran (-ian). *Add* : I. *to separate* objects already connected, (1) where there is intermixture :—þ melo ðurhcrýpþ ælc þyrel and þá siofoþa weorþaþ ásyndred, Bt. 34, 11 ; F. 152, 3. (2) where there is association, juxtaposition :—þá þe þæs wyrðe beóð hé ásyndreð (*segregat*) of cyriclican gemánan, Ll. Th. ii. 178, 34. Ásyndrað, 266, 7. Ásendraþ *separet* (*te a me*), An. Ox. 3407. þú ásyndrodest þinne críst *distulisti christum tuum*, Ps. L. 88, 39. Ðonne hí hæfdon þá eá oferfaren, þonne ásyndrede hine æghwilc feor fram óþrum, Hml. S. 23 b, 134. Se suiðra bôgh sceolde beón ásyndred from ðæm óðrum flæsce, Past. 81, 20. Hiera weorc ne wurdon from him ásyndred, Past. 269, 19. Ásyndrod gemaca *separ*, Ælf. Gr. Z. 43, 2. Ásyndred *spoliata t segregata*, An. Ox. 3648. (3) *to distinguish* :—Ásyndrede *sequestrantur* (*trifaria qualitate*), An. Ox. 1366. (4) *to except* :—Út ásyndredom *excepto*, R. Ben. I. 39, 12 : 40, 3 : 45, 5. II. where connexion is prevented, (1) *to place at a distance* :—Ásyndredre *in remoto*, Wrt. Voc. ii. 44, 29. Swá hí swíþor beóþ ásyndrode fram Gode *the farther they are from God*, Bt. 39, 7 ; F. 222, 32. (2) *to prevent intermixture*, *keep apart* :—Ðæs sácerdes weorc sculon beón ásyndred from óðerra monna weorcum, Past. 81, 21. (3) *to prevent association, participation, cut off* :—Seó syn þone man ásyndrað fram Godes ríce, Gr. D. 208, 1. Sê þe fram bróðerlicre geférrædenne byð ásyndrod *qui a fraterna societate secernitur*, Scint. 6, 7. Ásen[drede] *expertem* (*veritatis*), An. Ox. 2626.

á-syndrung. *For Cot. 68 l.* Wrt. Voc. ii. 28, 26.

a-tæfran. *l.* á-tæfran : á-tæglod. v. á-cæglod.

á-tælan *to blame* :—Þte nô átæled sié *ut non vituperetur*, Rtl. 11, 31.

á-tæsan ; *p. de To tear* with a weapon (lit. or fig.) :—Án scytta ásceát âne flan and átæsde ðone cyning betwux þære lungene, Hml. S. 18, 221. Gif ðú wære on fell scoten oððe ... on flæsc ... oððe ... on lið, næfre ne sý ðín líf átæsed, Lch. iii. 54, 8. Ðæt áhrêrede mód, ðonne hit ongiet ðæt him mon birgð, mid ðære gesceádlican andsware hit bið átæsed on ðæt ingeðonc *commotas mentes, dum et parci sibi sentiunt, et tamen responsorum ratione in intimis tanguntur*, Past. 296, 17.

á-talodlic. v. un-átalodlic.

áte. *Dele in bracket* : O. Nrs. *át food, and add* :—Áte *avena*, Txts. 43, 248. Átae, átte *lolium*, 74, 599. Áta t unwæstm *zizania*, Mt. L. 13, 38. In vv. 27, 30 of this chapter occur the forms *átihi, átia*, with which may be compared *oatty*=oats of very short stalks, a Nhb. Yks. word. v. D. D., s. v.

á-téfred. v. á-tífran : ate-gár. v. æt-gár.

á-tellan. *Add* : I. *to count, number, compute* :—Hé hié átellan ne mehte *numerum explicare non potuit*, Ors. 3, 10 ; S. 140, 30. Ne wêne ic þæt ænig wære þe þæt átellan mehte, þæt on ðâm gefeohte gefeóll, 3, 11 ; S. 150, 24. II. *to enumerate* :—Hé áteled him eall ðæt hê ær tô gôde gedyde *quod bene gessit enumerat*, Past. 463, 12. On manige óðre þingon þe earfoðe sindon tô áteallene, Chr. 1086 ; P. 222, 18. III. *to tell, relate, recount* :—Hig eall átealdon þ hig gesáwon, Nic. 2, 17. Hig hym eall átealdon be þâm wýtegum, 19, 30. Þ hig wyþ ús sprecon and ús átellon ealle þá gerýnu, 11, 29. Earfoðlic is tô átellanne seó gedrecednes, Chr. 1056 ; P. 186, 32. IV. *to reckon, repute* :—Bið áteled *reputatur*, Rtl. 100, 35. [O. H. Ger. ar-zellen *explicare, reputare*.] v. un-áteald.

á-tellendlic, -temedlic. v. un-átellendlic, -átemedlic.

á-temian. *Add* :—Ðæt hê unáliéfede lustas átemige, Past. 383, 6. Seó costung synlustes wæs átemed on him, Gr. D. 101, 34. Ðæs átemedan *edomiti*, Wrt. Voc. ii. 32, 19. Wudufuglas wel átemede, Bt. 25 ; F. 88, 16.

á-tendan. *Add* : I. *to light up* :—Swá swá seó sunne hine (*the moon*) âtent, Lch. iii. 266, 25 note. II. *to expose to severe trial* :—We wæron âtende grimlíce swýðe ær we mihton þis gerêna áspyrian, Angl. viii. 312, 48. III. *to excite, inflame* :—Fram átendendum his deófle *ab accensore suo demone*, Scint. 208, 4.

á-tendend. v. preceding word.

á-tending. *Add* :—Tô átendincgum gálnysse *ad incentiva libidinis*, Scint. 221, 17.

á-teón. *Add* : I. *to draw* (*out*), (1) with direction undetermined, (a) of movement :—Hê his sword áteáh, Hml. S. 27, 75. (b) fig. *to protract* :—Hú lange wylt þú áteón þás ýdelnysse, Hml. S. 8, 105. (2) with direction determined by an adv. or prep. (a) of movement :—Seó orþung þe wê in áteóð, Hml. S. 1, 215. þæt ic áteó þás hringan up of ðysum hlyde, 21, 66. Forþ átogene *prolata* (*suspiria*), An. Ox. 988. (b) fig. of withdrawal, derivation, production, &c. :—Fæla þe ic hæfde tô mê gewyld and tô átogen, ... ealle hê from ðê átýhð, Nic. 13, 40. Forþ áteáh *edidit* (*opera*), An. Ox. 2316. þæt hê ðá deádan fram mê ne áteó, Nic. 14, 23. Sió scyld hine suíðe feorr of ealra háligra ríme átuge, Past. 37, 9. Ic wille áteón fram ðone þone intingan ælcre tweónge, Gr. D. 9, 5. Ealle þás gôd beóð átogen of þæm mægene þære Hálgan Þrynnesse, Bl. H. 29, 12. II. *to deal with*, (1) *to treat* a person :—þá men hê áteáh swá swá hê wolde (dyde of heom þ hê wolde, *v. l.*), Chr. 1071 ; P. 208, 9. Gê hiene átugon swá swá gê woldon, Ors. 6, 37 ; S. 296, 24. Lícaþ þe þ we synt þus átogene, Gr. D. 43, 3. (2) *to employ* property, time, talents :—Heó áteáh ealle þá niht in wôpum *in fletibus noctem ducens*, Gr. D. 215, 21. Eal hê on onlíc weorc áteáh, Bl. H. 215, 5. þá æhta áteóh hú þ lícige, Hml. S. 9, 44. Hiá hit átuge yfter hira dege swê hit him rehtlicast wêre ... suê huelc swê lifes sié âgefe ðet feoh and áteé suê hit soelest sié, Cht. Th. 465, 22, 33. Áteón, 466, 6. Drihten wile witan hú gehwilc manna þá gife átuge þe hê him forgeaf, Hml. Th. ii. 552, 17. Se cynincg hine forgeaf Eádgife tô áteónne swá swá heó wolde *rex dedit eundem michi* (Eadgifu) *ut de eo facerem secundum quod promeruit*, Cht. Th. 202, 19. For ðæm giefum ðe him ðynceð ðæt hê suíðe wel átogen hæbbe *in bene oblato munere*, Past. 321, 24. [*Goth*. us-tiuhan : O. Sax. á-tiohan : O. H. Ger. ar-ziohan.]

á-teorian. *Add* :—Áteoriaþ *desistunt*, Wrt. Voc. ii. 28, 39 : 59, 51. Áteorada *defuit*, 138, 27. I. *to get exhausted, faint*, (a) lit. :—On ðisum lífe we áteoriað gif wê ús mid bigleofan ne ferciað, ... gif wê tô lange waciað we áteoriað, Hml. Th. i. 488, 32-4. Gif ic hí forlæte fæstende hâm gecyrran, þonne áteoriað hí be wcge, ii. 396, 27. Se dêma hêt him ætes forwyrnan þ hê swá áteorode, Hml. S. 22, 137. (b) fig. *to lose heart or energy, get weary, faint* :—Wíte com ofer ðê and ðú áteorodest, Hml. Th. ii. 454, 18. Ne ðú ne átiara (*nec deficias*) ðonne ðú bist ðreád, Kent. Gl. 38. þæt hê æt ðære bodunge ne áteorige, Hml. Th. ii. 534, 33. II. *to get exhausted, come to an end, fail, be wanting* :—Ne áteorað ús ná þearfa tô scrýdenne *we shall never want for a poor man to clothe*, Hml. S. 31, 924. Ðín gemynd ne áteorað *the memory of thee will not come to an end*, 15, 64. Nama þe næfre ne áteorað, Hml. A. 41, 428. Of manna muðum þín mærð ne áteorað, 112, 337. Lufu næfre ne áteorað, Hml. Th. ii. 564, 11. Se dæg and seó niht áteorað, þ ys þá feówer and twêntig tída tô nánum þinge gewurþað, Angl. viii. 309, 6. þonne ealle dagas áteoriað, þonne þurhwunað hê (*Sunday*) aa, 310, 29. Hí (*unexpected guests*) næfre áteriað minstre *nunquam desunt monasterio*, R. Ben. I. 89, 10. þá æhta ðe ús áteorað *transitory possessions*, Hml. Th. ii. 318, 26. Him áteorode se heofonlíca mete *deficit manna*, Jos. 5, 12 : Num. 11, 33 : Chr. 1087 ; P. 224, 20. Áteorode his líchaman mægn, Gr. D. 227, 11. þes dæg blinneð ær mê spell áteorige, 7, 29. Ne sceolde áteorian þæt cynecynn, Hml. Th. i. 82, 2. Wín weard áteorod, 58, 12. Se môna þe byð áðwæsced oððe áteorod III. Kl. Augusti, Angl. viii. 316, 38. Ne biþ áteored *non auferetur* (*sceptrum*), An. Ox. 432. Ðín mægn is áterod, Hml. S. 3, 611. Áteoredum *exhausta*, Hpt. Gl. 462, 26. II a. in grammar, *to be defective* :—On óðrum stôwum hí áteoriað, Ælfc. Gr. Z. 205, 13. v. un-áteoriende, -teorod, *and next word*.

á-teorigendlic. *Add* : I. *getting exhausted* or *wearied, failing* :—Áteoriendlicum (-ter-, Hpt. Gl. 493, 63) *lassabundis* (*viribus*), An. Ox. 3718. II. *transitory* as opposed to eternal, *perishable* :—For áteorigendlicere edwiste, Hml. Th. i. 56, 16. þá ðing ðe wê geseóð on ðisum lífe sind áteorigendlicu, 252, 6. Sê ðe forlæt ðá áteorigendlican ðing, hê underfêhð þá gástlican mêde, 398, 4 : Hml. A. 46, 536. III. in grammar, *defective* :—Reor is *defectivum*, þæt is áteorigendlic, Ælfc. Gr. Z. 161, 20. Sume word syndon gehâtene *defectiva*, þæt synd áteorigendlice, 203, 2. v. un-áteorigendlic.

á-teorigendlíce. v. un-áteorigendlíce.

á-teorodness, e ; *f. Exhaustion, coming to an end* :—þá hálgan scínað and on þære beorhtnysse hí beóð æfre wunigende búton áteorodnysse (*the brightness will never be exhausted*), Hml. A. 44, 495.

á-teorung. *Add* : I. *exhaustion, faintness, weariness* :—Áteorung heóld mê *defectio tenuit me*, Ps. L. 118, 53. Englas ne geðafiað þæt him hunger derige oððe ænig áteorung, Hml. Th. i. 456, 25. II. *wasting away, decay, failing* :—Mid áteorung men[niscnysse] forweornaþ *defectu mortalitatis marcescit*, An. Ox. 1270 : 5268. þær is êce líf búton áteorunge, Wlfst. 142, 28 : Hml. S. 15, 218. Heó scínð búton æteorunge hire beorhtnysse, Hml. Th. i. 444, 2. Getâcnað se môna áteorunge úre deádlicnysse, 154, 29.

â-teran *to tear away:*—Hié mid đǣm ānum yfele âteratð of đǣre menniscan heortan ealle đâ gôdan crǣftas *dum unam nequitiam perpetrant, ab humanis cordibus cunctas simul virtutes eradicant,* Past. 359, 20.

âtes-hwon; *adv.* At all; ullatenus, H. Z. 31, 19. v. â-wiht, II.

âþ. *Add:*—Hê cwæđ đæt hê nân ryhtre geđencan ne meahte þonne hê þone âđ âgifan môste gif hê meahte . . . and hê gelǣdde tô đon ândagan đone âđ be fullan . . . and cwæđ đæt him wǣre leófre đæt hê . . . đonne se âđ forburste . . . and wê gehýrdan đæt hê đone âđ be fullan âgeaf, Cht. Th. 171, 16-37. þâ witan gerehton Eádgife þæt heó sceolde hire fæder hand geclǣnsian be swâ miclan feó, and heó þæs âđ lǣdde on ealre đeóde gewitnesse, and geclǣnsude hire fæder þæs ǣgiftes be .xxx. punda âđe, 202, 1-6. Hî heora freóndscipe gefæstnodon ge mid wedde ge mid âđe, Chr. 1016; P. 153, 4. Mid âþum, 921; P. 103, 20. Hê him âþas swôr, 874; P. 72, 30. þâ salde se here him foregíslas and micle âþas, þæt hié of his ríce uuoldon, 878; P. 76, 13.

âþ-brice. *l.* -bryce, *and add:*—Syndan wîde þurh âđbrycas and đurh wedbrycas forloren and forlogen mâ þonne scolde, Wlfst. 164, 7.

â-þecgan. *Substitute: to take food, consume:*—Gif mon þung ete, âþege buteran and drince *let him take some butter, and wash it down by drinking,* Lch. ii. 154, 1. Willađ hý hine âþecgan, Rä. 1, 2, 7.

â-þegen. *Substitute:* [þegen, *ptcpl.* of þicgan *to take food*] *Filled with food:*—Âđegen *distentus,* Wrt. Voc. ii. 106, 59. Âþegin, 25, 75.

â-þencan. *Add:* Hwylc man âþôhte ǣrest mid sul tô erianne?, Sal. K. 186, 28. Âþôht *commentum,* Wrt. Voc. ii. 105, 12. Âđôht, 15, 16. [*O. Sax.* â-thenkean: *O. H. Ger.* ar-denchen *excogitari.*]

â-þeneness, e; *f. Extension;* extensio, Txts. 411, 48.

â-þenian. *Add:* , -þennan. **I.** of motion or direction in a line, *to stretch out, extend:*—Ic âđennu gescôe mîn *extendam calciamentum meum,* Ps. Srt. 59, 10: 107, 10. Hê âþenedon up heora handa tô Gode, Hml. S. 30, 425. Ân fýren swer stôd up âþenod of heofonan, 3, 500. Mid âđenedum earmum, Hml. Th. i. 372, 19. **I a.** *to stretch by pulling:*—Râp tô swîđe âđened, Past. 459, 8. **II.** fig. (1) *to extend notice, direct attention, effort,* &c.:—Đæt ne âđennen (*extendant*) rehtwîse tô unrehtwîsnesse hond hara, Ps. Srt. 124, 3. Đæt môd biđ âđened suîđe heálîce tô dê, Past. 85, 25. Âđened on đâ lufan Godes, 87, 15. Sié hê up âđened mid đǣre godcundan foresceáwunge, 97, 23: 99, 9. Heora willa tô nânum ôþrum þingum nis âđenod bûton tô gifernesse, Bt. 31, 1; F. 112, 7. (2) *to extend, prolong:*—Nû wylle wê furđor ûre sprǣce âþenian, Angl. viii. 309, 25. **III.** *to spread out, extend* superficially:—Ic âþenige *oppando,* Wrt. Voc. i. 22, 33. Wê âđennađ (*expandimus*) honda ûre, Ps. Srt. 43, 21. Hê âđenode (-đened, *Ps. Srt.*) geniþu *expandit nubem,* Ps. Spl. 104, 37. þâ âþenedon (-odon, *v. l.*) hî geteld ofer *extento desuper papilione,* Bd. 4, 19; Sch. 447, 19. Âđennende (*extendens*) heofon swê swê fel, Ps. Srt. 103, 2. Âþened *oppansum,* Wrt. Voc. ii. 63, 66: *distenta .i. extenta,* 141, 22. **III a.** *to stretch out, prostrate:*—þâ âþenede se biscop hine in cruce *incubuit precibus antistes,* Bd. 4, 29; Sch. 530, 1. Sceal hê beforan him hine âþenian *coram eo se prosternere debebit,* Ll. Th. ii. 130, 34. Hê hine hêt âþenian on îrenum bedde, Shrn. 116, 2. **III b.** of a space of time:—þâ þrý dagas (*the first three*) wǣron bûtan sunnan and mônan . . . gelîcere wǣgan mid leóhte and þeóstrum âþenede, Lch. iii. 234, 6. [*O. H. Ger.* ar-dennen *extendere, expandere, prosternere.*]

Athēniense; *pl. The Athenians:*—Sôna swâ Athēniense wiston, Ors. 2, 5; S. 78, 22. þâ bearn þâra Athēniensa, 1, 9; S. 42, 28: 2, 5; S. 82, 13. Of Atheniensium, 1, 14; S. 58, 5. Tô Athēniensum, 2, 5; S. 82, 20: 84, 20. ¶ Latin forms are also used:—Pelopensium and Athēniensium, Grēca þeóda him betweónum winnende wǣron *Peloponnensium Atheniensiumque bellum commissum est,* 1, 13; S. 56, 7. Wið þǣm Athēnienses, 2, 7; S. 90, 11. Wið Athēnienses, 2, 5; S. 78, 21. Hié âspônan him on fultum Athēnienses, 2, 7; S. 90, 7.

Athēnisc; *adj. Athenian:*—Tô Athēniscre byrig, Hml. S. 3, 11. Tô þǣre Athēniscan byrig, 29, 78.

â-þenung (-ing). *Add:*—Sió âþenung (*distension*) þæs magan, Lch. ii. 192, 17. On bedde âþeninge mînre *in lecto strati mei,* Ps. L. 131, 3.

â-þeódan. *Add:* , -þíedan, -þýdan:—þes ûs þisse worlde lufu âþeóde from þǣre lufu þæs ēcan lîfes, Bl. H. 57, 23. Âđiéde, Past. 351, 21. Hié beóđ from đǣre lufe âđiéd hiera niéhstena, 349, 6. Ne myhte hyra nâđer fram ôđrum beón âđýded, Shrn. 99, 8. Swâ swîđe swâ hî beóđ fram him âþeódde hî ne cunnon his dômas, Gr. D. 138, 27. Wê swâ micle fier beóđ đǣm hiehstan ryhte âđiédde, Past. 355, 8.

â-þeóstrian. *Add:* (1) *intrans.:*—Seó sunne eall âþeóstrađ (-þystrađ, *v. l.*), Lch. iii. 242, 21. þâm lāreówum âđîstriađ đâ flǣsclican eágan, Past. 29, 15. (2) *trans.:*—Gif his andgit âđîstriađ đâ flǣsclican weorc, Past. 67, 25. Hê âđeóstrade hié *obscuravit eos,* Ps. Srt. 104, 28. Âþeóstredan *caliginabant, obumbrabant,* Wrt. Voc. ii. 127, 68. Đæt đæt dust ne âđîsđrige (-điéstrige, *v. l.*) đæt eáge, Past. 131, 22. Se môna mæg đâ sunnan âþeóstrian (-þýstrian, *v. l.*), Lch. iii. 242, 25. (3) uncertain in the case of past ptcpl.:—Seó eorđe wæs gesworcen and âđýstrod, Ps. Th. 17, 9. Weard middaneard âđeóstrod, Hml. Th. ii. 256, 34. Siún hira eágan âđîstrode, Past. 29, 9. Âđeástrade sind *obscurati sunt,* Ps. Srt. 73, 20. Sié âđíostrado *tenebrantur,* Rtl. 125, 33.

â-þeówan (v. þeówan), -þéwan, -þýwan, -þýgan, -þýn. **I.** *to drive away, force away:*—þû ût âþýdest (*reppulisti*) ûs, Ps. L. 59, 3. Âþýgdest, 42, 2. Hê hié âweg âþêwde, Ors. 6, 36; S. 294, 2. Ût âþýde *egessit,* Wrt. Voc. ii. 32, 10. Ût âþýdum *depulsae,* Ps. L. 61, 4. **II.** *to press out, thrust out, squeeze out:*—Hê of đǣm geclystrum ût âþýde lytelne dæl wînes, Gr. D. 58, 19. Hî ne mihton ǣnigne eles wǣtan ût âþýn, 250, 14. Ût âþýde *elisi,* i. *expressi,* Wrt. Voc. ii. 143, 11. Hî (*the eyes*) wǣron ût âđýde (*printed* -dyde) of þâm eáhhringum, Hml. S. 21, 279. **III.** *to press into:*—Swâ hié on wexe wǣron âđýde, Bl. H. 205, 1.

âþer, â-þêwan. v. â-hwæþer, â-þeówan.

â-þerscan *to thresh out:*—Sum tûn wæs þe ǣlce geáre wæs âwēst þurh hagol, swâ þ̄ heora æceras ǣr wǣron âþroxene ǣr ǣnig ryftere þ̄ gerip gaderode, Hml. S. 31, 1217.

âđexe. *Add:*—Âđexe (âđexa) *lacerta,* Txts. 73, 1182.

â-þíedan, -þierran, -þíestrian. v. â-þeódan, þirran *in Dict.,* â-þeóstrian.

â-þindan. *Add:*—For đǣre orsorgnesse monn oft âđint on ofermēttum, Past. 35, 3: 113, 18. Hî âđindađ innane on îdlum gilpe, 439, 5. þâ þe âþindađ and âswellađ þurh þâ wîlnunge þæs îdlan gylpes, Gr. D. 40, 4. Đætte hié ne âđinden on heora môde, Past. 319, 17. On ofermēttum âđunden, 25, 6: 111, 1. Hê wæs mid oferhygdes gâste âþunden, Gr. D. 144, 28: 180, 16.

â-þindung. *Add:*—þ̄ deáh wið âblâwunge þæs miltes. Gif þonne sió âþindung þæs windes (*the swelling up from wind*) semninga cymđ, þonne ne magon þâs þing helpan, Lch. ii. 248, 5.

â-þístrian, -þíwan. v. â-þeóstrian, -þeówan: a-þoht. *Dele, and see* â-þencan.

â-þolian. *Add:* **I.** *intrans.* To hold out *under trial,* (1) of persons:—Hit bið twýlic hwæđer đæt cild on lîfe âđolige ođ þæt hit þâm lāreówe andwyrdan mage, Hml. Th. ii. 50, 24. þâ earman bearn ne mihton leng for sceame on þǣre byrig âđolian, ii. 30, 27. (2) of things:—þ̄ scyp byð gesund, gyf se streng âþolađ, Shrn. 175, 23. Seó upfiéring tôbærst . . . þæt hûs eal ansund âđolode, Hml. Th. ii. 164, 5. Wurdon gelæhte micele and manega fixas, and þæt net swâ đeáh âđolode, 290, 21. **II.** *trans.* To put up with, endure, suffer:—Ic wundrige hû seó sǣ âđolode mîne lustas, Hml. S. 23 b, 385. þâm ylcum gemete wuniaþ and gyt âþolede synt munecena mynstru, R. Ben. 139, 3. [*Goth.* us-þul(j)an.]

â-þracian. *Add:*—Hê âþracađ (*horrescit*) ǣlc yfel, Scint. 235, 4. Fýlđe gylta hwônlîce ic âđracude (*exhorrui*), Angl. xi. 118, 46. Binne nâ âþracude (*abhorrui*), Hy. S. 51, 7. Âþracigende *horrens,* 142, 32. **II.** *to frighten:*—Wîtu âþraciað þâ þe mēda nâ ingelaþiađ *poene terreant quos premia non invitant,* Scint. 115, 5.

â-þrǣstan. *Add:*—Âđrēsti, ath(r)aestae *extorti,* Txts. 61, 780. Âþrǣste, Wrt. Voc. ii. 29, 60: 146, 7.

â-þrâwan. *Add:* **I.** *to twist, twine, curl:*—Mid þrâwingspinle synd âþrâwene (*antiae frontis*) *calomistro crispantur,* An. Ox. 5329. Gyldne styþa hié ûton wreþedon and âþrâwene đâr ingemong stôdon, Angl. iv. 143, 100. þâ âþrâwenan goldþrǣdas *torta aurea fila,* Wrt. Voc. ii. 127, 19. Âþrâwenum þrǣdum *contortis,* 21, 18. Âþrâwenum *tortis* (*crinibus*), An. Ox. 2, 34. **II.** *to twist, give a different direction* to *a moving body:*—Seó flâ wende ongeán swilce mid windes blǣde âđrâwen, Hml. Th. i. 502, 19. ¶ for a proposed emendation to âþrowen in An. 1427 v. â-dreópan *in Dict.*

a-þreát. *Dele, and see* â-þreótan.

â-þreátian; *p.* ode To force away:—Đæt mon wielle æt ôđrum his yfel âđreátigan, and hine on ryhtum gebringan, Past. 293, 10.

â-þreótan. *Add:* To make weary. **I.** used impersonally with acc. of person, (1) alone:—Hwæđerne âþreóted ǣr *which will be tired out first,* Sal. 428. (2) with gen. of object of weariness:—Eów þæs lungre âþreát, El. 368. Âđreát đâ hiéremenn ryhtes lîfes, Past. 129, 4. Hû micel scyld đæt sié đæt monn âđreóte þǣre nætinge yfelra monna, 353, 11. His mê sceal âþreótan, Ors. 5, 2; S. 218, 21. (3) with a (negative) clause:—Đæt hiene nâ ne âdriét đæt hê hî tô him ne ladige *non cessat vocare,* Past. 405, 22. Ne âdreát hine nâ đæt hê đâ dysegan ne tælde *nec insanientes cessabat reprehendere,* 355, 16. Heó wile late âþreótan þæt heó fǣhđo ne týdre *she will be slow to weary of exciting enmity,* Sal. 447. (4) with dat. infin.:—Mê sceal âđreótan tô âsecgenne *taedet referre,* Ors. 1, 8; S. 42, 12. **II.** personal. *Dele the meanings given.* [*Goth.* us-þriutan: *O. H. Ger.* ar-driozan *impers.* with acc. of person and gen. of thing, also with *zi* and infin.] v. un-âþroten, â-þrîtan.

a-þrescan. v. â-þerscan.

â-þríettan; p. -þríettan, dele '*loathe any one.*' *and add:*—Ûs nǣfre ne âdrýt þæra gôda genihtsumnys, Hml. Th. ii. 588, 8. Hié đæt folc âþrýtton þæt hié him on hond eódon *they tired out the people so that they yielded to them,* Ors. 5, 11; S. 238, 10.

â-þringan. *Under* I. *dele* '*to conceal,*' *and for* 'Cot. 33' *substitute* Wrt. Voc. ii. 14, 22 (celatum = embossed), *and add:*—Hê his feorh

āþrang of þām līchaman, Gr. D. 136, 2. Ic wæs ūt āþrungen fram eallum þām folce oððe ic ǣnlīpigu oþstōd, Hml. S. 23 b, 409.

ā-þrīstian *to be bold, presume* :—Hū swīðe hē sceolde āþrīstigean (-þrīstian, *v. l.*) on myclum bēnum *quantum praesumere in magnis petitionibus deberet*, Gr. D. 70, 30.

ā-þroten. Substitute *wearied* for *loathed*.

ā-þrotenlīce. v. un-āþrotenlīce.

ā-þrotennes. Add :—Āþrotenes *fastidia*, Wrt. Voc. ii. 38, 72.

ā-þrotsum; adj. *Wearisome* :—Āþrotsum is *pertæsum est*, Wrt. Voc. ii. 85, 80. v. ǣ-þrot.

ā-þrowen. v. ā-dreópan *in Dict.* for a suggested emendation.

ā-þrowian. Add :—Sēcen hie him broc on onrāde oððe on wǣne oððe on þon þe hie āþrowian mægen, Lch. ii. 184, 14.

ā-þroxen, -þrungen. v. ā-þerscan, -þringan.

ā-þrūten; adj. (*ptcpl.*) *Swollen* :—Lege on þā stōwe þǣr hit āþrūten sié, Lch. ii. 44, 14. Bið þ heáfod āþrūten and sār, 218, 19. v. þrūtian.

ā-þryccan; pp. -þryht *To press, oppress* :—Wē bidon āðryht *premimur*, Rtl. 15, 30. Þte uē sié āðryht *opprimamur*, 82, 27.

āþryd. Substitute: ā-þrý(a)n; pp. -þrýd *To extort, rob* :—Āþrýid *expilatam*, Wrt. Voc. ii. 107, 61. Āþrīd, 29, 68. Āþrýd *expressum*, 30, 19: *expilatam*, i. *conquassatam*, 145, 12.

a-þrýpian. *Dele.*

ā-þrytnes, e; f. *Weariness* :—Āþrytnesse *fastidium*, Hy. S. 6, 8.

āþ-swara *an oath.* v. swara, *and next word.*

āþ-swaru. Add :—Hē mid āþsware him tō cwǣd, Gr. D. 17, 19. Be āþsware . . . þū āgylst Drihtne āðswara (*juramenta*) þīne, Scint. 135, 3-5. Þurh āþsware *per juramentum*, Confess. Pecc. 183, 1. Āðsware (*jus jurandum*) hē swōr, Cant. Zach. 73. Ðæs fæder (*Herod*) dyrstigan āðsware, Hml. Th. i. 482, 1. Āðsware sē þe fiýhð, Lch. iii. 186, 7. Āðswara *juramenta*, Cant. Ab. 9.

āþ-sweord. *Dele:* sweord *sword, and see* sweord *swearing.*

āþ-swerian (?) *to curse* :—Wyrgdan, āþsweredon (āþ sweredan?) *devotabant* (*se*, Ald. 38, 19), Wrt. Voc. ii. 26, 48.

āþum. Add: I. *a son-in-law* :—Bidde wē þ þū geceóse ǣnne of ūs hwilcne þū wille þē tō āþume habban, Ap. Th. 20, 3. Hē genam ðā dohtor of his āðumme, Hml. Th. i. 478, 26: ii. 24, 30. [II. *a brother-in-law*, Chr. 1091; P. 226, 22.] III. *uncertain* :—Þǣr wæs ofslægen Æðelstān þes cynges āðum (Fl. Wig. says *gener*, Hen. Hunt. *sororius*, v. P. ii. 188), Chr. 1010; P. 140, 10.

ā-þundennes. Add: I. *physical* :—Wiþ þæs magan āþundennesse, Lch. ii. 182, 24. II. *fig.* :—Þurh āþundennese *per contumaciam*, Kent. Gl. 1168.

ā-þweán. Add: pp. -þwagen, -þwægen, -þwogen. I. *to wash, cleanse* an object from impurity :—Ic eów fram synnum āðweá, Hml. Th. i. 464, 17. Gif ic ne āðoá ðē, Jn. L. 13, 8. Se storm āðwyhð swā hwæt swā þæt fyr forswǣld, Hml. Th. i. 618, 12. Āþwehð, ii. 48, 29. Āðweahð, 56, 7. Āðweáð iów, ðæt gē sīn clǣne, Past. 421, 14. Þ hē hī mid fulluhte āþwōge, Hml. S. 5, 126. Mid teárum ougann āðoá (*rigare*) foet his . . . and mid smirinise āðuóh (*ungebat*), Lk. L. 7, 38. Āðoá (-ðwǣ, R.) foet *lavare pedes*, Jn. L. 13, 14. Bið micel folc āðwægen hira scylda, Past. 105, 23. Bið suīðe wel āðwægen sió wund, 259, 25. Mid fulluhte āþwagen (āðwogen, v. l.) fram his dǣdum, Hml. S. 27, 194. Hē bið āðwægen fram his synnum, Hml. Th. i. 472, 5. Hē hæfde hyra fēt āþwogene, Jn. 13, 12: Hml. Th. ii. 260, 15. II. *to wash* impurity from an object :—Hit ðā gedōnan synna āweg āðwiehð, Past. 257, 21. Ðæt sār āðwiehð synna of ðǣre sáule, 259, 3. Ðæt hié yfelu mid hreówsunga āðweán, 413, 9. Scylda of āðueán, 73, 18.

ā-þweran. Add :—Mon ðā buteran āðwere, Lch. iii. 24, 14.

āþ-wyrþe. Add: *Entitled to make oath* :—Sē þe mānað swerige, and hit him on open wurðe, þ hē nǣfre eft āðwyrðe ne sý, Ll. Th. i. 212, 19.

ā-þýan. v. ā-þeówan.

ā-þyddan *to thrust, push* :—Þurh āþidde *transfigit, transfodit*, An. Ox. 50, 3.

ā-þyft, Wrt. Voc. ii. 144, 41. v. ā-þyffan: ā-þýn. v. ā-þeówan.

ā-þynnian. Add :—Nihte is āþinnod sceadu *noctis tenuatur umbra*, Hy. S. 8, 19.

ā-þýtan *to expel* :—Āðýtið *eliminat*, Wrt. Voc. ii. 107, 15.

ā-þýwan. v. ā-þeówan.

ā-tīdrian; p. ode *To grow weak* :—Hē him þ ondrēde þ hē sceolde innan ātýddrian *ne intus inanesceret*, Gr. D. 59, 26.

a-tiefran. *l.* ā-tiéfran, *and add* :—On þōðere ātéfred, Shrn. 174, 18, 35. v. ā-tǣfran, teáfor.

ātih, ā-tiht, ā-tillan. v. āte, ā-tyhtan, tillan.

ā-timbr(i)an. Add :—Babilon ðe ic self ātimbrede, Past. 39, 17. Hwylc man ātimbrode ǣrust ceastre?, Sal. K. 184, 33. Hē hēt ātimbran (-ian, v. l.) þā ciricean, Chr. 643; P. 26, 15: 913; P. 96, 20.

atol; adj. Add :—Atol *atrox*, An. Ox. 7, 291. Atole *deformem*, Wrt. Voc. ii. 91, 17: *cenidos* (= *cinaedos*), 96, 60.

atolhiwian. v. ge-atolhiwian.

atolian *to deform, disfigure* :—Atoliende *deturpans, maculans*, Wrt. Voc. ii. 139, 49. v. ge-atelod.

---

atol-lic. Add :—Seó sunne scīman ne hæfde and wæs atollic (eatolīce, v. l.) on tō beseónne, Bd. 3, 27; Sch. 316, 11. Deófol is atelic sceocca, Hml. Th. i. 16, 21. Þeáh ðe hē (*the leper*) atelic wǣre, 122, 6. Ān atelic sceadu on sweartum hīwe, ii. 508, 1. Seó sāwel bið atelic þurh leahtras, Hml. S. i, 155. Gesewen on ðām atelican hīwe, Hml. Th. i. 336, 35. On atelicum hīwe mid byrnendum mūðe and līgenum eágum, ii. 164, 22. Þā atelican *obscena*, An. Ox. 4959. Ateliecost kin *teterrimum genus*, R. Ben. I. 10, 6.

atollīce; adv. *Horribly* :—Hē wæs atelīce hreófiig, Hml. Th. i. 122, 17. Atelīcor, 23. Hwæt is atelīcor gedūht on menniscum gecynde þonne is ðæs hreófiian līc?, 336, 31.

ātor. Add :—Ātr *bile*, Wrt. Voc. ii. 101, 72. Āter, 11, 9. Ātur *venenum*, Ps. Srt. 139, 4. Āttre *bile, felle*, Wrt. Voc. 126, 21. Ātre *toxa*, An. Ox. 6, 14. Þū swylst mid ātre ācweald *morieris veneno*, Nar. 31, 28. Wyrtdrenc wið ātre *theriaca*, Wrt. Voc. ii. 77, 4. Āttre, i. 20, 20. Āttre gemǣled *lita*, ii. 52, 69. Ðæt āter (-or, v. l.) hiera āgenra mettrymnessa *virus suae pestis*, Past. 371, 10. Āttor sellan *pestiferum veneni poculum fundere*, 449, 27. Him mon sealde āttor drincan, Shrn. 90, 25: Gr. D. 158, 29. Ettre *virus* (*evomuit*), An. Ox. 11, 85. Þā āttru (*venenum*, v. l.) geondfērdon his innoþ, Gr. D. 187, 3. Wið ealle āttru, Lch. i. 170, 18, 19. Fācnes āttru *fraudis venena*, Hy. S. 16, 15.

ātor-bǣre; adj. *Poisonous* :—Ðone āttorbǣran drenc, Hml. Th. i. 72, 22.

ātor-berende. Add :—Seó ātterberende nǣdre, Wlfst. 192, 22.

ātor-coppe. Add: [Dan. edder-kop *spider*.]

ātor-cræft. Add :—Leásunga and āttorcræftas, Engl. Stud. viii. 479, 97. Bebeorh þe wið lyblācas and āttorcræftas *cave tibi a maleficiis et veneficiis*, Ll. Th. ii. 132, 9: Wlfst. 290, 30.

ātor-drinc, -drinca. *Dele.*

ātor-lāþe. Add :—Āterlāðe *bettonica*, Wrt. Voc. ii. 11, 6.

ātor-lic. Add :—Āterlicum oððe biter *gorgoneo*, Wrt. Voc. ii. 41, 56.

ā-trahtnian; p. ode *To treat, discuss* :—Ātrah[tnode] *exposuit*, i. *tractavit*, An. Ox. 2300. Þ wē rūmlīcor þās gerēnu ātrahtnion, Angl. viii. 324, 7. Wē habbað ymbe þǣre sunnan ryne manega þing gerādlīce ātrahtnod, 308, 15.

at(t)rum *a black liquid* or *pigment* :—Attrum *calecantum, vitrolum*, Wrt. Voc. ii. 127, 64. Syndran atrume *scoriae atramento* (*foedatos*), An. Ox. 7, 45: Angl. xiii. 28, 25 (where see note). ¶ Attrum *glosses* lodix, An. Ox. 18 b, 52, *the gloss to which in* Wrt. Voc. ii. 93, 2 *is* loða, *the line in each case being*: et nova de liquido sumatur gurgite lodix, Ald. 168, 13.

ā-tweógendlīce. v. un-ātweógendlīce.

ā-tweónian; p. ode *To cause doubt* in a person (*dat.*); impers. :—Gif hwām ātweónige, Angl. viii. 333, 6.

ā-týddrian. v. ā-tīdrian: a-tydran. *l.* ā-týdran.

ā-tyhtan. Add: I. *to stretch*; tendere, attendere, extendere, intendere :—Hī ātiht (*adtendit*) fram slǣwþe, Scint. 67, 2. Ātiht (*extende*) þā sōðan lufe gynd ealne embehwyrft, 2, 16. Þænne geþanc nā tō bebodum sōðre lufe byð ātiht (*tenditur*), 53, 7. Ātyht, Past. 301, 19. Oðer bið tō ungemetlīce ātyht *inordinate extenditur*, 293, 13. ¶ Ātyht *intent* :—Ātiht mid bígenge his gebedes *orationis studio intentus*, Gr. D. 71, 10: Scint. 36, 16. Ātihtre smeágunge *intenta meditatione*, 124, 2. His eágena ātihtan scearpnysse, Gr. D. 171, 14. Eárum ātihtum, Dóm. L. 69. II. *to persuade, incite* :—Wē ātihtaþ *suademus*, R. Ben. I. 84, 10.

ā-tyhtung, e; f. I. *intention*; intentio, Scint. 29, 10: 35, 14: 28, 13. II. *incentive* :—Ātihtinga *incentiva*, An. Ox. 2, 304.

ā-týnan. Add :—Ātýnið *explodit, excludit*, Wrt. Voc. ii. 107, 64. Ātýned, 29, 72. Ātýneþ *explodit*, 146, 2.

auerian. v. aferian: āwa. *l.* nāwa.

ā-wacan *to spring, arise*. Add :—Fram þan Wōdne eall ūre cynecynn āwōc, Chr. 449; P. 13, 25: 547; P. 17, 20. Odo þe þæs þyng of āwōcan 1087; P. 223, 25. Hū fela þeóda āwōcon of his iii. bearnum?, Sal. K. 182, 24, 26. Cf. on-wacan.

ā-wacian. Add :—Hī of ðām slǣpe āwacedon . . . þā hī āwacodon, Hml. S. 23, 441-3.

ā-wācian. Add :—Āwācaþ *uilesceret*, i. *contemptibilis esset*, An. Ox. 2087. Sē bið gesǣlig þe þonne ne āwācaþ, Wlfst. 85, 14. Þ þū mē ne forlǣte þeáh ic āwācode, Angl. xii. 502, 2. On heora nǣnigum se hiht ne āwācode, Guth. 66, 14. Āwācyge þǣra stapela ǣnig, sóna se stól scylfð, Wlfst. 267, 17. Hý willan þurh deófles lāre āwācian, 11, 14. Āwācian for wītum, Hml. S. 5, 22. Bið ðæt mōd āwācod *mens in mollitiem vertitur*, Past. 143, 8. Āsolcene and āwācode *tepidi*, R. Ben. 44. 22. Ðā wundra sind swīðe āwācode, for ðon ðe hī sind swīðe gewunelice, Hml. Th. i. 184, 25.

ā-wacnian, -wæcnian. Add: I. *to awaken* :—Hē geseah ān lytel fæt þā þā hē āwacnode, Hml. S. 18, 165. Āwæcnode se wer of slǣpe, 21, 251. Clypiað . . . þ hē āwacnige, 18, 120. II. *to arise, spring* :—Þæt þeós weoruld mihte of hym āwæcnian, Wlfst. 206, 28. Þanon wæs āwæcnod þ æþeluste cynn, Angl. xi. 3, 56.

ā-wǣcan. *Dele:* awæht (*l.* ārǣht) *porrectus*.

**á-wǽgan.** *Add*: I. *to deceive* :—Beswîcþ, âwǽgþ *eludit*, i. *decipit*,Wrt. Voc. ii. 143, 16. Âwǽgde *eluderet*, 29, 19. Âwǽged *fallitur (humanum judicium)*, An. Ox. 1734. Hê wæs âwǽged (*inlusus*) from þǽm tungul-kræftgum, Mt. R. 2, 16. II. *to make of no effect*, (a) *to fail to perform* :—Gif hê beswicen byð, þ hê his behât âwǽgð, R. Ben. 102, 3 : Hml. A. 34, 244. Forgyldan ealle þâ þing þe wê ofor his bebod gedydon oþþe þæs âwǽgdon þe wê dôn sceoldan, Bl. H. 91, 17. Âwǽgdon *fefellisset* (*pollicita*), An. Ox. 2, 237. Hî heora fullnhtes behât ðurh forgǽgednysse âwǽgdon, Hml. Th. ii. 338, 9. Ne sceall nân mann âwǽgan þ hê sylfwylles behǽt, Hml. S. 26, 269. (b) *to invalidate, nullify* :—Gif þû nelt hine tellan . . . þonne âwǽgst (-wǽst, *v. l.*) þû þone regol, Lch. iii. 264, 16. Swilc man swê hit âwǽge, C. D. i. 297, 13. Hû heó âna mihte ealle þâ gewytan âwǽgan mid âðe, Hml. S. 2, 225. Þonne wǽre seó rihtwîsnys âwǽged, gif hê hî neádunge tô his ðeówte gebîgde, Hml. Th. i. 112, 6. Ân stæf ne bið ne ân strica âwǽged *iota unum aut unus apex non praeteribit*, Thw. Hept. 159, 31. Âwǽgune (-ede ?) yrfebêc *inritum testamentum*, Wrt. Voc. ii. 49, 15.

**á-wǽlan.** *Dele paragraph* I, *and see* â-wiltan, â-wilwan.

**â-wǽrlan** *to avoid* :—Giduolo âwǽrle *errores declinet*, Rtl. 39, 25.

**â-wǽscan** *to wash* :—Âwæsc ealle, Lch. ii. 38, 16. Âwæsc on hâligwætre, 110, 14.

**â-wandian.** v. wandian, II.

**â-wanian.** *Add* :—Sê ðe hit âwanie, C. D. iii. 344, 23. Ðâ ðe âwonað biðon in lîchoma *qui macerantur in corpore*, Rtl. 15, 3.

**â-wannian.** *Add* : *to become livid* :—Hê gedyde þ eall his andwlita âwannode (weard âwannod, *v. l.*) *totum illius vultum lividum reddidit*, Gr. D. 20, 32.

**â-wansian.** v. wansian.

**â-wâr.** *Add* :—Þæt wê ôðrum mannum forgifon, gif hî âwâr ûs geǽbiligdon, Hml. Th. ii. 100, 33.

**â-weallan.** *Add* : I. *to well out* :—Ic upp âwealle *ebullio*, Ælfc. Gr. Z. 192, 4. Aweól *exundavit*, Wrt. Voc. ii. 29, 56 : 146, 36. II. *to spring, proceed* from a source :—Ealle undeáwas âweallað of deófle, Wlfst. 40, 22. III. *to swarm*, (1) *to exist in large numbers* :—Swâ þicce hié in þǽre eá âweóllon swâ ǽmettan *veluti formice efferbuere*, Nar. 11, 13. (2) *of production in large numbers, to swarm* with :—þ flǽsc wyrmum âwealleþ, Bl. H. 101, 3. Hê âweól eal wyrmum, Shrn. 111, 25. IV. *of movement caused by heat* :—Fûlnes wæs mid ðæs fŷres ðrosme upp âweallende, Bd. 5, 12 ; S. 628, 26. V. *to be hot* :—Âuueóll *incanduit*, Wrt. Voc. ii. 111, 69. Va. *of the heat of disease* :—Wiþ þâ âdle þe Grêcas *frenesis* nemnaþ, þ byþ ðonne þ heáfod âweallen byþ, Lch. i. 210, 2. Vb. *of violent passion, to burn, rage* :—Sê âbarn and âweóll (*exarsit*) nid þŷ bryne wælhreównesse ongeán þâ ǽfestan weras, Gr. D. 162, 23. [*O. H. Ger.* ar-wallan *fervere, effervescere, emanare.*]

**â-weaxan.** *Add* :—Wǽron of ðæm stâne âwexene bearwas, Bl. H. 209, 32. [*O. H. Ger.* ar-wahsan *oboriri, increscere.*]

**a-web.** *l.* â-web, *and add* :—Âwebb *subtegmen*, Wrt. Voc. i. 66, 22. Âweb *subtimen*, 282, 9. v. ô-web.

**â-weccan.** *Add* : I. *to wake* (trans.) from sleep, *raise from the dead* :—Hwîlon lâreow mîn âwecþ mê stîþlîce mid gyrde, Coll. M. 35, 31. Ic mîne frŷnd âweahte, Nar. 30, 32. God hine âweahte tô onlîesanne ðâ gehæftan on helle, Past. 443, 9. Iern and âwece hine, 193, 18. Âwece ûrne deádan brôðor, Gr. D. 84, 14. II. *to arouse* a person from quiescence, *to excite* to feeling or action, *stir up* :—Hê (*John*) þǽre môdor innoþas ongeán þâm Godes suna âweahte, Bl. H. 167, 6. Wearþ se drý âweht wiþ ðâm apostolum, 173, 18. Hig wǽron ongeán hyne mid yrre âwehte, Nic. 14, 17. Sceolan wê beón âwehte and onbryrde tô godcundre lâre, Bl. H. 33, 23. III. *to arouse, excite* passion, &c. :—Ðâs ilcan geornfulnesse Paulus âweahte (*excitat*), Past. 139, 1. Bið âweaht se anga ðǽre wrǽnnesse, 309, 15. Ealles lîchoman âdla weorþað âwehte, Lch. ii. 218, 21. Beóð âwecte (-wehte, *v. l.*) andan, saca and tala, R. Ben. 124, 17. [*Goth.* us-wakjan : *O. H. Ger.* ar-wecken.]

**â-weceness**, e ; *f. Incitement* :—Hwylc man ne âwundrað swylce wundru þâra deádra þâ beóð gedône fore âwæcenesse (-wec-, *v. l.*) and lâre þâra lifigendra (*quae fiunt pro exercitatione* (the translator has read *excitatione?*) *viventium*), Gr. D. 199, 7.

**â-wecgan.** *Add*: I. *of physical movement* :—Þæt folc mid râpum ðâ anlîcnysse bewurpon and mid stengum âwegdon (*tried to overturn it with poles*), ac hî ne mihton for ðâm deófle hî styrian, Hml. Th. i. 464, 19. Lytel wind mæg ðone cîð âwecgan (-wecggean, *v. l.*) (*agitat*), Past. 225, 6. Wâc hreód ðe ǽlc hwiða windes mæg âwecgan, 306, 6. Hêt hê spannan oxan tô, ac hî ne mihton âwecgan þæt mǽden swâ, Hml. S. 9, 107. Seó mycelnes þæs stânclifes weard upp âweged (*evulsa*) fram ðâm mannum þe hit ymb wunnon, Gr. D. 213, 27. II. *mental* :—Ðone yfelan fǽsdrǽdan willan nân wind ne mæg âwecgan (-wecggean, *v. l.*), Past. 225, 7. Ne lêten hié nô hié on ǽlce healfe gebîgean, ne furðum nô âwecggan . . . Paulus cwæð : ' Ne lǽte gê eów ǽlcre lâre wind âwecggan ' *non circumferamur omni vento doctrinae*, 306, 4-9. Heora mâgas þǽra cnihta môd fram Crîstes geleáfan woldon âwecgan, Hml. S. 5, 42. Ðwyrlîcra manna heortan, þe beóð ðurh unrihtwîsnysse

hôcas âwegde, ðurh regolsticcan ðǽre sôðan rihtwîsnysse beóð geemnode, Hml. Th. i. 362, 27. [*O. H. Ger.* ar-wegen *agitare, commuovere, quassare.*]

**â-wêdan.** *Add*: I. *to go mad* :—Sê þe þurh sleápleáste âwêt *freneticus*, Wrt. Voc. i. 75, 60. Þæs mannes sunu âwêdde, Shrn. 97, 15. Se cyng âwêdde þe hine cwellan hêt, and ealle þâ hǽþenan bisceopas âwêddan and swulton, 121, 3-5. Ðâ swîn ealle âwêddan, Hml. S. 17, 194. Ðâ weard Decius mid feóndlicum gâste âwêd, Hml. Th. i. 434, 7, 9 : ii. 510, 28. His dohtor is âwêdd, 110, 28. Drihten mihte hire âwêddan dohtor gehǽlan, 114, 7. Ia. *of pestilence, to rage* :—Tô ðâm swîðe âwêdde se cwealm, Hml. Th. ii. 126, 18. II. *to be mad* :—Âuoeded *insanit*, Jn. L. R. 10, 20.

**â-wefan.** *Add* :—Wæs âwefen *ordiretur*, Wrt. Voc. ii. 63, 5. His reáf wæs âwefen of olfendes hǽrum, Hml. Th. i. 352, 5. Mid orle of golde âwefen, Hml. S. 7, 36. Heó wæs gegyred myd golde âwefenum hrægelum, Shrn. 149, 21.

**â-weg.** *Add*: , -wege :—Hê com wund âweg *confossus vulneribus evasit*, Ors. 4, 6 ; S. 172, 24. Hê tôwearp þ deófolgild and weard him âwege, Hml. S. 25, 228. *Amauisti vel amasti*, hêr ys se *ui* âwege, Ælfc. Gr. Z. 147, 1.

**âweg-âdrîfan, &c.** *In this verb and in others with the same prefix* âweg *should be separated.*

**â-wegan.** *Add*: I. *to carry off* :—Hê hêt delfan his byrgene and þæt greót ût âwegan, Hml. Th. i. 74, 25. Helias wæs mid cræte up âwegen, 308, 16. Upp âwegen *evulsa*, Gr. D. 213, 27. Âwegen *evectus, sublevatus*, An. Ox. 1440. Ia. *to put away, renounce* (?) :—Bûtan heora hwilc wolde âwegan (-wǽgan? v. âwǽgan, II) his geleáfan, Hml. S. 35, 228. II. *to weigh*. (1) *to put in a balance* (lit. or fig.) :—Hê âwecþ ealle dûna mid ânre handa, Hml. Th. i. 8, 30. Hê âwæh ðîn rîce on wǽgan, ii. 436, 12. Gelîcere wâge âwæh *aequa bilance trutinabat*, An. Ox. 4603. Âwæg, Wrt. Voc. ii. 86, 4. Âweh wiþ ǽnne pening, Lch. ii. 88, 5. Oððe gemetan oððe getellan oððe âwegan, Ll. Th. i. 194, 8. Sié âwegen *expendatur*, Wrt. Voc. ii. 30, 32. Âwegen *perpensa, librata*, Germ. 394, 307. (2) *to estimate, consider* :—Mægenu hê âwyhð *vires pensat*, Scint. 10, 15. Âweget *appendit* (*corda*), Kent. Gl. 768. Hig ǽrest âpinsiað wǽrlicum môde þâ naman and þâ bînaman . . . Syððan hig þâ word âginnað tô âweganne mid þâm bîwordum, Angl. viii. 313, 4-7. (3) *to be equal in weight to* :—Se dinor âwehð *decem nummos*, Ælfc. Gr. Z, 285, 2.

**â-wegan** ; *p.* -wegede. *Dele, and see* â-wecgan.

**âweg-âworpenness**, e ; *f. Abortion* :—Ðâ wîf þe ðôð âwegâworpnesse (*abortionem*) heora bearna, Ll. Th. ii. 154, 34.

**âwegendlic.** v. un-âwegendlic.

**âweg-gewitenness.** *Add* :—Sârie for his âweggewitennysse, Hml. S. 30, 159, 226.

[*âweg-weard moving away* :—þiss wurld is âweigweard, Shrn. 17, 30.]

**awel.** *Add* : , es ; *m.* :—Awel *arpago*, Wrt. Voc. ii. 100, 78 : *fuscinicula*, 109, 31 : *tridens*, 122, 64. Awele *fuscinicula*, An. Ox. 7, 378. Þirlie hê his eáre mid ânum æle (*subula*), Ex. 21, 6. Man sceal habban . . . awel, Angl. ix. 264, 7. Awelas *fuscinicula*, Wrt. Voc. ii. 34, 60. Awlas *angulae*, An. Ox. 46, 43. Awlum *uncis*, Germ. 393, 110. v. awul, æl, eal *in Dict*.

**â-wemman** ; *p.* de. I. *to disfigure* :—Decennovennalis . . . ys gecîged of þrym âwemmedum dǽlum (*component parts altered from the forms of the original words*), þ ys of *decem* and *novem* and *annalis*, Angl. viii. 325, 17. II. *to defile* [:—þ mîn sâwle ne seó âwæmmod Hml. A. 172, 63]. v. un-âwemmed, -lic, -ness, *and next word*.

**â-wemmendness**, e ; *f. Corruption* :—Geseón âwemmendnysse *uidere corruptionem*, Ps. L. 15, 10.

**â-wênan** ; *p. de To consider* :—Âhwênende *existimantes*, R. Ben. I. 4, 12.

**â-wendan.** *Add*: I. *trans. To turn*. (1) *to give a certain direction to* :—Hê âwende eów fram Drihtne, Deut. 13, 5. Hê âwende hine sylfne tô Gode, Chr. 1067 ; P. 201, 34. Hû se deófol tô mislicum synnum heora môd âwende, Hml. S. 16, 222. Uton âwendan ûrne willan tô Gode, 28, 174 : Ælfc. T. Grn. 6, 29. (I a) *to return* :—Hê âwende his swurd intô ðǽre sceáðe, Hml. Th. i. 482, 32. (I b) *to reduce, bring into subjection* :— Darius âwende ealle Assirîæ eft tô Perséum *Darius Assyrios bello recuperavit*, Ors. 2, 5 ; S. 78, 6. (2) *to turn aside*, (a) *to remove, divert* :—Ðâ sunnan âwende of hiere stede, Bt. 19 ; F. 70, 4. Hê âwende ðæt swurd of ðâm wæge mid ealle, Hex. 28, 8. (b) *to avert* :—Mid his upstige se cwyde ûre brosnunge is âwend, Hml. Th. i. 300, 6. (c) *to pervert* :—Âwendende þâs ûre dômas, Ll. Th. i. 102, 11. Âwended *vitiatum*, Wrt. Voc. ii. 123, 63. þâ Dænescan þe wæs ǽrur geteald eallra folca getreówast wurdon âwende tô þǽre mêste untrîwðe (*became perverts to faithlessness*), Chr. 1086 ; P. 221, 30. (3) *to change* :—Stôwe hê âwent (*non mutabit*, Lch. i. 151, 16. Hig noldan nâ feohtan mid fægerum wordum ânum, swâ þæt hi wel sprǽcon and âwendon þæt eft so *that they spoke well and then did not act in accordance with their words*, Ælfc. T. Grn. 11, 29. þâ sceolcn habban þrittig nihta ealdne mônan bûton hyt âwende se embolis-

mus, Angl. viii. 312, 7. Ic ne mæg âwendan (*immutare*) Godes word, Num. 22, 18. Æfre on æfen byð his (*the moon's*) ylde âwend, Angl. viii. 309, 17. Âwende môde *mutata mente*, Past. 39, 22. Gelîcost þâm þe monna heortan âwende wurden, Ors. 5, 15; S. 250, 30. (4) *to turn* into something else, *transform* :—Drýmenn âwendon ûre dohtor tô myran, Hml. S. 21, 482. *Metaplasmus, þæt is* âwend spræc tô ôðrum hîwe, Ælfc. Gr. Z. 294, 18. Âwendre *transfigurati*, An. Ox. 158. Tô duste âwende, Hml. Th. 1, 72, 6. Cweð tô ðisum stânum þæt hî beón âwende tô hlâfum, 166, 14. (5) *to translate, reproduce* something with other material, (a) of language :—Sê þe âwent of Ledene on Englisc, æfre hê sceal gefadian hit swâ þ þ Englisc hæbbe his âgene wîsan, Ælfc. Gen. Thw. 4, 8. Rædinga þe wê âwendon, Angl. viii. 333, 9. Hî (*interjections*) ne mægon nâht eáðe tô ôðrum gereorde beón âwende, Ælfc. Gr. Z. 280, 1. (b) of statuary :—Deófla anlícnysse gê âwendað on âre and on stânum, Hml. S. 8, 60. (6) *to exchange* :—Hwâ âwent môdignysse mid sôðre eádmôdnysse, oððe hwâ druncennysse mid sýfernysse, bûtan strece ?, Hml. Th. i. 360, 4. Heó âwende *mutarit* (*bona corporis animi virtute*), An. Ox. 8, 261. **II.** *intrans. To turn, take a certain direction* (lit. or fig.) :—Þû eart of eorðan genumen, and þû âwenst tô eorðan. Þû eart dust, and ðû âwentst tô duste, Hml. Th. i. 18, 17. Hê âwent tô eorðan, Hml. S. 25, 263. Ne âwoendað (*redeant*) on bæcc, Lk. L. 17, 31. Ðæt teóðe werod âwende on yfel, Hml. Th. i. 10, 18. Ðâ gyldenan gyrda eft tô þan ærran gecynde âwendon, 68, 19. Somnite âwendan on ôþre wîsan *Samnites novum habitum sumentes*, Ors. 3, 10; S. 138, 30. Âwoended wæs *reversa est*, Lk. L. 1, 56. Âwoend woeron *reversi sunt*, 10, 17. [Goth. us-wandjan *to turn aside*: O. H. Ger. ar-wenten *avertere, reducere, immutare*.] v. un-âwended, -âwendende.

**â-wendedlic.** *Add* :—Gesceaft brosniendlic and âwendedlic (*capable of change*), Hml. Th. ii. 270, 8. Swurd âwendedlic (-endlic, *v. l.*) *gladium versatilem*, Angl. vii. 30, 286. *Mobilia* (*pronomina*), þæt is âwendedlice (-endlice, *v. l.*) fram cynne tô cynne, Ælfc. Gr. Z. 94, 13 : 20, 3, 9. v. un-âwendedlic.

**â-wendedlicness,** e; *f. Changeableness, mutability* :—Ælc gesceaft is ýdelnesse underðeód, þæt is, âwendedlicnysse, for ðan ðe hî beóð âwende fram brosnunge tô unbrosnunge, Hm. Th. ii. 206, 1.

**â-wendedness.** *Add* :—Hwæt is gôdra manna deáð bûton âwendednys and færr fram deáðe tô ðâm êcan lîfe ?, Hml. Th. ii. 232, 23. Gif hwâ ræde ic bidde þ hê þâs âwændednysse (*translation*) ne tæle, Ap. Th. 28, 18. On âwændednyssum (*commutationibus*) heora, Ps. L. 43, 13.

**â-wendendlic** (v. â-wendedlic). *Add* :—Ðæt ylce swurd wæs âwendendlic *the sword might be turned aside*, Hex. 28, 3. Mid âwendenlicum mêce *romphea versatili*, An. Ox. 1151. God âna unâwendendlic wunaþ and eallra ðâra âwendendlicra welt *rerum orbem mobilem rotat, dum se immobilem conservat*, Bt. 35, 5; F. 166, 10. v. un-âwendendlic, -lîce.

**â-wendendness,** e; *f. Changeableness, change* :—Ýdelnys † âwendendnys *vanitas*, Ps. L. 38, 6. Âwendennessa *permutationes*, An. Ox. 191.

**â-wending.** *Add* :—Âwendincg *subversio*, Scint. 188, 4 : *inmutatio*, 225, 15.

**â-wenian.** *Add* :—Hî unwære men beswîcaþ and âdwellaþ and hî âweniaþ from Godes gemynde, Bl. H. 61, 24. Âwende *suspenderat*, Wrt. Voc. ii. 121, 62. Âwæned cild *ablactatus*, Ps. L. 130, 2. Awened, Ps. Srt. 130, 2.

**â-weódian.** *Add* :—Ær man âweódige þâ unriht and þâ mânweorc þe man wîde sæwð, Wlfst. 243, 19. Ælc unriht bêtan and unweód âweódian and gôd sæd âræran, 73, 2.

**â-weorpan.** *Add* : **I.** *lit. to throw, cast, cause rapid* or *violent movement of a body.* (1) the agent personal :—Hê ût âwearp þâ sceomolas and þâ setl, Bl. H. 71, 18. Hê þone ealdan feónd on helle grund âwearp, 87, 20. Bûtan man ðâ mædene âwurpe of þâm bûre, Hml. S. 35, 69. Daniel wæs âworpen þâm leónum, Ælfc. T. Grn. 10, 4. Þæt hê wurde âworpen dâm here, Hml. Th. ii. 502, 14. (2) the agent not a person :—Se stranga wind hî on þ land âwearp, Chr. 1075; P. 209, 37 : 1009; P. 138, 26 note. Weard hê âdûne âworpen of his horse, Gr. D. 14. 17. **I a.** *to throw away* :—Heó âwearp þâ cartan, Hml. S. 3, 640. **I b.** *to throw up* food :—Þonne se man mete þigð, þonne âwyrpð hê eft, Lch. ii. 204, 9. **II.** *fig.* (1) of change in condition :—Heó on þis wræcwîte âworpen wæs, Bl. H. 5, 26. (2) *to throw off, free one's self from* :—Of him selfum âweorpan ðâ ðiôstro his môdes, Bt. 35, 6; F. 166, 26. (3) *to cast out, expel* :—Âwearp *expulit*, Wrt. Voc. ii. 146, 38. Ût âweorp ð(û) *ejice* (*derisorem*), Kent. Gl. 824. Þâ setl þe deófol of âworpen wæs, Bl. H. 121, 35. Hie hæfdun hiera cyning âworpenne, Chr. 867; P. 68, 19. (4) *to reject, cast away* or *off, renounce,* (a) with person as object :—Âwerpeð *exetratur*, An. Ox. 56, 89. Gif wîf âwyrpð hire âgenne wer, Hml. Th. ii. 324, 1. Ic hæne (*Saul*) âwearp, 64, 5. (b) object not a person :—Manege þâra þe mê ne lícodon ic âwearp, Ll. Th. i. 58, 19. Hî âwurpon þâ ealdan dysignesse *abjecta prisca superstitione*, Bd. 4, 13; Sch. 419, 13. Ne âwearp ðû *ne abjicias* (*disciplinam*), Kent. Gl. 37. Ælcne hæðendôm âweorpan,

Ll. Th. i. 166, 12. Âworpenne *reprobatum*, An. Ox. 40, 6. (5) *to cast down, trouble* :—Mâgos âweorpð *propinquos abjicit* (troubleth his own flesh, A. V.), Kent. Gl. 368. Bið âworpen *dejicitur* (*spiritus*), 518. Âworpenra *dejectior*, Wrt. Voc. ii. 140, 3. [Goth. us-wairpan *to cast out, off*: O. H. Ger. ar-werfen *e-, de-, re-jicere*.]

**â-weorpan.** *Add* :—Âwyrþ *tabescit*, An. Ox. 5487. Âworden *bigener*, Wrt. Voc. ii. 126, 19. ¶ in Northern Gospels = ge-weorþan :—Forð âwordað *peribunt*, Mt. L. 26, 52. Âwærd † gewærð *facta*, 13, 21. Âwarð (giwarð, R.), Mk. L. 15, 33. Ðte âworðe † þte hiú sê âworden *fieri*, Lk. L. 21, 31. The p. p. occurs frequently.

**â-weosung.** *Add* :—Âweosung *subsistentia*, Wrt. Voc. ii. 88, 60.

`â-werd.` *l.* â-werde, *and dele* = a-wered . . . a-werdan: **a-wergian.** v. â-wirgan.

**â-werian. I.** *Add*: (1) *to defend* against attack :—Þâ burg âwerede þæt folc þe þær binnan wæs, Chr. 921; P. 101, 9. Hié þâ ceastre âweredon, 885; P. 78, 12 : Ors. 4, 13; S. 210, 33. (2) *to protect* from hurt, *secure* :—Wê âweriað ûs mid þære segene, âweriað eów mid þære lâre fremminge, Hml. Th. ii. 402, 26. Wê willað âwerian ûs, Ll. Th. ii. 364, 13. (3) in the phrase *land âwerian*, v. werian, III c : —Hê mid his scette âwerede ðæt land, C.D. vi. 183, 10. [O. H. Ger. ar-werren.] â-werian, **II.** v. â-wirgan, â-werian, **III.** v. next word.

**â-werian** *to wear out* :—On sumera seó cûle sceal beón þynne oððe eald âwered, R. Ben. 88, 12.

**â-wêstan.** *Add* :—Ômm and moððan hit âwêstað *aerugo et tinea demolitur*, Hml. Th. ii. 104, 30. Âwoestun *desolaverunt*, Ps. Srt. 78, 7. Âwêstan *grassari*, An. Ox. 5343. Hî woldon âwêstan þâ Iudêiscan, Hml. S. 25, 386. Þâ burg âwêstan, Ors. 2, 7; S. 90, 14. Se cyng lêtt âwêstan þ land âbûtan þâ sæ, Chr. 1085; P. 216, 4. Þæne âwêstendan deófol, Angl. viii. 330, 25. Âwêstendum *populantibus*, An. Ox. 2715. Gehwilce ænlîpige sind mid færlicum slihte âwêste, Hml. Th. i. 124, 10. [O. Sax. â-wôstian: O. H. Ger. ar-wôsten *vastare*.]

**â-wêstedness,** e; *f. Desolation* :—Lâ hû sint hig gewordene tô âwêstednysse (*in desolationem*), Ps. L. 72, 19. v. â-wêstness.

**â-wêstend,** es; *m. A devastator, destroyer* :—Þone âwyrgedan engel þone men âwêstend hâtað, Wlfst. 200, 19.

**â-wêstness.** *Add*: *destruction, devastation* :—Hûses âwêstnes, Lch. iii. 168, 16. Âwêstnesse his gôda ðæt tâcnað, 176, 5. v. â-wêstedness.

**â-widlian;** *p.* ode. **I.** of physical impurity, *to contaminate, defile, pollute* :—Sê ðe âwiht þicge þæs ðe hund âwîdlige (*inquinaverit*), Ll. Th. ii. 216, 10. Be âwîdledum swýnum *de inquinatis porcis*, 130, 31. **II.** of moral impurity, *to profane, pollute* :—Âwîtlieude *profanando* (*pudicitiae jura*), An. Ox. 2743. Tunge mîn mid ælcere leásunge ys âwîdlud (*profanata*), Angl. xi. 117, 41. v. un-âwîdlod.

**â-wiht.** *Add* : , ô-wiht, ôht. **I.** substantive (1) alone :—Him þær ôwiht ne derede, Dan. 274. (2) with governed gen. :—Ne sceþþeð þê wôlberendes âwiht, Lch. i. 326, 19. Ne mæg ðæs unrihtes beón âwiht bedîgled, Bl. H. 111, 1. Ær þon ôht þisses æfre gewurde, Cri. 238. Unc ne gedælde nemne deáð âna ôwiht elles, Kl. 23. Nâge hió his ierfes ôwiht (âwuht, *v. l.*), Ll. Th. i. 66, 19. Gif hê æfre þæs organes ôwiht cûðe, Sal. 33. Heó ôwiht swylces ne hýrdon, El. 571. Ymbe ôwiht elles, Seef. 46. Æniges teónan ôht ongitan, Gr. D. 35, 27. Ôht (âht, ænig þing, *v. ll.*) wundorlices wyrcan, 45, 5. **I a.** predicate subst. or adj. *any good, good for anything* :—Deófol môt ælces mannes âfandigan, hwæðer hê âht sý oððe nâht, Hml. Th. i. 268, 12. Hwæðer heora geþanc âht sý, Wlfst. 11, 13. Þâ þe âhte syndon, hî sculon beón ofslagene, 295, 14. **II.** oblique cases used adverbially :—Nis þæt ôwihtes gôd *it is no good*, Dan. 429. Âtes-hwôn (v. nâtes-hwôn) *ullatenus*, Angl. xiii. 434, 987. Âreccan fier ôwihte *to recount any further*, Cri. 248. Leng ôwihte, 343 : An. 801. Lâðra ôwihte, B. 2432. Gif man þæt fýr sceal tô âhte âcwæncan *if the fire is to be effectually extinguished*, Wlfst. 157, 9. Ealle þâ ðe Crýst âwyht cûðon, Hml. A. 188, 208. Heó nân land hæfde þe him âht tô gebyrede *that in any way belonged to him*, Cht. Th. 337, 23. Wê sculon ôðrum mannum âht fremian *we shall somewhat benefit other men*, Ll. Th. ii. 8, 5, 1; Sch. 551, 16. Nâhwær næs nænigu smêþnes þ man mihte âht tô þan lytelne wyrttûn gewyrcan *ad quemlibet parvum hortum excolendum nulla patebat planities*, Gr. D. 49, 4. v. nâ-wiht, *and* âht, â-wuht *in Dict.*

**â-wildian.** *Add* : **I.** of persons :—Sume synd tô mândæde on dyrnlican gâlscipe inne âiðlode and ûte âwildode, Ll. Th. ii. 322, 15. **II.** of uncultivated growth :—Gif se wîngeard ne bið on hrade gesceádod, ne bið hê wæstmbære, ac for hrade âwildað, Hml. Th. ii. 74, 15.

**â-wilian.** v. â-wilw(i)an.

**â-willan.** *Substitute for references* Wrt. Voc. i. 290, 45, 56 : ii. 25, 69, *and add* :—Âwyl on sûrum ealad, Lch. ii. 34, 14. Âwylle on buteran, 17. Þonne hit beó æne âwylled, iii. 14, 15. On âwyldum ealað, ii. 114, 11.

**â-wille** (-ân-?, on-?); *adv. Boldly*; *procaciter*, Wrt. Voc. ii. 66, 43.

**â-wiltan;** *p.* te. **I.** *to roll* (trans.) :—Huâ eft † âwæltes (-wælte,

R.) ûs ðone stān *quis reuoluit nobis lapidem?*, Mk. L. 16, 3. Se engel āwylte þæt hlid of ðære þrýh, Hml. Th. i. 222, 8. Engel eft āwælte (*revolvit*) ðone stān, Mt. L. 28, 2. Hē āwælte (*aduoluit*) ðone stān tō ðær dura, Mk. R. 15, 46. Eft āwælted *reuolutum*, 16, 4. II. fig. *to harass, molest :*—In lytlum āwælteto *in paucis vexata*, Rtl. 86, 22. [*O. H. Ger.* ar-walzen *a-, con-, de-, e-vellere, revolvere.*] v. ā-wyltan *in Dict.*

ā-wilw(i)an; *p.* -wilede. *To roll* (trans.) :—Ængel āwælede (*revolvit*) þone stān, Mt. R. 28, 2. Sume wyrhtan āfundon ðone stān and hine āweg āwiligdon, Hml. Th. ii. 426, 2. Gesaeh þ stān genumen ł āuæled (*sublatum*) of ðæm byrgenne, Jn. L. 20, 1.

ā-windan. *Add:* I. *trans. To twist, plait, weave :*—Āuundun *intexunt*, Txts. 68, 507. Āwunden, Wrt. Voc. ii. 45, 49. Āuunden *torta*, Txts. 100, 985. Āuundenre suipan *verbere torto*, 104, 1051. Hrægl of olfenda hærum āwunden, Bl. H. 169, 2. Hróf mid gyrdum āwunden *culmen uirgis contextum*, Bd. 3, 10; Sch. 234, 6. Ðý āwundenan ryfte *plumario*, Wrt. Voc. ii. 77, 15. Āwundne *contexta*, 20, 31. Āwundene, An. Ox. 254. II. *intrans.* (1) *to slip away :*—Ūt āwundene gylt oþþe ūt āslidene synne *prolapsum nefas*, Germ. 388, 58. (2) *to become weak* (?) :—þā handa āwindaþ (-swindaþ? v. ā-swindan), þā þe ǽr hæfdon ful hwǽte fingras, Wlfst. 148, 3. [*Goth* us-windan *to plait : O. H. Ger.* ar-wintan *reverti, redire.*]

ā-windwian. *Add:*—Wē beþurscon ûre fýnd and āwindwedan, Ps. Th. 43, 7.

ā-winnan. *Add:*—Gié we wunnon, óðero āwunnon (*laboraverunt*), Jn. R. 4, 38. [*O. Sax.* ā-winnan *to gain : O. H. Ger.* ar-winnan *lucrari, vindicare.*]

ā-wirdan. *Add to* ā-wyrdan *in Dict.:* I. *to corrupt, spoil,* (1) a material object :—Gif ealo āwerd sié, Lch. ii. 142, 10. Gif mete sý āwyrd, 14. Āwyrd wīn *defrutum*, An. Ox. 4, 6. Heó weóp for ðære āwyrdan lǽne (*the broken sieve*), Hml. Th. ii. 154, 17. (2) a non-material object :—Se dióful ðæt mód āwiert (*corrumpit*), Past. 415, 24. Sé þe his āgene sprǽce āwyrt, hē wyrcð barbarismus, Angl. viii. 313, 19. Ðing swā mǽre þæt man ne mæg ðǽron ǽnig ðing āwyrdan, fulluht and hūslhālgung, Wlfst. 34, 5. Tó āwyrdenne *deprauandum*, An. Ox. 4493. Hyra regol ne sý ā ðe āwyrdra, Wlfst. 269, 14. II. *to injure, annoy, afflict a person :*—Ðā ilco ðone āwoerdon mið teáncuidum *illi hunc afficientes contumelia*, Lk. L. 20, 11. þæt wē (*devils*) hí (*men*) mid mislicum untrumnyssum āwyrdon, Hml. Th. i. 462, 21. Ne mæg þē nān man āttre āwyrdan, Lch. ii. 110, 11. Sāwel āwoerðedo *animam afflictam*, Rtl. 5, 24. Wē bidon āwoerdedo *affligimur*, 42, 27 : 23, 32 (*printed* -woend-). Āwoerdeno (-do?) *afflictos*, 40, 29. III. *to hinder :*—Ne wallað hiá āwoerda (werda, R.) *nolite eos uetare*, Lk. L. 18, 16. v. wirdan, ā-werde, un-āwirded.

ā-wirding, e; *f. Corruption, blemish :*—Āwyrdingum *maculis*, Hpt. Gl. 421, 57.

ā-wirdness. *Add to* ā-wyrdnys *in Dict.:* I. *corruption, blemish :*—Līchaman unbrosnigendlicne būtan eallum wommum and būtan āwyrdnysse, Hml. A. 45, 522. Ðā ðe tō Godes ríce gebyrigað nabbað nāðor ne womm ne āwyrdnysse on heora līchaman, Hml. Th. i. 236, 31. II. *injury, annoy, affliction :*—'Būton wē ðære sāwle derian magon, ðā līchaman þurhwuniað on heora āwyrdnysse.' Hē cwæð : 'Hū becume gē tō ðære sāwle āwyrdnysse?', Hml. Th. i. 464, 1-4. þonne bið geðúht swilce wē hí gehǽlon, ðonne wē geswícað ðæra āwyrdnyssa (cf. gedreccednysse, l. 25), 462, 27.

ā-wirg(e)an. *Add:*—Āwyrigdon *devotabant, pro male dicebant,* An. Ox. 2807. Āwerigdun (ōwoerigdon, L.) ł miscwēdun him *maledixerunt ei*, Jn. 9, 28. Āweredon ł tēldon ðā óðoro *aspernabantur ceteros*, Lk. L. R. 18, 9. Men habbað heó sylfe swyðe stranglíce wið God āwerged and wið his hālgan, Wlfst. 207, 9. ¶ the most frequently occurring form is the *pp.* used as adjective :—Se āwyrgeda *malignus*, Ps. Spl. 14, 5. Ðā costunga ðæs āwiergdan (-wirg-, *v. l.*) gāstes, Past. 268, 19. Hiera āwiergdan weorc, 268, 19. Āwoergedo (-wærgede, R.) *maledicti*, Mt. L. 25, 41. Āuoergado (-werged, R.), Jn. L. 7, 49. On gewill ðāra āwiergedena (-wierdena, *v. l.*), Past. 248, 23. Mid āwyridum gāstum *furiis, i. malignis spiritibus*, An. Ox. 4666. Ic geseah ðā āwyrigedan sceoccan, Hml. Th. i. 68, 1.

ā-wirgedlic. *Add to* āwyrgedlic : v. ā-wirgendlic.

ā-wirgedness. *Add to* ā-wyrgednes :—Seó āwyrgednes ofer eów wunað, H. R. 7, 21. Būton bletsunge, mid deófles āwyrigednysse, Hml. Th. i. 100, 33. Būtan āwyrgodnysse, Hml. A. 45, 522 note. Geheald þíne tungan fram āwyrgednyssum, Wlfst. 246, 14.

ā-wirgende; *adj.* (*ptcpl.*) *Execrable :*—þ ic beó gewrecen on þǽre āwyrigendan Gezabel, Hml. S. 18, 324.

ā-wirgendlic. *Add to* ā-wyrgendlic :—Hí heom betwýnan āwyrgendlic (-wyrged-, *v. l.*) geþeaht worhton, Hml. A. 185, 133.

ā-wirgung, e; *f. A curse :*—þām gelamp seó āwyrigung þe se wítega cwæð, Hml. S. 15, 115.

ā-wirpan; *p.* te *To recover* from illness :—Fǽrlíce āwyrpte se ādliga cniht, Hml. Th. i. 534, 28.

ā-wlacian; *p.* ode *To grow lukewarm :*—Hí on þām frumwylme heora gecyrrednesse hý sylfe fulfremede taliaþ, ac hý swíþe recene āwlaciaþ (*continuo tepefacti*), R. Ben. 135, 6. Þe lǽs þe þǽre hālgan ǽfestnesse welm āwlacige and mid ealle ācólige, Lch. iii. 442, 20.

ā-wlǽht *glosses* decolor, Germ. 397, 366 (=? āwlǽtt. v. *next word*).

ā-wlǽtan. *Add: To make loathsome, disfigure, pollute.* (1) physical :—Āwlǽtende *deturpans, i. foedans* (*elephantino tabo*), An. Ox. 3586. Fúlíce āwlǽt *turpiter deformatur* (*splendida argenti species*), 449. Āwlǽtte *deformatos* (*neuorum maculis*), 650. Hine ǽt se cancer and his weleras wǽron āwlǽtte mid ealle, Hml. S. 6, 285. (2) moral :—Ic mid sweartum synnum mīne sāwle āwlǽtte, Angl. xiii. 113, 53. Ðās gyltas ne magon ūre sāwle ofsleán, ac hī magon hī āwlǽtan, Hml. Th. ii. 590, 29. Āwlǽttre *pollutae, oblitae*, Germ. 397, 466.

ā-wlancian; *p.* ode *To grow haughty, insolent :*—Āwlancige *insolescat, i. superbiet*, An. Ox. 1159.

ā-wlencan; *p.* te; *pp.* ed *To make proud, splendid, rich, &c.* v. wlanc :—Hié āwlencedo sié ł giwoelgado *ditentur*, Rtl. 59, 1.

ā-woffian. *Add:* I. *to be or become mad :*—Amens byð āwoffod, Angl. viii. 331, 41. Āwoffod *freneticus*, An. Ox. 4668. Gif hwylc gedwola oððe āwoffod man, Hml. S. 1, 20. II. *to become insolent :*—Āwolfige ł woffie *insolescat, superbiat*, Hpt. Gl. 461, 56 : An. Ox. 2350.

ā-wōgian; *p.* ode *To woo :*—Ðā foreward ðe Godwine worhte wið Byrhtríc þā hē his dohter āwōgode, Cht. Th. 312, 11 : Hml. S. 7, 14, 299 : 9, 58.

ā-wōh. *Add:*—Beorge þ hē āwōh ne befó, Ll. Th. i. 290, 8. Cf. on wōh *under* wōh ; *n.*

ā-wolfian. v. ā-woffian.

ā-wordenness, e; *f. Weakness, worthlessness :*—Āwordenes *enervatio*, Kent. Gl. 1172.

ā-worpenlic. *Substitute: Worthy of rejection* or *reprobation :*—Ðæt líf byþ āworpenlic *vita reprobatur*, Past. 409, 36.

ā-worpenlíce; *adv. Vilely;* viliter, An. Ox. 2736.

ā-worpennes. *Add:*—Āworpennesse *reprobatione*, An. Ox. 40, 6. v. āweg-āworpenness.

ā-wrǽnan *to make* wrǽne (q.v.) :—Gif mon sié tō unwrǽne, wyl on meolce þā ilcan wyrt, þonne āwrǽnst þū, Lch. ii. 144, 21.

ā-wrǽstan. *Add:*—Āwrǽste *extorsit*, Wrt. Voc. ii. 32, 47.

ā-wrecan. *Add:* I. *to drive away :*—Āwrecen sý *expellatur*, Wrt. Voc. ii. 146, 4. II. *to strike :*—Būtan his heorte sý eall mid deófles strǽlum āwrecen, Wlfst. 214, 13. Āwrecenum, tōgedýddum *adacto*, Wrt. Voc. ii. 3, 54. IV. *to avenge :*—Hū hí mihton þæs cynges bismer āwrecan and ealles þeódscipes, Chr. 1048 ; P. 174, 8.

ā-wreccan. *Add:* I. *to raise up :*—Gemiltsa mīn and āwrecce (*resuscita*) mē, Ps. Spl. 40, 11. II. *to arouse,* (1) from sleep :—Heó gemētte þæt cild slǽpende and hit āwrehte, Hml. Th. i. 566, 18. þū mē āwrehtest, 23. Hine āwrehte Godes engel, Hml. S. 18, 162. Āwrǽhte (-wrehte), 15, 62. Man hí āwreccan ne mihte, 35, 69. Mid gehlýde hine āwreccan, Hml. A. 113, 361. Of slǽpe āwreht, Hml. Th. i. 60, 19. Wurdon ðā óðre āwrehte mid þām sange, ii. 518, 30. (2) from death :—Ðū āwrecst ðā deádan, Hml. S. 24, 93. Beóð ealle āwrehte of þæs deáðes slǽpe, Hml. Th. ii. 568, 33. (3) referring to the mind, *to arouse, excite,* (a) a person :—Se apostol ūs āwrehte þæt wē of slǽpe ūre āsolcennysse ārison, Hml. Th. ii. 568, 30. Āwrece ðe sylfne tō mīnre sprǽce, Bas. 34, 3. Hē his mód āwrecce of gedwyldum, Hml. A. 53, 74. Wæs āwræht ł āwæht swylce slǽpende Drihten *excitatus est tamquam dormiens Dominus*, Ps. L. 77, 65. (b) a feeling, energy, &c. :—Āwræc (*excita*) þíne mihte, Ps. L. 79, 3. þ hí āwræccan ne magon mid heora plegan ǽnige gálnysse, Hml. S. 35, 65.

ā-wreón. *Take here the passages given under* ā-wríhan, -wríohan, dele -wreóhan, -wríohan, and add: p. -wrāh, pl. -wrigon; pp. -wrigen :—Be þære deópnysse þe him Drihten āwreáh, Ælfc. T. Grn. 13, 1. Swefne sint gewisse, nelle þū āwreón, Lch. iii. 186, 19. On āwrigenre béc *in apocalypsi*, An. Ox. 5178. ¶ in the Lindisfarne Gospels the verb means *to cover :*—Wē āwrigon *cooperuimus*, Mt. 25, 38. Āwrigon gié *operuistis*, 43. Āwrigon *uelauerunt*, Lk. 22, 64. Āwuriáð *operite*, 23, 30. Āwriá *operit*, 8, 16. Āwrigen *uelatum*, 9, 45 : *opertum*, 12, 2. Fore āwrigen *obscuratum*, 23, 45.

ā-wreþian. *Add:* with dat. acc. :—Hē þære ýtemestan yldo his lífes mid medmiclum hlāfe and cealde wætere āwreþede *ultimam uitae aetatem pane cibario et frigida aqua sustentat*, Bd. 5, 12 ; Sch. 630, 20.

ā-wrídian; *p.* ode *To spring, descend :*—Of þām sunum weard onwæcnad and āwrídad eall manna cynn, Angl. xi. 2, 38. Of him weard āwrídad twā and hundseofontig þeóda, 45.

ā-wrigennes. *Add:*—Swā hē geseah on ǽr þurh Godes āwrygennysse, Hml. S. 3, 102.

ā-wringan. *Add:*—Ic of āwringe *extorqueo*, Ælfc. Gr. Z. 155, 17. Hāwiað hū bóceras āwringað up þæne saltus on heora cræfte, Angl. viii. 314, 12. Āwrang *expressit*, Wrt. Voc. ii. 145, 58. þonne hió gesoden sié, āwring þā wyrt of, Lch. ii. 30, 24 : 18, 13. Ele āwringan of byrgum, Gr. D. 250, 22. Tó āwringenne *exprimendos* (*racemos*), Wrt. Voc. ii.

79, 74. Wîn of berium âwrungen, Hml. Th. ii. 268, 10. Fîfleáfe âwrungenu, Lch. ii. 110, 19. Æscþrotu âwringen þurh clâð, 36, 20. Betonican seáw gebeátenre and âwrungenre, 30, 4.

**â-writ, es;** *n. A writing :*—Ðerh alle âwriotto *per omnes scripturas,* Rtl. 113, 22. Cf. ge-writ.

**â-wrîtan.** *Add :* **I.** *to write out* or *down, write words :*—Âurîtteð ł âurât (*scribebat*) on eorðe, Jn. L. 8, 6. Heora ælces naman âwrît (*superscribes*) on his girde, Num. 17, 2. Âwrîtt, eádgo deádo *scribe, beati mortui,* Rtl. 48, 5. Wê ne magon swâþeah ealle naman âwrîtan, ne furþon geþencan, Wrt. Voc. i. 86, 74. 'Nelle ðû âwrîta (-urîtte, L.) cyning Iudêana ' . . . Ondsuorade ðe groefa : 'þte ic wrâtt (âurât, L.) ic wrât (âurât, L.), Jn. R. 19, 21-2. Wæs âwriten (-uritten, L.) on Crêcisc, 20. Hira naman hêr sint âwritene, Num. 13, 5. Bôca mid golde âwritenra, Bt. 5, 1; F. 10, 18. **II.** *to transcribe, copy in writing :*—Bidde ic, gif hwâ þâs bôc âwrîtan wylle, þæt hê hî geornlîce gerihte be þære bysene, Hml. Th. i. 8, 10. **III.** *to state in writing :*—Swâ holde þ hié on monegum templum âwriten, þ ælc crîsten mou hæfde frið . . . and Antonius hêt forbærnan þ gewrit þe hit on âwriten wæs hwæt mon on geáre âgiefan sceolde, Ors. 6, 13; S. 268, 18-23. Hit is âwrieten on ðæm godspelle ðæt . . . , Past. 403, 1. **IV.** of authorship, *to write a book, letter, &c.* :—Âwrât *elicuit* (*tractatus*), Wrt. Voc. ii. 31, 58 : *edidit* (*opusculum*), 85, 82 : *digessit* (*librum*), 91, 48. Monige godspellas âwritton, Mt. p. 7, 1. Þæt hê âwrite *tenuisse* (*oraculorum seriem*), Wrt. Voc. ii. 77, 66. Hié næron on hiora âgen geðióde âwritene, Past. 5, 13. **IV** a. where quotation is made :—Swâ swâ âwrât *ut* (*Psalmista*) *cyrografatur,* An. Ox. 2789. Moses âwrât, Mk. L. R. 12, 19. **IV** b. *to write of* or *about something :*—Be þâm ic âwrát on ôðrum gewrite, Ælfc. T. Grn. 2, 20. Hê âwrât be heora misdædum, Wlfst. 166, 17. Swindrige of ôðrum âwuritun, Mt. p. 11, 9. Wille wê be him âwrîtan, Chr. 1086; P. 219, 18. **IV** c. *to write to :*—Gesegen wæs mê ðê âwrîto (-urîtta, L.), Lk. R. 1, 3. **V.** *to write an account of, describe :*—Þæs cyn is beforan âwriten, Chr. 716; P. 42, 13. Hæbbe wé âwriten þære Asian sûðdæl *meridianam partem Asiae descripsimus,* Ors. 1, 1; S. 14, 5. (*Subst. this for quotation in Dict. from Bos.* 17, 42.) Âwriten wæran *pinguntur* (*in tomo castae praeconia vitae*), Wrt. Voc. ii. 95, 42. **VI.** *to inscribe the name of a person :*—Wê wæron âdîlegode of þâm frumgewrite þe wé tô heofenum âwritene wæron, Wlfst. 252, 13. Hig wæron âwritene *ipsi descripti fuerunt,* Num. 11, 26. **VII.** *to write on material, cover with writing :*—Þæt hê Alexandres wîsan besceáwade, swâ hê hit him eft hâm bebeád on ânum brede âwriten, and siþþan hit âwriten wæs hê hit oferworhte mid weaxe *virum ad perscrutandos Alexandri actus, qui omnia civibus suis per tabellas scripta ; et post cera superlitas enunciebat,* Ors. 4, 5; S. 168, 14. **VIII.** *to make a symbol* other than a letter :—Þâ âwrât hê Crîstes rôde tâcen on þæs blindes mannes eágum, Gr. D. 77, 26.

**â-wrîþan.** *Add :* **I** :—Âwrîðeð (*alligat*) forðræstnisse heara, Ps. Srt. 146, 3. Genim sceápes mearh, lege on þ ôþer mearh, âwrîþ swîðe wel, Lch. ii. 96, 1 Gif þú ne mæge blôddolh âwrîþan (*staunch*) . . . lege þ dust on clâð, wrîþ mid þý þ blôddolh. Gif þú geótendædre ne mæge âwrîþan . . . lege on þâ ædre þ dust and âwrîð swîþe, 148, 12-19. **II.** *for awrîðe, l.* âwriðe, *and add :*—Âwrîþe (*or* -wrîþe ?) *soluret* [*altered from soluat*], Bl. Gl.

**â-writting, âwðer, â-wuht, awul.** v. in-âwritting, â-hwæðer, â-wiht, awel.

**â-wuldrian;** *p.* ode *To glorify :*—Âuuldrad wæs (*glorificatus est*) se Hælend, Jn. L. 12, 16. Âwuldrad sié *glorietur,* Rtl. 79, 30.

**â-wundrian.** *Substitute :* **I.** *to wonder, be astonished :*—Ic âwundrode *mirabar,* Gr. D. 244, 13. Âwundrode eall se lîchama in þâm wîfum *omne in eis corpus obrigesceret,* 284, 21. Âwundradon *mirabantur,* Lk. L. 1, 21 : 4, 22 : *mirati sunt,* 8, 25. Âwundrad wæs *miratus est,* 7, 9. þ hê woere âwundrad *ut miraretur,* Mk. L. 15, 5. Âwundrade woeron, *mirati sunt,* Lk. L. 2, 18 : *ammirati sunt,* 48 : 11, 14. **II.** *to wonder at, admire, magnify :*—Âuundradon God *magnificabant Deum,* Lk. L. 5, 26. ¶ *in* El. 581 âwundrad *seems corrupt; Zupitza* suggests âwended.

**â-wunian.** *Add :*—Ic stille and swâ swâ deád âwunade . . . ic swîgende eall þâ niht âwunade *quietus et quasi mortuus permanens . . . tacitus tota nocte perduro,* Bd. 5, 9; Sch. 578, 6-11. Heó ðær âwunode þone dæg and ðâ niht on hire gebede, Hml. A. 121, 145 : Guth. 34, 15. Seó beorhtnys þær âwunode oð dæg, 86, 22. Seó studu gesund âstôd and âwunade (*remansit*), Bd. 3, 10; Sch. 234, 16. Þâ brôhton bân ûte âwunedon (*permanerent*), 3, 11; Sch. 237, 1. Þæt hî on þâm geleáfan âwunedan (*persistere curarent*), 2, 17; Sch. 181, 14. Wê geâxiaþ nænig gôd âwunigende, Bl. H. 109, 2.

**â-wyllan, -wyltan, -wyrdan, -wyrgan** (*to curse*), **-wyrpan.** v. â-willan, -wiltan, -wirdan, -wirgan, -wirpan (*and* -weorpan).

**â-wyrcan.** *Add :*—Ænne tîman gebîdan, þonne ûs wære leófre þonne eall þ on middangearde is, þ wê âworhtan Godes willan, Ll. Th. i. 370, 19. Ælces unnyttes wordes hié sculon ryht âwyrcean (*reddent rationem*), Past. 281, 10. [*Goth.* us-waurkjan : *O. H. Ger.* ar-wurchen.]

**â-wyrgan** *to strangle.* *Add :*—Hê (*Judas*) þonan gangende âwyrgde (mid sâde âwrigde, L.) hine *abiens laqueo se suspendit,* Mt. R. 27, 5. Hê forgiet ðæt grin ðæt hê mid âwierged wirð (*stranguletur*), Past. 331, 19. Fugelas and ôðre nŷtenu þâ þe on nette beóð âwyrgede (*strangulantur*), Ll. Th. ii. 162, 18.

**â-wyrn.** *Substitute :* v. â-hwergen.

**â-wyrtwalian.** *Add :* **I.** *to pluck up* or *out by the root,* (1) lit. :—Onweg âcorfenum þâm tungum swylce hî âwyrtwalode wæron *abscissis radicitus linguis,* Gr. D. 241, 12. (2) fig. *to extirpate, eradicate, exterminate :*—Ic âwyrtwalie *extirpo* (*gaudia carnis*), An. Ox. 186, 26. Âwyrtwalað *exterminabit* (*viam peccatorum*), Bl. Gl. Âwyrtwala grædignysse of ðînre heortan, Hml. Th. ii. 410, 1. þ man âwyrtwalige æghwylc unriht, Ll. Th. i. 376, 9. **II.** *to pluck, draw away :*—Hê âwyrtwalað (*evellet*) of gryne fêt mîne, Ps. L. 24, 15. Sió slæwð ûs âwyrtwalað from ælcre lustbærnesse gôdra weorca, Past. 283, 4.

**â-ȳtan.** *Add :*—Âȳtte *eliminarat,* i. *expelleret,* An. Ox. 4080. Ðonne ârîseð þeód wið þeóde and hié beóð þonne âȳtte fram heora gemærum (quoted in note to preceding).

# B

**bacan.** *Add :*—þú erast and sæwst ; þú grinst and bæcst, Hml. Th. i. 488, 25. Sê þe hine hlâf baceð, Wlfst. 212, 27. In þâm ofne þâ wîf bôcon heora hlâfas, Gr. D. 251, 26. þæt man breád bace, Wlfst. 296, 8. þâ oflætan þe gê sylfe bacen, Ll. Th. ii. 404, 35. Hlâf bacan *panes coquere,* 160, 26. Ofen wæs gegearwod tô þon þ man wolde on bacan, Gr. D. 219, 12. v. asc-, eald-, ele-, ge-, heorþ-bacen.

**bâd.** *Add :* **I.** *a pledge :*—Be bâdum, Ll. Th. i. 354, 5. **II.** *expectation, waiting :*—Hwet is bâd (*expectatio*) mîn ?, Ps. Srt. 38, 8. Hê generede mê of þære bâde (*expectatione*) Judêa folces, Gr. D. 107, 26. For þære bâde his ændes, 282, 10. Hit neálæhte þære tîde his deáþes . . . Hine þâ on þære sâwle bâde (*while the soul expected its departure*) âcsode his wîf, 301, 25.

**bâdere.** v. nîd-bâdere, *and next word.*

**bâdian.** *Add :*—Tô gemôte hê côme ofþe hine man bâdode *he should come to the meeting or a fine might be exacted of him* (? cf. iii gemôt on geáre bûton hê hit gebicge oþþe gebidde, 433, 33), Cht. Th. 432, 32. Cf. bædan.

**bæc, bec;** *m. n.* : bæce, bece ; *m.* : bæc(c) ; *f. A beck, brook.* The word, which seems to occur only in lists of boundaries in charters (except in wîl-bec?), appears with varying gender and declension. (1) bæc ; *m.* :—In baka brycge ; of baka brycge, C. D. iii. 386, 15. In ðâ bakas ; of ðâm bakan, 382, 7 : 386, 11. (2) bæc, bec ; *n.* :—On ðæt heówbec ; andlang heówbeces, C. D. iii. 135, 16. On ðæt heówbæce ; of ðâm heówbæce, v. 358, 22. On ðæt bec ; ðonne andlang ðæs becæs ; of ðæm bæce . . . tô ðâm eástran bæce ; ðonne andlang bæces, 207, 16-20. On þ bec ; siþþan andlang beces, on Tæmese, 294, 27. (3) bece, bæce ; *m.* :—In Coddan hrycges bece ; andlang beces, C. D. iii. 461, 21. In wynnabæce ; of wynnabæce . . . in foxbæce ; of foxbæce, 386, 9, 16. Ymbe heáfca bæce ; of þan bæce, 121, 16. In earna bæce ; andlang bæces . . . æft on earna bæce, v. 121, 4, 11. In beka brycge ; of becha brycge (cf. 386, 15 *above*), iii. 382, 11. On ðâ lytlan becas . . . ; of grindlesbece, 80, 4. (4) bæc(c) ; *f.* :—On cyrtwara bæc ; andlang cytwara bæcce (cf. in another copy of the same boundaries :—Of citwara beca . . . on citwara mearce ; andlang bæces tô citwara becon, v. 358, 7, 27), C. D. iii. 135, 23. (5) uncertain :—In wynnabæces gemŷdan ; of wynnabæce, C. D. iii. 382, 5 : v. 297, 31. Andlang burgbeces, vi. 43, 19. Andlang ðæs beces ; of ðâm bece, iv. 68, 25. Tô ðâm bæce ; of ðâm bæce, vi. 234, 29. Tô gafærbæce (gaferbice, 302, 33), v. 306, 28. In cærsa bæc ; of ðâm bæce, iii. 380, 2. ¶ in one passage the word occurs apparently as fem. and masc. in the same line :—On cnollan gæte in ðâ (ðâm ?) diópan bæce ; of ðâm diópan bæce, C. D. iii. 460, 26. [*O. H. Ger.* bah : *Icel.* bekkr. These forms point to an English bece.]

**bæc.** *Add :*—Bæc *tergum,* Wrt. Voc. i. 44, 31 : *terga,* 65, 19 : 283, 44. Se hund tôtær his hæteru of his bæce, Hml. Th. 374, 9. Hê byrð byrðene on his bæce, 212, 5 : 336, 16 : Angl. xi. 112, 23. Him forburnon on þâm bæce his reáf, Hml. S. 31, 865. Hê hine scêt bæftan his bæce, 18, 336. Wæron his handa tô his bæce gebundene, Hml. Th. i. 466, 27. Heó wæs cumende æfter Drihtenes bæce (*post tergum Domini*), Bd. 1, 27 ; Sch. 82, 2. On ûrum bæcum, R. Ben. 27, 17. In scyldrum ł bæccum *in humeros,* Mt. L. 23, 4. ¶ *add to* Ll. Th. i. 156, 6 *the other version :*—Mid rihte faran, l. 9. ¶ phrases giving direction or position :—Hî him on bæce filigdon *persecuti sunt eos,* Jos. 7, 5. Under bæce *retrorsum,* Ps. Spl. 34, 5. Ðæt môd him on bæc lêt (*turned its back on*) þâs gewîtendlican þing, Gr. D. 4, 14. Hê him on bæc sette þâ lâre Benedictes, 135, 29.

**bæc-bord;** *n.* (not *m.*). *Add :*—Hê lêt him þâ wîdsæ on ðæt bæcbord, Ors. 1, 1 ; Swt. 17, 11, 27 : 19, 17, 25, 30. On bæcbord him wæs Langaland, 35. [*Icel.* bak-borði, -borð *larboard.*]

bæce *posteriora*, Wrt. Voc. i. 44, 63. v. ge-bæcu.

bæcere. *Add:*—Bæcere, hwǣm fremaþ cræft þīn, oþþe hwæþer būton þē wē magon līf ādreógan?, Coll. M. 28, 25. Hwæt cunnon þās þīne gefēran? Sume synt . . . bæceras, 19, 9.

bæcere *a baptist*. v. bæzere.

bæce-ring. *Substitute:* bæcering, es; *m. A gridiron:*—Bæcering *craticula*, Wrt. Voc. ii. 136, 53 : 42, 6.

bæc-ern. *Add:*—Bæcern *pistrina*, lytel bæcern *pistrilla*, Wrt. Voc. i. 58, 39, 40 : *pistrinum*, 83, 13. Þ ealle neódbehēfness, þ is wæter, myll, orceard, bæcern (*pistrinum*), oððe mistlice cræftas wiðinnan minstre beón gegānne, R. Ben. I. 112, 15. Ðæs bæcernes tācen is þæt mon snīd bām sāmlocone handum tōgædere, swilce þū dāh brǣdan wille, Tech. ii. 128, 4. Kycenan and bæcernes (*pistrinae*), Angl. xiii. 441, 1087. On kycenon oþþe on mynstres bæcerne, R. Ben. 71, 18.

bæcestre. *Add:*—Bæcestre *pistor*, Wrt. Voc. i. 83, 15. Hē becom tō þām ofne, in þām þā wīf bōcon heora hlāfas. þā lōcode hē in þone ofn, wēnunga hwylc hlāf ðǣr tō lāfe wunode æfter þām bæcestrum (*coquentibus*), Gr. D. 251, 27.

bæcling, -linga. *Add:*—Ðā gehýrde ic swēg mē on bæcling, Bd. 5, 12; S. 628, 29. Ðā gehýrde ic ðone biscop mē on bæclinga cweþan, 5, 6; S. 619, 13. v. on-, under-bæcling.

bæc-slitol. *Add:*—Sē ðe wǣre bæcslitol, weorðe sē wǣrsagol, Wlfst. 72, 16.

bæc-þearm. *Add:*—Baecþearm (becdermi) *exta, praecordia*, Txts. 61, 801. Bæcþearm *anus*, Wrt. Voc. i. 65, 35 : ii. 8, 4 : *extale*, 145, 30. Wiþ leahtras ðæs bæcþearmes, Lch. i. 294, 15. þā wambseócan men þrowiað on þām bæcþearme, ii. 232, 13. þurh bæcþearm blōd dropað, 278, 6. Gif hē on hire bæcþerm hǣme *si in tergo ejus coiverit*, Ll. Th. ii. 148, 7.

bǣdan. *Substitute for passages:*—Baedde *exactum*, Wrt. Voc. ii. 108, 9. Bǣdde, 30, 16. I. *to urge, press, compel, impel:*—Bǣdt *inpulerit*, Wrt. Voc. ii. 46, 28. Beadætþ (= bǣdeþ) *angarizaverit* (= *angariaverit*, Mt. 5, 41), 72, 17. Ðonne ðā sācerdas tō weorðunga ūres Āliesendes ne bǣdað (*exigunt*) ðā ðe him underðiedde bioð mid hira līfes geearnungum, Past. 135, 10. Mǣru cwēn bǣdde byre geonge (cf. v. 1182), B. 2018. Hió unc bǣddan tō gemangum *they urged us to marry*, Shrn. 40, 29. Stinge finger on mūð, bǣde tō spīwanne (cf. nēde hine tō spīwanne, l. 17), Lch. ii. 286, 20. Baeden(d)re, baedendræ, bēdændræ *inpulsore*, Txts. 71, 1100. Bǣdendre, Wrt. Voc. ii. 48, 79. Com hē tō mē bǣdendre uncre lufan (*caritate exigente*), Gr. D. 248, 16. Bǣdendum þām nýde þæs ylcan hungres *exigente ejusdem famis necessitate*, 251, 17. Wǣron wit bǣdde þ wit sceoldon hig wurþian, Shrn. 38, 21. II. *to require, exact* (with gen.):—þæs his lufu bǣdeð *love for him requires that*, Gn. Ex. 100. þā gebrōðra woldon þæs hūses wāh hwēne hērran getimbrian, forþon þæs swā sum neódþearflicu wīse bǣdde (*quia res ita exigebat*), Gr. D. 124, 23.

bǣd-dæg *glosses* epiphania, Rtl. 2, 1.

bǣdde. *Dele, and see* bǣdan.

bæddel (bǣddel?). *Add:*—Bæddel *andreporesis*, i. *homo utriusque generis*, Wrt. Voc. i. 17, 38. v. N. E. D., s. v. bad.

bǣdel. *Dele:* bǣdend. v. bǣdan.

bǣde-wēg. *Add:*—Ðā hī him betweónum bǣdewēg (beadowig, *v. l.*) scencton þæs heofonlican līfes *dum sese alterutrum caelestis uitae poculi debriarent*, Bd. 4, 29; Sch. 528, 13.

bǣdling (bǣd-?). *Substitute:*—*An effeminate person;* mollis (= qui alterius fornicationem sustinet):—Sē ðe mid bǣdlinge (*cum molli*) hǣme, oððe mid ōðrum wǣpnedmen, fæste .x. winter. On ōðre stōwe hit cwyð . . . sodomisce .vii. geár fæston. Gif se bǣdling mid bǣdlinge (*mollis cum molli*) hǣme, Ll. Th. ii. 228, 13–17. Bǣdling *cariar*, Wrt. Voc. ii. 129, 6. *Effeminati, molles* oððe bǣdlingas, 29, 7. Cf. bæddel.

bǣdling *tabellarius. Dele:* bǣdzere. v. bæzere : bǣfta; *m. Dele, and see* bæftan.

bæftan. *Add:* I. *prep.* (1) *local:*—Hē hine scēt bæftan his bæce, Hml. S. 18, 336. Bæftan þǣre healle, 36, 97. Oft cymð sē bæftan ūs þe ūs forestæpð, Hml. Th. ii. 82, 17. (2) *marking inferiority:*—Nis heora nān māre þonne ōðer, ne nān lǣssa ðonne ōðer; ne nān beforan ōðrum, ne nān bæftan ōðrum, Hml. Th. i. 287, 5. II. *adv.* (1) *behind,* (a) *in contrast with* before (lit. or fig.):—Ic geseah þone bæftan þe mē geseah *I saw him behind that saw me*, Gen. 16, 13. Ne ǣnig man ōþerne bæftan ne tǣle *let not any man backbite other*, Wlfst. 70, 14. Ælc ōðerne bæftan werige, Ll. Th. ii. 316, 19. Hē weard gebunden bæftan tō his bæce, Hml. S. 31, 155. (b) *in contrast with* advance *along with,* as in *to leave* behind:—þā tungelwītegan fērdon, and þā bōceras bæftan belifon, Hml. Th. ii. 108, 11 : Chr. 1050; P. 169, 20. Hē lēt þǣr bæftan Titum and forð seglode, Hml. S. A. 190, 274. (2) *after:*—þāra noman hēr stondað āwritene bæftan, C. D. B. ii. 267, 12. v. hēr-bæftan, be-æftan.

bæftian. v. hand-bæftian, beaftan.

bǣl. *Add:*—Bǣl *focus*, An. Ox. 17, 49. *Pyre* bēle, *id est* fýr, Wrt. Voc. ii. 82, 42. Bǣla *pyrarum*, 85, 39. On bǣl gearu, B. 1109. On bǣl dōn, hladan, āhebban, 1116 : 2126 : Gen. 2903.

bǣl-blǣse. *l.* -blǣse : bǣl-blys. *l.* -blyse (?); *m.* -blysu (?); *f.* (*the word occurs only in the acc.:*—In bǣlblyse gesyllan, scúfan). Cf. blysian.

bælca, balca (-e ?), an; *m.* (*f. ?*). *Some kind of wooden fetter* (? cf. D. D., s. v. balk, 'a wooden frame for securing the cow's head while being milked'):—Mistlice þreála gebyriað for synnum, bendas oððe dyntas, lobban oððe bælcan, Ll. Th. ii. 278, 27. þā Regulus hī swīðost forslagen hæfde, ðā hēt hē hī bindan and on balcan lecgan *Regulus plures Poenorum bello captos in vincula conjecerat*, Bt. 16, 2 ; S. 37, 8.

bælcan *to cry out. Add:* Cf. bealcan; (or ?) *to boast*, cf. bælc : bæeldu. v. bildu : bǣl-þræc. *l.* -þracu.

bǣnen; *adj. Of bone:*—Tēð sind bǣnene, Hml. Th. i. 532, 6 : Lch. iii. 104, 5. v. elpen(d)-, ylpen-bǣnen.

bær; *adj. Add:*—Bær *without clothes*, Rä. 32, 22. Bare (*nudam*) rōde bar (*nudus*) folgaþ, Scint. 218, 15. Hē læg on þǣre baran flōra, Hml. S. 31, 853. Wīsdōm geseón bærne, Shrn. 186, 30. Hine lyst bet cyssan ōðerne on bær līc þonne þēr þær clāðas betweónan beóð, 185, 31 : 186, 1. Hē eóde ofer byrnende glēda mid his barum fōtum, Hml. S. 5, 378. Hē tōbræc hire ceaflas mid his barum handum, Ælfc. T. Grn. 7, 17.

bǣr. *Add:* I. *a bier:*—Līc cadaver, bǣr feretrum, Wrt. Voc. i. 85, 55. Hī hreopode þā bǣre . . . Seó bǣr ðe þone deádan ferode, Hml. Th. i. 492, 26. Geneálǣcað ðǣre bǣre, 372, 6. Ofer þā bǣre þe his līc on wæs, Gr. D. 329, 23. II. *a litter,* &c.:—Beer *basterna*, Wrt. Voc. ii. 101, 43 : 10, 64. Hē sīðode on fōtum ðe on bǣre þider geboren wæs, Hml. Th. i. 150, 15 : Hml. S. 21, 398. þā þe under þā bǣre (*feretro caballario*) gesette wǣron, Bd. 4, 6; Sch. 383, 1. Bēre *pillentes* (pilens = pilentum), Wrt. Voc. ii. 117, 34. v. bed-, hors-bǣr, and bēr, beer *in Dict.*

bǣr, e; *f. A pasture* (?):—Ðis is seó bǣr ðertō hýrð, C. D. v. 179, 33. Ðis synt ðā gemǣra ðā[ra] bǣra ðe hiérað tō Hwītancirican, Fiscesburnan, and Felghyrste, 173, 25. Cf. den-, weald-bǣre.

bǣran. *Substitute:* bǣran. v. ge-bǣran : bær-beáh, *dele, and see* bær : baercǣe. v. bearce : bǣr-disc. *Add:* Wrt. Voc. i. 82, 65.

bǣre, es; *n. Gesture, movement:*—Bǣrum *gestibus*, An. Ox. 45. Styllum bǣrum *quietis lapsibus*, Germ. 400, 487. v. ge-bǣre.

-bǣre, es; *n.* v. den-, weald-bǣre.

-bǣre; *adj. Add:* ātor-, blōstm-, deáþ(-d)-, fiþer-, fýr-, gim-, hunig-, līg-, tungol-, þūf-, wīg-, wudu-bǣre, *and see* beran *in Dict.*

bǣren. v. beren : bǣrende *dele:* bær-fisce *see next word.*

bær-fōt. *Add:*—Deóplic dǣdbōt bið þ lǣwede man weallige bærfōt wīde, Ll. Th. ii. 280, 18. Nime hē stæf him on hand and gā bærfōt, 286, 20. Cume manna gehwilc bærefōt tō circan, Wlfst. 181, 1. Bǣrfisce (-fōt ?) *nudapes*, Wrt. Voc. ii. 62, 19.

bær-līc, es; *m.? Substitute:* bær-lic; *adj. Of barley:*—Of hlǣwe tō bærlice crofte, C. D. vi. 79, 10. [þ acersǣd hwǣte . . . þ (acersǣd) bærlic . . . þ acersǣd āten, Chr. 1124 ; P. 254, 15.]

bær-līc; *adj. Open, public:*—Bærlic *publicam*, Lk. p. 3, 8. [*Icel.* ber-ligr.]

bær-līce. *Add:* *plainly, manifestly, publicly:*—Bærlīce æteáwdon *declarant*, Mt. p. 7, 4. Bærlīce æteáwas *perspicue ostenditur*, 10, 8. Bærlīce ðū sprecest *palam loqueris*, Jn. L. 16, 29. Ne on dæge hāligum ł bærlīce *non in die festo*, Mk. L. 14, 2. [*Icel.* ber-liga.]

bǣr-man. *Add:*—Hē hreopode ðā bǣre, and þā bærmenn ætstōdon, Hml. Th. i. 492, 25 : ii. 150, 13. Hē beád him þ hī þ deófolgild ne bǣron nā furðor . . . and þā bærmen sōna stedefæst stōdon, Hml. S. 31, 374.

bǣrnan. *Add:* I. *to expose to the action of heat:*—Hý leomu rǣcað tō bærnenne synna tō wīte, Cri. 1622. Bærned *vel* gehyrsted *frigi*, Wrt. Voc. ii. 150, 77. I a. *to cauterize:*—Se lǣce cyrfð oððe bærnð, and se untruma hrýmð, Hml. Th. i. 472, 15. þ hine mon lǣde tō þām rīcum þ mon þǣr mæge snīþan and bærnan his unþeáwas, Bt. 38, 7 ; F. 210, 3. II. *of a lamp, to cause to give light:*—þ gē wacian mid mē and wē bærnan gāstlico leóhfato, Bl. H. 145, 4. III. *to consume by fire:*—Ic folcsalo bærne, Rä. 2, 5. Gif man ōðres wudu bærne, Ll. Th. i. 70, 4. Swā se byrnenda swefl ðone munt bærnþ, Bt. 16, 1 ; F. 50, 5. Hý hergiað and bærnað, Wlfst. 163, 12. Mann hergode and bærnde, Chr. 1014 ; P. 145, 20. Hī ǣlc þing bærndon and slōgon þ hī gemētton, 997 ; P. 131, 9. Beorndon, 870 ; P. 71, 10. Swā þā bærne þornas fýre, Ps. Th. 117, 12. Hē ongan bærnan sum deófolgild, Bl. H. 221, 6 : B. 2313 : Dan. 242. Mul wærð on Cent bærned, Chr. 687 ; P. 39, 34. v. breneþ.

bærne-lāc. v. berne-lāc *in Dict.*

bǣrnes. *Add:* bærn-ness:—Hē þ tācen þǣre bærnnesse (*signum incendii*) on his sculdre bær, Bd. 3, 19; Sch. 281, 13. Hī bærnesse gefeoht timbredan *incendia bellorum struere*, Sch. 280, 2.

bǣrnett. *Add:* I. *burning, cauterizing.* v. bærnan, I a :—Lǣce-dōm *medicina*, bærnet *arsura vel ustulatio*, Wrt. Voc. i. 74, 6. Mid bærnette gelācnian, Hml. Th. i. 472, 14. Hātum bærneytte *torrido cauterio*, An. Ox. 1983. Hāliga gewrita lācnunga, and āmānsumunge bærnet (*ustionem*), R. Ben. 52, 13. I a. *of the effect of cold:*—

Wið cile bærnettes *frigore exustis*, Lch. I. 228, 23.   II. *a burn :—* Wæs þæt bærnet þe hē gelæhte æt ðām were on his sculdre gesewen, Hml. Th. ii. 346, 25.  Gif hwā forbærned sȳ . . . lege tō þām bærnette, Lch. i. 216, 16.  Bærnytte (-ette, *v. ll.*), 298, 13.   III. *burning heat :*—Hātum bærnete *torrido chaumate* (*solis*), An. Ox. 3244.  Bærnette, swoleþe *chaumate*, i *ardore*, 3779.   IV. *consuming by fire :*— Be wuda bærnette, Ll. Th. i. 70, 3.  Hī wrohton þ mæste yfel on bærnette and hergunge, Chr. 994; P. 129, 6.  Hē hēt gearcian ðā tunnan tō heora bærnette, Hml. S. 4, 301.  Hē hēt hī forbærnan, ac þā bān belifon æfter þām bærnette, 11, 261.  Isaac bær ðone wuda tō his āgenum bærnete, Hml. Th. ii. 62, 22.

**bærning.** *Add :*—Ongan seó bryne (sió bærning, *v. l.*) beón gebīged in hī sylfe *coepit incendium in semetipsum retorqueri*, Gr. D. 48, 6. Hwæþer sȳ ān helle fȳr, þe manige bærninge (*incendia*) sȳn gegearwode, 333, 14.  Gedrecednessa on hergunga and on bærninge, Chr. 1104; P. 239, 16.

**bærn-īsen, es;** *n. A branding-iron;* cauterium, An. Ox. 7, 113.

**bærs.** *Add :*—Baers (bers (r *above the line between* e *and* s)) *lupus*, Txts. 74, 592.  Bærs, Wrt. Voc. i. 66, 2: 281, 65.  Bears, ii. 51, 21.

**bærstlung, bærwe.** v. brastlung, bearwe.

**bær-synnig.** *Add :*—Bærsynig (bearswinig, R.), Lk. L. 18, 10. Bærsuinnig, Mt. p. 8, 7.  Ðone bærsynnig *publicanum*, Lk. L. 5, 27. Bærsynnigo *publicani*, 15, 1.  Bærsuinnigo, Mt. L. 5, 46.  Bærsuinniho, 9, 10.  Bærsunigo, Mk. L. 2, 15.  Ðāra bærsynnigra *publicanorum*, Mt. p. 16, 1.  Bærsuinnigra, Mt. L. 11, 19.  Barsynnigum *publicanis*, Mk. L. R. 2, 16.  v. bear-, beor-swinig *in Dict.*

**bæst.** *Substitute for the quotation :*—Lind *vel* baest (best) *tilo*, Txts. 102, 1017.

**bæswi.** *Dele, and see* basu.

**bǣtan.** *Substitute :* I. *to bait, worry* with dogs, &c. :—Gif ðū mid wilddeórum mē bǣtan wylt, Hml. S. 8, 85.  [*Icel.* beita *to bait, hunt* with dogs, &c.]   II. *to beat, make way against the wind* or *current :*— Good scipstióra ongit micelne wind on hreóre sǣ ǣr ǣr hit geweorðe, and hæt fealdan þ segl, and eác hwīlum lecgan þone mæst and lǣtan þā bǣtinge; gif hē ǣr þweores windes bǣtte, warenað hē hine wið ðæt weder *a good pilot perceives a great wind on a rough sea before it comes on him, and orders the sail to be furled, and also sometimes the mast to be lowered and to leave off beating ; if he have before in an adverse wind beat, he guards himself against the storm*, Bt. 41, 3; S. 144, 28-32.  [*Icel.* beita *to go against the wind.*]

**bǣtan;** *p.* te *To spread a covering, to saddle* a horse :—Bǣttan *straverunt* (*vestimenta sua*, Mt. 21, 8), Wrt. Voc. ii. 73, 7.  Ongan his esolas bǣtan (*stravit asinum suum*, Gen. 22, 3), Gen. 2866.  Cf. Hē þ gebǣte (-el, *v. l.*) of āteáh *stramine subtracto*, Bd. 3, 9; Sch. 230, 4. Mid þām cynelican gebǣtum *stratus regaliter*, 3, 14; Sch. 257,14.  Of boetingum ūsum *de cubilibus nostris*, Rtl. 37, 1.

**bæþ.** *Dele* II, *and add :* I. *a bath* for washing :—Bæþ (*balnearum usus* baða brice, R. Ben. I. 68, 1) þām untrumum swā oft swā hit framige ; hālum and hūru þām geongum sȳ seldor and lator getīdod, R. Ben. 60, 22.  v. pænningas tō beðe (=bæðe?) *five pence for the expenses of the bath* (?), Cht. Th. 509, 19.  On bæðe *in thermas*, Wrt. Voc. ii. 95, 76.  Hwæt wille ic mā cwæðan be mete oððe be drince oððe be baðe (*de balneis*), Shrn. 183, 30.  Þ hē ne cume on wearmum bæðe, ne on sōftum bedde, Ll. Th. ii. 280, 22.  Þolige hē cold bæð, 284, 5.  Þær wæron gehæfde hāte baðu, Hml. Th. i. 86, 21 : Hml. S. 2, 397 : Ruin. 41 : 46.  Baþa hȳ næfre brūcaþ for heora līchoman luste, R. Ben. 137, 9.  Æt baða gehwylcum, Ph. 110.  Baða *thermarum*, An. Ox. 2, 384.  Baþena, 4777.  Baþu wið blǣce, Lch. ii. 8, 2. Wyrc baþo, 68, 3.   I a. *of baptism :*—'Gif gē willað āþwegene beón ðȳ hālwendan wylle fullwihtes bæðes (*fonte salutari*) . . . Gif gē līfes bæð (*lauacrum uitae*) oferhicgeaþ . . .' 'Wē ne willað on ðæt bæð (*fontem*) gangan,' Bd. 2, 5; Sch. 134, 13-19.  Hī hiene bǣdon ryhtes geleáfan and fulwihtes bæðes *they asked him for the true faith and baptism*, Ors. 6, 34; S. 290, 27.  Hraþe þæs þe hī of þām fulwihtes bæþe eóde, þā fæstte hē, Bl. H. 27, 24.  Onfón fullwihtes bæð, An. 1642 : El. 490.   I b. *of the sea, the bath* of fish or sea-fowl :— Ofer fisces bæð *across the sea*, An. 293: Rūn. 16.  Ofer ganotes bæð, 25 : B. 1861 : Edg. 46.   II. *of immersion that is intended to torment.* v. baþian, I b :—Sē hēt āfyllan āne cyfe mid weallendum ele . . hē (*John*) ungewemmed of ðām hātum bæðe eóde, Hml. Th. i. 58, 29. Baðe, Ælfc. T. Grn. 16, 20.  Belūcan on byrnendum baðe, Shrn. 150, 1.   III. *of* blood poured out (cf. *Ger.* blut-bad) :—Him heortan blōd, fāmig flōdes bæð, foldan geséced, Sal. 157.  v. ælmes-, heáfod-, stān-, stuf-bæþ.

**bæþ-ærn, es;** *n. A bath-house :*—Be bæðernes tācne, Tech. ii.126, 18.

**bæþ-fæt, es;** *n. A bath :*—Bæðfæt, Angl. ix. 264, 16.

**bæþ-hūs.** *Add :*—þā healle and þā ōþre gebytlu bæftan þǣre healle, bæðhūs and kycenan, Hml. S. 36, 97.

**bæþ-sealf, e;** *f. A salve to be used when taking a bath :*—Lǣcedōmas wiþ āslāpenum līce and bæþsealf, Lch. ii. 12, 17 : 302, 23.

**bæþ-stede.** *Add :*—Hē bær iungra manna plegan on handa tō ðām

bǣðstede belimpende and cliopode : 'Gehȳre gē . . . se bǣðstede is open' Ap. Th. 12, 17-21.

**bæþþan.** v. beþian : **bǣting.** *Dele : A cable*, &c., *and see* bǣtan.

**bæzere.** *Add :*—Bæcere *baptista*, Rtl. 56, 13, 25, 31 : 67, 36.  Bæchere, 56, 9.  Bæðcere, Mt. p. 14, 3.  v. bæstere *in Dict.*  [From Latin through Celtic.]

**balsam, balzam.** *Add :*—Balsames blǣd *carpo balsamum*,Wrt. Voc. ii. 128, 72.  Balzaman smiring, Lch. ii. 174, 7 : 288, 12.

**bān.** *Add :*—Bān os, Wrt. Voc. i. 44, 22 : 70, 46.   I. *bone :*— Þū eart mīn bān and mīn flǣsc, Gen. 29, 14 : Ps. Th. 138, 13.  Ne bān ne blōd, Dōm. 40.  Þæt gafol bið on hwales bāne, Ors. 1, 1 ; S. 18, 17. Hié habbað swīþe æþele bān on hiora tōþum, 17, 36.  Hrepa his bān and his flǣsc *tange os ejus et carnem*, Hml. Th. ii. 452, 19 : Ph. 221. I a. *of other hard material :*—Sió ecg gewāc on bāne (*the hide of the firedrake*), B. 2578.  Wæter wearð tō bāne (*ice*), Rä. 68, 3.   II. *a bone :*—Bānes byrst, Ps. Th. 108, 18: Gū. 670.  Gif man findeð ān bān unforbærned, Ors. 1, 1 ; S. 21, 12.  Gif hwā mid his fēt ofstepð ǣttrig bān snacan oððe næddran, Lch. i. 152, 2.  Hwær sint nū þæs Wēlondes bān ?, Bt. 19 ; F. 70, 5.  Ne synu ne bān lāgon, An. 1421. Þā gebrocenan bān, Ps. C. 81 : Hy. 7, 88.  Bāna *ossuum*, Kent. Gl. 571 : Ph. 575.  Manna bān *ossa hominum*, Ps. Th. 52, 6.  Bānu handlian, Lch. iii. 208, 24.   II a. *the bone of a limb, a leg* or *arm.* v. bān-beorg, -geborg. -rift :—Bān weornedon *their limbs failed them*, Sat. 468.  Bāna *coxarum*, Wrt. Voc. ii. 17, 66 : 75, 27.  Wǣron þā bendas forburnene, þ him on bānum lāgon, Dan. 435.  Fȳrdraca heals ealne ymbefēng biteran bānum, B. 2692.  v. heáfod-, hleór-, hring-, scin-, sweor-, wiþo- (*not* wīdo) -bān.

**bana.** *Add :* Used of a weapon with which death is caused :—Ne wæs ecg bona *he was not slain by the edge of the sword*, B. 2506. Heardrēde hildemēceas tō bonan wurdon *falchions were the death of Heardred*, 2203.  v. flǣsc-, mæsser-, sācerd-, self-bana.

**bān-beorgas ;** *m. Substitute :* bān-be(o)rg, e ; *f. A greave :*—Bān-beorgum *ocreis*, Wrt. Voc. ii. 63, 31.  Bānberge *ocreas*, 97, 35.  [*O. H. Ger.* pein-perga *ocreas*.]  v. bān-gebeorg.

**bān-bryce.** *Add :*—Bānbryce on heáfode, Lch.ii. 8,28.  Bānbrice, 92, 6.

**banca.** v. hō-banca : **bān-cōfa.** *l.* -cofa : bān-cōða, -cōþ, -cóþu, -cōþe.  *l.* -coþa, -coþu : **banda.** *Dele :* banden. v. un-banden.

**bān-ece, es;** *m. Pain in the thigh.* v. bān, II a :—Wið bānece, Lch. i. 252, 1 : ii. 68, 25 : 70, 1.

**bān-fāh.** *l.* bān-fāh *adorned with bone* (of a hall): **bān-gār.** v. bon-gār *in Dict.*

**bān-gebe(o)rg, es;** *n. A greave :*—Baangeberg[um] *ocreis*,Wrt.Voc. ii. 115, 35.  v. bān-beorg.

**bannan.** *Add :*—Man beónn ealle Cantware tō wīgge *expeditio praeparabatur per omnem Cantiam*, Cht. Th. 201, 20.  Hēt se cyning bannan ūt here, Chr. 1048 ; P. 174, 22.  v. next word.

**bannend, es;** *m. A caller, summoner :*—Bodiend, bannend *gerulus*, i. *portitor*, An. Ox. 55.  Bannend *contionator*, 5415 : 2, 465.  Bannendra *contionatorum*, 2321 : 2, 74.

**bannuc, es;** *m. A bannock, cake :*—Healfne bannuc (cf. Wrt. Voc. ii. 79, 21 *where the gloss is* cicel) *bucellam semiplenam*, An. Ox. 2402.  [Cf. *Gael.* bannach.]

**bān-rift ;** *n. A greave :*—Baanrift, -ryft *tibialis*, Txts. 102, 1031. Bānrift, Wrt. Voc. i. 289, 15.  v. rift *in Dict.*

**bān-sealf, e;** *f. A bone-salve, a salve for pains in the limbs :*—Tō gōðre bān-sealfe þe mæg wið heáfodece and wið ealra lyma tȳddernysse, Lch. iii. 12, 23.

**ban-segn.** *Dele. For* bansegn, Wrt. Voc. ii. 10, 76 *read :* ban (=bandum) segn, cf. 101, 57 : ban-snacan, Lch. i. 152, 2 *l.* bān snacan. v. bān, II.

**bān-wǣrc, es;** *m.* (not *n.*). *Add :*—Bānwǣrc *caradrum, dolor ossium*, Wrt. Voc. ii. 128, 83.  [*Icel.* bein-verkr.]

**bān-wyrt.** *Add :*—Bānwyrt *swige*, Wrt. Voc. i. 68, 14 : *viola aurosa et viola purpurea*, 41 : *filia aurisa*, ii. 39, 2.  v. ban-wort in E. D. S. Pub. Dict. of Plant Names.

**bar** *a bear.* *Dele.*

**bār.** *Add :*—Baar *porcus dimisus*, Txts. 110, 1163 : *berrus*, 44, 151. Bār, Wrt. Voc. ii. 11, 2 : 126, 1 : *verrus*, i. 286, 44.  Wilde bār *aper*, tam bār *verres*, 22, 70, 71.  On bāra brōc, C. D. iii. 82, 5.  Bāras fȳran, Lch. iii. 184, 19.

[**barc** *bark :*—Nim horsellenes rōta and eftgewæxen barc and drȳ swȳðe and mac tō duste, Lch. i. 378, 15.  [*Icel.* börkr.]]

**barda.** *Add :* , barþa :—Barþa *navis rostrata* (to be added in Wülck. Gl. 195, 36 ; v. Angl. viii. 451).  Barda, Wülck. Gl. 289, 12.  [*Icel.* barði *a ship, a sort of ram ;* barð *the armed prow of a ship.*]

**Barda,** an; *m. The Apennines :*—Fōr Hannibal ofer Bardan þone beorg, Ors. 4, 8 ; S. 186, 33.

**barian.** *Substitute :* I. *to lay bare, remove a covering :*—Twēgen diáconas barian (*nudent*) þ weofud, Angl. xiii. 417, 749.   II. *to strip, despoil :*—Leóðhatan þe þurh mansylene bariað þás þeóde, Wlfst. 310, 5.  v. ā-, ge-barian.

bar(r)ic(g)e, an; *f.?*:—Barriggae *baruina*, Wrt. Voc. ii. 101, 59. Bericge *baruhina*, 10, 77. Barice *braugina*, 102, 25: *brugina* (printed *brugma*), 127, 29.

bār-spere. *Add*:—Bārspere *venabulum*, Wrt. Voc. i. 73, 44. þeáh hine deófol mid bārspere beótíge tó ofsticianne, Angl. viii. 324, 19. Bārsperum *venabulis*, An. Ox. 737.

barþa. v. barda.

basing. *Add: A mantle*:—Ðes basingc *haec clamys*, Ælfc. Gr. Z. 60, 13. Hē (*St. Martin*) tōcearf his basing . . . þá hlógon ðá cempan ðæs basinges . . . mid ðām basinge gescrýdne, Hml. Th. ii. 500, 25-32: Hml. S. 31, 69-72. Basingce *melote*, An. Ox. 1471: *clamidem*, i. *vestem*, 2117. Mid twifealdum basinge *diploide*, Ps. L. 108, 29. Helias lēt áfeallan his basinge, Hml. S. 18, 290. Hī gemētton ðæra drýmanna basingas, Hml. Th. ii. 488, 24.

bāsnian (*from* bādsnian, cf. bídan). *Add*:—Meotud on mereþyssan bāsnode (*of Christ asleep in the storm*), An. 447. Weras bāsnedon wíteláces weán (*of the people of Sodom just before their destruction*), Gen. 2417.

bāsnung. *Add*:—Of allum bāsnungum *de omni expectatione*, Rtl. 58, 24. v. on-bāsnung,

baso(u), e; *f.*, baso-popig. *Dele, and see* basu.

basu. *Add*: , beasu, beosu:—Baeso, beoso (-u) *finicia*, Txts. 62, 411. Baso, Wrt. Voc. ii. 35, 46, 39, 4. Basu, hæwen (*or ?* basu-hæwen) *indicum*, 49, 55. Beasu *finicium*, i. *coccinum luteris*, 148, 59. Baso popig *astula regia*, i. 66, 65. Mið basewium *purpureo*, Hpt. Gl. 436, 49. Hē wæs gegyred mid baswum godwebbe and hwítum *induebatur purpura et bysso*, Gr. D. 310, 1. Mid baswe godwebbe, Bl. H. 207, 17. v. brún-, reád-, scír-, wealh-, weoloc-, wyrm-basu.

basu-reádian. v. beso-reádian in *Dict.*: baswian. v. ge-baswian:

bat *dele, and see* batt.

bāt *a boat. Dele:* e, *f., in first passage for* Deós, *l.* Ðes, *and add*:—Baat *linter*, Wrt. Voc. ii. 112, 81. Bāt, i. 47, 62: 56, 10: *barca*, An. Ox. 5457: 4, 91. Þríe Scottas cōmon on ānum bāte bútan ǽlcum gereþrum . . . Se bāt wæs geworht of þriddan healfre hýde, Chr. 891; P. 82, 18-22. Flota wæs on ýðum, bāt under beorge, B. 211. On bātes fæðm, An. 444: Bo. 5. Bāte *lembulo*, Germ. 399, 455: *lintre*, Wrt. Voc. ii. 76, 25: 52, 11. Lytle bāte *lintrum*, 52, 12. Bāt *lintrem*, 75, 9: 52, 24: *lembum, naviculum*, i. *ratem*, Wülck. Gl. 254, 25. Hī wurpon hine on þone bāt and reówan tó scipe, Chr. 1046; P. 169, 9. Bāt on sǽwe, Hy. 4, 99.

bāt *food. Dele:* Baðan. *Add*:—Wæs æt Baðum gerēfa, Chr. 906; P. 94, 20.

baþian. *Dele* beði(ge)an, *and add to* I. *v. trans.*:—þ bæð þ scā Maria þ cild on baþode, Shrn. 30, 17. Heó wolde seldhwænne hire líc baðian . . . heó wolde ǽrest ealle ðá baðian þe on ðám mynstre wǽron, Hml. S. 20, 44-7: 11, 151. I a. *with reflex. pron.*:—Swā culfre ðonne heó baðað hī on smyltum wætre, Shrn. 85, 21. ~ Ic mē nǽfre bet ne baðode, Ap. Th. 13, 21. Ðá baþode hē hine on gehálgedum wætre, Guth. 60, 2: Gr. D. 308, 22. Baþige hē hine on swētum wætre, Lch. ii. 244, 17, 23. Ongan hē hine baðian swā swātigne, Ors. 3, 9; S. 124, 30. Heó wolde hī sylfe baðian, Hml. S. 20, 48. I b. *to immerse in a liquid by way of torment*, v. bæþ, II :—On weallendum ele hēt hine baðian, Ælfc. T. Grn. 16, 17. [O. H. Ger. badōn: *Icel.* baðask *to bathe*.] v. ge-baþian.

batian; *p.* ode. I. *of recovery from ill health, to get better*:—Bataþ hē inneweard, Lch. i. 80, 20. Lege on þǽr hit heardige, hnescaþ hyt sōna and bataþ, 84, 4. Gif hrýðera steorfan . . . geót on ðone mūð, sōna hý batigeað, iii. 54, 33. Smire oþ þ batige, ii. 78, 17. Ne mæg him se líchoma batian, 206, 10. Gif hit nelle for þisum lǽcedōme batian, 354, 9. Gefēlde ic mē batigende and wyrpende beón *me melius habere sentirem*, Bd. 5, 6; Sch. 581, 5. II. *of improvement in healthy condition*:—Se fisc . . . swā hine swiðor ðá ýða wealcað, swā hē strengra bið and swiðor bataið, Hml. Th. i. 250, 18. Grasu . . . sumu neát batigað fore, sumu cuelað *herbae, quae haec animalia nutriunt, alia occidunt*, Past. 173, 20. v. ge-batian.

bātian. *Dele:* bāt-swān. *Dele, and see next word.*

bāt-swegen, es; *m. A boatman*:—On Wýcinges bātswegenes gewitnisse, Cht. E. 254, 5.

batt *a bat, club, cudgel*:—Batt *hec claua*, An. Ox. 18 b, 18.

be. *Add*: A. *dat.* I. *local*, (1) *nearness to a point*, (a) *rest*:—Wē be þǽm treówum stōdan, Nar. 29, 24. Caiphan mid þām ōþrum be (bi, *v. l.*) him (*juxta eum*), Bd. 5, 14: Sch. 645, 15. Se healfe mínum hláforde *beside my lord*, By. 318. Heó gesæt big Hǽlendes fótum, Bl. H. 67, 27. (b) *motion*:—Sum man rād be þǽre stōwe (*juxta locum*), Bd. 3, 9; Sch. 229, 20. Forþ bi þǽre eá siglan *to sail past the mouth of the river*, Ors. 1, 1; S. 17, 22. (2) *nearness along a line or surface, by, along*, (a) *rest*:—Hī gelógodon ðá untruman be ðǽre strǽt, Hml. Th. i. 316, 14. (b) *motion*:—Fōr hē be þǽm lande *he sailed along the coast*, Ors. 1, 1; S. 17, 9. Hē eóde be þǽre strǽt, Hml. S. 29, 51. (3) *where local conditions of an action are defined*:—Se here wið feaht ge be wætere ge be lande, Chr. 1016; P. 150,

12. þæt folc eóde be drīum grunde, Hml. Th. ii. 194, 20. Hwæt se wītega him be wege (*by the way, on the road*) sǽde, Hml. S. 18, 241. (4) *marking part handled*:—Sē wæs togen ofdūne be þām þeón and upp be þām earmum, Gr. D. 320, 19. Hē gefēng be eaxle Grendles mōdor, B. 1537. Heó genam hine be feaxe sīnum, Jud. 99. Hē gegrāp sweord be gehiltum, Gen. 2905. II. *temporal*, (1) *of a point of time, by, not later than*:—Ciricsceattas sīn āgifene be Scē Martines mæssan, Ll. Th. i. 104, 9. Be Pentecosten . . . be emnnihte, 262, 20. (2) *of a period, by, during*:—Ge be heora lífe ge æfter heora lífe, Cht. Th. 137, 30. Be Cnutes dæge cinges, 336, 23. (3) *of a period within which an event falls*, (a) *marked by reference to a person then living*, cf. III. 28:—Constantinus be Diocletiane lyfgendum (*vivente Diocletiano*) Gallia ríce heóld, Bd. 1, 8; Sch. 28, 25. þāra landa ðe unc Aðulf forgeaf be Ædelbolde lifiendum, Cht. Th. 485, 33. Gif ceorl ācwyle be libbendum wífe and bearne, Ll. Th. i. 30, 3. Be lifiendre þǽre (þǽre cwenan, Wlfst. 269, 33), 316, 10. Gif hý hit be þan libbendan habban wyllan *if they will have it in their lifetime*, Cht. Th. 491, 25. Gif man mid esnes cwynan geligeð be cwicum ceorle, Ll. Th. i. 24, 9: 406, 6. (b) *by reference to living memory*:—Be manna gemynde *within the memory of man*, Chr. 959; P. 114, 22. III. *in other relations*, (1) *association or companionship, by, with*:—Ne hē nā mā wīfa þonne ān hæbbe ac beó be þǽre ānre þā hwíle þe heó lybbe, Wlfst. 271, 15: Ll. Th. i. 318, 19. Wíf þ bið be ānum were (*vivente viro*), ii. 158, 5. Seó godcundnes mæg beón ungemenged wið ōþre gesceafta . . . ne mæg nān ōþer gesceaft be him selfum bión, Bt. 35, 5; F. 166, 7. (2) *conveyance, by* (in *to send by*):—Hē him onsænde be his cnihtum twā spyrtan, Gr. D. 203, 4. Man þ Rōmgesceot be him sende, Chr. 1095; P. 232, 10. Hē hēt cýðan þām arceb be Ðeódrēde biscop *he sent word to the archbishop by bishop Theodred*, Ll. Th. i. 240, 24. (3) *accompaniment*:—Be hearpan singan, Lk. 7, 32: Bd. 4, 24; S. 597, 6. (3 a) *marking accompanying circumstances*:—þ hē be leáfe ōðer wíf niman mōte *quod cum venia aliam uxorem ducere possit*, Ll. Th. ii. 190, 2. (4) *assistance*:—Gif hē gangan mæge bi stafe *if he can walk with a stick*, Ll. Th. i. 48, 10. (5) *marking presence*:—Dǽle man be scriftes and be tūnes gerēfan gewitnesse, Wlfst. 181, 6. (6) *subject to*:—Siððan ic mē hæfde þás þing be gewealdum *quibus in potestatem redactis*, Nar. 5, 17. Beó se þeóf ealles scyldig þæs þe hē age, and þeófa gewita beó be þām ilcan (*subject to the same penalty*), Ll. Th. i. 200, 24. Se þe be lytlum þingum beón mæge *he that needs little to be done for him* (qui minus indiget) . . . se þe be māran þingan beón scyle, R. Ben. 57, 23-58, 2. Hī leofodon be hungre seofon niht meteleáse, Hml. S. 16, 81. (7) *comparison*:—Hwelc gewinn be ðǽm þe nū sindon, Ors. 2, 6; S. 88, 32. Hū seó burh burne and hū lange be þǽre ōþerre, Bt. 16, 4; F. 58, 5. Swylc is wyrd be þām godcundan foreþonce swilce þ hweól biþ tō metanne wiþ ðā eaxe, 39, 8; F. 224, 3. (8) *marking the object with which a circumstance is connected, in the case of, in the matter of, with*:—Bi (be, *v. l.*) monnum *with men*, Past. 63, 11. Be (bi, *v. l.*) þām aldan þeódscype (*in testamento veteri*) þā ýttran weorc wǽron behealden, Bd. 1, 27; Sch. 84, 10. Seó wíse wæs unēþe be mínre seolfre nēdþearfe, Nar. 9, 24. Swā hit biþ be ælcum þāra þinga, Bt. 27, 4; F. 100, 17. þ ilce þū miht geþencan be ðām líchoman and be his limum, 190, 26. Suā hē ǽr be him wēnde *quod de eis jam certum tenebat*, Past. 241, 5. Gā ælc cyricsceat intō þām ealdan mynstre be (*in the case of*) ælcum frígan heorðe, Ll. Th. i. 262, 16. Se ǽð sceal bión healf be (*in the case of, with*) húslgengum, 112, 4. Bige ūs rūmlícor tō dæg be hláfe . . . and bring ūs bet be hláf *in your purchase for us to-day be more liberal with bread, and be a better provider for us in the matter of bread*, Hml. S. 23, 467. Ðá gebrōðra næfdon būton fíf hláfas. Benedictus . . . cwæð: ' Tō-dæg wē habbað hwōnlíce be hláf,' Hml. Th. ii. 172, 2. (9) *marking the object affected by a deed or event*, (to do) *by or about, to, with*, (to become) *of*:—Ðæt he onginne sume scande bi (be, *v. l.*) ðǽm ōðrum, Past. 225, 25. Hwæt dō ic be þām Hǽlende *quid faciam de Iesu ?*, Mt. 27, 22. Hwæt be ðē gedōn beón sceolde *quid de te fieri deberet*, Bd. 5, 12; Sch. 629, 6. Hwæt dō ic be Iudēa cininge *quid faciam regi Iudaeorum ?*, Mk. 15, 12: Nic. 18, 24. Dōð be ūs þ þ Drihten wile, Hml. S. 11, 133. Tō dōnne be him eall swā Iudas dyde be úre Drihtene, Chr. 1087; P. 222, 34. Hwæt be ðyssum þingum tō dōnne wǽre *quid de his agendum*, Bd. 2, 9; Sch. 1504: Shrn. 139, 24. Hwæt be mē geweorðe *quid de me fieri velit Deus*, Bd. 5, 19; Sch. 670, 14. Hū hyt be þē geworden ys, Nic. 10, 34. Hwæt geworden wǽre be þām biscope, Gr. D. 172, 10. Hwæt bið be ūs synfullum, Hml. S. 31, 1406. (10) *marking the object of thought, feeling, care*:—þá þe syrwdon be him, H. R. 107, 2. Bysige ðē be sumum men, Prov. K. 43. Geseoh þū be þǽre fiascan . . . ne drinc ðū of þǽre, Gr. D. 142, 3. Wyrd swā þīnum heáfde hafað ārǽded, Nar. 29, 13. Geortrūwian be þís andweardan lífe, Bt. 10; F. 30, 7. (11) *marking object of speech, hearing, knowledge, about, of*:—Hē líehð be (bi, *v. l.*) ðǽm gódum weorcum, Past. 55, 24. Sprec tō þīnum discipulum be þām mægenum þe þín láreów dyde, St. A. 8, 14. Be þæs forwyrde (*de cujus interitu*) se ealda feónd gelýfde þ hē mihte gebysmrian Benedictum, Gr. D. 126, 3. Gif hē hwæt be ōðrum gehýre,

Ll. Th. ii. 316, 18. Þá word þe wē be þām Hǣlende gesáwon and gehýrdon, Nic. 8, 40 : 2, 17. Ic wát eall be þām, Hml. S. 24, 152. (12) marking quarter in which something is sought :—Hwílum man céas wíslíce men folce tó hyrdum ... syððan hit man sōhte be þām þe nearwlícast cūðan swician, Ll. Th. ii. 320, 24. (13) marking source :— Hwæt sý be Gode (de Deo) ... hwæt sý be heom sylfum (de semet-ipsis), Gr. D. 146, 36–147, 3. (13 a) by (in to have a child by a woman) :—Be ðǣre hē hæfde āne dohter, Ap. Th. 1, 8 : Chr. 1057 ; P. 188, 14. (14) marking cause :—Hwanan sió ádl cume be misgewi-derum and of metta þiginge, Ld. ii. 244, 11. (15) marking ground of action, because of, on account of :—Ne gedyrstlǣce nán man be mægðhāde būtan sōðre lufe ; ne trūwige nán man be ælmesdǣdum oððe on gebed-um būtan lufe, Hml. Th. i. 54, 10–13. Sē be (propter, Lat. vers.) wítum geswícan nylle, Ll. Th. i. 210, 4. (16) marking reason :—'Be hwām (wherefore) cwest ðū þ?' Ðá cwæþ ic : 'For þām þe þū ǣr cwǣde ...,' Bt. 38, 3 ; F. 202, 11. Wē sǣdan hū wē hit reahtan and be hwý wē hit reahtan, Cht. Th. 171, 6. (17) for the sake of :—Nis ðis gewrit be ānum men āwriten ac ys be eallum, Hept. Thw. 163, 20. ¶ Be þām þ in order that :—Be þām þ ðū mihtest þý ēð ongitan, Bt. 36, 5 ; F. 180, 1 : 39, 9 ; F. 226, 8. (18) marking material from which an inference or knowledge may be drawn, by which judgement may be made :—Ælc treów is be his wæstme (de fructu suo) oncnāwen, Lk. 6, 44. Þá geseah þæt wíf þæt þæt treów wæs gōd tó etanne, be þan þe hire þūhte, Gen. 3, 6. Ne ceós ðū nánne man be his ǣhtum, Prov. K. 42. Be þisum litlum man mæg understandan, Ælfc. Gen. Thw. 3, 20. Be eallum þisum racum þū miht ongitan ex quo fit, Bt. 36, 6 ; F. 180, 26. Ðæt is sweotol tó ongitanne be sumum ǣðelinge, 16, 2 ; F. 52, 18 : 37, 3 ; F. 190, 19. Be þām wæs cweden unde dicitur, Bd. 1, 27 ; Sch. 79, 3 : 85, 10 : Past. 153, 8. Be þǣm man mehte ongietan ubi conjici datur, Ors. 3, 4 ; S. 104, 10. Be þan man wát þæt hē bið his hláford, Wlfst. 298, 4 : 152, 21. Ongitan be þām ðe nánne mon ne lyst þæs þinges to understand from the thing pleasing nobody, Bt. 34, 7 ; F. 144, 1. Ic wille secgon be hwǣm ic hit ǣrest ongeat, 35, 2 ; F. 156, 33. (19) marking means or material used, by, by means of, by the use of :— Hangað sweord be smalan þrǣde, Bt. 29, 1 ; F. 102, 27. Ic hæfde sweotole gereht be manegum tácnum, 11, 2 ; F. 34, 32. Ðá óðre be him libben, Past. 319, 19. Hē leofode be hláfe and be wætere, Hml. S. 3, 478. Be hwilcum þingum fēddest þū ðē?, Hml. S. 23 b, 517. Þæt eal folc fæste be hláfe and wirtum and wætere, Wlfst. 180, 24. (19 a) marking object used to typify or signify something :—Bi Judēum wæs gecueden ðurh ðone wítgan sub Judeae specie per prophetam dicitur, Past. 241, 5. Be ðám sceabbe sió hreófe getácnað ðæt wōhhǣmed, 71, 4. (19 b) by way of, in the form of :—Gif hē secge þ hē hæbbe hire freóndscipe, þ ys be lufe (amatorie), Ll. Th. ii. 230, 17. (20) marking agent :—Þá ðing þe be him wǣrun gewórdene quae fiebant ab eo, Lk. 9, 7. (21) marking the object that serves as model, after :—Swelcra mā bi ðǣre bisene, Past. 9, 14. On þára apostola drohtnunge, be þám muneca líf is geby-senod, R. Ben. 57, 6. Þǣre þeóde hē óþerne naman āscóp be him syluum, Ors. 1, 8 ; S. 40, 33 : Hml. Th. i. 478, 10 : Angl. vii. 44, 429. Oþer burh wæs hátenu be his horse Bucefal, Ors. 3, 9 ; S. 132, 26. (22) marking that which guides action or conduct, or which determines a statement, according to, after :—Ðǣm mannum þe be his lárum lifiaþ, Bl. H. 61, 13. Be ðám ðe hí tǣhton sylfe lybbende, Hml. Th. ii. 130, 3. Þǣra manna þe lybbað be ágenum lustum, i. 536, 22. Unrihtdēman þe dēmað ǣfre be þám sceatte unjust judges that are ever guided in their judgements by bribery, Wlfst. 298, 19. Hit oferstíhð, be ðæs wítegan cwyde, sandceoslas gerím, 34. (23) marking measure, rate, degree :— Beó gemeten nygon fēt be þæs mannes fótan (ad mensuram pedum ejus), Ll. Th. i. 226, 13. Fultum be swá manegum mannum swá ús cinelic þince, 236, 15. Þæt ylce gemet, þæt is be twelf sealnum, R. Ben. 35, 6. Hæbbe wē þæt feoh bróht be þám ylcan gewihte, Gen. 43, 21. Þá eá mehte wífmon be hiere cneówe oferwadan, Ors. 2, 4 ; S. 72, 33. Mǣre be ánum stæfe, Nic. 19, 21. Bið se ofsprinc gesǣdcundes cynnes be twám þūsendum, Ll. Th. i. 188, 12. Ðū be ðinere dægullícum geþingdest wið mē, Mt. R. 20, 13, 2. Steor-ran feóllan náht be ánan oððe twám, ac þiclíce, Chr. 1095 ; P. 230, 29. Drinc be dropan, Lib. ii. 130, 4. Rūde be healfan þǣre saluion, 292, 16. Be twyfealdum forgielde hē hit, Ll. Th. i. 50, 22 : 224, 13. Lēton heora fultum binnan beón be þǣm dǣle þæt hié ǣgðer mehton ..., Ors. 4, 5 ; S. 168, 24 : Bt. 34, 12 ; F. 152, 19. Be nánum dǣle, 39, 7 ; F. 222, 18. Be mǣstan at most, Hml. Th. i. 594, 25. Be fullan, Hml. S. 35, 29. (24) marking proportion :—Gif hē onsacan wille, dō hē þ be þám feó and be þám wíte, Ll. Th. i. 120, 8 ; 118, 15. Ǣlcan ǣnlýpium wæs geseald be ðám þe hē behófade, R. Ben. 57, 19. Bētan be his gyltes andefne, Bl. H. 45, 28. Wē syndon geómrigende be myclum gewyrhtum, St. A. 36, 2. (25) marking that from which action results, by the command, at the request :—Hē fērde be his hláfordes hǣse, Gen. 24, 10. Gif þeów mon wyrce on Sunnandæg be his hláfordes hǣse, Ll. Th. i. 104, 2. Sē gefreóde Ongelcynnes scōle be Ælfrēdes bēne, Chr. 885 ; P. 80, 6. (26) marking penalty, (a) by deprivation, under pain of losing :—Forgá hē þ´ýsðe be his feóre and be eallum þám

þe hē áge, Ll. Th. i. 210, 3. Hē bebeád eallum his folce be heora lífe þæt hí sceoldon hí gebiddan tó ðǣre anlícnysse, Hml. Th. ii. 18, 24 : Hml. S. 11, 6. Hē beád þ ǣlc man be his heáfde deófle sceolde offrian, 23, 29. Þ gehwilc man his teóðunge gelǣste be Godes miltse and be þæs cynges and be ealles crístenes folces, Wlfst. 272, 7 : Ll. Th. i. 342, 12. Beóde ic mínum gerēfan be mínum freóndscipe and be eallum þám þe hí ágon, 272, 5. (b) by infliction, under pain of suffering :—Healde man frcólsunga be þám wíte (under pain of suffering the penalty) þe seó dómbóc tǣcð, Ll. Th. i. 264, 20 : 342, 12. 'Hí man ðreátige þ hí be wíte hí ámeldian' ... 'Būton gē hí ámeldian, gē sceolon heora wíte āstundian,' Hml. S. 23, 293. Be þǣre steóre þe Eádgár gelagede, Wlfst. 272, 8. Be mýnre oferhýrnysse, Ll. Th. i. 196, 15. (27) adjuration, by :—Yc eów bidde on Godes naman and on ealra his háligra, and eác be mínum freóndscipe, Ll. Th. i. 194, 5. (28) with dative absolute, cf. II. 3 a :—Gif elles be cwicum mannum (nobody being killed) ciricgrið ābrocen beó, Ll. Th. i. 340, 20 : 360, 11. B. instr. :—Bi dýs (be ðǣm, v. l.) ilcan, Past. 169, 19. Be þý, Bt. 34, 1 ; F. 134, 13 : 34, 7 ; 142, 29. Þá men bi ðý lifdon, Nar. 26, 22. C. adverb :—Stódon him twēgen weras big, Bl. H. 121, 23. Þæt yrfe þe wē big leofiaþ, 51, 18. Meolc þe hý bi libbað, Ors. 1, 2 ; S. 30, 10. Þæs be eall þeódscype big sceall libban, Ll. Th. ii. 306, 36. Tó þǣm mere þe wē bí gewícod hæfdon, Nar. 12, 21. Būton hió hwǣr tó lǣne ˙sié, oððe hwá óðre bí wríte, Past. 9, 7. v. bí, in Dict., bí-libban, big-standan.

**beácen.** Add :—Beácen indicium, An. Ox. 345. Beácne prodigio, 2870. Hí ātendon heora beácna swá swá hí fērdon, Chr. 1006 ; P. 137, 2. Bēcen (-on, -un) signum occurs often in the Lindisfarne and Rush-worth glosses, where the W. S. version has tácn. v. ge-beác(e)n.

**beácen-fýr,** es ; n. A signal-fire, lighthouse :—Bæcenfýr farans (= farus), Txts. 180, 7.

**beacen-stán.** Add :—Farus beácanstán, in promontoria rupis posita, i. fýrtor, Wrt. Voc. ii. 76, 13. Beácenstán farus, 37, 3.

**beácnian.** Add : to make a sign :—Hig beácnað mid eágum an-nuunt oculis, Ps. L. 34, 9. v. bēcn(i)an, bícn(i)an ; deáþ-beácnigende.

**beácnung.** Add : I :—Beácnengum nutibus, Wrt. Voc. ii. 59, 62. II :—Beácnunge tropologian, Wrt. Voc. ii. 75, 36. [O. H. Ger. bouhnung.] v. ge-beácnung ; bícnung.

**beád** a prayer. l. bead. v. bed : **beáda.** Dele.

**beado-wrǣd,** es ; m. A war-company (? v. wrǣd, III. The epithet applies to a collection of plants to be used against a disease, and occurs in a charm) :—Ic binne (benne ?) āwrát betest beadowrǣda swá benne ne burnon ne burston I have written out the best troop for fighting disease, so that wounds may neither burn nor burst, Lch. ii. 350, 29.

**be-æftan.** Add : I. prep. (1) local, (a) in contrast with before :— Hē hæfde þriddan dǣl his firde beæftan him, Ors. 1, 12 ; S. 52, 33.. (b) in contrast with advance along with :—Hē forlēt hundeahtatig þūsenda beæftan him, Ors. 2, 5 ; S. 78, 17 : 5. 12 ; S. 240, 3. (2) figurative :— Ic forlǣte mínne āgene wyllan beæftan mē for nytnesse mínra freónda voluntatem meam postpono utilitati proximorum, Gr. D. 259, 16. II. adv. (1) behind, (a) in contrast with before, (α) local :—Tó þǣm folce þe þǣr beæftan wæs, Ors. 1, 12 ; S. 52, 35. Mē wæs se sūðerne wind beæften, Hml. A. 193, 24. (β) figurative :—Lǣten hí ðæt líf ðæs mægðhādes beforan ðǣm ōðrum and hine selfne bizæftan, Past. 409, 26. (b) in contrast with advance along with :—Micel þæs heres þe mid hiere beæftan wæs reliquae relictae cum regina, Ors. 1, 10 ; S. 48, 23. Hē beæftan gebád, 3, 10 ; S. 140, 20. Þæt hié sume hié beæftan wereden, and sume þurh ealle þá truman út āfuhten, 5, 7 ; S. 230, 21. Læg se leáp beæftan, gǣst ellor hwearf, Jud. 112. Heora proletarii ne mōstou him beæftan beón, Ors. 4, 1 ; S. 154, 16 : Chr. 755 ; P. 48, 12. Ætsǣton ðá Centiscan þǣr beæftan, 905 ; P. 94, 5. (2) after :—þára twelf noman hēr stondað āwritene beæftan, C. D. ii. 150, 35. v. bæftan.

**beaftan.** Add :—Hí hondum beóftun hine lamentabantur eum, Lk. R. 23, 27. [ᵺbe-haftian. v. hafetian in Dict., and see beft in N. E. D.] v. hand-bæftian.

**beágian.** Add : v. bēgian in Dict., where read biégodyst ; ge-, wuldor-beágian.

**beág-wíse,** an ; f. Ring-fashion, circular-form :—Ofiæthláfas on beágwísan ābacene oblationum coronas, Gr. D. 343, 15.

**beáh.** Add : (1) a crown, garland :—Beáh of hwítum blóstmum geworht, Gr. D. 338, 12. Mon sette ðyrnenne beág on ðæt heáfod, Past. 261, 14 : Bl. H. 23, 33. Wuldres beág, 171, 10. Bēg coronam, Ps. Srt. 20, 4 : 64, 12 : Mk. L. R. 15, 17. (2) a collar, necklace :— Baeg munila (=monile), Wrt. Voc. ii. 114, 33. Beáh, 55, 79. (2 a) a shackle for the neck :—Beágas boias (in collo), Wrt. Voc. ii. 81, 29 : 11, 74. (3) a bracelet :—Beáh armilla, Wrt. Voc. i. 74, 55. Hí him þá áþas swóron on þām hálgan beáge, Chr. 876 ; P. 74, 9. Hē (the king) sylþ mē hors oþþe beáh (armillam), Coll. M. 22, 35. Bēgas dextralia, An. Ox. 5260. (4) a circle. v. beáh-hyrne :—Eáge oculus, seó papilla, beág corona (cf. in a list of similar words :—Circulus ðæs seó hringc, ... corona vel circulus wulderbeáh, 42, 72–43, 5), Wrt. Voc. i. 282, 54: ii. 16, 48. v. gylden-, sweor-beáh.

**beáh-gifa.** Add :—Æðelstān cyning, beorna beáhgyfa (cf. Egils Saga,

c. 55: Aðalsteinn konungr tôk gullhring af hendi sér, ok drô â blôðrefilinn, ok rêtti yfir eldinn til Egils. *See also* Coll. M. 22, 35 *under* beáh (3)), Æðelst. 2. Þ him God forgyue . . . and eác swâ his beáhgifan, þ is se sêlesða sinces brytta Ælfryd, Gr. D. 2, 14.

**beáh-hyrne**, an; f. *A corner of the eye :—Yrqui* beáhhyrne *vel* agneras *volvos dicimus angulos oculorum*, Wrt. Voc. i. 43, 2. v. beáh (4).

**be-áhsian.** v. be-áscian.

**bealcan.** *Add :—*Dæg dæges bealceþ wurd, Ps. L. 18, 3. [To balke *ructo*, Wülck. Gl. 608, 31.]

**bealcettan.** *Add :* I. *to belch :—*Þonne þurh mûð bitere hræcð oþþe bealcet, Lch. ii. 192, 13. Hê sceal oft bealcettan, 236, 14. II. *to come forth :—*Of þrih balcetteþ (*cum*) *de* (*sepulchri*) *tumba* (*pulvis*) *ebulliat*, An. Ox. 1884. III. *to utter :—*Mîn heorte bealcet good word, Ps. Th. 44, 1. Bylcetteþ *eructuat*, i. *a corde emittit*, Wrt. Voc. ii. 144, 12. Ðâ lâre hê mid hunigswêttre þrotan bealcette, Hml. Th. ii. 118, 22.

**beald.** *Add :* (1) *bold, confident :—*Bald *fretus*, Wrt. Voc. ii. 109, 26: *fretus, confidens, presumptus*, 36, 12. Bealwes tô beald, Bl. H. 109, 28. Hê næs nâht beald him tô tô gânne, Gr. D. 132, 13. Se bealda Hieu, Hml. S. 18, 359. Hî hæfden on bendum ænne bealdne ðeóf, Barrabam (cf. ænne strangue (*insignem*) þeófmann, Mt. 27, 16), Hml. Th. ii. 252, 11. Wæron Somnite swâ bealde *in tantum abusus est victoriae securitate*, Ors. 3, 8; S. 120, 32. Wæs hê bealdra (baldra, *v. l.*) geworden on þære frignesse *constantior interrogando factus*, Bd. 2, 12; Sch. 157, 15. Þ hî þý baldran and þý unforhtran wæron, 3, 18; Sch. 274, 21. Ðæt hié (*elati*) ne sién bealdran and orsorgran ðonne hié scylen *ne plus quam decet sint liberi*, Past. 302, 14. Hié beóð bealdran ðâ gôdan tô suenceanne *se robustius bonorum afflictioni illidunt*, 361, 14. (2) *bold, impudent :—*Bald *frontuosus*, Wrt. Voc. ii. 109, 29: 151, 27. Siô balde *frontosa* (*impudentia*), 85, 27. v. heáfod-beald.

**bealdlíce.** *Add :* (1) *boldly, confidently :—*Baldlíce *instanter*, Wrt. Voc. ii. 44, 12: *fiducialiter*, Angl. xiii. 38, 313: Ps. L. 11, 6: Wlfst. 284, 23. Ballíce, Rtl. 66, 13: *audacter*, Mk. L. R. 15, 43. Bealdlíce, Gr. D. 212, 8. Hû dearst þû æfre þus bealdlíce læran *praedicare quomodo praesumis?*, 32, 10: 135, 30. Hê bealdlíce clypað : ' Dêm, lâ dêma,' Wlfst. 254, 7: 256, 6. Abræd Petrus bealdlíce his swurd, Hml. Th. ii. 246, 22. Hî Crîstes naman andetton bealdlíce betwux gedwolmannum, 558, 24. Baldlícor *fiducialius*, Wrt. Voc. ii. 148, 75. (2) *boldly, impudently :—*Bealdlíce *procaciter*, Wrt. Voc. ii. 66, 57. Bealdlíce *achariter*, 10, 17.

**beald-ness**, e; f. *Boldness :—*Hê mid micelre baldnesse cîðde þ se Hælend wære sôð Godes sunu, Shrn. 31, 34.

**beald-wyrde** ; adj. *Bold in speech, saucy :—*Se biscop him andwyrde : ' Ðû earning, . . .' Se cwellere mid gebolgenum môde cwæð : ' Gif ðes bealdwyrda biscop (*this saucy priest*) âcweald ne bið, siððan ne bið ûre ege ondrædendlic,' Hml. Th. i. 420, 2.

**bealo(-u)** ; n. *Add :* I. *hurt, mischief, destruction :—*Þær wæs þ brýdealo þ wæs manegra manna bealo (mannum tô beala, *v. l.*), Chr. 1075; P. 210, 35. Hit bið him sylfum tô beaiowe geðyged, Hml. Th. i. 266, 14. I a. *a noxious thing :—*Bollan mid bealuwe (*with a noxious draught*) âfylled, Hml. S. 14, 68. Þæt his yrþ sî geborgen wið ealra bealwa gehwylc, Lch. i. 402, 10. II. *malice :—*Þone lâreów selfne þæs bealwes *ipsum malitiae magistrum*, Gr. D. 121, 12. Ne nîþa tô georn, ne bealwes tô beald, Bl. H. 109, 28. Hê wæs bealwes full, Hml. S. 7, 396. Gebealh hine Acitofel and mid bealwe weard âfylled, 19, 208 : Ps. Th. 58, 2.

**bealo(-u)** ; adj. *Add :—*Swâ inc se balewa hêt handþegen helle, Sat. 484. Uton gescyldan ûs wið þâ bealewan synne, Wlfst. 145, 18. Ic bealuwara weorc gebiden hæbbe, sârra sorga, Kr. 79. Hine sâr hafað befongen balwon bendum (cf. bealo-bend), B. 977. Sê inc forgeaf balewe geþôhtas, Sat. 488.

**bealo-bend**, es ; m. *A grievous bond, chain :—*Swâ hwæt swâ gê gebindaþ hêr ofer eorðan fæstum bealubendum (cf. B. 977) for yfelum gewyrhtum, Wlfst. 178, 2.

**bealo-dæd.** *Add :* [O. *Sax.* balu-dâd : O. H. *Ger.* palo-tât *maleficium*.] : **bealo-full.** *Add :* v. un-bealofull : **bealo-hýdig.** *Add :* [O. *Sax.* balu-hugdig.]

**bealo-leás.** *Add :—*Wæs â blîðemôd bealuleás kyng (*Edward the Confessor*), þeáh hê wunode wræclâstum, Chr. 1065 ; P. 194, 3.

**bealu** ; adj. v. bealo ; adj. : **bealo(-u)-ware.** *Dele and see* bealo ; adj.

**beám.** *Add :* I. *a tree :—*Nim ælces treówcynnes dæl bûtan heardan beáman (cf. tree heard *arborem sicomorum*, Lk. L. 19, 4), Lch. i. 398, 8. v. ciris-, cist-, cisten-, cwic-, crâwan-, fúl-, hnut-, môr-, wanan-beám. V. *a beam, post :—*Beám *trabes*, Wrt. Voc. i. 82, 13 : *trabs*, 290, 6. Swâ swâ greát beám (*or tree?*) on wyda wyrcþ hlûdne dynt, Bt. 38, 2 ; F. 198, 9. Of beáme *de stipite*, Wrt. Voc. ii. 26, 10. Tô earnes beáme (*or tree?*) . . . fram earnes beáme, C. D. ii. 73, 25. Dûnstân âna ætstôd uppon ânum beáme (*in uno de laquearibus*), Chr. 978; P. 123, 3. Se leóma wæs swilce ormæte beám, 1106; P. 240, 21. Heora earmas

wæron swâ ormæte beámas, Hml. S. 4, 288. Gewyrcean tor of treówum and of mycclum beámum, Bl. H. 187, 12. Man þâ beámas gelegð and þâ ræftras tô þære fyrste gefæstnað, Angl. viii. 324, 9. v. sýl-, wínbeám. Va. *a beam as part of an implement :—*Borige hê on þâm beáme (*of the plough*), Lch. i. 402, 1. v. scear-, sulh-, web-beám. VI. *a beam of light :—*Blôdig wolcen on mistlice beámas wæs gehîwod, Chr. 979 ; P. 122, 26. v. sunn-beám.

**beám** *a trumpet.* v. bîme : -beámen. v. cwic-beámen : beámere. v. bímere.

**beám-weg**, es ; m. *A road made with logs, a corduroy road :—*On beámweg (cf. stânweg, 15), C. D. B. i. 417, 17.

**beán.** *Add :—*Beán *cicer*, Wrt. Voc. ii. 103, 82 : 14, 37 : *falla*, 35, 13 : *legumen*, 52, 14. Gegrunden beán *faba pressa*, 39, 68 : 146, 62. Fugles beán *vicium*, 123, 57. Beána *fabae*, Ælfc. Gr. Z. 84, 6. Heó hafað sæd swylce beána, Lch. i. 238, 19. Greáte beáne, iii. 56, 21. Alwan leáf swelc swâ biþ preó beána, ii. 228, 6. Ádrîge beána, 70, 20. Beána gesodene, 44, 17. Healde hê hine wiþ beána, 214. 3. Gif þu beána habban wile, Tech. ii. 123, 16 : Coll. M. 34, 27. Sum him mid bær beána mid wætere ofgotene, Hml. S. 23 b, 128. Beána sâwan, Angl. ix. 262, 7.

**beán-belgas.** *Add :—*Of beánbælgum, Lk. L. 15, 16. Þâ swîn æton beánbelgas (-bylgas, -coddas, *v.ll.*), Gr. D. 106, 31.

**beán-cynn**, es ; n. *A kind of bean :—*Beáncyn *cicer*, Wrt. Voc. ii. 131, 39.

**beán-land**, es ; n. *Land on which beans are grown :—*Ðone þriddan æcer beánlandes, C. D. iii. 366, 20.

**beán-melu**, wes ; n. *Bean-meal :—*Genim beánmela, Lch. ii. 84, 4.

**beán-sǽd**, es ; n. *Bean-seed, beans for sowing :—*Tô beánsæde xl. pene[ga], Cam. Phil. Soc. 1902, p. 15.

**beán-scealas.** l. -scealu, e ; f., *and add :—*Beánscalu *quisquiliarum*, An. Ox. 608. Bēnsceala (*printed* -sæala), Wrt. Voc. ii. 76, 16.

**beán-stede**, es ; m. *A place where beans are grown ? :—*Tô beánstede . . . of beánstede, C. D. iii. 425, 19.

**beard.** *Add :—*Beard *barba*, Wrt. Voc. i. 64, 42. Beard him beón bescoren hearm hit getâcnað, Lch. iii. 198, 28. Se beard and þ feax wæron oþ þâ fêt sîde, Shrn. 120, 25. Mid sîdum bearde, Hml. Th. i. 466, 24. Ælfsige mid þâm berde, Cht. E. 257, 1. Lædes mannes tâcen is þæt þu þe mid ealre hande be þinum cynne nime, swilce þu þe be bearde niman wille, Tech. ii. 129, 17. Wê lærað þ ænig gehâdod man . . . his beard ænige hwîle ne hæbbe, Ll. Th. ii. 254, 13. Þonne hê (*one entering a monastery*) his beard âlêde, Hml. S. 6, 2228. Hî habbað beardas oþ cneów sîde, Nar. 35, 2 : 38, 1. ¶ beardas (*used of a single person*) *beard and whiskers :—*þ hire wolden beardas weaxan on þâm andwlitan, Gr. D. 279, 10. Hê hæfð sîde beardas, hwôn hârwencge, Hml. Th. i. 456, 18. v. wang-beard.

**beard-leás.** *Dele* : ' *also a hawk or buzzard* ' ; *and add :—*Beardleás *inpubis*, Ælfc. Gr. Z. 56, 2. Beardleáses *effebi*, Wrt. Voc. ii. 31, 54. Beardleásum rince *effebo hircitallo*, An. Ox. 4, 57. Beardleásne *effebum*, Wrt. Voc. ii. 32, 16. Beardleáse *inuestes*, An. Ox. 16, 2.

**Beard-sǽtan(-e)** ; pl. *The people* (*or district*) *of Bardney :—*Æþelrêde, sê wæs ær cyning, wæs ðâ Beardsætena abbud, Bd. 5, 19 ; S. 641, 5.

**bearg.** *Add :—*Bearug, berg *majalis*, Txts. 78, 652 : *magialis*, Wrt. Voc. ii. 55, 51. Bearg *porcaster*, 97, 19. Bearh *magalis*, i. 78, 35. Worn berga . . . in ðâ bergas (ðâm bergum, L.) *grex porcorum :—*Sunor bergana *grex porcorum*, Lk. L. porcos, Mk. R. 5, 11, 12, 13. 8, 32. Ðâ bergas *porcos*, 15, 15. Berg, Mt. L. 7, 6. v. mæstel-bearg.

**bearhtm-hwæt.** v. berhtm-, breahtum-hwæt in *Dict.*

**bearhtm.** *A twinkling of an eye, an instant :—*On breahtme *in atomo*, Wrt. Voc. ii. 79, 27 : 46, 60. Þonne (*at the last day*) englas blâwað býman on brehtme (cf. 1 Cor. xv. 52), Cri. 882.

**bearhtm-hwîl.** *Add :—*Þ þ wæs ân brehtmhwîl (breahtm-, *v. l.*), þâ heó þ heáfod upp âbôf and se regn ofdûne feóll *quatenus unum breahtm que esset momentum, et levare caput et pluviam deponere*, Gr. D. 168, 6. Þâ hraðe on þâ ylcan tîd næs ân brehtmhwîl tô ðon þ se cniht geweard geswænced *hora eadem ac momento puer vexatus est*, 242, 30. Gif hê nihte on ânre bearhtmhwîle (berhtm-, *v. l.*) swâ feorr gefaran sí þæt longe potuit sub momento ire, 150, 12. Âne berhtmhwîle (bærht-, *v. l.*) âswygode seó stefn *parvo momento vox siluit*, 52, 28. v. beorht-hwîl.

**bearhtmian** *to resound.* v. breahtmian.

**bearm.** *Add :—*Bearm *gremium*, Wrt. Voc. ii. 41, 65. Hê hlenode on þæs Hælendes bearme, Shrn. 32, 19. Hosp þone ic behæfde on bearme (*sinu*) mînum, Ps. Spl. 88, 49. ¶ *with the idea of possession*, cf. hand :—Hê brôhte him tô bearme stânas, bæd him for hungre hlâfas wyrcan, Sat. 672. Him tô bearme cwom mâððumfæt mære, B. 2404. Hiá sellað on barm iuer, Lk. L. 6, 38.

**bearm-rægl.** l. -hrægl : **bearm-teág.** v. beorm-teáh.

**bearn.** *Add :—*Bearn *soboles*, bearn (mâ = *pl.*) *liberi*, Wrt. Voc. i. 72, 26, 27 : *pignus*, ii. 66, 64. Bearna bearn *pronepotibus*, 76, 69. Nefena bearnum, An. Ox. 850. Betwuh bearnum *inter natos*, Wrt. Voc. ii. 46, 46. v. wæpned-bearn.

**bearn-cennicge** *a mother;* genetrix :—Bearncennices *genetricis,* Rtl. 70, 17. Bearncen〃, 66, 35. v. sunu-cennicge.

**bearn-eaca;** *adj. Big with child, pregnant :*—Maria wæs þāgyt bearneáca, Hml. Th. i. 30, 9. Ðonne mon snīð ða bearneácan wīf (*praegnantes*), Past. 366, 14.

**bearn-eácen.** *Add :*—Bearneácen wīf *praegnans mulier,* Gr. D. 261, 10. Wīf þæt sȳ bearneácen, and heó cenne cniht, Wlfst. 2, 20. Gif wīf biþ bearneácen feówer mōnoð (*four months gone with child*), Lch. iii. 144, 19. Witan on bearneácenum wīfe hwæþeres cynnes bearn heó cennan sceal, 6. Bearneácnum, ii. 330, 6. Wīf þe bearneácne (-ene, *v. l.*) (*praegnantes*) wæron, Past. 366, 3. Ða bearneácnan wīf, 367, 14.

**bearn-eácnigende;** *adj.* (*ptcpl.*). *Being with child, pregnant :*— Bearneácnigende wīf forbūgan, Hml. Th. ii. 94, 3.

**bearn-le(á)st.** *Add :*—Bearnleás(t)e *orbitatis,* An. Ox. 4873.

**bearn-myrþra.** *Add :*—Ðider sculan wiccan and bearnmyrðran, Wlfst. 115, 1. Hēr syndan myltestran and bearnmyrðran, 165, 33.

**bearn-teám.** *Substitute :* I. *progeny, offspring, issue :*—Wlmēr and his bearntēm, Cht. Th. 592, 15. Hē bi þære fægerne bearnteám gestrȳnde, seó wæs Agathes gehāten, Chr. 1057; P. 188, 14. Seó geladung ācenð micelne bearnteám, Hml. A. 30, 161. þ hī heora bearnteám gebringon tō Crīste þurh fulluht, 34, 254. Þæt hié wolden fultumleáse beón æt heora bearnteámum *intercepta spe sobolis,* Ors. I, 14; S. 56, 22. II. *child-bearing, procreation of children :*—On ǣþrum is mægðhád and eác swylce bearnteám, and se bearnteám ne wanode þone mægðhád, Hml. A. 31, 165. Isaac ābæd hyre bearnteámes, 38, 344. Gesceafta ne beóð āstealde būtan for bearnteáme ānum, 20, 161. Swīðor for bearnteáme þonne for gālnysse *propagandi voluntas pia fuit, quia concumbendi voluntas libidinosa non fuit,* Angl. vii. 44, 443 : Hml. Th. ii. 54, 10 : 70, 20 : 94, 13. On gāstlicum bearnteáme, Hml. A. 29, 129. [*Scot.* barn-teme, &c. v. *Dict.*]

**bearo.** *Add :*—Bearwes *nemoris,* Wrt. Voc. ii. 61, 65. Bearuwæs, 151, 17. On bearwe *in nemore,* 46, 6. Hwæt ic āna sæt innan bearwe mid helme beþeht, holte tōmiddes, Dōm. L. 1. Þone godcundan bearo *divinum lucum,* Nar. 27, 10. Hrīmige bearwas . . . on ðǣm īsgean bearwum, Bl. H. 209, 32, 35. Bearewæs *saltus,* An. Ox. 2036. Bearewum *nemoribus, saltibus,* 1807. Bearwum, Wrt. Voc. ii. 78, 36. Be þysse wyrte ys sǣd þ heó of dracan blōde ācenned beón sceolde on ufeweardum muntum on þiccon bearwum, Lch. i. 322, 25. Ðū ādydes ða bearwas, Past. 355, 5 : Nar. 12, 18 : 26, 24. v. palm-bearo.

**bear-scipe.** v. beór-scipe.

**bearwe, an ;** *f. A barrow :*—Bærwan, Angl. ix. 263, 6. v. meox-bearwe.

**be-áscian ;** *p.* ode *To ask* a person (*acc.*) *for advice* (*gen.*), the question given in a clause :—Hié hine lāre beáhsodan, hwæt him þæs tō dōnne wǣre, Bl. H. 199, 29. Þæt hié ðone pāpan and þæt pāpseld beáhsodan, hwæt him þæs tō rǣde þūhte, 205, 20. [*O. Frs.* bi-áskia.] Cf. be-frignan.

**beátan.** *Add :* I. *trans.* (1) *of living creatures :*—Sume hī beóton *quosdam caedentes,* Mt. 12, 5. Hī beóton his heáfod *percutiebant caput ejus,* Mt. 27, 30. Hī beóton heora breóst, Hml. Th. ii. 258, 9. Gif man hine beáte, Ll. Th. i. 348, 5. Þone þe þē beáton sceolde, Hml. S. 4, 148. Sī beáten *pulsetur,* Angl. xiii. 390, 357. (1 a) *where the instrument is given, to beat with* (*mid*) :—Ic mid fȳste breóst mīne beáte, Dōm. L. 30. Hē hine mid his handum beót, Gr. D. 20, 25. Þone hālgan beátan mid heardun saglum, Hml. S. 4, 142. Heora neb beátan mid flintum, 11, 99. ¶ *to beat with the feet, to tread :*—Beáteþ *quatit* (*ungula campum*), An. Ox. 16. (1 b) *where the place of the blow is given :*—Hē beót Libertinum on þ heáfod and on þa ansȳne, Gr. D. 20, 29. (2) *of things :*—Beátendes hameres *tundentis mallei,* An. Ox. 480. Beátendra slecgea *tundentium malleorum,* Coll. M. 31, 7. (2 a) *with dat. to beat on :*—Ne se bryne beót mæcgum (cf. Milton's 'the torrid clime smote on him sore'), Dan. 265. II. *intrans. To beat on :*—Hē on his breóst beót, H. R. 15, 29. Þeáh man mid hameron beóte on þæt þell, Wlfst. 147, 6.

**beátere.** *Substitute :* I. *a beater :*—Hē hēt his cwelleras þone hālgan beátan mid saglum. Þā bærst sum sagol intō ānes beáteres eágan, Hml. S. 4, 143. II. *a boxer ;* pugil, Ælfc. Gr. Z. 39, 1.

**beáw** *a gadfly :*—Beáw *cretabulus,* Wrt. Voc. ii. 22, 77 : 136, 79. Beáw *vel* (v. Wülck. Gl. 121, 12) hymette *oestrum,* i. 23, 64.

**beáw-hyrnet.** *Dele, and see preceding word.*

**be-baþian.** *Add :*—Hē hine bebaðede, Gr. D. 308, 22 note. Ǣr þon hē bebaðod sié *priusquam lauetur aqua,* Bd. 1, 27 ; Sch. 76, 17 : Lch. ii. 334, 24. v. bi-baþian *in Dict.*

**bebbi** *in* Wrt. Voc. ii. 122, 60 (*tragoedia,* bebbi, *cantio*) *is a mistake for* belli (Lat.). Cf. tragoedia, belli *cantica vel fabulatio,* Goetz. v. 396, 8.

**bebbisc ;** *adj.* ? :—Se hǣlend nazarenisca ł (*in the margin* ðe bebbisca .i. all suā monn cuoeðas) *Iesus Nazarenus,* Lk. L. 18, 37.

**be-beódan.** *Under* I. *dele* ' *to give . . . generally,' and add :* with dat. of person and acc. or clause of the command, &c. I. *to order, enjoin :*—Þæt hē sprecende bebiét *quod loquendo imperat,* Past. 81, 10. Bebiót, Kent. Gl. 816. Swā him hāligu gewreotu bebeódaþ, Bl. H. 45, 6. Ic sylle þæt þū ǣr bebude, Ps. Th. 39, 7. Hē bebeád his suna þæt hē

tōwearp þæt templ, Ors. 6, 7 ; S. 262, 19. Hē bebeád þæt nān crīsten mon ne cōme on his hiérede, 6, 30 ; S. 282, 29. Hwæt yfela bebeád Drihten æfre, Bl. H. 41, 2. Bebudan *sancserunt,* An. Ox. 1301. Bebiód ðis *praecipe hoc,* Past. 385, 30. S. Paulus sægde þ Crīst sylfa bebude Moyse þ hē ōþrum lāreówum sægde, Bl. H. 45, 20. Windum stilnesse bebeódan, 177, 17. Healde man mæssedæg swā hē beboden beó, Wlfst. 117, 5. Hī wǣron bebodene *imperantur,* An. Ox. 4782. II. *to commit, commend :*—Ic mē þē bebeóde, Hml. S. 23 b, 448. Gif ðū gewītest, hwǣm bebeódest þū ūs ?, Bl. H. 225, 17. Þā þrē fǣmnan þe him Crīst bebeád, 145, 31. Þē Gode bebeód *te Deo commenda,* Ll. Th. ii. 226, 16. Bebeóde hē hine Gode, Lch. ii. 116, 8 : Bl. H. 47, 19. þ hī mīne forðfōre mid bēnum Dryhtne bebeódan (*commendent*), Bd. 4, 3 ; Sch. 357, 11. Tō bebeódenne *commendenda,* Wrt. Voc. ii. 79, 80. Beboden *commissus,* 132, 36. Þā bebodenan *credita,* 96, 73. Hē his ealdormen hæfde beboden þa clūsan tō healdanne, Ors. 6, 36 ; S. 292, 26. II a. *to offer to the gods :*—Þā cuman hē tō blōte dyde and hys godum bebeád *hospitum sanguinem diis propinabat,* Ors. 1, 8 ; S. 40, 23. II b. *to commit* into (on, *in*) :—His gāst on (in, *v. l.*) his handa bebeódende *spiritum suum in manus ejus commendando,* Bd. 4, 24 ; Sch. 491, 21. III. *to announce :*—Þæt hē Alexandres wīsan besceáwade, swā hē hit him eft hām bebeád (*omnia civibus suis enunciabat*), Ors. 4, 5 ; S. 168, 13. [v. bi-beódan *in Dict.* O. Frs. bi-biada : O. H. Ger. bi-biotan.]

**be-beódend.** *Add :*—Ðīn eágan weorðað gesiónde ðīnne bebiódend (*praeceptorem*), Past. 405, 25.

**be-beódendlic.** *Add :*—Ealle bebeódenlice þinc *cuncta sibi imperata,* R. Ben. I. 97, 3.

**be-beorgan.** *Substitute :* I. *to ward off* something (*acc.* or *inst.*) from one's self (*dat.*), *to guard* one's self *against.* (1) with dat. of person only, *to save* one's self :—Hī heom sylfum beburgon mid Godes fultume, Gr. D. 335, 24. þ hē mihte him bebeorgan, 109, 33. (2) dat. of person and (a) acc. of thing :—þ hié him sylfum heora synna bebeorgaþ, Bl. H. 63, 24. Hē bebearh him hī and warnode hine wiþ hī swā swā wið þone ealdan feónd *eam quasi hostem cavens,* Gr. D. 276, 2. Þā wītu þe hī him sylfum beburgon *supplicia quae evaserunt,* 335, 21. Bebeorh þē þone bealonīð, B. 1758. þ hī him þ wīte bebeorgen, Gr. D. 336, 16. Ūs syndon tō bebeorhgenne þā mycclan synna, Bl. H. 63, 33. (b) *dat.* or *inst.* of thing :—Hē him bebeorgan ne con wōm wundorbebodum wergan gāstes, B. 1746. II. *to guard* one's self (*acc.*) against (*wiþ*) something :—Bebeorh þē wið þā eahta heáhsynna *cave tibi ab octo capitalibus criminibus,* Ll. ii. 132, 5, 9. [O. H. Ger. bi-bergan *evitare.*]

**be-beran.** *Add :*—In rihte beborene *municipales,* Wrt. Voc. ii. 59, 16.

**be-bindan.** *Add :*—Gif hē mid deófles weorcum hine sylfne bebint, Hml. Th. i. 212, 13 : 332, 32. Dō on clāþ, bebind fæste, Lch. ii. 34, 25. Bebinde genōh wearme, 270, 9. Þæt Iudéisce cyn is yfele bebunden mid þām ðe hī cwǣdon be Crīstes blōde, Hml. Th. ii. 252, 31. [*Goth.* bi-bindan : O. Frs. bi-binda.]

**be-bītan** *to bite :*—Bibitnae (-e) *mordicos,* Txts. 76, 616.

**be-bīwan** (?) *to rub over :*—Þā wæs sōht, hwær se læce wære, þe cūþe wyrtgemang wyrcan, þ sē mihte hine (*the dead man*) besmyrwian and bebyrwan (-bȳwan ?) *cum medicus atque pigmentorius ad aperiendum eum atque condiendum esset quaesitus,* Gr. D. 318, 3.

**be-blāwan** *to blow upon :*—On beblēw hine *inflammavit eum,* Ps. L. 104, 20. Ne lǣte hine wind beblāwan þȳ dæge, Lch. ii. 288, 28.

**be-blonden.** *Dele.*

**be-bod.** *Add :*—Bebod *decretum,* Wrt. Voc. ii. 25, 46 : *imperium,* An. Ox. 1247. Man mōt wīfian æt þām þriddan cneó æfter þære ealdan ǣ bebode (*secundum veteris legis sanctionem*), Ll. Th. ii. 216, 21. Hē hē beódan þæt hié fōron ealle ūt ætsomne. Þā ætsǣton ða Centiscan beæftan ofer his bebod, Chr. 905 ; P. 94, 6. Tȳn bebodu *the decalogue,* An. Ox. 841. Ælicera bebodu *praeceptorum legalium,* 1017. Godes biboda weg, Past. 67, 9. [O. H. Ger. bi-bot.] v. bi-bod *in Dict.*

**bebod-dæg, es ;** *m. A day appointed* (by the church) :—On ðām beboddagum þīnra hāligra, Angl. xi. 102, 67.

**be-bodian** *to commend, entrust :*—Bebodadon ł gefeastadon *commendauerunt,* Lk. L. R. 12, 48.

**bebod-rǣden[n], e ;** *f. Command, authority :*—Of bebodrǣddenne ł of ðīnum bebodum *de mandatis tuis,* Ps. L. 118, 110.

**be-boren-inniht.** *Dele, and see* be-beran.

**be-brǣdan ;** *p.* de. *To be-spread, cover* with :—Se weg wæs bebrǣded mid hwītum ryftum, Shrn. 65, 23.

**be-brecan.** *Dele second passage, for which see* be-brūcan, *and for the rest substitute :* To break to pieces (*acc.* of object and dat. of part broken) :—Beám heó bebriceþ telgum *she breaks the tree to pieces in its branches* (cf. Sia (*acc.*) Iudéoliudi bēnon (*dat.*) bebrākon, Hēl. 5699), Sal. 295. [O. H. Ger. pi-brehhan *confringere.*]

**be-bregdan.** *Add :*—Sēteras ðā ðe hiæ sōðfæsto bebrugden (*simularent*).

**be-brūcan ;** *p.* -breác ; *pp.* -brocen. I. *to consume* food :—Hyra

hláfas wǽron forneáh ealle bebrocene (gebrocene, v. l.) panes pene omnes consumti fuerant, Gr. D. 145, 10. **II.** to practise :—Ealle þá gódnyssa þe hé bebreác, Hml. S. 23 b, 34.

**be-búgan** to avoid. Add :—Hé bebeáh hí and warnode hine wiþ hí swá swá wið þone ealdan feónd eam quasi hostem cavens, Gr. D. 276, 2. Ongan hé his freónd and his geféran bebúgan amicos coepit et familiares deserere, 181, 1.

**be-bycg(e)an.** Add :—Bebycgeð vendat, Lk. L. 22, 36. Bebyges (-ið, R.) vendit, Mt. L. 13, 44. Bebycgaþ veneunt, Wrt. Voc. ii. 73, 48. Hé bebohte his lond, Shrn. 90, 22. Hé Críst bebohte for feós lufon, Bl. H. 63, 7. Swá hwæt swá ðú hæbbe bibyge (bebyg, L. vende), Mk. R. 10, 21. Sylle ł bebycge (-byg, L.), Mt. R. 19, 21. Ðá bebycendo (bibyccende, R.) and ðá bycgendo . . . seatlas bebycgendra (bibyccendra, R.), Mk. L. 11, 15. Bebygendra, Mt. L. 21, 12. Tó bebycgendum (bibycendum, L.), Mt. R. 25, 9. Ðá bebyccendra (bibycgende, R. vendentes), Lk. L. 19, 45. Héht hine se hláford bebycgan (þte wére beboht vaenundari, L.), Mt. 18, 25. v. un-beboht.

**be-bycgung,** e; f. Selling :—Bibycgong distra(c)tio (cf. gloss of same passage: Distractio, i. venditio tódál, An. Ox. 4002), Wrt. Voc. ii. 84, 36 : 26, 65.

**be-byrd.** Substitute : be-byrdan to fringe, border :—Bebyrde clavatae (v. Ald. 77, 15), Wrt. Voc. ii. 20, 46. v. ge-byrdan, borda.

**be-byrg(e)an,** -byrian, -byrigan(-ean). Add :—Bebyrgað (bi-, R.) sepeliant, Lk. L. 9, 60. Hiene mon bebyrgde, Chr. 544; P. 16, 15. Bebyrgede, 1066; P. 197, 1. Bebyrigde, 979; P. 163, 7. Hí bebyrgdon his líchaman, Mt. 14, 12. Bebyrgedon, Chr. 1046; P. 169, 12: Mt. R. 14, 12. Bebyrigdon, Bl. H. 155, 7 : Chr. 1012; P. 143, 3. Bebyrig abbud Zosimus, Hml. S. 23 b, 749. Þ hē mōste his fæder bebyrgan, Bl. H. 23, 14. Hine besmyrwian and bebyrwan (-býwan?; -byrian, v. l.), Gr. D. 318, 3. Hé bebyrged wæs, Bl. H. 177, 25 : Chr. 789; P. 55, 18. v. un-bebyr(i)ged.

**be-byrg(e)an** to save :—þ hē mihte þá gedýglian and him bebyrgean (-beorgan, v. l.), Gr. D. 109, 33.

**be-byr(i)gednes** (-byrgen-, -byr(i)g-). Add :—Tó cýpnesse mínre bebyrgednesse, Bl. H. 69, 18. Tó bibyrgnisse (bebyrgennese, L. sepulturam), Mk. R. 14, 8. Bibyrignisa, Mt. L. 27, 7.

**be-byr(i)gung,** e; f. Burial :—Gearciað þá þing þe eów gewunelice synd tó bebyrigunge, Hml. S. 3, 584.

**bec** a brook. v. bæc : be-cæfian. Substitute :—Becæfed falerata, Wrt. Voc. ii. 34, 67 : bēcan to book. v. ge-bēcan : be-carcan. Dele.

**becca.** Add :—Ligo becca vel palus, vel fustis, Wrt. Voc. i. 16, 15. Becca ligo, 84, 67. v. becc in N. E. D.

**bece** a brook. v. bæc.

**bēce.** Add :—Boecae, boeccae, boece aesculus, Txts. 36, 22 : fagus, 62, 417. Bēccae, boece esculus, 60, 391. Bēce, Wrt. Voc. ii. 7, 9 : fagus, 34, 71. Tó þaere mearcbēcean, of ðære bēcean, C. D. B. i. 295, 9. On þá ealdan mearcebēcan, 296, 26. Bēcum fagis, Wrt. Voc. ii. 34, 72. v. mearc-bēce, and dele : v. bōcce.

**be-ceápian.** Add : **I.** to sell :—Heó beceápode þá gymmas wið licgendum feó, Hml. S. 9, 53. Beceápa ealle ðíne æhta, Bas. 56, 3. Ylpes bán becgan oðče beceápan, Lch. iii. 204, 3. **II.** to buy, purchase :—Gif hē mid þám gewítendlicum gestreónum beceápað him þæt ēce líf, Hml. Th. i. 204, 8. Hí mid heora feore þæt heofenlice ríce beceápodon, 476, 35. Ne beceápige hē mid his sáwle ðæs líchaman gesundfulnysse, 474, 26. Hæfde Zacheus beceápod heofonan ríce mid healfum dæle his æhta, 582, 7.

**be-ceás.** v. un-beceás : beceásan. Dele.

**bēcen.** Add :—On bēcenan treówes wyrttruman gewexen, Lch. i. 182, 2.

**be-ceorfan.** Add : to deprive a person (acc.) of something (dat.) by cutting :—Ic wolde þ ðú mē feaxe becurfe, Hml. S. 33, 123. Hát mē heáfde beceorfan . . . hē þá sceolde beón heáfde becorfen, Bl. H. 183, 16-20. Hē wæs heáfde becorfen, 173, 5 : Shrn. 123, 6 : Hml. Th. i. 420, 4.

**be-ceorian.** Substitute : to murmur at, complain of :—Gif hē hit mid muðe beceoraþ ore si murmuraverit, R. Ben. 21, 1. His ríce men hit mændon, and þá earme men hit beceorodan, Chr. 1086; P. 221, 13.

**be-cēpan;** p. te To be heedful, observant of (gen.) :—þæs becēpð se feónd quem attendit hostis, Ps. L. fol. 142, 4.

**bēcere.** v. bōcere : be-cerran. v. be-cirran.

**be-cídan;** p. de To complain of :—Ðá bōceras becíddon þæt Críst mid þám synfullum mannum hine gereordode, Hml. Th. ii. 470, 6.

**be-cípan** (-cýpan, q. v. in Dict.) to sell :—Swá hwæt swá hý heora geswinces becýpaþ, R. Ben. 136, 18. þú becēptest ł þú sealdest vendidisti, Ps. L. 43, 13. Becýp (vende) eall þæt þú áhst, Mt. 19, 21 : Scint. 59, 1. Gif man hwæt becýpan scyle . . . Gif hwylc neód sý tó becýpenne ænig þing, R. Ben. 95, 10, 16.

**be-cirran** (-cerran, -cyrran, q. v. in Dict.). **I.** to turn round, about :—Ðonne bið sió cweorn becierred (-cirred, v. l.) ðonne se monn bið geendod ; ðonne bið sió micle cweorn becierred (-cirred, v. l.) ðonne ðeós weorld bið geendod, Past. 31, 21. **II.** to go round, pass by, avoid :—Sume undeáwas ðæt mód ǽr gesihð and útan becierð (declinat) ;

ðæt is ðæt hit ðá ungedónan foreðoncelíce becierre, swá se stióra dēð ; sume ýða hē becerð mid ðý scipe, Past. 433, 4-7. Ðá se Hǽlend ðæt ongeat, ðá becierde (-cirde, v. l.) hē hié (fugit), 33, 15. Hē walde bicerra (praeterire) hiǽ, Mk. R. L. 6, 48. **III.** to turn, pervert, seduce :—þú ne miht mē becyrran of mínum rihtan geleáfan, ne fram mínum rihthláforde, Hml. A. 173, 103. **IV.** to beguile, deceive ; cf. colloquial to get round a person :—Hē cwæð þ hē gesícled wǽre, and swá þ folc becyrde (beswác, v. l.), Chr. 1003 ; Th. 252, 30. Cyrtenysse (wǽre) becyrred venustate caperetur, An. Ox. 5258. [þurh þe smel of þe chese he bicherreð monie mus to þe stoke, O. E. Homl. i. 53, 22. Þe deuel mid his hinderworde bicherde Adam, ii. 59, 19. Hii wolleþ us bicheorre (biwiȝelien, 1st MS.) þorh hire wise craftes, Laym. 969. Herkne nu, we nelleþ þe nouht bicherre, Misc. 46, 324. O. Frs. bi-kera.]

**be-clǽmed.** Substitute : be-clǽman ; p. de To beplaster, plaster over, poultice :—Gemeng wið æges þ hwíte, beclǽm þ lim mid, Lch. ii. 74, 26. Bewreóh þ wíf wel, and lǽt beón swá beclǽmed lange tíde, 330, 22. [O. H. Ger. pi-chleimen contaminare.] v. clǽm.

**be-clǽnsian** to cleanse :—Ic eom beclǽnsod emundabor, Ps. Spl. 18, 14. bēc-leden, Bt. F. p. viii, 1, see Bt. S. p. 1, 2 : be-clemman. Dele : ' Beclǽmed glutinatus, Lye,' see be-clǽman, and add : [O. H. Ger. pi-chlemmit obstructum.]

**be-clencan ;** p. te To beclinch, fix firmly :—Hí beclencton on fótcopsum fēt his, Ps. L. 104, 18.

**be-clipian** (-clypian, q.v. in Dict.) to challenge :—Gif Englisc man beclypað ænigne Frænciscne mann tó orneste, Ll. Th. i. 489, 5, 10, 12, 21. Gif se Englisca ne durre hine tó orneste beclypian, 24. [v. be-clepe in N. E. D.]

**be-clyppan.** Add :—Ic beclyppe conplector, Wrt. Voc. ii. 21, 48. His swiðre hand mē beclipð (amplexabitur), Past. 389, 11, 14. Grǽdum beclypte gremiis obuncabat, An. Ox. 2956. Heó beclypte hire neb mid handum, Hml. Th. ii. 184, 1. Hē beclypte hí ealle, Hml. S. 23, 823. Ic eom beclypt mid his earmum, 7, 46. [O. Frs. bi-kleppa.]

**be-clypping,** e ; f. Embrace :—Beclyppincge complexu, An. Ox. 1551. Beclyppinga amplexus, 3174.

**be-clýsan.** Add : **I.** to close, shut what is open :—Hē his duru beclýst, Lk. 13, 25. þá blóstman hý sylfe beclýsað, and eft hig hig sylfe geopeniað, Lch. i. 154, 1. þú beclýsedest þyses mannes mūð, Hml. S. 22, 86. Ðæs scræfes locstān hí wel fæste beclýsdon, Hml. S. 23, 346. Beclýsan recludere (paradisi valvam), An. Ox. 1149. þæt beclýsede geat, Hml. Th. i. 194, 5. Beclýsedre dura, ii. 166, 22 : i. 230, 12. þæt cweartern wē fundon fæste beclýsed, 572, 33. Mid beclýsedum eágum, 408, 22. **I a.** to close, put an end to :—þænne beclýsþ dæg dimnyss nyhta cum clauserit diem caligo noctium, Hy. S. 3, 1. **II.** to shut up in a place :—Beclýsde includit, An. Ox. 3148. Hē wæs on his inran būre, and hine sylfne ðærinne beclýsde, Hml. S. 23, 396. Hig hig sylfe on Hierusalem beclýsan woldon, St. A. 34, 11. On cwearterne beclýsan, Hml. Th. i. 86, 30 : Nic. 6, 36. þone deáð þe wyt gefyrn beclýsed hæfdon, 14, 3. Beón hí ðǽr beclýsede . . . on ðám scræfe beclýsde, Hml. S. 23, 326-9. ¶ mid inseglum beclýsan to seal up, Guth. 8, 15 : Wlfst. 259, 20. **III.** to shut out :—þá com Martinus tó þám cásere, ac man hine beclýsde wiðútan, Hml. S. 31, 660.

**be-clýsing,** e ; f. **I.** a closed place, an enclosure :—Beclýsincga clausa, An. Ox. 1522. **II.** a clause, conclusion, syllogism :—Beclýsinge clausula, An. Ox. 5357. Beclýsingum conclusionibus (sillogismi), 3210. Beclýsincga sillogismos, 4142.

**bēcnan.** v. bícnan.

**be-cnáwan.** Add :—þæt gehwá hine sylfne becnáwe (ge-, v. l.), R. Ben. 38, 17. [Mon, hwi nultu the bicnowe? R. S. 1, 31. O. H. Ger. pi-chnáen cognoscere.]

**be-cnáwe** in the phrase beón becnáwe (v. to be beknown = to avow, confess, N. E. D. s. v. be-know) :—Ic ne am bicnówe ðat ic (printed it ; but cf. ic ne eom ge-cnáwe þ ic ænigean menn geáfe þá sōcne ]anon ut, 222, 27) áni man ūðe ðenen ūt . . . hámsōcne, C. D. iv. 226, 4. Cf. ge-cnáwe.

**be-cnedan ;** pp. -cneden to knead up :—Merces sǽd on hláf becneden oþþe on wín gegniden, Lch. ii. 248, 4.

**bēcnend, bēcnung, bēcnydlic.** v. bícnend, bícnung, bícn(i)endlic.

**be-cneord** (?) diligent :—On willsumnesse háligra gebeda gecneord (begneord, v. l.), Bd. 4, 28 ; Sch. 525, 15.

**be-cnyttan.** Add : **I.** with acc. of what is tied, (1) to tie up in a bundle :—Ðæt hē Godes gifa ná ne becnytte on ðæm sceáte his slǽwðe, Past. 59, 15. (2) to tie round, surround with a bond :—Hí becnytton his swuran mid rápe, Hml. S. 15, 53. (3) to tie, attach with a string, &c. :—Gif hwá ðá wyrta on him becnitte, Hml. Th. i. 476, 5. þæt heó náme ænne wernægel and becnytte tó ánum hringe mid hire snóde, ii. 28, 18. **II.** with acc. of the fastening to tie a rope, &c. :—Hí becnytton ánne wriþan onbútan his swuran, Hml. S. 23, 607.

**becola** (-e ?), an ; m. (f.?) A spectre, witch :—Becolan, egesgríman larbam, Wrt. Voc. ii. 95, 64. [Cf. O. H. Ger. bechela brucia (cf. Span. bruxa a witch).] v. eges-gríma.

béc-ræding, e; f. Reading of books:—Se biscop in bēcrǣdinge (bóca rǣdinge, v. l. lectioni) geornfull wæs, Bd. 4, 3; Sch. 354, 15. v. bóc-rǣding.

be-craflan. Add: [Ðis maiden wile ic bicrauen, Gen. a. Ex. 1388.] v. un-becrafod.

be-creópan. Substitute: To creep, reach by creeping:—Becreáp (ge-, v. l.) þær inn tó þām hālgan men sum swýðe unhýre nǣddre, Gr. D. 211, 13. Hí Timotheum ācwealdon þǣr ðǣr hē becropen wæs, Hml. S. 25, 502: Met. 25, 36.

béc-treów, es; n. A beech-tree:—Bēctreów[um] fagis, An. Ox. 23, 30.

be-cuman. Add: I. to come, get, (1) local, of completed movement (arrival, traverse):—Ecbyrht becuman wolde on Germaniam ... ac hē ne mihte; ac Wihtbyrht ðyder becom ... and eft wæs hām hweorfende on Scotland, þanon hē ǣr becom, Bd. 5, 9; Sch. 589, 5-12. Hē lange wun-ode wræclāstum. . . . Syððan forð becom, Chr. 1065; P. 194, 10. Ðæt word becom tó Neróne, Bl. H. 173, 35. Siþþan eástan hider Engle and Seaxe up becōman, Chr. 937; P. 110, 4. Hí ofer sǣ becōmon, 1052; P. 182, 7. Hí becōman on ān convenerunt in unum, Ps. Spl. 2, 2. Farað gesunde and gesǣlige becumað have a good journey and a happy return, Hml. S. 6, 89. Gif þū wǣre wegfērende and þū þonne bæcóme on þeófsceole, Bt. 14, 3; F. 46, 26. Tógædere becuman, Hml. S. 23 b, 643. (I a) of attack:—Hié on Ahtēne ungearwe becōman and hié gefliémdon, Ors. 3, 1; S. 98, 15. (I b) of coming into the world, birth:—þā þū ǣrest tó monnum becóme cum te matris ex utero natura produxit, Bt. 7, 3; F. 20, 10. Hē hider becom of his Fæder rīce, Bl. H. 203, 2. (2) temporal:—Hē tó þām seofoþan dæge ne becymð he will not live till the seventh day, Lch. iii. 76, 23. Ða þā seó hālige tíd lenctenfæstenes becom on þone drihtenlican dæg when Lent had got to the Sunday, Hml. S. 23 b, 649. (3) where a state, condition, position, &c. is reached, to come to power, get into trouble:—Gif hē on rīce becymð si ad regiminis culmen eruperit, Past. 35, 12. Gē becumað on micle yfelu, Deut. 31, 29. Hē becom on hatunga his herges, Bl. H. 193, 1. Hē becom tó ðǣre cynelican geðincðe, Hml. Th. i. 80, 34. Þeós þ becom tó gýmeleáste this law fell into neglect, Angl. vii. 8, 71. Becum-an tó þǣm ēcean lífe, Bl. H. 77, 21. Ne magon ðider fullíce becuman ðā stæpas ðæs weorces ð eder ðe hē wilnað quo desiderium innititur, illuc gressus operis efficaciter non sequuntur, Past. 65, 17. Hí on his anwald becumene wǣron, Chr. 1067; P. 201, 22. ¶ becuman to to become:—Seó ēhtnys him ne becymð tó nānre eádignysse the persecution does not become a blessing to them, Hml. Th. i. 552, 32, 34. Seó leáse wyriung becymð þām rihtwísum tó bletsunge, 554, 22. Þ hit him tó forwyrde be-cume, Angl. vii. 28, 261. Þeúh þe hit ús becóme tó ēcere ālýsednysse, Hml. S. 27, 178. Him tó gemynde þā mihton becuman, Ælfc. T. Grn. 12, 30. (4) of acquirement, to come to, by:—Ǣrþon þe hē tó his leómum becóme, Bl. H. 167, 2. Hí him gefylstan þ hié eft tó hiora āgnum be-cōman vindicati sunt et restituti, Ors. 4, 3; S. 162, 21. Þ hié mósten tó þǣm sāwlum becuman, 3, 3; S. 102, 21. (4 a) where something is received, to come to a person:—Swā hwæt swā gē biddað ... hit eów becymð (-cymeð, L. R.), Mk. 11, 24. (5) of recourse:—On ðæs word ic becom þe lǣs ǣnig man leóge I had recourse to these words lest any man lie, Bl. H. 177, 33. II. of events, to come upon, to befall:—Þ wíte þe nǣnig ende ne becymeþ, Bl. H. 51, 31. Gif him ǣnig hearm of þām drence becymð, Ælfc. T. Grn. 21, 32, 38. Se grama þe ofer mannum becymð, Hml. Th. ii. 538, 28: Wlfst. 201, 6. Him siþþan becom on micel hungor ... him becom on þæt Deniscæ gewin, Ors. 6, 13; S. 268, 8-10. Þā sorga þe on woruld becumað, 89, 14. Ðā bisgu þe on þā rícu becōmon, Bt. proœm. 7. Þāra þinga þe ús on becṓme, Nar. 14, 23. Gif ús on niht uncúðes hwæt on becwóme si quis noctu oriretur pavor tumultusque aliquis novus, 13, 2. Ús wæs swælc ge-swencnis becymen, 14, 31. III. to become, behove:—Gif ic scile ł becyme mec þ ic efne gesuelta ðē etsi oportuerit me commori tibi, Mk. L. 14, 31. [Goth. bi-kwiman: O. Frs. bi-kuma: O. H. Ger. bi-queman.] v. ofer-becuman.

be-cumendlic. v. ofer-becumendlic: be-cunnian. Dele.

be-cwelan. p. -cwæl To die:—Hit becwæð and becwæl sē þe hit āhte he that owned it bequeathed it and died, Ll. Th. i. 184, 1.

be-cweþan. Dele II, and add: I. to say:—Þæt fægere becweðe folca æghwylc, 'Wese swā, wese swā' dicat omnis populus, 'Fiat, fiat,' Ps. Th. 105, 37. I a. with the idea of remonstrance or reproach; cf. be-sprecan:—Gif hwelc iów bicweðes, 'Hwæt dóað gē?', cueoðas ðætte Drihtne nédþarf is, Mk. R. 11, 3. Cweþað him þæt edwīt feóndas þīne, fæste ætwītað; and þæt þīnum crīste becweþað swíðe quod exprobraverunt inimici tui; quod exprobraverunt commutationem christi tui, Ps. Th. 88, 44. I b. to urge, press:—Inculcare, sepe repetere, et aliquando incul-care est in becweð an, Wrt. Voc. ii. 49, 43. v. yfel-onbecweþende. II. to speak for, pray for:—Ðā cōmon þā gebróðra tó ðī þæt hí his sāwle becwǣdon (cf. the same incident in Gr. D. 324, 16: Þā bróðra woldon hine scyldan mid heora gebedum and fore gebiddan (orando protegere), Hml. Th. i. 534, 10. III. to bequeathe, grant by will (cwide):—Hit becwæð sē ðe hit āhte, Ll. Th. i. 184, 1. Būtan þām dǣle þe uncer

gehwæþer his bearnum becwæð, Cht. Th. 486, 4. Hē becwæð his ðincg, and ācwealde hine sylfne, Hml. S. 19, 211. Þām se fæder becwæð ger-suman unātcallendlice, Chr. 1086; P. 219, 14. Gif his yldran him ǣhta becwǣdon, Hml. Th. i. 256, 21. Þæt þū becweðe þīne ðincg, for ðan ðe ðū sweltan scealt, Hml. S. 18, 414. Him þe ic feoh becweden hæbbe, Cht. Th. 490, 20. Þā menn þe ic mīne bócland becweden hæbbe, 491, 8. [O. H. Ger. bi-quethan praedicere.]

be-cwiddian. v. be-cwydded in Dict.

be-cwilman? to torment:—Ne bið þǣr ansýn gesewen ǣnigre wihte būtan þāra cwelra becwylmað (þe cwylmað?) ðā earman (cf. Wlfst. 139, 5: Būton þǣra deófla þe cwylmað þā earman), Dóm. L. 203.

be-cyme. Add: v. on-becyme: be-cýpan, -cyrran. v. be-cípan, -cirran.

bēd a prayer. l. bed, dele passage from Bede, and add:—Blinde men hē mid his bedum gehǣlde, Bl. H. 173, 27. Beaddum precibus, Rtl. 91, 31. Sing ļ.ū ðǣr þīne bedu, Wlfst. 290, 14. Gihēr beodo exaudi preces, Rtl. 97, 14: 103, 38: 90, 20. v. bedu.

bed(d). Add: I. a bed, couch:—Bedd, bed culcites, Txts. 50, 243. Bed culcites, culcitatum, Wrt. Voc. ii. 15, 52, 53. Wolde beddes neósan gamela Scylding, B. 1791: Jud. 63. Bedde culcita, Wrt. Voc. ii. 91, 14. Ic ārās of mīnon bedde (lectulo), Coll. M. 33, 23. Swalt hē sǣringa on his bedde, Chr. 1054; P. 185, 29. Hié restað būton bedde and bolstre quiescentes sine ceruicalibus stratisque, Nar. 31, 11. Drihten him bringð fultum tó his bedde þe hē an lið (super lectum), and eall his bedd (stratum) hē onwent, Ps. Th. 40, 3. Bed æfter būrum, B. 140. On bed stīgan, 676. On ðæt hnesce bed gesinscipes, Past. 397, 22. Reced geondbrǣded weard beddum and bolstrum, B. 1240. Ic syndrigra hūs and bedd (bed, v. l.) geseah singulorum casas ac lectos inspexi, Bd. 4, 25; Sch. 500, 12. v. brýd-, deáþ-, fór-, gærs-, hild-, hlin-, leger-, neó-, rest-, wælbed. II. a surface on which something rests?:—þers-wald limen, oferdyre superliminare, bed spatula, Wrt. Voc. i. 290, 18: Txts. 98, 971. III. of ground. v. grund-bed. III a. of ground where plants grow. v. fearn- (gearn-), rysc-, wīþig-bed. [O. H. Ger. betti areola.] III b. of ground occupied by insects. v. ǣmet-bed, bed-gerid.] See D. D. bed = ant-hill.

be-dǣlan. Dele third passage, and add: I. where attainment is prevented:—Hē hine wile selfne bedǣlan ðǣre bledsunge on ðǣm ýtemestan dæge ... weordað hié bedǣlede (-dǣlde, v. l.) ðæs ēcean ēðles, Past. 333, 3-6. Þ ic heora wurðmyntes ne wurde bedǣled that I might not be prevented from sharing their honour, Hml. S. 28, 103. Bedǣled ælces gōdes destitute of every good, Bt. 18, 1; F. 60, 29. Nis nān man swā swīþe bedǣled ryhtwīsnesse, þ hē nān ryht andwyrde nyte, 35, 1; F. 156, 7. II. where what is possessed is taken away:—Bescyrede vel bedǣlde fraudaverat, Wrt. Voc. ii. 150, 46. Cwyld ælc eorðlic līchama, gyf hē býð ðǣre lyfte bedǣled, Lch. iii. 272, 27. [O. Sax. bi-dēlian: O. H. Ger. bi-teilen privare, fraudare, frustrare.]

bed-bǣr, e; f. A portable bed:—Nim bedbeer ðīn tolle grabatum tuum, Jn. L. 5, 8. Bedbēr, 12.

bed-búr, es; m. A bedchamber:—Bedbūres (bec-, MS.) thalami, Hpt. Gl. 481, 49.

bed-cláþ, es; m. A bed-covering; pl., bed-clothes:—Heó bewand þ bodig mid ðām beddclāðum, Hml. A. 111, 306.

bed-clýfa, l. -cleofa (-clyfa). Add:—In bedcleofan (cubili) his, Ps. Srt. 35, 5. Bedcleofum cubilibus, 4, 5: 149, 5.

bed-cófa. l. -cofa; m.; -cofe; f., and add:—Bedcofa cubiculum, Wrt. Voc. i. 58, 8. Bedcof[a] cubile, Gern. 388, 10. Hyt ys belocen on mýnre bedcofan, Hml. A. 189, 242.

bedd-. v. bed-: bedd-arn(ern). v. beód-ærn.

beddian. Add:—Þā woldon ðā preóstas him wurðlíce beddian, and bǣron micel streáw tó his beddinga, Hml. S. 31, 848. [Dó hyne on wearme bidde, and bedde hys bed myd mórsecge, Lch. iii. 140, 25. He lette hine baðien and beddien feire, Laym. 6658. O. H. Ger. bettōn to make a bed for a person.] v. ge-beddian.

bedding. Add:—Beddingc stramentum, Wrt. Voc. i. 81, 57. On fellum heora bedding, Nar. 31, 12. Hí bǣron micel streáw tó his beddinga ... Þā tōwearp hé þ streáw of þære beddingce, Hml. S. 31, 849, 852. Him weard gebeddod mid hnescre beddinge, 37, 191: 205. Uppan mínre beddincge super stratum meum, Ps. L. 62, 7. Hē læg on his beddinge (in lectulo), Gr. D. 326, 8.

-beddod -bedded. v. þri-beddod.

be-deáglian. Add:—Bedeúhlian celare, Kent. Gl. 952.

bedecian; p. ode To beg:—Hē bedecað (mendicabit) on sumera, Hml. A. 230. 'Hē wile biddan on sumera ...' Hit is swíðe wel be ðǣm gecweden ðæt hē eft bedecige on sumera, Past. 285, 12. v. ā-bedecian.

be-delfan. Add: I. to dig a grave:—Þā byrgena mon feor on eorðan bedelfe, Ll. Th. ii. 408, 12. II. to dig about:—Þæt treów bið bedolfen, Hml. Th. ii. 408, 29. III. to bury, put under ground, (1) of things:—Āgróf se mon on ǣrenum brede drýcræftes word and bedealf under þone þerscwold þæs húses, Shrn. 141, 16. Bedealf ús (the

*crosses*) man on deópan seáðe, Kr. 75. Nim his lifre and bedealf æt þám ymbhwyrftum þínra landgemæra, Lch. i. 328, 22. (2) of persons (when there are no funeral rites):—Hié þá Rómáne cuce on eorþan bedulfan *Minucia viva obruta est in campo*, Ors. 3, 6; S. 108, 19. Hé hine lét ofsleán and deópe bedelfan, Chr. 1049; P. 168, 38. **IV.** *to bury, put in a grave or tomb*:—Git métað weal; bedelfað on ðám þone líchoman, Shrn. 139, 27. Bebyrge † bidelfa *sepelire*, Jn. L. 19, 40. [O. Sax. bi-delban: O. Frs. bi-delva: O. H. Ger. bi-telban.]

**bed-felt.** *Add*:—Tó bedreáfe (bedd-, *v. l.*) genihtsumige tó hæbbenne meatte and hwítel and bedfelt (*lena*) and heáfodbolster, R. Ben. 91, 16.

**bed-gemána,** an; *m. Cohabitation*:—Ðone ymbhogan hé ne forlét ðæs flæsclícan beddgemánan *nec stratum carnalium sollicitudine deserit*, Past. 99, 25.

**bed-gerid,** es; *n. An ants' nest*:—Nime æmettan mid hiora bedgeride, Lch. ii. 328, 8. v. æmet-bed *and* gerid.

**be-dífan;** *p.* de *To plunge* (trans.), *immerse*:—Heó weard gelædd tó sumre eá and on wætere bedýfed (*in aquam mersa*), Gr. D. 73, 24.

**be-díglian.** *Add*: **I.** *to conceal*, (1) with noun as object:—Hé þ sóð bedíglað, Hml. A. 148, 104. Bedíólað gelt *celat commissum*, Kent. Gl. 361: 425. Þíne rihtwísnesse ic on mínre heortan ne bedíglode (*abscondidi*), R. Ben. 11, 7: *operui*, 28, 20. Bedígla hit, Lch. iii. 188, 15. Heó hine bedíglian (*celare*) ne mihte, Ex. 2, 3: Hml. S. 2, 228. Bedígledes *secreti .i. occulti*, An. Ox. 1442. (2) with clause:—Hé ne bedíglode þ hé on Drihten gelýfde, Hml. S. 5, 160. **I a.** *to conceal from* (*dat.*):—Hé bedíglode his ðæda þám cásere, Hml. S. 5, 9. Nán þing Gode bedíglian, Angl. xii. 513, 14. Swilce his tócyme mancynne bedíglod wære, Hml. Th. i. 82, 30: Hml. A. 53, 84. Þý læs mé ówiht in þæm londe beholen oððe bedégled wære *ne quid mihi in ignotis subtraheretur locis*, Nar. 20, 21. **II.** *to be concealed, lie hid*:—Ic nelle þ þe þis bedíglige (-deóglige, *v. l.*) and sý bemiðen *hoc nolo te lateat*, Gr. D. 174, 30.

**be-dígling,** e; *f. Concealment, secret place*:—On bedíglingce hreóhnysse *in abscondito tempestatis*, Ps. Spl. 80, 7.

**be-dípan** *to dip, plunge*:—Bedýp on fontwætre, Lch. ii. 344, 23. Sié bideped (*intinguatur*) fót ðín in blóde, Ps. Srt. 67, 24. Se ráp wæs bedýped (-dyp-?) in þám wætre *funis tingeretur aqua*, Gr. D. 214, 26. Bedíped *inditus*, Wrt. Voc. ii. 48, 62. Hé biþ bedýped on þá neoþemestan helle wítu, Bl. H. 185, 6. Þysne bedíptan (-dyp-, *v. l.*) hláf, Hml. A. 163, 253. v. be-dyppan.

**be-dirnan** (-dyrnan, q. v. *in Dict.*) *to conceal*:—Se hord þe þú oþ nú bedyrndest, Hml. S. 23, 662. Bemíþan, bedyrnan *dissimulare, i. occultare* (*desiderium*), An. Ox. 983. Hí synd nú bedyrnde þ hí nán man ne mæg gefindan, Hml. S. 23, 290. ¶ *to conceal from* (*dat.*):—Wé willað ðæt andgit eów geopenian and ða dýgelnysse eów ne bedyrnan, Hml. Th. ii. 214, 18. Ne nihte ic hire bedyrnan mínes módes unrótnesse, Shrn. 41, 23. Eall þeós mennisce gebyrd Sancte Johanne bedyrned is *St. John knew nothing of (was not subject to) frailties natural to humanity*, Bl. H. 167, 27. [O. Sax. be-dernian: O. H. Ger. bi-tarnen.]

**bedol.** v. bedul.

**béd-ræden.** *l.* bed-ræden, *and substitute: Prayers*:—Bist ðú on úre bedrædene *we will pray for you*, Wlfst. 290, 17. Wé habbaþ heom geunnen þá bedræddene for life and for ðeþe *we have promised to pray for them while alive and after death*, Cht. Th. 436, 15. v. gebed-ræden.

**be-dragan.** *Dele, and see* be-dróg.

**bed-reáf.** *Add*:—Ic geann ánes beddreáfes mid ðám hryfte and mid hoppscýtan and mid eallum ðám ðe ðærtó gebyreð . . . and ic geann mínum suna ánes beddreáfes, C. D. iii. 294, 4, 35. Hió becwið eal ðæt bedréf ðe ðærtó gebyreð, vi. 133, 10. Búrþénon his beddreáf, Cht. Crw. 23, 30. *Fulcris, thoris, lectis vel* heáfodbolstrum *vel* bedreáfum, Wülck. Gl. 245, 30. Munecas bedreáf (*lectisternia*) onfón æfter heora drohtnunge gemete, R. Ben. 47, 3. Ðonne þú bedreáf habban wylle, þonne wege þú þín reáf, Tech. ii. 126, 4. v. bed-felt.

**bed-reda.** *Add*:—Bedrida *paraliticus*, Wrt. Voc. i. 45, 61. Beddreda oððe sé þe hæfð paralisin, 75, 48. Þín cniht lið æt hám bedreda (*paralyticus*. v. Mt. 8, 6), Hml. Th. i. 126, 6. His cépte sum beddryda þe læg seofon geár tóslopenum limum . . . þá bletsode hé þone beddrydan mann, Hml. S. 6, 254-7. Hé læg bæddryda sume nigon geár and of þám bedde ne mihte, búton hine man bære, 21, 339. Beddryda, 24, 84. Gemétte hé ánne bæddrydan (bed-, *v. l.*) for eahta geárum lama. Þá cwæð hé tó þám earman bæddrydan . . . þá gelýfde seó burhwaru þurh þæs bæddrydan hæle, 10, 41-50. Feówer bedrydan wurdon gehælede, H. R. 105, 1. Þearfgendum mannum and bedridan, Wlfst. 181, 14. Fela bedridan hé gehælde, Hml. Th. ii. 476, 10. Bedrydan, Hml. S. 24, 91. Beddrydan, 16, 140.

**bedrian,** Glostr. Frag. 10, 30. v. be-dydrian.

**be-drífan.** *Add*: **I.** *where movement is caused*:—Ne mæg beón gehæfd se mete, ac beóþ somod þá innoþas bedrifen, Lch. ii. 278, 15. His scip weard bedrifen and genýded tó þan eálande, Gr. D. 305, 27. **I a.** *of flight, banishment*, &c.:—Hí ealle þá áwergdan on helle grund bedrífaþ, Bl. H. 95, 8. Alfwold Æðelréd bedráf on (of?) lande, Chr. 778;

P. 53, 15. Hí sume on fleáme bedrifon on þone wudu, 477; P. 14, 9: 890; P. 82, 14: Ors. 3, 1; S. 98, 12. Hié hié gefliémdon and hié bedrifon intó Rómebyrg, 3, 10; S. 138, 29. Wæs þæs folces mycel on fleám bedrifen, Chr. 1066; P. 196, 35. Biþ hé on écne weán bedrifen, Bl. H. 95, 5. **I b.** *to drive game*:—Hundas bedrifon hyne tó mé *canes perduxerunt eum* (*aprum*) *ad me*, Coll. M. 22, 15. **II.** *where something is done or suffered under compulsion*:—Ðonne mon býð tyhtlan betygen and hine mon bedrífeð tó ceápe, Ll. Th. i. 142, 1, 5. Bedrífe man hine tó swingum, 132, 10. Witeþeówne monnan mon sceal bedrífan tó swingum (swinglum, *v. l.*), 138, 3. **III.** *to follow up a track*:—Gif mon trode bedrífð forstolenes yrfes of stæðe on óðer, Ll. Th. i. 352, 4. Gyf him hundred bedrífe trod on óðer hundred, 260, 3.

**be-drincan.** *Add*:—[Fort se ruse habbe bedruncan þat wyn, Lch. iii. 112, 7.]

**béd-ríp.** *l.* bed-ríp, es; *n., and add*:—Aelc man in Sce Eádmundes byri húsfast on his ówc land sal gifen tó þe hálegenes bidcríþe ón peni, Cht. Th. 438, 7. [v. *N. E. D.* bed-rip: Andrews' Old English Manor, p. 159.]

**be-drípan;** *p.* te; *pp.* ed *To moisten*:—Of bedrýpedum cláþe *linteolo madido*, Germ. 391, 18.

**be-dróg.** *Dele*: '*p.* of be-dragan,' *and add* = O. Sax. be-dróg, *p. of* be-driogan.

**be-drúgian;** *p.* oðe *To dry up*:—Meng wið ele, smyre, and þonne þ bedrúgud sý, eft þú hit geníwa, Lch. i. 336, 4.

**bed-streáw,** es; *n. Straw used for bedding*:—Of his bedstréwe man band on ánne wódne; þá gewát se deófol him of, Hml. S. 31, 572. (Cf. streáw tó his beddinga, 849.)

**bed-þén, -þeg(e)n.** *Add*:—Bedþegn *cubicularius, custos cubili*, Wrt. Voc. ii. 137, 37.

**bedu,** e; *f. Request, prayer*:—Góddra þinga bedu ys *bonarum rerum postulatio est*, Scint. 170, 13. Ðínre béne ic wille onfón, and for ðínre bede ic ne tóweorpe ðá burg, Past. 399, 31. [*Goth.* bida *a request, prayer.*]

**bed-wahrift.** *l.* -wáh- (-wág-).

**be-dydrian.** *Add*: **I.** *to delude*:—Bedydrode *lubricat, lubricos facit, decipit*, An. Ox. 50, 30. Se swicola feónd hí swíðe bedydrode, þ swilce ðær sum hús sóðlíce forburne, Hml. Th. ii. 140, 15: 166, 9. Þá dwolmen hine bedydrodon, Hml. S. 3. 316, 320. God sylf forbeád þ wé swefnum ne folgion, þe læs ðe se deófol ús bedydrian (bedrian, Glostr. Frag. 10, 30) mæge, 21, 413. **II.** *to conceal from* (*wið*):—Se swicola bedyddrað (-dyderað, -dydrað, *v. ll.*) his ðæda wið menn, ac hí beóð geopenode oft unþances, Hml. S. 19, 174. [Itt maʒʒ þe wrecche follc forrblendenn and bididdrenn, Orm. 15391.]

**be-dyppan.** *Add*:—Heó wæs gelædd tó ánre eá and bedypped in þ wæter (*in aquam mersa*), Gr. D. 73, 24.

**be-dyrnan.** v. be-dirnan.

**be-eástan;** *prep. To the east of*, (1) with dat.:—Be-eástan him, Ors. 1, 1; S. 16, 9 (and often). Him is be-eástan se Wendelsæ, S. 28, 15. Be-eástan Ríne, S. 14, 36. Be-eástan Selwyda, Chr. 878; P. 76, 7. Nóht feor be-eástan ðære byrig, Shrn. 66, 22. (2) with acc.:—On þæm londe be-eástan Rín, Chr. 887; P. 80, 23. Be-eástan ðá bircan, C. D. iii. 213, 3. [v. *N. E. D.* be-east.]

**be-eástan-norþan** *to the north-east of*, Ors. 1, 1; Th. 246, 16. v. norþan-eástan *in Dict.*

**be-efesian** *to cut the hair of* a person:—Hwá mæg mé beefesian?, Hml. S. 33, 84. v. be-ceorfan.

**be-fæstan.** *Dele passage under I, and add*: **I.** *to fix*, (1) *to place in security*:—Hié befæston hira wíf and hira scipu and hira feoh on Eást-Englum, Chr. 894; P. 88, 4. Þá Deniscan hæfdon hira wíf and bearn innan Eást-Engle, 896; P. 89, 22. Bið se þridda dæl in þæs wylmes grund líge befæsted, árleásra sceolu in gléda gripe, El. 1300. (1 a) of burial. v. II. (2):—Líchaman on eorðan befæstan, Hml. S. 23 b, 781, 786. (2) *to fix in the mind, implant*:—Ðæt ðú ðone wísdóm ðe ðé God sealde ðær, ðæt ðú hine befæstan mæge, befæste, Past. 5, 4. Eallum óþrum mannum þú mihtest þín unriht befæstan, Bl. H. 175, 28. (3) *to fix by promise or agreement, to pledge*:—Hé wrát his handgewrit þám deófle and him mannrædene befæste, Hml. Th. i. 448, 15. Bifæsted him wíf *desponsata sibi uxor*, Lk. R. 2, 5. **II.** *to commit*:—Ic befæste committo, Wrt. Voc. ii. 22, 6. Tó befæstenne *committenda*, 23, 76. (1) *to commit to a person's charge*:—Hym ic mé befæste, Shrn. 189, 33. An þíne handa ic befæste (*commendo*) míne sáwle, Ps. Th. 30, 5. Þás sceáp þú mé befæsttest, Bl. H. 191, 25. Þæt hé befæste þæt pund, þe him God befæste, sumum óðrum men, Ælfc. Gr. 2, 2, 26. Ðæt hié tó sláwlíce ðára ne giémen ðe him befæste sién *ut a commissorum custodia minime torpescant*, Past. 191, 24. (1 a) where purpose of committing is given:—Hé befæste þá burg Æþeréde tó haldonne, Chr. 886; P. 80, 13. Manega befæstan heora cild tó láre þám sóðfæstan bydele, Hml. S. 22, 64. Gif hwylc wile his lytlingas hiom tó láre befæstan, Ll. Th. ii. 414, 9. (2) *to commit to a place*:—Befæste *tradidit* (*orci faucibus*), An. Ox. 839. þ man mid sealmsange þ líc corðan befæste *ut cum psalmorum cantu corpus terrae committatur*, Ll.

Th. ii. 184, 7. Hí woldon þǽre byrgene hine befæstan (*tradere*), Gr. D. 154, 23. (3) *to set, betake* to an occupation :—His dohtor befæste se fæder tó láre, þ heó on woruldwýsdóme wǽre getogen, · Hml. S. 2, 19. III. *to commend, recommend*, (1) *implying appeal* :—Sum man wæs hine sylfne befæstende tó his gebedum *quidam se eius orationibus commendans*, Gr. D. 203, 4. (2) *to make acceptable* :—Se ofermete ne befæsð ús nǽfre Gode *esca nos non commendat Deo*, Past. 317, 19. Befæste hé mid his lífes bisenum ða láre ðǽm ðe his wordum ne geliéfen *quod a non quaerente suscipitur, vita commendet*, 25, 1. IV. *to trust* :—Befæstyd *creditus*, Ps. Spl. C. 77, 11. Befæst *credatur*, An. Ox. 1711. v. bi-fæstan *in Dict.*

be-fæstnian; *p.* ode. I. *to fix* :—Búton gé ða heáfodleahtras him on befæstnian, ne sceal hé for ðám lǽssan losian, Hml. Th. ii. 336, 21. II. *to pledge, betroth.* v. be-feastnian *in Dict.* [O. Frs. bi-festena.]

be-fædman. *Add* : -, fæþmian. I. *to embrace* :—Ic befæðme, Rä. 88, 19. Heó Sceppend seolf befæðmed, Sat. 310: 359. Ús befæðman wile freóbearn Godes, 289. II. *to enclose* :—God ealle þincg befehð and befæðmað, Hml. S. 23 b, 584.

be-fǽttian *to fatten* :—Ele ne áfǽttaþ ł ne be[fǽttaþ] heáfod mín *oleum non inpinguet caput meum*, Ps. L. 140, 5.

befangenlic. v. un-befangenlic.

be-faran. *Add* : *to come upon, surprise, catch* :—Ætsǽton ða Centiscan bæaftan . . . þa befór se here hié ðǽr, Chr. 905; P. 94, 7. Þa landesmenn hine befóron innan þǽre burh and hine ofslógon, 1068; P. 203, 21. Gif man hwilcne man teó þ hé þone man féde þa úres hláfordes grið tóbrocen habbe . . . and gif hine (*the man so accused*) man mid him (*the breaker of the peace*) befare, beón hig bégen ánes rihtes weorðe, Ll. Th. i. 298, 2. Þa cýdde man intó þǽre scipfyrde þet hí mann eaðe befaran mihte, gif man ymbe beón wolde, Chr. 1009; P. 138, 20. [O. Frs. bi-fara *to come upon, catch.*] v. be-féran, *and cf.* be-rídan.

be-fealdan. *Add* : I. *to fold up, roll up* :—Heofon biþ befealden swá swá bóc, Bl. H. 91, 25. Befalden swé swé geteld *convoluta quasi tabernaculum*, Ps. Srt. ii. p 184, 30. I a. *to bend the body* (?) :—Befealden (-feallen?) tó Hǽlendes cneówum hé cwæþ, Bl. H. 87, 36. II. *to fold up in something, wrap up* :—Hé þone líchaman on scýtan befeóld, Lk. 23, 53. Befeald hyt on caules leáfe, Lch. i. 106, 17. Befeald on wulle, 206, 1. II a. *fig.* :—Befealdon *contentum, sufficiens*, Germ. 402, 54. III. *to entwine* : *implicare* :—Befealdende hófringas hófum *inplicans orbes orbibus*, An. Ox. 17. III a. *fig. to involve, implicate* :—Befelt *involvet*, Kent. Gl. 1058. Ðæt hié ne sién tó wyrsan gecirde and ðǽron befealdne *deterioribus implicantur*, Past. 271, 12. IV. *to attach* :—Tó befeóld *applicavit*, Wrt. Voc. ii. 3, 43. Hé (*the town*) wæs tó þæs pápan ǽhte bifealden, Hml. A. 199, 150. [O. H. Ger. pi-faltan *involvere*.]

be-feallan. *Add* : I. *to fall*, (1) *literal* :—Hé on þone pytt befylð *in foveam incidit*, Ps. Th. 7, 15. (1 a) *to get into* :—Se deófol befylð intó Antecristes móder innoðe, Wlfst. 193, 16. Þ furðon án speatwa on gryn ne mæg befeallan forútan his foresceáwunge, Chr. 1067; P. 201, 25. (2) *figurative*, (a) *to fall* into sin, into the hands of a person, &c. :—Mé is leófre þ ic on Godes handa befealle, þonne ic on mannes handa befealle, Hml. S. 13, 248. Befeld *incidet* (*in malum*), Kent. Gl. 614. Hé befeóll on untrumnysse, Hml. S. 33, 261. Ðæt hé suá suíðe wið ðæt winne suá hó on ðæt óðer ne befealle, Past. 189, 11. On hwelce ðǽra synna hié befeóllen, 417, 33. Hé wæs on gítsunge befeallan, Chr. 1086; P. 221, 4. On þǽre frecednysse þe hé on befeallen wæs, Hml. S. 25, 785. Gif hé ǽnigne man wite on heáfodleahtrum befeal(l)enne, Ll. Th. ii. 246, 1. (b) *to fall* to action :—Weard hé tó manslehte befeallen, Hml. Th. i. 484, 13. (c) *to fall upon, take effect* on a person :—Þonne ðǽres mannes dǽd befylð on mǽ oððe on ðé, þonne byþ þæt *passivum verbum*, Ælfc. Gr. Z, 120, 11. On befeól hárnys *inrepsit canities*, Germ. 388, 23. (d) *to fall to, be assigned to* :—On scortne *ir* befylð án ágen nama, Ælfc. Gr. Z. 45, 11. On scortne *ar* befeallað þás naman, 42, 4: 48, 15: 49, 17. (Cf. sé gescyrta *es* underfehð fela naman, 51, 7.) Seó óðer *praeteritum* geendað on *ii*, ac on ðǽre ne befeallað ná má worda, 166, 9. II. befeallen (æt) *deprived* (*of*) :—Hí wǽron æt hiora yldran befeallen(n)e, Lch. iii. 424, 13. [O. Sax. bi-fallan: O. Frs. bi-falla: O. H. Ger. bi-fallan.]

be-fégan; *p.* de *To join* :—Hí fundon ǽlcne stán on óðerne befégedne, Hml. S. 23, 425.

be-felgan. *Dele, and take examples under* be-feólan: be-feohtan. *Add* : [O. Frs. bi-fiuchta.] v. un-befohten.

be-feólan. *l.* be-feólan, *dele first passage, and add* : *p.* -fealh, -feall, -feal, *pl.* ful(g)on. I. *trans.* (1) *to bury* :—Mon sceal morðor under eorðan befeólan þe hit forhelan þenceþ, Gn. Ex. 115. [Cf. O. Sax. Sia thena líkhamon befulhun an themo felise.] (2) *to bear, be pleased with* :—Ne eaþmódnesse iuc ná leng befeólan nellaþ *nec iugum humilitatis diutius sustinere contenti sunt* (*contendunt, v. l.*), R. Ben. 135, 8. Sé þe woruldlicra manna sprǽce gelómlíce wilnað, þonne ne mæg hé þa engeilican sprǽce befeólan, Guth. 52, 23. II. *intrans.* (1) *to apply oneself earnestly* to something (*dat.*) :—Hé mid geornfullnysse befealh his gebedum *annisu precibus incubuit*, Gr. D. 74, 18: 125, 27. Befeall,

Guth. 86, 20. Befeal, 26, 21: 42, 12: 46, 20. Ðára ðe spéda hæbben ðæt hié ðǽm (*learning*) befeólan mægen, Past. 7, 11. Ne mæg ic ðǽre stídnysse befeólan þe þú mé tó tíhst, Hml. Th. ii. 374, 15. (2) *to be urgent with* a person (*dat.*), *to press* :—Hé mid gemálicum bénum befealh þám hálgan wer þ him wǽre álýfed út tó farenne *importunis precibus ut relaxaretur imminebat*, Gr. D. 156, 1. Se kyng befealh georne hire bréðer oð þ hé cwæð iá wið, Chr. 1067; P. 201, 21. (2 a) *reflexive, to persist, persevere* with something :—Hí þone Godes wer gesáwon him befeólan mid þǽre cyllfyllinge *virum Dei ad implendum utrem sibi invertere videbant*, Gr. D. 250, 27. (3) *with prep. to persist in, continue* :—þ þæs Hǽlendes líc him wurde forstolen, mid ðám þe hí befúlon fæste on slǽpe *while they continued fast asleep*, Hml. A. 79, 159. [O. Frs. bi-fella: O. Sax. bi-felhan: O. H. Ger. pi-fel(a)han.] v. be-felgan, bi-felgan, -feolan *in Dict.*

be-feón; *pp.* -feoð *To deprive of property* (feoh), *to confiscate* :—þ hé wǽre benǽmed, befeóð (-fiód, Hpt. Gl. 480, 53) *infiscaretur*, i. *fraudaretur*, An. Ox. 3157.

befer. *For* ? *after* ponticus *substitute* : (*ponticus canis* = castor, Migne), *and add* :—Bebr *fiber*, Txts. 60, 399. Bebir(-er) *castorius*, 52, 272. Befer *fiber*, Wrt. Voc. ii. 35, 33 : *castor*, 129, 34. Befor, i. 66, 3. Beofer *fiber*, 78, 16. On beueres bróces heáfod, C. D. v. 48, 8. The word occurs in local names, v. C. D. vi. 257, col. 2.

be-féran. *Substitute* : I. *to go about, from place to place*, Mk. 6, 6 (*in Dict.*). II. *to come upon, overtake, catch* (of a pursuing force) :—Hé beférde þæt folc þǽr hig gewícode wǽron *cum persequerentur Aegyptii vestigia praecedentium, repererunt eos in castris*, Ex. 14, 9. Hé beférde Maximum binnan ánre byrig, Hml. S. 31, 647: Bl. H. 79, 24. II a. *intrans. To get, fall among* :—Hé beferde ł becuom on ða ðeáfas *incidit in latrones*, Lk. L. 10, 30. III. *to pass by* :—Ðára naman ic beférde (*praeterii*), Lch. i. lxxii, 11. v. be-faran.

be-fician. *Add* :—Swician and befician and mid leásbregdum earmum mannum derian, Ll. Th. ii. 320, 25.

be-filgan. *For* v. be-felgan *read* v. be-fylgan: be-fillan *to fell. See examples under* be-fyllan *in Dict.*: be-flagen flǽsc. *Dele, and see next word.*

be-fleán. *Add* : I. *to strip the skin or bark off* :—Berinde, beflóg *decorticavit*, Wrt. Voc. ii. 25, 47. Befleán *deglobere*, 138, 29. Behyldan, befleán *deglobere* .i. *decoriare*, An. Ox. 3280. Hét hé hine cwicne befleán, Shrn. 84, 29 : 121, 1. Tó befleánne *euiscerandum*, Germ. 393, 109. Befagen *excoriatus*, Wrt. Voc. i. 27, 33. Beflagen fǽ[s]c *flesh with the skin stripped off*; *viscera*, 45, 7. II. *to strip off* (skin) :—Befleh (fleah, *v. l.*) ǽnne þwang þám biscope fram þám hneccan oþ þene hóh *episcopo a vertice usque ad calcaneum corrigiam tolle*, Gr. D. 198, 4.

be-fleógan. *Substitute* : *To come by flying, fly* on to :—Beflugan (upp flugon *v. l.*) ða spearcan on ðæs húses hróf *the sparks flew on to the roof of the house*, Bd. 3, 10; Sch. 234, 4.

be-fleón. *Add* :—Beflugan *aufugiunt*, Wrt. Voc. ii. 2, 37. Bifleónde *subterfugiens*, 83, 8. I. *absolute, to flee* :—Ðá ðe hire tó befleóð hió geheald *fugientem salvet infirmum*, Past. 399, 15. II. *to flee from* (with. acc.) :—þ hié Godes erre beflugon, Bl. H. 169, 11. þæt hit æfc befluge, Guth. 20, 22. Ðeáh hé hæbbe beflogen ðone gesinscipe, næfð hé nó beflogen ða byrðenne, Past. 401, 21–2. II a. *to flee from*, (1) with dat. :—Heó befleáh þám gesettan gyfte tó Godes cyrican, Gr. D. 199, 15. (2) with prep., Bd. 4, 25; S. 599, 39 (*in Dict.*). v. bi-fleón *in Dict.*

be-flítan. v. un-beflíten.

be-flówan. *Add* : *To come by flowing, to flow* to :—Welan þeáh þe tó beflówan *dinitiae si affluant*, Ps. L. 61, 11.

be-fón. *Add* : I. *to seize, catch, take*, (1) of persons :—Ýþelíce þú his hond beféhst, Nar. 31, 24. Hé (þone méce) mid handa beféng, Exod. 415. (1 a) *to seize, take forcible possession of* :—Laumeneda beféng ealle Asirie, Ors. 3, 11 ; S. 142, 28. (1 b) *implying restraint* :—Se anwealda hæfð ealle his gesceafta mid his brídle befangene, Bt. 21 ; F. 74, 6. (1 c) *to seize* a criminal, lost property, &c. :—Mon forstæl ǽnne wimman Ælfsige . . . Ða beféng Ælfsige þone mann æt Wulfstáne, Cht. Th. 206, 23. Gif þiéfefioh mon æt ciépan befó, Ll. Th. i. 118, 13. Sé geypte déman þæt Tiburtius wæs crísten, and hé wæs befangen, Shrn. 116, 24. ¶ *to take in the act* :—In dernelegerscip beféon *in adulterio deprehensam*, Jn. L. 8, 3. (1 d) *to catch, get to see* a person :—Gang tó ðám Godes menn þ þu hine befó ǽr his forðsíðe, Hml. S. 3, 649. (1 e) *to get, attain to* :—Þte þá úe bifóe (*contingamus*) ðóhte, Rtl. 71, 21. (2) of things :—Cwaecung biféng (*adprehendit*) hié, Ps. Srt. 47, 7. Heó mid wundrunge weard befangen, Hml. S. 2, 251. Weard hé befangen mid hreónesse *he was caught in a storm*, Gr. D. 248, 18. Is tó ongietanne þæt hú micelre sclyde ðá beóð befangene *quanta culpa involvantur aspiciant*, Past. 377, 23. II. *to surround, encompass.* (1) *to enclose*, (a) *to serve as a covering for, contain* :—Beféhþ *circumgirat*, An. Ox. 696. Beféhð *ambit*, 23, 38. Þæs mǽdenes sex beféng hí eall abútan, Hml. S. 7, 145. Þone ne magon befón heofon and eorþe, Bl. H. 5, 34. Þeós circe mihte fíf hund manna befón, 207, 14. Be-

fangen *circumamicta*, An. Ox. 1024. Ylp is mid bánum befangen binnan þám felle, Hml. S. 25, 567. Heora breósta beóð mid byrnum befangene, Wlfst. 200, 13. (b) *to put into a covering* :—Eal folc Rómwara beféng þá líchoman on þære stówe Catacumbe, Bl. H. 193, 11. Befóh útan mid golde, Past. 169, 23. Swá micel swá þu mid twám handum mæge befón, Lch. ii. 238, 12. (2) *to encircle*, (a) *to lie round* :—Asia is befangen (*circumcincta*) mid þæm gársecge súþan and norþan and eástan, Ors. 1, 1 ; S. 8, 7 : 12, 12. Hié wæron on ælce healfe útan befangen, 5, 7 ; S. 230, 19. (b) *to place round* :—Befóþ *cingunt, circumdant*, An. Ox. 2040. Hé befénge *circumdedit* (*me gemmis*), 4294. Hé beféng mínne swíðran mid stánum, Hml. S. 7, 32. Hé mid his earmum beféng his cneówu, Gr. D. 36, 23. Hé nolde his heáfod befón mid cynehelme, Hml. Th. i. 162, 13. (3) *of abstract objects, to include, contain, comprise* :—Seó forme bóc beféhð þás racu, Ælfc. T. Grn. 3, 19. Helmstán þis eal on þon áþe beféng, Cht. Th. 170, 27. Befongen *compressa*, Wrt. Voc. ii. 22, 15. (3 a) *to surround with words, furnish* with a commentary :—Ús gedafenað þæt wé underfón Drihtnes trahtnunge, and ðá ðing þe hé læfde ús tó trahtmigenne wé sceolon mid scortre race ðá befón, Hml. Th. ii. 90, 5. III. *with prep.* on. (1) *to have to do with an object* :—Se fæder nyste hú hé beféng on hig *ille non sensit quando accubuit filia*, Gen. 19, 33. Gif hwylc man mid arwan deór ofsceóte . . . and hit man ymbe .iii. niht deád finde, and þær hund oþþe wulf on befangen hæbbe (*have had anything to do with it ; eam occupaverit*), Ll. Th. ii. 212, 22. (2) *to engage in an occupation, get involved in an action* :—Ðonne hwá on ðá leásunga beféhð, ðonne ne mæg hé of, Past. 239, 12. Ðonne se Godes ðíow on ðæt gemearr ðære woruldsorga beféhð *quem curarum secularium impedimentum praepedit*, 401, 21. Gif hwæm gebyrige ðæt hé on ðá tælinge his hláfordes befóo . . . on ðæs hwæt befóo ðe wið his willan sié, 199, 14, 23. Þte nænig mon ne geþrístlæce on þone hálgan dæg on nán weoruldweorc befón, Ll. Th. ii. 420, 22. Ær hé hæbbe godcunde bóte underfangen and wið ðá mægðe on bóte befangen (*set his hand to the work of making* bót *to the kin*), Ll. Th. i. 248, 25. [*O. Sax.* bi-fáhan : *O. Frs.* bi-fá : *O. H. Ger.* pi-fáhan.] v. bi-fón, æt-befón *in Dict.*

**be-fóndlic.** v. un-befóndlic.

**be-fóran.** l. be-foran, *and add* : A. *prep.* I. *local*, (1) *with dat.* (2) *in the presence of* :—Gif hit beforan þám hláforde wæs *si impraesentiarum dominus fuerit*, Ex. 22, 15. ¶ *where a particular part of a person is specified, before one's eyes, &c.* :—Þone mist ðe hangaþ beforan úres módes eágum, Bt. 33, 4 ; F. 132, 32. Beforan Drihtnes gesihþe, Bl. H. 157, 24. Beforan his fótum, 247, 11. (b) *in front of an object* :—Beforan þæs ecan Déman heáhsetle, Bl. H. 53, 7. Beforan ðære norðdura þære ciricean, 203, 34. Beforan Mermedonia ceastre, 235, 18. Beforan his ródetácne forhtigað heofen and eorþe, 245, 19. (c) *a-head of, over against* :—Gáþ on þá wíc þe beforan inc stondeð, Bl. H. 77, 22. (d) *marking relative position or order, before, in advance of* :—Oþre apostolas beóþ sende beforan hire bære, Bl. H. 147, 22 : 163, 34. Ic sende mínne engel beforan þínre onsýne, se gerweþ þínne weg beforan þé, 167, 29. Ðá ðe férdon beforan þære fyrde, Chr. 1016 ; P. 150, 9. (2) *with acc.* (a) *into the presence of* :—Hé beforan þone cyning gelæd wæs, Bt. 16, 2 ; F. 52, 22. In feccan beforan hine, Bl. H. 175, 2. Hé héht hié ealle þrý in beforan hine, 18. (b) *where something is put into position* :—Hé þone ásette beforan þ weofod, Gr. D. 51, 5. II. *temporal, with dat.* :—Beforan ðære cenninge, and on ðære cenninge, and æfter ðære cenninge, Hml. Th. ii. 10, 3. Beforan þám, Ll. Th. i. 86, 15. Beforan þissum, Chr. 937 ; P. 110, 1. III. *marking degree, rank*, (1) *with dat.* :—Swá micle swá se bið beforan ðe on ðæm stóle sitt ðæm óðrum ðe ðær ymb stondað *sicut assistentibus turbis praelati sunt qui cathedrae honore fulciuntur*, Past. 435, 27. S. Iohannes gæþ beforan (*takes precedence of*) eallum óþrum wítgan, Bl. H. 167, 22. Ðæs menniscan lífes gecynd is þ hí sién beforan eallum óþrum gesceaftum *humanae naturae conditio est, ut ceteris rebus excellat*, Bt. 14, 3 ; F. 46, 4. Beforan gesegnesse licwurðe *pleasing beyond expression*, Hml. S. 23 b, 73. (2) *with acc.* :—Ne sceal hé þone æþelborenan settan beforan þane þeówborenan, R. Ben. 12, 13. B. *adv.* I. *local, before, in advance* :—Hé his ærendracan beforan ásende tó þære ðeóde, Ors. 1, 10 ; S. 44, 7. Ðá eóde se man in beforan tó ðám cynge, Ap. Th. 14, 8. II. *temporal* :—Hié eal þ tóweard wæs beforan wítgodan, Bl. H. 161, 15 : 163, 26. ¶ *combined with* ær :—God hit wát eall beforan, ær hit gewyrþe, Bt. 41, 3 ; F. 248, 28. Wæs hé beforan ær þá þreó geár gecrístnod, Bl. H. 215, 35. Swá Antecríst ær beforan dyde, 95, 3. Eal hé þ ær beforan on onlíc weorc áteáh, 215, 5. [*O. Sax.* bi-foran.] v. bi-foran *in Dict.*

**be-forhtian** ; *p.* ode *To fear* :—Þá ðincg þe ic swíðe þearle sylf beforhtige, Hml. S. 23 b, 525.

**be-fótian.** *Add* :—Se cyning hét hine befótian, Hml. S. 25, 117.

**be-frignung**, -frínung, e ; *f. Enquiry, investigation* :—Befrínungum, smeáungum *sciscitationibus*, i. *interrogationibus*, An. Ox. 2309.

**be-frinan.** l. be-frignan, -frínan ; *p.* -frán, *pl.* -frúnon, -frinon ; *pp.* -frúnen, -frinen, *and add* : I. *to ask* a person a question, (a) *the question stated* :—Gif eówre bearn eów befrínað, 'Hwæt dóð þá stánas hér ?',

Jos. 4, 6. Þá befrán se cyning his cnihtas and cwæþ, 'Hwylce méðe hæfde Mardocheus ?', Hml. A. 98, 216 : 99, 257. (b) *question indirect* :—Hé befrán his witan hwæt him þúhte be þám, Hml. A. 93, 46 : 156, 115. Hé befrán ðá hwám ðá gebytlu gemynte wæron, Hml. Th. ii. 354, 34. Hé hí befrán on hwilcne tíman hí þone steorran gesáwon, i. 82, 8. Heó befrínen þone cásere hwæt heó scolden, Hml. A. 194, 37. Ðone pápan þ hié befrínon hwæt him tó ræde þúhte, Bl. H. 205, 20. II. *to ask, question*, (1) *a person* :—Ic gewréged ðé ne wiðsóc, befrínen (*when questioned*) ic ðé geandette, Hml. Th. i. 426, 3. (2) *to ask about something* :—Ðás alle cynna befraignes (*inquirunt*), Mt. L. 6, 32. Cúðberhtus cwæþ þæt hé ðá sceolde befrínan his nýdþearfnysse, Hml. Th. ii. 152, 7. (2 a) *with prep.* :—Hé befrán be Swýðúne, hwylce wundra hé worhte, Hml. S. 21, 197. Befrínað be ðám cilde, Hml. Th. i. 82, 16. (3) *to ask* a person about something :—Hwæt mec befregnes ðú of gód *quid me interrogas de bono ?*, Mt. L. 19, 17. Be þære láre þe þú mé befrúne, Bl. H. 185, 8. Hé angan tó befrínenne sume inlendisce ymbe þæs íglondes gewunan, Lch. iii. 432, 27. III. *to ask for something* :—Hé befrán his geféran rædes, Hml. S. 25, 397. Búton hé his godes rædes befrúne, Hml. A. 197, 77. IV. *to ask of* a person what one wishes to be told :—Befrán hé æt þám mæssepreóstum ðæs martires naman, Hml. Th. ii. 506, 28.

**be-fýlan.** *Add* :—Befýledum *infectis*, Wrt. Voc. ii. 43, 62. I. *physical* :—Befýled *caccabatum*, An. Ox. 4156 : *fuscatus*, 4682. II. *moral* :—Fornicatio befýlð þone mann, Hml. S. 16, 277. Hé on synnum hine sylfne befýleð, Wlfst. 78, 16. Hí befýlað fracodlíce hí sylfe, 305, 10. Ic mid synnum míne lima befýlde, Angl. xi. 112, 19. Ic on fúlum forligre mé sylfne befýlde ge on sáwle ge on líchaman, 113, 28. Þ nán man his geleáfan mid þisum gedwylde ne befýle, Hml. Th. i. 110, 20. Hine befýlan fúllíce mid leahtrum, ii. 380, 10. Ys befýled *sordidatur*, Scint. 227, 9. Befýled *impuratus*, Germ. 394, 191. Synd míne handa mid manna blódum befýlede, Angl. xi. 113, 37.

**be-fyl(i)gan** ; *p.* de *To follow up, persevere with* :—Gif þu him (*a medicine*) ænige hwíle befylgest, þú ongitst þ hé ys frymful tó begánne, Lch. iii. 60, 2. Gif mon þisum lǽcedóme befýligð, þonne biþ se man hál, ii. 88, 12. [Cf. *O. Frs.* bi-folgia.] v. be-filgan *in Dict.*

**be-galan.** *Add* : I. *to enchant, charm* :—Hé on deófla naman begól þone gramlican drenc, Hml. S. 14, 76. Þá beóð begalene *quae incantantur*, Bl. Gl. II. *to recite* a charm :—Sygegealdor ic begale, sigegyrd ic mé wege, Lch. i. 388, 15. [þe londes men hire (*a snake*) begaleð, O. E. Hml. ii. 197, 20. Aluen bigolen þat child (*Arthur*), Laym. 19256. O. H. Ger. bi-guol ; *p. t.*]

**be-gán.** *Dele passage* Deut. 21, 20, *and add* : I. *of movement*, (1) *trans.* (a) *to go round* a place :—Lǽssan ymbgang hæfð se mann þe gǽð ábútan án hús þonne sé ðe ealle ðá burh begǽð, Lch. iii. 248, 12. Iosue beeóde ðá burh seofon síðum, Hml. Th. ii. 214, 34. Ðeáh þá unrihtwísan ús úton begán on ælce healfe in *circuitu impii ambulant*, Ps. Th. 11, 9. (b) *to reach by going, come upon, get at* :—Hæfde se cyng hí fore begán mid ealre fyrde, Chr. 1009 ; P. 139, 19. (c) *to go or pass by* :—Hí bieódon (*praetergrediebantur*) Galileam, Mk. L. R. 9, 30. (2) *intrans.* (a) *to go, come, get* :—On beóde offendisset, i. inueniret, An. Ox. 3800. Beeóde heó intó ðám scræfe, Hml. Th. ii. 188, 16. (b) *to pass by* :—Ðe Hælend bieóde (*transiret*), Mt. L. 20, 30. I a. *figurative*, (1) *trans.* To come by, get at :—Hú þæt gewrit begán wæs *how they got at* the manuscript, Guth. 48, 20. (2) *intrans.* (a) *to come, fall to* one's lot :—Swá oft swá him tó begǽð, Ll. Th. i. 434, 14. (b) *to fall, get into debt, &c.* :—Ðú eart on borg begán ðínum friénd *incidisti in manus proximi tui*, Past. 193, 18. II. *of position*, (1) *to surround* :—Deáþes geómerunga mé beeódon (*circumdederunt*), and helle sárnyssa mé beeódon, Hml. Th. ii. 86, 16. (2) *to confine* :—Hé hine sylfne beeóde swá him þearf wæs bútan racenteáge in swá mycclum landsticce ungebunden swá hé ær gebunden on wunode *in tanto se spatio sine catena coercuit, in quanto et antea ligatus mansit*, Gr. D. 214, 15. (3) *to occupy* :—Beeóde incoluit, i. habitavit, An. Ox. 845. III. *of action, to go about* a business, (1) *to attend to* :—Wé sceolon on ðissum dagum begán úre gebedu, Hml. Th. i. 246, 27. Ðá ðing tó begánne and tó bewitanne ðe tó scipene belimpað, Angl. ix. 260, 3. (2) *to cultivate* (lit. and fig.) :—Hié wel begáð hira plantan and hiera impan, Past. 381, 16. Hé his folces ðeáwas beeóde, swilce hé on wíngeardes biggencge swunce, Hml. Th. ii. 74, 26. Bega *exerce* (*agrum tuum*), Kent. Gl. 940. On begánum stówum, Lch. i. 142, 7. (3) *to worship* :—Hwylcne god begǽst þú ?, Nar. 41, 9. Begǽþ colit, i. *venerat*, Wrt. Voc. ii. 134, 71. Þ hié beeódan ánne God, Bl. H. 185, 30. Þ hí beeóde dumbe deófolgeld, Nar. 39, 18. (3 a) *to honour, venerate* a place :—Hí þá stówe weorþodan and beeódan, Bl. H. 205, 7. Hiora hálignesse þe hí ær beeódan, Bd. 2, 13 ; Sch. 167, 17. (4) *to exercise, practise* an art, mode of life, &c. :—Hú begǽst þú (*hunta*) cræft þinne *quomodo exerces artem tuam ?*, Coll. M. 21, 11 : 19, 11. Beóde *exercuit* (*anachoreseos vitam*), An. Ox. 3639. Se man þe wicce-cræft, Lev. 20, 27. (5) *to practise* a religion, *follow the dictates of* :—Hé deófolgeld georne beeóde *nixus praecipuo cultu idolorum*, Ors. 6, 31 ; S. 294, 15 : Hml. S. 28, 6. Seó ǽfæstnes þe wé beeódon

(beódan, v. l.) religio quam tenuimus, Bd. 2, 13; Sch. 164, 18. Hió swípe gemetlíce þa gecynd beeódan (followed the dictates of nature), Bt. 15; F. 48, 8. Godes word mid weorcum begán, Hml. Th. ii. 554, 16. Crístendóm tó begánne, Ors. 6, 31; S. 286, 8. (6) to practise, carry on, do (habitually) :—þa unþeáwas þe seó þeód beeúde, Chr. 1067; P. 201, 30: Bl. H. 113, 2. þa hálgan weras þe góde weorc beeódon, Ælfc. T. Grn. 1, 9. Hí Godes ðeówdóm beeódan, Chr. 995; P. 129, 34. Hym álýfed ne byð þ hē on ceápstówe ænige cýpinge begá (mercaturam ullam exercere), Ll. Th. ii. 174, 19. Godes lof begán, Bl. H. 43, 5. þa gódan weorc þe wē for úre sáule hǽle begán sceoldan, 109, 5. þ weorc begán þe wē ongunnen habbað, Angl. viii. 303, 19. (6 a) to devote one's self to a practice :—Hē begæð unǽtas and oferdrincas and gálscipe commessationibus vacat et luxuriae atque conviviis, Deut. 21, 20. (7) to exercise a person; reflex. to behave :—Se man þe hine swá begǽþ swá hit hēr on segð, Lch. ii. 288, 25. Hira nán ðe hine unwǽrlíce begá, Past. 23, 14. (7 a) to exercise in something :—Hē hine sylfne on gódum weorcum beeóde, Bd. 3, 27; Sch. 320, 6. Hē hine beeóde on gódre líflǽde, Hml. S. 33, 328. Begá (exerce) þē sylfne on þisum, Coll. M. 31, 37. (8) to exercise, use, employ :—Ða ðe ðone anwald begáð, Past. 121, 4. Sē þe þone lǽcedóm begá, Lch. ii. 296, 3. (9) to profess, pretend [cf. (?) O. Sax. quiðit that hē Krīst sī, begihit ina so grótes] :—Manna geþóhtas nǽnig mon ne wát. Petrus begǽþ þ hē hit wite men's thoughts no man knows. Peter professes to have this knowledge, Bl. H. 181, 12. [O. H. Ger. pi-gân.] v. mis-, un-begán; be-gangan, and bi-gán in Dict.

**bégan.** v. bígan.

**be-gang.** Add: n. (1) exercise, labour, business :—On bigonge mínum in exercitatione mea, Ps. Spl. C. 54, 2. Mid micle bigeong magno studio, Mt. p. 10, 13. Bigongum exercitiis, i. laboribus, studiis, Wrt. Voc. ii. 144, 61: 29, 58. Hē hine onwende from ealre þisse worlde begangum, Bl. H. 113, 30. (2) cultivation :—Fram ǽlce bigonge (cultura) þis land liged tólýsed, Gr. D. 258, 18. (3) religious practice :—Ðǽre godcundnesse begang (bigong, v. l.) diuinitatis cultus, Bd. 2, 13; Sch. 164, 10. Bigeon[g] ðes cultus iste, Rtl. 24, 21. Hē hine nýdde tó deófolgylde begonge, Shrn. 76, 6. Tó úra goda bigange (begangum, v. l.) culturae deorum nostrorum, Bd. 2, 13; Sch. 164, 22. Þæt hí heora eald begang (culturam) forlēton and þæt níwe beeódon, 5, 10; Sch. 602, 9. [O. H. Ger. pi-gang.] v. land-begang, bí-geng, and bi-gang in Dict.

**be-gangan.** Add: I. of movement, (1) to go about :—Begangende forðan þe hē gewilnode þ hē sumne fæder on þám wēstene funde, Hml. S. 23 b, 156. (2) to go by :—Bigongende (-geong- L.) praetereuntem, Mk. R. 15, 21. II. of action, to go about a business, (1) to attend to, see after a person :—Hē bebeód María Josephe tó gēmenne and tó begeonganne, Mt. L. 1, 18 note. (2) to worship :—God þone Columbe begangeð, Shrn. 47, 8. Hiá mē begangaþ (colunt), Mt. R. 15, 9. His godas þe hē begongende (-gónde, v. l.) wæs, Ors. 4, 1; S. 154, 34. (2 a) to honour, celebrate a day :—Ealle þá dagas synt mid gelícere eáwfæstnysse tó begangenne, Ll. Th. ii. 438, 27. (3) to exercise, practise an art :—Þæt cræft mīnne ic begange (exerceam), Coll. M. 22, 34. Þæt ánra gehwylc cræft his geornlíce begange, 31, 33. (4) to practise a religion :—þá þe swelc deófolgild lufiad and bigongað, Ors. 4, 12; S. 210, 6. (5) to practise, do (habitually), commit sin :—Men þe beforan óþrum mannum hwæthuga gód begangaþ, Bl. H. 57, 2. þá þe galdorcræftas begangaþ, 61, 23. þá þe wóhhǽmed begangaþ, 14. Náht análýsedlíces begangan, Shrn. 65, 11. Hié angiennað smeágean suiðor ðonne him ðearf sié tó begonganne se in inquisitionibus plus quam necesse est exercentes, Past. 67, 4. Ne morðor tó begongenne (fremmenne, v.l.) . . . ne þeófenda tó begangenne, Wlfst. 253, 7, 9. Ne hē gálnysse næs begangende, Guth. 12, 16. (6) to exercise, use :—Wið ðá wiðerweardan ne ondrǽde hē ðæt hē begonge his ryhtwísnesse erga perversos jura rectitudinis exercere non formidet, Past. 107, 17. [O. Sax. bi-gangan to attend to; O. H. Ger. pi-gangan.] v. be-gán.

**be-gangnes** celebration :—Begeongnise kalendas (cf. begangan, II. 2 a) and : kalendae gehealddagas vel hálige dagas, Wrt. Voc. i. 53, 35), Rtl. 189, 33. Cf. be-gengnes, and see next word.

**be-gangol** a cultivator :—Tó ðæm bigeonle ad cultorem, Lk. R. 13, 7. II. a cult, worship :—Tó bigeongle ðínes nome ad cultum tui nominis, Rtl. 38, 9. Cf. æfter-gengel, and-fangol.

**begannes.** l. be-gánnes, and substitute: Celebration :—Begánnes kalende, Wrt. Voc. ii. 70, 38. v. preceding word.

**beg-beám.** Add :—Morarius begbeám morarius etiam celsa vocatur, mora haec commune nomen est bergena (cf. heorot-berge), Wrt. Voc. ii. 59, 1. Cf. beger.

**be-geát,** es; n. (f. in Laym.). I. attainment, acquisition :—For begeáte þæs ēcan lífes, Hml. Th. i. 240, 7: ii. 70, 22. For begeáte obtentu, An. Ox. 2698: 3915. II. what is acquired, possessions, property :—Cýð mildheortnysse earmum mannum mid þínum begeáte, Hml. Th. ii. 104, 27. Mid þínum begeátum, Wlfst. 286, 29. Hí lǽccað of manna begeátum lóc hwæt hí gefón magan, Ll. Th. ii. 328, 4. Unlytel on ǽhtum . . . mycele welan on manegum begeátum, Hml. A.

108, 202. [þe bizeate of heouene, A. R. 166. He bizet þeos þreo bizeaten, 160. For þære muchele bizæte (-zeate, 2nd MS.), Laym. 609 Towarrd erþlij bizæte, Orm. 16835.]

**be-geáte** (-gēte). v. eáþ-, tór-begeáte (-gēte).

**bęgen.** l. bēgen, and add :—þæt gefeoht wæs gedón mid micelri geornfullnesse of þǽm folcum bǽm (utrimque), and þǽr wǽron þá cyningas bēgen (ambo reges) gewundod, Ors. 3, 9; S. 126, 1–3. Gedé bēgea enisela on ampullan, Lch. ii. 30, 18.

**be-genga,** an; m. A cultivator :—þá begengu agricolae, Mt. R. 21 35, 38. Begengum agricolis, 33. Begængum, 34. v. eard-, land begenga in Dict., and bí-genga.

**be-gengnes.** v. eard-begengnes in Dict., bi-gegnes, and cf. be gangnes.

**be-geómerian;** p. ode To lament, bewail :—Sē bið wís þe ǽrrar gewyrhta georne begeómerað, Wlfst. 75, 15.

**be-geonan** beyond :—Bigeonan (-ginan, -genan) trans, Txts. 103 2053.

**be-geondan.** Add: I. prep. (1) local, (a) with dat. or uncertain :— Begeondan Wendelsǽ citra Pontum, Wrt. Voc. ii. 24, 52. Begeonda sǽ hē is ultra mare est, begeondan ðē ultra te, Ælfc. Gr. Z. 270, 8 Begiondan Humbre, Past. 3, 16. Begeondan (begienda ðæm streáme, L. Iordáne, Jn. 3, 26. Begeondan þisse sǽ, Chr. 885; P. 78, 31. Be gonden sǽ, 1013; P. 144, 20. Fram begeondan sǽ, 1041; P. 162, 8 (b) with acc. :—Begeondan Iordánen, Mt. 19, 1. (2) temporal :—Ne mæg beón ǽr þám dæge ne begeondan .xiii. Kl. Mai . . . ne mæg beón ǽr .xi. kl. Apr1., ne begeondan .vii. kl. Mai, Angl. viii. 309 38–40. II. adv. :—Eal þ his fæder þǽr begeondan hæfde, Chr 1091; P. 226, 10: 1013; P. 144, note 2.

**be-geótan.** Dele first passage, and add : I. to cover with a fluid anoint, besprinkle, drench :—Se wītega begeát his heáfod mid ele, Hml S. 18, 319. Hí beguton hine ealne mid ealdum miggan, 35, 153 Begeót ðæne andwlatan ðǽr mid, Lch. i. 200, 9: 272, 5. Hē hēt hine begeótan mid weallende leáde he ordered boiling lead to be poured upor him, Shrn. 83, 16: 154, 3. Hē weard begoten mid fantwætere, Hml Th. ii. 346, 24. Ic wæs mid blóde begoten of ðæs guman sídan I wa drenched with blood from the man's side, Kr. 49. þá stánas wǽron mic his blóde begotene, Hml. S. 15, 55. I a. to cover with molter metal :—Hí stánas synd, þá þe þū godas gecīgst, begotene mid leáde Hml. S. 34, 336. II. to cover with, bestrew with :—Heó begeá þá hand mid deórwyrðum wyrtum and bewand on godwebbe, Shrn. 59 34. [O. H. Ger. pi-giozan perfundere, proluere, infundere.]

**beger** (-ir), es; n. A berry :—Beger baccinia (begir bucina), Txts 43, 266. Begir baccinia, Wrt. Voc. ii. 10, 65. Cf. berige vacciniu (bacinia, Wülck. Gl. 296, 26), Wrt. Voc. i. 67, 25, and v. wín-beger ir Dict.

**be-gíman.** Add: with gen. acc. (1) to care for, see to the welfare or wellbeing of a person or thing, keep :—God þū þe begýmst mannar Deus qui gubernas hominem, Ps. L. fol. 142, 6. Hí míne heorde wǽcc begímdon, Wlfst. 190, 21. Begým þínes sylfes, Hml. A. 198, 109 Þæt hig begímon þæra þinga þe tó þære hálgan eardungstówe belimpac custodiant vasa tabernaculi, Num. 3, 7. Begýmendum gubernante, An Ox. 1993. Is begēmed gubernatur, Kent. Gl. 495. þ wín ge þ wæter sýn mid ealre clǽnnysse begýmde, Ll. Th. ii. 404, 39. (1 a) to tenc the sick :—Begýmed fotam, An. Ox. 4353. (2) to attend to (ir answer to appeal) :—Tó Drihtne ic cleopige and hē begýmð (intendit mē, Ps. Spl. 76, 1. Begím dóm mīnne intende judicio meo, 34. 26. Begím þū, God, mē tó fylste Deus, in adjutorium meum intende, R. Ben 60, 5. (3) to observe, keep a command, an appointed season, &c. :—þ offringdagas wē ná ne begýmaþ, An. Ox. 40, 24, 37. Begýmað þisse gesetednysse, Ex. 12, 25. þás niht sceolon Israhēla bearn begíman, 42 (4) to observe, watch a person :—Hig begýmdon hine, Lk. 14, 1. [O. H Ger. pi-goumen observare, providere.] v. be-gýman in Dict.

**be-gímen(n),** e; f. Care, observation :—Hīrēdes begímen aulicc cura, Lch. i. lx, 4. Mid begýmene cum observatione, Lk. 17, 20. Or his begēmene intuitu suo, Kent. Gl. 736. Of begýmenna optentu, i. intuitu, An. Ox. 3915. Begýmyne operam, i. studium, 7, 86.

**be-gímend,** es; m. A guide, ruler :—Begýmend rector, Scint. 122 19: 123, 12.

**be-gíming.** Add :—Begýming gubernacula, An. Ox. 4995. Reste dæges begýminge sabbati observationem, 40, 6. v. be-gíman.

**be-gínan.** Substitute: To take with wide-open mouth :—Ic (a key begíne þæt mē ongeán sticað, Rä. 87, 3. Se draca hæfþ beginen in hi múðe mín heáfod and forswolgen draco caput meum in suo ore absorbuit Gr. D. 324, 26.

**be-ginnan.** Add : I. to begin, (1) trans. (a) with acc. :—Gif hý hit beginnan (incipient) and ne gefremman, Ll. Th. ii. 164, 29. Se tídsang is swá tó beginnenne, R. Ben. 33, 2. Hē fulworhte þ mynster þe his mǽg begunnon hæfde, Hml. S. 26, 110. Geendadre bletsunge sý dægredsang begunnen, R. Ben. 35, 23. þá sýn mid alleluian begunnene, 15. (b) with infin. :—Ne beginnes cuoeða, Lk. L. R. 3, 8. (c) with dat. infin. :—Begann hē tó hrýmenne, Hml. Th. i. 152, 15: 258, 11 :

ii. 502, 29. (2) *intrans.* :—Æfter đǽm beginne se abbod, R. Ben. 35, 22. Þæt Assiria ríce æt Ninuse begunne, Ors. 2, 1; S. 60, 25. **II.** *to attempt, undertake,* (1) with acc.:—Se apostel, swá swá þá biscopas bǽdon, began þá feórđan bóc, Ælfc. T. Grn. 12, 43. Hí wurdon áblende þe þ bebod begunnon (*attempted to carry out the command*), Hml. S. 4, 361. (2) with infin.:—God him þæs tíþode, and hé began git biddan (*he attempted further intercession*), Hml. S. 13, 203. (3) with dat. infin.:—Gif hwá útácymen man beginne tó þénienne, swelte hé deáđe *externus, qui ad ministrandum accesserit, morietur,* Num. 3, 10. **II a.** *to attack* :—Ymbe þreó mónađ þæs þe hié mon ǽr ongon (began, *v. l.*), Ors. 5, 11; S. 238, 11. [O. Sax. bi-ginnan : O. Frs. bi-ginna: O. H. Ger. pi-ginnan.] v. under-beginnan; un-begunnen.

**be-gitan.** *Add :* (1) *to get* for one's self, (a) of acquisition, possession :—Ic begeat æt Denulfe þá windcirican, Cht. Th. 156, 21. Bigeat *obtenuit,* Txts. 81, 1409. Se bisceop wæs Scyttisc and Scē Oswald hine begeat on đás đeóde *the bishop was Scottish and St. Oswald got him into this country,* Shrn. 124, 10. Hé begeat Arues dohtor him tó wífe, Ors. 3, 7; S. 112, 9. Hé beget þá burg, Chr. 919; P. 100, 11. Hé begeat forđ mid him fela scipu, 1052; P. 178, 14. Hié him þǽr scipu begéton, 897; P. 89, 28. Namige man him .xiiii., and begyte [hē] .xi. (*let him take xi*), Ll. Th. i. 410, 11. Wulfnóđ cuconne ođđe deáđne begytan, Chr. 1009; P. 138, 23. Mid eallon þám genge þe hē begeotan mihte, 1065; P. 191, 27. Ǽce líf begeotan, Bl. H. 97, 28. Begitende *conquirens,* Wrt. Voc. ii. 91, 53. Begiotende *nactus,* 61, 23. Đǽre begitenan *ineptae,* 76, 55. Đá sócna đe intó đám mynstre nú begytene (*printed* betytene, C. D. B. iii. 561, 29) *causas omnium terrarum ad monasterium pertinentium,* C. D. iii. 61, 12. Hié hæfdon monega byrig begietena, Ors. 2, 2; S. 66, 24. Begetna *comprehensos,* Mt. L. 4, 24. (b) where a request, favour, &c., is granted :—Hé sende tó đám cyninge, and begeat þæt hé móste Iosiam beheáfdian, Hml. Th. ii. 422, 26. Hé begeat æt þám cásere þ hé ácwellan móste þá menn, Hml. S. 37, 24. Beget, Guth. 54, 5. Þáh þe Benedictus begeáte þ hé férde þurh þone gást, Gr. D. 150, 16. Begitan *impetrare,* Wrt. Voc. ii. 47, 51. Begeatta, Jn. p. 7, 11. Hí wilnodon ... ac hí ne mihton þ begitan, Bt. 29, 2; F. 104, 33. (2) *to get for another, procure* :—Hý nellađ þæs willan gewyrcan þe him ēce líf begeat, Wlfst. 185, 17. Gif hwá sleá his néhstan ... begite hē him lǽce, Ll. Th. i. 48, 10. Begyte hē him þá lácnunge *sanationem ei comparet,* ii. 210, 25. (3) *to get to, find* :—Đú onfindes þ begetes *invenies,* Mt. L. 17, 27. Begettes *invenit,* 10, 39. Soecađ gē and gē begeattas (*invenietis*), 7, 7. Begæt *invenit,* 12, 43. Gif hē hine begytan ne mæge *si eum invenire nequeat,* Ll. Th. ii. 212, 11. Begetna Ɫ begeten *inventa,* Mt. L. 13, 46. Bigetten, 1, 18. Bigetna *repertae,* p. 17, 6. (4) *to get, cause to be done :*—Þ ǽlc gegilda gesinge án fíftig oþþe begite gesungen, Ll. Th. i. 236, 37. Þá mynsterclǽnsunge man begite, 340, 19. (5) *to beget* :—Hē bið mid synnum begyten and mid synnum ácenned and on synnum áfédd, Wlfst. 193, 4. [Goth. bi-gitan *invenire :* O. Sax. bi-getan *to seize :* O. H. Ger. pi-gezzan *adipiscere.*] v. next word.

**be-gitend,** es; m. *One who gets* :—Begetend (-ende?) *conquirens,* i. *causans, meditans,* Wrt. Voc. ii. 136, 39.

**be-gleddian.** *Add: to besmear, bedaub :*—Spere mid blóde begleddod, Hml. Th. i. 452, 8. Franca fúle begleddod mid blóde, Hml. S. 3, 266. Þá stánas wǽron mid his flǽsce begleddode, 15, 55. Mid đégum begleddode *fucis illita,* Hy. Srt. 22, 5. Áfýledum, begleddedum *infectis,* i. *irrigatis,* An. Ox. 380.

**be-gnagan.** *Add :*—þ seó nǽddre hí ábítan sceolde and hire bán begnagan, Shrn. 103, 6.

**begne.** *Dele, and see* blegen: **be-gneord.** v. be-cneord.

**be-gnídan;** p. -gnád *To rub thoroughly* :—Genim meluwes smedman and wiccgan innel(fe), begníd (*or?* innelfe gníd) tósomne, Lch. i. 134, 5.

**be-grafan.** *Add:* [O. Sax. bi-graban: O. H. Ger. pi-graban *to bury:* Goth. bi-graban *to dig round.*]: **be-grindan.** *Dele* I, *and see* ginder *in Dict.*

**be-grípan.** *Substitute:* **I.** *to seize, lay hold of :*—Gif ic begrípe (*sumpsero*) feđera míne, Ps. L. 138, 9. Begrípat *capessunt* (*arma*), An. Ox. 11, 79. Begráp (*apprehendit*) hig fyrhto, Ps. L. 47, 7. Hig begripon (*coeperunt*) míne sáwle, 58, 4. Gif seó sáwul mid leahtrum begripen bið, Hml. Th. i. 122, 24. Þ wíf in argscipe begrippene *mulierem in adulterio reprehensam,* Jn. p. 5, 8. **II.** *to reprehend :*—Begripen (*increpuerunt*) mē lendene míne, Ps. Spl. T. 15, 7 (cf. Toc nemnn Sannt Iohan to bigripenn, Orm. 9752). [O. Frs. bi-grípa : O. H. Ger. pi-grífan.]

**be-grípendlic.** v. un-begrípendlic.

**be-gríwan;** (*only in*) pp. be-griwen *To steep in,* (1) of profound knowledge :—Hē wæs on đǽre ealdan ǽ getogen, and mid micelre gecnyrdnysse on đǽre begriwen wæs (*was deeply versed in it*), Hml. Th. 384, 27. (2) of guilt, *sunk in* :—On ánum dæge hē oft geworhte mirm scylda, and nǽnige gebétan ne wolde, and in oferfyllo hē wæs begriwen on unrihtum, Vercell. MS. fol. 21 b. Sē is hýra and ná nyrde đe bið begriwen (*so in MS. printed* -gripen) on woruldþingum,

Hml. Th. i. 240, 16. For đǽm mannum þe beóđ begriwene on middaneardlicum lustum, ii. 368, 2. Heortan begriwene (*printed* -gripene) on eorđlicum gewilnungum, i. 520, 22. [Prof. Skeat suggests comparison with χρίειν.]

**be-gyrdan.** *Add:* **I.** in reference to apparel, *to gird :*—Gif hwylc man hyne begyrdeþ mid þysse wyrte, Lch. i. 198, 5. Begyrd þē and sceó þē, Hml. Th. ii. 382, 9. Hý gewǽdode and begyrde resten, R. Ben. 47, 10. Mid begyrdum lendenum, Hml. Th. ii. 218, 6. **II.** *to surround, encompass :*—Sē Bretenlond mid díce begyrdde, Chr. 189; P. 8, 23. Gif eáđmódnes bið mid óđrum gódum đeáwum begyrded *si humilitas ceteris virtutibus cingitur,* Past. 47, 11. Útan begyrdd (*accincta*) mid đám feówer godspellum, 171, 5. Þá lendenu beóđ mid sáre begyrdedu, Lch. ii. 232, 8. [O. H. Ger. pi-gurten. Cf. Goth. bi-gairdan.]

**be-habban.** *Add:* **I.** *to surround, embrace :*—Asia ealne middan-geard fram þǽm eástdǽle healfne behæfđ *Asia per totam transversi plagam orientis extenditur,* Ors. 1, 1; S. 8, 9. Sinewealt crop brúnon blóstman behæfđ, Lch. i. 282, 17. **II.** *to hold, contain :*—Máran endebyrdnysse þonne dis godspel behæfđ, Hml. Th. i. 220, 25. Þeús circe mihte fíf hund manna behabban, Bl. H. 207, 14. Má đonne đæt undeópe mód behabban mæge, Past. 459, 14. Þeáh þe þ mód behæfd wǽre in líchaman, Gr. D. 4, 21. **II a.** *to hold, have* in a receptacle :—Þone ic behæfde on bearme *quod continui in sinu,* Bl. Gl. **III.** *to hold back, withhold :*—Behæfđ God mildheortnysse his ?, Ps. Spl. 76, 10. [O. Sax. bi-hebbian *to contain :* O. H. Ger. pi-habén *continere, retinere, ambire.*]

**be-hádian;** p. ode *To deprive of holy orders :*—Gif mæssepreóst ođđe diácon wífige, þoligon hyra hádes; and gif hig æfter þám hǽmedþing begáđ, ná þ án þ hig behádod synt (*ordine privuntur*), ac eác swylce fæston .vii. geár, Ll. Th. ii. 196, 14.

**be-hǽfednes.** *Substitute: Restraint, temperance :*—Behæfednes *parsimonia* (*cujus alimonia parsimonia tam frugalis fuisse ferebatur,* Ald. 51), Wrt. Voc. ii. 83, 26. Cf. for-hæfednefs.

**be-hǽftan.** *Dele.*

**be-hǽpsian;** p. ode *To fasten with a bolt, bolt* a door :—Hē hēt hí gán út and behæpsode þá duru, Hml. S. 31, 214.

**be-hǽttian;** p. ode. **I.** *to make bald :*—Behǽttod *decalvata* (*quamvis caesaries raderetur* et *decalvata traheretur,* Ald. 62), An. Ox. 4466. **II.** *to strip the skin from the head :*—Đá cwelleras hine behǽttedon *they pulled off the skin of his head with the hair* (2 Maccabees 7, 7), Hml. S. 25, 126. Behǽttian, 116. v. hǽttian *in Dict.*

**be-hamelian;** p. ode *To mutilate :*—Þá hēt hē his leásere hig behamelian, Shrn. 154, 6. Hí áxodon hwæđer hē etan wolde ǽr đan þe hē behamelod wurde *they asked him, wilt thou eat, before thou be punished throughout every member of thy body?* (2 Maccabees 7, 7), Hml. S. 25, 127. v. hamelian *in Dict.*

**be-hammen;** adj. *Clouted, patched :*—Gescód mid behammenum (ge-, geclútedum, *v. ll.*) scón *clavatis calceatus caligis,* Gr. D. 37, 13.

**be-hát.** *Add:* **I.** *a promise :*—'On sunnandæge þú cymst tó mē.' Se apostol blissode on đám behǽte, Hml. Th. i. 74, 20 : 466, 30. Hé gefylde his behát þe hē gecwæđ, ii. 284, 17. Hē þæt behát mid weorcum gefylde, 486, 24. Gif đú đás behát mid weorcum gefylst, i. 380, 13. **II.** *a promise* in religious matters, *a vow :*—Scyldig þæs clǽnan behátes (*vow of chastity*), Hml. A. 34, 245 : (*baptismal vow*), Ll. Th. ii. 338, 16. Be hire behǽte (*voto*) æfter hyre were, 130, 23. For heora hálgan þeówdómes behǽte, R. Ben. 19, 17. Gif þe þis behát ábrycđ, 99, 21. Behát (*vota*) wē tólésan þē, Hy. S. 7, 27. Ic ágylde þē behát (*vota*) mín, Ps. Spl. 65, 12. Gode man sceal dón þá betstan behát, Hml. A. 35, 273. **III.** *a threat* (cf. beót; *Icel.* heit; *pl. threats*) :—Đeós wyrt tó manegum þingon wel fremađ, þ ys ... wið gehwylce behátu and wið andan and wið ógan, Lch. i. 312, 25. [Goth. bi-hait *strife :* O. H. Ger. pi-heiz *devotio ; factio.*] v. munuc-behát.

**be-hátan.** *Add:* **I.** *to promise :*—Hú fela beháta behēt God Abrahame ?, Angl. vii. 42, 396. Embe þis wē sprecađ eft swíđor swá swá wē ǽr behēton, Lch. iii. 240, 8. Cantware heom seoh behēton, Chr. 865 ; P. 69, 4. Þ him man gafol behēte, 994 ; P. 129, 11. Tó đám behátenan earde, Hml. Th. ii. 282, 17. Þǽra forewearda þe him behátene wǽron, Chr. 1093 ; P. 228, 2. **II.** in religious matters, *to vow :*—Ne syngast gif đú sylf ne behátest ; ac gif đú þone behátest Gode, hē wyle habban đæt đú him behēte, Hex. 50, 3-5. Þ hí behēton *quod professi sunt,* An. Ox. 57, 7. Gelǽste man eall þæt man beháte on Godes ēst tó dónne, Wlfst. 172, 13. **III.** *to threaten :*—Se abbot dyde heom yfele, and behēot heom mycel, and behēot heom wyrs, Chr. 1083 ; P. 214, 21. Hē heom behēt ǽlcne hete, Hml. S. 23, 230. Behǽte hē swilc wíte swilc hē ús behǽte, 459. **IV.** *to give assurance, certify :*—Þú mē behēte hál and clǽne þ þ þú mē sealdest, Ll. Th. i. 180, 22. **V.** reflex. *to profess one's self ready for the doing of something* (*gen.*) :—Sē đe hine selfne máran gódes behát *qui fortiori studio intenderat,* Past. 403, 5. (Cf. O. H. Ger. sie bihiazun sih thera selbun kuanheiti.)

**behát-land,** es; n. *A promised land* :—Gelǽddum his folce tó þám behátlande *perducto ad terram repromissionis populo,* Gr. D. 204, 12. v. gehát-land.

**be-háwian.** _Add: to consider,_ (1) _trans._:—Beháues ðæt wyrt londes _considerate lilia agri,_ Mt. L. 6, 28. (2) _intrans._:—Uton beháwian be þám óþrum tídum _de sequentibus horis videamus,_ R. Ben. 40, 21.

**be-heáfdian.** _Add:_—Hí beheáfdodon þone cempan, Hml. S. 19, 123: Hml. Th. i. 402, 17. Beheáfdian hine [geseón] gestreón getácnað _to see one's self beheaded in a dream betokens gain,_ Lch. iii. 212, 13. Þ hí hine beheáfdian sceolde, Bl. H. 183, 21: Ors. 6, 30; S. 282, 32: Shrn. 57, 21. Hí lǽdan tó beheáfdianne, 75, 23. Tó beheáfdigenne, Hml. S. 19, 85. Beheáfdienne _obtruncandum,_ An. Ox. 5255. Tó beheáfdiende _decollandi,_ 3092. Wæs beheáfdod _capite truncatur,_ 3022: Ap. Th. 3, 11: Chr. 1076; P. 213, 1. v. un-beheáfdod.

**be-heáfdung.** _Add: decapitation_:—Heó mid beheáfdunge hine ácwealde, Hml. Th. i. 488, 2: Hml. S. 19, 83. Tó beheáfdunge gelǽd, Ap. Th. 3, 17. Beheáfdinge, Shrn. 154, 8. Lǽded tó þ ͤ re beheáfdunge, 72, 34. Ðá ǽræfnode hé þá beheáfdunge, 129, 11. Underfón hé beheáfdunge, Hml. Th. i. 420, 7. Beheáfdunge underhnígan _capitalem sententiam subire,_ An. Ox. 3042.

**be-heáfodlic;** _adj. Capital_:—Beheáfodlicne dóm _capitalem sententiam,_ An. Ox. 4042.

**be-healdan.** _Add_: I. _to hold, occupy,_ (a) a place:—Þá wíc beheóld hálig gást, hreðer weardode, El. 1144. Seó þe flóda begong beheóld hund missera, B. 1498. (b) an office:—Þegn nytte beheóld, B. 494. Seleweard sundornytte beheóld ymb aldor Dena, 667. II. _to hold, contain_:—Bihaldne contentus, Mt. p. 10, 15. (a) _to have efficacy_:—Ne beheóld hit nán þing seó scipfyrding búton folces geswinc _there was nothing in all this preparation but labour for the people,_ Chr. 999; P. 133, 10. Cweþað þá ðe syndan stunte þæt mycel forhæfednes lytel behealde _that there is very little in great abstinence,_ Wlfst. 55, 24. (b) _to have meaning, signify_:—Wit gesáwon swefen, ac wyt nyton hwá hyt unc átelle, hwæt hit behealde _what its meaning is,_ Gen. 40, 8. III. _to hold, keep_ a law:—Godes beboda utan wé behealdan, Bl. H. 39, 4. IV. _to hold, keep, maintain_:—Hí mé onhwyrfdon of þ ͤ re gecynde þe ic ǽr cwic beheóld, Rä. 72, 4. Þá woruldsælþa beheóldon on þe heora ágen gecynd _fortuna servavit circa te propriam constantiam,_ Bt. 7, 2; F. 16, 31. V. _to keep, guard, preserve_:—Hé hine nó ne beheóld wið ðá gǽstlican scylde _sese a spiritalibus vitiis minime custodit,_ Past. 315, 1. Engel þá menigeo beheóld, Exod. 205. Ðá ðe hiá seolfa hygdiglige beheóldon _qui seipsos castraverunt,_ Mt. L. 19, 12. Beheald þé on þínum lífe þ þú dó wel þínum bearnum, Nar. 50, 24. Behealdað eów wið leásum wítegum _attendite a falsis prophetis,_ Hml. Th. ii. 404, 3: Bl. H. 241, 9: Past. 317, 9: 449, 36. Ðæt hí hí behealden ðæt hí innan ne áfeallen, Past. 439, 9. Ðá ðe heá búta éghwoelcum flíta behaldan, Mt. L. 5, 9 note. Hié for duste ne mehton geseón hú hí hí behealdan sceolden, Ors. 5, 7; S. 230, 16. Hit ǽr hit nolde behaldan wið unnyt word _otiosa cavere verba negligit,_ Past. 279, 4. On sibbe behealden, Ps. Th. 75, 2. VI. _to take care, beware_:—Beheald þæt ðú ðás dǽde ne dó, Hml. Th. i. 38, 25: Lch. i. 332, 6: ii. 318, 19. Behealdað ðæt Adam ne ete of ðám treówe, Hex. 26, 15. Behaldas _attendite,_ Mt. L. 6, 1. Tó behaldenne _cavendum,_ 16, 12. Tó behaldanne _evitandum,_ Lk. p. 7, 15. VII. _to behold,_ (1) _intrans. To look_:—Gif se yrðlincg behylt underbæc, Hml. S. 16, 178. Beheald æfter þé, Bl. H. 245, 6. Beheald on mé, 229, 30. Hé hét his cnapan behealdan tó þ ͤ re sǽ, Lch. iii. 276, 24. Behealden(d)ra _prospicientium,_ Kent. Gl. 1030. (2) _trans._ (a) _to look at, gaze on_:—Ic þé beheóld, Bl. H. 235, 26. Hí beheóldon Moises _aspiciebant tergum Moysi,_ Ex. 33, 8: Kr. 64. (b) _to watch, observe_:—Hiá biheóldun (-heáld-, L.) hine _obseruabant eum,_ Mk. R. 3, 2. Ne behealdon gé heofenan ne sunnan, Deut. 4, 19. Mid ðí heó behealdende wæs (_intueretur_) mid hwylcum þingum hé upp togen wǽre, Bd. 4, 9; Sch. 394, 6. (c) _to see_:—Folc ðer wundor beheóld líge scínan, Exod. 109. Behealdan _videre,_ Wülck. Gl. 255, 31. (d) of the mind, _to regard, consider, observe,_ (a) with acc.:—Gif þú míne unrihtwísnesse behealdest, Bl. H. 89, 16. Beheald mé holdlíce and gehýr mé _intende in me et exaudi me,_ Ps. Th. 54, 1. (β) with clause:—Ǽlc gleáw mód behealt hwelcne ende hí habbaþ, Bt. 7, 2; F. 18, 23. Heó beheóld hú þæt þing gewurde _considerante eventum rei,_ Ex. 2, 4. Beheald hú ðás men þínum ðeówe dóþ, Bl. H. 229, 22: Bt. 36, 5; F. 180, 5. Behealdan gé hwæþer gé hit hire gecýþan willen, H. R. 9, 7. [_O. Sax._ bi-haldan: _O. Frs._ bi-halda: _O. H. Ger._ pi-haltan.] v. next word.

**be-healden;** _adj._ (_ptcpl._). I. _cautious, reserved_:—Ðonne hé wilnað ðæt hé sciele rícsian, hé bið swíðe forht and swíðe behealden, ðonne hé hæfð ðæt hé habban wolde, hé bið swíðe ðríste, Past. 57, 4. II. _intent, assiduous_:—Hé wæs geornfull and behealden (_intentus_) in Godes hýrnessum, Gr. D. 224, 13. v. bi-healdan _in Dict._

**be-healdend,** es; _m. A beholder, spectator_:—Gesíit cymeð þám behealdendum _in quaestionem ueniat intuentibus,_ Bd. 1, 1; Sch. 9, 18.

**be-healdenness,** e; _f._ I. _observance_:—Bihaldnisses _obseruantiae,_ Rtl. 16, 17. Bihaldnisse _obseruantiam,_ 9, 1. II. _continence_:—Bihaldennises _continentiae,_ Rtl. 104, 4.

**be-healdness,** e; _f. Observation_:—Bihaldnisse _obseruatione,_ Rtl. 14,

8. Hé mid þ ͤ re geornfullan behealdnysse up lócode, Hml. S. 23 b, 166. [_O. H. Ger._ bi-haltnessi.]

**be-heáwan.** _Add:_—Man þ timber beheáwð, Angl. viii. 324, 8. Hí hine sceoldon þy heáfde beheáwan, Gr. D. 254, 11. Hé wæs heáfde beheáwen, Shrn. 155, 6. [_O. Sax._ bi-hauwan: _O. H. Ger._ pi-hauwan.]

**be-hédan.** _Substitute:_ v. be-hýdan: be-héfe, es; _m. Dele._

**be-héfe;** _adj. Add: useful, needful_:—Behéfe (_utilis_) ic eom eallum folce, Coll. M. 26, 25. Cræft behéfe and neódþearf _ars utilis et necessaria,_ 27, 27: 18, 16. Sibling þé swá behéfe swá ðín hand, Hml. Th. i. 516, 15. Mé þingð behéfe þing þ ic gecýðe, Angl. viii. 335, 2: 303, 26. Drihtne bihoefe is _Domino necessarius est,_ Mk. R. 11, 3. Sýn gehwám behéfe þing (_necessaria_) gesealde, R. Ben. 57, 17: 132, 4. Land ðæ him gehændre beó and behéfre _terra quae eis uicinior sit uel utilior,_ C. D. v. 137, 21. Sélost and hire behéfast, Hml. S. 33, 252. Feówer þing synt ealra þinga behéfost þám árwyrðan men, Wlfst. 247, 11. Þing þe behéfuste synt tó witanne, Angl. viii. 321, 40. v. níd-, un-behéfe.

**be-héflic;** _adj. Useful, needful, necessary_:—Ús þingð wel behéflic þ wé hine gehandlion, Angl. viii. 308, 15. Hé ys behéflic tó cunnane, 314, 18.

**be-héfness,** e; _f. Utility, advantage, convenience_:—Behéfnes _commoditas,_ i. _utilitas,_ Wrt. Voc. ii. 132, 4. Lífes éces behéfnyssa (_commoda_), Hy. S. 5, 21: 114, 9. Behéf[nyssum] _commoditatibus,_ An. Ox. 56, 306.

**be-helan.** _Add:_—Seó beholene ondweardnes _the hidden presence,_ Bl. H. 77, 2. Þý lǽs mé ówiht in þ ͤ m londe beholen oððe bedégled wǽre _ne quid mihi in ignotis subtraheretur locis,_ Nar. 20, 21. From þ ͤ m uncystum ðe mé beholen synt _ab occultis delictis meis,_ Ps. Th. 18, 11. [_O. Sax._ bi-helan.]

**be-helendlíce.** v. un-behelendlíce.

**be-helian.** _Add:_—Ðæt mód mid ðære beheleð his fét, Past. 241, 20. Heofon behelað eal ðæt him beufan bið, Sal. K. p. 178, 9. Moyses behelede ðá bierhto his ondwlitan, Past. 459, 19. Þ fex hí behelede on ælce healfe, Hml. S. 7, 147. Þá heortan æt þínum burhgeatum behele (-a, v. l.), Lch. i. 328, 24. Se preóst þá húsell'áfe behelie mid corporale, Ll. Th. ii. 358, 24. Ðeáh hé his þeáwas behelie, Prov. K. 58. Ðæt ðá loccas ðá hýd behelien (-igen, v. l.), Past. 141, 9. Ðæt hié hié gehýden and beheligen under ðæm ryfte ðære leásunga, 239, 25. Behýd and behelod mid ðære eorþan, Bt. 15; F. 48, 25. Ðá tríowa ðe ðé sindon opene, hí sindon git mid manegum ðþrum behelede, 7, 2; F. 18, 4. Heora synna beóð behelede (_tecta_), Ps. Th. 31, 1. [_O. Frs._ bi-hella: _O. H. Ger._ pi-hellen _velare._] v. be-hylian.

**be-heófian.** _Add:_—Yfelu beheófian _mala plangere,_ Scint. 44, 5.

**be-heonan.** _Add: prep. dat. On this side of_:—Biheonan cis, Wrt. Voc. ii. 104, 5. Beheonan, 14, 31. Behionan Humbre, Past. 3, 14. Behienan Wendelsæ, Chr. 885; P. 78, 31. Behinon (-heonan, v. l.) sǽ, 878; P. 76, 9. Ge beheonan sǽ ge begeondan, Shrn. 114, 5.

**be-heopian.** _Add:_ cf. Gen. 2701: be-hicgan. v. be-hycgan.

**be-hindan.** _Add:_ I. _prep._ (1) dat.:—Behindan him sylfum tǽlan, Bl. H. 65, 1. Hé þ ͤ r wunode behindan óþrum mannum, Gr. D. 278, 21. Ðeáh hí sín behindan ðæm ðe læssan hádes bióð, Past. 411, 23. (2) with acc.:—Ðeáh hé dó God behindan hine, Past. 373, 1. Gong bihionda mec _uade retro me,_ Mk. R. 8, 33. II. _adv._:—Ðá Deniscan sǽton þ ͤ r behindan, Chr. 894; P. 86, 4. Hié gebunden his handa behindan, Bl. H. 241, 29. Behindon forlǽtan, Nar. 7, 3. Stód bihianda _stans retro,_ Lk. L. 7, 38. Cwom bihianda _venit retro,_ Mk. L. 5, 27. Behianda (bihionda R.), Lk. L. 8, 44.

**be-hípian** _to heap up_:—Behýpedan _ingesserunt,_ An. Ox. 3322. v. heápan.

**be-híwian** _to feign, dissimulate_:—Behíwiende _dissimulans,_ R. Ben. I. 16, 7.

**be-hlǽman.** _Dele, and see next word._

**be-hlǽnan.** _Add: to surround, encompass_:—Foldbúende se micla dæg mægne bihlǽned (-hlæmed, MS.), swá þeóf hæleð forsléð slǽpe gebundne, Cri. 870. Eal engla werod behlǽnað (cf. embtrymmað, Wlfst. 137, 15) ðone Metod, Dóm. L. 116.

**be-hleápan.** _Add:_—Ic on behleápe _insilio,_ Ælf. Gr. Z. 191, 4.

**be-hlígan.** v. be-leán, II.

**be-hóf,** es; _n._ I. _behoof, need, use_:—Þ hé ænne scylling hæfde tó his ágenum behófe (nytte, v. l.) _ut unum solidum in expensis propriis haberet,_ Gr. D. 158, 23. Hé sende æfter pallium tó arð. behóue (ad opus), Chr. 780; P. 52, 14. Þ feoh syllan tó þæs cynges behófe, 1094; P. 229, 23. II. _need, want_:—Tó behófe _ad indigentiam,_ An. Ox. 27, 34. Cf. Lk. p. 8, 18 _where_ behófe _glosses_ prodigi. v. níd-behóf.

**be-hófen.** _Dele._

**be-hófian.** _Dele:_ 'DER. 2-behófian,' _and add:_ I. _absolute_:—Ic swíðor ceorude þonne mín sáwul behófode, Angl. xi. 113, 40. Swá geornlíce ús gebiddan swá wé behófedon, Hml. Th. i. 156, 14. II. with gen.:—Ic myltse behófige, Hml. S. 3, 558. Gé mín behófiað, 376. Gehwæt þæs þe þá þríe geférscipas behófiaþ (-igen, v. l.), Bt. 17; F. 60, 5. Hé metes behófode, Hml. Th. i. 178, 10. Þá þe þæs behófodon

Hml. S. 30, 10. Đá đe gémnisse bihófadun *qui cura indigebant*, Lk. R: 9, 11. Behófdan, Chr. 1006; P. 136, 23. **III.** impersonal :—Đá đe behófað ł gehríseđ (*oporteat*) tó cuoeđanne, Lk. L. 12, 12. Behófað *expedit*, Jn. L. 16, 7: 18, 14. Behófes, Mt. L. 5, 30. Iúh behófes *indigetis*, 6, 32. Mid máran unráde þone him á behófode, Chr. 1093; Erl. 229, 3. [O. Frs. bi-hóvia.]

be-hóflic. *Add :*—Behóflic is *expedit*, Mt. L. 5, 29: *proderit*, 15, 5: *oportet*, Lk. L. 18, 1: *necessarium est*, 10, 42: *utile est*, Mt. p. 13, 6. Boóflic *necesse*, p. 7, 8. Đá đe behóflico sint *qui necessari sunt*, Lk. L. 14, 28. v. níd-behóflic.

be-hogadnes. For Cot. 114 *read :*—On behogadnesse *in exercitatione*, Wrt. Voc. ii. 48, 42.

be-hogian. *Substitute : to take care of, attend to, be solicitous about :*—Hé behogode þá tíde þæs nihtlican gebedes, Gr. D. 170, 28. Đá đe his líc behogodon *qui funus ejus curaverant*, 297, 17. Ealdor þe georne behogige (*curiose intendat*) hwæþer hé God geséce, R. Ben. 97, 14. Þ þá ofiætan ge þ wín sýn mid ealre clénnysse and geornfulnysse behogode and begýmde, Ll. Th. ii. 404, 39.

be-hogod *careful, prudent :*—Bihogodo ué sié *sobrii simus*, Rtl. 28, 27, 29.

be-hogodlíce; *adv. Carefully, diligently :*—Swá hwilc man swá Godes weorc clénlíce and behogodlíce wirceđ. . . . Sé þe hit réceleáslíce and unclénlíce wyrceđ, Hml. A. 168, 120. Hé ongan hí geornlícor and behogodlícor cwencean *eas sollicitius extinxit*, Gr. D. 237, 2.

be-hón. *Add :*—Seó cyrce wæs eall behangen mid criccum, Hml. S. 21, 431. Mædenheáp blóstmum behangen, Dóm. L. 289.

be-hreósan. *Substitute : to fall :*—Sé þe on đá wítu behreóseđ, Wlfst. 26, 12: Ll. Th. ii. 330, 12. Đá on helle behreósað *in gehennam incidunt*, R. Ben. 24, 3. Þæt wæs ungerím þæt intó helle behreás, Wlfst. 9, 1. v. be-hroren.

be-hreówsian. *Add :* **I.** absolute, *to repent :*—Þæra behreówsigendra heortan, Hml. Th. i. 550, 32. **I a.** with object, *to repent of*, (a) with acc. :—Þæt þæt wé ágylton, þæt wé nú bereówsiað, Hml. Th. i. 68, 27. Þám þe heora synna behreówsiað, Ælfc. T. Grn. 2, 17. Behreówsodon, Hml. S. 12, 34. Behreówsian heora yfelan dǽda, Hml. A. 8, 206. (β) with clause :—Hé behreówsode þ hé swá dyslice dǽde gedyde, Gr. D. 143, 19. **II.** *to pity, compassionate :*—Heora earfeđa behreówsian, Hml. S. 23, 90. Behreówsiendes *compatientis*, An. Ox. 5267. v. un-behreówsigende.

be-hreówsung. *Add :*—Behreósunge *penitudinis*, An. Ox. 4496. Ætwindan hellicum wítum mid sóđre behreówsunge, Hml. A. 34, 252 : Hml. Th. ii. 352, 23, 24. Þurh synna behreówsunge, Wlfst. 24, 18.

behreówsung-tíd, e ; *f. A time of penitence, penitential season* (*Septuagesima*) :—Fram đisum dæge oð Eástron is úre heófungtíd and bereówsungtíd úre synna, Hml. Th. ii. 86, 25 : 88, 3.

be-hringed. *Substitute : be-hringan ; p. de ; pp. ed To surround, encircle :*—On mínum earfoþum þe mé habbað útan behringed *a pressura quae circumdedit me*, Ps. Th. 31, 8. Behrincged, 48, 5. Burh útan behringed mid feóndum, 17, 28. Mid costungum wé sint æghwonon útan behrincgde (-hring-, *v. l.*), Past. 163, 16. Ábútan beringede mid leahtrum *circumdati vitiis*, Scint. 103, 11.

be-hrúmig. *Add :*—Hé clypte đá hweras and cyste þá pannan đæt hé wæs eall sweart and behrúmig, Shrn. 69, 30. v. next word.

be-hrúmod. *Substitute :* Behrúmod *caccabatum*, Wrt. Voc. ii. 84, 71. Berúmad, 18, 55.

be-hwearft, es ; *m. Change :*—On behwearftum *in commutationibus*, Ps. L. 43, 13.

be-hweorfan (-hwurfan, -hwyrfan). *Substitute :* **I.** *to attend to, see to the good condition of :*—Gif hé wáccor hý behwyrfð, þonne þ hé him tó ágenum teleð, Ll. Th. i. 272, 11. Þá leóhtfatu þe hé behwearf *lampades quas reficiebat*, Gr. D. 46, 31. Þæt manna gehwylc his ágen hús wel behweorfe, þæt is, þæt gehwá his heortan geclǽnsige, Wlfst. 280, 11. Scipena behweorfan, Angl. ix. 261, 18. Mæssereáf wurðlíce behworfen, Ll. Th. ii. 250, 28 : 252, 24 : 350, 22. Godes cyrcan sýn wel behworfene, i. 246, 12. **I a.** of funeral rites :—Mid myrran man behwyrfð deádra manna líc, Hml. Th. i. 116, 6. Ic his líc behwearf mid gewunelicre þénunge, Hml. S. 31, 1423 : Hml. A. 79, 167. Hig mǽrlíce þæt líc behwurfon mid niclum wópe *celebrantes exequias planctu magno*, Gen. 50, 10. Þá wíf behwurfon hire líc oþ þ heó bebyrged wæs, Hml. S. 10, 270. Ælc preósta æfter forðsíđe georne behweorfe and ne geþafige ǽnig unnit æt þám líce, Ll. Th. ii. 258, 12. Pilatus geþafode đám đegene (*Joseph*) þæt hé hine behwurfe, Hml. Th. ii. 260, 33. Hí móston his líc mid heora đénungum behwurfan, i. 564, 13. **I b.** of dressing animals intended for food :—Hig behwurfon þá fugelas *siccaverunt coturnices*, Num. 11, 32. Gýme swán þ hé æfter sticunge his slyhtswýn wel behweorfe (*corrediet*), Ll. Th. i. 436, 16. Đonne hé spic behworfen hæfð, 2. **II.** *to treat*, (1) an object :—Gif heora hwylc gýmeleáslíce mynstres þing behwyrfe *si quis negligenter res monasterii tractaverit*, R. Ben. 56, 12. (2) a person or matter :—Biscop đe mihte behwyrfan đá hálgan martiras mid sanguni and Godes gerihtum, Hml. Th. ii. 312, 29. Þæt þám banan ne wearð hleahtre

behworfen (*turned out no laughing matter*), An. 1705. **III.** *to exercise, practise :*—Begá (behwyrf) þé sylfne on þisum *exerce temet ipsum in hoc*, An. Th. 31, 37. [*Goth.* bi-hwairban : O. Sax. be-hwer-ban : O. H. Ger. pi-hwerban.]

be-hwerfan. *Substitute :* be-hwirfan ; *p.* de. **I.** *to turn :*—Đonēcan þe heó útan behwerfed sié, Bt. 25 ; F. 88, 35 : Met. 13, 77. **II.** *to surround, encompass :*—Ic wolde mid sumre bisne þé behwerfan útan *ego tibi corollarium dabo*, Bt. 34, 4 ; F. 138, 27. **III.** *to turn to, convert* into, *change :*—Hí hæfdon behwyrfed heora gestreón on gymstānum . . . Hit wæs gewunelic . . . þæt hí behwyrfdon heora áre on gymstānum, Hml. Th. i. 60, 22–28. Þú bist behwyrfed ł miswend *peruerteris*, Ps. L. 17, 27. Þæt teóðe werod tó áwyrgedum gástum behwyrfede wurdon, Hml. Th. i. 540, 3. **IV.** *to exchange, change* for :—Hé ealle his ǽhta behwyrfde wið ánum gyldenum wecge, Hml. Th. i. 394, 12. Úre unclǽnan weorc wé sceolon behwyrfan mid clǽnum, 138, 29.

be-hwylfan. *l.* be-hwilfan, *and substitute :*—Ne behwylfan mæg heofon and eorðe his wuldres word wíddra and síddra þonne befæđman mæge . . . eorðan ymbhwyrft and uprodor *heaven and earth cannot form a vault that shall cover his glory's word, too wide and too ample for the globe and the firmament on high to embrace*, Exod. 426.

be-hwyrfan. v. be-hweorfan *and* be-hwirfan.

be-hýdan. *Add :*—Sé þe behýt his leahtras, Angl. xii. 513, 16. Seó clǽnnys behýt (*recondit*) hyre swurd on đám temple, Prud. 16 b. Behýdde *oppilavit*, Wrt. Voc. ii. 82, 51. Hí þá goldhord on eorðan behýddan, Chr. 418 ; P. 11, 23. Behéd *reconde*, Kent. Gl. 176. Ne mæg hine nán man behýdan wið hine hǽto, Ps. Th. 18, 6. Nis mín bán wið þé behýded (*occultatum*), 138, 13 : Bl. H. 93, 35. Behéd lác *munus absconditum*, Kent. Gl. 780. Of þám díglum stówum þe hí on behýdde (*abditi*) wǽron, Bd. 1, 16 ; Sch. 44, 14. Behýdde *abstrusa*, An. Ox. 8, 308. Hí on þám scræfe lágon fram Decie behýdde, Hml. S. 23, 741. ¶ of *sheathing a sword :*—Hé hét Petrum behýdan his swurd, Hml. S. 25, 848 : 28, 65. Þá sweord on heora sceáđum behýdde wǽron (*reconduntur*), Prud. 72.

be-hýdedness, -hýdness, e ; *f. Concealment, secrecy ; a secret place :*—Mid behýdnysse *in occulto*, Ll. Th. ii. 148, 13. Behýdednesse his *latibulum ejus*, Ps. L. 17, 12.

be-hydelíce, &c. *l.* be-hýdelíce, be-hygdiglíce (bí-, bi-), *and add :*—Behigdelíce (-hýgdig-), bihýdiglíce, bighigdelíce *sollicite*, Bd. 4, 3 ; Sch. 361, 7. Behýdilíce, bihýdiglíce (-higde-), Sch. 363, 4. Þ gehérende behýdelíce hí mearcedon đone dæg, Shrn. 86, 2.

be-hydig. *l.* be-hygdig, -hýdig (big-, bí-, bi-), *and add :*—Wes þú behýdig and gemyndig Marian þinga, Bl. H. 67, 32. Heó weard behýdig be þissum, Hml. S. 33, 47. Mid behygdige móde *solerti animo*, Bd. 4, 3 ; Sch. 355, 21. Behýdigne and sorhfulne be þisse wísan, Guth. 84, 24. v. big-hýdig *in Dict.*

be-hýdignys (-hygdignes). [In Ps. Spl. C. 28, 7 the same mistake seems to have been made as in Ps. Srt. 28, 8, where *solitudinem* is glossed *bihygdignisse* (= solicitudinem).] *Care, anxiety, solicitude :*—Bihýdinys (bighýdignys, Hpt. Gl. 528, 41) *sollicitudo*, An. Ox. 5430. Carfulnesse, bihýdine(sse) *sollicitudinis*, 906. v. be-hygdness.

be-hýdness. v. be-hýdedness.

be-hygdness, e ; *f. Care, anxiety :*—Behygdnis weorulde þisse *sollicitudo saeculi istius*, Mt. R. 13, 22. Cf. be-hogadness.

be-hyhtan ; *p.* te *To set hopes on, trust* in :—Wá þám þe on God ne behyht *vae qui non sunt confisi super sanctum Israel*, Wlfst. 48, 8.

be-hyldan. *Add :*—Hí behyldon ǽnne oxan and besywodon Crisantum mid þǽre hýde tó his nacodum líce, Hml. S. 35, 158. Behyldan, besleán *deglobere*, i. *decoriare*, An. Ox. 3280 : Wrt. Voc. ii. 82, 13. Óðre wǽron cuce behylde, Hml. Th. i. 542, 29.

be-hylian ; *p.* ede *To cover, veil :*—Heó hire heáfod behylede mid hire cúlan, Hml. S. 33, 237. [O. Sax. bi-hullean : O. H. Ger. pi-hulit *tectus, amictus*.] v. be-helian.

be-hýran ; *pp.* ed *To let* or *hire out :*—Behýred feoh *locatio*, Wrt. Voc. ii. 54, 3 : *conductio*, 135, 70.

be-hýring. *Add :*—Behýrung *locatio*, Wrt. Voc. ii. 54, 3.

be-hýdelíce. *l.* be-hýþelíce, *and substitute :* Sumptuously :—Behýđelíce *sumptuosius*, Wrt. Voc. ii. 87, 24.

be-innan. v. binnan.

be-irfeweardian *to disinherit :*—Beyrfeweardige *exheredet vel exalienat de hereditate*, Wrt. Voc. ii. 144, 73. Beerfwerdige, R. Ben. I. 2, 4. Þí lǽs hé ús beyrfewerdige (-weard-, *v. l.*), swá swá fæder déþ his bearn, R. Ben. 1, 16.

be-irnan. *Add :* **I.** trans. (1) *to run over, traverse* :—Seó sunne beyrnð đá twelf tácna, Lch. iii. 262, 23. Đǽre sunnan geár is þ heó beyrne þone zodiacum, 244, 20. (2) *to overrun, cover* :—Drihtnes ród bið blóde beurnen, Wlfst. 183, 17. **II.** intrans. (1) of movement :—Sum cild bearn under ánum hweóle, Hml. Th. ii. 26, 24. (2) of action, *to run into danger, have recourse to* :—Gif ic on unriht bearn, Ps. 58, 4. Þú beurne on þone wyrstan feónd, Hml. Th. i. 66, 28. (3) of thought, *to occur to the mind :*—Ús bearn þis on mód, Hml. S.

10, 233: B. 67. [Goth. bi-rinnan: O.-H. Ger. pi-rinnan.] v. bi-rinnan *in* Dict.

**be-ládian.** *Add:* I. *to excuse, absolve* from an obligation, *let off:*—Ic ne beládige mīne āteorigendlican ylde, Hml. S. 31, 1346. Hī bǣdon ðone bydel þæt hē hī beládode. Hml. Th. ii. 374, 9. Belāda mē, 372, 20: Lk. 14, 19. Þ ðū mē beládige *habe me excusatum*, 18. Nǣnig sý belādod fram þǣre kycenan þēnunge, R. Ben. 58, 14. I *a. reflex.* (1) *to beg off:*—Ic ne beládige mē for ylde, Hml. Th. ii. 516, 27. Hē hine beládað, 374, 17. Hī hī beládiað, 372, 18. þā ongunnon hig hig beládian *coeperunt excusare*, Lk. 14, 18. (a) with gen.:—Ne mæg eówer nān hyne lāre beládian, Ll. Th. ii. 424, 24. (β) with (neg.) clause:—Nān man hine ne sceal beládian þæt hē Godes cyrcan ne gesēce, Hml. Th. ii. 444, 8. Hē for his wīfe ne dearr hine sylfne beládian ðæt hē ne scule faran, Hex. 34, 21. (2) *to offer as excuse:*—Þ nān man ne ðorfte hine beládian, þ hē fæt næfde *that nobody need offer as excuse, that he had not a vessel*, Hml. A. 141, 83. II. where a person is charged with something, *to excuse, exculpate:*—Þæt hyra nān þurh nytennysse hine beládian ne mæge, R. Ben. 127, 10. Hū hī hī willen beládian on ðæm miclan dōme, Past. 429, 4. (1) with gen.:—Heó eáþe miähte þæs forligeres unhlīsan hī beládian, Hml. S. 2, 205. Ðāra scylda hié wilniað ðæt hié scylen hié beládian, Past. 241, 2. (2) with (neg.) clause:—Hē mæg hine ðý lǣs beládian ðæt hē næbbe wīte gearnod *inexcusabiliter merebitur supplicium*, 347, 19.

**be-ládiendlic;** *adj. Apologetic;* apologeticus, An. Ox. 2299: 2793: 2957: 4233.

**be-ládung.** *Add:*—Beládung *excusatio*, Wrt. Voc. i. 83, 66. Ðæt ǣlcere neóde beládung sý āðīlegod, R. Ben. 92, 4. Gif þū woldest myltsian, and ne miähtest, þær is sum beládung on þǣre segene, Hml. S. 3, 185. Beóð þā hǣðenan būton beládunge (*no excuse can be made for them*) rihtlīce fordēmede, 11, 344. Mid þæs cāseres beládunge (*excuse or defence of his conduct*), 31, 624. Þū sēcest beládunge, þ þu ne þurfe getīðian þæs þe ic þē bidde, Gr. D. 28, 7. Beládunge habban uncyste *to have an excuse for parsimony*, Hml. Th. i. 330, 9: ii. 76, 10.

**be-lǣdan.** *Dele second passage, and add:*—Sē þe ōðerne man on synna belǣdeð, Wlfst. 78, 17. Þīne ýþa þū on belǣddest (*induxisti*) ofer mē, Ps. L. 87, 8. Hē him sume hefigtýmnysse on belǣdde, Hml. Th. ii. 546, 19. Hī ðǣre sáwle wynsumnysse on belǣddon, 334, 11. þū ūs on ne belǣd (*inducas*) on costnunge, Ps. L. fol. 198 b. Þe lǣs ūs se lytiga belǣde on his sylfes wīte, Hml. A. 195, 10. Nellan on belǣdan (*inferre*) swincgla ūs, Coll. M. 18, 22. Of rihtan wege belǣdan, Btwk. 196, 19. On belǣdan *inrogare, ingerere*, An. Ox. 3944. [O. H. Ger. pi-leiten.]

**be-lǣfan.** *Substitute:* I. *trans.* (1) *to leave, be survived by:*—Hē bearn ne belǣfð, Hml. Th. ii. 146, 20. (2) *to leave* unconsumed, undone, *to spare:*—Hē ne belǣfde nāne lāfe cuce *non dimiserunt ullas reliquias*, Jos. 10, 28. Nān hǣðengyld se hagol ne belǣfde, Hml. S. 4, 427: Hml. Th. ii. 194, 2. Þone sǣdere hē belǣfde ūs tō sēcenne, 90, 8. Næs nān ele belǣged tō his gebrōðra bricum, 178, 20. II. *intrans. To remain* [for intrans. use in later English v. N. E. D. s.v. *believe*]:—Ān of him ne belāf (-lǣfde, MS. C), Ps. Spl. 105, 11. Hē hēt ācwellan þā crīsteran, wolde þ nān man ne belǣfde crīsten, Hml. S. 29, 202. [Goth. bi-laibjan *to leave*.]

**be-lǣþed.** *Substitute:* be-lǣþan *to make detestable:*—Eów þe taliaþ biter ðing tō swēte and swēte belǣþað, Wlfst. 47, 7.

**be-lǣwa** *a betrayer:*—Iudas, Drihtnes belǣwa, Hml. S. 19, 228: Hml. Th. i. 398, 22.

**be-lǣwan.** *Add:* to betray, (1) a person:—Hē hine belǣwde tō deáþe, Wlfst. 18, 1: Hml. A. 153, 56. Hē belǣwde þone Hǣlend þām cwellerum, 74, 45: Hml. Th. i. 26, 25. Beleede (bilēde, R.) *proderet*, Mk. L. 14, 10. Sē þe unscildigne man belǣwe wið mēdscette, Deut. 27, 25. Þū hæfst ūs beswicen and belǣwed, Wlfst. 240, 26. Wē synd belǣwde tō ūre līfleáste, Hml. A. 99, 254. (2) a thing:—Sum leógere belǣwde þ feoh, Hml. S. 25, 756.

**be-lǣwend,** es; *m. A betrayer:*—Sý hē Iudas gefēra, Crīstes belǣwendes, C. D. iii. 350, 17. Þurh þone Iudas, Crīstes belǣwend, H. R. 15, 6.

**be-lǣwing** *betrayal. Add:*—Behlēing *proditio*, Mk. p. 5, 10. Belǣwincge *proditionis*, Scint. 90, 12.

**be-lagen.** v. next word.

**be-leán.** *Substitute: pp.* -lagen. I. *to restrain* a person (dat.) from something (acc.) *by blaming, to prohibit:*—Hē willnode þæt hē mōste mid him sweltan, þeáh se bisscop him þæt swīðe belōh (*tametsi ipso multum prohibente*), Bd. 5, 19; Sch. 661, 18. Þ preóstas oferdruncen georne beleán ōðrum mannum *that priests restrain other men from drunkenness by their earnest condemnation of it*, Ll. Th. ii. 256, 14. Næs nān wītega āsend tō hǣðenum folce, þe heora gedwyld belōge, Hml. Th. ii. 76, 6. Ne inc ǣnig mon beleán miähte sorhfulne sīð *nobody could keep you two from the grievous adventure by pointing out its folly*, B. 511. Ðǣm lytegan is ǣrest tō beleánne hiera selfīce, ðæt hié ne wēnen ðæt hié síen wiése *in hebetibus hoc primum destruendum est, quod se sapientes arbitrantur*, Past. 203, 9. Him sī belagen ðæt hī dōð

*sunt destruenda ea, in quibus nequiter versant*, 441, 7. II. *to charge* with (? v. be-hlīgan):—Wīdgongel wīf mon wommum bilihð, Gn. Ex. 65. [For to bileande þ no man werpe þe gilt of his sinne auuppen God, Hml. ii. 107, 10. O. H. Ger. pi-lahan.]

**be-lecgan.** *Add:*—Gif man mid tihtlan preóst belēde, Ll. Th. ii. 256, 39. Belege mid wulle *cover with wool*, Lch. ii. 262, 3. Mid unþeáwum belēd *subject to vices*, R. Ben. 121, 14. Līge belegde *enveloped in flame*, Dan. 296. [O. Frs. bi-lega: O. H. Ger. pi-leggen: Ger. be-legen.]

**be-lēd** *impelled*, be-lēgan. *Dele, and see preceding word.*

**belene.** *Add:*—Belonae (-e) *sinfoniaca*, Txts. 98, 975. Belune, Wrt. Voc. i. 289, 38. Beolone, 68, 43: *simphonia*, Wülck. Gl. 301, 23: *laterculum*, Wrt. Voc. i. 67, 52. Belene, ii. 54, 21.

**be-leógan.** *Add:*—Wē, ðe men syndon, beóþ ful oft belogene fram ōþrum mannum *fallimur qui homines sumus*, Gr. D. 40, 23. ¶ used impersonally, *to be mistaken:*—Gif þū wilt geþencean hū mycel hine beleáh (*how much he was mistaken*), Bl. H. 189, 24. [O. Frs. bi-liaga: O. H. Ger. pi-liogan: Ger. be-lügen *to deceive*.]

**be-leórendlic;** *adj. Past:*—Synne biliórendlica (*praeterita*), ondueardlica, and tōueardlica, Rtl. 170, 11. Of bileórendlicum *de praeteritis*, 123, 27.

**belg.** *Add:* I. *a bag:*—Bǣlge oððe bylge *bulga*, Wrt. Voc. ii. 12, 27. Tōbersteþ þā belgas (*utres*) and þā belgas tō lore weordaþ, Mt. R. 9, 17. II. *bellows:*—Swēgincga blāwendra byliga (*follium*), Coll. M. 31, 7. Ðeáh man þone gārsecg embsette mid byligeon . . . and tō ǣghwylcum þǣra byligea wǣre man geset . . . ond man bleówe mid þām byligeon, Wlfst. 146, 27–147, 6. Belgum *folliginis*, Wrt. Voc. ii. 150, 15. Bylgum, 97, 23: 36, 1: *follibus*, 89, 12. Bylium, Germ. 398, 70. v. blǣd-, blǣs-, blǣst-, hirde-belg.

**belgan.** *Add:* I. *reflex.:*—Hē hine bealg wið Samuel, Past. 35, 16. II. *intrans.:*—þāra wōhnes bealh for þām þeáwum his rihtwīsnysse *quorum tortitudo in norma ejus rectitudinis offendebat*, Gr. D. 104, 14. Hiá bulgon bituih him seolfum *indigne ferebant intra semet ipsos*, Mk. L. R. 14, 4.

**-belge, belgness.** v. íþ-belge, bǣlignis *in* Dict.

**bel-hringes beácn.** *Add:*—Sōna swā þæt beácn þæs belhringces gehýred bið, R. Ben. 67, 20.

**bel-hús.** *Add:*—Belle *clocca*, belhús *cloccarium* vel *lucar*, Wrt. Voc. i. 81, 37.

**be-licgan.** *Add:* I. *to surround:*—Ealne middangeard ymbfēran swā gārsecg beliged *orbi terrarum circumfluum nauigare oceanum*, Nar. 20, 15. Ðæt innlond beliged ān dīc ūtanc, Cht. E. 161, 29. Italia land belīð Wendelsǣ ymb eall ūtan, Ors. 1, 1; S. 22, 17. Seó heofon beligð on hyre bōsme ealne middaneard, Angl. viii. 309, 46. Be gemǣre swā ðā ealdan dīca beligcað, C. D. iii. 213, 6. II. *to appertain* (only late; *see* N. E. D. *be-lie*, 4):—Ic hebbe bicweðen Portland and eall ðæt ðǣrtō bilýð, C. D. iv. 229, 21. [O. Frs. bi-liga: O. H. Ger. pi-ligan *opprimere, comprimere*.]

**be-lífan.** *Add:* I. *to remain,* (1) *not to move* from a place:—Abraham belāf þǣr, Gen. 21, 32: Chr. 1018; P. 155, 13. Seó scipfyrd belāf *the fleet did not move*, 1052; P. 177, 23. xl. scypa belifon mid þam cynge, 1018; P. 154, 14. Him twā mǣgða belifon, Hml. A. 61, 238. (1 a) with adverb:—Ðā bōceras bæftan belifon, Hml. Th. i. 108, 11. Fíf belifan wiðæftan, Chr. 1047; P. 171, 7. Bæftan belífan *remorari*, R. Ben. I. 87, 9. Hig ealle in on þā burh fōron þæt ðǣr nānþyng þæs folces wyðūtan belyfen næs, St. And. 34, 14. (2) *to be left, not to be taken away, to survive:*—Hyt tōflēwð swā ðæt þǣr nānwiht belífed būton þā bān, Lch. i. 242, 27. Se gewuna belāf of hǣðenra manna biggenge, Hml. A. 146, 47. Ne ōwiht þine ne belífe heánra gylta, Dōm. L. 38. Ōðer dǣl scel belīuan ðām ðe hit findæð, Cht. Th. 318, 21. Belīfendra *remanentium*, Scint. 74, 8. Swā hwæt swā tōforan þām neádbehēfum belifen byþ *quidquid necessario victui superest*, R. Ben. 138, 16. þæt folc þæt on þǣre ceastre belyfen wæs, St. And. 34, 31. Beliuene *superstites*, Hpt. Gl. 484, 4. (3) with predicate noun or adj.:—God þē benǣmð þīnra gōda, and þū belífst siððan wǣdla, Hml. Th. ii. 102, 23. Þæt þæt cucu belāf, Ælfc. T. Grn. 3, 29. Nān ne belāf cucu, Hml. S. 18, 141. Hē belāf þǣr gesund, 29, 251. Þā līchaman belifon ungederode, 4, 395. II. *to die:* belifen; *pp. dead* [cf. O. H. Ger. bi-liban *mortuus*]:—Sca Maria wæs iii and sixtig geára eald ðā heó belyfen wæs, Sal. K. 184, 2. Mid þǣm miclan wōlbryne monucwealmes þe him raðe ðæs æfter com, swā ðæt hié healfe belifene wurdon, Ors. 2, 6; S. 86, 26. [O. Frs. bi-līva.]

**be-lífan** (ié, ē, ý); *p. de To believe:*—þone hálgan gāst þe þū on belēfst, Hml. 177, 266. þā þe on God belýfað, Hml. Th. i. 114, 8. Þone dracan þe wē on belýfdon, 570, 25. Hí on God belýfdon, 92, 33: 244, 4: ii. 20, 7: Hml. S. 23, 22. [Cf. ge-līfan, which is the earlier form.]

**be-lífed;** *adj. Endowed with belief, having belief:*—Theodosius fullīce on God wæs belýfed, Hml. S. 23, 412. Maria and Martha wǣron twā geswystru swīðe on God belýfede, Hml. Th. i. 130, 5. Cf. ge-lifed.

be-lífend, es; m. A survivor :—Belíuendras superstites .i. uini, An. Ox. 3313. Belífendes (= -as), 2, 190.

be-lífian; p. ode To deprive of life, kill :—Hé wæs wælbreáw cwellere, and fela belífode gelýfedra manna, Hml. Th. ii. 308, 5. Hé hæt his underðeóddan hine belífian, 36, 10. Belífian (vel beheáfdian), Hml. S. 12, 221.

be-líman; p. de To glue together :—Swylce sē þe belíme tigelan quasi qui conglutinet testam, Scint. 96, 19.

be-limp, es; n. An event, occurrence, case :—Belimp fors, An. Ox. 50, 22. Wið liþa sáre, gif hý of hwylcum belimpe oþþe of ænigum þincge gesárgude beóð, Lch. i. 312, 1. On horse hwítum sittan belimp gód getácnað, iii. 202, 28. Smyltum belimpum secundis successibus, An. Ox. 7, 170. Ælc þæra dǽda þe gedón wæs on þæs cyninges belimpum, Hml. A. 95, 124. Belimp (-limpas, An. Ox. 388) eventus (acc. pl.), Hpt. Gl. 415, 49: 511, 71. On goldes belimpu in auri casus, Scint. 111, 3. v. un-belimp.

be-limpan. Add: I. to belong to :—Belimpþ attinet, An. Ox. 27, 22. (1) of possession :—Se dæg (the extra day of leap-year) belimpþ ǽgðer ge tó ðǽre sunnan ge tó ðám mónan, Lch. iii. 264, 13. Þá termina gebyriaþ ꝉ belimpað tó Pentecosten, Angl. viii. 329, 2. (2) of subordination or subjection :—Þæt Witland belimpeð tó Éstum, Ors. 1, 1; S. 20, 6. Þá belimpað tó þám deófle þe grǽdignysse gefremmað, Scrd. 20, 10. Eal ðæt folc þe tó his ríce belomp, Shrn. 120, 33. Manege scíran mid weorce tó Lundenne belumpon, Chr. 1097; P. 234, 5. (3) to be of a class :—Þá þuneras ne belimpað tó ðám ðunere þe on þyssere lyfte brastlað, Lch. iii. 280, 12. Belimpende pertinentes (ad inferiorem gradum), An. Ox. 872. (4) to be proper for, adapted to :—Þás lǽcedómas belimpað tó eallum innoþa mettrymnessum, Lch. ii. 158, 1. Leóð þá þe tó ǽfestnesse belumpon carmina religioni apta, Bd. 4, 24; Sch. 481, 5. Ælc man, hwæt his hǽde tó belumpe, folgade, Chr. 1086; P. 219, 31. (5) to concern, be the concern of a person :—Hwæt belympð tó þé hwylcere mǽgðe ic sý, Hml. S. 19, 56. (6) to pertain to, relate to, have to do with :—Þá þing þe Gode belimpað, Ex. 4. 16. Ðá ðing ðe tó scipene belimpað, Angl. ix. 260, 5. Plegan tó ðám bǽdstede belimpende, An. Th. 12, 18. II. to happen, befall :—Belamp evenit, contigit, An. Ox. 3203. Belamp þ se arð férde tó Róme, Chr. 1070; P. 206, 7. Ðætte ne wyrsa ðé bilimpe (blimpe, L. contingat), Jn. R. 5, 14. Þæt him ne belimpe se egeslica cwyde that the terrible sentence be not applied to them, Hml. Th. ii. 536, 6. III. to become, attain the character of :—Þis godspel ús tó bysene belimpeþ éces lífes, Bl. H. 15, 32. Þá ælmessan þe gé syllaþ eów tó nánigere áre ne belimpaþ (-eþ, MS.), 41, 23. Ðæt bið unnyt word, ðætte gescédwíse menn ne magon ongietan ðæt hit belimpe tó ryhtwíslicre ðearfe otiosum verbum est, quod ratione justae necessitatis caret, Past. 281, 12.

be-listnian. Add :—Se engel hine belisnode (ꝉ geldede), Gr. D. 25, 30. Geseah hé Godes engel hine belisnian angelo eunuchizari se vidit, 26, 25 : Chr. 1096; P. 232, 22. Belisnud spado, Germ. 394, 197. Eunuchi, þ synd belisnode, Hml. S. 2, 46 : Lch. iii. 202, 34. ¶ In An. Ox. 4307 stupratur is glossed by wæs belisned. [O. H. Ger. pilistinôn derogare.]

bell (more usual form belle, q.v.). Add :—Þær nǽron ǽr búton VII. upphangene bella, and nú þá siud XIII. upphangene, Cht. Th. 430, 4. v. hand-, mót-bell.

bellan. Add :—Bellende rugiens, Mt. p. 9, 14.

belle. Add :—Belle clocca, litel belle tintinnabulum, mycel belle campana, Wrt. Voc. i. 81, 36–39. Belle campana, cimbala, ii. 127, 83. Hrýðeres belle bið ánes sciꝉ. weorð, Ll. Th. i. 260, 16. Bellan sweg, Shrn. 149, 9. Beácn þǽre bellan gehýran, Hml. A. 168, 107. Áheng se munuc áne lytle bellan on ðám stánclúde . . . Se deófol wearp ǽnne stán tó ðǽre bellan, þæt heó tósprang, Hml. Th. ii. 156, 4–10. Hostiarius . . . sceal mid bellan bícnigan þá tída, Ll. Th. ii. 346, 29. Bellan gehíran, Lch. iii. 174, 9. Bellan teón, ryngan, Tech. ii. 118, 18, 20. On ðæs sácerdes hrægle wǽron bellan hangiende, Past. 93, 15 : 95, 3 : C. D. B. iii. 660, 34. Feohbót gebyreð . . . tó bócan and tó bellan, Ll. Th. i. 328, 8. Þonne gé gehýran cyricean bellan (campanas), Coll. M. 36, 1. v. cyric-, hand-, non-belle.

bell-tác(e)n, es; n. A signal given by a bell :—Sóna swá hý belltácen gehýrað þǽre nigoðan tíde, þ is seó nóntíd, Hml. A. 140, 65.

bell-tíd, e; f. A canonical hour marked by the ringing of a bell (v. preceding word. bel-hringes beácn, and Ll. Th. ii. 346, 29 given under belle) :—Singuli servorum Dei xxx diebus canonicis horis expleto synaxeos æt vii beltídum Pater Noster pro eo cantetur (the English words seem to be a gloss on ' canonicis horis'), Haddan and Stubbs' Councils, ii. 584, 8.

belt. Substitute :—Belt baltheus, i. cingulum, An. Ox. 486. Gyrdel oððe belt baltheum, Wrt. Voc. ii. 11, 51 : baltheum, cingulum, 125, 15. Helmstán þá undǽde gedyde þæt hé Æðerédes belt forstæl, Cht. Th. 169, 20.

be-lúcan. Add: I. to shut up in a place, enclose :—Ic mé on þisse gyrde belúce, Lch. i. 388, 11. Hé wæs on hire innoðe belocen, sé ðe belícð ealne middangeard on his ánre handa, Hml. Th. i. 198, 3. Hiene

ðǽrinne ne belýcð (circumcludit) nán ege, Past. 220, 13. Ne þú ná beluce (conclusisti) mé on handum feóndes, Ps. Spl. 30, 10. Hé hine sylfne in þám scræfe beleác, Gr. D. 214, 18: Hml. S. 35, 36. Belúcað hine þæt hé licge þǽr ána, 37, 182. On his frið wunian belocun wiþ þám láþan, Lch. i. 390, 14. I a. to secure, protect :—Ic hig wigge beleác manegum mǽgða, B. 1770. II. to shut up a place, to prevent entrance into a place, close :—Hé þone hálgan hám beleác, Bl. H. 9, 7. Hí heora baða belucon, Ap. Th. 6, 13 : Ps. Spl. 16, 11. Hostiarius sceal þá cyrcan þám ungeleáffullun belúcan, Ll. Th. ii. 346, 30. Belocenum fenge sinu concluso, Wrt. Voc. ii. 135, 3. His múþ and his næsþyrla beóþ belocene, Bl. H. 59, 14. III. to close a road, door, &c., prevent passage through :—Hé sylf him belícð þǽre forgifenysse weg mid his heardheortnysse, Hml. Th. i. 500, 19. Eua ús beleác heofenan ríces geat, . . . gif wé hit nú ús ne belúcað, ii. 22, 25–27. Hié belúcað hiera módes eáran ongeán láre, Past. 337, 22. Seó ástrehte nǽdre his weg beleác, Gr. D. 24, 23. Hig belucan þá duran intó heom, Chr. 1083; P. 215, 5. Belúc heora wegas mid þínum sweorde, Ps. Th. 34, 3. Þæt mé þone ingang beluce, Hml. S. 23 b, 416. Belucen, 426. Þéh hié hiera clúsan him ongeán beluce Philippi ingressum Thermopylarum munitione repularunt, Ors. 3, 7 ; S. 114, 23. Seó duru biþ belocen þǽm synfullum mannum, Bl. H. 61, 10. Hié þá gatu him tó belocen hæfdon, Chr. 755; P. 48, 16. Mid þám þe þá burhgatu belocene wurdon cum porta clauderetur, Jos. 2, 5. Þá belocenan wega gelǽta conpeta clausa, Wrt. Voc. ii. 19, 55. III a. to stop, impede :—On þám oreðe belocen, Hml. S. 23 b, 235. IV. to shut out, exclude :—Belúc alleluia do not sing Alleluia (after Septuagesima Sunday), Lch. iii. 226, 15. Ðe lǽs ðe hire lufu ðé belúce fram Críste, Hex. 48, 7. Hét se árleása hine útan belúcan, Hml. S. 31, 656. Tó bilúcanne costunge ad excludendas temptationes, Rtl. 118, 9. Maria wæs belocen (exclusa) bútan þǽre wícstówe, Num. 12, 15. Sind wé úte belocene fram ðám leóhte, Hml. Th. i. 154, 13. V. to confine within certain limits :—Se arc wæs mid áare fæðme belocen ufewerd at the top the ark did not exceed a cubit, Angl. vii. 34, 356. V a. of speech, to put thought into few words, to express briefly :—Lucas beleác þis dægþerlíce godspel mid feáwum wordum, ac hit is mid menigfealdre mihte áfylled the gospel of this day is contained in few words, but is filled with manifold power, Hml. Th. i. 90, 8. Críst gesette þis gebed, and beleác mid feáwum wordum, 272, 15. VI. to contain, comprise, include :—Gehwylces weorces frig, bútan ðæs cericlican weorces ðe seó bóc belýcð (work, of which the charter contains notice, cf. 33, 1), C. D. vi. 34, 33. Seó heofon belýcð on hyre bósme ealne middaneard, Lch. iii. 232, 17. Þás syx casus befóð and belúcað swá hwæt swá nien embe sprecað, Ælfc. Gr. Z. 23, 14. Þás twá bebodu belúcað ealle béc (cf. Mt. 22, 40), Hml. Th. ii. 314, 9. Þ eall þ andgit beó belocen on þǽre ánfealdan gerecednisse, Ælfc. Gen. Thw. 2, 31. Ealle úre neóda ðǽron (in the Lord's Prayer) sind belocene, i. 272, 17. VII. to close, conclude, stop, (1) trans. To bring to an end :—Se apostol beleác þisne pistol mid þisum wordum, Hml. Th. i. 606, 8 : 616, 32. Hé geseah þ ealle þás þincg belocene wǽron (all work and play were stopped), Ap. Th. 6, 17. (1 a) to complete a transaction, bargain :—þ hé beleác on hálre tungon conclusit et omnino confirmavit totum quod pater suus in vita sua fecerat, Cht. E. 212, 9. (2) intrans. To come to an end :—Ðæt godspel belícð þus, Hml. Th. ii. 574, 4. [v. N. E. D. belouke. O. Sax. bi-lúkan to shut up : O. Frs. bi-lúka : O. H. Ger. pi-lúhhan con-, ex-, in-, prae-, re-cludere.]

be-lutian; p. ode To lie hid :—Befleáh hé in sum hol treów and þǽr belutode and hine sylfne áhýdde fugiens in cava arbore latebat, Gr. D. 293, 15.

be-lyrtan; p. te To deceive :—Bisuicen ꝉ bilyrtet inlusus, Mt. L. 2, 16. [Bilurt (bichard, v. l.), A. R. 280. v. N. E. D. be-lirt.]

be-lytegan. l. be-lytigian.

be-mǽnan. Add: to lament, bewail, (1) absolute :—Bemǽndon dúna doluerunt montes, Cant. Ab. 10. Wé ne sceolan ceorian ne sorhlíce bemǽnan, þeáh ðe ús ungelimp getíme, Hml. S. 13, 280. (2) with clause :—Hé bemǽnde þæt Maurus ðæs óðres deáðes fæguian sceolde, Hml. Th. ii. 164, 9. Hí bemǽndon sárlíce þ hí swylce yrmðe gesáwon, Hml. S. 25, 213. (3) to feel penitence for :—Þá þing bemǽnað ꝉ behreówsiað (compungimini), Ps. L. 4, 6. Synna bemǽnan, Wlfst. 133, 14. (4) to feel pity for :—Hé þá buruhware mid teáron bemǽnde, Hml. Th. i. 408, 2. Synt tó bemǽnenne þá ðe þá earman ofðricceað, Hml. A. 148, 119.

be-mancian; p. ode To maim, mutilate :—Gif þú gesihst [h]earmas þine bemancude gód getácnað, Lch. iii. 214, 20. [Cf. Prompt. Parv. mankin mutilo.]

be-meldian; p. ode To denounce a person, disclose, reveal a secret :—Þéh hit sume hwíle forholen beó, hit warð á bemeldod (cf. hit bið æt sumum cyrre open, Prov. K. 30), Prov. M. 27. [That thou me nout bimelde, An. Lit. 3, 27. Ger. be-melden.]

be-meornan. l. be-murnan: bémere. v. bímere.

be-míðan. Add: I. trans. To conceal :—Bemíþan, bedyrnan dissimulare, occultare, An. Ox. 983: Wrt. Voc. ii. 27, 35. Wé magon

monnum bemíðan ûrne geðonc, Past. 39, 12. Bemíþende *recludentes*, An. Ox. 2334. God gecýþde þ mannum bemiðen wæs, Bl. H. 199, 32 : Gr. D. 174, 31. In þám hláfe nán bemiþen (forholen, *v. l.*) þ wôl, 118, 10. Benedicte ne mihte beón nán þing bemiþenes, 144, 33. Bemiðenum *dissimulato*, Wrt. Voc. ii. 27, 36.      II. *intrans. To lie hid :*—Bemáþ *delitescit*, An. Ox. 4687: 5095. þ is bedíhlod ûs, and eác þám bemáþ þe hit geseah *nos et eum qui vidit latet*, Gr. D. 320, 23. Bemiðon *latuerunt*, Wrt. Voc. ii. 50, 6. þeáh seó stefn mannum bemíþe (*lateat*), Gode heó bemíþan (*latere*) ná mæg, Scint. 32, 18. Bemiþe *delitesceret*, An. Ox. 2089. Bemíþan *delitescere*, 4204 : Wrt. Voc. ii. 80, 38 : 26, 47. Bemiþendra *latentium, occultarum*, An. Ox. 2102. [*O. Sax.* bi-míðan : *O. H. Ger.* pi-mídan *evitare, effugere, delitescere*.]

**be-murcian**; *p.* ode To murmur, grumble, complain :—Hû ungemetlíce gê Rômware bemurciað, Ors. 1, 10 ; S. 48, 17. v. murcian.

**be-murnan.** *Add :* *p.* -mearn and -murnde :—þú earhlíce scealt gyltas þíne swíðe bemurnan, Dôm. L. 30, 55. *Take here passages given under* be-meornan *in Dict.*

**be-mútian.** *Add :* [From Latin.]

**be-myldan** :—Bemyldan *humare*, Wrt. Voc. ii. 43, 12. Bimyldan, 110, 48. [Cf. *Icel.* mylda ; ð-myldr *unburied*.]

**ben[n].** *Add :*—Sing þis gealdor ofer : ' Ic binne áwrát (benne áwráð?) betest beaduwræda, swá benne ne burnon . . . .' þás galdor mon mæg singan on wunde, Lch. ii. 350, 30. v. bealu-, dolg-, sár-, seax-, seono-, wæl-ben(n).

**bén.** *Dele* : ' Hence . . . boon,' *in bracket read* petition, *and add :*—Ælc ðæra ðe bitt, and þære bêne ne geswícð, Hml. Th. i. 250, 5. Boene *supplicationem*, Rtl. 46, 20 : *deprecationem*, 40, 21. Hê Drihtene his bêna bebeád, Dôm. L. 60. Boene *petitiones*, Ps. Srt. 19, 7. Boeno *supplicationes*, Rtl. 40, 27.      ¶ *as a technical term.* v. bên-ríp, -irþ (-yrþ) :—Hê sceal erian .iii. æceras tô bêne *arabit .iii. acras precum*, Ll. Th. i. 434, 16. v. ge-, on-bên.

**béna.** *Add :*, bêne (?) ; *f.* :—Hê áforhtode for ðære geornfullan bênan (for hire hálsiendlican bêne, *v. l.*) and wolde þ wíf forbûgan *expavit petitionis illius juramentum, declinare mulierem voluit*, Gr. D. 17, 30. v. fulwiht-bêna.

**be-næced** ; *adj.* (*ptcpl.*) *Stripped :*—Benæced *expeditum*, Wrt. Voc. ii. 144, 71. v. be-neced *in Dict.*

**be-néman.** *Add :*—þ. hê wære benæmed *infiscaretur, fraudaretur*, An. Ox. 3157 : 23, 60.   (1) with acc. of person, (a) gen. of thing :—God þe benæmð þínra gôda, Hml. Th. ii. 102, 22. God þe benæmde wurðmintes *privavit te honore*, Num. 24, 11. þeáh hê ús feores benæme, Hml. Th. i. 576, 10. Hê wæs benæmed manncynnes, 216, 17 : S. 2, 290. Hí wæron benæmode (-ede, -de, *v. ll.*) lífes, Hml. A. 69, 92. (b) with dat. (inst.) of thing :—Hí wæron heora æhtum benæmede (-nêmde, *v. l.*) *possessiunculis suis ejecti*, Bd. 1, 12 ; Sch. 35, 14.   (2) with dat. of person :—Seó nædre him (hí ?) benæmde wuldres, Hml. S. 37, 82. Cf. be-niman.

**benc.** *Add :*—Benc *spondeus*, Wrt. Voc. i. 290, 14 : *sponda*, ii. 121, 2. Wæs on beórsele benc gerýmed, B. 492. Wê on bence beót áhôfon, By. 213. Wæron bollan steápe boran æfter bencum, Jud. 18.

**bencian** ; *p.* ode To furnish with benches :—Hê mæig findan hwæt hê mæig on byrig bêtan . . . betweox hûsan bricgian, beóddian, bencian, Angl. ix. 262, 22. [þatt hus wase wiþþ þrinne bennkess bennkedd, Orm. 15231. *O. H. Ger.* gi-panchôt *stratus*.]

**bend.** *Add :*—Bend *columbar*, Wrt. Voc. i. 16, 44 : *lunula*, 62 : *vincula* vel *ligamen*, 86, 36. Ic geann mínum feówer cnihtum ánes bendes on twêntegum mancussum goldes, Cht. Th. 531, 3. Bende *repagulo, freno*, An. Ox. 2399. Gewriðen mid ðæm bende (*ligamine*), Past. 123, 14 : (*vinculo*), 433, 36. Gif hine mon geyflige mid slege oððe mid bende, Ll. Th. i. 62, 3. Deóf siþþan hê bið on cyninges bende, 112, 5. Healdan þone bróðerlican bend, Hml. Th. i. 260, 29 : ii. 318, 5. Bendas *lora*, Wrt. Voc. ii. 136, 76. Tôburstan þá bendas, Shrn. 54, 21 : Wlfst. 83, 8 : Bd. 4, 22 ; S. 591, 13, 22. Benda, S. 592, 7. Bende, 19. On oþer benda cynn, 6. Bendum *nexibus*, An. Ox. 4935. þone hié hæfdon mid him on bendum *quem captivum detinebant*, Ors. 4, 6 ; S. 178, 9. Ðá hálgan menn geðafeden monige bendas (*vincula*), Past. 205, 12. Bende *nodos*, Wrt. Voc. ii. 95, 27. [*Goth.* bandi ; *f.* : *O. Sax.* bendi ; *f.*] v. bealo-, heáfod-, in-, sceanc-, seonu-, wiþo-, wudu-bend.

**bén-dæg, es** ; *m. A rogation day :*—þá dagas synt geháten on Lýden *rogacionum dies*, and on Englisc bêndagas, Angl. viii. 329, 26.

**bendan.** *Add :* I. *to bend :*—þonne bende ic mínne bogan, Wlfst. 229, 8. Hí bendað, Ps. Th. 10, 2 : 36, 13. Bogan bendan oððe flán ásendan geswinc getácnað, Lch. iii. 198, 19. Bendende, Ps. Spl. T. 77, 12.      II. *to bind :*—Hý hergiað and heáwað, bændað and bismriað, Wlfst. 163, 12. Man Críst bænde . . . þá þe hine bændon, Ll. Th. ii. 386, 23–26. Gif man gehádodne man bænde oþþe beáte, i. 348, 5. Bende, 400, 19, 21. [*Icel.* benda *to bend*.]

**be-neced.** v. be-næced.

**be-nemnan.** *Add :* I. *to name :*—Wæs genemned ł benemned (*Matthaeum*) *nomine*, Mt. L. 9, 9.      II. *to appoint, settle :*—On

þám mônðe hý bleóton á ; þ is þæt hý betæhton and benemdon (-nemndon, *v. l.*) hyra deófolgyldum þá neát þá þe hý woldon syllan, Mart. H. 198, 11. Heregýð hafað ðás wísan binemned *Heregyth makes the following dispositions by her will*, Cht. Th. 473, 22. Ðet hié ðiss gelæsten ðe on ðissem gewrite binemned is, 474, 3.

**be-neótan.** *Add :* [cf. *O. Frs.* bi-nêta (*wk.*).]

**be-neoðan.** :—And beneoþan þám *et infra*, Wrt. Voc. ii. 71, 59. Swýþe feorr beneoðan þan (*valde infra*) ic gelýfde þ, Gr. D. 218, 20. Beniðan *inferius*, An. Ox. 580.

**bén-feorm.** *Substitute* : A bean-feast. Cf. winter-feorm.

**[be-nídan** ; *p.* de *To compel* :—Mín sár (m)ê benêt tô segen *dolor me compellit dicere*, Angl. xi. 110.] [*O. Frs.* bi-nêda.]

**be-niman.** *Add :* I. *to take away, deprive :*—Benumen *orbata*, Wrt. Voc. ii. 65, 25. Binumni *adempta*, binumini (-e) *ablata*, Txts. 42, 102, 104. (1) with dat. of person, (a) acc. of thing :—Hê heora feorh him benam *interfecit eos*, Jud. 8, 21. Benam hê him (hine, *v. l.*) his bisceopscíre *deposuit eum de episcopatu*, Bd. 4, 6 ; Sch. 381, 13. (b) gen. of thing :—Ne mæg þára yfiena yfel þám (þá, *v. l.*) goodan beniman heora goodes, Bt. 37, 2 ; S. 113, 4. (2) with acc. of person, gen. of thing :—Benimð Wisle Ilfing hire naman Ors. 1, 1 ; S. 20, 11. Hê eów benimað eówres lífes, Wlfst. 207, 16. Buton hié hié þæs naman benáme, Ors. 2, 8 ; S. 94, 4. Benámon, 7. Ðone beniman (-neoman, *v. l.*) þære aldorlicnesse *eum privare auctoritate*, Bd. 1, 27 ; S. 74, 8. Hê ðære hælo benumen wierð, Past. 251, 10 : Wlfst. 1, 11 : Chr. 919 ; P. 105, 32. Mê hæfþ þeós gnornung þære gemynde benumen, Bt. 5, 3 ; S. 12. 20. Hine hæfde Penda ríces benumenne, Chr. 658 ; P. 32, 6. Hié wæron benumene ceápes, 895 ; P. 88, 16.      II. *to comprehend, contain :*—Benumene *comprehensum*, Jn. p. 1, 7.      III. *to apprehend, take :*—Uíf benumen (*deprehensa*) in dernelegerscip, Jn. I. 8, 4. [*O. Sax.* biniman (*dat. pers. acc. thing, acc. pers. gen.* (or *inst.*) *thing*) : *O. Frs.* bi-nima : *O. H. Ger.* pi-neman.]

**be-niming, e** ; *f. Taking away, deprival, privation :*—Gimynde biniming *lethargiam*, Wrt. Voc. ii. 53, 73. [v. *N. E. D.* be-nimming.]

**bén-líc** ; *adj. That may be entreated :*—Boenlic uæs ðú *deprecabilis esto*, Rtl. 172, 39.

**bénlíce** ; *adv. Suppliantly :*—Boenlíce uê biddað *suppliciter exoramus*, Rtl. 103, 24.

**be-norþan.** *Add : prep.* (*adv.*) *Be-north.* v. *N. E. D.* (English gaugers that you have sent down *benorth* the Tweed, Rob Roy, c. 4) :—Benorðan Dalmatia sindon Pulgare, Ors. 1, 1 ; S. 22, 19. Him is benorðan Creticum se sæ, S. 26, 33. Beeástan him . . . and benorðan, S. 28, 1. Gallie benorþan muntum, 4, 7 ; S. 184, 4. Ne benorðan mearce, ne besûðan, Ll. Th. i. 232, 18.

**be-norþan-eástan, -westan.** v. norþan-eástan, -westan *in Dict.*

**bén-ríp.** v. Seebohm Vill. Comm. s. v. *Precariae*.

**bénsian.** *Dele bracket, and* ' To fall down in prayer ' ; *add* : To supplicate, implore :—Hine boensendu hwæthwugu from him *petens aliquid ab eo*, Mt. R. 20, 20. Folce boensandi *populo supplicanti*, Rtl. 93, 17 : 80, 9. Boensandra *supplicantium*, 40, 5 : *supplicum*, 41, 23. Boensendra, 39, 36.

**bén-tíðe.** *Add* : [Cf. We mugen mid one worde þese þrie þing bidden and ben bene-tiðe (bene tiðe ?), *O. E.* Homl. ii. 27, 27.]

**beó.** *Dele* ' *indecl. in s*,' *and add* : *dat. pl.* beón :—Sume gesceafta týmað bûton hæmede ; þæt sind beón, Hml. Th. ii. 10, 16. Beón, gif hí man ácwellað, cwelle hig man iaþe . . . and ete man þ hunig þ hig worhton, Ll. Th. ii. 164, 1. Bián *apes*, Ps. Srt. 117, 12. Beóna hunig, Hml. Th. ii. 136, 30. þes náhte náht ôþres bûton feáwa hýfa beóna ; þysum wolde gedôn sum man reáfiac on ðám ylcum beón, Gr. D. 229, 11–13. Be beón, gif hí mannan ofsticiað, Ll. Th. ii. 130, 30. Ne áspond nán man þíne beón, Lch. i. 397, 3. Genim deáde beón, gebærne tô ahsan, ii. 154, 19. Biá *apes*, Rtl. 119, 28. v. feld-beó.

**beó-breád.** *For meanings given substitute* : Honeycomb with honey, *and add* :—Beóbreád *favus*, Wrt. Voc. i. 27, 65 : *favum*, 284, 70 : *favi*, ii. 37, 62 : Beóbreád *favus*, Germ. 390, 72. Hwæt getácnode ðæs hunies beóbreád? Beóbreád is on twám ðingum, on weaxe and on hunie, Hml. Th. ii. 292, 13–15. Weredum beóbreáde *dulci favo*, Wülck. Gl. 225, 19. Sáwl áfylled trytt beóbreád, Scint. 50, 9 : Lch. ii. 126, 1. Hê æt huniges beóbreád, Shrn. 68, 31. Biábreád, Ps. Srt. 118, 103. Bióbreád, Rtl. 3, 34 : Lk. p. 11, 14. [*O. L. Ger.* bí-brôd : *O. H. Ger.* bí-brôt.]. v. beón-breád *in Dict.*

**beó-cere.** *Add* :—Beócere *apiarius*, Wrt. Voc. i. 284, 69 : ii. 8, 17. Hwíta hátte wæs beócere intô Hæðfelda, Cht. Th. 649, 27. [? Býcera sald, C. D. iii. 80, 11.]

**beód.** *Add* : I. *a table*, (1) at which a meal is taken :—Beód *mensa*, Wrt. Voc. i. 290, 19. Biód, Ps. Srt. 68, 23. Bûtan cræfte mínon (*the baker's*) ælc beód æmtig byþ gesewen, Coll. M. 28, 33. Be abbodes beódes gereorde *de mensa abbatis*, R. Ben. 93, 2. Críst gehálgode on his beóde þá gerýnu ûre sibbe, Hml. Th. ii. 276, 32 : Lk. 16, 21. þ heó buteran macige tô hláfordes beóde, Ll. Th. i. 438, 32. Of þám crumum þe of hyra hláforda beódum (*bead mensa* L.) feallað, Mt. 15, 27. Under beádum, Mk. R. 7, 28. Hê beheóld þá beódas and þá þenunga, Ap. Th. 14, 18. I a. *a table* as a place of social meeting :—

sȳ hē āscyred fram beódes gemǣnnesse, R. Ben. 49, 2. Se leása freónd bið mannes gefēra tō beóde, and nā tō neódþearfe, Sal. K. p. 206, 4. **I b.** *food eaten at table :*—Ic selle þis lond Agustines hīgum intō hiora beóde, Cht. Th. 123, 25. (2) *a table* for other purposes :—Beádas (beód, R.) ðāra mynetra, Mt. L. 21, 12. Beádo (beódo, R.), Mk. L. 11, 15. **II.** *a charger, dish :*—Beódas lances, Wrt. Voc. ii. 90, 51 : 52, 52. Man sceal habban beódas (dishes or tables?), butas, blēda, mēlas, cuppan, Angl. ix. 264, 16. v. wíg-bed.

**beódan.** *Add :* **I.** *to command,* (1) with dat. of person :—Æðelstān beót his biscopum, þ gē þone frið healdan, Ll. Th. i. 240, 12. Mín fæder mē bȳd, Gen. 50, 5. Ne budþū mē nā ælmessan tō syllanne, Ps. Th. 39, 7. Man beád him ūt binnan .v. nihtan *he was ordered to leave the country within five days,* Chr. 1048; P. 177, note 1. Man beád þā[m] folce þider, 1052; P. 175, 28. Ðæt hié him tō unāberendlíce ne beóden *ne plus justo jubeant,* Past. 189, 19. Se biscop sceal beódan mid þon mǣston bebode þām mæssepreóstum, Bl. H. 47, 24. (2) with acc. of person, *to summon :*—Ðonne beád man ealle witan tō cynge, Chr. 1010; P. 140, 27. Beád hē ūt scipfyrde, 1071; P. 208, 3. (3) *to levy* a tax :—His hūscarlas þe þ strange gyld budon, Chr. 1041; P. 162, 6. Se cyng lēt beódan mycel gyld ofer eall Englaland, 1083; P. 215, 24. **II.** *to offer,* (1) *to present* an object :—Ne þincð mē nā, þ þes sȳ munuc, þe þū mē beódest (commendas), Gr. D. 28, 4. Beódende (būd-, Hpt. Gl. 424, 5) *offerentes* (frontem armatam), An. Ox. 755. (2) *to propose to grant :*—Beád hē heom heora āgene dōm feós ... budon hī heora māgon þ hí heom gesunde fram eódon, Chr. 755; P. 49, 16-21. Hié him eáþmēdo budon, 827; P. 60, 33. Gafol beódan, 1011; P. 141, 19. (3) *to attempt to do :*—Gif him man bude þæt man beád þām martyrum *if they were treated as the martyrs were,* Hml. Th. i. 212, 27. Athēne budon gefeoht Alexandre, ac he hié sóna forslōg, Ors. 3, 9; S. 134, 3. Be þǣm þe nān ōðrum dynt ne beóde *ut non presumat quisquam alium cedere,* R. Ben. 8, 26. Ænig man ōðrum ne beóde būtan riht; þæt is, þæt gehwā ōðrum beóde þæt hē wille, þæt man him beóde, Wlfst. 29, 4-6: 112, 5: 179, 28. Gif hwā ǣnigum preóste ǣnig wōh beóde, Ll. Th. ii. 290, 2. þ hē bude *ut* (*virgini spurca ludibria*) *inrogaret,* An. Ox. 4319.

**beód-bolla;** *m. l.* -bolle, an ; *f., and add :*—Beódbollæ *cuppa,* Wrt. Voc. ii. 105, 71.

**beód[d]ian** *to make tables :*—Hē mæig findan hwæt hī mæig on byrig bētan ... beóddian, bencian, Angl. ix. 262, 22.

**beódende.** *Substitute :* **beódend,** es ; *m. A preceptor :*—Fram beódende *a preceptore,* Angl. xiii. 432, 967. v. be-beódend.

**beód-ern.** *Add :*—Beóddern *refectorium,* Wrt. Voc. i. 82, 18. Be beóddernes tácne, Techm. ii. 122, 15. On beódernne (beódd-, *v. l.*), R. Ben. 117, 10. Twā land ... ðām gebrōðrum tō bryce intō heora beódderne, C. D. iv. 72, 23, 28 : 305, 13. Intō hære bēddarn ... of hira bæddern, Cht. Th. 493, 7, 18. Riht is þæt ǣnige wǣpnen on mynecena beódderne ne etan ne ne drincan, ne lǣwede men on muneca, Wlfst. 269, 10. Gesealdum þǣre bellan tácne beóddærn inngān, Angl. xiii. 393, 399. Canonicas, þær seó ār sī þ hī beóddern and slǣpern habban magan, healdan heora mynster, Ll. Th. i. 306, 12. Brōðra beóddern (met-, *v.l.*) ārǣran, Gr. D. 147, 29.

**beód-fæt,** es ; *n. A table-vessel, cup :*—Ciatis, i. calathis, vasis vel beódfatum, Wrt. Voc. ii. 131, 17.

**beód-fers,** es ; *n.* (not *m.*) *Substitute : Grace before meat :*—Be ðām ðe tō late tō beódferse cumað (*ad mensam veniunt*), R. Ben. 67, 19. Sē þe tō his beódferse ne cume *ad mensam qui ante versum ne occurrerit,* 69, 9. Hē tō Furtunates mȳsan becom, ǣr þām þe hē his beódfers sunge (Gode þone lofsang āsægde, swā swā sume men gewuniaþ, þ hī singað ... ǣr hī etan, *v. l.*), Gr. D, 62, 9.

**beód-lǣs,** es ; *f. Table-allowance, provisions contributed* to a monastery :—Ðæt (a list of provisions to be granted has just been given) sié simle tō hīgum beódlēse (hīgum tō beódlēse?) ymb twelf mōnað āgefen, Cht. Th. 474, 6. Cf. beód, **I b,** beód-ern.

**beód-láf,** e ; *f. Food remaining after a meal :*—Sylle hē earmum mannum his beódlāfa, Bl. H. 53, 13.

**beód-land,** es ; *n. Land to defray the cost of the food consumed in a monastery :*—Ic ðæs land sælle ðām hīwum tō hira beódlandæ *ego has terras dono ad refectorium fratribus,* C. D. v. 218, 19. Āgefe mon tuuēnti hīda hīguum tō biódland, ii. 47, 3. Ðen hēwen tō bēdlonde, iv. 292, 18. Cf. beód, **I b.**

**beód-reáf,** es ; *n. A table-cloth :*—Mínum suna ic geann ānes būrreáfes mid beódreáfe, C. D. iii. 294, 36. Cf. beód-hrægl.

**beód-sceát,** es ; *m.* -scíte, an ; *f.* For Cot. 136 *substitute :*—Beódscȳte oððe beódsceát *mantile,* Wrt. Voc. ii. 58, 52.

**beóftun,** Lk. R. 23, 27. v. beaftan.

**beó-gang.** *Substitute :*—Beógang *ag*[*m*]*en,* Wrt. Voc. i. 284, 39 : ii. 8, 12.

**beó-mōder.** *Add :*—Seó beómōder *cosdrus,* An. Ox. 258. Beómōdra *principum* (*apum*), 240. [*O. L. Ger.* bī-mōdar : *O. H. Ger.* bī-muoder *construx.*]

**beón.** *Add :* to be :—Wesan and beón *fore,* Wrt. Voc. ii. 34, 61.

(1) absolute, (a) *to exist,* (of life) *to last :*—Ðū eart ēce and ā byst, Shrn. 199, 21. Þā hwíle þe mín líf byð, Cht. E. 230, 7. Gif ic lenge beó þonne heó, Shrn. 159, 27. Þ ǣlces mannes sāwl nū sí and ā beó, 199, 10. Ān is þū woldest beón; ōðer þ þū woldest lybban, 193, 27. Hī woldon ā bión ... willniaþ simle tō biónne, Bt. 34, 12 ; F. 152, 18-23. Wesendum, beóndum *existentibus,* Wrt. Voc. ii. 32, 63. (b) of position, lit. or fig.:—Ðēr ic biúm (bióm, R.), Jn. L. 7, 34. Beó hē be þǣre ānre þā hwíle þe heó lybbe, Wlfst. 271, 15. Hē mōste beón mǣrlíce mid him, Hml. Th. ii. 310, 19. An his hláforddōme wē bián mōten, C. D. i. 311, 22. Ðā ðe fore ōðrum bieón (beón, *v. l.*) sculon, Past. 107, 24. ¶ beón ymbe *to be about* a business :—Deófol byð ā ymbe þæt ān, hū hē on manna sāulum mǣst gesceaðian mæge, Ll. Th. i. 374, 25. Hī beóð ymbe þæt ān, hū ..., Hml. Th. i. 12, 11. Tō beónne ymbe ðeófas, An. Th. 124, 29. (c) *to happen :*—Ðū bist dumb oð ðæt ðē þis bið, Shrn. 133, 33. Swā bið þǣre sáwle and þǣre synne, Wlfst. 140, 4. (d) *to consist of* (*on*) :—þæt gafol bið on deóra fellum, Ors. 1, 1 ; S. 18, 17. (2) with predicate. (a) noun or adjective :—Ic dō þ gyt beóð (beóþan, R.) manna fisceras *faciam vos fieri piscatores hominum,* Mt. 4, 19: Mk. 1, 17. Beóð eów ānrǣde, Hml. S. 16, 244. þæt þās stānes hláfes beón *ut lapides isti panis fiant,* Mt. R. 4, 3. Lucius bæd hine crístenne beón (*christianum se fieri*), Bd. 1, 4; Sch. 16, 4. (b) oblique case of noun :—þ hí ne mihtan him sylfum nǣnige gōde beón, Bl. H. 45, 16: Ors. 6, 30; S. 282, 18. (c) gerundial infin. :—Se trȳwleása ne bið nānum hláforde tō hæbbenne, Hml. S. 12, 131. Hié beóð tō ðreágeanne, Past. 265, 15. (d) prepositional phrase :—Bið hit swíðe leáslíce on siolufres hiéwe, Past. 269, 4. Biá ðū mē in God *esto mihi in Deum,* Ps. Srt. 30, 3. Hié him on nānum fultome beón ne mæhte, Ors. 2, 4; S. 74, 31: 4, 10; S. 196, 7. (3) as auxiliary :—Ic bióm gelustfullad *ego delectabor,* Ps. Srt. 103, 34. Gif onstyred ic beám *si motus fuero,* 12, 5. Biáð þreáde *aporiamur,* Wrt. Voc. ii. 100, 44. Wē bióton wrigen *operiemur,* Mt. L. 6, 31. Forgefen bíðon (beóþan, R.) ðē synno *dimittantur tibi peccata,* Mk. L. 2, 9. Tōstrogden biáð scíp *dispargentur oves,* Mt. L. 26, 31. Rím wintra hine hæbbende beón *se numerum annorum fuisse habiturum,* Bd. 5, 8; Sch. 586, 17. ¶ beón has a specially future sense :—Ge þte ǣr wæs, ge þte nū is, ge þte æfter ūs bið, Bt. 42; F. 256, 28. Sē byð (bieð, L. *erit*) eówer þēn, Mk. 10, 43. Swā beóð (biðon, L. *erunt*) þā fyrmestan ȳtemeste ..., manega synt (*sunt*) geclypede, Mt. 20, 16.

**beór.** *For translation of Icelandic quotation substitute :* Ale is called among men, but among the gods beer, *and add :*—Beór ydromellum vel mulsum, Wrt. Voc. i. 82, 34. Æppelwín, beór *idromelum,* ii. 49, 57. Leóht beór *melle dulci,* 56, 49. Beóres tācen is þæt þū gníde þíne hand on þā ōþre, Tech. ii. 125, 21. Ne dranc hē beór ne ealu ne nān ðæra wǣtan ðe menn of dru:cniað, Hml. Th. ii. 38, 6. Biór *siceram,* Knt. Gl. 1128. Beár, Lk. L. R. i. 15.

**beór-byden,** e ; *f. A beer-barrel :*—Man sceal habban ... beórbydene, Angl. ix. 264, 16.

**beorc,** berc, byrc, byric *a birch-tree.* *Add :*—Beta berc *arbor dicitur,* Txts. 44, 132. Berc *bitulus,* 45, 298. Byrc *populus,* Wrt. Voc. i. 33, 2 : 80, 13. Byric *populus, betulus,* An. Ox. 56, 364, 365.

**beorc** *a bark :*—Wiþ hundes beorc (gebeorc, *v. l.*), Lch. i. 28, 20. [Sor is bite and sor is berk (*rhymes with* werk), Angl. iv. 197, 18.] v. birce.

**beorcan.** *Add :*—Beorceð *latrat,* Wrt. Voc. ii. 95, 83: 52, 68. Beorcan *latrare,* Past. 89, 17. Beorcende fox, Shrn. 141, 12. Hundas beorcynde, Lch. iii. 200, 25. ¶ beorcan on *to bark at :*—Clypa ongēn þissum deófles hunde þe þē on beorceþ, Shrn. 56, 32. Se wrítere sǣde þ sum hund burce hetelíce on ānne man, Hml. S. 31, 1132.

**beorc-rind** (berc-), e ; *f. Birch-bark :*—Nim bercrinde, Lch. ii. 332, 9.

**beór-drǣste,** an : -drǣst ; *pl.* -drǣsta ; *f. Dregs of beer :*—Clām of beórdrǣstan and of grēnre mucgwyrte, Lch. ii. 330, 16. Genim beórdrǣstan and sāpan, iii. 42, 27. Genim beórdrǣsta, ii. 98, 26.

**beorg.** *Add :* **I.** *a hill :*—Dūn *mons,* hyll oððe beorh *collis,* Wrt. Voc. i. 80, 43. Beorh ufeweard *monticellus,* 54, 7. Þa dūna dreósað and beorga hlíða myltað *montes ruent, collesque liquescent,* Dōm. L. 101. **II.** *an artificial mound :*—Beorh *agger,* Ælfc. Gr. Z. 43, 15 : *tumulus,* Wrt. Voc. i. 54, 5. Cumulus, i. tumulus, apex, acervus, coaceruatio beorg, Wlck. Gl. 216, 26 : An. Ox. 2496. .ii. beorgas litelra stāna hē gesēnode tō gymnum, Shrn. 32, 22. v. líc- (?), sealh-beorg.

**beorg** *protection.* *Add :* v. bān-, breóst-, heals-beorg.

**beorgan.** *Add :* **I.** *to protect,* (1) *to prevent the happening of evil* (*acc.*) to an object (*dat.*) :—Ic mē his hete berh, Bd. 2, 12; Sch. 155, 5. (1 a) with dat. of object alone, *to protect, save, guard :*—Hē bewand his heáfod mid ānum clāðe, and bearh him sylfum swíðe georne, Hml. S. 23, 526. Beorh ðē sylfum, Hml. Th. i. 418, 34. Þ ǣlc hláford his nȳdþeówum byrge, Ll. Th. ii. 314, 10. (2) *to protect* an object (*dat.*) against (*wið*) evil :—Wið hete bearh ic mē, Bd. 2, 12; Sch. 155, 5. Þæt hí beorgan heom silfum wið Godes yrre, Wlfst. 190, 10. Beorgian Ll. Th. i. 364, 12. Wið helle bryne beorhgan his sāwle, 30. Hí fleón woldon and heom beorgan wið þone here, Hml. S. 25, 658. **II.**

*to abstain from injury* to an object (*dat.*), *to spare* :—Þæt mód ongiet ðæt him mon birgð *mentes parci sibi sentiunt*, Past. 297, 17. Wē beorgað ðínre ylde, Hml. Th. i. 418, 31. **III.** *to prevent the doing of* ill (*acc. or clause*) by a person (*dat.*) :—Hé him slǽp beorge *let him take care not to sleep*, Lch. ii. 270, 11. Būtan wē ūs beorgan þ wē him ne ábelgan, Ll. Th. ii. 332, 7. **III a.** without dat. of person, (1) with acc. or clause, *to guard against, avoid* :—Beorge hē þ hé áwóh ne befó, Ll. Th. i. 290, 7. Beorge man georne þ man þá sáwla ne forfare, 304, 16. (2) with prep. :—Wið ǽlc wóh gestreón beorge man georne, Wlfst. 70, 2. (3) absolute, *to abstain from wrongdoing* :—Nis on ǽnigne tíman unriht álýfed, and þeáh man sceal on freólsstówan geornlícost beorgan, 398, 19. Gelíce þám dwǽsan þe for heora prýtan lēwe nellað beorgan, ær hý ná ne magan, Wlfst. 165, 10.

**beorgiht**; *adj. Hilly* :—Þá lond sindon swíþe beorhtte (beorhte, *v. l.*) *situ terrarum montoso*, Ors. 1, 1 ; S. 10, 24.

**beorh-hlíþ.** *Substitute : A mountain-slope; and take here the passages given under* burg- (burh-)hleoþ *in Dict.* : **beorh-leóde.** v. burg-leóde.

**beorht**; *adj. Add* :—Hé áwrát muneca regol mid beorhtre sprǽce, Hml. Th. ii. 186, 17. Heó hæfde seofon síþum beorhtran sáule þonne snáw, Bl. H. 147, 17. Þá beorhtestan wununga, Ll. Th. ii. 398, 32. v. sige-beorht.

**beorhtan** *to shine.* v. birhtan.

**beorht-blówende**; *adj. Bright-blooming* :—Ful æcer sódres beorhtblówende, Angl. i. 404, 9.

**beorhte.** *Add* : (1) of light (lit. or fig.) :—Þū gedēst þ hé scínaþ swíþe beorhte, . . . sume beorhtor, sume unbyrhtor, swá swá steorran, Bt. 33, 4; F. 132, 20. Steorran gebirhte, sume þeáh beorhtor, sume unbeorhtor, 34, 5; F. 140, 6. (2) *splendidly* :—Beorhte hine gescrýdan, Lch. iii. 198, 26. His geearnunga wǽron beorhte gecýþed, Shrn. 52, 11. (3) *clearly,* of physical or mental vision :—Hé weard hál, beorhte lócigende, Hml. S. 22, 182. His andgit bið tó ðon beorhte scínende, ðæt hé mæge ongietan sóðfæstnesse, Past. 69, 24. [*O. H. Ger.* berahto *splendide.*] v. un-beorhte.

**beorht-hwíl.** *Add* :—On beorhthwíle *in puncto*, An. Ox. 3247. Hí wurdon ábitene on ánre beorhthwíle, 2370, note. On ánre berhthwíle *uno momento*, Ll. Th. ii. 172, 33 : R. Ben. 20, 5. Breohthwíle, Gr. D. 150, 13. Breohthwíle (bearht-, *v. l.*), 160, 23.

**beorhtlíce.** *Add* : (1) *splendidly* :—Heálíce, beorhtlíce *conspicue, i. preclare*, Wrt. Voc. ii. 134, 15. (2) of sight, *clearly* :—Mihton men beorhtlíce sceáwian Drihtnes fóta swaðe, Shrn. 81, 14. Ic wæs blind bám eágum, nú ic beorhtlíce leóhtes brúce, Hml. Th. i. 422, 7.

**beorhtnan** *to grow bright* :—Beorh(t)neð (beorhtmeð, An. Ox. 534) *splendescit*, Hpt. Gl. 419, 24.

**beorhtnes.** *Add* :—Sē hátte Lucifer for þǽre miclan beorhtnisse his mǽran híwes, Ælfc. T. Grn. 2, 35. Seó earme sáwl geseah miccle beorohtnesse . . . þū gesyhst eallra háligra beorohtnessa, Ll. Th. ii. 398, 27–34.

**beorhtnian** *to make bright, to glorify* :—Ic berhtnade *clarificaui*, Jn. L. R. 12, 28. Ic ðec bertnade, R. 17, 4. v. ge-beorhtnian.

**beorhtu.** v. birhtu : **beorht-word.** v. byrht-word *in Dict.*

**beorma** (bearma. v. *next word*). *Add* :—Hæf *vel* beorma *fermentum*, Wrt. Voc. ii. 147, 72. v. and-bita ; ge-beormad.

**beorm-teág,** e ; *f. A yeast-box* :—Man sceal habban . . . bearmteáge, Angl. ix. 264, 20.

**beornan, beorning.** v. birnan, birning.

**beór-scipe,** es ; *m. A feast* :—Beárscip *convivium*, Mt. p. 16, 1. Æfter þæs beórscipes geendunge, Ap. Th. 17, 19. Gelaðod tó lustfullum beórscype, Hml. S. 8, 98. Hig wrohton him beórscipe (*cenam*), Jn. 12, 2. Hē ðone beórscipe mid blóde gemencgde, Hml. Th. i. 484, 2. Gē eówerne beórscipe brúcað on unriht, Wlfst. 297, 30.

**beór-sele.** *Add* :—Hearpe and pípe drēmað eów on beórsele, Wlfst. 46, 17.

**beorþ.** *Dele.*

**beorþor.** *Add* : **I.** *child-bearing,* (1) *bringing forth of a child;* partus :—Ær þám þe heó cenne, and æfter hire beorðre *antequam pariat, et post partum suum*, Ll. Th. ii. 154, 3. Gif hē mónðe ǽr þám beorþre (*ante partum*) hǽmð, 24. Ær þám beorðre and æfter þǽre ácenned-nysse *ante partum et post partum*, 190, 20 : Bl. H. 155, 33. Þurh hire beorþor sceolde beón gehǽled eall wífa cynn, 5, 23. Þ hé wære fram þám módorlicum beorðrum on þ mynster befæst, Hml. S. 23 b, 46. (2) *gestation* :—Þá ácende heó ðæt bearn on ðone seofoðan mónað þæs beorðres, Shrn. 61, 2. **II.** *what is born,* partus, foetus :—Þæs byrþres líc on hire innoþe, Lch. iii. 146, 14. Mid beorþre *foetu*, Wrt. Voc. ii. 36, 34. Drihten ingc syled myccle grównysse on ingcran beorðre, Hml. A. 124, 257. Þū sealdest eallum gesceaftum byrðor, 120, 121. v. byrþor *in Dict.*

**beorþor-cwe(a)lm.** *Substitute for* Cot. 11 : Beorðorcwelmas *abortivos*, Wrt. Voc. ii. 6, 27.

**beorþor-þinen.** *Add* : cf. byrþ-þignenu.

**beost.** *Add* :—Colostrum, i. lac novum beóst *vel obestum*, Wrt. Voc. ii. 134, 19. Beóst (beust, 116, 178) *colostrum*, Txts. 53, 541 : Wrt.

Voc. ii. 14, 79 : *colostrum,* 134, 56 : *lactantia,* Txts. 110, 1183 (cf. H. Z. 33, 244) : *obestrum,* 81, 1406 : Wrt. Voc. ii. 63, 19 : *obesca,* 20 : *cassan,* 14, 80. [*Germ.* biest.]

**beosu.** v. basu : beót, Chr. 1006; P. 137, 5. v. beótian.

**beót.** *Dele bracket, and add under* **III** :—Hié tó beóte (bote, MS.) balde gecwǽdon þæt hié þæs wíges wihte ne róhton, Dan. 200. Heó (*the vestal virgin*) hiere beót (*vow;* gehát, *v. l.*) áleág, Ors. 3, 6 ; S. 108, 19. [beút *from* bi-hát, v. be-hát.]

**beó-þeóf.** *Add* : cf. :—Wolde gedón sum man reáfiác on ðám ylcum beón, Gr. D. 229, 12.

**beótian.** *Add* : **I.** *to threaten,* (1) absolute :—Biótiaþ *intentatis,* Wrt. Voc. ii. 45, 62. Beótade *intentabat,* 47, 47. Beótode *comminatus est,* 73, 18 : 17, 51 : *intentabat,* i. *minabatur,* An. Ox. 4958. Þá gástas þisum wordum beótodon, Guth. 38, 21. Beótiende *comminatus,* Wrt. Voc. ii. 17, 46. Beótiende, 72, 40. Þone cwyde ne gespræc hē ná þý þe hē hit wolde forðbryngan, ac beótigende (*minando*); Gr. D. 152, 16. Beótende *minax,* Wrt. Voc. ii. 58, 43. Wǽran beótende *intentarentur,* 47, 48. [Yfium onbiótendum *malis imminentibus,* Rtl. 53, 3.] (2) threat expressed, (a) by a clause :—Beótaþ hē þ hé wile þá sáula sendan on éce wítu, Bl. H. 95, 3. Hí ongunnon beótian þ hí scoldon hine geniman, Gr. D. 325, 29. ¶ threat inferred from a clause :—Hí onbídedon beótra (= beótedra?) gylpa ; forþon oft man cwæð . . . þet hí nǽfre tó sǽ gán ne sceoldan *they waited for the great things that had been threatened ; for it had often been said . . . that they should never get to the sea,* Chr. 1006 ; P. 137, 5. (b) with dat. infin. :—þeáh hine deófol mid bárspere beótige tó ofsticianne, Angl. viii. 324, 19. (3) beótian tó *to threaten,* (a) absolute :—Þeáh wē beótiaþ tó, Bl. H. 33, 27. (b) with dat. of person :—Þám þe se deáð tó beótað *quibus mors imminet,* Bd. 1, 27 ; Sch. 80, 1. Ongan se seóca man swíðlíce beótian tó him *coepit ille vehementer inminere,* Gr. D. 314, 8. Hē wæs beótigende tó þám *cui minatus est,* 80, 29. Þá tó beóti(g)endan frecennesse þám eágan *inminens oculo exitium,* Bd. 4, 32 ; Sch. 545, 16. (b 1) *to threaten* with (*mid* or *instrumental*), (a) a weapon, &c. :—Hē mid his tuxum tó him beótode, Guth. 48, 1. (β) a penalty, &c. :—Þá Langbeardan ongunnon beótian (-igean, *v. l.*) heom tó deáðe *coepere Longobardi mortem eis minari,* Gr. D. 232, 14. God wæs beótiende (beótode, *v. l.*) mid þám ēcum wítum tó synfullum mannum *Deus peccantibus aeternam poenam minatus est,* 334, 12. (b 2) with clause of evil threatened :—Hié mē tó beótedan, þ hié mē gegrīpan woldon *minitabantur me comprehendere,* Bd. 5, 12 ; Sch. 621, 14. (c) with acc. of evil threatened :—Se swile þæs eágan forwyrd tó beótade *tumor oculi interitum minaretur,* Bd. 4, 32 ; Sch. 545, 6. **II.** *to promise* :—Ymbe þæne circul wē beótedon ymbe tó sprecanne, Angl. viii. 325, 14. v. ge-beótian.

**beótian** *to get better.* v. bótian.

**beót-lic** ; *adj. Threatening, arrogant* :—Hē sende tó þám cyninge beótlic ǽrende, þ hē ábūgan sceolde tó his manrǽdene, Hml. S. 32, 44. v. ge-beótlic.

**beót-líce.** *Substitute* : **I.** *threateningly* :—Hē fērde beótlíce mid wíge *ascendit vallatus auxilio pugnatorum,* Jos. 8, 10. **II.** *boastingly, vauntingly, arrogantly* :—'Ne fare gē, ic bidde' . . . Hig swaþeáh áblende beótlíce ástigon, Num. 14, 44. Hē beótlíce mid deóflicum fiðerhaman fleón wolde, Hml. Th. i. 380, 29. Gē beótlíce lǽtað, þæt gē mǽre magan, þonne hit genet sý, Wlfst. 46, 15. Bóceras beótlíce habbað dǽlas . . . þæs ðe hig gylpað gelóme, Angl. viii. 317, 27.

**beótung.** *Add* :—Gif wambe bið on innan wund, þonne biþ þǽr sár and beótunga (*threatening symptoms*) and gesceorf, Lch. ii. 220, 3. For hwon sceolon gē mid eówrum leásum beótingum mē egsian ?, Guth. 38, 27. v. word-beótung.

**beów,** es ; *n. Bigg* (v. D. D. s.v.), *barley* :—Hondful-beówes (beóuuas, beóuaes, baeues) *manticum,* Txts. 77, 1278. Beowæs, Wrt. Voc. ii. 55, 45. [*Icel.* bygg *barley.*]

**beówan.** v. bíwan : **Beó-wulf.** *Substitute* : v. Arnold's 'Notes on Beowulf.'

**beó-wyrt.** *Add* :—Biówyrt *apiastrum,* Wrt. Voc. ii. 100, 45. Beówyrt, 8, 6 : i. 284, 42 : *marubium,* 55, 54 : (bió-), 113, 66 : *acanton,* i. 67, 5. [Cf. *O. L. Ger.* bini-uurt *apiastrum, melisphilla* : *O. H. Ger.* bini-uurz.]

**be-pǽcan.** *Add* :—Bepǽcst *defraudas,* Scint. 109, 8. Bepǽhst *deludis,* Wrt. Voc. ii. 138, 53. Gif ðū Gode líhst, ne bepǽcst þū ná hine, Hml. S. 12, 99. Þis líf bepǽcð þá ðe hit lufiaþ, 5, 65 : Angl. viii. 330, 3. Sē ðe bepǽhð ánne Godes þeówena, Hml. Th. i. 516, 20. Þonne hí bepǽcaþ *cum pellexerint,* An. Ox. 3929. Wǽgde *vel* bepǽhte *fefellit,* i. *delusit,* Wrt. Voc. ii. 148, 27. Hē bepǽhte hí in tó his búre, Chr. 1015; P. 146, 1. Ne bepǽce hē eów mid leásum hopan, Hml. Th. i. 568, 8. Bepǽcan *dissimulari,* An. Ox. 5348. Þū wylt ealde witan mid þínan lote bepǽcan, Hml. S. 23, 711. Bepǽcendre gesǽlignesse *fallentis fortunae,* Wrt. Voc. ii. 146, 74. Bepǽcendre *inlecebroso,* An. Ox. 3190. Bepǽht *decepta,* 1826: 2378. Hwá byð bepǽht ?, Hml. A. 6, 143. Gewurdon on slǽpe Pictauienscisce, bepǽhte for swíðe *the Poitevins, utterly deluded, went to sleep,* Hml. Th. ii. 518, 25.

**be-pǽcend,** es ; *m. A deceiver* :—Bepǽcend *deceptor,* Wrt. Voc. i.

49, 16 : *seductor*, 8፝, 42 : *illecebrosus*, Hpt. Gl. 481, 34. Deófol is sáwla bepǽcend, Hml. Th. i. 102, 2 : ii. 496, 13.

**be-pǽcung.** *Substitute : Deception :*—Bepǽcunge *factione*, i. *fallitate*, An. Ox. 2898 : *lenocinio*, 4015. Gehíwedre bepǽcung(r)e *dissimulato negotio*, 4838.

**be-prenan.** *l.* be-príwan, -préwan, *and add :*—Swylce hwá his eáge bepríwe, Wlfst. 148, 13. v. preówt-hwíl. [In Bt. 18, 3 Cott. MS. has *beprewan* (*not -prepan*) ; in the other MS. the first *n* in *beprenan* is altered to *w*. v. Sedgefield 44, note 5.]

**bera.** *Add :*—Bera *vel* bár *berrus*, Wrt. Voc. ii. 126, 1. Bera sceal on hǽðe, eald and egesfull, Gn. C. 29. Hé hēt þ hine man wurpe berum tō fretanne . . . and þǽr wæs begyten se mǽsta and se rēþesta bera, Gr. D. 194, 20–25. Fearres gelícnysse and beran ansÿne, Guth. 48, 2. Wilde beran and wulfas, Hml. Th. i. 244, 18 : Nar. 12, 3. Ðá egeslícan beran, Hex. 14, 33. In menigo leóna and beran, Shrn. 133, 10. Mid wildum berum and leónum gewyldan, Hml. Th. 192, 24.

**be-rǽdan.** *Add : pp.* -rǽden (*and* -rǽd). I. *to dispossess, deprive* of power, *betray,* (1) with acc. of person :—Twēgen his burþéna woldon berǽdan swíðe unrihtlíce heora cynehláford *duo eunuchi voluerunt insurgere in regem*, Hml. A. 95, 111. Acitofel wolde berǽdan his rihtwísan hláford, Hml. S. 19, 214. Hū Boetius hí (*the Goths*) wolde berǽdan (cf. áferran, 1 ; F. 2, 19), Bt. tit. 1 ; F. x. 2. Birēdnae (-raednae) *prodimur*, Txts. 89, 1661. (2) with acc. of person and inst. (gen., or *æt*) of thing :—Þone gelpscaðan ríce berǽdan (cf. áfyrran, Bt. 16, 4 ; F. 58, 13), Met. 9, 50. I a. *to take by treachery :*—Se deófol á sǽtaþ hwǽr hé mæge unware men beswícan, and hé nǽfre tō þæs feala berǽdeð þæt hé ǽfre ful sié *daemones insidiantur incautis, capiunt nescientes, captos devorant exsaturarique non queunt devoratis*, Bl. N. 5, 32. Ðá Iudéiscan syrwiað and rūniað hū hí þé (*Jesus*) berǽdan magon, Hml. S. 24, 100. Hū hé mihte þæt manncynn berǽdan *quo aditu possit obtinere eos* (the people of besieged Bethulia), Hml. A. 109, 239. II. *to consult about* (v. N. E. D. *be-rede*) :—Þǽr ðá mihtigan wíf hyra mægen berǽddon, Lch. iii. 52, 22. [*O. Frs.* bi-rēda : *O. L. Ger.* be-rāden *consultus.*]

**be-rǽsan.** *Add :* I. *to rush upon, attack :*—Hé him on berǽsde *irruit super eos*, Gen. 14, 15. II. *to rush* into (extremes) :— Berǽst hē on ungemetlíce cuēminge *inordinate ad mollitiem rapitur*, Past. 143, 6. Ðætte ðæt mód ne berǽse on ungeðyld *ne ad inpatientiam spiritus erumpant*, 313, 21.

**be-rafan.** *l.* be-rebban (*related to* rapere *as* hebban *to* capere).

**beran.** *Add :—Fero* ic bere gēd ðus ; *fers* ðū berst (byrst), *fert* hē berð (byrð), Ælfc. Gr. Z. 199, 6. Bierð *bajulat*, Wrt. Voc. ii. 11, 66. Bireþ *gestat*, 41, 59. I. with sense of motion, *to carry, bring.* (1) with concrete object :—Hié mē on heofenas beraþ, Bl. H. 183, 6. Hié bǽron Marian líchoman oþþæt hié cōman tō þǽre byrgenne, 155, 6. Þá hié gesáwan þá deádan men tō eorþan beran, Ors. 3, 10 ; S. 138, 26. Cumað beorende reopan heara, Ps. Srt. 125, 6. (2) with abstract object :—Bǽr Godwine eorl ūp his mál *Earl Godwine brought up his cause*, Chr. 1052 ; P. 183, 6. Sceal ūre ánra gehwylc beran his dǽda beforan Crístes heáhsettle, Bl. H. 63, 30. Hwylc handleán wē him forþ tō berenne habban, 91, 14. (3) used impersonally ; cf. similar use in Icelandic :—Swá hwæt swá þé on eáge byreð (cf. mart (*acc.*) berr fyrir augu mēr) *whatever* (*the dream*) *brings to your sight*, Lch. iii. 154, 22. II. without sense of motion, (1) *to bear, support* a burden :—Sió eax byrþ eallne ðone wǽn, Bt. 39, 7 ; F. 220, 28. Hé bierð (byrð, *v.l.*) on his heortan ðá byrðenne ðæs bismeres, Past. 73, 12. Wyrþe þ hié heofoncining on heora heortum beran, Bl. H. 79, 33. (1 a) *to suffer :*— Ðá scylda ðára scamleásena hé tǽlde, suelce hé efnsuíðe him bǽre *quasi compatiens*, Past. 207, 17. (2) *to carry :*—Hié hine lǽtan heora seódas beran, Bl. H. 69, 11. (2 a) *to bear* arms, *wear* clothes, &c., *carry* a mark, &c. :—Hé bired on his mōde opena wunda, Past. 61, 1. Þriwa hé bær his cynehelm ǽlce geáre, Chr. 1086 ; P. 219, 32. (3) *to bear* a child, fruit, &c. :—Hē nánne wæstm ne bired, Past. 337, 13. Birð, 339, 13. Eua bær teáras on hire innoþe, Bl. H. 3, 12. Beorende *enixa*, Txts. 59, 751. Berende bið *effeta*, Wrt. Voc. ii. 30, 57. Berend(e) *ferax*, 35, 17. Þeós eorðe is berende missenlicra fugela *auium ferax terra*, Bd. 1, 1 ; Sch. 8, 11. Hit is berende on wecga ōrum *uenis metallorum fecunda*, Sch. 9, 3. Scēp beorende *oves fetosae*, Ps. Srt. 143, 13. Stánas ne sint berende, Sal. K. p. 186, 30. Sÿ swá boren swá hē sÿ *whatever his birth be*, Ll. Th. i. 248, 4. DER. bul-, wearg-, weax-, wōl-, yfel-berende ; ǽwisc-, síþ-, telg-, wæter-, wrōht-berend ; wudu-bǽre ; ǽht-, bet-, betst-, blind-, ceorl-, cifes-, cyne-, deór-, efen-, ful-, sám-, síþ-, þegen-, þeów-, un-, wel-boren.

**bera-scinn**, es ; *n. A bear-skin :*—iii berascin, Cht. Th. 429, 27.

**berc.** *Substitute :* v. beorc.

**Bercingas** *in on* (in) Bercingum *Barking :*—On Eástseaxena mǽgþe on stōwe seó is nemned in Bercingum (Byrc-, *v.l.*), Bd. 4, 6 ; Sch. 383, 19 : 4, 7 ; Sch. 384, 17. On Bercingum (Bercc-, *v.l.*) þám mynstre, 10. Ðæt fǽmna mynster þ is nemned on Bercingum, Shrn. 138, 2.

**bere** *barley.* *Dele first passage, and add :*—Sixecge bere *exaticum* (cf. *hoc exaticum* byge (v. beów), i. 233, 62), Wrt. Voc. ii. 144, 58.

Bere is swíðe earfoðe tō gearc¹genne, and þeáhhwæðere sēt ðone mann, þonne hē gearo bið, Hml. Th. i. 188, 4. Horse mete is bere, Hml. S. 3, 216. Gebūr sceal syllan .xxiii. systra beres, Ll. Th. i. 434, 11. Genim beánmela oððe ǽtena oððe beres, Lch. ii. 84, 5 : 82, 24. Of fíf hláfum beres (bere, L.) *ex quinque panibus hordiaciis*, Jn. R. 6, 13. Hláfas of bere (bero, L.), 9. Mid onlegene of wearmum bere, Lch. ii. 82, 15. Beras *ordea*, Ælfc. Gr. Z. 84, 6. v. gafol-, lencten-bere.

**bere-ærn** (-ern). *Add :*—Bercern (ber-, L.) *horreum*, Lk. R. 12, 24. Þá feówer hyrnan þæs berenes, Lch. iii. 290, 28. Bernes flór (berern, L.) *area*, Lk. 3, 17. Æt bernes dure, Ll. Th. i. 440, 2. On hláfordes berne . . . of his áganum berne, Ll. Th. i. 434, 16, 19 : Cht. E. 377, 6, 7. On bærene gebringan, Cht. Th. 144, 38. Tō hire byrene (bern-hūs, berne, *v.ll.*), Gr. D. 68, 22 : 69, 4 : 290, 20, 24. In berern, Mt. L. R. 13, 30 : Lk. L. R. 3, 17. Nabbað hig bern (beren, *v.l.*), Lk. 12, 24. Ic tōwurpe míne bernu (bererno, L., berern, R.), 18. **be-reáfere**, es ; *m. A* plunderer, pillager :—Bereáfre captator, i. raptor, An. Ox. 46, 36.

**be-reáfian.** *Add :*—Bereáfað *populatur*, An. Ox. 139. Bereáfiað *moliuntur fraudes*, Kent. Gl. 3. Bereáuedon *abegerant*, An. Ox. 7, 263. Bereáfian *grassari*, 5343. Bereáfed *frauderetur*, 1583. I. with acc. of person (or thing) *despoiled*, (1) alone :—Hé bereáfode hine sylfne *se expolians*, Gr. D. 68, 8. Hí ðæt mynster berēfodon, Chr. 794 ; P. 57, 12. Þ hē God bereáfige, Lch. iii. 444, 1. Þá wícstōwa and þæt wæl bereáfian *castrorum praedam percensere*, Ors. 3, 9 ; S. 128, 9. (2) with spoil, (a) in gen. :—Þū þá treówa heora leáfa bereáfast, Bt. 4 ; F. 8, 6. Se mōna þá sunnan heore leóhtes bereáfaþ, F. 8, 1. Háma bereáfod, Chr. 975 ; P. 120, 24 : 1065 ; P. 195, 6 : Cri. 558 : El. 910. (b) inst. (dat.) :—Sceab þ heáfod feaxe bereáfað, Lch. i. 322, 18. Hí hine wǽdon bereáfoden, Hml. Th. i. 430, 2 : 428, 5. Wæs hē lande bereáfod, Chr. 1065 ; P. 194, 4 : Hml. S. 23 b, 207 : B. 2746 : An. 1316. Wē sind bereáfod ūrum gódum *aporiamur bonis nostris*, Wrt. Voc. i. 54, 43. (c) with æt :—Hí bereáfodon Loth æt his ǽhton *predati sunt Loth*, Prud. 2 b : Chr. 1043 ; P. 163, 34. Þeáh se reáfere ūs æt ǽhtum bereáfige, Hml. Th. i. 576, 10 : Ll. Th. i. 180, 21. Gif man beó æt his ǽhtum bereáfod, i. 286, 16. Aaron hæfde bereáfod (*spoliaverat*) þ folc æt hira golde, Ex. 32, 25. II. with acc. of spoil and *on* with person :—Þ hē him ágeáfe þæt hē ǽr on him bereáfode (ge-, *v.l.*), Ors. 3, 11 ; S. 146, 30. [*Goth.* bi-raubōn : *O. Sax.* bi-rōbōn : *O. Frs.* bi-rāvia : *O. H. Ger.* bi-roubon *exspoliare.*]

**be-reáfigend**, es ; *m. A* spoiler, robber :—Eálá þū sǽ, manna bereáfigend and unscæððigra beswícend, Ap. Th. 11, 10. Cf. Bereáfgende grassatrix, An. Ox. 7, 136.

**be-reáfigendlic.** v. un-bereáfigendlic : **be-rebban.** v. be-rafan.

**bere-brytta**, an ; *m. The guardian of a granary :*—Be berebryttan (-e, MS.). Berebryttan gebyreð corngebrot on hærfæste æt bernes dure, Ll. Th. i. 440, 2.

**be-rēcan.** *Substitute : To besmoke* (v. N.E.D. s.v.), *expose to smoke, fumigate, and add :*—Berēc on glēdum, Lch. ii. 50, 21. Berēc hÿ on hāte ǽmergean, iii. 30, 18. v. be-reócan.

**be-reccan, II.** *Add :*—Berecce hē hine on folcgemōte, and gif hē láðleás beó . . ., Ll. Th. i. 220, 23. Sē þe fríóne forstǽle, . . . and hit hym on bestǽled sié, þ hē hine bereccean ne mæg, swelte sē deáðe, 48, 6. Of ðǽre scylde ðe hē hine berecc(e)an ne mǽge *ex eo quod defendere nequeunt*, Past. 209, 23.

**bere-corn.** *Add :*—Swá berecorn ðerscendum (ðerccedum, MS.) *quasi tipsonas feriente* (Prov. 27, 22), Kent. Gl. 1035. Berecorn beorende *ptysones* (Is this also a gloss of Prov. 27, 22 with *ferente* read instead of *feriente*?), Txts. 89, 1677.

**-bered.** v. á-, ge-bered.

**bere-flór.** *Add :* v. bǽre-flór : **bere-gafol.** Cf. gafol-bere.

**be-regnian.** v. be-rēnian.

**bere-healm**, es ; *n. Barley-straw :*—Genim æscrinde and berehalm, Lch. iii. 28, 7.

**bere-hláf.** *Dele :* beren *a barn.* v. bere-ærn.

**ber(e)-land**, es ; *n. Land where barley grows, bear-land* (D. D.) :— On berlandes heáfda, C. D. iii. 367, 9.

**beren** *of barley.* *Add :*—Beren gebered corn *tipsane*, Wrt. Voc. i. 20, 27. Cruman berenes hláfes, Lch. ii. 134, 8. Fæsten tō berenan hláfe, Wlfst. 173, 10. Genim beren mela gōd, Lch. ii. 50, 3. Beren eár, 54, 11. Þá hláfas wǽron berene, Hml. Th. i. 188, 4.

**beren** *of a bear.* v. biren : **berend** *ferox* (= -ax). v. beran, II. 3.

**berend**, es ; *m. A carrier :*—Berend *gestator*, Germ. 393, 149 : *gerula* (*floris*, Ald. 54, 16), Wrt. Voc. ii. 83, 82 : 41, 38. Berend *geruli* (Ald. 179, 19), 94, 23 : 41, 46. v. cpds. under beran.

**be-rendan** ; *p.* de *To strip off peel* or *husk :*—Gárleác gebrǽd and berend, Lch. ii. 50, 22. Nim feówertig lybcorna, berend wel and gegníd, 336, 2 : iii. 18, 29. Berende, 272, 6. Sundcorn wel berended, iii. 18, 13.

**berendlic.** *Add :* v. un-berendlic, *and next word.*

**berendlíce**; *adv. With fecundity :*—Berendlíce *fecunditate*, Rtl. 32, 15.

**berendnis.** *Add :*—Berendnis *fecunditas*, Rtl. 108, 23.

beren-hulu, e; f. A barley-husk:—Berenhula tipsanas, Scint. 95, 19.

be-rēnian. Add: to ornament, adorn:—Bōc mid sylure berēnod, and iii. rōde mid sylure berēnode, C. D. vi. 101, 24. v. ge-regnian.

be-reócan; p. -reác To smoke (trans.), fumigate:—Bereóce man mid rēcelse suffiatur thure, Ll. Th. ii. 164, 5. v. be-rēcan.

berere. v. wæter-berere.

bere-tūn (ber-). Add:—Ic wille rȳman mīnne bertūn, Hml. Th. ii. 104, 17: Wlfst. 286, 16. v. N.E.D. 286, D.D. s.v. barton.

bere-wæstm barley-produce, barley-crops:—Geunne þē Drihten þære (-a?) brādan berewæstma and þāre (-a?) hwītan hwætewæstma and ealra eorþan wæstma, Lch. i. 402, 6.

bere-wīc (and ?-wīce; f. cf. Lat. berewica):—Mid allen ðām berewīcan ðe ic habbe intō ðāre hālagen stōwe gegifen, C. D. iv. 211, 27: 192, 7. Medeshāmstede and tā berewīcan þa þār tō hēren, and Anlāfestūn and þā(m) berewīcan þār tō . . . Undelum and tō berewīcum þār tō gebyred, C. D. B. iii. 367, 12-17. v. N.E.D. berewick.

berg a swine. v. bearg: berge protection, antidote. v. wēde-berge.

berian to bare. Dele second passage: berian to beat, berry (v. N.E.D.). v. ge-bered.

bericge. v. bar(r)icge.

be-rīdan. Substitute: I. to surround, invest:—Hē hine þær berād, Chr. 755; P. 46, 29. Gif hē mægnes hæbbe, þæt hē his gefán berīde and inne besitte si vim habeat, ut hostem suum circumveniat et obsideat, Ll. Th. i. 90, 4. [Bruttes þa burȝen gunnen biriden, Laym. 10739.] II. to seize, arrest:—þā berād mon þæt wīf the woman was arrested, Chr. 901; P. 92, 12. Ic beóde þæt þū on mīnre stede berīde þās lond þām hǣlge tō hande, Cht. Th. 369, 21. Harold king lēt berīdan Sandwīc of Xpes cyrcean him sylfan tō handa and hæfde hit twelf mōnað, 338, 30.

berie. Add: I. a berry:—Berige vaccinia, Wrt. Voc. i. 67, 25. Bergan bacce, 285, 66 : ii. 10, 66. Mora commune nomen est bergena, 59, 4. Bergan corimbos, 104, 40. Berian, 14, 62. II. a grape:—Ne bið þæt wīn of ānre berian, ac of manegum, Hml. Th. ii. 276, 27. Wīn bið of manegum berium āwrungen, 268, 10. Bergeum racemis, Wrt. Voc. ii. 83, 58. Bergean racemos, 97, 32. Se wīngeard hafað berian (uvas), on ðām bergean beóð cende swylce meregrota, Nar. 37, 28. v. hæþ-, heorot-, laur-, mōr-beri(g)e.

be-rīfan. Take here passage under be-rȳfan in Dict., and cf. be-reáfian.

berigeblæ farcille [for beri-geblæ (= bere-gafie) furcille?? This form, however, which might be possible in the Erfurt Glossary, is quite out of keeping with the glossary in which it occurs], Wrt. Voc. ii. 40, 1.

be-rindan. Add:—Berinde decorticavit, Wrt. Voc. ii. 25, 47. Æppla berindede, Lch. ii. 178, 2. [O. H. Ger. pi-rinten decorticare.]

be-rindran to strip, peel:—Genim spracen berindred, Lch. ii. 58, 8. Cf. ge-rendrian.

be-rīpan; p. te To strip, despoil, plunder. I. with acc. of person (or thing) despoiled, (1) alone:—Hē berȳpð þā wannspēdigan, Hml. Th. i. 66, 11: 328, 20: ii. 102, 15. Hē berȳpte ðā unscæððigan, Hml. S. 19, 8 : 3, 444. Nā berȳp ðū þeów wīsne ne defraudes seruum sensatum, Scint. 190, 1. þæt hē ðā unstrangan berȳpe, Hml. Th. i. 164, 4. þ hē inne oþþe ūte cirican berȳpe, Ll. Th. i. 334, 31. Mīn folc is berȳped þurh reáferas populum meum exactores sui spoliaverunt, Wlfst. 45, 17. Wē habbað Godes hūs clǣne berȳpte, 157, 18. (2) with spoil, (a) in gen.:—Man Eádgife berȳpte ǣlcere āre, Cht. Th. 203, 11. Hī mē berȳpton rædes and frōfre, Met. 2, 12. (b) with æt:—þ mynster hig berȳptan and bereáfodon æt eallon ðingan, Chr. 1055; P. 186, 9. II. with acc. of spoil:—Swā hwæt swā ic mid sácne berȳpte si quid defraudavi, Hml. Th. i. 582, 3. [Biripe it alle, Ps. 79, 13. O. L. Ger. birōpian to strip: O. H. Ger. bi-roufen depilare.] Cf. be-reáfian.

ber-land, bern, bern-hús (Gr. D. 68, 22), -berst. v. bere-land, bere-ærn, ge-berst.

berstan. Add: I. (1) literal:—Seó eorþe wæs cwaciende and berstende, Ors. 88, 11. Berstende līc a body breaking out into eruptions, Lch. i. 272, 1. (2) figurative:—þ him nāðor ne burste ne ǣð ne ordāl, Ll. Th. i. 280, 10. (3) to break away, cf. æt-berstan:—Gelæhton þā weardmen his wealdleðer, þæt hē mid fleáme ne burste, Ælfc. T. Grn. 18, 15. Hū hē Hingware berstan sceolde, Hml. S. 32, 58. II. of noise:—Fióndes byrstende hroeðnise inimici rugientis sevitiam, Rtl. 122, 14.

bersting. Add: v. tō-bersting: berþestre, berþling, be-rūmað, -rȳfan, -rȳpan. v. byrþestre, byrþling, be-hrūmod, -rīfan, -rīpan.

ber-winde, an; f. Bearbine (-bind, v. N.E.D., D.D. s. vv.):—Berwinde umbilicum, Wrt. Voc. i. 68, 57.

be-sǣgan; p. de To sink (trans.):—Besǣgedum convolutis, lapsis, Germ. 388, 85. [Biseid and hent on þe grune of idelnesse, O. E. Homl. ii. 211, 21. Bisaid, 213, 36.]

be-sǣtian; p. ode To lie in ambush for:—Hē forsǣtade hié ðēr ðēr hió geþōht hæfdon þ hié hiene besǣtedon insidiantes insidiis capit, Ors. 3, 11; S. 146, 11.

be-sārgian. Add: I. with idea of pity, to be sorry for:—Tō besārgienne doletura, An. Ox. 5266. Besārgiendes conpatientis, 903. (1) a person, (a) with dat.:—Besārgode hē ðǣre sorhfullan mēder, Hml. Th. ii. 150, 17. (b) with acc.:—Hē spræc tō ðām ceastergewarum, þā hē mid fæderlicere lufe besārgode, Hml. Th. i. 402, 11. (c) with prep.:—Besārega for him dole pro eo, Scint. 12, 1. (2) an unfavourable circumstance, (a) with acc.:—Hē besārgað ūres mōdes blindnysse, Hml. Th. i. 158, 8 : Hml. S. 1, 220. Benedictus besārgode his fōstormēder sárnysse, Hml. Th. ii. 154, 18. þæt hē ōðres mannes ungelimp besārgige, i. 584, 6. Wē sceolon his yfel besārgian, 274, 11. (b) with acc. and infin. (from Latin):—Besāriga hæftlingas beón þīne þeówtlingas dole captivos esse tuos servulos, Hy. S. 125, 5. Besārigende losian worulde condolens perire seculum, 34, 20. II. with idea of regret:—Hē besārgode þ hē ne mōste læncg brūcan þæs leóhtes, Hml. S. 21, 252. Hē behreówsode þ hē swā rēðne dōm sette, and hit besārgode ǣfre, 32, 227. Sume besārgodon þ hī swilces nāht ne dydon, 31, 73. Hī noldon besārgian þæs Hǣlendes slege, ne mid dǣdbōte his mildse biddan, Ælfc. T. Grn. 21, 2. III. with idea of complaint:—Gif hē hit mid nūðe beceorað oþþe mid mōde besārgað non solum ore verum etiam in corde si murmuraverit, R. Ben. 21, 2. Hī gesāwon þ him næs ālȳfed unālȳfedlic þing tō dōnne, and hī besārgodon þ hī sceoldon hyra gewunan forlǣtan, Gr. D. 104, 18. Hȳ nā ne ceorien, ne mid mōde besārgien non murmurarent, R. Ben. 65, 9. Geswīce ānra gehwylc be Gode oþþe be gōdum besārgian (conquiri), Scint. 165, 10.

be-sārgung. Add: compassion:—Sȳ þē ārfæst ofer ūs besārgung (compassio). Hy. S. 126, 24. Ne bið nān besārgung ðǣra mānfulra yrmðe, Hml. Th. i. 334, 10.

be-sāwan. Add:—Ðā leahtras þe deófol besǣwð on ūs (cf. O. E. Homl. i. 107, 17), Hml. S. 16, 376. Sǣd on eorðan besāwen, Hml. Th. i. 184, 34.

be-scēad, es; n. Distinction:—Ðerh bischeád per (minii) distinctionem, Mt. p. 11, 13.

be-sceádan (, -scead(w)ian?) to overshadow. Add: [v. be-shade in N.E.D., and cf. O. L. Ger. be-scediwit obscuratus: O. H. Ger. piscatewen obumbrare.] v. be-sceadwung.

be-sceáden. Substitute: be-sceádan; p. -scēd. I. to separate, part from (gen.):—Sē þe gesyhð hine sylfne ryhtwīsnesse and ōðera gōdra weorca besceádenne, Ll. Th. ii. 430, 9. II. to sprinkle:—Genim ægerfelman, besceád mid pipore, Lch. ii. 54, 21. [O. Frs. bi-skēda.]

be-sceadwung, e; f. Overshadowing:—On besceadewunga, Ps. L. Spl. 67, 15.

be-sceafan; p. -scōf To scrape thoroughly:—Bescæf ūtan swīðe clǣne ðā moran, Lch. iii. 18, 28. [O. H. Ger. pi-scapan conradere.]

be-sceatwyrpan; p. te To betroth:—Besceatwyrpte desponsaret, An. Ox. 4555 : 2, 346. [Cf. O. H. Ger. scaz-wurf manumissio.] v. ge-sceatwyrpan.

be-sceáwere, es; m. An observer; speculator, Hy. S. 24, 31. [O. H. Ger. pi-scouwari.]

be-sceáwian. Add: I. to contemplate, behold:—Seó sāwel on ānre tīde besceáwað heofonan and ofer sǣ flȳhð, Hml. S. 1, 124. Besceáwiað contemplantur (Prov. 15, 3), Kent. Gl. 506. Besceáwede contemplarer, Hpt. Gl. 404, 34. II. to consider:—For hwig ne besceáwost þū on þȳnre heortan . . . hū Crȳst on Iudéa lande geboren wæs, St. A. 32, 13. Hē besceáwað considerat (Prov. 5, 21), Kent. Gl. 115. Hē besceáwode þ hī mid Drihtne habbað þā sēlestan gife, Hml. S. 25, 476. þæs mannes bīleofa is tō besceáwianne, Lch. ii. 210, 19. Besceáwiende considerans (medicus cicatrices), An. Ox. 371. III. with idea of examination, enquiry:—Ic besceáwie exploro (-do, MS.), An. Ox. 18 b, 24. Hē hēt besceáwian þā burh dixit eis: Explorate terram, Jos. 7, 2. Uton geþencan hū besceáwigende wē scylon beón ūre sāwle cogitemus quam perscrutantes esse debemus animae nostrae, Ll. Th. ii. 226, 34. IV. to see about, take care of:—Hālige fatu hē besceáwige vasa sacrata conspiciat, R. Ben. I. 62, 2. Besceáwige hē praevideat, R. Ben. 89, 17. [O. Frs. bi-skawia: O. H. Ger. pi-scouwōn conspicere, contemplari, considerare, perpensare, lustrari.]

be-sceáwiendlic; adj. Contemplative:—Besceáwendlicre contemplativae, An. Ox. 991.

be-sceáwod; adj. Considerate, thoughtful, circumspect:—On gleáwscipe swīþe bescáwede and forewittige, Lch. iii. 436, 11. v. un-, welbesceáwod; un-besceáwodlíce.

be-sceáwung, e; f. Contemplation:—Besceáwunge contemplationis, i. speculationis, i considerationis, An. Ox. 244 : 706 : Wrt. Voc. ii. 139, 62. On Godes besceáwunge in contemplatione Dei, R. Ben. 135, 1 : Gr. D. 4, 22.

be-sceófan. v. be-scúfan.

be-sceótan. Add: I. trans. (1) to dash, fling:—Ðā deóflu bescuton hī ānum dracan innan þone mūð, Wlfst. 141, 23. (2) to shut up:—Hē þā cyrican beleác, and mid scyttelum besceát and gefæstnode, Gr. D. 234, 18. II. intrans. (1) to dash, fling one's self:—Curtius þæroninnan besceát, Ors. 3, 3; S. 102, 31. (2) to happen, occur:—Gyf se terminus bescȳt on sumon dæge þǣre wucan, Lch. iii. 244, 16.

On ðisum dagum . . . būton sum heálic freólsdæg him on besceóte, Hml. Th. ii. 244, 28.

be-sceran. Add:—Besceoren decalvatum, decollatum, Wrt. Voc. ii. 138, 5. I. to shave a person, head, &c.:—Hē beáh tō ðām mynstre, and weard bescoren (received the tonsure), Hml. Th. ii. 348, 30. Sum wæs bescoren preóst quidam erat attonsus ut clericus, Bd. 5, 12; S. 628, 35. Hē weard bescoren tō Crīstes þeówdōme, Hml. S. 6, 240. Seó bescorene hālignes tonsa sanctitas, R. Ben. 135, 28. II. to cut off hair:—Bescear heó hire feax swā weras, Shrn. 31, 7. Beard him beón bescoren, Lch. iii. 198, 29. Samson besceorenum fexe (with shorn locks), Hml. Th. i. 488, 9. O. L. Ger. bi-sceran detondere: O. Frs. bi-skera: O. H. Ger. pi-sceran decalvare, depilare.] v. un-bescoren.

be-sceredness, e; f. Deprivation, abdication:—Bescyrednesse abdicatione, Wrt. Voc. ii. 7, 57.

be-scerian. Add: To deprive a person (acc.) of something (gen., dat. (inst.) or prep.):—Hē mēde hyne bescyrað (privat), Scint. 123, 16. Tō hwon bescyredest þū þē twyfealdre bletsunga?, Bl. H. 49, 35. Hwā bescirede mē mīnes hihtes?, Hml. S. 33, 96. Bescyrede fraudaret, Wrt. Voc. ii. 38, 24. Ic eom bescyred fraudor, 18. Bescered, 37, 58. Bescyred depeculatus, i. vastatus, depraedatus, depopulatus, 138, 78. [O. L. Ger. bi-scerian frustrare: O. H. Ger. pi-scerien privare, fraudare.]

be-scīlan to give a side look at. v. passage under be-scȳlian in Dict. Cf. sceolh.

be-scīnan. Add:—Godes beorhtnys hī besceán, Hml. Th. i. 30, 16. Warna þū þ hȳ nā sunne ne bescīne, Lch. i. 318, 15. [v. N. E. D. be-schine. Goth. bi-skeinan: O. Frs. bi-schīna: O. H. Ger. pi-scīnan circumfulgere.]

be-scītan. For Cot. 189 substitute Wrt. Voc. ii. 84, 71, and add: [O. H. Ger. pi-scizzan oblitus.]

be-screádian, be-scrifen. Dele.

be-screopan. l. -screpan, and add:—Hofe bescrepen . . . rinde clǣne and bescrepene, Lch. ii. 270, 3, 4.

be-scūfan, -sceófan. Add: I. to thrust, cast into a place:—Seó gȳtsung manega bescȳfð (precipitat) on fȳr, Prud. 60. þē se Ælmihtiga [on] heolstor besceáf, An. 1193. Hī hine on cwearterne bescufon, Hml. S. 18, 440. Hēt ontendan fȳr, and hī tōmiddes besceófan, 7, 219. Hēt hiera bescūfan iu þā eá DC jubeo ex his .dc. in flumen mitti, Nar. 11, 9; 24, 13. On dimhofe wæs bescofen in latibulum truditur, An. Ox. 3769. Sȳ þū on besceofen detrudere, on besceofene detrusis, Wrt. Voc. ii. 139, 41-43. Bescēofene praecipitata, Wülck. Gl. 254, 36. II. to force to something:—Gif hē hī neádunge tō his ðeówte gebȳgde, oððe gif hē hī tō yfelnysse bescufe, Hml. Th. i. 112, 7. Hwā dorste ðæs gewilnian, þæt se Ælmihtiga Cyning sceolde besceófan tō cwale his áucennedan æðeling?, ii. 6, 21. Bescūfende trudentes (ad erroris naufragia), An. Ox. 5477.

be-scyldigian. Dele: be-scylian. v. be-scīlan: be-scyrednes. v. be-sceredness: be-scyrung. Dele: be-seah, Dōm. L. 241. v. be-sencan.

be-secgan. Add: I. to announce:—Seó weard gebrōht and besæd þām cyninge, Hml. A. 94, 87. I a. with on, to bring a charge against, accuse:—Ðā leásan gewitan him on besǣdon: 'Ne geswicð ðes man . . . ,' Hml. Th. i. 46, 1. II. to deny a charge, excuse one's self, Bd. 5, 19; S. 640, 11. [Elch sinne him seluen biseið (declares), O. E. Homl. ii. 176, 3. O. Frs. bi-seka to deny a charge: O. Sax. bi-seggian to declare the truth: O. H. Ger. pi-sagēn addicere: Ger. be-sagen to mention.]

be-sencan. Add: pp. -senct To plunge, submerge, drown; v. N. E. D. be-sench:—Ðonne blindum beseah (-sencþ?) biterum lígum earme on ende tunc caecis merget flammis sine fine misellos, Dōm. L. 241. Weleras unwīses besenceað (praecipitabunt) hyne, Scint. 96, 3. Hē xiii scipa on sǣ besencte, Ors. 4, 6; S. 172, 10. God besencte Pharao, Hml. Th. i. 312, 5. Wē besencton obsorbuimus, Bl. Gl. Hī hine besencton on þā eá æt his cneówa, Bl. H. 43, 29. Besencean þǣre gecwylman mergere aut mortificare, Coll. M. 24, 33. Besencendum submergente, An. Ox. 1739. Besenced of ðæm yfemestum tō ðæm nieðemestan, Past. 134, 24. On helle besenct, Hml. Th. i. 330, 26. Besencedum summerso, An. Ox. 11, 99. Besente demersos, 3078. Besencte, Bl. H. 49, 8. [O. Sax. bi-senkian: O. L. Ger. be-sencan.]

be-sendan to send:—Ic on besende inmitto, Ælfc. Gr. Z. 172, 11. On ðām ðwyrnyssum þe ūs se Ælmihtiga on besent, Hml. Th. ii. 460, 15. Besende se deófol swilc geþanc on þone munuc, Hml. S. 31, 1073: 33, 161.

be-sengan. Add:—þā fūlan sceanda hē besengd on helle, Hml. A. 115, 439. [Wordes huerof he may berne oþer bezenge. þe prive cat bezengþ ofte his scin, Ayenb. 230, 4. O. H. Ger. pi-sengen concremare.] v. un-besenged.

be-seolfrian, -silfran to cover with silver:—Besi(l)frede deargentatae, Ps. Srt. 67, 14. Cf. ofer-seolfrian.

be-seón. Add: I. intrans. To look. (1) absolute, (a) physical:—Ne beseoh þū underbæc noli respicere post tergum, Gen. 19, 17. (b)

mental:—Mann þe hys hand āsett on hys sulh and on bæc besyhð, Lk. 9, 62. Beseoh (respice) and gehȳr mē, Ps. Spl. 12, 3. (2) with preps. (a) physical:—Beseó hē upp tō þǣre næddran, and hē leofað, swā hē besihð on hig, Num. 21, 8. Swā ðā eágan on besióð, Bt. 41, 4; F. 252, 13. Of heofenum beseah Drihten Dominus de coelo prospexit, Ps. Th. 52, 3. Þæt folc beseah on Faraones here, Ex. 14, 10. Hē beseah tō heofenum, Hml. Th. i. 62, 9: Ap. Th. 11, 18. Hē underbæc beseah wið þæs wælfylles, Gen. 2562. þonne hié besāwon on þā burg, Ors. 2, 8; S. 92, 32. Beó se canon him ætforan eágum, beseó tō, Ll. Th. ii. 250, 24. (b) mental, to look with favour, attention, expectation, &c.:—Hē nǣfre ne besyhð tō ðǣre uplican āre, Past. 67, 14. Beseah Drihten tō Abele and tō his lācum, Gen. 4, 4, 5. Hē beseah wið mīn, and gehȳrde mīn gebed, Ps. Th. 39, 1. Ealle heó on āne īdelnesse symle besēgan omnes declinaverunt, simul inutiles facti sunt, 52, 4. Beseoh tō mē, Ps. Th. 12, 3: 21, 1. Beseoh mē tō fultume intende in adjutorium meum, 37, 21. Beseoh þū mē on fultum respice in auxilium meum, 70, 11. Beseoh tō ūs, Gen. 47, 25. Þēh Godes bydel misdō, ne beseó man nā þǣrtō ealles tō swȳðe, Wlfst. 178, 11. reflexive, (1) absolute:—þā hē hyne beseah, þā geseah hē olfendas cum elevasset oculos, vidit camelos, Gen. 24, 63: 33, 1: Hml. S. 23 b, 772. þā beseah hē hyne ymbūtan hider and þider cum circumspexisset huc atque illuc, Ex. 2, 12. Ne beseoh þū þē nā, Lch. i. 202, 17. Þ hē hine underbæc ne besāwe, Bt. 35, 6; F. 170, 9. (2) with prep.:—Beseah hē hine underbæc wiþ ðæs wīfes, Bt. 35, 6; F. 170, 14. Þ hē hine ne besió tō his ealdun yfelum, 17. III. trans. To see about, care for, attend to, provide for:—Ealle fata and spēde hē sceal beseón omnia vasa cunctamque substantiam conspiciat, R. Ben. 55, 1. Hē wæs wel besewen on reáfe and yfele on þeáwum, Hml. Th. i. 534, 3. Hlāf well besewen and well gesyfled, C. D. iv. 278, 4. Behealde hē þæt his ofiētan ne beón yfele besewene, Ll. Th. ii. 360, 27. Manega mid upplicre besawene gyfe multi superna respecti gratia, Scint. 46, 15. [Goth. bi-saihwan: O. Frs. bi-sia: O. Sax. be-sehan: O. H. Ger. pisehan.]

be-seón; p. -sāh to strain upon, sprinkle:—Rōd blōde bestēmed, biseón mid swāte, Cri. 1088. v. seón to strain, and cf. be-siftan.

be-seóþan to boil away, reduce by boiling:—Wæter besoden oþ þone þriddan dǣl, Lch. ii. 188, 16. Seóþ þū hyt swā swiðe þæt se þridda[n] dǣl beó besodan, iii. 92, 19.

be-seowian (-siwian) to besew (v. N. E. D. s.v.), sew up:—Hī besywodon Crīsantum mid þǣre hȳde, Hml. S. 35, 159. Sēc stānas . . . beseowa hira .iii. on þon þe þū wile (sew them up in anything you please), Lch. ii. 306, 9. Bisiuuidi (-siudi) uuerci opere plumario, Txts. 80, 699. Besiwed feðergeweorc, Wrt. Voc. ii. 63, 45. Besiwodon suto, Germ. 399, 470. [O. H. Ger. pi-siuuit uuerdan insui.]

be-settan. Add: I. to set, place, (1) with on, (a) to put one thing in another:—Ic on besette insero, Ælf. Gr. Z. 166, 3. God ðā sāwle beset on ðone līchaman, Hml. Th. i. 292, 31. Hē him sāwle on besett, ii. 2c6, 25. þā hē on his geleáffulra heortan beset, 524, 12. (b) to place hope, reliance on, inflict persecution on:—Deófol Godes gecorenum ēhtnysse on besett, Hml. Th. ii. 200, 10. Wē besettað ūrne hiht on eów, i. 24, 2. Hī heora hiht on þissum līfe besettað, 172, 14. Ealne mōdes hiht on God sylfne besette man, Wlfst. 75, 5. On besettan inpingere, An. Ox. 4229. (2) with tō, to apply:—Nylle gē heortan tō besettan (apponere), Ps. L. 61, 11. II. to surround:—þæt līc læg mid mannum besett, Hml. Th. ii. 346, 5. Hīs līc læg ealle þā niht inne beset, 348, 19. Wītum besette on helle, Wlfst. 145, 31. II. a. to besiege:—Gē beóð lange inne besette, Deut. 28, 53. III. to set with something inserted:—Hē eall wæs beset mid heora scotungum, Hml. S. 32, 117. Hié wǣron ymb eal ūtan mid eágum besett, Past. 195, 19. [Goth. bi-satjan: O. H. Ger. pi-sezzen.]

be-sewen. v. be-seón, III.

be-sidian; p. ode To regulate:—Besceáwige se abbod and hāte besidian þǣra reáfa gemet, R. Ben. 89, 18. v. sydung in Dict.

be-siftan; p. te To sift over, cover by sifting, sprinkle with dust:—Ealle heora heáfda wǣron mid duste besyfte, Homl. S. 23, 155. Cf. be-seón to sprinkle.

be-sīgan; p. -sāh To rush:—On besīgendum ingruenti, An. Ox. 4126.

be-sincan. Add:—Hē besanc tō grunde he sank to the bottom, Hml. S. 25, 348. Gnīd swȳðe þ þā sealfa in besincen, Lch. ii. 282, 1. Forlēt hē his fēt on þā eorþan besincan, Bl. H. 127, 22: Ors. 4, 2; S. 160, 30. Hwonne hié on þā eorþan besuncene wurden, 2, 6; S. 88, 14. [O. Sax. bi-sincan.]

besining. Dele, and see bēsming.

be-sirwan (-si(e)rian); p. (e)de To ensnare, entrap, circumvent:—Hē ofslōg and besirede his getreówne ðegn devotum militem sub studio fraudis extinxit, Past. 393, 8. Hiene Artabatus besirede and ofslōg per Artabatum circumventus occiditur, Ors. 2, 5; S. 84, 24. Besierede, 4, 5; S. 170, 2: 6, 32; S. 274, 3. Pontius hæfde þone consul besired, 3, 10; S. 140, 22. S. 140, 22. Rōmane besierede wǣron, 3, 8; S. 120, 27. Earme men wǣron beswicene and hreówlīce besyrwde (-sirwde, v. l.), Wlfst. 158, 12. v. be-syrwan, -serian, -syrewian, -syrian in Dict.

**be-sittan.** Add:—Besitt obsidet, Scint. 148, 12. Đã hellican gāstas besittađ þæs mannes forđsīđ, Hml. Th. i. 410, 3. Þā þe þ lic besæton, Hml. S. 10, 59. Þā hǣþenan hæfdon hī besetene, 25, 391. [Goth. bi-sitan: O. Frs. bi-sitta to possess: O. Sax. bi-sittian to besiege: O. L. Ger. bi-sittian circumsedere, circumdare: O. H. Ger. pi-sizzen possidere.]

**be-siwian.** v. be-seowian.

**be-sleán.** Add: I. trans. (1) to strike, smite, (a) lit.:—Hē beslôh stān percussit petram, Ps. Spl. M. 77, 13. (b) fig. to strike with disease:—Hē gewende mid snāwhwītum hreófian beslagen, Hml. Th. i. 400, 29. (2) to deprive by a stroke (lit. or fig.) of something (gen. inst.):—Hē wæs freúnda gefylled on folcstede, beslagen (-slægen, -slegen, v. ll.) æt sæcce, Chr. 937; P. 108, 23. (3) to strike, place with violence, dash, inflict :—Ic on besleá incutio, Ælfc. Gr. Z. 169, 9. Đurh đone đyrnenan helm on đone Hǣlend beslagen, Hml. Th. ii. 254, 10. Mid on beslagenre wunde, 88, 23. II. intrans. (1) to strike, give a blow :—Ic on besleá illido, Ælfc. Gr. Z. 171, 4. Gif mon æt blôdlǣtan on sinwe besleá, Lch. ii. 148, 19. Gif mon đā sculdru in besleá if a blow is given that penetrates the shoulders, Ll. Th. i. 100, 1. (2) to strike, force a passage :—Þā beslôh se þorn on þone fôt, and swā strang wæs se sting þæs þornes, þæt hē eóde þurh þone fôt, Guthl. 68, 2. [O. Frs. bi-slā: O. H. Ger. pi-slahan stringere, verberare.]

**be-slītan.** Substitute: To deprive by tearing of something (inst.).

**besma.** Add: bisme, bysm :—Besma scopa, Txts. 95, 1794. Bisme scops, Wrt. Voc. i. 16, 5. Bysm verriculum vel scopae, 27, 11. Hē hæfde fiþru swylce þyrnen besma, Shrn. 122, 28. Hē sceal habban ... besman, Angl. ix. 263, 7. [O. L. Ger. besmo verriculum.]

**be-smeágan,** -smeán to consider about, examine into :—Cỹđ þū þæs mynstres abbude þ hē hine sylfne georne besmeáge, Hml. S. 23 b, 633.

**bésming,** e; f. Curving :—Bēsming (printed besining) sinuatio, Wrt. Voc. i. 55, 11. v. bôsm, ge-bésmed.

**be-smirwan** to besmear, rub with ointment, &c. :—Besmyra eall þ scīnende mid hunigteáre, Lch. iii. 292, 10. Þ se lǣce mihte hine besmyrwian (v. be-bīwan), Gr. D. 318, 3. Bismiride (-æ, -a) interlitam, Txts. 71, 1095. Besmyred, Wrt. Voc. ii. 45, 51. [O. H. Ger. pi-smerwan ungere.]

**be-smītan.** Add: I. in a physical sense :—Se salt bismiten (-smitten, L.) bið, Lk. R. 14, 34. II. moral :—Þæt ic ne sié besmiten ne violer, Wrt. Voc. ii. 61, 63. (1) of the action of a person :—Ic mīn fǣmnhād besmāt, Hml. S. 23 b, 328. Þū woldest þone besmītan þe þū nānwiht yfles on nystest, Bl. H. 85, 36. Ne mæg þ Godes templ beón besmiten, 73, 15. (2) of the effect of evil :—Hwanne besmāt hine seó scyld þære fealasprecolnesse?, Bl. H. 169, 4. Đætte nān unclǣnnes hine ne besmīte (polluat), Past. 75, 20. His hand næs besmiten mid āgotenum blôde, Hml. Th. ii. 304, 31. Bið se deáda besmiten (incriminated; in culpa, Lat. vers.), būton hē frīnd hæbbe þe hine clǣnsnian, Ll. Th. i. 290, 12. Hié beóþ besmitene mid firenluste, Bl. H. 25, 8. Besmitenum pullis (palmis), Wrt. Voc. ii. 92, 52. [Goth. bi-smeitan ungere: O. H. Ger. pi-smīzan circumlinere, foedare, violare, contaminare.]

**be-smiten(n)es.** Add:—Besmitenesse contagione, Wrt. Voc. ii. 15, 21: colludio, 22, 25. Besmitenessa contagia, 21, 49. I. physical:—Besmitenyse squaloris, i. inquinationis, An. Ox. 3482. II. moral :—Þ hire bið besmitennys (pollutio), Ll. Th. ii. 156, 9. Būton leahtra besmitenysse sine pollutione peccati, Hml. A. 112, 329. Būtan leahtra besmitenesse sine macula, R. Ben. 3, 18. Geclǣnsode fram deófolgilda besmitennysse, Hml. S. 30, 73.

**be-smiþian** to work in metal. Add :—Nim þās næglas and heó besmiþian hāt on þīnes sunu brīdle take these nails and order them to be set in thy son's bridle (cf. þū þās næglas hāt ... on his brīdels dôn, El. 1175. The Emperour dyde doo sette the nayles in his brydel, H. R. 158, 32), H. R. 17, 9. [O. H. Ger. pi-smidôn includere.] Cf. be-wyrcan.

**be-smittian;** p. od To pollute, defile, (1) physical :—Besmittod blæc caccabatum atramentum, An. Ox. 4156. (2) moral :—Heora formænig mid īdelum lofe byþ besmittad multos ex eis cenodoxiae morbus commaculat, R. Ben. 139, 19. v. smittian in Dict.

**be-smyred.** v. be-smirwan.

**be-snǣdan.** For first passage substitute :—Engel hēt þæt treów ceorfan, ... Hēt þonne besnǣdan seolfes blǣdum. [Cf. O. L. Ger. bi-snīđan putare: O. H. Ger. pi-snīdan demetere.]

**be-snīwed.** Add: [Piers P. bi-sniwe, -snewed: Ayenb. be-snewed.]

**be-snyðian.** Add: , -snyþþan. [Cf. Icel. snauðr bereft: sneyða to bereave of.]

**be-solcen.** Add:—Oft đā monnđwǣran weorđađ suā besolcne and suā wlace and suā slāwe for hira monnđwǣrnesse đæt hié ne anhagađ nāne wuht nyttwyrđes dôn saepe mansueti dissolutionis torpescunt taedio, Past. 289, 15: 239, 3.

**be-sône.** Dele, and see sôn.

**be-sorg.** For Anxious, careful, substitute cared about, and add :— þæs cnihtes sāwle þe mē besorh ys (cf. hē begann tô lufienne þone cniht,

16, 42), Ælfc. T. Grn. 18, 1. Ne sỹ nān đing swā besorh þæt hē his tīdsang fore forlǣte let him not care about anything so much, that he neglects his service for it, R. Ben. 68, 5. Hī nān þing him inmêdre ne lǣten, ne besorhre, þonne hira Drihten Christo omnino nihil preponant, 132, 9. Eall þ deórwyrđoste đætte þū đē besorgost hæfdes quod in omni fortunae tuae censu pretiosissimum possidebas, Bt. 10; S. 22, 2. Þeóda hláford, ūs se besorgesta, Hml. S. 23, 143. v. un-besorh.

**be-sorgian** to be troubled about. Dele passage from Bt., and add :— Þæs man mid sárlicum andwlitan, nāt ic hwæt hē besorgađ, Ap. Th. 15, 10. Swīđor Drihten besorgade þā heora synna þonne his āgene wunda, Hml. Th. i. 50, 25. Ne þurfan gē nôht besorgian hwæt gē sprecan, Bl. H. 171, 18. [O. Sax. bi-sorgôn to take care of; O. L. Ger. bi-sorgôn honorare: O. H. Ger. pi-sorgên curare, providere, honorificare.]

**be-spǣtan;** p. te To spit upon (v. N. E. D. be-spete) :—Hī hine bespǣtton (coɪperunt conspuere eum, Mk. 14, 65), Hml. Th. ii. 248, 24.

**be-spanan.** Add:—Hē wile āwendan of rihtan geleáfan and bespanan tô his unlārum, Wlfst. 95, 15. v. bi-spanan in Dict.

**be-sparrad.** Substitute be-sparrian; p. ad To bolt, shut up (v. N. E. D. be; ar):—Bisparrad oppilatae, Wrt. Voc. ii. 115, 68. Besparrade, 63, 47. [Cf. O. H. Ger. pi-sperren oppilare, claudere, obstruere.]

**be-sprecan.** Substitute: I. to speak about, mention. Cf. be-secgan, I :—Hit is ūs swīþor bismre gelíc þæt wē þæt besprecađ erubescunt de recordatione praeteritorum, Ors. 3, 11 ; S. 152, 30. Hē begeat sumne đe hine bespræc tô đām cāsere, Hml. Th. i. 374, 13. II. of legal proceedings, to claim :—Sette hē borh þ hē bringe his geteáman in þǣr hit besprecen bið (where the recovered property will be claimed), Ll. Th. i. 288, 17. III. in an unfavourable sense, (1) trans. To complain of, blame, speak ill of :—Fram stefne besprecendre a voce obloquentis, Ps. L. 43, 17. (a) with case :—For hwī besprecađ nū men þās crīstnan tīda, and secgađ þæt nū wyrsan tīda sién ?, Ors. 1, 12 ; S. 54, 33. (b) with clause :—Ūre crístne Rôma bespricđ þæt hiere weallas for ealdunge brosnien nostri incircumspecta anxietate causantur, si Romanae reipublicae moles imbecillitate senectutis contremiscunt, Ors. 2, 4; S. 74, 34. (2) intrans. To complain, make complaint :—Hū ungemetlíce gē bemurciađ and besprecađ, þ eów nū wyrs sié, Ors. 1, 10 ; S. 48, 18. [O. Sax. bi-sprekan to complain of, blame: O. Frs. bi-spreka: O. H. Ger. pi-sprehhan obloqui, detrahere, vituperare.]

**be-sprengan.** Add :—Besprengan men mid fantwætere, Ll. Th. ii. 390, 16. Hē hēt mid pice þæt mǣden besprencgan, Hml. S. 9, 118. v. N. E. D. be-spreng.

**be-stǣlan;** p. de To lay a charge of crime on a person, to convict a person (on with dat.) of crime :—Þæt mē nǣfre deófel nāht on ne mæge bestǣlan æt mīnum endedæge, Angl. xi. 101, 53. Þæt se deófol eów nāge nāht on tô bestēlenne ungeandettes, Wlfst. 135, 31. Sē þe friône forstele, and l.ē hine bebycgge, and hit hym on bestǣled, þ hē hine bereccean ne mæg, Ll. Th. i. 48, 6. v. stǣlan.

**be-standan.** Add: I. to surround :—Đā hǣþenan hine bestôdon, Hml. S. 28, 104. II. to attend the dead, perform funeral rites for :—Heó forđferde and Abraham hig bestôd on þā ealdan wīsan mortua est, venitque Abraham, ut plangeret et fleret eam, Gen. 23, 2. Þā wīf behwurfon hire lïc oþþæt heó bebyrged wæs, swylce hī for đan cômon þ hī þā fǣmnan bestôdon, Hml. S. 10, 271. Þ đā gegyldan cumon, and þ lïc wurđlíce bestandan, and tô mynstre ferian, Cht. Th. 607, 20. [v. N. E. D. be-stand. O. H. Ger. pi-standan circumstare, custodire.]

**be-stapan.** l. be-stæppan, and add: I. of motion, to step, &c. :—Ic gange oþþe on bestæppe incaedo, Ælfc. Gr. Z. 171, 12. Đæt đïn fôt ne bestæppe on his grinum, Hex. 52, 13. II. to tread, print a footstep :—Þā lāstas beóþ on þāre ilcan onsýne þe hié þǣr on forman on þā eorþan bestapene wǣron, Bl. H. 127, 21.

**be-stealcian;** p. ode To proceed stealthily so as to surprise (cf. deer-stalking) :—Hinguar swā swā wulf on lande bestalcode, and þā leóde slôh, Hml. S. 32, 40.

**be-stefnan.** v. stefnan in Dict.

**be-stelan.** Dele translation of passage from Chronicle, and add : I. to rob :—Môde bestolene, Rā. 12, 6. v. bi-stelan in Dict. II. to go secretly, stealthily, to steal, (1) with reflexive pronoun :—Hē ārās, and bestæl hine tô him and forcearf his mentles ǣnne læppan occulte surrexit, et oram chlamydis ejus abscidit, Past. 197, 21. Se here hiene on niht up bestæl, Chr. 865 ; P. 68, 11. Hē hiene āweg bestæl, Ors. 5, 2 ; S. 218, 31. (1 a) to steal away from (dat.) :—Hiene bestæl se here intô Werhām Wesseaxna fierde ... hié hié nihtes bestǣlon þǣre fierde, Chr. 876; P. 74, 7–11. (2) without pronoun :—Bistilđ sió slǣwđ on ūs mentis desidia furtim torpore mactatur, Past. 283, 3. Hē bestæl ūt mid his stæfe hoppegende, Hml. S. 21, 417. Se þearfa bestæl in tô Martine, 31, 910. Bestæl (-steal) se here ūp fram scipon, Chr. 1004; P. 135, 27. [v. N. E. D. be-steal.]

**be-stingan.** Add: Gif heó þ heáfod innan þām men bestincđ (-stingđ, v.l.), Angl. vii. 28, 259. Bestang se hālga his hand him on mūđ, Hml. Th. ii. 510, 34. Hire man bestang sweord on đā hracan, Shrn. 56, 13. Hē bestang þone hlāf on þ sealtfæt, Hml. A. 163, 254. Hē bestang fýr in þ corn, Gr. D. 290, 23. Hī bestungon him on mūđ

þone mete, Hml. S. 25, 34, 88. Beren eár bestinge on eáre, Lch. ii. 54, 11. Ðeáh hié mettas him on múð bestingon on fæstendægum *though they cram food into their mouths on fast days*, Hml. Th. ii. 330, 31. Gif sió lendenbræde bið on bestungen, Ll. Th. i. 98, 2. [*Goth.* bi-stiggkwan.] v. an-, in-bestingan *in Dict.*

be-stípan; *p.* te To deprive of :—Sē þe his suna bestéped and bereáfod wæs, Gr. D. 76, 18. [*O. H. Ger.* pi-stiufen *orbare.*]

be-streddon. *Substitute :* be-stregdan ; *p.* -strédde To bestrew, cover by scattering :—Hé þæt Crístes mæl on ðone seáð ásette, and hit heóld, oð þæt his ðegnas mid moldan hit bestreddon and gefæstnedon *donec adgesto a militibus puluere terrae figeretur*, Bd. 3, 2 ; Sch. 194, 20. v. be-streþþan.

be-streówian. *Add :* To cover by sprinkling, be-sprinkle :—Hé scrýdde hine mid hæran and mid axan bestreówode, Hml. S. 31, 445. Hí mid axum hí sylfe bestreówodon, 12, 35. On flóre licgende, bestreówod mid axum, Hml. Th. ii. 516, 30. Hí urnon ealle mid duste bestreówode, Hml. S. 31, 996.

be-streðan. *Substitute :* be-streþþan, -streþian (-strȳ-) ; *p.* ede To bestrew, scatter over, cover :—Oþ þæt his þegnas mid moldan hit bestrȳðedon (bestrȳðed hæfdon, v. l.) and gefæstnodon, Bd. 3, 2 ; Sch. 194, 19. (v. be-stregdan.) Biþ stānum bestreþed (v. Prehn, p. 253, desuper multis *sternor*), Rä. 81, 38. Þás geweorc stondað stíðlíce, bestrȳþed fæste miclum meahtlocum, Sch. 87.

be-strícan; *p.* -strác To make a stroke round :—Wið ōman. Genim āne grēne gyrde, and lǽt sittan þone man onmiddan hūses flóre, and bestric hine ymbútan (*draw a circle round about him with the rod*), and cweð .., Lch. iii. 70, 13. [Later the word (like *O. H. Ger.* pi-strîhhon il-, ob-linere) means to besmear. v. *N. E. D.* be-strike.]

be-strídan. *Add :*—Æfter ðisum wordum hé his hors bestrád, Hml. Th. ii. 136, 3.

be-strípan. *Add to* bestrýpan :—Hȳ wydewan bestrýpað, Ll. Th. ii. 320, 20. Hȳ wydewan bestrýptan, Chr. 975 ; P. 121, 33. Godes hús syndon innan bestrípte (-strýpte, v. l.) ǽlcra gerisena, Wlfst. 158, 8. [v. *N. E. D.* be-strip.]

be-strúdan. *For second passage substitute :*—Bestroden wǽre *infiscaretur*, Wrt. Voc. ii. 46, 69: be-strȳpan. v. be-strípan : be-styrian. *Add :* v. be-stregdan.

be-súpan ; *p.* -seáp To sup up, swallow :—Besúp scenc fulne þæs drences, Lch. ii. 312, 25. [*O. H. Ger.* pi-sûfan *demergere.*]

be-súpan. v. súþ *in Dict.*

be-sútian ; *p.* od To make foul, sordid :—Besútod *obsoletum*, i. *sordidum*, Germ. 403, 26. [Cf. Mi saule is suti, *O. E. Hml.* i. 185, 5. Hu swart þing ant hu suti is sunne, Marh. 15, 1. Þat suti sunne, H. M. 35, 17.]

be-swǽlan. *l.* -swǽlan, *and add :*—Beswǽled *ambustum, circumustum*, Germ. 391, 23. Ic wæs grimlíce beswǽled for þām micclan byrne, Hml. S. 23 b, 574.

be-swǽtan; *p.* te To sweat ; fig. *to toil* ; *desudare* :—Sē þe on gyrnendlicum wurðscypum mid onstandendum beswǽt (*desudat*) geswince, Scint. 111, 14.

be-swápan. *Substitute :* I. to sweep ; fig. *to sweep into the mind, inspire* with a resolution (cf. on-swápan *under* swápan, II *in Dict.*) :—Gif hwylc sȳ þ Rǽdwolde on mód beswápe, þ hē nāwiht lāþes ne dó si qui sit, *qui Redualdo suadeat, ut nec ipse tibi aliquid mali faciat*, Bd. 2, 12 ; Sch. 156, 21. II. to wrap up, cover up :—Heó hié mid scýtan besweóp *caput linteo cooperuit*, Bd. 3, 9 ; Sch. 232, 10. Hé mid healfum (sciccelse) hine sylfne besweóp, Bl. H. 215, 8. Bisweópun hine mið líne *ligauerunt eum linteis*, Jn. R. 19, 40. Biswápen mid hregle *amictus vestimento*, Ps. Srt. 103, 2. Hé bió wið ælce orsorgnesse besuápen mid ðyssum mægenum *contra prospera virtutum ornamenta muniatur*, Past. 83, 11. Hé bið besuápen mid swíðe wlitige elnbrǽdelse on bǽm sculdrum *quanta in utroque humero superhumeralis pulchritudine tegatur*, 21. [He iseȝð him selfe be senne beswapen, *O. E. Hml.* i. 239, 32. *O. H. Ger.* pi-sweifan.]

be-swemman. *Add :* To wash an animal by sending it into the water :—Þeáh swín beswemde weorðen, þonne sleáð hí eft on ðā solu and bewealwiað hí þǽron (*sus lota reversa in volutabro luti*). [Cf. *Ger.* schwemmen.]

be-swepian (-sweþþan). v. sweþian, bi-sweþian *in Dict.*

be-swíc. *l.* be-swic (big-, bí-, bi-) ; *n., and add :*—Biswíc *decipula*, Wrt. Voc. ii. 25, 15 : *supplantatio*, Kent. Gl. 347. Tó biswíce weorðan *offendiculum fieri*, Past. 451, 33. Him Arpellas tó beswíce wearð *Arpellas had played him false*, Ors. 1, 12 ; S. 54, 10. Būtan ǽlcen brǽde oððe beswíce, C. D. ii. 58, 27. Hé hié lǽrde þ hié fram his bigswice cyrdon, Bl. H. 173, 31. Biswíca *nequitiarum, fraudium*, An. Ox. 763 : *strofarum*, 785. Biswigca *deceptionum*, 787. Bigswíca, 2, 15. Biswicum *fomitibus, deceptionibus*, 1135. Faran bigswicæ getācnað, Lch. iii. 208, 12. [*O. H. Ger.* pi-swih *seductio, fraus, dolus.*]

be-swíca (big-, bí-, bi-), an ; *m.* A deceiver :—Biswíca *deceptrix, fallax, seductrix*, Wrt. Voc. ii. 138, 13. Hé sægde þ Petrus bigswíca wǽre, Bl. H. 173, 21. Heó gebær þone biswican, 149, 36. Git sindon bigswicon, 187, 30.

be-swícan. *Add :*—Beswícþ *eludit*, i. *decipit*, Wrt. Voc. ii. 143, 16 : *fellitat*, i. *decepit*, 148, 29. Beswác *lusit*, 53, 61. I. to decoy, ensnare, beguile, (1) of fowling :—Fugelere, hú beswícst þú fugelas? On feala wísan ic beswíce fugelas, Coll. M. 25, 9, 11. (2) of persons :—Beswác *inlexit* (Ald. 182, 32), Wrt. Voc. ii. 94, 49. Eádríc beswác Sigeferð and Morcær, Chr. 1015 ; P. 145, 31. Beswican *pellexerunt*, Wrt. Voc. ii. 84, 14. Ǽr he Beorn beswíce, Chr. 1050 ; P. 170, 8. Se beswícenda *pellax*, Wrt. Voc. ii. 88, 67. II. to betray :—Hió hȳ mid fācne beswác tó deáðe, Ors. 1, 2 ; S. 30, 31. Gezabel beswác Naboð tó his feóre þurh leáse gewitnysse, Hml. Th. i. 488, 5. Þisne æþeling Cnut hæfde forsend on Ungerland tó beswícane, Chr. 1057 ; P. 188, 10. III. to defraud, supplant, injure by treachery :—Rihte ys hē genemned Jacob, nū hē beswác (*supplantavit*) mē, Gen. 27, 36. Būton hí beswican *nisi supplantaverint*, Kent. Gl. 72. Ic nǽnigne man beswícan (*laedere*) ne mihte, Gr. D. 30, 23. Ōsréd wæs beswícen and of ríce ádrǽfed, Chr. 790 ; P. 55, 23. IV. to circumvent, overcome by wiles :—Beswác Hannibal twégen consulas and hié ofslóg *Annibal utrumque consulem insidiis circumventos interfecit*, Ors. 4, 10 ; S. 198, 19. Beswác *refellit* (*astus*), Wrt. Voc. ii. 94, 75. Beswícan *circumvenire*, 24, 68. þ hié mōston ðára feónda searo beswícan and ofercuman, Bl. H. 201, 29. Hé wearð swíþor beswicen for Alexandres searewe þonne for his gefeohte *non minus arte Alexandri superata quam virtute Macedonum*, Ors. 3, 9 ; S. 124, 19. Ðā þā seó cwēn þis gehȳrde, hyre hláford and sunu þus beswikene, Chr. 1093 ; P. 228, 13. V. to seduce, mislead :—Hí unwǽre men beswícaþ and ádweliaþ, Bl. H. 61, 24. Þæt eów nǽfre se deófol beswícan mōte, Wlfst. 135, 9. Wǽron mid gítsunge beswícene nā þ ān his frínd ac eác swilce his frínd, Ap. Th. 7, 12. VI. to fail a person, leave in the lurch :—Se mennesca fultum him beswác, Guth. 76, 18. Hé cweð þet hē gesíclod wǽre, and swā þ folc beswác, þ hē lǽdan sceolde, Chr. 1003 ; P. 135, 14. Wolde se ealdorman beswícon þone æþeling, 1015 ; P. 146, 14. Cnut gewende him út, and wearð þet earme folc þus beswícan þurh hine, 1014 ; P. 145, 22. [v. *N. E. D.* be-swike. *O. Sax. O. L. Ger.* bi-swíkan : *O. H. Ger.* pi-swíhhan *decipere, illaqueare, illicere, circumvenire, seducere.*]

be-swícend, es ; *m. A deceiver, impostor* :—Eálá þū sǽ, unscæððigra beswícend, Ap. Th. 11, 10. Bisuícend (-suuícend, -suiccend) *impostorem*, Txts. 70, 545. Biswícend, Wrt. Voc. ii. 45, 54.

be-swícende. *Dele, and see* be-swícan, I : be-swícian. *l.* -swician.

be-swícenness, e ; *f.* I. deception :—Oncierde þ scip on wônne síðfæt þurh deófles beswícennesse, Shrn. 60, 8. II. surrender ; cf. swícan, III :—Eal werod tó þǽre beswícenesse fóron *cuncta acies ad deditionem transil*, Prud. 45 a.

beswíc-fealle, an ; *f. A trap* :—Biswícfalle *decipula*, Wrt. Voc. ii. 105, 83.

be-swícol ; *adj. Deceitful* :—Se feónd ðæt mód ðurh ðā bisuiculan (-swicolan, v. l.) ōlicunga forlǽreð, Past. 239, 16. v. bi-swicol *in Dict.*

be-swícung, e ; *f. Deception* :—Lotwrænc, beswícung *deceptio*, i. *fraus*, Wrt. Voc. ii. 138, 14. Beswícung *deceptio, seductio*, 141, 32.

be-swilian (-swillan) ; *pp.* ed To beswill, cover with liquid :—Hit wæs mid wǽtan bestēmed, beswyled mid swātes gange, Kr. 23. v. swilian.

be-swincan. *Add :* I. to labour for :—Laboratores synd þā þe úrne bigleofan beswincað, Hml. S. 25, 815. Nim þín gold, þe lǽs þe hit þe losige þ þú lange beswunce, 12, 219. II. to labour at, perform with labour :—Beswanc *desudat*, An. Ox. 8, 257. Gedafenað esnum þām orpedan, þonne hē gód weorc ongynð, þ hē þ geornlíce beswynce, Angl. viii. 324, 18. II a. to till land :—Hé seów hwǽte on beswuncenum lande, Hml. Th. ii. 144, 10. [v. *N. E. D.* be-swink.]

be-swingan. *Add :*—Hé beswincgeð mid untrumnyssum his gecorennan, Hml. Th. i. 470, 25. Hí beswingað mē, 152, 9. Saulus beswang þā crístenan, 392, 1. Gif mon cierliscne mon unsynnige beswinge, Ll. Th. i. 84, 3. Mid gierde mon bið beswungen, and mid stæfe hē bið áwreðed, Past. 125, 25. Wǽre þū tó-dæg beswuncgen?, Coll. M. 34, 7, 15. [v. *N. E. D.* be-swinge.]

be-swylian. v. be-swilian.

be-sylcan ; *p.* ed To make languid, exhaust :—Hungre geþreátod, clommum beclungen, sārum besylced, El. 697. Cf. be-solcen.

be-sylian. *Substitute :*—Hé on synnum hine sylfne besyleð, Wlfst. 78, 16 *note*. Ic mē sylfe on þām adale forligeres besylede, Hml. S. 236, 343. Hér lið se ealdorman (*Holofernes*) mid his blóde besyled, Hml. A. 113, 369. Hū oft his sweord wǽre besyled on unscyldigum blóde *quoties iniquus additur saevo gladius veneno*, Bt. 16, 4 ; F. 58, 18. [Hie bisulieð hem on þe fule floddri of drunkennesse, *O. E. Hml.* ii. 37, 30. *O. H. Ger.* pi-sullen *illinere.*] v. sylian.

be-syrewian, -syrian, -syrwan. v. be-sirwan.

bet. *Dele bracket and* 'DER. abet,' *and add :* I. with wesan, weorþan and dat. of object :—Hire sóna wæs bet, Hml. Th. ii. 150, 6. Hwæt bið eów ðȳ bet?, Bt. 19 ; F. 70, 16. Hwæt bið þǽm gítsere on his móde þe bet (cf. hwelc fremu byþ þām gítsere, Bt. 26, 3 ; F. 94, 12), þeáh hē micel hæbbe, Met. 14, 2. II. with other verbs :—Būton hē hine

gelādige þ hē nā bet ne cūðe, Ll. Th. i. 384, 15. Þæt þū þe bet mæge āredian tō rodorum, Met. 23, 9. Mon ǣlcne ceáp mehte be twiefealdan bet geceápian þonne mon ǣr mehte, Ors. 5, 13 ; S. 248, 2.

**betǣcan.** Add : I. to entrust, commit to a person for safe keeping, guidance, &c. :—Ic betǣce committo (Dei mei potestati), An. Ox. 3395. Hwā betǣhð (credit) eów þ eówer ys ?, Lk. 16, 11. Eádmund betǣhte Glæstingaberi S. Dūnstāne, Chr. 943 ; P. 111, note 19. Se cing betǣhte þā fyrde tō lǣdene Ealfrīce, 992 ; P. 127, 10. Betāhte, Ors. 6, 36 ; S. 294, 31 : 6, 37 ; 5 : 296, 1. Hī betǣhton heora rǣd tō his willan, Hml. Th. i. 12, 7. Him wæs betǣht þe castel tō healdene, Chr. 1087 ; P. 223, 17. Gleáwum ūþwitum betǣhtne gymnosophistis traditum (i. commendatum), An. Ox. 3097. I a. of betrothal :—Betāht desponsata, Mt. L. 1, 18. I b. to entrust work, office, &c. :—Mon ðæt gewin nolde him betǣcan, Ors. 5, 11 ; S. 236, 4. II. in an unfavourable sense, to hand over, deliver :—On þīne handa ic hī betǣce in manus tuas tradidi illos, Jos. 10, 8. God betǣhte hig Chusan cyninge Dominus tradidit eos in manus Chusan regis, Jud. 3, 8. Būtan him man betǣhte Judan, Hml. S. 25, 614. Betǣhte grǣdigum ceaflum, An. Ox. 1479. Betǣhte (torquendas) traduntur, 4643. III. to put in a place for storage :—Āgifen ā þā ealdan and tō hrægelhūse beteán vetera vestimenta semper reddant reponenda in vestiario, R. Ben. 91, 2, 7. IV. to hand over, pay, give, (1) of concrete objects :—Ūs gebyreð þæt wē ǣlces þinges ūre teóðunge Gode betǣcan, Wlfst. 102, 20 : 208, 1. Lǣde hē heorðpenig tō Rōme and þærtóeácan .xxx. penega, and bringe þonon swutelunge þ hē þær swā micel betǣht hæbbe, Ll. Th. i. 264, 10. (2) to give a pledge :—Geþence hē word and wedd þe hē Gode betǣhte, Ll. Th. i. 306, 5. V. to assign, destine, (1) an office, function, &c. to a person :—Sȳ hē āna wunigende on betǣhtre note (tō weorce tō betǣhtum, R. Ben. I. 57, 3) solus sit ad opus sibi injunctum persistens, R. Ben. 49, 18. (2) a person (thing) to an office, &c. :—Ǣnig þæra þinga þe tō lācum betǣht bið, Wlfst. 157, 17. Bigencgum betǣhtne ceremoniis deputatum, An. Ox. 2225. Laboratores sind yrðlingas tō þām ānum betǣhte, þe hig ūs bigleofan tiliað, Ælfc. T. Grn. 20, 20, 22. Þeówdōme betǣhte servitio addictos, Bd. 4, 26 ; Sch. 507, 11. VI. to dedicate, devote to the gods :—Hē genam bollan mid bealuwe āfylled, and deóflum betǣhte ðone drenc, Hml. S. 14, 69. VII. intrans. To give one's self up to, yield to :—Basilius mēnde þ unriht swā þ se cāsere æt nēxtan betǣhte tō his dōme, Hml. S. 3, 323. VIII. to direct (?) :—Cildgeongum mannum eal gefērrǣden unþeáwas stȳre oð þæt fífteóþe gēr hyra ylde. . . Gif hwylc þara þurh gedyrstignesse on māran ylde betǣcþ and þreále gebȳt būtan þæs abbodes hǣse (if any one of the brethren from presumption directs and imposes punishment in the case of those of greater age than fifteen without the abbot's order. The Latin is : in fortiori aetate qui praesumpserit aliquatenus sine precepto abbatis), R. Ben. 130, 4. [v. N. E. D. be-teach.]

**bētan.** Add : I. to make good, put right, (1) to mend, repair, restore :—Hī bēttan heora scipa, Chr. 1009 ; P. 140, 4. Wyrcan wē brycge and þā bētan (cf. brycg-bōt), Wlfst. 239, 9. Uton þetan ūre cyrcean, 303, 5. (1 a) of a fire or light (v. beet in D. D.), to attend to a fire, lamp :—Hē þā leóhtfatu gȳmeleáslīcor bētte, Gr. D. 237, 1. Nā bēte nān man þ fȳr nā læncg þonne man þa hālgunge onginne, Ll. Th. i. 226, 25. Hēt bewindan heora fēt mid flexe, and þā innan bētan, Hml. S. 23, 308. Hē ārás tō bētanne þā leóht (ad melioranda luminaria), Gr. D. 227, 4. (2) in a medical sense, to do good, cure :—Scearpa þā stōwe, þonne bētst þū ðā, Lch. ii. 82, 13. Wel þæt bēt, 28, 17. Þā hōman hyt bēteþ, 36, 11. (3) to correct, emend an error, mistake :—Ic bēte sume leáse bōc corrigo, Ælfc. Gr. Z. 173, 10. Ðū boetas restitues, Mt. p. 3, 11. Wē boetas corrigimus, 2, 2. Trahteras tō boetanne interpretes emendasse, 12. (4) to amend, reform what is wrong, imperfect :—Bēto (castigo) līchoma mīn, Rtl. 6, 7. Hē folces frið bētte, Chr. 959 ; P. 114, 20. Þ wē synna bēton mid fæstenum and mid sōþre hreówe. Þ bið seó sōþe hreów þ mon synna andette and georne bēte, Bl. H. 25, 16–19. Þæt hē wolde ǣlc þæra þinga bētan þe hī ealle āscunedon, Chr. 1014 ; 145, 7. Yldende tō bētanne heora synna and mān differentes emendare scelera, Bd. 5, 12 ; Sch. 626, 15. II. to make good, make amends, reparation for, atone for :—Þā þe yfel dóð and þæt ne bētað qui nequiter agunt, Ps. Th. 36, 9. Ðā menn þe heora synna and unrihtes geswīcaþ, and hié heora scriftum geandettiaþ, and be heora dōme bētaþ, Bl. H. 193, 23. Ǣghwylc man sceal bētan his wōhdǣda be his gyltes andefne, 45, 28. Ælc þæra þe his gyltas wið God bētan (erga Deum emendare) wylle, Ll. Th. ii. 134, 2 : Ps. Th. 50, 5. II a. in the laws, to make 'bot,' pay the fine for a crime :—Gif se hund mā misdǣda gewyrce, and hē (the owner) hine hæbbe, bēte be fullan were, Ll. Th. i. 78, 7. Bēte man þ fullum were, 286, 27 : 110, 17.

**bet-boren ;** adj. Better-born, of higher-birth :—Gif æðelborenran (bett-, v, l.) wīfmen þis gelimpe, Ll. Th. i. 70, 1. v. wel-, betst-boren.

**bēte.** Add :—Bēte beta, Wrt. Voc. ii. 12, 68 : prosopes, i. 68, 31.

**-bētel, bētel.** v. twi-bēte, bītel.

**be-tellan.** Substitute : I. to clear a person of a charge, exculpate, excuse :—Nis nān man swā dyrstig on ðām micclum dōme, þæt hē durre

---

ōðerne betellan, Hml. Th. ii. 570, 35. I a. generally reflexive, (1) absolute :—Būton hē þider fērde and hine betealde, Chr. 1094 ; P. 228, 36. Gewende hē tō Rōme, þæt hē hine betealde, gif hē mihte. þā betealde hē hine swīðe geáplīce, Hml. Th. i. 80, 9. Hī hī sylfe earhlīce betealdon, Hml. S. 23, 308. Se Hǣlend nolde hine betellan, ðeáh ðe hē unscyldig wǣre, Hml. Th. ii. 250, 11 : 420, 1. (2) to clear one's self from (æt), in the matter of (be) a charge, excuse one's self to (wið) a person :—Godwine betealde hine wið Eádward be eallum ðām ðingan ðe him wæs on geled, Chr. 1053 ; P. 183, 28. Þ hē mōste hine betellan æt ǣlc þæra þinga þe him man on lēde, 1048 ; P. 175, 2. Þ hē mage wið Crist hine betellan, Hml. S. 27, 160. II. to prove one's self innocent, (1) with adj. :—Hē hine betealde unsynnine, Hml. Th. ii. 226, 12. (2) with clause :—Hē betealde hine wið Eádward, þæt hē wæs unscyldig, Chr. 1052 ; P. 183, 7. III. to excuse a fault, plead excuse for :—Hē ne mihte his māndǣda betellan, Hml. S. 9, 145. [N. E. D. be-tell.]

**bētende.** Substitute : bētend, es ; m. One who repairs (? v. bētan, I (1), burh-bōt, ge-bētung) :—Brosnade burgsteal bētend crungon the buildings were in ruins, those who should have repaired them were dead, Ruin. 28.

**be-teón,** I and II (v. teón to draw). Add : I. to cover :—Swilce hī heora fēt mid deádra nȳtena fellum beteón, Hml. Th. ii. 534, 3. Mid pælle betogen, Chr. 1075 ; P. 209, 31. II. to bestow, assign :—Eád-werd geaf Ulfe þ ðrīce, and hit yfele beteáh, Chr. 1049 ; P. 171, 26. Hēr swytelað hū Ælfric wille his āre beteón . . . Ic gean, Cht. Th. 567, 10. [v. N. E. D. be-tee. Goth. bi-tiuhan : O. Fr. bi-tiá : O. H. Ger. pi-ziohan.]

**be-teón,** III (v. teón to accuse). Add : to accuse a person (acc.) of a crime, (1) crime in gen. or dat. (inst.) :—Gif mon cyninges þegu beteó manslihtes . . . Gif man þone man betȳhð þe bið lǣssa maga, Ll. Th. i. 154, 5–7. Sē þe hlóðe betygen (-togen, v. l.) sié, 110, 16 : 112 2 : 140, 16. Betogen forligres, Hml. Th. ii. 490, 27. (2) crime stated in a clause :—Ðonne mon monnan betȳhð þ hē ceáp forstele, Ll. Th. i. 130, 12 : 132, 8. Sum wær wæs betogen þ hē wǣre on stale, Hml. S. 21, 265. [O. H. Ger. pi-zīhan arguere, criminari.] v. be-tīhan in Dict.

**betera.** Add :—Hē conn wel emn bión wið ōðre menn, ond hine nā bettran (betran, v. l.) ne dēð, Past. 113, 23. Ic mē bættran hām ne wēne, Sat. 49. Weorc micle beteran (betran, v. l.), Past. 75, 4. Þ heó beaduweorca beteran wurdun, Chr. 937 ; P. 109, 6. Þām lārum beterena witena, Gr. D. 262, 3. ¶ used substantively, (1) of persons :—His betera læg, By. 276. Hē seóþ his betran, Mōd. 36. Geseóð hī þā betran blǣde scīnan, Cri. 1292. (2) of things :—Ne mōtan gē mīne sāwle grētan, ac gē on betran gebringað, Gū. 349. [Goth. batiza : O. Sax. O. Fr. betera : O. H. Ger. pezziro.]

**beterian.** Add :—Hē ārás beterian þā leóht (ad melioranda luminaria) . . hē beterode þ leóht (refovebat lumen), Gr. D. 227, 4–6. Betriende meliorando, 283, 27. [O. Frs. beteria : O. H. Ger. pezzirōn.] v. betrian in Dict.

**beterung, e ; f.** Improvement :—Hē anbidað ūre betrunge, Hml. Th. i. 350, 19. Hē leofode on mynstre for neóde swiðor þonne for beterunge, 534, 2. For beterunge, 272, 1 : 414, 26. Ūs tō beterunge, 360, 20. Tō ūre beterunge, Hml. A. 8, 211. [O. Frs. beteringe : O. H. Ger. pezzirunga.] v. betrung, bettrung in Dict.

**betest.** Add :—Ðone betestan (betstan, v. l.) tīman, Past. 281, 22. [Goth. batists : O. Sax. betst : O. Frs. best : O. H. Ger. pezzist.]

**beþ, beþan, be-þancen, be-þearf.** v. bæþ, beþian, be-þencan, II, nīd-be-þearf.

**beþearfaþ.** Add : [cf. O. H. Ger. pi-derban prodesse, expedire.] v. be-þearflic.

**be-þearfende ;** adj. (ptcpl.) Needy, indigent :—Beðearfende mon homo indigens, Kent. Gl. 708. v. þearfan.

**be-þearflic ;** adj. Useful, profitable :—Syle mē þæt beþearflice gebed þīnre fulfremednysse, Hml. S. 23 b, 242, note. [O. H. Ger. pi-darblih utilis.]

**be-þearfod (-ed) ;** adj. (ptcpl.) Needy, brought to want :—Gif þū hwæne on neáðþearfe ongitst, and gif þū hwæne on wædle beþearfodne (-þreaf-, MS.) ācnǣwst, Engl. Stud. viii. 474, 50. Cf. þearfian, þearfan, þearfed-nes.

**be-þeccan.** Add :—Ðū bideces tegis, Ps. Srt. 103, 3. Beþeaþ contegit, beþeaht contecta, Wrt. Voc. ii. 135, 7, 8. Beþea[h]t contectæ, 17, 71. Feld mid feó oferbrǣded and beþeaht, Bl. H. 199, 3. Ic sæt innan bearwe mid helme beþeht arboris umbriferae sub tegmine sedi, Dōm. L. 2, 2. Beþæht (efne beðeht, L.) coopertus, Mt. R. 6, 29. Beðeahtum tectis, Wrt. Voc. ii. 88, 13. [Laym. bi-þæht, -þeht ; pp. : O. Frs. bi-thekka : O. L. Ger. be-þekkan (-ōn) : O. H. Ger. pi-decchen.]

**be-þencan.** Add : I. to think about, consider, (1) with acc. :—Sē þe sóð on his heortan beðencð, R. Ben. 3, 19. Beþencað dōmes dæg, Wlfst. 228, 31. Þ þū beþence ðone rǣdels, Ap. Th. 5, 7. Beþænce hē (cogitet) Godes edleán, R. Ben. 92, 12. Beþænce se fæder þone sunu and se sunu þone fæder būtan yrre, Wlfst. 228, 23. Þæt heó beþencen

Drihtnes ǽrendgewrit, 230, 33. Hit is earfoðe eall tó gesecganne þæt sé beðencan sceal ðe scíre healt, Angl. ix. 265, 5. Moniga tó biðencanne gehéht *multa cavenda praecepit*, Mt. p. 19, 15. (1 a) reflexive :—Beþenc þe *animadverte*, An. Ox. 56, 25. Þæt hý hý sylfe georne beþencan ... þæt hé hyne sylfne beþence, Wlfst. 179, 4-11. Eáw sumes fyrstes geann þ gé eów sylfe beþencean, Hml. S. 23, 188. Þæt hí hí beðencan bescoldon, Hml. Th. ii. 424, 15. (2) with clause :—Oð þ hí beðóhton hú hí hine ácwealdon, Hml. S. 15, 59. Beþence hé hine sylfne, and beðence hwæðer hine ne mæge ǽnig man getǽlan, Wlfst. 233, 22. (3) with prep. :—þ hé ǽfre ne beþence ymbe þá hreówsunge *de poenitentia nunquam cogitare*, Ll. Th. ii. 174, 25. II. *to entrust to* (for examples v. Dict.). A curious participial form, which seems related to *beþencan*, occurs with this sense in the following passage :—Seó heordelice gýming tó ðám beran wæs beþancenu *injungebatur urso cura pastoralis*, Gr. D. 206, 15. [*Goth.* bi-þaggkjan : *O.L. Ger.* bi-thenkian : *O. Frs.* bi-thanka, -thensa : *O. H. Ger.* pi-denchen.] v. ǽr-, un-beþóht.

be-þeódan ; *p. de To join, attack* :—þǽm hý mid clǽnum móde hý sylfe beþeóddan and for his lufan manna geþeódrǽdenne forsáwan *cui puris mentibus inheserunt, et propter cujus amorem hominum consortia reliquerunt*, R. Ben. 134, 20.

be-þeówan ; *p.* -þeówde, -þeódde (v. þeówan *to serve*) *To serve* :—Beþeóddan *inserviunt* (*v. l.* to *inheserunt* in passage given under previous word), R. Ben. 134, 20.

be-þerscan *to thrash thoroughly* :—Þurh þé wé beþurscon úre fýnd *in te inimicos nostros ventilabimus*, Ps. Th. 43, 7.

beþian, beþigean. *Take together, and add* : beþþan ; *p.* ede, ode ; *imperat.* beþe, beþa *To warm, foment* :—Beþede *fomentat*, Wrt. Voc. ii. 37, 57. Hí (*two seals*) mid heora blǽde his leoma beðodon, Hml. Th. ii. 138, 13. ¶ generally as a medical term :—Gesæt hé under sunnbeáme and his scencan beðode, Hml. Th. ii. 134, 26. Seóð on wætre. beþe mid þ lim, Lch. ii. 146, 5 : 148, 9 : 154, 17. Mon sceal mid wearmum springum and háte wætre beþian þá stówe .. þá sáran stówa beþe and lǽt reócan on, 202, 20-24. Mon sceal beþan (beþian ?, beþþan ?) þá breóst mid wíne, 232, 19. Is sió tó beðianne mid hátan wætre, 206, 14. Bædþenda smerwunga wyrce of ele and wíne, beþe ðonne, smire mid þý, 182, 16. [*v. N. E. D.* beath.] v. ge-beþian.

beðing. *Add* :—Wiþ lyftádle ... beþing and bæþsealf, Lch. ii. 302, 23. Beþinge *fotu*, Wrt. Voc. ii. 37, 56. Hí on wlacum ele gebeðedon ... hé wæs on ðissere beðunge geléd, Hml. Th. i. 86, 24. Genim wád, wyl on meolce, on buteran is betere, and wyrc beþinge, Lch. ii. 36, 24 : 200, 3. Þá ærgenemnedan beþunga, 210, 6. Hwí ne bidst þú beþunga and plaster lifes lǽcedómes *cur tibi non oras placidae fomenta medelae* ?, Dóm. L. 80. [*v. N. E. D.* beathing.]

be-þirfe. v. un-beþirfe.

be-þráwan *to twist* :—Riscene weocan beþráwene *fila scirpea conlita*, Germ. 391, 16. [*v. N. E. D.* be-throw.]

be-þridian. *Add* :—On ðǽm ǽrestan gewinne Amilcor wearð from Spénum beþridad and ofslagen *Amilcar ab Hispanis in bello occisus est*, Ors. 4, 7 ; S. 182, 31.

be-þurfan. *Add* : I. personal. (1) implying privation :—Beþurfendra *egentium*, Scint. 108, 15. (2) *to need* what will supply insufficiency, defect, what is beneficial :—Nánes þinges máran hé ne beþearf ðonne hé hæfþ, Bt. 31, 1 ; F. 122, 7. Sé þe micel inerfe ágan wile, hé beþearf micles fultumes, se ealda cwide is swíþe sóþ, þte þá micles beþurfon þe micel ágan willaþ, 14, 2 ; F. 44, 10-13. Geleánað hé hit ús, þær wé betst beðurfon *when it best serves our needs*, Wlfst. 41, 2 : 56, 23 : 111, 14. Þá þe dǽdbóte ne beðurfon (sé ðe (ðá ðe, L.) ne biðorfeð tó hreównisse, R.) *qui non indigent poenitentia*, Lk. 15, 7. Gif hé ǽniges fultumes beþorfte, ðonne næfde hé nó self genóg, Bt. 35, 3 ; F. 158, 17. Getímode his wífe wyrs ðonne hé beþorfte *his wife's condition was too bad to allow of his happiness*, Hml. Th. ii. 142, 3. Hí nabbað þá láre þe hí beþorftan, Ll. Th. ii. 328, 37. Gif þú ǽgera beþurfe, Techn. ii. 124, 1. Gif þú taperas (=es ?) beþurfe, 120, 16. Gif hé máran gærses beðyrfe, Ll. Th. i. 434, 17. Lege tó ðám sáre þe man beþurfe *apply it to the wound for which it is needed*, Lch. i. 322, 4. Ðeáh ðú heora nánes ne beþorfte, Bt. 33, 4 ; F. 128, 14. (3) *to need, be obliged, have cause* or *reason to do something* :—Þonne beþurfon hí þ hí óleccan þǽm, Bt. 26, 2 ; F. 92, 28. Hý mishýrdan Gode swýþor þonne hý beþorftan (*ought*), Wlfst. 13, 14. Ne wé ǽlmessan dǽlað swá swá wé beðorftan, 92, 10. II. impersonal :—Ðonne þé salteres beþurfe, Techn. ii. 121, 7. Gyf þé disces beþurfe, 122, 25 : 128, 1. [*O. Sax. O. L. Ger.* bi-thurban : *O. H. Ger.* pi-durban.]

be-þwyr. *Substitute* : be-þweorian, -þwyrian *to deprave* :—Beþwyrad *depravatum*, Wrt. Voc. ii. 26, 3.

be-tíhan. *l.* be-teón : be-tíhtlian. *l.* be-tihtlian : be-tilldon. v. be-tyllan : béting. v. bǽtau, II : bétl. v. bítel.

betryman. *Add* : -trymman :—Hig woldon þæs cynges scipa ábútan betrymman, Chr. 1052 ; P. 180, 20.

betst-boren. *Add* :—Ealle þá betstboren men þe wǽron innan þisan lande, Chr. 1087 ; P. 224, 29.

bétung. v. eft-bétung.

be-tweoh (i, y, u), -tuh. *Add* : A. *with dat.* I. *between*. (1) local, (a) of position within certain limits :—Weall tó settonne betweoh (-tuh, *v. l.*) ðám wítgan and ðǽre byrh, Past. 164, 10. (b) of extent between limits :—Eall hira land betwuh (-tweoh, *v. l.*) dícum and Wúsan, Chr. 905 ; P. 94, 2. Betuh þǽm clife ond ðǽm wætre wǽron swylce twelf míla, Bl. H. 211, 2. Wæs heora lár sáwen and strogden betuh feówer sceátum middangeardes, 133, 33. (2) temporal :—Betweoh (-twyh, *v. l.*) þám þe hine man lácnode *inter medendum*, Bd. 4, 26 ; Sch. 509, 18. (3) of mutual relation :—For ðǽre dǽde ðe hié dóð betwuh him, Past. 399, 27. (4) marking relation of abstract objects :—Micel tósceád is betwuh ðǽre beðóhtan synne and ðǽre ðe mon fǽrlíce ðurhtiéhð, Past. 435, 5. Betweoh (-tuh, *v. l.*) ðǽm twǽm, 118, 2. II. *among* :—Betuih (-twihc, R.) iúh, Mt. L. 20, 26. B. *with acc.* I. *between* :—Sete weall betuh ðé and ðá burh, Past. 165, 8. II. *among*. (1) local (lit. or fig.) :—Betwyh betweoh engla þreátas, Shrn. 50, 16. Betwyh, 118, 2. Betwih (-twyh, *v. l.*) þá óþer gód *inter cetera bona*, Bd. 2, 5 ; Sch. 131, 20. Betweoh þá wiðfeohtend *inter rebelles*, Sch. 135, 11 : 4, 26 ; Sch. 507, 8. Betuh ealle wífcyn and betuh ealle hálie gástas, Bl. H. 143, 18. (2) temporal, *in the course of* :—Swefen betwuh feówer dagas gewyrð, Lch. iii. 190, 1. Betwih þás þing *quo tempore*, Bd. 2, 18 ; Sch. 181, 23 : 5, 13 ; Sch. 636, 4.

betweoh-blinness *intermission* :—Bútan bituihblinnesse *sine intermissione*, Rtl. 12, 5.

betweoh-gangende *separating* :—Betwihgongendes lég *intercidentis flammam*, Ps. Srt. 28, 7.

be-tweohn (-twíhn (<-twíhn), -tweón. I. *prep. Between, among* :—Bituichn (-tuín) ældrum *inter primores*, Txts. 70, 546. Bituihn, 77, 1310. Hé gesibbode þá cyningas betweohn (-twyh, *v. l.*) him *pacatis alterutrum regibus*, Bd. 4, 21 ; Sch. 453, 23. II. *adv.* :—Gyf micel feorrnes sídfates betweohn ligeþ (*interjacet*), Bd. 1, 27 ; Sch. 72, 14.

betweohn-forlǽtness *intermission* :—Bútan bituínforlétnise *sine intermissione*, Rtl. 58, 3.

[be-tweohnum], be-tweónum. *Add* : I. *prep.* (1) *between*, (a) of interposition :—Eódon góde men heom betwénen and sahtloden heom, Chr. 1066 ; P. 199, 7. (b) of mutual relation :—Betwýnan him hí syllan lǽcedóm *invicem sibi dent remedium*, Angl. xiii. 393, 408 : 438, 1045. Under þám griðe þe heom betweónan beón sceolde, Chr. 1004 ; P. 135, 27 : 1016 ; P. 153, 1. Unseht betweónan Godwine and þám cynge, 1052 ; P. 183, 14. Se ríca and se þearfa sind him betwýnan nýdbehéfe (*needful to each other*), Hml. Th. i. 256, 30. (2) *among* :—Bið mycel gewinn betweónan him, Ors. 1, 1 ; S. 20, 18. Betweónan þyssum ðingum, Bd. 2, 18 ; Sch. 181, 23. II. *adv.* :—Man sealde gíslas betweónan, Chr. 1052 ; P. 175, 27. Betwínum *in invicem*, Ps. Srt. 33, 4. v. be-tweoh.

be-tweohs, -tweox. *Add* : A. *with dat.* I. *between*. (1) local :—Segor stód on midwege betweox ðǽm muntum and ðǽm merscum, Past. 399, 13. Betweox (-tux, *v. l.*) him and hiera hiéremonnum, 164, 12. (2) temporal :—Betwix hláfmæssan and middum sumera, Chr. 921 ; P. 101, 5. (3) of mutual relation :—þ hé frið betwux þǽm folcum findan sceolde, Ors. 4, 10 ; S. 202, 11. (4) marking relation of abstract objects :—Micel tódál ys betweohx þǽre ealdan ǽ and þǽre níwan, Ælfc. Gen. Thw. 2, 2. II. *among*. (1) local (lit. or fig.) :—Betweox (-twiux, *v. l.*) ðám gingestum monnum, Past. 300, 13. Betwix eallum hira yflum, 423, 6. Betux wífa gebyrdum, Bl. H. 167, 18. Betwyx óðrum þingum nis ná tó forgytane þ góde frið, Chr. 1086 ; P. 220, 12. Hé arn betwux þám eórode middan, Hml. S. 25, 583. (2) temporal, *in the course of* a period, *during* events :—Betwux hancréde, Hml. Th. ii. 344, 30. Betwyx þissum *meanwhile*, Chr. 1087 ; P. 224, 13. B. *with acc.* I. *between*. (1) local :—Sete weall betweox ðé and ðá burh, Past. 164, 9. (2) temporal :—Betwux hancréd and dagunge, Chr. 795 ; P. 57, 16. II. *among* :—Hé betweox þá óðre þegnas férde, Guth. 70, 11. Hí sóhton betwux sciplíþende and on mynstre, Hml. S. 33, 188. betweohs-fǽc *an interval* :—Betwyxfǽce *intervallo*, An. Ox. 3861.

be-tweohsn, -tweoxn, *prep.* I. *with dat.* (1) *among* :—Ne sié hit ná suá betweoxn eów ... ond suá hwelc suá wille betweoxn eów mǽst beón, Past. 121, 4-6. Betweohxn (-tweoxn, *v.l.*) eów ... betweohxn (-twuxn, *v.l.*) hǽdnum, 210, 7-8. Betwuxn óðrum sprǽcum, 461, 10. (2) of mutual relation :—Ne untreówsige gé nó eów betweoxn *nolite fraudare invicem*, Past. 99, 15. II. *with acc. Among* :—Ðæt hé mæg gáu betwuxn unðeáwas *ut inter passiones medias transeat*, Past. 453, 16.

be-tyllan ; *p. de To lure, decoy* :—Þá gelǽdde hé here in Peohtas, þá gelíccetton hí fleám for him, and hine betyldon (-tilldon, -telldon *v. ll.*) on nearo fæsten *cum exercitum ad uastandam Pictorum prouinciam duxisset, introductus est, simulantibus fugam hostibus, in angustias*, Bd. 4, 26 ; Sch. 506, 3. v. tyllan *in Dict.*

be-týnan. *Add* :—Betíened *conclusus*, Wrt. Voc. ii. 24, 38. I. *to enclose, surround* with a fence :—þú eorþan on þínre fýst betýndest, Nar. 47, 3. Bebbanburh wæs ǽrost mid hegge betíned and þǽræfter

mid wealle, Chr. 547; P. 17, 21. Heortan betýnede mid lytelicum lādungum, Past. 245, 21. II. where movement to or by an object is hindered, *to shut* in, out, *shut up* :—Hié hine betýndon on þām carcerne, Bl. H. 243, 3. Wæs Euan wōp ūte betýned (*excluded*), 7, 14. Þā ōman beóð inne betýnde, Lch. ii. 174, 23. II a. with the idea of concealment :—Betínþ *occultat, abscondit*, Wrt. Voc. ii. 138, 48. III. *to close, shut*, (a) a place :—Hé betýnde his eágan, Bl. H. 231, 12. Betýned wæs se hefon *clusum est coelum*, Lk. L. R. 4, 25. Beóþ his eágan betýnede, Bl. H. 153, 19. (b) a passage, door, &c. :—(Protan) betýnde (*gurguliones*) *oppilauit*, Wrt. Voc. ii. 65, 18 (cf. 82, 53). Hī betýndon þære ceastre gatu, Bl. H. 241, 11. Þā duru betýnan, 219, 16. Ðā duro wērun bitýnde, Jn. R. 20, 19. Betýndan wega gelætan *competa clausa*, Wrt. Voc. ii. 132, 52. IV. *to close, end* :—Hé fægere ende his līf betýnde and geendade *pulchro uitam suam fine conclusit*, Bd. 4, 24; Sch. 488, 8. Hé þā ýtemestan word on his herenesse betýnde, Sch. 491, 19. [*O. H. Ger.* pi-zūnen *sepire*.]

**be-týnedness.** v. in-betýnedness.

**be-týning,** e; *f. A conclusion* :—Betýningum *conclusionibus*, An. Ox. 3210.

**be-tyrnan;** *p.* de. I. *to turn round* :—On ānre wendinge, ðā hwīle ðe hé (*the firmament*) æne betyrnð, gæð forð feówor and twēntig tīda, Hex. 8, 13. Embhwerfte betyrndum *orbis volutus*, Hy. S. 96, 5. II. *to bend* the knee, *prostrate one's self* :—Betyrne þām sylfan fōtum *voluat se ipsius abbatis pedibus*, R. Ben. I. 78, 14. Betyrnan hý wið ealra geférena cneówa swā biddende þæt heom fore gebeden sý *provolutis genibus* (betyrndum cneówum, R. Ben. I. 66, 13) *ab omnibus postulent pro se orari*, R. Ben. 59, 20.

**be-tytene,** C. D. B. iii. 561, 29. v. be-gitan.

**be-ufan.** *Add* :—Eall ðæt him beufan bið, Sal. K. p. 178, 9. Ðā þing þe wē beufan writon, Lch. ii. 228, 24. v. hēr-bufan in *Dict.*

**be-wacian;** *p.* ode *To bewake* (v. N. E. D.), *to keep watch over* :—Gē him weardas settað þe hī bewaciað wið þeófas, Hml. S. 14, 22. Weardmenn his līc bewacedon, Hml. A. 78, 154. Bewacige *excubet*, Germ. 388, 80.

**be-waden.** *Substitute* : be-wadan *to reach, come upon, surprise?* :—Mīn hord warað hiþende feónd . . . bewaden (*when surprised?*) fēred, stepped on stíð bord, Rä. 88, 24. Cf. be-faran, -fēran, -rīdan.

**be-wǣfan.** *Add* :—Of þām Maria sumne hire līchaman bewǣfde, Hml. S. 23 b, 793. Bewǣfan *obvolvere*, Wrt. Voc. ii. 65, 41. Þ treów biþ ūton gescyrped and bewǣfed mid þære rinde, Bt. 34, 10; F. 150, 7. Þām scyccelse þe hē mid bewǣfed wæs, Hml. S. 23 b, 218. [*Laym.* bi-wæive, -weave, wefe: *R. Glouc.* bi-weve.]

**be-wǣgan.** *Add* : *to deceive* :—Bewǣg[de] *fefellisset*, An. Ox. 3660. Biwǣgan *fallere*, Ps. Srt. ii. p. 230, 39.

**be-wǣpnian.** *Add* :—Ðū bewǣpnast *exarmaueris*, An. Ox. 34, 6. Hēt se cāsere hine ungyrdan and bewǣpnian, Hml. S. 30, 409.

**be-wǣrlan.** I. *to pass by.* v. bi-wǣrlan in *Dict.* II. *to avoid, be free from* :—Bewǣrle ēlc unclǣnnisse *careat omni inmundicia*, Rtl. 121, 7, 36.

**be-warenian,** -warnian. *Substitute* : I. *to guard* one's self against, *keep* one's self from, *avoid*, (a) with prep. (*wiþ*) :—Gif hē hine ne bewarenað wið unþeáwas *miseras fugare querelas non posse*, Mæt. 16, 23. Ðā ðe hié wið scylda bewareniað *qui se a pravis custodiunt*, Past. 437, 6. Sýn hý eaþmōde, bewarnian hý wiþ mōdignesse, R. Ben. 140, 8. (b) with negative clause :—Hī bewarniaþ hī, þ hi hira mōd ne besmītaþ *mentem inquinare devitant*, Gr. D. 209, 8. Þ hī hī sylfe bewarnian, þ hī ne þurfan cuman *ne ipsi veniant*, 310, 21. II. *to ward off* from one's self :—Þā ōþre geseóð þi yfel, tō þon þ hī heom bewarnian þā, and þās beóð þe mā wītnode þe hī noldon heom bewarnian þā hellewītu *ut isti videant mala quae caveant, illi vero eo amplius puniantur, quod inferni supplicia vitare noluerunt*, Gr. D. 321, 7. II a. *to guard against* :—Sý bewarnod, þæt hit nā ne gesæle *caveatur ne proveniat*, R. Ben. 36, 5. III. *to watch, guard* :—Þū bewarnast *observaberis*, Ps. Spl. 129, 3. v. next word.

**be-warian.** *Substitute* : I. *to guard* one's self against (*wiþ*) :—Mon hine bewarige wið ðā leohtmōdness *mentis levitas caveatur*, Past. 308, 5. II. *to ward off* from :—Þū inc bām twām meaht wīte bewarigan, Gen. 563. III. *to guard, protect* :—He bewarað (*but the Latin word thus glossed is* cernit) þā burh, Hpt. 31, 15, 405. Bewarede *protexit*, Hpt. Gl. 489, 67 : 500, 73. Eádweard eðel bewarede, Chr. 1065; P. 195, 14. Heorda bewarian and bewerian, Ll. Th. i. 374, 29; Wlfst. 191, 15. [*O. Frs.* bi-waria : *O. H. Ger.* pi-warōn *servare, providere.*] v. preceding word.

**be-wāwan.** v. bi-wāwan in *Dict.* : be-wealwian. *Add* : v. N. E. D. be-wallow.

**be-weardian.** *Add* :—Englas beweardiað manna gehwylcne, Wlfst. 144, 18.

**be-weaxan.** *Add* : I. *to grow round, surround* with wood, &c. :—Wæs se mere eall mid wudu beweaxen *stagnum erat circumdatum habundanti silva*, Nar. 12, 8. II. *to overgrow, cover* with a growth :—Sumne dæl þæs meóses þe seó rōd mid beweaxen wæs, Hml. S. 26, 37.

**be-weddendlic;** *adj. Relating to espousals* :—Beweddendlice *sponsalia*, An. Ox. 1122.

**be-weddian.** *Add* : I. *to betroth* :—Ic beweddode (*desponsavi*) eów ānum were, þ gē ān clæne mæden gearcion Crīste, Hml. A. 30, 139 : Hml. Th. ii. 54, 14. Beweddede *subarravit* (*me annulo*), An. Ox. 4293 : *subarraret* (*nuptiali dote*), 4553. Ic wolde Crīste þē beweddian, Hml. S. 3, 394. Maria wæs Iōsēpe beweddod (biwoedded, L. *desponsata*), Mt. 1, 18. Beweddod *subarratam*, An. Ox. 3618. Bewedda̸d *arratam*, Wrt. Voc. ii. 9, 31. Heó wæs ǣr beweddad sumum æþelum were, Shrn. 86, 14. Gif bewerddodu fǣmne hié forlicgge, Ll. Th. i. 72, 10. Þ nān man nān mā wīfa næbbe būton .i., and seó beó mid rihte beweddod and forgifen, ii. 300, 13. Gif hió ōðrum mæn in sceát bewyddod sī, i. 24, 5. Ácenned of beweddodan mædene, Hml. Th. i. 196, 7. I a. used of a married woman :—Beweddod *nupta*, Wrt. Voc. i. 52, 34. Hē nā mā wīfa þonne ān hæbbe, and þ beó his beweddode wif, Ll. Th. i. 364, 28. II. *to assure by pledge, pledge, plight* :—Seó weddung wæs beweddod *the betrothal was made*, Nic. 3, 31. Beweddedum wǣrum *pactis sponsalibus*, An. Ox. 1398. III. *to give security* for, (1) with gen. :—Se biscop beweddade Eádwulfe þæs ādæs, Cht. Th. 71, 3. Siþþan hē weres beweddod hæbbe, Ll. Th. i. 174, 16: 250, 18. (2) with clause :—Ðā bewedddode mē Eádnōð and Ælfstān, þæt hió ōðer þāra dydon, Cht. Th. 167, 20. [*O. Frs.* bi-weddia.] v. un-beweddod.

**be-welde.** v. be-willan *to roll about.*

**be-wendan.** *Add* : *To turn about, round.* (1) of simple movement :—Se drý geband Philetum swā þæt hē bewendan ne mihte, Hml. Th. ii. 414, 18. Hine bewendan fram wīte tō wīte, Hml. S. 37, 180. (2) *to turn the face* to or from an object, (a) reflexive :—Þā bewende Nero hine tō Paulum, Hml. Th. i. 378, 8. (b) *intrans.* :—Þ Mōd wiþ his bewende, Bt. 3, 1; F. 4, 29. (3) denoting purpose, *to turn one's attention* :—Iudas hine bewende and wan wið ðā hǣðenan, Hml. S. 25, 385. [v. N. E. D. be-wend. *O. Sax. O. L. Ger.* bi-wendian : *O. H. Ger.* pi-wenten : *Goth.* bi-wandjan *to pass by, avoid.*]

**be-weorpan.** *Add* :—Oð þæt ic hit mid meoxe beweorpe, Hml. Th. ii. 408, 6. Bewurpan *conjiciunt*, Wrt. Voc. ii. 24, 21. Beón bēgen oxan beworpene mid wuda wiðneoðan . . . Ðā nāmon hī þone dunnan oxan, bewurpon mid wudu tō offrunga, Hml. S. 18, 106–113. Þæt folc mid rāpum þā anlicnesse bewurpon, Hml. Th. i. 464, 19. Þæt hig mid wyrtgemangum hine bewurpon *ut aromatibus condirent eum*, Gen. 50, 2. Hē hēt settan hī on sandpytte and bewurpan mid eorþan and mid weorcstānum, Hml. S. 35, 326. [*O. Sax.* bi-werpan : *O. H. Ger.* pi-werfan *obruere.*]

**be-weorþian;** *pp.* od *To dignify, grace, adorn* :—Helme beweorðod, Dōm. L. 118.

**be-wēpan.** *Add* :—Swā man bewēpð deádne, Hml. A. 77, 124. Rachel bewēop hire cildra, Hml. Th. i. 84, 26. Hē bewēop ungemetgodra manna līf, 604, 27. Þæt se Hǣlend bewēope ðære ceastre tōworpennysse, 402, 6. Synna bewēpan, ii. 602, 22. ¶ bewōpen *disfigured by weeping, woe-begone* (cf. That he you nat biwopen thus ne finde, Ch. T. C. iv. 916) :—Þā iermingas ūt of þǣm holan crupon, swā bewōpene swelce hié of ōþerre worolde cōme, Ors. 2, 8; S. 92, 30. [v. N. E. D. be-weep *and* be-wept. *O. Sax.* bi-wōpian : *O. Frs.* bi-wēpa.]

**be-wēpendlic;** *adj. Lamentable, deplorable* :—Bewēpendlic *atratus, lugubris*, Hpt. 31, 14, 370 : 17, 463. Bewēpendlic gewēd *deflenda dementia*, An. Ox. 40, 1. Hū earm and hū bewēpendlic is þæra manna līf, þe ofer þ riht onginnað, Hml. A. 146, 66.

**be-werian.** *Add* : I. with idea of hindering, restraint :—Bewerede *coercuit*, Wrt. Voc. ii. 23, 60. (1) *to keep* something from a person, *prohibit, forbid*, (a) with acc. :—Bewerede *arcebat* (*introitum*), Wrt. Voc. ii. 81, 22. Mē Godes wracu þā duru bewerede, Hml. S. 23 b, 417. Se Hālga Gāst hié ǣghwylc gōd lǣrde, and him ǣghwylc yfel bewerede, Bl. H. 131, 30. Þeáh þe se bysceop him þ swīðe bewerede *episcopo multum prohibente*, Bd. 5, 19; Sch. 661, 17. Him þæt swīðe hys frýnd beweredon, 4, 26; Sch. 505, 18. (b) with clause :—Ne wē eów bewerigeað (*prohibemus*) þæt gē ealle . . . tō ǣfæstnesse gecyrre, Bd. 1, 25; Sch. 55, 13. Wundurlic wīse bewerede (*prohibuit*) þ nōhwæþer þyssa beón sceolde, 4, 11; Sch. 408, 12. (c) with dat. infin. :—Seó ǣ monig þing bewerede tō etanne *multa lex manducare prohibeat*, Bd. 1, 27. (2) *to restrain* a person :—Ne bewere ne compesaris, Ps. Srt. 82, 2. Ic mē ne mihte bewerigean (*cohibere*), Bd. 5, 6; Sch. 576, 9. (2 a) *to restrain* from, (1) with prep. :—Bewere (*prohibe*) tungan ðīne fram yfele, Ps. Spl. 33, 13. Hē wæs bewered fram þære biscopþegnunge *ab administrando episcopatu prohibito*, Bd. 4, 5; Sch. 380, 16. (2) with gen. :—Mē þ godcunde mægen þæs ganges bewerede, Hml. S. 23 b, 408. II. with idea of defence, protection, (1) *to protect, defend* :—Becumað wulfas tō ðīnre eówode, and hwā bewerað hī?, Hml. Th. ii. 516, 22. Bewerede *protexit, custodivit*, An. Ox. 3557. Eádweard eðel bewerode, Chr. 1065; P. 194, 12 : Hml. S. 25, 744. Þā hī hié bewerian ne mehton, Ors. 4, 13; S. 212, 5. Þā heorda bewerian, gif hwilc þeódscaða scaðian onginneð, Wlfst. 191, 8. Nān brōðor ne gedyrstlǣce þæt hē ōþerne mid wordum bewerige (*defendere*), R. Ben.

129, 5. His āgenne rǣd tô bewerigenne, 15, 13. (1 a) *to protect against* (*wið* (dat. acc.), *ongeán*):—Þæt hē bewerede Corsicam wið Rômānum *pro Corsis defensandis*, Ors. 4, 6 ; S. 172, 14. Hē his fyrde bewerode wið fŷnd, Hml. S. 25, 281 : Ælfc. T. Gm. 7, 3. Beweriað wydewan wið ēhterum, Hml. Th. ii. 322, 8. Hié selfe wið ðeówdôm bewerian, Ors. 3, 1 ; S. 98, 4. Widewan bewerian wið hunger, Hml. S. 25, 755. Ongeán yfele wŷfmen þē bewerian, Lch. iii. 214, 10. Treów bewerod mid rinde wiþ þone winter, Bt. 34, 10 ; F. 150, 7. (2) *to ward off, keep* evil from a person :—Bewered wǣre *arceretur* (*crudelitas*), Wrt. Voc. ii. 86, 62. [O. Sax. O. L. Ger. bi-werian ; O. Frs. bi-wera : O. H. Ger. pi-wer(i)en.]

be-werigend, -wergend *a protector.* Add:—Hē sceal beón bewergend wydewena, O. E. Hml. i. 302, 34. Paulus wæs bewerigend þǣre ealdan ǣ, Hml. Th. i. 388, 32 : Hml. S. 7, 127. Ðæt gē sŷn beweriendras Crîstes landâre, C. D. iii. 350, 27.

be-werung. *Substitute* : *Defence, protection* :—Freónd getreówe bewerung (*protectio*) strang, Scint. 194, 11 : *munitio*, 35, 20. For mynstres bewerunge (*defensione*), Angl. xiii. 373, 114. Under rihtum dôme and bewerunge *sub jurisdictione atque tuitione*, C. D. B. i. 155, 20. Wǣpnu on swæfnum beran bewerunge hit getâcnað, Lch. iii. 198, 11 : 206, 4.

be-westan ; *prep.* with *dat.* or *adv.* *To the west of* :—Bewestan Achaie is Dalmatia . . . ; besûþan Istria is se Wendelsǣ, and bewestan þā beorgas þe man hǣt Alpis ... bewestan him Profentsǣ, Ors. 1, 1 ; S. 22, 12, 15, 30. Beeástan him is se Risca sǣ, and bewestan Addriaticum, S. 28, 1, 10. [v. N. E. D. be-west.]

be-westan-norþan, -westan-sûþan. v. westan-norþan, -sûþan *in Dict.*

be-willan ; *p.* de *To boil away* :—Dô on wylisc ealu, bewyl oþ þriddan dǣl, Lch. ii. 120, 15. Genim betonican, wyl in wætere, bewyll þriddan dǣl, iii. 43, 22. Wylle oþ sié twǣde bewylled þæs wôses, ii. 38, 11. Wylle on cetele oþ þ se wǣ:a sié twǣde on bewylled, 332, 17 : 266, 31. Gewyrce gemilscade drincan, þ is micel dǣl bewylledes wæteres on huniges gôdum dǣle, 202, 27.

be-willan, -wellan ; *p.* de *To roll about, mix* with ingredients :—Bewelledne (-weledne, *v. l.*) hlâf and mid ǣttre gemengedne *infectum veneno panem*, Gr. D. 118, 6. Confectos, i. compositos, mixtos *vel* bewelde, Wrt. Voc. ii. 133, 22. [Cf. O. Frs. bi-willa *to pollute* : O. L. Ger. be-uuillid *inficit* ; beuuollan *pollutus* ; O. H. Ger. wellan *volvere* ; pi-wellan *polluere*.] v. next word.

be-wilw(i)an. I. *to roll down* :—Þænne hē byþ þurh fyllas bewylwud *cum fuerit per precipitia deuolutus*, Scint. 107, 14. II. *to roll about, mix.* v. preceding word :—Geǣtredum, bewyledum, befŷledum *infectis*, Wrt. Voc. ii. 43, 62.

be-wimman. Dele.

be-windan. Add: I. *to wrap* an object in or with something :—Heó bewand þā hand on godwebbe, Shrn. 59, 35. Hē hine biwand in lîne *eum involvit sindone*, Mk. R. 15, 46. Biuundun (*ligauerunt*) mid hrægium, Jn. L. 19, 40. Bewindan (*involvant*) hî þæs cildes hand on weofodsceáte, R. Ben. 102, 14. Hēt bewindan heora handa mid flexe, Hml. S. 4, 392. Hē forðférde, and his lîc bewunden læg, Hml. Th. ii. 24, 22. þē God hæfde wǣre bewunden *God had kept thee on every side*, An. 535. Gē gemētað ān cild hrægium bewunden (*pannis involutum*), Lk. 2, 12. II. *to serve as covering, girdle,* &c. *to* an object, *encircle, surround* :—Hē ceastre weall geseah Sennera feld sîdne bewindan, Dan. 602. [v. N. E. D. be-wind. Goth. bi-windan : O. Sax. bi-windan : O. H. Ger. pi-wintan.]

be-witan. Add: I. in a general sense, *to take charge of, watch over* :—Wēn is þ hē wille bewitan ā his menn ge on lîfe ge on deáðe, Hml. S. 17, 187. II. *of official or professional action, to have charge* or *direction of,* (1) *persons* :—Se mágister þe þā cild bewât *the schoolmaster*, Tech. ii. 118, 12. þā hyndenmenn and þā þe teóðunge bewitan, Ll. Th. i. 236, 4. Ic wæs dæges and nihtes mid hyre and hî bewiste, and heó hlyste mînre lâre, Wlfst. 140, 18. Se yldesta bewiste þā nigene tô ǣlcum gelǣste, Ll. Th. i. 230, 22. þæt werod þe hē (*Lucifer*) bewiste, Hml. Th. i. 10, 17. Oðer bewiste his byrlas, ōðer his bæcestran *alter pincernis praeerat, alter pistoribus*, Gen. 40, 2. þâra geréfena þe þā men bewiston æt þām temple, Angl. xi. 9, 24. Hundredes ealdras þe ðā burhware bewiston, Hml. Th. ii. 418, 34. Se lǣce tilað ðæs gewundedan ðe hē bewitan sceal (*cui medicamentum adhibet*), Past. 457, 16. Se cyng sende Ælfun mid þǣm æþelingum, þ hē hî bewitan sceolde, Chr. 1013 ; P. 144, 15. Hē hié (*his sons*) betǣhte twǣm ealdormonnum tô bewitanne *singulis potissimis infantum cura commissa erat*, Ors. 6, 37 ; S. 296, 2. (2) *places, institutions,* &c. :—Se ealdor þe þæt mynster bewât *qui monasterio praeest*, Cht. Th. 333, 37. Hǣðen mundbora þe þā burh bewiste, Hml. S. 22, 99 : 3, 61. þā gôde mæn þe þis land bewiston, Chr. 1091 ; P. 226, 27. (3) *property* :—þā (*the senators*) wǣron simbel binnan Rômebyrg wuniende, tô þon þ hié bewiston eal þ licgende feoh, Ors. 2, 4 ; S. 72, 4. Hē betǣhte hit Eardulfe tô bewitenne *commisit manerium Eardulfo ad custodiendum*, Cht. Th. 271, 25. Ic an ðæs landes Æffan tô bewitanne, 496, 14,

(4) *implements, affairs, offices,* &c. :—Ælfrîc þā sôcne mînre môder tô handa bewiste, C. D. iv. 222, 20. Hē ealle his gemôt bewiste, Chr. 1099 ; P. 235, 1. þegn þe his ælmyssan bewiste *his almoner*, Hml. S. 26, 91. Se munuc þe þæs mynstres geat bewiste, 23 b, 66. Hē ungeorne bewiste hwæt hē dyde *he managed his business carelessly*, Bl. H. 183, 23. Hî gesettan him x consulas, tô þon þ hié hiera ǣ bewisten (*constituendarum legum gratia*), Ors. 2, 6 ; S. 88, 19. Swilce þū micel bewytan wille *as if you wish to see after much business* (?), Tech. ii. 121, 8. Ðā ðing tô bewitanne ðe tô scipene belimpað, Angl. ix. 260, 4. Mynstres ǣhta on tôlum oþþe on reáfum sŷn betǣhte tô bewitenne þām gebrôþrum, R. Ben. 56, 4.

be-witian. Add: I. *to watch, observe* :—Sē sceal þǣre sunnan sîð behealdan, . . . georne bewitigan, hwonne up cyme ǣðelost tungla, Ph. 92. II. *to have charge* or *direction of, see about* or *after,* (1) *living things* :—Be ðām ðe beón bewitað *concerning the beekeeper*, Ll. Th. i. 434, 35. (2) *places* :—þæs mægenþrymmes nān þe rîcebewitigað, þeódnes þrŷtgesteald, Cri. 353. (3) *affairs, proceedings, matters* :—Hî þā þegnunge beweotigað, El. 745. Hē ealle beweotede þegnes þearfe, B. 1796. Hē þŷ geornlîcar hire þearfa begā and bewiotige (*geþence*, MS. Vercel.) *that he see after the course of his soul*, Exon. Th. 367, 4. þæt hē (*the star*) þǣre sunnan sîð bewitige, hē sceal beforan fēran, Met. 4, 16. Ealle gesceafta môtan heora gewunan bewitigan bûtan mē ānum *all creatures may direct their customs except me only*, Bt. 7, 3 ; F. 20, 24 : Gû. 170. v. preceding word.

be-wlâtian. Add:—Hē bewlâtode ofor ealle *respexit super omnes*, Ps. L. 32, 14.

be-wreón. *Take here the examples given under* be-wrîhan, *and add* :—Hî mon mid wrigelse bewrîhþ, Bl. H. 61, 16. Biwrâh *revelabit*, Ps. Srt. 28, 9. Bewreogon *contexerunt*, Ps. Spl. 54, 5. Bewreóh ðē wearme *wrap yourself up warmly*, Lch. ii. 116, 19 : 118, 9. Bewreóþ þ wîf wel, 330, 21. Bewreów, 338, 17. Feallaþ ofor ûs, and ûs bewreóþ, Bl. H. 93, 33. Hē hēt þā fatu bewreón, Gr. D. 51, 16. Stân mid þynre tyrf bewrigen (*obtectus*), Bd. 5, 6 ; Sch. 577, 12 : Bl. H. 95, 15. Mid godwebbe bewrigen, 207, 16. Bewrogen, Lch. iii. 30, 1. Bewrigene, Ps. Th. 43, 20 : Ps. Spl. 31, 1 : Bl. H. 15, 15. Bewrogene, Ll. Th. ii. 226, 22. [v. N. E. D. be-wry.]

be-wrîtan. Add: *To score round* :—Bewrît þū hŷ (*the mandragora*) wel hraþe mid îserne, þŷ lǣs heó þē ætfleó . . . þū hŷ bewrît mid îserne, and swā þū scealt onbûtan hŷ delfan swā ðū hyre mid þām îserne nā æthrîne *make a score in the ground round it at once with iron, lest it escape thee . . . score round it with iron, and so must you dig round it as not to touch it with the iron*, Lch. i. 244, 17-23. v. Grmm. D. M. 1153 sqq., *and cf.* ymb-wrîtan.

be-wrixl(i)an. I. *to change* :—Hē bewrixlede þǣre stôwe eardunge *habitationem mutavit loci*, Gr. D. 119, 21. II. *to exchange* :—þū ûs bebohtest and bewrixledest *vendidisti populum tuum sine pretio*, Ps. Th. 43, 14. [Bi-wrixled, A. R. 310.]

be-wuna ; *adj. indecl.* *Wont, accustomed* :—Swā hié ǣr bewuna wǣron, þonne hié wælstôwe geweald âhton, Ors. 3, 7 ; S. 116, 32. Hî dydon eall swā hî bewuna wǣron, Chr. 1001 ; P. 133, 20. Cf. gewuna ; *adj.*

be-wyrcan. *After* wool (l. 6) *add*: cf. non sum setigero lanarum vellere facta (Aldhelm), *dele* : Hē . . . Jos. 2, 1, *and add* : I. *to build round, surround* :—Hē þone oxan beworhte mid wuda, Hml. S. 18, 124. Hî bronda lâfe wealle beworhton, B. 3162. Lǣmen fæt biwyrcan wudubeámum, Jul. 575. þā fôtlâstas wǣron beworht mid ǣrne hweóle, Shrn. 81, 12. I a. *of fortification* :—Hî hēhtan bewyrcean þā burh æt Weogernaceastre, Cht. Th. 137, 6. Iericho wæs mid seofon weallum beworht, Hml. Th. ii. 212, 26. Hē hēt sceáwian Hiericho, hû heó beworht wæs, Jos. 2, 1. II. *to cover over* with metal :—Heó þā cartan beworhte mid leáde, Hml. S. 3, 532. Hē beworhte ðā bigelsas mid gyldenum læfrum, Hml. Th. ii. 498, 2. Hió ðā rôde bewyrcan hēt mid golde and mid seolfre, H. R. 15, 13. Wǣpenu mid gyldenum þelum bewyrcean *arma aureis includere laminis*, Nar. 7, 12. III. *to furnish* with buildings :—Bufan ðǣm wealle ofer ealne þone ymbgong hē is mid stǣnenum wîghûsum beworht (*habitaculis defensorum dispositis*), Ors. 2, 4 ; S. 74, 21. IV. *to shut up* in a building :—Hēt hire fæder hî bewyrcean on ānum torre, Shrn. 105, 33. [v. N. E. D. bework.]

be-wyrded *defatu. l.* be wyrde *de fatu*, Wrt. Voc. ii. 27, 60 : be-yrnan. v. be-irnan.

bî. v. be.

biblioþēce, bibliþēca. Add: I. *a library* :—Heora bibliþēca (bibliotheoco, *v. l.*) wærð onbærned . . . on heora bibliþēcan forburnon IIII hund M bôca, Ors. 6, 14 ; Bos. 122, 19-23. Nime heora ǣlc sume bôc of þǣre bibliothēcan, R. Ben. 74, 13. II. *the bible* :—þis spel (*Judith*) nis on ðǣre bibliothēcan, Hml. A. 114, 405. Gyf þū bibli-ðēcan habban wille, Tech. ii. 120, 26.

bicce. Add:—Bicce *cuniculi*, Wrt. Voc. ii. 23, 8. Andlang eá on biccan pôl, C. D. iii. 456, 26.

bícnan (-ian). *Add*:—I. *to make a sign* to a person (*dat.* or *prep.* tō) *with something*:—Hē bícneð mid ðǣm eágum *annuit oculis*, Past. 357, 20. Hē bícnode hire tō mid his cynegyrde, Hml. A. 97, 180. Þā bēcnade Sanctus Petrus him, 162, 239. Hī bēcnodon eágan (mid eágum, *v. l.*), Ps. Spl. 34, 22. Ðæt hē bícne (biécne, *v. l.*) mid ðǣm eágum, Past. 359, 3. II. *to summon* by a sign:—Hē bícnode gehwanon mid blāwunge him fultum *he summoned help to himself from all sides by the blowing of trumpets*, Hml. S. 25, 635. Hig bícnodon hyra gefēran, þ hī cōmun and him fylston *they signalled their companions to come and help them*, Lk. 5, 7. III. *to shew by a sign, signify, indicate, portend*:—Iste ys æteówendlic and ðār bið, þār man swā bícnað be him, Ælfc. Gr. Z. 93, 9. Saeged ł bēcneð *indicat*, Lk. p. 3, 11. Bēcnade ł cýdde *notans*, 7, 11: *significans*, Jn. L. 12, 33. Swylce man býcnige him, þ him sēlre wǣre þ hý wunodon on clǣnnysse *as if to signify to them, that it were better for them to live in chastity*, Ll. Th. ii. 346, 20. Bēcnende *portendentes*, Wrt. Voc. ii. 66, 11. Bēcnendo *significantia*, Rtl. 103, 28. v. bēcnan, býcnian *in Dict.* [*O. H. Ger.* pouhnen.] v. and-, ge-bícnian.

bícnend (-i(g)end), es ; *m.* I. *of persons, one who shews, ind-cates*:—Bícnigend (*index*) rihtwīsnysse hē ys *he sheweth forth righteousness* (Prov. 12, 17), Scint. 135, 14. II. *of things, the forefinger*:—Bēcnend *index*, Wrt. Voc. ii. 46, 35: i. 283, 20. Býcniend, 64, 80. v. ge-bícn(i)end.

bícnend-líc (-i(g)end-); *adj.* I. *allegorical*:—Be ðǣre bícnend-lican gerece *alligoricae expositionis*, Bd. 5, 23 ; Sch. 696, 15. II. *indicative* (mood). [v. býcniend-líc *in Dict.*] v. ge-bícniendlíc.

bícnol ; *adj.* *Indicating, indicative*:—Bícnole *indices*, Germ. 398, 193.

bícnung. *Add*:—Gif hwilc neód beoð, mid býcnunge sumes tācnes sī gebeden *si quid opus fuerit, sonitu cujuscumque signi petatur*, R. Ben. I. 69, 16. v. ge-bícnung.

bí-cwide. For *Prov.* 22 *substitute* Kent. Gl. 813.

bídan. *Add*: I. *to wait, remain.* For exs. v. Dict. II. *to await, wait for, bide* one's time, (1) *with gen.*:—Hē bītt (bīt, *v. l.*) ðǣre tīde, hwonne . . ., Past. 226, 11 : 220, 10. Hē bídeþ þīnre geþafunga, Bl. H. 7, 34. Hē wyrde bídeþ, hwonne . . ., 109, 32. Hē bād westan-windes . . . þā sceolde hē bídan ryhtnorþanwindes, Ors. 1, 1 ; S. 17, 15–17 : Nar. 27, 15. Ðeáh hē bíde his tíman, Past. 275, 13. (2) *with acc.*:—Hwæt bídað gē?, Cri. 510. Heó bād þone ēcan sige *coronam expectabat aeternam*, Bd. 4, 23 ; Sch. 465, 9. Bād hē endedógor, Gū. 1258. Bídan gesceapu heofoncyninges, Gen. 842. (3) *with gen. and acc.*:—Hē hēht þæt wītehūs wrǣcna bídan, . . . gāsta weardas (cf. Hēl. 4829–30), Gen. 39. (4) *with a clause*:—Ic bíde . . . hwonne gæst cume, Rä. 16, 9. Hī bídaþ, hwæt him dēman wille tō leáne, Jul. 706 : Cri. 802. Bídan, hwæs him cyning unnan wolde, An. 145. Bídan, hwonne him betre líf āgyfen wurde, Gū. 751. (5) *uncertain*:—Bídende *suspensus* (Lk. 19, 48), Wrt. Voc. ii. 73, 70. Bídendum *prestulanti* (*eventus rerum*), 75. 62. III. *to attain by waiting, experience* (with gen.):—Hwæt gif ic bíde merigenes *what if I live to see the morning*, Hml. S. 3, 584. Þū scealt deáðes bídan, Gen. 922.

biddan. *Add*: I. *to ask, make a request*:—Hit bið swā þū bidest, Shrn. 89, 1. Biddað, and gē underfóð, Jn. 16, 24. Nele se slāwa erian on wintra, ac hē wile biddan on sumera, Past. 285, 6. Þ hē þon bid-dendan líf forgeáfe, Bl. H. 19, 35. II. *to ask, make request to a person* (*acc.*):—Gehýrð Drihten þā þe hine biddað, Ll. Th. ii. 394, 4. Hié mid hālsunga hine bǣdon and þus cwǣdon, Bl. H. 87, 8 : 247, 33 : 249, 6. Drihten wile þ hine mon bidde, 19, 34. Hī bedene wǣron, Bd. 2, 5 ; Sch. 206, 15. II a. (v. *also* IV) *with object of request given*, (1) by gen. (v. III. 1):—Hē ne biddeð ūs nānes þinges, Hex. 44, 1. Bide helpes hine, Dóm. L. 36, 14. Ne biddan wē ūrne Drihten þyses lǣnan welan, Bl. H. 21, 10. Hié þā burgware ongunnon ānwigges biddan, 201, 22. (2) by acc.:—Hwæne hē byddan mihte fultum, Ap. Th. 12, 14. (3) by a clause:—Ic ðæc biddo, ðæt him fiónd ne sceððe, Shrn. 73, 3. Bidde, Bl. H. 57, 33. Bide, 151, 23. Ic þe bidde for þīnum naman, þ . . ., 147, 10. Þone þū bæde, þæt hē āsende his englas, Hml. Th. ii. 416, 15. (3 a) *with ellipsis of þæt and subject of clause*:—Wilt þū fremdne monnan biddan þē gesecge, Sch. 4. (4) by infin.:—Hē bæd gangan forð gōde gefēran, By. 170. (4 a) *with ellipsis of infin.*:—Heó bæd hine blíðne (wesan), B. 617. (5), (4) *and* (3 a) *together*:—Hē bæd hine āreccan, hwæt seó rūn bude, hófe hālígu word, Dan. 542–3. (6) *with prep.*:—Hī ongunnon for his hreddinge God biddan, Hml. Th. i. 534, 27. II b. *to pray to* (*with prep.*):—þū tō omnes sanctos bidde, þ hī þe þingian, Dóm. L. 36, 23. III. (v. *also* IV) *to ask for* something, (1) with gen. (v. II a. 1):—Hē bideð (bidt, *v. l.*) ingonges, Past. 284, 15. Hē bideþ þæs ēcan leóhtes, Bl. H. 17, 35. Hié biddaþ þīnre onlësnesse, 81, 22. Se blinda ne bæd goldes, 21, 5. Ne bidde gē þæs, 227, 13. (2) with acc.:—Dō þæt ic bidde, Bl. H. 245, 20. Ne bǣde gē nān þing on mīnum naman, Jn. 16, 24. Wē sceolon infær biddan, Hml. Th. ii. 572, 9. Gif þæt byð beden, nā ou naman Hǣlendes byð beden, Scint. 32, 5. (3) with gen. and acc.:—Ne bæd se blinda nāðor ne goldes, ne seolfres, ne nāne woruldlíce ðing,

Hml. Th. i. 158, 20. (4) *with a clause*:—Wē biddaþ þ þū fram ūs ne gewīte, Bl. H. 145, 18. Hē bæd þ hē mōste faran, 23, 13 : 211, 29. Hī bǣdan þ ōþer seonað wǣre, Bd. 2, 2 ; Sch. 115, 22. III a. *to ask* something of a person, (1) with gen. of thing:—þ hī witon hwæs hī biddað æt Gode, Hml. S. 12, 266. Hē wæs biddende ānes lytles troges æt ānum earman men, Ors. 2, 5 ; S. 84, 14. (2) with acc. of thing:—Ne bideþ hē æt ūs edleán, Bl. H. 103, 20. Swā hwæt swā gē biddað æt mīnum Fæder, Hml. Th. ii. 526, 34. Hī bǣdon lǣfe æt mē, Guth. 62, 13. Uton biddan leóht æt ūrum Drihtne, Hml. Th. i. 158, 26. (3) with clause:—Hē bæd æt Gode þæt hē mōste fandian lōbes, Hml. Th. i. 6, 10. IV. *with the person for whom request is made*, (1) given by dat. (a) *with construction of III.* 1:—Wē ūs forgifnessa (*or acc.?*) biddaþ, Bl. H. 19, 29. Men him forgifnesse biddaþ, 77, 17 : 107, 22. Sum þearfa sæt nacod, and bæd him hrægles, 213, 33. Ðā cild bǣdon him hlāfes, ac næs nān mann ðe ðone hlāf him betwýnan tōbrǣce, Hml. Th. ii. 400, 26. Ær þām þe hē him ryhtes bidde, Ll. Th. i. 90, 3. (b) *with construction of II a.* 1:—Hē bæd him fultumes willgeþoftan, Gen. 2025. (c) *with construction of II a.* 4:—Hē bæd him þā rinces rǣd āhicgan, Gen. 2030. (d) *with construction of II b*:—þ þū him tō þeossum hālgum helpe bidde, Gr. D. 2, 11. (e) *with construction of III a.* 2:—Hwī ne bidst þū þe beþunga and plaster æt freán, Dóm. L. 80. Hē bæd þām treówe fyrst æt ðām hlāforde, Hml. Th. ii. 408, 17. Biddað eów þingunge æt þysum martyrum, i. 88, 33. (2) with prep.:—Bide for ūs, þæt God þās nǣddran fram ūs āfyrsige, Hml. Th. ii. 238, 14. V. *construction uncertain*:—Bæd *inprecabatur*, Wrt. Voc. ii. 80, 58. Hió wæs beden *interpellata*, 44, 70. v. un-beden, -biddende.

biddere. *Add*:—Bidderes *proci*, Wrt. Voc. ii. 84, 7. Hē hēt syllan þā scyllingas þām biddere (*petitori*), Gr. D. 158, 20. [*Piers P.* bid-deres and beggeres.]

biden-fæt, bide-ríp, -bidian. v. byden-fæt, bed-ríp, and-(on-)bidian.

bifian. *Add*:—Bifgedon *fremebant*, Mk. L. 14, 5. Wæs se munt bifigende mid ormǣtre cwacunge, Hml. Th. i. 504, 28. Biuiende *treme-bundus, pavidus*, An. Ox. 2994. Se bifigenda dōm *the tremendous judgement*, Wlfst. 227, 14 : 228, 31 : Bl. H. 57, 20. Fryhtendo ł bib-giende *trementes*, Rtl. 122, 16.

bifung. *Add*:—Wiþ hramman and wið bifunge, genime þās wyrte, Lch. i. 302, 8. Seó swuster eallum limum cwacode . . . hī þæt mihton tōcnāwan on ðǣre swuster bifunge, Hml. Th. ii. 32, 21, 33. [*O. H. Ger.* bibunga.]

bí-fylc. *l.* bí-fylce.

bígan. *Add*: I. *trans.* To bend, (1) of shape, attitude:—Ic bǣge mīne cneówa, Bl. H. 187, 18. (2) of direction, *to incline*:—þā gē hē bígede *cum* (*membra sopori*) *dedisset* .i. *inclinasset*, An. Ox. 2105. (3) figurative, (a) *to humiliate, subdue*:—Líchama mīn in nēdhērnisse ic bēgo *corpus meum in servitutem redigo*, Rtl. 6, 9. Suæ hwælc bēges hine *quicumque humiliaverit se*, Mt. L. 18, 4. (b) *to turn, incline*:—Bēgan wē ūre mōd fram ðǣre lufan þisse worlde, Bl. H. 57, 22. II. *intrans.* To bend, move in a curve:—Se ord bígde upp tō þām hiltum, Hml. S. 12, 226. Se hara bígde gelōme *the hare frequently doubled*, 31, 1058. [v. *N. E. D.* bey. *Goth.* us-baugjan: *O. Frs.* bēia : *O. L. Ger.* bōgian : *O. H. Ger.* bougen.] v. bēgan, býgan *in Dict.*

bíge; *n.?* *l.* byge; *m.*: bíge. *l.* byge, *q. v.*: bi-gegnes = bi-gengnes. v. be-gegnes.

bígels. *Add*: I. *an arch*, &c.:—Bígels *arcus vel fornix*, Wrt. Voc. i. 81, 14. Bígels, boga, incleofa *camera, arcus, fornax*, ii. 127, 78. Sē ðe gebígde þone heofenlican bígels, Hml. Th. i. 170, 23. Bígelsa *arcuum*, Wrt. Voc. ii. 76, 2. Hrófum ođđe bígelsum *arcibus*, 96, 79 : *fornicibus*, An. Ox. 512. Wyrcan twelf hūs mid gōdum bígelsum, Hml. S. 36, 99. Hē beworhte ðā bígelsas mid gyldenum læfrum, Hml. Th. ii. 498, 2. II. *inclination*:—Bōh mid wōgum āhyldne bígelse *stipitem obliqua reclinem curvatura*, An. Ox. 2228.

bígend-líc. v. býgend-líc *in Dict.*

bí-geng (bíg-). *Add*: *and* e ; *f.* (? *v.* An. Ox. 2283 *infra*.) I. *practice, exercise, doing*:—Líf mid gōdra weorca bígenge frætwian, Ll. Th. ii. 402, 5. Bígenge, Hml. Th. ii. 48, 28. Biggenge, R. Ben. 3, 7. For lārlicere bígenge *propter gymnicum* (*philosophiae*) *studium*, An. Ox. 2283. Onscuniendlice on biggen[g]on (*studiis*) heora, Ps. Spl. 13, 2. Þ man mid gōdum biggencgum Gode gecwēme, Hml. S. 13, 114. II. *cultivation, tillage*:—Hī swuncon on wīngeardes bígencge, Hml. Th. ii. 74, 33, 25. III. *religious* or *ecclesiastical practice, observance, worship*:—Bígenge *cultura* (*paganorum*), An. Ox. 4558. Ðis hǣðen-gyld deófles biggeng is, Hml. Th. i. 72, 4. On bíggenge Godes beboda, 544, 25. Tō þām bígenge his gebeda *ad orationis studium*, Gr. D. 26, 19 : 71, 10. Gāstlicre rǣdincge bígencge (*studio*), Angl. xiii. 392, 383. Regullicum bígencge, 388, 333. Se gewuna belāf of hǣðenra manna biggenge, Hml. A. 146, 47. Ænigne deófles bígencg tō dōnne, 143, 122. Þ hiora biggencgas ne wurdon ādwǣscte, Hml. S. 22, 195. Bígencgum *ceremoniis* .i. *legibus divinis*, An. Ox. 2224. Þā þe Godes beboda mid biggengum ne healdað, Hml. S. 16, 172. Godes biggencgum, 24, 10 : 25, 738. Mid wōlicum biggencgum, 18, 392. Mānfulles hǣþenscipes

bígengcas *cerimonias*, An. Ox. 2624. Hwí ðū ūre goda biggencgas forseó, Hml. S. 8, 57. Godes biggengas, Hml. Th. ii. 66, 16. Bysega and bígengas þysses Drihtenlican þeówdōmes, R. Ben. 5, 10. v. bí-genge.

bí-genga. *Add:*—Bígenga, tilia, inbûend *colonus .i. incola, cultor, inquilinus*, Wrt. Voc. ii. 134, 25. I. *an inhabitant :*—Heofenlic bígengca *celicola*, An. Ox. 3934: Guth. 40, 3. Ðā bígengean þæs londes *incolae regionis ejus*, Nar. 5, 26. Biggengan, Bl. H. 209, 3. Bígengcan, Guth. 20, 14. II. *a cultivator :*—Hē cwæð tō þæs wīngeardes biggengan (bígencga *cultorem*, Lk. L. 13, 17)... Se biggenga him andwyrde, Hml. Th. ii. 408, 2-5. Hē sende tō bígengum (*ad cultores*), Lk. L. R. 20, 10. III. *one who takes care of persons ;* cultor. v. be-ganga *in Dict.* IV. *a worshipper :*—Hē wæs deófles biggencga (bígenga, *v. l.*), Hml. S. 5, 10: 22, 206. Biggenga, 24, 20. Sē is sōð God þe swā gesceádwíse biggengan hæfð, 5, 286. [*O. H. Ger.* pígeng(e)o, -gango.]

bí-genge, es ; *n. Practice, worship :*—Bígenge *cultus*, An. Ox. 5153. On ídol wē āspendað bígencge *inane expendimus studium*, Scint. 2, 1. Þā bígengu (*neomenias*) þæs níwan mōnan wē nā ne healdaþ, An. Ox. 40, 34. Bodiað bígenga (*studia*) his, Ps. Spl. 9, 11. v. bí-geng.

bí-genge (?), an ; *f. A female worshipper, attendant :*—Bigencge (but cf. bígengcest, An. Ox. 2065, a gloss of the same passage) *cultricem, ministraticem*, Hpt. Gl. 455, 16. y. bí-genga, -gengestre.

bí-gengere (big-, *q.v. in Dict.*) *a worshipper :*—Fram bisceopum and Godes biggencgerum *a praesulibus et cultoribus Deo decretae Christianae religionis*, C. D. B. i. 154, 13.

bí-gengestre, an ; *f. A female attendant, worshipper :*—Bígengestre *cultrix*, i. *inserviens*, Wrt. Voc. ii.137, 46. Bígengcestre, An. Ox. 4431. Bígengestran, þēnestran *cultricem*, i. *ministram*, 1358 : 2065.

bí-geonan, -geongol. v. be-geonan, -gangol.

bíging, e ; *f. Bending ;* curvatura, Wrt. Voc. ii. 137, 54. v. cneówbíging.

big-leofa, -leofen. v. bí-leofa, -leofen: big-leofan. *l.* big-leofian. v. bí-leofian.

bíg-nes. *Add:*—Mid bígnysse his āgnes onrǣses *reflexione sui impetus*, Gr. D. 48, 7. Þæt fenn mid menigfealdan bígnyssum þurhwunað on norðsǣ, Guth. 20, 7. On liþa bígnyssum, 90, 21. v. on-, ymbbígness.

big-spǣc. *Dele :* big-spell, -swic, -swica, -wist. v. bí-spell, be-swic, -swica, bí-wist: big-standan. *l.* big standan : bi-hlǣman. v. be-hlǣnan.

bil, bill. *Dele Dut. and Ger. cognates, and add :* [I. *a falchion.* v. Dict.] II. *a bill, an implement for cutting* (wood, stone, weeds):—Sīðe *vel* bill *falcastrum*, Wrt. Voc. i. 16, 16 : 34, 16. Bill *bidubium* (ferramentum rusticum idem quod falcastrum, Migne), i. *marra*, ii. 12, 74 : *marra*, 57, 70. Se hālga man (*Benedict*) āgeaf þām Gotan þone gelōman (þæt bill, *v.l.*), and cwæð : ' Hēr is þīn bill (v. wudubill *falcastrum*, 113, 18), Gr. D. 114, 17. Bill *chalibem* (cf. 92, 7, a gloss on Ald. 159, 33 where the incident of the preceding passage is related),Wrt. Voc. ii. 20, 57. Hē sceal habban æcse, adsan, bil, Angl. ix. 263, 1. v. cweorn-bill: case-bill.

bildan (byldan, *q.v. in Dict.*) *to embolden, encourage :*—Nān mon his hiéremonna mōd ne bilt (bielt, *v.l.*) tō gǣstlicum weorcum *nulla subditorum mentes exhortatio sublevat*, Past. 129, 11. v. ge-byld *in Dict.*

bildu (-o) ; *indecl. :* bíld, e ; *f. Boldness, confidence :*—Ðæt ne weaxe tō ungemetlico beldo (*praecipitatio*), and swā ðrycce ðā belde ..., Past. 455, 21. Bielde *constantia*, Wrt. Voc. ii. 23, 58. Bældo *temeritate*, Mt. p. 9, 4. Mid hwylcre byldu mæg ic gān tō Godes temple ?, Hml. A. 134, 617. Mid bylde Godes gewinnes, Hml. Th. ii. 494, 31 : Hml. S. 25, 319. Ðæt hié habbað ðā arodnesse and ðā bieldo (bældo, *v.l.*) ðæt hié magon anweald habban *auctoritatis fortitudine erecti*, Past. 41, 17. Hē hæfde mid him myccle bælde (*fiduciam*) hīwcūþnesse, Gr. D. 140, 7. Baeldo, Rtl. 89, 3. Byldum *fiducia*, i. *confidentia*, Wrt. Voc. ii. 148, 74. v. un-bildu, *and* byld *in Dict.*

bile ; *m. Add:*—His breóst and his bile beorht syndon ... is se bile hwit, E. S. viii. 477, 29, 34. Bile *rostro*, An. Ox. 2410. Twēgen hremmas his hūs tǣron mid heardum bile, Hml. Th. ii.144, 21. Fugelas on heora blōdigon bilon ðæra martyra flǣsc bǣron, Hml. S. 23, 80.

biled-breóst. v. byled-breóst *in Dict.*

bí-leofa *subsistence, maintenance, provision ;* in a limited sense *victuals :*—Hē sǣde þ þ feoh wǣre widewena bigleofa of gōdra manna ælmyssan, Hml. S. 25, 765. Leahtras fōda, deáðes bigleafa, 7, 26. þæs mannes bíleofa is tō besceáwianne, Lch. ii. 210, 18 : R. Ben. 64, 3. Ne sý regoles strǣc gehealden on heora bíleofan (*alimentis*), 61, 15. Sýfre on bigleofan *sobrii*, Hml. A. 52, 52. þā ðe hæfdon sum þing lytles tō bigleofan, þ reáferas of þām mūðe him ābrūdon, 68, 72. Ælcum hlāforde gedafenaþ ðæt hē dō his mannum heora bigleofan on gesettum tīman, 55, 128 : 105, 90. Bigleafan (-leofan), Hml. S. 25, 815. þ man ne sceolde ǣnigne bigleofan hire dōn binnon seofon nihton, 10, 282. Bíleofan *stipem .i. alimoniam*, An. Ox. 2193. Bíwiste, bíleofan *stipendia*, Hml. S. 4833. Hē Godes cyrcan gegōdode mid landum and bigleofum, Hml. S.

27, 135. Hē fæste fram eallum bigleofum, Wlfst. 285, 26. [*A. R.* bi-leove : *R. Glouc.* bi-live : *Piers P.* bi-lif. Cf. *O. H. Ger.* pī-lipi *esca, panes.*] v. next two words.

bí-leofen. *Add:*—Bílifen, andlifen *pulmentum*, Wrt. Voc. ii. 78, 5. Āsmeáge hē on þām þrím iengctenum hwæt his biglifen (-leofi, *v.l.*) sý *computet per tres quadrigesimas quanti victus ejus sit*, Ll. Th. ii. 134, 31. Tōforan gesetre bigleofene (-leofan, *v.l.*) *super statutam annonam*, R. Ben. 59, 15. þone þriddan dǣl mē tō biglifene, Hml. A. 201, 190. Hē beget him biglyfne mid his weorce, Hml. S. 30, 214. þā gesettan bíleofene (*annonam*), R. Ben. 55, 11. Heó bíleofenǣ sundon, Hml. A. 85, 121. [*O. L. Ger.* bi-liðan *victus, stipendium* : *O. H. Ger.* pī-lipan.]

bí-leofian ; *p. ode To support :*—Fēng hē tō medmycclan bigleofan, þæt wæs tō þām berenan hlāfe, and þone þigede and his líf bíleofode, Guth. 34, 7. v. bí-leofa.

bile-wit. *Add :* -wite, -witt, -witte, -wet, -hwit. I. generally in a good sense :—Biluit *mansuetus*, Mt. L. 21, 5. Bilwit *simplex*, Lk. L. 11, 34. Bilewite *mitis*, Ps. Spl. 85, 4. Bilewite (bylehwit *later MS.*), Mt. 11, 29. Iacob wæs bilewitte (*simplex*) man, Gen. 25, 27. Basilius se bylewitta (-wyta, *v.l.*), Hml. S. 3, 100. Wē witum þē bilewite (*mansuetum*) wesan, Coll. M. 18, 22. Hlūtre mōde and bylewite (-hwite, *v.l.*) *simplici ac pura mente*, Bd. 4, 24 ; Sch. 491, 9. Sume ðe wǣron bylewyte and gōde, Nic. 3, 25. Ðā bilwitan (bili-, 6, bile-, 7) *simplices*, Past. 237, 4. þā bilewitan *mansueti*, Bl. Gl. Mid ðǣm bilwitum, Past. 243, 16. Bilehwitum *simplicioribus*, R. Ben. I. 13, 5. Moïses wæs se bilewitusta (*mitissimus*) mann, Num. 12, 3. II. in an unfavourable sense, *plausible, affecting simplicity :*—Ne trūwa ðū smyltum wedere, ne bilewitum men, Prov. K. 63. [v. *N. E. D.* bilewhit. *O. L. Ger.* bili-wit *aequanimus.* Cf. *M. H. Ger.* pil-wiz. v. Grmm. D. M. (trans.) ii. 472 sqq.]

bile-witlíce (-hwit-, v. *Dict.*) ; *adv. Simply, with simplicity, innocently, uprightly, gently :*—Hié nǣfre bilwitlíce willað monigean *numquam clementer admonent*, Past. 145, 1. Gif hwā gonge bilwitlíce (*simpliciter*) treów tō ceorfanne, 165, 25 : 167, 6. Bielwitlíce (bile-?, bil-, *v.l.*) libban *simpliciter vivere*, 239, 22. Ðætte sē libbe getreówlíce, sē ðe bilwitlíce libbe *qui ambulat simpliciter, ambulat confidenter*, 243, 12. Hē sylfa mē geandette swīþe bilwitlíce (*simpliciter*), Gr. D. 242, 5.

bile-witness. *Add:*—Biliwitnes (bil-, *v.l.*) and ānfealdnes weorca *simplicitas actionis*, Past. 243, 12. Bilewitnes *simplicitas*, i. *puritas*, An. Ox. 1827. Biluitnise *modestia*, Rtl. 105, 1 : *mansuetudo*, 100, 11 : *lenitas*, 111, 26. Biluitnise *sinceritatis*, 25, 19. Mid ðǣre culfran bilewitnesse (bil-, *v.l.*) *columbae simplicitate*, Past. 291, 8. þis ic dyde mid bilewitnysse (*in simplicitate cordis mei*), Gen. 20, 5 : Ælfc. T. Grn. 5, 1 (cf. Gen. 25, 27). Bilwitnesse (bylewyt-, bylwet-, v. *ll.*), Bd. 3, 27 ; Sch. 322, 7. Wǣron hí wundriende þā bilehwitnesse (bylwyt-, bilwit-, bylwyt-, v. *ll.*) þæs lífes, 1, 26 ; Sch. 57, 16. Ðǣre culfran biliwitnesse (bil-, *v.l.*) ... ðǣre nǣdran wǣrscipe, Past. 237, 22. On bōcum þe ungelǣrede menn þurh heora bilewitnysse tō micclum wísdōme tealdon, Hml. Th. i. 2, 21.

bilgan *to anger.* v. ā-, ge-bilgan (-bylgan) : bil-hergas. v. billere : bí-libban. *l.* bí libban, v. be ; C : býlyhte. v. býlihte : bi-lihþ. v. be-leán : II- : bille. v. twi-bille.

billere (, bil-here ? ; *pl.* bil-hergas) *a plant name* (v. N. E. D., D. D. bilders) :—Billere *bibulta* (in a list of plant names), Wrt. Voc. i. 286, 29 : ii. 11, 58. Billeru, 102, 4. Bilhergas *bibultum*, 126, 7.

Bilmigas ; *pl. The name of (a people occupying) some district in England :*—Bilmiga syx hund hýda, C. D. B. i. 414, 28.

biman (-ian) *to trumpet, blow a trumpet :*—David býmendre stefne hleóðriende cwæð, Angl. viii. 331, 12. [v. *N. E. D.* beme.] v. býmian *in Dict.*

bíme (ié, ē, ȳ), an ; *f. :* bíma ; *m. ?* I. *a trumpet* (in the first place of wood v. beám : cf. horn) :—Hefe ūp ðīne stefne suā bíme (biéme, *v. l.* tuba), Past. 91, 20. Bēma, Rtl. 5, 14. Býma, Wrt. Voc. i. 73, 58. Bēme *concha*, Txts. 53, 571 : *barbita*, Wrt. Voc. ii. 12, 28. Býme *salpix*, 96, 22. Hlūdstefne býme *grandisona tuba*, 42, 41. Býman *salpicis*, An. Ox. 5246 : *classica*, 742 : *bucina*, 4, 82. Mid býman (bēman, R., beám, L. *tuba*), Mt. 24, 31. Ne blāu þū bēman (nelle ðū bēma tstocc singa, L.) *noli tuba canere*, Mt. R. 6, 2. Gebreces and biémena dæg *dies tubae et clangoris*, Past. 245, 6. Býmum *classibus*, Hpt. Gl. 467, 27. II. *a tablet, billet :*—Beeme *thessera*, Txts. 101, 2015. [v. *N. E. D.* beme.] v. scip-bíme, *and* býme, bēme *in Dict.*

-bíme. v. ān-bíme.

bímere, es ; *m. A trumpeter :*—Bēmere *tubicen*, Wrt. Voc. i. 289, 56. Bēmeras *tubicines*, ii. 72, 38. Beámeres *tibicines*, Mt. L. 9, 23. [v. *N. E. D.* bemer.] v. býmere *in Dict.*

bin, binn. *Add :* binne, an ; *f.* I. *a receptacle* for food, a basket ; cofinus :—In binne *in cofino*, Ps. Srt. 80, 7. þāra hlāfgebroca wæs tō lāfe twelf binna fulle, Shrn. 48, 32. II. *a crib, manger :*—Se untígd eówer ælc his oxan fram þǣre binne (*praesepio*)?, Lk. 13, 15. ' Se assa oncneów his hlāfordes binne.' þā geseah heó þæt cild licgan on binne, ðǣr se oxa and se assa gewunelíce fōdan sēcað, Hml. Th. i. 42,

25. Geléd on þǽre binne, 40, 32. Ic sceal fyllan binnan (*praesepia*) oxan mid hīg, Coll. M. 19, 35. **III.** *a stall* :—Ne bið nȳten on binnum *non erit armentum in praesepibus*, Cant. Ab. 17. [v. *N. E. D.* bin.] v. hunig-, yrse-bin.

**bí-nama**, an; *m. A pronoun* :—Þā naman and þā bīnaman, Angl. viii. 331, 5. [v. *N. E. D.* by-name : *O. H. Ger.* pī-namo *pronomen*.] -bind. v. ge-bind.

**bindan.** *Add* :—Ic beó bunden *ligor*, Wrt. Voc. ii. 53, 30. (1) *to bind, tie up* in a bundle :—Gadriað þone coccel and bindað (*alligate*) sceáfmǽlum, Mt. 13, 30. (2) *to fasten to, on* :—Hig bindað hefige byrðena, Mt. 23, 4. Beágas bundan *boias* (*in collo*) *nectunt*, Wrt. Voc. ii. 81, 30 : 60, 63. (3) *to fasten together, knit* :—Bindende (cf. 61, 12) *nectentem* (*retia luxus*, Ald. 206, 16), Wrt. Voc. ii. 96, 66. (4) *to put bonds on* :—Hié hine bindað and swingaþ, Bl. H. 15, 10. Hé nam Simeon and band hine *tollens Simeon et ligans*, Ger. 42, 24. (4 a) *to be a bond on* :—Bundan *nodarent* (*vincla pios lacertos*), Wrt. Voc. ii. 90, 28. (5) *to restrain the action of* :—Onlegen tō trymmanne þone magan and tō bindanne, Lch. ii. 180, 25. (6) of obligation :—Hine ǽghwylc sylfne on forhæfednysse band, Hml. S. 23 b, 132. Mid gehāte hine sylfne bindende *uoto se obligans*, Bd. 3, 24; Sch. 307, 15.

**binde.** *Add* :—Þæt þū [strīce] mid foreweardum fingrum þīn forewearde heáfod fram þām ānum eáran tō þon ōþrum on bindan tácne (cf. strícan on róde tácne, 2) *trace out a fillet on the forehead with the tips of the fingers from ear to ear*, Tech. ii. 129, 20. [v. *N. E. D.* bind. *O. H. Ger.* biuta *vitta, zona, ligamen.*] v. wudu-binde.

**bindel(l)e.** *Add*: *a bandage* :—Bind his ȳtmestan limo mid byndellum, Lch. ii. 196, 12. v. wudu-bindelle.

**binding**, e; *f. Binding* :—Bindingce *stricturae*, An. Ox. 3246.

**binnan, be-innan.** *Add*: **I.** *prep.* (1) of position, (a) *within a place*, (α) *with dat.* :—Binnan ðǽm locum ūres módes, Past. 385, 6. Hié wǽron binnan þǽre byrig, Ors. 2, 8; S. 94, 2. Hé sæt binnan þǽm hām, Chr. 901; P. 92, 6. Hí ofslógon hine binnan his āganan heordæ, 1048; P. 173, 2. Hié þā scipu binnan Lundenbyrig gebróhton, 896; P. 89, 21. Sume þā scipu gewendon binnon Scépíge, 1052; P. 180, 1. Binnan byrig oþþon būton, Ll. Th. i. 286, 26. (β) *with acc.* :—Sume binnan þ fæsten oðflugon, Ors. 2, 8; S. 92, 23. Wulfas bróhton monnes líchoman binnan þā burg, 4, 2; S. 160, 21. Hé binnan þæt templ becom, Hml. Th. i. 456, 11. Þā þā hé his fót nyðer ásette binnon þone wyrttūn, Gr. D. 24, 32. Þā wíse menn ǽgðær ge binnan burh ge būton, Chr. 1052; P. 181, 1. (b) *within an enclosure, a fence, &c.* (α) *with dat.* :—Iéwde hé mé āne duru beinnan ðǽm wealle, Past. 153, 19. Ðā wuhta beinnan ðām wāge, 155, 21. In loco qui dicitur Binnaneá, inter duos riuos gremiales fluminis, C. D. i. 259, 8. (β) *with acc.* :—Bionna uallas nerxnawonges *infra menia paradisi*, Rtl. 13, 4. (2) in measurement (space, degree) :—Binnan feówertigum míla of Rómebyrig *within forty miles of Rome*, Gr. D. 219, 2. Binnan eahta mannum bēte man þ fullum were, Ll. Th. i. 286, 27. (3) temporal, *within a period* :—Binnan þǽm (geárum), Ors. 3, 9; S. 128, 23. Binnan six dagum, Ælfc. T. Grn. 2, 30 : Lch. i. 278, 10. Bynnan healfon geáre, 204, 3. Binnon feówertig geára fæce, Hml. Th. ii. 196, 12 : Chr. 947; P. 112, 25. Binnon þām fyrste, Hml. S. 5, 208. **II.** *adv.* :—Ðrīm binnan, ðrīm būtan, Wrt. Voc. ii. 84, 58. Hié ealle þǽr binnan wǽron, Ors. 2, 8; S. 92, 14 : Chr. 894; P. 86, 22 : 1004; P. 135, 33. Þte binnan (binna, L.) is *quod intus est*, Mt. R. 23, 26, 27. Binna (bionna, R.), Jn. L. 20, 26. Binna eóde *introivit*, 18, 15. Binna būtan ǽc *interius exteriusque*, Rtl. 16, 3. Bionna in halle *intrinsecus in aula*, 95, 25. v. be-innan *in Dict.*

**biótul.** *l.* biotul *a bridle.* v. bitol.

**birce**, an; *f. Barking* :—Bercae *latratus*, Wrt. Voc. ii. 112, 46. Byrce, 50, 63. v. beorc.

**birce.** *Add* :—Birciae, birce *populus*, Txts. 88, 792. Birce, Wrt. Voc. i. 285, 22. Byrce, ii. 68, 25. Birce *beta*, i. 285, 38 : ii. 11, 57. Byrce *betulus*, 12, 65. Beeástan ðā bircan, C. D. iii. 213, 3. In ðā twislihtran birícean, 391, 21. v. beorc.

**birc-holt.** *Add* :—Byrcholt *betule(t)um*, Wrt. Voc. ii. 12, 66.

**biren**, e ; birene, an (v. byrene *in Dict.*); *f. A she-bear* :—Ursa, þ is on ūre geðeóde byren . . . Bebeád seó fǽmne þǽre byrene . . . and seó byren hine lét gangan, Shrn. 47, 1-7. In loco que vocitatur birene-feld, C. D. ii. 76, 7. Byrene *urse*, Kent. Gl. 606. [*O. H. Ger.* berin *ursa*.]

**biren**; *adj. Of a bear* :—Byrenre *ursinae*, An. Ox. 1476. Byrenne (= -re; byorenne, Hpt. Gl. 508, 43), 4380. [*O. H. Ger.* birín *ursinus*.] v. beren *in Dict.*

**birgan** *to taste* :—Byrgeth *libat*, Wrt. Voc. ii. 53, 33. Ic þ wæter bergde *aquam gustavi*, Nar. 8, 28, 30. Seó swétnes ðe ic ǽr byrigde (bregde, *v. l.*) (*degustans*), Bd. 5, 12; Sch. 625, 12. Úser Drihten gallan berigde, Angl. xi. 173, 3. Bergað *gustate*, Ps. Srt. 33, 9. Þæt wæter tō bergenne (byrigenne, *v. l.*), Bd. 5, 4; Sch. 569, 4. Tō beorgenne (byrg-, *v. l.*), 4, 3; Sch. 366, 18. v. bergan, býrgan (-ean) (*l.* byrgan), byrigan *in Dict.*

**birging**, e; *f. Tasting, taste* :—Byrgincg (*gustus*) swēte ūt ānȳdde of neorxena wonge, Scint. 57, 2. Hnesce on æthrine and weredre on byrigincge (biriginge, byrincge, *v. ll.*), Lch. i. 108, 2. On byrgynge, 250, 22. v. on-birging, *and* býrging (*l.* byrging) *in Dict.*

**birgness**, e; *f. Tasting, taste* :—Birgnes *gustus*, Wrt. Voc. ii. 41, 20 : i. 282, 29. Byrignes, 64, 20. Be ðes gallan berignesse ðe úser Drihten berigde, Angl. xi. 173, 3. Mid byrinesse (byrig-, beorh-, *v. ll.*) ðæs wæteres *aquae gustum*, Bd. 5, 18; Sch. 649, 16. v. on-birgness.

**birhtan** *to shine*, (1) literal :—Eall mín weorod for ðǽre micelnesse ðæs goldes scān and berhte, Nar. 7, 15. Byr[htende] *coruscans*, An. Ox. 4203. (2) figurative :—Hé beforan manna eágum swā manigum wundrum sceán and berhte, Guth. 90, 11. Se noma mid him swā lange sceán and bryhte *nomen apud eos tam diu claruerat*, Bd. 1, 12; Sch. 33, 3. [*O. H. Ger.* berahten *splendescere.*] v. ge-, on-birhtan, *and* beorhtan, byrhtan *in Dict.*

**birhtu** (-o). *Add* :—Sió birhtu þæs sóþan leóhtes, Bt. 33, 4; F. 132, 34. Birhtu his *splendor ejus*, Ps. Srt. ii. p. 189, 19. Ðæt andgit ðǽre incundan byrhto (birhto, *v. l.*), Past. 69, 22. Hé scīnaþ beorhte swīþe mistlice birhtu, Bt. 33, 4; F. 132, 21. Hé geseah þæt hūs mid heofonlicre bryhto geondgoten, Guth. 88, 10. Tō ongietenne ðā bierhtu (birhtu, *v. l.*; bierhto, *l.* 24) ðæs sóðan leóhtes, Past. 69, 14. Ðæs dæges bierhto and ðǽre sunnan, 387, 15. Birhtu, Bt. 34, 8; F. 146, 2 : *claritatem*, Ps. Srt. ii. p. 159, 21. In birhtum *in splendoribus*, Ps. Srt. 109, 3. v. beorhtu, byrhtu *in Dict.*

**birla**, an; *m. The barrel, body* (of a horse) :—Gif hors sié ofscoten ; nim tóbrecenre nǽdle eáge, stinge hindan on þone byrlan, Lch. ii. 156, 30. [Cf. *O. H. Ger.* birila *cophinus : urna, quam rustici vocant biral.*]

**birnan**; *pp.* burnen *To burn* (intrans.) :—Ic byrne *ardeo*, ðū byrnst *ardes*, ic onginne byrnan *ardesco*, Ælfc. Gr. Z. 212, 6. (1) of fire, light, &c. :—Bir[n]ð *ardescit* (*ignis*), Kent. Gl. 573. Hé þā leóhtfatu onǽlde and hý burnon, Gr. D. 43, 19. Ðætte se spearca bierne (birne, *v. l.*) heálice líge, Past. 87, 6. Þæccille bearnende (biornende, R.) *lucerna ardens*, Jn. L. 5, 35. Fȳres biornendes, Rtl. 101, 37. Mon geseah swelce se heofen burne *coelum ardere visum est*, Ors. 4, 7 ; S. 184, 22. Swelce se hefon birnende wǽre, 2, 6 ; S. 86, 23 : Chr. 1098; P. 234, 28. (2) of that which is heated (metal, furnace, &c.) :—Birnendan bærnísene *torrido cauterio*, An. Ox. 7, 112. Of ðām byrnendum *de torrente*, Wrt. Voc. ii. 82, 46. Byrnendum ofne, Ælfc. T. Grn. 8, 26. (3) of that which is consumed by fire :—On ðison geáre barn Xpes cyrce, Chr. 1066; P. 196, 2. For þæs fȳres bryne eall se feld born, Nar. 23, 27. Ðet ne byrnan *ut non ardeant* (*vestimenta*), Kent. Gl. 164. Hé fleáh ðā biernendan (birnendan, 35) ceastre, Past. 397, 33. (4) *to suffer heat*, of fire :—Hé (*Dives*) wæs eall biernende, Past. 309, 10. (b) of inflammation :—His (*Herod*) líchama barn wiðūtan mid langsumere hǽtan, Hml. Th. i. 86, 4. Hé barn (*from the action of thorns and nettles*) ūtan, Gr. D. 101, 24. Swā benne ne burnon, Lch. ii. 350, 29. (5) *to have ardent, vehement feeling* :—Hé unālȳfedlīce barn innan, Gr. D. 101, 26. Hé barn (born, beorn, *v. ll.*) on geleáfan, Bd. 4, 27 ; Sch. 511, 10. Hié burnon þǽre Godes lufan, Bl. H. 133, 23. (5 a) of action or passion, *to be ardent, vehement* :—Hātode, barn *incanduisset, feruebat* (*ardor crudelitatis*), An. Ox. 4731. Byrnendes gálscipes *flagrantis furie*, Wrt. Voc. ii. 149, 36. Þ wæs gnornung þām þe on breóstum wæg byrnende lufan, Chr. 975; P. 120, 16. v. beornan, byrnan *in Dict.*

**birning**, e; *f. Burning, incense* :—Beorning (biorning, R.) *incensi*, Lk. L. 1, 11.

**birn-sweord**, es ; *n. A flaming sword* :—God his byrnsweord getȳhþ and þās world ealle þurhslyhþ, Bl. H. 109, 34.

**bí-sǽc** (bi-sæc ?) :—Bisǽc *peram*, Mt. R. 10, 10. [? *From Low Lat.* bisaccus.]

**bí-sǽce, I.** *Substitute*: bí-sǽc ( = soec, -séc), e; *f. A visitation* :—Stód seó stów īdel and ǽmen, bād bísǽce betran hyrdes, Gū. 188. [*O. H. Ger.* be-suoch.]

**bí-sǽce, II.** *Substitute*: bí-sǽc; *adj. Disputed, disputable, contested* :—Gif ðǽr hwæt bísæces sȳ, sǽme se biscop *if there be anything contested, let the bishop arbitrate*, Ll. Th. ii. 314, 9. Wē lǽrað þ preóst bísǽce ordél ǽfre ne geǽde, 258, 3. Cf. un-besacen.

**bisceop.** *Add under* **I.**—Dǣda folces dǣd oferstīgan scyl bisceopes (*praesulis*), Scint. 120, 16. Hū hé his apostolas tō biscpum gebletsode, Wlfst. 175, 21. *Under* **II.**—Aristobolus wæs ǣgþer ge heora cyning ge heora biscop, Ors. 5, 12 ; S. 238, 14. *Under* **IV** *substitute : a priest of any other religion*, and add :—Biscop *flamen*, Wrt. Voc. ii. 37, 11. Se bisceop þǽre stówe *antistes oraculi* (in India), Nar. 26, 27. Him (*Philip*) þā biscepas sǽdon þæt ealle godas him irre wǣren, Ors. 3, 7 ; S. 144, 4. Lundenwaran lufodon þæt heó þeówedan heora deófolgelda biscopum *idolatris magis pontificibus seruire gaudentes*, Bd. 2, 6 ; Sch. 138, 9. v. burh-, gedwol-, leód-, scīr-bisceop.

**bisceop-cynn**, es ; *n. An episcopal race* :—Þ mǣre biscopcyn þe com of Aarone . . . men ne ceósað nū of nānum biscopcynne óðerne biscop, ac of ǣlcum cynne, Ll. Th. ii. 380, 20-26.

**bisceop-dóm. I.** *add the v. l.* :—Sién hié bégen biscopes dóme scyldie *excommunicationi subjacebunt*, Bd. 4, 5 ; Sch. 377, 16. **II.** *add: the office of bishop, episcopate, pontificate* :—Biscopdóm *pontificatus*, An. Ox.

4134 : *pontificium*, 5055 : *flamina*, 7, 102. Ægelbryht onféng Wesseaxna biscōōmes, Chr. 650; P. 28, 5. Hlōþhere féng tō biscepdōme ofer
Wesseaxan, 670; P. 34, 12. On his biscepdōme (-hāde, v. l.) binnan
Affrican scīre, Hml. A. 5, 108. [v. *N. E. D.* bishop-doom. *O. H. Ger.*
piscof-tuom (bisc(e)-) *dioecesis, episcopatus, sacerdotium*.].

**bisceop-ealdor**, es; *m. A chief priest* :—þā bisceopealdras (*pontifices*) embe ūrne Drihten ræddon, Hml. A. 65, 2 : 67, 51.

**bisceop-folgoþ**, es; *m. The episcopal office, episcopate* :—Tō þām
þ hē þone bisceopfolgoþ and hād mid gebicgean þōhte *pro adipiscendo
episcopatu*, Gr. D. 65, 31.

**bisceop-hād**. *Add* :—Biscophād *pontificium*, Rtl. 59, 11 : *flaminium*.
An. Ox. 5056. Biscophādes *pontificatus*, i. *episcopatus*, 2989. Þ wē
þās þing cȳðon be þām tīman his bisceophādes, Gr. D. 67, 25. Se abbod
þes biscophādes gernde, Chr. 1048; P. 172, 10. Ðā geár gefilled
wǣron his bysceophādes (-hāda, v. l.), Bd. 3, 17; Sch. 267, 7: 4, 5;
Sch. 380, 13. Twēgen bisceophādes men, Hml. S. 23, 365. His sunu
on bisceophāde (*sacerdotem*), Ors. 4, 4; S. 164, 31. Tō bisscephāde teón,
Past. 61, 6. Hē féng tō his sweorde æfter his biscuphāde, Chr. 1056;
P. 186, 28. Hē þon bisceophāde onféng in Turnan, ... and hē his bisceophād gedéfelīce geheóld, Bl. H. 219, 24–31. Be bisceophādum ... hū
bisceophādas wurdan ǣrest āstealde ... hū bisceophād sceolde of manegan
cynryum āspringan, Wlfst. 175, 17–176, 6, 11. Biscophādas *flamina*,
Wrt. Voc. ii. 35, 58 : *flaminea*, i. *episcopali gradus*, 149, 7. [v. *N. E. D.*
bishop-hood. *O. H. Ger.* piscof-heit *sacerdotium*.]

**bisceop-hādung**, e; *f. Ordination as bishop* :—þā underféng se
hālga wer bisceophādunge, and þone hād geheóld, Hml. S. 31, 286.

**bisceop-hām**, es; *m. An episcopal estate* :—Ic gean þes landes æt
Hedhām ... intó Paulusbyrig æt Lundænæ tō bisceophāmæ, Cht. Th.
520, 14. Tō biscophāme, 523, 23. On ǣlcon bisceophāme ǣlcon
men freót þe wīteþeówe wǣre, Cht. Crw. 23, 28. Sæ biscop him dō
hira fullan fóstær of his bisceophāmum *episcopus eos de suis propriis
episcopalibus uillis pleniter pascat*, C. D. v. 219, 4. [Cf. *the place-name
Bispham.*]

**bisceop-heáfodlín**. v. biscop-heáfod-lín *in Dict.*

**bisceop-híred**, es; *m. The clergy subject to a bishop* :—Biscophírede
*cleri* (ad calumniam pontificis et infamiam cleri, Ald. 41, 2 : cf. gloss on
the passage, An. Ox. 3006 :—*Cleri*, i. *familie*, i. *populi preósthíredes),
Wrt. Voc. ii. 81, 28 : 18, 28. Se biscop þrowade martyrdōm mid ealle
his biscophírede, Shrn. 105, 18.

**bisceop-hyrde.** *Dele, and see preceding word.*

**bisceopian.** *Retain only : To confirm*; confirmare, *and add* :—Ne
hine (*one not knowing the Creed and Pater noster*) mon fulluhte fullian
ne mōste, ne biscopian, Ll. Th. ii. 418, 36. Se biscop is geset tō māran
bletsunge ðonne se mæssepreóst sȳ, þ is ... men tō biscopienne, 378, 22.
[v. *N. E. D.* to bishop.] v. ge-bisceopian, un-bisceopod, bisceopung.

**bisceop-lic.** *Add* : I. *bishop-like, proper to a bishop* :—Hē ne gefremede nāht biscoplices, Chr. 1050; P. 170, 20. II. *episcopal,
pontifical* :—Biscoplic wurðscipe *flamininus honor*, Wrt. Voc. i. 59, 54.
Biscoplic stól *pontificalis cathedra*, An. Ox. 2029. Tō biscoplicum syn-
oðe *ad pontificale (episcopale) conciliabulum*, 3, 1. [v. *N. E. D.* bishop-
like, -ly.]

**bisceop-ríce.** *Add* :—Leódbiscop *episcopus*, biscepríce *diocessis vel
parochia*, Wrt. Voc. i. 71, 72. Cūþ þām biscope þe seó hálige stów on
his biscepríce is *in notitiam episcopi ad cujus diocessim pertinet locus*,
R. Ben. 119, 9. Gedǣlen hí þæt feoh geond þā biscopríca, C. D. B.
iii. 75, 22. Biscopríca *parrochias, diocesis*, An. Ox. 2033. v. biscopscír.

**bisceop-ród**, e; *f. A cross worn by a bishop* :—ii. bisceopróde, C. D.
iv. 275, 11.

**bisceop-scír** *a diocese.* *Add* :—Biscopscír *diocessis*, Wrt. Voc. ii.
26, 28. Ealle þā witan þe in þǣre biscopscíre (-ríce, v. l.) (*episcopio*)
wǣron, Gr. D. 67, 30. Sumne híred on his (*St. Martin*) bisceopscíre,
Bl. H. 225, 6. Wæs tōdǣled in tuā biscēscíra West-Seaxna lond; ǣr
hit wæs ān, Chr. 709; P. 40, 26.

**bisceop-seonoþ**, es; *m. A synod of bishops* :—Se bisceopsinoð þæs
Nicēniscan geþeahtes, Angl. xi. 8, 1.

**bisceop-setl** *an episcopal see.* *Add* :—Landfranc wæs gehāded on his
āgenum biscsetle, Chr. 1070; P. 204, 4. Se apostol gesæt biscepsetl in
Antiochia, 35; P. 6, 15. Þæt biscepsetl on Hrofesceastre, 633; P.
24, 21.

**bisceop-stæf.** v. next word.

**bisceop-stól.** *Add* : I. *a bishop's chair* (cf. *chair* of St. Peter),
*episcopal authority* :—Cathedra is gereht bisceopstól on Englisc, and se
hālga Petrus wæs āhafen on þām dæge on his bisceopstól. þone stól hé
gesæt seofon geár, Hml. S. 10, 4–7. Candelstæf *candelabrum*, bisceop-
stæf (? *l.* -stól) *cathedra*, Wrt. Voc. i. 81, 5. On setl biscopstóles *in sedem
pontificatus*, Bd. 5, 23; Sch. 692, 1. Hē wæs tō bisceope gehālgod tō
þām bisceopstóle æt Seolesígge, Chr. 980; P. 122, 29. Hē gesæt þone
bisceopstól an þāra twégra apostola dæge on Wintanceastre, 984; P. 124,
5. Hē betǣhte his bisceopstól ōþrum bisceope, Hml. S. 29, 112. II.
*in a local sense,* (1) *a bishop's see, cathedral town* :—Geáfon hí him

tō bisceopstóle þā burh Dorcanceaster, and hé þǣr binnan wunode, Hml.
S. 26, 135. Ic tō ǣlcum biscepstóle on mínum ríce wille āne onsendan,
Past. 7, 25. Þ ǣlc biscop bið æt his biscepstóle (*in sede episcopali*),
Ll. Th. ii. 178, 1. Hē is bebyrged æt his ƀstóle, Chr. 1069; P. 204,
10. (2) *a bishop's palace* :—Fǣringa cómon þearfan tō þām bisceopstóle
(tō þām biscope, v. l.) *subito ad episcopium pauperes venerunt*, Gr. D.
63, 29. [v. *N. E. D.* bishop-stool.]

**bisceop-sunu**, a; *m. A spiritual son at confirmation* (v. bisceopian) :—
Gif hwā ōðres godsunu sleá ... Gif hit biscepsunu sié, Ll. Th. i. 150,
20 (cf. In baptismate et confirmatione unus potest esse pater, ii. 58, § 22).
Hē (*pope Leo*) hiene (*Alfred*) him tō biscepsuna nam (cf. Asser: ad
manum episcopi in filium confirmationis acceptus), Chr. 853; P. 64, 30.
(v. note ii. p. 79.)

**bisceop-þegnung**, -þenung *episcopal ministration.* *Add* :—Hē wæs
bewered fram þǣre biscopþegnunge *ab administrando episcopatu prohibito*, Bd. 4, 5; Sch. 380, 17. Hē forlét his bisceopþegnunge *relicto
episcopatus officio*, 3, 24; Sch. 312, 13. Hē him bisceopþéninge (*ministerium episcopale*) sēceað tō Westseaxna biscope, 5, 23; Sch. 691, 4.

**bisceopung**; *f. Confirmation* :—Se Hālga Gāst ðās gyfa tōðǣlð
... ealswā biscopas on biscpunge tō Gode sylfum wilniað, Wlfst. 51, 14.
Hí setton heora handa ofer geleáffulle men, and him com tō se Hālga
Gāst ðurh heora biscepunge. Biscopas sind þæs ylcan hādes on Godes
gelaþunge, and healdað ðā gesetnysse on heora biscepunge, and biddað
þæt se ælmihtiga Wealdend him sende ðā seofonfealdan gife his Gāstes,
Hml. Th. i. 328, 2–7. v. bisceopian.

**bisceop-wíte**; *n. Substitute : A fine payable to a bishop* (cf. e. g.
Ll. Th. i. 262, § 3 : 474, § 17) :—Ðæt ðe scȳrbiscop ... hādinge ne dó
on ðis abbotríce, būton seó abbod hit him bydde, ne biscopwíte *episcopus
dioceseos ... sine abbatis fauore arroget, ... neque ... in omni priuilegio ipsius juris quicquam praeter abbatis assensum accipiat vel faciat*, C. D. v. 28, 35.

**bisceop-wyrt.** *Add* :—Biscopuuyrt *hibiscum*, Wrt. Voc. ii. 110, 37.
Biscopwyrt *gerobotana*, 42, 26.

**bisceop-wyrtel** (?) *bishop's weed* :—Biscopwyrtil *gerobotana vel ver-
bena vel sagmen*, Wrt. Voc. i. 31, 14.

**bísen.** *l.* bisen, e; bisene, an; *f.* (also *n.* in North.), *and add* : I.
*example to be followed or avoided,* (1) *of persons* :—On hū monigfaldum
mǣgenum se sācerd scolde scínan mannum tō biesene (bisene, v. l.), Past.
85, 1. Riht is þ wydewan Annan bysenan fylian, Ll. Th. ii. 324, 6.
Mid bisseno Dauiðes *exemplo Dauid*, Mt. p. 16, 13. Sel ūs hiora bissene
giðia *da nobis eorum imitatione proficere*, Rtl. 62, 16. Ic eów sealde
bysene (bisen, L., bisine, R. *exemplum*), Jn. 13, 15. Nimað eów bysne
be ðām, Hml. S. 24. 79, 66. Ne sceal hé yfele bysne niman æt forðfarenum mannum, Hml. Th. ii. 532, 31. Uē bisen ginime *imitemur*,
Rtl. 57, 15. Biseno, 62, 23. Hē wolde ūs bisene āstellan, Past. 33, 18.
Gōde bisene, 191, 5. Hālgawara ðínra biseno (*exempla*), Rtl. 49, 11.
Hwelce bisena hé stellende wæs, Ors. 2, 2; S. 66, 24. (2) *of things* :—
Gelíce and seó burg wǣre tō bisene āsteald eallum middangearde, Ors. 2,
4; S. 74, 24. II. *an exemplar, a model, pattern* for the being,
doing or making of something :—Wē sint gesceapene æfter ðǣre biesene
(bisene, v. l.) ūres Scippendes ... sē ðe tō Godes bisene gesceapen is *ad
conditoris nostri sumus imaginem et similitudinem creati ... qui ad Dei
imaginem et similitudinem conditus*, Past. 249, 17–22. Mið ūser líchome bisene *cum nostrae carnis substantia*, Rtl. 4, 28. Mið ðȳ on
bisne Godes wæs *cum in forma Dei esset*, 21, 18. Gif hwā ðās bóc āwrítan
wylle, þæt hé hí gerihte be ðǣre bysne (*the original*), Hml. Th. ii. 2,
21 : Ælfc. Gr. Z. 3, 21. Hé monig tācen unwitende dyde on Godes
bisene, Ors. 5, 14; S. 248, 14. Hē hét forbǣrnan Rōme burh æfter
þǣre bisene þe Trōgiaburh barn, Bt. 16, 4; F. 58, 4. Ic hit mid yfelre
bysene inc forgylde *I will repay it you in evil fashion*, Bl. H. 189, 26, 31.
Magon gē geseón sweotole bysene, 99, 14. Wē wyllað eów ðēn bysne
of twām mōnðum, Angl. viii. 300, 37. Gif bisenum (*exemplaribus*) lufu
is tō gefanne ... swǣ monig aron bissena (*exemplaria*) swā monige
boec, Mt. p. 1, 13. Sealdon hí him bysne monige, hū hí him wǣpen
wyrcean sceoldan *praebent instituendorum exemplaria armorum*, Bd. 1,
12; Sch. 34, 9. III. *example, parallel case, precedent* :—Hē mā
cēgde ... wē sceolan beón gelǣrede mid þysse bysene, Bl. H. 19, 14.
On þisse bysene is gecȳþed þ ..., 35, 2. Hē nam bysne be mannum, hū
*exemplo bovis adquandi*, Lk. p. 8, 5. Hú ǣlc sunu bið gingra þonne se fæder, Hml. Th. i. 290, 7. IV. *a
rule, prescript, precept* :—Bysne *normam*, i. *regulam*, An. Ox. 997.
Bisne *normam*, i. *rectitudinem*, 2306. Bysnum *normulis*, i. *regulis*,
130. V. *a figurative example, parable, similitude, type* :—Bísen
fēwer nētna *similitudo quattuor animalium*, Mt. p. 9, 10. Ðió biseno
*parabola*, Lk. L. 8, 9. Ðiós bisseno, 11. Mið bisene from esne erende
*similitudine de seruo arante*, p. 9, 6. Būta biseno (bisene, R.) *sine parabola*, Mk. L. 4, 34. Ðæt hié magon be ðisse bisene ongietan þe him is
tō gecweden *quod intelligi figuraliter potest, illis dicitur*, Past. 188, 21.
Ic þé mæg gereccan be sumere bisne, þ þū miht ongiton ..., Bt. 27, 2;
F. 98, 17. Þis wæs ūs gedón tō lífes bysene (*as a type of life*), Bl. H.
73, 23 : 75, 27. Þis eástorlíce gerýno ūs ætéöweð þæs écean lífes

ṣweotole bysene, 83, 8. Ốđero biseno *aliam parabolam.* Mt. L. 13, 31. Ốđer bisen, 33. Bisin, p. 19, 1. Þ bisen (đā bisine, R.), Lk. L. 14, 7. Wē sculon manega bisna reccan . . . ne fō wē nā on đā bisena (bisna, *v. l.*) for đāra leásana spella lufan, Bt. 35, 5; F. 166, 13–16. [v. *N. E. D.* bysen.] v. býsen (*l.* bysen) *in Dict.*

**bisene**; *adj. Blind:*—On þǽre tīde hē wæs bysne (bysene, *v.l.*); þā sealde Drihten him gesyhđe, Gr. D. 275, 3. Hē āwrāt rōde tācen ofer þæs bysenan (blindan, *v. l.*) mannes eágan, and seó niht þǽre blindnysse gewāt fram þām eágum, 77, 28. Tuoege bisene ł blinde *duo caeci,* Mt. L. 9, 27. Bisena, 28. Biseno geseáđ *caeci vident,* 11, 5. [v. *N. E. D.* bisson.]

**bisenian**; *p.* ode     I. *to set* or *give an example* of something (*acc.* or *clause*) to a person (*dat.*) :—Gif hē wel lǽrđ and yfele mid weorce bysenađ, R. Ben. 11, 19. Hī bisnodon hiora æftergengum þ hī nǽren mid wītum oferswīþde *exemplum ceteris praetulerunt, invictam malis esse virtutem,* Bt. 39, 10; F. 230, 2. Bysnige hē ealle eáđmōdnesse eallum *magis humilitatis exempla omnibus det,* R. Ben. 107, 6. Gif se lāreów riht tǽce . . ., gif hē yfel bysnige, Hml. Th. ii. 48, 35. Þæt hỹ bodian and bysnian Godes riht georne, Wlfst. 179, 8. Þ hig mihton þām folce wel wissian tō Godes geleáfan and wel bisnian tō gōdum weorcum, Ælfc. Gen. Thw. 2, 28.     II. *to take example:*—Đā lāreówas đæt wæter gedrēfađ mid hira undeáwum, đonne đæt folc bisenađ on hira undeáwum, ɲals on hira lāre *cum subjecti non sectantur verba, sed exempla pravitatis imitantur,* Past. 31, 6. Ốđre men bi đām bieseniađ (bis-, *v.l.*) *ad subditos suos exempla transmittunt,* 191, 7. Hē gesyngađ đurh đā đe he him bisniađ (*per eos, qui se imitari fecerint, delinquant*) . . . đỹlǽs đā untruman be him bisneden, 451, 27–30.     III. *to take the model for, model, form* after a pattern. v. bisen,   II.:—Of þīnum rīce wē bysniađ eall þ wē gōdes dōđ, Shrn. 166, 23. Bisnide ł sceóp mec esne him *formans me servum sibi,* Rtl. 55, 32. Ne bysna þē be nānum ɟǽra þe yfel dōn, Ps. Th. 36, 8.     IV. *to express figuratively.* v. bisen, V :—Đæt ilce Dryhten ūs bisnade đurh Moysen, đā hē cuæđ *quod figurate Dominus per Moysen praecipit, dicens,* Past. 165, 24. [v. *N. E. D.* bysen.] v. bysnian *in Dict.*

**bisenung**, e; *f.* I. *example* (of conduct) :—þæt ōđre þurh his gōdan bysenunge gelǽrede sỹn, R. Ben. 109, 23. Nāþor ne hī mid bodengum wel nā lǽraþ ne mid bisnuncgum wel nā tǽcaþ, Wlfst. 276, 25. Hī mid bysnungum wel ne lǽdađ, Ll. Th. ii. 328, 2.     II. *example, proof:*—Bysnung *documentum,* An. Ox. 4539. [v. *N. E. D.* bysening.] v. bysning *in Dict.*; gelīc-bisning.

**bi-seón** *to see. l. to strain upon.* v. be-seón.

**bises.** *Substitute:* The intercalary day in leap year, bissext (v. *N. E. D.*) :—Būtan þænne bises geboden weorđe feórđan geáre *except when bissext is ordered every fourth year,* Men. 32. v. bissextus.

**bisgian.** *l.* bisgian, *and add:* I. *to occupy, employ:*—Đæt hē suā micle sorgfulra sié ymb hine selfne, suā hine lǽs ōđerra monna giémen bisegađ (bisgađ, *v.l.*) *tanto circa se sollicitius vivant, quanto eos aliena cura non implicat,* Past. 191, 21. Bisiga đē be sumum men; fordon biđ ǽlces mannes līf sumes mannes lār, Prov. K. 43. Se lāreów đe bodunge underfēhđ, ne sceal hē hine sylfne mid woruldþingum bysgian (*printed* bysnian), Hml. Th. ii. 532, 27.     II. *to harass, trouble:*—Wildeór ūs on þǽre nihte bisgodon, Nar. 15, 4. v. býsgian (*l.* bysgian) *in Dict.*

**bisgu.** *l.* bisgu, *and add: gen.* u, e, a; an :    I. *occupation:*—þonne hī mid eorđlicum teolungum hī gebysgiađ, þonne ne magon hī for đǽre bysga smeágan embe þæs Hǽlendes menniscnysse, Hml. Th. i. 524, 16. Gif hwā for bisgan oftor ne mæge, Btwk. 194, 7. Martha hī (*Mary*) wolde habban tō hire bysegan, Hml. Th. ii. 440, 21. Ongemang ōđrum bisgum đisses kynerīces, Past. 7, 18. Būton hwā mid bysegum ofset sỹ *nisi in causa gravis utilitatis quis occupatus fuerit,* R. Ben. 58, 15: 59, 3. Ic settan wille bysega and bīgengas þysses drihtenlican þeówdōmes *constituenda est a nobis dominici scola servitii,* 5, 10. Hỹ swā hwilce bysiga, swā hỹ on handa hæfdan, unfulworhte lǽtađ *ex occupatis manibus quod agebant relinquentes,* 20, 2.     II. *trouble:*—Eác đǽm ōþrum bisgum and geswencnissum cwom micel deór, Nar. 15, 10. Ic wolde for þǽm bysegum mīnes mōdes mē gerestan *ego animo aeger ad requiem vado,* 30, 21. v. býsgu (*l.* bysgu) *in Dict.*; weorold-bisegu.

**bisgung.** *l.* bisgung, *and add:*—Sió bisgung đæs rīces tōslīt đæt mōd đæs receres *occupatio regiminis solidaritatem dissipet mentis,* Past. 37, 11. Þeáh hē mid þǽre manigfealdnysse þǽre synne bysgunge ābysgod sỹ *licet multiplicitate negotii peccati suspensus sit,* Ll. Th. ii. 176, 8. For đāra bisgunge ne sié his giémen nā đỹ lǽsse ymb đā gehīrsuman *internorum curam in exteriorum occupatione non minuens,* Past. 75, 14. Ne sceal hē hyne ābysgian worldlicra bysgunga *non debet occupari mundanis negotiis,* Ll. Th. ii. 174, 28. v. á-, weorold-bisgung.

**bisig**; *adj. Busy, occupied:*—Oft biđ seó sāwul on ānum þinge swā bysig, þ heó ne gỹmđ hwā hyre gehende biđ, þeáh đe heó on lōcie, Hml. s. 1, 217. Se bisceop wæs bysig mid þām cynincge, 21, 235. Mīn dohtor is nū swīđe bisy ymbe hyre leornunge, Ap. Th. 20, 5. v. býsig (*l.* bysig) *in Dict.*; syn-, tiht-bisig.

**bisleásung.** *Dele:* bisme. v. besma.

**bismer**; *n. Add: m., f.*     I. *infamy, shame, an infamous deed :*—Bysmor, sceaniu *rubor,* An. Ox. 2933. Hē gehỹrde þæt bysmor mīnra worda, Hml. S. 23 b, 366. Tōeácan þǽm bismrum þe hē đōnde wæs, hē hēt onbærnan Rōmeburg, Ors. 6, 5; S. 260, 29.     II. *disgrace, ignominy, humiliation :*—Hwæþer . . . hē hié ācwealde, þe hié libbende tō bismre gerēnian hēte. Hié þā hē tō đǽm bismre getawade þe on đǽm dagum mǽst wæs, þæt hē hié bereáfade heora clāþa and heora wǽpna . . . hié him beforan drifen þā consulas swā swā niédlingas, þ heora bismer þỹ māre wǽre (*oneratos ignominia consules remiserunt*). Geornor wē woldon iówra bismra beón forsugiende, Ors. 3, 8; S. 122, 1–10. Ealne þæne bysmor þe wē þoliađ, wē gyldađ mid weorđscype þām þe ūs scendađ, Wlfst. 163, 9.     III. *scorn, contumely, insult :*—Bysmer *ludibrium,* Wrt. Voc. ii. 50, 35. Bysmeres ganniturae, An. Ox. 4757. Bysmires, Wrt. Voc. ii. 85, 67. Ofsceótan mid đǽm bismere . . . hē geman đæt bismer *commovere in contumeliarum jaculatione . . . injuriarum jacula ad memoriam reducit,* Past. 227, 9–16. Hē bær þā gatu upp tō ánum beorge tō bysmore his feóndum, Jud. p. 161, 11. Tō bismere, Bl. H. 201, 23. Hine bismriende mid myclere bismre, 243, 7. Hē manig bysmor geþrowade, 23, 31. Bismer (*ad*) *dedecus* (*natalium*), An. Ox. 4309. Hī wrohten ǽlc þǽra harme and bismere þæs cynges, mannan . . . hū hī mihton þæs cynges bismer āwrecan and ealles þeódscipes, Chr. 1048; P. 174, 1–8. Hē sǽde þā sār and đā bysmra þe hē ādreógan wolde, Bl. H. 15, 33.     IV. *blasphemy:*—Þū bysmor (-er, *v.l.*) spycst *blasphemas,* Jn. 10, 36. [v. *N. E. D.* bismer. *O. H. Ger.* bismer *opprobrium, ludicrum, insultatio, blasphemia.*] v. weoroldbismer.

**bismer-full.** *Add:*—Ābūgan tō bismerfullum (bysmor-, *v.l.*) deófolgylde, Hml. A. 28, 98. Būgan tō þām bysmorfullum godum, Hml. S. 29, 207.

**bismer-gleó[w]**, es; *n. Unseemly, disgraceful sport :*—Ic gehāte þ ic nǽfre ofer þis mīnne līchoman ne besmīte þurh þ grimme bysmergleów þæs mānfullan geligeres, Hml. S. 23 b, 451. Bysmergle(ó) *ludicra* (*prima juventutis calcans severe,* Ald. 158, 8 : cf. lascivam aetatis petulantiam crudeliter castigans, 33, 35), An. Ox. 17, 17.

**bismerian.** *Add:*—Bysmraþ *adludit,* An. Ox. 46, 37. Hē bysmraþ men mid his dreócræfte, Bl. H. 183, 35. Se synfulla bysmraþ (*irritavit*) Drihten, Ps. Th. 9, 23. Mec þās elreordegan nū bysmergeađ *illudi me a barbaris existimavi,* Nar. 25, 26. Bysmrode ic hine mid mīnum ondswarum, 18, 13. Hē hī tintrade and bismrade, oþ hié mid ealle wǽron dōn and forhiéned *cruentissimam victoriam exercuit,* Ors. 3, 7; S. 118, 25. Hē þā biscepas for þǽre sægene swīþe bismrade *irridens eos,* 3, 10; S. 140, 2. Hē hine bismerode *adortus est illum contumeliis,* Bt. 18, 4; F. 66, 28. Hié hine on þǽm tældon and bismrodan, þ . . ., Bl. H. 215, 9. Ne mīne fỹnd mē for đỹ ɲe bysmrian (*irrideant*), Ps. Th. 24, 2. Mihtest þū bismorian þās andweardan welan, Bt. 14, 3; F. 46, 32. Folces bysmri(g)endes (beosmr-, *v.l.*) *vulgi insultantis,* Bd. 5, 12 ; Sch. 620, 7. Gehispende, bysmriende *insultantes,* i. *exprobrantes,* An. Ox. 1474. Bismriende mid myclere bismre, Bl. H. 243, 7. Se mon biđ bismrod (-ad) (*inluditur*) swā swā đurh swefen, Bd. 1, 27; Sch. 93, 10. Bismrud, Lk. 18, 32. [He bismereþ and scorneþ þe guode men, Ayenb. 22, 20. *O. H. Ger.* bismarōn *illudere, blasphemare.*]

**bismeriend.** *Substitute:* A scorner, mocker, Kent. Gl. 60 : 298.

**bismer-leóþ.** *Substitute:* A contemptible, frivolous, ridiculous song :—Tweógendlicra gewrita bismerleóđ *apocryphorum naenias,* i. *vanitates,* Hpt. Gl. 522, 51. Bismærleóđ *naenias .i. vanitates* (*frivolorum*), 524, 71. Bismerleóđ *nenias,* Wrt. Voc. ii. 87, 14 : 60, 73. v. next word.

**bismer-lic.** *Dele: unpleasant,* and last passage, and add : I. *disgraceful, ignominious :*—Gewearđ seó mǽste sibb and seó bismerleceste, Ors. 3, 1 ; S. 94, 21. Hē heora ǽgþer ge mid bismere onfeng, ge hié eác on þone bismerlecestan eard gesette *cum foedissima ignominia dispersi sunt,* 3, 11; S. 146, 34.     II. *contemptible, ridiculous, frivolous :*—Bismerlic *frivolous,* i. *mendax, fictus,* Wrt. Voc. ii. 150, 81 : *ridiculosum* (*phantasma*), Hpt. Gl. 459, 35. Þ is swīđe bysmærlic *ridiculum est valde,* Gr. D. 321, 12.

**bismer-līce.** *Add:* I. *with ignominy :*—Man sceal þā geoguđe lǽdan gehæft heánlīce and swā bysmorlīce bringan of heora ēđle, Wlfst. 295, 18.     II. *irreverently, blasphemously :*—Hī ic besencte on helle grund, forþan hig sprǽcon bysmorlīce be mē, Wlfst. 295, 30. Þā hǽđnan bysmerlīce and synlīce heora godas him laþodan on fultum, Bl. H. 201, 30. [*O. H. Ger.* bismer-līhho *ridicule.*]

**bismer-nes.** *Substitute:* I. *disgrace, pollution :*—Seó bysmernes (besmitenes, *v.l.*) *inquinatio,* Bd. 1, 27 ; Sch. 95, 13. [Lendenu] mīn gefyllede synd on bysmyrnyssum, and nis hǽlo on flǽsce mīne, Ps. Spl. C. 37, 7.     II. *reproach, insult :*—God wolde đā bysmernyssa ūra feónda fram ūs ācerron, Hml. A. 126, 321.     III. *contemptibleness, pitifulness.* v. bismer-lic, II :—Hē forseah þā deófollican lāre, for þām þe hē ealle þā ỹdele ongeat . . . and þā bysmornysse forhogode heora lāra and heora costunga, Guth. 34, 4–12.

**bismer-sprǽc.** *l.* -sprǽc, *and add:* [*O. Sax.* bismer-sprāka *insulting, contumelious speech.*]

**bismer-sprecan.** *Dele, and see* bismer, IV.

**bismerung.** *Add: Mockery, scorn :*—Bismrung *cavillum, cavillatio,*

Wrt. Voc. ii. 129, 68. þæt hit cáðe mihte beón, ðæt hit þurh bysmrunge (biosm-, beosm-, *v.ll.*) ætýwde *ne forte inlusoria esset visio*, Bd.
5, 9; Sch. 593, 17. Fúle bismerunga *spurca ludibria (opprobria)*, Hpt.
Gl. 507, 21. [*O. H. Ger.* bismarunga *blasphemia*.] v. ge-bismerung.

**bí-spell.** *Add:*—Bíspel *paradigma*, Wrt. Voc. ii. 66, 3. Þreó
ðusend bigspella Salomon gesette *locutus est Salomon tria millia para-
bolas* (1 Kings 4, 32), Hml. Th. ii. 578, 3. Ídele býspellu forbúh
*inanes fabulas devita*, Scint. 213, 5. [v. *N. E. D.* by-spell.]

**bissextus**; *gen.* bissexte *The intercalary day of leap-year; also leap-
year* :—Sume preóstas secgað þ bissextus cume þurh þ, þ Iosue ábæd æt
Gode þ seó sunne stód stille ... Nis næfre þurh þ bissextus ... *Bis* is
twuwa, *sextus* se syxta, bissextus twuwa syx, for þám wé cweðað on
ðám geáre nú tódæg *sexta kl. Martii*, and eft on merigen *sexta kl.
Martii*, Lch. iii. 262, 7-18. Be rihte bissexte (bisexte, *v.l.*) *de ratione
bissexti*, Bd. 5, 23; Sch, 698, 1. þá tída maciað æfre ymbe þ feórðe
geár þone dæg and þá niht þe wé hátað bissextum, Lch. iii. 246, 14. [v.
*N. E. D.* bissext.] v. bises.

**bísting**, e; *f. Beestings* :—Býstinc (v. Angl. viii. 451) *colostrum*,
Wrt. Voc. i. 27, 31. Cúhyrde gebyreð, þ hé hæbbe ealdre cú meolc
.vii. niht syððan heó núge cealfod hæfð, and frymetlinge býstinge .xiiii.
niht, Ll. Th. i. 438, 19. v. býsting *in Dict.*

**bí-swíc** (bí-), -swíc-. v. be-swíc, -swíc-.

**bita** *a bit. Add:* bitu (-e) (?), e, an; *f.* :—Bita *frustum*, Wrt. Voc. ii.
151, 40. Drége bite *bucella sicca*, Kent. Gl. 587. Swá swá bita *sicut
buccellas*, Ps. Spl. M. 147, 6. [*O. Frs.* kor-bita: *O. H. Ger.* bizzo (-a)
*buccella, offa : Icel.* biti.]

**bita** *a biter. Add:* [*O. H. Ger.* wolf-bizo *liciscus*.] v. and-, hræd-,
næder-bita.

**bítan.** *Add:* I. *to bite with the teeth* :—Ic bíte *mandeo*, bítende and
slítende *mordax*, Wrt. Voc. ii. 57, 47, 56. Hé bítes and slítes hine
*adlidit eum*, Mk. R. 9, 18. Bítende (bídtende, L.) ł bát hine *discerpens
eum*, 1, 26. Ia. *to bite, gnash the teeth* :—Hí biton heora téð
him tógeánes, Hml. Th. i. 46, 27. II. *of a pungent substance* :—
Þone yfelan, bítendan wætan, Lch. ii. 60, 23. v. be-, for-bítan.

**bíte.** *l. bite, and add:* I. *a bite* :—Wiþ nædran bite, Lch. ii. 110,
19. Bite *morsum*, Wrt. Voc. ii. 57, 60. Swá hwilcne swá þær hors
mihte, hit slát and wundode hiora lima mid bitum, Gr. D. 78, 5. Ia.
*of the effect of cancer* :—Ealne þone bite þæs cancres heó áfeormað, Lch.
i. 296, 22. Ib. *fig.* :—' Eálá deáþ, ic beó þín deáþ, and ic beó þín
bite on helle.' Mycelne bite Drihten dyde on helle þá hé þyder ástág,
Bl. H. 67, 17. II. *the bite, cut of a weapon, &c.* :—Ðær is benda bite
and dynta dyne, Wlfst. 114, 23: 209, 17. Gif bánes bite weorð *if
the bone be cut*, Ll. Th. i. 12, 5. (Cf. *O. Frs.* bênes biti.) [*O. Frs.* biti:
*O. Sax.* biti (billes): *O. H. Ger.* biz *morsus: Icel.* bit; *n.*] v. grist-bite.

**bítel**, es; *m. A beetle, hammer* :—Nán monn ne gehiérde æxe hlem ne
biétles suég *absque mallei sonitu*, Past. 253, 17. Hé sceal habban
æcse, ... býtel, Angl. ix. 263, 7. þá blacan bétlas *nigro colore* (the
noun is unglossed), Wrt. Voc. ii. 61, 58. [*O. H. Ger.* stein-bôzil *latomus*.]
v. býtl *in Dict.*

**bítel** *a beetle. Substitute:* bitela, an; *m. A beetle, insect* :—Bitela
*mordiculus* (in a list of insects), Wrt. Voc. i. 24, 18: ii. 58, 11. Bitelum
*blatis*, 127, 10. Bitulum *blattis*, Txts. 45, 307. Cf. bita.

**biter.** *Add:* I. *bitter to the taste* :—Biter wyrtdrenc *picra*, Wrt.
Voc. i. 20, 18. Ðonne se læce bietre wyrta deð tó hwelcum drence, ...
ðonne bið se deáðbæra wæta ofslægen mid ðæm biteran drence, Past.
303, 12-17. Bitrum *rancidis*, Wrt. Voc. ii. 118, 62. II. *bitter
to the mind, painful* :—þá geogoðlustas him swíþe bitere þencaþ, Bl. H.
59, 11. Biterra *dirior*, Wrt. Voc. ii. 27, 76. Hwæt is ðienga ðe bietere
(biterre, *v.l.*) sié on ðæs láreówes móde?, Past. 165, 1. þú mé ne syle
on þone biterestan deáð, Bl. H. 229, 26. III. *bitter (of feeling),
acrimonious, ill-natured* :—Onbærude mid þære biteran æfeste, Bl. H.
25, 7.

**bitere.** *Add:*—þú scealt þá sáwle bitere forgyldan, Wlfst. 177, 7:
Bl. H. 195, 23. [*O. Sax.* bittro: *O. H. Ger.* bittaro.]

**biter-líc** (?); *adj. Bitter* :—Áterlicum oððe biter[licum] *gorgoneo*,
Wrt. Voc. ii. 41, 56. [*Icel.* bitr-ligr.]

**biter-líce.** *Add:*—Swíþe bitterlíce (biter- *v.l.*) weópende, Gr. D.
140, 12. Ðæt réðe flód biterlíce (*amare*) bærnð ðá earman sáula, Dóm.
L. 166. Weard seó móder biterlíce gegremod, Hml. Th. ii. 30, 3.

**biter-nes.** *Add:* I. cf. biter, I:—Ðá bieternesse ðære wyrte ...
se swæc ðære bieternesse, Past. 303, 14-15. II. cf. biter, II:—
Biternys *acerbitas (poenarum)*, An. Ox. 4816. Ágyld þú mé mid biternesse leán, R. Ben. 22, 19. Þes middangeard flýhþ from ús mid
mycelre biternesse, Bl. H. 115, 17. III. cf. biter, III:—Biternes
*accedia*, Wrt. Voc. ii. 10, 9. Yfel biternesse anda, R. Ben. 131, 12.
v. ofer-biterness.

**biter-wyrde.** *Substitute: Bitter of speech, given to bitter words,*
and add:—þ gé ne beón tó biterwyrde, ne bealufulle on móde, Hml. A.
48, 576.

**-bitian, -bitung.** v. grist-bitian, -bitung.

**bitol**; *m. A bit, bridle. Add:*—Biotul *bagulum*, Wrt. Voc. ii. 12,
51. On bytole *in freno*, Bl. Gl. [*Icel.* bitull (-ill); *m. a bit.*]

**bitt.** v. ge-bitt.

**bíwan** (eó, ý) *to rub, polish.* [Iesu Crist bæweþþ follc off sinness,
Orm. 19719. To clennsenn and to bæwenn, 15153. *O. H. Ger.* fer-
bouuit *confectus*; ge-beuuit *tritus*.] v. â-, ge-bíwan, *and* býwan *in Dict.*

**bi-windla**, an; *m. ?* :—Onbútan ðone gáran on ðone biwindlan (pi-
windlan, 15), C. D. v. 148, 16.

**bí-wist.** *Add: and* es; *m.* (cf. dæg-, hús-, neáh-wist). *Subsistence* :—Ðis is myngung manna bíwiste *quorum hoc viaticum sit*, Ll. Th.
i. 440, 29. Gif hwá hwæt lytles æniges bigwistes him sylfum gearcode,
reáferas ðone mete him of ðám múðe ábrúdon, Hml. Th. i. 404, 3. On
heora bíwiste and on hrægle gehealdene, Bl. H. 185, 16. þearfum
bigwiste syllan, Hml. S. 26, 276. þá þe on gemænum ðingum bigwiste habbað (*the monastic orders*), Hml. Th. i. 398, 13. Bíwiste *stipendia*,
An. Ox. 4833.

**bí-word.** *Dele:* -wyrd, *and second passage, and add: An adverb* :—
Hig ærest ápinsiað þá naman and þá bínaman, ... syððan hig þá word
(*verbs*) áginnað tó áwegenne mid þám bíwordum, Angl. viii. 313, 7. v.
bí-wyrde.

**bí-wrítan.** *l.* bí wrítan, *and see* be, C.

**bí-wyrde**, es; *n. A proverb, saying* :—Bíwyrde *proverbium*, Wrt.
Voc. ii. 68, 56. Bíwyrda *proverbiorum*, An. Ox. 5232. [v. *N. E. D.*
by-word. *O. H. Ger.* pî-wurti *proverbium, parabola*.]

**bixen, blac.** v. byxen, blæc.

**blác.** *Add:*—Blác *pallidus*, An. Ox. 11, 145. Ðæt bleoh ðæs wel-
hæwnan iacintes bið betera ðonne ðæs blácan carbuncules *coerulei coloris
hyacinthus praefertur pallenti carbunculo*, Past. 411, 29. (Cf. seó
bláce blegen *carbunculus*. v. blegen.) [v. *N. E. D.* blake. *O. Sax.*
blêk: *O. H. Ger.* bleih *pallidus: Icel.* bleikr.] v. flód-, heoru-,
weder-, wíg-blác; blác-hleór.

**blác-ern.** *Add:*—Blácern *lichinus*, Wrt. Voc. i. 81, 31. Swá is án
micel blácern *sicut lucerna*, Nar. 37, 18. Ðonne þú blácernes behófige,
Tech. ii. 126, 1. Man sceal habban ... leóhtfæt, blácern, Angl. ix. 264,
22. v. blæc-ern.

**blácian.** *Add:*—Ðá ongan hé cwacian and blácian (*pallescere*) and
swætan, Gr. D. 325, 31: Hml. Th. i. 414, 12. Blácigende *pallens*, Hy.
S. 24, 9. [v. *N. E. D.* blake, bloke. *O. H. Ger.* bleihhên *pallescere*.]

**blácung.** *Add:*—In blácunge (*pallore*) and on cwacunge þæs untruman mannes, Gr. D. 326, 5. Glædne andwlitan búton blácunge and
forhtunge, Hml. Th. i. 72, 27. Se móna blácunge (*pallorem*) healdende,
Hy. S. 35, 11.

**bladesian** (blat-); *p.* ode. I. *to flame, blaze, be hot* :—Bryne ł
bladesige on fíre sóþ lufu *flammescat igne karitas*, Hy. S. 10, 14. Bla-
desiendum (blat-, Hpt. Gl. 464, 51) *coquentibus, i. assantibus*, An. Ox.
2469. II. *to emit an odour* :—Bladesiað *redoleant, i. spirent*, An.
Ox. 554. v. next words.

**bladesnung** (blat-), e; *f. Scent, odour* :—Blatesnung *flagrantia* (cf.
stincende *flagrans*, 35, 73), Wrt. Voc. ii. 36, 38. v. previous word.

**bladesung**, e; *f. Flaming, blazing, sparkling* :—Blætesunge *coruscationes*, Ps. Spl. 76, 18.

**blæc** *ink. Add: black matter* :—Deorces sótes blæc *furvae fuliginis
atramentum*, An. Ox. 4159. [v. *N. E. D.* bleck. *O. L. Ger.* blac.] v.
bóc-blæc.

**blæc, blæc** *black. Dele last paragraph, and add:*—Blac *niger*,
Wrt. Voc. i. 46, 31: 76, 83. Blac wíngeard *brabasca*, 30, 16. Blac
purpur *ferrugo*, 40, 41. Hwæþer hé biþ ðe blac ðe hwít, Bt. 41, 4; F.
252, 11. Blacu rammes wul, Lch. i. 356, 11. þ deór wæs blæces
heówes (*atri coloris*), Nar. 15, 17. Ðú ne miht wyrcan án hær hwít
oððe blacc, Hml. Th. i. 482, 20. Blace berian *flavia vel mori*, Wrt.
Voc. ii. 38, 67. Blaco *pulla*, 118, 46. þá blacan, 87, 62. Him wæron
þá nebb and þá cleá swilce blace *rostro pedibusque nigris*, Nar. 16, 16.
Hió an Ceóldrýþe hyre blacena tunecena swá þær[a?] hyre leófre beó,
Cht. Th. 538, 5. Beátan mid blacum flintum, Hml. S. 11, 99.

**blæc.** *Add:* I. *bright* :—Lég onetteð blæc, byrnende, Dóm. 56.
þæs deóres híw, blæc brigda gehwæs, Pa. 26. II. *pale* :—Blæc
thrustfell *bitiligo*, Txts. 45, 296. [v. *N. E. D.* bleach; *adj.*, bleak.] v.
blác.

**blæcan.** *Add:* [*Icel.* bleikja]: **blæc-berie.** *l.* blæc berie. v. blæc.

**blæccan**, an; *f. Black matter* :—Speccan blæccan gefýlede *scoriae
atramento foedatos*, An. Ox. 652. [v. *N. E. D.* blatch.] v. blæc.

**blæce, blêce**, es; *n. An itching skin-disease* :—Wiþ blæce on andwlitan, Lch. ii. 52, 15, 18, 20, 23. Wið ðám micclan líce and wið
óðrum giccendum blêce, iii. 70, 28. [*Take here passages from Lchdms.
given in Dict. under* blæco.] Blêci *viti(li)ginem*, Txts. 105, 2117: 114,
107: *pruriginem*, 111, 24. [v. *N. E. D.* bleach; *sb.*] v. blæcþa, blác,
blæc.

**blæc-ern.** *Dele.*

**blæc-ern.** *Add:*—Blæcern *lucerna*, Wrt. Voc. i. 284, 25: ii. 51, 74.
Blæcern ælan, Past. 43, 2. þæra eágan scínað nihtes swá leóhte swá
blæcern (*lucernae*), Nar. 34, 14. Blæcernum *lichinis*, Wrt. Voc. ii. 51, 75.

blæc-feaxed. *l.* blæc-feaxede.

blæc-horn, es; *n. An ink-horn :*—Ðonne þ̣ū blechorn habban wille, Tech. ii. 128, 18. [*O. L. Ger.* blac-horn *atramentarium : Icel.* blek-horn.]

blǣco, es; *n. Substitute: indecl. f. Pallor :*—Blǣco *pallor,* Wrt. Voc. ii. 66, 42. On blǣco gecyrred, Guth. 88, 14. [*v. N. E. D.* bleach. *O. H. Ger.* bleihhî.] v. blǣce.

blǣc-pytt *a bleaching-pit* (?) :—On blǣcpit; of blǣcpytte (the *æ* is accented), C. D. v. 332, 14.

blæc-teru. *l.* blæc teru, *and see* teoru *in Dict. :* blǣcþa. *Substitute :*—Blēctha *vitiligo,* Wrt. Voc. ii. 123, 55. Cf. blǣce : blǣd *a cup. Dele.*

blǣd; *m. Add: ; f.* (v. Bd. S. 569, 8).     I. *a blowing, blast* of wind :—Swîðe mycel windes blǣd, Bl. H. 199, 21 : Hml. S. 23, 72. Blǣde *flamine,* Germ. 400, 496. Se wind him stôd ongeán mid ormǣtum blǣde, Hml. Th. ii. 378, 16 : i. 502, 19. Hē ðone windes blǣd áweg flîgde, ii. 140, 26. Zephirus blǣwð westan, and þurh his blǣd (blǣd, *v. l.*) ácuciað ealle blǣdu, Lch. iii. 274, 20. Blǣdas *flabra,* i. *flatus ventorum,* Wrt. Voc. ii. 149, 24 : *fla(b)ra,* 37, 21. Blǣdas (-es, MS.) *auras,* An. Ox. 50, 4. Tôworpen þurh windes blǣde (blǣde, blǣdum, *v. ll.*), Lch. iii. 276, 16.     I a. *figurative :*—Blǣdum *fasti vel superbiae flatibus,* Wrt. Voc. ii. 146, 43.     II. *breath, breathing :*—Blǣde *anhelitu,* An. Ox. 48, 5. Hî (*the seals*) mid heora blǣde his leoma beðedon, Hml. Th. ii. 138, 12. Ðurh ðæs dracan blǣd seó menigu wearð geuntrumod, 294, 22. Ðone lîflican blǣd *the breath of life,* 92, 12. Blǣdas *spiracula,* An. Ox. 4864 : *flabra* (*chelydri*), Wrt. Voc. ii. 86, 59.     III. *spirit :*—Hâlgostes blǣd onblâwende *sacrosancti flatus* (i. *spiritus) inspirans,* An. Ox. 1527.     IV. *inspiration :*—Of gerŷnelicum blǣde (*spiramine*) word Godes geworden flǣsc, Hy. S. 43, 36. Se Hâlga Gâst mid his blǣde onǣlde eorðlicra manna heortan, Hml. Th. i. 323, 13.     V. *of fire, flame, blaze; cf.* blǣst, blâwan, I. 4 :—Blaeed, blēd, bleð *flamma,* Txts. 64, 445. Fŷr *ignis,* lēg *flamma,* blǣd *flamina* (*flamma?*) (in a list 'de igne'), Wrt. Voc. i. 284, 13. Biscophâdas oððe blǣd *flamina,* ii. 35, 68.     VI. *prosperity :*—Gif him þince þ his hûs byrnð, micel blǣd and torhtnes him byð tôweard, Lch. iii. 170, 10. [*v. N. E. D.* blead.] Cf. blâwan.

blǣd (*properly* blēd, v. blôwan) *fruit. Add:*—Blǣd *coma,* Wrt. Voc. ii. 22, 41. Hē âbreác þæs forbodenan treówes æpples . . . hié þā blǣde þigdon, Angl. xi. 1, 19. Âbiteriað ðā blǣda *fructus amarescit,* Past. 341, 24. Âcuciað ealle eorðlice blǣdu (-e, -a, *v. ll.*) and blôwað (*printed* blâwað), Lch. iii. 374, 21. Hit ūt âspringþ on leáfum and on blôstmum and on blēdum, Bt. 34, 10; F. 150, 5. Beran ðā blǣda gôdra weorca *ferre fructum boni operis,* Past. 339, 21. Hē âbyrgde ðā forbodenan fîctreówes blǣda, Sal. K. 182, 34. Blēda, Nic. 17, 20. Ic sylle eów in eówrum bernum blǣde, Wlfst. 228, 15. Hî fretaþ eówre blǣde, þe gē big libban scylon, 229, 11. [*v. N. E. D.* blede. *O. H. Ger.* bluot *flos.*] v. plūm-blǣd; blēd *in Dict.*

blǣdan *to blow.* v. tô-blǣdan.

blǣd-belg, es; *m. Bellows :*—Blǣdbylig *follis,* Wrt. Voc. ii. 150, 16. Cf. blǣs-, blǣst-belg.

blǣd-dæg. *Add:*—Brúcaþ blǣddaga, Gen. 200.

blǣder-wǣrc, es; *m. Pain in the bladder :*—Wiþ blǣdderwærce, Lch. ii. 320, 3.

blǣd-fæst. *Add:* [*Laym.* blæd-fæst.]

blēd-horn. *Add:*—Ǣnne seolforhammenne blēdhorn (blēd-, C. D. iii. 362, 22), Cht. Th. 559, 29. Cf. blǣs-horn.

blǣdness (blēd-), e; *f. A blossom :*—Þeáh hē (*May*) wynsumlîce blôwe and blǣdnyssa fægere geyppe, Angl. viii. 311, 1.

blǣdre. *Add:*—Blēdrae (-e) *vessica,* Txts. 106, 1077. Wið blǣdran sáre . . . sôna seó blǣdder tô sēlran gehwyrfeð, Lch. i. 206, 12-15.

blǣgettan (blag-); *p.* te *To cry, squall :*—Se biscop ongan frēfrian þone hlŷdendan and blǣgettendan (blagettyndan, *v. l.*) cniht *episcopus stridentem vagientemque puerum consolari coepit,* Gr. D. 278, 12.

blǣ-hǣwen. *Add:*—Blǣhǣwenre *glauco,* An. Ox. 528.

blǣs, es; *m. Blowing, blast :*—Þurh ðæs windes blǣs, Angl. viii. 320, 33.

blǣs-belg, es; *m. Bellows :*—Blaesbaelg *follis,* Txts. 65, 910. [*O. H. Ger.* blâs-balch *follis.*] v. blǣd-, blǣst-belg.

blǣse. *Add:*—Blǣse *fax,* Germ. 393, 67. Ðeós wyrt scîneð on nihte swâ blǣse (blyse, *v. l.*), Lch. i. 300, 23. Blasan (-en, MS.) *globi,* An. Ox. 3085 : *facula,* 976 : 3, 39. Blæsan, 2, 22. Blǣsum *faculis,* 3522 : 4427. Blesum *tedis,* Wrt. Voc. ii. 122, 12. ¶ *figurative :*—Hē wearð mid þǣre blǣsan sôþere lufe ontend, Lch. iii. 432, 30. Onǣled mid þæs nîþes blǣsum *invidiae facibus succensus,* Gr. D. 117, 27. [*v. N. E. D.* blaze.] v. blysa.

blǣs-horn, es; *m. A horn for blowing :*—Blǣshorn bið ânes scill. weorð, and is melda geteald, Ll. Th. i. 260, 16. v. blǣd-, blǣst-horn.

blǣst *flame.* *l.* blǣst, *take with* blǣst *blast, and add :*—Ðæra lyfta leóma and þǣra ligetta blǣst, Wlfst. 186, 5. Cf. blǣd, V, blâwan, I. 4.

blǣstan; *p.* te.     I. *to blow* (v. N. E. D. blast). v. â-blǣst.     II. *to move impetuously, rush* [*or is this a different verb* blǣstan ? *cf.*

*O. H. Ger.* blesten *descendere ;* ana-blesten, *p.* -blasta *ingruere, inruere :* ar-blesten *erumpere ;* ana-blast (-blâst ?) *impetus*] :—Forð blǣstan *erumperant,* Wrt. Voc. ii. 30, 23. Þā deófla þā blǣstan hié ofer þone hâlgan Andreas (cf. the same scene in the poem : Hié wǣron reówe, rǣsdon on sôna gīsrum grāpum, An. 1336), Bl. H. 243, 11. [Cf. (?) *Mid. E.* bluster. v. *N. E. D. s. v.*] v. on-blǣstan *in Dict.*

blǣst-belg, es; *m. Bellows :*—Bloestbaelg *sublatorium* (= *sufflatorium*), Txts. 35, 28. Blēstbaelg *follis,* 64, 454. Blâstbelg, Wrt. Voc. ii. 35, 80. [Cf. *Icel.* blâstr-balgr.] v. blǣd-, blǣs-belg.

blǣt. *Dele:* -blēta (-e). v. hæfer-blǣta (-e).

blǣtan. *Add:*—Blētid *balatus* (*balat?*), Wrt. Voc. ii. 101, 61. Blǣted, 10, 79. [*O. H. Ger.* blâzen.]

blǣtesung, blagetung. v. bladesung, blǣgettan : blanc. *Take* B. 856 *under* blanca.

blanca. *Add : a steed :*—Þā hēt hē on ðæs pāpan ciericean gestællan his blancan and monig ôðer neát, Shrn. 51, 22. v. blonca *in Dict.*

blandan. *Dele:* 'þ. bleónd, -e, -on', (cf. *Icel.* þ. blett), *and add :*—Blondu *inficio,* Txts. 71, 1138.

blǣst-belg, blaster. v. blǣst-belg, plaster.

blāt. *Substitute for first passage :*—Þā cwom wôpes hring blât ūt faran, weóll waðuman streám *a flood of tears poured forth pale, a surging stream welled,* An. 1281. [Grein takes blât *as a noun, but cf. for the construction vv. 1271-3 :* Com hæleða þreât . . . wadan wælgīfre.]

blāte. *In first passage for* Helle fŷr, *substitute* Hit (*Etna*) ôðra stôwa : blatesian, blatesnung. v. bladesian, bladesnung.

blāwan. *Dele first passage, and add :* I. *intrans.* (1) *of the wind :*—Se wind hæfd mistlice naman on bôcum ; ðanon þe hē blǣwð him byð nama gesett, Lch. iii. 274, 12. Sūþan blâwan *to blow from the south,* Lk. 12, 55. (2) *of living creatures, to blow, breathe :*—Swā hwæt swā seó nǣddre gesihð, heó tô blǣwð and onǣleþ, Lch. i. 242, 21. Bleów *ructabat,* Wrt. Voc. ii. 96, 1. Þæs þe hē on mînne andwlitan bleóu (bleów, blēw, *v. ll.*) *exsufflante illo in faciem meam,* Bd. 5, 6 ; Sch. 581, 3. (2 a) *to breathe hard, snort, pant :*—Ðæt hors ongan blâwan and gremetian ungemetlîce (*immenso flatu et fremitu*), Gr. D. 183, 11. (2 b) *to blow, make a sound with a trumpet :*—Swiðlîce bleówan seofon sácerdas mid sylfrenum bŷmum, Hml. Th. ii. 212, 29 : Jos. 6, 13. Seofon sácerdas blâwon niid bŷmon (*clangent buccinos*), 6, 4. (3) *of things,* (a) *to emit air :*—Blâwendra byliga *flantium follium,* Coll. M. 31, 7. (b) *to blow, sound* (of a trumpet) :—Seó bŷme blǣwð, Hml. Th. ii. 568, 24. Blâwendre *clangenti sistro, sonanti tubae,* Wrt. Voc. ii. 131, 49. Þǣr com egeslic swēg and blâwende bŷman, Hml. Th. i. 312, 12. (4) *of fire, to flame, blaze.* v. blǣd, V, blǣst *flame :*—Ðonne fŷren lîg blâweð (-að, MS.) and braslað reað and rēðe *ignea tunc sonitus perfundet flamma feroces,* Dôm. L. 151.     II. *trans.* (1) *to drive by blowing :*—Blâw mid hreóðe þ seáw on þ dolh . . . blâw þa sealfe on þ dolh, Lch. ii. 332, 2, 11. (2) *to cause to sound by blowing, blow* a horn, trumpet :—Þā bleów man mîne bŷman, Nar. 13, 4. Hē nâwðer ne hrŷme, ne hē horn ne blâwe, Ll. Th. i. 42, 24. (3) *to fill with air, inflate :*—Þā bleówan wē þa kylla, Hml. A. 205, 347. v. be-, on-, wiþ-blâwan; þurh-blâwen.

blâwend, es; *m. An inspirer :*—God, lîchamena scyppend and sâwla Blâwend, Hml. Th. ii. 478, 8.

-blāwenness. v. tô-blâwenness : blâwere. *Add :* Past. 269, 18 : blâwness. v. â-, on-blâwness.

blāwung. *Add :* I. *of wind.* v. blâwan, I. 1 :—Ðæra winda naman and blâwunge (-a, *v. l.*) wē mihton secgan, Lch. iii. 276, 2.     II. *blowing* of a trumpet. v. blâwan, II. 2 :—Hwæt is se hreám būton ðæra engla blâwung ?, Hml. Th. ii. 568, 21. Hē bîcnode mid blâwunge him fultum, Hml. S. 25, 635. Ðurh ðæra sácerda blâwunge tôburston ðā weallas, Hml. Th. ii. 216, 2.     III. *inflation, cf.* blâwan, II. 3 :—Ealle þā blâwunge and þā welmas þā þe beóþ gehwǣr geond þone lîchoman, Lch. ii. 204, 14.

bleát. *Add :* [v. *N. E. D.* blete.] v. wæl-bleát.

bleáp. *Add :*—Siþþan hié welegran wǣron, hié eác bleáðran gewurdon *aurum Persicum prima Graeciae virtutis corruptio fuit,* Ors. 2, 5 ; S. 84, 22. [v. *N. E. D.* blethe.]

blec, blece. v. blæc, blæce : blēcþa. v. blǣcþa : bled. *Dele, and see* bledu : blēd. v. blǣd.

blēdan. *Add :*—Gif þæt wîf blēde tô swiþe æfter þām beorþre, Lch. ii. 330, 10. Slît mid foþorne oþ þæt hié blēden, 52, 8.

-blēde. v. or-blēde.

bledu. *Add :*—Bledu *patera,* Wrt. Voc. i. 82, 44 : *fiola,* 290, 79 : ii. 36, 63. Blede tâcen is þæt þū ārǣre ūp þîne swŷþran hand, Tech. ii. 125, 9. Man bær þām cāsere wîn on ânre blede, Hml. S. 31, 631. Hrer on blede, Lch. ii. 314, 3 : 308, 29. Drince hē gôde blede fulle, 118, 24. Hæbbe hē blede fulle hwēges, Ll. Th. i. 438, 24. On bleda *in pateras* (*fialas*), Germ. 389, 17. IIII cuppan and IIII bleda, Cht. Th. 519, 24. Man sceal habban beódas, bleda, mēlas, cuppan, Angl. ix. 264, 17. Dô twā bleda fulle wæteres tô, Lch. ii. 38, 2, 4 : 118, 6. v. helur-bledu.

blégen. _l._ blegen, _and add_: , blegne, an :—Blegnae (-æ), _vesica._ Txts. 106, 1094. Seó blāce b(l)egne _carbunculus_ (v. blāc), Wrt. Voc. i. 40, 52. Gif men eglað seó blāce blegen (_carbunculus_) . . . þis gebed man sceal singan on ðā blācan blegene, Lch. iii. 40, 19, 8 : 8. 31.

-blegned. v. ā-, ge-blegned : **blencan.** _Add_ : [v. _N. E. D._ blench.]

blendan (-ian). _Add_ :—Hine man sceolde blendian, Chr. 1086 ; P. 221, 8.

blend-ness, e ; _f. Blindness_ :—Blendnise _cecitate_, Rtl. 38, 9.

bleó-cræft. _For Cot._ 17 _substitute_ Wrt. Voc. ii. 9, 11.

bleodu ; _n. pl._ (?) _Corn_ :—Farra, i. _triticum, frumentum vel_ bleodu, Wrt. Voc. ii. 147, 45.

bleó-fæst ; _adj. Beautiful, pleasant._ v. bleó-fæstnes _in Dict._, _and cf._ hīw-fæst : **bleó-fæstnes.** _Add_ : cf. bleó-mete.

bleó-fāg. _Add_ :—Bleófāh _uersicolor_, An. Ox. 521. On þysne mislecan ymbhwyrft and bleófāgan _in orbem_, Wrt. Voc. ii. 48, 59. Bleófāge _multicolora_, Germ. 390, 104.

bleoh (bleóh ?). _Add_ : I. _colour_ :—Ðæt bleoh ðæs iacintes . . . carbuncules blioh, Past. 411, 28, 32. Hīwes, bleós _coloris_, An. Ox. 529. Þ heó (_Iris Illyrica_) þone heofonlican bogan mid hyre bleoge efenlæce, Lch. i. 284, 15. Hió scīnð on twǣm bleóm suā suā twēgea bleó godwebb, Past. 87, 9, 3, 13. Bleohga (bleóa, Hpt. Gl. 529, 64) _fucorum_, An. Ox. 5495. Ongemang ōðrum bleón (bleóm, _v. l._), Past. 89, 1. Mistlice bleoh _varios colores_, An. Ox. 5203 : Hy. S. 23, 13. II. _form_ :—Hū moniges bleós bið ðæt deófol and se Pater Noster ? Ðrītiges bleós . . . Ðæt deófol bið on cildes onlícnisse ; se Pater Noster on hāliges gāstes onlícnisse, Sal. K. 144, 1-7. Hé brǣd hine on feala bleóna þurh deófles þegnunga, Bl. H. 175, 5. v. twi-, un- bleoh.

bleó-mete, es ; _m. A delicacy_ :—Þu gegearwodest þē wiste and bleómettas _tu tibi delicias praeparas_, Gr. D. 99, 18. Cf. bleó-fæstnes _in Dict._

bleó-reád. _For Cot._ 135 _substitute_ Wrt. Voc. ii. 58, 8 : bleó- stǣning. _Substitute_ :—Bleóstǣning _musac_, Wrt. Voc. ii. 56, 7.

blere. _Substitute_ : blere ; _adj. Bald_ :—Blere _blurus, calvus_, Wrt. Voc. ii. 127, 13 : _blurus_, 12, 56. Blere _onix_, calo _calvus_, ūpfeax _recalbus_, i. 288, 55-7 : ii. 64, 18. v. next word.

blerig ; _adj. Bald_ :—Bleri pittel _scoricarius_, Wrt. Voc. i. 30, 6. Blerea pyttel _soricarius_, 63, 8 (cf. _bald_ as an epithet of birds, v. E. D. S. Bird-names). On Ælfstānes ðys blerian gewitnesse, Cht. Th. 174, 7. [v. _N. E. D._ bald.] v. preceding word.

bletsian (_from_ blēdsian, bloedsian). _Add_ : I. _to hallow, conse- crate_ :—Genom se Hǣlend hlāf and bletsade, Mt. R. 26, 26. Bloedsade, Mk. L. 14. 22. I a. _to make the sign of the cross as a protection against evil_ :—Gif hwā hit bletsað, þonne āblynd seó dydrung, Hml. S. 21, 469. Ah ne bloedsade (bletsadon, R.) uē ūsic ł uē sægnade ūsic, Jn. L. 8, 48. Mid þrym fingrum man sceall sēnian and bletsian, Hml. S. 27, 155. Þæt sum orfcyn sȳ þe man bletsigan ne sceole, Hml. Th. i. 100, 30. Wæter gihālsia, bloetsia _aquam exorcizare, benedicere_, Rtl. 119, 7. II. _to call holy, adore_ :—Mec gié bledtsiges, Jn. L. 13, 13. Hé bletsode Drihten, Bl. H. 245, 32. Bledsiað noman his, Ps. Srt. 95, 2. III. _to invoke divine favour upon_ :—Þæt ic þē bletsige, Gen. 27, 4. Isaac bletsode hine, 28, 1. Bletsiað (bloedsas, L.) þā ðe eów wiriað, Lk. 6, 28. IV. _to speak gratefully of a person_ :—Eal riht- gelýfed folc sceal hine (St. John) bletsian, Bl. H. 167, 14. V. _to benefit, prosper_ :—Ðonne ðū bledsas (_benefeceris_) him, Ps. Srt. 48, 19. Drihten bletsode his ǣhta, Gen. 39, 5.

bletsian, I :—Swā Thomas tó þām tīman āgeán fērde būton bletsunga (_without consecration_), Chr. 1070 ; P. 206, 6. Hé mid his bletsunge þæt wæter tó wīne āwende, Hml. Th. i. 58, 13. I a. v. bletsian, I a :—Sume cweðað þæt sum orfcyn þurh bletsunge misfarað, Hml. Th. i. 100, 31. Þā þā (hē) bletsunga mearcode on sǣlicum strandum _cum_ (_patibuli_) _signacula sulcaret in glarigeris litoribus_, An. Ox. 2490. II. v. bletsian, II :—Wyrþe þū eart, Drihten, þ þu onfō wuldor and blet- sunga, Bl. H. 75, 2. III. _benediction._ v. bletsian, III :—Æfter þæs engles bletsunga and hālettunge, Bl. H. 7, 15. Wulfrēd mid bled- sunge þæs pāpan hwearf eft tó his āgnum biscðóme, Chr. 813 ; P. 58, 18. _Benedicta et beata sis_ . . . Ðā hyre mōdor hī mid þyssere bletsunge onfangen hæfde, Lch. iii. 428, 8. Bloedsungas tó rēde _benedixiones i lectionem_, Rtl. 126, 1. IV. v. bletsian, V :—Dryhtnes is hǣlu and ofer folc ðīn bledsung ðīn, Ps. Srt. 3, 9. B(l)oedsung _benignitas_, Rtl. 123, 5. Bloetsunges ðīnes gefe onfōe wē, 81, 39. Tō hwon be- scyredest þū þē twyfealdre bletsunga ?, Bl. H. 49, 36. Bledsunge, Past. 331, 25. Folc ðīn bloetsung onfōe, Rtl. 79, 28. Bloedsung, 88, 14. Maria brōhte eallum geleáffullum bletsunga and ēce hǣlo, Bl. H. 5, 30. v. brȳd-, un-bletsung.

bletsung-bóc ; _f. A benedictional, a book containing the forms of episcopal benedictions_ :—Mæssebóc and bletsungbóc and pistelbóc, Cht. Crw. 23, 27. ii. ymneras and i. deórwyrðe bletsingbóc and .iii. ōðre, Cht. Th. 430, 14.

bletsung-sealm, es ; _m. The Benedicite_ :—Æfter þisum mou sceal singan þone bletsingsealm, þæt is ' _Benedicite_' _inde benedictiones_ (i. e. canticum trium puerorum) _dicantur_, R. Ben. 36, 18.

blīcan. _In bracket dele_ : _Laym._ blikien : _O. Nrs._ blika, _and add_ :— Blīcan, glitenian _rutilare_, An. Ox. 1196. v. blician.

blīce. _l._ blice, _and add_ : v. _N. E. D._ blick _brightness on silver or gold after refining._ _O. H. Ger._ blich ; _m. fulgor_ : _Icel._ blik ; _n. gleam, sheen._]

-blice (-a ?). v. ofer-blice.

blīcettan. _l._ bliccettan :—Blyccyt _vibrat_, An. Ox. 50, 52. Bliccette _vibrabat_, Wrt. Voc. ii. 96, 4. Bliccette _corusca_, Ps. Srt. 143, 6.

blīcettung. _l._ bliccettung :—Bliccetunge _coruscationes_, Ps. Srt. 76, 19 : 143, 6.

blician ; _p._ ode _To shine_ :—Blicede _enituerit_, An. Ox. 1499. [v. _N. E. D._ blik, blike. _Icel._ blika ; _p._ aði _to shine._ Cf. _O. H. Ger._ -blichen ; _p._ -blicte.]

blin. _Add_ : [Witouten blin, C. M. 881.]

blind. _Add_ : I. _physical_ :—Ic wæs blind bām eágum, Hml. Th. i. 422, 7 : Bt. 38, 5 ; F. 206, 26. _Palpo_ ic grāpige ; _hic palpo_ ðes blinda mann, _kujus palponis_ ðyses blindan, Ælfc. Gr. Z. 216, 10. (_Dele the rendering in Dict._) II. figurative, (a) of persons :—Ðā dysegan men sint ælces dōmes blinde, Bt. 32, 3 ; F. 118, 22. Hé hēt hī būgan tō his blindum godum, Hml. S. 25, 217. (b) of passion, &c. :—Blindre gyrninge _caecae cupiditatis_, An. Ox. 5288. Þæs blindan lustes, Bt. 7, 2 ; F. 18, 3. Blindre fyrhto _ceca formidine_, Wrt. Voc. ii. 130, 81. III. of a place, _without light, dark_ :—On blindum scrǣfe _in carcere caeco_, Dōm. L. 230. Sēcað ān blind cweartern, þǣr nān leóht ne mage inn, Hml. S. 37, 176. IV. _not shining, dim_ [v. _N. E. D._ blind, 7] :— Blindum līgum _caecis flammis_, Dōm. L. 241. V. _hidden from sight_ [v. _N. E. D._ blind, 9] :—On blindan wyll ; þanon on clǣnan splott, C. D. B. iii. 336, 22. VI. _blind_ (as in _blind_ alley. v. _N. E. D._ blind, 11), _closed at one end_ :—Blind þearm _blind gut_ ; cecum, Wrt. Voc. ii. 16, 59. VII. of a plant which is without some property, _not stinging_ (of a nettle-like plant) [v. _N. E. D._ blind, 12] :— Netel _urtica_, blind netel _archangelica_, Wrt. Voc. i. 79, 31. Blinde netele, An. Ox. 56, 402. v. stær-blind.

blindan. v. ā-blindan.

blind-boren ; _adj. Born blind_ :—Égo ðæs blindborenes, Jn. L. 9, 32. blind-fellian, blindian. v. ge-blindfellian, ā-, of-blindian.

blind-nes. _Add_ : I. physical, (1) of persons, (a) where faculty of vision is absent :—Hire eágan ðýstredon, þ heó nænigne dǣl leóhtes scīman geseón mihte. Mid þý heó sum fæc on blindnesse wæs, Bd. 4, 10 ; Sch. 401, 12. Ofslegene (slegene, 29) mid blindnysse, Bl. H. 153, 17. (b) _inability to see because of darkness_ :—Ðā ýttran þeóstru sind þæs līchaman blindnyssa wiðūtan . . . Hé bið wiðūtan āblend, and ælces leóhtes bedǣled, Hml. Th. i. 132, 10. (2) of darkness, _obscurity_ :—Ic wæs mid þā blindnesse þāra þýstra ūtan betýned, Bd. 5, 12 ; Sch. 621, 22. II. figurative, (1) of persons :—Hé þurh þā menniscan gecynd ūre stefne blindnysse gehýreþ, Bl. H. 19, 28. Eal þis menniscan cyn wæs on blindnysse, seoþþan þā ǣrestan men āsceofene wǣron of gefeán neorxna wanges, 17, 14. Ðā inran þeóstru sind þæs mōdes blindnyssa wiðinnan, Hml. Th. i. 130, 11. (2) of a condition :—Wē habbaþ nēdþearfe þ wē ongyton þā blindnesse ūre ælþeódignesse, Bl. H. 23, 2.

blinnan. _Add_ : [=be-linnan]. I. of persons, (1) absolute :— Cleopa and ne blin, Past. 91, 19. Blinnað _sinite_, Lk. L. 22, 51. (2) _to cease from action_, (a) with gen. :—Sē þe nǣfre ne blind ungestæððig- nesse _cui carnis petulantia sine cessatione dominatur_, Past. 70, 3. Hé þæs ne blann (blon, _v. l._) _existere non desistit_, Bd. 5, 20 ; Sch. 675, 20. Ic nā ðe ǣr þǣre ærninge blann _nihilominus coeptis instiui uetitis_, 5, 6 ; Sch. 576, 21. Heó ne blann cossetunges _non cessauit osculari_, Lk. L. 7, 45. (b) with infin. ; Bt. 1, 11 ; S. 480, 13 (in Dict.). (c) with clause :—Ne blinnis ðū þ ðū gisceáwia _non desinis intueri_, Rtl. 64, 33. Ne blan (blonn ; geswāc, _v. ll._) hē þ hē his geongran ne manode _nec discipulos suos admonere cessabat_, Gr. D. 27, 4. Blinn (blin, R.) þ ðū gefoeda ðā saturari filios, Mk. L. 7, 27. (d) with prep. :—Ne hē ōhte þý mā blan (bleon, _v. l._) fram gearwunge þæs sīðfætes _nec a praeparando itinere cessare uolebat_, Bd. 5, 9 ; Sch. 593, 21. Hé hēt blinnan fram ēhtnysse _cessari a persecutione praecepit_, 1, 7 ; Sch. 26, 20. II. of things, _to cease, come to an end_ :—Ic wēne þ þes dæg blinned (geendige, _v. l._) (_cessabit_), ǣr mē spell āteorige, Gr. D. 7, 29. Sōna se hwōsta blinneð, Lch. iii. 58, 11. Blinnes lufo _refrigescet caritas_, Mt. L. 24, 12. Him ælc mennisc fultum blonn _humanum cessabat auxilium_, Sch. 38, 5. Blan se wind _cessavit ventus_, Mt. R. 14, 32. [v. _N. E. D._ blin. _O. H. Ger._ pi-linnan _cessare._ Cf. _Goth._ af-linnan : _Icel._ linna (_vk._).]

-blinnend-lice, -ness. v. ā-, un-blinnendlíce, ā-blinnendness.

blinnes. _Substitute_ : _Cessation, intermission_ :—Fæste heó .xv. winter būtan blinnysse (_sine intermissione_), Ll. Th. ii. 156, 5. v. betweoh- blinness.

blis. _Add_ :—Blisse _jubilationis_, An. Ox. 2610. Þonne þǣr wæs blisse intingan (_laetitiae causa_) gedēmed, þæt hī ealle sceoldon be hearpan singan, Bd. 4, 24 ; Sch. 482, 16. Þū woldest mē laðian, þæt ic swiðor

drunce swilce for blisse ofer mínum gewunan, Ælfc. T. Grn. 21, 30. Blisse, gefeá *tripudio* .i. *gaudio*, An. Ox. 1346. Gá intó þínes hláfordes blisse (*gaudium*), Mt. 25, 21. v. un-, wyn-bliss.

**blissian.** *Add:* [= blíþsian, *q. v.*]    I. absolute :—þancaþ, blissaþ *gratatur* .i. *laetatur*, An. Ox. 5111. Blissaþ *gratatur*, Wrt. Voc. ii. 40, 50. Hé sæt mid þám gebeórum blissigende samod, Hml. S. 26, 227.    II. *to rejoice* at (with gen.) :—His fýnd þæs micclum wundrodon and blissodon, Hml. Th. ii. 26, 11. Ðis folc micclum blissigan wile mínes deáðes, i. 86, 32.

**blissigend-líc;** *adj. Joyous* :—Se dæg is heora sóðe ácennednys; ná wóplic swá swá seó ærre, ac blissigendlíc tó ðám écum lífe, Hml. Th. i. 354, 11.

**blíþe.** *Add:* I. *cheerful,* &c. :—Blíþe *letus,* Wrt. Voc. i. 83, 36 : *alacris,* 287, 66.    (1) of persons, *feeling gladness :*—þ hié ealle þá blíðe móde (*alacri animo*) lustlíce healdan woldan, Bd. 4, 5; Sch. 375, 15 : Bl. H. 39, 4 : 7, 1. Oft gebyreð ðætte sume bióð tó ungemetlíce blíðe for sumum gesǽldum *plerumque quis laetae nimis conspersionis existit,* Past. 455, 8. Wǽron þá burgware tó þon fægene and tó þon blíðe þæt hié feohtan móston, Ors. 5, 3 ; S. 222, 4. Blíþum *uoti compotibus,* i. *letis,* An. Ox. 809. Mycele blíþre bið seó sáwl, Bl. H. 41, 30. (1 a) *glad* at, of (with gen.) :—Gehwylc sý blýðe þæs þe him æt his cyrcan cume, Ll. Th. ii. 410, 34. Gehýrdon gehwilce hálige englas singan, blíðe þæs hálgan tócymes, Hml. Th. ii. 518, 9.    (1 b) *well-disposed* to, *ready* for ; alacer (ad) :—þá cempan hét Claudius heáfde beceorfan . . . , and hié wǽron blíðran tó ðám deáðe þonne hý her on hæðengilde lifden, Shrn. 132, 12.    (1 c) in encouraging exclamations :—Beó blíþe *euge,* An. Ox. 56, 134. Ealle blíðe *cuncti euax,* 14. (2) of things, *expressing gladness :*—Hí blíþre stefne cégdon, Bl. H. 89, 30. Hit frán blíþum wordum, Bt. 3, 1; F. 4, 28. Seó Gesceádwísnes him blíþum eágum on lócude, 5, 1; F. 8, 25.    II. *gentle,* &c. :—Milde ł blíðe ł bilwit *simplex,* Lk. L. 11, 34 : þ. 7, 9 : Mt. L. 6, 23 : *mansuetus,* 21, 5. Hé feól tó his fótum, and bæd þ hé hin blíþe wǽre (*ut sibi placatus esset*), Bd. 3, 14; Sch. 259, 3, 13. Hwæþer hí ealle smylte mód and bútan eallum incan blíðe tó him hæfdon . . . and hí hine bǽdon, þ hé him eallum blíðe wǽre (*placidam erga ipsos mentem habere*), 4, 24; Sch. 490, 5–13. Se cásere hét sendan hine of bendum, and him þá blíðe wæs, Hml. S. 3, 197. þ þú þám godum offrige, þ hí þe blýðe beón, 4, 131. Wosas gé blíðo ł mildo (*simplices*) suæ culfre, Mt. L. 10, 16. Blíþe word *delenifica,* Wrt. Voc. ii. 138, 61. Hié wilniað ðæt wé him geðwǽre sién, and hié ús ðe blíðran beón mægen, Past. 255, 2.

**blíþe ;** *adv. Add:*—Drihten on middangearde blíðe wunode, Bl. H. 9, 35. Gif wé blíþe and rúmmódlíce hí dǽlan willaþ earmum mannum, Bl. H. 51, 10. þæt hé blíþe þæs earman líchoman gefylle, 37, 29. þ hí blission blíþe mid Xpe, Chr. 1036; þ. 158, 29. v. ge-blíþe.

**blíþe-líc ;** *adj. Gentle, pleasant :*—Blíðelícum iocce *blando jugo,* Rtl. 108, 19. Blíðelícum égum ðínes árfæstnisse *serenis oculis tuae pietatis,* 123, 3. [*O. Sax.* blíð-lík : *O. H. Ger.* blíd-líh (muot, word).]

**blíþe-líce.** *Add : Cheerfully, willingly :*—Manna gehwylc his ælmessan blíðelíce syllan, Wlfst. 103, 5. Hé blíðelíce (*joyfully*) hám tó his earde férde, Chr. 1022; þ. 156, 6. Drihten swíþe blíþlíce mannum geleánað, Bl. H. 101, 22. Blíðelícor *propensius,* Rtl. 34, 30.

**blíþe-méde.** v. un-blíþeméde.

**blíþe-mód.** *Add : ,* blíþ-mód.    I. *of gladsome mind :*—þú blíðmód bidde, þ hí (*the saints*) þe þingian tó þeódne, Dóm. L. 36, 23.    II. *of kindly mind, kindly disposed :*—Hí cwǽdon þ hí ealle him swíðe blíðemóde wǽron . . . Hé cwæð, ' Ic eom swíðe blíðemód (blíðmód, blíðemóde, *v. ll.*) tó eów' *respondebant omnes placidissimam se mentem ad illum habere . . . Respondit, ' Placidam ego mentem erga vos gero,'* Bd. 4, 24; Sch. 490, 8.

**blíþ-nes.** *Add :*—On eádegum setlum brúcan blíðnesse bútan ende forð *sedibus semper gaudere beatis,* Dóm. L. 304. Hié mid micelre blíðnesse þæt wín drincende wǽron, Ors. 2, 4; S. 76, 17. [*O. H. Ger.* blíðnissa *deliciae.*]

**blíþs.** *Add :*—On gefeán blíðse, Ps. C. 79.

**blód.** *Add :*—Deád blód *cruor,* Wrt. Voc. ii. 16, 57. Heó sæde þ hire blód forléten wǽre on earme, Bd. 5, 3; Sch. 563, 2. Swíðe unwíslíce gé dydon, þæt gé sceoldon on feówernihtne mónan blód lǽtan, Sch. 504, 6 : Lch. iii. 184, 11. Ær him mon blód lǽte, þám þe fela blódes hæfþ, ii. 210, 16. Blód wanian, iii. 184, 16. Wer blóda *vir sanguinum,* Ps. L. 5, 8 : Ps. Spl. 25, 9. Handa mid manna blódum befýlede, Angl. xi. 113, 36. v. mónaþ-blód.

**blód-æx.** v. blód-seax.

**blód-dolg (-h),** es ; *n. A cut from which blood flows :*—Gif monnes blóddolh (-dolg, 16, 4) yfelige . . . Gif þú ne mæge blóddolh (-dolg, 16, 6) áwríþan . . . lege þ dust on cláð, wríþ mid þý þ blóddolh, Lch. ii. 148, 7–15.

**blód-dryncas.** *Substitute :* blód-drync, es ; *m. Blood-drinking, draught of blood :*—þær wæs gesiéne þæt seó eorþbeofung tácnade þá miclan blóddryncas þe hiere mon on þære tíde tó forlét *merito dicatur tantum humanum sanguinem susceptura terra tremuisse,* Ors. 4, 2 ; S. 162, 3.

**blódegian.** v. blódgian.

**blóden (?) ;** *adj. Bloody :*—Of blódene *de cruente,* Wrt. Voc. ii. 138, 15. [Cf. *O. H. Ger.* bluotín *sanguineus.*]

**blód-forlǽtan.** *Dele, and see* blód.

**blód-gemang,** es ; *n. A blood-mixture :*—Of blódgemongum *de sanguinibus,* Wrt. Voc. ii. 139, 28.

**blód-gemenged** *blood-stained :*—þone blódgemengedan middaneard, Wlfst. 182, 11.

**blód-geótan.** *Dele :* blód-geóte. *l.* -geót.

**blód-geótend,** es ; *m. A shedder of blood :*—Áles mé of blódgeótendum, Ps. L. 50, 16.

**blód-geótende.** *Add :*—Wer þe is blódgita ł (blód-)geótende *vir sanguinum,* Ps. L. 5, 8.

**blódgian ;** *p.* ode.    I. *to make bloody :*—Hé hys líchaman mid his tóþum blódgode, Guth. 56, 17. Hié mid heora múðe hié blódgodon, Nar. 11, 5. Hí ongunnon heora hors mid heora spurum blódgian, Gr. D. 14, 28.    II. *to become bloody :*—Reáwde *vel* blódgade *crudescit,* Wrt. Voc. ii. 137, 17. [*O. H. Ger.* pluotagón *cruentare.*]

**blód-gíta.** *Dele, and see next word.*

**blód-gyte** *bloodshed. Add :*—Wæs here and hunger, bryne and blódgyte on gewelhwylcon ende, Wlfst. 159, 8. Hé sægde þ ðæt næfre wæs álýfed ænigum men þ hé þær ænig nýten cwealde oþþe blódgyte worhte *negatat licere animal ullum interfici,* Nar. 28, 18. Tácnað þ micelne blódgyte on sumre þeóde, Lch. iii. 180, 12. Wer þe is blódgita ł wer blóda *vir sanguinum,* Ps. L. 5, 8. On blódgytum *in sanguinibus,* 105, 38. Tácnað þ gewinn and blódgytas, Lch. iii. 182, 3. [*Laym.* blod-gute.]

**blód-hrǽcan, -hrǽce.** *Dele.*

**blód-hrǽcung,** e ; *f. Inflammation of the lungs; peripleumonia,* Wrt. Voc. i. 19, 37.

**blódig.** *Add :*—Blódge *cruentos,* þǽm blódigum *cruentis,* Wrt. Voc. ii. 22, 7, 8.    I. *of the nature of blood :*—Ríneþ blódig regn, Bl. H. 91, 34. His micgge bið blódreád swilce hió blódig sié, Lch. ii. 198, 20. Swilce blódig wæter, 202, 2. Mid blódigum ríþum *sanguineis rivulis,* An. Ox. 3023.    II. *smeared with blood :*—þá eár wǽron blódege (*cruentae*), Ors. 4, 8 ; S. 188, 28. On blódigum limum, Hml. S. 31, 981. Blódigum (*cruentis*) handum, An. Ox. 11, 149.    III. of colour, *red as blood :*—Ástígeþ blódig wolcen, Bl. H. 91, 32 : Chr. 979 ; P. 122, 24.    IV. *of battle, attended with much bloodshed :*—þá blódgan *cruda* (*certamina belli,* cf. 90, 1 = Ald. 143, 34), Wrt. Voc. ii. 21, 65.    V. of persons, *bloodthirsty, given to bloodshed :*—Mid werum blódigum *cum viris sanguinum,* Ps. L. 25, 9. v. un-blódig.

**blódlǽs-tíd,** e ; *f. Proper time for bleeding :*—Nis nán blódlǽstíd swá gód swá on foreweardne lencten, Lch. ii. 148, 2.

**blód-lǽtan.** *Substitute :* blód-lǽs, e ; blód-lǽswu, e ; *f. Blood-letting :*—Blódlǽs is tó forgánne fíftýne nihtum ær Hláfmæsse, Lch. ii. 146, 8. Frægn hé hwonne hyre blódlǽs (-lǽswu, *v. l.*) ǽrest wǽre . . . þæt þǽre tíde blódlǽs (-lǽsewu, -lǽswu, *v. ll.*) wǽre frecenlíc, Bd. 5, 3; Sch. 563, 10–564, 11. On þǽre blódlǽs(e) (-lǽswu, *v. l.*), Sch. 563, 3. Hú mon scyle blódlǽse forgán, Lch. ii. 16, 2 : 146, 19. Æfter þon þe se líchoma sié þurh þá blódlǽse geclǽnsad, 210, 18. [v. *N. E. D.* blod-les.]

**blód-lǽtan.** *Dele, and see* blód : blód-orc. v. orc *in Dict.*

**blód-reád.** *Add :*—His micgge bið blódreád swilce hió blódig sié, Lch. ii. 198, 20. His fét syndon blódreáde, E. S. viii. 477, 34. [*Icel.* blód-rauðr.]

**blód-ryne.** *Add :*—Blódryne of nǽsþyrlon, Lch. i. 282, 12. Sum wíf wæs on blódryne þearle geswenct, Hml. S. 31, 1256. Gefór hé on blódryne *effusione sanguinis, quod Graece apoplexis vocatur, mortuus est,* Ors. 6, 33 ; S. 288, 27. Ðeós wyrt þone blódryne gewríð, Lch. i. 306, 22. Hé blódrynas áfeormaþ, 300, 16. [*O. Frs.* blód-rene. Cf. *O. H. Ger.* pluot-runs.]

**blód-sceáwung,** e ; *f. Supply of blood (?) :*—þ mon mæg gelácnian þenden of þære lifre sió blódsceáwung geondgét ealne þone líchoman, Lch. ii. 222, 9.

**blód-seax.** *Add :*—Blódsaex *flebotoma,* Wrt. Voc. ii. 108, 77. Blódseax *flebotomum, Graece namque fleps, vena, tomum vero incisio nominatur,* 39, 22 : *fletoma,* 33, 73. Blódsex *flebotomum,* 149, 42. Sé án blódseax (lǽceíren, *v. l.*) ásette on míne tungan, Gr. D. 32, 24. Se ealda feónd sittende on ánum múle on lǽces ansýne bær horn and blódsex (blódaexe, *v. l.*), 161, 2. [*O. L. Ger.* blód-sahs (-sax).]

**blód-seten** *a remedy to stop bleeding :*—Gif men yrne blód tó swíþe . . . Blódseten ; biscopwyrt nioþowearde ete . . . Blódseten ; genim hegeclífan, gebinde on sweoran, Lch. ii. 54, 4–8, 9, 10, 11, 16. Blódsetena ge on tó bindanne ge on eáre tó dónne ge horse ge men, 4, 11.

**blód-siht,** e. *Substitute :* blód-sihte, an :—Wiþ wífa blódsihtan, Lch. ii. 172, 20.

**blód-þigen,** e ; *f. Tasting blood :*—Be blódþigene *de esu sanguinis* (cf. Gif wíf þicgð (*gustaverit*) hire weres blód for hwylcum lǽcedóme, 156, 13), Ll. Th. ii. 130, 18.

**blód-wanian.** *l.* blód wanian : blód-wíte. *Add :* [v. *N. E. D.* blood-wite.]: blód-wyrt. *Dele.*

blōma a mass, lump:—Blōma metallum, Wrt. Voc. ii. 57, 77: massa (picea; massa is glossed by clyne, Wrt. Voc. ii. 90, 22), An. Ox. 18 b, 55. Blōman īsenes massam ferri, Scint. 97, 2. Hēt se gerēfa heora ǽlcum gebindan leádes blōman on heora swyran, Shrn. 54, 20. [v. N. E. D. bloom.]

blōstm, es; m. Add: (f. (?) Wülck. Gl. 240, 22):—Blōstm flos, Ælfc. Gr. Z. 312, 2: flosculus, Wrt. Voc. ii. 149, 58. Īseugrǽgum blōstme ferrugineo flore, 147, 67. Flores blōstma (-as?, -an?) s. nominati quod cito defluant de arboribus, Wülck. Gl. 240, 22. Feld full grōwendra blōstma (blōsma, v. l.), campus flosculorum plenus, Bd. 5, 12; Sch. 623, 20.

blōstma. In passage from Bd. for blōstma substitute blōstmena (blōsmana, v. l.), and add: blōstme; f. (?):—Swǽ swǽ blōstme (flos) londes, Ps. Srt. 102, 15. Swylce blōstme quasi flos, Scint. 70, 3. Wīntreówa blōstman beóð gimmum gelīce, Ælfc. Gr. Z. 295, 12. Blōstman ligustra, Wrt. Voc. ii. 53, 5. Sixte wæs blōstmena pund, ðanon him (Adam) wæs eágena missenlīcnes geseald, Sal. K. 180, 13. Hire leáf and blōstman meng tōgædere, Lch. ii. 24, 21.

blōstm-bǽre; adj. Flowery, blooming (lit. or fig.):—Blōstmbǽre floriferum, blōstmbǽres florigeri, Wrt. Voc. ii. 149, 53, 54. Blōst(m)bǽre florulenta, florida (tellus), An. Ox. 812. Ðeós blōstmbǽre stōw locus iste florifer, Hml. Th. ii. 352, 31. Ðā blōstmbǽran juguðe floritidam iuuentutem, Ælfc. Gr. Z. 295, 13. Blōst(m)bǽre, An. Ox. 442. Blōstmbǽre florulenta, i. floribus referta, 140.

blōstm-bǽrende. l. -berende flowery, in passage substitute blōstmberende (blōsm-, -bǽrende, v.ll.), and add:—þā blōstmberendan florigera, Wrt. Voc. ii. 34, 7.

blōstm-freóls, es; m. A floral festival:—Blōstmfreólsas floralia, An. Ox. 4720.

blōstm-gild, es; n. A floral festival:—Blōstmgeld floralia, Wrt. Voc. ii. 37, 52.

blōstmian. Add:—Swǽ blōsmæ lǽndes swǽ blōsmæþ sicut flos agri ita florebit, Ps. Spl. T. 102, 14. Þās treówa blōstmiað þurh þæs windes blǽd, Shrn. 67, 11.

blōstmig; adj. Flowery:—Blōsmige land florea rura, Wülck. Gl. 256, 3.

blōt. After gedyde add: and hys godum bebeád hospitum sanguinem diis propinabat; add also:—Hē his ágenne sunu his godum tō blōte ácwealde, and hine him sylf siððan tō mete gegyrede ipsum filium epulis Iovis non dubitarit inpendere, Ors. 1, 8; S. 42, 11. Hǽðenscipe dreógan on blōt, Ll. Th. ii. 296, 28.

blōt (?) itching:—Bloot proriginem, Hpt. 33, 251, 22.

blōtan. Add: [a weak past seems used (ofredon and blōtten (-on, Th., blōten, S. 162, 30)) in Ors. 4, 4; Bos. 80, 18; cf. O. H. Ger. plōzta libuit: Icel. blóta is strong and weak]:—Swelce hwā wille blōtan ðæm fæder tō ðance and tō lācum his ǽgen bearn quasi qui victimat filium in conspectu patris sui, Past. 393, 9. [O. H. Ger. blōzan: Goth. blōtan.]

blōtere, es; m. One who sacrifices:—Blōteras plutones, Germ. 398, 99. [Cf. O. H. Ger. bluostrari sacrificator.]

blōt-mōnaþ. Add:—Se mōnoð is nemned on ūre geðeóde blōdmōnað, Shrn. 144, 5. Se mōnað þe wē nemnað blōdmōnað, 153, 20. ¶ In Bede's 'De temporum ratione' it is said: 'November dicitur blōtmónath . . . Blōtmónath mensis immolationum, quod in eo pecora, quae occisuri erant, diis suis voverent. Gratia tibi, bone Iesu, qui nos ab his vanis avertens tibi sacrificia laudis offerre donasti.' [O. L. Ger. blōt-mánoth.]

blōt-orc. v. orc in Dict.

blōwan. Add:—Blōweð frondescit, Wrt. Voc. ii. 34, 8. Blēwþ florescit, blōwaþ florent, 149, 48, 49. Blōwendum frondente, 151, 10. I. of vegetation:—Þā wyrte man nimeð þonne heó blēþ (blēwð, v. l.) swiðust, Lch. i. 160, 14. Þ cyn mintan blōweð hwīte, iii. 16, 11. Þeáh Maius wynsumlīce blōwe, Angl. viii. 311, 1. Treówa hē dēð blōwan and eft āseárian, Wlfst. 196, 1. Blōwendre tyrf florei cespitis, blōwende eorþe florida tellus, i. florulenta terra, Wülck. Gl. 240, 27, 34. II. of other matter:—Heora hālgan līchaman hī gesáwon eall blōwende, Hml. S. 23, 439. III. fig.:—þeáh, bleów floruerit, An. Ox. 1500. Blōwende rīce, Dōm. L. 28, 2. v. beorht-blōwende.

blōwend-lic; adj. Flowery:—þā blōwendlican floralia, Wrt. Voc. ii. 149, 51.

blycgan. v. ā-blycgan.

blysa. Add:—Man mid blysum ontende his bare līc, Hml. S. 37, 159. Hē hēt ontendan blysan (blasan, v. l.) æt his sīdum, 14, 44. [Icel. blys a torch.] Cf. blæse.

blyscan to be red, shine:—Bliscan (blyscan) l glitian rutilare, coruscare, Hpt. Gl. 434, 75. [Or = blīcsan?; in An. Ox. 1196 the gloss is blīcan, glitenian. v. N. E. D. blush.]

blysian to burn, blaze:—Fýr blysede beforan his ansýne ignis a facie ejus exarsit, Ps. Th. 17, 8. v. ā-blysian; blysa.

blysige. Add:—Blysige facula, fax, Wrt. Voc. ii. 33, 53, 54.

blysung. v. ā-blysung.

blywnys (= blōwnys?) bloom, flourishing condition:—Forsearode swā swā blywnys l crocsceard mægen (crocsceard blywnys l mægen?) mīn aruit tamquam testa uirtus mea, Ps. L. 21, 16.

bōc a beech-tree. Add:—Bōc aesculus, Wrt. Voc. i. 285, 23.

bōc a book. Add: g. bēc, bōce, bōc; d. bēc, bōc. I. a document, register, catalogue:—Of boec (bōc, L.) līfgendra, Ps. Srt. 68, 29. Bēc in catalogo, An. Ox. 341. On cyninga bōcum in basileon, Wrt. Voc. ii. 87, 4. I a. a legal document, (1) a bill of divorce:—Hīwgedāles bōc libellum repudii, Mk. 10, 4. (2) a charter:—Hafingseotan boec, C. D. B. i. 402, 5. Lulla gebohte ðǽs boec and ðis lond, C. D. ii. 3, 10. II. a book, volume, literary work, pages; main division of a work:—Bōc liber vel codex vel volumen, Wrt. Voc. i. 80, 75: cartula, ii. 92, 47 : 19, 44. From ðǽre dura ðisse bēc, Past. 25, 11. Þā blōstman þǽre æftran bēc, Shrn. 200, 12: 129, 29 : Bt. 42; F. 256, 22. In heáfde boec (bōc, Spl.) in capite libri, Ps. Srt. 39, 8. Isaias hit on bēc sette, Ælfc. T. Grn. 2, 22. Capitel gemyndelīce būtan bēc gesǽd, R. Ben. 34, 1. On bœc in libro (Clementis), Scint. 17, 16. On boec ðāra salma, Lk. L. R. 20, 42. On Isaias bēc (bōc L.), Lk. 3, 4; Mk. 12, 26. On þǽre bōc þe ys Exodus genemned, Angl. viii. 335, 31. Bōc biblum, bōcum biblis, bēc biblos, Wrt. Voc. ii. 12, 30, 29, 38. Bōc opusculum, An. Ox. 4586. Bēc opuscula, 4535. þāra bōca indegitament(or)um (cf. An. Ox. 4442), Wrt. Voc. ii. 85, 52 : 47, 1. Ðāra bōcana librorum, Mt. p. 11, 12. Bōcum cartis, Wrt. Voc. ii. 91, 3 : 19, 29 : scedulis, 85, 77 : tomis, 93, 20. Of bōcum ex bibliothecis, An. Ox. 2027. Þ hī tō ǽlcon sinoðe habban bēcc and reáf tō godcundre þēnunge, Ll. Th. ii. 244, 11. ¶ Crīstes bōc a, the, gospel:—Wē habbað micele mǽran endebyrdnysse þǽre Crīstes bēc gesǽd þonne ðis dægðerlice godspel behæfð, Hml. Th. i. 220, 25. Æfter Crīstes bōce tǽcinge, R. Ben. 104, 19. v. canon-, ciric-, cneóres-, ge-rīm-, lǽden-, seonoþ-, spell-, traht-, þegnung-, wītegung-bōc; irse-bēc.

bōc-æceras. Add:—Hiis terminis circumdata terra . . . in acquilone, burhware bōcaceras, C. D. v. 186, 34.

bōc-blǽc, es; n. Ink:—þiús Dryhtnes ǽrendbōc ne wæs mid bōcblece, ne mid nǽnigum eorþlicum andweorce āwriten, Wlfst. 225, 1.

bōc-cest, -cist, e; -ciste, an; f. Substitute: A receptacle for books, (1) of books for reading:—Bēc of bōccystan codices de blibliotheca, R. Ben. I. 83, 3. Apollonius his bōcciste untýnde and āsmeáde þone rǽdels æfter ūðwitena wīsdōme, Ap. Th. 5, 24. Bōccysta armaria, An. Ox. 27, 19. (2) of books for sale:—Bōccest taberna (libraria), Wrt. Voc. i. 22, 7. [Cf. O. H. Ger. buoh-faz bibliotheca.]

bōc-cræft. Add:—þes mōnan oferhlýp wyxst wundorlīce æfter bōccræfte, Angl. viii. 308, 25. On þām bōccræfte fela hīw synt āmearcode, þā synd on Lýden figure gecīged, 331, 2. Men þe wǽron geswincfulleste on bōccræfte men that studied most laboriously, Ll. Th. ii. 322, 21. Mid mē þū bōccræft leornodest thou wert my scholar, Ap. Th. 21, 17. Hē wæs befæsted tō Rōmebyrig þæt hē sceolde bōccræftas and gewrita wīsdōmas leornian . . . forsægenum þām onginnum þāra bōccræfta Romae liberalibus litterarum studiis traditus fuerat . . . despectis litterarum studiis, Gr. D. 95, 12–26 : 96, 19. Ðā ðe nellað heora bōccræftas Godes folce nytte gedōn those who will not make their learning profitable to God's people, Wlfst. 213, 24. [O. Sax. bōk-kraft.]

bōc-cræftig. Dele 'learned in the Bible,' and add:—Bōccræftige weras (scholars) secgað þ þ syxtēte vers sceal habban feówer and twēntig tīman, Angl. viii. 335, 13.

bōc-cynn, es; n. A kind of book:—Saga mē hwæt bōccynna and hū fela sindon, Sal. K. p. 192, 8.

bōcere. Add: I. a bookman, an author, a scholar:—Nān bōcere ne mæg, þeáh hē mycel cunne, heora naman āwrītan, Hml. S. p. 6, 67. Ðus Bēda ðe brōema bōcere cuæð, Jn. 19, 37 margin. Þ andgit eów gecýðan on Englisc, þ þā bōceras cunnou on Lýden, Angl. viii. 314, 23. From boecerum a librariis, Mt. p. 2, 2. II. a (Jewish) scribe:—Ðā boecere scribae, Mk. p. 5, 3. Hē manige searwa ādreág æt þām unlǽdum bōcerum, Bl. H. 85, 1. Mið boecerum (bōkerum, R.) cum scribis, Mt. L. 27, 41. [Goth. bōkareis: O. L. Ger. bōkari : O. H. Ger. buohhāri.]

bōc-fel. Add:—Bōcfel pergamentum vel membranum, Wrt. Voc. i. 75, 14. Word on bōcfelle āwritene verba pitacio caraxata, Angl. xiii. 367, 31. Seó rǽding þe ys āwriten on þām bōcfelle, viii. 308, 2. Wrīt þis on swā langum bōcfelle þ hit mæge befōn ūtan þ heáfod, Lch. iii. 66, 7. Bōcfellum pitaciolis, i. membranulis, An. Ox. 4570. [O. H. Ger. buoh-fell membranum : Icel. bōk-fell.]

bōc-fōd(d)er a book-case. v. bōc-hord.

bōc-gesamnung, e; f. A collection of books, library:—Bōcgesamnunge celestis bibliothece, Wrt. Voc. ii. 130, 48.

bōc-gestreón. Add: [O. H. Ger. buoh-gistriuni bibliotheca.]

bōc-haga, an; m. A beech-haw, an enclosure of beeches:—On ðone bōchagan . . . on ðām sieran bōchagan, C. D. v. 70, 26, 32.

bōc-holt a beech-wood:—In bōcholte, C. D. B. i. 344, 11. An cinges bōcholte fīf wēna gang, C. D. ii. 103, 1. xii. manentium quae dicuntur bōcholt, i. 232, 20.

H 2

**bôc-hord.** *Add:*—Bôchord *bibliotheca*, Wrt. Voc. ii. 13, 3. Bôchord *vel* fôdder *bibliotheca*, i. *librorum repositio*, 126, 4.

**bôcian.** *Add:*—Þreó hída ðe Oswald bisceop bôcað Hêhstâne his þægne þreora monna dæg on ðâ gerâd . . ., C. D. iii. 19, 10 : 20, 32. [*O. Frs.* bôkia.]

**bôc-land.** *Add:*—Bôclandes *fundi*, Wrt. Voc. ii. 34, 50. Ic geseah englas ferigan gesælige sâwle of ðínum (*the abbess Ælflæd's*) bôclande (*de tuo monasterio*), Hml. Th. ii. 150, 26. An ic (*King Eadred*) mînre mêder ealra mînra bôclanda þe ic on Sûð-Seaxum hæbbe, C. D. B. iii. 75, 25. Twelf bôclanda æhte (*xii possessiones praediorum*) hê Gode geaf mynster on tô timbrianne, Bd. 3, 24; Sch. 308, 3. Bôcland *territoria*, Sch. 306, 11 : 2, 3; Sch. 124, 3 : *fundos*, Wrt. Voc. ii. 152, 18. ¶ used figuratively:—Gif þú (*the wealthy man*) wêne, þæt hit þín bôcland (*land exempt from the claims of charity*) sý, þæt þú on eardast, and on âgene æht geseald, Wlfst. 260, 3. [*v. N. E. D.* book-land. *O. Frs.* bôk-lond.]

**bôc-lâr.** *Add:*—Hê sceal bôclârum hlystan, Wlfst. 267, 6. [*v. N. E. D.* book-lore.]

**bôc-lêden.** *l.* -leden, *and add:* , -læden :—Se steorra þe mon on bôclæden (on Læden, *v. l.*) hæt *cometa*, Chr. 892; P. 82, 31. Seó dûn is on bôcleden gehâten Armenia, E. S. viii. 477, 4. [*v. N. E. D.* boc-leden.]

**bôc-lic.** *Add:*—Þurh âsmeágunge bôclicre snotornesse (*scholarly wisdom*) rædels rædan, Ap. Th. 3, 16. Basilius âwrât ðâ lâre ðe wê nú willað secgean . . . Hê cwæð on his bôclican lâre (*the advice contained in his book*), Hex. 32, 19. Underþeódd þære bôclican lâre, Hml. A. 41, 419. Þeáh wê hí æfter bôclicum andgyte âwríton *if we describe them scientifically*, Lch. iii. 244, 8. Gif þú wylle witan mid bôclicum getæle hwanon þá *regulares* cumon, Angl. viii. 305, 1. Uton þencan, þonne wê þyllic gehýrað, þ̃ wê þe beteran beón þurh þá bôclican lâre, Hml. S. 28, 120. Se cræft (*grammar*) is ealra bôclicra cræfta (*liberal arts*) ordfruma and grundweall, Ælfc. Gr. Z. 289, 13. Bôclican lâreówdômum *liberalibus studiis*, An. Ox. 3099 : 4141. Tô þysum wîfmannum âwrât Hieronimus trahtbêc, for ðan ðe hí wæron gecneordlæcende on bôclicum smeágungum, Hml. Th. i. 436, 12.

**bôc-rædere.** *Add:*—Bôcræderas *lectores*, Wrt. Voc. ii. 54, 8.

**bôc-ræding.** *Add:*—Bôcræding *lectio*, Wrt. Voc. ii. 54, 7. Hê his eágan upp âhôf fram þære bôcrædinge, Gr. D. 164, 7. Cf. bêc-ræding.

**bôc-reád.** *For* Cot. 75 : 176 *substitute:* Wrt. Voc. ii. 71, 45. Of bôcreáde *ex mineto*, 30, 61.

**bôc-stæf.** *Add:*—Bôcstæf *hoc gramma*, An. Ox. 18 b, 45. Ne cûþe hê nænige bôcstafas (*nequaquam litteras noverat*), ac swâþeáh hê gebohte him sylfum þâ bêc þæs hâlgan gewrites, and bæd þ̃ man rædde þâ bêc beforan him, Gr. D. 281, 22. [*v. N. E. D.* boc-staff. *O. Sax.* bôk-staf : *O. H. Ger.* buoh-stab *littera, character* : *Icel.* bôk-stafr.]

**bôc-stigel.** *v.* stigel : **bôc-sum, -ness.** *Dele.*

**bôc-tæcing,** -talu. *Substitute:* Teaching or direction contained in books :—Godcunde bôte sêce man georne and symble be bôctæcinge (bôctale, *v. l.*) according to the directions contained in books (e. g. Theodore's Liber Poenitentialis) (or *as books tell*), Ll. Th. i. 398, 22.

**bôc-treów.** *Add:*—Bôctreów *fagus*, Ælfc. Gr. Z. 29, 17.

**bôcung.** *Dele.*

**bôc-weorc,** es; *n. Literary work, study*:—Bisceopes dægweorc, þ̃ bið mid rihte his gebedu ærest, and ðonne his bôcweorc, ræding oððon rihting, lâr oððon leornung, Ll. Th. ii. 314, 19.

**bod,** es; *n. Add:* also *m.* in North. and in cpd. æ̂-bod. **I.** a command :—Se forðmesta bod *primum mandatum*, Mk. L. 12, 30, 25, 29. Boda *praecepta*, 7, 7. Bodo *mandata*, Lk. L. 18, 20. **II.** a message :—Burgwaras sendon bod (*legationem*) æfter him, Lk. L. R. 19, 14. **III.** preaching :—Ðæs godspellesca bodes *euangelicae praedicationis*, Mk. p. 1, 11. *v.* fore-, gewil-bod.

**boda.** *Add:*—Bodana *preceptorum*, Rtl. 95, 35 : 97, 8. *v.* brýd-bôda.

**bodan.** *v.* botm.

**bodere.** *Add:* ; *a preacher* :—Bodare, Lk. L. 9, 33. Sende twoelfe boderes *mittens duodecim praedicaturos*, Mk. p. 3, 10.

**bodian.** *Add:* **I.** to declare, proclaim, make known :—Ðâ geleáffullan bodiað (bodigeað, *v.l.*) be Gode ðæt sôð is *ecclesia ore fidelium de Deo, quaeque vera sunt, testatur*, Past. 367, 9. Sê . . . þe hê tôwearde sægde and bododo, Bl. H. 9, 16. Weorþian wê Sancta Marian, for þon þe heó engla þreátas eádige bododon, 11, 12. Ne sceal hê nô ðæt ân bodigan (-ean, *v.l.*) his hiéremonnum hû ðâ synna him wiðwinnað, ac hê him sceal eác cýðan mid hwelcum cræftum hê him wiðstondan mæg *non solum debent innotescere qualiter vitia impugnent, verum etiam quomodo custoditae nos virtutes roborent*, Past. 163, 2. **II.** to announce what is coming :—Fricca and forerynele hêr iernað beforan kyningum and bodigeað (bodiað, *v.l.*) hira færelt and hiera willan hlýdende. suâ sculun ðâ sâcerdas nû faran hlýdende and bodiende beforan ðæm egeslican dêman ðe him æfter gæð, Past. 91, 21–24. **II a.** to foretell, prophesy :—Bodiendra wîtedôma *vaticinantium, prophetantium*, An. Ox.

1524. **III.** to proclaim the excellence of, celebrate, praise (cf. bodigend-lic) :—Hê hine swâ orgellîce up âhôf and bodode, ðæs þ̃ hê úþwita wære, Bt. 18, 4 ; F. 66, 29. Agustinus wæs fram him eallum bodad and hered *ab omnibus praedicatur Augustinus*, Bd. 2, 2 ; Sch. 115, 14. **III a.** intrans. To boast about :—Ic mid getote be mê bodude, R. Ben. 22, 17 note. **IV.** of religious or moral teaching, to preach, (1) a person :—Scyppend ealra gesceafta, þone ic bodige, Bl. H. 187, 9. (2) a doctrine, belief, &c.:—Manige men þâ godcundan lâre gehýrað, and him mon þâ oft bodaþ and sægþ, Bl. H. 57, 19. Ðâ ðe swigiað ðæt hié ðâ hâlgan æ ne bodiað (bodigeað, 4) *qui sacrae legis verba non loquuntur*, Past. 365, 7. Birinus bodude West-Seaxum fulwuht, Chr. 634; P. 26, 1. Felix bodade Eást-Englum Crístes geleáfan, 636 ; P. 26, 5. Nâ ðæt ân dætte hê nân wôh ne bodige, ac eác ðæt hê ðæt ryht tô suíðe ne bodige *ab eis non solum prava nullo modo, sed ne recta quidem nimie proferantur*, Past. 95, 16. Rihtne crístendôm bodian, Wlfst. 175, 22. Suâ huêr suâ bodad bið þis godspell, Mt. L. R. 26, 13 : Bl. H. 69, 19. Þ̃ hâlige sæd him of þæs lâreówes múþe wæs bodad and sægd, 55, 30. (3) intrans. :—Se Hælend þe hê embe bodade, Hml. S. 22, 53. Boda heom be þâm Hælende, 21. *v.* be-bodian.

**bodi(g)end,** es; *m.* **I.** one who announces :—Bodiend, bannend *gerulus, portitor*, An. Ox. 56. **II.** a teacher, preacher :—On hâligre laþunge gelæred bodigend (*predicator*), Scint. 124, 9. Paulus wæs bodigend and âcoren lâreów, Hml. A. 149, 148. Bodiend *praedicator*, Kent. Gl. 1157 : *praeceptorem*, 132.

**bodi(g)end-lic;** *adj.* To be celebrated, praised. *v.* bodian, III; *praedicabilis* :—Ic bletsige ðê, Fæder, bodigendlic God, Hml. S. 7, 232. Cf. herigend-lic.

**bodig.** *For* II *and* III *substitute*: **II.** the main portion, (1) of the animal frame (opposed to head or limbs) :—Bodig *truncus*, Wrt. Voc. i. 283, 26. Bodeg, bodeʒ *spina*, Txts. 99, 1891. Bodig, An. Ox. 18 b, 89. Hí næfdon þ̃ heáfod tô þâm bodige, Hml. S. 32, 137, 165. Hí tyrndon mid bodige, and heora fôtwylmas âwendan ne mihton, Hml. Th. ii. 508, 19. Hí (*idols*) habbað dumne mûð and ungrâpigende hand, fêt bútan fêðe, bodig bútan lîfe, i. 366, 27. Heó bewand þ̃ bodig mid ðâm beddclâðum and nam þ̃ heáfod, Hml. A. 111, 306. Mon mæg gesión ægðer ge his (*the hedgehog's*) fêt ge his heáfod ge eác eall ðæt bodig (*corpus*), Past. 241, 10. Bodig *spinam*, Wrt. Voc. ii. 79, 37 : 97, 34. (2) of an implement :—Nim þ̃ sæd, sete on þæs sules bodig, Lch. i. 402, 2.

**bod-scipe.** *Add:* [*O. Sax.* bod-skepi : *O. Frs.* bod-skip : *Icel.* boð-skapr : *O. H. Ger.* bota-scaf ; *f.*] : **bodu.** *v.* þunor-bodu.

**bodung.** *Add:* **I.** annunciation, declaration, making known (cf. bodian, I), (1) announcement by a messenger (cf. bodung-dæg) :—Hê (*Antecrist*) sent his bodan geond ealne middaneard, and his hlîsa and bodung bið fram sæ tô sæ, Wlfst. 195, 20. (2) declaration by a witness, testimony :—Lôca hwonne se tîma cumen bið, þæt heora bodung geendod bið *cum finierint testimonium suum* (Rev. 11, 7), Wlfst. 199, 17. (3) interpretation :—Bodunge *conjectionis*, Wrt. Voc. ii. 23, 67. (4) glossing logical terms :—Bodunga *praedicamentorum*, An. Ox. 3129. Lâra, bodunga *cathegorias .i. nuntiationes* ɫ *praedicationes*, 3128. **II.** reciting, rehearsing :—Gif hwylc brôðor wægð and misfêhð on boduncge sealma oðþe ræpsa *si quis dum pronuntiat psalmum aut responsorium fallitur*, R. Ben. 71, 5. **III.** boastful assertion (cf. bodian, III) :—Þæt dîgle þing beón scolde, tô sige, þæt is tô bodunge and tô getotes gylpe hý gewyrcaþ, R. Ben. 136, 22. **IV.** preaching :—Seó bodung forestæpð, and Drihten cymð syþþan tô þæs mannes môde þe ðâ bodunge gehýrð, Hml. Th. ii. 530, 10. Heora (*the Apostles'*) bodunge swêg swêgde geond eall, and heora word be-cômon tô eorþan gemærum, Hml. A. 56, 144. Hê mê (*St. Paul*) tô bodunga sende, Bl. H. 185, 33. Críst clypode on his bodunge, Hml. S. 16, 130. Se cyning gerehte his witum þæs bisceopes bodunge, 26, 66. Þurh Paules bodunga, Bl. H. 173, 18. Bodunge, R. Ben. 4, 5 : Hml. Th. i. 58, 30. Hí mid bysnungum wel ne lædað, ne mid bodungum wel ne lærað, Ll. Th. ii. 328, 2. Bodengum, Wlfst. 276, 24. Hê âl his bodunga mid gebysnungum âstealde, Hml. Th. ii. 148, 26. *v.* fore-, godspell-bodung.

**boeting.** *v.* bætan.

**boga.** *Add:* , bog (? cf. boga *arcuum*, An. Ox. 511). **I.** a (rain-) bow :—Þ̃ heó þone heofonlîcan bogan mid hyre bleóge efenlæce, Lch. i. 284, 15. **II.** an arch, a vault :—Fornix boga (-o) *super columnis*, Txts. 64, 453. Bígels, boga, incleofa *camera, arcus, fornax*, Wrt. Voc. ii. 127, 78. Bogan *fornicem*, 37, 2. Bígelsa bogum (boga bígelsum, An. Ox. 511) *arcuum fornicibus* (of an aqueduct, v. Ald. 8, 32), Wrt. Voc. ii. 76, 3 : 37, 1. **III.** bow (as in saddle-bow) :—Boga *antena*, Wrt. Voc. ii. 100, 33 : 6, 65. Ioc *jugum*, boga *antena*, iocsticca *obicula*, i. 16, 32. Boga *postena*, ii. 117, 52 : *canda*, 103, 26 : 14, 8. Bogan *boiae* (cf. *boia, arcus vel geoc*, 126, 42), ii. 55. **IV.** a bow for shooting :—Flâ *sagitta*, boga *arcus*, Wrt. Voc. i. 35, 25 : 84, 30. Hê gebende his bogan and mid flân ðone fearr ofsceótan wolde, Hml. Th. i. 502, 18 : Bl. H. 199, 18. **V.** folded parchment [cf. Ger. bogen] :—Cine *quaternio*, boga *diploma*, Wrt. Voc. i. 75, 12.

[Bowa *diploma*, 89, 51.]    **VI.** the word occurs as a surname:—
Edwíg boga, C. D. B. iii. 536, 5.  v. geoc-, sadol-boga.

**bógan.** *Add:* , bógian, bón ; *þ.* bóde :—Sê þe hyne bógað *qui se jactat*, Scint. 152, 2.  Ic ne férde on mærðum, ne wundorlíce mid getote ne bóde, R. Ben. 22, 17.  þæt nán þing fíæsclices beforan Gode mid getote ne bógie *ut non glorietur omnis caro coram Deo*, 139, 2.  v. bón *in Dict.*; bógung.

**boge-fódder.** *Substitute in bracket* fódder *a case, and add :* [*O. L. Ger.* bogo-fódar : *O. H. Ger.* bogo-fuotor *coritus.*]

**bogen** *the name of some plant.* *Add:*—Bogen and redic and hwíte clǽfran, Lch. ii. 64, 3: 134, 17: 322, 21.  [*In* 310, 17 bogenes *is corrected to* boþenes.]  [Cf. (?) *D. D.* bowens *ragwort*; *groundsel.*]

**boget(t)ung.** *Add:*—Bogetungum *anfractibus*, Wrt. Voc. ii. 9, 53.

**bógian** *to inhabit.* v. búan : **bógian** *to boast.* v. bógan.

**bogiht[e]**; *adj. Full of bends* :—Bogehte woeg *arta via*, Mt. L. 7, 14.  Cf. bogettung.

**bógincel**, es ; *n. A small bough* :—Bóginclum *ramusculis*, i. *ramis modicis*, An. Ox. 1556.  Bóhginclium, 548.

**bog-timber**, es; *n. Wood for an arch* (? v. boga, II) :—Ic gegaderode mê bohtimbru and bolttimbru (bolt = bold? cf. boldgetæl (bolt-)) *I gathered me wood for building*, Shrn. 163, 7.

**bogung.** *Substitute :* bógung, bóung, e ; *f. Ostentation, arrogance, boasting* :—Bóung ꝉ gylp *jactantia*, Angl. xi. 118, 63.  Bóunge *ostentationis*, An. Ox. 5163 : 2, 427.  Swýðor begýman on bóunge ídeles gylþes þonne on árfæstum weorke *ostentationi potius intendisse quam operi*, Gr. D. 77, 4.  þæt Iudêisce folc wæs up áhafen and hí sylfe herodon . . . þæt Iudêisce folc gewát fram Gode forsewen þurh heora upáhefednysse and ágenre bógunge (*praise of themselves*), Hml. Th. ii. 428, 17.

**boh.** *l.* bóh, *and add :* [*a weak form* bóga *occurs*, Wrt. Voc. i. 33, 16, *and also weak forms of g. pl.*]    **I.** *a shoulder* of an animal :—Boog *armus*, Wrt. Voc. ii. 100, 82.  Bóg *armum*, 7, 17.  ðone suíðran bógh, Past. 81, 19.  Gif hors on hricge oððe on þám bógum áwyrd sý, Lch. i. 290, 10.  þegnas mǽton mílpaðas meára bógum, Exod. 171.    **II.** *bough* of a tree, *sprig, sprout* of a plant :—Bóg *frondus*, Wrt. Voc. ii. 151, 24.  Bóh *ramus*, i. 80, 5.  Bóga, 33, 16.  Pintreówes bóh *pini stipitem* (.i. *ramum*), An. Ox. 2223.  Bógas *frondes, s. dicuntur quod ferant virgultas*, Wrt. Voc. ii. 151, 8.  Bóga *stipitum, frondium*, An. Ox. 3084 : 7, 83.  Bógana, 1557 : 2457.  Bógum *comis vel ramis*, Wrt. Voc. ii. 132, 12.  Hyre (*leechwort*) stela byð mid geþúfum bógum, Lch. i. 248, 18.  þ óðer cyn (*of southernwood*) is greáton bógum and swýþe smælon leáfon, 250, 19.  Wæs Aarones gyrd gemétt grówende mid bógum, Hml. Th. ii. 8, 15.  Hit bið unnyt ðæt mon hwelces ysles bógas snæde, buton mon wille ðá wyrtruman forceorfan, Past. 222, 15.  Bógas wíngerdes *propagines uitis*, An. Ox. 2016.  Hpt. Gl. 496, 76.  v. wín-geard-bóh.

**boh-timber.** v. bog-timber.

**bol** (?), es ; *m. The bole, trunk* :—Scæf efic wið, þon[n]e bol, in meolc, Lch. iii. 18, 9.  [*Icel.* bolr.]

**ból** *glosses* murenula :—Bool *murenula*, Wrt. Voc. ii. 114, 31.  [Cf. (?) *N. E. D.* boul, bool *anything bent into a curve.*]

**bolca.** *Dele bracket, and add :*—Bolca *foros* (= *forus*, cf. *forus vel prorostra*, i. 36, 43 : *prorostris* hêhseldum, foreweard scip, ii. 68, 47), Wrt. Voc. ii. 35, 78.  Bolcan *foras*, 109, 8.

**bold.** *Add:* **I.** *a dwelling* :—þær wæs ðá kyninges bold (*uilla regia*), hêt Eádwine þær cyrican timbrian, on Donafelda, þá þá hǽðenan mid ealle þí bolde [bóðle, *v. l.*] forbærndon . . . For ðám þá æftercyningas him bold (*uillam*) worhton on ðám lande þe Loides hátte, Bd. 2, 14; Sch. 173, 14–22.  þ se líg náht þære burge boldes ne gehrínan ne dorste *ut flamma contingere quidquam aedificii non auderet*, Gr. D. 48, 11.  Hwá fêhð tó þám ðe þú lange samnodest, oððe hwám gearwadest þú þín bold and þíne getimbru, nú þíne erfeweardas lifian ne mótan?, Wlfst. 261, 8.  þ hê heora bold gedréfe, Angl. x. 146, 187.    **II.** *a town.* Cf. tún :—In þám bolde þe is háten Eoferwícceaster, Angl. x. 141, 13.  (The last two passages are from a 12th-century MS.)    ¶ *in place-names*, e. g. Wíc-bold, C. D. vi. 351.  Æt Nióweboldan *Newbold*, iii. 256, 11.  [*v. N. E. D.* bold.]  v. wer-bold.

**bold-getæl.** *Substitute :* *The collection of habitations subject to some single authority, a district, province* :—Of dælum þæs boldgetales (bolt-geteles, *v. l.*) þe hátte Apaulie *provinciae Apuliae partibus*, Gr. D. 185, 23.  Wæs sum wer in Samni þám boldgetæle (boltgetele, *v. l.*) . . . swá manige men swá cúðon Samni þ boldgetæl (-tel, *v. l.*) *erat in Samnii provincia quidam vir . . . quot Samnii provinciam noverunt*, 229, 6–11.  Manige men of manigum boldgetalum (scírum, *v. l.*) *multi ex diversis provinciis*, 45, 23.

**bold-wéla.** *l.* -wela : **-bolgenness.** v. á-bolgenness.

**bolla.** *Add:* ; bolle, an ; *f.* :—Bolle *aceti cotilla, vas*, Txts. 37, 65.  Bolla, bollae *cyatus*, 50, 234 : *scifus*, 98, 965.  Bolla *catus*, Wrt. Voc. ii. 129. 53 : *cotula vel catus*, 135, 27 : *cratus*, 136, 54 : *ciatus*, i. 29c, 80.  Bolle *cotilla*, ii. 135, 38.  Hê genam ǽnne mycelne bollan mid bealuwe áfylled, Hml. S. 14, 68.  Bolla full ꝉ copp full of æcced

---

spongiam plenam aceto, Jn. L. 19. 29.  Gê syttað ealle niht and drincað oð leóhtne dæg . . . ac wíte gê mid gewissan, þ eów wurdað þá mycclan bollan bytere forgoldene, Wlfst. 298, 1.  v. wæter-bolla.

**bolster.** *Add:*—Bolster *pulvinar*, Germ. 398, 179 : *compluta*, Wrt. Voc. ii. 133, 6.  Bolster *vel* wongere *cervical*, i. *capitale*, 130, 26.  Lang bolster *plumacium*, i. 288, 61.  Bolstor *pulvinar*, An. Ox. 56, 17.  Hié restað búton bedde and bolstre *quiescentes sine ullis ceruicalibus stratisque*, Nar. 31, 11.  Lecggeað bolster under ælcne hneccan . . . bið se hnecca underléd mid bolstre, Past. 143, 14–18.  Bolstrum *auleis*, Germ. 399, 366.

**bolstrian.** v. ge-bolstrod.

**bolt.** *Substitute :* *A bolt, an arrow* :—þær is ælc treów swá riht swá bolt *there is every tree as straight as a bolt* (cf. bolt-upright), E. S. viii. 477, 13.  Speru, boltas *catapultas* (cf. An. Ox. 4238 (*where the same passage is glossed*) arewan, gauelucas), Wrt. Voc. ii. 85, 16 : 18, 58.

**bolt-timber.** v. bog-timber : **bon-.** v. ban-: **bón** *to boast.* v. bógan.

**bón**, e ; *f. Ornament* :—Harold his heáfod þám kynge bróhte, and his scipes heáfod, and þá bóne (*ornaturam*, Fl. Wig. Plummer quotes the further description, 'Proram cum puppi pondus graue scilicet auri, Artificum studio fusile multiplici,' ii. 251) þêr mid, Chr. 1063 ; P. 191, 16.  [Cf. (?) *Icel.* búa *to ornament*; gull-búinn *ornamented with gold.*]  v. ge-bóned.

**bonda.** *l.* bónda, *and add :*—Æt ælcum fordfarenum gildan, sê hit bónda, sê hit wíf, þe on þám gildscipe sindon, Cht. Th. 609, 12.  Gyf frígman þæt fæsten ábrece, gebête þæt þus : bónda mid .xxx. penigan, þegen mid .xxx. scillingan, Wlfst. 172, 5.  Bunda, 181, 9.  Án his manna wolde wícian æt ánes bundan húse, Chr. 1048; P. 172, 22.  Swá þám bóndan sý sélost, Wlfst. 272, 1.  ¶ *A comparison of* Wlfst. 172, 5 : 181, 9 *with* L. Eth. viii. 2 : Si quis jejunium suum infringat, reddat liber pauper .xxx. d., *gives* liber pauper *as the translation of* bónda.  [*From Icel.* bóndi.]  v. *N. E. D.* bond.]  v. hús-bónda.

**bónde-land.** *Substitute :* *Land held by a* bónda *as tenant.* The Latin version of the charter cited is : terram x manentium (*manentes inquilini, coloni, sed proprie qui in solo alieno manent, in villis, quibus nec liberis suis invito domino licet recedere*, Migne).

**-bóned.** v. ge-bóned : **bool.** v. ból.

**bór.** *l.* bor, *and add :*—Boor *dasile*, Wrt. Voc. ii. 98, 7.  Bor *desile*, 26, 22 : 139, 24 : i. 287, 10.  Boor *scalpeum*, Txts. 117, 259.  Bor *scalpellum*, bore *scalpro*, 95, 1806, 1803.  Bor *scalprum*, Wrt. Voc. i. 289, 3.  v. næfe-, tym-bor.

**-bora.** *Add:* v. ceác-, ród-, sóþ-, strǽl-, wudu-bora.

**bord.** *Add:* **I.** *a board* :—Borda *gefêg commissura*, Wrt. Voc. i. 39, 65.    **II.** *side of a ship, board* (in larboard) :—Hí wurpon heora waru ofor bord, Hml. Th. i. 246, 2, 9.

**borda**, an; *m.*    **I.** *an ornamental border, a fringe* :—Borda *prinicula, ornatus vestimentorum*, Hpt. 33, 247, 105 : *clavia*, Wrt. Voc. ii. 104, 10 : 14, 40 : *clava*, 131, 53 : *lesta*, 112, 64 : 50, 76.    **II.** *embroidery* :—Fǽmne æt hyre bordan gerîseþ (cf. *Icel.* sitja við borða *to sit embroidering*), Gn. Ex. 64.  [*O. H. Ger.* borto *limbus* : *Icel.* borði *border* ; *embroidery*; *tapestry.*]  v. byrdan ; byrd-estre, -icge, -ing.

**bord-cláþ**, es ; *m. A table-cloth* ; mappella, An. Ox. 56, 22.

**borde.** *Dele, and see* borda, **II.**

**bord-haga.** [haga *a hedge.* *l.* *an enclosure.*]  *A shield-enclosure, phalanx.* Cf. scild-burh.

**bord-hreóða.**    **I.** For *the cover of the shield* substitute *a phalanx.* v. scild-hreóþa.

**bord-rima**, an ; *m. The edge of a plank* :—Bordremum *rimis* (the passage to which the gloss belongs is : 'Rimis patentibus intravit mare,' which is translated : 'Geoniendum þám ceólum se sǽ eóde inn,' Gr. D. 248, 27 ; sc that *bordremum* refers to the edges of the ship's planks which parted from one another, thus making a gap through which the sea entered), Txts. 114, 112.

**bord-ríþig** *a stream running in a channel made of planks* (?) :—Of sandbróce on bordríðig; of bordríðig on horpyttes ríðig, C. D. iii. 82, 23.

**bord-þaca.** *Substitute :* bord-þaca, -þeaca, an ; *m.*    **I.** *a board for roofing* :—Bordþacan *latrariis*, fierst *laquear*, fierste *laquearea*, hróf *lacunar*, Wrt. Voc. ii. 50, 52–55.  [Cf. *Icel.* borð-þak *a covering of planks*; borð-þekja *to cover with planks.*]    **II.** *a shield-covering, phalanx* :—Bordðeaca, borohaca, brodthaca *vel* sceldhrêða *testudo*, Txts. 101, 1999.

**bord-weall.** *Add:* **I.** *a line of shields.* Cf. scild-weall :—Hí bord-weal clufan, heówan heaþolinde, Chr. 937; P. 106, 13.    **II.** *the side of a ship* :—Wiht (*an iceberg*) cwom æfter wǽge líðan . . . bord-weallas gróf, Rä. 34, 6.

**borettan** ; *þ.* te *To move to and fro, brandish* :—Borettið, boreтtit *vibrat*, Txts. 107, 2147.  Cf. beran.

**borg-gylda**, -gilda, -gelda.  *Add :* *A debtor :*—Deáðes borggeldum *mortis debitoribus*, Ps. Srt. ii. 203, 29.  Borhgeldum, Hy. S. 33, 1.

**borgian.** _Add:_ **I.** _to borrow:_—Æfre borgiað þā synfullan, and næfre ne gyldað _mutuatur peccator, et non commodat_, Ps. Th. 36, 20. **II.** _to lend._ Cf. borgiend—Borgedan _commodarent_, Wrt. Voc. ii. 16, 8. **III.** _to be surety, bail_ for. Cf. byrg(e)a, and Icel. borga fyrir _to be bail for_:—Borgiendre _sequestra_, An. Ox. 3812. v. on-borgian.

**borgiend.** _Add:_—Borhgiend _fenerator_, Bl. Gl.

**borg-wed.** _Add:_—Borgwed (borg, wed ?) _vadimonium_, Wrt. Voc. i. 289, 66.

**borh.** _Add:_ **I.** _responsibility for performance, payment_, &c., by another, _suretyship, security:_—Borges andsaca (-u ?) _inficiatio, idem et abjuratio_, Wrt. Voc. ii. 49, 27. Feohlænung būtan borge _ypotheca_, i. 21, 9. Ðis synt þā men þe synt anburge (-byrge ? cf. _Icel._ ā-byrgð _responsibility ; or on_ borge ?) betwīnon Eádgyfe abbedysse and Leófrīce abbode æt þām lande æt stoctūne, Cht. E. 256, 7. Gilēbdae borg _concesserim vadimonium_, Txts. 106, 1090. Ðā ðe berað on hira greádum ðā fatu tō ðǣm temple on hira āgenne borg _qui ad templum vasa in sinu propriae sponsionis portant_, Past. 77, 7. Ðū eart on borg begān ðīnum friénd _incidisti in manus proximi tui_, 193, 17. Eóde þyses ealles on borh Ælfgār _Alfgar became responsible for the performance of all this_, Cht. Th. 313, 3. ¶ on, under borh sellan _to lend_ on security :—Gelēned feoh _vel_ on borh geseald _res credita_, Wrt. Voc. i. 20, 70. Gode on borgh geseald _foenerata Domino_, 55, 21. Ne þurfon gē wēnan þ gē þ orceápe sellon, þ gē under Drihtnes borh syllaþ, Bl. H. 41, 13. **I a.** _lending_ on security ; _what is so lent, loan, debt_ of a borrower:—Borh _foenus_, borge _fenore_, Wrt. Voc. ii. 35, 23, 24. Borg, 108, 42. Borg _vel_ lǣn _fenus_, i. _lucrum, usura_, 148, 23. Borge _mutuo_, 56, 5. þ man ǣlcne borh āgulde _ut quicquid in mutuo ab aliquo acceptum erat restitueretur_, Cht. Th. 550, 26. þā þe on fæstendagum willað hiora borga manian (_call in their loans_) ... gē āsēcað ealle eówre borgas (_loans_, not _debtors_ as in Dict.), Ll. Th. ii. 438, 33–36. Scytte man mīna borgas, Cht. Th. 568, 19. ¶ tō borge _on loan ;_ tō borge sellan _to lend :_—Tō borge (_qui accipit_) _mutuum_, Kent. Gl. 817. Se rihtwīsa syleð ōþrum tō borge _justus commodat_, Ps. Th. 36, 25. þā rihtwīsan syllað ǣgher ge tō borge ge tō gife, 20. Sum mon sealde ōþrum scilling seolfres tō borge, Shrn. 127, 26. **II.** of persons :—Sanctulus his borh (_fidejussor_) wæs, Gr. D. 253, 26. Se godfæder wæs þæs cildes forspreca and borh wið God, Hml. Th. ii. 50, 17. [v. _N. E. D._ borrow.] v. friþ-, hȳre-, in-, wer-borh.

**borh-fæst ;** _adj._ _Bound by the giving of security :_—Wolde hē gedōn þ ic him wǣre borhfæst ... and ætfæste hē mē mīne efenþeówene [_the marriage would be security for continued service_], Hml. A. 203, 254.

**borh-hand.** _Substitute ; m., f. A surety, bail, sponsor :_—þes borh-hand _hic vas_, Ælfc. Gr. Z. 50, 15 : _hic praes_, 60, 16. Borhhand _sponsor vel praes vel fidejussor vel vas vel vador_, Wrt. Voc. i. 60, 50. Borh-hond _fidejussor_, Kent. Gl. 742. Ic mīnre heortan eágan tō þǣre mīnre borhhanda (_the Virgin Mary_) up āhōf, hī biddende þ heó mē gefultumode, Hml. S. 23 b, 560. Borhhande _vades_ (cum his, qui _vades_ se offerunt pro debitis), Kent. Gl. 848.

**borian.** _Add:_ **I.** _trans._ (1) _to perforate :_—Ic borige _terebro_, Wrt. Voc. i. 84, 64 : [24, 8 _in Dict._]. þurhþȳnde, bori[gende] _transverberans_, An. Ox. 230. (2) _to insert into a hole bored_ :—Borige man on þām beáme stōr and finol, Lch. i. 400, 19. **II.** _intrans._ _To bore_ into :—Dō þū mid þīnum fingre swilce þū borige inn on þīne hand, Tech. ii. 123, 11. v. þurh-borian.

**bor-līce ;** _adv. Eminently, excellently, well :_—Hyt gerīst borlīce wel _it is eminently suitable_, Angl. viii. 302, 5. Wel borlīce hē forð stæpped _full nobly he steps forth_, 307, 28. Hē geswutelað borlīce _he shews admirably_, 329, 24. þā hīw rīmcræftige esnas borlīce foregylpað, 334, 27. Wolde ic þ þā æþelan clericas āsceócon fram heora andgites orðance ǣlce sleacnysse, þ hig þe borlīcor mihton gecýðan þǣra epactena gesceád, 315, 5. [v. _N. E. D._ burly. Cf. _O. H. Ger._ bur-līh _praestans, sublimis, excellens._]

**-borstenness.** v. tō-borstenness : **bósg.** _Dele_ bósg, _and add :_ [v. _N. E. D._ boosy.]

**bósmig ;** _adj. Sinuous :_—Bōsmigum bī(g)um _sinuosis (laterum) flexibus_, Hpt. Gl. 405, 35 ; An. Ox. 8, 2.

**bósum.** _Add:_ **I.** _bosom ; sinus, gremium._ (1) of persons :—Hē bær on his bōsme (sinu) Honorates scōh, Gr. D. 17, 9. Hī wurdon gegripene fram mōderlicum breóstum, ac hī wurdon betǣhte engellicum bōsmum, Hml. Th. i. 84, 9. (1 a) _personification :_—[Tō mōder]licum bōsme _ad maternum (sanctae ecclesiae) gremium_, An. Ox. 4162. (2) of things :—Seó sǣ wunað on ðǣre eorðan bōsme, Hex. 10, 31. Tunnena bōsmum _cuparum gremiis_, An. Ox. 3513. **II.** _womb ; uter_ :—þý syxtan mōnþe þæs þe Sct. Iōhannes on his mōdor bōsm onfangen wæs ... þ cild his Hlāford of his mōdor bōsme on þǣre fǣmnan bōsm hālette, Bl. H. 165, 24–30. Se Hālga Gāst wunode on þām æþelan innoþe and on þām betstan bōsme, 105, 15. þǣre mēder wæs on slǣpe ætȳwed, þā heó myd þām bearne wæs, þ hyre man stunge āne sȳle on þone bōsum, Shrn. 149, 2. v. segl-bōsm.

**bót.** _Add:_ **I.** _mending, repair, remedy, improvement_, (1) _repair_ of a structure :—Is ealles þæs landes .xxv. swulga and ān swulung þǣre cirican tō bōte, C. D. iii. 429, 19. Cf. ciric-bót. (2) _a medical remedy :_—Gē blindnesse bōte fundon, Gū. 600. Him tō laman limseóce cwōmon ... symle hǣlo þǣr æt þām bisceope, bōte fundon, El. 1217 : 299. (3) _rescue from evil_ or _peril, amendment_ of condition, _help :_—Hȳ tō anlicnessum hȳ gebǣdon, and wēndon þæt heom of ðām cōme bót ... ǣlc yfel cymð of deófle and ǣlc broc and nān bōt, Wlfst. 11, 6–15. Wæs frōfor cumen, earfoðsīða bōt, Gen. 1476 : B. 281. Is seó bōt gelong æt þe ānum, Cri. 152. Cume nū tō bōte, gif hit God wille. And git mæg þeáh bōt cuman, wille hit man georne on eornost āginnan, Ll. Th. i. 348, 22–24. Hē on Drihten blyssað, bōte gewēned (_sperabit in eo_), Ps. Th. 63, 9. Smeágende hwæt tō bōte mihte æt þǣm fǣrcwealme, Ll. Th. 270, 9. þ wyrð hē āgeaf tō ðāre ceastre bōte (cf. hē heora ceastre ge-stadolode, 16), Ap. Th. 10, 9. Weána bōte gebīdan, B. 934 : 909. (4) _improvement of moral condition, amendment :_—Hié nāne mildheortnesse þurhteón ne mehtan, ǣr þǣm him seó bōt of ðǣm crīstendōme com, Ors. 2, 1 ; S. 64, 18. Hē tō bōte gehwearf _he was converted_, El. 1126. Hī gegaderiað monifeald dysig, būtan heora hwilc eft tō rihtre bōte gecirre, Bt. 3, 1 ; F. 6, 5. Manige men þurh þ tō sōþre bōte gecyrraþ, and gōde geweorþaþ, Bl. H. 129, 23. þās tīda ūre Drihten ūs tō bōte and tō clǣnsunga ūrra dǣda forgifen hafaþ, 131, 1. Ic þā bōte gemon, cume tō gif ic mōt, Hy. 4, 19. **II.** _amends, reparation, compensation for injury_, (1) in a general sense :—Him eft cymeð bót in bōsme, Rä. 38, 7. Hié heora land tō bismere oferhergodan, and him ðæs nǣnige bōte dydon, Bl. H. 201, 23. (2) as a legal term :—Gif hwā ōðres godsunu sleá ... weaxe sió bōt be þām were, Ll. Th. i. 150, 14. Ne sȳ þǣr nān ōðer bōt būtan þ heáfod, 282, 1. Nān ōðer bō: būton þ man ceorfe him handa of, 394, 9. Nān man þ ne wrece, ne bōte ne bidde, 288, 3. Nǣnig witena wēnan þorfte bōte tō banan folmum, B. 158. Hē sealde him tō bōte, þæs þe hē his brýd genam, gangende feoh and seolfor, Gen. 2718. þ hire frýnd mōton beón bōte nýhst (i. e. _bōt was to be claimed from the guilty woman's relatives_), Ll. Th. i. 256, 4. þ hē hine sylfne inlagige tō bōte (i. e. _make himself entitled to offer bōt for a crime, which, but for the king's grace, would be_ bótleás (v. 8)) ... Gif hit þonne tō bōte gegā, 340, 13–16. Ǣr þām þe hī habban bōte āgunnen, 324, 13. Godcunde bōte underfangen, 248, 24. From alre nēweste geleáfulra sȳn heó āsyndrade nymðe heó hit hēr mid þingonge bōte gebēte (cf. nisi ante placita satisfactione emendaverit, 1c6, 9), C. D. i. 114, 27. (3) as a religious term, _amends for sin, repentance, penance_ (cf. dǣd-bót) :—Dōn wē ūrum Drihtne sōþe hreówe and bōte, þ wē þurh þ gegearnian ūra synna forlǣtnesse, Bl. H. 35, 36 : 79, 8. Dōn bōte ūre yfeldǣda, 99, 1 : 101, 9. v. ciric-, cyne-, dǣd-, eft-, geár-, god-, mǣg-, mann-, mōnaþ-, syn-, twi-, weorold-, wicu-bót ; twi-bóte.

**bótettan ;** _p._ te _To repair :_—Wē magon swýþe micele þearfe and ælmessan ūs sylfum gedōn, gif wē willað bricge macian and þā symle bótettan (cf. bētan, 239, 9), Wlfst. 303, 8. Bytlian, bótettan (_printed_ bote atan), tȳnan _to build, repair, fence_, Angl. ix. 261, 10.

**boðen** _thyme._ _Add:_—Boþene _thymo_, Germ. 390, 74. [v. _D. D._ bothen (-am).]

**bótian ;** _p._ ode _To get better, recover from illness :_—Sing ymb þone ceáp ... bærn ymb rēcels ... lǣt syþðan bótegean (beot-, MS.), Lch. iii. 56, 13. Gefēlde ic mē bótiende (_e before o erased in one MS._) and wyrpende _me melius habere sentiebam_, Bd. 5, 6 ; Sch. 581, 5.

**botl.** _Add:_ **I.** of any dwelling :—On middan ðǣre flōre his fægeran botles (_Cuthbert's hermitage_), Hml. Th. ii. 144, 3. þ se līg nāht þǣre burge botles ne gehrīnan ne dorste _ut flamma contingere quidquam aedificii non auderet_, Gr. D. 48, 11. Wē ceorfað heáh treówu on holte ðæt wē hī eft up ārǣren on ðǣm botle, ðǣr ðǣr wē timbran willen _altum silvae lignum succidimus, ut hoc in aedificii tegmine sublevemus_, Past. 433, 36. **II.** of a considerable (royal, monastic, &c.) dwelling :—On Donafelda, ðǣr wæs ðā cyninges botl (_uilla regia_), hēt Ēdwine þǣr cyricean getimbran, þā hī hǣpenan mid ealle þý botle forbærndon ... For þām þā æftran cyningas him botl (_uillam_) worhton on þām lande þe Loidis is hāten, Bd. 2, 14 ; Sch. 173, 13–21. þæs cynges botl, Hml. Th. i. 244, 19 : ii. 480, 6. Tō Melantian (cf. wīf wæligon æhtum, Melantia gecýged, 1) botle, Hml. S. 2, 262. Nabod hæfde ǣnne wīneard wið ðæs cynincges botl, 18, 172. Wið þæt botl Salustii, Hml. Th. i. 428, 10. Se biscop him ðǣr mynsterlic botl timbrian hēt, 508, 30. Hēt hē ontendan eal hire (_the abbess Effigenia_) botl, þǣr heó mid (mā ðonne twām hund, cf. 476, 20) mædenum on gebedum ðurhwunode, ii. 478, 35. ¶ _Bottle_ remains in local names, e. g. Newbottle. [v. _N. E. D._ bottle. _O. Sax._ bodl : _O. Frs._ bodel : _Icel._ bōl.] v. cyne-botl ; bold.

**bót-leás.** _Substitute : Not to be expiated by the payment of_ bót, _that cannot be compensated for by payment of_ bót ; _and add :_—þ his grið sý bótleás, þ hē mid his āgenre hand syld, Ll. Th. ii. 292, 4. Open þýfðe and hlāfordes searwu and ābǣre morð æfter woruldlagu is bótleás þing, Wlfst. 274, 24. Cf. bót-wyrþe.

**botm.** _Add:_—Bodan _fundus_, Wrt. Voc. ii. 98, 10. Cf. bytme.

**bót-wyrþe.** _Substitute : That admits of expiation by the payment of_ bót ; _and add :_—Gif man ābrece þæt þe bótwyrðe syg, bēte hit iorne if

ʒ man commit a crime for which the law allows bót, *let him make* bót *for it promptly*, Wlfst. 274, 22. Æt nánum bótwyrdum gylte ne forwyrce man máre þonne his wer, Ll. Th. i. 266, 12. Æt bótwurðan þingan bête man mid .v. pundum, 340, 28. Cf. bót-leás.

**bóung.** v. bógung: **box** *a box. Add:* v. sáp-box.

**box; m.** *A box-tree. Add:*—Box bux[us], Wrt. Voc. ii. 102, 27 : buxus, An. Ox. 56, 331. Þýfela *vel* boxa *belsarum*, Wrt. Voc. ii. 125, 14.

**bracan.** *Dele, and see* ele-bacen.

**brac-hwíl.** *Add:*—Swá ys seó brachwíl on þæs mannes eágan, heó ys sóðes *atomus*, Angl. viii. 318, 33.

**-brácian.** v. á-brácian: **bracigean,** *dele.*

**brád.** *Add:* I. *broad* (as distinguished from *long*) :—Se bráda wulfes lamb *cameleon alba*, Wrt. Voc. i. 67, 26. II. *of superficial extent,* (1) *where size is defined* :—Seó burh wæs hyre ymbeganges .xxx. míla brád, Ors. 4, 13 ; Th. 432, 22. Innewerdre (*printed* -ne) handa brádnæ hláf *a loaf as big as the flat of the hand*, Lch. i. 404, 6. (2) *of the hand, open* (v. brádlinga)—Brád hand *palma*, Wrt. Voc. i. 283, 14. Wé hors ðacciað and stráciað mid brádre handa, Past. 303, 11. Bráde hand *palmam*, Wrt. Voc. ii. 74, 22. (3) *of great extent, wide-spread, spacious* :—Ðære rúman a(u)guste, brád *augustum*, Wrt. Voc. ii. 5, 23 : 287, 78. Se bráda bryne ofer ealle woruld . . . þæt bráde bealo, Wlfst. 186, 8, 11. Hié þær gesetene sint mid brádum folcum (*amplissimis generis sui incrementis*), Ors. 3, 5 ; S. 104, 27. (4) *of great circumference in comparison with depth, flat* :—Brád hláf *a flat loaf* (? cf. O. H. Ger. breitinga *placenta*); pax(i)matium, Wrt. Voc. i. 288, 66. Braad ponne *cartago*, ii. 103, 23. Of brádre pannan *sartagine*, 26, 11.

**brád-æx.** *Add:*—Brádæx *dolatura*, Wrt. Voc. ii. 28, 28 : *dolatura, lata securis*, 141, 64. Brádacus *dolabella*, Txts. 116, 197. [v. N. E. D. broad-axe. Icel. breið-øx.] v. brádlást-æx.

**bráde.** *Add:*—Blinde gefettan, þæt hý lócedan bráde, Wlfst. 5, 2 : 47, 11. Þú hête him bysmere bráde healdan, Ps. Th. 103, 25.

**bráde-leác,** es ; n. *A plant-name* :—Brádelaec (brádæ-, -leác, -léc) *serpillum*, Txts. 97, 1835. Brádeleác *sarpulum*, Wrt. Voc. i. 68, 47. Genim rædices .iii. snæda and brádeleáces gelíce, Lch. ii. 268, 19. Gearwan and brádeleác, iii. 12, 31.

**brád-hláf.** v. brad, II. 4: **brádiende.** *Substitute:* brádian; *p. ode To become broad, extend (intrans.).*

**brádlást-æx,** e ; f. *A broad-axe* :—Braadlástæcus (braedlaestu aesc, Erf. Gl.) *dolatura*, Txts. 57, 703. v. brád-æx.

**brádlinga;** *adv. Flatly, with the hand open* (v. brád, I. 2)—Sete þíne hand brádlinga tó þínum leóre, Tech. ii. 120, 27. Brálinga, 121, 3. Dó brálinga þíne hand tó þínre nasan, 123, 12. Wend þú his hand brádlinga ádúne, 121, 26. [v. N. E. D. broadling.]

**brád-nes.** *Add:*—Fyðerscýte brádnys *triquadra (mundi) latitudo*, Hpt. Gl. 437, 7. On brádnysse *in superficie*, 451, 1. Brádnysse, *vastitatem*, 491, 73.

**brád-þistel.** *l.* brád þistel?. Cf. se unbráda þistel. v. þistel.

**bræc,** brec, es ; n. (?) *A brack, break* [v. N. E. D., D.D. *s. vv.*], *a strip of uncultivated land* (?) :—Of ðane ealdan máre innon ðá(m?) bræce ; of ðan bræce andlang beces innon ródstubban (*cf. the same boundaries in another charter* :—Of ðan ealdan mære innon ðám brece ; andlang breces innon ródstubban, iv. 129, 34), C. D. vi. 170, 36.

**bræc** *rheum. l.* bræc (v. ge-breec *pituita*, Erf. Gl. 775) : **-bræc.** v. ge-bræc.

**bréc,** e ; f. *Breach, breaking, destruction* :—His sunu cwæþ þ hé nolde geþafian þ man swá deórwurðne cræft (*an astronomical instrument*) tó-cwýsan sceolde, bútan man þá hálgan wurpe on háte ofnas, gif his fæder nære hæled æfter þære bréce, Hml. S. 5, 292. v. ciric-, frið-bréc.

**bræce** *trousers* :—Braeccę (*the second* c *is added above the line*) *sarabare*, Txts. 95, 1788. [*Latin* braccae.]

**bræc-cóþu.** *l.* bræc-coþu (bréc-?): **-bréce.** v. land-bréce.

**bræclian;** *p. ode To crackle, rattle, resound* :—Aweóx and bræclade mára swég and hefegra *gravior sonitus excrevit*, Gr. D. 236, 12. Cf. ge-bræc.

**bræc-seóc** (bréc-?). *Add:*—Bræcseóc *freneticus*, Wrt. Voc. ii. 40, 6. Bræccéc *lunaticus*, Mt. L. 17, 15. Bræcceic, p. 18, 1. Gif mon sý bræcseóc (*epileptic*), Lch. ii. 284, 31. Bræcseóca *caducus, demoniacus*, Wrt. Voc. ii. 127, 36. Wiþ bræcseócum men, Lch. ii. 138, 8. Bræcseólde *lunaticos*, Wrt. Voc. ii. 71, 74. Bræcséc, Mt. L. 4, 24. Heó hælde bræcseóce men and deófolseóce, Shrn. 103, 3.

**bræd.** *l.* bréd, *and see* brægd.

**bréd** (-u, -o) *breadth. Add:*—Wæs seó wícstów on lengo .xx-es furlonga *long*, and swá eác brédo, Nar. 12, 17. On lenge and on bréde, 33, 22. Mid braeda *extensione*, Mt. p. 15, 13. Mid wudu beweaxen míle brédo *circumdatum silua mille passus*, Nar. 12, 8. Seó eorþe wæs fíf æcra bréde tó axan geburnen *flamma quinque agri jugera in cinerem extorruit*, Ors. 4, ɟ ; S. 160, 25.

**bréd** *flesh* :—Þonne (*after the burning*) bréd weorþeð eal edníwe eft ácenned *inde reformatur qualis fuit ante figura*, Ph. 240. [O. H. Ger. brát *pulpa*; fleisc-brát *carnes*: Icel. bráð *flesh*.] Cf. bréde.

**brédan** *to broaden. Add:* I. *trans.* (1) *to make broad* :—Hiæ brædaþ (*dilatant*) þwænge heora, Mt. R. 23, 5. (2) *to extend, enlarge* :—Ðæt is ðæt mon his mearce bræde *terminum suum dilatare est*, Past. 367, 13. (3) *to spread out, unfold, pitch a tent* (v. bréding) :—Wé þær úre geteld bræddon ealle *cuncta erecta temptoria*, Nar. 22, 25. Ðió mengu giwédo hiora bræddan (*strauerunt*) on woeg, Mk. R. 11, 8. II. *intrans. To spread, increase* :—Ðá yfelan oferlíce swýðe brædað on worulde, Wlfst. 83, 14. Líccetéras árísað and brædað tó swýðe, 89, 18. v. á-, be-, fore-, under-brædan.

**brédan** *to roast. Dele last two passages, and add:* I. *to roast flesh* :—Ðú, earming, bræddest ænne dæl mínes líchaman, wend nú þone óðerne, and et, Hml. Th. i. 430, 16. Hine cwicne hirstan and brédan, Shrn. 116, 3. þæt lamb brédan, Hml. Th. ii. 40, 13. Brédan *frixiri*, i. *coqui*, Wrt. Voc. ii. 151, 3. Brédendum *assantibus (titionum globis)*, Wrt. Voc. ii. 80, 23 : 5, 8. Fisces brédedes *piscis assi*, Lk. p. 11, 14. II. *to toast cheese* :—Bréde man þone cýse and drígne hláf, Lch. ii. 278, 21. III. *to bake bread* :—Hé hláfas brædde and leác sette *in pistrino, in horto, gaudebat exerceri*, Shrn. 61, 20. v. á-brédan.

**bréde,** es ; m. *l.* bréde, an ; f., *and add* :—Bréde *assura*, Wrt. Voc. i. 82, 67 : *frixa*, Wülck. Gl. 243, 21. [v. N. E. D. brede.] v. lendenbréde.

**bréde,** an ; f. *Substitute:* -bréde. v. wearg-, weg-bréde: **brédels.** *Substitute* v. ofer-brædels : **brédan.** v. brægden.

**-brédipanne,** an ; f. *A frying-pan* :—Brédipanne (-pannae, breitibannæ) *sartago*, Txts. 95, 1762. Brédepanne *cartago*, Wrt. Voc. ii. 13, 54. On brédepannan *in frixerio*, 48, 54. Cf. hearste-panne.

**bréding** *a spreading. Add:* what is spread, a couch, bed :—Gif ic ástíge on legir brédinges mínes (*stratus mei*), Rtl. 181, 7. v. brédan, I. 3.

**bréding,** e ; f. *Roast meat* :—Gesod *cocturam*, brédingce *assaturam*, An. Ox. 3760.

**bréding-panne.** v. bréding-panne *in Dict*.

**bréd-ísen** (bréd-?). *Dele bracket, and substitute* : A chisel :—Brédísen *scalpellum*, Wrt. Voc. i. 288, 42. Bredísern (-aern), Txts. 95, 1793.

**bréd-lést.** v. brádlást-æx: **bréd-nys.** *Substitute:* -bréd-ness. v. tó-brædness: **bréd-panne.** *l.* bréde-panne.

**brægd** *fraud. Add:*—Bréd *astus*, Wrt. Voc. ii. 94, 68 : 5, 62. Bútan ælcen bréde, C. D. ii. 58, 26. Ne beó nænig man bregda tó full, Bl. H. 109, 29. Hý æt mé leornedan leáse bregdas, Wlfst. 255, 15. [v. N. E. D. braid. Icel. bragð ; n. a trick.] v. leás-bregd; bregdan, II. 3.

**brægdan.** v. bregdan: **brægd-boga.** *Dele in bracket* 'bræg d . . . bend.'

**brægde** (?), bregde; *adj. Fraudulent, done with fraud* :—Ús ne þincþ nán riht þ ænig man ágnian sceole þær gewitnysse bið, and man gecnáwan can þ þær bregde (bregden, brygde (or *dat.?* v. brygd) *v. ll.*) bið (*that the matter is conducted with fraud*), Ll. Th. i. 390, 13. v. leás-bregda, *and next word*.

**brægden,** bregden. *Substitute for translation of* Ors. 5, 7, *Marius non minore pene quam ipse praeditus erat astutia ; and add* :—Brædynes *non minore pene quam ipse praeditus erat astutia*, An. Ox. 8, 84. Brædnes, 7, 54: Angl. xiii. 29, 39. (*The passage to which all these refer is glossed by* swicfulles, An. Ox. 732.) þær man gecnáwan can þ þær bregden bið (*that there has been fraud*), Ll. Th. i. 390, 13. v. preceding word.

**brægen.** *Add:*—Brægen *cervellum*, Wrt. Voc. ii. 22, 55 : *cervellum*, i. *ceutrum*, 130, 31. Ærest þæs mannes brægen bið geworden on his móder innoþe. Þonne bið þ brægen útan mid reáman bewefen on þære syxtan wucan, Nar. 49, 24-26. Án stán hine slóh inn oð þæt brægen, Hml. Th. ii. 300, 24.

**brægen-loca,** an ; m. *The head, skull* :—Ic (*a lance*) þrísta sum under brægnlocan (hrægn-, MS.) [bealde þringe?], Rä. 72, 21.

**brægen-panne,** an ; f. *Brain-pan, skull* :—Brægenpanne (bræg-, Hpt. Gl. 472, 30) *cerebri*, An. Ox. 2815.

**brægen-seóc;** *adj. Brain-sick, frantic, mad* :—Brægenseóc (bregen-, Hpt. Gl. 514, 31) *freneticus*, An. Ox. 4668. Brægensécne (-seócne, Hpt. Gl. 520, 67) *freneticum*, 5011.

**brémbel-brær,** es ; m. *l.* f.: **bræs.** *Add:*—Bræs es, Wrt. Voc. i. 85, 9 : bræsian. *Add:* [v. N. E. D. braze.]

**bréþ.** *Add:* I. *odour* :—Bréþ *odor*, Wrt. Voc. i. 81, 26. Mære bréd þær stanc, swá þ þ wíf wundrode þæs wynsuman bréþes, and cwæð þ heó næfre ær næht swilces ne gestunce, Hml. S. 4, 347. Se bréd on heora nosðyrlum ne áteorode, Hml. Th. ii. 98, 9. Se wynsuma bréd beláf, 548, 7, 3. Wundorlíces brédes swæc, 352, 15. Bréd þ olfacium, i. odorem, An. Ox. 315 : *odoratum*, 3487. Bréþum swétum odoramentis nectareis, 3325. I a. fig. :—Mid bréðe háligra mihta . . . mid brédum gódra weorca, Hml. Th. i. 222, 4, 7. II. *exhalation, air impregnated with odour* :—Wynsum bréd stémde of þære hálgan róde, and þá lyfte áfylde, Hml. S. 27, 109. Weard þ brýdbed mid bréðe áfylled, swylce þær lǽgon lilie and rose, 4, 32. þes bréð is

of Críste, 42.　　　**III.** *hot vapour :*—Ðá brǽdas ðæs flǽsces stigon up eall swilc hit mist wǽre, Hml. S. 23, 36.　　　**III a.** in a medical sense :—Ne æppla ne wín nis tó sellanne, for ðon ðe hié habbað hátne brǽþ, Lch. ii. 212, 3.　　　**III b.** fig. :—Wylm, brǽþ *feruorem*, i. *ardorem* (*devotionis*), An. Ox. 2511.　v. wyrt-brǽþ.

**brǽw.** *Add :*—Brǽwas *palpebre*, i. *superciliarum loca*, An. Ox. 1731. On ðæs siwenígean eágum ðá brǽwas (*palpebrae*) greátigað, Past. 69, 2.　Dínum brǽwum *palpebre*, Kent. Gl. 79.

**brand.** *Add :* **I.** *a fire-brand, a piece of wood that is burning* or *intended for burning :*—Brand (brond) *titio*, Txts. 100, 987 : Wrt. Voc. i. 66, 40 : *torris*, 284, 19.　Cylle, brond *calbrum*, ii. 127, 70.　Nán brand nolde byrnan under þám wǽtere, Hml. S. 36, 399.　Brandas *p(re)usti*, Txts. 111, 18.　Branda *titionum*, An. Ox. 2470.　Brandum *flammantibus scindulis*, 2459.　Fýrum, brandum *torribus*, i. *ignibus*, 3520 : Wrt. Voc. ii. 94, 56.　Swilce sum hús forburne, brastligende mid brandum, Hml. Th. ii. 140, 16.　**I a.** *a torch :*—Mid brondum I ðæccillum *cum facibus*, Jn. L. R. 18, 3.　**II.** *burning* (v. Dict.).　**II a.** (?) *brand, blight causing leaves, &c. to look as though burnt* (v. N. E. D. brand, 7. Cf. O. H. Ger. wintbrant *rubigo :* Ger. brand *blight*):—Brond, oom (? or brand-oom, *q. v.*) *rubigo*, Wrt. Voc. ii. 119, 34.　Possibly the word occurs in the obscure gloss 'Et dedit erugini, i. brondegur̄ (=?? brond *erugo*),' An. Ox. 54, 2 (see the note).　**III.** *a blade, sword :*—Se hálga áleát and ástrehte his swuran under ðám scínendan brande, Hml. Th. ii. 510, 19.　[Ásleah .iiii. scearpan mid ǽcenan (ǽrenan ?) brande, geblódga ðone brand, weorp on weg, Lch. iii. 52, 2.?]

**brand-ísen, -íren.** *Substitute : Fire-dog, andiron, trivet, and add :*—Crocca *olla*, brandísen *andena*, Ælfc. Gr. Z. 25, 8.　Andlamena fela . . . pannan, crocca, brandíren, Angl. ix. 264, 10.　[v. N. E. D. brand-iron.] Cf. brand-rád.

**brand-óm** *rust that comes from exposure to burning*, or (?) *blight* (v. brand, II a) :—Brondoom *rubigo*, Wrt. Voc. ii. 119, 34.

**brand-rád.** *Substitute :* brand-rád, -rod, -red ; *f. :* -reda, -rida ; *m. A fire-dog, trivet :*—Brandrád (brond-), bran[d]rod *andeda*, Txts. 36, 4.　Brandred *andena*, Wrt. Voc. ii. 6, 62.　Brondreda *andeda*, i. 66, 36.　Brandrida, 284, 10.　[A brandrythe *hec tripos*, Wrt. Voc. i. 232, col. 2. v. N. E. D. brandreth.　O. H. Ger. brant-reita *andeda* (-na) : Icel. brand-reið *a grate.*]

**brand-stefn.** *Substitute : Having a prow with a beak?* Cf. Icel. brandr *a ship's beak ;* or [brand-=brant-?] *high-prowed.* Cf. heáhstefn, An. 266 :—Ne mæg wind áwecgan ne wæterflódas brecan brondstæfne, An. 507.

**brastl.** v. ge-brastl.

**brastlian.** *Add :*—Cracaþ, brastlaþ *crepat*, i. *sonat*, Wrt. Voc. ii. 136, 64.　Fýren líg bláweð and braslað reád and reðe *ignea sonitus perfundet flamma feroces*, Dóm. L. 151 : Wlfst. 138, 8.　Bærstlaþ *crepuerit*, Wrt. Voc. ii. 16, 12.　Brastlade *crepuit*, i. *sonuit*, 136, 71.　Brastlode, Wlfst. 147, 7 : *scintillat*, Germ. 398, 226 : *uerberat*, 401, 38.　Brastliende bendas *crepitantia lora*, Wrt. Voc. ii. 136, 76.　Brǽstlieude, Hpt. Gl. 508, 52.　Spyrcendum, brastliendum *scintillantibus (favillis)*, 499, 45.　[Cf. berstan.] v. á-brastlian.

**brastlung.** *Add :*—Bóh brastlunge hreósendlíc *stipes fragore cassabundus*, An. Ox. 2235.　Se hláf worhte ormǽte brastlunge (barstluncge, bærstlunge, *v. ll.*), efne swylce þǽr tóburste sum mycel crocca on þám fýre *immensum crepitum panis dedit, ac si ingens in ignibus olla crepuisset*, Gr. D. 87, 17.

**breád.** *Add :* **I.** *a bit, morsel (of bread) :*—Breádru *frusta (panis)* (cf. hláfgebrece, Ps. Th. 147, 6 : stycce hláfes, Ps. Srt.), Bl. Gl.　**II.** *bread :*—Breád *bacan*, Wlfst. 296, 8.　Þám mannum sceal man sellan beren breád, Lch. ii. 220, 7.　Þicge hé breád gebrocen on hát wæter, 264, 5.

**-bre(a)dian.** v. ge-bre(a)dian.

**breahtm** *a noise.* *Add :*—Braechtme, brectme, bretme *strepitu*, Txts. 99, 1916.　Áhleópon hildfrome heriges brehtme, An. 1204.　Cómon earnas . . . feðerum hrémige . . . feðrmum blíðe, 869.

**breahtmian ;** *p.* ode *To creak, whizz :*—Strengce bearhtmiendum *nervo stridente*, Hpt. Gl. 405, 74.　Brehtniende (*l.* -miende ; *the same passage as in previous example is glossed*), Wrt. Voc. ii. 74, 72.

**breahtmung, e ;** *f. Conuolatus*, Wrt. Voc. ii. 20, 46.

**breátan.** *Transfer the passage to* breótan, *and see remark at* á-breátan.

**breáþ ;** *adj. Brittle :*—Se wyrttruma byð breáþ and tídre þonne hé gedríged byð, and þonne hé tóbrocen byþ hé rýcþ, Lch. i. 260, 7. [O. H. Ger. bródi *fragilis, tener*.]

**breáw-ern** *a brew-house.* *Substitute :*—Breáwern *apoditerium* (? this word is glossed previously : Baðiendra manna hús, þǽr hí hí unscrédað inne), Wrt. Voc. i. 37, 11.　Cf. Brewarne *pandoxatorium*, 174, 14 : brywhowse *pandoxatorium*, 274, col. 1 : brewster *pandoxator*, 214, col. 1. v. N. E. D. brew-ern.

**bréc.** *Dele 'acc. s. and' :* breca. *Add :* v. lah-breca.

**brecan.** *In line 5 after* méce *add* helm, *dele* **II.** 2 *and* **III.** *and add :*—Brǽcan *friabant*, Wrt. Voc. ii. 38, 2.　Brecan *proteri*, 118,

---

12.　　**I.** *trans.* (1) *to separate into parts,* (a) *to break* a solid body into pieces :—Brec ðǽm hyngriendum ðínne hláf, Past. 315, 13 : Bl. H. 37, 20.　(β) with idea of destruction, *to shatter, demolish :*—Hé sum deófolgild brǽc and fylde, Bl. H. 223, 15, 4, 18.　Mid þǽm palistas hié weallas brǽcon, Ors. 4, 6 ; S. 174, 9.　(γ) *to break* land, *plough for the first time :*—Brocen land *novalis ager*, Wrt. Voc. i. 37, 53.　(δ) *to break* a chain :—Racentan brecan, Bt. 25 ; F. 88, 13.　(2) *to violate* a law, agreement, &c. :—Be þám þe ǽwe brecað, Ll. Th. ii. 180, 12.　Sé ðe hálignessa grið brece, Wlfst. 68, 1.　Hé cwæð þ hé ne cóme nó þás bebodu tó brecanne ne tó forbeódanne (*legem solvere*, Mt. 5, 17), Ll. Th. i. 56, 1.　(2 a) *to fail to perform :*—Banan grimme ongildað, ðæs hié gilp brecað, Sal. 132.　(3) *to subdue, tame :*—Úrne willan tó brecanne, Past. 307, 9.　(4) *to force a way into* a place, *break into* a house, *storm* a town :—Gif man þeóf geméte and hé hús brece *si effringens vir domum fuerit inventus*, Ex. 22, 2 : Ll. Th. i. 50, 18.　Gyf man hús brece, ii. 140, 34.　Hié þæt fæsten brecan woldon, Ors. 4, 11 ; S. 206, 13.　Hwænne se ðeóf cóme his hús tó brecenne, Hml. A. 50, 11.　(5) *reflex. to exert* one's self *violently* (cf. **II.** 3) :—Gif man hine brece ofer gemet tó spíwanne, Lch. ii. 268, 29.　Hé ongan hine brecan tó spíwenne, Chr. 1003 ; P. 135, 13.　　**II.** *intrans.* (1) *to force a way* out of confinement :—Úp brécon *erumperant (fontes aquarum)*, Kent. Gl. 264.　Hí nǽfre siððan út (*out of hell*) brecan ne magon, Hml. Th. i. 174, 3.　(2) *to force a way* through obstructions, *move impetuously :*—On bricþ *ingruerit (quasi tempestas)*, Kent. Gl. 13.　Se Wendelsǽ brycð swíðor on ðone súððǽl þonne hé dó on þone norðdǽl (*in meridiem magis vergens*), Ors. 1, 1 ; S. 24, 26.　Ofer bæþweg brecan *to force a way across the waves*, An. 223 : 513 : El. 244.　(3) *to exert* one's self *violently, to struggle, strive* (cf. **I.** 5) :—Se lég ongan sleán and brecan ongeán þone wind, and efne swá se wind swíþor slóg on þone lég swá brǽc hé swíþor ongeán þǽm winde, efne þǽm gelícost swylce ðá gesceafta twá him betweónan gefeohtan sceoldan, Bl. H. 221, 12–15.　Hé ágynþ tó brecanne þanne tó spíwanne, Lch. iii. 140, 2.　v. lahbrecende.

**brec-mǽlum.** v. bryc-mǽlum : **brecþ, e ;** *f.* *Substitute :* brecþa, an ; *m. :* -brecþ.　v. ǽ-, edor-brecþ.

**bred.** *Add :* **I.** *a board, plank :*—Bred *tabetum*, Wrt. Voc. ii. 121, 81.　Ic ðé bidde ðæt ðú mé on ðǽm scipgebroce ðisses lífes sum bred gerǽce, ðæt ic mæge on sittan, oð ic tó londe cume, Past. 467, 24.　Lege bred þweores ofer þá fét, Lch. ii. 342, 6.　Ðá ungesewenlican brega (breda ? cf. (?) breden) næglas *invisibiles sudum clavos*, Lch. i. lxxiv, 13.　**II.** *a tablet, table* for writing on :—Brede *albo*, i. *tabula*, Hpt. Gl. 477, 51 : An. Ox. 3032.　Brǽde, 2, 139.　Sé þæt fácn tó his cýþþe gebodade, and hit on ánum brede áwrát, and siþþan mid weaxe beworhte *quod per tabellas primum scriptas, deinde ceratas, suis prodidit*, Ors. 2, 5 ; S. 80, 2.　Ðá stǽnenan bredu ðe sió ǽ wæs on áwriten, Past. 125, 18.　On twelf breduu þe þá þeódwitan þǽrtó ámearcode, Angl. viii. 321, 41.　v. gyrdel-, hand-, nam-, pic-, rihte-, tæppel-, writ-bred.

**bredan.** *l.* brédan. v. bregdan.

**brédan ;** *p.* de *To cherish, nourish, hatch* an egg :—Feormat, broedeth *fovet*, Wrt. Voc. ii. 108, 79.　Brédeþ, feormaþ *fovit*, 35, 74.　Fugelas ne týmað swá swá óðre nýtenu, ac ǽrest hit bið ǽig, and seó módor siððan brét þæt ǽig tó bridde, Hml. Th. i. 250, 24.　Beón týmað heora teám mid clǽnnysse, of ðám hunige hí brédað heora bród, ii. 10, 17.　[O. H. Ger. bruoten *fovere*.]

**bréden** *broad.* *Substitute :* breden, briden, bryden ; *adj. Of boards* or *planks :*—Him ne widstent nán ðing, náðer ne stǽnen weall ne bryden wáh, Hml. Th. i. 288, 4.　Gewrohte hé (*Severus*) weall mid turfum and bredweall (breden weall, *v. l.*) ðǽronufon (cf. Bd. i. 5 *where speaking of the vallum made by Severus it is said*, 'vallum fit de cespitibus, quibus circumcisis, e terra velut murus exstruitur altus supra terram, ita ut in ante sit fossa, de qua levati sunt cespites, supra quam sudes de lignis fortissimis praefiguntur') *he made a wall of sods and a palisade on the top*, Chr. 189 ; P. 10, 25.

**bredende.** *l.* brédende. v. bregdan : **brédettan.** v. brogdettan : **bred-weall.** v. breden : **-bréfan.** v. ge-bréfan : **brega**, Lch. i. lxxiv, 13. v. bred.

**brégan.** *Add :*—Ús deófol brégð mid yfelum geðóhtum, Hml. Th. i. 156, 30.　Mid óðrum worde hé hierte, mid óðrum hé brégde (*terret*) Past. 53, 11.　Reðe forebécna þ folc earmlíce brégdon, Chr. 793 ; P. 55, 33.　Þæt hit leásung wǽre, þæt hí þæt folc mid brégdan, Wlfst. 100, 7.　Ðá óðre sint tó bréganne (-eanne, *v. l.*) *istis inferre metum debemus*, Past. 181, 7.　Brégende *terrentia*, An. Ox. 4419.　[O. H. Ger. bruogen *terrere*.]

**bregd.** v. brægd : **brégd**, brégda.　*Dele.*

**bregdan.** *Add :* **I.** *trans.* (1) with acc. (a) *to pluck, pull, draw, drag :*—Sáh hé niðer ealre his mihte benumen, and hine man ðá brǽc intó ðæs kinges búre, Chr. 1053 ; P. 182, 22.　Ealle men hine fram stówe tó stówe brúdon, Hml. S. 23, 653.　Ompran ymbdelf, bréd up Lch. ii. 116, 14 : iii. 38, 12.　Ne bréde gé nó ðá stengeas of ðám hringum, Past. 172, 10.　(b) *to move quickly to and fro :*—Brǽd þ heáfod hider

and geond ofer þ fýr, Lch. ii. 38, 3. (c) *to bind, knot :*—þā brūdon hig rāpas on hyre handa and on hyre fēt, Shrn. 154, 28 : 74, 30. (d) *to bring* a charge (*braid* in *up-braid*) :—þe lǣs þe God up brēde þone godspellican cwide *lest God bring up against you that saying of the gospel*, Wlfst. 248, 9. (e) *to change :*—þā brǣd se sceocca hine sylfne tō menn, Hml. S. 11, 222. On manegum ōþrum hīwum hine brǣd se deófol, 31, 718. Hē brǣd hine on feala bleóna, Bl. H. 175, 5. Se līchama ongan swǣtan and mislic hīw brēdan, Wlfst. 141, 3. (2) with dat. (cf. *Icel.* bregða with *dat.*), *to change :*—Hī gehērad hleóðrum brǣgdan ōðre fugelas *they hear other birds varying their notes*, Met. 13, 47. **II.** *intrans.* (1) *to move, be pulled :*—Ne bregden nō ðā stengas of ðǣm hringum *vectes a circulis numquam recedant*, Past. 173, 10. (2) of lightning, *to flash :*—Swilc leóht swilce þǣr līget brūde, Hml. S. 36, 226. (3) *to play a trick, act with guile.* v. brēdende, brægden, brægd. v. mis-, under-bregdan; þurh-brogden.

**brego** (-a). *Add :*—Sum ārleás cyningc, Cosdrue gehāten, wæs swā upāhafen, and swā ārleás brega, þ hē wolde bǔon God, Hml. S. 27, 27.

**brego-ríce.** *Add :*—Wē gehērdon þā on bregoríce *audivimus eam in Effrata*, Ps. L. 131, 6.

**brego-rōf;** *adj. Very valiant :*—Bold wæs betlic, bregorōf cyning, heá healle, Hygd swīðe geong, B. 1925.

**brehtnian.** v. breahtmian : brehtnung. *Dele.*

**brēme.** *Add :*—Brēmþ *concelebrat*, An. Ox. 2612. Brēmaþ *celebrant*, 4812. Weorþodan wē and brēmdon þone myclan symbeldæg, Bl. H. 131, 9. Eall cynn lofu brēme (*celebret*), Hy. S. 48, 9. Bletsien þec fiscas and fuglas, ealle þā þe onhrērað hreó wǣgas brēmen Dryhten, Az. 142 : 116. Brēmed *celebratur, honoratur*, Hpt. Gl. 470, 67.

**brēman;** *p.* de To rage :—Hine broemende *eum fervere*, Mt. p. 7, 5. [v. *N. E. D.* breme, II.]

**brēme.** *Add :*—Dæg brýme *dies celebris*, Hy. S. 38, 5. Se brēma cyng (*Cnut*), Chr. 1023 ; P. 156, 11. Bēda ðe bróema bócere, Jn. L. 19, 37 margin. Þā rīcu þæs brēman Fæder *Patris regna*, Dōm. L. 295. Heó ǣteówde hyre breóst þām brēman Philippe, Hml. S. 2, 234 : 18, 363. Þū tōbrýttest þone brēman here, 25, 370, 629, 658. Brýmest *celeberrimus*, Wrt. Voc. ii. 150, 64. Seó (*Athens*) wæs þā brēmost (brýmest, *v. l.*) on lāre, Hml. S. 3, 11. Se brēmesta ł wyrðfullesta *celeberrimus*, i. *nobilissimus*, An. Ox. 55 : *excellentissimus*, 2301 : *opinatissimus*, 4999. Hié Rōmāna brēmuste wǣron tō ðǣm cyninge *they were most illustrious of the Romans after the king*, Ors. 2, 2 ; S. 66, 32. [Is ðeos burch (*Durham*) breome geond Breotenrice, C. D. B. ii. 375, 36. Is ðerinne ... breoma bocera Beda and Boisil abbot, 376, 13. v. *N. E. D.* breme.]

**brēmel, brēmer** (v. brēmel-leáh). *Add :*—Brēmel *anguens*, Wrt. Voc. ii. 7, 20 : *murus*, 55. 82. Ðā hē fleáh, ðā tōrýpte hine ān bre[m]ber ofer ðæt nebb, Cht. Th. 172, 28. Hī hine lǣddon betwux þā þiccan gewrido þara brēmela, þæt him wæs eall se līchama gewundod, Guth. 36, 12. Of þiccum brēmelum *senticosis surculis*, An. Ox. 1268. Æcer þe æfter ðornum and brēmelum wæstmas āgifð, Hml. Th. i. 342, 7. Hwā gaderað ficæppla of brēmelum (*tribulis*) ?, ii. 406, 3. Sēcende geond þýfelas and brēmelas (brēmblas, brýmelas, *v. ll.*), Hml. S. 32, 143. v. heorot-brēm(b)el.

**brēmel-leáf.** *Add :*—Brēmbelleáf, Lch. ii. 50, 1.

**brēmel-leáh** (brēmer-) ; *m. A lea covered with brambles :*—On brēmerleáh ; of brēmerleá, C. D. iii. 80, 26.

**brēmel-þorn,** es ; *m. A bramble :*—Andlanges furh on brēmelþornan on ðā ealdan dīc, C. D. iii. 10, 22.

**brēmel-þýfel,** es ; *m. A bramble-thicket :*—Tō ðām brǣmbeldýfelan, C. D. v. 340, 24.

**brēmel-þyrne.** *Add :*—Of ðǣre þyrnan on ðā brēmbelþyrnan, C. D. iii. 419, 13.

**brēmel-wudu** (brēmber-) *a bramble-wood :*—Ūt þurch brēmberwudu, C. D. v. 13, 26 : 81, 1.

**brēmen.** *Dele, and see* brēman.

**brēmend-lic ;** *adj. Worthy to be celebrated :*—Brēmendlícum *celebrandis*, An. Ox. 7, 1. Brýmlícum (= brýmendlicum), 4614.

**bremman.** For *bremman* ... *192* substitute :—Bremmendra *rudentum*, Wrt. Voc. ii. 82, 84.

**bremung,** e ; *f. Roaring :*—Grymetung *vel* bremung *fremitus*, i. *mugitus*, Wrt. Voc. ii. 150, 61.

**breneþ.** *Substitute* = (*?*) berneþ, bærneþ. v. bærnan, *and add :*—Eolxsecg wundað grimme, blōde brened (*brings hot blood upon* ?) beorna gehwylcne þe him ǣnigne onfeng gedēð.

**breng(e)an.** *Add :*—Ic forð brenge *proferam*, Kent. Gl. 9. Ic brengo (*adduco*) hine ūt, Jn. L. R. 19, 4. Hū micelne unweorþscipe se anwald brengþ þām unmedeman, Bt. 27, 2 ; F. 96, 10 : 16, 3 ; F. 54, 25. Sē þe mē brengð (bring(ð), *v. l.*) lāc, Past. 342, 8. Hié Gode forhæfdnesse brengað (briengað, *v. l.*), 314, 21. Briengað, 395, 36. Bre(n)gað *conferunt*, Kent. Gl. 889. Bren, bryn *affer, affer*, 1086. Breng (bring, W. S.) þ lāc *offer munus*, Mt. R. L. 8, 4 : Lk. L. 5, 14. Brencgas (bringað, W. S.) hine, Mk. L. 9, 19. Brenges, 12, 15. Ne brengende uæstem ... sē ðe brenged þ uæstm ... þte þ uæstem brenge, Jn. L. 15, 2. Him

swelcra mā brengan, Past. 9, 14. Tō brenganne, Mt. p. 14, 13. Forð brengende, Kent. Gl. 152. Hit bið brōht (beorht, *v. l.*) tō lācum, Past. 216, 24. Brōht beforan ūres mōdes eágan, 259, 20. Tō Rōme brōht, Ors. 4, 11 ; S. 208, 19. Him þ sǣd brōht wæs, Bd. 4, 28 ; S. 605, 39. v. þurh-brengan, stenc-brengende, *and see* bringan.

**brenning.** *Dele :* breósa. v. briósa.

**breodwian.** *Add : to trample* ? :—Ofer ðý (= ðē) cwēne reodan ofer ðý (= ðē ?) brýde bryodedon (*or from* breodian ?), Lch. iii. 32, 11.

**breóst.** *Add :* [The word occurs of all three genders, and can be used in the plural (dual) when a single person is referred to.] **I.** *the front of the chest :*—Mid gildenum girdle his breóst wæs befangen ... hē silf wæs begird æt his hālgum breóste (*praecinctus ad mamillas zona aurea*, Rev. 1, 13), Ll. Th. ii. 370, 4-7. Oþ mannes breóst (cf. swyran, Shrn. 81, 13) heáh, Bl. H. 127, 6. Cumað deór ..., and heora breósta beóð mid byrnum befangene (*habebant loricas*, Rev. 9, 9), Wlfst. 200, 12. Hē hlinode ofer ðæs Hǣlendes breóstum (*onufa breóst supra pectus*, L. R.), Jn. 13, 25. Þæs lāreówes scōh hē ásette on ðā breúst (*pectus*) þæs deádan līchaman, Gr. D. 19, 12. **II.** *the chest, thorax :*—Breóst *thorax*, Wrt. Voc. i. 65, 6 ; 283, 27 : *pectus*, 28. On iugoðe bið se līchama þeónde on strangum breóste, Hml. Th. i. 614, 11. **III.** *the stomach, womb :*—Breúst crassum (*ventrem*, *v. l.*), Lch. i. lxx, 1. Wiþ innoþes sāre and þæra breósta (*or under* IV ?), Lch. i. 182, 21. Þis ofet is swā swēte, blīð on breóstum (*bonum ad vescendum*), Gen. 656. On þām hālgan breóstum hē eardode nigon mōnaþ, Bl. H. 105, 16. **IV.** *a breast ; mamma, mamilla :*—Hē hēt hī gewrīðan on ðām breóste, and hēt siððan of āceorfan. Heó him cwæð tō : 'Ne sceamode þē tō ceorfanne þ þ ðū sylf suce, ac ic habbe mīne breóst on mīnre sāwle ansunde' ... Heó beseah tō hyre breúste and wæs þ corsene breóst geedstaðelod, Hml. S. 8, 122-146. Þurh þæt swīðre breúst, Sal. K. 204, 25. Underneoðan ōþer breóst *sub mamma*, Ors. 3, 9 ; S. 134, 23. Sceal mon þis wrītan and dôn þās word on þā winstran breúst, Lch. ii. 140, 27. Breóstum *pipillis, papillis*, Wrt. Voc. ii. 94, 54. Bríóst *mamillas*, Lch. i. lxxii, 2. **V.** *breast* as seat of feeling, &c. :—Hū mycel se camp wæs in þæs mannes breoste ... Seó ārfæstnys oferswýðde þone strangan breóst, forðon nǣre se breóst oferfunden, gif hine seó ārfæstnes ne oferswýðde, Gr. D. 18, 2-22. Þurh þone hālegan breúsd ūres fæder, 2, 19. His breúsd sién simle onhielde for ārfæstnesse tō forgiefnesse *per pietatis viscera citius ad ignoscendum flectitur*, Past. 61, 12. v. ang-breúst.

**breóst-bān.** *Add :*—Bríóstbān *pectusculum*, Lch. i. lxii, 1.

**breóst-bedern.** *Substitute :* breóst-byden, e ; *f. The breast, chest :*—Breóstbydyn *thorax*, Germ. 393, 89. Foranbodig *vel* breóstbeden *torax*, Wrt. Voc. i. 44, 12.

**breóst-beorh,** -beorg, es ; *m. A breast-plate.* Substitute, e ; *f. A breast-work :*—Bríóstbiorg *propugnaculum*, Wrt. Voc. ii. 118, 30. v. breóst-gebeorh.

**breóst-cearu.** *Add :* [*O. Sax.* brióst-kara.] : breóst-cōfa. *l.* -cofa.

**breóst-gebeorh.** *Add :*—Breóstgebeorh *propugnaculum*, Wrt. Voc. ii. 66, 65. v. breóst-beorh.

**breóst-gehygd** (-hýd) *thought, mind.* *Add :*—Þoncsnottor guma breóstgehygdum (*prudently*) his bearn lǣrde, Fä. 22 : Gen. 1289. Gif gē hýraδ mē breóstgehygdum (*with purpose of heart*), 2316. Wē þe biddað geornlīce breóstgehygdum, Cri. 262. Hē his bēna bebeád breós:-gehigdum *verba precantia clamat*, Dōm. L. 60. Ealle þurhyrnð ōga breóstgehýda *singula percurrit pectora terror*, 172.

**breóst-gird,** e ; *f. A sceptre* ? :—Tǣnene breóstgyrde *sceptrinae virgae*, An. Ox. 3303 : 2, 188.

**breóst-lín.** *Add :*—Breóstlīnes *fasciae*, Wrt. Voc. ii. 37, 42.

**breóst-nirwett,** es ; *n. Oppression of the chest, angina pectoris :*—Wiþ breóstnyrwette, Lch. iii. 76, 3.

**breóst-rocc.** *Add :* [*O. H. Ger.* brust-roch *thorax*.]

**breóst-þing,** es ; *n. A part of the breast :*—On þām eahtoþan mōnþe him beóð þā breóstþing wexende (*the organs of the breast are developing*), Lch. iii. 146, 18.

**breóst-wǣrc,** es ; *n. Substitute :* ; *m. Pain in the chest :*—Wiþ breóstwǣrce, Lch. ii. 58, 20, 25 : 316, 5.

**breóst-weall.** *Add :*—Breóstweal *propugnacula*, Wrt. Voc. ii. 76, 71.

**Breoten** (-on). *Add :*—Albanum seó wæstmberende Bryton (-en, *v. l.*) forðbered, Bd. 1, 7 ; Sch. 19, 18. Micelne dǣl Breotone (Brytene, *v. l.*), 1, 5 ; Sch. 17, 3. Hī fērdon of ðisse Brytene, Shrn. 137, 3. Sē wæs on ðisse Brytene, 134, 12. Breotone, 93, 28. Ongla ðeód com on þās Breotone, 78, 1 : 87, 3. Bretene, 111, 33. Ofer ealle Brytene, 149, 2. Eádwine hæfde rīce ofer eall þā Brytene (eal(le) Brytene, Breotone, *v. ll.*) būton Cantwarum ānum, Bd. 2, 5 ; Sch. 130, 21. v. Breten, Briten, Broten *in Dict., and next word.*

**Breoten-ríce.** *Add : n. The kingdom of Britain :*—Basianus fēng tō Breotenríce (Brytene ríce, *v. l.*) *Bassianus regno potitus est*, Bd. 1, 5 ; Sch. 17, 25.

**Breoten-wealda,** an ; *m. The ruler of Britain :*—Ic Æðelstān Ongol-Saxna cyning and Brytænwalda eallæs ðyses īglandæs *ego Æðelstanus rex et rector totius hujus Britanniae insulae*, C. D. v. 218, 17. Ongol-

Saxna cyning and Brytenwalda ealles ðyses íglandæs *Angul-Saxonum necnon et totius Brittaniae rex*, 219, 9. Hē wæs se eahteþa cyning sē þe Brytenw(e)alda (Bretenan, *v. l.*) wæs *octavus rex qui rexit Bryttaniam*, Chr. 827 ; P. 60, 26 note. [v. *N. E. D.* Bret-walda.]

**breóþan.** *Substitute : To decay, waste away :*—Gif lungen breóþe, Lch. ii. 170, 4.

**-breótness.** v. ā-breótness : **breótun.** v. breátan.

**breoton ;** *adj. Spacious, ample :*—Fōh hider tō mē burh and breotone bold, Sat. 687. v. bryten-.

**breówan.** *Add :*—Dô on breówende wyrt, Lch. ii. 332, 22. v. ge-breówan.

**brēr,** es ; *m. l. e ; f., in bracket dele 'Fr.* bruyère ... Du Cange,' *and add :*—Breer *anguens*, Wrt. Voc. ii. 100, 27. Braer *murus*, 114, 48. Braere *tribula*, 122, 73. v. heorot-brēr.

**brerd.** *Add :*—Brerd *labrum*, Wrt. Voc. ii. 51, 54. Se sǣ gefylde þ scip oð þā ýfmestan þeolu þæs bryrdes (brerdes, *v. l.*) *mare usque ad superiores tabulas implevit navem*, Gr. D. 249, 1, 12. Wið tō briorde *usque ad summum*, Mk. R. 13, 27. Tō briorde upp, Jn. R. L. 2, 7. Crocca sý āsett on eorþan oþ brerd, Lch. iii. 292, 4. Se ele feóll ofer þā brerdas þǣre bydene *oleum ora dolii transiens*, Gr. D. 160, 13. [v. *N. E. D.* brerd.]

**brerd-full ;** *adj. Brim-full :*—Ǣfre wæs se būteruc brerdful wīnes, Hml. S. 6, 282. [v. *N. E. D.* brerd-full.]

**brēr-hlǣw,** es ; *m. A hlǣw* (q.v.) *with briers on it :*—On brērhlǣw, C. D. iii. 82, 21.

**brēr-þyrne,** an ; *f. A brier-bush :*—On brērðyrnan, C. D. vi. 221, 13.

**breting, bret-mǣlum.** v. bryting, bryt-mǣlum.

**Bret-walas.** *Add :*—Neáh ðǣre ceastre þe Bryttwalas nemdon Uerolamium, Shrn. 94, 2. On Brytwala dagum, 111, 33. v. Brytt-walas *in Dict.*

**Bret-walda.** v. Breoten-walda.

**Bret-wilisc ;** *adj. British, Welsh :*—Bryt-Wylsc, Chr. P. p. 3, note 10. Būton ānum Brytwyliscum gīsle, Chr. 755 ; P. 49, 10.

**brica.** *Dele :* bric-bót. v. brycg-bót : **brice.** *l.* bryce, *dele cognates, and see* bryce : **brīce** *use. l.* brice. v. bryce : **brícsian.** v. brýcsian.

**brid.** *Add :*—Brid *pullus*, Wrt. Voc. ii. 118, 45. Cicen oððe brid, i. 77, 37. Brid swalwan *pullus hirundinis*, Ps. Srt. ii. p. 185, 1. Fugla briddas, gif hié ǣr wilniað tō fleóganne ǣr hira feðra fulweaxene sīn, Past. 383, 29. Sellan wel meltende mettas, culfrena briddas, hænne flǣsc, Lch. ii. 196, 22. Swā earn his briddas (*pullos*) spænð tō flihte, Deut. 32, 11 : Ps. Srt. ii. p. 192, 31. On lencgten ic lǣte mīne hafocas ætwindan tō wuda, and genyme mē briddas on hærfeste and temige hig, Coll. M. 26, 3. v. bird *in Dict.*

**bridel.** *l.* brīdel (*from* brigdel), *substitute for first instance :*—Bagula brīdel, i. *frenum*, Wrt. Voc. i. 21, 35, *and add :*—Brīdel *frenum*, Wrt. Voc. i. 84, 7. Ðone brīdel ðīnre mettrymnesse, Past. 467, 2. Ic gesleá ænne brīdel on his weleras, Hml. Th. i. 568, 33. Þæt wíf sceolde him tógeánes gān and his brīdel onfōn, ii. 142, 18. *Lupatis* brīdlum *frœnis*, Wrt. Voc. ii. 49, 61. Īsenum brīdlum *ferratis saliuaribus*, An. Ox. 2188. v. next word.

**bridels.** *l.* brīdels, brigdels, *and add :*—Brīdils (-els), brigdils *bagula*, Txts. 44, 127. Brīdels, Wrt. Voc. ii. 10, 60. In brídelse *in fraeno*, Ps. Srt. 31, 9. Heó genam þæt hors be þām brídelse (brídele, *v. l.*), Gr. D. 17, 21. Hé breác hælftre for brídelse (brídele, *v. l.*) *capistro pro freno utebatur*, 34, 12. Ðone brídels ðæs eges, Past. 427, 31. Brídelsum *lupatis*, Txts. 75, 1248.

**briden, brid-gifu.** v. breden, brýd-gifa.

**bridlian.** *l.* brīdlian, *and add :*—Hī heofon mid heora mægenum brídlodan, Bl. H. 161, 18.

**brigd.** *Substitute :*—Þæs deóres (*the panther*) hīw blǣc brigda gehwæs beorhtra and scȳura *the beast's hue, splendid with every bright and beauteous variety of colour*, Pa. 26.

**brigdan** (?) ; *p. de To seize property improperly held by another :*—Ðus man sceal swerigean, ðonne man hafð his ǣhte gebryid ( = -brigd ?) (cf. þ orf þ ic mid N. befangen hæbbe, l. 15). Ðæs ōðres āð ðe mon his orf ǣt bryideð ( = bribgeð ?) . . . Ðæs āð ðe his ǣhte bryideð *thus shall a man swear, when he has seized his (stolen) property . . . The oath of the other party from whom a man seizes his (stolen) cattle . . . The oath of him who seizes his (stolen) property*, Ll. Th. i. 178, 10–180, 8. [*Icel.* brigða *to escheat* ; brigð *a right to reclaim.*]

**brihtan.** v. birhtan (*not* beorhtian) : **briig.** v. brīw.

**brim,** es ; *n.* (not *m.*), *dele passages from* An. 496, Edw. 12, *and add :*—Monnum bið ðonne (*in June*) gewunelic ðæt hí lðað on sǣs bryme, Shrn. 88, 2. Ofer sǣs brim, Bl. H. 143, 6. v. brymm.

**brim ;** *adj. ? :*—Brimne stōr and hwītne rýcels, Lch. iii. 14, 21.

**brim-flód.** *Add :*—Brimflóde *cataclismum*, Wrt. Voc. ii. 21, 5.

**brim-nesen.** *l.* (?) brim nēsen, *and substitute :*—Gif hié brim nēsen (cf. Gen. 1341) and gesunde sīð settan mōsten *if they came safe from the sea, and might make a prosperous passage*, El. 1004.

**brim-stæþ,** es ; *n. Sea-shore :*—Streámwelm hwīleð, beátaþ brimstæþo, An. 496.

**brim-þisa.** *l.* -þīsa.

**bringan.** *Add :*—Ic bringe *dono, ostendo*, Wrt. Voc. ii. 145, 2. Ic þē bringe mid mē tō heofonum, Bt. 3, 4 ; F. 6, 17. Lytel gestreón wiþerweardnes þē bringþ, 20 ; F. 72, 13. Ic nāt hwæt þā woruldlustas myrges bringaþ hiora lufigendum, 31, 1 ; S. 70, 14. Gif ðū wille ðīn lāc bringan (brengan, *v. l.*) . . . lǣt inc gesēman ǣr ðū ðīn lāc bringe (brenge, *v. l.*) ; brieng (breng, *v. l.*) siððan ðín lāc, Past. 349, 9–13. Hē þā sprǣce ne mihte bringan tō nānum ende, Bt. 41, 3 ; F. 246, 29. Bringende *delaturos*, Wrt. Voc. ii. 28, 56. Þ yrfe þ him brungen (brōht, *v. l.*) wæs, Gr. D. 201, 10. v. brengan.

**briosa.** *l.* briósa, *and add :*—Briósa *asilo*, Txts. 38, 27. Briósa, briusa *tabanus*, 102, 1016. [v. *N. E. D.* breeze.]

**brītan ;** *p.* te *To pound, bruise, crush :*—Gif ðū hyre blōsdman brýtest, hē hæfð swæc swylce ellen, Lch. i. 104, 20. Þæt hig grundon on cwyrne oððe britton *populus illud frangebat mola sive terebat in mortario*, Num. 11, 8. Genim wyrte leáf and brýt hý, Lch. i. 72, 4. Genim hý (*garclive*) drīge and dype on wearnum wætere, swā þū eáþelícost hý brýtan mæge, 130, 6. Brýtende *friens*, Wrt. Voc. ii. 37, 38 : 150, 74. v. for-, ge-, tō-brītan ; bryttan.

**-brītedness, -brītendlic.** v. tō-brītedness, -brītendlic.

**brīting,** e ; *f. Breaking to pieces :*—Brēting hlāfes *fractio panis*, Lk. L. 24, 35. v. tō-brīting.

**Brittisc.** *Add :* I. *British :*—Būtan ānum Bryttiscum gīsle, Chr. 755 ; P. 48, 10. Bryttiscne (Brettisc, *v. l.*) cining, 508 ; P. 15, 25. Brytiscne (Brettisc, *v. l.*) man, 501 ; P. 15, 23. On Bryttisc sprecende, Guth. 42, 17. On Brytisc, 7.

**brīw.** *Add :*—Briig *pulenta*, Wrt. Voc. ii. 118, 38. Brīu *puls*, An. Ox. 53, 35. Brīw wiþ þon ilcan and sealf, Lch. ii. 4, S. Brīwes tācan is þæt þu wecge þīne fýst swilce þū brīw hrēre, Tech. ii. 123, 13. Gebrīw wel swīþne brīw mid hwǣtemelwe, Lch. ii. 354, 11. Brīwas and drenceas and sealfa wiþ þǣre ádle, 8, 16.

**brīwan.** *Add :* v. ge-brīwan.

**brīw-lāc,** es ; *n. Dressing food :*—Ðā sceandlican wīglunga on brȳwlāce, Hml. S. 17, 103. v. preceding word.

**brīw-þicce ;** *adj. Thick as pottage :*—Wylle hit oð ðæt hit beó wel brīwþicce, Lch. iii. 76, 7.

**broc** *a badger. l.* brocc, *and add :*—Brocc *taculus*, Wrt. Voc. ii. 121, 78. ¶ in local names :—Agrum cui uo cabulum est *brochyl*, C. D. i. 97, 13. Brocceshám ðes dennes nama, ii. 74, 1. v. brocc-hol ; broccen.

**broc,** es ; *n. A fragment :*—Þā hǣðenan weras tōslōgon his glæsenne calic. þā gesomnode hē þā brocu (brycas, *v. l.*), Mart. H. 140, 12. [v. *N. E. D.* broke.] v. ge-broc.

**broc** *a kind of locust ? :*—Broc *ophiomachus* (v. Vulg. Lev. xi. 22), Wrt. Voc. ii. 63, 67. [v. *N. E. D.* brock *cicada spumaria*.]

**brōc** *a covering for the leg. Dele ' acc.* brēc,' *and add :*—Brooc *suricus* (cf. sura), Txts. 117, 256. Gyrdils *vel* broec *lumbare*, 72, 573. Gyrdel oððe brēc, Wrt. Voc. ii. 51, 15. Brēcena tācen is þæt þū strīce mid þīnum twām handum up on þīn þeóh, Tech. ii. 127, 8. Ðā þe on ȳtinge faráð nīman him brēc (*femoralia*) of hrægelhūse, R. Ben. 90, 8.

**brōc** *a brook. Add :*—Hleomoce hātte wyrt, sió weaxeð on brōce, Lch. ii. 92, 14. Þ wæter cymþ up æt ðām ǣwelme, wyrþ ðonne tō brōce, ðonne tō eá, ðonne andlang eá oþ hit wyrþ eft tō sǣ, Bt. 34, 6 ; F. 140, 19. Sum micel ǣwelm, and irnon manige brōcas of, 34, 1 ; F. 134, 10. On cocbrōc . . . on mylenbrōc . . . on beánbrōc . . . on ðan lace ðæt ðā brōcas twisliað, C. D. v. 198, 34. v. alor-, clǣg-, sealt-, wiþig-brōc.

**brōc** *affliction. l.* broc, *and add :* I. *labour, laborious effort :*—Hē mihte būtan broce ealra Cartaina anweald begitan, Ors. 4, 5 ; B. 83, 13. Mid ūtancumenum brocum gelǣred *exterioribus studiis eruditus*, Gr. D. 180, 10.    II. *misery, affliction, trouble :*—Swā gemune men wǣron ælces broces, Ors. 1, 10 ; S. 48, 12. Hwylc broc and hwylc sār (*laborem et dolorem*) wē þoliaþ, Th. 9, 34. Ic ādreáh mycel broc mid Petre *I have suffered much annoyance from Peter*, Bl. H. 175, 12. Deáh hine ðā brocu getýn and gelǣren *nam adversitatis magisterio sub disciplina cor premitur*, Past. 35, 12. Eówre brocu nū lǣssan sindon þonne heora þā wǣre, Ors. 3, 7 ; S. 120, 11, 14, 8. Ealle þā sār and þā brocu þe se man tō gesceapen is, Bl. H. 59, 33.    III. *disease, bodily trouble or hurt :*—Ǣlc broc cymð of deófle and nān bót . . . hē sent on unwǣre menn oððon on heora yrfe sum swiðlic brocc . . . byð þæt brocc liðre, Wlfst. 11, 15–12, 5. Þæt broc þæt hē āræfnode, Gr. D. 22, 5. Ansund eallum linum fram þām egeslican broce (*paralysis*), Hml. S. 26, 218. On his broke hē Gode fela behǣsa behēt, Chr. 1093 ; P. 227, 22. v. scip-, weorold-broc.

**broc,** es ; *n. Use, advantage :*—Fatu mennisces broces (bryces, *v. l.*) *uasa humani usus*, Bd. 3, 22 ; Sch. 291, 7. Sēcen hí him broc on ourāde and on wǣne *let them seek to benefit themselves by riding on horseback and in a carriage*, Lch. ii. 184, 13. v. weorold-broc, and cf. bryce.

**brōc** *a horse. Dele, and see preceding word :* brōc ? :—Brooc *thadalus*, Wrt. Voc. ii. 122, 31 : broca. v. wiþer-broca : **brocc** *a badger.* v. broc.

brocc-hol, es; *n. A badger's hole*:—On broccholes weg, Cht. E. 239, 18.

broccian *to tremble*:—Ongan se munuc forhtiende and broccsiende (*tremens et palpitans*) mid mycclum stefnum clypian, Gr. D. 156, 14, 21.

brôce. *Dele, and see* broc *use*: brocen. v. twilic-brocen: broc-heard. v. un-brocheard.

brôcian. *l.* brocian, *and add*:—Hê bebeád þæt mon Crístene men brocode *persecutionem in Christianos exercuit*, Ors. 6, 19; S. 272, 7. v. ge-brocian.

brôc-líc. *Substitute*: broc-lic; *adj. Miserable, laborious, full of trouble*:—Geþenc hû sceorte and hû broclice synt þisses lífes dagas, Wlfst. 248, 1.

brôc-minte. *Dele* brôc-mint, e; *f., and add*:—Brôcminte sisymbrium, Wrt. Voc. i. 69, 3. Brôcminte and ôþre mintan, Lch. iii. 6, 14.

brôcung. *l.* brocung.

brôd, e; *f. Substitute*: I. *a brood*:—Beócere *apiarius*, beóbreád *favum*, brôd *gratis* (cf. grates (e *over* i *which is struck out*), cellae apium, Corp. Gl. H. 61, 170), Wrt. Voc. i. 284, 71: ii. 41, 26. Of ðám hunige beón brêdað heora brôd, Hml. Th. ii. 10, 17. Brôd *foetibus*, An. Ox. 28, 25. II. *breeding, hatching* (v. brôdig):—Brôde *concretione* (cf. cennung *concretio*, 136, 25), Wrt. Voc. ii. 23, 19. [v. *N. E. D.* brood.]

brôd; *adv. Dele, and see previous word*: broddetan. v. brogdettan: broddian. v. brogdian: brodetung. *Dele, and see* brogdetung: brôdian. v. brogdian.

brôdig. *Substitute*: *Inclined to sit (of a hen)*:—Oft seó brôdige henn, þeáh heó sárlíce cloccige, heó tôspræt hyre fyðera and þá briddas gewyrmð, Angl. viii. 309, 25. [v. *N. E. D., D. D.* broody.] v. brôd, II.

broel. *Dele*: brôga. *Add*: v. wiþer-brôga.

brogdettan (brodd-, brôd-, brêd-, brott-?); *p.* te. I. *to shake, quiver*:—Brogdetteð *vibrat*, Txts. 107, 2132. Swá þ wæs æteówed, þ hê brôdette byfiende mid wundorlicre styrunge *ut apparuerit concussione mirifica tremendo palpitaret*, Gr. D. 166. 14. þá ongan hê ofdrædd bifian and broddettan (forhtiende and brêdetende, *v. l.*) and clypian . . . Hí þone munuc cwakiendne and broddettendne (brôd-, *v. l.*) gelæddon *coepit ipse tremens et palpitans clamare . . . trementem et palpitantem monachum reduxerunt*, 156, 13–21. Brogdetende *vel* cleppetende *campus* (can the English words be epithets applied to *campus* (=aequor, cf. Corp. Gl. H. A. 314, aequor, pelagus *vel* campus) referring to the quivering of the surface of the water ?), Txts. 49, 411. Brogdetende, brocdaettendi, brogdaethendi *palpitans*, 83, 1472. Brôdetende, Wrt. Voc. ii. 67, 54. II. *to glitter, be splendid* (cf. brogdian):—Mid dislicum glengcgum brottetende (v. brogdettung *for form*) *stolidis pompis indruticans*, Hpt. Gl. 435, 37.

brogdettung, e; *f.* I. *shaking, quivering*:—Mid unáblinnendlicre brogdettunge (brôtetunge, *v. l.*) ealles líchaman *incessanti totius corporis motu quassi*, Gr. D. 183, 12. II. *feigning, pretence*:—Gehýwunge ł brogdetunge (leásunga, Ps. Spl.) *figmentum*, Ps. Spl. C. 102, 13. v. bregdan, II. 3.

brogdian, broddian, brôdian *to glitter, be splendid*:—Scimerað, brôdað *vibrat* (minor modico Phoebi radiis qui vibrat atomo, Ald. 272, 32), An. Ox. 23, 51. Mid dislicum glengum broddiende *stolidis pompis indruticans*, 1218. Cf. bregdan, II. 2, brogdettan, II.

brogna (-e ?) *a leafy bough*:—Brognena *frondium*, Rtl. 95, 10. v. ge-brogne.

broht ?:—Broht *viscellum* (cf. ? viscellus *vivarium*, Migne), Wrt. Voc. ii. 123, 71.

brôm. *Add*:—Broom, brôm *genista*, Txts. 66, 465. Brôm, Wrt. Voc. ii. 41, 28. Brôma *genistarum, miricarum*, Hpt. Gl. 408, 60: An. Ox. 3, 7. ¶ the word occurs in many local names. v. C. D. vi. pp. 263–4.

brôm-fæsten. *Substitute*: *A place full of broom bushes*:—Brômfæsten *genescletum*, Wrt. Voc. ii. 41, 29.

brômig; *adj. Broomy*:—Se cnoll is styccemælum mid brômige (*printed* hsomige) wuda oferwexen *the knoll was overgrown with patches of broom*, Bl. H. 207, 27.

brondeguř. v. brand, II a: brond-hord. *Dele translation of passage*: brond-stæfn. *Substitute*: v. brand-stefn.

brord, es; *m. Add*: I. *a point*:—Brord, broord *punctus*, Txts. 86, 782. Brord *punctus*, Wrt. Voc. i. 288, 74: pun(c)tus, ii. 68, 53. II. *a spire of grass or corn*:—Þý læs þá ofþinenan corn in brord gehwyrfden (*should sprout*), Hml. A. 204, 320. Brordas *clumula* (spicarum glumula, Ald. 23, 10), Wrt. Voc. ii. 77, 51.

brosnian. *Add*:—Heó (*Rome*) weosnað and brosnaþ (*marcescet*) in hire sylfre, Gr. D. 134, 2. Næfre his líchama ne fúlode ne ne brosnode, Angl. xi. 1, 6.

brosniend-líc. *Add*:—þ flæsc is brosnigendlic and deádlic, Hml. S. 17, 13. Se heofonlica mete wæs gesewenlic and brosniendlic, Hml. Th. ii. 274, 29. Þis brosniendlice *corruptibile hoc*, An. Ox. 1250. Mid byrðenne þæs brosniendlican líchaman *carnis corruptibilis pondere*, Gr. D. 138, 21. In þám brosnendlican líchaman, 312, 8. Nú ðú unscrýddest þê þone brosnigendlican mann, Hml. S. 30, 113.

brosnung. *Add*:—Se cwyde úre brosnunge *the sentence that declared us to be dust*, Hml. Th. i. 300, 6. Oferfæreld of brosnunga tô unáwemmednysse, Angl. viii. 330, 10. Ne forrotige on brosnunge þeós hand, Hml. S. 26, 101. Se Hælend hæfde ðá (*after the resurrection*) oferfaren ðá brosnunga ðises andweardan lífes, Hml. Th. i. 222, 17.

brôþ. *Add*:—Brôð *jus*, Wrt. Voc. ii. 47, 66: *apozima, aqua cum uariis cocta condimentis*, Hpt. 31, 7, 95. Ælc broþ is tô forgánne, for þon þe hit biþ þindende, Lch. ii. 210, 21. Gif mon sý garleác on henne broþe, 276, 16. Haran lifer gesoden . . . mid þám broþe ðá eágan tô beþianne, i. 346, 19. Selle drincan mintan brôð oþþe moran, 62, 5. Pysena broþ, 278, 18. Sele geseáw broþu and geseáwe pysan, 264, 4. [*O. L. Ger.* broth *jus*: *O. H. Ger.* brod (-t): *Icel.* broð.] v. beón-broþ.

brôþor. *Add*: I. *of blood-relationship*:—His brôður (-or, *v. l.*) lác, Past. 235, 3. For Amilcores láre, Hannibales brôðor (brêðer, *v. l.*), Ors. 4, 11; S. 204, 11. Tô his brêðer, Past. 235, 7. þ his broðor nime his wíf and his brôðor (broeðre, L., brôðer, R. *fratri*) sæd wecce, Mk. 12, 19. þá wæron Arwaldes brôþor (broðra, *v. l.*), Bd. 4, 16; Sch. 426, 16. Brôþer (brôðero, L.) *fratres*, Mt. R. 12, 46. Broeþre (brôðra, L.), 1, 11. II. *of kindly relation, association, fellowship, &c.*:—Forwyrð ðín brôður for ðínum ðingum, Past. 451, 34. Hwí lá, brôðer dêst ðú þ . . .?, Angl. viii. 315, 4. Gesión cíð on ðínes brôður eágan, Past. 224, 1. Brôðres ðínes, Mt. L. 7, 3. Brôðeres, 18, 15. Brôðere *fratri*, 5, 22. Broeðer, 7, 4. Hwæt dô gê, brôður (-or, *v.l.*), dôð esnlíce, Past. 363, 2. Ðá Apostolas and þá eldran brôðor (brôðra, *v.l.*) *Apostoli et seniores fratres*, Ll. Th. i. 56, 13. Ealle þíne breþere (brôðor, *v.l.*), St. A. 4, 10. II a. *of monastic relation*:—Mid ôðrum gingran brêðer, Bd. 4, 6; Sch. 388, 2. On sumum þára mynstra þá brôðor him woldon sellan áttor drincan, Shrn. 65, 9. Of þám brôþrum (gebrôðrum, *v.l.*), Bd. 4, 13; Sch. 421, 22. Hát úre seofan brôþra (gebrôðor, brôðor, *v. ll.*) cuman, 4, 3; Sch. 356, 7. Biddað úre brôþro (brôðor, *v.l.*), 357, 9. v. wed-brôþor.

brôþor-dohtor; *f. A niece*:—Brôðerdochter *neptis*, Wrt. Voc. i. 51, 72.

brôþor-gefædred, -gemêdred. *Dele*.

brôþor-licness. *Add*: *A title used in addressing an ecclesiastical brother*:—Ðis mæg geþencean ðín brôþorlicnys, Bd. 1, 27; S. 490, 7. Is hê tô onbærnanne mid ðínre brôþorlicnysse lufan . . . Ealle Brytta biscopas wê bebeódaþ ðínre brôþorlicnysse, 492, 19, 24.

brôþor-lufu *charity, love*:—Mára ðisra is brôðerlufu (*caritas*), Rtl. 6, 23: 28, 31.

brôþor-ræden. *Add*: I. *fellowship*:—Sóþe lufe brôþerrædenne eów betwýnan lufiaþ *caritatem fraternitatis diligite*, Scint. 1, 7: 14, 3. Brôþorrædene, R. Ben. 132, 6. Wunige betwux eów lufu sôðre brôðerrædenne *let brotherly love continue*, Hml. Th. ii. 286, 10. Êstfulre brôðerrædene *devotae germanitatis*, Hpt. Gl. 403, 5. Brôð[er]rædene *sodalitate* (*apum*), An. Ox. 232. Lufige hê brôðerrædene betwux crístenum mannum, Hml. Th. i. 142, 11. Wê magon cúðlíce tô him (*Christ*) clypian, swá swá tô úrum brêðer, gif wê ðá brôðerrædene swá healdað . . . þæt wê ne sceolon ná geþafian þæt deófol ús gewême fram Crístes brôðorrædene, 260, 7–11. Ðurh uncer brôðorrædene (-nne, *v.l.*) ic secge sôð *per nostram fraternitatem, verum dico*, Ælfc. Gr. Z. 227, 6. II. *membership of a brotherhood*:—Þá canonicas innan Scs Petrus minstre habað underfangen þone gefêrscipe on brôðorrædenne mid ôðrum gebrôðrum, Cht. Th. 609, 4. Þe prior on Baþan and ealle þá gebrôþran habbaþ heom geunnen þá brôþerrædene and þá bedrædene for lífe and for dêþe, 436, 14. [v. *N. E. D.* brother-red.]

brôþor-scipe, es; *m. Brotherliness, kindness, love*:—Brôðerscip ł lufo *caritas*, Mt. L. 24, 12: Lk. L. R. 11, 42: *fraterna*, Rtl. 63, 34.

brôþor-sib. *Add*:—Brôðorsibbe *germanitatis*, Wrt. Voc. ii. 42, 33. Hê ofteáh his brêðer landes and æhta . . . Ðá for þære brôðorsibbe (*propter consanguinitatis fraternitatem*) geúðe hê him Wuldahâmes his dæg, Cht. Th. 272, 9.

brôþor-slaga. *Add*:—Cain, se brôðorslaga, þe Abel ofslôh, Hml. A. 60, 221.

brôþor-slege, es; *m. Fratricide*:—Brôþorsleges *fratricidi[i]*, Wrt. Voc. ii. 150, 42. Se anda wearð tô sæde ðæs brôðorsleges (-slæges, *v.l.*) *livor fratricidii seminarium fuit*, Past. 235, 8.

brôþor-sunu, a; *m. A nephew*:—Brôðorsunu *frat[r]uelis*, Wrt. Voc. ii. 109, 17. Brôðersune *nepos*, i. 51, 71. Cynegils, Ceólwulfes brôþursunu, Chr. P. 2, 14. Brôþursunu (brôðor-, *v.l.*), 887; P. 80, 17. Griffines brôðersunu, 1097; P. 233, 22. Mid brôðorsuna *cum fratrueli*, Wrt. Voc. ii. 87, 12: 19, 13: 34, 57.

brôþor-þinen. v. beorþor-þignen.

brôþor-wíf; *n. A sister-in-law*:—Brôþorwíf *fratrissa, fratris uxor*, Wrt. Voc. ii. 39, 54: i. 52, 30. Is bewered þæt mon hine ne menge wiþ his brôþorwífe (*cognata*) . . . þ him ályfed ne wære þ hê his brôðorwíf hæfde, Bd. 1, 27; Sch. 70, 7, 15. Steópmôðrum and brôþorwífum *nouercis et cognatis*, Sch. 68, 18.

brottetan. v. brogdettan.

brú. *Add*:—Brúwa *cilium*, Wrt. Voc. ii. 16, 47. Betwuh brúwum *intercilium*, 46, 34. Brúum mínum *palpebris meis*, Rtl. 181, 9.

brúcan. *Add*: dat., acc.     **I.** *to use*, (1) with concrete object :—
Hí welan habbaþ . . . and his ungemetlíce brúcað (*indigne acta felicitas*),
Bt. 39, 11 ; F. 230, 23.   Þú heora bruce, 7, 1 ; F. 16, 21.   Hé his
ágenes ungemetlíce breác, Past. 339, 2.   Brúc ðínra ǽhta, ðá hwíle ðe
ðú hál sý, Prov. K. 52.   Swá hwæt swá ús God sylle máre þonne wé
néde brúcan sceolan, Bl. H. 53, 15.   Ne mihte nánwuht libbendes ðǽre
eorþan brúcan, ne þæs wæteres, Bt. 33, 4 ; F. 130, 9.   Úre æfter his
bebodum tó brúcanne, 7, 5 ; F. 24, 9.   Wæs þæt folc þæs micclan welan
ungemetlíce brúcende *bonis male utens*, Ors. 1, 3 ; S. 32, 8.   Brúccendum
*utentibus*, Rtl. 98, 12.   (1 a) *to use* clothes, *wear* :—Hé wyllenra hrægla
breác, Shrn. 93, 7 : 94, 28.   Gesáwon wé men deóra hýdum gegyrede,
and nánes óðres brucon, Nar. 26, 15.   Heó nǽfre línenum hræglum
brúcan (*uti*) wolde, Bd. 4, 19 ; Sch. 443, 3.   (1 b) *to use* food, *eat or
drink* :—Flǽscmettum íc brúce *carnibus vescor*, Coll. M. 34, 21 : 35, 3.
Ne brúco (brúcco, L.) íc *non manducabo*, Lk. R. 22, 16.   Sé ðe ettað í
brúcað *qui manducavit*, L. 14, 15.   Sé ðe brúceð *qui manducat*, Jn. L.
6, 57.   Brúccað, 56.   Eów þe ne wyrtum eówrum bútan mé brúcaþ
(*utimini*), Coll. M. 28, 23.   Gé eówerne beórscipe brúcaþ on unriht,
Wlfst. 297, 30.   Eówre fýnd his brúcað *ab hostibus devorabitur*, Lev.
26, 16.   Huoelpas brúcas (*edunt*), Mt. L. 15, 27.   Þæra (hláfa) íc breác,
Hml. S. 23 b, 521.   Wé brécon í éton *manducavimus*, Lk. L. 13, 26 :
Mk. L. 6, 44.   Þæra ẽwena meolc gé brucon *ovium lacte fructi estis*,
Ll. Th. ii. 202, 23.   Ett í brúc *manduca*, Jn. L. R. 4, 31.   Brúce
(brýce, R.) *comede*, Lk. L. 12, 19.   Him weaxað untrumnyssa, þæt hé
ne mæg ætes oððe wætes brúcan, Hml. Th. i. 66, 9.   Brúcan his est-
mettas, 330, 15.   Brúca (brúcca, R.) *manducare*, Mk. 3, 20.   (1 c) *to
use* a person (of cohabitation) :—Þonne mæden weres brícð, þonne bið
hire mægðhád ádýlegod . . . Maria weres ne breác, Hml. Th. ii. 10, 6, 11.
His módor is mæden, and his fæder wífes ne breác, Hml. S. 7, 50.   (2)
with abstract object :—Breác hé ealdre hælsunge *uetere usus augurio*, Bd.
1, 25 ; Sch. 53, 25.   Þæs gemánan heó wæs twelf winter brúcende
(brýcende, *v. l.*), 4, 19 ; Sch. 440, 10.     **II.** *to possess* what may
cause pleasure, profit, &c., *to enjoy* :—Nán eówer blisse brýcþ *nemo
vestrum gaudio fruitur*, Coll. M. 28, 9.   Þæt þ he gesǽllíce brýcþ, hé
ondrǽt þ hé scyle forlǽtan, Bt. 11, 1 ; F. 32, 15.   Hé brécð *perfruetur*
(*abundantia*), Kent. Gl. 16.   Ne breác hé his cyneríces mid gesundfulnysse, Hml. Th. i. 84, 33.   Farað gé teala and his (*the horse*) wel brúcað
(*may the horse be of service to you*), Gr. D. 15, 22.   Ealra manna brúce
gé betst ǽgþres ge penega ge hláfa, Hml. S. 23, 583.   Þeáh þú wífes
brúce and blysse on lífe, 2, 161.   Brúce hé his gódes dǽl, Ll. Th. ii.
176, 23.   Bruce *potiretur*, An. Ox. 3757.   Seó sáwl mót brúcan þæs
heofenlican *coelo fruens*, Bt. 18, 4 ; F. 68, 17 : 24, 7 ; F. 82, 16 : Bl.
H. 39, 24.   Seó sǽ mót brúcan smyltra ýþa, Bt. 7, 3 ; F. 20, 23.     **III.**
*to perform the duties* of an office, *execute* an office :—Zacharias his
sácerdes hádes breác *he executed the priest's office*, Lk. 1, 8.   Hí brucon
sácerdhádes *functi sunt sacerdotio*, Num. 3, 4.   Brúcan ðǽre hirdelícan
áre *honore pastorali uti*, Past. 133, 3.   Þá hé bisceopðegnunge brúcende
wæs *cum episcopatus officio fungeretur*, Bd. 3, 23 ; Sch. 299, 1.   Þá
brúcende *fungentes*, i. *utentes* (*monachica professione*), An. Ox. 3766.   v.
á-, be-brúcan ; gást-brúcende.

brúcendlíce ; adv. *Serviceably, appropriately* :—Brúcendlíce *abusive*
(-*usive* only seems glossed), An. Ox. 53, 1.

brúcing (-ung). *Add* :—Fram ǽlcere gærsuman woruldlicra brúcunga
unmǽne *ab omni munere secularium functionum immunes*, C. D. B. i.
154, 15.

-brucol. [v. *N. E. D.* bruckle.]   v. ǽ-, on-, scip-brucol.

brún. *Add* :—Bruun *burrum*, Wrt. Voc. ii. 102, 30 : 11, 38 : *furbum*,
109, 33.   Brún *furvum*, i. *nigrum*, 36, 17 : *badius*, 11, 39 : *burrus*,
*rufus*, 126, 77 : *purpurea* (cf. ðý brúnan oððe þý brúnbasewan *punicio*,
Wrt. Voc. ii. 89, 26), An. Ox. 526 : 3, 36.   Ýð sió brúne (cf. Dante's
*onda bruna*), Rä. 61, 6.   Spíca is brúnes heówes, Bl. H. 73, 21 : *colore
fuluo*, Nar. 16, 15.   Wíf móton under brúnum hrægle (*sub nigro velamine*) tó husle gán, Ll. Th. ii. 162, 7.   Brúnne brerd *the black rim of the
inkhorn*, Rä. 27, 9.   Sweartum, brúuum beaduwǽpnum, 18, 8.   Brúne
helmas, Jud. 318.   [For brún *applied to metal* v. *N. E. D.* brown, 4.]

brún-basu. *Substitute for passages* :—Bruunbesu (-beosu) *ostriger*,
Txts. 82, 716.   Brúnbaso, Wrt. Voc. ii. 63, 58.   *Balla loca prasinum*
(cf. calcido ut ignis lucet haec est prasinum, Corp. Gl. H. C. 77) brún-
basu, 125, 16.   Bánwyrt ys brúnbasuw, Lch. i. 294, 10.   Brúnbasewum
*purpureo*, An. Ox. 1269.   Brúnbasum, 5139.   Brúnbaswere, 5072.
Brúnbasne *coccineum*, 5125.   Hé wæs hæbbende brúnbasone gegyrelan,
Shrn. 106, 10.   Mid brúnbæswe godwebbe, Gr. D. 310, 1.   Þý brúnbasewan *punicio*, Wrt. Voc. ii. 89, 26.   Brúnbasuum *purpureis*, An. Ox.
96.   Brúnbasewum, 2119.

brúnéða.   *l.* brúneþa.

brúnian ; *p.* ode *To get brown* :—Wylle on pannan oþ þ hit brúnige,
Lch. ii. 292, 24.

brún-wyrt.   *Add* :—Brúnwyrt *spimon* vel *reverion*, Wrt. Voc. i. 69,
25.   [Brounwort *consida*, Wülck. Gl. 575, 5.   v. *N. E. D.* brown-wort.]

bryce.   *Add* : **I.** *breaking, action of breaking* :—Hláfes brice, Lk.
24, 35.   **II.** *fracture* of a limb, &c. :—His scanca wæs tóbrocen,

þ þ bán wæs tódǽled on twá stycca . . . wearð se bryce eft gestaðelod,
Gr. D. 82, 27.   Wiþ bryce . . . lege on þone bryce, Lch. i. 368, 7.   Tó
gehwylcum bryce, 370, 18.     **III.** *breach, violation*, Ll. Th. i. 62,
9 (v. Dict.).     **IV.** *a fragment* :—Bryce *buccellam*, An. Ox. 56, 70.
Gesomnode se bisceop þá brocu (brycas, *v. l.*), Mart. H. 140, 12.     **IV a.**
*a tile, brick* (v. *N. E. D.* brick) :—Tigelum, brycum *imbricibus*, An.
Ox. 2256.   [v. *N. E. D.* bruche.]   v. lencten-, on-, regol-, scip-, þeccbryce.

brýce *use*.   *l.* bryce, *and add* : **I.** *use* :—Baða brice *balnearum usus*,
R. Ben. i. 68, 1.   Hí heora hors tó bryce (tó brúcenne, *v. l.*) onféngon,
Gr. D. 16, 3.   Sé ðe wíf hæfð for lícumlícre frófre, and ðeáh for ðǽm
bryce (v. brúcan, I. (1 c)) and for ðǽre lufe hine ne áwent from bettrum
weorcum *qui sic per uxorem carnali consolatione utitur, ut tamen numquam a melioris intentionis rectitudine ejus amore flectatur*, Past. 395,
16.   Ðǽm bisceope tó bryce *ad usum episcopi*, C. D. iii. 159, 29.   Hé
forgeaf him ðá twentig penega tó his ágenum bricum, Hml. Th. ii. 178,
10.   Hafa þe þ seolfor tó þínes sylfes bricum *argentum tuum sit*, Hml.
A. 96, 159.     **II.** *profit, advantage* :—Bryce *commodum*, Wrt. Voc.
ii. 24, 64.   Of bryc(e) *compendio*, *lucro*, Hpt. Gl. 484, 76.   Hé forgeaf
fǽla ǽhta þám Crístenum him tó gemǽnan brice, Hml. S. 2, 283.     **II a.**
*usufruct* :—Habban hí þone bryce (ðæs landes) healfne, and healfne þá
munecas, Cht. Th. 547, 18 : 545, 17.     **III.** *enjoyment* :—Seó
sáwul is on sibbe wunigende on hire dæge, þonne heó on gewítendlicere
tíde blissað, and on hwílwendlicum bricum bið ungefóh, Hml. Th. i. 408,
15.   v. níd-bryce.

brýce ; *adj.*   *Add* :—Gif þ ówiht brýce (bríce, *v. l.*) wæs *si hoc aliquid prodesset*, Bd. 5, 14 ; Sch. 643, 13.   His hýd is brýce hundum wið
wóles gewinne on tó dónne, Lch. i. 330, 3.   Hé bið bríce tó ðám uferan
dǽle þæs líchaman, 23.   [v. *N. E. D.* briche.   *Goth.* brúks *useful, profitable* : *O. H. Ger.* brúhhi.]

-brycel.   v. hús-brycel.   [v. *N. E. D.* britchel, brickle.]

brycg.   *Add* :—Brygc *pons*, Wrt. Voc. i. 80, 50.   Bricg, 54, 11.   Hét
Maxentius oferbricgian ðá eá mid scipum, and syððan ðylian swá swá
óðre bricge . . . hé ne gemunde ðære leásan bricge þe hé álecgan hét,
Homl. Th. ii. 304, 21–27.   Þære bricce geweorc, C. D. B. iii. 659, 2.
Of ðǽre bricge, C. D. iii. 259, 32.   Æt ðǽre brycge (brycg, *v. l.*), Ors.
6, 30 ; S. 282, 26.   Bricge gesihð carleáste getácnað, Lch. iii. 210, 5.
Ceastre and strǽta and brycge (-a, *v. l.*) geworhte wǽron, Bd. 1, 11 ;
Sch. 31, 1.     ¶ of the importance attached to bridges in early
England the following passages speak :—Sé þe þára mihta hæbbe . . .
gódige Godes cyrican, . . . and gódige folces fær mid bricgum ofer deópe
wæteru and ofer fúle wegas, Ll. Th. ii. 282, 10.   Wyrcan wé simle
brycge and þá bétan.   Ðeáh se man nime ǽnne stán and lecge on fúl
slóh, þæt se ælmesman mæge mid þám óðrum fét steppan on ðá clǽnan
healfe, þæt him bið micel mếd for Gode, Wlfst. 239, 9.   Wé magon
swýþe micele þearfe and ælmessan ús sylfum gedón, gif wé willað bricge
macian and þá symle bótettan, 303, 8.   v. þel-brycg.

brycg-bót.   v. bric-bót *in Dict., and see the following word*.

brycg-geweorc.   *Substitute* : *Work at the repairing* or *constructing
of bridges* :—Bryggeweorces, C. D. ii. 304, 7.   Bútan brycggewæorce, v.
218, 25.   Brigcgewurce, iii. 350, 10.   Bryggeweorce, vi. 202, 21.   Brycgeweorc, iii. 159, 30.   Brigcge-
worc, 50, 7.   Brycgeworc, 5, 13.   Ðegenes lagu is þ hé þreó ðinc of
his land dó, fyrdfæreld, and burhbóte and brycgeworc, Ll. Th. i. 432, 5.
*In C. D. B. iii.* 657–9 *are given Latin and Anglo-Saxon versions of the
regulations for the repair* (þǽre bricce geweorc) *of Rochester bridge,
which shew the character of the demands made by brycg-geweorc.*     ¶ In
Latin charters which state the terms of the *trinoda necessitas*, the
most frequently occurring renderings of that part of the formula which
refers to bridges are *pontis* (or *pontium*) *cocedificatio, constructio, instructio, restauratio*.   Besides these occur *aedificamen*, C. D. ii. 368 ;
*aedificatio*, iv. 60, 70 ; *aedificium*, ii. 240 : v. 259 ; *assolidatio*, v. 232 ;
*comparatio*, ii. 342 ; *conductio*, v. 155 ; *confectio*, ii. 247 : v. 290 ; *co-
operatio*, ii. 235 ; *emendatio*, ii. 80 : 104 : 326 ; *exercitium*, v. 327 ;
*extructio*, ii. 56 ; *fabrica*, v. 234 ; *factio*, i. 218 : ii. 48 ; *fundatio*, iv.
66 : 134 ; *instauratio*, vi. 96 ; *juvamen*, iv. 104 : 132 ; *munimen*, ii.
133 : 341 ; *munitio*, iii. 158 ; *obsequium*, iv. 140 ; *operatio*, i. 216 ;
*opus*, v. 9 ; *reaedificatio*, ii. 168 : 347 ; *recuperatio*, iii. 149 : 201 ;
*reformatio*, iv. 136 ; *renovatio*, ii. 177 : 180 ; *reparatio*, iii. 307 : 358 ;
*restructio*, iv. 82 : 146 ; *structura*, iii. 16 : 65 : 106.   *Pons* alone is also
used, ii. 268 : 306, and the rendering is sometimes given by the use of
verbs, *componere*, ii. 389 ; *construere*, iii. 319 : vi. 163 ; *munire* (cum
sua petunt pontis titubantia muniri uada), iii. 252 : iv. 85 : *recuperare*,
iii. 301 ; *renovare*, i. 271.

brycgian.   *Add* : *to make a causeway with planks* or *stones* (v. E. S.
xi. 511 ; *and cf.* Wlfst. 239, 9 *given under* brycg) :—Brycgaþ *calabit*
(cf. (?) cala *a billet* ; caladia via *via strata*, Migne), Wrt. Voc. ii. 127,
72.   Betweox húsan bricgian, Angl. ix. 262, 22.   [Þe children briggeden
þe wei mid here cloðes, O. E. Homl. ii. 91, 5.]   v. ge-brycgian.

brycgung.   v. líf-brycgung.

brycg-wyrcende *glosses* pontifex, Rtl. 194, 31.

brȳcian, brȳcsian. *Add:*—Swīðe brīcsað and helpeð þām sāwlum seó onsægdnes, Gr. D. 343, 38. Hē þām cynnum brīcsade (*profuit*), Bd. 3, 27; Sch. 322, 16. Gif þæt ōwiht brīccige (brȳciæ, *v. l.*) *si hoc aliquid prodesset*, 5, 14; Sch. 643, 13. Hē wolde monegum brȳcsian (brīcgian, *v. l. prodesse*), 5, 9; Sch. 589, 23. v. brȳce *useful*; ge-brȳcsian.

bryc-mǣlum; *adv. Piecemeal:*—Brecmǣlum *minutatim*, Hpt. Gl. 449, 47. v. bryt-mǣlum.

brȳd. *l.* brȳd, *and see* brygd.

brȳd. *Dele* 'one . . . purchased,' *and add:*—Brȳd *gamos*, Wrt. Voc. i. 50, 53: *nupte*, ii. 62, 14. On þone gemānan þæs brȳdguman and þǣre brȳde, Bl. H. 11, 6. Hē onfēng æþele brȳd, Shrn. 49, 2. Brȳda *beðāta pacta sponsalia*, Hpt. Gl. 498, 43.

brȳd-bed(d) *nuptial bed. Add:*—Wearð þ brȳdbed mid brǣðe āfylled, Hml. S. 4, 32. His brȳdbedd, 7, 43. Brūcan his dohtor ārleásan brīdbeddes, Ap. Th. 3, 7. On eówrum brȳdbedde, Hml. S. 4, 19. Swā swā brȳdguma of his brȳdbedde, Hml. Th. i. 200, 21 : ii. 10, 26: Hml. A. 27, 82. [*N. E. D.* bride-bed. *O. H. Ger.* brūt-betti *thorus, thalamus.*]

brȳd-boda, an; *m. A bridesman; paranimphus*, An. Ox. 18 b, 71. [*O. H. Ger.* brūti-boto.]

brȳd-būr. *Add: bridal-chamber:*—Brȳd *sponsa*, brȳdbūr *thalamus*, Wrt. Voc. i. 288, 84. Se Crīstes brȳdbūr (*the Virgin's womb*), Bl. H. 7, 31. Brēdbū[res] (brȳd-, An. Ox. 3376) *thalami*, Hpt. Gl. 485, 54. Se heofonlica cyning gearwaþ þinne innoþ his suna tō brȳdbūre, Bl. H. 9, 10, 26. Ðǣre forman brȳdniht, þā hī twā wǣron on ðǣm brȳdbūre, Shrn. 49, 3. On þǣre nyhte þā heú wæs ingelǣded on þone brȳdbūr, 149, 22. Gibloetsa, Drihten, brȳdbūre (*thalamum*) ðis, Rtl. 110, 38. His brȳdbūras and his heáhcleofan *talami cubiliaque*, Nar. 5, 2.

brȳd-cofa, an; *m. Bridal chamber, bedchamber:*—Brȳdcofa *thalamus, cubiculus*, Hpt. Gl. 445, 53.

bryddan. v. ge-bryddan: brȳdelic gewrit. *Dele, and see* brȳd-lic: brȳden wah. *Dele, and see* breden: brȳd-gifa. *Add:* [*O. H. Ger.* brūt-gebā *sponsalia.*]

brȳd-gifta; *pl. f. Espousals, nuptials:*—Ǣr ðām dæge mīnra brīdgifta ic eom besmiten, Ap. Th. 2, 14. Brȳdgifta, 17. Brīdgyftum (beweddedum brēdgiftum, Hpt. Gl. 439, 20) *pactis sponsalibus*, An. Ox. 1398. [Gelīc þam kynge þe makede hys sunes brīdgyfte (*nubtias*), Mt. 22, 2.]

brȳd-guma. *Add:* I. *a bridegroom:*—þone gemānan þæs brȳdguman and þǣre brȳde, Bl. H. 11, 6. Sǣde heó þām brȳdguman . . . gif hē hyre onhryne myd unclǣnre lufon, Shrn. 149, 23, 31. II. *a suitor:*—Brȳdguma *procus*, Wrt. Voc. ii. 118, 27: 67, 3. Brȳdguman *proco* (*desponsata virgo*), 94, 39. [*O. Sax.* brūdi-gumo: *O. Frs.* breid-goma: *O. H. Ger.* brūti-gomo *sponsus, procus: Icel.* brūð-gumi.]

brȳd-hlōp, -lóp, es; *pl.* -hlópa; *n. Marriage, bridal:*—Æt þām brȳdlōpe, Chr. 1076; P. 212, 24. Wērun sald tō brȳdhlōpum (-loppum, L.) *dabantur ad nuptias*, Lk. R. 17, 27. Brȳdhlōpum (-lópum, L.), 20, 34. In brȳdlōpum *in nubtiis*, Jn. p. 1, 8, 3. Tō brȳdloppum, Mt. L. 25, 10. Sē ðe dyde brȳdlópa (*nubtias*), 22, 2. [*Icel.* brūð-hlaup, brul-laup: *Dan.* bryllup. Cf. *O. H. Ger.* brūt-loufti *nuptiae: M. H. Ger.* brūt-louf.]

brȳdian. v. ge-brȳdian.

brȳd-lāc. *Dele* 'A marriage gift or feast,' *and add:* I. *married state, wedlock:*—Bærn nē āteoriað on ðām brȳdlāce; þēr is . . . singallic wæstmbærnyss, Hml. S. 7, 61. II. *in pl. marriage ceremony, nuptials:*—Is ǣlcum preóste forboden, þæt hī beón ne mōton on þā wīsan, þe hī ǣr wēran æt þām brȳdlācum, þær man ōðre sīðe wīfað *where a man marries a second time, priests are forbidden to attend in the way they did at the previous marriage*, Wlfst. 304, 32. Se cniht þā brȳdlāc geforþode *the young man had the marriage ceremony performed*, Hml. S. 34, 21. [v. *N. E. D.* bride-lock.]

brȳd-leóþ. *Add:*—Brȳdleóþes *epithalami(i)*, An. Ox. 3181. Brȳdleóðes, 7, 232 : Hpt. Gl. 481, 19. v. brȳd-sang.

brȳd-lic, brȳde-lic. *Add:*—Brȳdlicere gyfe *nuptiali dote*, An. Ox. 4551. Þȳ brȳdelican gewrite *sponsali dramate* (the Song of Solomon), Wrt. Voc. ii. 95, 34: 27, 25. Brȳdlice *sponsalia*, Hpt. Gl. 498, 43. Of brȳdlicum *genialibus*, Germ. 390, 144. [*O. H. Ger.* brūt-līh *sponsalis, hymenaeus.*]

brȳd-lóþ. v. brȳd-hlóþ.

brȳd-niht, e; *f. Bridal night, night after a wedding:*—Ðǣre forman brȳdniht, þā hī twā wǣron on ðǣm brȳdbūre, Shrn. 49, 3.

brȳd-ræst, -rest, e; *f. Substitute: Marriage-bed, nuptial couch:*—Brȳdrǣst *geneales*, Wrt. Voc. ii. 42, 18. Laþian tō ōðres mannes brȳdrǣste *ad iterandum thalamum vocare*, Gr. D. 278, 28. Ic nǣire gewemme Adrianes brȳdrǣste, Shrn. 60, 4.

brȳd-sang. *Add:*—Brȳdsang *epithalamium*, Wrt. Voc. ii. 70, 15 : 29, 10. [*O. H. Ger.* brūti-sang *carmen nuptiale.*] v. brȳd-leóþ.

brȳd-sceamol (?) *a bridal bed:*—Ānum brȳdsceaм (-sceamole ?) gifoegedo *uni thoro juncta*, Rtl. 110, 1.

brȳd-þing; *pl. n. Marriage. Add:*—Æt sumum brȳdþingum (*the marriage in Cana*), Shrn. 48, 27. Þ heú mihte fēran tō þǣm brȳdþingum,

87, 22. Ongunnon hys yldran hyne laþian tō brȳdþingum *his parents wanted him to marry*, 152, 22.

brygd, es; *m.* I. *drawing* a weapon. v. bryd *in Dict.* II. *something twisted,* a wick (?). v. candel-brygd. III. *a trick, fraud* (?). v. brægde, un-brygd.

brygdan. *Dele:* bryidan. v. brigdan: brym. *Dele second reference.*

brymme. *Substitute:* brym[m], es; *m. Sea, waves:*—Brym, sǣ *æquor*, Wrt. Voc. i. 53, 50. Brym *vel* holm *cataclismus, diluvium*, ii. 129, 42. Eorþe, brym (*pontus*), roderas, Hy. S. 74, 34. Se brym hwoðerode under his fōtswaðum, Hml. Th. ii. 388, 19. Of grunde brymmes (*pelagi*), Rtl. 61, 33. Of brymme *aequore*, Hy. S. 70, 31. Īgland beworpen mid sealtum brymme, Hml. Th. ii. 142, 29 : 138, 4. On þām heágan brymme, Hml. S. 2, 394. Hāwian tō ðǣre sǣ, gif ǣnig mist ārise of ðām mycclum brymme, 18, 146. Ofer ðone sealtan brym, Hml. Th. ii. 144, 20. Ðone brym *the sea of Galilee*, 378, 23 : 384, 19. Brymmas *aequora*, Hy. S. 38, 23. Sǣs brymmas *ponti freta*, 6, 28. Flōdes bremmas (brymmas, 2, 90) *cataclismi cerula*, An. Ox. 2478. Swā ymbclyppaþ cealda brymmas, Chr. 1065; P. 193, 35.

bryne. *Add:* I. *burning,* where there is destruction by, *or* exposure to, fire :—Wæs bryne and blōdgyte on gewelhwylcon ende, Wlfst. 159, 8. Biornendo byrno lēgo *aedaces incendii flammas*, Rtl. 64, 16. Hī hæfdon ælce scīre stīðe gemarcod mid bryne and mid hergunge, Chr. 1006; P. 137, 18. Seó cæster weard on bryne, Gr. D. 47, 24. On hiere (*Corinth*) bryne, Ors. 5, 2; S. 216, 1. Þæt þā elpendas fōran wēdende for þæs flexes bryne, 4, 1; S. 158, 7. Þone bryne seó sāwl þrowaþ, Gr. D. 304, 12. I a. *a conflagration, fire:*—Tō miclum bryne sceal wæter unlytel, gif man þæt fȳr sceal tō āhte ācwæncan, Wlfst. 157, 8. Hī woldon mid wætre dwæscan ðone byrne . . . ðā ne gemitton hī nǣnigne bryne, Shrn. 73, 37. II. *burning heat:*—Hǣto ł byrn *aestus*, Mt. L. 20, 12. Beswǣled for þām micclan byrne (*of the sun*), Hml. S. 23 b, 574. II a. *of disease, inflammation:*—Se bryne ðe on ðǣm innoðe bið, Past. 71, 5. III. *a fire, flame:*—Brenum *incendiis*, An. Ox. 1432. Ecelicum tinterge byrnum *aeternis gehenne incendiis*, Rtl. 64, 6. IV. *something burning, a brand, torch:*—Brynas (*rogorum*) *torres*, āla brynas *pyrarum faculas*, An. Ox. 4387-96. V. *a burn* or *scald:*—Wið wæteres bryne oððe fȳres, Lch. i. 368, 9. Lǣcedōmas wið bryne, ii. 12, 22. VI. *metaph. ardor, fervor, passion:*—Wilme and bryne *fervore*, Wrt. Voc. ii. 33, 42. Hātum bryne *torrido rigore* (*caenobialis vitae*), An. Ox. 2706. Hié burnon þǣre Godes lufan . . . Be ðǣm bryne wītgode Dauid, Bl. H. 133, 28. On þām bryne forligeres licgende, Hml. S. 23 b, 334. Godes lufu byrne *caritatis ardore*, Rtl. 64, 14. v. in-, wōl-bryne.

bryne brine. *l.* brȳne.

bryne-ādl. *Substitute for* Cot. 92:—Bryneādl *febris*, Wrt. Voc. ii. 148, 51. *Febris a fervore nominatur, id est* bryneādl, 39, 9.

bryne-ness, e; *f. Fierce trial:*—Hātum brynenesse *torrido rigore* (*caenobialis vitae*), Hpt. Gl. 469, 64. Cf. next word.

brynig; *adj. Burning, fiery:*—Wyrmas heora bān gnagað brynigum tuxlum (cf. byrnendum tōðum, Wlfst. 139, 10) *vermes lacerant ignitis dentibus ossa*, Dōm. L. 209.

brynige. v. heals-brynige.

brȳsan (-ian). *Add:* I. *to bruise, crush:*—Mid swiðran his nele brȳsan wanhydig gemōd wealdend engla *quassatos nec vult calamos infringere dextra*, Dōm. L. 49. II. *to pound, season:*—Weorcu nāne synd būtan of eádmōdnysse brȳsdde *opera nulla sunt nisi ex humilitate condiantur*, Scint. 20, 20. v. ge-brȳsan (-ian).

-brȳsedness. v. ge-brȳsedness: bryst *a bristle.* v. byrst: brystman. *l.* brystnian, *and see* brytsnian: brȳtan. v. brītan: bryðen. *Dele last reference, and see* byrþen: brȳtian. *l.* brytian.

bryt-mǣlum; *adv. By bits, gradually:*—Bretmǣlum *minutatim*, An. Ox. 1829. Bryt(mǣlum) *minutatim*, i. *gradatim* ł *ordinatim*, 1553.

brytnian. *Add:*—Þās suǣsenda ge reogolward brytniæ swǣ hīgum mǣst rēd sié, Cht. Th. 460, 37. Brytnian *inpendere*, i. *donare*, An. Ox. 7, 3. Brytniende *dispertiens*, Wrt. Voc. ii. 140, 73. Wæs brytnod *inpendebatur*, 44, 65. v. ge-brytnian.

brytnung, e; *f. Dispensation, distribution:*—Dispensatio dihtnung, brytnung, scīr, gedāl *vel* diht, Wrt. Voc. ii. 140, 64.

brȳtofta. *Add:* =brȳd-þofta; cf. þoft-rǣden, -scipe.

brytsnian; *p.* ode *To distribute, spend:*—Brytstniendum (brystmendum, Hpt. Gl. 458, 16) *erogantem*, i. *dividentem*, An. Ox. 2195. [Cf. brytsen.] v. ge-brytsnian.

brytta. *Add:*—Swegles brytta *rex supernus*, Dōm. L. 117. Sigores brytta (*Christ*), 277. [See Andrews' Old English Manor, p. 144.] v. bere-, hlāfo-, wīn-brytta.

bryttian. v. ge-bryttian.

bryttian. *Substitute:* bryttian, brytian. I. *to dispense, distribute, grant a share of:*—Exhibeo, i. *porrigo, prebeo, tribuo* ic bryttie, *dono, ostendo* ic bringe, Wrt. Voc. ii. 145, 2. Hē missenlīce monna cynne his giefe bryttað, Crä. 105 : Cri. 682 : B. 1726. Hē gumum gold brittade, Gen. 1181. Bryttade, 1236. Hē him gyfe bryttode,

welum weorðode, An. 755. Ic wisse cwēn giefe bryttian, Vīd. 102. Ðā þe hit him bryttian (brytian, *v. l.*) sceoldon ... ðā þe be hiora gifum libban sculon *qui dispensatores sunt ... qui ex aliena dispensatione subsistunt*, Past. 320, 4. Hē ðǣm ūtlican tō geleáfan bringan (brytian, *v. l.*) ne mihte *externis prodesse ad fidem non poterat*, Bd. 5, 9 ; Sch. 397, 2. **II.** *to dispose of, have control of, be master of, enjoy, use :—* Sǣda gehwilc þára þe hæleð bryttigað *every seed that men use*, Exod. 376. Hē lange siððan woruld bryttade *for long after he lived*, Gen. 1226. Hié wintra fela woruld bryttedon, 1724. His eaforan eád bryttedon *his children were masters of his wealth*, 1602 ; Dan. 672. Mē (*Abraham*) æfter sculon woruldmágas welan bryttian, Gen. 2178. Ne mihton hī mægyn bryttigan *they were powerless*, 52. Hī lēton him behindan hrā bryttian þone hrefn and þone earn ǣses brūcan, Ǣdelst. 60. v. ge-bryttian.

**brýttian.** *Dele, and see preceding word.*

**búan, būn, būgan** (-ian, -ean), **būian, būwian, bógian,** *q. v. in Dict. ;* býa *in N. Gospels ; p.* būde, būgede, bōgode, býede ; *pp.* būn, būd, býed. *Add :* **I.** *intrans. To dwell :—* Huēr būes (býes, R.) ðū *ubi habitas ?,* Jn. L. 1, 38. Þā būað oð Mēda burh *habitantes usque ad Medorum civitatem*, Nar. 33, 16. Þā þe in Norþhymbrum būgeað, Chr. 894 ; P. 86, 7 : 924 ; P. 104, 20. Gē bōgiað (būgiað, *v. l.*) on þam sīftan ðǣle healfum, Bt. 18, 1 ; S. 42, 15. Flēgendo býes (*habitant*) in tyggum his, Mt. L. 13, 32. Hē būde on Eást-Englum, Chr. 890 ; P. 82, 10. Manna þe mē ymbūtan būdon *circumhabitantium*, Ps. Th. 30, 15. Ðā ðe býedon in Hierusalem, Lk. L. R. 13, 4. Býa *habitare*, Mk. L. R. 4, 32. Allo býendo (*habitantes*) in ðǣm, Rtl. 100, 17. **I a.** *of land, to lie :—* Þ land būeð oð Mēda rīce *subjacet regionibus Medorum*, Nar. 34, 11. Heora landgemǣre būað neáh þam gársecge, 38, 20. **II.** *trans. To inhabit, occupy (and cultivate* land*), possess :—* Līf ēce hē býeð (*possidebit*), Mt. L. 19, 29. Gié býeð (*possidebitis*) sáuelo íuero, Lk. L. 21, 19. Būgede (bōgede, An. Ox. 845) *incoluit* (*terram*), Hpt. Gl. 426, 44. Þā þe ðā lond būdon, Nar. 17, 10. Þā burgware þe þā burg ær būdon, Chr. 919 ; P. 100, 12. Þæt mennisc þone eard bōgodan, Ælfc. T. Grn. 6, 12. Býes (*possidete*) rīc, Mt. L. 25, 34. Būian *inhabitare*, An. Ox. 11, 13. Godes templ būgian, Hml. S. 3, 353. Mæg ic býa *possidebo*, Lk. L. 10, 25. Tō býenna *possidenda*, p. 9, 16. Forgeaf God him and his ofspringe þone eard tō būgienne, Hml. Th. ii. 190, 14. Land tō būgianne *land to inhabit*, Bt. 17 ; F. 60, 4 : 18, 1 ; F. 62, 16.

**buc** *a buck. Dele, and see bucca.*

**būc.** *Add :* **II.** *a vessel :—* Būc *lagena*, An. Ox. 56, 54. Him weard geboren tō būc ful wæteres, Hml. Th. ii. 422, 29. Butas (būcas ?), blēda, mēlas, cuppan, Angl. ix. 264, 17. **III.** *glossing* buccula (*= a cheek ?, or the beaver of a helmet ?, or the boss of a shield ?;* more from the bulging shape) :—Buuc *buccula*, Wrt. Voc. ii. 102, 30. Būc, 126, 64. Būcc, 11, 41. [Wright gives the accent in the last two.] v. rēcels-būc.

**bucc.** v. *preceding word.*

**bucca.** *Add :—Cervus* vel *eripes* heort vel bucca (in the margin *hircacervus* bucheort) ; this is the proper reading, not that given in Wrt. Voc. i. 22, 63. v. Angl. viii. 450. Hī onsægdon deófle, swā heora þeáw wæs, buccan (*capræ*) heáfod, Gr. D. 232, 25. Hē wæs on buccan slege getācnod, Hml. Th. ii. 210, 23. Ðær mon ðane chiorl slōh for ðan buccan, C. D. iii. 434, 21. Buccan wē offriað oððe sceáp, gif wē ūres līchaman gālnysse oferswīðað, Hml. Th. ii. 210, 31. Fearra flǣsc oððe buccena blōd, i. 590, 15. v. wæter-bucca.

**bucce** *glosses* bulbile, Wrt. Voc. ii. 126, 72 : **būc-ful.** *l.* būc ful :

**buc-heort.** v. bucca.

**Buccingahām-scīr.** *Add :—*Innon Buccinghāmscīre be Cilternes efese, C. D. iv. 232, 32.

**būend and būende.** *Add :* būgend (-iend, -igend), býend *an inhabitant, a cultivator* of land :—Būend *accola*, Wrt. Voc. ii. 91, 51. Būgend, 3, 76 : *indigena*, An. Ox. 7, 292. Būgynd, 8, 220. Býed *habitator*, Rtl. 98, 8. Þā būendan *habitatores*, Cant. M. 14 : 15. Ðā būendo (býende, R.) *coloni*, Mk. L. 12, 7 : Lk. L. (R.) 20, 14. Būgendra *accolarum*, i. *habitatorum*, An. Ox. 2230. Ðǣm yrrestum būendum *colonis pessimis*, Mk. p. 4, 20. Būendum *cultoribus* (*uineæ*), Lk. p. 10, 7. Ðǣm būendum (býendum, R.) *colonis*, Lk. L. 20, 9. Be ðǣm būgendum his eardungstōwe *de habitatore tabernaculi ejus*, R. Ben. 4, 22. Stōdon āwēste hūs būton būgigendum, Hml. Th. ii. 122, 20. v. in-būend.

**bufan ;** *prep. adv. Add :* **A.** *prep.* **I.** *with dat.* (1) *local,* (*a*) *above, at a point higher than :—*Ætēowode leóht bufon ðām apostole, Hml. Th. i. 76, 9. Hangaþ bufan þǣm lāstum leóhtfæt, Bl. H. 127, 28. Hī licgað bufan eorðan on hyra hūsum, Ors. 1, 1 ; S. 20, 24. Gif se earm bið forad bufan elnbogan, Ll. Th. i. 94, 24. Hē ofwearp þone ent bufon ðām eágan, Hml. S. 18, 24. (*b*) *upon :—*Byrgenne, swelce hiera þeáw wæs þæt mon rīcum monnum bufan eorðan worhte, Ors. 4, 10 ; S. 202, 5 : 2, 4 ; S. 74, 19. (2) *of time, above, more than :—*Fram ānum mōnðe and bufan þām, Num. 3, 15. **II.** *with acc.* (1) *above, to a point higher than :—*Hē up gewāt bufan þā wolcnu, Bt. 7, 3 ; F. 22, 5. Tugon hié hrægl bufan cneów, Ors. 3, 5 ; S. 106, 16. (2) *upon :—*

Lege mīne tunecan bufon ðǣra deádra līc, Hml. Th. i. 72, 33. **B.** *adv. of previous mention :—*Preóst þe wē ǣr bufan emb sprǣcon, Bl. H. 43, 27. Swā hit bufan hēr āwriten is, Chr. 1052 ; P. 173, 21. Þæs gemynd ic dyde ǣr feorr bufan, Gr. D. 86, 20.

**bufan-cweden ;** *adj. Aforesaid, above-mentioned :—*Ðæs bufancwedenan mannes mægnu ... se bufancwedena wer, Gr. D. 14, 8. Þā landgemǣro ðæs bufancwedenan landes, C. D. ii. 265, 27. Þysum bufancwedenum gelīce, Gr. D. 90, 27.

**bufan-sprecen ;** *adj. Aforesaid :—*Þæs bufansprecenan ealdormannes here, Gr. D. 14, 23.

**bufantigera :—***Mitræ* hættes, bufantigera (*l.* hūfan *tigera.* Cf. *mitr*, i. *tigera* hūfan, An. Ox. 2, 440 ; *thiara* hætte, 325. So *tigera* from Latin *tiara*), Hpt. Gl. 525, 9.

**būgan** *to bow. Add :* **I.** *to bow, bend the body :—*Him būgað englas, Hml. S. 7, 50. **I a.** *to sink, fall :—*Dauid ofwearp mid his liþeran þone ent þ hē beáh tō eorðan, Hml. S. 18, 24. **II.** *to yield, give ground, give way :—*Beág *cedebat*, Wrt. Voc. ii. 20, 70 : *cessit*, 21, 33. Se stream beáh for his fōtum þ hē mihte drȳge ofergangan *uidit undam suis cessisse ac uiam dedisse uestigiis*, Bd. 1, 7 ; Sch. 24, 9. Sóna swā hī tōgædere fēngon, þa beáh seó Englisce fyrd, Chr. 1001 ; P. 133, 23. **III.** *to bend one's steps, turn, go :—*Þæt folc beáh ðyderweard, Hml. Th. ii. 32, 26. Nis ūs betere þæt wē būgon ongeán tō Egipta lande (*reverti in Aegyptum*) ?, Num. 14, 3. Heó nǣfre ne wolde on hūs būgan, Lch. iii. 34, 29. Wæs him in bogen bāncoða, Gū. 997. **III a.** *of retirement, withdrawal :—*Eádgár æþeling beáh fram him, ... and þæs æðelinges swuster beáh intō mynstre, Chr. 1085 ; P. 217, 11–15. Hē forlēt woruldþing and beáh tō ðām mynstre þe is Magilros gehāten, Hml. Th. ii. 348, 29. Gif hió mid bearnum būgan wille *if she wish to go away taking the children with her*, Ll. Th. i. 22, 6. **IV.** *of adhesion, submission, or abandonment, defection, to turn to or from :—*Sē ðe fram Gode bīchð tō deófle, Hml. Th. i. 110, 1. Seó geladung þe of Iudēiscum folce tō Crīstes geleáfan beáh, 44, 11. Ciningas and eorlas georne him tō bugon, Chr. 959 ; P. 114, 24. *Declina a malo,* þ is būh fram yfele ... Nis nā genōh þæt þū fram yfele būge, Hml. Th. ii. 602, 8 : Hml. S. 12, 147. Hē wolde būgan tō þam cynge (hē wolde his man beón, *v.l.*), Chr. 1050 ; P. 169, 17. It is mīne fulle unna ðat Ælfrich mōt būgan tō ðō tuēyen abboten, Cht. Th. 416, 8. Būgende *declinantia* (*a religionis tramite*), An. Ox. 3429.

**būgend.** v. būend : **būgian ; II.** *Dele, and see* būan : **būgi-(g)end(e).** v. būend.

**bul, bula ;** *m. An ornament, brooch :—*Bula *bulla*, Wrt. Voc. ii. 12, 34. Bulan *legulam*, An. Ox. 8, 319. Ic geann mīure goddohtor þone bule (bul ?) ðe wæs hire ealdermōder, Cht. Th. 548, 17. Bulum *bullis*, Wrt. Voc. ii. 12, 4. Bulas gyldenno gidōe wē ðē *murenulas aureas faciemus tibi*, Rtl. 4, 3. [From Lat.] v. bul-berende.

**bula, an ;** *m. A bull :—*On bulan wyllan, C. D. iii. 81, 31. On bulan dīc, vi. 62, 26. [*Icel.* boli.]

**bul-berende** *glosses* bullifer, Wrt. Voc. ii. 126, 71.

**Bulgarisc ;** *adj. Bulgarian :—*Bulgarisc man, Gr. D. 300, 21, 23. v. Pulgare *in Dict.*

**bulluca.** *Substitute :* **bulluc, es ;** *m. A young bull, bull-calf :—*Tō bulluce gemǣstum *ad uitulum saginatum*, Scint. 169, 15.

**bulot.** *Add :—*Bulut bresion, Wrt. Voc. ii. 127, 20.

**bund, e ;** *f.* (?). *A bundle :—*Bunda *fasciculos*, Mt. L. 13, 30. [*O.L. Ger.* bund.]

**bune.** *Add :* **I.** *a reed :—*Canna, harundo, calamus vel bune (cf. *calamus* vel *canna* vel *arundo* hreód, i. 79, 27 : cf. *too* Bun-hām *with* Hreód-hām *in local names, and see* N. E. D. bun. *Or is* bune *meant to give an alternative meaning for* canna, cf. *crater* vel *canna* canne, i. 24, 38?), Wrt. Voc. ii. 128, 3. **II.** *a cup :—*Bunan *carce*:ia, Wrt. Voc. ii. 103, 54 : 14, 15. *Carcesia, summitas mali, et genus poculorum,* vel buna[n], 128, 58. **III.** *the name of a stream* (?) :—Andlang ðǣre dīc ðæt intō bunon ; andlang bunan ðæt tō ðan ealdan forda, C. D. vi. 129, 27. ¶ *Buna* occurs as the name of a person, Txts. 156, 81 : 161, 277.

**būr, es ;** *m.* (not *n*). *Add : A* (*private, inner*) *chamber* (as distinguished from the *heall*) :—Būr *camera*, Wrt. Voc. i. 58, 6. Gemētton hī ðæs cnihtas on ānum būre tō Gode gebiddende, Hml. S. 23, 140. Hē wolde wyrcan þā healle on eástdǣle, and þā ōðre gebytlu bæftan þǣre healle, bæðhūs and kycenan ... and wynsume būras, 36, 98. (1) *a bedchamber :—*Būr þrybeddod *triclinium*, Wrt. Voc. i. 58, 5 : 83, 30. (1 a) *a bridal chamber* (cf. brȳd-būr) :—Būre (*nuptiali*) *thalamo*, Hpt. Gl. 511, 34. Ic eom nū in Crīstes būre, Shrn. 140, 28. (2) *a supper-room :—*Būre *triclinio, sede*, Hpt. Gl. 423, 36. On būr *in triclinium*, 480, 68. (3) *the chamber* of a great man :—Drihten behȳdde mē on his būre (*tabernaculo*), Ps. L. 26, 5. Hē (*the emperor*) wæs him āna on his inran būre, Hml. S. 23, 395. Com se apostol intō ðæs cyninges būre, Hml. Th. i. 458, 27. All hīgen eódan tō mīnum (*the bishop's*) būre on Weogorna ceastre, C. D. ii. 100, 29. Eádrīc ealdorman bepǣhte hī intō his būre (*in camera sua*), Chr. 1015 ; P. 146, 2. (4) *a lady's chamber, bower :—*Hē ābræc intō þām būre þǣr heó inne læg, Ap. Th. 2, 1, 8.

Eóde hē intó ðām būre þār his dohtor inne wæs, 22, 17. Geáscode hē þone cyning on wífcýþþe on Merantūne, and hine þǣr berād, and þone būr ūtan beeóde, Chr. 755; P. 46, 30. v. bed-búr.

-búr. v. ge-búr; ā-būrod, *and next word.*

búr-byrde; *adj. Of peasant birth* :—Wēron þǣr ðreó wíteþeówe men búrbærde, and ðreó ðeówborde, Cht. Th. 152, 19.

búr-cniht, es; *m. A chamberlain, servant of the bedchamber, eunuch:* —His búrcnihtas (*eunuchi*) woldon hine ámyrran, Hml. A. 98, 213. Án þāra búrcnihta, 100, 278.

búr-cote. *Substitute:* búr-cot, es; *n. A bedchamber:*—Búrcot cubile, Wrt. Voc. ii. 137, 39. Hē his mōdes scearpnesse eft gecierde tó ðām flǣsclican búrcotum . . . hē wæs gecierred tó smeáganne hū flǣsclicum monnum gedafonode on hira búrcotum and on hiera beddum tó dónne *ad cubile carnalium aciem mentis revocat . . . carnalium cubile perscrutatur*, Past. 99, 10–21.

burg, burh, burhg, buruh (-ug, -ig), byrg, byrig; *gen.* byrig, burge, burhge, burcge; *dat.* byrg, byrig, byrh, burh; *n. acc. pl.* byrg, byrig, burh, burga, burha; *gen. pl.* burga, burha; *dat. pl.* burgum, burhum, byrgum. *Add:* I. *a fortified place:*—Becom hē tó þǣre cynelican byrig (*ad urbem regiam*), seó is nemned Bebbanburhg (-byrig, -burh, -burg, *v. ll.*). Ðā hē þā geseah þ̄ seó burh (buruh, burg, *v. ll.*) wæs tó þan fæst þ̄ hē ne mihte hié ábrecan, hē áslát þā tūnas ymb þā burhg onweg, Bd. 3, 16; Sch. 265, 5–14. Tó burge and tó wealle *ad arcem et ad moenia*, Kent. Gl. 287. For íserne weall betuh ðǣm wítgan and ðǣre byrig (byrh, *v. l.*), Past. 165, 10. Hine wǣrlíce healdan on ðǣre byrg his mōdes *intra mentis castra se munire*, 431, 6. Hē tówearp ðā burg æt Hierusalem *destruxit muros Ierusalem*, 311, 6. Byrgum tómiddes þǣr þā ǣrendracan synd Godes *inter apostolicas arces*, Dōm. L. 284. Iα. *a residence surrounded by a wall* (v. burg-geat):—Þā geáscode hē þone cyning on Merantūne, and hine þǣr berād and þā burh ūtan beeóde . . . Hié þone æþeling on þǣre byrig mētton þǣr se cyning læg ofslægen, and þā gatu him tó belocen hæfdon, Chr. 755; P. 46, 28–48, 16. Áhē mæig findan hwæt hē mæig on byrig bētan, Angl. ix. 262, 16. Burh hegegian, Ll. Th. i. 432, 16. II. *where the idea of fortification is at least not prominent, a town, city* :—Burh *municipium*, Wrt. Voc. ii. 85, 8. Sió burg *Siracusas*, 84, 33. On þyssere byrig Babilonia, þe hwílon wæs æþelost burh ealra burha . . . on ðǣm twām burhum Bethsaida and Corozain . . . þā burha ðreáde Críst, Wlfst. 194, 9–14. Bǣdleem hātte seó buruh, Lch. iii. 60, 11. Ic nyste þ̄ ǣnig óþer byrig ūs wǣre gehende, Hml. S. 23, 542. Þ̄ þis sý Efesa byrig, 538: 677: 743. Ánre burge riht *jus civile*, Wrt. Voc. ii. 49, 7. Burge *municipii*, An. Ox. 5123. Ðǣre burcge nama, Bt. 18, 2; F. 64, 18. Ercebiscop Cantwara burhge, Bd. 2, 18; Sch. 182, 11. His gemynd is micel on twām burgum . . . In óðre birg . . . in óðre birg, Mart. H. 194. 11–14. Sē þe sit būton ðǣre berig *suburbanus*, Wrt. Voc. i. 84, 45. On þǣre burh in (*Tribulanum*) territorium, An. Ox. 4848. On þǣre burh þæs nama wæs Garganus, Bl. H. 197, 28. Biscop æt Florentie þǣre burh, Chr. 1059; P. 189, 5. Of burug in burig *de civitate in civitatem*, Mt. L. 23, 34. Hī Rōmāne burig ábrǣcon, Bt. 1; F. 2, 3. Monega byrg (byrig, *v. l.*) tó gafolgieldum wurdon, Ors. 4, 5; S. 170, 6. Ðás twā burh, Hml. Th. ii. 66, 28. Ðāra burga (buriga, L.), Lk. R. 4, 26. Þæt ígland hæfd on him X byrg (*decem civitates*), Ors. 1, 1; S. 10, 18. Monega byrig, 2, 2; S. 66, 23. Geond þā byrig. 3, 7; S. 114, 30. v. castel-, eardung-, sǣ-burh; burge?.

burg-biscop, es; *m. The bishop of a city:*—Hē fulluht underfēng æt þām burhbiscope, H. R. 15, 16.

burg-bót. *Add:* Cf. ge-bētung: burg-bryce. *Add:* v. *N. E. D.* burgh-breche.

burge (?), an = burg:—Of ðām burhgan geate, C. D. iii. 36, 18. Cf. burg-geat.

burg-ealdor (burh-). *Add:*—Hēt se burhealdor (*alt. to* burhge ealdor) þone bisceop him tó gefeccan, Hml. S. 22, 203.

burg-geat (burh-). *Add:* I. *the gate of a burg* (v. burg, Iα):—Ðus feor sceal beón þæs cinges grið fram his burhgeate þǣr he is sittende, Ll. Th. i. 224, 7. Þā heortan æt þīnum burhgeatum behele, Lch. i. 328, 24. [He wende tó þan burhȝate þer þe king on bure lai, Laym. 17670.] II. *a town-gate* (v. burg, II):—Hē fērde on ðā burg Ambinensus . . . þā sæt þǣr sum þearfa æt ðǣm burggeate, Bl. H. 213, 33.

burg-geat-setl. *Substitute* (*for entry under* burh-geat-setl): If burg-geat *is used in the sense given under* burg-geat, I, *the word would mean* 'jurisdiction over those belonging to the "burg," the owner's family and tenants'; *if as in* burg-geat, II, *it would mean* 'a seat (right to sit) in a court held at the gate of a town' (cf. Grmm. R. A. 804):—Gif ceorl geþeáh þ̄ hē hæfde fullíce fíf hída ágenes landes, cirican and kycenan, bellhús and burhgeatsetl, Ll. Th. i. 190, 16.

burg-gemet, es; *n. Measure used in a town:*—Ne sceall biscop geþafian wóh gemet, ac hit gebyreð þ̄ he rǣde fare ǣlc burhgemet (cf. gange ǣn gemet swilce man on Lundenbyrig and on Wintanceastre healde, i. 270, 1), Ll. Th. ii. 312, 20.

burg-gerēfa (burh-). *Add:*—Þā frægn se burhgerēfa (cf. Rōmeburge gerēfa, 28) hyne, Shrn. 96, 30. Se burhgerēfa (cf. ðǣre burge

gerēfa, 12), 120, 14. Ðæs burhgerēfan (cf. Rōmeburge gerēfa, 6) sunu (*praefecti filius*, Ald. 60, 5), 56, 10: Hml. S. 23, 770. Ðā cwæþ Neron tó his burhgerēfan, Bl. H. 189, 28. [A burhreue *urbis prefectus*, Kath. 1904.] [The word does not seem to occur as the title of an English official, though it is said in Ll. Th. i. 194, 2–4: Ic Æðelstān cýðe þām gerēfan tó hwilcere birig. In a Latin charter the praepositus of Oxford (praepositus ciuitatis Oxnaford, C. D. iv. 285) is mentioned, and in this and in similar cases Kemble supposes a *burh-gerēfa* to be meant. v. Saxons in England, ii. pp. 171–3.]

burg-hege, es; *m. The fence of a 'burg'* (v. burg, Iα):—Andlanges þǣre ceápstrǣte oð cyninges burghege (burge hege?), C. D. B. ii. 305, 26.

burg-hleop (*l.* -hlìþ). *Substitute:* =(?) beorg-hlìþ, *q. v.*

burg-lagu, e; *f. Civil law:*—Burglage *jus civile*, Germ. 388, 18.

burg-leód, es; *pl.* -leóde (-a); *m. A burgess, citizen:*—Burgliód (-leód) *municipes*, Txts. 79, 1334: 180, 17. Buruhliód, An. Ox. 8, 221. Beorhleód, 7, 293. Sicelic burleód (burh-, Hpt. Gl. 499, 37) *Siculus indigena*, 3958. Burgleóda *municipes*, 4852. Burgleóde, 5, 40. Hē gelende tó þǣre byrig, and mid micle gefeán þāra burgleóda (*cinium*) onfangen wæs, Ors. 3, 1; S. 98, 24. Siracussa cyning þāra burgleóda *rex Syracusanus*, 4, 1; S. 158, 14. Buruhleóda *oppidorum, ciuium*, Germ. 392, 65. Burhleóðum *civibus*, Hy. S. 112, 1: Bl. H. 241, 23. Of beorhleóðum *de popularibus*, Wrt. Voc. i. 54, 56. Beorleóðum *municipibus*, An. Ox. S, 358. [O. H. Ger. burg-liut; *pl.* -liuti *civis*.] *Take here* burh-leóde *in Dict., and see next two words.*

burg-leód(?), e; *f. The people of a town* :—Hié áspōnon him tó fultume Corinthum þā burgleóde (*or pl. from* burg-leód, es; *m.*?), Ors. 3, 11; S. 144, 24. Cf. land-leód.

burg-leóda, an; *m. A citizen, burgess:*—Burhleódan *municipes*, Hpt. Gl. 517, 70. Cf. land-leódan; *pl. under* land-leód; *m.*

burg-man (burh-). *Add:*—Hē wæs ánes burhmannes sunu on Ysrahéla lande, Hml. A. 181, 10. Hí wendon him tó þǣre burge (*Dover*) weard and ofslógon mā þanne .xx. manna, and þā burhmen ofslógon .xix. men on óðre healfe, Chr. 1048; P. 173, 4. Lǣde hine sum ealdormann hine geond þās burh and secge þām burhmannum, Hml. A. 99, 235. [v. *N. E. D.* borough-man.]

burg-rǣden (burh-). *Substitute for* Cot. 128:—Burhrǣddenne *municipatu*, Wrt. Voc. ii. 54, 67.

burg-riht (burh-). *Substitute: Town-right, law in a town:*—Ne sceall hē (*the bishop*) geþafian ǣnig unriht . . . ac hit gebyreð þ̄ be his rǣde fare ǣghwilc lahriht, ge burhriht ge landriht, Ll. Th. ii. 312, 20.

burg-rūne, an; -rūn, e; *f.* [*Substitute these for* burh-rūnan.] *A sorceress:*—Burgrūnan *furiae*, Wrt. Voc. ii. 39, 42. Burhrūnan, 151, 76. Burgrūnae (-e) *parcas*, Txts. 86, 761. Burgrūnan, An. Ox. 38, 2. Cf. hægtess(e).

burg-sǣta, -sēta (-seta?) (burh-). *Add:*—Burgsētan *oppidani*, Wrt. Voc. ii. 64, 71.

burg-scipe (burh-). *Add:*—Burgscipe *municipium*, Wrt. Voc. ii. 80, 13. Burhscipe, 54, 66. Burhscipe, eardung *municipatus*, An. Ox. 4853.

burg-scír (burh-). *Substitute: A township, town or city with the district belonging to it, and* add :—þǣre burhscíre *Hipponensis* (*pontifex*), An. Ox. 5400. Hē hine gesette tó bisceope þǣre burhscíre (*Alexandria*), Hml. S. 15, 24. Ealle ðā hysecild þǣre burhscíre *omnes pueros in Bethleem et in omnibus finibus ejus*, Hml. Th. i. 82, 11. Tó ánre burhscíre ðe is gecíged Cesarea Philippi *in partes Caesareae Philippi*, 364, 14: 366, 5: ii. 110, 6. Pictauienscisce woldon habban ðone ylcan þe hī ǣr álendon of heora burhscíre, 518, 21. Ne ára ðū nānum ríce ne ǣnigre burhscíre *non parcet oculus tuus ulli regno, omnemque urbem munitam subjugabis mihi*, Hml. A. 103, 48.

burg-síta (burh-). *Dele, and see* burg-wita.

burg-slǣd? :—Andlang burhslǣdes, C. D. vi. 137, 19.

burg-sprǣc, -spæc (burh-). *Substitute:* burg-sprǣc, -spǣc, e; *f. Elegant speech:*—Gleáwnesse burhsprǣce *dissertudinem urbanitatis*, Wrt. Voc. ii. 74, 52. Burhspǣce *urbanitatis, eloquentiae loquela*, Hpt. Gl. 404, 40: An. Ox. 9, 13. [*All are glosses of* Ald. 2, 6.]

burg-stal, -stól. *Dele.*

burg-staþol (burh-). *Substitute: The foundation of the wall of a burg* (v. burg, Iα):—Nim his lifre, tódǣl and bedealf æt þām ymbhwyrftum þīnra landgemǣra and þīnra burhstaþola, and þā heortan æt þīnum burhgeatum behele, Lch. i. 328, 23.

burg-steall (burh-). *Add: The site of a town* (?), *a hill* (?):—Helde, burhsteal *cliv(i)um*, i. *discensum* (cf. cum ascenderent clivum civitatis, 1 Reg. ix. 11. v. Angl. xix. 463), Wrt. Voc. ii. 131, 72. Cf. tūn-steall.

burg-þegen, es; *m. A thane living in a burg:*—Alle mīne burhðegnes on Lundene, C. D. iv. 213, 4: 214, 32: 221, 13.

burg-tūn. *Add:* [v. *N. E. D.* borough-town.]

burg-waran, -ware. *Add:* , -waras (-weras). [Though plural forms are most frequent, the singular seems to be used in the following :—Yldest burhwara *proceres*, burhwara *cives*, Wrt. Voc. i. 18, 40, 35 (cf.

ceaster-gewara)]:—Wǽron ealle þā burgware Cartaginenses mid wōpe anstyred, Ors. 4, 5; S. 166, 11. Hē weard from ðǽm burgwarum in ābrōden ... swāþeáh ealle þā burgware ne mehton hiene ǽnne geniéddan, 3, 9; S. 134, 17: 3, 1; S. 98, 13: Bl. H. 199, 24. Burhware, 77, 27: *municipes*, Wrt. Voc. ii. 54, 49. Alle burgwaras *omnis civitas*, Mk. L. 1, 33. Burgwaras (burugweras, R.) *cives*, Lk. L. 19, 14. Ðā burguaras *Hierosolyma*, Mt. L. 3, 5. Burgwǽras, 2, 3. Cirinensa gewinn þāra burgwarana, Ors. 2, 2; S. 66, 14. Hwylcra burgwara for worulde þū wǽre, Bt. 5, 1; F. 10, 4. Þāra uplicra burhwara and þæs ēcean gefērscipes, Bl. H. 197, 16. From Hierusolimiscum ðǽm burguærum (burugweorum, R.) *ab Hierosolimis*, Jn. L. 1, 19. Sē ðā burhware ofercynd, Past. 218, 18. v. underburh-ware.

**burg-waru.** *Add:*—Eall seó buruhwaru *populus civitatis*, Deut. 21, 21. Gyf hit binnan byrig gedōn bið, fare seó buruhwaru sylf tō and begyte þā banan, Ll. Th. i. 286, 21. Seó burhwaru gelæhton hine, Ap. Th. 26, 23. Seó burhwaru, þæt sind Turonisce ..., and Pictauienscisce ... būtū ðā burhwara (-waru, -waræ, Hml. S. 31, 1469) besǽton ðone hālgan, Hml. Th. ii. 518, 18–24. Burware gefeoht *civile bellum*, Wrt. Voc. i. 35, 17. Hreám þǽre burhware of Gomorra *clamor Gomorrhae*, Gen. 18, 20. Mid þisre scildigre burhware *in scelere civitatis*, 19, 15. Com se cyning mid þǽre burhware tō ðām temple, Hml. Th. i. 462, 6. Hē þa twā burhwara, Sodomam and Gomorram, forbærnde, 246, 25. Hié þa burgware (*here?* or under preceding word?), Beneuentius and Sepontanus hātton þa twā leóde, hié þa ongunnon ānwiges biddan (cf. Neapolite cwǽdon gefeoht tōgeánes þǽre burhware Sepontiniscre ceastre and tōgeánes Beneuentanos, Hml. Th. i. 504, 12–15), Bl. H. 201, 21. v. *next word.*

**burgwaru-mann, burg-wealda** (burh-). *Add:*—Aaron and Iulius wǽron burhwarumen (burhwaru, burhwealdan) on Ligeceastre *Aaron et Iulius Legionum urbis ciues*, Bd. 1, 7; Sch. 27, 17.

**burg-weall.** *Add:*—In Lucan þǽre cæstre ... seó eá flōweþ be þām burhwealle (*juxta urbis muros*), Gr. D. 192, 16. On ðā burhwalles; of ðām burhwallan ... on sūðwardne ðone burhwal, C. D. iii. 394, 28–30. Pharao hēt hī wyrcan his burhweallas (cf. hig getimbrodun Pharaones eardungburga *urbes tabernaculorum*, Ex. 1, 11), Hml. Th. ii. 190, 34.

**burg-weard** (burh-). *Add:* [*O. L. Ger.* burg-ward.] v. byri-weard *in Dict.*

**burg-weg, es; m. I.** *a road to a burg* (v. burg, I a):—Andlang burhslædes on burhwege, C. D. vi. 137, 20. **II.** *a road in a town* (v. burg, II), *a street:*—Hī nāmon ungerīme sceattas, and ealle ðā tōwurpon geond þās rūman burhwegas, Hml. S. 23, 289.

**burg-weorod,** -wered *body of citizens. Add:*—An gewitnysse ðes hīrēdes æt Crīstes cirican and ealles buruhweredes, C. D. ii. 3, 36.

**burg-wille,** -welle, an; *f. A spring that supplies a burg* (?):—Onlong brōces ðæt on burhwellan, of burhwellan on ðā burhwalles, C. D. iii. 394, 28.

**burg-wita** (burh-). *l.* -wita, *and add:*—Burhwita *urbanus*, Wrt. Voc. i. 84, 44. Burhwita (*printed* -sita) *vel* burhman *urbanus*, 34, 32. Þis cýdde se bisceop þām burhwiton on Exanceastre, Cht. Crw. 9, 130.

**burhrest** = (?) būr-rest *a bed in a separate chamber* (?). Cf. būr (I): —Ðonne þū burhreste haban wille, þonne wege þū þīne fȳst swilce þū wyrta cnocian wille, and lege þīnne scytefinger tō þīnum welerum, Tech. ii. 125, 23.

**būr-land, es;** *n. Land occupied by peasants* (? v. -būr):—Ðā landgemǽro ðæses būrlandes tō Abbendūne, Cht. E. 384, 25. Cf. geneátland.

**burn.** *Add:*—Burna woegas *rivulorum tramites*, Mt. p. 2, 9. Cf. On Winterburne, C. D. iii. 32, 28.

**burna.** *Add:*—Burna *latex*, Wrt. Voc. ii. 52, 10. On sumere stōwe wæs getācnod swilce fordrūwod burna ... þā sceát heó inn on þone burnan, Hml. S. 23 b, 197: 740. On þone burnan þe scýt tō culan fenne, andlang þæs burnan, ... andlang heges þe scýt of ðām burnan, C. D. iii. 458, 7–10. v. cweorn-, winter-burna.

**burne.** *Add:*—Burne *latex*, Wrt. Voc. ii. 112, 39: An. Ox. 1714: *fons*, Kent. Gl. 633. Ondlong ðǽre burnan, C. D. iii. 32, 29. Hē eóde tō þǽre burnan *accessit ad torrentem*, Bd. 1, 7; Sch. 24, 6. In ðā burnan, C. D. iii. 33, 8. v. wæter-, wǽde-burne.

**burn-stōw, e;** *f.*?:—Andlang burnstōwæ, C. D. iii. 175, 34. On ðā burnstōwæ; of ðǽre burnstōwæ, 176, 10.

**-būrod.** v. ā-būrod.

**burse, an;** *f. A bag, pouch:*—Bursan (burse, lxxiv, 28) *marsem* (=*marsupium*), Lch. i. lxxii, 4. [*O. L. Ger.* bursa: *O. H. Ger.* burissa *cassidile.* v. *N. E. D.* burse.]

**būr-þegen.** *Add:*—Būrþen *camerarius*, Wrt. Voc. ii. 127, 80. Būrþenon (hē becwiþ) his beddreáf, Cht. Crw. 23, 30.

**burþre.** *l. A mother.* v. byrþre: but. v. būc.

**būta** *unless. Add:*—Ne bið hit bletsung būta hē wyrce tācn, Hml. S. 27, 152.

**būtan.** *Add:* **A. prep. I. with dat.** (1) *outside of,* (a) local :— þā men þe hié foran forrīdan mehton būtan geweorce, Chr. 894; P. 88,

11. Būtan fæstenne gefeohtan, Ors. 4, 5; S. 168, 22, 2. Þætte nān būton þǽre gesomnunga ne sié, Bt. 24, 4; F. 86, 3. Þ good būton himselfum ... þ gōd oninnan himselfum, 37, 2; F. 188, 23. Þā eálond ūt on gārsecge būtan Breotone *insulas ultra Brittaniam in oceano*, Bd. 1, 3; Sch. 15. 6. Hē ne mihte būton ðām hrōfe ācuman, Hml. Th. ii. 184, 12. (b) in reference to state, condition, *free from, not in a state of:*—All Angelcynn þæt būton Deniscra monna hæftniéde wæs, Chr. 886; P. 80, 12. Þæm þe þeówdōme wǽron, Ors. 2, 4; S. 72, 7. (2) *without, free from, not provided with:*—Būtan ǽnigre hǽse *abs quolibet jussu*, Ælfc. Gr. Z. 271, 14. Būton geswince ic sitte hēr *sine labore hic sedeo*, būtan leahtre *sine crimine*, būtan ōgan hē hine gerest *absque terrore quiescit*, būtan twýnunge *absque ambiguitate*, 272, 10–13. Būton ælmessan and fæstenne lifian, Bl. H. 41, 32. Būton mete and drence, 57, 10. On ānum bāte būtan ǽlcum gerēþrum, Chr. 891; P. 82, 19. Agustuses lādteówas būton Agustuse selfum, Ors. 5, 15; S. 250, 8. (3) *except,* (all, none) *but* :—Þæs ōþres folces þone mǽstan dǽl hié him tō gecirdon būton þām cyninge Ælfrēde, Chr. 878; P. 74, 28. Hié wǽron simle healfe æt hām, healfe ūte, būtan þǽm monnum þe þā burga healdan scolden, 894; P. 84, 32. Ymbe .xli. wintra būtan ānre niht, 941; P. 110, 9. Ealle ofslagene wǽron būton feáwum, Ors. 4, 6; S. 178, 30. Hit nā næs on ðǽm dagum būton gewinne *there was nothing but fighting in those days*, 3, 10; S. 138, 19. (4) *besides, in addition to:*—Tōforan ðǽm oðde būtan þām *praeter illa*, Ælfc. Gr. Z. 270, 10. Mid allra ōðerra priústa būtan ðissum mæsseprióstum efen .lx., Cht. Th. 72, 3. Hē ofslōh mā þoune .xxx. gōdera þegena būtan ōðrum folce, Chr. 1052; P. 178, 19. Syx hund manna būtan þǽm þe hié mid heora wǽpnum ācwealdon, Bl. H. 203, 29. ¶ būtan þām þe *besides* :— Wurdon .viiii. folcgefeoht gefohten, and būtan þām þe Ælfrēd and ānlīpig aldormon oft rāde onridon þe mon nā ne rīmde, Chr. 871; P. 72, 13. Hē hæfde ealle Asiam on his geweald ...; būtan þǽm þe hē eác fōr mid gefeohtum on Sciððie, Ors. 1, 2; S. 30, 2. (5) *notwithstanding, in spite of, for all* (that) :—Þurcyl beád metsunga tō þām here ..., and būton þām (for eallon þām, *v. l.*) hī hergodan, Chr. 1013; P. 144, 10. Būton eallum þisum yfelum se cyning hēt gyldan þām here .xxi. þūsend punda, 1014; P. 145, 25. **II. with acc.** (1) *outside :*—Hē āwearp þ līc ūt būton þone weall, Gr. D. 198, 11. (2) *except,* (nothing) *but* (cf. **C. III.** 1):—Eal hē þ for Godes lufan sealde būton ðone dæghwāmlican andleofan ānne, Bl. H. 213, 19. Þeáh hit ne sȳ būtan feorðan dǽl hlāfes, Wlfst. 238, 27. **B.** *adv., or without following case.* (1) *outside:*—Hié genāmon ceápes eall þæt þǽr būton wæs, Chr. 894; P. 88, 10. Nǽre hit nō þ hēhste gōd, gif him ǽnig būton wǽre, Bt. 24, 1; F. 80, 15. Ge on hiora hīrēde ge būton, 29, 2; F. 104, 30. Hē hwearf æfter wegum ge būton geond þone wudu, Bl. H. 199, 13. (2) *without :*—Hié him tō getióð ðæt, ðætte hié eáðe būtan bión meahton, Past. 293, 18. Ðās bēc sceal hē nēde habban, and hē ne mæg būtan beón, Ll. Th. ii. 350, 16. Forlǽt hē þ scyp standan, for þām him þincð þ hē mæge ǽð būtan faran þonne mid, Shrn. 175, 13. **C.** *conjunction.* **I. with subj.** (1) *unless, except, if ... not :*—Būton Drihten gehealde þā burh *nisi Dominus custodierit civitatem*, Ælfc. Gr. Z. 262, 13. Būton (būta, L. R.) God beó mid him ... būton hwā beó edniwan gecenned *nisi fuerit Deus cum eo ... nisi quis natus fuerit denuo*, Jn. 3, 2, 3. Būton him geholpen weorðe, Past. 251, 18. Him þæt tō lytel yfel þūhte, būton hié hié þæs naman benāme, Ors. 2, 8; S. 94, 3: Bl. H. 37, 17: 43, 18. Ne bideþ hē æt ūs nǽnig oþor edleán, būton þ wē ūrne līchoman and ūre sāule unwemme him āgeofan, 103, 21. Hwæt mǽnde hit elles, būton þ wē gefyllon þæs þearfan wambe?, 39, 29. Ic wēne þ ic þē up āhōfe ... būton þū git tō full sȳ þæs þe lǽfed is, Bt. 11, 1; F. 30, 19. Būton hē gelȳfde þ hī ārīsan sceoldon, elles hē offrode on īdel, Hml. S. 25, 473. (2) *if only :*—Ne rōhtan hī hū synlīce hit wǽre begytan, būton hit cōme tō heom *did it but come to them*, Chr. 1086; P. 218, 11. **II. with indic.** (1) *except, but* (that), *if ... not :*—Būton þū woldest, ne cōme ðū *ni uelles, non uenisses*, Ælfc. Gr. Z. 262, 11. Hē wæs swīþe yfel monn ealra þeáwa, būton þ hē wæs cēne, Ors. 6, 14; S. 268, 27. Būton þ hē wið his hlāford won, 6, 35; S. 292, 16. Hwæt magon wē secgean, būton þ hī scotedon swīþe?, Chr. 1083; P. 215, 16: Bl. H. 19, 22. Nōht elles ne wunað, būton þ ān þ sē mæg hine sylfne lǽran, 101, 5. Næfde hé nōht on hire, būton þ ān þ heó hæfde mennisce onlīcnesse, 147, 15. Ymb twēntig wintra his rīces, būtan ān ðǽgyt næs gefylled *anno regni sui uicesimo necdum impleto*, Bd. 5, 5; Sch. 648, 19. (2) *adversative, but*:—Ne gēmdon hié nānes fyrenlustes, būton swīþe gemetlīce þā gecynd beeódan, Bt. 15; F. 48, 7. Ic ne girnde rīces, būton ic wilnod þeáh andweorces, 17; F. 58, 25. Ic nāt hūmeta, būton wē witon þ hit unmennislic dǽd wæs, 31, 1; F. 112, 16. Næs nān færeld tō Rōme, būton twēgen hleáperas Ælfred sende mid gewritum, Chr. 889; P. 82, 5. Ealle þā witan gefeóllan of ānre upflōran, būtan se hālga Dūnstān ætstōd, 978; P. 123, 2. (2 a) introducing the answer to a question, where the first clause is not expressed :—Ac hwonon wurde þū þus swīþe geswenced? Būton ic wāt þ þū ... hæfst tō hraþe forgiten, Bt. 3, 1; F. 4, 21. Hē ongan þā cnyhtas tō āxienne, for hwig þ folc þone Hǽlend swā yfele hæfde. Hig andswaredon : 'Būton hig habbaþ andan tō hym,'

Nic. 4, 18. 'Hwæt hæfð hē gedōn ꝥ hē sweltan scyle?' Hig sædon: 'Būton for þām þe hē sæde ꝥ hē Godes sunu wære,' 5, 36.　　**III.** without dependent verb (cf. Bl. H. 147, 15 under II. 1). (1) (*any, few*) *but* (cf. A. II. 2):—Hira feáwa onweg cōmon, būton þā āne þe ūt ætswummon, Chr. 918; P. 98, 30. Litel rihtwísnesse wæs mid ǣnige men, būton mid munecan āne, 1086; P. 218, 8. (2) after a negative clause, (*none, nothing*) *but* (cf. *nobbut* in dialects); ne ... būtan *but, only, not more than*:—Næfde ic nǣnne hiht on ōðerne næfre būton on ðe *spem in alium numquam habui, praeter in te*, Ælfc. Gr. Z. 270, 12. Næs gemētt sē ðe āgēnhwurfe, būton (būta, L. R. *nisi*) þes ælfremeda, Lk. 17, 18. Nis nān man gōd, būton God āna, 18, 19. Hié nǣron on hié hergende būton þríe dagas, Ors. 2, 8; S. 94, 1 : 3, 7; S. 120, 14. Ne mehte mon būton feáwa ofslagenra geāhsian *vix unquam requiri, qui perierit*, 2, 8; S. 94, 12. Hē wolde gewin findan, ac hē ne mehte būton sibbe, 6, 3; S. 256, 30. Hē næs būton seofontiéne-wintre, 4, 9; S. 190, 29. Nolde hē nā andswerian būton mid mon-þwǣrnesse, Bl. H. 33, 29. Nis nǣnig man ꝥ þurfe gesēcan, būton þā, 103, 16: 185, 9. Ðā gebrōðra næfdon būton fíf hlāfas, Hml. Th. ii. 170, 34. (2 a) after a comparative, *than, but*:—Nān man mā wísa nǣbbe būton .i., Ll. Th. ii. 300, 13. ꝥ ic ne þorfte nā māre āwendan þǣre béc būton tō Isaace, Ælfc. Gen. Thw. 1, 8. (3) after interrogative clause, (*who, what*) *but*:—Hwæt wæs seó ræste elles būton se hālga innoð?, Bl. H. 11, 20 : 59, 27. Hwylc bið hē būton swylce stān?, 21, 26. Hwæt is ðis líf būton weg?, Hml. Th. i. 614, 1. Tō hwæm cumaþ hī elles būtan tō tācnunge sorges?, Bt. 7, 2; F. 18, 21. Hwæt gelýfeþ se líchoma būtan þurh þā sāwle?, Bl. H. 21, 22. v. on-būtan; be-ūtan.

**butere.** *Add:*—Gemeng wið ferscre buteran, Lch. ii. 74, 21. On-legena geworhte of butran, 244, 20. Drincan āmylte buteran, 106, 3. Gif þū buteran habban wylle, þonne stríc þū mid þrím fingrum on þíne innewearde hand, Tech. ii. 123, 22. Hí ðicgað on ðām earde (*Italy*) ele on heora bigleofum, swā swā wē dōð buteran, Hml. Th. ii. 178, 18. v. cū-butere.

**buter-flége** (-fleóge). *Add:*—Buterflíege, buturflíógae, -fii[ó]go *papilio*, Txts. 85, 1507.

**buterian.** v. ge-buterod.

**buteruc.** *Add:*—Næfdon hí nān wín būton on ānum gewea+ dan butruce ... wæs se buteruc brerdful wínes, Hml. S. 6, 274–282. Sum man sende twégen butrucas mid wíne (cf. twā treówene fatu fulle wínes, on folcisc flascan gehātene *vino plena duo lignea vascula, quae vulgo flascones vocantur*, Gr. D. 141, 25), Hml. Th. ii. 170, 13.

**butsa-carlas.** Substitute: **butse-carl** (butsa-), es ; *m. A seaman.* ['The "butsecarls" stand in the same relation to the "scip-fyrd" that the housecarls occupy towards the "land-fyrd"; *i. e.* they are the king's standing force, as opposed to the national levies. This seems clear from a passage in Domesday: "quando Rex ibat in expeditione uel terra uel mari, habebat de hoc burgo aut .xx. solidos ad pascendos *suos buzecarlos*, aut unum homimem ducebat secum pro honore .v. hidarum."' Chr. P. ii. 239.]:—Þā butsecarlas (butsa-, *v.l.*) hine forsōcan, Chr. 1066; P. 197, 8. Hē nam of þām butsekarlon sume mid him, P. 196, 7. Hē gespeón him tō ealle þā butsecarlas (-karlas) of Hæstingan, 1052 ; P. 178, 25. [v. *N. E. D.* bus-carl, buss: *Icel.* buza *a kind of ship.*]

**buttuc**, es ; *m. A small butt* (? *butt*, a provincial term applied to such ridges as run out short at the sides of the field. A small parcel of land is often called the *butts*, v. *N. E. D.*):—Of ðām heáfdon on ðæne weg ; of ðām wege on ðā buttucas; of ðām buttucon on ðonebróc, C.D.iv.19,32.

**būtū.** *Add:*—Būtū binas, Wrt. Voc. ii. 126, 24.

**bȳ;** *n.? Add:* The Danish form *bȳr* is *m. Bȳ* in local names is found in Baddan-, Bad-, Bē-, Kirk-bȳ. v. C. D. vi.

**bȳa.** v. būan.

**bycgan.** *Add:* **I.** *to buy goods:*—Hwā bigþ hí?, Coll. M. 23, 25. Bege eme, Kent. Gl. 895. Þte metto bochton, Jn. L. 4, 8.　　**II.** in reference to marriage:—Be ðon ðe mon wíf bycgge, Ll. Th. i. 122, 3.　　**III.** *to hire* workmen:—Bycgæ wyrhta *conducere operarios*, Mt. R. 20, 1.

**bycgend,** es ; *m. A buyer:*—Beccen *emptor*, Kent. Gl. 738.

**bycgen(n), bȳcn-, bycera, -bycgung, bȳd.** v. bygen, bícn-, beó-cere, be-bycgung, beódan.

**byd?,** byd-incel?:—Andlang brōces on Bydincel, of Bydincele ... of thām forda on thā ealdan byd, andlang byd ... of thām hamme on Byd, andlang Byd, C. D. B. iii. 44, 24–38. On bydyncel ... ðæt on byd, C. D. iii. 81, 5–7.

**bȳdel.** *l.* bydel, *and add:* **I.** *a herald:*—Hē sende bydelas and beád eallum þām here *transierunt praecones per castrorum medium et clamare coeperunt*, Jos. 3, 2.　　**II.** *a beadle.* v. Andrews' Old English Manor, pp. 142–3:—Bydel gēd ætforan dēman, Hml. Th. i. 354, 34: Shrn. 95, 14. Hēte þū (*Pilate*) þynne bydel hym swā ongeán cuman?, Nic. 2, 15. Bydelum *exactoribus*, Wrt. Voc. ii. 30, 43. Sende se cāsere his bydelas and beád ꝥ man sceolde cēpan crístenra manna, Hml. S. 23, 47. [*O. L. Ger.* budil.]

**bydel-æcer,** es ; *m. Land allotted to a* bydel (cf. Bydele gebyreð sum

A.-S. SUPPL.

landstycce for his geswince, Ll. Th. i. 440, 7):—On ðæne bydelæcer, of ðām bydelæcere, C. D. vi. 152, 31.

**byden.** *Add:*—Bydin (-en) *cupa*, Txts. 52, 260. Byden *doleus*, Wrt. Voc. ii. 98, 6: *doleum*, 26, 24: i. 291, 6: *bunia*, ii. 102, 35: 11, 42: 126, 75: *cuba*, i. 34, 24. Wæs sum oferwrigen byden (*dolium*) eles æmtig ... ongan ꝥ wrigels þære bydene beón upp āhafen, Gr. D. 160, 9–12. Site on bydene ... geót on þā bydene, læt reócan on, Lch. ii. 76, 22–24: 78, 20. Eleberigan dön on bydene (*praelo*), Gr. D. 50, 30. Bydno *hydriae*, Jn. L. 2, 6. Bydena *cuparum*, An. Ox. 4, 60. Bydenum *cupis*, Wrt. Voc. ii. 47, 62. Bydena *cupas*, An. Ox. 17, 35. Ealle þā wínfatu and ealle þa bydenu (-a, *v.l.*) *cuncta vini vascula omnia-que dolia*, Gr. D. 57, 28. [*O. L. Ger.* budin. From *Lat.* butina.] v. beór-, breóst-, wæter-byden ; bydenestre.

**bydenestre.** v. glíw-bydenestre : **bydincel.** v. byd.

**byden-fæt,** es ; *n. A bushel, barrel:*—Hwēne wíddre þonne bydenfæt, Bl. H. 127, 6. VI. bidenfate and þrý trogas, C. D. B. iii. 367, 38.

**bȳdla,** an ; *m. A cultivator, worshipper:*—Sē ðe Gode bȳdla is (bȳdle, ꝥ is ðē ðe God wordias, L.) *qui Dei cultor est*, Jn. R. 9, 31. Cf. būan.

**bȳed, bȳencg, bȳend, bȳgan, byge.** v. un-bȳed, bȳing, būend, bígan, bige.

**byge.** *l.* byge, *and add:* **I.** of shape or direction:—Byge *sinus*, Wrt. Voc. ii. 120, 65. Andlanges ānre furh oð hit cymð tō ānum byge ; ðanone of ðæm byge, C. D. v. 153, 31. Tō ðære díce byge, 298, 12. On ðone byge ; of ðām byge, vi. 1, 20 : 2, 4. Sete þíne hand on earmes byge, Tech. ii. 128, 14. Bigum *anfractibus*, An. Ox. 3696. Wrǣda bíum *fasciarum ambagibus*, 3500. Hit bið drifen on swíðe nearwe bygeas, Past. 59, 6.　　**II.** of movement (lit. or fig.):—Bigas *circuitus*, Wülck. Gl. 232, 41. Se hara bígde gelóme, þóhte mid þāu bigum æterstan þām deáðe, Hml. S. 31, 1059. Hē gedyde bigeas (-ias, *v.l.*) and fleám, Gr. D. 122, 24.　　**III.** *something bent:*—Under býcnunge ðæs ēcan biges (beáges, *v.l.*) *sub figura coronae perpetis*, Bd. 5, 22 ; Sch. 682, 6. Hyrdle, bige *plecta*, An. Ox. 3888. [*Icel.* bugr.] v. fram-byge.

**bygen;** *f. Buying, purchase:*—On hernumena bygenum, Ll. Th. ii. 328, 11. v. gebed-bygen.

**byht** [cf. *būgan*]. *Add:*—Ðēr sæ díc ūtt scætt æt ðām bihtæ, C. D. v. 74, 2. On heges byhte ; of ðām byhte, iii. 419, 16. [*The poetical passages should be taken separately under* byht = *habitation, abode.* Cf. būan.]

**bȳing.** *Add:*—Bȳencgum *habitaculis*, Rtl. 123, 7. v. un-bȳing.

**bȳl.** *Add:* bȳle, an (?) ; bȳl, e (?) ; *f.:*—Wearte *vel* bȳl *furunculus*, Wrt. Voc. ii. 151, 75. Wearte, bȳle *frunculus (furunculus?* -*os?*), 34. Gif bȳl on men gebersteð, Lch. ii. 94, 24. Bȳlas *carbunculi*, Wrt. Voc. ii. 128, 56. Bȳlum *bullis*, 89, 47. On þǣre lifre bȳlum, Lch. ii. 204, 24. [*O. L. Ger.* būla ; *wk. f. struma.*] v. lifer-, wen-bȳl.

**bȳld** (-u, -o), **byldan** *to embolden.* v. bildu, bildan.

**byldan;** *p.* de To build, fence (?):—Onbūton ðone croft ðe Wynstān bylde ; on ðā díc ðe hē gedícte, C. D. iii. 367, 6. Tō werbolde ān fōðer gyrdo, oððe .viii. geocu byld, 451, 1. v. bylda, bold.

**bylg(e)an** *to bellow. Add:*—Hwílum ðā deófol hine bylgedon on swā fearras and ðuton swā wulfas, Shrn. 52, 29.

**bȳlihte;** *adv. In an ulcerous condition:*—Gif men bílyhte sié ymb þone þearm, Lch. ii. 170, 28.

**bȳme, bȳmian, byrc, byrce** *barking,* **Byrcingas.** v. bíme, bíman, beorc, birce, Bercingas.

**byrd,** e ; *f.* **I.** *birth:*—Gemildsa mē nacodum, forlidenum, næs nā of earmlicum birdum geborenum, Ap. Th. 11, 20. [*O. H. Ger.* burt.] v. læt-, lam-, mis-, sweart-byrd.　　**II.** *bearing.* v. ende-, for-, fore-, mund-, stefn-byrd.

**byrd,** e ; *f. A burden:*—Hē hæfde strengðe tō ādreóganne þā byrde, Gr. D. 215, 1. [*O. H. Ger.* burti *onus: Icel.* byrðr: *Goth.* baurþei.]

**byrdan** *to embroider.* [*Icel.* byrða.] v. be-, ge-byrdan ; borda.

**byrde.** *Add:* v. būr-, efen-, in-, þeów-, unge-byrde.

**byrdestre,** an ; *f. An embroideress:*—Byrdistrae *blaciarius, primicularius* (cf. *primicula, ornatus uestimentorum* borda, Hpt. 33, 247, 105), Txts. 109, 1153.

**byrdicge.** Substitute: *An embroideress.* Cf. byrdestre : **byrdig.** v. fore-byrdig.

**byrding,** e ; *f. Embroidering:*—Byrdingc *plumaria*, Wrt. Voc. i. 66, 22. v. byrdan.

**byrdling,** es ; *m. A tortoise:*—Byrdlingc *testudo*, An. Ox. 23, 21. Cf. bord.

**byre** *a son. Add:*—Eádweard cing ... byre Æðelrēdes, Chr. 1065 ; P. 193, 33.

**byre** *a time, season. l.* byre, *and add:*—Ǣr þām byre, þe hē wite eal, Wlfst. 123, 5. Oð ðone byre, þe hí God āwehte, Hml. S. 23, 336.

**byre;** *m. A strong wind, storm:*—Byre *aestu* (cf. ȳst), Germ. 400, 496. [v. *N. E. D.* birr. *Icel.* byrr *a favourable wind.*]

**bȳre,** es ; *m. A byre, shed, hovel:*—Bȳre *mapalia, magalia*, Txts. 77, 1292, 1294. Bȳrae *magalia*, 115, 155. Bȳre *vel* sceápheorden *magalia vel mappalia vei capanna*, Wrt. Voc. i. 58, 31. Of mearcwille on duddes bȳre, of duddes bȳre on þone clofenan beorh, Cht. E. 293, 26. [*Cealc-*

I

bȳras, C. D. i. 140, 14. Crangabȳras, wihtherincfaladstô, 248, 18. Aet Crangabȳrum, 216, 28.] v. cū-bȳre.

**byrele**, es; *m. Add*: byrele, an; *f.*:—Æt þām cnihte þe wæs þæs bisceopes byrele (byrle, *v. l.*) *the bishop's cupbearer*, Gr. D. 186, 22. Be đām byrle þe đone apostol eárplætte, Hml. Th. ii. 520, 13. Ælcan gesettan discđegne and gesettan biriele, C. D. B. iii. 75, 30. Gif wiđ eorles birele man geligeđ ... wiđ ceorles birelan, Ll. Th. i. 6, 11, 13. Hêt hê þone byrle beôdon Martine ǽrest, Hml. S. 31, 632. Đǽm birilum *ministris*; *the servants who bore the wine*, Jn. L. 2, 5. [v. *N. E. D.* birle.] v. wîn-byrele.

**byrelian**. *Add*: [v. *N. E. D.* birle. *Icel.* byrla.]: byren. v. biren.

**byres**, e; *f. A borer, chisel*:—Buiris *foratorium*, Txts. 35, 11. Byris, byrs *scalprum, scalpellum*, 94, 891, 907. Byres *faratorium*, Wrt. Voc. ii. 147, 47: *boratorium*, 11, 60: i. 287, 8. Byre[s] *baratorium*, 11. 125, 26. Hê sceal habban adsan, bil, byrse, scafan, Angl. ix. 263, 1. [*O. H. Ger.* bursa *scalprum*.]

**byrga**. *Substitute*: *A surety, bail*, and add:—Byrga (-ea) *presetuas*, Txts. 89, 1652: *sequester*, 97, 1840. Byrgea *sequestra*, Wrt. Voc. ii. 78, 42: 83, 40. Byrga *creditor*, 15, 50. [*O. L. Ger.* bur(i)go: *O. H. Ger.* burgeo *fiuejussor, sponsor*.]

**byrgan** *to bury*. *Add*: v. un-byrged: bȳrgan *to taste*. *l.* byrgan, *and see* birgan: **byrg(e)an** *to save*. v. be-byrg(e)an: byrgedness. v. ge-byrgedness.

**byrgels**. *Add*:—Ođ đone hêđenan byrgels, C. D. iii. 421, 35. In hǽđenan byrigels, 380, 24. On đâ hǽđenan byrigelsas; đonne of đâm byrgelsum, 407, 2. Byrgelsum *bustis*, Wrt. Voc. ii. 90, 2: 12, 6.

**byrgels-leóþ**, es; *n. An epitaph*:—Bergelsleóþ ł [bergels] sang *epitaphion, carmen super tumulum*, Hpt. Gl. 427, 71.

**byrgels-sang**, es; *m.* **I.** *a dirge*:—Wôpleóþ, lícsang, byrielssang *tragoediam*, i. *luctum*, An. Ox. 3504. **II.** *an epitaph*. v. preceding word.

**byrgen**. *Add*: es; *n.* **I.** *a burial-place*:—Byrgen *murilium*, Wrt. Voc. ii. 114, 43. Byrigen *monumentum vel sepulchrum*, i. 85, 77. Seó hefige byrþen þǽre byrgenne, Bl. H. 75, 8. Tô þǽre hâlgan byrigene, Hml. S. 7, 291. Nyman of þâm byrgene þone arceb, Chr. 1023; P. 156, 10. Ferede man âues cnihtes líc tô byrgene, Hml. Th. i. 490, 31. Of đǽm byrgenne *de monumento*, Jn. L. 20, 2. Tô đǽm byrgenne *ad monumentum*, 3. Âne tôbrocene byrgenne, swelce hiera þeáw wæs þæt mon rícum monnum busan eorđan of stânum worhte *sepulchrum dirutum*, Ors. 4, 10; S. 202, 4. Ofer ryhtwísra monna byrgenne *super sepulturam justi*, Past. 327, 2. Byrgenu openodon, Hml. Th. ii. 258, 4. Gif man openađ deáddra manna byrgynu, i. 256, 15. Ne fyllađ hié nô hûs, ac byrgenna (*tumulos*), Past. 383, 36. **II.** *burial*:—'þú gesettest ealle þíne apostolas tô mínre byrgenne' ... Heó þǽm apostolum æteówde ealne hire gegyrelan þe heó wolde æt hire byrgenne habban, Bl. H. 143, 29–36. Be his lífe and be his forđfóre and be his byr(i)genne (*sepultura*), Bd. 4, 3; Sch. 348, 14.

**byrgen-leóþ**. *Add*:—Byrgenleóđ *epitaphion*, Wrt. Voc. ii. 31, 3. v. byrg-leóþ.

**byrgen-song**. *Substitute*: byrgen-sang, es; *m. An epitaph, a dirge*:—Byrieusang *epitaphion*, i. *carmen mortuorum*, An. Ox. 902: 2, 20. v. byrg-sang.

**byrgen-stôw**. *Add*:—Byrgenstôwe *cimiterio*, Wrt. Voc. ii. 85, 32: 18, 60. Hit becôm tô Rôme and tô Scê Petres byrgenstôwe, Wlfst. 231, 30.

**byrgere**. *Add*:—Dorh buyrgeras *per vispellones*, Txts. 86, 760. Byrgeras, Wrt. Voc. ii. 68, 1.

**byrging**. *Dele* Jn. 20, 1, 4 Lye, *and add*:—Be Crístes líce and his byrgenge, Angl. xi. 173, 14. v. be-byrging.

**byrging**. *l.* byrging, *and see* birging.

**byrg-leóþ** (byrig-), es; *n. An epitaph, a dirge*:—Byrgleóđ *carmen funebre*, Hpt. Gl. 427, 63. Byregleóþ *epichedieon*, An. Ox. 901. *Epicedion* lícleóđ, *epitaphion* byrigleóđ, *utrumque est carmen super tumulum*, Wrt. Voc. ii. 76, 78. v. byrgen-leóþ.

**byrgness**. v. byrignes *in Dict.*: **byrgness** *tasting*. v. birguess.

**byrg-sang** (byrig-), es; *m. A dirge*:—Birisang *tragoediam, luctum*, Hpt. Gl. 488, 57. v. byrgen-sang.

**bȳrian** *to happen*. *l.* bȳrian *to taste*. *l.* byrian. v. birgan: **byrig** *tumba* (An. Ox. 4346; Hpt. Gl. 507, 66) = byrigen *or* byrigels: **byrig** (cf. byri-weard) *a city*. *Dele* e; *f. acc. s.* byrige. In the earlier MS. of the Chron. the form *burg* occurs in the passages; in the later the mutated form seems to have made its way into the nominative and accusative.

**byrig** *a mulberry tree?* In Ps. Spl. 77, 52 has the glosser read *muros?* or *moras?* (mora *mansio, habitatio*, Migne): in Lch. ii. 274, 17 *byrig eolonan* might be a compound?

**byrig-**, **byris**, **byrla**, **byrle**, **byrnan**. v. byrg-, byres, birla, byrele, birnan.

**byrne** *a corslet*. *Add*:—Byrne *lorica vel torax vel squama*, Wrt. Voc. i. 35, 6: *thoraca*, ii. 86, 81. Hringedu byrne *lorica hamata* (anata, MS.), 51, 37. Byrne gileúfes *lorica fidei*, Rtl. 28, 31. Byrnan

*thoracis*, Wrt. Voc. ii. 96, 25. Biđ se Pater Noster on heofonlicre byrnan onlícnisse, Sal. K. 146, 6. Gewǽpnod, nâ mid reádum scylde, ođđe mid hefegum helme, oþþe heardre byrnan, Hml. Th. ii. 502, 13. Gegyrede heó hȳ mid hǽrenre tunecan and mid byrnan, þ is mid lytelre hacelan, Shrn. 140, 30. Hê geann his ađume twêgra byrnena, Cht. Crw. 23, 16. [*O. L. Ger.* brunnia.] v. brynige.

**byrn-sweord**. v. birn-sweord: **byrn-wíga**, -wígende; *part. l.* byrn-wiga, -wígend, es; *m.*: **byrs**. v. byres.

**byrst** *a bristle*. *Substitute*: e; *f.*, *in passage from* Lch. *read* swínen ... *bristle, and add*:—Byrst *seta*, An. Ox. 51, 1. Brysti *setes*, Txts. 109, 1132. Manu, brystae (biriste, Hpt. 33, 244, 5) *juba, setes porci et leonis cabalique*, 110, 1182. Hí heora fíân him on âfæstnodon swâ þicce swylce íles byrsta, Hml. S. 5, 428 : 32, 118. Hê wæs đâra strǽla swâ full swâ igl biþ byrsta, Shrn. 55, 9. v. feþer-byrst.

**byrst** *loss*. *Add*: **I.** *injury*:—Se byrst wyrđ gemǽne, Wlfst. 159, 3. Fela byrsta (bersta), 157, 1 : 128, 4. **II.** *failure*. v. teám-byrst; cf. berstan, I. 2. **III.** *a crash*; cf. berstan, II :—Byrstum *creporibus*, Wrt. Voc. ii. 136, 83. [v. *N. E. D.* burst. *O. H. Ger.* brust.]

**byrstig**; *adj. Broken, rugged*:—Of byrstigum clúdum *preruptis cautibus*, An. Ox. 2037.

**byrþen**. *Add*:—Byrþen *sarcina*, Wülck. Gl. 257, 5. **I.** literal, (1) *material carried, a load*:—Ân bryþen mealtes, Shrn. 159, 7. Âne byrđene wudes, Cht. Th. 606, 15. Him læg onuppan fela byrđena eorđan, Hml. S. 12, 57. Heáwađ incre byrđene gyrda, Hml. Th. i. 62, 34. Hê gesênode .ii. birþena gyrda, Shrn. 32, 20. (1 a) in contrast with carriage by an animal or in a vehicle:—Ælce lâde, ǽgđer ge on wǽne, ge on horse, ge on byrdene, Ll. Th. ii. 298, 23. (2) *an oppressive weight*:—Seó hefige byrþen siteþ on þǽm deádan líchoman þǽre byrgenne, Bl. H. 75, 7. **II.** figurative, (1) in a favourable sense:—þurh þâ gife đæs Hâlgan Gâstes byrþenne, Bl. H. 135, 7. (2) of what is difficult or troublesome:—Seó unârǽsnedlice byrþen synna, Bl. H. 75, 9. Hefig byrđæn, Dôm. L. 28, 20. Be đǽre byrđenne (*pondere*) đæs reccendômes, Past. 33, 4. Hê bierđ đâ byrđenne (*pondus*) hira scylda, 153, 7. þâ myclan byrþenne þǽre mycclan langunga, Bl. H. 135, 7. Gebîgđ đæt folc hira hrycg tô hefegum byrđenum mauegum *ad portanda peccatorum onera*, Past. 29, 17. Hié underlútađ mid hira sculdrum ôđerra byrđenna *humerum opprimendus ponderibus submittit alienis*, 53, 1. (2 a) *a charge*:—Sê đe bryđene underfêhđ, and þ gecwême ne dêđ, Cht. Th. 606, 18. [*O. H. Ger.* burdin.] v. ge-byrþen.

**byrþen-mete**. *Substitute*: byrþen-mǽte; *adj. Burdensome*:—Byrđenmête *oncrosa*, Kent. Gl. 1011.

**byrþen-stân**, es; *m. A mill-stone*:—Asales byrđenstân *mola asinaria*, Mt. L. 18, 6.

**byrþestre**, an; *f. A female bearer*:—Berþestra *gerula, portatrix*, Hpt. Gl. 498, 18.

**byrþling**, es; *m. A carrier*:—Berþling *gerulum*, An. Ox. 4922.

**byrþra**. v. wudu-byrþra.

**byrþre**, an; *f. One who bears a child, a mother*:—Đurh đâ byrþran (burþran, *v. l.*) (Scā Marian) wê wǽron gehǽlede, and þurh þæt gebyrđor wê wurdon âlýsede, Wlfst. 251, 13. v. burþre *in Dict.*

**byrþ-þignenu**, -þínen, e; *f. A midwife*:—Byrđđínenu *obstetrix*, Germ. 392, 97. Gif wífmen hwæt swylces derige, dô hyre man fram hyre byrþþínene þone sylfan lǽcedôm, Lch. i. 236, 4.

**bȳsen** (*l.* bysen), **bȳsgian** (*l.* bysgian), **bysm**, **bysmer**, **bȳsting**, es; *m.* (*l.* e; *f.*). v. bisen, bisgian, besma, bismer, bîsting.

**byt**. *Add*: ; bytte, an [? cf. *Lat.* butta (buttam plenam, Cht. E. 119, 1)]:—Geworden ic eam swâ swâ bytte (*uter*), Ps. L. 118, 83. Æren byt *lenticula*, Wrt. Voc. i. 25, 17. Trȳwen byt *flasco*, ii. 149, 34. Bytte hlid *cordias*, 135, 80. Líchoma tôblâwen on ânre bytte gelícnysse, Hml. S. 31, 952. On bitte *in utre*, Ps. Spl. 77, 16. Swilce man siwige âne bytte, Hml. S. 34, 317. Trinnu ( = trîwenu?) byttæ *flasce, eadem et flascones*, Wrt. Voc. ii. 39, 78. In byttum aldum *in utres veteres*, Mk. L. 2, 22. [*Lat.* buttis. v. *N. E. D.* bit.] v. ele-, treów-byt.

**byþne**, **bȳtl**. v. bytme, bîtel: **bȳtla**. *l.* bytla, *and dele bracket*.

**bȳtlian**. *l.* bytlian, *and add*:—Wer þe ofer fæstum stâne bytlode, R. Ben. 4, 12. Man bytlode âne gebytla, Hml. Th. ii. 354, 32. 'Đâ synfullan bytledon uppe on mínum hrycge.' Hê sârette đætte hié sceoldon bytlan, Past. 153, 9. Hêt Harold bytlian on Brytlande, Chr. 1065; P. 190, 26. On sumor geneát sceal bytlian and burh hegegian, Ll. Th. i. 432, 15 : Angl. ix. 261, 10. Cf. botl, ge-bytlu.

**bytlung**. *Add*:—On þǽre bytlinge, Shrn. 164, 2. v. ge-byilung.

**bytme** (-ne), byþne, an; *f.* **I.** *the keel of a ship*:—Bythne *carina*, Wrt. Voc. ii.103, 5. Bytne, i3, 36. Bytme, i. 63, 39. Hí sǽton ufan on þǽm wætre swâ swâ scipes byđme (bytme dêđ, *v. l.*), þonne hit fleóted on streáme, Mart. H. 118, 20. Hê sæt ofer þǽre bytman þæs scipes, Gr. D. 347, 23. **II.** *the head of a dale*. Cf. *Icel.* botn:—On byttman díc, C. D. iv. 39, 7. On bitnan burnan, v. 84, 8. On đǽre dæne bytnan, 78, 12 : 137, 35. v. twi-bytme, botm.

**bytming**, e; *f. Ground-floor of the Ark*:—On đǽre nyđemystan bytminge wunodon þâ rêđan deór ... on đǽre bytminge wæs se arc rûm, Hml. Th. i. 536, 10–14.

**bytne.** v. bytme.

**bytt** a butt, piece of land?:—Innan Scrowes bytt, of Scrowes bytt betweox .ii. beorgas, C. D. iii. 85, 11. [v. N. E. D. butt (6).]

**býwan.** v. bîwan.

**byxen**; adj. Of box:—Sió bixne buxeus, Wrt. Voc. ii. 12, 21. v. bixen in Dict.

# C

**cac, cac-hûs, cæd.** Dele: cæfer-tûn. v. cafer-tûn.

**cæfester,** es; n.? Add:—Caebestr capistrum, Wrt. Voc. ii. 102, 72. Hælfter vel cæfster, 128, 45. Cæfester capisternum, 13, 27. [From Latin.]

**cæfian.** Add: v. ofer-cæfed.

**cæfing,** e; f. An ornament for the head:—Úplegen vel cæfing discriminale, Wrt. Voc. ii. 141, 1. Kævinge (printed -e; but v. Angl. viii. 450) redimicula, i. 16, 58. Eárpreónas, cæfinga discriminalia (capitum), hosebendas periscelides (crurum) (cf. discriminalia, capitis ornamentum, Corp. Gl. H. 44, 301), An. Ox. 4821 : 2, 389.

**cæfl** a bit, muzzle, gag:—Caefli capistro, Wrt. Voc. ii. 103, 48. Cæfli, 14, 11. [Cf. Icel. kefli a piece of wood, a gag. v. N. E. D. kevel.]

**cǽg.** For cǽge; f. l. cǽga; m., and add:—Cǽg clavis, Wrt. Voc. i. 81, 18. (1) lit.:—Se preóst nolde undón þa duru mid cǽge, Hml. S. 3, 484. Þæs wifes cǽglocan . . . þæra cǽgean (cǽgan, v. l.) heó sceal weardian, þ is hire hæddernes cǽge and hyre cyste cǽge and hire tǽgan, Ll. Th. ii. 418, 20. (2) fig.:—Ic ðē betǽce heofonan rîces cǽge.' Nis seó cǽig gylden, ne sylfren, ne of nânum antimbre gesmiðod, ac is se anweald þe him Crîst forgeaf, Hml. Th. i. 368, 35. Mid ðám unwemlican cǽgan virgineo clave, Wrt. Voc. ii. 91, 76. Wē rîmdon ðá cǽga (cǽgea, v. l.), wē ætiéwen hwæt hié healden, Past. 179, 11 : Wlfst. 176, 15.

**cǽg-bora.** Add: one who has charge of the keys of a jail, jailor:—Cǽgbora clavicularius, Wrt. Voc. i. 288, 45 : ii. 17, 11. Scs Heremus wæs cǽgbora in Rôme, Shrn. 121, 23. [Cf. N. E. D. key-bearer.] Cf. cǽg-hirde.

**cǽge.** l. cǽga. v. cǽg : cǽggian. Dele.

**cǽg-hyrde.** l. -hirde, and add:—Caeghiorde clavicularius, Wrt. Voc. ii. 104, 21. [Ðe heuenliche keiherde Sainte Peter, O. E. Hml. ii. 193, 16. Cf. N. E. D. key-keeper.] Cf. cǽg-bora.

**cǽg-loca.** Dele: 'The action . . . key-locking.' The cǽglocan in the passage are the repositories which the wife could lock up with keys (v. cǽg (1) supra); if the stolen property were not put into these, the keys of which were in her keeping, she was to be held guiltless.

**-cǽglod.** v. â-cǽglod : **cǽlan.** Dele: cǽle rostrum. v. cele : **cǽle** chill. v. cile : **cǽpe-hûs.** Dele the bracket.

**cæppe.** Add:—Placidus cwæð þæt hé gesáwe bufon his heáfde Benedictus cæppan (kæppan melotem, Gr. D. 116, 12), and him wæs geðúht þæt seó cæppe him átuge of ðám streáme, Hml. Th. ii. 160, 18. Hé geann Eádwine mæssepreóst his kæppan (cope), Cht. Crw. 23, 17. Se munuc bewand þone hreófsian mid his cæppan, Hml. Th. i. 336, 12. Sácerd, þonne hē mæssan singe, ne hæbbe hē on cæppan (cappam), Ll. Th. ii. 140, 9. Ðá dyde Albanus on hine þæs preóstes cæppan (caracallam, Bd. 1, 7), Shrn. 93, 31. Se bisceop brǽd of his cæppan (ceppan, v. l.), Hml. S. 31, 469 : 913. Þis synd þá mádmas þe Adeluuold bisceop sealde . . . þ is . . . iiii. cæppan, Cht. Th. 244, 6. Mid kæppum (cappis) gescrýdde, Angl. xiii. 427, 881. v. cantercæppe; cappa.

**cærse.** Add: cresse (-a):—Cressae (-a) sinapis, Txts. 96, 917. Cressa nasturcium, 108, 1121 : sinapiones, 109, 1133 : brittia, 45, 329. Cærse cardamon, Wrt. Voc. i. 32, 13 : 66, 68 : cresco, 79, 45. Kerse, 31, 23. Cærsan, An. Ox. 56, 414 : sinapdones (l. -iones?), Wrt. Voc. i. 68, 71. Ce[r]sena tâcen, Tech. ii. 123, 18. v. leác-, worþ-, worþig-cærse.

**cærsiht**; adj. Cressy, having much cress:—In cærsihtan wyll, C. D. iii. 121, 18. v. next word.

**cærs-will,** es; m. A spring where cress grows:—In cærswylle ; æfter cærswylles sîce, C. D. iii. 384, 19. v. preceding word.

**caerte, cæsternisc.** v. carte, ceasternisc.

**cǽf.** Add:—Cǽf praeceps, i. alacer, Germ. 393, 66 : efficax, 400, 547. Se eorðlica kempa bið æfre gearo and cǽf, swá hwyder swá hē faran sceal tô gefeohte mid ðám kininge, Hex. 34, 19. Þæt hý sýn cǽfran tô Godes þeówdóme, R. Ben. 68, 19. Petrus wæs cǽfost on Crîstes lufe, Hml. Th. ii. 388, 29. [v. N. E. D. cof; dele in bracket 'O. Nrs. â-kafr.']

**cǽfe.** Add: [v. N. E. D. cofe.]

**cǽfer-tûn.** l. cafer-tûn, dele ' DER. cîfan,' and add: (cæfer-, ceafr(-or, -ur)-):—Caebrtuun (ceber-) vestibulum, Txts. 105, 2094. Cavertûn, Wrt. Voc. i. 290, 1. Cafertûn atrium, ii. 7, 61 : mesaulum, 55, 65.

In midle ceafurtûnes ðînes in medio atrio tuo, Ps. Srt. 73, 4. Se biscop on his cafortûne hēt him medmicel hûs gewyrcan episcopus ei in conseptis ejusdem mansionis parvum tugurium fieri praecipit, Bd. 5, 2 ; Sch. 557, 21. Heó gewunode tô fēdenne henna on hire hûses cafortûne (in þám ingange hire hûses) in hospitii sui vestibulo, Gr. D. 69, 26 : Bl. H. 219, 20. Hē Laurentium tô ðæs cynges cafertûne gelǽdde, Hml. Th. i. 422, 26. On þám cafertûne (outside the door of the temple), Hml. S. 23 b, 410. Ic sæt binnan mînan cafertûne, 30, 372 : 5, 324. Cauertûne, Hml. Th. ii. 248, 27. In cæfertûn (atrium) þæs aldorsácerdas, Mt. L. R. 26, 3. Ceafertûn (cæfer-, R.), 58 : Lk. L. (R.), 11, 21. Ceafortûnum atriis, Ps. Srt. 133, 1. Ceafultûnum, 83, 11.

**cáf-lîce.** Add:—Cáflîce, scearplîce efficaciter, i. velociter, Wrt. Voc. ii. 142, 56. (1) of rapid movement:—Cáflîce cuman velociter pervenire, R. Ben. 23. 3. Hé rád ormǽte cáflîce, Hml. Th. ii. 304, 8. Hí cômon cáflîce rîdende, Hml. S. 27, 84. Se cásere cáflîce lîhte, 101. (2) of strenuous, energetic action:—Cáflîce viritim, Germ. 396, 162. Þæt folc cáflîce nid rápum ðá anlícnysse bewurpon, Hml. Th. i. 464, 18. Singaþ cáflîce (naviter), Hy. S. 57, 4 : An. Ox. 56, 258. Cáflîce naviter (coronam nancisci), Hpt. Gl. 405, 23. Hí sóna begyrdon hí cáflîce (with alacrity), Hml. S. 5, 247 : R. Ben. 47, 13. Hieu fērde mid fultume . . . Ioram áxode hwæðer hé côme mid sibbe swá cáflîce (with such a display of force), Hml. S. 18, 330. Hí gearcodon heora môd cáflîce tô campienne (to fight valiantly), 5, 151 : 25, 433. Hē ðone cásere cáflîce befrán he boldly asked the emperor, 14, 51. Myngunge þînes fæder cáflîce (efficaciter) gefyl, R. Ben. 1, 4. Geheald þine heortan cáflîce wið unþeáwas, Wlfst. 247, 3 : Angl. viii. 323, 36. [v. N. E. D. cofly.]

**cáf-ness,** e ; f. Alacrity, promptness, energy:—God onscunað þá sleacnysse on his ðegnum, and ðá hē lufað þe mid cáfnysse þæs ēcan lifes myrhðe secað, Hml. Th. ii. 282, 4.

**cáf-scipe.** Substitute: Alacrity, energy, promptness, boldness:—Mid Godes eges cáfscipe bútû þá þing beoð gefyllede in velocitate timoris Dei ambe res citius explicantur, R. Ben. 20, 6. Se man hýwað hine sylfne mihtine and unforhtne, þe náh on his heortan ǽnigne cáfscype, Wlfst. 53, 16. v. un-cáfscipe.

**-cafstrian.** v. ge-cafstrian.

**calan.** Add:—Caelith, cælid, kaelið infrigidat, Txts. 72, 561. Cælþ, Wrt. Voc. ii. 48, 10. Hátian, calan aestuare, algere, Bd. 1, 27 ; Sch. 82, 25.

**calc.** Dele Cot. 209, and add: [From Latin] : calc chalk. v. cealc.

**calca-træppe,** -trippe (colte-), an ; f. A plant name, caltrop (v. N. E. D. s.v.) :—Calcatrippe heraclea, Wrt. Voc. i. 68, 9. Coltetræppe ramnus, 285, 47.

**calc-rond,** -rand. Substitute: With shielding shoe, shod:—Tomes mcares, cûðes and calcrondes, Gn. Ex. 143.

**calend.** l. câlend : calian. Dele.

**calic.** Add : , celc:—Calic calix, Wrt. Voc. i. 81, 1. Calices calicis, Ps. Srt. 10, 7. Celces, 15, 5. Hē on ǽnne lytelne calic sende sumne dǽl þæs lîchaman, Hml. S. 23 b, 659. v. silfrene caliceas, Cht. Th. 429, 19. Gē clǽnsiað caliceas (calicas, v. l. ; cælces, L., cælcis, R. calicis) and dixas, Mt. 23, 25. v. symbel-calic.

**calu.** Add :—Calo calvus, Wrt. Voc. i. 288, 56 : ii. 17, 15. (1) of persons, bald :—Gif mannes feax fealle . . . and gif man calu sié, Lch. ii. 16, 28. Brichtrîc se calewa, C. D. iv. 234, 6. Catus cwydas þæs calwan esnes, Angl. viii. 321, 29. (2) of plants, trees, bare:—On þone calewan telgan, C. D. i. 258, 7. Oþ þone calewan stoc, ii. 216, 1.

**calwa.** Substitute: In Wrt. Voc. ii. 99, 80: 6, 54 occurs the gloss alapiciosa calwa. The latter word seems to be Latin ; cf. alapiciosus caluus in other glossaries. v. Corp. Gl. H. xli.

**calwer.** Add: , calwere:—Caluuaer, caluuer galmaria, Txts. 66, 471. Caluaer, calwer galbalacrum, 476. Calwere galmaria, calwer gabalacrum, Wrt. Voc. ii. 40, 61, 62. Cealre calmaria, 17, 19. [v. N. E. D. calver.]

**calwer-brîw.** Add :—Cealerbrîw calviale, Wrt. Voc. ii. 17, 21.

**calwer-clim** (? cf. clám) curds (?):—Caluuerclîm calvarium, Wrt. Voc. ii. 103, 45. v. next word.

**calwer-clympe** curds (?):—Calwerclympe calvarium, Wrt. Voc. ii. 127, 60. v. preceding word.

**calwere.** Dele, and see calwer.

**cáma,** an ; m. A bit:—Mid brîdle and mid cáman in freno et camo, Ps. Th. 31, 11. [From Latin.]

**camb.** Add: I. comb for the hair:—Genim þone camb þe heó âna hyre heáfod mid cemde . . . þ on þám cambe geþolige, gesomnige, Lch. i. 332, 11-15. Þ feax þe on þám cambe cleofige, 21. Ic his heáfod mid gambe gekamde, C. D. iv. 261, 2. II. crest, (1) comb of a bird:—Combas on fugele cristas, Wrt. Voc. ii. 137, 7. Cambas cristas (of cocks), An. Ox. 26, 16. Byð ôðer fugelcynn fênix hâtte, þá habbað cambas (cristas) on heúfde swá páwan, Nar. 39, 3. (2) crest of a helmet:—Cambe helmes crista cassidis, An. Ox. 5019. [For Cot. 46 in Dict. l. Wrt. Voc. ii. 19, 10.] v. hors camb.

cambiht(e); *adj. Crested :*—Cambihte helme *crista cassidis* ( =cristata casside ?; the passage is : Gigantem crista cassidis indutum, Ald. 71, 33; Wrt. Voc. ii. 86, 79 : 19, 10.

cammoc. *Add :*—Cammocc (*printed* -e ; v. Wülck. Gl. 300, 27) *peucidanum,* Wrt. Voc. i. 68, 63. Cammuc *gotuna,* ii. 42, 32. Snáda cammuces, Lch. iii. 28, 28. Commuc, 54, 21. Cammoc, ii. 270, 1.

camp *a fetter. Add :* [cf. *O. H. Ger.* champen *compedibus;* gechampeten *compeditos.*]

camp *a field* (?) :—Þis synt þá denbæra . . . gelecan camp, C. D. ii. 216, 6. Wæst tó rocggan campæs geatæ, v. 255, 32. Tó wigan campe, 313, 10: vi. 67, 9. On todan camp; of todan campe, iii. 425, 27. [*O. L. Ger.* kamp *an enclosure, field : O. Frs.* kamp *an enclosed piece of land.* v. Jellinghaus *s. v.* kamp, a word in place names, which is almost exclusively Saxon and Frisian ' Der kamp ist ein eingefriedigter als Ackerland, Weide, Wiese oder Holzung dienender grösserer Landfleck.' See also Midd. Flur. s. v. camp. From Latin.]

camp. *Add :*—Se camp (*certamen*) in þæs mannes breóste, Gr. D. 18, 3. Se stranga wiga, S. Paulus, sóhte þone feld þæs campes (*certaminis campum*), 110, 16. Fulfremede campe (compe) *perfecto agone,* Bd. 1, 7; Sch. 27, 22. Hé wolde deófol gelaþian tó campe wiþ hine, Bl. H. 29, 20. Mid heora geatwum gegyrede efne swá hié tó campe féran woldon, 221, 29. Ic wæs on dæm heardan campe hér on worlde, 225, 31, 32. Níwe campas and gewin *nova certamina,* Gr. D. 122, 22. [v. *N. E. D.* camp.] v. ge-, weorold-camp.

camp-dóm. *Add :*—Mannes líf is campdóm ofer eordan (*militia est vita hominis super terram*), for dan þe ælc . . . bid on gewinne wid done deófol, Hml. Th. ii. 454, 26 : i. 418, 9 : Hml. S. 23, 86. Campdómes *militiae,* An. Ox. 868 : 750. Compdómes, Txts. 180, 18 : Rtl. 8, 15. Wǽpnu campdóme[s] úres ná flǽsclice synd *the weapons of our warfare are not carnal,* Scint. 207, 16. Campian on Godes campdóme, Hex. 34, 12. Hét se cwellere þæs cáseres cempan geoffrian . . . þá wǽron on þám campdóme (*soldiery*) Cappadonisce cempan Hml. S. 11, 16. Hé wæs gewenod tó wǽpnum and campdóme fyligde (*followed the profession of arms*), 31, 17. Þæra cempena suna wurdon genamode tó þám ylcan campdóme (*military service*) þe heora fæderas on wæron, 32 : 100.

camp-ealdor, es; *m. A captain :*—Campealdra *magistri militum,* An. Ox. 4433.

camp-geféra, an; *m. A fellow-soldier, comrade-in-arms :*—Campgeférum *commilitonibus, sociis,* Wrt. Voc. ii. 132, 23 : An. Ox. 3578. [*A. R.* kemp-ifere.]

camp-hád. *Add :*—Camphâde *tyrocinio,* An. Ox. 616. Gúdlác of þǽre gedrésednysse þissere worulde wæs geléded tó camphâde þæs ēcan lífes, Guth. 24, 23. In camphád sendan *in militiam mittere,* Gr. D. 298, 8.

campian. *Add :*—Ic campude *certaui,* An. Ox. 1349. Campa *dimica,* Germ. 393, 175. Oumpadi (*alt. from* compadi) *decertarent,* Jn. L. 18, 36. Winnan and campian *militare,* R. Ben. 96, 23. Hé wǽpn gegráp mid tó campienne, Bl. H. 167, 1. Campiende *agonizans,* Wrt. Voc. ii. 2, 51. (1) *to fight for,* (a) with dat. :—Þá þe campiad cyningce eordlicum *qui militant regi terreno,* Scint. 61, 1, 2 : Hex. 34, 15, 17. Od þis ic campode þé, geþafa nú þ ic Gode campige, S. 31, 103. Gif dú wylle campian on Godes campdóme, ne campa dú ǽnigum búton Gode ânum, Hex. 34, 12. Nǽnig compigende Gode *nemo militans Deo,* Rtl. 60, 11. (b) *with* for :—Wé willad campian for dínre hǽlo, Ap. Th. 9, 20. Tó campienne for Crístes geleáfan, Hml. S. 5, 151. (2) *to fight with, serve with* :—Him ne dúhte fremfullic þ hé fénge tó þáre cyge, and syddan ne campode mid þám cásere, Hml. S. 31, 102. (3) *to fight with, against* (*wiþ, ongeán*), (a) with dat. :—Hé wid þám gástum campode, Guth. 24, 12. In him wunnon and campedon (*certabant*) þá yfel his líchaman wid þám weorce his ælmesdǽda, Gr. D. 122, 18. Campian ongeán dám deófle mid geleáfan, Hml. Th. ii. 402, 15. (b) with acc. :—Se eordlica kempa kampad mid his wǽpnum ongeán gesewenlice feónd, and dú sealt campian wid dá ungesewenlican fýnd, Hex. 34, 24. Mid gástlican wǽpnan campian wid deófol, Ll. Th. ii. 388, 5 : Hml. S. 17, 162. Campian wid leahtras, Hml. S. i. 360, 17. Tó campigenne ongeán þone feónd, Hml. S. 5, 242. v. ge-campian.

camp-lic ; *adj. Military :*—Camplic meniu *a body of soldiers,* Hml. S. 31, 1237. Camplicere mihte *tribunicae potestatis,* An. Ox. 11, 156 : 12, 9. Reþe, camplice *tyrannici* (*militonum commanipulares*), 858.

camp-róf. v. un-campróf.

campung, e; *f. Fighting, contest :*—Campung *certatio,* An. Ox. 7, 346. Compung *concertatio,* Wrt. Voc. ii. 20, 40. Ic mid þínum wǽpnum getrymed on þínum féþan fæste stande and for þínre campunga (*a better reading is :* for dé campige. v. Bl. N. 5, 40), Bl. H. 225, 34.

camp-weorud (-od), -wered. *Add :*—Dæt compweorod (-uearod, L.) *cohors,* Jn. R. 18, 12. Þæs hiofoncundan compwerodes *caelestis militiae,* Lch. i. lxviii, 5. Ymbseald mid þon heofonlican campweorode, Bl. H. 11, 24.

camp-wísa, an; *m. A superintendent of public games;* agonotheta, Hpt. Gl. 405, 4.

Cananéisc. *Add :*—þone Cananisca (Channanesca, L.). *Cananaeum,* Mk. R. 3, 18.

canc *mockery, derision :*—Cance *gannatura, irrisione,* Hpt. Gl. 510, 73. [v. *N. E. D.* cank.] v. ge-canc; cancettan; cincung.

cancer (-or). *Dele* 'II. *a crab &c.,' and add :*—Hine æt se cancor, and his weleras wǽron áwlætte mid ealle, and eác his nosu fornumen mid áttre, Hml. S. 6, 284. Hym of þám andwlytan nyder áfeóll se cancer þe hyne ǽr swýde ámyrred hæfde, Hml. A. 183, 70. Þone cancor (*άφθas*) þæra tóda, Lch. i. 294, 21.

cancer-hæbern. *Dele, and see* hæfern.

cancer-wund, e; *f. The wound made by cancer :*—Wid cancorwund, Lch. i. 370, 7. Wid cancorwunda, genim þás wyrte . . . lege tó dám wundum, ealne þone bite þæs cancres heó áfeormad, 296, 20.

cancettan. *Add :*, *to chatter, mock, deride :*—Cancet (*printed* -er) *clamet,* Wrt. Voc. ii. 23, 14. Cancettende *gannature,* 40, 51. v. canc, *and next word.*

cancet(t)ung. For Cot. 58 *substitute :*— Cancetunge *cachinnos,* Wrt. Voc. ii. 24, 16.

candel. *Add :*—Condel *funalia,* Wrt. Voc. ii. 109, 34. Candel *candela,* i. 284, 34 : 81, 34. Gif þé smælre candelle geneódige, þonne bláw þú on þínum scytefingre, Tech. ii. 120, 20. *Acolitus* is gecweden sé þe candele odde tapor byrd, Ll. Th. ii. 348, 4. Gyf man mǽte þ hé byrnende candele geseó, gód þ byd, Lch. iii. 176, 12. Ontend þreó candela, and drýp þ wex þriwa, 286, 6. Swá hwelc mon swá condella onbærne on ciricean of his gestreónum on mínum noman, Shrn. 101, 28. v. weax-candel.

candel-bryd ( = -bred?) *a flat candlestick* (?) :—Gyf þé smælre candelle geneódige . . . Donne þú candelbryd habban wille, ástrehte þínre winstran handa ofsete hý eclinga mid þínre swi(þ)ran, Tech. ii. 120, 20–23.

candel-leóht. For C. R. Ben. 53 *substitute :*—Se æfen swá sý gefadod þæt hý candelleóhtes æt dám gereorde ne behófien, ac eallu ding be dæges leóhte gefyllede sýn, R. Ben. 66, 7.

Candelmæsse-æfen *Candlemas-eve :*—Ærest on Eásteræfen, and ódre síde on Candelmæsseæfen, Ll. Th. ii. 256, 28.

candel-snytels. *l.* -snýtels. v. snýtan.

candel-stæf. *Add :*—Candelstæf *candelabrum,* Wrt. Voc. i. 81, 4. Leóht scínende ofer candelstæf hâligne *lucerna splendens super candelabrum sanctum,* Scint. 226, 1 : Gr. D. 99, 13. Man sceal habban candelstafas, Angl. ix. 264, 18. [*Wyc.* candel-staf : *O. H. Ger.* kentilastab.] v. next word.

candel-sticca. *Add :*—Gyf þú candelsticcan habban wille . . ., hald þíne hand sânlocene, swylce þú candelstæf hæbbe, Tech. ii. 120, 18. II. sylurene candelsticcan and II. ouergylde, Cht. Th. 243, 34. II. mycele gebónede candelsticcan, and VI. læssan candelsticcan gebónede, 429, 32.

candel-twist. *Add :*—Candeltwist, -thwist *emunctoria,* Txts. 59, 745. Candeltwist (*printed* camel-), Wrt. Voc. ii. 29, 31 : 143, 49.

candel-weoc, e ; *l.* -weóce, an, *and add :*—*Funalia, candela* odde candelweócan, Wrt. Voc. ii. 36, 18 (*cf.* funalia, i. lucernarum stuppae, 27).

cann. In translation of last passage for '*the church clearance right*' substitute '*the church's right of clearance.*'

cannon *seems to represent* Lat. coenum in :—Wæs þ lond ádrígad and cannon *palus sicca et ceno habundans,* Nar. 20, 23.

canon. *Add :*—Béte hé swá canon tæce, Ll. Th. i. 168, 7. On sumum canone hit cwyd .xii. geár, ii. 230, 5. Hí gesetton done canon þæt nán mæssepreóst on his wununge wífhádes mann næbbe, Hml. Th. i. 97, 29. Canones beódaþ, Hml. S. 36, 387.

canon-bóc *a book of canons :*—Hæbbe ǽlc bisceop canonbóc tó sinode, Ll. Th. ii. 316, 14.

canonic, es ; *m. Add :*—Ná þ ân be munecum, ac eác swylce be árwyrdum canonicum þe tó munuclífe cumad, R. Ben. 111, 6.

canonic ; *adj. Canonical :*—Sé de tóbrecd þá canonican gesetnysse, Hml. Th. ii. 96, 13.

cantel *a piece of wood placed obliquely to support a rafter* (? v. cantle, cant *in N. E. D.*) :—Ærest man ásmead þæs húses stede, and eác man þ timber beheáwd, and þá syllan man fægere gefégd, and þá beámas gelegd, and þá ræftras tó þǽre fyrste gefæstnad and mid cantlum underwridad, Angl. viii. 324, 10. [*From Low Lat.* cantellus.]

cantel-cap. *l.* -cáp, *and add :* [v. *N. E. D.* cantel-cape, -cope.] v. next word.

canter-cæppe (-cæpp?), an; *f. A cope :*—Se'abbud mid cantercæppan (*cappa*) gescrýdd, Angl. xiii. 403, 546. III. cantercæppa[n ?], Cht. Th. 429, 23. [Cf. A canturcope *hec dalmatica,* Wrt. Voc. i. 231, 25. *Icel.* kantara-cápa.]

cantere, es ; *m. One who sings the psalms in church :*—Fram cantere beó ongunnan antefn mid sealme *a cantore inchoetur antephona cum psalmo,* Angl. xiii. 428, 904. [From Latin.]

canter-stæf, es ; *m. A staff used by a cantor* (v. preceding word) :—III. canterstafas *III. baculi cantorum* (baculi quibus in ecclesia utebantur cantores, Migne), Cht. Th. 429, 23.

**cantic.** *Add:*—Cantic Deuteronomio, þæt is Adtende celum' . . . ôþrum dagum sý cantic gesungen, þæt is lofsang þe tô þâm dæge belimpð, R. Ben. 38, 2–5. Þæne saltere mid gewunelican cantican, 44, 20. Singan þrý canticas of wîtigena bôcum, 35, 13.

**Cantwara burg.** *Add:*—Cantwarabyrig forbarn, Chr. 754; P. 47, 20. Seó ceaster Cantwaraburge *civitas Doruuernensis*, Bd. 2, 7; Sch. 139, 16.

**Cantwara mægþ.** *l.* mægþ.

**Cant-ware (-an).** *Add:*—Cantwarena landes is fîftêne þûsend hýda, C. D. B. i. 414, 30. Sê wæs Cantwara (Cont-, *v. l.*) leód (leode, *v. l.*) *oriundus de gente Cantuariorum*, Bd. 3, 14; Sch. 253, 13. Paulinus huerf eft tô Cantwarum (gewât tô Cent, *v. l.*), Chr. 633; P. 24, 21.

**Cant-waru, e; *f. The people of Kent:*—**Eall Brytene bûton Cantware ânre, Chr. 617; P. 24, 28.

**capian.** *Substitute:* To look; ûp capian *to look up, lie on one's back :*—Gyf seó sunne hine (*the moon*) onâlð ufan, þonne stûpað hê, . . . gyf heó hine ontend neoðan, þonne capað hê ûp; for þan þe hê went æfre þone hricg tô þære sunnan weard, Lch. iii. 266, 20–24. Capiende *supinus*, Germ. 393, 172. [*O. L. Ger.* kapen: *O. H. Ger.* kapfên *to look; ûfschafta supinabat; ûfscafénder resupinus.*]

**capitol** *Add:* **I.** in connexion with books, (1) *a chapter:*—Hêr geendiaþ þâ capitulas *explicium capitula*, R. Ben. 8, 31: 6, 4. Hêr onginnað disse bôce capitulas, Ll. Th. ii. 128, 5, 7. Hêr onginð seó ôðer bôc mid hire capitulon, 180, 40. Mæg sê ðe wile þâ capitulas æfter ðære forespræce geendebyrdian *any one who likes can make an index to the chapters after the preface*, Hml. Th. ii. 2, 19. (2) *a short passage from Scripture*, (a) *a lesson:*—Fylige capitel (*lectio*) ð þæra apostola lâre bûtan bêc gesæd, R. Ben. 34, 1. Æfter geendunge þâra þreora sealma sié ân capitul (kapitol, R. Ben. I. 47, 9) gecweden *recitetur lectio una*, 41, 1. Sý ânes capitules ræding gecweden *lectio recitanda est*, 11. Feówer capitulas (*capitula*), þæt is feówer tôdâla angin þæs cxviii-an sealmes, 42, 1. (b) *an anthem:*—þrý capitulas (*capitula*) sýn gesungene, R. Ben. 42, 4. Tô nônsange sýn þrý capitulas gesungene of þâm nigan capitulum þe tô lâfe synt, 18. **II.** *a chapter, meeting of ecclesiastics:*—Þe abbot eóde intô capitulan, Chr. 1083; P. 214, 22. [*v. N. E. D.* capitle. *O. H. Ger.* kapital (-el, -ul) *inscriptio, titulus: Icel.* kapituli (*wk.*) *a chapter. From Latin.*]

**capitol-hûs, es;** *n.* *A chapter-house:*—Gyf þû hwæt be capitelhûse tæcan wylle, Tech. ii. 122, 4.

**capitulod.** v. ge-, un-capitulod.

**cappa.** *For '*Ælf. Gl. . . . 15*' substitute* Wrt. Voc. i. 40, 48, *and add :*—Caracalla cappa, Wrt. Voc. ii. 128, 84. Wyrpe him of heden oðÞe cappan *cucullum vel cappam dejiciat*, Ll. Th. ii. 140, 23

**Cappadonisc;** *adj. Cappadocian:*—Cappadoniscre scîre *Cappadocie*, An. Ox. 2302. Cappadonisce cempan, Hml. S. 11, 16.

**carbunculus;** *gen.* carbuncules; *m.* *A carbuncle:*—On gimma gecynde carbunculus bið diórra ðonne iacintus, and swâðeáh ðæt bleóh ðæs iacintes bið betera ðonne ðæs carbuncules; forðæm . . ðeáh ðe ðæt gecynd ðæs carbuncules hine ûp âhebbe, his blióh hine gescent, Past. 411, 27–32.

**carcern.** *Dele in bracket '* carc *care, or,' and add :*—Carcernes *lautumiae*, Wrt. Voc. ii. 52, 75: 83, 32. Heó ût eóde of þâm carcerne (*printed* carcernerne, Shrn. 30, 30, *but the MS. has* carcernes *with the first* cer *above the line*), Mart. H. 4, 17. In carcrænnæ *in carcere*, Mt. R. 25, 44. Tô cærcherne *carceri*, Lk. p. 4, 8. In cercerne, Mk. R. 6, 17. In carchern (carkærn, R.), Mt. L. 25, 36: Mk. L. 6, 27. þâ monegan cyningas on carcernum lægon, Ors. 5, 1; S. 214, 18. Ða hâlgan menn geðafedon monige bendas and carcernu (karcernu, *v. l.*), Past. 205, 12.

**carcern-ern.** v. preceding word.

**carcern-þeóstru, e;** *f. Prison-darkness, the darkness of the prison:*—Mistlice þreála gebyriað for synnum, bendas oðÞe dyntas oðÞe carcernþýstra, Ll. Th. ii. 278, 26.

**carcern-weard, es;** *m.* *A prison-warder, jailor:*—Hê wæs on carcern sænded . . , and æfter twelf dagum côm se carcernweard, Shrn. 54, 13, 16. Scê Arthemius wæs ær carcernweard, 89, 23, 27.

**care-lîce.** *Add:* [Cf. *O. H. Ger.* char(a)-lîh *lugubris.*]

**car-ful (care-).** *Add:* **I.** of persons, (1) *filled with anxiety, anxious, troubled:*—Ðû eart carful and bysig ymbe fela ðing *thou art careful and troubled about many things* (Lk. 10, 41), Hml. Th. ii. 440, 8. Ne beó ðû carful ymbe woruldlicum gestreónum, 344, 2. Fêrde se câsere swîðe carful, and gelôme beheóld wið heofonas weard, 304, S. Hê ongæn his fiónd fêrde mid carfullum môde, H. R. 3, 12. (2) *careful, attentive to the interests of, solicitous for :*—Hû abbod careful (*sollicitus*) beón sceal ymbe ðâ dædbêtendan, R. Ben. 50, 16. Se þên þe þâm untrumum gebrôðrum þênað sý careful (car-, *v. l.*), 60, 21. (3) *careful, painstaking, applying care to what one does, heedful :*—Carful gestaþeliend *zelotypus plasmator*, An. Ox. 364. Weorðe sê carfull, hû hê swýþast mæge gecwêman his Drihtne, Wlfst. 72, 10. Wer carfull (*studiosus*) and wîs, Scint. 206, 5. Hweþer hê carful sý tô godcundum weorcc *si solicitus est ad opus Dei*, R. Ben. 97, 16. Mæden

carful, þancful, nytwyrþe, Lch. iii. 188, 14. Drusiana ârâs, and carfull be ðæs apostoles hæse hâm gewende, Hml. Th. i. 60, 19. Hê sylf ælce tîd getâcnige, oðþe swylcum carefullan brêðer þâ gýmene betæce, þe nâne tîd ne forgýmeleásige, R. Ben. 72, 12. Undernimað ðæra apostola word mid carfullum môde, Hml. Th. i. 236, 4: ii. 284, 25. **II.** of things, (1) *fraught* or *attended with anxiety, troublesome :*—Carfull (heñ) bîhýdinys *scrupulosa* (*dubitata*) *sollicitudo*, An. Ox. 5429. (2) *shewing care* for or *attention* to a person's interests :—Hæfde se godspellere gýmene þære hâlgan Marian, and mid carfulre þênunge gehýrsumede, Hml. Th. i. 438, 15. (3) *careful, heedful :*—Mid carfulre gýmene *solerti cura*, Scint. 121, 2. v. cear-ful *in Dict.*

**carful-lîce.** *Add:*—Eálâ ðû gôde rôd, ðû wære gefyrn gewilnod and carfullîce gelufod, Hml. Th. i. 596, 15. þis wæs carfullîce (*sollicite*) gehealden, Gr. D. 126, 19. Carfullîcor *sollicitius*, R. Ben. I. 111, 9.

**carful-nys.** *Add:* **I.** *care, anxiety* (v. carful, **II.** 1) :—Is seó mæste þearf þ wê hwîlon ûre môd gebîgean tô þâm gâstlicum rihte betweoh þâs eorðlican carfulnysse (ymbhigdo, *v.l.*), Gr. D. 1, 11. **II.** *a charge, cure* of souls :—For þâm bysgum þysre bisceoplican carfulnysse (scîre, *v. l.*), Gr. D. 4, 29. **III.** *care, solicitude* for (v. car-ful; **I.** 2) :—Hîwcûþ carfulnys (*domestica sollicitudo*, An. Ox. 4184. **IV.** *carefulness* (v. car-ful, **I.** 3) :—Carfulnesse geornfulness *sollicitudinis sollertia*, An. Ox. 906. Agyfan Gode þinre carfulnysse weorc, Hml. Th. ii. 334, 24, 26. Ðâ geniðerunge mid carfulnysse foresceáwian, i. 408, 29. Heó mid carfulnysse þone hýrêd gewissode, Hml. S. 2, 127.

**carian.** *Add:* **I.** *to sorrow, be troubled :*—Ne ceara þû, ne ne wêp, Bl. H. 143, 3. **II.** *to care* for (*ymbe*), *see to the welfare* of, *be solicitous* about :—Se abbod mid ealre embhýdignesse carige embe þâ gyltendan gebrôðru *omni sollicitudine curam gerat abbas circa delinquentes fratres*, R. Ben. 50, 18. Restan hý mid heora ealdrum þe embe hý carien *cum senioribus, qui super eos solliciti sint, pausent*, 47, 8. **III.** *to take care, pains, thought*, (1) with a clause :—Hê carað dæges and nihtes þæt his feoh gehealden sý; hê gýmð grædelîce his gafoles, Hml. Th. i. 66, 9. Carian hî æfre hû hî swýðost magan Gode gecwêman, Ll. Th. ii. 322, 6. (2) with *ymbe* :—Mîne scêp sint tôstencte ðurh eówre gýmeleáste . . . Gê cariað embe eówerne bigleofan, and nâ embe þæra sceápa, Hml. Th. i. 242, 2. Ðâ sýn emhýdige and cariende embe heora ealdorscypas *qui sollicitudinem gerant super decanias suas*, R. Ben. 46, 11. **IV.** *to care* about, *be interested* in; with negative, *to be indifferent* to :—Hê hwônlîce carað ymbe Godes beboda and his sâwle ðearfe, Hml. Th. i. 342, 1. Hê nâteshwôn ne carað ymbe Crîstes teolunge, 412, 15. Riht is þ abbodas næfre ymbe woruldcara ne îdele prýda ne carian tô swýðe, Ll. Th. ii. 320, 35. [*Goth.* karôn : *O. Sax.* karôn : *O. H. Ger.* charôn (-ên).]

**caric[-a, -e?]** *a fig :*—Ænne lytelne tänel mid caricum gefylledne, Hml. S. 23 b, 661. v. fîc-æppel.

**cearig.** [*O. Sax.* karag : *O. H. Ger.* charag *sollicitus, lugubris.*] v. cearig.

**carl.** *Dele bracket, and add :*—Arcton hâtte ân tungol on norðdæle . . . þone hâtað læwede menn carles wæn, Lch. iii. 270, 11. [*O. H. Ger.* char(a)l, karl *vir, maritus : Icel.* karl *a man.*] [From Scandinavian.] v. butse-carl, *and cf.* ceorl.

**carl;** *adj.* *Dele :* carl-cat. *Dele :* car-leás. *For* R. Ben. 2 *l.* R. Ben. 11, 3.

**carl-fugol, es;** *m.* *A male bird :*—Nân man ne wât hweþer hit (*the Phenix*) is þe carlfugol þe cwênfugol, E. S. viii. 479, 90. [*Icel.* karl-fugl.]

**carl-mann.** *Add:*—Gif hwilc carlman hæmde wið wimman hire unðances, Chr. 1086; P. 220, 17. [*Icel.* karl-maðr.]

**carr.** *Add:* v. stân-carr.

**carte.** *Add:*—Hê sum gewrit âwrât on cartan . . . Sum hrefen þâ cartan genam . . . geseah hê þone hrefen þâ cartan beran . . . hangode seó carte on þâm hreóde . . . and hê sôna fêng tô þære cartan, Guth. 48, 22–50, 18. Hê sceáwode þâ cartan and clypode tô ðâm wîfe: 'þeós carte is âðilegod,' Hml. S. 3, 659. Heó ealle hyre mânlican dæda âwrât on ânre cartan and beworhte mid leáde, . . . þâ genam se biscop þâ cartan, 532. Ic oncnâwe þâs cartan; þis ic sylf âwrât, 456. Cartena, gewrita *scedarum*, An. Ox. 2308. Kærtena, 7, 142 : 8, 117.

**caru.** *Add:*—Caru câru, Wrt. Voc. i. 83, 60. **I.** *care, trouble :*—Gind ealne middangeard caru and gewin and ege *crudelis ubique luctus, ubique pavor*, Ors. 2, 4; S. 72, 21. Hwæt bewearp þe on þâs care and on þâs gnornunga *quid est quod te in moestitiam luctumque dejecit?*, Bt. 7, 2; F. 16, 26. Hî fâcnum wordum heora aldorþægn unreordadon on cearum (*d. pl.*) cwidum (? cwîðdun. Cf. in cearum cwîðað, Gú. 194), Sat. 67. Hê wiste ferhð guman cearum (*grievously;* cf. cearum cwîðende, Cri. 892) on clommum, Ger. 2794. **II.** *care* for (v. carian, **II.**) :—Hyrdelicere care *sollertia pastorali*, i. *sollicitudine*, An. Ox. 2986. **III.** *care, interest* in (v. carian, **IV.**) :—Ðâ andweardan myrhðe gewâcan mid nânre care þære tôweardan ungesælðe,

Hml. Th. i. 408, 21. Habban máran care úre sáwle þonne ðǽre scortan gesǽlde *to care more about our soul than about transitory happiness*, ii. 460, 16.

**case-bill** ( cáser-?) *a sceptre?* : — Casebill *clauam* i. *gestaṁ* (*for* ? cáserbill *gestamen;* gestamen *sceptrum*, Migne : billus *baculus, claua oblonga*, ib. : *so* cáser-bill *might be compared with* cyne-gird), Germ. 394, 285.

**cáser-dóm.** *Add :*—Cáserdómes *imperii*, An. Ox. 12, 13. Cáserdóm *rem puplicam*, Rtl. 191, 23. [*O. Sax.* késur-dóm : *O. H. Ger.* cheisar-tuom : *Icel.* keisara-dómr.]

**Cásere.** *Add :*—Cásere *imperator, Caesar, vel Augustus*, Wrt. Voc. i. 17, 45. Gaius Iulius se Cásere (Kásere, *v. l.*), Chr. P. p. 4, 23. Lóthwí se cásere, 840 ; P. 64, note 3. Odda Rómána cásere, 982 ; P. 124, 24. Þíne godas, cásere, synd manna handgeweorc, Hml. S. 14, 20. Féng Tiberius tó ríce se césar æfter Agustuse *post mortem Augusti Tiberius Caesar imperium adeptus est*, Ors. 6, 2 ; S. 254, 21. Cáseres reáf tó gefeohte *paludamentum*, Wrt. Voc. i. 40, 31. Hé begeat þæs cáseres mága tó wífe, Chr. 1057; P. 188, 13. Cáseres gæfel, Mt. L. 17, 24. Cǽseres, p. 19, 5. Ðæs casseres, 22, 21. Geldas ðá ðe sint caeseres (cáseras, R.) ðæm cásere, Mk. L. 12, 17. Cessares, Lk. L. 2, 1. Ðæm cásari (kásere, R.), Mt. L. 22, 21. Nabbo ué cyning búta ðone cáser, Jn. L. 19, 15. [*Goth.* kaisar : *O. Sax.* késur : *O. Frs.* keiser, kaiser : *O. H. Ger.* cheisar : *Icel.* keisari.]

**cásering** *a coin of the empire :*—Cásering ł cáseres gæfel *didrachma*, Mt. L. 17, 24. Cásering *dragma*, Lk. p. 8, 16.

**cáser-líc.** *For* Cot. 115 *l.:*—þæs cáserlícan húses *imperialis hypodromi*, Wrt. Voc. ii. 48, 45. [*O. Frs.* keiser-lik : *O. H. Ger.* cheisar-líh *imperialis.*]

**Cásern.** *Add :* [*O. H. Ger.* cheiserin *imperatrix.*]

**cassa?** *a net :*—Casses vel cassan *retia*, Wrt. Voc. ii. 129, 23.

**castel** *Substitute for the single form the two following :*—

**castel**, es ; *n. A village, town :*—On þ castel on naman Emaus, Lk. 24, 13. Drihten foresceáwode him þæt castel þá cynelícan Bethleem, tó ðan þæt he wolde ðǽr on ðǽre byrig menniscnesse underfón, Wlfst. 193, 27 : [Mt. 21, 2 : Mk. 6, 6. v. Dict.] [*O. Sax.* that kastel (*Emmaus*) : *O. H. Ger.* chastel, kastel (*Bethlehem, Bethany*). From Latin *castellum.*]

**castel** (-ell), es ; *m.*    **I.** *a castle :*—þá Frencyscan þe on þan castelle wǽron, Chr. 1052; P. 175, 13. Sume tó Pentecostes castele, sume tó Ródbertes castele, P. 181, 5. Æt ælcan castelle, 1075 ; P. 210, 25. His wíf wæs innan þám castele, and hine heóld swá þ man hire grið sealde, P. 211, 11. Hæfdon þá welisce menn gewroht ǽnne castel, 1048; P. 173, 16. Tó Eoferwíc fóron and þone castel tóbrǽcon, 1069; P. 204, 18. Hí þá castelas gewunnan, P. 203, 4. [From Norman-French. For native English usage, cf. þ woerc *castellum*, Lk. L. 24, 13.]    **II.** *an old British or Roman earthwork* (?). v. *N. E. D.* castle, 8:—On ánne castel at Swíndúne ; of ðý castele . . . tó ánne castel ; of ðí castele on ánne herepað, C. D. iii. 397, 18–21. v. stán-castel.

**castel-burg** *a fortified place? :*—Hec sunt confinia . . . inde in montem susibrem urbs antiqua et postea bi þǽre aldan cestelbyrig on nunnena beorgas, C. D. B. i. 205, 8. [Ne moste na mon cumen wiðinne þon castelburi, Laym. 6714.]

**castenere**, es ; *m. A cabinet, chest :*—Ic geann eallum mínum híréd-wífmannum tó gemánum ánes gódes casteneres wel gerénodes, Cht. Th. 537, 7. [Cf. *O. H. Ger.* chastanári *inclusor.*]

**casul.** For Som. Ben. Lye *substitute :*—Casul *byrrum*, Wrt. Voc. ii. 127, 33. [*From Lat.* casula. v. *N. E. D.* s.vv. casule, chasuble.]

**cásus.** *Add :*—Verbum ys word, án dæl lédensprǽce mid tíde and háde bútan cáse, Ælfc. Gr. Z. 119, 9. Tó sumum cásum, 107, 4.

**cat.** *Add :*—Catt *muriceps*, Wrt. Voc. ii. 56, 56 : 71, 31. Gif hwylcum mete hund oððe catt (*felis*) oððe mús oðhríne, oððe óðer unclǽne nýten hwylc, Ll. Th. ii. 164, 8. Cattes fleót, stán, stoke, C. D. vi. 267. v. catte.

**Catacumbé** *representing late Lat.* (ad) Catacumbas :—Eal folc Rómwara befeng þá líchoman (*of SS. Peter and Paul*) on þǽre stówe Catacumbé, Bl. H. 193, 11. Hine ferian tó Catacumbas, þǽr Petrus and Paulus bebyrgede wǽron, Hml. S. 5, 465.

**catte**, an ; *f. A she-cat :*—Catte *fellus* (=felis), Txts. 63, 863. And-lang eá on cattan ége, Cht. E. 294, 27. [Cf. *Icel.* ketta *a she-cat.*] v. cat.

**cattes mint.** *Dele.*

**cawel** (cáwel?). *Add :*—Cawel *caulus*, Wrt. Voc. ii. 129, 83. Caul *caula*, An. Ox. 56, 366. v. cál *in Dict.*

**cawl** *Add : a cawl* (v. *N. E. D.*) :—Cauuel, couel *corbus*, Txts. 51, 513. Lorg, couel *colum*, 110, 1172. Cawel *corvis*, Wrt. Voc. ii. 15, 9. Caulum *corbibus*, 79, 73. Caulas *corbos*, 83, 68 : 18, 53. v. ceofl, ceol, ceoul, ceowl *in Dict.*

**ceác.** *Add :*—Ceác *antulum*, Wrt. Voc. i. 291, 1 : 285, 13 : ii. 8, 34 : *urna*, An. Ox. 4322. Ágrafen ceác *expolita pelvis*, Germ. 403, 16. Ǽren fæt, læfel oþþe céc, Lch. iii. 292, 9. On ceáce (*concha*) fét ðwearde, Angl. xiii. 415, 716. Ðone ceák (*luterem*) . . . on ðǽm

ceáke, Past. 105, 17, 13. Hé (*David*) genam his (*Saul's*) ceác (*scyphum aquae*, 1 Sam. 26, 11), Ps. Th. 35, arg. Se gelýfeda cempa bróhte ceác fulne wæteres fulluhtes biddende, Hml. Th. i. 428, 1. Gedó on ceác fulne wínes (cf. ceác-full), Lch. ii. 30, 23. [Cf. (?) *N. E. D.* keach *to ladle out.*] [*From Lat.* caucus.]

**ceác-ádl** (ceóc-) *disease in the fauces* (v. ceáce, II):—Wiþ ceócádle and wiþ ceolwærce, Lch. ii. 300, 11. Wiþ ceócádle, nim hweorfan, bind on his sweoran, and swile innan mid háte meolce, 310, 21.

**ceác-bora.** *For* 'anhilus?' Cot. 13' *substitute :*—Caecbora *antulus*, Txts. 41, 171. Ceácbora, Wrt. Voc. ii. 7, 3.

**ceace** *a trial, &c.* *Dele, and see* ceáp, III a.

**ceace**, an ; *f.* (?) *A cake :*—Ceaum (ceacum ? cf. cyclum, *the gloss to the same passage*, An. Ox. 3859) *tortellis*, Wrt. Voc. ii. 83, 63. [Hire cake bearned o þe stan, H. M. 37, 36. *Icel.* kaka.] Cf. cicel.

**ceáce.** *Add :* ceóce.    **I.** *jawbone, cheek :*—In suíðra ceica ðín (in ðæt swíðran wonge ł céke þín, R.) *in dextera maxilla tua*, Mt. L. 5, 39. þæt wange wið þá ceócan ufan *mandibula*, Wrt. Voc. ii. 58, 3. On céce *in maxillam*, Lk. L. 6, 29. Ceácan *mala, maxilla*, Wrt. Voc. ii. 56, 23, 24 : i. 282, 58, 59. Ceócan *malae*, 64, 44. Ceácan *mandibulas*, An. Ox. 1206 : 17, 36. Gif monnes ceácan mon forslihð, þ hié beóð forode, Ll. Th. i. 94, 14. Ceócan *maxillas*, Bl. Gl. Céacan, Ps. Srt. 31, 9.    **II.** *chaps, fauces.* v. ceác-ádl :—Smire þone sweoran mid ; þ biþ strang sealf wiþ þára ceácna geswelle oððe ásmorunge, Lch. ii. 48, 11.

**ceac ful ;** *adj.* *Dele, and see* ceác.

**ceác-full** (?) *a jugful :*—Geseóð on þrím ceácfullum (ceácum fullum ? .v. ceác ; *but cf.* handful) wæteres, Lch. ii. 188, 24.

**ceacga**, an ; *m. Broom, gorse* (? v. *D. D.* chag ; cf. Chagford in Devon) :—On ceacgabróc, C. D. B. ii. 434, 38. On þone fearngáran . . . swá on ceacganseáð, C. D. v. 284, 17. Tó ceágganheale, 262, 8. On ceaggancum, iii. 411, 19.

**ceaclum.** v. ceafl.

**ceaf.** *Add :*—Þú deáðes bearn, ðú ceaf écum ontendnyssum gegearcod, Hml. Th. i. 594, 6. Sé ðe getimbrað ofer ðám grundwealle treówa, oþþe streáw, oððe ceaf (*ligna, foenum, stipulam*) . . . Ðurh ðám streáwe and ðám ceafe sind getácnode leóhtlíce synna, ii. 590, 9–14 : 322, 19. Swelce wé nimen ðone clǽnan hwǽte, and weorpen ðæt ceaf onweg, Past. 369, 9. Ánim þ ceaf onwcg *paleam tolle*, Gr. D. 276, 22. On ceafa *in paleas*, Scint. 57, 7. v. windwig-ceaf.

**ceafer.** *Add :*—Ceber *arpia*, Txts. 43, 214. Cefer, cefr *bruchus*, 45, 326. Ceafer, Wrt. Voc. ii. 11, 46. Ic sænde ceferas an eów, Wlfst. 221, 7. ¶ *in a local name* ceafor-leáh, C. D. iii. 77, 26.

**ceaf-finc**, es ; *m. A chaffinch :*—Ceaffinc *scutacis*, Hpt. 33, 241, 50.

**ceafl.** *Add :*—Þý fǽcnan ceafle *strophoso rictu* (*carpere*), Wrt. Voc. ii. 89, 66. Háwa hwæþer his ceaflas síu tóswollene, Lch. ii. 140, 8. Ceafla *faucium*, An. Ox. 3575. Grǽdigum ceaflum (*faucibus*), 838. Mid deórenum ceaflum *ferinis rictibus*, 3342 : 1478. Ceaflum (ceaclum, Hpt. Gl. 454, 65) *faucibus*, i. *labris*, 2048 : *rostris*, Wrt. Voc. ii. 88, 79. Ðá león mid grǽdigum ceaflum hí tótǽron, Hml. Th. i. 572, 18. Hí clumiað mid ceaflum þǽr hí sceoldan clypian, Ll. Th. ii. 308, 20. Ceaflan (*l.* -as) *mandibalas*, An. Ox. 5015. Ceaflas *rictus*, 5017. Ic úp áhóf míne nyþeran cæflas ł mínre undertungan *exaltavi sub lingua mea*, Ps. L. 65, 17.

**ceafl-ádl**, e ; *f. Disease of the jaws :*—Him becumað on missenlica ádla . . . sweorcoþu, ceafládl (ceaflf-, MS.), Lch. ii. 240, 20.

**ceahhe**, an ; *f. A daw :*—On ceahhan, C. D. iii. 48, 26. [Cf. *O. L. Ger.* ká *monedula* : *O. H. Ger.* kaha *cornicula*.]

**ceahhet(t)an.** *Substitute for the citation :*—Hié on þon swíðe blissedon and ceahhetton(-heton v. l.) *turba multum exultans et cachinnans*, Bd. 5, 12 ; Sch. 620, 14 : *and add :*—Cæh[hetende] *cachinnantes*, An. Ox. 5234. [Ceahhe]tendum *cachinnanti*, 4499.

**ceahhet(t)ung.** *Substitute for first citation :*—Gehýrde ic mycel gehlýd and ceahhetunge (-ttung, ceahetunge, v. ll.) swá swá ungelǽrdes folces and bysmriendes gehæftum heora feóndum *audio cachinnum crepitantem quasi uulgi indocti captis hostibus insultantis*, Bd. 5, 12 ; Sch. 620, 5 : *and add :*—Ceahhetung *cachinnus*, Wrt. Voc. ii. 127, 34. Ceachetunge, hospe *cauillatione*, i. *uituperatione*, An. Ox. 4500. Ic hí tó ceahhetunge bysmerlicum ástyrede *I excited them to shameless shouts of laughter*, Hml. S. 23 b, 375. Þá higeleáslican ceahhetunga *ineffrenatos cachinnos*, An. Ox. 3171. Forbeóde gé þá hǽðenan sangas þǽra lǽwedra manna and heora hlúdan cheahchetunga, Ll. Th. ii. 358, 3. [*O. H. Ger.* chachazunga *cachinnus*.] v. cehhettung *in Dict.*

**cealc.** *Add :*—Calc *calculus*, Wrt. Voc. ii. 102, 39. Cealc, 13, 6. Býð gefylled múð his mid cealce (*calculo*), Scint. 110, 14.

**Cealca-ceaster.** *Add :*—Heó gewát tó þǽre ceastre þe in Englisc is háten Cealcaceaster (Kalca-, v.l.) *secessit ad ciuitatem Calcariam, quae a gente Anglorum Kælcacaestir appellatur*, Bd. 4, 23 ; Sch. 466, 15.

**cealc-crundel**, *a chalk ravine :*—On cealccrundel, C. D. iii. 419, 17.

**cealc-pytt**, es ; *m. A chalkpit :*—On ðæuc chelcpyt, C. D. iii. 24, 3.

**cealc-seáþ**, es ; *m. A chalkpit :*—Tó cealcseáðan ; of cealcseáðan, C. D. iii. 82, 7. On ðá cealcseáðas, v. 325, 15.

**cealc-stán.** *Add:*—Cealcstán *calculus,* Wrt. Voc. ii. 89, 15. Geǽl cealcstán swíðe, Lch. ii. 98, 13.

**cealct.** v. níw-cealct.

**ceald;** *adj. Add:*—Mid cealdrum ēstum *frigidioribus aepulis,* Scint. 52, 1. v. ungemet-ceald.

**ceald, es;** *n. What is cold:*—Þām synfullum þinceð, þæt nān wiht ne sȳ þæs hātes ne þæs cealdes . . ., þæt hig nihte fram ūses Drihtnes lufan āsceádan, Wlfst. 184, 19. Dô on sumes cynnes cald (MS. B. *adds* seáw), Lch. i. 80, 19.

**cealde;** *adv. Coldly:*—Se feórða heáfodwind blǽwð norðan cealde, Lch. iii. 274, 23.

**cealdian.** *Add:*—Ic cealdige *frigesco,* i. *frigeo, algeo,* Wrt. Voc. ii. 150, 72.

**ceald-ness, e;** *f. Coldness, cold:*—Ic mænigfeald earfeðu dreáh, hwílum þǽre ísihtan cealdnysse þæs wintres, hwílum þæs unmǽtan wylmes þǽre sunnan hǽto; ic wæs beswǽled for þām micclan byrne and eft for þǽre micclan forstigan cealdnysse þæs wintres, Hml. S. 23 b, 571-5.

**cealf.** *Add:*—Caelf *vitulus,* Wrt. Voc. ii. 123, 76. Cealf *bucula,* 90, 4 : 12, 7. Cælfes *vituli,* Mt. p. 9, 11. Celfes, 15. Caelf *vitulum,* Ps. Srt. 28, 6. Ymbsaldon mē calfur monig (*vituli multi*), 21, 13. On cealfa leáge, Cht. E. 294, 25. Calfra *vitulorum,* Rtl. 21, 12. Calfero *vitulos,* 119, 28. Cealfru, Ps. L. 49, 9 : 50, 21. Cealfas, Ex. 24, 5 : Ps. Spl. 28, 6. Hē ðā cealfas tô cūum lǽdde, Shrn. 61, 19. v. cū-, hind-cealf ; cealfa hús *in Dict.*

**cealf-ādl.** v. ceasf-ādl.

**cealfian.** *Add:*—Ān cū wolde cealfian on gesihðe þæs folces, Hml. Th. ii. 300, 34. Ealdre cū meolc .vii. niht syððan heó níge cealfod hæfð, Ll. Th. i. 438, 19.

**cealf-loca, an;** *m. An enclosure for calves:*—Of ðǽm londe et cealflocan, C. D. i. 312, 6.

**cealf-wyrt:**—Calfwyrt *eruca,* Wrt. Voc. i. 31, 72.

**ceáp.** *Add:* I. *trading, bargaining, bargain, sale, purchase:*—Ceáp *distractio,* sala *venditio,* Wrt. Voc. i. 55, 54. Hē sealde his sweostor ān marc goldes . . . on geceápodne ceáp . . . þes ceáp wæs geceápod ætforan ealra scȳre *he was to give his sister a mark of gold . . . to complete the purchase . . . This purchase was completed before all the shire,* Cht. Th. 350, 14-22. Hí cêpes ne gȳmdon, ne nāht syllan ne mōston, Hml. S. 31, 324. Ceápe *negotio,* An. Ox. 4838. For ceápe *commertio,* 7, 227. Þæt tempel næs tô nānum ceápe ārǽred, Hml. Th. i. 406, 25. Sȳn on ǽlcum ceápe twēgen oþþe þrȳ tô gewitnysse, Ll. Th. i. 274, 19. Gif hē ceáp ǽredige ût on hwylcere faæ, 23. Gif man hwæt becȳpan scyle, warnien þā þe þone ceáp drífað, þæt hí nān þing fācenlices on þām ceápe ne dôn *si quid venumdandum est, videant ipsi, per quorum manus transigenda sunt, ne aliquam fraudem presumant inferre,* R. Ben. 95, 11. Hē hreówlíce his ceáp gedrífen hæfde *he had done his bargaining (for bread) miserably,* Hml. S. 23, 585. Ceápas *negotia,* Scint. 60, 10. Ðā ealdorbiscopas ðā leáslican ceápas' binnan ðām Godes hûse geðafedon, Hml. Th. i. 406, 15. ¶ tô ceápe *on sale:*—Gehírde Iacób secgan, þæt man sealde hwǽte . . . þā cwæð hē : 'Ic gehírde secgan, þæt hwǽte wǽre tô ceápe (*venumdetur*),' Gen. 42, 2: Hml. S. 19, 235. Man orf þæt tô ceápe hæfde, . . . ðæt man on gehendnysse tô bicgenne gearu hæfde, Hml. Th. i. 406, 21. II. *what is given for a commodity, price:*—Tô ceápe syllan *venumdare,* Gen. 37, 27. Man hláf sealde tô ceápe, Hml. S. 23, 563. Heó bohte Gladu wyð healfe punde tô cēpe and tô tolle, Cht. E. 254. 8 : Cht. Th. 633. 5. God mid deórwyrðum ceápe ús gebohte, Wlfst. 144, 1. Heardan ceápe, B. 2482. ¶ bûtan ceápe *gratis, without payment:*—Hē āgeaf hí bûtan ceápe (weorðe, *v.l.*) *sine pretio,* Gr. D. 83, 5. Scottas him andlyfene bûton ceápe (*sine pretio*) sealdon, Bd. 3, 27; Sch. 318, 4. Bûtan cēpe (*gratis*) gē underfēngon, bûtan cēpe syllaþ, Scint. 131, 11. II a. *the amount of a fine for redemption:*—Sceal sē þe hine (*a homicide*) āh . . . lx. sciłł. gesellan wið his feore. Gif hē þone ceáp nelle fore gesellan, Ll. Th. i. 148, 17. III. *what may be bought or sold, goods, chattels, stock:*—Mid hú wáclicum wurðe Godes ríce bið geboht. . . . Se ceáp ne mæg wið nānum sceatte beón geeht, Hml. Th. i. 582, 27 : B. 2415. Sunnandæges cȳpinge gif hwá āgynne, þolie þæs ceápes, Ll. Th. i. 170, 16. Nimð him man hyra ceápes (*rei*) wið hwæthwega, ii. 160, 3. Teóþan dǽl ealles þæs ceápes þe gē habban, Bl. H. 41, 25. Þæs þe wē on ceápe habban, 39, 16. Be his ceápe *according to the value of the (stolen) goods,* Ll. Th. i. 132, 10. Cyning sceal mid ceápe cwēne gebicgan, bûnum and beágum, Gu. Ex. 82. Gif man mægð gebigeð ceápi, Ll. Th. i. 22, 1. Crístene men . . . Godes āgenne ceáp þe hē deóre gebohte, 304, 21. Þǽr hē his hláfordes ceáp (*rem*) werige, ii. 150, 5. Gif ceorl ceáp forsteld, and bireð intô his ærne, i. 138, 15. Þæt mon ǽlcne ceáp mehte be twiefealdan þet geceápian *ut duplicia possessionum aliarumque rerum venalium pretia statuerentur,* Ors. 5, 13 ; S. 248, 1. Ǽlc þāra ceápa þe hē bigcge óðer sylle, Ll. Th. i. 274, 13. Ðonne his ceápa hwilcne man forstolenne (hæfð), Lch. i. 390, 17. Cf. iii. 60, 9. III a. *property given as pledge:*—Tô ceápe (ceáce, *v.l.*) fordrífan be-), Ll. Th. i. 140, 15 :

142, 1, 5. Se cierlisca mon, sē þe oft betygen wǽre þiéfðe, and þonne æt síðestan synnigne man gefô in ceápe (ceáce, *v.l.*) *and at last is caught offending when a pledge has been given for his good conduct* (cf. (?) Omnes accusationibus ingravati sub plegio redigantur, 253, 23), 124, 23. III b. *cattle, (live) stock:*—Ealra dūna ceáp *jumenta in montibus,* Ps. Th. 49, 11. Ceápes hierdas *pastores pecorum,* Past. 109, 4. Ceápes heorde *gregarius,* Nar. 18, 26. Be þæs ceápes (*swine*) weorðe, Ll. Th. i. 132, 16. Sum fearhrýþer þæs ôþræs ceápes gefērscipe oferhogode, Bl. H. 199, 4 : Lch. iii. 56, 8. Benumene ǽgðer ge þæs ceápes ge þæs cornes, Chr. 895 ; P. 88, 17. On ûrum wæstmum and on cwicum ceápe, Bl. H. 39. 20: Ll. Th. i. 197, 6 : Cht. Th. 492, 22. Hié nāmon þone ceáp onbûtan, Chr. 921 ; P. 101, 26. Sendan ādla on manna ceáp, Wlfst. 209, 29. Ceáp milcian, Lch. iii. 178, 30. On hrýþrum and on manigfealdum ceápum, Bl. H. 199, 2. v. lah-, teóþung-ceáp ; or-ceápes, -ceápe ; un-ceáp.

**ceáp-cniht.** *Substitute: A (young) man who has been bought, a slave:*—Ceápcneht *empticius,* Wrt. Voc. ii. 107, 18. Ceápcniht, 29, 28. v. cȳpe-cniht *in Dict.*

**ceáp-dæg.** *For* Cot. 142 *substitute:*—Ceápdagas *nonae, a nundinis,* Wrt. Voc. ii. 62, 26. v. cípe-dæg.

**ceáp-ealeðel.** *l.* ceáp-ealo-þelu (?). The passage cited occurs in a section headed 'Ut sacerdos tabernas fugiat.' *Tabernae* is glossed by *lytle hús* of bredan, Wrt. Voc. i. 37, 7 ; as þel=plank, a word containing a derivative of it might have served to translate *tabernae,* perhaps *ceáp-ealo-þelu;* cf. buruh-þeiu.

**ceáp-gyld, II.** *indemnity for stolen property. Add:*—Gecýðe hē þ hit wǽre forstolen, and bidde syþþan his ceápgildes, Ll. Th. i. 238, 13. 8. Þingie hē on þām ceápgilde, nāht on þām wíte, 210, 16. Þone þeóf ût niman be his were and be fullan ceápgilde, 228, 28. Þ wē niman eall þ hē (*the thief*) āge, and niman ǽrest þ ceápgyld oð þām yrfe, 228, 15. Sylle mon þ ceápgyld ðām ðe þ yrfe (*the stolen cattle*) āge, 258, 11. Healde se landhláford þ forstolene orf and þæs orfes ceápgyld, 276, 15. þ ceápgild (for)gildan, 200, 16: 208, 22.

**ceápian.** *Dele last passage, and add:* I. *to trade, traffic:*—Ceápigas (ceópigas, R.) *negotiamini,* Lk. L. 19, 13. Gif ciépemon uppe on folce ceápi(g)e, Ll. Th. i. 118, 12. II. *to buy, purchase* (with gen.):—Bycges ł ceápas (ceópias, R.) *emant,* Mk. L. 6, 13. Man wið þone here frides ceápode, Chr. 1004; P. 135. 24. Hē mid ælmessum him ceápode ēces ríces, Shrn. 110, 8 : Cri. 1096. Ceápa þe mid ǽhtum ēces leóhtes, Dóm. L. 30, 34. Þæt mon nāne burg ne mehte ieð mid feó geceápian, gif hiere ǽnig mon ceápode *O urbem venalem, si emtorem invenerit !* Ors. 5, 7 ; S. 228, 21. Bochton ł ceápadon *emerent,* Jn. L. 4, 8. Ceápigan *comparare,* i. *emere,* Wrt. Voc. ii. 132, 78. Ceápiendum *mercantibus,* i. *comparantibus,* An. Ox. 1647. v. un-ceápod; cípan.

**ceáp-man.** *Add:*—Ceápmanna del, C. D. vi. 41, 18. [*O. Frs.* káp-man : *O. H. Ger.* chouf-mann *mercator, negotiator.*] v. cípe-man.

**ceáp-scip.** *Add:*—Be ceápscypum.' Ǽlc ceápscip frið hæbbe þe binnan mūðan cuman, þēh hit unfriðcypa sȳ, gif hit undrifen bið, Ll. Th. i. 284, 19-21. [*O. H. G.* chouf-scef.]

**ceáp-stede, es;** *m. A market-place,* in the place-name *Chêpstede,* C. D. vi. 269. [*O. Sax.* kôp-stedi *market-place* (of the temple, v. Mt. 21, 12).]

**ceáp-stów.** *Add:*—Ceápstóu *commercium,* Wrt. Voc. ii. 104, 41. Ceápstów *emptorium,* i. *mercatus,* 143, 39. Him nā ālyfed ne byð þ hē on ceápstówe (*mercatu*) ǽnige cýpinge begá, Ll. Th. ii. 174, 18. Nis man on life, ðe ǽfre gehýrde ðæt man crasode hine on hundrede oððon āhwār on gemôte, on ceápstówe oþþe on cyricware, Lch. iii. 288, 5. Ceápstôwa *nundinarum,* Wrt. Voc. 79, 81 : 59, 63. Hí sēcað ðæt hí mon ǽrest grēte on ceápstówum (*in foro*), Past. 27, 7. [*Chepstow, a local name.*]

**ceáp-strǽt.** *Add:*—Ceápstrǽte *foro,* Wrt. Voc. ii. 149, 75. Wið ðā cēpstrǽt (cȳp-, ceáp-) *circa forum,* Ælfc. Gr. Z. 269, 9. Þæs hagan gemǽre . . . æt Wintanceastre lið . . . norð on þā ceápstrǽt, þonne eást andlanges þǽre ceápstrǽte, C. D. B. ii. 305, 22-26. v. cȳp-strǽt *in Dict.*

**ceápung.** *Add:*—þ tácnað ceápunge and hwearfunge, Lch. iii. 156, 5. Ceápunge *negotia,* Wrt. Voc. i. 20, 35: *commercia,* ii. 82, 61 : 18, 38. [*N. E. D.* cheaping ; Chipping in local names. *O. Frs.* kâping.] v. wôh-ceápung; or-, un-ceápunga ; cíping.

**ceápung-gemôt.** *For* Cot. 133 *substitute* Wrt. Voc. ii. 58, 62 : **ceápung-þing.** *Dele:* **cear;** *adi. Dele, and see* caru: cear-. v. car-: cearc. *Dele.*

**cearcet(t)ung** *creaking. Add:*—Heora grymetung bið gelíc crætena cearcetunge, Wlfst. 200, 18. Cf. next word.

**cearcian.** *Add:*—Ic cearcige *strideo* and *strido,* Ælfc. Gr. Z. 220, 9. Þā tēð, þe nū on oferæte blissiað, sceolon þǽr cearcian on þínungum, Hml. Th. i. 530, 32. Ne gestilde nǽfre stefen cearciendes wǽnes. Lch. iii. 430, 33. Cearciendum *crepante* i. *sonante* (*naucleri porticulo*), An. Ox. 31: 3, 20. Ðǽr beóð wēpende eágan and cearcigende tēð, Hml. Th. i. 132, 30. [v. *N. E. D.* chark.] Cf. circan.

**cearm**, es; *m. Clamour, noise :*—Se forhta cearm (cyrm, *v. l.*) and þǽra folca wôp, Wlfst. 186, 18. [v. *N. E. D.* charm.] v. cirm.

**cearricge** *a vehicle* (?):—Cearricge, cearruccae, cearricae *senon* (*cf.?* seno vel *tilia* lind, Wrt. Voc. i. 32, 46), Txts. 97, 1849. [From *Low Lat.* carrigium, carruca, carriga ?: cf. *O. H. Ger.* karruh *carruca.*]

**ceart**, cert, *chart*, '*a rough common overrun with gorse, broom, bracken,* &c.,' D. D. :—Haec sunt terrae ... Selebertes ceart, C. D. v. 62, 16. Silua quae dicitur cært, i. 261, 4. Cert, 273, 2. Cymeringes cert, 4.

**cearung.** *Dele, and see* ceorung : **cear-wund.** v. scear-wund.

**ceás**, e; *f. Add :* I. *strife, quarrel, contention :* — Dyslic bið mannes ceás ongeán Godes gôdnysse, Hml. Th. ii. 89, 26. Ðá wrôhtgeornan ðe ceáse wyrceað (cf. ðá ðe wrôhte sáwað, 357, 14) *seminantes jurgia*, Past. 177, 11. *Cǽsa insectationes, rixas,* An. Ox. 4, 54. II. *reproof, chiding, rebuke :*—Dauid anfeng eáðmôdlíce his ágnes ðegnes ceáse (*correptionem*), Past. 145, 19. 'Ðonne ic him cídde, ðonne oncúðon hié mê.' Hié oncúðon hiene for ðære ceáse, 355, 16. For ûre ceáse *ex nostra increpatione*, 23. [*O. Frs.* kâse. *Lat.* causa.] v. or-, unbe-ceás; *adj.* ; ceást.

**ceásan.** *Dele :* ceásness. *Substitute :* v. or-ceásness.

**ceást**, e; *f. Add :* I. *strife,* &c. :—Cêst *lis*, Hpt. Gl. 495, 32. Mid ceáste andswarian *cum jurgio respondere*, Gr. D. 64, 33. Ðá ðing þe heó nû tô sibbe talað, beóð hire ðonne tô ceáste áwende, Hml. Th. i. 408, 26. Hê forlêt his gingran tôgeánes þære ceáste *he left his subordinate to meet the tumult*, Hml. S. 7, 212. Þá ðe þá ceáste macedon, 222. Þá micclan ceáste ácuman, 243. Ceáste *contentionem*, R. Ben. I. 22, 6 : Hml. Th. i. 604, 35. Ceáste (â)styrian, ii. 420, 33 : 338, 11. Ceásta *litium*, Hy. S. 10, 29 : *sectarum*, Scint. 134, 15. Ceásta *lites*, 12. II. *reproof :*—Hogode hê hyra wâcmôdnysse tô þreágenne mid ungemettlicre ceáste (*increpatione*), Gr. D. 145, 18. Gefylledre þære cǽste (ceáste, *v. l.*) *qua increpatione completa*, 160, 7. [*v. N. E. D.* chest. *O. L. Ger.* caest *c(l)asma.*] v. lotwrenc-, un-ceást; ceás.

**ceastel.** v. stân-ceastel.

**ceaster.** *Dele passage from Chron. under* I, *and add :* I. used as a general term, or applied to foreign towns. [For the use of *burh, ceaster* respectively cf. the translation of Orosius, in which *burh* is always used in speaking of Jerusalem, Sodom, Gomorrah and Babylon (and of other towns), with the passages from the poetry in which *ceaster* is used of the same.] :—Cester *arx, civitas*, Hpt. Gl. 530, 2. Hierusalem ys mǽres cyninges ceaster (cester, *v. l.*, cæstra, R., burug, L. *civitas*), Mt. 5, 35. Hierusalem, ðû wǽre swá swá cýmlic ceaster (cester, Ps. Srt.) getimbred, Ps. Th. 121, 3. Sió ceaster (*Mermedonia*), An. 207. Ceastre weardas, El. 384. Hê ceastre weall, Babilone burh, geseah, Dan. 600. Cempan in ceastre (*Jerusalem*), 707. Hwǽr cýpst þû fixas þíne? On ceastre (*civitate*), Coll. M. 23, 23. In Antiochia þǽre ceastre (Antiochia ceastre, *v. l.*), Chr. 35; P. 6, 16. Of Caldéa ceastre, Gen. 2200. In þǽre ceastre Commedia, Jul. 21. Hê getimbrode ceastre (*civitatem*), Gen. 4, 17. Ic wât heáhburg, lytle ceastre, Gen. 2518. Sodoma ceastre (cf. Sodoman burg, 2402), 2425. Wæs hé tô þære mǽran byrig cumen in þá ceastre, An. 41. Hæleð tô Hierusalem cwômon in þá ceastre, El. 274. Nineuen ceastre, Sal. 188. On ceastre weallum beworhte *in civitatem munitam*, Ps. Th. 59, 8. Ðá fæstan ceastre *munitum castrum*, Wrt. Voc. ii. 58, 38. Ceaster timbran, Gen. 1057. Ceastra beóð feorran gesýne, ongean enta geweorc, Gn. C. 1. Cýmast ceastra, Ps. Th. 86, 2. On ceastrum (*Sodom and Gomorrah*), Gen. 2507 : 2546. Of ceastrum and cynestólum and of burgsalum, Pa. 49. ¶ with weak inflection :—Ceastran *civitatis*, An. Ox. 818. I a. used of heaven :—Þu, Dryhten God, wunast on þære upplican ceastre, Hy. 8, 19. Cestre, Sat. 258 : 657. Godes ealdorburg gesêcan, rodera ceastre, Rä. 60, 16. Wunian cestre and cynestôl, Sat. 298. I b. of hell :—Hê byrnwigend tô þám burggeatum lǽdan ne wolde ; ac þá locu feollon, clústor of þám ceastrum (*at the harrowing of hell*), Hö. 40. II. used of places in England [in place-names *gen.* -ceastres and -ceastre occur, and the *acc.* -ceaster seems more frequent than -ceastre] :—Aldwulf, Hrôfescæstre (Rôfeceastre, *v. l.*) biscop, Chr. 731 ; Th. i. 77, 5. On ânre wêstre ceastre, seó is Legaceaster gehâten, 894 ; P. 88, 6. On ðǽre ealdan byrig, Acemannes ceastre, 973 ; P. 118, 7. Hié ábrǽcon Wintanceastre, 894 ; P. 68, 3. Oþ ceaster (-ceastre, *v. l.*), 877 ; P. 74, 18 : 876 ; P. 74, 11. Hié ymbsǽton Andredesceaster, 491 ; P. 14, 15. Justo hê sealde Hrôfesceaster, seó is .xxiiii. míla from Dorwitceastre, 604 ; P. 23, 3. Hié genâmon .iii. ceastra, Gleáwanceaster and Cirenceaster and Baþanceaster, 577 ; P. 18, 32. v. neáh-ceaster.

**ceaster-æsc.** *Add :*—Ceasteræsc *eliforus*, Wrt. Voc. ii. 32, 30.

**ceaster-geat** ? :—Ðis is ðæs wuda gemǽre ... ðæt is, ǽrest æt ceastergeate tô ceasterwege; ondlong ceasterweges tô middelwege; of niddelwege eft tô ceastergeate; of ðæm geate tô longan leáge, C. D. iii. 260, 4-7.

**ceaster-gewara**, an; *m. A citizen :*—Ceastergewara (cestergewaru, *v. l.*) oððe portman *civis*, Ælf. Gr. Z. 318, 7. Þes and þeós ceastergewara *hic et haec civis*, 53, 12. Ceastergewara (-geware, -gewaran, *v. ll.*) *civis*, 11, 16. Cæstergewara *concivis*, Hy. S. 55, 31. Cæstergewaran rodorlice *cives aetherei*, 57, 4. Hê côm tô þære byrig . . . ðá ceastergewaran wundrodon, Hml. S. 24, 131 : Shrn. 98, 33 : 151, 34. Wé syndon þýne ceastergewaran, Ap. Th. 20, 1. Gê Tharsysce ceastergewaran, 26, 2. Godes ceastergewaran, Hml. Th. i. 38, 34. Ðá Rômâniscan ceastregewaran, 370, 30. Ðǽra heofonlicra ceastregewarena, 348, 33. Ceastriwarena, An. Ox. 329 : 703. Se cyncg hine sylfne ætýwde his ceastergewarum, Ap. Th. 3, 3. Sleán þá ceastergewaran, Hml. S. 13, 254 : 22, 167. Cf. ceaster-wara.

**ceaster-geware(-a)**; *pl. Citizens :*—Ealle cæstergewara heofonlice *omnes cives celici*, Hy. S. 118, 27. Cæstergewara blissigendra *civium gaudentium*, 56, 1 : 103, 25. Ceastregewara, Hpt. Gl. 452, 39. Ceast(re)gewara, 414, 7. v. ceaster-ware, *and preceding word.*

**ceaster-gewaru**, e; *f. The inhabitants of a city, citizens :*—Castergewaru *cives*, Hy. S. 105, 1. Seó ceastergewaru wundrode, Ap. Th. 26, 18. v. ceaster-waru.

**ceaster-herpaþ** *a high road* (?) :—Andlang furh on ceasterherpað, C. D. v. 217, 1.

**ceasternisc**; *adj.* ? :—.ii. blace rǽgl cæsternisce, and vi. uuâhryft, Cht. Th. 244, 13.

**ceaster-sǽtan, -sǽte**; *pl. Towns-folk :*—Ceastersǽtna preóst, Cht. Th. 140, 19 : 142, 1.

**ceaster-wara**, an; *m. A citizen :*—Se cyning wæs ceasterwara (cester-, *v. l.* ciuis) gefremed þæs êcan ríces, Bd. 3, 22 ; Sch. 293, 2. Þá earman ceasterwaran *miseri ciues*, 1, 12 ; Sch. 35, 12. Þá eádigan ceasterwaran (þǽre eádigan ceastre weras, *v. l.*), Wlfst. 265, 11. Hê cwæð tô ðám ceasterwarum : . 'Gê Tharsysce ceasterwaran,' Ap. Th. 9, 23 : 12, 19. v. efen-, ge-ceaster-wara; ceaster-gewara.

**ceaster-ware.** *Add :*—Ceasterware *civis*, Wrt. Voc. i. 34, 33. Eal seó burh wæs onstyred, and þá ceasterware cêgdon, Bl. H. 71, 13. Þǽre burge ceasterware (*cives urbis illius*) gecyrdon, Gr. D. 198, 15. Þæs êþles ceasterware wǽron englas, 260, 20. Þá ceasterwara (-e, *v. l.*) þǽre burge, 210, 12. Hwá bigþ fixas þíne? Ceasterwara *cives*, Coll. M. 23, 27. Seó cwên þara úplicra cesterwara, Mart. H. 146, 23. v. ceaster-geware.

**ceaster-waru.** *Add :*—Micele lufe hæfde eal seó ceasterwaru tô him, Ap. Th. 6, 11. Þeós ceasterwaru on heáfe wunað, 23. Mínre ceasterwaru nis nân hǽlo hiht, 9, 10. v. ceaster-gewaru.

**ceaster-weall**, es; *m. A city-wall :*—Sê wæs in þære ceastre Augustodonensi ... clypode his môdor of þám cesterwealle, Shrn. 119, 26.

**ceaster-weg?** v. ceaster-geat.

**ceaster-wíc**, e; *f. A village :*—Gangaþ on þás ceasterwíc (*castellum*, Mt. 21, 2) þe inc ongeán standeþ, Bl. H. 69, 35.

**ceaster-wyrhta.** *For* Cot. 156 *substitute :* Wrt. Voc. ii. 68, 27, 69: 69, 24.

**ceaster-wyrt.** *For* Lch. ii. 375, 24 *substitute :* Ceasterwyrte sǽd, Lch. ii. 102, 21.

**ceást-full** *contentious, quarrelsome :*—Ne beó ðú tô ceástful; of irsunge wyxt seófung, Prov. K. 23. Gâlful þing wín, and ceástfull (*tumultuosa*) druncennyss, Scint. 105, 5.

**ceat.** *Dele, and see* sceatt : **ceaum.** v. ceace : **ceber.** v. ceafer : **cêc.** v. ceác : **cêce.** v. ceáce.

**cecil** *a cooking-pot* (?) :—Cecil *suffocacium*, Wrt. Voc. ii. 121, 68. [Cf. *O. H. Ger.* chahhala *cacabus*.]

**cêcil** *a cake :*—Coecil *tortum*, Txts. 100, 993. [v. *N. E. D.* kechel.]

**cecin**(?) *a board :*—Cecin *tabetum*, Wrt. Voc. i. 289, 51.

**ced** *a boat.* *l.* ceól. v. An. Ox. 58.

**ceddran ?**:—Ic hopige þ cherubin se mǽra wylle . . . mid his gyldenan tange þǽre glêdan spearcan tô mínre tungan gebringan, and þæs dumbes mûðes ceddran æthrínan (*the passage seems based on Is.* 6. 6, 7 : Unus de seraphim, et in manu ejus calculus, quem forcipe tulerat, . . . et tetigit os meum, et dixit : Ecce tetigit hoc labia tua), Angl. viii. 325, 32.

**cedelc.** *Add :*—Cedelc *merculialis*, Wrt. Voc. ii. 59, 44: *mercurialis*, i. 67, 59. [v. *N. E. D.* kedlock.]

**ceder**; *f. n. Add :*—Cedara *cedri*, Bl. Gl.

**ceder-beám.** *Add :*—Fram ðám heágan cederbeáme, . . . tô ðære lytlan ysopan, Hml. Th. ii. 578, 5. Ceodorbeámas *cedros*, Ps. L. 28, 5.

**ceder-treów.** *Add :*—Neorxnawanges cedertreów, Gr. D. 191, 7. Cedertrýwes twyg, Angl. viii. 332, 37. Cedortreówu . . . þá myclan cedertreówu *cedros* . . . *cedros Libani*, Ps. Th. 28, 5.

**cedrisc**; *adj. Of cedar :*—Cedrisc *caedrus*, Rtl. 65, 31.

**cefer.** v. ceafer: **cefes.** v. cifes.

**ceir** (cêr, cír ?) *a cry, clamour :*—Irra and ceir *ira et clamor*, Rtl. 12, 35. Ceir mín tô ðê cyme. Of grundum ic geceigde *clamor meus ad te veniat. De profundis clamavi*, 183, 10-15 : 170, 27 : 171, 21 : 174, 23. Cf. cígan (ceigan).

**cêlan.** *Add :* v. *trans. To make cool, slake* thirst :—Se úplica sǽ cêleð ðǽra tungla hǽto, Shrn. 63, 7. Wæter célde þá ísena, Hml. S. 36, 392. Wolde ic mínne þurst cêlan, Nar. 8, 28. Scó âdl mid cealdum þingum biþ tô cêlanne . . . scealt þû ǽrest þá hǽto cêlan mid

cellendre, Lch. ii. 82, 3-6. [v. *N. E. D.* keel. *O. H. Ger.* chuolen: *Icel.* kœla.] v. ge-cēlan.

celc. v. calic: cēle. *l.* cele, *and see* cile.

celde, an; *f. A spring* (?):—Tō celdan, C. D. iii. 429, 13. In loco ubi nominatur Baccancelde, C. D. B. i. 402, 15. [*Icel.* kelda *a spring.*]

cele *the beak of a ship*:—Neb *vel* scipes caeli (cæle, celae) *rostrum*, Txts. 93, 1748.

celendre. *Add:*—Cellendre *coleandrum*, Wrt. Voc. ii. 105, 15: 15, 19: *coantrum*, i. 67, 21. [*O. H. Ger.* chullantar. *From Latin.*]

cēling. *Add:*—Þā mettas þe cēlunge and strangunge mægen hæbben, Lch. ii. 176, 16. Se þurstiga gewilnað wæteres cēlincge, Hml. S. 8, 25. Eówre glēda nāne hǣtan ne gedóð, ac swíðor cēlinge, Hml. Th. i. 430, 13. Wē fērdon þurh fýr and þū ūs lǣddest on cēlincge (kēlinge, Ps. L. 65, 12) *in refrigerium*, Hml. S. 4, 340.

celle. v. cyll.

cēl-nes. *Dele* cōl-nes, *and add:*—Hē wæs eall biernende, and ðeáh ðā tungan suíðust mǣnde, and him ðǣre kēlnesse bæd *totus ardens refrigerari se praecipue in lingua requirebat*, Past. 309, 11. Coelnisse *refrigerium*, Ps. Srt. 65, 12: Rtl. 36, 17. Cēlnessa *refrigeria*, Lch. i. lxxiii, 8.

cēlod. *l.* celod, *and substitute: Having a boss or beak* (? cf. cele, *and see* Worsaae's Primeval Antiquities, p. 52, for such a 'beak').

cemban. *Add:* (1) *to comb* hair:—Genim þone camb þe heó āna hyre heáfod mid cemde (cǣmde, v. l.), and nǣnig man ǣr mid cemde ne æfter cembe. Under ðām treówe cembe hyre feax . . . þ bið lǣce-dōm þǣre ðe hyre heáfod þǣr cembeþ (cæmbeð, v. l.), Lch. i. 332, 11-18. Stríc þū mid þīnum fingrum on þīn feax nyþerwearad, swilce þū cembe þē, Tech. ii. 127, 5. Hý sculan hiora heáfod cemban, Lch. ii. 30, 31. (2) *to comb* wool, &c.:—Be cemdan wearpe *de stuppe stamineo*, Wrt. Voc. ii. 26, 62. [v. *N. E. D.* kemb. *O. H. Ger.* chempen *pectere*: *Icel.* kemba.] v. ge-cemban.

cemes. *Substitute: A shirt*:—Ham, cemes *camisa*, Wrt. Voc. ii. 13, 23. Būtan his kemese and eác gelōmlíce būtan his tunecan hē eft cyrde *sine linea, crebro etiam sine tunica revertebat*, Gr. D. 68, 6. [*From Latin.*]

cempa. *Add:*—Cempa *agonista*, An. Ox. 4, 4: *tyro*, Wrt. Voc. i. 289, 14. Heánra cempa *miles ordinarius*, ii. 59, 14. Kempa *miles*, Coll. M. 31, 37. Sē wæs cāseres cæmpa under Paulino on Rauenna, Shrn. 76, 2. Cempan *agonitheta*, An. Ox. 1334. Caempan, cempan *gladiatores*, Txts. 66, 481. Cempan *manipulares*, Wrt. Voc. ii. 86, 38: 56, 76: *tirones*, 88, 63. Wǣpenboran, cempan *pugiles .i. gladiatores*, An. Ox. 751. Cemp[ena] *luctatorum*, 4735 (cf., 11, 188). Cempena *anthletarum*, Wrt. Voc. ii. 74, 62. Cempum *tirunculis*, An. Ox. 719. Bebeád sum hǣþen ealdormon his cæmpum (cf. hēt his þegnas *jussit milites*, Bd. Sch. 20, 19) . . . Albanus eóde ongeán þǣm cæmpan, Shrn. 93, 29-32. Ne forseah Críst his geongan cempan (*the Innocents*), Hml. Th. i. 82, 33. Seleucus hæfde ealle þā æðelestan men Alexandres heres . . . , and Cassander þā cempan mid Chaldēum *summa castrorum Seleuco cessit; stipatoribus regis satellitibusque Cassander praeficitur*, Ors. 3, 11; S. 144, 2. [v. *N. E. D.* kemp. *O. Frs.* campa, cempa: *O. L. Ger.* kempio: *O. H. Ger.* chemph(i)o: *Icel.* kappi.] v. aud-lang-, efen-, in-, rǣde-, weorold-cempa.

cempestre, an; *f. A female soldier*:—Cempestran *tyrunculae*, An. Ox. 3992.

cend-lic. v. cyn-lic.

cēne. *Add:*—Kēne *belliger*, An. Ox. 26, 42. Swíþe yfel mon ealra þeáwa, būton þ hē wæs cēne and oft feaht ānwíg, Ors. 6, 14; S. 268, 27. Sum cēne heretoga mid ormǣtre fyrde, Hml. S. 25, 431. Se cēna Iudas, 424. Cwæð Moyses tō þām cēnan Iosue, 13, 6. Hē ðrowode mid cēnum mōde tintregu, Hml. Th. i. 436, 1. Mid cēnum geleáfan, Hml. S. 5, 53: 29, 133: Hml. A. 114, 415. Hī wurdon swā gehyrte and swā cēne, Hml. Th. i. 232, 29. Ne beóð ongeán hine hundas cēne, Lch. i. 372, 5. Tigras and leopardos, þ syndan þā kēnestan deór, Nar. 38, 4.

cēne; *adv. In warlike wise*:—Cēne *belliter*, Wrt. Voc. ii. 125, 38.

cenep, es; *m.* I. *a bit* of a bridle:—Cenepum *lupatis* (cf. the gloss of the same passage in An. Ox. 12:—*Lupatis, frenis, mīdlum*), Wrt. Voc. ii. 75, 4. II. *a moustache*:—Cambas cenepes *cristas cerebri*, Germ. 401, 117. Leófgār werede his kenepas on his preústhâde, Chr. 1056; P. 186, 29 (v. note ,ii. 246). *For the two meanings* cf. (?) *Germ.* knebel, knebelbart. v. *N. E. D.* camp, kemp. *O. Frs.* kenep: *Icel.* kanpr.]

cen-lic. v. cyn-lic.

cēnlíce. *Add:*—Cēnlíce (kēn-, v. l.) feohtan, Hml. S. 16, 379: 26, 14. Cēnlíce sweltan for ðǣre hālgan ǣ, 25, 102.

cennan. *Add:* I. (1) *to beget*, &c., children:—On sāre þū cennest (cynnest, v. l.) bearn *in dolore paries*, Bd. 1, 27; Sch. 79, 6. Þonne þā wíf heora bearn cendon, Ors. 1, 10; S. 46, 10. Cenne hē ðæt bearn ðām gefarenan brēder *ad nomen fratris filios gignat*, Past. 43, 14. Þæt cennende (cynn-, v. l.) wíf *enixam mulierem*, Bd. 1, 27; Sch. 79, 8. Wið þ cennende lim, Lch. ii. 328, 22. Þā cennendan leomu *genitalia*,

Gr. D. 26, 27: Wrt. Voc. i. 65, 27. (2) of plants, *to produce*:—Of þām treówum balzamum bið kenned (*nascitur*), Nar. 36, 32. (3) *to produce, cause*:—Cynð wam *generat maculam*, Kent. Gl. 291. II. *to declare*, &c.:—Þā cende hē tēm, Cht. Th. 206, 27. Se abbot cænde þ Cnut cing gelōgode, 349, 14. Ǣlc be him sylfum cennan sceolde . . . Gehwilce ǣnlípige on heora burgum be him sylfum cendon, Hml. Th. i. 34, 2-5. Ǣlc man sceolde cennan his gebyrde and his āre, 30, 4. v. un-cenned.

cennend, es; *m. A parent*:—Eádge wǣron þā æþelan cennend Sancte Jōhannes, Bl. H. 161, 32. Be þǣra cennendra gefyrhtum, 163, 26. On þǣm cennendum, 16. v. word-cennend.

cennend-lic. *Add:*—þā cennendlican *genitalia*, Wrt. Voc. ii. 41, 24. Of his cennendlicum limum, Gr. D. 26, 27.

cen-ness, e; *f.* I. *child-birth*:—þ sār þǣre cennesse, Bd. 1, 27; Sch. 78, 24. II. *nativity, birthday*:—Dæg cennisse *die natalis*, Mt. L. 14, 6. Cennisse his *natalis sui*, Mk. L. 6, 21. v. ā-, symbel-cenness.

cennestre. *Add:*—Eálā ðū eádige Godes cennestre, symle mǣden Maria, Hml. Th. i. 546, 8. Cynnestre, 354, 20. Seó wæs cennnystre ūres Drihtnes Hǣlendes Crīstes, Hml. A. 117, 5. Þǣre hālgan Godes cennestran anlícnys, Hml. S. 23 b, 430. Seó cyrice is hāli þǣre eádigan Godes cennestran, Gr. D. 88, 4. Þæt eádige mǣden his cennestran, Hml. Th. i. 438, 18.

cennicge. v. ā-, bearn-, ge-, sunu-cennicge.

cenning. *Add:*—Cynnincg *nativitas*, Hpt. Gl. 442, 57. Cennung *concretio*, Wrt. Voc. ii. 136, 25. Mid wæstembǣre cynnincge *fetosa concretione . . . cennunge concrctione, creatione*, Hpt. Gl. 411, 56, 60. Cynninge (cenningce, An. Ox. 1764) *matrice*, 448, 4. Bið ðæt sǣd unnyt āgoten, næs tō nānre kenninge ðæs cynrenes, ac tō unclǣnnesse *non ad usum generis, sed ad immunditiam semen effundit*, Past. 97, 10. Seó gelaðung on gāstlicere cenninge ācenð bearnteám, Hml. A. 30, 160. Mǣden heó wæs beforan ðǣre cenninge, and mǣden on ðǣre cenninge, and mǣden æfter ðǣre cenninge. Ne bið nān mægðhād forloren on cenninge, ac bið forloren on hǣmede, Hml. Th. ii. 10, 2-5: i. 194, 10. Ðurh þīne clǣnan cenninge, 546, 12.

cenning-stān. v. cynning-stān.

cenning-stōw, e; *f. A birth-place*:—Hē befrān hwǣr Crīstes cenning-stōw wǣre *sciscitabatur ubi Christus nasceretur*, Hml. Th. i. 78, 11. Hī his cenningstōwe geáxodon, 80, 24.

Cent; *f.* (not *n.*). *Add:*—Is on eásteweardre Cent micel īgland *est ad orientalem Cantiae plagam insula non modica*, Bd. 1, 25; Sch. 51, 21. Se here oferhergeade alle Cent eástewearde, Chr. 865; P. 68, 11.

centaur, es; *m. A centaur*:—Þæs centaures *centauri*, Wrt. Voc. ii. 3, 47: 19, 48.

Centingas. *Substitute:*—Hi heafdon ofergān . . . ealle Centingas, Chr. 1011; P. 141, 16. Hē gespeón ealle Centingas (Kentingas, v. l.), 1052; P. 179, 17. v. Eást-, West-Centingas.

Cent-land. *Add:*—Hē wið þā Brettas gefeaht, and gefliémed weard on þǣm londe þe mon hæt Centlond. Raþe þæs hē gefeaht wiþ þā Brettas on Centlonde, and hié wurdon gefliémede, Ors. 5, 12; S. 238, 19-21.

Cent-rīce. *Add:*—Æðelbyrht cyning on Centrīce (*in Cantia*), Bd. 1, 25; Sch. 51, 15.

centur; *m. A centurion*:—Tō cuōm tō him ðe centur, þ is hundrades monna blāferd *accessit ad eum centurio*, Mt. L. 8, 5 (cf. ðe centurion, Mk. R. 15, 44). Ðæs centures *centurionis*, Mt. p. 15, 13.

ceó; *gen.* ceón (*not indecl.*). *Add:*—Chȳae (cȳhae?) cīae *cornicula*, Txts. 50, 240. Ció, Wrt. Voc. ii. 16, 20. Cyó, i. 62, 30. Tiope (ciohe?) *cornicula*, Hpt. 33, 241, 67.

ceód? ceóde? *a bag*:—Ceódas (seódas? cf. siódas *marsupia*, 84, 37: seódas, 92, 65: 55, 9) *marsuppia*, Wrt. Voc. ii. 113, 56. Man sceal habban cȳsfæt, ceódan, wilian, windlas, Angl. ix. 264, 12. [Cf. (?) kiot *bursa*, Grff. iv. 366.]

ceól. *Dele* 'The keel of a ship', *and add:*—Ceól *celox, species navis*, Wrt. Voc. ii. 130, 61: 103, 60: 14, 19: *ciula*, 131, 42: *liburna*, An. Ox. 28. *In* Gr. D. 248, 27, *for* ceólum *read* (?) þeolum.

ceola. *Dele, and see* ceole: ceolas. v. cile: ceolbor-lamb. v. cilfor-lamb.

ceoldre, an; *f. A milk-pail*:—Ceoldre *muluctra*, Wrt. Voc. ii. 114, 32.

ceole. *Add:* I. *a throat*:—Gif ðe þynce ðæt ðū tō wrǣne sý, wít ðæt ðīnre ceolan for ðām unnyttum lustum, Prov. K. 54. Ceolan *gurgustio* (cf. *gurgustio* ceolor (*omitted after* Wrt. Voc. i. 43, 34; v. Angl. viii. 451), Wrt. Voc. ii. 75, 49. II. *a channel, gorge* (?):—On ciolan weg . . . on ceolan ford, C. D. iii. 213, 2, 5. Tō ceolan heáfdan; of ceolon heáfdon, 462, 21. Ceolan hyrst, ii. 216, 5.

ceoler (-or). *Dele* '; *gen.* ceolre . . . or,' *and add:*—Ceolor *gurgustio.* (v. preceding word.) Chelor *gurgustium*, Txts. 112, 52. [*O. L. Ger.* kelor *gurgustium* (Gall. 464): *O. H. Ger.* celur. Grff. iv. 385. v. Job, c. 40. v. 26.] Cf. ceosol.

ceól-þelu; *f. Add:* -þel (?); *n.* cf. wǣg-þel.

ceorcing, e; *f. Complaining*:—Ceorcincg (ceorung?) *questio*, Germ. 398, 208.

**ceorfan.** *Add:* I. *to cut, cut off,* &c:—Cearf *cederet,* Wrt. Voc. ii. 25, 5. Cearf hine *abscide eum,* Mt. L. 18, 3 : 5, 30: *amputa illum,* Mk. L. 9, 44. Man ceorfe him þā handa of, Ll. Th. i. 394, 10. Hēt ic ceorfan ðā bearwas *jubeo cedi nemus,* Nar. 12, 18. Gyf þē syxes genyóðige, þonne sníð þū mid þínum fingre ofer þone óþerne swylce þū cyrfan wille *if you want a knife make a stroke with one finger on another as if you meant to cut it off,* Tech. ii. 123, 4. Ne sceamode þē tō ceorsanne þ þ ðū sylf suce, Hml. S. 7, 125. þ corfene breóst, 145. Ceorfende *infindens,* Wrt. Voc. ii. 47, 23. II. *to slay :*—Fióndas míno cearfas (ceorfas, R.) *inimicos meos interficite,* Lk. L. 19, 27. v. ge-ceorfan.

**ceorfing-ísen.** *Add :*—Fýld flǽsces ísene behófað and ceorfincg-ísene *putredo carnis ferro indiget et cauterio,* Scint. 43, 2.

**ceorf-ness.** v. ymb-ceorfness.

**ceorf-seax,** es ; *n. A surgeon's knife, scalpel :*—Ðeáh ðe se woruld-lǽce þone gewundodan mid bærnette oððe mid ceorfsexe gelácnige, Hml. Th. i. 472, 14.

**ceorian.** *Add:* I. *to murmur, complain without just cause.* (1) absolute :—Ic swíþor ceorude þonne mín sáwul behófode, þā ðā ic ǽhta forleás, Angl. xi. 113, 40. Manega ceorodon and fandoden Godes, Hml. S. 13, 230. Hý nā ne ceorien (cyrian, R. Ben. I. 72, 16) *non murmurent,* R. Ben. 65, 9. Ceoriende (cyrigende, R. Ben. I. 55, 12) *murmurans,* 48, 4. Ceriende *murmurosus,* R. Ben. I. 20, 15. Ne gestilde nǽfre stefen cearciendes wǽnes ne ceoriendes wales, Lch. iii. 430, 34. (2) *to murmur* about (*ymb*), against (*ongeán*) :—Hē ceorað ongeán God, Hml. Th. i. 472, 8. Gē ymb þæt ān gefeoht ceoriað, Ors. 3, 11 ; S. 142, 7. Ic ongeán þē dyrstiglíce ceorode, Angl. xi. 113, 42. Swā þæt wē ne ceorion ongeán Godes swinglum, Hml. Th. ii. 546, 10. (3) *ground of complaint given in a clause :*—þā sunderhālgan ceorodon þæt hē mid ðām synfullum æt, Hml. Th. ii. 472, 1. Ne þurfe wē ceorian þæt Drihten nis líchamlíce on ðyssere worulde wunigende nū, 438, 27. Ceorian hwí hí mōddru nǽron and eác swylce mǽdenu, Hml. A. 32, 207. II. *to complain with just cause :*—Be ðǽre gýmeleáste spræc se wítega mid ceorigendre stefne, Hml. Th. i. 404, 24.

**ceorig ;** *adj. Querulous, bitter* (complaint) :—Ceorigum murcnungum *querulosis questibus,* Hpt. Gl. 421, 8 : *raucidis (amaris) questibus,* 472, 61.

**ceorl.** *Dele first passage under* II, *and add:* I. *a man, male person :*—Ceorl *mas,* Wrt. Voc. ii. 58, 39. Ciorl *vir,* Kent. Gl. 1195. I a. poet. *a* (*noble*) *man :*—Snotor ceorl monig, B. 908. Gomelum ceorle, 2444 : 2972. Leóde míne þā sélestan, snotere ceorlas, 416 : 202 : 1591. I b. *a* (*married*) *man, husband :*—Ceorl þe wíf hæfð *maritus,* Wrt. Voc. i. 73, 13. Ceorl *uxorius,* ii. 124, 26. Weard fordféred sumes wífes ceorl . . . and sæt þ wíf ofer þām líchaman hire fordférdan ceorles, Gr. D. 215, 18 : Gn. Ex. 97. þū wilnast ceorles, Hml. S. 3, 396. Wǽron wydewan fornýdde on unriht tó ceorle, Wlfst. 158, 11. Ceorl *maritum,* An. Ox. 5166. Hæbbe ǽlc monn his wíf, and ǽlc wíf hiere ciorl, Past. 99, 12. Wóhhǽmed begangan nid óþerra ceorla wífum, Bl. H. 61, 14. II. *a man of inferior class, peasant, rustic :*—Hwæt is þes ceorl (*rusticus*)?, Gr. D. 35, 2 : 45, 24. Se mǽra landbegenga (*St. Paul*) underséng ðā hālgan gesomnunga tó plantianne, suā se ceorl ðeð his ortgeard, Past. 293, 4. Dūnhere, unorne ceorl (*simple peasant*), By. 256. Mon ðane chiorl slóh for ðan buccan, C. D. iii. 434. 21. Ceorla samnung *compita,* Wrt. Voc. i. 36, 32. Mid mycelre ceorla (*rusticorum*) mænigu, Gr. D. 213, 13. Eádwíg ceorla cyng, Chr. 1017; P. 155, 8. II a. *where ceorl is in contrast with* eorl :—Eóde ānrǽd eorl tó þām ceorle, By. 132. Cūð þeódum gewelhwǽr, ceorlum and eorlum, Men. 31. II b. *in contrast with* þeów :—þā oþūhte heora ceorlum (*libertinis*) þæt mon þā þeówas freóde, and hí nolde, Ors. 4, 3; S. 162, 16. II c. *a layman :*—Swā mæssepreóst, swā munuc, swā ceorl (*laicus*), swā cempa, Coll. M. 31, 37. Swylce hit nān pleoh ne sý þ se preóst libbe swā swā ceorl, Ll. Th. ii. 344, 18. þæt mæssepreóst lybbe his líf swā swā ceorl, Wlfst. 269, 29. II d. *as a term of contempt?:*—Wæs Eaxeceaster ābrocen þurh þone Frenciscan ceorl Hugon (far ānes Frencisces ceorles ðingan Hugo hætte, *v.l.*) *through the French fellow, Hugh,* Chr. 1003; P. 135, 5. III. *the legal status of the ceorl* is illustrated by the following passages:—Gif on eorles tóðe man mannan ofslæhð .xii. scill. gebéte . . . Ceorles mundbyrd .vi. scillingas, Ll. Th. i. 6, 9–12. Gesíðcund man gebéte .C. scill. Ceorlisc man gebéte .L. scill., 38, 4–7. Gesíðcund mon landágende geselle .cxx. scill. . . . unlandágende .lx. scill. . . . cierlisc .xxx. scill., 134, 8–10. Gif syxhyndum þissa hwæðer gelimpe þriefealdlíce áríse be þǽre cierliscan bóte ; .xii.-hyndum men twyfealdlíce be þæs syxhyndan bóte, 88, 2–5 : 9–11. Ceorles wergild is on Myrcna lage .cc. scill. Ðegnes wergild is syx swā micel, 190, 2. Cyninges þegn gilde .x. healfmarc; landágende .vi. healfmearc; ceorl .xii. ór., ii. 300, 10. v. beó-, hǽmed-ceorl.

**ceorl-folc.** *Add :*—þis rídende ceorlfolc *hoc equestre vulgus,* Ælfc. Gr. Z. 44, 15.

**ceorlian.** *Add :*—Nān wer ne wífað, ne wíf ne ceorlað, Hml. Th. i. 238, 1. Gif wíf þriwa ceorlað, Ll. Th. ii. 232, 4. Hit riht nis þæt wíf ceorlige oftur þonne ǽne, Wlfst. 305, 2. Heó hraðor wolde sweltan þonne ceorlian, Hml. S. 7, 303. v. ge-ceorlian.

**ceorlisc.** v. cirlisc.

**ceorl-leás ;** *adj. Without a husband, unmarried :*—Ðæt wudewe sitte .xii. mónðas ceorl(l)ǽs. Sitte ǽlc wuduwe werleás twelf mónað, Ll. Th. i. 416, 3.

**ceorl-líc.** *Substitute for citation :*—Heánra mann *vel* ceorlic (*l.?* heánra manna *vel* ceorlicra) ǽhta *peculium,* Wrt. Voc. i. 20, 59.

**ceorl-líce.** *For* 'Bridf' *substitute :*—On twām wísum is se dæg gecweden, *naturaliter et vulgariter,* þ ys gecyndelíce and ceorlíce, Angl. viii. 317, 8.

**ceorran ;** *p.* cearr, *pl.* curron *To creak :*—Cræte curran, Lch. iii. 32, 9. Cf. georran.

**ceorung.** *Add :*—Ceorung *murmur, murmuratio,* Ælfc. Gr. Z. 49, 4. Seó ceorung is swýðe lāð Gode, and hūru þ mann gremige him mid wordum, Hml. S. 13, 233: Hml. Th. i. 446, 10. Ceorunge yfelnes *murmurationis malum,* R. Ben. 58, 8. Būtan ceorunge *non cum murmurio,* 20, 19. Mid wóplicre ceorunge *with lamentable complaint,* Hml. S. 2, 355. Ceorunge (cear-, Hpt. Gl. 514, 67) *querimoniam,* An. Ox. 4692. Gif ǽnig ongeán sumne hæfð ceorunge (*querelam*), Scint. 24, 3.

**ceósan.** *Add :*—Ceóseþ *legit,* Wrt. Voc. ii. 53, 34. (1) *to choose a person as lord :*—Ic eom fyrmdig tó þām híwum þ hý hine ceósan, Cht. Th. 487, 28. Ic wylle þæt man āgyfe þām híwum hyra freóls swylce hand tó ceósenne swylce him leófast sý, 492, 17. (2) *to choose as, elect* to an office :—Man ceás Arnwi munec tó aðð., Chr. 1041; P. 163, 16. Ðā cusen þā munecas tó abbot Brand, 1066; P. 199, 1.

**ceosel ;** *m. Gravel, shingle.* *Add :*—Cisal *glarea,* Txts. 64, 461. Hē sang his gebedu on sǽlicere ýðe, . . . and syðdan his cneówa on ðām ceosle gebígde . . . Twégen seolas his bletsunge bǽdon licgende æt his fóton on fealwum ceosle, Hml. Th. ii. 138, 8–14. þæs wæs líc tó þām strande becōm, . . . and on þām ceosole gelæg, Hml. S. 37, 271. Ceoslum *glareis,* Wrt. Voc. ii. 40, 39 : An. Ox. 2, 287. Cyslum, 2879: 4102. Ceoslas *glareas,* 2, 51 : 7, 96. ¶ *The word is found in local names,* e. g. Cysel-hyrst *Chiselhurst* v. C. D. vi. 269. [v. *N.E.D.* chesil.] v. stān-ceosel.

**ceosel-bǽre ;** *adj. Gravelly, shingly :*—On ceoselbǽrum sandum *in glari(g)eris* (*sablonum*) *litoribus,* Angl. xiii. 32, 126.

**ceosel-stān.** *Add :*—Cisilstān *glarea,* Wrt. Voc. ii. 109, 74: 40, 69.

**ceosleg ;** *adj. Gravelly, shingly :*—On cioslegom *in glari(g)eris,* An. Ox. 4, 40. [v. *N. E. D.* chiselly.]

**ceoslen ;** *adj. Gravelly, shingly :*—On ceoslynum sandum *in glari-geris litoribus,* An. Ox. 7, 161.

**ceosol.** *Substitute :*—*Gullet; maw :*—Ceosol, cesol *gurgustium,* Txts. 67, 1001. Cesol, Wrt. Voc. ii. 41, 8. Ceōsol, cesol *ventriculus, stomachus avis,* Txts. 105, 2090. Cf. ceoler.

**ceósung.** *Dele.*

**ceówan.** *Add :*—Ceóweþ *ruminet,* Wrt. Voc. ii. 97, 15. Gnæhð, cíwþ *sulcat,* An. Ox. 23, 49. Ceúwð *ruminat,* 26, 48. Wyrm eówre líchaman cýwð, Hml. S. 4, 386. þā clǽnan nýtenu heora cudu ceówað, 25, 46. Hí ceówað Godes beboda mid smeágunge, 60. Ceówað (cýwat, An. Ox. 101) *decerpunt, rodunt,* Hpt. Gl. 408, 37. Ceáw *remordet,* Germ. 392, 27 : *momorderat,* 402, 57. Hē slāt and ceáw his ágene handa, Gr. D. 301, 3. Swín ne ceów his cudu, Hml. S. 25, 80. þ se draca mē mā ne ceówe, Gr. D. 324, 27. Swylce hí heora mete ceówan, Hml. S. 25, 49. Meng pipor wiþ hwítcwudu, sele tó ceówanne, Lch. ii. 24, 9. v. ge-ceówan.

**cépan.** *Add:* I. *to observe, notice.* (1) with acc. :—Zachēus cēpte þæs Hǽlendes fær, Hml. Th. i. 580, 28. (2) with clause :—Sē ðe his feóndum ofer sumne weall ætfleón wile, ðonne cēpð hē hwǽr se weall unhéhst sý, Hml. Th. i. 484, 10. þā ðenan cēpton hwǽr se godspellere mæssode, Hml. S. 15, 49. I a. *to keep, observe* a season :—Gē cēpað dagas and mónðas *dies observatis et menses,* Hml. Th. i. 102, 18. II. *cépan be to keep by.* (1) *trans. To regulate by :*—Hí cēpað be ðām mónan heora fær and heora dǽda be dagum, Hml. Th. i. 100, 24. (1 a) with clause :—Ne sceal nān man cēpan be dagum on hwilcum dæge hē fare, Hml. S. 17, 92. (2) *intrans. To regulate one's conduct by :*—Wē ne sceolan cēpan ealles tó swýðe be swefnum, 21, 403. III. *to take heed, be careful.* (1) with gen. :—Nýtenu etað swā ǽr swā hí hit habbað, ac se gesceádwísa man sceal cēpan his mǽles, Hml. S. 16, 318. (2) with (negative) clause :—Cēpe gehwá þ hē his líf on unnyt ne āspende, 12, 135. IV. *to attend to, be concerned about, see after.* (1) with gen. :—Wē forlǽtað ðone líchaman, and cēpað ðǽre sáwle, Hml. Th. i. 464, 7. Gif wē ðæs ðeces lífes cēpað, ii. 464, 33. þām þe ǽniges crístendómes cēpað on heora life, Ælif. T. Grn. 14, 10. (2) with clause :—Se deófol syrwð ymbe Godes gelaðunge, and cēpð hū hē mage crístenra manna sáwla fordón, Hml. Th. i. 240, 1. V. *to care*

about, desire to have. (1) with gen. :—Hé lufað ðá áteorigendlican edleán ... Hé cépð þæra sceatta, Hml. Th. i. 240, 18. Ne cépð nán man ðeórwyrðra reáfa búton for ýdelum gylpe, 328, 28. Ne cépð nán hungrig man næfre his gereordes ná swýðor þonne þá sceoccan dóð þære sáwle, Wlfst. 248, 23. Ne cép ðú swá swíðe þises middangeardes stylnysse, Hml. Th. ii. 392, 30. Þ we on gódum weorcum Godes lufe cépon, ná ídeles gylpes, Hml. S. 16, 362. (2) with acc.:—Hé cépte woruldlíce herunga, Hml. Th. ii. 154, 29. **VI.** to be intent on an action, seek, desire to do. (1) with gen. :—Gif we þæs cépað, Hml. Th. ii. 356, 14. Ic ðá fieámes cépte I sought to fly, Hml. S. 7, 351. Ðý læs he fleámes cépte ne aufugeret (Bd. 4, 22), Hml. Th. ii. 358, 2. Hí þóhton þ hí hyne ofslógon, and swíþe þæs cépton, Hml. A. 66, 21 : 71, 163. Hé wolde ðám biscope þances képan he would be very grateful to the bishop, C.D. vi. 184, 22. **VII.** to look out for, (1) a person (gen.): —Férde Martinus, and þæt folc his cépte, Hml. Th. ii. 506, 7. Rád Maurus tó þám lande, and his cépte sum beddryda, Hml. S. 6, 254. (1 a) with idea of hostility:—þá cwelleras cépton ðæra crístenra gehwær, Hml. S. 19, 18. Hét Syrian cyning his (Ahab) cépan, þ hé ána feólle, 18, 217. Se cásere beád þ man swíðe georne sceolde cépan crístenra manna, 23, 48. (2) an object, to seek. (a) with gen. :—Heó bæd þ heó faran móste, wolde swá cépan þæra crístenra láre, Hml. S. 2, 30. (b) with clause :—Ðá hæðenan cépton hú hí hine ácwealdon, Hml. S. 15, 48. Hé cépte symle hú he cwémde Gode, 18, 36. **VIII.** to keep, hold prisoner:—Swá hwylcne swá ic cysse, cépað his sóna (tenete eum, Mt. 26, 48), Hml. Th. ii. 246, 11. v. be-, ge-cépan.

cépe-, céping. v. cípe-, cípung: ceren a churn. l. cirn, q. v.

ceren. Add:—Caerin, coerim dulcis sapa, Txts. 57, 709. Ciern sapa (dulcisapa, Ald. 81, 1), Wrt. Voc. ii. 88, 40. Coerin defrutum, 105, 74 : 25, 10. Cærenes defruti, 27, 30. Cerenes, 96, 58 : carene (-i, Ald. 3, 34), 17, 65. Gedó on eald wín oþþe cæren, Lch. ii. 276, 9.

cerfille (-elle). Add:—Cerfelle cerefolium, Wrt. Voc. ii. 103, 73 : i. 69, 19. Cerville, 286, 13 : ii. 16, 71 : cerpillum, An. Ox. 56, 416.

cerlic. v. cirlic: cernan, dele: cerr. v. cirr: cerran. v. cirran.

certare a charioteer :—Crætwísa (glossed kertare) auriga, Hml. S. 18, 295. [A Scandinavian form (?). Cf. Icel. kartr a cart.]

cése, cése-lib, cesena, cest, cestian, céte, cetel, cheahchetung. v. císe, císe-lybb, cærse, cist, cistian, cíte, kitel, ceahhettung.

chor' es; m. A choir. Add: (1) local :—Chor sacrarium, i. sanctuarium, An. Ox. 2990. þá þénas inn gán tó chore ministri introeant chorum, Angl. xiii. 391, 370. Gelamp þ þá Frencisce men bræcen þone chor, Chr. 1083; P. 215, 8. (2) personal :—Tó þære mæssan offrige se swíþra chor (dexter chorus), se wynstra tó heáhmæssan, Angl. xiii. 384, 278. Andswarige eall chor, 410, 644. Oþ þæt chor endige, 646. Tó ðả swíþran chores, 645. Ne hé ne gedyrstlæce þæt hé hine þæm chore geþeóde, R. Ben. 69, 5 : 70, 13.

chroa, chuæt, chuelc, chýae, chýun. v. crocca, hwá, hwilc, ceó, cían.

cían; pl. Gills of a fish:—Cían branciae (braciae), Txts. 46, 158. Chýun brantie, 113, 61. Cían bracie, Wrt. Voc. ii. 11, 48. [Keho, kio brancia, Gall. 170, 174 : chiuua, kio brancia, Grff. iv. 534.]

cicel. v. cycel.

cicen (ciécen?). Add:—Cycen (cy added in another hand) pullus, Wülck. Gl. 286, 27. Ciacen, Hpt. 33, 241, 64. Cicina (-u, MS.) mete modera, An. Ox. 56, 411. Cicceno (ciken, R.) pullos, Mt. L. 23, 37.

cicropisc; adj. Cyclopean (?) :— Cicropisces cycropide, Wrt. Voc. ii. 137, 75.

cídan. Add: I. to chide, reprove, rebuke. (1) with dat. :—Wið ðone ðe him cít contra corripientem, Past. 185, 14. Mid eáðmóde ingeðonce ðú me cíddes humili intentione reprehendis, 23, 10. Seó menigu ... cíddon ðám blindan, Hml. Th. i. 156, 10. Cíð him increpa illum, Lk. 17, 3. Ge him sculon cídan swá bréðer corripite ut fratrem, Past. 357, 8. Cóm Nathan tó cídanne ðæm cyninge Nathan arguere regem venerat, 185, 17. (2) with acc. :—Cocc þá wiþsacendan cít gallus negantes arguit, Hy. S. 7, 3. (3) with preps.:—Ðá men cíddon ongeán ðone blindan (cf. 156, 10 above), Hml. Th. i. 152, 17. Wið ðone tó cídanne ðe yfel dêð si male acta corriperent, Past. 355, 22. (4) absolute :—Þreá and wítna and hálsa and cíd (increpa), R. Ben. 13, 9. Cíð mid wordum, Hml. A. 12, 307. On ðæs cídendan monnes móde, Past. 357, 1. **II.** to blame unjustly, speak against, speak angrily. (1) absolute :—Uncer hláford hlýdde þærúte and cídde, Hml. A. 207, 395. (2) with prep. :—Se mann geunrótsað for his æhta lyre, and cíd þonne wið God, Hml. S. 16, 292. Maria and Aaron cíddon wið Moises for his wífe locuta est Maria et Aaron contra Moysen propter uxorem ejus, Num. 12, 1. Þæt gê cíddon wið Moises detrahere Moysi, 8. **III.** to dispute, complain about :—Ne cíden (causentur) nó þá nunecas ymb þá deáge oþþe greátnesse hyra reáfa, R. Ben. 89, 14. **IV.** to quarrel :— Cídde altercaretur, Wrt. Voc. ii. 94, 62 : 5, 61. Getugun † cédun

litigabant, Jn. R. 6, 52. [Dele ' Ger. kiden ... sound.'] v. be-, ofer-cídan.

cider. Dele : ciele. l. ciele, and see cile: ciépe-mon, cier, cierlisc. v. cípe-mann, cirr, cirlisc.

cifes. Add :—Of cifise ex pellice, Hpt. Gl. 511, 56. Hé hæfde his bróþor wíf him tó cifese, Shrn. 123, 1. Hé hæfde cyfese under his rihtæwe, Scrd. 22, 22. Cebise, cebisae, caebis pelices, Txts. 85, 1540. Cyfesa, Wrt. Voc. ii. 84, 1. Cifesene (from sing. cefesen?), 67, 1. Cefissa concubinae, Rtl. 68, 41. Cifesan pelices, i. concubinas, An. Ox. 3904. [O. L. Ger. kevis, kievis pellex.]

cifes-boren; adj. Born of a concubine: — Ortrýwes ciuesdômes, cifesboren perfidi pelicatus, An. Ox. 5042. v. cyfes-boren in Dict.

cifes-dóm, es; m. Concubinage. v. preceding word. [O. L. Ger. keuis-dôm pellicatus.]

cifes-hád, es; m. Concubinage :—On cifesháde in pelicatu, Wrt. Voc. ii. 46, 26. Cyfesháde, 87, 6. [O. H. Ger. kebis-heit pellicatus.]

cígan. Add: I. with acc. :—Hé drihten ðone ceiged (uocat), Lk. L. 20, 44. Ic ceigde sona mín, Mt. L. 2, 15 : Mk. L. 3, 13. Stefn hine céde, Shrn. 88, 30. Cégdun vocauerunt, Jn. R. 9, 18. **II.** absolute :—Hig micelre stefne cíað, Ll. Th. ii. 396, 8. Cígende (ciggende, v. l.), Past. 379, 19. Ceigende clamantes, Rtl. 43, 29. v. ed-cígan; cégan, cýgan in Dict.

cíged-ness, cígend-lic, cíg-ness. v. ge-cígedness, -cígendlic, -cígness.

cígere, es; m. One who calls :—Ceigeras clamatores, Rtl. 194, 1.

cígung, e; f. Calling :—Ceigung vocatio, Mt. p. 12, 9. Æt þære cígingce, Gr. D. 53, 7. Mid ceigunge clamando, Jn. p. 6, 8. Of ceigeng Petres de uocatione Petri, Mk. p. 2, 10. Ceigunc vocationem, Mt. p. 13, 7. v. ge-, on-cígung.

cild. Dele in bracket all foreign forms but the Gothic, and add : I. a child :—Eahta-gen. pl. cilda, cildra ; dat. pl. cildum, cildrum. Fêng his bearn wintre cild ... ðrywintre cild, Hml. Th. ii. 134, 3, 7. Be fundenes cildes fóstre, Ll. Th. i. 118, 17. In cildes híw, Cri. 725. Heó weard mid cilde, Hml. Th. i. 24, 26. þá cild on Bethlem ofslægene wærun, Chr. 2 ; P. 2, 29. þá cild rídaþ on heora stafum and manigfealdne plegan plegiaþ, Bt. 36, 5 ; F. 180, 9. Gê sint giet cilderu, Past. 459, 17. Cildra pueri, R. Ben. I. 60, 16. Iung cildra lactantes, i. infantes, An. Ox. 2591. Cildas (cild, R.) parvoli, Mt. L. 19, 13. Ofer hiora dei, wífes and cilda, C.D. i. 316, 16. Of cilda (cildra, R., infantium) mûeð, Mt. 21, 16; Bl. H. 71, 17. Hé ealra ðæra cildra plegan gestilde, Hml. Th. ii. 134, 17. Ic Eádwine munek, cildre meistre, Cht. Th. 321, 26. Hê unborenum cildum líf syld, Hml. S. 23, 429. Gesceád wexð on cildrum, 1, 110. Cild parvulos, Ps. Srt. 114, 6. Cild (cildo, L., cild, R.) infantes, Lk. 18, 15. **II.** as a title of dignity :— Eádríc cild, Chr. 1067; P. 200, 35 (see note, vol. ii. p. 259). Fór Eádgar cild (Edgar Atheling) út ... and se cyng Melcolm genam þes cildes swuster tó wífe, P. 201, 1-3. Ælfsige cild, C. D. iv. 10, 29. Brihtríc forwrêgde Wulfnóð cild þone Suðseaxscian, Chr. 1009 ; P. 138, 17. v. cniht-, cradol-, fóster-, leornung-, munuc-, wæpned-, wíf-cild, and two following words.

cilda mæsse-dæg. Add :—On cilda mæssedæge, Chr. 963; P. 114, 10 : 1066; P. 195, 4.

cilda trog. Dele ' cunæ ... Lye,' and add :—Cilda trog conabulum, Wrt. Voc. ii. 104, 23. v. cild-trog.

cild-cláþ; m. (not n.). Add:—Cildcláðas cunae, Wrt. Voc. ii. 105, 67 : i. 25, 53 : cunabula vel panni infantiae, ii. 137, 26. In cild-cláðum in cunis, 91, 29 : in pannis, Shrn. 87, 7. Mid cildcláðum bewunden pannis obsitum, Hy. S. 48, 21 : Hml. Th. i. 36, 35.

cild-cradol. Add: I. a cradle :—Tó his cildcradele feallende ipsius ad cunabula cadentes, Hy. S. 48, 17. On cildcradelum ástreht in cunis supinus, An. Ox. 2156 : Wrt. Voc. ii. 44, 19. **II.** as symbol of infancy, the cradle :—Crísten fram cildcradole, Hml. Th. i. 428, 23. We ðe fram cildcradole tó Godes geleáfan cômon, ii. 76, 11. Fram cyldcradole, Hml. S. 7, 188.

cild-fédende child-feeding, nursing :—Cildfoedendum nutrientibus, Mt. R. 24, 19.

cild-geogoð, e; f. Infancy, childhood :—þá feówer tíman, lengten ..., and eác þá gelícnyssa, þ ys cildhád, ... lengtentíma and cildiugoð geþwærlæcað, Angl. viii. 299, 26. Swá hê ær behét on his cildgeogoðe, Lch. iii. 438, 10. Spræcon hí embe heora cildgeogoðe, Hml. S. 30, 320, 374.

cild-geong infant. Add:—Læg ic (the infant Jesus) cildgeong in crybbe, Cri. 1426. Mon cildgeong, Gn. Ex. 49: Lch. iii. 438, 5. Cildiung wíf puerpera (cf. puerpera, puella, Corp. Gl. H. 855), Wrt. Voc. i. 17, 17. Þysum cildgeongum cyningce calle þing underþeódde synt, Lch. iii. 436, 8. Samuhel and Danihel cildgeonge (pueri) forealdedum mæssepreóstum dêmdon, R. Ben. 114, 8. Be ealdum munecum and cildgeongum (infantibus), 61, 10, 12. Cildgeongum mannum infantibus, 130, 1. [Cf. O. Sax. kind-jung.]

cild-hád. Add :—Úres andgites merigen is úre cildhád, Hml. Th. ii.

76, 14. Sē þurh his cildhādes nytennysse þis ríce tōstencte, Lch. iii. 434, 26. Seó forme wæcce is on cildhāde, Hml. A. 52, 67. v. cild-geogoþ.

**cild-hama.** *Add:*—Cildhama *folliculus,* Wrt. Voc. i. 44, 40: *secundae,* 41. Cwið *vel* cildhama *matrix,* 45, 23. Cildhaman *matrice,* An. Ox. 1764: *matrice,* i. *puerperio,* 1245.

**cild-ildu(-o)** ; *indecl.* ; -ild, e ; *f. Childhood, infancy :*—Lengtentīma ys wǣt and wearm, þ lyft ys wǣt and wearm. Cildyld byð wǣt and wearm, and hyra blód byð wǣt and wearm, Angl. viii. 299, 28. v. cild-geogoþ.

**cildiung-wíf.** *Dele, and see* cild-geong.

**cild-líc.** *Add:*—Cildlíc *juvenilis,* Hy. S. 70, 13: *primaevus,* An. Ox. 56, 115. Cildlíc on geárum and ealdlíc on mōde, Hml. S. 7, 9. Se cildlíca heáp wolde þæs ānes cildes dreórignysse gefrēfrian, Hml. Th. ii. 134, 18.

**cildsung,** e ; *f. Puerility, trifling :*—Ne gerīseð ǣnig unnytt ǣfre mid bisceopum, ne doll ne dysig ne cildsung on spǣce, Ll. Th. ii. 314, 31.

**cild-trog,** es ; *m. A cradle :*—Ciltrog *cune,* Txts. 115, 154.

**cíle.** *l.* cile, *and add :*—Ciele *frigus,* Wrt. Voc. ii. 36, 64. Ccle *frigor,* 150, 82. Cæle *frigus,* i. 291, 10. Se cyle wiþ þā hǣto, Bt. 33, 4 ; F. 128, 33. Sió hǣte þæs sūðdǣles, se cyle þæs norðdǣles, Ors. I, 1 ; Swt. 24, 28. For ciele (cele, *v. l.*) nele se slāwa erian . . . for ðǣm ege ðæs cieles (ciles, *v. l.*), Past. 285, 5, 10. On cele *in frigore,* Wrt. Voc. ii. 48, 9. Cyle *algore,* Wülck. Gl. 254, 42. Sum for hǣto, sum for cyle, Bt. 18, 1 ; F. 62, 11. For ungemetlicum cyle, 33, 4 ; F. 130, 34: Lch. ii. 56, 17 : Hml. S. 31, 60. On middeweardan cyle ungeleáffulnysse, Hml. Th. i. 84, 14. Ðone cele ungetreównesse, Past. 447, 6. Fugelas and fixas þurh þone micelan cyle forwurdan, Chr. 1046 ; P. 164, 36. þec hergen byrnende fȳr and beorht sumor, wearme wederdagas . . . And þec ceolas weorðian, forst and snāw, winterbiter weder, Az. 103. v. cēle, cȳle (*l.* cele, cyle) *in Dict.* and *at* cȳle *dele foreign forms in bracket.*

**cíle-gicel.** v. cȳle-gicel (*l.* cyle-).

**cíle-wearte,** an ; *f. Goose-skin :*—Celewearte *oripilatio,* Wrt. Voc. ii. 115, 63. Cylewearte, 63, 50.

**cilfor-lamb.** *Add :*—Ceolborlomb *enixa,* i. *genuit agnam,* Wrt. Voc. ii. 107, 27. Cilforlamb oððe ācennende wæs *enixa est,* 29, 36.

**cílian.** *l.* cilian, *and* v. for-cilled : cillinesc. v. cyllenisc.

**cille,** an ; *f. A vessel for use with fire, a pan ; a lamp :*—Cellae *lancola,* Corp. Gl. H. 6, 197. Citel *cacabum,* hwer *lebes,* cille *lancona,* Wrt. Voc. i. 288, 35-37. Cylle *lancona,* ii. 52, 3. Cylle, brond *calbrum,* 127, 70. Stōd se leóma him of swylce fȳren cylle ongeán norðdǣl *portabant facem ignis contra Aquilonem,* Bd. 5, 23 ; Sch. 687, 22. Man sceal habban . . . leóhtfæt, blācern, cyllan, sāpbox, Angl. ix. 264, 22. Gefyllde hē mid wætere ealle þǣre cyrcean ciellan (cillan, cyllan, *v. ll.,* lampades ; cf. leóhtfatu, 43, 18), Gr. D. 244, 14. [*O. H. Ger.* kella *trulla* ; fiur-kella *receptaculum ignis* ; rouh-kella *thuribulum.*] v. cyll.

**Ciltern.** *Dele bracket, and add :*— Innon Buccingahāmscíre be Cilternes efese, Hrysebyrgan, C. D. iv. 232, 32. Cf. Hrisebeorgan margine luci Cilterni, iii. 347, 12.

**Ciltern-sǣte (-an)** ; *pl. The occupants of the Chiltern district :*— Cilternsǣtna landes is feówer þúsend hýda and ān hund hýda, C. D. B. i. 414, 25.

**cim, cim-stānas.** v. cimb-stān.

**cimbala (cym-).** *Add :*—On cimbalum *in cymbalis,* Ps. Spl. L. 150, 5. Cymbalan, cimbalan, Ps. Srt. 150, 5. Hē slóh cymbalan (cimbalan, *v. l.*) *percussit cymbala,* Gr. D. 62, 16, 23.

**cimbal-glíwere,** es ; *m. A cimbal-player :*—Hú Bonefatius foresǣde tō sweltenne þone cimbalglíwere, Gr. D. 61, 20.

**cimbing.** *Add :*—Cimbing *commisura,* Wrt. Voc. ii. 105, 1. Gefēg, cimbing *commisura, s. dicitur tabularum conjunctio,* 132, 10. v. cimbstān. [v. *N. E. D.* chime, chimb.] v. preceding word.

**cimb-íren,** es ; *n. A joining-iron (?), a clamp (?) :*—Hē sceal habban . . . cimbíren, tigehōc, Angl. ix. 263, 2. [v. *N. E. D.* chime, chimb.] v. preceding word.

**cimb-stān,** es ; *m. A stone into which a pillar is fitted (?), a base, pedestal :*—Sweras gyldene ofer cimstānas (*bases*) sylfrene, Scint. 226, 2.

**cin, cinn,** es ; *n.* (not *f.*). *Add :*—Cin *mentum,* Wrt. Voc. i. 43, 40. Cinn, ii. 56, 25. Cinne *mento,* Lch. i. lxx, 5. Lǣdes mannes tācen is þæt þū þe mid ealre hande be þínum cynne nime swilce þū þe be bearde niman wille, Tech. ii. 129, 17. Cinn *menta,* An. Ox. 46, 4.

**cínan.** *Add :*—Gif men cíne hwilc lim, Lch. ii. 148, 22. Cínendi (-aendi) *hiulca,* Txts. 67, 1020. Cínende, Wrt. Voc. ii. 42, 44. *De-hiscens,* i. *aperiens, inhians, patefaciens, scindens vel cinende,* 139, 80. [v. *N. E. D.* chine. *O. Sax.* kīnan *to germinate : O. H. Ger.* kīnan *dehiscere, patescere, pullulare, promere.* Cf. *Goth.* keinan (*wk.*) *germinare.*]

**cin-bán.** *Add : jaw-bone, jaw :*—Ān geswel weóx on hire swuran under þām cinbāne (cynn-, *v. l.*) (*sub maxilla,* Bd. 4, 19), Hml. S. 20, 52. Cinbān *maxillae,* Wrt. Voc. i. 64, 45 : *mandibulas,* ii. 77, 42: 86, 76 : 56, 26 : Hpt. Gl. 520, 73. þǣra cinbān þū scealt mid brídle

---

tō þē geteón *in freno maxillas eorum constringe,* Ps. Th. 31, 11. [*O. H. Ger.* kinni-bein *mentum, mandibula.*]

**cincing.** *Add :* [v. *N. E. D.* chink, kink, kench.] Cf. canc.

**cine,** es ; *m. Substitute : A folded sheet of parchment :*—Cine *quaternio* (quaternio *chartae invicem compactae,* Migne), Ælfc. Gr. Z. 35, 3. Cine *quaternio,* bod on cine *diploma,* Wrt. Voc. i. 46, 65, 67. Cine *quaternio, boga diploma,* 75, 10, 12.

**cíne.** *l.* cine (-u), *take here passage in Dict. under* cínu, *and add :* I. *a chink, crack :*—Cinena *rimarum,* Wrt. Voc. ii. 92, 5. Cinum *rimis,* An. Ox. 26, 11. Geoniendum þām cinum se sǣ eóde inn *rimis patentibus intravit mare,* Gr. D. 248, 27. Cinan *rimas,* Germ. 399, 307. þurh þā cinan (cynan, *v. l.*) þǣre dura *per rimas ostiorum,* Bd. 4, 7 ; Sch. 388, 4. II. *a chasm, cavern :*—Cinan *crypte,* Wrt. Voc. ii. 23, 61. Cinum *cavernis,* Germ. 399, 272. II a. fig. *a deep subject (?) :*—Ic warnige þæne þe þās cinan þengð tō āspyrianne, þ hē gelōme sceáwige þās seofon rǣdinga, Angl. viii. 333, 8. [v. *N. E. D.* chine. *O. L. Ger.* (Gall.) kina.] v. ciniht.

**cíne-líc.** v. cyn-líc : **cinecti.** v. ciniht : **cíne-wāþen.** v. cyne-wǣden.

**ciniht ;** *adj. Full of cracks :*—Cionecti *rimosa,* Wrt. Voc. ii. 119, 16.

**cín-líc.** *Dele.*

**cin-tóþ.** *For* 'Prov. 30, Lye' *substitute :*—Of his cintōþum *molaribus suis,* Kent. Gl. 1084. [*O. H. Ger.* kinni-zand.]

**cípa,** an ; *m. A merchant, trader :*—Cȳpa *mercator,* Germ. 389, 43. Se lāreów bið culfran cȳpa, Hml. Th. i. 412, 10. Ēdríc se cípa, Cht. Th. 637, 38. Cȳpan *institoris,* Kent. Gl. 1136. Gif þiéfefioh mon æt ciépan befō, Ll. Th. i. 118, 13. v. cēpa, cȳpa, I *in Dict.*

**cipe.** *l.* cípe, *and add :*—Cípae, cípe *caepa,* Txts. 52, 448. Cípe *scolonia,* 95, 1791 : Wrt. Voc. i. 69, 6 : *ascolonia,* 67, 7. Cípa *ascolonium,* 286, 7 : ii. 8, 46. [*From Latin.*] v. ciepe (*l.* ciépe) *in Dict.*

**cípe** *for sale.* v. ge-, un- cípe (-cȳpe) : **cípe-cniht.** v. cēpe-, cȳpe-cniht *in Dict., and* ceáp-cniht.

**cípe-dæg,** es ; *m. A market-day :*—Cȳpedaga *nundinarum,* An. Ox. 7, 1867 : 8, 144. v. ceáp-dæg.

**cípe-hús.** v. cǣpe-hús *in Dict.* : **cípe-leác.** *l.* cípe-leác, *and for* Cot. 55 *l.* Wrt. Voc. ii. 23, 4.

**cípe-mann (cíp-),** es ; *m. A merchant, trader :*—Cípemann *institor,* Wrt. Voc. ii. 48, 28. Ciépeman *agapa* (cf. agapo, qui negotia aliena anteambulant, Corp. Gl. H. 14, 383), i. 285, 8 : ii. 8, 28. Cēpemon *emptor, venditor,* 143, 37 : Shrn. 134, 4 : Mt. L. 21, 12. Gif ciépemon (cēpe-, ceáp-, *v. ll.*) uppe on folce ceápie, Ll. Th. i. 118, 12. Se iiii nihta mōna byð gōd þǣm cípemen his cípinge tō anginnane, Lch. iii. 178, 2. Æt cȳpmen (ceáp-, *v. l.*) befōn, Ll. Th. i. 118, 13. Hē penegas wið hlāfe þām cēpemen sealde, and þā cȳpemeu þā penegas sceáwodon, Hml. S. 23, 564. Ceápemenn *nummularii,* Mt. L. 21, 12 : *vendentes,* Mk. L. 11, 15 margin. Cípamonna riht *hrodia lex,* Wrt. Voc. ii. 43, 46. Be ciépemonna (cȳpe-, *v. l.*) fōre, Ll. Th. i. 118, 11. Cȳpmanna cȳpinga *nundinarum,* An. Ox. 2655. Be ciépemannum (cȳpe-, cȳp-, *v. ll.*), Ll. Th. i. 82, 9, 10. Seó landbūnes is swiðost cȳpe-monnum geseted *haec colonia est maxime negotiatorum,* Nar. 33, 15. ¶ *The word occurs in local names,* Cȳpmanna del, Chȳpmanna ford, C. D. vi. 269. v. cēp-, cēpe-, cȳp-, cȳp-, cȳpe-mann *in Dict.*

**ciper-sealf.** v. cyper-sealf : **cípe-þing.** v. cēpe-, cȳpe-þing *in Dict.* (*where for* Cot. 133 *l.* Wrt. Voc. ii. 58, 61).

**cíping,** e ; *f.* I. *trading, marketing :*—Se smið gemētte on cȳpincge þæs Eádzies mann *the smith met this Eadsige's man a-marketing,* Hml. S. 21, 75. þām dǣdbētan nis ālȳfed nǣnige cȳpinge tō drífenne *mercaturam exercere,* Ll. Th. ii. 170, 11. On ceápstōwe cȳpinge began *in mercatu mercaturam exercere,* 174, 19. Cȳpinge wyrcan, Cht. E. 231, 21. Cípinge anginnan, Lch. iii. 178, 2. I a. *dues paid for trading, market-dues :*—Uillae *mercimonium,* quod · Anglice ðæs tūnes *cȳping* appellatur, censusque omnis ciuilis æcclesiae, cum omnibus commodis, deseruiat, C. D. v. 158, 37. II. *merchandise :*—Cēping *mercimonium* (or under I, if a gloss on Ald. 56, 15 :—Spirituale exercetur mercimonium. Cf. An. Ox. 4807), Wrt. Voc. ii. 57, 18. III. *a market, market-place :*—Cēping *mercatum,* scipmanna myrt þe cēping *teloneum,* Wrt. Voc. i. 37, 9, 10. Hē cōm intō þǣre cȳpinge þǣr gehwilce men heora ceáp be[ceápod]an, Hml. S. 23, 527. Hí hine ātugan tōmiddes þǣre cȳpinge, 609. v. cēping, cȳping *in Dict. and* ceápung : flǣsc-cíping.

**cíp-líc ;** *adj. For sale :*—þes sáwle his cȳplíce hæfð *hic animam suam uenalem habet,* Scint. 98, 17.

**cipp,** es ; *n.? Substitute :* cipp, es ; *m.* I. *a beam, log, stock :*—Cip *cadurcus,* Wrt. Voc. ii. 127, 38 : *catercus,* 129, 49. Cyppes *stipitis, cippi,* Germ. 399, 271. þurh cwearternlice cyp *per carceralem stipitem,* 400, 552. þū ne gesáwe þone mǣstan cypp (cyp, cip. *v. ll.*) on þínum āgenum eágan, R. Ben. 12, 4. II. *the share-beam of a plough :*—Cipp *dentale,* Wrt. Voc. i. 15, 7. III. *a weaver's beam :*—Hē sceal habban . . . wulcamb, cip, Angl. ix. 263, 13. [v. *N. E. D.* chip. *From Latin* cippus.]

**cíp-strǣt.** v. cȳp-strǣt *in Dict.,* and *cf.* ceáp-strǣt : **circ-.** v. ciric-.

**circan** to roar (?):—Circinde wæter, Lch. i. 390, 11. [v. *N. E. D.* chirk.] Cf. cearcian.

**circan lād.** v. lād: **circol-wyrde.** *Add:* [wyrde = (?) wi(e)rde *a guard:* cf. *Goth.* wardjans, *acc. pl. from* (?) wardeis], *and for* Bridf. 63 *l.* Angl. viii. 306, 26. v. next word.

**circul.** *Dele 'the zodiac,' and add: a cycle, circular arrangement for computing:*—Sceal wintrum frōd on circule cræfte findan hālige dagas, Men. 67. Rīmcræftige men wyrcað heom fægere circul of þām fīf stafum ... on þām circule fīftȳne niht hig onfōð ... Ðys ys þ eahtoðe geár on þām circule, Angl. viii. 327, 36-47. Ðās circulas synt behēfe eallum gehādedum mannum. ... On þissum circulum ærest stent se circul þe gebyrað tō þǣre lengtenlican tīde, 328, 44-7. v. getæl-tācn-circul.

**circul-cræft.** *Dele, and see preceding word:* **cires-** v. **ciris-:** **ciric** v. **cirice: ciric-.** v. also **cyrc-, cyric-** in Dict.

**ciric-ǣ** (w) *church-marriage, the relation of the priest to the church on account of his orders:*—Þ syndon þā ǣwbrecan þe þurh heálicne hād ciricǣwe underfēngan and þ ābrǣcan ... Ciric is sācerdes ǣwe, Ll. Th. ii. 334, 14, 23.

**ciric-belle.** *Add:*—Of ciricbellum drincan, Lch. ii. 14, 6.

**ciric-bōc** *a church-book,* Wlfst. 171, 8. v. cyric-bōc in Dict.

**ciric-brēc,** e; *f. Church-breaking, breaking into a church:*—Þā heáfodleahtras sind cyrcbrǣce, leásgewitnyssa, stala, Hml. Th. ii. 592, 4. Cf. ciric-bryce.

**ciric-dōr.** *l.* -dor.

**cirice.** *Take here passages at* cyrice, circe, cyrce *in Dict. and add:*—Seó cierece, Shrn. 53, 25. Ciric is sācerdes ǣwe, Ll. Th. ii. 334, 23. Beforan ðǣre ciricean dura, Past. 105, 13. On ðæs pāpan ciericean, Shrn. 51, 21. On eallum ciericum, 54, 1. v. Angel-, feld-, neáh-, tūn-, wind-cirice.

**ciricend,** es; *m. An ecclesiastic:*—Ciricendum hlifiendum *ecclesiasticis vivis,* Mt. p. 10, 10.

**ciric-friþ.** *Add:* [O. Frs. kerk-fretho: Icel. kirkju-friðr *sanctuary.*]

**ciric-gang,** es; *m. Church-going, churching of a woman:*—Oþ cyricgange scā Marian *usque ad purificationem Sanctae Mariae,* Angl. xiii. 399, 484. [v. *N. E. D.* church-gang. O. Frs. kerk-gung: Icel. kirkju-ganga: Germ. kirch-gang.]

**ciric-gemāna,** an; *m. Church-communion, membership of a church:*—Sume men sculan of cyricgemānan āscādene weorðan for synnan, eal swā Adam weard of engla gemānan, Wlfst. 103, 23.

**ciric-georn;** *adj. Diligent in attending church:*—Beó circgeorn, and þe þǣr georne tō Gode bide and tō allum his hālgum, Wlfst. 290, 8. Beó ciricgeornn tō Godes cyrecan, Angl. xii. 518, 26. v. cyric-georn in Dict.

**ciric-grið.** *Add:* [v. *N. E. D.* church-grith. Icel. kirkju-grið.]

**ciric-hād,** es; *m. Ecclesiastical order, holy order:*—Sind on ānum hāde se biscop and se mæssepreóst, þ is on ðām seofoðan cirichāde, Ll. Th. ii. 378, 14. For þām seofon cirichādan (cyriclicum andebyrdnyssum, *v. l.*) þe se mæssepreóst geþeáh þ hē hæfde, i. 182, 15.

**ciric-hālgung,** e; *f. Dedication of a church:*—Hē þ mynster lēt hālgian ... and seó cirhālgung (cyric-, *v. l.*) wæs on Cildamæssedæig, Chr. 1065; P. 192, 22. Nīwe circhālgung *encenia* (cf. encenie, *nove dedicationis,* ii. 74, 16), Wrt. Voc. i. 16, 52: An. Ox. 56, 286. Tō cirichālgunge þæs gebedhūses *ad dedicationem oratorii,* Gr. D. 72, 1, 5, 16. Ðā lāc þe Salomon geofrode Gode æt þǣre ealdan cirichālgunge, Wlfst. 280, 21: 281, 7. v. cyric-hālgung in Dict.

**ciric-hata,** an; *m. An enemy of the church, a persecutor:*—Lā, hwæt fremað cyrichatan crīstendōm on unnyt; for ðām ǣlc þǣra bið Godes feónd þe bið Godes cyrcena feónd, Wlfst. 67, 18. Godes wiðersacan and cyrichatan hetole, 164, 11. Cyrchatan and sācerdbanan, 298, 14.

**ciric-hyll** *a hill near a church* (?) *or on which a church stands* (?) [Churchill occurs several times in England as a local name; cf. *Icel.* Kirkju-fell.]:—Of cirichylle ... on cirichylle, C. D. B. ii. 394, 30, 39.

**ciric-land,** es; *n. Church-land, land belonging to a church:*—'Ne þū nā geþrýstlǣce þ þū ūre cyricland (ciricean land, *v. l.*) derige' ... Se flōd gecyrde fram þan cyriclande '*nec terras ecclesiae laedere praesumas*' ... *Statim se a terris ecclesiae fluminis aqua compescuit,* Gr. D. 193, 25, 194, 3. [v. *N. E. D.* church-land. O. L. Ger. kiric-land: Icel. kirkju-land *glebe.*]

**ciric-lec, -lic.** *Add:*—Cyriclicre āwrigenesse *ecclesiasticae traditionis,* An. Ox. 178. Cyrclice tīdsang[as] *canonicas horas,* 56, 317.

**ciric-mǣrsung,** e; *f. Dedication of a church:*—Ic wylle eów cýðan ymbe cyricmǣrsunge, þæt gē understandan magan hū man cyrican weorþian scyle þe Gode tō wurðmynte gehālgod bið, Wlfst. 277, 10.

**ciric-pæþ.** v. cyric-pæþ *in Dict., and add:* [O. Frs. kerk-path.] Cf. ciric-stīg, -weg.

**ciric-rān** (-rēn), es; *n. Sacrilege:*—On fæstenbricon, on cyricrēnan,

and on mæniges cynnes misdǣdan, Ll. Th. i. 322, 20. [*Icel.* kirkju-rān *sacrilege.*]

**ciric-sang.** I. *a church-song;* Bd. 5, 20; S. 642, 8. (v. Dict.) II. *church-singing;* Bd. 2, 20; S. 522, 25 (cf. hē wæs mägister ciriclices sanges (*cantionis*), 27). v. Dict. Hē fērde and ciricsang lǣrde *ad docenda ecclesiae carmina diuertens,* 4, 12; S. 581, 7. [*Icel.* kirkju-söngr *church-music.*]

**ciric-sceat.** v. cyric-sceat *in Dict., and add:*—Gange ǣgðer ge cyricsceat ge teóðunge intō þām hālgan mynstre, Cht. E. 236, 2. Freoh ǣlces weoruldcundes þeówetes būton þreóm þingum, ān is circsceat, C. D. ii. 400, 29. On þæt gerād þe hē ǣlce geáre of þām lande geerige twēgen æceras, and þǣron his circsceat gesāwe, and þæt eft gerīpe and in gebringe, 398, 20. Þæt wē eal gelǣstan on geárgerihtan þæt ūre yldran ǣr Gode behētan, ðæt is ... cyricsceattas, Wlfst. 113, 11. On ðæt gerād ðet hē gesylle ǣlce geáre ... cyresceattas and cyresceatweorc, C. D. v. 162, 26. [v. *N. E. D.* church-scot.] Cf. circan lād *under* lād.

**ciricsceat-weorc,** es; *n. Work connected with the grain contributed as* ciric-sceat. v. C. D. v. 162, 26: ii. 398, 20 (*quoted under* ciric-sceat).

**ciric-sōcn.** *Substitute:* I. *going to church, attendance at church:*—Þæt crīstene men þæne egesan ǣfre ne dreógan þæt hȳ deófolgyld weorðian, for ðām ne fremeð ǣnig cyricsōcn ǣfre ǣnigum þēra þe þæt ōðer drýhð, Wlfst. 281, 5. Þeówetlingas weorces beón gefreóde wið cyricsōcne, 171, 20. Lufian cyricsōcne, 112, 17. Þisne dæg wurþian mid ciricsōcnum, H. R. 17, 26. Mid cyricsōcnum cealdum wederum, Dōm. L. 30, 4. II. *seeking a church for protection, a church as sanctuary.* v. sōcn, VI:—Be ciricsōcnum. Gif hwā sié deáðes scyldig, and hē cirican geierne, Ll. Th. i. 104, 12. III. *the territory of a church:*—Ic wille ðat se byrig æt Winintūne and feówer hīdan landes ðærtō mid ðāre cyrice and mid ðāre cyricsōcne ... and mid ðām lande æt ðǣre leá liggen intō Westmynstre, C. D. iv. 220, 19. [v. *N. E. D.* church-soken. *Icel.* kirkju-sōkn *church-attendance: a parish* (modern).]

**ciric-steall,** es; *m. The site of a church:*—Wē wrītað him ðā circan and ðone circstall and ðone wordig, C. D. iii. 52, 37. [Cf. Kirkstall *as a local name.*] v. next word.

**ciric-stede,** es; *m. Church-stead, site of a church:*—Ðonon on clǣgweg be ciricstede, C. D. iii. 81, 10. Ǣrest on ðone chiricstede; ðonne of ðām chiricstede ... on ðone chiricstede, 85, 7, 22. [Cf. Kirkstead *as a local name.*]

**ciric-stīg.** v. cyric-stīg *in Dict., and cf.* ciric-pæþ.

**ciric-þenung-þegnung.** *Add:*—On þām sinoðe wǣron gesette þā hālgan cyricþenunga, Ll. Th. ii. 344, 8. Cyrcþēnungum *orgiis, sacrificiis,* Germ. 395, 65. v. cyric-þēnung in Dict.

**ciric-þing,** es; *n. An article belonging to a church:*—Gif preóst on circan ungedafenlice þingc gelōgige, gebēte þ. Gif preóst ciricþingc ūtige, gebēte þ, Ll. Th. ii. 294, 12-14.

**ciric-wag.** *l.* -wāg.

**ciric-weard.** *Take here passages under* cyrc-, cyric-weard, *and add:*—Ðæs cyricweardes tācen is þæt mon sette his twēgen fingras on his twā eágan and dō mid his handa swylce hē wille āne hangigende bellan teón, Tech. ii. 118, 16. In þǣre cyricean hē breác and þeówode cyricweardes þēnunge *in ecclesia mansionarii functus officio deserviebat,* Gr. D. 44, 1. Sǣde se cnapa þām cyricwerde, Hml. S. 21, 163. Āxode hē þone cyricweard, 3, 258. Niman þā cyricwerdas (es, MS.) þā rōde *sumant editui crucem,* Angl. xiii. 426, 870. Hē ābæd him ingang fram þām cyricweardum þæt him wǣre āgifen leáf him tō gebidenne *ingressus ecclesiam a custodibus petiit, ut sibi licentiam concederetur orandi,* Gr. D. 200, 3. [O. H. Ger. chirih-wart *ecclesiae provisor: Icel.* kirkju-vörðr.]

**ciric-weg,** es; *m. Road to a church:*—Tō þām cyricwege, C. D. iv. 36, 10. [O. Frs. kerk-wei: Icel. kirkju-vegr.]

**ciris-** *cherry-.* [*From Lat.* cerasus.] v. cirse, *and next three words.*

**ciris-æppel** *a cherry:*—Ciseræpla *caricarum* (= ? ciresæpla *cerasorum;* cf. carica ficæppel, 21, 61), Wrt. Voc. ii. 15, 74. v. next word.

**ciris-beám.** *Add:*—Ciserbeám (cysir-, Erf.) *cerasius,* Txts. 49, 445. [O. H. Ger. chers(e)-, chriesi-poum *cerasus.*]

**ciris-treów.** v. cyrs-treów in Dict.

**cirlic, cerlic** *charlock:*—Cyrlic *mercurialis,* Wrt. Voc. i. 67, 59. [v. *N. E. D.* charlock.] v. cerlic in Dict.

**cirlisc.** *Add:* I. *in a technical sense, of the 'ceorl' class or rank:*—Gif mon hǣme mid twelfhyndes monnes wīfe, hundtwelftig scitt. gebēte þām were. Syxhyndum men hundteóntig scitt. gebēte. Cierlisum (ceorl-, cyrl-, *v. ll.*) men feówertig scitt. gebēte. Be cirliscere (cierl-, cyrl-, *v. ll.*) fǣmnan onfenge. Gif mon on cirliscre (ceorl-, cyrl-, *v. ll.*) fǣmnan breóst gefō, Ll. Th. i. 68, 9-14. II. *in a general sense, common, vulgar, rustic, plebeian, clownish:*—Hwæt is þeo ceorlisca wer *quis est iste vir rusticus*?, Gr. D. 35, 2. Ceorlisc bysmrung, 46, 18. Se feórþandæl byð *quadrans* gecíged, beó hyt penig oððe pund, swā þ wel wāt ceorlisc folc, Angl. viii. 306, 31. *Vulgaris dies,* þ byð ceorlisc

dæg, 317, 11. Cyrlisc *plebeia*, Germ. 393, 115: *barbarus*, An. Ox. 56, 228. Forseah Apollonius cyrlisces mannes grētinge æfter rīcra manna gewunan. Hellanicus cwæð: 'Ne forseoh ðū cyrliscne man þe bið mid wurðfullum þeawum gefrætwod,' Ap. Th. 7, 22–26. Of cyrliscum līfe and of folclicum gedeorfe *ex vita rustica et ex plebeio labore*, R. Ben. 138, 22. Mid cyrlisceum (ceorl-, *v. l.*) þeawe *rusticano usu*, Gr. D. 9, 16. On þām ceorliscean mōde *in mente rustica*, 46, 13. Interorina fram manegum mannum mid ceorliscum wordum (cyrlisceum worde, *v. l.*) (*verbo rustico*) is genemned Interocrina, 87, 32. Cierliscum *rusticis*, Wrt. Voc. ii. 86, 8.

**cirlisce**; *adv. As in the case of a 'ceorl'* :—Gilde man cirlisce, Ll. Th. i. 188, 14.

**cirm.** *Add:* *loud sound* of thunder, trumpet, &c. :—Suoeg, cirm *fragor*, Wrt. Voc. ii. 109, 27: 36, 13. Cyrm *strepitus, sonus conflictus*, i. *sonitus*, 136, 75. Æt middere niht cirm (*clamor*) geworden wæs, Mt. R. 25, 6. Se forhta ceorm (cyrm, *v. l.*) and þæra folca wōp, Wlfst. 186, 18. Cyrm *strepitus tonitruum*, Wrt. Voc. ii. 150, 26: *clangor, tubarum sonus vel vox tubae*, 131, 52: *clamor tubis*, 126, 49: *clangor* (*salpicum*), An. Ox. 1642. Cyrm *clangor*, Hpt. Gl. 445, 12. Þæra bȳmena cyrm, Hml. Th. ii. 202, 29. Se dæg is bȳman dæg and cyrmes, i. 618, 17. Of þunerlicum cirme (cerme, Hpt. Gl. 451, 46) *tonitruali fragore*, An. Ox. 1915. Cyrme (cerme, Hpt. Gl. 509, 23), 4417. Mid cyrme hlyhhan *cum strepitu ridere*, Scint. 172, 17. Cyrmum *clangoribus*, An. Ox. 5247. [*v. N. E. D.* chirm.]

**cirman.** *Add:*—Scylþ, cyrmþ *crepitat*, i. *resonat*, Wrt. Voc. ii. 136, 72. Cyrmende *confragosum*, 133, 20. Cyrmiende *stridulae*, An. Ox. 4605. Cyrmyndre, 8, 264. Cermenda *sonantia*, 46, 6. [*v. N. E. D.* chirm.]

**cirn, cirin, e**; *f. A churn* :—Cirm *sinnum* (= ? cirin *sinum*), Wrt. Voc. ii. 120, 57. Man sceal habban . . . cyrne, cȳsfæt, Angl. ix. 264, 11. v. ceren *in Dict.*

**cirnel.** v. cyrnel.

**cirps**; *adj. Curly* :—Cyrpsum loccum *crinibus crispantibus*, Hpt. Gl. 435, 10. Hē hæfde cyrpse (cyrspe, crispe, *v. ll.*) loccas fægere *capillis pulcherrime crispis*, Bd. 5, 2 ; Sch. 561, 3. [*From Latin.*] v. cyrps *in Dict.*

**cirpsian.** *For* 'Som. Ben. Lye' *substitute* :—Cyrpsaþ *asperat*, Germ. 394, 275. Cyrpsiendum *crispantibus*, An. Ox. 1201 : Hpt. Gl. 435, 9. v. ge-cirpsian.

**cirps-loccas.** *Dele.*

**cirr.** *Add:*—Æt ānum cierre *uno eodemque tempore*, Past. 455, 33. Hit gesælde æt sumum cierre, Met. 9, 23. Cyrre, Sat. 538. Cirre, Ors. 1, 1 ; S. 17, 7 : Chr. 897 ; P. 90, 20. Bestælon hié hié upp æt sumum twām cirron (cyrrum, *v. l.*), æt ōþrum cierre (cyrre, *v. l.*) beeástan Wæced, and æt ōþrum cierre æt Portlocan, 918 ; P. 98, 26–29. [*v. N. E. D.* chare.] v. ofer-, wiþer-, ymb-cirr, *and* cerr, cierr, cyrr *in Dict.*

**cirran.** *Add:* **I.** *trans. To turn, cause to move* :—Cerrende heáfda hiora *moventes capita sua*, Mt. L. 27, 39. Cærrende (cerr-, R.), Mk. L. 15, 29. Styrendum ł cerrendum *mobilibus*, Mt. p. 8, 7. **II.** *intrans.* (1) *of change in direction of motion, to turn* :—Cirdon hié ūp in on ðā eá, Ors. 1, 1 ; S. 17, 21. (2) *to come or go back, return, retire* :—Ic cearro ł ic willo cerre *revertar*, Mt. L. 12, 44. Deáð bið ælces yfeles ende, and ne cyrð hē næfre mā, Prov. K. 49. God bebeád þæt hí eft ne cyrdon tō Herōde, Hml. Th. i. 78, 29. Cerras *recedite*, Mt. L. 9, 24. Þá hī tō sæ cōman, þā hēt hī man cyrran, Chr. 1094 ; P. 229, 22. (2 a) *with reflex. dat.* :—Hē forlēt þā fyrde and cyrde him eft tō Lundene, Chr. 1016 ; P. 147, 12. (3) *of change in conduct, to turn, reform* :—Hí geeácniað heora wíta, gif hí ær ende ne cyrrað, Hml. S. 13, 311. (4) *to turn to a person in submission, for protection, &c.* :—Him all Angelcyn tō cirde, Chr. 886 ; P. 80, 11. Him cierde tō eall se þeódscype, 922 ; P. 103, 28. Cantware him tō cirdon, 823 ; P. 60, 15. v. cerran, cyrran (*where for bracket substitute*, v. *N. E. D.* chare) *in Dict.*, *and* from-, oþ-, under-cirran.

**-cirre.** v. earfoþ-, tōr-cirre.

**cirse, an**; *f. A cherry* :—Cyrsena tācn is . . ., Tech. ii. 124, 22. v. eiris-.

**cīse, es**; *m. Cheese* :—Cēse *formaticus*, Wrt. Voc. ii. 109, 13. Wit unc gefyldan niówes cēses, Hml. A. 207, 412. III. wēga spices and cēses, Cht. Th. 471, 14 : 474, 29. X. pund caeses gif hit fuguldaeg sié. Gif hit festendæg sié, selle mon uuēge cæsa, 460, 19–22. Ne ete niŵne cīse, Lch. ii. 88, 7. Đonne þū cȳse habban wille, Tech. ii. 123, 20 : Goll. M. 34, 27. XL. and CC. hlāba, I. wēge cēsa, Cht. Th. 468, 24. Cȳswyrhtan gebyreð hundred cȳse (-a?), Ll. Th. i. 438, 31. v. cȳse *in Dict.*

**cīse-fæt** (cīs-), **es** ; *n. A vessel in which the curds are pressed and the cheese shaped in cheese-making* :—Cȳsefæt *calathus*, Wrt. Voc. ii. 22, 42. Man sceal habban cyrne, cȳsfæt, Angl. ix. 264, 12. [*v. N. E. D.* cheese-vat. Cf. *O. H. Ger.* châsi-, châs-char *calatum, formella.*]

**cīse-lybb** (cīs-) *rennet* :—Cēselyb *coagolum*, Wrt. Voc. ii. 105, 8. Cēslyb, 133, 12. Cȳslyb, 15, 13. Ne cȳse ne cȳslyb, Angl. ix. 260, 13. Harau cȳslyb, Lch. i. 346, 11. Cȳslybbu *coagula*, Germ. 390, 68. [v. *N. E. D.* cheese-lip. *O. H. Ger.* châsi-luppa.]

**ciser-.** v. ciris- : cīse-wicu. v. cȳs-wuce *in Dict.* : cīse-wyrhte. v. wyrhte *in Dict.*

**cīs-ness** *squeamishness* :—Cīisniss *fastidium*, Txts. 62, 406. Cīsnes *fastidium, nausia*, Wrt. Voc. ii. 146, 47. Wē gelȳfað þæt genōh sȳ twā gesodene sufel for missenlicra manna untrumnesse ; gif hwā for hwylcre cīsnesse þæs ānes brūcan ne mæge, brūce hūru þæs ōðres *ut forte qui ex uno non potuerit edere ex alio reficiatur*, R. Ben. 63, 12.

**cist** *a chest. Add:* ciste, an (? v. bōc-cist). **I.** *a box, coffer, casket* :—Cest *capsis*, Txts. 50, 231 : *cista, arcula*, 110, 1168. Cyst oððe mederce *loculus*, Wrt. Voc. i. 80, 80 : *capsis*, ii. 13, 19. Seó rōd is on treówenre ceste belocen, and ðonne seó cest bið onlocen, þonne cymeð upp wunderlic stenc, Shrn. 67, 27. Hwæt fremað þē þæt ðīn cyst stande ful mid gōdum, and ðīn ingehȳd beó æmtig ælces gōdes?, Hml. Th. ii. 410, 11. On ciste *in capsella*, Wrt. Voc. ii. 45, 78. Ceste *capsulam* (*cum sanctorum reliquiis*, Bd. 1, 18), Txts. 181, 65. Man sceal habban piperhorn, cyste, mydercan, bearmteáge, Angl. ix. 264, 19. Funde mon on his māðmhūse twā cista (*arcas*), Ors. 6, 3 ; S. 258, 13. **I a.** *a coffin.* v. cistian :—Cest *arca funeris, sarcofagum*, Txts. 109, 1146. Heó wearð bebyrged on treówenre cyste, Hml. S. 20, 69. Hē hrān þ ceiste (*loculum*), Lk. L. 7, 14. **II.** *a basket or ark of rushes.* [v. *N. E. D.* chest, 4] :—*Cistula, sporta vel* cyst, Wrt. Voc. ii. 131, 19. **III.** *a horn* as a receptacle (?) :—Ceste *cornu*, Wrt. Voc. ii. 105, 34. Cyste, 15, 53. [*From Lat.* cista.] v. lǣce-, mæst-, māðm-, seód-cist.

**cist-beám.** v. cyst-beám *in Dict. for ex.*

**cistel** *a chestnut.* v. cystel, *and add* :—On swæce swylce grēne cystel (cysten, *v. l.*), Lch. i. 108, 3. v. stān-ceastel.

**cisten** *a chestnut.* v. preceding word. [v. *N. E. D.* chesten. *O. H. Ger.* chestinna *castanea.*] v. stān-cisten.

**cisten-beám.** *Add:*—Cistenbeám (cistim-) *castanea*, Txts. 47, 374 : Wrt. Voc. ii. 13, 25 : *castaneus*, 16, 69. [*O. H. Ger.* chesten(ne)-boum.]

**cistian** *to put in a coffin.* v. cist, **I a.** :—Forðferede þearfan mildheortlīce cestian (cystian, *v. l.*) and syððan bebyrian, Wlfst. 119, 10. Cystian, 209, 7. [v. *N. E. D.* chest, vb. 1, *and* chest, sb. 3.]

**cist-mēlum** ; *adv. Emulously, earnestly* ; *certatim*, An. Ox. 4, 32. Cf. ceást.

**cīte, an** ; *f.* **I.** *a hut, cabin, cottage* :—Cētan *gurgustione*, Wrt. Voc. ii. 110, 17. Gecōm hē tō hyre cȳtan (cf. Gr. D. 167, 6), Hml. Th. ii. 182, 26 : 184, 7. Settan Hierusalem samod anlīcast swā hī æppelbearu āne cȳtan *posuerunt Hierusalem velut pomorum custodiam*, Ps. Th. 78, 2. Hē lēt ārǣran ealle ābūtan ðā dūne his hyrdecnapan cȳtan, þ hī ðær gehende mid heora hlāfordes yrfe lāgon, and wið cyle and wið hǣton hī sylfe geburgon, Hml. S. 23, 418. **II** *a cell* of a monk, hermit, &c. :—Cȳte, hulce (hulce ł cēte, Hpt. Gl. 465, 45) *tugurio* .i. cella (the cell of John the hermit), An. Ox. 2515. Sȳ þām untrumum gebrōðrum synderlīce cȳte (hūs, cȳte, R. Ben. I. 67, 17) geset and tō þām ānum betæht *fratribus infirmis sit cella super se deputata*, R. Ben. 60, 20. Þæs muneces cȳte mid leóhte weard āfylled, Hml. S. 31, 811. Heó began faran tō ðæs foresǣdan wēstensetlan cȳtan, and on þære cȳtan duru cnocode, Hml. A. 196, 25. Hē eóde on þā cētan þær se līchoma wæs, Bl. H. 217, 25 : 219, 14. Se geatweard sceal cȳtan (hūs *cellam*, R. Ben. I. 112, 7) habban wið þæt geat, R. Ben. 126, 18. Gangende in þā cȳtan (*cellam*) Benedictes, Gr. D. 140, 10. ¶ *in a local name*, Cētwudu *Chetwood*, C. D. i. 292, 20. [v. *N. E. D.* chete.] v. cete, cyte (*l.* cēte, cȳte) *in Dict.*

**citel.** *Add:*—Cetil *caccabum*, Wrt. Voc. ii. 102, 40 : *caldaria*, 103, 21 : *enum*, 107, 24. Cetel *caldaria*, 127, 53. Citel, 13, 53 : *cacabum*, 7 : *enum*, 29, 35. Lytel cytel *lebes*, 54, 18. Olla aenea cytel ; *sed ideo additus aenea quia est et olla fictilis, id est crocca*, 65, 36. Cyteles *sartaginis*, An. Ox. 4127. Seóð on cetele, Lch. ii. 230, 7. Man sceal habban hwer, leád, cytel, hlædel, Angl. ix. 264, 9. Hē hēt mycel fȳr onǣlan and ǣnne cytel þǣrofer gesettan, and bæd þǣre fǣmne fēt and handan innen þone weallende cetel gesetton, Hml. A. 178, 286–9. Cytelas *lebetes*, An. Ox. 7, 319. [*From Latin.*] v. cetel, cytel *in Dict.*

**citelian, citelung.** *Add:* [v. *N. E. D.* kittle, kittling.]

**citere, citre, an** ; *f. A harp* :—Citere *cythara*, Ps. Spl. 56, 9. Citre *cithara*, 107, 3. In citran *in cythara*, 42, 4 : 70, 22. In citra, 32, 2. [*From Latin.*] v. cytere *in Dict.*

**cīþ.** *Add:*—Se smala ciið *festuca*, Past. 224, 3. Wæstm, cīþ *crementum*, i. *augmentum*, Wrt. Voc. ii. 136, 66. Hī habbaþ nænne cīð (*incrementum*) mægenes, Scint. 5, 18. Cīþas *gramina*, Wrt. Voc. ii. 42, 35. Cīðas *genimina*, Kent. Gl. 251. v. cor-cīþ.

**cīwung, e** ; *f. Chewing* :—Cīwung *vel* edroc *ruminatio*, Wrt. Voc. i. 54, 62.

**clā.** v. clawu.

**clacu, e** ; *f. Hurt, harm, injury* :—Sceal āspringan wīde and sīde sacu and clacu, hōl and hete, Wlfst. 86, 10. [3iff þatt ȝe ȝuw lokenn Fra clake ɫ sake (*do violence to no man, neither accuse any falsely*, Lk. 3, 14), Orm. 9317.] v. clæc-leás.

**clader-sticca**, an; *m. A rattle :—*Cladersticca (-stecca) *anate*, Txts. 42, 116. v. clædur.

**clǽc-leás**. *Substitute :* I. *free from evil, that has done no harm, innocent :—*Clǽcleáse, láþleáse *immunes*, Wrt. Voc. ii. 43, 68. [II. *free from injury, uninjured :—*Ic habbe getýþed sǽe Cúðberht þ land and all þ þǽrto belimpeþ clǽne and claclēs, Hick. Thes. i. 149, 57.] [*Icel.* klak-laust *unhurt.*] v. clacu.

**clǽdur** *a clapper, rattle :—*Crepacula clǽdur (cledr, cleadur), *id est tabula qua a segitibus territantur aves*, Txts. 48, 218.

**clǽfre.** l. clǽfre, dele ' n.' (in Lch. ii. 312, 20 reád clǽfre *is nominative*), *and add :*, clǽfer (?), clâfre. [*From* clǽfre *comes* claver (remaining only in dialects), *from* clâfre *comes* clover] :—Huíte clâfre (clâbre) calcesta, Txts. 47, 377. (*In* Lch. ii. 326, 21 hwíte-clǽfre *seems a compound* :—Nim hwíteclǽfran wísan.) Reáde clâfre (clâbre) *caltha vel genus floris*, 375. Rǽde clǽfer *calta*, Wrt. Voc. i. 288, 49. Clǽfre *viola*, 79, 61 : An. Ox. 56, 429. Cleáfre, Lch. iii. 305, col. 2. Clǽfra fetta, Wrt. Voc. ii. 38, 47. Clâfrena (clǽfran, An. Ox. 94) *caltarum*, 75, 22. v. þunor-clǽfre.

**clǽg.** *Add :* ¶ *as a component of words denoting places with a clayey soil*, Clay- *in local names :—*Of clǽgbróc . . . on clǽgbróc, C. D. vi. 52, 25, 29. Clǽigate, iv. 178, 2. On clǽghyrste, C. D. B. iii. 45, 7. On clǽgweg, andlang clǽgweges, 44, 25 ; C. D. iii. 81, 10. In clǽgwyllan ; of clǽgwyllan, 80, 18.

**clǽg-weg, -willa.** v. clǽg.

**clǽig ;** *adj. Add :* , clǽgig :—Of cleíian hîde (cf. *Clayhithe*), C. D. vi. 232, 11.

**clǽman.** l. clǽman, *and add :—*Mǽnge wið ele þ hit sý swylce clâm ; clǽm ðonne on ðâ sîdan, Lch. iii. 48, 19. Seó ðe clǽman sceal *litura*, Ælfc. Gr. Z. 256, 3. Clæmende *affirmans*, Wrt. Voc. ii. 115, 42. Clǽmende, 63, 37. [v. *N. E. D.* cleam.] v. be-, for-clǽman ; healf-, un-clǽmed (-od) : clâm.

**clǽmende.** *Dele, and see* clǽman: clǽmman. v. clemman.

**clǽmming.** *Substitute :* clǽming, e ; *f. Smearing :—*Clǽming *litura*, Ælfc. Gr. Z. 256, 4.

**clǽm-ness.** v. clem-ness.

**clǽne ;** *adj. Add :* I. *physical.* (1) *of metal, free from dross or alloy :—*Fífténe scillingas clǽnes feós, Cht. Th. 168, 16. Mid claene feó, ðæt wæs mid clǽne golde, Txts. 175, 5. (2) *of land, free from hurtful growth, clear :—*Ðone æcer ðe wæs mid ðornum âswôgen . . . ðone æcer ðe stent on clǽnum lande (*terram quae nullas spinas habuit*), Past. 411, 19. Ðǽm folce ðe on clǽnum felda (*in campo*) sige gefeohtað, 227, 24. (3) *fit for food :—*Ic genime mé clǽne fixas tô mete, Coll. M. 23, 17. Wyrta and ægra, fisc and cýse, buteran and beána and ealle clǽne þingc ic ete, 34, 29. (4) *clear, without defect :—*Þ eal se líchoma sý clǽnes hîwes and glades and beorhtes, Lch. ii. 296, 6. Habban eágan clǽne and hlûttre, Bt. 42 ; F. 256, 13. II. *free from impropriety :—*Wið clǽnum legere *if the death had not been a violent one* (it was by drowning), Cht. Th. 206, 30. þâ clǽnan þenunga *lauta munia*, Wrt. Voc. ii. 52, 51. III. *in a moral sense, pure, sincere :—*Âufeald, clǽne, hlûtor *simplex*, Wrt. Voc. ii. 74, 50. Se lâreów sceal biôn clǽne (*mundus*) on his môde, Past. 75, 18. þæt hié gehealdað hiera líchoman firenlusta clǽnne, 40, 14. Ne magon wé nǽfre gereccan þone yfelan mon clǽnne and untwîfealdne, Bt. 36, 6 ; F. 182, 19. Clǽne *lautos* (*biblos*), Wrt. Voc. ii. 92, 44. v. ge-clǽne.

**clǽne ;** *adv. Add :* I. *clean, so as to leave nothing remaining :—*Dô þ fâm of clǽne, Lch. ii. 94, 8, 20. Feormige man þone pyt clǽne *purgetur puteus*, Ll. Th. ii. 220, 20. Wé habbað Godes hûs inne and ûte clǽne berýpte, Wlfst. 157, 18. Nân gesceaft swâ clêne onwæg ne gewít, þæt hî æft ne cume, ne swâ clǽne ne forwyrð, þ hî tô hwanhwugu ne weorðe, Shrn. 198, 17, 18. Swâ clǽne hió (*learning*) wæs oðfeallenu, Past. 3, 13. Ælcere synne swâ clǽne âmerede, swâ æfre ǽnig gold mæg clǽnost âmerod weorðan, Wlfst. 96, 14. II. *in full, without reservation :—*Man sealde Godwine clǽne his eorldóm, swâ full and swâ forð swâ hé fyrmest âhte, Chr. 1052 ; P. 180, 29. [*O. H. Ger.* chleino.]

**clǽn-georn.** *Add :—Celibatus*, i. *sine uxore vir, vel viduatus, vel abstinentia virginitatis* clǽngeorn ; *celibes*, i. *casti, steriles celestem vitam ducentes* clǽngeorne, Wrt. Voc. ii. 130, 49-53. Sýn hý clǽngeorne, R. Ben. 140, 7.

**clǽn-heort.** *Add :—*Ic wæs unsceðþende and clǽnheort, Shrn. 139, 23. Se unscæððiga on handum and se clǽnheorta *innocens manibus et mundo corde*, Ps. L. 23, 4. Eádige synd þâ clǽnheortan þe on clǽnnysse lybbað, Hml. A. 47, 563 : 23, 222.

**clǽn-lic.** *Add : Splendid, excellent.* Cf. clǽne, II :—Deófol hine wile geteón in oferhigd, giſ se man ôht wundorlices oþþe clǽnlices wyrceþ ûtan þurh Godes gife, Gr. D. 45, 6. v. un-clǽnlic.

**clǽn-líce ;** *adv. Substitute :* I. *cleanly.* Cf. clǽne ; *adv.* I :—Âdríge clǽnlíce, Lch. ii. 214, 24. II. *clearly.* Cf. clǽne ; *adj.* I. 4 :—Clǽnlíce ꝥ bǽrlíce ꝥ lûtorlíce *perspicue*, Mt. p. 10, 10. III. *with propriety.* Cf. clǽne, II :—Se sâcerd sceal dôn clǽnlíce and carfullíce Godes þēnunga,

---

Hî Godes ðeówdôm clǽnlíce becôdan, Chr. 995 ; P. 129, 34. IV. *purely.* Cf. clǽne, III :—Ðæt is ðonne ꝥ hé sié clǽnes willan and goodes, ðæt hé clǽnlíce and ryhtwíslíce ongiete ðæt ðæt hé ongiete *pudica videlicet, quia caste intelligit*, Past. 349, 3. Ðæt wé ûrne crîstendôm clǽnlíce gehealdan, Wlfst. 112, 15. V. *entirely.* Cf. clǽne ; *adv.* I :—Giſ þǽr beón lǽs manna þonne þæt lamb mæge fretan, þonne nyme hé hys neâhgebûr . . . þ hé mæge þ lamb clǽnlíce fretan, Angl. viii. 322, 8. [*O. H. Ger.* chlein-lîhho *diligenter.*] v. un-clǽnlíce.

**clǽn-ness.** *Add :—*Clǽnnys *pudor*, An. Ox. 5176. Clǽnnysse *pudoris*, 4176 : *celibatus*, 9, 19. Clǽnnysse, geþincþe *propositi*, i. *gradus*, 3451. On clǽnnysse *in proposito*, i. *gradu*, 2565. Heortan clǽnnesse *cordis munditiam*, 40, 8.

**clǽnsere.** *Add :—*Sé ðe wǽre gâlsere on fûlan forligere, weorðe sé clǽnsere his âgenre sâwle, Wlfst. 72, 6. Sâcerdas, ðæt is on Englisc clǽnseras, Past. 139, 15.

**clǽnsian.** *Add :—*Clǽnsaþ hit onweg þ sâr eall, Lch. i. 86, 26. Clǽnsade *lustrat*, Wrt. Voc. ii. 53, 63. v. þurh-clǽnsian ; clǽsnian *in Dict.*

**clǽnsung.** *Add :* , clǽsnung. I. *physical.* (1) *cleansing from dirt :—*Clǽnsunga *purgamenta* (*latrinarum*), An. Ox. 3918. (2) *cleansing from impurity, disease :—*Clǽnsunga and swiling tô heáfdes hǽlo, Lch. ii. 2, 3. II. *with reference to moral impurity :—*Mid clǽsnunge forhæfednesse *abstinentiae castigatione*, Bd. 4, 28 ; Sch. 526, 4. Clǽnsunge, R. Ben. 76, 5. Stýran mid lícumlicre clǽnsunge (*corporis castigatione*), 13, 21.

**clǽnsung-dæg**, es ; *m. A day for taking cleansing medicine, day for purging :—*þis wilddeór well fremað, gif þû þînum clǽnsungdagum hys flǽsc gesoden etest, Lch. i. 330, 8. v. next word.

**clǽnsung-drenc**, es ; *m. A cleansing-drink, purgative :—*Ne bið âlêfed on ðyssum dagum ðæt mon blôd lǽte oððe [cl]ǽnsungdrenceas drince, Shrn. 80, 5. v. preceding word.

**clǽnu.** v. un-clǽnu.

**clǽppan** *to throb :—*Wið heáfodsâr . . . þis syndon þâ tâcnu þæs sâres, þ is ǽrest þâ ðunewenga clǽppaþ, Lch. iii. 88, 5. v. next word.

**clǽppettan** *to throb.* *Add :—*Wið þæt þæs mannes heáfod clǽppitað, Lch. iii. 92, 10. Clǽppette and sprangette *palpit*(*r*)*avit*, Wrt. Voc. ii. 69, 26. Brogdetende *vel* cleppetcnde (*printed* depp- ; *but see* Corp. Gl. H. p. 29) *campus*, 103, 27. v. preceding word.

**clǽþan ;** *p.* de *To clothe :—*Nacod ic wæs and gié clǽðdon meh *nudus eram, et operuistis me*, Mt. L. 25, 36. [v. *N. E. D.* clead.] v. clâþian.

**clâm.** I. l. clâm, es ; *m., and add :* I. *mortar, mud, clay, paste :—*Mǽnge wið ele þ hit sý swylce clâm, Lch. iii. 48, 19. Clâmes gefége *liturae compage*, An. Ox. 4439. II. *in medicine, a poultice :—*Clâm, clîpan *tiriaca*, An. Ox. 964. Clâm wiþ þon : þâ reádan tigelan geclâm cnuwa tô duste, gemeng wið grût, Lch. ii. 114, 24. Lǽcedôme, clâme *malagma*, Wrt. Voc. ii. 54, 38. Hafa þé ǽrgeworht clâm of beórdrǽstan, Lch. ii. 330, 16. [v. *N. E. D.* cloam.] v. clǽman.

**clâm.** II. l. clam[m], clom[m], es ; *m., and add :* I. *a bond, fetter :—*þ hé sý genered of þâm clammum *ut eripiatur*, Gr. D. 345, 27. Æfter þǽm bendum his deápes and æfter þǽm clammum helle þeóstra, Bl. H. 83, 22. Dryhten gescylde ûs wiþ þâ ēcan clammas, Wlfst. 226, 9. II. *a bond, pledge :—*Clam oððe wed *clasma* (v. mâl *in Dict.*), Wrt. Voc. ii. 21, 2. [v. *N. E. D.* clam.] v. nîd-clamm.

**clâne ;** *adj., adv.* v. clǽne ; *adj., adv.* : **clappan.** v. clǽppan.

**clâte.** *Dele German forms in bracket, and add :—*Clâtae (-e) *blitum* (*clitum?* cf. *clitum* clâte í clifwyrt, Lch. iii. 303, col. 1 : *cliton* clâte, 301, col. 2), Txts. 44, 144. Clâte, Wrt. Voc. ii. 11, 13 : *tubera*, Txts. 103, 2066. Clîfae, i. clâta, clâtacrop *personacia* (cf. *personacia* bête, Lch. iii. 304, col. 2), Hpt. 33, 250, 14. Clâtum *lappis*, Wrt. Voc. ii. 53, 40. [v. *N. E. D.* clote.]

**clâte-crop.** v. preceding word.

**clâþ.** *Add :* I. *a cloth :—*þu noldest þæt ǽnig clâð betweuh wǽre (*nullo interposito velamento*), Shrn. 185, 34. Stôd ân cýſ oferwrogen . . . hí brûdon of ðone clâð (*operimentum*), Hml. Th. ii. 178, 35. II. *a garment :—*God hyre âsende tunecan. Heó . . . ðone clâð hire on âdýde, Hml. S. 7, 156, 159. Hé hæfde genumen sumne clâð (*uestimentum*, Bd. 3, 19) æt ânum swyltendum men, Hml. Th. ii. 338, 28 : i. 286, 24. Hé forðférde under Crîstes clâðum (*cum adhuc esset in albis*), Chr. 688 ; P. 41, 4. Clâðum *metallis* (? as a gloss to : Stabant simulacra metallis, Ald. 172, 8), Wrt. Voc. ii. 57, 37. v. bed-, bord-, eaxl-, flyhte-, fôt-, sweor-, wæter-clâþ.

**clâþian.** v. ge-clâded *in Dict.* : **clâþ-scear.** *Dele.*

**clâþ-weóce**, an ; *f. A small piece of cloth used as a wick :—*Of bedrýpedum clâþe, of gedrýpdre clâþweócan *linteolo ebrio* (*madido*), Germ. 391, 18.

**clatrung.** *Substitute : Clattering, noise :—*Clatrunge *crepacula* (cf. *crepaculum, sonum dyne vel* geþun, 136, 63), Wrt. Voc. ii. 21, 36.

**clauster.** *Add :—*Clauster (*printed* claustre, Wrt. Voc. i. 82, 48) *claustrum*, Ælfc. Gr. Z. 316, 2. Claustres gýmenne dôn . . . ymbfaran þ *claustrum*, Angl. xiii. 433, 981. On mynstres claustre, R. Ben. 19, 9. [*Icel.* klaustr; *n. From Latin.*]

**clawan.** *Dele 'p. ede; pp. ed,' and add:* (clāwan? In Mid. E. p. *cleu, clew* is found) :—Clawe *scalpo,* Wrt. Voc. ii. 120, 36. [v. *N. E. D.* claw.] v. *next word, and* cf. cleweþa, clawu.

**clawian;** *p.* ode *To claw, scratch :*—Ic clawige *scalpo,* Ælfc. Gr. Z. 170, 11 note.

**clawu.** *Add :* (clāwu? *but* cf. Orm. Clawwess). I. *a claw,* (1) of a bird or beast :—Earnes clawa, Hml. Th. ii. 434, 9. Him (*birds*) wæron þa cleá blace (*pedibus nigris*), Nar. 16, 16. Clawa *ungularum,* An. Ox. 8, 385. Seó culfre is unrēđe on hire clawum, Hml. Th. ii. 44, 26. Þa fuglas þa fixas mid hiora clēum (cleam, Nar. 16, 20) tǣron, Angl. iv. 153, 378. (2) *claw-like nail* of a human being :—Mē cōman tō Silhearwan . . heora clawa wæron scearpe, Hml. S. 4, 289. II. *a hoof :*—þa ᵹe synd gehōfode on horses gelícnysse untōclofenum clawum, Hml. S. 25, 45. Eofores clawa oþþe ōþres swīnes gebærn tō ahsan, Lch. ii. 88, 21. Caelf fordlǣdende cleá (*ungulas*), Ps. Srt. 68, 32. III. *a hook :*—Clauuo *harpago,* Wrt. Voc. ii. 100, 78. Clawu, 7, 13. ˙ Hī man clifrode mid īsenum clawum, Hml. S. 12, 187. Ic ofercōm þæs cwelleres tintregu, scearp īsen and þa slītendan clawa, 8, 189. [v. *N. E. D.* claw, clee.]

**cleá.** v. clawu.

**cleac,** e; *f. A stepping-stone :*—On cleaca, C. D. iv. 36, 3, 12.

**cleacian.** *For* M. H. 115 a *substitute* Hml. S. 23, 493 : cleadur. v. clædur : cleáfa. *l.* cleafa : cleawen. v. cliwen.

**clemman;** *p.* de *To press, pinch :*—Clæm þu þīne handa tōgædere, Tech. ii. 122, 21. Clæm þu þīne wynstran hand þām gemete þe þu ōstran on handa hæbbe *shut your left hand as if there were an oyster in it,* 124, 12, 20. [v. *N. E. D.* clem.] v. *next word.*

**clemness,** e; *f. Pressure, pang, pain :*—Fram swā miclum clæmnessum onlēsed beón *a tantis cruciatibus absolui,* Bd. 4, 9; Sch. 396, 11.

**clencan.** *Add :* [O. H. Ger. klenchen.]

**clengan.** *Substitute : To adhere, remain :*—Dreám bið in innan, clengeđ, lengeđ *joy is within, remains, is prolonged,* Rä. 29, 8, [v. *N. E. D.* clenge.]

**cleófa.** *l.* cleofa, *dele* ' *That* . . . , *chasm,*' *and add :*—Hē hæfde ǣnne līcđrowere belocen on ānum clyfan . . . Đā eóde Basilius tō đām clyfan, ac se preóst nolde undōn þa duru mid cǣge, Hml. S. 3, 480–4. Sum dēma hēt hī belūcan on stǣnemum cleofan, Shrn. 103, 4. Cleofan *absidan,* Wrt. Voc. ii. 92, 51. Gefere þæne mannan on swīđe fæstne cleofan and wearmne, Lch. ii. 280, 11. [v. *N. E. D.* cleve. *Icel.* klefi, klifi *a closet.*] v. ealu-, heáh-, mađum-cleofa.

**cleófan.** *For first two references substitute* Germ. 399, 451 : 400, 498, *dele all derivatives but* tō-cleófan, *and add :*—Cleáfađ hearta iuero *scinditₑ corda vestra,* Rtl. 5, 4. On wintra erian and in miclum gefyrstum timber cleófan, Angl. ix. 261, 23. On þone cleofenan beorh, Cht. E. 293, 27. v. ā-cleófan.

**cleónede** *talaricus :*—Cneówede *genosus,* cleónede (ancleónede? *having large ankles?*) *talaricus,* hōnede *calcaneus,* Wrt. Voc. i. 45, 39–41.

**cleopian.** v. clipian : **cleopigend.** *Dele :* cleopung. v. clipung.

**cleót.** *Substitute : A tablet* (?) :—Clūt, cleót *pittacium,* Wrt. Voc. ii. 117, 32. [Cf. (?) *N. E. D.* cleat.]

**cleóþa.** *l.* cleoþa. v. cliþa : **clepung.** v. clipung.

**cleówe** *a clew :*—Cleóuuae, cleúuue, clōuue *glomer,* Txts. 66, 472. [O. H. Ger. chliuwa *globus.*] v. cliwen.

**clerc, cleric.** *Add : one of the secular* (*as opposed to monastic*) *clergy :*—Ic secge þē, lā cleric, on þīn eáre, Angl. viii. 300, 14. On gewitnesse Byrhtstānes mæssepreóstes and on clerices þe þis gewrāt, Cht. E. 255, 30. Wolde ic þ þā æđela(n) clericas āsceócon fram heora andgites orđance ǣlce sleacnysse, Angl. viii. 301, 14. Ūs þingđ tō langsum þ wē ealne þisne cwide on Englisc clericum geswutelion, 300, 7. Hē was underfange of þām hādesmannum þe him ealra uneáđest was, þ was clerican, Chr. 995; P. 128, 20. Hē ongan tō tellende þām pāpan eal embe þā clericas, P. 130, 31. [O. H. Ger. chlirih : *Icel.* klerkr.] v. cliroc *in Dict.*

**clerc-hád.** *Add : the state of a secular clerk :*—Đā đe clerichādes synd and munuchādes wilniađ *clericorum si qui monasterio sociari voluerint,* R. Ben. 106, 13. Swā sācerdhādes swā clerichādes *sacerdotum vel clericorum,* 110, 8. Clerochāde *cleratis* (ab clericatus gradu discedens, Ald. 51, 1), Wrt. Voc. ii. 83, 5 : 18, 43. Ceólwulf cining fēng tō Petres scǣre (tō clerichāde, *v. l.*), Chr. 737; P. 45, 20.

**cleric-mann,** es; *m. A clerk :*—Gif hwylc clericman gewundige *si quis clericum vulneraverit,* Ll. Th. ii. 210, 27.

**clibbor.** *Add :* [Cf. *N. E. D.* clibby.]: clibecti. v. clifiht.

**clidrenn,** e; *f. A clatter, noise :*—Bretme *vel* clidrinnae (cliderme) *strepitu,* Txts. 96, 928.

**clif.** *For translation of last passage substitute :* Fluvius Nilus de litore incipientis maris Rubri videtur emergere; *and add :*—Andlang clifes middeweardes, C. D. iii. 82, 21. Ođ đæs clifes norđhyldan, 418, 25. Tō đæs clifes westende, 419, 6. Fram þām heán clife *ab alta rupe,* Gr. D. 52, 22. Þ wæter wæs sweart under þǣm clife neođan,

---

Bl. H. 211, 2 : 209, 34. Đā stānas swā of ōđrum clife ūt sceoredon, 207, 20. On đǣm sǣs clife, Ors. 4, 13 ; S. 210, 31. Abies þ treówcyn þy clyfe weóx, Nar. 8, 22. Ofer clif *per preceps* (v. Mt. 8, 32), Wrt. Voc. ii. 72, 35. Ealle đa clifu (*rupes*) þe neáh þǣm sǣ wǣron forburnan tō ascan, Ors. 5, 4 ; S. 226, 4. Cliofum *cautibus,* Wrt. Voc. ii. 16, 16. Hī on heán clifum (cleofum, *v. l.*) wunedon *uitam in rupibus arduis agebant,* Bd. 1, 15 ; Sch. 44, 2. v. hnut-, sǣ-clif.

**clifæhtig.** v. clifihtig.

**clīfan.** *Add :*—On clīfende þām gāste se līchama *inhaerendo spiritui caro,* Gr. D. 264, 1.

**clife.** *Add :*—Clifae, clibe *lappa,* Txts. 76, 613. Clife, Wrt. Voc. ii. 49, 63 : glitilia, 40, 75 : Txts. 67, 978. Clife *personacia,* Hpt. 33, 250, 14. Clife *appasina,* Wrt. Voc. i. 67, 33. Cliue *apparine,* Lch. iii. 299, col. 2. [v. *N. E. D.* cleavers. O. H. Ger. chliba *lappa.*] v. clif-wyrt.

**clifer.** *Substitute for citations :*—Clifra *ungularum,* An. Ox. 5341 : Germ. 399, 337. 'Þū þis weorc nid þīnum clifrum dō' . . . Sōna seó leó mid hire clifrum scræf geworhte, Hml. S. 23 b, 786. C(l)ifras *ungulas,* Germ. 400, 551. [v. *N. E. D.* cliver.] v. next word.

**clifer-fēte;** *adj. Cloven-footed :*—Hara wæs unclǣne, for đan đe hē nis cliferfēte, Hml. S. 25, 79. v. clyfer-fēte *in Dict.*

**clif-hlēp.** *Substitute :* clif-hlīp (-hlēp, -hlȳp), es ; *m. A cliff-leap, a going headlong to destruction :*—Clifshlēp *pessum* (cf. *pessum, praeceps,* Corp. Gl. H. 92, 370 : *pessum* spilth, 90, 213 : ofer clif *per praeceps* (v. clif), Wrt. Voc. ii. 117, 6 (= Corp. Gl. H. 91, 307). Clifhlȳp, 68, 7.

**clifian.** *Add :*—On cliofađ *inheret,* Wrt. Voc. ii. 48, 15. Se gāst sylf cleofađ on Gode, Gr. D. 264, 3. Hī mid hyra mōde him on clīfađ (cleof-, *v. l.*), 138, 30. Of þām hege þe hē fæste on clifode (clyf-, *v. l.*), 25, 12. Hē cleofode on đǣre eorđan and ne mihte nā onstyrian his fēt tō gānne, 224, 22. Cleofede *lentesceret,* An. Ox. 3108. On cleofode, Wrt. Voc. ii. 50, 24. Āhryse þa moldan of, þ hyre nān wiht on ne clyfie, Lch. i. 70, 9. Þ feax þe on þām cambe cleofige (clyf-, *v. l.*), 332, 21. v. on-clifiende.

**clifig, clifiht.** *Substitute :* clifig ; *adj. Cliffy, steep :*—Clifig, tōhyld *clivosus,* Wrt. Voc. i. 19, 4.

**clifiht(e) ;** *adj. Cliffy, steep :*—Clibecti *clibosum,* Txts. 51, 478. Clifihte, Wrt. Voc. ii. 14, 39.

**clifihtig;** *adj. Cliffy, steep :*—Clifæhtig *clivosum,* i. *inclinatum,* Wrt. Voc. i. 131, 69.

**clifrian.** *Add :*—Clifrode *abradit,* An. Ox. 50, 20. Hī man clifrode mid īsenum clawum, Hml. S. 12, 187. Mid īsenum clawum clifrian his lima, 14, 43. v. clifer.

**clifrung,** e ; *f. A clawing ; a claw* (?) :—Clifrunga *ungulae,* Germ. 398, 61.

**clif-stān.** *Substitute :*—Clifstānas *cautes,* Wrt. Voc. ii. 18, 16. Neólnes tōweaxen mid mycelnessum þāra clifstāna *praecipitium saxorum molibus asperum,* Gr. D. 159, 26. Hē sceolde beón tōsliten for þām clifstānum (*scopulis*) þe þǣr gehwǣr ūt sceoredon of þām munte, 213, 4.

**clif-wyrt.** *Add :*—Clifwyrt *clitum,* Lch. iii. 303, col. 1. v. clyf-wyrt *in Dict.*

**clīm.** v. calwer-clīm : **climan.** *Dele.*

**clincig ;** *adj. Shrivelled with heat or cold, rough :*—Clincig sīþfæt *asperum iter,* Hy. S. 104, 35. [Cf. somer dryeth mareis and mores . . . and maketh hem rouȝe and harde and clynkery. v. *N. E. D.* clinkery.] Cf. clingan.

**clingan.** *Add : to shrink together from heat or cold.* [*Scot.* cling *to shrink in consequence of heat.* v. *N. E. D.* cling.] v. ā-clingan ; healf-clungen.

**clipian.** *Add :* I. *of persons :*—Ic tō þē cleopie, Bl. H. 89, 14. Clepađ *clamitat,* Kent. Gl. 6. Wē cliepiađ (clip-, *v. l.*) tō Gode, Past. 263, 23. Clipode *proclamat,* Hpt. Gl. 480, 17. Þes þearfa clepode (*clamavit*) tō Gode, Ps. Th. 33, 6. Hī for ege ne durron clypion (cleopian, *v. l.*), Past. 88, 11. II. *of animals :*—Assan clipiende, Lch. iii. 198, 12. v. ā-cleopian.

**clipol ;** *adj.* I. *sounding, vocal :*—Hig deóplīce þā stefna þæs lyftes swēge gesleađ, and mid þǣre tungan clypole þæne swēg gewynsumiađ, Angl. viii. 313, 15. v. hlūd-clipol. II. *vowel :*—þæne clypolan .a., Angl. viii. 314, 16.

**-clips.** v. ge-clips.

**clipung,** e ; *f. Take here* clypung, cleopung *in Dict., and add :* I. *crying, clamour :*—Gehȳrde hē mycele heáf and wōp, and manige cleopodan mid mycelre stefne. þā āhsode hē hwæt seó cleopung wǣre, Bl. H. 219, 10. Manegum stefnum and cleopungum (hreámum, *v. l.*) *vocibus clamoribusque,* Gr. D. 74, 4. II. *a cry, call, words of address, appeal, &c. :*—Cōm clypung of đām Hālgan Gāste, þus cweđende, Hml. Th. i. 388, 12. Se sunderhālga cwæđ : 'God ! ic đancige đē þæt ic ne eom nā swilce ōđre menn' : ealles tō micel clypung þæt hē nǣre ōđrum mannum gelíc . . . Mid ānre clypunge wearđ þes synfulla gerihtwīsod, ii. 428, 19–34. Hē clypode tō Gode : 'þū ælmihtiga God . . .' Æfter đisre clypunge, Hml. S. 18, 132. Cleopodon þā gāstas mid

mycelre cleopunge and þus cwædon, Guth. 38, 16.     **III.** *an appellation, name* :—Gecīednysse, clipunge *vocabulo*, i. *nomine*, An. Ox. 1503. Clypunge, naman *vocabulo*, 4847 : 4737. Clypunga *vocabulorum*, i. *nominum*, 878.     **IV.** *articulation* :—Þás syndon healfclypiende gecīgede, for ðan ðe hī nabbað fulle clypunge, Ælfc. Gr. Z. 6, 3. Hī ne synd nā mid ealle dumbe, ac hī habbað lytle clypunge, 3.     **V.** *form of address* (of pronouns). v. stefn, II :—Se ðridda hád (*the pronoun of the*) *third person* hæíð syx clypunga, Ælfc. Gr. Z. 93, 7.

**clipur.** *Add* : [v. *N. E. D.* clip *to ring a bell*.]

**clīþa.** *l.* clīþa, cleoþa, *and add* :—Clīþa cataplasma, *medicamentum*, Wrt. Voc. ii. 129, 38. Clyþa *malagma*, i. *medicamentum*, Hpt. 33, 239, 28. Lācnunge, clīþan *cataplasma*, An. Ox. 3050. Cleoþan, lǽcedóm, 1973. Éhsealfe, þone hālwendan cleoþan *malagma* .i. *colirium*, 3051 : malagma, i. *unguentum* í *medicina*, 5359. Clyþan, 2078. Wyrcan ǽnne clyþan (clīðan, *v. l.*) tó þæs cynincges dolge, Hml. S. 18, 430. Clám, clīþan *tiriaca*, An. Ox. 964. Cf. clīþan.

**clīþan** *to stick, cleave.* v. æt-clīþende.

**clíþe,** an ; *f.* Burdock :—Clīþae *lappa*, Txts. 76, 613. [v. *N. E. D.* clithe, clithers. *O. H. Ger.* chleta *lappa*.] v. clife, *and next word.*

**clíþ-wyrt,** e ; *f.* Clivers ; rubea minor :—Genim ðā smalan clīðwyrt, Lch. iii. 50, 8. v. clif-wyrt, *and preceding word.*

**clíwen, cleówen.** *Add* : (? clīwen, cleówen ; v. *N. E. D.* clew) :—Cleowen *glomer*, Wrt. Voc. ii. 40, 72. Clywen (*printed* clywe ; *but see* Angl. viii. 452), i. 59, 35. Swilce ān byrnende clīwen, Hml. S. 31, 937. Clīwenes *globi*, An. Ox. 492. Clīwene *glomere*, 457 : 3736. Gewint hē (*the hedgehog*) tó ānum clīwene (cliw-, *v. l.*), Past. 241, 11. On fȳrenum clīwene (cleow-, clyw-, *v. ll.*), Gr. D. 171, 17. Cleowne (cliowene, *v. l.*), 272, 15. Suelce se lāreów hæbbe ān clīwen on his honda, Past. 241, 24. Hī gesáwon fȳren cleowen (cleawen, Cockayne) gefeallan and óðre síðe gylden cleowen, Mart. H. 2, 13. Cleowena *globos*, An. Ox. 1658. v. cleówe.

**cloccettan ;** *p.* te To *palpitate, beat, throb* :—Gif se drinca mára biþ, sóna biþ seó wamb gehefegod and cloccet swā swā hit on cylle (fylle ?) slecgeð *fluctuationes habeant, si id quod redundat, innatet*, Lch. ii. 220, 18. [Cf. *O. H. Ger.* chlocchón *palpare, pulsare.*]

**cloccian.** *Add* : [v. *N. E. D.* clock.] : -clofa. v. ge-clofa.

**clofe,** an ; *f.* A buckle :—Clofae, clouae *mordacius*, Txts. 78, 653.

**clott** *a mass, lump* :—Clotte (clottum, Hpt. Gl. 488, 76) *massa* (*picis*), An. Ox. 3514. Clot *massas*, 3846. [v. *N. E. D.* clot.]

**clough.** *Dele.*

**clúd.** *Substitute for bracket at end* : [v. *N. E. D.* cloud], *and add* :—Cluud *scopulus*, An. Ox. 8, 219. Clúdes *collis*, 1548. Fram þām heán clúde (clife, *v. l., rupe*), Gr. D. 52, 23. Se heort āstāh on ānneh eáhne clúd, Hml. S. 30, 38. Hī gemētton ðone clúd swǽtende, Hml. Th. ii. 162, 6. *Cautes*, i. *aspera saxa in mari vel torres vel* clúdas *vel rupes*, Wrt. Voc. ii. 129, 30. Clúdas *praerupta*, Germ. 394, 331. Scylpa, clúda *scopulorum*, i. *saxorum*, An. Ox. 642. Clúdum *cautibus*, i. *saxis* í *petris*, 2039. Wǽron ðreó mynstru āsette on heálicum muntum, and wæs ðám gebróðrum micel frecednys tó āstígenne of þām clúdum tó wæterscipe, Hml. Th. ii. 160, 30. Clúdas *rupem*, Ps. Spl. 113, 8.

**clúdig.** *Add* :—Betwyx clúdige heollstru *inter recessus scrupeos*, Germ. 399, 447. [v. *N. E. D.* cloudy.]

**clufe.** *Substitute* : clufu, e ; *f., and add* :—Clufu *capiclum*, Wrt. Voc. ii. 128, 50. [v. *N. E. D.* clove. Cf. *O. H. Ger.* chlofo-louh *allium*.]

**clufeht.** *Add* :—Of þǽre clufihtan wenwyrte, Lch. ii. 128, 7. þā clufihtan wenwyrt, 276, 5. Clifihtan (cluf- ?), 266, 26.

**cluf-þung.** *Add* :—Clufþung *batrachium*, Wrt. Voc. i. 66, 70. Mid ǽttrigere clufþunge (clyf-, An. Ox. 896) *letali toxa*, Hpt. Gl. 427, 55. [v. *N. E. D.* cloffing.]

**cluf-wyrt.** *Add* :—Clufwyrt *batracion*, Wrt. Voc. i. 67, 29. [v. *N. E. D.* clovewort.]

**clugge.** *Add* : (clucggan, clucgan ; bellan, *v. ll.*), Sch. 477, 13.

**clumian.** *For* 'Wanl. Catal. 30, 14' *substitute* : Wlfst. 176, 30 : Ll. Th. ii. 308, 20, *and add* :—Clummiað, Wlfst. 177, 30 : 190, 27. [v. *N. E. D.* clum.]

**clúse.** *Add* : **I.** *a bar, bolt* :—Tóforan āsete tungan þīnre clúsan swīgean (*claustra silentii*), Scint. 214, 9.     **II.** *a place that may be locked up, closet ; prison* :—Clúsan (*intra animi*) *conclave*, An. Ox. 3110.     **III.** *a narrow passage, pass, defile* :—Hē búta þā clúsan on his gewealde hæfde *angustias Thermopylarum ingreditur, easque occupatas emuniit*, Ors. 3, 7 ; S. 114, 28, 23. v. mynster-clúse ; clȳse.

**clústor-loc ;** *pl.* -locu (*not* -loca). *Substitute for citations* :—Clústor-loc (clústorlocae, clústerlocae, Ep. Erf. Gll.) *clustella*, Txts. 51, 481. Clústerloc, Wrt. Voc. ii. 14, 42 : 131, 78. Clústerlocu *crustra* (ǽrea portarum *clustra*, Ald. 148, 30), 90, 57.

**clút.** *Add* :—Clút *pittacium*, Wrt. Voc. ii. 117, 32 : *commisura*, 132, 10. Man ledde tó his breóstum brāde ísene clútas swíðe glówende, Hml. S. 37, 162.

**clyccan ;** *p.* clyhte ; *pp.* clyht To *clitch* (v. *N. E. D.* s.v.), *to bend,*

---

*incurve* the fingers :—Clyce þīne fingras swilc þū blæchorn niman wille, Tech. ii. 128, 19. v. ge-clyccan.

**clȳfa.** *l.* clyfa, *and* v. cleofa : clyfer-fēte. v. clifer-fēte : **clyfian.** v. clifian : -clyft. v. ge-clyft.

**clympe** (?) *a lump.* v. calwer-clympe. [v. *N. E. D.* clump.] v. next word.

**clympre.** *Add* :—Clympre *metallum*, Wrt. Voc. ii. 56, 37. Climprum *fornicis*, Germ. 398, 243. [v. *N. E. D.* clumper.]

**clynan.** *l.* clynnan, clynian ; *p.* ede.     **I.** *intrans.* To *sound, resound* ; El. 51.     **II.** *trans.* To *cause to sound, knock at* a door :—Clyniga ðæt dor *pulsare ostium*, Lk. R. 15, 25.

**clyne.** *Substitute* : clyne, es ; *n.* A *mass, lump, ball* :—Clyne *massa*, Wrt. Voc. ii. 113, 66. Clyne *globus* (*astrorum*), An. Ox. 23, 40. Clynes *globi* (*lunaris*), 492. Trendles, clynes *spere* (clynes, trendles *sphaerae*, trendel, clyne *sphaera*, Hpt. Gl. 489, 22), 3527. Clyne, clotte (of clyne í clottum, Hpt. Gl. 488, 76) wǽran gecrammede *massa* (*picis*) *farciuntur*, 3514. Clyne *massam* (*piceam*), Wrt. Voc. ii. 90, 22. God him fram þæt fȳrene clyne ādyde þe ofer þā ceastre wæs on þām genipe hangiende, An. Ox. 492 note. Ælces kynnes weeg *vel* óra oððe clyna *metallum*, Wrt. Voc. i. 34, 67. Leádes clynum *mastigiis*, i. 54, 75. Clyno massas (*caricarum*), ii. 83, 56 : 56, 38. Clyna, An. Ox. 2, 260. Clyne, clyna, Hpt. Gl. 496, 68. Cnynas, An. Ox. 3846. Clyna, clystru *botros*, 2639. [Sile hym þan fæstende etan feówur dayes ǽlc dæ āne clyne, Lch. iii. 134, 33.]

**clynian** (?) *to make into a ball* (v. clyne), *to enfold* :—Clyniende *inplicans*, Germ. 401, 24.

**clypian, clypol.** v. clipian, clipol.

**clypp,** es ; *m. Embracing, embrace* :—On clyppe ge on hleahtre ge on spræce, Angl. xi. 99, 76 : 102, 61.

**clyppan.** *Add* :—Hē gelæhte hine be þām swuran and cyste and clypte, Hml. S. 30, 336. Þte clioppende (cliopende, R.) wæs *ut complexus esset*, Mk. L. 9, 36.

**clypping,** e ; *f. Embracing, embrace* :—Hē gefeóll on þæs ceorles clyppinge (hē þone ceorl beclypte, *v. l.*), Gr. D. 47, 1. v. be-, ymb-clypping.

**clȳse.** v. munt-clȳse ; clúse.

**clȳsing.** *Add* : **I.** *closing, stopping ; a bar* :—Higlísta ēcer[e] clȳsunga (cf. ēcum loce, R. Ben. 22, 5) wē fordēmað *scurilitates aeterna clausura dampnamus*, R. Ben. I. 26, 14.     **II.** *an enclosed place, cloister, closet* :—Út āgān mǽdenes módor clȳsinga *egressus virginis matris clausula*, Hy. S. 34, 34. Hē lēt þā módor tó þām suna on synderlicre clȳsincge, Hml. S. 4, 343. Clȳsunga mynstres *claustra monasterii*, R. Ben. I. 23, 2 : 114, 1. Binnon his mynstres clȳsingum *intra cellae suae claustra*, Gr. D. 124, 24. Hē nolde beón gehæfd binnon clȳsingum þǽre burge (binnan þǽre byrig, *v. l.*) *teneri intra claustra noluit*, 110, 14. þæt hī his sáwle mid him tó hellicum clȳsungum gegripon, Hml. Th. i. 414, 11.     **III.** *a clause, period, conclusion* :—Clȳsincg *syllogismus*, Hpt. Gl. 503, 58. Fulle cwydas, clȳsincga *periodos*, An. Ox. 2849. Clȳsinga *syllogismus*, 2, 291.

**clyster.** *Add* :—Clyster *botrus*, An. Ox. 7, 287. Clystri *botrum*, Txts. 45, 318. Clystre, Wrt. Voc. ii. 11, 30. þā feáwa clystru þǽra bergena, Gr. D. 57, 18. Clystrum *racemis*, An. Ox. 3850. Clystru *botros*, 2639 : *racemos*, 5, 29. Clystra, 2641 : *butros*, Wrt. Voc. ii. 126, 83. *Botros* .i. *uvarum globos* .i. glyster, An. Ox. 2, 99. Clistro *dactilos*, 2, 10. Clystro, fingerappla clystra, 472. v. wín-clyster ; ge-clystre.

**clywe.** *Dele.*

**cnæp[p].** *For third passage substitute* :—Ofer scittisce cneppas *trans* [s]*cotianorum juga*, Germ. 397, 539, *for bracket at end substitute* : [v. *N. E. D.* knap, knop], *and add* : **I.** *top* of a hill :—On þorndúnes cnep ; of ðane cneppe, C. D. iv. 8, 27.     **II.** *a button, brooch* :—Cnæp *fibula*, Wrt. Voc. ii. 148, 57.

**cnæpling.** *Add* :—Cnæplingc *puer* .i. *infans*, An. Ox. 2579. Hē syfonwyntre wæs . . . þā wunode se cnæplingc on Cappadoniscre byrig fíf geár on láre, Hml. S. 3, 9. Cf. cnapa.

**cnéwe.** *Add :* v. eáþ-, on-cnáwe.

**cnafa,** an ; *m. A boy, lad, young man* :—Gamenian mid cnafan *jocari cum parvulo*, Scint. 172, 19. Cnafan þínum *puero tuo*, Ps. Spl. C. 85, 15. Sȳn twēgen tó þām sylfan gescyfte cnafan (*pueri*), Angl. xiii. 410, 640. [v. *N. E. D.* knave. *O. H. Ger.* chnabo.] v. mǽg-cnafa. Cf. next word.

**cnapa, cnafa.** *Dele* cnafa (q.v.) *and bracket at end, and add* : **I.** *a lad* :—Cuðberht þá þā hē git cnapa wæs, Hml. S. 26, 279. Sende þone cnapan mid mē *send the lad with me*, Gen. 43, 8. Geonge cild and stíðe cnapan *pueri vel adolescentiores aetate*, R. Ben. 53, 21. Geongum cnapum *pueris minore aetate*, 64, 3. Of þám iungum cnihtum hī ālǽddon āweg . . . and of þám cnapum ys þæt kynn git gehwǽr, Ælfc. T. Grn. 21, 21.     **II.** *a (young) man* in service, *a servant* (take here Coll. M. 19, 27 : Gen. 22, 3, 5, 19 given under I in Dict.) :—Mín cnapa lið on mínum húse lama, Mt. 8, 6 : 12, 18. His cnapa wæs āwēd ðurh deófol . . . Se āwyrgeda gást gewāt of ðám

men, Hml. Th. ii. 510, 32. [v. *N. E. D.* knape. *O. Frs.* knapa: *O. L. Ger.* knapo: *Icel.* knapi.] v. hirde-, munuc-cnapa.

**cnáwan.** *Add: p.* (cneów), cnéw (v. oncnéw, Past. 295, 8):—Þ wē cnáwan wæg ðinne *ut cognoscamus viam tuam*, Ps. Spl. 66, 2. Þā beóð cnáwene *noscuntur*, An. Ox. 76. v. ā-cnáwan.

**-cnáwe.** v. be-, or-cnáwe, -cnǽwe: **-cnáwenness.** v. on-, tó-cnáwenness.

**cnáwlǽcung,** e; *f. Acknowledgement :*—Alle ðā gerihte and ðā cnáwelācinge ðā tó mē bilimpaddon, C. D. iv. 193, 14. [v. *N. E. D.* knowledging.]

**-cnáwlíce.** v. tó-cnáwlíce: **-cnáwness.** v. on-, tó-cnáwness.

**cneátian.** *Substitute for passages :*—Cneátiað ł cwiddiað ł secgeað *contendunt* .i. *dicunt,* Hpt. Gl. 450, 69: An. Ox. 2, 54. Cneátian *disceptare,* 927. Cneá[tiende] *indagantes* .i. *investigantes,* 1318. v. ge-cneátian; cnītan.

**cneátung.** *Add:*—Smeáunge, cneátunge *scrutinium,* i. *indagationem,* An. Ox. 1085. On cneátungum *in disputationibus,* Scint. 74, 20.

**cnedan.** *Add:*—Gāte tord cned swýþe þ hyt sý swylce sealf, Lch. i. 354, 19. v. be-cnedan.

**cneó.** v. cneów: **cneódan.** *Dele, and see* cnódan : **cneord.** *Add:* v. be-cneord: **cneord-lǽcan.** *For* 'M. H. 14 a *substitute :*—Seó lār ne mihte þām cneordlǽcendum cnihte cýðan be his Scyppende, Hml. S. 3, 27.

**cneord-nys.** *Substitute for citations :*—Cneordnesse *studio,* i. *in labore,* An. Ox. 2508. Cneordnysse *studio* (.i. *disciplina,* Hpt. 430, 2), 995. Cneorð[nesse] *studio,* 7, 30.

**cneór[e]d-ness,** e; *f. A generation, race :*—Drihten sibbe cneórdnesse tódǽlde . . . hē on ðreó tówearp þā cneórdnysse, þ wæs wælisc and on cyrlisc cynn and on gesýðcund cynd, Angl. xi. 3, 59–63. v. ge-cneóredness, *and following words.*

**cneóres.** *Add:*—Cneóris *familia,* Wrt. Voc. ii. 39, 44. *Familia* hiwrǽden *vel familiaritas* cneóres, 147, 31. Cneóres *propinquitas,* An. Ox. 4180. Cneóris *cognatio,* Ps. Srt. 73, 8 : *natio,* ii. 191, 40. Cneoreso (-reswo, R.) ðíos *generatio haec,* Mk. L. 13, 30: Rtl. 96, 25. Cneúreso, 108, 27. Cneúresu, Mt. L. 1, 18. Cnēwureso (cneórissa, R.), 24, 34. Cneúreso (cneórisse, R.), Mk. L. 8, 12. Cnēwreso, 9, 19. Cniúrisse, cneórissa (-æ) *sanguinis,* Txts. 95, 1780. Cneórisse cneórissa *nationis nationum,* Ps. Srt. ii. 192, 5. Cneóresse *genesi,* An. Ox. 2629. In cnērisse *in generatione,* Ps. Srt. 88, 2. Cneúresu, Mt. p. 12, 10. Cneóresse *posteritatem,* An. Ox. 585. Cneúresa (kneórisse, R.) *generationes,* Mt. L. 1, 17. Cneúresuu *generationum,* p. 13, 14. In cneúreswum ðassum, Mk. R. 8, 38. v. æfter-, eft-cneóres.

**cneórisn,** e; *f. A generation, race, family :*—Cneórisn Caines . . . mē þæt cynn hafað ābolgen, Gen. 1256. Þus wæs Crīstes cneóres (cneórisn, *v. l.*) *Christi generatio sic erat,* Mt. 1, 18. Mín Drihten, wē ealle forlēton úre cneórisne and wǽron þē fylgende, Bl. H. 229, 21. Mē eádige cwǽdon ealle cneórisna, 7, 5.

**cneórnis.** *Add:*—Cneórnesse *genesi,* An. Ox. 7, 178.

**cneów.** *Add:* I. *a knee :*—Mín ádlige cneów, Hml. Th. ii. 134, 32, 23. Þæt þā eá mehte wífmon be hiere cneówe oferwadan *amnem feminis vix genua tingentibus permeabilem,* Ors. 2, 4 : S. 72, 33. Cnēuo bēged *genu flexo,* Mk. L. 10, 17. Cnēw gebēged (knēu bēgende, R.) *genu flexu,* Mt. L. 27, 29. Cneówa *genua,* Wrt. Voc. ii. 41, 25. Cnyówu, i. 65, 40. Feóllan ealle on cneówum biddende, Hml. S. 18, 257. Ic wille þ gē beran eówer leóht tó mē, and licgað on cneówum (*kneel*), 21, 296. Cnēum gewælteno (cnēu bēgende) *genibus provolutus,* Mt. L. 17, 14. Mid gesetnum cneóum *positis genibus,* Lk. L. 22, 41. Gisettedum cnēum, Rtl. 44, 13. Settun on cneóm *ponentes genua,* Mk. R. 15, 19. Feól tó cnēuum ðæs Hǽlendes, Lk. L. 5, 8. Āstreccað eówru cneówu, Past. 65, 18. Þ man his cneówu gebíge sixtigum síðum tó eorðan, Ll. Th. ii. 284, 31. Cneówa, Hml. S. 23 b, 83. Hí bígdon heora cneówa, Mt. 27, 29 : Hml. Th. ii. 148, 9. Knēwa, Mt. L. 15, 19. II. *a generation, a degree of descent in a genealogy* [v. *N. E. D.* knee, ll. 11; Grmm. R. A. 468–70]:—On ðām feórðan cneówe hí gecyrrað hider ongeán, Hml. Th. ii. 190, 22. Feówertēne kneó (*generationes*), Mt. R. 1, 17.

**cneówade.** v. cneówede: **cneó-wærc.** v. cneów-wærc.

**cneów-bíging,** e; *f. Bending of the knee, genuflexion :*—Mid cneówbígincge *cum genuflectione,* Angl. xiii. 417, 743. Būton cneówbígincge, 418, 752. Mid cnēwbēging (mid cneú bēgende ł bēginge, R.) *genu flexo,* Mk. L. 1, 40.

**cneówede** (-ade); *adj. Having great knees :*—Cneówede *genosus,* Wrt. Voc. i. 45, 39. Cneówade, ii. 42, 14.

**cneów-gebed,** es; *n. Prayer on bended knees :*—þ heó mōste be leáfe gān on hyre gebedum tó gebiddenne hire Drihten on hire cneówgebedum *ut daretur ei copia egrediendi ad orationem et deprecandi Dominum,* Hml. A. 110, 277. Ealle feóllan heom on cneówgebedum, 179, 328. Clypode hē on cneówgebedum ðus : 'Gefæstna þis, Hǽlend,' Hml. S. 4, 49. [Cf. *O. Sax.* knio-beda.]

**cneów-holen.** *Add:*—Cnióholen (-aen) *ruscus,* Txts. 93, 1759: Wrt. Voc. i. 68, 51 : *victoriala,* 59 : *mirstillago,* ii. 58, 29. Cneówhole[n] *sinpatus,* i. 30, 29. [v. *N. E. D.* knee-holly.]

**cneówian.** *Add: ;* cneówan (?); *p.* de:—Hí cneówdon þā æft, Hml. S. 3, 522. Ðǽre cyningas tó him cneówodon, 24, 6. Se fiscere cneówige æt þæs cāseres gemynde, Hml. Th. i. 578, 9. Hí Godes hús sēce and cneówige þǽr úte, Wlfst. 155, 9. Man ne mót cneówian on Sunnandagum, Hml. S. 12, 7. Singe hē þreó hund sealma cneówigende (*genuflectens*), Ll. Th. ii. 134, 14. [v. *N. E. D.* knee. *O. H. Ger.* chniuwen.]

**cneówlian** *to kneel :*—Sylf hē on díglum stōwum gecneówige (cneówlie, *v. l.* v. *N. E. D.* kneel), Ll. Th. ii. 282, 30.

**cneów-rift,** es; *n. A napkin :*—Cneóribt *mappa,* Wrt. Voc. ii. 98, 24. [Cf. *O. H. Ger.* chnio-rest (-reft?) *mantile.*]

**cneówung.** *Add:*—Cneówuncge *genuflectione,* Angl. xiii. 433, 977. Mid cneówunge *genu flexo,* 434, 994. Singe hē þreó hund sealma cneówigende, oððe hund and twēntig būtan cneówunge (*sine genuflexione*) . . . mid cneówunga oððe būtan cneówunge *cum genuflexionibus vel sine genuflexione,* Ll. Th. ii. 134, 14–18.

**cneów-wǽrc;** *m.* (not *n.*): cneów-wyrste; *pl. f. Substitute :* cneów-wrist (-wyrst), e ; *f. A knee-joint.*

**cníf.** *Add:*—Wrít þysne circul mid þínes cnífes orde on ānum mealan stāne, Lch. i. 395, 3. [þā mann mid cnífun hǽle menn, iii. 82, 10.]

**cniht.** *Add:* I. *a youth :*—Scipia wæs cniht (*adolescens*), Ors. 4, 10 ; S. 196, 12. Ic eom cnioht (*puer*), Past. 49, 7. Hē his cnieht lǽrde : 'Sunu mín,' 287, 10. Se drý wearþ fǽringa geong cniht and sóna eft eald man, Bl. H. 175, 3. Hē þone cniht (*Hæsien's son*) āgef and þæt wíf, Chr. 894; P. 86, 31. Ðone cniht (*Alcibiades se æðeling,* 19) ðurhseón, Bt. 32, 2; F. 116, 23. Cnihtas, geonglingas *puberes,* Wrt. Voc. ii. 66, 12. Ealle ðā cnihtas and ealle ðā mǽdena (*the firstborn of Egypt*), Ors. 1, 7; S. 38, 15. I a. *an unmarried man.* v. cniht-hād, II.—Hit býð rihtlíc líf þæt cniht þurhwunige on his cnihthāde, oð þæt he on rihtre ǽwe gewífige, Wlfst. 304, 20 : Ll. Th. ii. 332, 28. II. *a servant, man, follower :*—Cniht *clitus* vel *clientulus,* Wrt. Voc. ii. 50, 32. Hit is níeððearf ðæt mon his hláford ondrǽde, and se cneoht his mǽgister, Past. 109, 13. Karl þæs cincges cniht, Cht. Th. 312, 33. Ic geann Wulfgāre mínan cnihte þæs landes, 545, 28 : 559, 10. Ic geann Ǽðelwine mínon cnihte ðæs swurdes þe hē mē ǽr sealde, 561, 20. Ic gean Wulmǽre mínum cnihte landes for his gōdra gearnunge, Cht. E. 238, 10. Cnihta *parasitorum,* An. Ox. 4165. II a. *a man engaged in military service, a soldier :*—Byrd se cniht his swurd *portat miles gladium,* Ǽlfc. T. Grn. 20, 26. Þū sylst ārleásum cnihte (*militi*) þæt þú nelt syllan sācerde, Scint. 109, 10. Þā cnihtas (*the two spies in Jericho*), Jos. 2, 14. Wǽron innan þām castele Oda ðs cnihtas, Chr. 1087; P. 224, 4. Seofen hundred þes cynges cnihta, 1094; P. 229, 17. Sume of ðām cnihtan, 1083; P. 215, 9. II b. *a disciple, scholar.* v. leorning-cniht :—Se hǽþena scop and his cniht *historicus ejusque breviator,* Ors. 1, 5; S. 32, 28. Paulus manode his cneoht (*discipulum*), Past. 97, 12. Cuiht, 169, 16. III. *a soldier of rank, a knight :*—Ealle þā ríce men, arcebiscopas, and leóðbs, abbodas and eorlas, þegnas and cnihtas, Chr. 1086; P. 220, 2. Swíðe gōde cnihtas, Eustatius þe iunga, and Rōgeres eorles þreó sunan, and ealle þā betstboren men þe wǽron innan þisan lande, 1087; P. 224, 28. v. búr-, ceáp-, cípe-, hel-, heorþ-, híréd-, hors-cniht.

**cniht-cild.** *Add:*—Hié ǽghwelcum cnihtcilde ymbsnidon þ werlice lim, Shrn. 47, 20.

**cniht-geogoþ,** e; *f. Boyhood, youth :*—þā feówer tíman . . . sumor . . . , and eác þā gelícnyssa . . . cnihtiugoð and sumor beóð gelíce . . . sumor byð wearm . . . cnihtiugoð byð wearm, Angl. viii. 299, 23–30.

**cniht-hād.** *Add:* I. *boyhood :*—Úre cnihthād is swylce underntíd, on þām āstíhð úre geogoð, Hml. Th. ii. 76, 15. Cnihthādes *pubertatis,* i. *adolescentie,* An. Ox. 2382. Seó forme wæcce is on cildhāde, and seó óðer wæcce is on weaxendum cnihthāde, Hml. A. 52, 68. Sum cild hāl geboren . . . ðíonde on cræftum þā hwíle þe hit on cnihthāde bið, and swā forþ eallne ðone giogoðhād, Bt. 38, 5 ; F. 206, 23. Fram cnihthāde *a pueritia,* Kent. Gl. 1066. Of his cnihthāde *ab annis puerilibus,* Gr. D. 11, 6. On his cnihthāde, Bl. H. 213, 27 : Shrn. 65, 8 : Ors. 2, 2 ; S. 66, 16. II. *unmarried state, celibacy.* v. cniht, I a :—Hē (*S. John*) on mægðhāde (cnihthāde, *v. l.*) on ēcnysse þurhwunode *virgo in eum permansit,* Hml. A. 14, 30. Iōhannes se fulluhtere þurhwunode ǽfre on cnihthāde . . . and Iōhannes se godspellere wunode on cnihthāde oð his lífes ende, Ll. Th. ii. 366, 35–39 : 332, 39 : Wlfst. 304, 20.

**cniht-iugoþ.** v. cniht-geogoþ.

**cniht-leás.** *For* 'M. H. 113 b' *substitute :*—Hē for ðǽre sārignysse wæs him āna cnihtleás on his inran búre, and hine sylfne ðǽrinne beclýsde, Hml. S. 23, 395.

**cniht-þeáw,** es; *m. Boyish habit :*—Placidus þāgyt heóld his cniht-

þeáwas and gebǽru *Placidus puerilis adhuc indolis gerebat annos*, Gr. D. III, 9.

**cniht-wesende.** *l.* (?) cniht wesende. v. wesan, II.

**cnítan** (?), **cnítian** (?) *to dispute* :—Full wamb éþelíce be fæstenum cnítað (-eð?) *plenus uenter facile de ieiuniis disputat*, Scint. 51, 12. Cf. cneátian.

**cnódan, cneódan**; *pp.* [ge-]cnóden. **I.** *to impute, attribute* :—Gif hwæt welgedónes bið, ðonne cnódað him ðæt ealle ðá ðe him underðiédde bióð mid herenesse *omnes subditi, si qua bene gesta sunt, laudibus efferunt*, Past. III, 3. **II.** *to attribute, call* by a person's name, *name* after a person :—Þone tún mon his naman cneóded (cweðeþ, *v. l.*) *cujus nomine vicus cognominatur*, Bd. 2, 20 ; Sch. 189, 8. Wæs se heretéma (*Theodoric*) Críste gecnóden (cf. hé wæs Crísten, Bt. I ; F. 2, 6) *the leader bore the Christian name*, Met. 1, 32. [*For meanings cf. Icel.* kenna *to impute ; to name*.]

**cnoll.** *Add* :—Cnol *jugum*, Wrt. Voc. ii. 112, 15. Wæs se cnoll swá hit nú cúð is þ se munt is mycel úteweard, Bl. H. 207, 26. Þæs muntes cnoll, 203, 8. On þǽm heán cnolle sumes muntes, 197, 18. Tó brynes cnolle, Cht. E. 267, 3. Tó Húnes cnolle, 381, 19. On cnolle *in vertice*, i. *in summitate*, An. Ox. 853. Cnol *apicem*, Wrt. Voc. 73, 64 : *arcem*, 7, 27. Þá mǽran cnollas *almos clivos*, Hpt. 31, 18, 515. Ofer þá pirescan cnollas *trans pirenas ninguidos*, Germ. 397, 540. v. mǽr-, stán-cnoll.

**cnop[p]** (?) *a knob, button* :—Cnop *ballationes*, Wrt. Voc. ii. 101, 55 : 7, 73. [*v. N. E. D.* knop. *O. H. Ger.* chnopf *bulla*.] v. cróp.

**-cnos.** v. ge-cnos.

**cnósl.** *Add* :—Óþer of hyre sylfe swylce hyre cnósl (*printed* cnoss) byþ upp sprungen *aliud ex ipso quasi sua soboles oritur*, Scint. 232, 9. Cnósl (cnol, MS., cnoll, Hpt. Gl. 521, 22) *proles*, An. Ox. 5033. ' Eal Adames cnósl *omnes homines*, Dóm. L. 129. Cnósle *stirpe*, An. Ox. 1601 : *progenie*, 7, 89 : *prolem*, 26, 31. Hig æton Jacobes cnósel *comederunt Jacob*, Ps. L. 78, 7. v. ǽ-cnósle.

**cnot-mǽlum** *glosses* strictim, Angl. xiii. 35, 201. v. next word.

**cnotta.** *Add* : **I.** *a knot, fastening* :—Hét hé þone wer gebindan and ǽnne mæssepreóst . . . mid heardum cnottum samod, Hml. S. 29, 214. Unbindan þá fæstan cnottan synna, 10, 47. Hé unband þá rápas and þá cnottan þára bænda, Gr. D. 165, 4. **II.** *a knotty point, difficulty* :—Hé hine befrán be gehwylcum cnottum þe hé sylf ne cúþe on þǽre hálgan béc, Angl. vii. 2, 13.

**cnucel.** *Dele.* v. cnycel.

**cnucian, cnocian.** *Add* : **I.** *intrans. To knock* at a door :—Sóna þænne cnucað (cnocige, cnucige, R. Ben. 126, 21) *mox ut aliquis pulsaverit*, R. Ben. l. 112, 9. Heó on þǽre cýtan duru cnocode, Hml. A. 196, 26. Gif hé þurhwunað cnuciende (*pulsans*), R. Ben. l. 95, 14 : Hml. Th. i. 248, 21. Cnucigende æt þám geate, Hml. S. 10, 110. **II.** *trans.* (1) *to knock, strike, hit* :—Þá stánas wendon swá þ ðá cwelleras hí sylfe cnucodon, Hml. S. 11, 101. Hét hé mid stánum ðæs hálgan múð cnucian, Hml. Th. i. 428, 32 : 432, 3 : ii. 422, 25. Sí cnucud *pulsetur* (*tabula*), Angl. xiii. 431, 951. (2) *to pound* :—Cnuca ealle tósomne swíðe smale, Lch. iii. 56, 21. Cnocie man þá bán mid æxse ýre, 14, 17.

**cnuwian.** *l.* cnúwian, *and add* :—Cnúa on wíne, Lch. ii. 32, 11.

**-cnycc.** [*v. N. E. D.* knitch.] v. ge-cnycc.

**cnyccan**; cnycte, cnyhte; *pp.* cnyht *To tie, bind*; nectere ;—Oft þræl þæne þegen þe ǽr wæs his hláford cniht swýðe fæste, Wlfst. 163, 2. Tó cnuicte (*printed* -cnutte) *adnexuit*, Mt. p. 10, 15. v. ge-cnyccan; -cnycc.

**cnycel** (? *to be inferred from* ge-cnyclede, q.v.) *a knuckle*.

**cnyll.** *Add* : **I.** *clang, sound* from metal :—S. Petrus þá duru belýcð . . . and hé þonne weorpeð þá cǽga ofer his exle intó helle. . . . Hlúd bið se cnyll ofer ealle eorðan, þonne sió cǽg fealleð innon helle, Hml. A. 169, 138. **II.** *the stroke, sound of a bell* :—Fram þám cnylle *a primo pulsu*, Angl. xiii. 432, 964. Siðþan hý þone forman cnyl (*signum*) tó nóne gehýren, R. Ben. 74, 5. Þone óðerne cnyll *secundum signum*, R. Ben. I. 82, 13. v. fore-cnyll.

**cnyllan.** *Add* : **I.** *to strike, knock, clap* :—Tósomne cnyllaþ *conliserint*, Wrt. Voc. ii. 134, 66. Cnyllan *complodere* vel *concutere*, *conlidere*, 133, 5. **II.** *to strike a door, knock* :—Cnyllas gé *pulsate* . . . ðǽm cnyllende (cnyllenda, p. 15, 7) *pulsanti*, Mt. L. 7, 7, 8. **III.** *to strike, ring a bell* :—Þonne þone óðerne cnyll cnylð (þonne mon eft cnylle, R. Ben. 74, 7) *dum secundum signum pulsaverit*, R. Ben. I. 82, 13. Þænne se cyrcwerd tácn cnylle, Angl. xiii. 398, 475. Swilce hé gehwǽde bellan cnyllan, Tech. ii. 118, 9. Sí cnylled þ forme tácn, Angl. xiii. 391, 374. v. ge-cnyllan.

**cnyllsan.** *Substitute* : **cnylsian,** cnylsian :—Mid ðý cymeð and cnyllsað (*pulsauerit*), Lk. L. 12, 36. Cnyllsað *pulsate* . . . ðǽm cnylsanda *pulsanti*, 11, 9, 10. Cnylsiga *pulsare*, 13, 25. Cnylsende *pulsandum*, p. 7, 4.

**cnyss** (?), e ; *f. A beating*; pulsus :—Cardiacus (glossed by *cardian*, i.e. *pulsum cordis patiens*) heortan cnysse (þrowiende), Hpt. 31, 13, 321. Or is heort-ancnysse (= -angnysse) *to be read* ? Cf. *cardiacus dicitur qui*

*patitur labor:m cordis, vel morbus cordis* heortcoþa *vel* ece, Wrt. Voc. i. 128, 64. v. cnyssan, ge-cnos.

**cnyssan.** *Add* :—Þú cnysest *elides*, Wrt. Voc. ii. 30, 30. Swá þ seó sǽ cnyste þá heofonlican tungla, Ap. Th. 11, 1. Cnyssaþ (cnysað, L.) *pulsate* . . . cnyssande (ðǽm cnysende, L.) *pulsanti*, Mt. R. 7, 7, 8. Ongan ic wépan and míne breóst cnyssan, Hml. S. 23 b, 428.

**cnyttan.** *Add* :—Cnyt(s)t *inlicias* (cf. *inlicias*, i. *nectis*, Hpt. Gl. 524, 8), An. Ox. 8, 333. Oft þrǽl þæne þegen þe ǽr wæs his hláford cnyt swýðe fæste and wyrcð him tó þrǽle, Wlfst. 163, 2. Cnytt, 224, 2. Þá cnitton hí rápas hire tó handum and fótum, Hml. S. 9, 100. Ðæt hé ne cnytte ðæt underfongne feoh on ðǽm swátlíne, Past. 59, 13. Tó cnyttende *annectens*, Angl. xiii. 406, 588.

**cnyttels** ; *m. For* ' Mone B. 2858 ' *substitute* An. Ox. 2935, *and add* : [*v. N. E. D.* knittle.]

**coc[c].** *Add* :—' Hwá sealde kokke wísdóm ? ' Ðæt getácnað ðætte ǽghwelc ðǽra láreówa . . habbað onlícnesse ðǽm kokkum . . . Ðonne grǽt se láreów swá swá kok on niht . . . Ðæs cocces ðeáw is . . . , Past. 459, 29–461, 2. Se kok ðe wé ymb sprǽcon, 12. Cuca *pullorum*, An. Ox. 4891. Cocca, 2, 398.

**cóc.** *Add* :—Cóc *culinia*, cycene *coquina*, Wrt. Voc. i. 291, 22. Cóces *coci*, ii. 21, 68. Of ðám þeówan mannan at Cinnuc . . . hió becwið Eádgyfe Ælfsige ðene cóc, C. D. vi. 133, 1. Cócas *culinia* (coacas, Erf. = (?) *sterculinia, cloacas*. v. Angl. xix. 102 ; *but see first citation, and next*), Txts. 55, 620. Cócas *culini*, Wrt. Voc. ii. 15, 56. Gebríwed swá cócas cunnon, Lch. ii. 220, 9. Kóka ealdormon *princeps cocorum*, Past. 311, 6, 7, 11.

**coccel.** *For last citation substitute* :—Lasera, coccela *loliorum, zizaniorum*, Hpt. Gl. 462, 24, *and add* :—Hyre corn beóð gelíce coccele (*a mistranslation of* cocci *simile*), Lch. i. 170, 2. Hé sǽwd ge lasor ge coccul on manna æceron, Angl. viii. 300, 24. Coccelas oferstígað hwæte *zizania transcendunt frumentum*, Scint. 101, 1.

**cocer** *a quiver. Add* :—Coker *faretra*, Wrt. Voc. i. 35, 23. Seó lufu cocor (*faretram*) and bogan and flán forlét, Prud. 51. Hí fyllaþ heora coceras mid flánum, Ps. Th. 10, 2.

**cócer-panne.** *For* ' Mone B. 4694 ' *substitute* Hpt. Gl. 514, 38, *and add* :—Hyrstepannan vel cócorpanne *frixorium*, i. *sartago, cremium*, Wrt. Voc. ii. 151, 2. Cócerpannan *sartagines*, An. Ox. 4673. Cócurpannan, 8, 278.

**cócnian** *to season food.* v. ge-cócnian ; cócnung.

**cócnunga.** *Substitute* : **cócnung,** e ; *f. Seasoning, seasoned food* :—Cócnung *quadripertitum*, Wrt. Voc. ii. 118, 49. Metegearwa and cócnunga *meat-dressings and seasonings*, Lch. ii. 210, 26. Sume of rigenum melwe wyrceað bríwas and cócnunga mid sealte, 236, 10. v. next word.

**cócor-mete** *seasoned food* :—Cócormete *quadripertitum*, Wrt. Voc. i. 290, 41. [Cf. *O. H. Ger.* choch-muos *dapes*.] v. preceding word.

**coc-ród,** e ; *f. A cock-road, a clearing in a wood where woodcocks could be netted* :—Oð ðá cocródæ ; swá of ðǽre cocród, C. D. v. 346, 26. v. ród.

**-cócsian.** v. ge-cócsian : **cócunung.** v. cócnung : **cod-æppel.** *For* Cot. 93 *substitute* Wrt. Voc. ii. 39, 72.

**codd.** *Add* :—Ne bere gé mid eów pusan oððe codd *nolite portare sacculum neque peram*, Hml. Th. ii. 532, 20. v. beán- (*not* bien-), leþer-codd.

**cófa.** *l.* cofa. *Add* : ; cofu (-e), an ; *f.* (v. bed-cofe.) **I.** *a chamber, closet* :—Cofa *pistrimum*, Wrt. Voc. ii. 117, 30 : 68, 15 : *pistrinum*, i. 288, 62. Lytel cofa *pistrilla*, 63. On cofan *in conclavi*, ii. 46, 14. Gá in þíne cofan (*cubiculum*), Mt. R. 6, 6. In cofum *in penetralibus*, Mt. L. R. 24, 26. **II.** *a cave, den* :—Cofa *spelunca*, Jn. L. R. 11, 38. Cofa ðeáfana *speluncam latronum*, Mt. L. 21, 13 : Mk. L. R. 11, 17 : Lk. L. R. 19, 46. [*v. N. E. D.* cove. *Icel.* kofi *a cell, hut*.] v. brýd-cofa.

**cóf-godas.** *l.* cof-godas (v. cofa), *and for second reference substitute* :—Cofgodas *penatum*, Germ. 402, 195.

**cofincel.** *l.* cofincel *a small chamber* :—Cofincel *pistrilla*, Wrt. Voc. ii. 117, 33 : 68, 16. v. cofa.

**-cofrian.** v. á-cofrian.

**cól** *coal. l.* col, *and add* :—Coll *carbo*, Ælfc. Gr. Z. 35, 2. Þæt fýr wearð ácwenced þ þǽr án col ne gléow, Hml. S. 7, 240. v. sǽ-col.

**cól** *cool. Add* :—Cól *frigidus*, An. Ox. 2, 409. Cól cwyld *frigida pestis*, Wrt. Voc. ii. 150, 76. Se þearfa bemǽnde þ him wǽre þearle cól, Hml. S. 31, 911. Hé bæþes brúce, ná swáþeáh cóles, ne hé cólne wǽtan þicge, Lch. i. 238, 9. Cólre *frigenti*, An. Ox. 5486. Cóle *algida* (*aequora*), 18, 15. Cólum *algosis*, 8, 8.

**-cole.** v. hæp-cole : **-cóle.** v. wín-cóle.

**cólian.** *Add* :—Ic cólige *algeo*, Ælfc. Gr. Z. 155, 9. Fram þám fistigoðan geáre cólað seó hǽte þæs líchaman, Gr. D. 102, 23. Cólaþ seó lufu þe wé tó úrum Hǽlende habban sceolde, Bl. H. 109, 3 : Wlfst. 82, 9. Wyrc swylc án lytel cicel . . . swá ðú hátost forberan mǽge . . . þonne se cicel cólige, Lch. iii. 30, 21. Cólgendre *frigenti*, Angl. xiii. 38, 318. [*O. Sax.* kólôn.]

collatio. v. æfen-collatio.

collecta, an; m. f. A collect :—Ǣr þām seó collecta (collecta) beó geended, Angl. xiii. 406, 590. Cweðe se sácerd þone collectan, and geendige þā mæssan mid ānre collectan, Ll. Th. ii. 360, 1-4. Collectan (gebedu, R. Ben. I. 42, 18) letania, R. Ben. 37, 2. Twā rǣdinga mid iwām collectum, Ll. Th. ii. 358, 19. Mid þysum collectum cum his collectis, Angl. xiii. 381, 223.

collen-ferhtan. In passage read gecollenferhtaþ for gē collenferhtaþ.

collon-crōh, -crōg. l. -croh, -crog, for Cot. 140 substitute Wrt. Voc. ii. 62, 41, and add :—Colloncroh achillea, Wrt. Voc. i. 67, 35 : nimphea, Lch. iii. 304, col. 1. v. croh.

cōl-māse. l. col-māse, and add :—Colmāse bardioriolus, Wrt. Voc. ii. 12, 61 : parrula, Hpt. 31, 241, 46. [M. H. Ger. kole-meise.]

cōl-pyt. l. col-pyt a place where charcoal is made [v. N. E. D. coal-pit], and add :—Forð bæ hæselholtæ on collpytt; of collpyttæ, C. D. iv. 27, 13. On þone ealdan collpytt þǣr.þā þreó gemǣru tōgædere gāþ, Cht. E. 206, 23.

col-sweart; adj. Coal-black :—Hwīlum hē bið collsweart, Nap. 13.

colt. Add :—x. mǣran mid .x. coltan....vi. mǣran mid .vi. coltan, Shrn. 159, 17, 29.

cōl-þrǣd. l. col-þrǣd, and add :—Colðrēd perpendiculum, Txts. 85, 1548. Colþrǣd, Wrt. Voc. ii. 68, 2.

coltræppe. v. calca-træppe.

columne (-a?), an; f. (m.?) A column :— Gyldene columnan columnae aureae, Nar. 4, 21. Greáte swā columnan, 14, 4. Ðæt godweb ymb mīnes fæder Dauides columban hangode on ðissum temple, Sal. K. p. 152, 25.

comb. Dele.

comēta. Add :—Hēr atīwede comēta, Chr. 1066 ; P. 196, 2. Hēr atēwoden twēgen comētan, 729 ; P. 45, 1.

consul. Add :—Hiene mon tō consule dyde, Ors. 5, 14 ; S. 248, 8. Agustus þone consul ... wearþ ǣlc ofslagen būton þǣm consule ānum, 5, 15 ; S. 250, 9-11. On þāra twēgea consula dæge, 3, 6 ; S. 108, 22 : p. 4, 10. Consula bēc fastorum libri, Wrt. Voc. ii. 39, 40.

cop a top. v. copp.

cōp a garment. Add :—Cōp ependiten, Txts. 59, 757, 760 : Wrt. Voc. ii. 29, 43.

-cōp ( = ceáp). v. land-cōp : -eōp fitting. v. ge-cōp.

copel ; adj. Unsteady, rocking (?) :—Ǣrest on copelan stān ... eft on copelan stān, C. D. B. iii. 624, 17, 22. [v. N. E. D. coppling, copple-stone.]

cope-man. Dele : copenere. Add : [v. N. E. D. copener a paramour ; copen to desire eagerly.]. copest. Dele.

copian. For Cot. 53 substitute Wrt. Voc. ii. 22, 32, and add : [v. (?) N. E. D. cop to lay hold of.]

cop-lic, -līce. v. ge-cōplic, -līce.

copor. Add :—Coper cyprum, Wrt. Voc. ii. 137, 71. Cøpor colos, i. color conciliatus, 134, 33.

copp a top, summit :—Coppe helmes cono (.i. summitate, Hpt. Gl. 443, 22) (sublimi) uerticis, An. Ox. 1563. Coppe cono, 32, 6 [v. N. E. D. cop.] v. hreác-copp.

copp a cup. Add :—Hē gefylde copp (spongiam) mið ǣcced, Mk. L. R. 15, 36. Bolla full ł copp full, Jn. L. 19, 29. [v. N. E. D. cop. O. H. Ger. choph crater, cyphus : Icel. koppr.]

copped. Add : [v. N. E. D. copped.] : cops. v. cosp : -cor. v. ge-cor: -cora. v. wiþer-cora: -coren. v. wiþ-, wiþer-coren.

coren-beág, es ; m. A crown :—Be þǣm þyrnenan corenbēge ofer Crīstes hǣfde on rōde, Angl. xi. 172, 32.

coren-scipe, es ; m. Election :—Corenscip electio, Mt. p. 12, 13. v. ge-corenscipe.

corflian. Add :—Swylce hē hine corflige swā swā mon ǣl dēð þonne hine mon on spite stagan wyle, Tech. ii. 124, 10.

Cor[r]inthisc ; adj. Corinthian :—Corrinthisce fatu Corinthia vasa, Ors. 5, 2 ; S. 216, 4.

corion. Dele.

corn. Add : I. a grain :—Þǣre lenticula, þ syndon pysan, heó on hire mūð sende þreóra corna gewyrde, Hml. S. 236, 716. Hwā gemenigfylt þæt gerip of feáwum cornum, Hml. Th. i. 184, 32. II. corn :—Beren gebered corn tipsana, Wrt. Voc. i. 20, 27. Heó sealde þǣm munucum corn genōg, Ors. 6, 4 ; S. 260, 11. v. bere-, lyb-, mold-, pipor-corn.

corn-æsceda. l. -æsceáda : corn-appla. Add : An. Ox. 3840 : corn-bǣre. Add :—Cornbǣrum granigeris, An. Ox. 2360.

corn-berende ; adj. Corn-bearing :—þā cornberendan granigera, Wrt. Voc. iii. 40, 22.

corn-gebrot, es ; n. Remnant of corn, corn dropped in carrying :—Berebryttan gebyred corngebrot on · hærfeste æt bernes dure, Ll. Th. i. 440, 2.

corn-gesceót. l. -gesceot : corn-hwæᵹca. Dele.

corn-lād, e ; f. Leading or carrying corn :—Æt cornlāde, Ll. Th. i. 440, 28.

cornoch. v. cranoc.

corn-sǣd, es ; n. A grain of corn :—Hē gemænigfealdað feáwa cornsǣda in unārīmede wæstmas æcra pauca seminis grana in innumera segetum frumenta multiplicat, Gr. D. 253, 1.

corn-teóþung, e ; f. Tithe of corn :—Sȳ cornteóðung āgifen be emnihte, Wlfst. 208, 5 : 116, 25.

corn-treów. Add :—Corntreówes corni, Wrt. Voc. ii. 20, 51 : 138, 5.

corn-weal. Dele.

corn-wurma. Substitute : A scarlet dye, and add :—Cornuurma ve[r]miculus, Wrt. Voc. ii. 123, 45. Cornuurma coccus, An. Ox. 1064, note. Cor[n]wurman murice, 1064. Be cornwurman de muricibus, 1067. Cornwurmum, 5141.

corōna, an ; m. A crown :—Hī geworhton þyrnene corōnan ... hæfde hē þā þyrnenne corōnan on his heáfde ... þone corōnan þǣra twelf steorrena, Nap. 13.

-corōnian. v. ge-corōnian : cors, corsian. Dele : cor-snǣd. Add : [cf. O. Frs. kor-bita.]

corte, an ; f. ? :—Andlanges ðǣr eá tō ðǣre wīc ; fram ðǣre wīc tō ðǣre cortan ; and swā andlanges tō Sūðsexan, C. D. vi. 217, 7.

corþer a whisk (?) :—Corthr verberatorum (cortr, cordr verberatorium), Txts. 105, 2099.

cor-wurma. v. corn-wurma.

cos. Add :—Gangge ǣlc æfter ōðrum tō cosse fratres accedant ad pacem, R. Ben. 114, 4. Syle mē sibbe coss, Hml. Th. ii. 422, 34. Cossas bassia, Wrt. Voc. ii. 94, 47 : 12, 37 : labra, An. Ox. 3180. Hē þā mǣdena onscunode, and forbeáh heora cossas, Hml. S. 35, 59.

cosp. Dele 'Lat. compes,' and add :—Puncto, foramine, in quo pedes vinctorum tenentur in ligno cubitali, spatio interjecto, id est cosp, Txts. 86, 765. Copses cippi, An. Ox. 3251. Copse cibbo, Wrt. Voc. ii. 82, 3 : 18, 32. Copsas (conpedes) synd on fōtum dysiges, Scint. 96, 16. Cospa cipporum, Wrt. Voc. ii. 93, 6 : 19, 46 : An. Ox. 17, 26. Būtan mīn līchama beó on þīnum bendum genyrwod and on þīnum copsum āgrāpod, Hml. S. 8, 121. [v. N. E. D. cops.]

cossettung, e ; f. Kissing :—Ðiós ne blann cossetunges haec non cessauit osculari, Lk. L. 7, 45.

cost costmary. Add :—Cost costa, An. Ox. 56, 392. [From Latin.]

cost, es ; m. Condition, mode :—Getīðode hē ðæs ... ðæs costes ðe (on condition that) heó ðis gelǣste, Cht. Th. 540, 34. Ǣnigum coste ullo modo, Rtl. 113, 34. Unāsæccendlicum costum ineffabilibus modis, 108, 27. Þǣr þegen āge twēgen costas, lufe oþþe lage, and hē lufe geceóse where a thane has two ways of settlement open to him, by amicable agreement or by appeal to law, and he choose the former, Ll. Th. i. 298, 5. [From Scandinavian, Icel. kostr. Goth. kustus trial. v. N. E. D. cost.]

costere. Add :—þā ðā hē āna wæs, þā com him tō se costere, Hml. Th. ii. 156, 22 : Gr. D. 100, 18. [O. H. Ger. chostāri tentator.]

costian. Add :—Hī costodon ł costnodon mē temptauerunt me, Ps. L. 34, 16. Ðāra ācorenra mōd hē wile costian, Past. 465, 11. Costtad conprobatur, An. Ox. 12, 7.

costigend. Add :—þone costigend on helle grund besencean, Bl. H. 33, 19.

costnere. Add :—þā geneálǣhte se costnere, Hml. Th. i. 166, 12. Sē befealt on ðæs costneres grinu, Hex. 52, 25. Hī gewyldað þā feóndlican costneras, Hml. Th. i. 344, 31.

costnian. Add :—Hit is āwriten þæt God āfandode Abrahames, and se apostol Jacob āwrīt þæt God ne costnað nænne man ; hū mæg beón ægþer sōð? ... God ne costnað nænne man, for þan þe hē nele nænne tō synnum gebīgan, Scrd. 22, 46-23, 10 : Hml. Th. ii. 560, 20. Ne lǣt ðū ūs costnian, ac ālȳs ūs fram yfele, Wlfst. 125, 13. v. ā-costnian.

costnung. Add :—'Ne geðafa þæt wē beón gelǣdde on costnunge.' Ōðer is costnung, ōðer is fandung.... Þurh ðā fandunge hē sceal geðeón, gif hē þām costnungum wiðstent, Hml. Th. i. 268, 6-19. Ōþer is seó fandung þe Jacob embe spræc, þæt is seó costnung þe gewemð þone man tō syngienne, Scrd. 23, 8.

costnung-stōw, e ; f. A place of temptation :—On þǣre costnungstōwe in loco tentationis, Deut. 6, 16.

cot. Add :—Ūt tō ðan coten, C. D. vi. 9, 5. Æt Sceolles ealdcotan, iv. 122, 21. v. būr-cot, and next word.

cote. Add :—Ne mæg nān wīf hire bōndan forbeódan þ hē ne mōte intō his cotan (-on, v. l.) gelōgian þ þ hē wille, Ll. Th. i. 418, 24. [Perhaps in the two instances given under cote the form cotan (-on, v. l.) is dat. pl., and the passages should be put under cot (q.v.). But see N. E. D. cote.]

coþa, an ; m. v. coþu.

coþig ; adj. Diseased :—Hit is neód þ hī man āscirie of þǣre gefērrǣdene eallswā coðige sceáp (oues morbidæ), Nap. 13.

cōþu. l. coþu, and add :—Hreóflige hē geclǣnsode fram ðǣre

inclǽnan coðe, Hml. S. 15, 6. Fram earmlicere coðe, Hml. Th. ii. 150, 3. Coða becumað *erunt pestilentiae*, 538, 29. Wurdon gehǽlede nettrume menn fram mislicum coþum, Hml. S. 26, 193: 27, 131. Ælcne man warnian wið þás deófollican coðe, þæt is wið þás hellican unþeáwas, Wlfst. 245, 21: Angl. viii. 337, 7. [v. *N. E. D.* cothe.] v. milt-coþu.

cot-líf. *Add:* I. *used of a single habitation :*—Ælcne man lyst, siððan hē ǽnig cotlýf on his hláfordes lǽne myd his fultume getimbred hǽfð, þ hē hine mōte þáron gerestan, and huntigan and fuglian and fiscian, Shrn. 164, 3. [Cf. Wo is him þat uvel wif bryngeþ to his cotlyf (cf. wif hom bryngeþ, 265), Misc. 118, 259.] II. *in the charters of Edward the Confessor the word seems used in the sense of manor ; the places to which it is applied are in the possession of individuals, and have landed property belonging to them ; they are in almost every case the subjects of grant to the church.* Thus the brethren of Westminster have ' ðat cotlif Aðguðe and ale ðare þnge ðe ðǽrtō nid richte gebirað, mid circe and mid milne, mid wode and mid felde, mid láse and mid máde, and on allen þngen swá ful and swá forð swá Ælfwine and his wíf it firmest ǽhten and intō ðare hálagen stōwe gáfan,' C. D. iv. 217, 7–13. Other instances are ' ðat cotlif Leosne ðe Atsere ǽhte and bequeð . . . tō ðera monece fōden ' with all belonging to it (cf. 178), 191, 13, and ' ðat cotlif Moleshám ðe Leófcild ǽhte and bequað,' 214, 6. In like manner the king grants ' ðat cotlif ðe ic was boren inne bi naman Giðslēpe,' 215, 31 : ' ðá cotlífe Perscore (cf. loco celebri . . . qui Persoran nuncupatur uocabulo, iii. 74 . . . in Perscoran . . . mansi, 75) and D(e)órhyrste (cf. nomina terrarum quas dabo ad locum qui dicitur Deórhyrst, i. 227) mid allen ðan landen, &c.,' 192, 6 : ' ðat cotlif Stáne (cf. cum coenobio quod Stána uocatur, ii. 367),' 211, 25 : ' ðat cotlif Euerslea,' 204, 19. In the last case it is said ' ic bebeóde ðat Paðu mí meodes wrichte and UUlnōð mín húscarl and Ælfríce Hort and Frēbern mín freósōcne men ðe ðat cotlýf healdeð heonneford . . . bēn on sainte Petres wealde and ðám hirde on ðám minstre hērsumian and þewwan.'

cot-sǽta. *Dele, but see N. E. D.* cotset : cot-setla. *See* Andrews' Old English Manor, *s. v.*

cot-stōw. *Add :*—Of ðam mere on Cúðulfes cotstōwe ; of ðam cotstōwum, C. D. v. 389, 17.

cottuc. *Add :*—Cottuc (cotuc, Ep.) *malva*, Txts. 77, 1288 : Wrt. Voc. ii. 56, 36.

-cow. v. ge-cow.

crá *the croaking sound made by frogs or crows :*—Coax i. crá, vox ranarum vel corvorum, Wülck. Gl. 208, 10.

crabba. *Add :*—Crabba *nepa*, Wrt. Voc. ii. 61, 48 : *cancer*, 128, 7.

cracettan. *Substitute :* crǽcettan, crǽccettan *to croak :*—Se hrefn mid openum mūðe ongann crǽkettan (crǽccettan, *v. l.*) ymbútan þone hláf *corvus aperto ore circa panem coepit crocitare*, Gr. D. 118, 25. v. crǽcetung.

cracian. *Substitute : To crack, sound, resound :*—Cracaþ, brastlaþ *crepat*, i. sonat, Wrt. Voc. ii. 136, 64. Craciendum, cearciendum *crepante*, i. sonante, An. Ox. 31. ¶ *In Ps.* 45, 3 *for* cracode *apparently should be read* cwacode (v. Angl. vi. 133), *but the former seems better to give the meaning of* the sonaverunt *in the Latin, and to agree with the preceding clause of the English :*—Ús ðuhte for þám geþune þæt seó eorþe sil cracode (?).

cradel. *Add :*—Hē lǽg on cradole (-ule, *v. l.*) bewunden ealswá ōðre cild dōð, Wlfst. 17, 1. Cradelas *cunabula*, Wrt. Voc. ii. 137, 27.

cradol-cild. *Add :* Wlfst. 158, 14 : crǽ. v. cráwe: crǽcetung.
v. crǽcetung, *and see* crǽcettan : crǽfian. v. crafian : crǽfing.
crafing.

cræft. *Dele* 'IV. *a craft, kind of ship*; navis qualiscunque,' *and add under I :*—Mid eallum Crēca cræftum *universam Graeciae lectam inventutem*, Ors. I, 10 ; S. 46, 31. *Under II :*—Hē leornode sumne cræft þe hine ásēt, Hml. Th. ii. 556, 32. *Under III :*—Hié wēnað þæt hiera unðeáwas sién sum gōd cræft *vitium virtus creditur*, Past. 289, 13. Hearpestrengas mid cræfte ástírian, Ap. Th. 17, 8. Cræftas *studia*, An. Ox. 9, 8. Lárlíce cræftas *scholares disciplinas*, 42. III a. *in a bad sense, a cunning trick, stratagem, artifice :*—Mid þám cræfte þe þá scondlicost wæs . . . þysne nyttan cræft, þēh hē árlic nǽre, funde heora tictator, Ors. 2, 8 ; S. 90, 28–92, 3. Wíf gif heó mid hwylcum cræfte (*molimine*) hire hǽmed gerēnað, Ll. Th. ii. 156, 7. Gif hē þurh druncen oððe þurh ōðerne cræft (*alio artificio*) man ofsleá, 150, 34. IV. *a machine, instrument, engine :*—Æþele cræft (*of a medicine*), Lch. ii. 28, 10. Hē hæfde án wurðlic weorc on mechanisc geweorc . . . Se cræft sceolde wissian se steorrum hwæt gehwilcum menn gelumpe, . . . on þám cræfte áspende mín fæder má þonne twá hund punda . . . Gif þú þisne cræft healst . . . Hē nolde geþafian þ man swá deórwurðne cræft (cf. weorc, 287) tōcwýsan sceolde, Hml. S. 5, 253, 263, 266, 290. Tōbærst seó hengen mid eallum ðam cræfte, 35, 314. Þǽne mǽnifealdan cræft *multiformem* (*favorum*) *machinam*, An. Ox. 120. Cræftas *machinas*, 1668. v. circul-, gedwol-, gramati(s)c-, meter-, morþ-, swēg-, tæl-, tōw-, wicg-, wynde-cræft.

cræfte-líce ; *adv. With art, skilfully :*—Hē his láre suá cræftelíce (*tanta arte*) tōsceád, Past. 291, 20. Hē sceal gemetgian swá cræftelíce (*tanta arte*) his stemne, 453, 12.

cræftig. *Add :* I. *powerful :*—Iulius se cræftega cásere *Caesar totis viribus*, Ors. 1, 10 ; S. 48, 16. Hiera cynn wæs ealra cræftegast *gloriosissima illa viribus familia*, 2, 4 ; S. 72, 10. II. *knowing a craft, art, trade :*—Gif cræftige men (*artifices*) on mynstre sýn, begán þane cræft and georne wyrcen, R. Ben. 95, 3. III. *skilful, cunning :*—Man on ǽnigum þingum cræftig oþþe on máran wísdōme oþþe on lǽssan, Bl. H. 49, 28. Hē wæs cræftig lǽce, Shrn. 138, 27. Wæs sum mǽden wundorlíce cræftig . . . on ūðwītegunge snoter, Hml. S. 35, 80. Cræftig[estan] *sollertissimae*, An. Ox. 56, 208. III a. *of books, dealing with art or science :*—Munecas þe heora cildhád habbað ábisgod on cræftigum bócum, Angl. viii. 321, 27. v. drý-cræftig.

cræftig, es ; *n. Strength :*—Drihten is mægen and cræftig ælces þǽra þe hine ondrǽt *firmamentum est Dominus timentibus eum*, Ps. Th. 24, 12.

cræftiga. *Add :* I. *a craftsman, &c. :*—Crǽfican (crǽftcan ?) *artifices*, R. Ben. I. 94, 10. Ðæt wǽron .iiii. stáncræftigan in Rōme, þǽr wæs samod .vi. hund cræftigena and xxii, and nǽron náne ōðre him gelíce, Shrn. 146, 14. Be mynstres cræftigum (*artificibus*), R. Ben. 95, 2. Hē gegaderode manige cræftigan, and eác má ōþra weorcmanna þe þám hýrdon *artifices multos ac plures subministrantes operarios adhibuit*, Gr. D. 251, 13. v. rím-, scín-, stán-, tungol-cræftiga.

cræftig-líce. *Substitute :* Skilfully, cunningly, ingeniously :*—Smiþlíce *fabrile*, cræftig[líce] *fabre*, i. perfecte, ingeniose, arteficiose, Wrt. Voc. ii. 146, 61. Smiþlíce *fabrile*, cræftiglíce *fabre* (MS. -i), 35, 15. v. sundor-, wundor-cræftiglíce.

cræft-leás. *Add :*—Cræftleásne þeówdōm ætiwað munecas *iners servitium ostendunt monachi*, R. Ben. I. 52, 1.

cræft-lic. *Substitute :* I. artificial :*—On twám wísum ys se dæg gecweden, naturaliter and vulgariter . . . Vulgaris vel artificales dies est, þ byþ ceorlisc dæg oððe cræftlic, fram þǽre sunnan anginne þ heó tō setle gá and eft cume mancynne tō blisse, Angl. viii. 317, 11. II. skilful, skilled :*—Ðá ōðre cræftigan sægdon þ hý þurh drýcræft dydon ða cræftlican weorc, Shrn. 146, 22.

cræft-searo. *Dele.*

cræft-wyrc. *Substitute :* cræft-weorc, es ; *n. Skilled work, art, profession :*—Be campdōme, be ceápe, be cræftwyrce ágyf teóþunga *de militia, de negotio, de artificio redde decimas*, Scint. 109, 5.

crǣt. *Add :* pl. gen. crætena, cratwa :*—Cræt *carcura* (=*carruca*), Wrt. Voc. ii. 102, 62. Cræt *carruca*, 13, 20. Ðá stód þǽre sunnan cræt mid feówer horsum of golde ágoten . . . ; on ōðre healfe stód ðæs mōnan cræt of seolfre ágoten and ðá oxan ðǽrto, Hml. Th. ii. 494, 22. Se þegen álýhte of his cræte (*de curru suo*), i. 400, 26. On cræte *in carruca*, Wrt. Voc. ii. 47, 42 : *esseda, uehiculo*, Germ. 393, 56. Hēlias weard on heofenlicum cræte tō heofenum áhafen, Hml. S. 16, 61. Cræta *bigarum*, An. Ox. 2185. Cratwa, Wrt. Voc. ii. 78, 76. Crætena cearcetunge, Wlfst. 200, 17. Cratum *bigis*, Wrt. Voc. ii. 89, 70 : 12, 5. Crætum *quadrigis*, 149, 14 : *curricis*, 28, 17 : *carpentis*, i. *curribus*, Wülck. Gl. 254, 12. Creatum *curribus*, Ps. Srt. 19, 8. v. hors-cræt.

cræt-wisa, an ; *m. A charioteer :*—Israheles cræt and his wissigend, þ is cr ætwísa *currus Israhel et auriga ejus*, Hml. S. 18, 293.

crafian, crǣfian. *Add :*—Hēr kýþ on þissere bēc þ Huberd cræfede ánne wífman þe Édit hátte mid unrihte . . . and Huberd wæs leósende þǽre wífmanne for his unrihtcrǽfinge, Cht. Th. 633, 17. Ðæt nán bisceop náne feorme ne crafige, bútan of ðám ðe him mid rihte gebyrað, C. D. iv. 290, 32. v. for-crafian.

crafing, e ; *f. Demand, claim :*—Saccles of ælcre crauigge, Cht. Th. 645, 5. Crauigge, 24. v. unriht-crafing.

crammian. *Add :*—Ic crammige *farcior*, Hpt. Gl. 489, 5. v. á-, ge-crammian ; crimman.

cramming-pohha, an ; *m.* The word translates *viscarium* in the following passage :—Gif wíf wunað mid werum, þǽr bið wēn deófles crammingpohha (*viscarium diaboli non deerit*), Nap. 13.

crampiht ; *adj. Crumpled, wrinkled :*—Crompeht *folialis*, Wrt. Voc. ii. 38, 58.

cran. *Dele.* 'e ; *f.,*' *and add : The word occurs in local names, e. g.* Cransleá, Craumere. v. cranoc.

cranc-stæf. *Substitute : A crank :*—Crancstæf (*in a list of weaving implements*), Angl. ix. 263, 14. Cf. crencestre.

cranic, es ; *m. A chronicle :*—Swá swá Hieronimus sǽde on his cranice, Hml. A. 79, 164. Man gesette on cranice (*mandatum est historiis et annalibus traditum*) ælc þǽra dǽda þe gedōn wæs mid him on þæs cyninges belimpum, 95, 122. Hē hēt forðberan þone cranic (*historias et annales*) and rǽdan ætforan nolde, 98, 210.

cranic-writere, es ; *m. A chronographer, chronicler :*—Cranicwrítera *chronographorum*, An. Ox. 7, 24.

cranoc, es ; *m. A crane :*—Cornoch *grus, gruis, cornuc gravis*, Wrt. Voc. ii. 110, 10, 11. Cf. *the local name* Cornuchom, C. D. vi. 275, col. 2. v. cran.

**crano-hawc.** *Dele, and see* Whitman, p. 45. Cf. *O. H. Ger.* 'accipiter, quem* chranohāri *dicunt*,' Grff. iv. 614.

**crās; m.** *Food* :—Swā picce hié in þǣre eá āweóllon swā ǣmettan đǣm crās, and swilc unrím heora wæs *major explicatus numerus beluarum quam prius affuit ad spem inde contingentis cibi, ubi cum apparerent veluti formice efferbuere*, Nar. 11, 14. [*Icel.* krās *a dainty.*]

**crat-hyrdel** (?) :—*Plecta* bige crathyrdle (*in marg.* hyrdle ł bige *plecta*), Hpt. Gl. 497, 70.

**crāwan.** *Add* :—Onlícnesse đǣm kokkum đe on đīstrum niehtum crāwađ, Past. 459, 32. Þonne coccas crāwan forman sýđe, þonne drince hē ǣne, Lch. iii. 6, 5. v. ge-crāwan.

**crāwe.** *Add* : crāwa; *m.* :—Crāuuae (-e) *cornacula*, Txts. 50, 241. Crāuua, crāwe *cornix*, 54, 308. Crē *curnicula*, 110, 1171. Crāuue *garula*, Wrt. Voc. ii. 109, 52 : 40, 58 : *carula*, 103, 17 : 13, 49.

**crāw-leác.** *Add* :—Crāwanleác *poloten*, Wrt. Voc. i. 69, 11 : *hermodoctula vel tidolora*, 79, 57.

**Creácisc.** v. Crēcisc.

**creás; *adj. Fine, elegant* :—Ne beó gē tó creásum reáfum (*cultis vestibus*) gefrætwade, ac medemlicum, Nap. 13.

**creás-lic; *adj. Dainty, rich* (of food) :—Sume þá preóstas þe woroldwelan habbađ . . . scolon māran and creáslicran fódan (*maiorem annonam*) habban on mynstre, Nap. 13.

**creás-ness, e; *f.* *I. fineness, elegance* (of dress) :—Wē mid heortan creásnysse (*cultu cordis*) sceolon God sēcan swiđor þonne mid reáfes prýton . . . reáfes creásnysse (*cultum uestium*) . . . an reáfes creásnysse (*studio uestium*), Nap. 14. *II. elation, pride* :—*Elationis* orgelnysse ł creásnysse, Hpt. Gl. 432, 54.

**Crēcas** (-e). *Add* :—Crēcas *Graeci*, Rtl. 194, 17. Criécna *Graecorum*, Mt. p. 2, 15. Mid Crēcum *apud Grecos*, 11.

**Crēcisc.** *Add* :—Crēcisc noma *Graecum nomen*, Rtl. 194, 21. On Crēcisc, Ors. 1, 10; S. 46, 14 : Jn. R. 19, 20. On Crēgisc *Graece*, Jn. L. 19, 20. In Crēgesc, 20, 24. Stafum Crēciscum *litteris Graecis*, Lk. L. R. 23, 38. Þā Creáciscan *Argolicas*, Wrt. Voc. ii. 95, 39 : *Pelasgos*, 41.

**crēda.** *Add* :—Se lǣssa crēda. Ic gelýfe on God, Fæder ælmihtigne . . . on flǣsces ǣrist and þæt ēce líf, Angl. x. 100, 7. Se mǣssepreóst sceal secgan Sunnandagum . . . be þām Paternoster and be þām crēdan eác, swā hē oftost mage, Ll. Th. ii. 350, 30. Gif hē song his crēdon odđe Paternoster on untrumue mon, hē wæs sóna hál, Shrn. 116, 20.

**credic** (?) *a bowl* :—Credic *fiala* (v. Bd. 3, 27 : Lac iu *fiala* ponere solebat), An. Ox. 29, 3.

**crencestre.** *Add* : Cf. cranc-stæf : **creódan.** *l.* crūdan.

**creópan.** *Add* : *I. of reptiles* :—Eall đæt on sǣ and on eáuum crýpđ, Hex. 14, 8. Nǣddran crupon on þ hūs, Shrn. 152, 28. Wurmas crupon cuce of his líce, Hml. S. 4, 430. *II. of human beings.* (1) *literal* :—Heó creáp on þām handum, and dróh on đǣre eorđan ealne hire líchaman, Gr. D. 228, 10. (2) *to walk* with crutches :—Hē árás and mid twām criccum creáp him tó Wynceastre, Hml. S. 21, 101. (3) *of humble, abject movement* :—Þá iermingas ūt of þām holan crupon þe heó on lutedan, Ors. 2, 8; S. 92, 30. Uton creópan tó Críste, Wlfst. 166, 38. v. ge-creópan.

**creopel.** v. crypel.

**creópere.** *Add* :—Se cnapa wæs creópere (cf. þām healtan cnapan, 28.), Hml. S. 6, 20. Læg þǣr sum creópere lama fram cildhāde, 10, 25.

**creópung.** *For* Cot. 144 *substitute* : — Criópungae, cr[i]úpungae, cr[i]úpunge *obreptione*, Txts. 80, 696. Creópunge, Wrt. Voc. ii. 63, 16.

**crepel.** v. crypel : **crib**[b]. v. cryb (*in Dict.*) : **cricc.** v. crycc.

**crīgan; *p.* crīde *To bubble up* :—Criid *scaturit*, Wrt. Voc. ii. 120, 3. Crīđ *ebulliat*, An. Ox. 7, 101 (where see note). Crīþe *scaturiat*, 8, 104. Crīđ (*after which a letter is erased*), Angl. xiii. 31, 93.

**crimman.** *Substitute* : *To cram, stuff, insert* :—Hornes sceafoþan swiđe smale gesceaf, crim on þ dolh innan, Lch. ii. 132, 12. Cram *inseruit, immisit*, Germ. 401, 22. v. ge-crimman ; crammian.

**crinc** *a kind of shoe* (?) :—Crince *cuturno*, Hpt. 33, 250, 2. Cf. (?) crencestre.

**crisma.** *I. Add after* 'baptism': *and at other times* :—Đonne se sácerd smyređ mid þām hālgan crisman breóst and sculdru, þonne befēhđ hē þæne man mid Godes scylde, Wlfst. 35, 16. Āsprungenra manna líc (*cadavera*) man byređ on ciricean and mid crysman smyređ his breóst, Ll. Th. ii. 162, 1. Ne crismena *nec balsamorum* (*sacris chrismatibus unctum*, Ald. 154), Wrt. Voc. ii. 91, 34 : 61, 1. *I a. the sacred character conferred by unction* :—Se biscop forlēt his crisman and his róde and his gástlican wǣpnu, and fēng tó his spere and tó his swurde, Chr. 1056 ; P. 187, 24. *II. Add* :—Under crisman ádle forgripen *in albis adhuc positus, langore correptus*, Bd. 5, 7 ; Sch. 584, 2. Under crismum *in albis*, An. Ox. 6, 48. Crysmum, 2127.

**crismal**(e ?), es; *m. or n. A chrisom-cloth* :—Mid þām crismale þe man him on utan þæt heáfod dēđ, man tácnađ þæne cristenan cynehelm þe hē on heofenum áh, Wlfst. 36, 17. [*Lat.* crismale.]

**Crist.** *l.* Crīst, *and add* :—Crīsđ, Past. 27, 5. Krīsđ, 103, 11. Manega lcáse Crīstas cumađ, Hml. Th. i. 4, 2.            ¶ Crīstes mǣl,

*mæsse* :—Opiéwde reád Crīstes mǣl (*a cross*), Chr. 773 ; P. 50, 20. Tóforan Xþes mæssan, 1038 ; P. 161, 14 : 1043; P. 165, 9 : 1076; P. 212, 20.

**cristalla.** *Add* :—Anlícnyssa of cristallan, Hml. S. 4, 166.

**cristallisc; *adj. Of crystal* :—Cristallisce dryncfatu, Nar. 5, 13.

**cristel-mǣl (cýrstel-), es; *n.* *I. a cross* :—On wearddūne þǣr þæt crīstelmǣl stód, Cht. E. 294, 21. Tó þām cýrstelmǣle ; of þām cýrstelmǣle, Cht. Crw. 25, 24. Tó đām langan cýrstelmǣle, C. D. v. 297, 15 : 298, 9. *II. the sign of the cross* :—Wyrce mon crýstelmǣl on his heáfde foran mid his þūman, Tech. ii. 119, 8.

**cristelmǣl-beám, es; *m. A tree on which a cross is fixed* (?) :—On crīstelmǣlbeám (*in a list of boundaries*), C. D. v. 389, 13.

**cristen.** *Add* :—Heó wæs crīstenu, Shrn. 86, 15. Ūre crīstne Rōma, Ors. 24; S. 74, 34. Hē bæd hine crīstene beón . . . bæd þ hē đurh his bebod crīstene gefremed wǣre, Bd. 1, 4; Sch. 16, 3, 16. Cristenum þēnungum þeówian, 1, 7; Sch. 22, 6. Se crīstenesta (crīstena, *v. l.*) cyning, Ors. 6, 38; S. 296, 30. v. efen-, un-crīsten.

**cristen-dōm.** *Add* : *I. the state or condition of being Christian* :—Fram fremþe þīnes crīstendómes, Angl. xii. 515, 21. Deáh þrǣla hwylc of crīstendóme tó wícinge weorđe *though any thrall from being a Christian become a pirate*, Wlist. 162, 6. For heora crīstendóme *because they were Christians*, Ors. 2, 1 ; S. 62, 28 : 2, 4; S. 76, 1. Sē is geūtlagod for his crīstendóme, Hml. S. 34, 132. Heora crīstendóm gehealdan, Ll. Th. ii. 350, 32.            *II. time when or place where Christianity prevails* :—Þā þe secgađ þæt þeós world sý nū wyrse on đysan crīstendóme þonne hió ǣr on þǣm hǣþenscype wǣre . . . Hwǣr is nū on ǣnigan crīstendóme betuh him sylfum þ mon him þurfe swilc ondrǣdan ?, Ors. 1, 8 ; S. 40, 24-8. Nū is đes dæg gehālgod on ealium crīstendóme, Hml. A. 25, 30. *III. the Christian faith* :—Hwelc mildsuug siþþan wæs, siþþan se crīstendóm wæs, Ors. 2, 1 ; S. 62, 34. Āwācyge se crīstendóm, sóna scylfđ se cynedóm, Wlfst. 267, 23. Þæt sixte muneca cyn āsprang on anginne crīstendómes, R. Ben. 136, 7. Hē gesette ān þūsend bóca . . . be đām crīstendóme, Hml. A. 5, 107. On þām crīstendóme þe Crīst sylf āstealde, 16, 74. Healdan rihtne crīstendóm, Wlfst. 78, 9. Se apostol bodade ealne crīstendóm, Hml. Th. i. 460, 8.

**cristen-lic; *adj. Christian* :—Folc crīstinlic *plebs Christiana*, Rtl. 91, 39.

**cristen-mann, es; *m. A Christian* :—Hē gerǣsde on þā fǣmnan ir crīstenmonna (crīstenra monna, *v. l.*) midle, Mart. H. 170, 25.

**cristen-ness, e; *f. Christianity* :—Þ hē ūs āhebbe on þā sóþan crīstennesse, Nap. 14. v. crīst-ness.

**cristian.** v. crīstnian.

**cristnere, es; *m. A catechist* :—Seó tíd sancte Petres þæs crīstneres, Shrn. 89, 6. v. crīstnian.

**crist-ness (cristen-?), e; *f. Christianity* :—Ic eów hālsige . . . foı đǣre crīstnesse đe gē underfēngan, Rtl. 114, 16.

**cristnian.** *Add* : *I. to instruct in the Christian religion previous tc* (*adult*) *baptism, to catechize* :—Þā crīstnade hē mē (*me cathecizare ipsi curavit*) . . . and æfter medmiclum fæce . . . ic gefullad wæs, Bd. 5, 6 Sch. 581, 1-19. Hē gelýfde on ūrne Drihten and lēt hine crīstniaı (*had himself catechized*), and æfter lytlum fyrste hē wearđ gefullod, Hml S. 31, 523. Hē nǣfre þ þēnunge tó crīstnienne (crīstigenne, crīstienne *v. ll.*) odđe tó fullianne geleornian mihte *nullatenus potuit cathecizandı uel baptizandi ministerium discere*, Bd. 5, 6; Sch. 580, 19.            *II. to perform the ritual that precedes baptism* :—On đǣre crīstnunge þe maı dēđ ǣr đām fulluhte is mycel getācnung. Þonne se sácerd crīstnađ þonne orđaþ hē on þone man . . . and mid þæs sácerdes hālsunge se deófol wyrđ āflýmed fram þǣre menniscan gesceáfte . . . þæt sealt þæt s; sácerd þām men on mūđ dēþ þonne hē crīstnađ, þæt getācnađ godcundne wisdóm . . . and đonne se sácerd him æftoran singđ *credo in deum*, þoun trymeđ hē his geleáfan . . . đonne se sácerd æthrinđ mid his spátle þæ mannes nose and eáran . . . and smyređ mid þām hālgan crisman breós and sculdru . . . And đonne þis gedón biđ eal fullíce wel, swā tó đǣr crīstnunge gebyređ, þonne is æfter eallum þisum mid rihtum geleáfaı tó efstanne wiđ fontbæđes, Wlfst. 33, 16-36, 1. Þonne se preóst crīst nađ, þonne ādrǣfđ hē đone deófol of đām cilde; for đan đe ælc hǣđeı man biđ deófles, ac þurh fulluht hē biđ Godes, Hml. Th. i. 304 33. *IV. to baptize* (?) cf. crīstnung, II :—Þā hǣþenan feóllon tó his cneówum biddende hine þ hē dyde hī crīstene. Hē ne wandode oı þām wīdgillan felda þā hǣþenan tó cristnigenne . . . ac hē hī ealle són; samtinges gecrīstnode, Hml. S. 31, 1036. v. ge-crīstnian.

**cristnung, e; *f.* *I. performing the ritual that precedes baptism* v. crīstnian, II. *II. baptizing* :—Pāpa gesette . . . þ þæs Hālgaı Gástes þēnung wǣre in þǣre gife þæs fulluhtes, nalæs þæs mannes in crist nunge (*in baptizando*), Ll. Th. ii. 140, 17.

**croc, crocc, es; *m. Substitute* :—crocc, e; *f. A pot* :—Man scea habban . . . pannan, crocca, Angl. ix. 264, 10.

**crocca.** *In bracket dele all but Scandinavian forms, and add* crocce (?), an; *f.* : — Crocha, chroca, chroa, croha *citropodes*, Txts 46, 171. Crohha *luteum*, Wrt. Voc. ii. 113, 27. Crocca, 51, 24

olla fictilis, 65, 38 : anfora, i. 25, 9. Swylce þær tôburste sum mycel crocca (olla), Gr. D. 87, 19. Hwer † crocce lebes, Ps. L. 107, 10. v. cryccen, and next word.

croco-hwer (?), es ; m. An earthen pot :—Crocchweras (croccan, hweras? ; cf. citiles . crocc . hweres, Hpt. Gl. 514, 35) cacabos, An. Ox. 4672.

-croced. v. ge-croced : croc-hwær. v. crocc-hwer.

croft. Add :—Ondlong ðæs croftes heáfodlandes . . . ðæt tô bercrofte, C. D. iii. 259, 34. On hwætecroft ; of ðém crofte on grênan hylle, C. D. B. iii. 135, 25. Tô bærlice crofte, C. D. vi. 79, 10. Oubûton ðone croft ðé Wynstân bylde, iii. 367, 6. Croftas praedia, An. Ox. 3790 : Hpt. 31, 11, 233.

crog. Substitute : crôg, es ; m. A pot, vessel : — Croog, crôg lagoena, Txts. 74, 584. Crôg lagena, Wrt. Voc. i. 67, 77 : legythum, i. 83, 69. Crôh lagena, legythum, 50, 47, 48. Crôges oþþe ampellan lenticule, 94, 26 : 52, 62. [v. N. E. D. croh. O. H. Ger. chruog lagena, amphora.] v. wæter-crôg.

crôg-cynn, es ; n. A kind of vessel :—Collatum, i. vas in quo deportatur vinum, vel crôgcyn, Wrt. Voc. ii. 134, 51.

crôh ; gen. crôs (?) ; m. Tendril : — Crôs, crôus pampinus (crôas pampinos?), Txts. 86, 773.

croh. Add : v. collon-, geola-croh : crohh. l. crohha. v. crocca : crompeht. v. crampiht.

crop. Add : I. a sprout, berry, &c. :—Crop caulon, Wrt. Voc. ii. 130, 1. Þ cropp uvam, Lk. L. 6, 44. Bergan vel croppas bacce, Wrt. Voc. ii. 135, 73. Croppas corimbos, 21, 67 : racemos, An. Ox. 2641 : botros, 5, 28. II. a (round) pebble :—Croppas (teretes) glareas, An. Ox. 1812. v. clâte-crop.

crôp (?) bleating, Wrt. Voc. ii. 125, 8. [Cf. (?) N. E. D. croup to cry hoarsely.] v. cnop[p].

crop-leác. Add :—Cropleác serpulum, Wrt. Voc. i. 286, 7. Croplêc cipus, ii. 131, 48.

croppa. Add : v. îsig-croppa.

crûc, es ; m. A cross :—Nime hê his (of petroleum) dæl and wyrce Crîstes mæl on ælcum lime, bûtan crûc on þám heáfde foran sê sceal on balzame beón, Lch. ii. 288, 22. Hine ymbwrît mid sweorde on .iiii. healfa on crûce, 346, 27. [v. N. E. D. crouch. O. Sax. krûci : O. Fri. crioce : O. H. Ger. chrûzi ; n. From Latin.]

cruce. l. crûce, and add :—Crûcae, crûce trulla, Txts. 100, 989. Crûcena urceorum, Wrt. Voc. ii. 73, 35. [v. N. E. D. crouke. O. L. Ger. krûka.] v. fýr-, wæter-crûce.

crûdan. v. creódan in Dict.

cruft. Substitute for examples :—Cruftas (e written over the a : cf. cruftan (es written over the au), Hpt. Gl. 454, 62) crypte, An. Ox. 2046. Cruftan (so Hpt. Gl. 485, 3) (in) crypta, 3350. Crufte, 4907 (so Hpt. Gl. 518, 77). Crufte (scrufte, An. Ox. 4889) (ad) spelaeum, antrum, Hpt. Gl. 518, 47. [O. H. Ger. chruft crypta, spelunca. From Latin.]

crumb, crump. Substitute : Bent, crooked :—Crump obunca, Wrt. Voc. ii. 115, 21 : 63, 21. Þá crumban obunca (of a hook), 87, 70. v. hnifol-crumb ; crymbing.

crundel. For the meaning of crundel v. D.D.: ' Crundel. Sus. Hmp. A ravine ; a strip of covert dividing open country, always in a dip, usually with running water in the middle.' For additional examples v. Cht. E. pp. 471-3. [He (John the Baptist) turnde fro mennes wuninge to wilde deores, and ches þere crundel to halle and eorðhole to bure he chose a ravine for his hall and a cave for his bedchamber, O. E. Hml. ii. 139, 15.] v. cealc-crundel.

crusene. l. crûs(e)ne, and add :—Crûsne vel heden cocula (cf. mastruca, cocula, de pellibus siue de pilibus, Corp. Gl. H. 76, 65 : cappa, capsula, cocula, 27, 108), Wrt. Voc. ii. 135, 39 : 136, 49. [O.H. Ger. chursina, chrusina mastruga. Cf. Ger. kürschner a furrier.]

crycc. Add :—Lituus, baculum augurale in prima parte curvum, id est crycc (cryc), Txts. 72, 571. Cryc baculum, Ps. Srt. 22, 4. Se biscop slôh mid his cricce on ðá eorðan, Shrn. 70, 14. Hê mid twám criccum creáp him tô Wynceastre, Hml. S. 21, 101. Seó ealde cyrce wæs eall behangen mid criccum, 431.

cryccen ; adj. Earthen :—Cryccen fictile, Germ. 398, 162. v. crocca.

crymbing. For Cot. 56 substitute Wrt. Voc. ii. 23, 66. v. crumb.

crymian, crymman. v. ge-crymian, -crymman : crympan. v. gecrympan.

crypel, es ; m. A cripple :—Hê cuoeð ðæm cryple (paralytico), Lk. L. 5, 24. [Heó creopeles wurðon, Hml. A. 177, 240. Sume wæron crypeles, 180, 363.] [O. L. Ger. krupil : Icel. kryppill.] v. eorþ-crypel.

crypel ; adj. Crippled [:—Nán unhál cild, ne crypol, ne dumb, Hml. A. 179, 322.] [v. N. E. D. cripple ; adj.] v. crypel-ness.

crypel, es ; m. I. a narrow passage, burrow, drain :—Crypeles (crepeles cuniculi, i. latrinae, Hpt. Gl. 484, 21) cuniculi, An. Ox. 3320. Crypelas, 2, 191. Crypel (crepel, in margin crypell altered to crypele cuniculum, foveam, domunculam, Hpt. Gl. 473, 34) cuniculum, 2856 :

cuniculum, i. domunculam, 2, 113. Cripel cuniculum ,i. foramen, 5, 33. II. crypelas ; pl. glosses cancelli :—Durh crepelas per cancellos (prospexi ; I looked through my casement, Prov. 7, 6), Kent. Gl. 180. v. creópan.

crypel-ness, e ; f. Crippleness, lameness, paralysis :—From crypelnise gehæled a paralysi curat, Lk. p. 5, 1.

cryppan ; p. te To crook a finger, close the hand, bend :—Crypte plecteret, An. Ox. 52, 2 ; E. S. xi. 64 (where see note). Crip þinne þûman, Tech. ii. 119, 4. Ðonne þê æpples lyste, þonne cryp þû þînne swiþran þûman tô middewearde þînre handa and befôh hine mid þînum fingre and rær up þîne fæste, 124, 15. [Cf. Ger. krüpfen, kröpfen to crook, bend.] v. ge-cryppan.

cû. Add :—Cuu vacca, Wrt. Voc. ii. 123, 16. Ealdre cû meolc, Ll. Th. i. 438, 18. Æt ânes heówe[s] cý, Lch. iii. 24, 13. Hê ðá cealfas tô cûum lædde, Shrn. 61, 19. Betwih cýe inter vaccas, Ps. Srt. 67, 31.

cubit a cubit :—Þîn seáð bið twégea cubita wîd and feówra lang, Nar. 50, 29.

cû-butere. Add : Lch. ii. 124, 2.

cû-bŷre, es ; m. A cow-byre, cow-shed :—Land æt cûbýrum . . . Oxena gehæg . . . cûbýra[s?], C. D. iv. 77, 26, 29.

cû-cealf. Substitute : I. a cow-calf, young cow :—Cûcaelf vitula, Wrt. Voc. ii. 123, 77. II. A cow's calf :—Gif man of myran folan áðríþ oððe cûcealf (or cû (gen.) cealf), Ll. Th. i. 70, 23.

cuceler. Add : ; cucelere :—Cucelere coclear, Wrt. Voc. ii. 17, 22. Cuc(el)ere, i. 290, 39. Twêgen cuculeras, Lch. i. 86, 25.

cucelere ? capo, Wrt. Voc. ii. 22, 82.

cucler-mæl. Add :—Diles preó cuclermæl, Lch. ii. 184, 17, 18 : 250, 26.

cucon. Dele. v. cwic : cucu. v. cwic.

cucurbite, an ; f. A gourd :—Lâcnian mid lactucan and clâtan and cucurbitan, Lch. ii. 244, 17. [From Latin.]

cud. Dele. v. cwudu : cuffle. Add : [v. N. E. D. coif. Cf. O. H. Ger. chuppha mitra] : cufel. v. cyfel.

cufle, an ; f. A cowl :—Cufle cuculla, R. Ben. I. 93, 9. Cufian cucullas, 92, 9, 15. [v. N. E. D. cowl. Cf. Icel. kufl ; m. a cowl.] v. next word.

cugele. Add :—Cugele, R. Ben. 92, 3. Þæt hê hæbbe cugelan (cûlan, v. l.) . . . sŷ on wintra seó cuhle (cûle, v. l.) of þiccum hrægle, R. Ben. 89, 11. Heó hire heáfod behylede mid hire cûlan, Hml. S. 33, 237 : Angl. xiii. 443, 1115. Ofer þa cûlan super cucullam, 1116. Sŷn on hrægelhûse gehealden cugelan (cûlan, v. l.), R. Ben. 91, 11.

cû-hyrde. Add :—Cûhyrdas bubulcos, An. Ox. 2450.

culfre. Add :—Culfran sunu Bar Jona (cf. Bar Jona filius columbae, Corp. Gl. H. 3, 48), Wrt. Voc. ii. 12, 15. Eádig eart þû Simon culfran bearn beatus es Simon Bar Jona, Mt. 16, 17.

culpa ; m. Add : (? culpe ; f.) : culpian. Add the Latin original :—Poscendi humilitate vilesces.

culter. Add :—Culter culter, Ælfc. Gr. Z. 27, 6 : cultrum, Wrt. Voc. ii. 22, 49 : Angl. ix. 263, 4.

cuma. Add :—Se âwerigda cuma Antecrîst nûget hider on middangeard ne côm, Bl. H. 117, 33. Cymð sió blis seldhwanne, suelce hió sié cuma oððe elðeódig quasi peregrina veniens laetitia, Past. 313, 24. Hê cwæð, 'cuma,' for ðan ðe wê ealle sind cuman on ðisum life, and ûre eard nis ná her, Hml. Th. i. 248, 14. Bæd hê ðá ælðeódigan weras ðe on cuman hîwe him mid wunodon peregrinos viros atque in hospitalitatem susceptos admonuit, ii. 96, 35. Ne aron giê gestas and nîwe cumo non estis hospites et advenae, Rtl. 82, 30. [O. Sax. [wis-]kumo : O. H. Ger. [aftar-]quemo.]

cuman ; p. côm, coom. Add : I. of movement, (1) to a place :—On þyssum eálande côm upp Agustinus in hac insula adplicuit Augustinus, Bd. 1, 25 ; Sch. 52, 8. Hannibal him côm þwyres on, Ors. 4, 8 ; S. 188, 15. Hê hiene raðe gefliémde þæs hié tôgædere cômon, 5, 13 ; S. 246, 5. Þá cwômon wê tô þæm mere, Nar. 12, 6 : 13, 10. Mon cymen wæs of Alexandres herewîcum, 18, 8. (2) from a place, to get away :—Þæt hié nysten hû hié þonan cômen, Ors. 2, 5 ; S. 78, 16. I a. with infinitive :—Of þære côm gân micel draca, Shrn. 88, 23. Côm ðær gân in tô mê Wîsdôm, Bt. 3, 1 ; F. 4, 17. II. to be transferred to another state :—Þá ne wiste hê hwær hê côm (cwôm, v.l.) he did not know what had become of him ; disparuit, Gen. 2, 12 ; Sch. 159, 1. Ne wiste ic hwær mîn lâdþeów côm (becôm, v. l.), 5, 12 ; Sch. 619, 1. Hwær côm seó frætwodnes heora húsa ? . . . oþþe hwær côm heora snyttro ?, Bl. H. 99, 27, 31. Hwær côm middaneardes gestreón ? hwær côm worulde wela ? hwær côman þá þe geornlícost æhta tiledan ?, Wlfst. 263, 21-3 : Wand. 92. III. to come to. (1) of persons, to reach a state, condition :—Oft þá forcúþestan men cumað tô þám anwealde, Bt. 16, 3 ; F. 54, 21. Hwelc sê bión sceal ðe tô reccenddôme cuman sceal, Past. 61, 5. (2) of things, to come to be, become, turn out, amount to :—Hit cwæð eów tô wuldre, Hml. S. 25, 250, 253. Þ cymð tô gefeán, Lch. iii. 154, 16. Ne côm seó hreówsung tô nánre þrowunge usque ad cruciatum non perveniret poenitentia,

Past. 419, 14. Hit côm tô þám, . . . þæt hê geceás him leorningcnihtas, Wlfst. 17, 9. Þá côm hit tô wítenne þám eorlum, Chr. 1052; P. 177, 13. **IV.** (1) *cuman of* to *come from*, (a) to *be derived from* :—Oferspræc cymeð of ðære oferwiste, Past. 313, 10. Hira demm ðe him of ðæm gestreónum cymð oððe coom (côm, *v. l.*), 345, 2. (b) *to leave* :—Wilnian æt þám cásere þ hê of þám campdôme cuman môste, Hml. S. 31, 100. (c) *to escape from* :—Of þám cnihtum þe cômon of þám hungre, Ælfc. T. Grn. 21, 19. (2) *cuman úp to be born in a country* :—Hilarion wæs úp cymen in Palistina mægðe, Shrn. 141, 6. (3) *cuman forþ to be carried out successfully, succeed* :—Gif se áð forð cume, Ll. Th. i. 392, 30. Gif seó lád forð cume . . . gif heó forð ne cume, 394, 22, 23. **V.** *to happen* :—Hit cymð him sáre, Ps. Th. 7, 14. Cymen mê mildse ðíne *veniant mihi miserationes tuae*, Ps. Srt. 118, 77. **VI.** in address :—Hê cwæð hire tô : ' Wel þú côme ; ac cum tô ús on êce reste, Shrn. 60, 19. **VII.** *to come to, to recover* :—Hê læg bútan andgite. Eft ðá ðá hê côm, þá hêt hê hine ferigan tô Hiericho, Hml. Th. i. 86, 27. **VIII.** with dat. of object, *to put, bring* (cf. Icel. koma *with dat.*) :—Hê hine áhsode hwær hê his mægcildum cumen hæfde, Lch. iii. 426, 1. **IX.** with past ptcpl., *to become, get* :—Þá côm Gallicanus eác tô Gode gebogen *then Gallicanus also got converted*, Hml. S. 7, 336. Nim wulle þe ne côm næfre áwaxen *take wool which never got washed*, Lch. iii. 122, 14. v. efen-, under-cuman ; tô-cumende, útan-cumen, -cymen, *and* cwom *in Dict.*

**cumb.** *I and II should be taken as separate words* (but see *N. E. D.* coomb). *Add to cumb,* I :—On cumb middeweardne, C.D. iii. 411, 11. On wulfcumb úseweardne, 403, 19 : 446, 22. *But also neuter* (?) ; cf. Innan rigecumb norðewærd, 449, 27. *Add to cumb,* II :—Cumb *dolium*, An. Ox. 56, 30.

**cumbol.** *I and II should be separated ; to* I *add* : v. eofor-cumbol. *For* II *see* cumul.

**cû-meoluc.** cû meoluc (?). v. meoluc.

**Cumere** (-as ?) ; *pl. The Britons of Strathclyde* :—Ealle ðá cyningas þe on þysum íglande wæron Cumera and Scotta cômon tô Eádgáre, Hml. S. 21, 451. v. Cumber-land *in Dict.*

**cum-feorm.** *Add : For the nature of this exaction* v. eafor.

**cum-líþe.** *Add* :—Beón manþwære and cumlíþe *esse mansueti et hospitales*, Ll. Th. ii. 224, 26. þ mæssepreóst his hýremen lære þ hig cumlýðe sýen, and nænegum farendum men hyra húsa ne wyrnen, 422, 6. Beón wê æfre cumlíðe ; úre sáwel bið Crístes cuma on dômes dæge, Wlfst. 239, 5. v. un-cumlíþe.

**cum-líþian.** *Substitute : To be a guest* :—Þá geond mistlicora hús cumlíðiað *qui per diversorum cellas hospitantur*, R. Ben. I. 11, 1.

**cum-líþness.** *Add :* —þ hê lufige cumlíðnysse, and nánum cuman ne forbeóde þ hê ne môte on his húse gerestan, for ðan ðe manega Gode gelícodon þurh þ þ hí cuman onféngon, Hml. A. 147, 83 : Ll. Th. ii. 422, 13. **II.** *a living as a guest, sojourn* :—Mon meahte his líf tôcnáwan on þan fyrste þe hê on cuman húwe on mynstre wunade. Gif hine mon leahtorfulne ongit on þone tíman his cumlíðnesse *tempore hospitalitatis potuit ejus vita dignosci. Si vitiosus inventus fuerit tempore hospitalitatis*, R. Ben. 109, 17. On þære cumlíðnesse, 21.

**cumul.** *Add* :—Wiþ calle yfelu cumlu, Lch. i. 60, 10. [Cf. *Icel.* örkuml *a maim ;* kumla *to bruise, wound*.]

**-cund.** *Add* : -cundd- (v. sió godcundde, Past. 91, 7). v. yfel-cund.

**cunelle.** *Add* :—Cunillae (-elle) *cerefolium*, Txts. 50, 246. Cuncla *rutam*, Lk. L. R. 11, 42.

**cunnan.** *Add* : **I.** *to know.* (1) *absolute* :—Ge þá þe cunnon, ge þá þe ne cunnon, Bt. 21 ; F. 72, 31. (2) *with acc.* :—Seó óþru leofað, þá ic cann on ansýne and ne can ná hire naman *altera superest, quam facie scio, sed nomen nescio*, Gr. D. 283, 12. Þá cann eal ðis wêsten, and wást hwær wê wîcian magon *tu nosti in quibus locis per desertum castra ponere debeamus*, Past. 304, 15. Swylce hê andgytful sý þe lytel can tô geráde on ænige wîsan, Wlfst. 53, 5. Hié woldon ðæt hér ðý mára wísdôm on londe wære ðý wê má geðeóda cúðon, Past. 5, 25. Leófre ys ús beón beswungen for lâre þænne hit ne cunnan (*nescire*), Coll. M. 18, 22. Hê wilnade mê tô cunenne *cupidus me nosse*, Nar. 18, 1. Ic gemune . . . cunnendum [mê] *memor ero . . . scientium me*, Ps. L. 86, 4. (3) *with acc. and predicate genitive* :—Hwá hine þæs wið-scipes cúðe *who knew him* (to be) *of that dignity*, Angl. viii. 308, 22. (4) *with gen. To know of* :—Þæt folc ne cúðe ðæra gôda *the people knew not of those benefits*, Hml. Th. i. 190, 31. (5) cunnan on *to be skilled in, have knowledge of* :—Ic þær nán þing on ne cann, Hml. A. 182, 42. Gif þú canst on cræftum swá swá þú cwæde, hwí wolde þín hláford þe álætan tô mê?, Hml. S. 36, 64. Þá þe on stáne cunnon and gecwêmlíce on treówe, 38. Ealle þá eásternan and þá Egiptiscan þe sêlost cunnan on gerímcræfte, Lch. iii. 256, 7. Sumne wyrhtan þe wel cunne on cræfte, Hml. S. 36, 24. On cunnende wæs *expertus sit*, Wrt. Voc. ii. 31, 13. **II.** *to be able* :—Wê him ne cunnon æfterspyrigean, Past. 5, 16. Hwæðer hê cúðe gán, Hml. S. 10, 33. Swíðe fêawa wæron ðe hiora ðeninga cúðen understondan on Englisc, Past. 3, 14. v. á-cunnan.

**cunnian.** *Add* : **I.** *with gen.* (1) *to try, test* :—Þæs cunnede sum

láece *a certain doctor tested that statement*, Lch. iii. 152, 6. Ðæt wê his cunnedon hwæþer hit swelc wære, Nar. 26, 2. Hí woldon cunnian heora mihte on þæs cáseres fyrde ær þám þe hig féngon tô sibbe, Jud. Thw. 162, 31. Þá apostolas hine lêtan heora seódas beran þ hié woldan mid þon his gítsunga cunnian, Bl. H. 69, 12. Hê hleóp cunnigende his fêdes, hwæðer hê cúðe gán, Hml. S. 10, 33. (1 a) *of medical examination* :—Hê côm and cunnode (cf. fandode his, 434) þæs mannes. Hml. S. 3, 430. Án æþele láece . . . cúðe tôcnáwan, gif hê cunnode þæs mannes, be his ædrena hrepunge hweðer hê hraðe swulte, 568. Neósode hê mín and cunnode, Bd. 5, 6 ; Sch. 579, 19. (2) *to have experience of, to feel* :—Hê cunnode his mihte, þæt hê mihtig wæs gesceapen, Ælfc. T. Grn. 2, 33. **II.** *with acc.* (*or absolute*). *To try a plan, put into practice* :—Geseah hê áidlian his smeágunge, and wolde þágyt cunnian ánes cynnes wíte, Hml. S. 4, 400. Hê nán ryhtre geþencan ne meahte þonne hê þone áð ágifan môste . . . Ðá cwæð ic þæt hê wolde cunnigan, Cht. Th. 171, 19. **III.** *with clause.* (1) *to seek to know, enquire* :—Hí bædon his rædes, cunnodon hwæðer hê wolde þæs óðres willan gefremman, Hml. S. 6, 117. Hê côm tô Críste cunnode hwæðer hê ænig þing his on him gecneówe, Angl. vii. 30, 276 Hê wolde cunnian hwæt þ wære þ hê ær gehýrde, Gr. D. 142, 10 (2) *of attempted action, to try* :—Se deófol cunnað hû hê mæge tôbrecan þá gebedu, Hml. S. 13, 55. Hié bædon þ hié ealle cunnoden, mehten hi heora gemænan fiénd him from áðôn, Ors. 3, 7 ; S. 118, 14. Cunnan hwæðer ðú mæge áðôn ðone cíð of ðínes bróður eágan, Past. 225, 8 Hê wolde cunnian gif hê mihte hí gebígan fram Godes biggencgum, Hml. S. 29, 281 : Chr. 992 ; P. 127, 12. Ic wolde cunnian, meahte ic ealne middangeard ymbféran, Nar. 20, 9. v. for-cunnian.

**cunning.** *Substitute* : cunning (-ung), e ; f. *Knowledge* :—Ánum brýdsceamole gísoegedo cunnunga (cf. Cri. 198, *given under* cunnan) ðæ unclænlíco gísíiæ *uni thoro juncta contactus inlicitorum fugat*, Rtl. 110 1. v. on-cunning.

**cunnung.** *Add* : **I.** *trial, probation* :—Þeós cunnung (*probatio*) wæ in þære brycge, þ swá hwylc unrihtwísra manna swá wolde ofer þá fêran hê sceolde áslídan on þá þýstran eá, Gr. D. 319, 12. **II.** *trial proof, experiment, experience* ; experimentum :—For þære cunnunge (*experimento*) þæra twêgra gebeóda hí gelýfdon him, Gr. D. 300, 26 For þon þe hí ne magon þá ungesewenlican þing witan þurh cunnunge and áfandunge *quia illa invisibilia scire non valent per experimentum* 261, 1. Þá þe nabbað ne nyton nænige gewislíce cunnunge be þær forðgewitenan wísan *nullum de praeterito experimenti tenent*, 8.

**cuopel.** *Add* : [v. *N. E. D.* coble.]

**cuppe.** *Add* :—Gif wê þám þearfan geræcað cuppan fulle côle wæteres, Hml. A. 141, 82. Hê genam áne cuppan mid cwealmbærun drence . . . and begôl þone drenc, Hml. S. 14, 73. Ne mage gê samod drincan úses Drihtnes calic and ðæs deófles cuppan, 17, 218. Man sceal habban . . . mêlas, cuppan, Angl. ix. 264, 17. v. drenc-cuppe.

**curs.** *For first passage substitute* :—Bisceopum gebyreð þ hí æfre on ænine man curs ne settan, bútan hý nýde scylan, Ll. Th. ii. 318, 5 *and add* :—Bietsung fæder . . . curs môder *benedictio patris . . . maledictio matris*, Scint. 174, 6. Ná ágyldende curs for curse *non reddente maledictum pro maledicto*, 24, 6.

**cursian** (?) *to plait* :—Slænde ł cursende (cursendo ł slægendo, L.) ðyrnenne bêg *plectentes spineam coronam*, Mk. R. 15, 17.

**cursumbor** *incense* :—Cursumbor *tus*, Mt. L. 2, 11. [Cf. corzumber *pretiosum suffimenti genus*, Du Cange.]

**cursung.** *Add* :—Sunu cursunges *filium gehennae*, Mt. L. 23, 15 Ðæs onfôæð cursung(e) (*damnationem*), Lk. L. R. 20, 47. In stôue cursungra *in locum tormentorum*, 16, 28.

**cusceote.** *l.* cusceote, *and add* :—Cúscotae (-e) *palumbes*, Txts. 90. 829. Cúscote *palumba*, Hpt. 33, 240, 40. [v. *N. E. D.* cushat.]

**cû-sealf**, e ; *f. Suet, fat* :—Cúself *arvina, pinguedo*, Germ. 392, 9.

**cû-slyppe.** *Add* :—Cúslyppe *brittanica*, Wrt. Voc. ii. 12, 69 : cúsnis. *l.* ciisnis.

**cuter.** *Add* : cudu (?). Cf. hwît cwuda *mastix*, Wrt. Voc. i. 68, 8.

**cúþ.** *Add* : **I.** —þ heora eágum se weg wære úp tô heofenum cúþ tô lôcienne, Bl. H. 125, 29. Gif þ þone ceorl cúð byð *si hoc de maritu manifestum sit*, Ll. Th. ii. 146, 20. þ hê þ feoh undeornunga hi cúðan ceápe (*with property known to be his*) gebohte, i. 34. 10. Hæfde Marcellus Rômánum cúð gedôn þæt mon Hannibal gefliéman mehte Ors. 4, 9 ; S. 192, 14. Hí ácwellað heora cild . . . þ hí cúðe ne beón ne heora forligr ámeldod ne wurðe, Hml. S. 17, 152. **II.** —Cúð *conpertum*, Wrt. Voc. ii. 21, 45. Hwæt is cúðost mannum tô witanne ? Nis nænigum men nánwiht swá cúð swá hê sceal deáð þrowian, Sal. K 188, 3-5. Be ongytenesse þære cúþan eástortîde *de agnitione certe temporis paschalis*, Bd. 5, 22 ; Sch. 684, 20. Cúþum *experto*, Wrt. Voc. ii. 32, 22 : An. Ox. 2488. Tô sôðan ł cúðan *pro certo*, Hpt. Gl 416, 42. Hió nænige cúðe (*certum*) andsware findan mihte . . . heó þá cúþestan (*certissimum*) andsware onfêng, Bd. 4, 7 ; Sch. 386, 7-12. Se cúþesta læcedôm, Lch. ii. 26, 2. **III.** —Gesio *vel* cúþ *cognata* i. *conjuncta, propinqua*, Wrt. Voc. ii. 133, 33. Mid cúðre stefne, Bl. H. 215, 21. Áwrítan his wundra mid cúðum gereorde, Hml. Th. ii

514, 30. Heora cūðan (cūþe, v. l.) menn and heora geféran illorum socii, Bd. 5, 10; Sch. 603, 20. Cūðra manna cognatorum, Nar. 37, 5, 1. dæg-, mæg-, seld-cūþ.

cūþa. Add:—Acsodon hine his cūþan (noti sui), Gr. D. 277, 1. Ðine cūðan cognatos tuos, Past. 323, 20.

cūþe-lic. v. cūþ-lic: cūþe-menn. l. (?) cūþe menn. v. cūþ, III.

cūþian; p. ode To become known:—Cūðas innotesceris, Ps. Srt. ii. p. 189, 6. Nū openaþ mē and cūþað seó rihte gesceádwīsnis patet ratio, Gr. D. 305, 13. Ðū cūðades him innotuisti ei, Ps. Srt. 143, 3. Cūðie (hit cūþie ł gesweotelien, Ps. L.) innotescat, 78, 10.

cūþ-læcan; p. -læhte To make friends with:—Hē sende tō Rōme recorene ærendracan, wolde cūðlæcan wið hī, Hml. S. 25, 644. v. ge-cūþlæcan.

cūþ-lǣtan. Dele, and see preceding word.

cūþ-lic; adj. Certain, evident:—Ūre Dryhten cwæð: 'Saga hym... ič ic hym gylde hys mēde'... Hē ymbe þā cūðlican mēde gehŷrde, Shrn. 98, 20. Heó onfēng swā cūþlicra gehāta, 99, 37. Bið þis þā cūðlæcestan (-lec-, v. l.) tācnu habet evidentissime signa sua, Gr. D. 13, 10. [Laym. cud-lich friendly.] v. un-cūþlic.

cūþ-līce. Add: I. (1) with verbs denoting either the possession or the imparting of knowledge, certainly, well, clearly:—Dèah hit mon cūðlíce wite, hit is tō forberanne aperte cognita toleranda, Past. 151, 10. Cūðlíce wē witon (wē witon, þ ūs eallum cūþ is, v. l.) mihi luce clarius constat, Gr. D. 8, 29. Ic hæbbe cūðlíce (gearolíce, v. l.) ongiten, 1, 3. Þis folc oncnāwe cūðlíce þ þu eart Dryhten, Hml. S. 18, 130. Cūðlíce gesēne cognoscitur, Jn. p. 3, 11. Hē þā tōweardan mannum cŷdde swā cūðlíce (cf. 62, 17) swā þā andweardan, Guth. 60, 21: Bl. H. 127, 28. Cūðlíce gewissian, Hml. Th. i. 440, 1. Bī ðæm præc Dauid swíðe cūðlíce on psalmum, swā hē hit oft ācunnad hæfde, Past. 375, 1. Ic wylle eów gyt cūðlícor secgan, þæt gē hit magon þe wutelícor ongytan, Wlfst. 15, 7. (I a) with verbs of guidance, with kill, expertly:—Ic mēde gehēt þæm þe ūs cūþlíce gelæddon þurh þā incūðan land pollicitus his praemia qui nos periti regionum ducebant per gnota loca, Nar. 6, 11. (2) evidently, certainly:—Cūðlíce is constat, Wrt. Voc. ii. 21, 34. Sceoldan þā word beón ealle cūðlíce gelæste ðe se Hælend cwæð, Wlfst. 261, 11. II. (adverbial) conjunction (cf. óþlíce):—Cūðlíce nemphe, Wrt. Voc. ii. 61, 55. Cūðlíce ł for ðon þonne ł cūþlíce, R.) igitur, Mt. L. 12, 28: p. 9, 8: ergo, 1, 17: tutem, 19: 5, 37. Cūðlíce (for þon, v. l.) wē magon nū gehŷran, 2, 22. Cūðlíce hē wæs freóh fram leahtre liber quippe a vitio, 102, 7. Cūþlíce þ vuldor þysses middangeardes is sceort, Bl. H. 65, 14: 61, 30: 81, 3. Swā hwæt swā bið on marmstāne ic sóþlíce wyrce, and ic him cūðlíce æce, Hml. S. 36, 76. III. (1) in a friendly manner:—Clipode seó vimman cūðlíce him tō, Jud. 4, 22. Hī tō him cūðlíce sprǣcon... Wē nellað þe leng swencan, Guth. 30, 17: Hml. S. 25, 104: 17, 69. (2) familiarly, as an acquaintance:—Wunode Dionisius mid Clemente cūðlíce, Hml. S. 29, 125. Clemens Dionisium him cūðlíce tō lēt and mid lufe geheóld, Hml. Th. i. 560, 1. Wē māgon cūðlíce tō him clypian, swā swā tō ūrum brēðer, 260, 7. Martha sprǣc cūðlíce tō ðām Hælende, ii. 440, 5. Ðe cūðlícor tō him clypian, gif heora lífes drohtunga eów cūðe beóð, i. 556, 29. Nō hēr cūðlícor (less as strangers) human ongunnon lindhæbbende, B. 244. [v. N. E. D. couthly.] v. un-cūþlíce.

cūþ-nes. For 'Scint. 38 . . . to know' substitute:—þinges cūðnesse, Hml. A. 200, 165.

cuðudyst. Substitute: v. cūþian.

cū-wearm; adj. Warm from the cow (of milk):—Scenc fulne cū-wearmre meolce, Lch. ii. 354, 2. Mid cūwearmum [meolcum], 15. Ðn cūwearme meolce, 358, 24.

cwacian. Add:—Ðonne þu pipor habban wille, þonne cwoca þu mid þinum scytefinger ofer óþerne, Tech. ii. 123, 14. Gif sino clæppette and wacige, Lch. ii. 6. 15. Eal hit bið bifiende and cwaciende, Wlfst. 6, 1. Cwacende (cuaciende, L.) tremens, Lk. R. 8, 47. Cuacende bifigende febricitantem, Mt. L. 8, 14. Þā cwacigendan heortan, Bl. H. 07, 19. v. ā-cwacian.

cwacung. Add:—Cwaecung tremor, Ps. Srt. 47, 7: 54, 6. Seó urg on swelcre cwacunge wæs, Ors. 3, 2; S. 100, 21.

cwala. v. self-cwala.

cwalu. Add:—Ūs stalu and cwalu . . . derede swýðe þearle, Wlfst. 59, 10. Him næs on þām hlāfe forholen seó cwalu (wōl, v. l. pestis), ir. D. 118, 9. Hwæt bið unāberendlicre tō gesiónne ðonne ðæs earnes cwalu (mors) beforan ðæs fæder eágum?, Past. 343, 11. Mæstð hié hié selfe on hiera niéhstena cwale in proximorum nece grassantur, 335, 15: Bl. H. 193, 1. Tō his cwale ad interfectionem ejus, Kent. Gl. 703. Cwale exitio, Wrt. Voc. ii. 33, 4. Hē his sunu āsende tō cwale for ūs, Ælfc. T. Grn. 4, 32. Dōn tō cwale to put to death, Hml. S. 21, 372. v. morþor-, sūsl-cwalu.

cwānian. Add: v. weá-cwānian.

cwānung, e; f. Lamentation:—Grānung and cwānung, Nap. 15.

cwatern, quatern glosses quaternio:—Quatern, quaterni quaternio, Txts. 90, 847.

cwead. l. cweád, and add:—Cwēd vel meox stercus; of cweáde ārærende de stercore erigens, Bl. Gl. Cweád purgamenta, Wrt. Voc. ii. 84, 8.

cwealm. Add:—Cwealm nex, Wrt. Voc. ii. 62, 21. Þæt fīfte (the fifth plague in Egypt) wæs hyra nŷtena cwealm (pecorum et jumentorum strages), Ors. 1, 7; S. 38, 6. Æfter þæra cilda cwealme (the murder of the Innocents), Mart. H. 10, 10. Mid hungre oþþe mid cwealme with famine or with pestilence, Hml. S. 13, 143. Generian from þon ēcan cwealme, Bl. H. 25, 28. Hē lēcnode monigo of cualmum (plagis), Lk. L. 7, 21. Nelle wē nā þ þū swelte þurh missenlice and mænigfealde cwealmas and tintergu nolumus te per varios cruciatus mori, Gr. D. 254, 6. v. beorþor-, mæg-, mann-, slit-cwealm.

-cwealmbǣran. v. ge-cwe(a)lmbǣran (-cwylm-).

cwealm-bǣre (cwelm-). Add: (1) of persons:—Dioclitianus wæs tō cāsere gecoren þeáh ðe hē cwealmbǣre wǣre, Hml. S. 19, 2. Hē ne mihte widcweðan þām cwealmbǣrum folce, 7, 217. Cōmon cwealmbǣre deófiu, Hml. Th. ii. 326, 12. Judas cōm mid þām cwealmbǣrum . . . and belǣwde þone Hǣlend þām ārleásum cwellerum, Hml. A. 74, 43. (2) of things:—Seó cwealmbǣre ēhtnyss, Hml. S. 19, 16. Ā-cwellan mid cwealmbǣrum swurde, 7, 244. Mid cwealmbērum (-bǣrum) drence, 14, 73. Lǣdan tō leóhtleásum cwearterne . . . tō þām cwealmbǣrum hūse, 29, 258. Cwealmbǣrne (cwelm-, An. Ox. 4882) wom letiferam (mortiferum) luem, Hpt. Gl. 518, 38. Cwealmbǣre pestiferum (virus), An. Ox. 11, 83. Cwylmbǣre perniciosa, i. mortifera (fruteta), 920. Hine forhabban fram cwylmbǣrum mettum, Hml. Th. i. 360, 23.

cwealm-bǣrnes. Add:—Heó heóld þā líc oþ þ seó ēhtnys geswāc, and se crīstendōm ācucode æfter þǣre cwealmbǣrnysse, Hml. S. 29, 330.

cwealmberend-lic; adj. Pernicious, pestiferous:—Syndon twā cynnryno unrōtnesse, ān hālwendlic and óðer cwylmberendlic (cwyldbærendlic, v. l.), Nap. 15.

cwealm-full. v. ge-cwealmfull: cwealm-ness. Add: v. mann-cwealmness: cwealm-stede. For reference substitute Germ. 398, 213.

cwealm-stōw. Add:—Cualmstōu calvariae locus, Wrt. Voc. ii. 98, 2. Ðā cempan hine (Jesus) gelǣddon tō ðǣre cwealmstōwe þær man cwealde sceaðan, Hml. Th. ii. 254, 15. Hī lǣdde Maximus mid ōþrum cwellerum tō þǣre cwealmstōwe, Hml. S. 34, 226. Tō ðǣre ealdan cwalmstōwe (cwealm-, Cht. E. 290, 29), C. D. iii. 404, 27. Inn an ðā cwealmstōwe, of ðǣre cwealmstōwe, v. 107, 22. [Omnia qualstowa, i. occidendorum loca, totaliter sunt regis, Ll. Th. i. 519, 11.]

cweartern. Add:—Cweartern, cwearten carcer, Ælfc. Gr. Z. 318, 11. Cwærtern earcer vel ergastulum vel lautumia, Wrt. Voc. i. 58, 32. Þ stǣnene cweartern, Hml. A. 79, 170. Cweartenes ergastuli, An. Ox. 2553: lautomiae, latrinae, Hpt. Gl. 513, 57. Lǣdan tō leóhtleásum cwearterne, Hml. S. 29, 257. Gebringan on þām blindan cwearterne, Hml. A. 8, 204. On fæstum cwearterne (cwearten, v. l.) beclŷsan, 187, 185. On cwearterne gesettan, 189, 236. Þǣre-gehæftan wylne cild þe sǣt on cwerterne, Ex. 12, 29. On cwearterne settan, Hml. A. 79, 165. Hē (St. Paul) wæs on manegum cwearternum, Hml. Th. i. 392, 9.

cweartern-lic. For reference substitute Germ. 400, 552.

cweartern-weard, es; m. A warder of a prison, jailor:—Cweartenweard manceps (i. servus) carceris, Germ. 399, 345.

cweccan. For first reference substitute Germ. 397, 504, and add:—Þā cwehte se dēma his deóflice heáfod, Hml. S. 8, 91. Se cwellere slōh swíðe . . . him ætfeóll fǣrlíce his gold þā þā hē swā hetelíce his handa cwehte, 12, 217. Cwahte vibrabat, Ps. Spl. T. 7, 13. [v. N. E. D. quetch.] v. ge-cweccan.

cweccung. Add:—Cwecging (c written over first g) vibramen, An. Ox. 18 b, 94.

cwece-sand, es; m. A quick-sand:—Cwecesond aurippus, Wrt. Voc. ii. 10, 48.

cweddian. v. cwiddian: cweden. v. bufan-, sōþ-cweden: cwedenness. v. wiþ-cwedenness.

cwedol, cwidol; adj. Ready of speech, talkative, eloquent:—Dicax, i. facundus, qui verbis jocatur in quamlibet rem, vel cwedel, Wrt. Voc. ii. 140, 11. Quedol dicam (-x ?), quedole, dicas, 106, 48, 49. Ne sŷ nān tō þæs cwedol wíf ne tō þæs cræftig man þæt āwendan ne mæge word þus gecwedene, Lch. i. 402, 13. v. hearm-, wearg-cwedol (-cwidol).

-cwedolian. v. wearg-cwedolian: -cwedolness. v. wearg-, wiþer-cwedolness.

cwelan. Add:—Hī libbað óðrum monnum and cwelað him selfum vivunt aliis et sibi moriuntur, Past. 449, 19. Þū scealt ǣrest óðerne geseón drincan and ðǣrrihte cwelan, Hml. Th. i. 72, 15. Þ spere him eóde þurh ūt, and hē feóll cwelende, Hml. S. 12, 55. Lífes lǣcedōmes forwirnan ðǣm cwelendum monnum, Past. 377, 6. [v. N. E. D. quele.] v. be-cwelan.

cwelde-rǣde (?) an evening-rider (?), a bat:—Vespertilionem quæl-

dǽrǽde, Shrn. 29, 8. [Cf. *Icel.* kveld *evening*; kveld-ríða *a night-hag.*]

**cwellan.** *Add:*—Đá men đe wēnað đæt hí cwēman Gode đonne hí cwellað hyra oxan, Prov. K. 67. Cwealdon *necarent*, Wrt. Voc. ii. 61, 53. Tō cwellene (-ende, An. Ox. 4508) *truncanda, decollanda, occidenda*, Hpt. Gl. 511, 2. Hí [wǽron] cwealde *mactarentur*, 478, 47. [v. *N.E.D.* quell.] v. ge-cwellan.

**cwellend.** *For reference substitute* Germ. 400, 529.

**cwellere.** *Add:*—Aurelianus wæs wælhreáw cwellere crístenra manna, and fela belífode gelýfedra manna, Hml. Th. ii. 308, 4. Hē (*St. Paul*) wæs crístenra manna ēhtere ǽr and cwellere, Shrn. 58, 27. Đæs cwelres hand . . . đǽm cwelre syllan, 129, 9–12. Cwelres *lictoris*, Germ. 393, 72. Tō đām hǽđenan cwellere, Hml. Th. ii. 424, 13. Ne bið þǽr ansýn gesewen bútan þára cwelra þe cwylmað đã earman *non nisi tortorum facies ibi cernitur ulla*, Dōm. L.'204. Hē belǽwde þone Hǽlend þām cwellerum, Hml. A. 74, 46.

**cwelm-.** v. cwealm-: **cwelman.** v. cwilman.

**cwēman.** *Add:* (1) *absolute:*—Ic cwēme *blandior*, Wrt. Voc. ii. 12, 44. Þ¢h þe þes middangeard cwēme *etiam si mundus blandiretur*, Gr. D. 258, 26. (2) *with dat.*:—Ic wilnige đæt ic monnum cuēme and lícige (*placeo*), Past. 147, 19. Þ wē Gode cwēmon and deófol týnan, Bl. H. 47, 11. Đã men đe wēnað đæt hí cwēman Gode đonne hí cwellað hyra oxan, Prov. K. 67. Manege tiligaþ Gode tō cwēmanne, Bt. 39, 10; F. 228, 13. Cuoemendra đē *placentium tibi*, Rtl. 91, 31. [v. *N.E.D.* queme.]

**cwēmed-ness,** e; *f. Pleasure, satisfaction:*—Hí ǽlc gód árǽrdon Gode tō cwēmednesse, Hml. S. 21, 462.

**cwēming.** *Add:*—Mid fullum geþance and cwēmingce *satisfactione*, Gr. D. 303, 10: 316, 13. Đonne đæt selflíce gegriépð đæt mód đæs recceres, and hē wilnað ungemetlíce lícigean, đonne berǽst hē oft on ungemetlíce cuēminge and bið hwílum tō ungemetlíce smēđe *amor proprius, cum rectoris mentem ceperit, aliquando hanc inordinate ad mollitiem rapit*, Past. 143, 6.

**cwēm-líc;** *adj. Pleasing, agreeable, satisfying:*—Cuoemlíc (*placabilis*) sié đē điós âsægdnis, Rtl. 124, 38. Đã đe đē aron cuoemlíco *quae tibi sunt placita*, 39, 3. Cuoemlíc *sufficientiam* (-*tem?*), 7, 27. v. next word.

**cwēm-líce;** *adv.* (1) *graciously, kindly:*—Drihten, bihald cuoemlíce *Domine, intende placatus*, Rtl. 41, 39. (2) *humbly:*—Cuoemlíce wē biddas *suppliciter exoramus*, Rtl. 93, 21. [v. *N.E.D.* quemely.]

**cwēmnys.** *Add:* [Singe songes . . . Gode to quemnesse, O.E. Hml. ii. 55, 27. þe (God) ine cwemnesse, i. 213, 32.]

**cwēn.** *For* cwēne (*wk.*) *l.* cwene, *q.v., and add:* **I.** *a woman:*—Cwēna geligr *adulterium*, Wrt. Voc. i. 21, 33. **III.** *a queen:*—Ealra fǽmnena cwēn, Bl. H. 105, 17. Coen (cwoen, R.) sūđđǽles *regina austri*, Lk. L. 11, 31. Đió cuoen *reginam*, p. 7, 8. Cuoeno *reginae*, Rtl. 68, 41. **III a.** *a king's wife:*—Þæs cyninges nama wæs Eilippus, and his quēne noma wæs Eufenisse, Shrn. 131, 31. **III b.** *a king's daughter:*—Þæs cynges dohtor cwæð: 'Ic gife þe . . .' Đis weard þus gedón æfter þǽre cwēne hǽse . . . þã men ealle grētton þone cyngc and đã cwēne . . . Apollonius cwæð: 'Đū gōda cyngc . . . and þū cwēn.' Hē cwæð: 'Nimað þãs þing þe mē seó cwēn forgeaf,' Ap. Th. 17, 16—18, 15. v. port-, rihtæþel-cwēn.

**cwēne.** *l.* cwene, *for last reference substitute* Wlfst. 161, 20, *and add: a quean, woman* (with unfavourable sense):—Hiene ân cwene sceát þurh þæt þeóh, Ors. 3. 7; S. 118, 3. Nis preóstes cwene ǽnig óðer bútan deófles grin, Ll. Th. ii. 336, 25. Wylt đū hit eal đǽre cwenon syllan?, Lch. iii. 428, 2. Sume mæssepreóstas habbað twâ [wíf] odđe mâ, and sume forlǽtað þã hig ǽr hæfdon, and be lifiendre cwenan eft óðre nimað, Wlfst. 269, 23. Unrihthǽmeras, þã fúlan þe forlǽtað heora cwenan and nimað óðre, and þã þe habbað mâ þonne heora rihtæđelcwēne, 298, 17. [*Goth.* kwinō.] v. hōr-cwene.

**cwēn-fugol** (cwen-? *cf. Icel.* kvenn-fugl). *For* 'Som . . . Lye,' *substitute:*—Nân man ne wât hweþer hit (*the Phenix*) is þe carlfugol þe cwēnfugol, E.S. viii. 479, 91.

**cwēn-hirde,** es; *m. A keeper of women, eunuch:*—Cuoenhiordo *eunuchi*, Mt. L. 19, 12.

**cweorn.** *Add:*—Đurh đã cweorne (*molam*) is getâcnod se ymbhwyrft đisse worolde . . . Đonne bið sió cweorn becierred đonne se monn bið geendod; đonne bið sió micle cweorn (cwiorn, *v. l.*) becierred đonne đeós weorld bið geendod, Past. 31, 18–22. Wolde hē grindan mid his hondum . . . þã sóna þã hē þǽre cweorna neálǽhte, and þ corn þǽron lǽgde, þã orn (grand, *v. l.*) seó cweorn þurh godcunde miht, and se abbod . . . stód be þǽre cweorna, Mart. H. 200, 22–26. Coern (cwearne, R.) *mola*, Mk. L. 9, 42. Stân coern (cern, R.) *lapis molaris*, Lk. L. 17, 2. Æt cweorne (on coernæ, L.) *in mola*, Mt. R. 24, 41. On coern, Lk. p. 9, 11. Se IIII. nihta mōna, se byð gōd þǽm ergendan hys sul ût tō dóne, and þēm grindere his cweorn, Lch. iii. 178, 1. v. pipor-cweorn.

**cweorn-bill.** *For* Cot. 125 *substitute* Wrt. Voc. ii. 53, 43.

**cweorn-burna,** an; *m. A mill-stream:*—Andlang mearcellan þ hit

cymđ þǽr cwyrnburna and mearcella sceótað tōgædere; þonne forđ andlang cwyrnburnan, C.D. iii. 458, 12–14. [Cf. *Icel.* kvern-â *a millstream.*]

**cweorn-stân.** *Add:*—Cweornstân *scopulum*, i. *lapis* (*collo connexum*), An. Ox. 4457. Coernstân *mola*, Mt. L. 18, 6. Curnstânes *molaris*, Germ. 400, 489. Lǽt niman ǽnne greátne cwurnstân and hǽtan hine and lecgan hine under þone man, Lch. iii. 38, 15. [v. *N.E.D.* quern-stone. *O.H.Ger.* quirn-stein *mola asinaria: Icel.* kvern-steinn.]

**cweorn-tōþ.** *Add:*—Cweorntōđum *molaribus*, Wrt. Voc. ii. 76, 40. -cweorra, -cweorran. v. mete-cweorra, â-cweorran.

**cweorþ.** *The name of the* q-(cw-)*rune:*—Cweorð (q), at the end of the Runic poem Hickes' Thesaurus i. 135: see also Wimmer's Runenschrift, p. 85.

**cweþan.** *Add:* **I.** *to say.* (1) *of a particular statement:*—Ne cweðo ic nō đæt đæt ic ǽr cwæð bebeódende, ac lǽrende, Past. 397, 27. Salm ic cweoðu *psalmum dicam*, Ps. Srt. 17, 50. Se yfela þeów cuið on his móde, Past. 121, 11. Gē cweađað *dicitis*, Ps. Srt. 138, 20. Cweoðað *dicite*, 65, 2. (2) *of a general statement, as in it says, books say:*—Wē cweðaþ on gerímcræfte Cathedra Sancti Petri seofon nihton ǽr þãm mōnđe þe wē Martius hâtað *according to our calendar Cathedra S. Petri is seven days before March*, Hml. S. 10, 1. Sýn hý þæs wyrđe þe on þãm canone cwæð, Ll. Th. i. 244, 13. Þæs ylcan scyldige þe hit hē beforan cwæð, 248, 18. Æt þãm táum . . . ealswâ æt þãm fingrum ys cwiden, 20, 4. Se mon bið, þæs þe swâ tō cweþanne sié (*so to say*), ǽghwæþer ge gehæfted ge freó, Bd. 1, 27; Sch. 98, 17. **II.** *to call, name:*—Þone tûn mon his naman cweðeþ *cujus nomine vicus cognominatur*, Bd. 2, 20; Sch. 189, 8. Mē eádige cwǽdon ealle cneórisna Bl. H. 7, 4. **III.** *to declare:*—Hí cwǽdon gefeoht tōgeánes þǽre burhware (*cf.* þã burhware hí ongunnon ânwígges biddan, Bl. H. 201 22), Hml. Th. i. 504, 13. **IV.** *introducing a question:*—Cweðsþū lâ yrsað hē *numquid irascitur?*, Ps. L. 7, 12. Ac lâ ic þe bidde, cwys þū (cwysđu, *v. l.*) hwæþer hit tō gelýfenne sý?, Gr. D. 146, 1. Cweþ wē is þes Dauides sunu *numquid hic est filius David?*, Mt. 12, 23. Gē ceastergewaran, cweðe gē þ ic eów dide ǽnigne unþanc?, Ap. Th. 26 3. v. wearg-, wiþer-, yfel-cweþan; un-cweþende; -cweden. -cweþness. v. wiþer-cweþness.

**cwic.** *Take here the* (accusative) *forms given under* cwicen *and those under* cwicu, *and add:*—Nât nǽnig man hwæþer se Jōhannes sí þ cwicu þe deád, Shrn. 32, 30. Cwucu *vivus*, Scint. 37, 16. Đeós wyr is swylce heó symle cwicu (cwice, cuca, *v. ll.*) sý, Lch. i. 270, 19. Hí wunade on þãm wundum cucu, Hml. S. 2, 306. Hié wēndon þ heor hláford wǽre on heora feónda gewealde odđe cuca odđe deád, Ors. 3, 9 S. 134, 29. Mǽnende þ hē tō him cuco (cucan (*dat.*), S. 244, 5) n cóm, and þ hē swylcon deáđe swealt, Ors. 5, 12; Th. 462, 16. Cuc *vivus*, Wrt. Voc. i. 28, 67. Genim cwicenne (cwicne, *v. l.*) fox, Lch. i 340, 25. Þone câsere cwicenne (*altered from* cwicne) forbǽrnan, Bl. H 191, 12. Heora godas bǽdan þæt him mon sealde ǽnne cucne (cuceunne Th. 330, 23) mon, Ors. 3, 3; S. 102, 28. Hē nãnne ne lēt cucn (cucune, Th. 472, 27), 6, 2; S. 256, 1. Hine cucene þe deádne, Shrn 47, 3. Cucenne hine forbǽrnan, Hml. Th. i. 372, 10. Cukenn (cwicne, *v.l.*), Gr. D. 17, 22. Scealt þú eal þ deáde of âsníþan oþ þ cwice líc, Lch. ii. 82, 27. Þã Rōmâne hié cuce bebyrgdan. Ac . . . hi mid hiera cucum onguldon þæt hié ungyltige cwealdon, Ors. 4, 7; S 184, 6–10. v. ed-cwic.

**cwic-beám.** *Add:*—Cuicbeám *cariscus*, Wrt. Voc. ii. 102, 6; Cwicbeám, 129, 8. Quicbeám *juniperum*, 46, 19.

**cwic-beámen;** *adj. Of quickbeam:*—Mid cwicbeámenum sticcan Lch. iii. 14, 25.

**cwicclian** *to totter* (?):—Cwiccliende (wiccliende, Hpt. Gl. 459, 6 *nutabundum*, An. Ox. 2234.

**cwice,** an; *f. Add:* cwice, es; *m.:*—Quiquae, quicae, quice *grame* Txts. 66, 464. Cwice, Wrt. Voc. ii. 41, 64. Quicae, cuique *virect* Txts. 106, 1088. Cwice *gramis birecta*, Wrt. Voc. i. 68, 75. Cwica *gramina*, Hpt. Gl. 433, 30: *frutecta*, i. *arbusta*, An. Ox. 2, 28.

**cwicen.** v. cwic: **cwic-feoh.** *Dele.*

**Cwichelmingas;** *pl. m. Descendants of Cwichelm:*—Penda and c đãm Pending and Pendingas; Cwicelm and of đãm Cwicelmingas, Ælf Gr. 2. 15, 4.

**cwician.** *Add:* **I.** (1) *to become living:*—Ealle treówa cuciað c lenctenes tíman, Hml. S. 12, 31. (2) *to become sensitive, recov feeling, power:*—Gif wund on men âcōlod sý . . . heó cwicaþ and wea mað, Lch. i. 194, 25. Wæs sum mǽden licgende on paralisin . . . eal hire lima cucodon, Hml. S. 31, 504. **II.** *to make alive:*—Se fǽd đã deádo cuicað (*vivificat*), Jn. L. 5, 21. Þǽre sâwle mægen cwica þone líchoman, Gr. D. 268, 18.

**cwic-lâc,** es; *n. A living sacrifice:*—Cuiclâcum (cwicum lâcum, R *holocaustomatibus*, Mk. L. 12, 33.

**cwic-líc;** *adj. Living, vital:*—Cuiclíc *vitalis*, Rtl. 94, 29.

**cwic-rind,** e; *f. Rind of quickbeam:*—Nim æpsrinde, cwicrind Lch. ii. 332, 8. Cwicrinda hand fulle, 358, 15.

**cwic-seolfor.** For Cot. 16 *substitute* Wrt. Voc. ii. 8, 54, *and add :*—Cwicseolfor *vel* mæstling *electrum*, Wrt. Voc. ii. 142, 77. [*O. H. Ger.* quech-silpar *argentum vivum, electrum.*]

**cwic-sūsl.** *Add :*—On þǣm hellefŷre[s?] cwicsūsle his līf geendaþ, Bl. H. 61, 2. Seó menigo hāligra sāula wǣron of þǣm cwicsūsle āhafena, 87, 19. Intō ēcere cwicsūsle, Wlfst. 289, 9. Uncyst hine besencte on cwycsūsle, Hml. Th. i. 328, 22. On deorce cwicsūsle *in tetra tartara,* An. Ox. 1249.

**cwic-sūslen;** *adj. Of hell, of Hades :*—Gif ǣnig andgit sŷ on helle, lǣt þū þæt cwicsūslene hūs, and gehīr ðu ðīnes fæder stæfne, Ap. Th. 26, 12.

**cwic-treów.** *Add :*—Cwictreów *cresis,* Wrt. Voc. ii. 137, 1 : *gnesis,* 42, 17. [v. N. E. D. quick-tree.]

**cwicu.** v. cwic : -cwicung. v. ge-cwicung.

**cwic-wille** (-welle); *adj. Living* (of water):—Wæter cwicwelle (līfwelle, L.) *aquam vivam,* Jn. R. 4, 10, 11.

**cwida.** v. wiþer-cwida : **cwid-bōc.** *Add :*—Cuidbōcum, Past. 257, 25.

**cwiddian,** cweddian, cwydian (*q. v.* in Dict.); *p.* ode, ede *To say :*—Cwiddiaþ (cwyddiaþ, An. Ox. 1881) t secgcað *contendunt, dicunt,* Hpt. Gl. 450, 70. þā hī cweddiað (cwyddiaþ, An. Ox. 1953) *quam dicunt,* 452, 43. Cwedd(iað), cwyddiað *ferunt, dicunt,* 504, 60. Befrān hē hū woruldmenn be him cwyddedon . . . His apostoli him andwyrdon : ' Sume men cwyddiað (cf. sume men cweðað, 364, 16) þæt ðū sŷ Jōhannes, Hml. Th. i. 366 5-10. [*O. H. Ger.* [harm-]quetôn.] v. be-, hearm-, teón-, wiþer-cwid[d]ian.

**cwide.** *Add :* I. *a saying, words :*—Se cwide Dauides þe hē cwæð, Bl. H. 139, 27. Drihten is gemyndig þæs his cwides þe hē gecwæð . . . and hē wolde þone cwide getrymman on þǣre godcundan dǣde, 215, 24. Getrymede mid Jōhannes cuide *Johannis voce roborati,* Past. 85, 20. Cwyde *sententia,* An. Ox. 4629 : Hpt. Gl. 522, 62. Cwide, Kent. Gl. 532. Se gecyrreda sceaða on his deaðes cwyde (*by his dying words*) þæs ēcan līfes mēde gearnode, Hml. Th. ii. 124, 33. Ealdra manna cwidas and dǣda *priorum gesta sive dicta,* Bd. praef. ; Sch. 1, 12. I a. *a wise saying, adage, proverb, sentence :*—Se cwide þe þū mē sædest þ se wīsa Plato cwæðe, Bt. 3, 4 ; F. 6, 20. Se cwide ðe hē cwæþ : ' Swā mon mā swincþ, swā mon māran mēde onfēhþ,' 41, 3 ; F. 248, 1. Of Salomonnes cuidum wē nāmon, Past. 259, 8. Catus cwydas *Catonis disticha,* Angl. viii. 321, 29. Cwidas *sententias,* Kent. Gl. 993. II. *a* (*grammatical*) *sentence, period :*—Bebeád hē þæt him mon lengran cwidas (*sententias*) cwæðe, Bd. 5, 2 ; Sch. 559, 9. Stæfcræfti(g)ra fulle cwydas (cwedas, Hpt. Gl. 473, 19) *grammaticorum periodos,* An. Ox. 2849. III. *a* (*judicial*) *sentence :*—Se sārlica cwide þe ūre Drihten tō þǣm ǣrestan men cwæþ : ' Terra es, et in terram ibis,' Bl. H. 123, 7. Se cwyde ūre brosnunge, Hml. Th. i. 300, 6. On dōmes dæg hī beoð þysne cwide gehērende, Bl. H. 63, 26. Datianus gedihte þisne cwyde : ' Nimað þisne scyldigan . . . and ofsleað hine, Hml. S. 14, 151. Þone cwyde þæs slāwan þeówes *the sentence on the slothful servant,* 23 b, 14. IV. *a decree, decision :*—Ǣr se dæg cyme þæt sŷ cwide ārunnen, Sal. 479. *Condicta,* i. *decreta vel* cwidas, Wrt. Voc. ii. 135, 57. V. *a proposal, proposition :*—þā cwæð se apostol tō ðām hǣðengyldum : ' Gað ealle tō Godes cyrcan . . . ' þā hǣðengyldan ðisum cwyde geðwǣrlǣhton, Hml. Th. i. 70, 34. VI. *a discourse, sermon, homily :*—Ne mage wē āwrītan ealle his wundra on ðisum scortan cwyde, Hml. Th. ii. 514, 30 : Hml. S. 18, 474. Ic āwende on Englisc sumne cwide (*the homily on Job*), Ælfc. T. Grn. 11, 1. VII. *a will, testament :*—Cwyde *testamentum,* Wrt. Voc. i. 83, 3. On cwyde þīnum lǣf þearfum *in testamento tuo relinque pauperibus,* Scint. 146, 13. v. folc-, fore-, samnung-, sealm-, spell-cwide.

**cwidele.** For *examples see* cwydele *in Dict., and add :* [*O. H. Ger.* quedila *pustula, varix.*]

**cwide-leás.** *Add :*—Gewāt Eádrīc ǣr Ælfēh cwideleás, and Ælfēh ēng tō his lǣne, Cht. Th. 272, 20.

**cwidian.** *Dele, and see* cwiddian : **cwidol.** v. cwedol.

**cwiferlīce.** *Substitute : Actively, zealously :*—Ðonne hē wel þēnaþ and ūres Drihtnes heorde cwiferlīce gealgað and tō rihte manað, R. Ben. 122, 2. [v. N. E. D. quiverly.]

**cwild.** *Add :*—Cwyld *clades, pestes,* Wrt. Voc. ii. 131, 60. Cuild cualm *valitudo,* Rtl. 146, 35. Fǣrlic cwyld *clades,* Dôm. L. 258. Cwyldes *pestilentiae,* i. *necis,* An. Ox. 2787. Cwilde *internicionis,* Wrt. Voc. ii. 43, 72. Cwilde flōd *diluvium,* Ps. Srt. 28, 10. Ic ofsleá hig mid cwylde and fordō mid cwealme *feriam eos pestilentia atque consunam,* Num. 14, 12. Cwylda *pestilentiae* (n. pl.), An. Ox. 61, 42. Sē þe mid gesyntum swylce cwyldas mæg wel forbūgon *qui illas effugiet prospere clades,* Dôm. L. 248.

**cwild-bǣre.** *Add :*—Swā hwæt ofer gemet ys, cwyldbǣre (*perniciosum*) hit byð, Scint. 55, 2 : 192, 17. Orsorhnesse cwyldbǣr(r)e *securitatis pestiferae,* 92, 14. Cwyldbǣre fægernyssa *perniciosas pulchritudines,* 168, 15.

**cwild-bǣrlīce.** *Add :*—Synne āttor hālwendlīce byð geopenud on ndetnysse, þæt cwyldbǣrlīce lutude on geþance *peccati virus salu-*

**cwildberend-lic.** v. cwealmberend-lic.

**cwild-full;** *adj. Pernicious, deadly :*—Cwyldfulle *perniciosum,* i. *mortiferum,* An. Ox. 1223. v. ge-cwildfull.

**cwild-seten.** v. cwyld-seten *in Dict., but substitute for citations :*—Cwylsetene (cwylseten *conticinium,* Hpt. Gl. 495, 6) *conticinio,* An. Ox. 3771. Cwyldsetene, 2, 250 : 8, 198. Cwuldsetene, 7, 273. Cwyldsetene (*conticinio, gallicantu,* Hpt. Gl. 514, 17), 4658 : 2, 363 : 8, 271. v. next word.

**cwild-tīd,** e ; *f. Even-tide, evening :*—Cwyldtīd *conticinium,* Wrt. Voc. ii. 135, 14. [Cf. *Icel.* kveld-tīmi *eventide.*]

**cwilman.** *Add :* I. *to torment :*—Ansŷn þara cwelra þe cwylmað ðā earman *tortorum facies,* Dôm. L. 203 : Wlfst. 139, 5. Þ se draca mē mā ne ceówe ne ne cwelme, Gr. D. 324, 27. Ic eom cwielmed on ðŷs liége, Past. 309, 7. Cwylmed, Bl. H. 63, 6 : Dôm L. 216. I a. *to mortify the flesh :*—Hē on monigum ðrowungum his līchoman cwilmð, Past. 61, 7. II. *to kill :*—Dryhten cwælmeð and geliffesteð *Dominus mortificat et vivificat,* Ps. Srt. ii. p. 186, 21. Se lēg hié cwylmde, Bl. H. 203, 16. Ðæt hié cwælmen (*trucident*) ðā rehtheortan, Ps. Srt. 36, 14. His hīred wæs gestanden mid cwylmendre ādle and wǣron deáða ægðer ge his þeówas ge þeówena, Hml. S. 30, 142. Cwylmed on rōde *crucified,* Dôm. L. 54. Bið cwelmed *mortificabitur,* Kent. Gl. 698. II a. cwilman tō deáþe *to put to a cruel death :*—Cwylm hig ealle tō deáðe, Hml. A. 188, 197. v. ā-cwilman ; cwābitan.

**cwilmend,** es ; *m.* I. *a tormentor :*—Tō þǣm þ se his cwylmend his gelŷfde *dum hoc a torquente creditur,* Gr. D. 163, 10. II. *a slayer, destroyer :*—Hē ongann clypian þ hē his cwylmend wǣre *se interfectorem illius clamare coepit,* Gr. D. 89, 5.

**cwilmian.** *See* cwylmian *in Dict., and add :* I. *intrans. To suffer torment :*—Hī cwylmiað on ēcum fŷre, Hml. Th. i. 132, 16, 22. Hē sceal beón cwylmiende mid deófle, Angl. viii. 337, 9. Ðā sceaðan ðāgyt cwylmigende cuce hangodon, Hml. Th. ii. 260, 8 : i. 334, 6. Hī wurdon tōcwŷsede and cwylmiende lāgon, Hml. S. 6, 94. II. *trans.* (1) *to torment :*—Þ hē mē mā ne ceówe ne ne cwelmie (*cruciet*), Gr. D. 324, 27. (2) *to kill :*—Hē sēcð tō cwilmianne hine *quaerit mortificare eum,* Ps. L. 36, 32. (3) *fig. to crucify* the flesh :—Gif wē ðā flǣsclican lustas cwylmiað, Hml. Th. i. 118, 11. þā þe Crīstes synd cwylmiað heora flǣsc *qui sunt Christi carnem suam crucifixerunt* (Gal. 5, 24), Hml. S. 17, 61. v. cwilman ; deáþ-cwylmmende.

**cwilming.** *See* cwylming *in Dict., and add :* I. cf. cwilmian, I, II. 1 :—Bearn mid ormǣtre cwylminge cwacigende eallum limum, Hml. Th. ii. 30, 20. Cwylmingce tō tintreigenne *cruciatu torquendus,* An. Ox. 3235. II. cf. cwylmian, II. 2 :—Cwylmminge Hǣlendes *mortificationem Jesus,* Scint. 161, 3. III. cf. cwylmian, II. 3 :—Flǣsclicra leahtra cwylminge *carnalium vitiorum mortificationem,* An. Ox. 40, 22.

**cwinod.** *l.* ormōd : **cwis.** *l.* un-cwisse (*at end*).

**cwīsan.** *See* cwysan (*l.* cwŷsan) *in Dict., where substitute for bracket :* [v. N. E. D. quease], *and add* v. ge-cwīsan.

**cwiþ, cwiþa.** *Add :*—Cwiþ *matrix,* Wrt. Voc. ii. 90, 41 : i. 45, 23. Quitha, ii. 55, 55. Wið cwiþan sāre, Lch. i. 152, 17. Cwiðan *matrice,* Wrt. Voc. ii. 56, 67. Wiþ wīfes cwiþan tō feormienne, Lch. i. 54, 15.

**cwīþan.** *Add :* I. *to lament :*—Severus cwŷþed and mǣneþ his sāwle (hine bewēpð and heófað, v. l.) *Severus plangit,* Gr. D. 89, 34. Þ ic mæge mīne synne cwīþan, Angl. xii. 508, 13. Hē wæs cwīþed fram þām ymbstandendum *a circumstantibus plangeretur,* Gr. D. 191, 19. Þonne synne beoð cwīþde and bewōpene, 244, 26. Cwīðde *lamentatae,* Ps. Srt. 77, 63. II. *to make a legal complaint against, bring a charge against :*—Nis se man on līfe ðe ǣfre gehŷrde ðæt man cwīdde (cwŷdde, Ll. Th. i. 184, 11) oððon crafode hine on hundrede oððon on gemōte, on ceápstōwe oþþe on cyricware, ðā hwīle hē lifde. Unsac hē wæs on līfe, Lch. iii. 288, 4. v. un-cwīð[d].

**cwīðend-līc.** *Substitute :* **cwiþen-lic ;** *adj. Native, natural :*—Cwiþenlicre *genuini* (*perhaps* Aldhelm 73, 11 ' genuini (partus),' *glossed by* gecyndelicere, An. Ox. 5092. Cf. *also* genuina matrice *glossed by* ācennendlicum cildhaman, 1243), Wrt. Voc. ii. 40, 49. v. cwiþ.

**cwīþ-ness.** *Add :*—Gecyrran tō cwīðnesse þǣre sōðan dǣdbōte *ad lamentum poenitentiae redire,* Gr. D. 257, 5. Hē sealde hine sylfne in wōp and in cwīðnesse *sese in lamentis dedit,* 207, 8. In hefige cŷpnesse (cwīðnesse, v. l.) *in gravibus lamentationibus,* 120, 7.

**cwīþung,** e ; *f. Lamentation, complaint :*—Quiðungum *questibus,* Wrt. Voc. ii. 76, 19.

**cwudu.** *Add :*—Cwudu *rumen,* An. Ox. 20, 3. Swīn wæs unclǣne for ðan þe hit ne ceów his cudu, Hml. S. 25, 80, 46 : Lch. iii. 120, 27. ¶ hwīt cwudu *mastich :*—Huuít quidu, huít cudu *mastice,* Txts. 78, 655. Hwīt cweodu, Wrt. Voc. ii. 55, 53. Hwit cudu *mastica,* i. 286, 33. Hwit cwudu *mastix,* 68, 8.

**cwy-.** v. cwi- : **cwyrn.** v. cweorn.

**cycel,** cs ; *m. A small cake :*—Cicel *bucellam,* Wrt. Voc. ii. 79, 31 :

11, 73. Cyclum *tortellis*, Hpt. Gl. 497, 16: An. Ox. 3859. Cielum, 2, 262: 7, 288: 8, 212. Cicelum *tortis*, 17, 40. [v. *N. E. D.* kichel.] v. cicel *in Dict.*

**cycene**, an. *Add:* cycen, e; *f.*:—Cicen *coquina* vel *culina*, Wrt. Voc. i. 57, 55. Ciacene *coquina*, Hpt. 33, 241, 63. Þæs abbodes cicene (kicene, *v. l.*), R. Ben. 85, 7. Belâdod fram þǣre kycenan (cicene *coquine*, R. Ben. I. 65, 7) þênunge, 58, 14. Ðǣre kycenan wicþênas, 59, 6. Cycenan *culinae*, An. Ox. 8, 274. Cycene *culine*, Wrt. Voc. ii. 83, 29: Hpt. Gl. 494, 56. Cicene, An. Ox. 3755. Fram cycene *de culina*, 56, 76. Tô kicenan, Hml. S. 12, 60. In þâ cycenau, Gr. D. 123, 25.

**cycen-þegnung**, e; *f. Service in the kitchen*:—Se ǣrcediácon and se prâuost môton beón âspelode fram þǣre cycenþênunge, Nap. 15.

**cycgel**, es; *m. A strong stick, a cudgel*:—Mid ðǣm kycglum (kyclum, *v.l.*) hiera worda worpian *verborum jacula reddere*, Past. 297, 1. Ic gaderode mê kigclas and stuþansceaftas, Shrn. 163, 5.

**cȳf**. *Dele* 'cȳfe, an; *f.*' *and citation from* Wrt. Voc. 83, 25, *and add*:—Cȳf *dolium*, Ælfc. Gr. Z. 316, 17. Hû seó ǣmtige kȳf (*dolium*) weard mid ele gefylled, Gr. D. 93, 26. Hig gebrôhton Iôhannem binnan þǣre cȳfe, Ælfc. T. Grn. 16, 19. Wæs geset wearm wæter on cȳfe, Hml. S. 11, 150. Cȳue *dolium* (acc.), An. Ox. 2, 236. Hêt hê þ man ealle þâ kȳfa (bydenu, *v. l.* dolia) gegearwode, Gr. D. 57, 28. Man sceal habban .. cȳfa, Angl. ix. 264, 11. [v. *N. E. D.* keeve.]

**cȳfel** (cȳfel?), es; *m. A tub*:—vi. bidenfate and .ii. cuflas and þrȳ trogas, C. D. B. iii. 367, 39. Man sceal habban cyflas, Angl. ix. 264, 11. [v. *N. E. D.* cowl. *O. H. Ger.* milich-chubili: *Ger.* kübel.]

**cȳfes**. v. cifes: **cylcende** (bylcende? cf. bealcan, bealcettan) *ructans*, An. Ox. 20, 2: cȳle. *l.* cyle. v. cile.

**cylen**. *Add:*—Cyline, heorðe *fornacula*, Wrt. Voc. ii. 109, 7. Cylene, heorþe, 35, 77: *culine*, 18, 46. On odene cylne macian, Angl. ix. 262, 2. [*From Lat.* culina.]

**cylenisc**. *Dele:* cylew. *For* Cot. 99 *substitute* Wrt. Voc. ii. 42, 13: cyle-wearte. v.cile-wearte: cyle-wyrt. *Dele:* cyline heorþ. *Dele.*

**cyll**. *Add:*—Kylle *ascopa*, Wrt. Voc. ii. 101, 14. Cylle *culleus*, Germ. 399, 458. Hê teáh ford ðâ cyllan (cillan, *v.l.*) *utrem protulit*, Gr. D. 250, 18. Wit geworhton þâ hȳde tô twâm kyllum . . . and wit dydon þæs flǣsces hwylcnehwugu dǣl in þâ kylla . . . þâ bleówan wit þâ kylla and âstigon þǣron, Hml. A. 205, 342–348. [*From Lat.* culeus, culleus.] v. cille, *and next word.*

**Cyllenisc**; *adj. Of Cyllene*:—Cillinescum *cyllineae*, Wrt. Voc. ii. 22, 19.

**cyll-fylling**, e; *f. The filling of a bottle* (cyll):—Hî þone Godes wer gesâwon him befeólan mid þǣre cyllfyllinge (þâre cillan fylling, *v. l.*) *virum Dei ad implendum utrem sibi insistere viderent*, Gr. D. 250, 27.

**cymbala**. v. cimbala.

**cyme**. *Add:*—Tâcun þînes cymes *signum adventus tui*, Mt. R. 24, 3. [*Goth.* kwums: *O. Sax.* kumi: *O. Frs.* keme: *O. H. Ger.* quumi.] v. hâm-cyme.

**cyme**; *adj. l.* cȳme, *and add:* [cf. *O. H. Ger.* chúmo *vix*; chûmig *infirmus.*] v. cȳm-ness.

**cymen**. *Add:*—Cymin *cinnamomum, resina*, Txts. 51, 475. Cymen *cinnamomum*, Wrt. Voc. i. 67, 48. Cimen *ciminum*, 79, 38.

**cȳm-lîc, -lîce.** *l.* cȳm-lic, -lîce.

**cȳm-ness**, e; *f. Fastidiousness, daintiness*:—Cȳmnis (ciisnis, Ep., ciinis, Erf.) *fastidium*, Txts. 61, 829.

**cyn.** I. *Add:*—Cyn *propago*, Wrt. Voc. ii. 67, 33. Gê sint âcoren kynn (*genus*), Past. 85, 18. Cinnes *stirpis*, An. Ox. 4587. Cynnes *gentis*, 26, 32. On mæniges cynnes misdǣdan, Ll. Th. i. 322, 20. Mid ælces cynnes gimmum geglenged, Bt. 28; F. 100, 27. Ælces cynnes gimcyn, 32, 3; F. 118, 18. Nânes cynnes hæftnung, Hml. Th. ii. 358, 20. Mid his âgnum cynne and mid his âgnum burhwarum, Bt. 5; F. 10, 11. Cyn *sobolem*, An. Ox. 4517. Hwæt þâ cynn (*the peoples of Sodom and Gomorrah*) dydon, Gen. 1944. Feorheáceno cynn, þâ þe flôd wecced, 204. On manegra cynna hrǣglum, Bt. 37, 1; F. 186, 3. I a. (*noble*) *family*(?):—Swâ mǣre (mǣres?) cynnes menn (cf. on ðissere byrig yldest getealde, 151) swâ swâ hî wǣron, Hml. S. 23, 272. v. æppel-, Angel-, biscep-, bôc-, crôg-, cyning-, ealdhlâford-, eall-, earn-, eft-, hafoc-, hreód-, môdor-, riht-fædren-, riht-mêdren-, sibb-, sprǣc-, stân-, tynder-, wîf-, wilde-, wîn-, wudu-cyn. II. *in line 6 for* cynd *read* cynn. v. Ælfc. Gr. Z. 18, 14. III. *Add:* v. hê-cyn.

**cyn**; *adj. Add:* *and subst.*:—Suâ is cynn ðæt sió giémen sié ðâm beboden *dignum est, ut cura ei imponatur*, Past. 43, 24: 45, 2, 5: 185, 6. Suâ hit is cynn ðætte . . . , 195, 20. Hit is cynn (*justum est*) ðæt wê ðæs gemǣnelîce brûcen, 337, 3. Hit is cyn ðæt wê ûre scomigen *debemus erubescere*, 407, 15. Þonne is hit cyn þ gê þone mid eádmêdum gesêcen, Ll. Th. ii. 410, 25. ¶ *as substantive, a worthy, proper proceeding*:—Is hit swȳde micel cyn þ gehwylc crîsten man þone dæg weordige, Ll. Th. ii. 420, 31. Nis hit nân cyn þ mon þ for nâuht telle, Bt. 24, 4; F. 86, 19. Eóde ford cwên Hróðgâres cynna gemyndig, grêtte guman, B. 613. Hê grêtan eóde cuman cûðlîce, cynna gemunde riht and gerisno, Gen. 2431. Þû mîn costadest cynnum (*properly*), Ps. Th. 138, 1.

**cynce** (-a P), an; *f.* (*m.* ?) *A small bundle, bunch* (?):—Genim dweorge dwostlan and gyþrifan kyncean (*a bunch of cockle*), Lch. ii. 58, 22. [Kynch *fa*(s)*ciculus*, Wrt. Voc. i. 229, 49. Halliwell gives *kinch*=a small quantity as a Lincolnshire word.]

**cynd**. *Substitute:* cynd, e; *f.*: es; *n.* I. *nature*:—Nis nân gesceaft ðe hê tiohhige þ hió scyle winnan wiþ hire Scippendes willan, gif hió hire cynd (gecynd *v. l.*) healdan wile *nihil est quod naturam servans Deo contraire conetur*, Bt. 35, 4; F. 160, 23. Cniht weóx and þâg, swâ him cynde wǣron ǣdele from yldrum (*he inherited noble natural qualities from his parents*), Gen. 2771. v. môdor-cynd. II. *a kind; genus*:—Sǣgdon ûs þâ bîgengean þæt wê ûs warnigan scoldon wid þâ missen[l]ice cynd nǣdrena and hrifra wilðeóra *praedixerant nobis incolae ne serpentes et rapida ferarum genera incideremus*, Angl. iv. 144, 113. v. ge-cynd.

**cynde**; *adj. Dele, and see preceding word:* cynd-lic. v. cyn-lic: cȳne *a chink*. v. cine (-u).

**cyne**(?); *adj. Royal*:—Cyne sâcerdlic (cynesâcerdlic?) *regale sacerdotium*, Rtl. 25, 31. Menn cyni (=cynig(e)?; cyninge, R. Cf. cynemann) *homini regi*, Mt. L. 18, 23.

**cyne-**. *Add:* Occurs frequently in proper names. [*O. H. Ger.* chuni-.]

**cyne-bænd**. *For* 'Som. Ben. Lye' *substitute*:—His þegnas geworhton þyrnene beáh for cynebænd, Nap. 15.

**cyne-bearn**. *Add:* *a prince*:—Ðǣr sitte sum cynebearn, Sal. K. p. 85, 38: Lch. iii. 166, 28. Siððan rîxadon West-Seaxna cynebarn (-beam, *v. l.*) of þâm dæge, Chr. 519; P. 17, 3. Hêr Oswiu ofslôh Penda and .xxx. cynebearna (*duces regii xxx interfecti*, Bd. 3, 24) mid him, 654; P. 29, 4. Tâcnað þ cynebearna (cyme-, MS.) cwealm, Lch. iii. 180, 10. [*Laym.* kine-be(a)rn: *O. E. Hom.* kine-bern (cune-).]

**Cynebellingas**; *pl. m. The settlers at Kimble*:—Innan Cynebellinga gemǣre, C. D. B. ii. 259, 10. Cf. *the proper name* Cynebill, Bd. 3, 23.

**cyne-boren**. *Add:*—Sum cyneboren mǣden, Hml. S. 2, 326. Þ kyneborene mǣden, 351. Hê ût âflȳmde twêgen cyneborene mæn (cyningas, *v.l.*), Chr. 944; P. 111, 6. [*Laym.* kine-boren.]

**cyne-botl.** *Add:*—Þæt hî on Rômânisce wîsan ârǣre his cynebotl, Hml. S. 36, 39.

**cyne-cyn.** *Add:*—Fram þan Wôdne âwôc eall ûre cynecynn, and Sûðanhymbra eác, Chr. 449; P. 13, 25. Norþanhymbra cynecyn (-kyn, *v.l.*), 547; P. 16, 17. Ælcne þâra þe hió geácsian myhte þæt kynekynnes wæs *omnes regie arcessitos*, Ors. 1, 2; S. 30, 30. Næs hê ædelboren, ne him nâht tô þâm cynecynne ne gebyrode, Hml. Th. i. 80, 33. Hî gecuron heora kynecinn aa on þâ wîfhealfa, Chr. p. 3, 16. Hire fæder wæs Eádward æþeling, Eádmundes sunu kynges, Eádmund Æþelreding . . . and swâ ford on þ cynecynn, 1067; P. 202, 21. v. riht-cynecynn, *and cf.* cyning-cyn.

**cyne-dôm.** *Substitute:* I. *a royal ordinance* or *law*:—Þte ryhte ǣw and ryhte cynedômas þurh ûre folc gefæstnode wǣron, þte nǣnig ealdormonua . . . wǣre âwendende þâs ûre dômas, Ll. Th. i. 102, 9. II. *supreme authority, especially royal authority, royalty, empire*:—Cynidôm, cynedoom *respublica*, Txts. 92, 859. Cynedôm *sceptrum*, Wrt. Voc. i. 42, 7. Stande in crîstendôm and cynedôm on þeóde, Ll. Th. ii. 302, 8: Wlfst. 267, 24. Cynedômes *potestatis*, i. *imperii*, An. Ox. 3943. Hê wæs mid ungemete girnende þæs cynedômes *dominationis hausti cupiditatem*, Ors. 4, 5; S. 166, 25. Hê mid gôdum weorcum geglengde his kynedôm and his kynedômes geweold feówertig geára, Ælfc. T. Grn. 7, 11: Ps. C. 149. Kynedôme *regio*, An. Ox. 43, 3. Claudius Orcadas ðâ eáland geþeódde tô Rômwara cynedôme (cf. rîce, 15, 7) (*Romano imperio*), Bd. 1, 3; Sch. 14, 5: Chr. 47; P. 6, 24. Eardwulf fêng tô Norþanhymbran cinedôme (rîce, *v.l.*), 795; P. 57, 18. Wê under ânum cynedôme ǣnne crîstendôm healdan willað, Ll. Th. i. 304, 8. Crîstendôm and cynedôm healdan and wealdan, 350, 3: Ælfc. T. Grn. 8, 6. Þone cynedôm ciósan *to accept the crown*, B. 2376. Cynedômas *fasces*, i. *honores, dignitates*, Wrt. Voc. ii. 146, 51: 35, 11. Cynedômum *sceptris*, An. Ox. 12, 14. III. *noble estate, royal rank* or *dignity*:—Apollonius forlêt his þone wurdfullan cynedôm (cf. Apollonius wæs ealdorman on Tiro, 3, 24), and mangeres naman genam, Ap. Th. 10, 7. III a. *the fine paid for the offence to the royal dignity where a king is slain*:—Nordleóda cynges gild is .xxx. þûsend þrymsa. fîftêne þûsend þrymsa bið þæs wergildes, .xv. þûsend þæs cynedômes. Se wer gebirað mâgum, and seó cynebôt þâm leódum, Ll. Th. i. 186, 2–5. For þâm cynedôme (*for the offence done to the royal dignity*) gebirað ôðer swilc tô bôte on cynegilde, 190, 7. IV. *royal property* v. cyne-lic:—Cynedômes *fisci* (cf. *fiscus* kyninga seód, 39, 80), Wrt. Voc. ii. 37, 60. [v. *N. E. D.* kin-dom.]

**cyne-gerela.** *Add:*—Ðâ âlêde ic (*Alexander*) mînne kynegyrylar *posi*⊃ *meo cultu*, Angl. iv. 155, 410. Cf. cyning-gierela.

**cyne-gild.** *Substitute: The fine paid for slaying a king.* It consisted of two parts, the *wergild*, which belonged to the kindred (*mâgas*) and the *cyne-bôt*, of like amount, which belonged to the people (*leóde*):—For þâm cynedôme gebirað ôðer swilc tô bôte on cynegilde (cf. cynegild, 180, 2), Ll. Th. i. 190, 8. [Cf. the entry in the Chronicle under

the year 694, which mentions the payment made to Ine by the men of Kent in atonement for the burning of MuL]

**cyne-gird.** *Take here exs. under* cyne-gyrd *in Dict., and add:*—Swíðe ryht is seó cynegyrd þínes ríces *virga recta est virga regni tui,* Ps. Th. 44, 8. Hé bícnode hire tó mid his cynegyrde *extendit contra eam virgam auream,* Hml. A. 97, 181. [*Orm.* kineȝerrde.]

**cyne-gold.** *Add:*—Kynegold mid deórwyrþum gimmum ástæned *coronam de lapide pretioso,* Ps. Th. 20, 3.

**cyne-hád.** *In first passage for* '[MS. cyneháde]' *read*] cynelica hád, *v. l.*] *and add:*—Hé nolde beón cyning . . . Ðá weorðmynde cynehádes (kyne-, *v. l.*) hé fleáh *rex fieri noluit; . . . oblatam gloriam culminis fugit,* Past. 33, 20.

**cyne-helm.** *Add:* I. *a crown:*—Cynehelme *palma,* i. *corona,* An. Ox. 3093. Þ Vashti cóme tó him mid hire cynehelme, swá swá heora seodu wæs þ seó cwén werode cynehelm on heáfode, Hml. A. 93, 37. Þriwa hé bær his cynehelm ælce geáre, Chr. 1086; P. 219, 32. Ðone écean cynehelm underfón, Hml. S. 23, 209. Cinehelm *coronam,* R. Ben. I. 31, 14. II. *the crown, royal power:*—Ealle ðá gyltes ðá belimpeð tó míne kinehelme (*ad regiam coronam meam*), C. D. iv. 209, 16. [*Laym.* kine-helm. Cf. *O. H. Ger.* chuninc-helm *diadema.*]

**cynehelmian;** *p.* ode *To crown:*—Se geleáfa cynehelmode (*coronat*) þá mægnu, Prud. 10 a.

**cyne-hláford.** *Add:*—Þ him nán leófre bláford nære þonne heora cynehláuord, Chr. 1014; P. 145, 3 note. Se cyning . . . cwæð þ hé sylf wolde geseón ðá stówe. . . . Férde Florus tó ðám mynstre and his kynehláford cóm swá swá hí cwædon, Hml. S. 6, 230. God hine áwende of Godes dreáme sé ðe ðis áwende, bútan hit mín áne cynehláford sý, C.D. vi. 149, 31. Ærest his cynehláforde ænne beáh . . . and ðære hlædigan ænne beáh, ii. 380, 25. Him láð nære þ hí ongeán heora cynehláford standan sceoldan, Chr. 1048; P. 174, 16. Se Pontisca Pilatus grét his cynehláford Claudium, Nic. 19, 36. [*Laym.* kine-louerd.]

**cyne-hof,** es; *n. A royal residence, palace:*—Cynehof *regiam, palatium,* Germ. 391, 5.

**cyne-lic.** *Add:*—Cynelic toll *fiscale tributum,* mid cynelicere lage *fiscali jure* (cf. cyne-dóm, IV.), An. Ox. 1454: 4844. Þes weg is kyne´ic (*but v.* cyn-lic) *this is the king's highway,* Angl. viii. 322, 44. Gé sint kynelices preósthádes *vos regale sacerdotium,* Past. 85, 19. Cynelicere *tyrannicae* (*potestatis*), An. Ox. 673. Cynelice gesettnesse *augusto* (i. *regali*) *textu,* 3447. Wið cynelice ádle, Lch. i. 370, 5. Þá cynelican *puplica* (*strata*), Wrt. Voc. ii. 96, 68. Tó cynelicon geseton *ad palatinas* (i. *regales*) *zetas,* An. Ox. 2996. [*Laym.* kine-lich.]

**cynelíce.** *Add:*—Hé wel cynelíce gefeaht *he fought right royally,* Ors. 5, 13; S. 244, 25. Se cyng him cynelíce gifode, Chr. 994; P. 129, 19.

**cynelic-nys.** *Substitute:*—*Royalty, kingliness, royal excellence:*—Fore his cynelicnesse ge módes ge onsýnes and his geearnuncge wyrþnesse *ob regiam ejus et animi et vultus et meritorum dignitatem,* Bd. 3, 14; Sch. 256, 9.

**cyne-mann,** es; *m. A royal person, a king:*—Gelíc geworden wæs ríc heofnæ cynemenn (cyninge, R. *homini regi*), Mt. L. 22, 2.

**cyne-ren.** *v.* cyn-ren.

**cyne-ríce.** *Add: royal power or authority:*—Óswoldes cyneríce weard gerýmed swá þ feówer þeóda hine underféngon tó hláforde, Hml. S. 26, 104. Næs nán eorðlic cyninceg ofer hí cyneríce underféncg, 18, 7. [Laws for a haill country and kinrick, Rob Roy i. 216. *v. N. E. D.* kin-rick. *O. H. Ger.* chuni-ríchi *regnum, res publica.*] Cf. cyning-ríce.

**cyne-riht,** es; *n. A royal right, right belonging to the crown:*—Myrce gecuran Eádgár tó cynge, and him anweald gesealden ealra cyne-rihta, Cht. E. 202, 18.

**cyne-sácerdlic** *of a royal priest. v.* cyne.

**cyne-scipe.** *Dele* 'honour,' *and add: royal dignity:*—Feala óðra cásera ríxodon on heora cynescipes wuldre and on heora anwealdes myrhþe, Hml. S. 23, 350. Hí hine on cwearterne bescufon tó sceame his kynescipe, 18, 440. For his micclan cynescipe, Hml. A. 101, 300. Heó hiræ cinehláford bitt for cynescypæ þæt heó móte beón hyre cwydes wyrðe, Cht. Th. 552, 30. Ic (Cnut) beóde þ hý fylstan þám biscopum tó Godes gerihtum and tó mínum kynescype . . . Gif hwá swá dyrstig sý . . . þ ongeán Godes lage gá and ongeán mínne cynescype, Cht. E. 230, 16–21. ¶ *as a form of address, majesty, royal highness:*—Stópon in tó ðám cásere ðá yldestan . . . and þus spræcon : 'Ealra manna hláford, wé biddað þínne cynescipe þ þú ne beó dreórig . . . Gyf ðín cynescipe swá cwyð, hit geworden bið sóna þ . . ., Hml. S. 23, 281–292. Ic gréte þé, leóf, and ic bidde þínne þrymfullan cynescype, 794.

**cyne-setl.** *Add:*—Cynesetl *solium,* Kent. Gl. 557. Ne cóm hé (*Christ*) tó ðý þæt hé wære on mærlicum cynesetle áhafen, Hml. Th. i. 82, 24. Seó sáwul is þæs líchoman hlæfdige, and heó gewissað þá fíf andgitu swá swá of cynesætle, Hml. S. 1, 196. [He set o kineseotle, Kath. 45.]

**cyne-stól.** *Add:* I. *a throne:*—Hé eall mid reádum golde his

cynestól geworhte, H. R. 101, 2. II. *a seat of government, capital:*—Hierusalem, Iudéa cynestól, Hml. Th. ii. 300, 26. Babilon ðe ic self átimbrede tó kynestóle *Babilon quam ego aedificavi in domum regni,* Past. 39, 17. [*Laym.* kine-stol *a throne.* Cf. *O. Sax.* kuning-stól: *O. H. Ger.* chuning-stuol.]

**cyne-strǽt.** *Substitute: The king's highway, a high road:*—Cyne-strǽte *puplicum,* Wrt. Voc. ii. 67, 16.

**cyne-þrym.** *Add:* I. *royal power:*—Ðú áðenes bogan ðínne ofer cyneðrym (*super sceptra*), Ps. Srt. ii. p. 190, 5. II. *royal glory, great glory:*—Eádweard kingc wunode þráge on kyneþrymme (kine-, *v. l.*), Chr. 1065; P. 192, 30. Sancta Hyldan gást wæs gelæded on heofenes cyneþrym, Mart. H. 206, 32.

**cyneþrym-lic;** *adj. Very glorious:*—Swíðe cyneþrymlica tácen him beforan samod síðedon, Nap. 15.

**cyne-wáden** (?); *adj. Purple:*—Hyre cinewaðenan (-wád-?) cyrtel, Cht. Th. 538, 10. [Cf. *O. H. Ger.* weitín *purpureus.*]

**cyne-wirþe;** *adj. Royal, noble:*—Kynewyrðe ræd hyt ys geþúht and trumlic, Angl. viii. 308, 33. [His kineworþe (kineliche, 1st MS.) lond, Laym. 11026. Of kinewurðe cunne, al of kingen icume, 20768. Swiþe kinewurðe (worþlich, 2nd MS.) hom, 19455. Kineworþe king, C. L. 14. Wið kinewurðe ȝeoues ȝelden hehliche *altis muneribus donare,* Kath. 568.]

**cyne-wise.** *Substitute for translation of first passage* 'nihil omnino in re militari ausus est,' *and add:*—Sum eorðlic æ is in þære Rómániscan cynewísan (cynne-, *v. l.*) *quaedam terrena lex in Romana republica,* Bd. 1, 27; Sch. 68, 24. Ðeós cwén on þám lande manege nytwyrðe dǽda gefremede Gode tó lofe, and eác on þá kynewísan wel geþéh (*she proved too of great advantage to the state*), Chr. 1067; P. 202, 17.

**cyne-wiþþe.** *Substitute for references:*—Cynewiððan, cyniuuithan *ridimiculae,* Txts. 93, 1743. Wrædas, cynewiþþan *redimicula* (*habent mitrae*), An. Ox. 5241 : Wrt. Voc. ii. 87, 44. Cynewiððan, Hpt. 33, 239, 16.

**cyning.** *Add:* , cynig (-eg):—Cynig (kining, R.) *rex,* Mt. L. 2, 2. Cynig (king, R.), 3. Ðone cining *regem* . . . cinig *rex,* 1, 6. Salomones móder ðæs cyniges, 1, 6, margin. Cyningces *regnatoris,* An. Ox. 4472. Ðæs cyninges tácen is þæt þú wende þíne hande ádúne, and besóh þín heófod ufeweard eallum fingrum on cynehelmes tácne. Cyninges wífes tácen is þæt þú strece onbútan heófod, and sete syððan þíne hand bufon þín heófod, Tech. ii. 128, 23–27. Ne mæg nán mau hine sylfne tó cynge gedón, ac þæt folc hæfð cyre tó ceósenne þone tó cyninge þe him sylfum lícað; ac siþþan hé tó cyninge gehálgod bið, þonne hæfð hé anweald ofer þæt folc, Hml. Th. i. 212, 6–9. Tó cynige *ad regem,* Mk. L. R. 6, 25. Cynegas (-ingas, *v. l.*) hine wurðodon, Hml. S. 25, 729. *v.* æfter-, eást-, under-cyning, and cyneg *in* Dict.

**cyning-ǽþe;** *adj. Entitled to make a king's thane's oath* (?) :—Sé þe onsacan wille þæs sleges mid áðe, þonne sceal bión on þære hyndenne án kyningǽðe (-æðe, *v. l.*) (cf. ládige hé hine mid .xi. his gelícena and mid ánum cyninges þægne, 154, 9), Ll. Th. i. 136, 12. [For -æþe cf. *Goth.* uf-aiþjai ; *pt. Or* cyning-ǽþe *might be a neuter noun* (ja-stem): *the old Latin version has* 'unum regium jusjurandum.']

**cyning-cyn.** *Add:*—Of Francena cyningcynne *de gente Francorum regia,* Bd. 1, 25; Sch. 53, 8.

**cyning-dóm.** *Dele* 'a kingdom,' *substitute* 'kingship,' 'sovereignty' *for* 'thy, the kingdom' *in extracts, and add:* [*O. Sax.* kuning-dóm: *Icel.* konung-dómr.]

**cyninge,** an; *f. A queen:*—Æfter þære bysne þære hálgan Godes cyningan, Bl. H. 13, 1.

**cyninges wyrt.** *Add:*—Cyninges wyrt *samsuhthon,* Wrt. Voc. i. 69, 7. Cinges wyrt *samsuchon,* Lch. iii. 305, col. 1.

**cyning-gereord(e).** *Substitute:*—Cyninggereordo *fercula,* Wrt. Voc. ii. 40, 4.

**cyning-gierela.** *Substitute: Royal apparel:*—Tenia, *honore vel* cyninggierela, Wrt. Voc. ii. 89, 68. Cf. cyne-gerela.

**cyning-ríce,** es; *n. A kingdom:*—For ælre ðere kynga sáwle ðe æfter mé ðyses kynyngríches wældeð, C. D. iv. 229, 26. [*v. N. E. D.* king-rick. *O. H. Ger.* chuning-ríchi *sceptrum, res publica : Icel.* konung-ríki.] Cf. cyne-ríce.

**cyn-lic** *convenient. Add:*—Þ ne beó behýdd þæs cynlica weg, Angl. viii. 302, 40 (cf. 322, 44). Suá cenlic (cendlic, Ep. Erf) *percommode,* Txts. 85, 1534. *v.* un-cynlic, *and* cine-lic *in* Dict.

**cynlíce.** *Add:*—Forlǽtan þá gebróðru þe hé ǽr cynlíce underféng *fratres deserere quos semel suscepit,* Gr. D. 108, 29.

**cynnestre, cynning.** *v.* cennestre, cenning.

**cynnig;** *adj. Of good family, noble :*—Of cynnigum *generosis* (*natalibus*), An. Ox. 7, 299: 8, 230. Cynningum, æþelum, 4149. Cynnegum, Angl. xiii. 36, 240. [All are glosses on Ald. 58, 23.]

**cynn-recceniss.** *Add:*—Crístes cynnreccenise (*generatio*) suǽ wæs, Mt. L. 1, 18. Bóc cynnreccenisse *liber generationis,* p. 9, 13.

**cyn-recen.** *Dele.*

**cyn-ren.** *Add:* I. *a family, stock, race :*—Mid cynrene, mǽgþe

*prosapia*, An. Ox. 1297 : 1664. Hē ne gecȳst nū be nānum cynrene, ac of ǽlcere mǽgðe, Hml. A. 17, 85. Of mōdignesse cynrene, R. Ben. 22, 14. Wé gesāwon Enachis cynryn (*stirpem*), Num. 13, 29. Bisceophād sceolde of manegan cynrynan āspringan, Wlfst. 176, 12.    II. *progeny* :—Tō kenninge ðæs cynrenes *ad usum generis*, Past. 97, 10. Eówre wíto and eówres cinrenes (*seminis tui*) wíto, Deut. 28, 59.    III. *a nation* :—Dryhten rīnað ofer eall cynrynu (*gentes*), Ps. Th. 46, 8.    IV. *a kind, species* :—Synderlicere cynrene *singulari* (*tincturae*) *genere*, An. Ox. 1057. Syx synt muneca cynerena, R. Ben. 134, 3. Ðysse wyrte syndon twā cynrenu, Lch. i. 298, 5. Twā cynnryno unrót-nesse, Nap. 15. Ðū fyldest þās eorþan mid mistlicum cynrenum nētena, Bt. 33, 4 ; F. 132, 26. v. fore-, wyrt-cynren.

**cyn-resu** *a generation* :—In cynreswu *in generationi*, Mt. p. 12, 10. Cynnresuu *generationum*, 13, 14. Cf. cneó-res.

**cyp** *a beam*. v. cipp.

**cȳp** *a tub*. For second passage substitute :—Byden, cȳpe *dolium* (*in* Hpt. Gl. 492, 32 *the same form occurs, but in another gloss of the same passage the form is* cȳue, An. Ox. 2, 236), An. Ox. 3657, *where see note*.

**cȳp(e)-, cȳpa, I.** v. cīp(e)-, cīpa.

**cȳpa, II.** *Substitute* : cȳpe, an ; *f. A basket* :—Cȳpan *corbes*, An. Ox. 18, 3. Þǽr tō lāfe wǽron XII cȳpan fulle, 3657 note : Lk. 9, 17 (*in Dict.*). [v. *N. E. D.* kipe.]

**cyp^en.** *Add* : , cypren :—Cypren *cyprinus*, Wrt. Voc. ii. 137, 72. Cyperene *æreum*, Ps. Spl. T. 17, 36.

**cyper-sealf**, e ; *f. Henna-ointment* :—Cipersealf *ciprum*, Wrt. Voc. ii. 131, 47. [Cf. *N. E. D.* cypre.]

**cypresse.** *Add* : Cf. : þā wǽron wunderlíce fægere, and cypressus styde hié ūtan wreþedon *nitebant testudinibus cupressinis*, Nar. 5, 7. [*From Latin.*]

**cyre-.** v. ciric- : cyrc-brǽce. v. ciric-brǽc.

**cyre.** *Add* : I. *choice, &c.* :—Cyri (*printed* cyni, Wrt. Voc. ii. 106, 27) *delectum vel electio*, Txts. 57, 664. Cyre *optio*, Germ. 396, 217. Freólicum sylflíces willan cyre (*munus quod*) *libero spontaneae voluntatis arbitrio* (*offertur*), An. Ox. 1290. Þæt folc hæfð cyre tō ceósenne þone tō cyninge þe him sylfum lícað, Hml. Th. i. 212, 7.    II. *free will in a theological sense* :—Hwī wolde se Scyppend þone mannan tō his āgenum cyre lǽtan *cur homo factus est in liberum arbitrium?*, Angl. vii. 24, 232 : An. Ox. 1315 : 2682. Hē ūs forgeaf āgenne cyre. Hē sealde swíðe fæste gife . . . þ is seó gifu, þ se man mōt dón þ hē wile, Hml. S. 17, 250. Gehwilc man hæfð āgenne cyre, ǽr ðām ðe hē syngige, hweðer hē wille fílian deófles willan oððe wiðsacan, Hml. Th. i. 212, 11. [*Laym.* cure : *Gen. and Ex.* kire. Cf. *O. H. Ger.* churi ; *f. : Icel.* kør ; *n.*]

**cyre-líf.** *For* ' A choice . . . eligunt ' *substitute* : I. *the condition of life which allows a person to choose his lord, the state of dependence on a lord whom a person has chosen* :—Gehicgon hig eác þ hig gehealdon heora clǽnnysse, oððe beón gefērlǽhte þǽre gefæstnuncge ðæs gesynscipes, būtan þām canonican þe on cyrelífe sittað (*those who are dependents of the bishop* ; exceptis his canonicis qui victu et vestitu potiantur), Nap. 15,    II. *a person in such a condition*.

**cyrf.** *Substitute* : cyrf, es ; *m.* I. *a cutting. act of cutting* :—Notige se abbod cyrfes and mid īsene þone uncoðan āceorfe *abba utatur ferro abscisionis*, R. Ben. 52, 19. ' Ǽlc treów ðe ne wyrcð gódne wæstm bið forcirfen.' . . . þe ðisum cyrfe sprǽc se Hǽlend, Hml. Th. ii. 406, 33. v. of-, ymb-cyrf.    II. *what is cut off* :—Tōdāl ł cyrf *comma*, An. Ox. 18 b, 9. v. æ-cyrf *in Dict., where read* ǽ-cyrf, es ; *m.* [v. *N. E. D.* kerf.]

**cyrfel.** *In* l. 2 *read* sagul *for* stigul : cyric-. v. ciric- : cyric-ǽwe. v. ciric-ǽ(w) : cyric-sócn. v. ciric-sócn : cyrin. v. cirn : cyrlic. v. cirlic : cyrn. v. cirn.

**cyrnel.** *Add* : [*and* cimel ? cf. *O. H. Ger.* cherno *nucleus, granum : Icel.* kjarni.] I. *a kernel* of a nut, *&c.* :—Hnutu *avilina, cynel nuclium*, Wrt. Voc. i. 285, 26. Cyrnel *nucleus*, cyrnlas *nucli*, ii. 60, 26, 25. Cirnlas *nucli*, 115, 6.    II. *a kernel* in the neck, *a tonsil ; a glandular swelling* :—Cirnel *glandula*, Wrt. Voc. ii. 109, 80 : 41, 1. Cyrnel *tolia*, i. 289, 62. Cyrnla *toles* (cf. grynlas *toles*, 64, 60), 282, 80.

**-cyrnod (-ad), -cyrnlod (-ad).** v. ge-cyrnod, -cyrnlod.

**cyrographum** *a writ* :—Mid his ūpstige is ādȳlegod þæt cyrographum ūre geniðerunge, Hml. Th. i. 300, 5.

**cyrps, cyrpsian, cyrr, cyrran.** v. cirps, cirpsian, cirr, cirran.

**cyrriol, kyrriol** *the Kyrie Eleison* :—Þā munecas þǽre tíde lof mid kyrriole and engla lofsange gewurðiað (cf. sȳ gecweden lofsang of ðām godspelle, þæt is ' Magnificat,' hālsung, þæt is ' Kyrrieleison,' R. Ben. 41, 13), Angl. viii. 320, 6. [v. *N. E. D.* kyriel[le].]

**cyrse** *cherry*. v. cirse : cȳrstel-mǽl. v. crīstel-mǽl : -cyrtan. v. ge-cyrtan.

**cyrten** (?) *decoration, ornament* :—Cyrten *crustus* (cf. *crustu*, i. *ornatu* frætwunge, 25, 8 : *crustu* glenge, An. Ox. 7, 370 : 8, 371), Wrt. Voc. ii. 137, 24. v. next word.

**cyrten ;** *adj. Add* : I. *comely in person* :—Se seofoða heáfodleahter is gehāten īdel wuldor . . . þonne se man gewilnað þæt hē sȳ cyrten, and nele foresceáwian þæt ūre líchaman beóð āwende tō duste, Hml. Th. ii. 220, 29. Heó (*Esther*) wæs on wæstme cyrten, Hml. A. 95, 99. Þā geceás man þā twēgen cnihtas, for þām þe hī wǽron cǽflice and cyrtene, Hml. S. 30, 300.    II. *as a complimentary epithet* (cf. later use of *fair*) :—Wē willað heora gerēna kyrtenum (cf. lā, ārwurðan preóstas, 330, 2 : 314, 12 : wite þū, gerāda preóst, 330, 17 : wynsume preóstas, 329, 19 : wynsume bóceras, 313, 37) preóstum gecȳðan, Angl. viii. 326, 2.

**cyrten-líce.** *Add* : *elegantly, fitly, fairly, well* :—Cyrten[líce] (*si tu te sumptuosius comas et per publicum*) *notabiliter* (*incedas*), An. Ox. 5185. Eall þ cyrte[n]líce (*subtiliter*, i. *eleganter*) wē þenceað, Scint. 140, 7. Tō þām bócerum þe beóð cyrtenlíce getȳdde, Angl. viii. 313, 33, 30. Þā þing þe beóð cyrtenlíce geset, 330, 36 : 298, 33 : 300, 23 : 306, 15 : 317, 28 : 320, 5. Þæt gē cyrtenlíce eów gewarnion and geornlíce gȳmon, 329, 19.

**cyrten-ness**, e ; *f. Beauty, elegance, comeliness* :—Cyrtenysse (cert-, Hpt. Gl. 431, 18) *uenustati*, i. *ornamenti*, An. Ox. 1053 : 5108 : *venustatem*, 4644.

**cyrtlan ?**—On cyrtlan geat, of cyrtlan gate, Cht. Crw. 3, 10.

**cȳse.** v. císe : cyspan. *Add* : v. ge-cyspan.

**cyssan.** *Add* :—Hió cyst *deosculatur*, Kent. Gl. 192. Ne cys þū mīne fēt, Hml. S. 5, 301. Cyssan *bassiare*, Wrt. Voc. ii. 86, 19. Ǽlc þāra manna þe óðerne swíðe lufað, hine lyst bet cyssan ðonne óðerne on bær líc, þonne þēr þǽr clāðas betweóna beóð, Shrn. 185, 31. Sylle heom eallum cyssan bóc, Ll. Th. i. 226, 25. Cyssende handa *osculans manus*, Angl. xiii. 416, 730.

**cyst.** I. *dele last two passages*.    II. *substitute for* ' *with gen. pl. . . . æstimatio*,' *an excellent, precious thing ; with gen. the best* of any-thing, *best* of its class (cf. colloquial *the pick* of), *and add* :—Gif wē þām dǽdlican þās cyste (cf. ungerīm feós, 231) geúðan, Hml. S. 3, 281. Ne hī for āwyht eorþan cyste (*the pick of earth*) þā sēlestan geseón woldon *pro nihilo habuerunt terram desiderabilem*, Ps. Th. 105, 20.    III. *add* :—Hit ne beóð nāne cysta ne nān cræft *non virtutis est donum*, Past. 347, 16. Þǽm ðe word bið in lāre and in ðǽwum and in clǽnnisse and in cystum, Mt. L. 10, 8 *note*. Beóð gesomnad on þā swīðran hond þā clǽnan folc Críste gecorene bi cystum (*by their virtues*), Cri. 1224.    III a. *liberality, bounty, munificence* :—God āsend his rēnscūras ofer ðā rihtwīsan menn and ofer ðā mānfullan for his mycclan cyste (cf. *God that giveth to all men liberally*, Jam. 1, 5), Hml. S. 11, 334. Cyste *munificentiam*, Wrt. Voc. ii. 75, 57 : 56, 61. Ðā uncystgan cysta man lǽre *tenacibus infundatur tribuendi largitas*, Past. 453, 27. Hē weorðeð eádig, sē þe hine God cystum geceóseþ, Ps. Th. 64, 4.    III b. = (?) stæf-cyst :—Stæfcræftes, cyste (cyste, stæfcræftas, Hpt. Gl. 477, 49) *litteraturae*, An. Ox. 3031.    IV. *a troop*. v. cist *in Dict*. v. stæf-, unriht-cyst.

**cyst ;** *adj.* Dele, *and see* cyst, II : cystel, cysten. v. cistel, cisten : cyste-líce. v. cystig-líce.

**cystig.** *Add* :—*Devotus*, i. *largus, honorabilis* cystig *voluntarius*, Wrt. Voc. ii. 139, 48. Cystig *devota*, 106, 33. Ōswold weard swíðe ælmesgeorn and eádmód on þeáwum and on eallum þingum cystig (cf. *Osuald pauperibus et peregrinis semper humilis, benignus et largus fuit*, Bd. 3, 6), Hml. S. 26, 84. Nā cystig *non prodigus*, R. Ben. l. 61, 6. Cystigre sylene *prodiga liberalitate*, Hpt. Gl. 517, 35. Cystigan *muni-fica*, Wrt. Voc. ii. 114, 29. Hī fēdað yfle gliigmenn and beóð tō unge-metlíce kystige *effusis largitatibus nutriunt histriones*, Past. 327, 7. Swā hē ðā cystgan on merringe ne gebringe *ut prodigis effusionis frena minime laxentur*, 453, 27. [*O. H. Ger.* kustig *bonus*.]

**cystig-líce** (cyste-) ; *adv. Liberally* :—Cystiglícor *largius*, Hy. S. 29, 21. v. cyste-líce *in Dict*.

**cystig-ness.** *Add* : I. *liberality* :—Largitas, þ is cystignyss on Englisc, Hml. S. 16, 326. Cystinesse *liberalitatis*, An. Ox. 2576 : *munificentiae*, 3833. Þ wyrð hē āgeaf tō ðāre ceastre bóte. Ðæt folc weard fagen his cystignissa, Ap. Th. 10, 10. Sē ðe him for Godes lufon bigwiste foresceáwað, þonne hæfð hē mēde his cystignysse æt Gode, Hml. Th. i. 334, 14. Cystignesse *liberalitati*, Wrt. Voc. ii. 50, 21.    II. *abundance* :—Hē metta mid cystignysse weald *aescarum largitate feruescit*, Scint. 56, 2.

**cyst-ness (?)** *munificence* :—Cystnysse (cysti-, An. Ox. 1183) *munifi-centiam*, Hpt. Gl. 434, 50.

**cȳta.** *Add* :—Cȳta *buteo*, Wrt. Voc. ii. 11, 35 : *butium*, 126, 81.

**cyte, cote.** *l.* cīte, *q. v.* : cytel. v. citel : cytere. v. citere : cȳp. v. cȳþþu.

**cȳþan.** *Add* : I. *to make known* in words, (1) *to tell* a matter, (a) *with acc.* :—Se cyng sende and kȳdde heom þ ilce, Chr. 1064 ; P. 192, 3. Nǽnig mon his geþóht openum wordum ūt ne cȳðe *nemo palam pronunciet*, Nar. 28, 30. Hit nǽnig mon ūt cȳþan ne móste, 32, 17. (b) *with clause* :—Hēr cȳþ on hū seóc man móð his fæsten ālȳsan, Ll. Th. ii. 284, 24. Þā cȳdde man intó þǽre scipfyrde þet hī man befaran mihte, Chr. 1009 ; P. 138, 20. Kȳdde, 1067 ; P. 202, 30. Hié him

cýþdon þæt hiera mǽgas him mid wǽron, 755; P. 48, 18. (c) uncertain:—Ypte and cídde ederet, Wrt. Voc. ii. 32, 5. Tó cýðenne intimandum. 112, 3. Cýþende indicans (somnium), An. Ox. 2139. Cýþendes disserentis, i. narrantis, 4364. (2) to tell about a person:—Cýðeð (priscos tantum cur patres pagina) prodat?, Wrt. Voc. ii. 90, 34. (2 a) to tell about (be, ymbe):—Cýþ him ymbe þē tell him about yourself, Hml. S. 3, 561. þám cnihte cýðan be his Scyppende, 3, 27. (3) with complementary adj. (?):—Ne cýþ ðū witod on wēn dīn; wite māran þanc ðæs ðe ðū hæbbe, ðonne ðæs ðe ðū wēne don't count your chickens before they are hatched; a bird in the hand is worth two in the bush, Prov. K. 22.　　II. to shew feeling, capacity, exercise, practise:—Cýð him mildheortnisse swā swā ic cýðde þē juxta misericordiam quam feci mihi faci es mihi, Gen. 21, 23. God cýþæ his sāule mildheortnisse, Chr. 1086; P. 221, 21. Ðū wāst þ nān mon ne mæg nǽnne cræft cýðan būtan tōlum and andweorce, Bt. 18; F. 58, 29. [v. N. E. D. kithe.] v. fore-, on-cýþan.

cýþere. Add:—Swilce ðǽr gereste sum hālig cýðere. þā befrān Martinus ðæs martires naman, Hml. Th. ii. 506, 28. [O. H. Ger. chundāri nuntiator.]

-cýðig. Substitute: cýþig; adj. Known:—Cýðig cognitus, Jn. p. 6, 2. Cýðic dōn manifestum facere, Mt. l. 26, 73. Cýðigo nota, Jn. L. 15, 15. [Laym. cuði: O. H. Ger. kundig: Icel. kunnigr.] v. gecýþig; un-andcýþigness.

cýþing, e; f. A making known, telling, narration:—þā word mínre kýðinge (segene, v. l.) narrationis meae verba, Gr. D. 86, 14. [v. N. E. D. kithing.]

cýþ-lǽcan. For 'Mone B. 4286' substitute An. Ox. 4284, and add: v. ge-cýþlǽcan: cúþ-lǽcan: cýð-lic. Dele: cýþ-ness, Gr. D. 120, 7. v. cwíþ-ness.

cýþ-ness. Add: I. witness, testimony:—Seó cýðnes þǽre ealdan ǽ testamentum ueteris legis, Bd. 1, 27; Sch. 92, 21. Men feówer stānas ālegdon tó gemynde and tó cýþnesse þæs siges, Bl. H. 189, 16: 69, 18. Críst be him cýðnysse gecýðde, Hml. Th. i. 476, 31. Cýðnessum adstipulationibus, Wrt. Voc. ii. 3, 64.　　II. (the Old, New) Testament:—þǽre ǽrran cýþnyssa prioris instrumenti, An. Ox. 1676. Cýþnesse ealdre testamenti ueteris, 40, 2. Rǽde man ǽgðer ge of þǽre ealdan cýðnesse ge of þǽre nīwan, R. Ben. 33, 19: 34, 12.　　III. knowledge, acquaintance:—þæs hālignysse hlýsa hine sylfne gemǽrsode feor and wíde and hine gelǽdde tó manigra manna cýþnesse cujus sanctitatis opinio sese ad notitiam hominum longe lateque tetenderat, Gr. D. 44, 5. Hū swýðe neáh Godes cýðnysse Dei notitiae quantum propinqui, 56, 10. v. and-cýþness.

cýþþu (-o). Take here cýþ, cýþþ in Dict., and add: I. knowledge of, acquaintance with, (1) a matter, subject, &c. :—Cýð notitia, Scint. 139, 8. Cýððe notitiae, An. Ox. 4214. Cýþþe, Wrt. Voc. ii. 59, 72. Ic þ for ðínre cýðde, and þē weorðne wiste þyses tó gewitanne I send it for your information, and as knowing you worthy to know this, Lch. i. 326, 8. God eal þæt tó cýþþe and geswutelunge bröhte, iii. 432, 14. Tó manegra manna cýðde (v. cýþ-ness, III), Gr. D. 44, 5. Hæbben þá ungelǽredan inlendisce þæs regules cýþþe þurh āgenes gereordes anwrigennesse, Lch. iii. 442, 8. þurh cýðde þǽre ealdan ǽ, Hml. Th. i. 106, 20. (2) a person:—Hū neáh hī wǽron Godes cýðde (v. cýþ-ness, III), Gr. D. 56, 11. For þǽre ealdan cýðde Philippes, Hml. S. 2, 318. On þínre cýþþe wē, rǽste habbaþ (cf. peace ... through the knowledge of God, 2 Pet. 1, 2), Bl. H. 141, 10. þurh þæs (the bishop's brother) cýþþo (cýðþo, cýðde, v. ll.) gelamp þæt se cyning þone biscop lufade per cujus notitiam rex ad diligendum episcopum pervenit, Bd. 3, 23; Sch. 300, 7. (2 a) familiar, intimate knowledge, friendliness. v. cúþ III :—Heó geladode þá cwelleras swilce for cýðde hire tó, Hml. S. 29, 326. ¶ habban cýþþe tó to stand in relations of intimacy, familiarity, friendliness, &c. to a person:—Sum eáwfæst man hæfde micele cýðde tó Cūðberhte and gelōmlíce his lāre breác, Hml. Th. ii. 142, 1. Sum hæfð sume cýðde tó rícum men; ðonne sceal se earmum ðingian tó ðām rícan men þe hē cýðde tó hæfð, 558, 1-3. þá þurh geleáfan ūs gelenge beóð, and þurh crístendōm ūs cýðde tó habbað, 314, 14. Abraham ... tó Gode cýðde hæfde (cf. Abraham was called the friend of God, James 2, 23), 190, 12. Māran cýðde habbað englas tó Gode þonne men, i. 10, 3: ii. 112, 29. þá hæðenan nāne cýðde tó Gode nǽfdon, i. 396, 28. Cídde, 25. Gif hē tó þām cyninge furðor cýðde hæbbe, Ll. Th. i. 414, 17.　　II. native country, home:—Hē hine bæd þ hē sǽde hwæt hē on his cýðþe wǽre (quid in terra sua fuisset), nalæs hwæt hē þǽr wǽre, Gr. D. 181, 30. Ic wille faran tó mínre cýðde and tó ðǽm londe ðe ic on geboren wæs revertar in terram meam in qua natus sum, Past. 304, 14. Hié budon him þæt hē on cýþþe mid him wunade, Ors. 4, 6; S. 178, 19. Colman mid his geférum fōr tó his cýðde (cf. Colman ... in Scotiiam regressus est, Bd. 3, 26), Chr. 664; P. 34, 5. Hē of his cýþþe gewāt and of his earde. ... þá ongan hine eft langian on his cýþþe, Bl. H. 113, 12-15. On cýþþe cuman, Ors. 1, 11; S. 50, 11.　　III. fellow countrymen:—An wræccea þæt fācn tó his cýþþe gebodade (suis prodidit), Ors. 2, 5; S. 80, 2. Hī hēton hine cýðan on his cýðde æt hām Godes wundor ... Hē þæs Ælmihtigan mihte

his hlāforde cýdde and his leódum eallum, Hml. S. 25, 792.　　IV. kinsfolk:—In cýððo his in cognatione sua, Mk. L. R. 6, 4. In cýððo ðínre in cognatione tua, Lk. R. L. 1, 61. [v. N. E. D. kith. O. H. Ger. chundida notitia, denotatio.] v. sundor-, un-, wíf-cýþþu.

cyt-wér. l. cyt-wer, and add: v. Seebohm Vill. Comm. p. 152, and N. E. D. kit.

cýwung. v. cíwung.

# D

dǽd. Add:—Deid effectum, Wrt. Voc. ii. 107, 4. Dǽd effatum (effectum?), 142, 41. Se hwæl hine ābær tó Niniuea birig, and seó dǽd getācnode ūres Drihtenes deáð, Ælfc. T. Grn. 10, 13. Mid þanca dǽde cum gratiarum actione, Scint. 50, 5. Dǽde factum, i. opus, An. Ox. 2502. Ealle þás dǽdạ (facta) and mǽrsunga, 40, 10. Dǽdum gestibus, 45: effectibus, i. operibus, Wrt. Voc. ii. 142, 53. Gif monnes tunge bið of heáfde ōðres monnes dǽdum, Ll. Th. i. 94, 21. Mid dǽdum gelǽstan to carry into effect, Ors. 2, 4; S. 72, 34: 76, 25. v. ælmes-, forþ-, fracod-, lāc-, sceaþ-, un-, unriht-, weorc-, weoruld-, wil-, wōh-, wundor-dǽd.

-dǽda. v. nīd-, unriht-, yfel-dǽda.

dǽd-bēta. Add:—Se dǽdbēta (poenitens) æfter his dǽdbōte hreównysse ne sceal gecyrran tó þysse worulde, Ll. Th. ii. 170, 13, 11, 15, 20. 'Wylt þū būgan eft tó Chrīste?' Se wyþersaca cwæð: 'Ic wylle georne' ... Cwæð se dǽdbēta: 'þā deófiu cumað tó mē,' Hml. S. 3, 423. Sind mænige rihtwíse unscyldige wið heáfodleahtras, and habbað hwæðere stíðe drohtnunge ... þām ne mæg nān dǽdbēta beón geefenlǽht, for ðan ðe hī sind rihtwíse and behreówsigende, Hml. Th. i. 342, 12. Drihten cwæð þæt micel blis wǽre on heofenum be ānum dǽdbētan, 350, 8. þæt forbod hūslganges and inganges intō cyrican sie eal þearflic þām dǽdbētan, Wlfst. 155, 3. Be dǽdbētan, Ll. Th. ii. 278, 1.

dǽd-bētan. Add: I. in a general sense, to repent:—Būtan geþeahte nāht þū dō, and æfter dǽde þū nā dǽdbētst (peniteberis), Scint. 200, 12.　　II. as an ecclesiastical term, to be penitent, do penance:—þolige se preóst his hādes and dǽdbēte georne, Wlfst. 120, 11. Gif hit gelimpe, dǽdbēte sē Gode on his gebedhūse þe hit þurh his gýmelēste gelamp si contigerit, satisfaciat Deo in oratorio per cujus evenerit neglectum, R. Ben. 36, 6. Sý hē gelícum gelimpe āniānsumad and on gelícre wrace dǽdbēte similem sortiatur excommunicationis vindictam, 50, 14. Āstrecce hē hine eallum limum on þām stede þe hē stande, and on þá wīsan mid hreówsunge dǽdbēte oð se abbod hine geswīcan hāte proiciat se in terram in loco quo stat, et sic satisfaciat usque dum ei jubeat abba ut quiescat ab hac satisfactione, 70, 18. Be ðām āmānsumedan hū hī dǽdbētan (satisfaciant), 70, 2, 21. God wyle gemiltsian ǽghwylcum synfullum menn þe his synna andet his scrifte and dǽdbētan wyle, Wlfst. 150, 2. Būtan hē beforan eallum hine dǽdbētende geeáðmēde nisi per satisfactionem coram omnibus humiliatus fuerit, R. Ben. 71, 7. Be þām dǽdbētendum (poenitentibus), on hwylcum tīman him man forgifnysse dōn scyle, Ll. Th. ii. 170, 23. Be ðām þe ... wið ðā dǽdbētendan ðeódað ðe is qui ... junguntur excommunicatis, R. Ben. 50, 9, 17. Ūre Drihten gelǽt þá dǽdbētendan (the penitent) æfter sōðre dǽdbōte tó ðǽre ūplican Hierusalem, Hml. Th. ii. 68, 24.

dǽd-bētere, es; m. A penitent:—Ne mæg man nā dǽdbēterum þis dōn, Nap. 16.

dǽd-bōt penitence, penance. Add:—Hī clipodon tó Gode mid sōðre dǽdbōte, Ælfc. T. Grn. 6, 24. Būtan hē mid fulre dǽdbōte his ungeþanc gebēte si non cum satisfactione emendaverit, R. Ben. 21, 6. þá men þe dǽdbōte underfōð for hefelicum gyltum homines qui poenitentiam pro gravibus peccatis suscipiunt, Ll. Th. ii. 174, 17. Hreówe and dǽdbōte dōn þæs mycclan yfeles and mānes, Bl. H. 79, 5.

dǽd-bōt-lihting, e; f. Mitigation of penance:—Ðis is mihtiges mannes dǽdbōtlihtinge, ac ān unmaga ne mæg swilc gefordian, ac þ hē mōt on hine sylfne hit sēcan þe geornor, Ll. Th. ii. 288, 21.

dǽd-bōtnys. For Scint. 9 substitute:—Be dǽdbōtnysse de penitentia Scint. 41, 4.

-dǽde. v. ār-, earfoþ-, eáþ-, īþ-, mān-, unriht-, yfel-dǽde.

dǽd-lǽt; adj. Slow to act, slothful. v. next word.

dǽd-lata, an; m. One slow to act, a sluggard:—Oft daedlata dōmẹ foreldit sigisītha gahuēm, Txts. 152, 8.

dǽd-lic. Add:—Dǽdlicere practicae, i. actualis, An. Ox. 994.

dǽftan. For Glos. ... 73 read Germ. 400, 476, and add:—Se fæder hēt feccan þone cniht, and hine sōna scrýdde mid deórwurðum reáfum, and hēt dæftan his būr mid pallum and mid wāhryftum wurðlíce þām cnihte, Hml. S. 35, 49.

dæg. Dele daga, an; m., and add: inst. dæg, dæge; pl. gen. daga, dagena. I. day, period of twenty-four hours:—Wē habbað oft gehýred þæt men hātað þysne dæg geáres dæg, swylce þes dæg fyrmest sý on geáres ymbrync, Hml. Th. i. 98, 17. Ys on bōcum geteald tó ānum

dæge fram þǽre sunnan úpgange oð þ heó eft becume þǽr heó ǽr úp stáh on þám fæce synd getealde feówer and twěnti tída, Lch. iii. 236, 3. On þám forman dæge dagena ealra, Hy. S. 4, 2. Dæge ǽr þridie, Wrt. Voc. ii. 68, 50. Ðá cóm se arceð fram Róme áne dæge ǽr Scs Petrus mæsseǽfene, Chr. 1048; P. 172, 3. Fram dæge tó dæge, Wlfst. 79, 12: Hml. S. 23, 33. Ðá ðe ǽlce dæg symblað, Past. 309, 8: Ors. 2, 6; S. 88, 11. Farað six dagas simble ymbe þá burh ǽlce dæg ǽne (semel per diem), Jos. 6, 3, 12: Lch. ii. 108, 6: Bt. 26, 2; F. 92, 14. Hé ǽlce dæge symblede, Past. 309, 5. Hé sǽde þæt hé þone dæg forlure þe hé nóht tó góde on ne gedyde, Chr. 81; P. 8, 7. Þrý dagas wǽron ǽr þám dæge bútan sunnan and mónan, Lch. iii. 238, 19. ii. móuðas and .xxi. daga, Chr. 643; P. 27, 34. Mǽstra daga ǽlce, 894; P. 84, 29. Seofon dagena fæsten, Hml. Th. i. 434, 21. **I a.** day (as in one day), time of an occurrence :—Ánes dæges þe abbot eóde into capitulan, Chr. 1083; P. 214, 22. Þá sume dæge rád se cyng be þǽre eǽ, 896; P. 89, 11. Hyt wæs þá on dæg restedæg it was the sabbath at that time, Nic. 7, 5. Hyt wæs on dæg þá gé mé beclýsdon it was at the time when you shut me up, 10, 35: Chr. 1083; P. 215, 7. Oþ þisne andweardan dæg up to the present time, 851; P. 64, 23. (See also tó dæge, dæg under tó.) In dægum hungres in diebus famis, Ps. Srt. 36, 19. **II.** day as opposed to night :—Ðá hwíle ðe se rodor ǽne betyrnð gǽð forð feówor and twěntig tída, ðæt is ealles án dæg and án niht, Hex. 8, 32. Aþiéstrode sió sunne áne tíd dæges, Chr. 879; P. 76, 25. Matutinum úhttíd sive beforan dæge, Wrt. Voc. ii. 58, 64. Geéfenedan deige advesperescente die, Kent. Gl. 186. Ðonne hit neálécð dæge, ðonne singð se cocc smælor, Past. 461, 3. Þ Scs Petrus on dæge folce sǽde, þonne wrát Scs Marcus þ on niht, Shrn. 74, 19. Gé hwyrfað niht tó dæge, Wlfst. 47, 8. Eall swá þicce is þeó heofon mid steorrum áfylled on dæg swá on niht . . . Wé hátað ǽnne dæg fram sunnan úpgange oð ǽfen, Lch. iii. 234, 31–236, 2. **III.** day, time. (1) lifetime :—Ðæt hió hæbbe ðæt land hire dæg . . . and efter hire dæge geselle hit . . . ðám hírode, C. D. ii. 58, 22. Tó syllanne on dæge and æfter dæge (in his lifetime and after it) þám þe him leófust sý, iv. 117, 20. ¶ in pl. days of life :—Swegen geendode his dagas, Chr. 1014; P. 144, 27. (2) time during which an office is held, reign of a king :—Ic wearð ásend on Æþelrédes dæge cyninges tó sumum mynstre, Hml. Th. i. 2, 14. Féng Æþelbryht tó þám ríce . . . on his dæge cuóm micel sciphere, Chr. 860; P. 68, 2. Mauricius and Valentines onféngon ríce, and rícsodon .vii. winter; and on hiera dagum Hengest and Horsa gesóhton Bretene, 449; P. 12, 5. On þríora consula dæge cóm Hasterdal, Ors. S. 4, 10. On þára twégea consula dæge, 3, 6; S. 108, 22. ¶ in pl. days of a reign :—On his (Beorhtric) dagum cuómon ǽrest .iii. scipu, Chr. 787; P. 54, 4. (3) time during which something exists :—Hé geseah þá ceastre and cwæð : ' Eálá, gif þú wistest on þysum þínum dæge,' Lk. 19, 42. v. ár-, bæd-, bebod-, bén-, ceáp-, cípe-, clénsung-, eáster-, eáster-freóls-, foran-, fugol-, gearwung-, gefyrn-, gereord-, hádung-, heáhfreóls-, heáhmæsse-, offrung-, palm-, reste-, resten[d]-, swǽsend-, sweotolung-, swíg-, teóþung-, þeorf-, weorþung-, wól-, ymbrendæg ; dæges.

**dæg-cúþ** ; adj. Clear as daylight, perfectly known :—Ne þǽr ówiht inne ne belífe on heortscræfe heánra gylta, þ hit ne sý dægcúð, þ þ díhle wæs, openum wordum eall ábæred nec lateat quidquam culparum cordis in antro, omnia quin luci verbis reddantur apertis, Dóm. L. 91.

**dǽge**, an ; f. A maker of bread, baker :—Pistrilla lytel cofa, pristris dǽge, panis hláf, . . . sparrum daag, Wrt. Voc. i. 288, 63–67. Godwíg hæfð geboht Leófgife þá dǽgean (dágean, C. D. iv. 271, 16) æt Norðstoke and hyre ofspring . . . tó ěcan freóte, Cht. Th. 641, 23. Áne dǽgan, Cam. Phil. Soc. 1902, p. 15. [v. N. E. D. dey. Icel. deigja a dairy maid. Cf. Goth. deigan to knead.] Cf. dáh dough.

**dǽgen-líc** ; adj. Of this day :—Fram þyssum dægenlícan dæge ab hodierno die, Angl. xvii. 121, 7.

**dæges** ; adv. Substitute : By day, during the day, day :—Se sunnan seáð bið dæges hát and nihtes ceald, and se mónan seáð bið nihtes hát and dæges ceald, Nar. 36, 26. Ymb his ǽ smeágende dæges and nihtes, Ps. Th. 1, 2 : Bl. H. 47, 11. Hí fóron ánstrecces dæges and nihtes they marched day and night without stopping, Chr. 894 ; P. 88, 5 : 1066; P. 196, 30. Ægðer ge dæges ge nihtes, Bt. 35, 6; F. 168, 7. v. þý-dæges.

**dæges eáge.** Add :—Dæges ěge consolda, An. Ox. 56, 385.

**dæg-fæsten.** Add :—Gif man wylle his dægfæsten álýsan mid ælmessan, gesylle twám mannum oððe þrým dægswǽsendo si aliquis iejunium suum eleemosynis redimere velit, duobus vel tribus hominibus det cibum unius diei, Ll. Th. ii. 220, 29.

**dæg-feorm.** Add :—Yc wille þ man gelǽste ǽlce geáre áne dægfeorme þám hírēde intó Ælíg, Cht. Th. 559, 30.

**dæg-gehwámlic** ; adj. Daily :—Dægihuǽmlíce hérnisse cotidiano officio, Rtl. 74, 35. Dægihuǽmlíce wordunge cotidiana veneratione, 18.

**dæg-gehwámlíce** ; adv. Daily :—Dægihuǽmlíce cotidie, Rtl. 74, 18 : 171, 5.

**dæg-gehwelc** ; adj. Daily :—Sé ðe nǽfde dægihuoelc néddarf qui non habet cotidie necessitatem, Rtl. 90, 36.

**dæg-hwam.** l. -hwǽm, and add :—Dæghuǽm cotidie, Mt. L. 26, 55.

**dæg-hwǽmlic.** Add :—Úrne dæghwomlican hláf, Angl. xi. 100, 3. Ǽfre on dæghwǽmlicum tídum semper diurnis horis, R. Ben. I. 48, 11. Gemunon wé úre dæghwǽmlican synna, Bl. H. 25, 15. [Ure dagghwammlike bræd, Orm. 5434.]

**dæg-hwǽmlíce** every day. Add :—Hé dæghwǽmlíce wæs blótende diófolgildum, Ors. 6, 37 ; S. 296, 13 : Bl. H. 127, 14. Wé him gyldað singallíce, and hý ús hýnað dæghwǽmlíce, Wlfst. 163, 11 : 156, 12 : Gen. 41, 56. Dæghwǽmlíce (-hwom-, v. l.) ðæs mónan leóht býð weaxende, Lch. iii. 242, 6. Ǽne ðrowade Críst ðurh hine sylfne, ac dæghwomlíce bið his þrowung geedníwod þurh gerýnu þæs húsles, Hml. Th. ii. 276, 10. Dæghwonlíce, i. 44, 20 : 46, 18. Dæghuǽmlíce, Rtl. 75, 5. [Orm. dagghwammlike.]

**dæg-lang.** Add :—Day-long. [Icel. dag-langr.]

**dæg-langes.** Add :—Ac gyf unc swá þince uton gebyddan unc hǽr dæglanges and spurian tó morgen furður sed hodie satis, ut puto, scripsimus, Shrn. 188, 17. [Cf. Icel. dag-lengis all day long.]

**dæg-líc.** Substitute : Daily ; diurnus :—Diurnum, i. unius diei dægrynum vel dæglicum, diurne psalmodie þæs dæglican sealmsanges, Wrt. Voc. ii. 141, 58–61 : R. Ben. 44, 9. Sýn simle þá dæglican tída begunnene mid ferse semper diurnis horis dicatur versus, 41, 21. On þém dæglicum tídum, 69, 2. Dæglicum dédum diurnis actibus, Rtl. 162, 23. v. twá- (twi-), þri-dæglic.

**dæg-mǽl.** Add :—Dægmǽl horologium, dægmǽles píl gnomon, Wrt. Voc. i. 86, 41, 42. Seó sunne ástíhð pricmǽlum on þám dægmǽle . . . se sticca on þám dægmǽle áriht stent, Angl. viii. 317, 15–21. Seó emniht is on .xiimᵃˢ kl. April., swá swá þá geleáðullan rǽderas hit gesetton, and eác gewisse dægmǽl (-mælas, v. l.) ús swá tǽcað, Lch. iii. 256, 22.

**dægmǽl-sceáwere.** Substitute : An observer of the dial, an observer of times and seasons, an astrologer, diviner :—Dægmǽlsceáwere aruspex, Wrt. Voc. i. 17, 12 : horoscopus, 60, 11. v. tíd-sceáwere.

**dæg-mete.** Substitute : A day-meal (?), breakfast or dinner :—Dægmete agapis, Wrt. Voc. i. 284, 36 : ii. 8, 9. [O. H. Ger. takemaz, laba refectio : cf. taga-muos prandium. Cf. also Icel. dag-verðr morning meal, nátt-verðr evening meal : Goth. nahta-mats supper.]

**dæg-réd.** Add : , dæge-réd (-red ?) :—Degred (crepusculum) mód nyte, degred (aurora) ryne forðweged, degred (aurora) all forðyped, Ps. Srt. ii. p. 201, 25. Ðæt leóht þe wé hátað dægred (dæge-, v.l.), Lch. iii. 234, 29. Gongað þá .vii. steorran on dægered on setl, Shrn. 146, 8. Se cocc hlúdor singð on úhtan ðonne on dægred, Past. 461, 2. On dægred siþþan hit frumlýhte, Bl. H. 207, 35. On þæt dægred sylf, Jud. 204. [þe engles in þe daired blewed heore beme, Misc. 162, 17. O. H. Ger. taga-ród crepusculum, aurora: M. L. Ger. dage-rát : M. Du. daghe-raet : Icel. dag-ráð. v. Grmm. D. M. (trans.) 747.]

**dægred-leóma.** m. The light of dawn :—Þá se ðægredleóma beorhte scymrode, þá Drihten of helle árás, Nap. 16.

**dægréd-sang.** Add : (dæge-) : Matins :—Þæt lytel fæc gehealden sý betwyh þém úhtsange and þém dægredsange . . . and úpásprungenum dægriman dægredsang sý begunnen (matutini subsequantur), R. Ben. 33, 1. Dægeredsang (dæg-, v. l.), 35, 23. Dægredsanges weorðung matutinorum sollempnitas, 37, 5. Hú dægredsangas tó healdenne sýn. On þém dægredsangum (dæge-, v.l.) . . . qualiter matutinorum sollempnitas agatur. In matutinis . . . , 36, 9–11. Dægredsanga bēcnu matutinorum signa, Angl. xiii. 426, 869. Æfter degredsangum post matutinos, 392, 388.

**dæg-rima.** Add :—Dægrim[a] aurora, An. Ox. 18, 19. Dægrima crepundia (?), 18 b, 15. Úpásprungenum dægriman incipiente luce, R. Ben. 33, 1. Þú getimbradest dægriman tu fabricatus es auroram, Ps. L. 73, 16. [Þæt fir hi seagon in ðe dæirime, and læste swa lange þ hit wæs liht ofer eall, Chr. 1122; P. 250, 33. v. N. E. D. day-rim.]

**dæg-ryne** ; adj. For or of a day :—Diurnum, i. unius diei dægrynum vel dæglicum . . . diurnae aescae dæghryne mettas, Wrt. Voc. ii. 141, 58, 62.

**dæg-sang**, es ; m. Daily service :—Þē ðe his dægsang cunne, singe þone swá hé oftest mage, Wlfst. 290, 22. [Hiss Drihhtin to cwemenn wiþþ daggsang, Orm. 6360.]

**dæg-sceald** the sun (? cf. Icel. himin-targa the sun) :—Dægscealdes hleó (the protection from the sun i.e. the pillar of cloud) wand ofer wolcnum ; hæfde witig God sunnan síðfæt segle ofertolden, swá þá mæstrápas men ne cúðon, Exod. 79.

**dæg-steorra.** Add :—Hé wæs ásend tóforan Drihtne, swá swá se dægsteorra gǽð beforan ðǽre sunnan, Hml. Th. i. 354, 33. Ðú geworhtest dægsteorran (auroram) and sunnan, Ps. Spl. 73, 17.

**dæg-swǽsendo** food for one day ; cibus unius diei, Ll. Th. ii. 220, 30. v. dæg-fæsten.

**dæg-ðerlic.** Add : , of the day :—Genihtsumian tó dægþerlicere reordunge sufficere ad refectionem cotidianam, R. Ben. I. 70, 11. On dægþerlicum tídum diurnis horis, 76, 16. On dægþerlicum dǽdum in diurnis actibus, Hy. S. 9, 6 : Angl. viii. 319, 47.

**dæg-þern.** Add :—Dægþerne leng þonne .xii. mónaþ a day longer than twelve months, Lch. ii. 348, 19. Cf. nihterne.

**dæg-þerne**; *adj. Day, for use in the day time :*—Gân hí and hí mid dægþernum (*diurnalibus*) tyslian gescýum, Angl. xiii. 383, 259. Tô unscrýdende dægþerne scós *ad exuendos diurnales calceos*, 392, 390. [*Diurnales* dicuntur calcei quibus interdiu utuntur monachi, qui *calciamenta diurna* appellantur in Capit. Ludovici Pii. Migne.] Cf. nihterne.

**dæg-tíd** *day, time. For* 'On dægtídum *in the day-time*' substitute: Dægtídum *at times, some days; and add :*—Ðonne beóð ealra gesweotolude dígle geþancas on þære dægtíde (*doomsday*), Dóm. L. 135. Unbecweden and unforboden wið ælcne man tô þære dægtíde, Cht. Th. 209, 2. Nyste ic on þám þingum þe þú ymbe specst fúl ne fâcn tô þære dæigtíde þe ic hit þé scalde, Ll. Th. i. 182, 4.

**dæg-weorc**. *Add :*—Bisceopes dægweorc, þ bið his gebedu ǽrest, and ðonne his bôcweorc . . . , Ll. Th. ii. 314, 18. Gê hwyrfað niht tô dæge and dægweorc tô nihte, Wlfst. 47, 8. [v. *N. E. D.* day-work. O. Sax. dag-werk.]

**dæg-wine**. *Add :*—Daeguuini *expensa*, Wrt. Voc. ii. 107, 77. Dægwine oððe andliofen, 30, 5. Dægwine *expensa, i. substantia, census*, 145, 43. Dægwi[ne] *inpensum*, An. Ox. 56, 122. [Cf. (?) *Goth.* winja bigitan *pascua invenire*.]

**dæg-wist**, e; *f. Substitute :*, e; *m. A meal, food :*—Hê ðone hálgan (Cuthbert) grétte, biddende þæt hê him dægwistes tíðode (*that he would give him a meal*). Cûðberhtus cwæð : ' Ic wolde ðíne ðénunge sylf nú gearcian, gif ic mê mid feðunge ferian mihte,' Hml. Th. ii. 134, 30. Him syððan sig dægwistes (wegnestes, *v. l.*) getíðode, gif hig þæs gewilnion, and swâ hâm gecyrran, R. Ben. 102, 22. Cf. dæg-mete.

**dæl**. *Add :*—Dael *baratrum*, Wrt. Voc. ii. 101, 53. Dæl *vel færseáþ baratrum, i. terre hiatus*, 125, 24. Dæl (dell, den, *v. ll.*) lígum full, Bd. 5, 12; Sch. 616, 4. Of þám hylle dûn in þæt dæll ; þ ollung þæs dæles ; þ úp on þone hyll, Cht. E. 235, 2 : C. D. iii. 52, 22. Oð ceápmanna del ; of ceápmanna dele, vi. 41, 18. On þet deópe del, iii. 130, 32. v. dell.

**dǽl**. *Add :* pl. dǽle (gelimplice daele *conpetentes portiunculas*, Wrt. Voc. ii. 104, 79), dǽlas. **I.** *a part* (in contrast with the whole) :—Tôdǽlde se here on tú, óþer dǽl eást, óþer dǽl tô Hrófesceastre, Chr. 885 ; P. 78, 9. Sumursǽtna se dǽl sé þær níehst wæs, 878 ; P. 76, 5. Se êcea dǽl, Bl. H. 111, 32 : Gú. 352. Se eorðan dǽl (*the body*) . . se wuldres dǽl (*the soul*), 1340-2. Hié micel þæs folces ofer sǽ ádrǽfdon, and þæs óþres þone mǽstan dǽl hié geridon, Chr. 878 ; P. 74, 27. Hê tôbærst on feówer dǽlas, Bl. H. 189, 14. **II.** *denoting amount, quantity, &c., some* (in contrast with none), *a deal, lot, portion :*—Nǽnig dǽl regnes ne ungewidres in cuman ne mæg, Bl. H. 125, 33. Ne wund ne lâðes dǽl *neither wound nor any hurt*, An. 1476. Bicgað ûs sumne dǽl metes (*pauxillum escarum*), Gen. 43, 2. Sumne dǽl tyrwan *modicum resinae*, 11. Tô feormianne sumne dǽl hwǽtes *ad purgandum triticum*, Gr. D. 97, 2 : Hml. S. 23, 473 : Chr. P. p. 5, 1. Syle sumne dǽl (þæs fisces) ðám earne, Hml. Th. ii. 140, 7. Hwæðer sǽ dǽl ǽnigne grênre eorðan ofgifen hæfde, Gen. 1453. Nǽnigne dǽl leóhtes scíman geseón *ne minimam quidem lucis alicujus particulam videre*, Bd. 4, 10 ; Sch. 401, 10. Tô gôde gedôn þone dǽl þe wê dôn magon (*as much as we can*), Wlfst. 188, 13. **II a.** *a great quantity*, (cf. *deal, lot* in mod. E.), *a (great) deal :*—Dryhtmâðma dǽl, B. 2843. Oferhygda dǽl *much pride*, 1740. Lífwynna dǽl, Cri. 807 : Deór. 30. Þæt is wundres dǽl *it is a great wonder*, Rä. 61, 10. Beran wunden gold and seolfres dǽl, 56, 4. Weána dǽl, B. 1150 : 2028 : Vy. 67. Ne mæg weorðan wís wer, ǽr hê âge wintra dǽl (*many years*) in woruldríce, Wand. 65. Leóðworda dǽl reccan, An. 1490. ¶ sum-dǽl *some-what, some* (cf. *Chauc.* som-del ; *adv.*) :—Hê gewât fêran út sum-dǽl óðres weorces (sum weorc, *v. l.*) tô wyrcanne *ad exercendum opus aliquod discessit*, Gr. D. 63, 28. þ heó mihte sum-dǽl (sumne dǽl, *v. l.*) hwǽtes geclǽnsian, 97, 3. ¶ in adverbial phrases :—þæt lond þe mon Ongle hǽt, and Sillende and sumne dǽl Dene, Ors. 1, 1 ; S. 16, 7. Sume daeli *partim*, Wrt. Voc. ii. 115, 80. Be dǽle *somewhat, in some measure :*—Bútan hit gelimpe þæt man be dǽle (*aliquid*) rǽdinga gescyrte, R. Ben. 36, 4 : 94, 6. Hí be dǽle hí gereordodon, Hml. S. 23, 240. Nim hunig be dǽle *take a little honey*, Lch. iii. 58, 30. Hê cúðe be dǽle Lýden understanden *he knew a little Latin*, Ælfc. T. Grn. 22, 14. Be sumum dǽle *to some extent*, Past. 231, 2, 15 : Wlfst. 166, 4. Be ǽnigum dǽle *in any measure*, 165, 2 : Bt. 38, 7 ; F. 210, 9. Be nánum dǽle gefæstnode tô Gode, 39, 7 ; F. 222, 18. Be (þám) dǽle (þæt) *in so far as, to the extent that :*—Be dǽle ðe wê mǽgen *in quantum possumus*, Past. 231, 4. Be þám dǽle þe hê mǽge *quantum possit*, Ll. Th. ii. 182, 10 : Bt. 34, 12 ; F. 152, 19 : Shrn. 163, 8 : 186, 16 : 194, 14. Be þǽm dǽle þæt (þe, *v. l.*) mehton, Ors. 4, 5 ; S. 168, 24. Wê nú gehýrdon of hwylcumhugu dǽle secggan be . . . *we have now in some sort heard say about . . .*, Bl. H. 103, 18. þæt hê Grécisc gereord of miclum dǽle cúðe *ut Graecam linguam non parva ex parte noverit*, Bd. 5, 20 ; Sch. 673, 27. **III.** *part, share, portion :*—Eart þú on lifigendra lande mín se gedéfa dǽl *tu es portio mea in terra viventium*, Ps. Th. 141, 5. Mê ys on dǽle þæt ic wylle þíne ǽ healdan *portio mea custodire legem tuam*, 118, 57. þú môst heonon hûde lǽdan ealle bútan dǽle þissa drihtwera, Gen. 2150. Ðú miht habban dínne dǽl ðæs sóþan leóhtes, Bt. 36, 2 ; F. 174, 17 :

Crä. 7. Synd foxes dǽlas *partes vulpium erunt*, Ps. Th. 62, 8. **IV.** *part* (where there is community, association) :—Sýn hí â fram ælcum Godes dǽle (*from any part in God*) âworpene, Ll. Th. i. 246, 15. Nǽfst þú nânne dǽl in myd mê, Jn. 13, 8. **V.** *part, way of life :*—Sié hira dǽl scired mid Marian, El. 1232. Maria geceás þone sêlestan dǽl, Lk. 10, 42 : Bl. H. 67, 35. **VI.** *in a local sense, part, region, quarter, district :*—Dǽles *climatis, i. partis*, An. Ox. 1443. Hwider mæg ic þinne andwlitan befleón eorðan dǽles *a facie tua quo fugiam*?, Ps. Th. 138, 5. On þǽm dǽle þe Decius on ofslagen wæs, Ors. 3, 10 ; S. 138, 15. In þǽm dǽle þe hê mid tân geeóde, Bl. H. 121, 9. Geond þisse eorðan ǽghwylcne dǽl *in universa terra*, Ps. Th. 104, 7. Fison foldan dǽl bebúged, Hebeleat, Gen. 222. On þás niþeran dǽlas þisse ceastre, Bl. H. 239, 6. Worolde dǽlas, síde ríce, B. 1732. On Indêa ôþre dǽlas, Ap. 51. On þone wyrsan dǽl *to the left hand*, Cri. 1226. Of þǽre ylcan stôwe dǽlum (sumum dǽle, *v. l.*) *de ejusdem loci partibus*, Gr. D. 67, 1 : 70, 35. Neáh þám dǽlum Tuscie þǽre mǽgðe, 71, 23. **VI a.** *part, particular :*—Gif hié on ǽnigum dǽle wôlíce libban heora líf, Bl. H. 109, 19. **VII.** *part* (*in for my, your, &c., part*), *side, behalf :*—Mænigfealde þearfe ge Godes dǽle ge worolde dǽles, Cht. Th. 167, 17. Ic geseah of dǽle þ mê þá earfeðu becwóman *ego cernens ex parte mea id accidisse*, Nar. 6, 24. Bið sê his dǽl synnig *he for his part will be guilty*, Ll. Th. i. 138, 17. **VIII.** *in numeration, time :*—Is ânra gehwylc synderlíce xxx-tigum ðúsendum dǽla lengra ðonne eal middangeard, Salm. K. 150, 13. v. eástsúþ-, middel-, neáh-, twi-dǽl.

**dǽlan**. *Add :* **I.** *to divide*. (1) *to separate* into parts :—Ic tôclǽfe ł dǽle (= tô-dǽle?) *findo*, An. Ox. 18 b, 38. Holmas dǽlde Waldend úre, Gen. 146. Ic wille dǽlan ðá yfelan ðám yfelum on twá ; óþer dǽl þára yfena hæfð êce wíte, . . . óþer dǽl sceal beón geclǽnsod, Bt. 38, 4 ; F. 202, 27. (2) *to break up* union, association :—Ne ceara þú fleáme dǽlan somwist incre, Gen. 2279. **II.** *intrans.* (1) *to separate* (intrans.) into parts, *be torn to pieces* :—On þreó dǽleð folc ânra gehwylc, El. 1286. Sceal þín hrâ dǽlan, An. 954. (2) *to separate one's self* from another, *to part, depart* (cf. sie fan irð drohtne dǽlian skoldun, Hél. 4774) :—Ic feor gewíte, fleáme dǽle *elongavi fugiens*, Ps. Th. 54, 7. **III.** *to distribute*. (1) *to give to many* :—Hú þrymlíce þú þíne gife dǽlest, An. 548. þú dǽlest mete þínum mannum, Hy. 7, 70 : 10, 57. Hê dǽleð help and hǽlo hæleða bearnum, Sat. 581 : Cri. 428. Hê mâdmas dǽleð, B. 1756. Tungel heora wlite wíde dǽlað, Gen. 2191. Ofer ûs dǽl rumnôdnise *super nos effunde clementiam*, Rtl. 41, 5. Sum licgende feoh hê hêt ðǽm folce dǽlan, Ors. iv. 10 ; S. 196, 21. Cyning sceal on healle beágas dǽlan, Gn. C. 29 : B. 1970 : Gen. 2829. Fremsumnesse folcum dǽlan, Ps. Th. 64, 2. Mid þí þe hé deád sié, uton wê dǽlan his líchaman úrum burhleódum (*the cannibal Mermedonians*), Bl. H. 241, 22. **II a.** *especially used of alms-giving* :—Him bið be hundfealdum êcelíce geleánod swâ hwæt swâ hí be ânfealdum hwílwendlíce dǽlað . . . Hê sumne dǽl his ǽhta dǽlð, Hml. Th. i. 398, 17-29. Wê ælmessan dǽlað, Wlfst. 92, 10. Dǽl of ðám ðe ðú God forgeaf . . . Gif ðú forgýmeleásast tô dǽlenne ælmessan, Hml. Th. ii. 102, 20. Welan beceápian and þæt wurð ðearfum dǽlan, i. 62, 3. His wǽstma þone teóþan dǽl for Godes naman dǽlan, Bl. H. 49, 23. Miclum feoh dǽlan *to give alms liberally*, Rún. 1. (2) *to give a variety of things* :—Ðú dǽlst eall gód swâ swâ ðú wilt, Bt. 33, 4 ; F. 128, 25. God dǽlþ manega and mistlice gemetgunga eallum his gesceaftum . . . Sió wyrd dǽlþ eallum gesceaftum andwlitan and stôwa and tída and gemetgunga, 39, 5 ; F. 218, 19-33. Dǽleð, Vy. 65. Meotud monnum dǽleð, syleð sundorgiefe, Crä. 4. Regnþeófas dǽlað yldo oððe ǽrdeáð, Exod. 538. þeáh úre Drihten þá eorþwæstmas mannum missenlíce dǽle, Bl. H. 39, 18. (3) *to spend* :—Man gehylt þæt hê hæfð, gif hê him ondrǽt þæt hit him odsceóte. Ðý mon dǽld spǽrlíce, ðe mon nele þæt hit forberste *a man spends sparingly from fear of failing*, Prov. K. 19. Gefrægn ic Hebrêos eádge lifgean goldhord dǽlan (*to spend lavishly*), Dan. 2. **IV.** *to share with* (*wiþ*). (1) *to grant a share* :—Hê him gehét þæt hê his ríce wið hiene dǽlan wolde, and hiene under ðǽm ofslôg *Titum Tatium, mox ut in societatem regni adsumpsit, occidit*, Ors. 2, 2 ; S. 66, 11. Hêt hê þe dǽlan þíne goldhordas wið hine, Hml. S. 32, 52. Se ríca berð mâre þonne hê behófige . . . ; for ðí sceal se ríca ðǽlan his byrdene wið þone ðearfan, Hml. Th. i. 254, 31. Swâ nô man scyle his gǽstes lufan wið Gode dǽlan *not in such measure is the spirit's love to be given to God*, Dan. 21. (2) *to obtain a share* :—Nǽfre Ismael wið Isáce, wið mín âgen bearn, yrfe dǽlan, Gen. 2788. Wið Drihtne dǽlan wuldorfæstan wíc, 26. Hê smeáde hú hê mihte dǽlan ríce wið God, Hml. Th. i. 12, 1 : 172, 1. (3) *of common action* :—Nis þæt gemet mannes þæt hê wið ǽglǽcean eofoðo dǽle (*take part in conflict, fight with*), eorlscype efne, B. 2534. Betere þonne wê hilde dǽlon *better than our fighting with one another*, By. 33. v. twi-dǽlan ; þri-dǽled, -dǽle, -dǽledness. v. of-dǽle, tô-dǽledness : **dǽlend**. *Add:* v. on-dǽlend.

**dǽlere**. *Add: an almsgiver.* v. dǽlan, III 1 ¶ :—Cýð mildheortnysse earmum mannum mid begeáte, sê ðe dǽl tô dǽlere gesette, Hml. Th. ii. 104, 28 · Wlfst. 286, 30.

L

dǽling. *Add: sharing, participation* :—Dælin[ge? v. dælni, An. Ox. 707] *participio, parte, communicatione*, Hpt. Gl. 423, 15.

dǽll. v. æf-dæll, dell, dæl.

dǽl-leás. *Add : destitute* of, *without* :—Bist þū dælleás mīnes rēnes, Wlfst. 260, 9.

dǽl-mǽlum. *Add* :—Sticmælum, dælmælum *frustratim*, i. *particulatim, minutatim*, Wrt. Voc. ii. 151, 37. Dælmælum *particulatim, per partes*, An. Ox. 3587: *partim*, Angl. xiii. 375, 141. Of wæterum ūpásprungen cynn dælmælum (*partim*) þū ongeánsændst wæle, dælmælum þū ūp áliefst on lyftum, Hy. S. 25, 6. Genim þás wyrte, syle hý dælmēlum etan oðfe on drince þicgean, Lch. i. 198, 24.

dǽl-ness, e ; f. *Division, breaking* (of bread) :—On dælnise hláfes *in fractione panes*, Lk. p. 11, 11. [*O. H. Ger.* teil-nussa *scissura*.]

dǽl-niman. *Add* :—Dǽlnimende ic eam *particeps sum*, Ps. L. 118, 63. Bistū daelniomende alra gōda, Txts. 174, 11. Dælnimende *participes*, Rtl. 35, 35. Þæt hié sȳn dælnimende þinra geofena mid mē, Bl. H. 191, 25. Hē ūs gedyde dælnimende þæs heofonlican ríces, 11, 2. Se Hælend his ðægnas ðæs godcundlican gereordes dælnimende dyde, Hml. S. 23 b, 632.

dǽl-nimend. *Add* :—Daelniomend *particeps*, Ps. Srt. 118, 63. Dælnimendras *consortes*, i. *participes*, An. Ox. 1902.

dǽl-nimeness, e ; f. *Participation* :—Dælniomenis *participatio*, Ps. Srt. 121, 3.

dǽl-nimung. *Add* : , *participation* :—Fram sōþre lufe dǽlnimincge *a caritatis participatione*, Scint. 6, 7. Daelneomencge, C. D. i. 114, 24. Fram beóde dælnimunge *a mense participatione*, R. Ben. I. 56, 8 : 77, 13.

dǽrst, dǽrstan. *Take these together under* : dǽrste, dræste, an : dærst, dræst, þræst, e ; f., *and add* : I. *mostly in pl. dregs, lees* :—Þræst (drosne derstan, Ps. Srt.) is *faex* Ps. Spl. 74, 8. Of lāme dærstan (derstan, Ps. Srt.) *de luto faecis*, Ps. Spl. C. 39, 2. Nim wīnes dræstan, Lch. ii. 102, 7 : 296. 8. Ecedes dræstan, iii. 42, 22. [v. *N. E. D.* drast, drest. *Cf. O. H. Ger.* trestig *acinum, quisquiliae*.] v. beór-dræste ; dærstig. II. *in the Northern specimens leaven, barm* :—From dærste ł ðærie *a fermento*, Mt. L. 16, 11. Tō ðærste *fermento*, 13, 33. Tō dærsto, Lk. p. 8, 6. From dærsto (dærstum, R.), Mk. L. 8, 15. Daege ðaere dærstana *die azymorum*, Mk. L. 14, 12 : Lk. L. R. 22, 1, 7. From dærstum ł ðærfe *a fermento*, Mt. L. 16, 6, 12 : Lk. p. 7, 12. Daerstum, Rtl. 25, 17. On dærstum ł on ðearfum *in azymis*, 19. Giclænsað ða alde dærsto (o *from* a) *expurgate vetus fermentum*, 13.

dǽrstig, dræstig ; adj. *Full of dregs, feculent* :—Dræstig (printed dræsig, Wrt. Voc. ii. 148, 45) *feculentus*, i. *fece plenus*, Wülck. Gl. 238, 20. [v. *N. E. D.* drasty.]

dafen. v. ge-dafen : dafen-lic. *Substitute for citation* :—Þæslicum, dafnlicum *congruis* i. *oportunis*, An. Ox. 1331.

dág, es ; m. (?). *Substitute* : *Dough* :—Daag *sparsum*, dáges hlǽfþe (lǽiþe ?) *sparsio*, Wrt. Voc. i. 288, 67, 68. Dág *massa*, An. Ox. 56, 58. Hit sié swilc swā dāh, Lch. ii. 118, 14. Ðæs bæcernes tácen is þæt mon mid bām sámlocone handum tōgædere swilce þū dáh brǽdan wille, Tech. ii. 128, 5. [*Take here the instances given under* dáh *in Dict.*]

dagian. *Add* :—On morgne mid þý hit dagode þa onbrǽd ic *postero die matutino expergefactus diluculo*, Nar. 30, 30 : Hml. S. 21, 172. On niht ǽr hyt dagige, Lch. i. 398, 4. Ðá hit þá on mergen dagian wolde *on the morrow when day was about to break*, Guth. 40, 23 : Hml. S. 21, 123 : Chr. 979 ; P. 122, 26.

dagung. *Add: crepusculum* :—Hwæðer hit sí þe æfenglommung ðe on morgen d(e)agung (*e written above* ; dagung, *v. l.*) *utrum crepusculum adhuc permaneat uespertinum, an jam advenerit matutinum*, Bd. 1, 1 ; Sch. 9, 21. Ǽr þæs uppcumendan leóhtes dagunge *ante exsurgentis lucis crepusculum*, Gr. D. 84, 29. [v. *N. E. D.* dawing.]

dáh. v. dág.

dál. *Add* : I. *a dole, share, lot, destiny* :—Sortis supremae, i. *distributionis* þǽre ȳtemeste hlȳtes, dáles, An. Ox. 2294. II. *distribution* of charity :—Ðȳ læs hié for ðǽm dále (gedále, *v. l.*) ðæs fiós wilnigen ðysses lǽnan lofes *ne ex impenso munere transitoriam laudem quaerant*, Past. 322, 12.

dalc. *Add* :—Oferfengc, dalc *ligulam*, i. *fibulam*, Hpt. Gl. 523, 3. [*Icel.* dálkr *a pin for a cloak* ; *Dan.* dolk. *From* (?) *O. Ir.* delc.]

dál-mǽd, e ; f. *Meadow-land held in common and divided into doles or shares among the holders* :—Gebirað se fífta æcer ðǽre dálmǽd we tō ðǽre híde, C. D. iii. 260, 3. [v. *N. E. D.* dole-meadow.] Cf. gedál-land.

dalmatice, an ; f. *A dalmatic* :—Man álegde ofer þá bǽre his dalmaticau (*dalmaticam*), . . . and sum man gehrán þǽre dalmaticau, Gr. D. 329, 24.

darian ; p. ode *To lurk, lie hid* :—Fare man swíðe hraðe tō þām scræfe ðǽr þá wiðersacan inne dariað behȳdde, Hml. S. 23, 322. [v. *N. E. D.* dare.] Cf. dirnan.

daroþ-hæbbende *javelin-holding, armed with a javelin*, Jul. 68.

daroþ-sceaft. v. deoroþ-sceaft *in Dict.*

daru. *Add:* I. *injury, hurt* :—Māran him hȳnþa oþþe dara (*detri-* menta) hē dēþ . . . þǽr þǽr gestreón, þǽr daru (*damnum*) ; gestreón on cyste, daru (*damnum*) on ingeþance, Scint. 208, 8-10. Þæt sǽd þe feóll be ðám wege mid twyfealdre dare losode, ðá ðá wegférende hit fortrǽdon, and fugelas tōbǽron, Hml. Th. ii. 90, 14. Dare *noxam*, Wrt. Voc. ii. 61, 64. Án gecyndelic ǽ is gesett, þ nǽn man ne gedó dare ōðrum menn, Hml. S. 11, 349 : Wlfst. 11, 1. Dere (dare, *v. l.*), Gr. D. 207, 14. Dara *noxas*, Hy. S. 15, 7. II. *loss, deprivation* :—Þonne se mon bið blind, þeáh hē mycel áge, þ him bið mycel daru, gif hē hit geseón ne mæg, Bl. H. 21, 8. [*O. H. Ger.* tara *damnum, laesio*. v. *N. E. D.* dere.]

datárum ; *indecl. m. Date* :—Be þám datárum nonarum Aprilium, Angl. viii. 304, 46. Gif man rǽt þæne datárum on Sunnandæge, 302, 20.

Dauític ; *adj. Of David* :—Of ðám Dauíticum sealmum, Lch. iii. 428, 17.

deád. *Add:* I. *physical.* (1) *of an animal or a vegetable* :—Ðá hē onfunde þ hē deád beón sceolde *when he found that he must die*, Bt. 29, 2 ; F. 104, 20. Án cild arn under wǽnes hweowol and weard sōna deád, Shrn. 32, 12. Ðeáh þá yfian nǽire ne wurden deáde, Bt. 38, 2 ; F. 198, 13. (2) *of flesh, dead, without sensation* :—Gif þ líc tō þon swíþe ádeádige þ þǽr nán gefelnes on sié, þonne scealt þū sóna eal þ deáde of ásníþan oþ þ cwice líc, þ þǽr náwiht þæs deúdan líces tō láfe ne sié, þæs þe ǽr ne ísen ne fȳr gefélde, Lch. ii. 82, 25-29. Wiþ deádum líce, 78, 3. Wiþ deádum swile, 74, 12. (3) *of blood,* (a) *congealed* :—Hū mon þ deáde blōd áweg wenian scyle, Lch. ii. 8, 14. (b) *blood away from the body, gore* [cf. *Icel.* dauda-blōð *gore*] :—Deád blōd *cruor*, Wrt. Voc. i. 283, 79 : ii. 16, 57. II. *fig. dead* to, *insensible* to :—Heó bið deád ǽlcere duguðe and gesǽlðe, and bið gehealden tō ðám ēcan deáðe, Hml. Th. i. 160, 15.

deád-bǽre, -bǽrness. v. deáþ-bǽre, -bǽrness.

deád-boren. *Add: still-born* :—Gyf deádboren cyld sȳ on wífes innoðe, Lch. i. 206, 6. [v. *N. E. D.* dead-born.]

deád-hrægel, es ; n. *A garment of a dead person* :—Deádraegelum *palearibus*, Wrt. Voc. ii. 116, 12. v. deáþ-reáf.

deádian ; p. ode (*in Northern specimens*) *To die* :—Ne bið deád ł ne deádaged (deádað, R.) *non moriatur*, Jn. L. 6, 50. Gié deádaged (deódigað, R.) *moriemini*, 8, 21. Deádade ł deád wæs Heródes *defuncto Herode*, Mt. L. 2, 19. Ðiós deádade (deódade, R.) *haec moriebatur*, Lk. L. 8, 42. Þte deádege *ut pereat*, Mt. L. 5, 30. Þte ne deádige (deódige, R.) ł nére deád *quia non moritur*, Jn. L. 21, 23. Uoe deádige (deódige, R.), 11, 16. Þte ðes ne deádade (*moreretur*), Jn. R. 11, 37. Þte deádedo *mori*, Rtl. 86, 14. Deádade (-iga, R.) *mori*, Lk. L. 20, 36. Deádege (deódiga, R.), Jn. L. 4, 47. Gē biðon deádade (deádo, L.) *moriemini*, Jn. R. 8, 24. [*O. H. Ger.* tōdēn *mori*.] v. á-, gedeádian.

deád-lic. *Add:* I. *causing death, deadly, mortal, dire* :—Gif deádlic (*mortiferum* ; deódlic, R.) huæt gedrincas, Mk. L. 16, 18. Ðá deádlicustan (thā deátlicostan, ðá deudlicustan) *funestissima*, Txts. 65, 942 : Wrt. Voc. ii. 36, 25 : 151, 61. II. *subject to death, mortal, perishable* :—Þū bist deádlic, gif ðū þæs treówes wæstm geetst, Hml. Th. i. 14, 2. Se líchama is deádlic þurh Adames gylt, 16, 17. On myrran wæs getácnod þ hē wæs deádlic mon, Shrn. 48, 22. Lífes deádlices *vitae mortalis*, Rtl. 39, 25. In líchoma úsra deádlicum *in carne nostra mortali*, 13, 5. Ic wát þ ic on libbendum men and on gesceádwísnesse eom and þeáh on deádlicum *scio me rationale animal atque mortale esse*, Bt. 5, 3 ; F. 12, 28. On ðissum deádlican flǽsce, Past. 159, 5. Þára gimma oðfe æniges þára deádlicena ðinga ðe gesceádwísnesse næfþ, Bt. 13 ; F. 40, 7. On þissum lǽnan and on ðísum deádlicum ðingum, 32, 3 ; F. 118, 25. II a. *subject to immediate death, about to die* :—Esne wæs deádlic *servus erat moriturus*, Lk. L. 7, 2. Manu deádlicne *hominem moriturum*, Scint. 17, 8. Cf. deáþ-lic.

deád-líce. *Substitute: So as to cause death, mortally.* v. deádlic, I :—Deádlíce *loetaliter*, Wrt. Voc. ii. 52, 38. Dǽdlíce *letaliter*, i. *mortaliter*, An. Ox. 379. Þá beóð ádwealde þe wēnað þæt se man scyle deádlíce swyltan (*die and have no life after death*), efne swā nýten, Wlfst. 5, 9.

deád-licnys. *Add: mortal state, this life* :—Hopa deádlícnysse þyssere . . . hopa ēce *spes mortalitatis hujus . . . spes aeterna*, Scint. 219, 15.

deád-rægl, -synnig. v. deád-hrægel, deáþ-synnig.

deád-wille ; adj. *Unproductive, barren* :—Ðá beorgas tōdǽlað þ wǽsmbǽre land and þæt deádwylle sand *mons dividit inter vivam terram et arenas*, Ors. 1, 1 ; S. 26, 19. Cf. cwic-wille.

deáf. *Add:* I. *deaf, without hearing* :—Deáffra manna eáran, Hml. Th. ii. 16, 17. II. *imperfect in some essential quality, sterile* :—Se æker ðe bið unwæsðmbǽre oðfe ungefynde corn bringð oðfe deúf *terra quae sterilem segetem gignit*, Past. 411, 20. [Cf. *Icel.* daufr *insipid* ; *and see N. E. D.* deaf, § 6.]

deáfu. *Add:* [*and* diéfu, dífu (?). Cf. *Goth.* daubei, *and* v. beorhto, bi(e)rhto *for the absence as well as presence of mutation*] : deáfung. v. á-deáfung.

**deág(-h)**, e ; f. *A dye, colour :*—Telg, deág *fucus,* Wrt. Voc. ii. 36, 66. Deág *vel* telg, 151, 52. Deáh, 70, 19. Dēch *murex,* An. Ox. 18 b, 56. Telge, deáge *ostro,* Wrt. Voc. ii. 64, 37 : 87, 10. Of hǽwenre deáge *ex iacintho,* An. Ox. 1058. Deáche *stibio,* 4645. Dǽge *fuco,* 2, 23. Ne cîden nó þa munecas ymb þa deáge (dēge, *v. l.*) (*de colore*) hyra reáfa, R. Ben. 89, 15. Deáhum *sucis,* An. Ox. 5218. [*Take here examples under* deáh *in Dict.*] v. fisc-deág.

**deágan.** v. dígan (díegan).

**deágian.** *Add :* , dēgan :—Gewēsan, deághian *inficere,* i. *miscere* ł *fucare,* An. Ox. 5196. Dēgian (dēgan *tingere,* Hpt. Gl. 524, 59), 5220. Deágedum *coloratis,* 5330.

**deáh** *dye.* v. deág : **deapung.** *Dele.*

**dearf.** [= *W. S.* deorf] ; *adj. Bold :*—Dearfe ł dyrstige *audaci,* Mt. p. 9, 3. [v. *N. E. D.* derf. *O. Sax.* derbi : *O. Frs.* derfe : *Icel.* djarfr : *Dan.* djerv.]

**dearf-lic** ; *adj. Bold, presumptuous :*—From dearflicum *a praesumtoribus,* Mt. p. 2, 1. [v. *N. E. D.* derfly. *Icel.* djarf-ligr.]

**dearf-scipe**, es ; *m. Boldness, presumption :*—Dearfscip *praesumtio,* Mt. p. 1, 4. Dearfscipes *temeritatis,* 8, 2. Dearfscipe ł bældo *temeritate,* 9, 4. [v. *N. E. D.* derfship.]

**dearnunga.** *Add :*—Hé ongan hî hatian dearnunga and wrēgean tó þam cyninge, Lch. iii. 424, 19. Þeáh hé dearnunga forlicge *etiamsi adulteretur,* Ll. Th. ii. 156, 11. Hé forfieáh deornunga þa fôstormôdor, Hml. Th. ii. 154, 30. Dernunga, Mt. L. 19, 18. Twá cynn sind martirdômes, ân dearnunge, ôðer eáwunge, Hml. Th. ii. 544, 14. Dernunge *in occulto,* Jn. L. 18, 20. Dernunga *clam,* Mt. R. 2, 7. Hé begeat mid his smeáwrencan ealł dyrnunga æt Steorran þ him gewearð se þridda penig of þære tolne, C. D. iv. 56, 29. [*O. Sax.* darnungo. Cf. *O. H. Ger.* tarningun *latenter.*]

**dearr-lic, -scipe.** *Dele.* v. dearf-lic, -scipe.

**deáþ.** *Add :* gen. es and (?) a, *as being an old* u-*stem noun.* v. deáða gedál (cf. deáþgedál, 936) dreógan, Gū. 206. I. *death,* (1) *of an individual :*—Þa langan tíd þæs dimman ·deáðes *mortis inamabile tempus,* Dôm. L. 14. Hé bið mid wîtum þreád æfter his deáþe, Bl. H. 49, 25. Seó culfre ne leofað be nânum deáðe, Hml. Th. ii. 406, 18. Deáða swælteþ *morte moriatur,* Mt. R. 15, 4. Giniðrias hine tó deóða, Mk. R. 10, 33. Of deóða his *de morte ejus,* Jn. R. 11, 13. Deóðe, Lk. R. 23, 15. Hé lîchomlicne deáþ geþrowode, Bl. H. 103, 10. Oþ þone deáþ hé hine tintregaþ, 59, 30. Oð deáð *letotenus,* Wrt. Voc. ii. 83, 41. Oþ deáþ beswungen, Hml. S. 25, 782. (1 a) *a particular mode of death :*—Hé eall tôbærst . . . Iulius wæs wâniende þ hé swelce deáðe swealt, Ors. 5, 12 : S. 244, 5 : Jn. 12, 33. Ceás hé him þone deáþ þ him mon ofléte blôdes on þâm earme, Bt. 29, 2 ; F. 104, 23. Hwelc moncwealm wæs mid monigfealdum deáðum, Ors. 2, 5 ; S. 84, 33. Wê geáxiað ungecyndelico wîtu and ungecynelice deáþas, Bl. H. 107, 26. (2) *in the abstract :*—Gif hit ǽnige hwîle wunaþ, se deáþ hit hūru ǽfírreþ. Hwæt syndon þa woruldsǽlþa ôþres būton deáþes tácnunge, for þæm se deáþ ne cymð tó nânum ôþrum þingum būtan þ hē þ líf áfyrre, Bt. 8 ; F. 26, 3-7. Hwæt is þ líf elles buton lytelu ylding þæs deáþes ?, Bl. H. 59, 28. Ealle men geendiaþ on þâm deáþe, Bt. 11, 2 ; F. 34, 35. Heó þone deáþ forleás, and þ ēce líf gemētte, Hml. S. 7, 11. (3) *personified (or localized) :*—Se deáþ him tó cymeþ Godes dôm tó ábeódenne, Bl. H. 59, 11. Frecces deáðes *ambronis orci (faucibus),* An. Ox. 11, 107. Deáðe *orco,* Wrt. Voc. ii. 64, 69. II. *state of being dead :*—Seó hefige byrþen siteþ on þǽm deádan lîchoman þære byrgenne and þæs deáþes, Bl. H. 75, 8. Hé of deáþe árîseþ, 15, 12 : 67, 25. Swylce wē on deáðe lâgon, Hml. S. 11, 240. II a. *state after death of those not in heaven :*—Genere mē (*Eve in hell*) of þysses deáþes bendum, Bl. H. 89, 24. Tô þon ēcan deáþe, 61, 8. III. *cause or occasion of death* (as in to be the *death* of a person) :—Eálá deáþ, ic beó þín deáþ, Bl. H. 67, 17. IV. *a dead person, departed spirit :*—Ic gedyde þ man hyne on rôde áhēng . . ., and nū ic wylle hys deáþ tó þē gelǽdan, Nic. 14, 21. Deádas *manes,* Wrt. Voc. ii. 57, 57. Gegang þa deáða bearn þe hî dēmað nū *posside filios morte punitorum,* Ps. Th. 78, 12. Þurh deáðes(-as ?) wîtgung *nicromantia,* Wrt. Voc. ii. 62, 30. v. fǽr-deáþ.

**deáþ-bǽre** (deád-). *Add :*—Deáðbǽre (deád-, An. Ox. 1872) *letale, mortiferum,* Hpt. Gl. 450, 52. Se deáðbǽra wǽta, Past. 303, 16. Þæt on ūs deáðbǽres is ðurh synna, 445, 25. Deáðbǽre (deád-, An. Ox. 2020) *letiferas, mortiferas,* Hpt. Gl. 454, 17.

**deáþbǽr-lic** (deád-). v. deáðbǽr-lic *in Dict.*

**deáþbǽr-ness**, e ; f. *Deadliness, destructiveness :*—Slîtinc, geter, deáðbǽrnes *dilaceratio,* i. *mortificatio,* An. Ox. 3946. [*Take here* deáþbērnis *in Dict.*]

**deáþ-beácnigende** ; *adj. (ptcpl.) Threatening death :*—Cumað of heofenum deáðbeácnigende tâcn *de coelo venient signa minantia mortem* (Dôm. L. p. 23, 56), Wlfst. 137, 13 : Dôm. L. 112.

**deáþ-berende.** *Add :*—Þæs rēþan and þæs deáðberendan *funesti,* Wrt. Voc. ii. 34, 52. Fram ðǽm deáðberendum *a funesto,* 2, 30. I. *of things.* (1) *physical, deadly, pestilential :*—Deáðberende smîc gǽð of heora mūðe, Wlfst. 201, 1. Se deáðberenda drinc *pestifer potus,* Gr. D.

104, 29. Wæs þæra wyrma oroð swîðe deáðberende and ǽterne *halitus erat pestifer,* Nar. 14, 16. Ǽttres uoercdēðo deáðberendo *viri operationes mortiferas,* Rtl. 125, 37. (1 a) *figurative :*—Hē cwæð ðæt sió tunge wǽre deáðberendes ǽtres (*veneno mortifero*) full, Past. 281, 7. þæs biteran ǽttres þa deáþberendan wæter (*evil thoughts*), Guth. 46, 6. (2) *moral or spiritual :*—Þeó deáþberende uncyst (*envy*), Bl. H. 65, 13. II. *of living creatures :*—On fǽdme þæs deáðberendan dracan þe is deófol genemned, Wlfst. 188, 10. Þæt deáðberende deófol, 185, 13.

**deáþ-dæg.** *Add :*—Huaet his gāstae aefter deóthdaege doemid uueorthe, Txts. 149, 20. [v. *N. E. D.* death-day. *Icel.* dauþ[a]-dagr.]

**deáþ-godas.** *Substitute : The infernal deities :*—Manes deáðas and deáðgodas, Wrt. Voc. ii. 57, 57.

**deáþ-lic.** *Substitute :* I. *mortal, subject to death :*—Ǽnig deáþlic man, Bt. 7, 3 ; F. 20, 7. Ælc deáþlic man, 24, 1 ; F. 80, 6. Hē cōm deáðlic . . . hē árās undeáðlic, Hml. Th. i. 222, 10 : Bl. H. 21, 31. On þyssum deáðlican (deád-, *v. l.*) lîchaman *in hac mortali carne,* Bd. 1, 27 ; Sch. 82, 18. Þára sôþena gesǽlða wilniaþ ealle deáþlice men tô begitanne *est mentibus hominum vere bona inserta cupiditas,* Bt. 24, 2 ; F. 80, 30 : Bl. H. 197, 16. II. *mortal, grievous :*—Underlūtan þ deáþlice geoc (*mortale jugum ;* cf. þæt swǽre gioc, Met. 10, 20), Bt. 19 ; F. 68, 27. III. *dead :*—Hrǽwas oððe ðá deáþlican *morticina,* Ps. L. 78, 2. [*O. H. Ger.* tôd-lîh *mortalis, mortifer, funebris.*] v. un-deáþlic ; deáð-lic.

**deáþlice.** v. un-deáþlice.

**deáþlicness**, e ; f. *Substitute : Mortality.* I. *liability to death :*—Þonne se môna wanað, þonne tácnað hē ūre deáþlicnesse, Bl. H. 17, 24. II. *mortal life, this world :*—Tô þinre mildheortnesse becuman of þisse deáðlicnesse, Angl. xii. 509, 19.

**deáþ-reáf**, es ; *n. A garment of a dead person :*—Deáþreáf *exuvias* (cf. *exubiae, uestes mortuorum,* Corp. Gl. H. 52, 524 : *exuviae, spolia* reáf, i. *uestes mortuorum,* Wulck. Gl. 233, 44), Wrt. Voc. ii. 32, 32.

**deáþ-scyldig.** *Add :*—Of unrehtwîsnisse ūsa deáðscyldego uosa uē ongēton *ex iniquitate nostra reos nos esse cognovimus,* Rtl. 78, 14. v. scyldig, V ; deáþ-synnig.

**deáþscyldig-ness.** v. deáþsynnig-ness.

**deáþ-synnig** ; *adj. Guilty of death, liable to the punishment of death :*—Sē ðe ofslaeð deáðsynig (*reus*) bið tô dôme, Mt. L. 5, 21.

**deáþsynnig-ness**, e ; f. *Guiltiness of death :*—Deáðsynnignise ł [deáþ-?] scyldignise *reatum,* Rtl. 42, 33.

**deáþ-þēnunga.** *Substitute :* deáþ-þegnung, e ; f. *Ministration to the dead ;* pl. *exequies :*—Deáþþēnunga *exequias,* Wrt. Voc. ii. 30, 24. Hū mæg ic ðē ána gedēfelîce deáðþēnunga gegearwian nymðe mîne brôþor hider sîn gesamnode ? . . . Ðá þreó fǽmnan þâm Maria hire deáþþþenunga bebeád, Nap. 16.

**deáþ-wyrda.** *Substitute :* deáþ-wyrd, e ; f. *Fate, death :*—Deáþwyrde *fata* (cf. *prolis luxerunt fata parentes,* Ald. 176, 18), Wrt. Voc. ii. 38, 34.

**deáw.** *Add :*—Seofoðe pund wæs deáwes pund, ðanon him (*Adam*) becôm swât, Sal. K. 180, 14 : Rtl. 192, 17. Of deáuwe *rore,* Kent. Gl. 46. *Roscido* deáwe (wǽtum ? : *the immediately preceding gloss is* roscida, rore madida (v. Corp. Gl. H.), *and* deáwe *seems to be due to* rore), Wrt. Voc. ii. 119, 29. Būtan iēnscúrum and reócendum deáwe, Hml. S. 18, 57. Swilce hē wǽre on wynsumum deáwe, 31, 888, 876. Þyses fýres hǽto sý gecyrred on wǽtne deáw, 30, 441. Deáwas and rîmforst *rores et pruina,* Hy. T. P. 68.

**-deáw** ; *adj.* v. ge-, un-deáw.

**deáwian.** *Add :* [*To be inferred from* deáwigend-lic ? v. *N. E. D.* dew ; *vb. O. Frs.* dawia : *O. H. Ger.* towôn(-ēn) : *Icel.* döggva.]

**deáwig.** *Substitute for first passage :*—Deáwig sceaftum *with the dew on their spears,* Exod. 344 ; *and add :*—Deáwigre *roscido,* An. Ox. 84. Mid dēwium (dǽwigum, Hpt. Gl. 421, 65) *roscidis, rore madidis,* 655.

**deáwi(g)endlic (?)** ; *adj. Dewy :*—Dǽáweinlicre *roscido,* Hpt. Gl. 408, 4.

**deáw-wyrm.** *Add :* [*Du.* dauw-worm *ring-worm.*]

**decan**, decanon, es ; *m. One who has charge of ten monks :*—Fram decane sî boren *a decano portetur,* Angl. xiii. 414, 701 : 433, 980. Þurh decanonas *per decanos,* R. Ben. 125, 8. Cf. teóþung-ealdor.

**dēcan** ; *pp.* dēced *To smear, daub :*—Dēc ânne clāð, Lch. i. 150, 19. [v. *N. E. D.* dag.] v. ge-dēcan.

**decan-hâd**, es ; *m. Dignity of a dean* (decan, *q. v.*) :—Ofor heora wican heora decanhâdes *super decanias suas,* R. Ben. I. 54, 2.

**decanon.** v. decan : **deccan.** *Dele, and see* dēcan.

**declínian** ; *pp.* od *To decline* (in grammar) :—Mæg man on ǽgðrum ende hine (*a compound noun*) declínian, Ælfc. Gr. Z. 88, 6. Wē habbað nū declínod þa eahta frumcennedan pronomina, 100, 6.

**declíni(g)endlic.** *Add :*—Bið se nama declíniendlic, Ælfc. Gr. Z. 88, 9 : 86, 9. v. un-declínigendlic.

**declínung.** *Add :*—Þá naman and þa bínaman and heora declínunga, Angl. viii. 313, 5.

defe? :—Of þām þorne tô þǽre defe; of þǽre defe tô beorclīge, Cht. Crw. 25, 55.

dēfe. Add :—Gif þū wilt doefe beón si vis perfectus esse, Mt. R. 19, 21.

delan. Dele, and for the passage substitute :—Ǽr þon engla weard (weard, MS.) for oferhygde dǽl on gedwilde; noldan dreógan leng heora selfra rǽd ere of the angels part from pride fell into error; they would not longer do what was best for themselves, Gen. 23.

delf. Add: v. under-delf.

delfan. Add: I. absolute, to dig :—'Ic nât mid hwī ic delfe . . .' ongan þā þǽrmid delfan, Hml. S. 23 b, 765. Þā dulfon hī in þǽre ylcan stōwe, Shrn. 113, 13. II. to dig the ground :—Genam hē āne spada and dealf þā eorþan, H. R. 13, 13. Hē hēt delfan þā eorðan, Hml. S. 27, 37. Þā eorþan delfan æfter golde, Bt. 15; F. 48, 23. III. to extract by digging, dig gold, &c. :—Þā ǽmettan delfað gold ūp of eorðan, Nar. 35, 8. IV. to excavate, dig a pit :—Bið dolfen seáð fodiatur fovea, Ps. Srt. 93, 13. V. to bury :—Ic ásende ofer eów mancwealm, . . . and þā deádan man nât hū man delfe, Wlfst. 296, 16. v. for-delfan; un-dolfen.

delfín a dolphin :—Delfín pina, Wülck. Gl. 293, 13.

delf-ísen. Add :—Delfísen fusorium, Wrt. Voc. ii. 38, 49.

dell (dæll), es; n. m. A dell, deep hollow or vale :—Dell (den, v. l.) weallendum lēgum full, Bd. 5, 12; Sch. 616, 4. Forð be deópan delle, Cht. E. 290, 30. On scipdel; of scipdelle on cȳpmanna [del]; of cȳpmanna delle andlang weges, C. D. v. 48, 13. On ðæt twigbutme del; of ðǣm delle on beran del, 86, 20. Of ūlan delle, 180, 3. On ðet del; of ðǣm dellæ, 242, 28. Oð ðane myclan del, C. D. B. ii. 202, 8. [Cf. Goth. [ib-] dalja.] v. æf-dæll (-dell), wæter-dell; dæl.

dem. Add :—Hȳnð vel lyre vel hearm vel demm dispendium vel damnum vel detrimentum, Wrt. Voc. i. 47, 29. (v. Angl. viii. 451.) For þȳ dæmme (demme, v. l.) þæs wāges fylles damno parietis, Gr. D. 125, 11. Þone wōl (dem, v. l.) þiure gedrēfednesse perturbationum morbum, Bt. 5, 3; F. 12, 17.

dēma. Add :—Dēma praetor, An. Ox. 17, 58: þreses, 45, 1. Doema arbiter, Wrt. Voc. ii. 9, 50: judex, Ps. Srt. 7, 12 : Lk. L. R. 12, 14. Dēman satrat̨e, i. iudicis, An. Ox. 4760. Dēman presbiteri, i. iudices, 4245: proceres, 7, 64. Dēmena praetorum, i. iudicum, 31, 8, 249. Mid him (Judas) byrnan sceolan þā þe heora sylfra sāula forhycggaþ for feós lufan . . . Hī habbaþ dēmena naman and sceaþena dǽda. . . . Þonne hié for feós lufan earmne fordēmaþ būton scylde, Bl. H. 63, 9. v. self-, unriht-, weorold-, yfel-dēma.

dēman. Add: I. to judge. (1) absolute :—Ic dēme (doemo, L.) swā swā ic gehȳre sicut audio judico, Jn. 5, 30. Gif ic dēme (doemu, R.) mīn dōm is sōð, 8, 16. ' Mē þynceþ unscyldiglicre þ him man heáfod of áceorfe,' þā cwæþ Neron : ' On ðā betstan wīsan þū dēmest,' Bl. H. 189, 35. Yfele gerēfan þā þe on wōh dēmaþ, 61, 26. Dēme gē swā swā gē willon þ eów sȳ gedēmed, 28. (2) to judge a person, (a) with dat. :—Ic ne dēme (doemo, L., doemu, R.) nǽnum men, Jn. 8, 15. Se mon þe dēmeþ þǽm earmum būton mildheortnesse, Bl. H. 95, 35. Ic dēmde twelf þeódum, 155, 29. Hē gecȳðde ðæt hē him dēman nolde, ðā hē gedyde ðæt hī him selfe dēmdan . . . eft hit wæs gecweden : ' Ðǽr wē ūs selfum dēmden, ðonne ne dēmde ūs nō God' constat quod a suo judicio abscondere voluit quos sibimetipsis judices fecit . . . Hinc dicitur : 'Si nosmetipsos dijudicaremus, non judicaremur,' Past. 415, 3-8. Samuel and Daniel cildgeonge forealdedum mæssepreóstum dēmdon (judicaverant), R. Ben. 115, 8. Dēm folcum judica populos, Ps. Th. 7, 8. Hē him symle rihte dēme, Bl. H. 43, 11. (b) with acc. :—Þū hī on rihtum rǽdum dēmest judicas populos in aequitate, Ps. Th. 66, 4. Hē dēmeð fyrhte þearfan judicabit pauperes, 71, 4. Hié gescyldaþ þā unscyldigan, and þā scyldigan þearlwíslíce dēmaþ, Bl. H. 63, 20. Dēm þū þīn folc, Ps. Th. 71, 2. (3) to judge a cause, crime :—Dēm.þine ealde intingan judica causam tuam, Ps. Th. 73, 21. Ðonne hié ðā scylda on him selfum dēmen and wrecan cum culpas se judice puniat, Past. 151, 17. (4) where the matter of judgement is given :—Ic sōð symble dēme ego justitiam judicabo, Ps. Th. 74, 2. Hē riht folcum dēmeð, 95, 10. Dēmað ǽlcon men riht quod justum est judicate, Deut. 1, 16. (4 a) with cognate acc. :—Hié dēmaþ heora dōmas they give their judgements, Bl. H. 63, 18. Sē þe þā gebregdnan dōmas dēmde, 99, 32. Dēm mīnne dōm judica judicium meum, Ps. Th. 118, 154. Dēmað steópcildum dōmas sōðe judica pupillo, 81, 3. (5) to sentence a person to punishment :—Dēm þū hī tô deáþe, Jul. 87. Nō hȳ hine tô deáþe dēman mōston, Gū. 521. Deáþe dēman, El. 303. (6) to adjudge, assign reward, punishment, &c., to a person :—Hē eallum dēmað leán æfter ryhte, Cri. 846. On swā hwæðere hond Dryhten mǽrðo dēme swā him gemet þince, B. 687. Hwæt mē God dēman wille, Sat. 109 : Cri. 803 : Jul. 707: An. 75. (7) to settle, appoint, decree :—Heora scriftbēc tǽcan swā swā hié ūre fæderas dēmdon, Bl. H. 43, 9. God wolde hyra nȳdwræce dēman God would decree their exile, Gū. 526. (7 a) of decision by lot :—Heora ǽlcum his dǽl, swā him dēmde seó tā, Hml. Th. ii. 254, 31. Hleótan man mōt . . . þ him dēme seó tā, gif hī hwæt dǽlan willað, Hml. S. 17, 86. II. to deem, think, suppose :—

Doemo ic arbitror, Jn. L. 21, 25. Doema censeo, Wrt. Voc. ii. 103, 58. Ne dēmeð hē non retur, 61, 57. III. to estimate, value :—[Swā] þearle hē dēmde tantopere (i. tam valde) taxauerat (i. iudicauerat), An. Ox. 2014. IV. to proclaim something noble, celebrate :—Hī eahtodon eorlscipe and his ellenweorc dēmdon, swā hit gedēfe bið þæt mon his dryhten wordum herge, B. 3175. Is árlic þæt wē ǽfæstra dǽde dēmen, secgan Dryhtne lof, Gū. 498 : Sat. 299. Hié Dryhtnes ǽ dēman sceoldon, reccan fore rincum, Ap. 10 : An. 1196: 1405. Wē þæt hȳrdon hǽleð eahtian, dēman dǽdhwate, þætte gelamp, Jul. 2. Dēman, meldan, Rä. 29, 11.

dēmed-líc; adj. That may be judged :—Hwæthugu dēmedlíces aliquid judicabile, Gr. D. 336, 20. v. for-dēmedlic.

-dēmedness. v. for-dēmedness.

dēmend. Add :—God is dēmend Deus judex est, Ps. Th. 49, 7. Sē ðe fore ūs doemend (adjudicandus) tô cuōm, fore ūs doemend bið (adjudicaturus) tô cyme, Rtl. 35, 7-9. v. for-dēmend.

dēmere. Add :—Se doemere judex, Lk. L. 12, 58. Hī beóð ðā dēmeras and him ne bið nān dōm gedēmed, Hml. Th. i. 396, 19. Doemeras judices, Mt. L. 12, 27. Hwǽr syndon dēmra dōmstōwa?, Wlfst. 148, 31.

dēmon a demon, devil :—From dēmonum a demonibus, Rtl. 146, 1.

den. v. denn : Dena lagu. v. lagu in Dict.

den-bera; pl. n. Lat. Substitute : den-bǽre, es ; n. A swine-pasture (used only in pl.) :—Ðis synt ðā denbǽra ðe tô ðissum londe belimpað, C. D. ii. 195, 15. Þis synt þā denbǽra on wealda, 216, 4. Þā denbǽro, 265, 33. Mid ðǽm denbǽrum in Limenwero wealdo and in burhwaro wealdo and in bôcholte, C. D. B. i. 344, 10. ¶ Add to the Latin forms given in Dict. :—Adiectis IIII daenberis in commune saltu, C. D. i. 140, 12. v. weald-, wer-bǽre; denn, II.

den-berende a swine pasture :—Tresdecem denberende on Andrede, C. D. i. 229, 14. v. preceding word.

dencgan. v. dengan: dene; f. v. denu.

dene; m. Add :—On Duddingdene; andlong denes, C. D. iii. 449, 11. On ðām dene (convalle) ðe Mambre wæs hāten, Prud. 6 b : Gen. 18, 1.

Dene. Add : Dena, Dǽne, Denan; gen. pl. Dena, Deni(g)a :—þæt lond þe mon Ongle hǽt, and Sillende and sumne dǽl Dene, Ors. 1, 1; S. 16, 8. Hēr Ængle and Dene gefuhton, Chr. 910; P. 97, 5: 1018; P. 155, 14. Dena him mycel feoh guldon, 1048; P. 167, 17. Dena (Deona, v. l.) weóldon rīce Englalandes, 1065; P. 194, 7. Þā Denan sige áhton, 943; P. 111, 13. Under Dena onwalde, 901 : P. 91, 28 : 921; P. 103, 14. Denia leóde, B. 2125. Mægen Deniga, 155: 271. Fram Anglum ge fram Denum, Chr. 1039; P. 161, 25. Hē Dene weorðode, B. 1090. [Icel. Danir.] v. Beorht-, Eást-, Gār-, Hring-, Norþ-, Sǽ-, Sūþ-, West-Dene; Dene-mearc; Dǽne in Dict.

dene-land. v. dene-land in Dict.

Dene-mearc. Dele the bracket, and add :—Wæs him on þæt bæcbord Denamearc, Ors. 1, 1 ; S. 19, 26. Sume fērdon tô Dænmarce (tô Dænmercan (Denmarcon, v. l.), 30), Chr. 1070; P. 207, 16. On Denemearcon, 1036 ; P. 159, 18. Tô Denemarcon, 1076; P. 211, 2, 36. Tô Dænemearcon (Denmearcan, v. l.), 1005; P. 136, 5. Tô Denamarcon, 1049; P. 167, 19. Tô Denmarcon, 1045 ; P. 165, 23 : 1046; P. 165, 28. Of Denmearcon, 1075; P. 211, 16. Tô Denmearcon, 1019; P. 155, 17. Of Dænmarcon, 1069; P. 202, 12. On Dænmearcan, 1076; P. 212, 12. Hē betǣhte þurcille Denemearcan tô healdenne, 1023 ; P. 157, 30. Magnus gewann Denmarcon, 1047; P. 165, 24. [Icel. Dan-mörk.]

dengan; p. de To ding, beat, strike :—Ælcum gemete ne sceal ārung beón þǽre gyltendan geogoðe, ac swiðor man sceal heora sīdan mid giterdon gelōmlíce dencgan (sed potius eorum latera virgis assidue tundenda sunt), Nap. 17. [v. N. E. D. dinge.]

Denisc. Add :—Æfter þǽm him becōm on þæt Deniscæ gewinn mid eallum Germānium cum insurrexissent gentes innumerabiles, hoc est, Marcomanni atque omnis pene Germania, Ors. 6, 13 ; S. 268, 10.

denn. Add : I. a den, lair of a beast :—Haran den lepusculi cubile, Kent. Gl. 1107. Denn lustra (ferarum), An. Ox. 26, 47. v. feóf-denn. II. a woodland pasture for swine :—Hī geúðen Ælfwolde ānes dennes wið his lícwyrðan scætte, þ is .MCCCC. and L denarios. Ðis dǽn is genamod Hȳringdænn, C. D. B. iii. 490, 11-13. Þis synt þā denbǽra on wealda . . . þe norþan ea . . . ceorla den, C. D. ii. 216, 6. Belimpað tô ðām lande fíf denn, ān on ūtwalda, brocces hām ðæs dennes nama, and þæs ōðres dennes nama sængethryc . . . þonne twā den an glæppan felda, iii. 227, 31-4. Ðis synt ðā den ðe ðǽrtô gebyrigeað, v. 313, 14. ¶ the word occurs in many local names :—Adiectis quattuor denberis . . . Heáhden . . . helman hyrst, i. 317, 20. Hec sunt pascua porcorum quot nostra lingua denbǽra nominamus, lamburnanden, orriceden, teligden, stānehtandenn, ii. 65, 5-8 : 75, 26-8 : 228, 2-3. Adiectis deuberis in commune saltu, otanhyrst . . . et haeseldaen, i. 248, 18. Aet Haeseldenne, 216, 28. Inn on ðæt eádenn; of ðām eúdenne, iii. 385, 4. v. dænn in Dict.; den-bǽre, -stōw.

**den-stów,** e; f. A place of pasture:—Þis sint þá denstówa, brochyrst . . . , C. D. B. iii. 144, 21. v. preceding word.

**denu.** [Though a nominative dene occurs weak forms of the oblique cases are not found.] Add:—Deuu myrtea, Wrt. Voc. ii. 57, 20. On middan þære dene, Iosaphat. Seó dene is betwux þære dáine Sion and þám munte Oliueta, Hml. Th. i. 440, 15. Án ðeóstorful dene, ii. 338, 5. Bituih iúih and úsih dene micel (chaos magnum) gefæstnad is, Lk. L. 16, 26. Hé mǽwð gærs on þysse dene (valle), Gr. D. 36, 2. Andlang weterdene tó ðære deópan dene; of ðære dene tó ðan reádan stáne, C. D. vi. 8, 16. On þære dene eádmódnesse, Bt. 12; F. 36, 22. Dena getácniað þá eádmódan, Hml. Th. i. 362, 18. In deanum in convallibus, Ps. Srt. 103, 10. ¶ the word occurs often in local names:— Ðá denbǽra . . . hlósdionu, swánadionu, C. D. ii. 195, 16. In hæsldene; of hæsldene, iii. 401, 2. On hwǽtedene norðeweardre; of hwǽtedene, Cht. E. 293, 22. See also Txts. 545. v. eorþ-, mór-, wæter-denu.

**deófel-, deóf-lic, -líce.** v. deóful-lic, -líce.

**deófol.** Add: In sing. both masc. and neut., in pl. neuter (except in northern specimens), pl. nom. deófol, deóflu (-o, -a). I. the devil:— Ðæt lytige dióful (hostis callidus) ðonne hé gesihð . . . Swá dêð ðæt dióful (diabolus) . . . Swá ðæt dioful (corruptor) . . . Swá ðêð ðæt dióful, Past. 415, 10-30. Se dióbul (dióful, v. l.), 227, 5. Þæt deófol cwæð tó þam folce, Bl. H. 243, 2, 4, 9, 14. Þ wæs þæt deófol þ seó þeód hyre for god beeódon, and hí nemdon þone Astaróþ, Shrn. 120, 31. Forlêt se deófol (diówl, L., þ deóful, R. diabolus) hine, Mt. 4, 11. Gyf se deóful ádrífð út þone deóful si Satanas Satanan eicit, 12, 26. Hú mæg hê ðe wiðerworda diówul (ðe diówl, L. Satanas) ðone diówul (ðone diówl, L.) fordrífa, Mk. R. 3, 23. Dióbul, Mt. L. 4, 5. Cunnung diábles temtatio diaboli, Mk. p. 1, 16. Satanase ðám ealdan deófle, Nic. 14, 1. Ne maga gié Gode gehêra and dióble (Mamonae), Mt. L. 6, 24. Díwle and englum hes, 25, 41. II. a devil, an evil spirit:—Ðá deófol hine swungan, Shrn. 52, 27. Ðæt deófol genam mid him óþre seofon deóflo . . . þá deófla blǽstan ofer hine, Bl. H. 243, 4-11: Sat. 319. Deófla (diówla, L. R.) ealdor princeps demonum, Mk. 3, 22. Deófla (diówla, L.) of manegum, 4, 41. Ðá diówblas, Lk. L. 8, 33. Ðá deófla (þá deoful, R.) bǽdon, Mt. 8, 31. Gyf ic ádrífe út deófla (dióules, L., deóful, R.) . . . Gyf ic áwurpe deóflu (diówles, L., deóful, R.), 12, 27, 28. Diúlas, Lk. p. 7, 4. II b. a devil as object of worship, false god. Cf. deófol-gild:—Alle godas ðioda dióful omnes dii gentium daemonia, Ps. Srt. 95, 5. Hiera deófla sum Proserpinam, Wrt. Voc. ii. 85, 3. Godes ǽ ús forbiét diófulum (deóflum, v. l.) tó offrianne lex Dei sacrificia Satanae prohibet, Past. 369, 3. Þær hǽþene men deóflum onguldon, Bl. H. 221, 3. III. applied to a human being. (1) a wicked person:—Eówer án is deófol (diúl, L., diówul, R.), Jn. 6, 70. Diúbul, p. 5, 3. On þám gé deóflu drincan ongunnon, Dan. 750. (2) as a term of abuse or contempt:—Hé cleopode rêceleaslíce tó his þeówtlinge: 'Cum, deóful, hider and unscó mê' (veni, diabole, discalcea me), Gr. D. 221, 21. v. ealdor-, hell-deófol.

**deófol-cræft.** Add:—Se moncwealm wæs swá ungemetlic, ðæt hié mid deófolcræftum sóhton hú hié hit gestillan mehte, and gefetton Escolafius þone scínlácan, Ors. 3, 10; S. 140, 7.

**deófol-gild.** Add: I. idolatry; an idolatrous practice:—Deófolgild bið þ man his Drihten forlǽte and his crístendóm, and tó deófollicum hǽðenscype gebúge . . . Oðer deófolgild is . . . ðonne se man þá sceandlican leahtras begǽð þe se sceocca hine lǽrð, Hml. S. 17, 47-51. Se crístendóm weóx and þ ealde deófolgield wearþ ádwêsced, Jud. p. 162, 4. Ðæt hié Godes ǽ ne gehwierfen tó deófulgielde ne legem Dei in Satanae sacrificium vertant, Past. 369, 4. Þ man hine forhæbbe fram deófolgylde (ab idolatria), Ll. Th. ii. 162, 35. Þá Crístenan þe swelc deófolgild lufiað and bigongað, Ors. 4, 12; S. 210, 6. Deófolgild lustramina, Wrt. Voc. ii. 50, 3. Deófelgylda, An. Ox. 1899. Þá hêðnan heora þá leásan godas mid mislicum deófolgeldun (cf. mid lácum and offrungum, Hml. Th. i. 504, 18) him laþodan on fultum, Bl. H. 201, 31. II. an idol:—Se cásere ongan timbrian deófolgyld on cirican . . . ðær ðær ǽnig deófolgyld wæs árǽred . . . ðá hǽþenan . . . deófle offrodon, Hml. S. 23, 27-36. Hêt se gerêfa hí lǽdan tó þúres deófulgeldum ond hêt hí þ weorðian . . . þá feól þ deófolgild tó hire fótum, Mart. H. 166, 14-16. Syxtum nêdde se cásere tó Tíges deófolgilde. Þá cwæð hê tó þám deófulgylde: 'Tówyrpe þê Críst'; þá sóna gefeól þæs deófolgyldes húses sum dǽl, 140, 2-5. Hé eóde intó ðam temple tó ðám deófolgylde Astaróð, Hml. Th. i. 454, 16. Búton þǽm deófolgelde þe hê bærnan ongan, Bl. H. 221, 17. Þ hê weorðode sunnan deófolgyld. Þær wæs þære sunnan anlícnys geworht of golde, ond heó wæs on gyldenum scryde, ond æt þám wǽron gyldene hors, Mart. H. 220, 28: 206, 4. Hé bebeád þæt mon áfielde diófolgielda þá cirican, and þæt mon his ágen deófolgield þær tómiddes ásette, þæt wæs his ágen onlícnes sacrarium repleri statuis simulachrisque imperavit, seque ibi ut Deum coli

praecepit, Ors. 6, 3; S. 258, 8. Hiora ágnum godum, þ sint diófolgild idolis suis, 1, 5; S. 34, 20. Deófolgylda (deófulgilda, v. l.) begang idolorum cultus, Bd. 2, 3; Sch. 125, 20. þis tempel mid eallum þám deófolgyldum þe him on eardiað, Hml. Th. i. 72, 3. Deófulgildum, Lev. 26, 30.

**deófol-gilda.** Add:—Se ðeóda láreów sǽde þæt deófolgyldan (idolis servientes, 1 Cor. 6, 9) nabbað Godes ríce, Hml. Th. ii. 330, 25. Þá deófolgildan (the prophets of Baal), Hml. S. 18, 112. þá leásan deófolgildan þe Baal wurðodon, 369.

**deófol-gítsung,** e; f. Unrighteous mammon:—In unrehtwíso, i. ðæt is díwlgíttsungo in iniquo mamonae, Lk. L. 16, 11.

**deófol-lic (deóf-);** adj. Take here examples under deóf-lic in Dict., and add: I. of the (a) devil:—Se freódóm ðæs deófollican onwaldes freedom from the power of the devil, Bl. H. 137, 13. Dióflices fanaticae (lustrationis), An. Ox. 2058. Deóuolicre, 7, 125. Deóflices galdres necromantiae, i. demonum invocationis, 1927. On þám deófollican (deóflican, v. l.) tíman in Antechrist's time, Wlfst. 86, 4. Tó deófollicum hǽðenscype to the worship of the devil, Hml. S. 17, 48. Deóflicere ǽigælþe fanatica superstitione, An. Ox. 3232. Deófelicum (deóff-, Wrt. Voc. ii. 138, 65) gefærscipe demonico globo, Wülck. Gl. 218, 42. Diówlica onerninge diabolica incursione, Rtl. 36, 1. His weorc syndon deófollicu his works are of the devil, Bl. H. 177, 1. Hé ne ondrêd heora deófellican híw, Hml. Th. ii. 512, 21. II. of other than spirits, like the (a) devil, devilish, diabolical, evil, cruel:—Mennisclic is ðæt mon on his móde costunga ðrowige . . . ac ðæt is deófullic ðæt hê ðone willan ðurhteó, Past. 71, 14. Hí sendon tó Domiciane þám deófellican (deóflican, v. l.) cásere, Hml. S. 29, 190. Mid wealhr(e)ówre, deóflicere mihte tyrannica potestate, An. Ox. 1157. Þone deófollicon abbod þe cwæð þ úres Drihtenes líchama and his godcundnes wǽre ánes gecyndes, Ll. Th. ii. 374, 23. Ðæne deófollican unðeáw . . . gedón þ óðre men námað máre ðonne hit gemet sý, Hml. A. 145, 22. Tó deóflicum weorcum, Angl. xi. 112, 19. Wið þás egeslican and þás deófollican coðe, þæt is wið þás hellican unþeáwas, Wlfst. 245, 21: Angl. viii. 337, 7. Wyrto yfelwyrcendo and dióublica (diabolicas), Rtl. 103, 1. [v. N. E. D. devilly; adj. O. H. Ger. tiufal-lîh diabolicus: Icel. djóful-ligr.]

**deófol-líce (deóf-);** adv. I. as a devil. v. deófol-lic, I:—Antecríst áginð leógan deófollíce (deóflíce, v. l.), Wlfst. 85, 1: 200, 11. II. like a devil, furiously, cruelly. v. deófol-lic, II:—Datianus deófollíce (deóflíce, v. l.) geyrsode ongeán ðone hálgan wer, Hml. S. 14, 23. Hé deóflíce weard geháthyrt, 22, 220. [v. N. E. D. devilly; adv.]

**deófol-scín.** For the citations see under scín, scinn in Dict., and add:—Utan wið deófolscín scildan ús georne, Wlfst. 188, 34. [He dide mare inoh off deofelschine o life, Orm. 8110. v. N. E. D. devilshine.]

**deófol-scipe,** es; m. Idolatry:—Crístes apostolas wǽron onsende on þysne middaneard for ðí þ hí sceolon menn trymman and lǽran and fullian, and deófolscipe nyðerian, Nap. 17.

**deófol-seóc.** Add:—Deófelseócne inerguminum, An. Ox. 4934. Hé deóflum bebeád þ hié of deófolseócum mannum út ferdon, Bl. H. 173, 28. Heó deófulseóce gehǽlde, Shrn. 33, 13. Gewítleáse, deófelseóce inergumenos, i. amentes, An. Ox. 3057: larbatos, 4936.

**deófol-seócnes.** Add:—Wið gewítleáste, þ is wið deófulseócnysse, genim of þám líchoman þysse ylcan wyrte mandragore, Lch. i. 248, 3.

**deóg.** v. dígan (diégan).

**deón;** p. de To suck:—Of múðe cildra and súkendra í díendra ex ore infantium et lactantium, Mt. R. L. 21, 16. [O. H. Ger. tāen lactare: Dan. die to suck; dægge to suckle: Swed. di to suck; dägga to suckle: Goth. daddjan to suckle.] v. ge-deón, meoloc-deónd (not -teónd).

**deóp.** Add: I. literal:—Dióp seáð fovea profunda, Kent. Gl. 829. II. metaph.:—þes pistol is . . . eów swíðe deóp tó gehýrenne, Hml. Th. i. 448, 8. His deópe rihtwísnys his infinite righteousness, 112, 3. Deópum ceápe at a high price, Ll. Th. i. 370, 10. Þ hé swá deópe friðsócne (so inviolable a sanctuary) gesêce, 340, 10. For ðínum deópum gyltum for your grievous sins, Hml. S. 22, 177. On manegum landum gebyreð deópre (more onerous) swánriht, Ll. Th. i. 436, 15. Be þám deópestan áðe by the most solemn oath, 324, 19.

**deóp** the deep. Add:—Þreó ásæton on ðá healfe þæs deópes ðe ðá Deniscan scipu áseten wǽron, Chr. 897; P. 91, 3. Deóp (trans) fretum (Mt. 8, 18), Wrt. Voc. ii. 72, 30: 36, 71. Cf. dípe.

**deópe,** an; f. v. dípe.

**deópe;** adv. Add: I. literal:—Hé hine hêt sleán and deópe bedelfan, Chr. 1050; P. 170, 3. II. metaph.:—Ús is deópe beboden we are most solemnly bidden, Wlfst. 282, 22: Ll. Th. ii. 328, 27. Hit is forboden on hálgum bócum swýþe deópe, Shrn. 162, 26. Þá dǽde wrecan swíðe deópe to punish the deed very severely, Ll. Th. i. 174, 10: 400, 8. Hé syngað swýðe deópe he sins very grievously, Hml. S. 19, 254. Swá man bið mihtigra . . . , swá sceal hê deóppor synna gebêtan, Ll. Th. i. 328, 14. [O. H. Ger. tiufo alte, funditus, penitus.]

**deópian**; *p.* ode *To get deep:*—Swâ dolh ne deópian, Lch. ii. 352, 2. [þer waxeð wunde and deopeð into þe soule, A. R. 288.]

**deóp-lic.** *Add:* I. *where great knowledge is shewn or required:*—Ðis fers is swîðe deóplic eów tô understandenne, Hml. Th. ii. 386, 3. Hit wile þingcan ungelæredum mannum tô deóplic, Lch. iii. 244, 10. Deóplicu (depp-, MS.) is seó âcsung and winsumu tô witanne þâm þe hyt witan mæg, Shrn. 191, 20. God geswâc ðæs dihtes ðæs deóplican cræftes, Hex. 20, 15. II. *grievous, terrible:*—Deóplice, egeslice *minacem,* An. Ox. 3523.

**deóp-líce.** *Add:* I. *of mental operations:*—Hê deóplíce undernam Drihtnes lâre . . . and wunode deóplíce gelæred, Hml. S. 29, 76, 81. Deóplícor (*profundius*) þû smeágst þonne yld ûre anfôn mæge, Coll. M. 33, 11. II. *in other connexions:*—Hî Godes þeówas deóplíce griðedan *they most effectually protected God's servants,* Ll. Th. i. 334, 24. Tô ðâm ëcan life ðe hê deóplíce geearnode *to the eternal life that he most thoroughly deserved,* Hml. Th. ii. 154, 7.

**deópnes.** *Add:* I. *a deep place:*—Diópnis *chaos,* Wrt. Voc. ii. 20, 53. Deópnysse *voragine,* An. Ox. 4340. II. *depth of meaning, mystery:*—Þæt ðâm gódum ne sŷ oftogen seó gâstlice deópnyss, Hml. Th. ii. 96, 5. Diópnise ríces heofna *mysteria regni coelorum,* Mk. L. 13, 11. III. *cunning, subtlety:*—Þâra gerêfena unriht and reáfiâc and deópnessa and wôge dômas and prættas, Wlfst. 245, 2 : Angl. viii. 336, 40.

**deóp-þancol.** *Substitute: Deep-thoughted, profoundly thoughtful:*—Þæt þû scealt deópþanclum geþance âsmeágan, Wlfst. 248, 7. Witan mid deópðanclum môde, Angl. viii. 329, 11.

**deóþþancol-líce;** *adv. With depth of thought, with profound learning:*—Bûton ôðrum trahtbôcum ðe hê mid gecneordum andgite deópðancollíce âsmeáde, Hml. Th. i. 436, 20.

**deór** *an animal. Add:*—Deór *ferus,* Ælfc. Gr. Z. 236, 11. God biþ þonne rêðra þonne ænig wilde deór, Bl. H. 95, 31. Þæt græge deór wulf on wealde, Chr. 937; P. 109, 22. Ûr byð . . . fela frêcne deór, Rûn. 2. Se camal þ micla deár, Lk. L. 18, 25. Se micla deár, Mk. L. 10, 25. Of camele ðæm deáre, Mt. p. 19, 11. Wildu diór þær woldon tô irnan and stondon swilce hî tamu wæron, Bt. 35, 6 ; F. 168, 1. Deór and neát *bestiae et universa pecora,* Ps. Th. 148, 10. Wildu deór and neáta gehwilc, Dan. 389. Hâlig feoh and wilde deór, Gen. 202. Holmes læst and heofonfuglas and wildu deór, 1516. Manna pað *semita,* deóra pað *callis,* Wrt. Voc. i. 37, 42. Dióra, Met. 26, 92. Leó, deóra cênost, Exod. 322. Fugel oðde fisc on sæ, oðde on eorðan neát, feldgangende feoh, oðde on wêstenne wildra deóra þæt grimmeste, Seel. 82. Sum bið on huntode . . . deóra dræfend, Crä. 38. Þû þurh deóra gripe deáðe sweltest, Jul. 125. Deárum *bestiis,* Rtl. 178, 7. v. wilde-deór.

**deór** *brave. Add:* [v. N. E. D. dear, dere.]

**deorc.** *Add:* I. *without light:*—Deorc *tenebrosus,* Wülck. Gl. 246, 3. Eal bið ûpheofon sweart and gesworcen, deorc and dimhîw *tristius coelum tenebris obducitur atris,* Dôm. L. 106 : Wlfst. 137, 9. Þeós deorce niht getâcnaþ micel leóht tôwerd, Hml. S. 29, 14. II. *of colour:*—Deorc, dungræg *fuscus,* i. *niger,* Wülck. Gl. 246, 3 : *furua, fusca, nigra,* 245, 41. Ceruleus, i. *glaucus* grênehæwen, fâh, deorc. *Color est inter album et nigrum, subniger. Cerulei profundi* diórcre dýpan, 203, 1-4. Deorces sôtes *furue* (i. *nigre) fuliginis,* An. Ox. 4157. Deorcre *caerula,* Germ. 389, 73. Geolwum oðde deorcum *fuluis,* Wülck. Gl. 401, 39. III. *gloomy, dreadful, horrible:*—Duerc *teter,* Wrt. Voc. ii. 122, 13. On deorce cwicsûsle *in tetra tartara,* An. Ox. 1248.

**deorce-græg;** *adj. Dark grey:*—Deorcegræg *elbus,* Wrt. Voc. i. 46, 48 : ii. 32, 56. *Elbus,* i. *medius color* dyrcegræg, s. *inter nigrum et album,* 143, 20.

**deorc-full.** *For* Scint. 59 *substitute* Scint. 186, 8, *and add:*—Eall líchama þîn deorcfull (derkful, Wick. Mt. 6, 23 : Lk. 11, 34) byð, Scint. 187, 14. [v. N. E. D. darkfull.]

**deorcian.** *Substitute: To become dark, to grow dim* (of sight):—Deorcaþ gesihð *hebet visus,* Ps. L. fol. 142, 2. [Hise iȝen derkeden (*caligaverant*), Wick. i. Sam. 4, 15. v. N. E. D. dark ; *vb.*] v. â-deorcian.

**deorc-líce.** *For reference* 'Glos. . . . 7' *substitute* Germ. 391, 22.

**deorc-ness, e; f. Darkness, obscurity:*—On swâ micelre deorcnysse *in tanta obscuritate,* Scint. 228, 3.

**deorcung.** *Add:*—On þeorcun(c)ge *in crepusculo,* Angl. xiii. 398, 475 : 400, 508. [*In Mid. E. a variant of* derk *is* þerk. v. N. E. D. *s. v.* dark.]

**deór-cynn** *a species of* (*wild*) *beast. Add after* deórcynn (l. 4) :—and ealle nŷtena þe on feówer fôtum gâð (cf. God geworhte þære eorðan deór (*bestias*) æfter hira hîwum and þâ nîtena (*jumenta*), Gen. 1, 25).

**deóre.** *Add:* , diére, dŷre. I. *beloved:*—Se deóra þegn *the beloved disciple,* Bl. H. 67, 22. Sunu mîn leáf t dióra *filius meus dilectus,* Mt. L. 17, 5. II. *of great value:*—Hê ûs swâ dŷran cêpe gebohte, Angl. xii. 517, 35. Ic bidde þê þæt ðû læte hûru ðê ðîn líf deórre

þonne ðîne sceós *I pray thee at any rate set thy life higher than thy shoes,* Hml. Th. ii. 410, 18. Ðâ fatu sint fægran and diérran þonne ænegu ôþru, Ors. 5, 2 ; S. 216, 5 : Bt. 14, 2 ; S. 32, 16. Deórran, 31, 11 note. Diórrest fet *vas pretiosum,* Kent. Gl. 741. III. *of great excellence:*—Dióres gâstes *pretiosi spiritus,* Kent. Gl. 623. v. efen-dîre.

**deóre;** *adv. Fiercely, cruelly* [v. deór ; *adj.*]:—Deáð se bitera swâ deóre (deórne ?; *but cf.* þone deóran sîð = *death,* Sal. 361) genam æþelne of eorðan, Chr. 1065 ; P. 194, 14.

**deóre;** *adv. Dearly. Add:* I. *in reference to payment:*—Deóre bebohte *care vendidit,* Wrt. Voc. ii. 129, 16. His ceáp þe hê deóre gebohte, Ll. Th. i. 304, 22. Hî sculon deóre âgildan eal, Wlfst. 190, 22. Hygeteónan seolfre deóre bêtan, Gen. 2732. Ælce misdæda deórar âgyldan, Ll. Th. i. 328, 15. Se cyng sealde his land tô mâle swâ hê deórost mihte, Chr. 1086 ; P. 218, 12. II. *with kindness, as holding a person dear:*—Dêm þû þîn folc deóre mid sôðe *judica populum tuum in tua justitia,* Ps. Th. 71, 2 : 117, 24. Drihten, mîn gebed deóre gehŷre, and onfôh georne mîne hâlsunge, 142, 1 : 118, 154. [v. N. E. D. dear ; *adv.* O. H. Ger. tiuro.]

**deóren.** *Add:*—Deórenum *ferinum, ferinis,* Wrt. Voc. ii. 148, 8, 9. [O. H. Ger. tiorîn *ferinus.*]

**deorf;** *adj.* v. dearf ; mân-deorf.

**deór-fald.** *Substitute:* I. *an enclosure or cage for wild beasts:*—Deórfald *cavea, domus in theatro,* Wrt. Voc. ii. 129, 64. [II. *a deer-park:*—Se king râd in his dêrfald, Chr. 1123; P. 251, 5. Þis wæs segon on þe selue derfald in þâ tûne on Burch and on ealle þâ wudes, 1127; P. 258, 21.]

**deorfan.** *Add:* I. *to labour:*—Ic dearf *exercebor,* i. *laboravi,* Wrt. Voc. ii. 144, 67. Ic nelle deorfan (*laborare*) ofer hig, Coll. M. 26, 17. II. *to be in peril:*—On frecednesse hê dyrfð *periculo periclitat,* Lch. iii. 151, 10, 15. Manega for êhtum durfon *multi propter opes periclitauerunt,* Scint. 215, 13. [O. Frs. for-derva *to perish:* O. L. Ger. far-durvon *perierunt.*] v. dirfan.

**deór-geat, es;** *n. A gate for deer to pass through:*—Of stapolwege on ðæt deórgeat ; of ðâm deórgeate, C. D. v. 270, 15. Eást be hagan tô ðâm ealdan deórgeate, 281, 25.

**deór-haga (?), an; m. A deer-enclosure, deer-park:*—Ic an mîne cnihtes þat wude at Aungre bûten þat dêrhage, Cht. Th. 574, 20. [O. H. Ger. Teorhage (*local name*). Cf. Ger. wild-gehäge.] v. next word.

**deór-hege.** *Add:*—Deórhege heáwan, Angl. ix. 262, 8.

**deór-líce.** *Add:* [O. Sax. diur-lîko : O. H. Ger. tiur-lícho *gloriose, pompatice.*]

**deór-ling.** *Add:* , *a* (*king's*) *favourite:*—Drihtnes deórling (dŷr-, *v.l.*) Benedictus, Gr. D. 176, 7. Dauide ðæm Godes dîrlinge, Past. 393, 3. Dŷrling, Hml. S. 6, 326. Leóf cyningc . . . hêr syndon þe þîne deórlingas beón sceoldon, 23, 148. His (*Godwin's*) sunan wæron eorlas and þæs cynges dŷrlingas, Chr. 1052 ; P. 176, 24. Dŷrlingas *penates,* Germ. 397, 448. Se wela þe hê (*the king*) gifþ his deórlingum, Bt. 29, 1 ; F. 102, 3. Hê (*Nero*) weorþode his deórlingas mid welum, 28 ; F. 100, 29. Sumne king and his deórlingas, Shrn. 200, 29. ¶ *as a nickname:*—Eádríc ealdorman and Ælmær Deórlingc (Dŷrling, *v.l.*), Chr. 1016 ; P. 150, 3.

**deór-net.** *Add:*—Deórnett *cassis,* Wülck. Gl. 183, 12.

**deór-tûn.** *Add:*—Deórtûn *broel, hortus cervorum,* Wrt. Voc. ii. 127, 22. Deórtuun *broel,* 190, 20.

**deór-wyrþe.** *Add:* I. *of persons, of great worth, excellent, noble:*—Dionisius se deórwurða martyr, Hml. S. 29, 6. Dauid se deórwurða sealmwirhta, Ælfc. T. Grn. 7, 5. II. *of things, of great value, precious, costly:*—Deórwurðe wæfels *regillum vel peplum vel palla,* Wrt. Voc. i. 40, 32. Sealfbox deórwyrþes (diórwyrðes, L., diórwyrdes, R. *pretiosi*) nardes, Mk. 14, 3. Ân pund deórwyrþre smerenesse, Bl. H. 69, 1. Diórweorþum stâne, Kent. Gl. 250. Hê his þ deórwyrðe blôd âgeát, Bl. H. 97, 12. Glengas deórwyrþra hrægla, 99, 19. Þincg dŷrwyrþe *res pretiosas,* Coll. M. 26, 33. Þ is þ eallra deórwurðost feoh *pretiosissimum divitiarum genus,* Bt. 20 ; F. 72, 26. v. diór-, dŷr-wurþe *in Dict.* [v. N. E. D. dearworth.]

**deórwyrþ-lic (-wi(e)rþ-);** *adj. Precious, costly:*—Hî him deórwurðlíce anlícnyssa ârærdon, Hml. Th. i. 366, 21. Mid þînum deórwyrðlícostan blôde *praetioso sanguine,* Hymn. ad Mat. 20.

**deórwyrðlíce (-wi(e)rþ-);** *adv.* I. *richly, sumptuously, splendidly, gloriously:*—Þ mann his godas deórwurðlíce frætewode, Hml. S. 14, 129. Hê geseah ðone rícan deórweorðlíce geglencgedne, Hml. Th. i. 330, 14. Hê geseah Drihtnes rôdetâcn deórwurðlíce scînan, ii. 304, 11 : Hml. S. 27, 92. Se dêma deórwurðlíce bebyrigde his líchaman, 215. II. *in high esteem, as of great value:*—Þî hê elcað ðæt wê sceolon deórwyrðlíce healdan Godes gife. Swâ hwæt swâ man eáðelíce begyt, þæt ne bið nâ swâ deórwyrðe swâ þæt þæt earfoðlíce bið begyten, Hml. Th. i. 248, 28. Heó wæs sumne dæl hæbbende of þâm reáfe þæs Hælendes and hyt swŷðe deórwyrðlíce heóld, Hml. A. 187, 179. Se bisceop underfêng þone cniht and hine deórwurðlíce heóld . . . and hê

(the young man) wunode swā mid him (the bishop) on ārwurðnysse, Ælfc. T. Grn. 17, 8. [v. N. E. D. dearworthly.]

deóþ death. v. deáþ: dépan. v. dípan: dépe. v. dípe: Dera (mægþ, ríce), Dere. l. Dēra (-e): dere (Gr. D. 207, 14). v. daru.

derian. Add:—Dereð ledet, Kent. Gl. 283. Deraþ, Wülck. Gl. 257, 7. Sió ilce lār ðe ōðrum hielpeð, hió dereð ðæm ōðrum saepe aliis officiunt quae aliis prosunt, Past. 173, 19. Ne dereð nān mon suíðor ðære hālgan gesomnunge nemo amplius in Ecclesia nocet, 31, 10. Nān gōd ne dereþ þæm þe hit āh, Bt. 14, 3; S. 32, 32. Deraþ, 14, 1; S. 30, 15. Monnum derian (derigean, v. l.), Past. 363, 16. ¶ with acc. (late):—Seó unrōtnes deraþ ægðer ge mód ge líchaman, Shrn. 190, 5. v. ā-derian.

deriend-líc. Add:—Bið swýþe derigendlic (-iend-, v. l.) þ bisceop beó gýmeleás, Hml. S. 13, 125. On ælcum mōnðe beóð æfre twēgen dagas þa syndon swíðe derigendlíce ænigne drenc tō drincanne. On þām ōðrum mōnðe se teóða dæg is derigendlic, Lch. iii. 152, 1-12. Wē āwurpon þa derigendlican ealdnesse, Hml. Th. i. 194, 25. Feralia, i. lugubria, tristia, noxia, luctuosa, mortifera, mortalia vel deriendlican, rēplican, Wrt. Voc. ii. 147, 50. Þa deófiu æteówiað þære synfullan sāwle ða derigendlican spræca and ða mānsullan dæda. Hml. Th. i. 410, 7. ¶ with dat. of object exposed to hurt:—Óðer deófolgild is derigendlic þære sāwle, Hml. S. 17, 49. v. un-derigendlic.

derne. v. dirne.

derung. Add:—Swilce hē næfre nāne derunge (-inge, v. l., laesionem) his líchaman ne þolode, Gr. D. 82, 33. Swylce hit fleónde wære þæs Godes weres deringe (laesionem), 214, 1.

déping. v. díping.

deþþan (?); p. deþede To suck:—Þā breóst ða ðū deðedes (gedēdes?; L. has gediides) ubera quae suxisti, Lk. R. 11, 27. v. deón.

dex. v. dosc.

diácon. Add:—Diácon diaconus vel levita, Wrt. Voc. i. 42, 25. Æt Scī Laurentie þām deácone, Shrn. 117, 11. v. heáh-, sub-diácon.

diácon-gegirela, an; m. A deacon's vestment:—Bysceopgegirelan and diácongegyrelan sacerdotalia uel clericalia indumenta, Bd. 1, 29; Sch. 90, 20.

diácon-hád. Add:—On ælcre hādunge, ge on diáconhāde ge on preósthāde. æfre sē ðe gehādod bið, hē bið gesmyrod mid gehālgodum ele, Hml. Th. ii. 14, 26.

diácon-rocc, es; m. A dalmatic:—Diácone mid diáconrocce gescrýddum diacono dalmatica induto, Angl. xiii. 416, 722.

díc, es, e, and indecl.; m. f. [The instances given in Dict. under díc; m. and díc; f. may probably be taken together.] Add: I. an excavation, ditch, pit; fossa, fovea:—Díc fossa, pyt puteus, Wrt. Voc. i. 84, 57. Ðær fyxan díc tō brōce gǣð. C. D. ii. 29, 1. Of ðǣm pytte on ðone díc... ondlong díces ðēh sió díc forscoten wǣre, iii. 168, 35. On ðā ealdan díc; andlang díce... andlong díc... andlang ðære miclan díc... andlang díc, 78, 10-18. Oð Ordstānes díc; ðæt andlang díc; of ðære díc... tō ðære díc ðære se æðeling mearcode, ðæt andlang díc... tō ðære lytlan díce ende... andlang ðære díc byge, v. 297, 36-298, 13. Andlang díc (per longum foveam illam)... on ða hōcedan díc; of þære hōcedan díc, C. D. B. ii. 260, 35-6. Tō cynninges díc; andlang þære díc ad regiam foveam; per longum foveam illam, 386, 23. Hē hit begyrde mid þære díc magnam fossam duxit, Bd. 1, 5; Sch. 17, 19: Chr. 189; P. 8, 23. On ða ealdan díc; of ðære díc, C. D. iii. 82, 27. On ðone díc ðær esne ðone weg fordealf, ii. 28, 33. Be gemǣre swā ða ealdan díca beligcað, iii. 213, 6. Ðeós wyrt bið cenned on dícon and on hreóðbeddon, Lch. i. 98, 13. Hē hēt delfan þā eorðan swā þ hors urnon embe þ hús þurh þa dígelan díca, Hml. S. 27, 39. II. an earthwork with a trench:—Gihaðrigað ðec fióndas ðine mið díce (dícg, L.) circumdabunt te inimici tui uallo, Lk. R. 19, 43. Hē oferhergade eall hira land betwuh dícum aud Wūsan (terras illorum quae inter terrae limitem sancti regis Eadmundi et flumen Usam sitae sunt devastat, Flor. Wigorn. The limes is the Recken or Devil's Dyke. v. Lappenberg, England under the A. S. Kings i. 242), Chr. 905; P. 94, 2. v. mær-; mearc-, wcall-díc. See al·o Leo. A. S. Names, pp. 123-6, Midd. Flur. s. v. dike.

dícian. Substitute: To make a ditch:—Se cāsere hēt dícian and eorðweall gewyrcan Seuerus uallum fecerat, Bd. 1, 12; Sch. 33, 27 (cf. Sch. 17, 19 under díc). Harald lēt dícian ðā díc ābūtan þ port, Chr. 1055; P. 186, 14. Wíngeard settan, dícian, deórhege heáwan, Angl. ix. 262, 8. [v. N. E. D. dike.]

díc-sceard, es; n. A gap in a ditch:—Dícsceard bētan, Angl. ix. 262, 20.

díc-walu, e; f. A ditch-bank (?):—On ða eástlangan dícwale, C. D. v. 334, 28. v. walu.

díc-weall, es; m. A ditch-wall:—Directe uersus occidentem usque la dichewalle; et sic per fossatum directe usque in riuulo de Tamyse, C. D. iii. 408, 20.

dídan; p. de To put to death; Ll. Th. i. 172, 13. [v. N. E. D. dead; vb. II. Goth. dauþjan mortificare: O. H. Ger. tōden to kill: Icel. deyða.] v. dýdan in Dict.: ā-dídan.

díend. v. deón.

dífan to make deaf or dull, to deaden sound. [v. N. E. D. deaf; v. trans., deave. Goth. ga-daubjan to dull, harden the heart: O. H. Ger. touben: Icel. deyfa to blunt, stupefy.] v. ā-dífan; deaf.

dífan (causal to dūfan); p. de To plunge (trans.), immerse. [v. dýfan in Dict. for citations.] [v. N. E. D. dive. Icel. deyfa.] v. be-, ge-dífan.

dífing, e; f. Immersion:—þā ðreó dýfinga on fontbæðe, Wlfst. 36, 9.

dígan (?); p. deóg To die:—Deáðfæge deóg, siððan dreáma leás in senfreoðo feorh ālegde, hæðene sāwle deathdoomed he died, after he joyless in the fensfastness life laid down, his heathen soul, B. 850. [H. R. N. deȝen: Laym. deȝen: A. R. deien. v. N. E. D. die. Icel. deyja; p. dō: O. Frs. deia: O. Sax. dōian: O. H. Ger. touwan.]

dígle, dēgle, díegle, deigle, deágol, dǣg-, dēg-, deóg-, dióg-, dýg-ol (-el), deáhle, díhle; adj. Secret. Add: I. of that which might be seen, hidden from sight:—Dígle hús secessus, Wrt. Voc. i. 26, 39: 57, 57. Deágol obstrusus (of John yet unborn), Wrt. Voc. ii. 90, 36; 64, 40. Se dígla (dígla, v.l.) Dēma gehírde and suíðe undeógollíce geandwyrde judex prius invisibiliter vidit, quod postea publice reprehendit, Past. 39, 19. On díglum hole in clandestino speleo, An. Ox. 2045. On āne dígle stōwe, Ors. 2, 4; S. 76, 13. On dígle crypel in obstrusum cuniculum, An. Ox. 2855. þā díglan wiðgilnysse abstrusam (heremi) vastitatem, 2798. Díglum feolstrum clanculis (i. occultis) latebris, An. Ox. 4211. Díhlum dimhofum latebrosis (i. intimis) latibulis, 819. Of ðæm díglum de obstru·is (pharetrae latibulis), Wrt. Voc. ii. 74, 68: ii. 26, 28. Seó sunne stígþ on þā dǣglan wegas (secreto tramite), Bt. 25; F. 88, 26. II. of thought, action, concealed from the knowledge or notice of others:—Weorc, swā open swā dēgle, Past. 451, 14. Dígle (dēgle, L. R.) occultum, Mk. 4, 22. Ðegn dēgle (deigle, L.) discipulus occultus, Jn. R. 19, 38. þ hit ne sý dægcūð, þ þ díhle wæs, Dóm. L. 40. Deáhle secretum, Kent. Gl. 1126. Dígelre latentis, An. Ox. 4209. Mid díglum cum secreta (oratione), 1842. Díhlum fācne clandestina fraude, 5128. Sege hwæt ic þence oþþe hwæt ic dō on déglum gerece, Bl. H. 181, 14. þurh his díhlan miht, Dóm. L. 20. Beóð gesweotolude dígle geþancas arcana patebunt, 135. Hié wæron gewitan Godes dēgolra dóma, Bl. H. 161, 16. Ondrǣd þū þē díhle wīsan, Dom. L. 30, 51. ¶ on díglum in secret:—þā yfelu on díglan þurhtogene, R. Ben. 28, 14. Hē líð him on dígelan, Hml. S. 34, 131. On díglum, on díhlum in abscondito, Mt. 6, 4. III. hard to get knowledge of. (1) of a fact or circumstance:—Wē leorniaþ þ seó tíd sié tō þæs dēgol þ nære nænig mon þe þ wiste hwonne..., Bl. H. 117, 25. Huā nāt ðæt ðā wunda ðæs mōdes bióð dígelran ðonne ðā wunda ðæs líchaman quis cogitationum vulnera occultiora esse nesciat vulneribus viscerum?, Past. 25, 19. (2) of things to be understood, abstruse, occult:—Gimærsiga dægla girýne celebrare misterium, Rtl. 2, 41. þǣm díglum opacis (biblis), Wrt. Voc. ii. 95, 40. þā díglan clancula (dicta), 94, 28. Ðū woldest ælcum mōde díglu ðing tǣcan and seldcūþe latentium rerum caussas evolvere, velatasque caligine explicare rationes, Bt. 39, 4; F. 216, 13. v. dígol; adj. in Dict.

dígle, dígol, es; n. I. a secret place:—Of þām þýstorfullon díglum de latebrosis recessibus, An. Ox. 4, 23: Wrt. Voc. ii. 138, 56. Of heolhstrum, of díglum de recessibus, i. de occultis vel de secretis, 139, 5. On deóhlum in secretioribus (ventris), Kent. Gl. 765. II. a secret:—þ man mancynnes dígle geopenige, Hml. S. 23 b, 10: 25, 467. Hē ārǣdan ne mihte þæs apostoles dēgol, Bl. H. 181, 18. Geryna vel dígla sacramentum vel mysterium, Wrt. Voc. i. 47, 26. Díglu archana, i. mystica, An. Ox. 1506: Angl. xi. 119. 67. Yppan dígla ūre pandere secreta nostra, Coll. M. 34, 15. Dióhla archana, Kent. Gl. 359. Deiglo abscondita, Mt. L. 13, 35. Hē heora heortena deágol ealle smeáþ, Bl. H. 179, 26. v. dígol; n. in Dict.

dígle; adv. Add:—Deágle opace, Wrt. Voc. ii. 64, 41. Dígle furtim, Germ. 394, 208 (= Glos. Prudent. Record. 144, 30).

díglian, díglan. Add: I. to hide:—Gif hē his abbode ne díglað (celaverit) ealle þā geþōhtas, R. Ben. 28, 13. Dēgelde abscondit, Mt. L. 13, 33. II. to lie hid:—Dēgla latere, Jn. p. 8, 5. Dēglendes fióndes latentis inimici, Rtl. 121, 40. [O. H. Ger. tougalen occultare.] v. ge-díglian, -díglan.

díg-líce. v. dígol-líce: -dígling. v. be-dígling: dígneras. v. dínor: dígol. v. dígle.

dígol-líce, dígelíce. Add: Secretly, (1) so as to take others unawares or at a disadvantage:—Hē gesette twā folc díegellíce on twā healfa his, Ors. 4, 6; S. 174, 32: 4, 10; S. 200, 13. Hē díegellíce for þǣm gewinne V geár scipa worhte, 2, 5; S. 78, 32. Hē nolde geþarfian þæm þeófe þ hē underdulfe dígellíce his hús, Hml. A. 50, 13. Hē gegaderode his fyrde díglíce, Chr. 1004; P. 135, 31. (2) so as to avoid publicity, exposure, detection:—Hē wearð díegellíce crīsten, for þon hē eáwenga ne dorste, Ors. 6, 21; S. 272, 18. Hē sende dígellíce ærendgewritu tō þām Cāsere, Bt. 1; F. 2, 20. Lǣran openlíce oððe digollíce, Hml. A. 12, 297. Dígellíce absconse, R. Ben.

I. 33, 5. Ðeáh hē hit openlíce dō . . . Ac sē ðonne sē hit dēgellíce (*in secreto*) dēð, Past. 451, 18. Þ hiora fýnd hit deágollíce (*occulto*) genōmon, Nar. 7, 4. Hié in heora húsum deágollíce hié miþan *inter tectorum suorum culmina delituerunt*, 10, 18. Hié genāman deógollíce his líc, Bl. H. 191, 32. Hē wolde hī díglíce forlǣtan, Hml. Th. i. 196, 17. Dígelíce (díhlíce, *v. l.*, deiglíce, L., dēgullíce, R.) *occulte*, Mt. 1, 19. Díglíce (dēglíce, L., dēgullíce, R.) *secreto*, 17, 19. Dēglíce (dēgullíce, R.), Mt. L. 20, 17 : *clam*, 2, 7. Dēglíhe *secreto*, 24, 3. Díhlíce (dígellíce, *v. l.*), Wlfst. 88, 21. Hē sý dýhlíce (dýglíce, *v. l.*) gemyngod *ammoneatur secrete*, R. Ben. 48, 6 : 51, 2. Hý swā díhlíce wuniende hý fram manna gesyhðe áscyriaþ, 134, 18. (3) so as to confine an action to one's self :—Ðā scylda ðe hié diógollíce (diégollíce, *v.l.*) on him selfum forberað *culpas quas in se tacite tolerari considerant*, Past. 151, 15. Þā þōhte hē dígollíce *he thought to himself*, Hml. A. 134, 622. Hió cueð deiglíce *dicebat intra se*, Mt. L. 9, 21. v. un-dígollíce.

**dígolnes.** *Add* : **I.** *secrecy, privacy, solitude* :—Hwý hié þára geearnunga hiora dígelnesse (diég-, *v. l.*) and ānette bet trūwien ðonne ðǣre hū hié ōðerra monna mǣst gehelpen *qua mente utilitati ceterorum secretum praeponit suum*, Past. 46, 2. **II.** *a secret, mystery* :—Heó þurhwunode on þām wǣrlicum hīwe . . . and hyre cnihtas hyre dígolnysse eallum bedyrndon, Hml. S. 2, 103. Þēh þe ǣgþer þissa burga þurh Godes diégelnessa (*arcana*) þus getācnod wurde, Ors. 2, 1 ; S. 62, 25. Hē árīmde ðā diógolnesse (dígol-, *v.l. secreta*) ðæs ðriddan hefones . . . hē geimpod wæs tō ðǣm hefenlicum diógolnessum (dígol-, *v. l.*), Past. 99, 7, 18. Dígelnyssa *abstrusa*, An. Ox. 1952. Wē habbað ðās race ánfealdlíce gereht ; wē willað eác þæt andgit eów geopenian, and ðā dýgelnysse eów ne bedyrnan, Hml. Th. ii. 214, 18. **III.** *a secret place* :—On dígelnesse *latibulo*, i. *secretorio*, An. Ox. 392. Hē hæfde behýdd on his dígolnysse án wurðlic weorc, Hml. S. 5, 250. Hē him cýtan árǣrde on sumere dígelnysse swylce hē ancersetla beón mihte, 31, 1069. Dígelnesse *latibulum*, i. *obscurum*, An. Ox. 3318. Deágelnesse *abyssum*, Wrt. Voc. ii. 9, 29. Of dēgolnessum *de recessibus*, 28, 51. Dígelnessum, An. Ox. 2952. ¶ Dýgelnyssum *anastasis*, Wrt. Voc. i. 17, 35. v. díligness. [*O. H. Ger.* in *tougalnesse in absconso*.]

**diht**, es ; *m*. *Add* : **I.** *order, arrangement, disposition* of material :—God geswāc ðæs dihtes ealra his weorca . . . Hē gedihte ealle gesceafta . . . and on ðām deópan dihte stōdon ealle þā ðing ðe ðāgyt nǣron ; Witodlíce wē wǣron on þām dihte, Hml. Th. ii. 206, 8–19. **I a.** of composition :—Fíf béc hē áwrāt mid wundorlicum dihte, Ælfc. T. Grn. 3, 18. Hē gesette þurh his sylfes diht án þūsend ðára, Hml. A. 5, 105. **II.** *direction* of action, conduct :—Wē ne beóð be ágenum dihte ácennede, Hml. Th. ii. 230, 30: 232, 1. Hī leofodon him be heora ágenum dihte, be nānes ealdres wissunge, Hml. A. 44, 502 : Ælfc. T. Grn. 20, 8. **II a.** *direction* by one in authority, (1) of men :—Benedictus sǣde þæt heora þeáwas ne mihton his dihte (*his rule as abbot*) geðwǣrlǣcan, Hml. Th. ii. 158, 7. Hý bedreáf onfón æfter heora abbodes dyhte (*dispositionem*), R. Ben. 47, 5. Þæt hī drohtnian on mynstre be heora ealdres dihte, Hml. Th. ii. 318, 9. Be Maures dihte ádreógan his líf, Hml. S. 6, 221. (2) of the Deity :—On þām micclan dihte Godes foresceáwunge, Hml. A. 70, 120. Æfter Godes dihte, 24, 14. Ealle gesceafta ðeówiað hyra Scyppende, for ðon þe hī farað æfter Godes dihte, Hml. Th. i. 172, 17. Hē áwrāt ðā ealdan ǣ be Godes dihte, 312, 14 : 40, 33. Marcus be Godes dihte gefór tō Ægypta lande, Hml. S. 15, 1. Seó sunne gǣð be Godes dihte, Lch. iii. 234, 19. On bócum þe ðurh Godes dihte gesette wǣron, Hml. Th. ii. 444, 19. Þurh Godes diht, 594, 23. **III.** *the office of* a director :—Scír *vel* diht *dispensatio*, Wrt. Voc. ii. 140, 65. Gesette hē þæne and gehādige tō ðām dihte abbodhādes þe Godes hús wel fadige (gesetton þone tō abbode and gehādian tō ðām dihte þ hē Godes hús wel fadige, *v. l.*) *domui Dei dignum constituant dispensatorem*, R. Ben. 119, 11. **IV.** *an order, precept* :—Ditio *vel* arbitrio, *judicio vel ratione, lege* vel diht, Wrt. Voc. ii. 140, 9. Dōmas and dihtas rihte man geornlíce, þæt leód and lagu trumlíce stande, Wlfst. 74, 8. v. ge-diht.

**diht**, e ; *f*. *A saying, dictum, oracle* :—Dihta oððe saga *presagia*, Wrt. Voc. ii. 67, 46. Dihta *oraculorum*, An. Ox. 7, 81 : 8, 96. [*O. H. Ger.* dihta ; *f.*]

**dihtan.** *Add* : **I.** *to order, regulate, arrange, direct* :—Dih[t(eð)] *dispensat*, An. Ox. 17, 1. On þā wísan þe se abbod dyht (diht, *v. l.*) *prout abba disposuerit*, R. Ben. 125, 10. Wē andbidodon ðīn þæt þū ūs þæs mynstres gebytlu dihtan (*disponere*) sceoldest, Hml. Th. ii. 172, 23. Sculon bisceopas mid worulddēman dōmas dihtan, þ hī ne gebafian þ ǣnig unriht úp áspringe, Ll. Th. ii. 312, 31, 36. Dihtende *dispensans* (*ecclesiae rudimentum*), An. Ox. 11, 130. **II.** *to give direction* to a person, *dictate, direct* a person (*dat.*) :—Swā swā him diht se abbod, Ll. Th. ii. 372, 5. Benedictus on swefne . . . hī gewissode ymbe ðæs mynstres gebytlungum . . . 'Árǣrað þæt mynster swā swā ic eów on swefne dihte,' Hml. Th. ii. 172, 28. Hē dēð be þām þe his willa him dihte, Hml. S. 27, 175. **III.** *to dictate* what is to be written :—Þā fíf béc God sylf dihte, and Moyses hī áwrāt, Hml. Th. i. 186, 20.

þās endebyrdnysse þe Moyses áwrāt swā swā him God self dihte, Ælfc. T. Grn. 3, 14. Aman dihte gewritu be þām Iudēiscum tō ǣlcere scíre *scriptum est ut jusserat Aman, et litterae missae sunt ad universas provincias*, Hml. A. 97, 162. [*v. N. E. D.* dight.] v. dihtian.

**dihtend**, es ; *m*. *A director, ruler* :—Dihtend cercan *dispensator* (i. *gubernator*) *ecclesiae*, An. Ox. 1997. [Almihti God, shuppende and wealdende and dihtende of alle shafte, O. E. Hml. ii. 123, 14.]

**dihtere.** *Add* : *One who dictates* :—Ne tweóge ic áht þā míne dihteras þæt hī mihton gemunan þā wundru þises weres *non ambigo illos dictatores non omnia facta illius potuisse cognoscere*, Guth. 6, 8. The Latin translated at 4, 23 is : Prout a dictantibus idoneis testibus audivi. [*v. N. E. D.* dighter.] v. dihtian.

**dihtian** ; *p*. ode *To dictate*, (1) what is to be done :—Seó lufu þ gemet þǣre þreáunge dihtað (*dictat*), Bd. 1, 27 ; Sch. 67, 13. (2) what is to be written :—In þām folclārum þe ic wrāt and dihtode, Gr. D. 290, 11. Se Drihtnes wer him tō gehēt his wrítere and him dihtode (*dictavit*) þus cweðende, 193, 22. Se Hālga Gāst dihtode ealle þā þing þe hālige men writon, Bl. H. 133, 1. Dihtade *instigavit*, Lk. p. 2, 6. [*Lat.* dictare.]

**dihtnere.** *Add* :—Dihtnere *dispensator*, Wrt. Voc. i. 74, 14. Dictator, i. *dictor, relator, praeceptor, imperator, dihtnere, ordinator, prescriptor*, ii. 140, 5. Hīwrǣddene wurðe gesetton dihtneran (-as ?, e ?) *domui Dei dignum constituant dispensatorem*, R. Ben. I. 107, 12. Getreówne dyhtnere his hālegra cyricena (*Dunstan*), Lch. iii. 434, 21. Se cyningc him tō gecígde his dihtnere, Ap. Th. 5, 13.

**dihtnian** ; *p*. ode. **I.** *to order, dispose* :—Fram leahtrum ásyndrian hē dihtniað *a vitiis separare se disponunt*, Scint. 17, 4. **II.** *to direct, dictate* :—Þā hē sylf dihtnode *quam ipse dictavit*, Angl. xiii. 426, 869. v. ge-, tō-dihtnian.

**dihtnung.** *Add* :—Dihtnung *dispensatio*, Wrt. Voc. ii. 140, 64. Dehtnunge *dispositione*, Kent. Gl. 919.

**dihtung**, e ; *f*. *Disposition, regulation, ordering* :—Wunderlic dihtung upplices tōdāles *mira dispositio supernae distributionis*, Scint. 227, 8. Æfter gesetnesse oððe dihtinge abbodes *secundum dispositionem abbatis*, R. Ben. I. 54, 13. [*v. N. E. D.* dighting.]

**dile.** *Add* :—Dili, dil *anetum*, Txts. 41, 159. Dile, Wrt. Voc. i. 30, 46: *anethum*, 66, 71.

**díl(e)gian.** *Add* :—Naman heora ðū dýlegodest *nomen eorum delesti*, Ps. Spl. 9, 5. Ðonne þū niicel weaxbred habban wille, þonne stríc þū mid þīnum twām fingrum on þīne breóst forewearde swilce þū dýlige (*as if you were wiping out something*), Tech. ii. 128, 13. [*v. N. E. D.* dilghe.] v. ge-dílgian.

**dílig-ness**, e ; *f*. *Destruction, extermination* :—Dílignissum *anastasis* (= ἀνάστασις *overthrow, destruction*), Txts. 41, 163. Dýgelnyssum (= ? dýlegnyssum), Wrt. Voc. i. 17, 35.

**dim.** *Add* : **I.** *dark, without light, gloomy* :—Þ under þǣre brygce urne swýþlíce sweart and dim (*niger et caliginosus*) eá, Gr. D. 318, 28. Dimne and deópne hellewítes grund, Wlfst. 48, 2. Of dymmum díglum *de latebrosis recessibus*, Wrt. Voc. ii. 138, 55. **II.** *dark-coloured*. v. dim-híw :—Seó byrgen is bewrigen mid dimmum stānum and yfellicum, Shrn. 66, 24. **III.** *wretched, grievous, sad, unhappy* :—Of dimre, earmre *calamitosa* (*fames atrocitate*), An. Ox. 3853. Dymre, 2, 261. On ðǣre dimman ádle *in that miserable malady*, Gū. 1135. **IV.** *dark, wicked* ; Gen. 685.

**dimma**, Sat. 606. v. dyne.

**dim-híw** ; *adj*. *Dark-coloured, gloomy* :—Eal bið ūpheofon sweart and gesworcen, deorc and dimhíw and dwolma sweart *tristius coelum tenebris obducitur atris*, Dōm. L. 106 : Wlfst. 137, 9.

**dim-hofe**, an ; *f. Add* : dim-hofu (?), e ; *f.* : -hof, es ; *n.* :—On dimhofe (*dat.* or *acc.* ?) *in latibulum* (on dimhoue ; dimhof *latibulum*, Hpt. Gl. 494, 77-8), An. Ox. 3768. Dimhoua *latibula*, i. *secreta*, 1677.

**dim-hús**, es ; *n. A prison, dungeon* :—Dimhúses *lautumiae*, i. *carceris*, An. Ox. 3774. Dimhús *latibula* (*ergastuli*), 4993.

**dim-lic.** *Add* :—Se bearnede dæg tōdrǣfð þā dimlican þeóstru ðǣre sweartan nihte, Hml. Th. i. 604, 1 : Hml. S. 5, 108.

**dimmian.** *Substitute* : *To be or become dim* :—Dymme[n]de *caligans*, Wrt. Voc. ii. 127, 65. Hyt fremað dimgendum eágum tō þý þ seó beorhtnys ágyfen sý, Lch. i. 136, 1. Wið dymgendum eágum, 178, 4. [*v. N. E. D.* dim ; *intrans.* : Icel. dimma *to become dim, grow dark.*]

**dim-nes.** *Add* : **I.** *darkness, want of light* :—Dimnis (*caligo*) under fótum his, Ps. Srt. 17, 10. Þýstreful dimnys *tenebrosa caligo*, An. Ox. 3297. Utan wē geþencan dómes dæg and dimnessa helle grundes, Hml. A. 168, 113. **II.** *a dark place* :—On sweartum dimnessum *latibulis carceralibus*, An. Ox. 3144. **III.** *dimness* of sight :—Wiþ eágena dymnysse, Lch. i. 176, 16. Dimnesse gāstas *chao*, Wrt. Voc. ii. 20, 1 : 95, 81.

dincge. v. dynge : dīner. v. dínor: ding *to a dungeon*. v. dung : ding *sound*. v. dyng : dinne. v. dynge.

**dínor** (-er), es ; *m. A coin* :—*Denarius* is se dínor þe áwehð *decem*

*nummos*, þæt sind týn penegas, Ælfc. Gr. Z. 285, 2. þā mæstan digneras *folles*, Wrt. Voc. ii. 40, 2. Dīnra beorh (*a hill where money had been found?*), C. D. v. 332, 18. [*Lat.* denarius.] v. digneras in *Dict.*

**dīpan**; *p.* te. I. *to dip, immerse* :—Sē ðe dēpið (ðēpeð, L.) honde in þäs parabside *qui intingit manum in parapside*, Mt. R. 26, 23. Hafa þū þīne þrī fingras swīlce þū dýpan wille . . . Swilce þū feþere hæb(b)e and hī dýpe, Tech. ii. 128, 18–22. II. *to baptize* :—Ic eówic dēpu (*baptizo*) wætere . . . sē eówic dēpið (*baptizabit*) fýre, Mt. R. 3, 11. Þte hē wære dēpid *ut baptizaretur*, 3, 13. Wērun dēpte *baptizabantur*, 3, 6. [*v. N. E. D.* deep, *vb.* 4. *Goth.* daupjan:—*O. Sax.* dôpian: *O. H. Ger.* toufen.] v. be-, in-dīpan.

**dīpan** *to deepen.* v. dýpan in *Dict.*

**dīpe**, an: **dīpu** (-o), *indecl.* or *gen.* e; *f.* I. *depth, deepness*; Mt. 13, 5. II. *the deep, deep part of water (sea, lake, river), deep water, a deep place in water* :—Deorcre dýpan *cerulei profundi*, Wrt. Voc. ii. 130, 37. Þreó āsæton on ðä healfe ðære dýpan ðe ðä Deniscan scipu āseten wæron, Chr. 897; P. 91, 3. Deópan (dēpan, Hpt. Gl. 492, 48) *gurgitis*, An. Ox. 3667. Dēpan (-en, MS.) *alveo*, 4794. Hī becōman tô ānre dýpan *they had reached a deep place in the river*, Hml. S. 11, 271. Ofer dýpe, Rä. 4, 21. III. *a deep place on land* :—On dīgelre dýpe [dýpen (= -an), Hpt. Gl. 516, 28] *in latebroso* (*carceris*) *fundo*, An. Ox. 4767. [*v. N. E. D.* deep; *sb. Goth.* diupei: *O. L. Ger.* diupî *profundum* : *O. H. Ger.* tiufi : *Icel.* dýpi.]

**dīran** *to hold dear.* v. deóran in *Dict.*, *and add* : [*O. Sax.*] diurian: *O. H. Ger.* tiuren *glorificare.*] v. ge-dīran (-dýran).

**dīregað** = *Lat.* dirigat :—*Vibrat* borettið *vel* diregað (the corresponding gloss. in Epinal and Erfurt glossaries is :—*Vibrat, dirigat* boretit), Txts. 107, 2147.

**dīrfan**; *p.* de; *pp.* ed *To afflict, molest* :—Ús deriað and ðearle dyrfað fela ungelimpa, Wlfst. 91, 18. [*v. N. E. D.* derve.] v. ge-dīrfan; deorfan.

**dīrfung**, e; *f. Affliction, molestation* :—Dyrfingum *subactionibus*, Germ. 395, 78.

**dīrige.** *The first word of the antiphon* (v. Ps. 5, 8) *at Matins in the Office of the Dead, used as a name for that service* :—Dirige for forþférdum *vigilia pro defunctis*, Angl. xiii. 433, 975: 444, 1131. [*v. N. E. D.* dirge.]

**dīr-ling.** v. deór-ling.

**dīrnan**; *p.* de *To conceal, hide* :—Dyrnþ *occultat, abscondit.* Wrt. Voc. ii. 138, 48. (1) *with acc. of thing* :—Gif hē hit dierneð (dirneð, dyrned, *v. ll.*), and weorðeð ymb long yppe, Ll. Th. i. 116, 6. Wä mē þ þū swā lange þē sylfe dyrndest, Hml. S. 33, 308. Gif hē hit dierne (dyrne, *v.l.*), Ll. Th. i. 124, 8. Þēh hié hit ær swiþe him betweónum diernden, Ors. 5, 10; S. 234, 1. Noldan hī heora synna dyrnan, Ps. Th. 77, 4. Dyrnan Meotudes mihte, An. 693: El. 971: Hy. 7, 93. (2) *with dat. of person from whom a thing* (*acc.*) *is concealed* :—Seó rôd þe gē mannum dyrndun, El. 626. On yrre wille hē his milde môd mannum dyrnan *numquid continebit in ira sua misericordiam suam?*, Ps. Th. 76, 8. [*v. N. E. D.* dern. *O. Sax.* dernian: *O. H. Ger.* tarnen *occultare, dissimulare.*] v. dyrnan in *Dict.*

**dīrne**; *adj. Add to examples given in Dict. under* dyrne: I. *secret, hidden* :—Dyrne hordas (gerýna) *abdita archana*, An. Ox. 4215. Dyrnum pricelsum *clandestinis stimulis*, 4655. Of dymmum dīglum *vel* of dyrnum *de latebrosis recessibus*, Wrt. Voc. ii. 138, 56. II. *secret* (so as to escape detection), (1) *of adultery* :—Hē bið diernes gelīres scyldig, Past. 143, 2. *Spiritus fornicationis*, þ is dernes geligeres gāst, Shrn. 52, 27. Dēmde hē ðäm bisceope for his dyrnum geligrum, 130, 14. From dernum geligerum, Ll. Th. i. 56, 26. (2) *of stolen goods, concealed* :—Ænigne þära þe ymbe þäs smeágunge bið and þ dyrne orf āmeldað, Ll. Th. i. 276, 33. v. following compounds; in some cases the passages given under them may belong to the simple adjective.

**dīrne-forlegen**; *adj. Guilty of fornication, adulterous* :—Gif man sý fram dyrneforlegenum (*fornicante*) preóste gefullod, Ll. Th. ii. 144, 19.

**dīrne-gelegerscipe**, es; *m. Adultery, fornication* :—In derne-gilegerscipe (*adulterio*) ginumen, Jn. R. 8, 3. Fleás dernegilegerscipe *fugite fornicationem*, Rtl. 106, 34.

**dīrne-geligere**, es; *m. A fornicator* :—Dernegileigere *fornicator*, Rtl. 107, 1.

**dīrne-geligere**, es; *n. Adultery, fornication* :—Druncennes and dyrnegeligere, Dôm L. 30, 43. Diernegeligres (diernes gelīres, *v.l.*) scyldig, Past. 142, 2. Dyrnegeligres leahtor *fornicationis crimen*, Ll. Th. ii. 152, 21. Wíf fornumen in dernegiligro (*adulterio*), Jn. R. 8, 4. Mid þäm heó hæfde diernegeligre *quem flagitiose cognitum*, Ors. 3, 11; S. 148, 3. Dernegiligero *adulteria*, Mk. R. 7, 21. Dernegiligru and arognisse, 8, 38. Tô dernegiligrum, 10, 11.

**dīrne-leger**, es; *n. Adultery, fornication* :—For dernelegere ob *fornicationem*, Mt. L. 19, 9. Derneleger *adulterium*, Mk. L. 10, 11. Dernelegero *adulteria*, 7, 21.

**dīrne-leger**; *adj. Adulterous* :—Ðerneleger *adultera*, Mk. L. 8, 38. Dernel'e *adulteri*, Lk. L. 18, 11.

**dīrne-legere**; *adv. Licentiously* :—Dernelegere *luxuriose*, Lk. L. 15, 13.

**dīrne-legerscipe**, es; *m. Adultery, fornication* :—In derneleger-scip (ðerne-, v. 3) *in adulterio*, Jn. L. 8, 4.

**dīrne-licgan.** v. dirn-licgan.

**dīrn-gewritu**; *pl. n. The Apocrypha* :—Dyrngewrita *apocrifa*, Wrt. Voc. ii. 6, 4.

**dīrn-hǣmende**; *adj.* (*ptcpl.*) *Fornicating, adulterous* :—Dyrn-hǣmendra [*in*]*cestarum*, Wrt. Voc. ii. 24, 61.

**dīrn-līce**; *adv. Secretly* :—Hē hī on niht gemartirode swā hē dyrn-lícost mihte, Lch. iii. 424, 30.

**dīrn-licgan** *to fornicate, commit adultery* :—Alle ðä dernliggað *omnes qui fornicantur*, Ps. Srt. 72, 27. Þ ðū ne dernelice ne *adulteris*, Mk. L. R. 10, 19. Dyrnlicendra *mecharum*, Wrt. Voc. ii. 55, 12. v. dyrn-licgan in *Dict.*

**dīrn-maga**, an; *m. One who presides at mysteries* :—Dyrnmaga *mysteriarches*, Germ. 397, 350.

**dīrsian.** v. ge-dīrsian.

**disc.** *In passage from Bede for* disce *l.* disc, *and add* :—Disc *patena* (-*ina*), Txts. 86, 786: *ferculum*, 63, 852. Þær stôd micel sylfren disc (*discus*) on, Bd. 3, 6; Sch. 209, 14. Discas (-es?) *ferculi*, swæsende *fercula*, Wrt. Voc. ii. 35, 18. Sende se cyning þäm þearfum þone sylfrenan disc mid sande mid ealle, and hēt tôceorfan þone disc and syllan þäm þearfum, Hml. S. 26, 96. Ânnæ dics an þrým pundom, C. D. iii. 127, 19. Man sceal habban . . . pannan, crocca, dixas, Angl. ix. 264, 10. v. offrung-disc.

**disc-berend.** For Cot. 65 read Wrt. Voc. ii. 82, 83: 94, 2: 26, 60.

**discipul.** *Add* :—Gif þū sý his discipul . . . sprec tô þīnum discipulum, Bl. H. 233, 35. Hira discipulas wæron wel gelærede, Bd. 4, 2; Sch. 344, 19. Discipulas *discipuli*, Mt. L. 26, 8. Bædon hine his discipulos, Bl. H. 227, 11. Wē synd discipuli Drihtnes, 233, 15. Ofer ænne his discipula, 235, 12. Micelne þreát discipula, Bd. 4, 2; Sch. 344, 14. Hē monige him tô discipulum genam, 3, 5; Sch. 205, 12. Hēht hē him his discipulos tô, Bl. H. 225, 13. Hē lærde his discipuli, 231, 18.

**discipula** *a female disciple* :—Seó cyninges dohtor wæs discipula and leoruingman regollices lífes, and eft wæs mägister and lāreów, Bd. 3, 24; Sch. 311, 2.

**discipul-hād.** *Add* :—Swā swā níwe discipulhāda underðeódde *quasi novo discipulatui subditam*, Bd. 5, 21; Sch. 680, 12.

**disc-þeg(e)n**, -þēn. *Add* :—Discþegn *discifer*, Wrt. Voc. i. 82, 23. An ic ælcan gesettan discðegne hundeahtatig mancusa goldes, C. D. B. iii. 75, 30. Ic geann Ælmære mīnon discþēne þära ehta hīda æt Cateringa-tūne, Cht. Th. 560, 36.

**disme.** *Add* : moss (?) :—Peregrino *pulvere*, i. *musco. Muscus est mus peregrinus* þ is disme (*muscus*, in the sense of moss, seems to be rendered by disme), An. Ox. 46, 4.

**distæf.** *Add* :—Distæf *colus*, Ælfc. Gr. Z. 30, 2. Disstæf, Wrt. Voc. i. 59, 39.

**dīping** (dēp-), e; *f. Killing, putting to death* :—Rôdes dēðinges *crucis mortificationem*, Rtl. 72, 30.

**dob-fugel.** v. dop-fugel: dobgendi. v. dofian.

**dôc** *a bastard, mongrel, hybrid* :—Doóc, hornungsunu *nothus*, Wrt. Voc. ii. 61, 66. Âworden *vel* dôc *bigener*, 126, 19. v. dôc-incel.

**docce.** *Add* :—Docce *lappatium*, Wrt. Voc. ii. 54, 22. Ompre, docce *rodinaps*, i. 68, 53. Docce *dilla vel acrocorium*, 30, 45: *dilla*, An. Ox. 56, 371. Docca, Wrt. Voc. i. 79, 1.

**-docce** (-a?) v. finger-docce.

**docga.** *For reference substitute* Germ. 398, 147.

**dôc-incel**; *n. A bastard child* :—Dôcincel *nothus* (the reference is to the illegitimate brother of Ecgfrið. v. Nap. 17), Hpt. 33, 238, 4. v. dôc.

**dofian**; *p.* ode *To be doting, stupid* :—Dobgendi, dobende *decrepita*, Txts. 55, 638. [*v. D. D.* dove *to be in a doting state, be stupid. O. H. Ger.* tobôn (-ēn) *delirare.* Cf. *Icel.* dofna *to become dead* (of a limb); dofi *torpor.*] v. next word.

**dofung.** *Substitute: Absurdity, stupidity* :—Dofunge, dwolunge *deleramenta*, Wrt. Voc. ii. 28, 46. Dofuncga (dofunga *deliramenta*, i. stoliditates, Hpt. Gl. 444, 18), An. Ox. 1614. Dofunga *deliramenta*, 4194: (*frivola*) *machinamenta*, 2801. [*O. H. Ger.* tobunga *deliramentum.*] v. ge-dofung.

**dôgor.** *Add* :—Âuðer oððe eft uferran dôgore oððe ðonne *either afterwards or at the time*, Past. 281, 13. Wið þan ðe mīn wiif þær benuge inngonges swæ mid mīnum líce swæ sioððan yferran dôgre (*either with my body or afterwards at a later date*), Cht. Th. 470, 37. Æfter tuæm dôgrum ł dagum *post biduum*, Mt. L. 26, 2: p. 20, 1; Mk. L. 14, 1. Driô dôgor *triduo*, 8, 2. Ðerh ðreó dôgor *per triduum*, 14, 58. v. feoþor-, feówer-dôgor.

**dohter** *doctor :*—Dohter gód (*bonus doctor*, L.) *rabboni*, Jn. R. 20, 16.

**dôhtor.** *l.* dohtor, *and add :*—Dogter mín *filia mea*, Mt. R. 15, 22. Ic bidde þínre dohtor, Ap. Th. 4, 4. Mýnre dohtor gifta, 8. Sǣcgaþ dohter (doehter, L.) Sione *dicite filiae Sion*, Mt. R. 21, 5. Of dohter (doehter, R.) his *de filia ejus*, Mk. L. 7, 26, 29. Móder on doehter (dohter, R.) and dohter on moeder *mater in filiam et filia in matrem*, Lk. L. 12, 53. Docter *filiam*, Mk. p. 3, 17. Dohtra (dohtero, L., dohter, R.) *filiae*, Lk. 23, 28. v. bróþor-, freó-dohtor.

**dohtor-sunu** *a grandson :*—Leódulf wæs þæs ealdan Oddan sunu and Eádweardes cininges dohtorsunu, Chr. 982 ; P. 124, 32.

**dohx.** v. dox.

**dol** ; *adj.* For Cot. 193 *l.* Wrt. Voc. ii. 85, 6, *and add :*—Tô dol þu wǣre and tô gedyrstig þá þú wêndest þæt þínra feohgestreóna ende ne gewurde, Wlfst. 260, 21. Dysig † dole (ðú ídle † unwís) *fatue*, Mt. R. 5, 22. Gelíc were dysig † dolum *similis viro stulto*, 7, 26. Him ne ondrǣdað ðá dolan ðæt hié sién ofer ôðre *praecipites ceteris praeferri non metuunt*, Past. 51, 19. Ðá dolan . . . ðá wísan *hebetes . . . sapientes*, 203, 3.

**dol**, es ; *n. Folly, stupidity :*—Ne geríseð ǣnig unnytt ǣfre mid bisceopum, ne doll ne dysig, Ll. Th. ii. 314, 31. Sê ðe eall his môd bið áflogen tô gǣglbǣrnesse and tô dole *qui totis cogitationibus ad lasciviam defluit*, Past. 73, 12. Gif se gilda mid dysie and myd dole stleá, bere sylf þ hê worhte, Cht. Th. 612, 2.

**dolg** ; *n. and m.* (Hml. S. 20, 67). *Add to instances given under* dolh : I. *a wound :*—Wiþ hundes dolge *for a wound made by a dog*, Lch. ii. 144, 11. Þú ætýwest þínra honda dolh and þínre sídan and þínra fóta, Angl. xii. 510, 14. II. *a boil, tumour :*—Se lǣce sceolde ásceótan þ gesweil . . . hcô gewát of worulde on þám þriddan dæge syððan se dolh wæs geopenod, Hml. S. 20, 67. Hêt Isaias wyrcan ænne clyþan tô þæs cyninges dolge *jussit Isaias ut tollerent massam de ficis et cataplasmarent super vulnus* (Is. 38, 21), 18, 431 : Hml. Th. i. 476, 1.

**dolg-drenc.** *Add to* dolh-drenc :—Dolhdrenc *antidotum*, An. Ox. 383. Wryc gôdne dolhdrenc, Lch. ii. 326, 25.

**dolg-rune.** *l.* dolg-rûne.

**dolg-swæþ** ; *n.* : -swaþu ; *f. Add to examples under* dolh-swæþ : I. *neut.* :—Dolgswæð *cicatricis uestigia*, Bd. 4, 19 ; Sch. 449, 7. Eáðe mihte Críst árísan of deáðe bútan dolhswaðum, ac hê heóld þá dolhswaðu, Hml. Th. i. 234, 26. Hí grápodon ðá dolhswaðu, 302, 2. II. *fem.* :—Nán dolswaþu næs gesýne, Hml. Th. ii. 492, 9. Hê hæfde áne dolhswaðe on his hneccan, Hml. S. 30, 268. Dolgswaþhe *plagae uestigia, cicatrices*, Bl. Gl. Dolcswaðan *cicatrices*, Hpt. Gl. 510, 57.

**dol-líce.** *Add :*—Oft mon rǣsð suíðe dollíce on ælc weorc and hrædlíce, and wênað men ðæt hit sié for hwætscipe *saepe praecipitata actio velocitatis efficacia putatur*, Past. 149, 12. Seó beó dollíce hyre cynesetl gestíhð, Angl. viii. 324, 15.

**dol-sceaþa.** *Add :* dol(h)-sceaþa (?) *a robber who wounds.* Cf. dolswaþu *for* dolh-swaþu : **dol-scipe.** *Add the Latin passage :* aversio parvulorum interficiet eos : **dol-sprǽc.** *l.* dol-sprǽc : **dol-willen.** Cf. druncen-willen : **dol-wíte.** *Add :* dol(h)-wíte (?) *pain of a wound.* The Latin on which this part of the riddle (dryhtfolca helm, nales dolwíte) seems based is 'sanis victum et laesis praestabo medelam.'

**dôm.** *Add :*—Dôm *censura*, Wrt. Voc. ii. 21, 35 : 24, 5. I. *judgement.* (1) *where an opinion is formed :*—Ðá dysegan men sint ælces dômes swá blinde, þ hí nyton hwǽr ðá sôþan gesǽlþa sint gehýdde, Bt. 32, 3 ; F. 118, 22. Þætte ealra heora dôme (*judicio*) gecoren wǽre, hwanone þ cymen wǽre, Bd. 4, 24 ; Sch. 485, 8. (2) *where sentence is passed :*—Mycel egsa gelimpþ eallum geceaftum, þonne se dôm neálǣceþ, Bl. H. 91, 19. Ealle sceolan forþ gán tô þám dôme, 95, 18. Se vfela dêma onwendeþ þone rihtan dôm, 61, 31. (2 a) *of an unfavourable sentence, condemnation :*—Þá láreówas beóþ dômes wyrþe, gif hí nellaþ þ folc lǣron, Bl. H. 47, 23. II. *direction, ruling :*—Hié heora scriftum fullíce geandettiaþ, and be heora dôme bêtaþ, Bl. H. 193, 23. III. *will, discretion ; arbitrium :*—Mid cyre, dôme *arbitrio*, i. *judicio*, An. Ox. 1315. Hí rícsiað of hira ágnum dôme, næs of ðæs hiéhstan dêman *ex se et non ex arbitrio summi rectoris regnant*, Past. 27, 16. Sié þ on cyninges dôme, swá deáð swá líf, Ll. Th. i. 66, 10. Ic hine tô heora sylfra dôme ágeaf, Bl. H. 177, 25. Þú lǣtst eal eówer fǽreld tô þæs windes dôme *quo flatus impellerent, promovereris*, Bt. 7, 2 ; F. 18, 33. Gebeád hê him hiera ágenne dôm feós and londes, Chr. 755 ; P. 48, 17 : By. 38. Þá teóþan sceattas wǽron on úrum ágnum dômum, Bl. H. 51, 7. Wese hit be eówrum dômum, 157, 7. IV. *authority :*—Dôme *auctoritate*, An. Ox. 5149. Swá hê dêmð ús on dômes dæg, swá wê hêr demað þám mannum þe we on eorþan dóm ofer ágon, Wlfst. 300, 11. Dômas *magistratus*, i. *principatus*, An. Ox. 260. IV a. *an authority, a judicial body, court* (cf. Icel. dômr *a court for judgement*) :—Dôme *senatu* (a Romano *senatu* capitalem sortitus sententiam), An. Ox. 8, 229. V. *reputation, glory :*—Sê geworhte micelne dôm on ðæm gefeohte, Ors. 2, 5 ; S. 78, 27. Þ hê him swilcne dôm ne on-

drêde, ne his mægnes micelnysse ne wundrode, Hml. S. 30, 40. VI. *an ordinance, a decree :*—Nis nán rihtra dôm, þonne úre ælc ôðrum beóde, þæt wê willan, þæt man ús beóde, Wlfst. 112, 4. Dôme, rǽde *decretum*, i. *judicium*, i. *secretum*, An. Ox. 2676. 'Canst ðú þone dôm mýnre dohtor gifta ?' Ap. Th. 4, 8–10. Þis synd þá dômas (*judicia*) þe þú him tǣcan scealt, Ex. 21, 1. Dôma *decretorum*, An. Ox. 2, 329. Dômum, gesetnessum *sanctionibus*, i. *judiciis*, 842. Gehír nú godcunde dômas *audi ceremonias atque judicia*, Deut. 5, 1. Bebodu and godcunde ǣ and dômas *mandata et ceremonias atque judicia*, 31. Gescriíu, dômas *ceremonias*, Wrt. Voc. ii. 23, 54. VII. *a sentence, doom :*—Se dôm þæt hire wæs tô gecweden, þ heú cende on sáre, Bl. H. 3, 8. Se mon þe nú dêmeþ þǣm earmum bûton mildheortnesse, þonne biþ þám eft heard dôm geteód, 95, 36. Se deáð him tô cymeþ Godes dôm tô ábeódenne, 59, 11. Heardne dôm gehýran, 83, 17. Beheáfodlicne dôm *capitalem sententiam*, An. Ox. 4043 : 4803. Iudas geseah þone rêðan dôm, Hml. Th. ii. 250, 13. VIII. *a case for settlement, question :*—Áworden wæs doom (dôm, L.) from clǣnsunge *facta est quaestio de purificatione*, Jn. R. 3, 25. Dôme *examini*, i. *judicio*, An. Ox. 1313. Geáxode dômas *responsa*, Wrt. Voc. i. 20, 68. Dômum *scissitationibus*, Wrt. Voc. ii. 79, 14. IX. *state, condition :*—Geceás hê Laurentium tô þám háde þæs biscopes dômes *ad pontificatus ordinem Laurentium elegit*, Gr. D. 329, 17. Álýsede fram bende ælces mennisces dômes *nexu humanae conditionis exuti*, C. D. B. i. 154, 15. On þeówum dôme † tô þeówan geseald *in servum venundatus*, Ps. L. 104, 17. Yfel se cyning wiþ þám Crístenan dóma dyde, Bt. 1 ; F. 2, 15. Wê sculan ǣnne Crístendôm healdan and ælcne hǽðene dôm oferhogian, Wlfst. 274, 16. v. dryht-, un-, unriht-, weoruld-, wôh-dôm.

**dôm-bôc.** *Add :*—Ic gedô þ man sceall þe wel fæste gewríðan, and þe, eall swá seó dômbôc be swilcum mannum tǣcð, oft and gelôme swingan, Hml. S. 23, 714. [v. *N. E. D.* doom-book.]

**dôm-dæg.** *Add :*—Ondrǣde man dômdæg, Wlfst. 75, 6 : 179, 16. [*O. Sax.* dôm-dæg : *O. H. Ger.* tuom-tag.]

**dômere.** *Add :*—Þe mon tô dômere geceás, Bt. 8 ; F. 24, 30. [v. *N. E. D.* doomer.]

**dôm-ern, -ærn.** *Add :*—Dômærn *pretorium*, Wrt. Voc. ii. 85, 64. Dômern, An. Ox. 4498. Þæs dômernes cæfertún *atrium praetorii*, Mk. 15, 16. Hê eóde in þæt dômern ðǣr ðǽr Caluisianus wæs in miclum gemôte, Shrn. 116, 31.

**dôm-hús.** *Add :*—Dômhús *pretorium*, Wrt. Voc. ii. 85, 64. [*Prompt. Parv.* dome-howse.]

**dômisc** ; *adj. Of the final judgement, of doomsday :*—Mid ðý dômiscan fýre onǣled, Sal. K. 148, 30.

**dôm-lic.** *Add :*—Dômlicum *synoþum decretis synodalibus*, An. Ox. 2889. Tída dômlice *horas canonicas*, Angl. xiii. 384, 268. [*O. H. Ger.* tuom-líh.]

**dôm-líce.** *Add :*—Sê hæfde áre on eorþríce, sê þe ælmyssan dǣlde dômlíce, Lch. i. 400, 9. Bið deóplícor gehwyrfed ðæt deófol on deádes onlícnisse . . . Dômlícor bið ðonne se Pater Noster gehwyrfed on Dryhtnes onlícnisse, Sal. K. 146, 25.

**domne.** *Add :*—Þá wæs domne Leó pápa on Rôme, Chr. 853 ; P. 64, 29. Tô ðæs bisceopæs mearcæ . . . swá tô domnes hlincæ, C. D. v. 84, 16 : 243, 22. Cf. (?) domni pôl, vi. 221, 30 : iii. 377, 24.

**dôm-setl.** *Add :*—Beforan dômsetle *ante tribunal*, Dôm. L. 123. Hê gearwað his dômsetl *paravit in judicio sedem suam*, Ps. Th. 9, 8. Tô dômsetlum *ad subsellia, ad tribunal*, Germ. 393, 61. Þæt hí on ðám micclum dôme ofer twelf dômsetl sittende beóð tô dêmenne eallum mannum, Hml. Th. i. 542, 20. [*O. H. Ger.* tuom-sedal *tribunal.*]

**dôm-settend.** *Substitute : One who ordains judgement* (v. settan, VI), *a lawyer :*—Jurisconsultus, jurisperitus, id est rihtscrífend *sive* dômsettend, Wrt. Voc. ii. 49, 13.

**dôm-stôw**, e ; *f. A judgement-place, tribunal :*—Hwǽr syndon dêmra dômstôwa ?, Wlfst. 148, 31.

**dôm-weorþung**, e ; *f. Honour, glory :*—Sige forgeaf Constantíno cyning ælmihtig, dômweorðunga, El. 146 : 1234.

**dôn** (?) :—Dôn *damulus* [dán *damulus* ?], Wrt. Voc. ii. 28, 30.

**dôn.** *Add :* [*Forms from the Northern Gospels and Vespasian Psalter are :* ic dóam, dôem, doom, dôm, dóe, þú dôas, dóes, dôest, hé dóas, dóes, dôað, dóeð, *pl.* dôas, dôað ; *subj.* dóe ; *infin.* dôa, dôe, tô dôanne, dôenne ; *pp.* dôen, dǽn. *In a Mercian charter a subjunctive* dê *occurs ;* deodan, *p. pl. indic.,* dede *faceret*, Kent. Gl. 257, *are Kentish forms.*] I. *absolute, to do, act :*—Sê bið Godes andsaca þe Godes láre forlǣt and þurh deófles láre of ðám deð ðe his cristendôme tô gebyreð (*acts in a way that is not consistent with a proper regard to his Christianity*), Wlfst. 78, 15. Ðegn ðone hláferd suá dôende (dônde, R.), Mt. L. 24, 46. Ealle unrihtlíce dôende *omnes inique agentes*, Ps. Spl. 24, 3. II. *to do, perform an action, make war :*—On hwælcum mæht ðás ic dôe † dôam (*faciam*), Mk. L. 11, 29. Ic dôam, 33. Ðoncunge ic dôem (dôm, R.) *gratias ago*, Jn. L. 11, 41. Þ ic doom (dôe, R.) *quod ego facio*, 13, 7. Ðás tácено ðá ðe ðú dôas

(dóes, R.), Jn. L. 3, 2. Dóæs (dóes, R.), Mk. L. 11. 28. Dóes *facit*, Mt. L. 7, 24. Sē ðā unrehtan dóeð *qui iniqua gerit*, Ps. Srt. 9, 24. Hwæt forðor gié dóas (dóaþ, R.)? ah ne ēsuice ðis dóas (dóaþ, R.)?, Mt. L. 5, 47. On Thessali hē þæt gewinn dyde *Thessaliam invasit*, Ors. 3, 7; S. 112, 2. Him mon wrenc tō dyde, 4, 1; S. 156, 8. Ðæt wit deodan for Godes lufan, Txts. 175, 6. Ðæt ic dóe (*faciam*) willan ðinne, Ps. Srt. 39, 9. Wite hē þ hē hit dē ofer Godes ēst, Cht. Th. 131, 36. Noldan hié dón þone triumphan beforan hiora consulum *triumphus consuli denegatus est*, Ors. 4, 7; S. 182, 1. Hē māre mæg doon ðonne ōðre menn, Past. 111, 17. Hréowe dóan *paenitentiam facere*, Bd. 5, 13; Sch. 641, 2. þ ic wille dóan (dóa, L.) *quod volo facere*, Mt. R. 20, 15. Ðæs is rehtlic tō dóanne *haec oportuit facere*, Mt. L. 23, 23. Hē wæs monega gefeoht dónde *plurima bella gessit*, Ors. 4, 8; S. 188, 19. Oft būtan synne bið dón (dóen, *v. l.*) þ of synne cymeð, Bd. 1, 27; Sch. 84, 3 : 13. **II a.** *to do, practise, exercise, pass time, lead a life* :—Būtan þē ic dede þone hālgan dæg (*I spent the day*) æt Drihtnes ācennisse, ac ic dō mid þē ðone hālgan dæg æt Drihtnes ætýwnesse, Shrn. 48, 8–10. Ðā ðe dóð forhæfdnesse *qui parce cibo utuntur*, Past. 308, 13 : *abstinentes*, 16. Mid ðý hē þæt langre tíde forðéold and dyde *quod dum multo tempore sedulus exsequeretur*. Bd. 4, 25; Sch. 497, 13. Hē āncorlíf dyde (on āncorlíf drohtode, *v. l.*) *anchoreticam vitam egerat*, 5, 9; Sch. 596, 6. Þær dydon Rōmāne lytla tríewþa, Ors. 5, 2; S. 218, 16. Tō dóanne (-enne. L.) mildheortnisse *ad faciendam misericordiam*, Lk. R. 1, 72. **II b.** *with preps., to do about, with* :—Þā menn ealle hē tóc, and dyde of heom þ hē wolde, Chr. 1072; P. 208, 29. Dóð be ūs þ þ Drihten wile, Hml. S. 11, 133. Hwæt tō dónne wǽre be þām stalle cyrícean, Bd. 3, 29; Sch. 327, 20. **III.** *to make.* (1) *with acc.* :—Mið ðý ðū dóest (dóes, R.) gebærscip, Lk. L. 14, 13. Dydon hí þā mǽstan gebeórscype, Hml. S. 30, 387. Sum ārgeótere mehte dón missenlíce anlícnessa, Ors. 1, 12; S. 54, 20. (2) *to cause.* (a) *with acc. and infin.* (α) *where noun is subject of infin.* :—Swā ðū dydest mínne bróðor his god forlǽtan, swā dō ic eác ðē forlǽtan ðinne god, Hml. Th. i. 468, 21. (β) *where noun is object of infin.* :—Þone ōðerne dǽl he dyde gehealdan (-en, MS.) *he had the second part kept*, Hml. S. 3. 123. (b) *with clause* :—Gif se sācerd dēð þæt þæt folc syngie, Lev. 4, 3. Hē dyde þæt gē dwelodon, Deut. 13, 5. Dóð þæt þæt folc sitte, Hml. Th. i. 184, 16. (c) *to do harm* :—Séo léase wyrd ne mæg þām men dón nǽnne dem, Bt. 20; F. 70, 22. (3) *with complementary adjective* :—Ic dō þinne ofspring menigfealdne, Gen. 13, 16. Men hāle ðū dóes, Ps. Srt. 35, 7. Hāl dóeð hē folc, Mt. L. 1, 21. Ðing ðe heora hlāfordas dóð geswencte, Hml. Th. ii. 92, 16. Dō þín mōd hlūttor, Hml. S. 5, 216 ; Lch. i. 72, 8. (4) *with acc. and tō, to make an object (into) something, make something of an object* :—Hrýðra þāra þe mon tō mete dyde *armentorum ad usum carnis*, Nar. 9, 13. Þā hí men woldon him tō mete dón, St. A. 4, 18. Hē hēt dón tō geblote ealle þā cuman, Ors. S. 1, 19. Hine dón niédenga tō cyninge *eum rapere et regem facere*, Past. 33, 14. **IV.** *to put, bring, take.* (1) *literal* :—Suā oft suā wē ūre hand dóð tō ūrum mūðe, Past. 313, 14. Hyne man dyde ūp *eductum decarcere Joseph*, Gen. 41, 14. Se biscop dyde ūp (*took up from the grave*) þone sanct, Hml. S. 21, 140. Þone ðryddan dǽl hē dyde onsundor *the third part he put aside*, 3, 125. Dō *appresenta*, An. Ox. 56, 73 : *applica*, 135. Mon hæfde anfiteatrum geworhte, þæt hē mehte Godes þéowas on dón (*objiceret*), Ors. 6, 31; S. 286, 12. Dón þā elpendas on þæt gefeoht *introductos inter concurrentia agmina elephantos*, 4, 1; S. 156, 7. Uton dón hine on þone pytt *mittamus eum in cisternam*, Gen. 37, 20. Hē hió niman þā nǽdran and dón tō hire earme, Ors. 5, 13; S. 246, 24. Hē lēt dón ūp þær þā gíslas *he had the hostages put ashore there*, Chr. 1014; P. 145, n. 8. Teter of andwlitan tō dónne *to remove tetter from the face*, Lch. i. 336, 3. (2) *fig., to put to use, change, death, &c., bring into a state* :—Dyde hē him þā rícu tō gewealdon *he brought the kingdoms into subjection to him*, Ors. 3, 7; S. 114, 29. Þā twégen dǽlas hē dyde tō þæs mynstres neóde *the two parts he applied to the needs of the monastery*, Hml. S. 3, 287. Þā ðe hine dydon tō cwale, 21, 372. Hí dóð mē tō bysmore, Hml. Th. i. 152, 8. Tō hiéran hāde dón *to elevate to a higher rank*, Past. 7, 15. Tō lāre dón *to send to school*, Ll. Th. ii. 414, 3. Þā gife ic wylle tō þon dón *I will put the gift to that use*, Guth. 84, 12. (2 a) *where there is combination or separation* :—Dō tō endlufon (*add eleven*) . . . tō twām and twēntigum dō endlufon . . . gyf þū dēst twelf þærtō, Angl. viii. 301, 13–20. Ōðres mannes man þe hē for hys yfele him fram dō (*turns away, dismisses from service*), Ll. Th. i. 220, 20. þ hit nǽfre næs his dǽd þ man sceolde ǽfre Sandwíc dón ūt of Xpes. cyrc. *that Sandwich should be taken away from Christchurch*, Cht. Th. 340, 6. **V.** *to give, supply, furnish* :—Tācn mínes weddes þæt ic dō betwux mē and eów *signum foederis quod do inter me et vos*, Gen. 9, 12. Ne behófiað ūre líchaman nānre strangunge eorðlicra metta, ac se Hǽlend ūs dēð ealle ūre neóda mid heofenlicum ðingum, Hml. Th. i. 296, 31. Him se bisceop forgyfennysse dēð (*remissionem dat*), Ll. Th. ii. 178, 9 : 18 ; 266, 18. Absolutionem dēð, 266, 12. Gif hý him ne dōþ mete ne munde, i. 248, 7. Him mon dyde feówer síþan þone

triumphan, Ors. 5, 12 ; S. 244, 8 : 262, 25. Gē swylc leán dydon eówrum witan, 6, 4 ; Bos. 105, 7. Dō him þis tō lǣcedóme, Lch. i. 350, 23. Gif him þyrste, ðū dō him drincan, Hml. S. 21, 376. Man ne sceolde ǽnigne bigleofan hire dón, 10, 282 : Ll. Th. ii. 372, 30. Hí noldon Juliuse nǽnne weorþscipe dón, Ors. 5, 10 ; S. 234. 30. Seó léase wyrd ne mæg þām men dón fultum, Bt. 20 ; F. 70, 22. Doonde *laturi* (*praesidium*), Wrt. Voc. ii. 79, 9. **VI.** *to make* (*much, nothing*) *of, to make out to be so* and *so, consider, esteem* :—Sē ðe conn wel emn bión wið ōðre menn, and hē hine nā bettran ne dēð, Past. 113, 23. Þonne wē ūs for nōwiht dóð þ wē earme menn reáfiað *cum infirmiores spoliare pro nihilo ducimus*, Bd. 3, 19; Sch. 279, 6. Ðætte hē on nánum ðingum hiene betran ne doo ðǣm gódum *ut bonis in nullo se praeferat*, Past. 106, 11. Hwý hié hiene swā unweorðe on his ylde dyden *why they had such contempt for him in his old age*, Ors. 5, 4 ; S. 224, 26. **VII.** *almost with the force of the later auxiliary.* (1) *with a verb in apposition* :—Se mōna dēð ǽgðer ge wycxð ge wanað, Hml. Th. i. 154, 26. Hié dydon ǽgðer ge cyninga rícu settan ge níwu ceastra timbredon, Ors. 1, 10; S. 48, 9. Dō gā and ne synga þū nǽfre mā *uade et amplius jam noli peccare*, Jn. 8, 11. (2) *with a clause* :—Dydon þā hǽðenan þ hí buden sybbe and hí sylfe þǽm cǽsere, Hml. S. 31, 118. **VIII.** *representing a preceding verb* :—Monige beóð blíðe and eác unblíðe ðāra ðe for nánum woruldðingum nāhwæðer dóð, Past. 187, 24. Hē sníð swíðe hrǽdlíce. Suā se wítga dyde ðone cyning, 187, 2 : 185, 8. Þā behídde Adam hyne and his wíf eác swā dide, Gen. 3, 8. Se man nolde gān, swā swā ōðre men dydon, Hml. S. 12, 43 : 15, 82. þ mon lufode þone gódan swā swā riht is þ mon dō, Bt. 39, 1; F. 212, 7. Gif Ænglisc man Deniscne ofsleá, gylde-hine mid .xxx. pundum, and dō se Denisca þone Engliscan eal swā gif hine ofsleá, Ll. Th. i. 286, 23. v. wel-, yfel-dón ; riht-, unriht-, wel-, yfel-dónde.

-dónd. v. ælmes-, wel-, yfel-dónd.

dón-líc. For Cot. 149 substitute :—Þǽre dónlecan (*printed* dor-) *practicae*, Wrt. Voc. ii. 65, 74. On dónlicum þingum *in faciendo*, R. Ben. I. 23. 12. Dónlicum *agendis*, 44, 14.

-dónness. v. wel-dónness : dooc. *Dele* : 'The . . . Lye,' *and see* dóc.

dop-enid. *Add* :—Doppaenid (dop-) *fulix*, Txts. 65, 936. Dopened, Wrt. Voc. ii. 36, 20.

dop-fugel. *Add* :—Dopfugel *mergus*, Hpt. 33, 240, 23. *Mergulum, niger avis, mergit sub aquam pisces quaerere*, i. e. dobfugel, Shrn. 29, 4. Ðæs gífran dopfugeles *voracis mer*[g]*ule*, Wrt. Voc. ii. 76, 7 : 56, 61. [*O. L. Ger.* dop-fugul.]

doppa. v. dūfe-doppa.

Dor. *Add* :—Swā Dor scadeþ, Hwítan wylles geat, Chr. 942; P. 110, 15.

dór . . . dūru. *Substitute* : dor, es ; *n., and add* :—Tō dore ł geat (tō duru ł tō gæt, L.) *ad januam*, Mk. R. 1, 31. Bifora ðǽm dore (dor, L.) *ante januam*, 11, 4. Ongegn ðǽm dore (ðæs dores, L.), 12, 41. Sete dor þone ostium, Ps. Th. 140, 4 : Rtl. 179, 9. Cnylsiga þ dor *pulsare ostium*, Lk. L. R. 13, 25. ⁋ Of secbróce tō þan heán dore (*gate*, Kemble : *pass*, Earle, Chr. p. 328) ; of þan (heán, C. D. iii. 79, 3) dore tō brýdbróce, Cht. E. 447, 8. v. ciric-, wōþ-(?) -dor.

dora. *Add* :—Dora *atticus*, Txts. 43, 236 : *attacus*, Wrt. Voc. ii. 7, 39 : *adticus*, 66. Foxes geallan gemencged mid doran hunige, Lch. i. 342, 6.

dor-weard, es ; *m. A doorkeeper, porter, janitor* :—Dorweard, ðā in aldum gecýðnise dorweardas *hostiarius, qui in veteri testamento janitores*, Rtl. 193, 39. Ðǽm dorworde (*janitori*) bibeódes þ hē wæcce, Mk. R. L. 13, 34. v. duru-weard.

dott. *Add* : [Cf. *O. H. Ger.* tutto(-a) *mamma, mamilla, pupilla*.]

dox, dosc (?) ; *adj. Dark-coloured* :—Dohx *furva*, Angl. xiii. 28, 18. Of glæteriendum *vel* scylfrum híwe *vel* doxum *flava specie*, Wrt. Voc. ii. 149, 21 : An. Ox. 532 (*printed* dexum, Hpt. Gl. 419, 24). [v. *N. E. D.* dusk.] v. next word.

doxian ; *p.* ode *To become dark-coloured* :—Hwílum hē (*the dead body*) bið swíðe láðlicum men gelíc ; þonne wannað hē and doxaþ, ōðre hwíle hē bið blǣc and ǣhíwe, Verc. fol. 23 b. [v. *N. E. D.* dusk ; vb.]

drabbe. *Dele.*

draca. *Add* :—Draca, droco, draco *tipa*, Txts. 103, 2027. Draca *dracus*, Wrt. Voc. i. 78, 54. Se draca *leviathan*, ii. 76, 50. Ðegnas his gifuhton wið ðǽm drǽcce (*dracone*) and se drǽcca gifæht, Rtl. 70, 21. Hēr is cumen ān draca þe mē forswelgan sceal . . . Mín heáfod hē hæfð mid his ceaflum befangen, Hml. Th. i. 534, 15. Ic eom forðrycced mid þām scyllum þisses dracan (*draconis*) . . . Ðes draca nū fleáh, Gr. D. 325, 5–9. Dracan *gypsam* (-*um*, Ald.), Wrt. Voc. ii. 91, 69 : 41, 41. Deósterfulle wununga mid dracum āfyllede, Hml. Th. i. 68, 5.

dracu, e ; *f. Trouble, affliction* :—Eal hit is for synnum and gyt weorþeð māre, þæs þe bēc secgað, wracu (dracu, *v. l.*) and gedrecednes, Wlfst. 91, 7. v. dreccan.

**drǽdan.** *Add:*—Gong ût sâwl, hwæt drǽdest (ondrǽdest, Mart. H. 194, 4) ðû ðê?, Shrn. 141, 29. Mann wîs on eallum drætt *homo sapiens in omnibus metuit*, Scint. 67, 1. ꝥ wolde hine ofsleán ꝥ dreórd him ꝥ folc *et volens illum occidere timuit populum*, Mt. R. 14, 5. þâ leorneras wundradun ꝥ dreórdun *discipuli mirabantur*, 19, 25. ꝥ soecende hiá ꝥ hine genôman ꝥ dreórdun him mængu *et quaerentes eum tenere timuerunt turbas*, 21, 46. [*Perhaps in the last three examples the symbol ꝥ may represent the prefix in* ondrǽdan, *under which verb they would then belong.*]

**drǽf** *a drove.* v. drâf.

**drǽfan.** *Add:*—Hêr drǽfde Eádgâr þâ preóstas on Ceastre of Ealdan mynstre, Chr. 964; P. 116, 1. Ǽghwæþer oþerne ût drǽfde, 887; P. 80, 29. Hêr man drǽfde ût Ælfgife, 1037; P. 161, 9. Æþelrêd man drǽfde ût of his earde, Wlfst. 160, 14. Tô drǽfene *pulsaturam*, An. Ox. 4865. [*Goth.* draibjan : *O. H. Ger.* treiben.]

**drǽge,** es ; *n.? l.* drǽge, an ; *f., and add :* [v. *N. E. D.* drayman.]

**drǽg-net.** *Add :* [v. *N. E. D.* dray-net.]

**drǽgtre ?** :—Wesan draegtre *exerceri*, Wrt. Voc. ii. 108, 6.

**drǽst(e), drǽs[t]ig.** v. dærst[e], dærstig.

**drâf, drǽf.** *Add :*—Hêt se hâlga wer þæt seó cû gewende tô þǽre heorde, and heó swâ bilewite swâ scêp beáh tô þǽre drǽfe, Hml. S. 31, 1055. Se geneát sceal lâde lǽdan, drâfe drîfan, C. D. iii. 450, 33. Sum fearhrýþer þæs ôþræs' ceápes gefêrscipe oferhogode . . . Hê þæs hyrdes drâfe forhogode and him on ꝥ wêsten gewunode, Bl. H. 199, 7. [*Add to passage from* Hml. Th. i. 502, 10, *cf.* hwî se fearr his heorde forsâwe, 17.]

**dragan.** *Dele the derivatives and the passage from* Gû. *given under* II, *and add :*—Heó creáp on þâm handum and drôh (*trahebat*) on ðǽre eorðan ealne hire lîchaman . . . þâ ongan heó hider and þider dragan hî selfe (*se trahere*) geond þâ cyrican, Gr. D. 228, 10–18. Wildu hors hyne drôgon on gorstas and on þornas, Shrn. 117, 13. Hî becnytton his swuran mid râpe and drôgon (cf. tugon, 54) hine swâ swâ hî ǽr dydon, Hml. S. 15, 82. Drôgun (trôgun, R., cf. trôg, v. 11) *segni trahentes rete*, Jn. 21, 8. Dragað hine niwelne his neb tô eorðan, 14, 155. Ongon þâ leófne sîð dragan Dryhtnes cempa tô þâm eorðan dǽle, Gû. 699. Hê lêt dragan ûp þæne deádan Harald, Chr. 1040; P. 162, 3. Hî fêrdon æfter heom intô þâm mynstre and woldon hig ût dragan, 1083; P. 215, 6. v. â-dragan.

**dreahnian.** *l.* (?) dreáhnian (*Kluge compares N. Fris.* druugin *to strain*), *and add :*—[Nim hyt â morgen and dreáhne hit þurh lînnen clâþ, and syle hym drinca, Lch. iii. 130, 22.] [v. *N. E. D.* drain.]

**dreám, drêm, drîm.** *Add :* **I** *joy :*—God ælmihtig hine âwende of eallum Godes dreáme, Cht. Th. 548, 16. Tealte beóð eorðan dreámas, Wlfst. 264, 3. **II.** *joyous sound, jubilation :*—Drêmes *jubilationis* (cf. swêges, 8, 141), An. Ox. 7, 176. On drîme *in jubilo*, Wrt. Voc. ii. 46, 15. **II a.** *musical sound of voice or of instrument :*—Efenhleóþrung *vel* dreám *concentus*, i. *adunationes multarum vocum*, Wrt. Voc. ii. 136, 8. Dreámes *melodiae*, An. Ox. 402 : *psalmodiae*, 982. Ic wynsume stemne ormǽtes dreámes gehýrde *uocem cantantium dulcissimam audiui* (Bd. 5, 12), Hml. Th. ii. 352, 15. Býman bleówan mid swiðlicum dreáme . . . Betwux þisum dreáme clypode Drihten (v. Ex. 19, 19), 196, 26. Swinsunge, dreáme *armonia*, An. Ox. 2594. Drême, 7, 174. Se æfensang sý geendod mid feówer sealma dreáme *vespera quattuor psalmorum modulatione canatur*, R. Ben. 43, 8. Swinsunge, dreám (swinsunge ł dreám, Hpt. Gl. 438, 8) *melodiam*, An. Ox. 1342. Dreám, swinsunge *armonia* (cf. swinsunge *armonia* (*harmoniam*, Ald.), 90, 61), Wrt. Voc. ii. 3, 29. Hû manige dreámas and lofsangas hleóþriaþ in heofonum *quantae resonent laudes in coelo*, Gr. D. 282, 14. Godes þeówas þe þâ cyrican mid godcundum dreámum weorþiað . . . þâ þe forhycggaþ þâ Godes dreámas tô gehêrenne, Bl. H. 41, 27–36. Dreámas *armonias*, i. *sonos*, An. Ox. 3053. Dreámas and tyrnende swêgas *iambicos et rotatiles trocheos*, Germ. 403, 7. Þâ eáran âslâwiað þe wǽron ful swifte tô gehýrenne fægere dreámas and sangas, Wlfst. 148, 3. v. æfen-, pîp-, sang-, wôden-dreám.

**dreám-cræft.** *Add :*—Musica, ꝥ ys dreámcræft, Shrn. 152, 15. In Bt. 16, 3 *the original Latin is :* Musica musicos facit.

**dreám-lic.** *For* Cot. 133 *substitute* Wrt. Voc. ii. 78, 6 : 56, 65, *and add :*—Dreámlic swinsung *organica armonia*, An. Ox. 3923.

**dreámness.** v. wyn-dreámness : **dreám-swinsung.** *Dele, and see* dreám.

**dreáriend** *the inrushing tide* (?) :—Dreáriende *dodrante*, Wrt. Voc. ii. 142, 3. Cf. êgor.

**dreccan.** *Add :*—Gif þû þis dôn ne miht, drece ûs lôca hû þû wylle, Hml. S. 7, 115. Gewǽce *vel* drecce *fatigat*, Wrt. Voc. ii. 147, 27. Hî gefêngon tô dreccenne þone fîftan brôðor, Hml. S. 25, 148.

**dreccing.** *Add :*—Bûtan dreccunge *sine uexatione*, Scint. 217, 6.

**drêfan.** *Add :*—Hê sceal drêfan dimne and deópne hellewîtes grund *he shall be plunged into hell's dim and deep abyss*, Wlfst. 48, 2 : Ll. Th. ii. 320, 5. Drêfende *turbulentus*, R. Ben. I. 61, 6 : R. Bén. 120, 12. Drêfende *turbida* (*aequora turgida*, Ald.), Wrt. Voc. ii. 91, 70.

**drêfedness.** *Add :*—For hwî forgetst þû ûre drêfednesse (*tribulationis*), Ps. L. 43, 24.

**drefela,** an ; *m.* A *driveller* (?), *slobberer :* — Ic geann Godwine Dreflan (Drefelan, l. 28), Cht. Th. 561, 14. v. dreflian.

**drêfend,** es ; *m.* A *disturber, turbulent person :*—Se mynstres hordere sî . . . nâ drêfend (*non turbulentus*), R. Ben. 54, 8. Drǽfend, 121, 12.

**dreflian.** *l.* dreflian *to drivel, slaver.* [v. *N. E. D.* drivel; *vb.*] v. drefela.

**drêfre ;** *adj. l.* drêfre, drêfere, es ; *m.* A *disturber, turbulent person :*—Ne sý hê drêfre (drǽfend, drêfende, *v.ll.*) *non sit turbulentus*, R. Ben. 121, 12. v. drêfend.

**drehnigean.** v. dreahnian : **dreman.** v. drîman.

**drenc.** *Add :* **I.** *drinking :*—Sê þe ôðerne neádað ofer his mihte tô drincenne, sê môt âberan heora bêgra gilt, gif him ǽnig hearm of þâm drence becymð, Ælfc. T. 21, 32, 38. Gýfernyss dêð ꝥ man tô micel nimð on wǽte . . . and þone mann tô deáðe gebrincgð for ðâm ormǽtan drænce (ormǽtum drenceum, *v. l.*), Hml. S. 16, 273. v. ofer-drenc. **II.** *drink, liquid taken as nourishment :*—Þæt genôh sý ǽnlýpigum munuce tô dæges drence (drænce, *v. l.*) þæs wînes gemet þe is emina gehâten, R. Ben. 64, 14. Se lîchoma bûtan mete and drence leofian ne mæg, Bl. H. 57, 10. Drenc, fôdan *haustum, pastum*, Hy. S. 103, 35. **III.** *a draught, cup :*—Drences *potationis*, An. Ox. 4990. Deáðes scencende drenc *mortis propinans poculum*, Hy. S. 31, 15. Drencas *biberes*, R. Ben. I. 66, 8. **III a.** *what is drunk as medicine :*—Hit is se lǽcedôm and se drenc ðe ðû wilnodest, Bt. 39, 12 ; F. 232, 21. For hwî se gôda lǽce selle ðâm hâlum men sæftne drenc, 39, 9 ; F. 226, 11. [v. *N. E. D.* drench. Cf. *Goth.* draggk; *n.* : *O. Sax. O. Frs.* drank : *O. H. Ger.* tranch.] v. âc-, clǽnsung-, eced-, medu-, morgen-, spiw-, wece-, wîn-drenc ; drence.

**drencan.** *Add :* **I.** *to give drink to :*—Swâ hwâ swâ ôðerne drencð (ðrencð, *v. l.*), hê wirð self oferdruncen *qui inebriat, ipse quoque inebriabitur* (Prov. 11, 25), Past. 381, 4. God ûs drencte mid teárum *potum dedit nobis in lacrymis*, 413, 11. Drynctun mec mid ecede *potaverunt me aceto*, Ps. Srt. 68, 22. Swelcum mannum deáh ꝥ hié hié selfe drencen, Lch. ii. 224, 1. **II.** *to plunge into water :*—Heó þǽre rôde tâcn on þâ wætru drencte, Hml. S. 23 b, 684. **II a.** *to plunge, sink :*—Þæt hý wið deáða dûru drencyde wǽran, Ps. Th. 106, 17. **III.** *of water, to drown :*—Hî ne mihte fýr bærnan ne wæter dræncean, Shrn. 66, 17. **IV.** *intrans.* To *sink in water, drown :*—Þû Petre ðǽm drencende hond girahtest *Petro mergenti manum porrexisti*, RtL 101, 42. [v. *N. E. D.* drench.] v. geond-, under-drencan ; scip-drencende.

**drence,** an ; *f.* (?) A *drink, potion :*—Gesing .xii. mæssan ofer ealle þâ drencan þe tô þǽre âdle belimpaþ, Lch. ii. 138, 21. [*Icel.* drekka ; *wk. f.* Cf. *O. H. Ger.* trencha ; *f.*]

**drenc-fæt.** *Add :* drence-fæt :—Gyf þû lytel drencefæt habban wylle, Tech. ii. 125, 12.

**drenc-horn.** *Add :* v. drinc(e)-horn : **dreng.** *Add :* [v. *N. E. D.* dreng.] : -dreóg. v. ge-dreóg.

**dreógan.** *Add :* **I.** *to do, perform ; commit, perpetrate :*—Sê þe dêð ǽnig unnyt, hê drýhð deófles willan, Wlfst. 279, 2. Wâ eów þe oferdrenc dreógað, 46, 15. On gedwimerum þe men on dreógað fela þæs þe hî nâ ne sceoldan, Ll. Th. ii. 248, 7. Ne dreáh ic nâne ôþre dæda, bûtau Dryhtne þâs lâc offrode, Hml. S. 9, 64. For þen hêðenscipe þe hî drugon, Chr. 634 ; P. 27, 7. God sceáwað hwæt þær man dreóge wordes oððe weorces, Wlfst. 278, 31. Hǽðenscipe dreóge, Ll. Th. ii. 296, 28. Wê lǽrað ꝥ preóstas on ciricþênungum ealle ân dreógan (*there is to be uniformity of practice in the church services*), 254, 23. Godes lof on cyricean dreógan *to perform divine service*, Cht. Th. 355, 3. **I a.** *to do battle, wage war :*—Hî gewin ûp hôfon and þæt drugon op hî mid ealle ofslegene wǽron, Ors. 1, 4 ; S. 32, 18. Hió þæt ylce gewin twâ and feówertig wintra wæs dreógende, 1, 2 ; S. 30, 17. Hî him brôhton ongeán eahta C M feþena and LX M gehorsades folces. And hié lange wǽron þæt dreógende ǽr heora âðer mehte on ôþrum sige geræcan (*commisso praelio diu anceps pugna*), 3, 9 ; S. 134, 7 : 1, 14 ; S. 58, 4 : 4, 7 ; S. 182, 4. **II.** *intrans.* (1) *to act :*—Tôgênes ǽ dreógendes *contra legem agentis*, Ps. L. 70, 4. (2) *to labour :*—On hû grundleásum seáðe ꝥ môd drîgð (cf. swinceð, Met. 3, 2), þonne hit bestyrmað þisse worulde ungeþwǽrnessa, Bt. 3, 2 ; S. 9, 11. Nǽnig manna wât hû mîn hyge dreógeð, bysig æfter bôcum, Sal. 60. **III.** *to suffer :*—Ðæt hié ne fleón yfel, suelce hié hit âdrîogan ne mægen, for ðon ðe hit oft gôde menn dreógað *mala nequaquam velut intolerabilia fugiant, quibus plerumque bonos affici non ignorant*, Past. 263, 14. Seó gedrecednes ꝥ geswinc and manna fyll and eác horsa þe eall Engla here dreáh, Chr. 1056 ; P. 186, 33. Þâs ðing wê drugon *quae res nos sollicitos tenuit*, Nar. 13, 26. Þ hié wîte drugon *ut uterentur supplicio*, 17, 2. For þâm ermðum ðe hî drogan, Bt. 38, 1 ; S. 116, 26. Hié mon slôg and hiênde and on ôþru land sealde . . . Ispânie þæt ilce wǽron dreógende, Ors. 5, 1 ; S. 214, 15. [v. *N. E. D.* dree.] v. þurh-dreógan.

-dreóglǽcan (-dreóh-). v. ge-dreóglǽcan: dreóhlíce. v. ge-dreóhlíce.

dreópan. Substitute for 'stillare ... a-dreópan':— Drupon distillauerunt, Bl. Gl. Driópende hrófas tecta perstillantia, Kent. Gl. 1021: 689. [v. N. E. D. dreep. O. Sax. driópan: O. Frs. driapa: O. H. Ger. triofan: Icel. drjupa.] v. ā-, ge-dreópan.

dreópian. Dele dropian, drupian and last two passages. v. dropian.

dreópung, e; f. Dropping, dripping:—Dreápung stillicidia, Ps. Srt. 71, 6. In dreápungum in stillicidiis, 64, 11.

dreórgian, dreórig(i)an to be or become dreary. Dele 'to fall, perish,' and add:—Hī dreórigende þóhton and mid heora módes unrótnysse teáras āléton they grew dismal as they thought and in the sadness of their hearts shed tears, Hml. S. 23, 445. [v. N. E. D. dreary; vb.]

dreórig. Substitute: I. dreary, mournful, sad, sorrowful:—Dreórig maestus vel maerens, Wrt. Voc. i. 51, 2: 83, 38. Se mann ðe bið dreórig, hē behófað sumes frófres, Hml. Th. ii. 370, 20: Wand. 25. Begann se wer dreórig wēpan, Hml. Th. ii. 142, 13. Maria stód wið ðā róde ðearle dreórig ... Đā clypode Drihten tó his dreórian mēder, 256, 25. Đā ðā Jóseph undergeat þ Maria mid cilde wæs, ðā wearð hē dreórig, i. 196, 16. Gewitan him þā Norðmen, dreórig daraða lāf, Chr. 937; P. 109, 12. Sceal þes dreórga heáp þrowian, Sat. 394. Dreórigne hyge, Gū. 1112: Wand. 17: Met. 22, 33. Hig wurdon swíðe dreórige and cyrdon eft illi scissis vestibus reversi sunt, Gen. 44, 13. Beón dreórige contristari, Mk. 14, 19: Hml. Th. i. 60, 15: 62, 28. Dreórge, Jul. 482. Dǽle man frófer þām dreórigum, Wlfst. 74, 5. Se deópa seað dreórge fēdeð, Cri. 1545. II. causing grief, cruel, horrid, grievous, (1) of persons:—Spreceð grimlíce se gāst tó þām duste: '... dreórega (dreórga, v. l.), tó hwan drehtest þū mē?', Seel. 17. Þæt mē ne mótan þā dreórgan deófla mínne synna on stǽlan, Angl. xi. 100, 93. (2) of things:—Seón cyning swylt dreórig (or III) fornam, Ps. Th. 135, 20. In þās dreórgan tíd, Gū. 1058. III. bloody, gory:—Wæter under stód dreórig and gedrēfed. ... Flód blóde weól, hātan heolfre, B. 1417-23. Hē dryhten sinne driórigne (cf. 2692-3) fand, 2789. IV. headlong (? cf. dreórung, dreósan):—Ic geseah ðone sceoccan swā swā sc'nende līget feallende ādūn dreórig of heofonum, Hex. 18, 6. [v. N. E. D. dreary. Cf. O. Sax. drórag: Icel. dreyrigr bloody.] v. heoru-dreórig.

dreórig-lic; adj. Sad, mournful:—Dreórilic frecednys triste periculum, Germ. 402, 66. v. next word, and dreór-lic.

dreórig-líce. Add:—Mid biterum teárum dreóriglíce wēpende, Hml. Th. ii. 134, 16: S. 31, 996.

dreórig-mód. Add: [v. N. E. D. dreary-mood.]

dreórignys. Add:—Jóhannes ofhreów þǽre mēder dreórignysse, Hml. Th. i. 66, 21. Mid micelre dreórignysse, ii. 174, 25. Þonne weópon and geómredon hí and on ðǽre mǽstan dreórignysse wunedon, þ hí swilce yrmða geseón sceoldon, Hml. S. 23, 41. Þæs cildes dreórignysse gefrēfrian, Hml. Th. ii. 134, 18. Dreórinyssa fletus, Germ. 401, 39.

dreór-lic. Dele II (v. dreórig-lic), and add: cruel, horrid. Cf. (?) dreórig, II:—Manige wǽron gewende fram þām dreórlican (= deór-?) móde multi a bestiali mente mutati sunt, Gr. D. 100, 12.

dreósan. Add: I. to fall, not remain suspended:— Hē meledeáwes dǽl gebyrgeþ, sē dreóseð oft æt middre nihte ambrosios libat coelesti nectare rores, stellifero teneri qui cecidere polo, Ph. 261. II. to fall, not remain standing (lit. or fig.), fall down, fall to pieces:—Þes middangeard ealra dógra gehwām dreóseð and fealleð, Wand. 63. Þā dúna dreósað and hreósað montes ruent, Dóm. L. 100. Druron deófolgyld, Exod. 47. III. to fall, not remain alert, droop, fail, sink:—Nǽnig manna wāt hū mín hyge dreóseð, bysig æfter bócum, Sal. 60. v. tó-dreósan; be-droren.

drepan. Add:—Drihten hine drep mid līchamlicere untrumnesse Dominus corporali hunc molestia percussit, Gr. D. 325, 26. Heó weard drepen and gestonden on þā breóst mid cancre þǽre wunde cancri ulcere in mamilla percussa est, 279, 26. Mid cwylde drepen and slægen mortalitate percussus, 289, 11. Drepen and gestelled, 298, 27. Hē weard drepen in þā sceare percussus in inguine, 324, 14. Hē wæs in feorh dropen, B. 2981. On gemynd drepen stupefied, Gen. 1571. [Hī drāpen (killed) heom swā ... Mani þūsen hī drāpen mid hungær, Chr. 1137; P. 264, 14, 23. v. N. E. D. drepe. With pp. dropen cf. O. H. Ger. troffan; with pp. drepen cf. Icel. drepinn.]

drí. Dele, and see drý: drían. Dele, and see be-dydrian.

drif. Add: dríf(?). Cf. with passage from Chronicle William of Malmesbury's statement that a contagious fever destroyed more than half the people. v. drífan, IV.

drífan. Add:—Onstyredan, drífan agitabant, Wrt. Voc. ii. 3, 39. I. to force living beings to move. (1) to force men or animals to move forward from one:—Hié mon beforan hiera triumphan drifon, Ors. 5, 1; S. 214, 17. Dríf þā sceáp in heora lǽse, Gr. D. 20, 12. Se æþeling bebeád þæt hié heora witan him beforan drifen swā swā niédlingas, Ors. 3, 8; S. 122, 7. (2) to cause to flee before one's pursuit, to

chase, hunt, pursue:—Hé nolde ðane sleán ðe hine drāf ... Đā ðā hē ongeán ðone cirde ðe hine drāf persequentem non vult ferire ... Cum contra persequentem substitit, Past. 297, 3, 10. Drífan heora hundas swýðe ænne haran geond þone brādan feld, Hml. S. 31, 1057. (2 a) to follow a track:—Gif mon trode bedrífð forstolenes yrfes ... mid mearce gecýþe þ man riht drífe ... Gif mon secge þ man þ trod āwōh drífe, Ll. Th. i. 352, 6, 10. Drífan þā menn þ spor oð hit man þām gerēfan gecýðe ... ādrífe hē þ spor ūt of his scíre, 236, 21. II. to impel by physical force. (1) to cause something to move by application of force:—Se wind drífeð ðæt wolcn, Past. 285, 21. Drífende agens (liburnam remorum tractibus trudit, Ald. 3, 2), Wrt. Voc. ii. 1, 3. (2) to force by a blow, thrust, &c.:—Genim geoluwne stān and saltstān and pipor ... and dríf þurh clāð, Lch. i. 374, 15. Ālege þone man ūpweard, dríf 11. stacan æt þām eaxlum, ii. 342, 5. Gif hwā drífe stacan on ǽnigne man si quis acus in homine aliquo defixerit, Ll. Th. ii. 208, 26. III. to carry on vigorously, transact, prosecute, conduct, practise, exercise, do:—Mē is lāð tó tǽlenne Godes freónd gyf hē Godes riht drífð, Hml. A. 13, 9. Sē þe wōh drífð and geswícan nele, Wlfst. 283, 13. Wā ðæs mannes sāwle þe þā ungemetlican hleahtras drífð innan cyrcan, 233, 26. Đā wiglunga þe gedwǽsmenn drífað, Hml. S. 17, 101. Gif man hwæt becýpan scyle ... warnien þā þe þone ceáp drífað (ipsi per quorum manus transigenda sunt), R. Ben. 95, 11. Hī nāne sprǽce ne drifon būtan ǽfre embe Crístes naman they carried on no conversation except ever about Christ's name, Hml. S. 23, 530. Man ne mót sprǽce drífan binnan Godes cyrican, 13, 69. Þām dǽdbētan nis ālýfed nǽnige cýpinge tó drífenne (mercaturam aliquam exercere), Ll. Th. ii. 170, 12. III a. to speak often of a matter, bring up, agitate; cf. colloquial to trot out a subject:—Eówer brocu þe gē ealneg drífað your troubles that you are always bringing up, Ors. 3, 7; S. 120, 14. IV. to go through what is painful, suffer, undergo:—Fefer drífende febricitans, Mk. R. 1, 30. (Cf. drif.) [v. N. E. D. drive, V.] V. intrans. To proceed with violence, act impetuously:—þā þe hlystan nellað ... ac willað forð on wōh and gewill drífan and geswícan nyllað those that will not listen ... but will rush on wrongly and wilfully and will not stop, Wlfst. 304, 13. v. un-urifen.

drigian. Add: [Cf. Icel. drýgja.]: driht-ealdor. v. dryht.

driman I. intrans. To make a joyous sound with voice or with instrument, to rejoice. (1) of living creatures:—Ic drēme psallam, Ps. L. 107, 2. Seldan snottor guma sorgleás blissað, swylce dol seldon drýmeð sorgful ymb his forðgesceaft, Fä. 55. Anna and Simeon sungon and drýmdon, Lch. iii. 428, 20. Uton drēman (jubilemus) Gode ... on sealmum wē drýman him, Ps. Spl. 94, 1, 2. (2) of musical instrument:—Hearpe and pípe and mistlic gliggamen drýmað eów on beórsele. II. trans. To sing a song:—Ealle singende hý drýman omnia psallendo modificentur, Angl. xiii. 371, 78. Seó beó ne murnð leóflic leóþ tó drýmanne, Angl. viii. 324, 17. Wynsume swinsunge tó drēmene dulcem melodiam modulaturus (i. canaturus), An. Ox. 1344. Getwinnum sangum hǽle Gode drē(mende) geminis concentibus Osanna persultans, 2608. [Take here drēman, drýman in Dict.] v. ge-dríman.

drime. Take here drēme in Dict.: drinc. v. drync: drinca. v. ge-drinca.

drinca. Add:—Heó ðām biscope bær drincan and ūs eallum þēnode and scencte obtulit poculum episcopo et nobis, coeptumque ministerium nobis propinandi ... non omisit, Bd. 5, 4; Sch. 569, 15. Gif him ðyrste, ðū dó him drincan, Hml. S. 21, 376. Drince hē betonicam on wætre ǽr óþerne drincan, Lch. ii. 152, 5. Gebryte on drincan ... swā þū scealt þā óþre ǽtas gend drincan sellan, 90, 10-12. Of metta and drincena þiginge, 244, 12. Þāra metta cyn ge þone rím þāra drincena (potionum), Gr. D. 127, 17. Tó scencenne drincan ad haurienda pocula, Angl. xiii. 393, 395. [Under DER. dele on-.]

drincan. Add: [druncaþ prs. pl., Seel. 114; druncan bibere, tó druncenne ad bibendum, Scint. 107, 1, 3. I. absolute. (1) to take a draught of a liquid:—Druncðū (drunce, v. l.) bibisti?, Ælfc. Gr. Z. 226, 13. Drince hē gelóme, Lch. ii. 314, 14. Syle drincan on wíne, i. 316, 5. Þū scealt ǽrest óðerne geseón drincan, Hml. Th. i. 72, 14. (2) to take liquid as nourishment or to quench thirst:— Gif þū ofer gemet itst oþþe drincst, Bt. 14, 1; F. 42, 15. (3) to drink intoxicating liquors convivially, to feast (cf. Icel. sitja við drykkju to banquet, carouse):—Gif cyning æt mannes hām drincæð, Ll. Th. i. 4, 1. Đā ðe wódlíce drincað, and heora gewitt āmyrrað, Hml. A. 6, 145. Gif man wǽpn ābregde þǽr mæn drincen, 32, 11, 8. Ne mót nān preóst drincan æt wínhūsum ealles tó gelóme, ii. 386, 8. Sē ðe wylle drincan and dwæslíce hlýdan, drince him æt hām, 357, 39. II. trans. (1) to imbibe a liquid:—Hié þone drenc druncon, Bl. H. 229, 13. Þ man is betste wín on gebeórscipe drince, 57, 6. Drince hē wearmes scenc fulne, Lch. ii. 316, 16. Būton Jóhannes āttor drunce, Hml. Th. i. 72, 11. Hié him sealdon āttor drinccan, Bl. H. 229, 16. (2) to swallow the contents of a cup:—Mæge gyt drincan þone calic þe ic tó drincenne hæbbe? Gyt mínne calic drincað, Mt. 20, 22, 23: Mk. 10, 38-39. (3) to use as a beverage:—Ne drincþ hē wín ne ealu, Bl. H.

165, II. Se cyning and þā rícostan men drincað myran meolc, and þā unspēdigan and þā þeówan drincað medo, Ors. 1, 1; Swt. 20, 16. Nalles scír wín hí ne druncan . . . hlúterra wella wæter hí druncon, Bt. 15; F. 48, 10, 13. Hí wæter ne druncon, ac manna blód druncon, Bl. H. 229, 8. (4) *to inhale* smoke (cf. *to drink* tobacco) :—Lege on hātne stān, drinc þurh horn þone rēc, Lch. ii. 316, 11. (5) of porous material, *to absorb* :—Elpendes hýd wile drincan wætan gelíce and spynge dēð *elephanti corium, cujus ea natura est, ut imbrem tamquam spongia ebibat*, Ors. 5, 7; S. 230, 26.

**drincere.** *Add : drunkard, wine-bibber* :—Drinceras, þ synd þā þe druncennysse lufiað *ebriosi*, Hml. S. 17, 41 : Hml. Th. ii. 330, 26. [*O. H. Ger.* trinkāri *potator*.]

**drīpan**; *p.* te *To drop, cause to fall in drops* :—Ontend iii. candella and drýp ðriwa þ weax, Lch. i. 392, 11 : iii. 286, 6 : ii. 138, 29. Drýp ealo on oðде win, 274, 7. Drýp on þā eáran, 310, 6. Drýpe on þ eáre, i. 268, 5 : 72, 9 : ii. 40, 5, 24, 28, 30. [From this form *drype* an infin. *dryppan* is inferred in the *N. E. D.* (v. *drip* :) but the form may be taken as a subjunctive, cf. the following instances of that mood in Lch. :— Nime þysse wyrte wōs, dô on, i. 266, 8. Ceáces sure wið wín *gemenge*, ii. 32, 9. Gewyrce (cf. wyrc, 32, 5) him . . . finul, wyl þā wyrta, 34, 9. Læt reócan þone steám on þ eáre and fordýtte mid þære wyrte, 44, 3.] Læt drýpan wearm on þ eáre, 310, 12. [v. *N. E. D.* dripe. *O. H. Ger.* troufen *distillare : Icel.* dreypa.]

**drisn.** *Add :*—Rāwe, drisne *capillamenta* (rūwe, drysne? *the hair-like filaments that hang from the root of a plant? Cf.* rūh, I, and dreósan), Wrt. Voc. ii. 128, 39.

**-drītan.** v. ge-drītan, *and next word.*

**drīting,** e ; *f. The voiding of excrement* :—Drīting *degestio*, i. *egestio*, Wrt. Voc. ii. 138, 37. Miggung *minctio*, drīting *digestio* (omitted by Wright, v. Angl. viii. 451), i. 46, 9. v. ge-drītan.

**drōf.** *Take first passage under* drōfig, *and add :*—Gyf hē fæger wæter geseó. . . . Gyf hine mēteð þ hē drōf wæter geseó, Lch. iii. 168, 27. v. drēfan.

**drōf-denu.** *Dele.*

**drōfe**; *adv. Grievously, with trouble* :—Hý þ drōfe onguldon, Lch. iii. 286, 14.

**drōfig**; *adj. See first passage under* drōf *in Dict.* : drōf-lic. *Add :* [Mid drofliicen witan, Laym. 1026. *O. H. Ger.* truob-líh *turbidus*.] : drōf-man. *Dele* : drōf-nys. *Dele.*

**droht.** *Add* (?) :—Droht *conversationis* (*but cf.* drohtnunge *religionis*, *conversationis*, 466, 34. An. Ox. 2507 has droh), Hpt. Gl. 465, 29 : 428, 49 ; An. Ox. 933.

**droht** *drawn. Substitute* : droht, drōht (?) *pull, draught* (cf. *Prompt. Parv.* drawte or pulle *tractus*) :—Drohtum (*remorum*) *tractibus*, Wrt. Voc. ii. 75, 15. [Cf. *Icel.* drāttr *pulling*.]

**drohtaþ.** *Add :*—In lífe and in hāde hāliges drohtoðes *in vita atque habitu sanctae conversationis*, Gr. D. 205, 17. In þā geornesse hāliges lífes and drohtoðes, 27.

**drohtian.** *Add :* I. *to live a life* :—Ic drohtige *conversor*, i. *locum uto, utor, habito, maneo*, Wrt. Voc. ii. 135, 50. Git hē self drohtað on ðām eorðlicum tielongum *si in terrenis negotiis ipse versatur*, Past. 133, 4. Menn wēndon ðæt hē æfæsðlíce drohtode (*degere religiose*), 24. Lifde oðдe drohtode *degebat*, Wrt. Voc. ii. 27, 47. Drohtadun þā hié *conversantibus eis*, Mt. R. 17, 22. Hū hē ðæron drohtian (-igean, v. l.) scyle *qualem se in ipso regimine debeat exhibere*, Past. 75, 2. Drohtiende *degens*, Wrt. Voc. ii. 28, 45. II. *to carry out* a practice :—þ hē þ (*the right observance of Easter*) inihte mid ðý māran ealdorlicnesse drohtian (þurhteón, v. l.) and gefremman *quod ut majore auctoritate perficeret*, Bd. 5, 21 ; Sch. 676, 24. [Godefrihte muneces þā wolden drohtien here líf on ankersetle, Chr. 656 ; P. 31, 17.]

**drohtnian.** *Add :*—Of cyriscum lífe . . . men . . . swā micele eáðelícor and sēl drohtniaþ (*live as monks*), swā hý stíðlíce āfēdde wēron, R. Ben. 138, 24. Hē cwæð be ðām Hælende: 'Mid mannum hē drohtnode,' Hml. Th. ii. 12, 32. Mid sōðre lufe hē drohtnode on ðisum lífe, 44, 23. Bæd hē þ hē mōste healdan heora æceras and him mēde earnian ; and hē ðær drohtnode fíftýne geár, Hml. S. 30, 216. Hē fērde tō Burch tō Sē Petres mynstre and þær drohtnode .xii. geár, Chr. 1072 ; P. 209, 2. Drohtniende *degens*, i. *conversans*, An. Ox. 1446. Drihtelm wunode on ðæs mynstres dígelnysse stíðlíce drohtnigende, Hml. Th. ii. 354, 16. v. ge-drohtnian.

**drohtnoþ** (= drohtaþ, q. v.) *life, way of life* :—Seó sāwl sceal mid deóflum drohtnoð (drohtoð, v. l.) habban in morðre and on māne, Wlfst. 187, 18. Næfre ic gefērde heardran drohtnoð, An. 1404.

**drohtnung.** *Dele* '*in great renown*' l. 10, *and add :*—þæt þū fare tō wēstene þær ðær nānes mannes drohtnung nis (*where nobody lives*), Hml. Th. i. 466, 32. Drohtnunge *religionis*, i. *conversationis*, An. Ox. 2567. Se gewuna þisse hālgan drohtnunge (*conversationis*), R. Ben. 5, 18. Angin gōdre drohtnunge, 132, 16. Mid godre drohtnunga Godes ríce geearnian, Hml. S. 28, 122. Hē wæs mæres lífes man on munuclícre drohtnunge, 26, 54. Iōhannes heóld þā clǣnnysse . . . on

micelre drohtnung (*living an excellent life*), Hml. A. 14, 23 : 16, 64. Hlísful þurh his drohtnunga, 195, 16. Hwæt wille gē mē syllan, gyf ic āmyrre þisne wēstensetlan and ālecge his miclan drohtnunga ?, 196, 23. Hē āstealde þā stíðan drohtuunge *he founded the ascetic life*, Hml. S. 16, 99. [Se hālge wær fērde tō his wæterseáðe and þær his drohtnunge and his salmsanges on þan wætere hnacoden leomen ādreáh swā his gewune wæs . . . Hē nolde þ his drohtnung ǣnigen eorðlice mæn cūð wurðe on his líf, Shrn. 14, 5–11.]

**drohtung.** *Add :*—Drohtunge *conversationis*, Wrt. Voc. ii. 23, 36. Disse eorðlican drohtunge gewuna *humanae conversationis usus*, Past. 169, 7. On langsumere mynsteres drohtunge (drohtuunge, v. l.), R. Ben. 9, 6.

**dropa.** *Add :* I. *a drop* :—In þ ilce scip nān regnes dropa ne gefeóll *in navem eamdem una pluviae gutta non cecidit*, Gr. D. 196, 6. þ nǣfre in þǣm londum regnes dropa ne cwōme *nunquam in his locis pluuiam adire*, Nar. 28, 5. *Gutta*, þ ys hunigswēte dropa, Angl. viii. 299, 48. Mid dropum *imbribus*, An. Ox. 646. Geondgoten mid swātes dropum, Hml. S. 23 b, 233. II. *humour, choler* :—Cwyld tōgeneálǣhð oð ðæne dropan *pestilentia adpropinquabit usque ad coleram*; surfeiting turneth to choler (Ecclus. 37, 30), Scint. 170, 2. Genihtsumnysse blódes and dropena and manega seócnyssa metta of rūmgyfulnysse wē þoliað *abundantiam sanguinis et colerarum* (cf. colera, umores, Corp. Gl. H. 34, 619) *et plurimas egritudines escarum largitate patimur*, 56, 4. III. *gout*. (? v. *N. E. D.* drop 11.) *See passages under* II *in Dict.* v. ge-, mǣl-dropa.

**drop-fāg** *stronius*. v. next word.

**drop-fāh.** *Add : name of the starling from its markings* :—Dropfaag *stornus, stronus*, Txts. 96, 924. Dropfāg *stronius* (cf. stærn *stronus*, 29, 39), Wrt. Voc. i. 289, 27.

**dropian.** *Add :*—þurh bæcþearm lytel blód dropað, Lch. ii. 278, 6. Blód of his sídan dropian, iii. 210, 22. v. mǣl-dropiende : drop[p]an *in Dict.*

**drop-mǣlum.** *Add :* [v. *N. E. D.* drop-meal.]

**drop[p]ettan.** *Add :*—Dropeteð blód swā þon gelícost þe tōbrocen fæt, Lch. ii. 230, 25. Dropetende *stillantia*, Ps. Srt. 71, 6. [*O. H. Ger.* trof[f]ezzen (-ōn) ; troffezunga *stillicidia*.]

**dropung.** *Add :*—Hē wæs geondgoten mid þæs swātes dropunge, Hml. S. 23 b, 233.

**dros.** *Substitute* : drōs *dross, ear-wax* :—Drōs *auriculum*, Txts. 38, 39 : Wrt. Voc. ii. 7, 40 : 8, 59. [*M. L. Ger.* drōs : M. Du. droes *dregs*.]

**drosen-líc.** *Dele.*

**drosna.** l. drōsna, *and add : a wk. sing. gen.* drōsnan *occurs* (cf. *O. L. Ger.* drōsnon) :—Of fenne drōsnan *de luto faecis*, Ps. L. 39, 3. Fex, i. *virus vel* drōsna, Wrt. Voc. ii. 148, 50. Drōsne, Ps. Srt. 74, 9. [v. *N. E. D.* drosen.] v. ele-, med-drōsna.

**drugaþ**; *f.* drūgaþ ; *m., and add ,* drūgoþa, an ; *m.* I. *drought* :— Drūgoða eów cymð, þonne gē rēnas behōtedan, Wlfst. 297, 10. Drūgaþe (-a ?), Wrt. Voc. i. 53, 43. II. *a dry place* :—Hí dweledon on wēstene on drūgoþe *erraverunt in solitudine in inaquoso*, Ps. L. 106, 4.

**drugian.** l. drūgian, *and add :*—Drūgað l wisnað *aruit*, Jn. R. 15, 6. v. be-drūgian.

**drugung.** l. drūgung, drūwung, *and add :*—Seó lange drūgung (drūwung, v. l.) mid mycelre hǣte bærnde þā eorðan *aestu nimio terram longa siccitas exurebat*, Gr. D. 210, 16. Hit wæs ǣr þām singal drūwung, and sōna æfter þām cōm geþuhtsum rēn, Shrn. 113, 20.

**druh** *dust. Substitute* : drūhþu (?), drūguþu (? cf. drūgoþ(a)) *something dry* :—Spreced grimlíce se gāst tō ðām duste : 'Hwæt ! drūhðu dreórega (drūguþu dreórega, Exon. Tb. 368, 5) . . . eorðan fúlnes eal forwisnad, lāmes gelícnes' *fiercely the spirit speaks to the dust of the body, 'Ah ! wretched quintessence of dryness, earth's mud with the moisture dried out of it, clay's very image*, Seel. 17.

**druncen**; *adj. Add :*—Druncen *lentus* (the epithet applies to Nabal, Ald. 205, 28), Wrt. Voc. ii. 96, 62 : 53, 9 : *paponius* (paponius =ebriosus, v. Goetz, s. v.), i. 61, 2. Is tō wyrnanne bearneácnum wífe þ hió beór drince, ne wínes flæsc ete, ne druncen gedrince (*get drunk*), Lch. ii. 330, 8. Wín, þ is ælces cynnes drinc þe man mæg of (fore, v. l.) druncen beón, Ll. Th. ii. 134, 21. Wíne druncen *crapulatus a vino*, Ps. Th. 77, 65 : Gen. 1563 : Jud. 67 : B. 1467. Beóre druncen, 531. Se druncena (*ebriosus*) wín onfēhþ, Scint. 107, 8. þære druncnan *madidae*, Wrt. Voc. ii. 57, 54. Hié dydon swā drucnnum (*Lot*), Gen. 2598. þā hié druncne æt heora symble sǣtan, Ors. 3, 9 ; S. 130, 25 : B. 1231. Hæðene swæfon dreóre druncne, An. 1005. Hié wlenco anwōd æt wínþege, druncne geþóhtas, Dan. 18. Hē drincð mid druncenum (ðruncnum, L., druncennum, R. *ebriis*), Mt. 24, 49.

**druncen** *drunkenness. Add :* Mid druuncen (druncennisse, R.) *ebrietate*, Lk. L. 21, 34. Ne ǣnig nan lufige druncen tō swýðe ne fúle oferfylle, Wlfst. 70, 20. Dru[n]cen, Mōd. 12. [þæt folc þurh heora drunken moni þusend swulten, Laym. 6070. þa þe luueden hordom and drunken, O. E. Hml. i. 175, 253. *Goth.* druggkanei : *O. H. Ger.* truncheni.]

**druncen-georn.** *Add:*—Ne môt nân preóst tô druncengeorn wurðan, Ll. Th. ii. 386, 9. Ne sceal mon beón druncengeorn ne oferæte (*non vinolentus, non multum edax*), R. Ben. 17, 15. Næfre druncengeorne (*ebriosi*) nâgon Godes rîce, Hml. A. 145, 39. Besceáwigen ðâ druncengeornan þ hî synt micele mættran ðonne nýtenu, 26. Gif ðâ druncengeornan men heora druncennyssa geswîcan nellað, 33.

**druncenig;** *adj. Drunken:*—Druncgnia i þte sê druncenig *inebriari*, Lk. L. 12, 45.

**druncen-læt** *lentus*, Cot. 124. *This seems to be the gloss given as:*—*Lent*... dru... dryncwîrig, Wrt. Voc. ii. 53, 9. v. druncen; *adj.*

**druncennes.** *Add:*—Wînes druncennes and synlustas synt forbodene, næs meoloc ne cýse, Ll. Th. ii. 438, 17. Ðâ ðe wôdlîce drincað... swâ þ hî dwæsiað for heora druncennyssum. . . . Ûre Hælend forbeád þâ druncennysse, Hml. A. 6, 148. Gif ðâ druncengeornan men heora druncennyssa geswîcan nellað, 145, 34. v. ofer-druncenness.

**druncen-scipe.** *Substitute for* ' Som. Ben. Lye ':—Gif ðâ druncengeornan men heora druncenscipes geswîcan nellað, Hml. A. 145, 34. [*v. N. E. D.* drunken-ship.]

**druncen-wille.** *Add:*—Hê drincð him mid ðæm druncenwillum monnum, Past. 120, 13.

**druncen-willen;** *adj. Drunken:*—Ne ðâ giétseras, ne ðâ druncenwillan, Past. 401, 29.

**drunc-mennen.** *Add:*—dunc-mennen (?). [*v. O. L. Ger.* (Gall.) dunc (-g, -ch) *textrina*: *O. H. Ger.* tunch *textrinum* (-a).]

**druncnian.** *Add:* I. *to get or be drunk:*—Nelle gê druncnian wîne *nolite inebriari vino*, Scint. 105, 3. Lof ys micel druncan and nâ druncnian (*bibere et non inebriari*), 107, I. Nîwum wîne druncnian *musto madere*, Hy. S. 94, 13. Wîn, þ is ælces cynnes drinc þe man mæg fore druncnigan *vino, hoc est, omnis generis potu quo quis inebriari possit*, Ll. Th. ii. 134, 21. Druncniga (druncgnia, L.) *inebriari*, Lk. R. 12, 45. II. *to make drunk:*—Swâ hwæt swâ druncnað (*inebriat*) swâ wîn, Scint. 106, 7. [*v. N. E. D.* drunken; *vb. O. H. Ger.* trunkanên, -ôn.]

**druncning.** *For* ' A drinking ' *read* ' A making drunk.'

**drût** *a friend, beloved one:*—Ænlicu Godes drût . . . Maria *alma Dei genetrix*, Maria, Dôm. L. 290. [*v. N. E. D.* drut. *O. H. Ger.* trût (drût) *amicus, sodalis, dilectus.*]

**drý.** *Add:* gen. drýes, dat. drýe, dat. pl. drým:—þâ Iudêas þone Hælend genâmon . . . and sædon þ hê drý wære, Nic. 19, 40. Nectanebases þæs drýs, Ors. 3, 9 ; S. 126, 25. Hê weard âlýsed fram þæs drýes bendum . . . and arn bysmrigende þæs drýes yfeldædum, Hml. Th. ii. 414, 24 : 412, 30. Ânes drýes folgere, i. 468, 8. þâ deóflu gecyrdon tô ðâm drýe . . . Cwæð se apostol tô ðâm drý, 416, 9-13. Drýas *marsi*, An. Ox. 4476. Drîas, 2, 338. Drêas *arioli*, Kent. Gl. 868. Mon sægð þ drýas tô heora cræftum þysse wyrte (*vervain*) brûcen, Lch. i. 170, 20. Drýra *magorum*, An. Ox. 4019. Hî befæston þ wîf drým (drým, *v. l.*) *puellam maleficis tradiderunt*, Gr. D. 73, 16. [*O. Ir.* drui.]

**-drycnan.** v. ge-drycnan.

**drý-cræft.** *Add:* I. *sorcery, magic:*—Syxte mægen is þ drýcræft þâm men ne dereþ þe hine (*agate*) mid him hæfð, Lch. ii. 298, 10. Ðîn drýcræft ðe tô nânre freme ne becymð, Hml. Th. ii. 414, 14. Âgrôf se mon on ærenum brede drýcræftæs word, Shrn. 141, 16. ' Miht þû âdwæscan þæra crîstenra drýcræft ?' . . . 'Beó ic scyldig gif ic his scýncræft ne mæg âdwæscan mid mînum drýcræfte,' Hml. S. 14, 54-58. Gif wîf drýcræft begæð *si mulier artem magicam exerceat*, Ll. Th. ii. 130, 15. Drýcræft wyrcan, 154, 8. II. *a magic art* or *practice:*—Drýcræftas *necromantiae*, An. Ox. 4, 29. Hê sæde þ hê (*Joseph*) ðær (*in Egypt*) drýcræftas geleornode and of þæm drýcræftum þ hê gewunode monige wundor tô wyrcenne, and þ hê mihte swâ wel swefn reccan . . . and hê sæde þ hê of þæm drýcræfte geleornode godcundne wîsdôm, Ors. 1, 5 ; S. 34, 3-8. Se deófol geswutelað þære wiccan hwæt heó secge mannum, þ þâ beón fordône þe ðæne drýcræft sæcað, Hml. S. 17, 113. Hê wæs fyrmest on þâm drýcræftum *in magicis operibus primus fuit*, Gr. D. 27, 20 : Hml. Th. ii. 414, 4. Soroaster cûðe manna ærest drýcræftas (*magicae artis repertor*), Ors. 1, 2 ; S. 30, 11. III. *magical apparatus:*—Se drý nam þone stæf and gewende hâm, and genam ealne his drýcræft and brôhte tô ðâm apostole, and began hî tô forbærnenne, Hml. Th. ii. 418, 3. [*Orm.* driȝcræfft.] v. dreó-cræft *in Dict.*

**drý-cræftig;** *adj. Add:* **drý-cræftiga,** an ; *m. A sorcerer:*—On þâm ylcan tîman þe þâ drýcræftigan (*malefici*) wurdon ârâsode, Gr. D. 27, 15.

**drýegge.** v. drýicge.

**drygan.** *l.* drýgan, *and add:* I. *to make dry.* (1) of a person's action. (a) *to dry by wiping, rubbing, &c.:*—Heó his fêt mid hire loccum drýgde. Bl. H. 69, 2. Drêgde, 73, 19. Hê geseah Godes engel drýgan mid sceátan Sci Laurentius limu, Shrn. 115, 23. Drêgende *tergens* (*os suum*), Kent. Gl. 1067. (b) *to dry by exposure to heat, air:*—Drîg hî on sceade swýþe þearle, Lch. i. 70, 10. Nim heortes

sceallan, drýg, wyrc tô duste, 336, 16. Drîg tô duste, 20. (2) *of the action of heat, air, &c.:*—Seó hætu drýgð, and seó beorhtnys onlýht, Hml. Th. ii. 284, 35. II. *to become dry:*—Drýgeð i wisneð *aruit*, Jn. L. 15, 6.

**dryge.** *l.* drýge. *Take here the examples given under* drige, *and add:*—Sumor byð wearm and drîgge, Angl. viii. 299, 29. Drêge bite *bucella sicca*, Kent. Gl. 587. Drîg (*corrected from* driu) geward *arefacta*, Mt. p. 18, 18. Gangende swâ swâ on drîgum, Hml. S. 23 b, 685. Of drýggium (drýgum, *v. l.*) felle, Past. 346, 5. Gîtsung gedrinceð tô drýggum welan, Met. 7, 16. Hond drýgi *manum aridam*, Mk. L. 3, 1, 3. Drûgi, Lk. p. 5, 4. Drýi, Mt. L. 12, 10. Driu, p. 16, 14. Druige, Mk. L. 11, 20. Ðerh stôwa drýia *per loca arida*, Mt. L. 12, 43.

**dryg-nes.** *l.* drýg-nes, *and add:*—Drîgnes *arida*, Wrt. Voc. ii. 7, 25.

**drýg-scôd;** *adj. Dry-shod:*—þæt folc fôr betwux þâm twâm wæterum on þâm grunde ealle drýgsceóde, Wlfst. 293, 17.

**dryht.** *Take here last two passages given under* driht-ealdor *in Dict.*

**dryht-dôm,** es ; *m. Noble judgement:*—Dryhten dryhtdômas dônde *Dominus judicia faciens*, Txts. 196, 17.

**dryht-ealdor.** *For* brýdguma *l.* dryhtguma, *and add:* v. drihtealdor *in Dict.*

**dryht-ealdormann,** es ; *m. A bridesman:*—Brýdguman and brýde mid gebedum and mid ofringum mæssepreóst sceal bletsian . . . and þâ drihtealdormen hî healdon, Nap. 17.

**dryhten.** *Add:* I. *a lord:*—Æþelstân cyning, eorla dryhten, Chr. 937; P. 106, 9. Drihtenna i hlâforda *dominorum*, Ps. L. 135, 3. II. *the Deity:*—Æt ðæm uferran ende Dryhten hlinode, Past. 101, 20. Dryhtna Dryhten *Deus deorum Dominus*, Ps. Th. 49, 1. Godes, êces Drihtnes, Chr. 937; P. 106, 24. Tô ûres Drihtenes byrgene, 1058; P. 189, 19. Eall swâ Iudas Scarioth dyde be ûre Drihtene, 1087; P. 222, 35. Wê geleofað on Drihten þyses ælþeódigan mannes, Bl. H. 247, 4. [*v. N. E. D.* drightin.]

**dryhten;** *adj.* (?) *Lordly, royal:*—Drihtenum Gode *domino Deo*, Wülck. Gl. 253, 8. Drihtnum Crîste, sôðum cyninge *domino Christo, vero regi*, R. Ben. 1, 9. v. in-dryhten.

**dryhten-hold;** *adj. Loyal to one's lord:*—Wes drihtenhold, Gen. 2282. [*Icel.* dróttin-hollr.]

**Dryhten-lic.** *Add: Of the Lord:*—Eálâ þû drihtenlica cempa *O tu herilis miles*, Hpt. 31, 17, 473. Se drihtenlica ærist *anastasis dominica*, An. Ox. 2753. Drihtenlic gebed, þæt is Pater noster, R. Ben. 41, 13. þysses drihtenlican þeówdômes *dominici servitii*, 5, 11. Læran mid ðære drihtenlican lâre, Hml. A. 12, 298. Dôn æfter þære drihtenlican bisene, 160, 198. ' þû eart Crîst, þæs lifigendon Godes suna.' On ðære drihtenlican andetnysse (*in that confession of the Lord*), 156, 118. Drihten þe gebletsode on his drihtenlican mihte, 112, 334. þurh his drihtenlican mihte, 4, 81 : Hml. S. 29, 40 : Ælfc. T. Grn. 10, 15 : Hex. 10, 4. Crîst on his godspelle cwæð . . . understande hê þisne drihtenlican cwyde, Hml. Th. i. 132, 29. þ hûsel . . . þone drihtenlican hlâf, Ll. Th. ii. 392, 6. þâ drihtenlican þênunge *the Lord's supper*, Hml. A. 151, 11. [*O. H. Ger.* truhtin-lîh *dominicus* : *Icel.* dróttin-ligr.]

**dryht-folc.** *Add:* [*Laym.* driht-folk : *O. Sax.* druht-folk.]

**dryht-guma.** *Add: A bridesman:*—Dryhtguma *paranimphus*, Wrt. Voc. ii. 116, 4, 45 : 78, 33 : 66, 16 : i. 50, 42 (*read* dryhtguma *for* brýdguma). [*O. H. Ger.* truhti-goma *paranymphus*.] v. dryhtmann.

**dryht-lic.** *Add: Of the Lord:*—Bûtan þâm drihtlican (drihtenlican, *v. l.*) gebede, þæt is Pater noster, R. Ben. 38, 15. [*Laym.* drihtlich.]

**dryht-mann,** es ; *m.* I. *a bridesman:*—Drihtmon *paranimphus*, Wrt. Voc. i. 288, 79 : An. Ox. 7, 94. II. *a warrior, retainer.* [Hengest mid his drihtmonnen, Laym. 14715.] v. dryht-guma.

**dryht-scipe.** *Add:* [*O. Sax.* druht-skepi.]

**dryht-wémend, -wémere,** es ; *m. A bridesman;* paranymphus, An. Ox. 1774. Cf. dryht-guma, -mann.

**dryht-weorþ;** *adj.* -weorþa, an ; *m. Divine; a divine, theologian* [as epithet of St. John (θεολόγος) :—Se drihtwurðe (*Iohannes*) *theologe*, Hy. S. 126, 14. Iôhannes se drihtwurða wrîtere, Hml. S. 15, 200.

**drýicge,** an ; *f. A sorceress:*—Cwædon Rômware þ heó wære drýegge, Shrn. 56, 13. þâ þe hêr biôð þâ mæstan drýicgan, and gealdorcræftigan, Nap. 43.

**drý-lâc (?)** *sorcery, magic:*—Gif þîne æceras nellaþ wel wexan oþþe þær hwilc ungedêfe þing on gedôn bið on drý (= drýlâce) oððe on lyblâce, Lch. i. 398, 3.

**drý-lic;** *adj. Of magic, magical:*—Mid drýlices fâcnes galdre *magicae fraudis necromantia*, An. Ox. 2907. Mid drýlicum sciulâce *magica praestigia*, 3261 : 4699. Mambres ontýnde ðâ drýlican bêc (*libros magicos*) his brêðer, Nar. 50, 13.

**drý-man[n],** es ; *m. A magician, sorcerer:*—Hê eóde tô ânum drýmen . . . þâ gebrôhte se drýman þone cnapan tô his deófle, Hml. S. 3, 367. Fela sædon þâ drýmen þurh deófles cræft, Iamnes and Mambres, 17, 114. Drýmen þe mid dydrunge farað, Hml. Th. ii. 330, 27. þurh

drýmanna dydrunge, Hml. S. 21, 474. Antecrīst hæfð mid him drýmen, Wlfst. 194, 17 : Hml. Th. ii. 472, 14. [Magy sinndenn . . . drigmenn. Orm. 7076. An defless þeww Symon Drigmann (*Simon Magus*) ʒehatenn, 16051.]

**drýman.** v. drīman : **drýme.** v. drīme.

**drync.** *Take here examples under* drinc, *and add:* **I.** *drink, liquid taken as nourishment :*—Be drinces gemete *de mensura potus*, R. Ben. 64, 9. Wel āfēdd mid ðæm drynce (drence, *v. l.*) mislicra and manigfaldra gifa (*potu multiplicati muneris*), Past. 380, 8. **II.** *a kind of drink, beverage :*—Þæm folce uncūðe wæron wīnes dryncas, Ors. 2, 4 ; S. 76, 12. **III.** *a draught, cup :*—Drync *haustum*, Wrt. Voc. ii. 110, 23 : 42, 24 (cf. 78, 43 :—Mortiferum poculi haustum, Ald. 25, 14). Ðætte hié ðone hālwendan drync ðæs ædelan wīnes ne gehwyrfen him selfum tō āttre *quia saluberrimum vini potum in veneni sibi poculum vertunt*, Past. 365, 9. Wyrc tō duste, dō hys dǣl on wīnes drinc, Lch. i. 336, 16. Drync *poculum*, Ps. Srt. 22, 5. Hē sǣde þām brōðrum drincea (*potionum*) getel (cf. þus fela scencea, 11), Gr. D. 127, 16. v. blōd-, spiw(e)-, wæter-drync.

**drync-fæt.** *Add :*—Cristallisce dryncfatu *crystallina uasa potatoria*, Nar. 5, 13. v. drenc-fæt.

**drync-gemet,** es ; *n. Measure of drink :*—Þ man ne mæge þ drincgemett bringan forð, Nap. 17.

**drync(e)-horn,** es ; *n. A drinking-horn :*—Ic ann Æþelwerdæ ānæs gerǣnodes drincæhornæs, Cht. Th. 555, 6. Cf. drinc-horn.

**drync(e)-leán.** *Take here* drince-leán, *and add :*—Drynceleán, Ll. Th. i. 422, note 1. The word occurs under the heading: De officiis domino debitis.

**drync-wērig;** *adj. Weary of drinking, stupid with drink :*—Dru[ncen], dryncwīrig *lent*[*us*] (v. *first passage under* druncen), Wrt. Voc. ii. 53, 9.

**drypan.** *l.* drýpan, *and see* drīpan : **drype.** *Add :* Cf. dropen, *pp. of* drepan : **dryppan.** v. drīpan : **dryre.** *Add :* [*Goth.* drus *a fall*] : **dryrmian.** *l.* (?) drysmian : **drysn** (?). v. drisn.

**drysnan.** *Add :*—Ne drysnes *non extinguet* (*linum fumigans*), Mt. L. 12, 20. v. ā-drysnan.

**dubban.** *l.* dubbian : **duce.** *Add :*, dūce (?) : **dūfan.** *Add :*—Bil in dufan, El. 122.

**dūfe-doppa.** *Add :* [v. *N. E. D.* dive-dap, -dop] : **dūfian.** *Dele.*

**dugan.** *l.* deáh, deág, *and add :* subj. prs. dyge, duge. **I.** *absolute :*—Biþ se wela þý wyrsa, gif sē ne deáh þe hine āh, Bt. 27, 2 ; F. 98, 15. Gif þū hunig tō dēst, þ deáh, Lch. ii. 30, 22. Ne dohte hit nū lange inne ne ūte, ac wæs here and hunger, Wlfst. 159, 7. Þ ys tō gelýfenne þ hit dyge, Lch. i. 84, 19. Ān hrīðer dugunde (cf. *Icel.* dugandi(s)-a prefix to nouns, denoting *doughty*), Cht. Th. 460, 17. Lǣcedōmas wiþ þon gif hunta gebīte mannan . . . sex dugende cræftas, Lch. ii. 14, 20. Þām ealdan gedafeniað dugende þeáwas, O. E. Hml. i. 300, 3. **II.** *to do, be good.* (1) *for a person* (*dat.*) :—Seó deáh gehwæþer ge þæs mannes sāwle ge his līchoman, Lch. i. 70, 3. Ðæs wǣtan þing breóstum and innoþum ne dugon, ii. 246, 4. Sē mē dæge, i. 388, 16. Ic secge þ sió forespræc ne dyge (*prosit*) þām scyldigan, Bt. 38, 7 ; F. 210, 6. (2) *for a purpose :*—Deah hit wið æghwylcre innancundre unhǣlo, Lch. i. 86, 18. Seó wyrt deáh tō drincanne, ii. 238, 27.

**dugeþ;** *adj. Dele :* **dugunde.** v. dugan.

**duguþ.** *Add: The word is sometimes masc.* **I.** *virtue, excellence :*—Sinope tō eácan hiere hwætscipe and hiere monigfealdum duguþum hiere līf geendade on mægðhāde *Sinope singulorum virtutis gloriam perpetua virginitate cumulavit*, Ors. 1, 10 ; S. 46, 25. Sē wǣre wierðe ealra Rōmāna onwaldes for his monigfealdum duguðum *vir strenuus et probus, atque Augusto dignus*, 6, 35 ; S. 292, 16. **II.** *power, strength :*—Þonne land wurðeð for sinnum forworden and þæs folces duguð swiðost fordwīneð, þonne fēhð seó weálāf synna bemǣnan, Wlfst. 133, 12. God lēt Engla here . . . Brytta dugeðe fordōn mid ealle, 166, 20. **III.** *in a collective sense of persons.* (1) *a strong body of people, host* (especially in a military sense) :—Duguðes (duguðe, Wülck. Gl. 442, 1), *militiae*, Wrt. Voc. ii. 55, 18. Gehýr mē, dugoþa cāsere, Bl. H. 175, 11. Þū, þonne, dugoþa cyning, 177, 1. (2) *a body of great men, nobility, retainers of a chief, a senate :*—Ealdermanna duguð *senatus*, Wrt. Voc. i. 18, 38. Ælfsūn abbod and þegenas ǣgðer ge of Eást-Cent ge of West-Cent, eal seó duguð, Cht. Th. 302, 30. Hē beád þ eall þ folc cōme and eal seó dugoþ Rōmāna folces, Bl. H. 187, 13. Eóde Porrus se kyning mē on hond mid ealle his ferde and dugoþe, Nar. 19, 17. Þǣr gelīfde sum rīce man mid ealre his dugeðe, Chr. 627 ; P. 25, 24. Dugheþe senatu, An. Ox. 4041. (3) *men who are good for something, the flower of a people :*—Þǣr wearð ofslagen Eádnoð biscop and Wulsige abb. and Godwine ealdorman . . . and eall se dugoð (seó duguð (-að), *v. ll.*) on Angelcinne, Chr. 1016 ; P. 152, 8. On swicdōme wearþ Numantia duguð gefeallen *Numantini, interfectis suorum fortissimis, bello cedunt*, Ors. 5, 3 ; S. 222, 8. **IV.** *a benefit, good, what does good to a person :*—Þām hē geūðe ǣlcere dugeðe gif Maxentius him wolde ābūgan, Hml. Th. ii. 304, 19. Ús gedafenað tō

dōnne dugeðe on sibbe mid ēstfullum mōde menniscum gesceafte, 318, 16. [v. *N. E. D.* douth.]

**duguþ-gifu.** *Add :*—Dugeþgifu *munificentia*, An. Ox. 3063. Mid gecwēmre dugeþgyfe *cum gratuita munificentia*, 2577. Dugeþgyfe *munificentiam, liberalitatem*, 1183. Dugaðgife, 362.

**duguþ-lic;** *adj. Noble, chief.* v. duguþ, III. 2 :—Ealdorlicere, dugoþlice(re) mihte *tribunicie potestatis*, An. Ox. 4544. Duʒuþlicre, 2, 345. [Cf. þ heo maʒen drihten duʒeðliche hǣrien, Laym. 16844.]

**duguþ-miht,** e ; *f. Supreme power :*—Ealdordōmas and duguðmihta *principatus et potestates*, Lch. i. lxviii, 11.

**duguþ-nǣmere,** es ; *m. One who takes a benefit* (as a gloss to *municeps*, v. duguþ, IV) :—Dugutnaemeras *municipes*, An. Ox. 7, 62.

**dumb.** *Add :*—Sum þegn wearð fǣrlice dumb, Hml. S. 22, 73. Dumbre swīgan *mutae taciturnitatis*, An. Ox. 1936. Spǣcleáse ł dume *elinguia*, Germ. 398, 72.

**dumbness,** e ; *f. Dumbness :*—Úre Drihten gehǣlde þone wōdan fram his dumbnesse, Nap. 18.

**dumle.** v. rāre-dumbla (-e) : **dumnys.** v. dumbness.

**dun.** *Add :*, dunn :—Dun *balidus*, Wrt. Voc. ii. 125, 4. Dunn (*printed* dunu) *natius*, 62, 6. On horse dunnan sittan ferðrunge getācnað, Lch. iii. 202, 30. Ðā nāmon þā deófolgildan þoue dunnan (dumban, *v. l.*) oxan, Hml. S. 18, 112. Hyre betstan dunnan tunecan, Cht. Th. 537, 31. On ðā twēgen dunne stānes . . . ðone dunnan stān wiðforan ðām burggete, C. D. iii. 85, 10, 13.

**dūn.** *Add :*—Æt þære dūne þe man hæt Assandūn, Chr. 1016 ; P. 152, 12. Æt ðære dūne þe mon hætt Morotthonie (*campis Marathoniis*), Ors. 2, 5 ; S. 78, 25. Þæm gelīcost þe ic sitte on heáre dūne and geseó on smēðum felda fela fýra byrnan *quasi de specula montis adspectans, nihil in magno campi spatio praeter innumeros focos cernam*, 3, 11 ; S. 142, 14. On Lucaniam on Arosinis þære dūne *apud Lucaniam in Arusinis campis*, 4, 1 ; S. 158, 23. Micelne fultum hī gegaderodon on Thraci þære dūne *Dyrrachium gerendi bellum sedem delegerunt*, 5, 12 ; S. 240, 15, 23. Ge on tūne ge on dūne, ge on wuda ge on wætere, Angl. ix. 259, 25. Dūna swioran *juga*, Wrt. Voc. ii. 48, 18. Nōht elles būton þā wēstan feldas and wudu and dūna be ðǣm gārsecge *nihil praeter desertos in oceano campos siluasque ac montes*, Nar. 20, 10. v. neáh-, weard-, winter-dūn ; dūne.

**dūn;** *adj. Dele.*

**dūn-ælf,** e ; *f. A mountain fairy :*—Þā castalidas *nymphas*, þ synt dūnylfa þā þe wuneðon on Elicona þære dūne, Angl. viii. 325, 27. Dūnælfa *castalidas nymphas*, Wrt. Voc. ii. 88, 84 ; 19, 22. Dūnelfa, 129, 33.

**dunc-mennen.** v. drunc-mennen.

**dundre ?, duntre ?** :—Dundre stefne *bombosae vocis*, Hpt. Gl. 440, 56. *The same passage* (Ald. 20, 35) *is glossed* duntre stefne, An. Ox. 1463, þære thundendan (stefne), Wrt. Voc. ii. 77, 59, *and* bombose *is glossed by* ðære þūtendan, Wrt. Voc. ii. 11, 71. *A participial form of one of the verbs* dynian, þunian (*q. v.*), þeótan *seems to have been corrupted into these two forms.*

**dūne;** *adv. Down :*—Dūne āstāg *discendit*, Lk. L. 4, 31. [Clumben upp to þe stepel, brohton dune þ hæcce, Chr. 1070 ; P. 205, 30.] v. ā-, of-dūne, *and next word.*

**dūne-stīgende** *descending :*—Mid ðǣm dūnestīgendum in seáð *cum descendentibus in lacum*, Ps. Srt. 87, 5.

**dun-falu.** *Add :*—Dunfealu *cervinus*, Wrt. Voc. ii. 22, 72 : 130, 24.

**dung** dung. *Add :*—Dung (*printed* dinig) *fimus*, Wrt. Voc. i. 15, 6.

**dung;** *dat.* dyng ; *f. A subterranean chamber, a dungeon :*—Cōm hæleða þreát tō ðære dimman ding, An. 1272. [*O. L. Ger.* dung, dunc *textrina : O. H. Ger.* tunc *hypogeum, genecium, textrina.* Cf. *Icel.* dyngja *a lady's bower.*] v. drunc-mennen.

**dun-grǣg;** *adj. Dark-grey :*—Dungrǣg *fuscus*, i. *niger vel tenebrosus*, Wülck. Gl. 246, 4.

**dun-hof,** Hpt. Gl. 494, 78 : **dun-hūs,** 495, 11. *l.* dim-hof, -hūs.

**dūn-hunig,** es ; *n. Down-honey :*—Mid doran hunige oððe mid dūnhunige, Lch. iii. 4, 24. Cf. wudu-hunig.

**dūnian;** *p.* ode (?) *To fall down.* v. next word.

**dūniend-lic** (?) ; *adj. Falling down, tottering :*—Dunondlice (dūniendlice ?) ł tealniende (tealtriende ?) *nutantes*, Ps. L. 108, 10.

**dūnig** (?) ; *adj. Down, mountain :*—Tō dūnian mere *to the mere on the downs* (?), C. D. v. 245, 22.

**dūn-land.** *Add :*—Genim swīnes scearn þæs þe on dūnlande and wyrtum libbe, Lch. ii. 62, 28. Deós wyrt (*betony*) biþ cenned on mēdum and on clǣnum dūnlandum, i. 70, 2. Hē hine geond ealle eorðan sōhton, ge on dūnlandum gē on wudalandum, Ap. Th. 7, 14.

**dūn-lic;** *adj. Mountain :*—Þā dūnlican *castalidas*, Wrt. Voc. ii. 20, 49. Cf. dūn-ælf.

**dunn.** v. dun.

**dunnian.** *Substitute: To grow dark, become invisible :*—Swā dēð se mōna mid his blācan leóhte, þ þā beorhtan steorran dunniað *the stars become invisible when the moon shines*, Bt. 4 ; F. 6, 35.

dunond-lic. v. duniend-lic : dún-scréf. *l.* -scræf : dún-strǽt. *Dele :* duntre. v. dundre : dunung. *Dele :* dúr. *Dele :* dúre. v. duru : dure-. v. duru-: dúre-leás. *Dele.*

dúreras. *Substitute :* dur-here, es ; *m.* *A folding-door :*—Durhere sualdam, Txts. 96, 925. Durheri *valvam,* 104, 1053. Dureras *vualbas* (aulae coelestis *valvas,* Ald. 139, 15), Wrt. Voc. ii. 89, 16.

durran. *Add : subj. prs.* dyrre, durre :—Ich darr *audeam,* Mt. p. 1, 9. Ne dear man gewanian, Wlfst. 157, 15. Hælda ic ni darstæ, Txts. 126, 5. Húmeta dorstest ðú gán ?, Hml. Th. i. 530, 2. Darston (-un, R.) *audebant,* Lk. L. 20, 40. Ðæt ic ðé ne dyrre ofstingan, Past. 295, 16. Nis nán þe ic him módsefan mínne durre ásecgan, Wand. 10. Gebíd oþ þ þú mæge oððe dyrre, Lch. ii. 254, 4. Gif þú dón ne durre, 252, 27. Oðsace sé, sé þe wille oþþe sé þe dyrre, Ors. 6, 4 ; S. 260, 5 : Ll. Th. i. 154, 6 : Shrn. 176, 32. Þ hé gán dyrre and mæge, Lch. i. 176, 9. Ic nát hwá hit dyrre (durre, *v. l.*) secgan, Bt. 40, 2 ; F. 238, 5. Þ hé þé leógan ne durre, Bl. H. 179, 29 : Ll. Th. i. 418, 11. Ðætte unlǽrde ne dyrren (*audeant*) underfón láreówdóm, Past. 25, 14 : 427, 18 : 467, 16. v. ge-durran.

dúr-stodl. *l.* dur-stodl. v. stodl.

dúru. l. duru, *dele* dure, *and add :* gen. a ; *dat.* u, dyru (-e), *and a wk.* duran ; *pl. nom.* e, u ; *gen.* a ; *dat. pl.* dyrum (-an) :—Duru *hostium,* Wrt. Voc. i. 81, 11 : *valva,* 290, 12 : *limen (olympi),* ii. 93, 36 : 52, 5. Þǽre forscytlican dura *vectiferae valvae,* 90, 56. From ðǽre dura selfre ðisse béc *in ipsa locutionis nostrae janua,* Past. 25, 11. Beforan ðǽre ciricean dura (duru, *v. l.*) . . . on ðá duru, 105, 13, 14. Æt heofona ríces dura, Bl. H. 41, 35. Fram ðǽre byrgenne duru, 157, 9. Tó óðres mannes dure . . . tó óðres mannes húses dura (duru, *v. l.*), Ll. Th. i. 418, 1, 5. Tó þæs carcernes dyru (duru, l. 20), Bl. H. 237, 18. Ǽtforan þǽre cyrican dyre (dyran, R. Ben. I. 78, 10) *ante foras oratorii,* R. Ben. 70, 5. Binnan circan dyre, Ll. Th. ii. 254, 9. Tó þǽre duran (dura, *v. l.,* tó duru, L.) *ad januam,* Mk. 1, 33. Duru (duru, L.) helle ne ofereswíðiaþ *portae inferi non praevalebunt,* Mt. R. 16, 18. Ðá dure (dura, *v. l.,* duro, L. R.) wǽron belocene *fores essent clausae,* Jn. 20, 19. On ærne þ næbbe þon má dura þonne sió cirice, Ll. Th. i. 64, 15. Hí mid æxum duru (*januas ejus*) curfan, Ps. Th. 73, 6. Lufude Sione duru (*portas*) Drihten, 86, 1. Undóð mé duru (*portas*) sóðfæstra . . . sóðfæste on þá duru (*portam*) séceað inngang, 117, 19. v. norþ-, súþ-duru, *and the following compounds.*

dúru ; *pl. n. Dele.*

duru-healdend (dure (-a)-), es ; *m. A door-keeper :*—Durehaldend (dura-, R.) *i* dureueard *ostiaria,* Jn. L. 18, 17.

duru-stod ; (*n.?*). *For* Cot. 157 *l. :*—Durustod *postes,* Wrt. Voc. ii. 68, 70, *and add :* [Dorstodes *gyrneaus,* Wrt. Voc. i. 170, note 2. *Icel.* dura-stoð *a door-post.*]

duru-weard. *Add :*—Duruweard *janitor,* Wrt. Voc. ii. 45, 10. Hwæt mín fæder þé gedyde þá hé wæs duruweard, Bl. H. 151, 25. Dureweard *janitor,* An. Ox. 5147. Ðe duruard *ostiarius,* Jn. L. 10, 3. Ðegn cuæð ðæm duruuardæ (duroworde, R. *ostiariae*) . . . cuoeð dureweard, Jn. L. 18, 16, 17. Duruweardas *ostiarii,* Wrt. Voc. ii. 65, 43. Férde hé tó hire húse and forbeád ðæm duruweardum þ heó hine hire gesægde, Shrn. 86, 16. [v. *N. E. D.* door-ward. *O. H. Ger.* turiwart.]

dust. *l.* dúst, *and add :* I. *dried earth reduced to powder :*—Dyslicre ðonne hwá lufige hwelcre wuhte spor on ðæm dúste, and ne lufige ðæt ðætte ðæt spor worhte, Past. 353, 1. Seó eorðe wearð manegum tó bóte. Mid þám dúste wurdon áflígde deófla, Hml. S. 26, 198. Hé on axan and on dúste licge, Bl. H. 227, 15. II. *other dry material reduced to powder :*—Ofenbacen hláf *clibanius,* dúst of ðæm . . . *amolium,* Wrt. Voc. i. 41, 22. Færlíce áhreás þæt templ mid eallum his anlícnyssum tó dúste áwende, Hml. Th. i. 72, 6. Genim þás wyrte and cnuca tó swíþe smalan dúste, Lch. i. 240, 4. Genim of ðysse wyrte swýþe smæl dúst, 11. III. *applied to the mortal frame of man :*—Þú eart dúst and tó dúste wyrst, Gen. 3, 19. Ic eom dúst and axe, 18, 27. Hwæt ofermódgað ðiós eorðe and ðis dúsð ?, Past. 299, 22.

dústig ; *adj. Dusty :*—Dústigne *puluereum,* An. Ox. 15 : 3, 9. v. dýstig.

dúst-swearm, es ; *m. A cloud of dust* (of the motes in the sunlight) :—Dústswerme *atomo* (modico Phoebi radiis qui vibrat atomo, Ald. 272, 32), An. Ox. 23, 52.

duphamor. *l.* dúþ-hamor, *and add :*—Malleoli tyndercyn, *id est* dýphomer, Wrt. Voc. ii. 78, 9. [*In* An. Ox. 1655 *and* Hpt. Gl. 445, 39, *where the same passage* (Ald. 23, 8) *is glossed the form is* dúþhaman, *which seems a corruption of* dúþhamar.] v. dýþ-hamar *in Dict., and* dýþ.

dwǽs. *Add :*—Se portgeréfa nam tó Malche graman, and him mid eallum hete cídde, and hine þus áxode : 'Þú stunta and se mǽsta dwǽs þe ǽfre on þissere byrig mǽst wæs (*the biggest blockhead that ever was in this town*), on hwilce wísan sceole wé þé gelýfan ?, Hml. S. 23, 696. Gelíce þám dwǽsan þe for heora prýtan léwe nellað beorgan, Wlfst. 165, 9.

dwǽscan. *l.* dwǽscan, *dele* '*p.* dwæscede,' *and add :*—Ongunnon

hió weorpan wæter and hlýdan, swá þá dóð þe fýr dwǽscað (-eað, *v. l.*), Gr. D. 124, 1. v. on-dwǽscan.

dwǽsian ; *p.* ode *To become foolish, stupid :*—Ðá ðe wódlíce drincað and heora gewitt ámyrrað, swá þ hí dwǽsiað for heora druncennyssum, Hml. A. 6, 146.

dwǽs-lic ; *adj. Foolish, silly, stupid :*—Ongeán Godes ege se gromlica deófol syleð dyrstignysse mid dwǽslicum gebǽrum réceleásum man, Wlfst. 59, 20.

dwǽs-líce ; *adv. Foolishly, stupidly :*—Sé ðe wylle drincan and dwǽslíce hlýdan, drince him æt hám, Ll. Th. ii. 357, 40.

dwǽs-nys. *Add : Insipientia,* þæt is dysig oððe dwǽsnyss, Wlfst. 58, 15 : Angl. xi. 109, 37. Ic wénde þ þú sceoldest ðín mód fram dwǽsnysse áwendan . . . Dyslic bið þæt man hine sylfne tó tintregum ásende, Hml. Th. i. 592, 25.

dwalian. v. dwolian : dwás-líht. *Dele.*

dwelian. *Add :* I. *intrans.* (1) *to go astray.* (a) literal :—Hé on ðám holte dwelode (*wandered*), oð þæt hine wulfas tótǽron, Hml. Th. i. 384, 10. Hé án (sceáp), þe ðǽr losode and dwelede, sóhte, R. Ben. 51, 19. Heó began faran . . . swilce heó dweliende þyder cóme . . . Heó cwæð mid wóplicre stefne : ' Dweliende, leóf, ic cóm hyder,' Hml. A. 196, 24–29. Dweli(ende) *erraneam,* i. *errantem (ovem),* An. Ox. 347. (b) figurative :—Nú ic wæs of þám rihtan wege mínes ingeþances, ac betere hit bið þ ic eft fare út of þysum porte, ðy læs ic tó swíðe dwelige, Hml. S. 23, 553. Ðá ðe fyligað þǽre gýtsunge, hí dweliað fram Godes geleáfon, Hml. Th. i. 256, 18. Ðá, þe lífes weg lǽdan cunnan, gebringan on rihtwege þá, þe ǽr dweledan (-odan, *v. l.*), Wlfst. 75, 2. Sé ðe færð on sóðre lufe ne mæg hé dwelian ; heó gewi·sað and gelǽt, Hml. Th. i. 52, 15. Dweliende *exorbitans (a recto religionis tramite),* An. Ox. 3697 : 4619. (2) *of inaccurate conception, to mistake, err :*—Swíþe raþe þe bið cúþ þ wit ne dwelgaþ, Bl. H. 189, 6. Sume gedwolmenn cwǽdon . . . ac hí dwelodon ·mid þǽre segene (*they were mistaken in what they said*), Hml. Th. i. 486, 7. Ne dwela ðú on idel . . . and ne wén ðú ná be þ þ þú ungewítnod beó, Hml. S. 25, 157. (2 a) *of madness :*—Seó dohtor on wódum dreáme læg dweligende, Hml. Th. ii. 110, 19. (3) *of wrong conduct, to err :*—Þ dwelast, geneálǽc and geoffra þíne lác, Hml. S. 14, 33. Mid þám Francum þe þá swíðost dweledon on deófles biggencgum, 29, 165. Hié on hǽðnum þeáwum dwelgende wǽron, Bl. H. 201, 20. Dryhten, þú gecyrst ðá dweliendan, Hml. S. 30, 68. II. *trans. To lead astray.* (1) physical :—Ðá genipu hit dweliað, Sal. K. 148, 5. (2) moral :—Hý dwelode deófol, Wlfst. 11, 8 : 156, 8. Hí ne gelýfdan on riht . . . ac mid manegum gedwyldum dwelodan (-edon, *v. l.*) þá Crístenan, Hml. S. 3, 357. Þá dwolmen dwelodon þone cásere, 312. Cf. dwolian.

dwellan. *Dele* '*p.* dwelede,' *and* III (see dwelian, I. 1 a), *and add :* I. *trans. To lead astray, lead into error :* — Unwǽrlicu sprǽc menn dweleð *incauta locutio in errorem pertrahit,* Past. 89, 8. Ðæt hí ðǽre lícettunga óðre men ne dwellen, 449, 24. II. *intrans. To go astray, wander :*—Dwelet *obambulat,* An. Ox. 47, 1. Álýse mé of ðám gedwolan þe ic on oð þisum dwealde, Shrn. 170, 17. Hí dweldon on wéstene *erraverunt in solitudine,* Ps. Spl. 106, 4.

dwel-lic ; *adj. Erroneous, heretical :*—Be þám men þe dwellice þing begéð *de homine qui res haereticas committit,* Ll. Th. ii. 180, 35. Dwællice *palladios,* Germ. 397, 511.

dwelsian ; *p.* ode *To stray, wander :*—Of ðínum bebodum ic ná ne dwelsode (*erravi*), Ps. L. 118, 110.

dweorg. *Add :*—Duerg *nanus vel pumilio,* Txts. 80, 686. Duerh, 110, 1176. ¶ Dwarfs were supposed to be able to injure living creatures. v. Grmm. D. M. (trans.), pp. 460 sqq. :—Dweorg on weg tó dónne . . . syle etan þám untruman men ǽr þære tíde hys tócymes, swá on dæge swá on nihte, swæþer hyt sý, his tógan(g) bið ðearle strang, Lch. i. 364, 13–17. (The disease meant is convulsions, Cockayne.) Wrít ðis ondlang ðá earmas wið dweorh, iii. 38, 29. Wið [d]weorh man sceal niman .VII. lytle oflǽtan . . . , 42, 3. [v. *N. E. D.* dwarf.] v. werc *in Dict.*

dweorge-dwostle. *Add :*—Duuergaedostae (duergae-), duergedostle *pulegium,* Txts. 90, 831. Dweorges dwostle, Wrt. Voc. i. 68, 61. v. *in Dict.* dwyrge-dwysle.

dwild. *Add :* [Mikell hæþenndom and hefig dwilde, Orm. 9736.]

dwilman. *l.* dwylman. Cf. dwolma : dwimor. *Add :*—Dwimer *portenta* (?), An. Ox. 50, 1. [Cf. *Laym.* dweomer-cræft, -lac.] : dwínan. *For* Cot. 190 *read* Wrt. Voc. ii. 84, 42, *and add :* v. tó-dwínan.

-dwol ; *adj.* v. ge-dwol.

dwola *error. Add :* , dwala (*q. v. in Dict.*) :—Duola *error,* Mt. L. 27, 64. Dwola, Þs. p. 3, 4. Unwísdómes i duoles blendnise *ignorantiae cecitate,* Rtl. 38, 9. On dwolan gebringan þá þe Gode gecorene wǽron, Wlfst. 196, 9. Mið dwala *errore,* Mt. p. 3, 10. Þ in duala (gedwolan, R.) inn biðon gelǽded *ut in errorem inducantur,* 24, 24. Þone dwolan þára manna [þe wénaþ þ] sáwle nǽbben nán edleán æfter þisse worulde heora gearnunge *eorum errorem, qui animarum merita nulla esse apud te putant,* Shrn. 167, 27. [v. *N. E. D.* dwele ; *sb.*]

**dwola**, an; *m.*   I. *one who errs, a person without understanding* :—Líf dwolan *uita uecordis* (cf. gedwolenum *uecordi*, Kent. Gl. 308), Scint. 223, 3.    II. *a heretic, schismatic* :—Dwola *hereticus*, An. Ox. 27, 14. Dwolan *seismatici*, 2854.   v. ge-dwola.

**dwol-cræft.**   *Add* : v. gedwol-cræft.

**dwolian.**   *Add* :   I. *to stray.*   (1) literal :—þá þá heó swá wídgál swíðe dwolode *dum vaga nimium erraret*, Gr. D. 176, 21. Scípa ðá ðe ne duoladon *oves quae non erraverunt*, Mt. L. 18, 13. On wudum dwolgende, Bl. H. 193, 8. Swylce hwylc man urne þǽr geond dwoliende *ac si in eis aliquis erranda discurreret*, Gr. D. 236, 11. (2) figurative :—Of ðínum bebodum ic ne dwolade *de mandatis tuis non erravi*, Ps. L. 118, 10.   II. *of inaccurate conception.*   (1) *to mistake, err* :—Bið se here eal ídel, ðonne hé on óðer folc winnan sceal, gif se heretoga dwolað *in exploratione hostium frustra exercitus velociter sequitur, si ab ipso duce itineris erratur*, Past. 129, 9. Gé dwoligas (duolas, L. *erratis*), ne wutun gé giwriotu, Mk. R. 12, 24. Gié duolages, L. 27. (2) *to be out of one's senses.*   Cf. dwolung :—Ic dwolie *deliro*, þú dwolast *deliras*, Wrt. Voc. ii. 28, 5, 6. Wénde se cniht þ̌ hé dwolode ... Hé cwæð : 'Wite þú þ̌ ic náht ne dwolige' *cum hunc puer insanire crederet ... dicens* : '*Non insanio*,' Gr. D. 314, 7-10.   III. *of wrong conduct, to err* :—Álýse mé of ðám gedwolan þe ic gyt on dwolige, Shrn. 170, 17. Ne dwolað *non errabit*, Kent. Gl. 555. Dwoliað *errant*, 491.   v. dwalian *in Dict.*, and cf. dwelian.

**dwol-líc.**   *Add* :—þæs flǽsces weorc ... dwollíc lár (*sectae*, Gal. 5, 20), Hml. S. 17, 26. Se biscop þá dwollican sócne (v. sócn, V) á-dwæscte, Hml. Th. ii. 508, 5.

**dwol-líce.**   *Add* : *erroneously, ignorantly, stupidly* : — Dwollíce, (dollíce, *v. l.*) etan binnan Godes húse, Hml. S. 13, 72. Þurh ðone deófol þe hé dwollíce gehýrsumede, 7, 172 : 18, 391 : Hml. Th. ii. 140, 19. Þá deófiu oncneówon Críst, and þæt Iudéisce folc hine dwollíce wiðsóc, 380, 2. Woruldmen ðus dwollíce (*so erroneously*) mé oncnáwað, i. 366, 13. Ðú lufast druncennysse and dwollíce leofast ... ðá ðe wódlíce (dwollíce, *v. l.*) drincað, Hml. A. 6, 140, 145. Hé deófolgild beeóde dwollíce libbende, Hml. S. 28, 6.

**dwolma.**   *Add* : *a state* or *place of confusion* :—Duolma, dualma *chaus, chaos, prima confusio omnium rerum*, Txts. 49, 457. Dwolma *chaos* (*abstrusum, et torpens confusio rerum*, Ald. 150, 10), i. *tenebre*, An̄. Ox. 17, 9. Eal bið úpheofon sweart and gesworcen, deorc and dimhíw and dwolma sweart *tristius coelum tenebris obducitur atris*, Dóm. L. 106 : Wlfst. 137, 10. Dwolma *cahus* ( = *chaos*, Lk. 16, 26), Wrt. Voc. ii. 73, 65 : 17, 56. Dwolman (*in antiquum*) *chaos*, An. Ox. 2483.   v. ge-dwolma.

**dwol-mann**, es ; *m.*   *A heretic* :—þá dwolmen hine bedydrodon, Hml. S. 3, 316.   v. gedwol-mann.

**dwolung**, e ; *f.* *Absurdity, folly* :—Dofunge, dwolunge *deleramenta*, Wrt. Voc. ii. 28, 46.   v. dwolian, II. 2, *and* dofung.

**dybbian** *to pay attention to* :—Dybbian *incumbere* (*fletibus*), An. Ox. 645.

**dyd.**   *Dele* : dýdan.   v. dídan.

**dyderung.**   *Add* :—Manega drýmen maciað menigfealde dydrunga þurh deófles cræft, and bedydriað menn, swylce hí soðlíce swylc þincg dón ; ac hit is dydrung mid deófles cræfte, and gif hwá hit bletsað, þonne áblynð seó dydrung, Hml. S. 21, 464-9. Drýmen mid dydrunge farað, Hml. Th. ii. 330, 27. Forhogian þæs deófles dydrunga, Hml. S. 17, 165.

**dýfan.**   v. dífan : **dyfen.**   *Dele, and see* andefn, II : **dýfing.**   v. dífing : **dýgan.**   *Dele, and see* dugan : **dýgel** (-ol).   v. dígle.

**dylsta?**   *pl.* dylstan.   *l.* dylsta, dylstan ; *pl.*

**dyncge.**   *Substitute* : dyncge, dynge, an ; dyncg, e ; *f.*   I. *dung, manure, litter* :—Dincge *letamen*, An. Ox. 4773. Dinig (*l.* dincg or dung ?) *fimus*, Wrt. Voc. i. 15, 6. Of dincge *gramine*, An. Ox. 46, 16. Sceáphyrdes riht is þ̌ hé hæbbe twelf nihta dingan (ðingan, MS. ; the Latin version has *dingiam*) tó Middanwintra, Ll. Th. i. 438, 22.   II. *manured land* :—Dincge *navalium* (cf. *naualis, campi culturae dediti*, Corp. Gl. H. 80, 3), Wrt. Voc. i. 66, 56. Dyncgum *noualibus*, i. *inrigationibus*, An. Ox. 1409. Dincgum, 2367. On dengum *in novalibus*, Kent. Gl. 466.   v. mixen-dyncge ; dung.

**dyne.**   *Add* :—Dyne *clangor*, Wrt. Voc. ii. 131, 52 : *crepaculum, sonum*, 136, 63. Dynta dyne, Wlfst. 114, 23. Heora fyðera swégað, swá swá wæteres dyne, 200, 16. Dine *clangor*, An. Ox. 22, 1. Dyne *fragore*, 17, 55. Dinna (dimma, MS.) mǽst hlúd gehýred, Sat. 606.

**-dýne.**   v. æf-dýne : **dýneras.**   v. dínor : **dyng** *to a dungeon.*   v. dung : **dyng(e)** *manure.*   v. dyncge.

**dynge** *a storm.*   *Substitute* : dynges mere ? :—Gewitan him þá Norþmen nægledcnearrum on dinges (dynges, dyniges, dinnes, *v. ll.*) mere ofer deóp wæter Difelin sécan, Chr. 937 ; P. 109, 12. [*With the reading* dinnes *cf. fram* dinmeres *múþan ...* Oþ dinmeres fleót, C. D. B. ii. 526, 6, 5 : tó dinnes hangran, C. D. v. 226, 12 : on dinnes ... dynnes hlince, vi. 36, 12, 13 : dynningden, ii. 228, 3 ; *the last form seems to point to a proper name.*]

**dyng(i)ung.**   v. dingiung *in Dict.*

**dynian.**   *Add* :—Feld dynede, Chr. 937 ; P. 106, 20. Dynedan and þunedan *crepitabant*, Wrt. Voc. ii. 21, 17. Dynigende *concrepans*, An. Ox. 7, 104. Dynigendum *crepante*, 8, 5. Dynegendum, 7, 11. Hors urnon þurh þá díca dynigende mid fótum, Hml. S. 27, 39.

**dynige** (dýnige ?).   *Substitute* : *The name of a plant.*

**dynt.**   *Substitute* :   I. *a blow, stroke* :—Slóh hine án heora mid ánre æxe ýre on þet heáfod, þet hé mid þám dynte niðer ásáh, Chr. 1012 ; P. 142, 24. Án ðára ðegna salde dynt (*alapam*) ðǽm Hǽlende, Jn. R. L. 18, 22. Ðone dynt *ictum* (*securis*), Past. 339, 15. Be ðám ðe nán óðrum dynt ne gebeóde *ut non presumat aliquis alium cedere*, R. Ben. 129, 12. Mistlice þreála gebyriað for synnum, beudas oððe dyntas, Ll. Th. ii. 278, 26. Gif is benda bite and dynta dyne, Wlfst. 209, 17 : 114, 23. Hí habbað sweopan, swenga ne wyrnað, deórra dynta, Sal. 122. Mid fýstum ł dyntum geslaa *colaphis caedere*, Mk. L. 14, 65. Dyntas *alapas*, Jn. L. 19, 3. Martianus hét his cwelleras þone hálgan beátan mid saglum ... Ðá cwæð Martianus ... 'Ðú þás dyntas náht ne gefrētst,' Hml. S. 4, 147.   II. *mark made by a blow, bruise* :—Gif man óðerne mid fýste in naso slæhð, .iii. scill. Gif dynt sié, scilling. Gif hé heáhre handa dyntes onféhð, scill. forgelde. Gif dynt sweart sié búton wǽdum .xxx. scætta gebéte. Gif hit sié binnan wǽdum, gehwilc .xx. scætta gebéte *if a man strike another on the nose, a fine of three shillings. If there is a mark, a shilling. If the person struck get a bruise* (or *blow?*) *on an arm raised for protection* (?), *a shilling must be paid. If the bruise be black in a part not covered by clothes, there shall be a fine of thirty scatts. If it be in a part covered by clothes, for each bruise there shall be a fine of twenty scatts*, Ll. Th. i. 16, 17-18, 5.   III. *the sound made by a blow, thud* of a body striking the ground :—Swíþe oft se micla anweald ðára yfelena gehríst swíþe fǽrlíce, swá swá greát beám on wyda wyrcþ hlúdne dynt (*strikes the ground with a loud thud*), ðonne men lǽst wénaþ, Bt. 38, 2 ; F. 198, 9.

**dýp.**   v. dípe : **dýpan** *to baptize.*   v. dípan : **dýpan** *to deepen.*   *l.* dípan : **dýpe.**   v. dípe : **dyppan.**   *Dele the forms given as cognates, and see* dípan : **dýr.**   *Dele, and see* duru : **dýran.**   v. díran : **dyrce-grǽg.**   v. deorce-grǽg : -dyre.   v. fore-, ge-, ofer-dyre : **dyrfan.**   v. dírfan : **dyrfing.**   v. dirfing : **dyrne.**   v. dirne : **dýrsian.**   *l.* dírsian : **dyrste-líce.**   v. dyrstig-líce.

**dyrstig.**   *Add* :   I. *bold, daring* :—þá men þe tó ðám dyrstige beóð þ̌ hí þæt gold nimen *homines qui audaces sunt aurum tollere*, Nar. 35, 10.   II. *audacious, presumptuous* :—Dyrstig *procax*, Wülck. Gl. 250, 29. Swíðe dysig is se man and dyrstig sé þe syngað gelóme, Angl. xii. 513, 27. Hé þá hálgan róde genam hám tó his earde árleáslíce dyrstig, Hml. S. 27, 26. þæt heofonlíce hors wearp áðúne þone dyrstigan Heliodorum, 25, 777. Gif huætd ungebyredlic bidda dyrstigo ué sindon *si aliquid incongruum rogare ausi sumus*, Rtl. 179, 34.   v. fore-dyrstig.

**dyrstigan.**   *l.* dyrstigian.

**dyrstig-líce.**   *Add* :   I. *boldly, daringly* :—Dyrstelíce (deorster-, Hpt. Gl. 424, 19) *audacter*, An. Ox. 753.    II. *presumptuously, with temerity* :—On swá hwilcum dæge swá þu dyrstilíce geþristlæcst þ̌ þu þone hálgan sácerdhád underféhst *quacumque die sacrum ordinem temerare praesumeris*, Gr. D. 135, 12. Se gedwola dirstilíce cwæð þ̌ on Críste wǽron twégen hádas, Ll. Th. ii. 374, 18. Dyrstelíce, Hml. Th. i. 170, 35. Úre nán be him sylfum tó dyrstelíce ne trúwige, ii. 82, 26. [*Orm.* dirrstiglike *boldly.*]

**dyrstig-ness.**   *Add* :—Se synfulla man ... þe geþristlæcð tó mæssianne ... and wát hine sylfne tó fúlne ... his dyrstignes dereð him sylfum, Wlfst. 34, 18. Temeritas, þæt is dyrstignys, 52, 20. Temeritas, þ̌ is dyselic dyrstignys, Angl. xi. 109, 41 : Hml. Th. ii. 220, 15 : Hml. A. 66, 34. Dyrstynnys *presumptio*, Angl. viii. 331, 5. Hé wearð deád for þǽre dyrstignysse þ̌ hé dorste onginnan þǽra sácerda þénunga, Hml. A. 59, 188. Se ealda feónd onféng swilce dyrstinysse (bylde, *v. l.*, *ausum*) tó ácwellanne, Gr. D. 75, 32. Gif hé þurh dyrstignysse hine onhefð mid módignysse *si presumpserit*, R. Ben. 129, 12. Hé þǽra gedwolmanna dyrstignesse ádwæscte, Hml. Th. i. 70, 7.

**dyrsting-panne.**   *l.* hyrsting-panne.

**dyrst-lǽcan** *to presume* :—Ne dyrstlǽce (*presumat*) se gingra þ̌ hé mid þám yldran sitte, búton hé hine háte, R. Ben. 116, 5 : 128, 4. Ne dyrstlǽcen hí þæt hý út of mynstre etan *non presumant foris manducare*, 79, 16.

**dyrst-líc.**   *Dele.*

**dysegian.**   *Add* :—Suá micle suá hé má wát and wísra bið ðonne óðre menn, suá hé má dysegað and suíður wiend wið ðone cræft án-módnesse *quo plus sapiunt, eo a concordiae virtute desipiscunt*, Past. 347, 12. On Nóes dagum ðá ðá menn dysgodon tó swýðe, Hml. S. 13, 185.   v. á-dysgian ; ge-dysegind.

**dysig** ; *adj.*   *Add* :—Dysig *buccum* (cf. bucco, stultus rusticus, Corp. Gl. H. 26, 219), Wrt. Voc. i. 287, 79. Desiges *susurronis*, Kent. Gl. 998. Gelíc þám dysigan (dysge, L.) men *similis viro stulto*, Mt. 7, 26. Mid dysigum geswince *stulto labore*, Ex. 18, 18. Dysine *vecordem*,

Kent. Gl. 183. Dysige *butra* (cum *bruta* mente, Ald. 202, 5), Wrt. Voc. ii. 96, 10: 12, 18. Dysige *hebeti*, 42, 75. Nys drenc cilda ne dysigra (*stultorum*), Coll. M. 35, 19. Þú dysegost manna, Hml. Th. ii. 416, 13. v. yfel-dysig.

**dysig**; *n.* *Add* :—Bigspellbóc, ná swilce gé secgað, ac wísdómes bigspell and warnung wið disig, Ælfc. T. Grn. 7, 38. v. frum-dysig; dysigu.

**dysig-dóm.** *Add* :—Andswaru stuntan æfter dysigdóme his (*juxta stultitiam suam*), Scint. 95, 14. Dysigdóme gelettendum *imperitia impediente*, Angl. xiii. 372, 97.

**dysig-nes.** *Add* :—Eálá on hú micelre dysignesse men nú sindon *O dura mens hominum et cor semper inhumanum*, Ors. 3, 9 ; S. 136, 17. Swá hwæt swá wé þurh hwylce dysignesse gedón habban, Hml. A. 143, 137.

**dysig** (-o); *indecl.* or *gen.* e; *f. Folly, stupidity* :—Neátum gelíce for eówre dysige, Bt. 26 ; F. 90, 3. v. dysig; *n.*

**dys-lic.** *Add* :—Dyslic *absurdum*, Wrt. Voc. ii. 2, 32. Dyselic, An. Ox. 7, 130. Dyslic bið þæt hwá woruldlice spéda forhogige for manna herunge and beó on Godes dóme geniðerod, Hml. Th. i. 60, 32 : Bt. 34, 3; F. 136, 28. Dys(e)lic dyrstignes. v. dyrstignes. Hit ðincð ungelæredum mannum dyselig tó gehýrenne, Hml. Th. i. 94, 35. Fela dyslice dǽda deriað mancynne, Hml. S. 13, 91. Hé ádreáh his líf on dyslicum weorcum, 26, 245. Mid dislicum glencgum *stolidis* (*i. stultis*) *pompis*, An. Ox. 1216.

**dys-líce.** *Add* :—Dyslíce *fatuiter*, Wrt. Voc. ii. 38, 41. Þá férdon his men dyslíce æfter inne, Chr. 1052 ; P. 173, 24. Nú dóð menn dyslíce, þ hí willað wacian and wodlíce drincan, Hml. S. 13, 75. Sume menn dyslíce fæstað ofer heora mihte, 93.

**dystig.** *l.* dýstig, and for Cot. 183 *substitute* :—Ðý dýstgan *pulverulenta*, Wrt. Voc. ii. 89, 31. v. dústig.

**dýþ**, e; *f. Fuel, tinder* :—Dýþe *malleoli* (ambustas *malleoli* machinas, Ald. 23, 8. Cf. malleolus, genus fomenti aput Persas: malleolus, sarmenta, Corp. Gl. H. 75, 2, 5), An. Ox. 2, 43 : Hpt. 445, 39. v. dúþhamor.

**dyphomar.** *l.* dýþ-homar. v. dúþ-hamor ; dýþ: **dyttan.** *Add* : [v. *N. E. D.* dit.]

# E

**eá** *a river. Add:* *gen.* ié, é; *dat.* ié, ee ; *dat. pl.* eáuum, éum :—Eá *amnis*, Wrt. Voc. i. 80, 56. Eá mid treówum ymbset *amnis*, 54, 16. Seó eá (ēa, MS.) Danai, Ors. 1, 1 ; S. 8, 16 : Nar. 35, 5. Se múþa þǽre ié (íe, MS.), Ors. 1, 1 ; S. 10, 13. Ælfe múþa þǽre ié, 16, 6. Cymþ þ wæter úp æt ðám ǽwelme, wyrþ ðonne tó bróce, ðonne tó eá, ðonne andlang eá oþ hit wyrþ eft tó sǽ, Bt. 34, 6 ; F. 140, 20. On twá healfe þǽre é, Chr. 894 ; P. 87, 22. On ǽgþere healfe eás, 918 ; P. 100, 6. In Danai þǽre ié (íe, MS. *fluvio*), Ors. 1, 1 ; S. 8, 10, 11, 14. Forþ bí þǽre eá, S. 17, 22. Æt þǽre ee, S. 24, 33. Tó ánre eá (ēa, MS.), Hml. S. 30, 328. Be þǽre eá, Chr. 896; P. 89, 11. On þǽre ǽ þines willan *torrente voluntatis tuae*, Ps. Th. 35, 8. Ofer þá eá (ēa, MS.), Ors, 1, 1 ; S. 8, 30. Ic ána wát eá rinnende, Lch. iii. 36, 25. Monega eá (ēa, MS.) sindon be noman nemnede, 2, 4; S. 72, 12. Ðá eá stódon, Bt. 35, 6 ; F. 168, 8. Ealle eán (ēán MS. *flumina*) eft gewendað þanon þe hí ǽr cómon, Angl. vii. 36, 343 : Hml. S. 15, 176 : Lch. iii. 254, 23. On ǽghwelcra eá múþum, Bt. 32, 3 ; F. 118, 19. Ealdor eá *caput fluviorum*, Nar. 35, 20. On þǽre stówe þe genemned is æt eá mótum, Chr. 926 ; P. 107, 24. On sǽ and on eáuum, Hex. 14, 7. Betux þǽm twám eán, Ors. 3, 11 ; S. 144, 4 : Nar. 35, 18. Æt Tweoxn-eám (Tweoxnám, *v. l.*), Chr. 901 ; P. 92, 4. [v. *N. E. D.* ea.] v. neáh-eá.

**eá**; *interject. Add* :—Eálá eá ! is þ þonne forweorþfullic wela ?, Bt. 29, 1 ; F. 102, 14. Eálá wuldor þisse worulde, eá ! for hwí ðe hátan dysige men wuldor ?, 30, 1 ; F. 108, 2. Eálá (eá, *v. l.*) mín cild, eá !, 34, 12 ; F. 154, 9.

**eác**; *prep. Dele* 'DER. tó-eác ', *and add* :—Swiðulf biscop and Ceólmund ealdorman . . . and Eádulf cynges þegn . . . , and manige eác him (tó eácan him, *v. l.*), Chr. 897 ; P. 90, 9. Monige eác him (eác tó him, eác mid him, *v. ll.*), 905 ; P. 94, 10, 15. Þæt is nú þæs líchoman gód, þ mon sié fæger and strang . . . and manegu óþru gód tó eác þǽm (eác þǽm, *v. l.*), Bt. 34, 6 ; F. 140, 32. ¶ eác þǽm (þon) *besides, moreover* :—Aec ðon *quin etiam*, Wrt. Voc. ii. 118, 54. Eác þon *ceterum*, Nar. 9, 14. Eác þǽm (*moreover*) monega eá sindon be noman nemnede for þǽm gefeohte, Ors. 2, 4 ; S. 72, 12. Eác þan, Ll. Th. i. 36, 9.

**eác**; *conj. l. adv.*, *and add* : I. where there is addition of objects :—þǽr weard Síulf ealdorman ofslægen . . . and Eádwold, and manige eác tó him, . . . swíðe mænige eác mid him, Chr. 905 ; P. 95, 16, 20. Þ cinges þegnas . . . , ge eác sum dǽl þæs Norð-Wealcynnes, 894 ; P. 87, 18. Hý habbaþ eall þ ðá unstyriendan habbaþ, and eác máre tó, Bt. 41, 5 ; F. 252, 26. II. where there is addition of condition or circumstance :—Hét ic ǽlcne mon hine gegerwan, and faran forð, and þ

---

eác bebeád ðæt . . . , Nar. 9, 27. Drihten is mid þé on þínre heortan and on þínum innoþe and eác on þínum fultome, Bl. H. 5, 12. Salde se here him micle áþas þæt hié of his ríce uuoldon, and him eác gehéton þæt . . . , Chr. 878 ; P. 76, 14. Be westan Sealwuda ge be eástan, ge eác be norþan Temese, 894 ; P. 87, 17 : Bl. H. 15, 4 : 21, 10. Hié beóð úpáhafene and eác beóð onbærnde . . . ge eác beóð besmitene, 25, 7. Hé for þon ús gesette þ wé hine biddan sceoldan, þý wé sceolan þonne eác úre heortan gecl ǽnsian, . . . Gehýran wé eác þ . . . , 21, 2–5. III. *combined with* (1) swá :—Fóron micel dǽl þára burgwara, and eác swá óþres folces, Chr. 896 ; P. 89, 5. Línsǽd sáwan, wádsǽd eác swá, Angl. ix. 262, 11. Beóð henna ácende . . . eác swá (*preterea*) beóð wildeór ácennede, Nar. 34, 4. Wæs ic sáriges módes and þá míne frýnd swá eác, 30, 15. (2) swilce :—Ac eác swylce *uerum*, An. Ox. 2917 : *uerum etiam*, 4096. Næs nó on gesundum þingum ánum, ac eác swylce on wiðerweardum þingum, Bl. H. 13, 8.

**eáca.** *Add* : I. addition, increase :—Ðonne ys ðis se eáca on landum ðæt hé hæfð of his ágenum ðæt mynster mid gegódod, C. D. iv. 274, 32. Hwæt se eáca is ðe ic geunnen hæbbe, 51, 23. Nán nis swá welig þ hé sumes eácan ne þurfe, Bt. 33, 1 ; F. 120, 16. Seó gnornung is mé eald for·gewunan, níwe for (þurh, *v. l.*) eácan (*per augmentum*), Gr. D. 4, 9. Eácan au(g)menta, Kent. Gl. 66. I a. addition to something :—Tó eácan mínum sáre *in augmentum mei doloris*, Gr. D. 6, 20. Ic fíftýne geár þé tó fyrste lǽte ðínum dagum tó eácan, Hml. S. 18, 429. Þæt gástlicum mægenum gearwige eácan (*incrementum*), Scint. 209, 12. Ænigne eácan tó úrum friðgildum, Ll. Th. i. 238, 16. I b. *increase* of something :—þæt hé his ǽwe healde and álýfedlíce for folces eácan bearn gestreóne, Hml. Th. ii. 94, 20 : Ælfc. Gen. Thw. 2, 6. Melu on swefnum handlian eácan ceápas getácnað, Lch. iii. 204, 4, 31. I c. in various special applications. (1) *increase of goods* :—Wylspring on húse his gesihð beón geopenad eácan oððe blisse getácnað, Lch. iii. 204, 16. (2) *a reinforcement* to an army :—Him cóm micel eáca tó ǽgþer ge of Eást-Englum ge of Norþhymbrum, Chr. 894 ; P. 87, 11. (3) *additional words, a supplement, appendix* :—Swíðe ryhtlíce wæs se eáca ðér tó gedón, ðá mon cuæð : 'Wyrceað fæsten ymb ðá burg,' Past. 163, 4. Hér is git óþer wel gód eáca, Wlfst. 180, 1. (4) *a suffixed particle* :—Þrý eácan synd *met, pte, ce*, Ælfc. Gr. Z. 107, 3. II. *something in excess, overplus* :—In þǽre tócnáwnesse ǽgðres gedáles weaxeþ se éca (*cumulus*) þæs edleánes, Gr. D. 311, 12. II a. with numbers, *more* :—Ehta fóta and lytel eáca, Lch. ii. 218, 24. Ymb VII c wintra and ymb lytelne eácon, Ors. 6, 1 ; S. 252, 20. Hé ofslóh án hund þúsend manna and hundeahtatig ðúsend and sumne eácan ðærtó, Hml. S. 18, 404. [v. *N. E. D.* eke ; *sb.* Icel. auki.] v. æt-, mann-eáca ; tó-eácan.

**-eáca**; *adj.* v. bearn-eáca.

**eácan, eácen**; *adj. Substitute for these*: **eácan** ; [*p.* eóc, *pl.* eócon] ; *pp.* eácen, ēcen *to increase* (trans.) :—Hí sculon ǽlce dæg eácan (ýcan, *v. l.*) þ mon ǽlce dæg wanaþ, Bt. 26, 2 ; F. 94, 1. Nó þæs bebodu tó brecanne, ac mid eallum gódum tó eácanne (ícanne, *v. l.*), Ll. Th. i. 56, 2. ¶ **eácen**; *ptcpl.* (adj.). (1) *increased, augmented* :—Eácne egesan, Sal. 473. Mé ecga dolg eácen weorðað þurh deáðslege dagum and nihtum *wounds from the swords are increased upon me by deadly stroke day and night*, Rä. 6, 13. (2) *endowed with excellent qualities* or *properties, noble, excellent, great* :—Higelá ces þegn, gód mid Geátum . . . wæs mægenes strengest, . . . ǽdele and eácen, B. 198 : Rä. 34, 11. Eácen feoh (cf. hálig feoh, 201), Gen. 1517. Hé eácenne gást in sefan sende, snyttro cræftas, Dan. 485. Beorhtne sunu, bearn eácen Godes, Cri. 205. Eald sweord eácen, B. 1663. Eácne eardas, 1621. Ic heáfde forcearf Grendeles módor eácnum ecgum, 2140. (2 a) *endowed, inspired* with something :—Eácen *afflatus* (*praesago spiritu*, Ald. 35, 13), Wrt. Voc. ii. 79, 48 : 5, 6. Adam weard of Godes múðe gáste eácen, Gen. 1001 : Rä. 10, 8. Bið seó móddor mægene eácen, 81, 15. Cræfte eácen, 21. Néron gé swá eácne módgeþances, Dan. 136. (3) *pregnant* :—Eácene *feta* (*coelesti pignore*, Ald. 182, 5), Wrt. Voc. ii. 94, 40 : 37, 40. Eácenu *foeta*, i. *fecunda, plena, gravida*, Wülck. Gl. 238, 8. On ðone dæg Sca Maria eácen geworden, Shrn 67, 9 : Cri. 38. Deór. 11. Heó wæs magotimbre be Abrahame eácen worden, Gen. 2236 : 2766. Of ēcnum *ex fecundo* (*utero*), Hpt. Gl. 404, 67. Idesa wurdon eácne, eaforan bröhton on woruld, 2606. Wá éknum *vae praegnantibus*, Mt. R. 24, 19. [*Goth.* aukan : *Icel.* auka> *p.* iók : *O. Sax.* ōkan *pregnant* : *O. Fris.* áken.] v. bearn-, feorh-, mægen-eácen ; cf. ícan.

**eácian** ; *p.* ode *To increase* (intrans.) :—Hé him eác gesǽgd hú ðǽm monnum ðe him mægen and cræft wiext, hú him eác hwílum eákiað æfter ðǽm mægenum ðá costunga *crescente virtute plerumque bella tentationis augentur*, Past. 163, 8. Ðonne hié geseóð ðára óðerra gesǽlða eáciende *dum augmenta alienae prosperitatis aspiciunt*, 231, 19. [Cf. *O. H. Ger.* auhhón *augere:* Icel. auka ; *p.* aði.]

**eácnian.** *Add* : I. *to add* :—Þrý eácan synd þe man eácnað tó sumum casum, Ælfc. Gr. Z. 107, 3. II. *to conceive, be pregnant* :—Ðá Maria eácnigende wæs, Hml. Th. i. 42, 2. Ðá eácniendan wíf *praegnantes*, Past. 366, 9. Wá eácniendum *vae praegnantibus*, Mt.

M 2

24, 19. **III.** *to produce, bring forth:*—Eácnaꝺ *parturiet,* Kent. Gl. 341. Eácniendra and elniendra æcera, Lch. i. 402, 5. [Þe beggere ecneꝺ his bode *the buyer increases his offer,* O. E. Hml. ii. 213, 30. *R. Glouc.* ekni. *Goth.* auknan *to be increased.*] v. bearn-eácnigende, -eácnod.

**eácni(g)end-lic;** *adj. To be increased:*—For eácniendlicum *pro augendis,* An. Ox. 1078.

**eácnung.** *Add:* **I.** *increase:*—Eácnunge *supplemento,* i. au(g)mento, An. Ox. 1000. Eácnungum *incrementis,* 3629. **II.** *conceiving, conception,*—Ēcnung *conceptio,* Lk. p. 3, 13. **III.** *bringing forth, birth:*—On ꝺám brýdláce (*the bridal with Christ*) is eácnung būton sāre (cf. in dolore paries filios, Gen. 3, 16), Hml. S. 7, 62. Mid mōꝺerlice cennincge ꝼ eácnuncge *materna matrice,* An. Ox. 1764 : 2, 48. Eácnunga *partum,* Kent. Gl. 1091. Of mēꝺernum eácnungum (*antequam) maternis (ederetur) partubus,* An. Ox. 1487. Of tūdderfullum eácnungum *fetosis partubus (editur),* 2, 161.

**eáꝺ.** *Add:* **I.** *happiness, felicity, prosperity:*—Ne biꝺ him hyra yrmꝺu ān tō wīte, ac ꝼára ōꝺerra eáꝺ tō sorgum, Cri. 1294. Ic ꝼe gōꝺa swā fela forgiefen hæfde, and ꝼē on ꝼām eallum eáꝺes tō lyt ꝼūhte, gif ꝼū meahte spēꝺ efenmicle Gode āgan ne mōste, 1401 : 1199 : Gū. 1165. Forber oft ꝺæt ꝺū wrecan mæge; geꝼyld biꝺ middes eáꝺes, Prov. K. 25. Eáꝺes hleótan, Fä. 89. Þær (*in Paradise*) him nænges wæs eáꝺes onsȳn . . . him bitter wearꝺ yrmꝺu æfter æte, Ph. 398. Næs his frymꝺ æfre, eáꝺes ongyn, 638. Wæs hyra tīres æt ende, eáꝺes and ellendæda, Jud. 273. Þá hyra tȳr and eáꝺ ȳcaꝺ, Rä. 27, 23. **II.** *wealth, riches:*—Siꝺꝺan his eaforan eáꝺ bryttedon . . . him wæs beorht wela, Gen. 1602. Hié eáꝺ bryttedon, oꝺ ꝼæt hié ne meahton leng somed . . . heora bēgra ꝼær æhte habban, 1891. His aferan eáꝺ bryttedon, welan, wunden gold, Dan. 672. Hē lēt weaxan heora eáꝺ and æhta, Gen. 2756. Frumbearnes riht, eáꝺ and æꝼela, Exod. 339. Beorn monig seah on sync, on sylfor, on searogimmas, on eáꝺ, on æht, on eorcanstān, Ruin. 37. Se rinc āgeaf eorꝺcunde eáꝺ (*earthly possessions*), Gen. 1627.

**eáꝺ;** *adj. Substitute:* **eáꝺ;** *adj.* (?):—Ic ꝼe eáꝺ mæg (eáꝺge (-ig) mæg? *or* eáꝺ-mæg, cf. wyn-mæg?) yꝼa gehwylces ōr gecȳꝺe oꝺ ende forꝺ, Jul. 352. On ꝼæt eáꝺe (ealde?) riht *according to the ancient right,* Exod. 186. [Cf. (?) ki-ōter, gi-ōder *praeditus,* ke-aota *beati,* Grff. i. 149.]

**eáꝺan.** *For second passage substitute:*—Þonne is gromra tō fela æfestum eáꝺen hæbbe ic ꝼonne æt freán frōfre *when fate maliciously brings too many foes, then may I have comfort from the Lord,* Hy. 4, 46. *Add:* [*O. Sax.* ōdan : *Icel.* auꝺit [-inn] *granted by fate.*]

**eáꝺgian.** *Substitute:* **eáꝺgian,** eáꝺigan, eáꝺigan; *p.* ode. **I.** *to make happy:*—Hand unhāl wīf seó ꝼe nā eáꝺigaꝺ wer hyre *manus debilis mulier quae non beatificat uirum suum,* Scint. 224, 4. **II.** *to bless, enrich with something (gen.):*—Sē ꝼe eáꝺgaꝺ ūs siges, ōꝺrum forwyrneꝺ wlitigan wilsīꝺes, Cri. 20. **III.** *to call blessed:*—Hī (*the Virgin Mary*) englas eáꝺigaꝺ and ealle ꝼeóꝺa, Hml. A. 136, 690. Heó is ūs tō herianne and tō eáꝺgienne, for ꝼon ꝼe heó eugla ꝼreátas eáꝺige bodedon, Bl. H. 11, 11. [*Goth.* audagjan *to call blessed:* O. H. Ger. gi-ōtagōn *ditare:* Icel.* auꝺga *to make happy; to enrich.*] v. ge-eáꝺgian.

**eáꝺig.** *Add:* **I.** *blessed, happy;*—Eáꝺig is heora (*the Innocents*) yld . . . eáꝺige sind ꝼá innoꝼas ꝼe hī gebǣron, Hml. Th. i. 84, 2, 15. Sē ꝼe gōꝺ biꝼ, sē biꝼ gesǣlig, and sē ꝼe gesǣlig biꝼ, sē biꝼ eáꝺig, Bt. 36, 6; F. 182, 13. Ðis wæs sōꝺlīce eáꝺig wer *uere beatus vir,* Bl. H. 223, 31. Mid eáꝺire forestihtunge *beata praedestinatione,* An. Ox. 1488. Þone eáꝺegan hlīsan *fau(s)tam famam,* Wrt. Voc. ii. 92, 16 : 37, 31. Mē eáꝺige cwǣdon ealle cneórisna, Bl. H. 7, 4. Eáꝺige (*beati*) synt ꝼá gāstlican ꝼearfan, Mt. 5, 3. . . . 11. Se Hǣlend sægde ꝼurh hwæt seó sāul eáꝺegust gewurde, Bl. H. 159, 28. Þ ic sȳ seó eáꝺgoste fǣmne, 6. Eáꝺgeste, 13, 15. **I a.** *as epithet of a sainted person, or of the memory of such:*—Se eáꝺiga Jōhannes, Bl. H. 141, 17. Se eáꝺiga Michael, 30. Se eáꝺiga engel Micahel, 201, 32. Se eáꝺ ga Petrus, 153, 24. Se eáꝺiga apostol Sanctus Petrus, 179, 24. Se eáꝺiga Petrus se apostol, Chr. 35; P. 6, 15. Seó eáꝺige Maria, Bl. H. 11, 14. Seó eáꝺige fǣmne Sancta Maria, 9, 18. ꝼæs eáꝺigan weres Sancte Martines, 211, 14. Be ꝼǣre his (*St. Michael*) eáꝺgan gemynde, 197, 5. **I b.** *as epithet of a special season:*—On ꝼam eáꝺgan dæge . . . Pentecostenes dæg, Chr. 973; P. 118, 10. **II.** *rich, opulent, prosperous:*—ꝼ ǣlc man sȳ folcrihtes wyrꝺe, ge earm ge eáꝺig, Ll. Th. i. 266, 4. Eallum gemǣue, earmum and eáꝺigum, Hml. Th. i. 64, 33. On ōꝺre wīsan mon sceal manian earme, on ōꝺre eáꝺige (*locupletes*=ꝺā welegan *divites,* 181, 3), Past. 175, 14. Þætte ꝼonan ꝺe hī teohhiaꝼ ꝼ hī scylan eáꝺigran weorꝼan, ꝼ hī weorꝼaꝼ ꝺonan earmran and eargran *nam quae sufficientes sibi facere putabantur opes, alieno praesidio faciunt indigentes,* Bt. 26, 2; F. 92, 27. **II a.** *of rank, or position, great.* cf. rīce :—Wæs gesamnad eáꝺigra geꝼeahtendlic ymcyme : ꝼær wæs Birhtwald Bretone heáhbisceop, and se ærnæmda cyning; eác ꝼan Hrōfceastre bisceop andweard wæs; and cwæꝺ ǣlc hād ciricean ꝼǣre mægꝺe ānmōdlīce mid ꝼy hērsuman folcy. Ðær ꝼá eáꝺigan fundon ꝼás dōmas, Ll. Th. l 36, 7-12. v. hlīs-, sēft- (?) eáꝺig.

**eáꝺig-lic.** *Add:*—Godes anweald nǣre full eáꝺiglic (*nec beatum regimen esse videretur*), gif ꝼá gesceafta hiora unwillum him hērden, Bt. 35, 4; F. 160, 18. Him se bisceop eáꝺiglice and hālwendlice geꝺeaht forꝺbrōhte, Bl. H. 205, 18.

**eáꝺig-līce.** *Add: blessedly:*—Eáꝺiglīcur *beatius,* Scint. 156, 8.

**eáꝺig-ness.** *Add:*—On eallum ꝼisum līchamlicum gesǣlignessum men sēcaꝼ ānfealde eáꝺignesse. . . . Ne onsace ic nāuht ꝼ ꝼá gesǣlꝼa and ꝼeó eáꝺignes sié ꝼæt hēhste gōꝺ ꝼises andweardan līfes *quibus omnibus solam beatitudinem desiderare liquet . . . Sed summum bonum beatitudinem esse definivimus,* Bt. 24, 3 ; F. 84, 9-15 : 34, 6 ; F. 142, 7. Sē ꝼe ꝼæt ēce līf begyteꝼ, ꝼon biꝺ ēce eáꝺignes geseald, Bl. H. 97, 30. Seó upplice eáꝺignes, 101, 35. Seó eáꝺignes ꝼæs heáhengles tīde, 197, 3. Éces eáꝺignesse meardo *aeterne beatitudinis premia,* Rtl. 51, 19. Hī wilniaꝼ ꝼurh ungelīce earnunga cuman tō ānre eáꝺignesse *ad unum beatitudinis finem nititur pervenire,* Bt. 24, 1 ; F. 80, 9. Ðæt hālige godspel (Mt. c. 5), geendebyrt ꝼá eahta eáꝺignyssa (*beatitudes*), Hml. Th. i. 548, 9.

**eáꝺ-lufe.** *l.* -lufu: **eáꝺ-mēd-,** -mōd-. v. eáꝼ-mēd-, -mōd-: **eáꝺ-nes.** v. eáꝼ-nes.

**eá-docce.** *Add:*—Eádocca *nimphea,* Wrt. Voc. i. 31, 71. [*v. N. E. D.* edocke.]

**eador-geard.** v. ealdor-geard.

**eáꝺ-wacer.** *Substitute:* **eáꝺ-wacer,** eáꝼ-wacer (?); *adj. Easily roused* (?), *alert, vigilant.* As a proper name, Rā. 1, 16.

**eáꝺ-wēla.** *l.* -wela, *and add:* [*O. Sax.* ōd-welo.]

**eá-fisc.** *Add:*—Ryslas ealra eáfisca, Lch. ii. 30, 1.

**eafor,** es; *m. n.* (?). *The obligation to carry goods and convey messengers, due to the king from a tenant* (?) :—Sit liberatum et absolutum illud monasterium ab illis causis quas *cumfeorme* et *eafor* uocitemus . . . ab omni illa incommoditate *aefres* et *cumfeorme* nisi istis causis quas hic nominamus : praecones si trans mare uenirent ad regem uenturi, uel nuncii . . . de gente Northanhymbrorum . . . si uenirent supra nonam horam, tunc dabitur eis noctis pastum, et iterum de mane pergent in uiam suam, C. D. ii. 30, 33-36, 9. Cf. Erat antea in illo monasterio pastus unius noctis regi . . . et quicquid rex uellet inde ducere usque ad Curig . . . cum plaustris et equis, et si aduenae de aliis regionibus aduenirent debebant ducatum habere ad aliam regalem uillam quae proxima fuisset in illorum via, v. 159, 3-11. v. aferian, *and see* Sax. Engl. i. pp. 294 sqq., *N. E. D.* aver ; *sb.* 3.

**eafora.** *Add: gen. pl.* eafora (?) :—Eáꝺmundes eafora, Chr. 973; P. 118, 22 : B. 2358. Sethes eafora se yldesta, Gen. 1133. Eafora æfter yldrum, 1129. Of idese biꝺ eafora wæcned, 2392. Is his eafora (-an, MS.) heard hēr cumen, B. 375. Þám eafera wæs æfter cenned, 12. Zebedes afera, Men. 136. Afera (afora, eafora, *v.ll.*) Eádweardes, Chr. 942; P. 110, 24. Ne ꝼearf ꝼē ꝼæs eaforan sceonigan, Gen. 2327 : B. 2451. Hē ꝼám yldestan eáforan lǣfde folc, frumbearne, Gen. 1214. Ne ꝼearf ic yrfestōl eaforan bytlian ǣnigum mīnra (*for any child of mine*), 2176. Cniht, eaforan ꝼīnne, 2915. Sunu, eaforan geongne, An. 1112. Hire bearn, āngan eaferan, B. 1547. Aferan, Chr. 975; P. 121, 3. His eaforan wōcan, bearn from brȳde, Gen. 1061. Eaferan, B. 2475. Aforan, Gen. 967. Aferan, Dan. 672. Afaran (eaforan, aforan, eoforan, *v. ll.*), Chr. 937; P. 106, 15. Hē bearna strȳnde him byras wōcan eafora (*n. pl. parallel* to byras, *or gen. pl. parallel* to bearna?) and idesa, Gen. 1234. Nǣfre gerēfan rǣdaꝼ ꝼīne eafora yrfe, 2187. Lǣd eaforan ꝼīne, frumgāran ꝼrȳ, 1333. Idesa eaforan brōhtan heora ealdan fæder, 2606.

**eafor-heáfod-segn.** v. eofor, II.

**eafoꝼ.** *Add:*—Eafoꝺes cræftig, B. 1466. Nū is ꝼīnes mægnes blǣd ; eft sōna biꝼ ꝼæt ꝼec ādl oꝺꝺe ecg eafoꝺes getwǣfeꝺ, 1763. Wē frēcne genēꝺdon eafoꝺ uncūꝺes ; ūꝺe ic ꝼæt ꝼū hine selfne geseón mōste, 960. Hine God mægenes wynnum, eafeꝺum stēpte, 1717. Cf. afol.

**eá-gang.** *Dele, and see* gang.

**eág-brǣw,** es ; *m. The eye-lid:*—Mid ꝼá eágbrǣwas, Lch. i. 352, 6. [*v. N. E. D.* eye-bree. *O. H. Ger.* oug-brāwa *palpebra.*]

**eág-dūru.** *l.* -duru, *and add:*—Glád ꝼæt deófol ūt swā swā smȳc æt his eágdura, Shrn. 52, 33. Geseah hē sittan ꝺone Hālgan Gāst on culfran hīwe on ꝺæs carcernes eágdura, 54, 15. Þurh ꝼá eágduru, 78, 27. [*Goth.* auga-dauro : *O. H. Ger.* oug-tora *fenestra.*]

**eáge.** *Add:* eáge, es :—Eáge yfel *oculus malus,* Scint. 102, 15. On prince eáges *in ictu oculi,* 43, 16. Hī ne mōston cuman on his eágon gesihꝺe, Chr. 1048; P. 174, 10. Þū gesāwe mot on ꝼīnes brōꝺ ur eáge, and ne gesāwe cyp on ꝼīnum āgenum eágan, R. Ben. 12, 4. Fram ꝼám swȳdran næsꝼyrle oꝺ hit cōm tō ꝼám eáge, Hml. A. 181, 8. Wiꝼ eágna ece, Lch. ii. 34, 14. Egna *occellorum,* Wrt. Voc. ii. 64, 44. Ægna (ætna, MS.), 92, 27. Þá sūrigan eágan *lippos oculos,* 22. v. cū-eáge.

**-eáge** (-ēge, -īge). v. an-, glæsen-, niht-, sceolh-, siwen-, sūr-, toren-eáge (-ēge, -īge). [*O. L. Ger.* -ōgi : *O. H. Ger.* -ougi : *Icel.* -eygr.]

**eág-ece.** *Add:*—Wiꝼ miclum eágece, Lch. ii. 32, 4, 10 : 34, 11.

**-eágede.** v. ān-, sceolh-, sūr-eágede.

**eág-fleáh;** *n. Add:*—Eágfleá *albugo,* Wrt. Voc. i. 43, 63 : ii. 6, 37 : *macilia,* 55, 60.

eág-gemearc, es; n. Limit fixed by sight:—Eal ꝥ ús þincð ǽmtig eáhgemearces all that seems to us empty as far as the eye can reach; quo aer gremium diffundit inane, Dóm. L. 148. [Cf. N. E. D. eye-mark.]

eág-hill. l. -hyll, and add:—Eághyll from þǽm ognoran glebenus, Wrt. Voc. ii. 42, 7.

eág-hlid (?), es; n. An eye-lid [:—Égælid palpebrae, Ælfc. Gr. Z. 298, 4 note (12th cent.). Ase þin ehelid tuneð ant openeð, O. E. Hml. i. 265, 5.]

eág-hringas. Substitute: eág-hring, es; m. The socket of the eye; also the pupil:—Éhringa pupillarum, Hpt. Gl. 405, 68. Éghringum (eáhringum, lxxiv, 7) rotis, Lch. i. lxx, 6. Eáhringum oculorum orbibus, An. Ox. 4686: 3690. Þá eágan wǽron út ádyde of þám eáhhringum, Hml. S. 21, 280. His blód geglende míne eáhhringas, 7, 48. Se Hǽlend ðá ungesceapenan eáhhringas (of the man born blind) mid his hǽlwendan spátle geopenode, Hml. Th. i. 474, 8.

eág-mist, es; m. Dimness of the eye:—Wið eágna miste ... þis tódrífþ þá eáhmistas þeáh þe hié þicce synd, Lch. ii. 30, 9.

eágor. v. égor: eago-spind. v. hago-spind.

eág-sealf. Add:—Ðis is seó séleste eáhsalf wið ēhwærce, Lch. i. 374, 1. Ðeós eáhsealf mæg wiþ ǽlces cynnes broc on eágon, iii. 292, 1 : 4, 4. His man brúceþ on eágsealfe, i. 334, 4. Ðis mæg tó eáhsalfe, 374, 14. Nim þær góde eáhsealfe, iii. 292, 15, 18. Éhsealfe malagma, i. colirium, An. Ox. 3051. Éhsealue, 2, 141. Heáhsealuæ, 7, 224. Eágsealfe colliria, Wrt. Voc. i. 20, 24. [O. H. Ger. oug-salba collyrium.]

eág-seóung. Add: cataract:—Eágsióng glaucoma, Wrt. Voc. ii. 92, 21. Eágs(eó)ung, 78, 18. Eágseóung, 41, 34.

eág-séung. Dele: eág-sȳne (-síne). Add: [O. H. Ger. oug-siuni evidens: cf. oug-siunig evidens: Icel. aug-sȳniligt evident.] v. next word.

eág-sínes; adv. With one's eyes, ocularly, evidently:—Swilce ic hine mid mínan eágan eáhsȳnes beheólde as if I beheld him plainly with my eyes, Hml. S. 23, 828. Hé geseah ēhsȳnes þæs lifigendan Godes sunu and hine gecneów, Hml. Th. ii. 18, 20. [v. N. E. D. eye-sene. O. H. Ger. oug-siuni vultus, species : Icel. aug-sȳn sight : cf. O. H. Ger. oug-siuno evidenter, ad liquidum : Icel. aug-sȳniliga evidently, visibly.]

eág-þyrl. Add:—Éhðyrl fenestra, Wrt. Voc. i. 81, 10. Næs duru ontȳned, ne eáhþyrl geopened, Shrn. 99, 7. Heofones eáhþerl, Hy. S. 76, 7. Æt ðǽm eáhðyrle, Hml. Th. ii. 178, 29 : 184, 27. On ánum ēgðyrle, Hml. S. 31, 1126. Þurh þæt eáhþyrl (ēgðyrl, v.l.) ... under þám ylcan eáhþyrle (ēh-, v.l.), Gr. D. 159, 21, 25. Ontȳnde se bysceop ꝥ eágþyrl (eágh-, eáh-, eághþyrel, v. ll.), Bd. 4, 3; Sch. 355, 22 : 5, 12; Sch. 623, 11. Ehta eágþyrelu of glæse geworht ... þá leóhtfatu scínaþ þurh þá eágþyrelo, Bl. H. 127, 33, 36. Swá swá culfran tó heora ēhðyrlum ... Úre ēhðyrla sind úre eágan, Hml. Th. i. 584, 28, 32. Þurh ðá ēghþyrl (-þyrla, eághþyrelu, v. ll.), Bd. 4, 7 ; Sch. 388, 5. [v. N. E. D. eye-thurl.]

eág-wræc, -wærc, es; m. (not n.). Add:—Eáhsalf wið ēhwærce, Lch. i. 374, 1. Eáhsealf wið eáhwyrce, iii. 4, 5. [Cf. Icel. augna-verkr pain in the eye.]

eág-wund, e; f. A wound in the eye:—Be monnes eáhwunde ... Gif mon men eáge of ásleá, Ll. Th. i. 94, 1. Eáhwunda egilopia (uulnera oculorum, lxv, 10), Lch. i. lxi, 10 ; Hpt. 31, 9, 180.

eaht. Substitute: eaht, æht, eht, es ; m. I. council, deliberation:—Þonne úðweotan æht besǽton (sat deliberating), on sefan sóhton hú hié sunu Meotudes áhēngon, El. 473. II. estimation, consideration:—Bið ðæt ædeleste híw onhworfen, ðonne se æht ðára gódra weorca ðe hé ǽr beeóde bið gewanod color optimus commutatur, cum quorundam, qui degere religiose credebantur, aestimatio anteacto minuitur, Past. 133, 23. Hwæt is mannes sunu, þæt hit gemet wǽre, þæt þú him aht (äht ?) wið ǽfre hæfdest quid est filius hominis, quoniam reputas eum ?, Ps. Th. 143, 4. Ne gewuna wyrsa(n) ǽngum eahta (gen. pl. cf. ǽnige þinga) don't make a companion of an inferior on any consideration, Fä. 24. III. reckoning, valuation :—Micel ígland, ðǽr synt syx hund hȳda æfter Angelcynnes æhte (juxta consuetudinem aestimationem Anglorum), Bd. i. 25 ; Sch. 52, 2. v. æht, eht in Dict., and ymbeaht.

eahta. Add: I. as adjective:—Eahta eádignyssa synd ... þá eahta eádignyssa belimpað tó mannum, Hml. Th. i. 554, 9, 13. Eahta (ehta, v. l.) hund míla lang, Bd. 1, 1 ; Sch. 8, 2. Ehta (æhto, L., æhtowe, R.) dagas, Lk. 2, 21. Æfter eahta (æhtuo, L., dæge æhtowum, R.) dagum, Jn. 20, 26. Æfter dagum æhtuu, p. 8, 6. Æhtu ōra seulfres, p. 188, 9. Eahtu and ðritðeih uintra .xxxviii. annos, p. 4, 8. II. as substantive:—Ðá tēno and ðá æhtou (æhtowe, R.) illi decem et octo, Lk. 13, 4. Mid feáwum bróþrum, ꝥ is seofonum oðða æhtum (eahtum, v. l., þæt wǽron seofon oðða eahta, v. l.), Bd. 4, 3 ; Sch. 351, 7. Ne weard má þonne him eahtum, Angl. xi. 2, 39. Cf. seofon.

eahta-feald ; adj. Eightfold :—Þurh ðá eádignyssa þæs eahtafealdan geteles, Hml. A. 45, 528. Ehtafealdum octenis, An. Ox. 3716. Hehtefealde bis quaternos, 774.

eahta-hyrnede ; adj. Eight-cornered, octagonal :—Seó cyrce wæs eahtahyrnede, Hml. Th. ii. 496, 33.

eáhtan. Substitute the two following words:

eahtan to estimate, appreciate :—Wile fæder eahtan hú gesunde suna sáwle bringen of þám ēðle þe hí on lifdon the father will estimate how sound the sons bring their souls from the land where they lived, Cri. 1074. Þæt wē magon eahtan (this point we can appreciate) ... þæt se sáwle weard lífes wísdóm forloren hæbbe, sē þe nú ne gíemeð hwæðer his gǽst sié earm þe eádig, 1550. v. eahtian.

eahtan to persecute, pursue :—Brægdwís bona eahteð ánbūendra, Gú. 59. Swá sceal ōretta Gode compian and his gǽst beran on ondan þám þe eahtan wile sáwla gehwylcre, 317. v. eahtend, eahtness; ēhtan.

eahta-nihte ; adj. Eight days old :—Se eahtanihta mōna, Lch. iii. 178, 14.

eahta-teóða. Add:—Se eahtateóða octavus decimus, Ælfc. Gr. Z. 283, 5. On þone eahtategþan dæg, Shrn. 71, 5 : 92, 7. Eahtateogðan, 85, 23. Eahtategeþan, 105, 22.

eahta-tȳne. -tí(é)ne. Add:—Eahtatȳne decem et octo, Ælfc. Gr. Z. 281, 14. Eahtatiéne sexies terna, Wrt. Voc. ii. 85, 78. Þreó wǽron ofslagene tó deáðe and eahteteóne gewundade, Chr. 1083 ; P. 215, 20. Þeós smerenes wæs geworht of ehtaiēne cynna wyrtum, Bl. H. 73, 20. Gif þú dēst twelf tó þám eahtatȳnum epactum, Angl. viii. 301, 21. v. ehta-tȳne in Dict.

eahta-wintre ; adj. Eight years old :—Sanctus Iustus wæs .viii. wintre þá hē martyrdōm þrowode, Shrn. 139, 17. Ðá ðá hē wæs eahtawintre cild, Hml. Th. ii. 134, 3.

eahtend ; m. A persecutor :—Mē syndon eahtend ungemete neáh appropiaverunt persequentes me, Ps. Th. 118, 150. v. eahtan and cf. ēhtend.

eahtend-líc. v. ge-eahtendlíc.

eahtere, es ; m. A valuer :—Echtheri censor, rimator, pretiator, Txts. 110, 1167. Æhtere aestimator, Wrt. Voc. i. 61, 6.

eahtian. Add: I. to deliberate, consider :—Aecta[t]h, aechtath, aehtað perpendit, Txts. 88, 836. II. to estimate, fix the character, quality of something :—Hē suíðe ungemetlíce eahtað eall ðæt him ǽr gedón wæs, and hit suíðe unáberendlíc talað cuncta, quae sibi illata sunt, vehementer exaggerans intolerabilia ostendit, Past. 227, 17. Eahtige hé hine selfne on his inngeðonce suelcne suelcne hé ondrætt ðæt hē sié servent interius quod de sua aestimatione pertimescunt, 119, 8. Ðætte hié mægen geteóu ðurh ðá eahtunge ðe hié mon eahtige hira níehstan tó ðǽre sóðfæstnesse lufan ut suae aestimationis dulcedine proximos in affectum veritatis trahant, 147, 8. Ðȳ lǽs hié eahtigen óðerra monna dǽda (cf. that hi ahtóie óðres mannes saka, endi habad im selbo mēr firinwerkō gefrumid, Hēl. 1716), and forgieten hié selfe ne insequentes aliorum facta se deserant, 371, 3. Wē þæt hȳrdon hæleð eahtian, dēman áðdhwate, þætte in dagum gelamp Maximianes, Jul. 1. Þæs bisceopes líf swá swíðe swá mannum riht is tó eahtienne (eht-, æht-, v. ll.) uitam illius quantum hominibus aestimare fas est, Bd. 5, 6 ; Sch. 573, 21. [O. Frs. achtia : O. Sax. ahtôn : O. H. Ger. ahtôn putare, censere perpendere, deliberare, computare, judicare.] v. ge-eahtian; eahtan.

eáht-ness. l. eaht-ness, and add :—Þæt wē mid geþylde earfeþa and eahtnesse (eht-, v. l.) þolien, R. Ben. 6, 2. Cf. ēht-ness.

eahtoþa. Add:—Se eahteoða (-oþa, -eþa, eht-, v. ll.) octauus, Ælfc. Gr. Z. 282, 18. On ðone sextan dæg þæs mōnðes bið þára apostola eahtæþa dæg, Shrn. 100, 11. Þæt eahteoðe bebod, Hml. Th. ii. 208, 26. On ðám eahteoðan dæge, 68, 31 : i. 554, 11, 17.

eahtung. Add:—Æhtungc aestimatio, Wrt. Voc. i. 61, 7. Þ bið seó sóðe æhtung þæs mannes lifes in þám mægne his gódra weorca, nalæs in æteównysse þára foretácna vitae vera aestimatio in virtute est operum, non in ostensione signorum, Gr. D. 90, 29. Ðurh ðá eahtunge ðe hié mon eahtige suae aestimationis dulcedine, Past. 147, 8. [O. H. Ger. ahtunga opinio, existimatio.]

eal, eal-. v. eall, eall-.

eálá. Add:—Eálá ðú láreów O magister ... eálá, gif hē gecyrde intó ðǽre byrig þro, si remeasset in urbem, Ælfc. Gr. Z. 280, 4-8. Eálá reówlic tíd wæs þæs geáres, Chr. 1086 ; P. 218, 26. Eálá hú leás is þysses middaneardes wela, 219, 6. Eálá men þá leófestan, mycel wæs þes ǽrendwreca, Bl. H. 9, 12. Eáwlá, Ps. Srt. 117, 25.

eá-land. Add:—Delo(s) swá hwæt þæt eáland, Wrt. Voc. ii. 89, 2. Eálondes insule, Rtl. 55, 26. Claudius þone mǽstan dǽl þæs eálondes onfēng, and eác swelce Orcadus þá eálond Rōmána cynedōme underþeódde, Chr. 47 ; P. 6, 22-25. On Híí þám eálande, 565 ; P. 18, 11. Hié genámon Wihte eáland, 530 ; P. 16, 6. v. neáh-eáland.

eald. Add: I. of great age. (1) of living creatures :—Ald senex, Wrt. Voc. ii. 120, 47. Hú mæg man beón eft ácenned þonne hē bið eald (ald, L. R.)?, Jn. 3, 4. Ic eom eald tó híwigenne I am (too) old to pretend, Hml. S. 25, 94. Þá cyld ... and eác ðá ealdan ceorlas, Bt. 36, 5 ; F. 180, 7. Wín nys drenc cilda, ac ealdra (senum), Coll. M. 35, 21. Ealdra cwēna spell anilis fabula, Wrt. Voc. i. 55, 24. Ic lǽre ge geonge ge ealde, Bl. H. 107, 11. (1 a) used substantively:—Ongan seó leó fægnian wið þæs ealdan weard, Hml. S. 23 b, 778. (2) of material things :—

Sylle hé earmum mannum his ealde hrægl, Bl. H. 53, 13.    **I a.** *where two people of the same name or of the same office are distinguished by difference of age* :—Sidroc eorl se alda and Sidroc eorl se gioncga, Chr. 871 ; P. 70, 25. Forðférde seó ealde hlǽfdige, Eádwerdes cinges móder, 1051 ; P. 172, 32.    **I b.** *of long experience* in :—Presbiter is ealdwita ; nā þ ǽlc eald sý, ac þ hé eald sý on wísdóme, Ll. Th. ii. 348, 21.    **II.** *of (a certain) age* :—Ðæt cild þ ne wæs ánre nihte eald, Shrn. 142, 33. Byð se móna feówertýne nihta eald, Angl. viii. 326, 8 : Lch. iii. 182, 10 (and often). On ánre nihte ealdne mónan, 5.    **III.** *that belongs to a time long past* :—Sume sǽdon eald wítega (*propheta unus de antiquis*) árās, Lk. 9, 8. On þā ealdan wísan *antiquitus*, An. Ox. 4243. Þāra ealdena treówa *antiquorum foederum*, Ors. 2, 5 ; S. 82, 18. Ealdra manna byrgenu, Hml. Th. ii. 258, 26. On ealdum dagum, 11. Swā se wudu on ældum tímum (*antiquis temporibus*) gelægd wæs, C. D. iv. 202, 13.    **IV.** *that dates from a time long past* :—Se ealda cwide þe mon gefyrn cwæþ, Bt. 14, 2 ; F. 44, 11.    **V.** *that has lasted long* :—Fióndes aldes *hostis antiqui*, Rtl. 95, 14. Hé gefylde þone ealdan feónd, Bl. H. 87, 19.    **VI.** *where difference of date is marked, old as opposed to new, earlier, former* :—Hlóþwíg wæs þæs aldan Carles sunu, Chr. 885 ; P. 80, 3 : 982 ; P. 124, 32. Tó ðæs cynges dómerne Heródes ; sé wæs þæs ealdan Heródes suna sunu, Hml. Th. ii. 422, 1. Ǽaldere gesuntfulnessa *pristinae incolomitate*, An. Ox. 11, 148. Cýþnesse ealdre *testamenti ueteris*, An. Ox. 40, 2. Aldes, Rtl. 113, 22.    **VI a.** *great-, grand-* in terms denoting relationship, v. eald(e)-fæder, -móder :—Ealda fæder *avus*, Wrt. Voc. i. 72, 20. Ealde fæder, 51, 51. Ealde móder *avia*, 51, 54. Bearn Ælfrices ... cwæð ... ' Wæs mín ealda fæder Ealhelm háten, By. 218. Ruth weard geǽwnod Iessan ealdan fæder (*Boaz was Jesse's grandfather*), Ælfc. T. Grn. 6, 32. Eádmund is byrged mid his ealdan fæder Eádgār, Chr. 1016 ; P. 153, 12. [On Willelmes kinges dege mínes furþur ealdefader, and Henrices (*Henry I*) kinges mines (*Henry II*) ealdefader, Angl. vii. 220, 8. He wes Mærwales fader, Mildburʒe aldefader, Laym. 31009. Of hir fader and of hir eldefadir, Chauc. Boeth. 40, 1042. *O. Frs.* alde-, ald-fader.]    **VII.** *that has been done (habitually) before* :—Seó gnornung is mé eald for gewunan, Gr. D. 4, 7. Man hine gehádede efter þan ealdan gewunan, Chr. 1070 ; P. 204, 8. Healdaþ þā tunglu þā ealdan sibbe ðe hí on gesceapene wǽron, Bt. 39, 13 ; F. 232, 26. Þ hé hine ne besió tó his ealdum yfelum, 35, 6 ; F. 170, 18. Hé teáh forð his ealdan wrenceas *he brought out his old tricks*, Chr. 1003 ; P. 135, 11.    **VIII.** *denoting rank or position, an elder, great (man), chief* person :—Ælda ðæs folces *seniores populi*, Mt. L. 21, 23. Ðā aldu (ældo, L.) *pharisaei*, Mk. R. 2, 16 : 7, 1. Ðā aldo, Mt. L. 16, 1. Ðā aeldo, Lk. L. 7, 30. Ðā alde wearas, Jn. R. 4, 1. Æfter gesetnisse ældra (*seniorum*), Mk. L. R. 7, 5. From ældum *a senioribus*, 8, 31. v. niht-eald ; ildra, ildest, *and* eald-*cpds.*

**eald-a-wered.** v. á-werian.

**eald-bacen** ; *adj. Baked long ago* :—Behealde hé þ his oflétan ne beón ealdbacene, Ll. Th. ii. 360, 27.

**eald-cot.** v. cot : eald-cwén. *Dele.*

**eald-cýþþ[u].** *Add :* **I.** *old (native) country* :—Conon gelende tó Ahténa þǽre byrig, his ealdcýþþe, Ors. 3, 1 ; S. 98, 24.    **II.** *old acquaintance* :—Þā bǽdon ðā cwelleras for heora ealdcýððe þ hí móston him beran unforboden flǽsc, Hml. S. 25, 90.

**eald-dagas.** *Add :*—Be ðām ðe hit of ealddagum witan geræddan, Angl. ix. 259, 6. Þ hié gemunden þāra ealdena treówa ... þe hié hæfdon ... ær on ealddagum, Ors. 2, 5 ; S. 82, 20. On ealddagum wæs ān hús árǽred Gode tó lofe binnan þǽre byrig Gerusalem, Wlfst. 277, 13.

**ealde-móder** *a grandmother.* Cf. eald, VI a :—For mínes leófan fæder sáwle and for mínre ealdemódor *for my dear father's soul and for my grandmother's,* Cht. Th. 562, 27. Þone bule ðe wæs hire ealdermóder, 548, 8. [*O. Frs.* ald-móder (alde móder *according to Richthofen is more correct than* alde-móder).]

**eald-fæder,** ealde-fæder. *Substitute the two following :*

**ealde-fæder** *a grandfather.* Cf. eald, VI a :—On Arcestrates cyneríce his ealdefæder, Ap. Th. 28, 9. Se cing Eádmund ys bebyrged mid his ealdefæder Eádgāre, Chr. 1016 ; P. 153, 22.

**eald-fæder** *an ancestor ;* in pl. *fathers, forefathers* :—Ealdfædera cnósle *auita stirpe,* An. Ox. 1600. Þu forðfærst tó þinum ealdfæderum *tu ibis ad patres tuos,* Gen. 15, 15. Swā hé behét hira ealdfæderum (*patribus eorum*), Jos. 21, 41. [Hir aldfadir cal I Adam, Met. Hml. 122, 17. *O. Sax.* ald-fader (*Abraham*) ; *O. H. Ger.* alt-fater (*Adam*) ; in pl. *the pa'riarchs.*]

**eald-feónd.** *Add :* [*O. H. Ger.* alt-fiant *the devil.*]

**eald-gefá,** an ; *m. An old foe* :—Métte hiene his ealdgefāna sum and hiene otstang, Ors. 3, 7 ; S. 118, 34.

**eald-geféra,** an ; *m. An old comrade* :—Hié hæfdon þritig cyninga ofslagen heora āgenra ealdgeférena, Ors. 3, 11 ; S. 152, 24.

**eald-geriht,** es ; *n. Ancient right* :—Waldon ðā swāngeréfan ðā lǽswe foður gedrífan ... ðonne hit aldgeryhta wéron, Chh. Th. 70, 22. v. eald-riht.

**eald-gestreón.** *Add :*—Þæt wæs ān ealdgestreóna, B. 1458. Hié

ne ūþon þ hiera fiénd tó hiera ealdgestreónum féngon, Ors. 5, 3 ; S. 222, 11. Brond ǽleð ealdgestreón, Cri. 813.

**eald-gewyrht.** *Substitute :* **I.** *what has been done of old, a deed of old :*—Wuldres beám þe God on þrowode for mancynnes manegum synnum and for Adames ealdgewyrhtum, Kr. 100.    **II.** *what has been deserved of old, desert for deeds of old* :—Ic wât geare þæt nǽron ealdgewyrht þæt hé āna scyle gnorn þrowian *I know well that for past deeds he has not deserved to suffer sorrow alone,* B. 2657.

**eald-hláford.** *Substitute: An old lord, a lord whose right to rule is of ancient date, a rightful, liege lord* :—Hiera ealdhláfordes sunu *regis filium,* Ors. 3, 11 ; S. 148, 33. Hwelce hláfordhylda hí þóhton tó gecýþanne on hiora ealdhláfordes bearnum, 6, 37 ; S. 296, 5. Dauid cearf læppan of Saules mentle his ealdhláfordes, Past. 199, 11. Bill ǽr gescód ealdhláfordes (*Beowulf's, who was Wiglaf's liege lord*) þām þāra māðma mundbora (*the fire-drake*). Cf. weard unhióre goldmādmas heóld, 2413) wæs, B. 2778. Hé gemunde þāra ealdrihta ðe hí under ðām Cāserum hæfdon heora ealdhláfordum, Bt. 1 ; F. 2, 17 : Met. 1, 63.

**ealdhláford-cynn,** es ; *n. The old royal family, the rightful royal line* :—Se cāsere wæs heora ealdhláfordcynnes, Bt. 1 ; F. 2, 22.

**eald-hríþer** (?) *an old ox* :—Æt .x. hídum tó fóstre ... tú ealdhríðeru (eald hríðeru ? .ii. ealde hrýðeru, twā ealda rýðeru, twā ealda rýðeru, *v. ll.*) oþþe .x. weðeras, Ll. Th. i. 146, 17. iiii. aldhryðra, Shrn. 159, 9. v. next word.

**eald-hryter-flǽsc.** *l.* eald hrýþerflǽc (v. Angl. viii. 451) = ealdhrýþer-flǽsc ? *or* eald hrýþerflǽsc ? v. preceding word.

**ealdian.** *Add :* **I.** *to grow old, be old* :—Ic wæs geong and nū ic ealdige *junior fui, etenim senui,* Ps. Th. 36, 24. Ðonne hé ealdað *cum senuerit,* Kent. Gl. 815. Þonne se sunu wyxð, þonne ealdað se fæder, Hml. Th. i. 278, 25. Ic aldade *senui,* Ps. Srt. 36, 25. Ðā ðā hé ealdode, and his sunu wífian sceolde, Hml. Th. ii. 234, 24. Siððan hé ealdode (*jam persenilis aetatis*), Jos. 23, 1 : Hml. S. 25, 246 : Shrn. 145, 20. Mon sceal on eorðan geong ealdian, Gn. Ex. 8. Ðæs ealdigendan mannes mægen bið wanigende, Hml. Th. ii. 76, 21.    **I a.** *to grow old in a pursuit, continue long* :—On weorce beboda þínra ealda *in opere mandatorum tuorum veteresce,* Scint. 90, 9.    **II.** *to grow feeble with age, or as with age, be worn out with age, decay* :—Se líchoma ealdaþ and his fægernes gewíteþ, Bl. H. 57, 29 : Seef. 89. Fultum heora aldað (*veterascet*), Ps. Srt. 48, 15. Seáðo ðā ðe ne aldagiað (aldigað, R. *ueterescunt*), Lk. L. 12, 33. Ic ealdode (*inveteravi*) betweox feóndum mínum, Ps. Spl. 6, 7. Þe lǽs þe hí þurh eorþlice dǽda ā ealdodon (āealdodon ?: hí ne ealdodon nǽfre, *v. l.*) fram hyra módes níwnysse *ne per humanos actus a novitate mentis veterascerent,* Gr. D. 6, 32. Aldadon bān mín *inveteraverunt ossa mea,* Ps. Srt. 31, 3. Þā cyricsangas ðe mid langre gýmeleásnesse ealdian (-igan, *v. l.*) ongunnon *carmina ecclesiastica, quae longo usu ne negligentia inueterare coeperunt,* Bd. 5, 20 ; Sch. 675, 9. Sele sceal stondan, sylf ealdian, Gn. Ex. 158. [*v. N. E. D.* old ; *vb. O. H. Ger.* altēn *senescere, antiquare.*] v. ge-, on-ealdian ; æt-ealdod.

**eald-land,** es ; *n. Old-land, land that has remained long untilled* : (cf. *old-land* ground that has lain untilled a long time and is now ploughed up ; arable land which has been laid down in grass more than two years. D. D.) :—Feówer æceras be-westan exan fornāgeán Eádferðes ealdlande, C. D. iii. 411, 28.

**eald-letre,** Wrt. Voc. ii. 2, 57. v. next word.

**eald-lic.** *Add :* **I.** *proper for mature years, of the character that should belong to age* :—Cildlic on geárum and ealdlic on móde, Hml. S. 7, 9. Sé of þære tíde his cnihthádes wæs berende ealdlíce heortan (*cor gerens senile*), Gr. D. 95, 1. Biscopum gebirað ealdlíce wísan, Ll. Th. ii. 318, 29.    **II.** *belonging to early times, original, authentic* (?) :—Mid ealdlecre (*printed* -letre, *but for* -lec =-lic v. ll. 1, 12 *on same page*) autentica *veterum* (*the passage glossed is :* Authentica veterum auctoritate, Ald. 35, 26. Cf. An. Ox. 2597 *which has:* authentica .i. auctoritate plena mid heálicum ; *so perhaps* ealdlic *should be rendered* authoritative. Cf. eald, VIII), Wrt. Voc. ii. 2, 57. [Cf. Oxe aldelike lateþþ *behaves with gravity,* Orm. 1229. Full aldeliʒ to fraʒʒnenn *with all proper seriousness to ask,* 2553.]

**eald-móder.** *Dele, and see* ealde-móder.

**eald-ness** *old age. Add :*—Seó endlyfte tíd bið seó forwerode ealdnyss, þām deáðe geneálǽcende ... Sume beóð gelǽdde tó rihtum lífe on forweroдre ealdnysse, Hml. Th. ii. 76, 21-26. Ealdnesse *vetustatem,* R. Ben. I. 91, 16.

**ealdor.** *Dele bracket at end, and add :* **I.** *one occupying a position of superiority.* (1) *of human beings.* (a) *one (man or woman) having authority over others.* (α) *of public authority* :—Manna ealdor *tribunus,* þusendes ealdor *ciliarcus,* fíftiga ealdor *quinquagenarius,* fíf hund cempena ealdor *princeps,* Wrt. Voc. i. 18, 8, 10, 13, 14. Ic eom ealdor and lätteów Drihtnes heres *sum princeps exercitus Domini,* Jos. 5, 14. Geneálǽhte ān ealdor (*princeps*), Mt. 9, 18. Æþered Myrcena ealdor (cf. Æþered ealdormon, 894 ; P. 87, 14), Chr. 910 ; P. 95, 4. Ðā wæs hyre gecýd þe ðǽr ealdor wæs, Ap. Th. 23, 11. Ealdre *tribuno,* An. Ox.

2523: *chiliarco*, 2, 379. Ealdor *monarchum*, i. *dominatorem*, 3906. Aldur *dictatorem*, Wrt. Voc. ii. 106, 15. On Iuda ealdrum *in principibus Iuda*, Mt. 2, 6. (β) *of domestic authority, head* of a household (applied to man or woman):—Sarai . . . is gereht, ' Mín ealdor,' ac God hi hêt syððan Sarra, þæt is, 'Ealdor,' þæt heó nǽre synderlíce hire híredes ealdor gecíged, ac forðrihte ' Ealdor,' þæt is tó understandenne ealra gelýfedra wífa móder, Hml. Th. i. 92, 16–20. (γ) *of marital authority*:—Bútan þám wífe, forþon heó sceal hire ealdore (ealdre, hláforde, *v. ll.*) hiéran, Ll. Th. i. 138, 18. (δ) *of ecclesiastical authority*:—Se ealdor (aldor, L.) þǽra sácerda *princeps sacerdotum*, Mt. 26, 62. Hé wæs mænig geár ealdor þæs mynstres *annis multis monasterio praefuit*, Gr. D. 96, 9. Geworhtum beácne fram þám ealdre *facto signo a priore*, R. Ben. 46, 3. Sýn þá ealdras (*decani*) swylce gecorene, þæt se abbod his byrðenna on hý tódǽlan mæge, 12. Gesetton cyricena aldoras þ fæsten, Bl. H. 35, 7. Sume men forhogiað þ hí hýran godcundan ealdran, Ll. Th. i. 332, 34. Ealderas *seniores*, R. Ben. 18, 23. (b) *an authority, a master* in a subject, *one having superior knowledge*:—Þysse wyrte onfundelnysse manega ealdras geseðað, Lch. i. 140, 10. (2) *of superhuman beings*:—On þone aldor deófla, Bl. H. 83, 23. Gehýrstú, úre aldor?, 85, 18, 29. þæt ðǽra ðeóstra ealdras mē ne geméton, Hml. Th. i. 76, 4. (3) *of things, the chief, principal of its kind, head*:—Seó Níl is ealdor fallicra (ful-?) eá *Nilus est caput fluuiorum*, Nar. 35, 19. II. *a parent.* v. ealdor-leás *orphan*:—Cóm ǽrest Cam in síðian, eafora Nóes, þær his aldor læg, Gen. 1578. Þín aldor *thy father*, Dan. 754. Se ǽresta ealdor þisses menniscan cynnes *Adam*, Bl. H. 23, 4. Eardcundes aldores *terreni parentis*, Rtl. 33, 36. III. *an author, source*:—Hé Martinum wurðode, for þan ðe hé wæs ealdor his hǽle, Hml. S. 31, 526. III a. *a primitive, that from which something is derived*:—*Rex* cyning is frumcenned nama, and *regalis* cymð of þám and hæfð ealle þá ðing þe his ealdor hæfð, Ælfc. Gr. Z. 245, 4. [v. N. E. D. alder. *O. Frs.* alder *parent*.] v. bisceop-, burg-, camp-, dryht-, heáh-, teóþung-ealdor, *and cpds. with* ealdor-.

**ealdor** *eternity. Add*:—In écnisse ł in aldre *in sempiternum*, Mt. L. 21, 19.

**ealdor-bisceop.** *Add: a chief priest, high priest* of the Jews:—Cwæð se ealdorbiscop *dixit princeps sacerdotum* (Acts, 7, 1), Hml. Th. i. 46, 6 : ii. 422, 20. Ðá gýtsigendan ealdorbiscopas, i. 406, 5. Þám weardmannum þe wǽron ásænde fram þám ealdorbisceopum tó Crístes byrgenne, Hml. A. 78, 153. Hé gesamnode ealle þá ealdorbiscopas *congregans omnes principes sacerdotum* (Mt. 2, 4), Hml. Th. i. 78, 10.

**ealdor-bold,** es; *n. A chief residence, court* of a king:—Be Deorwentan þǽre eá, ðǽr wæs þæs cyninges ealdorbold (aldor-, *v.l.*) *juxta amnem Deruuentionem, ubi tunc erat uilla regalis*, Bd. 2, 9; Sch. 146, 21. v. ealdor-botl, -burh *in Dict.*

**ealdor-botl.** v. preceding word.

**ealdor-burh.** *Add*:—Ealdorburh *metropolis*, Wrt. Voc. ii. 58, 24: Hpt. 33, 239, 19.

**ealdor-deófol,** es; *m. The prince of the devils*:—Þonne þú gesyxt þone ealdordeófol þe líð on bæc gebunden . . . and siððan heó bið gelǽdd tó þám ealdordeófle, Nap. 18.

**ealdor-dóm.** *Add*: I. *greatness, power, authority*:—Ðá wurdon æteówode fela ðúsend engla, ðý lǽs ðe wǽre geþúht ánes engles ealdordóm tó hwónlic tó swá micelre bodunge, Hml Th. i. 38, 5. Ealdordóme *auctoritate*, An. Ox. 2598. Ealderdóm *auctoritatem*, i. *praerogativam*, 2873. Þurh lǽreówa ealdordóm, Wlfst. 285, 28. II. *state of superiority, pre-eminence, primacy*. (1) *of persons*:—Claudius him wæs on teónde ealdordóm ofer þá óþere *primus ex decemviris solus Appius Claudius sibi continuauit imperium*, Ors. 2, 6; S. 88, 20. Hé lǽred aldordóm ne sié tó soecanne *docet primatum non esse quaerendum*, Mk. p. 4, 8. (2) *of things*:—Swylce eác be ðám heán muntum and dúnum, þá þe heáh standað ofer ealne middaneard, þá hwæðere wíte habbað þæs ealdordómes, þæt heó beóð genehhe mid heofonfýre geþreáde, Wlfst. 262, 14. Hwilce þe geþúht betwux woroldcræftas healdan ealdordóm *quales tibi videtur inter seculares artes retinere primatum?*, Coll. M. 30, 25. III. *rule, government, any official position involving command of others*:—Þis ealdordóm sette on eaxle *factus est principatus super humerum ejus* (Is. 9, 6), Ælfc. T. Grn. 9, 14. Licge se ealdordóm on unfriðe, Ll. Th. i. 286, 34. Ealdordó[me] *municipatu*, i. *principatu*, An. Ox. 3030. Ðǽm aldordóme ðæs undercyniges *principatui praesidis*, Lk. R. 20, 20. Hé him æfter fyligde on ðæs mynstres ealdordóme (*regimine*), Gr. D. 96, 7. Israhéla folc geceás Ionatham, biddende þæt hé wǽre heora heáfod and heretoga; and hé féng ðá tó ealdordóme swá swá hí bǽdon, Hml. S. 25, 718. Hér forðférde Ælfere ealdordóm, and féng Ælfríc tó þám ilcan ealdordóme, 983; P. 125, 6. Óslác féng tó ealdordóme (*was made earl of Deira*), Ch. 966; P. 119, 2. Óslác eorl and eal here þe on his ealdordóme wunað, Ll. Th. i. 278, 6. Willelm cynge geaf Rôdbearde eorle þone ealdordóm ofer Norðhymbra land, 1067; P. 203, 20. Ealdordóm *tribunatum*, i. *principatum*, Hpt. Gl. 427, 22. Ealdordóm *monarchiam*, i. *principatum*, An. Ox. 1994. Geðence hé ðone ealdordóm his onwealdes; and . . . forsió hé his ealdordóm . . . *potestatem sui*

*prioratus agnoscat; et honore suppresso* . . . , Past. 107, 13. *Fasces,* i. *honores* cynedómas *vel* aldor[dómas], Wrt. Voc. ii. 146, 51. Þá gecorenan ðe . . . þá lǽssan gebróðru oferstígað mid ealdorscipe, þá habbað heora dǽl betwux ðám heofenlícum ealderdómum (*principalities*, Col. 1, 16), Hml. Th. i. 344, 33. IV. *a beginning*:—Þis is ealdordómm uncres gewinnes on fruman gefongen (cf. þis is a beginnunge of þe sar þ tu schalt . . . drehen, Jul. 27, 8), Jul. 190. [He (*Christ*) ræfeþþ þe (*John*) þín alderrdom, Orm. 18278.]

**ealdor-dóm-scipe** (?), es; *m. Aldermanship*:—Hér forðférde Ælfhere ealdorman, and féng Ælfríc tó þám ilcan ealdordómscipe (ealdormanscipe?: ealdordóme, MS. E.), Chr. 983; P. 124, 35.

**ealdor-geard** (?) *the house of life, the body*:—Lǽtað íren ecgheard eadorgeard (ealdor-? cf. feorh-bold, -hús) sceoran, An. 1183.

**ealdor-lang.** *Add: eternal.* [*O. Sax.* aldar-lang: *O. Frs.* alderlang *eternal*.] v. ealdor *life*, II.

**ealdor-leás.** *Substitute*: I. *without a lord.* v. ealdor, I:—God fyrenþearfe ongeat, þæt hí ǽr drugon aldorleáse, B. 15. II. *without parents, orphan.* v. ealdor, II:—Ne forlǽte ic eów aldorleáse (=aldorleása *orfanos*, Jn. L. 14, 18), Bl. H. 131, 21. [*O. Frs.* alderlás *orphan*.]

**ealdor-leg,** es; *n. Substitute*: ealdor-legu, e; *f. Course of life, life*:—Gé mé sægdon þæt gé cúðon míne aldorlege, swá mé ǽfre weard oððe ic furðor findan sceolde *you told me that you knew the course of my life, whatever has befallen me, or what I was yet to experience*, Dan. 139. Nelle ic lǽtan þé ǽfre unrôtne æfter ealdorlege mínre (*after my life's course is ended*) geweorðan, Gú, 1234. [Cf. *O. Sax.* aldar-lagu; *pl. life*.]

**ealdor-lic.** *Add*: I. *of an ealdor.* v. ealdor, I:—Ealdorlícere mihte *tribunice potestatis*, An. Ox. 4544. Ealdorlícere *tribunica*, 4010. II. *chief, principal, princely*:—Seó ceaster wæs héh and aldorlíc, Bl. H. 77, 25. Swá ealdorlíces hádes *principalis tanti sexus*, An. Ox. 3890. Ic hálsige þá Crístes þegnas fór hiora ealdorlícan setle (cf. þæt gé sitton ofer þrymsetl, Lk. 22, 30), Angl. xii. 503, 17. Mid gáste alderlíce *spiritu principali*, Ps. Srt. 50, 14. Twá and hundseofontig þeóda ealdorlícra mægða . . . xv mǽgða ealdorlícera (-e, MS) and mycele, Angl. xi. 2, 46, 48. III. *authentic.* v. ealdor, III:—Ealderlícum *authentico*, An. Ox. 5151.

**ealdor-líce.** *Add*:—Ealdorlíce (*principaliter*) syndon tú cyn þǽre inbryrdnesse, Gr. D. 244, 26. Aldorlíce, Rtl. 9, 15.

**ealdorlicness.** *Add*:—Ic þé þá wísan secge mid bysene þǽre hálgan ealdorlícnysse *ea narro sacrae auctoritatis exemplo*, Gr. D. 8, 30. Ealdorlícnesse *auctoritate*, An. Ox. 216: 40, 3. Ælalderlícnessa, 11, 8. Ðæt on his ealdorlícnesse hié ongieten ðæt hié him mægen ondrǽdan, Past. 119, 12. Gefultumiende mid his cynelícre ealdorlícnesse (aldor-, *v.l.*), Bd. 5, 10; Sch. 598, 13. Hé hafað him sylfum genumen þá ealdorlícnysse þǽre hálgan láre (*auctoritatem praedicationis*), Gr. D. 35, 3.

**ealdor-mann.** *Add*: I. *in a general sense.* (1) *used of a person of high position, a prince, ruler, leader, magistrate*:—Ealdorman *princeps vel comes*, Wrt. Voc. i. 42, 12. Eoldorman *princeps*, 72, 59. Se ealdormonn (*rector*) sceal lǽtan hine selfne gelícne his hiéremonnum, Past. 107, 8. Sié ðú aldormon tó gehæld *sis praesul ad custodiam*, Rtl. 180, 12. In aldormonnum (aldur-, R) . . . aldormon ł lǽtua ðe rícses *in principibus . . . dux, qui reget*, Mt. L. 2, 6. Ðú haldormon *praeceptor*, Lk. L. 5, 5. Achilles se aldorman, Lch. i. 308, 8. Geonduearde Nicodimus se aldormonn (cf. Nicodemus aldormonn (*princeps*) Judéana, 1) *respondit Nicodemus*, Jn. L. 3, 9. Tó ealdormenn ðú eart gesett *ducem te constituerunt*, Past. 119, 22. Mið ðý ðú gást mid wiðerworde ðínum tó aldormen (*principem*), Lk. L. 12, 58. Se cyning sende him tógeánes ánne ealdormann (*principem*), Jud. 4, 7. Eorðcyningcas and ealdormenn (*principes*), Ps. Th. 2, 2: 23, 7. Yfelra ealdormanna geþeaht *consilia principum*, 32, 9. Ealdormanna riht *jus publicum*, Wrt. Voc. i. 20, 63: ii. 49, 10. Ealdermanna duguð *senatus*, i. 18, 38. Ealdormanna *procerum*, An. Ox. 4546: *magestratibus*, Wrt. Voc. ii. 55, 17. Cyningum and yfelum rícum ealdermannum wiþstandan, Bl. H. 161, 17. Hié eft hwirfdon tó hiora ealdormannum, 239, 26. Gegaderode Pharao his ealdormen and here, Ex. 14, 6. Twégen ealdormen *duos viros*, Jud. 7, 25. .xii. Wilisce aldormenn, Chr. 465; P. 12, 27. (2) *a master, overseer* of workmen:—Cóm hé tó þám túngeréfan, sé þe his ealdormon wæs *veniens ad uillicum, qui sibi praeerat*, Bd. 4, 24; Sch. 484, 22. Berebryttan gebyred corngebrot . . . gif him his ealdorman ann, Ll. Th. i. 440, 3. I a. *with gen., chief of a class or profession*:—Michael se heáhengel wæs ealra engla ealderman, Bl. H. 147, 2. Aldormon beorswingra *princeps publicanorum*, Lk. R. 19, 2. Sum heora cræftes ealdorman *quidam artis eorum primus*, Gr. D. 342, 5. Sce Petres apostola ealdormannes, Bl. H. 171, 4. Aldormonnes sácerda *principis sacerdotum*, Lk. L. R. 22, 50. Þá ealdormen þára sácerda, Bl. H. 77, 7. II. *used of the holder of a particular office.* (1) *referring to other than English officials; or in glossaries.* (a) *of secular office*:—Ealdorman *judex vel consul*, Wrt. Voc. i. 50, 4: *pretor*, ii. 95, 26: *comes*, An. Ox. 4712. Dêma ł ealdorman *preses*, 45, 1. Cempena ealdormon *tribunus scutariorum*, Ors. 6, 33; S. 288, 5. Ðe aldormon *tribunus*, Jn. L. 18, 12: *architriclinus*, 2, 9.

Ealdermen *preside*, i. *judice*, An. Ox. 3453. Ðām haldormenn *centurioni*, Mt. L. 8, 13. Be þām ealdormen þǣre burge *de urbis comite*, Gr. D. 301, 16. Cwǣdon þā Judēiscan tō heora ealdormenn Pilate (cf. pro- curante Pontio Pilato, Lk. 3, 1), Hml. Th. i. 220, 5. Ðǣm aldormen *Pilato*, Mk. L. R. 15, 1. Ealdormanna *pretorum*, Wrt. Voc. ii. 85, 70. Ealdormen *quinquagenarios*, 66, 5. (b) of ecclesiastical office :—Ðæs folces aldormon *archesynagogus*, Lk. L. 13, 14. Ðæs aldormonnes *archesynagogi*, Mk. L. R. 5, 38. From ðǣm folces aldormenn, 35. Cūð ðǣm aldormenn ( *pontifici* ) . . . on worðe ðæs aldormonnes *pontificis*, Jn. L. R. 18, 15. Caifa ðæs aldormonnes *Caiaphae*, 13. (2) of English officials :—Ǣðelstān ealderman *ego Æðelstan senator*, C. D. v. 253, 26. Beorhtrīc cyning forðfērde and Worr aldormon, Chr. 800 ; P. 58, 3. Hēr Cūþrēd cyning gefeaht uuiþ Æþelhūn þone ofermēdan aldormonn, 750 ; P. 46, 11. Hē ofslōg þone aldormonn þe him lengest wunode, 755 ; P. 46, 21. ¶ used of Saxons coming from or living on the con- tinent :—Hēr cuōmon twēgen aldormen on Bretene, Cerdic and Cynrīc his sunu, Chr. 495 ; P. 14, 18. þā hī on Ealdseaxe cōmon, þā eódon hī on sumes tūngerēfan gestærn, and hine bǣdon þ hē hī onsende tō þām ealdormen (*ad satrapam*) þe ofer hine wæs . . . þā Ealdseaxan næfdon āgenne cyning ; ac manige ealdormen (*satrapae plurimi*) wǣron heora þeóde foresette, and þonne seó tīd gewinnes cōm, þonne hluton hī mid tānum tō þām ealdormænnum, and swā hwylcne heora swā him se tāu ætȳwde, þonne gecæron hī þone him tō heretogan, and him hȳrdon. þonne þ gewin geendad wæs, þonne wǣron hī eft efenrīce, wǣron ealle ealdormen (*satrapae*), Bd. 5, 10 ; Sch. 600, 4–601, 3. v. dryht-, þūsend-ealdormann.

**ealdor-ner.** *l.* eald-neru, e ; *f., and add :* [cf. Icel. aldr-nari *fire* (poet.)] cf. feorh-neru.

**ealdor-sacerd.** *l.* -sǣcerd, *and add :*—Aldursācerd *princeps sacerdotum*, Mt. R. 26, 62. Esne ðæs aldorsācerdas (-os, R) *servum principis sacer- dotum*, Mt. L. 26, 51. Gesomnad wēron aldorsācerdas in cæfertūn ðæs aldorsācerdas, 3. Ætteáw þe ðǣm aldorsācerd, Mk. R. 1, 44. Aldor- sācerdas *principes sacerdotum*, Mt. R. 21, 23 : Mt. L. 27, 62. Tō aldorsācerdum, 26, 14, 47.

**ealdor-scipe.** *Add :*—Abbod sceal ā gemunan hwæt hē gecweden is, and þæs ealdorscipes noman mid dǣdum gefyllan (*nomen majoris factis implere*), R. Ben. 10, 10. Teóðingealdras sȳn hȳdege embe heora ealdorscypas (*decanias*) . . . Gif heora hwylc þurh þǣne trūwan his ealdorscipes tōdint . . . hē sȳ of ðām ealdorscype āworpen, 46, 10–19. Se biscop is geset tō māran bletsunge ðonne se mæssepreóst . . . Preóstum gedafenað for ðām ealdorscipe þ hī heora biscope beón underþeódde, Ll. Th. ii. 378, 25 : Hml. Th. i. 344, 32. Petre þæne ealdorscipe hē ǣrest betǣhte, Wlfst. 176, 14. Sōð lufu on eallum bebodum Godes ealdorscype (*principatum*) healt, Scint. 4, 5. *Principatus* sind ealdor- scipas, Hml. Th. i. 342, 30.

**ealdoþ** (?) *a trough* (?), *a channel* (?) :—Aldaht, aldot *alviolum*, Txts. 39, 124. [Cf. *Bavarian* alden *a furrow*. v. Beib. 15, 71.]

**eald-riht.** *Add :* cf. eald-geriht.

**Eald-Seaxe.** *Add :*—þāra cynna monig hē wiste on Germanie wesan, þanon Engle and Seaxan cumene wǣron þe nū on Breotone eardiað. Wǣron Frysan, Dene, Ealdseaxan (Ald-, *v. l.*), Bd. 5, 9 ; Sch. 590, 9.

**eald-spræc.** *Substitute :* eald-sprǣc, e ; *f. An old form of words, a proverb, byword :*—þū hæfst ūs gedōn tō ealdsprǣce, þæt ðe ðeóda nyton hwæt hȳ elles sprecon būton ūre bysmer *posuisti nos in similitudi- nem gentibus*, Ps. Th. 43, 16. v. eald, **IV.**

**ealdung.** *For translation of passage substitute :* Nostri causantur, si Romanae reipublicae moles imbecillitate propriae senectutis contremescant, *and add :*—þā getimbru þissere burge wē geseoð mid langre ealdunge gewācode *hujus urbis aedificia longo senio lassata videmus*, Gr. D. 134, 10. Se gegyrla þe ic hæfde . . ., mid swīðlicre ealdunge tōtorene, for- wurdon, Hml. S. 23 b, 571. [Wyþoute zyknesse and wyþoute ealdinge, Ayenb. 95, 17.]

**eald-wita.** *Substitute :* An elder, senior, principal person. v. wita, **III** :—Presbiter is mæssepreóst oððe ealdwita ; nā ðæt ælc eald sȳ *presbiter is priest or senior ; not that each is old in years*, Ll. Th. ii. 348, 20. Mē sǣde sum ārwyrðe mæssepreóst, þæt him sǣde sum ealdwita, þ hē wǣre gefullad fram Paulino *narravit mihi presbyter quidam retulisse sibi quendam seniorem, baptizatum se fuisse a Paulino*, Bd. 2, 16 ; Sch. 178, 19. Manige ūre ealdwitan wǣron clǣnsiende þ eáge heora mōdes *multi nostrorum mentis oculum mundantes*, Gr. D. 272, 1.

**eald-wrītere.** *Add :*—Ealdwrīterum *antiquariis*, i. scribis (*scriptori- bus*, Hpt. Gl. 528, 73), An. Ox. 5449.

**ealgian.** *Add :*—Ðonne hē wel þēnað and ūres Drihtnes heorde ealgað, R. Ben. 123, 2. Hī ealle on andwyrdnysse stōdon, ðā ðā se ān ðē tȳnde, and noldon ðē ealgian wið heora brēðer, Hml. Th. ii. 30, 13 : B. 796.

**eall.** *Add :* **I.** with another word in agreement. (1) noun, adj., numeral. (a) *all* :—Forðfērde Decius and ǣfre ælc dǣl eall his cynnes (*one and all of his race*), Hml. S. 23, 349. Hwī wæs Adame ān treów forboden, þā þā hē wæs ealles ōðres hlāford (*lord of all else*)?, Angl. vii. 6, 42. þæt þū ðē mid ealre hande be þīnum cynne nime, Tech. ii.

129, 16. Hī cunnon eall mennisc gereord *nationum linguis loquentes*, Nar. 37, 3. Hī þā ealle feówertig ætforan him stōdon, Hml. S. 11, 55. Yfel monn ealra þeáwa, Ors. 6, 14 ; S. 268, 27. Sum wydewe næfde ealra ǣhta būton ænne feórðling, Hml. Th. ii. 106, 9. Ealra geára hē stōd on ðǣm wēstenne seofon and feówertig, Shrn. 109, 12. Wyl ealle feówer on buteran, Lch. ii. 128, 8. Hē wæs on sumre fōre ealle þrȳ dagas, Bl. H. 217, 17. (b) *quite* :—Hī cōmon unwær on heom on ealne ǣrnemergen, Chr. 1050; P. 170, 14. (2) pronoun :—Hē wæs eall biernende, and ðeáh ðā tungan suīðust mǣnde and him ðǣre kēlnesse bæd *qui totus ardens refrigerari se praecipue in lingua requirebat*, Past. 309, 10. Sē wæs reád and eall rūh *rufus erat et totus in morem pellis hirsutus*, Gen. 25, 25. Hē bið eal (or *adv.?*) unwrenca full, Wlfst. 97, 15. Hē sāmcucu læg and fleów eall blōde, Hml. S. 6, 165. þæt is ungeliéfedlic tō gesecganne hwæt þæs ealles wæs (*how much there was of it all*), Ors. 5, 12 ; S. 240, 17. Ealle wē witon, Past. 63, 11. Fram eallum ūs, Bd. 4, 5 ; Sch. 375, 2. **II.** alone :—Syððan hine forlēton ealle būtan .ii., Chr. 1049 ; P. 171, 21. ¶ oblique cases or prepositional phrases with adverbial force. (1) genitive (a) with superlative adj. or adv. :—Hié wǣron micle swīþor gebrocede mid ceápes cwilde and monna, ealles swīþost mid þǣm þæt . . ., Chr. 897 ; P. 90, 1. *Justus* rihtwis, *justior* rihtwīsre, *justissimus* ealra rihtwīsost, Ælfc. Gr. Z. 16, 1 (and *often*). (b) with a numeral, *in all, altogether* :—þ ðǣr sȳn ealles fīftig æcera, Cht. Th 563, 25. Hī wunedon on fulre sibbe ealles feówertig geára, Jud. 3, 11 : 4, 3 : Hml. S. 3, 23 : 19, 10. Feówor and twēntig tīda, þæt is ealles ān dæg and ān niht, Hex. 8, 32. Fērde Jacob mid his twelf sunum and his suna sunum ealles hund- seofontig manna, Hml. Th. ii. 190, 30. þā hæftlingas ealles sixtȳne, Hml. S. 5, 134. Hundteóntig muneca and feówertig ealles, 6, 264. Ealles fīftȳne lǣcedōmas *fifteen recipes in all*, Lch. ii. 8, 5 ; 15 : 10, 26. Gif þæt beóþ seofon ealra, Angl. viii. 326, 26. (c) *entirely, quite :*—þeáh þū nū fier sié þonne þū wǣre, ne eart þū þeáh ealles of þām earde ādrifen Bt. 5, 1 ; F. 8, 35. Mē næfre wæs ealles swā ic wolde, 26, 1 ; F. 90, 28. Sē þe on ðā wītu ealles behreóseð, Wlfst. 26, 12. þ mau crīstene men for ealles tō lytlum tō deáðe ne fordēme, Ll. Th. i. 304, 19. Wurdon hig ealles tō oft on yfel āwende,- Jud. pref. 8. (2) dat. inst. *entirely, altogether :*—Ealle hē wæs swelce Rōmāne þā wyrþe wǣron *qui vere dignus Romanis punitor adhibitus videretur*, Ors. 6, 3 ; S. 256, 23. Ne bæd hē nō ðæt hē hine elle (mid ealle, *v. l.*) fortȳnde, Past. 275, 22. (2 a) mid eallum, mid ealle. (a) *quite, altogether :*—Ðā ðā ic myd eallum untrum wæs, Nic. 13, 15. þæt gē forwurðað mid ealle *quod omnino dispereas*, Deut. 8, 19. (β) along with noun governed by *mid*, and *all* :—Forweard nō lǣs þonne .xx. scipa mid monnum mid ealle, Chr. 897 ; P. 90, 20. Āwurpan ūt þæt fæt mid ele mid ealle, Hml. Th. ii. 178, 27 : 304, 29. Drīg hī and mid wyrttruman mid ealle gewyrc tō dūste, Lch. i. 70, 11. (3) acc. (a) alone, *all, quite* :—Bētende eall be bisceopes dōme emendans *omnino juxta sententiam episcopi*, Ll. Th. ii. 188, 28. Wālā þǣre yrmðe and wālā þǣre woruldscame þe nū habbað Engle eal þurh (eall for, *v. l.*) Godes yrre, Wlfst. 163, 4. Hit biþ eall ōþer, Bt. 27, 3 ; F. 98, 23. þā līchaman geborene wǣron þurh eall feówertig mīla (*per xxxx fere milia passuum*), Bd. 5, 10 ; Sch. 603, 19. xxx. þūsenda eal farena and oxna, Nar. 9, 10 (v. faru, **IV**). Ne mihte se pāpa þæt geþafian, þeáh ðe hē eall wolde (*though he was quite willing*), Hml. Th. ii. 122, 12 : Wlfst. 165, 10. þeáh ic eal mǣge, B. 680. (β) with prepositions :—Crīstendōm næs þāgyt geond eall cūð (*known everywhere*), Hml. S. 2, 13. Man ārǣrde ðyrcan on his rīce geond eall, 26, 85. Ofer eal gewidmǣrsude *late crebresceret*, An. Ox. 2584. Ofer eall, Gen. 45, 16. Hē hēt geáxian ofer eall sumne drȳ, Hml. S. 14, 49 : 23, 266. Hē sende ofer eall intō ǣlcan lande, Chr. 1086 ; P. 221, 1 : 1067 ; P. 203, 11. *See the compounds with* eall.

**eallencten.** v. eall-lencten : **eallenga.** v. eallinga : **ealles** ; *adv.* v. eall : **eall-fela,** -felo. v. eal-fela, -felo *in Dict.*

**eall-gōd** ; *adj. All-good, infinitely good* :—God sylf ys eallgōd, and ǣlc gōd cimð of him, Ælfc. T. Grn. 2, 29. [v. *N. E. D.* all-good. *Icel.* all-gōðr.]

**eall-godwebb** ; *adj.* (or *noun?*) *All of silk* (or *a garment made all of silk?* Cf. oloserica .i. vestis tota ex serico, Hpt. Gl. 480, 64) :—Ealgodwebbum *eloséricis* (*l.* olo-), Wrt. Voc. ii. 31, 17.

**eall-godwebben** ; *adj. All of silk* :—Ealgodwebnum *elosericis* (*l.* olo-), Wrt. Voc. ii. 81, 70.

**eall-gylden.** *Add :*—Wyrc feówer hringas ælgyldene *facies quatuor circulos aureos*, Past. 169, 21.

**eall-hālig.** *Add :* [v. *N. E. D.* all-holy.]

**eall-hwit.** *Add :*—Eallhwīte wȳsan *gesce*, Wrt. Voc. ii. 42, 18. [*O. Sax.* ala-hwit.]

**eal-lic.** v. eall-līc.

**ealling.** *Add :*—Ne inlīhteð nā ealling (alning, simle *v. l.*) se wītedōmes gāst þā mōd þæra wītegæna *prophetiae spiritus prophetarum mentes non semper irradiat*, Gr. D. 146, 8 : 280, 10. Hē wolde ealling (alning, *v. l.*) beón betweoh earfeðum, and hē symble lufode þā geþyldu ; hē wæs fieónde ealling woruldlicra manna gemētinge and symble gyrnde þ hē wǣre geǣmtigod tō his gebede *inter adversa semper patientiam*

*amplectens, conventus secularium fugiens, vacare semper orationi concupiscens*, 290, 14–17 : 324, 11. Eallinc *jugiter*, Hpt. 31, 13, 307.

**eall-lencten**, es ; *m. The season of Lent :—*Fram idus Septembris oð lenctenes anginne hȳ on ān mǣl tō nōnes gereorden ; ofer ealllencten (eal-, *v. l.*) oþ Ēástran hȳ oð ǣfen fæsten *ab idibus Septembris usque ad capud quadragesime ad nonam semper reficiant ; in quadragesima usque in pasca ad vesperam reficiant*, R. Ben. 66, 5.

**eall-líc, eallic** ; *adj.* I. *of all, universal :—*Regol þæs eallican dēman *the rule of the judge of all* (*the Deity*), Gr. D. 336, 27. II. *Catholic :—*Þá dōmas þæs allican geleáfan *catholicae fidei decreta*, Bd. 4, 18 ; Sch. 435, 15. Weras þǣre ǽallǽcan cyrican *catholicae ecclesiae viros*, Gr. D. 162, 25. Tō þám eallican (allican, *v. l.*) geleáfan *ad fidem catholicam*, 237, 20 : 239, 7.

**eall-mǽst**. v. mǣst ; *adv.* II.

**eall-meaht, -miht**, e ; *f. Omnipotence :—*On mihtigre handa and on eallmihte earmes *in manu forti et brachio excelso*, Ps. Th. 135, 12. [*O. H. Ger.* ala-maht : *Ger.* all-macht.]

**eall-mihtig**. *Add :* [*O. Sax.* ala-, alo-mahtig : *O. H. Ger.* al-, ala-mahtig.] v. æl-mihtig *in Dict.*

**eall-niwe**. *l.* -níwe, *and add :—*Seó burhwaru bebyrigde hire líc on eallníwere þrȳh, Hml. S. 8, 198. Eallníwne croccan, Lch. iii. 292, 3.

**eallnunge**. v. ealnunga.

**eall-offrung**, e ; *f. A holocaust :—*Ealoffrung *holocaustum*, Wrt. Voc. i. 28, 51.

**eall-rihte** ; *adv. Quite directly, exactly :—*Ealswá yfel anda lǣt tō helle, ealrihte swá gōd anda lǣt tō Gode, R. Ben. 131, 13.

**eall-rúh**. *Dele, and see* eall, I. 2.

**eall-seolcen** ; *adj. Made all of silk :—*Mid eallseolcenum *olosericis*, Wrt. Voc. ii. 62, 71. Of eallseolcenum, An. Ox. 2, 164. Of ealseolcenum (eall-, eal-, Hpt. Gl. 480, 62–3), 3161. v. eal-seolcen *in Dict.*

**eall-swá**. *Add :* I. *adv.* (1) *with adj. or adv., just as or so :—*Ealswá feala mǣrþa ic geríme *tot ego glorias numerabo*, An. Ox. 4762. Ic wylle þysum ȳtemestan syllan eallswá mycel swá þē *volo huic novissimo dare sicut et tibi*, Mt. 20, 14. Eallswá mihtig swá hē nú is, Swt. A. S. Rdr. 57, 39. (2) *with verb, likewise, in just the same way :—*Hí gefēngon ðone feórþan and eallswá getintregedon, Hml. S. 25, 143. Se wítega wæs ealswá genumen tō ðám ōðrum lífe, Swt. A. S. Rdr. 61, 140. II. *adverbial conjunction.* (1) *as :—*Ealswá *ut*, An. Ox. 316. Hí dydon eallswá hí bewuna wǣron, Chr. 1001 ; P. 133, 20. Tō dōnne be him eallswá Judas dyde be ūre Drihtene, 1087 ; P. 222, 34. Stande hē eallswá (eal-, *v. l.*) wē ǣr cwǣdon, R. Ben. 69, 4. Hē sȳ on swēge gelencged eallswá (eal-, *v. l.*) on Sunnandæge, 37, 8. (2) *as* (*if*) *:—*Hí ridon tō Bosanhām eallswá hí sceoldon tō Sandwíc, Chr. 1049 ; P. 168, 35. (3) *correlative forms :—*Eallswá bealdlíce mōt se ðeówa clypigan God him tō Fæder ealswá se cyning, Hml. Th. i. 260, 23–24. Eallswá (eal-, *v. l.*) yfel anda lǣt tō helle, ealrihte swá gōd anda lǣt tō Gode, R. Ben. 131, 12. v. swá.

**eall-swilc** ; *adj. Just such :—*Eallswylc (or eall swylc) is Basilius swylce þes fȳrena swer, Hml. S. 3, 502. Tō eallswilcre gehȳrsumnesse swá hē ǽr his fæder dyde, Chr. 1091 ; P. 227, 3.

**eallunga**. *Add :* I. *entirely, altogether, completely :—*Ne fulgá hē eallunga ðæs líchoman wilnunga, ðȳ lǣs hē eallunga áfealle *nec totum se ad hoc, quod agit, conferat, ne funditus cadat*, Past. 395, 10. Ne sculon gé nō eallunga tō swíðe lufian ðisne middangeard *nolite constanter mundum diligere*, 28. Eallunga *penitus*, Kent. Gl. 1094. Swá emnes mōdes þæt ic eallunga wǣre orsorg, þ ic swá orsorg wǣre þ ic nāne gedrēfednesse næfde, Bt. 26, 1 ; F. 90, 26 : 10 ; F. 28, 8. Hē þá bernesse eallinga (*funditus*) ádwæscte, Bd. 4, 21 ; Sch. 453, 19. Ne liged hē eallinga on ðǽre eorðan, ac bið hwæthwugu ūp áhæfen, Past. 155, 25. Templ eallinga Gode weorþe, Bl. H. 163, 14. II. *with a less definite sense, certainly, indeed, now :—*Slápað eallunga *dormite jam*, Mt. 26, 45 : Gr. D. 167, 9 : 168, 4 : An. Ox. 40, 13, 15 : Angl. xiii. 410, 639 : *forte*, 396, 437. Swá eallunga *ita prorsus*, i. *omnino*, An. Ox. 4081. Eallunge, 2901. Eallenga, Wrt. Voc. ii. 43, 59. Eallunga *profecto*, An. Ox. 27, 4. Ne wilt þú þú ondrǣdan ; þín bēn is eallunga fram Gode gehȳred. . . . Hē bið eallunga swíþe mycel beforan Gode *ne timeas, quoniam exaudita est depraecatio tua . . . Erit autem magnus*, Bl. H. 165, 7–11. Ðá wearþ se drȳ eallunga áweht *then the sorcerer did indeed get roused*, 173, 19. Hwæt þonne hūru eallunga . . . *why then and at least* . . ., 123, 3. Witodlíce ðæs mōnan trendel is symle gehāl, þeáh ðe eall endemes eallunga ne scíne *certainly the disc of the moon is always complete, though to be sure the whole of it does not continuously shine*, Lch. iii. 242, 5. Ðætte ðá untruman mōd mon ne scyle ellenga tō heálíce lǣran *quod infirmis mentibus omnino non debent alta praedicari*, Past. 459, 4.

**eall-wealda**. *Add :—*Hæfð se alwealda ealle gesceafta gebǽt, Met. 11, 22. [*O. Sax.* ala-, alo-walda ; *adj. and subst.*] v. al-wealda *in Dict.*

**eall-wealdend**, es ; *m. The omnipotent, the Deity :—*God ðe āna gewylt ealra gesceafta . . . swá swá eallwealdend (eall-, *v. l.*) God, Hml. S. 17, 142. Swá swá se eallwealdend heom ūðe, 26, 26. Gif hē

gewilnaþ þæs eallwealdendes miltsunge, 19, 187. [*O. Sax.* ʾalo-waldand.]

**eall-wealdende** ; *adj.* (*ptcpl.*) *Omnipotent :—*Se eallwealdenda God, Hml. Th. i. 344, 1. Se eallwealdenda Hǣlend, Hml. S. 19, 181. Se eallwealdenda Drihten, Wlfst. 144, 30 : 146, 7. Se ealwealdenda Dēma, Hml. S. 16, 343. [*Goth.* all-waldands.]

**eall-writen** ; *adj. All written with one's own hand :—*Eallwritene yrfebēc *olographum testamentum*, Wrt. Voc. ii. 65, 39.

**ealneg**. *Add :—*Hē nǽfre ne besyhð tō ðǣre ūplican áre, ac ealneg (ealne weg, *v. l.*) fundað tō ðisum eorðlicum, Past. 66, 15 : 395, 29. Gē ymb þæt án gefeoht alneg ceoriað, Ors. 3, 11 ; S. 142, 7. Ealneg (-ig, Bos. 88, 2), 4, 7 ; S. 182, 16 : 5, 1 ; S. 214, 4. Hit God wrǣc on him swá hē ǽr ealneg dyde, swá oft swá mid monnum ofredan, 4, 7 ; S. 184, 8. Alneg (ealling, *v. l.*), Gr. D. 280, 10. Beóð his wegas ealneh unclǽne *polluuntur viae ejus in omni tempore*, Ps. Th. 9, 24. v. eallneg *in Dict.*, weg ; V.

**ealning**. *Add :—*Ðú wuldres God ealning ábidde þ hē þē ne forlǣte lāðum tō handum, Dōm. L. 30, 28. Alning (ealling, *v. l.*), Gr. D. 146, 8 : 290, 14 : 324, 11. v. ealling.

**eal-nósu**. *Dele, and see* nosu : ealoþ. v. ealu.

**ealnunga** ; *adv. Altogether, entirely :—*Hē gange in, þæt him se tīdsancg ealnuncge (-nunga, eallunge, *v. ll.*) ne losige *ingrediatur intro, ut nec totum perdat*, R. Ben. 68, 23.

**ealu** (-o, -a). *For ' generally indecl. in sing.'* substitute : *gen.* ealoþ (-aþ, -eþ), alþes (Rtl.) ; *dat. inst.* ealoþ (-aþ, -eþ) ; *acc.* ealu (-o, -a) ; *gen. pl.* ealeþa, *and add :* I. *ale :—*Ealo *coelia*, Wrt. Voc. ii. 17, 24 : i. 290, 61. Ealu *celeum, cervise*, ii. 130, 47. Ǽþele alu *carenum*, 23, 1. Gif ealo áwerd sié, Lch. ii. 142, 10. Twēgen fǽtels full ealað oððe wæteres, Ors. 1, 1 ; S. 21, 16. Lytel níwes ealu, Lch. i. 388, 8. Healde hē hine wiþ geswet eala, drince hlūttor eala, and on þæs hlūttran ealað wyrte wylle ácrinde, ii. 292, 21. Dō healfne bollan ealoð tō . . . and gehǣte þ ealu, 268, 24. Aefne alðes *materiam cervise*, Rtl. 116, 42. Twá flaxan mid ælað gefylde, Guth. 64, 16. Wyl on ealoþ oððe on beóre, Lch. ii. 102, 27. Ealað, 104, 2. On áwyldum ealað, 114, 12. On sūrum ealað, 34, 15. On twybrōwnum ealað, 120, 10. On ealdum ealað, 292, 12. Mid strangum ealað, 314, 14. Mid hlūttre ealoþ, 116, 5. Gníd on eala, 100, 22 : 114, 23. On ealo, 102, 18, 21, 22. On þ eala, 142, 13. Hē nāne þinga beór ne drince, and gemetlíce wín and eala, 88, 11. Hlūttor ealu, 104, 17. On strang hlūttor eala, 314, 23. On wylisc ealo, 118, 4. Hwæt drincst þú ? Ealu (*cerevisiam*), gif ic hæbbe, oþþe wæter, gif ic nǽbbe ealu, Coll. M. 35, 11 : Bl. H. 165, 11. II. *an intoxicating drink :—*Ne oferdrincað gē eów wínes ne ōðera ealeða, Ll. Th. ii. 438, 20. v. æfter-, brȳd-, mealt-ealu.

**ealu-benc**. *Add :* [*Icel.* öl-bekkr.]

**ealu-clȳfe**. *Substitute :* ealu-cleofa, -clyfa, an ; *m. A place for storing ale :—*Ealuclyfum *apothecis* (*coelestibus defruta recondenda*, Ald. 36, 9), An. Ox. 36, 9.

**ealu-gafol**. *Substitute : A tribute paid in ale, and add :—*Cf. Hér synd gewriten ðá gerihta ðæ ðá ceorlas sculan dōn tō Hysseburnan. Ǽrest æt hilcan híwisce feówerti penega tō herfestes emnihte, and vi ciricmittan ealað, C. D. vi. 147, 15. Sylle se gebūr .vi. penegas ofer Éstre, healfne sester hunies tō Hláfmæssan, .vi. systres mealtes tō Martines mæsse, iii. 451, 6. See also Seebohm, Vill. Comm. p. 157.

**ealu-gálness**, e ; *f. Drunkenness :—*Forlǣtan . . . ǽrætas and ealugálnessa (ealo-), Nap. 5.

**ealu-geweorc**, es ; *n. Brewing :—*Hié hié selfe mid ealoð oferdrencton . . . On þǣre byrig wæs ǽrest ealogeweorc ongunnen, for þon þe hié wín næfdon *larga prius potione usi, non vini, cujus ferax est locus non est, sed succo tritici per artem confecto*, Ors. 5, 3 ; S. 222, 7. [*Icel.* öl-verk *brewing*.]

**ealu-hús** *an alehouse*. [Ðe werc of þesternesse . . . ben oueretes and untimeliche eten alehuse, O. E. Hml. ii. 11, 30. *Icel.* öl-hús.] v. eala-hús *in Dict.*

**ealu-sceop**. *Dele :* ealu-scerwen. v. scerwen.

**ealu-scóp**. *Substitute :* ealu-scop, es ; *m. One who recites poetry where there is drinking :—*Wē lǣrað þ ǽnig preóst ne beó ealuscop ne on ǽnige wísan glíwige mid him sylfum oþ[þe mid] ōðrum mannum, Ll. Th. ii. 256, 15. Gif preóst oferdruncem tealige, oþþe glíman oþþe ealascop wurðe, 296, 12. Cf. *the section*, ' Ut sacerdos ebrietatem et tabernas fugiat, et inordinata etiam convivia,' 410, 13.

**eám**. *Add :—*Wæs sum æðele cyning Óswold . . . wearð ofslagen Eádwine his eám (*cf. erat Osuald nepos Aeduini regis ex sorore Acha*, Bd. 3, 6), Hml. S. 26, 7. Rōdbert þæs cynges sunu Willelmes hleóp fram his fæder tō his eáme Rōtbryhte (*this Robert was brother of Matilda, William's wife*) on Flandron, Chr. 213, 33.

**eánian**. *Add :—*Wolde seó cú cealfian, ac heó eánode lamb ongeán hire gecynde, Hml. Th. ii. 302, 1. [v. *N. E. D.* ean.]

**eá-ófer**. *Add :—*Be ǽófrum, Bt. 32, 3 ; F. 118, 17.

**ear** *ocean*. *l.* eár *and add :—*In eáre (me are, MS.), Dan. 324. Cf. eá *water*.

**ear** *an ear of corn.* *l.* eár, *and add :*—Eár spica, Wrt. Voc. i. 38, 47 : 287, 20. In eher (æhher, R.) *in spica,* Mk. L. 4, 28. Genim beren eár, Lch. ii. 124, 17. þá hié heora corn ripon ealle þá eár (*spicae*) wǽron blódge, Ors. 4, 8 ; S. 188, 28. Ðára ehera *spicarum,* Mk. p. 2, 16. Eára, An. Ox. 1411. Cornbǽrum eárum *granigeris spicis,* 2361. Eár *spicas,* Wrt. Voc. ii. 120, 84. Ehera, Mt. p. 16, 13. þá ehera (æchir, R.), Mt. L. 12, 1. Ehras, Lk. L. 6, 1. v. æhrige.

**ear** *a harrow :*—Ear occa, An. Ox. 2359 : 2735.

**eár** *an ear.* v. eáre. v. racu.

**earan,** Bl. H. 227, 10. *l.* hǽran. v. hǽre.

**earbe.** *Add :*—Earbe rolon (?·a corruption of *orobus* (=ὄροβος)), Wrt. Voc. i. 68, 22.

**eár-blæd** *the blade of an ear of corn.* v. er-bleadd *in Dict.*

**earc,** e; *f.* *Add :* arc, es; *m.* **I.** *a chest :*—Hú seó earc (*arca*) wæs áworpen of Æquities byrigene ... Sum ceorl ásette his earce mid hwǽte gefyllede ofer his byrgenne ... þoden feorr áwearp þá earce, Gr. D. 41, 23–42, 6. **II.** *the ark of Noah.* v. arc *in Dict.:*—Hú wæs Nóes arc (earc, *v.l.*) gesceapen? Se arc (earc, *v.l.*) wæs fýðerscýte, Angl. vii. 34, 322. Se swymmenda arc, Hml. Th. ii. 60, 2, 9. God beleác hí þynnan þám arce. ... Ðæt flód ábær úp þone arc, i. 22, 1–5 : 20, 31. Se wæs geboren in þære earce, Chr. 855; P. 66, 28. In ðā arkæ (ærce, L.) *in arcam,* Mt. R. 24, 38. In ærce (erce, R.), Lk. L. 17, 27. **III.** *the ark* of the covenant :—Dryhten bebeád Móyse hú hé scolde beran ðā earce ... 'Áhóh hringas on ðā hyrnan ðære earce ... and sting stengas út þurh ðā hringas hí ðære earce sídan ... ' Hwæt mæg seó earc tácnian?, Past. 169, 19–171, 2. Ðerh aerca cýðnisse *per arcam testamenti,* Mt. p. 8, 6. Ðā aerce, Rtl. 194, 15.

**earce.** *Add :* **I.** *a chest :*—Sum ceorl ásette his earcan (*arcam*) mid hwǽte gefylde ofer þæs hálgan mannes byrgene ... þá semninga wæs geworden þoden, þ hé áhóf upp þá earcan and hí forð áwearp, Gr. D. 41, 32–42, 8. **II.** *the ark* of the covenant :—Ðā hyrnan ðære earcan ... bí ðære earcan sídan, Past. 168, 22, 24 (v.p. 506).

**eár-clǽnsend.** *Add :* cf. eár-finger : eár-cóðu. *l.* -coþu.

**eard.** *Add :* **I.** *a land, country, region :*—Óðres eardes landseta, *colonus,* Wrt. Voc. i. 18, 49. Eall gærs and wyrta ealles eardes *omnem herbam regionis,* Gen. 2, 5. Ne þú ne ætstande on þisum earde *nec stes in omni circa regione,* 19, 17. Ealne þone eard Asiam, Hml. Th. i. 68, 34. þone eard Chanaan landes *terram Chanaan,* Num. 13, 3. þone Judéiscan eard, Hml. S. 25, 734. Se cyning wolde þone eard (*Northumbria*) mid ealle fordón, Chr. 448; P. 112, 32. Eord, Shrn. 156, 1. Hé (*St. Clement*) gehwilce eardas namcúðlíce on gemynde hæfde, and þá wanspédigan crístenan ðæra earda ne gedáfode þæt hí openre wǽdlunge underðeódde wurdon, Hml. Th. i. 558, 24. **II.** (1) in connexion with persons. (a) *the country where a person lives or is going to live :*—Eardes álýsednys *patrie liberatio,* Hml. S. 8, 204. For hiora eardes lufan, Bt. 38, 1; F. 194, 28. Ic gewende tó mínum earde, þær ic geboren wæs *revertar in terram, in qua natus sum,* Num. 10, 30. Se kyning ðe hine (*David*) on suā heardum wræce gebróhte, and of his earde ádrǽfde, Past. 37, 4. þ hié on wræcsíþas fóran and þ ellþíéde ... þæt hié mon tó hiora earde forléte, Ors. 4, 4; S. 167, 27 : 6, 30; S. 282, 20 : 6, 34; S. 290, 19 : Wlfst. 120, 13, 14. Férde Godes folc fram ðeówte tó ðām behátenan earde, Hml. Th. ii. 282, 17. Seó sunne scínd on Hierusalem and on Rómebyrig and on þisum earde and on eallum eardum, i. 286, 35. Tó þysan earde, Chr. 959; P. 115, 13. Hú man þisne eard werian sceolde, 1010; P. 140, 29. On þá gerád þ hý nǽfre eft on eard ne cuman. And gif heó man ǽfre eft on earde geméte, Ll. Th. i. 220, 8–10. Beó hé útlah, búton him se cyng eard álýfe (*allow him to remain in the country*), 258, 20. Siþþan Engle and Seaxe Brytene sóhtan, eard begeátan, Chr. 937; P. 110, 7. Oð hié him þær eard genámon, Ors. 1, 10; S. 44, 27. Eard gesécan *to return to their country,* 2, 4; S. 70, 15. (b) *of a more limited area, the place where a person lives, habitation, dwelling, home :*—Hé leng on þám lande gewunian ne mihte, ac of his cýððe gewát and of his earde, Bl. H. 113, 12. þú, Drihten, forgeáfe þám sáwlum eard on hiofonum, Bt. 33, 4; F. 132, 19. Úre ealra bliss eard hæbbendra on ánum þé éce standeð *the joy of us all having habitation in thee alone stands for ever* ; laetantium omnium nostrum habitatio est in te, Ps. Th. 86, 6. (2) in connexion with things, *natural place, native soil* (of plants) :—Ǽlc þing biþ fullost on his ágenum earda, Bt. 34, 1; F. 134, 24. [v. *N. E. D.* erd.] v. úp-eard.

**eard-éðel-riht.** *Dele :* **eard-éðel-wyn.** *Dele.*

**eard-fæst.** *Dele* 'earth-fast,' *and add :* domiciled : **I.** of human beings :—On ðære dene Drihten selfa þára eádmétta eardfæst wunigað (cf. Crist eardað on þære dene eádmódnesse, Bt. 12; F. 36, 22), Met. 7, 38. þá Seaxan wǽron eardfæste néh þǽm gársecge *Saxones, gens in Oceani litoribus sita,* Ors. 4, 13; S. 288, 22. **II.** of things :—Fýr fiólan ne mæg eft æt his éðle, þær þ óþer fýr úp ofer eall þis eardfæst wunað, Met. 20, 156.

**eard-gyf,** es; *n.* *l.* (?) **eard-gifu,** e; *f.* v. gif, An. 575: **eardhæbbendra.** *Dele, and see* eard, II. 1 b.

**eardian.** *Add :* **I.** *intrans.* (1) of human beings. (a) *to live, dwell,*

*be inhabitant* of a country, city, &c. :—Seó mégð þe nú eardaþ on Wiht, Chr. 449; P. 13, 18. On þæm mórum eardiað Finnas (cf. the word used for less permanent dwelling :—On feáwum stówum styccemǽlum wíciað Finnas, 17, 5), Ors. 1, 1; S. 18, 28. On þæm landum eardodon Engle ǽr hí hider on land cóman, 19, 29. Ælle and Cissa ymbsǽton Andredes cester, and ofslógon ealle þá þe þær inne eardedon, Chr. 491; P. 14, 16. Wé witon óþer égland, þér gé magon eardian, pref.; P. 3, 12. (b) *to live, pass one's life :*—Seó cyrice sceal fédan þá þe æt hire eardiaþ, Bl. H. 41, 28. Hú good is þ mon eardige on ðára gebróðra ánnesse *quam bonum habitare fratres in unum,* 139, 30. (c) of the unborn child in the womb :—On þám hálgan breóstum hé eardode nigon mónaþ, Bl. H. 105, 16. (2) of an in-dwelling spirit :—Geleáffulle menn gearwiaþ clǽne wununga on heora heortum Críste. Hé cwæþ: 'Ic eardige on him' . . . God sécþ þá clǽnan heortan him on tó eardienne, Bl. H. 73, 13. On his hálgum God eardaþ (*habitat*), An. Ox. 40, 38 : Bl. H. 11, 28. (3) of beasts :—Stréd þær nǽdran eardien, Lch. i. 366, 9. (4) of things :—þ þær mæge yfelu uncyst eardian, Bl. H. 37, 10. **II.** *trans.* To inhabit, occupy *a country :*—þæt is seó þeód þe Wihtland eardað *gens quae Vectam tenet insulam,* Bd. 1, 15; Sch. 41, 18. [v. *N. E. D.* erde. *O. Sax.* ardón *to inhabit: O. H. Ger.* artón *habitare.*] v. efen-eardigende.

**eardiend,** es; *m. A dweller, an inhabitant :*—Se unclǽna eardiend (*habitator*) eóde of þære ilcan stówe, Gr. D. 236, 8. þá eardiend þære ceastre *inhabitatores civitatis illius,* 192, 3. v. in-, on-eardiend.

**eard-lufiende,** Lch. i. lxi, 4. v. sceand-lufiende.

**eardung.** *Add :* **I.** abstract, *living, dwelling.* (1) of men (or spirits) :—Eardung wæs *municipatus fuerat,* An. Ox. 2, 395 : 4853. Ne biþ Crístes eardung (*or* **II**?) on þære heortan, Bl. H. 13, 23. Nú se áwyrgda gást tó þon férde in þ hús þ hé manna eardunge of þám húse ádrífe *si hanc domum spiritus malignus invasit, et ab ea hominum inhabitationem repulit,* Gr. D. 184, 26. (2) of beasts, v. eardian, I. 3 :—Úre wæs þurh þá lond and stówe þe missenlicra cynna eardung in wæs nǽdrena and wildeóra *per bestioa serpentiosaque loca nobis iter erat,* Nar. 10, 5. Wið nǽddrena eardunge and áflygennysse *to prevent snakes living in a place, and to drive them away,* Lch. i. 366, 8. **II.** concrete, *a dwelling-place, an abode.* (1) of men (or spirits) :—þú, mínes wuldres eardung, Bl. H. 157, 12. Hié gearwiaþ deóflum eardunga, 77, 6 : 151, 11. (2) *a lair* of beasts :—Under ðǽm stáne wæs niccra eardung, Bl. H. 209, 34.

**eardung-hús.** *Add :*—þ hús wæs geworden geleáffullra manna eardunghús (*habitaculum*), Gr. D. 185, 16. Of ðǽm eardunghúse his *de habitaculo suo,* Ps. Srt. 32, 14 : ii. p. 188, 29. Hé funde áne wéste stówe, in þære hé him sylfum geworhte tela unmycel eardunghús, Gr. D. 201, 5. Eádig þú eart, Maria, for ðan on þínum móde þú gearwodest Drihtnes eardunghús, Hml. A. 133, 574.

**eardung-stów.** *Add :*—Háligum werum on þisum middanearde eardungstów (*tabernaculum*) nys, Scint. 62, 9. Betwix deádum mannum bið þín eardingstów, Nar. 50, 28. Uton gebeorgan ús wið swilce eardungstówe (*hell*), Wlfst. 141, 27 : 147, 10. Eardungstówe *tabernaculum,* Ps. L. 18, 6. Hé him sylfum þær (*Canterbury*) eardungstówe sette and his æfterfiligendum eallan, Chr. 995; P. 128, 39. Hié sceolden habban éce eardungstówe on ðæs Fæder húse furðor ðonne his ægnu bearn *in domo Patris aeterna mansione etiam filiis praeferuntur,* Past. 409, 4. Symbelnessa eardungstówa *sollemnitates tabernaculorum,* An. Ox. 40, 37.

**eard-wunung,** e ; *f. Living in one's native land :*—þolige sé ðe hit on gelang sý ǽlcere eardwununge and wræcnige of earde, oððon on earde swíðe deópe gebéte, Wlfst. 120, 13 : 300, 24.

**eáre.** *Add :* eár, es : **I.** *an ear* (part of the head) :—Inneweard eáre *auris,* útweard eáre *auricula,* Wrt. Voc. ii. 10, 22, 23. *Parotides* eár-cóðu, *ota, g.* (=ὦτα, *graece*) eár, i. 20. 1. Hé cearf of heora handa and eáran and nosa, Chr. 1014; P. 145, note 9. Égo, eára *oculos, aures,* Rtl. 125, 39. **II.** with reference to its function, *the organ of hearing :*—Of eáres hlyste hé hýrsumode mé, R. Ben. 19, 20. þ gé on eáre (in eáre, L. R.) gehýrað *quod in aure auditis,* Mt. 10, 27. Ic secge þé on þín eáre, Angl. viii. 300, 14. þte in eáre sprecend gié woeron *quod in aurem locuti estis,* Lk. L. 12, 3. Eówer þonne eádige ége þe hiæ geseoð and eáran (eáro, L.) eówre þe hiæ gehērað, Mt. R. 13, 16. Se ðe hæfes eáro (eára, R.) tó hérenne, Mt. L. 13, 9. Heáro, 43. Eóro, Lk. p. 8, 15. **III.** as channel of information, as in to come to the *ears* of a person :—þá becóm þ tó eáran þæs ealdormannes *peruenit ad aures principis,* Bd. 1, 7; Sch. 20, 16. þá cóm him tó eáran þe Agathes drohtnunge, Hml. S. 8, 7. þis cóm þá tó eáran þam cnihte, 9, 57. **IV.** *ear,* as in favourable *ear, attention* to what is heard :—Sé is fram Gode þe Godes beboda mid gehýrsumum eáre gehýrð, Hml. Th. ii. 228, 23. Hié forgytaþ þ hié hwéne ær ymbhygdigum eárum gehýrdon reccean, Bl. H. 55, 27. Hé him mildheortnesse eáron ontýnde, 107, 1. **V.** *a handle* on a pot. Cf. *Icel.* eyra *a handle* on a pot, see *N. E. D.* ear, II. 8, *and next word.*

**eárede ;** *adj. Having a handle :*—Eárede (*printed* earde, but see Angl. viii. 450) fæt *cratera,* Wrt. Voc. i. 24, 25. v. eáre, V.

**eáre-finger.** ·v. eár-finger : **eáre-lippric.** v. eár-liprica(-e).

**earendel.** *Add:* eorendel :—Leóma *vel* earendil (oerendil, Erf., earendel, Corp.) *jubar,* Txts. 72, 554. Eorendel *aurora,* Hy. S. 16, 35 : 30, 2. Se níwa eorendel Sanctus Jóhannes, Bl. H. 163, 30. [Cf. *Icel.* Örvandill, *and* v. Grmm. D. M. (trans.), 374 sqq.]

**earfe.** v. earbe: **earfed-nyme.** *Dele:* **earfede.** v. earfoþe.

**eár-finger,** es ; *m. The little finger.* Cf. Quas tua fert auris sordes trahit auricularis (*lytil finger*), Wrt. Voc. i. 179, 25 :—Eárfinger *auricularis,* Ælfc. Gr. Z. 298, 15 : Wrt. Voc. ii. 10, 25. [*O. H. Ger.* örfinger.] v. eár-clænsend.

**earfoþ-cirre ;** *adj. Hard to turn, difficult to convert:*—Hé wæs swíðe earfaðcierre tó Godes geleáfan, Shrn. 100, 17.

**earfoþ-dǽde ;** *adj. Hard to do, difficult:*—Hit is ðeáh swíðe earfeðdǽde (earfoð-, v. l.) ðæt mon lustlíce ðone láreów gehiéran wille ðe mon ne lufað *difficile est, ut quamlibet recta denuntians praedicator, qui non diligitur, libenter audiatur,* Past. 147, 12. Cf. íþ-dǽde.

**earfoðe,** es ; *pl. nom. acc.* a, u, o, e ; *n.* [*A feminine* earfoþu ; *gen.* e, a, *or indecl. seems to occur in the following :*—Hú ne witon wé þ nán nearewnes, ne nán earfoþu, ne nán unrótnes, ne nán sár, ne nán hefignes nis nán gesǽld, Bt. 24, 4 ; F. 86, 21. Is him óðer earfeðu . . ; þ hí scoma mǽste dreógað, Cri. 1273. Þæt hís earfeðu eal gelumpe, módcearu mǽgum, Gú. 165. Orsorg ðises andweardan lífes earfoþe (-a, v. l.), Bt. 39, 7 ; F. 222, 31. Þæt him Dryhten tó hyra earfeða ende gerýme, Gú. 196. Ic merestrengo máran áhte, earfeðo on ýþum, B. 534. Nele hé þá earfeþu (*or pl.?*) habban, þæt hé on þysne síð fare, Gen. 513.] **I.** *tribulation, affliction, trouble :*—Him ne wæs nænig earfoþe þ líchomlice gedál, Bl. H. 135, 30. Þ þú mid earefoþe sum eofel ne geféldest, Bt. 7, 3 ; F. 22, 19. Manifeald earfoþe (-u, v. l.) þrowian, 39, 10 ; F. 228, 15. Monige earfoþa ús becuman sceoldan, Bl. H. 85, 35. Mistlíce wíta (-u, v. l.) and manigfealde earfoþa (manigfeald earfoþu, v. l.) cumaþ, Bt. 39, 2 ; F. 212, 28. Þæt synt þás andweardan earfoþa, Ps. Th. 31, 7. Mé synt earfoðu swýðe néh *tribulatio proxima est,* 21, 9. Mé on dæge deorc earfoðe cnyssedan *in die tribulationis,* 85, 6. Orsorg ðises lífes earfoþa, Bt. 39, 7 ; F. 222, 31. Wépan míne wræcsíðas, earfoða fela, Kl. 39. Þæt sý endeleás earfoða dǽl, Deór. 30. Sumum eádwelan, sumum earfeða dǽl, Vy. 67 : Wand. 6 : Jul. 626 : Gú. 178. On hwylcum earfoþum þær wé úres feóres ne wénaþ, Bl. H. 51, 28. Efenþrowgende óþres earfoþum, 75, 19. Of earfoðum eallum *ex omni tribulatione,* Ps. Th. 53, 7 : 59, 10. Of ðám earfoðum eallum *de necessitatibus,* 106, 12. Earfeðum, Men. 224. Þ hé him tó earfeðum cwóme *that he came to trouble them,* Gú. 403. Wið earfeðum gescildan, 428. Sume him ondrædaþ earfoþu . . , ðeáh hí hí eáþe ádreógan mægen, Bt. 39, 11 ; F. 228, 26 : Sal. 374. Earfoða, Deór. 2. Earfeðu, Cri. 1172. Tó þe ástígan þurh ðás earfoþu þisse worulde, Bt. 33, 4 ; F. 132, 28 : Met. 20, 254. Gemunan eal þá earfeþu, Cri. 1202. Eall þá earfeðo, An. 1488. His earfoðo ealle, Sat. 127. Hí ne magon nán earfoþa (-u, v. l.) áberan, Bt. 39, 10 ; F. 228, 2. Ðe ðú him earfoðu ǽnig geáfe *quem percussisti,* Ps. Th. 68, 27. Ic wíte þolade, yfel earfeðu, Cri. 1453. Gearfoðu, Bt. 31, 1 ; F. 110, 26. **II.** *labour, pains, trouble of laborious work :*—Naenge earbeðe *nullo negotio,* Wrt. Voc. ii. 115, 7. Þæt hí ágon on ágenan hwílan mid earfeðan gewunnen, Wlfst. 159, 19. Bútan earfeðum *easily,* Jul. 359 : Gú. 216 : El. 1292. **III.** *bodily pain, labour of childbirth, disease, hardship :*—Sió áheardung is on twá wísan gerád. Oþer biþ on fruman ǽr þon þe ǽnig oþer earfeþe on lífre becume ; óþeru æfter óþrum earfeþum þǽre lífre cymð, Lch. ii. 204, 5–8. Hé (*Adam*) sár ne wiste, earfoð dǽl, ne cóm blóð of benne, Gen. 180. Weorc þrowade, earfoða dǽl, Rä. 71, 13. Þirst and hungor . . . ǽghwylc þissa earfoða éce standeð, Sal. 474. Hí cleopigan ongan, méðe and meteleás : ' Ic eów hálsie þæt gé mé of þyssum earfeðum úp forlǽten,' El. 700. Sceal mon blóð lǽtan ; þá þe þ ne dóþ on micel[um] earfeþum becumað, Lch. ii. 210, 12. Wíf ácenþ bearn and þrowaþ micel earfoþu æfter þám ðe heó ǽr micelne lust þurhteáh, Bt. 31, 1 ; F. 112, 2. **IV.** *work, labour :*—Geseón on him selfum synne genóge, atol earfoða ǽrgedénra, Cri. 1266. **V.** *what is difficult, the difficult v. next word :*—Þám synfullum þinceð þæt nán wiht ne sý þæs hátes ne þæs cealdes . . . , ne þæs eáðes ne þæs earfoðes, ne þæs leófes ne þæs láðes, þæt hig mihte fram úres Drihtnes lufan ásceáden, Wlfst. 185, 1.

**earfoþe ;** *adj. Dele* 'Bt. proœm ; Fox viii. 7,' *and add :* **I.** *difficult :*—Earfoðe *difficilis,* earfoðre *difficilior,* ealra earfoðust (-ost, v. l.) *difficillimus,* Ælfc. Gr. Z. 16, 6. Hé nǽre ná ælmihtig, gyf him ǽnig gefadung earfoðe wǽre, Lch. iii. 278, 15. Drihten, nis ðé nán ðing earfoðe, Hml. Th. i. 62, 11. Se gewuna gedéþ eáþe þæt ðe ǽr earfoðe þúhte, R. Ben. 5, 19. Tó earfoðe þyncan, Wlfst. 284, 10. For ðǽm ðe hit swá earfoðe is ǽnegum menn tó witanne hwonne hé geclǽnsod sié *quia valde difficile est purgatum se quemlibet posse cognoscere,* Past. 51, 5. Hú hefig and hú earfoþe (gearfoþe, v. l.) þis is tó gereccanne, Bt. 39, 4 ; F. 216, 33. Hit is earfoð tó witane, Chr. 1050; P. 170, 25. Þæt gástlice angyt is earfoþe tó understandende, R. Ben. 66, 19. Ðú mé áhsast micles and earfoþes tó ongitanne, Bt. 42 ; F. 256, 11. Ðis fers is swíðe deóplic eów tó understandenne . . . Seó Godcundnys gefylde þysne earfoðan cwyde ðurh ðá ánnysse Crístes hádes, Hml. Th. ii.

386, 20. Earfoðu *difficilia,* Kent. Gl. 1093. Wæter and eorþe sint swíþe earfoþe tó geseónne on fýre, Bt. 33, 4 ; F. 130, 27 : 34, 11 ; F. 150, 24. Manige óðre þe earfoðe sindon tó áteallene, Chr. 1086 ; P. 222, 18. Earfeþe, P. 218, 21. On þá earfoþestan sprǽce tó gereccenne, Bt. 39, 4 ; F. 216, 15. **II.** *laborious, toilsome :*—Hit bið swíðe geswincful ðæt mon ǽlcne mon scyle onsundrum lǽran, hit is ðeáh earfoðre ealle ætsomne tó lǽranne *valde laboriosum est unumquemque . . . instruere ; longe tamen laboriosius est auditores innumeros uno eodemque tempore instruere,* Past. 453, 11 : 455, 6. Earfeðran *difficiliore,* i. *graviore,* Wrt. Voc. ii. 140, 19. Uton niman þone earfoðran weg, þæt wé hér sume hwíle swincon, tó ðý þæt wé écelíce beón bútan geswince, Hml. Th. i. 164, 12. **III.** *grievous :*—Micel éhtnys wæs þá þá hí wǽron gemartyrode, ac git cymð earfoðre éhtnys on Anticrístes tócyme, Hml. S. 35, 347. [v. *N. E. D.* arveth. *Icel.* erfiðr.]

**earfoþ-fére.** *l.* -fére *hard to travel, and for* 'Scint. 10' *substitute :*—Sume cumað swíðe feorran and habbað swíðe yfelne weig and swíðe earfoðférne, Shrn. 187, 10. Cf. eáþ-fére.

**earfoð-fynde ;** *adj. Hard to find :*—Earfoðfynde wæs ðár se man þe swilc ne mihte hreówan, Hml. S. 23, 82.

**earfoþ-hylde.** *Substitute :* earfoþ-hilde ; *adj. Hard to incline, that does not readily relinquish old habits :*—Sé ðe on muneclícere drohtnunge earfoðhylde bið, and gyrnð ðǽra ðinga ðe hé to woruldlicere drohtnunge nǽfde, him geneálǽhð se hreófla Giezi, Hml. Th. i. 400, 1.

**earfoþian.** v. exrfoþian *in Dict. and* ge-earfoþian.

**earfoþ-lǽre.** *Substitute : Hard to teach, indocile :*—Benedictus forlét þá earfoðlǽran bróðro *Benedictus indociles deseruit,* Gr. D. 110, 19.

**earfoþ-lic.** *Take Deut.* 1, 17 *under next word, and add :* **I.** *difficult :*—Ðæt is wundorlic þ ðú segst, and swíþe earfoþlic dysegum monnum tó ongitanne *mira et concessu difficilis illatio,* Bt. 38, 2 ; F. 198, 17. Earfoðlic (*or under* II ?) is tó áctellanne seó gedrecednes . . . and þ geswinc and manna fyll, Chr. 1056 ; P. 186, 31. **II.** *grievous :*—Earbetlicust (earbed-) *molestissimum,* Txts. 79, 1320. Earfoðlicost, Wrt. Voc. ii. 56, 13. [þe erueðliche (arueð-, 127, 11) herbiwist *the hard life* (of John the Baptist), O. E. Hml. ii. 125, 11. *Icel.* erfiðligr.]

**earfoþ-líce.** *Add :* **I.** *with difficulty, hardly :*—Earfedlíce (erabedlícae, Erf.) *egre,* Txts. 59, 729. Earfoðlíce, Wrt. Voc. ii. 29, 15 : 142, 71 : *difficulter,* Wülck. Gl. 251, 42. Earfoþli[ce] *quoquomodo,* An. Ox. 56, 151. Ðone þurst wé earfoðlíce (*vix*) áberon, Nar. 7, 30 : Homl. Th. i. 86, 8, 14. Se eorl earfoðlíce gestylde þ folc, Chr. 1052 ; P. 180, 10 : 1075; P. 209, 38. ¶ *used instead of a complementary adjective :*—Gif eów ǽnig þing þince earfoðlíce *si difficile vobis visum aliquid fuerit,* Deut. 1, 17. Earfoðlíce *difficile (est),* Scint. 33, 4. **II.** *grievously, painfully :*—Earfoðlíce *graviter, dolenter,* Wrt. Voc. ii. 142, 71. Þá gelomp ús þæt wé wurdon earfoðlíce mid þurste geswencte *accidit nobis siti laborare,* Nar. 7, 29. [v. *N. E. D.* arvethliche. *Icel.* erfið-liga.]

**earfoþnes.** *Add :*—Sýn him gebodod eal seó stíðnes and seó earfoðnes þe tó Gode lǽt *predicentur ei omnia dura et aspera per que itur ad Deum,* R. Ben. 97, 19. Se bisceop and se eorl gebidan mycele earfoðnysse þá hí hámward fóran *the bishop and the earl underwent much hardship on the journey home,* Chr. 1061 ; P. 191, 2. Áfyrseþ hé þás earfoðnesse (*a flood*) fram ús, Bl. H. 247, 4 : (*St. Andrew's imprisonment*), 243, 18. For þissum earfoðnessum þe wé þissum mannan dydon *for the hardships we have inflicted on the man,* 247, 18. Be þisse worlde earfoþnessum *about the troubles of this world,* 109, 6. Manega earfoðnessa hié þé magon on gebringan, ah áræfne þú þá ealle, 237, 7. [þu scealt mid ærfeðnesse þe metes tylian (*in laboribus comedes ex terra,* Gen. 3, 17), O. E. Hml. i. 223, 34.]

**earfoþ-recce.** *For* 'Lupi . . Lye' *substitute :*—Hit is on rǽdinge earfoþrecce hwæt hé gesewenlicra wundra geworhte, Wlfst. 22, 14.

**earfoþ-rihte ;** *adj. Hard to correct, incorrigible :*—Gif hé þwur sý . . . oðde earfoðrihte, Nap. 19.

**earfoþ-sǽlig.** *Add :* , *having hard fortune. After* moldan *add :* þæt hine se árgifa ealles bescyrge módes cræfta. Cf. heard-sǽlig.

**earfoþ-þrag.** *l.* -þrág.

**earfoþ-wilde ;** *adj. Hard to subdue :*—His foregengan þe wǽron . . . on ǽnegum gewinne earfoþwylde nǽfre þisne andweald on swá micelre sibbe smyltnesse gehealdan ne mihton, Lch. iii. 436, 12.

**earg.** *Add :* **I.** *cowardly, timid, spiritless :*—Earh *tremibundus,* i. *pavidus,* An. Ox. 1865 : 4896. Þone ungemetlíce eargan þe him ondræt mǽre þonne hé þurfe *pavidus ac fugax non metuenda formidat,* Bt. 37, 4 ; F. 192, 21. Earge *ignavi,* Wrt. Voc. ii. 46, 13 : *inertes,* 92, 36. Eálá gé eargan and ídelgeornan, hwý gé swá unnytte sión and swá áswundene, Bt. 40, 4 ; F. 238, 30. Eargra *timidorum,* i. *timentium,* An. Ox. 739. Mid eargum *formidilosis,* 4894 : *meticulosis,* i. *tremebundis,* 5271. Þá consulas noldon hié selfe swá earge geþencan swá hié þá wífmen forcwǽdon, Ors. 4, 10 ; S. 194, 15. Þá eargan mengo *fugaces turmas,* Wrt. Voc. ii. 151, 48. Þonan ðe hí teohhiaþ þ hí scylan eádigran weorþan, þ hí weorþan ðonan earmran and eargran, Bt. 26, 2 ; F. 92, 27. **II.** *vicious, profligate, prodigal.* v. earg-ness, -scipe :—

Geddung from ðǽm argæ sune *parabola de luxurioso filio*, Lk. p. 8, 18. v. arg, earh *in Dict.*

**ear-geát.** v. earn-geát: **ear-gebland.** *l.* eár-gebland.

**eár-gespreca.** *Substitute: A confidential speaker, a counsellor :—* Eárgespeca *auricularius* (cf. auricularium, consiliarium, Corp. Gl. H. 23, 945. a gloss on 2 Sam. 23, 23 (?) :—Fecit eum sibi David auricularium a secreto), Wrt. Voc. ii. 7, 46.

**eargian.** *Substitute: To grow timid, turn coward, lose heart :—* Ðumbe beóð þá bydelas þe for ege oððe ǽnigre worldscame eargiað and wandiað Godes riht tó sprecanne, Wlfst. 191, 5. Þá eargode heora án for þám ormǽtum cyle, Hml. S. 11, 156. His geféran eargodon bútan eahta hund mannum þe him mid fuhton, 25, 654. Ne dēð hē náht, eargie hē oððon hine forsceamige riht tó sprecanne, Ll. Th. ii. 326, 21. Eargian for woruldege, 310, 20. Sculon cówre heortan eargian swíðe (*animam uestram tabescentem faciam*), and eówra feónda mǽgen strangian þearle, Wlfst. 133, 4. [v. *N. E. D.* argh; *vb.* Cf. *O. H. Ger.* ir-argēn *obstupescere.*] Cf. ge-irgan.

**earg-líc;** *adj. Cowardly, craven. timid :—*Ne gewurðe hit ná on lífe ꝥ wē álecgan úre wuldor mid earhlicum fleáme, Hml. S. 25, 661. Ful earhlíce lága (*laws that only cowards would submit to*) and scandlice nýdgyld ús synt gemǽne, Wlfst. 162, 10. Cwæð hē earhlicon wordum *he said with timid words*, Hml. S. 23, 580.

**earglíce** *in a cowardly manner. Add to* earhlíce :—Earhlíce † nīðlíce *muliebriter* (i. *enervit*er, An. Ox. 744), Hpt. Gl. 424, 1. Gē tósesede swíðe áfirhte oft litel werod earhlíce forðúgað *fugistis nullo persequente*, Wlfst. 133, 6. Hē eóde in earhlíce (*fearfully*), Jud. 4, 18 : Hml. S. 3, 160 : 23, 493. Se smið eóde tó his byrgene and genam áne hringan, earhlíce swaþeáh, 21, 63. Hý hī sylfe earhlíce betealdon, 23, 307. þú earhlíce (*with fear and trembling*) scealt gyltas þíne bemurnan, Dóm. L. 30, 54. v. arhlíce *in Dict.*

**earg-ness,** e; *f. Profligacy :—*Dernegiligru and arognisse *adultera et peccatrice*, Mk. R. 8, 38. [v. *N. E. D.* arghness.] v. earg, II, *and next word.*

**earg-scipe.** *Substitute:* I. *cowardice, pusillanimity.* v. earg, I :—Ongeán módstaðolnysse and módes strencðe se mánfulla deófol sendeð wácmódnesse and lyðerne earhscype (*base cowardice*), Wlfst. 53, 12. II. *profligacy.* v. earg, II :—ꝥ wíf in argscipe begrippene *mulierem in adulterio reprehensam*, Jn. p. 5, 8. [Heo mid ærhscape arnden to heolde and letten slæn heore folc, Laym. 12411. *Icel.* arg-skapr *cowardice.*]

**earh.** *Add:* v. arewe: **earhlíce.** v. earglíce.

**eár-hring.** *Add:—*Eárhring *inauris*, Wrt. Voc. ii. 48, 26. Wǽron þá eáran him þurhþyrelode and eárhringas on hongedon of mænigfealdan gimcynne geworhte *perforatis auribus, ex quibus uniones dependebant*, Nar. 26, 31. [*O. L. Ger.* ōr-hring.] v. eár-preón.

**eá-risc.** *For ‘ Cot. . . . Lye ’ substitute :—*Eórisc *papirum*, Txts. 85, 1503 : *scirpea*, 98, 960. Eórisc, *leber*, 95, 1823. Eárisc *bremium*, Wrt. Voc. ii. 12, 67 : i. 31, 32 (*printed* eáric). v. eá-rixe *in Dict.*

**eá-ríþ.** *l.* eá-ríþ. **eár-læppa.** *Add:* [v. *N. E. D.* ear-lap.]

**eár-lip[p]rica (-e).** [The gender is uncertain, the word occurring with masc. fem. and neut. pronouns.] *The flap of the ear* (used only in the Northern specimens) :—Ðió eárliprece *auricula*, Lk. p. 11, 6. Eárlipprico his ðió suiðro (eárliprica his ðæt swiðra, R.) *auriculam ejus dextram*, Lk. L. 22, 50. Eárliprico (-a, R.), 51. Ðone ꝥærliprica (ðá eáreliprica, L.) *auriculam*, Mk. R. 14, 47. Eárlipprica ꝥ (*altered from* ðió) suiðra (eárliprica ðæt swiðra, R.), Jn. L. 18, 10. Eórlipprico (eárliprica, R.), 26. Eároliprice, Mt. L. 26, 51. In eárliprico (-a, R.) *in auriculas*, Mk. L. 7, 33. [Cf. (?) *O. L. Ger.* lepor *a lip, and* -ic- *diminutive suffix* ]

**eár-loccas.** *Substitute:* eár-locc, es; *m. An ear-lock* (v. *N. E. D.*), *a lock of hair over* or *above the ear :—*Eárloccas *antiae*, Wrt. Voc. i. 40, 49.

**earm.** *Add:* I. *an arm :—*Se earm betweónan elnbogan and hand-wyrste *cubitus*, Wrt. Voc. ii. 22, 61. Sum man feóll on íse ꝥ his earm tóbærst, Hml. S. 26, 34. Weard Pirrus wund on óþran earme *Pyrrhus transfixo brachio saucius*, Ors. 4, 1 ; S. 158, 2. Earma *lacertorum*, An. Ox. 5458. Hé áþenedum earmum ongan fleógan, Bl. H. 187, 27. II. *a foreleg of an animal :—*Seó leó mid hire earmum scræf geworhte, Hml. S. 236, 787.

**earm.** I. *wretched, unhappy.* (1) of persons :—Earm *calamitosum* (*vulgus*), An. Ox. 4868. Ne meht þú cwedan ꝥ þú earm sē and ungesǽlig (*te existimari miserum*), Bt. 8 ; F. 24, 23. Ic earm tó þē cleopie ; for þon on sáre míne geár syndon fornumene, Bl. H. 89, 13. Hí ácwealdon eall þæt hí fundon þæs earman folces, Jos. 10, 37. Help nú þínum earmum moncynne, Bt. 4 ; F. 8, 11. þē þincþ sē earmra sē ꝥ yfel dēþ ðonne sē þe hit þafað *miserior tibi injuriae illator, quam acceptor esse videretur*, Bt. 38, 6 ; F. 208, 1. Hí sint earmran and dysigran and ungesǽligran, 32, 3 ; F. 118, 28. (1 a) in a moral sense :—Hit is scondlic ymb swelc tó sprecanne hwelc hit þá wæs, þá swá earme wíf and swá elðeódge (*mulieres patria profugae*) hæfdon gegán þone cræftgestan dǽl ealles þises middangeardes, Ors. 1, 10 ; S.

48, 5. (2) of things :—Of earmre *calamitosa* (*atrocitate*), An. Ox. 3853. II. *poor, destitute :—*Swá earm ꝥ hē næfþ furþon þá neódþearfe áne, ꝥ is, wist and wǽda, Bt. 33, 2 ; F. 124, 16. ꝥ hē blíþe þæs earman líchoman gefylle . . . God him worldspēda syleþ, ꝥ hí þæs earman helpan sceolan, Bl. H. 37, 29, 36. Earman wífe *pauperculae mulierculae*, An. Ox. 3646. Winnan on swá earm folc swá hí wǽron *adversus inopes sumsisse bellum*, Ors. 1, 10 ; S. 44, 12. Hié for feós lufan earmne fordēmaþ, Bl. H. 63, 11. Úre teóþan sceattas sýn earmra manna gafol. Ágifaþ teóþan dǽl ealles þæs ceápes þe gē habbaщ earmum mannum, and tó Godes cyrican, þǽm earmestan Godes þeówum þe þá cyrican mid godcundum dreámum weorþiað . . . Gē seóþ hū blíþe þá earman beóþ, þonne hí mon mid mete and mid hrægle rēteþ, 41, 24–29. Swá feala earmra manna swá on þæs rícan neáweste and þæs welegan sweltaþ, 53, 5. Sýn wē earmum ælmesgeorne, 109, 14. Eallum gemǽne, earmum and eádigum, Hml. Th. i. 64, 32. þǽm earmestum mannum, Bl. H. 53, 19. II a. *poor in something, destitute of* (*with gen.*) :—Hú earne wē bióð ðára ēcena ðinga *ab aeternis nos miseros cernimus*, Past. 389, 8.

**earm-beág.** *Add:—Dextrocerium, armillum, vel torium*, i. *brachiale* earmbeág, Wrt. Voc. ii. 139, 86. Armbāges [=earmbeágas] *dextralia*, Hpt. 33, 250, 4. [*O. L. Ger.* arm-bōg : *O. H. Ger.* arm-pouc *armilla, brachiale.*]

**earm-boga.** *Add.* **Dele.**

**earme.** *Add :—*Judas wæs on ðæra twelf apostola rím geteald ǽr hē hine sylfne swíðe earme and unlǽdlíce of ðære gemánan ealra Godes gecorenra ádwǽscte and ádílgode, Hml. A. 153, 48.

**earmella,** an ; *m. A sleeve :—*Wege þú þínne earmellan, Tech. ii. 127, 16. Hý habbaþ síde earmellan (*fluxas manicas*), R. Ben. 136, 23. [*O. H. Ger.* armilo ; *m. manica.*]

**earm-full ;** *adj. Wretched, miserable :—*Hí for hellewítes ōgan and for Crístes lufan þis earmfulle líf forlǽtaþ, Lch. iii. 440, 34.

**earm-gegírela.** *For* Cot. 59 *substitute* Wrt. Voc. ii. 26, 9.

**earm-heort.** *Substitute :* I. *poor-spirited, faint-hearted :—*On ôðre wísan sint tó monianne ðá ofermódan and ðá úpáhæfenan on hira mōde, on ôðre wísan ðá earmheortan and ðá wácmódan (*pusillanimes*), Past. 209, 2. II. *pitiful, tender-hearted :—*Hē wæs tó þám earmheort (*swá mildheort, v. l.*) ꝥ him ofhreów ꝥ ástēpede wíf, gif hē ne gehulpe hire dreórinysse, Gr. D. 18, 13. [Cf. Mildhertnesse is nemned ec arm-hertnesse. Armbeorted is þe man þe reoweð his sinne and milce bit, O E. Hml. ii. 95, 29. *Goth.* arma-hairts *misericors : O. H. Ger.* arm-herz *misericors.*]

**earmian.** *Substitute : To cause pity* in a person (*dat.*). [For con-structions cf. of-hreówan.] (1) used impersonally with gen. of cause :—Hwám ne mæg earmian swylcere tíde *to whom will there not be pity for such a time?*, Chr. 1086 ; P. 218, 4. (2) with cause of pity as subject :—Him earmode þær[e] ungesǽligan angin *the unhappy woman's enterprise was a cause of pity to him*, Hml. A. 196, 29. [Cf. *Goth.* arman *to pity : O. H. Ger.* parmēn *miserari.*] v. of-earmian ; earmung ; *and* cf. irman.

**earming.** *Add :* (1) with the idea of suffering :—Nū is seó tíd, earmincg Zosimus, ꝥ þú gefremme ꝥ þē beboden is, ac . . . ic nát mid hwí ic delfe, Hml. S. 23 b, 763. Earming, ne geýc ðú swýðor þíne yrmða, Hml. Th. i. 594, 27. Wē spreacð ymbe God, earmingas be mildheortum, 286, 9. (2) with idea of reprobation :—Ic, earming, míne lima áwende tó deóflicum weorcum, Angl. xi. 112, 18. Hwæt ðú (*the impenitent thief*) lá, earming, ne ondrǽtst ðú ðē God?, Hml. Th. ii. 256, 12. Ðá áwrát se earming mid his ágenra hande swá swá se deófol him gedihte þone pistol, Hml. S. 3, 382. (3) with idea of contempt, *a poor thing :—*Gē sind earmingas gewordene, gē ðe wǽron mǽre and strange, Hml. Th. i. 64, 24. ¶ The word seems to occur in local names :—Þrý hámas . . . þus gehátene . . . Earmingaford, C. D. iii. 60, 34. Earmingtūn, iv. 292, 11. [v. *N. E. D.* arming. *O. H. Ger.* arming *pauper.*] v. irming.

**earm-lic.** *Add :* I. *miserable.* (1) *attended with misery :—*Ne wēnaþ hí nō ꝥ ꝥ gōd wyrd sié, ac wēnaþ ꝥ hió sié swíþe earmlico (*populus judicat esse miserrimam*), Bt. 40, 2 ; F. 236, 27. Bið earmlic gedál líces and sáwle, Wlfst. 187, 15. Æfter þære earmlycan eówre geendunge, 295, 20. On þære earmlican tíde *ea tempestate*, An. Ox. 3938. Ðý earmlican *calamitosa* (*atrocitate*), Wrt. Voc. ii. 83, 61. Earmlicne deáþ geðolian, Wlfst. 97, 5. (2) *expressing misery, piteous :—*Wēpendre stefne and earmlicre, Bl. H. 87, 27. (3) *pitiable, deplor-able :—*Sárlic tó cwepene, earmlic tó se[cganne] *dolendum dictu*, i. *gemendum*, An. Ox. 1730. Hit is swíþe earmlic ðing ꝥ ðá dysegan men sint ælces dōmes swá blinde, Bt. 32, 3 ; F. 118, 21 ; An. 1137. Ic eom mycd earmlíre ofergiotolnesse ofseten, Solil. H. 63, 4. Ð þær wǽre sum man earmlíce deáþe áswolten, swá ꝥ hē hine sylfne áwyrde, Bl. H. 219, 11. II. *poor, mean, sorry :—*Mid earmlicum *cum paupertinis*, An. Ox. 46, 15. Gemildsa mē nacodum forlidenum, næs ná of earm-licum birdum geborenum, Ap. Th. 11, 20. [v. *N. E. D.* armlich. *O. Sax.* arm-lik *pitiable : O. H. Ger.* arma-líh *miser.*]

**earmlíce.** *Add:* I. *miserably.* (1) cf. earm-lic, I. 1 :—Rēðe sorc-

bēcna þ folc earmlíce brēgdon (drehtan, v. l.), Chr. 793; P. 55, 33. Hū earmlíce hit gefaren is gynd þás ðeóde, Wlfst. 166, 11. Hī earmlíce fērdon swā þ se hālga wer hī wundorlíce geband, Hml. S. 32, 206. (2) *piteously*, cf. earm-lic, I. 2 :—þēh þe heó earmlíce hiere feores tō him wilnade *quamvis miserabiliter pro vita precantem*, Ors. 3, 11; S. 150, 33. (3) *pitiably*. Cf. earm-lic, I. 3 :—Sume hreówlíce on fōtan gangende, sume earmlíce rídende, Chr. 1075; P. 210, 17. þá ealdan sculan earmlíce licgan heápmælum æt hām hungre ācwolene, Wlfst. 295, 15. II. *meanly*. Cf. earm-lic, II :—ðū woldest beón foremǽre on weorþscipe . . . þonne scealt þū ōleccan swíþe earmlíce and swíþe eádmódlíce þām þe þē tō þām gefultumian mǽge *dignitatibus fulgere velis? danti supplicabis; et poscendi humilitate vilesces*, Bt. 32, 1; F. 114, 11. Hū mæg mon earmlícor gebǽron, þonne mon hine underþeóde his weregan flǽsce *quis non spernat atque abjiciat vilissimae fragilissimaeque rei, corporis, servum?*, F. 114, 23. [v. N. E. D. armliche. O. H. Ger. armelicho.]

**earm-sceape**, Dóm. L. 196. v. next word.

**earm-sceapen.** *Substitute: Miserable, wretched.* (1) *suffering misfortune, hardship*, &c. :—Gewāt þā earmsceapen (Nebuchadnezzar) eft sīðian, nacod nýdgenga, wundorlic wrǽcca tō mancynne, Dan. 632. Ne mihte earmsceapen (*the youth about to be eaten by the cannibals*) āre findan æt þām folce, An. 1131. (2) *in a moral sense* :—Saga, earmsceapen unclǽne gǽst, Jul. 418: An. 1347. Earmsceapen on weres wæstmum (*Grendel*), B. 1351. Se earmsceapena man, Antecríst, Wlfst. 54, 16. Se sylfa deófol . . . wyrð on þām earmsceapenan men, Antecríste, 101, 7. Þis atule gewrixl earmsceape (-sceapene? cf. *the same passage in* Wlfst. 138, 30: þá earmsceapenan men) men on worulda woruld wendað *his miseris vicibus miseri volvuntur in aevum*, Dóm. L. 196. Mǽrðe þára hāligra, earmsceapenra wítu *gaudia sanctorum, poenas malorum*, 23. Ðā micelan wíta þe þǽr beóð þām earmsceapenan for heora ǽrdǽdum gegearwode, Wlfst. 137, 1. [O. Sax. arm-skapan *unhappy, unfortunate.* Cf. Icel. arm-skapaðr *miserable*.]

**earm-slífe.** Add: R. Ben. I. 93, 9.

**earm-stoc**, es; m (?). *A sleeve* :—Feald þū mid þínre swíðran hande þane hem þínes wynstran earmstoces ofer þinne wynstran scytefinger, Tech. ii. 128, 2. [Cf. O. H. Ger. stūcha *manica: Icel.* stuka *a sleeve.*]

**earm-swíþ.** For Cot. 123 : 200 *substitute* :—Ðǽm earmswíðum *lacertosis (viribus)*, Wrt. Voc. ii. 76, 41 : 52, 27.

**earm-þenning.** v. þenning : earmþu. v. irmþ.

**earmung.** *Substitute : Pity, compassion* :—On mildheortnyssa and earminga (*printed* earnunga) *in misericordia et miserationibus*, Ps. Spl. 102, 4. v. of-earmung.

**earn.** *Add* :—Fleáh sum earn ætforan him (*Cuthbert*) on síðe . . . Hē cwæð : 'God mæg unc þurh þisne earn ǽt foresceáwian' . . . Se earn on ðam ófre gesæt mid fisce geflogen, þone hē ðǽrrihte gefēng, þá cwæð hē . . . 'Yrn tō ðam earne and him of ānim þæs fisces dǽl . . . Syle swaðeáh sumne dǽl ðam earne tō edleáne his geswinces, Hml. Th. ii. 138, 30–140, 8. Þonne him þynce þ his earn ēhte, þæt bið deáð, Lch. iii. 168, 20. Se earn ūp gewít bufan þá wolcnu styrmendum wederum, þ him þá stormas derian ne mahan, Bt. 7, 3; F. 22, 4. þæs earnes gelícnys belimpð tō Jōhanne, for ðan þe se earn flýhð ealra fugela ufemest, and mæg starian on þǽre sunnan leóman, Hml. S. 15, 198 : Jn. 1, heading. Tō earnes beáme, C. D. ii. 73, 25. On earnes beorh, iii. 427, 18. (Earn *occurs in many local names*, v. C. D. vi. 282, col. 2.) þæt feórðe nýten wæs fāgum earne gelíc, Hml. S. 15, 184. Gif þū gesihst earn fleón wíf þín gegrípan, deáð getácnað, Lch. iii. 214, 11.

**earn-geáp, earn-geát.** *Substitute:* earn-geáp, -geát, -geúp, -geót *a vulture* :—Earngeát, -geót, aerngeúp, arngeús *arpa*, Txts. 38, 40. Earngeát *arapa*, 43, 232. Earngeár *vultur*, Wrt. Voc. i. 29, 51. Earngeáp (-geát, Wülck. Gl. 284, 2) *arpa*, 62, 2. Ear[n]geát, 280, 2 : ii. 7, 58. Arngeát, Hpt. 33, 239, 8.

**earnian.** *Add:* I. *to labour* for, *strive after* (*with gen., or prep. or clause*) :—Eádig eorl ēcan dreámes, heofona hāmes earnað on elne, oð þæt ende cymeð dōgorrímes, Ph. 484. Ǽlc hæfð be þām andefnum þe hē hǽr æfter æarnað, Solil. H. 65, 27. Gē earnigaþ (-iaþ, v. l.) þæs and forseoþ þá cræftas eówres ingeþonces, Bt. 18, 4; F. 66, 23. Þá þe rǽsnaþ hēr wordum and weorcum wuldorcyninges lāre, earniaþ on eorþan ēcan lífes, Gū. 767. Hwæs þū earnodest oððe hwæt þū habban woldest *quid scire vis?*, Solil. H. 14, 13. Þte ælces monnes ingeþanc wilnaþ tō þǽre sōþan gesǽlþe tō cumenne, ðeáh hē ungelíce hiora earnige (-ien, v. l.) *intentionem omnem voluntatis humanae, quae diversis studiis agitur, ad beatitudinem festinare*, Bt. 36, 3; F. 176, 21. Þæt wē geornlíce earnian þæt wē Godes miltse habban mōton, Wlfst. 180, 20. II. *to deserve* as the reward of labour :—[Ear]naþ *merebitur*, An. Ox. 1338. Sumum monnum God selleþ ǽgþer ge gōd ge yfel gemenged, for þǽm hí ǽgþres earniaþ *aliis mista quaedam, pro animorum qualitate, distribuit*, Bt. 39, 11; F. 228, 21. Ic lyt earnode ārna, Hy. 4, 48. Earna þē ára, Gen. 2281. Gyf wē ǽnige bōte gebídan sculan, þonne mōte wē þæs tō Gode earnian bet þonne wē ǽr ðison dydon, Wlfst. 157, 3. Wiþ þām þe hē mē healde swā ic earnian wille, Ll. Th. i. 178, 8. III. *to obtain* as the reward of labour, *to earn* wages (*with acc. or clause*) :—Dū

miht ongitan be þām þe nānne mon ne lyst þæs þinges þe hine lyst, ne þæs þe hē dēþ, ac þæs þe hē mid þām earnaþ . . . Hū ne wāst ðū þ nān mon for þý ne rít ðe hine rídan lyste, ac rít for þý þe hē mid þǽre rāde earnaþ sume earnunga. Sume mid þǽre rāde earniaþ þ hié sién ðý hālran; sume earniaþ þ hié sién þý cáfran si *salutis causa quispiam velit equitare, non tam equitandi motum desiderat, quam salutis effectum*, Bt. 34, 7; F. 144, 1–8. Ne suā wēre losad þte ǽrest earnade *ut nec sic perderet quod prius meruerat*, Mk. p. 2, 1. Oxan hyrde mōt earnian mid ðám scós and glófa him sylfum, Ll. Th. i. 438, 15.

**earning-land.** *The passage is* : Ðá nam Ealdulf hit and sealde ðám ðe hē wolde tō earningclaude. Cf. *the expression in the same charter* : Wē wrítað him ðone croft . . . ðæt hē hæbbe hit swā rūm tō bóclonde, swā hē ǽr hæfde tō lǽnlonde, C. D. iii. 258, 27.

**earnung.** *Dele last passage, and add* : I. *labour* to obtain something :—Ǽlc deáþlic man swencþ hine selfne mid mistlicum and manigfealdum ymbhogum, and þeáh williað ealle þurh mistlice paþas cuman tō ānum ende þ is þ hí wilniaþ þurh ungelíce earnunga cuman tō ānre eádignesse *omnis mortalium cura, quam multiplicium studiorum labor exercet, diverso quidem calle procedit, sed ad unum tamen beatitudinis finem nititur pervenire*, Bt. 24, 1; F. 80, 9. II. *merit, desert* :—Earnunga *merito*, Rtl. 42, 27. Hearnunge, Jn. p. 7, 10. For his hálgena earnunge, Hml. S. 23, 314: Solil. H. 1, 21. Earnunga *meritorum*, Rtl. 39, 32. Edleán heora geearnunga (earnunga, v. l.), Bt. 31, 1; F. 112, 1. Mid miclan earnungan wē geearnodon þá yrmða . . ., and mid swýðe miclan earnungan wē þá bóte mótan æt Gode geræcan, Wlfst. 157, 3–6. Ðerh Sancti Cūðberhtes earnunga, Jn. p. 188, 12. III. *recompense* :—Hē rít for þý þe hē mid þǽre rāde earnaþ sume earnunga, Bt. 34, 7; F. 144, 7. [O. H. Ger. arnunga *meritum.*]

**eár-plætt** *a blow on the ear* :—Eár[plættum] *colaphis*, An. Ox. 61, 58. v. plætt *in Dict., and next word.*

**eár-plættan.** *l.* -plættan, *see* plættan *in Dict., and* ge-eárplættan.

**eár-preón.** *Add* :—Eárpreónas *discriminalia*, An. Ox. 4821.

**ears.** *Add* :—þæs earses *ani*, Wrt. Voc. ii. 92, 30.

**eár-scrypel.** *l.* -scripel *and add* :—Eórscripel *applare*, Wrt. Voc. ii. 100, 50.

**eár-sealf.** *Add* : Lch. ii. 2, 14.

**ears-ende** ; m. *Substitute* : ears-endu; *pl. n. The buttocks* :—Earsendu *nates*, Wrt. Voc. i. 65, 36 : Lch. i. lxxi, 9. Earsenda, lxxiv, 19 : Wrt. Voc. i. 283, 61 : ii. 60, 38.

**ears-gang**, es; m. I. *a privy.* v. gang, II :—Hwílum þurh þá nosa hym yrnþ þ blōd, hwílum þanne on arsganga sitt hyt hym fram yrnþ, Lch. iii. 138, 5. Þonne hē tō arsganga gǽþ, þanne þ hym from gǽþ byþ swýþe wyþ blōde genineged, 140, 18. Ar[s]ganga *latrinarum*, An. Ox. 3917. II. *faecal discharge* :—Wið þon þe man þurh hys argang (arsgange, v. l.) blōde út yrne, Lch. i. 82, 3 : 4, 19. Gif hyt byð of þan þerman, þanne myht þū þurh þane arsgang hyt gecnāwan, iii. 138, 16.

**eár-slege**, es; m. *A blow that strikes off an ear* :—Be eárslege. Gif him mon āsleá ōðer eáre of, geselle .xxx. scill. tō bóte, Ll. Th. i. 92, 21. [O. L. Ger. ōr-slegi : O. H. Ger. ōr-slac *alapa.*]

**eár-spinl.** For Prov. 25 *substitute* :—Gylden eárspinl *inauris aurea*, Kent. Gl. 963.

**earþ**, earþ-land. v. irþ, irþ-land.

**eár-þyrel**, es; n. *The ear-passage* :—Eárþyrel (ears-? v. ears-þerl *in Dict.*) *fistulas*, i. *arterias*, Wrt. Voc. ii. 148, 54.

**earu.** *In the passage for* earne *might be read* earmne? *or* earhne, eargne? *timid* : earwian = gearwian. v. ge-gearwian.

**eár-wicga.** *Add* :—Eárwicga *auriculum*, Wrt. Voc. ii. 7, 40. Eárwicga (*printed* eor-, *but see* Angl. viii. 450) *blatta*, i. 24, 24.

**earwunga.** *Dele references to* earnung.

**eáse** (?) *wild carrot* (?) :—Eáse *vel* nǽster *caucale*, Wrt. Voc. ii. 129, 74. v. nǽster.

**eá-spring.** *Add* :—Sió eorþe rínde of hire eásprencgum, Wlfst. 217, 2.

**Eást**, es; m. *Substitute* : eást; *adv. East, to the east*; *dele first passage, and add* : I. *marking direction*, (1) *of movement* :—Hēr fōr se here eást, Chr. 891; P. 82, 16. Swegen gewende eást tō Baldewines lande, 1046; P. 171, 2. Hē is eást irnende (*orientem versus*), Ors. 1, 1; S. 12, 26, 22 : Lch. iii. 74, 13. (2) *of measurement* (of a road, boundary, &c.) :—þæs hagan gemǽre lið eást on þone ealdan welig . . . eást andlanges þǽre ceápstrǽte, C. D. B. ii. 305, 22–26. (3) *of looking* :—Wend þín heáfod eást, Lch. iii. 154, 25. þæt hē ymbsáwe sūð, eást, and west, Met. 10, 5. II. *of relative position*, *east, to the east, in the east* :—þá beorgas onginnað westane . . . and endiað eft eást in Dalmatia, Ors. 1, 1; S. 22, 21. Rufinus wolde habban þone anwold þǽr eást, and Stileca wolde sellan his suna þisne hēr west, 6, 37 ; S. 296, 6. Eást mid Crēcum, Met. 30, 1. Secga sitlu sūð, eást, and west, 9, 42 : 14, 7. v. norþ-, sūþ-eást; cf. west; *adv.*

**eást**; *adj. Substitute* : [*the positive is uncertain*] ; cpve. eástra ; spve. eást(e)mest :—þǽre eástan Eoae (*the passage is* : Eoae tripertitas Indiae

provincias illustravit, Ald. 25, 31, the glosses to which in Hpt. Gl. 451, 13, 16 are, *Eoae* i. *orientis* þára eástan (in margin) . . . *Indiae* þǽre eástan : in Wrt. Voc. ii. 31, 73 *Eoae* is glossed by eástdǽlas), An. Ox. 1894. Andlanges þæs eástran mylengeares, C. D. B. ii. 305, 240. On þonæ eásteran weg, C. D. v. 319, 19 : Cht. Crw. 4, 36. Is sió eástemeste þeód háten Libia, Ors. 1, 1 ; S. 24, 33. On þǽm eástemestan onwalde, 6, 1 ; S. 252, 5. Cf. west ; *adj.*

**eásta.** *Dele, and see* be-eástan : eá-stæþ. v. eá-steþ *in Dict. for passage.*

**eá-stán,** es ; *m. A stone taken from a river* (?) :—Eác hylpð gif mon mid eástánum onbærnedum þá meoluc gewyrð, Lch. ii. 218, 23.

**eástan** ; *adj. Dele.*

**eástan** ; *adv.* *Add* : I. marking direction of movement :—Forð ofersóran folcmǽro land eástan ǽfæste men, Gen. 1802. Eástan hider Engle and Seaxe úp becómon, Chr. 973 ; P. 110, 3. Gotan eástan of Scidþia sceldas lǽddon, Met. 1, 1 : Víd. 8. **I a.** of wind :—þone stearcan wind norþan and eástan, Bt. 4 ; F. 8, 6 : Met. 12, 15. **I b.** of light :—Syððan God eástan sende leóhtne leóman, Jud. 190. þis ne dagað eástan, Fin 3. **II.** marking direction of measurement, giving quarter from which measurement is made :—Affrica ongind eástan westverd fram Egyptum æt þǽre ee þe man Nilus hǽt *measured from the east westwards Africa starts from Egypt at the river Nile*, Ors. 1, 1 ; S. 24, 32. Se morgensteorra cymþ eástan úp, Bt. 39, 13 ; F. 234, 4 : Met. 29, 20, 26. [*O. Sax.* óstan : *Icel.* austan.] v. be-, norþan-, súþan-, wiþ-eástan ; cf. westan.

**eástane (-ene)** ; *adv.* I. marking direction of movement, *from the east* :—Gif hé eástane of Asiam Italiam gesóhte, Ors. 3, 8 ; S. 122, 28. þonne hé eft wǽre eástane (-ene, *v. l.*) hámweard, 6, 31 ; S. 286, 10. **II.** marking direction of measurement. v. eástan, II :—þá beorgas onginnað ǽrest eástane of þǽm gársecge and þonne licgað westryhte, 1, 1 ; S. 14, 8. Dioclitianus and Maximianus bebudon ēhtnesse, Dioclitianus eástane (-ene, *v. l.*) (*in oriente*), 6, 30 ; S. 280, 18. [*O. Sax. O. H. Ger.* óstana.]

**eástan-norþan** ; *adv. From the north-east* :—Eástannorþan *ab borea*, Wrt. Voc. ii. 98, 30. Eástannorþan, 4, 16. v. be-eástannorþan.

**eástannorþan-wind** ; es ; *m. A north-east wind* :—Eástannorðanwindes *chori*, Wrt. Voc. ii. 14, 25.

**eástan-súþan.** *Substitute : adv. From the south-east* :—Eástansúdan *ab euro*, Wrt. Voc. ii. 98, 20. Eástansúðan, 4, 18. [*O. H. Ger.* óstan-sundan.]

**eástansúþan-wind,** es ; *m. A south-east wind* :—Eástansúþanwind *vulturnus*, Wrt. Voc. i. 36, 12.

**eástan-wind,** es ; *m. An east wind* :—Eástenwind *subsolanus*, Wrt. Voc. i. 36, 12. [*O. H. Ger.* óstan-wint : *Icel.* austan-vindr.]

**eást-cyning,** es ; *m. An eastern king* :—Wið Seleucus þone eástcyning (cf. Seleucus begeat ealle þá eástlond, S. 144, 1), Ors. 3, 11 ; S. 148, 35.

**eást-dǽl.** *Add* :—Dioclitianus in eástdǽle middangeardes *in oriente*, Bd. 1, 6 ; Sch. 18, 14. Cómon fram eástdǽle middangeardes þrý tungelwítegan . . . 'Wē gesáwon his steorran on eástdǽle,' Hml. Th. i. 78, 4–7. Of eástdǽle, Chr. 2 ; P. 4, 28. Heofon biþ open on þǽm eástdǽle, Bl. H. 93, 1. Mathēum hē gedyde gangan tó þam eástdǽle, 239, 16. Hē is eást irnende from eástdǽle þurh Æthiopica wēstenne (*orientem versus per Aethiopica deserta prolabi*), and þǽr mon hǽt þá eá Ion oþ þone eástdǽl, Ors. 1, 1 ; S. 12, 27. Eástdǽlas *Eoae*, Wrt. Voc. ii. 31, 73. v. west-dǽl.

**Eást-Dene** ; *pl. The East-Danes* :—Aldor Eást-Dena, B. 392 : 616. Eást-Denum, 828 : Rún. 22.

**eáste,** an ; *f.* (?) *The east. See first passage under* eást ; *adj.*

**eást-ende.** *Add* : , *the east part* of a country, of the earth, *the east* :—On eástende þǽre heofonan, Angl. viii. 310, 10. Seó eorþe on þǽm norþende and on þǽm eástende sprecaþ him betweónum, Bl. H. 93, 11. Asia ongén middeldǽle on þám eástende *Asia ad mediam frontem orientis*, Ors. 1, 1 ; S. 10, 6. On ðǽm eástende þisses middangeardes *orientem*, 3, 9 ; S. 128, 33. Hē nom Iliric, and begeondan þǽm þone eástende and þone mǽstan dǽl þisses middangeardes *Illyricum, Asiam, et Orientem*, 6, 30 ; S. 280, 26. Hē gespeón him tó ealle Kentingas, and ealle þá butsecarlas of Hǽstingan and ðǽr ǽghwǽr þe þǽre sǽ riman, and eallne þæne eástende and Súð-Sexan, Chr. 1052 ; P. 178, 26.

**Eást-Engle.** *Add* : (the word may often be translated by) *East Anglia* :—Norþhymbre and Eást-Engle hæfdon Ælfrēde cyninge áþas geseald, and Eást-Engle foregíslas .vi., Chr. 894 ; P. 84, 20. Eást-Engla cyning and seó þeód gesóhte Ecgbryht . . . and Eást-Engle slógon Beornwulf, 823 ; P. 60, 17–19. Eást-Engla (-e MS.) landes is þrittig þúsend hýda, C. D. B. i. 414, 29. Ofer Norðhymbra lond and Eást-Engla, Chr. 895 ; P. 88, 20. Ðǽr wærð Eást-Engla folces seó yld ofslagen, 1004 ; P. 135, 36. Hē búde on Eást-Englum, and þæt loud ǽrest gesæt, 890 ; P. 82, 10. Hí winterseti námon on Eást-Englum, and hié him friþ wiþ námon. Hēr fór se here of Eást-Englum, 866–7 ; P. 68, 14–16. On Lindesse and on Eást-Englum and on Cantwarum

wurdon monige men ofslægene, 838 ; P. 64, 1. Felix bodade Eást-Englum (-Eanglum, *v. l.*), 636 ; P. 26, 5. Se here on Eást-Englum (Ést-, *v. l.*), 885 ; P. 80, 8. Rád se here ofer Mierce innan Eást-Engle, 870 ; P. 70, 5. Fór se here on Eást-Engle and gesæt þæt lond and gedǽlde, 870 ; P. 76, 26. Sende Ælfrēd cyng sciphere of Cænt on Eást-Engle, 885 ; P. 79, 18. Eást-Englan, 1017 ; P. 154, 4.

**eáster.** *Substitute* : **Eástre,** an (es *in North*) ; *pl.* an, on, un. [*In W. S. the* (*wk.*) *pl. is almost always used, in the North sing. and pl., strong and wk. forms occur.*] **I.** of the Jewish festival, *the passover* :—Freólsdæg azimorum is gecweden Eástre (-on, *v. l.* : Eóstro, L., Eóstru, R. *pascha*), Lk. 22, 1. þte wēre geslægen Eóstro (Eóstru, R.), Lk. L. 22, 7. Eástran on ǽfen *Paschae vespere*, Hy. S. 82, 19. þone Eástres dæg *pascha diem*, Bd. 5, 22 ; Sch. 685, 4. Eástres (Fástra, R.), Lk. L. 2, 41 : Mk. p. 5, 11 : Jn. p. 6, 11. Eástres (Eóstro, R.), Jn. L. 13, 1. Eóstres, Mk. p. 5, 18 : Lk. p. 11, 16 : Jn. 12, 1. þinne Eástran geseón *tuum Pascha videre*, Hy. S. 56, 25. Æfter twám dagum beóð Eástro (-on, *v. l.*, Eástran, R. Eástro bið *Pascha fiet*, L.), Mt. 26, 2. Wǽron Eástron (wæs Eástro (Eóstru, R.)), Mk. 14, 1. Judēa Eástron (nēh wæs Eástro (Eóstrum, R.)) wǽron gehende, and manega fóron ǽr þám Eástron (Eástra, L., Eóstrum, R.) *proximum erat Pascha Iudaeorum, et ascenderunt multi ante Pascha*, Jn. 11, 55. Eástrun, An. Ox. 40, 30, 29. Eástran úre Críst is *pascha nostrum Christus est*, Hy. S. 82, 27. Eástro úsra, Rtl. 25, 15. Ðæra eóstruna *azymorum*, Mk. R. 14, 12. Ǽr Judēa Eástrum, Bl. H. 67, 24 : 71, 24. Tó Eástron, Mt. 26, 17. Neáh Eástron (Eóstrum, R.), Jn. 2, 13. On Eástron, 23. Ǽr þám Eástron (Eóstrum, R.), Jn. 12, 1. þonne ytst ðú þíne Eástru mid grēnum lactucum, Angl. viii. 323, 21. þæt ic wyrce míne Eástro (Eástron, *v. l.*, Eástra, R.), Mt. 26, 18. Híæ gearwadun Eástran (Eástro, L.) *paraverunt Pascha*, 19. þá hí Eástron (Eóstro, L., Eóstru, R.) offrodon, . . . þ ðú Eástron (Eástro, L., Eóstru, R.) ete, Mk. 14, 12. **II.** of the Christian festival, *Easter* :—In swá hálgum dæge þǽre Eástron (þára Eástrena, *v. l.*), Gr. D. 308, 24. ' Arís . . . nú tó dæg wǽron Eástran ' . . . ' Ic wát þ hit Eástron wǽron,' 99, 27–29. Hē wæs gefullod on Eástrum . . . þá wǽron Ēstran on .ii. idus Apr., Chr. 626 ; P. 25, 16. þá wǽron Eástron on .iii. Nᵒ Apr., 1042 ; P. 163, 19. Tó þám Eástran þe wǽron ǽfter þám middanwintre þe se cyng forðfērde, and wǽron þá Eástran on þone dæg .xvi. kl. Mai, 1066 ; P. 195, 29. On þisan Eástron cóm se kyng tó Wincestre, and þá wǽron Eástra on .x. kl. Apr., 1067 ; P. 202, 28. Eástron, Angl. viii. 330, 14, 15, 16. þǽre ylcan nihte þára hálgan (þǽre hálegan) Eástrena *eadem nocte sacrosancta dominici paschae*, Bd. 2, 9 ; Sch. 147, 18. Eástran *þase*, Wrt. Voc. ii. 68, 80. Ǽr Eástrum, Ll. Th. ii. 438, 25. Ǽr þám hálgan Eástron *ante sanctum Pascha*, 190, 18. Nēhst Eástron (-um, *v. l.*), Gr. D. 308, 15. Tó rihtum Eástrum, Chr. 716 ; P. 43, 15 : 627 ; P. 25, 29. Æfter Eástron, 875 ; P. 73, 6. Ofer Eástron, 878 ; P. 76, 6. þæt hié Eástron onryht heóldon, 716 ; P. 42, 15. Fram þǽre hálgan Eástertíde oð eft Eástron *from the holy Eastertide until Easter again*, Lch. iii. 248, 23. **III.** of a season of the year, *spring* :—Hwæþer þū fægerra blóstmæna fægnige on eástran swelce þū hié gescópe . . . hwæþer hit dínes gewealdes sié þ se hærfest sié swá welig on wæstmum *an vernis floribus ipse distingueris? aut tua in aestivos fructus intumescit ubertas?*, Bt. 14, 1 ; F. 40, 24–28.

**eáster** ; *adj. Dele.*

**eáster-ǽfen.** *Add* :—On Sæternesdæge on þám hálgan Eásterǽfenne *ipso sacratissimo vesperascente Sabbato Paschali*, Gr. D. 83, 31. On Eásterǽfen *Sancto Sabbato*, Chr. 1047 ; P. 171, 12 : Wlfst. 117, 2. On Ðunresdæg ǽr Eástrum and on Frigedæg and on Eástorǽfen, Ll. Th. ii. 438, 25. Oð ðet Eástreǽfen, Chr. 1097 ; P. 233, 13.

**eáster-dæg.** *Add* : I. *the day of the Passover* :—Eásterdæg wæs se forman þá on þǽre ealdan ǽ, þonne se móna wæs .xiiii., and þá seofon dagas þe þǽr æfter wǽron wǽron gecíged *dies azimorum*, Angl. viii. 330, 19. On Eásterdæges freólstíde *in die solemni Paschae*, Lk. 2, 41. Hí woldon habban þone hálgan Eásterdæg geblódegodne mid þæs Hǽlendes blóde, Hml. A. 67, 61. **II.** of the Christian festival. (1) *a day in Easter-week* :—Se forma Eásterdæg *Easter Sunday*, Guth. 82, 12. Ǽr þám drihtenlican Eásterdæge *before Easter Sunday*, Hml. S. 23 b, 622. þám forman Eástordæge, Chr. 685 ; P. 39, 18. On ðóran Eásterdæge *on Easter Monday*, 1053 ; P. 182, 20. On forman Eásterdæg (on Eásterdæg, *v. l.*), 1043 ; P. 163, 31. On ðone forman Eásterdæg, Bd. 5, 23 ; Sch. 685, 16. þá Eásterlican dagas tácniaþ þá ēccan eádignesse . . . swá magon þe mǽran blisse habban þá Eásterdagas, Bl. H. 35, 34. (2) *Easter Sunday* :—On Martius ofer .xii. kl. Apr. lóca hwǽr þū finde .xiiii. nihta ealdne mónan, ofer þ se niésta Sunnandæg bið Eástordæg, Lch. iii. 226, 20. Nǽfre ne sý se hálga Eásterdæg gemǽrsod ǽr þám þe seó lenctenlice emniht sý ágán, 256, 11 : Angl. viii. 309, 37. Wæs Ǽsterdæg þá on ðám datarum Idus Apr., Chr. 1012 ; P. 142, 14. þý hálegan Eásterdæge (Eástor-, *v. l.*) *die sancto Paschae*, Bd. 3, 6 ; Sch. 209, 10 : Hml. S. 26, 88. On Eástorǽfen and on Eástordæg, Ll. Th. ii. 438, 25. þone Eástordæg, Bd. 5, 22 ; Sch. 685, 5. [*O. H. Ger.* óstor-tag *pascha*.]

**eáster-fæsten** *Lent.* *Add* :—Ercenbriht . . . ǽrost Engliscra cininga

gesette Eástorfeasten (Eásterfæsten, *v. l.*) (cf. hē bebeád þæt feówertiglice fæsten ǣr Eástrum, Bd. 3, 8 ; Sch. 219, 20), Chr. 639 ; P. 27, 19.

**Eáster-freólsdæg**, es ; *m. The feast day of the Passover :*—Ǣr þām Eásterfreólsdæge *ante diem festum Paschae*, Jn. 13, 1.

**Eáster-gewuna**, an ; *m. An Easter custom :*—Hē tō þām mynstre fērde on þǣre ylcan tíde þe heora Eástergewuna wǣron (wæs?) tōgædere becuman, Hml. S. 23 b, 643.

**Eáster-líc.** *Add :* I. v. Eáster, I :—Ymbe þæne eásterlican dæg wē eów wyllað gecýðan þ hē wæs on þǣre ealdan ǣ *tribus argumentorum indiciis preceptum*, Angl. viii. 330, 4. II. v. Eáster, II :—Þis eástorlíce gerýno, Bl. H. 83, 7. Þæs eásterlican mōnðes angin *the beginning of the lunar month in which Easter falls*, Angl. viii. 330, 1. On beorhtre eásterlicre gefeán *claro paschali gaudio*, Hy. S. 86, 13. Þā eásterlican mǣrsunge Crístes ǣristes, Angl. xii. 514, 4. Þā eásterlican tíd, Lch. iii. 238, 29. On þā hālgan eásterlicon tíd, Ll. i. 244, 3. Þā eásterlican dagas, Bl. H. 35, 31. III. v. Eáster, III :—Æfter þǣre eásterlican emnihte, Angl. viii. 330, 6.

**Eáster-mōnaþ.** *Add :*—Þone mōnaþ man nemneð on Læden Aprelis, and on ūre geþeóde Eástermōnaþ, Shrn. 69, 16. [*O. H. Ger.* ôstarmânot.]

**eást-ern.** *Substitute :* **eásterne ;** *adj.* I. marking position. (1) *in the east :*—Leóht eásternes tungles *lux eoi sideris*, Hy. S. 22, 9. (2) *of the east part of the world, eastern :*—Of Asian lande þæs eásternan ríces, Hml. S. 25, 752. Eásterne tungelwítegan *eoi magi*, Wrt. Voc. ii. 143, 58. Þā eásternan tungelwítegan, Hml. Th. i. 106, 24. Þā eásternan and Grēciscean munecas, Hex. 32, 6. Of eásternum leódum, Hml. S. 28, 9 : Hml. Th. i. 486, 10. (2 a) used substantively, *an Eastern, an oriental :*—Ealle þā Eásternan and þā Egiptiscan, Lch. iii. 256, 6. Þone regol ðā Eásternan and eác swylce Grēcas healdað, Hml. S. 3, 146. Se wer (*Job*) wæs swíðe mǣre betwux eallum Eásternum, Hml. Th. ii. 446, 15. II. marking direction of the wind, *east, from the east :*—Feówer heáfodwindas synd : se fyrmesta is eásterne wind, Lch. iii. 274, 13 : Gen. 315. [*O. Sax.* ôstroni : *O. H. Ger.* ôstrôni : *Icel.* austrænn.] v. sūþ-, sūþan-eásterne.

**Eáster-sunnandæg**, es ; *m. Easter Sunday :*—Ic an heofonas ástáh an þone hālgan Eástorsunnandæg, Wlfst. 222, 21.

**Eáster-symbel**, es ; *n. The Passover :*—On ðǣm dæge gearuadon hiora mett tō Eástrosymble, Jn. 19, 42 margin.

**Eáster-tíd.** *Add :* I. v. Eáster, I :—Wæs seó tíd þām folce geset tō Eástertíde . . . Nū is his ðrowung and his ǣrist ūre Eástertíd, Hml. Th. i. 312, 8, 19. Hyt wæs gehende heora (*the Jews*) Eástertíde, Hml. A. 67, 60. II. v. Eáster, II :—On sumum geáre byð se mōna twelf síðon geníwod fram þǣre hālgan Eástertíde oð eft Eástron, Lch. iii. 248, 22. Is beboden on ðām regole þe ūs gewissað be þǣre Eástertíde þ nǣfre ne sý se hālga Eásterdæg gemǣrsod ǣr þan þe seó lenctenlíce emniht sý ágán, 256, 11. On Eástertíd, Chr. 774 ; P. 51, 28. Ðām mannum ðe ic nū on Eástertídum feoh sealde, C. D. ii. 115, 21.

**Eáster-wucu.** *Add :*—Gestód hine seó ádl þon Wōdnesdæg nēhst Eástron and þā eft þan ylcan dæge on þǣre Eástorwucan hē þæt líf of þām líchaman sende, Guth. 80, 7. Innon þǣre Eásterwucan on .xiiii. k. Mai, Chr. 1061 ; P. 190, 2. Ǣr þām hālgan Eástron and ealle þā Eásterwucan *ante sanctum Pascha et per totam hebdomadam paschalem*, Ll. Th. ii. 190, 18.

**eáste-weard.** *Substitute :* **eáste-weard ;** *adj. Eastward, east, eastern part of the noun to which the word is applied :*—Þæt býne land is eásteweard brādost. Eásteweard hit mæg bión syxtig míla brād, Ors. 1, 1 ; S. 18, 29, 30. Būton gewaldenum dǣle eástewerdes þæs folces, Chr. 894 ; P. 86, 13. From eástewearde middangearde *ab oriente*, Nar. 25, 24. On eásteweardre (eástwarde, *v. l.*) Cent *ad orientalem Cantiae plagam*, 893 ; P. 84, 5 : Bd. 1, 25 ; Sch. 51, 18. On ðā forryðe eástewerde, C. D. iii. 449, 32. Se here oferhergeade alle Cent eástewearde, Chr. 865 ; P. 68, 11. Hié cōmon on Eást-seaxna lond eásteweard, 895 ; P. 88, 21. Eást on ðā ealdan díc oð ídel híwisce eásteweard, C. D. v. 319, 22. Oð Indéas eásteweard, Met. 16, 18. ¶ used substantively :—Þæt Babylonicum (ríce) wæs þæt forme and on eásteweardum *Babylonium regnum ab oriente*, Ors. 2, 1 ; S. 60, 2. v. westeweard.

**Eást-folc.** *For* Som. Ben. Lye *substitute :*—Eástfolcum *eeois*, Wrt. Voc. ii. 31, 75.

**eást-gársecg**, es ; *m. The eastern ocean :*—Þ hē his ríce gebrǣdde oþ þone eástgársecg *ut oceano ultimoque oriente finiret imperium*, Ors. 3, 9 ; S. 132, 5.

**eást-gemǣre**, es ; *n. An eastern boundary :*—Hē cōm on India eástgemǣra, Ors. 3, 9 ; S. 132, 29.

**eást-healf.** *Add :*—Seó Asia on ælce healfe is befangen mid sealtum wætre būton on eásthealfe *Asia absque orientali parte undique circumdata est mari*, Ors. 1, 1 ; S. 12, 12. On eásthealfe þæs landes líþ gársecg, S. 14, 2. [*O. H. Ger.* ôst-halba (ôstar-) : cf. *Icel.* austr-hálfa.]

**eást-healh.** v. healh.

**Eást-land.** *Substitute :* **eást-land**, es ; *n.* I. *an eastern land ;* in pl. *eastern lands, the East :*—Hē cōm tō þām eástlande *venit in terram*

---

*orientalem*, Gen. 29, 1. Hē monega anwealdas mid gewinnum geeóde on þǣm eástlondum *plurima per orientem bella gessit*, Ors. 3, 11 ; S. 150, 17. Gewinn on eástlondum *Orientis bella*, 5, 2 ; S. 218, 21. Maximianus hē gesette on þā eástlond *Maximium in Oriente constituit*, 6, 30 ; S. 280, 33. Hē begeat ealle þā eástlond, 3, 11 ; S. 144, 1. [Cf. *O. H. Ger.* ôstar-lant *oriens : Icel.* austr-lönd ; *pl. the East.*] II. *Esthonia :*—Eástan of Eástlande . . . þæt Eástland is swýðe mycel, Ors. 1, 1 ; S. 20, 10, 14. Cf. Ôsti, 16, 29. [*Icel.* Eist-land *Esthonia.*] v. Este.

**eást-lang ;** *adj. Lying in an easterly direction :*—On ðā eástlangan dícwale, C. D. v. 334, 28. v. west-lang ; *adj.*

**eást-lang ;** *adv. Dele bracket, and add :* v. west-lang ; *adv.*

**eást-leóde ;** *pl. m. Eastern people, orientals :*—Hē scare hæfde eástleóda þeáwe *habuerat tonsuram more orientalium*, Bd. 4, 1 ; Sch. 339, 15.

**eást-norþ ;** *adv. North-east :*—Ryhte be-eástan him sindon Bǣme, and eástnorþ sindon þyringas, Ors. 1, 1 ; S. 16, 4 : 8.

**eást-norþerne ;** *adj. North-east :*—Cōman eástnorþerne windas, Ap. Th. 11, 2.

**eástnorþ-wind**, es ; *m. A north-east wind :*—Eástnorþwind, eústnorduind *boreus*, Txts. 46, 162. Eóstnorðwind *chorus*, 51, 460. Eástnorðwind, Wrt. Voc. ii. 126, 52.

**eást-portic**, es ; *n. An east porch or portico :*—Þæt eástportic wæs on lenge twēntig fǣdma be þæs temples wídnysse and wæs týn fǣdma wíd, Hml. Th. ii. 578, 12.

**eá-streám.** *Add :*—Eástreám ýða, Dan. 385.

**eá-streám-ýþ.** *Dele, and see preceding word :* -eástrian. v. geeástrian.

**eást-ríce.** *Substitute :* I. *an empire in the east, the East :*—Ðæt eástríce in Asiria gefeóll . . . Ninus rícsade on ðon eástríce lii wintra, Ors. 2, 1 ; S. 62, 7, 13. Constantinopolis is nū þ hēhste cynesetl and heáfod ealles eástríces *Constantinopolis nunc imperii sedes et totius caput Orientis est*, 3, 7 ; S. 116, 13. Asia on eástríce, Affrica on sūððǣle, Ælfc. T. Grn. 4, 39. Genāman þāra apostola líchaman Grēcas and woldan lǣdon on Eástríce, Bl. H. 193, 10. II. *a kingdom that lies to the east of another :*—Fór se here of þǣm eástríce (*the kingdom of the East Franks*) westweard, Chr. 893 ; P. 84, 2. [Cf. *O. H. Ger.* ôstar-ríchi *oriens : Icel.* austr-ríki.]

**eást-rihte.** *Add : due east :*—Beág þæt land þǣr eástryhte, Ors. 1, 1 ; S. 17, 14.

**eást-rihtes ;** *adv. Due east :*—Of fótmǣle ēstrihtes on wulfputt, C. D. iii. 449, 31, 27.

**eást-sǣ.** *Add :*—Eástsǣ *mare eoum*, Wrt. Voc. i. 41, 65.

**Eást-Seaxe.** *Add :*—Eást-Sexena landes is syofon þūsend hýda, C. D. B. i. 414, 30.

**eást-stæþ**, es ; *n. The east bank of a stream :*—Of Afenan eáststaðæ, C. D. v. 216, 35.

**eást-sūþ ;** *adv. South-east :*—Eástsúth *ad euronothum*, Wrt. Voc. ii. 98, 21. Eástsūð, 4, 19. Be-eástan him is Wineda lond . . . and eástsūþ Maroara, Ors. 1, 1 ; S. 16, 10.

**eástsūþ-dǣl**, es ; *m. The south-east part :*—Fram eástsūðdǣle heofones, þæt is fram heánnesse þǣre winterlícan sunnan uppgange *ab Euroaustro, id est ab alto brumalis exortus*, Bd. 4, 3 ; Sch. 355, 1.

**eástsūþ-lang.** v. westnorþ-lang *in Dict.*

**eást-þeód**, e ; *f. An eastern people :*—þǣm eástþeódum gewelgode *orientis provinciis ditati*, Nar. 3, 26.

**Eást-þyringas ;** *pl. The East Thuringians*, Víd. 86.

**eást-weard.** *Substitute for the example :*—Eástweard *orientem uersum*, Ælfc. Gr. Z. 225, 9. (1) defining direction of motion :—Gewende se here eástweard intó Frommūðan, Chr. 998 ; P. 131, 12. Hí wendon eástweard tō Lundene, 1013 ; P. 143, 25. (2) defining direction of measurement :—þǣr scýt se ende ūp of þām gársecge betuh þām twām beorgum eástweard, Ors. 1, 1 ; S. 26, 23. (3) defining position, attitude, *so as to face to the east :*—Wē wendað ūs eástweard þonne wē ūs gebiddað, Hml. Th. i. 262, 5. Wende þē eástweard . . . and cweð . . . 'Eástweard ic stande,' Lch. i. 398, 26–28. Tō middes mergenes stande eásteweard, ii. 116, 8. v. west-weard.

**eást-weardes ;** *adv. Eastwards.* (1) of direction :—Án scínende weg mid rihte stige eásteweardes wæs áþæn tō heofonum, Gr. D. 176, 2. (2) of position :—Hē oðstód eástweardes wendende, Hml. S. 33 b, 162. Hē geseah þæs wífes líchaman orsáwle licgende, and þā handa . . . eásteweardes gewende, 743. v. preceding word.

**eást-weg.** *Substitute : A way to or in the east ;* in pl. *eastern parts, the east :*—þonan mæg hē on eástwegum síð behealdan hwonne swegles tapur hǣdre blíce (cf. hwan sie (*the Magi*) an ôstarwegun gisáhin kumbal liuhtian hēdro, Hēl. 634), Ph. 113. Hí gelǣddon on langne síð Israēla cyn on eástwegas tō Babilonia, Dan. 69. Ofer eástwegas *travelling from the east*, El. 255 : 996. [Cf. *Icel.* austr-vegr *used especially of Russia, Wenden, the East Baltic.*]

**eást-Wille (-as?) ;** *pl. The people of some district in England :*—Eást-Wlla landes is syx hund hýda, C. D. B. i. 414, 29.

**Eást-Wixan.** v. Wixan.

eáþe = (1) eáþe; adv. Easily, Gen. 2058 : Gū. 528. (2) íþ; cpve. More easily :—þæt hē þe eáð (iéð, S. 68, 14) mihte winnan, Ors. 2, 3 ; Bos. 42, 6 : An. 368. þæt mæg engel þīn eáð gefēran, 194.

eáþ-. Umlauted forms (íþ-, iéþ-, ēþ-, ȳþ-) occur, the compounds with which are taken under íþ-.

eáþ-bēde. l. -bede, and add : [cf. Icel. auð-beðinn easily entreated.]

eáþ-begeáte (? cf. Icel. auð-gætt), -begete ; adj. Easy to get :—Gyf þȳ æfteran dæg sunne scȳneþ, þonne byð on Ængelcynne gold eáðbegeáte, Lch. iii. 166, 1. þās wȳrta sindon betste tō þon and eáðbegeátra[n], ii. 226, 25. v. ēþ-begete, tōr-begete, eáþ-gete.

eáþ-bylgness, e ; f. Readiness to anger, irascibility :—Eáðbylhnyssa gāst, Nap. 24.

eáþ-bylige. v. íþ-belig in Dict.

eáþ-cnǽwe, -cnáwe ; adj. Easy to recognize :—Seó ōðer conjugatio ys ful eáðcnǽwe (-cnáwe, v. l.), for ðan ðe ǽlc ðára worda þe geendað on eo, and se ōðer hæð on es, ys þǽre ōðre geðeódnysse, Ælfc. Gr. Z. 147, 8.

eáþ-dǽde ; adj. Easy to do :—Wæs hit hyre eáðdēde, Lch. iii. 428, 30. v. íþ-dǽde.

eáþe ; adj. Add :—Eáðre facilior, ealra eáðost facillimus, Ælfc. Gr. Z. 16, 6. (1) of action :—þ wæter and sió lyft bióþ swīþe eáþe tō tōdǽlenne, Bt. 34, 11 ; F. 150, 28. Eáðre mē þincð on drígum lande tō farande, Solil. H. 21, 23. (2) of persons, easy to be entreated, gentle :—þū eart eáðe God . . . þū eart sōð Metod . . . þū eart Hǽlend God, Hy. 3, 4–9. [v. N. E. D. eath.] v. íþe, and next word.

eáþe, es ; n. What is easy, the easy :—þæt nān wiht ne sȳ þæs eáðes ne þæs earfoðes, Wlfst. 185, 1.

eáþe ; adv. Add : I. of action, easily. (1) as being well within one's power :—ðæt wē gedón, swǽ wē swīðe eáðe magon mid Godes fultume, ðætte . . . , Past. 7, 9. ðet hī mann eáðe befaran mihte, Chr. 1009 : P. 138, 20. Eáðe beþencan, Wlfst. 165, 21 : Gen. 48 : Cri. 173 : Mōd. 9. Eáða ongeota cognosci, Mt. p. 16, 18. Eáðe gecnáwan, Met. 19, 31. þæt hē ðe iéð mehte winnan wið Brutuse, Ors. 2, 3 ; S. 68, 14. Eáður facilius, Mt. L. 19, 24 : Mk. L. R. 2, 9. Eáðor, eðor, 10, 25. (1 a) as being within proper limits :—þ gewin mon eáðe mæg tō þǽm mǽstum gewinnum getellan bellum merito inter maxima bella referendum, Ors. 4, 11 ; S. 208, 5. (2) without discomfort or trouble, conveniently, readily, at ease :—þū ofer aspide miht eáðe gangan and bealde nū basiliscan tredan super aspidem et basiliscum ambulabis, Ps. Th. 90, 13. Cumað ǽalle tō ānum hlāforde, sume ǽð, sume unēð ; nāðer ne hī þeder gelíce eáðe cumað, ne hī þēr gelíce eáðe ne beóð. Sume becð on māran āre and on māran ēðnesse þonne sume, Solil. H. 44, 10–13. Him þincð þæt hē mæge ǽð būtan faran þonne mid, 21, 22 : 39, 18. Heó listum ālēde lāðne mannan, swā heó þæs unlǽdan eáðost mihte wel gewealdan, Jud. 102 : 75. (3) without reluctance, willingly, readily :—þ swurd læg þer him ætforan and heora nān nolde nāht eáðe hine sleán, Hml. S. 19, 106. Se deófol þe beswāc ðoue þeóf . . . nele nāht eáðe on his ende geðafian þ hē þonne gecyrre . . . tō þām Hǽlende, 190. II. of event, easily, possibly, perhaps :—Swīþe eáðe þ mæg beón þ sume men þencan . . . very possibly some men may think . . . , Bl. H. 21, 17. Swā hit eáþe beón mæg þ se heáhengel of heofenum cumen wǽre, 197, 12. Gif huæt eáða (forte) gemitte, Mk. L. R. 11, 13. ¶ Eáþe mæg, (1) perhaps, may be :—Eáða mæhte t eáðe mæge forte, Mt. L. 11, 23. Eáðe (ēðe, R.) mæg forsitan, Jn. L. 8, 19 : alioquin, Mt. L. 6, 1. (2) lest ; ne forte :—Eáðe mæg t ðȳ lǽs ne forte, Lk. L. 12, 58. Dȳ lǽs t eáðe mæg, Mt. L. 4, 6. Eáðe mæg, 25, 9. Eáða maeg, 13, 29. Eáða (-e, L.) mæge, Lk. L. 21, 34. Eáðe mæg, Mt. L. 27, 64. Eáðæ (eóðe, R.) mæge, Lk. L. 4, 11. Eóðe mæge (ǽðe mæg, R.), 14, 8. [O. Sax. ōðo : O. H. Ger. un-ōðo.] v. eáþ, íþ, íþost.

eáþe-lic. Add :—Eáðelic facilis, Ælfc. Gr. Z. 16, 5. I. easy, presenting little difficulty :—Gif hē ðæt eáðelice beþod geheólde, Hex. 24, 16. Seó ealde ǽ wæs eáðelicre þonne Crīstes gesetnys sȳ, Hml. Th. i. 358, 28. II. inconsiderable, slight. (1) of living things, weak, tender :—Swilce hē tōtǽre sum eáðelic ticcen, Jud. 14, 6. Wyrta siud eáðelice gesceafta, and ðurh winterlicne cyle symle forseariað, Hml. Th. ii. 464, 6. God ðone mōdigan cyning (Pharaoh) mid þām eáðelicum gesceaftum (insects) geswencte, 492, 23. (2) of lifeless matter, mean, poor, scanty :—Se Hǽlend becōm intō sumere eáðelican byrig intrauit Jesus in quoddam castellum, Hml. Th. ii. 438, 10. Hē hæfde mid him eáþelicne fōdan . . . hē þā eáðelican þénunga heom þénode, Hml. S. 23, 234, 239. Bring ūs bet be hlāf . . . for þon þe þā hlāfas wǽron swīðe eáðelice þe ūs gyrstanǽfen cōmon, 469. (3) of an abstract object, slight, trifling :—Mōd āstyred þeáh hit for gehwǽdum and eáþelicum þincge sié animum commotum quamvis modice, R. Ben. 131, 4. [v. N. E. D. eathly. O. H. Ger. ōd-līh facilis.] v. íþe-lic.

eáþelíce. Add : I. cf. eáþe ; adv. I. 1 :—Sē mihte hine eft ārǽran eáðelíce tō life, Hml. A. 67, 39 : 107, 152 : 109, 239. On sumre stōwe se hróf wæs þ man mihte eáþelíce mid heáfde gehrínan, Bl. H. 207, 23. II. cf. eáþe ; I. 2 :—Eáþelíce facile, Wülck. Gl. 252, 2. Ne sȳ him nō eáþelíce þæs infæres getíðod non ei facilis tribuatur ingressus, R. Ben. 97, 4. Hwænne þū eáðelícost miht tō þam folce becuman Hml. A. 110, 257. III. cf. eáþe ; I. 3 :—þ hié þe

eáþelícor and þe wysumlícor þā myclan byrðenne āberan mihton, Bl. H. 135, 7. IV. fickly, weakly. v. eáþe-lic ; II :—Hī geáðelíce (cf. (?) geáþ ; but for form cf. gearfoþe under earfoþe) forlēton Godes gesetnysse fecerunt malum in conspectu Domini, Jud. 3, 7. [v. N. E. D. eathly. O. H. Ger. ōð-līhho.] v. íþelíce.

eáþ-fere. l. -fēre easy to travel. Cf. earfoþ-fēre.

eáþ-fynde. Add : [Icel. auð-fyndr.] Cf. earfoþ-fynde.

eáþ-gete. Substitute : eáþ-gete, -geáte (?) ; adj. Easy to get :—Him wæs eáðgete ele tō þām baðe oil for the bath was easy for him to get, Ælfc. T. Grn. 16, 18. Gyf þȳ .viii. dæge sunne scȳneð, ðonne byð cwicseolfor eáðgeáte, Lch. iii. 166, 10. [Us is eþgete (rimes with lete (< lǽtan), bete (< bētan), swete) helle, Misc. 74, 71. Icel. auð-gætt.]

eáþ-hylde. Substitute : eáþ-hilde (-hylde) ; adj. Lit. easy to hold (cf. ge-healden), content :—Gif munuc eáðhylde bið and geþæf si contentus sit monachus, R. Ben. 29, 2 : 109, 6. Ðǽre sáwle miht is ðæt heó . . . beó hire eáðhylde, Hex. 40, 4. v. íþ-hilde.

eáþ-lǽce. -lǽcne (-lāc-) ; adj. Easy to cure :—Biþ hē þȳ eáðlǽcra (printed -na) . . . hit bið þe uneáþlǽcra, Lch. ii. 258, 26. Biþ hit þȳ eáþlǽcre, 260, 2. Bið þ eáðlǽcnere, 284, 23, 29. v. un-eáþlǽce, -lǽcne.

eáþ-mēd. l. -mēdu (q. v.).

eáþ-mēdan (-ian). Dele eáð-mēdan in Dict., and add : to humble :—Swā hwā swā eáðmēdaþ hine quicumque humiliaverit se, Mt. R. 18, 4. þā ðeóde þe mid ūs ārísan hē wolde eáðmēdigan, Hml. A. 126, 316. [O. H. Ger. ōtmōten humiliare.] v. eáþ-mēde.

eáþ-mēde. Add :—Eáðmēdde (-mēded? v. eáþ-mēdan) ic eom humiliatus sum, Ps. Spl. 38, 3. Ðū mē dydest eáðmēdne (or from eádmēd, pp. of eádmēdan?) humiliasti me, Ps. Th. 118, 75. Ic gebrenge þā heofonlican gōd æt þām eáðmēdum (-mōdum, S. 18, 11), Bt. 7, 3 ; F. 22, 3. [Ðe modie wreccha . . . þe edmeda riche, O. E. Hml. i. 115, 10. O. Sax. ōd-mōdi : O. H. Ger. ōt-, ōð-mōti.]

eáþmēdlíce ; adv. With humility, humbly :—Hē eal þ se arb. æt him cræfede eáðmēdlíce gefylde, Chr. 1070 ; P. 206, 17.

eáþ-mēdu ; f. : -mēde, es ; n. (Cf. ofer-mēde.) Take instances given under eáþ-mēd, -mēdum in Dict., and add : I. humility, lowliness :—Hē his blǽd Gode þurh eáðmēdu ealne gesealde, Gū. 74 : Cri. 1443. Eádmēdu, Gū. 748. þæt wē mid eáðmēdum ūrum Drihtne hȳron, and mid eáðmēdum ūrum scrifte ūre synna andetton, Wlfst. 134, 12–16. Hī hī (Judith) mid eáðmēdum in forlēton, Jud. 170. Mid eallum eáðmēdum regollíce libban, Ll. Th. ii. 322, 3. þū eallum eáðmēdum þíne bēne onsend, El. 1088 : 1101. þū ūs tō eáðmēdum gebrōhtest nos humiliasti, Ps. Th. 89, 17. Hē on eáðmēdum bād on beorge, wæs him botles neód, Gū. 299. I a. submission to a conqueror :—Hié him þær eáþmēdo (eád-, v. l.) budon, Chr. 827 ; P. 60, 33. II. graciousness, gentleness, condescension :—Ne gedæfenað þe, nū þe Dryhten geaf welan and woruldspēde, þæt þū andsware mid oferhygdum sēce ; sēlre byð æghwǽm þæt hē eáðmēdum ellorfūsne oncnáwe cūðlíce, An. 321. Gewāt him þā sēcan eallra cyninga cyning þone clǽnan hām eáðmēdum upp, 981. [Heo ȝeornden Arðures æðmeden (cf. we ȝeorneð þine milzce, 21889), Laym. 21866. Heo hine beden þurh his ædmeden þæt he nomen heom tō þrallen, 10013. O. Sax. ōð-, ōd-mōdi : O. H. Ger. ōð-, ōt-muotī humilitas.]

eáþ-metto. l. -mētto, and add :—þā hwíle þe Agustus þā eáðmētto wiþ God geheóld þe hē angunnen hæfde, Ors. 6, 1 ; S. 254, 7. Heora eáþmētto ne mihton nāuht forstandan, ne hūru heora ofermētta, Bt. 29, 2 ; F. 104, 34. On þǽre dene Drihten selfa þára eáðmētta wunigað, Met. 7, 38. Gebūge hē intō mynstre mid eallum eáðmēttum, Ll. Th. i. 306, 3.

eáþ-milte ; adj. Easily digested :—þā ȳtmestan leomo swína beóð eáðmelte, Lch. ii. 196, 24. Sele þū him eáðmelte mettas, 182, 15. Eáðmylte, 220, 12. v. un-eáþmilte.

eáþ-mōd. Add : I. humble, lowly ; submissive :—Eádmōd humilis, Wrt. Voc. i. 76, 27. Hnitol vel eádmōd cernuus, pronus, vel inclinatus, 19, 1. Eádmōd āstāg in middangeard mægna goldhord, Cri. 786. þū (Hagar) eádmōd ongin dreógan, Gen. 2281 : Seef. 107 : An. 270. Eom ic eáðmōd his ombiehtþēra, þeów geþyldig, Gū. 571. Wel gerás þ heó wǽre eáðmōd þā heó þone eáþmōdan cyning bær, sē be him sylfum cwæþ, 'Ic eom mildheort and eáþmōd,' Bl. H. 13, 16–19 : 129, 12 : Cri. 255. Weard Ōswold eádmōd on þeáwum, Hml. S. 26, 84. Ne byð se eádmōda (humilis) ǽfre gecyrred, Ps. Th. 73, 20. Se eádmōda biscop wæs swīðe geðyldig wið þwyrum mannum, Hml. Th. ii. 514, 10. Hē hié tō eáþmōdre (eádmōdre, v. l.) hērsumnesse gedyde, Chr. 828 ; P. 62, 3. Ábogene, eádmōdre cernua, i. humilis, An. Ox. 1278 : suplici, 1329. Eádmōdne on gāste humilem spiritu, Scint. 82, 16. Ðā eáðmodan humiles, Past. 299, 1. Uton beón eáþmōde and mildheorte, Hml. Th. 95, 26. þām eádmōdum mediocribus, An. Ox. 4121. Wæs heó on eallum þingum þe eáþmōddre, Bl. H. 13, 3. II. gracious, gentle, condescending :—þū (the Deity) eádmōd eart ealre worlde, Hy. 7, 57. Leófa Hǽlend, þū eart se miccla and se eádmōda, 3, 39. [v. N. E. D. edmod. O. H. Ger. ōt-mōt humilis, abrogans.] v. eáþ-mēde.

eáþ-módig (?); adj. Humble. [Þe edmodies monnes bonen þurlen þe weolcne, A. R. 246. O. H. Ger. ôd-muotig.] Cf. ofer-módig, and v. next word.

eáþ-mód(i)gian, -módi(g)an. I. to be humble, obey:—Uindas and saes eádmódas him (obediunt ei), Mt. L. 8, 27. Eádmódigad (eádmódad, R.), Mk. L. I, 27. Eádmódad (eád-, R.), 4, 41. II. to make humble, to humble:—Swǽ hwælc eádmódiges hine quicumque humiliaverit se, Mt. L. 18, 4. Eáþmódgiaþ eów sylfe under ჴǣre mihte Godes handa, Bl. H. 99, 2. [Crist eadmode hine seolfne, O. E. Hml. i. 17, 27. Eadmodied (maked edmod, v.l.) our heorte, A. R. 278. O. H. Ger. gi-ôtmuotigôn, (-ôd-) humiliare.] Cf. eáþ-médan.

eáþ-módlic; adj. Humble:— On Crístes sôþre eáþmódlicre and-etnesse in true, humble confession of Christ, Bl. H. 171, 12. Eádmódlice uē biddad supplices deprecamur, Rtl. 101, 32. Gif wē ásmeágaþ þá eádmódlican dǣda þá þe hē worhte, Bl. H. 33, 6.

eáþ-módlíce. Add:—Þæt hié ongieten dæt hié mon tǽle, and dæt eádmódlíce gedáfigen, Past. 151, 14: R. Ben. 17, 14. Eádmódlíce (eád-, v.l.) humiliter, 22, 18. Sancta Maria forhtode and bifigendre stefne eáþmódlíce ondswarode, Bl. H. 9, 19. Gē eáþmódlíce (eád-, v.l.) his word gehýrad obtemperanter illum audite, Bd. 2, 2; Sch. 117, 15. Eáþmódlíce, Bl. H. 133, 7. Eádmódlíce, 43, 15. Abúgaþ eáþmódlíce (suppliciter) tô hálgum wefodum, Coll. M. 36, 3. Þá þe nolden ǽr tô his libbendum líchaman onbúgan, þá nū eádmódlíce on cneówum ábúgad tô his dǣdum bánum, Chr. 979; P. 123, 26. Eádmódlíce humiliter, Angl. xiii. 369, 50: 383, 255. [O. E. Hml. edmodliche: Laym. ǽdmodliche: A. R. edmodliche: Orm. æddmodliჳ.]

eáþ-módnes. Add: I. humility, meekness:—Eádmódnys humilitas, Wrt. Voc. i. 76, 28. Þæt wæs ánrǽdlicu eáþmódnes þ heó sylf hié þeówen nemde, Bl. H. 13, 13. Eádmódnisse humilitas, Rtl. 100, 11. Be dám twelf stæpum ealre eádmódnesse, R. Ben. 23, 16. Eallon þám tô hǽlde þe his hálgan líchoman mid ealre eádmódnysse sēcead, Chr. 1023; P. 156, 26. Hē geseah his þínene eádmódnesse (eádmódnisse, R.), Lk. I, 48. Eádmódnisse humilitatem, p. 8, 10. Hē him ongeán cômon and his mid eáþmódnessum anfēngon, Ors. 3, 9; S. 126, 14. II. gentleness, graciousness, kindness:—Secggan wē Gode þanc ealra his miltsa and his eádmódnessa and bis geofena, Bl. H. 103, 26. Ealra his eádmódnessa and fremsumnessa, 115, 23. Be þǽm eádmódnessum and mildheortnessum, 103, 18. [O. E. Hml. eadmodnesse: A. R. edmodnesse: Orm. æddmodnesse.]

eáþ-nes. Add: I. ease, freedom from trouble, suffering, &c.:—Eorla gehwám eáduys and tôhyht, Rún. 1. II. ease, freedom from difficulty:—Eádnise facultatem, Lk. p. 9, 6. III. gentleness:—Ongan hē wurdigan þá gódan þeáwas þára gódra on þám life, eádnysse and hýrsumnysse, geþyld and þolemódnysse, Guth. 18, 16. v. un-eáþness; íþ-ness (eþ-).

Eatole, Eatol-ware. v. Eotol, Eotol-ware: eáw-brǽce. v. ǽ-brǽce: eáwed-ness. v. íwed-ness.

eáwesclíce. Add:—Eáwislíce sié manifestum fiat, Rtl. 114, 1. v. next word, and cf. eáwunga.

eáwisc-lic; adj. Manifest, displayed:—Eáwisclica monstra, Rtl. 78, 32. v. preceding word.

eáwis-firina. The word has been given under ǽwisc-firen (q. v.), but perhaps it belongs here, and the first part, eáwisc, =public-anus, see the two preceding words, and cf. bǽr-synnig.

eáw-lá. v. eá-lá.

eáwunga. Add:—Ðá ðe dearninga yfel dôd, and gôd eáwunga (publice), Past. 179, 8. Twá cynn sind martirdômes, án dearnunge, ôder eáwunge, Hml. Th. ii. 544, 14. Hí þá sceattas eáwunga and dearnunga spendon, Hml. S. 23, 199. Þæt hē ǽnige sprǽce wiþ hý áge, eáwunga oþþe dearnunga, R. Ben. 141, 1. Ðá synfullan sýn eáwunga (-e, v.l.) geþreáde beforan ealre gefērrǣdenne peccatores coram omnibus arguantur, 129, 17. Eáwunga manifestum, Mt. L. 12, 16. Eáwunge (eówunga, R.), Mk. L. 6, 14. Ēwunga (eáwunga, R.) manifeste, 1, 45. Eáunge (eówunga, R.), Jn. L. 11, 14. Ǽunge, 7, 10: palam, 10, 24. Eáunga, 16, 29. Eáwungæ, 18, 20. Ǽwunge in publicum, i. manifeste, An. Ox. 3536. ¶ used as the case of a noun:—On eáwunge in propatulo, i. manifeste, An. Ox. 2826. On openysse, on ǽwunge, 1485: 47. In eáuung (in eówunga, R.) cymed in palam veniat, Mk. L. 4, 22. On eáwung, Lk. L. 8, 17. In eáunge, Jn. L. 7, 4. On eáunge (eówunga, R.), 11, 54.

eax. Add:—Aex axis, Wrt. Voc. ii. 101, 38. Eax, 7, 54: i. 284, 51. Swylce ex wendende quasi axis versatilis, Scint. 97, 4. Áhôh þæt heáfod nyþerweard ofdæt seó ex sý gesóht hang the head downwards until the vertical axis is reached (until it is hanging vertically downwards?), Lch. iii. 2, 11.

eaxel. Add:—Exel humerus, Wrt. Voc. ii. 43, 40. Eaxla (=-e) humerus, ufeweard exle dæs æftran dǽles ola, 43, 45, 46. His ealdordôm ys on eaxle (super humerum), Ælfc. T. Grn. 9, 14. Þú mid þinre brǽdre hand þá nunnan ofer hire eaxle þaccodest, Gr. D. 190, 14. Hine þonne ofer eaxle besihd se dēma tô þám forwyrhtum, Wlfst. 256, 8. Eaxla humeri, Wrt. Voc. i. 64, 67: 283, 5. Eahslum scapulis, Bl. Gl.

A.-S. SUPPL.

eax-faru an expedition in carriages (?):—Aexfaru aparatu (perhaps a gloss on Ald. 64, 10:—Scythicae gentis impetum, quae cum infinito duelli apparatu proficiscens. In An. Ox. 4560 the word is glossed by fyrdungce), Txts. 41, 186.

eaxle-gespan. Add: the beam of a cross which passes behind the shoulders.

eaxl-gestealla. Add: a competitor (?):—Mid exlistealle cum aemulo, Hpt. Gl. 405, 33.

ebba. Add:—On þís ylcan geáre wæs swa mycel ebba ǽghwǣr ánes dæges swa nán man ǽror gemunde, and swá þ man fērde rídende and gangende ofer Tǽmese be-eástan þǣre brigge on Lunden, Chr. 1114; P. 244, 13. iii. ebban tȳne he must put three fences to correspond to the heights of spring, middle and neap tides (v. Seebohm Vill. Comm. p. 155), C. D. iii. 451, 2.

ebbung. v. æbbung: ebolsian. v. eofulsian.

Ebréas; pl. m. The Hebrews:—Ebrēos, Jud. 218. Ebreá God, Bl. H. 177, 14. Ebréa leód, Gen. 2165: Dan. 97. Æfter Ebréum, 78. For Ebréum and Israhélum swylce ... Judēa galdorcræftum, An. 165.

Ebréisc. Add:—þám Ebriscan eorle, Gen. 2021. Ebréiscre stefne, Bl. H. 153, 2. On Ebréisc (Ebr[e]isc) gedióde, Past. 6, 1. On Ebréisc, Bl. H. 245, 4. On Ebresc, Jn. L. 19, 20: Cri. 133. On Ebrisc Hebraice, Jn. R. L. 5, 2: 19, 13, 17. Weras Ebréisce, Jud. 241. Ebresce, El. 559. Ebriscum stafum, Mt. p. 2, 8.

Ebréisclíce; adv. In Hebrew:—Ebresclíce Hebraice, Jn. L. 19, 13, 17. ēcan. v. íean.

ece. Add:—Hē wæs geþreád mid fefre ... þá ælce dæge weóx se ece and seó ádl hefegode correptus febri ... Cum per dies singulos languor ingravesceret, Gr. D. 175, 17. Dǣr (in hell) is ēce æce (ece, v.l.), Wlfst. 114, 4. Nis þǣr (in heaven) ǽnig sár gemēted, ne ádl, ne ece, Bl. H. 25, 30. Heora sina forscruncon ... þ hí hrýmdon for ece, Hml. S. 35, 318. Hē biþ ece hál, Lch. ii. 308, 2. Manig man hæþ micelne ece on his eágum, Lch. ii. 32, 4. Wiþ bánece ... Beþe tô fýre swíde þone ece, 70, 4. Ne sceal mon þisne drincan sellan on foreweardne (in the early stage of) þone ece and þá ádle, ac ymb fela nihta, 256, 19. Hē mid sáre geswenced bid, mid mislicum ecum, Bl. H. 59, 8. v. bán-, eág-, fôt-, síd-, tôþ-, þeóh-ece.

ēce; adj. Dele bracket, and add: I. perpetual, to all time:—Od done fyrst þe hē bócland and æce yrfe geearnige, Solil. H. 2, 12. Hē on feorhgebeorh foldan hæfde eallum eordcynne ēce láfe frumcneów gehwæs túddorteóndra he (Noah) to save life for all that lives on earth had a remnant that should perpetuate it, to wit, the primal generation of everything that has offspring (i. e. from the creatures saved in the ark would come a progeny that would last till the end of time), Exod. 370. On þæt gerád þæt hié him siþþan ēce þeówas wǣren, Ors. 3, 8; S. 122, 4. Ecum rictum jure perpetuo, An. Ox. 11, 114. II. eternal:—Hú ēce dæt is dæt hié wilniad, lū gewítende dæt is dæt hié onscuniad ... hū ēciu (ēcu, v.l. aeterna) dá ding sint, Past. 299, 8–10. Deádlic and gewítendlic, þe á libbendu and ēcu, Solil. H. 3, 5. Reste þǣre ēcean quietis aeternae, An. Ox. 40, 19. On ēcium fýre, Past. 328, 9. Ne synt dreó ēcean, Ath. Crd. 21. Gooda gifu, þeáh hí ēca ne sién, Solil. H. 53, 4. Þára ēcena háma, 2, 14. [v. N. E. D. eche. Cf. Goth. ajuk-duþs.] v. þan-ēcan, and cf. wídefeorh-lic.

ēce; adj. Add:—Ēce esenlic comperennis, Wrt. Voc. ii. 132, 61. Wē beód mid úrum sáwlum ēce symle earme odðe eádige, Wlfst. 145, 13.

eced. Add:—Dá arn tô dám ecede sum árleás cempa, Hml. Th. ii. 256, 32. Mid æcced (ecedes, R.) aceto, Mt. L. 27, 48. Æcede, Mk. R. 15, 36. Of æcced (æcedes, R.), Jn. L. 19, 29. Hí æcced (æced, R.) bróhton him, Lk. 23, 36. [From Latin.] v. next word.

eced-drenc, es; m. A potion in which vinegar is an ingredient:—Oxumelle, súderne eceddrenc, ecedes and huniges and wæteres gemang, Lch. 284, 32: 150, 8: 254, 17. Þæs eceddrences swá geworhtes, 286, 8. v. wyrt-eceddrenc.

eced-fæt. Add:—Ecedfæt (ecet-, v.l.) acitabula (uas, quo fertur acetum), Hpt. 31, 11, 217.

ēce-lic. Add:—Ēcelices perpetuae, Rtl. 35, 17. On gemynde ēcelice ł ēcum in memoria aeterna Ps. L. 111, 7. Þá ēcelican wuldor perhenni doxa, Hpt. 31, 18, 524. Ēcelicum aeternis, Rtl. 18, 21. Ēce-lica sempiterna, 46, 22. ¶ hodiernus is glossed by ēcelic, Rtl. 4, 26: 57, 4: 126, 3: 174, 33. [v. N. E. D. echelich.]

ēcelíce. Add: I. to all time, perpetually:—Þætte ēcelíce mín gemynd stonde perpetuum statuimus monimentum, Nar. 33, 1. II. to eternity:—Ēcelíce lifian, habban, forweorþan, gehealden beón, Gr. D. 337, 1: Bl. H. 111, 22: Wlfst. 96, 20: Hml. A. 168, 121. Þæt hí ēcelíce árǽrede synd that they will never die after their resurrection, Hml. Th. i. 440, 26, 28. Sý him wuldor á on ealra worulda woruld ēcelíce, Hml. A. 72, 181. Beód welige hwílwendlíce, þæt gē ēcelíce wǽdlion, Hml. Th. i. 64, 16.

ecg. Add. Dele twý- at end, and add: I. of weapons:—Egc acies, hiltan capulum, Wrt. Voc. i. 84, 20. Ecge mucrone, An. Ox. 52, 3. Scearp sweord dá wunde tôsceát, and gǽd geháire ecge ford, Past. 453, 17. Hē ealle ofslôh mid swurdes ecge, Hml. S. 25, 415. Hí þá Bryttas

fardydon þurh fȳr and ðurh swyrdes egge, Chr. 448; P. 12, 38.    **II.** *an edge, verge, brink* of high ground:—Of ðam slæde ūp on ða ecg; ðæt andlang ecge, C. D. iii. 438, 33. Ūp on wādhām; ðonne be ecge, 406, 23, 34, 35. Of cumbes sūðecge . . . ðonan sūð on ecge oð ðæt niéhste slæd, 416, 21. Ūp ofer feld . . . tō wuda; of wuda be ecge . . . ā norð be ecge; of ecge eást, 446, 18–23. On Wilbaldes ecge; of Wilbaldes ecge, 439, 2. Á be ecge on ðā medemunga; of ðǽre mǽdemunge nydǽr on ðone ealdan wiðig, v. 286, 31. Be ðæs hlinces niðerecge, iii. 418, 19. Ādūn ofer ðā ecge ðæt hit cymð tō Crimes hylle, 389, 29. v. scír-ecg; -ecge.

**ecgan**; *p.* egede *to harrow*:—Egide *occabat*, Wrt. Voc. ii. 115, 39. Egede, 63, 33. [*Piers P.* eggen oþer harwen. *O. H. Ger.* ecken *arare, aequare*.] v. ecgung, egþe.

**ecg-clif.** *Add: A cliff with an edge* or *brink* (? v. ecg; II). -ecge. v. feówer-, six-, twi-ecge: -ecgede. v. feówer-, fíf-, fiþer-, ge-, scearp-, twi-ecgede(-ode).

**ecg-lást.** [The gender is doubtful, the word occurring both *m.* and *f.* in the only passage where it is found: *lást* a track is *m.*] *A sword's edge*:—On ðæs Paternosters ðǽre swíðran handa is gyldenes sweordes onlícnis . . . and ðæs dryhtenlican wǽpnes seó swíðre ecglást (*gender influenced by that of* ecg?) hē (*the true gender of* -lást?) is mildra ðonne middangeardes swétnissa; and seó winstre ecglást ðæs ilcan wǽpnes hē is scearpra ðonne eal middangeard, Sal. K. p. 150, 14–22.

**ecglinga, eclinga**; *adv. Edgeling* (v. N. E. D. s. v.), *on the edge*:—Ðonne þū handlín habban wille, þonne stríc þū mid þínre swýþran hand eclinga ofer þíue wynstran, Tech. ii. 120, 2. Ástrehte þínre winstran handa ofsete hý eclinga mid þiure swí[þ]ran, 23. Stríc þū eclinga mid ǽgðere hande ofer ǽðerne earm, 127, 19. Cf brádlinga.

**ecg-plega.** *Add:* [cf. *Icel.* egg-leikr *battle*.]: ecg-prǽc. *l.* -þracu. **ecgung**, e; *f. Harrowing*:—Egcgung *occatio*, Wrt. Voc. i. 15, 9. [*O. H. Ger.* egunga *occatio*.] v. ecgan.

**ecilma.** *l.* ēcilma, *and see* ǽ-celma: **ēcilmehte.** v. ǽcelmehte: **eclinga.** v. ecglinga: ēcndóm, Bl. H. 121, 20. *l.* (?) ece dóm.

**ēc-nes.** *Add:* I. *all time*:—Nǽfra from ðec wæstm accenned bið in ēcnisse (ēk-, R.) (*in sempiternum*), Mt. L. 21, 19: Hml. Th. i. 58, 8. On ēcnesse *in aeternum*, Mk. 11, 14.    **II.** *eternity*:—On ēcnesse in ealra worlda world ā būton ende, Bl. H. 53, 32. In ēcnesse *in aeternum*, Jn. L. 4, 14.

**ed-byrdan, -cenned.** v. ge-edbyrdan, -edcennan.

**ed-cenning, -cynning.** *Add:*—'On ðǽre edcynninge . . .' Edcynninge hē hēt þæt gemǽnelice ǽrist, on ðām beóð ūre líchaman geedcynnede tō unbrosnunge, Hml. Th. i. 394, 23–27.

**ed-cer.** v. ed-cir: **ed-cígan.** v. ge-edcígan.

**ed-cir[r].** *Add to* ed-cer:—Gewiss edcyrr (-cyr, *v. l.*) (*certus redditus*) þára beorhtra wera, Gr. D. 298, 14. Hē him ðǽre ádle edcier suíður ondrǽde ðone fruman *languorem plus reserpentem timeat*, Past. 229, 6. Forbodenne edcyr *interdictum postliminium*, An. Ox. 4, 43: Hpt. Gl. 470, 21.

**ed-cwic**; *adj. Restored to life*:—Edcwicum *redivivis*, Angl. xiii. 400, 499.

**ed-cwician.** *Add to* ed-cucian:—þū cwæde þ þū hæfdest tō ācwellene anweald and tō edcucigenne, Hml. S. 34, 329. Se edcukeda seóca *aeger redivivus*, Gr. D. 90, 7.

**ed-cwide.** *Add:*—Edcuide *relatio*, Wrt. Voc. ii. 119, 6.

**eder-gong.** *Substitute: A going into an enclosed place* (?), *a taking refuge*:—Þǽr (*in heaven*) nǽfre hreów cymeð, edergong fore yrmþum, Cri. 1676. [*Parallelism with* hreów *suggests* (?) *a connexion between* edergong *and* Goth. idreigôn, idreiga.]

**ed-freólsian.** v. ge-edfreólsian.

**ed-geong.** *Add:*—Árísed se Fénix of dǽðe and bið edgung . . . ā emb þūsend wintra hē hine forbærneþ and eft ediung ūp áríseþ, E. S. viii. 479, 85–89.

**ed-gifan.** *Dele:* ed-gift. *Add:*—Hē bæd þ hē him geþingude wiþ Eádgife his bôca edgift *requisivit ut pro eo me* (Eádgifu) *rogaret quatinus ei redderem libros terrarum suarum*, Cht. Th. 202, 33. Cf. ǽ-gift.

**ed-gild.** *Dele.*

**ed-gildan**; *p.* de *To requite, remunerate*:—Hē edgylt *remunerat*, i. *reditat*, Scint. 162, 11.

**ed-gildend**, es; *m. One who requites, remunerates*:—Edgyldend *remunerator*, i. *redonator*, Scint. 127, 17.

**ed-grówung.** *Add:* [cf. N. E. D. ed-grow.]: ed-hirtan, -híwian. v. ge-edhirtan, -edhíwian.

**ed-hwyrft.** *Substitute:* I. *return* to a place:—Ús is āléfed edhwyrft tō þǽm ēcean life, Bl. H. 137, 14. Gesǽligum edhwyrftum *felici reditu*, Wrt. Voc. ii. 148, 30.    **II.** *return, recovery* from a condition:—Oftigen bið him torhtre gesihðe . . . þæt him bið sár in his móde . . . ne wéneð þæt him þæs edhwyrft cyme (*he does not expect to recover from his blindness*), Gn. Ex. 42.    **III.** *return* to a condition:—þā þǽr sóna wearð edhwyrft eorlum siððan inne feallh Grendles módor *there was a return to the old state of things for the men after Grendel's mother had forced her way in*, B. 1281.

**edisc.** *Substitute:* edisc, es; *m. An enclosed pasture, a park*:—Edisc, deórtuun *broel*, Wrt. Voc. ii. 102, 20. Broel, *hortus cervorum* deórtūn *vel* edisc, 127, 23. Ad illum agellum qui dicitur Tatan edisc, C. D. iii. 383, 11. Greótan edesces lond, i. 273, 3. Wē his sceáp syndan, ðā hē on his edisce āfēdde *nos oves pascuae ejus*, Ps. Th. 99, 3: 94, 7. Tō Wynburhe edisce, C. D. iii. 78, 34. Tō sundran edisce, v. 401, 33. Ad Griman edisc; ab Griman edisce, iii. 388, 7, 8. On brādan edisc, 30. Per hídes edisc, 407, 33. On fearnedisc, C. D. B. i. 519, 2. v. fearn-edisc. Cf. e(o)dor; ersc.

**edisc-hen.** *Add:*—Edischen (-hæn) *ortigome(t)ra*, Txts. 83, 1460. Edischenn *cicius* (*ciaus*?), Wrt. Voc. i. 281, 23. Edischen *ciaus* (*cicius*?), ii. 16, 22: *coturnix*, 22, 76.

**edisc-weard.** *Add:*—Ediscueard (-uard) *broellarius*, Txts. 45, 525. Ediscweard, Wrt. Voc. ii. 127, 24: 11, 64.

**ed-lǽcan.** *Add:*—Cild swíþran chores edlǽcean (*repetant*) þā ufran, Angl. xiii. 410, 645, 646. Edlǽcendum *reciprocis, iteratis*, Hpt. Gl. 460, 45: 462, 3: 470, 64: 516, 56. Edlǽhtum *reciprocis, iteratis*, 484, 5. v. ge-edlǽcan.

**ed-lǽsian.** v. ge-edlǽsian, ed-lesende, -lesung.

**ed-leán.** *Add:*—Edleán *recompensatio*, Wrt. Voc. i. 47, 28. Wiðerriht *vel* edleán *hostimentum*, 22, 24. Sigeleán ł edleán *palma*, Hpt. Gl. 482, 5. Edleánes *recompensationis*, 432, 71. Efenhlyttan þæs ēcan edleánes, Hml. Th. i. 84, 20. Ne bideþ hē æt ūs nǽnig óþor edleán, Bl. H. 103, 21. On ðǽm dieglan edleánum *in occulta retributione*, Past. 105, 11. Edleán *retributiones*, Ps. Spl. 102, 2: Bl. Gl. [*O. H. Ger.* it-lôn.]

**ed-leánian.** *Add:* [*O. H. Ger.* it-lônôn *retribuere*.] v. ed-leánian *in Dict.*, ge-edleánian.

**ed-leániend**, es; *m. One who rewards, recompenses, remunerates*:—Se ordfruma and edleániend þæs ēcan lífes *auctor ac retributor vitae*, Gr. D. 286, 6. Edleáni[ende] *remuneratore*, i. *largitore*, An. Ox. 2549. v. ge-edleániend.

**ed-leánung.** *Add:*—Edleánung *compensatio*, Wrt. Voc. i. 29, 2. Edleánunge *compensationis*, ii. 23, 40. On edleánunga *in retribuendo* Bl. Gl.

**ed-lesende**; *adj. Reciprocal*:—Edlæsendum *reciproco*, An. Ox. 1885. Sume noman synd *diuidua*, þā getácniað tōdāl mid edlesendre sprǽce, Ælfc. Gr. Z. 13, 13. v. ge-edlesende.

**ed-lesendlic.** *Add:*—*Relatiuum*, þæt ys edlesendlic (-læs-, *v. l.*), Ælfc. Gr. Z. 99, 1: 116, 16.

**edlesendlíce**; *adv. Relatively*:—Seó sāwul oððe þ líf synd gecwǽdene tō hyre sylfra, and þ gemynd oððe þ andgit beóð gecwǽdene tō sumum þinga edlesendlíce, Hml. S. 1, 119.

**ed-lesung.** *Substitute: Relation*:—Hwylc getácnað þreó ðingc . . . *relationem*, þæt is, edlesunge (-læs-, *v. l.*), Ælfc. Gr. Z. 116, 10. Edlesunge (-lys-, *v. l.*), 117, 5.

**ed-mǽle**, es; *n. A season which recurs* (?), *festival*:—Edmélu *sacra orgia*, Wrt. Voc. ii. 119, 69. [*O. H. Ger.* it-máli; *f. festivitas*; it-mál(i) *solemnis, festus*.]

**edmǽl-tíd**, e; *f. A festival-time*:—Ælce geáre tō ðǽre edméltíde (cf. man his gemynd dô, 15), Cht. Th. 158, 21.

**ed-níwan.** *l.* -níwan, *and add*:—Edníwan *identidem*, An. Ox. 8, 292: 7, 332. God gescípð symle edníwan of þām ǽrran þ hí ne āteorian *ex primordialibus seminibus non incognitae oriuntur naturae, sed notae saepius, ne pereant, reformantur*, Angl. vii. 10, 99. Ðæs landes bóc ðe Eádrēd cyngc ednýwon gebócade, C. D. iii. 428, 2. v. edníwe; *adv.*

**ed-níwe**; *adj. Add:*—Se heofonlica mete him dæghwomlíce edníwe (*or adv.*?) of heofenum cóm, Hml. Th. ii. 196, 1: Ælfc. T. Grn. 5, 33. Ðeáh ðe eal middangeard sý fram Adames frymðe edníówe geworden, Sal. K. 150, 1. Tō geeácnienne heora ealdan synna mid edníwum synnum *peccatis veteribus jungentes nova*, Jud. 10, 6. [*O. H. Ger.* it-niuwi *redivivus*.] v. next word.

**ed-níwe**; *adv. Add:*—God gescípð ælce geáre ôðre edníwe (cf. Angl. vii. 10, 99 *under* edníwan) ðæs ylcan gecyndes, for ðan ðe ðā ǽrran āteoriað, Hml. Th. ii. 206, 29. (*This and* Ph. 253 *might be taken under* ed-níwe; *adj.*) [Cf. *O. H. Ger.* it-niuwes *denuo*.]

**ed-níwian.** *Add:*—On dómes dæge ūre Drihten edníwaþ ealle gesceafte, Shrn. 64, 24. Ongunnan hí þā heargas edníwian (-níwan, *v. l.*) þā þe ǽr forlǽtene wǽron *coeperunt fana, quae derelicta erant, restaurare*, Bd. 3, 30; Sch. 331, 15. [*O. H. Ger.* it-niuwôn.]

**ed-níwigend**, es; *m. A restorer, repairer, renewer*:—God, scyppend and edníwigend (*reparator*) mennisces cynnes, Angl. xi. 115, 9.

**ed-níwinga, -niówunga.** *Add:*—Wē ðǽr eft edniówunga hæfdon micel gefeoht, Nar. 17, 21.

**ed-níwung.** *Add:*—Gerýnu mancynnes edníwunge, Hml. Th. i. 590, 1. In eftcynnes edníwung *in regeneratione*, Mt. L. 19, 28. Ðā edníwunge and ðā lāre hí forsāwen, ðǽr hí ǽr ne ongéten ðone hryre and ðā ðorwpennesse *aedificationis verba contemnerent, nisi prius ruinam suae destructionis invenissent*, Past. 443, 16. v. ge-edníwung.

**ed-rec.** v. ed-roc.

**ed-recan.** *Substitute:* ed-reccan, eodorcan (*q. v. in Dict.*); *pp.* ed

*To ruminate:*—Edreceð, ceóweþ *ruminet,* Wrt. Voc. ii. 97, 15. [*O. H. Ger.* it-ruchen (itar-) *ruminare : M. L. Ger.* ed-, id-ricken.] v. ed-roc.

**ed-recedroc.** *Dele, and see* ed-roc: ed-rine. *l.* -ryne : ed-ric. v. ed-roc: edring. v. íþring.

**ed-roc.** *Substitute:* ed-roc, -rec, -ric. **I.** *the gullet:*—Wäsend *vel* edroc *rumen,* Wrt. Voc. i. 43, 43. Edroc, -ric *rumen* (-*ex,* MS.), Txts. 92, 876. Edrec, edroc *rumen,* Wrt. Voc. ii. 97, 18. **II.** *ruminating:*—Cíwung *vel* edroc *vel* áceócung *ruminatio,* Wrt. Voc. i. 54, 62. [*O. L. Ger.* idrig *rumen: M. L. Ger.* ederic.] v. ed-reccan.

**ed-sceaft.** *Substitute:* **I.** *a new creation:*—Edscaeft (-scaept) *palingenesean,* Txts. 83, 1488. Oþ edsceafte, Dan. 112. **II.** *a new creature:*—His gesceafta ... of heora sǽde weorþaþ eft geedníwade, swylce hí þonne weordon tó edsceafte; ... hí ǽlce geáre weorþaþ tó ædsceafte, Bt. 34, 11 ; F. 150, 12–16.

**ed-sihþ,** e; *f. A looking again, respect :*—Etsith *respectus,* Wrt. Voc. ii. 119, 11.

**ed-staþelian.** *Add:*—Beó sé áwirged þe ǽfre gedó [þæt man?] edstaðelige þás burh Hiericho *maledictus vir, qui suscitaverit et aedificaverit urbem Iericho,* Jos. 6, 26. v. ge-edstaþelian.

**ed-staþelig.** v. preceding word.

**ed-staþeli(g)end,** es; *m. A restorer :*—Hé is þín edstaþeligend, Hml. S. 5, 201. v. ge-edstaþeli(g)end.

**ed-staþelung** *restoration. For* R. Ben. 36 *substitute :*—Mancynna Ealdor for úre edstaðelunge þǽre róde gealgan underféng, Hml. Th. i. 588, 19. Tó edstaþelungum *ad lumina vitae,* An. Ox. 2214. v. ge-edstaþelung.

**ed-þingung.** *Add :* cf. eft-þingung : **ed-þráwen.** v. ge-edþráwen. **ed-walle** (-a). v. ed-wille.

**ed-wendan.** *Substitute: To turn back, cease to affect :*—Gyf him edwendan ǽfre scolde bealuwa bisigu, bót eft cuman *if worry from woes should cease to trouble him, better times come again,* B. 280.

**ed-wenden.** *Substitute for first passage :*—Hyne Géata bearn gódne ne tealdon, ne hyne on medobence micles wyrðne drihten wereda gedón wolde ... edwenden cwóm tíreádigum menn torna gehwylces *there came for the glorious man an end to all griefs,* B. 2188. *Add :*—Hwæt mé þæs edwendan (-en?) cwóm, gyrn æfter gomene *ah! for me of that happiness an end there came, mourning after mirth,* B. 1774. v. previous word.

**ed-wendu.** *l.* -wend : ed-wielle. v. ed-wille.

**ed-wille,** es; *m.:* -wille, -walle (-a), an ; *f. (m.) A whirlpool :*—Eduuaelle (-uella, -uelli) *toreuma,* Txts. 103, 2034. Eduaelle *alveum,* 39, 137. Eduuelle (-walla, -ualla, -ualle) *vertigo,* 105, 2096 : *Scylla,* 95, 1798. Edwelle *fortex,* 65, 908. Edwielle, Wrt. Voc. ii. 35, 79. Eduualles *Carybdis,* An. Ox. 53, 11. Ýþ, ædwella *flustra,* i. *unda,* Wrt. Voc. ii. 149, 67.

**ed-wilm** *a fiery whirlpool :*—þonne se fǽcna (*the devil*) in þám fæstenne (*hell*) gebróht hafað æt þám edwylme (cf. Milton's 'floods and whirlwinds of tempestuous fire') þá þe him on cleofiaþ, Wal. 73. Cf. preceding word.

**ed-winde.** *Substitute :* ed-winde, an: -wind, e; *f. A vortex, whirlpool, abyss :*—Deópnyss *abyssus,* edwinde *vortex,* swelgend *vorago,* Wrt. Voc. i. 54, 36. Edwindan *uoraginis,* An. Ox. 4, 10. Swyliendes, eadwindan, 636. Edwindan *uoraginem,* i. *foveam,* 701 : 4, 20. Edwinde *voragines,* 5474. [Cf. *O. L. Ger.* ed-windan *rotare.*]

**ed-wirpan,** -wirping. v. ed-wyrpan, -wyrping *in Dict.*

**ed-wist.** *Add :*—Ǽdwist *substantia,* An. Ox. 50, 57. Ǽlc edwist þætte God nys, þæt is gesceaft, Hml. Th. i. 276, 21. Seó sunne hæfð ðreó ágennysa; án is seó líchamlice edwist, þæt is ðǽre sunnan trendel, 282, 8. Án sáwul is and án líf and án edwist ... ná þreó ædwiste ... seó edwist, Hml. S. 1, 115–117: Hml. Th. i. 288, 24. Edwiste *substantia,* Hpt. Gl. 407, 6. Ne on ágenre edwiste ne on óþrum híwe, Hml. S. 31, 709. Tó gewitendlicum ǽhtum ... for áteorigendlicere edwiste, Hml. Th. i. 56, 16. 'Se stán wæs Críst.' Hé cwæð 'wæs' for ðǽre getácnunge, ná for edwiste (*figuratively, not as indicating material*), 98, 12. þæt Godes sunu become on mínne innoð, and mennisce edwiste of mé genime, 200, 20: 360, 9. Nama mæg beón on ðám forman háde on ðám worde ðe getácnað edwiste : *Priscianus sum ic eom Priscianus,* Ǽlfc. Gr. Z. 128, 10.

**edwistlian.** *Dele:* ge-edwis.ian. v. ge-edwis.ian.

**edwistfull.** *Dele:* ge-edwis.ian. v. ge-edwis.ian.

**ed-wít.** *Add :* **I.** *a source* or *cause of disgrace :*—Edwít *probrum,* Wrt. Voc. ii. 87, 21. Þý lǽs him ætwite and on edwít sette (*should make it a reproach to him*) his gebóftan þ hé for ege þæs deáþes þá þing dyde *ne exprobrarent sibi sodales, quod timore mortis faceret ea,* Bd. 5, 13; Sch. 636, 18 : Gen. 2728. On edwít ásettan, Sat. 639. In edwít settan, Gú. 459. Eall hí mé þæt on edwít oncyrdan *factum est mihi in opprobrium,* Ps. Th. 68, 10. **II.** *disgrace, shame, blame incurred by a person :*—Hé sǽde þ hit þǽm cyninge lǽsse edwít wǽre (*sine regis infamia*), Ors. 2, 5 ; S. 82, 33. Hé him ætfæste éce edwít *opprobrium sempiternum dedit illis,* Ps. Th. 77, 66: Bl. H. 101, 7. Hé forfleáh þone woruldlican wurðmynt, ac hé ne forfleáh ná þæt edwít and ðone hosp, Hml. Th. i. 162, 12. Ic þec hálsige þæt þú furður mé fracebu ne

wyrce, edwít for eorlum, Jul. 542. On edwít sellan *in opprobrium dare,* Ps. Th. 56, 3. Þú mé scealt edwítt mín of áwyrpan, 118, 39. **III.** *blame directed against a person.* (1) expressing disapproval :—Edwít *exprobatio,* i. *improperatio, objurgatio,* Wrt. Voc. ii. 146, 9. Donne hé hine on ormódnesse gebringð mid his edwíte, ðeáh hé hit for lufum dó, Past. 167, 12. (2) expressing scorn, contempt :—Teónan hospe i edwíte (*of unrihtum edwíte*) *calumniae improperio,* Hpt. Gl. 505, 16. Gefylled mid edwíte, Ps. Th. 122, 5. Ic edwít for þé oft árǽfnade *propter te supportavi improperium,* 68, 8. Edwít þolian, 73, 6: Jud. 215. Hí edwít on þé hæfdon *exprobraverunt tibi,* Ps.Th. 78, 13. Hí hine hysptun, sprǽcon him edwít, Cri. 1122. Þurh edwít *in scorn* (?), Sat. 681. **IV.** *an expression* (1) *of disapproval :*—Edwít *apostropha de muliere nequam,* Scint. 223, 1. (2) *of scorn, contempt, opprobrious term :*—Cweþað him þæt edwít feóndas þíne *quod exprobraverunt inimici tui,* Ps. Th. 88, 44. Fram ðám Godes men ádrígde þá edwítu þǽre bysmrunge (*irrisionis opprobria*) se fisc of ðám munte, Gr. D. 11, 29. Ealle þá sáran edwíta þé hé ádreág, Bl. H. 97, 15. Edwít *opprobria,* Ps. Srt. 68, 10. **V.** *an object of scorn :*—þú ús gesettest tó edwíte úsum neáhgebúrum *posuisti nos opprobrium vicinis nostris,* Ps. Th. 43, 15. Hé on edwít weard ymbsittendum *factus est in opprobrium vicinis suis,* 88, 34. [v. *N. E. D.* edwit. *Goth.* id-weit: *O. L. Ger.* ed-wít *opprobrium: O. H. Ger.* it-wíz (ita-) *opprobrium, exprobratio, insultatio.*] v. hearm-edwít.

**ed-wítan.** *Add :*—Edwiton (-un) *exprobraverunt,* Ps. Srt. 41, 11 : 88, 52. Eft-edwidon *reprobaverunt,* Mt. L. 21, 42. [v. *N. E. D.* edwite.] v. next word.

**ed-wítan ;** *p.* te *To reproach :*—Edwítte *improperavit,* Ps. Srt. 73, 18. Edwíttun *exprobraverunt,* 34, 7. [*Goth.* id-weitjan : *O. H. Ger.* ita-wízen, -wízôn.] v. ed-witian, *and preceding word.*

**edwít-full ;** *adj. Shameful, disgraceful, ignominious :*—Edwítfull *ignominiosus,* Scint. 173, 15. Eadwítfulne (-wíd-, An. Ox. 2783) *probrosum, vitiosum, nefandum,* Hpt. Gl. 471, 36. Edwítfullum *probrosis, vitiosis* (i. *inhonestis,* An. Ox. 2913), 474, 54.

**edwítfull-líc ;** *adj. Disgraceful :*—Edwídfullic *probrosum,* Wrt. Voc. ii. 80, 47.

**ed-witian** (-wet-), -wítian (?), *p.* ode, ede *To reproach, revile :*—Edwetede *improperavit,* Ps. Srt. 73, 10. Edwitadun (eð-, L.) *reprobauerunt,* Lk. R. 20, 17. Eðwetendes *exprobrantis,* Ps. Srt. 43, 17. v. ed-wítan.

**edwít-sprǽc.** *l.* -sprǽc : **éd-wylm.** v. ed-wilm : **ed-wyrpan,** -wyrping. *l.* ed-wirpan, -wirping: **ed-yppol.** v. ge-edyppol.

**efen.** *Add :*—Efnum *aequatis,* Txts. 39, 92. **I.** *level:*—Ðá ðe ne magon uncwaciende gestondan on emnum felda *qui in planis stantes titubant,* Past. 41, 7. **I a.** *of sounds, harmonious, not discordant :*—Efnum sónum *consonantibus,* Mk. p. 1, 13. **II.** *unruffled, undisturbed :*—Gyf eówer hwylc bið geunrótsod, hé hyne gebidde mid emnum móde (*aequo animo*), Ll. Th. ii. 354, 19. Mid efnum móde, R. Ben. 55, 16: R. Ben. I. 62, 15. **III.** *equal, just, impartial :*—Mid þá efnan helurbléde *justa lance,* Wrt. Voc. ii. 48, 40. Hé démð rihtne dóm and emne dóm, Wlfst. 253, 20: 254, 9. **IV.** *equal, of like condition :*—Sé ðe conn wel emn bión wið ôðre menn, ond hé hine ná bettran ne ðéð *qui scit ceteris aequalitate componi,* Past. 113, 23. þ ilce þ hé lifde in líchaman, hit wǽre efen þan þe hé eallinga bútan þám líchaman eall wǽre *totum jam extra carnem est, hoc ipsum quod vivit in carne,* Gr. D. 218, 12. Efnum ðegnum (*altered from* eðegnum) *conseruis,* Jn. p. 7, 1. ¶ efen ; *n. as substantive :*—On efne *directly ;* e *regione,* Mt. p. 4, 6. Ǽlc þǽra þinga þe man mæg tódǽlan on feówer on emne *everything that can be divided into four exactly,* Angl. viii. 306, 30. v. on-efn, emn *in Dict.*

**efen ;** *adv. Add :*—(1) with an adverb :—Efen (em) swá feala *totidem,* Hpt. Gl. 493, 70. (2) with a numeral :—Mid allra ôðerra priósta bútan ðissum mæsspeprióstum efen LX *with just sixty other priests besides these* (*already named*), Cht. Th. 72, 4. Hé wunode on his ágenum mynstre em feówertig geára, Hml. S. 6, 360. On þám frummynetslæge wǽron twá and sixtig penega, and on þǽm æftran em sixtig, 23, 480. v. *following compounds with* efen-.

**efen-ámeten ;** *ptcpl. Compared :*—Efenámeten hé is neátum *comparatus est jumentis,* Ps. Srt. 48, 13.

**efen-apostol** *a fellow-apostle :*—Efneapostol *coapostolum,* Rtl. 61, 31. Hér cumað míne efnapostolas ... Mid mínum efnapostolum, Nap. 19. Efneapostolas, 16.

**efen-beorht.** *Add :* [*Icel.* jafu-bjartr.]

**efen-bisceop.** *Add :*—Laurentius mid his efnebiscopum (*coepiscopis*), Bd. 2, 4 ; Sch. 126, 1.

**efen-blissian.** *Add :*—Is sǽd þæt se cining wǽre swá efenblissiende (efnblissende, *v. l.*) *ita congratulatus esse rex perhibetur,* Bd. 1, 26; Sch. 59, 4. Efenblissiende hyre wuldres *ejus gloriae congaudens,* Gr. D. 169, 10.

**efen-blíþe ;** *adj. Rejoicing with another :*—Ne wépað git mé ná swá ic deád sý, ac beóð mé efenblíðe *weep not for me as if I were dead, but rejoice with me* (*rejoice as I do*), Shrn. 56, 19. [*Icel.* jafn-blíðr.]

N 2

**efen-boren**; *adj.* *(ptcpl.)* *Of equal birth :*—þ se mæssepreóst nǽre, gif hē wíf hæfde, ǽnigre ōþre láde wyrþe būtan eallswā lǽwede sceolde þe efenboren wǽre, Ll. Th. ii. 256, 38. [*Icel.* jafn-borinn.]

**efen-brád**; *adj.* *Equally broad, as broad (as long)* :—Paradisus is eall efenlang and efenbrád, E. S. viii. 477, 7. [*O. H. Ger.* eban-breit: *Icel.* jafn-breiđr.]

**efen-byrde**; *adj.* *Of equal birth :*—Hē genam him gemeccan efenbyrde his cynne *he took a wife of as good family as his own*, Hml. S. 33, 3.

**efen-ceasterwearan.** *Add :*—Efenceasterwaran (efn-, *v. l.*), Bd. 1, 26; Sch. 59, 10. Of hyra efenceasterwarum *civibus suis*, Gr. D. 205, 1.

**efen-cempa**, an; *m.* *A fellow-soldier :*—Embe his efencempan hē hæfde welwillendnysse . . . and his efencempan hine árwurđodon, Hml. S. 31, 44, 49: Hml. Th. ii. 500, 15.

**efen-cristen** *a fellow-christian.* [*v. N. E. D.* even-christian. *O. Frs.* ivin-kerstena, -kristina: *O. H. Ger.* eban-christani: *Icel.* jafn-kristinn.] v. em-crīsten *in Dict.*

**efen-cuman.** *Add :*—Efnecwōm (*convenit*) điú menigo, Mk. L. 3, 20. Efnecwōmon (-cōmun, R.) đā apostolas *convenientes apostoli*, 6, 30. Efencōmon (efne-, -cwōmon, *v. ll.*) wē *convenimus*, Bd. 4, 5; Sch. 373, 17. Seofon bysceopas tō his hālgunge efencōman (efnecōmon, *v. l.*), 4, 28; Sch. 524, 13.

**efen-dīre, -dȳre.** *Add :*—Mæssepreóstes áđ and woruldþegenes is geteald efendȳre, Ll. Th. i. 182, 15. [*Icel.* jafn-dȳrr.]

**efen-eádig.** *Add :* [*Icel.* jafn-auđigr.]

**efen-eald.** *Add :* (1) adjective :—Hē is efeneald his Fæder . . . Seó beorhtnys is efeneald þām fȳre . . . ealswā eald swā þæt fȳr, Hml. Th. i. 278, 20–32. Lǽswede heó sceápum mid ōþrum mægdenum hire efnealdum (*with other maidens of like age with herself*), Shrn. 101, 16. Heó tǽhte þām mægdene hire efenealde mægdenu *coaevas ei puellas ostendit*, Gr. D. 287, 13. His efenealdan lytlingas hē ácwealde, Hml. Th. i. 88, 12. (2) substantive, efen-ealda *a coeval :*—Efenealda *con-senior*, Wrt. Voc. ii. 133, 58. Hē his efenealdan áđȳlegode, Hml. Th. i. 82, 19. [*v. N. E. D.* even-old. *O. H. Ger.* eban-alt *coaevus*; eban-alto *consenior*.]

**efen-ēce.** *Add :*—Efenēce *coeternus*, Wrt. Voc. ii. 136, 40. Godes Sunu is efenēce (efn-, *v. l.*) his Fæder and þām Hālgan Gāste, Gr. D. 60, 15 : Hml. Th. i. 198, 15 : 278, 21. Euenēce, 32, 6. Efnēce, Bl. H. 111, 8 : 29, 3. Ān Godcundnys and gelíc wuldor and efenēce mægen-đrymnys, Hml. Th. i. 276, 26. Đurh đīnum euenēcum wīsdōme, ii. 598, 31. On mec his efenēcne sunu, Shrn. 106, 13. [*Orm.* efenn-eche.]

**efen-ēhþ, -nēhþ.** *Add : Three of the four MSS. have efennehþe, and this form points to connexion with* efen-neáh, *and to the idea of neighbourhood. For this sense cf. the later* efen-nexta *neighbour :*—Gif þū agultest wiđ þine efennexta, O. E. Hml. i. 17, 32.

**efen-fela** (em-). *Dele 'indecl.', and add :* (1) substantive with gen. :—Man ne mihte nānne mete gegyrwan, þ þāra wyrma nǽre emfela þæm mete, Ors. 1, 7 ; S. 36, 28. Gān inn emfela manna of ǽgđre healfe, Ll. Th. i. 226, 20. Dō bēga emfela, Lch. ii. 20, 24. Ealra emfela, 28, 14. (2) adjective :—Mid efenfealum (-feol-, Hpt. Gl. 511, 4) reádum rosum *cum purpureis totidem rosis*, An. Ox. 4509.

**efen-gedǽlan.** *Add :* [Cf. *O. H. Ger.* eban-giteilo *consors.*]

**efen-gefeón.** *Add :*—Efengefeónde his hǽlo *cujus sanitati congaudens*, Bd. 5, 2; Sch. 560, 15. Efengefeánde (-feónde, *v. l.*) hire micclan wundres, Gr. D. 169, 10. Cf. efen-blissian.

**efen-gelíc.** *Substitute :*—Efnegelíc hine dōende Gode *aequalem se faciens Deo*, Jn. p. 4, 9. v. next word.

**efen-gelíca**, an ; *m.* *A coequal, fellow :*—Þúhte him (*Lucifer*) þæt hē mihte beón þæs efengelíca đe hine gescōp, Wlfst. 84, 4. Godes euengelíca, 306, 26. Þæt ungesǽlig man mǽđe ne geseó on his under-þeóddum ne on his efengelícan, 53, 25 : Mt. 11, 16. (*In Dict. under* efen-gelíc.)

**efen-gemæcca.** *Substitute : An equal, a fellow, consort :*—þe lǽs gif hyra (*suna*) hwylc wǽre hyre oferstealla þ sē ne myhte on heofenum beón hyre efngemæcca, Shrn. 151, 14. Gif hié ne ongietađ đæt đā beóđ hira gelícan and hira efngemæccan on hira gecynde, đā đe him under-điédde beóđ đurh Godes gesceafte *si eos, quos per conditionem tenent subditos, aequales sibi per naturae consortium non agnoscunt*, Past. 201, 17. [Cf. *Icel.* jafn-maki.]

**efen-gemynd** (efne-) *commemoration :*—Efnegimyndes *commemo-rationis*, Rtl. 57, 13. On mīnum efnegimynde (-gemynd, L.) *in meam commemorationem*, Lk. R. 22, 19.

**efen-gemyndig**; *adj.* *Commemorative :*—Ealle þā syndon nū from heora eágum gewitene, and nǽfre efngmyndige hider eft ne cumaþ (*will never come back here to commemorate them*), Bl. H. 101, 1.

**efen-gōd.** [*O. H. Ger.* eban-guot: *Icel.* jafn-gōđr.] v. emn-gōd.

**efen-hāda-bisceop.** *Substitute :* efen-hāda, an; *m.* *One of like rank with another, a co-bishop :*—Sumes bisceopes mīnes efenhādan *cujusdam coepiscopi mei*, Gr. D. 43, 22.

**efen-hæfdling.** *l.* -heáfodling. v. heáfod-ling, efen-heáfda.

---

**efen-hālig**; *adj.* *Equally holy :*—Se biscop biþ efenhālig Godes apostolum, Bl. H. 45, 18. [*O. H. Ger.* eban-heilag : *Icel.* jafn-heilagr.]

**efen-heáfda**, an; *m.* *A fellow, comrade :*—þā wæs ōđer man, þæs mannes efenheáfda (*unus de conservis suis*, Mt. 18, 28), þætte him sceolde ān hund peninga . . . hē nāne líđe þām his efenheáfdan gedōn nolde, Nap. 19. v. efen-hæfdling.

**efen-heáh.** *Add : equally exalted :*—Hē dyde hine efenheáhne Gode, and get hēgran wolde dōn. [Wiþþ hiss Faderr efennheh, Orm. 15720. *O. H. Ger.* eban-hōh : *Icel.* jafn-hárr.]

**efen-heáp.** *Substitute : A band of comrades :*—Efenheápas *commani-pulares*, efenheápum *commanipularibus*, Wrt. Voc. ii. 20, 21, 27. Cf. efen-weorod.

**efen-heort**; *adj.* *Concordant, harmonious.* v. next word.

**efen-heort** (-e, -ness?) *concord, harmony :*—Æfnehearta *concordiꝗ*, Rtl. 108, 21. Efneheortā *concordiam*, 164, 24.

**efen-hērenis.** *l.* -herenis : **efen-hērian.** *l.* -herian, *and add :*—Hergađ Dryhten alle đióde and efenhergađ (*conlaudate*) hine alle folc, Ps. Srt. 116, 1 : **efen-hleóþor**; *n.* (not *m.*)

**efen-hleóþrian**; *p.* ode *To sing together :*—Gyf þā deóflu þæt ongytađ . . . beóđ hí ealle efenhleóþriende and swȳđe blíđe, Nap. 19.

**efen-hleóþrung**, e; *f.* *A singing together, concert :*—Efenhleóþrung *vel* dreám *concentus*, i. *adunationes multarum vocum*, Wrt. Voc. ii. 136, 8.

**efen-hleta.** *Substitute :* efen-hlíte, -hlēte, -hlȳte; *adj.* *Having like lot with* another ; efen-hlíta, an ; *m.* *A partner.* (1) *adj.* :—Se biscop biþ efenhālig Godes apostolum, and efenhlēte his wītgum, Bl. H. 45, 18. (2) *substantive* :—Hæfde se cyning efenhlētan (-hlȳtan, *v. l.*) þǽre cynelican wyrđnesse *habuit Oswiu consortem regiae dignitatis*, Bd. 3, 14; Sch. 253, 18. Mid þām efenhlētum (-hlyttum, *v. l.*) his hādes *cum consortibus sui gradus*, 5, 8; Sch. 587, 7. v. hlēt, hlȳt.

**efen-hlytta.** *Add : a partner :*—Sē þe ne mæg lustlíce Godes word gehȳran, hē biđ đǽra árleásra Judēiscra efenhlytta, Hml. Th. ii. 228, 26. (1) with gen. of thing shared :—Efenhlytta fæderlices leóhtes *consors Paterni lucis*, Hy. S. 18, 1. Neód is þæt hí beón efenhlyttan þæs edleánes, þonne hí wǽron gefēran đǽre đrowunge, Hml. Th. i. 84, 19. Gefērscipes efenhlyttum *sodalitatis consortibus*, Hpt. Gl. 506, 41. (2) with prep. :—Efenhlytta on martyrdōme hē wæs *consors martirio fuit*, Hy. S. 38, 17. Swā swā đū underfēnge ǽr his gōd, swā đū scealt beón his efenhlytta on his wītum, Hml. Th. ii. 344, 22. [*O. H. Ger.* eban-(h)lozzo *consors.*] v. preceding word.

**efen-irfeweard**, es; *m.* *A co-heir :*—Efnyrfeweard *coheres*, Wrt. Voc. ii. 136, 41. Efenyrfeweardum *coheredibus*, Scint. 30, 8.

**efen-íþe.** v. efn-ēđe *in Dict.*

**efen-lǽcan.** *Add :*—Efenlǽcende, Hml. A. 39, 386 note. [Nis nan mon wel cristene butan þe þe Criste euenlecheđ, O. E. Hml. i. 113, 21.] v. following words.

**efen-lǽce** (?); *adj.* *Imitative :*—þe lǽs þe gē syndon efenlǽce (-lǽcend?, -lǽceras?) þæs hǽđenscypes þe hȳ þǽr begád, Ll. Th. ii. 358, 4.

**efen-lǽcend.** *Add :*—Godfader efenlǽcend *Dei Patris imitator*, Scint. 13, 11. þæt forme werod biđ þāra apostola and heora efenlǽc-endra, Hml. Th. i. 396, 18. Hwæđer þes árwurđa wer lǽfde ǽnie efenlǽcendras (*imitatores*) his mægena, Gr. D. 23, 1.

**efen-lǽcere**, es; *m.* *An imitator, follower :*—Efenlǽceras *sequipedas*, i. *sequaces*, An. Ox. 1957.

**efen-lǽcestre.** *Add :* v. ge-efenlǽcestre.

**efen-lǽcung.** *Add :*—Efen lǽcinge hāligra mægena *imitatione virtutis*, R. Ben. 139, 7. þā Judēiscan wǽron yfele đurh euenlǽcunge, nā đurh gecynde, Hml. Th. ii. 226, 35. [Efenlǽcunge (*wrongly*) *glosses* suggillationis, i. *vituperationis*, An. Ox. 5353.] v. ge-efenlǽcung.

**efen-lang**; *adj.* *Equally long.* (1) *of the same length, coextensive with, stretching all along :*—Se milte biđ emlang and gædertenge þǽre wambe, Lch. ii. 242, 15. Licgađ wilde mōras wiđ eástan emnlange þǽm bȳnum lande, Ors. 1, 1 ; S. 18, 28. (2) *as long (as broad).* v. efen-brád. [*O. H. Ger.* eban-lang: *Icel.* jafn-langr.]

**efen-láste.** *Substitute for 'The everlasting' The herb mercury, and add :* [*Mercurialis* euenlesten, mercurial, Wrt. Voc. i. 141, 8].

**efen-leóf**; *adj.* *Equally dear :*—Nȳdþeówas sind Gode efenleófe and þā đe syndon freólse, Ll. Th. ii. 314, 11. v. em-leóf *in Dict.*

**efen-lic.** *Substitute :* I. *equal in extent :*—þǽm wintrum tōdǽldum efenlíce dǽle *quibus (annis) aequa portione divisis*, Bd. 4, 23 ; Sch. 463, 17. II. *of equal degree, of like condition :*—Ēce efenlíc *comper-ennis*, Wrt. Voc. ii. 132, 61. Nǽnig efenlíc þām on worlde geweard *wífes gearnung woman's merit to match that was none in this world*, Cri. 39. Āna God on đrīm hādum efenlíces wuldres (*aequalis gloriae*), Bd. 4, 17 ; Sch. 432, 20. Wē sint emnlíce on đām đe wē ongietađ đæt gē stondađ *aequales vobis sumus, in quo vos stare cognoscimus*, Past. 117, 1. Efenlíce englum *aequales angelis*, Scint. 69, 1. þrý hādas synt efenlíce (*coaequales*), Angl. ii. 362, 12. Ne synd nā emlíce þissere tíde þrowunga þām tōweardum wuldre *non sunt condignae passiones hujus temporis ad futuram gloriam*, Hml. A. 77, 109. [*v. N. E. D.* evenly. *Goth.* ibna-leiks : *Icel.* jafn-ligr.] v. ge-, un-efenlíc.

**efenlíce.** *Substitute :* I. *evenly, without inequalities of surface :—* Man þǽre cyrcean flór emlíce gewyrce, þ þǽr nán byrgen gesýne ne sý, Ll. Th. ii. 408, 12. II. *without disagreement, without discrepancy :—* Seó lár mæg unc emlíce sēman (*bring us to complete agreement*), Hml. A. 13, 12. III. *on equal terms, as equals :—* Hé cwæð þæt him tó micel ǽwisce wǽre þæt hé swā emnlíce wrixleden, Ors. 4, 6 ; S. 178, 16. IV. *in like manner, in like degree, equally :—* Emlíce *simili modo*, Wrt. Voc. ii. 143, 61. Efenlíce Godes mon til *vir aeque Deo devotus*, Bd. 3, 23; Sch. 300, 4. V. *with equanimity, calmly :—* Efulíce (emn-, *v. l.*) *aequanimiter*, Past. 100, 3. Emlíce, Wrt. Voc. ii. 143, 61. Geþyld sóð ys fremede yfelu emlíce þolian, Scint. 10, 3 : 12, 5 : 114, 16. Emlíce forberan, Hml. Th. i. 526, 33 : 534, 5 : Hml. S. 13, 291. *v. emn-, em-líce in Dict.*

**efen-lician.** *v. ge-efenlícad.*

**efen-licnes.** *Add :—*Hiá onfoeð sceld unáfæhtendlic efennlíce (efenlicnisse?) *sumet scutum inexpugnabile aequitatem*, Rtl. 92, 18. *v. em-licnes in Dict.*

**efen-ling.** *Add :* [Luuien þi cristen euenling alswa þe seoluen *to love thy neighbour as thyself*, O. E. Hml. i. 57, 39. Þin sunful efenling luue 57, 222.] Cf. efnung.

**efen-mǽssepreóst,** es ; *m.* *A fellow-priest :—*Speciosus mīn efenmǽssepreóst *compresbyter meus*, Gr. D. 283, 3 : Bd. 4, 25; Sch. 503, 2.

**efen-meahtig ;** *adj.* *Of equal might :—*Ðeáh hé him efnmihtig (emmiehtig, *v. l.*) sié on his godhāde *quamvis divinitate esset aequalis*, Past. 260, 16. Habban geleáfan on God ælmihtigne. . . Hé wæs ǽfre efenmihtig, and Hé gyt is, and Hé ā swā byð, Wlfst. 16, 7. [*Icel.* jafn-máttugr. Cf. *O. H. Ger.* eban-maht Gotis *aequalitas Dei.*]

**efen-medume ;** *adj.* *Equally worthy :—*Onfóh deápe þ þū sí efnmedome þīnum bróþrum (cf. *being worthy of thy brethren, take thy death*, 2 Macc. 7, 29), Shrn. 111, 18.

**efen-metan ;** *pp.* -meten *To compare :—*Mon efenmeten wes neátum *homo comparatus est jumentis*, Ps. Srt. 48, 21. [Cf. *O. H. Ger.* ebanmezōn *comparare*.]

**efen-micel.** *Add : just as much.* (1) *adj. :—*Hé bið genied mid ðǽm folgoðe ðæt hé sceal heálíce sprecan . . . him is efnmicel niéd ðæt hē suā doo suā suā hē lǽrð *qui loci sui necessitate exigitur summa dicere, hac eadem necessitate compellitur summa monstrare*, Past. 81, 7. Hwæðer se spiwða sý swā micel swā hē ǽr gedranc. Gif hē māra sý . . . gif hē emmicel sý þām þe hē ǽr gedranc, Lch. ii. 286, 24. (2) *subst. :—*Genim þysse wyrte seáw, and eles efenmycel, Lch. i. 312, 3. Gemeng wið huniges emmicel, 26, 11. Saluie, rūde he healfan þǽre saluian, feferfugian emmicel þāra twēgea wyrta, ii. 292, 17. [*O. H. Ger.* ebanmichel *aequalis : Icel.* jafn-mikill.] *v. emn-, em-micel in Dict.*

**efenmódlíce ;** *adv. With equanimity, calmly :—*Efenmódlíce *aequanimiter*, i. *fortiter* (*patienter*, Hpt. Gl. 476, 26), An. Ox. 2978.

**efen-neáh.** *Add :—*Middeweard se spaca bið ǽgþrum ende emneáh, Bt. 39, 7 ; F. 222, 8. [*Icel.* jafn-nær.] *v. emn-neáh in Dict.*

**efen-niht.** *Substitute :* **efen-niht,** e ; *f. :* -nihte(?), es ; *n.* *An equinox :—*Emniht *aequinoctium*, Wrt. Voc. i. 53, 38. Gif hit wǽre rihtlíce emniht on Scā Marian mæssedæge, Lch. iii. 256, 14. Seó lenctenlíce emniht (-nyhte, *v. l.*), 12. Seó hærfestlíce emniht, 24. Seó emniht byð on .xii. kl. Octobris, Angl. viii. 311, 26. Fram þǽre emnihte þe . . . ys *vernale* geháten, þ ys sēo lenctenlíce emniht, 322, 40. Þurh þæs lenctenlícan emnihtes dæg, for þon se emnihtes dæg ys se feórþa dæg þissere worulde, 310, 14 : Lch. iii. 238, 17 : 256, 26 : 240, 5. Þæs hærfestlícan emnihtes ryne, 238, 28. Þæs emnihtes circul, 24 : 264, 1. Be efennihte (em-, *v. l.*) *de aequinoctio*, Bd. 5, 23; Sch. 698, 2. Ǽr emnihte and oferswīðdum ðeóstrum, Lch. iii. 256, 18. Be þissere emnihte, 25. On lenctenlícre emnihte, 246, 18, 22. Æfter þǽre eásterlican emnihte, Angl. viii. 330, 7. Rīmcræftige on þā ylcan tíd emniht healdað, Men. 45. Ymb þæs emnihte sprecan, Lch. iii. 240, 1. Macað heó lenctenlíce emnihte, 250, 26 : 252, 2. Twēgen sunstedas synd and twā emniht on þām twelf mónðum, Angl. viii. 311, 9. Hé geendebyrde þā twelf mónðas on twām emnihtum, 299, 18. [*O. Frs.* euen-nacht : *Icel.* jafn-nætti ; *n.*] *v. em-niht in Dict.*

**efen-nys.** *Add :* I. *equity :—*In efennisse *in aequitate*, Ps. Srt. 95, 13. Efennisse *aequitatem*, 36, 37. Efnesse *veritatem*, Ps. Th. 36, 36. II. *comparison :—*Mið efennesse *comparatione*, Mt. p. 15, 12 : 17, 6. *v. efnes, emnes in Dict.*

**efen-rēþe ;** *adj.* *Equally cruel :—*Romulus heora forma cyning and Brutus heora forma consul wurdon emnrēðe *Brutus, primus consul, primum regem Romae exaequare parricidio studuit*, Ors. 2, 3 ; S. 68, 6.

**efen-ríce.** *Add :* [Wiþþ enngless efennrike, Orm. 11868. *O. H. Ger.* eban-ríchi : *Icel.* jafn-ríkr.]

**efen-sácerd,** es ; *m.* *A fellow-priest :—*Leóf bróðer and ūre efensácerd, Angl. xi. 7, 4. Cf. efen-mǽssepreóst.

**efen-sáre ;** *adv.* *Equally bitterly :—*Hé ne magon ealneg ealle on āne tíd emnsáre hreówan, ac hwīlum ān, hwīlum ōðru cymð sárlíce tó gemynde *neque uno eodemique tempore aeque mens de omnibus dolet ; sed nunc hujus, nunc illius culpae memoria acrius tangitur*, Past. 413, 29. [Cf. *Icel.* jafn-sárr ; *adj.*]

**efen-sárgian ;** *p.* ode *To compassionate, sympathize :—*Eálā þ mín sāwl efensárgaþ þises wífes sáre *dolori hujus mulieris anima mea compatitur*, Gr. D. 216, 1. Þā rihtwísan þe lifgende beóþ ne efensárgiað (*compatiuntur*) nā þām unrihtwísum mannum deádum, 336, 18. Se Godes man efensárgode (efensárgende, *v. l.*) hire sáre, 215, 22. Se abbod him efensárgode, Hml. S. 33, 16. Hé hæfde frýnd þ hine frēfrodon and him efensárgodon, 30, 202.

**efen-sárgung,** e ; *f.* *Compassion :—*þā heó þis gehýrde, heó wēnde þ hit mā wǽre bysmrung þonne efensárgung *quod audiens irrisionem potius credidit quam compassionem*, Gr. D. 180, 8.

**efen-sárig.** *Substitute :* (1) *feeling compassion or pity :—*þā þā hē geseah his fóstormóder wēpan hē wæs sóna hire sáre efensárig (*ejus dolori compassus*), Gr. D. 97, 16. (2) *equally sorry :—*þā wurdon hiora wíf sárige . . . hié woldon þte þā óþere wíf wǽren emsárige him (*ut omnibus par ex simili conditione animus fieret*), Ors. 1, 10 ; S. 46, 3.

**efen-scearp.** *Add :* [*Icel.* jafn-skarpr.]

**efen-scolere,** es ; *m.* *A fellow-pupil :—*Chalisten his emnscolere *Callisthenem sibi apud Aristotelem condiscipulum*, Ors. 3, 9 ; S. 132, 1.

**efen-scyldig.** *Add :—*þ cild þe læg on cradele þā gýtseras lǽton efenscyldig (eal swā scyldigne, *v. l.*) and hit gewittig wǽre. [*O. H. Ger.* eban-sculdig.]

**efen-sorgian ;** *p.* ode *To compassionate, be sorry for :—*þā ongan mín mód efnsorgian (*compati*) þām forðfērdan brēþer and mid hefigum sáre þæncan ymb his wíte, Gr. D. 345, 18.

**efen-spēdiglic.** *Add :—*Efenspēdelice *consubstantialem* . . . efenspēdelice (efne-, *v. l.*) *consubstantialibus*, Bd. 4, 17; Sch. 432, 18, 21.

**efen-sprǽc** *confabulation :—*þ efnesprēc *confabulationem*, Lk. p. 11, 11.

**efen-stálian.** *v.* stálian : **efen-swíþ.** *Dele.*

**efen-swíþe ;** *adv.* *Just as much :—*Him sculan eglan ōðerra monna brocu suelce hē efnsuíðe him ðrowige *singulis compassione proximus*, Past. 75, 10. Ðā scylda ðāra scamleásena hē tǽlde suelce hē efnsuíðe him bǽre *culpas verecundantium quasi compatiens reprehendit*, 207, 17. Ond suaðeáh oft ágyltað ðā ealdormenn efnsuíðe on ðām ðe hē bið tó eáðmód *et tamen nonnunquam gravius delinquitur* . . . , 121, 20. Manigu óþru gesceaft efnswīðe him (*the elements*) winnað betweox him (cf. manega óþru gesceafta beóþ ā swā ungeþwǽra betwux him, Bt. 21; F. 74, 16), Met. 11, 44.

**efen-teám,** es ; *m.* *A pulling together, conspiracy :—*Getugun conspirauerant (in marg. *conspiratio* efneteám (esne-, MS.)), Jn. L. 9, 22.

**efen-þegen,** es ; *m.* *A fellow-servant :—*Efneþegn *conservus*, Mt. L. 18, 29. Efneðegnas *conservi*, 31. Ēnne of his efneðegnum, 28.

**efen-þeówa, -þeów.** *Add :* (1) *strong forms, subst. and adj. :—*Ðæm hláforde is tó cýðanne ðæt hē ongiete ðæt hē is efnðeów his ðeówe *ut cognoscat se conservos esse servorum*, Past. 201, 20. Uncer efenþeów wæs forworden, Hml. A. 207, 393. Ēnne æfnþāra his . . . se his efnþeúw . . . Geseónde æfnðeúwe his *unum de conseruis suis . . . conseruus ejus . . . Videntes conserui ejus*, Mt. R. 18, 28, 29, 31. Mínne hláford and míne efenþeówas, Hml. A. 207, 240. (2) *weak forms :—*Ic eom eówer efnðeówa (emn-, *v. l.*) *consenior*, Past. 136, 16. Hwī wylt þū cweðan þ ðū sý mín þeówa ? Ac þū eart mín efenþeówa, for ðan ðe wit syndan ānes Godes þeów, Hml. A. 123, 204 : Hml. Th. i. 38, 25. Se góda þeówa þe hwæte gedǽlde his efenþeówum, R. Ben. 127, 9.

**efen-þeówen,** e ; *f.* *A female fellow-servant :—*Ætfæste hē mē mīne efenþeówene, Hml. A. 203, 256.

**efen-þrowian.** *Add :—*Ne beóð gē unróte . . . þanc ic dō for þon þás sceáp mē efenþrowiaþ, Bl. H. 191, 24. Ongan heó emþrowian his staþolfæstnesse, Hml. S. 23 b, 243. Eallum monnum efnðrowiende on hiora earfoðum *singulis compassione proximus*, Past. 97, 20, 23. Bið hē ūs efenþrowiende and miltsiende, Bl. H. 19, 30. Beón efenþrowgende óþres earfoþum, . . . on óþres góde beón gefeónde, 75, 19.

**efen-þrowung.** *Add :—*Be efenþrowunge níhstan *de compassione proximi*, Scint. 147, 8 : 148, 12.

**efen-þwǽr.** l. -þwǽre, *and add :—*Efenþwǽre *concordes*, Angl. xiii. 367, 32.

**efen-twá** *in the phrase* on efen-twá *into two parts :—*Þæt hrīdder tóbærst on emtwā (cf. weard tóbrocen and tódǽled on twā styccu *in duabus partibus divisum*, Gr. D. 97, 7), Hml. Th. ii. 154, 16. Seó eá on emtwā tóeóde, 212, 21. *v.* em-twá in Dict.

**efen-unwemme ;** *adj.* *Equally inviolate :—*Sí ǽlc ciricgrið binnan wāgum and cyninges handgrið efenunwemme, Ll. Th. i. 318, 25.

**efen-wǽge,** an ; *f.* *An equipoise :—*Ebnwǽge *aequipensum*, Wrt. Voc. ii. 99, 47. Efenwǽge *equipensium*, 143, 71.

**efen-weaxan** *to grow together :—*Emnweaxende (efenwexende, lxxiv, 21) *concrescentes*, Lch. i. lxxi, 13.

**efen-wel** *as well.* *Add :—*Riht is þ preóstas, and efenwel nunnan, regollíce libban, Ll. Th. ii. 324, 2. [*Icel.* jafn-vel.]

**efen-weorþ.** *Substitute :* **efen-weorþ,** -wirþe ; *adj.* I. *of equal worth or dignity :—*Heó efenwyrþe hī ou eallum þingum þām bysceope gegearwade, Bd. 4, 6; Sch. 384, 3. þ preóstas beón efenweorþe on eallum ciricþēnungum, Ll. Th. ii. 254, 23. II. *of adequate worth,*

*very worthy;* condignus:—Hē þone hād mid efenwyrþum (-weorðum, *v. l.*) dǣdum frætwade *gradum condignis ornans actibus,* Bd. 3, 27; Sch. 321, 23. Hē þ bysceopsetl efenwyrðum (efenwyrðe, *v. l.*) dǣdum his hādes heóld *episcopalem cathedram condignis gradu actibus seruat,* 5, 12; Sch. 632, 3.

**efen-werod.** *Substitute:* **efen-weorod,** es; *n. A band of comrades:*—Efenwerod *commanipulares,* Wrt. Voc. ii. 23, 35. Cf. efen-heáp.

**efen-wiht.** *Substitute: One of equal condition* (?), *fellow, associate:*—Sceóte man ælmessan . . . hwīlum þe mannes efenwihte, hwīlum þe freótmen, hwīlum þe healffreón *sometimes in the case of a man's equal* (?), *sometimes in that of the freedman or the half-free,* Wlfst. 171, 4. Hī woldon efenwihte (-wyhton, -wyrhtan, *v. ll.*) beón on sǣ and on lande, Chr. 972; P. 119, 11.

**efen-wyrcan.** *Substitute: v. next word.*

**efen-wyrcend,** es; *m. A co-operator:*—Adrianus wæs efenwyrcend on Godes worde Theodora arcebiscopes *Hadrianus co-operator in uerbo Dei Theodori Episcopi,* Bd. 5, 20; Sch. 673, 10. [Cf. *O. H. Ger.* eban-wirkenti *co-operans.*]

**efen-wyrhta.** *Add:*—Hī woldon efenwyrhtan beón on sǣ and on lande, Chr. 972; P. 119, 11. Ic gewilnode mid him tō farenne þ ic þe mā emwyrhtena on þǣre þrowunge mīnes wynlustes hæfde, Hml. S. 23 b, 358. Gemang þām emnwyrhtum, 97.

**efen-wyrþe, -yrſeweard.** v. efen-weorþ, -irſeweard: **ēfern.** v. ǣfen.

**efes, efesc.** *Add:*—Be Cilternes efese, Hrysebyrgan (cf. Hrisebeorgam margine luci Cilterni, iii. 347, 12), C. D. iv. 232, 33. Tō ðæs wudes efese, iii. 389, 27. Ūt of ðām wudu; of ðæs wudes efese, 390, 2. Be ðǣre æfesce . . . be efæsce, 460, 15, 18. Innan hangran; swā forð be æfise . . . be efise (æfisc, efisc, C. D. B. ii. 304), v. 184, 11, 13.

**efes-drypa.** v. yfes-drype.

**efesian.** *Substitute:* (1) *absolute, to cut hair:*—Ic efesige *tondeo,* Ælf. Gr. 2, 157, 9. Sceára tācen is þæt þū wecge þinne scytefinger and þone midemistan on þīnre swīðran hande ymb þīn heáfod swilce þū efysian wille, Tech. ii. 127, 25. (2) *with acc. of person, to cut the hair of a person:*—Ne efesiað eów, Deut. 14, 6. Ne gē eów ne efesion *neque in rotundum attondebitis comam,* Lev. 19, 27. Man ne mōt hine efsian oððe besciran *non tanget caput ejus novacula,* Jud. 13, 5. Seó wolde efsian ǣlce geáre þone sanct, Hml. S. 32, 192. (2 a) *with head as object:*—Wæs wel gecweden ðæt se efsigenda (efsienda, *v. l.*) efsode his heáfod *bene dicitur : 'Tondentes tondent capita sua,'* Past. 141, 3. Ða sácerdas ne scoldon nō hiera heáfdu scieran mid scierseaxum, . . . ac hié scoldon hié efsigean (efsian, *v. l.*) mid sceárum, 139, 14. (3) *with acc. of hair:*—Sē þe on þām dæge hine baðað oððe his fex efesað, Wlfst. 212, 27. [v. *N. E. D.* evese.] v. be-, ge-, mis-efesian.

**ēfest.** *l.* efest *haste, and add:*—Inn eóde sōna mið oefeste (*festinatione*), Mk. L. R. 6, 25. Mið oefeste (-iste, R.), Lk. L. 1, 39. v. ofost.

**ēfestan.** *l.* efestan, *and add : I. intrans. To hasten:*—Efstan *properare,* Wrt. Voc. ii. 67, 17. (1) *of movement:*—Hwider sīdast ðū būtan ðīnum bearne? hwider efst ðū būtan ðīnum diácone?, Hml. Th. i. 418, 1. Swā efst fugel *ut si avis festinet,* Kent. Gl. 219. 'Oefesta (eofesta, R.) ādūne stīg' . . . And oefistade (eofestade, R.) ofstāg ādūne '*festinans descende*' . . . *et festinans descendit,* Lk. L. 19, 5, 6. Cuómon oefistande *uenerunt festinantes,* 2, 16. Hē fērde efstende tō his discipulum, Bl. H. 249, 20. (2) *referring to rapid passage of time :*—Ælc fægernes tō ende efsteþ, Bl. H. 57, 28. Þes middangeard tō ende efsteþ, 59, 26. Ǣtwesan efestaþ tīda *adesse festinant tempora,* Cant. M. ad. fil. 35. Hē geseah his ágen līf dæghwāmlīce tō þām ende efstan and scyndan, Guth. 14, 25. (3) *of prompt action, exertion :*—Līg efested hū hē synfullum sūsle gefremede *flamma festinans scelerum ulciscere causas,* Dōm. L. 152. Tō gefultumiende mē oefeste (*festina*), Ps. Srt. 69, 2. Oefestig, Rtl. 175, 3. Efste (eftsf, MS.) *contendat,* Kent. Gl. 1160: An. Ox. 27, 11. Utan samod efestan *concurramus, i. certemus,* 1333. Oefistia *festinare,* Rtl. 96, 7. Þē gedafenað tō efestenne þ þū mē þīne trýwa gehealde, Hml. S. 30, 124. Tō ðǣm heistum ibodum oefistende *ad altiora festinans,* Mt. p. 9, 17. **II.** *trans. with gen. To strive after, endeavour to do, undertake:*—Þā gōdan weorc wē ānforlǣtaþ . . . Uton wē nū efstan ealle mægene gōdra weorca, and geornfulle beón Godes miltsa, Bl. H. 109, 9. Ic nāht gehýdes hæbbe þis weorc tō begangenne, ne ic efstan ne mæg swā myccles sīðfætes hider tō bringanne *I have nothing convenient for doing this work, and I cannot undertake such a long journey to bring tools hither,* Hml. S. 23 b, 784.

**efestlīce;** *adv. In haste, hurriedly:*—Hrædlīce ł oefestlīce *per praeceps,* Mt. L. 8, 32. Oefestlīce, Lk. L. 8, 33. Oefestlīce ādūne stīg *festinans descende,* 19, 5.

**efestung,** e; *f. Haste:*—Swā þæt nānra þinga mid ǣnigre efestinge mannes hī mihton beón undōn *ut dissolvi tam concite nulla hominum festinatione potuissent,* Gr. D. 164, 15. Mid oefestunge *cum festinantia,* Ps. Srt. 77. 33.

**efesung.** *Substitute : Hair-cutting, clipping, polling :*—Oefsung *circinatio,* Wrt. Voc. ii. 104, 7. Efesung *circinnatio,* 14, 29. Efesunge *tonsura,* An. Ox. 4174. Man geswīce higeleásra gewǣda and bismorlicra efesunga, Ll. Th. ii. 248, 16. [Ase oft ase me euesede Absalom me solde his euesunge vor two hundred sicles, A. R. 398.]

**efete.** *Add:*—Efete *lacertus,* Wrt. Voc. ii. 71, 16: 52, 18. Efete (-a, *v. l.*) *lacerta,* Ælfc. Gr. Z. 310, 3.

**eficisc ?** :—Zenodotus se eficisca esne, Angl. viii. 334, 17.

**efn-.** *For compounds with* efn- *v.* efen-.

**efnan.** *Take* I *and* II *separately.*

**efnan, I.** *Substitute : To even.* **I.** *to level, bring to a level with :*—Ic (*mead*) eom weorpere (q. v. *in Dict.*), efne tō eorðan (*lay flat on the ground*) ealdne ceorl ; sōna þæt onfindeð, sē þe mec fēhð ongeán, þæt hē hrycge sceal hrūsan sēcan, Rä. 28, 8. [v. *N. E. D.* even; *vb.* I. 2. Cf. *O. H. Ger.* ebanōn *sternere.*] **II.** *to make equal :*—Ðū efnes ðā ūs *pares illos nobis fecisti,* Mt. L. 20, 12. [v. *N. E. D.* even; *vb.* I. 5. Cf. *Icel.* jafna *to make equal.*] v. ge-efn(i)an.

**efnan, II.** *Add :*—Ic ðīn bebod efnede, Ps. Th. 118, 131. Hī his bebodu efnedan *custodiebant praecepta ejus,* 98, 8. þæt heó his word efnan (*faciant*), 102, 17. þā þe þīne ǣ efnan nellað *contra legem agentes,* 70, 3 : 88, 27. Dōmas efnan *judicium custodire,* 105, 3. Ne bið swylc cwēnlic þeáw idese tō efnanne, B. 1941. [*Icel.* efna *to perform.*]

**efne.** *Add :* **I.** *evenly.* (1) *uniformly, regularly.* Cf. efen, I :—Mē is metegung on mōdsefan hū ic ǣ þīne efnast healde *lex tua meditatio mea est,* Ps. Th. 118, 77. (2) *with equanimity.* v. efen, II :—Hē hit emne and gedyldelīce (*aequanimiter*) forbær, Past. 227, 22. (3) *equally, justly, fairly.* v. efen, III :—Dǣm þū swīþe emne, Ll. Th. i. 54, 11. Hié bǣdon þæt hē hié ymb þæt rīce gesēmde, and on þǣre gewitnesse wǣre þæt hit emne gedǣled wǣre, Ors. 3, 7 ; S. 114, 18. (4) *equally.* v. efen, IV :—Emne unwemme, Ll. Th. i. 166, 21. **II.** *as intensive or emphatic particle.* (1) *exactly, just.* (a) *with a numeral :*—Efne nigon hund wintra and lxxi. on þýs geáre, Bl. H. 119, 2 : 129, 16. (b) *of manner, degree :*—Mid wīne and hunige gemenged gelīce efne (*just alike*), Lch. i. 362, 14. ¶ *followed by* swā, swelce :—Cirican mundbyrd is efne swā cynges, Ll. Th. i. 330, 21. Emne suelce (*just as if* ; quasi) hié him on ðæt nebb spǣten, Past. 45, 3. Efne swylce *ac si,* Gr. D. 216, 18 : 220, 16. Efne swā seó byrþen siteþ . . . swā sæt seó byrþen, Bl. H. 75, 7 : 221, 12. Hié cwǣdon . . . Efne swā swā hié openlīce cwǣdon . . . , 81, 19. Efne þæm gelīcost swylce . . . , 221, 14. (c) *of time, just now, directly :*—Wyrcað dǣdbōte, for ðan þe heofonan rīce efne geneálǣchð, Hml. S. 16, 133. Uton ūs gesettan efne nū (*even now, at once*) heretogan, Num. 14, 4. (2) *just, only, no other than :*—Wundurlic wīse and efne heofonlic *mira res et non nisi caelitus facta,* Bd. 4, 11 ; Sch. 408, 11. Efne þā ān þā þe tō ǣfæstnesse belumpon *ea tantummodo quae ad religionem pertinent,* 4, 24; Sch. 482, 7. Ne gedafenað þ hē elles dō, būtan swā hē efne on axan and on duste licge, Bl. H. 227, 14. Efne þ gē mē sylfum dōð, 215, 26. Him ne bið nǣfre nān rest seald būton emne þý dæge, Ll. Th. ii. 396, 37. (3) *even :*—Hit āwriten is be Salamonne hū hē āfióll emne oð ðæt hē dióflum ongan gieldan *Salomon usque ad idololatriam cecidisse describitur,* Past. 393, 14. Simle ic beó gemyndig efne (*etiam*) betweoh tweóndan frecnisse ūra gefeohta, Nar. 1, 9. þ hé efne munuclīfe gytʒ swīþor liſde þonne lǣwedes mannes, Bl. H. 213, 10. Manige men . . . ge efne eác manige hǣþene men, 129, 24. (4) *lo, indeed, now :*—Efne *ecce,* An. Ox. 40, 2, 36. Efene en, 9, 16. Efne ðā ðā se apostol sprecende wæs, Hml. Th. i. 66, 15 : Hml. S. 15, 60 : 22, 75. Efne þū eart gelǣred, 22, 16, 43. Ðū gōda cyngc, efne þes man þe þū swā wel wið gedēst, hē is æfestful for ðīnum gōde, Ap. Th. 14, 23. Heó efne and heóld þæs lichaman lustes forhæfdnesse, ac hwæðre . . . *carnis quidem continentiam habuit, sed . . . ,* Gr. D. 340, 15. Efne . . . , ac . . . , Hml. S. 22, 107. Mīn se leófesta lāreow, and efne tō mīnre mēder . . . se leófesta freónd *my dearest teacher, and indeed, next to my mother, my dearest friend,* Nar. 1, 11 : Bl. H. 217, 18. Ond efne swīðe mīn weorod wæs gewelgod *et esne miles locupletatus est,* Nar, 7, 5. (4 a) *with* nū :—Efne nū en, Kent. Gl. 9. Efene nū ic eom geara tō eówere neóde *ecce adsum,* R. Ben. 3, 2. Efne nū is ðeós giſu eów ætbrōden, Hml. Th. i. 64, 23. [*O. H. Ger.* ebano *aeque, ordinate, aequanimiter, aequaliter, pariter.*] v. un-efne.

**efne,** es; *n. Material :*—Aefne ðiss alðes *materiam istam cervise,* Rtl. 116, 40. [v. *N. E. D.* evene. *Icel.* efni; *n. material.*]

**efne-.** This form is used in the Northern specimens to render the prefix con- in many Latin verbs, e. g. efne-ārīsa *con-surgere,* efne-ceiga *con-vocare,* efne-fornioma *com-prehendere,* efne-senda *com-mittere.* For other compounds v. efen-.

**efnes;** *adv. Quite, just :*—Efnes hit bið gelīc rēna scūrum, Wlfst. 149, 5. Eal þ ūs þincð ǣmtig . . . bið emnes mid þý eal gefylled, Dōm. L. 150.

**efn-etan.** v. next word.

**efnettan;** *p.* te. **I.** *to make even, square, adjust :*—Emnettan *quadrare,* An. Ox. 2, 311. **II.** *to be equal, imitate :*—Ic mēsan mæg

meahtelícor and efnetan ealdum þyrse (-re, MS.) (cf. mando dapes mordax lurcorum more cyclopum, Prehn 217), Rä. 41, 63. Emnyttende *equiparando*, Angl. xiii. 421, 803. v. emnettan *in Dict.*

efnian. v. efnan.

efning, es; m. *A consort, partner :*—Hæfde se cyning efning (*consortem*) þære cynelican wyrðnesse, Bd. 3, 14; Sch. 253, 18. [v. *N.E.D.* evening. Cf. *Icel.* jafningi *an equal, a match.*]

efolsian. v. eofulsian : efstan. v. efestan.

eft. *Add.* I. of repetition, *again :*—Eft gelíce *identidem*, Wrt. Voc. ii. 47, 50. Eft rædende *lectitando*, 50, 23. Wé nú gehýrdon þis godspel rædan, and þéh wé hit sceolan eft ofercweþan, Bl. H. 15, 31. Wæs culufre eft (*a second time*) of cofan sended, Gen. 1464 : B. 1377. Eft . . . níwan stefne, Gen. 1885 : An. 1304. Eft . . . óðre síðe, 706 : 1677 : Sat. 75. Eft swá ǽr, An. 1276 : 1343. Eft swá ǽr . . . níówan stefue, B. 1787. I a. of replacement, restoration, renewal :—Geðwegenum fótum eft sceógian hí *lotis pedibus recalcient se*, Angl. xiii. 413, 687. Sceal beón se ingang eft geopenod, Bl. H. 9, 8. Hú hé eft gesette seld sélran werode, Gen. 94 : Dan. 641. þá wæs eft swá ǽr þeód on sælum, B. 642 : An. 1478. II. of return, reversal, *back, again* (a) to a place :—Hí eóden and eft cómon, Hml. Th. i. 64, 7 : Gen. 1478. Hám eft becuman, El. 143. Se heofonlica ærendwreca eft hám cerde, Bl. H. 9, 24. Wæron Egypte eft oncyrde, Exod. 451. Nú wille ic eft þám líge neár, Gen. 760. Hig æðelinges eft ne wéndon *they did not expect the prince back*, B. 1596. (b) to a condition :—þú tó eorþan scealt eft geweorþan, Cri. 624. Willflód ongan lytligan eft, Gen. 1413. (c) of giving :—Hé hâteþ þá eorþan eft ágifan þ heó ǽr onféng, Bl. H. 21, 30. (d) reversal of order :—Agof is mín noma eft onhwyrfed, Rä. 24, 1. III. *afterwards*, (a) in reference to the past :—Sió ǽ wæs ǽrest on Ebrisc geðióde funden, and eft Creácas wendon hié on hiora ágen geðióde, and eft Lædenware swǽ same, Past. 7, 1-3. Swá hié eft dydon, Cri. 455 : Exod. 389 : Sat. 374. Ic sóna eft mé sylfum andwyrde, Past. 5, 21. Gesceóp God Adam and Evah eft siððan . . . Beswác se deófol siððan eft ðá men, Ælfc. T. Grn. 3, 4–8. Hé spræc tó Abrahame . . . Cwæð þá eft raðe tó Sarran, Gen. 2726 : Sat. 229. Hé eft æfter fæce geþrowade, Bl. H. 23, 30. Eft ufaran dógrum, B. 2200. (b) in reference to the future, *hereafter :*—þæt þú ne secge eft, 'Ic gewelegode Abram,' Gen. 14, 23 : Gen. 2145. Ǽr seó mengeo eft tófaran sceolde, 1663 : 2702. Wâ eów þe nú hlíhaþ, for þon gé eft wépað on écnesse, Bl. H. 25, 23, 20 : 55, 24 : B. 1753. Wé wǽron on wrǽcsíþ sende, and nú eft sceolon óþerne éþel sécan, Bl. H. 23, 6 : Sat. 212 : Gú. 1159. III a. *afterwards, in a later part of a book :*—Eft rehþ *infra subdit*, An. Ox. 5167. IV. where there is a sequence of propositions, statements, *again :*—Wæs gecueden ðætte ðá sácerdas ne scoldon nó hiera heáfdu scieran . . ., ne eft hí ne scoldon hira loccas lætan weaxan, Past. 139, 13. Sé ðe ágiémeleásað ðá giémene . . ., oððe eft folgað ðǽre giémenne, 87, 11 : 321, 16. Gehíeren hwæt áwriten is . . . and eft gehíerað ðone cwide, 323, 10 : Met. 7, 27 : 11, 26. Hwîlum . . . hwîlum eft, 20, 215 : Cri. 648 : B. 2111. Nænig eft . . . *again no one* . . ., Crä. 13. Swá hit eft be eów Esaias mælde *so, again, Isaiah said it of you*, El. 350. ¶ In the Northern glosses the prefix *re-* in many Latin verbs is rendered by *eft*, but the English word is separable ; cf. eft tó cerranne *reuerti*, Lk. R. L. 19, 12.

eft-ácenned *re-born, born again :*—Eftácenned *renatus*, Jn. p. 3, 14. Eftácennedum *renatis*, Rtl. 32, 3. Eftácenndum, 33, 22.

eftácennedness, -cennes *regeneration :*—Eftácennednisses *regenerationis*, Rtl. 35, 15. Æftákenuisse *regeneratione*, Mt. R. 19, 28.

eft-ǽrist *resurrection :*—Eftérest *resurrectionem*, Mt. L. 22, 23.

eft-bétung, e; f. *Restoration* to health :—Eftboeteng *restitutio* (*manus aridae*), Mk. p. 2, 17.

eft-boren *re-born, born again :* renatus, Jn. L. R. 3, 5.

eft-bót, e; f. *Restoration* to health :—Eftboete *restitutio*, Mk. p. 2, 17. Eftbóte *reparationis*, Rtl. 33, 17.

eft-cennes *regeneration :*—Eftcynnes, edníwung *regeneratione*, Mt. L. 19, 28. v. eft-ácennedness.

eft-cneoreso *regeneration*, Rtl. 108, 29.

eftern (?) *evening :*—Forðon þ eftern lócað (forðon ǽfern longeð ðú wâst, R.) *quoniam aduesperascit*, Lk. L. 24, 29. [The glosser seems to have read *uesper aspicit*.] [Cf. (?) *Icel.* aptan, aftan.]

efter-sóna; *adv. Again :*—Eftersóna *iterum*, Mk. L. 8, 25. Efðsóna (æfter-, R.), 2, 1. Efðsóna (efter-, R.), 7, 31. Efðsóna (æfter-, R.), *rursus*, 2, 13. [Frequent in Northern Gospels, in L. generally with the symbol for *er*, in R. written in full.] v. eft-sóna.

eft-flówende *glosses* redundans :—Eftflówende wætera *redundantia flumina*, An. Ox. 506.

eft-flówung, e; f. *Redundance :*—Eftflówu[nga] *redundantia*, i. *flumina*, Hpt. Gl. 418, 45.

eft-for(e)gifnes *glosses* remissio, Mk. p. 2, 14 : L. 3, 29 : Lk. L. R. 24, 47 : Rtl. 119, 38 : reconciliatio, Mt. p. 14, 13.

eft-gadrian. v. ge-eftgadrian.

eft-geearnung *remuneration :*—Eftgearnunge *remuneratione*, Rtl. 59, 1.

---

eft-gemyndig; *adj. Remembering :*—Eftgemyndig wæs Petrus *recordatus est Petrus*, Mk. L. 14, 72 : Lk. L. 22, 61. Eftgemyn(d)ig, Mt. L. 26, 75. Eftgimyndig, Mk. R. 11, 21 : Rtl. 55, 30. Eftgemyndig *reminiscens*, Jn. p. 7, 16. Eftgemyndig wé aron, Mt. L. 27, 63. Eftgemyndigo (-myndge, R.), Lk. L. 24, 8 : Jn. L. (R.) 2, 17. Eftgemyndgo (-e, R.), 22. Wosað gié eftgemyndgo *reminiscamini*, 16, 4.

eft-gemynd(i)gian *to remember :*—Ic nó eftgimyndga *ego non recordabor*, Rtl. 19, 5. Eftgimyndga milsa ðinra *reminiscere misericordiarum tuarum*, 167, 27. v. eft-myndig.

eft-gewæxen; *adj.* (*ptcpl.*) *Grown again :*—Eftgewæxen barc, Lch. i. 378, 15.

eftgian; *p.* ode *To repeat, iterate :*—Hit is áwriten : ' Ne eftga ðú ðín word on ðínum gebede.' Ðæt is ðæt mon eftgige his word *scriptum est : ' Ne iteres uerbum in oratione tua.'* *Verbum iterare est*, Past. 421, 11, 12. v. ge-eftgian.

eft-hweorfan. *Add :*—þí hálgan lenctenfæstene efthwyrfende *when Lent returns*, Hml. S. 23 b, 613.

eft-leániend, es; m. *A remunerator, recompenser :*—Eftleániend *remunerator*, Rtl. 89, 30.

eft-lésing, -lísing. *Add :* Lk. L. R. 24, 21 : Rtl. 123, 35.

eft-lócung *glosses* respectus, Rtl. 86, 30.

eft-myndig; *adj. Remembering :*—Eftmyndig *recordatus*, Mk. L. 11, 21. Eftmyndigo *recordati*, Jn. L. 12, 16. v. eft-gemyndig.

eft-níwung, e; f. *Renewal, restoration :*—Eftnívuwunges *reparationis*, Rtl. 7, 27. Eftníwawnges, 31, 1.

eft-onfónd (?) *a receiver :*—Eftonðfóende *receptorem*, Mt. L. p. 16, 8.

eft-ryne, es; m. *A running back, return :*—Útgong his and eftyrn his *egressio ejus et occursus ejus*, Ps. Srt. 18, 7.

eft-sel(e)ness, e; f. *Requital, retribution, recompense :*—Dæge eftselenise (eftðselenisse, R.) *diem retributionis*, Lk. L. 4, 19. Ðá ilcu dóe ðé eftselnisse (-selenise, L.) *fiat tibi retributio*, Lk. R. 14, 12. Alle eftselnisses *omnes retributiones*, Rtl. 169, 27.

eft-sóna. *Add :*—Eftsóna *ibidem*, An. Ox. 7, 289 : 8, 213 : *iterum*, Mt. L. 5, 33 : 13, 45 : 20, 5. Ne þincð mé nǽfre þ hit sóð sý þ þis sý Efesa byrig . . . ac ic nât eftsóna, ne ic nǽfre git nyste þ ǽnig óþer byrig ûs wǽre gehende bûton Ephese ânre *methinks it cannot be true that this is Ephesus, but again I do not know, nor ever yet did I know, that any other town were near us but Ephesus only*, Hml. S. 23, 542. v. eft, efter-sóna.

eft-spellung. *For* Cot. 271 *l.* Wrt. Voc. ii. 77, 36.

eft-þingung, e; f. *Reconciliation :*—Eftðingung *reconciliatio*, Rtl. 88, 10. Cf. ed-þingung.

eft-tóseleness. v. eft-seleness.

eft-wyrd. *Add : A becoming again* (v. weorþan, I), *a renewal of existence, resurrection at doom's day* (?) :—Swá nú regnþeófas ríce dælað, yldo oððe ǽrdeáð; eftwyrd cymð, mægenþrymma mǽst *now mighty robbers hold sway, eld or early death; renewal of life shall come, greatest of God's glorious powers*, Exod. 539.

ég-clif. v. ecg-clif.

ege. *Add :*—Nis þǽr (*in heaven*) ege, ne geflit, ne yrre, Bl. H. 23, 31. Orsorg ǽlces eorþlices eges, Bt. 10 ; F. 28, 18. For ðǽm ege ic hine innecundan déman, Past. 79, 7. For ríces mannes ege, Bl. H. 43, 10. Þysne ege þrowian æt þyssum englum, 93, 34. Ofergytende þisse sǽwe ege, 235, 1. Hú mycelne ege wé sceolon witan (hú micel ege sí tó hæbbenne, v. l.) tó þám hálgum werum *quantus sit viris sanctis timor exhibendus*, Gr. D. 63, 5. Wíf ic lǽrde þ hié heora weras lufedan and him ege tó wiston, Bl. H. 185, 23 : Wlfst. 220, 27. v. weorold-ege.

egean. v. ecgan.

ege-full. *Add :* I. *fearful, inspiring fear, terrible*, (1) of persons :—Egeful hláford *metuendus dominus*, R. Ben. 2, 2. Côm rídende sum egefull ridda, Hml. S. 25, 773. Swá egefull wæs Alexander þá þá hé wæs on eásteweardum þissum middangearde þte þá from him ondrédan þe wæron on westeweardum *tantus timor in summo Oriente constituti ducis populos ultimi Occidentis invaserat*, Ors. 3, 9 ; S. 136, 6. Alexander se egefulla cyning, Hml. S. 25, 1. Hí geseoð egefulne þone ðe hí eádmódne forhygedon, Hml. Th. i. 300, 19. (2) of things, *terrible, tremendous :*—Beó him swíðe egefull ðæt éce wíte *aeterna supplicia perhorrescant*, Past. 263, 16. Seó sǽ is hwîlon swíðe hreóh and egeful on tó beónne, Hml. Th. i. 182, 33. Tó þám egefullan Godes dóme *tremendo judicio Dei*, R. Ben. 31, 10. Þone egefullan cwide *terribilem sententiam*, 49, 19. II. *fearful, timorous*. (1) *feeling fear, expressing fear :*—Mid eargum, egefullum gebǽrum *formidilosis*, i. *stupefactis gestibus*, Hpt. Gl. 518, 58.

egefullíce; *adv. Fearfully, awfully, in a way that inspires awe :*—Se Hǽlend egefullíce and hálwendlíce clypað on his godspelle, Hml. Th. i. 94, 9.

ege-healdan. *l.* ege healdan : ege-láf. *Dele, and see* éce, I.

ege-leás; *adj. Without fear, without awe.* Cf. ege-full, II, *and see two following words.*

egeleáslíce; *adv. Without fear, unconcernedly :*—Ðý lǽs hié siððan

geearnigen swá micle hefigre wîte suá hié nū egeleáslícor and unnytlícor
brúceð Godes giefe *eo postmodum supplicia graviora mereantur, quo
nunc largioribus bonis Dei male uti non metuunt*, Past. 247, 10.

**egeleásness**, e ; *f. Confidence, presumption :*—þá þíne welan þe þú
(the devil) on fruman begeáte æt þæs ǽrestan mannes egeleásnesse (*from
his not having the fear of God before his eyes*) and unhýrsumnesse,
Bl. H. 85, 31.

**ege-lic** ; *adj. Terrible :*—þú egelic (*terribilis*) eart, Ps. Spl. 75, 7.

**egenu.** *Substitute:* egenu, e ; *f. A husk, chaff :*—Gewrid, egenu
oððe scealu *glumula*, Wrt. Voc. ii. 40, 23. [Cf. *N. E. D.* awn : *Goth.*
ahana *chaff : O. H. Ger.* agana *arista*, *festuca*, *palea : Icel.* ǫgn.]

**egenwirht.** *Substitute:* egnwyrht :—Egnwirhtæ (gen-?) *mercis.*

**ege-nys.** *Substitute:* eg-ness (ēg-? cf. ēgan), e ; *f. Fear :*—
Egnesse *formidinem.*

**egesa.** *Add :* I. *fear, terror :*—Fēhð ōðer tō sē þe unmurnlíce
máðmas dǽleð, egesan ne gýmeð (*does not cherish fear*), B. 1757. Mid
þon egsan and þǽre lufan Drihtnes, Bl. H. 119, 17. Uton wē þæs dæges
fyrhto and egsan on úre mód settan, 125, 6. II. *what excites fear
or horror, a terrible thing :*—Mannum þincþ heora deáð leófra þonne
ðone egesan tō gehýranne *it will seem to men better to die than to hear
that awful tempest*, Wlfst. 196, 7. Micel þearf is þæt crístene men þone
egesan ǽfre ne dreógan, þæt hý deófolgyld weordian *it is very needful
that Christian men never commit the horrible sin of worshipping idols*,
281, 4. Leahtra egesan forbúgan *uitiorum monstra diuitare*, Angl. xiii.
381, 226.

**ēgesa.** *Dele, and see preceding word :* egese-gríma. v. eges-gríma.

**eges-ful, ege-ful.** *l.* eges-ful, *omit the instances of* ege-ful, *and
add :*—Mereflódes weard (*the Deity*) yrre and egesfull, Exod. 505. Ne
bið ús (*devils*) freá milde egesful ealdor (*the Devil*), Jul. 329. Egesful
eorla drihten (*Holofernes*), Jud. 21. þæt egesfulle *horrendus*, Wrt. Voc.
ii. 42, 43. Egesfulra *terribilium*, Ps. L. 144, 6.

**egesfullíce** ; *adv. Terribly :*—Egesfullíce *terribiliter*, Ps. L. 138, 4.
Óþer dæl wæs weallendum lígum ful swíðe egesfullíce *flammis feruentibus nimium terribile*, Bd. 5, 12 ; Sch. 616, 5.

**eges grime.** *Substitute:* eges-, egese(-i)-gríma, an ; *m. A horrible mask, a creature that has assumed a horrible form, a spectre :*—
Egisgríma (egisi-) *larbula*, Txts. 73, 1168. Egesegríma, Wrt. Voc. ii.
50, 46 : *musca* (*l. masca*), 55, 47. Egesgríma, 114, 44. Hē wæs eall
sweart and behrúmig, and flogon hine his ágene mæn, and wēndon þæt hit
wǽre larbo, þ is egesgríma (cf. *atrum phantasma*, Ald. 66, 31), Shrn.
69, 31. Egesgríman *larbam* (v. Ald. 197, 5 : this and the preceding
passage refer to the same incident), Wrt. Voc. ii. 95, 64. Egesgrímana
*mascarum*, An. Ox. 21, 7. [See Grm. D. M. (trans.) p. 1045.]

**egesian.** *Add :* I. *to terrify, inspire (with) fear or awe.* (1) absolute :—Oft Scyld Scēfing monegum mǽgðum meodosetlá ofteáh, egesode
eorl (*the hero inspired (men with) fear*), B. 6. Hē egesiende stiérð
*terroribus retrahet*, Past. 53, 16. (2) *with acc. :*—Hié ofergietað ðǽre
hirdelícan lufan and egesiað hié and ðreátigeað mid onwalde suá suá
hláfordas hos, *pastoralis mansuetudinis obliti, jure dominationis ierrent*,
Past. 145, 2. Hē egesode ða ðe on unryht hǽmdon *fornicationis metum
praemisit*, 397, 20. Hē ðæt mód his hiéremonna ōliccende egesige and
ðreátigende ōlicce *corda subditorum et terrendo demulceat, et tamen ad
terroris reuerentiam demulcendo constringat*, 127, 7. II. *to
threaten :*—Egsude *minaretur*, An. Ox. 2481.

**eges lic.** *l.* eges-lic, *and add : threatening :*—Egeslic *terribilis*, Wrt.
Voc. i. 61, 43. Egeslic nýten on sǽ oððe on lande *belua*, 77, 74.
Egslic *horrida*, An. Ox. 50, 55. Se egeslica dōmes dæg, Bl. H. 27, 27.
Egeslices *horrentis*, An. Ox. 3635. Mid egeslicum gebode *imperio
terrente*, i. *tremefaciente*, 1940. Egislicum gehlýde *furibundo strepitu*,
3810. Cyrme egeslicum (-o, MS.) *fragore horrisono*, 4418. [E]gislicere
*horrendo* (*apparatu*), 777. Harðacnut fǽringa feóll tō þǽre eorðan mid
egeslicum anginne (*with a horrible convulsion*), Chr. 1042 ; P. 162,
14. Egeslicere heáhnysse *minaci proceritate*, An. Ox. 4435. Egeslice
*minacem*, 3525. Egislican *ferinam*, i. *bestialem* (*ferocitatem*), 2984.
Þæt forme scip þæt egeslice spell gebodade *the first ship told the terrible
tale*, Ors. 4, 5 ; S. 166, 10. Egeslice *truculenta*, i. *horrida* (*venena*),
An. Ox. 1852. Egeslice dǽda, Wlfst. 161, 9. Mid egislicum *cornutis*
(*vultibus*), An. Ox. 163. Eislicum (egislicum, An. Ox. 4831) *furibundis*,
Hpt. Gl. 517, 37. Egislice orleahtras *horrida discrimina*, 1366 : *horrida*,
i. *formidolosa*, 3480. Cwōman nǽdran wunderlicran þonne þá
ōþre and egeslicran, Nar. 14, 1. þæt wē wǽre beón þæs egeslican tíman
þe tōweard is . . . þæt bið se egeslicesta þe ǽfre gewearð, Wlfst. 95, 2.

**egeslice.** *Add : horribly :*—Hé egeslice hweós, Hml. Th. i. 86, 7.
þǽr manna líc lágon and egeslíce stuncon, Hml. S. 4, 212. þá wyrhtan
tōtǽron hí sylfe and egeslíce grymetedon, 6, 197.

**egesung.** *Add :*—Send hē him tō swá fela eóroda þe mihton gebígan
þ mennisc him tō, oþþe mid egsunge þæt hig bugon tō sibbe, oþþe mid
wíge þ hí wurdon gewylde, Jud. Thw. 161, 37. Hē ondrǽde [þæs
wítegan] egesunge *metuat prophete comminationem*, R. Ben. I. 58, 13.

**egeþe**, an ; *f. For ‘ Som. . . . Lye ’ substitute :*—Egðe, egdae *erpica*,
Txts. 59, 761. Egþe, Wrt. Voc. ii. 144, 15. Egeþe, 29, 44. Egiðe

*raster*, 118, 61. Egþe (-a, MS.) *hircipes* vel *tribula*, i. 16, 25. Eiþe
(*printed* ciþe) *traha*, 15, 11. [Theose foure harowede . . . with to
eythes (harwes, MS. B.), Piers P. C. 22, 273. *O. L. Ger.* egiða :
*O. H. Ger.* egida *erpica*.] Cf. ecgan.

**egeðere.** *Substitute:* egeþere, es ; *m. One who harrows or rakes :*—
Egðere, egderi *erpicarius*, Txts. 59, 762. Egþere, Wrt. Voc. ii. 114, 16.
Egeþere, 29, 45. [*O. L. Ger.* egiðari : *O. H. Ger.* egiðâri *erpicarius*.]

**egeþ-getigu** ; *pl. n. The apparatus belonging to a harrow :*—Man sceal
habban wǽngewǽdu, sulhgesídu, egeðgetigu, Angl. ix. 264, 5. v. ge-teóh.

**ege-wilm**, es ; *m. A terrible surge :*—Ofer egewylmum, Ps. Th.
106, 24.

**eggian.** v. ge-eggian : **egile.** v. egl.

**Egipte.** *Add : gen.* (e)na :—Egiptena land, Angl. viii. 322, 3.
Egiptna, Nar. 34, 34 : 35, 20. Geseah ic miccle meniu Affricána and
Egypta, Hml. S. 23 b, 346,

**Egiptisc.** *Add :*—Ealle þá eásternan and þá Egiptiscan, Lch. iii. 256, 7.

**egl.** *Add :* egle, an ; *f.* I. *an ail, awn, beard of barley :*—Egle,
eglae, egilae *glis*, Txts. 67, 973. Glis *fonfyr* (*furfur?*) oððe egle,
Wrt. Voc. ii. 40, 71. Egle *aresta*, Wrt. Voc. i. 287, 21. Egle (-a,
MS.) *arista*, 38, 48. Eára scale (hule, egle) *spicarum glumula*, An. Ox.
1412. Eglan *fistucam* (v. Mt. 6, 3), Wrt. Voc. ii. 72, 25 : 36, 69.
Elgum *aristis*, 96, 50. Eglum *gliribus* (prava seges *gliribus* densescit
acerbis, Ald. 210, 37), 97, 10 : 41, 50. Eglum oððe eárum, 5, 69.
Eárum, eglum *spicis*, An. Ox. 2361. II. *a talon, claw :*—Egl
unheóru, B. 987. [v. *N. E. D.* ail.] Cf. egenu.

**eglan(-ian).** *Add :*—Him nán þing ne eglað ǽnigre brosnunge. Hml.
Th. ii. 552, 28 : Lch. iii. 40, 19. Wið untrumnysse ðe eágan eigliað,
16, 28. Wiþ þám wyrmum þe innan eglað monnum, ii. 12, 4 : 120, 18.
For eówre forhtnysse and yrhðe þe eów eglað *propter cordis tui formidinem qua terreberis*, Deut. 28, 67. Him (Cain) eglde ðæt hē (Abel)
wæs betra ðonne hē *meliorem se esse doluit*, Past. 235, 8. Gif ðám
gífran ungemetlicu sprǽc ne eglde *nisi gulae deditos immoderata
loquacitas raperet*, 309, 3. Swelce ōþrum monnum ǽr þ ilce ne eglede,
Bt. 7, 2 ; F. 16, 28 : Hml. Th. ii. 514, 11. Hē cwæð þ him þ nánuht
ne eglode *dixit quod ei nihil noceret*, Ll. Th. ii. 164, 10. Ðá ðe hira
hláfordas diégellíce tǽlað, and ðeáh suá suá hit him nō ne derige, ne ne
egle *dum praelatae dignitati saltem innoxie et latenter derogant*, Past.
199, 13. Him sculan eglan ōðerra monna brocu, 75, 10.

**egle** *grievous, painful. Add :*—Sē ðe eów hrepað, hit mē bið swá
egle swylce hē hreppe ðá seó mínes eágan, Hml. Th. i. 390, 15 : 516,
22. Ne mæg þē ǽnig yfel egle weordan *non accedent ad te mala*,
Ps. Th. 90, 10 : Rūn. 29. Cleopian wē in eglum móde and inneweardre
heortan *let us cry with painful thoughts from the bottom of the heart*,
Bl. H. 19, 2. Frēcne þúhton egle eálāda, An. 441. Hē ús gescildað
wið sceððenda eglum earhfarum, Cri. 762 : Gū. 376. [v. *N. E. D.* ail ;
*adj.*] v. elra.

**egle**, an ; *f.* v. egl : **egor** *nine ounces. Dele, and see next word.*

**egor**, es ; *m. High tide, flood :*—Ēgur, aegur *dodrans*, Txts. 57,
702. Ēgur *dodrans*, i. *malina*, Wrt. Voc. ii. 142, 2. Ēgor *dodrans*
(de-, MS.) : *detrans*, 70, 3. Ēgores *cataclismi, genus fluctus*, An. Ox.
7, 159. Eógra, eógora *dodrantium*, 13, 1. [v. E. S. 27, 223.]

**egor-streám.** *Add :*—Hwanon eágorstreám ofer ýða gewealc eówic
bróhte ?, An. 258. Ǽnig . . . þára þe . . . on eágorstreám ceól gesōhte,
379. þǽr git eágorstreám earmum þehton, B. 513. Mere . . . eágorstreámas, An. 492.

**egsian, egsung.** v. egesian, egesung : **egþa.** v. egeþe.

**egþ-wirf :**—Hundehtetig ǽcera gesáwen and án egþwirf and vi.
bidenfate, C. D. B. iii. 367, 38.

**ehennys.** *Dele :* eh-heóloþe. v. heáh-heoloþe : **ēh-syne.** *Dele, and
see eág-sýnes :* -eht(e). v. -iht(e).

**ēhtan, ēhtian.** *Add :* Ēhtende *insectatum*, Wrt. Voc. ii. 47, 8. I.
*to pursue an enemy, a criminal :*—Ic ēhtige fýnd míne *persequor
inimicos meos*, Ps. L. 17, 38. For ðǽm mín mon ēht þe ic bodige ymb
ðone tōhopan deádra monna ǽristes *de spe et resurrectione mortuorum
judicor*, Past. 362, 3. Hē ſérde and ēhte þǽra hǽþenra and mid ealle
ádrǽfde, Hml. S. 25, 244. þá Egyptiscan þe hira ǽr ēhton, Ex. 14, 31.
Gif ǽnig man Godes ciricgrið ábrece . . . ēhte his ǽlc þára þe Godes
fréond sí, Ll. Th. i. 340, 8. Ðý lǽs hwelc ðára niéhstena his ēhte
(*persequatur*) and gefóo, Past. 167, 4. Engel ēhtiende hig *angelus
persequens eos*, Ps. L. 34, 6. Ēhtendum *insequente*, i. *persequente*, An.
Ox. 4749. Ēhtende *persequente*, Kent. Gl. 1042. II. *to chase
an animal :*—Ǽteówde án ormǽte heort . . . Placidas him geornlíce æfter férde . . . Placidas stód . . . and áblan his ēhtan . . .
‘ Eálá Placida, hwí ēhtest þú mín ?’, Hml. S. 30, 28-45. II a.
*of animals :*—Geseah hē scealfran doppetan tō grunde ēhtende þǽra fixa,
Hml. S. 31, 1316. III. *to assail, attack,* (1) *with weapons :*—Hié
his wǽran swíðe ēhtende ge mid scotum ge mid stāna torfungum, Ors. 3,
9 ; S. 134, 14. (1 a) *of an animal :*—Gyf his nǽdre ēhte, Lch. iii. 168,
19. (2) *with words, abuse, reproaches :*—Tō hwon ēhtest þú þás men ?,
Bl. H. 175, 23. þá þe hí yrre gesáwene beóð ēhtan and wítnian *quos
irati insequi uidentur*, Bd. 1, 27 ; Sch. 67, 11. (3) *of things :*—Ðeáh

hine ôhtan (= ēhtan ?) ealle ðā yfela and ealle ðā brōgan, Sal. K. p. 84, 11. **IV. to persecute, act with malevolence towards :**—Ic ēhtige infesto, Wrt. Voc. i. 22, 34. Ofslāð and oehteð (oehtad biðon, L.) occident et persequentur, Lk. R. 11, 49. Mið ðy oehtas iúch (eówer hēhtende beóþan, R.) cum persecuti uos fuerint, Mt. L. 5, 11. Þā þe ēhtiað mē, Ps. L. 34, 3. Ēhte t ēhtigende is (persecutus est) feónd sāwle mīne, 142, 3. Hig ēhton t big ēhtegende wǣron, 68, 27. Saulus, hwæt ēhtesðū mē? ic eom Ihs þone þū ehtest, Shrn. 58, 29. Gif mec oehtende (-o, L.) wērun and iówih hiá oehtadun, Jn. R. 15, 20. Rōmāne crīstenra monna ēhton, Ors. 6, 6; S. 262, 11. Hē hēt crīstenra monna ēhtan ad persequendos Christianos feralia dispersit edicta, 6, 22; S. 274, 4. Þā ēhtegende mē, Ps. L. 118, 150. Fram ēhtiendum mē, 30, 16. Oehtigendum, 141, 7. Ēhtendum (oehtendum, L.), Mt. R. 5, 44. Oehtendum adversantibus, Rtl. 176, 33. [O. Sax. āhtian : O. H. Ger. āhten persequi, insectari.] v. ā-, ge-, oþ-ēhtan (-ian).

**ēhtend.** Add: **I. a pursuer, assailant** (cf. ēhtan, I, III) :—Scipia sǣde þæt hē þāra ǣlces ēhtend wolde beón, swā swā his feóndes, þe þæs wordes wǣre þæt from þōhte Scipio said he would pursue with relentless hostility every one who voted for leaving Rome, Ors. 4, 9; S. 190, 24. Gyf man mēte þ hē geseón ne mæge, lǣre ic hine þ hē him wið his ēhtend beorge, Lch. iii. 174, 28. **II. a persecutor :**—Hē (Nero) wæs monna ǣrest ēhtend crīstenra monna, Ors. 6, 5; S. 262, 5. Oehtende persecutore, Rtl. 64, 16. Hié wǣren crīstenra monna ēhtend, Ors. 6, 10; S. 264, 27. Oehtendum persecutoribus, Mk. L. R. 10, 30. v. eahtend.

**ēhtere.** Add :—Domicianus, crīstenra manna ēhtere, Hml. Th. i. 58, 26. Sauwlus wæs crīstenra manna ēhtere and cwellere, Shrn. 58, 27. Ēhtere Crīstes ǣ, Bl. H. 187, 5. Godes circena ēhtere, Hml. A. 149, 147. On ðām ēcan wuldre ne wunað nān wiþerwinna, ne nān yfel ēhtere þe ūs dreccan mage, 78, 146. Se Hǣlend for his ēhterum gebæd, 47, 567. Fore oehterum (persecutoribus) gibidda, Rtl. 44, 30. [O. H. Ger. āhtāri persecutor, apparitor.]

**ēhtian.** v. ēhtan.

**ēhting.** Add :—Yrmþa ēhtinga calamitatum insectationes, Hpt. Gl. 476, 16. [O. H. Ger. āhtunga persecutio.] v. on-ēhting (?).

**ēht-nes.** Add :—Oehtnisses persecutionis, Mt. p. 14, 10. Ðā ðe þoliað ēhtnysse for rihtwīsnysse, Hml. Th. i. 552, 29. On ēhtnessum, Bl. H. 171, 17. Oehtnissum, Mk. p. 4, 13. Ēhtnesse insectiones (insectationes, Ald. v. ēhtung), Wrt. Voc. ii. 81, 16 : 46, 68. [O. H. Ger. āhtnessi persecutio.

**eiseg.** Add : cf. eislic = egislic, Hpt. Gl. 517, 37. v. eges-lic.

**el ; pl. elle** other :—Elle (ðā oðero, L.) genōman æsnas his reliqui tenuerunt servos ejus, Mt. R. 22, 6. v. elles.

**el-boga.** v. eln-boga : elch. v. eolh.

**elcian.** Add : to procrastinate. **I. absolute :**—Elcaþ differt, i. moratur, Wrt. Voc. ii. 140, 13. Ylde, elcode distulit, moram fecit, 141, 47. Ne hē lange ne elcode, Lch. iii. 434, 24. Elkede (ilkede, ylcodan þā dēman) man fram dæge tō dæge, Chr. 999; P. 133, 5. Hī þágit elcodon, Hml. S. 31, 1166. God behēt ǣlcum behreówsigendum his synna forgifennysse, ac hē behēt nānum elcigendum gewiss līf oð merigen, Hml. Th. ii. 602, 29. Elciendum, Hml. S. 12, 1166. Nellen gē elciende eówere heortan āhyrdan, R. Ben. 2, 10. Behreówsigendum mannum hē miltsað, ac hē ne behēt þām elcigendum gewiss līf oð merigen, Hml. Th. i. 350, 13. **II. with gen. :**—Hē elcað his tōcymes, Hml. Th. ii. 566, 25. Hē elcode his sleges, 380, 31. **III. with prep. :**—Hī elciað ongeán ðone deáð, and mid ealle ne forfleóð . . . on ende þisse worulde hī deáðes onfóð. Ûre Ālȳsend ne elcode nā ongeán þone deáð Enoch and Elias delay to meet death, and do not avoid it . . . at the end of this world they will receive death. Our Saviour did not delay to meet death, Hml. Th. i. 308, 2–7. Þæt se Ælmihtiga forgeáfe gōdne willan þām seócan hǣðenan, þæt hē leng ne elcode tō His geleáfan that the Almighty would give a good will to the sick heathen, that he should not put off longer coming to a belief in Him, ii. 26, 1. **IV. with clause :**—Nān man ne sceal elcian þæt hē his synna gebēte, Hml. Th. ii. 602, 27 : Hml. S. 12, 164. v. ildcian.

**elcor.** Add : else :—Ælcor (ellicor, v.l.) alias, Ælfc. Gr. Z. 239, 2. **I. besides :**—Ic genom mid mec þreó þūsendo and forlēt mīne fyrd elcor (the rest of the army) in Fasiacen, Nar. 26, 5. Næs nāht elcor (nōht elles, nān þing elles) tō ealles geáres andlyfne būton þ ān (nihil aliud . . . nisi . . .), Gr. D. 57, 2 : 290, 21. **II. otherwise, in another way :**—Gif nasu þyrel weorð . . . Gif nasu ælcor sceard weorð, Ll. Th. i. 14, 13. Gif mē seó godcunde gyfu forgyfan wile . . . ; gif hit hwæt ælcor (elcor, elles, v.ll.) bið, ic eft hweorfe (sin alias rꜹuertar), Bd. 4, 28 ; Sch. 519, 7. Hē ne mihte elcor gewearmigan būton æt fȳre, Nar. 18, 15. Hī ne magon elcor beón būton mīnre gemynde geendebyrded non sine magna cura ordinata, 3, 15. Hū mæg þ beón ylcor (elles, v.l.) ongyten būton . . . quid sentiri aliud potest, nisi . . . , Gr. D. 315, 1. **III. as an alternative, as a substitute :**—Wyrc tō duste oþþe elcor gnīd on wīn, Lch. i. 368, 15. Þā þe wē ne magon ongytan in þām godcundan dōme wē sculan ūs þe mā ondrǣdan þonne elcor reccan (timere

magis quam discutere debemus), Gr. D. 301, 12. **IV. if not, under other conditions, on another supposition :**—Gif hē bið cealdre gecyndo, þonne cymð æfter feówertigum ; elcor cymð æfter fīftigum wintra, Lch. ii. 284, 21. Þæt weorc byþ of þǣre gife geseald, nalles seó gifu of þām weorce, elcor (elles, v. l., alioquin) ne byþ seó gifu Godes gifu, Gr. D. 33, 5 : 274, 16. Elcor si quo minus (v. Jn. 14, 2), Wrt. Voc. ii. 74, 20. **IV a. after a negative clause, if so :**—Behaldeþ þ gē eówre sōþfestnisse ne dōan fore monnum . . . elles t elcur (alioquin = elcor elioquin, Wrt. Voc. ii. 72, 20 : 30, 63) gē ne habbaþ leán, Mt. R. 6, 1. Ne menn geótaþ wīn neówe in wīnbelgas alde ; elcur t elles (alioquin) tōbersteþ þā belgas ealde, 9, 17. Elcur nū, Lk. L. 5, 36, 37. **V. elsewhere :**—Seó fǣmne on mynster oððe ælcor on hire clǣnnysse hig healde eat puella in monasterium, vel alibi in castitate se contineat, Ll. Th. ii. 148, 4. v. ælcor in Dict., and elcra ; elles.

**elcora, elcra ;** adv. **Else, otherwise :**—Ac elcra, elles hū sed secus, i. aliter (ellcra, Hpt. Gl. 481, 47), An. Ox. 3202. Hwylc beren mǣnde hē ðonne elcora (elles, Bl. H. 39, 27) būtan heofona rīce ?, ib. note. Wæs his rest on his hǣran oððe elcora (elles, Bl. H. 227, 11) on nacodre eorðan . . . 'Ne gedafenað crīstenan men þ hē elcora (elles, Bl. H. 227, 14) dō,' Nap. 20. Gif hē elcra (ælcra, v. l.) þurh tōþundennesse gedyrstlǣcð si aliter presumpserit, R. Ben. 113, 12. v. elcor ; elles.

**elcra ;** adj. Substitute (?) : elcran ; adv. Otherwise :—Wið manegum ādlum þ deáh, ðā ðe cumað of oferfyllo and of yflum wǣtum. Gif hié cumen of oferfyllo, mid spiweðan hȳ mon sceal lytlian. Gif hié þonne cumað of ōþrum biterum and yfelum wǣtum, þā þe wyrceað ōman, þonne beóþ þā elcran tō stillanne the inflammations are to be reduced by other means (than emetics), Lch. ii. 178, 14. v. elcra ; adv.

**elcung.** Substitute :—Hȳrsumnes būtan elcunge obedientia sine mora, R. Ben. 19, 14, 19 : 47, 12. Būtan ælcere elcunge, 131, 5. Hāt mē nū fullian būtan elcunge, Hml. S. 3, 607. Þū ūs mid elcunge geswænctest, Ap. Th. 19, 26. Hē wiðcwæð mid langsumere elcunge diu negando distulit, Hml. Th. ii. 158, 6. v. eldcung in Dict.

**eld.** v. ild : eldcung. Add : v. ildcian, elcung : elde. v. ilde : eldcend-lic. v. ildend-lic.

**eldne ?** :—Eldne hinnuli capini (= ? elone (elene) hinnula campana), Wrt. Voc. ii. 43, 54.

**eldo.** v. ildu : eldra, eldran. v. ildra, ildran : eldre dele. v. ildra : eldung. v. ilding.

**ele, es ; m.** Add : and n. :—Balzamum se deórweorðesta ele, Nar. 36, 32. Wē tō dæg sceolan dǣlan ūrne ele on þreó wīsan gehālgodne . . . hālig ele, ōþer is crisma, and seóccra manna ele : and gē sceolan habban þreó ampullan gearuwe tō þam þrým elum, Ll. Th. ii. 390, 2–7. Grēnes eles, Lch. ii. 180, 11. Eles gecynd bið þ hē beorhton scīneþ þonne wex on sceafte, Bl. H. 127, 36. Oeles olei, Lk. L. 16, 6. Of ole de oleo, Mt. L. 25, 8. Mið ole (oele, R.), Mk. 6, 13. Seóþ on ele . . . dō þonne weax on þ ele, Lch. ii. 234, 10. Ðone ele (oele, v.l.), Past. 369, 19, 11. Ele āwringan of byrgum, Gr. D. 250, 22. Hī ðicgeð on ðām earde ele on heora bigleofum swā swā wē dōð buteran, Hml. Th. ii. 178, 16. Ne genōmun oele, Mt. L. R. 25, 3. v. fulluht-, smirwung-ele.

**ele-bacen.** Add :—Þā sceolon beón elebacene (æle bracene, Thw.) and wearme in sartagine oleo conspersa frigetur ; offerent eam calidam, Lev. 6, 21.

**ele-beám.** Add :—Oelebeám oliva, Rtl. 65, 35. Úp tō ðām ealdan elebeáme, C. D. v. 194, 3. Tō ðām elebeáme, 297, 20. On ǣnne elebeám, 374, 21. Andlang hagan oð ðone elebeám, 70, 23. Mōr oelebeáma (-beómes, R.) mons oliuarum, Mk. L. 11, 1 : 14, 26. On mōre oelebeáma (-beóma), 13, 3. [O. H. Ger. oli-baum.]

**elebeám-stybb** the stump of an olive tree :—On þone elebeámstyb, C. D. iii. 430, 26.

**ele-bearu (-o), wes ; m. An olive grove :**—Oelebearwes dūn mons Oliueti, Mt. R. 21, 1 : 26, 30. Mōr oelebearwes (olebearua, L.) mons oliuarum, Lk. R. 22, 39. Mōr elebearues mons Oliveti, Mt. L. 26, 30. Oelebearuu, Lk. L. 19, 29. Olebearu, 21, 37.

**ele-berge.** Add :—Seó tīd þ man sceolde eleberigean somnian colligendae olivae tempus, Gr. D. 50, 10. Eleberigan (-berian), 22. Men wrungun elebergean (olivas) on þǣre treddan . . . Hī nāht ne gehāwedon flōwan þæs eles of þām elebergum, 250, 13–26. [O. L. Ger. oli-beri : O. H. Ger. oli-beri oliva.]

**ele-byt.** For example substitute :—Ǣrenu elebyt lenticula, Wrt. Voc. ii. 50, 75. v. byt : elehtre. v. elehtre.

**ele-drósna ; pl. Lees of oil, oil-dregs :**—Genim þysse wyrte seáw mid eledrōsnum gemencged, Lch. i. 310, 17. [O. H. Ger. oli-truosin amurca.] Cf. eles drosna under ele.

**ele-fæt.** Add :—Gē sceolan habban þreó ampullan gearuwe tō þām þrým elum, for ðan ðe wē ne durran dōn hī tōgædere on ānum elefate, Ll. Th. ii. 390, 8. Ampellan oððe elefæt legithum, Wrt. Voc. ii. 52, 76. Genim þysse wyrte sǣdes an elefæt ful and twēgen bollan fulle wæteres, Lch. i. 300, 2. Āfyll ðīn elefæt (imple cornu tuum oleo, 1 Sam. 16, 1), Hml. Th. ii. 64, 6. Hē hēt āwurpan ūt þæt glæsene fæt mid ele mid ealle . . . hēt eft āhebban þæt elefæt, 178, 31. Oelefæt

full smirinise *alabastrum ungenti*, Lk. L. 7, 37. [*O. H. Ger.* oli-faz *alabastrum.*]

**ele-greófa**, an; *m. An oil-pot* (v. greófa); *or fibrous material saturated with oil* (?) (cf. *O. H. Ger.* griubo v. pfanna *frixorium, cremium* vel *siccamina lignorum : Ger.* griebe *fibrous remains of lard, &c. after being fried*) :—Elegreóuena *naptarum* (the passage is: incendia *naptarum* fomite succensa: cf. heordena, tyrwena *naptarum*, An. Ox. 1649. The glosser may have thought of the fire as fed by oil from cans, or by tow soaked in oil), An. Ox. 7, 87 : 8, 99.

**ele-horn**, es; *n. A horn for oil* :—Elehorn *lecitho*, Wrt. Voc. ii. 51, 43.

**elehtre**. *Add* : electre, elot(h)r :—Elotr, elothr *electrum*, Txts. 59, 735. Elehtre, Wrt. Voc. i. 31, 5. Electre, 79, 10: An. Ox. 56, 382. Elehtre *maliterre*, Wrt. Voc. i. 67, 68 : *maura*. ib. 58, 30.

**ele-lǽnde**. *Add* : v. el-lende : **ele-land**. *Add* : v. el-land : **ele-leáf** (?) :—Eleleáfes stelan, Lch. ii. 272, 23. Heleleáfes moran, Lch. iii. 18, 26.

**ele-leást**, e; *f. Lack of oil* :—For eleleáste, Gr. D. 44, 21.

**ele-lendisc**. *Add* :—On stówe elelendiscre *in loco peregrinationis*, Ps. L. 118, 54. Elelendisc *extorrem*, Hpt. Gl. 412, 74. Elendisc, An. Ox. 275. Ǽelelendiscne, 11, 21. [Kumeð þes helendisse Mon . . . Mon elelendis he is icleped for he is of unkuþe þode, O. E. Hml. i. 81, 32.]

**ele-sealf**. *Add* :—þǽre getreówan elesealfe *nardi pistici*, Wrt. Voc. ii. 86, 41. Elesealfe *ambrosia*, 2, 34 : *nardo*, 74, 67 : 60, 54 : Hpt. Gl. 405, 48.

**eleþ**. *Substitute* : eleþ. *l.* ēþel.

**ele-tredde**, an; *f. An oil-press, press in which olives are crushed* :—Wǽron feáwa eleberian . . . hēt hé þá gegaderian and dón on eletreddan (*in praelo*), Gr. D. 50, 29. Of þǽre eletreddan (*ex prelo*) nǽnige gemete ǽnig dǽl eles ūt eóde, 251, 2.

**ele-treów**. *Add* :—Ne ættýwde ǽnig wæstm on þám eletreówum *fructus in oleis nullus appareret*, Gr. D. 50, 11. Treówcynn eletreówum *gelíce arbores similes oliuae*, Nar. 36, 31.

**ele-twig**. *l.* -twig, *and add* :—Eletwiges *oleastri*, Wrt. Voc. ii. 64, 7.
**elfetu**. v. ilfette: **elh, elha**. v. eolh.

**el-hygd**. *Substitute* : *Alienation of mind, ecstasy*, and add :—Se engcel his mód gegráp and gelǽdde iu ellhygd būton him sylfum *angelus ejus mentem in ecstasim rapuit extra se*, Gr. D. 108, 4.

**Elíg**. *Add* :—On ðǽm londe þe wē nemnað æt Elíe, Shrn. 94, 27.
**Elíg-mynster** *the monastery of Ely* :—Heó weard gehádod tó abbadissan on Elígmynstre, Hml. S. 20, 38.

**ell**, es; *m.* (v.u.) *The letter l* :—Uelim on ánum elle . . . *uellem* on twám ellum, Ælfc. Gr. Z. 200, 5, 6.

**el-land**. *Add* : [Til eillandes þir þam drou, C.M. 2189.] v. eleland : **ellarn**. *l.* ellaern, *and see* ellen : **elle** *others*. v. el : **elle** *elder-tree*. v. ellen.

**ellen** *strength*. *Add* :—In elne *in agonia*, Wrt. Voc. ii. 46, 48. Hé áweóx in gástlicum elne *in spirituali zelo excreverat*, Gr. D. 205, 19. Swá hwæt swá wē tó góde dóþ on elne gástlices mægenes, Bl. H. 29, 9. Swá hwylc swá on elne oþ his ende wunað *qui perseueraverit usque in finem*, 171, 25. Bǽd ic þá fyrde þ hié hæfdon gód ellen þára þinga þe ūs on becwōmon *orabam Macedones ne aduersis casibus cederent*, Nar. 14, 22. Ic syngode þurh ásolcennysse þá þá mē gód ne lyste dón ne nán ellen niman tó ǽnigum godan weorce *did not apply myself zealously to any good work*, Angl. xi. 113, 45. [v. N. E. D. elne.]

**ellen** *elder-tree*. *Add* : ellern (-aern), elle :—Ellaen, ellae, ellaern *sambucus*, Txts. 94, 893. Elle *sambuca*, 109, 1131. Ellen *sambucus*, Wrt. Voc. i. 285, 67 : *actis vel sambucus*, 69, 31. Elnes rind, Lch. ii. 230, 14. In tó gryddeles elrene, of gryddeles elrene in tó ðára smalan āc, C. D. B. i. 117, 27. Usque ad ellerne, C. D. iii. 447, 31. Tó ðám ellene, v. 226, 14. On ðæt ellen : of ðám ellenne, iii. 85, 8. On ðæt ǽnlýpe ellyn ; ðonne of ðan ellynne, v. 398, 28. Petram recte contra le ellarne, iii. 393, 5. Þá gemearr þe man drífð . . . on ellenum and eác on óðrum mislicum treówum (for the elder as a sacred tree see Grmm. D. M. p. 651 (trans.)), Ll. Th. ii. 248, 5. [*For* ellen *in place-names v.* ellen-beorh (ellern-, elle-, elles-), -crundel, -cumb, -ford (elle-), -wyl, -worþig, C. D. vi. 284.]

**ellen-asce**, an; *f. Elder-ash* :—Wyrc him leáge of ellenahsan, Lch. ii. 338, 25.

**ellen-campian**. *Substitute for quotations* :—Ellencampedon *agonizarunt*, Wrt. Voc. ii. 3, 5.

**ellen-dǽd**. *Add* : [*O. Sax.* ellean-dâd.]

**el-lende**; *adj. Dele last two quotations, and add* :—Afiniculum ellende *a finibus procul*, Txts. 39, 99. [*O. Sax.* eli-lendi : *O. H. Ger.* el(i)-lenti *peregrinus, exul.*]

**el-lende**, es; *n. Foreign parts* :—Oþþe on ellende (ælþeóde, *v. l.*) oðče on heora āgenre gecýþþe, Bt. 27, 3 ; F. 98, 34. On ellende *apud exteras nationes*, 27, 4 ; F. 100, 10. In ellende ł in eldióde gefoerde *peregre profectus est*, Mt. R. 21, 33. On ellende fǽrende *peregre proficiscens*, 25, 14. [*O. Sax.* eli-lendi : *O. H. Ger.* el(i)-lenti *transmigratio, exilium.*]

**ellenga**. v. eallunga.

**ellen-gráfa**, an; *m. An elder-grove* :—On ellengráfan ; fram ellengráfan, C. D. B. ii. 469, 27.

**ellen-hete**, es; *m. Jealousy* :—Ic ondette . . . ellenhete and níð, Angl. xi. 98, 26.

**ellen-lǽca**. *For* 'pugil . . . Cot. 15' *substitute* :—Ellenlǽca (-e, MS.) *agoneta* (=agonotheta), Wrt. Voc. i. 284, 38. Ellenlǽca *agontea*, ii. 8, 11. Cf. ellen-campian.

**ellen-leás**. *Add* : [Herrsummnesse iss unstrang wiþþutenn meocnesse, meocnesse iss ellennlæs wiþþutenn herrsummnesse, Orm. 10908.]

**ellen-lic**; *adj. Courageous, valiant* :—Ellenlic gewinn, Hml. S. 23 b, 2.

**ellen-róf**. *Add* : [*O. Sax.* ellean-róf.]

**ellen-stybb, -stubb**, es; *m. An elder-stump* :—Æt þæne ellenstyb; of ðám stybb, C. D. iii. 24, 3. On ðone ellenstyb, 437, 19. Ellenstub, 10, 17 : 25, 21. Of ðā(m) ellenstubbe on ðane óðerne ellenstubbe, vi. 102, 25. Usque le ellerne stubbe, iii. 407, 25. On þá ellenstybbas ; þonne of þám ellenstybban, C. D. B. iii. 396, 30.

**ellen-tán**, es; *m. An elder-twig* :—Ellentānas and āctānas, Lch. ii. 322, 19.

**ellen-treów**, es; *n. An elder-tree* :—Tunc in uiam publicam usque sambucum quam uocitant ellentreóws, C. D. iii. 379, 15.

**ellen-wód**; *adj. Add* :—Andig, ellenwód *zelotypus*, An. Ox. 364.
**ellen-wódian**. *Add* :—Emulari, i. imitari, *vel* ellenwódian, Wrt. Voc. ii. 143, 43.

**ellen-wyrttruma**, an; *m. A root of elder* :—Ellenwyrttruman rind, Lch. ii. 270, 3.

**el-leoht**, es; *n. The incorrect use (elision?) of l* :—Elleohtes *lautacismi* (= *labdacismi* ; cf. *laudacismi* ðǽre uncyste, Wrt. Voc. ii. 88, 33), An. Ox. 5471. Cf. em-leoht.

**ellern**. v. ellen.

**elles**. *Add* : I. with indef. or interrog. pronouns, or indeterminate numeral words :—Būton hit mid ūrum hláforde sý, oððon elles hwylc þe māran Godes ege habbe, Wlfst. 269, 12. Gif him sylfum ælles hwæt sǽle . . . elles hwæt, C. D. i. 311, 12, 13. Mid elles hwám gerēnod, Bt. 14, 3 ; F. 46, 14. Hwæt is elles ðiós gewītendlice sibb būton swelce hit sié sum swæð ðǽre ēcean sibbe ?, Past. 351, 24. For hwām wæs elles . . . būton for ðǽm de ? , 389, 32. Elles ǽlc oþer þing būtan þysum sý gehealden *reliqua omnia impleantur*, R. Ben. 34. 13. Ne gehýrde nǽnig man on his mūþe óht elles nefne Crístes lof, Bl. H. 223, 36. Wæs se bigleofa gemětt and nán ðing elles, Hml. Th. i. 76, 19. Hē elles nán þincg ne cwæð, Hml. S. 23 b, 616. Nán mann ne mihte ðencan embe nǽht elles būtan . . ., Chr. 995; P. 130, 10. Eall þæt manncynnes elles wæs, eall hit ādranc, Wlfst. 10, 13. I a. referring to a substantive with pronominal &c. adj. (cf. I) :—Hwylc beren mæðm hē elles būton heofona ríce ?, Bl. H. 39, 27. Þ man ǽlc beboden fæsten healde, sí hit Ymbrenfæsten, sí hit Lengtenfæsten, sí hit elles óðer fæsten, Ll. Th. i. 368, 22. Elles óðre fæstena healde man, 308, 18. Hwæþer þys sý Ephesa byrig þe elles ǽnig óþer, Hml. S. 23, 743. Hit wæs elles feáwum mannum cūð, Chr. 1043; P. 164, 3. II. with pronominal adverbs. (1) local :—Wæs eorðstyrung on Deórbý and elles gehwǽr . . . and eác þ wilde fýr on Deórbýscíre micel yfel dyde and gehwǽr elles, Chr. 1049; P. 167, 25, 27. Elles hwider *aliorsum*, Wrt. Voc. ii. 3, 25. Áwhyder oþþe elles hwyder *usquam aut aliorsum*, An. Ox. 7, 276. Elles hwanune *aliunde*, Scint. 33, 2 : R. Ben. I. 70, 1. (2) of manner :—Elcra, elles hū *secus*, i. *aliter*, An. Ox. 3202. Hit ne sý þ se lāreów þe him tela tǽce him sylf elles hū dó, Ll. Th. ii. 418, 4. III. *otherwise, differently* :—Elles *aliter*, An. Ox. 1380: *ceterum*, 5183. Ne gespræc hē nā þý þe hē hit wolde 'forðbringan, ac elles beótigende *non proferendo, sed minando*, Gr. D. 152, 16. Būton þū elles wylle *sin aliter tibi videtur*, Num. 11, 15. Gif hē elles dēð, Hml. Th. i. 266, 14: Hml. S. 27, 73. Gehwā dyde swā, and elles ne dorston, 23, 30. Saul elles ne meahte his wambe geclǽnsigan, būton hē tó feltúne eóde, Past. 197, 23. Ne gedafenað þ hē elles dó, būton swā hē on axan licge, Bl. H. 227, 14. Oððe mid rihte oððe elles, Chr. 1085; P. 217: Ll. Th. i. 236, 4. III a. *elsewhere* :—Elles *aliorsum*, An. Ox. 2, 252. IV. *else, under other conditions* :—Ne mæg ðæt scip nō stille gestondan, būton hit ankor gehæbbe, oððe mon mid róðrum ongeán tió ; elles hit gelent mid ðý stréame, Past. 445, 13. V. *else, as an alternative* :—Wæs his seó æþeleste ræst on his hǽran oþþe elles on nacodre eorðan, Bl. H. 227, 11. v. el ; *adj.* ; elcor.

**ellm**. *Dele, and see* ellen : ellor. *Add* : [*O. Sax.* ellior.]
**elm**. *Add* :—Elm *ulmus*, Wrt. Voc. ii. 124, 4. Genim elmes rind, Lch. ii. 52, 9. Elmes drǣnc *a drink made with elm rind*, 66, 25. Cf. Elmleáh *as a place name*, C. D. iv. 70, 3, 13.

**elm-boga**. v. eln-boga : elmestlic. v. ælmes-lic.

**Elmed-sǽte** (-a), *pl. The inhabitants of Elmet, the ancient British Loidis, an independent district in Yorkshire* :—Elmedsǽtan (Elmet-, Elmeth- *in Latin MSS.*) landes is syx hund hýda, C. D. B. i. 414, 17. Cf. In monasterio . . . quod est in silua Elmete, Bd. 2, 14.

**eln**. *Add* :—Eln *ulna*, Wrt. Voc. i. 283, 10. *Cubitum* fæðm betwux

elboga[n] and handwyrste, *palmus* span *vel* handbred, *ulna* eln *vel* spanning betwux þūman and scitefingre, 43, 51–53. Hē geseah hī ūp āhefene swā swā mannes elne fram þǣre eorðan, Hml. S. 23 b, 274.

**eln-boga.** *Add :*—Elnboga *cuba*, se earm betweónan elnbogan and handwyrste *cubitus*, Wrt. Voc. ii. 22, 60, 61. Elnboga *vel* fæþm *cubitum*, elnboga *vel* hondwyrst *cuba*, i. *ulna*, 137, 38, 40. Elboga *cuba*, i. 43, 50. Gif men sié se earm mid honda mid ealle of ācorfen beforan elmbogan (el-, *v. l.*), Ll. Th. i. 96, 29. An elmbogan *in ulmam*, Germ. 396, 156. v. ele-, elm-boga *in Dict.*

**elnian.** *Add : to gain strength :*—Geunne þē ēce Drihten æcera wexendra and wrīdendra, eácniendra and elniendra, Lch. i. 402, 5. [v. *N. E. D.* elne. *Goth.* aljanon *aemulari : O. H. Ger.* ellinōn *aemulari*, *agonizare : Icel.* elna *to grow stronger* (of disease).]

**elnung.** *Add :* I. *encouragement, comfort :*—Hē æfter þysum geþance teáh him elnunge tō be dæle *after this thought he took comfort to himself in some measure*, Hml. S. 23, 524. II. *zeal :*—Hē mid geornfulre elnunge ūp ārīsende wæs, Hml. S. 31, 251. [Mi Iesu, þu beodest þin elning . . . and we wendeð us þer from and bugged worldes froure, O. E. Hml. i. 201, 2. *O. H. Ger.* ellinunga, elnunga *aemulatio.*]

**elotr.** v. elehtre : **elpen-bǣnen, -bān.** v. elpend-bǣnen, -bān.

**elpend.** *Add :*—Ylpend *elefans*, Wrt. Voc. ii. 142, 81. On horsum and on mūlum and on olsendum and on elpendum *equis et mulis et elephantis et camelis*, Nar. 9, 15. [*O. H. Ger.* helfant. From Latin.] v. elpend-bān ; ylp.

**elpend-bǣnen ;** *adj. Ivory :*—Of þīnum elpanbǣnenum hūsum . . . þā elpanbǣnenan hūs tācniað rihtwīsra manna heortan, Ps. Th. 44, 10. From stepum elpanbaennum *a gradibus eburneis*, Ps. Srt. 44, 9. [*O. H. Ger.* helfent-peinīn *eburneus.*] v. ylpen-bǣnen *in Dict.*

**elpend-bān, es ;** *n. An elephant's tusk, ivory :*—Elpendbaan, elpendesbān *ebor* ; Txts. 59, 713. Elpanbān oððe elpend ( =elpendbān ? ; *but cf. O. H. Ger.* elafant *ebor* ; elefant-īn, -isc *eburneus*) *ebor*, Wrt. Voc. ii. 28, 73. Ūton his brýdbūras wǣron elpendbānum geworhte, Nar. 5, 5. [*O. H. Ger.* helfent-bein *ebur.*] v. ylpen-bān *in Dict.*

**elpend-tōþ, es ;** *m. An elephant's tusk :*—Elpendtōþ *eburneus dens*, Wrt. Voc. ii. 32, 37.

**elra.** *Add :* ēlra (?) =eglra ; *cpve.* of egle.

**el-reord.** *Add :*—Mid þý hī þā ellreordan (elreordigan, ell-, *v. ll.*) ongēton *qui cum cogniti essent a barbaris*, Bd. 5, 10 ; Sch. 601, 10. Ne myhton ælreorde þeóde hergian on þā, Shrn. 156, 24. [*O. H. Ger.* eli-rart *alienigena.*]

**el-reordig.** *Add :*—þā oferhygdlican gedyrstignesse þæs elreordgan kyninges *the overweening presumption of the barbarian king*, Nar. 19, 12. Mec þās forealdodan elreordegan bysmergeað *me illudi a barbaris senibus existimavi*, 25, 26. Micel fyrd þǣra elreordigra (*barbarorum*), 17, 9. Þ syndon þā wyrstan men and elreordigestan, 36, 25. v. el-reord.

**el-þeód.** *Add :*—Hē in eldióde gefoerde *peregre profectus est*, Mt. R. 21, 33. ¶ *especially in reference to enforced absence from a person's native country :*—Đolian earfeðu suā suā mon sceal on eldióde *labores velut in aliena pati*, Past. 253, 11. On elþeóde ādrǣfan *in exilium agere*, Ors. 5, 9 ; S. 232, 20. Hē hēt þā crīstnan . . . gebringan on elþeóde . . . þā hēt hē þæt mon þā crīstnan eft gebrōhte on heora earde (*de exsiliis revocavit*), 6, 30 ; S. 282, 17. Sume hē on eldióde him wið feó gesealde 3, 9 ; S. 126, 16. Eall þæt folc on ellþeóde him wið feoh gesealde *reliquos sub corona vendidit*, Bos. 64, 11. On ellþeóde forsendan, 3, 7 ; Bos. 62, 35 note. [Alþeodene gold, Laym. 2327.]

**el-þeódgian, -þeódian ;** *p.* ode *To be in foreign parts, to travel to* or *live in a foreign land :*—Foerde fearr ł eldiódegde *peregre profectus est*, Mt. L. 21, 33. Elldeódigde ł fearr fǣrende wæs, Lk. L. 15, 13. Elldiódade, Mk. L. 13, 34. Wilnade hē eldiódigan (-þeódigan, -þeódian, *v. ll.*) cupiens peregrinari, Bd. 5, 7 ; Sch. 585, 15. v. ge-elþeódian.

**el-þeódgung, -þeódung, e ;** *f. A being in a foreign land, living* or *going abroad :*—In foresetenesse elþeódgunge (-þeódunge, *v. l.*) *proposito peregrinandi*, Bd. 4, 23 ; Sch. 465, 15.

**el-þeódig.** *Add :*—Ælþeódig *peregrinus*, Wrt. Voc. i. 74, 65. Đā eldeódigan *bargina* (cf. bargine, peregrine ; barrigenae, peregrinae, Angl. xiii. 332), Wrt. Voc. ii. 94, 29 : 12, 13. I. *of persons,* (1) *expressing relation to one person of another, of another race, foreign, stranger :*—Githro, ðeáh hē hǣðen and elþeódig (-ðeód-, *v. l.*) wǣre, tǣlde Mōyses *Moyses Iethro alienigenae reprehensione judicatur*, Past. 131, 13. Wē geleófað on Drihten þyses ælþeódigan mannes, Bl. H. 247, 4. Sēcaþ sumne ælþeódigne man þæs nama is Andreas, 239, 33. Hē lǣdde þe eldeódgan (æll-, *v. l.*) ǣrendracan on his mǣdmhūs *venientibus ad se alienigenis aromatum cellas ostendit*, Past. 39, 3. (2) *of local relation, living in another land than one's own :*—Hē wende tō Scottum, þæt hē ælþeódig on lǣre geðuge, Hml. Th. ii. 148, 19. Hē dǣlde þǣre cyrcan mādmas ælðeódigun ðearfum, i. 418, 17. ¶ *figuratively :*—Swelce hē sié eldiédig (æl-, *v. l.*) on ðissum middangearde, Past. 140, 20. Wē synd on þisse worlde ælþeódige, Bl. H. 23, 3. (3) *stranger to, alien from :*—Eldídig (ælðiódig, *v. l.*) from Gode *auctori extraneus*, Past. 140, 21. I a. *used substantively, a foreigner, stranger :*—Fordwān se foresǣda ælðeódiga, Hml. Th. ii. 286, 22. Þās ealle ūp cōman for þissum ælþeódi-

gum (*St. Andrew in Mermedonia*), Bl. H. 245, 35. Swā wē dydon on þisne ælþeódigan, 247, 13. In bibyrignisa elldiódigra (eldeódigra, R.) *in sepulturam peregrinorum*, Mt. L. 27, 7. From helldiódigum *ab alienis*, 17, 26. Sume hē on elþiódige forsende, Ors. 3, 7 ; S. 120, 13. Hē þæt folc on ellþeódge him wið feó gesealde *reliquos sub corona vendidit*, 3, 9 ; S. 124, 6. II. *of a country, foreign :*—Sum rīce man wolde faran on ælðeódigne eard, Hml. Th. ii. 548, 26.

**el-þeódige ;** *adv. In* or *to foreign parts, abroad :*—Ðe gingra suno eldiódge foerende wæs (*peregre profectus est*), Lk. R. 15, 13.

**el-þeódiglic ;** *adj. Foreign, strange :*—Twēgen Godes þeówas on ælþeódiglicum gegyrlan, Shrn. 99, 32.

**el-þeódiglīce.** *Add :*—Ælþeódilīce *peregre*, Mk. 13, 14. Ælþeódelīce, An. Ox. 284.

**el-þeódignes.** *Add : absence from one's own country, generally that which is a result of compulsion* or *of a sense of religious duty, exile, banishment, pilgrimage :*—Wrǣcsīð *exilium*, ælðeódignes *peregrinatio*, Wrt. Voc. i. 51, 37. I. *literal :*—In forsetenesse elþeódignesse *proposito peregrinandi*, Bd. 4, 23 ; Sch. 465, 15. Tō eldeódignesse *ad incolatum*, Wrt. Voc. ii. 75, 47. Tō ælþyódinessa, An. Ox. 11, 25. Þrié Scottas cōmon of Hibernia, þonon hī hī bestǣlon, for þon þe hī woldon for Godes lufan on elþiódignesse beón, hī ne rōhton hwǣr, Chr. 891 ; P. 82, 21. Hē wolde for Godes lufon on elþeódignesse lifian (*peregrinam ducere uitam*), Bd. 3, 19 ; Sch. 276, 7. Hē (*St. Luke*) wæs Paulus gefēra in ælce eldeódignesse, Shrn. 138, 28. Hē his eard forlǣte for Godes lufon, and on ælþeódignysse fare (*peregre proficiscatur*), Ll. Th. ii. 224, 9. II. *figurative, of this world :*—Elðeódignysse his on þyses līfes langfērnysse *peregrinationis suae in hujus vitae longinquitate*, Scint. 29, 1. Wē habbaþ nēdþearfe þ wē ongyton þā blindnesse ūre ælþeódignesse ; wē send on þisse worlde ælþeódignesse, Bl. H. 23, 2. On ðisse eldiódignesse (ælðeód-, *v. l.*), Past. 252, 18. Đý lǣs ūs weorðe tō wōpe and tō eldiódignesse ðæt ēcean līfes ðæt ðæt ūs on ðisse eldiódignesse tō fultume gelǣned is, 389, 5. Hē ūs gesōhte on þǣs ælþeódignesse, Bl. H. 11, 35.

**el-þeódisc.** *Add :*—Ǣghwylc man þe on þǣre ceastre cōm ælþeódisc, hié hine genāmon and his eágan ūt āstungon, Bl. H. 229, 10. Of elþeódiscre bargina (v. elþeódig), Wrt. Voc. ii. 12, 13. [*Laym.* alþeodisc.]

**el-þeódlīce ;** *adv. Abroad :*—Ælfþeódlīce *peregre*, Hpt. Gl. 413, 10. v. el-þeódiglīce.

**el-þeódung.** v. el-þeódgung : **el-wiht.** v. æl-wiht *in Dict.:* **emban.** v. ymb : **embe-fær.** v. ymb, ymb-fær *in Dict.:* **embehtian.** v. ambehtan.

**emb-rin.** *Substitute :* embrin (-en), æmbern *an urn :*—Embrin *bothoma* (the m is altered into ni, Corp. Gl. H. 25, 146), Wülck. Gl. 9, 18. Embren *bothoma*, 358, 19. Æmbern *bothonia*, 195, 20. Embrin *balus*, 275, 12. [*Cf. O. H. Ger.* eimberin *urna* ; *bothoma, urna*, i. eimber, E. S. viii. pp. 153, 154.] v. amber.

**emb-stemn.** *Dele, and see* stefn *a turn, in Dict.:* **emdenes.** v. endemes.

**emel.** *Substitute :* es ; *m., and add :*—Emil, æmil *curculio*, Txts. 55, 613 : *gurgulio*, 67, 1003. Emel, Wrt. Voc. ii. 16, 26 : i. 281, 47 : *brucus*, Ps. Srt. 104, 34. Hū Bonefatius āsīgde þā emelas . . . Gemētte hē þone wyrttūn beón oferwrigenne mid micelre menio emela . . . Hē þā bewende hine tō þām emelum (*ad erucas*), Gr. D. 66, 31–67, 11.

**emer.** v. omer *in Dict.:* **emertung,** *l.* smertung. v. smeortung.

**em-leoht, es ;** *n. The incorrect use* (*elision?*) *of* m :*—Emleohtes *motacismi* (=*metacismi*), An. Ox. 5473. Cf. el-leoht.

**emm, es ;** *m. The letter* m. v. *preceding word, and cf.* ell : **em-nettan.** v. efnettan.

**ēnd.** *l.* end *in.* [Cf. *O. Frs.* end, ande *in.*]

**ende.** *Add :* I. *local.* (1) *the extremity* or *outermost part, boundary of space :*—Se mōna went his hrigc tō þǣre sunnan, þ is se sinewealta ende þe þǣr onlýht byð, Lch. iii. 242, 14. Ic wæs āheáwen holtes on ende, Kr. 29. Sǣfæsten landes æt ende, Exod. 128. Wæges æt ende, 466. Æt meres ende, An. 221. On Rōmwara rīces ende ymb þæs wæteres stæð, El. 59. Fram þysse eorðan ende *ab extremo terrae*, Ps. Th. 134, 7. Seó sunne gǣð on ǣfnunge under þyssere eorðan . . . heó eft on ōþerne ende ūp āstīhð, Lch. iii. 240, 17. (1 a) *a limit of magnitude* or *multitude :*—Micelnise his nisse *magnitudinis ejus non est finis*, Ps. Srt. 144, 3. (1 b) *the part of a surface near the boundary :*—Hægcwerde gebyreð þ man his geswinces leán gecnāwe on þām endum ðe tō etenlǣse licgan (*in eam partem segetis que pascuis adjacet*), Ll. Th. i. 440, 13. (2) *a region, quarter, cf. side.* (a) *of the world :*—On feówer endum þyses middangeardes (*per quatuor mundi cardines*) . . . on eásteweardum . . ., Ors. 2, 1 ; S. 58, 31 : Bl. H. 93, 5 : 95, 13. (b) *a district* of a country, especially an official division :—Hē hié on þone bismerlecestan eard gesette, þæt wæron on ðǣm ýtemestan ende his monna foedissima ignominia in exercitu Antigoni dispersi sunt, Ors. 3, 11 ; S. 146, 35. Bidde ic mīne arceð and ealle mīne leóð., þ hý ealle neódfulle beón ymbe Godes gerihta ǣlc on his ende þe heon betǣht is, Cht. E. 230, 15. Hæsten hergode on his rīce þone ilcan ende þe his cumpæðer healdan sceolde, Chr. 894 ; P. 87, 1. Hē cōm intō Afenan mūðan and hergode ofer eall þone ende, 1067 ; P. 203, 12. (c) *a division* of an army :—Hē fōr on þone ende Hannibales folces þe hē self on wæs, Ors.

4. 9; S. 192, 12. Hé beseah tó þǽre swýðran healfe ... and hí tódrifon þone ende, ac him æfter eóde þ óðer gefylce, Hml. S. 25, 669. (d) *quarters* in a building:—Heó is genyrwed on þone ende þe þá gesceádwísan wuniað, Hml. Th. i. 536, 19. (e) in an indefinite sense, *side*, *quarter*:—Beó man georne ymbe seós bóte ǽghwǽr on earde, and ymb burhbóte on ǽghwylcan ende, Ll. Th. i. 310, 23 : 322, 32 : Wlfst. 268, 6. (3) *the extremity* of a line or long object:—Ðá stánas licggeað æt ǽlcre strǽte ende, Past. 133, 9. Hwílum ic on wicge ríde herges on ende, Rä. 78, 8. Ende calcem, Wrt. Voc. ii. 25, 34. Æfter strǽta endum, Past. 135, 3. (3 a) *part of the human body* (?):—Gif nýten sig mannes ende besmiten *si bestia a viro sit polluta*, Ll. Th. ii. 144. 10. (4) *part*, *proportion* (v. *N. E. D.* end, 5 c):—Hé him ánum deádum lytle mildheortnesse gedýde . . . þe hé siþþan nánum ende (*not at all, in no instance*) his cynne gedón nolde, Ors. 3, 9; S. 128, 17. Hé ofslóh mycelne ende þes folces (mycel folc, má þonne .xxx. gódera þegena bútan óðrum folce, *v. ll.*), Chr. 1052; P. 178, 9. II. with reference to time or serial order. (1) *close* of a period, *conclusion* of an action or continuous state or course of events:—Aldres ende, B. 822. Him weorðeð ende lífes, Ph. 365. Ende cymeð dógorrímes, 484. Wuldres ende, An. 1059. Ende nǽfre þínes wræces weorðeð, 1384. Þ wíte þe nǽfre nǽnig ende ne becymeþ, Bl. H. 51, 31. Geseá bútan ende, Hml. Th. i. 460, 19. Á bútan ǽnigum ende, Nar. 49, 19. Þá wæs hyra tíres æt ende, Jud. 272 : Dóm. 2 : Cri. 1030. Is nú ende feor þæt wé sceolun ætsomne súsel þrowian *it is far from the end of the time during which we must suffer together*. i. e. *our sufferings will never end*, Sat. 40. Oð his lífes ende, Chr. 709; P. 41, 35. Þes dæg hæfð ǽlcere wucan frymþe and ende, Bl. H. 133, 6. Gewinnes ende gereccan, Gú. 106. Ðisses eorðweges ende gescrífan, Ps. Th. 118, 87. Oþ ende *in finem*, 102, 9 : 111, 8. Wiþ ende, 67, 16 : 73, 10. (1 a) *the end of* all things:—Beóð fela frecednyssa on mancynne ǽr þan þe se ende becume, Hml. Th. i. 2, 30. Hé eft æt þám ende eallum wealdeð monna cynne, Gn. Ex. 137. (2) *the concluding part* of a period, action, &c.:— On ðínum endum *in novissimis tuis*, Kent. Gl. 707. Endas extrema, 483. (3) *the terminal point* of a series, in phrases expressing completeness:—God is fruma and ende ǽlces gódes, Bt. 80, 10. Cyninga wuldor, fruma and ende (cf. Ego sum α et ω, principium et finis, dicit Dominus Deus, Rev. 1, 8), An. 556. Ic þe secgan wille ór and ende, 649. Ongeat cyning ord and ende þæs þe him ýwed wæs, Dan. 162. From orde oþ ende forð, El. 590. Ór gecýðan oð ende forð, Jul. 353. (4) *termination of existence*:—Ealle þá gewítaþ swá swá wolcn . . . þyllic bið se ende þæs líchoman fægernesse, Bl. H. 59, 21. Ælc fægernes tó ende esfteþ, 57, 28 : 59, 26. Bútan ǽr God ende worulde wyrcan wille, Seel. 13. (4 a) of persons, *death*:—Þurh hwelces monnes hond mín ende wǽre getiód *cujus mortem percussoris manu cauendam habeam*, Nar. 31, 18. Oþ þæt ende becwóm, swylt æfter synnum, B. 1254. Ær þám syxtan dæge his endes (ǽndes, *v. l.*) . . . hé his ende (ǽnde, *-v. l.*) getrymede *ante sextum exitus sui diem . . . exitum suum muniuit*, Gr. D. 175, 14, 18. Hé him æt his ende grim geweorþeð, Bl. H. 25, 13. Hé þær wunode tó his ende, Chr. 633; P. 26, 23. Ær his ende, Shrn. 50, 13. Mon heora líchoman ætsomne ne byrgde at heora ende, 35, 21. (4 b) (*latter, last*) *end*:—þám ýtemestan ende *suprema sorte*, An. Ox. 1990. þæt him feóndes hond æt þám ýtmestan ende ne scóde, Gú. 414. (5) *final state*:—Ic (*the soul*) uncres gedǽles onbád earfoþlíce; nis nú húru se ende tó gód, Seel. 38. (6) *completion* of action, æt ende *finished*:—Swefn wæs æt ende, Dan. 524 : Exod. 267. Eall þ mon untídlíce onginþ, næfþ hit nó ǽltǽwne ende, Bt. 5, 2; F. 10, 28 : Hy. 2, 13. Þus þá æðelingas ende gesealdon *thus those noble ones made end*, Ap. 85. (7) *issue*, *event*:—Hé in eóde þæt hé gesáwe ðone ende, Mt. 26, 58. Hú gelíce onginn þá twá byrg hæfdon . . . ac hiora anwalda endas wǽron swíþe ungelíce *similis Babyloniæ ortus et Romæ . . . tamen non similis exitus similisue defectus*, Ors. 2, 1; S. 64, 5. (8) *end* to be attained, *goal*:—Sege hwelces endes ǽlc angin wilnige . . . Hú mæg þæt beón, nú þú þ angin wást, þ þú eác þone ende nyte, Bt. 5, 3; F. 12, 18, 24, 35. Willniað ealle þurh mistlíce paþas cuman tó ánum ende, þ is þ hí wilniaþ þurh ungelíce earnunga cuman tó ánre eádignesse *omnis mortalium cura diverso quidem calle procedit, sed ad unum tamen beatitudinis finem nititur peruenire*, 24, 1; F. 80, 8. (9) in phrases. (a) æt (þám) ende *in the end, ultimately*:— Æt þám ende ne behéold hit nán þing seó scipfyrding búton folces geswinc, Chr. 999; P. 133, 9. Weard hit fram dæge tó dæge lætre and wyrre swá hit æt þám ende eall geférde, 1066; P. 200, 6. Ǽfre hí æt ende sige áhton, 998; P. 131, 16. Húru æt þám ende ne tweóde þes leánes þe heó lange gyrnde, Jud. 346. (b) in ende *always, to the last*:—Nales in ende *in finem* ofergeotulnis bið ðearfena, Ps. Srt. 9, 19. (c) on (þám) ende *in the end, ultimately*:— þéh þá hláfordas on ðǽm ende hæfdon heánlíce sige, Ors. 2, 6; S. 88, 1. Ðæs ðý wyrse wíte hié sculon habban on ende *gravius quippe extrema ultione feriendi sunt*, Past. 231, 14 : Ps. Th. 58, 12. (d) on ende *continuously, consecutively, without omission or intermission*:— Hit man ǽfre on ende for áne híde werian scolde, C. D. iii. 112, 23 : Ps. Th. 78, 5. Heó eorlum on ende (*to all in succession*) ealuwǽge bær, B. 2021. III. *kind, sort*:—Hé sealde þ betste hors and þæs

fægerestan endes (heówes, híues, eondes, *v. ll.*) Aidane *donauerat equum optimum Aidano*, Bd. 3, 14; Sch. 257, 1. Ne hæfdon wit monig óþer uncýmran hors and óðres endes (eondes, híwes, *v. ll.*) *numquid non habuimus equos uiliores uel alias species*, Sch. 258, 4. v. norþeást-, norþwest-, rihtwest-, súþeást-, úp-, westsuþ-ende.

**ende-byrd**, e; *f.* (*not* es; *n.*). *Add*: (cf. Mid hwilcere endebyrd-nesse Drihten gemetgað ealle gesceafta *quibus immensum legibus orbem natura seruet*, Bt. 25; F. 88, 4.) v. ende-byrdes.

**ende-byrdan**. *Add*: , -byrdian:—þá þe endebyrdiaþ (*ordinant*) gecýðnesse his, Ps. L. 49, 5. Gif hwám þises sealmsanges endebyrdnes mislícaþ, endebyrde (*ordinet*) hé sél, R. Ben. 44, 15. Mynster tó endebyrdienne *ordinandum monasterium*, Bd. 4, 23; Sch. 467, 12. Endebyrde *digesta*, i. *ordinata*, An. Ox. 185. v. ge-endebyrdan (-ian).

**endebyrdend**, es; *m. One who orders* or *arranges*:—Endebyrdend *conditor*, An. Ox. 8, 335 : 7, 351.

**ende-byrdes**. *Substitute for* 'for order' *in order, and for the second passage*:—Ðú þysne middangeard from fruman ǽrest forð oð ende tídum tódǽldes endebyrdes (*in order, in regular succession*; cf. the corresponding prose : Ðú ðe tída fram middaneardes fruman oþ þone ende endebyrdlíce gesettest, Bt. 33, 4; F. 128, 7), Met. 20, 12. v. ende-byrd.

**ende-byrdian**. v. ende-byrdan : **ende-byrdlic**. *Add*:—Endebredlices *originalis* (misread by glosser as *ordinalis*?), Rtl. 109, 27.

**ende-byrdlíce**. *Add*: I. of action, conduct, &c., *in accordance with prescribed* or *requisite order*:—Ðæt is tó tacne ðæt mon endebyrd-líce (-byrð-, *v. l.*) ðone biscepdóm halde, Past. 52, 23. Sé ðe gedafen-líce and endebyrdlíce tó cymð *qui ad regimen ordinate peruenerit*, 75, 1. Ne gelýfe ic nó þ hit geweorþan mihte swá endebyrdlíce *nullo existima-uerim modo, ut fortuita temeritate tam certa moueantur*, Bt. 5, 3; F. 12, 4. Nǽron nó swá gewislíce ne swá endebyrdlíce heora stede and hiora ryne funden on hiora stówum and on hiora tídum *non tam certus naturae ordo procederet, nec tam dispositos motus locis, temporibus explicaret*, 35, 2; F. 158, 2. Sió godcunde foreteohhung welt ǽlces þinges endebyrd-líce, 39, 6; F. 220, 17. Wé sprecað be ðǽre heofonlícan cwéne endebyrdlíce æfter wífháde *we are quite in order in speaking of the heavenly queen as if she were woman*, Hml. Th. i. 546, 14. Ic hohgie swá ændebyrdlíce gedǽlan swá ic ændebyrdlícost mæg (*sapientissime atque cautissime administrare*), Solil. H. 35, 19. II. of narration, where circumstances are given in due order:—Béda þises hálgan líf endebyrdlíce áwrát, Hml. Th. ii. 132, 28. Swíðe endebyrdlíce þú hyt recst, Solil. H. 59, 10. Wé wyllað nú secgan endebyrdlíce be eallum þisum, Ælfc. Gr. Z. 119, 17. v. ge-endebyrdlíce.

**ende-byrdnes** (-bred-, *in Northern specimens*). *Add*: I. *a row*, *series, rank of objects on the same level*:—Ðá xii apostolas and siððan ealle ðá endebyrdnessa ðára biscopa ðe ðæræfter fylgeað *uniuersus pastorum ordo*, Past. 105, 6. Heó hæfð on ǽghwylcum leáfe twá ende-byrdnyssa fægerra pricena, Lch. i. 188, 13. II. *a rank, grade, degree, body of persons of the same status*:—Ǽlc endebyrdnes on mynstre sceal beón gefadod be heora gecyrrednesse, R. Ben. 113, 21. II a. *rank, position, degree*, (1) of persons:—Menn magon on ǽlcere ende-byrdnysse ðám Ælmihtigan gecwéman, Hml. Th. ii. 318, 31. *Quotus* and *totus* gebyriað swýðost tó endebyrdnysse. *Quotus es in ordine monachorum?* hwylcere endebyrdnysse eart ðú betwux munecum? Ic cweþe *secundus uel tertius*, Ælfc. Gr. Z. 117, 15–118, 1. Ná be gebyrdum ánum þis is tó healdenne, ac be ealles mynstres endebyrdnysse, R. Ben. 12, 18. Hé sý onfangen on úteweardre endebyrdnesse *in ultimo gradu recipiatur*, 53, 11. Swá bið on ðisse menniscan gecynde manige on beteran háde and on beteran endebyrdnesse wyrsan, and on wyrsan háde and on wyrsan endebyrdnesse beteran *sic in humano genere et quidam in meliori ordine deteriores sunt, et quidam in deteriori ordine meliores*, Past. 411, 32–34. (2) of things:—Ðæs ðe seó endebyrdnes and ðæt gecynd forwiernð ðæm iacinte, se wlite his beorhtnesse hit eft geíceð, and eft ðeáh ðe ðæt gecynd and sió endebyrdnes ðæs carbuncles hine úp áhebbe, his blioh hine gescent *hyacintho, quod naturae ordo subtrahit, species decoris adjungit, et carbunculum, quem naturalis ordo praetulerat, coloris qualitas foedat*, Past. 411, 29–32. III. *an order, a body of persons of the same occupation in a community*:—On þysre worulde synd þreó endebyrdnysse on ánnysse gesette, þ synd *laboratores, oratores, bellatores*, Hml. S. 25, 813. IV. *a class of beings distinguished from others by nature* or *character*:—þǽr beóð feówer werod . . . þæt forme werod bið þǽra apostola . . . Óðer endebyrd-nys bið geleáffulra woruldmanna . . . Án endebyrdnys bið þǽra wiðer-corenra . . . Óðer endebyrdnys bið þǽra hǽðenra manna, Hml. Th. i. 396, 15–28. Se Drihten þe on engla endebyrdnesse wæs gehered þá hé wæs on Betleem ácenned, Bl. H. 93, 8. V. rank in specific depart-ments. (1) *one of the nine orders of angels*:—Mid þám ix endebyrd-nyssum heofonwara, Wlfst. 183, 16. Uton biddan ðá nigen endebyrd-nessa ðára hálgra engla, Bl. H. 209, 27. (2) *rank in the church*:—Hwæt getácniað ðá stánas ðæs hálgan húses búton ðone hád ðǽre hálgan endebyrdnesse *quid sanctuarii lapidibus nisi sacrorum ordinum personae signantur?*, Past. 133, 17. Preóstas ðe synt þǽre micclan endebyrdnysse þ hí sceolon óðrum mannum ðǽre sýfernysse God

bodian, Hml. A. 146, 60. Cyrclicre endebyrdnysse *ecclesiasticis gradibus*, Guth. 90, 16. Hē weóx on endebyrdnysse (*ordini*), Gr. D. 67, 28. Đā đe đā endebyrdnesse underfóð đæs hálgan hādes *qui ordinem sanctitatis habet*, Past. 31, 11. **VI.** *succession in place or time*. (1) *arrangement in which one thing follows another* :—Gif hwām þises sealmsanges fadung and endebyrdnes mislīcað, R. Ben. 44, 14. Hwilcre endebyrdnesse þā sealmas tō cweþenne sȳn, 6, 25 : 35, 13. Æfter endebyrdnesse *per ordinem*, Bd. 4, 5 ; Sch. 375, 9. Æfter þære endebyrdnesse þe se abbod gestaþelað gange ǣlc æfter óðrum tō cosse, 115, 2. Gesinge hē fīftig sealma be endebyrdnysse (*juxta ordinem*), Ll. Th. ii. 134, 12. Sindon twā bēc gesette on endebyrdnisse tō Salomones bōcum, Ælfc. T. Grn. 8, 41. In endebrednesse *in ordine* (*uicis suae*), Lk. R. L. 1, 8. Hī ealle sceoldan þurh endebyrdnesse be hearpan singan, Bd. 4, 24 ; Sch. 482, 17. (2) *succession* of events :— Mishwyrfedre endebyrdnysse *ordine prepostero*, An. Ox. 4870. Eall þās þing of endebyrdnysse (*ex ordine*) gefyllede wǣron, Bd. 3, 15 ; Sch. 263, 2. (2 a) *course of life* :—Hē him mid sōðe wītegunge his līfes endebyrdnysse sǣde, Hml. Th. ii. 148, 14 : Hml. S. 5, 254. (3) *with reference to narrative or statement in which circumstances are stated in proper order* :—Wit gerehton æfter endebyrdnysse be ealre uncer fōre, Hml. A. 107, 414. Hē þis æfter endebyrdnysse sǣged, 162, 238 : 152, 12. Hē him sǣde his sīð be ændebyrdnysse, 107, 159 : Hml. Th. ii. 486, 4 : Hml. S. 7, 344. Mid endebrednisse āwrīta *ex ordine scribere*, Lk. R. 1, 3. Þurh (be, *v.l.*) endebyrdnesse, Gr. D. 144, 26. (3 a) *a regular narrative, a series of statements* :—Wē oferrǣddon þis godspel for gereccednysse þære godspellican endebyrdnysse . . . nū wille wē eft oferyrnan þā ylcan godspellican endebyrdnysse, Hml. Th. i. 104, 3-8. Nū syndon hit þās dagas swā swā hit hēr on segð. Se forma dæg on Martio . . On Februarius mōnðe se .iiii. dæg . . . Wē gesetton on foreweardan þissere endebyrdnesse Martius, Lch. iii. 152, 8-31. Wē nymað of þām bōcum þās endebyrdnysse þe Mōyses āwrāt, Ælfc. T. Grn. 3, 13. Wē habbað nū miccle māran endebyrdnysse þære Crīstes bēc gesǣd þonne ðis dægðerlice godspel behæfð *we have mentioned many more circumstances than are contained in the gospel for the day*, Hml. Th. i. 220, 24. (4) *where superiority is marked by position, order* ; *place* in a series or company :— On nānum stōwum ne sȳ endebyrdnes be nānre ylde gefadod . . . Būtan þām ānum þe of hyra endebyrdnysse ūtor āscofene synd, oðþe innor genumene, ǣlc ōþer healde his endebyrdnesse, R. Ben. 115, 5-11. Ne stande hē on his stede and endebyrdnesse, ac stande hē ealra ȳtemest, 68, 10. Wē tōgædere cōman and æfter endebyrdnesse (*juxta ordinem*) ætsomne sǣton, Bd. 4, 5 ; Sch. 374, 15. **VII.** *order, condition in which a thing performs its proper functions* :—Ic ongite þ ealle gesceafta tōhleówon swā swā wæter, and nāne sibbe ne nāne endebyrdnesse ne heóldon, Bt. 34, 12 ; F. 154, 3 : 39, 5 ; F. 218, 15. **VIII.** *order, suitable means to attain an end, method* :—On hwylcere endebyrdnysse magon wē Jōseph tō ūs geladian and hym wyþ sprecan *by what means shall we bring Joseph to us to speak with him*? (Nic. H. 11, 7), Nic. 10, 3. **IX.** *regular mode of procedure* :—Sē ðe eall gefyllan mæg þ on þǣre bēc gecweden is, þ biþ swȳðe gōd, and hit bið riht endebyrdnys (*rectus ordo*), Ll. Th. ii. 134, 11. Þæt hī dæghwomlīce Godes þēnunge mid þæslīcere endebyrdnysse gefyldon, Hml. Th. i. 588, 29. Mid gelimplicre endebyrdnesse, Bl. H. 207, 33. Þā gefadunge þe snotorlīce geset is be incūþra þinga endebyrdnysse *the disposition which is prudently appointed concerning procedure in the case of strange matters*, Lch. iii. 440, 26. Hē rihte endebyrdnesse līfes (*rectum uiuendi ordinem*) ætȳwde, Bd. 4, 2 ; Sch. 344, 2. Hī Gode lāc brōhton . . . and on heora yldrena endebyrdnysse Gode gecwēmdon. Nū is gemēted þæt Maria hæfð nīwe endebyrdnysse ongunnon Gode mid tō gecwēmanne, cweð þæt heó wile hire mægðhād bringan, Hml. A. 129, 442-130, 449. **IX a.** *a stated form of a rite, order of service* :—Þā gefullode hine mon on ðǣre ciricean endebyrdnesse, Bl. H. 215, 35 : 213, 14. **X.** *order* of nature, *system in which things proceed according to fixed laws* :—Ðāra unstillan gesceafta styring ne mæg nō weorþan onwend of ðām ryne and of þǣre endebyrdnesse þe him geset is, Bt. 21 ; F. 74, 5. Hī ne mōton tōslūpan of heora endebyrdnesse, 39, 5 ; F. 218, 32. Hē gesceóp englas and heáhenglas and ealle heofenlīce miht and endebyrdnysse, Wlfst. 293, 11. **XI.** *the action of putting* or *keeping in order, regulation, ordering* :—Hī sylfe ealdras geworhton on swylcere fadunge and endebyrdnesse. . . . Eal mynstres fadung and endebyrdness on þæs abbodes dōme stande, R. Ben. 125, 4-8. Mid hwilcere endebyrdnesse hē gestaþolaþ and gemetgað ealle gesceafta *quibus legibus orbem servet*, Bt. 25 ; F. 88, 4. Þte middangeardes erning sibsum ūs dīnum endebrednisse sié gerihtad *ut mundi cursus pacificus nobis tuo ordine dignatur*, Rtl. 39, 9. **XII.** *an injunction, ordinance* :—Ūs is tō understandenne ðās endebyrdnyssa, Hml. S. 16, 228. v. riht-, tō-endebyrdnes.

endebyrdnian. v. ge-endebrednian in Dict.

ende-dæg. *Substitute: The day when the end comes.* (1) cf. ende, II. 1 :—Ðā wæs endedæg ðæs ðe Caldēas cyningdōm āhton *then the power of the Chaldeans was at an end*, Dan. 679. (2) *þæt se gūðcyning*

swealt, B. 3035. Him wearð bām samod ān endedæg *they died together the same day*, Ap. 79. Æfre hē him gehende endedæges wēne *let him ever think his last day at hand*, Wlfst. 75, 9. Hit nū swīþe neálǣceþ ūrum endedæge, Bl. H. 51, 35. Heó becōm tō hire ændedæge (ende-, *v. l.*) *ad diem pervenit extremum*, Gr. D. 286, 17. Þrīm dagum ǣr his endedæge, Shrn. 134, 19. Hē þæt wunode oþ his endedæg (*to his dying day*), Chr. 688 ; P. 41, 6. Hwelcne endedæg mīn mōdor oþðe mīn geswuster gebīdan sceoldon *quem exitum mater mea sororesque mee habituri sint*, Nar. 31, 19. Ic gefremman sceal eorlic ellen oððe endedæg mīnne gebīdan *I will do or die*, B. 637. (3) *the last day*, cf. ende, II. 1 a :—Ne lǣt lāðe cwellan and bærnan sāwla ūre . . . ne lǣt swā heánlīce þīn handgeweorc on endedæge forwurðan, Hy. 7, 112. [*v. N.E.D.* end-day. Cf. *O. H. Ger.* endi-dago *the last day*.] Cf. ende-dōgor.

ende-deáþ. *Substitute: Death that is the end of life. Perhaps however the passage should read* :—Līf būtan deáþe or līf būtan ende ; *either form would suit the metre better, and* (*the former especially*) *would be parallel with the contrasts that follow*, gioguð būtan ylde, hǣlu būtan sāre, &c.

ende-fæstend, es ; *m.* *One who puts the last touches to a work, a finisher* :—On wyrhte gileáfes and endefæstend *in auctorem fidei et consummatorem* (Heb. 12, 2), Rtl. 27, 29.

ende-furh *an end-furrow, bounding trench* :—Inn on ðære endefureh ; of ðēre endefureh, C. D. iii. 384, 18.

ende-leás. *Add* :—Hwæþer þe ēce līf and ēce blisse, þe ēcne deáþ and endeleáse yrmðe, Wlfst. 23, 20. Ðerh endeleáso uoruldo *per infinita saecula*, Rtl 180, 3.

endeleás-lic ; *adj.* *Endless, everlasting* :—Heora yfel is egeslic and endeleáslic morð, Hml. S. 17, 154. v. next word.

endeleáslīce. *Add* : (1) *everlastingly, to eternity* :—Gē beóð engla gefēran endeleáslīce, Hml. Th. ii. 90, 1. Þā mānfullan beóð ǣfre cwylmigende on helle sūsle endeleáslīce, 608, 11. Endeleáslīce losian, Hex. 22, 12. Endeleáslīce orsorh beón on gefeán, 52, 9. (2) *without making an end, without stopping* :—Ortrūwige sē āna ðe endeleáslīce syngað, and ǣr his endenēxtan dæge dǣdbōte ne gewyrcð, Hml. Th. ii. 316, 30.

ende-mǣst. v. endemestnes.

ende-mann, es ; *m.* *A person living in the latest age of the world* :—Wē endemenn ðyssere worulde (*for the ideas of the time as to the end of the world* cf. Wlfst. 156, 4 : Ðeós woruld is on ofste and hit neálǣcð þām ende), Hml. Th. i. 476, 18. Fela hālige menn fram frymðe middaneardes wǣron beforan ūs, þām wē nū endemenn geefenlǣcan ne magon, Hml. S. 12, 281.

ende-mes. *Add:* , emdenes, emdemes. **I.** *together.* (1) in respect to quantity or number, marking completeness, *without exception* :—His efencempan hine endemes wurðodon (cf. *the rendering of the same in* Hml. S. 31, 49 : His efencempan ealle hine ārwurðodon), Hml. Th. ii. 500, 16. Wearð gefullod se cnapa and his fæder cempan endemes, Hml. S. 4, 239. (1 a) *combined with* eall :—Ic ne mæg eal þā monigfealdan yfel emdenes (*altered to* endemes) ārecceau, Ors. 2, 5 ; S. 86, 15. Seó swearcigende sunne and ðā gesceafta ealne middaneard endemes āðeóstrodon, Hml. Th. ii. 258, 16. Hī ealne middaneard onlīhton, swā swā þā feówer eán ealne þisne embhwyrft endemes wæteriað, Hml. S. 15, 177. God ealne þone eard endemes tōwende and ealle þā burhwara forbærnde ætgædere *Dominus subvertit omnem circa regionem, universos habitatores urbium*, Gen. 19, 25. Ealle heora bigleofan endemes hī ætbrūdon *nihil omnino ad vitam pertinens relinquebant*, Jud. 6, 4 : Lch. iii. 236, 13 : 242, 5. Hī ealle endemes ūt fērdon swā þ furðon ān ne belāf *ita omnes egressae sunt, ut ne una quidem remaneret*, Gr. D. 67, 16. Nǣron hī ealle endemes ungeleáffulle, Hml. Th. i. 108, 25. þæt hit eal ne forwurde endemes ætgædere, Wlfst. 86, 1 : 198, 10. Hȳ forwyrndon ealle tōgædere endemes, Cht. E. 299, 1. (2) *marking combination, coincidence* :—þā hié swā monega gewin hæfdon emdenes underfongen *eo tempore quo tria bella fuerunt suscepta*, Ors. 4, 9 ; S. 192, 29. Þā Israhēla bearn endemes hrīmdon, Num. 13, 31. Sceamien hȳ heora and him eác ondrǣdon ǣgðer endemes *erubescant pudore et revereantur simul*, Ps. Th. 34, 24 : 39, 16. (2 a) *combined with* eall :— Hī hīwe fleóð ealle endemes (*omnes simul*), Ps. Th. 13, 4 : Hml. S. 18, 96 : 32, 142 : Hml. Th. i. 70, 26 : ii. 516, 13. Þā ōþre ealle endemes (-mest, *v. l.*) fērdon āweg, Hml. S. 5, 345 : Bt. 37, 2 ; F. 188, 10. Hī ealle eódon endemes tō cyrcan, Hml. S. 21, 226. Hī forlēton ealle endemes þone sang, 234. Eall seó meniu endemes weóp sōna, Num. 14, 1 : Hml. Th. ii. 516, 18. Se ælmihtega waldend his āgen weorc eall geondwlīteð, endemes þurhsyhð ealle gesceafta *omnia uno mentis cernit in ictu* . . . *respicit omnia solus*, Met. 30, 16. Ændemest, Bt. 41, 1 ; F. 244, 12. Hī ealle sceoldon endemes forwurðan, Hml. S. 13, 278. Hī him ondrǣdan hū hī wið him eallum emdemes mehten, and siredon hū hī hié tōtwǣman mehten, Ors. 3, 10 ; S. 138, 6. **II.** *straightway, at once* :—þæt folc eall hrȳmde, þā burston þā weallas endemes tō grunde *omni populo vociferante muri illico corruerunt*, Jos. 6, 20. Þonne hig ūt farað tō ūs, wē fleóð endemes, 8, 6. Cumað endemes tō mē gē ealle þe swincað *venite ad me omnes qui laboratis*, Hml. A. 10, 244. Hī cēpton hwǣr hē mæssode, and urnon endemes tō,

and hine gelæhton, Hml. S. 15, 62.     III. *in like manner :*—Ne tódǽl ðu on tó fela ðin mód, and ðin weorc endemes, Past. 37, 17.

**endemestness.** *Substitute :* **endemest-ness** (? ende-nēhstness) *extremity :*—Æftergencnysse oððe endemestnesse (-nēst-?) *extremitate*, R. Ben. I. 33, 15. v. next word.

**ende-nēhst.** *Add :*   I. *of place, most remote :*—On eallum middangearde oð þæt endenēxte land, Hml. Th. i. 294, 28.     II. *of number, order, last :*—Módignys is endenēxt gesett on getele ðæra heáfodleahtra, Hml. Th. ii. 222, 3.   Ǽr ðan þe þu forgelde þone endenēxtan feórðling (*novissimum quadrantem*, Mt. 5, 26, *where* R. *has* þone nǽhstu feórþan dǽl), Hml. A. 4, 100.     III. *of rank, position, degree, last, lowest :*—þeáh ðe hē endenēxt on Godes ríce sȳ geendebyrd, Hml. Th. ii. 82, 2.     IV. *of time.* (1) *last, final :*—þes tíma is endenēxt and ende þyssere worulde, Hml. S. 13, 294. Se endenēxta dæg þises andweardan lífes, Hml. A. 53, 85. þæt endenēcste gelimp *supprema* (*ultima*) *sors*, An. Ox. 1834. Sum hláford becóm tó his endeniéxtan dæge, Gr. D. 88, 7. þā þe nellað Gode lybban oð heora endenēxtan ylde, hī standað ȳdele oð ðā endenēxtan tíde, Hml. Th. ii. 78, 9. On þám endenȳhstan dagum þissere worulde *in novissimis diebus*, Wlfst. 81, 11. On heora ǽndenȳhstum, Ps. L. 72, 17. Onsóh þás endenēhstan lác þínes láreówes, Hml. S. 6, 76. (2) *latest, most recent :*—Oð þ hit becóm tó ús endenēxtum mannum, Hml. A. 5, 117.

**ende-spǽc.** *Substitute :* **ende-sprǽc, -spǽc,** e ; *f. An epilogue :*—þysse lyttlan bóce endespǽce *hujus libelluli epilogum*, Angl. xiii. 447, 1166.

**ende-stæf.** *Substitute :* *An end, conclusion :* especially with reference to the end of life ; *death* (violent or natural) :—Endestaeb *exito, perditio*, Wrt. Voc. ii. 107, 57. Endestæf *exito*, 29, 65. *Exitus, finis, effectus, terminus, egressus* útgong, endestæf, 144, 83. Endestæf *exterum*, 32, 51. Se endestæf earfeðmæcgum weálic weorðeð, Vy. 11. Hyre endestæf weordan sceolde, líf ālȳsed, Jul. 610. þú for his deáþe plegodest, and þú ús æt endestæfe mycel herereáf gehéte, Bl. H. 85, 19. Hit on endestæf eft gelimpeð þæt se líchoma lǽne gedreóseð, B. 1753. Him þæt gehreówan mæg, þonne heó endestæf eft gesceáwiað, Sat. 541. Hæfdon hī on rímcræfte āwriten wera endestæf *they had written down the date of men's death*, An. 135.

**ende-prēst,** e ; *f. An end, destruction :*—Heó þrowað deáð bútan deáþe and āsprungennesse and ændeþrēste bútan ænde þæs wítes *mortem sine morte, et defectum sine defectu, et finem sine fine patitur*, Gr. D. 337, 9.

**ende-tíma,** an ; *m. Last day, last hour :*—Ne geþristlǽce hē þ hē Drihtenes líchaman underfó ǽr his endetíman (*ante diem suum extremum*), Ll. Th. ii. 268, 25. On úrum endetíman, Btwk. 220, 37.

**endian.** *Add :* I. *to make an end of, to complete, finish :*—Hǽlo ic endigo *sanitates perficio*, Lk. L. 13, 32. Endað *terminat*, Kent. Gl. 986. Tó endanne ł sié endade *consummari*, Mk. R. 13, 4. Hē his líf wæs endiende, Bd. 5, 19 ; Sch. 654, 4. Endedre *finito*, v. l. expleto, An. Ox. 1336.     II. *to come to an end :*—Hér endaþ seó æftre fróferbóc, Bt. 21 ; F. 76, 2 : 35, 6 ; F. 170, 23. On heora endunge þonne hié endiaþ, 16, 3 ; F. 56, 26. Ðā beorgas endiað æt þǽm sǽ, Ors. I, I ; S. 22, 20. þes middangeard on ðás eldo endian sceal þe nú andweard is, Bl. H. 117, 35 : 119, 1. [*O. Sax.* endôn, -iôn : *O. Frs.* endia : *Icel.* enda.]

**endigend-líc, endod-líc.** v. un-geendigendlic, un-geendodlic.

**endleofan.** *Add :*—Endleofan (-leofon, -lufan, -lufon, *v. ll.*) *undecim*, Ælfc. Gr. Z. 281, 10. (1) adjectival :—Ðā férdon þá endlufun (-leofen, *v. l.* ; ællefno, L., þá enleftan his, R.) leorningcnihtas, Mt. 28, 16. Endleofon daga færeld, Deut. 1, 2. Endleofan síþum hundteóntig þúsenda, Bl. H. 79, 19. (2) substantival :—Hig cýddon eall þis þám endlufenum (-leof-, *v. l.* ; ællefnum, L. R.), Lk. 24, 9. Hig gemétton endlufan (-leofen, *v. l.* ; ællefno, L., ællefne, R.) gegaderude, 33.

**endleofan-gilde ;** *adj. Entitled to elevenfold compensation :*—Is arcebiscopes feoh endlifangilde, Ll. Th. i. 330, 19. Biscopes feoh .xi. gylde, 2. 4.

**endlyfta.** *Add :*—Se endleofta (-lyfta, *v. l.*) *undecimus*, Ælfc. Gr. Z. 282, 19. Sió endlefte tíd dæges, Nar. 11, 16. On þám endleoftan dæge Crístes úpstiges, Hml. Th. i. 298, 5. Embe þá endlyftan (ællefta, L. R.) tíde, Mt. 20, 6 : Bl. H. 93, 6.

**-endu.** v. ears-endu.

**endung.** *Add :*—Swā hwæt swā þe on eáge byreð æfter tíde cymð seó endung (*fulfilment*), Lch. iii. 154, 22. Neár worulde endunge, Past. 213, 6. On endunge *in consummatione*, Ps. L. 58, 14. On heora endunge þonne hié endiaþ, Bt. 16, 3 ; F. 56, 26. From endung *a perfeccione*, Lk. p. 2, 15. Æt þæs godspelles endunge *qua perlecta*, R. Ben. 35, 21.

**ened.** *Add :*—Enid, aenid, aenit ane*t*a, Txts. 41, 158. *Aneta* æned, *vel anax* (= *anas*?) æned (*perhaps from a misreading of this or a similar gloss comes the* larax *in the following :*—*Anatis* ened, *aneta* ened, *larax* ened, 280, 7–9. Ened larax, ii. 51, 58), Wrt. Voc. i. 62, 8, 9. Fuglas þá þe heard fiæsc habbað, pāwa, swan, æned, Lch. ii. 196, 20. On eneda wylle, C. D. B. iii. 203, I. ¶ *in local names :*—Tó ænedwille, C. D. v. 179, 36. Tó enedforda, 216, 35. [*v. N. E. D.* ende.] v. dop-ened.

**engan.** v. ge-engan.

**enge.** *Add :*   I. *narrow, confined :*—þes ænga stede (*hell*), Gen. 356. Se Hǽlend mē in þám engan hám getȳnde, El. 921.     II. *painful, grievous, cruel :*—Se enga deáð *mors crudelis*, Ph. 52. Under enge treówe *sub ipso stipite*, Germ. 395, 24. Nearusorge dreáh, enge rúne, El. 1262.

**engel.** *Add :*—Encgel *angelus vel nuntius*, Wrt. Voc. i. 41, 51 : Lk. L. 22, 43. Se angel, 1, 30. Sum swíðe fæger æncgel, H. R. 3, 18. Ðurh ðone ængel (engel, *v. l.*), Past. 69, 10.

**engel-líc.** *Add :*—Hē þone apostol on engellicre fægernysse geseah, Guth. 28, 27. Of engcellicre sprǽce, 72, 11. Hí wurdon betǽhte engellicum bósmum, Hml. Th. i. 84, 9. Tó engelicum sprǽcum, 544, 31. Engellicum, Guth. 86, 8. Engcellice sangas hē gehȳrde, 88, 14.

**Engla land.** *Add :*   II. *England, the country occupied by the Teutonic invaders of Britain :*—Ic Eádwerd cyng and Engla landes wealdend, C. D. iv. 232, 3. Eall Engla landes ríce, West-Seaxan, Eást-Englan, Myrcean, and Norþhymbran, Chr. 1017 ; P. 154, 2. Hér cóm Augustinus and his geféran tó Engla lande, 597 ; P. 20, 35. Hér Landfranc cóm tó Ængla lande, 1070 ; P. 204, 1. Willelm gewann Ængla land, 1066 ; P. 196, 1. Cf. Angel-cynn.

**Engle.** *Add :*   I. *Angles in contrast with Saxons :*—þanon Engle (Ongle, *v. l.*) and Seaxan cumene wǽron þe nú on Breotone eardiað, Bd. 5, 9 ; Sch. 590, 5. Siþþan Engle and Seaxe Brytene sóhtan, Chr. 937 ; P. 110, 4. Englum and Sæxum, 1065 ; P. 193, 34.     II. *the English :*—Engle (Myrce and West-Seaxe, *v. l.*) and Dene gefuhton, Chr. 910 ; P. 94, 33. Dene and Engle wurdon sammǽle, 1018 ; P. 155, 14. þá Normen wurdon on fleáme, and þá Engliscan hí hindan slógon . . . þ þǽr wæs lyt tó láfe, and Engle āhton wælstówe geweald, 1066 ; P. 199, 17. þá wyrte Rómāne *astula regia* nemnað, and Ængle (*v. l.* Engle: cf. Angle, 152, 21) wudurofe hātað, Lch. i. 156, 11. Eádgar, Engla cyning (Angla reccent, *v. l.*), Chr. 975 ; P. 118, 27. Eádward, Engla (Englene, *v. l.*) hláford, 1065 ; P. 192, 26. Engla waldend, 973 ; P. 118, 5. Eádmund, Engla þeóden, 942 ; P. 110, 12. Engla þeód, 596 ; P. 21, 17. Hē ealle Engla þeóde gesamnade, 1016 ; P. 150, 19. Ængla þeód, Shrn. 94, 2. Eall Engla here, 1056 ; P. 186, 33. v. Eást-, Norþ-, Súþ-Engle.

**Englisc.** *Add :*   I. adjectival :—þǽr ādranc mycel Ænglisces folces, Chr. 1016 ; P. 151, 18. On Engliscre sprǽce, H. R. 105, 10. In Englisc gereorde (on Englisce reorde, *v. l.*) *in lingua Anglorum*, Bd. 4, 24 ; Sch. 481, 12. Ǽr wǽrun Rómānisce biscepas, siþþan wǽrun Englisce, Chr. 690 ; P. 40, 11. Eall þæt folc on Mercna lande geseten, ægþer ge Denisc ge Englisce, 922 ; P. 104, 5. Ǽlc man . . . Frencisce and Englisce, 1087 ; P. 224, 34. Ǽrost Engliscra cininga Ercenbriht gesette Eástorfæsten, 639 ; P. 27, 18. Ealra monna, Fresiscra and Engliscra, 897 ; P. 91, 11.     II. substantival. (1) of persons, (*the*) *English :*—Ealle þá þe on Norþhymbrum búgeaþ, ægþer ge Englisce ge Denisce ge Norþmen, Chr. 924 ; P. 104, 20. þá Normen wurdon on fleáme, and þá Engliscan hí hindan slógon, 1066 ; P. 199, 15. Twā mynstro, óðer þám Scottum, óðer ðām Engliscan (*Anglis*), Bd. 4, 4 ; Sch. 367, 19. (2) Englisc, es ; *n. the English language :*—þ Léden and þ Englisc nabbaþ nā āne wísan. Ǽfre sé þe āwent of Lédene on Englisc, ǽfre hē sceal gefadian hit swā þ þ Englisc hæbbe his āgene wísan, elles hit biþ swiþe gedwolsum tó rǽdenne þám þe þæs Lédenes ne can, Ælfc. Pref Thw. 4, 7–11. (2 a) *English form* of a word :—Ealle ðás (*et, que, ac, ast, at, atque*) habbað ān Englisc (i. e. and), þeáh ðe hí tor fægernysse fela synd on Lédensprǽce, Ælfc. Gr. Z. 295, 12.

**eno.** v. heonu.

**ent.** *Add :*—þone swȳþlican ent Goliam, Hml. S. 18, 18. Hí worhton him anlícnyssa, and sceópon him naman, þǽra manna naman þe wǽron entas and yfeldǽde, Hml. Th. i. 22, 31 : 366, 21. Nembroð and ðā entas worhton þone wundorlican stȳpel, Wlfst. 105, 3. Enta *cyclopum*, An. Ox. 23, 16. On hlǽwe hord, eald enta geweorc, B. 2774. ¶ in local names :—Ænta díc, C. D. iv. 34 11. On enta (entan, *v.* 265, 20) hlǽwe, 49, 4. [Cf. *O. H. Ger.* Anzo, Enzo, Enziwíb, *and see* Grmm. D. M. s.v. ent.]

**eodorcan.** *Add :* v. ed-reccan.

**eofole** (?), an ; *f. A plant-name :*—Twā snāda eofolan (*but cf. the same recipe in* Lch. ii. 324, 20 :—ii. snǽda elenan. *See, however :*—Ebule ł eobulum wealwyrt ł elenwyrt, iii. 302, Col. 1), Lch. iii. 28, 27.

**eofor.** *Add :* I :—Eobor *aper*, Wrt. Voc. ii. 100, 43. Eofur, Ps. Srt. 79, 14. Genim eoferes blǽdran, Lch. i. 360, 4. Eoferes tuxas *aprorum dentes*, Nar. 34, 31. Eofor *aprum*, Wrt. Voc. ii. 94, 33.     II :—Hē hēt in beran eafor, heáfodsegn, B. 2152. ¶ in local names. Efer-bróc, Eferæs cumb, Efer-dún, Eofor-sol, C. D. vi. 284, 285.

**eofor-fearn.** *Add :*—Eoforfearn *filix minuta*, Wrt. Voc. ii. 38, 76 : *filicina*, 39, 1 : *radiolum*, i. 68, 30.

**eofor-hwæt ;** *adj. Bold as a boar :*—Eoforhuaet (*a proper name*), Txts. 160, 1.

**eofor-spere,** es ; *n. A boar-spear :*—Eofursperum *venabulis*, An. Ox. 7, 56. Cf. bār-spere.

**eofor-spreót.** *For* Cot. 200 *substitute :*—Eoborspreót (ebor-) *vena-*

*bula*, Txts. 105, 2089. Eoforspreótum (cf. eofursputum, Angl. xiii. 29, 40) *venabulis*, Wrt. Voc. ii. 76, 44. [Cf. *O. H. Ger.* ebar-spioz *lata hasta*.]

**eofor-þring.** *Add:*—Eburðring *orion*, Txts. 83, 1464.

**eofor-þrote.** *Add:*—Eoburþrote, aebordrotae *colicum*, Txts. 53, 558. Eborðrote, -throtae *scasa*, 95, 1816. Eoforþrote *scisca*, 35, 27. Eoforðrote *colicus*, Wrt. Voc. ii. 15, 8.

**Eofor-wíc.** *Add:*—Hér forbarn Eoferwíc, Chr. 741; P. 45, 32. Of Eoferwíc, 774; P. 51, 28: 1075; P. 201, 23. Tó Eoferwíc, 1041; P. 163, 27: 1068; P. 202, 6. Tó Eoforwíc weard, 1016; P. 148, 4: 1066; P. 196, 27. Hér Regnold gewan Eoforwíc (Eofer-, *v. l.*), 923; P. 105, 12. Heoforwíc, 948; P. 112, 30. [*Icel.* iór-vík.]

**Eoforwíc-ceaster.** *Add:*—On Eoforwícceastre *apud Eboracum oppidum*, Bd. 1, 5; Sch. 17, 23. On Eoforwícceastre (Eofer-, *v. l.*) *Eburaci*, 2, 14; Sch. 170, 5: Chr. 738; P. 44, 20. Tó Eoforwícceastre, 867; P. 68, 17: 869; P. 70, 3. Æt Eoforwícceastre (Eofer-; on Eoforwíc, *v. ll.*), 867; P. 68, 23. Fram Eoforwícceastre *ab Eburaco*, Bd. 2, 13; Sch. 169, 11.

**Eoforwíc-scír.** *Add:*—Eádweard cyng grét Tostig eorl and ealle míne þegenas on Eoferwícscíre, C. D. vi. 203, 22.

**Eoforwíc-stól**, es; *m. The see of York:*—Féng Ealdulf abb of Burch tó Eoferwícstóle, Chr. 992; P. 127, 21.

**eofot.** *Dele ' debt ' (the various readings to the passage from the Laws are:* Be cynincges geréfan þýfðe, be þeófes andettan, *and* þeófðe *for* eofot), *and add :*—Flítere in eobotum (in ebhatis, *v. l.*) *rabulus*, Txts. 93, 1705. [*O. L. Ger.* (Gall.) efat *epiphonima, causa*.] [*From* ef-hát.]

**eoful-sæc.** *Add:* Cf. yfel-sacian, -sacung: eofulsian, eofulsung. [*From* ef-hálsian, ef-hálsung.] v. yfelsian, yfelsung: eógor. v. ægor: **eoh-bígenga.** v. feoh-bígenga: eóla. v. eolh: eolene. v. eolone.

**eolh.** *Substitute:* eolh; *gen.* eóles; eóla, elha, an; *m. An elk:*—Elh, elch *cer(u)us*, Txts. 49, 443. Elch *tragelafus vel platocerus*, 100, 1001. Elha *damma*, 115, 139. Eóla *damma, bestia*, Wrt. Voc. ii. 105, 73. On elchene seáð, C. D. iii. 440, 28. [*O. H. Ger.* elaho, elch *tragelaphus, alx*. Cf. *Icel.* elgr.]

**eolh-sand.** *For* Cot. 75 *substitute :*—Eolhsandes *electri*, Wrt. Voc. ii. 77, 25: 31, 4. Eolcsandes, An. Ox. 1071.

**eolhx.** *Substitute:* eolh-secg, es; *m. Some kind of sedge :*—Eolxsecg *papilluum*, Wrt. Voc. i. 286, 36. (*See other instances under* secg, *and* v. Lch. iii. 324.) ¶ the word occurs as the name of a rune :—Eolx-secg eard hæfð oftust on fenne, wundað grimme beorna gehwylcne þe him ænigne onfeng gedéð, Rún. 15. See Wimmer, Runenschrift, p. 132.

**eolone.** *Add:*—Eolone, elonae *oridanum*, Txts. 83, 1453: *inola*, Wrt. Voc. ii. 45, 47: *innula*, i. 67, 44: *orianthum*, 68, 21. Eolene *inola*, Txts. 69, 1057: *ybys*, Germ. 394, 258. Elone *horidanum*, Wrt. Voc. i. 286, 21. Elene, il. 43, 18: 63, 48: *inula* (*mula*, MS.), 59, 41.

**eom.** *Add:*—Hú ne iom ic monn suá ilce suá ðú ?, Past. 115, 12.

**eonu.** v. heonu.

**eorcnan-stán.** *Add:* I. literal, *a jewel, topaz, pearl :*—Ofer gold and þone baswon stán (gymcynn *l* eorcnanstán, MS. C.) *super aurum et topazion*, Ps. Spl. 118, 127. Gelíc is ríce heofunas menn ceápe sóhte góde ercnanstánas (*margaritas*). And gemoetend þá ænne ercnastán (*margaritam*) diórwyrðe, Mt. R. 13, 45, 46. Goldes and eorcnanstáne (-a?) micel gemet *auri margaritarumque non paruam praedam*, Nar. 6, 32. His brýdbúras wæron eorcnanstánum unionibus and carbunculis þæm gimcynnum swíðast gefrætwode *talami margaritis unionibusque et carbunculis nitebant*, 5, 3. II. figurative. (1) of persons :— Cwæþ úre Drihten tó þære eádigan Marian líchoman, ' Ne forláte ic þé næfre, mín meregrot, ne ic þé næfre ne forláte, mín eorclanstán,' Bl. H. 149, 3. (2) of things :—Ne geweorpaþ ercnanstánas (*margaritas*) eówre beforan swínum, Mt. R. 7, 6. [See Grmm. D. M. (trans.) p. 1217.]

**eóred.** *Add:* f.:—Eóred ðín *equitatus tuus*, Ps. Srt. ii. p. 190, 1. *Equitatus* ferdwerod *vel* eóred, gerid, i. *equitatio*, Wrt. Voc. ii. 143, 72. Án eórod (*legion*) is on bócum geteald tó six ðúsendum, Hml. Th. ii. 378, 29. Wæs án synderlic eórod . . . Án eórod is gecweden on ðám ealdan getcle six ðúsend manna and six hund and six and syxtig; swá sela manna wæron on þám foresædan eórode . . . þá gewende seó eórod, Hml. S. 28, 9–30. Hé arn betwux þám eórode middan oð þæt he tó þám ylfe cóm, 25, 583. Eóroda *legionum*, Hpt. Gl. 413, 2. Yroda, An. Ox. 11, 24. Eórodum *equitatum*, Wrt. Voc. ii. 31, 40 : *cohortibus*, An. Ox. 279. ¶ *a chariot?* cf. eóred-mann, ¶ :—Twá þúsenda horsa and cccc. búton þæm eóreda and xx. þúsenda féþena (*the Latin which this should translate is:* Quadringente quadrige equorum omnes falcate. bige ii mille . ducente equitum turme . xx milia peditum. *The numeral seems to connect* eóreda *with* quadrige, *but the meaning of* eóred *elsewhere with* equitum turme), Nar. 9, 8. [*From* eoh-rád.]

**eóred-heáp**, es; *m. A troop, host :*—Þonne cumað upplice eóred-heápas, stíþmægen ástyred *tum superum subito veniet commota potestas*, Dóm. L. 113.

**eóred-mann.** *Add:*—Áfýred olbenda *dromidus*, se eórodmon (orit-) *dromidarius*, Txts. 57, 708. Eóredmen *Cerethei*, foreirnerum *Feletei* (*Pelethi*, Ald.), Wrt. Voc. ii. 76, 51. Eóredmen, rædehere *Cerethi*, 15, 76. (*In the gloss to the same passage in* An. Ox. *the renderings are transposed :*—) Hleáperes, rædehere *Cerethi*, eóredmen, féþeheres *Felethi*, An. Ox. 776. Tuu and ðrittih eóredmonna *xxxii equites*, Jn. 18, 12 margin. Hét ic þá hors gerwan and eóredmen hleápan úp *imperaui equitibus ut ascenderent equos*, Nar. 21, 22. ¶ *a man riding in a chariot?* cf. eóred, ¶ :—Sixténe þúsend monna and eahta hund eóred-manna ealle mid heregeatwum gegerede *xvi milia equitum, octingente quadrige, omnes falcate*, Nar. 4, 13.

**eóred-menigu** *a legion :*—Micel eóredmeniu (deófla) *legio*, Gr. D. 73, 33. Þone ormætan truman þára deófla eóredmenigeo (þ weorod þára deófla mænigeo, *v.l.*) *legionis aciem*, 74, 21.

**eóred-weorod.** *Substitute for citation :*—Swá þ hé þára deófla eóredweredu (weoredu, *v.l.*) ádræfde *ita ut legiones daemonum pelleret*, Gr. D. 71, 6.

**eorl.** *Add:* I. *a man of rank* or *gentle birth :*—Eorl *herus*, An. Ox. 53, 6. Weorðscipes wyrðe, ælc be his mæðe, eorl and ceorl, þegen and þeóden, Ll. Th. i. 190, 13. Gif wið eorles birele man geliged .xii. scill. gebéte. Gif wið ceorles birelan man geliged .vi. scillingum gebéte, 6, 11. Þræl weorð tó þegene, and ceorl weorð tó eorle, 334, 8. II. used of Scandinavians, = *Icel.* jarl:—Ælfred gefeaht wiþ þára eorla getruman, and þær wearþ Sidroc eorl ofslægen se alda, and Sidroc eorl se gioncga, and Ósbearn eorl, and Hareld eorl, Chr. 871; P. 70, 24–27: 918; P. 98, 10, 20. II a. of a Scandinavian acting with the English :—Se cyng betæhte þá fyrde tó lædene Ealfríce ealdorman and þórode eorl, 992; P. 127, 11. III. as a title in England, taking the place of *ealdorman*. [The transition may be illustrated by the following passages referring to Oslac :—Óslác féng tó ealdordóme, Chr. 966; P. 119, 2. Óslác ealdorman, 963; P. 117, 19. Óslác se mæra eorl, 975; P. 122, 6. Óslác eorl and eal here þe on þís (his, *v.l.*) ealdordóme wunað, Ll. Th. i. 278, 5.] :—Se cyng and Þúrkyl eorl (cf. Cnut cyng eall Englalandes ríce tódælde on feówer; him seolfan West-Sexan, and Þúrkylle Eást-Englan . . . , 1017; P. 154, 4), Chr. 1020; P. 154, 24. Ðá cóm Godwine eorl and Swegen eorl and Harold eorl . . . þá wælisce men forwrégdon ðá eorlas, 1048; P. 174, 3, 9. Æt cynges spæce lecge man .vi. healfmearc wedd; æt eorles and bisceopes .xii. óran wedd, Ll. Th. i. 296, 26. Eorles heregeata, 414, 4. Ærcebisceopes and eorles (æðelinges, *v.l.*) wærgild bið .xv. M. þrimsa, 186, 19. Gif þegen geþeáh þ hé wearð tó eorle, 192, 7. Beó hé scyldig wið þone be hit áge, swá wið cyningc .cxx. scill., swá wið eorl .lx. scill., 384, 18. Man sette Oddan tó eorle ofer Defenascíre and ofer Sumersæton and ofer Dorséton and ofer Wealas, Chr. 1048; P. 177, 2. v. eorl-dóm. IV. *a hero, &c.* v. eorl-lic.

**eorl-cund.** *Add:*—Mund þáre betstan widuwan eorlcundre .l. scillinga gebéte; ðáre óðre .xx. scill.; þáre þriddan .xii. scill.; þáre feórðan .vi. scill., Ll. Th. i. 20, 10.

**eorl-dóm.** *Add:*—His fæder ne wolde him lætan his eorldómes on Normandíge, Chr. 1079; P. 214, 23. Undernam Godwine eorl swýðe þ on his eorldóme sceolde swilc geweorðan, 1052; P. 175, 7. Mann sette Ælfgár Leofríces sunu eorles ðane eorldóm on handa þe Harold ær áhte, P. 177, 4. Willelm geaf Róðberde eorle þone eorldóm on (ealdordóm ofer) Norðhymbra land, 1068; P. 202, 2. His fæder wæs geboren on Norðfolce, and se kyngc geaf for þí his suna þær þone eorldóm and Súðfolc eác (þone eorldóm on Norðfolc and Súðfolc, *v.l.*), 1075; P. 210, 33. v. eorl, III.

**eorl-gebyrd.** *Add:*—Ðeáh hwa æþele sié eorlgebyrdum (cf. þeáh hwá wexe mid micelre æþelcundnesse his gebyrda, Bt. 19; F. 68, 31), Met. 10, 27.

**eor-lic.** v. ir-lic: **eorlíce.** *Substitute:* v. irlíce.

**eorl-lic.** *Add:*—Mid eorllicum *heroicis*, Wrt. Voc. ii. 42, 55.

**eormen.** v. irmen: **eornan.** v. irnan: **eorness.** v. ir-ness: **eornigende.** *l.* (?) eorsigende. v. irsian.

**eornost**, es; *n.* (not *f.*) *Add:*—Heardlíc eornost and wíslic wærscipe and steðefæst módstaþol . . . bið witena gehwilcum weordlicre micle þonne hé his wísan fágige tó swíðe, Ll. Th. ii. 318, 37. Ne healde gé mid suelcum eorneste (*studio*) ðá heorde suelce hirdas scoldon, Past. 89, 14. Beóð ánræde and habbað sum eornost. Sé ðe eornost næfð, earfoðlíce hé sceal æfre gedeón tó ænigre geðingðe, Hml. A. 48, 582–4. Hé mid geleáfan clipode on his eornost tó Gode, Ælfc. T. Grn. 11, 38. Eornisti (-esti, -ęsti) *serio* (the form might be instrumental adjective), Txts. 97, 1845. ¶ on eornost (1) *in earnest, seriously :*—On eornyst *serio*, An. Ox. 7, 203. Git mæg þeáh bót cuman, wille hit man georne on eornost áginnan, Ll. Th. i. 348, 24. Ús eallum tó woruldscame, gyf wé on eornost ænige cúðan *to the shame of 'us all, if we really could feel any*, Wlfst. 163, 8. (2) with weakened force, *indeed*. Cf. eornostlíce :—Sóðlíce on eornost ic eów secge *amen quippe dico vobis*, Mt. 17: 20. v. eornoste; *adv.*

**eornoste;** *adv. Add:*—Swá hwæt swá hé æfre gecwæð bodiende, þeáh þe hé hit ná eorneste (on eornost, *v.l.*) gecwæde *siquid umquam non jam decernendo, sed minando, diceret*, Gr. D. 151, 8. v. eornost.

**eornoste;** *adj. Add:*—Heornested *seria*, Wrt. Voc. ii. 92, 32. v. preceding word.

**eornostlíce.** *Add:* (1) *adv.:*—Eornstlíce *serio*, An. Ox. 2, 116.

Eornestlíce, 2891. Wiðstandaþ þám eornostlíce (georne, *v. l.*) strange on geleáfan, Hml. A. 52, 56. (2) (*adverbial*) *conj.* :—Sume (*conjunctions*) sind gecwedene *rationales . . . ergo, igitur . . . tulit ergo Dominus hominem* eornostlíce Drihten genam þone mann : *igitur perfecti sunt caeli* eornostlíce heofenas wæron fulfremedlíce geworhte, Ælfc. Gr. Z. 263, 8–14. Nú eornostlíce (witodlíce, Jn. 16, 22) hæbbe gé sume unrótnysse *vos igitur nunc quidem tristitiam habebitis*, Hml. A. 74, 30. Waciað eornostlíce (witodlíce, Mt. 24, 42) *vigilate ergo*, 49, 7. Beó ðú eornostlíce gebeógul *esto consentiens*, 4, 92. Swá eornestlíce *ita duntaxat*, An. Ox. 3211. Geornustlíce *igitur*, Angl. xiii. 439, 1062. [*O. H. Ger.* ernustlícho *strenue, veriter, certissime.*]

**eorre, . . . eorsung.** v. irre, . . . irsung: **eór-scripel.** v. eár-scripel: **eorþ.** *Dele.*

**eorþ-æppel.** *Add* : [*O. H. Ger.* erd-apfel *pepo.*]

**eorþ-ærn.** *Add* :—Eorþern *apogium* (cf. eorþ-hús), Wrt. Voc. ii. 7, 19. Geond eorðærn, Nap. 20.

**eorþ-beofung.** *Add* :—Wæs in Achie eorþbeofung, and twá byrig on eorþan besuncon *terrae motu Achaia concussa est, et duae civitates abruptis locorum hiatibus devoratae sunt*, Ors. 3, 2 ; S. 100, 18 : 3, 9 ; S. 132, 13.

**eorþ-beri(g)e**, an ; *f. A strawberry* :—Streábergan *vel* eorþbergan *fragium*, i. *pumorum*, Wrt. Voc. ii. 150, 31. [*O. L. Ger.* erth-beri *fragum* : *O. H. Ger.* erd-peri *fraga.*]

**eorþ-bigegnys.** *l.* eorþ-bígengnes.

**eorþ-bígenga.** *Add* : [*O. H. Ger.* erd-bigengio *rusticanus.*]

**eorþ-brycg**, e ; *f. A bridge made by placing poles across a stream and laying earth and sods on them* :—Of eorthbrycge, C. D. B. iii. 223, 24. [Cf. In termino latine vocitato Pons Terrestris, anglice Orthebrygge (the earlier English form of the charter has Eorthebyrg), C. D. B. ii. 251, 4.]

**eorþ-búend.** *Substitute:* **eorþ-búend, -búgend, -búgi(g)end (-ende)** *an inhabitant of earth; inhabiting earth* :—Ealle eorðbúend Drihten herian *jubilate Deo, omnis terra*, Ps. Th. 65, 1. Ealle eorðbúend *gentes*, 101, 13. Þeóda, ealle eorðbúend, 65, 7. Þá nú æðelingas, ealle eorðbúend, Ebréi hátað, Gen. 1648 : Cri. 1279. Eorðbúend ealle, 422. Óðre þára mægða Moabitare eorðbúende ealle hátað, óðre weras nemnað, æðelinga bearn, Ammonitare, Gen. 2617 : 1759. Gylt þe men gefremedon, eorðbúende, 1000. Þá ýtmestan eorðbúende (cf. ðá útemestan ðíoda, Bt. 19 ; F. 68, 29), Met. 10, 25. Ylde eorðbúende, folcweras, Gen. 221. Ealle eorðbúgiende *omnes habitatores terrae* (Dan. 4, 32), Hml. Th. ii. 434, 14. Gehwilce eorðbúgiende sind ætbródene, 124, 16. Gehwilce eorðbógiendan *quique terrigenae*, Ps. L. 48, 3. Eal Adames cnósl eorðbúendra *omnes homines*, Dóm. L. 129. Eorðbúgiendra, Wlfst. 137, 24, Fore eágum eorðbúendra, Cri. 1324. Ænig eorðbúendra, Gen. 1754 : Met. 10, 36. Þú hæleðum eart, eallum eorðbúendum, weard and wísa, Dan. 565. Þ hé rénas forgeáfe eorðbúgiendum (-búgigendum, *v.l.*), Hml. S. 18, 144. Ofer ealle eorðbúende *super omnem terram*, Ps. Th. 82, 14. Þú eorðbúende ealle healdest *gentes in terra dirigis*, 66, 4. Ofer geleáfulle eorðbúgiende *super fideles terrae*, 100, 6 : Hy. 3, 8. [*O. Sax.* erð-búandi.]

**eorþ-burh, -byr(i)g.** *Dele* ' or *burying-place;* humatio,' *and add: earth-work* :—Scídwealles eorðbyri *vallum*, Wrt. Voc. i. 37, 34. On eorðburge geat, C. D. v. 256, 11. Of ðære díc besúþan ðære eorðbyrg, vi. 129, 21. Ðone wudu æt ðære eorðbyrig, iii. 4, 11. Anlang hrycges tó ðære eorðburh middeweardre, 411, 23. On lythlan eorðbeorg; of ðære byrig, 48, 26.

**eorþ-byrgen(n)**, e ; *f. A grave* :—Eorðbyrgenna wurdon opene *monumenta aperta sunt* (Mt. 27, 52), Nap. 20.

**eorþ-cafer.** *Substitute:* **eorþ-ceafer, es ; m. An earth-beetle** :—Eorðceaperas (printed -caferas, *but see* Angl. viii. 450) *tauri* (cf. a kind of earth-beetles called tauri, i. Buls, Holland's Pliny), Wrt. Voc. i. 24, 26.

**eorþ-cenned.** *Add* :—Eorðcende *terriginae*, Ps. Srt. 48, 3.

**eorþ-cræft**, es ; *m. Geometry* :—Eorðcræft *geometrica*, Hpt. Gl. 479, 46.

**eorþ-cund.** *Add* :—Eardcundes aldores *terreni parentis*, Rtl. 33, 36. Ealre eorþcundre gesceafte *totius terrestris* (i. *terrene*) *creaturae*, An. Ox. 691. [*Goth.* airþa-kunds.]

**eorþcund-líc** ; *adj. Earthly, of earth* :—Þá wilnunga ðissa eorðcundlícra ðinga *terrenarum rerum cupidinem*, Past. 78, 18.

**eorþ-cyn.** For ' each terrestrial species' *substitute* ' all that lives on earth,' *and add* : [*O. H. Ger.* alliu aerdchunni *omnes terrae tribus.*]

**eorþ-cyning.** *Add* :—Eorðcyningcgas *reges terrae*, Ps. Th. 2, 2. Eorðkyningas, 47, 4. Se sélesða sinces brytta, Ælfryd mid Englum, ealra cyninga þára þe hé secgan hýrde, oððe hé hiorðcyninga ænigne gefrugne, Gr. D. 2, 16. Oðrum eorðcyningum tó bysne, Nar. 33, 2. Eorþcyningas ofercuman, Bl. H. 119, 21.

**eorþ-denu**, e ; *f. A valley* :—Þonne ealle eorðware úp árísað of ðæm ealdum eorðscræfum and of ðæm ealdum eorðdenum, Nap. 20.

**eorþ-dyne.** *Add* : [v. *N. E. D.* earth-din.]

**eorþe.** *Add* : I. *the ground.* (1) as a surface :—Hé ástrehte his líchaman tó eorðan, Hml. Th. i. 66, 22. Wæs his ræst on nacodre

eorðan, Bl. H. 227, 11. Þín blód fléwþ ofer eorþan swá swá wæter, 237, 6. Þá lástas on þá eorþan bestapene wæron, 127, 21. (1 a) of a part of the surface which has special characteristics, (*rough, &c.*) *ground* :—Hé hleóp on unsméðe eorðan, Shrn. 152, 2. (2) as a solid stratum :—Eorþu hroernis *terrae motus*, Mk. R. 13, 8. Eorþo, Lk. R. 21, 11. From burgum and from túnum on eorþan besuncen, Ors. 2, 6 ; S. 88, 13. (2 a) as a place of burial :—Hié ne mehton þá gefarenan tó eorþan bringan, Ors. 2, 6 ; S. 86, 28. His ne cóm furðon án bán tó eorðan, Shrn. 54, 29. Heora líchoman licggað on eorðan, Bl. H. 101, 2. (3) as suitable for cultivation, *soil, land* :—Dæl rénas ofer þíne eorðan . . . syle wæstmas þínre eorðan . . . bið þín eorðe ídel and unnyt, Wlfst. 260 6–10. (3 a) as productive :—Ðiós eorðe, ðe him ðæt gestreón of cóm, eallum mannum is tó gemánan geseald and eallum mannum bringð gemænne fóster, Past. 335, 9. Þá wæstmas þe eorþe forþbringeþ, Bl. H. 39, 17. Regnas eorþan wæstmas weccaþ, 51, 20. II. *the world we live in.* (1) *dry land* as opposed to sea :—Heofon and eorþe and sǽ, Bl. H. 91, 21. Seó sǽ ne mót þone þeorscwold oferstæppan þǽre eorþan . . . hié ne mót heore mearce gebrǽdan ofer þá stillan eorþan, Bt. 21 ; F. 74, 27. Gé befarað sǽ and eorðan (eordu, R.), Mt. 23, 15. Þá neólnessa þá eorþan willaþ forswelgan, Bl. H. 93, 12. (2) *earth* as opposed to the material heaven :—þone ne magon befón heofon and eorþe, Bl. H. 5, 34. Heofon biþ befealden swá swá bóc, and eorþe biþ forbærned tó axan, 91, 26. (3) as the abode of man :—Æt þám ýtmestan eorþan gemǽrum, Bl. H. 119, 25. Gié aron salt earðes, Rtl. 118, 3. Mé is geseald ælc anweald on heofonan and on eorþan (eorðo, L., eorþe, R.), Mt. 28, 18 : Bl. H. 49, 16. Wé æt þǽm ýtmestan dæge eall ágyldan sceolan þe hé ús ær on eorþan sealde, 51, 25. (3 a) in intensive phrase :—Nyste ic náwár eorðan hú ic ongynnan wolde *I shouldn't know how on earth to set about it*, Shrn. 182, 13, 19. (4) *the earth* as a planet :—Seó eorðe stent on ælemiddan, Lch. iii. 254, 15. Seó sunne gǽð . . . on dæg bufon eorðan and on niht under ðysse eorþan . . . Æfre heó byð yrnende ymbe ðás eorðan . . . Æfre byð on sumre sídan þǽre eorðan dæg, and æfre on sumre sídan niht, 234, 18–28. Eorðan ymbhwyrft, 236, 7. Úre eorðlíce niht cymð þurh ðære eorðan sceade, 240, 13. III. *a land, country* :—Bethlem, eorðu (Iudéa land, W. S.) *Bethleem, terra Juda*, Mt. L. 2, 6. Zabulones eorðu and Neptalimes eorþe *terra Zabulon et Neptalim*, Mt. R. 4, 15. Heofenas and eorðan (*terrae*) wæron geworhte, Ælfc. Gr. Z. 263, 13. Ymbhwyrft eorðana *orbis terrarum*, Ps. L. 97, 7. India mǽgþ is ealra eorðena seó ýtemyste, Shrn. 120, 19. IV. *the material of which the surface of the ground is composed, soil, mould, dust* :—Reád eorðe *glarea*, An. Ox. 18 b, 40. Swá seó hefige byrþen siteþ on þǽm deádan líchoman þǽre byrgenne, and hié se stán and seó eorþe þrycce, Bl. H. 75, 9. Þú eart eorþe, and þú scealt eft tó eorðan weorðan, 123, 9. Se eorðan dǽl *the body*, Gú. 1340. Wyrcað weófod of eorðan, Ex. 20, 24. Loccas mínes heáfdes mid þisse eorðan synd gemengde, Bl. H. 243, 35. V *one of the four elements* :—Ðeáh þú ealle gesceafta áne naman genemde, ealle þú nemdest tógædere and héte woruld ; and þeáh ðone ánne noman ðú tódǽldest on feówer gesceafta ; án þæra is eorþe, oþer wæter, þridde lyft, feówrþe fýr, Bt. 33, 4 ; F. 128, 9. Feówer gesceafta synd þe ealle eorðlice líchaman on wuniað, þ synd *aer, ignis, terra, aqua* . . . *Terra* is eorðe, Lch. iii. 272, 16. v. þeód-eorþe.

**eorþen** ; *adj. Of or in the earth* :—Grafe eorþenum *cuniculo subterraneo*, An. Ox. 3312. [*A. R.* eorþen. Cf. *Goth.* airþeins : *O. H. Ger.* irdîn.]

**eorþ-fæst.** *Add* :—Sume men synd swá áblende þ hí bringað heora lác tó eorðfæstum stáne, Hml. S. 17, 130. Hig læddon þone cyning tó ánum eorðfæstum treówe and tígdon hine þǽr tó, 32, 109. [v. *N. E. D.* earthfast. *Icel.* jarð-fastr.]

**eorþ-gealla.** *Add* :—Heorðgealla *centauria*, Wrt. Voc. i. 67, 14. Eorðgealla *fel terre uel centaurum*, An. Ox. 56, 423. Nim centaurian, þ is hyrdewyrt, óðre naman eorðgealla, Lch. ii. 248, 14. Hirdewyrt, þ is eorðgealla, 202, 23. [*O. H. Ger.* erd-galla *centaurea.*]

**eorþ-geberst, -gebyrst**, es ; *n. A chasm in the ground, land-slip* :—In ðæt eorðebyrst ; of ðám eorðgebyrste, C. D. iii. 52, 10. Úp tó ðám eorðgeberste tó foxes beorge, v. 297, 30. On eorþgeberst, Cht. Crw. 3, 17. [On ðár eordebriste, C. D. vi. 262, 15.] [Cf. *O. L. Ger.* undar theru erthbrusti *subter terranea* : *O. H. Ger.* erdprust *interruptio, vorago.*]

**eorþ-gemǽre**, es ; *n. An end of the earth* :—Eall eorðgemǽru *universi fines terrae*, Ps. Th. 21, 25.

**eorþ-gemet.** For Cot. 95 *substitute* :—*Geometrica*, þ ys eorðgemet, Shrn. 152, 15. Eorþgemet, Wrt. Voc. ii. 40, 41 : An. Ox. 55, 2. Eorþgemete *geometrica*, 2, 157. Eorþgemet *geometricam, terram mensuram*, 5442.

**eorþ-grǽf.** *Substitute for citation* :—Eorþgræf pædeþ it (*the bucket of a draw-well*) *makes its way through a passage dug in the earth*, Rä. 59, 9. [*O. Sax.* erð-graf *a grave*. Cf. *O. L. Ger.* erth-gróba *lacus vel cisterna.*]

**eorþ-gráp.** *After* wyrhtan *add:* forweorene, geleorene, heard gripe hrúsan, *and for* ' mighty workmen' *substitute* ' masters and (?) makers.'

**eorþ-hele.** *Substitute:* A covering of the ground (?) :—Wæs þæt

deáw swilce hit hagoles eorðhele wǽre *the dew was as if there were a covering of hail upon the ground;* ros jacuit ... in similitudinem pruinae super terram, Ex. 16, 14. Cf. helian.

**eorþ-hífign.** v. eorþ-ífig: eorþ-hnutu. *Add:* [*O. H. Ger.* erd-nuz tubera.]

**eorþ-hrērness,** e; *f. An earthquake:*—Mycel eorþhrērnes bið on ðǽm dæge geworden, Bl. H. 93, 14. Eorðhroernisse, Mt. L. 28, 2. Geséende eorðhroernise *viso terrae motu,* 27, 54. Biðon eorðhreoerniso (*the first* e *in* -hreoerniso *is marked for erasure;* -hroernisse, R.), 24, 7. Eorðhroernisso miclo, Lk. L. 21, 11. [Wearþ micel eorþhrǽrnesse geworden, Nar. 46, 13.]

**eorþ-hús.** *Add:*—Se cāsere hēt hine gelǽdan intó ānum eorðhúse, and hēt āne strange leó lǽtan in tó him, Hml. S. 30, 415. [He hehte hine makian an eorðhus . . . wes Astrild i þissen eorðhuse þat na mon heo þer nuste, Laym. 2360, 2381.] [*Icel.* jarð-hús.]

**eorþ-ífig.** *l.* -ífig, -ífegn, *and add:*—Eorðífig *hedera nigra,* Wrt. Voc. i. 68, 11 : ii. 43, 51. Suoelce earðhífign (*terebintus*) ic gerahte telgo mīno, Rtl. 68, 32. Þá cyrnlu þæs eorþífiges, Lch. ii. 248, 26. [Cf. *O. H. Ger.* erd-ebuh.]

**eorþ-lic.** *Add:* I. cf. eorþe, I. 3, 3 a :—Seó culfre ne leofað be wyrmum, ac be eorðlicum wæstmum, Hml. Th. ii. 44, 26. Þá gewideru ealle eówre wæstmas and eorðlice tilþa gebētað, Wlfst. 132, 14. Gescóp se Ælmihtiga God sǽ and eorþan and ealle eorðlice spryttinga, Lch. iii. 234, 3. II. cf. eorþe, II. 3 :—Eorðlic æðeling *a prince of men,* Dan. 525. Á þin dóm wunað eorðlic (*on earth*) mid aldum, Cri. 406. Ǽnig eorðlic þincg (= ǽnig ðing, Bt. 35, 1 ; F. 154, 20) *anything in the world* (cf. eorþe, II. 3 a), Met. 22, 5. Ǽfter eorþlicre wīsan *after the manner of men,* Bl. H. 135, 20. For eorþlicra manna gebedum, 47, 8. On ealra eorþlicra gebedrǣdenne þe Crīstene wǽron, 45, 37. Dryhten clipode eorðlice menn tó geleáfan *Dominus vocavit terram,* Ps. Th. 49, 1. II a. where a contrast is expressed or implied with heavenly, spiritual :—Nān eorþlic man ne mehte swelce sibbe ofer eallne middangeard gedón, Ors. 3, 5 ; S. 106, 27. Hēr sceal mīn wesan eorðlic ēðel, Gū. 232. Of eorþlicum gestreóne *de terreno* (i. *seculari*) *mercatu,* An. Ox. 2654. Tó þǣm eorþlican ðeápe, Bl. H. 145, 10. Ǽgþer ge eorþlice mēðe ge heofenlice, 49, 33 : Hml. Th. i. 82, 21. Hī þone eorðlican egsan forsāwon, and hē him forgeaf ēces līfes hyht, Bl. H. 137, 7. Þyses lǽnan welan ne þyssa eorþlicra geofa, 21, 11. Þissa eorþlicena góda, Bt. 34, 1 ; F. 134, 25. III. cf. eorþe, V. 4 :—Úre eorðlice niht cymð þurh ðǽre eorðan sceade, Lch. iii. 240, 13.

**eorþ-ling.** *Substitute for* 'A farmer; terrae cultor' '*A bird,*' *and add* : v. irþling, II.

**eorþ-mata** (-maþa?), an; *m. An earth-worm:*—Eorþmata *vermis,* Wrt. Voc. ii. 123, 44.

**eorþ-rest.** *For* 'A resting . . . , Cot. 31' *substitute :*—A *bed on the ground :*—Eordraestae, -restae, -reste *caumeuniae,* Txts. 48, 219. Eorðreste, Wrt. Voc. ii. 13, 16. Hlýwþa *vel* eorðreste *caumene,* 130, 7.

**eorþ-ríce.** *Add:* I. *the earth :*—Sē hæfde āre on eorðríce, sē þe ælmyssan dǽlde dómlíce, Lch. i. 400, 8. II. *an earthly kingdom, earthly power :*—Críst fleáh eorðríce tó underfónne *regnum percipere vitavit in terris,* Past. 33, 12. [Nan eorþliʒ kinedom here upponn eorþeriche, Orm. 12132. *O. Sax.* erð-ríki *the earth; earthly power: O. H. Ger.* erd-ríchi *terra; regnum mundi: Icel.* jarð-ríki *the earth.*]

**eorþ-scræf.** *Add:* I. *a cave :*—Dauid wæs gehýd on ānum eorðscræfe (*spelunca*) . . . Ðá fór Saul forð bī ðæm scræfe, Past. 197, 12. II. *a cave for burial, tomb, grave :*—Ne þearf þæs nān mau wēnan þ his líchama mæge þá synbyrþenna on eorþscrafe gebētan, Bl. H. 109, 31. Ealle eorðware ūp ārísað of ðǣm ealdum eorðscræfum, Nap. 20.

**eorþ-slihtes.** v. sliht *in Dict.*

**eorþ-styren(n),** e; *f. An earthquake :*—Gewordenre eorðstyrene *facto terrae motu,* Gr. D. 182, 20. For eorðstyrenum heó (*Rome*) byð geswenced, Gr. D. 134, 1.

**eorþ-styrung.** *Add:*—Wæs mycel eorðstyrung wíde on Englalande (on Wygracestre and on Wíc and on Deórbý and elles gehwǣr, v. l.), Chr. 1048 ; P. 166, 24: 1089; P. 124, 1 : Hml. S. 15, 60. Hē sǽde þ his hūs feólle fǽrlíce mid eorðstyrunge, 25, 842. Eorðstyrungum geswenced *terrae motu fatigata,* Gr. D. 134, 1.

**eorþ-tilia.** *Add:*—Nele nān gód eorðtilia niman his góde sǽd and sāwan on þæt land þǣr hē wāt þæt hit nǽfre weaxan nele, Wlfst. 305, 31. Hē gesette his wīngeard mid eorðtilium (*agricolis*), Mk. 12, 1. Eorþtilian *agricolas,* An. Ox. 2449. [*Laym.* eorðe-tilien (-es, 2nd MS.); *pl.*]

**eorþ-tilþ.** *Add:* [erþe-tilþe *agricultura,* Wick. 2 Chron. 26, 10.]:

**eorþ-tudor.** *l.* -túdor.

**eorþ-wæstm.** *Add:*—Usus nittung *vel* notu *vel* eorðwæstmas (*printed* -wæstm, cess) tó ǽte ālýfed, Wrt. Voc. i. 21, 39. Sý ǽlcere geoguðe teóðung gelǣst be Pentecosten, and þāra eorðwæstma be emnnihte, Ll. Th. i. 262, 21 : Wlfst. 116, 3. Þá teóþunga ǽgðer ge on cwicum ceápe ge on þæs geáres eorðwæstmum, Ll. Th. i. 194, 7. Gif mon æppla hæbbe oðþe hwylces ōþres cynnes eorðwæstmas (*poma aut nascentia leguminum*), R. Ben. 63, 14.

**eorþ-waru,** &c. *Add:* (1) -waru :—Eall eorðwaru, Wlfst. 25, 11.

(2) -ware :—Forhtiaþ ealle gesceafta, ge heofonware ge eorþware, Bl. H. 11, 4. Heofonwara hyht and eorþwara, 87, 10 : Ors. 3, 5 ; S. 106, 20.

(3) -waran :—Samson wæs ealra eorðwarena strengest, Wlfst. 147, 1.

(4) uncertain :—Ætforan eorðwarum, Hml. Th. ii. 604, 5. Hē his þone hālgan sunu sendan wolde tó eorþwarum, Bl. H. 177, 13. [*A. R.* eorðe-ware.]

**eorþ-weall.** *Substitute:* I. *a rampart, mound made by the earth taken from a dyke and raised along it :*—Hē hit begyrde and gefæstnade mid dīce and mid eorðwealle *magnam fossam firmissimumque uallum duxit,* Bd. 1, 5 ; Sch. 17, 20. Mid dīce and mid eorðwealle ūtan ymbsealde *circumvallante aggere,* 4, 28 ; Sch. 520, 1. Se cāsere hēt dīcian and eorðwall (-weall, *v. l.*) gewyrcan *uallum fecerat,* 1, 12 ; Sch. 33, 27. II. *a wall formed by the ground, the side or roof of a cave :*—Hē beáh under eorðweall *he went into the cave,* B. 2957. Inn under eorðweall, 3090. (Cf. under wealle, 3060. Beorges getrūwode, wīges and wealles, 2323.)

**eorþ-weard.** *Substitute for* '*An earth-guard,*' *what guards a land, a fortress, and add* leóda fæsten *after* lígdraca.

**eorþ-weg.** *Add: the earth* (cf. weg, VI) :—Worulde kyningas þá ou eorðwege ealle syndan *omnes reges terrae,* Ps. Th. 71, 11. Wutun symbeldagas Drihtnes on eorðwege ealle tówurpan *comprimamus omnes dies festos Domini a terra,* 73, 8. On eorðwege, ūp on heofenum *in caelo et in terra,* 112, 5 : 91, 8. [*Icel.* jarð-vegr *the earth.*] Cf. fold-weg.

**eorþ-wéla.** *l.* -wela, *and add :*—Mon nōhtes wyrþe his sāule ne dēþ ne his goldes ne his seolfres ne his eorþwelena (*earthly wealth or* (?) *wealth derived from the earth*), Bl. H. 195, 6.

**eorþ-weorod,** es ; *n. The inhabitants of the earth, mankind :*—Ðǽr (*at the day of judgement*) bið gryre se mǽsta, for ðǽm þurh Godes mihte bið eal āstyred ge heofonwered ge eorðwered ge hellwered, Wlfst. 25, 21.

**eor-wicga.** *Dele, and see* eár-wicga: eosel. v. esol : eoseh. v. esole : eosen. v. gesen : eóten *a giant. l.* eoten, *and add* : [*v. N. E. D.* eten.] : eotendan. v. etan: eótenisc. *l.* eotenisc, *and add* : [*v. N. E. D.* etenish.]

**Eotol, Eatol, Etol** (-el, -ul), es ; *n. Italy :*—Eotoles Hesperie (= *es-perie,* i. *italie* westdǽles, An. Ox. 2583 (Ald. 35, 21)), Wrt. Voc. ii. 79, 55 : 43, 23. On Eotole Hesperie, 91, 28. In Eatole *in Latio,* 93, 60 : 47, 34. On Eatule, Víd. 70.

**eotol-ware.** *Add:*—On Italia mǽgðe, þ is on Etelwara lande, Mart. H. 90, 10. Tó Etelwara (Eten-, *v. l.*) mǽgðe, 84, 19. v. Italie.

**eoton-weard.** *l.* (?) eoton weard. *See* ā-beódan (2 a).

**eówan, eówian.** *Add:*—Eóweð (-að, *v. l.*) hē ūtan eádmódnesse, Past. 313, 2. Ðæt ðæt hē ūtan eówað (iówað, *v. l.*), 55, 13. Eáuað *ostendit,* Lk. L. 3, 7. Hē eówode þǽm hundum þone hlāf, Bl. H. 181, 22. Suelce hē nacodne hine selfne eówige tó wundigeanne his feóndum, Past. 277, 17. Hwelce hié hié selfe eówien (-igeu, *v. l.*), 273, 4. Hē hine sceal eówian (eówan, *v. l.*), 118, 7 : 449, 31, 32 : Bt. 35, 3 ; F. 160, 9. Ðū eáuande arð *manifestaturus es,* Jn. L. 14, 22. v. ge-eówan ; īwan.

**eówd, eówde.** *Add:* (1) *neuter* (*or uncertain*) :—On miclum ēwede, Shrn. 130, 24. Hē Godes ýwde gescylde, 129, 10. Ic befǽste þē þ eówde . . . þurh þē ic þ ýs eówde stýran ne mæg, Bl. H. 191, 26. Of eówedum þīnum *de gregibus tuis,* Ll. S. 49, 9. (2) *feminine* :—Eówde sceápum, Ps. Th. 64, 14. Hē hēt nýtenu faran tó þǽre eówode þe hī of ādwelodon, Hml. Th. ii. 514, 23. Ðý lǽs ðe ān wannhāl scēp ealle ðá eówde besmīte, i. 124, 33 : Gr. D. 109, 11. [*Goth.* awēþi *ovile : O. H. Ger.* ewit *grex;* ewida *caulas.*] v. ēde.

**eówer, eówre** *of you.* *Add:* (1) as personal pronoun :—Þá Gotan eów hwōn oferhergedon, and iówer feáwe ofslōgon, Ors. 1, 10 ; S. 48, 20. Eówer ǽlces ācennednesse, Bt. 30, 2 ; F. 110, 18. Drihten fandað eówre, Deut. 13, 3. (1 a) with noun in apposition :—Eówer Rōmāna brocu ðe ge ealneg drīfað, Ors. 3, 7 ; S. 120, 14. (2) as possessive :—Hwæþer gē eówer hundas and eówer net ūt on ðá sǽ lǽdon, Bt. 32, 3 ; F. 118, 13.

**eówer** *your.* *Add:* I. qualifying a noun, *your :*—Ðiós eówru leáf, Past. 451, 32. Eóweres andleofan, Bl. H. 169, 16. Eówres Fæder, 171, 21. Mid eówrum (eórum, *v. l.*) āgenum willan gē sculon ðencean for eówre heorde, Past. 137, 19. For eówere fortrūwodnesse, 211, 12. For eówere mengu, Gū. 679. Gē onfóð eówerra synna forgifnessa, Bl. H. 49, 21. On eówerum heortum, Hml. Th. ii. 542, 4. Āstreccað eówre āgālodan honda and eówru cneówu, Past. 65, 18. II. predicative, *yours :*—Nis þ eówer þ ge witan þá tīde *non est vestrum nosse tempora,* Bl. H. 117, 23. III. where in place of an inflected form of the adjective the genitive *eówer* might be expected :—Eóweres ǽlces ācennednesse, Bt. 30, 2 ; F. 110, 18 note. In nǽniges eóweres mūð *in nullius vestrum ore,* Gr. D. 243, 5. Þ heó sylf geceóse hwilcne eówerne heó wille, Ap. Th. 20, 9. Þ ic eówerne sum mē tó begeáte, Hml. S. 33, 109. Iówra selfra anwaldes, Ors. 1, 10 ; S. 48, 21. Cf. úre.

**eówestras.** *Substitute:* eówestre, es ; *m.* : an ; *f. A sheepfold :*—On ðǽre ylcan circan wǽron onfæste þā eówestran (locu, *v. l.*) þára brōðra sceápa (*caulae ovium*) . . . Se þeóf eóde in ðā eáwestran (locu, *v. l.*), Gr. D. 224, 16–20. Tó ēwestrum *ad caulas,* Wrt. Voc. ii. 4, 38.

A.-S. SUPPL.

Eóuuistras *mandras*, 113, 48. Eówestras, 81, 21. [Cf. *Goth.* þis awistris *ex hoc ovili*: *O. H. Ger.* ewist; *m. ovile, caula.*]

**eówocig.** *Add*:—Mid eówcigre wulle, Lch. ii. 182, 4. Eówecigre, 18.

**eówo-meoluc** *ewe-milk*:—Wearme eówomeoluc, Lch. ii. 188, 12.

**eówu.** *Dele* '*dat.* eówenum; ewe, an', *and add*: eowu (?):—Hé ēwa mealc, Shrn. 61, 19. v. eáwu, ēwe *in Dict.*

**epactas** (-e, -an?); *gen. pl.* epacta, epactana, *epacts*:—Þæs geáres ne beóđ nāne epactas, Angl. viii. 301, 29. Tō geáre synd feówertýne epactas, 327, 11. Hū fela epactas beón on geáre, 329, 35: Lch. iii. 228, 5, 8. On grēcisc hī synt gecwedene epacte, Angl. viii. 302, 32. Swā fela epacte beóđ, 301, 21. Swā fela epacta þū sĉealt habban þý geáre, Lch. iii. 226, 28. Þisra epacta gerýnu āpinsian, Angl. viii. 300, 48. Þæra epactana gesceád, 301, 5. Tō þām epactum, 11: 21. Dō þærtō þrittig epactas, 301, 24, 30: 300, 44.

**epegītsung.** *Dele, the MS.* has ewe gītsungæ.

**epistol,** es; *m.* (not e; *f.*): epistola, an; *m.* (1) strong forms:—Hēr is seó gesetenis Alexandres epistoles . . . Cwæþ hē in fruman þæs epistoles, Nar. 1, 2, 9. On þǣm ǣrron epistole, 3, 28. (2) weak forms:—Hē cuæđ on his epistolan tō Galatum, P. 117, 7. Sealde hē mē ǣnne epistolan, Nar. 18, 28. (3) uninflected:—Þū geare canst þæs eádegan Paules epistola þone hē wrāt tō Timotheo, in þām hē hine týde, Bd. 1, 27; Sch. 61, 17. v. pistol.

**eran.** v. ǣren: erce-. v. ærce-: ercnan-stān. v. eorcnan-stān: **erd-ling.** v. irþ-ling: -ere. *Dele*: ēre. v. īr: erfe. v. irfe.

**erian.** *Add*:—Of đām tīman đe man ǣrest eređ ođ Martinus mæssan hē sceal ǣlcre wucan erian .i. æcer . . . His gafolyrđe iii. æceras erige, Ll. Th. i. 434, 14–19. Wæs se mere ǣwend tō felda, swā þ man erode ealne þone fixnoþ, Nap. 22, 28. Þeáh hē erige his land mid đūsend sula, Bt. 26, 3; F. 94, 14. Þeáh him mon erigan scyle ǣghwelce dæg æcera đūsend *quamvis rura centeno scindat optima bove*, Met. 14, 4. Man mæg on wintra erian, Angl. ix. 261, 22. Ælce dæg ic (*the ploughman*) sceal erian fulne æcer oþþe māre, Coll. M. 19, 21. Hwylc man āþōhte ǣrest mid sul tō erianne? Đæt wæs Cham, Noes sunu, Sal. K. p. 186, 28.

**erming.** v. irming: ermþu. v. irmþu: -ern. *Dele*: ērndian (C. D. i. 222, 35). v. ǣrendian: ērndung. v. ǣrendung: ernþ. v. irþ: erre. v. irre.

**ersc.** *Substitute*: ersc, ærsc, es; *m. Arrish, ersh* (*arrish* a stubble-field; stubble of any kind after the crop has been cut, D.D. See also N. E. D. *arrish, earsh*):—Tō brādan ersce, Cht. E. 290, 29. Tō crāwan ersce, C. D. iii. 123, 6. Tō wudan ærscæ; fram wudan ærscæ, v. 255, 37. For bealdan ærsc eásteweardnæ, 174, 1. Ad locum qui dicitur langan ersc . . . ubi dicitur heán ersc, iii. 373, 9, 18.

**ersc-hen.** *Add*:—Erschen *ortigomera*, Wrt. Voc. ii. 63, 53.

**erþ-ling.** v. irþ-ling: ēsa, Lch. iii. 54, 9. v. ōs: ē-sceapa. v. scip.

**esne.** *Add*: I. *a man of the servile class* (cf. esne-cund, -wyrhta, and see Andrews' *Old English Manor*, pp. 192 sqq.):—On esnes ham, of esnes hamme, C. D. iii. 425, 21. II. *in a more general sense, a servant*:—Nis esne (*servus*) ofer lāferd his. Genōh biþ þte esne sié swā swā lāford his, Mt. R. 10, 24, 25: Shrn. 196, 11. Þū esne nāwiht, Mt. R. 18, 32. Eádgo biđon esnes (*servi*) đā đā đe se drihten gemoetađ wæccendo, Lk. L. 12, 37. III. *a young man*:—Đe esne *adolescens*, Mt. L. 19, 20, 22. Ging esne, Mk. L. R. 14, 51: *juvenis*, 16, 5. Esne *juvenis*, Lk. p. 6, 13. IV. *a man*:—Þū scealt beódan Israhēla folce, þæt esne bidde æt his frýnd and wīf æt hire nēhgebūran, Ex. 11, 2. IV a. *a man of mark, a learned, brave, &c. man.* Cf. esnlīce:—Zenodotus se eficisca esne, Angl. viii. 334, 17. Catus cwydas þæs calwan esnes, 321, 29. Þā hīw þe þā rīmcræftige esnas borlīce foregylpađ, 334, 27. v. efen-esne.

**esne-cund;** *adj. Of the servile class*:—Esnecund *conditiorius*, Wrt. Voc. ii. 135, 59.

**esne-mann,** es; *m. A servant, hireling*:—Đe aesnemonn *mercenarius*, Jn. L. R. 10, 13.

**esne-teám.** v. efen-teám.

**esne-wyrhta.** *Add*:—Hū manige esnewyrhtan (fela esnewyrhtena, *v. l.*) wǣron in mīnes fæder hūse *quanti mercenarii in domo patris mei*, Gr. D. 107, 4.

**esn-līce.** *The Latin translated in the passage* Past. 363, 2 *is*: Viri fratres.

**esol.** *After* sæt, l. 2, *add*: Đæt wæs for đǣm đe se assa geseah đone engel. *Add*:—Eosol *asina*, Wrt. Voc. i. 287, 50. Se eosol þe Crīst on sittan wolde, Bl. H. 71, 29. Ānes esoles cinbān, Sal. K. p. 186, 32. Esules, Mt. R. 18, 6. Hý habbađ eoseles eáran *auribus a:ininis*, Nar. 36, 6. On eoseles gelīcnisse *onagro similes*, 20. Sittende on eosule *sedens super asinam*, Mt. R. 21, 5. Ysle asello, An. Ox. 3663. Hī læddon him tō þone eosol, Bl. H. 71, 6. Eoselas (assan, *v. l.*) þā habbađ swā micle hornas swā oxan *onagri cornua boum habentes*, Nar. 34, 15. Eosola gehlýd *ruditus asinorum*, Gr. D. 185, 3. v. esole, asal.

**esol-cweorn,** e; *f. A mill turned by an ass, mill-stone*:—Esulcweorn *mola asinaria*, Past. 31, 17: *asinaria*, Wrt. Voc. ii. 72, 79: 8, 72. Eosulcweorn *mola asinaria*, Ll. Th. ii. 236, 11.

**esole** (-ele), an; *f. A she-ass*:—Ofer eoselan folan sittende, Bl. H. 71, 5. Gyt gemētaþ eoselan (*asinam*) gebundene and hire folan, 79, 28: 69, 35. Eosula and fola *asinam et pullum*, Mt. R. 21, 7. Eoslena *asinorum*, Gr. D. 185, 3. v. esol.

**ess,** es; *m. The letter s*:—Premo ic ofđrycce macađ *pressi* on twām essum, Ælfc. Gr. Z. 170, 3. *Fissum* on twām essum . . . *fusum*, ān s for đan đe se *u* is lang, 178, 5.

**ēst.** *Dele* 'Andr . . . 483,' *and add*: I. (1) in the following glosses:—Oest, gifu *gratia*, Wrt. Voc. ii. 41, 5. Ēst *munificentia*, 58, 18. Oeste *devotione*, Rtl. 8, 25. Oest *devotionem*, 15, 1: *votum*, 169, 7. Oesto *vota*, 29, 34. (2) *good pleasure, favour*:—Sum him Metudes ēst ofer eorđwelan ealne geceósed, Cri. 87. Þæt þæt heom on Godes ēst (*in accordance with God's good pleasure*) gōde men geūđon, Wlfst. 159, 19. Eal þæt wē sceoldan on Godes ēst gelǣstan *all that according to the will of God we ought to do*, 92, 12: 103, 5: 172, 7: 181, 11. Dunn hafađ đās bōc gesald his wīfe an Godes ēst, C. D. ii. 58, 21. (3) *where favour is shewn by gifts, gracious, liberal gifts*, cf. II:—Ic eów gōda gehwæs ēst āhwette, An. 339. Mē þis hildesceorp Hrōđgār sealde, hēt þæt ic his ǣrest þē ēst gesægde (*that I should describe to thee his gracious gift*), cwæđ þæt hyt hæfde Hiorogār cyning, B. 2157. Hē him ēst geteáh meara and mādma, 2165. II. *luxuries* (*especially food*):—Ýsta *diliciarum*, An. Ox. 11, 35. Ætlicum ēstum *edendis dapibus*, Wrt. Voc. ii. 142, 33. Gif wē willađ becuman tō đām ēstum þæs ēcan gereordes, Hml. Th. ii. 374, 8. Ēstas *delicias*, Kent. Gl. 1063. Hē sende him sanda and ēstas, ac se cniht forseah þā sanda and drencas, Hml. S. 35, 56. Se fiscere đā ēstas him beforan legde þe hē him tō beóđenne hæfde, Ap. Th. 11, 25. [v. *N. E. D. este.*] v. æf-ēst, ēstum *in Dict.*

**ēstan;** *p.* te *To feast, give luxurious food to.* cf. ēst, II:—Wā þām hirdum þe ēstađ heom silfum swā heom betst līcađ *vae pastoribus qui pascebant semetipsos* (Ezech. 34, 2), Wlfst. 190, 17.

**estas?**:—On þeodherpoþ oþ þā estas, C. D. B. ii. 270, 7.

**ēste** *liberal. Add*:—Gif þū lidwērigum lārna þīnra ēste (est, MS.) wyrđest, An. 483. Oestum *devotis*, Rtl. 9, 13. [v. *N. E. D. este; adj.*]

**Ēste.** *Add*:—Þǣr is mid Eástum ān mægđ þæt hī magon cyle gewyrcan, Ors. 1, 1; S. 21, 13. v. Īstas.

**ēste-līce.** *Add*: I. *graciously*:—Suā micle suā hió ēstelīcor of dūne āstīgeđ, suā hió iéđelīcor ūp āstīgeđ *quo benigne descendit ad infima, valenter recurrit ad summa*, Past. 103, 18. Hié hié sculon suā micle ēstelīcor dǣlan suā hié ongietađ đæt him unāgenre bir đæt hié đǣlađ *tanto humiliter praebeant, quanto et aliena esse intelligunt, quae dispensant*, 321, 8. Oestelīce *devote*, Rtl. 31, 34. II. *delicately, luxuriously*:—Ēstelīce fram cnihthāde fēdan *delicate a pueritia nutrire*, Kent. Gl. 1065. Genōh estelīce (*delicate*) hine grāpađ sē þe wyle būtan geswince leahtras oferswīþan, Scint. 103, 20.

**ēst-full.** *Add*: I. cf. ēst, I:—Oestful *voluter, cupido votium*, Txts. 107, 2161. Ēsteful *votibus* (l. *votivus*), Wrt. Voc. i. 289, 67. Ēstful mǣden *devota* (*Christi*) *virguncula*, An. Ox. 4358. Enoch wæs ēstful on mōde, Hml. S. 16, 17. Martirius wæs swīđe ēstfull þeów Gode *devotus valde Dei famulus*, Gr. D. 86, 27. Ēstfulre brōđerrǣdene *devotae germanitatis*, Hpt. Gl. 403, 4. Þ ic þē mid ēstfullum mōde sylle *ea ego tibi devotus dabo*, Gr. D. 25, 23: Wlfst. 287, 18: Chr. 1023; P. 156, 25. Ēstful *votivum*, i. *optativum*, An. Ox. 2509: *divitem* (*virginem*), 4591. Geoffrian þā ēstfullan onsægednessa, Hml. S. 18, 376. II. cf. ēst, II:—Deliciosa, i. *amabilior, leta* þþgeorn vel ēstful, *delicius*, i. *in deliciis amatus* ēstgeorn, ēstful, Wrt. Voc. ii. 138, 42–45. Ēstfulles *delicatae*, An. Ox. 1088. Hwǣr beóđ đā ēstfullan swǣsnessa, Hex. 50, 26. Ēstfullum *delicatis*, R. Ben. I. 84, 2. Ēstfulle *delicatas*, An. Ox. 3166: *diliciosas*, 1135. [v. *N. E. D. estful.*]

**ēstful-līce.** *Add*:—Ealle þā þe ēstfullīce Drihtne fyliađ *omnes qui devote Dominum sequuntur*, Gr. D. 138, 15. Hē mē þus ēstfullīce æt þisum bađe þegnađ *mihi solet tam devotissime ad lavandum obsequi*, 343, 13.

**ēstfulnes.** *Add*: I. cf. ēst-ful, I:—Devotio, i. *obsequio, bonitas, honor* ēstfulnes, Wrt. Voc. ii. 139, 51: Scint. 29, 11. Ēstfulnese *devotione*, i. *humilitate*, An. Ox. 369: Hy. S. 88, 17. Mid ēstfulnysse, Gr. D. 138, 18. Hē mid ealre ēstfulnesse (*tota devotione*) lufađ đæt þeó līf, Past. 389, 15: Lch. iii. 442, 12. Uton mid ealre ēstfulnysse ūres mōdes đās freólstīde wurđian, Hml. Th. i. 446, 28. Ic þē þæt mid ēstfulnysse sylle *id ego tibi devotus dabo*, Gr. D. 25, 23. Gode mid geornfulnysse and ēstfulnysse þēnian, Ll. Th. ii. 360, 21. II. *luxury, lasciviousness.* Cf. ēst-ful, II:—Swutele synd þæs flǣsces weorc, þ is forligr and unclǣnnyss, ēstfulnyss ođđe gālnyss, hǣđengyld ođđe unlybban (*fornicatio, immunditia, impudicitia, luxuria, idolorum servitus, veneficia*, Gal. 5, 19), Hml. S. 17, 24.

**ēst-georn.** v. ēst-full, II.

**ēstig.** *Add*:—Cirica đīn oestigo (*devota*) đerhwunige, Rtl. 72, 18. Uē bigaađ oestigo *colimus devoti*, 30, 23. Oestigo ūsig *votivos nos*, 85, 35 [*Goth.* ansteigs: *O. H. Ger.* ensig *gratiosus, benevolus, gratus: Icel.* āstigr.]

**ēst-lic;** *adj.* I. *devout.* v. ēst, I:—Fæstine oestlico *jejunia votiva*,

Rtl. 18, 15. Oestlicum ðóhtum *devotis mentibus,* 9. 19. Oestlicere *devotius,* 13. II. *delicate, dainty.* v. ēst, II:—Éstlicost *delicatissimum,* An. Ox. 56, 298. [v. *N. E. D.* estlich; *adj.*]

éstlíce. *Add:*—Hig sceolon swíðe lustlíce hig onfón and him éstlíce tǽcan, Ll. Th. ii. 414, 10. [v. *N. E. D.* estlich; *adv.*]

ést-mete. *Add:* I. *of food* (lit. or fig.):—Éstmet[tas] *grata fercula,* An. Ox. 56, 77. Éstmetta *ferculorum,* 3169. Hire þénian of his ágenum þénungum and his éstmetum *dare illi de convivio suo,* Hml. A. 110, 269. Éstmettas (*delicias*) mon ne sceal lufian, ac fæsten mon sceal lufian, R. Ben. 16, 23. Lazarus geseah ðone rícan brúcan his éstmettas (*fare sumptuously*), Hml. Th. i. 330, 15. Éstmettas þæs ēcan gereordes, ii. 372, 17. II. *of other things:*—' Geoffra ðíne lác úrum godum, oððe ðú bist mid eallum ðisum þínungtólum getintregod,' Se diácon cwæð: 'þás éstmettas ic symle gewilnode,' Hml. Th. i. 424, 23. [He mid estnieten his innað ne gefýllde, Angl. iii. 107, 55.]

esul-cweorn. v. esol-cweorn: é-swíc, -swíca. *l.* é-swic, -swica.

etan. *Add:* I. *of living creatures.* (1) *to take food, take a meal :*—Sē itt and drincð mid ðǽm synfullum, Past. 327, 3. Eatað ðearfan *edent pauperes,* Ps. Srt. 21, 27. Ðá þá se Godes wer æt (ætt, *v. l.*), se munuc stód him ætforan, Gr. D. 144, 1. Ðíne suna and ðíne dohtra ǽton and druncon mid heora yldestan bréðer, Hml. Th. 450, 16. Hí ǽton ǽne on dæg, Bt. 15; F. 48, 8. Éton *manducaverunt,* Ps. Srt. 21, 30. Et (*comede*) and drinc and gewista, Lk. 12, 19. Ne gedyrstlǽcen hí þæt hý áhwǽr út of mynstre etan, þeáh hý hwá bidde, R. Ben. 79, 17. Et(a)n *aepulari,* An. Ox. 56, 81. (2) *to eat food, &c. :*—Ic eton flǽsc ferra *manducabo carnes taurorum,* Ps. Srt. 49, 13. On ǽrmergen hē yted (eted, ited, *v. ll.*) hlóþe, Bd. 1, 34; Sch. 104, 13. Ðæt folc ætt þæs lambes flǽsc, Hml. Th. ii. 266, 15. Drinc þ wæter and et þá wyrta, Lch. ii. 110, 9. Etað þisne hláf, Hml. Th. ii. 266, 33. þ man gódne mete ete, Bl. H. 57, 5. (2 a) *to eat habitually, as a regular article of food:*—Nǽbbe gē líf on eów búton gē eton mín flǽsc ... Sē ðe et mín flǽsc, hē wunað on mē ... Sē ðe et ðisne hláf, hē leofað on ēcnysse, Hml. Th. ii. 266, 25-32. Ælcne mete hē onscunedon þe men etaþ, and wilnodon ðára þe deór etaþ, Bt. 38, 1; F. 196, 4. Treówa wæstmas hí ǽton and wyrta, 15; F. 48, 9. Hí hláf ne ǽton ..., ac ǽton manna líchaman, Bl. H. 229, 8. (2 b) *to eat of something :*—Fela monna ǽton of ðám heofonlican mete on ðám wēstena, Hml. Th. ii. 274, 20. Sittað under ðám fictreówe and etað of his wæstmum, Bl. H. 239, 7. (3) *to provide food* for a person (*dat.*):—Hí ǽton (eoton, *v. l.*) him of Hamtúnscíre and of Súð-Seaxum, Chr. 998; P. 131, 17. (4) *to devour, consume, destroy :*—þú etst (etest, *v. l.*) úre æceras *nostri agros depastas,* Ælfc. Gr. Z. 104, 19. Deóf eteð and spilleð *fur mactat et perdat,* Jn. R. L. 10, 10. Ic et *exedi,* Wrt. Voc. ii. 32, 36. II. *of things.* (1) *of the action of physical agents,* (a) *where it is gradual :*—Hine æt se cancor, Hml. S. 6, 284. Seó sealf wile þ deáde flǽsc of etan, Lch. ii. 332, 25. (b) *where it is rapid :*—Sió onlícnes sendde mycel wæter þurh hiora múþ and hié (hit?) æt manna líchaman, and hit ácwealde heora bearn ... þæt wæter weóx, and swíþe hit æt hyra líchaman, Bl. H. 245, 24-33. Ðá eotendan *edaces* (*flammas*), Wrt. Voc. ii. 92, 11: 31, 53. (2) *of passion, &c. :*—Þínes húses anda mē et (*comedit*), Jn. 2, 17. Ited, Ps. Srt. 68, 10.

ete, es; *m. Eating:*—Etes (ētes = ǽtes?. v. ǽt) first *manducandi spatium,* Mk. L. R. 6, 31. Sē þe hine laðode tó ete (*ad manducandum*), Gr. D. 128, 33.

Etel-ware. v. Eotol-ware.

eten-lǽs, (w)e; *f. The common pasture land :*—Þæt landstycce sceal beón nýhst etenlǽse (*vicina compascuis,* Latin version; cf. *compascuus ager* gemǽne lǽs, Wrt. Voc. i. 53, 54), Ll. Th. i. 440, 15. Ofer wudu ofer feld ofer ecen lǽse (etenlǽse ?), C. D. v. 262, 18.

etere. *For* Prov. 18 *substitute* Kent. Gl. 1044, *and add:*—Ettere *devorator,* Lk. L. 7, 34.

éþ-, éþe. v. íþ-, íþe.

éþel. *Add:*—Éþl *clima,* i. *plaga,* Wrt. Voc. ii. 131, 74. I. in connexion with human beings. (1) *a person's native country, fatherland :*—Æþel *patria,* Wrt. Voc. i. 80, 40. All lond þ oeðel *omnis regio,* Mt. L. 3, 5. Þín wræcstów is þám monnum éþel þe þǽron geborene wǽran, Bt. 11, 1; F. 32, 28. Seó burg (*Tyre*) wæs on ǽrdagum heora (*the Carthaginians'*) ieldrena éðel, Ors. 4, 5; S. 168, 11. þæt wíf wæs áfaren fram gemǽrum hire éðeles, Hml. Th. ii. 110, 13. Swá gemindige mínes gódes swá bið manna gehwilc metes and éþeles (*of food and fatherland*), Lch. i. 384, 26. Hē bebeád þæt ælc þára þe on elðeódignesse wǽre cóme tó his ágnum earde and tó his fæder oeþle, Ors. 5, 14; S. 248, 24. In eard í oeðel (oeþel, R.) his *in patria sua,* Mt. L. 13, 57. In oeðel í lond hiora *in regionem suam,* 2, 12. Sume naman synd *patriae,* þá geswuteliað þæs mannes éþel, Ælfc. Gr. Z. 13, 4. Ic hæfde bróþer and éðel on Egyptum, Hml. S. 23 b, 324. Þín wræcstów is þú fērdest þú ne uiuus in patriam non reuerteris amplius, Nar. 29, 12, 19. Ðá kyningas hiora onweald innanbordes gehióldon, and eác út hiora éðel gerýmdon, Past. 3, 8: Vald. 1, 31. Alle oeðlas ðeóda *omnes terrae gentium,* Ps. Srt. 21, 28. (1 a) *the land* of the living,

*this world :*—On éþele í earde lifigendra *in regione uiuorum,* Ps. L. 114, 9. (1 b) *an adopted country :*—[Mi]d elþeóde éðel healdan *to settle in a foreign country,* Bo. 36. (1 c) fig. *proper condition :*—Ic ongeat þ ðú wǽre út áfaren of þínes fæder éþe'e, þ is of mínum lárum, Bt. 5, 1; F. 8, 29. (1 d) *used of heaven* (or *hell*) *as the home of man after death :*—Ðæt wuldor ðæs úplican éðles, Past. 159, 23. þæs heofonlican éþles, Bl. H. 81, 30: 131, 15. Wē sculon cuman of þisse worolde tó úres fæder oeðle, þ is tó heofonríce, Ors. 5, 14; S. 248, 28. Wē wǽron on þysne wræcsíþ sende, and nú eft sceolon óþerne éþel sēcan, swá wíte, swá wuldor, swá wē nú geearnian willaþ, Bl. H. 23, 6. þone ēcean éþel í Englas 209, 24. II. *the land, abode* of spirits. (1) oí heaven :—Englas wiston þ heora éþel þǽr on heofenum sceolde geseted weorþan mid hálgum sáwlum, Bl. H. 121, 33. Engla éðel, An. 642: Cri. 630. Gǽsta éþel, 1407. Wǽron gesōme þá þe swegl buán, wuldres éðel, Gen. 83. (2) of hell :—Atolan éðles, Sat. 327. Ic móste in þeossum atolan oeðele gebídan, 108. III. *used in poetry of the sea as the home of fishes or birds :*—Fisces éðel, Dóm. 39. Ofer hwæles éðel. Seef. 60: An. 274: Edg. 48. Mere sēcan, mǽwes éðel, Bo. 25. ¶ The Rune is used instead of the word, which is its name, in Ors. 4, 5; S. 168, 11, and Vald. 1, 31. v. riht-éþel.

éþel-ríce. *Add:*—Wið ðæs úplican éþelríces *towards heaven which is our home,* Dóm. L. 32, 73.

éþel-riht. *Add:*—Him wæs on þám leódscipe lond gecynde, eard, éðelriht, B. 2198.

éþel-stól. *Add:* Gen. 1748: Cri. 516.

éþel-wyn. *Add:*—Hē mē lond forgeaf, eard, éðelwyn, B. 2493.

éþian. *Add:*—Se gást éþað (*spirat*) þǽr hē wile, Gr. D. 146, 12. Oeðað (oeðiga, R.) *spirat,* Jn. L. 3, 8. Swá swá se man swelteþ, swá swylteþ eác þá nýtenu, and gelíce hí ealle éþiað (*spirant*), Gr. D. 264, 20. þonne þá wyrmas éðedon, þonne eóde him of þý múðe mid þý oroðe swylce byrnende þecelle, Nar. 14, 13. Éþgiendra *anhelantium,* Wrt. Voc. ii. 1, 1. [Leowse þi fot of mi neche ... þ ich eði mahe, Marh. 13, 2.] v. ge-éþian.

-éþrian, éþring. v. ge-íþrian, íþring.

éþung. *Add:* I. *breathing, panting :*—Mid þæs rynes éðgunge (éþunge) *with panting from running,* R. Ben. 68, 3. I a. *flatulency* (?) :—Wiþ áþundenesse and éþunge magan, Lch. ii. 188, 19. I b. fig. *inspiration :*—Éþunge *inspirationis,* R. Ben. I. 53, 12. II. *breath :*—Oroþ vel éþung *flatus,* Wrt. Voc. ii. 149, 32. Ðridde wæs windes pund, ðanon him (*Adam*) wæs seó ǽðung gesealg, Sal. K. p. 180, 10. Wæs þǽra wyrma oroð and éþung swíðe deáðberende *serpentum halitus erat pestifer,* Nar. 14, 15. III. *the emission of a smell.* cf. éþian, II:—Éðung *obolitio* (cf. *oboleo*), Wrt. Voc. ii. 115, 9: 63, 15. [or does éþung = ieþung, *and* obolitio = abolitio (v. á-íþan)?] IV? :—Éþungum *safumentio,* Wrt. Voc. ii. 147, 18. v. on-éþung.

eting, e; *f. Eating :*—On etincge *in edendo,* Scint. 170, 5.

et-lic (ēt-=ǽt-?); *adj. To eat, for eating :*—Huoethuoego þte ētlic (etlic, R.) se *aliquid quod manducetur,* Lk. L. 24, 41. Cf. ǽt-lic.

etol. *Add:*—Etol, gísre *edax,* i. *vorax, vorator,* Wrt. Voc. ii. 142, 29. [O. H. Ger. ezzal *edax.*]

etol-ness, e; *f. Gluttony, voracity :*—Ettulnysse mid leahtre *edacitatis vitio,* Scint. 55, 6.

ettan. *Substitute :*—To consume the produce of land, to graze land :—Gif ceorlas gærstún hæbben gemǽne oþþe óðer gedǽland . . . and etten hiora gemǽnan æceras oþþe gærs (*and* (cattle) *eat up their crops or grass*), Ll. Th. i. 128, 7. Hē sǽde þæt Norðmanna land wǽre swýþe lang and swýþe smæl. Eal þæt his man áþer oððe ettan oððe erian mæg (*all of it that can be grazed or ploughed*), þæt lið wið ðá sǽ, Ors, 1, 1; S. 18, 25. [O. Frs. etta: O. H. Ger. ezzen *depascere.*] v. á-ettan.

ettulnys. v. etol-ness.

euwā *alas ;* va(e), Wrt. Voc. ii. 98, 32. v. eów *in Dict. :* ēwan. v. íwan: ēwunga. v. eáwunga: ex. v. exe: -ex? v. þri-ex.

exe, an (?), e; *f. The brain :*—Cerebrum brægen vel exe, Wrt. Voc. ii. 130, 21. Exon þǽre ðryfealdan (brægene þám þryfealdan, *v. l.*) *cerebro triformi,* Lor. H. 183, 1. Se drǽnc is gód wið heáfodecce and wið brægenes hwyrfnesse and weallunge, wið seóndre exe, Lch. iii. 70, 21. [Take here also (?) Lch. iii. 2, 11 given under eax.]

exen. v. oxa.

exlypsis *eclipse :*—þonne þ exlypsis wǽre, þ is ðæs sunnan ásprungnis, Nar. 28, 9.

# F

-fá. v. ge-fá.

fácen. *Add:*—Fácni *astu.* Wrt. Voc. ii. 101, 13. Fácne, 8, 62. Cóm Swegen mid fácne, and bæd Beorn þ hē his gefēra wǽre . . ., cwæð þ hē him hold beón wolde. Ðá wēnde Beorn þ hē him swícan nolde, Chr. 1049; P. 168, 31. þonne gemētst ðú bútan fácne (*without fail*) þæs mónðes angin, Angl. viii. 327, 10. Hié hit tó nánum fácne ne tó þæs mónðes angin, Angl. viii. 327, 10. Hié hit tó nánum fácne ne tó nánum láðe nǽfdon *they did not hold it any wrong or injury,* Ors, 1, 10;

S. 48, 12. Fǎnc *strofam*, i. *fraudem*, An. Ox. 3650. Ælc fracodlic fǎcn áweorpan, Wlfst. 73, 17. Þ hé þǣr nán fǎcn (fācen, *v. l.*) gefremede, Ll. Th. i. 50, 31. Þēh hié him eft fācen gelǣsten *though they played him false afterwards*, Ors. 2, 5; S. 82, 12. Hē forgeaf him eallum þ unryht and þ fācn þ hē him dǒn þōhte *omnium factorum dictorumve in eo veniam sanxit*, 6, 4; S. 258, 29. Heora tungan wyrcaþ mycel fācn *linguis suis dolose agebant*, Ps. Th. 13, 5. Sē þæt fācn (*the secret preparation of a fleet*) tō his cȳþþe gebodade, 2, 5; S. 80, 2. Fācnum *factionibus*, i. *falsitatibus*, An. Ox. 2914. Fācn *factiones*, Wrt. Voc. ii. 33, 64. Fācnu, An. Ox. 7, 191: *strofas*, 204. Fācna, 2896. His (*the devil's*) swicolan fācna, Hex. 52, 12.

**fācen-ful.** *Add:*—Inwitful *vel* fācenful *dolosus*, i. *insidiosus, fraudulentus, callidus*, Wrt. Voc. ii. 141, 66: *subdola*, 150, 48. Fācenful *gewita testis fraudulentus*, Kent. Gl. 415. Fācenfulles *strofosi*, An. Ox. 2708. Þone fācenfullan *factiosum*, Wrt. Voc. ii. 33, 63. His fācenfullan syrewunge, Hml. Th. i. 82, 17. Fācenfullum *probrosis*, Wrt. Voc. ii. 66, 41. Heora nēhstan beswícan þurh þā fācenfullan word, Bl. H. 55, 18.

**fācenful-líc;** *adj. Deceitful* :—Nǎht ne sprece wē fācenfullíces *nichil loquamur subdolum*, Hy. S. 24, 19.

**fācenfullíce;** *adv. Deceitfully, cunningly* :—Fācenfullíce *dolose*, Ps. Spl. 5, 11: 35, 2. Fācnfullíce, 13, 5.

**fācen-gecwis.** For Cot. 46 *substitute* :—Fācengecwis *conspiratio*, Wrt. Voc. ii. 86, 73: 19, 8. Fācengecwys *conspicatio*, i. *conspirago*, 134, 9.

**fācen-geswipere.** *Dele, and see* geswipere.

**fācen-leás.** *Add*: *of precious metals or jewels, not sham* :—Mid golde and mid gimmum ǣc mid suulfre ofergylded, fāconleás feh, Jn. p. 188, 5.

**fācen-líc.** For 'R. Ben. . . . Lye' *substitute* :—Hū sió bysmerlíce sibb and fācenlíce weard betweónum Lǣcedemonium and Persum, Ors. S. 2, 28. Warnien hí þæt hí nán þing fācenlíces ne dōn *videant ne aliquam fraudem presumant inferre*, R. Ben. 95, 12, 15. Fācenlícu *dolore* (misread *dolosa* ?), Ps. L. 106, 39.

**fācen-líce.** *Add:*—Fācenlíce *fraudulenter*, Wrt. Voc. ii. 36, 14: *astute*, Wülck. Gl. 242, 21. Hȳ þenceað swíde fācenlíce (faecen-, Ps. Srt.) *dolose cogitabant*, Ps. Th. 34, 20: 35, 2. Sum fǣmne hí fācenlíce híwode sǎrlíce seóce, Hml. Th. ii. 506, 5. v. fǣcen-líce.

**facg.** *Add:* [cf. *N. E. D.* fadge *a large flat loaf.*]

**facian.** *Substitute:* fācian; *p.* ode. **I.** *trans. To wish for, desire to obtain* :—Pirrus him for þām swíþost fylste þe hé him selfum fācode Mæcedonia anweald *Pyrrhus helped them chiefly for the reason that he wanted the kingdom of Macedonia for himself*; his se Pyrrhus jungit, sperans Demetrium Macedonia posse depelli, Ors. 3, 11; S. 152, 7. **II.** *intrans. To arrive at a point* (?), *reach* :—Andlanges þæs ealdan mylegeares od hit fācad on þǣm íþhtan æsce (*until the boundary reaches* (?) *the ivy-clad ash-tree*), C. D. B. ii. 305, 27. [Cf. *Icel.* fíkjask á *to desire, be eager for*; fíkinn *greedy*.] v. fǣcan.

**fācne.** *Add:*—From men unrehtum and fācnum (*doloso*), Ps. Srt. 42, 1. Fācnum *fictis*, Wrt. Voc. ii. 108, 66: 35, 58. v. un-fācne.

**fācnes-full;** *adj. Deceitful* :—Ealle þā fācnesfullan weoloras *universa labia dolosa*, Ps. Th. 11, 3.

**fadian.** *Add:*—Fadode *digessit*, An. Ox. 56, 326. (1) *absolute* :—Seofon þing gedafenad rihtwísum cyninge . . . seofode, þ hé be freóndan and be fremdan fadige *gelíce* on rihtlican dōme (*that in the matter of just judgement his ordering be the same for friends and for strangers*), Ll. Th. ii. 306, 29. (2) *with acc.* :—Se prǎfast þæt fadaþ and gegearewaþ *praepositus omnia disponens*, R. Ben. 137, 22. Hē wíslíce his líf ne fadad *he orders not his life wisely*, Wlfst. 52, 28. Fadode, 159, 18. Gesette man þæne þe Godes hús wel fadige *domui Dei dignum constituant dispensatorem*, R. Ben. 119, 12. Gif hé his líf rihtlíce fadige, Ll. Th. i. 346, 18. Heora ágene wísan rihtlíce fadian *to order their conversation aright*, ii. 318, 13: Wlfst. 143, 22: 144, 22. [v. *N. E. D.* fade.]

**fadiend,** es; *m. One that directs, regulates, &c., a moderator* :—Fadiend *moderator*, An. Ox. 56, 308.

**fadung.** *Add:*—Þises sealmsanges fadung (fandung, *v. l.*) and endebyrdnes *haec distributio psalmorum*, R. Ben. 44, 14. On swylcere fadunge (fandunge, *v. l.*) . . . eal mynstres fadung (*ordinatio*), 125, 4–7. Þ Lēden and þ Englisc nabbaþ nā āne wísan on þǣre sprǣce fadunge (fandunge, MS.), Ælfc. Gen. Thw. 4, 8. Þæt is gedōn þe Godes fadunge, Hml. Th. i. 518, 31: Hml. S. 23, 257: Hex. 40, 26.

**fǣc.** *Add:* (*n.* and) *m.* **I.** *temporal* :—Fǣce *intercapedine*, An. Ox. 2401. Þū byst æfter fǣce þ ic nū eom, Bl. H. 113, 24: 23, 30. Ofer ealne geáres fǣc, Wlfst. 102, 15. Þā lǣcedōmas ne sculon on āne þrāge tō lange beón tō gedōne, ac sculon fǣc habban betweónum, Lch. ii. 186, 13. Ymb lytel fǣc *paulo post*, Past. 283, 1. Ymb tela micel fǣc (mycelne fyrst, *v. l.*), Chr. 942; P. 110, 26. Facum *spatiis*, i. *intervallis*, An. Ox. 3723: *lustris*, Wrt. Voc. ii. 50, 27. **II.** *local*, (1) *distance* :—On ōþere healfre míle fǣce *unius miliarii et dimidii spatio*, Bd. 5, 2; Sch. 556, 5: 5, 4; Sch. 567, 11. (2) *space of two or three dimensions.* v. fǣc-full :—Þæt ǣmtige fǣc bufon þǣre lyfte, Lch. iii. 242, 17. Hí ne beód mid ǣnigum fǣce fram him sylfum tōtwǣmede, Hml. Th. i. 500, 4. Betwux þā cealdan faca þǣre lyfte, Guth. 36, 15. Faco, 88, 15. (2 a) *room* :—Fec *spatium*, Kent. Gl.

649. **III.** *difference* of condition :—Swíþlic fǣc and micel rúmes faces tōdǎl *grande intervallum et larga spaciosae intercapedinis differentia*, An. Ox. 1177–1182. v. geár-, líf-, wræc-fǣc.

**fǣcan** *to desire to go.* Cf. willan; **II** d. 1 :—Gyf þ geneódige þ úre ǣnig tō ódrum fǣce (*the other version has* : Gif gebyrige þ for neóde heora hwilc wid úre bige habban wille, oþþe wē wid heora) mid yrfe and mid ǣhtum *if from necessity it happen that one of us wants to go to another* (*and trade*) *with cattle and goods*, Ll. Th. i. 156, 10. v. fācian.

**fǣcele.** *Substitute:* fǣcele, fecele, an; *f. A torch* :—Fǣcilae, faecile *fax*, Txts. 62, 407. Fǣcele, Wrt. Voc. ii. 95, 77. Fecele, 33, 54: *facula*, 53. [*O. H. Ger.* facchela *fax.*] Cf. þæcele.

**fǣcen-líce;** *adv. Fraudulently, deceitfully* :—Faecenlíce *fraudulenter*, Wrt. Voc. ii. 109, 28. v. fācenlíce.

**fǣcen-nes** (?) *deceit, guile, wile* :—Wā middangeard from fǣknissume *vae mundo a scandalis*, Mt. R. 18, 7.

**fǣc-full;** *adj. Spacious* :—Fǣcfull ys weg *spatiosa est via*, Scint. 185, 15.

**fǣcne.** *Add:*—Faecni *subscivum*, Txts. 96, 938. Fǣcne *fribula*, An. Ox. 7, 189. Fǣ[cne] *versuta*, 36, 2. Ne sȳ hé fǣcne *non sit nimis suspiciosus*, R. Ben. 121, 13. Fǣcne *unriht iniquitas*, Ps. Th. 72, 6. Se fǣcna *the devil*, Wal. 71. Þæs fǣcnan *strofose*, Wrt. Voc. ii. 80, 29: 76, 43. Faecnum *veterno*, 123, 43. Þȳ fǣcnan *strophosa*, 89, 65. From tungan faecenne *a lingua dolosa*, Ps. Srt. 119, 2, 3. Fǣcne *factiosam*, Au. Ox. 11, 121. Đā fǣcnan, Wrt. Voc. ii. 77, 46. Đā faecnan *dolosi*, Ps. Srt. 54, 24. In weolerum faecnum *in labiis dolosis*, 16, 1. Þā fǣcnan *fraudulentas*, Wrt. Voc. ii. 150, 47. [*v. N. E. D.* faken. *O. Sax.* fēkni: *Icel.* feik(in)n *monstrous.*] v. fācen.

**fǣcne;** *adv. Add:*—Fǣcne (fācne? *v.* fāceu) *astu*, Wrt. Voc. i. 287, 69.

**fǣcnig;** *adj. Crafty*, Nap. 78.

**-fǣd.** v. ge-fǣd.

**fæder.** *Add:* **I.** *of human beings.* (1) *a parent* :—Þonne hwylcum men gelimpeþ þ his ful leóf fæder gefærþ, ne mæg þ nā beón þ þā bearn þe unblíþran ne sȳn, Bl. H. 131, 24. Þæs fæder and þǣre mōdor mægen, 163, 25. Hwæðer þāra twēgra dyde þæs fæder (fadres, L., fæderes, R.) willan?, Mt. 21, 31. Nǣfre ácennede from fæder ne from mēder, Bl. H. 93, 28. Ic fare tō mínum fæder (feder, L.) and ic secge him: 'Eálá fæder (fader, L.),' Lk. 15, 18. Cwæd se yldra tō his fæder (fæder, L., feder, R.): 'Fæder,' 12. Úre worldcunde fædras (fæderas, *v. l.*), Past. 253, 25. Úre flǣslican fædras, 255, 10. Fæderas ic lǣrde þ hié heora bearnum þone þeódscipe lǣrdon, Bl. H. 185, 18. (1 a) *a step-father* :—Þā þe steópcildum wesen strange fæderas, Ps. Th. 67, 5. (2) *a male ancestor, forefather*; mostly plural, *fathers, ancestors* :—Wē habbad Abraham ús tō fæder, Mt. 3, 9. Hit is gesǣd þæt úre ealdan fæderas (fædras, *v. l.*) wēron ceápes hierdas, Past. 100, 4. Úre fæderas (fedras, Ps. Srt.) bit ús sǣdon, Ps. Th. 43, 1. Fadoras, Lk. L. 6, 23. Fadero ł aldro úsero, Jn. L. 6, 31. Oþ cneórisse fæderena (feddra, Ps. Srt.) heora *usque in progenies patrum suorum*, Ps. L. 48, 20. On úre fædera (fædra, R., fadora, L.) dagum, Mt. 23, 30. Se Hǣlend wæs sprecende tō úrum fæderum, Bl. H. 159, 25. Fædrum (fadorum, L.), Lk. R. 1, 72. Tō fadrum his, Jn. p. 2, 2. (2 a) *where degree of relationship is given, father* (as in grand-*father*, &c.) :—Yldra fæder *avita*, fífta fæder *atavus*, Wrt. Voc. ii. 4, 71, 72. Bearn Ælfríces cwæd: 'Wæs mín ealda fæder Ealhelm hāten,' B. 218. Fēng Carl tō þām westríce . . . swá hit his þridda fæder (*his great-grandfather*) hæfde, Chr. 885; P. 78, 32. Félix wæs his (*Gregory's*) fífta fæder *Felix ejus fuit atavus* (Bd. 2, 1), Hml. Th. ii. 118, 9. On þām is swiotol ealla þā duguþa hiora fæder and heora eldran fæder *vel paterni vel aviti specimen elucet ingenii*, Bt. 10; F. 28, 32. Eádmund is byrged mid his ealdan fæder Eádgáre, Chr. 1016; P. 153, 12. Ǣnne for mē, ōþerne for mínne fæder, þriddan for mínne ieldran fæder, C. D. ii. 176, 7. (3) *a god-father* :—On þām fulluhte ān fæder (*sponsor*) mæg beón, gif hit nýdþearf bid, Ll. Th. i. 140, 18. (4) *one of the early church* :—Wē rǣdad þæt þā ealdan fæderas on ānum dæge þæt stídlíce gefyldon, þǣr wē ásolcene on āre wucan gelǣsten, R. Ben. 44, 21. Þā gesetton hālige fæderas and Godes folces lāreówas þā tíd þæs fæstenes, Bl. H. 27, 25. Hē dā bisene þāra fordgefarena federa (fædra, *v. l.*) sceáwad, Past. 77, 19. (5) *one who exercises fatherly care, a patron* :—Aðelwold muneca fæder, Chr. 984; P. 125, 8. Se árwurda muneca feder Landfranc, 1089; P. 225, 8. Hine (Eádweard) gecēs tō fæder (fædere, *v. l.*) and tō hláforde Scotta cyning and eall Scotta þeód, 924; P. 104, 18. (6) *the head of a family* :—Þæs mynstres fæder (*the abbot*, cf. l. 39), Hml. S. 33, 13. Cuoeðas gié ðǣm fædir (feder, R.) hiórodas, Lk. L. 22, 11. **II.** *of the Deity.* (1) *the first person of the Trinity* :—Fæderes *Patris*, Hy. S. 96, 22. Drihten, þū de āstíhst ofer tungla mid Fæder, 88, 35. Sȳ lof Fæder mid Suna, 96, 19. (2) *the Father* of Jesus :—Mínes Fæder (Fador, L., Fædres, R.) willa, Jn. 6, 40. Fædores, Mk. p. 3, 3. Faderes, Mt. L. 12, 50. Ic wæs sended fram mínum Fæder, Bl. H. 155, 24: 157, 21. (3) *the heavenly Father* of men :—Fæder úre þū þe eart on heofenum, Mt. 6, 9. Úre se heofonlica Fæder, Bl. H. 131, 27. Úre gǣsta Fæder, Past.

255, 9. On ðæs Fæder hûse, 409, 5. þînum Fæder (Federe, L.), Mt. 6, 18. v. ealde-, fêster-, fulluht-, mynster-, neáh-fæder.

**fædera.** *Add:*—Faedra *patruus,* faedran sunu *patruelis,* Wrt. Voc. ii. 116, 24, 25. Mînes fæderan fæder *patruus meus magnus,* i. 52, 14. Harald, Magnus fædera (*Sigurð, Harald's father, was stepfather to Olaf, the father of Magnus*), Chr. 1049; P. 167, 20. Acsicheles sunum, Aarones fæderan (*patrui*; cf. Ex. 6, 18–22), Lev. 10, 4. Ðâ Eádwine wæs ofslegen, þâ fêng tô rîce his fæderan (*patrui*) sunu Ælfrîces, Osrîc wæs hâten (*Ælfric and Ælle, the fathers of Osric and Eadwine respectively, were sons of Yffe*), Bd. 3, 1; Sch. 190, 9. Osrîc wæs Ælfrîces sunu Ædwines federan, Chr. 634; P. 27, 1. Ôswine, Édwines fedran suna sunu Ôsrîces, 643; P. 27, 34. Ceólwulf sealde his rîce Edberhte his federan sunu (*Leodwald, great-grandfather of Ceolwulf, was Edberht's grandfather, so that C. and E. were first cousins once removed.* v. Chr. ann. 731, 738); 737; P. 45, 21. Wæs Ecgbriht heora (*Eormenred's two sons*) fæderan sunu, Eorcenbrihtes (*Eorcenbriht and Eormenred were sons of Edbald.* v. Chr. 640), Lch. iii. 424, 14. þâ twêgen Scipian gefuhton wið Hasterbale, Hannibales fædran and hiene ofslôgon *Scitiones Asdrubalem bello oppresserunt,* Ors. 4, 9; S. 192, 19. þâ Scottas Dunecan (Melcolmes sunu, P. 228, 18) ofslôgan, and heom his fæderan, Dufenal (Melcolmes brôðer, P. 228, 16), tô cynge genâmon, Chr. 1094; P. 230, 10.

**-fædera(-e).** v. ge-fædera(-e).

**fæderen.** *Add:*—Gâlnyss forspillednyss ys fædrenre (*paternę*) yrfe-wyrdnysse spêde, Scint. 87, 2. v. ge-fæderen.

**fæderen-brôþer.** *In l. 2 for* fram ðe *l.* framþe.

**fæderen-cnôsl.** *Add:*—Fæderencnôsles *parentelae,* Wrt. Voc. ii. 67, 11.

**fæderen-cyn.** *Add:* v. riht-fæderencyn.

**fæderen-feoh;** *gen.* -feós; *n. Property given by the father to the daughter on her marriage, dowry* (cf. quicquid de sede paterna secum attulit, lex alam, 55. v. Grmm. R. A. 429):—Fædrenfeoh *dos,* Wrt. Voc. ii. 141, 80. v. fæder-feoh *in Dict.*

**fæderen-mæg.** *Add:*—Swâ hwylc mînra fædrenmêga swâ þæt sió, þ hine tô þan gehagige, Cht. Th. 481, 24. v. fædering-mæg.

**fæder-êþel.** *Add:*—In his faderoeðel *in sua patria,* Mt. p. 17, 8.

**fæder-eðel-stôl.** *l.* fæder eðel-stôl, *and see* êþel-stôl: **fæder-feoh.** v. fæderen-feoh.

**fæder-gestreón.** *Add:*—Fædergestreón *patrimonium,* An. Ox. 4818: *patrimonia,* 4624. Fædergestreóna *patrimonium,* Wrt. Voc. ii. 66, 69.

**fæder-leás.** *Add:*—Feadurleásum (*pupillo*) ðû bist fultum, Ps. Srt. 9, 35. þû eart fæder ealra þæra þe fæderleáse syndon, Hml. A. 175, 174. Fylstan fæderleásum cildum, Wlfst. 228, 22. Feadurleásum his *pupillis ejus,* Ps. Srt. 108, 12. Hî feadurleáse (*pupillos*) ofslôgun, 93, 6.

**fæder-lic.** *Add:* I. *of a father :*—Hê ðeign from faederlica forbeád byrgen *discipulum a paterna vetuit sepultura,* Mt. p. 15, 17. I a. *referring to the Deity.* v. fæder, II :—Birhtu federlices (*paternae*) wuldres, Ps. Srt. ii. p. 200, 31. Of hêhþe þæs fæderlican þrymmes, Bl. H. 65, 31. Úre Hælend tô þæm fæderlican setle eóde, 115, 33 : 5, 15. II. *ancestral ; of succession, lineal.* v. fæder, I. 2, 2 a :—þîne suna ge-sittað þ cynesetl oð ðâ feórðe mægðe mid fæderlicre æftergengnysse (*son shall succeed father for four generations*), Hml. S. 18, 385. III. *of feelings or conduct, proper to a father.* v. fæder, I. 5 :—Fadorlico ðingo *patrocinio,* Rtl. 63, 3 : 62, 1 : 50, 15. Hê æteówde fæderlice lufe, Hml. Th. i. 392, 16.

**fæder-lîce;** *adv. As a father :*—þæt Cûðberhtus his fyrwitnysse fæderlîce miltsode *that Cuthbert like as a father would pity his curiosity,* Hml. Th. ii. 138, 19. v. un-fæderlîce.

**fæder-rîce.** Dele.

**fæder-swica,** an; *m. A traitor to a father :*—Swâ geendode se fæderswica (*Absalom*) mid his feore his unræd, Hml. S. 19, 224.

**-fædlic, -lîce.** v. ge-fædlic, -lîce : **-fædred.** v. ge-fædred: **faedun.** v. fægan.

**fægan;** *p.* fæde; *pp.* fæged *To paint :*—Faehit *pingit,* Txts. 86, 785. ¶ *In the following glosses there seems to be confusion either between the Latin verbs* pangere *and* pingere *or between the English verbs* fægan *and* fêgan :—Fêgð *pingit* (cf. gefêgað *conpingite,* 15, 43), Wrt. Voc. ii. 68, 14. Fægde (foegde ?) *pangit* (nec glus murorum moenia pangit, Ald. 173, 32), 93, 66. Faedun, fædun *pangebant* (*pingebant ?*), Txts. 85, 1504. [v. N. E. D. fay. O. H. Ger. gi-fêhen *tingere, pingere* Icel. fâ *to paint.*] v. â-fægan; fâg.

**fæge.** *Add:* I. *doomed to death, fey :*—þonne þ wîf seó mid bearne . . . cweþe heó : 'Ic gonge . . . mid cwican cilde, nalæs mid cwellendum, mid fulborenum, nalæs mid fægan (*with one that will be born alive, not with one that is to be still-born*), Lch. iii. 66, 30. Fæge *praecipitem,* Germ. 402, 43. Hê fægra manna forðsîð foregleáw sæde, Hml. Th. ii. 152, 2. II. *doomed to eternal death, damned :*—Æt heldore þær firenfulra fæge gæstas æfter swyltcwale sêcan onginnað ingong, Gû. 532. [v. N. E. D. fey.]

**-fæge.** v. ge-fæge.

**fægen.** *Add:* , fagen *glad.* (1) absolute:—Faegen *conpos,* Wrt. Voc. ii. 104, 73. Fægen *voti compos,* 124, 11. (2) *with cause of gladness given,* (a) in genitive:—Hilarius hine underfêng, fagen his cymes, Hml. Th. ii. 504, 19. Fægen (fagen, *v. l.*) his gecyrrednysse, Hml. S. 26, 133. Fægen wæron sîðes, lungre leórdan, An. 1043. (b) in a clause :—Hê wæs fægen þ hê tô scypum ætfleáh, Chr. 1076; P. 211, 28. Wæron þâ burgware tô þon fægene and tô þon blîðe þæt hié feohtan môston, Ors. 5, 3 ; S. 222, 4. Weaxad hraðe feldes blôstman, fægen þ hî nióton, Met. 6, 10. (c) *with gen. of pronoun and clause :*—Lyt monna weorð lange fægen ðæs ðe hê ôðerne bewrencð *few men are glad for long that they have tricked others,* Prov. K. 34. Wæron ealle þæs fægen þæt Drihten wolde him tô helpe hâm gesêcan, Sat. 435. v. feorh-fægen.

**fæger, es;** *n.* (*not* e ; *f.*). Dele bracket, *and add:* I. *beauty :*—Gif hit fæger is, þ is of heora âgnum gecynde, næs of ðînum ; heora fæger hit is, næs þîn. Hwæt fægnast þû þonne heora fægeres ? hwæt belimpþ his tô þe ?, Bt. 14, 2 ; F. 42, 32–36. Hwæþer ðû beó â þý fægerra for ôðres mannes fægere, 30, 1 ; F. 108, 28. II. *what is beautiful :*—þeáh he mycel âge und feala fægeres, him bið mycel daru gif hê hit geseón ne mæge, Bl. H. 21, 8. [v. N. E. D. fair; *sb.*]

**fæger.** *Add:* I. *beautiful to the eye :*—Swâ manega gesceafta und swâ micla und swâ fægra, Bt. 42 ; F. 256, 8. (1) *of persons :*—Fæger man *pulcher homo,* Wrt. Voc. i. 72, 14. Fæger *formosa,* An. Ox. 3410. Ân þæra nunnena þe wæs swýþe fægru (*speciosa*) æfter þæs lîchaman gesceape, Gr. D. 28, 25. On fægeres cildes heówe, Bl. H. 235, 29. Mid wlite und mid wæstmum fægerum, 113, 17. Fægerne bearnteâm, Chr. 1057; P. 188, 14. Ðeáh þû wære eallra monna fægrost, Bt. 32, 1 ; F. 114, 27. (1 a) *of the body and its parts :*—þæt feax âfealled þe ær wæs fæger on hîwe und on fulre wæstme, Wlfst. 148, 5. Þîn se fægresta fæþm, Bl. H. 7, 25. Fægre leomu on tô geseónne, 113, 22. (1 b) *of a period of life :*—Fægre *uenustae* (*pubertatis*), An. Ox. 2115. þonne se geogoþhâd ærest blôweþ und fægerost biþ, Bl. H. 59, 6. (2) *of inanimate things :*—Hwæþer ðe lîcigen fægeru lond ? . . . Hwî ne sceolde mê lîcian fæger land ? hû ne is þæt fægeresta dæl Godes gesceafta ? *an vos agrorum pulcritudo delectat ? quidni ? est enim pulcerrimi operis pulcra portio,* Bt. 14, 1 ; F. 40, 17. þes middangeard wæs fæger, Bl. H. 115, 10. Þ þ templ wære þrymlic geweorc und fæger, 77, 32. On þæm fægran neorxnawange, 143, 25. Fægerra blôstmena, Bt. 14, 1 ; F. 40, 24. (3) *of appearance :*—Fægereste *pulcherrimae* (*venustati*), An. Ox. 1052. II. *of moral beauty :*—Wæs fæger eáðmôdnes gemêted on þære sæmnan, Bl. H. 9, 21. Fægeran *formosiore* (*virginitate*), An. Ox. 4978. III. *fig. as an epithet of sound, odour, &c. :*—Ðâ eáran wæron hræde tô gehýrenne fægere dreámas, Wlfst. 148, 2. IV. *fair, desirable, handsome* (*of amount*) :—þîn mêd is on mê fæger, Hml. A. 167, 99. Gemun ðû ðæs miclan and þæs fægran edleánes, Bt. 37, 2 ; F. 188, 30. V. *fair, plausible* (*of words*) :—Mê nædre beswâc þurh fægir word, Gen. 899. VI. *fair, not disturbed, not stormy :*—Gyf hê fæger weter geseó, oððe ofer færeþ, þ byð orsorgnyss, Lch. iii. 168, 25. VI a. *free from trouble, pleasant :*—þûhte fæger and wlitig heora lîf and wynsumlic, Bl. H. 107, 30. VI b. *free from impropriety :*—Heó hâdunga underfêng mid fægere drohtnunga, Hml. S. 7, 284. v. for-fæger.

**fægere.** *Add:* I. *beautifully to the eye :*—Fægere gefrætewod, Seel. 139. Fægere gegyrwed, Râ. 21, 2. Cyrice geworht swâ fægre swâ hit men fægrost geþencean meahton. Synd þær þrý porticas swîþe fægere ufan oferworhte, Bl. H. 125, 22. þæt on foldan fægre stôde wudubeám wlitig, Dan. 498. II. *of sound :*—Hî singað fægre, Cri. 390. III. *of composition, elegantly :*—Ic þâ ged ne mæg gefêgean swâ fægre (cf. ic sceal mid ungerâdum wordum gesettan, Bt. 2 ; F. 4, 7), Met. 2, 6. IV. *of gentle movement or procedure, without haste or violence, gently :*—Fægre *pedetemptim* (= sôfte, Wrt. Voc. ii. 81, 39), An. Ox. 3046 : Wrt. Voc. ii. 40, 47 : 66, 49. Se læce grâpað suiðe fægre ymbûtan ðæt ðæt hê snîðan wile, Past. 187, 1. þær mê sôfte byð, þær ic beó fægere beþeaht fiðerum ðînum, Ps. Th. 60, 3. Hî hine mid ealre smyltnysse on heora fiðerum feredon, þæt hê ne mihte ne on scipe fægeror gefered beón, Guth. 40, 18. V. *of gentle, courteous, kindly treatment :*—Onfôh þû þînum esne fægere, Ps. Th. 118, 122. Swâ fæder ðenceð fægere his bearnum milde weorðan, 102, 13. VI. *of gentle speech, cf. to speak a person fair :*—Ongan Abraham sprecan fægere tô Lothe, Gen. 1900 : 2497. Fægre grêtan, 2104. Fægre fricgean, B. 1985. Fægre gehâtan *to make fair promises,* 2989. Hê swæslîce sibbe gehâteð, frêfreð hî fægre (*speaks words of kind comfort*), Cri. 1341. Hê ðâm folce fægere bodade *with kindly words he warned the people,* Hml. Th. ii. 140, 10. Hê hî gefrêfrode, þus fægre tihtende, 328, 3. Mid fæderlicre lufe fægere tihtende, Hml. S. 13, 313. VI a. *in a bad sense, plausibly, speciously :*—Hê spreceð fægere beforan and þæt fâcen hafað in his heortan, Leás. 5. VII. *so as to be without impurity :*—Hê mec fægre feormað, Râ. 72, 18. VIII. *without defect, thoroughly, nobly, splendidly, with happy result.* v. fægerlîce :—Hû mæg se ungelêreda læwedum folce fægre bodian ?, Hml. Th. ii. 320, 12. Fægere gereorded *splendidly entertained,* B. 1788. Hê

fylde þīnne willan fægere mid gōde *satiat in bonis desiderium tuum*, Ps. Th. 102, 4. Heofonas syndon fægre gefylled þīnes wuldres, Ph. 627 : Gū. 625. Gefultuma mē, þonne beó ic fægere hāl, Ps. Th. 118, 117. Gefultuma mē fægere, 118, 86. Fægre, Jud. 301. Þā gefetredan fægre Drihten ālȳseð *the Lord makes deliverance fair of the fettered*, Ps. Th. 145, 7. Seledreáme fægre onþeón, Rä. 64, 2. Fægere āfréfran, Ps. Th. 125, 1. Git mid þȳ fullwihte fægre onbryrdon ealne þisne middangeard *gave splendid incitement to all this earth*, Hö. 136. Hē him fægre leán geaf *he rewarded them splendidly*, Cri. 472 : 1361. Þū þe Maria fægere ākende *thou whom Mary in happy hour brought forth*, Hy. 3, 26. IX. *with propriety, in a becoming manner* :—God sceal mon ǣrest hergan, fægre fæder ūserne, Gn. Ex. 5. Wese God ā gebletsad, and þæt fægere becweðe folca ǣghwylc, Ps. Th. 105, 37. X. *justly, in equity* :—Sceal wearh hangian, fægere ongildan þæt hē ǣr fācen dyde, Gn. C. 56. [v. *N. E. D.* fair ; *adv.*]

fæger-līce ; *adv. Splendidly, sumptuously* :—Hē gehriordade fegerlīce *epulabatur splendide*, Bl. H. 16, 19.

fægernes. *Add* : I. *beauty* that is visible. (1) of a person. v. fæger, I. 1 :—Se līchoma ealdaþ and his fægernis gewīteþ, Bl. H. 57, 29. Fægernesse *venustate* (*membrorum*), Hpt. Gl. 516, 50. Wlitig mǣdenmann on wundorlicre fægernysse, Hml. A. 94, 82 : 2, 26 : Ælfc. T. Grn. 2, 24. (2) of other living creatures :—Sió fealwe fægernes (*fulva venustas* (*pavonis*), Wrt. Voc. ii. 89, 62. (3) of things :—Hwæt belimpþ þe heora (*sun, moon and stars*) fægernesse? hwæþer ðū durre gilpan þ heora fægernes þīn sié?, Bt. 14, 1 ; F. 40, 22. Fægernes *venustas* (*marmoris*), Wrt. Voc. ii. 75, 73. Þes middangeard wæs ealre fægernesse full, Bl. H. 115, 6. Þā hié emb þā fægernesse þæs temples sprǣcan ... hē cwæþ : 'Hwæt gē geseóþ ealle þā fægernessa þissa getimbra,' 77, 31. Þā fægernes þæs londes, Nar. 26, 25. (3 a) *a beautiful thing, ornament* :—Beorhtra ðonne ealra heofona tunglu oððe on ealre eorðan sȳn goldes and seolfres frætwednissa and fægernissa, Sal. K. p. 150, 18. II. *beauty, elegance* of diction :—Āwend sprǣc tō ōðrum hīwe, hwīlon for fægernysse, hwīlon for neóde, Ælfc. Gr. Z. 294, 18. Fægernessa on lēdensprǣce, hū heó betst gelōgod beó, 295, 4. III. *pleasantness, a pleasant, delightful condition* :—Ne mæg nān man hit āsecgan ymbe þā fægernessa þe God hafað gegearwod þām mannum þe hine lufian willað, Hml. A. 167, 100. IV. *moral or spiritual beauty* :—Seó fægernes þǣre sāule, Bl. H. 57, 31. Brūcan his wuldres fægernesse, 39, 24. [*O. H. Ger.* fagar-nessi *claritas*.] v. un-, weorold-fægerness.

fæg-lic. v. un-fæglic.

fægnian. *Add* : I. *to rejoice, exult*. (1) absolute :—Ic fægnige and þē herige *exaltabo te*, Ps. Th. 29, 1. Fægnian ealle on ēcnesse *omnes in aeternum exultabunt*, 5, 12. Cōmon ealle ... swīðe fægengende, Chr. 1069 ; P. 204, 17. (2) with cause of joy, (a) in gen. :—Hē fægnode (fægenode, *v. l.*) ðæs miclan weorces *dum magna se fecisse gauderet*, Past. 39, 14. Hē fægnode Godes fultumes, Ps. Th. 4, arg. Hē fægnode his tōcymes, Hml. S. 18, 77 : 26, 60. Ic lǣre þ ðū fægenige ōþerra manna gōdes, Bt. 30, 1 ; F. 108, 30. Ðæt hié fægenigen (fægenien, *v. l.*) ōðra monna gōðra weorca *ut alienis bonis congaudeant*, Past. 229, 13. Ðæs gōdes his nīhstena hē sceal fægnian (fagenian, *v. l.*) *in bonis proximi laetatur*, 61, 17. Fagnian, Hml. Th. i. 88, 2. (b) by clause :—Gē fægniaþ þ gē mōton sceppan þone naman, Bt. 16, 4 ; F. 56, 24. Hī fægnodon þ heó wæs þām brēþer gelīc, Hml. Th. ii. 32, 32. Ic wolde fægnian mid swīþe ungemetlice gefeán ... þ ic hit mōste geseón. Bt. 34, 9 ; F. 146, 11. (c) with gen. of pronoun and clause :—Heó fægnað (ïagenaþ, *v. l.*) þæs þæt heó mōt brūcan þæs heofonlican, Bt. 18, 4 ; F. 68, 16. Hē fægniaþ þæs þ hē heora wealt, 39, 13 ; F. 234, 29. Deáh hē þæs fægnige þ hē his naman brǣden, 30, 1 ; F. 108, 11. (d) with prep. :— Ic fægnie on þīnre hǣlo *exultabo in salutari tuo*, Ps. Th. 9, 14. Dȳ lǣs for ðǣm giefum his mōd fægnige *ne in oblato munere animus hilarescat*, Past. 321, 24. Dȳ lǣs hē tō ungemetlice fægnige (fægenige, *v. l.*) for his gōdum weorcum *ne in benefactis immoderatius gaudeant*, 323, 6. Þæt hē on his gesundfulnysse fægnige, Hml. Th. i. 584, 6. II. *to make a movement that expresses joy*. (1) of persons :—Þā fahnude (fægnode, *v. l.*) (*exultavit in gaudio*) mīn cild on mīnum innoðe, Lk. 1, 44 : Shrn. 95, 17. Fægnian mid folmum *plaudere*, Ps. Th. 97, 8. (2) of animals :—Cerverus ongan fægenian mid his steorte, Bt. 35, 6 ; F. 168, 17. Ongan seó leó fægnian wið þæs ealdan weard, and hine mid his leoþum styrgendum grētte *the lion came towards the old man fawning, and with its limbs quivering greeted him*, Hml. S. 23 b, 777. III. *to receive with pleasure, welcome* :—Se cyng cwæð þ hē þ lustlīce fægnian wolde *the king said that he would welcome such a proposal with pleasure*, Lch. iii. 426, 30. [v. *N. E. D.* fain, fawn. *Goth.* faginōn : *O. Sax.* faganōn : *O. H. Ger.* faginōn, feginon : *Icel.* fagna.]

fægnung. *Add* :—Fægnung *jubilatio*, Hy. S. 106, 23. Fægnunge, blisse *jubilationis*, i. *laudis*, An. Ox. 1345. Fægnunge *tripudio, gaudio, exultatione*, Hpt. Gl. 433, 2. Mid blisse and mid fægnuncge *in laetitia et exultatione*, Ps. Th. 44, 16. Ongan for ðon gefeán (fægnunge, *v. l.*) weópan *coepit ex gaudio flere*, Gr. D. 216, 20. Þæt folc mid micelre fægnunge and singalre herunge hī gelǣddon tō ðǣre stōwe, Hml. Th. ii. 32, 30.

fæg-nys. v. fāg-nes : fǣgon. v. feón *to rejoice*.

fægrian. *Add : to make fair, adorn* :—Fægeredre *falerata*, An. Ox. 5309. [v. *N. E. D.* fair ; *vb. Icel.* fegra *to aðorn*.] v. ge-fægerian ; æ-fægred.

faehit. v. fǣgan.

fǣhþ ( =fǣgþ? cf. fǣge) *feyness* :—Dol seldon drȳmeð sorgful ymbe his forðgesceaft, nefne hē fǣhðe wite *a fool in his life of pleasure is seldom anxious about his future, unless he knows that death is at hand*, Fä. 56. [*Icel.* feigð *feyness*.]

fǣhþ *feud*. *Add* : I. in a general sense :—Themistocles gemyndgade Iōnas þǣre ealdan fǣhþe þe Xersis him tō geworht hæfde, hū hē hié mid forhergiunge and mid heora mǣga slihtum on his geweald geniédde, Ors. 2, 5 ; S. 82, 16. Hié forgeáfon þǣm Cāsere þā fǣhþe þe his mǣg hæfde wið hié geworht, 6, 4 ; S. 258, 27. Samson hæfde fǣhðe tō ðām folce *Samson was at feud with the folk (the Philistines)*, Hml. Th. i. 226, 23. II. as a law term :—Be fǣhðum, Ll. Th. i. 90, 1. v. un-, wer-fǣhþ.

fælde-stōl. v. filde-stōl : fǣle. *Add* : [v. *N. E. D.* fele:] fǣlging. v. filging : fǣll, fǣllan. v. fill, fillan.

fǣlsian. l. fǣlsian, *and add* :—Fǣlsende *lustrans*, Wrt. Voc. ii. 53, 53. v. fǣle.

fǣman. *Add* : (1) of fluids, (a) when boiling :—Wyl wæter on croccan, dō hunig on, fleót simle þ fām of oþ hit nelle mā fǣman, Lch. ii. 104, 20. Se fǣmenda seáþ *puteus ille flammivomus*, Bd. 5, 12 ; Sch. 627, 12. (b) when in violent motion :—Fǣmendre wīdsǣ *spumantis pelagi*, Hpt. Gl. 409, 68. (2) of living creatures, *to foam* at the mouth :—Hē fǣmeð (*spumat*) and gristbitteð mid tōðum, Mk. L. R. 9, 18. [þe reue ... feng on to feamin (femin, *v. l.*) and gristbeatien up o þis meiden, Jul. 69, 17. þe geant vemde and grunte, as yt were a strong bor, R. Glouc. 208, 7. *Scot.* feam : *O. H. Ger.* feimen *spumare*.] v. līg-fǣmende.

fǣmne. *Add* :—Ungehǣmed fǣmne *innupta*, i. *uirgo*, An. Ox. 1174. Scylcen, fǣmne, meówle *iuuencula*, i. *uirguncula*, 2112. Ceorlstrang fǣmne *virago*, Wrt. Voc. i. 17, 18. Þā cwæð Adam : 'Beó hire nama Uirago, þæt is fǣmne, for ðan ðe heó is of hire were genumen,' Hml. Th. i. 14, 24. Fram wǣpenleásre fēmnan *e virgine inermi*, Wrt. Voc. ii. 144, 39. ¶ referring to the Virgin Mary :—Heó is seó clǣneste fǣmne, and heó wæs fǣmne ǣr hire beorþre and heó wunaþ fǣmne æfter hire beorþre, Bl. H. 155, 33. Þū wǣre symle fǣmne oncnāwen ... þone Hǣlend þū fēmne (fǣmne, *v. l.*) geeácnodest, eác swilce fǣmne ācendest ... ðā hē līchaman onfeng. Æt Scā Marian, þǣre unwemman fǣmnan, Wlfst. 251, 8–13. v. nunn-fǣmne.

fǣmnenlic. *Substitute*: fǣmnen-lic (fǣmn-) ; *adj. Virgin, virginal* :—Clǣnnys fǣmnenlicre sāwle *puritas virginalis animae*, Scint. 69, 13. Of þām fǣmnendlican (fǣmned-, *v. l.*) līchaman *ex virgineo corpore*, Gr. D. 288, 15. Ic fǣmnenlicne (fǣmne-, *v. l.*) innoð gesōhte, Nap. 21. Þone fǣmnlican bōsm, Bl. H. 165, 27.

fǣmn-hād, es ; *m. Add* :—Fǣmnhād līchaman *virginitas corporis*, Scint. 69, 7. Fǣmnhādes *uirginitatis*, An. Ox. 574. Fǣmnhādes men hī geneósiaþ *apud hos ... visitatio virginum*, R. Ben. 136, 24. Be faemnhāde *de uirginitate*, Scint. 68, 13. Ic mīnne fǣmnhād besmāt ... ne forleás ic mīnne fǣmnhād for æniges mannes gyfum, Hml. S. 23 b, 328, 335.

fǣmnhād-lic ; *adj. Virgin, virginal* :—Fǣmnhādlices *uirginalis*, An. Ox. 1483. Fǣmnhādlicere, 1717. Fǣmnhā[d]licum *uirginali*, 535 : 2280.

fæng-tōþ. v. feng-tōþ : fæniht. *Dele*: Fæppingas. v. Færpingas : fænucæ. v. fen-ȳce.

fær. *Dele* 'fær ; *gen. dat. acc.* fǣre ... *f.* ?,' *and add* : I. of movement. (1) *going, passing* :—Faru ł færr *transitus*, Ps. L. 143, 14. Hī bǣdon þ hī mōston faran þurh ðā burh, ac ðā burhware noldon þæs færes him getȳðian, Hml. S. 25, 445. Þā þā hē gehȳrde þæs folces fær mid þām Hǣlende, ðā ācsode hē hwā þǣr fērde. Hī cwǣdon him tō þæt þæt wǣre ðæs Hǣlendes fær, Hml. Th. i. 152, 13–15. Hwæt is þæs Hǣlendes stede, oððe hwæt is his fær?, 156, 33. Hē cēpte þæs Hǣlendes fær *he was on the look-out for the passing of Jesus*, 580, 28. (1 a) *mode of going* :—Hī habbað blióh and fær bū ungelīce (cf. hī sint swīþe ungelīces hīwes and ungelīce faraþ, Bt. 41, 6 ; F. 254, 25), Met. 31, 4. (2) *a going away* (of change of abode) :—Be unālēsedum fære from his hlāforde. Gif hwā fare unālíefsed fram his hlāforde, Ll. Th. i. 126, 8. Be gesīðcundes monnes fære. Gif gesīðcund man fare, þonne mōt hē habban his gerēfan mid him, 144, 1. (2 a) fig. of change of state :—Hwæt is gōðra manna deáð būton ... færr fram deáðe tō ðām ēcan līfe?, Hml. Th. ii. 232, 27. (3) *a journey, course*, (on water) *a voyage*, (of an army) *a march* :—Syx daga fær ofor sǣ, Lch. iii. 260, 3. Hwæt is ðeós ðe hēr āstīhð ... swā egeslic swā fyrdtruma? ... Hire fær (*her ascension*) is wiðmeten fyrdlicum truman, Hml. Th. ii. 444, 5. Hē fērde ofer langne wæg ... Hit gelamp for his langsumum fære, Hml. S. 29, 115. On fære mid þǣre scīre þe mid him fierdedon, Chr. 894 ; P. 86, 2. Geong ł fær *iter*, Lk. L.

10, 33. Manega cēpaþ be ðām mōnan heora fær (cf. on xvi.-nihte mōnan far ofer sǣ, Lch. iii. 180, 3; see also 176, 21: 178. 23, 27), Hml. Th. i. 100, 24. Þurh his langsume fær (gewende hē tō Rōme, 7), 80, 27: Lch. iii. 434, 4. Hē (Gehazi) bedīglode his fær . . . Se wītega hine befrān: 'Hwanon cōme ðū?,' Hml. Th. i. 400, 22. Ic ne cūðe hira fær nesciebam unde essen', Jos. 2, 4: Hml. S. 3, 637. (3 a) fig. of the coming of a season :—Embe feówer wucan se solmōnað sīgeð tō tūne, swā hit getealdon geó Februarius fær frōde gesīðas, Men. 18 : 167. (4) an expedition, enterprise :—Heó (Judith) bebeád þām folce þ hī ná ne hogedon embe hire fær ac gebǣdon for hī, Hml. A. 109, 233. II. a place where passage is possible or admissible, a passage, thorough-fare, road, entrance :—Hē him tǣhte þone wæg ofer ānum brādum fenne þær nān fær ǣr næs, Jud. Thw. 162, 18. Wæs þær ān burh, and næs nānes mannes fær on nāþre healfe þǣre byrig, Hml. S. 25, 441. Ðū fær eft biluce aditum reserasti, Rtl. 29, 34. Hī fordytton ǣlc fær upp tō þām muntum praeoccupaverunt omnes vertices montium, Hml. A. 104, 70. III. a means of transport, carriage, vessel :—Æt hȳðe stōd hringedstefna, īsig and ūtfūs, æðelinges fær, B. 33. Fōr fānig scip, . . . siððan fær seleste (the ark) flōd ūp āhōf, Gen. 1419. IV. of persons, a body of persons who journey, (1) on land, a troop :—Cōmon him tōgeánes þǣra cempena fær on cynelicum cræte, Hml. S. 31, 968. Hē geseah þǣra sceaþena fær. Ælfc. T. Grn. 18, 14. Hī ūt færdon mid folclicum truman, oð ðæt ðā Syriscan gesāwon heora fær, Hml. A. 113, 358. (2) on sea, a crew :—Hof seleste (the ark) fōr mid fearme; fære ne mōston wǣglīðendum wætres brōgan hrīnan, ac hié God ferede and nerede, Gen. 1394. V. of action or condition, fare (in welfare), proceedings, course of life, path in life :—Nū eom ic cnæpling, and nytende mīnes færes ignorans egressum et introitum meum (1 Kings 3, 7), Hml. Th. ii. 576, 15. Hē leornode on hālgum bōcum be þæs Hǣlendes fære, Hml. S. 3, 34. Ongan hē tō secgenne be ðæs Hǣlendes fære, hū hē worhte wundra fela, and siððan deáð þrowode, 10, 155. Crīst wolde þæt manega wītegan sceoldon cȳðan his fær, Hml. Th. ii. 20, 31 : Ælfc. T. Grn. 4. 4. Tō ðȳ þæt ic wolde witan ymbe ðīn fær, hū se Ælmihtiga embe ðē wolde ut, quid de te fieri deberet, agnoscerem (Bd. 5, 12), Hml. Th. ii. 354. 9. Man gesette on cranice his leóde fær, Hml. A. 95, 124. [Icel. far travel; a ship; life, conduct.] v. fram-, sīþ-, tō-, wæg-, ymb-fær; faru.

fær. Add: a calamity, disaster, evil, accident :—Fēr casus, Wrt. Voc. ii. 103, 35. Fǣr cassus, 14, 2. Cassibus, calamitatibus vel fērum, cassus, scelus, malum vel fǣr (cf. excidium, casus, ruina, 145, 8), 129, 27–30. Land, leóhtes leás and līges full, fȳres fǣr micel a land without light and full of flame, a huge destroying fire, Gen. 332. Ǣr him fǣr Godes aldre gesceóde ere the calamity sent by God destroyed them, Dan. 592. Ne con hē yfles andgiet, ǣr hit hine on fealleð. Hē þonne onfindeþ, þonne se fær cymeð, Dōm. 73. Ic þæs færes ā on wēnum sæt, hwonne mē wrāðra sum aldre beheówe I was ever expecting disaster, the stroke that should rob me of life, Gen. 2699. Hē sōna deád wæs. Ðā gesāwon ðā burgware, ðā wurdon hié swīðe forhte for ðǣm fære, Bl. H. 199. 24. Preóstas magon būtan fēre (without ill result?) þæs mōnan ylde findan mid gerāde, Angl. viii. 332. 46. Hié þurh flōdes fær (the destruction caused by the flood) feorh āleton, Andr. 1631 : 1532. Hī flugon forhtigende, fær ongeton they fled in terror, knowing the calamity that had come upon them, Exod. 452. Gif se ǣrra fær genam if the former got hurt, Rä. 54, 12. ¶ attack of disease ? :—Lǣcedōmas wiþ feferādle . . . wiþ þriddan dæges fǣre (cf. fefre, 134, 21) and feórþan dæges fǣre (cf. fefre, 134, 22) and wið ǣlces dæges fēre (cf. fefere, 134, 24), Lch. ii. 12, 26–28.

fǣr a fever. v. preceding word: fær; adj. Dele: fær for. v. for:

fǣr-. v. for-.

fǣr-ærning; es; f. Rapid riding :—Se here mid fǣrærninge (cursu rapido) becōm tō sumre eá, Gr. D. 14, 24.

fǣran. Add: I. to terrify :—Ðæt hē swā egesige ðā ofermōdan ðæt hē ðā eáðmōdan tō swīðe ne fēre (ut timidis non augeatur metus), Past. 453, 19. [v. N. E. D. fear, vb.] II. to take by surprise, seize quickly (?) :—Unlfes fērende lupi rapaces, Mt. L. 7, 15. [Cf. O. Sax. fārōn to lie in wait : O. H. Ger. fārēn desiderare, insidiari.] v. fǣring, fǣringa, fǣr-lic.

fǣr-bēna. Substitute : fær-bēna (-u), an; m. I. one that has to ask leave to go (faran) from his lord (? v. fær; I. 2), a person of the churl class :—Gif ǣni man āgiten wurðe þ hé ǣnisse hǣdenscipe dreóge . . . gif hé sī cynges þegn . . . Gif hit sī elles landāgende man . . . Gif hit sī færbēna . . . Gif cyninges þegen ǣtsace . . . Gif landāgende man ǣtsace . . . Gif cyrlisc man ǣtsace, Ll. Th. ii. 296, 27–298, 13. II. one that asks for passage on a ship (? cf. fær; I. 3; III; IV. 2) :—Faerbēnu epifates (= ἐπιβάτης), Txts. 108, 1112.

fǣr-blǣd. v. fēr-blǣd in Dict.: fǣrbu. Dele, and see fær; I. (1 a):

fǣr-clamm. v. fēr-clamm in Dict.

fǣr-cōþu. Substitute : fǣr-coþu, -e; f. Apoplexy (?) :—Wiþ fǣrcoþe, Lch. ii. 276, 10: 170, 16. Cf. fǣr-deáþ.

fǣr-cwealm. Add :—Gif hwæt fǣrlices on þeóde becymð, beón hit hererǣsas, beón hit fǣrcwealmas, Wlfst. 271, 2.

fǣr-cȳle. l. fǣr-cile, -cyle: fǣrd. v. fird.

fǣr-deáþ. Substitute: Sudden death, apoplexy :—Fǣrdeáþ apoplexia, Wrt. Voc. ii. 7, 63. Sǣde Cecilia þām brȳdguman þ heó gesāwe engel of heofenum, and sē wolde hyne sleán myd fǣrdeáþe (he would strike him dead), gif hē hyre onhryne, Shrn. 149, 24. [Fǣrdeáð mors repentina, Angl. xi. 387, 396.]

-fǣre. v. lang-fǣre.

fǣred-lic; adj. Sudden :—Wundrodon ealle men þ on swā lytlan fæce hine nān man findan mihte . . . and se cāsere and his þegnas wǣron sārie for his fǣredlican (cf. fǣrlican, 225) āweggewitennysse all men wondered that all of a sudden nobody could find him . . . and the emperor and his thanes were sorry for his sudden departure, Hml. S. 30, 158.

fǣr-eht. v. fǣr-riht.

fǣreld. Add : (n. and) m. I. of movement. (1) going, walking, &c. :—Fǣrelde cursu (rapidissimo abscessit), An. Ox. 4903. Þū on hrædum fǣrelde þone heofon ymbhweorfest rapido coelum turbine versas, Bt. 4; F. 6, 31. (1 a) a particular mode of travel :—Mōt hē swā rīdan, swā rōwan, swā swilce fǣrelde faran swylce tō his wege gebyrige, Ll. Th. ii. 420, 24. (1 b) ability to walk :—Hē gesundfull his fǣreldes breác, Hml. Th. ii. 136, 5. Healtum hī forgeáfon fǣreld, i. 544, 33. Underfōd þā healtan fǣreld, Hml. S. 29, 337. (2) a going, course, journey :—þes mōnan fǣreld, on hwilcum tungle hē nū is oþþe on hwilce hē ðanon gēð quo cras signo luna cursura sit, Solil. H. 17, 18 : 20, 16. Ðæt wǣre getācnod ðurh Balaham on ðǣre lettinge his fǣreltes (in ipsa ejus itineris retardatione), Past. 255, 20. Hig æfter ridon īdelum fǣrelde, Jos. 2, 7. Faran þreóra daga fǣreld, Ex. 3, 18. Gif þet Godes wille seó þæt heó þ fǣreld āge (that she be able to make the journey), Cht. Th. 481, 13. Se cwyrnstān tyrnð singallīce and nǣnne fǣreld ne ðurhtīhð the millstone turns continually and never moves a step from its place, Hml. Th. i. 514. 20. Fǣreltu meatus, fǣreð meat, Wrt. Voc. ii. 57, 32. Fǣreldum meatibus, An. Ox. 4857. Mid fingelum fǣreldum fugitiuis discursibus, 263. (2 a) a military expedition :—Hē wæs biddende . . . þ hē mōste on Ispānie firde gelǣdan, and hē þ fǣrelt þurteáh . . . Rōmāne wǣron þæs fǣreltes swā geornfulle . . . þæt hié eall him gesealdon þæt hié þā hæfdon on þǣm fǣrelte tō fultume, Ors. 4, 10; S. 196, 12–20. Sendon Rōmāne hiene þæt hē þæs fǣreltes consul wǣre consul creatus in Africam transiit, S. 200, 2. Hē gegaderade fierde, and wolde faran on Perse . . . ac God gewrǣc on þǣm fǣrelte . . . his ārleáse geþōht, 6, 31; S. 282, 29 : 4, 10; S. 194, 4. II. of space traversed, a way, road :—Seó sǣ him gerȳmde þreóra mīla drīes fǣreldes, Hml. Th. i. 564, 18. II a. the run, track of an animal :—Denn ł fēreldu lustra (vaga venatrix (the cat) rimabor lustra ferarum, Ald. 265, 7), An. Ox. 26, 47. Fǣreltu lustra (cf. ryne lustro, 50, 42), Wrt. Voc. ii. 53, 21. III. a means of transport, carriage, vehicle :—Fǣrelde, wǣne uehiculo, An. Ox. 4164: 2, 378: 11, 189. IV. people (and things) in movement, an expeditionary force, a train, retinue :—Fōr se consul on Affrice and mid eallum his fǣrelte on sē forweard universam classem naufragio amisit, Ors. 4, 6; S. 180, 2. Hē bebeád þæt nān crīsten mon ne cōme on his hiérede ne on his fǣrelte omnes Christianos e palatio suo jussit expelli, 6, 30; S. 282, 29. V. of conduct, course, way of life, proceeding :—Ic ǣlcum sylle æfter his fǣrelde do unicuique juxta viam suam (Jer. 17, 10), Hml. Th. i. 114, 17. His wiðerwinna wæs on eallum his fǣrelde sum drȳ, 370, 32. Se līchoma ðǣm mōde wierneð his unnyttan fǣrelta, Past. 257, 9. VI. referring to the Passover :—Pascha is on Lēden transitus, and on Englisc fǣreld ; for ðan on ðisum dæge fērde Godes folc ofer ðā Reádan sǣ, Hml. Th. ii. 282, 15. [Icel. farald.] v. fram-, hām-, onweg-, sǣ-, scip-, ūp-, wealh-fǣreld; fereld in Dict.

fǣreld-bōc an itinerary :—Sīðbōc, fōre bōc, fereld[bōc] itinerarium, Hpt. Gl. 454, 20.

fǣreng. v. fǣring.

fǣren-ness, e; f. A passage, migration :—Tō fǣrennisse . . . from fǣrennisse ad transmigrationem . . . a transmigratione, Mt. R. 1, 17. v. fǣr-ness.

fǣre-sceat. v. fere-, fǣr-sceat.

fǣr-fyll. Substitute: fǣr-fill, es; m. A sudden fall, headlong fall :—On fǣrfyll head foremost, headlong; in praeceps, Wrt. Voc. ii. 47, 44.

fǣr-haga. Substitute : Calamity that compasses about :—Wæs se bāncofa ādle onǣled . . . leomu hefegedon sārum gesōhte . . . hē his mōdsefan wið þām fǣrhagan fæste trymede the body was inflamed with disease . . . the limbs grew heavy attacked by pains . . . he fortified his mind firmly against the ills that compassed it about, Gú. 933.

fǣring. v. fering.

fǣring, e; f. I. ecstasy, rapture. v. fǣran; II Fǣringa extaseos, Wrt. Voc. ii. 32, 67. II. accusation :—Fēringe insimulatione (v. accusantes publica insimulatione (ǣswice, wrōhte, An. Ox. 4842), Ald. 69, 5), Wrt. Voc. ii. 111, 20.

fǣringa. Add : I. without warning or notice, unexpectedly, of a sudden, all at once :—Fēringa improvisu, Wrt. Voc. ii. 110, 64 Fǣringa, 45, 41. Fēringa extimplo, Kent. Gl. 146. þī fǣringa

(*repete*) stôd þǽr ætforan þǽre dura sum man, Gr. D. 62, 9: Bl. H. 173, 24; 175, 2: B. 1414. Fǽringa ymbe þá herehûðe hé hlemmeð tôgædre grimme gôman, Wal. 60: 44. Hé fǽringa feóll tô þǽre eorðan ... and hé forðférde, Chr. 1042; P. 162, 14: Bl. H. 223, 11. Swealt Ôsgod fǽringa swâ swâ hé on his reste læg, Chr. 1054; P. 184, 21: Jul. 477. II. *without premeditation:*—Sume ic lârum geteáh tô geflite ... þæt hý fǽringa ealde æfþoncan ednîwedan. Jul. 484. III. *soon, at once, without delay, early:*—Hé cwæþ: 'Cuman nû mycele hundas forþ'; and þá fǽringa côman hundas forþ, Bl. H. 181, 20. Eft fǽringa (cf. eft sôna), 129, 9. Fǽrunga hig cômon tô him *diluculo veniebant ad eum,* Ps L. 77, 34. Biscope is forbod þ hé onfóe nîwe cumenum preóst and tô gehǽlgenne fêrunga, Mt. L. 10, 14 note. Hit fǽringa fŷre byrneð, Ph. 531. IV. *by chance;* forte:—Man slǽtte ǽnne fearr fǽringa (fêr-, *v. l.*) þǽrûte, Hml. S. 12, 72. Gif heora hwylc fǽringa (*forte*) tôðint, R. Ben. 46, 16. Fǽrunga, R. Ben. I. 16, 13: 54, 6: 87, 3. Begŷmaþ þæt [ne] fǽrunga beón gehefegude heortan eówre *attendite ne forte grauentur corda uestra,* Scint. 105, 1. [*O. Sax.* fârungo: *O. H. Ger.* fârunga *subito, casu.*] v. fǽran; II.

**fǽr-lic.** *Add:* I. *sudden, that is unexpected, that happens without warning:*—Ðý lǽs eów hrǽdlíce on becume se fǽrlíca (*repentina*) dômes dæg, Past. 129, 21. Feerlic (fêr-, R.), Lk. L. 21, 34. Gif hit gewyrþe þæt on þeódscipe becume fǽrlic coþa oþþe fǽrlic deáþ, Wlfst. 172, 19. Fǽrlic ende, Bl. H. 113, 8. Hwæt þis ǽfre beón sceole fǽrlices *whatever can this sudden change be,* Hml. S. 23, 516. Gif hwæt fǽrlices on þeóde becymð *if any sudden ill befall the nation,* Wlfst. 271, 1. Ðá ðe mid fǽrlíce luste (*repentina concupiscentia*) beóð oferswîðde, Past. 429, 33: 417, 5. Mín Drihten, ne lǽt mé nǽfre fǽrlicum deáðe of þissum life gewîtan, Angl. xii. 499, 5. For his fǽrlican âweggewitennysse, Hml. S. 30, 225. Fǽrlican ôgan *repentino terrore,* Kent. Gl. 49. II. *sudden, quick in operation* (of poison):—Hé ðygde unlybban, ac hé ðá frecednysse ðæs fǽrlican âttres (cf. þ attor sôna hine swîðe þreáde forneán tô deáðe, Hml. S. 31, 198) âsîgde, Hml. Th. ii. 504, 15. III. *that occurs without design, fortuitous:*—On fǽrlicum gelimpe *fortuitu casu,* R. Ben. I. 69, 3. Fǽrlicum gelimpum *fortuitis casibus,* An. Ox. 4185. Þá fǽrlican âwendennissa *fortuitas permutationes,* 190. [*v. N. E. D.* ferly; *adj.* fâr-ligr *disastrous.*]

**fǽrlíce.** *Add:* I. *suddenly, of a sudden, all at once, unexpectedly:*—Cômon fleógende fǽrlíce englas, Hml. Th. ii. 510, 15. Hé swâ fǽrlíce swealt þæt hé on fulluhte underfangen næs, 504, 23: Bl. H. 217, 19. Manegum men fǽrlíce gelimpeþ þ hé hine wiþ þás world gedǽleþ, 125, 10. Mið ðý gecymmes feerlíce (*repente*), Mk. L. 13, 36. Fǽrlíce cliopað *subito clamat,* Lk. R. L. 9, 39. II. *soon, immediately, in a hurry:*—Hwî hête ðû mé feccan þus fǽrlíce tô þe *why did you send for me in such a hurry?,* Hml. S. 14, 52. Hé ôðre fyrde hêt feárlíce âbannan *he had another force called out at once,* Chr. 1095; P. 231, 19. Hé nâ mihte swâ fêrlíce munecas findan *he could not find monks at such short notice,* 870; P. 284, 4. III. *by chance.* (1) *not of set purpose:*—Bûtan hit fǽrlíce swâ gelimpe þæt man lator ârîse *nisi forte tardius surgatur,* R. Ben. 36, 3. (2) *without forethought, haphazard:*—Ne man ne gedyrstlǽce þæt hé fǽrlíce bôc gelǽcce and þǽr bûtan foresceáwunge onginne tô rǽdenne *ne fortuitu casu qui arripuerit codicem legere audeat,* 62, 4. [*v. N. E. D.* ferly; *adv. O. H. Ger.* fârlícho *subito.*]

**fǽr-nys.** *Add:* v. fêr-ness.

**Færpingas, Fæppingas;** *pl. The people of a district of Mercia:*—Færpinga landes is þreó hund hŷda (*in margin:* Is in Middel-Englum Færpinga), C. D. B. i. 414, 27. [*In Latin forms of this list* Fferpinga, Ferpinga, Ferwinga, Fearfinga *are variants of the word.*] Hé (*Diuma*) forðférde on Middel-Engluu on ðám þeódlande ðe is genemned in Fæppingum (Fepp-, *v. l., quae vocatur in Feppingum*), Bd. 3, 21; Sch. 289, 9. Cf. [Ad Fepsetna tûne, C. D. ii. 326, 3.

**fǽr-rǽden.** v. fêr-rǽden.

**fǽr-rǽs, es;** *m. A violent rush:*—Mið fêrrǽs eóde þ sunor oefistlíce *impetu abiit grex per praeceps,* Lk. L. 8, 33. v. next word.

**fǽr-rǽsende** *rushing impetuously;* repens:—Feerrǽsende *repentia,* Rtl. 125, 31. v. preceding word.

**fǽr-riht, es;** *n. Due payment for passage, fare:*—Ðá cwæð hé: 'Gif þû hæfst þ færriht (fǽreht, *v. l.*), ne forwyrnþ þe heora ǽnig.' Ðá cwæð ic tô him: 'Brôðor, næbbe ic nân fǽrriht (fǽreht, *v. l.*) tô syllanne, ac ic wille faran and ân þæra scypa âstîgan' *then said he:* 'If you have the fare, not one of them will refuse you.' Then said I to him: 'Brother, I haven't any fare to give, but I want to go and to embark on one of those ships,' Hml. S. 23 b, 352. Cf. fǽr-sceatt.

**fæers** *furze* (?). v. fyrs.

**fǽr-sceat(t), es;** *m. Passage-money, fare:*—'Âstîgap on þis scip tô ûs, and sellað ûs eówerne fǽrsceat (fêr- (fêr- ?), Bl. H. 233, 13).' Hé him andswarode: 'Nabbað wê fǽrsceat (fêr-, Bl. H. 233, 15), St. A. 6, 22, 24. Cf. fǽr-riht, fere-sceat.

**fǽr-seáþ, es;** *m. A gulf, abyss:*—Fǽrseáþ *baratrum,* i. *terre hiatus,* Wrt. Voc. ii. 125, 25.

**fǽr-spryng, es;** *m. A sudden pustule, ulcer of a rash:*—Wið fleógendum âttre and fǽrspryngum, Lch. iii. 6, 26.

**fǽr-steorfa, an;** *m. Murrain:*—Gif sceáp sŷ âbrocen, and wið fǽrsteorfan, Lch. iii. 56, 15. Wið swîna fǽrsteorfan, 25.

**fǽr-stice, es;** *m. A stitch, sudden pain:*—Wið fǽrstice (cf. *the refrain of the charm that follows:* Ût lytel spere, gif hêr inne sié), Lch. iii. 52, 11.

**fǽr-stylt** *amazement, stupor:*—Feerstylt forgráp alle *stupor apraehendit omnes,* Lk. L. 5, 26.

**fǽr-swile, es;** *m. A sudden swelling:*—Wiþ fǽrswile, Lch. ii. 74, 8. **faerucae.** v. fen-ýce.

**fǽr-weg, es;** *m. A cart-road:*—Andlang þǽre dîc tô cnictes ferwege; of þám wege on ealdan stânwege, C. D. B. i. 417, 15. Ondlong heges on fǽrweg, C. D. iii. 213, 1. [*Ger.* fahr-weg.]

**fǽr-wyrd.** *Dele,* and see fêr-wyrd.

**fǽs.** *Add:*—Þte fæse giwêdum his gehrionon *ut fimbriam uestimenti ejus tangerent,* Mk. R. 6, 36. Þone munuc sum sweart cniht teáh ût be þám fæsce (*per fimbriam*) his hrægles, Gr. D. 11 J, 28. Gihrân fæste tetigit fimbriam, Lk. R. 8, 44. Heó gehrân þ fes (fæs, *v. l.*) his hrægles, Bd. 1, 27; Sch. 82, 3. Feasum *fimbriis,* Ps. Srt. 44, 15. [Cf. *Prompt. Parv.* fasylle *of a clothe fractillus. O. H. Ger.* faso(-a) *fimbria.*]

**fæsce.** v. fæsceaft-ness. v. feásceaft-ness.

**fæst.** *Add:* I. *firmly fixed.* (1) in *a place* (lit. or fig.):—Âlŷs mé of lâme þe lǽs ic weorþe fæst (*ut non inhaeream*), Ps. Th. 68, 14. Ancor on eorþan fæst, Bt. 10; F. 30, 6. Biþ ôþer eude fæst on þǽre nafe, ôþer on ðǽre felge, 39, 7; F. 222, 3: Rä. 22, 13. Wudu wyrtum fæst *the wood firm fixed by its roots,* B. 1364. Sió godcunde gesceádwîsnes is fæst on þám heán Sceppende *divina ratio in summo omnium principe constituta,* Bt. 39, 5; F. 218, 27. Þá gôd sindon fæste on þám hêhstan gôde; swâ swâ ælces hûses wâh biþ fæst ægðer ge on ðǽre flôre ge on þǽm hrôfe, swâ biþ ælc gôd on Gode fæst, 36, 7; F. 184, 10–13. Timbrian hûs on þám fæstan stâne, 12; F. 36, 22. (2) to or *by something, firmly attached, closely bound, fixed to a spot:*—Weard his ôðer fôt be his scô fæst on ânum hegesahle *ejus þes per calceamentum in sude sepis inhaesit,* Gr. D. 24, 28. Scip on ancre fæst, B. 303. Segl sâle fæst, 1906. Foldærne fæst *laid in the grave,* Cri. 730: El. 723. Hé wæs reste fæst *he lay on his couch without stirring,* Gen. 178. Se lêgdraca ... glêdum beswǽled ... wæs deáðe fæst *the firedrake ... scorched by the flames ... lay a captive to death,* B. 3045. Hí âslôgan ân geteld on westhealfe þǽre cyricean on þǽre cyricean fæst (*ita ut ipsum tentorium parieti hereret ecclesiae*), Bd. 3, 17; Sch. 268, 3. Hé rom geseah brêmbrum fæstne, Gen. 2928. Bendum fæstne, An. 184. Scip oncerbendum fæst, B. 1918. Ceólas bi staðe fæste, Wal. 18. Ceólas æt sǽfearoðe oncrum fæste, El. 252. (2 a) *of a band, tie, &c., not easily loosed:*—Ðeáh seó leó fæste racentan hæbbe, Bt. 25; F. 88, 9. þǽm fæstestum *tenacissimis* (*vinculis*), Wrt. Voc. ii. 86, 2. (2 b) *of alliance, agreement, &c.:*—Ðá wiþerweardan gesceafta ægþer ge hié betwux him winnað, ge eác fæste sibbe betwux him healdaþ, Bt. 21; F. 74, 14: Met. 11, 41. Þæt þú wið Wealdend heólde fæste treówe, Exod. 422. II. *of persons or their attributes, constant, firm, steadfast:*—Mid fæstum sefan, Hy. 10, 40. Þone ic ǽr on firenum fæstne talde, El. 909. Ic hæbbe fæstne geleáfan, Gen. 543. Freóndscipe fæstne, B. 2069. Wê ûs naman Drihtnes neóde habbað on fultume fæstne and strangne, Ps. Th. 123, 7. Ic þá leóde wât ge wið feónd ge wið freónd fæste geworhte, B. 1864. II a. *of abstract things.* (1) *fixed, unchangeable:*—Nâuht woruldríces fæstes and unhwearfiendes beón ne mæg, Bt. 8; F. 26, 11. Hé sealde swîþe fæste gife and swîþe fæste æ, 41, 2; F. 246, 2. Ænig ðing swâ fæst getiohhod ... þ hit nǽfre onwended weorþe, 41, 3; F. 250, 6. Niman fæstne eard *to reside permanently,* Ps. Th. 86, 3. Geheald mîne fæste æ *keep my law that changes not,* 77, 1. (2) *firm, secure:*—Fæst *tuta,* i. *firma* (*prosperitas*), An. Ox. 793. (3) *stubborn, unyielding:*—Ic ælcne wiccecræft eáðelíce oferswîðde ... and ic nǽfre ne âfunde swâ fæstne drŷcræft, Hml. S. 35, 179. III. *firm.* (1) *firmly joined together, strongly built* or *made:*—Bold eal inneweard îrenbendum fæst, B. 998. Glôf ... searobendum fæst, 2086. Fæstostan eardungstôwe *firmissimo habitaculo,* Ps. L. fol. 189, 4. (2) *solid, compact:*—þ þæt hnesce and flôwende wæter hæbbe fiôr on þǽre fæstan eorðan, Bt. 33, 4; F. 130, 4. (3) *of a joint, strong, firm:*—Fæstes *forti* (*compage*), Wrt. Voc. ii. 85, 50: 93, 39: 37, 14. IV. *of places that can resist attack, strong, fortified:*—Beorh ... neácræftum fæst, B. 2243. Fæst is þæt êglond fenne biworpen, Rä. 1, 5. Ðá fæstan ceastre *munitum castrum,* Wrt. Voc. ii. 58, 38. Leonida tôr on ânum londfæstenne ... Xersis hêt þ fæste lond ûtan ymbfaran ... Leoniþa his fierd gelǽdde on ân ôþer fæstre land, Ors. 2, 5; S. 80, 14–29. Þá hié ongeáton þæt þæt festen sceolde âbrocen bión, hí sendon on ôðer fæstre fæsten, 3, 11; S. 148, 23. Seó burg (*Babylon*) wæs ealra weorca fæstast, 2, 4; S. 74, 24: 3, 7; S. 114, 11. IV a. *of a chamber, closely shut up:*—Gefere þæne mannan on swîðe fæstne cleofan and wearmne, Lch. ii. 280, 11. IV b. *of a vessel, that does not leak, water-tight:*—Fæstne kylle, Past. 469, 9. V. *of sleep, rest, unbroken, undisturbed:*—Þú eart sió fæste ræst (cf. seó sêfte ræst, Bt. 33, 4; F. 132, 34) eallra sôðfæstra *tu requies tranquilla piis,* Met. 20, 271. Bið se slǽp tô fæst, B. 1742. Þá Langbearde ealle wǽron on

fæstum slǽpe (*somno gravi depressi*), Gr. D. 253, 18. Of slǽpe þý fæstan, Cri. 890: An. 796. **VI.** *of established reputation* (?), *standard* (of books) ?:—Hē forbeád openlīce þæt mon nāne fæste bóc ne leornode *aperto praecepit edicto, ne quis Christianis docendorum liberalium studiorum professor esset*, Ors. 6, 31; S. 286, 4.

-fæst. *Add:* ǽrend-, eorþ-, sceam-, weder-, wíf-, wíte-, word-fæst.

**fæstan; I.** *Add: to make fast.* v. ende-fæstend. **II.** *to entrust, commit:*—ln hondum ðínum ic fæsto (*commendo*) gāst mīnne, Lk. L. 23, 46. [v. *N. E. D.* fast; *vb.*] v. borh-, on-fæstan.

**fæstan; II.** *to fast. Add:* **I.** in a general sense. (1) absolute, *to abstain from food:*—Hē fæste feówurtig daga, Mt. 4, 2: Sat. 667. Fæstte, Bl. H. 27, 24, 29. Móyses and Hēlias fæston, Guth. 32, 2. Fæstende *jejunius*, Wrt. Voc. i. 83, 44. (2) *to abstain.* (a) *with gen.:*—Ðæt hié selfe ne fæsten ðæs hláfes ryhtwīsnesse *ne ipsi remaneant a justitiae pane jejuni*, Past. 137, 25. Þonne hié woldon sylfe firene fæstan (*abstain from sin*), Dan. 592. (b) *with prep.:*—Þā fram middangeardes gyrninge fæstað *qui a mundi ambitione jejunant*, Scint. 53, 18. Hē fæste fram eallum bigleofum, Wlfst. 285, 24. **I a.** *to fast as a remedy:*—Gif sió ādl sié weaxende, fæste .ii. dagas tógædere, Lch. ii. 218, 1. **II.** *to fast as a matter of ecclesiastical discipline.* (1) absolute:—Ic fæste tuwa on wican, Past. 313, 6. Nā Gode ac him sylfum gehwylc fæst (*jejunat*), Scint. 53, 9. Ðonne wē fæstað oððe ælmessan sellaþ, Bt. 41, 2; F. 246, 2. Hwī fæste wē ... sóðlīce þīne leorningcnihtas ne fæstað, Mt. 9, 14. Fæstest þū on foldan, Seel. 144. Fæst tō nónes, and forgang hwīt, Ll. Th. ii. 132, 4. Sē ðe fæstan wille, ne tǽle hē nō ðone ðe ete, Past. 311, 24. Ðā dagas syndon rihtlīce tō fæstenne, Shrn. 80, 2. (2) *with cognate acc.:*—Stuntlīce fæst sē lenctenlic fæsten, sē ðe hine sylfne mid gālnysse befȳlð, Hml. Th. ii. 100, 16: Wlfst. 285, 31. Þæt fæsten þe þā Ninivete fæston, fæstað þā, 227, 29. Fæstað eówer lenctenfæsten tō nónes, 136, 16. v. un-fæstende.

**fæste.** Dele II, and add: **I.** *so as not to be moved* or *shaken, firmly, fast* (in to stand *fast*) (lit. and fig.):—Þæt treów fæste stód, Dan. 557. Nānwuht nis fæste stondendes weorces on worulde, Bt. 9; F. 26, 21. Ic fæste stande for þīnre campunga, Bl. H. 225, 34. Him þā fērend on fæste wuniað *the travellers fix their abode on him*, Wal. 25: 36. Oþ þæt þín fót weorðe fæste on blóde, Ps. Th. 67, 22. Þ man Godes cyricean fæste tremede, Bl. H. 43, 6: 111, 4: An. 1673. Þ ge stemn mōte þȳ fæstor standon, Bt. 34, 10; F. 148, 34. **I a.** *of sleeping:*—On middre nihte þā men fæstost slēpon, Hml. S. 31, 857. **I b.** *expressing fixity of intention, attention* or *purpose:*—Gerēfa mín fæste mynteð þæt mē æfter sīe eaforan sīne yrfeweardas *my steward quite means his children to be heirs after me*, Gen. 2182. Hwæþer þū ǽnig þing swā fæste getiohhod hæbbe þ hit nǽfre þínum willum onwended weorþe, Bt. 41, 3; F. 250, 6. Þā þing þe wē handledon and fæste wǽron *þe matters that we handled and with which we were diligently engaged*, Angl. viii. 304, 24. **I c.** *expressing vigorous action* or *thoroughness of condition:*—Hī fæste tōgedere fēngon *they attacked each other vigorously*, Chr. 999; P. 131, 21: Cri. 980: Ps. Th. 70, 6, 4. Hī mē georne ær fæste feódan *they hated me fiercely and violently*, 85, 16. Fæste wiðhycgan, Jul. 42. Fæste wiðsacan, El. 933. Swīðe fæste gesoden ǽgra *very hard-boiled eggs*, Lch. ii. 194, 5. Fæste geþūf *luxoriante* (*prosperitate*), Wrt. Voc. ii. 77, 76: 52, 18. Beóð Godes strēamas gōde wætere fæste gefylde *flumen Dei repletum est aqua*, Ps. Th. 64, 10. Gif geliórade fæst *if he were quite dead*; si jam obisset, Mk. L. 15, 44. **II.** *with firm grasp* or *attachment, fast* (in to bind, hold *fast*) (lit. and fig.):—Dō on þ dolg and bind fæste, Lch. ii. 132, 18: Sat. 324. Oft þrǽl þegen cnyt swȳðe fæste, Wlfst. 163, 2: Gen. 374. Hē þone cniht genam fæste mid folmum, Exod. 407: B. 554. Sié fæste genæglad on róde *crucifigatur*, Mt. L. 27, 22. Gefēg fæste, Gen. 1310: Crä. 66. Nim þe fæste þ ic sprece *fixum tene quod loquor*, Gr. D. 172, 33. Hē nam of hire eall þ heó āhte, for ðām heó hit heóld ǽr tō fæste wið hine, Chr. 1043; P. 162, 26. Fæste bewunden, An. 58: El. 937. Fæste genearwod, Gen. 2603. **II a.** *of command, promise, urgently, strictly, solemnly:*—Ðā ilca lufu suīðe fæst bebeád *eandem dilectionem instantius commendans*, Jn. p. 7, 11. Þā senatus him hæfden þā dǽd fæste forboden, Ors. 4, 10; S. 196, 8: Gen. 895. Hē him fæste gehēt þ..., Met. 1, 35. **II b.** *of concealment, securely:*—Þēh þe hē hit fæste wið þā senatus hǽle *though he succeeded in keeping it secret from the senate*, Ors. 4, 10; S. 196, 16. Þū him fæste hel sōðan sprǽce *be sure to keep the truth from them*, Gen. 1836. Þū heora fyrene fæste hǽle, Ps. Th. 84, 2. Wǽron hié þý swȳðor āfyrhte and hié fæstor hȳddan *tanto magis cunctis propter timorem abditis, diu apparente nemine*, Nar. 10, 26. **II c.** *fast* (as in to stick *fast*), *so as to be unable to move:*—Hē þæs þeófes fót onlýsde of þām gærde þe hē ǽr fæste on clyfode *pedem furis a sepe in qua inhaererat solvit*, Gr. D. 25, 11. **III.** *fast* (as in to shut *fast*):—Stód on merigen þæt cweartern fæste belocen, Hml. Th. i. 230, 22. Hē þā grimman gōman bihlemmeð fæste tōgædre, Wal. 77. Weard sē hālga wong þurh feóndes searo fæste bitýned, Ph. 419. **IV.** *so as to make secure.* Cf. fæst; **IV** :—Seó burg wæs ungemettan fæste mid clūdum

ymbweaxen *the town was so surrounded by rocks that it was exceedingly strong*; saxum mirae asperitatis et altitudinis, Ors. 3, 9; S. 132, 10. **V.** *speedily, at once:*—Ricene weorðe his feóuda gehwylc, fæste tōworpen, Ps. Th. 67, 1. Ic mē helpe fand þæt ic fæste ne feóll (*that I did not straightway fall*), 117, 13. Þæt þone māndrinc geceápað wer fæste feóre sīne, Rä. 24, 14. v. fæstlīce.

**fæsten; I.** *Add:* **I.** *abstinence from food:*—Fæsten, behæfednes (*q. v.*) *parsimonia*, Wrt. Voc. ii. 83, 26. Fæstern *jejunium*, Mk. p. 1, 16. **I a.** *a fast on grounds of health.* v. dæg-fæsten; fæstan; **I a.** **II.** *a fast as ecclesiastical discipline:*—Hié gulpon hiera fæstennes (-enes, *v. l.*), Past. 313, 1. Gif hwā for his untrumnysse þ fæsten āberan ne mæg ... him ys ālýfed þ hē mōt his fæstan ālýsan, Ll. Th. ii. 220, 26. Man ǽlc beboden fæsten healde ... tō Philippi et Jacobi mæssan wē ne beódað nān fæsten ... ælces Frigedæges fæsten, Wlfst. 117, 8-13. Gif hī þæt fæsten rihtlīce ne gefæstan ... gyf hē þæt fæsten ābrece, 172, 1-2. Fæstinum *jejuniis*, Rtl. 8, 17. Heó lufude fæstenu, Hml. Th. i. 148, 1. ¶ Fæsten dreógan *to do penance* (?), *suffer scarcity* (?):—Þæs fæsten dreáh fela missera Egypta folc, þæs þe hié wyrnan þóhton Móyses māgum sīðes *for many a year the Egyptians did penance* (?), *suffered scarcity* (?), *because they thought to refuse the Israelites leave to depart*, Exod. 49. [v. *N. E. D.* fasten; *sb.* Cf. *O. Sax.* fastunnia; *f.: Goth.* fastubni.] v. ǽ-, dæg-, easter-, ge-, gecwed-, lār-, lencten-, riht-, ymbren-fæsten.

**fæsten; II, III.** *Add:* **I.** *a firm place, firmament:*—Hē geworhte roderas fæsten.... Flōd wæs āðǽled ... wæter of wætrum þām þe wuniað under fæstenne folca hrōfes, Gen. 147-153. **II.** *in a military sense, a strong place, one fitted to resist attack.* v. fæst; **IV.** (1) *a place of permanent residence, citadel, fort, fortified town:*—Faestin arx, Wrt. Voc. ii. 100, 71. Fæsten *oppidum*, sē þe on fæstene sit *oppidanus*, i. 84, 41, 47. Fæsten *municipium*, i. *oppidum*, An. Ox. 2443: *municipium*, i. *civitas*, 3990. Burge, fæstenes *municipii*, 5123. Fæstennes arcis, Wrt. Voc. ii. 10, 1. Beforan Numentia fæstennes geate, Ors. 5, 2; S. 218, 32. Hē gefōr tō ānum fæstenne, þā ne mehton hié nānne monn on ðæm fæstenne ūtan geseón *exercitum ad urbem duxit. Et cum murum escendisset, vacuam civitatem ratus*, 3, 9; S. 134, 10: 3, 11; S. 148, 19. Palistas, mid þæm hié weallas brǽcon, þonne hié on fæstenne fuhton, 4, 6; S. 174, 9. Martinus wæs geboren on þām fæstene (cf. on þǽre byrig, Hml. Th. ii. 498, 23) Sabaria, Hml. S. 31, 10. Tō þām fæstenne ... under burhlocan, Gen. 2534. On þām fæstene (*Exeter*), Chr. 877; P. 74, 19. Hē forneáh ealle þā betste of þes eorles hīrēde innan ānan fæstene (*in a fortress called New Castle*, Hen. Hunt.) gewann, 1095; P. 231, 3. Hí fōron on þæt fæsten (*Rome*), Met. 1, 20. Hē þæt fæsten (*urbem Pydnam*) ābræc, and þā burgleóde ... hī sendon on ōðer fæstre fæsten (*in arcem Amphipolitanam*), Ors. 3, 11; S. 148, 20-23: 2, 6; S. 88, 4: 3, 9; S. 124, 4: 5, 7; S. 230, 4. Fæstena worn (*Babylon*; cf. Ors. 2, 4; S. 74, 24), Dan. 692. Faestinnum arcibus, Txts. 42, 110. Hī manige festena and castelas ābrǽcon, Chr. 1094; P. 230, 3. (2) *a fortification, entrenchments, fortified camp, place strengthened to resist attack:*—Ðanan eást ūp suae ðet ealde(n) fæstan scāðe (*as the old earthwork makes a line of separation*); andlang ðes fæstenes, C. D. v. 70, 30. Hié þone here besǽton on ānum fæstenne (cf. *they threw up a fortification*, Hen. Hunt.), Chr. 894; P. 87, 21. Hī wīcstōwn nāmon on twām stōwum ... Scipia geāscade þ þā foreweardas wǽron feor ðǽm fæstenne gesette ... hē feáwe men tō ōþrum þāra fæstena onsende ... þæt þā ōþre onfundon þe on ōðrum fæstenne wǽron, Ors. 4, 10; S. 200, 8-19. Hié on þǽm īglande fæsten worhton (*castra posuerunt*), 4, 6; S. 176, 15. Þ hī fæsten geworhten him tō gescyldnesse, stǽnene weal, Bd. 1, 12; Sch. 33, 23: 34. 8. (2 a) *used with reference to siege-works:*—'Wyrceað fæsten ymb ðā burg.' Fæsten wyrcð se hālga lāriów '*aedificalis munitiones.*' *Munitiones sanctus praedicator aedificat*, Past. 163, 5: 161, 5. Hī ymbsǽton ðā ceastre aud worhton oþer fæsten ymb hié selfe ... se here forlēt þæt geweorc, Chr. 885; P. 78, 11. ¶ *a siege* (?):—Fæstenne *obsidione* (cf. in arta Betuliae *obsidione*, Ald. 76, 25), Wrt. Voc. ii. 62, 13. (3) *a place naturally strong against attack, fastness, stronghold:*—Faestin Termofilas (cf. Ors. 2, 5; S. 80, 14), Txts. 104, 1042. Grendel mōras heóld, fen aud fæsten, B. 104. Hē swīþe þæs loudes fæstenum trūwode þonne his gefeohte, Nar. 17, 28. Hæfdic þæs kyninges wīc and his fæstenu gesceáwod þe hē mid his fyrde in gefaren hæfde, 19, 13. **III.** *a place that can be shut fast.* (1) *a place of security, closet, strong room:*—Fæstene gehæft (*in arto carnis*) clustello continetur, An. Ox. 5396. Hī hȳdað heáhgestreóna, healdað georne on fæstenne, Sal. 318. (2) *a place of confinement.* (a) *a prison:*—Hē on þām fæstene (cf. beinnan þām carcere, Bt. 1; F. 4, 2) frōfre ne gemunde, Met. 1, 79. Gelǽdan of leoðobendum fram þām fæstenne, An. 1036: 1070. (b) *a sepulchre:*—Út eóde engla Drihten of þām fæstenne, Sat. 521. (c) *Hell:*—In þām fæstenne gebróht *brought to Hell*, Wal. 71. **IV.** *an implement that closes* or *confines*; claustrum:—Ōstiges copses fæstene *in nodosi cippi claustrum*, An. Ox. 3252. Heó fēged mec (*hemp*) on fæsten, Rä. 26, 9. Fæstenu *claustra* (*coelestis*

*regni reserare*), Hpt. Gl. 433, 58 : An. Ox. 57, 6. [*O. H. Ger.* festin(a), fastinna *munitio, septum, praesidium*.] v. brōm-, heáh-, land-, mōr-, wæter-fæsten.

**fæsten-behæfednes.** *Dele, and see* behæfednes : **fæstend.** v. endefæstend.

**fæsten-dæg.** *Add* :—Gif hit tuguldæg sié ; gif hit festendæg sié C. D. i. 293, 10. Gif hit fæstendagas beón *si jejunii dies fuerint*, R. Ben. 67, 3. Gif wē on þǣm syx wucan forlǣtaþ þā syx Sunnandagas þæs fæstennes (*Lent*), þonne ne bið þāra fæstendaga nā mā þonne syx and þrítig, Bl. H. 35, 24. On ðām fæstendagum *in quibus diebus quadrigesimae*, R. Ben. 74, 12. On eówrum fæstendagum *in diebus jejuniorum vestrorum*, Past. 315, 2. Þā fæstendagas þe men eów beódad tō healdenne, Wlfst. 230, 34. [v. *N. E. D.* fasten-day.] v. riht-fæstendæg.

**fæsten-geat.** *Add* :—On ðet fæstergeat, C. D. iii. 130, 32.

**fæsten-gewerc.** *Substitute* : **fæsten-geweorc,** es ; *n. Work at the repairing* or *construction of fortifications*: one of the three obligations included in the *trinoda necessitas*. v. burh-bót, brycg-geweorc :—Būtan fæstengewerce and fyrdsōcne and brycggeweorce, C. D. ii. 111, 16. Fæstengeworce, 24. Freódōm from æghwelcum eordlecum þeówdōmæ būtan firdæ and fæstængewæorcæ and bryccggewæorce *excepto expeditione et arcis pontisque constructione*, v. 218, 25. Fyrðe and brycge and festergeweorc hēwe swā mon ofer eall folc dō, 151, 30.

**fæsten-lic** ; *adj. Of a fast, Lenten* :—Fæsternlicre bihaldnisse *quadrigesimali observatione*, Rtl. 14, 8.

**fæstennes.** *Dele, and see* fæsten.

**fæsten-tíd.** *Transfer the last two passages to* riht-fæstentíd, *and add* :—Freólstída and fæstentída rihtlíce understandan, Wlfst. 113, 2.

**fæsten-wicu,** an ; *f. A week of fasting, a week in Lent* :—On þām drihtenlican dæge þǣre forman fæstenwucan *on the Sunday of the first week in Lent*, Hml. S. 23 b, 111.

**fæster-.** v. fæsten-geat, -geweorc : **fæstern.** v. fæsten, fæsten-lic.

**fæstes** ; *adv. Dele, and see* fæst ; **III. 3** : **fæst-gongel.** *For* '*faithful*' *substitute* '*steady-going*,' *and for* '*faithful soul*' *substitute* '*constant mind*.'

**fæst-hafol.** *Add* : **I.** *that holds fast* :—Fæsthafellæstum (-nestum, An. Ox. 4595) gerǣpod *tenacissimis* (*vinculis*) *inretita*, Hpt. Gl. 512, 63. **II.** *strong, firm, steadfast* :—God, fæsthafol strængð unāstyred on þē þurhwunað *Deus, tenax vigor inmotus in te permanet*, Hy. S. 11, 2. **III.** *tenacious, retentive* :—Fæsthaful *capax* (cf. capax memorie, An. Ox. 3101), Wrt. Voc. ii. 21, 47. Mid fæsthafelre race *tenaci* (*memoriae*) *textu*, An. Ox. 192. Hē gefæstnode his lāre on fæsthafelum gemynde, Hml. Th. ii. 118, 20. **IV.** *parsimonious, closefisted* :—For hwí wǣre þū swā fæsthafol mínra gōda þe ic þe sealde ?, Wlfst. 258, 12. Were grǣdigum and fæsthafelum *uiro cupido et tenaci*, Scint. 110, 15. Sint tō manianne ðā fæsðhafula[n] (*tenaces, qui sua retinent*), Past. 339, 7.

**fæst-hafolnes.** *Add* :—Fæsthafolnes *dira cupido*, Dōm. L. 236. Swā ðā rūmmōdan fæsthafolnesse lǣren, swā hī ðā uncystegan on yfelre hneáwnesse ne gebrengen *sic prodigis praedicetur parcitas, ut tenacibus periturarum rerum custodia non augeatur*, Past. 453, 28.

**fæst-heald** ; *adj. Having fast hold, firmly joined, firmly cemented* :—Hí swíðe fæsthealdne weorcstān upp āhwylfdon, and ǣfre swā hī neár and neár eódon hī sundon ǣlcne stān on ōðerne befēgedne, Hml. S. 23, 423. [*Icel.* fast-haldr *tenacious*.]

**fæsting.** *Add* :—Hē wilnode þ hē befæste þām biscope his ōðerne sunu . . . þā gefyllede þǣre fæstinge hē wæs forðfēred *episcopo filium suum commendare curavit . . . Qua commendatione expleta defunctus est*, Gr. D. 239, 15. ¶ *As a technical term, the quartering of officials upon a monastery when these were travelling on the king's business* :—*Liberabo monasterium a pastu et refectione illorum hominum quos saxonice nominamus* Walhfæreld *and heora* fæsting, C. D. ii. 60, 30. v. rǣde-fæsting ; fæsting-men, *and see* Sax. Engl. i. 294 sqq., ii. 58 sqq.

**fæstingan** = fæstnigan : **fæsting-men.** *Add* : v. fæsting.

**fæst-land,** es ; *n. Land adapted to resist attack, that is hard to invade* :—Fōran wē þurh ðā fæstlond and þurh þā ungefērenlican eorþan we marched through country which could easily have been defended and over ground that was almost impassable, Nar. 17, 6. v. fæst ; **IV.**

**fæstlic.** *Add* : **I.** lit. *firm, solid* :—Geseah ic wíngeard trumlicne and fæstlicne *vineam solidam miratus sum*, Nar. 4, 28. **II.** *resolute, vigorous* :—Fæstlic on færelde, Rūn. 27. Suelce hē fæsdlicu and stranglecu weorc wyrce *quaedam robusta exerceat*, Past. 235, 18. Þæt hē þý fæstlecre gewinn mehte habban wið hiene, Ors. 5, 12 ; S. 240, 8. [*O. H. Ger.* fast-líh *fixus, tutus : Icel.* fast-ligr.]

**fæstlíce.** *Add* : (1) *fast.* Cf. fæste ; **I** :—Ðū gestaþoladest eorþan swíþe fæstlíce þ heó ne helt on nāne healfe, Bt. 33, 4 ; F. 130, 36. Hié þā ingehygd heora heortan ful fæstlíce on þone heofonlican hyht gestaþelodon, Bl. H. 135, 29 : Jul. 270 : El. 427 : Hy. 4, 37. Hī man swýðe fæstlíce widstōd and heardlíce, Chr. 1001 ; P. 133, 19. Þe fæstlícor þǣm wergan gāste wiþstondan, Bl. H. 135, 10. (2) *expressing firmness of purpose.* Cf. fæste ; **I b** :—Hié swíþe fæstlíce hié sylfe tō

Crístes lufan gecyrdon, Bl. H. 173, 14. Synna fæstlíce geswícan, 193, 22. (3) *expressing vigorous action, thoroughness.* Cf. fæste ; **I c** :—Hí þær fæstlíce feohtende wǣron, Ch. 1001 ; P. 133, 18 : By. 254. Fæstlíce, Chr. 994 ; P. 127, 33. Hí tōgædere feastlíce fēngon, 1004 ; P. 135, 35 : S. 25, 489. Fæstlíce gesǐtan and gewinnan, Bl. H. 173, 2. Fæstlíce werian, By. 82. Ic fæstlíce fyrenwyrcende elnode *zelavi in peccatoribus*, Ps. Th. 72, 2. Hē fæstlíce ealle þā costunga of his líchaman ādrígde *omni carnis tentatione funditus caruit*, Gr. D. 190, 23. Ic þín wundur eall sæcge, swā ic fæstlícast mæg befōn wordum (*as completely as ever I can express them in words*), Ps. Th. 74, 2. (4) *firmly, constantly.* Cf. fæst ; **II** :—Būton fæstlíce (*firmiter*) hē gelýfe, Ath. Crd. 42 : Shrn. 195, 3. Hí fremmað fæstlíce Freán ēce word, Sch. 50. Þæt gē fæstlícor gelýfdon, Wlfst. 231, 32. (5) *expressing permanence, persistence.* Cf. fæste ; **II a** :—þær hié fæstlíce eard genāmon *they settled there*, Gen. 1653. Gif hit on ǣnegum men ǣnige hwíle fæstlíce wunaþ, Bt. 8 ; F. 26, 4. Hī nǣfre fæstlíce ne þurhwuniaþ swelca swelce hí ǣr tō cōman, 11, 1 ; F. 30, 28 : Bl. H. 171, 27. Hē fæstlíce (*pertinaciter*) widsōc, Gr. D. 190, 15. Hí fæstlíce (*constanter*) gehēndon hine, Lk. L. R. 23, 10. (6) *fast* (in hold *fast*). Cf. fæste ; **II** :—Uton wē his lufe fæstlíce on ūrum heortum healdan, Bl. H. 131, 3. Hē hēht fæstlíce healdan þone hererinc, Met. 1, 70 : Rtl. 58, 1. Nim þē fæstlíce þæt ic sprece, Gr. D. 172, 33. Hí þeódað hí fæstlícor tō þǣre rihtwísnesse *ipsi justitiae arctius inhaerebunt*, Gr. D. 336, 23. Fæstlícor *artius*, Wrt. Voc. ii. 9, 26. Þ wē ūre gesibsumnesse fæstlícost ūs betweónan healdan, Ll. Th. i. 246, 22. (7) *strictly* (of command). Cf. fæste ; **II a** :—Ic þæt fæstlíce bebeád ðæt se mon sé ne wǣre mid his wǣpnum gegerwed, þæt hine mon scolde mid wǣpnum ācwellan *legem dixi me in eum animadversurum qui non indutus armis deprehensus esset*, Nar. 9, 27 : Bl. H. 47, 20. (8) *speedily, at once.* Cf. fæste ; **V** :—þonne fæstlíce flǣsc onginneð cōlian, Rūn. 29. (9) *as a particle of vague meaning* :—Sume fæstlíce (wutudlíce, R., *the West-Saxon version has nothing*) cuoedon *quidam autem dicebant*, Jn. L. 7, 41. Ǣc ↑ fæstlíce (*W. S. has nothing*) *quidem*, 16, 9 : 11, 6 : Lk. L. R. 11, 4. Ðes fæstlíce (*etiam*) synna forgefeð, Lk. L. 7, 49 (*W. S. has nothing*) : L. R. 9, 5. Fæstlíce *jam*, L. 8, 27 (*W. S. has nothing*) : Jn. L. R. 3, 18 : 9, 22 : 13, 2. [v. *N. E. D.* fastly. *O. H. Ger.* fastlíhho *firmiter, solide : Icel.* fastlíga.] v. ge-, un-fæstlíce.

**fæst-mōd** *of constant mind, steadfast.* *Add* :—Hē tōmiddes þām líge tō Gode ānmōdlíce clypode, and on þǣre frecednysse fæstmōd þurhwunode, Hml. S. 31, 872. [The Latin in Ors. 6, 33 is : Tantam constantiam pro retinenda fide quondam habuisset.']

**fæstmōd-staðol.** *Dele, and see* mōd-staþol.

**fæstnes.** *Add* : (1) *stability.* v. fæst ; **III** :—Þæs wealles micelness and fæstness *murorum firmitas et magnitudo*, Ors. 2, 4 ; S. 74, 14. (2) *tenacity.* Cf. fæst ; **I** [:—Seó fastnysse þæs yfeles wǣtan on þan heáfede, Lch. iii. 130, 7.] (3) *resolution, vigour, firmness.* Cf. fæst ; **II** :—Sameramis fēng tō þām ríce mid mycelre fæstnesse (reþnesse, *v. l.*) and wrænnesse (cf. Ors. 1, 2 ; S. 30, 14-35), Ors. 1, 2 tit. ; Th. 513, 4. v. ymb-fæstness.

**fæstnian.** *Add* : (1) *to fix firmly in.* v. fæst ; **I. 1** :—Fæstniað eower mōd on his wundrum *ponite corda vestra in virtute ejus*, Ps. Th. 47, 11. (2) *to attach firmly to.* v. fæst ; **I. 2** :—Tō þām lifgendan stāne staðol fæstniað, Jul. 654. (2 a) *to betroth.* Cf. Icel. fastna :—Fæstnad *desponsatam*, Lk. L. 1, 27. (3) *to make firm* or *steadfast.* v. fæst ; **II** :—Scyle deóphýdig mon fæstnian ferðsefan, Sch. 20. (4) *to confirm an agreement, statement, ratify peace, &c.* :—Ic fæstnige (*printed* fæstinge) mín wedd mid eów *firmabo pactum meum vobiscum*, Lev. 26, 9. Ðās godspelles ðæs wítges bōc sōðeð ↑ fæstnaagið *haec euangelia Ezechielis volumen probat*, Mt. p. 9, 9. Mon fæstnode þone frið ǣgðer ge wið Eást-Engle ge wið Norðhymbre, Chr. 906 ; P. 94, 21. Se here hine gecēs him tō hláforde, and þæt fæstnodon mid āþum, 921 ; P. 103, 20. Wēre trume fæstnie *pactum firmum feriat*, Lch. i. lxix, 4. Sume syndon *confirmativa* þæt synd fæstnigende, Ælfc. Gr. Z. 226, 10. (4 a) *where a document is signed* :—Write hē ðā fæstnunga mid his āgenre handa, and on ðām gewrite rōdetācn mearcige and hý swā fæstnigende uppan ðām altare ālecge, R. Ben. 100, 6. ¶ *in the case of charters* :—Ego Ceólnoð mid Crístes rōdetācne festnie and write ( = confirmo et subscribo *or* roboro et subscribo, p. 295, 13, 15), C. D. i. 296, 15 : 299, 25. Ic ðās míne gesaldnisse trymme and faestna (cf. roboravi, l. 15) in Crístes rōdetācne, ii. 5, 33. Ic ðās word and ðās wísan fæstnie and write, 122, 2. Ic ðis write and ðeafie and mid Crístes rōdetācne hit festnie, i. 311, 24. [*O. Frs.* festna : *O. Sax.* fastnōn : *O. H. Ger.* fastinōn (fest-) : *Icel.* fastna *to pledge, betroth*.] v. be-, on-, rōd-, þurh-fæstnian.

**fæstnung.** *Add* : (1) *the condition of being fast, stability, fixity.* v. fæst ; **I** :—Hē gekýdð on ðǣre styringe ðāra telgena ūtane ðæt ðǣr ne bið nān fæstnung on ðǣm wyrttruman innan *exteriori mobilitate indicat, quod nulla interius radice subsistat*, Past. 359, 3. Nǣfde hē (*Lucifer*) nāne fæstnunge, ac feóll sōna ādūn, Hex. 18, 2. (2) *the condition of being closed.* v. fæst ; **IV a** :—Seó fæstnung ðǣre hellican clýsinge ne geðafað þæt hí ǣfre ūt ābrecon *the prison of hell is shut too*

*fast to allow them ever to break out*, Hml. Th. i. 332, 20. (3) *a making strong, fortifying*. v. fæst; IV:—Festnunge *munificentiam* (? as if connected with *munire*), Wrt. Voc. ii. 54, 37. (4) *a fastening, binding*. v. fæst; I. 2:—Hé þá tungan onlýsde, þá se heáhengel mid þære swígunge fæstnunga geband þone fæder, Bl. H. 167, 11. (5) *a making steadfast, an exhortation.* v. fæst; II:—Fæstnunges *i trymnisses exortationis*, Mk. p. 2, 5. (6) *protection, security.* Cf. fæst; II a. 2, IV:—Þte sié esnum dínum fæstnung scíldnise æc giscíldnisses *ut sint servis tuis munimentum tutelaque defensionis*, Rtl. 117, 27: Wrt. Voc. ii. 56, 3. Wel bið þám þe him frófre tó fæder on heofonum séced, þær ús eal seó fæstnung stondeð, Wand. 115. (7) *confirmation, ratification.* v. fæstnian, (4):—Fæstnung *confirmatio*, Wrt. Voc. ii. 130, 6. Be þám his beháte sette hé fæstnunga mid gewrite tó ðæs abbodes naman and ðæra hálgena þe heora bán on ðære stówe restað. Wríte hé ðá fæstnunga mid his ágenre handa, R. Ben. 100, 1–4. Ðá ðá Landfranc crafede fæstnunge his gehérsumnesse mid áðswerunge, þá forsóc hé and sæde þ hé hit náhte tó dónne *when Lanfranc required that his profession of obedience should be confirmed by an oath, he refused and said that he was not obliged to do it*, Chr. 1070; P. 204, 9. (7 a) *a document that contains a confirmation:*—Se godspellere wæs fæstnung ægþer ge þære ealdan æ ge þære níwan, Bl. H. 163, 24. Ðerhwunadon mid tó ondword tít fæstnunga bærlíce æteáwdon *perseverantia usque ad praesens tempus monumenta declarant*, Mt. p. 7, 4. (8) *a covenant, assurance:*—Ic sette mín wed tó him and tó his ofspringe on écere fæstnunge *constituam pactum meum illi in foedus sempiternum et semini ejus post eum* (Gen. 17, 19), Hml. Th. i. 92, 8. Þá sealdon hí heom fæstnunge betweónan, þ hí ealle þis woldon healdan, Hml. S. 23, 211. (9) *a strong place, a closed place* (?). Cf. fæsten; III:—In byrgennum i fæstnungum *monumentis* (*has munimentis been read?*), Mk. L. 5, 5. [*O. H. Ger.* festinunga *affirmatio, confirmatio, assertio.*] v. ge-, hand-, ymb-fæstnung.

**fæst-ræd[e].** *Add: of firm counsel.* (1) *of persons or personifications:* —Sió wiþerwearde wyrd is sió sóþe gesælþ, þeáh hwæm swá ne þince, for þám heó is fæstræd and gehæt simle. Þte sóþ biþ *adversa fortuna semper vera est, cum se instabilem mutatione demonstrat*, Bt. 20; F. 70, 32. Drihten is fæstræd and fremsum *benignus est Dominus*, Ps. Th. 134, 3. Jacobus fród and fæstræd folca láreów *James wise and firm teacher of men*, Men. 135. Se wísa and se fæstræda folces hyrde ... Caton *rigidus Cato*, Met. 10, 49. Hé cwæð mid olecunge þ hí æþele cempan wæron, and on ælcum gefeohte fæstræde him betwynan (*constant to one another*), Hml. S. 11, 21. (2) *of human attributes:*—Ongon hé æresð herigean on him ðæt ðæt hé fæstrædes wiste *prius in eis, quae fortia prospicit, laudat*, Past. 213, 8. Uton habban fulne hyht and fæstrædne geleáfan on úrne Drihten, Wlfst. 282, 5. Ánrædne geleáfan and fæstræde geþanc tó úrum Drihtne, 101, 23. Hí ne magon áfyllan mín fæstræde geþanc *they cannot cast down my constant mind*, Hml. S. 8, 20. [He is nu ripe and fastrede, ne lust him nu to none unrede, O. and N. 211. Cf. *Icel.* fast-ráðinn *determined*.]

**fæstræd-líc;** *adj. Constant:*—Wénst þú þ on ænigum menniscum móde mæge áuht fæstrædlices beón búton hwearfunga *ullamne humanis rebus inesse constantiam reris?*, Bt. 8; F. 26, 3.

**fæstrædlíce** *with constancy, firmly:*—Mycel þearf is crístenum mannum þæt hý rihtne geleáfan cunnan and ðæne fæstrædlíce healdan, Wlfst. 123, 1.

**fæstrædnes.** *Add:* (1) *constancy of mind:*—Mon forlæt ðone ege and ðá fæstrædnesse ðe hé mid ryhte on him innan habban scolde *a timoris intimi soliditate vacuatur*, Past. 37, 17. Ðonne mon ðá fæstrædnesse his módes innan forlíst *qui statum mentis perdidit*, 359, 6: Bt. 5, 3; F. 10, 34: 5, 1; F. 8, 30. (2) *constancy, unchangeableness:*—Þá woruldsælþa on heora wandlunga gecýþdon heora fæstrædnesse *servarit in ipsa sui mutabilitate constantiam*, Bt. 7, 2; F. 16, 32.

**fæt.** *Add:* (1) *a vessel, utensil:*—Fæt *vas*, drenccuppe *poculum*, Wrt. Voc. i. 82, 41. Þ fætt, Jn. L. 19, 29. Glæsen fæt ðæs wætan onféng, Bl. H. 209, 4. Fætes botm *fundum*, Wrt. Voc. ii. 39, 37. Fæte *acerra*, 5, 66. Dó on cyperen fæt oþþe on ærenum fate hafa, Lch. ii. 36, 1. Heald on cyperenum fæte, 38, 12. On læmenum fæte *in vase fictili*, An. Ox. 11, 120. Under fæt *sub modio*, Mk. p. 3, 4. Fæte (fætt, L.), Mk. R. 4, 21. Fatte, Lk. L. 8, 16. Stænino fatto í bydno *lapidae hydriae*, Jn. L. 2, 6. Fato *phialas*, Mt. p. 10, 2. Ðás fato (*vascula*) cræfte gihrínado hæðenra, Rtl. 97, 27. Hí geáfon him manega gærsama on gyldenan faton and on seolfrenan, Chr. 1075; P. 209, 33. Þá gersuman ... on golde and on seolfre and on faton, 1086; P. 222, 16. (2) *a receptacle, box, casket.* v. bán-, hord-, máþm-, sinc-fæt:—' Drihten, þú þe gecure þ fæt (*the body of the Virgin Mary*) on tó eardienne ' ... þ wæs Drihten cweþende tó Marian líchoman : ' þú eart lífes fæt, and þú eart þ heofenlíce templ,' Bl. H. 157, 1–13. Stænne fæt (þ stænna fæt, R) *alabastrum*, Mk. 14, 3. (3) *a compartment:*—þes circul (*the zodiac*) ys tódæled on twelf and seó sunne geyrnð þæs twelf fætu binnan twelf mónðum, Angl. viii. 298, 16. [v. *N. E. D.* fat.] v. æppel-, ál-, bæþ-, beód-, byden-, císe-, drenc(e)-, eced-, ele-, fant-, gemet-, gléd-, melcing-, meolc-, scip-, sealt-, seolfor-, stór-, þegnung-, wearp-, wín-, wyrt-fæt.

**fæt** *a going. Substitute:* fæt *a going.* v. síþ-fæt *and cf. Icel.* feta *to*

*step:* fæt *fat. l.* fæt, *and see* fætt : fæt *ornament. l.* fæt. *For* 'fæ:um, *befeallen* ... *with ornaments, shall be fallen off*' *substitute* fætum befeallen ... *shall be stripped of ornaments; and see next word.*

**fætan;** *p.* te; *pp.* fæted, fætt. I. *to lay as a burden, pack:*—Swá bið ðæm ðe ðá gedónan yfelu hreówsiað, ðonne hí ðæt yfel mid ondetnesse him of áweorpað ðætte hira módes innað yfele and hefiglíce mid gefylled wæs, and ðonne eft fóð tó ðæm ilcan and fætað in æfter ondetnesse ðæt ilce yfel (*they burden themselves within after confession with the same evil*) ðæt hí ær áwurpun *qui admissa plangunt, profecto nequitiam, quae mentis intima deprimebat, confitendo projiciunt, quam post confessionem, dum repetant, resumunt*, Past. 419, 33. Hié dóð swelce hié hit on ðyrelne pohchan fæten (sætten, *v. l.*) *in pertuso sacculo mercedes mittunt*, 343, 24. [Cf. *O. H. Ger.* fazzón *to load; fazza a burden.*] v. ge-fætan; fætels. II. *to adorn, ornament. Take here* fæted (*l.* fæted) *in Dict.:*—Hé genóh hafað fædan (=fættan?) go[l]des, Bo. 35. Þeáh hé geþeó þ hé hæbbe helm and byrnan and golde fæted sweord (ofergyldene sweord, *v. l.*), Ll. Th. i. 188, 9. Hé hét úp beran æðelinga gestreón, frætwe and fæt gold, B. 1921. Fædde (fætte?) beágas, 1750. [*Goth.* ga-fétjan *to adorn; ga-féteins ornament.*] Cf. (?) hroden *for ideas of load and ornament.*

**fætels.** *l.* fætels *and* (?) fætel, *and add:* (1) *a vessel:*—Fylle nú his fætels sé ðe fæstne hider kyl:e bróhte, Past. 469, 9. Forleort fétels (*altered from* fételcs) hire *reliquit hydriam suam*, Jn. L. 4, 28. In fételsum *in vasa*, Mt. L. 13, 48 : 25, 4. Ðás fételsco (*altered from* fætelsco) *haec uascula*, Rtl. 97, 39. (1 a) *applied to persons:*—Wé beóð tempel and fætels þæs Hálgan Gástes, Hml. Th. i. 212, 1. Hé (*St. Paul*) is mé gecoren tætels *vas electionis est mihi iste*, 386, 24 : An. Ox. 5112. Deáðes dohtor and deófles fætels, Hml. S. 2, 175. (2) *a bag:*—Ne fætels *non peram*, Wrt. Voc. ii. 72, 44 : 60, 48. Fætel, 73, 56. In fætelsum *in sitharciis*, 45, 79. Twá hund mittan meluwes on fætelsum (on saccum *in saccis*, Gr. D. 145, 27), Hml. Th. ii. 172, 4. v. leóht-fætels.

**fætere.** *Dele.*

**fæt-fellere.** *Substitute:* fæt-fyllere, es; *m. One who fills a vessel, who pours wine into a cup:*—Fætfellere *abatis* (cf. fert *abatis* orcam, 176, 41), Wrt. Voc. i. 60, 25. Þá gebígde hé þæs fætfylleres (fylleres, *v. l.*) mód tó þon þ hé gemengde áttor tó ðæs wínes drynce *cum vini fusoris ejus animum corrupisset, ut mixtum vino veneni ei poculum praeberet*, Gr. D. 186, 19. Gelæste man Ægelríce IIII pund míre fætfylre, Cht. Th. 568, 3.

**fæt-gold.** *l.* fæt gold, *and see* fætan; II.

**fæþel** (?), es; *m. A player:*—Fæþelas [*hi*]striones, An. Ox. 39, 2.

**fæt-hengest.** *l.* fæt hengest.

**fæþm.** *Add:* (1) *a bosom, lap:*—Faethm *gremium* (gremen, MS.), Wrt. Voc. ii. 110, 3. Faeðm *sinus*, 120, 66. Openige nú þín se fægresta fæþm and se clæna, Bl. H. 7, 25. On fæþme *gremio*, An. Ox. 32, 11. On fæðme (in fæðm, L.) fædres *in sinu patris*, Jn. R. 1, 18. (2) *the fore-arm:*—Eln *ulna*, fæðm *cubitus*, hand *manus*, Wrt. Voc. i. 64, 72 : 283, 11. (2 a) *as a measure of length, a cubit:*—Genim medmicle moran glædenon fæðme longe and swá greáte swá ðín þuma, Lch. iii. 18, 24. Se arc wæs mid ánre fæþme ufeweard belocen, Scrd. 21, 5. Seó earc wæs .ccc. fæðmena lang and .l. fæðmena wíd and xxx fæðmena heáh, Sal. K. 184, 29. (3) *an arm which embraces;* in pl. (*embracing*) *arms, bosom:*—Sceal beón seó góde sáwel on Abrahames fæðmum oð dómes dæg, Wlfst. 238, 7 : Ps. 188. (4) *the distance covered by the arms outstretched, a fathom:*—Faeðm *vel* twégen stridi *passus*, Wrt. Voc. ii. 116, 40. (5) *a closed hand, fist:*—Hand *manus*, fæþm *pugnus*, bräd hand *palma*, Wrt. Voc. i. 283, 13.

**-fæþme.** v. síd-, wíd-fæþme.

**fæþm(i)an.** *Add:*—Boden æfter burgum, swá brimo fæðmeð(-að?), in ceastre gehwære *told through all towns round which circles the sea, in every city*, El. 972. Faeðmendi, faetmaendi, faedmendi *sinuosa*, Txts. 97, 1862. [*O. H. Ger.* fademón *nere: Icel.* faðma *to embrace.*] v. ymb-fæþm(i)an.

**fæþm-líc;** *adj.* I. *embracing, encompassing:*—Sý þín þæt fæþmlíce hríf mid eallum fægernessum gefrætwod, Bl. H. 7, 28. II. *sinuous:*—Ðæm fæðmlíce sinuosis (*flexibus*), Wrt. Voc. ii. 74, 65.

**fæþm-ness.** v. on-fæþmness.

**fætnes.** *l.* fætnes, *and add:*—Fætnys *crassitudo*, Wrt. Voc. i. 51, 12 : pinguedo, 83, 46. Fætnesse *sagina*, i. *pinguedine*, An. Ox. 2395 : 3179. Hig wæron gemæste and wiðerodon for hira fætnisse, Deut. 32, 15. Hé onféhð innan ðæs inngedonces fætnesse (*pinguedinem*), ðæt is wísdom, Past. 381, 5.

**-fætnian.** v. ge-fætnian.

**fætt.** *l.* fætt, *and add:* I. *of animals or human beings.* (1) *in a well-fed condition, plump:*—Hine oxa ne teáh, ne fæt hengest, Rä. 23, 14. Þæt þæt gé fæt sáwon (þæt gé fættas gesáwon, R. Ben. 51, 15) gé underféngon, and þ wanhäl wæs gé wiðsócan *quod crassum videbatis, assumebatis; et quod debile erat, proiciebatis*, R. Ben. I. 56, 14. Þá men beóð mægre, þeáh þe hié ær fætte wæron, Lch. ii. 242, 4. Culfrena briddas, hænne fixsc, and góse fiþru, swá betere swá fætran sién, 196, 23. (2) *in an overfed condition, corpulent, obese:*—Bearg fæt þorcaster *obesus*,

Wrt. Voc. ii. 97, 20 : 64, 50. ¶ as a nickname :—Ealdrēd hæfð geunnen Æðestān fættun sumne dǣl landes, C. D. iv. 262, 13. (3) of animals intended to be eaten, *fatted* :—Fǣt heáhfore *altilium*, Wrt. Voc. i. 23, 50. Tō fēttum stiorce *ad vitulum saginatum*, Kent. Gl. 525. II. of things, *plump, full-bodied, substantial* :—Ðā beóð fulle of fǣttum leáfum and wel wōsigum, Lch. i. 258, 3. Hafað seó lǣsse smæle leáf and gehwǣde, and seó óðer hafað mǣran leáf and fǣtte, 264, 20. Sió hæfð fǣtte and þicce ǣdra, ii. 242, 16. III. *containing fatty matter, consisting of fat* :—Genim fǣttes flǣsces, sele twā snǣda, Lch. ii. 268, 30. Bið swā sēlre swā hē fǣttron mete ete, and gif hē mǣge gedrincan ge ðǣre buteran, iii. 22, 14. III a. referring to fluids, *oleaginous, unctuous* :—Ðȳ fǣttan *crasso* (*crassa olei pinguedine*, Ald.), Wrt. Voc. ii. 83, 67 : 18, 52. IV. *rich* (of food) :—Fǣtt broþ *pingue jus*, Coll. M. 29, 13. Fētto *pinguia*, Kent. Gl. 788. V. *fertile, productive, rich* (soil) :—Ðeós wyrt byþ cenned on fǣttum landum and begānum, Lch. i. 254, 11. VI. *well supplied with what is needful* or *desirable, rich* in good things :—Ǣt fruman ðes middangeard wæs ðeónde, . . . on spēda genihtsumnysse fǣtt, Hml. Th. i. 614, 19. v. frǣ-, ofer-fǣtt.

fǣtt, es ; *m. Fat* :—Fīfte wæs gyfe pund, ðanon him (*Adam*) wæs geseald se fǣt and geþang, Sal. K. p. 180, 12.

fǣttian. *Add* : (1) *to grow fat* :—Fǣttiað endas *pinguescent fines*, Bl. Gl. Fǣt geworden wes and faettade *pinguis factus est et incrassavit*, Ps. Srt. ii. p. 193, 11. (2) *to make fat, anoint* :—Ðū faettades in ele heáfud mīn *inpinguasti in oleo caput meum*, Ps. Srt. 22, 5. [v. *N. E. D.* fat ; *vb.*] v. ā-, be-fǣttian.

fǣx *deceit. Dele, and see* telg.

fāg. *Add* :—Faag *arrius*, Wrt. Voc. ii. 100, 68. Fāg, 7, 21. Faag *farius*, 108, 27. Fāg, 35, 9. Fāh *barius, varius*, 125, 24. *Ceruleus,* i. *glaucus,* fāh, deorc, *color est inter album et nigrum, subniger*, 130, 35. Hwītes heówes and eác missenlices, on bringwīsan fāg *candido versi colore in modum ranarum*, Nar. 16, 2. Þ feórðe nȳten wæs fāgum earne gelīc, Hml. S. 15, 184. On fāgan stāne ; of fāgan stāne, C. D. iii. 180, 32. Tō fāgan flōran, 404, 9. [v. *N. E. D.* faw.] v. drop-, hring-, nǣder-, spec-fāg.

fāgettan. *Add* : (1) literal, *to change colour, grow dark* (cf. Wrt. Voc. ii. 130, 35. v. fāg) :—Se fulla mōna fāgettað, þonne hē ðæs sunlican leóhtes bedǣled bið þurh ðǣre eorðan sceadwunge, Hml. Th. i. 608, 33. (2) *to quibble, use with double meaning* :—Cwæð Ualerianus tō ðām cȳðere : 'Āgif ðā mādmas.' Se cȳðere him andwyrde : 'On Godes ðearfum ic hī āspende, and hī sind ðā ēcan mādmas.' Se gerēfa cwæð : 'Hwæt fāgettest ðū mid wordum?' (*why do you use this word treasures with double meaning ?*), Hml. Th. i. 422, 34. Cf. fāgian.

fāgetung. *Substitute :* fāget[t]ung, e ; *f. A changing colour, growing dark* :—' Ōgan of heofenum.' Hēr is þǣre lyfte fāgetung ðurh mislice stormas, Hml. Th. ii. 538, 33.

fāgian. *Substitute :* (1) *to grow dark* (of a stormy sky) :—Tōdæg stearm, fāgas for ðon unrōtlic heofon *hodie tempestas, rutilat enim triste coelum*, Mt. L. 16, 3. (2) *to vary* :—Swā hit nū fāgað, Freán eald geweorc þætte winnende wiðerweard gesceaft fæste sibbe forð anhealdað (cf. swā hī hit fāgiaþ þ . . . , Bt. 21 ; F. 74, 13) *quod mundus stabili fide concordes variat vices, quod pugnantia semina foedus perpetuum tenent,* Met. 11, 40. Ðæt fāgas *quod variat*, Mt. p. 1, 11. Betwih him fāgas t fāgegas *inter se variant*, p. 1, 2. Ānfealde wīse bið witena gehwylcum weorðlicre micle þonne hē his wīsan fāgige tō swīðe, Ll. Th. ii. 318, 40. v. ge-fāgod, and cf. fāgettan.

fāgnys. *Add* ; *fāhness variety of colour* :—Mid fāgnesse *varietate*, Ps. L. 44, 10. Ymbscrȳd mid menigfealdre fāhnysse, Hml. Th. ii. 586, 16 : An. Ox. 1019. Mid geolewere fāhnysse *crocea qualitate*, 525. On ðisum getelde (*the tabernacle*) wǣron menigfealde fāhnyssa and frætwunga ; swā beóð eác on Godes gelaðunge menigfealde fægernyssa, Hml. Th. ii. 210, 10. Mid fāhnyssum *varietatibus*, Hml. A. 28, 109. Fǣgnessum, Ps. L. 44, 15.

fāgung. *Substitute :* (1) *variety of colour* :—Pund blōstmes, of ðon is fāgung ēgena *pondus floris, inde est varietas oculorum*, Rtl. 192, 19. Hē āwænde eallre þǣre hȳde hīw swā þ seó fāgung (*varietas*) wæs tōbrǣded geond eallne his līchaman, þ hē wæs geþūht swylce hē hreóf wǣre . . . sōna swā hine gehrān se hālga wer, hē gefȳmde ealle þā fāgunge (*varietatem*) swā þ, Gr. D. 158, 31–159, 9. (2) *a diversity* :—Fāgungum *diversis*, Mk. p. 5, 7.

fāg-wyrm, es ; *m. A basilisk* :—Ofer nēdran and fāgwyrm *super aspidem et basiliscum*, Ps. Srt. 90, 13.

fāh. *Add* : *exposed to the vengeance of a slain man's kin because of the murder* :—Gif fāh mon (gefāh mon, *v. l.*) cirican geierne, hine seofan nihtum nān mon ūt ne teó *if a criminal fly for refuge to a church, for seven days no one shall drag him out*, Ll. Th. i. 64, 9. v. un-fāh ; ge-fā, -fāh.

fahame (?) :—Fahame (-ae, Ep. Gl.) *polentum*, Wrt. Voc. ii. 117, 68 : *pullentum*, 118, 42.

fāh-man. *l.* fāh man, *and see* fāh : **fāhness.** v. fāgness : **fahnys.** *Dele :* fala *many.* v. fela.

fala (?) *a plank* :—Fala *tabula*, Ep. Gl. 27 A, 11. [*The Erfurt Glossary has* fala *tabulo, the Leiden and Corpus Glossaries have* fala *tubulo, and in* Wrt. Voc. i. 289, 60 *the gloss is* fealo *tubulo.* If the Epinal Glossary gives the correct form *fala* may be connected with *falod, fald,* if the Latin forms with *tub-* are correct, *fala* might be compared (?) with Icel. *falr* the socket of a spear's head in which the handle is put. v. Ld. Gl. H. s.v. tubulo.]

fald, es ; *m.* (not *f.*). *Add* : , falod (-ud, aed) :—Falud (-aed) *bobellum*, Txts. 45, 310. Falod, Wrt. Voc. ii. 11, 21. Falaed *stabulum*, Txts. 99, 1920. Fald *volio* (*l.* (?) *ovile*), Wrt. Voc. i. 287, 62. Mid swylcum monnum byð hell gefylled swā swā fald mid sceápum, Ps. Th. 48, 13. On ðone ealdan fald ; of ðām ealdan falde . . . On Bunningfald ; of Bunningfalde on æscfald ; of æscfalde . . . on Wufincgfald, C. D. vi. 56, 9–15 : Cht. E. 290, 31. Gebūr sceal licgan of Martinus mæssan oð Eástran æt hlāfordes falde, Ll. Th. i. 434, 13. Wāc byð se hyrde æt falde þe nele þā heorde þe hē healdan sceal mid hreáme bewerian, . . . gyf þǣr hwlyc þeódsceaþa sceaþian onginneð, ii. 326, 10. Þæs þe tō tūne belimpð . . . ge on felda ge on falde, Angl. ix. 260, 1. Fald weoxian, 261, 18. On wifilingsfalod westeweardne, C. D. ii. 172, 25. Byringfalod, fæstanfalod, 195, 20. Falodleáh, v. 70, 24. [*O. L. Ger.* faled *bovellium.*] v. deór-, hind-, pund-, stód-, wudu-fald.

fald-gang. *Substitute : The pasture land grazed by the animals belonging to a fold* (?). (Cf. fold-course *a sheep-walk*, N. E. D.) :—Sceóte man ælmessan, swā æt heáfde peninc, swā æt sulhgange peninc, swā æt faldgange pening, Wlfst. 170, 37.

fald-gang-penig. v. preceding word.

fald-hrīper (?), es ; *n. A beast kept in a fold* (?) :—.xvi. oxan, faldrēþere, and .iii. hund scēpa, C. D. B. iii. 367, 35.

faldian ; *p.* ode *To make a fold* :—Me mǣig on sumera . . . faldian, fiscwer and mylne macian, Angl. ix. 261, 12.

fald-weorþ, -wyrþe ; *adj. Bound to send sheep to the folds of the lord* :—Uolo ut . . . abbas et fratres Ramesiae habeant socam in omnibus super omnes homines qui sunt motwrði, ferdwrði, et faldwrði (-wurði, 208, 32), C. D. iv. 210, 14.

falewende. v. fealwian : **falletan.** v. feallettan : **fallic.** v. fullic : **falod.** v. fald.

fals, es ; *n. Add* :—þ deófol his falses tō fela ongemang þǣre heorde ne gesāwe. Ne wyrð nǣfre folces wīse wel gerǣde on þām earde þe man mǣst falses lufað, Ll. Th. ii. 312, 26–29. Buton ǣlcon false, Wlfst. 272, 3.

fals ; *adj. False* (of weight or coinage) :—Fals *pening* (*printed* flas pennig) (*or?* fals-pening, cf. Icel. fals-penningr) *paracaraximus*, Wrt. Voc. i. 57, 34. Swicollice dǣda and lāðlice unlaga āscunige man swȳðe ; þ is false gewihta and wōge gemeta, Ll. Th. i. 310, 13. Wōge gemeta and false gewihta rihte man georne, Wlfst. 272, 4.

falthing. v. feal-þing.

fām. *Add* :—Leásung *vel* faam *famfaluca*, Txts. 62, 426. Fām, Wrt. Voc. ii. 34, 75. Fām, hwastas *molles*, 55, 72. (1) *foam of living creatures* :—Mid fāmæ *cum spuma*, Lk. L. 9, 39. Dō þertō bāres fām, Lch. i. 360, 1. (2) *foam, froth of boiling liquid* :—Dō on pannan, wyl swīðe, dō þ fām of clǣne, Lch. ii. 94, 8, 20.

fām-blāwende. *In l.* 2 *read :* se lēgfāmblāwenda.

fāmgian. *Add* :—Fēmgendes *spumosis*, An. Ox. 3, 23. [*O. H. Ger.* feimigōn.] v. next word.

fāmig, fǣmig. *Add* :—Fāmbige melcingfata *spumea mulctra*, Germ. 390, 66. Ðǣm fāmigum drohtum *spumosis* (*remorum*) *tractibus*, Wrt. Voc. ii. 75, 13 : Hpt. Gl. 406, 67. Fǣmigum, An. Ox. 34 : 4334 : Hpt. Gl. 507, 71.

fāmwǣstas. *Dele, and see* fām.

fana. *Add* : fanu(-e) ; *f.* I. *a flag* :—Pater Noster hafað gyldene fonan, and seó fone is mid .xii. godwebbum ūtan ymbhangen, Sal. K. 152, 17. Fanan *uexillo*, An. Ox. 4804. Fanan *labara*, 1762. [v. *N. E. D.* fane *a banner.*] v. wind-fana. II. *fane, flower de luce* :—Fana (fanu, *v. l.*) *citsana* (a 12th cent. MS. has fæarn *gitsana*), Ælfc. Gr. Z. 311, 2 : An. Ox. 56, 397. Fanu *cittasana*, Lch. iii. 301, col. 2. Fane, Lch. ii. 136, 30. Fone nioþoweard, 350, 24. Uane iii. 12, 25. Fanu, 58, 20. Fanan, 24, 6. [v. *N. E. D.* fane (plant-name). Cf. *O. L. Ger.* rēni-fano *tanacetum* : *O. H. Ger.* reine-uano.]

fan-byrd, e ; *f. Banner-bearing* (v. fana ; I) :—Fanbyrde *vexillationis*, An. Ox. 1744.

fandere, es ; *m. One who tries, tests, &c.* (v. fandian) :—Nā swylce leornungcniht ac swylce fandere (*temptator*), Scint. 206, 4. [v. *N. E. D.* fander.]

fandian. *Dele passage from Runic poem, and add :* (1) *to try, test the quality* or *character of* an object (*gen.*) :—Gāð tō smiððan, and fandiað þises goldes, Hml. Th. i. 64, 6. Ou ðǣm anbīde ðe hē hira fandige *interveniente correptionis articulo*, Past. 153, 15. God āfandað þæs mannes, nā swilce hē nyte ǣlces mannes heortan ǣr hē his fandige, Scrd. 23, 2. (1 a) *to tempt* :—Se lytega fiónd wile fondian ǣlces monnes mid ðǣre ūpāhæfennesse for gōdum weorcum, Past. 465, 9. (2) *where a* (doubtful) *point is to be determined, the point being given in a clause,*

*to try* whether, if, &c. (a) of the action of persons :—Fandode forð-weard scipes, hwæðer sincende sǽñôd þǽgyt wǽre, Gen. 1436. Man scolde fandian, gif man mihte betræppan þaue here, Chr. 992 ; P. 126, 21 : Met. 9, 12. Hê wolde fandian hû longe þæt land norþryhte lǽge, oþþe hwæðer ænig mon be norðan þǽm wêstenne bûde, Ors. 1, 1 ; S. 17, 7. (b) of the action of things:—Gârsecg fandaþ, hwæðer âc hæbbe ædele treówe, Rûn. 25. (3) combining the constructions of (1) and (2):—Wolde se wîsa mon his fandigan, hwæðer hê swâ wîs wǽre swâ hê self wênde þ hê wǽre, Bt. 18, 4 ; F. 66, 32. (4) *to try, have experience of, taste, feel* (lit. or fig.). (a) *absolute :*—Fandiað nû þonne gustate, Ps. Th. 33, 8. (b) *with gen. :*—Se lǽcecræft þê tirþ on þâ þrotan þonne ðû his ærest fandast *degustata mordent*, Bt. 22, 1 ; F. 76, 30. Hê cwæð þ þ heora weorce nânum men ǽr ne gerise bet tô fandianne þonne þǽm wyrhtan þe hit worhte *he said that for no one was it more fitting that he should be the first to try the machine* (the bull of Phalaris) *than for the man who made it*, Ors. 1, 12 ; S. 54, 30. (c) *acc. :*—Hiê þone bryne fandedon, Dan. 455. (5) *to try, have recourse to, seek the help* of a person (*gen.*):—Man ne sceal fandian Godes þâ hwîle þe hê mæg mîd ænigum gesceáde him sylfum gebeorgan. Sê fandað Godes, sê þe his âgen gesceád forlǽt þe him God forgeaf, and swâ bûtan gesceáde sêcð Godes fultum, Scrd. 22, 2–4. (6) *to visit :*—Ic wæs on cearcerne, and gê mîn noldon fandian *in carcere eram, et non visitastis me*, Past. 329, 5. Gif þê ǽfre gewyrð þ þû wilt eft fandian þâra þióstra þisse worulde *si terrarum placeat tibi noctem relictam visere*, Bt. 36, 3 ; S. 105, 29. (7) *to try the patience* of a person (*gen.*), *tempt, provoke:*—Manega oft ceorodon, and faudodon Godes and gremedon mid sprǽcon, Homl. S. 13, 231. (8) *to try to do something, attempt :*—Þeáh hit ûre mæþ ne siê þ wê witan hwæt hê sié, wê sculon be ðæs andgites mǽðe ðe hê ûs gifð fandian, Bt. 42 ; F. 256, 4. [v. *N. E. D.* fand.]

**-fandigendlic.** v. â-fandegendlic : **fandlíc.** *Dele* : -fandod, -fand-dodlíc, -líce. v. â-fandod, â-fandodlíc, -líce.

**fandung.** *Add* : (1) *trial, testing :*—Oðer is costnung, ôðer is fandung. God ne costnað nænne mannan ; ac hwæðere nân man ne cymð tô Godes ríce, bûton hê sý âfandod ; for ðî ne sceole wê nâ biddan þæt God ûre ne âfandige, ac wê sceolon biddan þæt God ûs gescylde, þæt wê ne âbreóðon on ðǽre fandunge . . . Âfandað God þæs mannes môd on mislicum fandungum . . . Wel God wât hû hit getîmað on ðǽre fandunge . . . þurh ðâ fandunge se man sceal geþeón, gif hê þâm costnungum wiðstent, Hml. Th. i. 268, 7–19. (2) *trial, experiment :*—Þâ þe wê nû gyt ne magon mid gewislicre fandunge witan *quae adhuc scire per experimentum non possumus*, Gr. D. 261, 29. [v. *N. E. D.* fanding.] v. ge-fandung.

**fang.** *Add :* [v. *N. E. D.* fang.] v. and-, on-fang ; gearu-fang (?): **fangend.** v. on-fangend : **fangen-nes.** *Add :* v. â-fangennes : **fan-gian.** v. ge-fangian : **fangol.** v. and-fangol, under-fangelnes.

**fann, e ; f.** *Add :*—Fon *vanna*, Wrt. Voc. ii. 123, 15. Hý habbað micelne mûð swâ fann (swǽ fon, *v. l.*) *ore amplissimo sicut uannum*, Nar. 35, 31. Hî habbað eáran swâ fann (fan, *v. l.*) *aures habentes tamquam uannum*, 37, 11. Man sceal habban . . . fanna, trogas, æscena, Angl. ix. 264, 14. Cf. wind-fana.

**fannian ; p. ode** *To winnow corn :*—Nâ fanna þû þe on ǽlcum winde *non uentiles te in omni uento*, Scint. 186, 17. [v. *N. E. D.* fan ; *vb.*]

**fant.** *Add :* (1) *a fount :*—Font *gurges*, An. Ox. 358. (2) *a font :*—Heó eóde tô ðǽm fantfæte, and tôlýsde hire feax, and bedýpte on ðâm fante, Hml. Th. ii. 30, 17. Hî on fante gefullode wurdon, Hml. S. 2, 90. On þâm hâligan fante, Ll. Th. ii. 390, 14. Se ængel gehâlgode þæt wallende wæter (on þâm cytele) tô fonte, Hml. A. 178, 293. Se sâcerd orðunge on þæt wæter orðað þonne hê font hâlgað, Wlfst. 36, 4.

**fant-bæþ, es ; n.** *The baptismal font, font with water in it ready for baptism, the rite there performed :*—Þonne is æfter eallum þisum mid rihtum geleáfan tô efstanne wið fontbæðes georne . . . Þâ ðreó dýfinga on fontbæðe getácniað . . ., Wlfst. 36, 1–10. Geléstan þæt þæt wê behêtan þâ wê fulluht underfêngan, oððon þâ þe æt fontbæþe (fulluhte, *v. l.*) ûre forespecan wǽran, 67, 8. Hê eóde in (ðâ eá) nacod. Þæt gefullode hine se bisceop . . . and hê eóde of þǽm fantbæðe sôna, Hml. S. 3, 76.

**fant-fæt.** *Add :* v. *first passage under* fant.

**fant-hâlgung, e ; f.** *Consecration of a font preparatory to baptizing a person :*—Wæter gehâlga fonthâlgunge *hallow water in a font* (?), Lch. iii. 24, 17. Þurh þâ fonthâlgunge gewyrð sôna Godes midwist, and ðurh ðâ orðunge þe se sâcerd on þæt wæter orðað, þonne hê fout hâlgað, wyrð deófol þanon âfyrsad, Wlfst. 36, 2. v. next word.

**fant-hâlig ; adj.** *Consecrated in a font :*—Fanthâlig [wæter], Lch. iii. 14, 21.

**fant-wæter.** *Add :*—Ǽr þan þe gê þæt hǽþene cild fullian on þâm fantwætere, ofergeót ðinne lîchaman mid fantwætere, Hml. Th. ii. 346, 14, 24. Bedýp on fontwætre gehâlgodum, Lch. ii. 344, 23.

**fanu.** v. fana : **fara.** *Add :* [*O. L. Ger.* ofar-faro : *Icel.* fari.] v. nîw-fara.

**faran.** *Add :*—Ic fare *eo*, ic ût fare *exeo*, ic tô fare *adeo*, Ælfc. Gr. Z. 193, 3. Færeð *meat*, Wrt. Voc. ii. 57, 33. Sîþien and færen *comitentur*,

22, 14. **I.** *expressing movement*. (1) *of persons*. (a) *to travel, journey :*—Wê beóþ mid þê swâ hwyðer swâ þû færest, Bl. H. 233, 33. Wê faraþ tô Gerusalem, 15, 7. Far . . . and þæt land gesêc þe ic þê ýwan wille, Gen. 1748. Oþer næfþ his fôta geweald þ hê mæge gân, and wilnaþ þeáh tô farenne *the other has not the use of his feet so that he can walk, and yet wants to make the journey*, Bt. 36, 4 ; F. 178, 14. [On my]nster tô ganganne oððe sûð tô faranne, Txts. 447, 17. Hê þanon wæs farende, Bl. H. 249, 2. ¶ figurative :—Gif gê on mînum bebodum wæs farað, Hml. S. 13, 157. Þǽr þû þines fæder êþele fôre of, ðâ ðû ðîne fæstrædnesse forlête, Bt. 5, 1 ; F. 8, 30. Of þǽm wege þe wit getiohhod habbaþ on tô farenne, 40, 5 ; F. 240, 19. Þâ ðing forgif mê tô Crîste farendre (*to me who wish to be the bride of Christ, to remain a virgin*), Hml. S. 9, 40. (a a) *of a military expedition, to march :*—Hê gegaderode fierd, and wolde faran on Perse (*he intended to march on Persia*) ; *bellum adversus Parthos parans*, Ors. 6, 31 ; S. 286, 9. (a β) of troops on board ship :—Octauianus hæfde xxx scipa and cc þâra micelna þrierêðrena on þǽm wǽron farende eahta legian, and Antonius hæfde eahtatig scipa on þǽm wǽron farende x legian, Ors. 5, 13 ; S. 246, 5–8. (b) *to go :*—Ic cweðe tô ðisum, 'Far ðû,' and hê færð ('vade', *et vadit*) . . . 'Far ðe hâm' (*vade*), Hml. Th. i. 126, 11–21. Far (gaa L fær, L.) and gâ heonon *exi et uade hinc*, Lk. 13, 31. Hê bæd þ hê môste faran and his fæder bebyrgean, Bl. H. 23, 13. (b a) of the movements of troops by land or sea :—Hié on ðǽm sǽ tôgædere fôran, and gefuhton *they joined battle and fought*, Ors. 3, 1 ; S. 96, 31. Fôron tô-somne wrâðe wælherigas, Gen. 1982. (c) *to go, depart* from this life :—Ic fearu (*vadam*) tô gete helle, Ps. Srt. ii. p. 184, 24. Hyra waldend fôr of lîchoman, Cri. 1186. Gâst fearende and nô eft cerrende *spiritus uadens et non rediens*, Ps. Srt. 77, 39. (2) *of animals, to go, move*. v. (4):—Manig wyht is mistlíce fêrende, and sint swîþe ungelíces hîwes and ungelíce faraþ, Bt. 41, 6 ; F. 254, 25. Þû (the serpent) scealt faran fêðeleás, Gen. 908. Heaðorôfe hleápan lêton, on geflit faran, fealwe meáras, B. 865. (3) *of things*, (a) *that move naturally*. v. (4):—Fǽred æfter foldan fýrswearta lêg *the flame shall run along the ground*, Cri. 984. Færþ se mete ût þurh ðone lîchomon, Bt. 34, 11 ; F. 150, 35. Sceal faran flôde blôd *blood shall flow in streams* (*from wounds*), An. 956. (b) *that move by artificial means, to go* (of a machine), *fly* (of a missile) :—Mê (*a bow*) of bôsme færeð ætren onga, Rä. 24, 3. Sió nafu færþ micle fæstlícor ðonne ðâ felgan dôn, swelce sió eax sié . . . God, and ðâ sêlestan men faran nehst Gode . . . Ðâ felga farað ungerydelícost, sió nafu færþ gesundlícost, Bt. 39, 7 ; F. 220, 30–222, 23. (c) of abstract things, *to come :*—Gesweorc ûp færeð, cymeð hægles scûr, færeð forst on gemang, Gen. 809. Yldo him on faræð, Seef. 91. (d) *to pass away, depart :*—Þeós woruld faraþ, Hy. 11, 6. Ðû tîda endebyrde gesetteð, swâ þte hî ægðer ge forþ faraþ ge eft cumaþ, Bt. 33, 4 ; F. 128, 8. Ealle gesceafta faraþ and æft cumað, and weorðað eft tô ðâm ylcan wlite, Solil. H. 62, 31. (4) *special constructions*. (a) *with pres. ptcpl.* :—Þû færsð wôrigende and bist flýma geond ealle eorðan *uagus et profugus eris super terram*, Gen. 4, 12. Wind wêdende færeð, El. 1274. Hî (*clouds*) farað feohtende . . . winnende fareð atol eóredþreát, Rä. 4, 46, 48. Sume wyhta licgaþ mid eallon lîchaman on eorþan, and swâ snîcende faraþ, Bt. 41, 6 ; F. 254, 26. (b) with accusative of road :—Hió fôr flôdwegas, Rä. 37, 5. foldweg tredan, An. 774. **II.** of action, behaviour. (1) *of persons, to go on :*—Sê ðe mid lufe bið âfylled, sê færð on smyltnesse, and sê ðe hatunge hæfð, sê færð mid yrsunge *he that is filled with love goes on quietly, and he that has hatred in his heart gives way to anger*, Hex. 44, 20. Hê fôr swâ *he so behaved*, Gr. D. 324, 11. Hî ne môston þurh unâlýfedlice weorc faran (cf. heom næs âlýfed, þ hî ǽnigu unâlýf-edlicu weorc worhton (unâlýfedlíc þing tô dônne, *v. l.*), Gr. D. 104, 17), swâ swâ hî ǽr gewunode wǽron *they might not go on with their unlawful acts, as before they had been wont*, Hml. Th. ii. 158, 12. (I a) faran mid *to act with, make use of, practise :*—Ðonne se man mid lícetunge hæfð, Hml. S. 16, 302. Drýmen þe mid dydrunge farað, Hml. Th. ii. 330, 28. Hwæðer þe God mid inweardlícre heortan lufige, oððe hê mid hîwunge fare, i. 268, 14. Þeáh þû mid ligenum fare, Gen. 531. Godes þeówas nâgon mid wigge ne mid worldcampe âhwâr tô farenne, ac mid gâstlican wæpnan campian wið deófol, Ll. Th. i. 388, 5. (2) *of things and animals :*—Æceras farað on sumera swâ swâ sǽ ýdigende, Ælfc. Gr. Z. 295, 11. Ealle gesceafta, sunne and môna and ealle tunglan, land and sǽ, and nýtenu, ealle hî farað æfter Godes dihte, Hml. Th. i. 172, 17. **III.** *to go well or ill, happen, turn out :*—Hit fareð yfele ealles tô wîde, Ll. Th. ii. 322, 18. Swâ mâ witena beóð, swâ hit bet færð, Hml. S. 13, 130. Þwyrlíce færð æt ðâm hûse þǽr seó wyln bið ðǽre hlǽfdian wissigend, 17, 10. Ðeáh ûs þince þ hit on wôh fare, Bt. 39, 8 ; F. 224, 21. Þû segst þ hit scyle eall faran swâ hê getiohhod habbe, 41, 2 ; F. 244, 19. Gif hit oftor gewyrð, nyte wê hû þæt faran mæg *if a man marries oftener than four times, we do not know what will happen*, Wlfst. 305, 6. **IV.** of procedure, *to go according to a rule :*—Wit wæs hwîlum on Engla lagum þ leód and lagu fôr be geþincðum, Ll. Th. i. 190, 11. **V.** *to get on well or ill :*—Se man þe ne can þæs gescâd, hê ne færð nâht, Wlfst. 123, 12. **VI.**

in greeting :—Faraþ nū gesunde, and gesǣlige becumaꝺ, Hml. S. 6, 89. **VII.** of money, to be current, be in use :—Hit mǣre is þonne ccclxxii wintra syꝺꝺan ꝺyllic feoh wæs farende on eorꝺan, Hml. S. 23, 702. v. simbel-, wīd-farende.

**farend.** v. scip-farend.

**Farisēisc.** Add :—Hū ne eom ic Farisēisc swā same swā gē?, Past. 363, 3. Þǣre farisēiscre farisaice, An. Ox. 1259. v. next word.

**Farisēos** ; gen. o ; pl. The Pharisees :—Swā dydon Farisēos, Past. 59, 24. Þā Farisēos (Farissēos, v. l.) geliéfdon, 362, 6. Ꝺæt folc Farisēo (Pharisēo, v. l.), 360, 25.

**farnian** ; p. ode To prosper. Cf. faran, **V** :—Hāl mē dō uel farniga salvum me fac bene prosperare, Rtl. 176, 25. [Cf. Icel. farnask to speed well ; farnaꝺr furtherance, speed.]

**faroþ.** Substitute : **faroþ,** es ; m. **I.** water in motion [? cf. faran ; **I.** 3 ; and for connexion of a noun denoting water with a verb denoting motion, v. wǣg wave, and wegan to move], surging sea, ocean, waves : —Brādne hwyrft oꝺ þæt brim faroþæs (cf. the phrase sǣs brim. The MS. has oꝺ þ brim faroþæs : in Az. 38 the reading is oꝺ brimflōdas) the spacious vault of heaven down to the waters of ocean (i. e. to the horizon), the entire expanse of the sky, Dan. 322. Mec sǣ oꝺbær æfter faroꝺe the sea bore me along on its waves, B. 580. Wæs æt holme gearo, fūs æt faroꝺe, 1916. Bāt on sǣwe, fleót on faroꝺe, Hy. 4, 100. Hī hyne ætbǣron tō brimes faroꝺe they bore him to the water, B. 28. Gewāt him ofer sandhleoꝺu tō sǣs faroꝺe, An. 236. Brimþisan æt sǣs faroꝺe sēcan, 1660. **II.** the land bordering the sea, shore :—Hē on greóte stōd, fūs on faroꝺe, An. 255. [Perhaps some passages given under **I** should be taken here.] v. compounds with faroþ-.

**faru.** Substitute : **I.** of movement. (1) going, passing :—Ꝺǣr manna faru mǣst wæs juxta publicos viarum transitus, Bd. 2, 16 ; Sch. 180, 5. Hit is Godes faru est transitus Domini, Ex. 12, 11 : Ps. Spl. 143, 18 : Ps. L. 143, 14. Næs ꝺǣr nān man on fare (in transitu) þe gryre fore ne stōde, Hml. S. 23, 83. Seó scamu hyre forbeád þā fare (processionem) tō þǣre cyrichālgunge, Gr. D. 72, 15. (1 a) going by sea, sailing :—Hē him mid fare gehwearf eft tō Centlande rediit Cantiam nauigio, Bd. 2, 20 ; Sch. 186, 24. (2) a journey, voyage :—Be þām preóste þe forwyrnꝺ fulwihtes for neóde his fare (itineris), Ll. Th. ii. 128, 16. Seó wīteguno be ꝺǣre fare, Hml. Th. i. 80, 3. Se pāpa hī tō ꝺǣre fare tihte, ii. 128, 1. Ꝺā yldestan ealdras Israhēla ꝺeóde geendodon heora līf on ꝺǣre langsuman fare (the journey in the wilderness), 212, 12 : 198, 25 : 200, 26. Siꝺꝺan þū fram ūs sīꝺodest on fare since you went from us on your journey, Hml. S. 6, 83. Lucas mid Paule siꝺꝺan sīꝺode on his fare, Ælfc. T. Grn. 12, 39. ' Hwanon cōme ꝺū ?' Hē andwyrde : ' Leóf, næs ic on nānre fare ' (non ivit servus tuus quoquam), Hml. Th. i. 400, 24. Sume scypmen reówan . . . swā man fǣrꝺ tō Rōme . . . þā wæs on þǣre fare sum mangære, Hml. S. 31, 1138. ' Āsende ūre Hǣlend his engel mid þē, sē þīne fare gewissige ' . . . Appollonaris ꝺā fērde, 22, 29. Hī ꝺā fare fērdon būton wiste, Hml. Th. ii. 138, 33. Hē gearcode his fare and tō Englelande cōm, Chr. 1091 ; P. 226, 29. (3) an expedition :—Wē him his geswinces geþancedon of ūrum gemǣnum feó þe þām þe seó fare (the search for stolen property) wurꝺe wǣre, Ll. Th. i. 234, 28. Se cyng geāxode þ his feónd ge!ǣtte wǣron and ne mihten nā geforꝺian heora fare, Chr. 1085 ; P. 216, 7. Ꝺurh þās fare (the crusade) wearꝺ se cyng and his brōꝺor sehte, 1096 ; P. 232, 30. Micel is þeós menigeo, mægenwīsa trum, sē þās fare lǣdeꝺ, Exod. 554. **II.** of action or conduct. (1) of persons, proceedings, course of life, path :—Hī wītegodon be þām Hǣlende and heora bēc setton be ealre his fare, Ælfc. T. Grn. 10, 33. Hī wǣron mid him on eallum his weorcum and on ealre his fare, Hml. Th. i. 286, 7. Twā bēc hē self gesette be his fare, Ap. Th. 28, 14. Þenc ǣfre embe God on eallum ꝺīnum wegum, and hē sylf gewissaꝺ wel þīne fare in omnibus viis tuis cogita illum, et ipse diriget gressus tuos, Hml. S. 13, 321. (1 a) procedure in a single instance :—Hī gameniíce rǣddon and mid geáplicre fare fērdon callide cogitantes perrexerunt, Jos. 9, 6. (2) of things :—Þā concurrentes þe þý geáre yrnaꝺ, þǣra fare wē hēr bufon ætýwdon, Angl. viii. 304, 9. Wē cwǣdon hwanon se bissextus cymꝺ, and manega þing wē cýꝺdon ymbe his fare, 312, 46. **III.** in a collective sense, a body of people who go with a person. (1) the train of one who goes on a mission :—Nāāmān gecyrde mid ealre his fare (cf. reversus cum universo comitatu suo, 2 Kings 5, 15) tō his āgenre leóde, Hml. Th. i. 400, 14. Sum cwēn cōm tō Salomone mid micelre fare, ii. 584, 10. Cōm Flaccus mid mycelre fare tō Petronellan, wolde hī niman tō wīfe, Hml. S. 10, 253. (2) the troops of a general :—Hwænne þū (Holofernes) eáꝺelícost miht tō þām folce becuman mid ealre þīnre fare tōmiddes Hierusalem be mīnre wissunge ut ego adducam te per mediam Jerusalem, Hml. A. 110, 258. (3) the followers of a teacher :—Se hālga wer fērde mid his fare, Hml. S. 31, 1011. (4) the household and live stock of one migrating :—Abram fērde of Aran and Loth fērde mid him mid ealre fare and mid eallum ǣhtum egressus est Abram, et ivit cum eo Lot, tulitque universam substantiam quam possederant, Gen. 12, 5. Abram fērde mid ealre his fare (omnia quae habebat), 20. Gewīt þū fēran and þīne fare (cf. Gen. 12, 5) lǣdan, ceápas tō cnōsle (cf. egredere de terra tua . . . faciamque te in gentem

magnam, Gen. 12, 1, 2), Gen. 1746. God gemunde Nōes fare and þǣra nýtena recordatus Deus Noe cunctorumque animantium et omnium jumentorum, Gen. 8, 1. **III** a. the attendants on a number of persons :—Wand fýr of heofonum and forbærnde þā fíftig manna mid ealre heora fare (cf. descendit ignis de coelo, et devoravit quinquagenarium et quinquaginta qui erant cum eo, 2 Kings 1, 10), Hml. S. 18, 250. **IV.** a means of transport (?), carriage or beast of burden :—Þonne wæs þridde healf þūsend mūla ꝺe þā seámas wǣgon, and xxx. þūsenda eal (a second l has been erased) farena and oxna þā þe hwǣte bǣron (quite xxx. thousand carriages and beasts of burden and oxen that carried wheat?) twā þūsenda olfenda (the Latin which corresponds to this passage is : Duo milia sub armis mulorum castrensium et ad sarcinas militum uehendas curruum duo milia. Camelorum dromedarumque et boum duo milia qui frumenta uehebant), Nar. 9, 11. [v. N. E. D. fare. O. Frs. fare : Icel. för.] v. cild-, earh(-g)-, eax-, fyrd-, gār-, hægl-, huntaþ-, mann-, nīd-, streám-, ūt-, wǣg-, wægn-, wolcen-, ȳþ-faru ; fær.

**faster-mann.** v. fester-mann : **fatan.** Dele.

**faꝺu.** Dele e ; f. : and add :—Faꝺe amita, Wrt. Voc. ii. 6, 36. Sēe Emeliana wæs sēe Gregorius faꝺe, Shrn. 48, 6. Faꝺu oꝺꝺe mōdrige, Ll. Th. ii. 344, 14. Be Tassillan mīnre faꝺan de Tharsilla amita, mea, Gr. D. 286, 8.

**fatian** ; p. ode To fetch :—Ꝺā ne sinigaꝺ ne fatas wīfo illi neque nubunt neque ducunt uxores, Lk. L. 20, 35. Ꝼæt nān man wyrte in lēhtūne ne fatige, Wlfst. 227. 8. v. fetian.

**fatu** in Wrt. Voc. ii. 79, 63 : 41, 35 is Latin (=fato). v. An. Ox. 2627.

**fēā.** Dele 'indecl. n. Fee . . . , S. 549, 10 ' : **feá** ; adv. Add : [cf. Icel. fātt.]: **feágan.** Add : v. ge-feón : **feala-fōr.** v. felo-for : **feala-hīw.** Dele, and see ıela ; **II.** I.

**fealcen,** es : fealca (?), an ; m. A falcon :—Tō fealcnes forda (cf. Hafucíord, C. D. v. 103, 37), C. D. B. ii. 220, 14. Ꝺæt land æt Fealcnahām (cf. æt Habeccahām, i. 315, 23. On heafoces hamme, vi. 75, 33), C. D. ii. 381, 20. Cf. Wilgīsi Westerfalcing (-falcning, v. l.), Westerfalca (-falcna, v. l.) Sǣfugling, Chr. 560 ; P. 18, 5. [O. L. Ger. falko : O. H. Ger. falcho : Icel. fālki.] From Latin.

**feald** a fold. Dele , es ; n. . . . , Lye.

**feald** fold (as a multiplicative) :—Þæt man ælcne ceáp mihte be twām fealdum (be twiefealdan, S. 248, 2) bet geceápian þonne man ǣr mihte ut duplicia quam usque ad id fuerant rerum venalium pretia statuerentur, Ors. 5, 13 ; Bos. 113, 37. [O. H. Ger. falt plica : Icel. faldr.] v. fela-, þic-feald ; fild.

**feald** (?) :—Lyt muneca wæs on feáwum stōwum þe be rihtum regule lifdon ; næs þæt nā fealdre (manigfealdre ?) þonne on āre stōwe, Lch. iii. 438, 22.

**fealdan.** Add :—Þonne þū fyldstōl fyalden wylt, Tech. ii. 122, 22. Fealdendum volventibus, Wrt. Voc. ii. 92, 42. v. on-, twi-fealdan.

**-feald-líc, -líce, -ness.** v. twi-feald-lic, -líce, -ness : **feale-for.** v. felo-for.

**fealgian** ; p. ode To fallow, break up land :—Me mæig on sumera fealgian, myxendincgan ut dragan, Angl. ix. 261, 8. v. Andrews' Old English Manor, p. 260, n. 4. [v. N. E. D. fallow ; vb.] v. next word.

**fealh.** Substitute : fealh, fealg, felg, e ; f. Fallow land :—Fealh (felh, Hpt. Gl. 461, 75) occa, An. Ox. 2359 : 2, 75. Felg, 10, 5. Felch, 4, 36. Wealh (l. fealh), Wrt. Voc. ii. 79, 25. Walh (l. falh), 62, 63. [All these are glosses on : Foecunda conversationis occa, Ald. 32, 29.] Fealga occas, Txts. 82, 713. Fealge, Wrt. Voc. ii. 89, 58. Fealga, 65, 32. Felga, An. Ox. 15, 1 : 17, 2. [Most, if not all, of these are glosses on : Graculus segetum glumas et laeti cespitis occas depopulare studet, Ald. 142, 20.] [v. N. E. D. fallow ; sb.]

**feall** a trap. v. fealle.

**feall** a fall :—Feallo torres foretreden ruina turris oppressi, Lk. p. 8, 3. Þā getimbru wǣron gehrorene nnid gelōmlicum feallum, Gr. D. 134, 12. [Icel. fall ; n.] v. ge-feall ; fill.

**feallan.** Add : **I.** of a body that can move freely :—Sum sceal on holte of heán beáme fiꝺerleás feallan, . . . hē fealleꝺ on foldan, Vy. 21-26. Se feónd mid his gefērum feóllon of heofonum on helle, Gen. 360. Teáras feóllon, El. 1134. Feall nū āðūn (mitte te deorsum), Mt. 4, 6), Hml. Th. i. 166, 8. Hié cwepaþ tō þǣm dūuum : ' Feallaþ ofor us,' Bl. H. 93, 33. Nis þǣre eorþan eþre tō feallanne ofdūne ꝺonne ūp, Bt. 33, 4 ; F. 130, 38. Se feallenda deófol, Hml. Th. i. 214, 23. **I** a. fig. of immaterial things :—Mē feall:ꝺ on fyrhtu deáꝺes, Ps. Th. 54, 4. Dōm. 72. Feól him ege on, Bl. H. 193, 5. **II.** of that which becomes detached and drops :—Þone cancor þǣra tōꝺa, of ꝺām for oft ꝺā teþ feallaꝺ, Lch. i. 294, 22. Feól tō foldan swurd, ne mihte hē gehealdan mēce, By. 166. Þā locu feóllon, Hō. 39. Wiþ þ ꝺæt mannes feax fealle, Lch. i. 110, 15. **III.** of the direction of a stream, to run :—Fylꝺ swýꝺe mycel sǣ ūp in on ꝺæt lond, Ors. 1, 1 : S. 19, 22. **IV.** where an erect position is lost :—Ꝺā feól hē fǣringa onbǣcling, Bl. H. 223, 11. Hié feóllan tō eorþan, and grāpodan mid heora handum on þā eorþan, 151, 5. **IV** a. fig. to be overcome :—Ic wæs

hearde cnyssed, and ic ne feóll, Ps. Th. 117, 13. **IV b.** *to prostrate oneself in reverence :*—Gif þū feallest tō mē and mē weorþast (*si cadens adoraveris me*, Mt. 4, 9), Bl. H. 27, 18. Englas gebǣfedon þæt mennisce men him tō feóllon, Hml. Th. i. 38, 28. Hī feóllon on foldan and tō fōtam hnigon, Sat. 533. Hē clypode: 'Uton feallan tō ðǣre rōde, and þone Ælmihtigan biddan . . .' Hī feóllon þā ealle mid Oswolde on gebedum, Hml. S. 26. 19-24. Hié on gebed feóllon, Gen. 847. Tō gebede feóllon, 777. **IV c.** *to drop wounded or dead :*— Mycel wæll feóll on ægðre healfe, Chr. 1016; P. 150, 2 : By. 303. Hē blōde fāh feóll on foldan ; næs hē fǣge þā gyt, B. 2975. Feóllon wergend bennum seóce, Gen. 1971 : Hml. S. 26, 154. **IV d.** *to stumble, fall* into a pit, snare, &c. :—Gif ðæt swīn fild on ðæt sol, Past. 421, 2. Feallað firenfulle on heora sengnettum, Ps. Th. 140, 2. **V.** *to fail, fall away, decay, crumble away.* v. feallend-lic :—Þes middangeard daga gehwylce fealleþ and tō ende efsteþ, Bl. H. 59, 26: Wand. 63. Foldwela fealleð, eorðmægen ealdað, Reim. 68. Eáðre is þ heofen and eorðe gewīton þonne ān stæf of þǣre ǣ fealle, Lk. 16, 17. Feal[l]endne *nutabundum*, i. *corruendum*, An. Ox. 2778. Þes middangeard fīyhð from ūs, and wē him fieóndum fylgeaþ, and hine feallendne lufiaþ, Bl. H. 115, 18. v. for-, forþ-, ofer-feallan.

**fealle**, an; *f. A trap* :—Feallan *muscipulam*, An. Ox. 4979. Feallum *muscipulis*, i. *decipulis*, 4074. [*v. N. E. D. fall a trap. O. L. Ger. O. H. Ger.* falla *muscipula, decipula.*] v. beswic-fealle (*or* ? beswic, fealle), mūs-fealle.

**feallend-lic**; *adj. Perishable. transitory, frail.* v. feallan ; V :— Þeós world is gebrosnodlic and feallendlic, Bl. H. 115, 4 : Wlfst. 136, 27. Þysse worulde wela is hwīlwendlic and feallendlic and gebrosnadlic, 263, 12.

**feallettan**; *p.* te *To fall to the ground :*—Falletande *concidens*, Mk. L. 5, 5.

**feallung.** v. feax-feallung : fealo *tubulo.* v. fala.

**fealo**; *adj. Add :*—Falu *gilvus*, Wrt. Voc. ii. 109, 69. Fealu *rubeum, rubicundum*, 15, 80 : *busius*, 126, 76. Feala, 12, 57. Sió fealwe fægernes *fulva venustas* (*pavonis*), 89, 61 : 33, 40. Nim þonne þ seax þe þæt hæfte sié fealo hryþeres horn, Lch. ii. 290, 22. Þæs fealaweris *flava*, Wrt. Voc. ii. 33, 39. Gyf him þince þ hē on fealawan horse rīde . . . oððe grǣgan, Lch. iii. 172, 29. Licgende on fealwum ceósle, Hml. Th. ii. 138, 14. Fealewum *fulvis* (*cineribus*), An. Ox. 5485. v. æsc-, dun-, mūs-fealo.

**feá-lōg.** *Add :* [Cf. *O. H. Ger. fō(h)-lōgī raritas, paucitas.*] **feal-þing**(?) *a great mass, a great weight* (?) :—Falthing *moles*, Wrt. Voc. ii. 114. 23.

**fealwian.** *Add :*—Falewende *flavescentibus* (*botris*), Wrt. Voc. ii. 83, 60 : 37, 15. [*v. N. E. D. fallow ; vb. O. H. Ger.* falewēn.]

**fearh.** *Add :*—Faerh *porcellus*, Wrt. Voc. ii. 117, 61. Fearh, 68, 31. [*O. H. Ger. farh porcellus : Lat. porcus.*] v. stig-fearh ; ge-fearh.

**fearn.** *Add :*—Fearn (feran, Erf.) *filix*, Txts. 62, 420. *Filix, fearn cujus radix utilis est ad soluendam difficultatem pariendi*, Wrt. Voc. ii. 39, 35. *Filicumque* and fearnes oððа fearna, 37, 48. Wiþ þeóhhece, smīce mid fearne swīþe þā þeóh, Lch. ii. 64, 26. [The word forms the first part of many local names, v. C. D. vi. pp. 286, 287.]

**fearn-bed.** *For* 'R. 85, Lye' *substitute :*—Fearnbed *filicetum*, Wrt. Voc. ii. 35, 50 : 148, 53 (gearn-, MS.). Andlang weges oþ hit cymþ tō fearnbedde, C. D. B. ii. 386, 13.

**fearn-bracu**, e ; *f. A fern-brake, bed of fern :*—On fearnbraca sūðeweardæ, C. D. v. 173, 18. [*Promp. Parv.* brake bushe or fernebrake *filicetum, filacarium.*]

**fearn-edisc**, es ; *n. A fern-pasture :*—On sacecumb, swā on fearnedisc, C. D. B. i. 519, 2. Cf. fearn-lǣs.

**fearnig**; *adj. Ferny, full of fern :*—On ðā fearnigan hylle, of ðǣre fearnigan hylle, C. D. B. ii. 246, 21. On ðā fearnige leáge, C. D. iii. 376, 5.

**fearn-lǣs**; *gen.* -lǣswe ; *f. A fern-pasture ; the right to pasture swine in such a pasture :*—Illam terram liberabo a pascua porcorum regis quod nominamus *fearnlesuae*, C. D. ii. 59, 19. v. Sax. Engl. ii. 87, *and* cf. fearn-edisc.

**fearr.** *Add :*—Fear *taurus*, Wrt. Voc. ii. 122, 5. *Et suovetaurili(a)* oðða þā þe æt þǣm geldum þǣr wæs swīn and sceáp and fear, 31, 35 : Bl. H. 199, 7. Fearr, Wrt. Voc. i. 287, 59. Hwæþer gē sién strengran ðonne leó oððe fearr, Bt. 32, 1 ; F. 114, 26. Sum mōdig fearr wearð āngeucga . . . Garganus ðone fearr gehwǣr sōhte . . . heora nān ne dorste ðām fearre geneálǣcan, Hml. Th. i. 502, 11-22. Flǣsc ferra *carnes taurorum*, Ps. Srt. 49, 13. Se micela ylp þe ðā mōdigan fearras mid ealle ofbeát, Shrn. 133, 12. ¶ *in local names :*—Fearrhām, C. D. iii. 233, 31. Fearres cumb, v. 232, 24. Sunt rura haec . . . Fearresheáfod . . ., iii. 101, 15: v. 342, 23.

**fearr-hrīþer**, es ; *n. A bull :*—Sum fearhrýþer (cf. se fear, 6) þæs ōþræs ceápes geférscipe oferhogode, Bl. H. 199, 4. Gif him þince þ hē hæbbe ferrhrýðer, Lch. iii. 174, 21.

**fearrian.** v. feorrian.

**fearr-lic**; *adj. Of a bull :*—[Æt] swīnenan and æt sceáplican and æt fearīc (= fearlican) *suovetaurilia*, An. Ox. 11, 187.

**feásceaft-ness**, e ; *f. Poverty :*—Fǣsceaftnes *paupertas*, An. Ox. 1171.

**feáwa.** *Add :*—Feára *paulorum*, Wrt. Voc. ii. 65, 54. **I.** substantival. (1) *few persons or things :*—Syndon feáwa þe þǣm deádan getreówe weorþon, Bl. H. 53, 1. On þām folce feáwe wǣran ǣnige *there were few only in that folk*, Ps. Th. 104, 11. Hwæt ðā feáwa syndan þe his willan wyrcean willen, R. Ben. 2, 17. Hē cýdde fela þe Crīstes godcundnysse . . . feáwa hē āwrāt be his menniscnysse, Hml. Th. i. 70, 21. (1 a) followed by a pronoun in the singular :—Feáwa siént tō þām gesceádwīse, gif hē wyrþ on ungeþylde, þ hē ne wilnige þ his sǣlþa weorþan onwende, Bt. 11, 1 ; F. 32, 32. Manegum is forgifen ðæt hē sprecan mæig, and swīþe feáwum (or sing. ? v. (2)) ðæt hē sý gesceádwīs, Prov. K. 5. (2) with gen., in sing. *a few, small number* of, in pl. *few* of :—Manige weras þe swīþe feáwa manna ā ongit, Bt. 19 ; F. 70, 12. Feá ǣnig wæs monna cynnes *there was only a few of mankind*, Rä. 61, 3. On þām fenlande synd feáwa weorcstāna, Hml. S. 20, 77. Ic hæbbe āne feáwa geférena, 23, 733. Sprecan āne feáwa worda, Nic. 5, 40. **II.** adjectival :—þā frýnd . . . þe hine for þām welan lufiaþ . . . þā feáwan þe hine for lufum lufedon, Bt. 29, 2 ; F. 106, 11. Feám wordum, Past. 73, 19. Feám (feáum, *v. l.*), 75, 16. Feáum, 395, 12 : Bt. 19; F. 70, 11. Feáwum, 11, 2 ; F. 34, 7. Binnan feágum (feáwum, *v. l.*) tīdum, Lch. i. 100, 12. Mid feáwum þām getrýwestum mannum, Ap. Th. 6, 5. Gesāwon wē mennisce men feá (*paucos homines*) . . . hēt ic feá strǣla (*paucas sagittas*) sendan, Nar. 10, 16, 22. Þās feáwan cwidas sōna, Ll. Th. ii. 402, 2. Þās feáwan dagas, Bl. H. 37, 11. Hī lǣtaþ þīne feáwan getreówan mid þē, Bt. 20 ; F. 72, 17. Þā feástan *paucissimi*, Ps. Srt. 104, 13. Feáwoste, Bl. Gl. **II a.** undeclined :—Æfter feáwa dagum, Lk. 15, 13. Æfter feáwa (feáwum, *v. l.*) dagum, Mart. H. 176, 4. v. ān ; V a.

**feáwnes.** *Add :*—Feáuisse *paucitatem*, Ps. Srt. 101, 24.

**feax.** *Add :*—Feax *coma*, Wrt. Voc. i. 282, 36 : ii. 22, 56. Wiþ þ ðæt mannes fex (feax, *v. l.*) fealle, Lch. i. 110, 15. Þ fýr ne fornam ne ān hǣr heora feaxes, Hml. S. 30, 465. Fexe, hǣre *capillatura*, An. Ox. 1214. Heó hire wætres bæd, and hī þwōhg, and hyre feax gerǣdde (*crines composuit*), Bd. 3, 9 ; Sch. 232, 9. Hī habbað beardas oþ cneów and feax oð hēlan (*comas usque ad talos*), Nar. 35, 2. Monig man hæfð micel feax on foranheáfde, and weord fǣrlīce caluw, Prov. K. 42. Fexa, hǣra *cincinnorum*, An. Ox. 1199: 4172. Feaxum *comis*, Wrt. Voc. ii. 95, 45. ¶ *a bush* (?). v. feaxede (2) [cf. (?) *Icel.* vallar-fax *the wood* (poet.).] :—Oð ealdan hege ; on westhealfe ealdan hege tō feaxum ; ðonne west from feaxum, C. D. iii. 429, 12. [*v. N. E. D. fax.*] v. fore-, loc-, wīf-feax ; feax-wund ; -feaxe.

**feax-clāþ.** *For* Cot. 93 *substitute :*—Feaxclāð (*printed* seax-) *fascia*, Wrt. Voc. ii. 39, 74.

**-feaxe.** *Add :* -feax. v. and-, gylden-, sīd-feax(e) ; feax.

**feax-eácas.** *Substitute :* feax-eáca, an; *m. A forelock :*—Loccas oððe feaxeácan *antiae frontis* (*calamistro crispantur*, Ald. 77, 16), Wrt. Voc. ii. 3, 66.

**feaxede.** *Add :* (1) *having hair :*—Ðeós wyrt is greáton bōgum and swīþe smælon leáfon swylce heó mā fexede gesewen sý *this plant is with thick boughs and very narrow leaves, it looks rather as if furnished with hair*, Lch. i. 250, 20. (2) *bushy, full of foliage* (?), cf. feax ; ¶ *of ācynnendlicum* i *fexedum* (wexendum? *The gloss to the passage in* An. Ox. 2420 *is:* Of ācennendlicum, wexendum) þyrnetum *de spinetis nascentibus*, Hpt. Gl. 463, 35. [*v. N. E. D. faxed.*] Cf. sceacgede.

**-feaxen.** v. fȳr-, ge-feaxen : feax-gerǣdian. *Dele, and see* feax.

**feax-ness**, e ; *f. Hair :*—Faexnis *capillatur(a)* (cf. fex, hǣr *capillatura*, An. Ox. 1214), Wrt. Voc. ii. 102, 60. Locgewind *vel* fexnes *capillatura*, 128, 38.

**feax-sceacga.** *Dele, and see* sceacga : feax-sceacged. *Dele :* feax-sceára. v. sceár.

**feax-wund**, e ; *f. A wound at a place covered by the hair of the head :*—Be feaxwunde. Gif in feaxe bið wund inces lang, geselle ānne scill. tō bōte. Gif beforan feaxe bið wund inces lang, twēgen scill. tō bōte, Ll. Th. i. 92, 17.

**febrende.** v. feferian : febrig. *Add :* v. feferig.

**feccan.** *Dele :* 'þ. feahte . . . feht,' *and add :*—Hē hēt hī ardlīce feccan, Hml. S. 8, 39. Men gesōhton þone stede heora hǣle feccende, 26, 238. v. fetian (*the earlier form of* feccan).

**fecgan.** *Dele.*

**fēdan.** *Add :* I. of living creatures. (1) *to give food to* (lit. or fig.) :— Gif hié mon ongemang ðǣre ðreátunga fēt mid sumere heringe, Past. 303, 1. Wiþ feóndseócum men, þonne deófol þone monnan fēde oððe hine innan gewealde mid ādle, Lch. ii. 136, 25. His mǣgas hine fēden, gif hē self mete næbbe. Gif hē mǣgas næbbe, fēde cyninges gerēfa hine, Ll. Th. i. 60, 10-12. Ofǣtum wǣre fēd *holusculis vesceretur*, Hpt. Gl. 494, 50. Seó sāul, gif heó ne bið mid Godes worde fēded, Bl. H. 57, 11, 10. (1 a) *of feeding infants, to suckle, nurse :*—Fæddæ hiǣ (*Romulus and Remus*) wylif in Rōmæcæstri, Txts. 127, 2. Þonne þā wīf heora bearn

cendon, þonne fēddon hié þā mædencild, and slōgon þā hysecild *editos mares mox enecant, feminas nutriunt*, Ors. 1, 10; S. 46, 10. Gemeng þ dūst wiþ wīses meoluc þe wæpned fēde, Lch. ii. 338, 8. Unryht gewuna is ārisen þ wīf forhicgaď heora bearn fēdan (*nutrire*), and hī ōþrum wīfum tō fēdanne (*ad nutriendum*) syllaď, Bd. 1, 27; Sch. 80, 9-14. (2) *to put food into* the mouth :—Biď fēd of ungleáunesse (*os stultorum*) *pascitur imperitia*, Kent. Gl. 519. (3) *to feed up, fatten* :—Foede ł fuglas mīne *altilia*, Mt. R. 22, 4. (4) *to support, maintain* :—Fēdeþ *fovet*, Wrt. Voc. ii. 38, 12. Se Metod eallra gesceafta fēt on eorþan ealle grōwende westmas and ealle forþbrengþ *alit ac profert quidquid vitam spirat in orbe*, Bt. 39, 13; F. 234, 18. ¶ where the subject is a personification :—Seó cyrice sceal fēdan þā þe æt hire eardiaþ, Bl. H. 41, 28. (5) *to bring up* the young, *nurture, educate, foster* :—Ēstelíce fram cnihthāde fēt *delicate a pueritia nutrit*, Kent. Gl. 1076. Hē (*Micipsa*) hiene (*Jugurtha*) on his geogoðe underfēng, and hiene fēdan hēt and tyhtan mid his twām sunum *Jugurtha, Micipsae adoptivus*, Ors. 5, 7; S. 228, 8. Gyf þū wille fēdan cyniges bearn, oððe æðeles monnes, geleód hine on pīn hūs, and fēd hine, Lch. iii. 178, 11. Þā seó mōdur onsende on Gallia rīce tō fēdanne Dægbrehte þām cyninge *quos mater misit in Galliam nutriendos regi Daegberecto*, Bd. 2, 20; Sch. 187, 13. Ðā wæs ic (*Bede*) seald tō fēdanne and tō lǣranne abbude Benedicte *datus sum educandus abbati Benedicto*, 5, 23; Sch. 694, 23: Ap. Th. 24, 25. (5 a) *to rear* fowls :—His mōdor gewunode tō fēdenne henna, Gr. D. 69, 25. II. *of things, to nourish, sustain*. (1) of material things :—Bere is swīðe earfoðe tō gearcigenne, and þeáhhwæðere fēt ðone mann þonne hē gearo biď, Hml. Th. i. 188, 5. Saga mē ðás iiii wæteru ðe ðás eorðan fēdaď, Sal. K. p. 192, 4.' Wel fēdende mettas *very nutritious food*, Lch. ii. 224, 10. (2) of immaterial things :—Seó oferfyll simle fēt unþeáwas, Bt. 31, 1; F. 110, 27. Ǣlc oferfyll and ǣlc ýdel fēt unhǣlo, Prov. K. 60. III. *to bring forth* :—Ðā ðe ne foedaď ł ne alaď *quae non parent*, Lk. L. 11, 44. IV. *intrans. To graze* :—Wæs worn berga michil foedende *erat grex porcorum magnus pascens*, Mk. L. R. 5, 11. Sunor bergana foedendra, Lk. L. 8, 32. v. cild-fēdende.

fēdels, fēdesl. *Add*: I. *a fatling* :—Foedils *altilia*, Txts. 39, 134. II. *feeding*. The word occurs as a technical term in the following :—Cyninges fēdesl .xx. scillinga forgelde, Ll. Th. i. 6, 8. [*O. L. Ger.* foedils *altile saginatum* : *O. H. Ger.* fuotisal *pastio*. Cf. *Icel.* fœdsla *food*.] v. next word.

fēdels-swin, es; *n. A fatted swine* (?) :—.i. fēdelsswīn, C. D. B. i. 367, 40.

fēdes. v. feþer: fēdesl. v. fēdels.

fefer. *Add* :—Þǣr (*in heaven*) ne byð fefor ne ādl, Wlfst. 139, 28. Eft cume ān lytel febbres (fefres, *v.l.*), Past. 229, 3. Mid þreóra daga fefre, Bt. 32, 2; F. 116, 31. Gedreht mid langsumum feofore, Hml. S. 2, 135. Þā hors þā þe sȳn on feofre (fefore, *v. l.*) oþþe on ǣnigre ādle, Lch. i. 328, 9. Ðǣm febere *febri*, Lk. L. 4, 39. Of feber *febre*, Mk. p. 2, 12. Fefer drīfende *febricitans*, Mk. R. 1, 30. Hāl from februm, Mk. L. 1, 31.

fefer-ādl. *Add* :—þ feferādol (feber-, L.) *febris*, Jn. R. 4, 52. þā folc būtū on seferādle mid ungemete swulton *gravissima pestilentia uterque exercitus angebatur*, Ors. 4, 10; S. 198, 35. Wearð hē untrum on feforādle, Bl. H. 217, 16: 227, 5: 209, 11. Miclum feberādlum *magnis febribus*, Lk. L. 4, 38 : Mt. L. 8, 15.

fefer-cynn, es; *n. A kind of fever* :—Fefercynnes gealdor, Lch. ii. 14, 10.

fefer-fuge. *Add* :—Feferfuge *febrifuga*, Wrt. Voc. ii. 38, 68 : *febrefuia*, An. Ox. 56, 373. Feferfugie (-fugia, -fuge, *v. ll.*) *febrefugia*, Ælfc. Gr. Z. 310, 9. Feferfugian emmicel, Lch. ii. 292, 17. Gebeáte feferfugean and pipor, 80, 6. Feferfugian, 350, 7. [*From Latin*.]

feferian; *p.* ode *To be feverish, suffer from fever* :—Febrende wæs *febricitans*, Mk. L. 1, 30. Gyf hē feforgende (fefrigende, *v. l.*) sȳ, Lch. ii. 220, 18. Syle drincan fefergindum, 122, 15. Tō þām fefergendan (-um, *v. l.*), 138, 5: 212, 13. Wið feforgende (feforgendne, fefrigende, *v. ll.*), 226, 26.

feferig, febrig (*q.v. in Dict.*); *adj. Feverish* :—Gif hē feforig sȳ, Lch. i. 334, 21. [*v. N. E. D.* fevery.] v. un-feferig.

fefer-seóc *sick of a fever*. For Cot. 88 substitute :—Feferseóce *febricitantem* (Mt. 8, 14), Wrt. Voc. ii. 72, 29. Feferseócne, 36, 70.

-fēg. v. ge-fēg.

fēgan. *Add* : I. *to join, connect* :—Ne fēgde ic eówre lima, ne ic eów līf ne forgeaf, Hml. S. 25, 164. Wē ceorfað treówun on holte ðæt wē hī ūp ārǣren on ðǣm botle . . . swā swā hī swīður ādrȳgde beoð on eorðan, swā hī mon mæg orsorglícor ūp fēgean, Past. 445, 3. [v. fǣgan.] II. *to compose* :—Hēr mæg findan foreþances gleáw hwā þās fitte fēgde, Hpt. 33, 72, 3. [v. *N. E. D.* fay; *vb.*] v. ā-fēgan.

fēgedness. v. ge-fēgedness.

fēging. *Add* : I. *a joining* :—Foeging *junctura*, Wrt. Voc. ii. 112, 16. II. *as a grammatical term, composition* :—Ealle ðā eahta dǣlas underfóð fēginge, būton *interjectio* āna, and gif se nama bið gefēged of twām ansundum dǣlum . . ., Ælfc. Gr. Z. 88, 3: 266, 11. [v. *N. E. D.* faying.] v. ge-, treów-fēging.

fēgness. v. ge-fēgness: feht ? :—.xx. lamba and .xx. fehta, C. D. ii. 64, 32.

fel. *Add* : (1) *human skin* :—Fel ufan eágan *praefolium*, Wrt. Voc. i. 43, 3. Fel sceal for felle *pellem pro pelle* (Job 2, 4), Hml. Th. ii. 452, 17. Eft ic beó mid mīnum felle befangen *rursum circumdabor pelle mea* (Job 19, 26), i. 532, 13 : ii. 270, 19. (2) *a beast's skin* or *hide* :—Gif hrȳðera hwelc sié þe hegas brece . . . nime se āgenfrīgea his fel and fiǽsc, Ll. Th. i. 128, 15. Nān scyldwyrhta ne lecge nān scēpes fell on scyld, 208, 10. Hē breác weðera felle for sadele *vervecum pellibus pro sella utebatur*, Gr. D. 34, 13. (3) *a purple garment* (= pæll. v. felle-reád. v. *Gall.* s. v. fello) :—Welige mid felle *divitem purpuratum*, Lk. p. 9, 2. v. bōc-, þrust-fell.

fela. *Add* : I. *as substantive* (v. also III). (1) alone. (a) singular :—Fela ofslagen weard on ǣgðere healfe *multis populis deletis*, Ors. 4, 7; S. 182, 34. Ðǣm fealo (feolo, R.) gesald wæs *cui multum datum est*, Lk. L. 12, 48. Feolo (feola, R.) gespreca *multum loqui*, Mt. L. 6, 7. (b) plural :—Se godspellere āwrāt þæt fela ārison mid Crīste (*multa corpora sanctorum surrexerunt*, Mt. 27. 52), Hml. Th. i. 226, 4. Dryhten sceáwað . . . hē fela findeð, feá béoð gecorene, Gū. 30. Spreccende wæs him feolo (feola, R.) ł monigo (*multa*), Mt. L. 13, 3. Fala, Wülck. Gl. 250, 10. (c) uncertain :—Hē cýdde fela be Crīstes godcundnysse . . . feáwa hē āwrāt be his menniscnysse, Hml. Th. i. 70, 18. (2) with gen. (a) gen. sing. :—Hrippes sōðlíce feolo (feolu, R.) *messis quidem multa*, Lk. L. 10, 2. Mē onsāh unrihtes feala *declinaverunt in me iniquitates*, Ps. Th. 54, 3. Is þæs fela tō secgenne, þæs þe hē ādreág, Gū. 509. Ne wundriaþ hī nō fela þæs þe hī nū wundriaþ, Bt. 39, 3; F. 216, 6. Þeáh hē āge feala fægeres, Bl. H. 21, 7. Bitres fela, Gen. 479. Fela gelīces, Th. 387. Hī gesáwon wyrmcynnes feala, B. 1425. ¶ where the noun in genitive is a noun of multitude the verb may be plural :—Fleóhcynnes feala flugan on gemǣru, Ps. Th. 104, 27. (b) gen. pl. (a) where *fela* is nom. to a verb in sing. :—Heora fela ðūsenda gefongen wæs *octo millia sunt capta Tuscorum*, Ors. 3, 4; S. 104, 11. Fela monna wāt þætte . . ., Met. 20, 83. Mā þonne fela manna gelýfan mæge *majora quam credi potest*, Bd. 3, 24; Sch. 306, 23. Feala, Bl. H. 41, 14. Fela weard tōdrǣfed Godes ðeówa, Chr. 975; P. 120, 14: Gen. 1638. þæt eówer fela geseah, Dan. 412. Wæs māðma fela gelǣded, B. 36 : Cri. 43 : Crä. 1. (β) where *fela* is nom. to a verb in pl. :—For þon gebode gewurdon fela martyra, Ors. 6, 30; S. 280, 19. Mē fela þīnra edwīta on gefeóllon *opprobria exprobantium tibi ceciderunt super me*, Ps. Th. 60, 9. Þē þanciað þūsenda fela, Hy. 7, 49. Bregowearda fela rōfe ārīsaþ, Gen. 2333. (γ) other cases than nom. :—Mid wīta fela, Cri. 1548. Feala, Ps. Th. 77, 43. Hié fela wucena sǣton, Chr. 894; P. 87, 22. Fela geára, Bd. 5, 15; Sch. 652, 15. Hē brǣd hine on feala bleóna, Bl. H. 175, 5. þā sǣde ic þ ic his þinga feola ne cūþe *respondi me ignorare quid faceret Alexander*, Nar. 18, 24. II. *adjective* (v. also III). [*a dat. pl. in* -um *occurs*. v. efen-fela.] (1) *singular or uncertain*. Cf. monig :—Unc sceal worn fela māðma gemǣnra, B. 1783. Gelýfdon fela ðūsend manna, Hml. Th. ii. 296, 22. Feala hīwes hrægel *polymita*, Wrt. Voc. i. 40, 14. Hē fela þing wiste ǣr þan þe hit gewurde, Hml. S. 31, 1009. Þū worn fela sprǣce, B. 530. Hē ofslōg fela þūsend monna, Ors. 6, 13; S. 268, 17. Hió inuwit feala ȳwdan, Ps. Th. 108, 2. Þū scealt fela gewinn habban, Hml. Th. i. 426, 18. (2) *plural* :—Fela wītegan bodedon, Hml. Th. i. 358, 6.· Wurdon fela cyrcan ārǣrede, 562, 24. Fela hundas, ii. 114, 17. Se Hǣlend . . . beheóld hū þæt folc heora ælmyssan wurpon intō ðām māðmhūse, and ðā fela rīcan brōhton miccle ðing (*multi divites jactabant multa*, Mk. 12, 41), Hml. Th. i. 582, 14. Oðre fela bisceopas, Hml. S. 3, 631. Fela ōþre, 28, 19. Hī āgutan blōd bearna feala (or I. 2 b. γ), Ps. Th. 105, 27. In feolo wiðirweardnisum *in tot adversis*, Rtl. 23, 1. Fela (feola, *v.l.*) geár, Bd. 5, 15; Sch. 652, 15. Fela ōðre gecorene hālgan, Hml. Th. ii. 112, 31 : Hml. S. 6, 304. Feala, Hex. 16, 1. III. *with qualifying adverbs*. (1) v. I. 1 a :—Drincan ðreó swā feala ge feówer swā feala swā his neád wǣre, Hml. A. 145, 29. Swā feolu (*quotquot*) hæfde aidulo, Mk. R. 3, 10. Hē salde swā feolo swā (*quantum*) hiǽ waldun, Jn. R. 6, 11. Huu feolo āht ðū tō geldanne *quantum debes?*, Lk. L. 16, 7. Huu fela (feolu, R.) ēghuelc geceópad wēre, 19, 15. (2) v. I. 1 b :—Suā feolo (*quotquot*) hiá hæfdon uncūð ādlo, Mk. L. 3, 10. (3) v. I. 2 a :—Nǣs nā for ðǣm þe þæs landes swā fela wǣre, Ors. 1, 1; S. 24, 25. Hē hearmes swā fela Adam gespræc, Gen. 579. Feala, 322. Nǣire man þǣre moldan tō þæs feale nimeþ, þ . . ., Bl. H. 127, 17. Ālȳfan landes tō fela, By. 90. Tō fela micles Deniga leóde, B. 694. (4) v. I. 2 b a :—Ðeáh ðām feohgītsere cume swā fela welena swā þāra soudcorna beoþ, Bt. 7, 4; F. 22, 26. Heó nyste þæt hearma swā fela fylgean sceolde, Gen. 708. Þāra micles tō feala wind wið gecynde, Met. 13, 16 : Hy. 4, 45. (5) v. I. 2 b β :—Swā fela manna wǣron on þām eórode, Hml. S. 28, 14. Swā feala geára synd nū āgāne, 23, 727. (6) v. I. 2 b y :—Swā feala (*gen. or nom.*?) earmra manna swā on þæs rīcan neáweste sweltaþ . . ., biþ hē ealra þāra manna deáþes sceldig, Bl. H. 53, 5. Ic mæg swā fela wundra gewyrcean, Gen. 279: An. 710. Hū fela hlāfa hæbbe gē?, Mk. 8, 5. Swīðe feala cynna, Hy. 9, 20. (7) v. II. 2 :—Wytað hū fela epactas beón, Angl. viii. 339, 35. Em swā

feala facum *totidem spatiis*, An. Ox. 3722. Ealswā feala mærþa ic geríme *tot ego glorias numerabo*, 4762. Hū fela dagas and hū fela ída seó sunne wunað on ǣlcum tācne, Angl. viii. 318, 1. Foregíslas swā fela swā hē habban wolde, Chr. 877; P. 74, 20. (8) v. II. 2 and I. 2 b a:—Wǣron swā fela gereord swā ðǣra wyrhtena wæs, Hml. Th. 318, 22, (9) v. II. 2 and I. 2 b β:—þā wǣron swā fela gereord swā ðǣr manna wǣron, Hml. Th. i. 22, 23. IV. adverb:—Sélre bið ǣghwǣm þæt hē his freónd wrece, þonne hē fela murne, B. 1385. Gif ií fulle ne beóð, fela gnorniað (*murmurabunt*), Ps. Th. 58, 15, Hí fêt habbað, ne magon feala gangan *they cannot walk much;* non ambulabunt, 13, 15. Fela, Rä. 32, 8. Heó wíde ne fêrcð, ne fela ríded, 59, 3. ee the compounds.

**féla;** B. 1032. v. feól.

**fela-ǣte;** adj. *Eating much:*—Felaǣte *mordax* (*luscorum more* *Cyclopum*), An. Ox. 23, 15. Cf. micel-ǣte.

**fela-feald.** *Add:*—Ðeós woruld is gemǣncged mid mænigfealdan nāne and mid felafealdan fācne, Wlfst. 82, 6. [v. *N. E. D.* felefold.]

**felage.** v. feó-laga : **fela-geong.** *Dele, and for citation substitute:*—'rōd guma sægde fela geongum *the wise old man said much to the young* ne (cf. sægde eaforan worn, 66), Fä. 53.

**fela-ídelsprǣce;** adj. *Talking very idly:*—Ðā felaídelsprǣcan -sprǣcean, *v. l.*) *multiloquio vacantes*, Past. 175, 25.

**fela-leóf.** *Add:* [cf. *Goth.* filu-gálaubs *precious.*]

**félan.** *Add:*—Sume lator fēlað þāra lǣcedōma, sume raþor, Lch. ii. 4, 25. Gif se maga þæs ne fēle, 192, 21. Nēdmægn ǣc stences ðínes mægn hiá foele *vimque odoris tui vel virtutem sentiant*, Rtl. 117, 27. . un-fēlende.

**fela-sinnig.** *l.* -synnig : **fela-specol, -specolness.** v. fela-sprecol, sprecolness.

**fela-sprǣc,** e; *f. Much speaking:*—In heora feolasprēce *in multiloquio* uo, Mt. R. 6, 7. [*O. H. Ger.* filu-sprāhha.]

**fela-sprǣce;** adj. *Speaking much, loquacious, using many words with* itent *to deceive:*—Felospraeci, felusprēci *trifulus, trufulus*, Txts. 102, 009. Huelc wíte wēne wē ðæt se felasprǣce (-sprǣca, *v. l.*) scyle habban e simle on ofersprǣce syngað *pensemus quae poena multiloquium maneat,* i quo etiam per noxia verba peccatur, Past. 281, 14. On ōðre wīsan ion sceal manian ðā bilwitan (*simplices*), on ōðre ðā felasprǣcan (*impuri;* f. ðā lytegan, 237, 6), 175, 21. [*O. H. Ger.* filu-sprāhhi *procax, ver-* osus, linguosus. Cf. *Icel.* fjöl-málugr *tattling;* fjöl-mæli *tattle, slander.*]

**fela-sprecol;** adj. *Talkative, loquacious:*—Móna se ehteóða . . . cild cenned . . . ofermód, felasprecol, Lch. iii. 192, 22.

**felasprecol-ness,** e; *f. Loquacity:*—Symle ēstum felaspecolnyss *loquacitas*) fyligð, Scint. 170, 18. Hwanne besmāt hine seó scyld þǣre ralasprecolnesse? oþþe hū sceþede hine seó synn þǣre swígunge?, Bl. H. 69, 5. Sē þe hatað felaspeculnysse, hē ācwencð yfelnysse, Scint. 79, 9.

**fela-wyrde;** adj. *Of many words, talkative:*—Ne beón gē tō fela-'yrde ne ealles tō hlagole, Wlfst. 40, 18. [Cf. *Goth.* filu-waurdei *multi-* quium : *Icel.* fjöl-orðr *tattling, talkative.*]

**felawyrd-ness,** e; *f. Talkativeness:*—Ac hū byð þ gif hit gelimpeð se man þ wyrignesse word ne gecwið tō his þām nehstan for hete and iþe, ac hit sceóteð forð þurh his tungan (for his felawyrdnesse and his ingan, *v. l.*) gýmeleásnesse *quid si homo non fortasse ex malitia, sed ex* nguae incuria, maledictionis verbum jaculatur in proximum?, Gr. D. 08, 4.

**fel-cyrf,** e; *f.? l.* fel-cyrf, es; *m., and add.* v. cyrf; II.

**feld.** *Add:* gen. felda (v. Licetfelda):—Feld *gotium*, feldas *gotia*, /rt. Voc. ii. 42, 4, 5. (1) *open country.* (a) *land free from wood,* lain (as opposed to mountainous):—Hí fērdon on wudu and on felda, hr. 1071; P. 207, 36. On þām felda (*campo*), sē wæs genemned ǣdfeld, Bd. 4, 17; Sch. 429, 14. Nǣnig oþer stān on eallum þām lda (-e, *v. l.*) gemēted beón mihte *neque ullus alter in tota illa campi* lanitie *lapis inueniri potest*, 5, 6; Sch. 577, 13. Ælc man sý his untnoðes wyrðe on wuda and on felda on his āgenan, Ll. Th. i. 420, 5. Nefrod hēt wyrcan ǣnne tor on ðām felda þe Sennar hātte, Bt. 35, ; F. 162, 19. Þǣm gelícost þe ic sitte on ðǣre dūne and geseó a smēðum felda (*in magno campi spatio*) fela fýra byrnan, Ors. 3, 11 ; 142, 14. Gif hié (*the Danes occupying wooded country*) ǣnigne feld ícan wolden, Chr. 894; P. 84, 26. Sum gemyndleás wíf fērde wōri-nde geond wudas and feldas, Hml. Th. ii. 188, 15. Ne gesāwon wē ðht elles būton þā wēstan feldas and wudu and dūna þe þǣm gārsecge ihil praeter desertos in oceano campos, siluasque ac montes, Nar. 20, 10. ) *field* as opposed to garden:—Mid þǣre lactucan þe on felda wixð *im lactucis agrestibus*, Ex. 12, 8. (c) *land free from buildings:*—Gif ǣ on hūse gefeohte . . . And þeáh hit sié on middum felda gefohten, l. Th. i. 106, 10. (2) *land that affords pasture* or *that may be culti-* ated:—Nētenu feldes *pecora campi*, Ps. Srt. 8, 8. Ic (*the ploughman*) i ðý þywende oxan tō felda, and jugie hí tō syl, Coll. M. 19, 15. Þæs untes cnoll is sticmǣlum mid wuda oferwexen, and eft sticmǣlum mid ̄ēnum felda oferbrǣded, Hml. Th. i. 508, 24 : Bl. H. 207, 28. Geond es muntes feld mid þý feó oferbrǣded, 199, 3. On middum ūrum intra beóð hyra (*the Egyptians'*) feldas mid wyrtum blówende, Lch. iii.

252, 21. Feltha *saltuum*, Wrt. Voc. ii. 119, 76. (3) *a place suitable* *for fighting, field* of battle :—Feld *scamma*, Wrt. Voc. ii. 119, 75. Feld dænnede, Chr. 937; P. 106, 20. Ðǣm folce ðe on clǣnum felda weorðlicne sige gefeohtað, Past. 227, 25. Se Godes stranga wiga Sanctus Paulus nolde beón gehæsd binnan þǣre byrig Damasco, ac sōhte þone feld þæs campes, Gr. D. 110, 16. (4) *used figuratively:*—Mon on þām feldum þāra hāligra gewryta þā wǣpnu mētan mæg mid þām mon þā uncysta ofercuman mæg, Ll. Th. ii. 44, 13. [The word often occurs, alone or in composition, in the charters. v. Midd. Flur. s. v.] v. pæþ-, scín-feld : felde; feld-land.

**feld-ǣlfen.** v. feld-elfen.

**feld-beó.** *Dele 'locust,' and add:*—Feldbeó, dora *adticus*, beó *apis*, Wrt. Voc. ii. 7, 66. Feldbeón hunig, Lch. ii. 308, 6 : 312, 4. Feld-beóna hunig, i. 348, 7 : 366, 14. Cf. dora.

**feld-biscopwyrt** *name of a plant*, Archiv. 87, 325.

**feld-denu,** e; *f. A valley in which there is pasturage* (?):—On feld-dene; andlang dene tō wuda, C. D. v. 86, 20. On feldene; andlang feldene on ðone hagan, 356, 9. v. feld, (2).

**felde?** :—Of þiccum āsodenes wínes þēfele t felde *lento careni defruto* (the same passage (Ald. 3, 35) is glossed in Wrt. Voc. ii. 138, 59 thus: *De lento fruto* of þiccum felde, *de denso campo*), An. Ox. 104.

**feld-elfen.** *Add:*—Feldælbinne oððe elfenne *amadriades*, Wrt. Voc. ii. 8, 14.

**feld-gangende.** *Add: going about the fields,* (a beast) *of the field:* —Ealdes swínes tord þæs þe feldgangende sié, Lch. ii. 62, 22. Hē hine gedîdde tō feldgongendum deórum (*agri bestiis*), Past. 38, 23.

**feld-hrýðer.** *Substitute:* **feld-hríþer,** es ; *n. A beast out at pasture :* —iiii feldhrýðera (*pascuales vituli*), Nap. 56, 7. v. feld-oxa.

**feld-land.** *Add:* opposed to wood-land :—Ðæs landes gemǣra ðe gebyriað intó ðǣre westmestan hîde feldlondes and wudulandes, C. D. iii. 262, 19. Ðone þriddan æcer feldlandes and healfne ðone wudu, 4, 10.

**feldlic.** *Add:* applied to plants, *field, wild* (v. feld, (1 b)):—Mid feldlicere lactucan *cum lactucis agrestibus*, Hml. Th. ii. 264, 3. Mid feldlicum lactucum, 278, 19.

**feld-minte.** *Add:*—Feldminte *mentasri*, Wrt. Voc. ii. 59, 46.

**feld-oxa,** an; *m. An ox out at pasture* (opposed to a fat ox):—His bigleofa wæs ǣlce dæg . . . twelf fǣtte oxan and twēntig feldoxan (*oxen out of the pastures;* boves pascuales, I Kings 4, 23), Hml. Th. ii. 576, 33. v. feld-hríþer.

**feld-seten[n],** e; *f. Country occupied as pasture-land:*—On felda t on feldsætennum *in campo Taneos*, Ps. Lamb. 77, 12. Cf. land-seten.

**feld-swamm.** For Cot. 87 *substitute:*—Swamm oððe feldswamm *fungus*, Wrt. Voc. ii. 36, 22.

**feld-swop.** *Substitute:* **feld-wōp,** es ; *m. A peewit* (?):—Felduðop, felduðop *bradigabo*, Txts. 44, 131. Feldwuðop, Wrt. Voc. ii. 11, 45. Feldwōp *bradigatio, ploratio campi*, 127, 16. [Cf. *O. L. Ger.* feld-hoppo *bradigabo*: widu-hoppo *upupa.*]

**feld-wyrt.** *Add:*—Feldwyrt *gentiana*, Wrt. Voc. ii. 42, 39. v. felt-wyrt.

**-fēle.** v. ge-fēle: **fele-ferð.** v. felo-ferþ.

**felg.** *Add:*—Felge, faelge *canti*, Txts. 54, 292. Felga, Wrt. Voc. ii. 13, 18 : 16, 1 : 128, 15. Felg, i. 284, 48. Felgan, 66, 5. v. sadol-felg.

**fellen.** *Add:*—Hē hæfde fellenne gyrdel (gyrdils fillenu *sonam pelliciam*, L.) enþe his lendenu, Mt. 3, 4. Hē lǣdde his hālgan bēc mid him in fellenum sæccum *pelliceis sacculis*, Gr. D. 34, 14. [*Goth.* filleins : *O. H. Ger.* fellín.]

**felle-reád** (1) *adj. Purple:*—Gegearwodon hine mið fellereáde (-reóde, R.) hrægle *induunt eum purpura*, Mk. L. 15, 17. Mið felle-reádum uoede *ueste purpurea*, Jn. L. 19, 2. Þ fellereád (-reóde, R.) uoede, 5. Tunuc fellereád *tunicam purpuream*, Mt. L. 27, 28. (2) *subst. A purple garment:*—Gehreáfadon hine ðæs fellereádes *exuerunt illum purpura*, Mk. L. R. 15, 20. Mið fellereáde *purpura*, Lk. L. 16, 19. Mið fellereáde, Mk. R. 15, 17 : Jn. R. 19, 2. v. fell, (4).

**fell-stycce,** es ; *n. A piece of skin :*—Hafa þǣre hýde fellsticceo on þínum sceón, Lch. i. 330, 5.

**felma.** v. ǣger-felma, *and cf.* filmen, fell : **fel-nys.** *Dele.*

**félnyss.** *Add:*—*Sensus,* þ is andgit oððe fēlnyss, Hml. S. 1, 183. Foelnese *sensum*, Rtl. 177, 3.

**felo-ferþ,** fele-, feolu-, -feorþ *a breast, stomach, maw* of an animal:—Feleferð *centumpellia* (=? centipellio *the second maw of* *ruminating animals*), Wrt. Voc. i. 22, 4 : centumpellis, 22, 64 : cen:umcilio, i. *pellis* vel centumpellis, 130, 44. Felofearth, felufrech, feoluferð *torax*, Txts. 102, 1027. Feolufor (-ferð ?), Wrt. Voc. i. 289, 17. Gescyld feoluferð mid lungenne (feleferð mið ðǣre lungene, *v. l.*) *tege toracem cum pulmone*, Lch. i. lxxii. 29. [*O. H. Ger.* uile-fart *omasus* (= *ventriculus qui continet alia viscera.* v. Angl. xxx. 254. Cf. (?) *Icel.* fel *the rough inside of an animal's maw :* fill *or* fela *a maw*, Ivar Aasen.]

**felofor.** *Substitute:* **felofor,** feal(e)-, fe(o)lu-, -fer *a bittern;* onocrotalus, porphyrio (v. Lev. 11, 18):—*Onocrotalum, avis quae* *sonitum facit in aqua*, rāredumlǣ *vel* felufor, Shrn. 29, 6 (a list of glosses on Lev. 11). Feolufer *onocrotallus*, Txts. 83, 1445. Felofor, feolufer

*porfyrio*, 88, 807. Fealfor, Wrt. Voc. ii. 68, 28. Fealefor *onocratulus*, 63, 44. Fealuor *porphyrio*, i. 280, 17. ¶ feolufor *torax*. v. feloferþ. [*O. H. Ger.* felefor, -fer *onocrotalus*.]

**felsan.** *l.* felsian, *and see* fælsian.

**felt.** *Add:*—Felt *centuclum*, Wrt. Voc. ii. 130, 43. Sadol *sella*, felt *mento* (*a saddle-cloth?* cf. sadol-felt *pella*, 291, 15; or cf. (??) pelltaria, pellis quae a *mento* bobis pendent, Corp. Gl. H. 91, 276), i. 83, 71.

**fel-tún.** *Add:*—Hē gecierde inn tō ðǣm scræfe and wolde him ðǣr gān tō feltúne *ad purgandum ventrem speluncam ingressus est*, Past. 197, 15, 24.

**feltún-grēp**, e; *f. The drain of a privy:*—Wyrse is þæt mon ðæs ofer riht brūce þonne hine mou on feltúngrēpe wiorpe; on þǣre grēpe hē wiorðed tō meoxe, Nap. 21.

**felt-wurma.** *Add:*—Feltwurma *origanum*, Wrt. Voc. ii. 65, 45.

**felt-wyrt.** *Add:*—Feltwyrt (feldwyrt, *v. l.*) *anadonia*, Ælfc. Gr. Z. 310, 10 (= Wrt. Voc. i. 79, 5). Feldwyrd *anadonia*, Wrt. Voc. i. 30, 48. Feltwyrt *anadona*, An. Ox. 56, 376. Feldwyrt *anadonia*, Lch. iii. 300, col. 1.

**fen.** *Add:* (1) *mud, mire, dirt:*—Fennes *coeni*, Wrt. Voc. ii. 21, 7. Fenne *luto*, An. Ox. 2, 435 : Past. 277, 10. Hī āstōdon . . . þe. on ðām fænne (fenne, *v. l.*) ǣr lāgon, Hml. S. 10, 22. Hē worhte fenn (*lutum*) of his spātle, and smyrede mid þām fenne ofer his eágan, Jn. 9, 6. Fenn strǣta *lutum platearum*, Ps. Spl. 17, 44. Sió hond . . . ðe wille ðæt fenn of óðerre ádierran *manus quae diluere sordes curat*, Past. 75, 23. Wā ðǣm ðe gaderað an hine selfne ðæt hefige fenn (*densum lutum*) . . . ðæt ðicke fenn, 329, 18, 19. (2) *fen:*—Cenum, i. *luti vorago vel lutum sub aquis fetidum*, i. wāse *vel* fæn, Wrt. Voc. ii. 130, 75. Wæs ðæt lond . . . ádrígad and fen (fien, *v. l.*) and cannon and hreádwæteru *palus erat sicca et ceno habundans*, Angl. iv. 157, 5. Mid sǣ, mid fænne, Bt. 18, 1; F. 62, 23, 26. Mid wudum and mid muntum and mid fænnum, 18, 2; F. 62, 35. Fuglas þe on fennum ne sién, Lch. ii. 254, 20. Swā se hrefen þurh þā fennas upp áflígeð, swā þū him æfter rōw, Guth. 50, 10.

**fen-ampre**, -ompre, an; *f. Water-dock:*—Nim fenompran, Lch. ii. 100, 23.

**fenester**, es; *n. A window:*—Þ scamléase wíf gewāt fram þām ēhþyrle (fenestre, *v. l.*) his cýtan (*a fenestra cellulae illius*), Gr. D. 212, 13. Þ wæter becōm upp tō þām fenestrum (*ad fenestras*), 220, 15, 22. [*v. N. E. D.* fenester : *O. H. Ger.* fenster; *n. fenestra.*]

**fen-fixas.** *Substitute:* fen-fisc, es; *m. A fish living in the water of a fen:*—Ne þicgen hié fenfixas, ne sǣfixas þā þe habbað heard flǣsc, Lch. ii. 254, 22.

**feng.** *Add:* (1) *a taking:*—Faengae, fenge *pro captu*, Txts. 82, 727. (1 a) *a taking hold by way of greeting, embrace:*—Ou fænge (fenge, 102, 61) ge on clyppe, Angl. xi. 99, 76. (1 b) *a taking* of fish, game, &c. :—Feng *fisca captura piscium*, Lk. p. 4, 17. In feng ðǣra fiscana *in captura piscium*, Jn. p. 8, 9. (1 c) *capture, seizure* of a person :—Sē þe ne sealde ūs on gehæfte ī tō fǣncge (*in captionem*) tōðum heora, Ps. L. 123, 6. (2) of concrete things. (a) *that which grasps, embraces, catches:*—Arpax geara feng *vel lupus, arpago* hooc, Wrt. Voc. i. 16, 42. Geara feng *peeris* (cf. gearufang *proceris*, 63, 75), 57, 14. Belocenum fenge *contenta sinu, concluso*, ii. 135, 4. (b) *that which is formed as a clasp:*—Foreweard feng ðǣre lippena tōgædere *rostrum*, Wrt. Voc. i. 43, 26. (c) *what is taken* captive :—Feng gilǣdde gefeng *captivam duxit captivitatem*, Rtl. 83, 3. [*v. N. E. D.* feng. *O. Frs.* feng: *Icel.* fengr.] *v.* æt-, ge-, mis-, þeóf-, ymb-feng; fang; on-feng.

**-fenga**, -fenge. *v.* and-fenga, and-, on-fenge: **-fengend.** *v.* and-fengend.

**fen-gemirce** (?), es; *n. The boundary of marsh-land:*—Þis sint þā fangemerca . . . tō binguuellan æt clibe ūt on ðone brōc midne, . suǣ . . . ūt on mōr . . . þanon andlangæs brōces middesweardes, C. D. B. i. 295, 27.

**feng-tōþ** (?) *a molar tooth:*—Dens quem Angli vocant fengtōð (cf. Ll. Th. i. 94, 11, on which this passage is founded where the word *wongtoþ* is used), Schmid. 426, 18.

**fen-hōp.** *Substitute:* fen-hop, es; *n. Land in the midst of fens* (*v. N. E. D.* hope):—Fleón on fenhopu, B. 764.

**fēnix.** *Add:*—Án fugel fæger Fēnix gehāten, E. S. viii. 475, 21 (*and see* pp. 474-477).

**fen-land.** *Add:*—On þām fenlande synd feáwa weorcstāna, Hml. S. 20, 77. [Þet Englisce folc of eall þā feonlandes cōmen tō heom, Chr. 1070; P. 205, 8.]

**fen-lic.** *Add: miry, muddy, dirty:*—Ðā swýn ðā deófiu gecuron for ðǣre fūlnysse fenlices adelan, Hml. Th. ii. 380, 8. Se Hǣlend hí (*the disciples*) áðwōh fram fenlicere fūlnysse (*from muddy impurity*), 242, 30.

**fen-minte.** *Add:*—Fenminte *mentrati*, Wrt. Voc. ii. 59, 37.

**fennig.** *Add:*—On wege fennigum lǣdan oððe gān teónan hefige getácnad, Lch. iii. 212, 7. Cenosas þā fennigan meras, i. *paludes paludosas vel adelihtan*, fūlan *lutosas, fetidas, immundas*, Wrt. Voc. ii. 130, 67. Fennegan *stagnosa*, An. Ox. 36, 13.

**fon-þæc**, es; *n. Thatch consisting of reeds taken from a fen:*—Mið ðǣm fenðacum *palustria arundine* (v. Bd. 1, 19 : Consumptis domibus quae palustri harundine tegebantur), Txts. 181, 70.

**fen-ȳce.** *Substitute:* fen-ȳce, -úce, an; *f. A snail* (?), *tortoise* (?):—Fænúcæ *testudo* (cf. *limax* snægl, *testudo* gehúsed snægl, Wrt. Voc. i. 24, 5; *lumbricus* rēnwyrm, *chelio*, *testudo* sǣsnæl, 32), Txts. 100, 997. Mē is snægl swiftra, snelra regnwyrm, and fenýce fóre hreðre *lumbricus et limax et tarda testudo palustris me vincunt certamine currus* (Ald. 272, 2), Rä. 41, 70.

**feógan.** *Add:*—Hē ðőerne fiáð ī hateþ *unum odio habebit*, Mt. R. 6, 24. Ne mæg midengeord gifióge iówih, mec fiáð (*odit*), Jn. R. 7, 7. Gefeð ða (oðða?) fiáð (gefiið, L.), 15, 19. Sē ðe mec fiáð and fæder mīnne fiáð, 23 : Ps. Srt. 10, 6. Ðā ðe ðē fígað *qui te oderunt*, 20, 9 : 33, 22, Ic fióde *odivi*, 25, 5. Ðū fēdest *odisti*, 5, 7. Fiéde *odivit*, 35, 5. Feódon hine þā hæþnan, Shrn. 125, 9. Fiáð yfel *odite malum*, Ps. Srt. 96, 10. Dōeþ wæl þǣm þe eówic hateþ ī fiégæ, Mt. R. 5, 44. Figende hine *odientes eum*, Ps. Srt. 88, 24. Þā fígendan mē, 17, 41. Fígendra *odientium*, 105, 10. Of ðǣm fígendum mec, 68, 15. *v.* ge-feógan.

**feógaþ** *hatred:*—Fiégaþ hæbbende *odio habebunt*, Mt. R. 24, 10. [Cf. *Goth.* fi(j)aþwa.]

**feógaþ**; *prs. pl.* (*we*) *rejoice.* v. feón: feó-gýtsung. v. feoh-gītsung.

**feoh.** *Add:* I. *cattle*, *tame beasts* as opposed to wild :—Fugel oððe fisc on sǣ, oððe on eorðan neát, feldgangende feoh būtan snyttro, oððe wildra deóra þæt grimmeste, Seel. 81. Inc is hālig feoh and wilde deór on geweald geseald, Gen. 201 : 1517. Feoh and fuglas, 1299. Feld mid þý feó oferbrǣded, Bl. H. 199, 3. II. *property, wealth, money.* (1) in a general sense :—Is betere þæt feoh þætte nǣfre losian ne mæg, þonne þ þe mæg and sceal, Bt. 11, 2; F. 34, 18: 13; F. 38, 18, 20. Hweþer micel feoh oððe weorþscipe oððe eall þes andwearda wela mæge ǣnigne mon dōn swā gesǣline, 26, 1; F. 90, 12: Wand. 108. Ne sceal hē beón tō georn deádra manna feós, Bl. H. 43, 13 : Ors. 1, 1 ; S. 20, 27-21, 4. For feós lufon, Bl. H. 63, 7, 8. Godes feós ðeófð *sacrilegium*, Wrt. Voc. i. 20, 31. Sel mē ðǣl fǣes (feás, R.) and dǣlde ðǣm þ feh *da mihi portionem substantiae et diuisit substantiam*, Lk. L. 15, 12, 13. Gif ðū þisses mannes feá (cf. gōde, 3, *and:* Hē his hrægle onfēng, 280, 21) ne onfēnge, Bd. 3, 19; Sch. 281, 8. Gif hié feoh (fioh, *v. l.*) habbað and his him oftióð *si quas haberent pecunias absconderent*, Past. 377, 2. For ðý hī wilniaþ anwealdes þe hié woldon ormǣte feoh gegaderian *potentiam pecuniae causa petunt*, Bt. 24, 2; F. 82, 17. Heó forsalde all feh (*substantiam*) hire, Lk. R. L. 8, 43. (1 a) of an article of property :—Gif hē (*the slain slave*) ánne ðæg gelifað ofer þæt, hē (*the owner*) bið unscildig, for þām hit ys his feoh (*pecunia*), Ex. 21, 21 : Ll. Th. i. 48, 15. Ǣlcere synne ǣrre ys gýtsung and lufu feóna (*pecuniarum*), Scint. 112, 2. (1 b) of valuable property, *riches, treasure*, an article or material of value:—Wela, hord, feoh *gazofilacium* (cf. in Temples feh *in corbanan*, Mt. R. 27, 6), Wrt. Voc. ii. 74, 24. Þ is þ eallra deórweorþeste feoh *pretiosissimum divitiarum genus est*, Bt. 20; F. 72, 26. Mið golde and mið gimmum ǣc mið suulfre ofergylded, fáconléas feh, Jn. p. 188, 5. Deórwyrþe feoh *opes*, Bt. 20; F. 72, 23. Geblōdon him tō hūde hordwearda gestreón, feá and freós, Dan. 66. ¶ licgende feoh *gold and silver, treasure, money* :—þæt hié bewisten eal þæt licgende feoh under ánum hrófe þæt hié begeáton oþþe on gafole oþþe on hergiunga, Ors. 2, 4 ; S. 72, 4. Þǣr hé geáscade þæt Geoweorþan goldhord wæs, and þā burgleóde him ágeáfon eall þ licgende feoh þ þær binnan wæs, 5, 7 ; S. 230, 6. Hié sealdon Demostanase licgende feoh *Demosthenes auro corruptus*, 3, 9; S. 124, 1. (2) property dealt with in business transactions :—Gehýred feoh *locatio*, Wrt. Voc. i. 20, 60. Behýred feoh, ii. 54, 3 : *conductio*, 135, 70. Gelēned feoh *vel* on borh geseald *res credita*, i. 20, 70. Ālēned feoh *pignus*, gylden wed *vel* feoh *arra*, forweddad feoh *fiducia*, 21, 5-8. (3) *price paid.* v. sellan ; IV :—Feh blōdes hit is *praetium sanguinis est*, Mt. L. 27, 6. Mid hū micelan feó woldest þū þā habban geboht þ . . . , Bt. 20; F. 72, 19, 21. Sume hí gebycgaþ hlísan mid heora ágnum deáþe, for þǣm hí wēnaþ þ hí næbben nán óþer fioh ðæs hlísan wyrþe būton hiora ágnum feore *nonnulli venerandum nomen gloriosae pretio mortis emerunt*, 39, 11 ; F. 228, 29. (4) property given as wages, bribe (v. feoh-fang) or gift :—Ðȳ lǣs hié for ðǣm gedále ðæs feós wilnigen ðisses lǣnan lifes *ne ex impenso munere transitoriam laudem quaerant*, Past. 323, 12. Se yfela dēma onfēhð medmycclum feó and onwendeþ þone rihtan dōm for þæs feós lufon, Bl. H. 61, 31: 43, 10. Hié feoh sealdon þǣm weardum *they bribed the keepers*, 177, 28. Þ feoh þe mon ðām ferdmonnum sellan sceolde, Bt. 27, 4; F. 100, 14. (5) (*coined*) metal, coin. v. sleán ; II a :—Feoh *pecunia vel nummus*, Wrt. Voc. i. 83, 11. Fíftēne scillingas clǣnes feós, Cht. Th. 168, 16. Mid uncre claene feó, ðæt wæs mid clǣne golde, Txts. 175, 5. Hwanon þū þus eald feoh gemēttest, and þus ealde penegas hider brōhtest, Hml. S. 23, 587. Swíðe eald feoh þe man on fyrndagum slōh, 614. Hwæt begytst þū of þínum cræfte ? Scrūd and feoh (*pecuniam*), Coll. M. 23, 5. Feóna *sestertiorum*, Germ. 395, 76. v. ælmes-, fæderen-, forfang-, lǣce-, land-, meld-, Rōm-, scrūd-, þífe-, wudu-feoh.

**feohan.** *Dele, and see* feón: **feoh-behát.** v. feoh-gehát.

**feoh-bígenga**, an; m. A herdsman:—For þon þe ic wǽre his ceápes heorde and wǽre his [f]eohbígenga (gregarius), Nar. 18, 27.

**feoh-fang.** Substitute: (1) taking money as a bribe. v. feoh; II. 4:—Sé þe undóm gedéme for feohfange (-fancge, v. l.), beó hé wið þone cyningc .cxx. sciłł. scyldig, Ll. Th. i. 384. 10. (2) the fine inflicted for bribery, the right to receive such fines:—Huic libertati concedo additamentum, in qua nomina consuetudinum Anglice praecepi ponere ... fyhfænge, Cht. Th. 411, 31.

**feoh-gafol.** Add:—Ne higion hí on feohgafole usuris nequaquam incumbant, Nap. 21.

**feoh-gehát**, es; n. A promise of money:—Cantware him feoh gehéton (behéton, v. l.) ... and under þám feohgeháte (-beháte, v. l.) se here hiene úp bestæl, Chr. 865; P. 68, 10.

**feoh-georn.** Add:—Leófan men, beorgað eów wið deófles lára ... ne beón gē tó feohgeorne, Wlfst. 40, 17 note. Bisceopum gebyreð þ hí ne beón tó feohgeorne æt hádunge, ne æt hálgunge, ne æt synbóte, ne on ǽnige wísan on unriht ne strýnan, Ll. Th. ii. 316, 31.

**feohgeorn-ness**, -gyrness, e; f. Covetousness:—Ne teó ic N. ne for hete ne for unrihtre feohgyrnesse, Ll. Th. i. 180, 11.

**feoh-geréfa**, an; m. A steward, bailiff:—Fehgroefa (fehugeroefa, L.) dispensator, Lk. R. 12, 42.

**feoh-gestreón.** Add:—Feohgestreón enteca (pecunia, lxiii. n. 17), Lch. i. lix, 1. Hé forlét þá scríne his feohgestreónes scrinium deseruit, Gr. D. 52, 7. Þú wéndest þæt þínra feohgestreóna ende ne gewurde, Wlfst. 260, 22. Feohgestreón gazas, Wrt. Voc. ii. 42, 37.

**feoh-gítsere.** Add: An avaricious, a covetous person:—Gehiére gē feohgiétseras (-gídseras, v. l.) hwæt he eów gecweden is. ... 'Ne wyrð se gítsere nǽfre full feós' cum augendis pecuniis inhiat, audiant quod scriptum est: 'Auarus non impletur pecunia,' Past. 331, 6.

**feoh-gítsung**, e; f. Avarice, covetousness, miserliness:—Monig mon déð micel fæsten and hæfð ðone hlísan ðæt hé hit dó for forhæfdnesse, and déð hit ðeáh for hneáwnesse and for feohgítsunge (-gídsunge) saepe sub parsimoniae nomine se tenacia palliat, Past. 149, 6. For feohgýtsunge (feó-, feágítsunge, v. ll.) forleósan amore pecuniae perdere, Bd. 2, 12; Sch. 160, 12.

**feoh-gód**, es; n. Property consisting of cattle, cattle considered as property:—Mid .ix. sciłł. gebéte, and þ sié on cwicǽhtum, feógódum, and mon nǽnigne mon on þ ne selle (i. e. the fine was to be paid in livestock, but cattle only, not human beings (slaves)), Ll. Th. i. 72, 13. Cf. ǽht; I d, ǽhte-mann.

**feoh-gyrnes.** v. feohgeorn-ness: **feoh-gýtsung.** v. feoh-gítsung:

**feoh-hof, -hord.** Dele.

**feoh-land**, es; n. Pasture-land:—Hé mé geset on swýðe good feohland in loco pascuae me collocavit, Ps. Th. 22, 1.

**feoh-lufu**, an; f. Love of money:—For feohgýtsunge (feó-, v. l.) and [feoh] lufan amore pecuniae, Bd. 2, 12; Sch. 160, 13.

**feoh-spéd**, e; f. Money, property; pl. riches, wealth:—Þá gebróðra áhton myccle feohspéda for worulde multas pecunias in hoc mundo possederant, Gr. D. 273, 2.

**feoht.** Add:—Hé gehýrde þæs feohtes hreám, Hml. S. 25, 422. Eall úre folc mid fleáme ætwand, búton wé feówertig þe on ðám feohte stódon, 11, 74. Cynig farende tó gesettanne feht rex iturus committere bellum, Lk. L. 14, 31. v. gescot-feoht.

**-feoht (?)** joy. v. ge-feohtsumness.

**feohtan.** Add:—Þú simle fihtest wið manna cyn, Bl. H. 241, 4. Hió self fieht (fiht, v. l.) wið hié selfe, Past. 277, 25. Hér fegtaþ Títus end Giáþeasu, Txts. 127, 3. Feaht (feht, fæht, v. ll.) him on seó hæþene ðeód Myrcna inpugnatus ab pagana gente Merciorum, Bd. 3, 14; Sch. 252, 16. Cwóman hié tó þon þ hié on ðá úre wíc feohtan (woldon?) (ad expugnanda castra), Nar. 21, 21. Mon alne deg fehtende (bellans), Ps. Srt. 55, 2.

**feohte.** Add:—Þá wæs feohte (fohte, MS.) néh, tír æt getohte, By. 103. Æt feohtan in battle, Gen. 2116. Þæt ðú tó fyrenlice feohtan sóhtest, ... óðres monnes wígrædenne, Vald. 1, 20, 18. Þú gúðe findest, frécne feohtan, An. 1352.

**feohtend**, es; m. A man of war, warrior, fighter:—Feohtend bellicosus, gladiator, An. Ox. 3805. Ealle feohtendras cuncti bellatores, Jos. 6, 3. v. wiþ-, wiþer-feohtend.

**feoht-gegírela**, an; m. An article of warlike apparel:—Feohtgegyrelan falarica, Wrt. Voc. ii. 33, 46.

**feól.** Add: fiil, fél, e; feóle, an:—Fiil lima, An. Ox. 53, 34: Wrt. Voc. ii. 113, 7. Feól, 78, 28: 49, 75: i. 287, 2: An. Ox. 1769. Feole, Wrt. Voc. i. 86, 17. Býð fremedre feóle þwyrnysse erit aliene lima prauitatis, Scint. 150, 5. Sum heora mid feólan feólode ábútan, Hml. S. 32, 203. Þæt him féla láf (weapons) frécne ne meahton scúrheard sceddan, B. 1032. [O. L. Ger. fíla.]

**feó-laga**, an; m. A fellow, colleague, partner:—Án marc goldes míne félage ... on his félowes witnesse, Cht. Th. 573, 15, 21. Þá cyningas (Edmund and Cnut) wurdon feólagan and wedbróðra (heora freóndscipe gefæstnodan, v. l.) ... and féng þá Eádmund cyng tó Westsexan and Cnut tó þám norðdǽle, Chr. 1016; P. 152, 26. [Icel. fé-lagi a fellow, partner.]

**feólag-scipe**, es; m. Fellowship, partnership:—Ic wille þat mín and Ulfketels félageschipe stonde ... and Ulfketel hauið leyd þerwith four marc, Cht. Th. 573, 25. Gif Eádwyne mín ém wille helden se félageshipe mid mé and mín ém Uulfríc ymbe þat lond at Meþeltúne, 582, 24. [Icel. félag-skapr.]

**feolan.** l. feólan, take here passages under felgan, and add: p. fealh, feal(l), pl. fulgon, fúlon To make one's way, press to or from a place, get (lit. or fig.):—Nú mé fealh on móde it has come into my mind, Gr. D. 17, 32. Hé hét rǽdan oð ðæt hé fulge on slǽpe he bade them read till he could get to sleep, Hml. A. 98, 211. Swá swýðe swá hí ǽr þám folce þæs útfæreldes wyrndon, swá micle hý wǽron geornran þæt hí him fram fulgen (that they should hasten their departure; cf. urgebant Aegyptii populum de terra exire velociter, Ex. 12, 33), Ors. 1, 7; S. 38, 20. Þæt fýr fiólan ne mæg eft æt his éðle (cf. ne mæg cuman tó his earde, Bt. 33, 4; F. 130, 32), Met. 20, 154. v. oþ-, wiþ-feólan.

**feól-heard.** For 'hard like a file' substitute: hardened by the file. v. passages under feól, and cf. fýr-heard.

**feólian**; p. ode To file:—Sum heora mid feólan feólode ábútan, Hml. S. 32, 203. [O. H. Ger. fílón limare: O. L. Ger. ge-fíled politus.]

**feó-lif.** Dele.

**feologan** to become many (? v. fela) or to become fallow (? v. fealu):—Swá benne ne burnon ne burston, ne fundian ne feologan, Lch. ii. 352, 1.

**feolufer.** v. felofor: **feolu-ferþ.** v. felo-ferþ: **feolu-fór.** l. -for, and see felofor.

**feón**; p. feah, pl. fægon; pp. fegen, fægen To rejoice:—Swá mycle má wē feógað on ðám tóweardan lífe, An. Ox. 1118 note. Þý lǽs on þ fægon þ ic swá lytle hwíle lifgean móste, Nar. 32, 20. v. fægen, feowung, gefeón.

**feón** to gain. v. be-, ge-feón.

**feónd.** Add: (1) an enemy, foe:—Fram stemne fýndes a voce inimici, Ps. L. 54, 4. 'For ðínum feóndum ic áswand on mínum móde, and ic hié hatode, for ðǽm hié wǽron eác míne find (fiénd, v. l.).' Swá mon sceal Godes fiénd hatigean, Past. 353, 5–8. Feónda emulorum, i. inimicorum, An. Ox. 22, 42. Feóndum emulis, 5367. (1 a) of things, what is prejudicial:—Bewreóh hine wearme, for þon þe cile biþ þǽre ádle feónd, Lch. ii. 234, 1. (2) a malevolent person (or animal):—Hé (Nero) wæs witena gehwelcum láð. ... Se feónd swá þeáh his diórlingas duguðum stépte, Met. 15, 7. Se feónd (the raven; cf. hrefen ... wæliel, El. 53) gespearn fleótende hréaw, Gen. 1447. Nelle ic þyssum fýnd leng árian, Bl. H. 179, 16. (3) a hostile spirit, fiend, devil:—Wē witan þ þyses menniscan cynnes fýnd áblende eówre heortan, Bl. H. 151, 33. On ðá ealdon unryhtwísnesse ðæs lytegan fióndes (feóndes, v. l.), Past. 233, 18. Wið ðǽm lytegan fiénd, 433, 17. Ðeów ðǽm Godes feónde (fiónde, v. l.), 361, 1. Be onsægdnysse feóndum (cf. gif man deófilum onsægð, 156, 15) de sacrificio daemonibus, Ll. Th. ii. 130, 20. (3 a) a devil as a cause of illness. Cf. deófol-seócness:—Fiénda ádl, Lch. ii. 174, 26.

**feónd-gild**, -gyld. Add: (1) idolatry, an idolatrous practice:—Arrianus se gedwolbiscop næfde hús þ hé mihte his feóndgyldes symbelnesse (solemnia sua) inne gedón, Gr. D. 234, 11. Mið fióndgeldum tormentis, Mt. L. 4, 24. (2) an idol:—Hé tóscynde þæt feóndgyld (deófol-, v. l.) contriuit idolum, Gr. D. 121, 24. Sum ǽren feóndgyld, 123, 24. Þ flǽsc þe hí heora feóndgyldum onsægd hæfdon immolata, 232, 15. Hé him swíþe ondréd þá feóndgyld þe in þám temple wǽron, 189, 2.

**feónd-lic.** Add: (1) hostile:—Feóndlic emulus, Wrt. Voc. ii. 32, 12. Genumen fram ðám mannum ðæs feóndlican weredes (hostilis exercitus), Bd. 4, 22; Sch. 455, 18. Seó wan þurh geleásan wið þá feóndlican ealdras, Hml. S. 7, 10. (2) diabolic, of the devil:—Feóndlices nearaþances spiritalis nequitiae, An. Ox. 377. Þiune feóndlican drýcræft, Hml. S. 7, 183. Feóndlicra spiritalium, An. Ox. 762: 856. Feóndlicum æfgælþum superstitiosa cultura, 3933. Ðá fióndlico wóghfulniso hostiles nequitias, Rtl. 122, 16. (3) devilish, outrageous:—Feón[d]licere furibundae (libidinis ferocitas), An. Ox. 4312. [v. N. E. D. fiendly: O. H. Ger. fiant-líh emulus: Icel. fjánd-ligr.]

**feóndlíce.** Add: [Of þan fehte þe was feondliche stor, Laym. 85.]

**feónd-mann**, es; m. An enemy:—Ðe fyóndmonn (or? fyónd monn) ðis dyde inimicus homo hoc fecit, Mt. L. 13, 28. [Icel. fjánd-maðr a foeman.]

**feónd-rǽden.** Add:—Swutele synd ðæs flǽsces weorc ... feóndrǽden and geflit (inimicitiae, contentiones, Gal. 5, 20), Hml. S. 17, 25.

**feónd-rǽs.** Substitute: A hostile attack, an onslaught, assault:—Ic fracoðlíce feóndrǽs gefremede ... and reáfode beám on bearwe I (Eve) wickedly made onslaught and despoiled the tree in the garden, Gen. 900. [Frolle him to fusden mid his feondrǽse (reasde mid his feondreases, 2nd MS.), Laym. 23960.]

**feónd-sceaþa.** Add: ['Aris feondscaðe' ... þe eotend up asturte, Laym. 26039.]

**feónd-scipe.** Add:—þæs lǽþþu and feóndscipe forðweox tó þon swíðe cujus ad hoc usque odium prorupit, Gr. D. 158, 27. Þ wē wǽron

ealle swā on ānum freóndscype swā on ānum feóndscype *that we should all be united alike in friendship and in enmity*, Ll. Th. i. 234, 22. Of þǣm feóndscipe þe ūs ǣr betweónum wæs þ hē seoðþan wæs mē freónd and eallum Grēca herige *factus amicus ex hoste Macedonibus*, Nar. 19, 19. Brutus gecwæð ānwíg wið þone cyning ymb heora feóndscipe, Ors. 2, 3; S. 68, 16. Tōwurpende ðā ǣrran feóndscipas (*inimicitias*), Hml. Th. i. 106, 18. [Ȝif on uolke feondscipe arerð betweone twoin monnen, Laym. 22966. *O. Sax.* fiund-skepi : *Icel.* fjánd-skapr : *O. H. Ger.* fiant-scaf ; *f.*]

**feónd-seóc.** *Add :—*Wiþ feóndseócum men, þonne deófol þone monnan fēde oððe hine innan gewealde mid ādle, Lch. ii. 136, 24, 28. Cf. deófol-seóc.

**feónd-seócnes.** *Dele.*

**feóndulf?** *Substitute :* **feónd-ulf** (ulf < wulf ; cf. ulf *in proper names*, e. g. Swíð-ulf, Beorht-ulf, Eád-ulf, Beorn-ulf, Ecg-ulf, Chr. 897 ; P. 90, 4–9, *and see* Kl. Nom. Stam. p. 17), es ; *m. A felon, villain :—* Feóndulf *furcifer, furca dignus*, Germ. 396, 317. Cf. wearg.

**feor;** *adv. Add :* I. *at a great distance.* (1) of space, (a) absolute :—Þū feorr gehogodest sæcce sēcean, B. 1988. Hē wæs him feor (suíðe fearr, L., swíðe fear, R.) *ipse peregre fuit*, Lk. 20, 9. (b) where point from which distance is measured is given, (a) in dative :—Þā foreweardas wǣron feor ðǣm fæstenne gesette, Ors. 4, 10 ; S. 200, 12. Swā se mōna bið þǣre sunnan fyrr, Mart. H. 44, 2. þā se mōna wæs þǣre sunnan firrest, Ors. 6, 2 ; S. 256, 18. (ß) by adverb or with prep. :—Feor þonan, Ph. 415 : B. 1805. Feor heonon, Gen. 2279 : 2513 : Seef. 37. Nǣht feor from þæs mæssepreóstes sīdan, Bl. H. 43, 26. Hit is swíþe feor (swā fyrr, *v. l.*) of uncrum wege, Bt. 40, 5 ; F. 240, 18. (2) of time :—Þæt wæs oft bodod feor ǣr beforan, El. 1142. (3) figuratively of alienation, avoidance, &c. :—Ðeáh seó godcunde sibb him feorr (fior, *v. l.*) sié, Past. 363, 19. Ys heora heorte feor fram mē, Bl. H. 69, 25. Þē firina gehwylc feor ābūgeð, Cri. 56. (4) of remoteness of relationship :—Þā þe beóð feor (feorr, *v. l.*) heora cneórisse fram him ācende *quae sunt ab illis longa progenie generata*, Bd. 1, 27 ; Sch. 68, 4. (5) in deprecatory phrases :—Feor sí *absit*, An. Ox. 5115. Ac feor (feorr, *v. l.*) þæt lā sié, þ . . . *sed absit, ut . . .*, Bd. 1, 27 ; Sch. 67, 19. Fearr, Mt. L. 16, 22 : Rtl. 100, 37. Gif hit þ wǣre, swā hit feor þām sȳ, Hml. S. 33, 222. II. *to a great distance.* (1) of space, (a) absolute :—Fearr fǣrende wæs *peregre profectus est*, Mt. 21, 33. Feor (fearr, L.), Mk. R. 12, 1 : 13, 34. Firr gāa *longius ire*, Lk. L. 24, 28. Ǣrendian fyr swā nȳr swā hwyder swā him mon tō tǣcð, Ll. Th. i. 432, 18. (b) where point from which distance is measured is given, (a) in dative :—Hē hwearf mondreámum feor, B. 1715. (ß) with a prep. :—Nō hē wiht fram mē feor fleótan meahte, B. 542. Hē hine feor forwræc mancynne fram, 109. Of þan feán feor āworpen, Cri. 1405. (c) where direction is given :—Feor ūp ofer wolcnu windan, Met. 24, 9. (d) *far in various directions, widely* :—Feor *longiuscule*, i. *late*, An. Ox. 3939 : Wrt. Voc. ii. 50, 31. (e) with verbs of seeing :—Hī ne magon feor geseón, Ps. Th. 113, 13 : 134, 16 : B. 1916. Wiþ eágna miste monige men lōciað on ceald wæter, and þonne magon fyr geseón, Lch. ii. 26, 14. (f) figuratively :—Ne þū mē fram þīnum bebodum feor ādrífe *ne repellas me a mandatis tuis*, Ps. Th. 118, 10. Wē beóð suā micle fier (fierr, *v. l.*) gewitene fram ūrum æfterran mǣge, suā wē oftor āslīdað on ðæm unðeáwe, Past. 313, 16. (2) of time, *to a distant past* :—Hē feor oft gemon wælsleahta worn *his thoughts go back to a time long past and he remembers many a fatal fight*, Wand. 90 : B. 1701. III. *of progressive action or condition* :—Ne wæs hē nōht feor on oferhygd āhafen, Bl. H. 215, 32. Hē fōr siððan firr an Grēcas and gewin upp āhōf wið Athenienses *deinde in Athenienses impetum fecit atque arma direxit*, Ors. 2, 5 ; S. 78, 21. IV. *marking separation, by a great space, widely* (lit. or fig.) :—Hwanne besmāt hine seó scyld þǣre fealasprecolnesse, þone þe swā feor from eallum monnum ādǣled wæs?, Bl. H. 169, 5 : Gen. 2322. Wē micle fier (fierr, *v. l.*) beóð ðǣm hiéhstan ryhte āðiédde, Past. 313, 8. IV a. *marking inequality or unlikeness.* (1) *far* (more), *far* (other) :—Feorr on ōþre wīsan *longe aliter*, Gr. D. 326, 27. Fior *porro* (*omnia fabrorum porro molimina vincit*, Ald. 142, 25), Wrt. Voc. ii. 89, 63. (2) as predicate with dat., *quite different* from :—Þincþ þām ungelǣredum þæt eall þ angit beó belocen on þǣre ānfealdan gerecednisse, ac hit is swíþe feor þām, Ælfc. Gen. Thw. 2, 32. 'Mē gecýð hwilc se wer wǣre' . . . Cwæð se þearfa : 'Se man wæs swíþe feorr and ungelíc þysum mannum' '*mihi qualis vir fuerit innotesce.' Qui ait : 'Homo ille longe fuit ab istis hominibus,*' Gr. D. 79, 29. V. *to or from a distant source* :—Wē āreccan ne magon þæt fædrencynn fier ōwihte *we cannot trace the pedigree further*, Cri. 248. VI. *where the distance is determined :* (1) by accompanying adverbs or phrases :— Þā wæs hē swā feor norþ swā þā hwælhuntan firrest faraþ. Þā fōr hē swā feor swā hē meahte on þām ōþrum þrim dagum gesiglan, Ors. 1, 1 ; S. 17, 11–13. Swā feor ofdūne swā man geséon mihte feorst (fyrrest, *v. l.*), Gr. D. 212, 24. Nū gé þus feor hider on ūrne eard in becōmen. By. 57. Ic wiste þ þū ūt āfaren wǣre, ac ic nyste hū feor, Bt. 5, 1 ;

F. 8, 33. (2) by numerals :—Hē of þǣre ylcan stōwe wæs uneáðe gefaren tȳn mīlum feor (feorr, *v. l.*) *a loco eodem vix decem millibus aberat*, Gr. D. 120, 4. Þæt hē on twēntigum fōtmǣlum feor funde El. 831. VII. *almost with force of substantive* = *a great distance.* Cf. IV. a 2. (1) of space :—Nis þæt feor heonon þæt se mere standeð, B. 1361. (2) of time :—Hē frægn hū nēh þǣre tīde wǣre þ æt te þā brōþor ārīsan sceoldon . . . Andswaredon hī : 'Nis hit feor tō þon' (*non longe est*), Bd. 4, 24 ; Sch. 490, 25. Wē witon þ hit nis nō feor tō þon (*the end of the world*) . . . Nis þ feor tō þon þ þ eá geweorþan sceal, Bl. H. 117, 29–34. Nis þe ende feor *it is not far to the end for thee*, Gū. 1179 : 1139. Nis nū ende feor þ wē sceolon ǣtsomne sūsel þrowian, Sat. 40. v. fyrr, fyr, fier, fyrrest *in Dict.*

**feor;** *adj. Add :*—Hē fæder forlēt and feorr (feor, *v. l.*) land (feorrland? v. feor-land) sōhte *in longinquam regionem abiit*, Gr. D. 106, 26. Hē foerde on lond unnēh i suiðe fearr (feor, R. *adv.?*) *abiit in regionem longinquam*, Lk. L. 19, 12. Þæt folc nolde geliéfan ðeáh him mon feorr lond (feorrland?) on fierste gehēte, gif him sōua ne sealde sum on neáweste sē him ðæt māre gehētt *neque populus promissionibus Dei in longinquo crederet, si a promissore suo non etiam e vicino aliquid percepisset*, Past. 389, 33. Gehwylce men þe þǣr landleód wǣron, ge þā nearran ge þā feorran (fyrran, *v. l.*) *vicini vel longe positi ejusdem loci accolae*, Gr. D. 230, 8. Munecas of feorrum stōwum, Hml. S. 23 b, 29. Seó fyrre Ægyptus . . . seó ūs neárre Ægyptus *Aegyptus superior . . . Aegyptus inferior*, Ors. 1, 1 ; S. 14, 1. Hē sceolde fara tō þǣre fyrran India, Hml. S. 36, 256. In ðone firran *in citeriorem* (*alvei marginem*), Wrt. Voc. ii. 82, 82. [*O. Frs.* ferr, firr : *O. Sax.* ferr : *O. H. Ger.* ferr(i).] v. firra, fyrra *in Dict. ; feor-nes.*

**feoran.** *Dele.*

**feorh.** *Add :—*Ic cweþe tō eów þ gē ne sorgige eówrum fer (*animae*) hwæt gē etan . . . ah nis māre þ ferh (*anima*) þonne se mete?, Mt. R. 6, 25. On earfoþum þǣr wē ūres feores ne wēnaþ Bl. H. 51, 28. Nān ōþer fioh ðæs hlīsan wyrþe būton hiora āgnum fiore Bt. 39, 11 ; F. 230, 1. On þām teóþan mōnþe þ wíf ne gedíge hyre feore (*will not escape with life*), gif þ bearn ācenned ne biþ, Lch. iii. 146, 22. Ælc crīsten mann sceolde be his āgenum feore (*under pain of death*) þām Hǣlende widsacan, Hml. S. 11, 6. Ðæt hié hí selfe tō feore ne gewundigen *ac vulnere mortali se feriunt*, Past. 365, 11 Grame tō feore, Hml. S. 7, 242. Tō feore āfyrht, Hml. Th. i. 384, 7. Þæt wíf beswāc Naboð tō his feore, 488, 6. Þ wē mōtan tō wīdan feore hí onsȳne sceáwian, Bl. H. 103, 29. Ā tō wīdan feore sȳ ūrum Drihtne lof, 6, 24. Manig man his feorh for cyle gesealde *many a man died of cold* 213, 32. Uneáðe ic mihte begytan æt Gode þ mē wǣron befæste of þǣre stōwe þā feorh þāra gebrōðra *vix obtinere potui, ut mihi ex hoc loco animae concederentur*, Gr. D. 140, 29. v. mid-feorh.

**feorh-ādl.** *Add : the last illness* :—Hit (*an unborn child*) in þām maga wyrð tō feorhādle, oftost on Tīwesniht, Lch. iii. 146, 23. Full oft þā sweltende an men on heora feorhādle secgað beforan fela þinga swā hit æfter āg plerumque morientes multa praedicunt, Gr. D. 296, 21. Hē læg on hi feorhādle and hit wæs swíðe neáh hīs līfes ænde *ad extrema vitae venien* 314, 3.

**feorh-bana.** *Add :—*Feorhbona *carnifex, interfector*, Wrt. Voc. i 128, 75. Feorhbanena *carnificium*, i. *interfectorum*, An. Ox. 2356.

**feorh-cwalu.** *Add :—*Ferhqualu *internicies*, Wrt. Voc. ii. 48, 39 [*O. Sax.* ferah-quala *violent death.*]

**feorh-fægen;** *adj. Glad to live* :—Ðā hí ðus hí sylfe earhlíc betealdon, þā hēt se cāsere hí faran swā hwider swā hí woldon, and h feorhfægene him fram sōna ðanon eódon, Hml. S. 23, 309.

**feorh-gifa.** *Add :* [Cf. *Icel.* fjör-gjafi *one who saves another's life.*]

**feorh-hama,** an ; *m. Some part of the body* :—Seó ūtre wam venter, fearhhama *cauliculus*, cwið *vel* cildhama *matrix*, Wrt. Voc. 45, 22.

**feorh-hyrde,** l. **-hirde,** *and add :—*Se cyning wile his treówe and h gehāt wið ðē gehealdon, and þē feorhhyrde beón, Bd. 2, 12 ; Sch 159, 23.

**feorh-lāst** *a step stained by one's life-blood* (?) :—Hē fǣge an gefȳmed feorhlāstas bær he (*Grendel*) *death-doomed and fleeing dye the earth with his life-blood*, B. 846.

**feorh-leán.** *Substitute : Recompense for life saved* :—Se yldr cyning weard yrfeweard ingefolca . . . Woldon hié (*the Egyptians*) þa feorhleán (*what was due in consequence of the saving of life effected l Joseph when famine threatened, the reward for life saved*) fācne gyldan Ex. 141–150. [Compare this passage with Gen. 47, 20–25 : Em Joseph omnem terram Aegypti, subjecitque eam Pharaoni . . . Dix Joseph ad populos : 'En et vos et terram vestram Pharao possidet' . . Qui responderunt : 'Salus nostra in manu tua est.']

**feorh-lege.** *Substitute :* **feorh-lege,** es ; *m. Life-laying* [cf. lecgan II. *to slay*], *death* :—Hū wolde þæt geweorðan þæt on þone hālga handa sendan tō feorhlege fæderas ūsse *how should that come to pass th our fathers should lay hands on the holy one to the end that they mig slay him*, El. 458. Ic þanc wuldurcyninge secge þæs þe ic mōste mid leódum ǣr swyltdæge swylc gestrȳnan. Nū ic on māðma hord minr

bebohte frôde feorhlege *I to the king of glory give thanks that I might for my people ere the day of death so much gain. Now a hoard of treasures have I prudently got as the price of my death*, B. 2800. [Cf. Icel. fjör-lag *death* (poet.).]

**feorh-ner, -nere**, es; *n. Substitute*: feorh-neru, e; *f.*, and *add* :—þ hié oncnáwan mihton hwá him tô hǣle and tô helpe and tô feorhnere on þâs world ástâg, Bl. H. 105, 32. Tô hwon fêddest þû þê ǣnne of þǣm þe ic inc bâm gesceóp tô welan and tô wiste and tô feorh-rere?, Wlfst. 259, 17. Cf. ealdor-neru.

**feorh-seóc.** *Add*: [Icel. fjör-sjúkr *sick unto death*] : feorran. v. feorrian.

**feorht, ferht**; *adj. Honest, honourable* :—Ferht (ferth, fert) *probus*, Txts. 89, 1639. [O. Sax. feraht.]

**feorht-lic**; *adj. Honourable, just.* [Cf. O. Sax. fer[a]htlîko *honourably, equitably.*] v. ferht-lic *in Dict.*

**feor-land, -lond.** *Add to* feor-lond :—Geâcsode se foresprecena wrǣcca on feorlandum þæs hâlgan weres forðfôre, Guth. 94, 2. [Se gingre sune ferde wrǣclice on feorlanden (*in regionem longinquam*), Lk. 15, 13. Cf. N. E. D. far-land; *adj.*] v. feor; *adj.*

**feorlen**; *adj. sb.* v. firlen.

**feorm.** *Add* : I. *provisions, stores* :—Ðrîtig ombra alâð, and ðreó þund hlâfa . . . feówer weðras . . . sex gôsfuglas . . . ðrîtig leapera . . . ǣster fulne saltes . . . and hió forgifeð fîftêne pund for ðý ðe mon ðâs feorme ðý soel gelǣste, C. D. i. 312, 5–18. **I a.** *dead stock in contrast with live stock* :—þû sweltan scealt mid feó and mid feorme *norte morieris tu et omnia quae tua sunt* (Gen. 20, 7), Gen. 2659. Hit (*land*) becwæð sê þe hit âhte swâ swâ hit his yldran mid feó and mid feore (feorme?) rihte begeáton, Ll. Th. i. 184, 2. þ hê âðer oþþe ... þeó oþþe feorme (freme, *v. l.*) þâ wyrse sý *that he be injured in respect to anything that is his*, 384, 24. Ǣhta lǣdan, feoh and feorme, Gen. 1650. **I b.** *stores furnished to a person as his due* :—Ðâ nam hê his feorme on Wuldahâm, and on ðâm ôðran wolde *he took the provision that was due to him in Wuldaham, and intended to do the same in the other places*, C. D. vi. 127, 21. ¶ *of provision due to the king.* Cyninges feorm, cyning-feorm (q.v.) :—Þâra mynsterhâma hwelcne þe cyninges feorm tô belimpe, Ll. Th. i. 60, 24. Fram twâm mînra (*Athelstan's*) feorma (*de duabus meis nihtfirmis*, Lat. vers.) âgyfe mon âne ambra meles . . . , 198, 6. Cf. trium annorum ad se (*Offa*) pertinentes pastiones, id est, vi. convivia, C. D. i. 174, 3. Erat in illo monasterio pastus unius noctis regi . . . et pastus novem noctium accipitrariis regis, r. 159, 4. v. Sax. Engl. i. 294 sqq., ii. 58 sqq. **II.** *a feast, an entertainment* :—Eallum ǣhtemannum gebyreð Midwintres feorm and Eástorfeorm, Ll. Th. i. 436, 33. Feorma (farma, L.) giworden wæs *cena facta*, Jn. R. 13, 2. Tîd farmes *hôra caenae*, Lk. L. 14, 17. Tô feorme *ad agapem*, An. Ox. 4834. Æt ânre feorme *convivio*, Ors. 337, 4. Aman unþances côm tô þǣre cwêne feorme, Hml. A. 99, 247. Ârâs from ðǣr farma (feorme, R.) *surgit a cena*, Jn. L. 13, 4. Fǣrma, 1, 20. Ðonne ðû feorme (forme, *v. l.*) gierwe on ælmessan *cum facis convivium*, Past. 323, 22. Hié þâ miclan feorme þigedon Crîstes þonces þe hié ǣr þigedon æt hiora diófolgildum deófla þonces *magnificis ludis sic natalis annus a Christiano imperatore celebratus est*, Ors. 6, 21; 272, 22. Man þǣre sunnan feorme worhte, Hml. Th. ij. 494, 6. Feorme *prandium*, Mt. 22, 4. Fearme *cenam*, Mk. R. 6, 21. Farma *convivium*, Lk. L. 5, 29. Ðâ fǣrmo *nuptiae*, Mt. L. 22, 10. Hǣmdo feorme (fǣrmo, L.), Jn. R. 2, 1. Ðâra farmana *nubtiarum*, Jn. p. 1, 1. Farma, p. 3, 12. Æt feormum (farmum, L.) *in cenis*, Mk. R. 12, 9. **III.** *furnishing with food, entertainment.* v. flŷman feorm *in Dict.* v. cum-, dæg-, gift-, niht-feorm.

**feormend**, es; *m. An entertainer* :—Sum sceal on fêðe on feorwegas lŷde gongan and his nest beran . . . âh hê feormendra lyt lifgendra, Vy. 30. v. feormian *to entertain.*

**feormend**, es; *m. A furbisher.* v. feormynd *in Dict.*, and feormian *to cleanse.*

**feorm-fultum** *aid towards obtaining provisions*; firme adjutorium, Ll. Th. i. 412, 22 (Lat. vers.) :—Geselle hê cc. peninga êghwylce gêre ô Ceortesêge tô feormfultume, Cht. Th. 481, 34. Hêr stent ðâ orwarde ðǣ Æþeric worhte . . . þ is iii sceppe mealtes . . . Leófstân bbod dôð tô þis feormfultum, ân sceppe malt . . . , Nap. 55, 32.

**feormian.** *Dele* II, *take* III *separately, and add*: I. *to maintain, foster* :—Feormat, broedeth *fovet*, Wrt. Voc. ii. 108, 79. Brêdeþ, feormaþ *fovit*, 35, 74. Feormeþ *fomet*, 150, 8. Brond . . . fealo líg feormað *flammam parturit ipse calor*, Ph. 218. Fûl nâwâr friðian ne feormian, Ll. Th. i. 162, 26. **II.** *to entertain a guest* :—Gif man þuman feormæð .iii. niht an his âgenum hâme, Ll. Th. i. 32, 16. Hê ongæt hwæne hê sylfa feormode (underfêng, *v.l.*) *quem ipse susceperit ignovit*, Gr. D. 75, 29. Cuma ic wæs and gê feormadun mec *hospes eram et collegistis me*, Mt. R. 25, 36. þ ne geweorðe þ hine man læng feormige, Ll. Th. i. 38, 14. **III.** *to harbour* a criminal, fugitive :—Sê ðon ðe cierlisc man fliéman feormige, Ll. Th. i. 120, 16 : 210, 12 : 224, 5 : 248, 8. Sê þe þeóf dearnunga feormige, 228, 21. Lôc hwâ þone flŷman fêde oþþe feormige, 382, 21. Gif hwâ þæne friðleásan

man healde oþþe feormige, 384, 8. **IV.** *to maintain* a dependent, servant, *take* a person as a servant :—Gif mon wille of boldgetale in ôðer boldgetæl hlâford sêcan. . . . Gif hê hit bûtan þæs ealdormonnes gewitnisse dô, geselle sê þe hine tô men feormie .cxx. scill. tô wîte, Ll. Th. i. 86, 5. Gif hwylc landleás man folgode on ôðre scîre and eft his mâgas gesêce, þ hê hine on þâ gerâd feormige, þ hê hine tô folcryhte gelǣde, 204, 7. **V.** *to supply with food* as an obligation :—Ic wille þ Æffe feormige of þǣm þrîm dǣlum æt Ingepenne þâ Godes þeówas æt Cynetanbyrig þrié dagas on twelf mônþum, Cht. Th. 497, 8, 19 : 496, 1. **V a.** *where the obligation is to the lord* :—On sumon landum se geneát sceal hlâford feormian, Ll. Th. i. 432, 14. **VI.** *to feast* :—Feormode se ealdorman his heáhþegnas *fecit cenam servis suis*, Hml. A. 111, 282. Balthasar feormode ealle his witan *Baltassar fecit grande convivium optimatibus suis*, Hml. Th. ii. 434, 29. v. swíþ-feormende.

**feormian** *to cleanse. Add* : (1) *to clean* a place :—Sê þe on Sunnan-dæge his hûs feormað, Wlfst. 212, 26. Flôr feormian, Angl. ix. 262, 23. (2) *to cleanse* material :—Lege tô þǣre wunde, ðonne yt heó and fæormað, gyf þǣr hwæt horwes on sý, Lch. i. 100, 3. Hwîtlas on sǣ wacsan and feormian, Bd. 4, 31 ; Sch. 540, 12. Tô feormianne (geclǣnsian, *v. l.*) sumne dǣl hwǣtes, Gr. D. 97, 2. (3) *to furbish, polish* a weapon, vessel :—Seó hâlige clǣnnes þæt sweord feormað (*purificat*), Gl. Prud. 15. Hê mec (*a lance*) fægre feormað, Rä. 72, 18. Fe(o)r(mie) wǣge, B. 2253. [v. N. E. D. farm.] v. un-feormigende.

**-feormness.** v. or-feormness : feorm-riht. *Dele.*

**feormung; I.** *Add* :—Seó feormung (underfangennys, *v. l.*, *susceptio*; cf. sum man hine geladde þ hê sǣte mid him in his hûse æt þâm glêdan, 75, 17) næs nâ bûtan scylde, Gr. D. 76, 22. v. feormian *to entertain.*

**feormung; II.** *Add* :—Feormunga *purgamenta*, An. Ox. 609.

**feorran**; *adv. Add* : I. of space (lit. or fig.). (1) *from a distance* :—Gefetadne feorran *arceri porro*, Wrt. Voc. ii. 92, 35. Sume cumað swîðe feorran and habbað swîðe længe weig, Solil. H. 44, 5. Sume hî cômon feorran (fearre, L., feorra, R. *de longe*), Mk. 8, 3. Þâ wíf wǣron feorran (fearra, L. R.) behealdende *erant mulieres de longe aspicientes*, 15, 40. Fearra, Rtl. 55, 28. (2) *at a distance* :—Ús ðe feorran (*longe*) wǣron, Hml. Th. i. 106, 16. Ðâ stôd se mânfulla feorran (fearra, R., fearra tô, L.) *publicanus a longe stans*, Lk. 18, 13 : 23, 49 : 17, 12 Petrus him fyligde feorran (feorra, R., fearre, L. *a longe*), Mk. 14, 54. Hê feorran (feorra, R., fearra, L. *a longe*) geseah ân fîctreów, 11, 13 : Lk. 16, 23. **II.** of time. (1) of a distant past :—Frumsceaft fira feorran reccan *to tell the origin of men from the most remote past*, B. 91 : 2106. (2) of a distant future :—Hê wolde feorran and lange ǣr cŷðan his ðrowunge, Hml. Th. i. 152, 29. Fela wîtegan bodedon Drihten tôweardne, sume feorran, sume neán, 358, 7. Hê fela þing feorran wiste ǣr þan þe hit gewurde, Hml. S. 31, 1009. [v. N. E. D. ferren. O. Sax. ferran : O. H. Ger. ferron.] v. feorrane.

**feorran** *to remove.* v. firran.

**feorran-cumen**; *adj. Come from far, stranger* :—Gif feorrancumen man oþþe frǣmde bûton wege gange, Ll. Th. i. 42, 23. Gif freóndleás man oþþe feorrancuman geswenced weorðe . . . Sê þe freóndleásan aud feorrancumenan wyrsan dôm dêmeð þonne his geféran, 396, 25–29. Be feorrancumenum men bûtan wege gemêtton, 114, 13. Hêr syndon geferede feorrancumene (feorran cumene?) Geáta leóde, B. 361. Hié fira flǣschoman feorrancumenra þêgon, An. 24. Hwæt sié freóndlufu ellþeódigra uncer twêga feorrencumenra, Gen. 1836. þ hî ælþeódige men and feorrancumene ne tyrian, Ll. Th. i. 326, 27. Cf. feor-cumen.

**feorrane**; *adv. From a distance, from afar* :—Drihten, þû angeáte mîne geþôhtas feorrene (-one, *v.l.*; forrane, R. Ben. I. 29, 13) *intellexisti cogitationes meas a longe*, R. Ben. 24, 16. Feorrane (-one, *v. l.*) ðû meaht geseón, gif se wâh bið ðyrel, Past. 157, 17. Gehŷrde ic feorran (feorranne, *v. l.*) âne stefne clypigende, Hml. S. 23 b, 483. [O. Sax. ferrana : O. H. Ger. ferrana(-o).] v. feorran.

**feorred-lic**, Lch. i. lxi, 1. *l.* weored-lic (v. Hpt. 31, 8, 133) : feorren. v. feorran-cumen.

**feorrian**; *p.* ode; *pp.* od *To go far away, depart* :—Fearras *discedit*, Lk. L. R. 9, 39. Hiá fearrageð l fleáð *recedunt*, 8, 13. Feorriað hî and fleóð *longe fugiunt*, Nar. 35, 32 : 36, 22. Ic feorude fleógende *elongavi fugiens*, Ps. Spl. C. 54, 7. Ic feorrode symle fleónde *I fled always farther and farther away*, Hml. S. 23 b, 510. Feorrade (fearrade, L.) from hire ðe engel *discessit ab illa angelus*, Lk. R. 1, 38. Ðió hriófol of fearrade from him *lepra discessit ab illo*, Lk. L. 5, 13. Feorradun (fearradon, L.) from him ðâ englas, Lk. R. 2, 15. Þte ne fearrade *ne discederet*, Lk. L. 4, 42. [O. H. Ger. ferrên.] v. â-, æt-, ge-feorrian ; firran.

**feorrung**, e; *f. Departure, retirement, withdrawal* :—Þâ gebrôðru fundon þone stân of þǣre stôwe feor gewitenne, and for his feorrunga (*secessu*) gewearð genôh rûm stôw wyrta on tô settane, Gr. D. 49, 16.

**feorsian.** v. firsian.

**feor-sibb**; *adj. Distantly related*; *sbst. A distant relative* :—Ne bið nâ gelíc þ man wið swustor gehǣme and hit wǣre feorsibb, Ll. Th. i. 404, 18. Cf. neáh-sibb.

**feor-studu.** *Substitute:* **feor-studu,** -stuþu, -stud (feór-?), e, u ; *f.*
*A sloping beam, stay, buttress:*—Ferstud *continuus,* Txts. 108, 1110.
Feurstud *destina* (cf. seó wrǽdstuðu (*destina*) þām wāge tō wreþe geseted
wæs, Bd. 3, 17; Sch. 269, 22), 123, 18. Flōr *pavimentum,* feorstuþu
*obstupum* (*obstipum?* cf. (?) *obstipum, oblicum,* Corp. Gl. H. 84, 81 :
*obliquat* fyreð, Wrt. Voc. ii. 64, 67), duru *valva,* Wrt. Voc. i. 290, 11.
Feorstuðu, ii. 64, 19.

**feórþa.** *Add:* (1) ordinal :—Ðe feárða *quartum,* Mt. p. 10, 5.
Cuōm feórþe healf hund scipa, Chr. 851 ; P. 64, 16. Wæs xxxiiii wintra
and þæs feórþan dæl þæt hē līfes wegas tācnode *for 33 years and part of
the thirty-fourth he pointed out the ways of life,* Bl. H. 129, 16. Feórðe
(ðiú feórða, L.) þære wacone *quarta vigilia,* Mt. R. 14, 25. Ðā feárða
wacan, Mk. L. R. 6, 48. Feórðe healf geár se deófles man rīxað,
Wlfst. 197, 14. (1 a) genealogical :—Feórþa fæder *proavus,* Wrt. Voc.
i. 72, 22. Feórþa sunu *abnepos,* ii. 4, 73. Feówerðe dohter *abneptis,*
i. 51, 74. v. feówerþa(-e) *in Dict.* (1 b) in combination with another
numeral :—þȳ twēntigoðan dæge and þȳ feórþan Septembris mōnðes, Bd.
4, 5 ; Sch. 373, 19. Sē wæs feórða eác feówertigum fram Agusto *loco
ab Augusto quadragesimo quarto,* I, II ; Sch. 30, 15. (2) fractional.
v. next word :—Feórþan dæles aldor *tetrarca,* Wrt. Voc. ii. 74, 37. Eall
moncynn and ealle nētenu ne notigað nāwer neáh feórþan dæles ðisse
eorþan þæs þe men gefaran magon . . . Dō nū of ðām feórþan dæle . . .
*hujus in mundo regionis quarta fere portio est, . . . quae a nobis cognitis
animantibus incolatur. Huic quartae si . . . subtraxeris,* Bt. 18, 1 ; F.
62, 8–12.

**feórþan-dæl,** es ; *m. A fourth part, a fourth :*—Ðes feórðling oððe
feórðandæl ðinges *hic quadrans,* Ælf. Gr. Z. 61, 6. *Quadrans* ys
fýrðling oððe feórðandæl ; ælc þæra þinga þe man mæg tōdælan on
feówer on emne se feórðandæl byð *quadrans* gecīged, Angl. viii. 306,
28–30. Ǽr þon þū āgefe þone nǽhstu feórþandæl (*novissimum quadrantem*), Mt. R. 5, 26.

**feórþes fōt.** *Dele:* **feórþing.** v. feórþung.

**feórþling.** *Dele* 'feórþung, e ; *f.* . . . *example,' and last two examples,
and add:*—*Quadrans* ys fýrðling, Angl. viii. 306, 29. Oþ þæt gē cumon
tō ānum feórðlincge *until you are brought to your last farthing,* Hml. Th.
i. 268, 1. Sum earm wydewe næfde ealra ǽhta būton ǽnne feórðling,
ii. 106, 9. Ǽr ðan þe ðū forgelde þone endenēxtan feórðling, Hml. A.
4, 100. Syx tīda wyrcað ānne fýrðling, and feówer fýrðlingas wyrcað
ānne dæg, Angl. viii. 318, 47.

**feórþ-rīce.** *Dele.*

**feórþung,** e ; *f. Substitute:* **feórþung** (-ing), es ; *m. A quarter,
fourth part, farthing :*—Feórþung peninges *quadrans,* Mk. L. R. 12, 42.
Feórðung *quadrantem,* Mt. L. 5, 26. Feórðungas twoege (feórð ī ān
feórðunge, L.) *minuta duo,* Lk. R. 21, 2. [*Icel.* fjórðungr.]

**feorwe.** v. mid-feorh : **feor-weg.** *Add:* [*O. Sax.* fer-weg.] : **feoþer.**
v. fiþer.

**feóung.** *Add:*—Sōðfæstnysse feóung (fēung, *v. l.*) and seó lufu
leásunge *odium ueritatis amorque mendacii,* Bd. 1, 14 ; Sch. 38, 19 :
Past. 222, 2. Bið ðæt fýr onǽled ðære feóunga (fíóunga, *v. l.*), and sió
feóung (fíóung, *v.l.*) ādwǽscð ðā sibbe, 279, 11. Ðæt gebreátude mōd bið
swīðe hræde gehwierfed tō feóunga *correpti mens repente ad odium
proruit,* 166, 14. Feóunga *exosa,* Wrt. Voc. ii. 86, 72 : 31, 38.
Becōm on hatunga his herges and on feóunga Rōmāna folces, Bl. H.
193, 2. Gē beóþ in fiunge allum monnum, Mt. R. 10, 22 : Jn. L. 15,
18. Fīonge, Jn. R. 15, 25 : 17, 14. Ic ondette feóndscipe and feó-
wunge, Angl. xi. 98, 41. v. ā-feóung.

**feówer.** *Add:* I. adjectival. (1) uninflected :—Wǽron feówer (feór,
L.) þūsend manna, Mt. 15, 38. Bisen fēwer nētna *similitudo quattuor
animalium,* p. 9, 10. Gesceapen of feówer gesceaftum, Bl. H. 35, 5.
From fēwer (feówre, R.) windum, Mt. L. 24, 31. Fēwor streámas,
p. 8, 5. Fēuor dagas, Jn. L. 11, 17. Fēuoer dǽlo, 19, 23. (1 a) with
pronoun or indef. numeral adj. :—Sume feówer cyninges þegnas, Chr.
896 ; P. 89, 7. Þā feówer onwealdas þāra feówer heáfedrīca, Ors. 6, 1 ;
S. 252, 2. Ðā feówer hringas on ðām feówer hyrnum, Past. 171, 3.
Þā lāra þāra feówer godspellera, Bl. H. 35, 11. Æt þissum feówer
endum, 95, 13. Þā feówer (feówðer, MS.) wordias, C. D. iv. 171, 7.
Þā feówer gesceafta, Bt. 39, 8 ; F. 224, 8. (1 b) combined with a
multiple of ten :—Bituih ðǽm feóer and feórtigum and hundð ðūsenda
*inter illa* CXLIII *milia,* Rtl. 104, 12. (1 c) as part of an ordinal :—On
þissum feówer and feówertigoþan sealme, Ps. Th. 44, arg. Þysne feówer
and twēntigoðan sealm, 24, arg. : 34, arg. (2) inflected, cf. II. 1 a :—
Fēuero mōneðo sint, Jn. L. 4, 35. Wǽron feówere forð gewitene dagas,
Gū. 1107. Þīn seáð bið twēgea cubita wīd and feówra lang, Nar. 50,
29. Mid feówrum gesceaftum, Angl. viii. 299, 19. Fēwere hwommas
and hringas hæfis *quattuor angulos et anulos habet,* Mt. p. 8, 5. Bifora
feóro nētno *ante quatuor animalia,* Rtl. 47, 28. (2 a) with a pronoun :
—Ðās fēwera godspelles *haec quattuor evangelia,* Mt. p. 9, 8. I a.
as multiplicative, *four times :*—Se earma man wile drincan feówer swā
feala swā his neád wǽre, Hml. A. 145, 29. II. substantival. (1)
inflected :—Hannibal oþfleáh feówera sum *Annibal cum quatuor equitibus
confugit,* Ors. 4, 10 ; S. 202, 16. Gange hē feówra sum tō, and beó him

sylf fīfta, Ll. Th. i. 286, 18. Hē from feówrum wæs geboren, Mk. L. R.
2, 3. (1 a) in apposition to a noun. Cf. I. 2 *and* sum ; II. 2 :—þ
feáwa þe ic secge ic ongæt æt feówrum his gingrum (æt his feówe
gingrum, *v. l.*) *pauca quae narro quatuor discipulis illius referentibu
agnovi,* Gr. D. 96, 4. (1 b) with a pronoun :—Eádfrið and Æðilwal
and Billfrið and Aldred, ðās feówero ymb woeson ðās bōc, Mk. p. 1, ;
(2) uninflected :—þāra sint feówer þe þā þegnunge beweotigaþ, El. 74.
Tōdǽlan on feówer, Angl. viii. 306, 30. (2 a) with a pronoun or inde
numeral adj. :—Hē him wegas tǽcneð feówer eallum, Rä. 52, 7. W:
ealle feówer on buteran, Lch. ii. 128, 8. (2 b) with a multiple of ten :-
Weaxeð þ flōd ðæs sǽs feówer and twēntigum sīða, Shrn. 63, 29.

**feówer-dōgor ;** *adj. Lasting four days :*—Feówerdōgor (feóerdōge
L.) *quadriduanus,* Jn. R. 11, 39. Cf. fiþer-dōgor.

**feówer-ecge ;** *adj. Four-edged :*—Heó of hyre manega bōgas āsende
and þā lange and feówerecge, Lch. i. 306, 7.

**feówer-ecgede ;** *adj. Four-edged :*—Heó hafaþ feówerecgedne stela
Lch. i. 290, 19.

**feówer-feald.** *Add :*—Mid feówerfealdum *quaterno,* An. Ox. 154
Feárfald *quadruplum,* Lk. L. 19, 8.

**feówer-fealdlíce ;** *adv. Quadruply :*—þ ic forgylde feówerfealdlíce
*reddo quadruplum,* Ll. Th. ii. 136, 9 : 232, 22 : Bl. H. 11, 8.

**feówer-fēte.** *Dele* ' fiðer-fēte . . . , -fōtte,' *and* ' Eádbyrht . . . feówe
scyte,' *add:* [*O. H. Ger.* fior-fuozi *quadrupes.*] Cf. fiþer-fēte, *and :*
*next word.*

**feówer-fōt[e] ;** *adj. Four-footed :*—Feówerfōttra nȳtena (feóworfō!
neátna, *v.l.*) þone teóþan dǽl *decimam quadrupedum partem,* Bd. 4, 2
Sch. 532, 21. Cf. fiþer-fōt[e].

**feówer-fōted[e] ;** *adj. Four-footed* [ :—Mid feówerfōted nȳtene, Hr
A. 177, 246.]

**feówer-gild.** *l.* feówer-gilde. *In the passage the word might be tak*
*as the case of a noun, or as an adverb.* v. twi-gilde.

**feówer-hweohlode ;** *adj. Four-wheeled :*—Fýrhweohlodum (or f
<fyþer) crætum *quadrigis,* Nap. 80.

**feówer-nihte ;** *adj. Four days old :*—Hit wæs on feówornihtne (feów
nihta ealdne, *v.l.*) mōnan *in luna quarta,* Bd. 5, 3 ; Sch. 564, 2, 5.

**feówerteóða.** *Add :*—On ðone feówertegðan dæg þæs mōnðes, Shı
103, 24. Þȳ feówerteogeðan (-tegeðan, -teóðan, *v. ll.*) geáre *an
decimo quarto,* Bd. 1, 23 ; Sch. 48, 5.

**feówertig.** *Add:* I. substantival. (1) alone. (*a*) as a neut
sing. with adj. inflections (?) :—þǽr weard Somnita and Gallia feówer
M (=þūsenda? *but cf.* Past. 409, 9 *below for a number taken
singular*), Ors. 3, 10 ; S. 138, 14. Bið feórtiges cæmpena ðrowur
Shrn. 61, 27. Þ fæsten þyses feówertiges daga, Bl. H. 35, 5, 30.
þyssum feówertigum (*or pl. ?*) nihta, 35, 17. Daga feówertigum (dagu
feórtih, L.) *diebus quadraginta,* Lk. R. 4, 2. Fēuortig daga and feów
tig næhta, Mt. L. 4, 2. Feóertig daga and feórtig næhta, Mk. L. 1, 1
Ymb feówer hunde wintra and ymb feówertig, Ors. 2, 2 ; S. 64, 2
þis feówertig daga on forhæfdnesse lifgean, Bl. H. 35, 9. Þ feówer
wintra, 79, 4. (β) as plural :—Hī ealle feówertig ætforan him stōdc
Hml. S. 11, 55. Gif þær beóð gemētte feówertig rihtwīsra, Gen. 18, 2
Him eódon on hand feówertig burga, Ors. 4, 10 ; S. 198, 1. Wæs
feówertiga (feówertigra, *v. l.*) sum *viri, ut ferunt, ferme* XL, Bd. 1, 2
Sch. 52, 10. Hē wæs wunigende betwux him þās feówertig daga, Hr
Th. i. 296, 21. (2) combined with units, and the number treated [
as singular :—Þā beóð eahta and feówertiges elna lange, Ors. 1, 1 ;
18, 6. (β) as plural :—Gif þær beóð fīf and feówertig rihtwīsra, Ge
18, 28. Þǽr wǽron twā hund and eahta and feówertig wera and nig
and feówertig wīfa, Bl. H. 129, 14. (3) *the forty days of Lent :*—
þām þrim feówertigum *per tres quadragesimis,* Ll. Th. ii. 228, 13. I
adjectival :—Ðone sang ðe nān mon elles singan ne mæg būton ð
hun[d]teóntig and feówertig and feówer ðūsendo, Past. 409, 9. Feów
tigra daga fyrst, Hml. Th. i. 28, 6. Æfter þǽm þe Rōmeburg getimbr
wæs v hunde wintrum and feówertigum, Ors. 4, 9 ; S. 188, 30. II
used as ordinal :—On þone feówertegan dæg ofer midne winter, C
763 ; P. 50, 16. III. used in forming ordinals :—Sē wæs feórða eá
feówertigum fram Agusto *loco ab Augusto quadragesimo quarto,* Bd.
11 ; Sch. 30, 15. Fīfta eác feówertigum, 1, 13 ; Sch. 36, 9. Syxta e
feówertigum, 1, 15 ; Sch. 40, 15. Þ gēr wæs fram Crīstes hidercyme
sixte eác feówertigum, 1, 3 ; Sch. 15, 12. v. fīftig.

**feówertigeða.** *Add :* feówerteóþa. (1) alone :—Wē sceolon unc
þǽm feówerteóþan gerīme (*during Lent*) syllan þone teóþan dǽl ī
worldspēda, Bl. H. 35, 18. On þone feówerteg[ð]an dæg, Chr. 76
P. 50, 16. (2) with units :—On þǽm twǽm and feówerteóþan (-tigþ:
*v. l.*) wintra Agustuses rīces, Ors. 5, 15 ; S. 250, 23. On þǽm twǽm a
on feówerteóþan (feówertigan, Bos. 116, 7) wintra, 6, 1 ; S. 252, :
On þǽm twǽm and on feówerteogþan (-tigeþan, *v. l.*) geáre *anno quad:
gesimo secundo,* 254, 4.

**feówertig-feald.** *Add :*—Þis feówertigfealde fæsten (*Lent*) w
āsteald . . . ðā ðā Mōyses fæste feówertig daga and feówertig nil
tōsamne, Hml. Th. ii. 100, 1 : Wlfst. 285, 15.

**feówertyne.** *l.* -tīne, *and add :* I. substantival :—Twīa seof

eóð feówertýne, Angl. viii. 302, 45. From feówertiénum oþ hundnig-ntig *quinquies bilustris*, Wrt. Voc. ii. 79, 44. **II.** adjectival :—
ʾeówertêne (-têno, L.) kneórisse, Mt. R. 1, 17. Gif se môna bið xiiii ihta eald, Lch. iii. 182, 17. xiiii dagum, Chr. 538 ; P. 16, 11. Hî ʾeówertiéne geár hit tôtugon, Ors. 3, 11 ; S. 142, 23.

**feówertíne-wintre** ; *adj. Fourteen years old* :—Feówertýnewintre ian hine sylfne mæg þeówne gedôn *quatuordecim annorum homini licet ʾservum facere*, Ll. Th. ii. 152, 27.

**feówer-wintre** ; *adj. Four years old* :—Feówerwintre *quadrimus*, Ælfc. Gr. Z. 287, 19.

**feowðer.** v. feówer : **feówung** *hate.* v. feóung.

**feowung** *rejoicing.* *l.* feówung, feóung, e ; *f. Rejoicing, delight* :— ʾeówunge *gaudio*, An. Ox. 1118. v. feón.

**fera.** *l.* fêra, *and add* :—Of foera his *a socio ejus*, Lk. p. 11, 10. Ne ʾærun wê sôeran (*socii*) eora in blôdgyte, Mt. R. 23, 30. Foerano ʾociorum, Lk. p. 4, 18. Ðæm foerum *sociis*, Lk. L. 5, 7. [v. *N. E. D.* ʾere *a companion.*]

**feran.** *l.* fêran, *and add :* **I.** of motion. (1) literal :—Hwæt is þes iihtiga þe þus mærlîce fêreþ (*cometh like an honoured guest*)?, Bl. H. 1, 14. Hê mid fierde fêrde, Chr. 835 ; P. 62, 17. Hê foerde ðona ʾbiit inde, Mt. L. 19, 15. Þ hrýðer geond þ wêsten fêrde, Bl. H. 199, ʾò. 'Faraÿ þider' . . . Hié þa ealle fêrdon, 239, 12. Fêrdon *abscedunt*, ın. Ox. 3590. Hî fêrdon æfre forÿ æfter, Chr. 999 ; P. 133, 9. Fêr 1 mont *transmigra in montem*, Ps. Srt. 10, 2. Fêran *properare*, Wrt. ʾoc. ii. 85, 66. (1 a) with reflex. dat. :—Hê him hâmweard fêrde tô is âgnum rîce, Ors. 2, 4 ; S. 74, 33. Fêrde ælc man him hâm, Chr. 016 ; P. 147, 24. Hî him fêrdon onbûton swâ swâ hî sylf woldon, ʾoo1 ; P. 133, 27. Þû mihtest þê fêran betwyx þâm tunglum, Bt. 36, ; F. 174, 10. (1 b) with road by which motion is effected in dat. or ʾast. :—Ic þæm wegum fêrde, Nar. 6, 28. Fêrdon wê forÿ þý wege þe ʾê ær ongunnon, 8, 18. Ic wolde þæm frêcnan wege and sîðfatum ʾoeran, 6, 3. (2) figurative. (a) of course taken :—Fêrdon betwux *intervened*) Rôdbeard eorl and Eádgar æðeling and þæra cinga sehte ʾemacedon, Chr. 1091 ; P. 226, 37. Fulfremednesse weg þe wê on ʾêran sceolan, Bl. H. 21, 17. (b) of going from this world, *to depart* his life :—Ær hê of worulde fêrde, Bl. H. 225, 9. Fêrdon forÿ ʾatwine and Biéda, Chr. 734 ; P. 44, 14. Gif ceorl and his wíf bearn ʾæbben gemæne, and fêre se ceorl forÿ, Ll. Th. i. 126, 4. **II.** of ction, behaviour, *to go on, proceed* :—Heó fêrde fracodlîce on forlygre *she hamefully practised adultery*, Hml. S. 2, 217. On wlence ic fêrde þurh ʾ îdele wuldor, Angl. xi. 113, 50. Wæs hê mid yrre onstyred, for ðon þe ʾ hrýðer swâ ofermôdlîce fêrde, Bl. H. 199, 17. Hê fêrde swâ swâ his ʾorcuÿa fæder and swâ swâ his fracode môdor him yfele gebysnodon, ʾml. S. 18, 229. Sum leódscipe þe God wolde gewîtnian for heora ʾewîtleásum dædum ; þ wæron ÿa Niniuitiscan þe wôdlîce fêrdon, 13, ʾ75 : Ælfc. T. Grn. 8, 8. Litel rihtwîsnesse wæs . . . bûton mid ʾnunecan âne þær þær hî wæll fêrdon, Chr. 1086 ; P. 218, 9. **III.** ʾ *fare, go on, succeed.* (1) of persons :—Hî swuncon on îdel and earm-ice fêrdon, Hml. S. 32, 206. (2) impersonal :—Hû wel hit fêrde mid is þâ ÿâ þis îgland wæs wunigende on sibbe, Hml. S. 13, 147. Hê wæs meágende hû hit on ÿæs cáseres hîrêde fêrde, 23, 222. **IV.** *to ʾome, be derived* :—Ic wêne þ þu næfre tô ÿus mycles mægnes læcedômum ʾecôme swylcum swâ ic gefregn ÿâ þe fram Æscolapio fêrdon, Lch. i. ʾ26, 7. [v. *N. E. D.* fere *to travel, behave, fare.* O. *Frs.* fêra : ʾ. *Sax.* fôrian : *O. H. Ger.* fuoren : *Icel.* færa. All these, though ʾgreeing in form, are used with a causative force *to carry, bring.*] v. ʾore-, ymb-fêran ; forþbig-, wið-fêrende.

**fer-bed.** *Substitute : A litter* :—Ferbed *bajanula*, Wrt. Voc. i. 41, 32.

**fercian.** *Add :* **I.** trans. (1) *to bring, carry, conduct* :—þâ ealdor-ʾnenn forlêton þâ scipo and þet folc, þâ þe on ÿâm scipe wæron, færcodon fercodon, *v. l.*) ÿâ scipo eft tô Lundene, Chr. 1009 ; P. 139, 5. (2) *to ʾupport* :—Wyrtum fercian *leguminibus* (*vitam*) *sustentare*, An. Ox. 635. Ælcon men is âlýfed þ hê of his yldrena gestreóne hine sylfne ʾercian môte, Hml. S. 23, 597. (2 a) figuratively :—Man sceall þê oþer ʾecýþan þ þû ûs nâ lencg ne þearft mid þînre leásunge fercian (*you need ʾot try to make us swallow any more of your lies*), Hml. S. 23, ʾ13. **II.** intrans. *To go, make one's way* :—On þâm forman geáre ʾæt seó sunne on ærnemergen on þ tâcen þe ys *aries* genemned . . . þý ʾriddan heó sîhð tô þâm tâcne oÿ æfen, and on þâm feórÿan geáre heó ʾerecaÿ on middre nihte tô þâm foresprecenan tâcne, Angl. viii. 307, 21. v. *N. E. D.* firk. For double sense cf. *a similar case in O. H. Ger.* ʾuora *profectio* ; *sustentatio.* v. next word.

**fercung,** e ; *f. Provisions, food* :—Heó nolde his sanda brûcan . . . : ʾc heó hæfde gebrôht on hire þînene fætelse hire fercunge *non potero ʾnanducare ex his quae mihi praecipis tribui . . . ; ex his autem quae mihi ʾletuli manducabo*, Hml. A. 110, 272.

**fercuþ.** v. for-cûþ : **ferd.** v. fird.

**fere.** *l.* fêre, *and add* : (1) of persons, able, *fit for service* :—þâ ʾeád man fyrde be fullum wîte, þæt ælc man þe wære forÿ wende, ʾChr. 1016 ; P. 147, 26. Sôna þæs hî fêre wæron, hî worhton castel æt ʾHæstinga port, 1066 ; P. 199, 25. Hê sylf and his fêrestan menn

fêrdon ongeán tô Scotlande, 1075 ; P. 210, 16. (2) of ships, *sea-worthy* :—Swâ fela scipu swâ þær fêra wæron, Chr. 1052 ; P. 178, 14. ¶ of a ship which is the subject of a riddle :—Wiht . . . moncynne nyt, fêre fôddorwelan folcscipe dreóged, Rä. 33, 10. [v. *N. E. D.* fere. *O. Frs.* fêre : *Icel.* fœrr *able* ; *seaworthy.* Cf. *O. H. Ger.* gi-fuori *aptus.*] v. lang-, twi-, þurh-, unofer-fêre.

**-fêre.** v. ge-fêre ; *m. A companion* : ge-fêre ; *n. A society :* fered-ness. v. forþ-feredness.

**ferele,** an ; *f. A rod* :—þâ beran hê slôh mid þære telgan (færelan, *v. l.* ferula) þe hê wunode þ hê bær him on handa . . . þâ rêþan deór . . . ondrêdon þære ferelan (*ferulae*) slegas, Gr. D. 229, 21, 25. [*O. H. Ger.* ferala. From Latin.]

**ferend.** *l.* fêrend, *and add :* v. scip-fêrend.

**fêrende** ; *adj.* (*ptcpl.*) *Mobile* :—Se gâst is styrigendlîcran and fêrendran gecyndes þonne se lîchoma *mobilioris naturae est spiritus quam corpus*, Gr. D. 149, 35.

**fêrende,** Mt. L. 7, 15. v. fêran ; **II.**

**fere-sceat.** *Substitute :* fere-sceat[t], es ; *m. Fare, passage-money :* —Ferescaet *nabalum*, Wrt. Voc. ii. 114, 57. Feræscæt, 60, 8. [*O. H. Ger.* feri-scaz *naulum.*] Cf. fær-sceatt.

**fere-soca.** *Substitute :* fere-sôca ? :—Feresôca *sibba* (cf. (?) sigl *sibba*, Wrt. Voc. ii. 120, 49), Wrt. Voc. i. 289, 1. [Cf. (?) *O. H. Ger.* suohun v. furhi *occa.*]

**fergan ; II.** *Dele, and see* ferian : **fergen-berig.** v. firgen-beorh : **ferht** *honest.* v. feorht : **ferhþ.** *Add :* v. leás-, mid-ferhþ.

**ferhþ-bana.** v. fyrst, (2) : **ferht-líc.** v. feorht-líc.

**ferhþ-loca.** *Add* :—þær ic môste môd gefeÿran, þinne ferÿlocan, feÿrum mînum *pennas sibi cum mens induit*, Met. 24, 5.

**ferian.** *Dele bracket at end, and add :* **I.** *to carry, move, convey.* (1) the subject a person, and (a) the object not moving itself :—Hê forÿfêrde . . . hine man ferede tô Sĉa Marian mynstre, Chr. 977 ; P. 122, 12 : 1023 ; P. 157, 9. Hâm feredan *advectabant* (*manipulos*), Wrt. Voc. ii. 79, 28. Feredon ÿone eorÿcrypel *ferentes paraliticum*, Mk. L. 2, 3 : Hml. Th. i. 492, 28 : Chr. 1012 ; P. 143, 2. Hî âweg feredon þæs godspelleres líc, Hml. S. 15, 98. Hine mon bere oþþe on wæne ferige, Lch. ii. 30, 30. Hiora cyning wæs gewundod, þæt hî hine ne mehton ferian, Chr. 894 ; P. 86, 6. Wegfêrende môton for neóde mete ferian, Ll. Th. ii. 298, 26. Ic seah ræpingas on ræced fergan *I saw captives carried into a house*, Rä. 53, 1. Synna âna mid him ferigende, Hml. Th. i. 66, 14. (b) the object moving itself, *to lead, conduct* :—Fergaÿ swâ and fêþaÿ fæder and môdor *father and mother lead the child and walk with it* (?), Vy. 7. Hê færode folc his þurh þ wêsten *traduxit populum suum per desertum*, Ps. L. 135, 16. (b I) reflexive :—Gif ic mê mid fêdunge ferian mihte *if I could walk*, Hml. Th. ii. 134, 24. (c) where (a) and (b) are combined :—Hî hyra herehûÿe tô sæ færedon (feredon, *v. l.*) . . . mæte and mâdmas, Chr. 1006 ; P. 137, 10. þâ hié gefêngon micle herehýÿ and þâ woldon ferian norþweardes, 894 ; P. 85, 17. (2) the subject a vehicle :—Seó bær ÿe þone deádan ferode, Hml. Th. i. 492, 26. (2 a) figurative :—Ðâ ferede hine Godes hond þider þær hine men âredon, Shrn. 57, 5. **II.** *to direct the course of* :—Hê mid ÿæm ûre líf liÿelíce and getæslíce fered *vitam nostram blanda lenitate disponit*, Past. 369, 13. Þon gelícost swâ wê on laguflôde ofer cald wæter ceólum líÿan, geond sîdne sæ sund-hengestum flôdwudu fergen, Cri. 854. [v. *N. E. D.* ferry. Goth. farjan *to go by sea :* O. H. Ger. ferren : Icel. ferja *to carry by sea.*] v. for-ferian.

**fering,** e ; *f. Carriage, vehicle* :—Ne beþearf seó sâwul swâ gerâdre wege and færinge *anima vehiculo non eget*, Gr. D. 314, 25.

**fering** *going.* *l.* fêring : **fêrlécan.** v. ge-, twi-fêrlæcan : **fer-lêt.** v. for-lét.

**fernes.** *l.* fêrnes, *and add* :—In foernisse (fôrnissæ) *in transmigra-tionem*, Txts. 71, 1091.

**fern-líc.** v. firen-líc.

**fêr-ræden[n],** e ; *f. Society, fellowship* :—Fêrrædene *consortii*, An. Ox. 5037 : *sodalitate*, i. *familiaritate*, 2354. Of brôÿorlícere fêrrædene *fraterna ex acie*, R. Ben. I. 10, 2. Fêrrædene *consortium*, i. com-munionem, An. Ox. 2662.

**fêrrece.** v. fýr-ræce.

**fers.** *Add :* **I.** *a verse* of poetry :—Engla sum . . . þâs vers him mid gyldenum stafum âwritene on þâm handum betæhte . . . þæra versa anginne þe benyÿan þâm forman verse stant, healfe þâ vers gebyriaÿ tô þâm termene, Angl. viii. 325, 46–326, 10. **II a.** *sentence, verse* of the Bible :—Stynt on þære bêc on þâm forman ferse, Ælfc. Gen. Thw. 3, 4. Æt þâm ferse þe man æfter gereorde cwiÿ, R. Ben. 69, 16. Cweþe ærest þis fers, 'Deus in adiutorium meum intende,' 33, 8 (and often). [From Latin.] v. beód-, getel-, meter-fers.

**fersc.** *Add :* **I.** of water. (1) *fresh* as opposed to salt :—þær sint swîÿe micle meras fersce, Ors. 1, 1 ; S. 19, 5. (2) *fresh* as opposed to stagnant :—Wê æfter ferscum wætre hié frinon . . . hié cwædon þ wê fundon sumne swîÿe micelne mere in þæm wære fersc wæter and swête genôg (*dulcissima aqua*) . . . wæs ic gefeónde þæs swêtan wætres and þæs ferscan, Nar. 11, 22–12, 10. Ne fersc ne mersc, Lch. iii. 286,

**24.** II. of food, *fresh* as opposed to salted :—Ete sealtne mete and nówiht fersces, 28, 24. Gemeng wið ferscre buteran, ii. 74, 21. Ne ete fersce gōs, ne ferscne æl, ne fersc swín . . . gif hē hwilc þissa ete, sié þ sealt, 88, 7–10.

**fer-sceat.** v. fær-sceat : ferscian. v. á-ferscian : fēr-scipe. *Add :*—Fērscype *matrimonii sortem*, i. *coniugii*, An. Ox. 2544. Fērscipe *societatem*, 3596 : fer-scrifen. v. for-scrífan.

**fersian.** *Add :* fyrsian, uersian, *v. ll.*, Ælfc. Gr. Z. 218, 3.

**ferþe**, es ; *m. Skin :*—Wiþ tōbrocenum heáfde . . . gespæt þā wunde, and gif se hāla ferþe wille habban reádne hring ymb þā wunde, wite þū þonne þ þū hié ne meaht gehǽlan, Lch. ii. 22, 22. Cf. felo-ferþ.

**fer-tín.** v. for-tín : fēsian. v. físian.

**fēster-bearn.** *Substitute for passage :*—Gregorius is úre *altor* and wē syndan his *alumni*, ðæt is ðæt hē is úre fēsterfæder on Crīste, and wē syndon his fēsterbearn on fullwihte, Shrn. 62, 21.

**fēster-fæder.** *Add :*—Fēsterfæder *nutritor*, Gr. D. 228, 22. Drihtnes engel hine gelǽdde tō sumum sǽ and his fēsterfæder mid hine, Shrn. 91, 1. v. preceding word.

**fēsterling**, es ; *m. A foster-child, pupil :*—Fēsterlincgum *alumnis*, An. Ox. 3021. v. fōstorling.

**fēster-man.** *l.* fester-, *and add :*—De emptionibus sine fidejussoribus, quod Anglice dicitur *fastermannes*, Ll. Lbmn. 668, 18. [Cf. (?) *Icel.* festar-maðr *a betrothed man.*]

**fēster-mōdor.** *Add :*—Fēstermōdor *altrix*, Wrt. Voc. ii. 8, 19. Lǽswede heó hire fēstermōdor sceápum, Shrn. 101, 15. v. fæster-mōdor *in Dict.*

**fēstre.** v. cild-fēstre : fēstr[i]an. *Add :*—Of godcundum spǽcum inra mann byþ fēstrud and byð gefēdd (*nutritur ac pascitur*), Scint. 222, 15. v. ge-fēstr[i]an : fetan. *Dele.*

**-fēte.** *Add :* v. clifer-, six-fēte : -fētede. v. fíf-fētede.

**fetel.** *Add :*—Mínes swyrdes mid fetele, C. D. iii. 304, 29. [v. *N. E. D.* fettle.] v. next word.

**fetels**, es ; *m. A belt :*—Þat suerd on hundtuelftian mancusas goldes and four pund silueres on þan fetelse, Cht. Th. 505, 32. Ic gean þæs swurdes mid þām sylfrenan hylte . . . and þone gyldenan fetels, 558, 12. v. sweord-fetels ; fetelsod.

**fētelsco.** v. fǽtels.

**fetelsod** ; *adj.* (*ptcpl.*) *Provided with a belt :*—Tuēye suerde fetelsade, Cht. Th. 505, 21. v. ge-fetelsod.

**feter.** *Add :*—Feotur, fetor *pedo vel paturum*, Txts. 85, 1552. (1) *a fetter* for a person :—Sum man gesette his ðeówan man on fetera. Hē sæt lange on þām lāðum bendum, oð þæt hē bestæl ūt mid his stafe hoppende and gesōhte ðone sanct . . . Se scyttel ðā āsceát of þǽre fetere, Hml. S. 21, 414–419. Gebundene feterum *vinculis ligatos*, Ps. Th. 106, 9. Mið feoturum (feotrum, *L. compedibus*) gibunden . . . ðā feoturo (fattro, *L. compedibus*) forbræc, Mk. R. 5, 4. Mið fatrum, Lk. L. 8, 29. (2) *a shackle* for an animal :—Gyf feoh sý underfangen. Gif hit hors sý sing on his feteran oþþe on his brídele, Lch. iii. 286, 5. On his fetera oððe on his brídel, i. 392, 9. v. fōt-, ísen-, ísern-feter.

**fēþa.** *Dele* II, *and add :* I. *a footman :*—Fēða *pedester* (*nunquam pergo pedester*, Ald. 272, 34), An. Ox. 23, 54. Rīdende oþþe fēþan fær dōnde *equitando vel pedites iter agendo*, Angl. xiii. 373, 116. Fēþan *pedestres*, An. Ox. 61, 17. Fēþena *peditum*, 826. Foeðan *statores*, Ps. Srt. ii. p. 187, 16. II. of soldiers. (1) *a foot-soldier* (perhaps some of the passages might be put under (2)) :—Hē hæfde III C þusenda fēðena and ān hund þusenda gehorsedra, Ors. 3, 9 ; S. 124, 34 : Nar. 9, 9. Būton unārīmedīcan fēþum *permultae peditum copiae*, 4, 11. (2) *a troop* of foot-soldiers :—Foeða *falanx*, Wrt. Voc. ii. 108, 26. Fēða, 96, 41. Fēþa, 37, 44. Of foeðan *ex phalange*, 107, 59. Of fēþan, of þreáte *ex falange*, 29, 66. (2 a) in a collective sense, *troops* on foot, *infantry, an army* of foot-soldiers :—Tō þǽm gefeohte hæfde hē brōht LXM gehorsedra būtan fēþan, Ors. 5, 7 ; S. 124, 32. Ic mid þínum wǽpnum getrymed on þíuum fēþan fæste stande *armed with thy weapons I will stand fast in thine army*, Bl. H. 225, 34 ; Jul. 389. Fēðan *aciem*, Wrt. Voc. ii. 7, 15. Hē wǽpn gegráp mid tō campienne, ǽr þon þe hē tō his līchoman leomum becōme, and hē ǽr þone fēþan sōhte (*he joined the army*), ǽr þon þe hē þ leóht gesāwe, Bl. H. 167, 2. [*O. H. Ger.* fendo *pedes, pedestris ;* fendeo *falanx.*] v. next word.

**fēðan.** *Substitute for* fēþan ; *p. de To travel on foot, walk :*—Fergað and fēþað fæder and mōdor *father and mother lead [the child] and walk (with it)*, Vy. 7. Hí nāmon þā hors þe hí þyder brōhton, and wǽron ðā rīdende ðe ǽr wǽron fēðende, Hml. A. 116, 449. v. fēþung, fēþa.

**fēþe.** *Add :*—Se foreda fōt ā bið ǽlces fēðes bedǽled, Past. 67, 12. Læg þěr sum creópere lama fram cildhāde . . . Petrus cwæð : ʼ Áris hāl on þínum fótumʼ . . . and hē hleóp sōna cunnigende his fēðes hwæðer hē cūðe gān, Hml. S. 10, 33. Mengu folgedun him on foeðe *turbae secutae sunt eum pedestres*, Mt. R. 14, 13. Þæt hē fǽrlīce his fēðe forlure, Hml. Th. i. 380, 30. Wer . . . þæs fēþe getugon mycle fótswylas and fornāmon *vir . . . cujus gressum dolore nimio podagra contraxerat*, Gr. D. 47, 21.

**fēþe-gest.** *Add :*—Hwonne sincalda sǽ . . . ēce staðulas neósan cōme, fāh fēðegast, Exod. 475.

**fēþe-here.** *Add :*—Fēþehere *felethi* (= *Pelethi*, Ald. 11, 37), Wrt Voc. ii. 33, 45 : 148, 32 : An. Ox. 776.

**fēþe-leás.** *For* ʼ *Footless* ʼ *substitute : Without the power to walk and add :*—Sum deáf man and fēþeieás, ofer þone man becōm godcun wracu . . . þ hē ne meahte ne gehýran ne gangan. Ac hē gecreáp i þæs eádgan Berhtinus ciricean . . . þā meahte hē gehýran and gangan Shrn. 126, 22.

**fēþe-mann.** *Substitute :* (1) *one who goes on foot, a pedestrian :*—Fēþemen *pedestres*, Wrt. Voc. ii. 72, 67. Foeðemen, Mt. L. ʼ14, 13 Mk. L. R. 6, 33. (2) *a foot-soldier :*—Fēþemen *felethi* (cf. fēþe-here) Wrt. Voc. ii. 33, 45.

**fēþe-mund.** *For* ʼ*foot-hand*ʼ *substitute : walking-hand.*

**feþer.** *Add :*—Feþere *pluma*, Wrt. Voc. ii. 66, 61. I. *feather :*—Þæt gafol bið on deóra fellum and on fugela feðerum . . . S byrdesta sceall gyldan . . . týn ambra feðra, Ors. 1, 1 ; S. 18, 16 21. II. *a wing :*—Fugla briddas, gif hié ǽr wilniað tō fleóganne æ hira feðra fulweaxene sint *pulli avium, si ante perfectionem pennarun volare appetant*, Past. 383, 30. Under feðrum (feþran, R.) *sub alas*, Mt 23, 37 : *sub pinnis*, Lk. L. R. 13, 34. Fugel hæfde micele feðra Shrn. 57, 3. Feðra earnes *pennas aquilae*, Mt. p. 9, 17. II a. *wing* of an army (?) :—Here *exercitus*, getrimmed feða *cuneus*, fēþ (printed fedes, *but see* Angl. viii. 450. Should feþre *be read*? *or is* feþ *plural of* fēþu *q.v.*?) *alae*, Wrt. Voc. i. 18, 32. III. *a pen, quill :*—Fiþere tācen is þæt þū geþeóde þíne þrí fingras tōsomne swilce þū feþer hæbe . . . and styre þíne fingras swilce þū wrítan wille, Tech. ii. 128, 21 Mín tunge ys gelīcost þæs wrīteres feþere þe hraðost wrīt *lingua me calamus scribae velociter scribentis*, Ps. Th. 44, 2. Swylce sum getýd we sum meterves mid his feðere āwríte, Angl. viii. 317, 23. v. plūm-feþei

**feþer-bǽre** ; *adj. Feathered :*—Feþerbǽre *plumigeram*, Germ. 390, 44

**feþer-berende.** *Substitute :* feþer-berend, es ; *m. A feather bearer, a feathered creature :*—Feþerberend *penniger*, Wrt. Voc. ii. 66, 3c

**feþer-cræft.** *For* ʼ Som. Ben. Lye ʼ *substitute :* — Feþercræft *plumario* (*arte plumaria*, Ald. 15, 26), Wrt. Voc. ii. 77, 15.

**feþer-geweorc.** *Substitute for passage :*—Besiwed feðergeweor *opere plumario*, Wrt. Voc. ii. 63, 45.

**feþer-hama.** *Add :*—His geðōht is swiftra ðonne xii ðusend hāligra gāsta, ðeáh ðe ānra gehwylc gāst hæbbe synderlīce xii feðer homan, and ānra gehwylc feðerhoma hæbbe xii windas, Sal. K. p. 152 1–2. Feðrhoman *talaria*, Wrt. Voc. ii. 122, 4. [*O. Sax.* feðer-hamc Cf. *Icel.* fjaðr-hamr, ālptar-, vals-hamr. See the story of Loki's captur when flying with Freyja's *vals-hamr : see also* Grmm. D. M. pp. 327 425 (trans.).] v. fiþer-hama.

**feþor-byrste.** v. fiþer-byrste.

**fēþre** ; *adj. Laden, loaded :*—Sēlre byð oft fēðre þænne oferfēðr *better is often loaded than overloaded ; meliora plura quam gravi honera fiunt*, Angl. ii. 373. v. fōþor ; fēþre.

**fēþrian** ; *p.* ode *To become feathered, be fledged :*—Feðriað *plumescu (grandia membra miħi* (the ostrich) *corpore denso*, Ald. 255, 26), An. O 26, 27.

**fēþrian** ; *p.* ode *To load.* [þu hauest imaked uoðer to heui uort uedren mide þe soule, A. R. 140,] v. ge-fēþrian ; fēþre.

**feþriht** ; *adj. Feathered, winged :*—Feðrihtæ foet *pennati pedes*, M p. 9, 19.

**fēþu.** *l.* (?) fēþa, *but see* feþer, II a.

**fēþung**, e ; *f. Going on foot, walking :*—Weard his cneów ālēfe swā þæt hē mid criccum his fēðunge underwreðode . . . Hē cwæð : ʼ ] wolde ðíne ðēnunge sylf gearcian, gif ic mē mid fēðunge ferian miihte Hml. Th. ii. 134, 23–32. v. fēþan.

**fetian.** *Dele* ʼ fet,ʼ *and passage from* Prov. Kmbl., *and add :*—H wæter fette, Hml. S. 6, 14. Man him fette sumne dǽl þæs meóses, 2( 36. Þæt Ceaddes sáuwl cōme of heofonum and fette his brōþor sāwle t heofonum, Shrn. 59, 19 : Chr. 1049 ; P. 168, 38. Hí mæte (mete, *v. l* and mādmas ofer L. mīla him fram sǽ fættan (fetton, *v. l.*), 1006 P. 137, 12. Feta, gif ðū dyrre, æt ðus heaðuwērigan hāre byrnan, Val 2, 16. Fetige hē him mā, Solil. H. 1, 10. Fetod, fettad, feoto *arcessitus*, Txts. 42, 103 : Wrt. Voc. ii. 7, 31. [v. *N. E. D.* fet. C *Icel.* feta *to step, find one's way.*] v. fatian.

**fēt-lāst.** v. fōt-lāst : fexe. v. síd-fexe : fic. *Add : v.* ficol, fician

**fíc.** *Add :* I. *a fig :*—Hē sæh treów fices *videns fici arborem*, M R. 21, 19 : 24, 32. Of unberendum trēes fíc de *sterili arbori fic* Lk. p. 8, 3. Fīca *cariarum*, An. Ox. 8, 209. II. *a fig-tree :*— Forwisnade se fíc *arefacta est ficulnea*, Mt. R. 21, 19, 20. Be fíce ( *ficulnea*, 21. [*Hec ficus* a fyke or a fykes, Wrt. Voc. i. 227, col. (15th cent.).]

**fíc-æppel.** *Add :*—Fícæppel *carica*, Wrt. Voc. ii. 21, 61 : *dactulu* 83, 53 : 26, 63. Fīcæppla *caricarum*, An. Ox. 2, 259. Fīcapplan 3845. Hwā gaderað fīcæppla of brēmelum?, Hml. Th. ii. 406, : [*O. H. Ger.* fig-apful *carica.*]

**fíc-beám.** *Add :*—Se fíicbeám, Past. 337, 6. Fícbeám (-beóm, R *ficus*, Mk. L. 11, 21. Ðone fícbeóm *fici arborem*, . . . fícbeá *ficulnea*, Mt. L. 21, 19. Tíd ðāra fícbeáma (-beóma) *tempi*

icorum, Mk. L. 11, 13. Fýcbeámas *ficos*, Mt. L. 7, 16. [*O. H. Ger.* ig-boum *ficus, carix, ficulnea.*]

**fícian** *to deceive.* [Cf. *N. E. D.* fike.] v. be-fícian; ficol, ge-fíc, fácen.

**ficol.** *Substitute: Crafty, deceitful, false:*—Ficol *versipellis*, Kent. Gl. 493. Ne beón gē nāðor ne tō swicole ne tō ficole ne leáse ne ýðerfulle, Wlfst. 40, 4. Sume weorðað swicole and swǽslíce ficole and ūtan getrýwðum forscyldgode on synnan, 82, 3. [v. *N. E. D.* fickle.] v. fíc.

**fíc-treów.** *Add:*—Fictreów *ficus*, An. Ox. 56, 362. Hē (*Adam*) ibyrgde ðā forbodenan fictreówes blǽda, Sal. K. p. 182, 34. Under ðǽm ficbeóme † fictrēe *sub ficu*, Jn. R. 1, 48.

**fiell.** v. fill: **fíen.** v. feu: **fíend-wíc.** *l.* fierd-wíc: **fíer[r]** *farther.* r. feor: **fíer[r]** *distance.* v. fir[r]: **fíerd.** v. fird: **fíeran.** v. firsn: **fíerst.** v. first.

**fíf.** *Add:* I. adjectival. (1) uninflected:—Fíf gēra fæc *quinquennium*, An. Ox. 3035: B. 545. Nam hē fíf stānas, Bl. H. 31, 17. (1 a) with pronoun or indefinite numeral:—Þā fíf dysegan, Mt. 25, 3. Wē onféngon þā hālgan fíf seonoþas, Bd. 4, 17; Sch. 433, 5. (1 b) as part of an ordinal:—Þisne fíf and twēntigoðan sealm, Ps. Th. 25, arg.: 35, arg. (2) inflected:—Fífo ídlo *quinque fatuae*, Mt. L. 25, 3. Stearas fífe (fífo, L.) cōmun *quinque passeres ueniunt*, Lk. R. 12, 6. Mōnoðas fífe, 1, 24. Fífo cræftas, Mt. L. 25, 15: Jn. L. R. 4, 18. Cuuhoru bið twēgea pæninga wurð. Oxan tægl bið sciłł. weorð; cuus bið fífa [peninga], Ll. Th. i. 140, 3. Weorc crístes mǽl fífo, Lch. iii. 56, 8. (2 a) with pronoun or indefinite numeral adjective:—Þā fífe dysige, Mt. R. 25, 3. Of ðǽm hlāfum fífum, Jn. L. 6, 26. Sē ðe þā fíf pund underfēng gestrýnde ōðre fífe (fífo, L., féfe, R.), Mt. 25, 16, 20. II. substantival. (1) inflected:—Ealle þā syndon āgangen buton þǽm ānum . . . fífe þāra syndon āgongen, Bl. H. 117, 36. Fífe (fífo, L.) þāræ wērun dysige and fífe snottre, Mt. R. 25, 2. Fífum *lustris*, Wrt. Voc. ii. 92, 41. Nime fífe and beó him sylfa syxta, Ll. Th. i. 394, 5. (1 a) *in a series a member whose number is five or a multiple of five:*—Hū mon scule blōdlǽse on þāra six fífa ǽlcum on mōnðe forgān, Lch. ii. 146, 19: 148, 2. (2) uninflected and with a multiple of ten where the number is treated (a) as singular:—On þǽm geáre bið þreó hund daga and fíf and syxtig daga, Bl. H. 35, 22. Þǽr on ríme forborn fíf and hundseofontig hǽðnes herges, Jul. 588. (b) as plural:—Gif þǽr beóð fíf and feówertig rihtwísra, Gen. 18, 28. Cf. feówer *for construction.*

**fífalde,** an; *f. A butterfly:*—Fífaldae, uíualdra, fiffalde *papilio*, Txts. 86, 768. Fiffalde, Wrt. Voc. ii. 67, 56. *Spalagius, musca venenosa est, aut similis fifeldae, (saxonice),* Txts. 109, 1134. Fífaldae *animalus*, 115, 135. [Cf. *O. L. Ger.* fifaldra *papilio: O. H. Ger.* fífalter (-tra).]

**fífel-dór.** *l.* -dor, *and add:* v. Grmm. D. M. 239 (trans.).

**fífele?** *Substitute:* fífele, an; *f. A buckle:*—Sigel oððe hringe, fífele *fibula*, Wrt. Voc. ii. 35, 42. [From Latin.]

**fíf-feald.** *Add:*—Fíffealde *quinas*, Angl. xiii. 424, 848.

**fíf-fealde.** v. fífalde.

**fíf-fétede;** *adj. Having five feet (of a verse):*—Mid fíffétedum *brachicatalectico*, An. Ox. 130.

**fíf-lǽppede;** *adj. Having five laps or lobes:*—Hió (*the liver*) biþ fíflǽppedu (cf. sió lifer hæfð fíf læppan, 198, 1), Lch. ii. 160, 12.

**fíf-leáf,** es; *n.:* -leáfe, an; *f. Substitute:* fíf-leáfe, an; *f.*

**fíf-nihte;** *adj. Five days old:*—Sē on V-nihtne mōnan bið geboren gung hē gewítað, Lch. iii. 160, 22.

**fífta.** *Add:* (1) ordinal:—Þurh fíftan fótes tōdāl *per pentimemerem*, An. Ox. 203. Fíftan síþe, Bl. H. 47, 18. Þý fíftan dæge, 73, 4. (1 a) genealogical:—Fífta fæder *atavus*, Wrt. Voc. i. 72, 23. Fífte fæder *tritavus*, 51, 59. Fífte mōder *tritavia*, 60. Fífta sunu *adnepos*, ii. 8, 23. Fífte dohter *adneptis*, i. 51, 76. (1 b) in combination with another numeral:—Sē wæs fífta eác feówertigum fram Agusto, Bd. 1, 13; Sch. 36, 9. (2) fractional:—On þām fíftan dǽle healfum (cf. ofer þone teóþan dǽle, 25), Bt. 18, 1; F. 62, 22. Þone fíftan dǽl ealra hiora eorðwæstma, Ors. 1, 5; S. 34, 23.

**fíf-teóþa.** *Add:*—Sē fífteóða *quintus decimus*, Ælfc. G. Z. 283, 3. Under þām fífteóðan (-teogeþan, -tigeþan, -tegþan, -teþan, *v. ll.*) geáre, Bd. 4, 17; Sch. 430, 22. Gēr ðe fíftegða (ðió fífteiðe, L.) *anno quinto decimo*, Lk. R. 3, 1. Ðió fífteiðo, Lk. p. 4, 6. On þone fíftegðan dæg, Shrn. 104, 12.

**fíftig.** *Add:* I. substantival. (1) alone, (a) as a neuter singular with adj. inflection (?):—Wæs ālesen fíftig cista, Exod. 229. Þā mǽstan beóð fíftiges elna lange, Ors. 1, 1; S. 18, 6: Gen. 1307: B. 3042. Sē bið on fíftegum (or *pl.?*) mancessa, Past. 9, 1. (a a) distributive:—Hig sǽton hundredum and fíftegum (ðerh fíftigum, L. R. *per quinquagenos*), Mk. 6, 40. (β) as plural:—Gif on þǽre byrig beóð fíftig rihtwísra manna *si fuerint quinquaginta justi in civitate*, Gen. 18, 24. Þás fíftig daga sind ealle gehālgode, Hml. Th. i. 312, 22. Fíftiga ealdor *quinquagenarius*, Wrt. Voc. i. 18, 14. Under fíftiga (fíftigan, *v. l.*) cyninga ríce *per quinquaginta reges*, Ors. 1, 10; S. 42, 4. Fýr forbærnde þā fíftig manna, Hml. S. 18, 250. (γ) uncertain:—Þæs ymbe fíftig daga (*but* cf. *l.* 22 *v. supra*), Hml. Th. i. 312, 10: Bl. H. 133, 14. Án sceolde

fíf hund penega and ōðer fíftig (fífteiþ, L.), Lk. 7, 41. Writ fíftig (fíftih, L.), 16, 6. (2) with other numerals, and the number treated (*a*) as singular:—Þæra wæs hundteóntig and ðreó and fíftig, Jn. 21, 11. (β) as plural:—Wǽron gesomnode hundteóntig and fíftig bisceopa, Bd. 4, 17; Sch. 433, 14. Hē wífa ānes wana ealra fíftig forhte gefreoðode, An. 1042. (γ) uncertain:—Hundteóntiges fótmǽla and fíftiges lange, Nar. 36, 12. (3) *a set of fifty psalms:*—Þ ǽlc gegilda gesinge ān fíftig oþþe begite gesungen, Ll. Th. i. 236, 37: 222, 19. Ǽghwilc Godes þíow gesinge twā fíftig fore his sāwle, Cht. Th. 461, 27. II. adjectival. (1) alone:—Fíftig mancus goldes, Ll. Th. i. 414, 19. Árian þǽre stōwe for þām fíftigum rihtwísum, Gen. 18, 24. Fíftigum cempum *L. militibus*, Rtl. 193, 17: Sal. 70. (2) with other numerals:—Twā and fíftig wucan, Lch. iii. 246, 11. Mid fíftigum sciłł. and hundteóntegum, Ll. Th. i. 70, 19. II a. as ordinal:—Wē sceolon þone fíftigan sealm syngan, oððe þone .xxiiii., Ll. Th. ii. 426, 25. III. helping to form ordinals:—Sē wæs feórða eác fíftigum fram Agusto *ab Augusto quinquagesimus quartus*, Bd. 1, 23; Sch. 47, 21. IV. uncertain constructions:—Wealh gafolgelda .cxx. sciłł . . . ðeówne .lx.; somhwelcne fíftegum; weales hýd twelfum, Ll. i. 118, 4. Fíftig monna lātwu *quinquagenarius*, Rtl. 193, 17. Fíftig fæðma wíd, Scrd. 21, 4.

**fíftigoþa.** *Add:* (1) alone:—Fram þām fíftigoðan (-tiog-, *v. l.*) geáre, Gr. D. 102, 23. On ðǽm fíftegoðan psalme, Past. 425, 25. Þysne fíftigoðan sealm, Ps. Th. 50, arg. (2) with units:—On ðǽm feówer and fíftiogoðan psalme, Past. 429, 3.

**fíftig-wintre;** *adj. Fifty years old:*—Gyt þū ne eart fíftigwintre *quinquaginta annos nondum habes*, Jn. 8, 57.

**fíftíne-nihte;** *adj. Fifteen days old:*—On xv-nihte mōnan, Lch. iii. 180, 1.

**fíftíne-wintre;** *adj. Fifteen years old:*—Ðā hē wæs fífténewintre, Bl. H. 213, 1. Þ man nǽune gingran mann ne slóge þonne xv-wintre man, Ll. Th. i. 240, 28.

**fíf-týne.** *l.* -tíne, *and add:* (1) with a noun in agreement:—Þæt wǽron fíéftiéne hund þūsend monna, Ors. 3, 9; S. 128, 22. Fíftēna stōd deóp se drencefłōd moannes elna, Gen. 1397. Ofer fýftýne furlang (suælce spyrdum fíftēnum, L., swelce spyrdas fíftēne, R.) *quasi stadiis quindecim*, Ju. 11, 18. Fíftēne geár, Ors. 1, 10; S. 44, 19. (2) governing a noun:—Ymb seofon hund wintra and V-tiéne, Ors. 1, 14; S, 58, 11. Sē wæs fíftēne geára, Shrn. 84, 12.

**fíf-wintre.** *Add:*—Fífwintre swígan *quinquennem taciturnitatem*, An. Ox. 4144.

**fígan** *to fry.* v. ā-fígen: **figel?** *Dele, and see* fífele.

**fíhle,** es; *m.? n.? l.* fihl, es; *m., and add:*—Fihles ðæs alde *panni ueteris*, Mk. p. 2, 16.

**fíht (?)** *a mane:*—Deórenum fihtum *ferinis jubis*, Wrt. Voc. ii. 148, 9.

**fíhtan** *to moisten.* v. fýhtan: **fíhte-horn.** v. fyhte-horn.

**fíhtling,** es; *m. A warrior:*—Fihtling *bellator*, Wrt. Voc. ii. 125, 39. Sē bið unearh fihtling, Lch. iii. 158, 11. Se stranga Godes fyhtling (wiga, *v. l.*) *fortis praeliator Dei*, Gr. D. 110, 13.

**fíht-wíte.** *Substitute:* fíht-wíte (fihte-, fyht-, fyhte-), es; *n.* (1) *the fine paid to the crown for fighting (and slaying);* cf. Ll. Th. i. 66, 7: 106, 1:—Gif man ofslægen weorðe . . . on .xxi. nihtan gylde man þā manbóte, þæs on .xxi. nihtan þ fyhtwíte (fyhto-, *v. l.*), Ll. Th. i. 174, 28. Se fyhtwíte and manbóte. Ic nelle þ ǽnig fyhtewíte oþþe manbót forgifen sý, 248, 20. On Denalage se cynincg āh fyhtewíta (fihtwíte, *v. l.*) and fyrdwíta, 384, 5. (2) *the revenue derived from, or the right to receive, such fines:*—Se wagnscilling gonge tō þæs cyninges handa . . . ah elles ge landfeoh ge fihtewíte . . . ge ǽlc þæra wónessa þe tō ǽnigre bóte gebyrie, þ hit āge healf þǽre cyrcean hláford, Cht. Th. 328, 16. Ic habbe gegeofen . . . Ælfwine abbod intó Ramesége saca and sócna . . . fihtwíte and ferdwíte, 421, 31: 411, 31.

**fiil, fíl.** v. feól.

**fild;** *adj. l.* filde, *and see* fild-burne, -denu; ge-filde.

**fild,** es; *m.* (1) *a fold, plait, wrinkle:*—On fyld *in rugam*, An. Ox. 34, 1. Fyldas *uolumina*, i. *reuolutiones*, 3746. (2) *fold* (multiplicative):—Gē dōþ hine sunu helles twǽm fældum (*duplo*) māre þonne eów, Mt. R. 23, 14. v. feald.

**-fildan.** v. ge-, geþic-, manig-, twi-, þri-fildan.

**fild-burne** (-a?), an; *f. (m.?) A stream in a plain (?):*—Of ðǽm aldan felde . . .; swā ondlang bróces on ðone gemǽrhagan; ofer fild-burnan, C. D. iii. 393, 27.

**fild-denu (?)** *a valley with a flat bottom (?):*—Andlang bróces on fildena wyllan, C. D. iii. 15, 30. Of hlǽwe on fildena weg; andlang weges on ðone ealdan ford, 289, 3. Ondlong longan hylles on fildena weg; ðonan on holan dene, 400, 15. Tō fildene lane uppende, 410, 20. Andlang dene on fildena wuduweg, vi. 137, 10. v. feld-denu.

**filde.** v fild; *adj.*

**fild[e]-stól,** es; *m. A folding seat, camp-stool:*—Fyldestól (fælde-, *v. l.*) *cliothedrum, sellam plectibilem*, Hpt. 31, 10, 195. Gif þū fyldstól habban wille, þonne clǽm þū þíne handa tōgædere and wege hí þām

gemete þe þū dēst þonne þū hīne fyalden wylt, Tech. ii. 122, 20. [Cf. N. E. D. fald-stool. O. L. Ger. feldi-stôl clithedra.]

**fileþe** hay:—Hī swȳþe hraþe forséariað swā fileþe sicut foenam velociter arescent, Ps. Th. 36, 2. ¶ the word occurs in compound forms in the charters:—Tō filedléaȝe forda, C. D. v. 394, 12. In filiðléaȝe, iii. 383, 8. On ðā āc on filedcumbe, vi. 43, 21. Of Stokwei, tō Filed-hamme, iii. 445, 29. Also (?) in:—Andlang dīces ūp on fileþa, C. D. B. ii. 519, 11.

**filging**, e; f. Fallow land:—Faelging occa, Wrt. Voc. ii. 115, 67. Fylging, 62, 67. Faelging naualia (l. noualia), Wrt. Voc. ii. 114, 77. v. fealh.

**filian**, p. ode To file, rub with a file:—Fīliende fricans (lima . . . fricans informe metallum, Ald. 252, 22), Wrt. Voc. ii. 38, 10. [O. H. Ger. fīlôn limare.]

**filican** ?:—On filican slǣd, Cht. E. 389, 7: fīliende. v. fīlian.

**fill**, fiell, es; m. I. a fall from a higher to a lower point, or from an erect position:—Engel hēt þæt trēow ceorfan and þā wildeór onweg fleón . . . þonne his fyll cōme, Dan. 513. Fǣll hūses ruina domus, Mt. L. 7, 27. Faell, Lk. L. 6, 49. Feallo torres ruinâ torris, p. 8, 3. Fylle lapsu, An. Ox. 26, 44. Geswell þe wyrþ of fylle oððe of slege, Lch. ii. 6, 27. Hē on fylle weard he slipped and fell, B. 1544. Hē næs ācweald ðurh ðām héalican fylle (the fall from the pinnacle of the temple), Hml. Th. ii. 300, 20. Mid þȳ fylle (hryre, v. l. ruina) ðæs wāges, Gr. D. 125, 5. þā getimbru wǣron gehrorene gelōmlīce mid fyllum (ruinis), 134, 12. Se druncena . . . þurh fyllas bewylewud ebriosus . . . per precipitia deuolutus, Scint. 107, 14. I a. figurative:—Hē gǣd on ðone weg, ac hē nāt on hwæt hē gǣd, ac hē wird suīðe raðe on fielle (citius corruit), Past. 287, 17. II. fall in battle, death, destruction:—Manna fyll and eác horsa, Chr. 1056; P. 186, 33. Fyll and feorhcwealm, Gen. 1103: 2062: B. 2912. Micel here for þæs cynges fielle fléah, Ors. 3, 7; S. 118, 7: 3, 10; S. 138, 13. Mid heora twēgea fielle duorum morte, 6, 36; S. 294, 6. On his fylle, Hml. S. 26, 161. Līf edniwe, feorh æfter fylle, Ph. 371. Eal gesceaft cwīðdon cyninges fyll, Kr. 56. III. a fall in a moral sense:—Hī ðone fiell fleóð ðǣre synne, Past. 399, 17. v. fǣr-fill; ge-fill; and see fell, fyl, fyll in Dict. for other passages.

**fillan**. Take here passages given under fyllan, and add: I. to cause to fall to the ground, to pull down, throw down. (1) lit.:—Hē cwealde Crīstne men, circan fylde, Jul. 5. Hē sum deófolgild brǣc and fylde . . . hié mid heora handum þā īdlan gyld fyldon, Bl. H. 223, 15, 21. Hēt ic ceorfan ðā bearwas and þone wudu fyllan jubeo cedi nemus, Nar. 12, 19. (1 a) to make bellows collapse by driving the air out (?):—Ic wiht (bellows) geseah . . . þegn folgade . . . and micel hæfde gefēred þǣr hit felde (when he made the swollen bellows subside?), Rä. 38, 4. (2) fig. to be a stumbling-block to:—Gif honde þīne fælleþ þec, Mt. R. 18, 8. I a. to cast into:—Hē ūs on þæt fȳr fylde, Gen. 747. II. to fell, destroy:—Þonne ic hiora fȳnd fylde and hȳnde ad nihilum inimicos eorum humiliassem, Ps. Th. 80, 13. Ic fylde mid folmum fæder Enoses, Gen. 1096. Hūðe āhreddan and hæleð fyllan, 2113. II a. to put down error, &c.:—Hē deófulgild tōdrāf and gedwolan fylde, An. 1690. v. wind-filled.

**fille**. Add:—Fil[le] cespillum, An. Ox. 56, 38. Fille and finul, Lch. iii. 36, 30. Genim reáde fillan, 40, 17. v. wudu-fille, cerfille.

**fillen** (?), e; f. A dropping:—Biþ se þost hwīt and micel gif þū hine nimest and gaderast æt fylne, þonne ne biþ hē tō unswēte tō gestincanne, Lch. ii. 48, 14.

**fille-seóc**. Take here examples under fylle-seóc, and add:—Fylleseóc commitialis, Wrt. Voc. i. 19, 26.

**fille-seócness**. For examples see fylle-seócness.

**fille-wærc**, es; m. Epilepsy:—Þ deáh wiþ heortece and wiþ fellewærce Lch. ii. 194, 31. v. fylle-, felle-wærc in Dict.

**fill-wērig**. v. fyl-wērig: **film, filma**. Dele, and see next word.

**filmen**. Take here examples given in Dict. under fylmen. The gender varies, with meaning foreskin it is masc. or neut., membrane fem. I. of animal material, skin, membrane, scale:—Filmen (filṁ, MS.) omentum, centipillium, Wrt. Voc. ii. 130, 46. Se milte hæfð þynne filmene . . . and sió filmen biþ þeccende þā wambe, Lch. ii. 242, 14–17. Be þæs miltes filmene, 166, 13. Filmena membra[na]rum (laterum membranarum tenui velamine facta, Ald. 142, 6), Wrt. Voc. ii. 89, 51: 57, 4. On þǣre lifre on þām filmenum, Lch. ii. 204, 18, 5. Þrié filmenua on bridda wambum, 228, 27. II. of vegetable, skin, shell, husk:—Fylmenum cittis, i. tenuis pellis inter grana, An. Ox. 464. Fylminum, 11, 63. Filmenum, Wrt. Voc. ii. 75, 75. Vilmenum, æþelscealum ymb ðā cyrnlu, 17, 69. [These four are glosses on:—Mala punica cittis granisque rubentibus referta, Ald. 8, 15.] III. a crack (?):—Filmena oþþe cinena rimarum (capisterium rimarum fragmine ruptum, Ald. 159, 29), Wrt. Voc. ii. 92, 5. [O. Frs. filmene; f. skin.] v. felma.

**fin** a fin. Add:—Finnum squamis (the word occurs in a riddle on the cuttle-fish (loligo), Ald. 251, 28), An. Ox. 26, 10.

**fin** a heap. Substitute: fīn, e; f. (1) a heap of wood:—Fīn lignarium, ligneum, Txts. 110, 1186. Fīne strue (pyram strue stipitum in edito constructam, Ald. 34, 11), An. Ox. 7, 157 : 8, 125. (1 a) a wooden hut (?):—Fīn cella lignaria, Txts. 110, 1169. (2) a heap of other material:—On cyniges limfīne; of ðǣre fine, C. D. B. i. 518, 41. [O. H. Ger. [witu-]uīna.] v. līm-, wudu-fīn.

**fīna**. l. fīna, and add:—Fīna marsopicus (pīna marpicus), Txts. 78, 648. Fīna vel hiȝrae picus, 88, 808 : sturfus, 99, 1938 : marsopicus, Wrt. Voc. ii. 55, 49 : Hpt. 33, 240, 41. Tō fīnan mǣdwum, C. D. iii. 386, 1.

**finc**. Add:—Finc fringella, Txts. 62, 423 : cintus, Wrt. Voc. ii. 22, 74. On finces stapel, C. D. iii. 135, 20. v. ceaf-finc.

**findan**. Add : I. to come upon by chance or in the course of events. (1) to come across, meet with a person or thing:—Ðū findst (fintst, v. l.) wið hwone ðū meaht flītan contra quos valeatis vos extendere, semper invenitis, Past. 331, 5. Ic gehātan dearr þæt þū þǣr trēowe findest, Bo. 11. Ne þǣr mon his feónd findeð, Bl. H. 105, 1. Ic gōdne funde beáȝa bryttan, B. 1486. Iudas funde, þā ðā hē fram fyrde gecyrde, gold and seolfor and fela óðre herereáf, Hml. S. 25, 358. Līg eall fornam þæt hē grēnes fond, Gen. 2549. Nō wē oferhyȝdu ānes monnes māran fundon, Gū. 241. Þā fundon hié óþre flocrāde, Chr. 917; P. 98, 4. Nāmon hī menn, and swā hwæt swā hī findan mihtan, Chr. 1046; P. 166, 16. Ðā dysegan menn nāne lustbærnesse nabbað ðā sóþan ȝesǣlþa tō sēcanne, ac wēnaþ þ hī·mæȝon hī on þissum deádlicum ðingum findan, Bt. 32, 3; F. 118, 25. Bān bið funden on heortes heortan, Lch. i. 338, 5. Gestreón swilc þǣr funden wæs, Dan. 66. Ic eom wīde funden, Rä. 28, 1. Gif him cwicum sié funden þ hē ǣr stæl, Ll. Th. i. 50, 22. (1 a) with a complement to the object:—Hȳ æt hām findað witode him wiste, Rä. 44, 8. Hē dryhten sīnne dríorigne fand ealdres æt ende, B. 2789. Fleáȝ fugla cyn þǣr hȳ feorhnere witude fundon, Gū. 890. (1 b) to find in records:—Werþeóde on gewritum findað dōma ȝehwilcne, Exod. 519. ¶ where the record is the memory:—Findan on ferhðe, An. 1487: El. 641 : 632. (2) to find (and carry off) something hidden or hitherto unnoticed:—Swelce hwā nū delfe eorþan and finde goldhord . . . Gif nán mon ǣr þ gold þǣr ne hȳdde, þonne ne funde hé hit nó; forðȳ hit næs nā weás funden, Bt. 40, 6 ; F. 242, 5–9. Seó bóc on þǣre ciricean funden wæs, Bl. H. 197, 26. Syððan hē ǣrest weard feásceaft funden, B. 7. Tō fundenes cildes fóstre, Ll. Th. i. 118, 18. (3) to obtain, find favour, credit, &c.:—Hié þǣr helpe findað, godcunde gife, El. 1032. Ic fultum fand venit auxilium mihi, Ps. Th. 120, 1. Wǣre hié þǣr fundon, Exod. 387. Hī æt þām bisceope bōte fundon, El. 1217. Þ heó funde and ābǣde æt þæs Scyppendes mildheortnesse, þ heó fram swā miclum cwylmnessum onlȳsed beón mōste ut apud misericordiam conditoris inpetraret, se a tantis cruciatibus absolui, Bd. 4, 9; Sch. 396, 8. (4) to meet with, experience, be exposed to, find difficulty, &c.:—þǣr þū gúðe findest, An. 1351. Hē þǣr nāht ne funde þæs þe him þe bet wǣre he met with no success, Chr. 1072; P. 208, 15. Mīne aldorlege, swā mē ǣfre weard oððe ic furðor findan sceoide, Dan. 140. Se folctoga findan sceolde earfoðsīðas, 656. (5) to find, discover on inspection or consideration:—Ic andette þ ic hæbbe funden duru þǣr ǣr ic ǣr geseah āne lytle cynan, Bt. 35, 3; F. 158, 27. (5 a) with complement to the object or infin.:—Sume ic funde būtan Godes tācne, þā ic slōg, Jul. 490. Ic on bōcum fand cȳðan þe þām sigebeácne, El. 1255. Hē in þæt būrȝeteld nēðde, funde on bedde blācne licgan his goldȝifan, Jud. 278 : B. 118 : 2270. Hī eódon wundur sceáwian, fundon on sande sāwulleásne hlinbed healdan þone þe him hringas geaf, 3033. Carcernes duru hī opene fundon, An. 1078. (6) to find by trial or experience, find an object (to be) so and so:—Hine nǣnig man yrne ne funde, Bl. H. 223, 34. Sē fand wæccendne wer wīges bīdan, B. 1267. Symle hȳ Gūðlāc gearone fundon, Gū. 885: 861. þæt hē ūs gearwe finde, Bl. H. 83, 1. Ic wundrige hwī wīse men swā swīþe swuncen mid þǣre sprǣce, and swa litel ȝewis fundon, Bt. 41, 4; F. 250, 20. Nō hī findan meahton æt þām ædelinge, þæt hē þone cynedōm cíósan wolde, B. 2373. Eádiglicre funden, Seel. 132. Wace beóð ðā hirdas funden þe nellað þā heorda . . . bewerian, Wlfst. 191, 7. II. with the idea of search or effort. (1) to discover or obtain by searching:—For þī ne fint ǣlc mon þ hē sēcþ, for ðȳ hē hit on riht ne sēcþ. Gē sēcaþ þǣr ȝē findan ne magan, Bt. 33, 2; F. 122, 29. Heó wyrte sēceð, ā heó þā findeð, Rä. 35, 6 : 85, 26. Gē gold on treówum ne sēcaþ, ne finde ȝē hit nó, Bt. 32, 3; F. 118, 9. Se forma ȝītsere þe ǣrest þā eorþan ongan delfan æfter golde and þā frēcnan deórwurþnessa funde, Bt. 15 ; F. 48, 24. Wīc sceáwian oð þæt hié eorðscræf fundon, Gen. 2595. Eáȝan mīne georne sceáwedun, hwǣr ic treówe funde, Ps. Th. 100, 6. Wīȝan æȝhwilcne þe hē on þām fyrste findan mihte, Exod. 189 : Sal. 8. Hordweard sōhte æfter grunde, wolde guman findan, B. 2294. Gif wē fundne weorðen, Jul. 335. (1 a) to recover something hidden away or lost:—Swā hwā swā ungemyndig sié rihtwīsnesse, gecerre hine tō his gemynde, ðonne fint ðǣr þā ryhtwīsnesse gehȳdde mid þæs līchoman hæfignesse, Bt. 35, 1; F. 156, 11. Hē hine hēt sleán and deópe bedelfan. Hine man funde eft, and ferede hine tō Wincestre, Chr. 1050; P. 170, 4. Sume þā goldhord hī on eorþan āhȳddon þæt hié nǣnig mon siþþan findan meahte, 418; P. 10, 19. Mīn wīsdōm mē forlēt . . .

þin ðeów hæfð nū funden his wīsdōm, Past. 273, 15. (2) *to succeed·in obtaining* something needed or desired, *procure* :—Syle mē ðinne vineard, and ic þē ōðerne finde, Hml. S.18, 174. Þā funde se arcedeácon :t þām cnihte þ̄ hē þone geættredan drync him tō bær, Gr. D. 186, 21. Hē funde fīf mædena him tō . . . tō wunigenne mid him, Hml. S. 35, 51. ſe ord bígde upp tō þām hiltum . . . Him gewearð þ̄ man funde nīwe wurd and nīwne slagan þærtō, 12, 233. Hī fundon leáse gewitan þe orlugon Naboð, 18, 196. Hē biddende wæs þæt hē mōste wið Scipian precan, and wilniende wæs þ̄ hē frið betwux þǣm folcum findan ceolde, Ors. 4, 10; S. 202, 11. Wið swylcan sceatte swylce hē hit þā findæ mihte, C. D. B. i. 544, 5. (2 a) *in law phrases, to find* surety, &c. :—Finde hē borh, Ll. Th. i. 390, 19 : 332, 20. Finde hē verborh, 250, 18. Finde hē him borh, 268, 16. Hē þæs borh finde, ʒ68, 7. Hē him borh finde þ̄ hē swilces geswíce, 346, 13. Finde him ǣlc man þ̄ hē borh hæbbe, 268, 7. Ǣlc preóst finde him .xii. festermen, i. 290, 15. Seó mǣgþ þām hláfordleásan men hláford finden, i. 200, 8. þ̄ hē þone āð funde þe sē gelýfan mihte, 158, 17. (2 b) *to find resolution, courage, heart to* do something, *to bring* oneself *to do* something :—[þæt hē] in hige funde tō gesecganne hwæt se beám bude, Dan. ʒ43. Ic ne mæg findan æt mē seolfum þ̄ ic hine ǣfre geseó, Ors. 5, 12; S. 244, 1. Ne meahte hē æt his hige findan þæt hē Gode wolde þeówian, Gen. 266. Hē uneáðe mihte on his mōde findan þ̄ hē swā leófne freónd fram him lǣtan sceolde, Hml. S. 6, 225 : 31, 394. (3) *to visit, reach* a place :—Hī flugon forhtigende, woldon hāmas findan, Exod. 453. Sceal se gāst cuman symble ymbe seofon niht findan þone līchoman, Seel. 10. (4) *to ascertain, attain by mental effort, discover by study, find* an excuse, a remedy, &c. :—þæt gē blindnesse bōte fundon, Gū. 600. þonne se lǣce þ̄ ongit, þonne mæg hē þone lǣcedōm þe raþor findan, Lch. ii. 204, 22. þū sēcest belādunge, hū þū mage þ̄ findan þ̄ þū ne þurfe mē týdian þæs þe þū gebeden eart, Gr. D. 28, 8. þæt hē andsware ǣnige ne cunne findan on ſerhðe, Met. 22, 52 : Cri. 184. (5) *to come to the knowledge of* a fact, *learn* :—Hē fand þurh lārsmiðas hwǣr āhangen wæs rodora waldend, El. 202. (6) *to ascertain* by calculation :—Swā hit ūðwitan fundan, Men. 166. Sceal wintrum frōd on circule cræfte findan hālige dagas, 67. Nū gē findan magon hāligra tīd, 228. (7) *to devise* a plan, *arrange, settle* :—Gestihtade hē and funde þ̄ hē wolde landfyrde þider gelǣdan and eft on scyplāde hām hweorfan *terrestri itinere illo uenire, sed nauigio redire disponebat*, Bd. 3, 15; Sch. 262, 1. Se biscop funde him tō rǣde þ̄ hī mid fæstene swutelunge bǣdon, Hml. Th. i. 502, 24. Fand, Bl. H. 199, 30 : 201, 25. Funde hē swiðe yfel geðeaht *consilium praebuit*, Past. 423, 15. þysne cræft funde Camillis, Ors. 2, 8; S. 92, 2. Hié þ̄ tō rǣde fundon þ̄ hié ciricean ārǣrdon, Bl. H. 205, 13. Tō rihtan gafole oððe tō ōðran forewyrdan, swā hit man findan mage wið þone arcebisceop, Cht. Th. 355, 26. Hū hē sārlīcast meahte feorhcwale findan, Jul. 573 : B. 3163. Nǣron nō swā endebyrdlīce hiora stede and hiora ryne funden, Bt. 35, 2; F. 158, 3. (8) *to compose* poetry :—Ic þysne sang fand, Ap. 1. Ic sceal nū mid ungerādum wordum gesettan, þeáh ic hwīlum gecōplīce funde *carmina quondam studio florente peregi*, Bt. 2; F. 4, 8. (9) *to determine, provide* as a regulation :—Hié fundon þæt Antigones him sceolde mid firde ongeán cuman, Ors. 3, 11; S. 146, 15 : 148, 7. Fundon Rōmāne þæt hié scipa worhton *Romani classem fabricari praeceperunt*, 4, 6; S. 172, 1. Ðǣr þā eádigan fundon þās dōmas, Ll. Th. i. 36, 12. Swā witan tō rihte finden, 50, 2. Gif hīt bið ðus funden, 440, 17 : 220, 4. Beón þā herigeata swā fundene, 414, 4 note. III. *to supply, provide, furnish* :—Gif mīnra gerēfena hwylc þis dōn nylle, . . . ic finde ōðerne þe wile, Ll. Th. i. 214, 1. Him þæt sōðcyning sylfa findeð *Deus providebit sibi uictimam*, Gen. 2894. Farao him funde lādmen, Gen. 12, 20 : Prud. 1 b : Hml. S. 29, 143. Fundon, Nic. 9, 6; Dan. 88. Find mē nū æftergencgan, Hml. S. 7, 372. þæt man finde of þām yrfe healfes pundes wyrþne sāulsceat, Cht. Th. 534, 12. þæt hī findon betweox him twā scencingcuppan intō beóðern, 536, 6. þ̄ hē him bysceop funde and sealde *episcopum dari*, Bd. 4, 3; Sch. 348, 20. þ̄ man funde ǣnne man, Ll. Th. i. 232, 13. Ðætte hió him funden londāre, C. D. i. 222, 30. Wē him sculon mete findan þā hwīle þe hý mid ūs beóð, Ll. Th. i. 284, 16. Se scīrgerēfa . . . lēt him findan mete and fōddor æt ǣlcan castelle þǣr hī tō cōmon, Chr. 1075; P. 210, 24. v. rǣd-findende.

**findele.** v. fyndel.

**findend**, es; *m. A finder, discoverer* ; repertor, Germ. 391, 9. v. on-findend.

**findig.** *Dele.*

**finding**, e; *f. A device, invention* :—Nān āgenre findincge dōn geþrīst-lǣce *nullus propria adinventione agere presumat*, Angl. xiii. 441, 1081. [*O. H. Ger.* findunga *experimentum.*]

**finger.** *Add* :—Gif se midlesta finger sié of āslegen, sió bōt bið .xii. scitt. Gif se lytla finger bið of āslegen, þām tæl tō bōte .viiii. scitt., Ll. Th. i. 96, 3–8. Lǣt gān þ̄ getæl swā wē nū cwǣdon, þ̄ þū cume tō þæs lǣstan fingres nægle *go on counting as we have just said, till you come to the nail of the little finger*, Angl. viii. 326, 31. Gif man þone lytlan finger of āslæhð, .xi. scitt. gebēte, Ll. Th. i. 16, 12. Mec (*a book*)

fingras feóldon, Rä. 27, 7. Folm mec mæg bifōn and fingras þrý ūtan eáðe ealle ymbclyppan *in media concludor parte pugilli*, 41, 52. Genim cymenes swā micel swā þū mæge mid þrīm fingrum foreweardum geniman, Lch. ii. 180, 20. Æt þām ōðrum tāum healf gelde, eal swā æt þām fingrum ys cwiden, Ll. Th. i. 20, 4. v. scytel-finger.

**finger-æppel.** *Add* :—Tænel gefylledne mid palmtreówa wæstmum þe wē hātað fingeræppla, Hml.-S. 23 b, 662. Fingerapplu *palmeti*, Hpt. Gl. 496, 63.

**finger-docce(-a ?)**, an; *f.* (*m. ?*) *A finger-muscle* :—Fingirdoccana (-do[c]cuna, Erf.) *digitalium musculorum*. Txts. 57, 687.

**finger-liþ**, es; *n. A finger-joint* :—Lið ł fingerlið *articulus*, Nap. 79. **-fingre.** v. twi-, þri-fingre: **finig.** v. fynig: **finiht.** *Dele, and see* finiht.

**finol.** *Add* :—Finulae (finugl, Ep. Erf.) *finiculus*, Txts. 63, 880. Finul *finiculis*, Wrt. Voc. ii. 35, 55 : *fenuculum*, 38, 67.

**fint.** v. fynt: **finta.** *For passage under* I *substitute* :—þonne is se finta fægre gedǣled, sum brūn, sum basu, sum blacum splottum searolīce beseted *caudaque porrigitur fulvo distenta metallo, in cujus maculis purpura mista rubet*, Ph. 295,

**firas.** *l.* fīras.

**fird** (faerd, ferd, fierd, fyrd(e) ). *Add* : **I.** in glosses or referring to other than English forces. (1) *an expedition, campaign* :—Faerd (fertd, Erf.) *expeditio*, Txts. 61, 790. Fird, Wrt. Voc. ii. 29, 69. Fird *expeditio*, i. *praeparatio*, 145, 41. Fyrda *expeditionum*, 76, 62 : 29, 70. Firdum *expeditionibus*, 30, 8. Ðā gesægdon Rōmāne Bryttum þ̄ hī nō mā ne mihton for heora gescyldnysse swā gewinnfullicum fyrdum swencte beón, Bd. 1, 12; Sch. 33, 17. (2) *an army* :—Ferd *exercitus*, Wrt. Voc. ii, 145, 41. Hī cōmon tō Mōise þær hē mid þære firde wæs *venerunt ad Moysen et ad omnem coetum*, Num. 13, 27. Cōmon þā fīf cynegas mid firde (*cum exercitibus suis*), Jos. 10, 5. Eneas mid his firde fōr in Italiam, Ors. 1, 11; S. 50, 24. Mid lytelre firde, 3, 7; S. 118, 1. Hē mid firde wæs farende þær Constantinus wæs mid ōþerre fierde, 6, 31; S. 284, 32. Philippus gelǣdde fird on Lǣcedemonie, 3, 7; S. 118, 24. Hē gegaderade fierd *bellum parans*, 6, 31; S. 286, 9. Eóde Porrus mē on houd mid ealle his ferde and dugoþe, Nar. 19, 17. Swylce man fyrde trymme and samnige, Bl. H. 91, 31. Fyrdum *exercitibus*, Wrt. Voc. i. 145, 42. (3) *a camp* :—Ær þām gefeohte, þā hié on firde wǣron, Ors. 4, 1; S. 156, 34. Hannibal bestæl on þone consul, ðǣr hē on firde sætt (*where he was encamped*), 4, 10; S. 198, 12. **II.** used in reference to the English militia. [The military part of the *trinoda necessitas* is variously rendered in Latin charters, e. g. *expeditio*, C. D. ii. 291, 7: *expeditionis profectio*, 352, 1: *expeditionis juvamen (adjuvamen, obsequium, subsidium, auxilium, labor, exercitium)*, 318, 26: 183, 2: 292, 19: iv. 142, 22: 45, 12: v. 181, 29: 327, 25: *exercitus aditus*, v. 259, 18: 283, 23: *bellicae multitudinis additio*, iii. 358, 31: *agonis obsequium*, ii. 268, 27: vi. 166, 17: *agonis militia*, ii. 389, 31. Other forms are more descriptive of the general character or object of the obligation, *regni defensio*, iv. 149, 11: *expeditio popularis*, 74, 17: *communis expeditionis labor*, 98, 8: *communis (rata, justa, si necessitas exigat) expeditio*, v. 102, 6: iv. 35, 27: ii. 362, 18: iv. 115, 24: *hostium expeditio*, iii. 316, 17: *expeditio contra (in) hostes patriae*, iv. 95, 12: 92, 19: *communis publicae rei expeditio*, iii. 194, 33: 242, 34: *expeditio contra hostes*, 245, 11: *communis (publica) contra hostes expeditio*, 232, 26: 246, 14: *generalis expeditionis necessaria societas*, v. 232, 7. Cf. too, *si contingat expeditionem promoueri*, C. D. iii. 301, 13: 319, 36: *expeditionis militia augenda*, v. 234, 17: *cum glomerata sibi alternatim expeditioni compulerit populari commilitonum confligere castra*, iii. 252, 10: iv. 85, 12.] :—Besæt sió fierd hié þær ūtan þā hwīle þe hié þær lengest mete hæfdon. Ac hié hæfdon þā heora stemn gesetenne and hiora mete genotudne . . . þā se cyng wæs þiderweardes mid þære scīre þe mid him fierdedon . . ., sió ōþeru fierd wæs hāmwardes, Chr. 894; P. 85, 22–86, 4. Seó fird, P. 88, 7, 20. Gesomnode man ormǣte fyrde Defenisces folces and Sumorsǣtisces . . . beáh seó Englisce fyrd, 1001; P. 133, 23. Wæs þæs cynges fyrde hindan, 948; P. 112, 30. Cōm seó Centisce fyrde, 999; P. 131, 21. Hē hēt ōðre fyrde ābannan, . . . and his fyrde tōscyfte . . ., seó fyrde eall tōgædre cōm, 1095; P. 231, 21. Sende hē his sunu of þære fierde micle werede, 823; P. 60, 12. Mid West-Seaxna fierde, 851; P. 64, 21. Of þære fierde, ge eác of þǣm burgum, 894; P. 84, 30. Cōm Byrhtnōð ealdorman mid his fyrde, 993; P. 126, 5: 1001; P. 133, 22. Sceóc hē on niht fram þære fyrde him sylfum tō mycelum bismore, 992; P. 127, 16 (cf. Ll. Th. i. 310 below). Ecgbryht lædde fierd, 827; P. 60, 32. Ferde, 605; P. 23, 5. Gegaderode Ælfred cyning his fierd, 894; P. 84, 23. Fird, 905; P. 94, 1. Hēt hē beódan ofer ealle þā fird, 94, 4. Hē sende firde ge of West-Seaxum ge of Mercum, 910; P. 94, 28. Fyrde, 993; P. 127, 27. ¶ regulations concerning the *fird* (see, too, the compounds) :— Gif þisses hwæt gelimpe þenden fyrd ūte sié, hit sié twybōte, Ll. Th. i. 88, 11. Gif hwā būtan leáfe of fyrde gewende þe se cyning sylf on sý, plihte him sylfum . . ., and sē þe elles of fyrde gewende, beó sē .cxx. scill. scyldig, 310, 28–30 (cf. 420, 7). Gif hwā on fyrde griðbryce fulwyrce, þolige

līfes, 408, 22. ¶ an instance of a person receiving and responding to a summons to the *fird* is given in the following:—Gelamp emb þā tīd þæt man beónn ealle Cantware tó wigge tó Holme. þā nolde Sigelm tó wīgge faran mid nānes mannes scette unāgefnum . . . Hē on wīgge āfeallen wæs, Ch. Th. 201, 19–28. ¶ a case of assessment for the *fird*, that of Abingdon, is given in the following:—Expeditionem cum xii. uassallis et cum tantis scutis exerceaut, C. D. i. 272, 2. v. land-, scip-fird.

**fird-esne, -færeld.** v. fyrd-esne, &c., *in Dict.*

**fird-faru.** *Take here* **fyrd-faru,** *and add:*—Frig ælces woruldlican weorces būton đām đe eallum folce gæmēne is, đæt is fyrdfara, sig hit on scipfyrde, sig hit on landfyrde, C. D. iv. 51, 18.

**fird-fōr,** e; *f. Going on the* fird, *military service:*—Ælces þinges freóh būton ferdfōre and walgeweorce and brycgeweorce, C. D. iii. 20, 4.

**fird-geatwe, -gemaca, -gestealla, -getrum, -ham, -hrægl, -hwæt.** v. fyrd-geatwe, &c., *in Dict.*

**firdian.** *Take here passages under* **fierdian, fyrdian,** *and add: To go on an expedition, march, be on active service:*—Swā oft swā hȳ fyrdedon ođđe tó gefeohte woldon, þonne offrodon hȳ heora lāc, Wlfst. 106, 28. (1) *used of a leader:*—Fyrdode (mid fierde férde, *v. l.*) hē him tōgeánes, Chr. 835; P. 63, 15. Đā wearđ se cyning swā gram þ hē wolde eft in fyrdian, and þone eard fordōn, 948; P. 112, 32. (2) *of troops:*—Wæron on þære fyrde fela crīstene menn . . . for þan þe hī sceoldon fyrdrian (fyrdian?) swā swā eall folc dyde, Hml. S. 28, 11. Geánlæhte Lisias fīf and sixtig þūsenda fyrdendra þegena, 25, 363.

**firding (-ung).** *Add:* (1) *military operations, military service, fighting, marching:*—Earfođlic is tó ātellanne seó gedreċednes and seó fyrdung and þ geswinc, Chr. 1056; P. 186, 32. Menn wyrcađ wīghūs him (*elephants*) onuppan, and of đām feohtađ on heora fyrdinge, Hex. 16, 12. Beó đē stille dæglanges đīnre fyrdinge *stop your march for a day,* Hml. Th. ii. 482, 29. Geceás man þā twēgen cnihtas . . . tó þære fyrdunga, Hml. S. 30, 300. Hī lāgon ūte on fyrdinge ongeán þone here, Chr. 1006; P. 136, 16. (1 a) *figurative:*—þā concurrentes gehwyrfađ mid sōđre fyrdunge, þ ys mid fullum gesceáde, Angl. viii. 302, 30. (1 b) *an expedition:*—Se cāsere his fyrdinge gendode, Hml. S. 28, 118. Fyrdincga *expeditionum,* An. Ox. 825. Fyrdunga, 2, 16. Fyrdunga āginne man georne þonne þearf sȳ for gemænelicre neóde, Ll. Th. i. 382, 1. [(1 c) *the right to compel service in the* fird:—Nān man ne haue nān onsting ne geold ne feording, Chr. 975; P. 36, 10.] (2) *militia, troops, armament, military forces:*—Se here férde swā hē sylf wolde, and seó fyrding dyde þære landleóde ælcne hearm *the Danes went as they pleased, and the English levies did their countrymen all kinds of damage,* Chr. 1006; P. 136, 18. Eal seó fyrding tōhwearf *all the troops dispersed,* 1094; P. 229, 30. Sende þa cyning heretogan mid mycelre fyrdinge, Hml. A. 103, 46: 104, 55. ' Hæbbe hē mid him tó þære fyrdincge Jōhannem and Paulum . . . ' Se heretoga férde mid þære fyrdincge, Hml. S. 7, 313, 318: 28, 2: 18, 215, 397. Fyrdungce (ferdungc, Hpt. Gl. 512, 9) *apparatu (duelli),* An. Ox. 4560. Fyrdinga *cateruarum,* 5080. [v. *N. E. D.* ferding.] v. land-, scip-firding.

**fird-lāf,** e; *f. The remnant of an army, the survivors of a battle:*—Þær feóllon đā hæþenan fīf đūsend ofslagene, and Lisias fleáh mid þære fyrdlāfe, Hml. S. 25, 377. Cf here-lāf.

**fird-leás, -leóþ.** v. fyrd-leás, -leóþ *in Dict.*

**fird-lic.** *Take here* **fyrd-lic,** *and add:*—Feohte se cempa on fyrdlicum truman, and wīf hī gehealde þinnan wealle trymmincge, Hml. S. 31, 1098.

**fird-man.** v. fyrd-man *in Dict.:* **firdrian.** v. firdian: **fird-rinc, -sceorp, -scip, -searu,** v. fyrd-rinc, &c., *in Dict.*

**fird-sōcn.** *Take here* **fyrd-sōcn,** *and add: attendance in the* fird, *cf.* sōcn, V:—Hió hit hæbben tó friön ælces þinges būtan wealgeworce and brycgeweorce and ferdsócne, C. D. iii. 255, 18: 256, 17: iv. 263, 6: Cht. E. 242, 17.

**fird-strǣt,** e; *f. A military road, high road:*—Ūp tó cynges ferd-strǣte, C. D. iii. 174, 8. Andlang bróces on đā fyrdstrǣt, 443, 5. Cf. here-strǣt.

**fird-tiber** (?), es; *n. A sacrifice made when military operations were to be undertaken* (?):—Hostia, proprie fyrdtimber (-tiber?) hostia, *properly speaking army-sacrifice* [the glosser might have had the idea which is expressed in the following passage: Đysne yrming (*Mars*) wurđodon þā hæþenan, and swā oft swā hȳ *fyrdedon* ođđe tó gefeohte woldon, þonne *offrodon hȳ heora lāc* tó weorđunge þissum gedwolgode, Wlfst. 106, 26], Wrt. Voc. ii. 43, 48.

**fird-truma, -wēn, -weard.** v. fyrd-truma, &c., *in Dict.*

**fird-weorod.** *Take here* **fyrd-werod,** *and add:*—Firdwerod *phalanx,* Wrt. Voc. ii. 65, 70. Fyrdwerod *falarica,* 33, 48. Ferdwerod *equitatus,* 143, 72.

**fird-weorþ, -wirþe;** *adj.* (1) *fit to serve in the* fird:—Ealle đā men đā beón mótwurđi, ferdwurđi (ferduurđi, 210, 14), C. D. iv. 208, 32. (2) *fit to bear arms, mighty in war:*—Fyrdwyrđe man (*Beowulf*), B. 1316.

**fird-wīc.** *Take here* **fyrd-wīc,** *and add:*—Fyrdwīc ārās *the camp was pitched,* Exod. 129. Ferdwīc *castra,* Ps. Srt. 28, 3. Tó midlunge fyrdwīcana heora *in medio castrorum eorum,* Ps. L. 77, 28. Hē funde

herereáf on þām fyrdwīcum, Hml. S. 25, 360. Wīf ne sceal faran tó wera fyrdwīcum, ac wunian æt hām, 31, 1096. Hē āstyrede his fyrdwīc *movit castra,* Jos. 3, 1. Cf. here-wīc.

**fird-wīsa, -wīse.** v. fyrd-wīsa, -wīse *in Dict.*

**fird-wīte.** *Take here* **fyrd-wīte,** *and add:*—Gif cierlisc man forsitte fyrde, .xxx. sciłł. tó fierdwīte, Ll. Th. i. 134, 10.

**firen.** *Add:*—Hié nænigo firen ne gewundode, ne yfel gewitnes ne wrēgde, ne hié nænig leahter ne drēfde, Bl. H. 161, 33. Firena forgifnes, 163, 23. Ealra fyrena leás, 135, 2. Hē gyt feola cwide firna herede *he spoke of many troubles,* Sat. 160. Þeáh đe hī gelíce fyrene fremmen *etsi similia crimina committant,* Ll. Th. ii. 132, 29. v. deáþ-ñren, Cri. 1207; firnum, fyrenum *in Dict.;* ǣwisc-firen; *adj.*

**firen-dǣd.** *Add:*—Fyrendǣda, māndǣda *flagitia,* i. *vitia,* i. *spurcitia, scelera,* Wrt. Voc. ii. 149, 28. Ic fyrendǣda wræc, deáđcwealm Denigea, B. 1669. [*O. Sax.* firin-dād.]

**firenend.** v. ǣwisc-firenend.

**firen-full.** *Take here* **fieren-full** *in Dict., and add:*—On þære fernlican, [fern]fullum māndǣde *ab originali,* i. *principali piaculo,* i. *peccato,* An. Ox. 2005. Fyrenfulle *flagitiosum,* i. *maculosum,* 875. Fyrenfullum māndǣdum *flagitiosis facinoribus,* 2922: 917. Fyrnfullum, 4, 49. ¶ *used substantively, a sinner:*—Geheald mē wiđ firenfulles folmum *custodi me de manu peccatoris,* Ps. Th. 139, 4. Ne forhtige gē for đæs fyrnfullan þreátum, Hml. S. 25, 260. Gebeda for þone fyrenfullan *preces pro peccatore,* Ll. Th. ii. 136, 27. [*O. H. Ger.* firn-fol *publicanus.*]

**firen-hycga,** an; *m. A person of sinful purpose, an adulterer:*—Fyrenhycga *adulter,* Germ. 389, 24. v. following words.

**firen-hycge** (firenicge?), an; *f. An adulteress, a harlot:*—Fyrnhicge (-hicgce, Hpt. Gl. 475, 29), An. Ox. 2940. Fyrynycgyna *moecharum,* 8, 235.

**firen-hycgend** *a harlot:*—Fyrnhicgiendra *scortarum,* i. *meretricum,* An. Ox. 3327. Fyrnhicgendra, 2, 192. v. preceding words.

**firenian.** *Take* Seel. 103 *under* II, *and add to* I:—Ic firinode *peccavi,* Mt. L. 27, 4. Gif firnige brōđer đīn *si peccaverit frater tuus,* Mt. R. 18, 15. Fyr[n]gende flǣsc *caro luxurians,* Dōm. L. 214. v. ge-firenian.

**firen-leahter** (fyrn-), es; *m. Great sin, crime:*—Bewēpađ eówere fyrnleahtras, Hml. Th. ii. 420, 16. Cf. syn-leahter.

**firen-lic** (fyrn-). *Add: flagitious, criminal, gross, grievous* (of sin):—On þære fernlican māndǣde *ab originali* (i. *principali*) *piaculo* (i. *peccato*), An. Ox. 2005. Fram fyrnlicere synne đæs frumsceapenan mannes, Hml. Th. ii. 260, 15. Hē bæd þone Ælmihtigan for đām ārleásum cwellerum, þæt hē him forgeáfe þā fyrnlican synne, 300, 22. Þā fæstan cnottan fyrnlicra synna, Hml. S. 10, 47. Fyranlicra, C. D. iv. 51, 33. Sume æfter fyrnlicum leahtrum, . . . sume æfter manslihte, tó sōđre dǣdbóte gecyrrađ, Hml. Th. ii. 398, 3. Gefullod fram fyrnlicum synnum, Hml. S. 29, 61. [*O. H. Ger.* firin-līh *cruentus.*] v. next word.

**firenlīce.** *Add: flagitiously, criminally, grossly* (of sinning):—For his fūlum dǣdum þe hē fyrnlīce geedlǣhđ, Hml. Th. ii. 380, 13. Hē geclēnsod hæfde þ hālige templ fram eallum þām fýlđum þe hē fyrnlīce ārǣrde, Hml. S. 25, 538.

**firen-lust.** *Add: sinful pleasure, lust:*—Đǣm oferblīđan oft folgađ firenlusđ (*luxuria*), Past. 189, 5. Fierenlusđ, 7. Firenlust (fieren-, *v. l.*), 310, 3. Ælces unþeáwes and firenlustes (*luxuriae*) full, Bt. 28; F. 100, 28. Se oferæt wierđ oft gehwierfed tó fierenluste *usque ad luxuriam,* Past. 311, 14. Besmitene mid þǣm unclǣnan firenluste, Bl. H. 25, 8: Ors. 1, 2; S. 30, 33. Maria cende on blisse; Eua cende þurh firenlust, Bl. H. 3, 19. Hwær cumaþ þonne his willan and his fyrenlustas?, 113, 1. Đæt hié gehealdađ hira līchoman firenlusta clǣne *studio castitatis,* Past. 41, 14. Fyrenlusta and synlicra dǣda, Wlfst. 56, 6. Mid manigfealdon firenlustum, Ors. 1, 2; S. 30, 16. Þurh firenlustas (fieren-, *v. l.*) *per luxuriam,* Past. 311, 13. [*O. H. Ger.* firin-lust.]

**firenlust-georn;** *adj. Luxurious, voluptuous, lascivious:*—Ne sȳn wē tó gifre ne tó firenlustgeorne ne tó æfestige, Wlfst. 253, 5.

**firen-synn,** e; *f. Gross sin:*—Fyrnsynna fruma (*the devil*), Jul. 347. [*O. Sax.* firin-sundea.] Cf. firen-leahter, -synnig.

**firen-tācn** (?) *a sin-mark, pollution of sin.* (Cf. firen-full *maculosus*). v. next word.

**firen-tācnian** *to pollute with sin:*—Hȳ fyrentācnodon *conpulluerunt,* Ps. Rdr. 288, 21. Cf. tācnian; I.

**firen-þeóf,** es; *m. A robber:*—Firinđeáfum *latronibus,* Rtl. 119, 18.

**firen-weorc.** *Add:* [*O. Sax.* firin-werk.]

**firgen.** *Add:*—Fled þf (fleó þ ?) on fyrgen, hæfde hāl westu *may the pain flee to the hills, and you have your head sound* (? ?), Lch. iii. 54, 17.

**firgen-beorh** (?):—Fisc flóđu āhóf on fergenberig, Txts. 127, 5. (Cf. ? đone feórđan ǣcer æt Feregenne, C. D. iv. 264, 12.)

**firgen-gāt.** *Add:*—Firgengæt, firgingaett *ibices,* Txts. 69, 1037. Firgengǣt, Wrt. Voc. ii. 49, 3. Firgingāta *hibicum,* Txts. 112, 49. Firgengātum *ibices,* Wrt. Voc. ii. 46, 7.

**firht** *divination.* v. friht: **firhþ** *a frith.* v. fyrhþ.

**firlen;** *adj. Take here* **fyrlen;** *adj. in Dict., and add:*—Fyrlen *longinquus,* Ælfc. Gr. Z. 14, 20. Wē cōmon of fyrlenum lande (*de terra*

*onginqua*), Jos. 9, 6. Wē wǣron swīðe fyrlyne, ǣgðer ge stōwlíce ge ꝥurh uncýððe, Hml. Th. i. 106, 21. Him onbugon þā fyrlenan norðnenn, Hml. S. 29, 177. Tó fyrlenum landum, Hml. A. 106, 132 : Jos. 11, 18 : Jud. 6, 2. Of fyrlǣnum scīrum *de longinquis provinciis*, R. Ben. I. 101,12. ¶ On fyrlenum *at a distance :*—On ðǣre hwīle þe hē ꝺu fyrlenum wæs, Hml. S. 6, 47. On fyrlenum wunigende, 35, 26.

**firlen** *distance.* *Take here* **fyrlen** *in Dict., and add :*—Þā gebrōðra þe feorr beóð on geswince and hig ne magon for ðām fyrlene heora cyrcan gesēcan, R. Ben. 78, 5. Þeáh þe hē on fyrlene wǣre, Hml. S. 6, 110 : 18, 174. Sum dǣl þæs folces on fyrlene wæs fram Mathathiam, 25, 237.

**firl[u]** (?) ; *f. Distance :*—Ne þincð ús hwílum se mōna þe brǣdder þe ān scyld for þǣre firle, Solil. H. 66, 32. Se ylca þorn efne swā swā strǣl of bogan ǣstelleþ, swā hē of þām man āfleáh, and on þā fyrle gewāt, Guth. 68, 23.

**firm** *cleansing :*—Hū hē yrde mǣge fyrme gefordian, Angl. ix. 261, 5. v. feorman, firmþ.

**firm**, es ; *m. A fixed contribution* of food :—Leófstān dóð tó þis fermfultum ān sceppe malt . . . tó fyllincge intó þan ealdan fyrme, Nap. 55, 33. v. feorm.

**firmdig.** v. frimdig : **firmetan.** *l.* firmettan, *and add* Cf. frimdig : **firmþ.** v. fiíma, ¶, *and* fyrmþ *in Dict.* : **firn** *old.* v. fyrn : **firr** *distance.* v. ofer-firr : **firr** *farther.* v. feor ; *adv.* : **firra.** v. feor, *adj.*

**firran** ; *p.* de. *Add :*—Hit fyrþ *tollit*, An. Ox. 61, 6. [v. *N. E. D.* far ; *vb.* : *O. H. Ger.* firren : *Icel.* firra.]

**firredness.** v. ā-firredness.

**firsian** ; *p.* ode *To remove to a distance.* *Take here* **feorsian, fyrsian** *in Dict., and add :*—Ne feorsa ðū fultum ðīnne *ne elongaveris auxilium tuum*, Ps. Spl. 21, 18. [v. *N. E. D.* ferse.] v. ā-firsian.

**firsn.** *Take here* **fiersn** *in Dict., and add :*—Fyrsne *calce*, Wrt. Voc. ii. 15, 66. Fyrsnum *calcibus*, 127, 48.

**first** *a rafter.* *Substitute :* **first**, e ; *f. I. a ceiling, inner roof :*—Fierst (first, hróf (firsthróf ?), Corp. Gl.) *laquear*, Txts. 74, 595 : Wrt. Voc. ii. 50, 53. Fyrst, i. 26, 42 : 82, 15. Tóbærst þæs temples wāhryft fram ðǣre fyrste ufan oð ðā flór neoðan, Hml. Th. ii. 258, 3. Firste *laquearia*, Wrt. Voc. ii. 112, 45. Fierste, 50, 54. II. *the ridge-pole of a roof :*—First *tigillum*, Wrt. Voc. ii. 122, 43. Hróf *camara*, first *paratica*, i. 290, 3 (*in a list '* de domibus'). Fyrst on hūse *hoc tignum uel tigillum*, An. Ox. 18 b, 92. Ǣrest man āsmeað þæs hūses stede, and eác man þ timber beheáwð . . . and þā ræftras tó þǣre fyrste gefæstnað, Angl. viii. 324, 9. [v. *N. E. D.* first. *O. H. Ger.* first *culmen, pinna, tolus.*] v. first-hróf.

**first time.** *Take here* **fyrst** *in Dict., and add :* (1) *a space of time :*—Fyrst *intercapedo*, Ælfc. Gr. Z. 275, 7. Huu longes tídes ł huu long firstes *quantum temporis*, Mk. L. 9, 21. Beó hē feówertig nihta on carcerne . . . Gif hē ūt oðfleó ǣr þām fierste, Ll. Th. i. 60, 15. Gewurdon fela martyra on x wintra firste, Ors. 6, 30 ; S. 280, 19. Of fæce, fyrste *intercapedine*, i. spatio, An. Ox. 2967. Fyrst *intercapedinem*, 5428. Ne ētes firste hæfde *nec manducandi spatium habebant*, Mk. R. 6, 31. (2) with idea of postponement, delay, *respite*, (*additional*) *time*, time granted for doing something :—Þū wilt siofian þ hī swā langne fyrst habbaþ leáf yfel tó dónne, and ic þē sǣde þ se fyrst biþ swíþe lytle hwíle, and . . . him wǣre ealra mǣst unsǣlþ þ, þ se fyrst wǣre oþ dómes dæg, Bt. 38, 4 ; F. 204, 13–17. Wolde ic gebētan, gif ic ābídan mōste, . . . ic ne com wyrðe þæs fyrstes, Hml. S. 26, 254. Hē hæfde fyrst āne feáwa geára, Hml. S. 12, 121. Āge hē þreóra nihta fierst him tó gebeorganne, Ll. Th. i. 62, 1. Hē ongan cleopian : ‘ Fyrst lā oð morgen’ *coepit clamare :* ‘ *Inducias vel usque mane*,’ Gr. D. 326, 13. Him ðyncð ꝥ hē hæbbe fierst genōgue tó hreówsianne *tempus subsequens ad poenitentiam pollicetur*, Past. 415, 34. Tó fyrstan *ad inducias*, An. Ox. 58, 7. ¶ on firste *in time* (as opposed to *immediately*) :—Ðone weg ðǣre bōte ðe him on fierste becuman meahte *viam sibi subsequentis meliorationis*, Past. 383, 23. Ðæt folc nolde geliéfan ðeáh him mon feorrland on fierste gehēte (*neque populus promissionibus in longinquum crederet*), gif him sōna ne sealde sum on neáweste sē him ðæt māre gehētt, 389, 33. Swā sint hié tó beweorpanne ǣrest . . . tó ðǣm ðæt hī sién eft on firste (*postmodum*) ārǣrde, 443, 35. Se deófol wile on fyrste, gif hē æt fruman ne mag, þone man beswícan, Scrd. 20, 19.

**first-hróf**, es ; *m. The ridge-pole of a roof ; a ceiling* (? v. first ; I) :—On fyrsthrófe *tigillo*, An. Ox. 2812.

**first-mearc.** *Take here* **fyrst-mearc** *in Dict., and add :* (1) *a space of time, an interval.* v. first, (1) :—Firstmaerc, fristmearc *intercapido*, Txts. 71, 1108. Firstmearces *intercapidinis*, Wrt. Voc. ii. 44, 7 : *intercapidine*, 77, 37. Fyrstmearce *capidinae*, 23, 73. Þā æfter fyrstmearce bletsode hē eft Marian līchoman, Bl. H. 153, 3. Firstmearc *capidinem*, Wrt. Voc. ii. 24, 73. Fyrsmearce *intercapidinem*, An. Ox. 7, 134. Him wǣron gehātene þurh þā swefn lange fyrstmearce þises lifes *ei per somnium longa spatia hujus vitae promissa sunt*, Gr. D. 339, 26. (2) *a respite.* v. first, (2) :—Ðā ongan hē-willian fyrstmearce *coepit inducias petere*, Gr. D. 325, 31. Hē wilnode fyrsþmearce (*inducias*) . . . hē gewilnode þāra fyrstmearca, ac hē þā nā ne onfēng, 326, 18–20.

**firwet.** *l.* firwit (fer-, feor-, fǣr-, fyr-, fyrt-, -wet), *take here* **fyrwet** *in Dict., and add :*—Módes fyrwet *mentis ardor*, Hy. S. 14, 30. Ferwyt, 10, 16. [Cf. *Goth.* fair-weitjan *to be inquisitive.*]

**firwit** ; *adj. Take here* **fyrwit** *in Dict., and add :*—Fyrewyttre *curiose*, Wrt. Voc. ii. 137, 57 : An. Ox. 905. Fyrwittre, Hpt. Gl. 427, 77.

**firwit-full** ; *adj. Curious, careful, anxious :*—Fǣrwitfulla (ferwettfulle, R.) menn gié sint *solliciti estis*, Lk. L. 12, 26.

**firwit-georn.** *Add :*—Fyrwetgeorn *curiosus*, Wrt. Voc. ii. 137, 55.

**firwitgeornlíce** ; *adv. Carefully, studiously :*—Sume his wísan fyrwetgeornlíce (*studiose*) ic forgange, Gr. D. 174, 28.

**firwitgeorn-ness.** *Take here* **fyrwetgeornnes** *in Dict., and add :*—Feorwitgeornis, feruuitgeornnis, feruitgernis *curiositas*, Txts. 55, 609. Firwetgeornes, Wrt. Voc. ii. 25, 7. Feruitgiornis, Lk. p. 3, 9.

**firwit-ness.** *Take here* **fyrwitnes** *in Dict., and add :*—Ferwetnes *curiositas*, Wrt. Voc. ii. 137, 56. Fyrewitnesse (feortwitnysse, Hpt. Gl. 429, 43) *ardoris* (cf. Hy. S. 14, 30 *under* firwit), An. Ox. 975.

**fisc.** *Add :* (1) *a fish :*—Gif þū finde fisc on ōþrum fisce innan, genim þone and gebrǣd swíþe, Lch. ii. 90, 9. Wel meltende mettas, scellihte fiscas, Lch. ii. 196, 22. (2) in a collective sense :—Ðā munucas habben þriddan dǣl ðæs fisces, and hē ðā twā dǣl, C. D. vi. 147, 27. (3) *fish* as food, opposed to flesh or fowl :—Gif hit on Lencten gebyrige ðæt ðǣ ðonne ðǣre flǣscun geweorð on fisce gestriéne, C. D. v. 164, 33. v. ǣl-, fen-fisc.

**fisc-bryne.** *l.* -brýne.

**fisc-cynn.** *Add :*—Saga mē, hū fela is fisccynna on wætere ? Ic ðē secge vi and xx, Sal. K. p. 190, 20 : 204, 9.

**fisc-deág(-h)**, e ; *f. Purple dye obtained from a shell-fish :*—Fiscdeáh, weolces *conquilii*, An. Ox. 5193.

**fiscere.** *Add :* I.—Wæs ðǣm cyninge (*Xerxes*) swíþe ange on his móde . . . þæt hē ofer ðā eá cuman ne mehte. . . . Him þā tó cōm ān fiscere and hiene ǣnne ofer bróhte *piscatoria scapha trepidus transit*, Ors. 2, 5 ; S. 84, 10. Wearð geworden, swā swā God wolde, fiscere tó biscope, Ll. Th. i. 334, 12. Tó hwon þū sceole for ōwiht þysne man (*S. Peter*) habban, ungelǣredne fiscere þone leásostan, Bl. H. 177, 14. II. Cf. stæþ-swealwe.

**fisc-fell** ? :—Ofer ðǣr burge fiscfell (-pōl, L.) *super probatica piscina*, Jn. R. 5, 2.

**fisc-hús.** *Substitute : A place for storing fish :*—Flǣschūs *carnale*, wínhūs *apotheca*, feohhūs *aerarium*, fischūs *piscinale*, Wrt. Voc. i. 58, 20. [*O. H. Ger.* fisc-hús *gurgustium, casa brevis in qua pisces reponuntur.*]

**fiscian.** *Add :*—Ofer þone man becōm fǣringa godcund wracu for þām þe hē ficsode on Sunnandæg, Shrn. 126, 23. Hī mid nette fixodon on sǣlicum ýðum, Hml. Th. i. 576, 21. Ælcne man lyst, siððan hē ǣnig cotlýf . . . getimbred hæfð, þæt hē hine móte . . . huntigan and fuglian and fiscian, Solil. H. 2, 10. Ic gǣ fisciga *uado piscari*, Jn. L. R. 21, 3. [*Goth. O. Sax.* fiskōn : *O. Frs.* fiskia : *O. H. Ger.* fiscōn : *Icel.* fiskja.] v. ge-fiscian.

**fisc-lacu**, e ; *f. A fish-pond :*—Andlang mōres on fisclace, C. D. B. ii. 374, 16.

**fisc-mere.** *Dele* ‘ *vivarium*, . . . Lye,’ *and add :*—Fiscmere *piscina* (v. Jn. 5, 2), Wrt. Voc. ii. 74, 11. v. fisc-pōl.

**fisc-net.** *Add :* [He segh þos tweie brodren werpinde ut here fišhnet, *O. E. Hml.* ii. 175, 3. *O. Sax.* fisk-net : *Icel.* fiski-net.]

**fisc-noþ.** *Substitute :* **fiscnoþ** (-naþ), fixnoþ, es ; *m. I. fishing, the action* or *practice of taking fish.* (1) by persons :—Heora fixnoðe gelamp micel earfoðnys . . . Wē rǣdað . . . þæt Drihten hēte tuwa āwurpan net on fixnoðe, ǣne ǣr his ðrowunge, and ōðre síðe æfter his ǣriste . . . Se ǣrra fixnoð getācnode þās andwerdan gelaðunge . . ., and se æftra fixnoð getācnode þā tōwerdan gelaðunge gecorenra manna tó ðām ēcan life. On ðǣm ǣrran fixnoðe wurdon swā fela gelæhte þæt þæt net tóbærst . . . On ðǣm æftran fixnoðe wurdon gelǣhte manega fixas, and þæt net swā þeáh ādolode, Hml. Th. ii. 290, 5–21. Lǣrde hē þ hī on fiscnaðe him andlyfene sōhton . . . ; ac seó þeód þone cræft ne cūþe ðæs fiscnoþes nemne tó ǣlum ānum *docuit eos piscando uictum quaerere . . . ; sed piscandi peritia genti nulla nisi ad anguillas tantum inerat*, Bd. 4, 13 ; Sch. 420, 5–11. Petrus gecyrde eft tó his fixnoðe . . . ōðer is þæt man him ðurh fixnoðe bigleofan tilige, and ōðer þæt man ðurh toll feoh gegadrige, Hml. Th. ii. 288, 17–20. Hē hēt hý āweorpan heora net on fixnoðe, Nap. 22, 32. Far ðē on fiscnoð mid mē, Ap. Th. 12, 6. (2) by other living creatures :—Geseah hē scealfran . . . ēhtende þǣra fixa . . . þā bebeád hē þām scealfrum þ hī geswicon þæs fixnoðes, Hml. S. 31, 1323. II. *a place where there is fishing, a fishing-ground :*—Wǣron twēgen gebrōþra . . . and hæfdon ǣnne fixnoþ on ānum brādum mere . . . ac þǣr wurdon eft æt þām wæterscipe micele gefeoht for þām fixnoþe. Se bisceop . . . ābæd æt Gode þ hē worhte þone wæterscipe tó yrþlande, oð þ wæter gewænde of þām fixnoðe, and wæs se mere āwend tó felda, swā þ man erode ealne þone fixnoþ, Nap. 22, 21–28. Hē stód mid ðām folce swā wið ænne fixnoð, þ wæs ān brād mere Genesareð gehāten, 30. Sí ðis mynster fram eallum eorðlicum þeówdōme freóh . . . , ꝥæt is on feldum and on lǣsewum, . . . and on sealtum merscum, and on fiscnoðum, C. D. iii. 350, 8. Mid allum ðǣm

nytnessum ge on fixnoðum ge on mēdwum, v. 186, 5. **III.** *what is caught, a catch, draught of fishes:*—Cwæð hē: 'Wurp ūt þīn net, and þē fixnoð (fiscnoð, *v.l.*) becymð.' . . . Wearp þā ūt his net, and þær weard oninnan ān ormǣte leax, Hml. S. 31, 1273. Ne bærst heora net on ðisum fixnoðe . . . ; and þes fixnoð getācnað þā hālgan gelaðunge, þ is eall crīsten folc . . . Se fixnoð æfter his ǣriste getācnode þā gesǣligan Crīstenan . . . þā þā Petrus geseah swylcne fixnoð mid hym, þā feól hē tō þæs Hǣlendes cneówum . . . His geféran . . . wǣron eác āfyrhte for þām fixnoðe, Nap. 22.

**fiscoþ**, es; *m.* *Add:* I. *the action* or *practice of catching fish.* v. fiscnoþ; I:—Lǣrde hē þæt hī on fisceoðe (fiscaðe, *v.l.*) him andlyfne sōhton . . . Seó þeód þone cræft þæs fiscaðes ne cūðe, Bd. 4, 13; Sch. 420, 5–10. II. *a place for fishing.* v. fiscnoþ; II:—Ic an þæt lond at Sūðerēye mid alle ðe fiscode ðe þērtō bireþ, Cht. Th. 513, 6. [*R. Glouc.* visceth.]

**fisc-pōl**, es; *m.* *Add:*—Fiscpōl *piscina*, Jn. L. 5, 2. In þ fiscpōl (ðone fiscpōll, R.) *in piscinum,* 7. On fiscpōl, C. D. B. i. 518, 38. [Si quis furatus fuerit pisces in stagno quod Angli dicunt *fiscpól,* Ll. Th. ii. 544, 28. v. *N. E. D.* fish-pool.]

**fisc-þrūt**, es; *m.* *A small fish:*—Huðn fiscðrūtas *paucos pisciculos,* Mt. L. 15, 34.

**fisc-wēr.** *Substitute:* **fisc-wer,** es; *m.* I. *a weir for catching fish:*—Fiscwer and mylne macian, Angl. ix. 261, 12. II. *a fishing-ground;* captura :—Lǣtað eówre nett on þone fiscwer *laxa retia uestra in capturam* (v. wer *in Dict.*), Lk. 5, 4. [v. *N. E. D.* fish-weir. Cf. *Icel.* fiski-ver *a fishing-place.*]

**fisc-wille**, an; *f.* *A fish-pond:*—Fiscwelle *bifarius* (= *vivarius*) vel *piscina,* Wrt. Voc. ii. 126, 15 : *bisarius* (l. *bifarius*), i. 66, 8.

**fisc-wylle.** l. -wille, *and dele last passage.*

**fīsian.** *Take here* **fēsian, fȳsian** *in Dict., and add:*—Oft on gefeohte ān fēseð tyne, Wlfst. 162, 18. Hī munecas tōdrǣfdon and Godes þeówas fēsedon, Chr. 975; P. 121, 29. Fēsigende *exagitans, persequens,* Germ. 390, 163. [v. *N. E. D.* feeze.]

**fisting.** *Substitute:* **fisting,** e; *f.* *Breaking wind (silently)* :—Fīsting *fesiculatio,* Wrt. Voc. ii. 148, 16 : i. 46, 23. [v. *N. E. D.* fisting.]

**fit strife.** *Add:* [v. *N. E. D.* fit.]

**fit** *a poem.* *Add:*—Nū ic fitte ymb fisca cynn wille wōðcræfte cȳðan, Wal. 1. Hēr mæg findan sē ðe hine lysteð leóðgiddunga hwā þās fitte fēgde, Hpt. 33, 71, 2. [v. *N. E. D.* fit: *O. Sax.* fittia (*inferred from the Latinized form* vittea (*omne opus per* vitteas distinxit) *in preface to* Héliand.]

**fitel-fōta**; *adj.* *Having white feet:*—Brūn *badius,* fitelfōta *petilus* (cf. *petulus* whytfoted *et dicitur de equo,* Wülck. Gl. 602, 32 (15th cent.), Wrt. Voc. i. 46, *omitted after* 42 (v. Angl. viii. 451). [v. (?) *N. E. D.* fitel-foot, an epithet of the hare. *O. L. Ger.* fitil-fōt *petilus.* Cf. *O. H. Ger.* fizzil-fēh *petilus* (*equus*), *qui albos pedes habet.*]

**fiter-sticca.** *Add:* [Cf. *O. L. Ger.* fiteri *fimbria.*] : **fiþer.** *Add:* v. þri-feoþor.

**fiþer-bǣre**; *adj.* *Feathered, winged:*—Fiþerbǣre *penniger, uelox,* An. Ox. 2404. Fiþerbǣre heápas *pennigeras* (*volucrum*) *turmas,* 1565.

**fiþer-berende.** *For* 'Cot. 9: 170' *substitute:*—Fiðerberende *aliger,* Wrt. Voc. ii. 5, 53.

**fiþer-byrste** (?) ; *adj.* *Having four bristles* (? of a stick split into four at the end) :—Genim ǣnne sticcan and gewyrc hine feðorbyrste . . . styre mid ðȳ sticcan ðā buteran, Lch. iii. 24, 18.

**fiþercian**; *p.* ode *To flutter* :—Se fugel ongann flogettan and fiþercian ymb his ansȳne *avis circa ejus faciem volitare coepit,* Gr. D. 100, 19.

**fiþer-dǣled**; *adj.* *Divided into four parts:*—Fiðerdǣledre *quadripartitae, in quatuor partes divisae,* Hpt. Gl. 448, 68. þæne fiðerdǣledan *in quatuor partes divisam,* 418, 23. þā fyðerdǣledan *quadrifaria,* 410, 15.

**fiþer-dōgor**; *adj.* *Lasting four days;* quadriduanus :—Latzarum feoðordōger deád *Lazarum quadriduanum mortuum,* Jn. p. 6, 8. v. feówer-dōgor.

**fiþere.** *Take here* **fyþera** *in Dict., and add:* (1) *a wing* of a living creature :—Cumað egeslīce mycele deór . . . heora fyðera swēgað swā swā wæteres dyne; hī fleóð swiftlīce, Wlfst. 200, 15. Fiðerum *alis,* Wrt. Voc. ii. 89, 55. Se kok, ǣr ðǣm ðe hē crāwan wille, hefeð ūp his fiðru, Past. 461, 13. Seó brōdige henn tōsprǣt hyre fyðera and þā briddas gewyrmð, Angl. viii. 309, 26. Hē hæfde fiþru swylce þyrnen besma, Shrn. 120, 26. (2) *a wing* to be eaten :—þū scealt sellan wel meltende mettas, . . . hænne flǣsc and gōse fiþru, Lch. ii. 196, 22.

**fiþer-ecgede**; *adj.* *Four-edged:*—[Genim twēgen] sticcan feðerecgede, and wrīt on ǣgðerne sticcan ān paternoster, Lch. i. 388, 5. v. feówer-ecgede.

**fiþerede.** v. twi-fiþerede.

**fiþer-feald** *four-fold* :—Ic forgeldo feoðorfald *reddo quadruplum,* Lk. R. 19, 8.

**fiþer-fēte, -fōte.** *Take here* **fyþer-fēte, feþer-fōte** *in Dict., and add:* -fōt:—Fiðerfōte fugel *griffes,* Wrt. Voc. i. 22, 44. Eall ðæt fiðerfōte byð, Hex. 14, 30. Fiþerfēte[s] *quadrupedis,* An. Ox. 1854. Fiþer-

fētum *quadripedante,* 14. Gyf man forstele feoðerfōt (feðerfēte, *v. l.*) neát, Ll. Th. ii. 140, 33. Ūre feþerfōt niétenu *animalia quadrupedia,* Nar. 16, 7. Wæs þǣra feðerfōta niétena micel mænigeo, 9, 4. Se wind ūsse feþerfōt niétenu swencte *quadrupedia uexabantur,* 22, 30. ¶ *used substantively*—Feoðorfōta (-o, R.) his ï néteno *pecora ejus,* Jn. L. 4, 12. Fyþerfēte swā hwilc swā gesihð, uneáðnysse getācnað . . . Fyþerfēte sprecan feóndscipas cingas getācnað, Lch. iii. 210, 9, 11.

**fiþer-flēdende**; *adj.* *Flowing in four parts, running in four streams:*—Fyþerflēdendre eá *quadrifluo amne,* Germ. 390, 105. v. next word.

**fiþer-flōwende**; *adj.* *Flowing in four parts, running in four streams:*—Fyþerflōwendre eá *quadrifluo* (*quatuor fluminibus currens*) *amne,* An. Ox. 48, 2. v. *preceding word.*

**fiþer-hama**; *m.* *A covering of feathers with wings, plumage:*—Godes engel standande mid gyldenum fyþerhaman, Hml. S. 34, 74. Hē mid deóflicum fiðerhaman fleón wolde, Hml. Th. i. 380, 29. Genāmon twēgen englas his sāwle, and fleógende mid hwītum fyðerhaman betwyx him ferodon, ii. 334, 7. v. ge-fiþerhamod, feþer-hama.

**fiþer-hīwe**; *adj.* *Having four forms:*—Mid fiðerhīwum *quadriformis,* An. Ox. 177.

**fiþer-hweohlode.** v. feówer-hweohlode.

**fiþerian.** *Add: to flutter* :—Sum fugel ongon fleógende and fiðergende ymbe his onsyne *avis circa ejus faciem volitare coepit,* Gr. D. 100, 19.

**fiþerling**, es; *m.* *A quarter* :—Quadrans, þ ys fyðerlinc . . . *quadrans* byð se feórða dǣl þǣra þinga þe man mæg rihtlīce tōdǣlan on feówer, Angl. viii. 298, 10.

**fiþer-rīca.** *Take here* **fyþer-rīca** *in Dict., and add:*—Fiþerrīca *tetrarca,* An. Ox. 1799. Philippus se fyðerrīca, Hml. Th. i. 364, 30.

**fiþer-rīce**, es; *n.* *A tetrarchy:*—Philippus and Heródes Iudēam feþerrīcum (fyþer-, on feówer tetrarhchan, iiii rīcu, *v. ll.*) tōdǣldun, Chr. 12; P. 7, note 2.

**fiþer-sceát.** *Take here* **feþer-sceátas** *in Dict.*

**fiþer-scīte.** *Take here* **feþer-scétte, -scīte, fyþer-scīte** *in Dict., and add:*—Fiþerscȳte *triquadra* (*mundi latitudo*), An. Ox. 1295. Ān fæt fyðerscȳte and brād, Hml. S. 10, 85. Gefēgde feoþerscētte *quadratur* (*durus scopulus calcis compage*), Wrt. Voc. ii. 93, 68. Fiþerscȳtes *quadrati,* An. Ox. 1702. On fiþerscītum dǣle *in quadrata pagina,* 1589. On þām fyðerscȳtum stānum, Hml. Th. i. 466, 14.

**fiþer-sliht, -sleht**, es; *m.* *Wing-flapping:*—Scyllendre coca fiþerslehte *concrepante pullorum plausu,* An. Ox. 4892.

**fiþer-tīme**; *adj.* *Having four horses abreast:*—Feoðurtēmum *quadrigis,* Ps. Srt. ii. p. 188, 15.

**fiþer-tōdǣled**; *adj.* *Divided into four parts:*—Fyðertō[dǣledre] *quadripertitae,* Angl. xiii. 30, 83. Cf. fiþer-dǣled.

**fittan.** *Dele, and see* **fit** *a poem.*

**fitung.** *Add:* Ll. Th. i. 310, 14. [Cf. (?) Hē feng to fiten his mawmez and lasten his lauerd, Jul. 70, 8.] Cf. **fit** *strife.*

**fixen** *a vixen.* *Dele:* **fixen;** *adj.* v. fyxen: **fixnoþ.** v. fiscnoþ.

**fiā.** *Add: a strong dat.* fiā *occurs: dat. pl.* fiān (?) :—Hē gebende his bogan and mid geǣttrode flān (strǣle, Bl. H. 199, 18) ðone fearr ofsceótan wolde; ac seó geǣttrode fiā wende ongeán . . . Se mann mid his āgenre fiān ofscoten wæs, Hml. Th. i. 502, 17–20. Hē weard mid ānre flān ofscoten *telo e muris jacto perfossus occiditur,* Ors. 3, 11 ; S. 144, 27. Hē weard gescoten mid ānre fiā on ðām cneówe, Hml. Th. ii. 492, 5. Weard se cyng Willelm ȝn huntnoðe fram his ānan men mid ānre fiā ofsceoten, Chr. 1100; P. 235, 17. Flā ï *gafeluca jaculo,* i. *sagitta,* Hpt. Gl. 432, 43. Micel līget fleáh swilce flān . . . and hī wurdon mid þām fȳrenum flānum ofscotene, Hml. Th. i. 504, 29–506, 1. Wurdon hī mid deófles flān (*or sing.*?) þurhscotene, 62, 28. Hē ðā ǣttrigan flān costnunge ādwǣscte, ii. 140, 26. Hē lǣteð strǣle fleógan, farende flān, Rä. 4, 57. [v. *N. E. D.* flo.]

**flacea.** *Dele.*

**flacge.** *Substitute:* **flacg** *a poultice, plaster:*—Flacg *cataplasma,* Wrt. Voc. ii. 28, 3. [Cf. (?) flagge of þe erthe *terricidium, cespes,* Prompt. Parv. 163.]

**flacor** *fluttering.* *Add:* [v. *N. E. D.* flacker *to flutter.*] Cf. flicerian.

**flǣsc.** *Take here* **flǣc** *in Dict., and add: pl.* flǣscu : flǣsce (?), an; *f.* (v. C. D. v. 164, 32 *below*) (1) *the soft material of an animal body, often in connexion or contrast with skin or bone* :—Tōða flǣsc *gingiuae,* Wrt. Voc. i. 43, 33. Bān of mīnum bāne and flǣsc of mīnum flǣsce, Gen. 2, 23. Gemolsnad flǣsc *vel* forrotad *tabes,* Wrt. Voc. i. 20, 16. Deád flǣsc, Lch. iii. 292, 3. Heora līchoman licggað on eorðan . . . and þ flǣsc āfūlað, Bl. H. 101, 3. Gāst næ[þ] flǣsc and bān, Lk. 24, 39. þæs cealfes flǣsc (*carnes*) and fell þū bærnst, Ex. 29, 14 : Ll. Th. i. 128, 15. þ flǣsc þæs deádan oxan, 50, 11. (1 a) *figurative* :—Tō swutulunge þ man wite þ man clǣne flǣsc (*carnes,* ii.) hæbbe (*that one is acting without fraud*), Ll. Th. i. 156, 6. (2) *flesh* as food :—Gebrēded flaesc *viscera tosta,* Wrt. Voc. ii. 123, 67. Fiðerfēte flǣsc *carnium quadrupedum,* R. Ben. I. 71, 11. þā git wæs flǣsc (*carnes*) on hira tōðum, Num. 11, 33. Flǣsces hī bǣdon *petierunt carnes,* Ps. Th. 104, 35. Gif mon his heówum in fæsten flǣsc gefe, Ll. Th. i. 40, 9. Mon geselle

tū hriéðeru . . . and feór fliccu; gyf hit on Lencten gebyrige, ðæt ðǽ ðonne ðǽre flǽscun geweorð on fisce gestriéne, C. D. v. 164, 32. Æfter þisum ne et þū nǽfre flǽsc (*carnem*), Gr. D. 135, 9. Wile monna sum mín flǽsc etan, felles ue réceð, Ra. 76, 5. þæs lambes flǽsc gebrǽd etan, Angl. viii. 323, 47. Ic eotu figsc ferra (*carnes taurorum*), Ps. Srt. 49, 13. Flǽsca æt *carnium esus*, R. Ben. I. 68, 3. (3) *the visible surface of the body*, with reference to its colour or appearance :—' Teóh eft þíne hand ' . . . and heó wæs gelíc þám óðrum flǽsce, Ex. 4, 7. (4) *marking near kinship* :—Hē ys úre bróðor and úre flǽsc, Gen. 37, 27. (4 a) *of the marriage relation* :—Beóð twégen on ánum flǽsce. Witodlíce ne synt hig twégen, ac án flǽsc, Mt. 19, 5, 6. (5) *that which has corporeal life, animals*, in more limited sense, *human beings* :—Ælc flǽsc gesihð Godes hǽle, Lk. 3, 6. For ðē sceal ǽlc flǽsc forð síðian, Ps. Th. 64, 2. Hē seleð mele ylcum figsce, Ps. Srt. 135, 25. (6) *the human frame, the corporeal part of man* in contrast with soul or spirit :—Hwæt biþ se líchoma elles búton flǽsc seoððan se ēcea dǽl of biþ, þ is seó sáwl?, Bl. H. 111, 31. þonne þín flǽsc ligeð, Gen. 2188. Ic þone ǽrist ealra getreówe flǽsces on foldan, Hy. 10, 56. þú sáwle sendest in tō þǽm flǽsce, 7, 5. Nó þon lange wæs feorh ǽðelinges flǽsce bewunden, B. 2424. Ic beó eft mid mínum felle befangen, and ic on mínum flǽsce God geseó, Hml. Th. ii. 456, 18. Se líchama ðe Críst on ðrowode wæs geboren of Marian flǽsce, 270, 18. Foldbúendra flǽsc and gǽstas, Rä. 2, 13. Wē sceolon syllan þýne flǽscu heofanes fugelum, Nic. 6, 39. (7) *the animal or physical nature of man* :—Hit þe ne onwreáh flǽsc (flēsc, L.) and blōd, Mt. 16, 17. þ word wæs flǽsc geworden, Jn. 1, 14. Mín flǽsc on ðē getreóweð, Ps. Th. 62, 1 : 72, 21. (8) *the sensual appetites* :—Ðū woldest brúcan ungemetlicre wrænnesse ; ac ðē willaþ ðonne forseón Godes þeówas, for þám þe þín wérige flǽsc hafaþ þín anweald, nalæs þū his. Hū mæg mon earmlícor gebǽron þonne mon hine underþeóde his weregan flǽsce, and nelle his gesceadwísan sáule *voluptariam vitam degas; sed quis non spernat atque abjiciat vilissimae rei, corporis, servum?*, Bt. 32, 1 ; F. 114, 20-24. Hwæt is unstrenge ðonne se mon þe bið tō ungemetlíce oferswíþed mid þám tēdran flǽsce, buton hē eft geswíce and winne wiþ þá unþeáwas, 36, 6 ; F. 182, 4. v. eald-hryter-flǽsc.

**flǽsc-ǽt.** *Substitute: The eating of flesh* :—Flǽscǽt (*carnium esus*) þám untruman sý geðafod ; sóna swá hý geedwyrpte beóð, þám flǽscǽte (*a carnibus*) forhæbben, R. Ben. 61, 1-3. Ealle fram flǽscǽte hī forhæbben *carnium quadrupedum ab omnibus abstineatur commestio*, 64, 6.

**flǽsc-bana,** an ; *m. A slayer, executioner* :—Se flǽscbana (*interfector*) þe tō his cwealme gecoren wæs . . . se wælhreówa flǽscbana (*carnifex*), Gr. D. 254, 26, 33. Se ylca flǽscbana (*carnifex*), þám wæs ályfed þ hē slóh þone diácon lifigendne, him næs ná ályfed þ hē móste ofer hine deádne gefeón, 294, 19. v. flǽsc-cwellere.

**flǽsc-cíping.** v. flǽsc-cyping *in Dict.*: **flǽsc-cófa.** *l.* -cofa.

**flǽsc-cwellere.** *Substitute: A slayer, an executioner* :—þára flǽsc-cwellera *carnificum*, Wrt. Voc. ii. 24, 9. Wítniendra þíowa oððe flǽsccwellera *lictorum*, 52, 78. v. flǽsc-bana.

**flǽsceht (-iht).** *Add* :—On þám flǽscehtum stōwum, Lch. ii. 222, 7.

**flǽscen;** *adj. Of flesh* :—Eágan sind flǽscene and tēð bǽnene, Hml. Th. i. 532, 6. Flǽscene *carnulenta, carnea*, Germ. 394, 372. [*O. H. Ger.* fleiskîn.]

**flǽscen-ness,** e ; *f. Incarnation* :—þá hálgan flǽscennysse úres Drihtnes, Angl. viii. 324, 1. v. flǽsc-ness.

**flǽsc-gebyrd.** For Mone B. 499 *substitute* An. Ox. 429.

**flǽsc-hama.** *Add*: (1) *the material body, body* in contrast with soul :—Ne mæg him þonne se flǽschoma, þonne him þæt feorg losað, swēte forswelgan, Seef. 94. Ýða wrǽcon árleásra feorh of flǽschoman, Gen. 1385. Sáwle of flǽschoman scyndan, Jul. 489. (2) *corporeal state of man* :—Biþ se flǽschoma áscýred swá glæs, ne mæg ðæs unrihtes beón áwiht bedigled, Bl. H. 109, 36. þurh leáslíce líces wynne, earges flǽschoman ídelne lust, Cri. 1298. þú synna tō fela gefremedes in flǽschoman, Gū. 558.

**flǽsc-hús.** *Add:* [*O. H. Ger.* fleisk-hús *carnificina*.]

**flǽsc-líc.** *Add:* (1) *pertaining to the material body, human, mortal* :—þú wæst þ ic eom flǽsclic man, Bl. H. 231, 25. þú ǽr gesáwe æfter flǽsclicre gecynde fægre leomu on tō seónne, 113, 21. (1 a) *animal* in contrast with human :—Mýs and fixǽ sint flǽsclicu nýtenu, Solil. H. 16, 8. (2) *connected by, or based upon, ties of flesh and blood, natural* :—þám filigde sum flǽsclic bróðor tō mynstre, ná for gecnyrdnysse góddre drohtnunge, ac for flǽsclicere lufe. Se gástlica bróðor . . . and his flǽsclica bróðor, Hml. Th. i. 532, 31-35. (3) *carnal* in contrast with spiritual, *worldly* :—His þegnas wǽron þágyt flǽsclices mōdes, and nǽron mid gástes mægene getremede, Bl. H. 17, 6. (4) *pertaining to bodily appetites, carnal, sensual* :—Flǽslicra leahtra cwylming *carnalium uitiorum mortificatio*, An. Ox. 40, 22. Seó menego tácnode þá flǽsclican willan and þá ungerēclícan uncysta, Bl. H. 19, 6. (4 a) *sexual* :—Flǽslicum gemange *carnali commercio*, Wrt. Voc. ii. 128, 73.

**flǽsclíce;** *adv. According to the flesh, in a physical sense* or *manner, carnally* in contrast with spiritually :—Ðæt ðæt gē gǽslíce underfēngon,

gē willað geendigan flǽsclíce *cum spiritu coeperitis, nunc carne consummemini*, Past. 207, 16. Ne synd wē ná Abrahames cynnes flǽsclíce, ac gástlíce, Hml. Th. i. 204, 22. For þý flǽsclíce wē ne beóþ ymbsnidene *ideo carnaliter non circumcidimur*, An. Ox. 40, 16. [v. *N. E. D.* fleshly ; *adv.*]

**flǽslicness** *incarnate condition. Add* :—Flǽsclicnysse *incarnatione*, An. Ox. 1530. þ flǽsclicnysse (*incarnationem*) úres Drihtnes Hǽlendes Crístes hē gelýfe, Ath. Crd. 29 : Hml. Th. i. 194, 26. His hand getácnað his mihte and his flǽsclicnysse, 122, 28. [v. *N. E. D.* fleshliness.]

**flǽsc-mangere.** *Add* :—Flǽscmangere *lanio*, Wrt. Voc. ii. 53, 38. Macerarii, quos Angli uocant flaismangeres (fleis-, fles-, *v. l.*), Ll. Lbmn. 669, 17. [v. *N. E. D.* fleshmonger. *O. L. Ger.* flēs-mongere *macellarius*.]

**flǽsc-mete.** *Add: Flesh* (as opposed to fish and vegetables) *as food* :—þonne mē hingrigan ongan, þonne wǽron mē þá flǽscmettas on gewilnungum ; ic gyrnde þára fixa þe on Egyptum wǽron ; ic gewilnode þæs wínes, Hml. S. 23 b, 533. Ðæt hié ne wilnoden flǽscmetta *cibos carnis non appetere*, Past. 319, 8. Gyt flǽscmettum (*carnibus*) ic brúce, for þám cild ic eom, Coll. M. 34, 21. Unrihtlic bið þæt se crístena man flǽsclice lustas gefremme on þám tíman þe hē flǽscmettas forgán sceal, Wlfst. 286, 2.

**flǽsc-ness.** *Add* :—þætte flǽscnesse (*incarnationem*) Drihtnes úres hē gelýfe, Angl. ii. 363, 2. [*O. H. Ger.* in-fleisknessa *incarnatio*.] v. ge-, on-flǽscness ; flǽscen-ness.

**flǽscod.** v. ge-flǽscod.

**flǽsc-sand,** e ; *f. A portion* or *dish of meat* :—Gif man næbbe smeámettas, sylle man twám and twám twá flǽscsande ; and tō heora ǽfenþēnunge sylle man twám and twám flǽscsande oððe óðre smeámettas, Nap. 23.

**flǽsc-þegnung,** e ; *f. Allowance of animal food* :—Gif hit gebyrað on geáre þæt náðer ne byð on þám earde ne æceren ne bóc ne óðer mæsten þæt man mæge heora flǽscþēnunge forð bringan, Nap. 10, 30.

**flǽsc-tōþ** *one of the teeth* :—Se flǽsctōþ wiþæftan þone tux *gigra*, Wrt. Voc. ii. 42, 9.

**flǽp** *a fleece* (?), *wool* (?) :—Flǽd *nimbus* (the line is: Candidior nivibus dum ningit vellere *nimbus*, Ald. 272, 19 : *perhaps* flǽd *is gloss to* vellere), An. Ox. 23, 37 (where see note). v. fixþe-camb.

**flagg.** v. flacg.

**fláh.** *Substitute: Hostile, fell, cruel* :—Flách *infestus*, Wrt. Voc. ii. 110, 78. þonne þæt gecnáweð fiáh feónd gemáh . . . hē him feorgbona þurh slíðen searo weorþeð, Wal. 39. Fláh máh fítteþ, Reim. 62. Wið fiáne feónd werigean, Exod. 237. [If the word agrees in meaning as well as in form with *Icel.* flár (hygyja fiátt *to think false*) in one or two of the passages it might be translated by *treacherous, crafty*.]

**fláh.** *Add* :—Flaan *catapulta*, Wrt. Voc. ii. 102, 48. Fláne *obolisci*, An. Ox. 3524. Fram fláne fieóndre, Bl. Gl. þ yrre hit sylf mid fláne (*sagitta*) ofstang, Prud. 24 a. Ágeót út fláne *effunde frameam*, Bl. Gl. Flánas *tessa, pila*, Wrt. Voc. ii. 97, 1, 8. Flána *jacula*, Bl. Gl. þá þóhton hié þ hié sceoldon ǽrest . . . hié gebígan mid heora flána gescotum, ac . . . hié ne mehton from him nǽnne flán ásceótan, ac ǽlc cóm . . . on hié selfe (*tela . . . retrorsum coacta ipsos configebant*). . . . Theodosius fultum mehte mǽstra ǽlcne heora flána on hiora feóndum áfæstnian, Or. 6, 36 ; S. 294, 22-28. Swá him mǽre gescot and má fiána tō cymð *eo crebrioribus sagittis impetuntur*, Past. 407, 23. Flánum *spiculis*, Txts. 96, 937. Ðæt mód ðætte ne mæg gesión ðá fiáne ǽr hit sié gewundad *cor, quod praevidere vulnera non potest*, Past. 431, 3. Flána *sagittas*, Ps. Spl. 7, 14 : 10, 2. [v. *N. E. D.* flane.]

**fianc,** es ; *m. A flank* :—Flances *ilia*, An. Ox. 50, 35.

**flán-geweorc.** *Substitute: Arrows, javelins, a flight of arrows* :—Sumum hē wíges spēd giefeð æt gúðe, þonne ofer scildhreádan sceótend sendað flacor flángeweorc (*fluttering flights of arrows*), Cri. 676.

**fián-hred, -hræd.** *Substitute: Swift as an arrow* :—Flánhred dæg (*the day of death. Cf. My days are swifter than a weaver's shuttle*, Job 7, 6), Reim. 72.

**flániht.** *Substitute: Provided with darts* or *points* (?) :—þá flánihtan *jaculatas* (*fraude sagittas*), Wrt. Voc. ii. 92, 76 : 47, 29.

**flán-þræc, -pracu.** *Dele* -þræc.

**flasce,** an ; *f. Take here* flaxe *in Dict., and add* :—Flasce, trýwen byt *flasco*, Wrt. Voc. ii. 149, 33. Flaxe oððe cylle *asscopa*, i. 17, 32. Hū Bonefatius þám Gotan gefyllde þá flaxan . . . þá sealde hē heom áne trýwene flascan (flaxan, *v. l.*) wínes fulle (*parvum vas ligneum vino plenum*), Gr. D. 66, 3-10. Twá fatu on folcisc fiascan gehátene, . . . hē óðre þára fiascena (flaxena, *v. l.*) bróhte, óðre hē áhýdde, 141, 25-30. Hæfdon hī mid heom twá flaxan mid ælað gefylde, Guth. 64, 15, 24.

**fleá.** *Take* II *under* fleáh *albugo* ; *with* I *take* fleó *in Dict., and add :* Strong and weak forms occur of which the former seem the older :—Fleáh, fiþ *pulix*, Txts. 88, 813. Hine byton lýs and lyftene gnættas and eác swylce fleán, Hex. 24, 31. Hwí ne lufast þú fixá (*pulices*)?, Solil. H. 16, 7.

**fleah.** *l.* fleáh, *take here* II *under* fleá *in Dict., and add:* Strong

and weak forms occur, cf. fleá :—Flió *albugo*, Txts. 36, 12. Fleó on eágum *cimosis*, Wrt. Voc. ii. 131, 43. Ðeós eáhsealf mæg wiþ ælces cynnes broc on eágon, wiþ fleán on eágon, Lch. iii. 292, 2.

**fleám.** *Add*:—Fleám *fuga*, i. *fugatio*, Wrt. Voc. ii. 151, 46. Fleámas *fuge*, 38, 39. (1) *the flight* of a defeated force :—Wearð æfre þurh sum þing fleám ástiht, Chr. 998; P. 131, 16. Flugon Pēne ... For þæm fleáme Hanna mid his folce wearð Rōmānum tō gasolgieldum, Ors. 4, 6; S. 170, 25. Hē wearð gefliémed, and on ðæm fleáme hiene oftyrfdon his geféran, S. 172, 27. Be heora sige ge eác be þára hæþenra manna fleáme, Bl. H. 203, 4. Hī tōgædere fēngon and sōna þet wærod on fleáme gebrōhtan, Chr. 1006; P. 137, 9. Onstealdon þā heretogan ærest þone fleám, 993; P. 127, 28: 1010; P. 140, 12. (2) *the flight* of a fugitive, criminal, &c. :—Būton hē hine gelādige þ hē hine fleáme (flēma, *v. l.*) nyste, Ll. Th. i. 382, 23. [v. *N. E. D.* fleme.] v. tō-fleám.

**fleám-dóm**, es ; *m. The condition of a fugitive* :—Ðā fleáh se Siba mid fleámdōme āweg *he fled away as a fugitive*, Nap. 23.

**fleám-lást**, es ; *m. The track of a fugitive, apostasy* (cf. *apostata* āflíged mon, Kent. Gl. 141) :—Fleámlāstes *apostasie*, Wrt. Voc. ii. 81, 38.

**fleán.** *Add*:—Fleán *deglobere*, Wrt. Voc. ii. 25, 30: 106, 23. v. á-fleán.

**fleard.** *Substitute*: *Wicked folly, absurd error* :—Unwemme fiearde *immunis* (*ab illecebrarum*) *colludio*, An. Ox. 1517. Gif friþgeard sī on hwæs lande ābūton stān oððe treów oððe wille oððe swilces ænige fleard (*any wicked follies of a like kind*), Ll. Th. ii. 298, 17. [v. *N. E. D.* fierd.] v. ge-fleard, *and next two words*.

**fleardere**, es ; *m. One who acts with* (*wicked*) *folly, wantonly* :—Warnige hē eác þ hē þurh geþafunge ne wurðe þæra fleardera geféra, Nap. 23. v. next word.

**fleardian.** *Substitute*: *To act with* (*wicked*) *folly, act wantonly, to stray in the paths of folly* :—Sē þe preágincga forlæt, hē fleardað *qui increpationes relinquit errat*, Scint. 113, 16. Wā þām þe cyrican mid ídele sēcað ; þæt syndan þā ungesǽligan þe ðǽr fleardiað mid ídelre spǽce and hwílum mid ídelre dǽde, Wlfst. 279, 7. Hī ne swincaþ ā swíþe ymbe ǽnige þearfe, ac maciað eall be luste ... wōriað and wandriað and ealne dæg fleardiað, spelliað and spiliað and nænige note dreógað, Ll. Th. ii. 322, 24. Mid dislicum glengum fleardiende *stolidis pompis indruticans*, An. Ox. 1218.

**fleáþe.** *Cf.* fleathor-wyrt *nimpha*, Lch. iii. 304, col. 1.

**fleax.** *Add*:—Fleax *linum*, Wrt. Voc. ii. 51, 53. Flex, An. Ox. 1379. Hié nāmon treówu and slōgon on ōþerne ende næglas, and hié mid flexe bewundon and onbærndon hit, and beþýddan hit on þone elpend hindan, þæt hié fōran wēdende on þæs flexes bryne, Ors. 4, 1; S. 158, 4-8. Þone wlacan smocan wāces flæsces *lini lepidos fumos*, Dōm. L. 51. Hē hēt bewindan heora handa and fēt mid gesmyredum flexe, and fýr under bētan, Hml. S. 4, 393.

**fleax-æcer**, es ; *m. A flax-field* :—On ðā flexæcyras, C. D. v. 389, 16.

**fleaxen.** *Dele.*

**fleax-gesc[e]ot**, es ; *n. A contribution of flax paid to a church* :—Sceóte man ælmessan ... swā elles hwæt swā witan tō þearfe gerǽdan, hwílum weaxgescot, hwílum flexgescot, Wlfst. 171, 27.

**fleax-hamm**, es ; *m. An enclosure where flax is grown* :—On flexhammas ; of flexhamman on minthammas, C. D. v. 374, 25.

**fleax-líne**, an ; *f. A cord for hanging flax on* (?) :—Hē sceal fela towtōla habban ; flexlínan, spinle, reól, Angl. ix. 263, 10.

**fleax-waran ?** :—Andlang burnan on ðā flexwaran ; on ðone hagan, C. D. v. 382, 1.

**flecgan** v. fleógan : **fled** *a dwelling*. *Dele* : **flēd.** *Dele, and see* in-fiēde : flēdan *to flow*. [v. *N. E. D.* flede. *Icel.* flæða.] v. fiþer-fiēdende : flēde. *Add*: v. in-flēde ; flōde.

**flēge**, floege *a ship* :—Floege ł lyttel scipp ōðer ne uæs ðēr *nauicula alia non erat ibi*, Jn. L. R. 6, 22. [From Scandinavian (?). Cf. *Icel.* fley *a ship*.]

**fiehtre**(-a ?), an ; *f.* (*m.* ?) *A hurdle* :—Flehtran *cratem*, Wrt. Voc. ii. 136, 52. v. fleohtan.

**-fienod.** v. ge-fienod.

**fleógan.** *Add*: I. *to fly* with wings (lit. or metaph.) :—Nō ic fleóge *non trano*, Wrt. Voc. ii. 61, 49. Hwelc seled mē fiðru swē swē culfran and ic flíigu (*volabo*), Ps. Srt. 54, 7. Hē āstág on þone torr, and āþenedum earmum ongan fleógan on þā lyfte, Bl. H. 187, 28. Hē geseah hine fleógendne, 189, 1. Hē symble mid his mōde wæs fleógende (flēgende, *v. l.*) þā heofonlican tō lufianne *ad caelestia semper amanda peruolans*, Bd. 2, 7 ; Sch. 139, 11. II. of other (rapid) movement :—Ýfies seáw þæs þe eorþan flíhð *that runs along the ground*, Lch. ii. 40, 27. Hē eóde tō þære burge wealle, and fleáh ūt ofer (*he threw himself over*), þæt hē eall tōbærst, Ors. 5, 12 ; S. 244, 3. Flugon þā lēgetu swylce fýrene strǽlas, Bl. H. 203, 9. Gif mon ōðrum þā hond ūtan forsleá ... gif hió heaif onweg fleóge, Ll. Th. i. 98, 9. III. *to flee*. [v. fleón.] (1) lit. :—Þ man gingran mann ne slōge ... būton hē hine weriaʋ wolde oþþe fleóge, Ll. Th. i. 240, 29.

(2) *to avoid, refrain from* :—Por and cawel sind tō fleóganne, Lch. ii 26, 19. IV. *to cause to move* (?), *put to flight*. Cf. fleón, III :—Se mōna næfð nānre mihte wiht þ hē þære nihte genipu mæge fleógan (fiecgan, MS.) *pallida nocturnam nec praestat luna lucernam*, Dōm. L. 110. v. tō-fleógan.

**fleóge.** *Add*:—Flēge *musca*, Wrt. Voc. ii. 114, 47. Ðæt hī wiðbleówen ðære fleógan (*culicem*), Past. 439, 25. Flēgan hundlice *muscam caninam*, Ps. Srt. 77, 45. Lytle fugelas ofsleáð sum ðing, hūru ðás fleógan, Hml. Th. ii. 46, 17. v. must-fleóge.

**fleóg-rift.** *Add*: *A mosquito-net* :—Nette, fleógryfte *conopio*, Wrt. Voc. ii. 87, 50: 19, 18.

**fleohtan** ; *p.* fleaht, *pl.* fluhton ; *pp.* flohten *To weave, plait* ; plectere. [*O. L. Ger. O. H. Ger.* fiehtan *plectere, flectere, intexere*. Cf. *Goth.* in fiahtōm ἐν πλέγμασιν.] v. flohten-fōt, fiehtre, flyhte.

**fleón.** [*In the following passages given under I in Dict.* fleón *is intransitive* :—By. 247 : Ps. L. 54, 8 : Gen. 2080 : Bt. F. 116, 17 : Ælfc. Gr. 36 : 28, 6 : Ps. Th. 103, 17 : Ps. L. 113, 3 : Met. 1, 20 : Mt. 8, 33 : Ps. L. 30, 12 : El. 134 : Gū. 228.] *Add*: I. *intrans.* (1) *to flee* from conflict :—Ne āblinnan wē þ wē deófol týnan, þonne fiyhþ þ deófol fram ūs, Bl. H. 47, 12. (1 a) in case of soldiers :—Nān heáfodman fyrde gaderian wolde, ac ælc fleáh swā hē mæst myhte, Chr. 1010; P. 141, 1. Hié flugon ofer Temese būton ælcum forda, 894; P. 85, 21. Þā Brettas mid micle ege flugon tō Lundenbyrg, 457; P. 12, 25. Hī bugon and flugon *they turned and fled*, 999; P. 131, 22. Þā flugon Pēne, and his wundredan, þæt hié ǽr flugon ǽr hié tōgædere geneálǽcten, Ors. 4, 6; S. 170, 23. (1 b) where legal process is to be executed :—Gif se friðman fleó oþþon feohte, Ll. Th. i. 286, 13. Þ man nænne ne slōge ... būton hē fleón wille oþþe hine werian, 242, 9. (2) *to flee* from captivity, danger, evil, &c. :—From onsiéne ðinre hwiðer fleóm ic (*fugiam*) ?, Ps. Srt. 138, 7. Se hýra fiyhþ (fiiið, L., flēs, R.), Jn. 10, 13. Hī fleóþ tō muntum, Bl. H. 93, 25. Fleáh hē tō Godes ciricean, 211, 28. Flaeh (flēh, R.), Jn. L. 6, 15. Þū fleóh þanan, Dōm. L. 30, 30. Flēh, Mt. L. 2, 13. Ne dýde man ... forwyrhtne man, būton hē fleó, Ll. Th. i. 402, 12. Hié ealle woldon fleón of þære ceastre, Bl. H. 245, 26. Hwylc æteówde eów tō fleónne fram ðon tōweardan erre ?, 169, 9. Þ hē hine fleóndne for þeóf slōge, Ll. Th. i. 124, 7. (3) *to run away, be a deserter* :—Be ðām ðe fíihþ fram his hláforde. Se man þe ætfleó (fleó, *v. l.*) fram his hláforde oþþe fram his geféran for his yrhðe, sý hit on scypfyrde, sý hit on landfyrde, Ll. Th. i. 420, 5-9. (4) *to go into banishment* :—Gielden þā mēdrenmægas þæs weres þriddan dǽl, þriddan dǽl þā gegyldan. For þriddan dǽl hē fleó ... for healfne hē fleó, Ll. Th. i. 78, 23, 25. (5) *to refuse assent* :—Mín mōd fiyhþ nū gyt, þ hit ne mæg gelýfan þ hit geseón ne mæg mid þæs líchaman eágum *mens refugit credere, quod corporeis oculis non valet videre*, Gr. D. 269, 11. (6) of things. (a) *to pass away* :—Seó unwæstmfæstnes fram him fleáh, Bl. H. 163, 18. Oft ðæt yfel ðæt forholen bið, hit bið fleónde *plerumque culpa, dum absconditur, effugatur*, Past. 427, 22. (b) of that which is fugitive, elusive, transitory :—Þes middangeard flyhþ from ūs, and wē him fleóndum fylgeaþ, Bl. H. 115, 17. Ealle þā þing ðe hēr líciaþ on þisum andweardum lífe sint eorþlice, for ðý hī sint fleónde, Bt. 34, 8 ; F. 144, 36. Fleóndu, Met. 21, 30. Þā fleóndan *fugacia*, Wrt. Voc. ii. 38, 42. (7) *to fly* ( = fleógan) :—On ðære lyfte fleóð fugelas, Hex. 8, 22. Sume gesceafta fleóð mid fyðerum, Hml. S. 1, 54. Fleónde næddre *loppe*, Wrt. Voc. i. 24, 1. II. *trans.* (1) *to run away from* a person from fear :—Þū fluge Esau *fugiebas* Esau, Gen. 35, 1. Dauid fleáh Absalon his sunu, Ps. Th. 3, arg. Þā Walas flugon þā Englan swā fýr, Chr. 473; P. 14, 4. Geceós ān wíte ... oððe þrý mōnðas gewinn, þ ðū swā lange fleó þíne fýnd, Hml. S. 13, 245. Ne ēht God nānre wuhte, for þý hine nān wuht ne mæg flión, Bt. 42; F. 258, 4. (2) *to avoid* a person from dislike :—Se wísdōm wille sōna fleón ðone ðe hine fiiéhð (fííhð, *v. l.*), Past. 247, 18. Þā þe mē gesāwon, hī mē flugon, Ps. Th. 30, 14. (3) *to decline, refuse to allow.* (a) with acc. :—Rōmāne him woldon ofrian ..., and sǽdon þ sió sibb of his mihte wǽre ; ac hē ǽgðer fleáh ge þā dǽd ge þā sægene, Ors. 3, 5 ; S. 106, 32. (b) *with clause* :—Ðæt mōd fíihð ðæt hit sié gebunden mid ege and mid lāre *se per disciplinam ligare dissimulat*, Past. 283, 18. Hē fleáh and forbeád þ hiene mon god hēte, Ors. 6, 1 ; S. 254, 8. (4) *to avoid* something, eschew, keep aloof from. (a) with acc. :—Hatiaþ yfel and flióþ ... lufiaþ cræftas and folgiaþ ðæm, Bt. 42 ; F. 258, 24. Gemānan fleónde *contubernia subterfugiens*, An. Ox. 3703. (b) *with dat. infin.* :—Hē fleáh eorðríce tō underfōnne *regnum percipere vitavit in terris*, Past. 33, 12. (5) of things, *to keep apart from* :—Hwílum fíihð se wǽta þ drýge, Bt. 39, 13 ; S. 136, 12. III. *to cause to flee, put to flight.* v. flīgan :—Tō fleánne ælc mæht fióndes *ad effugandam omnem potestatem inimici*, Rtl. 100, 31. v. fore-fleón.

**fleót** *an estuary.* *Add*:—On brādan fleót; andlang brādan fleótes ūt on sǽ, C. D. iii. 179, 28. On mearcfleótes mūþan, ... tō mylenfleótes mūþan, 429, 4, 5. On seolcingfleót; eást andlang fleótes on hagganfleót ; andlang hagganfleótes, C. D. B. ii. 519, 14, 15. Fleótas, fleútas *aestuaria*, Txts. 42, 107. Fleótas, Wrt. Voc. ii. 7, 36 : 144, 24.

Fleótes tô nette, i. 57, 9. Bi fiítum *fluctris* ( *flactris* ? fiactra *locus coenosus*, Migne), ii. 36, 43. Binnan twâm fiiátum sind genemde pirifiiát and scipfiiót, ðâ gesceádað þæt land westan and eástan oð ðæt weallfæsten, C. D. ii. 86, 25.

**fleót** *a boat.* v. fleóte.

**fleótan.** *Add:* I. *to float.* (1) *to be supported on the surface of a liquid :*—Heó fieát âweg ofer þ wæter tô lande, Shrn. 31, 21. Eahta daga fulla þ ilce scip fieát (*enatavit*) wætres full, Gr. D. 249, 11. Nim eádoccan moran þâ þe fleótan wille, Lch. iii. 6, 28. Fleótende *fluitans*, Germ. 401, 12. (2) *of fish, to swim :*—Eall fleótendra fixa cyn and fleógendra fugla, Shrn. 65, 31. Þæt heó gesáwe fleótende fixas and fleógende fugelas, Wlfst. 3, 5. II. *to flow :*—Ðâ streámas ðe on neorxna wange fleótað, Sal. K. 190, 26. [v. N. E. D. fleet.] v. tô-fleótan.

**fleótan** ; *p.* fieót To skim, *remove what floats on the surface :*—Seóð swíðe, fieót of þ fâm, Lch. ii. 96, 4, 8 : 104, 19. Seóðe and fleóte þ smeru, iii. 14, 12. [v. N. E. D. fleet to skim.] v. â-fleótan.

**fleóte, fliéte, flýte** *a float, flat-bottomed boat, raft, punt. Take here* **flýte** *in Dict., and add :*—Fliute *ratis*, Txts. 108, 1126. Fliétum *ratibus*, Wrt. Voc. ii. 76, 23. v. fieót ; II *in Dict.*

**fleóte** *cream.* v. fliíte.

**fleoþoma** (?) *a marsh* (?) :—*Flactris* (fiactra *locus coenosus*, Migne), i. *pontibus vel* fleoþomum, Wrt. Voc. ii. 149, 23.

**fleótig.** *For passage substitute :*—Swift wæs on fôre, fuglum frumra (fromra ?), fleótgau lyfte *swift was it* (a dragon) *in its course, outstripping the birds and the nimble air*, Rä. 52, 4. [Cf. *Icel.* fijótr.]

**-fléra(-e).** v. middel-fiéra : -fiére. *Add :* v. þri-fiére.

**fiéring.** *Add :* I. *a flooring, story of a building :*—Paulus wæs gelæd tô heofonan oð ðâ ðriddan fiéringe (*raptus usque ad tertium coelum*, 2 Cor. 12, 2), Hml. Th. i. 392, 13. [II. *a stratum, layer :*—Dô on ænne pott ân fiéring of ðâ hârhuna, and oðer of ysopo and ðridde of fersc buter, Lch. i. 378, 21.]

**fleswian.** *For* 'To mutter, whisper' *substitute: To profess to do something* (?). *In the passage* lícettende wrehte *and* leáse fleswede *seem equally to render* simulatam (legationem) volveret, *and for the latter* leáslíce ongann *occurs in one MS. Another various reading is* fieosewade.

**fiet** ; II. In l. 5 for 'L. In.' *l.* L. Alf., *and add :*—Hraðe wæs gerýmed féðegestum fiet innanweard, B. 1976. Ic on flette mæg rincum secgan naman þâra wihta, Rä. 43, 5 : Víd. 3. Ic seah in heall, þér hæleð druncon, on fiet beran wudutreów, 56, 2 : 57, 12 : B. 1647 : 1036. Hé mid témnan on fiet gæð, 2034 : 2054. Þæt hié him óðer fiet eal gerýmdon, healle and heáhsetl, 1086. Land eal geondhwearf, . . . Mêda mâddumselas, . . . Filistina fiet, Sal. 192. [v. N. E. D. fiet.]

**fiéte** *cream.* v. fliíte.

**fiet-gefeoht**, es ; *n. Fighting in a house :*—Be cierlisces monnes fiet-gefeohte. Gif hwâ on cierlisces monnes fiette gefeohte, Ll. Th. i. 86, 20. Cf. fletgefohth, 589, 5.

**fiet-mon.** *Dele* 'fiet-rest.' *Dele* 'Domestic couch,' *and add :* See description of the Icelandic hall in Dasent's Story of Burnt Njal, pp. cii, ciii.

**fiéwsa.** *Add :*—Mê þæs blôdes fiéusa twelf geár eglode, Hml. A. 189, 228. Fram þæs blôdes fiéusan gehæled, 187, 178. Þâ þe on hyra líchaman witan fiéwsan (*fluxa*) gálnysse wealdan, Scint. 121, 19.

**fiían** *to put to flight.* v. fiígan.

**fiicce**, es ; *n. Add :*—Flicci *perna*, Txts. 86, 774. Flicii, 88, 804. Flicci *feusa* (perna, quod rusticae *fiosa* dicunt), An. Ox. 53, 44 (and note). Mon selle .IIII. scép and tuâ fiicca, C. D. i. 293, 9. Feówer swín and feór fiiccu, 164, 31.

**fiicerian.** *Add :*—Hé cwæð þæt hê geseáge âne culfran fiyceriende ofer his heáfod, Hml. A. 198, 108. [v. N. E. D. flicker.] Cf. fiacor.

**fiiét.** v. fleóte : fiiéte *cream.* v. fliíte.

**fiígan, fiían.** *Add :*—Flicþ (printed fiiþ, Wrt. Voc. ii. 151, 50) *fugat*, fiýmþ *aufert*, Wülck. Gl. 244, 27. Hê ðone windes blæd âweg fiígde, Hml. Th. ii. 140, 26. Ðâ fuglas we ne onweg fiégdon *quas nos aues non fugare ausi eramus*, Nar. 16, 22. v. for-fiígan.

**fiigel**, es ; *m. A flail :*—Man sceal habban tô odene fiigel, Angl. ix. 264, 8. [*Orm.* fie33l. O. L. Ger. O. H. Ger. fiegil *tribulum* (-a). *From* (?) *Lat.* fiagellum.]

**fiige-wil.** *l.* fiyge-píl : fiigul. v. fiugol : **fiihte-cláþ.** v. fiyhte-cláþ.

**fiíma.** *Take here* fiéma, *and add :*—Fliíma *profugus*, Wrt. Voc. ii. 66, 44. Flýma, i. 50, 57. (1) *one who flees from danger :*—Flýma (*aemulorum vesaniae cedens*) *profugus*, An. Ox. 7, 212. God mê fiíman hider tô eówrum gemæran gelædde, Ap. Th. 9, 13. (2) *a run-away, deserter :*—Fliéma *transfuga*, Ors. 6, 31 ; S. 286, 15. Ic þê hálsie, Drihten, þæt þû mê underfô, ðinne fiýman (*fugitivum tuum*), Solil. H. 11, 21 : Angl. xii. 511, 21. (3) *one who deserts a faith, an apostate :*—Flýmena *apostatarum*, An. Ox. 4494. (4) *in a legal sense, one who flees from justice, an outlaw, exile, a banished person :*—Gif hí hine þonne begytan . . . ne mægen . . . þonne beó hê syþþan fiýma (*forisbannitus*,

Lat. version), and hine lecge for þeóf sê þe him tô cume, Ll. Th. i. 200, 10. Ælc fiýma beó fiýma on ælcum lande þe on ânum sý, 296, 21. Pastio latronum latitantium in siluis qui spoliant et occidunt alios, quos Angli uocant fiéman, Ll. Lbmn. 614, 1. Gif hine (*a criminal*) hwâ feormige, bête swâ . . . sê scyle þe fiýman (*id est forisbannitum*, Lat. version) feormige, Ll. Th. i. 164, 6 : i. 382, 21. Ðâ forstæl hê ðâ oxan . . . and tû hine hête ðâ fiýman, Cht. Th. 173, 7. (4 a) *a fugitive from ecclesiastical law :*—Be Godes fiýman. Gif hwâ Godes fiýman (fiíman, *v. l. Dei fugitiuum*, Lat. version) hæbbe on unriht, âgife hine tô rihte, 410, 15. ¶ fiíman feorm *harbouring an outlaw. Take here* fiiéman feorm, fiýman feorm *in Dict.* ¶ fiímena firmþ. [v. N. E. D. fiemens-firth.] (1) *as a right of royalty, the right to the penalty due from one who sheltered an outlaw* (fiíma) :—Ðis syndon þâ gerihta þe se cyng âh ofer ealle men on Wesseaxan . . . þ is mundbryce and hâmsócne . . . and fiýmena fyrmðe (cf. lôc hwâ þone fiýman feormie, gylde fíf pund þâm cyninge, 382, 21 ; *and :* On Dena lage hê âh griðbryce and hâmsócne . . . and gif hwâ þæne friðleásan man feormige, bête þ swâ hit ær lagu wæs, 384, 5–8. Cf. Hec sunt jura que rex Anglie solus super omnes habet in terra sua . . . hamsocna . . . fiemenfyrme, 519, 2), Ll. Th. i. 382, 14. (1 a) *as a subject of grant by the king :*—Ic (*Cnut*) cýðe eów þ ic hæbbe geunnen him (*the archbishop*) þ hê beó wyrðe griðbryces and hâmsócne and fiýmena fyrmðe ofer his âgene menn binnan byrig and bûtan, Cht. E. 233, 4. (2) *the privilege of sheltering an outlaw* (?), *right of asylum :*—Ic au heom þ hý habben . . . fiémenefyrmþe (?), right of asylum :—Ic au heom þ hý habben . . . fiémenefyrmþe *cum priuilegio fugitiuos suscipiendi*, C. D. iv. 202, 8. (5) *an outcast, wretch :*—Ðâ cwæþ seó hell tô Satane : ' Lâ ðû ordfruma ealra ysela, and lâ þû fæder ealra fiýmena ' (O Satan, *thou prince of all the wicked, father of the impious and abandoned*, Nic. H. 18, 7), Nic. 17, 5. [v. N. E. D. fieme.]

**fiíman** *to put to flight.* Take here fiýman *in Dict., and add :*—Fugat fiicþ. *aufert* fiýmþ, Wülck. Gl. 244, 27. (1) *to rout :*—Seó rôd nû on middangearde âwergde gâstas fiémeþ, Bl. H. 91, 25. (2) *to banish, exile :*—Ealdbriht wrecca gewât . . . Ine ofslôh Ealdberht þe hê ær ût fiémde, Chr. 725 ; P. 43, 28. Man fiýmde Godwine eorl and ealle his suna of Englalande, 1051 ; P. 172, 28. [v. N. E. D. fieme.] v. next word.

**fiíme** ; *adj. Fugitive :*—Þás biscopas wurdon swâ fiéme (fiýmed, *v. l.*) oð þ hí becômon tô Constantinopolim þære byrig *hi itaque profugi ad Constantinopolitanam urbem venerunt*, Gr. D. 241, 4. v. ge-fiíme (-fiéme).

**fiíming**, es ; *m. A fugitive, a banished person, an exile, outlaw :*—Flými[n]g *profugus*, i. expulsus, An. Ox. 2965.

**fiind.** *For* 'Cot. 98, Lye' *substitute :*—Flind *genitrix*, Wrt. Voc. ii. 41, 71.

**fiint.** *Add :*—Seó clænnes þâ fûlnesse mid fiinte torfað (*saxo percutit*), Prud. 12 a. God hêt þæt Abraham nâme scearpecgedne fiint, Hml. Th. i. 92, 34 : Wlfst. 195, 9. Hêt se ealdorman heora neb beátan mid blacum fiintum . . . þâ gelæhte se ealdorman ænne ormetne fiint, wearp tô þâm hâlgum. ac hê wand tô þâm heáhgeréfan and his heáfod tôbræc, Hml. S. 11, 98–104. ¶ with special reference to its fire-producing property :—Fiint *petra focaria*, Wrt. Voc. ii. 117, 9 : 68, 8.

**fiinten** ; *adj. Flinty, of flint :*—Heó wæron fiintenre heortan, Wlfst. 252, 1 note.

**fiís.** *Take here* fiýs *in Dict., and add :* (1) *fleece of a sheep :*—Swâ miclum snîwde swelce micel fiýs feóll *cadere in modum uellerum immense ceperunt niues*, Nar. 23, 13. Flýs *uellera*, An. Ox. 5192. Flýss, 5207. Uullan fiiásum, Txts. 150, 3. (2) *used of other animals :*—Twêgen seólas mid heora fiýse his fêt drýgdon, Hml. Th. ii. 138, 12. (3) *wool, down :*—Flýse *lanugine*, Wrt. Voc. ii. 51, 64. (4) *what resembles, or serves the purpose of, a fleece :*—Hié of sunnan treówcynne and of his leáfum and of his fiýse þæs treówes spunnon and tô godewebbe wæfon *foliis arborum ex siluestri uellere uestes detexunt*, Nar. 6, 17. v. wull-fleós (-fiýs).

**fiít.** *Add :*—Ðâ friðgeorne, ðâ ðe heá bûta êghuoelcum fiíta behaldan *pacifici*, Mt. L. 5, 9. Fram fiítum a *contentionibus*, Kent. Gl. 728. [v. N. E. D. fiite.]

**fiíta.** *l.* fiita, *and dele* 'wið-,'.

**fiítan.** *For* wiþer *at end l.* wiþ, *and add :*—Flítað *disceptant*, Wrt. Voc. ii. 106, 41. *Disceptant, lacerant*, i. contendunt fiítaþ, 140, 59. Ic fiât *certavi, contendi*, 130, 28. Wê fiitan *disceptavimus*, 28, 20. I. *of action.* (1) *to strive as an opponent :*—Æfre gê fiiton and wunnon ongeán Drihten *semper adversum Dominum contendisti*, Deut. 9, 7. Æfre gê fiiton ougén God *semper contentiose egistis contra Dominum*, 31, 27. Hý fiiton *exercebantur* (*adversum me*; cf. mê wiðerwearde wæron ealle, Ps. Th. 68, 13), Bl. Gl. Ðû findst wið hwone ðû meaht fiitan *contra quos valeatis vos extendere semper invenitis*, Past. 331, 5. (1 a) *of abstract objects :*—Hû micel wære þ gecamp þe wann ou þæs mannes breóstum ; þær fieát (feaht, *v. l.* pugnabat) betweoh him seó eádmôdnys . . . and seó ârfæstnys, Gr. D. 18, 6. (2) *to strive as a competitor :*—Ðâ hâlsade ic þ mê wære lýfnes seald tô ærnenne and tô fiítanne mid him *obsecrans ut mihi: certandi cum illis copia daretur*,

Bd. 5, 6; S. 575, 19. (3) *to strive* after, *strive* to gain :—Ðā ðe hira gōd sellað . . . , ðā ðe flīctað (flītað, *v. l.*) æfter ōðerra monna and hié reáfiað (*qui aliena rapere contendunt*), Past. 319, 15 : 177, 6. II. of speech or opinion. (1) *to be quarrelsome, contentious* :—Hē ne flāt ne ne hrŷmde, ne nān mann his stemne on strǣtum ne gehŷrde, Hml. Th. i. 592, 5. Nān crīsten man ne sceal sceandlīce flītan, Hml. S. 13, 122. (2) *to dispute, argue, have a controversy, oppose the opinions* of a person, *be at variance* :—Paulus þ ilce lǣreþ, and wiþ mē flīteþ, and þ ilce spreceþ and mid him (*S. Peter*) bodaþ, Bl. H. 175, 13. Arrius hātte ān gedwolman, sē flāt wið ænne bisceop þe wæs genemned Alexander, wīs and rihtgelȳfed, Hml. Th. i. 290, 3. Hī flītun betwux him (*facta est contentio inter eos*) hwylc hyra wǣre yldest, Lk. 22, 24. Sume cwǣdon . . . sume cwǣdon . . . and hig flīton him betweónan (*schisma erat in eis*), Jn. 9, 16. Flītan *disceptare (de vitiorum radicibus)*, Wrt. Voc. ii. 76, 83 : 26, 43. Flītende *disputans*, An. Ox. 3002. Of flītendum trachterum *a vitiosis interpretibus*, Mt. p. 1, 14. Flītende *certantes* (conflictum gessit contra bis senos *certantes* arte magistros), Wrt. Voc. ii. 91, 7. (3) *to bring a charge, accusation* against, *lay blame* on :—Andreas mē on flīteþ wordum for wera menigo *Andrew with abusive words lays blame on me before the multitude of men*, An. 1201. Þā flīton him on ðā werian gāstas and mid gelōmlicum oncunningum tiledon þ hī him ðone heofonlican weg forsetton *spiritus maligni crebris accusationibus inprobi iter illi caeleste intercludere contendebant*, Bd. 3, 19 ; Sch. 278, 7. Heó feóll tō eorðan flītende wið þone hālgan þ hē hī āsende on swā mycelne weg and ne weard gefrēfrod *she fell to the ground quarrelling with (blaming) the saint for sending her such a long way and she had got no comfort*, Hml. S. 3, 652. [*v. N. E. D.* flite.]

**flīt-cræft.** For 'Mone B. 3030' substitute :—Flītcr[æft] *dialectica*, An. Ox. 3116. Flītcræfte, 2, 155. Mid flītcræftum *dialecticis artibus*, 3207.

**flītcræftlic.** For 'Mone B. 3147' substitute Hpt. Gl. 481, 62 : **flíte** *a raft.* v. fleóte.

**flīte** *cream.* Take here flēte in Dict., and add :—Flēte(-i, -u) *verberatrum*, Txts. 105, 2100. Flēte *crama*, Wrt. Voc. ii. 105, 48 : 15, 46. Fleóte, 136, 58. Geþuorne flete (-i) *lectidiclatum*, Txts. 75, 1205. Geþworen flŷte, Wrt. Voc. ii. 50, 72 : *lactudiclum*, 52, 6. Ete ealdes spices iii snǣda, and sūpe mid flētum, Lch. ii. 316, 13.

**flītend.** *Dele, and see* flītan : **flīter-cræft.** *Dele, and see* flīt-cræft.

**flītere.** *Substitute for the passages* :—Flītere in eobotum *rabulus*, Wrt. Voc. ii. 118, 64. On helle beóþ þeófas and flŷteras and gītseras, Bl. H. 61, 21. Flītera *scismaticorum*, An. Ox. 2895. [*v. N. E. D.* fliter.]

**flīt-ful.** *For references substitute* :—An. Ox. 3356 : 3222.

**flīt-gāra,** an ; *m.* A gāra (*q. v.*) *where some kind of contest took place?* :—On ðone flītgāran ; of ðām flītgāran, C. D. 217, 15, 22.

**flīt-georn.** *Substitute* : **flīt-georn** ; *adj. Contentious, quarrelsome* :—Flītgeor[n] *litig[i]osa (mulier)*, Kent. Gl. 1022. Mid flītgeornan wīfe *cum muliere litig[i]osa*, 972. Ne beón gē tō nīðfulle ne tō flītgeorne, Wlfst. 40, 17. Cf. gefiit-georn.

**flītlīce.** *Add* : [*O. Sax.* flītlīko *eagerly* : *O. H. Ger.* flīzlīcho *curiose.*] **flīt-mǣlum.** *For passage substitute* :—Flītmǣlum, tō geflītes *certatim*, i. *strenue*, An. Ox. 106. Flī[t]mǣ[lum] *certatim*, 56, 210.

**flītme.** v. un-flītme.

**flītme, flŷtme,** an ; *f. A fleam, lancet* :—Blōdsexe, flŷtman *flebotomo*, An. Ox. 1984. [From Latin. Cf. blōdsaex *fledomum*, Txts. 114, 110, *and under* blōdseax *see the Latin words which it translates. O. L. Ger.* (Gall.) flētma : *O. H. Ger.* fliodema (Grff. iii. 360) *phlebotomum* : *Ger.* fliete. v. *N. E. D.* fleam.]

**flōc** *a fluke. Add* :—Flooc *platissa*, Wrt. Voc. ii. 117, 47 : 68, 22.

**flocan.** *Substitute* : **flōcan** ; *p.* fleóc *To beat together, clap* with the hands, as an expression of joy or grief :—Oft ic (*a sword*) wīfe ābelge, wonie hyre willan : heó mē wom spreceð, flōced hyre folmum . . . ungōd gæleð, Rä. 21, 34. Flōcende *conplosis*, Wrt. Voc. ii. 16, 14. [*Goth.* faiflōkun ἐκόπτοντο, *plangebant.* Cf. *Lat.* plangere *for form and meaning.*]

**flocc.** *Add* : I. of people. (1) *a company* :—Hē sōhte his gelīcan, ac hē ne mihte hine findan on ðām flocce *he looked for his match, but could not find him in that company*, Ap. Th. 12, 25. Hē geseah Crīst standan and þone clǣnan flocc mid him, hundteóntig þūsenda and feówer and feówertig þūsenda, Hml. A. 18, 115. (2) *a troop of soldiers, band, legion* :—Cwæð se lǣwa tō ðām lāðum flocce (cf. *cohors*, Jn. 18, 3), Hml. Th. ii. 246, 11. Hē mid þām ōðrum flocce fērde mid wīge, Jos. 8, 10. Swā fela manna (6666) wǣron on þām eúrode . . . On þām flocce wǣron ðā fyrmestan menn . . . , Hml. S. 28, 17. (3) *a band of* robbers :—Sceaðan āfīigdon ðā līcmenn, þ hī urnon āweg swā hraðe swā hī besāwon on ðone rēþan floc, Hml. S. 18, 306. II. of animals, *a flock, herd* :—Geseah hē micelne floc heorta . . . ān ormǣte heort . . . gewende fram þām flocce and rǣsde intō þām wudu, Hml. S. 30, 26-31.

**flocc-mǣlum.** *Add* :—Hiē wǣron flocmǣlum þiderweard þǣm ōþrum tō fultume *they were flocking to the place to the help of the others*, Ors.

4, 10 ; S. 200, 19. Hī flocmǣlum fērdon mid heora hīwum, Hml. S. 25, 235.

**flocgan** *to spring forth* :—Flocgest *emices*, Germ. 399, 461.

**flōd.** *Add* : (1) *flood, flowing of the tide* :—Flood *adsida*, Wrt. Voc. ii. 98, 1. On ǣlcum ānum geáre weaxeð þ flōd ðæs sǣs feówer and twēntigum sīða, and swā oft wanað, Shrn. 63, 29. Ðonne hit bið full flōd, C. D. iv. 24, 1. God him ðā sylle āsende mid þām sǣlicum flōde ; and þæt flōd hī āwearp . . . on ðām sealtum ōfre, Hml. Th. ii. 146, 4. Gewrixle þæs flōdes and þæs ebban, Bt. 21 ; F. 74, 29. (2) *a body of flowing water, a river, waves* of the sea :—Flōd oððe hærn *flustra*, Wrt. Voc. ii. 33, 32. Be þæs flōdes (*the Nile*) ōfre *ripae fluminis*, Ex. 2, 3. Þises flōdes (*fluminis*) wæter . . . þā fixas þe synd on þām flōde (*fluvio*), 7, 17, 18 : Gr. D. 193, 16. Deópan flōd oferlīþan (*Nilotica*) *gurgitis fluenta transire*, An. Ox. 3668. Ýstendre sǣ flōdas *feruentis oceani flustra*, 2476. (2 a) *a (fiery) stream* :—Ðæt rēðe flōd biterlīce bærnð ðā earman sáula *fluvius ignivomus miseros torquebit amare*, Dôm. L. 165. (3) *water* as opposed to land or fire :—Eádweard cwæð : 'Lǣt mē þ land.' Ðā cwæð Æðelstān þ him leófre wǣre þ hit tō fŷre oððe flōde gewurde þonne hē hit ǣfre gebide, Cht. Th. 207, 14. Hǣðenscipe bið þ man weorþige fŷr oþþe flōd, Ll. Th. i. 378, 20. (4) *a flood, deluge, an overflowing of land* :—His deácon sǣde þ seó eú wǣre of hire rihtryne on þǣre cyrican yrðland ūp yrnende . . . þā andswarode se biscop : 'Gā and cweð tō ðǣre eá : "Geblin ðū þyses flōdes," ' Gr. D. 193, 19. Flōdes *cataclismi*, i. *diluuii*, An. Ox. 2477. Ðā cōm rēn, and mycele flōd, Mt. 7, 25. Seó eú þ land oferfleów mid fōtes þicce flōde, Ors. 1, 1 ; S. 32, 6. (4 a) *the Deluge* :—Ðæt flōd weóx and ābær ūp þone arc, Hml. Th. i. 22, 4. Þæt ȳðgende flōd þe þā synfullan ādȳlegode, ii. 60, 4. (4 b) figurative :—Þæt flōd (*diluvium*) þǣra myclena wæterena, þæt synt þās andweardan earfoþa, Is. Th. 31, 7. On cwilde flōd, Ps. Srt. 31, 6. (5) *a great outpouring of water, a torrent* :—Flōd *compluvium*, Wrt. Voc. ii. 22, 66. Swīðe lytle beóð ðā dropan ðæs smalan rēnes, ac hī wyrceað ðeáh swīðe micel flōd and swīðe strongne streám ðonne hī gegadrode beóð *altos gurgites fluminum parvae sed innumerae replent guttae pluviarum*, Past. 437, 13. (5 a) *a flood of* tears :—Heó gebīgde þ heáfod in þā handa and āgeát þone flōd hire teára, Gr. D. 168, 1. (6) ? :—Flood ? flooc. Cf. *platissa* flōc id(*em*) *et bubla*, i. 65, 70, 71) *bubla*, Wrt. Voc. ii. 102, 36. Flōd, 11, 43. v. flylleþ-flōd.

**flōde** *a channel. Add* :—Flōdae (-e) *lacunar*, Txts. 74, 597. Flōda *lacuna* 111, 8. Flōde *lacunar*, Wrt. Voc. ii. 50, 55 : *lucunar*, 53, 68. Oð dīc tō ðǣre flōdan ; from ðǣre flōdan of dūne ðǣr fyxan dīc tō brōce gǣð, C. D. ii. 28, 36. On ðone stān æt ðǣre flōdan, 29, 14. Of ðǣre leúge on scyteres flōdan ; of flōdan on hriscmere, iii. 13, 34. Tō ðǣre flōdan æt swīnweges slō, v. 297, 28. Flōdena *cloacarum*, Wrt. Voc. ii. 82, 19 : 18, 34. ¶ in compounds :—Tō mearflōdan, C. D. iv. 66, 8 : v. 245, 27. Tō cytelflōdan, iv. 66, 14.

**flōde** ; *adj. Abounding in water* (?) :—Flōde *conpluviosus*, Wrt. Voc. ii. 22, 67. v. flōd, (5), flēde.

**flōden** ; *adj. Of a river* :—Flōdenum *fluviali*, flōdenes þweáles *fluminei lavacri*, Wrt. Voc. ii. 149, 65, 66.

**flōd-hamm,** es ; *m. A place surrounded by water* (?), or *protected against water* (?) :—Flōdhammas, C. D. i. 289, 18. Cf. wæter-hamm.

**flōd-lic** *of a river. Add* :—Flōdlic *fluminalis*, An. Ox. 56, 198.

**floege.** v. flēge : -**flog.** [*Icel.* flog *a flying ; a shooting pain.*] v. ge-flog.

**flogettan.** *Substitute* : (1) *to fly about, flutter ;* volitare :—Sum lytel fugel ongann flogettan (*volitare*) ymb his ansȳne, Gr. D. 100, 19. (2) *to be uncertain, waver, vacillate* :—Sēlre ys on eádmōdrum trum faran þænne hangendum grāde on heágrum flogettan (*fluctuare*), Scint. 205, 18. [*O. H. Ger.* flogezzen *volitare.*]

**flogoþa,** an ; *m. Liquor ;* liquor, Germ. 402, 42.

**flōh.** *Substitute* : A bit of stone :—Stānes flōh *gleba silicis*, Wrt. Voc. ii. 42, 27. [*O. H. Ger.* fluoh *rupes, scopulus* : *Icel.* flō *a layer, stratum.*]

**flōr.** *Add* : flōre. v. ūp-flōre :—Flōr *excusorium, pavimentum*, Wrt. Voc. ii. 146, 10. Flōr on hūse, 32, 59. Hē ārās of þǣre flōra and of þām sæcce þe hē onuppan wæs sittende, Hml. S. 23, 802, 823. On þæs hūses flōre (*in habitaculi pauimento*) seað ādelfan, Bd. 4, 28 ; Sch. 520, 8. Lǣt sittan þone man onmiddan hūses flōre, Lch. iii. 70, 13. On flōre *in area*, An. Ox. 3432. Flōr *feormian*, Angl. ix. 262, 23. Ðā wearp ic mē sylfe forð on þā flōr, Hml. S. 23 b, 469. Mon þǣre cyrcean flōr emlīce gewyrce, Ll. Th. ii. 408, 12. Tōbærst þæs temples wāhryft fram þǣre fyrste ufan oð ðā flōr neoðan, Hml. Th. ii. 258, 3. Þ þæt flōwende wæter hæbbe flōr on þǣre fæstan eorðan, Bt. 33, 4 ; F. 130, 4. Ne mihte seó his swaðu nǣfre beón þǣm ōðrum flōrum geonlicod *his footstep could never be made like the rest of the floor*, Shrn. 80, 39. Andlang rīðiges ðæt hit cymð tō fāgan flōran ( =flōrum, *or sing.? from* flōre) (*the tesselated pavement(s)?* cf. flōr-stān) ; ðonne be ðām twām lytlan beorgan, C. D. iii. 404, 9. v. niþer-flōr.

**flot.** *Add* :—Spēda unrihtwīsra eall swā flot (*fluuius ;* flōd?) beóð ādrūgude, Scint. 179, 15. Swā ðæt ðonne hit bið full flōd and ðæt scip

biđ ā-flote *ita ut natante naue in flumine cum plenum fuerit*, C. D. iv. 24, 1.

**flota.** *Add*: (1) *a ship*:—Gewāt fiota fāmigheals fugle gelīcost, B. 218. (2) *a collection of ships with their crews, a fleet*:—Flota *classis, navis collectae*, Txts. 110. 1170: *clasis*, Wrt. Voc. ii. 104, 16: 14, 45. þonne flota (*or under* (1)?) stonded; bið his ceól cumen and hyre ceorl tō hām, Gn. Ex. 96. Ðæt man sceolde Swegen underfōn ðā hē ǣrest mid flotan cōm, C. D. iii. 315, 3. Wæs se cyning mid þām flotan þe on Temese læg (wǣron, *v. l.*) . . . Se cyning gewende fram þām flotan, Chr. 1013; Th. 272, 12, 19. (2 a) *the crews of the ships*:—Se flota eall gecuron Cnut tō cyninge, Chr. 1014; P. 144, 28. Lǣgun seofene eác. eorlas Anlāfes, unrīm heriges, flotan and Sceotta, 937; P. 108, 13. (3) *a sailor*:—Hē mid orde ānne gerǣhte flotan on þām folce, By. 227. v. unfrið-flota.

**floterian.** *Add*: (1) *to be tossed on the waves*:—Flotorode *fertur fluctibus*, Germ. 400, 492. (2) *to flutter, make short, quick flights*:—Flotorodon *praeuolant*, 499. (3) *to move* (intrans.) *restlessly with excitement*:—Him wæs swā uneáðe, and þā eágan floterodon *he was ill at ease, and his eyes moved restlessly from one to another*, Hml. S. 23, 655. Hī cōmon mid floteriendum eágum for ðǣre micclan angsumnysse, 23, 153.

**flot-herge.** *l.* -here, *and add*:—Se flothere (*the Danes that had killed Edmund*) fērde eft tō scipe, Hml. S. 32, 130.

**flotian.** *Add*: [*Icel.* flota *to float*.]

**flot-lic;** *adj. Of a fleet, naval*:—Flotlicum, *sciplicum classicis*, Wrt. Voc. ii. 131, 63.

**flot-man.** *Add*: (1) *a seaman, sailor*:—Sciplicum rēþra ł flotmanna herium *classicis nautarum cohortibus*, An. Ox. 22. Flodmanna, 3, 14. (2) *a pirate*:—Flotman *archipirata, i. summus latro*, An. Ox. 4039. (2 a) *used of the Scandinavians ravaging England*:—Engle tō swyðe geyrgde, and flotmen swā strange, Wlfst. 162, 16. þās flotmenn cumað and þē cucenne gebindað . . . ofslægene fram þysum flotmannum, Hml. S. 32, 70, 77. *Justum bellum* is rihtlic gefeoht wið ðā rēðan flotmenn, 25, 708.

**flot-scip.** *Add*:—Flotscipu *liburnas*, Wrt. Voc. ii. 49, 73. [*Cf. O. H. Ger.* flōz-scif *barcha, cimba, liburna*.]

**flot-smere.** *Substitute*: **flot-smeoru,** wes; *n. Floating fat, fat or grease floating in a vessel in which meat is cooked*:—Gýme hē ǣgðer ge ðæs sēlran ge þæs sǣmran, þ nāðor ne misfare . . . ne flǣsc ne flotsmeru. ne cýse ne cýslyb, Angl. ix. 260, 13. [*Cf. Icel.* flot *fat, grease of cooked meat*.] Cf. flīte *cream*.

**flōwan.** *Add*:—Fleów *fluxit, decurrit, manavit*, flōwen *fluitent*, flōwendum *fluido, i. fluenti*, Wrt. Voc. ii. 149, 70, 64, 63. (1) *to flow as a stream in its bed, or a fluid over a surface*:—þīn blōd flēwþ ofer eorðan swā swā wæter, Bl. H. 237, 6. Flōwed (flēwed, *v. l.*) seó eá betwyh *interfluente amne*, Bd. 5, 2; Sch. 556, 5. þæt hnesce and flōwende wæter, Bt. 33, 4; F. 130, 3. Mid flōwendum teárum, Hml. S. 3, 626. (2) *to be or become fluid*:—Weax þe fleúwð ł melteþ *caera quae fluit*, Ps. L. 57, 9. Flȳwð, 67, 3. (2 a) fig.:—þæt deúde flǣsc rotað leahtorlīce, þonne se deádlica līchama ðeówað þære flōwendan (*fluid, and so capable of rotting?*) gālnysse, swā swā se wītega be sumum cwæð: ' Ðā nȳtenu forrotedon on heora meoxe,' Hml. Th. i. 118, 14. (3) *of persons, to resort in great numbers, come or go in streams*:—þā him fleówon tō forwel menige, Hml. Th. ii. 158, 30. (4) *of (immaterial) things, to pass away, be transitory*:—Se wlite þæs līchoman is swīþe flīonde (flōwende, *v. l.*) *formae nitor rapidus est*, Bt. 32, 2; F. 116, 17. (5) *to issue from a source*:—Ðanon flēwð eallum mildheortnys and gifu, Hml. Th. i. 448, 2. Of his innoðe fleówð līflic wæter . . . þæt wæter þe of ðām stāne fleów, ii. 274, 4-9. Of his sīdan ūt fleów blōd and wæter samod, 260, 12. Hē eft cymþ tō þām ilcan æwelme þe hē ǣr ūt fleów, Bt. 24, 1; F. 80, 27. Ðæt of ðǣm innoðum ā libbendu wætru fleówen, Past. 467, 30. (6) *to flow* (opposed *to to ebb*):—Seó sǣ symle feówer prican oððe fīf lator flōwð. Ðonne se mōna ūp ārīst, þonne onginð seó sǣ tō flōwanne, Angl. viii. 327, 27. Flēwð, Lch. iii. 268, 16. (7) *to be flooded, be covered with a fluid*:—Oft of ðinnum rēnscúrum flēwð seó eorðe, Hml. Th. ii. 466, 8. Hē bāt his tungan þæt heó on blōde fleów *he bit his tongue, so that it was bathed in blood*, 312, 25. Feól sum preóst of þām weorce, swā þ hē sāmcucu læg . . . and fleów eall blōde, Hml. S. 6, 165. (8) *to flow with.* (a) *of a stream, where the material of the stream is given*:—Ðeáh ðe him eall streámas hunige fleówan, Sal. K. p 86, 4. (b) *of other things, to abound*:—Tō gōdan lande, þæt ðe fleówð mid meolce and mid hunige, Hml. Th. ii. 192, 8. Flōwendre (blōwendre?) *praepollenti, i. florenti* (*gazarum affluentia*), An. Ox. 3602. v. ge-flōwan; eft-, fiþer-, singal-, tō-flōwende.

**flōwend-lic;** *adj. Liquid, melting*:—Flōwendlice hē dēþ þā liquefaciet ea, Ps. L. 147, 18. v. ofer-flōwendlic.

**flōwend-ness.** v. ofer-flōwendness.

**flōwing** (-ung), e; *f. A flowing, flux*:—Wīf sum wæs in flōwing (*fluxu*) blōdes . . . Āstōd þ flōwing (*fluxus*) blōdes, Lk. L. 8, 43, 44. Flōwing *fluxum*, Mt. L. 9, 20. v. eft-flōwing.

**flōw-nys.** *Add*: (1) *a flow, flux*:—Āstōd ðiú flōwnis (*fluxus*) blōdes, Lk. R. 8, 44. Sió unrōtnes ðe cymð of yfles blōdes flōwnesse, Past. 455, 14, 23. (2) *a stream*:—Ðāra lāra flōwnisa *doctrinarum fluenta*, Mt. p. 8, 17.

**fiugol** (-ul, -el). *Add*:—Flugul *fugitivus, i. interdum qui fugit*, Wrt. Voc. ii. 151, 10. Flygul (*printed by Wright* fiigul) *fugax, i. fugitiva, fugiens*, Wülck. Gl. 244, 24. Se freóndscipe of næfte scort ys and fiugol (*fugitiua*), Scint. 198, 8. Mid fiugelum færeldum *fugitiuis discursibus*, An. Ox. 262. Flugulum, 7, 28: 11, 17.

**flustrian.** *For example substitute*:—Flustriende, windende *plectentis* (= -es. v. Mk. 15, 17), Wrt. Voc. ii. 74, 32.

**flycge;** *adj. Able to fly, fledged.* [*v. N. E. D.* fledge; *adj. O. H. Ger.* flucchi: *Ger.* flügge.] v. un-flycge.

**flyge.** *Add*:—Mid þan þe se strǣl on flyge wæs, þā cōm windes blǣd foran ongeán, þ seó strǣl weard eft gecyrred, Bl. H. 199, 20. [*O. L. Ger.* fiugi *volatus*.] v. on-flyge.

**flygen.** v. on-flygen: **flygenness.** v. ā-flygenness.

**flyge-pīl,** es; *m. A flying dart. See passage in Dict.* at flege-wīl, *where pīl should be read for wīl.* v. An. Ox. 7, 165 *note*.

**flygul.** v. fiugol.

**flyht.** *Take here* flyþ *in Dict., and add*:—Swēg swā swā micelra fugla swēg . . . þ wæs ðāra engla flyht, Shrn. 74, 5. Ðe mā ðe ǣnig fugel his flyhtes gewylt, gif his ōðer fiðere forod bið, Hml. Th. ii. 318, 28. On flyhte wesan, Shrn. 112, 7. Mid hiora feðra flihte, 71, 21. Hē sealde ðām fixum sund, and ðām fugelum fliht, Hml. Th. i. 16, 7. Flihtas *convolatus, alatus*, Wrt. Voc. ii. 135, 52. Flyhtas *convolatus*, An. Ox. 5482: 2, 488. Wīdgillum flihtum *passiuis uolatibus*, 11, 19.

**flyht-clāþ.** v. flyhte-clāþ.

**flyhte;** *m. A patch of cloth*:—Nīwes flyhtes (*assumentum*) *panni rudis*, Mk. L. R. 2, 21. Nǣnig mon setteþ clāþflyhti neówenne in hrægl ald *nemo inmittit commissuram panni rudis in vestimentum vetus*, Mt. R. 9, 16. v. fleohtan, *and next word*.

**flyhte-clāþ,** es; *m. A patch of cloth*:—Flycticlāð *commisura*, Wrt. Voc. ii. 104, 22. Flyhteclāþ *commissura*, 22, 35. Clūt *vel* fiihteclāþ, 132, 11.

**flȳma,** &c. v. flīma, &c.

**flyne.** *Add*:—Flyne *fleba*, Wrt. Voc. ii. 149, 40.

**flȳs.** v. flīs: **flȳte** *cream.* v. flīte: **flȳte** *a raft.* v. fleóte: **flȳtme.** v. flītme.

**fnæd.** *Add*:—þone munuc sum sweart cniht teáh ūt be þām fnæde his hrægles (*per vestimenti fimbriam*), Gr. D. III, 28: Hml. Th. ii. 160, 23. Heó hrepode his reáfes fnædu, 394, 12. Fnæda, Hml. S. 31, 570. Sume heora fnada (*fimbrias*) gemicclaþ, R. Ben. 135, 26. v. ge-fnæd.

**fnæran;** *p. de To snort*:—Fearras fnærdon (*printed* fnæsdon, *but see* Grn. Wlkr. i. 321, 10), Lch. iii. 32, 12. Cf. fnesan.

**fnærettan;** *p. te To snort, neigh, make a loud sound with the breath*:—Frendens hnægende, fnærettende (*printed* fnæs-, *but see* E. S. xi. 511), *vel* grymettende, frendit i. stridet dentibus, rugiet grymetteþ, Wrt. Voc. ii. 150, 52-55.

**fnæs.** *Add*:—þte fasne gewoede his gehrinon *ut fimbriam uestimenti eius tangerent*, Mk. L. 6, 56: Lk. L. 8, 44.

**fnæst.** *l.* fnǣst, *dele last passage and bracket, and add*: (1) *breath of living creatures*:—Orþes, fnǣstes *spiritus* (*draconis*), An. Ox. 2452. Fnǣste *anhelitu, i. suspirio*, 2050. Deóres fnǣstum *bestiae flatibus*, 2472. (2) *blast of frost, fire*:—Ne forstes fnǣst, ne fȳres blǣst, Ph. 15. [Wel neȝ hire (*the owl's*) fnast atschet, O. and N. 44.] v. fnesan.

**fnæstian;** *p. ode To breathe hard, pant*:—þā men beóð mægre . . . fnæstiað swīþe (*breathe with great difficulty*), Lch. ii. 242, 7. [*v. N. E. D.* fnast. *O. H. Ger.* fnāston *anhelare*.]

**fnæstiaþ.** v. preceding word.

**fneósan;** *p.* fneás, *pl.* fnuron; *pp.* fnoren To sneeze. [*v. N. E. D.* fnese. Cf. *Icel.* fnȳsa to snort.] v. fneósung, fnora.

**fneósung.** *In bracket dele.* 'Icel. . . . sneezing', *and add*: v. preceding word.

**fnesan.** *Substitute*: fnesan; *p.* fnæs To breathe hard, pant, gasp:—þā þā hē sceolde ālǣtan þ nīhste oroð and āgyfan his gāst . . . þ gyt in þām breóste ānum fnæs hwylchugu līflic hǣtu þæs oreþes *in solo pectore vitalis adhuc calor anhelabat*, Gr. D. 324, 19. [*Cf. Icel.* fnasa to snort: fnasan *snorting*; fnœsa *to snort. Also cf. O. H. Ger.* fnehan *anhelare*.] v. ge-fnesan.

**fnora.** *Add*:—Fnora *sternutatio*, Wrt. Voc. ii. 121, 15: *coriza sternutatio*, 128, 80. Nebgebræc *vel* fnora, 135, 77. Se drinc wyrcð micelne fnoran, and sē hine bēt. þonne se geohsa of þære īdlan wambe cymð, ne bēt þone se fnora, Lch. ii. 60, 27-62, 1. Sē ðe gelȳfð wiglungum oððe be fugelum oððe be fnorum, Hml. S. 17, 89. v. fneósan.

**foca.** *Add*:—Hē geseah þær licgan ǣnne snāwhwītne focan (*glossed* kake) *he looked, and, behold, there was a cake baken on the coals* (*subcinericius panis*, 1 Kings 19, 6), Hml. S. 18, 164. Hē āsende him ǣnne focan (cf. hlāf, Gr. D. 118, 5), Hml. Th. ii. 162, 20. [*Cf. O. H. Ger.* fochenza *lagana, crustula: Lat. focacia panis sub cinere coctus*.]

**fōda.** *Add:* (1) *victuals, provisions:*—God forgifð ūs ðone hwīlwendlican fōdan . . . se fōda nis nā ūre mēd, Hml. Th. ii. 466, 1–3. Se eorðlica līchama behōfað þæs fōdan, i. 252, 27. Fōdan *uictus*, An. Ox. 3862. 'Hē beád ūs nȳtena fōdan (cf. ðrȳ berene hlāfas, 2), underfō hē gærs.' Basilius underfēng þæt gærs ðus cweðende: 'Ðū ūs sealdest nȳtena andlyfene, nā ūs tō fōdan, ac tō hospe, Hml. Th. i. 450, 4–8. On binne ðær se oxa and se assa gewunelīce fōdan sēcað, 42, 27. Gif hē næsð þone līchamlican fōdan, ii. 442, 26. Þ se līchama hæbbe hlȳwðe and fōdan, Hml. S. 11, 358. Þ seó eorþe fōdan (*pastum*) gecwēmne āgeáfe, Hy. S. 20, 3. Man heom fōdan geaf (hī man fædde, *v. l.*) of West-Seaxana rīce, Chr. 994; P. 128, 6. (2) *sustenance, support:*—Æt him wæs gelang eall heora fōda; sē heom on ealre hwīle metes tilian sceolde, Hml. S. 23, 218. Mid gestreónfullum bīleofena fōdan *sumptuosa pabulorum alimonia*, An. Ox. 1572. Ðæt cotlīf licge intō ðāre munece fōdan, C. D. iv. 214, 8. Fōdan *stipendium*, An. Ox. 4636. (3) *a particular kind of food:*—Of fōdum *de alimentis*, Scint. 53, 13. On fōtum *in alimentis*, R. Ben. I. 68, 15. Mīnre wylne ic sylle fōdan (*alimenta*), Ælfc. Gr. Z. 101, 2. (4) *figurative:*—Mid wordes fōdan (*pabulo*) geþanc gereordian, Scint. 53, 1. Ðām hē forgifð ðone gāstlican fōdan, Hml. Th. i. 184, 10. (5) *food* for a thing, *material that increases* or *strengthens:*—Fōda fȳres holt, and fōda wambe mete micel *incrementum ignis silua, et incrementum uentris esca multa*, Scint. 56, 17. Tyrwena tendre and sprota fōdan *naptarum fomite sarmentorumque nutrimine*, An. Ox. 1652. Tyrewan fōdan *resinae fomentum*, i. *nutrimentum*, 4028. v. fȳr-fōda.

**fōdder; I.** *Add:*—Fōdre *sagina* (*epularum*), Wrt. Voc. ii. 81, 71. Se scīrgerēfa fērde mid him and lēt him findan mete and fōddor æt ælcan castelle, Chr. 1075; P. 210, 25. Ātīh ł wilde fōter *zizania*, Mt. L. 13, 27.

**fōdder; II.** *Add:*—Fōdre *theca*, Wrt. Voc. ii. 82, 34. Hē bær Crīstes godspel in fōdre ofer his sculdrum swā hwæder swā hē eóde, Shrn. 116, 29. Tēgum, fōdrum *tehis* (=*thecis*), Txts. 101, 2010. [*O. H. Ger.* fuotar *theca: Ger.* futter.] v. bōc-, stic-fōdder.

**fōdder (?):**—*Falcastrum*, i. *ferramentum curvum a similitudine falcis vocatum* wudubil *vel* fōdur, Wrt. Voc. ii. 146, 83.

**fōdder-hec** *a rack* or *manger to hold fodder:*—Man sceal habban . . . fōdder-hec, Angl. ix. 265, 1.

**fōddernoþ, es; m.** *Sustenance, nourishment:*—Ealle þā stōwe þe þær ðam mannum tō fōddornoþe beón sceoldon *tota illic loca nutriendis hominibus profutura*, Gr. D. 193, 17. v. next word.

**fōdnōþ.** *Substitute:* fōdnoþ, es; m. (1) *sustenance, support, food:*—Þā land beón ðām gebrōðran tō fōdnoðe and tō scrūde, Cht. Th. 370, 27. (2) *a stock of provisions;* annona:—Fōdnaðas annonas (*printed* fodraðus *annonas; but see* Bd. Sch. 42, 36, *the passage here glossed*), Txts. 180, 20. [Mon sulleð his elmesse þenne he heo ȝefeð swulche monne þe he ahte mid rihte helpe tō fodneðe and to scrude, O. E. Hml. i. 137, 15.] v. *preceding word,* and fōsternoþ.

**fōdrere.** *Add: The Latin has:* pabulatores tempestas fulminibus exussit. [*O. H. Ger.* fōtarari *pabulator*.]: **fōend.** v. on-fōnd: **fōgere.** *Dele* 'A suiter . . . 4287': **fol.** v. full: -fol. v. ge-fol.

**fola.** *Add:*—Ylp is ormǣte nȳten . . . feówer and twēntig mōnða gǣð seó mōdor mid folan, Hml. S. 25, 569. Gemēte gyt eoselan and hire folan, Bl. H. 69, 36. Lǣdað hȳ mid him olfenda myran mid hyra folan and stēdan; þā folan hȳ gesǣlað ǣr hȳ ofer þā eá faran *tollent aput camelos masculos et feminas quae habent foetas; foetas trans flumen alligatas relinquunt*, Nar. 35, 11.

**folc.** *Add:*—Folc *populus*, Wrt. Voc. i. 50, 22.      **I.** where no dependence is implied. (1) *a people, the inhabitants of a state, a nation:*—Folc, cynn æfter cynne, Exod. 350. Þenden þæt folc (*the Hebrews*) hiera fæder wǣre healdan woldan, Dan. 10. Hī geridan West-Seaxna land . . . and mycel þæs folces ofer sǣ ādrǣfdon, Chr. 878; P. 75, 27. Ealles folces weg *the high-way*, C. D. B. i. 586, 15. Þǣm of-þynceþ þ hié synd Judēa folces, Bl. H. 175, 20: 187, 14. Folces Sodoma, Gen. 2489. Wǣron rēðe forebēcna cumene ofer Norðanhymbra land, and þ folc earmlīce brēgdon, Chr. 793; P. 55, 33. Ūt on elþeódig folc tō bebycganne, Ll. Th. i. 46, 14. Tō bihaldað gié folco (*populi*), 55, 28. Beforan ansȳne eallra folca, Lk. 2, 31. Folca hrōf *the sky*, Gen. 153: 2539. Folca leófost, Exod. 279. On folcum . . . ; geond þeóde *in populis* . . . ; *inter gentes*, Ps. Th. 56, 11. On landa gehwām folcum fracoðe, An. 409: Gū. 792. On þissum folcum (*the peoples of Sodom and Gomorrah*), Gen. 2499. Sodoma and Gomorra fȳre gesyllan, and þās folc sleán, cynn on ceastrum, 2506. Hē slōh þeóde folc manige *percussit gentes multas*, Ps. Th. 134, 10. (1 a) *the people bearing arms, an army:*—Þeáh þe feónda folc fēran cwōme herega gerǣdum, Dan. 698. On þǣm gefeohte . . . an Persum Darius hæfde siex hund M folces *sexcenta millia Persarum in acie fuere*, Ors. 3, 9; S. 124, 18. Geslagen on folces gefeohte, Ll. Th. ii. 386, 16: 150, 32. Ne getrūwade Geoweorþa his āgnum folce *diffidens propriis rebus et viribus Iugurtha*, Ors. 5, 7; S. 230, 7. Bið se here īdel, ðonne hē on ōðer folc winnan sceal *in exploratione hostium frustra exercitus sequitur*, Past. 129, 9. Hē ūs on þæt fȳr fylde folca mǣste, Gen. 749. Wurdon þā Gallie Rōmānum wiðerwearde . . and raþe þæs

heora folc tōgædere gelǣddon (*varia forte bellatum est*), Ors. 4, 7; S. 180, 25. (2) *a race, tribe, sect:*—Hē geseah ðæt folc Pharisēo and Saducia his ēhtan, Past. 361, 25.      **II.** where subordination or inferiority is implied. (1) *a body of people in relation to a ruler*, (a) *a human ruler:*—From ðæm folces (folches, R.) aldormenn *ab archesynagogo*, Mk. L. 5, 35. Folces rǣswan, Gen. 1669. Folces weard, 2666: An. 1070: El. 157. Worldwitan woroldlaga settan folce tō steóre, Ll. Th. i. 348, 14. Þā Dænescan þe wæs geteald eallra folca getreówwast . . . Cnute cynge āðas swōron, and syððan hine ofslōgon, Chr. 1086; P. 221, 29. (b) *a divine ruler.* (a) with a general application:—Wē þec bletsiað, Freá folca gehwæs, Dan. 401. (β) used of the Israelites:—Tō þīnes folces wuldre Israhel *ad gloriam plebis tuae Israel*, Lk. 2, 32. Metodes folce, Exod. 102. Forlǣt mīn folc þæt hit mæg offrian mē, Ex. 5, 1. (γ) used of Christians:—Gif se biscop ne geþafaþ þ Godes folc heora līf on wōh lybban . . . Gode is his folc swȳþe leóf, Bl. H. 45, 19, 35: 47, 21. Hē monige Crīstes folces dēmde tō deáðe, El. 499. (δ) used of those in heaven:—Is dreám on heofonum, þǣr is Dryhtnes folc geseted tō symle, Kr. 140. (2) *lay-folk, the laity* in contrast with the clergy. (v. *also* folcisc) :—Ne sceolan þā lāreówas āgīmeleásian þā lāre, ne þ folc ne sceal forhycggan þ hī tō him hī geeáþmēdon, Bl. H. 47, 29. Oþer wundor þ folc ongeat, ōþer þa sācerdas oncneówon . . . þā folcu cōmon mid mycelre mænigeo, and wē wǣron . . . singende herenesse Gode . . . þā þræng seó mænigeo þæs folces, Gr. D. 235, 15–26. Ne gedafenað biscope þæt hē beó on dǣdum folces mannum gelīc, Hml. Th. ii. 134, 12. Gif hit folces man sig . . . gif hit mynsterman sig *si secularis homo sit . . . si monasticus sit* (cf. 42, 5, 7 where *saecularis* and *laicus* are in contrast with *clericus*), Ll. Th. ii. 166, 9. Gif folces mannes esne tihte cirican mannes esne, i. 42, 10, 11. Ælc hād ciricean ānmōdlīce mid þȳ hērsuman folcy, 36, 11. Folce, 374, 28. Gif preóst folce miswissige, ii. 292, 11. (3) *the people, followers, attendants* of a person :—Ne ceara þū, Maria, þ þīn folc ne sȳ ādrēfed, Bl. H. 143, 4. (4) *the general body of a population, the people, the common people:*—Eall folc (*omnis plebs*) Gode lof sealde, Lk. 18, 43. Þ folc (*uulgus*) hine geseah, Bd. 2, 13; Sch. 168, 21. Þæt Iudisce folc, Bl. H. 69, 20. Beforan þæs folces mengeo, 173, 13. Ne wend þū þē nō on þæs folces unrǣd *non plurimorum acquiesces sententiae*, Ll. Th. i. 54, 6. Eádsige foran eallum folce hine well lǣrde, Chr. 1042; P. 163, 20. Onfēng Eádwine cyning mid eallum þām æþelingum his þeóde and mid micle folce (*plebe*) Crīstes geleáfan, Bd. 2, 14; Sch. 170, 1. Hē ādrēd him þ folc (*populum*), Mt. 14, 5. Ðā lǣrdon þēra sācerda ealdras and þā hlāfordas þæt folc (þǣm folce, R., ðæm folcum, L. *populis*), 27, 20. (5) *country-folk.* v. folc-stōw :—Be ciepemonna fōre uppe on londe. Gif ciépemon uppe on folce ceápie, Ll. Th. i. 118, 12.      **III.** in an indefinite sense. (1) *folk, men, people;* also in pl. *folks:*—Swā micel folc . . . forwurdon, þæt wæs nigon x hund þūsenda, Ors. 2, 5; S. 84, 28. Sūð-Mercna rīce, þā syndon fīf þūsendo folces *regnum Australium Merciorum, qui sunt familiarum quinque milium*, Bd. 3, 24; Sch. 314, 5. Hē āhlōd of feónda byrig folces unrīm, Cri. 569. Ealles folces Frēfrend, and ealles middangeardes Hǣlend, and ealra gāsta Nergend, Bl. H. 105, 17: Sal. 80. Folkes Scippend, Hy. 2, 1. Forebeácen folce manegum *prodigium multis*, Ps. Th. 70, 6. Hē þær gemētte swīþe manig folc, Bl. H. 141, 32. Folca bearn (cf. niðða bearn, 1135), . . . burgsittende, Gen. 1087. Folca rǣswa, Caldēa cyning, Dan. 667. Folca gehwylcum (cf. monna gehwām, Jul. 729) Scyppend scrīfeð, Cri. 1219. Eorlum cūð, . . . rīcum and heánum folcum gefrǣge, Rä. 89, 3: Men. 179: 218. (2) *a crowd, company, troop:*—Cōm him tō micel folc manna, Hml. S. 31, 1012. Menigo cwōm, folc unlytel, El. 872. Forlētte ðæt folc (mengu, R.) *dimissa turba*, Mt. 15, 39. His englas . . . ealra folca mǣst, wereda wynsumast, Gen. 607. (2 a) *a military troop, body of soldiers:*—Æfter him folca þrȳðum sunu Simeones sweótum cōmon; þūfas wundon ofer gārfare, Exod. 340. Fēran foldwege folca þreáte, tō Iudēum sēcan wigena þreáte, El. 215: 27. Faraon mid his folcum, Exod. 501. Hē þā folc gelǣdde þǣr hié tōgædere gecweden hæfde, and gesette twā folc diēgellīce on twā healfa his, and þridde beæftan him; and bebeád þǣm twām folcum . . . on fōre, Ors. 4, 6; S. 174, 30–176, 3. (3) *(a particular class of) people*, the class determined by a word or phrase, (*such and such*) *folk* ; in pl. *folks :*—Eal þ folc (cf. seó menigo, 9) þ þǣr beforan fērde, Bl. H. 71, 7. Hī genāman þæs folces þe þǣr tō lāfe wæs . . . Ealles þæs folces þe se cāsere innon Ierusalem befērde, 79, 20, 24. Hē ne wæs þearfendum folce *non erat de paupere vulgo*, Bd. 4, 22; Sch. 458, 17. Ne filig þū þām folce þe yfel wylle dōn, Ex. 23, 1. For eal crīsten folc, Bl. H. 45, 32. Þ geleáffulle folc Iudēa, 79, 30. Þā clǣnan folc *the righteous*, Cri. 1223. Þ se cyning and se bisceop sceoldan beón crīstenra folca hyrdas, and hī from eallum unrihtwīsum āhweorfan; and gif mon ne mihte . . . , þonne sceal æghwylc man bētan his wōhdǣda be his gyltes andefne, Bl. H. 45, 25. Israhela folca rīce *the kingdom of the men* (or *tribes?*) *of Israel*, 117, 12. Þ wē ealle Gode līcian, swā hit eallum geleáffullum folcum beboden standeþ, næs nā þām ānum þe Gode sylfum underþeódde syndon mid myclum hādum, 109, 21. v. Angel-, ceorl-, eást-; norþ-, sīd-, unrīm-folc.

**folc-ágende** *ruling.* *Add:* For force of āgende cf. Breca gesōhte swǣsne ēđel, leóf his leódum, lond Brondinga, . . . þǣr hē folc āhte, burh and beágas, B. 522.

**folc-cwide**, es; *m. A popular saying:*—Swā eald folccwide cwyđ *ut uulgo dicitur*, Nap. 23.

**folc-cyning.** *Add:* [ȝit beođ icumen from þon kinge Aruiragune, faređ aȝen to þan folckinge, Laym. 9501.]

**folc-dryht.** *For first passage substitute :*—Þonne sió bȳman stefen and se beorhta segen . . . folcdryht wera biforan bonnađ, sāwla gehwylce *when the voice of the trumpet and the bright banner . . . summon to the presence the multitude of men, every soul,* Cri. 1067.

**folce-firen.** *Perhaps the passage given here might be read :*—Wǣrlogona sint folca firene hefige (folca *being taken as parallel to wǣr-*logona, *and each referring to the people of Sodom and Gomorrah :* cf. on þissum folcum, l. 2499, þās folc, 2506) *of the traitors, of the peoples, are the sins heavy.*

**folce-getrum.** *The passage is :*—Him þā Abrahani gewāt and þā eorlas þrý þe him ǣr treówe sealdon mid heora folce getrume. *Perhaps for the last half-line might be read* trume mid heora folce.

**folce-egsa.** *For* 'Folk-terror' *substitute:* Terror felt by a people *or that which causes terror in a people.*

**folc-frig, -freó.** *After* 'Folk-free' *add: having the rights of a freeman.*

**folc-gedréfness**, e; *f. Troubling of peoples :*—Mycel folcgedréfnesse biđ đonne ǣr dōmes dæg (cf. Mt. 24, 7), Nap. 23.

**folc-gefeoht.** *Add:* (1) *a war carried on by the forces of one people with those of another :*—Gif man ofsleá ōþerne on folcgefeohte (folces gefeohte, *v. l.*) *si quis alium in bello publico* (cf. in publico bello cum rege, 24, 11 : cf. also p. 5, § 17) *occiderit*, Ll. Th. ii. 150, 4. Æt þrīm folcgefeohtum forwurdon nigon x hund þúsenda of Persa ānra anwealde *de uisceribus unius regni decies novies centena millia virorum tria bella rapuerunt,* Ors. 2, 5 ; S. 84, 28. (2) *a battle fought in such a war :*—Hié gecwǣdon folcgefeoht him betweónum *they (the Romans and Jugurtha) agreed to fight a pitched battle,* Ors. 5, 7 ; S. 230, 10. Philippuse gepūhte þæt hē leng mid folcgefeohtum wiđ hié ne mehte, ac hē wæs mid hlōþum on hí hergende, 3, 7 ; S. 118, 18.

**folc-geréfa.** *Add:* Folcgeroebum *actionaris,* Wrt. Voc. ii. 98, 38. Folcgerēfum *actionariis* (printed *ac dignariis*), 4, 22.

**folc-gesíþas.** *Substitute:* **folc-gesíþ**, es ; *m. An officer of the nation* (in contrast with dryht-gesíþ ?) :—Folcgesíđas þe mē mid sceoldon mearce healdan, Gen. 2134. Þæt ehtode ealdor þeóde wiđ þām nēhstum folcgesíđum : 'Þæt eówer fela geseah, þeóde mīne . . .' Þā cwæđ sē þe wæs cyninges rǣswa . . ., Dan. 412. Þeódrīc hēht folcgesíđas healdan þone hererinc, Met. 1, 70.

**folc-gestealla.** *Substitute: A comrade in arms* (? cf. fyrd-gestealla) :—Bigstandađ mē strange geneátas, þā ne willađ mē æt þām strīđe geswícan . . . hié habbađ mē tō hearran gecorene . . . mid swilcum mæg man rǣd geþencean, fōn mid swilcum folcgesteallan (=-um ?) *with such may one devise counsel, take (counsel) with such comrades,* Gen. 287.

**folc-getæl.** *Substitute: The number of a people or army* (v. folc ; I. 1 a) :—Wæs on ānra gehwām ālesen under lindum on folcgetæl fíftig cista *in each tribe were picked out for service, elected into the number of the folk that should fight, fifty troops,* Exod. 229.

**folc-geþrang.** *Dele. See ge-þringan.*

**folc-her[e]paþ,** es ; *m. The public road, highway :*—On đone folchearpađ ; ondlang đæs hearpađes, C. D. iii. 393, 14 : 463, 17. Cf. þeód-herpaþ.

**folcisc.** *Add:* (1) *popular, with which all people are concerned :*—Folcisc gemót, Ll. Th. i. 326, 21. (2) *of the common people :*—Folcisce men secgaþ þ ǣlce rēþu wyrd sié yfel, Bt. 40, 2 ; F. 248, 6. ¶ on folcisc *in common, popular language :*—Lytel fugel, sē is on folcisc (*vulgo*) þrostle gehāten, Gr. D. 100, 19 : 141, 27. (3) *of the clergy, secular* (in contrast with *regular*) :—Gif man folciscne mæssepreúst mid tihtlan belecge þe regollíf næbbe (cf. gif man mæssepreúst tihtlige þe regollíce libbe, 11), Ll. Th. i. 344, 19.

**folc-lagu** *a law that is valid for all the people of a country, a law of the nation :*—Godes gerihta wanedan innan þysse þeóde on ǣghwylcum ende, and folclaga wyrsedan (*the laws deteriorated*), Wlfst. 158, 6.

**folc-land.** *Add:*—Gif se cyning mīnum suna geunnan wille đes folclondes tō đǣm bóclonde, đonne habbe and brúce, C. D. ii. 120, 35. Cyninges folcland, 65, 1. *See also p. ix, and N. E. D.* folk-land.

**folc-lár.** *For* 'Cot. . . . Lye' *substitute:*—Folclāre *omeliae verba,* Wrt. Voc. ii. 65, 42. In þām folclārum þæs godspelles (*in homiliis euangelii*), Gr. D. 290, 10 : 286, 7.

**folc-leásung.** *Add: uttering false and slanderous statements such as are prejudicial to the public welfare.* Slander, as affecting an individual, which entailed the same penalty as that for *folc-leásung*, is treated in the following :—Sē þe ōđerne mid wōge forsecgan wille, þ hē ađor oþþe feó oþþe freme þe wyrsa sȳ . . . sȳ hē his tungan scyldig, Ll. Th. i. 266, 22-25 : 384, 23-26 (*de poena conviciatorum*). See also L. Hen. I. c. 34. § 7 : 59, § 13. *Folcleásung* seems to be the same crime as that referred

to in later lawbooks, quoted Ll. Th. i. 82, 'Sunt quaedam atroces injuriae . . . sicut de inventoribus malorum rumorum, unde pax possit exterminari.' Cf. too *leasing-maker* in Scotch law, one who utters untrue and slanderous statements such as are likely to prejudice the relations between the king and his subjects. But perhaps the public character of the crime, indicated by *folc*, may consist in the false and slanderous statements being made to a court of law. Cf. L. Hen. I. c. 34, § 7 : Qui aliquem erga justiciam accusabit . . . et mendacium denique pernoscatur, linguam perdat. Cf. folc-wōh.

**folc-lic.** *Add:* (1) *that concerns the whole people, public, national :*—Hī woldon ferian mid folclicum wurđmynte þone hālgan līchaman, and lǣcgan innan þǣre cyrcan *they wanted to give the body a public funeral,* Hml. S. 32, 174. Hī gewǣpnode ūt fērdon mid folclicum truman *accepit unusquisque vir arma sua et egressi sunt,* Hml. A. 113, 356. Đone feórđan pening on folclicre steóre *omnem quartum nummum reipublicae,* C. D. iii. 61, 15. Hē nolde forlǣtan þone folclican campdōm *he would not give up the army,* Hml. S. 31, 92. (2) *of the great mass of people, common, general :*—Folclice *vulgata* (*traditio*), An. Ox. 5097. Fela wundra wē gehȳrdon on folclicre sprǣce, Hml. S. 32, 247. (3) *public* (in contrast with *secret*) :—Tō ansȳne folclicre (*ad faciem publicam*) geþyld hī hīwiađ, and on geþance yrsunge āttor hī behȳdađ, Scint. 9, 12. (4) *of the common people, plebeian, common :*—Of cyrliscum lífe and of folclicum gedeorfe *ex vita rustica et ex plebeio labore,* R. Ben. 138, 22. Ān his þeówa his gesīđa wæs . . . and samod hī gereordoden swā swā gelícan. Þreó geár hē fērde mid þām folclicum cempum, Hml. S. 31, 40. (4 a) *like the common people, common, without distinction or excellence :*—Mōna se þri and twēntigođa cild ācenned folclic, Lch. iii. 194, 22. Hē næs begangende īdele spellunge folclicra (-ric-, MS.) manna, Guth. 12, 17. (5) *having many people, populous :*—Folclicere *populosae* (*civitatis*), An. Ox. 4887. Betwyx twām folclicum *inter duo populosa* (*praedia*), 3789. [O. H. Ger. folch-līh *popularis, plebeius.*]

**folc-mǽgen.** *Substitute: The forces of a people, a people, tribe :*—Folcmǣgen fōr æfter ōđrum *tribe followed tribe* (of the twelve tribes passing through the Red Sea), Exod. 347. Hǣđne þeóde . . . efnedon unrihtdōm, swā hyra aldor dyde . . . fremde folcmǣgen (*the people of Babylon*), swā hyra freá ǣrest unrǣd efnde, Dan. 185. Gewāt him Andreas inn on ceastre gangan tō þæs þe hē gramra gemōt, fāra folcmǣgen (*the Mermedonians*), gefrægen hæfde, An. 1062. Cf. þeód-mǣgen.

**folc-mǽgþ.** *Add:*—Steápe stānbyrig . . . folcmǣgđa byht, Gen. 2213.

**folc-mǽre.** *Add:* Cf. folcum gefrǣge.

**folc-rǽden.** *Add: people* (?) :—Folcrǣdenne (*gen. sing.* or *n. pl.* ?) *sive ealles folces gesetnes lex,* Wrt. Voc. ii. 53, 79. [Þet we maki oure guode dedes touore þe uolkerede (*coram hominibus*), Ayenb. 196, 16.] Cf. folc-scipe.

**folc-riht.** *Add:*—Ne lǣte hē nǣfre his hȳrmen hync ofer wealdan (oferwealdan ?), ac wilde (wille, MS.) hē ǣlcne mid hlāfordes creafte and mid folcrihte, Angl. ix. 260, 29. [þæt hē] wiþ heora folcrihte feala worhte (cf. hunc inuenimus subuertentem gentem nostram . . . commouet populum, Lk. 23, 2, 5), Bl. H. 177, 22. Đǣr ne gebyređ an đām landæ an folcæs folcryht tō lēfænnæ rūmæs būtan twigen fȳt tō yfæsdrypæ, C. D. ii. 89, 7. Đæt hyra nān ne wandode ne for mīnan lufan ne for mīnum ege đæt hȳ đæt folcriht ārehton *that none of them either for love or fear of me hesitated to declare the law,* 114, 1.

**folc-scearu.** *Add:*—Þis þinceđ gerisne þæt þū þe āferige of þisse folcsceare ; þū þās werþeóde feorran gesōhtest, Gen. 2477. Is cūđ hwanon þām ordfruman ǣđelu onwōcon ; hē wæs āfēded on þysse folcsceare, An. 684. Wæs gefrǣge in þǣre folcsceare, geond þā werþeóde wīde lǣded, mǣre morgenspel, El. 968. ¶ in B. 73 Kemble would take *folc-scearu* = *folc-land* public land, C. D. ii. p. ix.

**folc-sóþ** *the plain truth* (?) :—Ic secge hēr beforan eów eallum folcsóđ *I say here before you all the plain and simple truth,* Hml. S. 23, 666. Cf. folc-wōh.

**folc-stede.** *Add: a battle-place, battle-field* (v. folc ; I. 1 a) ; Æđelst. 41 : Jud. 320 : Rä. 6, 11 : B. 1463 : Gen. 2000.

**folc-stów.** *Add:* v. folc ; II. 5.

**folc-toga.** *Add:* (1) *of a temporal leader :*—Hē (*Moses*) wæs leóf Gode, leóda aldor, herges wīsa, freom folctoga, Exod. 14. Se folctoga (*Nebuchadnezzar*), Dan. 656. Þæs folctogan (*Holofernes*') bed, Jud. 47. þām folctogan, Jul. 225. (2) *of a spiritual leader :*—Dryhtnes cempa, from folctoga (*Guthlac*), Gū. 874.

**folc-wélig.** *l.* -welig, *and add :*—þǣre folcwelegan *populose,* Wrt. Voc. ii. 67, 25.

**folc-wóh** *a public wrong :*—Nis his talu nān þineg sóþ, ne drífđ hē būtan folcwóh *there is no truth in his tale, he is but wronging the public,* Hml. S. 23, 691.

**fold-bold.** *For the passage substitute :*—Se winsele on hrúsan ne feól, fæger foldbold.

**folde.** *Add:*—Hāl wes þu, folde, fira mōdor, Lch. i. 404, 2. Se līchama in þǣre cealdan foldan (eorđan, moldan, *v. ll.*) gebrosnađ, Wlfst. 187, 12. Wæs Waldendes lof āfylled on foldan, Chr. 975 ; P. 120, 14.

**fold-hrérende.** *Add:* *earth-stirring*, epithet of an animal that stirs the ground with its feet, *making foot-prints on the ground, treading the ground.*

**fold-ræst.** *Substitute:* **fold-rest**, e; *f. A resting-place in the earth, a grave*; or *rest in the earth* (of the buried dead):—Þonne eall Adames cynn onfehð flæsce, weorðed foldræste, eardes æt ende *then* (*at the resurrection*) *all the race of Adam shall receive flesh, it will be at end with the grave, their dwelling-place,* Cri. 1029.

**folgend.** v. sunn-folgend.

**folgere.** *Add:* (1) *one who walks in the steps of another* (lit. or fig.):— Oft cymð sē bæftan ûs þe ûs mid swyftnysse gôdre drohtnunge fore-stæpð; and wē earfoðlîce him filiað tô merigen, sē ðe nû tô dæg is ûre folgere gedûht, Hml. Th. ii. 82, 19. (2) *one who succeeds to the office of another, a successor:*—Þæt gewinn betux Alexandres folgerum *bella inter successores Alexandri,* Ors. 3, 11; 148, 27. Þæt gewinn Alexandres folgera, S. 150, 27. (3) *a follower, adherent,* (a) of a prince:—Nâ mâ ne lifde þâra þe Alexandres folgeras wæron *extinctis Alexandri ducibus,* Ors. 3, 11; S. 152, 15. (b) of a teacher, example, opinion, &c.:— Ðâ wrôhtgeornan sint tô manigenne ðæt hié geðencen hwæs folgeras (*sequaces*) hié sindon, Past. 357, 16. Seó sôþe gesælþ mæg ælcum hire folgera sellan þurhwunigendne welan, Bt. 33, 3; F. 126, 12. (4) as a legal term, in contrast with *heorþfæst man.* [v. Andrews' Old English Manor, s.v.] The word is used of women as well as of men:—Gif hwâ mid his lotwrencum ôðres mannes folgere (*pedisequam*) fram him âþæce for hæmedþinge, Ll. Th. ii. 186, 22. [*O. H. Ger.* folgari *sequester, sectator;* folgara *pedisequa.*]

**folgian.** *Add:* (1) *to move behind and in the same direction as another object:*—Petrus folgade hine feorran, Mt. R. 26, 58. (1 a) *to follow with the intention of overtaking, to pursue:*—Ðâ hâtheortan folgiað hwæm suâ suâ Assael dyde Æfnere, Past. 297, 4. Ne folga mê *noli me persequi,* 295, 15. Gif him hwilc mon folligende biþ, þonne feorriaþ hî and fleóð, Nar. 35, 32. (1 b) *to journey* with an object:— Æteáwdan twêgen weras ... and cwædon þ hié of Hierusalem cômon and for him folgedan (*they had come to fetch him?*), Bl. H. 191, 32. (2) *to accompany, be attendant upon.* (a) of persons:—Cum and folga mê, Mk. 10, 21. Ic wille folgian þe hwider swâ þû ganges, Mt. R. 8, 19. (b) of things:—Ðæm oferbliðan oft folgað firenlusð and ðæm unrôtan ierre *habent laeti ex propinquo luxuriam, tristes iram,* Past. 189, 5. Þæra twelf mônða naman, and ... eall þ gerâd þæt heora gehwylcum folgað, Angl. viii. 305, 28. Þâ þing þe heora âgene gecynd þe gedydon fremde ... nis hit nô þe gecynde þte þû hî âge, ne him nis gebyrde þ hî ðe folgien, Bt. 14, 1; F. 40, 34. Ne þurfon gê ðâm anwealde æfter þringan; gif gê wîse biþ and gôde, he wile folgian eôw, þeáh gê his nô wilnian, 16, 1; F. 50, 31: 16, 3; F. 54, 10. (3) in a more or less technical sense, *to be a folgere* (v. folgere, (4) (3)) *to have no house of one's own, live as a dependent with strangers:*—Ic geondférde fela fremdra londa ... freómægum feór, folgade wîde, Vid. 53. Willfrið wæs on þâ tîd of his êðle âdrifen and in Mercna land folgade *Uilfrid tunc patria pulsus in Merciorum regionibus exulabat,* Bd. 5, 11; Sch. 608, 5. (4) *to follow* a teacher, *take as a guide* or *model:*—Þâ hâlgan apostolas þe ðâm Hælende folgodon, Hml. A. 56, 141. Þâ men þe Simone folgodan, Bl. H. 173, 33. (5) *to yield to, comply with the will of:*—Folgað *obsequitur,* Wrt. Voc. ii. 64, 76. (5 a) of persons:—Côm þâm cynge word þ se aðð. Wulfrîc forð gefaren wæs, þâ geceás he Æðelsige munuc þær tô ... , folgode þâ Stîgande arcb., and weard gehâlgod tô aðð., Chr. 1061; P. 190, 4. Hî môston þes cynges wille folgian, 1086; P. 221, 16. (5 b) of things:—Gif seó hringe him folgað æt þâm forman tige, Hml. S. 21, 45. (6) *to follow* an opinion, instruction, direction, *act in accordance with* a rule, *be guided by, follow* footsteps (fig.):—Hit is ælces môdes wîse þ sôna swâ hit forlæt sôþcwidas, swâ folgaþ hit leásspellunga, Bt. 5, 3; F. 14, 16. Folgiað his rædum, Hml. S. 25, 265. God sylf forbeád þ wê swefnum ne folgion, 21, 412. Þ gié folgiaþ swæðe his, Rtl. 26, 5. Uton wê his lâre folgian, Bl. H. 169, 18. Eád-gâres lagan geornlîce folgian, Ll. Lbmn. 278, 16, col. 3. (7) *to follow,* practise a profession, *devote one's self* to a pursuit:—Fela ôðre forférdon þe folgodon drýcræfte, Hml. S. 17, 122. Lufiaþ cræftas and folgiaþ ðâm, Bt. 42; F. 258, 25. Hwý wênst þû þ hî forlætan ðâ cræftas and folgian ðæm unþeáwum?, 36, 6; F. 180, 29. (8) used absolutely, *to follow the monastic profession:*—Þis land wæs swîðe âfylled mid munecan, and þâ leofodan heora lîf æfter scs Benedictus regule; and Xpendôm wæs swilc on his dæge þ ælc man, hwæt his hâde tô belumpe, folgade, sē þe wolde *such was the condition of religion in his time, that every man, whatever considerations there might be with regard to his rank, who wished to, followed the profession of a monk,* Chr. 1086; P. 219, 31.

**folgoþ.** *Dele bracket and first three passages, and add:* I. with the idea of service. (1) *to the king or state, service, office:*—Tô his folgaþe and tô his þenunge þâ æþelestan côman *ad eius* (Oswine) *ministerium uiri nobilissimi concurrerent,* Sch. 256, 14. Hê (*the centurion*) forlêt his folgoð, Hml. S. 27, 192. (1 a) *the district in which office is held:*—Se biscop âmanige þâ oferhýrnesse æt þâm geréfan þe hit on his folgoðe sý, Ll. Th. i. 214, 3. Ænne castel on Herefordscîre on Swegenes

eorles folgoðe, Chr. 1048; P. 174, 1. Him (*Godwine*) wæs lâð tô âmyrrene his âgenne folgað (*comitatum suum*), P. 173, 13. (2) to a lord:—Sêlre him (*the reeve*) is æfre of folgoðe ðonne on, gyf hine magan wyldan ðâ ðe hê scolde wealdan, Angl. ix. 260, 30. II. with the idea of independent rule. (1) *authority, official dignity:*—Ðâ ofersettan mon sceal suâ manian ðæt se hiera folgoð hî ne oðhebbe (*ne locus superior istos extollat*), Past. 189, 17. Monige wilniað folgoðes and ealdordômes *praedicationis officium nonnulli appetunt,* Past. 47, 23. On ðý seofoðan geáre ðæs ðe Ôswald bisceop tô folgaðe fêng, C. D. iii. 5, 17. Folgoðe, 21, 28. Hû hê on ðone folgoð becume *ad culmen regiminis qualiter veniat,* Past. 23, 20. Ðâ ðe ... him mon swelcne folgað beóded and hié him wiðsacað *qui culmen regiminum si vocati suscipere renuunt,* 41, 20. Ðonne hié underfôð ðone folgoð *cum regiminum loca percipiunt,* 289, 5. (2) *the district over which authority is exercised:*—Heom gebirað tô bestandenne þâ men þe hîrað intô heora mynstre, and ne sceal nân faran on ôðres folgoð, Ll. Th. ii. 386, 5. v. bisceop-, prâfost-, sundor-, weorold-folgoþ.

**folme, -an.** *Add:* folma(?); *m.:*—Of werlicum folman *sine uirili uolo,* An. Ox. 1549: fol-neáh. v. ful-neáh.

**fôn.** *Add:* I. *trans.:*—þ sý fang[e]n *ut reprehendatur,* An. Ox. 27, 27. (1) *to take, catch:*—Hwæt fêhst þû on sæ? ... wilt þû fôn sumne hwæl?, Coll. M. 24, 7, 15. Swâ swâ man deór oððe fugelas fêht, Solil. H. 46, 11. Hý fôð þâ wildan hrânas mid, Ors. 1, 1; S. 18, 12. Þonne eów fôn lysted leax, Met. 19, 11. (2) *to take, arrest, apprehend* a criminal:—All swâ tô ðeófe gî foerdun mid swordum tô fôenne mec, Mk. R. 14, 48. (3) *to get, gain.* (a) *with acc.*:—Ræd gemincean, fôn, Gen. 287. (b) *with gen.*:—Wê moniges fêngon, Sal. 432. (c) *with dat.*:—Hê þâm frætwum fêng, B. 2989. (4) *to get, suffer, experience.* (a) *with acc.*:—Hê fêng swâ stîð weðer þ hê uneaðe âwæig côm, Chr. 1052; P. 176, 15. (b) *with gen.*:—Seó wiht heaðoglemma fêng deópra dolga, Rä. 57, 3. (5) *to begin:*—Fêhð seó weâlâf synna bemænan, Wlfst. 133, 13. II. *intrans.* (1) *to begin:*—Se circul fêhð on Ianuario and þær eft geendað, Angl. viii. 300, 18. (2) *to take up* a subject:—Ic wolde þæt wit fêngen eft þider wit ær wêron *I should like us to take up the subject again at the point we were at before,* Solil. H. 58, 17. III. with prepositions or adverbs. (1) *fôn on to lay hands on.* (a) with a concrete object:—Se cyng lêtt âwêstan þ land âbûtan þâ sæ þet gif his feónd cômen ûpp þ hî næsdon nâ on hwâm hî fêngon, Chr. 1085; P. 216, 5. (b) *to take* matter for discourse:—Ne fô wê nâ on þâ bisena for ðâra leásana spella lufan, ac for þâm þe wê woldon mid gebeácnian ðâ sôþfæstnisse ... Platon cwæþ þ se mon se sceolde fôn on tô ungelíc bispell ðære spræce ðe hê ðonne sprecan wolde, Bt. 35, 5; F. 166, 15–21. Uton fôn nû on þæt godspel ðær wê hit ær forlêton, Hml. Th. i. 148, 32. (c) *to set about, betake one's self to, have recourse to, undertake.* (a) *with acc.*:—Ðû â ymbe sticce fêhst eft on ðâ ilcan spræce þe þû ær spæce, and forlætst eft ðâ, ær ðû hî geendod hæbbe, and fêhst on uncûþe, Bt. 35, 5; F. 164, 14: Solil. H. 26, 4. Ic on mýne gebedu fêng, Nic. 10, 36. Him fêng God on fultum *God put forth his hand to help them,* Jud. 300. Þe Metod fô on fultum, Dôm. L. 36, 9. Lâdige hê hine mid geséran, oþþe on fæsten fô, Ll. Th. i. 362, 25. Ælc man sceal on his fæsten fôn (*jejunium suum ordiri*), ii. 224, 33. Ðý læs ænig unclænsod dorste on swâ micelne hâligdôm fôn ðære clænan ðegnenga ðæs sâcerdhâdes *ne non purgatus adire quisque sacra ministeria audeat,* Past. 51, 2. Hê gestîhte his werod ... hû hî on þone huntað fôn sceoldon (*how they should set about the hunting*), Hml. S. 30, 27. Uton fôn on ôðre bôc forewearde *aggrediamur librum secundum,* Solil. H. 55, 4: Hml. Th. i. 206, 21. Ic sceal fôn on fitte, Met. Einl. 9. (β) *without* a case, *to set to work:*—Gif him ænig man misboden hæbbe, fôn hí ealle on (*let them all set to work*) swilce hit heom eallum gedôn beó, and gefilstan, Ll. Th. ii. 244, 19. Fô hê on mid fultume, 286, 22. (d) *to attack* (with dat.):—Iosue him þâ fêng on mid gefeohte *irruit Iosue super eos repente,* Jos. 10, 9. Eall folc gearu wæs heom on tô fônne, Chr. 1009; P. 139, 21. (e) *to begin at* or *with:*—Fôh on .iiii. nôn. April. and æfter id. fôh on .xvii. Id. Aprl., Angl. viii. 326, 35. Ærest wê wyllað fôn on Ianuarium, 305, 29. (2) *fon to take into the hand, get for one's self, take:* —Þâ hê tô wæpnum fêng, By. 10. Wæs geboden þ wê wæpenu nôman (*ut arma caperemus*) ... þâ dýdon wê swâ, fêngon tô ûssum wæpnum swâ ûs geboden wæs, Nar. 21, 16. Hî fêncgon tô mete *acceperunt cibos,* Gr. D. 167, 10. (b) *to set to work at, deal with* a subject:—Nû hæbbe wê âwriten þære Asian sûþdæl; nû wille wê fôn tô hire norðdæle, Ors. 1, 1; S. 14, 5. (c) *to take* what is given, *receive, accept* what is offered:—Hê fêng tô Karles dohter (him Carl his dohtor geaf him tô cuêne, v. l.) *he received Charles' daughter in marriage,* Chr. 855; P. 67, 9: 852; P. 67, 3. Fæla þæra gedwolmanna fêngon tô geleáfan, Hml. S. 3, 351. Þ se hlâford tô his gafole bûton wîtnunge fô *that the lord accept his* (*overdue*) *tribute without penalty,* Ll. Th. i. 270, 19. Gif ûre geréfan ænig ænigne eácan gedeacan mæge ... þ wê þærtô lustlîce fôn, 238, 17. Hê gesætte þet hî tô metsunge fêngon and tô gafie he *arranged that they should receive food and tribute,* Chr. 1002; P. 133, 35. (d) *to take* what is entrusted, *take charge of:*—Fô tô þâm

borge sẽ þe þæs weddes waldend sȳ, Ll. Th. i. 254, 21. (e) *to take* what is gained, *take possession of* a conquest :—Eádweard cyning fếng tố Lundenbyrig and tố Oxnaforda and tố eallum þám landum þe þǽrtố hȳrdon, Chr. 910; P. 97, 6. Hié ne úþon þ hiera fiếnd tố hiera ealdgestreónum fếngon, Ors. 5, 3; S. 222, 11. (f) *to take* what is forfeited or comes as a legal right :—Agife mon þám mǽgum þ treów ... oþþe him fố sẽ tố sẽ þone wudu áge, Ll. Th. i. 70, 11. Fố se landhláford tố þám hwearfe, 204, 21. Fố se hláford tố þám ǽhtan and tố his lande þe hế him ǽr sealde, 420, 10. Tố healfum fố se cyng, tố healfum se geférscipe, 228, 18: 264, 3: 274, 30. Fố Críst and cyning tố fulre bốte, ii. 300, 7. Fốn þá nếhstan frȳnd tố þám lande and tố þám ǽhtan, i. 416, 10. (g) *to take, undertake* an office :—Hếr heom metes tilian sceoldon, and hế mid eádmốdnysse fếngc tố đǽre gehȳrsumnysse, Hml. S. 23, 220. (h) *to take* office or property in succession to another, *to succeed to* a throne, inheritance, &c. :—Seố sáwl fếhð tố þám þe se líchama geworhte, Angl. viii. 336, 28. Hếr Æþelbald cyng forþférde ... and fếng Æþelbryht tố allum þám ríce his brốþur, Chr. 860; P. 66, 36. Sigebyrht tố þám ríce fếng *accepit regnum Sigberct*, Bd. 2, 15; Sch. 176, 1. Æfter hiere fếng tố đǽm ríce (*regno potita est*) Pentesilia, Ors. 1, 10; S. 48, 2. Sum cyning þe unrihtlíce fếng tố ríce *tyrannus*, Bt. 29, 1; F. 102, 26. Fếng Constantius tố þǽm onwalde *adeptus imperium*, Ors. 6, 31; S. 284, 13. Æfter his deáþe his cwến fếngc ǽgþer ge tố þǽm gewinne ge tố þǽm ríce, 1, 2; S. 30, 14. Gif hwá gefare and nán bearn ne gestriéne, gif hế brốðor lǽfe, fố sẽ tố his wífe, Past. 43, 13. (h a) *without a case* :—Hếr Ædwine ... forðférde, and fếng Wulfgár tố, Chr. 989; P. 125, 18. (h β) *with reflex. dat.* :— Philippus þá cyningas bốgen ofslốg and fếng him tố þǽm rícum bǽm, Ors. 3, 7; S. 114, 20: 6, 31; S. 284, 18. Decius beswác þone cásere and fếng him siððon tố þon anwalde, 6, 21; S. 272, 27. (i) *to take to, allow of* a condition, *make* peace :—Se cynincg fếng tố friðe wið hí, Hml. S. 25, 590. Engle and Dene tố friðe and tố freóndscipe fullíce fếngon, Ll. Th. i. 166, 8. Ne lǽt đú đæt yrre licgean on đínre heortan ofer sunnan setlunge, ac fốh tố sibbe ǽror, Hex. 46, 14. Tố sibbe fốn *in pacem redire*, R. Ben. 19, 1 : Ll. Th. ii. 182, 3. Se man þe ... tố þon stíð bið þ hế aðas sylð þ hế tố nánre sybbe fốn nelle æt þám de wið hine ágylt hæfð ... Gif hế þonne gecyrran wyle and tố sybbe fốn *homo qui ... adeo durus sit ut juramenta praestet se nullam pacem admittere velle cum eo qui in eum deliquerit ... Si autem resipiscere velit et pacem admittere*, Ll. Th. ii. 194, 8–11. (j) *to take to* doing something, *set about, set to, begin.* (a) *with dat.* :—Hí fếngon tố gereorde mid fulum handum, Hml. S. 28, 89. Gif wẽ willað fốn tố dǽdbốte, Wlfst. 228, 13. (β) *with dat. infin.* :—Hig fếngon eft tố gremienne God, Jud. 13, 1. Hí fếngon tố clypienne, Hml. S. 3, 344. (γ) *without a case* :—Englisce men fếngon tố þám cynge heora hláforde on fultume *English men set to work to help their lord the king*, Chr. 1087; P. 223, 34. Gif hȳ sammǽle beốn, þonne fốn mágas tố and weddian heora mágan tố wífe *if they are agreed, then let the kinsmen set to work and betroth their kinswoman*, Ll. Th. i. 254, 19. (k) *to take to, make customary* :—Hí fếngon tố ciningum, Jud. Thw. p. 161, 19. (3) fốn tốgædere. (a) *to attack one another, join battle* :—Sốna swá hí tốgædere fếngon, þá beáh seó Englisce fyrd, Chr. 1001; P. 133, 22. Hí tốgædere heardlíce fếngon, 1016; P. 152, 2. Hí cốmon tố gefeohte bốgen and fếngon tốgædere oð þ þǽr feốllon þá crístenan, Hml. S. 26, 156. (b) *to join together* to do something :—Fếngon hí tốgædere and worhton áne cyrcan, Hml. S. 32, 170. (4) fốn wiþ *to struggle with* :—Ic þæt forhicge þæt ic sweord bere tố gūðe, ac ic mid grápe sceal fốn wið feốnde *I am to grapple with the foe*, B. 439. (5) fốn ymb *to treat of, deal with* a subject :—Nú wẽ sculon fốn, cwæð Orosius, ymb þæt Punica gewinn, Ors. 4, 4; S. 164, 8.

**fona.** v. *fana :* **-fốnd.** v. *on-, under-fốnd :* **-fốndlic.** v. *under-fốndlic :* **fonfyr.** v. *egle :* **font.** v. *fant.*

**for.** Take here examples under **fốr** (*l.* for), *and add :* A. *with dat.* I. *local.* (1) *before, in front of.* (a) *where there is movement* :—Se stréam beáh for his fốtum swá þ hế mihte drȳge ofergangan *uidit undam suis cessisse ac uiam dedisse uestigiis*, Bd. 1, 7; Sch. 24, 9. Se forrynel cymeð eástan úp ǽr for sunnan (*cf.* widforan þá sunnan úp, Bt. 39, 13; S. 136, 3), and eft æfter sunnan on setl glídeþ, Met. 29, 26, (b) *of fixed position* :—Swá swá wex formylt for (*or* III. 1 ?) hátan fȳre, Hml. S. 14, 138. Berað bord for breốstum, Jud. 192. (2) *before* a person, *or* the eyes of a person, *within sight or hearing of* :—þæt wíf geseah for Abrahame Ismael plegan, Gen. 2778. Him Abraham andswarode for eorlum, 2137. Hế for þám folce spræc, Jul. 184: Met. 26, 85. Ic for dugeðum Dæghrefne weará tố handbonan, B. 2501. Áhleốp for hæleðum hildecalla, Exod. 252. Sió Circe wæs háten for herigum (*cf.* þǽre nama wæs Kirke, Bt. 38, 1; F. 194, 19), Met. 26, 57. Hí woldon lícian for manna eágum, Past. 449, 10. Wǽre þú gewurðod for þæs eágum þe þe tír forgeaf, Gen. 2108. II. *temporal.* (1) *marking length of time since an event, before, since, ago.* Hit is for seofon and feówertigum wintrum ... þ ic of đǽre byrig út fốr, Hml. S. 23 b, 515. þá de for hund wintrum mid eorþan moldan bewrogene wǽron *qui ante centum annos pulvere terrae obtecti sint*, Ll. Th. 226, 21. Hế cwæð þæt hế wǽre gefullod for hundseofontig geára, and

tố mæssepreốste gehálgod for manegum geárum, Hml. Th. ii. 310, 18. Hit wæs gedốn mǽre þonne for hundtiốntigum gǽrum *it was done more than a hundred years ago*, H. R. 11, 20. (1 a) nú for :—þone mann þe wæs gegripen nú for feówertȳne geárum *hominem ante annos quatuordecim raptum*, Hml. Th. ii. 332, 18: i. 104, 3 : Ælfc. Gr. Z. 3, 12. Nú for lyttlum fyrste (nú unfyrn, *v. l.*), Gr. D. 71, 13. Nú hit is for eahta and þrȳttiðan geáran þ mín dohtor mẽ losode, Hml. S. 33, 270. (2) *marking length of a period, for, in the course of* :—Ic ne árás of þysum bedde ána nú for nigon geárum *I have not risen from this bed without help for the last nine years*, Hml. S. 21, 345. Nú on þisne tíman geþencan, oððe ǽr for fela geárum gemunan, 23, 709. Oft getímað yfelum teala for life, Hml. Th. i. 332, 15. III. *figurative.* (1) *marking cause, as the result of, as the effect of, owing to the action of, from, through.* (a) *where a condition is brought about* :—Ic eom wếrig for þám langan wege, Gr. D. 38, 17: Gú. 1083. Unhále for fæstenum ... for fægrum ele onwended *infirmata a jejunio ... immutata propter oleum*, Ps. Th. 108, 24. For mundgripe mínum licgean lífbysig, B. 965: Gen. 602. For his ægsa áfirde *prae timore exterriti*, Mt. R. 28, 4 : An. 457. (b) *where action takes place* :—Sẽ wæs gecyrred tố geleáfan for Benedictes láre *Benedicti admonitione conversus*, Gr. D. 140, 5. For láre and trymnysse Benedictes (þurh Benedictus láre, *v. l.*) *Benedicti exhortatione*, 142, 23. Hế wiþ his hláford won for ốðra monna láre, Ors. 6, 35; S. 292, 17. For đæs ríces heánesse him weốxon ofermếtto *in tumorem superbiae culmine potestatis excrevit*, Past. 113, 6. For eốwerre fortrúwodnesse *per proterviam*, 211, 12. Monige for hiora wundum swultan, Nar. 16, 8. Ȳþa for-winde þá sǽ hrếraþ, Bt. 39, 1; F. 210, 25: Met. 27, 4. ¶ *marking the agent* :—Oþsace ... sẽ þe dyrre, þ þ angin nǽre gestilled for þæs crístendốmes Gode, Ors. 6, 4; S. 260, 5. (2) *marking reason, ground, on account of.* (a) *reason for being so and so* :—Ægþer þára folca wæs þæs gefeohtes georn, Somnite for þǽm anwalde ..., Rốmáne for þǽm bismere, Ors. 3, 8; S. 122, 22. Yrre for þǽre synne, Gen. 2742 : Dan. 666. Wierðe onwaldes for his duguðum, Ors. 6, 35; S. 292, 15. (b) *reason for doing* :—For eáðmốdnesse hế wæs áhæfen, ond fær (for, *v. l.*) ofermếttum hế wæs áworpen, Past. 113, 6–8. Noe eúde in tố þám arce for (*propter*) þæs flốdes wæterum, Gen. 7, 7. Hí cíððon wið Moises for (*propter*) his wífe, Num. 12, 1. Hế wæs geswenced fram his maniende for twelf scillingum, Gr. D. 157, 33. Ánra gehwylc hæfde sweord ofer his hype for nihtlicum ege, Bl. H. 11, 19. Wẽ þec for þreáum and for þeónȳdum árna biddaþ, Dan. 294: Exod. 575. ¶ *the construction in the following seems anomalous* :—Hit þếh God for heora crístendốme ne geþafode, náþer ne for heora cáseras ne for heora selfra, Ors. 2, 1; S. 62, 28–30. (3) *marking motive, for, from, through* :—þæt líf ic þẽ for lufan gecȳpte, Cri. 1471. Hế mycel for úre lufan geþrowode *from love of us he suffered much*, Bl. H. 25, 3 : Men. 86. Hig hyne for andan (*per invidiam*) him sealdon, Mt. 27, 18. Swá gecwæð se deốfol for hole and for æfste, Gr. D. 122, 19 : An. 610. Hí for wlence cȳðdon cræft heora, Gen. 1673 : Dan. 298. Seố þeód gesốhte Ecgbryht tố mundboran for Miercna ege, Chr. 823; P. 60, 19 : Ph. 461. (4) *marking substitution, where one object takes the place that should be occupied by another, instead of, in place of.* Cf. B. 1 :—Scs Albanus for đám cuman (*pro hospite*) gegyrede hine his munucgegyrelan, Bd. 1, 7; Sch. 20, 22. þis wræcfulle líf þe wẽ on sind wẽ lufiað for đám heofonlícan eðele, Hml. Th. ii. 540, 13. Mẽ nú þis geswel scȳnð for golde, and þæs háta bryne for heálicum gymstánum, Hml. S. 20, 59–60. Gif hwá þingie for ordále (ordal, *v. l.*), Ll. Th. i. 210, 16. (5) *where one object takes the place vacated by another, to take the place of.* Cf. B. 2 :—Be forðfốre Iustus ...; and þ Honorius for him gecoren wæs, Bd. 2, 18; Sch. 181, 17. (6) *marking object for which payment, requital is made.* (a) *reward for service, &c.* :—þ hế wǽre .xii. pæng þe betera for þǽre dǽda, Ll. Th. i. 234, 24. Đú scealt underfốn đá heofonlícan gife for đám gástlican gewinne, Hex. 36, 22. Brốhton Rốmáne þone triumphan angeán Pompeius for þǽm lytlan sige, Ors. 5, 10; S. 234, 29 : B. 951. Ic þám gốdan sceal for his mốdþræce mádmas beốdan, 385. (b) *compensation for loss.* Cf. B. 3 :—Tốð for tếð, Ll. Th. i. 48, 21. (c) *in exchange for, in return for* :—Hí mẽ feốunge settan for mínre lufan, Ps. Th. 108, 4. (d) *as punishment for.* Cf. B. 5 :—Hú mycel yfel þẽ gelamp for þínre gítsunga and oforhȳdo and for þínum ídlan gilpe, Bl. H. 31, 13 : Gen. 2670 : Dan. 657. (e) *in expiation of* :—Hế þrowode on þám gealgtreốwe for guman synnum, Kr. 146. (f) *in redemption for.* Cf. B. 4 :—Sí þreốra án for his feốre, wergild, ..., Ll. Th. i. 332, 17. (7) *marking object for which one is ready to do or suffer, for the sake of.* Cf. B. 6 :—Eal hế for Gode gesealde, Bl. H. 215, 5. Wẽ for úrum Drihtne árefnedon, 25, 2: Gú. 312: Ps. Th. 68, 8. Hế deáþ for ús geþrowode, Sat. 665. For Dryhtnes naman deáþes onbyrigan, Kr. 113 : Hml. S. 28, 137; 131 : Ps. Th. 108, 21. For þínes naman áre, Hy. 8, 35. Hếr lét Harðacnut hergian eall Wihraceastre scíre for his twếgra húscarla þingon, Chr. 1041; P. 162, 5. (8) *on behalf of, in support of.* Cf. B. 7 :—Hế ǽfre wan for willan þæs Ælmihtigan, Hml. S. 25, 683 : Ors. 5, 4; S. 224, 28. Gebiddað for tælendum eốw, Mt. 5, 44. (9) *in respect to, in relation to, as regards.* Cf. I. 2 :—Đǽr đú gemunan

woldest hwylcra burgwara þū wǣre for worulde, oþþe eft gǣstlīce hwilces gefērscipes ðū wǣre, Bt. 5, 1; F. 10, 4: 10; F. 30, 15. Gif þū gemunan wilt eallra þāra ārwyrþnessa þe þū for þisse worulde hæfdest siððan þū geboren wǣre, 8; F. 24, 20. Dohtor mīn ānge for eorþan, Jul. 95: Gū. 905. Hē is for eorþan ǣðeles cynnes, El. 591. Wē beóð mid Gode (apud Deum) swā micle suīðor gebundne suā wē for monnum (apud homines) orsorglícor ungewítnode syngiað, Past. 117, 23. Gif hē wile for Drihtne dōmes hleótan, Rūn. 1. Hyra sinscipe healdan for Gode and for worlde conjugium suum tenere coram Deo et coram mundo, Ll. Th. ii. 190, 15. Hē wīslīce rǣdde for Gode and for worulde (with regard to religious and secular matters) eall his þeóde, Chr. 959; P. 115, 7. Þæt him bið for worulde weorðmynda mǣst, and for ūssum Dryhtne dōma sēlast, Alm. 3-4. (10) marking object of fear, anxiety:—Ne forhtige gē for ðæs fyrnfullan preátum, Hml. S. 25, 260: Ps. Th. 113, 7: Ll. Th. i. 374, 16. Unforht wesan for þām worde, Kr. 111. Hē nalles for ealdre mearn, B. 1442. Sorgian for his sīde, Gen. 800: Gū. 209. (11) marking object against which protection, from which release, &c., is required, against, from:—Wið stede and for gebinde heortes hǣr beóð góde, Lch. i. 338, 3. Gistas mīne ic wille gemundbyrdan for eów, Gen. 2473. Hē brōhte him stānas, bæd him for hungre (for protection against hunger) hlāfas wyrcan, Sat. 673. For leahtrum ālēs þīne gesceft, Hy. 8, 33. Sió sāwl fǣrð tō hefonum siððan hió for (of v. l.) þǣm carcerne þæs līchoman onlēsed bið, Bt. 18, 4; S. 45, 28. (12) marking obstacle, for. (a) where a person is the obstacle:—Hī ne mōstan for him nāht unālȳfedlices begangan, Shrn. 65, 11. Se wulf for Gode ne dorste þæs heáfdes ābyrian, *Hml. S. 32, 156: Cht. Th. 202, 21: Gen. 359. Hī in ne mihtòn for þǣre micclan menigu, Hml. A. 31, 177. (b) the obstacle a thing:—Þæt folc ne mæg beón geteald for ðǣre micclan menigu, Hml. Th. ii. 576, 16: Bl. H. 245, 30: Bt. 18, 1; F. 62, 10-11: Gen. 1457. Ne dorste hē for Freán egesan leng eardigean, Gen. 2590: B. 462. Geornor wē woldon beón forsugiende þonne secgende, þǣr wē for eówerre āgenre gnornunge mōste, Ors. 3, 8; S. 122, 10. Hū mihtū for sceame ǣniges ðinges æt Gode biddan?, Hml. Th. i. 256, 5. (13) marking favouring circumstance:—On his dagum for his iugoðe Godes wiþærsacan Godes lage brēcon, Chr. 975; P. 121, 21. (14) in spite of, notwithstanding:—Gif hē for hungre libban mæge, Ll. Th. i. 64, 13. Ac for eallum þissum se here fērde swā hē sylf wolde, Chr. 1006; P. 136, 17. For eallon þām hī hergodan swā oft swā hī woldon, 1013; P. 144, note 3. Nā ðe lǣs for eallum þisum gride and fride and gafole hī fērdon æghwider and hergodan, 1011; P. 141, 21. (15) in accordance with, according to:—Hē hine sylfne tō þon geeáþmēdde for his ðǣre mycclan mildheortnesse þ hē ūs gesōhte, Bl. H. 11, 34. Feorma mec, Meotod, for þīnre miltse, Hy. 4, 26: Chr. 942; P. 110, 23: Ps. Th. 76, 7: An. 1287: Gū. 611. (16) marking purpose, end:—For ðǣre getácnunge hē wæs æteówod on culfran and on fȳre, Hml. Th. i. 322, 18: Hy. 6, 26. For góde hē dēþ eall þ hē dēþ, Bt. 39, 6; F. 220, 9: B. 382: 458: Gen. 598. (17) as representative of, for. Cf. B. 8:—Þonne þū for unc bǣm andwyrdan scealt, Seel. 87. (17 a) where there is responsibility:—Þonne ne biþ nǣnig tō þæs lytel lið on lime āweaxen, þæt þū ne scyle for ānra gehwylcum (for æghwylc ānra, v. l.) on sundrum riht āgildan, Seel. 97. (18) with verbs of appeal, promise. Cf. B. 9:—Ic bidde ðē for þīnre micelan mildheortnessan, and for þǣre hālegan rōde tácne, and for Scam Marian mægþhāde . . . and for ealra þīnra hālgena lufan and heora earnungum, Bt. 42; F. 266, 2-5. Sum þearfa bæd him for Gode hrægles, Bl. H. 213, 33: Met. 1, 64. Ic þē hālsige for þām hīrēde . . . þæt ic ūp heonon mæge, Sat. 423. Ic þē gehāte for þām hālgan þe heofena is āgendfreá, Gen. 2140. B. with acc. (1) marking substitution. Cf. A. III. 4:—Ic beó þīn þeówa for hine, Gen. 44, 33: Gen. 2930. Þā sende him mon āne blace hacelan angeán, him on bismer, for triumphan, Ors. 5, 10; S. 234, 22. Þæt fæt weard swā tōbroken swylce hē on ðǣm fæte āsende sumne stān for rōdetāken, Gr. D. 105, 9. (2) to take or fill the (vacant) place of. Cf. A. III. 5:—Aaron forðferde and his sunu wæs sācerd for hine, Num. 20, 28: Bd. 2, 8; Sch. 141, 15. (3) in compensation for. Cf. A. III. 6 b:—Drihten mē sealde þisne suna for Abel þe Cain ofslōh, Gen. 4, 25. (4) marking object to be redeemed or rescued. Cf. A. III. 6 f:—Þū ne forslāwodest þ þū þīn āgen līf for hine ne sealdest, Bt. 10; F. 28, 15. Abraham sealde wīg tō wedde, nalles wunden gold, for his suhtrigan, Gen. 2071. (5) as punishment for. Cf. A. III. 6 d:—Ne habbað hī wiht for þæt, þeáh hī wom dōn, Fü. 70. (6) for the sake of. Cf. A. III. 7:—Hē wolde þrowian for þis mennisce cynn, Bl. H. 77, 13. (7) on behalf of, for the benefit of. Cf. A. III. 8:—Gebiddað for eówre ēhteras orate pro persequentibus vos, Mt. 5, 44: Bt. procem. 11. For mīne brōðru (propter fratres meos) ic bidde, þæt wē sibbe on þē habbon, Th. 121, 8. Þone sēlestan dǣl for hine sylfne Gode gedǣlan, Bl. H. 195, 7. Þone feórþan dǣl þām Godes þeówum for mīne sāwle and for mīnes fæder and for mīnes ieldran fæder, C. D. ii. 175, 26. Ǣnne dæg for mē, ōþerne for mīnne fæder, þriddan for mīnne ieldran fæder, 176, 6. (8) as representative of. Cf. A. III. 17:—Hē for ealle spræc feónda mengu, Gū. 171. Hē sceal andwyrde āgifan for þyslicne þreát, El. 546: Seel. 87. Hē mōt swerian for syxtig hīda, Ll. Th. i. 114, 11. (8 a) where

there is responsibility. v. A. III. 17 a. (9) marking asseveration. Cf. A. III. 18:—Gistas mīne ic for God wille gemundbyrdan, gif ic mōt, Gen. 2472. (10) marking comparison:—Heora beorhtnes ne beoð nān beorhtnes for hire (compared with hers; cf. hiora birhtu ne bið āuht tō gesettanne wið þǣre sunnan leóht, Met. 6, 7), Bt. 9; F. 26, 17. Fulneáh swilce ān prica for þæt ōðer, 18, 1; F. 62, 20: Met. 10, 9. (11) marking superiority, preference, before, above:—Ðæt mōd ðætte wilnað for ōðre beón mens praeesse volentium, Past. 55, 14: 106, 24. Sié hē for ealle ūpāðened sit prae cunctis suspensus, 97, 23. Hit is micel cræft ðæs mōdes for ðone līchoman (cf. mægencræft micel mōda gehwilces ofer līchoman, Met. 26, 106), Bt. 38, 1; F. 196, 11. Hē his mōdor Marian for ealle men geweorðode, ofer eall wīfa cynn, Kr. 93. (12) marking object in relation to which a certain character is predicated of another object:—Hit nān gōd nis for eów selfe, Bt. 13; F. 40, 11. (13) marking estimate formed, character attributed:—Hē mōt gecȳdan þ hē hine for þeóf ofslōge, Ll. Th. i. 116, 5: 124, 7. Hig hæfdon Iōhannem for ānne wītegan habent Iohannem sicut prophetam, Mt. 21, 26, 46: Ph. 344. Þæt hǣþene folc þā anlīcnessa weorðedon heom for godas, Wlfst. 98, 25. Þās men wǣron getealde for ðā mǣrostan godas . . . hē is geteald ārwurðost ealra þǣra goda þe þā hǣþenan for godas hæfdon, 106, 15-21. Ic nolde þ unc beswice ǣnegu leás anlīcnes for sōþa gesǣlþa (any false appearance taken for true happiness), Bt. 34, 1; F. 134, 8. Hī hine for deádne lēton, Hml. Th. i. 392, 4. Hiǣ āworden wēron suelce for deádo facti sunt velut mortui, Mt. L. 28, 4. Hwæþer gōd hlīsa sié for nāuht tō tellenne? . . . Nis hit nān cyn þ mon þ for nāuht telle, Bt. 24, 4; F. 86, 17-19: Ps. Th. 55, 4: 117, 6. Wīte þū for sōþ, Bt. 7, 3; F. 20, 17: 14, 3; F. 46, 16. For sōþ secgan, Gn. C. 64. Þis andwerde līf hē nemde for weg, Ll. Th. ii. 432, 23. (13 a) marking the function discharged, acknowledged character:—Eall þeódscipe hine heafde for fullne cyning, Chr. 1013; P. 144, 6. Habban for fæder, Hml. S. 5, 15. Beón for fæder, 25, 265. For sunu freógan, B. 947. Beó hē flȳma, and hine lecge for þeóf sē þe him tō cume, Ll. Th. i. 200, 10. Beó Crīstes geleáfa for byrnan ðē sylfum, Hex. 36, 5. Mē wǣran mīne teáras for hlāfas fuerunt mihi lacrymae meae panes, Ps. Th. 41, 3. (14) marking destination (?):—Strȳc of ufwerdum heáfde mid þīnum scytefingran nyþerweard forð for (so as to reach?) þīne earmas, Techm. ii. 119, 17. C. with instrumental:—Ic eom wērig for þȳ (þām, v. l.) langan wege, Gr. D. 38, 16. For hwī drēfe gē eówru mōd . . . oððe for hwȳ ætwīte gē eówerre wyrde . . . oððe hwī ne magon ge gebīdan deáþes?, Bt. 39, 1; F. 210, 24-27. v. hwā, sē. D. with gen. ?:—Hē underfēht gife eorðlices gestreónes for his eorðlices geswinces, Hex. 36, 21. Hit God for heora crīstendōme ne gebafode, naþer ne for heora cāseras ne for heora selfra, Ors. 2, 1; S. 62, 29.

for-. Other forms of the prefix are fær, fer: e. g. faer-tyhted, Txts. 51, 483: fær-rēd (fer-), 89, 1635: fer-uuaenid, for-uuened, 70, 548: fær-hæfdnes (for-), Past. 41, 14: fær-wyrd (for-), 133, 20: fer-ðrycednis, Ps. Srt. 31, 7.

fōr; prep. l. for, q.v.

fōr. Add: (1) the action of going:—Hē wæs unāblinnendlīce on fōre geseted he was incessantly travelling, Hml. S. 23 b, 156. On fōre uehiculo (ad praediolium suum basternae uehiculo properabant, Ald. 67, 28), An. Ox. 4742. Fōre uehiculo (spreto basternae uehiculo, Ald. 58, 28. In An. Ox. 4164 the word is glossed by færelde), Wrt. Voc. ii. 84, 74. (2) a journey:—Gif þe fōr (foor, v. l.) gelimpe on Gallia mǣgðe si contingat ut ad Galliarum provinciam transeas, Bd. 1, 27; Sch. 74, 9. Fōre bōc itinerarium, Hpt. Gl. 454, 19. Swā hwylc preóst swā farende byð (iter faciat), and hine man on his fōre (in itinere ejus) fulwihtes biddeð, and hē wyrne for ofste his fōre (itineris), Ll. Th. ii. 138, 19-21. Be cíepemonna fōre uppe on londe, i. 118, 11: 82, 15. Cōm hē tō Rōme . . . hē oft ǣr on þǣre fōre wæs, Bd. 4, 18; Sch. 436, 12. Hē wæs on sumre fōre ealle þrȳ dagas, Bl. H. 217, 17. (3) an expedition of armed persons. (a) march of an army:—Heora hergende and bærnende þætte Cartainense mehton geseón of heora byrg þ fȳr and þone teónan, þonne hié on fōre wǣron, Ors. 4, 5; S. 168, 35. Be þǣre wīdgalnisse his (Alexander's) sīðfata and his fōra þe hē geond middangeard hergode, Nar. 1, 7. (b) of private war:—Sē þe on þǣre fōre wǣre þǣr mon monnan ofslōge, getriéwe hine þæs sleges, and þā fōre gebēte, Ll. Th. i. 122, 16: 74, 7 note. [v. N. E. D. fore. O. H. Ger. fuora profectio.] v. ūt-, weg-fōr.

fōr a hog. Add:—Foor, fōr porcaster, Txts. 88, 810. Foor, Wrt. Voc. ii. 68, 30. Fōr, An. Ox. 20, 4: porca (but the passage glossed is the same as in the preceding), 22, 3.

fōran; prep. adv. Substitute: foran, forn. I. prep. Before:—Ealdsige foran eallum folce hine lǣrde, Chr. 1042; P. 163, 20. II. adv. (1) alone. (a) marking position, in front:—Hié fortendun þæt swīðre breóst foran, Ors. 1, 10; S. 46, 12: Rä. 45, 2. Sē þe foran lǣdeð brīdels he that in front guides the bridle, El. 1184. (b) in front of that which is defended:—Hē hiene foran forstōd he stood in front and defended him, Ors. 4, 8; S. 186, 25. (c) in front of that which is obstructed or interfered with:—Hī þā men ofslōgun þe hié foran forrīdan mehton būtan geweorce they slew the men whose retreat they could cut

*off*, Chr. 894; P. 88, 10. Hié forfóron him þone múðan foran *they blockaded the mouth of the river for them*, 897; P. 90, 24. On þǽm wintregum tídum wyrþ se múþa fordrifen foran from þǽm windum, Ors. 1, 1; S. 12, 34. Gemêtton wê ús ǽghwanon storm foran onsettende *inuenimus nos undiqueuersum tempestate praeclusos*, Bd. 5, 1; Sch. 552, 10. þá ungesǽligan menn ne magon gebídon hwonne hê (*death*) him tó cume, ac forscéotaþ hine foran (*they rush in his way*), Bt. 39, 1; F. 212, 3. Leahtras mid gedwolmiste fortîð môd foran, Met. 22, 34. (d) *in front, before all, in a conspicuous place* (?) :—þæt tréow sceolde foran áfeallan *the tree should fall where all might see* (?), Dan. 557. (e) *in the front rank* (?) :—þæt wæs án foran ealdgestreóna, B. 1458. (2) *with prepositions*. (a) on. (α) *with dat.* :—Wrít þám horse on þám heáfde foran Crístes mǽl, Lch. ii. 290, 24. (β) *with acc.* :—Hê wearp his tungan on ðæt neb foran *linguam in os tyranni abiecit*, Bt. 16, 2; F. 52, 25. Gif men synd wænnas gewunod on þ heáfod foran, Lch. iii. 46, 21. (b) ongeán *opposite, over against*. (a) *as preposition with dat.* :—Hetware him foran ongeán linde bǽron, B. 2364. Gesæt Benedictus forn ongeán ðám Riggon, Hml. Th. ii. 168, 15 : Lch. iii. 248, 17 MS. S. Feówer æceras forn ágeán Eádferðes ealdlande, C. D. iii. 411, 27. (β) *with acc.* (*or uncertain*) :—Ic fare foran .ongeán þá burh *ego accedam ex adverso contra urbem*, Jos. 8, 5. þ castel þ foran ongên eów (*contra uos*) ys, Mt. 21, 2. Foran ongên (fora ongægn, L.) Galilêam, Lk. 8, 26. Foran ongên wylle ; of ðǽre wylle, C. D. vi. 129, 25. Foron ongeán stængedelf, 144, 9. Macian forn angên Mildryþe æker ænne hwerf, iv. 57, 37. (γ) *as adverb* :—Foran ongeán *eminus, cominus*, Ælfc. Gr. Z. 239, 13. Côm mycel windes blǽd foran ongeán, þ seó strǽl weard eft gecyrred *the arrow was met by a great blast of wind and turned back*, Bl. H. 199, 21. (c) tô. (α) foran tô. (αα) *as prep. Before. Take here* fôran-to (*l.* foran tô) *in Dict., and add* :—Foran tô his þrowunga and foran tô þon tôcyme dômes dæges, Bl. H. 35, 7 : 27, 26. Foran tô þyssum ondweardan dæge, Bl. H. 131, 11. Foran tô ðǽre tíde, C. D. i. 293, 24 : Chr. 918; P. 100, 3 : 1053; P. 182, 39. (αβ) *as adv. Beforehand, before* :—Him se reogolweord gebeóde foran tô hwonne sió tîd sié, C. D. i. 293, 28. Wê secgaþ eác foran tô þ seó bôc is swíþe deóp, Ælfc. Gen. Thw. 2, 29. Forsprecað hî foran tô *denounce them beforehand*, Hml. Th. ii. 494, 10. þá þe foran tô unriht wyrceð, oþþe on þám dæge him hláf baceþ, Wlfst. 212, 26. His gebídan ne magon burgsittende, ungesǽlige men hine (*death*) ǽr willað foran tô sciótan (*will anticipate death*), Met. 27, 19. (β) tô ... foran *before, to the presence of* :—þá þrý cômon tô þeódne foran, Dan. 93 : 434. (d) wiþ. *with acc. Before, in front of* :—Hî beóð wið þæt môd foran mistes dwoleman, Met. 5, 43. Hwý hí ne scînen beforan ðǽre sunnan, swá hí dôð wið ðone mônan foran (*cf. beforan þám mônan*, Bt. 39, 3; F. 214, 30), 28, 47 : 20, 265. Wið þone segn foran þengel rád, Exod. 172. [*v. N. E. D.* forne. *O. Sax.* foran.] *v. æt-, be-*(bi-), *on-, tô-, wiþ-foran; forane*.

**for án.** *Add* :—Heom for án þá wítu gemynte wǽron, Hml. S. 23, 112 : Lch. i. 286, 10. *v.* án; IX. 2 d.

**fôran-dæg.** *Substitute* : **foran-dæg,** es ; *m. The early part of the day* : —Ælc man sylð on forandæge his gôde wîn (*omnis homo primum bonum uinum ponit*, Jn. 2, 10), Hml. Th. ii. 70, 26 : Nap. 23. Cf. foran-niht.

**forane, forne ;** *adv. Take here* **forne, fôrne** (*l.* forne) *in Dict., and add* : I. *alone.* (1) *denoting anticipation, prevention, beforehand* (*as in to be beforehand with a person*) :—Forne forðþ *anticipet*, An. Ox. 603. Sý forne forfangen *preoccupetur*, ... *precedat*, 1236. Forne forgán, gelettan *praepedire*, i. *praeoccupare*, 3949. Heó þone ealdan forene forfêng, and him ne geþafode fulfremodlíce on þá eorðan astreccan *she anticipated the old man, and did not permit him to prostrate himself completely*, Hml. S. 23 þ, 605. Ic þ hæbbe mid Godes fultume forene forfangen, þ eów nǽfre heonforð þanon nán unfrið tô ne cymð *I have with God's help taken measures to prevent hostility ever from this time forth coming to you from Denmark*, Cht. E. 230, 4. (2) *denoting* defence :—Gif hwá þeóf fríðige oðða forena forlicge (*interpose in his behalf*), Cht. E. 230, 33. II. *with prep. Opposite, in front of, against.* (1) geán :—Ðǽre wyrte wyrtruman áhôh ... swá þ hé hangie forne geán ðá miltan, Biccenclife, C. D. iii. 4, 12. Forne gên hys ágen land, iv. 221, 6. (2) ongeán (á-) :—Oð þ hé eft cume hyre forne ágeán, Lch. iii. 248, 17. (3) tôgeánes :—Ic him eft wille sændan fleógende fláne forane tôgeánes, Lch. iii. 52, 25. [*v. N. E. D.* forne. *O. Sax.* forana.]

**foran-gengel.** *v.* fore-gengel.

**foran-heáfod.** *Add* :—Monig man hæfð micel feax on foranheáfde and weorð fǽrlíce caluw, Prov. K. 42. Bútan hê on his foranheáfde habbe his mearce, Wlfst. 200, 4. On foranheáfdum *frontibus*, Ps. Srt. ii. p. 203, 23. Wê mearciað eówere foranheáfdu, Hml. Th. ii. 488, 1.

**foran-niht.** *Add* :—Hit gelamp on þǽre nihte þ se cyning læg wæccende lange on forannihte, Hml. A. 98, 209. *De completorio* (Forannihtsang) On foranniht wê sculon God herian ǽr wê tô bedde gán, Btwk. 218, 34 : 194, 14.

**forannïht-sang.** *v.* preceding word : **fôran-onsettende.** *l.* foran onsettende. *v.* foran ; II. 1 c : **fôran-to.** *l.* foran tô. *v.* foran ; II. 2 c.

**fora-scýwung.** *v.* fore-scýwung.

**for-bærnan, -bernan.** *Add* : I. *to consume by heat* :—Forbærnde *extorruit*, An. Ox. 1434. Hié woldon þone cásere cwicenne forbærnan, Bl. H. 191, 12. Forbernende *crematuros*, Wrt. Voc. ii. 24, 41. Eorþe biþ forbærned tô axan, 91, 26. Ðæt land weard fram heofenlicum fýre forbærned *regionem arsisse igne caelesti Tacitus refert*, Ors. 1, 3; S. 32, 3. Forbærnd *torreretur*, An. Ox. 4120. II. *to injure by heat, burn, scald* :—Gif hwá forbærned sý, genim þás wyrte ... lege tô þám bærnette, Lch. i. 216, 10. Wiþ bryne. Gif mon sié mid fýre áne forbærned. ... Gif mon sié mid wǽtan forbærned, ii. 324, 12–14. [*v. N. E. D.* forburn. *O. H. Ger.* fer-prennen *comburere, consumere.*] *v.* un-forbærned.

**for-bærnednes.** *Substitute* : *Injury by burning, a burn* :—Ðeós wyrt gehǽleþ mænigfealde untrumnyssa ðæs líchoman ... forbærnednysse, Lch. i. 272, 2 : 5610. Wið forbærnednysse. Genim þysse wyrte wyrtruman ... lege tô þám bærnytte, 298, 10 : 62, 19.

**for-bærning,** e ; *f. Burning, heat of inflammation* :—Fleó hê þá mettas þá þe him forbærnunga and stiém oninnan wyrcen, Lch. ii. 226, 10.

**fôr-bed[d],** es ; *n. A litter* :—Fôrbed (-bæd, *v. l.*) *badanola* (*lectus in itinere, lectus itineralis : cf.* banadola *lectus quo in itinere fertur*, Gl. Isidor), Hpt. 31, 6, 80.

**for-belgan ;** *p.* bealg(-h), *reflex. To get angry, get in a rage* :—Forbealh hê hine for þon þe þ hrýþer him þúhte on wêdenheorte, Bl. H. 199, 10.

**for-beódan.** [*In N. Gospels* fore-beáda :—Forebeádas *prohibens*, Mt. p. 14, 16. Forebeád (for-, R.) *praecipiebat*, Mk. L. 7, 36.] I. *to forbid.* (1) *to order that something shall not be done* :—Forbodenne ágeáncyme *interdictum* (i. *prohibitum*) *postliminium*, An. Ox. 2720. þá forbodenan gyfta *uetitos hymeneos*, 1780. (2) *with acc.* :—Hé bodode geleáfan, and unriht forbeád, Ælfc. T. Grn, 9, 20. Ælc uuriht geold hê forbeád, Chr. 1087; P. 223, 32. Heora bisceopas sǽdon þæt hié (*the gods*) ðæt gefeoht forbuden, Ors. 3, 10; P. 140, 1. Hê cwæð þ hé ne côme nô þás bebodu tô brecanne ne tô forbeódanne (*to order that these commands should not be obeyed*), Ll. Th. i. 56, 1. Ege wæs forboden ofer menn, ðá hê wæs áliéfed ofer niétenu *terror esse super animalia praecipitur, profecto esse super homines prohibetur*, Past. 109, 8. (a a) *with dat. of person to whom it is forbidden* :—Ic him firene forbeád, Cri. 1486. Ic him þá þenunge forbeád *illum ab hujus praesumtione ministerii cessare praecepi*, Bd. 5, 6; Sch. 580, 21. Se pápa hit him forboden hæfde, Chr. 1048; P. 172, 8. (b) *with a clause.* (a) affirmative :—Ðæt ús on óðerre stôwe forbiét ðæt wê hit beforan mannum dôn, on óðerre lǽrð ... Ðǽr ðǽr God ús forbeád ðæt wê úre ryhtwísnesse beforan monnum dyden, Past. 451, 2–6. Nis eów forboden ðætte ǽhta habban, Bl. H. 53, 27. (β) negative :—Hê forbeád him ðæt hit ne scolde suá weordan *he forbade them to let it be so*, Past. 213, 25. God forbeád þæt mon ná ðær eft ne timbrede, Ors. 6, 7; S. 262, 22. Hê forbeád þæt mon náne fæste bôc ne leornode (*praecipit ne* ...), 6, 31 ; S. 286, 3 : Chr. 1012; P. 142, 19. (c) *combining* (a) *and* (b β) :— Forbeád hit se bisceop þ hí ne weópon, Nar. 32, 12. (d) *with gerundial infin.* :—Godes ǽ ús forbiét diófulum tô offrianne, Past. 369, 3. Hê forbeád him ǽlc wedd tô syllanne, Ll. Lbmn. 214, 25. (2) *to order that something shall be left alone* :—Hê forbeád þá heortas, swylce eác þá báras, Chr. 1086; P. 221, 9. Ánes treówes wæstm hé him forbeád, Wlfst. 9, 7. Hê breác forbodenes, 154, 2. Hé onbirigde þæs forbodenan æpples, Hml. Th. ii. 220, 2 : Ph. 404; Gú. 819. (2 a) *of time, in which it is forbidden to do something* :—Gif frí man an þane forbodenan tíman wyrce, Ll. Th. i. 40, 1. II. *to restrain, check, prevent the action of* :—Ðeós wyrt forbýt yfele lácnunga, Lch. i. 102, 9. Heó þone þurst forbýt, 146, 15. Forbeád *compescuit* (*rabiem*), An. Ox. 2498. Ðá lufe mon mæg swíþe uneáþe, oððe ná, forbeódan, Bt. 35, 6; F. 170, 11. II a. *to prevent* action in the case of a person (*dat.*). (1) *with acc.* :—Wênst þú þæt se anwald ne meahte Godes ... him his yfeles gestióran? Eálá, gif hê wolde þæt hê meahte þæt unriht him forbiódan, Met. 9, 54. (2) *with a negative clause* :—Godes swýðra forbeád Abrahame þ hê his sunu ne ofslôge, Prud. 1 b. *with* construction :—Forbude *compesceret* (*foeminas a pretiosarum uestium appetitu*), An. Ox. 5159. [*O. Frs.* for-biada : *O. H. Ger.* fer-biotan : *Ger.* ver-bieten : cf. *Goth.* faur-biudan : *O. H. Ger.* furi-biotan : *Icel.* fyrir-bjóða.] *v.* un-forbeóden.

**for-beornan.** *Add* :—Gif hwæs weorc forbyrnð, hê hæfð þone hearm *si cujus opus arserit, detrimentum patietur*, Hml. Th. ii. 588, 30. Lígýðum forborn bord, B. 2672. Forborn þurh þæs fíres fnæst fíf and hundseofontig herges, Jul. 587. Ealle ðá clifu forburnan tô ascan, Ors. 5, 4; S. 226, 5. His weorc sceal on ðám fýre forbyrnan, Hml. Th. ii. 590, 11. þá þá seó ceaster swýþlíce barn ... heom þúhte þ eall seó burh forbyrnan sceolde *cum civitas vehementer arderet ... ut flamma totius urbis interitum minari videretur*, Gr. D. 47, 27 : Bl. H. 221, 9. þ hús weard forburnon buton þám ánum poste, Hml. S. 26, 232. [*v. N. E. D.* forburn. *O. H. Ger.* fer-brinnan *uri, ardere*.] *v.* unforburnen.

**for-beran.** *Add*: (1) *to bear* pain, hardship, &c., *endure, sustain.*
(a) *with acc.* :—Forbær *perferebat,* i. *sustinebat (calamitatum insectationes)*, An. Ox. 2979. Se Hǽlend micel forbær for ūs, Hml. A. 72, 177.
Hwæđer đū þone ēcan bryne forberan mage, 196, 47. Tō forberende
*laturus (caumata solis),* An. Ox. 18 b, 53. Geol(s)ter forberende *uirus
ferentes,* An. Ox. 4856. (b) *with clause* :—Ic ne mæhte þeáh forberan
þæt ic æmbe me specce, Solil. H. 20, 5. Heó ne mihte forbæran þ heó hit
leng forhǽle, Hml. S. 30, 348. (c) *absolute* :—Hǽte oþ þ hit sié swā hāt
swā þīn finger forberan mæge, Lch. ii. 236, 28. Lege tō þǽm setle swā
đū hātost forberan mæge, iii. 30, 20. (2) *to bear with, tolerate, not to
stop* :—Hī setton mē in edwīt þæt ic eáđe forbǽr rūme regulas, Gū. 459.
Hwīlum đeáh hit mon cūđlīce wīte hit is tō forberanne *aliquando vitia
aperte cognita mature toleranda sunt,* Past. 151, 10. Mīne witan secgađ
þ ic hit tō lange forboren hæbbe, Ll. Th. i. 220, 4. (3) *to bear with
patiently, without getting angry, put up with, not to resent, not to
punish* :—Forberet *dissimulat (injuriam),* Kent. Gl. 411. Gif hē ge-
þyldelīce forbyrđ ǽgđer ge hosp ge edwītu *si inlatas sibi injurias visus
fuerit patientes portare,* R. Ben. 97, 6. Hī wǽron geþyldige and ǽlcne
hosp hī forbǽron for þæs Hǽlendes naman . . . wē neóllsađ forberan ān
bysmorlic word, Hml. S. 28, 131, 136. Gif on gebeórscipe hié gecīden,
and ōđer hiora mid geþylde hit forbere, Ll. Th. i. 106, 12. (3 a) *with
dat. of person to whom forbearance is shewn* :—Đæt hié nō lǽs ne
geđencen hwæt ōđre men him forberađ and geđafiađ, đonne hié geđenc-
eađ hwæt hī ōđrum monnum forberađ *ut non tam, quae ab altero tolerat,
quam quae ab ipso tolerantur, attendat,* Past. 397, 5–6. Him mon
geđyldelīcor forbær hiera irre, 295, 1. Đǽm monnum đe wē for geđylde
hwæt forberan sculon, đæt wē hié sculon eác lufian *quos ex patientia
tolerat, amare etiam non cessat,* 222, 6 : 294, 10. Đā wǽron ungesǽligran đe him unrihtlīce hiora yfel forboren wǽre, þonne þā wǽren þe
him hiora yfel ryhtlīce on gewrecen wǽre, Bt. 38, 4; F. 204, 18. (4)
*to endure the absence or privation of something, to do without* :—Mon
scel ǽr geđencean, ǽr hē hwæt selle, đæt hē hit forberan mæge būtan
hreówe, Past. 325, 18. (5) *to abstain from* action, *desist from.* (a)
*with acc.* :—Gif hwelc mon forbiređ his synna for đǽm ege ānum đæs
wītes *si a prava actione formidata poena prohibet,* Past. 265, 1. Hē
forberađ ǽghwelce unryhte tǽlinge *ab omni se peste obtrectationis
abstinentes,* 199, 4. (b) *with negative clause* :—Hē forbiređ đæt hē ne
syngađ, Past. 407, 5. Suā suā Dauid forbær đæt hē Saul ne dorste
ofsleán for Godes ege . . . suā suā Dauit forbær đæt hē ne slōg mid
his suerde Saul, suā hié forberađ đæt hié mid đǽm suerde hiera
tungna tǽlinge ne sleáđ hira hlāfurdes đeáwas . . . Gif hié eallunge
forberan ne mægen . . . đæt hié hit ne scīren *Saul Dauid ferire
metuit . . . subditorum mentes . . . praepositorum vitam nullo linguae
gladio percutiunt . . . Qui siquando sese abstinere vix possunt, ut . . .
loquantur,* 199, 2–9. Þ gē forberen þ gē deófolgyld ne weorđien. ne
blōd ne þicgen, Ll. Th. i. 56, 25. Hwā mæg forbæran þ hē þ ne siofige,
Bt. 36, 1; F. 172, 13. (5 a) *to abstain* :—Þ gē forberen from đernum
geligerum, Ll. Th. i. 56, 25. (6) *to refrain from using* :—Đā fæstenan
ne forsāwen đā etendan, for đǽm đe hié đǽre Godes giefe brucađ đā đe
ōđre forberađ, Past. 319, 10. (7) *to restrain.* Cf. wyrt-forbor :—Gif
mon sié wyrtum forboren . . . wiþ þon þe mon sié forboren . . . ne mæg
[man] hine wyrtum forberan, Lch. ii. 114, 8–12. Gif hyt mid geswelle
on forboren byđ *if the poison be kept in with the swelling,* i. 92, 8.
[O. H. Ger. fer-beran *abstinere, continere.*]

**for-, fōre-beran.** *Dele, and see* for-beran, fore-beran.

**for-berendlíce**; *adv. In a way that may be borne, tolerably* :—For-
berendlīcnr *tolerabilius,* Scint. 137, 6.

**for-bernan.** v. for-bærnan.

**for-berstan.** *Add* : (1) *of material, to burst asunder, be torn asunder* :
—Godwebba cyst (*the veil of the temple*) ufan eall forbærst, þæt hit on
eorđan læg on twām styccum, Cri. 1138. Đonne đā twigo forburston,
þonne gewitan þā sáula niđer þā þe on đǽm twigum haugodan, Bl. H.
211, 3. Đý lǽs se rāp . . . forberste *ne chorda rumpatur,* Past. 459, 8.
(2) *of property, to be dissipated, exhausted* :—Đý mon dǽlđ spærlīce đe
mon nele đæt hit forberste, Prov. K. 19. (3) *of legal proceedings, to
fail, break down, come to nothing* :—Gif hit tihtle sí and lād forberste *if
it be a prosecution and the defence fail,* Ll. Th. i. 406, 10. Him wǽre
leófre đæt hē . . . đonne se ađ forburste, Cht. Th. 171, 26. Þā cende
hē tēm and lēt þone forberstan (*let it go by default*), 206, 28. [Him
the rug forberst, Laym. 1912.]

**for-bīgan.** *Take here* for-bēgan *in Dict., and add* :—Assiria weard
bælc forbīged, Jud. 267.

**for-bītan**; *p.* -bāt *To bite to pieces, destroy by biting* :—Āhleóp ān
leó and hió swengde on hine and forbāt him þone sweoran, Hml. A. 206,
391. [v. N. E. D. forbite.]

**for-blāwan.** *Add* :—Đe sǽ winde miclum forbleów (forblāuene, L.)
ārās *mare uento magno flante exsurgebat,* Jn. R. 6, 18. [v. N. E. D.
forblow.]

**fōr-bōc.** *Substitute* :—Sīþbōc, fōr-bōc *itinerarium,* i. *librum quem in
itinere habebat,* An. Ox. 2023.

**for-bod.** *Add* :—Forbod *conspiratio,* An. Ox. 2975. Þæt forbod

hūslganges and inganges intō cyrican, Wlfst. 155, 2. Godes forboda wē
forbeódađ, Ll. Th. ii. 290, 6. [v. N. E. D. forbode; sb.] v. fore-bod.

**for-boda.** *Dele passage, and see* for-bod, fore-boda : **for-bodian.**
v. fore-bodian : **for-bor.** v. wyrt-forbor.

**for-brecan.** *Add* : (1) with a material object :—Đeós wyrt (*saxi-
frage*) þā stānas on blǽdran forbrycđ, Lch. i. 212, 15 : Ps. Th. 28, 5.
Hē đā feoturo forbrǽc ł tōscǽnde (tōbrǽc, W. S.) *compedes comminuisset,*
Mk. R. L. 5, 4. Ic wille þ palmtwig gegrīpan, . . . and forseáredum him
bēgen dǽlas forbrecan and forbǽrnan, Bl. H. 151, 16. Ic hēt hié gebindan and him þā bān and sconcan forbrecan *crurifragio punire
jussi,* Nar. 16, 27. Swylce mē wǽre se hrycg forbrocen, Ps. Th.
31, 4 : Ll. Th. i. 16, 8 : 18, 15. (1 a) fig. *to crush a person,
oppress* :—Ne forbrec đū *non conteras (egenum),* Kent. Gl. 843. (2)
with a non-material object. (a) *to break power,* &c., *destroy* :—Hié
Judēa blǽd forbrǽcon, Dan. 709. (b) in a moral sense, *to break a
promise, command,* &c. :—Wit Waldendes word forbrǽcon, Gen. 798.
[v. N. E. D. forbreak. O. H. Ger. fer-brechan *confringere; praeter-ire,
-gredi.*]

**for-bredan, for-bregdan.** *Substitute* : for-bregdan, -brēdan ;
*p.* -brægd, -brēd, *pl.* -brugdon, -brūdon ; *pp.* -brogden, -brōden. (1)
*to destroy by dragging about.* v. bregdan ; I. 1 a :—Hē wæs fram deófium forbrōden and hē sweolt *he was dragged about by devils and he
died,* Mart. H. 214, 31 : 28, 2. (2) *to hurl to destruction* :—Forbrægd
*praecipita,* Ps. Srt. 54, 10. (3) *to snatch away* :—Oft ic sȳne ofteáh
. . . misthelme forbrægd eágna leóman, Jul. 470. (4) *to change for the
worse, transform.* v. bregdan, I. 1 e :—Hī sǽdon þ hió sceolde mid
hire drȳcræft þā men forbrēdan, and weorpan hī an wildedeóra līc, Bt.
38, 1 ; F. 194, 31 : Met. 26, 75. Wearđ ān mǽden forbrōden þurh
drȳmanna dydrunge . . . þæt mǽden wæs swā forbrōden swylce heó ān
myre wæs, Hml. S. 21, 473. (5) *to corrupt* :—Forbrōdenum *muculentis,*
Germ. 396, 282. [v. N. E. D. forbraid.]

**for-brict.** *Substitute* : for-brīcan (?) ; *p.* te *To use up, consume,
destroy* :—Mid þissum wǽpnum beóđ ǽlce uncysta forbrīcte (-brītte ?)
and mid þyssum andlyfenum biđ ǽlc mægen gefēd, Ll. Th. ii. 404, 5.
[Cf. O. H. Ger. fer-brūchen : Ger. ver-brauchen.]

**for-brittan, for-bryttan.** *Take the passages under these under
for-brītan, and add* :—Forbrȳt, tōbrecþ *conterat,* Wrt. Voc. ii. 135, 5.
Forbrȳte *diruet,* i. *diuidet,* Germ. 398, 144. (1) with a material
object :—Dryhten forbrycđ and forbrȳt þā myclan cedertreówu *confringet
Dominus cedros Libani,* Ps. Th. 28, 5. Ne forbrȳte hē nā þæt
tōcnysede hreód, R. Ben. 121, 5. (2) *to crush, destroy a person* :—Hē
biđ forbrēt *conteretur,* Kent. Gl. 147.

**for-būgan.** *Add* :—Wæs forbūgende *cedens,* Wrt. Voc. ii. 24,
3.     I. *with acc. or clause.* (1) *to avoid.* (a) *not to come in
contact with, not meet with, get or keep out of the way of* a material object :
—Rar mid emfare forbūgaþ *balenam circilo declinant,* An. Ox. 670.
Swican hē forbeáh *decipulam declinavit,* Hpt. Gl. 520, 31. Hē nā ne
forbeág mid his nebbe monna spātl, Past. 261, 8. Đā suelcan wē magon
ealra betest geryhtan mid đȳ đæt wē hié forbūgen, 293, 22. Hié sindon
swǽ micle wærlīcor tō ferbūgonne (? oferbūganne, Hatt. MS.), 294, 21.
(b) *not to be exposed to, not be subject to* :—Yrre Godes þā hwīle þe wē
lybbađ forbūgan (*uitare*) wē magon, Scint. 233, 20. Đæt wē mægen
forbūgan đæt wīte, Past. 255, 5. Unsibbe mon ne mehte mid nānum
þingum forbūgan, Ors. 6, 3 ; S. 256, 33. Beón forbogen *uitari,* Scint.
234, 1. (c) *to abstain from* an action, practice, &c. :—Barbarismum hig
on heora gesetnyssa forbūgađ, Angl. viii. 313, 18. Swā þ heó (*the soul*)
leahtras forbūge, Hml. S. 1, 154, 237. Swā heó syngige, swā heó synna
forbūge, Hml. Th. i. 292, 33. Đæt wē orsorgnesse ūs ondrǽden, and hī
forbūgen, Past. 35, 2. Đæt wē ǽlce hǽđendōm georne forbūgan, Ll.
Th. i. 314, 9. Hē ne mæg forbūgan þ hē þæt ilce yfel ne geþafige
ōþrum monnum þe hē ǽr ōþrum dyde, Bt. 16, 2 ; F. 54, 5. Þā swylce
micele leahtras synd forbogene (*euitantur*), Scint. 231, 5. (2) *to fail to
attend* a meeting, *fail to keep* an appointment :—Forbēh þone āndagan,
Cht. Th. 206, 28. Sē þe þās gemōt forbūge þrywa, Ll. Th. i. 268, 15.
Gif preóst sinođ forbūge, ii. 296, 16. (3) *to escape from, evade* an
obligation, *neglect, not to obey* a command :—Gif hwā riht forbūge and
ūt hleápe, Ll. Th. i. 260, 7. Gif hē ūt hleápe, and þ ordāl forbūge,
282, 2 : 294, 16. Gif preóst biscopes āgen geban forbūge, ii. 290, 20.
Ne mihte hē forbūgan þæs cāseres hǽse, Hml. Th. i. 80, 26. (4) *to
pass by, pass over, leave unnoticed* :—Forgēman, i. forbūgon *praetergredi,* Kent. Gl. 685. Tō forbūgenne, forgitenne (*nec) praetereundum
(arbitror . . . Benedictum),* An. Ox. 2558. (4 a) *to pass by with dis-
favour, shun, eschew* :—Đǽra ungeleáffulra manna heortan God forbȳhđ
and oncunađ, Hml. Th. i. 288, 9. Se Hālga Gāst đā clǽnheortan lufađ,
and đā mānfullan forbīhđ, ii. 580, 34. Idele bȳspellu forbūh, Scint.
213, 5.     II. *with dat. To avoid, not to follow* :—Sē gehealt his
fulluht rihtlīce sē þe gehealt Godes beboda, and forbūhđ deófles unlārum,
Ll. Th. ii. 330, 27.     III. *absolute, to turn aside* :—Ne se wrecenda
brynæ wīle forbūgan, Dōm. L. 154. [v. N. E. D. forbow.] v. for-cirran.

**for-būgendlic,** -līce. v. un-forbūgendlic, -līce : **for-būgennys.**
*Dele.*

**for-byrd.** *Substitute:* **for-byrd (fore-),** e; *f.* (*in* Hml. S. 33, 203 *the word seems neuter*). (1) *bearing* pain, &c., *endurance.* v. for-beran (1) :—Ne mihte Pafnuntius nân forbyrd habban, ne nâne frôfre onfôn, Hml. S. 33, 203. Nû wille ic God biddan þ hê þe forgife fore-byrd and geþyld, 251. (2) *bearing patiently, forbearance.* v. for-beran (3), for-byrdig :—Ðæt hî beóð on ǽlengum ðingum and on ǽlcre longunge geðyldige and on foreƀyrde eáðmôde *patientiae longanimitate humiles,* Past. 41, 17. (3) *abstention.* v. for-beran (5) :—Hió gesette ofer eall hyre rîce þæt nân forbyrd nǽre æt geligere betwuh nânre sibbe *praecepit ut inter parentes ac filios, nulla delata reverentia naturae, de conjugiis adpetendis, ut cuique libitum esset, liberum fieret,* Ors. 1, 2; S. 30, 35.

**for-byrdig (fore-);** *adj. Patient, forbearing.* v. for-byrd (2) :—Hêr hê is swîðe forbyrdig (fore-, *v. l.*) for ûs, ac hê bið eft ûs swîðe rêðe, Nap. 23. Hêr hê is swîðe foreƀyrdig ofer ûs, ac hê is þǽr swîðe rêðe, Ll. Th. ii. 394, 5. v. un-foreƀyrdig.

**forca.** *Add:* **force,** an; *f.* (v. meox-force) :—Ðâ cwelleras tugon þâ glêda under ðæt bedd, and wiðufan mid heora forcum (cf. geaflum, l. 5) hine ðýdon, Hml. Th. i. 430, 11.

**forcel,** es; *m. A fork with two or three prongs* (?), *a pitch-fork* (cf. furculus *tridens,* merga, Migne) :—Þæt hûs (*hell*) is mid swîðe egeslican fýre âfylled, and helle hûs hafað forclas miccle, Nap. 23. Cf. twi-fyrclede.

**for-ceorfan.** *Add:* (1) *to cut up, cut asunder* :—Hê gelæhte his sex and forcearf his basing . . . þâ hlôgon his gesêran þæs forcorfenan basinges, Hml. S. 31, 69–72. Heó wæs forcorfen on middan on twâ styccu *per medium secabatur,* Gr. D. 340, 20. (2) *to cut off, out, away* :—Hió forcearf *sapientia excidit (columnas septem),* Kent. Gl. 284. Hî his eáran forcurfon, Hml. S. 21, 268. Heó bæd þ hî hyre fæx for-curfon, 2, 50. Hê hêt forceorfan his tungan . . . and his handa forceorfan, 25, 115. Heora ælces sweordfǽtelsas hê hêt forceorfan, 23, 178. Croppas forceorfende *racemos succidens .i. praecidens,* An. Ox. 2642. Hê ðone læppan forceorfenne hæfde, Past. 199, 17. Swâ swâ ðæt treúw ðe ðâ wyrtruman beóð færcorfene (for-, *v. l.*) forseárað, swâ hié magon ondrǽdan ðæt him weorðen ðâ wyrttruman færcorfene (for-, *v. l.*), 339, 19. (3) *to cut down* :—Forcorfen *succisa (arbor),* An. Ox. 1578. (4) *to deprive by cutting of* (*dat.*) :—Sume wǽron handum and fôtum forcorfene *some had their hands and feet cut off,* Hml. Th. i. 542, 32. [v. *N. E. D.* forcarve.]

**for-cilled;** *adj.* (*ptcpl.*) *Chilled* :—Wiþ forcillede wunda, Lch. i. 310, 15 : 66, 5.

**for-cinnan.** v. for-cuman.

**for-cippian;** *p.* ode *To cut off* :—Forcyppud *precisa,* Nap. 79.

**for-cirran;** *p.* de. *Take here* for-cyrran *in Dict., and add:* (1) *to turn* (intrans.) *aside from, get out of the way of, avoid* :—Ǽghwylce yfele fôtswaðu him ongeán cumende hê forbûgeþ, for ðon se yfela man hyne forcyrreþ, Lch. i. 318, 23. Barbarismum hig forbûgað, and eác barbara lexin hig forcyrrað, Angl. viii. 313, 19. Hý wǽron mid strǽlum scotode, ac ðâ strǽlas forcyrdon hý and slôgon ðâ hǽðnan, Shrn. 135, 29. Hî eft ne cyrdon tô ðan cyninge, ac þurh ôðerne weg hine forcyrdon, Hml. Th. i. 78, 30. Gif hê âgiémeleásað ðæt hê ðâ lytlan hreówsige and hwîlum forcierre *qui peccata minima flere ac devitare negligit,* Past. 437, 22. (2) *to turn* (trans.) *aside* :—For hwon onsíéne ðîne ðû forcerrest (*avertis*)?, Ps. Srt. 43, 24. Hê for-cerred (*avertit*) heftneð folces his, 52, 7 : 13, 11. Ðû forcerdes ûsic on bec *avertisti nos retrorsum,* 43, 11. (3) *to turn in a wrong direction, pervert, subvert* :—Ðû bist forcerred *subverteris,* Ps. Srt. 17, 27. Cneóris forcerredu *natio perversa,* ii. p. 191, 40. Ingeþanc wôh and forcyrred (-cerred, *v. l.*) *intentio perversa,* Gr. D. 76, 11. Mid heora þâm for-cyrdan (-cerdan, forhwyrfedum) cræfte, 73, 32.

**for-cirredness,** e; *f. Perversity* :—Hî onǽldon þǽra geongrena môd tô forcyrrednesse (-cerr-, *v. l.*) heora synlustes (*ad perversitatem libidinis*), Gr. D. 119, 15.

**for-cirring,** e; *f. A turning aside* :—On forcitringe *in convertendo,* Bl. Gl. Forcerringe, Ps. Srt. 9, 4 : 125, 1.

**for-clǽman;** *p.* de *To plaster up, stop up* :—Forclaemid (*printed* fol-) *obturat,* Txts. 81, 1419. Forclaemde *opilavit,* 83, 1446.

**for-clingan.** *Add:* —Forclingendu *rigentia,* Wrt. Voc. ii. 119, 21. [v. *N. E. D.* forcling.]

**for-clyccan;** *p.* -clyhte *To stop up, close* :—Swâ nǽdran forclyccende eáran heora, Nap. 79.

**for-cneów.** *Dele.*

**for-cnîdan.** *Add:* —Hê forcnýdeþ hî *comminuet eas,* Ps. Spl. 28, 6.

**for-corfian** (?) *p.* ode *To cut off* :—Ðâ hê ðone læppan forcorfedne (-ceorfedne, -corfenne, *v. ll.*) hæfde, Past. 198, 17.

**for-crafian;** *p.* ode *To demand* :—Neódbehêfnes stôwe giforcrafað (= gif forcrafað) *si necessitas loci exegerit,* R. Ben. I. 82, 3.

**for-cuman.** *Add:* (1) *to seize, get hold of* :—Forcuóm, bigeat *obtenuit,* Wrt. Voc. ii. 115, 19. Forcuóm (-cômun, R.) hiá ondo and fyrhto *invaserat eas tremor et pavor,* Mk. L. 16, 8. Forcumen sint *apraehensi sunt,* Mt. p. 13, 8. (2) *to overcome, conquer* :—Hine for-

cumað (*printed* -cinnað) þâ cirican getuinnas, Sal. 107. Ic forcuóm ðone middangeard *ego vici mundum,* Jn. L. 16, 33 : p. 7, 17. Forcuóm *conuincit,* Lk. p. 5, 4 : p. 10, 8 : *devicit,* Rtl. 64, 16. Gif strongra forcyme hine *si fortior vicerit eum,* Lk. R. 11, 22. Ðte forcuóme *ut vinceret,* Rtl. 81, 8. Forcumen sié *vincitur,* 125, 29. Forcuman, Sal. 206. Mið forcumenum deáðe *devicta morte,* Rtl. 29, 34. Forcum-men *deuicto,* Lk. p. 7, 6. Mið ðý ðôhte gelegeno ł forcumeno (-cumne, R.) woeron *dum mente consternatae essent,* Lk. L. 24, 4. (3) *to consume, destroy.* Cf. Goth. fra-kwiman :—Ne mæg hit (*fire*) nâne þâra gesceafta eallunga [f]orcuman (cf. hit waldan ne môt þ hit ǽnige eallunga fordô, Met. 20, 130), Bt. 33, 4 ; F. 130, 18. Ðǽm forcummenum (-cumnum, R.) monnum fore egisa *arescentibus hominibus prae timorum,* Lk. L. 21, 26. (4) *to reject* :—Forcuóm (-côm, R.) ł fordráf *exprobrauit,* Mk. L. 16, 14. Stân forcuómon *lapidem reprobauerunt,* 12. 10 : Lk. L. 20, 17. Forcuma from ældum *reprobari a senioribus,* Mk. L. R. 8, 31. Forcumman from aldum, Lk. L. 9, 22. Ðte hê sé forcumen, Lk. L. R. 17, 25.

**for-cuman.** *l.* for-cuman, and see **fore-cuman.**

**for-cunnian;** *p.* ode *To tempt, try* :—Huæt meh gé forcunnas *quid me temtatis?,* Mt. L. 22, 18. Of ðon forcunned sint *quo appraehensi sunt,* p. 13, 8.

**for-cúð.** *Add:* (1) *of human beings* :—Uncystig oððe heamol, fer-cúð *frugus,* Wrt. Voc. ii. 36, 5 : 70, 22. Ne bið hê nâ crîsten, ac bið forcúð wiðersaca, Hml. S. 17, 91. For þon Antiochus giémde hwæt hé hæfde monna gerîmes, and ne nôm nâne ware hûlice hié wǽron, for þon hiera wæs mâ forcúþra þonne altǽwra *qui cum in exercitu centum millia armatorum habere uideretur, ducenta millia amplius calonum atque lixarum inmixta scortis et histrionibus trahebat,* Ors. 5, 4 ; S. 224, 22. Þâ cyningas þe ǽfter Romuluse rîcsedon wǽron forcúðran and eargran þonne hé wǽre, 2, 2 ; S. 66, 25. Forcúðran *deteriores,* Past. 339, 25. Án ðǽra cyninga wæs heora eallra forcúðost, Hml. S. 25, 6. Eálâ þú forcúðost manna, 12, 197. (2) *of human actions or qualities* :—Hwæt segst ðú þ sié forcúðre ðonne sió ungesceádwîsnes?, Bt. 36, 6 ; F. 180, 31. Wið ðæt ðe forcúðre (*deterius*) bið, . . . ðæt is fierenlusð, Past. 189, 7 : Wlsft. 52, 28. (3) *of animals.* (a) *unclean* :—Þâ ðe tela nellað . . . syndon unclǽne swâ swâ ðâ forcúðan nýtenu, Hml. S. 25, 54. (b) *good for nothing, worthless* :—Hé wolde sittan on þâm horse þe hé on þâm mynstre forcúðost findan mihte *jumentum sedere consueverat quod despicabilius omnibus jumentis in cella potuisset reperiri,* Gr. D. 34, 11. [v. *N. E. D.* forcouth.] v. fracoþ.

**for-cúþe;** *adv. Infamously, evilly, wickedly* :—Wê wyllað nû sæcgan be þâm ungesǽligum Crîstes cwellerum, hû forcúðe hî ðôhton þâ ðâ hî feoh sealdon eallum þâm weardmannum, Hml. A. 78, 150.

**for-cúþlic;** *adj.* (1) *infamous, ignominious, ignoble, despicable, disgraceful* :—Forcúðlic hit bið þ cyning beó unrihtwîs, Hml. S. 13, 124. Hê cwæþ þ him forcúðlic þúhte, þ se ân Iudéisca hine forsáwe, Hml. A. 98, 196. Forcúðlic *absurdum,* An. Ox. 2081. (2) *worthless, poor, bad.* v. for-cúþ (3 b) :—On þâm horse þe hé mihte findan forcúðlocost on þâm mynstre, Gr. D. 34, 10.

**for-cúþlíce.** *Substitute:* (1) *in a way that excites contempt, contemptibly, ignominiously, feebly* :—Ortrýwes ciuesdômes forligere forcúþlíce bepǽht *perfidi pelicatus stupro enerviter deceptus,* An. Ox. 5044. (2) *in a way that expresses contempt, that inflicts disgrace, ignominiously* :— 'Teóð þâ cynegas ût of þâm scræfe, and gauge þâ yldostan tô and of-stæppað heora swuran swîðe mid fôtum.' Þâ dydon þâ ealdormen swâ . . . and þǽra cynega swuran forcúþlíce trǽdon, Jos. 10, 24. v. un-forcúþlíce.

**for-cweþan.** *Substitute:* I. *to reproach* a person, *upbraid, blame, reprove, rebuke* :—Ðâ fortrúwodan, ðonne hié him selfum tô swîðe trúwiað, hié forsióð ôðre menn and eác forcuéðað *protervi, dum valde de se praesumunt, exprobrando ceteros dedignantur,* Past. 209, 6. Forcueð ł tēlað *exprobrat,* Mk. p. 5, 3. Ðe ôðer forcwæð (-cuoæð, L.) ł ðreáde hine *alter increpabat illum,* Lk. R. 23, 40. Forcuoæð *arguit,* Jn. p. 5, 11. Forcuoeð *redarguit,* Lk. p. 7, 6. Ðâ aldu forcwédun (-cuoedon, L. *vituperauerunt*) hiæ, Mk. R. 7, 2. Forcuoeða *exprobrare,* Mt. L. 11, 20. Lǽran sceal mon geongne monnan, trymman and tyhtan . . . ; ne sceal hine mon cildgeongne forcweðan, ǽr hé hine âcýðan môte *a young man must be taught, encouraged and incited . . . ; when a child he must not be rebuked, before he can shew his character,* Gn. Ex. 49. Þ forcuoedne middangeard *arguendum mundum,* Jn. p. 7, 13. I a. *where cause of reproach is given.* v. I b :—Hû Nonius wæs forcweden for þâm gyldenan scridwǽne, Bt. F. xiv. 21. I b. *to call hard names.* v. I a :—Se wîsa Catulus, swâ ungefrǽglice forcwæð Nonium *Catullus Nonium strumam appellat,* Bt. 27, 1 ; F. 94, 32. Þâ wîfmen cwǽdon þ hié þâ burg werian wolden, gif þâ wǽpnedmen ne dorsten . . . Ac þâ consulas noldon hié selfe swâ earge geþencan swâ hié þâ wîfmen ǽr forcwǽdon *the consuls would not believe themselves such cowards as the women had called them,* Ors. 4, 10 ; S. 194, 15. II. *to reprove* a person's action :—Iudas tôslitnise forcuoeden bið *Judae murmur arguitur,* Jn. p. 6, 12. Ðte ne sié forcwedeno (-cuodeno, L.) werc his *ut non arguantur opera ejus,* Jn. R. 3, 20. III. *to refuse, decline* to do :—

Hē forcwið ðæt hē ne sēde Godes heorde *gregem Dei renuit pascere*, Past. 43, 6. Hē wilnode hine geðiédan tō ðǽre lufan his Scippendes, and for ðǽm hē forcwæð and nolde ðæt hine mon sende tō lǽranne *ne mitti ad praedicandum debeat contradicit*, 49, 17.   III a. *to excuse* one's self from doing. [Cf. *Goth*. faur-kwiþan, Lk. 14, 18] :—Sē ðe hine forcuoede *qui se excusare*, Lk. p. 8, 13.   III b. *to refuse to receive, to reject, disapprove of* :—Dryhten forcwæð swelce ælmessan *ipsa sacrificia Dominus reprobat*, Past. 343, 1. [Þū forcweðest ure godes, and seist ha beoð empti of gode, Kath. 389. *Goth*. faur-kwiþan *abjicere, excusare* : fra-kwiþan *maledicere, spernere* : O. H. Ger. ferquedan *abdicere, renuere, repellere*.]

**for-cyrran.** v. for-cirran.

**for-cӯpan.** Substitute : *To reprove, rebuke* :—Geðreátas ł forcӯðas of áðe . . . ēc forcӯðas ł geðreátas þ hiá getimbredon byrgenna ðára wītgena *increpat pharisaeos de juramento . . . Item arguit pharisaeos aedificantes sepulchra prophetarum*, Mt. p. 19, 11, 12. Forcӯðde *arguit* (*Sadducaeos*), 7. Of ðon forcunned ł forcummen ł forcӯðed sint and þ hié sié forcӯðed gegíuas *quo appraehensi sunt et apprehendere expetunt*, 13, 8, 9. Forcӯðed *reprobus*, Mk. p. 1, 20. Hæfde se snotra sunu Dauides forcumen and forcӯðed Caldéa eorl, Sal. 176: 206.

**ford.** Add :—Cōm Timotheus mid fyrde, and gesæt æt ánum forda. Ac Iudas him cōm tō . . . and oferférdon ðone ford, and fuhton wið þá hæþenan, Hml. S. 25, 432. ¶ The word occurs very frequently in the Charters both in composition and as an independent word. v. Midd. Flur. s. v.

**for-delfan** *to destroy by digging* (?), *to dig up* :—On ðone díc ðær esne ðone weg fordealf, C. D. ii. 28, 33.

**for-déman.** Add : I. *to give judgement against* a person. (1) in a general sense, *to condemn, express disapproval of* :—Hē (St. Martin) nǽnigne man unrihtlíce fordémde, ne nǽnigum yfel wiþ yfele geald, Bl. H. 223, 32. (2) in a civil case :—Þӯ lǽs ǽnig man cwede þæt ic míne mǽgcild mid wó fordémde, Cht. Th. 486, 28. (3) in a criminal case, *to condemn, sentence to punishment* :—Hwǽr synd þá ðe þe wrēgdon? Ne fordémde (*condemnauit*) þe nán man . . . Ne ic þe ne fordéme (*condemnabo*), Jn. 8, 10, 11. Hī habbaþ démena naman, and . . . hié for feós lufan earmne fordémaþ búton scylde, Bl. H. 63, 11. Heó nolde seccgan unsóð and hī sylfe fordéman, Hml. S. 12, 241. 'Ðū eart fordémed.' Ðá cwæð Apollonius: 'Hwá mihte mē fordéman, mínre ágenre þeóde ealdorman? . . . For hwilcum intingum hæfð hē mē fordémed? . . . Micclum ic eom fordémed, Ap. Th. 8, 1–7. Scyldig *reus*, fordémed *damnatus vel condempnatus*, Wrt. Voc. i. 86, 62 : 49, 2. Ealle þá þe fordémede wǽron . . . hié hit eall forgeáfon, Ors. 4, 9 ; S. 190, 35. Fordémendra *dampnatorum*, An. Ox. 3479. (3 a) in a spiritual sense :—Sē þe mē forsyhð . . . hē hæfð hwá him déman sceal. Mín word sceal hine fordéman (*judicabit*, Jn. 12, 48), Hml. A. 9, 219. Se fordémda þrowað on þám ӯttrum þeóstrum, Hml. Th. i. 530, 24. Hī ne beeódon heora geleáfan . . . ðás beóð fordémede, 396, 27. Fordémde, Bl. H. 87, 2. (3 b) where the punishment to which a person is condemned is stated :—God fordémð þá dyrnan forligeras on helle súslum, Hml. A. 19, 144. Mon fordémde ealle þá Bryttas . . . sume hī wurdon forblende, and sume wrecen of lande, Chr. 1076 ; P. 212, 24. Se cásere hine fordémde þyder (*to Patmos*), Hml. S. 29, 96. Hī hine fordémdon tō deáþe, Hml. A. 75, 70. Hī wurdon deádlíce and fordémde tō helle, 3, 58 : 80, 184.   II. *to confiscate, sequestrate*. v. for-déming :—Fordémet *addicit*, Wrt. Voc. ii. 4, 51. Fordémde *proscriberentur* (*possessiones earum fiscali jure*), An. Ox. 4845. [He let him fordéme lif and lime, O. and N. 1098.]   III. *to give judgement on, decide, determine* :—Hē ǽr on him fordéme gif lif his on wyrþscype si wel þæslic *ante in se discutiat si uita honore sit condigna*, Scint. 125, 5. Swá segð se apostol (v. 1 Cor. 11, 29) ná fordémiende (*dijudicantes*) líchaman Drihtnes, Angl. xiii. 389, 344. [v. N. E. D. fordeem.]

**fordémed-lic** ; *adj*. *To be condemned, deserving condemnation* :—Hú swíþe fordémedlic (*damnabilis*) þ word byþ þe ne byð bútan hete and níðe gesprecen, Gr. D. 208, 9.

**fordémed-nes.** Add :—Swá hí lífgendan bróðra seó myccle fordémednes (*damnatio*) bewerede, þ hí ne dorston hí gemǽngan in þá scylde þǽre gӯtsunge, Gr. D. 345, 3. Tō fordémednesse þæs Arrianiscan gedwolan *ad Arianae haereseos damnationem*, 235, 14. On ēcre fordémednesse hē sӯ fordémed *ad sempiternam damnationem condemnetur*, Ll. Th. ii. 238, 9.

**for-démend,** es ; *m*. *An accuser* :—Wíf ne from fordoemendum gedoemedo *mulierem nec ab accusatoribus condemnatam*, Jn. p. 5, 9.

**for-déming,** e ; *f*. *Confiscation, sequestration* :—Fordéming æhta proscriptionem rerum, An. Ox. 3149. v. for-déman ; II.

**for-dician.** Substitute : **for-dícian** ; *p*. ode *To barricade, block up* a path :—Hē wilnað ðæt hē ús ðone weg fordíkige (-dícige, *v. l.*), ðæt wē ne mǽgen ástígan *iter ascensionis abscidit*, Past. 361, 4. Ðӯ læs hié himselfum fordíkigen ðone weg ðǽre bóte *ne viam sibi meliorationis abscidant*, 383, 23.

**for-dilgian.** *l*. for-dílgian, *and add* :—Swá þæt hӯ þonne on ðǽm

hálgum dagum fordíligen þæt hӯ ǽr on óþrum tídum mid gémelēste forlēton *omnes negligentias suas aliorum temporum his diebus sanctis diluere*, R. Ben. 76, 6. Se hindsið mancynnes and þ heáflice gewrit þ weard þӯs dæge fordílegod, Bl. H. 123, 7. Sӯn ealle þá æhta þe þám cilde gebyrien swá fordӯlegade and tódǽlede *ita omnia obstruantur*, R. Ben. 105, 2.

**for-dimmian.** For ' R. Conc. 1 ' substitute :—þ hí ná mid þrӯstnesse hӯrsumnysse gearnunge fordimmian *ne praesumptione obedientiae meritum obnubilent*, Angl. xiii. 383, 263. Add :—Þænne his mód ne feóndes hatunge byð fordimmode *cum eius animus nec inimici odio fuscatur*, Scint. 24, 19. Sē þe gaderað seolfcr biþ fordimmod oðde áþӯstrod (*obscurabitur*), 99, 19.

**for-dōn.** Add : I. *of physical destruction* :—Hē fordyde *exterminavit*, Bl. Gl. Seneca and Papianus wurdon fordóne *Nero Senecam ad eligendae mortis coegit arbitrium. Papianum militum gladiis Antoninus objecit*, Bt. 29, 2 ; F. 104, 30. Hié mid ealle wǽron fordón and forhiéned *cruentissimam victoriam in eos exercuit*, Ors. 3, 7 ; S. 118, 26. Fordónra *interemptorum*, Bl. Gl.   II. *of moral or spiritual destruction* :—Ðá hálgan spēdað þá fordónan (*the damned*) micclum fram him geælfremode, Hml. Th. i. 332, 24.

**for-drǽfan** ; *p*. de *To drive, compel* to do or undergo :—Be ðon ðe mon tō ceápe fordrǽfe. Ðonne mon bið tyhtlan betygen and hine mon bedrífeð tō ceápe, Ll. Th. i. 140, 15.

**for-drencan.** Add :—Heó gelaðode þá cwelleras swilce for cӯððe and fordrencte hí mid wíne, Hml. S. 29, 327. Holofernis fordræncte hine sylfne mid þám strangum wíne . . . and ealle his þegnas wǽron fordræncte, Hml. A. 111, 294. [v. N. E. D. fordrench.]

**for-drífan.** Add : I. *to drive away, off, out* an object from a position of rest :—Hē fordráf (*eiecit*) of ðæm temple ðá scípo and ðá exin, Jn. L. R. 2, 15 ; Mt. L. 21, 12. Mid ðӯ fordrifenum (-drínum, R.) allum ł mid ðӯ alle úte fordráf *eiectis omnibus*, Mk. L. 5, 40. Hine fordrifon búta ðæm wíngeard, Mt. L. 21, 39. Fordriofon (-un, R.) hine út *eiecerunt eum foras*, Jn. L. 9, 34.   I a. *to drive away* illness, &c., *cast out* a devil :—Gif ic fordrífo (*eicio*) dióules, Mt. L. 12, 27. Feber fordráf *febre depulsa*, Mk. p. 2, 12. Forcuóm ł fordráf ungeleáfsulnise hiora *exprobrauit incredulitatem eorum*, Mk. L. R. 16, 14. Cynn ðæt mið gebed tō fordrífenne (*pellendum*), Mt. p. 18, 2. Unclǽnnise fordrífeno (*depulsa*), Rtl. 97, 31. Fordrífenum ús miste *depulsa nobis caligine*, 38, 7.   II. *to drive out* from a permanent position, *to banish, expel* :—Hēr Æþelstán cyning fordráf Gúðfrið cyning, Chr. 927 ; P. 107, 1. Gif mon gesíðcundne monnan ádrífe, fordrífe þӯ botle, næs þǽre setene, Ll. Th. i. 146, 7. Þte hine ne fordrífe búta ðæt lond *ne se expelleret extra regionem*, Mk. L. R. 5, 10. Sume þá munecas hē hēt ofsleán, sume on elþiéde fordrífan, Ors. 6, 34 ; S. 290, 5. Alle wítgo inngeonga in ríc Godes gié fordrifeno (-drífne, R.) úta (*expelli foras*), Lk. L. 13, 28 : Mt. p. 15, 14. Þte of ðær somnung néræ fordrífeno ([man] ne fordrife, R.) *ut de synagoga non eicerentur*, Jn. 12, 42.   III. *of a moving object, to drive aside* from its course :—Ðá gestód hine heáh weder ; wearþ ðá fordrífan on án íglond út on ðǽre Wendelsǽ, Bt. 38, 1 ; F. 194, 11.   IV. *to subject to excessive toil or hardship, to overtask* :—Eálá hú earmlíce and hú reówlíc tíd wæs ðá, ðá ðá wreccæ men lǽgen fordrífene full neáh tō deáðe, and syððan cōm se scearpa hungor and ádyde hí mid ealle, Chr. 1086 ; P. 218, 1. [v. N. E. D. fordrive.] v. for-drǽfan.

**for-drincan, (fore-).** Add :—Wiþ þon þe mon hine fordrince, Lch. ii. 152, 4 : 16, 17. Ælces cynnes drinc þe man mæg foredruncen beón *omnis generis potus quo quis inebriari possit*, Ll. Th. ii. 134, 21 note. For fordruncenes kyninges wordum, Mart. H. 156, 19. [v. N. E. D. fordrunken.]

**for-drugian.** *l*. for-drúgian, *and add* :—Áwisnade ł fordrúgade *aruit*, Lk. L. 8, 6. On þǽre stówe wæs getácnod swilce fordrúwod burna, Hml. S. 23 b, 197. [v. N. E. D. fordry.]

**for-druncnian (fore-)** ; *p*. ode *To be made drunk* :—Forgange hē wín, þ is ælces cynnes drinc þe man mæg foredruncnigan (*potu quo quis inebriari possit*), Ll. Th. ii. 134, 21.

**ford-wer,** es ; *m*. *A weir at a ford* :—Be súðan fordwere, C. D. iii. 437, 11.

**for-dwilman.** Add : Cf. dwolma.

**for-dwínan.** Add :—Ic fordwíne *evanesco*, i. *evaneo*, Wrt. Voc. ii. 144, 27. Fordwínþ *fatescit*, i. *evanescit, lacessit*, 147, 23.   I. *to vanish, pass* from sight :—Fordwán *disparuit*, Hpt. Gl. 502, 1. Fǽrlíce fordwán se ældeóðiga of his gesihðum, Hml. Th. ii. 286, 22. Hē ðǽrrihte of hyra gesihðum fordwán, i. 452, 15 : Hml. S. 6, 315. Se deófol ðǽrrihte fordwán on his gesihðe *the devil straightway vanished while he was looking at him*, 31, 178. Þá hundas ðǽrrihte of heora gesihðe fordwinon, Hml. Th. i. 378, 1.   I a. *to pass from knowledge, become unknown* :—Bemiþe, fordwíne *delitesceret*, i. *diu lateret*, An. Ox. 2089. Fordwínan *delitescere*. i. *latere*, 2152.   II. *to fade away, dwindle away, pass away, come to an end, decay* :—Gif se salt fordwínde ł fordwíneð *si sal euanuerit*, Lk. L. 14, 34. Þæs folces duguð fordwíneð, Wlfst. 133, 12. Fordwán *cassaretur*, An. Ox. 4711. Fordwinan

*tabuerunt*, 4032 : *euanuerunt*, i. *defecerunt*, 1679. Swylce sceádu gewitan, swylce swefen fordwinan (*euanuerunt*), Scint. 215, 11. Fordwínan *euanescere*, i. *deficere*, An. Ox. 3272. [v. *N. E. D.* fordwine.]

**for-dyslic**; *adj. Very foolish* :—Is þ þonne fordyslic geswinc, Bt. 18, 1 ; S. 42, 10.

**for-dyttan.** *Add* :—Fordytte *obstruit*, Wrt. Voc. ii. 115, 24. Fordyttat *obtrudite*, Germ. 398, 95. Fordyt *oblitum, coopertum*, 397, 378. **I.** in a literal, physical sense :—þá geoniendan ceáfla þrotbollan fordytte *hiulcos* (i. *apertos*)*faucium gurguliones oppilauit* (i. *obturauit*), An. Ox. 3577. Bescufon hí þone man in þone ofn and fordytton þone ofn (*clibanum clauserunt*), Gr. D. 219, 13. Hí fordytton ælc fær upp tó þám muntum *praeoccupauerunt omnes vertices montium*, Hml. A. 104, 70. Fordytte þ eáre mid þære wulle, Lch. ii. 42, 25 : 44, 3. Hé hét fordyttan þæs scræfes múð mid weorcstánum, Homl. Th. ii. 424, 26. Fordyttum scyttylsum *obseratis uectibus*, Germ. 399, 349. **II.** figurative, where there is obstruction of the mind or senses :—Líchamlicere forspennincge fordyt *carnalis* (*caligo*) *inlecebrae optundit* (i. *obfuscat*), An. Ox. 1725. Sé fordett *qui opturat* (*aurem suam*), Kent. Gl. 777. Heó simble heora eáran fordyttan and hit gehýran noldon, Wlsst. 255, 7. Heora módes andgytu hí fordytton, Hml. S. 23, 379. Forduttende (*obturantes*) eáran hire, Ps. Srt. 57, 5. Fordytt *obstructum*, Bl. Gl. Mid swige fordyt *silentio oppilatum* (i. *obturatum*), An. Ox. 2086. Fordytte þinc *abstrusa*, 2335. [v. *N. E. D.* fordit.] v. un-fordyt[t].

**fore.** *Take here* fóre (*l.* fore), *and add* : **A. with dat. or uncertain. I.** local, *before, in front of* :—Gif him wan fore wolcen hangað (cf. þonne sweartan wolcnu him beforan gáþ, F. 14, 22), Met. 5, 4. Ásetton on gesyhðe sigebeámas þrý eorlas fore Elenan cneó, El. 848. **I a.** figurative :—Næs ðær nán man þe gryre and ege fore ne stóde *no one who had not horror and terror before his eyes*, Hml. S. 23, 83. **I b.** of position, degree, *at the head of, acting as ruler of* :—Hé manega gær wæs fore þám mynstre (ealdor þæs mynstres, *v.l.* praefuit), Honoratus tó dæge is fore þám ylcan mynstre (*praeest*), Gr. D. 96, 10, 15. Ealle ðá ðe fore óðrum bieón sculon, Past. 107, 23. Hié beóð óðrum bróðrum ofergesett and him fore beón sculon on godcundum ðingum *fratribus animarum causa praelati sunt*, Past. 126, 17 : 129, 6. Sácerdas ðám geleáffullum sculon fore beón *sacerdotes fidelibus praesunt*, 139, 16. Hí gewilnodon þ he þám mynstre beón scolde fore (hyra mynstres ealdor beón sceolde, *v. l. eis praeesse deberet*), Gr. D. 103, 30. **I c.** *within sight* or *hearing of.* Cf. for; **A. I c** :—Hé heom fore sæde his neóde, Chr. 1087 ; P. 223, 30. **II.** temporal, *before* :—Is nú feala fordgewitenra ... þe ús fore wæron, El. 637. **II a.** of previous action :—Hí férdon tó heora geférum þe him fore stópon, Hml. S. 4, 416. **III.** figurative. (1) marking cause, *for, from, through, because of.* v. for; **A. III.** 1 :—Hí forhte beofiað fore fæder egsan, Cri. 1015 : Gú. 310. Him tó móde fore monlufan sorg gesóhte, 324. Hé sceal fore hæðenra handgewinne gást onsendan, An. 186, 1034. (2) marking reason, ground, *on account of.* v. for; **A. III.** 2 :—Geswænced from his moniendum fore .xii. scillingum, Gr. D. 157, 33. Hé fore góddædum glade blissiað, Cri. 1287. Adames cynn cwíðeð nales fore lytlum, ac fore þám mæstan mægenearfeðum, 963. Þ þing ðe mon eall gód fore déþ, Bt. 34, 7 ; F. 142, 36. Þý læs fore þære mærðe him mód ástíge, Crä. 101. Tó ðære genihtsumnisse þe hié ús ealneg fore gielpað *to the abundance on account of which they are always boasting to us*, Ors. 4, 7 ; S. 182, 16 : S. 4. 18. (3) marking motive, *for, from, through.* v. for; **A. III.** 3 :—Hé wið don won fore (for, *v.l.*) geornfullnesse and for lufan þæs árfæstan gewinnes *renitentem studio et amore pii laboris*, Bd. 4, 3 ; Sch. 349, 19. Þú fore monna lufan þínre módor bósm gesóhtes, Hö. 110 ; Fa. 78. Gif seó æfstum on his wergengan wíte legdon, Gú. 684 : Mód. 37. (4) marking substitution, *in place of, instead of.* v. for; **A. III.** 4 :—Dyde ic mé tó gomene ganetes hleóðor, mæw singende fore medodrince, Seef. 22. Fore hundum tigras and leópardos hí fédað, Nar. 38, 3. Sé þe hors nabbe wyrce þám hlátorde þe him fore ríde, Ll. Th. i. 232, 21. (5) with verbs expressing or implying payment, requital. v. for; **A. III.** 6. (a) marking compensation :—Gif hwá óðrum his eáge oþðó, selle his ágen fore (for *v. l.*) ; tóð fore (for, *v.l.*) téð, honda wið honda, fét fore fét, bærning fore bærninge, Ll. Th. i. 48, 20–22. Gif oxa óðres monnes oxan gewundige, and hé þonne deád sié ... selle him óðerne oxan fore, 50, 13. (b) marking expiation :—Hé on þone beám áhongen wæs fore moncynnes mánforwyrhtum, Cri. 1095. Se þegn fore fæder dædum blóðfág swefeð, B. 2059. (c) where an obligation is discharged :—Hé náh self nánwiht tó gesellanne ... þonne gæð óðer man, seleð his ceáp fore ... sé þe him ær ceáp fore sealde, Ll. Th. i. 142, 2–6 : 7. Gif hé nyte hwá him fore béte, 164, 12. Gif seó mægð him fore gyldan nellen, 248, 5. Sé þe áhte þ yrfe þe wé fore gildað (*the property in connexion with which the reward is given*), 234, 25. v. sceótan ; **VII.** (6) *for the sake of.* v. for ; **A. III.** 7 :—Þá earfeðu þe hé fore ældum ádreág, Cri. 1202. Deáðe mínum þe ic ádreág fore þé, 1476. Hé earfeðu geþolade fore þearfe þeódbúendra, 1173. (7) *on behalf of, for the advantage of.* **A. III.** 8 :—þ man ne mót him mæssian fora, ne him openlíce fora gebiddan, Ll. Th. ii. 386, 16–18. Biddende þæt heom fore gebeden sý

*postulent pro se orari*, R. Ben. 59, 21 : 62, 8 : 127, 18, 19. Hé bæd mé ðæt ic him wære forespeca ... Ðá spæc ic him fore, Cht. Th. 169, 29. Ic ne tóweorpe ðá burg ðe ðú fore spriceð *non subvertam urbem pro qua locutus es*, Past. 399, 31. Fore þencan, Past. 75, 11 : 97, 21. Gif bád genumen sý on monnes orfe for óðres monnes þingum, þonne begyte þá báde hám sé þe heó fore genumen sý, i. 354, 7. Blíþre bid seó sáwl þæs mannes, þonne hire man þá ælmessan fore dæleþ, Bl. H. 41, 33 : Gú. 373. Hé him (v. Angl. vi. p. 136 of Anzeiger) worhte fore wundur mære, Ps. Th. 77, 14. (7 a) *to the honour of* :—On þære hálgan Þrynnesse naman þe seó stów is fore hálig *in the name of the holy Trinity to which the place is dedicated*, Cht. Th. 559, 1. (8) marking object of fear, &c. v. for; **A. III.** 10 :—Hié ealle þreátas oforhogodan, and him nówiht fore ne ondrédon, Bl. H. 119, 16. Hý beofað fore Freán forhte, Cri. 1231. Ne þreodode he fore þrymme þeódcyninges æniges, Ap. 18. (9) marking obstacle. v. for; **A. III.** 12 :—Ic ne mæg fore mínum wonæhtum willan ádreógan, Hy. 4, 103. Hé staþolfæst ne niæg fore leahtra lufan leng gewunian, Jul. 375. (10) marking end to be attained :—Wé sellað ðæt lond ... fore hyhte and fore aedleáne ðaes aecan and ðaes tówardon lífes, and fore uncerra sáula héla, C. D. i. 292, 22–26. (11) with verbs of appeal. v. for; **A. III.** 18 :—Ic þé hálsige fore þínum cildháde, ... and fore þære wunde, Hö. 118–120 : 122. Fore Godes sibbum, Jul. 540. (12) with verbs of speaking, hearing, *of, about; de* :—Ealle men ðá ðe ðyses weres líf cúþon oþþe fore hýrdon, Bl. H. 219, 34. His fyrngefliitan þe ic ær fore sægde, Pa. 34. **B. with acc.** (1) with verbs of movement, *before, into the presence of* :—Mín gebed fore sylfne þe becume *oratio mea praeveniet te*, Ps. Th. 87, 13. Cuman fore heofona cyning, Cri. 1039 : 796 : 1114. Heafde se cyng hí fore began mid ealre fyrde, Chr. 1009 ; P. 139, 19. (2) *marking substitution.* v. for; **B.** (1) :—Dyde ic mé tó gomene ganetes hleóðor and huilpan swég fore hleahtor wera, Seef. 21.

**fore**; *adv. Substitute*: fore; *adv.* **I.** local (lit. or fig.), *in front, at the head, as chief* :—Fore tó yrnenne *prodeundi*, Scint. 224, 7. Eorðcyningas þe folcum hér fore wísian *kings that, placed at their head, direct the peoples*, Ps. Th. 148, 11. **II.** temporal, *before* :—Fore ic cueð t ær ic sægde *praedixi*, Mt. L. 28, 7 : Mk. L. 13, 23. *See also* fore; *prep., and verbs with* fore *as prefix. In the Northern specimens many Latin verbs with the prefixes* prae, pro *are glossed by* fore *and the verb which translates the simple Latin verb, e. g.* foregearuiga *praeparauero*, Jn. L. 14, 3 : foregebécnade *praefigurat*, Mt. p. 9, 16 : foreseóll *procidit*, Mk. L. 7, 25 : foresended *promittit*, Jn. p. 6, 16. *Such forms for the most part are not cited. The Latin* ob *is also rendered by* fore *e. g.* foregedistrat *obcecatum*, Mk. L. 6, 52 : foragémnis *observatio*, Lk. L. 17, 20 : foresuíge *obmutesce*, 4, 35.

**fore-ádihtian**; *p.* ode *To arrange beforehand, pre-arrange* :—Ðis ærendgewrit Agustinus bróhte, swá hit ær foreádihtode Róme pápa, Past. 9, 9.

**fore-andfenge** *glosses praesumtus* :—Foreoundfengca *praesumta*, Lk. p. 2, 13.

**for-eald.** v. for-ealdian : **for-ealden.** v. for-healdan.

**for-ealdian.** *Add* : (1) of living material, animal or vegetable, *to grow weak with age* :—Æpla, græs, and wyrtan foraldiað and forseriað ... Ge furþum manna líchaman forealdiað ... hý árísað on dómes dæge swá þæt néfre syððan þá líchaman ne geendiað ne ne forealdiað, Solil. H. 10, 3–12. Ic eom forealdod *inveteravi*, Ps. Th. 6, 6. Þá þá Dúnstán iung man wæs, and se swurdbora wæs forealdod man, Hml. S. 32, 6. Ic him sæde þ hé forealdod wære, and tó þæs eald wære þ hé ne mihte elcor gewearmigan búton æt fýre, Nar. 18, 14. Swá forealdod mon *decrepitus senex*, 21. Foreald[od] *decrepita*, An. Ox. 2109. On fótum forealdudes (*ueterani*), Scint. 223, 13. Mec þás forealdodan elreordegan bysmergeað *illudi me a barbaris senibus existimavi*, Nar. 25, 25. Samuhel and Danihel cildgeonge forealdedum mæssepreóstum démdon *Samuel et Daniel pueri presbiteros judicaverunt*, R. Ben. 114, 8. (2) of dead matter, *to get worn out with long use, to decay through being kept too long* :—Warnige hé þ þ húsl ná foreaidige ; gif hit for[h]ealden sí, þ his man brúcan ne mæge, forbærne hit man, Ll. Th. ii. 252, 7. Hé funde on þam mynstre ... I. forealdodne nihtsang ... and II. forealdode rædingbéc swíþe wáke, Cht. Th. 430, 25–31. (3) of abstract things :—Mín mægn forealdode, Ps. Th. 31, 3. (4) of a period of time, *to run out, expire* :—Seó syxte yld þe nú ys hyre geendung ys swýðe ungewis, ac hyre yld sceal forealdian and hwíd worulde ende beón geendod, Angl. viii. 336, 13. [v. *N. E. D.* forold.]

**fóre-áþ, fór-áþ.** *l.* fore-áþ, for-áþ, *and add* :—Hé móste mid his foráðe his hláford áspelian, Ll. Th. i. 192, 2.

**for-eáþelíce**; *adv. Very easily, without inconvenience* :—Hú mihtú for sceame æniges ðinges æt Gode biddan, gif ðú forwyrnst ðínum gelícan þæs ðe ðú foreadlíce him getíðian miht ?, Hml. Th. i. 256, 7.

**fore-beácen.** *Add* :—Hér wæron réðe forebécna (-býcna, *v. l.*) cumene ofer Norðanhymbra land ... þ wæron orméte ligræscas, and wæron geseowene fýrene dracan on þám lyfte fleógende, Chr. 793 ; P. 55, 32. Forebeácna *portentorum*, An. Ox. 4969. Forebeácuum *signis*, i. *prodigiis*, 2068. Stephanus worhte forebeácena (*prodigia*, Acts 6, 8)

and micele tācna, Hml. Th. i. 44, 24. Ic sylle mīne forebeácn (*prodigia*, Acts 2, 19), 314, 26. Forebēcun *prodigia*, Mt. R. 24, 24.

**fore-beódan** *to announce, preach* :—Forebodan (= -bodad ? v. forebodian) bið *praedicabitur*, Mt. L. 24, 14.

**fore-beódan** *to prohibit.* v. for-beódan : **fóre-beón.** *l.* fore beón, *and see* fore ; **A. I b.**

**fore-beran.** *Add :—*þætte nǣnig biscopa hine ōþrum forbere *ut nullus episcoporum se praeferat alteri*, Bd. 4, 5 ; Sch. 378, 17.

**fóre-bētan.** *l.* fore bētan, *and see* fore ; **A. III.** 5 c.

**fore-bisceop,** es ; *m. A high priest* :—Abiathar wæs in ðǣm tīd forebiscop, Mt. L. 1, 18 note.

**fore-bisigian** *to pre-occupy* :—Sȳ forebisegod *preoccupetur*, An. Ox. 1236.

**fore-bod,** es ; *n.* (1) *preaching* :—Forebod *praedicatio*, Mk. p. 2, 9 : Mt. L. 12, 41 : p. 14, 3. (2) *prohibition* ( = for-bod ; *q. v.*) :—Him forebod cōm fram eallum Rōmānum þ hē þ fær beginnan mōste, ne him swā gecwēme folc gefaran, Lch. iii. 434, 3.

**fore-boda** (for-), an ; *m. A herald, crier* :—þæt syndan forbodan and Antecrīstes þrǣlas þe his weg rȳmað, Wlfst. 55, 8. v. for-boda *in Dict.. and next word.*

**fore-bodere,** es ; *m. A herald, crier* ; praeco :—Forebodere *praeconium*, Rtl. 48, 10. Foreboderas *praecones*, 194, 1.

**fore-bodian.** *Add :—*Forebodas *praedicat*, Mt. p. 14, 7. Forebodade, 9. Forebodadon (for-, R.) *praedicabant*, Mk. L. 6, 12. Forebodages *praedicate*, Mt. L. 10, 7.

**fore-bodung,** e ; *f. Preaching* :—Forebodung *predicatio*, Rtl. 60, 27 : Mk. p. 5, 14.

**fore-brǣdan** ; *p.* de *To overshadow* :—Wolcen forebrǣde hiá *nubis obumbrans eos*, Mk. L. 9, 7. Cf. ofer-brǣdan.

**fore-breóst.** *Add :—*Forebreóst *praecordia*, Wrt. Voc. ii. 67, 49 : Ælfc. Gr. Z. 85, 12. His (*the Phenix*) forebreóst is fægre gehīwod swylce marmorstān, E. S. viii. 478, 58. Forebreóstu *precordia*, Scint. 97, 3.

**fore-burh.** *Add : a principal town* (?) :—Foreburga *praedia* (lis satis cruenta inter duo populosa *praedia* gerebatur, Ald. 52, 16), An. Ox. 3790. [Cf. *O. L. Ger.* fora-burgi ; *n.*]

**fore-byrd, -byrdig.** v. for-byrd, -byrdig.

**fore-cneóres** *glosses progenies* :—Of forecneówresse on forecneóressa *a progenie in progenies*, Ps. Rdr. p. 296, 50.

**fore-cnyll,** es ; *m. The first signal given by a bell* :—Gewordenum forecnyll þære nóntíde *facto primo signo hore none*, R. Ben. I. 82, 12.

**fore-cuman** (for-). *Take here* **fōr-cuman** (*l.* for-) *in Dict., and add :—*Forcōmon mē grinu deúþes *praeoccupaverunt me laquei mortis*, Ps. Spl. 17, 6. Forecuðmon *procedebant*, Lk. L. 4, 22. Forcyme *procedens*, Mt. p. 3, 20. Hiora forðfōre mid gōdum weorcum forecuman (*praeuenire*), Bd. 4, 3 ; Sch. 357, 16. [*Goth.* faura-kwiman.]

**fore-cweþan.** *Add :* (1) *to foretell, predict* :—Forecueð *predixit*, Rtl. 56, 5. Forecueð *praedicit*, Mt. p. 19, 19 : Mk. p. 4, 14. Forecwoedena *praedicta*, Mt. p. 9, 9. (2) *to preach* :—Forecwoedende *praedicantem*, 8, 12.

**fóre-cwide.** *Substitute :* **fore-cwide,** es ; *m.* (1) *a prediction* :—Wæs his sōð syn wītnad æfter forecwide (*juxta praedictum*) ðæs Godes weres, Bd. 3, 22 ; Sch. 296, 11. Forecwida ðæs wītges *praedicta Ezechielis*, Mt. p. 9, 9. (2) *heading of a chapter* :—Forecwide *capitulum*, Mt. p. 4, 1. Forecuido capitulae, Mk. p. 1, 1. Forecuido ðāra rēda capitula lectionum, 2, 7.

**fóre-cynn.** *Dele.* **fore-cynrēd** (?) *glosses* progenies :—Oþ on forecynrēd (-ren ?) *usque in progeniem*, Ps. Rdr. 48, 20.

**fore-cynren.** *For* Cot. 154 *substitute* :—Forecynren heora *propago eorum*, Ps. Rdr. p. 290, 32. On ealre cneórisse and forecynrene (*progenie*), 44, 18 : 48, 12 : 89, 1. Fram forecynrene on forecynren *a progenie in progeniem*, 84, 6 : Wrt. Voc. ii. 69, 44.

**fore-cȳpan** ; *p.* de *To make known beforehand, foretell, predict* :—Hē gewunað þ hē forecȳþeþ on þām swefnum manige sōðe wīsan *solet multa vera praedicere*, Gr. D. 339, 21.

**fore-dēman** *to pre-judge* :—Ne hē ne foredēme *nec prejudicet*, R. Ben. I. 105, 6.

**fore-druncen, fore-druncnian.** v. for-drincan, for-druncnian.

**fóre-dūru.** *Substitute :* **fore-duru,** e, a ; *f. A vestibule, porch* :—Tō foredure *ad vestibulum*, An. Ox. 2999. Foredura, infærelda *uestibula*, i. *introitum*, 135. v. next word.

**fore-dyre,** es ; *n. A vestibule, porch* :—Tō foredere *ad uestibulum*, Hpt. Gl. 476, 63. Foredyre (foredera ł infærelda, Hpt. Gl. 409, 33) *uestibula*, Wrt. Voc. ii. 75, 34 : 83, 79. [*Goth.* faura-dauri : *Icel.* for-dyri *a vestibule.*]

**fore-dyrstig** ; *adj. Presumptuous* :—Foredyrstig *presumptuosus*, Rtl. 100, 39.

**fóre-fæder.** *Dele.*

**fore-feax,** es ; *n. The hair growing on the front of the head, forelocks* :—Forefex antiae, crines, Hpt. Gl. 526, 43, 44. v. fore-locc.

**fore-féran** ; *p.* de *To precede, go in front of* :—Hē foreforde hiá

antecedebat eos, Lk. L. R. 22, 47. þā foreférendan *qui praeibant* (Lk. 18, 39), Bl. H. 15, 20.

**fore-fleón** ; *p.* -fleáh *To flee away* :—Hē forefléh from ðǣm *profugit ab eis*, Mk. L. 14, 52.

**fore-fōn.** *Add :—*Forefōe *anticipiat*, Rtl. 178, 15. Forefēnge *presumpserit*, 102, 21. v. for-fōn.

**fore-fréfrend** *glosses* pro-consul :—Forefroefrend *proconsul*, Rtl. 100, 17.

**fore-gān.** *Add :—*Forecáde *praeteriit*, Mt. L. 14, 15. Foreeádon ł foreeád wērun *praecedebant*, 21, 9. Foreeódon *praeibant*, Mk. L. 11, 9.

**fore-gangan.** *Add :* (1) *to precede* (in time) :—þā foregangendan hlǣfdian (*praecedentes matres*) gewunodon þ hī hit sǣdon þām gingrum nunnum, and nū þā gingran nunnan hit reccaþ, Gr. D. 280, 26. Gōdra foregangendra (*praecedentium*) wera, 8, 20 : 277, 10. (2) *to take precedence of, rank higher than* :—Ðes Iōhannes wæs māra ðonne ænig ōþer mon būton Crīste . . . ealle þā apostolas and martyras hē foregongeð, Shrn. 95, 11. [*Goth.* faura-gaggan.]

**fore-gearwung,** e ; *f. Preparation* :—Foregeorwunge (-gearuung, L.) *parasceue*, Lk. R. 23, 54. Metes foregearuung *praeparatio cibi*, Jn. L. 19, 14. Foregearuung *praeparatione*, Mk. p. 5, 10.

**fore-geblind** ; *pp. Blinded* :—Foregeblind *obcecatum*, Mk. L. 6, 52.

**fore-geceósan** *to choose beforehand* :—Ic mē sylfe myngode . . . þære mundbyrdnysse þe ic ǣr foregeceás, Hml. S. 23 b, 543.

**fore-gefnes.** v. for-gifnes.

**fore-gegán** (1) *to precede* :—Stearra foregeeáde heá *stella antecedebat eos*, Mt. L. 2, 9. (2) *to pass away* :—Tīd is foregeeád ł tīd eáde *hora praeteriuit*, Mk. L. R. 6, 35.

**fore-gehát.** *Add :—*Ic mē sylfe myngode mīnes foregehātes, Hml. S. 23 b, 543.

**fore-gehátan** (1) *to order* :—Foregehēht *praecipit*, Mt. p. 14, 11 : *praecepit*, 18, 9. (2) *to promise* :—Hiá foregehēhton him feh þte hiá sealla walldon *promiserunt ei pecuniam se daturos*, Mk. L. R. 14, 11. [*Goth.* faura-gahaitans *promised before.*]

**fore-geleóran** *to pass away* :—Þte foregeleóre *praeterire*, Lk. L. 16, 17.

**fore-genga.** *Add :* (1) *one who goes before* :—Forgencga *antecessor*, An. Ox. 619. (1 a) implying *interiority, an attendant* :—On þām fætelse þe hyre foregenga, blāchleór ides, heora bēgea nest þyder on lǣdde, Jud. 127. (2) *a predecessor* :—Se cyng Willelm wæs strengere þonne his foregenga wǣre, Chr. 1086 ; P. 219, 22. Mid ðǣre lāre ðe ic leornode æt ðām hālgum fæderum ðe wǣron ūre foregengan, Hex. 34, 7. Hī gesāwon heora foregengan swā dōn, Hml. Th. ii. 534, 1. (3) *a leader, ruler* :—Gemunað eówerra foregengena ðāra ðe eów bodedon Godes word *mementote praepositorum vestrorum, qui vobis locuti sunt verbum Dei*, Past. 205, 14. [*Goth.* faura-gaggja *a steward.*]

**fore-genge.** *Dele, and see preceding word.*

**fore-gengel** (for-), es ; *m. A predecessor* :—Ealle þā forgiuenesse þe mīne forgengles geáfen, Chr. 963 ; P. 117, 5, 9. Be cinga dagan mīnra forgenglan (foren-, Chr. 693 ; Th. 66, n. 2), and be mīnra māgan dagon, C. D. B. i. 137, 19. v. æfter-gengel.

**fore-gesǣgd** *predestined* :—Foregesægd *praedistinatum*, Mk. p. 1, 9.

**fore-gesceáwung,** e ; *f. Providence, forethought* :—þæt sȳ on ðæs abbodes foregesceáwunge *in abbatis sit providentia*, R. Ben. 66, 1. v. fore-sceáwung.

**fore-gesettan.** *Add :—*Foregeseted tal *propositum numerum*, Mt. p. 12, 1.

**fore-geteohhian, -teohgian** (?) *to destine* :—Tō foregetihtgedre (-tihgedre ? -stihtedre ?) stōwe *ad destinatum locum*, Hpt. Gl. 405, 77. v. teohhian.

**fore-geþeóstrod** ; *pp. Darkened* :—Foregeðístrat *obcecatum*, Mk. L. 6, 52.

**fóre-gewītnys.** *Dele.*

**fore-gidd, -gedd** *a proverb* :—Foregeddum (geddum, L.) nān ðū cweðes *prouerbium nullum dicis*, Jn. R. 16, 29.

**fóre-gilpan.** *Dele, and see* fore ; **A. III.** 2.

**fore-gimness,** e ; *f. Observation* :—Mið foragēmnisse *cum obseruatione*, Lk. L. 17, 20.

**fore-gisel.** *Substitute : A hostage given as security for the performance of a promise* :—Eást-Engle hæfdon foregísla .vi. geseald and þēh ofer þā treówa . . . fōron hié, Chr. 894 ; P. 84, 20. Hié him þǣr foregíslas saldon, swā fela swā hē habban wolde, and micle áþas swóron, and þā gódne friþ heóldon, 877 ; P. 74, 20. Salde se here him forgíslas (gíslas, *v. l.*) and micle áþas þæt hié of his rīce uuoldon, and him eác gehētou þæt hiera kyning fulwihte onfōn wolde ; and hié þæt gelǣston swā, 878 ; P. 76, 13. [*Icel.* for-gísl.]

**fóre-gleáw.** *Substitute :* **fore-gleáw** (for-) (1) *fore-seeing, fore-knowing, knowing what is to happen*, (a) *by natural means* :—Swā hit foregleáwe ealde ūðwitan ǣror fundan, Men. 165. (b) *by supernatural means, prophetic* :—Hē fægra manna forðsíð foregleáw sǣde, wīs ðurh wītegunge wīsdōmes gǣstes, Hml. Th. ii. 152, 2. Mid foregleáwre

clypunge *presago vocabulo*, An. Ox. 4846. Æfter forewittigum (foregleáwe) gydde (wîtedôme) *secundum praesagum uaticinium* (i. *prophetiam*), 3707. (2) *having forethought, provident, prudent* :—Sŷ hé â foregleáw (for-, R. Ben. I. 108, 16) on his gebodum *sit in imperiis suis providus*, R. Ben. 121, 15. Tô æfengereordunga lambes foregleáwes (*providi*), Hy. S. 82, 3.

foregleáwlíce *with forethought* :—Sê þe þê gescôp foregleáwlíce *qui te creavit provide*, Hy. S. 75, 41. Foraglæwlíce and rihtlíce ealle þinc gedihtan *provide et juste cuncta disponere*, R. Ben. I. 18, 7. Foregleáwlíce and wislíce wissian and dihtan *provide dispensare*, C. D. B. i. 154, 33.

fore-glendra *glosses* praecipitare, Lk. p. 4, 15.

fore-heáfod (for-). *Add* :—Mearciaô rôdetácen on eówrum foreheáfdum, Hml. Th. i. 466, 20. On forheáfdum *in frontibus*, Hy. S. 32, 29. v. foran-heáfod.

fore-hradian. v. for-hradian.

fore-irnan (for-). *Take here* for-yrnan, *and add* :—Heó foram ðam folce. Hml. Th. i. 566, 11. Ðe ôðer ðegn foream Petre *ille alius discipulus praecurrit Petro*, Jn. R. L. 20, 4: Lk. L. 19, 4. Forearn *procurrens*, Mk. L. R. 10, 17. Foreiorne *prorumpere*, Mt. p. 9, 4.

fore-irnend, es; *m. A forerunner* :—Foreiernend *antecessor*, Wrt. Voc. ii. 1, 18.

fore-irnere, es; *m. A forerunner, precursor* :—Foreiornere *precursor*, Rtl. 56, 3, 20. Foreirnerum *feletei*, Wrt. Voc. ii. 76, 52. Fêþemen, fêþehere *felethi*, foreirnerum *felethei*, 33, 46. [The passage glossed is Ald. 11, 37 where the word is *Pelethi*. Cf. An. Ox. 776.]

fore-lâdtéow, es; *m. A leader* :—Forelâtuu (-lâtow, R.) *praecessor*, Lk. L. 22, 26.

fore-lǽrende *acting as guide and teacher* :—þâ cwæð Petrus tô Paule, 'Brôðor Paulus, arîs þu and gebide þê ǽr . . .' [þâ cwæð hê], 'Ealle þâ þe ymbe standaþ hié syndan betran þonne ic; and þû eart forelǽrende on ðâra apostola gebede *then said Peter to Paul, 'Brother Paul, do thou arise and pray first . . .' [Then said he], 'All those that stand about me are better than I; it is for thee to take the lead when the apostles pray*, Bl. H. 141, 2.

fore-lâr, e; *f. Preaching* :—Forebod î forelâr *praedicatio*, Mt. p. 14, 3.

for-elcian *to put off too long, delay unduly* :—þ sume þâ gecoreime . . . beón gemanede tô Godes þênunga þe heó forelcodan, Nap. 24 (12th cent. MS.).

fore-leóran (1) *to precede* :—Ic forlióro (foregâ, R.) iówih *praecedam vos*, Mt. L. 26, 32. Foreliórað îwih *praecedit vos*, 28, 7. (2) *to pass in front of, pass by* :—Foreliórende *praetereuntes*, Mt. R. 27, 39.

fore-locc, es; *m. A fore-lock* :—Foreloccas *antiae (frontis)*, An. Ox. 7, 375 : 8, 378. v. fore-feax.

fore-mǽre. *Add* : , for-mǽre. (1) *of persons* :—Sum swîðe ænlic wer and foremǽre *quidam spectabilis vir*, Gr. D. 307, 1. þ wæs swîðe foremǽre man for Gode, and his gôd wæs swîðe gecŷðed, Bl. H. 217, 2. þus heálices and ðus foremǽres ûres mundboran lâre folgian, 169, 17. þ mycele and þ foremǽre bearn, Lch. iii. 428, 21. Wîtgan myccle and foremǽre. Bl. H. 161, 13. þâ federas scealon beón foremǽre on andgite, on þylde, on gesceáde (*omnibus rebus excelsi*), R. Ben. 137, 25. (2) *of things*, (a) material :—On þǽre dûne wæs gefyrn foremǽre templ, Hml. S. 3, 236. þæt wæs foremǽrost receda, B. 309. (b) non-material :—Is þ seó foremǽre gebyrd Sancte Iôhannes, Bl. H. 161, 6. Foremǽran (foræmeran, MS.; fore mǽran ?) *ob potiorem (virginitatis gloriam*, Ald. 58, 24. Cf. *potiorem* mǽran, An. Ox. 4153), Wrt. Voc. ii. 63, 7.

fore-mǽrnes. *Add* :—Hwæþer gôd hlîsa and foremǽrnes sié for nauht tô tellenne ? . . . Hî wênaþ . . . þ him ne sié wana nâþer ne anwealdes ne foremǽrenesse *an claritudo nihili pendenda est ? . . . sibi sufficientiam . . . potentiam, celebritatem . . . credunt esse venturam*, Bt. 24, 4; F. 86, 17–31.

fore-manig *glosses* promultus :—Foremonig *promultam*, Mt. p. 16, 5. v. for-manig.

fore-meahtig. *Add* :—Foremihtig *prepotens*, Hy. S. 74, 9. v. next word.

fore-meahtiglic (-miht-); *adj. Very strong, strenuous* :—þâ strangan oðđe foremihtiglice *strenua* (the corresponding gloss in Hpt. Gl. 405, 29 is : *strenua* þâ foremih[tigan ? or -tiglican?), þâ stra[n]gan î foremihti[gan ? or -glice ?]), Wrt. Voc. ii. 74, 60.

fore-mearcod. For Cot. 157 *substitute* :—Foremearcod *praenotatus*, Wrt. Voc. ii. 68, 64, *and add* :—Mid foremearcedum collectum *cum prenotatis collectis*, Angl. xiii. 391, 378.

fore-mearcung, e; *f. Heading of a chapter, title* :—In foremercunc *in titulo*, Mt. p. 12, 1. Foremercungo *capitulae*, Mk. p. 1, 1.

fore-mihtiglíce. *Dele, and see* fore-meahtiglic : fôre-mûnt. *Substitute* : fore-munt *a promontory* :—Foremunte *promontorio*, Wrt. Voc. ii. 65, 65.

fore-nama *glosses* pronomen :—Tô forenaman *pronomine*, R. Ben. I. 11, 13.

forene. v. forane.

fore-nyme, es; *m. glosses* presumtio, Wrt. Voc. ii. 118, 29.

fore-onfang *glosses* praesumtio :—Foreonfong *praesumtio*, Mt. p. 1, 4. Foreonfoeng, 8, 2.

fore-ridel. v. fôr-rídel *in Dict*. [*For the vowel in* ridel cf. bydel, rynel.]

fore-rynel *a harbinger*. *Add* :—Eádmôdnyss forrynel (*precursor*) ys sôðre lufe, Scint. 23, 8. Sê sê ðe ðone sácerdhâd onfêhð, hê onfêhð friccan scîre and foreryneles; ðâ hêr iernað beforan kyningum and bodigeað hira færelt, Past. 91, 21. On þǽre cyrcan þæs hâlgan forryneles and fulluhteres, Hml. S. 23 b, 505.

fore-sægdness, e; *f. A preface* :—Ðis ondweard foresaegdnis *haec praesens praefatiuncula*, Mt. p. 2, 14. Onginnes foresægdnise *incipit praefatio*, 10, 11. Foresægdnisse, 12, 6.

fore-saga (?) (1) *a prologue, preface* :—Forerîm î [fore]tal î [fore]-saga [ =-sagu ?) *prologus*, Mt. p. 1, 1. In foresaga *in prochemio*, Jn. p. 187, 12. Mið forasaga *praefatione*, Lk. p. 3, 11. (2) *translation* :—Of foresaga *de translatione*, Lk. p. 9, 6.

fôre-scéawere. *Substitute* : fore-sceáwere (for-) *glosses* provisor : —Gôd and forsceáwere (*prouisor*) hê bið, E. S. 39 (December).

fore-sceáwian. *Add* : (1) *to observe beforehand, consider* the future :—Se man gewilnað þæt hê hlîsful sŷ, and nele foresceáwian þæt ûre lîchaman beóð âwende tô dûste, Hml. Th. ii. 220, 29. þæs abbodes on hâdunge þ sî forasceáwod gesceád *in abbatis ordinatione illa consideretur ratio*, R. Ben. I. 106, 17. (2) *to foresee, have knowledge of* the future :—Wê sculon ûs ondrǽdan ðone endenêxtan dæg, þone þe wê ne magon nǽfre foresceáwian, Hml. Th. ii. 574, 11. (2 a) *of the Divine foreknowledge* :—þâ se tîma côm þe God foresceáwode, þâ âsende hê his engel, Hml. Th. i. 24, 21. Hit weard swâ geworden swâ God foresceáwode on ǽr, Chr. 1067; P. 201, 23. On foresceáwudum tîdum, Lch. iii. 432, 13. (3) *to provide for, take the steps necessary to secure* something. (a) *with acc.* :—Paulus nolde ðâ âlŷfdan bigleofan onfôn, ac mid âgenre teolunge his and his geférena neóde foresceáwode, Hml. Th. i. 392, 23. God wile foresceáwian ûre gesundfulnysse and sibbe mid ûs, Hml. S. 13, 136. (b) *with clause* :—Se Hǽlend foresceáwode þ hê sende þâm cyninge *the Saviour made provision for sending to the king*, Hml. S. 24, 125. (4) *to provide, give for use* to a person (*dat.*) :—Ic foresceáwode of his sunum mê gecorenne cyning *providi in filiis ejus mihi regem* (1 Sam. 16, 1), Hml. Th. ii. 64, 7. Crîst him lîf sealde and andlyfene foresceáwode, Hml. S. 11, 347 : 5, 325. Swâ swâ ûre Âlŷsend foresceáwode him þæt castel . . . swâ se deófol þâm forlorenum men (*Antichrist*) foresceáwað *gelimplice* stôwe, Wlfst. 193, 26–194, 6. Symle sceal þæt lǽwede folc gewilnian . . . þæt God him gôde lâreówas foresceáwige, Hml. Th. ii. 530, 22. God mæg unc þurh ðisne earn æt foresceáwian, 138, 35 : 462, 17. [v. *N. E. D.* foreshow.] v. un-foresceáwod.

fore-sceáwodlic; *adj. Considerate*. v. un-foresceáwodlic, *and next word*.

fore-sceáwodlíce; *adv. Considerately, with due consideration, with foresight* :—God swŷþor tô yrsunge unbesceáwudlíce hî forþ clypian þænne foresceáwudlíce tô synna forgyfenyssa innlaþian *Deum potius ad iracundiam inconsiderate prouocent, quam provide ad peccaminum ueniam inuitent*, Angl. xiii. 370, 76. v. un-forsceáwodlíce.

fore-sceáwung. *Add* : (1) *consideration, contemplation* :—Foresceáwung *consideratio*, Wrt. Voc. ii. 133, 73 : *contemplatio*, 134, 82. þeós foresceáwung (*consideratio*) mid þâm abbude is, R. Ben. I. 91, 13. Forasceáwung, 64, 13. Æfter forasceáwunga *juxta considerationem*, 37, 5. Foresceáwunge, R. Ben. 32, 11. Ne nân ne gedyrstlǽce þæt hê fǽrlíce bôc gelǽcce and þǽr bûtan foresceáwunge onginne tô rǽdenne *ne fortuitu casu qui arripueret codicem legere audeat*, 62, 5. Hê âtihtinge his on Godes foresceáwunge gefæstnað *intentionem suam in Dei contemplatione defigit*, Scint. 28, 14. Sié hê for ealle ûpâðened mid ðǽre godcundan foresceáwunge his inngeðances *prae cunctis contemplatione suspensus*, Past. 97, 24. (2) *foreseeing, foreknowledge* :—Ðâ arn hê tô cyrcan bûton his freónda foresceáwunge (*his friends had no idea of his intention*), Hml. Th. ii. 498, 29. (2 a) (*supernatural*) *foreseeing* :—Godcundlic forscáwung *praesagium*, i. *praescientia î divinatio*, Hpt. Gl. 466, 25. Hê ongeat þ heó mid þǽre godcundan foresceáwunge onlîht wæs, Hml. S. 23 b, 216. Ân spearwa on gryn ne mæg befeallan forûtan his foresceáwunge, Chr. 1067; P. 201, 26. (3) *forethought, foresight, providence* :—þæs abbotes hit sî on forascâwunga *in abbatis sit providentia*, R. Ben. I. 73, 11. Ðînum hǽse and foresceáunge *tua jussione et providentia*, Rtl. 98, 35. Foresceáuunge *prudentia*, 108, 25. (3 a) *divine providence* :—Hî wǽron gemynte on þâm micclan dihte Godes foresceáwunge tô his sceápa getele, Hml. A. 70, 121.

fore-scending, Lk. L. 21, 25. v. for-scending: fore-scêt, C. D. vi. 183, 10. v. sceótan ; VII : fore-scip (for-), es ; *n. The fore-part of a ship, the prow*. v. fôr-scip (l. for-) *in Dict*. [v. *N. E. D.* foreship.]

fore-scunian, -scûwa, -scúwung, -scŷa. v. fore-scynian, -scŷwa, -scŷwung, -scŷwa.

fore-scynian *to give way before evil, danger, &c.* :—Yflo monigo forescyniga (*for this form* cf. scyniga, 7, 12: onscynað. Jn. L. 14, 27) *mala plurima praecessura*, Lk. p. 10, 14.

**fore-scýwa** (=-scúwa), an; *m. A shadow:*—Forescýa *umbra*, Rtl. 13, 27.

**fore-scýwung**, e; *f. Over-shadowing:*—Forascýwung *obumbratio*, Rtl. 28, 11.

**fore-secgan.** *Add:* I. with reference to the past:—Hé hí gefréfrode swá swá wé hér foresǽdon (*as we have already mentioned in this narrative*), Hml. A. 78, 138 : Hml. S. 26, 169. Þæs Cýres sunu þe wé ǽr foresǽdon, Hml. A. 103, 24. Se foresǽda wiðerwinna *the aforesaid adversary*, S, 210. Þæne foresǽdan *praephatum*, An. Ox. 2461. Foresǽde cempan *praedictos tyrunculos*, 3044. II. referring to the future. (1) of natural knowledge, *to mention beforehand* what is to take place:—Foresǽgeð (*praenuntiat*) eástro æfter tuǽm dógrum (cf. scitis quia post biduum Pascha fiet, Mt. 26, 2), Mt. p. 19, 18. (1 a) with the idea of warning or command:—Hé ǽr inngeðonce his hiéremonna foresǽgð ðá diéglan sǽtenga ðæs lytegan feóndes *intentioni audientium hostis callidi insidias praedicit*, Past. 163, 13. Ealle þá þing þe ic eów foresǽgde þ̄ gé dón sceoldon, Bl. H. 131, 34. Tó wæccenne foresǽgde ðǽm ðe nyston tíd tócyme his *vigilandum praedicit nescientibus horam adventus sui*, Mt. p. 19, 15. (2) of supernatural knowledge, *to foretell, prophesy:*—Ic hyt eów foresǽde (*praedixi*), Mt. 24, 25. Gé magon hyne geseón swá swá hé eów ǽr foresǽde, Hml. A. 188, 222. Úre Drihten foresǽde þá tóweardan frecednyssa, Hml. Th. ii. 538, 6 : Wlfst. 151, 32. Hé foresǽgde hine ðrouende *ipse praenuntiat se passurum*, Lk. p. 6, 6 : Mt. p. 17, 17 : Mk. p. 5, 7. Þá wæs gefylled þ̄ se wítga foresǽgde, Bl. H. 203, 12. Þá wítgan þe Crístes tócyme wiston and foresǽgdon, 81, 10. Is gefylled þ̄ hí foresǽdon, Hml. A. 69, 91. Hyt syððan gelamp swá swá hí foresǽdon, 68, 67. Forestihtes ł foresǽdes *praedestinatae, antedictae*, Hpt. Gl. 425, 22. III. *to tell in the hearing of others, proclaim, pronounce, declare:*—Geðiódsumnise tó ðǽm fíonde on woeg foresǽgeð *consentiendum adversario in via pronuntiat*, Lk. p. 8, 1 : 9, 12 : 10, 2. Wordo his gǽst and líf foresǽgeð *uerba sua spiritum uitamque pronuntiat*, Jn. p. 5, 2. Foresǽgde, 6, 4. Oðero biseno foresǽgde him *aliam parabolam proposuit illis*, Mt. L. 13, 24, 31. III a. *to preach:*—Foresǽgdon þ̄ hreáwnise dédon *praedicabant ut paenitentiam agerent*, Mk. L. 6, 12.

**fore-sendan.** *Add: to send in advance:*—Hé foresende *premisit* (*thesauros*), Angl. xiii. 448, 1184.

**fore-seón.** *Add:* (1) *to foresee:*—Be þám sáwlum þe foreseóð and forewiton monige wísan *de animabus quae multa praenoscunt*, Gr. D. 301, 14. (2) *to despise* = for-seón; P. 217, 7.

**fore-setednes** *a proposition:*—Foresetednessa *propositiones*, Ps. Rdr. 77, 2. v. fór-settednys (*l.* for-) *in Dict.*

**fore-setl**, es ; *m. A chief seat, seat of honour:*—Þá formo ræsto ł foresedlo (þ̄ ǽreste sætil, R.) *primos recubitos*, Mt. L. 23, 6.

**fore-setnes.** *Add:*—Hé nǽfre þá foresetenesse his munuchádes ánforlét (cf. hé heóld his mune[c]lice ingehýd, Hml. Th. ii. 506, 13), Bl. H. 219, 32.

**fore-settan.** *Take here* fór-settan (*l.* for-), *and add:*—Foreset *praepositus*, Wrt. Voc. i. 50, 19. (1) of order in time or place, *to put before:*—Foresettaþ *praeferant*, An. Ox. 2001. Hé swór God him tó gewitan on his wordum foresettende *he prefaced his oath by taking God to witness*, Hml. S. 23 b, 271. Ðis Englisc ætýwð hwæt seó foresette rǽding mǽnð, Angl. viii. 298, 9. (2) of degree, rank. &c., *to put at the head, prefer:*—Foresette *praeposuit* (*omnibus gradibus*), An. Ox. 344. Foresettan *preferre*, 17, 51. Sí foreset *preferatur*, 8, 36. [*O. H. Ger.* furi-sezzen *pro-, prae-ponere, praeferre.*]

**fore-settendlic.** *For* 'Som. Ben. Lye.' *substitute:*—*Praepositinae*, þæt sind foresettendlice, Ælfc. Gr. Z. 267, 6.

**fore-sittan** *to preside at or over.* (1) *with dat. For first passage substitute:*—Be þám sinoðe ... æt Heortforda, þám wæs foresittende se arcebiscop (*cui praesidebat archiepiscopus*), Bd. 4, 5 ; Sch. 371, 13. (2) *with acc.:*—Þone sinoð foresæt scé Leó, Chr. 1050; P. 170. 25.

**fóre-smeagan, -smeágean.** *l.* fore-smeág(e)an, *for last line substitute:*—Foresmeágende *rimando*, An. Ox. 193. *For* foresmeá[gende] *ob indaganda*, 1504, *and add:*—Ne foresmeáge gé hwæt gé specan *nolite praecogitare quid loquamini*, Mk. 13, 11. Foresmeánde *praecogitandum*, Lk. p. 10, 14.

**fore-spǽc, fóre-spǽc.** *l.* fore-spǽc *and take instances to* fore-sprǽc.

**fore-sprǽc, fóre-sprǽc.** *Take these together under* fore-sprǽc, *ndudd:* (1) *speech on behalf of a person* or *thing.* (a) *advocacy:*—Hé ús gefreóð mid his foresprǽce from écum wítum *advocatione sua nos ab aeternis suppliciis liberans*, Past. 261, 10. Cam Putrael tó Boia and bed his forespéce tó Ælfríce. Þá sette Boia þás spéce wið Ælfríce ; þ̄ wes þ̄ Putrael sealde Ælfríce viii oxan ... and ... gef Boia sixtig penga for þére forspǽce, Cht. E. 274, 3-6. Tó foresprǽce þ̄ se cwyde standan móste, Cht. Th. 501, 13. Ryhtes wyrðe for míre forspǽce, 170, 4. (b) *excuse:*—Forespréc nabbas *they have nothing to say for themselves*; excusationem non habent, Jn. L. 15, 22. (2) *speech by the representative of another, what is said by a sponsor:*—Ðeáh þæt cild sprecan ne mæge þonne hit man fullað, his freónda foresprǽc (forspǽc, *v. l.*) forstent

him eall þæt ylce þe hit sylf sprǽce, Wlfst. 110, 4 : 38, 16. (3) *what has been already said, the contents of a document:*—Ðeós forespréc and þás gewriotu ðe hér beufan áwreotene stondaþ (*the reference is to the provisions of a will*), Cht. Th. 483, 8. (4) *preliminary speech, a preface, prologue:*—Foresprǽce in *prologo*, i. in sequentis operis praefatione, An. Ox. 2298. Þéra lǽreówa naman ic áwrát on ðǽre Ledenan foresprǽce (v. Hml. Th. i. 1), Hml. Th. ii. 2, 9 : Hml. S. 15, 108. [*v. N. E. D.* fore-speech. *O. H. Ger.* fora-sprǽhha *prologus, praefatio.*]

**fore-spreca.** *Add:* (1) *an advocate, defender:*—For[e]sprec[a] *patronus*, An. Ox. 56, 335. Forspeca *orator*, Germ. 400, 548. Hé bæd mé ðæt ic him wǽre forespeca, Cht. Th. 169, 26. Þá nyste Paulus ðá gástlican getácnunge ðǽre ǽ, and wæs forðí hyre forespreca, Hml. Th. i. 390, 3. Hí blissodon þ̄ hí swilcne forespræcan him áfunden hæfdon, Hml. A. 101, 317. (2) *a sponsor:*—Se godfæder wæs þæs cildes forspreca and borh wið God, Hml. Th. ii. 50, 17. Þá þe æt fontbæþe úre forespecan (-sprecan, *v. l.*) wǽran, Wlfst. 67, 9 : 109, 16. Foresprǽcan, Ll. Th. ii. 338, 8.

**fore-stæppan.** *Take here the instances given under* fore-stapan, **fore-steppan**, *and add:*—Forestepþ *procedit*, An. Ox. 51, 65. Hig þæne forman dæg forestæppað, Angl. viii. 330, 23. Se dæg forestóp þá niht eall oð Crístes ǽriste ; ac syððan hé þá niht gewuldrode mid his ǽriste, heó forestóp þæne dæg, 319, 40. Hé hí forestóp on heofenan ríce, Hml. Th. i. 50, 3. Forestópun mé grynu deáþes *praeoccupauerunt me laquei mortis*, Ps. L. 17, 6. Forestæpe hine *praeueni eum*, 16, 13. Steorran folgiende forestæppendne *stellam sequentes previam*, Hy. S. 51, 36. Of wiðmetennysse forestæppendra gódra wera *ex praecedentium comparatione*, Gr. D. 8, 20.

**fore-stæppend.** *Add:*—Forstæp[pend] *antecessor*, An. Ox. 619.

**fore-stæppung.** *For* 'Som. Ben. Lye.' *substitute:*—*Anticipatio* vel preoccupatio vel presumtio, þ̄ ys on Englisc forestæppung oððe dyrstynnys, Angl. viii. 331, 5.

**fore-standan.** *For* Cot. 149 *substitute* Wrt. Voc. ii. 65, 63, *and add: to hold one's ground, prevail* against:—Geatt helles ne forestondes wið ðá ilca *portae inferi non praevalebunt adversum eam*, Mt. L. 16, 18. v. for-standan.

**fore-stapan.** *l.* fore-stæppan.

**fore-stapol**; *adj. Going before, previous:*—Forestapulum *preuio*, Germ. 396, 147.

**fore-steall** (for-). *Add:* (1) *prevention, hindrance* to free progress :—Fǽrð fýr ofer eall, ne byð þǽr nán foresteal, ne him man náne mæg niht forwyrnan *ignis ubique suis ruptis regnabit habenis*, Dóm. L. 146. (2) *fine for the crime of* fore-steall. v. for-steal *in Dict.*:—Ic hæbbe geunnen him þ̄ hé beó his saca and sócne wyrðe, ... and forstealles, Cht. E. 233, 3. [*v. N. E. D.* forestall ; *sb.* cf. *O. L. Ger.* fora-stelli *constipatio.*]

**fore-stemman** (for-); *p.* de To *hinder, prohibit:*—Ðá ðá ðe infoerdon forestemdon (for-, R.) gié *eos qui introiebant prohibuistis*, Lk. L. 11, 52.

**fore-steóra.** *For* Cot. 149 *substitute* Wrt. Voc. ii. 65, 56 : fore-steppan. *Dele* ' *p.* stepede ... stept ?', *and see* fore-stæppan.

**fore-stíg** (?), -stigu (?), e ; *f.:* -stige (?), es ; *m. An entrance, a vestibule:*—Forestíge (-stige ?) *vestibulum*, i. introitum, Hpt. Gl. 514, 59.

**fóre-stihtod.** *Substitute:* fore-stihtan ; *p.* te ; *pp.* -stiht, -stihted ; -stihtian ; *p.* ode ; *pp.* od To *fore-ordain, predestine:*—Seó menniscnys wæs ǽfre forestiht ... swá swá Paulus cwæð, ' Qui predestinatus est Filius Dei ' ; þæt is, ' Sé þe is forestiht Godes Sunu ' ... Be ús cwæð se ylca apostol, þæt wé wǽron forestihte, ðus wrítende, ' Quos autem predestinavit ...' ; þæt is, ' Ðá ðe hé forestihte,' Hml. Th. ii. 364, 25-366, 1. Hé ne forestihte nǽnne tó yfelnysse ... Hé forestihte ðá gecorenan tó ðám écan lífe ... Hé nolde forestihtan þá árleásan tó his ríce, i. 112, 28-33. Þá þe God forestihte on frymðe þyssere worulde, Hml. A. 45, 514. God ǽr forestihtode (*praedestinaverat*) þ̄ hé Abrahames sǽd wolde gemanifealdigan ... þus wæs forestihtod seó manigfealdnys, Gr. D. 55, 15-24. Forestiht tó ðám écum deáðe, Hml. Th. ii. 232, 32. Forestiht cwyde *prefinu* (*prefinitam ?*) *sententiam*, Scint. 42, 15. Þére forestihtes *praedestinate*, An. Ox. 790. Faran tó ðám forestihtan kynehelme, Hml. S. 5, 80. Mannes sunu gǽð æfter þám ðe him forestihtod wæs *filius hominis secundum quod definitum est uadit*, Lk. 22, 22. Forestihtod, Guth. 10, 12. Tó hwylcum sýn ende forestihtude (*predestinati*), Scint. 227, 7. Forestihtode, Gr. D. 54, 17 : Hml. S. 30, 134.

**fore-stihtung.** *Add: predestination:*—Seó forestihtung (*praedestinatio*) þæs écan ríces, Gr. D. 54, 19, 30. Be forestihtinge (*predestinatione*). Twyfeald is forestihtung, sam þe gecorenra tó reste, sam þe wiþercorenra tó deáþe, ǽgþer mid godcundum dóme ys gedón, Scint. 226, 12-15 : An. Ox. 1489 : Hml. A. 70, 119. Þurh Godes forestihtunge ne hors ne his sylf gewérgod wæs, Hml. S. 30, 35, 310.

**fore-styltan.** v. for-styltan : **fore-swerian.** *Dele, and see* swerian : **fore-swígan.** v. fore ; *adv.* : fore-swíþan. v. for-swíþan.

**fore-tácen.** *Add:*—Fortácen *portentum* vel *prodigium* vel *ostentum*,

Wrt. Voc. i. 17, 19. Foretácna *portentorum*, ii. 66, 10. Fela þæra foretácna þe Críst foresǽde, þæt cuman sceolde, Wlfst. 151, 32. Fortácna, 18, 18 : 90, 17. Hiá seallas bēceno and foretáceno (*prodigia*), Mt. L. 24, 24. Foretácun *signa*, Jn. R. 6, 26. [v. *N. E. D.* fore token. *O. L. Ger.* furi-tēkin *prodigium : O. H. Ger.* fora-zeichan *prodigium, portentum, monstrum.*]

**fore-tácnian.** *Add : to foretoken :*—Foretácnas *informat*, Mt. p. 16, 7. His háliges wæs foretácnod on his cnihtháde, Shrn. 78, 24. [*O. H. Ger.* fora-zeichenen.]

**fore-tal.** v. tæl.

**fore-teohhian** ; *p.* ode ; *pp.* od To foreordain, *destine :*—Destinatus, ordinatus, deputatus, i. missus vel foreteohhad, Wrt. Voc. ii. 139, 9.

**fore-þanc.** *Add :* (1) *consideration of the future :*—Forþances gleáw, Hpt. 33, 71, 1. Of embehýdigum foreþance *sollerti prescientia*, An. Ox. 7, 355 : 8, 344. Ðonne ðá hátheortan hié mid nāne foreðonce nyllað gestillan *cum iracundi nulla consideratione se mitigant*, Past. 297, 3. Ðone foreðonc his gesceádwísnesse forlǽtan *intentionem providam non tenere*, 431, 36. Hē ne meahte mód oncyrran, fǽmnan foreþonc, Jul. 227. Hē nǽfð nǽnne forðanc be his deáðe, Ps. Th. 48, 8. (2) *what is thought beforehand, a preconceived idea :*—On þone foreþonc . . . þý þe hý (*the apostate angels*) him sylfum sēllan þūhton þonne Críst, Hy. 4, 53.

**foreþanc-full** ; *adj. Full of forethought, prudent, provident :*—Dō mē rihtwísne and foreþancfulne (*justum prudentemque*), Solil. H. 14, 6.

**foreþanc-líc** ; *adj. Provident, cautious :*—Ðæt hí ongiten mid foreðonclícre gesceádwísnesse *provida consideratione perpendant*, Past. 433, 33.

**foreþanclíce.** *Add : with forethought, carefully :*—Ðá gódan weorc ðe hē longe ǽr foreðonclíce timbrede *quidquid diu labore provido construxit*, Past. 215, 18. Ðæt hí foreðonclíce ongieten *ut provide perpendant*, 429, 3. Ðæt hit ðá ungedónan unðeáwas foreðoncelíce becierre *alia providens declinat*, 433, 6. Þæt se ealdor swíðe rihtlíce and foreþanclíce (*provide*) eal gestyhtige, R. Ben. 15, 18. Hē wærlíce and forðonclíce háwode *caute ac sollicite attendit*, Gr. D. 203, 17.

**foreþancul** (-ol). *Add :*—Se foreðancula wer *vir providus*, Past. 305, 2. Dō mē rihtwísne and forþancolne (*prudentem.* v. foreþancfull), Angl. xii. 513, 3.

**fore-þencan.** v. for-þencan.

**fōre-þencan.** *l.* fore-þencan, *and add :*—Hē smeáþ ł foreþæncð *meditabitur*, Ps. Rdr. 1, 2. Ne gié foreðencgæ *non praemeditari*, Lk. L. 21, 14. Nælle gié foreðence *nolite praecogitare*, Mk. L. 13, 11. [The Latin original of Past. 15, 5 ; S. 95, 16 is : *Providendum est sollicita intentione rectoribus.*]

**fore-þeón** (for-) *to excel, surpass :*—Ealle wē sind gelíce ætforan Gode, būton hwá ōþerne mid gódum weorcum forðeó, Hml. Th. i. 260, 26. Hū hē læssan gife hæbbe, ne andige hē on ðam foreðeóndum, for ðan ðe . . . sume englas mid underþeódnysse ōðrum hýrsumiað, and sume mid oferstígendre wurðfulnysse ðam ōðrum sind foresette, 346, 32.

**fore-þingere.** *Add :*—Hē wæs getreówe on neóde and strang foreþingere, Hml. S. 5, 6.

**fore-þingung.** *Add :*—Hēhbiscopes foreðingunge wuldrigo ūsig gescilde *pontificis intercessio gloriosa nos protegat*, Rtl. 49, 34. Seó ceaster weard áhred þurh Agathen foreþingunge, Hml. S. 8, 234. Seó burh hæfð Agathen miccle foreþingunga, 9, 135.

**fore-tíge.** v. tíg *in Dict. :* **fore-timbrigende.** *Add :*—Gemētton wē ūs ǽghwanon gelícne storm foran onsettende and foretimbrigende *inuenimus nos undiqueuersum pari tempestate praeclusos :* **fore-trymman.** v. trymman.

**fōre-týnd.** *l.* fore-týned : **fore-warde,** an. *Dele '* , an '.

**for-war[e]nian** ; *p.* ode. **I.** *to forewarn :*—Be ðám treówe Críst sylf forewarnode Adam, Nap. 24. Ealle þás þing him wæron ætýwede tó ðám þ hí sceoldon ūs forewarnian, *ib.* **II.** *to take heed beforehand :*—Forewarna þū *uideas*, Hpt. 31, 9, 160.

**fore-weall.** *Add :*—Wíghūs, foreweal *propugnaculum*, An. Ox. 3972. Foraeuuallum (fore-) *vel* tindum *rostris*, Txts. 92, 873.

**fore-weard,** e ; *f. Dele '* , an ', *and add :* es ; *n.* (?) :—Se cyng þǽre forewarde gyrnde þe him behǽten wæs, Chr. 1093 ; P. 227, 31. Būtan se cyng gelǽstan wolde eall þet hí on forewarde hæfdon ǽr gewroht, 1094 ; P. 228, 34. Hēr swutelað on ðysan gewrite ðá foreward ðe Godwine worhte wið Byrhtríc, C. D. iv. 10, 16. Twēgra manna dæg ealswá ðá foreward spreocað, iii. 333, 25. Hū man mǽden weddian sceal and hwylce forewarde þǽr ǽghon tó beónne, Ll. Th. i. 254, 23. Ne mihte hē beón weorðe þǽra forewarde þe him ǽr behátene wǽron, Chr. 1093 ; P. 228, 2. [þá þreó þūsend marc þe him seó cyng be foreweard ǽlce geáre gifan sceolde, 1103 ; P. 238, 24. Tó þ forewearde þ ǽfter his dæi scolde þ land in tó þe minstre, 852 ; P. 65, 22.] [v. *N. E. D.* foreward.] v. fore-word.

**fore-weard** ; *adj. Add : fore-part of* (noun in agreement). (1) *local :*—Foreweard scip *prorostris*, Wrt. Voc. ii. 68, 47. On foreweardre þisse bēc *principio libelli*, Ors. 6, 1 ; S. 252, 1. Mid forewearde orde stingan

*ex mucrone percutere*, Past. 297, 11. Mid þrim fingrum foreweardum geniman *to take with the tips of three fingers*, Lch. ii. 180, 21. (2) *temporal :*—Ne sceal mon þisne drincan sellan on foreweardne þone ece and þá ádle, ac ymb fela nihta, Lch. ii. 256, 18. On forewearde þá ádle, 260, 16 : 22, 1. On foreweardne sumor, Chr. 918 ; P. 96, 35. ¶ *substantive use.* v. æfte-weard :—Swā wē ǽr on foreweardan þysse race rehton, Hml. S. 23, 790. Malchus eóde on foreweardan (*in front*) in tó his geféran, and se bisceop æfter him inn eóde, 752. On ælces mannes tungan Crístes nama is ǽfre on foreweardan, 536. On forwerdum *in fronte*, i. *in facie*, An. Ox. 772. ¶ in the Northern specimens the prefix *for-* is used :—Onginneð forwueard *incipit capitula*, Mt. p. 13, 13. Foruard *initium*, Rtl. 174, 31. Forueard ł fruma *principium*, 38, 7. Foruuard, Mt. p. 12, 12. Ðæs forueardes *principii*, Mk. p. 1, 8. Of forueard *ex principio*, p. 5, 4 : Lk. p. 2, 7. Foruearde *capitulo*, Mt. p. 11, 17. In foruuard *in fronte*, p. 12, 2. Ðá foruearda ł ðá fruma *principia*, p. 12, 10. v. for-weard *in Dict.*

**fore-wís.** *For* Cot. 149 *substitute* Wrt. Voc. ii. 65, 79, *and add :*—þá áforhtode uncer mód, for þan hit bið ælces yfeles forewís, Hml. A. 206, 363. [v. *N. E. D.* forewise.]

**fore-witan.** *Add :*—Be þám sáwlum þe forewiton (*praenoscunt*) monige wísan, Gr. D. 301, 14. [v. *N. E. D.* forewit.]

**fore-witegian.** *Add :*—Stephanus . . . wē cweðað on Englisc, Gewuldorbeágod ; for ðan þe hē hæfð þone ēcan wuldorbeáh, swā swā his nama him forewítegode, Hml. Th. i. 50, 13. Heortan forewítegendra *corde presago*, Hy. S. 104, 1. Wæs forewítegod *praefiguratur*, An. Ox. 1541.

**fore-wítegung,** e ; *f. Foretelling, prophesying :*—Forewítegung *praesagium*, An. Ox. 2563. Forewítegunge *praesagio*, 949. Dionisius hine gefrēfrode mid forewítegunge, and sǽde þ hē wiste þurh God þ Iōhannes sceolde síþian of þám íglande, Hml. S. 29, 97 : Angl. iii. 110, 104, 115. Forewítegunga *praesagiorum*, An. Ox. 431.

**fore-wítig, -wíttig.** *Add :* (1) *sagacious :*—þá forewittigan *sagacissimam*, An. Ox. 70. His foregengan wǽron on gleáwscype swíþe bescáwede and forewittige, Lch. iii. 436, 12. (2) *foreknowing :*—Drihten cwæð tó ðǽre byrig, 'Gif þu wistest hwæt þē tóweard is . . .' Gif seó buruhwaru ðǽre yrmðe forewittig wǽre, Hml. Th. i. 404, 33. Basilius weard gebrōht on legere tó his forðsíðe, forewittig swá þeáh, Hml. S. 3, 565. (3) *presaging, prophetic :*—Mid forewittigum þurhblǽwen gáste *presago afflatus spiritu*, Angl. xiii. 370, 64. Æfter forewittigum gydde *juxta praesagum uaticinium*, An. Ox. 3707 : 2868. Mid forewittigere gelícnysse *praesago simulacro*, 1968.

**fore-witol.** *Add :*—Se forewitola Scyppend wiste on ǽr hwæt hē of hyre gedón habban wolde, Chr. 1067 ; P. 201, 26.

**fore-wittiendlic** ; *adj. Foreknowing, prophetic :*—Forewittiendlicere gecíednysse *presago* (i. *prescio*) *uocabulo*, An. Ox. 1502.

**fore-witung.** *Dele.*

**fore-word,** es ; *n. Take here* for-word *in Dict., and add : A proviso, condition :*—Ðæt land ǽr Áctúne twēgra manna dæg, ealswá ðá foreword sprecað, C. D. vi. 148, 30. Standan ðá forword betweónan ðan abbode and Ceólríce, iii. 352, 3. Syndon ðis þá forword þe Orecy and þá gegyldan gecoren habbað, iv. 277, 30. [Cf. *Dan.* for-ord *a proviso.*] v. fore-wyrd, fore-weard.

**fore-wrēgan.** v. for-wrēgan.

**fore-wrítan.** *Substitute :* **fore-writen** ; *pp. Above-written :*—Seó forewritene endebyrdnes *suprascriptus ordo*, Angl. xiii. 402, 540. ¶ the word also glosses *praescriptus* :—Mid forewritenum collectum *cum prescriptis collectis*, 391, 372 : 384, 276 : 444, 1129.

**fore-writennes.** *Add :*—Forewritenesse *proscriptionem*, Wrt. Voc. ii. 66, 56 : **fore-wyrcan.** *l.* fore wyrcan.

**fore-wyrcend,** es ; *m. One who works for another, a servant, slave :*—Hyre wer lǽfde unlytle ǽhta on lande and on feó and on forewyrcendum (wyrcendum mannum, *v. l.*), Hml. S. 2, 156.

**fore-wyrd.** *Substitute :* **fore-wyrd, -wyrde,** es ; *n. What is said before, a proviso, agreement, condition :*—Forewyrde *antefata* (cf. wǽrword), Wrt. Voc. ii. 100, 28. þá Pyhtas heom ábǽdon wíf æt Scottum on þá gerád (þ forewyrd, *v. l.*) þ hí gecuron heora kynecinn on þá wífhealfa, Chr. P. 3, 16. Hēr swutelað on þisum gewrite embe þá forewyrd þe Ægelríc worhte wið Eádsige . . . þis synd þá forewyrd . . . būtan sum heora freónda þá land ofgán mage tó rihtan gafole oððe tó óþran forewyrdan, C. D. iv. 86, 7–32. v. fore-word, ge-forewyrdan.

**fore-wyrdan.** v. ge-forewyrdan.

**for-fæger** ; *adj. Very beautiful, surpassingly fair :*—Hē (*the Phenix*) hine forbærneþ and eft forfæger eidung ūp áríseþ, E. S. viii. 479, 89.

**for-fang.** *Add :* ¶ *for-fang* occurs in a list of emoluments accruing to the king (Edward the Confessor) and granted by him to Westminster :—Huic libertati concedo additamentum :—mundbryche, burhbryce . . . forfænge . . . aliasque omnes leges et consuetudines quae ad me pertinent, Cht. Th. 411, 31.

**for-faran.** *Add :* **I.** *intrans. To perish :*—þū wást þ ic ne wiðsace þ ic sylf ne forfare, Hml. S. 12, 194. Micel gesǽlð bið þe þæt þū on ðinre gesǽlðe ne forfare, Hml. Th. ii. 392, 33. Fýse hí man ūt of

þissan earde, oþþe on earde forfaran hí mid ealle, Ll. Th. i. 378, 9. Gé sceolon forfaran, Hml. Th. ii. 494, 13. **II.** *trans. To destroy:* (1) the object a person :—Tó eácan óðran þe man unscyldige forfór, Wlfst. 160, 37. Þurh þ . . . þe hí heom sylfe ælc óðerne forfóre, Chr. 1052; P. 180, 25. Hé (*Jupiter*) wolde his ágene fæder forfaran, Wlfst. 106, 11. Is folces forfaren máre þonne scolde, 46, 18. Gif hæðen cild binnon .ix. nihton þurh gímeliste forfaren sí *if a child die and be lost, because through carelessness it is not baptized within nine days after birth, and so dies a heathen*, Ll. Th. ii. 292, 7. Cóm strang wind tó swá þ hí wæron ealle forfarene búton feówer, Chr. 1050; P. 169, 27. (2) the object a thing :—Timbrunge forfarene *muri consumti*, An. Ox. 2126. (2 a) where passage is obstructed, *to blockade :*—Hét se cyng faran mid nigonum tó þára níwena scipa, and forfóron him þone múðan foran on útermere þá ræd ordered nine of the new ships to go, and by lying out at sea in front of the mouth they were to stop the passage of the Danish ships, Chr. 897; P. 90, 24. [v. N. E. D. forfare. O. Frs. for-fara *to die:* O. H. Ger. fer-faran *praeterire, obire.*]

**for-faran.** See preceding word.

**for-feallan;** *p.* -feóll *To destroy by falling, overwhelm :*—Ðá cwóm micel snáw . . . Ðá ic þá unmætnisse ðæs snáwes geseah, ðá þúhte mé þ ic wiste þ hé wolde þá wícstówe forfeallan *cadere immense ceperunt niues, quarum aggregationem metuens ne castra cumularentur*, Nar. 23, 16.

**for-feored.** v. un-forfeored.

**for-feran.** *l.* -féran, *and add:* **I.** of physical death. (1) natural :—Se cing (*Ethelred*) forférde (geendode his dagas, *v. l.*) on S. Georgies mæssedæg æfter miclum geswince, Chr. 1016; P. 148, 21. (2) of violent or untimely death, *to perish :*—Forférde Hácun eorl on sæ (*comes Hacun in mari periit*, Fl. Wig.), Chr. 1030; P. 157, 36. Hé féng stíð weder and him þær micel forférde, 1052; P. 176, 16: Hml. S. 11, 202: 28, 118: Hml. A. 46, 549. Ealle þá forférdon þe æt þám ræde wæron, Chr. 1076; P. 212, 16: Hml. Th. ii. 384, 4: Hml. S. 4, 379: 17, 122: Forférdon *naufragauerant*, An. Ox. 4490: 4621. **II.** of spiritual perdition, *to be lost, perish :*—þæt teóðe engla werod forférde, Hml. Th. i. 344, 15. [v. N. E. D. forfere.]

**for-ferian** *to bring to an untimely end :*—Gif hwá óðrum his unmagan oðfæste, and hé hine on þære fæstinge forferie (*if the person accepting the charge cause the death of the person committed to his charge. Cf. Si quis alterius puerum, qui ei commissus sit . . . , occidat, vel dormiens opprimat*, 595, § 7), Ll. Th. i. 72, 5. Cf. for-faran.

**for-fleón.** *Add:* **I.** *intrans. To flee away :*—Forfleáh *aufugit*, An. Ox. 4992. þæt forfleó næddre feor *ut fugiat gorgon eminus*, Hpt. 31, 11, 241. Gif ænig wære þe fyrfluge þe on ðæm gefeohte wæs *si quis e praelio cedere moliretur*, Ors. 1, 12; S. 52, 34. **II.** *trans.* (1) where there is movement. (a) *to flee from* a person or place :—Forfleáh Hélias þæt fracode wíf út tó ánum wéstene, Hml. S. 18, 160. (b) *to flee from* danger :—Hé (*Jacob*) forfleáh ðá frecenfullan þeówracan þe his bróþor gecwæð, Hml. S. 11, 178. Hé mé sirwde tó ofsleánne. Mid þám þe ic þ forfleáh, þá weard ic on sæ forliden, Ap. Th. 24, 16. (2) *to get free from* unfavourable conditions, *escape from* difficulty :—Forflióh[ð] *effugiet* (*justus de angustia*), Kent. Gl. 408. (3) *to avoid being reached* or overtaken by, escape a pursuer :—Nán man Godes mihte ne forsihð on nánum heolstrum heofenan oþþe eorðan, Hml. Th. ii. 146, 30. (4) *to avoid intercourse with* a person, *keep out of the way of :*—Hí God lybbende forfleóð *Deum uiuendo refugiunt*, Scint. 152, 13. Þíne deórlingas þe sylfne forfleóð, Hml. S. 23, 148. Cæsterwara heápas forfleónde *ciuium turmas fugiens*, Hy. S. 103, 25. (5) *to avoid a state or condition, avoid* suffering :—Hé forfleáh þone woruldlican wurðmynt . . . ; ac hé ne forfleáh ná þæt edwít, Hml. Th. i. 162, 10–12: ii. 546, 16. Hí forflugon woruldmanna gesihðe and herunge, i. 544, 29. Ná for ðí hé deáð forfluge, 82, 27. Hí forfleón móston þæra árleásra éhtnysse, Hml. A. 72, 174. (5 a) *with acc. and infin.* :—Forfleóh wesan ealdor *fugeas fore corcula*, Hpt. 31, 4, 6. (6) *to avoid* action, *abstain from* doing :—Hí forflugon þ deófolgild, Hml. S. 28, 31. Gif hé þ ordál forfleó, Ll. Th. i. 296, 5. þæt þá unstrangan heora þeówdóm ne forfleón (*refugeant*), R. Ben. 121, 24. Uton ælc yfel forfleón and gód gefremman, Hml. Th. i. 602, 29: Wlfst. 115, 8. [O. H. Ger. fer-fliohan *effugere*.]

**for-flígan;** *p.* de *To put to flight :*—Forflýcð *aginat, fugat*, Hpt. 31, 16, 418.

**for-fón.** *For* 'I. *to be deprived of* . . . MS. H.]' *substitute:* **I.** *to take away, take as forfeit :*—Gif hine (*a man who has sought asylum in a monastery*) on þám fierste geyflige . . . lête mid ryhte þeódscipe . . . and þám hiwum hundtwelftig scitt. ciricfrides tó bóte, and næbbe his ágne forfongen (hæbbe his ágen forfangen, *v. l.*) (*the prosecutor shall not* (or *shall*) *have what is due to him from the fugitive forfeited on account of the injury done to the fugitive while entitled to the benefits of asylum*). **II.** *Add:* *to seize, arrest* an accused person :—Hé (*the accuser*) hine (*the accused*) forféhð, Ll. Th. i. 142, 7. **III.** *to anticipate, take measures to prevent.* v. fore-fón :—Ic lære þ þú beó hrædra mid hreówlicum teárum, and þ yrre forfóh éces déman *suadeo praevenias lacrymis modo judicis iram*, Dóm. L. 76. ¶ *with*

for[a]ne :—Forne forféþ *anticipet*, An. Ox. 603. Ðá arn se ealda wið hire weardes mid gebígedum cneówum tó þon þ hé hine on þá eorþan ástrehte . . . Heó þá þone ealdan forene forféng, and him ne geþafode fulfremodlíce on þá eorðan ástreccan, Hml. S. 23 b, 605. Sý forne forfangen *preoccupetur*, An. Ox. 1236. Ic þ hæbbe forefangen þ eów næfre heononforð þanon nán unfrið tó ne cymð *I have taken measures to prevent any trouble ever coming to you henceforth from that quarter*, Cht. E. 230, 5.

**for-fylden.** *Substitute:* for-fyllan; *p.* de *To fill up, stop up, obstruct :*—Forfyldan *obstrictas* (for? *obstructas*), Wrt. Voc. ii. 65, 22.

**for-gǽgan.** *Add:* **I.** of wrong done, *to go beyond* due bounds, *exceed, transgress :*—Gecyndes gemet ic forgǽgde *naturae modum excessi*, Angl. xi. 116, 20. Gemet tó specenne ná forgǽg þú, Scint. 81, 13. Wolde Eleazarus sweltan ǽr þan þe hé Godes ǽ forgǽgan wolde, Hml. S. 25, 86, 95. Tó forgǽgenne, 113. Forgǽgende (cf. oferlióende, Ps. Srt.) ic talode þá árleásan *praeuaricantes reputaui peccatores*, Ps. L. 118, 119. **II.** of right not done, *to pass by, omit to do, neglect :*—Se cniht þe wát hwæt his hláfordes willa bið, and hé þæt forgǽgð *seruus sciens uoluntatem domini sui et non faciens*, Wlfst. 248, 12. þ nán forgǽge *quod nemo pretermittat*, Angl. xiii. 440, 1065. Ná hé beboda þá lǽstan forgǽge (*pretereat*), 441, 1090. Náne þá tó dónne synd gódu forgǽgean *nulla quae facienda sunt bona preterire*, Scint. 68, 5. Herelof bócfellum ne sí forlǽten ł forgǽged ł forgýmeleásod *nequaquam rumusculus* [*a nostris*] *pitaciolis excipiatur*, An. Ox. 4571. Án strica oððe án stæf ðære ealdan ǽ ne bið forgǽged (*iota unum aut unus apex non praeteribit a lege*, Mt. 5, 18), Hml. Th. ii. 200, 1. **III.** *to pass away :*—Bebod hé gesette and hit ne gewíteþ ł hit ne forgǽgð (*non praeteribit*), Ps. L. 148, 6.

**for-gǽgednys.** *Add :*—Bið seó ealde forgǽgednys geendod (*ut consummetur praeuaricatio*, Dan. 9, 24), Hml. Th. ii. 14, 12. Þurh heora ágene forgǽgednysse and ðwyrnysse, i. 112, 34. For heora forgǽgednissum *pro suis excessibus*, Hy. S. 65, 1. þæt folc for heora mándǽdum and forgǽgednyssum wurdon gehergode, Hml. Th. ii. 84, 32: 64, 35: þá wyrcendan forgǽgednyssa *facientes praeuaricationes*, Ps. L. 100, 3.

**for-gǽging,** e; *f. Transgression, excess :*—Hí be hyra forgǽgincgum beóð geþreáde *de suis excessibus arguuntur*, Scint. 115, 9.

**for-gán** *to forgo. Add :* (1) *to abstain from, not to use, go without, not to take :*—Hé cuæð ðæt hit wǽre good ðæt mon foreóde flǽsc and wín *bonum est non manducare carnem neque bibere uinum*, Past. 319, 4. Hé eft ett þæt hé ǽr mid forhæfednysse foreóde, Hml. Th. i. 180, 9. Wæs ælc þæs wordes þ him leófre wǽre þ hé land foreóde þonne hé þæne hád underfénge *every one declared that he would sooner go without the land than take orders*, Cht. Th. 167, 33. Forgá ælc man mínne huntnoð, Ll. Th. i. 420, 25. On þám tíman þe hé flǽscmettas forgán sceal, Hml. Th. ii. 100, 9: Wlfst. 286, 2. Hwæt him sié tó forgánne on liferádle, hwæt foreóde, hwæt him sié tó healdanne ge on lǽcedomum ge on mete, Lch. ii. 210, 13. (2) *to abstain from* action, *not to do :*—Gémnise mettes and woedes forgáes fuglas *sollicitudinem cibi uestique carent aues*, Lk. p. 7, 15. Heó ðá scearpnesse dysiglicra sprǽca on hire ágenre tungan ná bebeáh ne ne foreóde *linguae procacitatem atque stultiloquium non declinavit*, Gr. D. 340, 17. Ðæt mon ðá lytlan forgá and ðá miclan dó, Past. 439, 23. Man forgá þýfðe, Ll. Th. i. 210, 3. Muneca þe woroldlica þing forgán sculon and wǽpna gefeoht *monachi qui ad unum fidei opus, dimissa secularium rerum actione, se redigunt*, Ors. 6, 34; S. 290, 1. Hwæt him sý tó dónne and hwæt tó forgánne, Wlfst. 123, 15. [O. H. Ger. fer-gán *transire, praeterire.*] v. next word.

**for-gangan** *to forgo, abstain from :*—Forgang þæt ic þe forbeóde. Hwæt mæg hit beón þæt þú forgán sceole? Ic ðé secge, forgang þú ánes treówes wæstm, Hml. Th. i. 14, 8–10. Forgang hwít *abstine te ab albo*, Ll. Th. ii. 132, 5. Forgange þ wíf hire wer abstineat se mulier a marito suo, 154, 2. Hé sceal fæstan tó nónes, and forgange (forgán, *v. l.*) flǽsc and wín *jejunare debet ad nonam, et abstinere se a carne et vino*, 134, 20. [O. Sax. far-gangan *to pass:* O. H. Ger. fer-gangan *transire, praeterire.*] v. preceding word.

**for-geara(-e);** *adv. Very well :*—Ic nát ná forgeare hú ic hit þus macige, Hml. S. 23, 556.

**for-gebind.** v. ge-bind: **for-gedón.** *Dele:* forgend. v. forglendrian: **for-genga.** v. fore-genga.

**for-genge;** *adj. Going with difficulty (?); of an arrangement, hard to carry out, impracticable (?) :*—Gyf hit on lencten gebyrige, þ þæ þonne þære flǽscun geweorð on fisce gestriéne, búton þ þis forgenge sié *if it (the time for giving a contribution of food (including flesh meat)) happen in Lent, that then the value of the meat may be taken in fish, unless this arrangement be impracticable*, Cht. Th. 159, 2. Cf. un-genge; forþgenge.

**for-gengel.** v. fore-gengel.

**for-georne;** *adv. Very diligently :*—Geseó wé nú forgeorne, Bl. H. 111, 23.

**for-gifan.** *Add:* **I.** *to give, bestow, grant, dispense :*—Gewelegade, forgæf *donat*, Wrt. Voc. ii. 141, 72. Forgeaf *contulit*, hié forgeáfan

*contulerunt*, 24, 26, 7. Hwā mæg þām gýtsere genóh forgifan? Swā him mon māre selþ, swā hine mā lyst, Bt. 7, 4; F. 22, 34. Forgyfende *dispensans*, i. *disponens*, An. Ox. 1776. (1) *to give* in answer to request :—Biód gearwe tō lǣranne and tō forgiefanne ǣlcum ðāra ðe iów bidde, Past. 173, 8. (2) *to give* as reward, retribution, &c. :—Wulderbeáh þǣne forgyſþ *corona quam reddet* (i. *restituet*), An. Ox. 1354. Wē sceolan dōn sōðe bōte, þonne forgifeþ ūs Drihten ūre synna forgifnesse, Bl. H. 99, 1. Se þe eft gylded þā þū him ǣr forgeáfe, and ūs eallum gesealdest *qui retribuet te retributionem tuam, quam tu retribuisti nobis*, Ps. Th. 136, 8. Sié þ on cyninges dōme, swā deád swā líf, swā hē him forgifan wille, Ll. Th. i. 66, 10. (3) *to give, allow as a matter of right* :—Eallum frióum monnum þās dagas sién forgifene, Ll. Th. i. 92, 2. (4) *to give up, hand over, deliver up, commit,* (a) to a living creature :—Forgeaf hē hym Barrabban, Mt. 27, 26. þām þe is recedōm forgyfen † befæst *cui regimen commissum est*, An. Ox. 274. Forgyfene *oblatam*, i. *deditam (praedam)*, 3572. Ðeówum monnum sién forgifen ǣghwæt þæs þe him ǣnig mon geselle, Ll. Th. i. 92, 9. (β) to a place, practice, &c. :—Ðā ðe hié selfe forgiefað gīfernesse *gulae dediti*, Past. 308, 14. Monge lifgað gyltum forgiefene, Gū. 432. Hē wāt æðelinga bearn eorðan forgiefene (*committed to the earth*), Seef. 93. (5) *to give back* what has been forfeited, *restore* :—Se cyng forgeaf þām eorle (*Godwin who had just cleared himself*) his fulne freóndscype and fulne eorldōm and eall þet hē ǣr āhte, Chr. 1052; P. 183, 10. þ hē wǣre his feores scyldig, buton se cyng him his feorh forgifan wolde, Ll. Th. i. 230, 7. (6) *to give* a woman in marriage, *to marry* a woman to some one :—Æþelstān his sweostor him forgeaf, Chr. 925; P. 105, 20: B. 2997. þām tō hām forgeaf hē āngan dohtor, 374. Se fæder þōhte hwām hē his dohter mihte heálícost forgifan, Ap. Th. 1, 13. þ nān man mā wīſa næbbe būton .i., and seó beó mid rihte beweddod and forgifen, Ll. Th. ii. 300, 14. Æt his mēdder þe wǣre tō ǣwum wífe forgifen his fæder, i. 90, 29. Forgifen Eádwine tō cwēne, Lch. iii. 422, 9. Forgyfen twām werum *twice married*, 430, 13. Hió wæs forgifen Aldferþe, and hié be him liſgendum hié gedǣldun, Chr. 718; P. 42, 19. Forgiefene *nuptae*, Wrt. Voc. ii. 135, 47. (7) Of the dispensation of Providence, *to give* powers of body or mind, conditions of being, &c. :—Þā gesceapu þe him ǣr forgeaf God, Gen. 844. Him wundra fela Alwalda in ǣht forgeaf, Ex. 11. Him liffreá woroldāre forgeaf, B. 17: Gen. 2109. Sige forgeaf Constantine cyning ælmihtig, El. 144. Forgif mē leóht on þissum lífe, An. 76. Forgif mē ondgiet, Hy. 4, 21. Se sceoppend eallra gesceafta hæfþ forgifen ān gecynd eallum his gesceaftum, Bt. 34, 12; F. 152, 17: 41, 5; F. 254, 3, 14. Forgiefen, Gū. 1106: Cri. 1400. Forgyfen, 1388. Sib is forgifen Godes geladunge, Hml. S. 9, 130. Ic eom forgifen fram Gode þyssere byrig, 136. Manegum men bióþ forgifene þās woruldgesælþa, Bt. 39, 12; F. 230, 24. (7 a) the object a clause :—Forgeaf him moncynnes fruma þæt hē weordan sceolde . . . , Ph. 377. Hafað þām treówe forgiefen Meotud þæt hē is ealra beáma beorhtast geblōwen, 175. Eów weorþeþ forgifen hwæt gē sprecaþ, Bl. H. 171, 19. **II.** *to grant.* (1) *to grant leave to do, permit, allow.* (a) without object expressed :—Forgeaf *permitteret*, i. *licentiam daret*, An. Ox. 2573. Gode forgyfendum fōr Æþelflǣd, Chr. 913; P. 96, 33. (b) with clause :—Forgifeþ hē ūs þ wē mōtan his onsýne sceáwian, Bl. H. 103, 28. Forgif ūs þæt wē þine onsýne gemēten, Jul. 729. þ hē him ālýfde and forgeáfe þ hē mōste hī gelǣran *ut eos liceret inbui*, Bd. 4, 16; Sch. 427, 17. (c) with pronoun :—Forgeaf se cyning him þ and lýfde *concessit rex*, Bd. 4, 16; Sch. 427, 20. (d) with pron. and clause :—Him þæt Críst forgeaf þæt hý mōten his ǣtwiste brūcan, Cri. 391. (e) with infin. :—Hē forgeaf (*permisit*) iúh forlēta wífa iúra, Mt. L. 19, 8. Forgef † lēf meh fara *permitte me ire*, 8, 21. (2) *to grant leave to have* :—Ne wæs se fyrst micel þe hī Gūðlāce forgiefan þōhtan, Gū. 298. (3) *to grant* a request, *cause to be done.* (a) with clause :—Forgif ūrum mōdum þ hī mōton tō þē cuman, Bt. 33, 4; F. 132, 27. Forgif mē þæt ic weorðe blíðe *vivifica me*, Ps. Th. 118, 107. (b) with infin. :—From sceððendum woerdnissum giblinna forgef *a noxiis vitiis cessare concede*, Rtl. 16, 27. (c) with a coordinate clause from which an object may be inferred :—Forgif mē, beága weard, hāt sīðian Agar, Gen. 2782. **III.** of action that produces an effect upon an object, *to give, cause* :—Þū eallum oferhýdigum eáþmōdnesse forgifest, Bl. H. 141, 12. Hē inc bām forgeaf balewe geþōhtas, Sat. 488. Hē him þā wunde forgeaf, By. 139. **III a.** *to give battle, deliver* an attack :—Hē mægenrǣs forgeaf, B. 1519. **IV.** *to forgive.* (1) *to remit* a fine, obligation, &c., *not to insist upon* what is due :—Ēghwelc scyld forgeaf ic ðē *omne debitum dimisi tibi*, Mt. L. 18, 32. þæt him nān þing þæs tigolgeweorces forgifen *non minuetur quidquam de lateribus*, Ex. 5, 19. Sié him sió swingele forgifen, Ll. Th. i. 104, 16. Ic nelle þ ǣnig fyhtewíte forgifen sý, 248, 20. Ne beó ǣfre ǣnig forað forgifen, 388, 18. Beón þā heregeata forgyfene, 420, 16. (2) *to give up* claim to reparation for wrong doing, sin, offence, the object a noun :—Se Hālga Gāst manna synna forgifð, Ælfc. T. Grn. 2, 16. Þū forgeáfe ðā ārleásnesse mínre heortan, Past. 419, 8. Hié forgeáfon þǣm cāsere þā fǣhþe þe his mǣg hæfde wið hié ǣr geworht, ond hē forgeaf him þ unryht and þ fācn þ hí him dōn

þōhton *Claudius omnium factorum dictorumve veniam sanxit*, Ors. 6, 4; S. 258, 27–29. Sié hit (gylt) healf forgifen, Ll. Th. i. 64, 22. Anweald synna tō forgifanne (-gef-, L.) *potestas dimittendi peccata*, Mt. 9, 6. Monig is tō forgeafanne (*ad ignoscendum*), Rtl. 10, 34. (b) the object a clause :—Hē forgifeþ eall swā hwæt swā þes middangeard wiþ hine ǣbyligda geworhte, Bl. H. 9, 11. Forgif mē þ ic tō þe sprecende wæs swā tō men, 235, 31. (c) absolute :—Gyf mín brōðor syngað wið mē, mōt ic him forgyfan (ic forgefo *dimittam*, L.), Mt. 18, 21. Eáðor tō forgeafanne *remissius*, Lk. L. 10, 12. **IV a.** *to give up* resentment for injury received, *dismiss* ill-will, anger, *remove* one's displeasure from a person :—Hē him forgeaf þone nīð þe hē tō him wiste, Ors. 5, 15; S. 250, 15. Gif hwylce þǣr beóð þāra þe hwæt ǣbylhða wið ōðre habbað, þonne sceolan hig þā forgyfan, Ll. Th. ii. 434, 8. [*Goth.* fra-giban : *O. Sax.* far-geban (for-): *O. H. Ger.* fer-geban.] v. for-gifen.

**for-gifedness (-gifen-?)** *forgiveness* :—Andetnys synne forgyfednysse syld *confessio peccati ueniam donat*, Scint. 40, 13.

**for-gifen**; *adj.* (*ptcpl.*). **I.** *forgiven, pardoned* :—Þē georne tō Gode bide and tō his hālgum, wið þām ðe þine synna þæs ðe forgifenron beón, Wlfst. 290, 10. **II.** *mild*; *remissus*. (1) of persons, *gentle, indulgent* :—Hē wæs Rōmānum swā forgiefen and swā milde swā him onwald næs ǣr þæm *Tiberius cum magna et graui modestia reipublicae praefuit*, Ors. 6, 2; S. 254, 22. Hié sume heora þeówas gefreódon, and eác him eallum wurdon tō milde and tō forgiefene *cum licentia in consuetudinem prorogata servos suos passim liberos facerent*, 4, 3; S. 162, 15. (2) of discipline, punishment, &c., *not hard* :—Sodomum forgefenra † eaðor tō forgeafanne bið *Sodomis remissius erit*, Lk. L. 10, 12, 14. Forgefenro, Mt. L. 11, 22. Forgefenre, 24. v. un-forgifen.

**for-gifend(?)**, es; *m. One who grants* :—Unnend † forgefend *prestabilis*, Rtl. 5, 10. v. for-gifestre.

**for-gifendlic** *dative. Take this apart from* for-gifenlic.

**for-gifenlic.** For 'forgiving, . . ., bearable' substitute : that is freed from an oppressive obligation, easy. v. for-gifen, and next word.

**for-gifenlice**; *adv. Easily, without hardship from burdensome claims* :—Tyro and Sydone bið forgifenlícor (*remissius*) þonne eów, Mt. 11, 22.

**for-gifestre**, an; *f. A female giver* :—Hāligre forgifestre gyfe *sancti datrix karismatis*, Hy. S. 49, 11. v. for-gifend.

**for-gifnes and for-gifennes** (-gifenes). *Add* : **I.** *remission* of a fine, tax, &c. :—Ic wille þ ealle þā freódōm and ealle þā forgiuenesse þe mīne forgengles geáfen, þet hit stande, Chr. 963; P. 117, 5. **II.** *release* :—Tō bodanne hæftedum forgefnisse *praedicare captiuis remissionem*, Lk. R. L. 4, 18. **III.** *forgiveness* of sin, offence, &c. :—Hē him þone eádigan wer forgifnesse bæd, Bl. H. 223, 13. Mæht forgefnisse synna *potestas dimittendi peccata*, Mt. L. 9, 6. Forgefenise, p. 15, 20. Forgifnesse, Past. 399, 18. In forgefnisse synna *in remissionem peccatorum*, Lk. R. L. 1, 77. Ðǣm hōendum forgefnise from feder of gebæd *crucifigentibus ueniam a patre deposcens*, Lk. p. 11, 7. On synna forgifenysse (-gyfenesse, v. l., -gefnisse, L. R.) *in remissionem peccatorum*, Mk. 1, 4. Hié nǣfre forgifenesse æt Gode ne biddaþ, Bl. H. 65, 13. Þū sealdest mannum synna forgifnessa, 87, 12. **IV.** *mildness, lenity, indulgence*; in a bad sense, *laxity* :—Oft ungemetlico forgifnes bið gelícet ðæt mon wēned ðæt hit sié mildheortnes *saepe inordinata remissio pietas creditur*, Past. 149, 9. Milsia † forgefnise *miseratione*, Mt. p. 18, 8. Of forgefnise *de indulgentia*, Mk. p. 5, 17: Rtl. 97, 39. Būtan miltsunge † forgyfenysse *sine respectu*, An. Ox. 3462. Forgifenysse, 4795.

**for-gildan.** **I.** *to pay back, restore* what has been taken :—Gif man forstele feoðerfōt neát . . . fæste ān gear and forgylde þ hē forstolen hæbbe (*quod furatus fuerit reddat*), oððe .ii. geár fæste, Ll. Th. ii. 140, 34. **II.** with idea of compensation. (1) absolute, *to make compensation* to a person (*dat.*), *pay damages* at law :—Gif mon wíf gebycgge and sió gyft forð ne cume, āgife þ feoh, and forgielde, and gebēte þām byrgean, Ll. Th. i. 122, 6. Gif hwā Godes fíyman hæbbe on unriht, āgife hine tō rihte, and forgylde þām þe hit gebyrige, and gylde þām cyninge be his weregilde, 410, 16. Gif hwā wrace dō . . . þ hē him on nime, āgife, and forgielde, and gebēte mid .xxx. scitt., 108, 5. Gif hwā reáflāc gewyrce, āgife, and forgylde (cf. āgife hē þone reáflāc, and geselle .lx. scitt. tō wīte, 108, 9: *and see first passage under* (1 a)), and beó his weres scyldig wið þone cynincg, 410, 2. Man wolde biddan þæs reáflāces þ hē hit sciolde āgyfan, and forgyldan, and þām cyninge his wer, Cht. Th. 289, 28. Gif ic gesealde ǣnigre wífhanda þ hé gestrýnde, þonne forgyldan míne māgas . . . Forðon ic cwepe þ hí hit gyldan, for þon hý sōð tō mínum be ic syllan mōt, 491, 23. (1 a) where the rate or manner of payment is given :—Bæd Ælfsige ǣgiftes his mannes (*a woman who had been stolen*), and Æðelstān hine āgef, and forgeald him mid twām pundum, Cht. Th. 206, 31. Meduman leódgelde forgelde, Ll. Th. i. 4, 9. Mid weorðe forgelde, 12, 2. (2) with acc. of object for which compensation is made. (a) the object a person slain or injured :—Gif hē ǣnig lande næbbe, forgilde hine nian mid .lxx. scitt. (cf. sī his wer .lxxx. scitt., 2), Ll. Th. i. 188, 3 : 6 : ii. 294, 7. Gif man æt unlagum man bewǣpnige, forgilde hine be his

healsfange; and gif hine man gebinde, forgilde be healfan were, i. 408, 18-20. Gif hwā fǣmnan beswīce unbeweddode, and hire mid slǣpe, forgilde hié, 52, 6. Hē þone ǣnne hēht golde forgyldan, þone þe Grendel ācwealde, B. 1054. (b) the object a thing lost or destroyed or damaged :—Gif . . . sié funden þ hē ǣr stæl, be twyfealdum forgielde hē hit (cf. gilde be twifealdon *duplum restituet*, Ex. 22, 4), Ll. Th. i. 50, 23. Gif mon āfelle on wuda wel monega treówa . . . , forgielde .iii. treówu ǣlc .xxx. sciłł., 128, 20. Gif fyrdscip man āmyrre þ hit ǣnote weorðe, forgilde hit fullíce, 324, 7. Ðeáh ūre heorda hwylc ān sceáp forgȳme, wē willað þ hē hit forgylde, ii. 326, 25. (c) the object an undischarged obligation :—Ciricsceat gelǣste man be Martinus mæssan, and se þe þ ne gelǣste, forgilde hine mid twelffealdan, Ll. Th. i. 342, 28. Forgylde hine .xi. sīðan, 366, 20. (d) the object a misdeed :—Sceolan wē mid ūre ānre sāule forgyldan and gebētan ealle þā þing þe wē ǣr ofor his bebod gedydon, Bl. H. 91, 16. (3) with acc. of compensation paid :—Gif man mannan ofslæhð . . . ealne leód forgelde . . . þā māgas healfne leód forgelden, Ll. Th. i. 8, 6, 8. Ealle forgielden þone wer gemǣnum hondum, 80, 16. III. with idea of release, redemption. (1) *to pay for* a criminal to save him from punishment :—Gif hine (*the criminal*) mon eft gefó, forgielde hē hine selfa be his wergilde, Ll. Th. i. 66, 11. Sȳ hē his tungan scyldig, būton hē hine mid his were forgilde, 384, 27. Sié se hláford ofslegen oþþe forgolden, i. 50, 1. (2) *to pay to get immunity from, buy off* :—Eów betere is þæt gē þisne gārrǣs mid gafole forgyldon, By. 32. IV. with idea of recompense, retribution, *to repay, pay out, requite* a person (*dat.*). (1) absolute :— Hē forgylt ānra gehwylcum æfter his āgenum gewyrhtum *reddet Deus unicuique secundum opera sua*, Wlfst. 184, 9. Wæs him forgolden æfter his āgenum gewyrhtum, Bl. H. 45, 2. (2) with acc. of action that is recompensed :—Ic heora synne swinglum forgylde *visitabo in verberibus peccata eorum*, Ps. Th. 88, 29. Forþon þū ūs þus dydest, wē hit þē forgyldaþ, Bl. H. 241, 18. Hȳ him grimme forguldon þone wīgcræft þe hȳ æt him geleornodon *vincere, dum vincitur, edocuit*, Ors. 1, 2; S. 30, 7. Mid hwām hié hit ðē forgielden (*retribuant*), Past. 323, 24. Hē wolde Grendle forgyldan gūðrǣsa fela, B. 1577. Hē wile hit him mid yfele eall forgyldan, Bl. H. 55, 25. Hit weorþeþ forgolden, 195, 23. (2 a) the object a clause :—Hē ūs forgyldeþ swā wē nū hēr dōþ ge gódes ge yfeles *he will requite us for both the good and the evil that we do here*, Bl. H. 51, 26. ¶ with acc. of object which has been the subject of action to be requited :—Beorges hyrde wolde līge forgyldan drync fæt dȳre *the fire-drake wanted to repay (the robbery of) the precious cup with flame*, B. 2305. V. *to pay* what is due, *perform* a vow :— Ðū forgeldes Drihtne gihāta ðīne, Mt. L. 5, 33. þæt ic ðē forgulde ealle þā gehāt, Ps. Th. 65, 13. [v. *N. E. D.* foryield : *Goth.* fra-gildan : O. Sax. O. L. Ger. far-geldan : O. Frs. for-ielda : O. H. Ger. fer-geltan.] v. un-forgolden.

**for-gilpan**; *pp.* -golpen *To boast of* :—Ne rēcð God þǣre forgolpenan ælmessan, Wlfst. 234, 16.

**for-gíman.** *Add*: (1) *to neglect* a concrete thing :—Gyf hē for slǣwðe his hláfordes [land] forgȳmð, ne bið his āgnum wel geborgen, Ll. Th. i. 440, 16. Gif preóst hūsl forgíme, ii. 292, 23. Ðeáh ūre heorda hwylc ān sceáp forgȳme, 324, 16. Ne sceolde hē nān ðing forgȳman ðe ǣfre tō note mehte, ne forða mūsfellan, Angl. ix. 265, 7. (2) *to neglect* to do (*dat. infin.*) :—Oferhogie hē oððe forgȳme ðā ðing tō begānne and tō bewitanne ðe tó scepene belimpað, Angl. ix. 260, 3. (3) *to disregard* evil :—Forgēman *praetergredi* (*iniqua*), Kent. Gl. 685. [v. *N. E. D.* foryeme.]

**for-gímeleásian.** *Add*:—*Excesserit*, i. *culpaverit, fregerit vel* forgēmeleásaþ, Wrt. Voc. ii. 145, 70. Sī forlǣten, forgȳmeleásod *excipiatur*, An. Ox. 4571. [O. L. Ger. far-gōmalōson *negligere*.]

**for-gitan.** *Add*:—On ðǣre gesundfulnesse mon forgiett (-git, *v. l.*) his selfes, Past. 35, 6. Hit forgiteð his āgenes gódes, Gr. D. 6, 11. Heó forgeat þ heó hine mid rōdetācne gebletsode (ne gebledsode, *v. l.*) *eam signo crucis benedicere oblita est*, 30, 34. þ hié forgeátan þāra ūtera gefeohta, Ors. 2, 6; S. 88, 24. Forgeotta *oblivisci*, Rtl. 169, 25. Tō forgitenne *praetereundum*, An. Ox. 2558. Ādíligiende, forgitende *obliterantes*, Wrt. Voc. ii. 62, 49. þū hæfst ðāra wæpna forgiten, Bt. 3, 1; F. 4, 22. Forgetne woeron tō onfōane hlāfas *obliti sunt sumere panes*, Mk. L. R. 8, 14. [O. Sax. far-getan : O. H. Ger. fer-gezzan.] v. for-giten, un-forgitende.

**for-gitel.** *Add* : [v. *N. E. D.* forgetel.]

**for-gitelian** (-geot-) ; *p.* ode *To forget* :—Ðū forgeotelas *obliviisceris*, Ps. Srt. 43, 24.

**for-gitelness.** *Add* :—Foregytelnysse *oblivionem*, R. Ben. I. 28, 15. [v. *N. E. D.* forgetelness.]

**for-giten** ; *adj. Forgetful* :—Críst nelle gehȳran þæs gímeleásan and þæs forgytenan mannes gebedrǣdene, Bl. H. 57, 4. Ealra þǣra worda hí wǣron forgytene, Hml. S. 23, 389.

**for-giting** ; *f. Forgetting* ; oblivio :—Forgitincge *obliuionis*, Angl. xiii. 440, 1064. On forgytincge *in obliuione*, Scint. 174, 13.

**for-glendrad** *and* **for-glendran.** *Substitute*: **for-glendrian** (**-gleddrian**) *p.* ode *To devour, consume* :—In þām dæge ligettas forglendriaþ (-gleddriað, *v. l.*) middaneard and mancyn, Wlfst. 182, 11. Byrnende līgræscas forglendriað eówre wæstmas, 297, 9. Swā hwæt manncynnes swā fȳr forbærnde and forglendrede, 183, 33. Forglendrian (?-glendra? *Wright prints* forgend, *Wülcker* forgle[ndrian] *lurcare*, Wrt. Voc. ii. 52, 72. Se líchoma byð from wyrmum freten and forglendred, Bl. H. 99, 9. Ealle heora snytru beóð yfele forgledred *omnis sapientia eorum devorata est*, Ps. Th. 106, 26. Seó grāniende neowelnys and seó forglendrede (-iende (?) : -glændrede, -gleddrede, *v. ll.*) hell, Wlfst. 187, 1. Forglendrad *conglutinatus* (confounded by glosser with *glutitus*?), Ps. L. 43, 25. ¶ forglendred (-end? *a voracious person* ; lurco?) *serviunculus*, Wrt. Voc. i. 290, 49.

**for-gnagan.** *Add*:—Forgnagen *conrosus*, i. *deuoratus*, An. Ox. 3820. Mid deórenum ceaflum forgnegen, 3343. Forgnagene *roderentur*, 3565. [v. *N. E. D.* forgnaw.]

**for-gnídan.** *Add*:—Ic forgníde *extricor*, wǣron forgnidene *extricabantur*, Hpt. Gl. 494, 39, 37. Bið forsworfen *vel* forgniden *demolitur*, i. *exterminatur*, Wrt. Voc. ii. 138, 64. [v. *N. E. D.* forgnide. O. H. Ger. fer-gnītan *delere*.]

**for-gnidennys.** *Add* :—Forgnidennes *contritio*, Wrt. Voc. ii. 134, 79.

**for-gnísednys.** *Dele* : for-grind. v. next word.

**for-grindan.** *Dele first two citations, and add* :—þu forgrindesþ *commolitis*, Wrt. Voc. ii. 15, 14. Forgrindet *commolitio* (? *commolit* ; *for the inflexion* -et, cf. menget *confundit*, 11. Or (?) *the* -et *might be a noun suffix*, cf. onǣlet: or (?) for-grind (cf. ge-grind) *might be taken*), 105, 9. Forgrundenum *commolitis*, 132, 6. ¶ *with dat.* :—Ic forgrand gramum, B. 424.

**for-grípan** *and* **fór-grípan** (*l.* for-). *Take these together, and add* : (1) *with acc.* To seize, seize and carry off :—Ic ætbrēde *vel* ic forgrípe *diripio*, i. *rapio, abstraho, eripio*, Wrt. Voc. ii. 140, 48. Ealle hí se stranga deáð forgríped and nymð, Guth. 78, 15. Genom ł forgráp *appraehendit*, Lk. L. 5, 26. Hē wæs mid hrædlice deáðe forgripen *morte immatura praereptus est*, Bd. 4, 23 ; Sch. 472, 5. (2) *with dat.* To destroy, B. 2353 : Gen. 1275 (v. Dict.).

**for-gríwan** ; *pp.* -griwen *To sink* in vice :—þā þe on unrihttīdum on oferfylla bióð forgriwene, Nap. 27, 30. v. be-gríwan.

**for-grówan.** *Substitute* : *To grow to excess*, Reim. 46. [v. *N. E. D.* forgrow.] Cf. for-weaxan.

**for-gryndan** ; *p.* de *To send to the bottom, destroy* :—Hit eall se gífra flód forswealh and forgrinde, Angl. xi. 2, 40.

**for-gyltan** ; *p.* -gylte ; *pp.* -gylt *To make guilty* (occurs as reflexive or in passive) :—þā ðe on openlican synnan (mid openan heáfodgyltan) hȳ sylfe forgyltan, Wlfst. 104, 12 : 153, 10. þ man freóge ǣlcne wítefæstne man þe on his tíman forgylt wǣre, Cht. Th. 551, 15. þone cwide þe se apostol be swā forgyltum cwyþ, R. Ben. 50, 1. [v. *N. E. D.* forguilt.]

**for-gyrd.** v. forþ-gyrd.

**for-gyrdan** ; *p.* de *To girdle, enclose* :—Hē Bretenlond mid díce forgyrde from sǣ oþ sǣ, Chr. 189; P. 9, note 4.

**for-habban.** *Add* : I. *intrans.* To abstain, refrain :—Ne þū ne forhafa *neque conpescaris*, Bl. Gl. Ne mihte hē þā forhabban, B. 2609. ¶ for-hæbbende *abstinent, continent* :—Hine þā brōðra hatedon, þȳ hē swā forhæbbende wæs, Guth. 16, 26. Forhæbbendra *continentium*, i. *virginum*, An. Ox. 1002. Ðā forhæbbendan *continentes*, Past. 453, 30, 31. I a. *to abstain from*. (1) *with dat.* :—Sóna swā hȳ geedwyrpte beóð, þām flǣscǣte forhæbben (-habban *v. l.*) *a carnibus abstineant*, R. Ben. 61, 3. (2) *with prep.* :—From giriordum forhabba, Rtl. 16, 25. Scolde heó forhabban fram ingange Godes hūses, Hml. Th. i. 134, 19. Gód is tō forhæbbenne fram unālȳfedlicum styrungum, ii. 564, 7. Fram mettum forhæbbende, Hy. S. 65, 37. II. *trans.* (1) reflexive, *to restrain* one's self from, *keep away*. (a) *with prep.* :— Ælc ðæra manna ðe hine forhæfð fram unālȳfedlicere gesihðe, Hml. Th. ii. 564, 3. Forhæfde hē hine fram his gebeórscipe, Hml. S. 31, 613. Heó ne mihte hí sylfe forhabban fram hire were *a viro suo sese abstinere non potuit*, Gr. D. 72, 10. (b) *with clause* :—Gehwā hine forhæbbe þ hē hí nā fæstende ete, Lch. i. 228, 14. (2) *to keep back*. (a) *not to pay* a due :—Gif cyninges þegn hit (Rōmpænig) forhæbbe, Ll. Th. ii. 300, 3, 6. (b) *not to mention* :—Hē worhte mā wundra mid eów þonne hē mid ūs dyde, and þeáh wē fela forhebbon (-habbæn, *v. l.*), Hml. S. 31, 1456. (3) *to restrain, check, stop, put difficulties in the way of* :—Cum ymb geáres rynu . . . ic þē bidde þ þū þis ne forhæbbe, ac þ þū cume, Hml. S. 23 b, 708. Hí ne mihton forhabban merestreámes mōd, ac hē managum gesceód, Ex. 487. Gif mon innan forhæfd sié *if a man be costive*, Lch. ii. 276, 4.

**for-hæbbend**, es ; *m. One who is continent, an unmarried person* :— þā eorþlican forhæbbendras *terreni celebes*, An. Ox. 1254.

**for-hæfednes.** *Add*: *and* -hæfnes :—Forhæfednys *parsimonia*, i. *abstinentia*, An. Ox. 3748. Forhæfdnes *continentia*, Wrt. Voc. ii. 23, 30. On færhæftnisse *abstinendo*, Rtl. 14, 12. Hine æghwylc sylfne on forhæfednysse band, Hml. S. 23 b, 131. On ðǣre forhæfednysse fram unālȳfedlicum styrungum, Hml. Th. ii. 564, 16. Ðā ðe dóð forhæfednesse *qui*

*parcius cibo utuntur, abstinentes,* Past. 308, 14, 16. Swâ hié ꝺâ forhæb-bendan lǽren forhæfdnesse *sic continentibus laudetur virginitas corporis,* 453, 31. Forhæfnisse *abstinentiam,* Rtl. 163, 13. Mid fæstenum and for-hæfdnessum, Dôm. L. 30, 46. Forhæuenessum *parsimoniis,* An. Ox. 47, 2.

**for-hǽlde.** *Substitute :* for-hǽlan; *p.* de *To make unsound* (?), *injure :*—Forhǽlde *offensa,* Wrt. Voc. ii. 65, 53.

**for-hǽtan;** *p.* te *To make too hot, overheat :*—Se mon wyrꝺ tô swîþe forhǽt, Lch. ii. 244, 8.

**for-hǽpan;** *p.* de; *pp.* ed *To parch up, burn out, consume :*—For-swǽld, forhǽþed *exustus,* i. *spoliatus,* Wrt. Voc. ii. 146, 34. v. hǽþa.

**for-hâtan.** *Add :* I. *to promise or vow not to do, to renounce :*—Bûtan synne hê mæg gehîwian, gif hê hit ǽr ne forhêt *sine culpa ad conjugium veniunt si necdum meliora voverunt,* Past. 401, 35. Ne lyst mê nâwiht ꝺâra metta þe ic forhâtan habbe *ea quae statui non edere nihil me commovent,* Solil. H. 37, 4. II. *to declare criminal, out-law, proscribe* (? cf. þû hine hête flîyman, Cht. Th. 173, 6) :—Se forhâtena (*the devil who tempted Eve*) sprǽc, Gen. 609. [v. *N. E. D.* forhight.]

**for-hâtena.** v. *preceding word :* for-heáfod. v. fore-heáfod.

**for-healdan** *and* for-healden. *Substitute :* for-healdan; *p.* heóld; *pp.* -healden. I. *to hold improperly, withhold, keep back what should be paid :*—On hǽþenum þeódum ne dear man forhealdan lytel ne mycel þæs þe gelagod is tô gedwolgoda weorꝺunge; and wê forhealdaꝺ ǽghwǽr Godes gerihta, Wlfst. 157, 12–14 : 229, 19. Hý forheóldon teoꝺunge, 211, 2. Gif hwâ teoꝺunge forhealde . . . Gif hwâ Rômfeoh forhealde, Ll. Th. i. 170, 1, 2. I a. *to keep too long :*—Preóst hûsl on clænnesse healde, and warige þ hit nâ forealdige. Gif hit þonne for[h]ealden sî, þ his man brûcan ne mæge, þonne forbærne hit man, Ll. Th. ii. 252, 7. II. *not to shew proper regard to, disre-gard, neglect* (1) *a person or personal attribute :*—þû forleósest þâ forhealdaꝺ þê *perdes omnes, qui fornicantur abs te,* Ps. Th. 72, 22. Hê onfêng for worlde mycelne noman, and þ eal forheóld and his Scyppend, Bl. H. 43, 35. Eall hî forheóldan heáh weorc Godes, Ps. Th. 105, 29. Hæfdon hý forhealden helm Scylfinga, B. 2381. (2) *a command, not to keep a command :*—Nǽfre bebod ꝺîn ic forheáld *nunquam mandatum tuum praeterii,* Lk. L. 15, 29. III. *not to keep in good condition.* (1) *not to keep in safety, not to preserve :*—Eálâ eá is þ forweorþfullic wela þe nâuþer ne mæg ne hine selfne gehealdan ne his hlâford, tô ꝺon þ hê ne þurfe mâran fultumes, oꝺꝺe hî beóþ bêgen forhealdan *O praeclara potentia, quae ne ad conservationem quidem sui satis efficax invenitur,* Bt. 29, 1 ; F. 102, 17. (2) *not to maintain in one's rights, to treat unfairly :*—Monige men ryhtan ge on londum ge on mâ þâra þinga þe heó on forhaldne wêran, Cht. Th. 139, 28. (3) *not to keep morally pure :*—Se wer unrihthǽmed wreceþ gif his wîf hié forhealdeþ, Bl. H. 185, 27. Forhealden *incestus,* Wrt. Voc. ii. 44, 45. On wrâꝺra (*the fallen angels*) gield þâra þe forhealdene (cf. the phrase used by Dante of the sin of the angels ' superbo strupo,' Inf. c. vii. 12) hê of hleó sende, Gen. 102. (4) *to abuse a privilege,* &c. :—Gif hî ꝺone frýdôm tela gehealdon . . . gif hî ꝺone frýdôm forheólden, Bt. 41, 3 ; F. 248, 11. [v. *N. E. D.* forhold. *O. H. Ger.* far-haltaniu *prostituta.*]

**for-healden.** v. *preceding word.*

**for-healdness,** e ; *f. Incontinence, unchasteness :*—Manna forheald-nessa, þ is unrihthǽmed . . . Gâstes ꝺe manna hyrtan beswîcaꝺ, þ is . . . forhealdnyssa gâst . . . Ne gewemmaꝺ eówre lîchaman ꝺurh forhealdnesse, Nap. 24.

**for-heard.** *Add :*—þu mê forhærdne lǽrst *thou dost teach me a very hard doctrine,* Solil. H. 42, 18.

**for-heardian.** *Add :*—Ǽr þon ꝺe hê þone forheardodan swile gehnesce, Lch. ii. 212, 18.

**for-heáwan.** *Add :*—Drihten forheáweꝺ ꝺ forcyrfeꝺ hnollas synfulra *Dominus concidet ceruices peccatorum,* Ps. L. 128, 4. [v. *N. E. D.* forhew. *O. Sax.* far-hawan : *O. H. Ger.* fer-houuan *vulnerare, excidere.*]

**for-helan.** *Add :* (1) *with acc. :*—Gif hwilc tûnes man ǽnigne þearf forhele oþþe forhæbbe, Ll. Th. ii. 300, 5. Nǽnne sacleásan man forsec-gean, ne nǽnne sacne forhelan, i. 294, 6. Hû magan þâ cyningas forhelan hiora unmihte, Bt. 29, 1 ; F. 104, 13. Ic þê ârecce, nâht ne forhelende (-hæl-, *v. l.*), Hml. S. 3, 319. Hit forholen beón ne mihte, Gr. D. 60, 20. Hû nytt biꝺ se forholena cræft ?, Past. 377, 7. (1 a) *with dat. of person from whom something is concealed :*—þ hê ꝺæs hâlgan hǽse forhule (-hæle, *v. l.*) his hlâforde, Hml. S. 21, 81. (2) *with clause* (*and dat. of person*) :—Hê forhæl him þæt hê hine eft ꝺreátian wolde, Past. 185, 24. [v. *N. E. D.* forhele. *O. Sax.* far-helan : *O. H. Ger.* fer-helan *celare, occultare, abscondere.*]

**for-helian;** *p.* ede *To cover up :*—Forheledum *tectis,* Hpt. Gl. 528, 16. [v. *N. E. D.* forhill. *O. H. Ger.* un-ferhelit *infronitus.*]

**for-hergend,** es ; *m. One who lays waste, ravages, devastates :*—Ferhergend, forhergen[d] *grassator,* Txts. 66, 467.

**for-hergian.** *Add :* (1) *of action by persons, to lay waste a country, carry captive people :*—Æfter þǽm þe hê Egyptum forhergede, hê gefôr siþþan on Judana lond and hiera fela forhergeade ; siþþan on Ircaniam hê heora fela gesette *post transactum in Aegypto bellum plurimos Judaeo-rum in transmigrationem egit, atque in Hyrcania habitare praecepit,*

---

Ors. 3, 5 ; S. 104, 23–26. (2) *of the action of natural forces :*—Se wîngeard wæs forslagen and forhergod mid onhreósendum hægle *vinea grandine irruente vastata est,* Gr. D. 57, 5. [*O. H. Ger.* fer-heriôn *depraedare.*]

**for-hergung.** *Add :*—Forheriunge (*printed* sor-) *infestatione,* Wrt. Voc. ii. 45, 43. Hwæt forwearþ . . . on þeóda forhergiunge *nationes vastationibus terebantur,* Ors. 5, 11 ; S. 238, 5.

**for-hînan.** *Take here* for-hýnan, *and add :*—Hê Scê Petres mynster tô bysmere macede, and ealle þâ ôꝺre forhergode and forhýnde, Chr. 1068 ; P. 203, 28. Hê hî miclum tintrade and bismrade, oþ hié mid ealle wǽron fordôn and forhiéned *cruentissimam victoriam in eos exercuit,* Ors. 3, 7 ; S. 118, 26. Mid þǽm bryne hió (*Rome*) wæs swâ swîþe forhiéned þæt hió nǽfre siþþan swelc næs *nec unquam majore incendio vastata est,* 6, 1 ; S. 252, 24.

**for-hirdan.** *Take here* for-hyrdan, *and add :* [*O. H. Ger.* fer-herten *obdurare.*] : for-hladan *to exhaust.* v. un-forhladen.

**for-hogd ;** *adj.* (*ptcpl.* v. for-hycgan). *Despicable, contemptible :*—Forhogd *irritum, inanem,* Wrt. Voc. ii. 112, 7. þâ burhware him wǽron for heora ungeleáfan swîþe forhogde and ungecorene, Bl. H. 77, 28. v. for-hogod, *and next word.*

**for-hogdlíce ;** *adv. With contempt, contemptuously :*—Crîst þâ mycclan burh swâ forhogdlíce nemde, Bl. H. 77, 26. v. preceding word.

**for-hogdness ;** e ; *f. Contempt :*—Tô worulde forhogdnisse *ad contem-tum saeculi,* Bd. 4, 24 ; Sch. 481, 15 : Ps. Srt. 78, 4 ; Rtl. 103, 28. Cf. for-hogodness.

**for-hogian.** *Add : to disdain :*—Ic forhogige *dedignor,* Wrt. Voc. ii. 139, 67. (1) *to hold in contempt* a person or thing :—Hê ânum folgaꝺ and ôꝺerne forhogaꝺ (-eꝺ, L. contemnet!), Lk. 16, 13. Forhogaꝺ *accusat,* Jn. R. 5, 45. Forogas, Mt. L. 6, 24. Gié forhogas bebod Godes *vos transgredimini mandatum Dei,* 15, 3. Forhogede *contem-serit,* An. Ox. 3920. Hié forhogodan ege ealra eorꝺlicra cyninga, Bl. H. 137, 5. Ne forhogiaþ wîsdôm, Bt. 16, 1 ; F. 50, 26. Forhogot *spreta,* An. Ox. 11, 72. Biꝺ forhoged *confunditur,* 520. Nâ sî forhugud *non aspernatur,* Angl. xiii. 441, 1085. (2) *to disdain to do.* (a) *with clause :*—Swâ hê lǽs forhogaꝺ ꝺæt hê ûs ꝺonne giet tô him spane, siꝺꝺan wê hine oferhycggeaꝺ *quanto contemtus adhuc vocare non dedignatur,* Past. 407, 18 : Bl. H. 83, 15. Sume men for heora prýtan forhogiaꝺ þ hî hýran godcundan ealdran, Ll. Th. i. 332, 34. (b) *with infin. :*—Hê forhogode tôgênes grêtan, Gr. D. 34, 6. (c) *with dat. infin. :*—þætte wîf forhogiaꝺ heora bearn tô fêdanne *ut mulieres filios nutrire contemnant,* Bd. 1, 27 ; Sch. 80, 12. þ hê his synna ne for-hogige tô andettanne *ut non negligat peccata sua confiteri,* Ll. Th. ii. 174, 12. [v. *N. E. D.* forhow.] Cf. for-hycgan.

**for-hogiend,** es ; *m. A despiser, contemner :*—þearfena lufiend and his sylfes forhogiend *cultor pauperum et contemptor sui,* Gr. D. 329, 13.

**for-hogiendlic ;** *adj. Contemptible, despicable :*—Forhogigendlic con-temptibilis, Scint. 62, 7 : 125, 9.

**for-hogness** (-hoh-), e ; *f. Contempt :*—Tô worolde forhohnesse (-hoge-, *v. l.*) *ad contemtum saeculi,* Bd. 4, 24 ; Sch. 481, 15.

**for-hogod ;** *adj.* (*ptcpl.*) *Despised, despicable, good-for-nothing :*—Se unnytta and forhogoda *inrita,* Wrt. Voc. ii. 48, 65. v. for-hogd.

**for-hogodlic ;** *adj. Denoting scorn or contempt :*—Drihten þâ cyne-lican burh forhogodlíce naman nemde, Bl. H. 77, 23.

**for-hogodness.** *Take here* for-hogednes, *and add :*—Forhogaꝺnis *contemptio,* Ps. Srt. 106, 40 : 122, 3 : *contemptus,* 30, 19. Forhogod-nesse *contemptum,* Bd. 4, 24 ; Sch. 481, 15. Cf. for-hogdness.

**for-hogung.** *Add :*—Forhogung *contemptus,* i. *contemptio,* Wrt. Voc. ii. 134, 81. Of forhogunge *ex contemptu,* Kent. Gl. 1167 : Angl. xiii. 440, 1067 : Scint. 203, 13. On forhogunge *subsannationem,* Ps. Spl. 43, 15.

**for-hôrwade.** *l.* for-horwade.

**for-hradian.** *Add :* I. *to go too quickly, hurry :*—þâ ꝺe nabbaꝺ ildo tô ꝺon ꝺæt hié mǽgen lǽran, and hî ꝺeáh forhradiaꝺ ꝺæt hié hit ongiennaꝺ *quos a praedicationis officio aetas prohibet, et tamen praecipi-tatio impellit,* Past. 383, 22. II. *to anticipate :*—Forhradode Godes engel þæs ârleásan geþeaht, Hml. Th. i. 82, 30. Forhrada hine *praeueni eum,* Ps. L. 16, 13. ꝺæt hié tô unwǽrlîce ne onetten, ꝺý lǽs hié forhradian ꝺone betestan tîman *ne dum bonorum tempus incaute festinando praeveniunt,* Past. 281, 21 : R. Ben. 61, 13. Hê wênde þæt hî woldon his cynedôm forseón and wolde ꝺâ forhradian, Hml. Th. i. 480, 2. Úrne endenêxtan dæg mid dǽdbôte forhradian, 482, 6. Beó forehradod *anticipatur,* An. Ox. 1232.

**for-hrǽdlíce ;** *adv. Very quickly, suddenly :*—Wê hî forhrǽdlíce tô ꝺǽm weorce dôn ne mægen *non repente in fabrica ponitur,* Past. 445, 1.

**for-hraþe.** *Add :*—Hê wearꝺ þâ gefullod forhraꝺe, Hml. Th. ii. 502, 1 : Hml. S. 29, 149. Æꝺelstân cyng gefreóde Eádelm forraꝺe þæs ꝺe hê ǽrest cyng wæs *very soon after he first was king,* C. D. B. ii. 315, 18.

**for-hrepian,** -hreppan (?) *to catch :*—In argscipe begrippene ꝺ forrepene (*reprehensam.* Cf. repaꝺ *reprehendit,* R. Ben. I. 102, 2, *and*

*Icel.* hreppa *to catch. The strong form of the participle might be formed on the analogy of a verb like* drepan), Jn. p. 5, 8.

**for-hréred.** *Add :* Wrt. Voc. ii. 129, 22 : **forhswebung.** *l.* (?) forþ-swebung. v. forþ-swebbung.

**forht.** *Add :* I. *feeling fear :*—Swíðe forht and bifiende *multum tremens et pauida,* Bd. 5, 12 ; Sch. 613, 17. Swíðe forhte *trepidi,* Gr. D. 132, 8. Frohto í forhto *timidi,* Mk. L. 4, 40. Forhtra *formidolosorum,* i. *timidorum,* An. Ox. 4733. Forhtum *tremebundis,* i. *formidantibus,* 3773. I a. *where the occasion of fear is given.* (1) *with* for :—Hú forht hé sceal bión for ǽlcre orsorgnesse, Past. 32, 5. Wurdon hié swíðe forhte for ðǽm fǽre, Bl. H. 199, 24 : Guth. 16, 8 : Dóm. L. 160. (2) *with dat. infin. :*—Nelle ðú forht beón tó onfóanne Maria *noli timere accipere Mariam,* Mt. L. 1, 20. II. *expressing fear :*—Þá blácan andwlitan and þæt bifiende wered, se forhta cearm and þǽra folca wóp, Wlfst. 186, 18.

**forhte;** *adv.* v. un-forhte.

**forhtian, frohtian.** *Add :* I. *intrans. To fear :*—Forhtode *obstipuit,* Wrt. Voc. ii. 63, 9. Ne wallas gé forhtiga (frohtiga, L.) *nolite expauescere,* Mk. R. 16, 6. Ðæt wíf ondrǽdende and forhtigende *mulier timens et tremens,* Mk. 5, 33. Swíðe forhtigende þæt hí his fandian dorston *in great fear because they had dared to try him,* Hml. Th. ii. 168, 19. Frohtende *timens,* Mt. R. 25, 25 : *metuens,* Mk. p. 2, 11. Ondo frohtendes (*pauescentis*) Petres, Lk. p. 4, 18. Forhtigendum *formidilosis,* Wrt. Voc. ii. 34, 53. Forohtandum ðegnum *pauentibus discipulis,* Jn. p. 4, 16. I a. *with the occasion of fear given with a preposition :*—Ic ne forhtige for ðínum gebeóte, Hml. S. 14, 101. Þæt hé forhtige for synnum, Wlfst. 179, 15. Þý lǽs wé ... lǽs tó Godes dóme forhtigen and ús ondrǽden *ne forte nos ... minus Dei judicium formidantes,* Bd. 4, 25 ; Sch. 503, 17. II. *trans.* (1) *with acc. :*—Egislíce orleahtras forhtude *horrida discrimina expauit* (i. *formidauit*), An. Ox. 1869. Forhtige *horrescas* (*voluntatem parentum*) 3406. Fortiende *obstupescens* (*prodigia*), 4800. Þý lǽs wé ... lǽs Godes dóm forhtige, Bd. 4, 25 ; Sch. 503, 18. Þone forhti[g]endan (*tremendum*) dóm, 1, 27 ; Sch. 71, 5 : Wlfst. 239, 6. (2) *with gen. :*—Þ þú mé ne genýde tó áreccenne míne gescyndnysse ; God wát þ ic heora forhtige, Hml. S. 23 b, 361. [*O. Sax.* forhtôn. Cf. *Goth.* faurhtjan : *O. Sax.* forhtian : *O. H. Ger.* forhten *to fear.*] v. be-forhtian ; un-forhtigende.

**forhtiendlic.** *Substitute :* (1) *fearful, timorous :*—Þǽm forhtiendlicum *meticulosis* (a gloss on Ald. 76, 27, *meticulosis municipibus* ? Cf. An. Ox. 5271), Wrt. Voc. ii. 55, 22. (2) *fearful, terrible :*—Hé heora líchaman sealde tó swá swíðe forhtigendlican deáþe (*in tam pauenda morte*), Gr. D. 249, 8.

**forhtig;** *adj. Timid, abashed :*—Licgan hý ætforan þére cyrican dyre and forhtige ástrehte tó ðára gebróðra fótum þe út of cyrican gangen *ante fores oratorii prostratus jaceat . . . posito in terra capite prosternatur þronus omnium de oratorio exeuntium pedibus,* R. Ben. 70, 5. [*O. H. Ger.* forhtag(-ig) *adtonitus, timoratus, timens.* Cf. *N. E. D.* frighty.]

**forht-lic.** *Add :* (1) *fearful, feeling fear.* v. Dict. (2) *fearful, inspiring fear, terrible :*—Se stranga and se forhtlíca wind, Shrn. 81, 31. (3) ? :—Hý sculan nyttian lytlum and forhtlicum metum, Lch. ii. 30, 30. [*O. H. Ger.* forht-líh *formidabilis, metuendus, tremendus.*]

**forhtlíce.** *Add :*—Hé þá fǽringa forhtlíce ábréd . . . hé wæs forhtlíce geworden for þére ungewunelican gesihþe, Guth. 94, 20–23. Gif hwæt bið beboden ne forhtlíce (*trepide*), ne lætlíce bið geworden, R. Ben. I. 24, 17. [*O. H. Ger.* forhtlicho *timide. N. E. D.* frightly.] v. un-forhtlíce.

**forht-mód.** *Add :*—Ástrehte se Riggo hine tó eorðan mid eallum his geférum swíðe forhtigende . . . and gecyrdon tó heora hláforde forhtmóde (*trepidi*). v. Gr. D. 132, 8 *under* forht), Hml. Th. ii. 168, 21 : i. 504, 31. v. un-forhtmód.

**forhtnys.** *Add :*—Þá gefór on Iulianes mód unácumendlic forhtnys (*intolerabilis pavor*), Gr. D. 37, 26. Wárð his leóhtbora áfyrht . . . and mid þére forhtnæsse . . . slæp, Vis. Lfc. 38.

**forhtung.** *Add :*—Hé forgífð trúwan úre forhtunge, Hml. Th. ii. 124, 27. Mid forhtunge eges *metu timoris,* Scint. 228, 7.

**for-hwǽga.** *Substitute :* **for-hwega** (-hwæga) ; *adv. Where position is only vaguely determined, somewhere :*—Him gebúht þ hí behýddon þ heáfod on þám holte forhwega (-hwæga, *v. l.*) *it seemed to him that they hid the head in the wood somewhere,* Hml. S. 32, 141. Syle mé ðínne wíngeard, and ic þé óðerne finde on fyrlene forhwega (hwǽrhwega, *v. l. glossed* parum) *give me thy vineyard, and I will find thee another a little further off,* 18, 174. Hí álecgað hit ðonne forhwæga on ánre míle fram þém túne . . . Ðonne sceolon beón gesamnode ealle ðá menn . . . forhwæga on fíf mílum oððe on syx mílum fram þém feó, Ors. 1, 1 ; S. 20, 30–36. Cf. tó-hwega.

**for-hweorfan ;** *p.* -hwearf *To pass away, be destroyed :*—On þám dæge on þám fýrenan wylme sé forhwyrfeð (-hwirf-, *v. l.*) and eorðe and heofonas, Wlfst. 183, 4.

**for-hwirfan.** *Take here* **for-hwerfan, -hwyrfan,** *and add :*—Storm landu forhwyrfð *imber arua subuertit,* Scint. 51, 17. Hié hiera

andgit forhwirfað (-hwerf-, *v. l.*) mid hiera wóre láre, Past. 369, 18. Forhwerfed bið *vertitur,* Kent. Gl. 990. Se forhwierfeda (-hwirf-, *v. l.*) gewuna, Past. 79, 19. Ðæs forhwirfdan (-hwirfed, *v. l.*), 67, 16. Forhwierfdan, 435, 24. [*O. Sax.* far-hwerbian.]

**for-hwirfedlic ;** *adj. Perverse :*—Se forhwyrfda gást spræc forhwyrfedlice word, Bl. H. 31, 4.

**for-hwirfedness, e ;** *f. Perverseness :*—Ðú lufodest ealle forhwyrfednesse word, Nap. 24.

**for-hycgan.** *Take here* **for-hicgan** (*where dele* -higan), *and add :* p. -hogde, -hygde, -hygede ; *pp.* -hogd (v. for-hogd). I. *to despise, scorn a person or thing :*—Hé hine ne forhygeð (*contemnit*), Past. 407, 5. Nalle gié woenæ þte ic forhycgende (-hyccende, R. *accusaturus*) sié, is sé ðe forhycað (*accusat*) iúih, Jn. L. 5, 45. Þá þe heora sáula forhycgaþ for feós lufan, Bl. H. 63, 8. Þú ðæra gield forhogdest, Jul. 146. Þú forhygdest ðá gewítendan *sprevisti discedentes,* Ps. L. 118, 118. Ne forhogde hé hí, Past. 405, 32 : 421, 6 : 441, 29 : Jul. 620 : Gú. 713. Forhygde, Bl. Gl. Forhygede, Ps. Spl. 52, 7. Hí his gebod forhogdon, Past. 405, 31. Forhygedon, Hml. Th. i. 300, 19. Ne forhyge þú *non despicies,* Ps. L. 50, 19. Ne forhycgað wísdom, Bt. 16, 1 ; F. 50, 26. Þý lǽs hé forhycge heúnspédigran, Crä. 26. Forhyggean (-hycgean, *v. l.*) ðone geférscipe ðára synfulra, Past. 103, 14. Forhycgan *spernere,* Th. 68, 34. Forhyccan, Dóm. L. 90. Scylda héht forhycganne *vitia praecepit abscidenda,* Mt. p. 18, 5. Tó forhygcanne *contemnendum,* Jn. p. 7, 12. I a. *intrans. To feel or shew contempt :*—Forhegeþ *contempsit,* Kent. Gl. 631. Ðá uetelíce torhogdon *illi autem neglexerunt,* Mt. L. 22, 5. II. *to disdain, scorn to do something.* (1) *with a case :*—Ðás gerás tó wyrcanne and ðá ilco ne tó forhycganne (*omittere*), Lk. L. R. 11, 42 : Mt. L. 23, 23. (2) *with a clause :*—Ne forhogde (-hogode, *v. l.*) hé ðæt hé hit eft gecierde, Past. 99, 10. Hé forhogde ðæt hé hit gehiérde *audire contemsit,* 295, 16. Þ folc ne sceal forhycggan þ hí tó him hí geeáþmédon, Bl. H. 47, 30. (3) *with a case and a clause in apposition :*—Ic þæt forhicge, þæt ic sweord bere, B. 435 : Ph. 552. (4) *with infin. :*—Wíf forhycgeaþ (-hicgaþ, *v. l.*) heora bearn fédan *mulieres filios nutrire contemnunt,* Bd. 1, 27 ; Sch. 80, 11, 19. (5) *with dat. infin. :*—Þá þe cyrican forlǽtaþ, and forhycgaþ þá Godes dreámas tó gehérenne, Bl. H. 41, 35. Góddǽda hý forhogdun tó dónne, Cri. 1288. [*O. Sax.* far-huggian : *O. H. Ger.* ferhuggen *contemnere, spernere.*] Cf. for-hogian.

**for-hycgend, es ;** *m. A despiser, contemner :*—Forhycgend (-hicg-, *v. l.*) úra goda *contemtor diuum,* Bd. 1, 7 ; Sch. 21, 13. Forhicgend, R. Ben. I. 55, 13.

**for-hýdan.** *Substitute :*—Forhýddan oferhygde mé inwitgyrene *absconderunt superbi laqueos mihi,* Ps. Th. 139, 5. Hú nytt bið se forholena cræft oððe ðæt forhýde (-hýdde, *v. l.*) gold *sapientia abscondita et thesaurus invisus, quae utilitas in utrisque?,* Past. 377, 7. [v. *N. E. D.* forhide.]

**for-hylman.** *Substitute : To cover up, leave unperformed, neglect :*—Cwæð Dryhten : ' Ic bebeóde . . . þæt þeós onlícnes eorðan séce ' . . . Ne dorste þá forhylman Hælendes bebod wundor fore weorodum, ac of wealle áhleóp fyrngeweorc, An. 736. v. ofer-hylmend, *and* cf. for-gǽgan.

**for-hýnan, for-hýrdan.** v. for-hínan, for-hirdan.

**for-ildan.** *Take here* **for-yldan,** *and add :* (1) *to put off* action. (a) *with a case.* (a) *acc. :*—Se sláwa ágǽld and forielt (-ield, *v. l.*) ðæt weorc ðe him niéddearf wære tó wyrcanne *piger necessaria agere negligit,* Past. 283, 25. Ðætte mon ðurhteón mæge, ðæt hé ðæt ne forielde (-ilde, *v. l.*) *ne, quae praebenda sunt citius, sero praebeantur,* 323, 24 : 151, 1. Þ hé ǽnig þára góda forylde þe hé þý dæge gedón mihte, Bl. H. 213, 24. (β) *dat. :*—Oft dǽdlata dóme foreldit, *sigisðina gahuēm,* Txts. 152, 1. (b) *with (negative) clause :*—Ðý lǽs hí tó lange torelden ðæt hí hí ne anbinden *lest they too long delay to unbind them,* Past. 413, 9. (2) *to put off* time :—Þe lǽs wé foryldon þás álýfdon tíd, Bl. H. 95, 25. Ðæt hié ne forielden ðone tíman ðe hié teola on dón mægen, Past. 281, 19.

**for-ildu** (-o) ; *indecl. :* -ild, e ; *f. Great age :*—Samuhel and Danihel cildgeonge forealdedum mǽssepreóstum démdon. For þig . . . ǽlc, forylde (oferylde, *v. l.*) and iugoðe, healde his endebyrdnysse, R. Ben. 114, 11. v. ofer-ild(u).

**for-inlíce ;** *adv.* v. in-líce *in Dict. :* **for-inweardlíce.** v. inweardlíce *in Dict.*

**for-irman.** *Take here* **for-yrman,** *and add :*—Wǽron tó mænige foryrmde, Wlfst. 158, 11.

**for-irnan.** v. fore-irnan.

**for-irþ, e ;** *f. A headland* (heáfod-land, *q. v.*) *in the case of land whose furrows are at right angles to those of the adjacent land* [cf. *forera* (other Latin forms are *forertha,* -erda, -erdum, v. Philol. Trans. 1898, p. 530); *vox agrimensorum, apud quos in agrorum distinctionibus pars ea dicitur quae latus suum alterius fini, fronti seu capiti opponit,* Migne]:—Andlanges ðǽre fyrh tó ánum andheáfdum, tó ðáre forierðe, and seó forierð gǽð intó ðám lande, C. D. v. 153, 21. Andlang herpaðes oð ðǽre foryrðe úpende (cf. oð ðæs furlanges úpende, 418, 23): ð nne áðúne be ðáre foryrðe westeáge, iii. 419, 33. Of ðáre ác on ðá fo yrðe eástewerde, 449, 32. v. Seebohm, Vill. Comm. pp. 4–5.

for-lǽdan. Add:—*to lead so as to injure* or *destroy, bring to harm, destruction, &c., betray*:—Þer hē wæs ǽrost geswenced mid grimmum gefeohte and micelne dǽl his heres forlǽdde (*ubi acerba primum pugna fatigatus, deinde . . . non paruum numerum . . . disperdidit*, Bd. 1, 2), Chr. P. 5, 6. Hē mid firde fōr . . . and sōna þæs folces þone mǽstan dǽl fleónde forlǽdde and mid searwe þǽm cyninge on onwald gedyde *acceptum exercitum statim Cyro per proditionem tradit*, Ors. 1, 12 ; S. 52, 27. Hié forlǽddan tō þām lindplegan swǽse gesīðas and hyra sylfra feorh *they carried themselves and their comrades to a fight that was fatal to all*, B. 2039. Mē þās woruldsǽlða on þis dimme hol forlǽddon, Met. 2, 11. Ðæt mōd ongit hine selfne on swelcre frecennesse and on swelcne spild forlǽd *mens sese in praecipitium peruenisse deprehendit*, Past. 441, 27.

for-lǽdan (?) *to bring forth*:—Gelíc þām hláforde þe forlǽt (forþlǽt? cf. forðbringð (forðbereð, R.), Mt. 13, 52) of his goldhorde ealde þing and nīwe *similis est homini qui profert de thesauro suo noua et uetera*, Ælfc. T. Grn. 19, 29.

for-lǽran. Add:—Se feónd ðæt mōd ðurh ðā bisuiculan olicunga forlǽreð *animum per blandam inquietudinem exerit*, Past. 239, 16. Monigo hiá forlǽræþ *multos seducent*, Mt. 24, 5, 11. Far nū geond þǽra manna hūs ðe þū mid þīnum drýcræfte forlǽrdest, and gebíg hī eft tō heora Drihtne, Hml. Th. ii. 418, 16. þā beswāc deófol and forlǽrde his (*Adam's*) wíf, and heó hine, Wlfst. 9, 8. þæt nǽnig eów forlǽre (*seducat*), Mt. R. 24, 4. Hē (the devil) tiolode menn forlǽran, Past. 233, 22. [v. *N. E. D.* forlere.]

for-lǽt (?), es ; m. *A going away*:—Ferlēt *transitus*, Ps. Spl. 143, 14. [Cf. *Goth.* fra-lēts.]

for-lǽtan. Substitute: I. *to let, permit, allow, suffer.* (1) absolute:—Forlǽt nū þus *sine modo* (Mt. 3, 15), Wrt. Voc. ii. 71, 67. (2) with acc., *to suffer an object to be or act*:—Forlǽt hē eów, Mt. 21, 3. Forlēt (-leort, L.) hē hine *dimisit eum*, Mt. 3, 15. Swā hwā swā unþeáwas forlǽtan wile, Bt. 31, 1 ; F. 110, 25. (2 a) where a verb of motion may be supplied, *to let in* or *out, admit to, put under*:—Ūsic þe hē tō wuldre forlǽt, Cri. 30. Hí hí in forlēton, Jud. 170. þæt hē under ānes meaht ealle forlǽte, Crä. 23. (3) *to let an object do something.* (a) with acc. and infin. (α) where the action is prompted or caused by the subject:—For hwí forlǽtst (*permittis*) þū þā getemedon ǽtwindan fram þē?, Coll. M. 26, 7. Dryhten forlǽt þone deófol of dūne gehreúsan, áfylde hine under foldan sceátas, Sal. 457 : Gen. 1405 : An. 837. Forlēt ūre Drihten his fēt on þā eorþan besincan, Bl. H. 127, 22. Hē of earce forlēt fleógan culufran, Gen. 1450. Hē gār forlēt windan on þā wícingas, By. 321. Hī þurh sweordgripe sáwle forlǽtan of flǽschoman scyndan, Jul. 488 : B. 3167. (β) where the action is not so prompted:—Nǽfre ic lufan sibbe þíne forlǽte āsānian, Gū. 1147. Nǽfre forlǽteð Drihten tān furðor gangan, Ps. Th. 124, 3. þū mē ne forlēte ūt gangan, Bl. H. 249, 15 : 75, 26 : Sat. 545 : El. 598. Hē hine sylfne forlēt beón āhangenne, Bl. H. 33, 10. Forlǽt mē hý on wíta lǽdan, Wlfst. 256, 3. Forlǽtað (*sinite*), forlǽtað mē heofon geseón, Bl. H. 227, 21. Forlǽte hē hetenīða gehwone sīgan, Sch. 101. Hine God forlǽtan nele eþelíce lifian, Bl. H. 59, 29. (b) with clause:—Sum ǽ forlǽteð (*permittit*) þæt oððe bróðor oððe swustur . . . gemengde wǽron in gesynscype, Bd. 1, 27 ; Sch. 68, 23. II. *to allow to have, grant*:—Him rūm forlǽt rodora waldend, Met. 10, 30. II a. with prep. tō:—Hē him þæt gerūm tō forlǽt, Bt. 21 ; F. 74, 9. Þancien wē Drihtne þǽre āre þe hē on twelf mōnðum tō forlǽteð, Wlfst. 234, 15. Tō forlǽteþ, 262, 1. Hió mē hiora landes sumne dǽl in ēce ærieweardnesse tō forleortan, Cht. Th. 130, 10. þæt wæs gesiéne þæt seó eorþbeofung tācnade þā miclan blóddryncas þe hiere mon tō forlet *ut merito dicatur tantum humanum sanguinem susceptura terra tremuisse*, Ors. 4, 2 ; S. 162, 3. Siððan him se wísdóm tō forlǽten wæs *concessa sapientia*, Past. 393, 17 : Bl. H. 37, 35. III. *to leave.* (1) of deceased persons, *to have remainder*:—Ðā deád wæs and ne forleort sēd ī teám . . . Ðā seofona ne forleorton sēd, Mk. L. R. 12, 21, 22. (2) *to leave property at death to successors, bequeath*:—Ūrum cildum . . . ðe wē eft tiochiað ūre ierfe tō te forlǽtanne, Past. 391, 29. (2 a) figurative:—Ic forlǽte mīne sibbe tō eúw, Bl. H. 157, 28. Forlēto (-lētto, L.), Jn. R. 14, 27. (3) *to leave, abstain from taking, consuming, &c.*:—Hié forleortun ðā tō lāfe wērun lytlingum heara, Ps. Srt. 16, 14. Forlǽt ðonne ān ðín lāc beforan ðǽm weófude, Past. 349, 11. Ne bið forlǽten stān ofer stān, Bl. H. 77, 36 : Ll. Th. i. 172, 16. (3 a) with complementary word or phrase giving condition in which a thing is allowed to remain:—Ne forlǽte ic þē ǽrna léase *I will not leave thee unhonoured*, Gen. 2256: Bl. H. 131, 21. Ne forlǽt ūre Drihten þysne middangeard būton lāreówum, 71, 26. Hié hié sylfe forlēton on ídelnesse, 159, 19. Hī for heora slǽwþe forlēton unwriten þāra monna þeáwas, Bt. 18, 3 ; F. 64, 34. Ne forlǽt þū mīne sáule mid hellwarum, Bl. H. 87, 32. Hē nolde þone cwealmcuman cwicne forlǽtan, B. 792. Būton mēde forlǽten (-an, MS.) *left unrewarded*, Hml. S. 30, 20. ¶ with infin.:—Āhōfon hié hine of þām wíte, forlēton mē þā hilderincas standan (*they left me standing*), Kr. 61. Ne forlǽt þū ūs on wītum wunian, Bl. H. 87, 14. IV. *to leave alone, leave undone, abstain*

from. (1) *to abstain from doing, not to attempt.* (a) *with acc.*:—For hwon forlēte þū líf þæt scýne?, Cri. 1470. Ealle þā gōde laga hē forlǽt þe hē ūs ǽr behēt *he made none of the good laws he had promised us*, Chr. 1093; P. 227, 29. Ðā hē þis leoð āsungen hæfde, þā forlēt hē þone sang *he sang no more*, Bt. 24, 1 ; F. 80, 4. Gē forlēton (-leortun, L.) þā þing þe synt hefegran þǽre ǽ . . . þās þing hyt gebyrede þ̄ gē dydon, and þā ōðre ne forlēton (*omittere*), Mt. 23, 23. Hié hit (*translating books*) forlēton, Past. 5, 24. Hwæt hī gōdes forlēton ðæs ðe hí dōn meahton, 403, 28. Hwý wēnst þū þ̄ hī forlǽtan ðā cræftas and folgian ðām unþeáwum, Bt. 36, 6 ; F. 180, 28. þū scealt druncen fleón and þā oferfylle ealle forlǽtan, Dóm. L. 32, 75. (b) *with (negative) clause*:—Hē forlǽt ðæt hē hwæthwugu gōdes ne dō *he never attempts to do any good*, Past. 287, 1. Hí forlǽtað ðæt hié yfel ne dóð (cf. hí libbað unsceaðfullíce, 7), 263, 2. Forlǽt ðæt ðū næbbe tō ōðres mannes gōde andan *refrain from envying another man's good*, Prov. K. 33. (c) *with dat. infin.*:—Ðæt hié ne forlǽten tō wilnianne ðāra ðe Godes sién *ut appetere quae Dei sunt non omittant*, Past. 393, 28. (2) *to leave uncared for, neglect*:—Sē þe cræft his forlǽt, hē byþ forlǽten fram þām cræfte, Coll. M. 31, 33. þā þe heora sylfra rǽd forlǽtaþ, Bl. H. 103, 17. þā þe heora cyrican forlǽtaþ, 41, 35. Forlǽtan æcer *squalidus ager*, Wrt. Voc. i. 37, 55. Mynstru forlǽtene *coenobia destituta*, Angl. xiii. 366, 13. (3) *to leave out, omit from narration or enumeration*:—Ic forlǽte *praetereo* (*plura*), An. Ox. 3348. Gif wē on þǽm syx wucan forlǽtaþ þā syx Sunnandagas, Bl. H. 35, 23. Ic sceall ealle forlǽtan (*praetereo*) þā þe of Cathma gesǽde syndon, Ors. 1, 8 ; S. 42, 15. Nys tō forelǽtenne þæt wundor, Guth. 76, 9. Ne sí forlǽten *ne excipiatur*, An. Ox. 4571. Forlǽtenne *omissa*, 317. Nānum forlǽtenum tācne *nullo excepto signo*, Angl. xiii. 383, 255 : 407, 597. (4) *not to take, to spare*:—Se scearpa deáð þe ne forlēt ne rīce menn ne heáne, seó hine genam, Chr. 1086; P. 219, 1. Nāne forlēt deáþ, Met. 10, 66. Nele hió forlǽtan libbendes wuht, nimð eall þæt hió fint, 13, 33. (5) *to leave unused, not to use*:—þā þe mē ryhtoste þūhton ic hēron gegaderode, and þā ōþre forlǽt, Ll. Th. i. 58, 27. Niótað þæs ōðres ealles, forlǽtað þone ǽnne beám, Gen. 235. Hē ðæs āliéfdan nānwuht nolde forlǽtan, ac his swīðe ungemetlīce breác, Past. 339, 5. Leáfe tō forlǽtene *ueniam dimittendi*, Angl. xiii. 406, 594. V. *to leave so that an object may be dealt with by another, leave*:—Hē ne forlēt tō gýmeleáste his apostol, Hml. Th. i. 58, 33. þ̄ hē þē ne forlǽte lāðum tō handa, Dóm. L. 30, 29. VI. *to leave, quit.* (1) *to leave a person.* (a) *to leave the presence* or *society of*:—Ne þǽr mon his feónd findeð, ne his freúnd forlǽteþ, Bl. H. 105, 1. Ðā forlēt (-leort, L. *reliquit*) se deófol hine, Mt. 4, 11 : Bl. H. 27, 21. Hē hié grētte and hié swā forlēt, 247, 36. His þegnas him ne mihton leng mid gewunian, ac tihodon hine tō forlǽtanne, Bt. 38, 1 ; F. 194, 29. (b) *to leave a person to whom allegiance, devotion, &c. is due, to abandon, forsake*:—Gif þū þā godu forlǽtest, Jul. 122. Hē forlǽt þone fæder þe hine gesceóp, Met. 17, 24. Norðhymbra witan forlēton Hyryc, Chr. 948; P. 112, 33. (c) *to leave unprotected, destitute, &c., desert, abandon*:—For hwon forlǽtest þū ūs *cur nos deseris?*, Bl. H. 225, 16 : An. 1415. Flýhð hē and forlǽt (-lettas, L. *dimittet*) þā sceáp, Jn. 10, 12. Hē ūs nō forlǽteð, ah líf syleð, Sat. 292. Hē ðē gefultumade þæt ic þín gewit ne forlēt, Bt. 5, 3 ; F. 14, 9. Tō hwí forlēte (-leorte, L., -lētes, R. *dereliquisti*) mē, Mt. 27, 46. Forleortes, Mk. L. 15, 34· Forleorte, Ps. Srt. 21, 2. Hē forlēt his man, Chr. 1090; P. 225, 32. Godríc þone gōdan (*Byrhtnoth*) forlēt, By. 187. Gif hine seó mǽgð forlǽte, and him fore gyldan nellen, Ll. Th. i. 248, 5 : 164, 11. Heó nā sí forlǽten fultumum *non destituatur auxiliis*, Angl. xiii. 381, 230. (c a) the subject a thing:—Ne forlēton mec deserant, Kent. Gl. 28. (d) *to leave, give up the society of, break the ties binding to*:—Forlǽt se man fæder and mōder, Gen. 2, 24. Gif hwelc wíf forlǽt hiere ceorl, Past. 405, 11. Hē his brýde forlēt, Hml. Th. i. 58, 17. Wē forlēton ūre cneórisne, Bl. H. 229, 21. Gif preóst cwenan forlǽte, and ōðre nime, Ll. Th. ii. 296, 1 : 300, 23 : i. 316, 10. (2) *to leave a place, office, position.* (a) *to cease to occupy*:—Se here forlēt þæt geweorc . . . and ofer sǽ gewiton, Chr. 885; P. 78, 13. Eádsige forlēt þet biscoprīce, 1043; P. 163, 26. Hē forlǽt þone woroldfolgaþ, and gewāt tō Sancte Hilarie, Bl. H. 215, 36 : Hml. S. 27, 192. Gif preóst þā circan forlǽte þe hē tō gehādod wæs, Ll. Th. ii. 294, 15. Hys clauster forlǽtende (*deserens*) . . . þ̄ hūs forlǽtende (*derelinquens*), Angl. xiii. 398, 467. ¶ *to leave the world, die*:—Seó sáwl forlǽteð þās lǽnan dreámas, Cri. 1668. Hē forlēt líf þis lǽne, Chr. 975; P. 118, 28. þās world forlǽtan and Críst geseón, Bl. H. 225, 20. (b) *to cease to attack* or *to defend, to abandon*:—Hí forlēton (-lǽttan) ðone weal and heora byrig, and flugan āweg, Bd. 1, 12 ; Sch. 35, 4. Hié forlēton (*abandoned the siege of*) þā burg, Chr. 921; P. 101, 10. (c) *to give up possession of*:—Manige men forlēton heora land and fērdon ofer sǽ, and se cyng geaf heora land þām þe him holde wǽron, Chr. 1087; P. 225, 5. (3) *to leave a thing.* (a) *to abandon* property:—Wē forlēton (-leorton (-un, R.), L.) ealle þingc, and folgodon þē, Mt. 19, 27. (b) *to leave a subject of talk, not to continue*:—Ðū ā ymb sticce fēhst on ðā ilcan sprǽce þe þū ǽr sprǽce, and forlǽtst eft ðæt ǽr ðū hí geendod hæbbe, Bt. 35, 5 ; F.

164. 15. **VI a.** with complementary words indicating place or condition of object quitted :—Hit forlǣteđ þás gesceaft mid cele ofercumen, Met. 20, 157. Hí hí forlǣtaþ on þám mǣstan sáre, Bt. 7, 1 ; F. 16, 13. Þǣr hé hine ǣr forlét, B. 2787. Hé his folme forlét tó lífwraðe lǽst weardian, 970. Se storm þ scyp forlét betwyh þá ýþa on sídan licgende, Bd. 5, 9 ; Sch. 595, 14. Hé nǽnigne forlét bendum fæstne, An. 1039 : Chr. 937 ; P. 108, 23. Þone man þe hié ǣr deádne forléton, Bl. H. 219, 1. **VII.** *to leave off, give up.* (1) *to abandon* a habit, pursuit, course of life. (a) *with acc.* :—Forlǣtaþ hí þá sibbe þe hí nú healdaþ, Bt. 21 ; F. 74, 33, 35. Đá þú đíne fæstrǣdnesse forléte, 5, 1 ; F. 8, 30. Heó weoruldhád forleort (-lét, *v. l.*), Bd. 4, 23 ; Sch. 464, 14. Forlǣtaþ *relinquite (infantiam)*, Kent. Gl. 288. Is đearf đæt hié forlǣten đæt dysig hiera slǽwđe, Past. 339, 17 : Bt. 39, 10 ; F. 228, 5. Hé geþóhte þ hé forléte þá ongin þéra bóccrǣfta, Gr. D. 96, 19. Unþeáwas forlǣtan, Dóm. L. 32, 79. (b) *with dat. infin.* :—Þá þá hé eallunga forlét tó leornienne þá bóccrǣftas *relictis litterarum studiis*, Gr. D. 96, 17. (2) *to cease to regard* a law, *abandon* a faith, principle, &c. :—Sé đe forlét *qui deserit (disciplinam)*, Kent. Gl. 454 : 1049. Sé đe aþor forlǣt, ǣ and godspel, Hml. S. 25, 68. Sóna swá hit forlǣt sóþcwidas, swá folgiaþ hit leásspellunga, Bt. 5, 3 ; F. 14, 15. Forlǣteþ, El. 929. Þonne forlǣte wit ǣlce gesceádwísnesse and ǣlce rihtwísnesse, Bt. 40, 2 ; F. 236, 29. Gé forlǣtađ Godes bebod, and healdađ manna laga, Mk. 7, 8. Hé forlét his fulluht, Chr. 616 ; P. 23, 17. Hié forléton Drihtnes dómas, curon deófles cræft, Dan. 31. Forlǣten, Gen. 429. (3) *to cease* an action, a proceeding, *desist from, stop.* (a) *with acc.* :—Bútan þú forlǣte þá leásunga *unless you stop lying*, El. 689. Gehwæđer þ hǣmed forlǣte, Ll. Th. i. 38, 8. Đæt man ne forlǣte nǽne ǣscan, 232, 18 : 234, 25. Sóna byþ seó untrumnys forlǣten, Lch. i. 206, 26. (b) *with (negative) clause* :—Se vultor sceolde forlǣtan þ hé ne slát þá lifre Tyties, Bt. 35, 6 ; F. 170, 2. **VIII.** *to let go.* (1) *to cease to hold* or *to restrain* :—Siþþan mé (*a bow*) se waldend leopo forlǣteđ, ic beó lenge ǣr, Rä. 24, 7. Hé þ gewealdleþer forlǣt þára brídla, Bt. 21 ; F. 74, 31. Hé þá eá upp forlét an feówer hund eá and on lx *in quadringentos sexaginta alveos amnem comminuit*, Ors. 2, 4 ; S. 74, 1, 5. ' Ic bebeóde þ gé hine leng ne beran' . . . hié sóna hine forlǣtan, and hé gefeól, Bl. H. 189, 12. (1 a) *to let* blood :—Hý of his sídan swát forlǣtan, Cri. 1112. Forlǣt blód of earme, Lch. ii. 130, 6. Gif þu wille on snide blód forlǣtan, 148, 10. (1 b) *to relax efforts to do* something :—Sé đe for his slǣwđe forlǣtt his gódan weorc *qui mollis est et dissolutus est in opere suo*, Past. 445, 17. (2) *not to detain* :—Hié mon forlǣteþ tó mé, Bl. H. 71, 2. Forlétes, Mt. L. 21, 3. Hié þá ǣrendracan siþþan hám forléton, Ors. 4, 1 ; S. 154, 13. (3) *to release* a prisoner, captive, *restore* an exile :—Wallas gé ic forléto iów cynig Judéa, Mk. R. L. 15, 9. Hé forlét Phtolomeus (cf. hé weard gefangen, 22) tó his ríce, Ors. 5, 12 ; S. 242, 24. Hié hié út forléton *obsidionem solvisset*, 2, 6 ; S. 88, 9. Be đeófes onfenge and hine man þonne forlǣte, Ll. Th. 124, 15. Þæt gé mé of þyssum earfeđum úp forlǣten, El. 700. Mon ealle þá wrǣccan an cýþþe forlǣte *jussit omnes exsules patriae restitui*, Ors. 3, 11 ; S. 144, 15 : 4, 4 ; S. 164, 27. Utan gangan on þissum carcerne and hine út forlǣtan, Bl. H. 247, 2. (4) *to give up* property, power, &c., *relinquish* :—Hé forlét his ríce eall, Bt. 38, 1 ; F. 194, 26. Þæt wé ne lufian tó swýþe þ þ wé forlǣton sceolan, ne þæt ne forlǣtan tó swíþe þ wé écelíce habban sceolan, Bl. H. 111, 21. Þing ne getrêwe tó habbenne, ne êđe tó forlǣtanne, Bt. 7, 2 ; F. 18, 16. (5) *to remit, forgive* :—Swá swá wé forlǣtađ leahtras, Hy. 6, 23. Unriht þú forléte (*remissisti*) þínum folce, Ps. Th. 84, 2. Forlǣtna synna, Past. 163, 20. Forlétne, Ps. Srt. 31, 1. (6) *to lose* :—Hé Breotena ríce forlét *Brittaniam amisit*, Bd. 1, 3 ; Sch. 15, 25. Gemong þǣm gewinnum hé forlét his xv suna *amissis xv liberis*, Ors. 3, 11 ; S. 152, 26. Hé forlét his eágena gesyhđe, Gr. D. 77, 20. Þá handa álýse oþþe forlǣte, Ll. Th. i. 404, 10. Þeáh hé þæt ríce forléten, ne forleton hí nó þ gecyndelíce gód, Bt. 27, 3 ; F. 100, 6. Ne hí wǣstm forléton (*amitterent*), Angl. xiii. 369, 56. Gif hé hine underbæc besáwe, þ hé sceolde forlǣtan þæt wíf, Bt. 35, 6 ; F. 170, 10 : 11, 1 ; F. 32, 15. Wé habbađ ǣgđer forlǣten ge đone welan ge đone wísdóm, Past. 5, 17 : Bt. 35, 2 ; F. 156, 20. (7) *to put away, dismiss, lay aside* :—Swá hwylc man swá his wíf forlǣt (*dimiserit*), Mk. 10, 11. Forleites, Mt. p. 14, 16. Forlét Wǣfod amittit pallium*, Kent. Gl. 967. (8) *to send* forth words :—Hé egeslicne cwide ofer þæt folc forđ forlǣteđ, Cri. 1518. Þá ídlan word hé út forlét, Bl. H. 59, 19. Þǣr ic hearme word út forlǣte, Ps. Th. 140, 5. [*v. N. E. D.* forlet. *Goth.* fra-lêtan : *O. Sax. O. L. Ger.* far-lâtan : *O. H. Ger.* fer-lâz(z)an : *Icel.* fyrir-láta.] *v.* án-forlǣtan ; tó-, un-forlǣten.

**for-lǣtedness**, e ; *f. Intermission* :—Bútan forlǣtednesse (-end-?-en-?) *sine intermissione*, Gr. D. 227, 16. *v.* next two words.

**for-lǣtende**, *adj.* (*ptcpl.*) *To be relaxed* or *remitted* :—Tiro and Sidone forlétendre biđ þonne eów *Tyro et Sidone remissius erit quam vobis*, Mt. R. 11, 22.

**for-lǣtenness.** *Add* :—Synna forlǣtennysse, Hml. A. 158, 155. *v.* forþ-, tó-forlǣtenness.

**for-lǣtere**, es ; *m. One who leaves, forsakes,* &c. :—Forlétrum *relinquentibus*, Lk. p. 9, 17.

**for-lǣting**, e ; *f.* **I.** *leaving, quitting.* *v.* for-lǣtan, **VI.** 2 a :—Gif þú gesihst beón fleón on húse þínum forlǣtincge getácnaþ, Lch. iii. 214, 9. **II.** *leaving off, intermission* :—Búton forlǣtincge *sine intermissione*, Angl. xiii. 439, 1049 : 444, 1121.

**for-lǣtnes.** *Take instances from* **for-lǣtennes** *in Dict., and add* : **I.** *abandonment, desolation.* *v.* for-lǣtan ; **IV.** 2 :—Forlétnis desolatio*, Lk. R. L. 21, 20. **II.** *neglect.* Cf. for-lǣtan ; **IV.** 2, **VI.** 1 c :—Of aldra in forlétnisse *de parentum inspretione*, Mk. p. 3, 15. **III.** *abandonment* of principle, &c. *v.* for-lǣtan ; **VII.** 2 :—Seó anfengnes mêdsceata on dómum ys sóđfæstnesse forlǣtnes, Ll. Lbmn. 476, 31. **IV.** *cessation, intermission.* *v.* for-lǣtan ; **VII.** 3 :—þ hié wacedon búton forlǣtnesse, Bl. H. 145, 32. **V.** *relaxation of effort, remissness.* *v.* for-lǣtan ; **VIII.** 1 b :—Sió forlǣtnes đæs gódan weorces *ipsa operandi remissio*, Past. 445, 14. **VI.** *remission, pardon.* *v.* for-lǣtan ; **VIII.** 5 :—Wé sceolan gelýfan synna forlǣtnessa and líchoman ǣristes, Bl. H. 111, 10. Tó forlétnise *ad ueniam*, Rtl. 103, 19. In forlétnisæ (*remissionem*) synna, Mt. L. R. 26, 28. Forlétnesse, Bl. H. 35, 36 : 129, 28. **VII.** *loss.* *v.* for-lǣtan ; **VIII.** 6 :—Æfter þára eágena forlǣtnysse, Hml. S. 23 b, 7. **VIII.** *putting away, dismission, divorce* :—Of boec forlétnise *de libello repudii*, Mt. p. 18, 8. *v.* án-, betweohn-forlǣtness.

**for-lange** (? for lange) ; *adv. Long ago* :—Forlonge (*olim*) þte heá gehreáwsadon, Lk. L. R. 10, 13. Forelong, Mt. L. 11, 21. Forelonge *dudum*, Rtl. 194, 1.

**for-leán** *to reprehend strongly* :—Þú scealt úpáhyfeđnysse forleón, Angl. xii. 517, 22.

**for-lecgan** *to cover up* :—Wiđ foredum lime, lege þás sealfe on þ forode lim, and forlege mid elmrinde, Lch. ii. 66, 22. [*O. H. Ger.* fer-legen *to cover up* the face with a mask.]

**for-legen.** *Add*: *guilty of fornication, adulterous* :—Cneórisse yfel and forlegene (*adultera*), Mt. R. 12, 39. Eallswá scyldig byđ geteald se forlegena cniht swá þ forlegene mǣden, Hml. A. 20, 152. For mé earmlicre forlegenre, Hml. S. 23 b, 598. Fúle forlegene hóringas, Wlfst. 165, 33. ¶ weak form used substantively :—þá forlegnan (-legenan, *v. l.*) mid þám forlegenan (-um, *v. l.*) *luxuriosi cum luxuriosis*, Gr. D. 316, 6. Æwbrecan and đá fúlan forlegenan, Wlfst. 26, 16. [*v. N. E. D.* forlain. *O. H. Ger.* fer-legan *adulter.*] *v.* dirne-forlegen.

**for-legenes**, -legen[n]es. *Add* :—For intingan dyrnre forlegenesse (dyrneforlegenesse, *v. l.*), Bd. 4, 5 ; Sch. 379, 8. Ásliden in forlegenesse, Gr. D. 241, 15. Unálýfedre forlegenesse, Bd. 2, 5 ; Sch. 133, 9. Þurh dyrne forlegennesse (-legenesse, *v. l.*), 1, 27 ; Sch. 87, 22. Cf. for-ligenes.

**for-legere.** *Dele* : **for-leges.** *v.* next word.

**for-legis.** *Add* : -leges, -liges, -lís *an adulteress, a prostitute* :—Forliges *prostituta*, Wrt. Voc. ii. 81, 5. Forlegese *scorti*, Kent. Gl. 162. Forlegisse *mecham*, Wrt. Voc. ii. 92, 38 : 55, 13 : Past. 353, '19. Eówer nebb sint swǣ scamleáse swǣ đára wífa đe bióđ forelegissa, 206, 9. Forlegesum *prostitutis*, Wrt. Voc. ii. 87, 23. Forlísum, An. Ox. 8, 324. Cf. for-legniss.

**forlegis-gleng** *the attire of a harlot* (Prov. 7, 10) :—Of forlísglenge *ornatu meretricio*, An. Ox. 8, 361.

**forlegis-wíf**, es ; *n. A prostitute* :—Ic þe háte lǣdan tó forlegeswífa húse, Shrn. 154, 21. *v.* forliger-wíf.

**for-legness**, e ; *f. Fornication* :—Þæt yfel forlegness *fornicationis vitium*, Past. 401, 25 : Bd. 2, 5 ; Sch. 133, 9. Cf. for-legen[n]es.

**for-legniss**, e ; *f. A harlot* :—Forlegnisse *meretrices*, Mt. R. 21, 31. Forlǣgenisse, 32. Eówer nebb sint suá scamleás suá đára wífa forelegnissa *frons mulieris meretricis facta est tibi*, Past. 207, 9. Cf. for-legis.

**for-legor.** *v.* for-liger : **for-legystre.** *Dele.*

**for-leógan.** *Dele* : ' *To lie greatly,*' *and add* : *to accuse falsely, bear false witness against* :—Ic nelle secgan unsóđ on mé sylfe, þ ic wiđ þé ne syngie, gif ic mé sylfe forleóðe, Hml. S. 12, 196. Se cniht hine sylfne forleáh, 208. Đá sǣdon þá hýredmen þ hit sóđ wǣre, and ealle mid đâe Eugenian forlugan, 2, 222. Hí fundon leáse gewitan þe forlugon Naboð (*cf. viri diabolici dixerunt contra eum testimonium*, 1 Kings 21, 13), 18, 196. *v.* for-logen.

**for-leórness**, e ; *f. Transgression* :—Foreliórnesse *praevaricationes*, Ps. Sp. 100, 3. *v.* ofer-leórness.

**for-leorning**, e ; *f. Learning wrongly, error* :—Þæs leásung and forleornung cymþ tó him þe hé hine sylfne dêþ tó þon þe hé nis *therefore will falsehood and error come to him that he makes himself out to be that which he is not*, Bl. H. 183, 34. [Cf. *Ger.* ver-lernung.] Cf. for-lǣran.

**for-leósan.** *Add* : **I.** *to lose.* (1) *with acc.* :—Ne forleósaþ hí þone willan, Bt. 36, 7 ; F. 184, 27. Titus sǣde þæt hé þone dæg forlure þe hé nóht tó góde on ne gedyde, Chr. 81 ; P. 8, 8. (2) *with dat.* (*inst.*) :—Hé nǣfre forlýst đám leánum, Bt. 36, 7 ; F. 184, 25. Forliést, 37, 2 ; F. 188, 25. Hé dóme forleás, B. 1470. Þæt hé elne forleóse, Gn. Ex. 188. Ic þám leánum forloren hæfde, B. 2145. Sý his spǣce forloren

*his case shall be lost*, Ll. Th. i. 294, 19. **II.** *to destroy.* (1) physical:—Hié gesworen hæfdon ðæt hié óþer forleósan woldon, oþþe hira líf, oþþe þæs cyninges, Ors. 2, 3; S. 68, 28. (2) spiritual, moral, &c.:—Þurh áðbrycas forloren, Wlfst. 164, 8. Hwæt wille ic ðisum forlorenum wiðersacan geandwyrdan, Hml. Th. i. 378, 11. [v. *N. E. D.* forlese. *Goth.* fra-liusan: *O. Frs.* for-liasa: *O. Sax.* far-liosan: *O. H. Ger.* fer-liosan.]

**for-licgan.** Add: **I.** *intrans. To lie in an improper manner or place.* (1) *to lie unnoticed, to be neglected:*—Þý læs seó mynugung forlæge, Ll. Th. i. 234, 29. (2) *of illicit intercourse, to commit fornication with* (*wiþ* or *mid*):—Forligeð *meretricabitur*, Wrt. Voc. ii. 57, 66. Gif gehádod man forlicge, Ll. Th. i. 168, 5. Gif hwá wið nunnan forlicge, ii. 300, 20. Yfel æwbryce bið þ æwfæst man mid æmtige forlicge, and mycele wyrse wið óðres æwe, i. 404, 22. Gif twégen gebróðra wið án wíf forlicgan, 168, 19. Forlicgean *fornicari,* Scint. 89, 2. **II.** *to injure by lying.* (1) *to lie with a person, defile by illicit intercourse:*—Þú on læces hiwe hí forlicgan woldest, Hml. S. 2, 203. Forlycgan, 186. Wæs forlegen *stupratur,* An. Ox. 4307. Be twelfhyndes monnes wífe forlegenum. Gif mon hæme mid twelfhyndes monnes wífe, Ll. Th. i. 68, 8. ¶ forlegen beón, wesan, weorþan *fornicari:*—Thamar ys forlegen *fornicata est Thamar,* Gen. 38, 24. Se bið forlegen *fornicatur,* Past. 465, 2. Hit wyrð forlegen *ad fornicationem ducitur,* 463, 29. Gif se líchoma forlegau weorðed unrihthæmede, Met. 18, 9. Ðú eart forlegen wið manigne cópenere *tu fornicata es cum amatoribus multis,* Past. 405, 13. Be ðæm forlegenan wífe *de fornicante muliere,* 15. Hí wæron forlegene *fornicatae sunt,* 403, 34. (2) *reflexive* (cf. *Icel.* fyrirliggja sér *to fall* (of a woman):—Be þám wífmen þe hig forligð (*fornicatur*), Ll. Th. ii. 180, 2. Gif mæden hí sylfe forligð, Hml. A. 34, 247. Ðú forlæge ðé *fornicata es,* Past. 463, 26. Hé hine forlæg wið ðá Madianiten, 353, 19. Gé eów forlægon *fornicata es,* 463, 33. Hine mon sæde þæt heó hié wið forlæge, Ors. 126, 26. Þæt hí hí forlægen, Past. 403, 33. **III.** *to lie in the way of, to defend.* Cf. for-standan:—Gif hwá þeóf friðige oððe forena forlicge, Cht. E. 230, 33. [v. *N. E. D.* forlie. *O. H. Ger.* fer-ligan *moechari.*] v. for-legen.

**for-licgend,** es; *m. A fornicator:*—Ælc forlicgend (*fornicator*) oððe unclæne, Scint. 98, 10. Gewemmend and forlicgend *mechus,* Wrt. Voc. ii. 57, 58.

**for-liden;** *adj. Much-travelled, that has travelled far and wide:*—Se ilce Nathan wæs forliðen (cf. gelyðen, 26, 13), þæt hé wæs gefaren fram ælcen lande tó óðren, ðæm sæ tó sæ, swá þæt hé hæfde ealle eorðe gemæren þurhfaren, St. A. ix. 11.

**for-liden** *shipwrecked.* v. for-líþan.

**for-lidennes** (-líþ-). Add:—Forliþennysse *naufragio,* An. Ox. 629. Þ ic forlidennesse gefare, Ap. Th. 12, 10. Forlidenesse ic þolie, Coll. M. 27, 1. Forlyðenisse, An. Ox. 56, 342. v. for-líþan.

**for-ligenes.** Add:—For intingan dyrnre forlignesse (-lige-, *v. l.*), Bd. 4, 5; Sch. 379, 8. Ðurh dyrne forligenesse, I, 27; Sch. 87, 20. v. for-legenes.

**for-liger;** *n.* Add: , -legor, -lír; *pl.* -ligr:—Forligr *fornicatio,* Scint. 86, 17. Forligre[s?] *fornicationis,* 57, 4. Forligres, 88, 5. Forligeris *prostibuli, fornicationis,* Hpt. Gl. 435, 42. Forligeres, hæmedes, An. Ox. 4219. Fúles forligeres *lupanaris incesti,* 4221. Forligres, 2, 307. Forlegores wíf, Mart. H. 140, 19 note. Forligere stupro, An. Ox. 5043. Beswícan mid forligre, Hml. S. 2, 202. Féran on forlygre *to commit fornication,* 217. Forleigere (-legere, R.) *fornicatione,* Jn. L. 8, 41. Hwá þæt forligr gefremode, Hml. Th. ii. 492, 1. Num. 14, 33. Ðínre módor mánfullan forligr (*fornicationes,* 2 Kings 9, 22), Hml. S. 18, 332. Þurh sibblegeru and ðurh mistlice forligru, Wlfst. 164, 6. Forligeru, 165, 32. [*O. H. Ger.* fer-ligari (-leg-) *stuprum, fornicatio.*]

**for-liger;** *m.* Add: for-liger, e; *f.* (?): es; *n.* (?:—Gynd forligeru *per scorta,* Germ. 396, 236) *an adulteress* [The masc. (neut.?) is used of a woman]:—Forligt *adulter,* Ælfc. Gr. Z. 27, 14. Forliger *prostituta, meretrix,* Hpt. Gl. 475, 26. Heó næs dyrne forligr, Hml. S. 12, 227. Þ þu ne beó forliger (-ligr, -lír, *v. ll.*), ne þín æwe ne brece, Hml. A. 6, 155. Forligeres *prostitutae,* An. Ox. 5292. Forligre, 8, 363. Forligras cwylmiað mid forligrum, Hml. Th. i. 132, 22. Forlíra *luparum,* An. Ox. 7, 350. Forligrena, 8, 351. Forligrum *scortis,* 18, 18. Forligerum ł unrihthæmerum *adulteris,* Ps. L. 49, 18. Of þám dyrnum foriigrum gescyppan lybbende cild, Hml. A. 36, 307. Þá fúlan forligeras Sodomitiscra ðeóda, Hml. S. 13, 191. v. next word.

**for-liger;** *adj.* Add:—Forliger *mechus, cha, chum,* An. Ox. 18 b, 57: *adulter* (cf. later glossary:—*Adulter* forliʒer *vel* æwbræche, 95, 76), Wrt. Voc. i. 86, 68. Swá hwá swá his æwe forlæt and óðer genimð, hé bið þonne eáwbræce and eác forligr, Hml. Th. ii. 322, 34. (Perhaps the last two examples belong to previous word.)

**forliger-bed.** Add:—Ná on forligerbeddum and unclænnyssum *non in cubilibus et impudicitiis* (Rom. 13, 13), Hml. Th. i. 602, 4.

**forligeren;** *adj. Adulterous, whorish:*—Forlírinys *lupanaris* (*incesti piaculum*), An. Ox. 8, 232.

**forliger-hús,** es; *n. A brothel:*—Forligerhús *lupanar,* An. Ox. 5293. Tó forligerhúsum *ad prostibula,* 3328.

**forliger-lic;** *adj. Adulterous:*—Þære forligerlicere *adulterinae,* An. Ox. 4246. Forligerlicum *incesto,* 4249. Forligerlicum húsum *prostitutis,* 5174.

**forligerlíce;** *adv. Adulterously* (lit. and fig.):—Hé áwearp his rihtæwe and forligerlíce mánfulles sinscipes breác, Hml. Th. i. 478, 28. Ðær is þæs geleáfan mægðhad þe wurðað ænne sóðne God, and nele forligerlíce tó leásum hæðengylde búgan, ii. 566, 10.

**forliger-wíf** (-legor-), es; *n. A prostitute:*—Affra wæs forlegorwíf (forlegores wíf, *v. l.*), Mart. H. 140, 19. Þu eart *meretrix,* þæt is forlegorwíf (-legos-, *v. l.*), 23. v. forlegis-wíf.

**forlig-gang;** *m. Adultery:*—Forliggange *prostibuli* (the passage is '*prostibuli stupro*' (Ald. 40, 6), and the gloss, which is in the dative, seems to belong to *stupro*), Wrt. Voc. ii. 81, 6.

**for-lis.** v. for-legis.

**for-líþan;** *p.* -láþ, *pl.* -lidon, -liþon; *pp.* -liden, -liþen *To suffer shipwreck:*—Forliþan *naufragaverant,* An. Ox. 4490: 4621. v. for-liden *in Dict.*

**for-liðednes.** *Dele, and see* for-lidenness: **for-liþen.** v. for-liden.

**for-logen.** *Substitute:* for-logen; *adj.* (*ptcpl.*) *Guilty of bearing false witness:*—Syndan ðurh mistlice leásunga forloren and forlogen má þonne scolde, Wlfst. 164, 7: 130, 6. Fela sýn forsworene and swíðe forlogene, 129, 7: 268, 27. [*O. H. Ger.* fer-logan *levis: Ger.* ver-logen *given to lying.*] v. for-leógan.

**for-lor;** *n.* (not *m.*). Add:—Ðone lætteówdóm ðæs forlores *ducatum perditionis,* Past. 33, 9. Ðæt forlor hira frecennesse *perditionis suae discrimina,* 403, 13. Forlor *amisionem,* Wrt. Voc. ii. 100, 10. [*O. H. Ger.* ferlor *interitus, perditio.*]

**for-lorennes.** Add:—Deg forlorenisse (*perditionis*) heora, Txts. 413, 1. [*O. H. Ger.* fer-loran[n]issa *perditio, dispendium.*]

**for-lorian** *to lose:*—Gif forlorað ł losað ænne *si perdiderit unam,* Lk. L. 15, 4.

**for-losian** *to destroy:*—Tó forlosanne hine *ad perdendum eum,* Mt. L. 2, 13.

**for-lytel;** *adj. Very little:*—Byð forlytlu wynsumnes æt þám lýfe, Solil. H. 64, 20. Oþþe hit nán gód nis for eów selfe, oþþe forlytel gód wiþ eów tó metanne, Bt. 13; F. 40, 11. Forlytla sælþa oððe náne, 11, 2; F. 34, 30. [*Icel.* for-lítill.]

**forma.** Add:—In fruma ł in forma *in principio,* Jn. p. 3, 2. Sylle mé þín forme bearn *primogenitum filiorum tuorum dabis mihi,* Ex. 22, 29. [cf. *Icel.* for-mál; *n. a preamble;* for-máli; *m. a stipulation, condition;* for-mæli; *n. a formula.*]

**for-maneg.** Add:—Heora formænig foremære wearþ, R. Ben. 138, 26: 139, 19. Wénde þæs formonig man ... þæt ..., By. 239. Hí þone Hælend wrégdon formanegum yfelum dædum, and hé ne wearþ næfre náne wyrcende, Nic. 1, 18.

**for-meltan.** Add:—Formelteþ *liquitur,* Wrt. Voc. ii. 53, 22. Þ ís formealt on eallum þám mere and þ wæter weard áwend tó wynsumum baðe, Hml. S. 11, 198. v. un-formolten.

**for-mengan.** For 'Past. . . . Lye' *substitute:*—Hé mæg hine formengan tó ðæm ecum mid his willan *aeternis se conjungere per desiderium valet,* Past. 395, 4.

**formesta.** *Dele, and see* from.

**for-mete.** Add:—Hig lédon on his sacc fórmete *datis cibariis in viam,* Gen. 42, 25. Hé sealde him fórmete (or for mete?), hláf and wæter *tollens panem et utrem aquae imposuit scapulae ejus,* 21, 14. Sile him fórmete *dabis viaticum,* Deut. 15, 14. Sum óðer wegférend bær fórmete (mettas tó þicgenne in þám wege, *v. l.*) *alter viator sumendos cibos in itinere portabat,* Gr. D. 128, 10. Se ríca berð máre þonne hé behófige tó his fórmettum, Hml. Th. i. 254, 30.

**for-micel;** *adj. Very great:*—Is ðæt formicel scyld *quanta sint mala,* Past. 349, 17: Lch. iii. 436, 8. Þú miht witan þ þ gecynd is swíþe micel. Ys þ formicel gecynd þ ..., Bt. 34, 11; F. 150, 33. Hé áh þæs formycle þearfe þ ..., Ll. Th. i. 372, 13.

**for-miltan;** *p.* te *To cause to melt:*—Formylte *liquefactas,* An. Ox. 3976: 2, 278.

**for-mogian;** *p.* ode *To decay:*—Sume cwædon þ se líchama þe æne bið formogod and tó dúste gewend and wíde tósáwon, þ hé næfre eft tógædre ne cóme, Hml. S. 23, 375.

**for-molsnian.** Add:—Manna líchaman formolsniað tó dúste, Hml. S. 12, 28. Hire líchama ne mihte formolsnian on eorðan ... God mæg áræran ðá formolsnodon líchaman, 20, 108–110. Seó anlícnys tófeól tó heora fótum formolsnod, 2, 374. v. un-formolsnod.

**formolsniend-lic.** v. un-formolsniendlic.

**for-molsnung,** e; *f. Corruption:*—Formols[n]unge *corruptionem,* An. Ox. 1251.

**for-myrþrian.** Add: -myrþran:—Gif hwylc wíf hyre cild ámyrð innan hire ... oððe eft formyrþreþ (*occiderit*) siþþan hit forð cymð, Ll. Th. ii. 182, 25. Þær (at doom's day) swutelað ælc cild hwá hit formyrðrode, Wlfst. 137, 28.

**forn** *a trout.* Add: [*O. L. Ger.* forna *tructuria;* forna, forchna *tructa.*]: fŏrn, fŏrne. *l.* forn, forne. *v.* foran, forane.

**for-næman;** *p. de To consume :*—Þonne heó byð mid langre nearonesse þære gnornunge forht and geswænced and fornæmed *cum longa moeroris anxietudine fuerit formido consumta,* Gr. D. 245, 3. Cf. for-niman.

**for-neáh.** Add :—Forneáh þā mæstan, Ors. 2, 6 ; S. 88, 29. Fornæh ealle Weast-Centingas, Chr. 999 ; P. 133, 2. Forneh *circiter* (X *millia*), An. Ox. 3421. Hē forneáh hungre swealt, Ors. 4, 6 ; S. 170, 30. Seó dæd weard forneáh Rōmānum tō dæm mæstan hearme, 4, 13 ; S. 210, 10. Forneh *propemodum* (*satis cruenta*), An. Ox. 3788. Forneáh wyrs bereáfode, Ll. Lbmn. 475, 14. Forneáh oþ þā beorgas, Ors. 1, 1 ; S. 12, 1. Forneáh oð August, Chr. 1097 ; P. 233, 18. Forneáh mid ealle, Ors. 1, 10 ; S. 48, 7. Forneáh tō náuhte gedōn, Bt. 38, 3 ; F. 190, 19.

**for-neán.** *Take here instances under* forneáh *in Dict., and add:*—Forneán *propemodum,* i. *pene* (*inuestigabile*), An. Ox. 2674. Unsprecende forneán, Hml. S. 3, 481. Forneán þ ýtemeste īglond, Lch. iii. 432, 18. Forneán. *circiter,* i. *pene* (*quingentorum*), An. Ox. 3719 : Angl. vii. 36, 335. Wē swincan nellað nānþincg forneán, Hml. S. 28, 133. Fornión *paene,* Kent. Gl. 100.

**for-nefe.** *Dele.*

**for-neted** cli (fornaeticli, Ep. Gl., fornetiali, Erf. Gl.) *glosses* cyprinus, Wrt. Voc. ii. 105, 72. Cf. (?) forn *a trout.* v. Angl. xxi. 242.

**Fornétes folm.** Add :—Forneótes (*printed* -reotes) folm *manus færne,* Wrt. Voc. ii. 59, 40. v. Grmn. D. M. p. 240 (trans.).

**for-nēþan;** *p. de* (*reflex.*) *To risk one's life :*—Him leófre wæs þæt hié hie seolfe fornēðdon þonne hié þā iermþo leng þrowedon, Ors. 5, 3 ; S. 222, 1.

**for-nídan,** -nýdan, Wlfst. 158, 10. v. for-nýdan *in Dict.*

**for-niman.** Add: I. *to seize and hold.* (1) lit. of a criminal or captive :—Ic eom mid racenteágum fornumen, Hml. Th. i. 462, 31. Ðis wíf fornumen is (*deprehensa est*) in dernegiligro, Jn. R. 8, 4. (2) of that which affects the body or mind, e. g. disease or fear :—Se unclǽna gāst fornōm (*arripiebat*) hine, Lk. L. 8, 29. Ádl þe fornime þ þu ne beó hāl ne gesund, Ap. Th. 21, 16. Lǽg heó swilce mid slǽpe fornumen, Hml. Th. ii. 32, 29. Seó mōdor mid murcnunge wæs fornumen, Hml. S. 2, 105. Mid fyrhte fornumene, 3, 138 : Hml. Th. ii. 382, 3. Mið costungum fornumena *tormentis comprehensos,* Mt. L. 4, 24. (3) *to comprehend* :—Ðióstro hiá ne fornōmon (*compraehenderunt*), Jn. L. R. 1, 5. II. *to seize and take away, carry off, do away with :*—Fornymþ *aboleuerit,* Germ. 388, 30. Fornoom *intercepit,* Wrt. Voc. ii. 111, 18. Sume þā wyrta wæron mid sótum fortredene, sume hý wæron mid ealle fornumene (*direpta*), Gr. D. 23, 30. Freóriht fornumene, Wlfst. 158, 15. I a. of death :—Hine swā fǽrlice deáð fornam ðæt hē ungefullad forðfērde, Bl. H. 217, 19. Þæt hié deáð fornōme, Ors. 4, 6 ; S. 174, 26. III. *to take from a person, defraud :*—Ne fornime incer nōðer ōðer *nolite fraudare invicem,* Past. 399, 34. IV. *to seize and devour, consume :*—Fornumen *exesum vel commessum,* Wrt. Voc. ii. 144, 77. (1) of living creatures :—Hié (*the hippopotamuses*) þā men mid heora mūðe sliton and hié ealle fornāmon (*assumpserunt*), Nar. 11, 5. Hē (*Herod*) mid wyrmum fornumen gewāt of life *consumptus a vermibus exspiravit* (Acts 12, 23), Hml. Th. ii. 382, 34. Fornumene *exesa, consumpta,* An. Ox. 50, 39. (2) of the destruction wrought by a person (or weapon) :—Þin sweord fornymeð þine ða wiþerweardan, Guth. 78, 2. Hē ðā ōþre wered fornōm (-nām, -nam, *v. l.*) and fordīlgode *ceteras copias deleuit,* Bd. 2, 2 ; Sch. 121, 19. Fornōmun mec *consummauerant me,* Ps. Srt. 118, 87. (3) of natural agents, fire, disease, &c. :—Ragu and meós fornymð (*consumet*) ealle wæstmas, Deut. 28, 42. Fýres gecynd is þæt hit fornimð swā hwæt swā gehende bið, Hml. Th. i. 320, 27. Þ fýr ne fornam ne ān hǽr heora feaxes, Hml. S. 30, 464. Tō fornumene *voraturos* (*ardores*), An. Ox. 3979. God is fornymende fýr (*ignis consumens*), Hml. Th. i. 322, 9. Líchama mid hreófnisse fornumen (*devoratum*), Num. 12, 12. Úre hors wæron swíðe mid þurste fornumene, Nar. 12, 14. (4) of the passage of time :—On sāre and on geómrunga mín líf and míne geár syndon fornumene, Bl. H. 89, 15. [v. *N. E. D.* fornim. *Goth.* fra-niman : *O. Sax.* far-niman : *O. H. Ger.* fer-neman.]

**for-nirw(i)an** *to check the growth of* (?) :—Ðǽre .x. niht (*after Christmas*) gif wind byð, treów byóð fornerwede (*will come into leaf late?*), Lch. iii. 164, 24.

**for-nytlíce;** *adv. Very usefully:*—Fornytlíce (full nyttlíce, *v. l.*) *utiliter,* Gr. D. 174, 20.

**forod.** Add :—Gif hōhsino forod (-ad, 146, 4) sié, Lch. ii. 14, 27. Ðe mā ðe ænig fugel his flyhtes gewylt, gif his ōðer fiðere forod bið, Hml. Th. ii. 318, 29. Heora fæder feóll foredum swyran, 326, 7. Man hine foredum sceancum intō þære eá wurpe, Hml. S. 27, 58. v. sceanc-, un-forod.

**forod-fōt[e];** *adj. Having a broken foot, broken-footed :*—Se forud-fóta, Past. 66, 9 (note on p. 505).

**forod-lic.** v. un-forodlic.

**for-oft.** Add :—Se Hǽlend hēt hine sylfne mannes sunu foroft, Hml. A. 55, 118 : 58, 169 : 50, 26 : 71, 169. Þā unrihtwísan dēman beóð wyrsan þonne heregende here : here man mæg foroft befleón, ac þā dēman man ne mæg befleón, Ll. Lbmn. 475, 23.

**for-pǽran.** Add :—Hē ne mæg ūs ætbrēdan ūrne geleáfau ne þæt ēce líf, gif wē ūs sylfe mid āgenum willan ne forpǽrað, Hml. Th. i. 576, 12. Hī mid swicdōmum hī sylfe and ōðre forpǽrað, 514, 33. Sume swefna beóð of deófle tō sumum swicdōme, hū hē ðā sāwle forpǽre, Hml. S. 21, 407. Wē ne mōtan nā furðor embe þis (*the nature of God*) smeágan, gif wē nellað ūs sylfe forpǽran (*if we do not wish to work our own destruction*), 1, 71.

**for-pyndan.** *Substitute : To preclude, shut up, stop, prevent the action of :*—Críst onwrāh in Dauides dýrre mǽgan þæt is Euan scyld eal forpynded *Christ revealed that in the Virgin Mary Eve's guilt is closed,* Cri. 97.

**fōr-racu,** e ; *f. An itinerary :*—Fōrrake *itinerarium,* An. Ox. 7, 121. v. fōr-bōc.

**for-rǽdan.** Add :—Faerrēd (fer-, Ep.) *proscripsit,* Txts. 89, 1635. Forrǽdde, Wrt. Voc. ii. 68, 36. Iudēisc folc þurh deófles lāre hine forrǽdde (fordēmde *on margin of a later MS.*), Wlfst. 17, 19. Hē geþafode þæt hine man tō deáþe forrǽdde, 22, 20. [v. *N. E. D.* forrede. *O. L. Ger.* far-rādan *tradere* : *O. H. Ger.* fer-rātan *prodere, tradere, machinari.*]

**for-raþe.** Add : v. for-hraþe.

**for-rēceleásian;** *p. ode To neglect :*—Þā þe swā Godes bebodu forrēceleásiað, þ hig þisne egeslican cwide (*the sentence on the wicked at the resurrection*) gehýran sculon, Ll. Th. ii. 396, 21.

**for-repen.** v. for-hrepian : fōr-rídan *to ride and stop, cut off. l.* for-rídan : fōr-rídel. *l.* for-rídel.

**for-rotian.** Add :—Forrotað *putrescet,* Kent. Gl. 324. Fultum heora forrotað (*ueterescet*) on helle, Ps. Rdr. 48, 15. Ðā nýtenu forrotedon on heora meoxe, Hml. Th. i. 118, 15. Ne forrotige on brosnunge þeós hand, Hml. S. 26, 101. Deúh ðā bān for æfste forrotigen *putredo ossium invidia,* Past. 235, 14, 25. Ne þinne gehālgodan þu ne lætst forrotian ne forweorðan *nec dabis sanctum tuum videre corruptionem,* Ps. Th. 15, 10. Forrotad tōð *dens putridus,* Kent. Gl. 966. [v. *N. E. D.* forrot.]

**for-rotigendlic,** -rotodlic. v. un-forrotigendlic, -forrotodlic.

**for-rotodnes.** Add :—Forrotadnes *putredo,* Kent. Gl. 395. Forrotodness *caries,* An. Ox. 18 b, 17. Áfylled mid deádum bānum and forrotodnysse *plenus ossibus mortuorum et omni spurcitia* (Mt. 23, 27), Hml. Th. ii. 404, 19. Forrotodnesse *corruptionem,* Ps. L. 15, 10. Wyð þæs mūþes and gōmena fūlnysse and forrotudnysse, Lch. i. 264, 1.

**for-sacan.** Add :—Ic forsace *detracto,* ne forsace ic *non detracto,* Wrt. Voc. ii. 70, 1, 2. Forsooc *detractavit,* 106, 15. Forsóc, 25, 24. I. *to refuse to receive* what is offered :—Hē forsóc þā feáwa axan (cf. þ hē underfēnge þā gerýnu, 46), Hml. S. 12, 58. Mid ārwurðnysse underfōn þone þe hī ǽr forsócon, 26, 189. I a. *to decline to bear* :—Se lǽce wile ðæt se untruna his lǽceseax gefrēde ǽr hē hit geseó, for ðæm he wēnð, gif hē hit ǽr geseó, ðæt hē hit wille forsacan *ut secantem gladium sentiret aeger antequam cerneret, ne, si aute cerneret, sentire recusaret,* Past. 187, 11. II. *to refuse* to do what one is called upon to do :—Hē hine ful oft ǽr tō him cleopað, and hé forsæcð ðæt he him tō cume *quos prius diutius renuentes vocavit,* Past. 247, 19. Ðā ðā Landfranc crafede fæstnunge his gehērsumnesse, þā forsóc hē and sǽde þ hē hit nāhte tō dōnne, Chr. 1070 ; P. 206, 1. II a. *to refuse to give* what is due :—Forsæcð hē ðone wæstm his gāstes *ferre fructum spiritus recusat,* Past. 344, 13. III. *to refuse allegiance to, renounce, abandon, forsake :*—Hē deófol and his gemānan ealne forsæcð and him mid ealle fram býhð and Críst gecýst, Wlfst. 33, 8. Man geceás Harald tō cinge and forsóc Harðacnut, Chr. 1037 ; P. 160, 13. Þā butsecarlas hine forsócan, 1066 ; P. 197, 8. [v. *N. E. D.* forsake. *O. Sax. O. L. Ger.* far-sakan : *O. H. Ger.* fersahhan (ab-, de-) *negare,* (ab-)*renuntiare.*]

**forsǽðan** ? :—Of horgan wege tō forsǽðan pylle ; ðonne of forsǽðan pylle, C. D. iii. 245, 26.

**for-sǽtian;** *p. ode To catch by lying in ambush, take by surprise :*—Hē forsǽtade hié ðǽr ðǽr hié geþōht hæfdon þ hié hiene besǽtedon *insidiantes insidiis capit,* Or. 3, 11 ; S. 146, 10.

**for-sǽtnian.** v. for-setnian : for-sǽwennes (-sæw- ?). v. for-sewennes.

**for-sǽwestre** (-sæw- ?), an ; *f. A woman who despises :*—Forsǽwestre *contemtrix,* An. Ox. 4430.

**for-sāwend** (-saw-?), es ; *m. One who despises :*—Forsāwendrum *contemtibilibus,* i. *despicientibus,* An. Ox. 5438.

**for-sāwenlic** (-saw- ?) ; *adj. Contemptible :*—Forsāwenlicne *contemptibilem,* i. *despectibilem,* An. Ox. 470 : 935. Cf. for-sewenlic.

**for-sāwenness** (-saw- ?) ; *f. Contempt :*—On forsāwennesse *in abusione,* Ps. L. 30, 19. Cf. for-sewenness.

**forsc.** v. frosc : for-scæncednys. *l.* for-screncednys.

**for-scapung.** *Substitute : Mishap, calamity, destruction* (?) :—þ sió

hǽte nǽre for hiora synnum, ac sǽdon þ̄ hió wǽre for Fetontis forscapunge, Ors. 1, 7 ; S. 40, 9. Ungetíma and tibernessa ǽgðer ge on monslihtum ge on hungre ge on scipgebroce ge on mislicre forscapunge *diuturnitatem illius obsidionis, eversionis atrocitatem, caedem, captivitatemque*, 1, 11 ; S. 50, 20. Cf. scippan ; III.

**for-sceádan.** [*In* Past. 18, 4; S. 135, 16 forsceádne *translates dispersi.*] *Add :*—Gif hér ðegna hwelc ðyrelne kylle bróhte tó ðȳs burnan, béte hine georne, ðȳlǽs hé forsceáde scírost wætra, Past. 469, 11.

**for-sceamian.** *Substitute : To be* or *to make greatly ashamed :*—Forscamed *confusum*, Wrt. Voc. ii. 133, 48. **I.** *to be greatly ashamed.* (1) *with prep. :*—Be his synnum forsceamigean *de peccatis propriis erubescere*, Scint. 40, 9. (2) *with clause :*—Hé forscamað þ̄ [hé] hit ánan men andette, Angl. xii. 513, 29. Eall þæt hé forsceamode þæt hé ǽnigum men gecýdde, Wlfst. 138, 1. (3) *with infin. :*—Wē forsceamiað dǽdbóte dôn *erubescimus paenitentiam agere*, Scint. 49, 10: 19, 18. (4) *with dat. infin. :*—Ic forsceamige tó secganne míne ungeleáffulnesse, Hml. A. 201, 189. **II.** *to make ashamed* (used impersonally) :—Hié on him selfum ðá scylda dēmen and wreccæn, and hié forscamige ðæt hié eft suā dón (*augere culpas erubescant*), Past. 151, 17.

**for-sceamung, e ;** *f. Shame :*—Forscamung *pudor, verecundia*, Germ. 390, 120.

**for-sceap.** *Dele bracket :* for-sceóppan. *l.* for-sceoppan.

**fōr-sceótan.** *l.* for-sceótan *to rush in the way of, prevent, stop :*—Ðā Petrus wolde befrínan þone Hǽlend, þá forsceát se Hǽlend hine, Hml. Th. i. 510, 31. Ðēh sió dīc forscoten wǽre, C. D. iii. 168, 35. Cf. for-scīt[e], -scyttan, -scytlic.

**for-sceppan.** v. for-scippan : **for-scéta.** v. for-scīt[e] : **fōr-scip.** v. fore-scip.

**for-scippan** *to transform, change for the worse. Take here* for-sceoppan, -sceppan *and add :*—Forsceóp . . . þet líc . . . wurdon tó hundum, An. Ox. 26, 61. Þurh ðá ofermódignesse mǽre englas on heofonum wurdon forsceapene tó atelicum deófium, Wlfst. 145, 23. Scinnan forscepene *spirits from angels changed to devils*, Sat. 72. [v. *N. E. D.* forshape.]

**for-scīt[e] ?** *a flood-gate, sluice :*—Catracte forscéta (*cataracte aquam concludunt*), Bl. Gl. Cf. Icel. skeyti *a missile, and see* for-sceótan.

**for-screncan.** *Add :*—Iacôb is gecweden forscrencend, and sē bið unleás forscrencend þe mid gleáwnysse his flǽsclican leahtras and deófles tihtinge forscrencð, Hml. Th. i. 586, 24. Wīgstealla forscre[n]cen[u]e (*ad*) *propugnacula subruenda*, An. Ox. 865. ¶ *to cause to shrink up :*—Mid forscrencedre (-screcendre, MS.) *arida (manu)*, An. Ox. 4926. [*O. H. Ger.* fer-screncen *impedire.*]

**for-screncedness.** v. for-scǽncedness *in Dict. :* for-screcend. v. for-screncan.

**for-scrīfan.** *Dele* II, *and add :* **I.** *to condemn :*—Forscrifen (faerscribaen, -scrifen) *addictus* (cf. *addicit* fordémet, Wrt. Voc. ii. 4, 51 ; *addicti, damnati*, 77, 54), Txts. 37, 69. Ferscrifenum *abdictis*, Wrt. Voc. ii. 7, 59. **II.** *to blunt a weapon by a charm written on it* (cf. Eggjar ek deyfi mínna andskota, bítað þeim vápn an velir, Hávamál 58) :—Áwrîteð hē on his wǽpne wælnota heáp, bealwe bôcstáfas, bill forscrífeð mēces mǽrðo *he (an evil spirit) writes on his weapon a number of deadly marks, baleful letters, he blunts the blade, dulls the glaive's glory*, Sal. 162.

**for-scrīhan.** v. screón (?).

**for-scrincan.** *Add :*—Swā hwæt swā heó gesyhð, hyt forscrincð and gewîteþ, Lch. i. 242, 24. Hond forscriuncen *manus arida*, Mt. L. 12, 10.

**for-scúfan.** *Substitute : To drive away, drive to destruction :*—Werud (*the Israelites*) wæs wígblác, oð þæt wlance (*the Egyptians*) forsceáf mihtig engel, Exod. 204.

**for-scunian.** *Dele.*

**for-scyldig ;** *adj. Very guilty, wicked, flagitious :*—Mid forscildigum *sceleratis (manibus)*, An. Ox. 4707. On forscyldegodum (-scyldigum, *v. l.*) monnan, Hml. A. 58, 170.

**for-scyldigian.** *Add : To make* or *become* scyldig. **I.** v. scyldig ; I :—Þá þe wǽron forscyldegode oþþe þurh manslihte oððe þurh morðdǽda, Hml. S. 37, 113. Sume weorðað swicole . . . forscyldgode (-scildeg-, *v. l.*) on synnan, Wlfst. 82, 3. **II.** *to condemn.* v. scyldig ; **V** :—Se sceaða þe forscyldgod (-scyldgod, -scyldegod, *v. ll.*) hangode mid þām Hǽlende, Hml. S. 19, 164. Hé cýdde þ̄ heó forscylgod wǽre for hire crístendóme, 7, 89. Biþ ofspringc forscyldegod þurh forðfǽdera mándǽda, gif hē mid yfele him geefenlǽhð, Hml. Th. i. 114, 22. Fultuman ðám forðfarenum þe on wîtnunge sind, gif hí mid ealle forscyldgode ne beóð, ii. 356, 16. v. next word.

**for-scyldigod ;** *adj. (ptcpl.) Guilty, wicked, infamous :*—Fǽrlíce gewítt hē of ðissere worulde, nacod and forscyldigod, Hml. Th. i. 66, 13. Ðæt forscildgode wíf, Ap. Th. 26, 17. Sege, þū forscyldeguda, Hml. S. 2, 201. God gewrecð his forsewennysse on forscyldegodum mannum, Hml. A. 58, 170. Ðū forscyldegodesta cyningc, Hml. S. 25, 131.

**for-scytlic ;** *adj. That may be shut* or *bolted :*—þǽre forscytlican dura *vectifere valve*, Wrt. Voc. ii. 90, 55. Cf. next word.

**for-scyttan.** *Add : to shut off* or *out, preclude :*—Forscytte *praeueniet*, Ps. L. 58, 11. Forscyttende *obdensa*, i. *opponens*, Germ. 397, 480. [v. *N. E. D.* forshut.] Cf. for-sceótan.

**for-seárian.** *Add :* **I.** *intrans.* (1) *of material :*—þás cynehelmas nǽfre ne forseáriað, Hml. S. 34, 82. Ðȳ lǽs ðá treówu tó ðǽm forweóxen ðæt hié forseáreden (-oden, *v. l.*), Past. 293, 7. Þ̄ palmtwig tó eorþan áfyllan, and forseáredum him bēgen dǽlas forbrecan, Bl. H. 151, 16. Hē ðá forseáredon bān wecð of deáðe, Hml. S. 23, 431. (2) *of persons :*—Hī forseáriað swā filede, Ps. Th. 36, 2. Menn forseáriað for ôgan (v. Lk. 21, 26), Hml. Th. i. 610, 19. **II.** *trans. To cause to wither :*—Forseárigende sáwle his *arefaciens animam suam*, Scint. 110, 18.

**for-seáþ ?** :—Be eástan forseáðas, C. D. v. 173, 16.

**for-sécan.** *Add : to seek with hostile intent, to attack.* v. sécan ; III.

**for-secgan.** *Add : to say ill of a person, accuse (falsely) :*—Sum wer his wíf forsǽde, swā þ̄ heó sceolde hī sceandlíce forlicgan . . . Se cniht forsǽde hī bûtá. . . . 'Hwī woldest þū forsecgan unc unscyldige swā ?', Hml. S. 12, 181-198. Biddað leáse gewitan þ̄ hī Nabóð forsecgan ðus : 'Nabóð wyrigde God,' 18, 191. Þ̄ hig nellan nǽnne sacleásan man forsecgan, Ll. Th. i. 294, 5. Ne sceal nán acolitus forsecgan (*accusare*) nánne subdiácon, ne nán exorcista forsecgan nánne acolitum . . . mid nánre wrôhte (*accusatione*), ii. 166, 21. Heó begann hī tó wrǽgenne and wolde forsæcgan, Hml. S. 2, 184.

**for-segness.** v. for-sewenness.

**for-sellan ;** *pp.* -seald *To give up, sacrifice, lose :*—Gif hē nylle hȳ niman, hæbbe forseald þ̄ hē sealde *si ille eam accipere nolit, perdat pecuniam quam dederat*, Ll. Th. ii. 148, 31. [Cf. *O. L. Ger.* for-saldun *distractis (patrimoniis).*]

**for-sencan ;** *p.* te *To let fall, drop :*—Forsencð hē ðone wǽsðm his gǽstes *ferre fructum spiritus recusat*, Past. 347, 13. [v. *N. E. D.* forsench. *O. H. Ger.* fer-senchen : *Ger.* ver-senken.]

**for-sendan.** *Add :* **I.** *to send away from a country, exile, banish :*—þisne æþeling Cnut cyng hæfde forsend on Ungerland, Chr. 1057 ; P. 188, 9. **II.** *to throw away, cast away.* (1) *lit. :*—Hēt hē hym gebyndan ánne ancran on hys sweoran and hyne forsendan on sǽ, Shrn. 150, 20. (2) *fig. to send to destruction, destroy :*—Dauid miclum his ágnes herges pleh and monigne forsende, Past. 36, 8. [*O. H. Ger.* fersenten *amittere, relegare : Ger.* ver-senden.]

**for-seón.** *Add :* **I.** *to despise, hold in contempt* a person or thing :—Hē forsiehð (-sihð, *v. l.*) ðá ðe him underðiódde beóð *subjectos despicit*, Past. 111, 13 : Bt. 19 ; F. 68, 32. Forsiohð, Kent. Gl. 490 : 1090. Forsióð, 529 : 541. Forseó ðysse worulde wlence, gif ðū wille beón welig on ðínum móde *thou shalt despise this world's pride, if thou wilt be rich in thy mind*, Prov. K. 50. Gif ðæt mód ǽr ne forsáwe ðá ecan edleán, Past. 435, 3. Forseónde *spernendo*, R. Ben. I. 61, 11. Hē ne mæg gebyldgian ðæt hē for ðisse worlde sié forsewen (fore-, *v. l.*), Past. 216, 7. Forsáwen (-saw-?), Chr. 975 ; P. 120, 18 note. Hē sǽde þ̄ se abbot him heafde forsegon *he said that the abbot had treated him with contempt*, 1066 ; P. 199, 7. **II.** *to reject with scorn.* (1) *to reject* what is offered :—Hēr bræc se here þone frið, and forsáwon ǽlc frið þe Eádweard and his witan him budon, Chr. 911 ; P. 96, 4. Iugelera orþancscytæs forsáwe *magorum molimina ammitteret* (i. *respueret*), An. Ox. 4091. (2) *to reject* a state or condition :—Forsíþ contemsit (*matrimonii commercia*), An. Ox. 1399. Hē wilnode synderlices ealdordómes, and forsieh (-seah, *v. l.*) ðá geférrǽddene ôðerra engla and hira líf, Past. 111, 23. Forsǽgenum (-sewenum, *v. l.*) þám onginnum þára bôccræfta *despectis litterarum studiis*, Gr. D. 95, 25. (3) *to refuse* to do. (a) *with acc. :*—Hī sceoldon þone lofsang singan, and sē þe hit forsáwe, sceolde hit gebētan, Hml. S. 21, 161. (b) *with clause :*—Ðeáh hē forsió ðæt hē him on lócige, Past. 111, 20. (c) *with dat. infin. :*—Sume fæston swā þ̄ hí forsáwon tó etanne bûton on ðone ôðerne dæg, Hml. S. 13, 96. [*O. H. Ger.* fer-sehan *despicere, spernere.*]

**for-seóþan ;** *pp.* -soden *To boil away ; fig. to consume by affliction.* Cf. seóþan ; II. 2 :—Hī (*the Innocents*) sind gehátene martyra blóstman, for ðan ðe hí wǽron swā úpáspringende blóstman on middeweardan cyle ungeleáffulnysse swilce mid sumere ehtnysse forste forsodene, Hml. Th. i. 84, 15. [v. *N. E. D.* forseethe. *O. H. Ger.* fer-sotan *discoctus : Ger.* ver-sieden *to boil away.*]

**for-setnian ;** *p.* ode *To besiege :*—Forsetnode *obsedit*, forsætnodon *obsederunt*, Ps. Rdr. 21, 17, 13.

**for-settan.** *Substitute :* **I.** *to stop up, block, obstruct :*—Dype ánne cláð and forsete þá nǽsðyrlu þǽr mid, Lch. i. 180, 2. Hī tiledon þ̄ hí him ðone weg forsetton and fortýndon *iter illi intercludere contendebant*, Bd. 3, 19; Sch. 278, 9. Sume hī wurpon þá moldan úp and hió wǽron forsettende þǽra wætera rynas, Shrn. 41, 4. Þone lǽcedóm þe þá forsettan þing ontȳne and út teó, Lch. ii. 212, 17. **II.** *to press down, oppress, repress :*—Seó sóðfæstnes forseteþ heora sweoran and gebígeð þurh þá eáðmódan men *eorum cervicem veritas per humiles*

*premit*, Gr. D. 197, 15. Hē forsette (*repressit*) þā rēdnisse þæs Gotan, 165, 3. þā hē þone witan forsette (*premeret*) mid þām ūttran þȳstrum his eágena, 274, 25. Hit byð mid manigum swingum forseted *flagellis premitur*, 258, 28. Ic eom forseted and forðryced mid þām scyllum þisses dracan *squamis hujus draconis premor*, 325, 5. [v. *N. E. D.* forset. *M. H. Ger.* ver-setzen.]

**fōr-settan.** v. fore-settan.

**for-sewen**; *adj.* (*ptcpl.*) *Despised, abject:*—þū hæfst ūs gehwyrfde on bæclincg and ūs forsewenran gedóne þonne ūre fȳnd *avertisti nos retrorsum prae inimicis nostris*, Ps. Th. 43, 12. Ðonne óðrum monnum ðyncð ðæt hié mǽste scande ðrowigen, and hié forsewenuste bióð for worulde *cum exterius perpeti abjecta cernuntur*, Past. 87, 1.

**for-sewen**[n], e; *f. Contempt :*—Forsǽwennesse ł forsewenne *despec-tio*[ne], Ps. L. 122, 4.

**for-sewenlic**; *adj.* (1) *deserving contempt, contemptible :*—Forsewenlic biþ þ werod þ wífmenn feohtað *that army is contemptible in which women fight*, Hml. S. 31, 1097. Ðā ungedyrstigan wēnað ðæt ðæt suíðe forsewenlic sié ðætte hié dóð *vehementer despecta putant esse quae faciunt*, Past. 209, 11. Forsewenlicra *dispectior*, Wrt. Voc. ii. 140, 63. (2) *exciting contempt, abject, despised :*—Hē wæs swā forsewenlic (*ita despectus*), þēh þe hit gelumpe þ him hwilc man . . . ongēn cóme, and sē wǽre gegrēted, þ hé forhogode tōgēnes grētan, Gr. D. 34, 2. Gehwilce untrume and forsewenlice on ðisum middanearde, Hml. Th. ii. 376, 5.

**for-sewenlīce.** *Add:*—Forsewenlīce deáð þrowian, Mart. H. 156, 20. Hȳ habbað mē swȳðe forsewenlīce ūtan ymbstanden *projicientes me circumdederunt me*, Ps. Th. 16, 10.

**for-sewennes.** *Add:*—Ðā swelcan mon sceal forsión mid eallum forsewennessum (-sewenissum, *v. l.*) . . . for ðæm ðætte sió forsewennes (-sewenis, *v. l.*) him ege on gebringe, Past. 265, 19. Swylce tō forsewennysse woruldlicra ǽhta *as if in contempt of worldly possessions*, Hml. Th. i. 60, 25 : Ps. Th. 43, 15. Forsǽwennesse (-sæw-? cf. forsewenne, *v. l.*) *despectione*, Ps. L. 122, 4. Mid forseawennesse *spernendo*, R. Ben. 54, 14. For þæs dæges forsegnesse *ad contemtum diei*, Ll. Th. ii. 236, 4. God gewrecð his forsewennysse (-segenesse, -segenesse) *God punishes contempt of himself*, Hml. A. 58, 170 : 62, 256.

**for-sewestre.** v. for-sǽwestre.

**for-sīþ.** *Add :*—Ūtsīþe, forsīþe *exitia*, An. Ox. 4128.

**for-sittan.** *Add:* I. *trans.* (1) *to stop up :*—Gif eágan forsetene beoþ . . . drȳp on þ eáge, Lch. iii. 2, 20. (2) *to lose by sitting, to fail to go and do something, neglect* or *defer a duty :*—Gif preóst fulwihðe untrumes forsitte, Ll. Th. i. 38, 10. Gif hwā burhbóte oþþe bricgbóte oþþe fyrdfare forsitte, 410, 9. Gif hwā hreám gehȳre and hine forsitte, 392, 17 : 236, 31 : 260, 5 : 258, 14 : 284, 4. II. *intrans. To remain unmoved :*—Gif se ūtgang forsitte, Lch. ii. 200, 2, 14. Gif him se ūtgang forseten sié, oþþe gemígan ne mæge, 260, 10. Gehnescige mid þȳ þ forsetene yfel, 212, 16. [Wah swa hit forsete þat þe king hete, Laym. 28518. *Ger.* ver-sitzen.]

**for-slǽwan**; *p. de To make too slow, hinder, impede, make reluctant :*—Ðæt hē nōht unryhtlíce hit ne forslǽwde (-ðe, *v. l.*) *quod in otio quasi non injuste torpescat*, Past. 284, 3. Nā þē forslǽwe geneósian untrumne *non te pigeat uisitare infirmum*, Scint. 202, 4. [v. *N. E. D.* forslow.] v. next word.

**for-slǽwian.** *Substitute :* (1) *to lose by sloth, neglect through laziness :*—Ðonne wē forslāwiað ðone gecōpestan tīman . . . ðonne bistilð sió slǽwð on ūs, Past. 283, 1. (2) *to be slow to do :*—þū nāht ne forslāwodest þ þū ðín āgen feorh for hine ne sealdest *thou wert not slow to give thine own life for him*; vitae pretio ne segnis emeres, Bt. 10; F. 28, 15. [v. *N. E. D.* forslow.] v. preceding word.

**for-sleán.** *Add :* I. *to injure by striking, cut through* or *break with a stroke, wound with a blow :*—Heó slóh tō his hneccan, and mid twām slegum forslóh him þone swuran *percussit bis in cervicem ejus et abscidit caput ejus*, Hml. A. 111, 305. Gif mon óðrum þā hond ūtan forsleá . . . gif hió healf onweg fleóge, Ll. Th. i. 98, 7. Gif mon óðrum rib forsleá . . . gif sió hȳd sié tōbrocen, and mon bān of ādó, 11 : 21. Hēt se cāsere him forsleán þone sweoran, Shrn. 145, 6. Mid stengum heora sweoran forsleán, 134, 7. Gif sió lendenbrǽde bið forslegen (-slægen, *v. l.*), Ll. Th. i. 98, 1. I a. *to slay, kill :*—Weard hē gefliémed and his folces fela forslagen, Ors. 5, 12 ; S. 240. 28. Mid sweordum and mid mancwealme hī wǽron forslægene (-sleg-, *v. l.*) *gladiis et pestilentia vastati sunt*, Gr. D. 192, 4. I b. *to destroy a thing, lay waste :*—Se wíngeard wæs forslagen (-sleg-, *v. l.*) and forhergod mid hægle *vinea grandine vastata est*, Gr. D. 57, 5. I c. *to put an end to, finish* (?) :—Forslægenum *expletis* (cf. expuncta, expleta, Corp. Gl. H. 482), Wrt. Voc. ii. 32, 1. II. *to make slaughter of, defeat with slaughter, beat* an enemy. (1) as a military term :—Hié mon gefliémde and swíþe forslóg, Ors. 2, 5 ; S. 84, 20 : 3, 9 ; S. 124, 3. Eft wǽron Rōmāne forslægen and gefliémed *iterum Romani pari clade superati sunt*, 4, 8 ; S. 186, 28. Gefliémed and swíþor forslagen *amisso exercitu*, 32. Rōmāne wunnan wið Fulcisci and wurdon swíþe forslægene *consulem Volsci superarant*, 2, 6 ; S. 88, 3. (2) figurative, *to rout, overthrow :*—

Forslaegen *proflicta*, Txts. 89, 1662. Forslaegenum (forsleginum, Ep., faerslaeginum, Erf.) *profligatis* (v. (?) profligatis tenebrarum principibus, Ald. 54, 6), 1637. Forslægenum, Wrt. Voc. ii. 68, 37. III. *to condemn.* Cf. *O. H. Ger.* fer-slahan *damnare :*—Forslegen *adictus* (v. for-scrīfan ; I), Wrt. Voc. ii. 9, 69. [*O. H. Ger.* fer-slahan *re-, suc-cidere, perimere, jugulare, necare.*]

**for-slegenlic**; *adj. Shameful, ignominious :*—God hine (*John the Baptist*) forlēt swā forslegenlicne (cf. (?) for-slegen *profligatus*. v. for-sleán; II. 2 ; or (?) *l.* for-segenlicne (= -sewen-) *one MS. has* forsewenlīce) and swā orwyrðlicne deáð þrowian, Mart. H. 156, 20.

**for-sliet.** *Substitute :* for-sliht (-slieht, -sliét), es ; *m. Massacre, total slaughter :*—Forsliét *intrinicio*, Wrt. Voc. ii. 111, 71 : 45, 65.

**for-smorian.** *Add :*—Forsmored[um] *suffocato*, An. Ox. 1481.

**for-sorged.** *Substitute :* **for-sorgian**; *p.* ode *To be too anxious :*—Ne ǽnig ðurh worldhoge forsorgie tō swȳðe, Wlfst. 69, 16.

**for-spǽc.** v. fore-sprǽc : **for-spǽn**[n]**endlic.** v. for-spennendlic.

**for-spanan** *to lure to evil, allure.* *Add:* (1) *to lure :*—Forspend hē hit mid ðǽre wōlberendan ōliccunge *mentem securitatis pestiferae blanditiis seducit*, Past. 415, 12. Forspa[nendre?] *illecebroso* (v. for-spennan), Angl. xiii. 34, 174. Forspanendum *lusum illecebrosis amplexibus*, Angl. xi. 117, 33. Weard þæt wíf forspanen þurh ðæs deófles lāre, Hml. Th. i. 18, 8. [Warþ þ wíf forspannen, O. E. Hml. i. 223, 28.] (2) *to lure* to evil action :—Ðā ðe mid mislicum lustum hī tō ðām leahtrum forspeónon, Hml. Th. i. 410, 33 : ii. 478, 31. Forspanen tō forligre, i. 306, 7. Ðe lȳs ic sió forspanen tō wiðsacenne *ne inliciar ad negandum*, Kent. Gl. 1079. (3) *to lure* to destruction :—Hū fela hē forspanan mæge tō ēcan forwyrde, Wlfst. 85, 7. On ðone ilcan deáð hié wilniað eal moncynn tō forspananne and tō forlǽdanne, Past. 249, 20. [*O. H. Ger.* fer-spanan *al-, in-licere*.] v. for-spennan.

**for-spanincg.** *Add:*—Forspanninge *lenocinio*, An. Ox. 3192. On forspanegum *inlecebris*, Kent. Gl. 301. Forspanincga *inlecebras*, Scint. 87, 4. v. for-spenning.

**for-speca.** v. fore-spreca : **for-speçan.** v. for-sprecan.

**for-spendan** *to spend entirely, exhaust* property. *Add:*—Hī ūre sceattas forspenden geond ealle eorðan, Hml. S. 23, 304. [Hit were wel god moste ic alunges festen swa þet ic mine oðre goð al ne forspende, O. E. Hml. i. 31, 34. Cf. *O. H. Ger.* fer-spentōn *impendere*.]

**for-spennan** *to allure, entice :*—Bepæcendre, forspennendre *illecebroso*, An. Ox. 3190. Forspennende *lenocinantes*, 4626. v. for-spanan.

**for-spennen.** For Mone B. 671 *substitute* Hpt. Gl. 420, 66 : **for-spennend.** For Mone B. 3130 *substitute :*—Bepæcend ł forspennend *illecebrosus*, Hpt. Gl. 481, 34, *and see* forspennan.

**for-spennendlic**; *adj. Alluring, enticing :*—Forspæunendlicum (-spænend-, Hpt. Gl. 525, 65) *lenocinante*, An. Ox. 5283. Forspennendlice gefērrǽdene *inlecebrosa consortia*, 222.

**for-spenning.** *Add:* (1) *luring* to evil action :—Forspenning *inlecebra*, Hy. S. 64, 31. Līchamlicere forspennicge (-spynnincge, Hpt. Gl. 447, 16) *carnalis inlecebre*, An. Ox. 1724. Mid forspennincge *lenocinio*, 3159. Forspenningce (-spenincge, Hpt. Gl. 512, 71) *illecebras*, 4599 : *lenocinia*, 5245. Forspennincge (-ingce, Hpt. Gl. 520, 34), 4985. Forspenninga *inlecebrosa*, Wrt. Voc. ii. 138, 2. þurh þǽra myltestrena forspennincgæ, Hml. S. 8, 13. Forspennigum *illecebris*, R. Ben. I. 11, 3, (2) *luring* to destruction, cf. for-spanan, (3) :—Forspenningce *anathe-mate*, i. *perditione*, An. Ox. 5122.

**for-spild.** *Add :*—Onlícnesse . . . ðára ðe hiera hātheortnes hié suíðe hrædlíce on færspild gelǽd *typum eorum quos vehementer arripiens furor in praeceps ducit*, Past. 295, 19. Cf. for-spildness.

**for-spildan.** *Add:*—Ðū forspildes alle *perdes omnes*, Ps. Srt. 72, 27. Ne forspild ðū mē *ne perdas me*, 27, 3. Ne forspild ðū ūsic oð ende *ne repellas nos usque in finem*, 43, 23. Ðæt ðū hī forspilde and tōstence *ut disperdas et dissipes*, Past. 441, 32. Ðæt hē forspilde (*perdat*) gemynd heara, Ps. Srt. 33, 17. Hē soeceð forspildan (*perdere*) hine, 36, 32. [*O. H. Ger.* fer-spildan *expendere, effundere.*]

**for-spildness**, e; *f. Destruction, perdition :*—þȳ lǽs hit gelumpe þ hē sylfa æfter þon eall geeóde in mycele forspildnysse (-spildnyssum, -spilnisse, -spillednysse, *v. ll.*) *ne ipse postmodum in immane praecipitium totus iret*, Gr. D. 95, 24. Seó nǽdre sende hī selfe in forspildnesse (*in praecipitium*), 211, 24. v. for-spild.

**for-spillan.** *Add :* I. *to destroy :*—Land hȳ āwēstad and burga forbærnad and ǽhta forspillad, Wlfst. 133, 10. Forspil hȳ *disperde eos*, Ps. Rdr. 53, 7. þ ic forspille (*disperderem*) of ceastre ealle, Ps. Srt. 100, 9. Is nēdðearf þ hié man forspille, and mid ordum hié man sleá, Bl. H. 189, 29 : Ll. Th. i. 304, 20. Hī eów wyllað forspyllan and eówre rȳce tōwurpan, Hml. A. 185, 118. II. *to destroy by extravagant use, consume wastefully, waste.* (a) of material objects :—Hē on ānum dæge mid ungesceáde forspilð þreóra daga oððe feówera andlifene . . . ðeáh seó andlifen forspilled wurde, Hml. A. 145, 29–32. Forspil feoh for brōþor and freónd *perde pecuniam propter fratrem et amicum*, Scint. 148, 5. (b) of personal or abstract object :—Gē eów sylfe and eówre ðeóudan geogoðe fordóþ and forspillað on wíton and on yrmðum, Hml. S. 23, 186. III. *to lose :*—þ ic nānne þǽra

ne forspille þe ðū mē sealdest *quia quos dedisti mihi non perdidi ex ipsis quemquam*, Jn. 18, 9. Hē (*Zacharias*) forspilde (*perdidit*) dreámas sprǽce, Hy. S. 103, 9. Ic þe londe richtlike bigat and ic it siðen nāwer ne forswat ne forspilde (nāþer ne forspæc ne forspilde (?) ; *see next passage but one*), Cht. Th. 584, 5. Hī heortan clǽnnesse forspildun (*perdiderunt*), An. Ox. 40, 9. Hē ðæt land ne mæg nāðer gifan ne syllan, ne forspecan ne forspillan (*forfeit*. Cf. nec cogi debet rectum ejus forspeken nec forspillen, Ll. Th. i. 562, 1) ūt of ðām minstre, C. D. vi. 190, 17, þæt īsen befeóll on ðone seáð . . . forspilledum (-lorenum, *v. l.*, *perdito*) þām īsene, Gr. D. 114, 2.

**for-spillan** (-spilian?) *to wanton* (?) :—Forspillendes forligres *lenocinantis prostibuli*, An. Ox. 4964. Forspillendra þēna, glīwra *parasitorum*, 4165. v. spilian.

**for-spillednes.** *Add* :—Mē þe swā manega sāwla on forspillednysse (-spillend-, *v. l.*) grin gelǽdde, Hml. S. 23 b, 388. On forspillednesse *in perditione*, Kent. Gl. 356 : R. Ben. I. 110, 11. Hig þ rīce myd forspyllednysse gewǽhton, Hml. A. 185, 111.

**for-spillendnes.** v. for-spillednes : **for-spilness.** v. for-spildness : **for-spircan.** v. for-spyrcan *in Dict.* : **for-spornen.** v. un-forspornen : **for-sprǽc.** v. fore-sprǽc : **for-spræca,** -spreca. v. fore-spreca.

**for-sp[r]ecan** ; *p.* -sp[r]æc, *pl.* -sp[r]ǽcon ; *pp.* -sp[r]ecen. **I.** *to speak against, speak ill of, denounce* :—Forsprecað hī foran tō ðisum folce, þæt 'swā hraðe swā hī becumað tō ðyssere byrig, gehǽftað hī,' Hml. Th. ii. 494, 10. [Fra steven of forspekand *a voce obloquentis*, Ps. 43, 17.] **II.** *to misrepresent a case, state wrongly* :—Ne sȳ forspecen ne forswigod . . . þ wē þǽrtō lustlīce fōn *do not let the fact be stated wrongly or passed over in silence*, . . . *that we gladly accept it*, Ll. Th. i. 238, 15. **III.** *to lose that which is the subject of a suit* :—Cnut cyng lēt ðæt land intō Crīstes cyrcean . . . tō ðām forewearde ðæt Eádsige hit hæbbe his lifes tīman . . . and hē hit ne mæg nāðer gifan ne syllan, ne forspecan ne forspillan (*lose it by a suit at law or by forfeiture*; cf. nec cogi debet rectum ejus forspeken nec forspillen (cf. perdere vel forisfacere placitum, 561, 24), Ll. Th. i. 562, 1) ūt of ðām hālgan minstre, C. D. vi. 190, 17. v. for-spillan ; Dict. **IV.** *to speak to no purpose, waste one's words.* v. for-specan *in Dict.* [*O. H. Ger.* fer-sprehhan *repudiare, abnuere, renuntiare.*]

**for-spurned.** v. un-forspurned.

**forst.** *Add* : **I.** *frost, intense cold* :—Forst, frost, frots *gelum*, Txts. 67, 964. Æfter Candelmæssan cōm se stranga winter mid forste and mid snāwe, Chr. 1046 ; P. 164, 33. Se mere wæs mid forste oferþeaht, and se winterlica wind wan mid þām forste, Hml. S. 11, 143. **II.** *hoar frost, rime* :—In forste *in pruina*, Ps. Srt. 77, 47.

**for-standan** *and* **fōr-standan** (*l.* for-). *Take these together, and add* : **I.** *intrans.* (1) *to stand in the way* of an object (*dat.*), *lie in the line of advance* :—Oð þæt sǽfæsten landes æt ende leódmægne forstōd, Exod. 128. (2) *to come to a stand, stop* :—Gif se man āspīwð þone yfelan wǽtan onweg, þonne forstent se geohsa, Lch. ii. 60, 23. Wiþ þon þe wīfum sié forstanden hira mōnaþgecynd, 330, 13. **II.** *trans.* (1) *with the idea of hindrance.* (a) *to stop the advance of, hinder, resist, withstand* :—Breóstnet wið ord and wið ecge ingang forstōd, B. 1549. Uton forstandan hī (*the soul*) foran mid gefeohte, Hml. Th. ii. 336, 7. Tō forstondanne *resistendum*, Lk. p. 5, 8. (b) *to stop passage through* or *along, block* a door, a way for a person (*dat.*) :—Se biscop mid Crīstene folce forstōd cirican dura ā[geán] . . . ðǽm kāsere, Shrn. 58, 7. Seó leó forstōd him þā duru, Hml. S. 35, 267. Ongan se fæder wyrnan hire and wolde forstandan þone weg þæs ēcan lifes *ei pater ad viam vitae resistere conatus est*, Gr. D. 222, 22. (c) *to stop* a person (*dat.*) *doing something* :—Hī mec willað oðfergan . . . Ic him þæt forstonde *they want to carry me off* . . . *I stop them doing that*, Rä. 17, 8. Hī woldon feore beorgan . . . him þæt engel forstōd, An. 1542 : Gen. 2748 : Mōd. 65. Hē hyra mā wolde ācwellan, nefne him God wyrd forstōde, B. 1056. (2) *with idea of defence, to defend, protect* :—Betǽc ūs Daniel . . . Gif ðū hine forstenst, wē fordȳlegiað þē, Hml. Th. i. 570, 25. Hine God forstōd, An. 1337. Scipio ofslagen wǽre, gif his sunu his ne gehulpe mid þǽm þ hē hiene foran forstōd oð hē on fleáme fealh *Scipio per Scipionem filium ab ipsa morte liberatus evasit*, Ors. 4, 8 ; S. 186, 25. Se lytla cniht geseah bifiendum eágum þā āwyrgdan gāstas cuman in tō him. Þā ongan hē clypian, 'Lā, fæder, forstand mē (*obsta, pater*),' Gr. D. 289, 16. (2 a) *to protect from* (*dat.*) :—Hine God forstōd hǽðenum folce, An. 1145. Hē þæt folc forstōd feónda mægene, Ps. Th. 105, 19. Heaðolīðendum hord forstandan, bearn and brȳde, B. 2955 : Met. 1, 22. Hē sceal þȳ wonge wealdan : ne magon gē him þā wīc forstondan, Gū. 674. Gif gē þæt fæsten fȳre willað forstandan, on þære stōwe wē gesunde magon sǽles bīdan, Gen. 2522. **III.** *to avail, profit, be good for* :—Hwæt forstent his gehlȳd ?, Past. 91, 25 : Ps. Th. 2, 4. Habbe ic nū forbærned ðā ealdan gewritu ðe ic geāhsian mihte. Gif hyra hwilc funden bið, ne forstent ðæt mē, C. D. ii. 116, 3. Witan hwæt gerīmcræft forstande, Angl. viii. 312, 44. Þēh hit æt þām ende nāht ne forstōde, Chr. 1066 ; P. 196, 18. Cwæð hē tō mē ðæt hē freólsas genōge hæfde, gif hī āht forstōdan, C. D. iv. 10, 2. Heora eáþmetto ne mihton nāuht forstandan, Bt. 29, 2 ; F. 104,

34. **III a.** *to avail* a person (*dat.*) :—Hwæt forstondes (fore-, L.) menn ðēh . . . *quid proderit homini si* . . ., Mk. R. 8, 36. Ne forstent hit him nōht, Past. 163, 19 : 421, 21. Hwæt forstōd seó mengu þāra freónda þām deórlingum ?, Bt. 29, 2 ; F. 106, 6. Ūre Drihten cwæð þ þām men nāwiht ne forstōde þeáh hē ealne middangeard gestrīnde, Ll. Th. ii. 424, 10. **IV.** *to stand for, be the equivalent of, be as good as* :—Sē þe þis gebed singð on cyrcean, þonne forstent hit him sealtera sealma. And sē þe hit singð æt his endedæge, þonne forstent hit him hūselgang, Lch. iii. 288, 13–16. His freónda forspǽc forstent him eal þæt sylfe swylce hit sylf spǽce, Wlfst. 38, 16. [Ān messe forstant .xii. daga feasten, Lch. iii. 166, 17.] **V.** *to understand* :—Ne sēce ic nō hēr þā bēc, ac þ þ þā bēc forstent, þæt is, þīn gewit (*non libros, sed id quod libris pretium facit*), Bt. 5, 1 ; F. 10, 20. Siððan ic ðā bōc geliornod hæfde, swǽ swǽ ic hié forstōd . . . ic hié on Englisc āwende, Past. 7, 23. Ic wēne þeáh þ þū ne forstande hwæt ic ðē tō cwæþe *nondum forte quid loquar intelligis*, Bt. 20 ; F. 70, 26. Ic geanbidode oþ ic wiste hwæt þū woldest, and hū þū hit understandan woldest, and eác ic tiolode swīþe geornfullīce þ ðū hit forstandan mihtest *I waited till I knew what you wanted, and what idea you had formed of it* (cf. understandan ; III), *and I laboured earnestly that you might understand it*, 22, 1 ; F. 76, 27. [v. *N. E. D.* forstand. *O. Sax.* far-standan *to defend* ; *to stop* ; *to understand* : *O. H. Ger.* fer-standan *protegere* ; *intelligere, cognoscere.*]

**for-stelan.** *Substitute for meanings* : *To steal away, and add* : **I.** *of criminal theft, to take* the property of another :—Ðēr ðeáfas forstealas, Mt. L. 6, 19. Forstæl *conpillat*, Wrt. Voc. ii. 21, 8 : *subripuit*, 87, 19. Se ceorl forstæl ǽnne oxan *furatus est uir bouem*, Ælfc. Gr. Z. 146, 13. Se fruma wæs þ mon forstæl ǽnne wimman Ælfsige *the beginning was that a woman was stolen from Ælfsige*, Cht. Th. 206, 19. Þū hit nā hū elles begitan ne miht būton þū hit forstele oððe gereáfige *eripies habenti*, Bt. 32, 1 ; F. 114, 8. Þ ðū ne forstele *ne fureris*, Mk. L. 10, 19. Gif hwā forstele esne oððe mannan, fæste .ii. winter, Ll. Th. ii. 140, 37. Þā ofdrīfenan oððe þā forstolenan *depeculata*, Wrt. Voc. ii. 26, 59. **I a.** *with* cognate acc. (or *dat.*) :—Gif preóst mycele stale forstele *si presbyter furtum magnum commiserit*, Ll. Th. ii. 140, 14. Gif man mycelre þȳfðe forstele, feoðerfōt neát . . . forgylde hē þ hē forstolen hæbbe . . . Gif māran stalan forstele *si homo magnum quid furatus fuerit, animal quadrupes . . . quod furatus fuerit reddat . . . Si majus aliquid furatus fuerit*, 33–36. **II.** *to obtain surreptitiously, take away without the knowledge of another.* [Cf. *Ger.* ver-stohlen.] :—Heó creáp bæftan þām Hǽlende, and forstæl hire hǽlu, Hml. Th. ii. 394, 12. Hū Bonefatius forstæl þone hwǽte his mēder, Gr. D. 67, 21. Secgað þ his þegnas gereáfodan his līc on ūs and forstǽlan, Bl. H. 177, 30. Heó hēt dearnunga faran tō þām scipe and forstelon þā līc, Hml. S. 29, 328. [*O. Sax.* far-stelan : *O. H. Ger.* fer-stelan *furare.*]

**for-stemman.** v. fore-stemman.

**forstig** ; *adj. Frosty* :—Ic wæs beswǽled for þām micelan byrne, and eft for þǽre micclan forstigan cealdnysse þæs wintres, Hml. S. 23 b, 575. [*O. H. Ger.* frostag (-eg) *algens, algidus*.] v. fyrstig.

**for-stoppian** ; *p.* ode *To stop up* :—Mid þære wulle forstoppa þæt eáre, Lch. ii. 42, 12. [v. *N. E. D.* forstop. *O. H. Ger.* fer-stoppōn : *Ger.* ver-stopfen.]

**for-strogdnes** *dispersion* (?). Forstrogdnis *is given as the gloss to* praecipitationis *in* Ps. 51, 6, Nap. 25. *This word is glossed by* fortrūgadnisse *in* Ps. Srt. 51, 6 : Ps. Spl. T. 51, 4 : *could* for-strogdnis *be an error for this form?*

**for-styltan** ; *p.* te *To be overcome with astonishment* :—Forstyltun (forestyldton, L.) *obstupuerunt*, Mk. R. 5, 42 : (forstyldton, L.), 10, 24 : (forestylton, L.), 16, 5.

**for-styntan.** *For* Cot. 48 : 177 *substitute* :—Forstynt *contudit*, i. *domavit, fregit, compressit*, Wrt. Voc. ii. 135, 25. Forstyntaþ *contundunt* (*virtutes tela sparorum*, Ald. 204, 1), 96, 32 : 20, 7.

**for-sūcan** ; *p.* -seác ; *pp.* -socen *To suck up, devour* :—[þæt se] wemmend mid deórenum ceafum wǽre forsocen (forgnegen) [*ut*] *scortator ferinis rictibus suggillaretur* (i. *rapietur*), An. Ox. 3343.

**for-sūgan.** *Substitute* : *To suck in* (used of the spasmodic action of the stomach in hiccough ? Cf. sūgan ; II, sogoþa) :—Lǽcedōmas wið ādeádodum magan and gif hē forsogen sié, Lch. ii. 158, 14. Wiþ forsogenum magan oþþe āþundenum *for a stomach troubled with hiccough or wind*, 186, 17.

**for-swǽlan.** *l.* -swælan, *and add* : **I.** *to injure* or *destroy with heat.* (1) *of the action of fire.* (a) *to consume, burn up* :—Fȳr cymð and forswǽlð fela þinga on eorðan, Wlfst. 195, 26. Þæt fȳr slōh ūt of ðām ofne, and forswǽlde þā cwelleras, Hml. Th. i. 570, 16. Forswǽlan *cremare*, An. Ox. 3086. Heora bendas wurdon forswǽlede, Ælfc. T. Grn. 8, 27 : Hml. S. 7, 231. Sume wǽron on līge forswǽlede, Hml. Th. i. 542, 10. (b) *to scorch, pain* or *damage with fire, singe* hair :—Fȳr byrnð on his gesihðe, and bið swiðlīc storm.' Se storm āðwyhð swā hwæt swā þæt fȳr forswǽlð, Hml. Th. i. 618, 12. Se līg ne mōste furðon heora fex forswǽlan, Hml. S. 16, 76. Þæt heora fex næs furðon forswǽled *quoniam capillus capitis eorum non esset adustus* (Dan. 3, 27), Ælfc. T. Grn. 8, 29. Hylie on fȳrum wē beóð for-

swǽlede teartlícor *Averni ignibus crememur acrius*, Hy. S. 5, 15. (2) of the effect of the sun :—Sunne ne forswǽle þé *sol non uret te*, Ps. L. 120, 6. (3) of the effect of disease :—Hine gelæhte ádl; hís líchama barn wiðútan mid langsumere hǽtan, and hé eal innan forswǽled wæs, Hml. Th. i. 86, 5. (4) uncertain :—Forswǽld, forhǽþed *exustus*, i. *spoliatus*, Wrt. Voc. ii. 146, 34. II. *intrans.* (?) *To flame, burn* :—Forswǽl-ende *combustos*, i. *flagrantes*, An. Ox. 1434. v. [v. *N. E. D.* for-sweal.] un-forswǽled.

**for-swarung**, e ; *f. Perjury* :—Forswarung, þ is mǽne áðas, Nap. 25.

**for-swat**, Cht. Th. 584, 5. v. for-spillan ; III : **for-swelan.** For '*kindle*' *substitute* '*be consumed.*'

**for-swelgan.** *Add :* (1) of living creatures. (a) lit. :—Se fisc for-swylcð þone angel forð mid þám ǽse, Hml. Th. i. 216, 12. Þe lǽs wulfas forswelgen (*devorent*) míne sceáp, Coll. M. 20, 15. Forswelgan *lurcare*, An. Ox. 3573. (b) fig. :—Forsweld *devorat* (*os impiorum iniquitatem*), Kent. Gl. 719. (2) of inanimate objects. (a) material. v. swelgend :—þá neólnessa þá eorþan willaþ forswelgan, Bl. H. 93, 13. Wæterǽddrum forswelgendum *cataractis vorantibus*, An. Ox. 516. (b) non-material :—þæt hé þurh mycele gnornunge ne sý on lyre forswolgen *ne habundantiori tristitia absorbeatur*, R. Ben. 51, 6. (3) denoting destructive action. (a) of material agents :—Blódig regn and fýren fundiaþ ]ás eorþan tó forswylgenne and tó forbærnenne, Bl. H. 93, 4. (b) of non-material agents :—Se deáð hý forswylcð on ēcnesse *mors depascet eos*, Ps. Th. 48, 13. Oððæt hí mid ealle deáð forswelge, Hml. S. 23, 326. [*O. L. Ger.* far-suelgan *absorbere* : *O. H. Ger.* fer-swelhan *deglutire*.]

**for-swelgend**, es ; *m. A devourer* :—Forswelgend *grassatrix*, i. *deuoratrix* (*parcarum non ulli parcentum atrocitas*), An. Ox. 2209.

**for-sweltan.** *Add :* (1) of persons, *to die, perish.* [He shal þe makie to forswelten, Jul. 19, 7.] (2) of a (visible) thing, *to die away, fade away, disappear* :—Forswealt *disparuit* (*omnis praestigiarum scaena . . . ut fumus evanescens disparuit*, Ald. 57, 13), Wrt. Voc. ii. 84, 50 : 26, 66.

**for-sweorcan** *to grow dark.* For *Prov.* 7 *substitute* Kent. Gl. 185, *and add :*—Seó sunne forswyrcð sóna on morgen *Titan tenebrescit in ortu*, Dóm. L. 108 : Wlfst. 137, 11. Ásweartad, forsworcen *fuscatus*, i. *denigratus, obnubilatus*, Wrt. Voc. ii. 152, 7 (cf. An. Ox. 2, 369 *infra*). Beón forsworcene (*obscurentur*) eágan heora þ hí ne geseón, Ps. L. 68, 24. Betwyx forsworcenum sweartum nihtum *obscuras inter noctes*, Dóm. L. 198. ¶ a wk. form occurs, *to make dark* (?) :—Forsweorced *fuscatus* (*velut Aethiopica nigritudine*, Ald. 66, 23), An. Ox. 2, 369. (Cf. Wrt. Voc. ii. 152, 7 *supra*.)

**for-sweorfan** *to wipe out, destroy.* See sweorfan *in Dict.* [*O. H. Ger.* fer-swerban *terere.*]

**for-swerian.** *Dele first passage, and add :* I. *to commit perjury* :—Swerian ne sceal mon þý lǽs mon forswerige *non jurare ne forte perjuret*, R. Ben. 17, 9. I a. *reflex. To perjure* one's self :—Ná swerian þe [lǽs] hé hine forswerige (v. *preceding passage*), R. Ben. I. 20, 8. Ne ǽnig man hine sylfne nid máne ne forswerie, Wlfst. 70, 10. Þú wylt besyrwian óðerne and þé sylfne forswerian, Hml. A. 7, 164. ¶ for-sworen *forsworn, perjured* :—Fela synd forsworene. Wlfst. 268, 27. II. *to constrain by swearing, to bewitch* :—Forsuór defotabat (v. áþ-swerian, wirgan), Txts. 57, 660. Þone synscadan (Grendel) gúðbilla nán grētan nolde, ac hé sigewǽpnum forsworen hæfde, ecga gehwylcre (cf. *the power attributed to Odin, who is called* ljóða snidr, *of making his enemies' weapons useless :* Óðinn kunni svá gera at vápn þeira bitu eigi heldr en vendir. This power seems attributed to Grendel), B. 804. [*O. Sax.* for-swerian (sik) : *O. H. Ger.* fer-swerien (sih) *perjurare.*]

**for-swigan.** v. swígan *in Dict.* : **for-swigian.** *l.* -swigian.

**for-swigung** -suwung, e ; *f. Silence, a passing over in silence* :—Of forsuwunge *silentio*, Hpt. Gl. 455, 55.

**for-swíþan.** [The Latin original of Past. 50, 1 (Swt. 387, 22) is : Prosperitatem apud judicium cordis non reprimit.] *Add :* (1) *to over-come, conquer* :—Þte stronga ðú forsuíðes *ut fortia confundas*, Rtl. 50, 13. Þ forswíðed middangeard *vincit mundum*, 28, 1, 3. Þte ðá ðe ué giðoligað foresuíðe ué *ut ea quae patimur vincamus*, 7, 40. [Eal þat sár heó forswýhþ, Lch. iii. 86, 24.] (2) *to surpass, excel* :—Of ðon ðerhcyme ēðmódnisse ēdes ðona forsuíðde heáhnisse hiordes *eo perveniat humilitas gregis, quo praecessit celsitudo pastoris*, Rtl. 32, 21. (3) *to drive away, force away* (?) :—Gif wíf forswýð hire wer hyre fram *si mulier virum suum a se rejiciat*, Ll. Th. ii. 152, 1. v. un-forswíþed.

**for-swíþe.** *Add :*—Þú eart án forswíðe leás man, Hml. S. 23, 687. Ic ealles forswíþe ne girnde þisses eorþlican ríces, Bt. 17 ; F. 58, 24. Cf. for-wel.

**for-sworcenlic** ; *adj. Obscure* :—Wealcan wé forsworcenlices náht *volvamus obscurum nichil*, Hy. S. 24, 21.

**for-sworcenness**, e ; *f. Obscurity, darkness* :—On forsworcennesse sweartes þrosmes and ðæs weallendan pices, Wlfst. 139, 1. Næfð mín niht náne forsworcennysse, Hml. Th. i. 428, 30. Forsworcennyssa *obscura*, Hy. S. 23, 31 : 37, 4.

**for-sworennys.** *Add :*—Of ðisum leahtre (gítsung) beóð ācennede leásunga . . . and forsworennys, Hml. Th. ii. 220, 11. Gítsung (*avaritia*) macað leásunga and forsworennyssa, Hml. S. 16, 283.

**for-syngian.** *Substitute : To make sinful* ; reflex. *to sin* :—Gif hé hine sylfne wið God forsyngað, Wlfst. 280, 8. ¶ forsyngod *burdened with sin, sinful* :—Swá se man sý swýðor forsingod, swá hé geornor Godes hús sēce, Wlfst. 155, 8. Weard þes þeódscype swýðe forsyngod þurh mænigfealde synna, 163, 19. Forsyngodes mannes nýdhelp, Ll. Th. ii. 278, 2. On forsyngodre þeóde, Wlfst. 45, 13 : 166, 8. Þurh mistlice forligeru forsyngode swýðe, 165, 32.

**for-tácen.** v. fore-tácen.

**for-teón.** *Substitute :* for-teón ; *p.* -teáh, *pl.* -tugon ; *pp.* -togen. I. *to pull and hurt, to gripe* :—Fortogen *turminosus*, Wrt. Voc. i. 16, 10. Þá men . . . fnǽstiað swíþe, beóð fortogene, Lch. ii. 242, 7. II. *to pull in the way of, obscure, cover up*; *obducere* :—Þæs líchoman hefignes mid gedwolmiste fortíhð mód foran monna gehwelces, þ hit beorhte ne mót blícan, Met. 22, 34. Þeáh sió swǽrnes ðæs líchoman mid þám gedwolmiste þ mód fortió þ hit ne mæge beorhte scínan, Bt. 35, 1 ; F. 156, 1. III. *to draw away, lead astray* ; *seducere* :—Tó þám ríce þonan ús ǽr þurh synlust se swearta gǽst forteáh, Cri. 270. [Þenne com þe fule gost and forted þat child to here wille, O. E. Hml. ii. 87, 33. *O. H. Ger.* fer-ziuhan.]

**forþ.** *Add :* (1) *forwards.* (a) from an upright position :—Hé leát forð tó ðǽm men ðe hine sleán mynte, Bl. H. 223, 9. Forþ fællende *procidens*, Mt. R. 18, 26, 29. Forþ álotene *cernui*, Hy. S. 5, 29. Forð onloten tó his fótum *provolutus ejus pedibus*, Gr. D. 53, 23. Ásitte hé þonne úplang, hníge þonne forð, Lch. iii. 2, 13. (b) from a point of rest :—Se engel hié lǽrde ðæt hié æt þǽre þriddan tíde hié forð trymedan ongeán heora feóndum, Bl. H. 201, 35. (2) denoting con-tinuity of movement or direction, *on* :—Þá on dæg hé mehte cuman tó ealra Rómána anwealde, þér hé forþ gefóre (*if he had marched on*) tó ðǽre byrg, Ors. 4, 9 ; S. 190, 11. Ðá fór hé forð bí ðǽm scræfe, Past. 197, 13 : Ors. 1, 1 ; S. 17, 22. Ferdan hié ealle forð be him, and heora nǽnig him tó cerran nolde, Bl. H. 213, 34. Of þǽm ǽwielme non hæt þæt wæter Nilus, and þonne forþ þonan west iernende heó tólíþ on twá, Ors. 1, 1 ; S. 12, 31. Forð be mearce tó Culesfelda ; forð be gemǽre tó Stódleagg swá tó Ticnesfelda . . . swá tó Tæppeleage ; swá forð tó scipleage . . . ðæt forð be deópan delle, C. D. iii. 404, 23–28 (*and often in charters*). (2 a) forþ mid *along with* :—Se fisc forswylcð þone angel forð mid þám ǽse, Hml. Th. i. 216, 13 : ii. 320, 31. Þý lǽs wé sylfe losigon forð mid eów, Ll. Th. ii. 356, 23. Gif seó heord for-wurð and hé sylf forð mid, 326, 23 : Hml. Th. i. 68, 15 : Chr. 1070; P. 206, 8. (2 b) of action continued to completion :—Gif se hund losige, gá þeós bót hwæðere forð *this fine must still be paid*, Ll. Th. i. 78, 6. He ne mihte ná forð hérmid *he could not carry out his plan*, Cht. Th. 341, 4. Se híred him forwyrnde þæs forð út mid ealle *the convent refused him that out and out*, 10. ¶ and swá forþ *and so on* :—Ðá cwæð se Hǽlend, 'Dóð þæt þæt folc sitte,' and swá forð on swá wé eów ær rehton, Hml. Th. i. 184, 16. (3) *forth*, as in *henceforth* :—Á fordh (forthe, forht) *in dies crudesceret*, Txts. 70, 529. Á forð, Wrt. Voc. ii. 48, 75. v. heonan, þanan, I. 6. (3 a) expressing continuity of action, *on* as in to go *on* doing :—Petrus cnucode forð oð þæt hí hine inn léton *Peter went on knocking till they let him in*, Hml. Th. ii. 382, 23. Ðá stód seó fǽmne forð on hire gebede *she went on with her prayers*, Shrn. 103, 7. Drince hé forþ þone drenc feówertýne niht, Lch. ii. 118, 22. Gif hine forð nelle forstandan sē þe him ǽr ceáp fore sealde, Ll. Th. i. 142, 6. Suelce hé wel libban wolde, gif hé forð móste *if he might continue to live*, Past. 251, 15. Þæt godspel cwyð forð gyt *the gospel goes on further to say*, Hml. Th. i. 396, 34 : Wlfst. 222, 33. Hé sæt ðá ðǽr swá forð, Hml. S. 27, 44 : Guth. 26, 14. Diácon forþ folige (*prosequatur*), Angl. xiii. 416, 728. (4) marking position in place or time, *at an advanced point, a later part of a book* :—Þá gestód hé æt ánum ēhðyrle oð forð nihtes (*until far on in the night*), Hml. Th. ii. 184, 27. Be þám wē eft forð (*hēr æfter, v. l.*) on þysse bēc secgean willaþ *de quibus in sequentibus suo tempore dicendum est*, Bd. 3, 18; Sch. 275, 19. (5) *forth, out, so as to be seen or known* :—Of swearan forð hlífað (*promineat*) seó reádnes ðæs swyles, Bd. 4, 19; Sch. 450, 10. Swát sprong forð under fexe, B. 2967. Se wuldorcyning cwóm forþ ofer þeóde þǽre fǽmnan, Bl. H. 9, 33. Beóþ þeóstra forþ gewordene ofer ealle world, 93, 18. Hwylc handleán wē him forþ tó berenne habban, 91, 13 : 53, 12. Hé hine lǽdde forþ tó þon cafor-túne, 219, 20. Forþ reccean and secggean, 83, 8. (5 a) expressing accomplishment :—Gif mon wíf gebycgge, and sió gyft forð ne cume, Ll. Th. i. 122, 5. Gif Englisc onstal gá forð (*take place*), 130, 15. (6) *forth, away* from a place, *out* :—Se here fór forþ (*marched out of its winter quarters*), Chr. 887 : P. 80, 29. Faran ealle forð, ðǽr him God wísige þ hí tó cuman móton, Ll. Th. i. 258, 8. Se Hǽlend fērde forþ forþ, Bl. H. 19, 17. (6 a) of death or decay :—Gif ceorl and his wíf bearn hæbben gemǽne and fēre se ceorl forð (*and the husband die*), Ll. Th. i. 126, 4. Þá wuduwyrta forþ gewítaþ for þæs sumores hǽton, Bl. H. 59, 3. (6 b) of the course of the seasons :—Þá tída ǽgþer ge forþ

faraþ, ge eft cumaþ, Bt. 33, 4; F. 128, 8. (7) expressing extent or degree, to (such) a degree:—Swá forð hý wæron forworhte, Wlfst. 14, 8: 110, 11: Ll. Th. ii. 424, 17. God swá forð geherian swá hé wyrðe is, Btwk. 194, 15. Hæfð hé his sceoppendes onlícnesse swá forþ swá swá ænegu gesceaft fyrmest mæg hiere sceppendes onlícnesse habban, Bt. 14, 2; F. 44, 27. Þ his grið stande swá forð swá hit fyrmest stód on his yldrena dagum, Ll. Th. i. 292, 3. Swá ful and swá forð swá hé hit mé tó handa lét, C. D. iv. 58, 25: 172, 1. Hig sceoldan habban Sandwíc swá full and swá forð swá hig hit æfre hæfdon on ænies kinges dæge . . . on eallon þám þingan þe hit æfre ænig king fyrmest hæfde, 57, 24. Anweald habban swá forþ þ hé ná máran ne þorfte, Bt. 33, 1; F. 120, 33. On wísum scrifte bið swíðe forð gelang forsyngodes mannes nýdhelp, Ll. Th. ii. 278, 2: 280, 12. Swíðe forð hí wæron gehrorene, Gr. D. 134, 11. Man oft herede þæt man scolde hyrwan, and tó forð hyrwde þæt man scolde herigan, Wlfst. 168, 12. Tó forð þeós þeód is bedæled rædes and rihtes, 243, 5. Hé ða lufan tó ðæs forð wið heó gecýdde þ . . ., Hml. A. 152, 30. Sé þe hine sylfne þus forð forscyldigað, Ll. Th. ii. 280, 28. *See also the verbs given with forþ as prefix in Dict., and forþmest.*

**forþa** [=furþum], Angl. ix. 265.

**forþ-ágoten**; *adj.* (*ptcpl.*) *Poured forth, profuse*:—Mid forðágotenum bénum, Hml. S. 23 b, 789.

**for-ðam.** v. se; V. 3 b: for-þanc, -þanclíce, -þancol. v. foreþanc, -þanclíce, -þancol: forþ-atineg. v. for-þeahtung: forþ-bǽre. v. forþ-bǽro: forþ-bǽro(-u). *Substitute*: *Productivity, and add:* cf. wæstmbǽru(-o).

**forþbig-férende** *passing-by*:—Þá forðbigférende, Nap. 79.

**forþ-bilding.** v. forþ-bylding *in Dict.*: **forþ-blǽstan.** *For Cot.* 74 *substitute*:—Forð blǽstan *erumperant*, Wrt. Voc. ii. 30, 23: **forþ-blǽwan.** *For Cot.* 78 *substitute*:—Forþ bláwaþ *eructant*, Wrt. Voc. ii. 32, 20.

**forþ-dǽd**, e; *f. Profit, advantage*:—Mid his handcræfte hé (*S. Paul*) teolode his and his geférena forþdǽda, Hml. Th. i. 392, 17. Cf. þá munecas náht syllan ne móston búta þám ánum þe heora bigleofan forð dydon (*were of service to their sustenance*), Hml. S. 31, 325. v. forþian; III.

**for-þeahtung,** e; *f. Advice, exhortation*:—Gesceádwíslicre forþahtincge mynegunge *rationabili exortationis monitu*, Angl. xiii. 447, 1167.

**for-þearle.** *Add*:—Hé weard geblyssod forþearle, Hml. S. 3, 463. Hí geswencton hí sylfe forðearle, 13, 99. Se micela ylf ondrǽt him forþearle, gif hé gesihð áne mús, Hml. A. 64, 287.

**fór-þearlíce.** *Substitute*: for-þearllíce, -þearlíce; *adv. Very sternly or severely*:—Hé bið forþearlíce áworpen *ipse reprobus invenietur*, R. Ben. 11, 19.

**for-þencan.** *Substitute*: *To despise*; used reflexively, *to despise one's self, to despair*; *pp.* for-þóht *desperate, in despair*:—Þú eart fulneáh forþóht. Ac ic nolde þ þú þe forþóhte . . . for ðæm se sé ðe hine forþencð, sé bið ormód *thou art wellnigh desperate. But I would not that thou shouldst despair . . . for he that is without hope is without heart*, Bt. 8; S. 19, 29–31. Þú þe ús sealdest þæt geþyld þæt wé ús ne forþóhton on nánum geswince ne on nánum ungelimpe *Deus per quem non cedimus adversitatibus*, Solil. H. 7, 15. Hé lǽrde þæt þá ðearfan hý ne forðóhton ne ne wénden þæt God heora ne róhte *he taught that the needy should not despair, or suppose that God did not care for them*, Ps. Th. 48 arg. Þý lǽs hé hine for ðǽre wynsuman wyrde fortrúwige, oððe for ðǽre réðan forðence *ne vos aut tristis fortuna opprimat, aut jucunda corrumpat*, Bt. 40, 3; S. 138, 27. Ne scealt þú þe forðencan þæt þú tulraðe ne mæge becuman tó ðám ðe ðú wilnast, Solil. H. 30, 20. Hé fela word sprǽc, forþóht ðearle (cf. ormód, Bt. 1; S. 8, 4), ne wénde ǽfre cuman of ðǽm clammum, Met. 1, 82. Hwæt mæg ic, earm, forðóht, mǽre geðencan?, Hml. S. 23 b, 477. Wǽron Rómane swá swíðe forþóhte *usque ultima desperatio Reipublicae apud Romanos fuit*, Ors. 4, 9; S. 190, 17. Wurdon hié swá swíþe forþóhte þætte . . . hié him heápmǽlum selfe on hand eódon, 4, 5; S. 170, 5. [O. H. Ger. fer-denchen *contemnere*.]

**for-þeófian.** v. for-þiófan, þeófian *in Dict.*: for-þeón *to surpass.* v. fore-þeón: for-þeóstrian. *Add*:—Forþrýstrede *obscuravit*, Bl. Gl.

**for-þerscan** *to destroy by beating*:—Se wíngeard weard forðorscen mid onreósendum hetolum hagole, Gr. D. 57, 4. (v. for-sleán; I b.) [O. H. Ger. fer-droskan *attritus*.]

**forþ-fǽderas.** *Add: Fathers.* (1) in a natural sense:—Eówre forðfæderas (*patres uestri*, Jn. 6, 58) ǽton þone heofonlican mete, Hml. Th. ii. 266, 30: i. 558, 20. Heora heortan gerihtlǽcan mid heora forðfædera gebysnunge (v. Acts, c. 7), 46, 9. Bið gelóme ofspring forscyldegod þurh forðfædera mándǽda, 114, 22. Forþfæderas *tritavos*, An. Ox. 847. (2) in an ecclesiastical sense:—Þára drohtnunge ic gesweotelige swá swá úre forþfæderas hit gesettan *quorum (monachorum) conversationem, ut patrum edocet institutio, intimabo*, R. Ben. 136, 29. [v. N. E. D. forthfather.]

**forþ-faran.** *Dele first passage, and add*:—Forðfǽrð *defungitur*, forðfaren *defunctus*, Wrt. Voc. i. 28, 71, 70. Ádwǽsced, forþfaren,

ácweald *extinctus*, i. *peremptus, mortuus*, ii. 145, 20. Þá forðfarenan *obeuntem*, 63, 6. Bysne niman æt forðfarenum mannum, Hml. Th. ii. 532, 31.

**forþ-feran.** *l.* -féran, *and add*:—Forðférende *obeuntem, morientem*, Hpt. Gl. 501, 31. Ðá ðe wæron forðférede for hund geárum oððon gyt firnor, Wlfst. 96, 7.

**forþ-fering.** *l.* -féring, *and add*:—On dæge forðféringe *in die defunctionis*, Scint. 65, 8.

**forþ-fór.** *Add*:—Be ðon hálgan lífe and forðfóre Sancte Martines, Bl. H. 211, 14: Gr. D. 20, 20. Hé bodode hire forðfóre (*obitum*), 169, 14: Guth. 94, 3. ¶ where death is commemorated:—On ðone endlyftan dæg þæs mónðes bið þǽre hálgan abbodissan forðfór, Shrn. 137, 32. Hí mǽrsodon þǽre eádigan forðfóre dæg, Hml. S. 23 b, 800. [Pasche, forðfor on engle tunge, Gen. and Ex. 3158.]

**forþ-framian, -fremian.** *Substitute*: (1) *to grow up*:—Weaxende, forðframiende *pubescens*, Wrt. Voc. ii. 66, 20. (2) *to make progress, thrive*:—Hí forðfremedon (-fremedun, v. l.) and þungon *profecerunt*, Gr. D. 205, 5.

**forþ-fromung.** *l.* -framung, -fromung, *and dele bracket.*

**forþ-gang (-geong).** *Add*: (1) *a going forth* of a place:—Forðgang *egressio*, Ps. L. 18, 7. (2) *a going forth* to a place:—Hire forbeád þone forðgang (-gong, v. l.) seó sceomu tó þǽre cyrichálgunge *cum processionem imperaret verecundia*, Gr. D. 72, 16. (3) *a going on, course, progress*:—Forðganges nép, Exod. 469. In forðgange (-geonge, v. l.) þæs ǽrendgewrites *in processu epistolae*, Bd. 1, 13; Sch. 36, 25. (3 a) *successful progress, success*:—Þe ágen cyre næfð nǽnne forðgang, búton hé beó gefyrðrod þurh þone Ælmihtigan, Hml. Th. i. 210, 12: ii. 340, 28. Gif hé on þám gástlican gefeohte forðgang habban sceall, Hml. S. 26, 856. Þte hé hæbbe ondfong on heofnum, seel and sibb on eorðo, forðgeong and gidyngo, Jn. p. 188, 11. (4) in a local sense, *an exit, a passage* (of part of the body):—Him eóde se innoð út æt his forðgange, Hml. S. 16, 207. Se deófol ne móste faran þurh þone múð út, ac fúllíce férde þurh his forðgang út, 31, 547. (4 a) *a privy*:—Forðgang *secessum*, Hpt. 33, 239, 22. v. út-gang.

**forþ-geclypian.** *Add*: Scint. 105, 15.

**forþ-gefaren**; *adj.* (*ptcpl.*) *Departed, deceased*:—Ðá bisene ðára forðgefarenra federa, Past. 77, 19.

**forþ-gegyrd** *an ornament on the martingale* (forþ-gyrd, q. v.) of a horse:—Forþgegyrdu *bullas, ornamenta cinguli* (cf. bulla, nodus in cingulo, i. 175, note 3), Wrt. Voc. ii. 126, 73.

**forþ-gelang.** *l.* forþ gelang. v. forþ, (7).

**forþ-geleóred**; *adj.* (*ptcpl.*) *Departed, deceased*:—In þǽra forðgeleóredra fædera dǽdum *in patrum praecedentium factis*, Bd. 4, 3; Sch. 356, 201.

**forþ-geleóredness**, e; *f. Departure, decease, death*:—For þǽre báde his ændes and forþgeleórodnesse *pro expectatione sui exitus*, Gr. D. 282, 11.

**forþ-genge.** *Substitute*: (1) *going forwards, progressing, having success.* Cf. forþ, 1 b:—Hú mæg se geleáfa beón forðgenge, gif seó lár and ðá láreówas áteoriað?, Ælfc. Gr. Z. 3, 8. Hé mid his bénum fylste þæt ðǽra bydela bodung forðgenge and Gode wæstmbǽre wurde, Hml. Th. ii. 126, 30. (2) *going on to completion, carried into effect.* v. forþ, 2 b:—Ðæt hé sprecende bebiét, þæt wyrcende oðíéwe, þæt his ðurh ðone fultum síé forðgenge *quod loquendo imperat, ostendo adjuvat, ut fiat*, Past. 81, 11. Þæs cáseres hǽs weard forðgencge *the emperor's order was carried into effect*, Hml. Th. i. 560, 22. (3) *going on continuously, in full operation, flourishing.* v. forþ, 3 a:—Ðínre módor forligr and fela unlybban syndon forðgenge *adhuc fornicationes matris tui et veneficia multa vigent* (2 Kings 9, 22), Hml. S. 18, 333.

**forþ-gesceaft.** *Add*: III. *a condition that continues* (? cf. forþ, 3), *the state of the angels whose tenure of heaven was to continue for ever*:—God þá nigon engla werod gestaþelfæste swá þæt hí nǽfre ne mihton fram his willan gebúgan, Hml. Th. i. 12, 8:—Engel Dryhtnes ealle fægere þurh forðgesceaft, Kr. 10.

**forþ-gewiten**; *adj.* (*ptcpl.*) *Past*:—His forðgewitenan yfelu hé sceal andettan, R. Ben. 18, 10.

**forþ-gewitenes.** *Add*:—Forðgewitenes *transmigratio* (v. 106, 10), Angl. xi. 7, 9.

**forþ-gyrd.** *Add*:—Forðgyrde *antela*, Wrt. Voc. ii. 10, 19. Mid forgyrdum *antelis*, Hpt. 31, 14, 335.

**forþ-heald.** *Add*: (1) *bent forwards, inclined from the perpendicular*: fig. *prone to*:—Andgit and geþóht menniscre heortan syndon forðhealde tó yfele (*in malum prona*), Gen. 8, 21. (2) *sloping, inclined to the horizontal*:—Se weg is rúm and forðheald þe tó deáðe and tó hellewíte lǽt, R. Ben. 5, 20.

**forþ-here, -herge.** *Dele* -herge, *and substitute*: *A host that marches forth*:—Hié getealdon on ðám forðherge féðan twelfe . . . on ánra gehwám . . . fíftig cista, hæfde cista gehwilc gárberendra týn hund (*the passage corresponds with Exodus* 12, 37: *Profecti sunt filii Israel* sexcenta fere millia peditum virorum), Exod. 225.

**forþ-hreósan**, Scint. 101, 13: for-ðí. v. se; V.

**forþian.** *Add:* I. *to send forth* or *out, dispatch:*—Mann sceolde forðian ūt tō Sandwīc scipu, Chr. 1052; P. 177, 8.     II. *to forward, promote the well-being of.* Cf. forþ-dǣd:—Hē friðige and forðige ǣlce tilðe, Angl. ix. 259, 14. Yrðe georne forðian, 261, 21. Þā menn gehabban and gehealdan þe ic forðian sceal, Solil. H. 35, 18.     III. *to carry out, accomplish, perform:*—Ealle Godes gerihto forðige man georne, Ll. Th. i. 168, 25. Forðige hē ofer þ geár ealle gerihtu ðe him tō gebyrigean, 434, 25. Se cyning betǣhte þām wyrhtan ungerim feós tō forðigenne þ weorc, Hml. S. 36, 105. [v. *N. E. D.* forth; *vb.*]

**for-þindan;** *pp.* -þunden *To swell up:*—Gif men sié maga āsūrod and forþunden, Lch. ii. 356, 11. v. for-þunden *in Dict.*

**forþ-leoran.** *l.* -leóran.

**forþlíce;** *adv. In a state of forwardness:*—Swā hit ǣfre forðlícor beón sceolde swā weard hit fram dæge tō dæge lætre and wyrre, Chr. 1066; P. 199, 37. [Cf. *N. E. D.* forthly; *adj.*]

**forþ-lífan.** *Dele, and see* hlīfian: forþ-loten. *See next word.*

**forþ-lūtan.** *For* Scint. 6: Prov. 29 *substitute*—Forþloten tō sārgungum *pronus ad lamenta*, Scint. 29, 9, 10. Forðloten *proclivior (ad peccandum)*, Kent. Gl. 1068.

**forþ-mann,** es; *m. A man of rank:*—Hē cwæð þ sum forðman wǣre on Myrcna lande, Nap. 25. Cf. forþ-þegn, -wíf.

**forþmest;** *adj. First.* (1) *of order in place or time:*—Swelc in endebrednisse forðmest ł ǣrest (*primus*) geseted is godspell ǣrest ł forðmest (*primus*) āwrāt, Mt. p. 12, 8. Cuoæð ðæm forðmesto (*primo*), Lk. L. 16, 5. Ða forðmesto (*primi*) hlætmest and ðā hlætmesto forðmæsto, p. 8, 7 : Mt. L. 20, 10. Wið ðæm forðmestum *usque ad primos*, 20, 8 : *prioribus*, 21, 36. Ða forðmesto sōðfæste *priores justos*, Lk. p. 6, 18. (2) *of age:*—Wēron seofo brōðro and ðe forðmest wíf lǣde, Mt. L. 22, 25. De foerðmesta, Mk. R. 12, 20. Tō ðǣm forðmest (*ældra,* R., yldran, W. S.), Mt. L. 21, 28. (3) *of rank or importance:*—Sē ðe wælle betuih iúh forðmest wossa, Mt. L. 20, 27. Foerðmest, Mk. R. 10, 44. Se forðmesta (foerð-, R., mæste, W. S.) bod, Mk. L. 12, 28. On ðæm forðmestum (foerð-, R.) seatlum sitta and ðā formesto setla, 12, 39.

**forðmest;** *adv. First:*—Cueð tō ðǣm apostolum and biscopum æfter him forðmest, Mt. L. 10, 8 note.

**forþ-onloten.** v. forþ, I a.

**for-þrǣstan.** *Add: to destroy by pressure.* (1) *to crush, break to pieces:*—Toeð synfulra ðū forðrǣstes (*conteruisti*), Ps. Srt. 3, 8. Forðrǣst (*contere*) earm ðes synfullan, 9, 36. Boga bið forðrǣsted, 36, 15. Reód forþrēst *calamum quassatum*, R. Ben. I. 108, 8. Forþrǣste *obtruncati*, An. Ox. 805. (2) *to strangle, choke:*—Forsmored, forþrǣstum *suffocato*, An. Ox. 1481. Woruldcara forsmoriað ðæs mōdes ðrotan . . . swilce hī ðone líflican blǣd forðrǣstne ācwellon, Hml. Th. ii. 92, 12. [v. *N. E. D.* forthrast.]

**for-þrǣstednes** and **for-þrǣstnes** *a crushing, breaking to pieces;* contritio :—Forðrēstednis *contritio*, Ps. Srt. 13, 3. Forðrēstnisse *contritiones*, 146, 3. Forðrāstnisse, 59, 4.

**forþ-riht.** *Substitute: Straight forward, direct, without variation or modification, plain:*—Forðrihte lēden leóðcræfte gelōgod, Ælfc. Gr. Z. 295, 15. Forðrihte *directanei* (directaneus *unico vocis tono, nulla modulatione dictus psalmus*, Migne), Wrt. Voc. ii. 140, 51. [v. *N. E. D.* forthright; *adj.*] *See* forþ-rihtes.

**forþ-rihte.** *Substitute:* (1) *of direction, straight on, without swerving :*—Forðrihte tō foregetihtgedre stōwe *indeclinabiliter ad destinatum locum,* Hpt. Gl. 406, 3. (2) *of manner, without modification or qualification, plainly, simply, directly.* (a) *of a title:*—Sarai is gereht ' Mīn ealdor,' ac God hí hēt syððan Sarra, þæt is, ' Ealdor,' þæt heó wǣre synderlíce hire hīrēdes ealdor gecíged, ac forðrihte ' Ealdor,' Hml. Th. i. 92, 19. Ne cwǣdon hī nā Ūre Hláford, ne Dīn Hláford, ac forðrihte Hláford, 210, 2. (b) *of the service in church.* Cf. forþ-riht; *adj.:*—Gif hit mycel gefērrǣden is, sýn hý mid antefene gesungene, gif seó gefērrǣden lytel is, sýn hý forðrihte (*in directum*) būtan sōne gesungene . . . ðā sealmas sýn gesungene forðrihte (*directanei*) būtan antefene, R. Ben. 41, 7–16. Forþrihte fram cilde gecwedenum *directo a puero prolato,* Angl. xiii. 429, 914. [v. *N. E. D.* forthright; *adv.*]

**forþ-rihtes;** *adv. Straight on :*—Þā sealmas forðrihtes būtan antemne sint tō singanne *psalmi directanei sine antiphona dicendi sunt,* R. Ben. I. 48, 6. v. forþ-riht, forþ-rihte, 2 b.

**for-þringan.** *Add: to thrust aside, crowd out :*—On nānum stōwum ne sý endebyrdnes be nānre ylde gefadod, ne seó yld þā geogoðe ne forþringe, R. Ben. 115, 7.

**for-þryccan.** *Add:* (1) *to injure* or *destroy by pressure.* (a) *literal:*—Mid þý fylle ðæs wāges forþryccende (*opprimens*) hē geþrǣste ǣnne þāra muneca, Gr. D. 125, 6. Ic wille mē segnian, ac ic ne mæg, for ðon ðe ic eom forseted and forðrycced (*premor*) mid þām scyllum þisses dracan, 325, 5. (b) *to torture:*—Beóð þā earman sāwla āhangene ofer þā hātestan līgeas, and þǣr ðonne beóð forþriccende (-ede ?) and gebundene, Ll. Th. ii. 400, 22. (2) *to close up* an opening:—Þā tōslitenan wunda heó forþrycceþ, Lch. i. 356, 15. Mūð his forðrycca (-ðrycga, L., dyttan, W.S. *opprimere*), Lk. R. 11, 53. [O. H. Ger. fer-druccen *premere, opprimere.*]

**for-þryc[c]ednes.** *Take here* for-þriccednes *in Dict., and add:*—Geberg from ferðrycednisse *refugium a pressura*, Ps. Srt. 31, 7.

**for-þrycness,** e; *f. Oppression, extortion :*—Þa unrihtwísan dēman him of hira ceasterwarena forðrycnesse gestreón gaderiað, Ll. Lbmn. 475, 26.

**for-þrysmian.** *Add:* -þrysman. (1) *to choke* as with smoke:—Þā Judēas Crýst mid stengum and myd blāsum hyne forþrysmodon and ūre leóht ofslōgon, Hml. A. 191, 291. Þæt sǣd mid þǣra þorna wæstme forðrysmod weard, Hml. Th. ii. 92, 6. Forðresmedon *suffocato*, An. Ox. 11, 100. (2) *to darken with smoke, cloud :*—Āsweartad, forsworcen, forþ[r]ysmed *fuscatus,* i. *denigratus, obnubilatus,* Wrt. Voc. ii. 152, 7.

**forþ-scencan.** *For* Cot. 149 *substitute* Wrt. Voc. ii. 65, 57.

**forþ-sige(?),** es; *m. Departure from this world to the lower regions* (?):—Efter his āwyrgedan forðsige (-síþe ?) ligce hē ǣfre on helle grundleásan pytte *post maledictum exitum suum crucietur jugiter in profundissimo puteo,* C. D. iv. 52, 8.

**forþ-síþ.** *Add:—Exitium,* i. *periculum* forþsíþ, ūtsíþ *mors perdictio,* Wülck. Gl. 231, 10. Ðonne him forðsīð gebyrige gýme his hláford ðæs hē lǣfe, Ll. Th. i. 434, 27. Behealdað hiera líf and hira forðsiíð, Past. 205, 16. Hē þām brōðrum cýðde hyre forðsíð (*obitum*), Gr. D. 169, 14 : Hml. Th. ii. 184, 19. v. for-síþ.

**forþ-stæppung,** e; *f. A stepping forth, proceeding, process :*—Þeáh ðe tō ðām Suna belimpe seó ācennednys, and tō þām Hālgan Gāste seó forðstæppung, Hml. Th. i. 500, 8. Mid forðsteppinge (*processu*) drohtnunga, R. Ben. I. 6, 8 : Hy. S. 80, 27.

**forþ-stefn.** *Add:*—Far ofer sǣ, and site on þes scipes forðstefna, ðonne . . . þū freónd findest begeondan þǣm sǣ, Lch. iii. 180, 4.

**forþ-swebbung(?)** *a storm:*—Forhswebung *procella,* Ps. Spl. T. 106, 25. [Cf. (?) *O. H. Ger.* swep (-b) *aer, vanum, gurges.*] v. forþ-swebban *in Dict.*

**forþ-tēge.** v. tīg *in Dict.:* forþ-teón. v. teón.

**forþ-þegen,** es; *m. A thane of high rank, a great noble :*—Sum forðþegn wæs welig Florus gehāften (cf. Se Florus wæs ðā fyrmest þǣra Francena þegna, 140), Hml. S. 6, 125 : 22, 38. Cf. forþ-mann.

**forþ-tíhan.** *l.* -teón, *and see* teón: forþ-tihting. *Dele:* for-þunden. v. for-þindan.

**forþung.** *Substitute: Forwarding, furtherance, promotion :*—Gold on swefnum handlian forðunge ceápes getācnað, Lch. iii. 198, 23. v. scip-forþung; forþian.

**forþ-weard;** *adj. Add to* III : *continued, carried on.* Cf. forþ, 3 : Þæs sylfa þeáw lange on Angelcynnes mynstrum forþweard wæs, Lch. iii. 434, 20. *For* I *and* II *substitute:* (1) *of direction in position, inclined forwards.* Cf. forþ, 1 a :—Mē (*a plough*) þurh hrycg wrecen hongað under ān orþoncpíl, ōðer on heáfde fæst and forðweard fealleð on sīdan, Rä. 22, 13. (1 a) *fig. inclined towards:*—Ontýn eárna hleoðor, þæt mín gehērnes hehtful weorðe . . . forðweard tō þē, Ps. C. 79. (2) *of direction of motion, advancing.* Cf. forþ, 1 b :—Ic (*a lance*) hwílum eðelfæsten forðweard brece, Rä. 72, 23. (3) *expressing state reached, forward, advanced.* Cf. forþ, 4 :—Ā swā hit forðweard[r]e (-werdre, -wærdre, *v. ll.*) beón sceolde, swā hit lætre wæs, Chr. 999; P. 133, 6. (4) *departed, deceased.* Cf. forþ, 6 a :—Þ him lifiendum wǣre þ tō wite þ þām forðweardan (forðfarenum, *v. l.*) men bið tō reste, Mart. H. 162, 8.

**forþ-weard;** *adv.* (1) *expressing motion, moving onwards :*—Mid þí þe hig ongunnon rōwan and hī forðwerd wǣron on heora weg (*they were making way*), Ap. Th. 10, 24. (1 a) *with a verb of motion, on, onwards :*—Nathan wæs forðwerd farende tōweard Rōmāna ríce, Hml. A. 181, 17. (2) *temporal.* (a) *continuously:*—Hē þeáh fægere forðwerd *he went on thriving,* Wlfst. 17, 8. (b) *prospectively, looking to the future:*—Þis gemet (*the imperative mood*) sprecð forðwerd (-weard, *v. l.*) and næfre praeteritum, for þan þe nán man ne hǣt dōu þæt ðe gedōn byð, Ælfc. Gr. Z. 125, 5. [v. *N. E. D.* forthward. *O. Sax.* forð-werd.] v. next word.

**forþ-weardes;** *adv. Forwards, on :*—Volosianus hym þā wæs forðwerdes farende and on ānes dæges færelde tō sǣ becōm, Hml. A. 188, 203. [*O. Sax.* forð-wardes, -werdes.] v. preceding word.

**forþ-weardness,** e; *f. Progress, growth in excellence :*—Se nídfulla mæssepreóst ne mihte wiðstandan þæs hālgan weres forðweardnesse and gōdum weorcum (*ejus profectibus obviare*), Gr. D. 117, 19.

**forþ-weg.** *Add:*—Hē his gāst āgeaf on Godes wǣre, fūs on forðweg (*desirous to depart*), Men. 218. [*O. Sax.* forð-weg.]

**forþ-werd, -werdes.** v. forþ-weard, -weardes.

**forþ-wíf.** *Substitute: A woman of rank, a great lady :*—Hláford *dominus,* forðwíf *matrona* (cf. þæs hláfdian *matrone,* ii. 54, 65), hlǣfdige *domina,* Wrt. Voc. i. 72, 78. v. forþ-mann, -þegn.

**for-þwyrftan (-þwyrtan)** *to cut off, cut down;* obtruncare :—Forþwyrtan *obtruncasse,* An. Ox. 5028. Fortþerty (= forþwyrte) *obtruncati,* 11, 75. Hí man forðwyrftum limum tō wæfersýne tucode, Hml. S. 28, 128.

**for-þyldian, -þyldigian.** *These two forms may be taken separately:* for-þyldian *to bear, suffer, take patiently :*—Gif syngiende gefýstlude

gē forþyldiaþ (*suffertis*), Scint. 7, 16. Forþyldigaþ *tollerant*, An. Ox. 4270. Forþyldiað mildheortnysse his *sustinete misericordiam ejus*, Scint. 65, 16. Forþildian *sustineant*, 114, 16. Forþyldian *tolerare*, 10, 10: *sufferre*, R. Ben. I. 20, 11. Gē wǣron forþyldiende costnunga, Hml. S. 30, 446. [Cf. *O. H. Ger.* fer-dulten *ferre, perferre.*]

**for-þyldigian.** *Add :*—Forþyldigað *suffert*, Hpt. Gl. 31, 14, 354. Forþyldigað *sustinebit*, Ps. L. 129, 3 : *tolerat*, Scint. 60, 9 : 150, 1 : 162, 11. Forþyldigiað *·tolerant*, 61, 16. Forðelgiað *sustinuere*, Kent. Gl. 1018. 'Forþyldiga þinne Drihten,' þæt is þola eall þæt God be þē geþafað . . . hī ealle līfes wiðerweardnesse forþyldigian (-þyldigan, *v. l.*) scylun, R. Ben. 27, 5–8. Tō forþyldigenne synd *tolerandi sunt*, Scint. 150, 6.

**for-þylman.** *Add :* ,-þylmian *to choke :*—þā māran wyrttruman beóð swýðe bittere on byrgincge, and hý habbaþ tō þām swýþlice mihte and frecenfulle þ hý foroft hrǣdlīce þone man forþilmiaþ (-þilmað, *v. l.*), Lch. i. 260, 13. Ðī lǣs strengð þǣre wyrte þā gōman bǣrne and for-ðylme, 316, 20.

**forþ-yppan.** For Cot. 150 *substitute :*—Forð yppeð *promulgatur*, Wrt. Voc. ii. 66, 7 : **for-þyrrian.** For þyr *l.* þyrre : **for-tīhan.** *Dele :* for-tihtend. v. for-tyhtend.

**for-timbr(i)an** *to obstruct, stop :*—Fortimbred is (*obstructum est*) mūð spreocendra, Ps. Srt. 62, 12. v. for-tymbrian in *Dict.*

**for-tīn(?),** es ; *n. A portent :*—Bēcun and fortīna (bēceno and fertīno, L.) *signa et portenta*, Mk. R. 13, 22. [Cf. (?) *Icel.* jar-tign, -tegn, -tein.]

**for-tog,** es ; *n. Gripes, colic :*—Wiþ innan fortoge [innanfortoge?] and smælþearma ece, Lch. ii. 300, 27 : 324, 8. v. for-togenness.

**for-togen.** v. for-teón ; I.

**for-togennes.** *Add :*—Wiþ fortogenysse, Lch. i. 370, 1. Fortog-onysse, 368, 3.

**for-togian ;** *p.* ode *To contract :*—þā sina fortogiað, Lch. iii. 120, 8.

**for-tredan.** *Add :*—*Contrivit* geþrǣste *minuit* fortræd, Wrt. Voc. ii. 134, 80. Þte hiá ne fortrēdon (-un, R.) hine *ne compremerent eum*, Mk. L. 3, 9. [*v. N. E. D.* fortread. *O. H. Ger.* fer-tretan *proterere, conculcare.*] v. un-fortreden.

**for-treddan ;** *p. de To tread down, destroy by treading :*—Swā swā rīpe yrð hī fortreddon and fornāmon and hī ealle foryrmdon *quasi maturam segetem obuia quaeque metunt, calcant, transeunt*, Bd. 1, 12 ; Sch. 32, 22. [*O. H. Ger.* for-tratta *proterit.*]

**for-treding.** *Add :*—Mūð dysiges fortredincg (*contritio*) his *a fool's mouth is his destruction* (Prov. 18, 7), Scint. 95, 10.

**for-trendan ;** *p. de To obstruct by rolling, stop* an opening :—Hī nāmon swīðe micelne stān and fortrendon þǣre byrgenne ðuru *they took a very big stone and stopped the sepulchre's mouth by rolling the stone to it*, Nap. 62.

**for-trūwian.** *Add* [-trūwan] ; *p.* trūwde ; *pp.* trūwed (cf. for-trūwed-nes) :—Ðonne hī hié fortrūwiað on ðǣm cræftum ðe hī hæbbað *cum de confidentia uirium inordinate securi sunt*, Past. 463, 7. Ðā for-trūwdes ðū ðe for ðǣm *habens fiduciam in pulchritudine tua*, 463, 25. Ðæt hié ðencen tō him selfum and ne fortrūwigen hié for óðerra monna weorcum *ut ad suum cor redeant, et de alienis actibus non praesumant*, 231, 12.

**for-trūwodnes (-ed-).** *Add :*—Word fortrūgadnisse *verba praecipitationis*, Ps. Srt. 51, 6. Ðā ðe for hira fortrūwodnesse and for hira hrǣdwilnesse beóð tō (ðǣre lāre) gescofene *quos praecipitatioimpellit*, Past. 375, 20. Hē bið genēd mid sumre fortrūwodnesse *temeritate impellitur praecipitationis*, 453, 19. Ðurh ðā fortrūwednesse *per hanc fiduciam*, 463, 28.

**for-trūwung.** *Add :*—Gerest ðæt mōd hit orsorglīce on ðǣre for-trūwunga (*confidentia*), Past. 463, 11. For ðǣre fortrūwunga (*fiducia*) his cræfta, 27.

**for-tyhtan.** *Add :*—Fǣrtyhted *clinici*, Wrt. Voc. ii. 104, 14. [Þe fule gost and seuene oðre gostes . . . fortehten þ child . . . swo þ it eft bifel on his oðer wune, O. E. Hml. ii. 87, 30. Cf. þe deuel mid his for-tihtinge (*per suggestionem*) bringeð unnut þonc on mannes heorte, 107, 5.] v. next word.

**for-tyhtend, -igend,** es ; *m. A seducer, an unchaste person :*—Wrǣne fortyhtigend (-tiht- *corruptor*, Hpt. Gl. 484, 56) *petulcus incestator* i. *maculator*, An. Ox. 3337. Fortihtend *clinice*, i. *lectus tetrus*, Wrt. Voc. ii. 131, 71. [Cf. (?) for-liger *for the sense in which* clinicus *has been taken.*] v. preceding word.

**for-tyllan.** v. tyllan : **for-tymbrian.** v. for-timbrian.

**for-tȳnan.** *Substitute :* To *shut up, prevent passage along a road, into or out of a place :*—þā scearpan þing sint fortȳende þā innoþas, Lch. ii. 212, 1.

**for-ūton.** *Substitute :* **for-ūtan ;** *prep.* (1) *without :*—Ān speorwa on grȳn ne mæg befeallan forūtan his forescēawunge (cf. būtan eówrum Fæder, Mt. 10, 29), Chr. 1067 ; P. 201, 25. Forūtan ǣlces cynnes riht, 1070 ; P. 207, 25. [(2) *except :*—Ealle þā gersumes forūton feáwe bēc, Chr. 1122 ; P. 250, 18.] [*v. N. E. D.* forout.]

**for-wandian.** *Add :* I. *to reverence :*—þ mǣden mid forwandi-gendre sprǣce cwæð *the maid speaking respectfully said*, Ap. Th. 15,

17. II. *to hesitate from fear* to do something (with a negative clause) :—Sume seóce menn forwandigað þ hý nellað geþafian þ hī man smyrige on heora untrumnysse, Ll. Th. ii. 354, 14. Ne forwandede (fore-, An. Ox. 466, 3) *non vereretur* (*violenter irrumpere*), Hpt. Gl. 514, 22.

**for-wandigendlīce, -wandodlīce, -līce.** v. un-forwandigendlīce, -wandodlīce, -līce.

**for-wandung.** *Add :*—Forwandunge *pudore*, Ps. Rdr. 34, 26. For-wandunga *verecundiam*, 6S, 20.

**for-weallen.** *Substitute :* **for-weallan ;** *pp.* -weallen *To boil away :*—Wylle eft oþ þ þæt eced sié forweallen, Lch. ii. 252, 23.

**for-wealwian ;** *p.* ode *To wither up, wither away.* [v. *N. E. D.* forwelewe.] v. un-forwealwod.

**fōr-weard ;** *adv.* l. for-weard, *and see* forþ-weard.

**for-weaxan.** *Add :*—Gif wamb forweaxe on men, Lch. ii. 238, 29. Ne eft hē ne lǣte forweahsan (-weaxan, *v. l.*) tō swīðe tō unnytte . . . hē mǣge hié ȳðelīce of āceorfan ðæt hié tō ungemetlīce ne forweaxen *nec rursum ad crescendum nimis relaxet . . . recidantur citius, ne immoderatius excrescant*, Past. 141, 1–6. [*The Latin to* Past. 40. 3 [=Swt. 293, 6] *is :* Ne immoderate crescendo fructus amittant.] Cf. for-grōwan.

**for-wel.** *Add :*—Forebeácn forwel manegum *prodigium multis*, Ps. L. 70, 7 : Hml. S. 30, 7. Forwel oft *interdum*, i. *aliquando*, An. Ox. 3346.

**for-wemman ;** *p. de To defile :*—Hē manega his māgan mānlīce forwernde, Sal. K. p. 121, 38.

**for-wēnan ;** *p. de To suspect, think ill of :*—Forwēned *suspecta*, Nap. 25.

**for-wēnan** *to overween.* *Substitute :* **for-wened** *glosses* insolens :— Feruuaenid, foruuened *insolens*, Txts. 70, 548. þā forwenedan *insolentiam*, Wrt. Voc. ii. 87, 53. Cf. ofer-wenian, *and next word.*

**for-wenedness** *glosses* insolentia :—Forwenednessa *insolentiam*, Nap. 25. v. preceding word.

**for-weoren.** *Substitute :* **for-weoren** (-wer-, -wor-) ; *adj.* (*ptcpl.*) *Withered away, very old, decrepit, worn out with age :*—Decrepita i. *vetula* forweren *valde senex*, Wrt. Voc. ii. 137, 76. Forwered, forworen *decrepita*, i. *inueterata*, An. Ox. 2109. Eorðgrāp wyrhtan hafað for-weorone geleórene, Ruin. 7. v. next two words.

**for-weorenness,** e ; *f. Extreme old age, decrepitude :*—Forwerennisse *senium*, Ps. Rdr. 70, 18. Cf. for-weredness.

**for-weornian.** *Add :*—Forweornaþ (-wurnað, Hpt. Gl. 436, 53) *marcescit*, i. *arescit*, An. Ox. 1273. Hraðe se līchama āswint and for-weornað, gif him oftogen bið his bigleofa, Hml. Th. i. 266, 3. Rōme burh on hire sylfre forweornað (weosnað and brosnaþ, *v. l., marcescet*), Gr. D. 134, 2. Forwærniað *marcescunt*, Wrt. Voc. ii. 55. 35. þæt mænnisce cynn forslagen forweornode *humanum genus succisum aruit*, Gr. D. 258, 13. Forweornodon *tabuerunt*, An. Ox. 8, 227. Forwurn-ende *polluta, maculata*, Hpt. Gl. 448, 45.

**for-weorpan.** *Add :* I. *to throw away :*—Mið ðȳ forwarp *rejecta* [*sindone*], Mk. L. R. 14, 52. I a. *fig.,* of reckless or fruitless expenditure :—Ðȳ lǣs mon unnytlīce mierre ðæt ðæt hē hæbbe, gehíeren menn ðisne cwide : 'Heald ðīne ælmessan, ðȳ lǣs ðū hié forweorpe,' Past. 325, 4. God nele þ wē beón grǣdige gȳtseras, ne eác for woruld-gylpe forwurpan ūre ǣhta, Hml. S. 16, 330. His feoh þe hē wēnð þ him forwurpen sȳ (*lost to him by useless expenditure*), 36, 150. II. *to throw out, cast out :*—Dióblæs wē forworpon *daemonia ejecimus*, Mt. L. 7, 22. Ðegn forworpes (*eicite*), 25, 30. þ hē foruorpa *ut eiciat*, 9, 38. þte ðone diówl hē forwurpe (*eiceret*), Mk. L. R. 7, 26. [v. *N. E. D.* forwerpe.]

**for-weorpness,** e ; *f. Ejection, expulsion :*—Tō forworpnise Babilones *ad transmigrationem Babylonis*, Mt. L. 1, 17. v. preceding word.

**for-weorþan.** *Add :* (1) *to become ill :*—Philippus forweard on mōde, Hml. S. 2, 104. (1 a) of food, *to go bad :*—Gif salt forworðes *si sal evanuerit*, Mt. L. 5, 13. (1 b) *to come to a bad end :*—His geféran ealle forwurdon tō deáðe, Ap. Th. 11, 6. (2) *to perish.* (a) of death :— Ealle þā ðe sweord nymað, mid swurde hig forweorþað (-wurþað, *v. l. peribunt*), Mt. 26, 52. Fugla briddas forweorðað *pulli avium in ima merguntur*, Past. 383, 41. Wyrþigre wrace hié forwurdon, Ors. 6, 2 ; S. 256, 12. þȳ lǣs wēn sié þæt wē yfele forweorþon, Bl. H. 247, 2. Hȳ sculon æt Seaxena handa forwurðan, Chr. 605 ; P. 23, 7. Hié fornǣh mid ealle forslægene and forwordene wǣron, Ors. 2, 2 ; S. 64, 33. (a a) of an animal's death :—Ic gedwolede swā swā þ sceáp þ forwearþ, Bl. H. 87, 31. (b) of the destruction of things :—Ne an loc of eówrum heáfde forwyrð, Bl. H. 243, 33. þǣr forweorþ .cxx. scipa, Chr. 877 ; P. 74, 16. Healdan heora forweorðendan welan *perituras divitias custodire*, Gr. D. 201, 15. (b a) *fig.* :—Forweorð *peribit* (*lingua pravorum*), Kent. Gl. 342. (c) in a moral or spiritual sense :—Ðonne forwyrð ðīn brōður for ðīnum ðingum, Past. 451, 33. Hē eóde on wēsten þǣr ǣr Adam forwearþ, Bl. H. 29, 18. þȳ lǣs gē forwyrþen (*pereatis*) of wege ryhtum, Ps. Rdr. 2, 12. Wē scoldan forweorðan ēcan deáðe nǣre þæt Crīst for ūs deáð þrowode, Wlfst. 111, 7. On mē earmre is mīnes fæder nama reówlīce forworden, Ap. Th. 2, 22. [v. *N. E. D.* forworth. *Goth.* fra-wairþan : *O. Sax.* far-werðan : *O.H. Ger.* fer-werdan.]

**for-wered.** *Take here* **for-werod** *in Dict., and add : Used up :*—Foruerit *abusus*, Txts. 109, 1135. (1) of material, *worn out :*—In wéde ald **ł** foruered *in vestimentum vetus*, Mt. L. 9, 16. (2) of persons, *decrepit :*—Forwered *decrepita* (*anicula*), An. Ox. 2109. Eald wíf . . . þonne heó forwerod býð and teárnes ætealdod, Hml. A. 20, 158. Cild oððe forwerod man, Hml. Th. i. 236, 25. Wæron hí bútan cilde oð þæt hí wæron forwerede menn, 202, 1. Hit is swíðe ungedafenlic þæt forwerode menn and untýmende gifta wilnian, ii. 94, 11. (2 a) of advanced age :—Forweredre *decrepitae* (*uetustatis*), An. Ox. 2522. Seó þridde wæcce is on forweredre ylde, Hml. A. 52, 69. þá forweredan *decrepitam* (*senectam*), An. Ox. 2411. [v. *N. E. D.* forwear.]

**for-werednes.** *Add : decrepitude.* Cf. for-weorenness : **for-weren.** v. for-weoren : **for-wernedlíce.** v. for-wirnedlíce : **for-werod.** v. for-wered : **forwest.** v. forwost.

**for-wiernan.** *Take here* **for-weornan, -wernan, -wyrnan** *in Dict. and add :* (1) *to refuse* something (*gen.*) *to a person* (*dat.*), *deny :*—Hé þæs teóþan dǽles Gode forwyrneþ, Bl. H. 51, 5. Hié him þára béna forwierndon, Ors. 2, 2 ; S. 64, 27. Him ǽtes forwyrnan, Hml. S. 22, 137. Him nánes willan næs forwyrnd, ne nánes lustes, Ps. Th. 48, 11. (1 a) with gen. of thing only :—Welena forwyrned, frófre bedǽled, Dóm. L. 30, 27. (1 b) with dat. of person only (*a*) *to refuse to give :*—Hé heóld his ǽhta him tó weán, and forwyrnde (-on, MS.) þám Drihtnes þearfum . . . þ man þǽm earman forwyrne, þ is mycel synn, Bl. H. 53, 8–22. (β) *to refuse admittance :*—Hé slóg on þæs húses duru and heó him ne forwyrnde, ac heó hié ontýnde, Bl. H. 141, 31. (1 c) construction not given :—Forweornde *denegabam* (*gloriam*), An. Ox. 4796. (2) *to refuse* to do something (*clause*) :—Hé forwirnð (*recusat*) ðæt hé his helpe, Past. 377, 19. (3) *to restrain* a person (*dat.*) from something (*gen.*), *prevent, prohibit :*—Se assa geseah ðone engel . . . him ðæs fǽreltes forwiernan *prohibitione immorata asina angelum videt*, Past. 255, 25. Ðá ðe welena wilniað, and mid sumum wiðerweardum brocum hiora him bíð færwirned, 387, 8. Him wæs forwyrned ðæs inganges, Hex. 26, 17. Seó wrænnes bíð ǽlcum men gecynde, and hwílum ðeáh hire biþ forwerned hire gecyndes ðurh þæs monnes willan *gignendi opus, quod natura semper appetit, interdum coercet voluntas*, Bt. 34, 11 ; F. 152, 13. (3 a) *to hinder, prevent* a person (*acc.*) :—Búton hine þǽra þinga hwylc forwyrne, Wlfst. 285, 14. (3 b) *to prevent* something (*clause*) :—Hé wile forwyrnan (-weornan, v. l.) þ hit ne gewyrþe *he will prevent its happening*, Bt. 41, 3 ; F. 250, 12. (3 c) construction not given :—Forwyrnende *conpescens*, i. *uetitans*, An. Ox. 1782.

**for-wirdan ;** *p. de To corrupt, destroy :*—Heora forwyrdendan (-weorðendan, v. l.) welan *perituras divitias*, Gr. D. 201, 15. [*Goth.* frawardjan *to corrupt : O. H. Ger.* fer-warten *corrumpere, demoliri.*] v. un-forwirded, *and cf.* (?) for-wyrþendlic.

**for-wirnedlíce ;** *adv. With restraint, abstemiously :*—Se man ðe wile on ǽlce tíd heardlíce and forwernedlíce lyfigean, sé bið fulfremed. Gyf þæt þonne hwylc mon sý, þæt him on his móde tó earfoðe þince, þæt hé on ǽlce tíd swá forwernedlíce lyfige, tylige hé þonne húru þæt hé þis fæsten sélost afæste, Wlfst. 284, 7–12.

**for-wirnedness,** e ; *f. Restraint, continence, abstemiousness :*—Hé þá fægerestan bysene forlét, þæt hé wæs micelre forhæfdnesse and forwyrnednesse lífes *saluberrimum abstinentiae uel continentiae exemplum reliquit*, Bd. 3, 5 ; Sch. 202, 11. Hé hæfde forwyrnednesse on his líchoman ǽghweder ge on mete ge on hrægle ge on ǽghwylcum þinge, Bl. H. 219, 29.

**for-wisnian.** *Add :*—Forwisnode *emarcuit*, Wrt. Voc. ii. 30, 36. Forwisnade sónæ se fíc *arefacta est continuo ficulnea*, Mt. R. 21, 19. For þon þe hié næfdan wyrtryme forwisnadun (*aruerunt*), 13, 6. Forwisnende (-werniende, An. Ox. 59) *corruptibilem*, Hpt. Gl. 407, 34. þá forwisnedon *marcida*, Wrt. Voc. ii. 55, 36. Forweosnodon *arescentibus*, 73, 71.

**for-witolnes.** *Add :*—Scel se abbod mid ealre glǽwnesse and forwitolnesse gelácnian ǽnig of sceápum þ hé ná forlure *debet abbas omni sagacitate et industria curare ne aliquam de ovibus perdat*, R. Ben. I. 58, 10.

**for-word** *glosses* iota :—Foruord **ł** pricle *iota*, Mt. L. 5, 18.

**for-wordenlic ;** *adj. Substitute : Corrupt :*—þysse worulde wela is wyrslic and ýsellic and forwordenlic, Wlfst. 263, 13. v. un-forwordenlic.

**for-woren.** v. for-weoren : **for-worhta.** *Dele, and see* for-wyrcan : **for-worpness.** v. for-wyrpness.

**forwost,** es ; *m. A chief person, prince, captain :*—Diówla foruost Beelzebub, Mt. L. 10, 25. Forðmest **ł** foruost wosa *primus esse*, 20, 27. Ofer ðrím hundradum *tribunus* bið forwost, Mk. L. 6, 21 rbc. Aldormonn **ł** foruost *princeps* (*publicanorum*), Lk. L. 19, 2. Ðe aldormonn **ł** is cynnes heáfuduærd **ł** foruost *tribunus*, Jn. L. 18, 12. Forwostum ðæra sácerda, Mt. L. 20, 18. Forwostum (forwestum, R.) Galilæas *primis Galilaeae*, Mk. L. 6, 21.

**for-wracnian ;** *p. ode To be an exile :*—þám forwracnedum elþeódigum *peregrinis*, R. Ben. 82, 2.

**for-wrecan.** *Add :*—þám forwrecenum elþeódegum *peregrinis*, R. Ben. 83, 1. [*Goth.* fra-wrikan.]

**for-wrégan.** *Add :*—Forwréged *publicatus, abdicatus*, An. Ox. 7, 146. [v. *N. E. D.* forwray. *Goth.* fra-wróhjan : *O. H. Ger.* fer-ruogen *accusare.*]

**for-wríþan.** *Add :*—Hafa þé línenne wǽtlan gearone þ þú þ dolh sóna mid forwríðe, Lch. ii. 208, 22.

**for-wundorlic ;** *adj. Very wonderful :*—Is þ forwundorlic wíse and in úrum tídum tó wafienne *res mira et nostris stupenda temporibus*, Gr. D. 240, 4 : 255, 25 : 229, 20.

**for-wurnian.** v. for-weornian : **for-wynned.** v. for-wyrned.

**for-wyrcan.** *Add :* p. -wyrhte ; *pp.* -wyrht. **I.** *to do wrong, be guilty :*—Búton hé forworhte, þ hé þǽre hádnote notian ne móste, Ll. Th. i. 192, 16. **II.** *to injure* or *destroy by wrongful working.* (1) *to treat improperly, use badly :*—Hié witan willað hwæt hié sellað, and nyllað wietan mid hwelcum woo hié hit gestríendon oððe forworhton (*wasted it*), Past. 343, 24. þæt hé néfre ne mugen forwerken míne quide (*fail to carry out my bequest*), Cht. Th. 508, 20. (2) *to bring to an end :*—On worulde geendunge bið seó gálnys forwyrht, and on ðære áblind ǽlc hǽmed, Hml. Th. ii. 70, 2. (3) *to ruin :*—Ðá sibbe hé forlét and hine mid ðǽm forworhte, Past. 361, 3. Ðurh mænigfealde synna heora eard hý forworhton, Wlfst. 166, 30. Seó mennisce gesceaft þe ðurh Adam forworht wæs, 34, 1. Hæfdon hý forworhte hý sylfe and wurdon of þǽre myrhðe áworpene, 9, 11. Wé wǽron forwyrhte, Hml. Th. ii. 6, 8. (4) *to make guilty :* reflex. *to commit crime* against (*wiþ*) :—Swegen forworhte hine wið Denum, Chr. 1050 ; P. 169, 16. þeáh hwá ágylte and hine sylfne deópe forwyrce (*commit grievous crime*), Ll. Th. i. 376, 16. Gif man hine forwyrce mid deáðscylde, 400, 27 : ii. 290, 8. þæt hé hine sylfne openlíce wið God forwyrce mid heálicre misdǽde, Wlfst. 154, 25 : Ll. Th. ii. 312, 32. Ealle þá þe fordémede wǽron oþþe hié selfe forworht hæfdon *homines quicunque sceleribus obnoxii essent*, Ors. 4, 9 ; S. 190, 36. ¶ for-worht, -wyrht *guilty, criminal, sinful.* (*a*) as regards human law :—Wið cyning forwyr[h]t *majestatis reus*, Wrt. Voc. i. 21, 13. Se scyldiga man þe býð wið sumne king forweorht, Shrn. 200, 28. Wið his hláford forworht, Past. 143, 3. Gif hé náne gewitnysse hæbbe þ hé forworht síg (*eum malefactorem fuisse*), Ll. Th. ii. 182, 30. Sum forworht wíf dón on carcern, Wlfst. 2, 19. Hé monegum ýselum wið hine selfne forworhtum geárode *malis noverat parcere*, Past. 37, 1. (*b*) as regards divine law :—þ se rihtwísa man hreówsige hine sylfne swylce hé wið God forwyrht síg *ut justus homo poenitentiam agat eorum quae erga Deum deliquerit*, Ll. Th. ii. 174, 7. Forworht, Wlfst. 14, 2. Synnum tó fúlne and swýðe forwyrhtne, 34, 16. Ðú, forwyrhte (*the lost soul*), 240, 9. þá forworhtan (*the wicked*) Bl. H. 101, 4 ; P. firnedon, Sat. 620. þá forwyrhtan (forworhtan, fordémde, v. ll.), Wlfst. 24, 21 : 26, 3. **II a.** *to bring* to an ill condition :—Eal mancyn wæs þurh deófles láre . . . forworht intó helle wíte, Wlfst. 22, 1. **III.** *to lose by evildoing, to forfeit.* (1) in a general sense :—Hé hefonríce mid his ágenre scylde forworhte *ipse coelum perdidit*, Past. 233, 20 : Hex. 18, 11 : Wlfst. 103, 25. Hé nolde niman mancyn neádunga of ðám deófle, búton hé hit forwyrhte, Hml. Th. i. 216, 6. Tó ðám earde wé wǽron gesceapene, ac wé hit forwyrhton, ii. 222, 12. (2) as a legal term :—þá .iii. hída þe Wístán forworhte wið þone cyning mid unrihtum monslihte, Cht. Crw. 20, 27 (see note p. 113 on crimes for which forfeiture of land was a penalty). Hæbbe hé hit . . . bútan hé hit forwyrce, Cht. E. 238, 24. Hit wæs his lǽn ðæt hé on sæt, hé mearkte ná his forwyrcan, C. D. ii. 134, 35. Heó hit náge mid nánon þinge tó forwyrcenne, ac hæbbe heó ðone bryce, vi. 147, 35. Sí forworht eal þe hé áge, Ll. Th. i. 330, 23. Gif hé bócland hæbbe sý þ forworht þám cyninge tó handa, 382, 19. **IV.** *to bring about, cause* what is evil :—Wé geedníwiað and gemyndgiað ðǽre scylde ðe úre ieldesta mǽg ús on forworhte *parentis primi lapsus iteratur*, Past. 312, 15. [v. *N. E. D.* forwork ; forwrought. *Goth.* fra-waurkjan *to sin* (also reflex.) ; fra-waurhts *sinful : O. H. Ger.* fer-wurchen ; fra-wurht *flagitiosus.* Cf. *O. Sax.* far-werkôn, -wirkian *to sin* (reflex.) ; *to forfeit.*] v. un-forworht.

**fŏr-wyrcan.** l. for-wyrcan, *and add :*—Wé ðone biteran wille æt ðǽm ǽsprynge forwyrceað and ádrýgað, Past. 307, 1. Hé hét þæs scræfes ingang ðǽr hí inne lágon eall hit mid weorcstánum forwyrcan . . . Hé clypode : ' Hí man mid weorcstáne on ǽghwilce healfe ðǽrinne forwyrce, þ hí sunnan leóman nǽfre lengc ne geseón,' Hml. S. 23, 315–24. Hé hét þ scræf forwyrcan, 758. Hét ic eft þá ðyrelo mid golde forwyrcean and áfyllan (*metallo complevi*), Nar. 20, 4. [*O. H. Ger.* furiwurchen *obstruere.*] v. un-forworht.

**for-wyrd.** *Add :* (1) *f.* or *uncertain :*—Deós forwyrd *perditio haec*, Mt. R. L. 26, 8. Is án forwyrd and ænde (*interitus*) þæs mannes and nýtena, Gr. D. 264, 16. Cwilde, forwyrde *internicioni*, Wrt. Voc. ii. 43, 72 : Guth. 38, 22. Forwirde dæg *dies perditionis*, Deut. 32, 35. Weg ðe lǽt tó færwyrde (for-, v. l.), Past. 133, 20 : 457, 11 : 463, 6, 8. In écere forwyrde, Wlfst. 188, 8. Fram þǽre écan forwyrde, Gr. D. 348, 19. On éce forwyrde, Bl. H. 101, 13 : 159, 20. Tó écum forwyrdum, Hml. Th. i. 516, 3. (2) *n.* :—On seað forwyrdes *in puteum interitus*, Ps. L. 54, 24. Sleges, forwyrdes *internitionis*, An. Ox. 835 : Wlfst. 193, 22 : R. Ben. 68, 22 : Hml. Th. i. 194, 30. þá bydelas

þæs ēcan forwyrdes, 4, 12. Tô ûrum forwyrde, ii. 546, 11: Chr. 1052; P. 175, 27. On ēcan forwyrde, Wlfst. 8, 9. [*O. H. Ger.* ferwurt *interitus.*] v. on-forwyrd.

**for-wyrdende.** v. for-wirdan: **for-wyrht** *criminal.* v. for-wyrcan.

**for-wyrht.** *Substitute:* e; *f. Evil-doing, crime, sin:*—Būton forwyrhtum *sine malefactis*, Ll. Th. ii. 238, 11. [*Goth.* fra-waurhts: *O. Sax.* far-wurht.]

**for-wyrnan, -wyrnednes.** v. for-wirnan, -wirnedness.

**for-wyrþendlic;** *adj. Perishable:*—Forwyrþendlice welan *perituras divitias*, Scint. 43, 11. Cf. (?) for-wirdan.

**for-yldan, -yrman, -yrþ.** v. for-ildan, -irman, -irþ: **Foss** *the Roman road.* v. C. D. vi. 288, col. 2.

**fôster;** *m.* (not *n.*). *Dele first passage, and add:* (1) *food, nourishment, sustenance:*—Sió lifer is blôdes timber and blôdes hûs and fôstor, Lch. ii. 198, 2. Seó sôðe lufu is þǽre sāwle fôstor, Ll. Th. ii. 428, 38. Geunn ûs tô þissum dǽge dæghwāmlices fôstres, Wlfst. 125, 11. Wǽron earme men besyrwde æt fôstre, 158, 31. Mid ðām fôstre (*nutrimento*) ðǽre Godes lufan weaxan, Past. 263, 17. Ðiós eorðe eallum mannum bringð gemǽnne fôster *terra alimenta omnibus communiter profert*, 335, 11. Fôster *alimoniam*, An. Ox. 3863. (2) *feeding, giving food:*—His discipuli woldon þæt folc fēdan, ac hî næfdon mid hwām; se Hǽlend hæfde þone gôdan willan tô ðām fôstre, and þā mihte tô ðǽre fremminge, Hml. Th. i. 184, 22. (3) *bringing up, fostering.* Cf. fēdan; I. 5:—Wǽron þā æþelingas befæste Egcbrihte tô fôstre, Lch. iii. 424, 12. Hē eftwunade from his fôstre (? *the MS. has* fost *with a curl over the* o. v. *note, p.* 249) *he remained behind out of the care of his parents* (?); remansit a suis, Lk. p. 4, 4. (4) *bringing forth progeny.* Cf. fēdan; III:—Ic gegaderige in tô þē of deórcynne and of fugelcynne symble gemacan, þæt hî eft tô fôstre beón (cf. ut salvetur semen super faciem terrae, Gen. 7, 3), Hml. Th. i. 20, 35. [v. *N. E. D.* foster.] v. tûdor-fôster.

**fôster-bearn.** *For Cot.* 9 *substitute:*—Fôstorbearn (fôstar-, fôstribarn, *v. ll.*) *alumnae*, Txts. 39, 131. Fôsterbearn, Wrt. Voc. ii. 88, 62: 5, 45.

**fôster-brôþor.** *Add:*—Fôsterbrôðor *alumnus*, Wrt. Voc. ii. 8, 20.

**fôster-cild.** *Add:* (1) lit. *a foster-child:*—Fôstorcild *alumnum, seruum*, Germ. 391, 48. Ic eom untýmende; nim mîne þinene tô þînum bedde, þæt ic hûru underfó sum fôstercild of hyre, Gen. 16, 2. Hēr synd þā cnihtas . . . þine fôstercyld, Hml. S. 2, 243. (2) fig. (a) *of a disciple, scholar, &c.:*—Hē (*St. Martin*) sǽde his gyngrum þæt hē sceolde gewîtan. Hî hine befrinon: 'Hwî forlǽtst þû, fæder, ðîne fôstercild?,' Hml. Th. ii. 516, 20. (b) *of a provincial in his relation to Rome:*—Æfter menniscum gebyrde ic eom Hispaniscis, Rômānisc fôstorcild, Hml. Th. i. 428, 22.

**fôster-fæder.** *Add:* (1) *of human beings.* (a) lit.: Fôsterfæder *altor*, i. *nutritor* (Alexander, who brought up Athanasius), An. Ox. 2841: Wrt. Voc. ii. 80, 62: 92, 28. Fôstorfæder, 100, 7. Jôseph, Crîstes fôsterfæder, Hml. Th. i. 30, 6: 42, 4. Fôstorfæder, 148, 34. Côm hire fôsterfæder (cf. se cing þæt mǽdencild hēt ût āweorpan— and Theothimus gefand þ cild and hē hit wel befæste tô fēdenne, 170, 13–16), Hml. A. 175, 178. (b) *of a teacher or tutor:*—Ûre hyrde and ûre fôsterfæder (fêster-, *v. l.*) Sanctus Petrus *pastor et nutritor noster beatus Petrus*, Gr. D. 228, 22. Neron wolde hātan his āgenne mǽgistre and his fôsterfæder (*Senecam familiarem praeceptoremque suum*) ācwellan, Bt. 29, 2; F. 104, 19. (2) *of superhuman beings:*—Crîst, fôsterfæder (*altor*) ealra þinga, Hy. S. 65, 35. [*Icel.* fôstr-faðir.]

**fôster-land.** *Add: Land assigned for the support of monks* (ad cibum monachorum) [:—Ich Æðelstān . . . grantye . . . xxx. hýden on Sidemyntone tô fôsterland, and tô at Chelmyntone, and six at Hylsfelde, C. D. v. 236, 10.]

**fôster-leán.** *Add:* [*Icel.* fôstr-laun.]: **fôsterling.** *Add:* v. fêsterling: **fôsterman.** *Dele.*

**fôster-môdor.** *Add:*—Þeós fôstormôdor *haec nutrix*, Ælfc. Gr. Z. 71, 3. (1) lit.:—His fôstormôdor (*nutrix*) āne wæs him fylgende, for þon þe heó hine swýðe geornlíce lufode, Gr. D. 96, 20: 152, 28. Fôstermôder, Hml. A. 171, 49. (2) fig.:—Sió fôstermôdur ælces cræftes *virtutum nutrix*, Past. 215, 23. Nytenyss leahtra fôstermôder (*nutrix*), Scint. 98, 1. [*O. L. Ger.* fôstir-môdar *nutrix: Icel.* fôstr-môðir.]

**fôster-nôþ;** *m.? l.* fôstemoþ; *m.*, *and add: food, provisions:*—Fôsternoð *pulmentum*, Wrt. Voc. ii. 66, 13. Wæs neódþearf þ heom wǽre bûtan yldinge gegearwod se mete and fôstornoð (-nað, *v. l.*) þǽre dæghwāmlican andleofne *necesse erat ut quotidiani sumtus laborantibus sine dilatione praeberentur*, Gr. D. 251, 16. Sceáp fôstornoþes (*pascue*) his, Ps. Rdr. 94, 7. Etan of þām fôstornoþe mînre môdur *de nutrimentis matris meae manducare*, Gr. D. 70, 7. Fôstern[oþ?] *alimoniam*, An. Ox. 2, 263. Cf. fôdnoþ, fôddornoþ.

**fôst-raþ.** *For Som. Ben. Lye substitute:* Wrt. Voc. ii. 32, 41: **fôstre.** *Add:* [v. *N. E. D.* foster *a nurse. Icel.* fôstra *a fostermother, nurse.*]: **fôstrian.** *Add:* [*Icel.* fôstra *to foster.*]

**fôstring,** *es; m.* I. *a fosterchild of the place where one is brought up, a native of a place:*—Ðǽre burge fôstring, Lk. p. 2, 1. II. *a fosterchild of the person by whom one is educated, a disciple:*—Discipul ł lārcneht ł fôstring ðāra postola *discipulus apostolorum*, Lk. p. 2, 2.

**fôt.** *Add: gen.* fêt; *inst.* fêt. I. *the foot of a living creature:*—Sete þū þinne scytefinger uppon þinne fôt and stríc on twā healfa þînes fêt, Tech. ii. 126, 9. Mid foet *pede*, Ps. Srt. 65, 6. Mid ðǽm fêt, Past. 357, 21. Mid ðý fêt, 358, 4. Oðre fêt onscôd, 44, 8. Seldon hē wolde rîdan, ac síðode on his fôtum, Hml. S. 26, 80. Gebindað him foet and honda, Mt. R. 22, 13. ¶ *where a humble position or condition is expressed:*—Heó tô his fôtum hî āstrehte, Mk. 7, 25. Sum sceal mid hearpan æt his hlāfordes fôtum sittan, Vy. 81: B. 500: 1166. Ealle gesceafta þū legst under his fêt, Ps. Th. 8, 7: 46, 3. II. *a foot as a measure of length:*—Seó eá þæt land oferfleów mid fôtes þicce flôde, Ors. 1, 3; S. 32, 6. Eahta fôta brādne and twelf fôta heánne, Bd. 1, 12; Sch. 34, 2. Twigen fýt tô yfæsdrypæ, C. D. ii. 89, 7. III. *the lowest part of an object:*—Ânes fôtes (cf. fôt·rāp) segl *sipara*, Wrt. Voc. i. 56, 61.

**-fôt** (-e, -a). v. feówer-, fiþer-, fitel-, fiohten-, forod-, lytel (?), sceáf-, wann-fôt (-e, -a). Cf. -fête: -fotad. v. ge-fetian.

**fôt-ádl.** *Add:* men. I. *gout; podagra:*—Ðā geuntrumade hē mid þǽre mettrymnesse podagre, þæt is on ûre geþeóde fôtádl, Shrn. 100, 19. His handa and his fêt wǽron swellende and āþundene for þý wǽtan þǽre fôtádle (*podagrae*), Gr. D. 302, 8. Wið ðǽre miclan siéndan fôtádle þǽre de lǽceas hātad podagre, Lch. iii. 48, 26. Hē sunne mann gehǽlde fram þām miclan fôtádle, Hml. S. 24, 163. Gif hwā mid fôtádle swýþe and hefelíce geswenced sý, Lch. i. 104, 8. Wið fôtádle þeáh ðe heó hefegust sý, 246, 22. Heó fôtádle geliðigað, 304, 25. II. *as a translation of* regia pestis, regius morbus:—Fôtádles, fôtcoþu *regie pestis* (*virulenta incommoditate populari*), An. Ox. 2792. Fôtádla, fôtcoþa *morbo regio* (*turgescens . . . foetidum exhalavit spiraculum*), 2817. [*Morbus regius* is jaundice, but in these two passages it seems to be taken as in the following:—Wið þā cynelican ādle þe man auriginem nemneð (*ad morbum regium hoc est, auriginem*), þ ys on ûre geþeóde þæra syna getoh and fôta geswel, Lch. i. 190, 14.] Cf. fôt-swyle.

**fôt-ádlig;** *adj. Having the foot diseased, gouty:*—Wǽron gehǽlede þrý fôtádlige men, Hml. Th. ii. 26, 19.

**fôt-claþ,** *es; m. A patch:*—Fôtclāð *commissuram*, Mt. L. 9, 16.

**fôt-cops.** *Add:*—Hī gesettan hine on ǽnne heardne stocc and his sceancan gefæstnodon on þām fôtcopsum, . . . ac se fôtcops āwende tô dûste, Hml. S. 35, 150. 'Ne binde þǽ seó racenteág' . . . hē tôbræc þone fôtcops (-cosp, *v. l.*) *eamdem compedem solvit*, Gr. D. 214, 13. Fôtcopsas *conpedes*, Scint. 190, 6: Hml. S. 21, 173. Fôtcopsas *nervi*, Wrt. Voc. ii. 62, 25. *Nervi, boia* fôtcopsa[s] *vel* sweorscacul, i. 21, 15. Fôtcospum, Ps. Spl. C. 104, 17.

**fôt-copsed** *fettered, shackled:*—Fôtcopsede *compeditos*, Hy. S. 125, 7.

**fôt-côðu.** *l.* fôtcoþu, *and see* fôt-ádl: II. -fôte. v. -fôt (-e, -a): -fôted[e]. v. feówer-, horn-, þri-, wôh-fôted[e]: fôter. v. fôdder.

**fôt-feter,** e; *f. A fetter for the feet:*—Fôtfetera *compedes*, Wrt. Voc. i. 21, 14.

**fôt-gangende;** *adj. Going on foot, foot* (soldiers):—Fôtgangendum here *peditatu*, An. Ox. 5254. [*Icel.* fôt-gangandi.]

**fôt-gemearc.** *Add: measurement by feet.* Cf. mîl-gemearc.

**fôt-geswell,** es; *n. A swelling of the foot:*—Wið cneówwrǽce and fôtgeswelle, Lch. iii. 70, 27. Cf. fôt-swyle.

**fôt-gewǽde.** *For R. Ben.* 55 *substitute:*—Hæbben hý tô fôtgewǽdum hosa and meón *indumenta pedum pedules et caligas*, R. Ben. 89, 14.

**fôþer.** *Add:* I. *food, nutriment:*—Fôthur *alitudo* (? *altitudo*. v. III), Wrt. Voc. ii. 100, 6. II. *a covering:*—Fôthr, fôdor *emblema*, Txts. 59, 744. Fôþer *emblemma*, Wrt. Voc. ii. 29, 30. III. *the body of a waggon* (?); *the amount contained in a waggon, a waggon-load:*—Fôþer *altitudo*, wǽngehrado *tabula plaustri* (in a list ' de plaustris et de partibus ejus '), Wrt. Voc. i. 284, 52. Fôder *altitudo* (? *alitudo*, v. I), ii. 8, 13. Man āgeaf of six tûnan æt ǽlcere sylh ān fôðer cornes, C. D. B. iii. 367, 24. Ân fôðer gyrda, C. D. iii. 451, 1. IIII. fôðra weada, i. 297, 2. IIII. fôðera āclofenas gauolwyda, v. 147, 20. Ælce geáre of burhwuda fiftig fôðra wudes, and fiftig swîna mæsten, Cht. E. 293, 30. [*Goth.* fôðr *a sheath.*] v. feþre, feþring: fôdder (fôþer *and* fôdder *seem to have become confused with one another*).

**-fôtian.** v. be-fôtian.

**fôt-lǽst.** *Add:* e; *f.* (1) *a foot-print:*—Þā fôtlāstas wǽron swutole on þǽm stāne, swā hié on wexe wǽron āðýde, Bl. H. 203, 36. Hwæþer þū mage tôcnāwan hwæs fôtlǽsta þū geseó on þissere flôre āstapene, Nap. 79. Gesāwon hî on þām marmanstāne swilce mannes fôtlǽsta fæstlíce on ðām stāne geðýde, Hml. Th. i. 506, 12. Fôtlǽste, 508, 11. (2) *where movement is spoken of, a step:*—Hige ne myhton hig þā git ǽnne fôtlāst furður āteón, Shrn. 154, 30. Ælc þǽra stæpa and fôtlǽsta þe wē tô cyrican weard gestæppað, Wlfst. 302, 26. (3) *the sole of the foot, the foot:*—Sôna swā hî gesetton heora fôtlǽst on þǽre eá ôfre *as soon as they set foot on the bank of the river*; ingressis sacerdotibus Jordanen et

pedibus eorum in parte aquae tinctis, Jos. 3, 15. Hē hēt hī hine ferian þǣr Petrus and Paulus bebyrgede wǣron, and lecgan his līc æt heora fôtlǣstum, Hml. S. 5, 467. Geseah hē león wið þǣre hālgan līchaman standan, and hit his fôtlāstas (-es, MS., fētlāstas, *v. l.*) liccode, 23 b, 773.

**fôt-lǣst, -leást,** e ; *f. See* læs-hosum *in Dict.*

**fôt-lic ;** *adj.* I. *on foot, that is done on foot :*—Folga mē nā þæt ān on fôtlicum gange, ac eác swilce on gôdra ðeáwa geefenlǣcunge, Hml. Th. ii. 468, 21. II. fig. *pedestrian, low in style :*—Fôtlic *pedestre,* i. uile, Germ. 403, 12.

**fôt-mǣl.** *In* l. 3 *for* foot-mark *read* foot, *and add :* (1) *a foot as a measure :*—Men on lenge syx fôtmǣla lange *homines statura pedum .vi.,* Nar. 35, 2. On lenge hundteóntiges fôtmǣla and fiftiges lange, 36, 12. (2) *some kind of cross* (? v. mǣl ;) II :—Of ðām hamme tô fôtmǣle ; of fôtmǣle ēstrihtes on Wulfputt, C. D. iii. 449, 30. v. furh.

**fôt-mǣlum.** *For* R. Conc. 5 : Cot. 95 *substitute :*—Fôtmǣlum *gradatim,* Wrt. Voc. ii. 40, 47 : *pedetemptim,* Angl. xiii. 427, 883.

**fôt-rāp.** *Add :* v. sceát-līne.

**fôt-sceamel.** *Add :*—Fôtscoemel, Mt. L. 5, 35. [*O. H. Ger.* fuoz-scamal : *Icel.* fôt-skemill.]

**fôt-sceanca,** an ; *m. The leg from the knee downwards, the shank :*—Nim blæces hundes deádes þone swȳþran fôtscancan (fôten (fôtes ?) sceancan, *v. l.*), Lch. i. 362, 27.

**fôt-setl,** es ; *n. A footstool :*—Sæt hē mid ðām cyningce æt gereorde. Þā fǣringa sāh hē niðer wið ðæs fôtsetles sprǣce benumen (cf. mutus in ipsa sede declinavit, Florence of Worcester), Chr. 1053; P. 182, 21.

**fôt-setla,** an ; *m. One who sits on a footstool* (?), *an inferior member of a company :*—Gif cniht binnan stig sitte, gylde ānne syster huniges : and gif hwā fôtsetlan hæbbe, dô þ ylce, Cht. Th. 612, 34. Cf. fôt ; I. ¶ **fôt-sīþ-gerif, fôt-sīþ-sticcel.** *Substitute :* fôt-sīd ; *adj. Reaching to the feet* (of a garment) :—Fôtsīd gerif *limus* (printed *limes* ; but see Nap. 25, *where is given Isidor's definition of* limus, 'vestis, quae . . . ad pedes producitur'), Wrt. Voc. i. 16, 45. Hacele *vel* fôtsīd sciccel (printed fôtsīð sticcel, *but see* Nap. 25) *clamis,* 40, 67. [*Icel.* fôt-sīðr *reaching down to the leg,* of a garment.] Cf. lenden-sīd.

**fôt-spor.** *Add :* [*O. H. Ger.* fuoz-spor *vestigium : Icel.* fôt-spor *footprint.*]

**fôt-stappel,** es ; *m. A footstep :*—Fôtstaplas mīne *uestigia mea,* Ps. L. 17, 37. Cf. sīþ-stappel.

**fôt-swæþ, -swaþu.** (1) of the track (lit. or fig.) of living creatures. (a) *neut. or uncertain :*—Ne bið nǣnig wonung on þǣm sande ðæra Drihtnes fôtswaða, Mart. H. 74, 21. Hē āstrehte hine tô Iôhannes fôtswaðum, Hml. Th. i. 68, 14. Ic sceolde his fôtswaðum fylian, 382, 18. Ǣghwylce yfele fô:swaðu him ongeán cumende hē forbūgeþ, ge for ðon se yfela man hyne forcyrreþ oððe him onbūgeþ, Lch. i. 318, 22. (b) *fem. :*—Fylian his fôtswaðe *ejus vestigia sequi,* Gr. D. 60, 26. Hē nāne fôtswaðe on ðām snāwe ne geseah, Hml. Th. ii. 136, 32. (2) of the trace of things :—Nāu synne fôtswæð (*uestigium*) on his sāwle belīfð, Scint. 25, 12.

**fôt-swyle.** *Add :*—Þæs fēþe getugon mycle fôtswylas (-swilas, *v. l.*) and fornāmon *cujus gressum dolore nimio podagra contraxerat,* Gr. D. 47, 21. Cf. fôt-geswell.

**fôt-þweál.** *Add :* ¶ the washing of the feet of the poor, enjoined by the Church :—Biscoepes dægweorc . . . þearfena fôtþweál, Ll. Th. ii. 314, 21. Se ercediácon geáxode mā crīstenra manna, and hī . . . mid fôtðweále geneósode, Hml. Th. i. 418, 27. Sceóte man ælmessan . . . hwīlum þearfena fôtþweál, Wlfst. 171, 2. Fēde man Godes þearfena swā fela swā man mǣst mæge, and . . . baðige man ealle . . . and sylf se dǣdbēta beó ymbe heora fôtþweál, Ll. Th. ii. 288, 8.

**fôt-wærc ;** *m.* (not *n.*) *Add :* [*Icel.* fôt-verkr.]

**fôt-welm.** *Add :* e ; *f.* (? v. Kent. Gl. 165 below ; or has the glosser taken *plantae* to be dative?) : -welma, an ; *m.* :—Fôtwelma, Wrt. Voc. i. 65, 46. Fôtwylm *planta,* Germ. 396, 151. His fôtwelme (*ut non comburantur*) *plantae ejus,* Kent. Gl. 165. Heó (*Jezabel*) wæs eall freten būtan þām handum . . . and þām fôtwylmum (*nisi pedes et summas manus,* 2 Kings ix. 35), Hml. S. 18, 354. Mid drīum fôtwylmum ofer ȳða gān, Hml. Th. i. 108, 16. Wǣron his fēt niðer āwende . . . āwendað mīne fôtwelmas tô ðan heofonlican wege, 382, 13. Āwendan ūre fôtwylmas fram deádbǣrum sīðfæte, 96, 25. Oþ þā fôtwylmas (-mylmas, MS., -welmes, Hpt. Gl. 472, 32) *plantatenus,* i. *usque ad plantas,* i. *pedes,* An. Ox. 2816.

**fox.** *Add :*—Hwīlum swā þeótende wulf, hwilum swā beorcende fox, Shrn. 141, 12. Fox is geápest ealra deóra, 14, 19. Ðone leásan lytegan þū scealt hātan fox, max mann, Bt. 37, 4 ; F. 192, 17. Hū Bonefatius ādȳdde þone fox þe bāt his môdor henna . . . His môdor gewunode tô fēdenne henna, ac hig gelômlīce āweg bær and ābāt ān fox cumende of þām neáhlande . . . Þā côm se fox, swā his gewuna wæs, and gelæhte āne henne, Gr. D. 69, 22–70, 2. Gedôn foxes gelyndes dǣl on þā eáran, Lch. ii. 308, 1 : i. 338, 20 : 340, 4 (and often). Wið liþādle, genim cwicenne fox and seóð þ þā bān āne beón lǣfed, 340, 25. ¶ the word occurs in place-names. v. C. D. vi. 288. Cf. also :—Tô ðǣre foxēc ; of ðǣre foxēc, C. D. iv. 90, 9.

foxes glôfa. *Add :*—Foxes glôfa *buglosse,* Wrt. Voc. i. 67, 24.

**fox-hol,** es ; *n. A fox-hole, fox's earth :*—Tô ðām foxhole ; of ðām foxhole, C. D. iii. 384, 13. Æt ðǣm hwītan foxholum, v. 83, 28. On ðā foxhola, 340, 18.

**foxung,** e ; *f. A foxlike trick :*—Cwæð se Hǣlend him tô : 'Foxas habbað holu' . . . Crīst geseah his prættas, for ðan þe hē mid sôðfæstnysse ne sôhte þone Hǣlend, ac foxunga wǣron wunigende on him, Hml. S. 16, 162. [In ure skemting he (the devil, compared here with the fox) doð raðe a foxing, Misc. 14, 435.]

**fracoþ.** *Add :*—Nis se mæssepreóst on worulde swā synfull ne swā fracod on his dǣdan . . ., þeáh hē ǣlc unriht dreóge on his life, Wlfst. 34, 6. Gif preóst mid fūlum dǣdum hine fracoðlice gedēð, Hml. Th. ii. 320, 22. Þ fracode wīf (*Jezebel*), Hml. S. 18, 160. Hē cwæð þ hīe fracuþe (-coðe, *v. l.*) and earme wǣron *dicens contemnendos esse eos et miseros,* Bd. 3, 21 ; Sch. 288, 11. Fela is fracodra getrȳwða (*bad faith*) mid mannum, Wlfst. 243, 15. Fracodum *turpibus,* Germ. 389, 23. Tô helle faran for fracodum dǣdum, Hml. S. 26, 250. Tarquinius hira eallra fracoþast wæs, Ors. 2, 2 ; S. 66, 28. Þā fūlan forligeras þæs fracodostan mennisces Sodomitiscra ðeóda, Hml. S. 13, 191. Cf. forcūþ.

**fracoþ,** es ; *n. Add :* fracoþu ; *f. Infamy, wickedness :*—Ignominium sconde hlēwung *sive* fraceþu, *idem et infamium,* Wrt. Voc. ii. 49, 31. Sume men beóð swā gehīwode līceteras, swylce hȳ Godes ege habban, and bið eal heora ingeþanc mid fracoðe āfylled, Wlfst. 54, 7. Mið frǣceðo geyfled *contumelia adfectus,* Mt. L. 22, 6. Unclǣnnessa ł fracede *squalores, immunditias,* Hpt. Gl. 509, 76. Þ hē wið swā mycelre geearnunge man swylce wælhreównysse fraceþa (fraced, teónan, *v. ll. contumeliam*) gefremede, Gr. D. 21, 34.

**fracoþ-dǣd,** e ; *f. A foul deed :*—Uton mān and morðor forbūgan, and ealle fracoddǣda swīðe āscunian, Wlfst. 188, 15.

**fracoþ-lic.** *Add :* foul (language), *filthy* (lucre) :—Of gālnysse cumað higeleás and fracodlic sprǣc, Hml. Th. ii. 220, 7. Ne sȳ seó syn nǣfre tô ðām fracodlic, Wlfst. 135, 13. Ǣlc fracodlic fācn āweorpe man, 73, 16. Hī ongunnon hine onscunian mid māran orwyrðum fracodlicra (fraced-, *v. l.*) worda *majoribus hunc verborum contumeliis detestari coeperunt,* Gr. D. 251, 1. For fracedlecum (fracoðlicum, *v. l.*) gestreónum *turpis lucri gratia,* Past. 137, 21.

**fracoþ-līce.** *Add :*—Swā wer sē fracodlīce (*fraudulenter*) derað frȳnd hys, Scint. 194, 1.

**fracoþ-nes.** *For* Cot. 143 *substitute :*—Fracoðnesse *obscenitatis,* Wrt. Voc. ii. 62, 58. Hī gālnysse onscunedon . . . and þā fūlan forsāwon for heora fracodnysse, Hml. A. 23, 214. Unclǣnnessa, fracedn[essa] *squalores,* An. Ox. 4455.

**fracoþ-scipe,** es ; *m. Shameful conduct :*—Þæt him nān unhlīsa ne fylge þurh ǣnigne fracodscype *boni sint testimonii ob detractionem vitandam,* R. Ben. 141, 5.

**fracoþ-word, -wyrde,** es ; *n. An abusive word, an insult, bad language :*—Hē sǣde hū manigne teónan and orwyrdu þāra nunnena fracodwyrda (-worda, *v. l.*) hē geþrowode *quantas pateretur verborum contumelias enarravit,* Gr. D. 152, 7.

**fracu.** v. frecu.

**frǣ-beorht.** *Take here* freá-beorht, *and add :*—Freábeorht *limpida,* An. Ox. 1716. Freáberht *praeclarum,* Ps. Srt. 22, 5. Þā clypiað freábrihtum stefnum, Wlfst. 212, 20. Þǣre freábeorhtestan *limpidissimi,* i. *clarissimi,* An. Ox. 87.

**frǣ-bodian.** v. freá-bodian *in Dict.* : frǣc, Wrt. Voc. ii. 7, 22. *l.* wræc : frǣc-genga. v. frǣt-genga : frǣclíce. v. freclíce : frǣclíce. v. frēcenlíce.

**frǣ-drēman.** *Take here* freá-drēman *in Dict., and add :*—Wē singaþ and wē freádrēmaþ strengða þīne *cantabimus et psallemus uirtutes tuas,* Ps. L. 20, 14. Cf. frǣ-þancian.

**frǣ-fætt.** *l.* frǣ-fǣtt, *and for* Cot. 177 *substitute :*—Frǣfǣttum *prepinguibus,* Wrt. Voc. ii. 96, 47.

fræfel *cunning, craft :*—Fācni *vel* fraefeli *astu,* Wrt. Voc. ii. 101, 13. **fræfele ;** *adj. Saucy. Substitute :* **fræfel ;** *adj. Cunning, crafty ; wanton :*—Fræfol oððe litig *procax,* Wrt. Voc. ii. 67, 48. v. following words.

**fræfelian ;** *p.* ode *To be cunning :*—Fraefeleo *calleo,* Wrt. Voc. ii. 103, 48. Fræfele. 14, 13. Ic frefelie *calleo, decipio,* 127, 62.

**fræfel-líce.** *Substitute : Cunningly, craftily ; wantonly :*—Frǣfellíce (frefelíce *sollerter, astute,* Hpt. Gl. 479, 75), gleáwlíce *sollerter,* An. Ox. 3131. Freulíce (frǣflíce, Hpt. Gl. 405, 50) *sollerter, curiose,* 1. Frefelíce hiene gesôhte seó cwēn mid þrīm hund wīfmonna tô þon þæt heó woldon wið Alexander . . . bearna strienan *regina, excitata suscipiendae ab eo subolis gratia, cum trecentis mulieribus procax invenit,* Ors. 3, 9 ; S. 130, 9.

**fræfel-nes.** *Substitute : Cunning, craftiness :*—Frǣfelnyssa (-e, Hpt. Gl. 512, 37) *sollertia,* An. Ox. 4579. Frǣfelnesse *sollertiam,* 46. Þā mānfullan fræfelnesse *nefandum astum,* Hpt. 31, 18, 511.

**frǣ-gleáw.** *Take here* freá-gleáw *in Dict.*

**frægnian ;** *p.* ode *To ask :*—Hwæt ðū mec geáxast ł frægnast þe gôde *quid me interrogas de bono ?,* Mt. R. 19, 17. v. ge-frægnian.

**frǽgnian.** v. ge-frǽgnian.

**frǽgning,** e ; *f. Asking, enquiry, questioning* :—Mē nāht nū tō lāfe ne wunað þǽre frǽgninge and ācsunge be þām wīsum, in þām ic wæs tweógende ǽr *de his in quibus dubius fui nihil mihi quaestionis remansit*, Gr. D. 323, 23. Mid fraignung *interrogando*, Mk. p. 4, 19. v. frignung.

**frǽ-hrǽd;** *adj. Very quick* :—Fraehraedae (-hraede) *praepropera*, Txts. 84, 733. Freáhrǽde *propera*, Wrt. Voc. ii. 68, 35.

**frǽ-mǽre.** *Add* :—Frǣmēre *eximia*, Wrt. Voc. ii. 91, 64 : 31, 52. þæt frǣmēre *eximiam*, 66.

**frǽ-micel.** *For Cot.* 178 *substitute* :—þæt frǣmicle *eximiam*, Wrt. Voc. ii. 95, 53.

**frǽmsum.** v. fremsume : **frǽne,** Wrt. Voc. ii. 63, 55, *is Latin*. Cf. oreae, frenae, Corp. Gl. H. 87. 259. Cf. *too* Wrt. Voc. ii. 116, 43 *where Latin frena is given as an English gloss to* pugula.

**frǽ-ofestlíce.** *For Cot.* 178 *substitute* :—Frǣofestlíce *propere*, Wrt. Voc. ii. 95, 44.

**frǽppigan** *to be afraid of, to accuse* :—Tēldon ł fræppigdon *verebuntur*, Mt. L. 21, 37. v. ge-fræppigan.

**frǽt;** ... *superbus. Substitute*: **frǣte;** *adj. Wanton, shameful, foul* ; fedus, turpes, *and add* :—þæt ne blissige [þē] frǣte bǽr *ne letetur te fedus* (*obscenus, turpis*) *sandapila*, Hpt. 31, 4, 12. þæt bið feóndes bearn ... , hafað frǣte līf, Mód. 48. Frǣtum *fugitivus* (-*is ?*), Wrt. Voc. ii. 38, 40. Cf. earg *cowardly*; *evil.* [Cf. *O. H. Ger.* frâza *obstinatio*; frâzar *procax, protervus.*]

**frǽte[w]ness,** e ; *f. An ornament* :—Frǣtenisse *stemmate*, Wrt. Voc. ii. 92, 50. Frǣtenessa (*printed* wrǣt-) *discrimina*, 27, 61. v. heáfod-frǣtewness.

**frǽt-genga** (frǣt-? cf. frǣtum *given under* frǣte) *glosses* apotas[s]ia (=apostasia ?) :—Fretgenga *apotassia*, Wrt. Voc. i. 285, 11 : ii. 8, 32. Fraetgengian *apotasia*, 100, 47. Frǣtgengan, 7, 8.

**frǽ-pancian** (freá-) *to rejoice greatly, exult* :—Freáþancað se gecorena *exultavit Jacob*, Ps. Rdr. 52, 7. Cf. frǣ-drēman.

**frǽtig.** *l.* frǣtig. *and see* frǣte.

**frǽ-torht;** *adj. Very brilliant, very splendid* :—Freátorht *luculentus*, An. Ox. 11, 73. Mid freátorhtum *limpidis*, freátorh[t] *limpida*, Hpt. Gl. 511, 37. þā freátorhtestan *limpida, clarissima*, 446, 22.

**frǽtwe.** *Add* :—Nelle wē þ þǣr mon ǽnig þing inne healde, būtan þā þe tō þǽre cyrcean frǣtwum belympað, þ is, hālige bēc and hūselfata and mæssereáf, Ll. Th. ii. 406, 33.

**frǽtwed-nes.** *Add* :—Hwǣr cōm seó frǣtwodnes heora hūsa, Bl. H. 99, 27. Beorhtra ðonne on ealre eorðan sȳn goldes and seolfres frǣtwednissa, Sal. K. p. 150, 18. Frǣtwednessa *crepundiorum*, Wrt. Voc. ii. 23, 63.

**frǽtwian.** *Take here* **frǽttewian** *in Dict., and add* :—Frǣtwian *comere*, Wrt. Voc. ii. 20, 47. v. un-frǣtewod.

**frǽtwung.** *Add* :—Frǣtwunge *crustu*, i. *ornatu*, Wrt. Voc. ii. 25, 8. Frǣte[wunge] *ornatu*, An. Ox. 5109. Hwā mæg ðǣre heofenan freatewunge āsecgan?, Hml. Th. i. 286, 18. Frǣtwunga *crepundia*, i. *insignia, indicia, cunabula*, Wrt. Voc. ii. 136, 70. Frǣtewunge, preónas *lunulas*, An. Ox. 2204. Frǣte[wunge] *ornamenta*, 540. Frǣtewunga, Prud. 52. Hē mē beád bǣteran frǣtegunga and his hring mē lēt tō wedde, Hml. S. 7, 29. v. ge-frǣtwung.

**frǽ-wlitig;** *adj. Very beautiful* :—þā syndon freáwlitige deór *isti formosi sunt*, Nar. 38, 15.

**fragian** *to ask.* [Cf. *O. Frs.* fregia.] v. ge-fragian.

**fram.** *Add*: I. *with dat.* (1) *denoting departure and marking point from which movement takes place* :—Hēr for se here tō Lundenbyrig from Reádingum, Chr. 872 ; P. 72, 18. From (of, *v. l.*) Lindesse, 874 ; P. 72, 24. Hēr cuōm se here intō Escanceastre from (fram, *v. l.*) Werhām, 877 ; P. 74, 14. Cōmon þā tungolwītegan fram Eástdǣle, Mt. 2, 1. (2) *indicating a starting-point in measurement.* (a) *where the two boundaries of an extent are given* :—Fram eorþan ūp tō heofonum, Bl. H. 5, 17. Fram eásteweardum oþ westeweardne, Bt. 16, 4 ; F. 58, 11. (b) *where the limits of a series are given* :—Fram þām men oþ þā nȳtenu, fram þām slincendum oð þā fugelas, Gen. 6, 7. (3) *indicating a starting-point in time* :—From ðǣm dæge hē mehte eallra Cartaina onwald begietan, Ors. 4, 5 ; S. 170, 11. Wæs ǣlcum fram dæges orde drync gearu, An. 1537. (3 a) *where the two limits of a period are given* :—From (fram, *v. l.*) frymþe middangeardes oþ þis geár, Chr. 6 ; P. 6, 1 : Bt. 18, 3 ; F. 66, 14. Ðā āgangen wæs tȳn ᵈhund wintra fram gebyrdtíde brēmes cyninges, Chr. 973 ; P. 118, 16. Fram Abrahame oð Dauid, Mt. 1, 17. Fram þǣre sixtan tíde oð þā nigoðan tíd, 27, 45. (4) *indicating an object which is left behind by an object which withdraws* :—Ðā hē him from wolde, ðā gesēng hē hine, Past. 35, 19. Sceal ic þē nihtes gesēcan and fram þē hweorfan on hancrēd, Seel. 67. Āstāg hē on þysne ymbhwyrft fram þām heáhsetle, Bl. H. 11, 29. (4 a) *where there is desertion or flight* :—Hiera mǣgas him mid wǣron þā þe him from noldon, Chr. 755 ; P. 48, 19. Hē āsceacen wæs fram Ǽðelrēde cyncge ofer ealle ðā getrȳwða ðe hē him gesealde hæfde, 1001 ; P. 132, 13. þāra ǣlces þe þæs wordes wǣre þæt from Rōmebyrg þōhte, Ors. 4, 9 ; S. 190, 25. þonne flȳhþ þ deófol fram ūs, Bl. H. 47, 12 :

Hml. S. 25, 435. Lyt eft becwōm fram þām hildfrecan hāmes niósan *few escaped from him and saw home again*, B. 2366. (5) *indicating an object from which another turns aside or away* :—Sceoldon Crístenra folca hyrdas hí from eallum unrihtwīsum āhweorfan, Bl. H. 45, 26. Hí wǣron in gedwolan ācyrred fram Críste, El. 1120. Ic fram ðǣm synnum gecerre, Ps. C. 64 : Hex. 52, 3. Lōcað fram þām unlǣdan ǣngan hlāford *the lord turns his look from the luckless solitary*, Sal. 382. (6) *denoting distance, absence, away from, apart from, absent from* :—Of wealle āhleóp frōd fyrngeweorc, þæt hē on foldan stōd, stān fram stāne, An. 739. Hwæt wolde ic fram þē wyrcean ?, Ps. Th. 72, 26. (6 a) *with words indicating extent of distance* :—iiii. mīla fram þǣm mūþan, Chr. 893 ; P. 84, 10. Nāht feor from þæs mǣssepreóstes sídan, Bl. H. 43, 26 : 69, 25 : B. 541. (7) *denoting removal, separation, deliverance, expulsion, cessation, &c. from.* (a) *a concrete object.* (a) *where the object removed is concrete* :—Fram sylle ābeág medubenc monig, B. 775. Se hyrde āsyndrað þā scēp fram tyccenum, Mt. 25, 32 : Sat. 177. Hē eów fram unclǣnum generede gāstum, El. 301. (β) *where the object removed is abstract* :—Āsceacan slǽp ūs fram, Hml. Th. i. 602, 15. Āfyr fram þē þā yfelan sǽlþa, Bt. 6 ; F. 14, 32 : Ps. Th. 118, 22 : Bl. H. 67, 35 : Bt. 16, 3 ; F. 56, 5. Eówre wǣdle eów fram ādōn, 26, 2 ; F. 94, 9. (b) *an abstract object* (*condition, action*, &c.) :—Hē bið gefríðod from his āgnum costungum *a sua tentatione eripitur*, Past. 107, 2. þæt hē ūs generige from þon ēcan cwealme, Bl. H. 25, 28 : 31, 23 : El. 296. Ūre heortan geclǣnsian from ōþrum geþōhtum, Bl. H. 21, 4 : Ps. C. 38 : El. 1309. þæt gē mē of þyssum earfeðum ūp forlǣten, heánne from hungres genīðlan, 701. Hē ācwæð hine fram his hyldo, Gen. 304 : 1032. Befreó mē fram blōdgete, Ps. C. 111. Ðæt ðīn heorte beó onliht mid his scínendom leómum fram ðǣre sweartan dymnysse *that thy heart be delivered from darkness, being illumined by his shining rays*, Hex. 52, 5. Āblinnan from unrihtum gestreónum and gītsunga, Bl. H. 25, 5. (8) *indicating a state which is abandoned or changed for another* :—Hē færð fram deáðe tō līfe, Jn. 5, 24. (9) *denoting distinction, difference* :—Se godcunda dōm gedēncð ðætte ealle men gelíce beón ne magon, ac wile ðæt simle se ōðer beó ārǣred from ðǣm ōðrum, Past. 107, 23. (9 a) *denoting unlikeness, incongruity, alien from* :—Se leó cwæð : ' Ic for ðē sprece from mínre gecynde,' Shrn. 118, 24. (10) *indicating the place, quarter, &c., whence something is brought or obtained* :—Ic eom ālǣded fram leóhte in þone lādan hām, Sat. 178 : An. 1036 : El. 712. (11) *indicating a place where action is originated, while the originator is fixed there* :—Fram hām gefrægn Higelāces þegen Grendles dǣda, B. 194. (12) *indicating a person as a source from which comes or is obtained something* :—Onsōþ hí from Gode māran mēde þonne hí from ǣnigum ōþrum lācum dōn, Bl. H. 45, 34. Heora biscopas from hiora godum sǽdon (*their bishops gave as a message from the gods*) þæt hié ðæt gefeoht forbuden, Ors. 3, 10 ; S. 138, 34. Ǽlc wuht from Gode wiste his rihttíman, Bt. 5, 3 ; F. 12, 8. (13) *indicating the agent, by* :—Hē weard ofslagen from his āgnum monnum, Ors. 6, 16 ; S. 270, 19. Hē wæs gelǣred from ānum biscope, 6, 33 ; S. 288, 13 : El. 190. Ic eom genȳded from Godes englum þæt ic sprece, Shrn. 118, 23. Bist þu gehǣled fram him, Bl. H. 151, 34 : Chr. 625 ; P. 24, 5. Fram deófle costud, Mt. 4, 1 : Bl. H. 27, 5. Dǣda gedōne from Drihtne, 31, 20. From þū lǣst wēnst þū bist beswicen, Nar. 30, 12 : Bt. 29, 2 ; F. 104, 17 : Bd. 3, 14 ; Sch. 256, 11 : Ps. Th. 113, 23. Weard Cartainum frið ālíefed from Scipian (*per Scipionem*), Ors. 4, 10 ; S. 202, 20. Wyrþ se mūþa fordrifen foran from þǣm windum, 1, 1 ; S. 12, 34. (14) *indicating the person who causes a feeling, state, or condition* :—Hié ungemetlicne ege from him hæfdon, Ors. 3, 9 ; S. 124, 4. Wæs swā micel ege from ðǣm wīfmonnum *gentes tanta formido invaserat*, 1, 10 ; S. 46, 27. Weard Rōmānum se mǣsta ege from Sceltiuerin *cum Romanos ingens Celtiberorum metus invaisset*, 4, 12 ; S. 208, 24 : 4, 10 ; S. 198, 32. Ǽghwǣðrum wæs brōga fram ōðrum, B. 2565. Him þæs egesa stōd gryre fram þām gāste, Dan. 526. Heora wíse on nǣnne sǽl wel ne gefōr, nāþer ne iunan from him selfum, ne ūtane from ōþrum folcum *nulla unquam tempora vel foris prospera vel domi quieta duxerunt*, Ors. 4, 4 ; S. 164, 14. (15) *denoting derivation, source* :—þū fram mínre dohtor onwōce, Sat. 439. Swā him geæþele wæs from cneómǣgum, Chr. 937 ; P. 106, 16. Fram þan Wōdne āwōc eall ūre cynecynn, Chr. 449 ; P. 13, 24. (16) *indicating an object after which another is named* :—From þām heó sind genemnode Dæl Reodi, Chr. P. 5, 2. From (fram, *v. l.*) þām hit naman onfēng, Bd. 1, 1 ; Sch. 10, 13. (17) *denoting ground, reason, cause, because of, on account of, as a result of* :—Lǣcedōm is ālȳfed from líchamena tȳddernysse, Hml. S. 17, 213. Ic gelýfe þæt hit from Gode cōme, brōht from his bysene, Gen. 680. Regn þe þeós eorðe fram æfter grōweð, Ps. Th. 146, 8. (17 a) *indicating the ground of judgement, belief, &c.* :—Fram hyra wæstmum gē hí undergytað, Mt. 7, 16. (18) *indicating the object spoken of, of ; de* :—Se diácon sǽde fram þysum fȳre, emne swā wē rǣdað on Sunnandæges spelle, Wlfst. 205, 24 : Bl. H. 169, 24. Mon cōm unārímedlíce oft and him sǣdon from burgum and from tūnum on eorþan besuncen *ut de innumeris quassationibus ac ruinis villarum oppidorumque Roma nuntiis fatigaretur*, Ors, 2, 6 ; S. 88, 13. Hié

from gesælgum tídum gilpað, 5, 2 ; S. 220, 10. **II.** *with instru-mental* :—Fram þis wígplegan wendan, By. 316. **III.** *with pre-positional phrase* :—Côm Eustatius fram geondan sǽ, Chr. 1048; P. 172, 15. Fram begeondan sǽ, 1066 ; P. 194, 34 : Mt. 4, 25. **IV.** *as adverb* :—Budon hié þæt hiera mǽgum þæt hié gesunde from eódon, Chr. 755 ; P. 48, 22. Hé nô þý ǽr fram meahte, B. 754. Fram ic ne wille, By. 317. *See also verbs given in Dict. as compounds with* fram, from.

**fram**; *adj. Take here* from *in Dict., and add* : (1) *stout, bold* :—From, fraam *acris, fortis*, Txts. 37, 60. From *efficax*, 59, 727 : Wrt. Voc. ii. 29, 13. From, snel *explicitus, liber, efficatus*, 145, 35. Sum from wer *uir strenuissimus*, Bd. 4, 23; Sch. 471, 21. Fra[m] hys æcerweorce *agresti bonus* [*exhibebat arte*], Germ. 391, 60. Sume . . ., frame, fyrdhwate, feorh ofgêfon, Ap. 12. Fromra *prestantior*, Wrt. Voc. ii. 118, 9 : 67, 47. Se fromesta (fyrmesta, *v. l.*) esne *vir strenuissimus*, Bd. 2, 20; Sch. 183, 18 : 5, 20; Sch. 674, 4. (2) *chief*. Cf. from-rinc :—Ealdra ł fromra feónda *principum inimicorum*, Ps. Rdr. p. 292, 42. v. swíþ-from.

**fram-byge**, es ; *m. A turning aside from what is right, backsliding, defection, default* :—Ðín frambige þe sceal gederian *aversio tua increpabit te* (Jer. 2, 19), Wlfst. 49, 12. Hig sýn ǽfre underðeódde and gehêrsume and ðám hláfordscipe folhgien ðe ðonne bisceop beó, and gif hig ǽnigne frambyge dôn, þolian ðǽre âre, C. D. iv. 137, 23.

**fram-cyme.** v. from-cyme *in Dict.*: **fram-cynn.** v. from-cynn *in Dict.*

**fram-fǽr**, es ; *n. A going away, departure* :—Se hálga wer wende âweg fram ðǽre stôwe . . . se preóst stôd fægnigende ðæs ôðres framfǽres, Hml. Th. ii. 164, 3. Ic ðê bebeóde þæt ðú (*a dragon*) gewîte of ðyssere stôwe, and far tô wêstene . . . and þú nânum men on ðínum framfǽre ne drece, 296, 5.

**fram-fǽreld**, es ; *n. Departure* :—Þá hyrdas sprǽcon him betweónan æfter ðǽra engla framfǽrelde *ut discesserunt ab eis angeli in coelum pastores loquebantur ad invicem* (Lk. 2, 15), Hml. Th. i. 40, 5.

**fram-faru.** v. from-faru *in Dict.*

**fram-fundung**, e ; *f. A going away to another place* :—Se Hálga Gást wæs þǽm apostolum tô frôfre gehâten for þǽre miclan langunga Drihtnes framfundunga, Bl. H. 131, 14. Se Hǽlend wiste þ his gingran woldan unrôte beón for his framfundunga, 135, 15. Cf. Se Hǽlend fundigende of ðissere worulde tô his Fæder sprǽc, Hml. Th. ii. 360, 3.

**fram-hycgend** (?) *one whose thoughts are turned from right* (?), *a froward person* :—Framhicgendra *scortorum*, Hpt. Gl. 484, 35. v. firen-hycgend.

**framian.** *Take here* fromian *in Dict., and add* : **I.** *to do good, benefit*. (1) *absolute* :—Framað *ualebit*, Hpt. 31, 18, 495 : Scint. 30, 13: *proficit*, 20, 8 : 160, 7. Hwæt framaþ *quid prodest*, Wülck. Gl. 255, 34. Gif hé ongyt þæt eal his hogu and gleáwscipe náht framað *si viderit nihil suam prevalere industriam*, R. Ben. 52, 14. Hyt framað (fremað, *v. l.*), Lch. i. 270, 4. Ne fromiað *non proderunt*, Kent. Gl. 313. Furþor þonne hit framige (fremige, *v. l., expedit*), R. Ben. 22, 4 : 60, 23 : Angl. xiii. 373, 111 : 411, 666. (2) *to do good to an object*. (a) *with dat.* :—Þú náht frámast (*profices*) heortan þínre, Scint. 7, 4. For dý þe hé be dǽle þǽre stôwe framaþ *eo quod videatur aliquid con-ferre monasterio*, R. Ben. 95, 7. Þæt hit him eal framað *sibi expedire*, 128, 18. Framað (fremað, *v. l.*), Lch. i. 300, 14. Hí framigaþ heora bearnum, R. Ben. 137, 26. Framedon *profuerunt*, Scint. 153, 10. Framige (*prosit*) ânra gehwylc ôþron on cræfte hys, Coll. M. 31, 25. Hú hé swýþor þám sáulum framian (fremian, *v. l., prodesse*) mæge, R. Ben. 119, 19. Framian (fremian, *v. l.*) *expedire*, 121, 9. (b) *with prep.* :—Heó framað (fremað, *v. l.*) tô eallum drenceom, Lch. i. 110, 4. **II.** *to get good, derive benefit, profit, make progress* :—Swá micelum ǽnig on gewrite háligum framaþ (*proficit*) . . . swá micelum swá þú framast (*proficeris*), Scint. 219, 1–3. Nôwiht fromað se fiónd in him *nihil proficiet inimicus in eo*, Ps. Srt. 88, 23. Fromedon *proficiebant*, Bd. 3, 19 ; Sch. 278, 10. Wê ne mid segele ne mid rôunesse ôwiht fremian (fromian, fromgan, *v. ll., proficere*) mihton, 5, 1 ; Sch. 551, 15. **II a.** *to prevail* :—Ne framige mon *non praeualeat homo*, Ps. Rdr. 9, 20. Sê þe framian (*proficere*) higð, þeáh þe hé stæpe fulfremed-nysse âtilþ, symle swá þeáh hé fint þ hé wexe, Scint. 100, 14. v. forþ-framian ; fremman.

**frami[g]endlic.** *Add* :—Framiendlic *profuturum*, An. Ox. 8, 343. Framliendlic, 2, 434. Framendlic, Hpt. Gl. 524, 28. Lege tô ðǽre miltan, hyt bið hyre nytlic and framgendlic, Lch. i. 300, 19. v. fremi-[g]endlic.

**fram-lád.** v. from-lád *in Dict.*

**fram-lêce**; *adj. Having the looks averted* :—Framlêce *aversa*, Germ. 401, 41. Cf. lêc.

**fram-lic** (freom-); *adj. Stout, bold* :—Hé (*Nero*) nôht fromlices (freom-, *v. l.*) ongan on ðǽre cynewísan *nihil omnino in re militari ausus est*, Bd. 1, 3; Sch. 15, 21.

**framlíce.** *Take here* fromlíce *in Dict., and add* :—Framlícae, fromlícae *strenue*, Txts. 96, 946. Fromlíce *efficaciter*, Wrt. Voc. ii.

107, 2 : 29, 12 : *perstrenue*, 116, 62. Framlíce, 67, 71. Fromlíce *nauiter*, i. *uiriliter* ł *fortiter*, An. Ox. 738. Ongan hê framlíce (from-, *v. l.*, *strenuissime*) þá staþolas ýcean, Bd. 2, 4 ; Sch. 127, 2 : 1, 5; Sch. 17, 13 : 4, 10; Sch. 400, 1. Fromlíce, 5, 7; Sch. 583, 1. v. swíþ-framlíce.

**fram-ness.** v. fromnis *in Dict.*

**fram-rinc** (from-), es ; *m. A chief man, prince.* v. fram, (2) :—Fromrincas *principes*, Ps. Rdr. 282, 115.

**fram-scipe.** *Substitute* : **fram-scipe** (from-), es; *m.* **I.** *energy, vigour, vigorous action* :—On geswince (bígonge ł fromscype, MS. C.) mínum *in exercitatione mea*, Ps. Spl. 54, 2. Fram ðyssa munuca fram-scype (freóndscipe, *v. l.*) tô lǽrenne Crístes geleáfan Angelþeóde wæs sended Aidan *thanks to the energy of these monks* (but the Latin is : ab horum collegio monachorum) *Aidan was sent to teach belief in Christ to the English*, Bd. 3, 5 ; Sch. 202, 4. **II.** *advancement, success* :—Wæs for his fromscipe (forþscype, *v. l.*) onstyred Ædon *motus ejus pro-fectibus Aedan*, Bd. 1, 34; Sch. 104, 14. Þý lǽs hié ormôde wǽron . . . ðæs hié mid mec tô fromscipe gefêran scoldon *lest they should despair . . . of coming to advancement with me*, Nar. 32, 25. Þ þú gefeó in þǽm fromscipe mínes lífes and eác blissige in þǽm weorðmyndum *that you may be glad at the success of my life, and rejoice in my honour*, 31. v. fromnis *in Dict.*

**fram-síþ.** *Substitute* : **fram-síþ** (from-), es; *m. Absence on a journey* :—Ne dorste nán þǽra munuca on hyra ealdres framsíþe (æfweard-nysse, *v. l., in Patris absentia*). Cf. hê on færelde wæs, 28, 21) gangan inn tô þǽra fǽmnena gesomnunge, Gr. D. 29, 2. Ful oft mec hêr wráðe begeat fromsíð freán, Kl. 33.

**fram-slitnes** (-slit- ?). v. from-slit[t]nis *in Dict.* : **fram-swengan.** *l.* fram swengan, *and for* Cot. 179 *substitute* Wrt. Voc. ii. 31, 55 :

**frampe.** v. fremede.

**framung, fromung** (*q. v. in Dict.*), e ; *f. Profit, advancement* :—Ælc framung (*profectus*) of rædincge and smeáunge forþstæpþ, Scint. 219, 9. On hâligre spǽce framunge þú gemêst *in sacro eloquio profectum inuenies*, 2 : Angl. xiii. 398, 480. v. forþ-framung.

**fram-weard.** *Substitute: With the face turned away, having the back turned* to another :—Geseoh þ hé sié tôweard þonne þú ingange . . . ; gif hé þe sié framweard, ne grêt þú hine, Lch. ii. 352, 20. Ðone fromweardan hé ciéged *aversum revocat*, Past. 407, 11. v. from-weard, -weardes *in Dict.*

**fram-werende** *absent* :—Brôðrum ûsum fromuoesen[d]um *fratribus nostris absentibus*, Rtl. 178, 35.

**fram-wísum.** *Dele*: fran; *p. of* frinan. *l.* frán; *p. of* frínan [= frignan].

**franca.** *Add* :—Stód his franca begleddod mid Julianes blôde, Hml. S. 3, 266. Ic geann mínum hláforde mínes swyrdes mid fetele and ðártô twá targan and twêgen francan, C. D. iii. 304, 30.

**Francan.** *Add* :—Bucellinus côm mid Francum (Froncum, *v. l.*) . . . Ongunnon þá Francan (*Franci*) gangan in tô cyrican, Gr. D. 16, 8–16. Far tô ðǽra Francena ríce, Hml. Th. i. 564, 4. Florus wæs fyrmest þǽra Francena þegna, Hml. S. 6, 140. Hê mid þám Francum wunode, 29, 164. Mid Froncum ic wæs, Víd. 68 : 24 : B. 2912.

**Franc-land.** *Add* :—Ðeós wyrt byþ cenned in Gallia, þ is on Franc-lande, Lch. i. 238, 13: Hml. Th. i. 560, 7 : Hml. S. 28, 2 : 26, 240.

**frásian.** *Add* : *to question, interrogate* :—Ne gebelg þú þe wið mê, þeáh ic þe frásige and ðín fandige, Solil. H. 35, 7. Ne gidarste ǽnig monn frásiga (*interrogare*) hine, Jn. L. 21, 12. Ðǽm frásendum Judêum *interrogantibus Judaeis*, p. 3, 4.

**freá.** *Add*: v. frígea : freá-. *See compounds under* frǽ-.

**freá-meaht**, e ; *f. Lordly power* :—God mín and freámiht mín *Deus meus et fortitudo meus*, Ps. Rdr. 42, 2.

**frec.** *Add* :—Frec wǽsend *gulosa ingluvies*, An. Ox. 3569. Frǽc, 2, 225. Gyf fríg man swá frǽc sý þæt hê þæt fæsten âbrece, Wlfst. 172, 2. Frecces *ambronis*, An, Ox. 11, 106. Frǽcum *gulosa*, 2445. Þý frettan (freccan ?) *gulosa*, Wrt. Voc. ii. 96, 64. Hí mettas him on mûð bestingon on swilcum fæstendagum mid frǽcere gýfernysse, Hml. Th. ii. 330, 31. Ðǽm frecum *ambronibus*, Wrt. Voc. ii. 76, 33 : 4, 69: 1, 23. [*v. N. E. D.* freck.] v. wôd-frec, *and* fric *in Dict.* See E. S. 39, 327 sqq.

**frêced-lic**; *adj. Perilous* :—Hit ûs is frêcenlic (frêcedlic, *v. l.*), Hml. A. 139, 24. v. frêcend-lic.

**frêcedlíce**; *adv. In peril* :—Scipu frêcedlíce geyrnað, Archiv cxx. 298, 6.

**frêcednes.** *Add* :—Dreórilic frêcednys *triste periculum*, Germ. 402, 66. Of þǽre wídgyllan sídan þæs muntes wæs swíðe hefgu frêcednys (frêcenes, *v. l.*) for ege þám niþerstígendum *e devexo montis latere erat grave descendentibus in timore periculum*, Gr. D. 112, 20 : Hml. Th. ii. 160, 30. Hit is eów micele mǽre frêcednes, þ . . ., Hml. A. 139, 25. Be frêcednesse *de periculo*, Kent. Gl. 220. Frêcced[nysse] *discrimine*, An. Ox. 4952. On frêcednesse (frǽcnisse, *v. l.*) hê dyrfð *periculo periclitat*, Lch. iii. 151, 9: Hml. Th. ii. 160, 6: Hml. A. 97, 177. Beón hý âlýsede fram ǽlcere frêcednysse, Hml. S. 30, 437. Búton

frǣcednysse, Ll. Th. ii. 370, 27. Frēcednysse *discrimen*, An. Ox. 1595. On heora frēcednyssum and on earfoðnyssum hī wǣron getrȳwe Gode, Hml. A. 109, 222. Frǣcednyssum, Hml. Th. i. 354, 7.

frēcelness, e; *f. Peril, danger*:—For ðyssa tīda frēcelnisse *turbatis rebus Nordanhymbrorum*, Bd. 2, 20; Sch. 186, 21. Hālo from ǣlcum froecelnisse *sanos ab omni periculo*, Rtl. 116, 9. In miclum froecelnissum *in tantis periculis*, 7, 36: 69, 13, 38: 79, 24. Froecilnissum, 17, 19.

frēcelsod. *Substitute:* frēcelsian; *p.* ode *To endanger, imperil:*— Frēcelsod *periclitatur*, Wrt. Voc. ii. 66, 35. v. *preceding word, and cf.* frēcnian.

frēcen *peril.* v. frēcne.

frēcend-lic. *Add:*—Ǣgðer is swíðe frēcendlic, ge þ him hwā unmedomlíce onfoo, and eác þ him hwā tō lange būtan sȳ, Ll. Th. ii. 440, 21. Uneáðe þā frēcendlícan nȳdþearfnysse ādreógende, Hml. S. 23 b, 538.

frēcen-ful. *For* Mone B. 685, 686 *substitute* An. Ox. 628.

frēcen-lic. *Add:*—Hū frēcenlic ðæt is *quam perniciosa sint ea*, Past. 441, 8. Froecenlic dearfscip *periculosa praesumtio*, Mt. p. 1, 4. Hit ūs is frēcenlic, þ wē hit eów ne cȳðen, Hml. A. 139, 24. Gif þās tācn lange wuniað, þonne biþ seó ādl tō frēcenlico, Lch. ii. 258, 21. þ bið swíþe frēcenlic, iii. 182, 18. On ðām endenȳhstan dagum þissere worulde beóð frēcenlíce (frǣcen-, *v. l.*) tīda (*tempora periculosa*, 2 Tim. 3, 1), Wlfst. 88, 11.

frēcenlíce. *Add:* frǣclíce *in peril:*—Sē þe hine ādl gestandeð, sē bið frēcenlíce gestanden, Lch. iii. 182, 6, 22. Frǣclíce bið his þing, E. S. 39, 328.

frēcennes, frēcnes. *Take here* frēcnes *in Dict., and add:*—Seó frēcennes (frēcenes; frēcnes, *v. ll.*) þyses yfeles *cujus periculi malum*, R. Ben. 125, 3. Frēcennes, Past. 51, 21: Bt. 22, 1; F. 76, 15. Lege tō ðǣre wunde, oþ ðæt þū ongite þ seó frēcnys (frǣcen-, *v. l.*) sȳ ūt ātogen, Lch. i. 92, 19. Ungecyndelic is ǣlcre wuhte þ hit wilnige frēcennesse oððe deápes, Bt. 34, 11; F. 152, 8: 20; F. 72, 6. Betwuh ðā frēcnesse stówe *inter Scyllam*, Wrt. Voc. ii. 88, 28: 47, 11. Sceaþa frǣcnesse *predo pellax*, 88, 67. Frēcennysse *discrimine*, Hpt. Gl. 421, 41. Gif monn mīnne noman nemneð in ǣnigre frēcennisse, Shrn. 73, 6. Ðætte hié ongieten under hū micelre frēcennesse (frēcenesse, *v. l.*) hié licggeað and hū hié iéceað hiera forwyrd *ut cognoscant quantis lapsibus succrescentis ruinae subjaceant*, Past. 232, 24. Frǣcnysse *exitio*, Hpt. Gl. 450, 53. On frǣcnisse *periculo*, Lch. iii. 151, note 4. Hyra āgne sáula þurh þās frēceness (frēcennesse, frēcnesse, *v. l.*) losiað *ipsorum animas periclitari*, R. Ben. 124, 20. þā þe ne mihton ādreógan þæs hungres frǣcnesse (frēcen-, *v. l.*) *qui famis periculum ferre non poterant*, Gr. D. 197, 25. Frēcnysse *discrimen*, Hpt. Gl. 443, 71.

freceo. *Dele, and see* frecian.

frec-full; *adj. Gluttonous, greedy:*—Frǣcfulre *gulosa*, An. Ox. 2445.

frecgenga. v. fræt-genga.

frecian *to be greedy, eat voraciously:*—Freceo (*for the verbal inflexion* cf. fraefeleo, 103, 49, mengio (= ic menge, 58, 42) *lu[r]cor*, Wrt. Voc. ii. 113, 13. Freced(-o?), 51, 14.

freclíce; *adv. Greedily:*—Geseah heó ǣnne leahtric . . . heó hine freclíce bāt (*avide momordit*), Gr. D. 31, 1.

frec-mǣse. *Add:*—Frecmǣse *laudariulus*, Wrt. Voc. ii. 112, 47: (*printed* fret-) *lardariulus*, 50, 64.

frēcne; *adj. Add:*—Frecmǣse he man wel sprecan . . ., ne biþ þeós ādl hwæþere tō frēcne, Lch. ii. 46, 13. Ðȳ lǣs ðā gongen on suā frēcne stíge *ne in praecipiti pedem ponant*, Past. 41, 7. Ðonne se hirde gǣð on frēcne wegas *cum pastor per abrupta graditur*, 29, 23. Forlēton wē þā frēcnan wegas and síðfato *relictis periculosissimis locis*, Nar. 17, 13. Gif sié þǣra ādle bryne innan . . . sió biþ ðȳ frēcenre, Lch. ii. 46, 20. Ðonne hit ðē frēcnost þynce, wēn ðē ðonne frófre, Prov. K. 75.

frēcne, es; *n. Peril. Take here* frēcen *in Dict., and add:*—Byþ lytel frēcne (frǣcne, *v. l.*) fram fȳre, Lch. i. 330, 2.

frēcnen-sprǣc. *l.* -sprǣc. *But perhaps the word might be taken as adjective* frēcnen-sprǣce (frēcen- *or* frēcne-?) *Using dangerous or mischievous speech.*

frecnes? *glis. Substitute:* frec-ness, e; *f. Greediness, gluttony, voracity:*—Frecnis *glus*, Wrt. Voc. ii. 109, 78. Frecnes, 40, 74. Frecnesse *ingluviae*, 44, 27. Of gīfre frecinesse (frecennesse, Angl. xiii. 32, 119) *gulosa inglunies*, An. Ox. 4, 38. Frecnesse *ingluuiem*, 19, 1.

frēcne-stíg. *Dele, and see* frēcne.

frēcnian; *p.* ode *To endanger, imperil:*—On his heortan unhǣlo cymð, and hē bið frǣcnoð, E. S. 39, 328. Moni wíf sweltað and scíp beóð frēcnode and ciningas forweardað, Lch. iii. 164, 1. v. ge-frēcnian.

frecu *greediness.* [*Goth.* faihu-frikei *avarice*: O. H. Ger. frechī *avaritia.*] v. scyld-frecu: frēdan. *Add:* [v. *N. E. D.* frede]: frēdelíce, frēdendlic, frēdmǣlum, frēdnes. v. ge-frēdelice, &c.: frēfel. v. fræfel.

frēfer-ness, e; *f. Consolation, comfort:*—Gié habbað froefernise *habetis consolationem*, Lk. L. 6, 24.

frēfran. *Take here* frēfrian, *and add:*—Se Hālga Frófforgāst ūs frēfrað mid his gife, Hml. A. 1, 14. Hig frēfrodon (-edon, *v. l.*, froe-

fredon, L., freófradun, R.) *consolabantur*, Jn. 11, 31. þ hī Godes þearfan frēfriau and fēdan, Ll. Th. i. 326, 24. Froefra *consolari*, Mt. L. 2, 18. Frófran, Ps. Srt. 76, 3. Ðā wǣdlan sint tō frēbranne (frēfranne, *v. l.*) and tō rētanne (*offerre consolationis solatium*), Past. 180, 6. Froefrende mec *consolantem me*, Ps. Srt. 68, 21.

frēfrend. *Take here* frēfriend, *and add:*—Paraclitus, þæt is Frēfrigend, Hml. Th. i. 550, 31. Hēr is se frēfrigend ūres geswinces and weorces, 560, 34: 562, 18. v. fore-frēfrend.

frēfrung. *Add:*—þīne frēfrunge geblissodan mīne sāwle *consolationes tuae laetificabuntur animam meam*, Ps. L. 93, 19.

fregen? *The form seems to have an intensive force in the two following words.*

fregen-seldlic, -syllic; *adj. Very strange, very wonderful:*—Nys þis fregensyllic þinc tō rǣdenne, Wanl. Cat. 223, col. 1.

fregen-pearle (fregn-); *adv. Very much, excessively:*—Hī swíþe georne þā penegas sceáwodon, and hī swilces feós fregnþearle (fregen-, *v. l.*) wundredon *they looked very earnestly at the coins, and were excessively astonished at such money*, Hml. S. 23, 566.

freht. v. friht.

fremdian. *Substitute:* (1) *to alienate, make indifferent to:*—Fram weoruldwilnungum hine sceal gehwā fremdian *a seculi actibus se facere alienum*, R. Ben. 17, 4. (2) *to deprive of:*—Ne fremda (cf. l. 443) þ [mē] þǣre gesihþe þe þū mē ǣrest æteówdest, Hml. S. 23 b, 670. (3) *to make an alien* of a person, *excommunicate:*—Fremdiga *anathematizare*, Mk. R. 14, 71. Fremdian (frendian, MS. *The word is a gloss on* Mk. 14, 71), Wrt. Voc. ii. 74, 31. [*Goth.* framaþjan *to alienate.*] v. ā-, ge-fremdian.

fremdung. v. ā-, æl- (Ps. Rdr. 285, 14) fremdung: freme, an. *Take the passages under* fremu: fremed. v. full-fremed.

fremede. *Add:*—*Extra* vel ultra, aliena, alia, plus, praeter vel fremde, Wrt. Voc. ii. 145, 32. Fremde *exter, alienus*, 61. Fremdra *externorum*, 30, 44. (1) *of another family, stranger:*—Ne bearh nū gesib gesibban þe mā þe fremdan, Wlfst. 159, 16. Ðū hit becweðe swā gesibre handa swā fremdre swaðer ðe leófre sȳ, C. D. ii. 114, 7. Sceolon beón gesamnode ealle ðā menn ðe swyftoste hors habbað on ðǣm lande . . . þonne ærnað hȳ ealle tōward þǣm feó . . . ðā fremdan tō ærnað anð nimað, Ors. 1, 1; S. 21, 10. Ðȳ lǣs fremde menn (*extranei*) weorðen gefylled of ðīnum gesuince, Past. 249, 11. For bearnlēste þone welan hī lǣfað frǣmdum tō brúcanne, Bt. 11, 1; F. 32, 7. (2) *of another race* or *country:*—Hwā is ðonne from ūs fremde būtan ðā āwiergdan gǣstas, ðā ðe from ðæs hefencundan Fæder ēðle ādrifene sindon *qui namque alieni a nobis sunt nisi maligni spiritus, qui a coelestis sunt patriae sorte separati*?, Past. 249, 14. (3) *not natural* or *native* to a person, *foreign, external:*—Ic āna eom benumen mīnra þeáwa and eom getogen tō fremdum þeáwum, Bt. 7, 3; F. 20, 25. Gē wēnaþ þæt gē nān gecyndelic gōd ne gesǣlþa on innan eów selfum nabbaþ, for þām gē hī sēcaþ būtan eów tō fremdum gesceaftum, 14, 2; F. 44, 17. Fremdum, 14, 3; F. 46, 10. Hwī lufost ðū þā fremdan gōd swelce hī sién þīn āguu, 14, 1; F. 40, 30. (4) *unknown:*—Gē woldon habban eówerra gōdena weorca mēde æt frǣmdra monna cwiddunge *de alienis praemia sermunculis postulatis*, Bt. 18, 4; F. 66, 25. (5) *not friendly, estranged, not in the society of:*—Ic framþe weard fæderenbrōðrum *exter factus sum fratribus meis*, Ps. Th. 68, 8. (6) *free from, not participating in, deprived of.* (a) *with case:*—þȳ lǣs þ þæs heofenlican lofes fremde wǣre, Hml. Th. ii. 142, 26. Hē weard fremde þǣre costunge *alienus extitit a tentatione*, Gr. D. 26, 28. þ ic ne wurðe fremde geworden þǣre rōde gesihðe, Hml. S. 23 b, 443. (b) *with prep.*:—Hē fram þǣre costnunge weard fremde, Gr. D. 26, 30. Swæ fremðe (*extraneus*) from wærc deáðes swælce from unclæmnise wæs fremðe (*alienus*), Jn. p. 2, 2, 3. Hē willnode hine sylfne fram eallum begangum fremde (fremðne, *v. l.*) gedōn *cupiens se ab omnibus negotiis alienare*, Bd. 3, 19; Sch. 282, 19. [v. *N. E. D.* fremd.]

fremed-lǣcan *to alienate, estrange:*—Fremdlǣcede (-lǣtede, MS.) *alienati*, Ps. Rdr. 57, 4.

fremed-lic. v. full-fremedlic.

fremedlíce; *adv. Perfectly:*—þurh þæt fremedlíce (*perfecte*) ys geherud, Scint. 129, 3. v. full-fremedlíce.

fremednes. *Add:* v. full-, ge-fremednes.

fremfull. *Add:*—Fremful *beneficus, benefactor*, Wrt. Voc. ii. 125, 31. Fremfulra *utilium*, An. Ox. 56, 310. (1) *of persons, beneficent, benignant:*—Drihten wiste hū fremful hē beón wolde, Lch. iii. 436, 21. Hī syndon fremfulle (*benigni*) menn, Nar. 38, 22. (2) *of things, useful, beneficial, advantageous:*—Ðysse wyrte wōs ys swýðe fremful, Lch. i. 152, 15. Se drænc is frymful tō begānne, iii. 60, 2. Wē foresceáwiað and fremful taliað tō gehealdsumnesse gemǣnre sibbe þæt mynstres fadung on ðæs abbodes dōme stande *nos previdimus expedire propter pacis custodiam in abbatis pendere arbitrio ordinationem monasterii*, R. Ben. 125, 5. Mid mycelum and fremfullum (*subtili*) gesceádes tōdāle, Angl. xiii. 369, 52. God cwæð be synfullum mannum twā word swíðe fremfulle, Hml. Th. ii. 602, 7: Hml. S. 12, 146. [v. *N. E. D.* fremeful.] v. un-fremful; fremfulnes.

**fremful-lic**; *adj.* *Profitable, advantageous, beneficial :*—Is swíðe fremfullic þæt gehwá hine gelóme and geornlíce tó Gode gebidde, Hml. Th. ii. 430, 3. Him ne ðúhte ná fremfullic þ hé fēnge tó þǽre gife, Hml. S. 31, 101.

**fremfullíce.** *Add : to profit* or *advantage :*—Drihten ealle gód him fremfullíce (*to his profit*) tōwearde dyde, Lch. iii. 436, 22. Fremfullíce (*only* fremfi *is left in MS.*) effica[citer], R. Ben. I. 1, 5. [þ drihten fulste me to seggen wat it bitocned, and heu fremfulliche to understonden (*to understand to your profit*), O. E. Hml. ii. 175, 15.]

**fremfulnes.** *Substitute :* (1) *beneficence, benignity, action that profits another.* v. fremfull, (1) :—Beó him gegearewod eal mennisclic fremfulnes (-fullnyss, *v. l.*) *omnis ei exhibeatur humanitas*, R. Ben. 83, 18. Ic sille eówrum ceasterwarum hundteóntig þúsenda mitta hwǽtes . . . Ic gelíse þ gē willan beón gemindige þissere fremfulnesse, Ap. Th. 9, 25, Hé behēt þám þe hine funden micelne wurðscipe and fremfulnesse, Hml. S. 30, 229. (2) *usefulness, beneficial operation.* v. fremfull, (2) :—Genim þás wyrte, syle etan ; þú wundrast hyre fremfulnysse, Lch. i. 236, 16.

**fremian.** *Add :* (1) *absolute :*—Fremað *proficit*, An. Ox. 56, 347. Genóg frēmað *sufficit*, Rtl. 191, 37. Fremet *expedit*, Kent. Gl. 605. Hú micclum fremige þǽre sóðan lufe gebed, Hml. Th. i. 50, 35. Wið fýre fremiende *contra ignem valens*, Bd. 3, 10 ; Sch. 232, 16. (2) *with dat. of object benefited :*—þ him ne fremað náht, Hml. S. 13, 310 : 11, 301. Him fremað swíðor þ þá ungesewenlícan fýnd beón oferswýðde þonne þá gesewenlican, 25, 829. Hig ne fremiað mē ealle *non mihi expediunt omnia*, Ll. Th. ii. 174, 10. Hé wæs swíðe wís . . . , þ fremode eallre þisse ðeóde, Chr. 1057 ; P. 118, 25 : Hml. S. 10, 239. Hwæt eów betst fremige, 11, 35. Him sylfum fremian *sibi prodesse*, R. Ben. I. 107, 17. Fremian (framian, *v. l.*) his underþeóddan, R. Ben. 120, 9 : Hml. Th. i. 62, 8. Þurh lufe óðrum fremigan, 252, 20. (2 a) *where the particular is given in respect to which benefit is done :*—þá ðing þe him fremað tó nitwyrðum þingum and tó þǽre ēcan hǽle, Hml. S. 1, 101. Hit him náwiht tó hǽlo ne fremede, Guth. 96, 16. (2 b) *where means or manner of benefit is given :*—þæt hē óðrum fremige on worde and on weorce, Hml. Th. ii. 556, 15. Ne mihte se ēhtere mid nánre ðēnunge þám lytlingum swá micclum fremian, swá micclum swá hē him fremode mid þǽre ēhtnysse hætunge, i. 84, 11. [Ne ligge nefre on þine heorde þ hauelese monnam meie fremian, O. E. Hml. i. 111, 8. Þing þet ham wolde ureomien, A. R. 284.] [Fremian *seems to be distinguished in meaning and form from* fremman.]

**fremi[g]endlíe**; *adj. Beneficial :*—Fremiendlíc *profuturum*, An. Ox. 5199. Hyt bið hyre nytlic and fremgendlíc, Lch. i. 300, 19. v. frami[g]endlíc.

**fremman.** *Add :* I. *intrans. To advance, get on, prevail :*—Fremet *proficiet* (*radix justorum*), Kent. Gl. 406. Gúðlác wítedómlíce gáste weóx and fremede, Guth. 60, 22. Hé nówiht on þon fremede *nec ipse proficere aliquid ualebat*, Bd. 3, 11 ; Sch. 241, 3. Nó hí ówiht on ðám fremedon *nec quicquam proficiebant*, 3, 19 ; Sch. 275, 10. þæt hē gewyrce. ǽr hē on weg scyle, fremman on foldan wið feónda níð *that he succeed by his labours, ere he must depart, in prevailing on earth against the fiends' malice*, Seef. 75. II. *trans.* (1) *to advance, further, promote :*—Fremid *provehit*, Wrt. Voc. ii. 118, 17. (2) *to perform, commit* a crime :—Gif hē unrihthǽmed fremeþ wiþ óþer wíf, Bl. H. 185, 26. Heálíce synna þá ðe woruldmen fremmað, 213, 6. Fremmaþ *facessunt*, Wrt. Voc. ii. 95, 31. Fremede *facessit*, 93, 30 ; *exercebat*, 144, 69. Freme nú þ þú ongunne, Bl. H. 189, 2. Ne mæg hē mid þám óþrum nánwuht fremman *nihil est quod explicari queat*, Bt. 36, 3 ; F. 176, 8. Þá geogoðlustas tó fremmenne, Bl. H. 59, 9. Mínne willan tó fremanne, Hml. S. 23 b, 419. Gelígre fremmende, Ors. 1, 2 ; S. 30, 29. Tugon hié hiene þæt hē heora swicdómes wið Alexander fremmende wǽre *quasi urbem regi venditasset*, 4, 5 ; S. 168, 17. Fremmendum *prestante*, Wrt. Voc. ii. 118, 11. [v. *N. E. D.* freme.] v. full-fremman, wel-fremmende.

**fremming.** *Add :* I. *progress, advance.* v. fremman ; I :—Hé ne nihte wiðwiþerian þæs hálgan mannes fremmingum (*profectibus*), Gr. D. 117, 20. II. *a doing, accomplishing.* v. fremman; II. 2. (1) *the doing, operation of an agent :*—Swá hwæt swá on ðám húsle is þe ús lífes edwist forgifð, þæt is of ðǽre gástlican mihte and ungeswenlicere fremminge, Hml. Th. ii. 270, 26. Miht þú witan þæt weorc sprecan swíðor þonne þá nacodan word þe nabbað náne fremminge, Ælfc. T. Grn. 21, 25. (1 a) *with gen. of agent :*—Gif ic on Godes fingre deófla ádrǽfe ' . . . Nis ná tó understandenne be ðæs limes micelnysse, ac be ðǽra fingra fremminge, Hml. Th. ii. 204, 6. Þurh ðæs Hálgan Gástes fremminge wearð Críst ácenned on ðǽre menniscnysse, i. 198, 31. (2) *the doing* of an action :—Se Hǽlend hæfde þone gedwlan willan tó ðǽre fóstre and þá mihte tó ðǽre fremminge, Hml. Th. i. 184. 22 : 306, 8 : Hml. A. 11, 272. (2 a) *with gen. of what is done :*—þǽre lufe fandung is þæs weorces fremming, Hml. Th. ii. 314, 29. Ágyfan Gode þínre carfulnysse weorc and fremmincge . . . Æfter ðínre carfulnysse gódre fremmincge, 334, 23-27. Wē áweriað ús mid þǽre segene, áweriað eów mid þǽre láre fremminge, 402, 27. For ðǽre synne fremminge, Hex.

22, 29. Se Hálga Gást is genemned tó ðǽre fremminge Crístes menniscnysse, Hml. Th. i. 196, 22 (cf. 198, 31 *supra*). Ðurh geswicenysse yfeles and ðurh fremminge gódes, 332, 4. Fremmincgum *effectibus* (*operum*), An. Ox. 1332. Tó gódum fremmingum fulfremedra dǽda, Hml. A. 48, 581. v. ge-, wel-fremming.

**fremnes** *glosses* effectus, Rtl. 63, 20 : 68, 3. v. full-, ge-, wel-fremnes.

**fremsum.** *Add :*—Gedéfe is þín milde mód, mannum fremsum *benigna est misericordia tua*, Ps. Th. 68, 16. Siexte is ðæt hí beóð fremsume *pietatis gratia benigni sunt*, Past. 41, 18. Eálá þú fremsumeste hlǽfdige þe mē þíne árfǽstan mildheortnysse æteówdest, Hml. S. 23 b, 472.

**fremsume**; *adv. Benignly, kindly :*—Gedó nú frǽmsume frófre þíne tó þínum gódan gástes willan *benigne fac in bona voluntate tua*, Ps. C. 130. v. fremsumlíce.

**fremsum-líc**; *adj. Benign :*—Býcnode hē tó hyre mid onhyldum heáfde swý þe fremsumlícre ansýne, swá hē ealling byð *cui ille benignissimi ut est vultus inclinato capite annuit*, Gr. D. 280, 10.

**fremsumlíce.** *Add :*—Suíðe freóndlíce and suíðe fremsumlíce ðú mē tǽldesð *me benigna atque humili intentione reprehendis*, Past. 23, 9. Geþafode hē þ swíðe fremsumlíce (*benigne*), Gr. D. 242, 12 : 249, 7. Fremsumlíce ðóa, Dryhten *benigne fac, Domine*, Ps. Srt. Spl. T. 50, 19. Hié ús fremsumlíce and luflíce onféngon *benigne excepti*, Nar. 17, 17 (v. Angl. i. 510).

**fremsumnes.** *Add :*—Fremsumnes *benignitas*, Wrt. Voc. ii. 125, 35. Wē ongytaþ þ hit þus byð in ðám mundbyrdum háligra martyra, þ hí ná ne cýðað swá manige fremsumnesse þurh heora líchaman swá hí gód eówiað þurh heora reliquias (*ut non tanta per corpora sua quanta beneficia per reliquias ostendant*), Gr. D. 177, 2.

**fremu.** *Take here* freme *in Dict., and add :* (1) *Kindness, kind deed, benefit, good :*—Fremu, freomu *beneficium*, Txts. 44. 135. Frēme *affectus* (cf. *affectum* hyldo, Wrt. Voc. ii. 1, 12), Rtl. 187, 17. *Beneficium* freme, i. *donum* gife, Wrt. Voc. ii. 125, 29. (2) *profit, advantage :*—Hwelc fremu bið menn ðæt hē gestríene eal ðæt him ymbútan sié *quid prodest homini, si totum, quod extra se est, congregat ?*, Past. 333, 10. Gyf hē máre geearnian mæig, him byð sylfum fremu *si plus deservit, ipsi commodum erit*, Ll. Th. i. 438, 7. Sē þe óðerne mid wóge forsecgan wille, þ hē aðor oþþe feó oþþe freme þe wyrsa sý, 266, 23. Freme (feorme, freomu, *v. ll.*), 384, 24. Wǽron earme men besyrwde ge æt freme ge æt fóstre ge æt feó, Wlfst. 158, 30. Eádsige hine wel lǽrde tó ealles folces freme *docuit eum ea quae facienda erant ad utilitatem sibi subjecti populi*, Chr. 1042 ; P. 162, note 6. Ðæt hē sumne hearm geswigode ðǽr ðǽr hē freme gecleopian meahte *that he had done harm by silence where he might have got profit by calling out*, Past. 49, 22.

**frence**, an; *f. A rough cloak :*—Frence coculus (cf. amphibalum; coculus, Ll. Gl. H. 43, col. 2, 18, *and* rúh hrægel *amphibalum*, Wrt. Voc. i. 25, 65), Wrt. Voc. ii. 135, 41. [Cf. (?) Francan.]

**Francisc.** *Add :*—Frenciscra wyrþlíce cyrcena gewunan *Galliarum honestos aecclesiarum usus*, Angl. xiii. 368, 43. ¶ *French speech :*—Sprecan on Frencisc, viii. 313, 21.

**frendian.** v. fremdian.

**freó.** *Add :* (1) *free, not in subjection to a master, having liberty of action :*—Ægylmǽr bohte Sǽdrýðe æt Sǽwolde abbude . . . and ofer his dæg and his wífes dæg beó se man freóh, C. D. vi. 210, 17. Þeówie hē six gēr and beó him freóh on þám seofoðan, Ex. 21, 2. Gif frig man frēum stelð, Ll. Th. i. 6, 2. Mægðbót sí swá fríges mannes, 20, 9. Eall sió gioguð ðe nú is on Angelcynne fríóra monna, Past. 7, 10. Eallum fríóum monnum þás dagas sién forgifene, Ll. Th. i. 92, 2. (1 a) *free as regards* (*wiþ*) *another :*—Ðǽm ðeówan is tó cýðonne ðæt hē wiete ðæt hē nis freóh wið his hláford, Past. 200, 19. (1 b) *not in subjection* to sin :—Gif sunu íow gefríoð sóðlíce fríó (freó, L.) gē bióðon, Jn. R. 8, 36. Hē ús freó gedyde, Bl. H. 83, 31. (2) *of studies, liberal :*—Wæs hē on gelǽrednesse gewrita ge freóra (*liberalium*) ge cyriclicra tó wundrienne, Bd. 5, 15 ; Sch. 651, 14. (3) *at liberty, not in confinement or custody :*—Álýs ðú hine fram deóflum gehæftne, and lǽt hine gán frígne, Hml. Th. ii. 416, 28. Hē hēt hí unbindan . . . þ hí fríge móston faran swá hwider swá hí woldon, Hml. S. 23, 191. (4) *free from obligation or restraint upon action* (*with gen.*) :—Ðá ðe beóð mid synscipe gebundene . . . ðá ðe beóð fríó ðǽra benda, Past. 177, 21. Freó, 393, 11. Ic wolde beón þí freóra Gode tó þáwianne, Solil. H. 36, 11. (5) *free from work, disengaged :*—Hié wilniað ðæt hié beóu freó and ǽmetige . . . and noldon beón ábisgode on eorðlicum ðingum, Past. 135, 25. Bydele gebyrað þ hē for his wycan sý weorces ðíng ðonne óðer man, Ll. Th. i. 440, 6. Swá swá ðú freóra byst þissa weorlde ðinga, swá ðú sweotolor ongytst be ðám wísdóme, Solil. H. 46, 13. (6) *free from guilt, innocent :*—Tó hwon lǽddest þú þeosne freóne and unscyldigne hider ?, Bl. H. 87, 1. (7) *of action, movement, &c., unimpeded, unhindered :*—Mid freóre and unforwandodlicre stefne, Past. 89, 23. (8) *acting of one's own will, unforced :*—Simle hē (*God*) bið freóh, ne biþ hē tó nánum weorce geneded, Bt. 42 ; F. 258, 10. God

moncynne forgeaf ðæt hié môston stondan on fríðum anwalde, Past. 405, 28. Fríum cyre *libero arbitrio*, An. Ox. 1287. (9) *free* from trouble, &c., *exempt, immune* :—Hē wæs freó (freóh, *v. l.*) fram þǣre uncyste deófles costunge, Gr. D. 102, 6. Hī gehrínð hēr sumu wracu ðæt hī ne sién freó ne orsorge, Past. 429, 18. (10) *free, not liable* to a tax, &c. :—Cyningas nimað gafol of fremedum . . . þā bearn synt fríge (freó, L. R.), Mt. 17, 26. (10 a) of land :—Sī hyt ælces þinges freóh būton ferdfóre . . ., C. D. iii. 20, 4. Æghwæs tô brúcenne tô freón . . . būtan ðǣm circsceatte, 254, 12. Hió hit hæbben tô frión ælces þinges būtan wealgeworce . . ., 255, 17 : 256, 16 : Cht. E. 242, 16. (10 b) of property, *at one's own disposal*. v. freó-sceatt. v. folc-, gafol-, healf-, scot-, toll-freó.

**freó** *a lady*. Cf. frowe.

**freó-bearn.** *Add :* (1) of human beings :—Hié (*the descendants of Abraham*) gesittað be sǣm tweónum . . . leóde þíne, freóbearn fæder, folca sēlost, Exod. 445. Abraham andswarode '. . . Gǣð gerēfa mín fægen freóbearnum,' Gen. 2182. (2) of Christ :—Hálígne Gást swā ēcne swā Fæder oððe Freóbearn, Hy. 10, 43. Āhangen wæs cyninges freóbearn, Godes gāstsunu, El. 672. Hū þē (*Christ*) rodera weard æt frymðe genôm him tô freóbearne, Cri. 223. Cf. freó-dohtor.

**freó-bearn-fæder.** *Dele, and see preceding word :* **freód.** *Add :* [Cf. *Goth.* frijaþwa *love.*]

**freó-dohtor** *a freeborn, legitimate daughter :*—His fæder hine (*Antichrist*) strýnð be his ágenre freódehter, Wlfst. 193, 6.

**freó-dôm.** *Add :* (1) *freedom* from spiritual bondage. v. freó, (1 b) :—Ðǣr se Dryhtnes gást is, ðǣr is freódoom, Past. 265, 1. Se freódôm þæs unāræfnedlican þeówdómes, þ is ðæs deófollican onwaldes, Bl. H. 137, 12. Wilnigende mid þissum þeówdôme cuman tô ēcum freódóme, Angl. viii. 320, 9. Fríódôm gifylga, Rtl. 31, 9. (2) *freedom* from obligation, *release* from restraint. v. freó, (4) :—Selle hir bôc freódômes *det illi libellum repudii*, Mt. L. 5, 31 : 19, 7. Ðæt ðæt môd suā bald sié for his freódóme ðæt hit ne gewende on selflíce, ðonne his hláford him tô ungemetlicne anwald forgiefð his sprǣce, Past. 147, 2. (3) *freedom* of activity, *absence of restraint*, or *hindrance*. v. freó, (7) :—Hē mid freódóme (*deliberatione*) geþances yfel dēþ, Scint. 229, 11. (4) *freedom to do, liberty* of action :—On þyssum lífe for ān hreówsunge geopenað freóhdóm *in hac vita tantum pænitentiæ patet libertas*, Scint. 48, 15. (5) *freedom* in expenditure, *liberality* :—Freódóme oððe cystignesse *liberalitate*, Wrt. Voc. ii. 50, 21. Ðonne hié hit eall ryhtlíce gedǣled hæbben, ðonne ne teón hié nānwuht ðæs lofes tô him . . . ne him selfum ne tellen tô mægene hiora freódóm (frió-, *v. l.*) *ne sibi virtutem suae liberalitatis deputent*, Past. 323, 3. (6) *freedom, frankness* :—Sié in ðær hygdigo fríódóm *sit in ea casta libertas*, Rtl. 105, 3. (7) *freedom* from trouble, &c. v. freó, (9) :—þu ūs freódôm gief from yfla gehwām, Hy. 5, 10. (8) *freedom* from a tax, &c. v. freó, (10) :—Mín ærfelond ðe ic et Aeðeluulfe cyninge begæt and gebohte mid fullum fríódóme on ǣce ærfe, C. D. i. 316, 5. Hē gebohte æt Æðere . . . ðis gewrit and ðis land mið ðy fríaðóme ðe hit hēr gefriád wæs tô Crístes cyrican on ēc erfe, C. D. B. ii. 154, 17. Heó æt him gebohte his dǣl ðæs eardes tô freódôme intó ðām mynstre *she bought of him his share of the district and enfranchised it, and granted it to the monastery*, Lch. iii. 432, 4. (8 a) *the charter granting freehold land :*—Ðes fríódôm waes bigeten aet Wíglāfe cyninge (cf. *hoc munus et hanc libertatem scripsi et scribere precipi*, 314, 32) mid ðaem twēntigum hîda aet iddeshale, end ðaes londes fríódôm aet habeccahām mid ðy tēn hîda londes aet felda . . . Ðis is heánbirige fríódóm, C. D. i. 315, 21-29. Hió him tô spraecon ymb ðæt lond, ðæt hē his him geūðe, ðæt hió maehten ðone freódôm begeotan, 222, 28. Ic Eádweard cyngc mid ðære hālgan Crístes rôde tácne ðis hēt getrymman and gefæstnian, ðisne freódôm . . . Ic fæstlíce bebeóde ðæt hine nǣnig mínra æfterfyligendra eft ne onwende, vi. 203, 2. v. sundor-freódôm.

**freó-scipe** (?), es ; *m. Friendship, kindness :*—Gif him mǣte þ his earmas beón fægere gegerede, þ bið freódscipe (freónd-?), Archiv cxx. 304, 30. [Sē þe] Herculem gesihð freódscipe fēgð, Lch. iii. 206, 4. Hláf wexenne niman freódscipas getácnað, 210, 1.

**freógan** *to free*. *Add :*—From dióble friáð (*liberat*), Mk. p. 3, 17. Frēwed, Mt. p. 16, 16. Þys sint þāra manna naman ðe man freóde for Ordgār ðā hē læg on ádle, Cht. E. 255, 7. Mon þā þeówas freóde, Ors. 4, 3 ; S. 162, 16. Sume þā men þe hié on ðeówdôme hæfdon, þā þe heora hláfordas freógean noldon . . . þā consulas . . . freódon, 4, 9 ; S. 190, 35. v. ā-freón, *and* friá *in Dict*.

**freógend, frígend** *a liberator*. v. ge-freógend : **freó-gyld**. v. friþ-gild : **freó-lác** *might be feminine*. v. lác.

**freó-lǣta** (*and* -lǣte, an ; *f.* ?). *Add :*—Fríólēta *vernaculus*, Wrt. Voc. ii. 123, 35 : *libertus*, 112, 80. Fríglǣta, 51, 2. Fríólētan *libertabus*, 112, 72. Fríglǣtan, 51, 1. [Cf. *O. H. Ger.* frî-lâz *manumissio*. Cf. *also Goth.* fra-lēts *libertus*.]

**freólic.** *Add :* (1) *free* as in *free* will. v. freó, (8) :—Freólicum cyre *libero arbitrio*, An. Ox. 1287 : 1312. (2) *liberal, unstinted in quantity :*—Of frílicum gestríóne *fenore liberali*, Kent. Gl. 1046. [v. *N. E. D.* freely ; *adj. O. H. Ger.* frî-lîh *liber*.] v. ge-freólic.

**freólíce.** *Add :* (1) *without constraint* or *reluctance, willingly :*—Þonne se man syngað freólíce būtan ælcere sceame, Angl. vii. 46, 451 : Cri. 1291. Heó þæt ǣrende onfēng freólíce, Hy. 10, 15. (2) *without restraint* or *reserve* in regard to speech :—Ðā unwaran lāreówas ne durron ryht freólíce lǣran and unforwandodlíce sprecan, Past. 89, 12. Suā micle freólícor hē tǣld ôðre menn suā hē lǣs ongitt his ágene uncysta, 273, 1. (3) *without restriction upon action, without let* or *hindrance :*—Hē cwæð þæt hē môste freólíce ðā heofonlican lāre his leóde bodian (*licentiam praedicandi non abstulit*, Bd. 1, 25), Hml. Th. ii. 128, 28. (4) *with impunity :*—On mægenfæstum eardum man mæg fæstan freólícor ðonne hēr, Hml. S. 13, 109. (5) *with freedom from control, rule, &c.* : —Ic gife þās landes . . . freólíce, swā ðet nān man nā have þǣr nān onsting būton seó abbot, Chr. 656 ; P. 30, 26 : 963 ; P. 116, 18. (6) *nobly, splendidly :*—Forð becôm freólíce in geatwum (cf. *Laym.* freoliche iwapned) kyningc, Chr. 1065 ; P. 194, 10.

**freóls.** *Add :* I. *freedom* in respect to land granted, *grant of land that enjoys immunity ; libertas :*—Þis is ealra þāra landa freóls þe Eádgár cyning geedfreólsade Wulfríce his þegene (cf. *Dedit minister regi cxx mancusas causa hujus libertatis*, 360, 35), C. D. ii. 361, 26. Æðerēdes cyninges frióls and his handseten and sǣlen, 89, 11. Ðes freóls ā ēcelíce forð þurhwunige, vi. 203, 6. Ic on ðysum gewrite geswutelie þe Ciltacumbes freúlse, v. 113, 22. II :—Freóls *iubileus ; s. annus*, An. Ox. 3831 : 2, 256. Of ðære stôwe weard ārǣred þises dæges freóls, Hml. Th. i. 502, 7. On mǣrum dæge eówres freólses (*sollemnitatis*), Ps. L. 80, 4. Ealle dagas freólses Godes *omnes dies festos Dei*, 74. 9. Eásterlíces freólses *paschalis sollempnitatis*, Angl. xiii. 401, 515 : *festivitatis*, 522. Gemunað þisne dæg and wurðiað hine Drihtne tô freólse (*celebrabitis eam solemnem Domino*), Ex. 12, 14. Būton drihtenlicum and freólsum *exceptis dominicis et festivitatibus*, Angl. xiii. 396, 450. v. blôstm-, færeld-, hríþer-freóls.

**freóls ;** *adj. Add :* I. *free*. (1) of persons, *not in bondage :*—Hē dide hine sylfne and his ofspreng ǣfre freóls and sacclēs, Cht. Th. 628, 23. Ælc hláford his nýðþeówum byrge . . . for ðām hí sýn Gode efenleófe and þā ðe syndon freólse, Ll. Th. ii. 314, 11. (2) of places, *exempt from jurisdiction, &c.* :—Ic wille ðat ðat mynster . . . beó swā freóls swā ǣnig ôðer mynster is æt eallan þingan, C. D. vi. 203, 27. II. of a feast or festival :—Būton dæg freóls hit beó *nisi dies festiua fuerit*, Angl. xiii. 374, 119. Freóls ǣnig dæg *festiua aliqua dies*, 389, 349. (Cf. dagum freóls *diebus festis*, 437, 1029.) Freólsne dæg *diem festum*, Ps. L. 75, 11. [*Icel.* frjáls *free.*]

**freóls-bóc.** *Add :*—Ðis is seó freólsbôc tô Cheolcar and ealra ðǣre landa ðe intó ðǣ mynechina lífe æt Wiltûne forgifene synt, C. D. iii. 117, 24.

**freóls-bryce.** *Add :*—Syndan freólsbrycas (-bricas, *v. l.*) and fæstenbrycas wîde geworhte oft and gelôme, Wulfst. 164, 9.

**freóls-dæg.** *Add :*—Hû on freólsdagum (*in sanctorum natalitiis*) seó nihtlíce wæcce tô healdenne sý . . . sealmas sýn gesungene þe tô þām freólsdæge belimpað, R. Ben. 39, 4-9. v. Eáster-freólsdæg.

**freóls-dôm.** *For* 'Ciricean . . . [MS. freólsdôme]' *l.* Cirice an freólsdôme.

**freóls-geár.** *For* Cot. 106 *substitute :*—þæt freólsgēr *jubelemus* (l. *jubeleus annus*. v. 83, 47, and cf. freóls ; II), Wrt. Voc. ii. 44, 64.

**freóls-gefa.** *Add :* [*Icel.* frjáls-gjafi.]

**freólsian.** *Add :* I. *to free*. (1) *to deliver* from bondage :—Drihten mancyn freólsode, Bl. H. 83, 24. (2) *to enfranchise* land. v. geedfreólsian. II. *to celebrate* a festival :—Ðone fíftan dæg hí freólsodon Ioue tô wurðmynte, ðām mǣrostan gode, Sal. K. p. 124, 134. [v. *N. E. D.* trels. *Icel.* frjálsa, frelsa *to free.*]

**freólsiend.** v. fríolsend *in Dict*.

**freóls-lic ;** *adj. I. free*. v. freolslíce ; I. [*Icel.* frjáls-ligr *free.*] II. of a festival :—Godspell nā freólslicum þēawe (*festiuo more*) sî rǣdd, Angl. xiii. 402, 529. Dagum freólslicon *diebus festiuis*, 390, 350. Freóls[l]icum symeltîdum, 397, 451.

**freólslíce.** *Substitute :* I. *freely, without hindrance, without restraint :*—Hē him synderlíce wîc getimbrede, þ hē mihte on ðam freólslíce (freólíce, *v. l.*) Gode þeówian (*in quo liberius caelestibus studiis uacaret*), Bd. 3, 19 ; Sch. 277, 14. Þæt hí āblinnen fram gewinnum hwîlwendlicra þinga, þæt hí for willunge þāra ēcra gôda freólslícor (freólícor, *v. l., liberius*) gewinne, 4, 25 ; Sch. 500, 7. II. in a manner proper to a festival, solemnly :—Seó wucu freólslíce (*sollempniter*) byþ gewyrþud, Angl. xiii. 436, 1017. [*Icel.* frjálsliga *freely*.]

**freóls-mann.** *Add :* [Cf. *Icel.* frjálsmann-ligr.]

**freóls-niht.** *Add :* f. *The night before a festival :*—þā cildra þe beóð begiten on Sunnanniht and on þām hālgan freólsnihtum, hí sceolan beón geboren būtan eágon, Nap. 26.

**freóls-stôw.** *Add :* Ll. Th. ii. 260, 30.

**freóls-tíd.** *Add : a festival* of the Church, *an anniversary :*—Ðāra seofen hāligra slǣpera freólstíd bið on geáre fíf nihton ǣr hláfmæssan, Hml. S. 23, 7. On þurhhāligere freólstíde *in sacrosancta* (*palmarum*) *solemnitate* i. *festiuitate*, An. Ox. 2601. Tô dæg Godes gelaðung mǣrsað þāra eádigra cildra freólstíde (*natale innocentium infantum*),

Hml. Th. i. 76, 28. Hú dægredsangas on freólstídum tó healdenne sýn *qualiter matutinorum sollempnitas agatur*, R. Ben. 36, 9. On Godes hálgena freólstídum *in sanctorum festiuitatibus*, 39, 4. Freólstída and fæstentída rihtlíce understandan, Wlfst. 113, 1.

**freólsung.** *Add :*—On freólsungum oððe on eallum symelnyssum *in sanctorum festivitatibus vel omnibus sollempnitatibus*, R. Ben. I. 45, 3.

**fræó-man.** *For last passage substitute :*—Hwæt gifest þú me, gásta Waldend, freómanna tó frófre . . . ne sealdest þú mé sunu . . . Gæð geréfa mín fægen freóbearnum *what freeborn children wilt thou give me, Ruler of spirits, for my comfort ?* . . . *Thou hast not granted me a son* . . . *My steward goes rejoicing in fair sons and daughters*, Gen. 2175. *Add :*—Eallum freómannum (fríoum monnum, *v. l.*) þás dagas sién forgifene, Ll. Th. i. 92, 2. ¶ *in some cases where* freó-man *is given as a compound perhaps* freó man *should be read*. e. g. frígman *is printed* Ll. Th. i. 4, 3, *but cf.* frígne mannan, l. 6. Gif . . . frígman (fríg man ?) frígne ofsleahð, 286, 21. Gif fríman (frí man ?) wið fríes mannes wíf geligeð, 10, 6.

**freomlic.** v. framlic.

**freó-nama.** *Add :*—Cwénburh wæs þære fæmnan noma (freónama, *v. l., nomen*), Bd. 5, 3; Sch. 565, 15. Freónaman *cognomine*, Wrt. Voc. ii. 15, 79.

**freónd.** *Add : dat.* friénd, frínd, frýnd, freónde. (1) where mutual affection is felt or professed :—Eálá þú freónd and mín mæg (cf. his néhmága sum and his worldfreónda hine lufode, 9), Bl. H. 113, 22. Ðá getreówan freónd (friénd, *v. l.*), ic secge, seó þæt deórweorþeste ðyng þissa woruldgesælþa . . . ælcesóþres þinges mon wilnað . . . tó sumum woruldluste bútan ðæs getreówan freóndes, Bt. 24, 3; F. 82, 34. Ðú eart on borg begán ðínum friénd, Past. 193, 18. Tó his friénd (fríend, *v. l.*), 325, 1. Friénd (frynd, freónd, *v. ll.*), Ll. Th. i. 50, 29. Frýnd, Hml. Th. i. 248, 4, 13 : Th. Ap. 16, 13. Hwæt forstód seó mengu þára freónda . . . þá friénd cumaþ mid ðám welan, Bt. 29, 2; F. 106, 8. His freónd him ætfeallað, oððe his feoh him ætbyrst, Wlfst. 142, 6. Æghwylcum men biþ leófre swá hé hæbbe holdra freónda má, Bl. H. 123, 1. Seó lícetung heora freónda, 99, 33. Hé gegæderaþ frínd and geféran, Bt. 21; F. 74, 38. Friénd, 84, 1. (2) used to a stranger as a mark of goodwill or kindly condescension :—Eálá þú freónd, ne dó ic þé nænne teónan, Mt. 20, 13 : 22, 12. Freónda gehwilc mid rihtan getrýwðan óðerne lufige, Ll. Th. i. 350, 13. Wé willað biddan freónda gehwylcne . . . þ hí ænne God lufian, 316, 17. Word and weorc freónda gehwylc fadige mid rihte, 322, 10 : 372, 1. (3) *a relative, kinsman :*—Mæg ł freónd *amicus*, Mt. L. 11, 19 : Jn. L. 11, 11. Áríseþ suna wið freóndum *insurgent filii in parentes*, Mt. R. 10, 21. Fríondum and mégum *cognatis et amicis*, Lk. L. R. 21, 16. Betuih freúndo (-e, R., mágas, W. S.) and cúðo *inter cognatos et adnotos*, 2, 44. (3 a) where the duties or benefits consequent upon kinship are referred to :—Gif man mædan weddian wille, and hit swá hire and freóndan gelícige . . . áborgian his frýnd þ, Ll. Th. i. 254, 2-7 : 10 : 256, 2. Fón þá nehstan frýnd (frínd, *v. l.*) tó þám lande, 416, 10. Licge hé águlde eallum his freóndum, 312, 12. (4) *a lover :*—Juliana, þú wiðsæcest þínum brýdguman . . . hé is tó freónde gód, Jul. 102. Sceal fæmne hire freónd gesécean, Gn. C. 44. (5) *one who wishes well* to another, *favours, supports, helps :*—Gif þú hine forlætst ne eart ðú ðæs cáseres freónd (friónd, L.), Jn. 19, 12. Ne þearf hé þær næfre wénan þæs freóndes þe hine of þæs deófles gewealdum álésan mæge, Bl. H. 63, 2. Þone hé tealde him tó frýnd þe him sume hefigtýmnysse on belædde, Hml. Th. ii. 546, 18. Dryhten, sint geweorðode mid mé ðíne friénd, Past. 85, 24. Gefáh wið þone cyning and wið ealle his frýnd, Ll. Th. i. 248, 13. Wid ealle his freónd, 210, 11. ¶ Godes freónd *an upholder of religion, a pious person, a true Christian* :—Éhte his ælc þára þe Godes freónd sí, Ll. Th. i. 340, 9 : 358, 24. Hé wæs swýðe Godes freónd, Chr. 654; P. 29, 14. Feówer þing synt behéfost þám árwyrðan men, þám Godes frýnd þám þe þencð tó þám écan lífe, Wlfst. 247, 12. Gé þe Godes frýnd synd, Bl. 191, 36. Sculan Godes freónd ælc unriht álecgan, Ll. Th. ii. 312, 30. Eallum Godes freóndum gebireð þ hí Godes cirican lufian, 240, 4. (5 a) in the laws, *one who undertakes responsibility on behalf of another :*—Niman hine on borh þá þe hine ær hláforde befæston . . . oððe óðere frýnd gif hé hæbbe, Ll. Th. i. 162, 18. Bið se deáda besmiten búton hé frínd hæbbe þe hine mid rihte clænsnian . . . Gif hé þæra freónda hæfd þe þ tó þon durron, 290, 12-15. Selle hé his wæpn his freóndum tó gehealdanne, 60, 8. His mægum and his fríondum, 90, 9. (5 D) *of* things, *anything helpful :*—Mé gelyste þære deóglan stówe þe ic ær on wæs in mynstre, seó is þære gnornunge freónd *secretum locum petii amicum moeroris*, Gr. D. 3, 13. (6) *one who is on good terms with* another, *not at variance :*—Áworden woeron fríondas Heródes and Pílatus, Lk. L. R. 23, 12. (6 a) *one who is on the same side* or *of the same party* as another, *an associate :*—Ne sé wé freóndas (*socii*, geféran, W. S.) hiora in blód ðára wítgana, Mt. L. 23, 30. Oft ic (*a sword*) óðrum scód frécne ær his freónde, Rä. 21, 16. ¶ *in contrast with* feónd :—Of þæm feóndscipe þe ús ær betweónum wæs, þ hé seoððan wæs mé freónd *factus amicus ex hoste*, Nar. 19, 21. Feúnd on freóndes anlícnesse, Bt. 29, 2; F. 106, 15. Freónde ne feúnde, Met. 25, 16.

Mid ðís andweardan welan mon wyrcþ oftor feónd ðonne freónd, Bt. 24, 3; F. 84, 4. Tócnáwan þíne frínd (frénd, *v. l.*) and þíne fýnd (fiénd, *v. l.*), 20; F. 72, 20. Ne friénd ne fiénd, 37, 1; F. 186, 7. v. neáh-, níd-, wíf-freónd; ge-frínd.

**freóndheald-lic;** *adj. Related :*—Of gesibbum *vel* of freóndheadlicum *de consanguineo*, Wrt. Voc. ii. 138, 10.

**freónd-leás.** *Add : without relatives, orphan :*—Doem ðæm freóndleásan *judicare pupillo*, Ps. Srt. 9, 39. Ne forlét ic iúih freóndleása ł aldorleása (*orfanos*), Jn. L. R. 14, 18. [*Icel.* frænd-lauss *without kinsmen*.]

**freónd-leást.** *Dele ' indigence.'*

**freónd-lic.** *Add : amicable :*—Mid freóndlicre and mid bróþorlicre geþeahte *amicali et quasi fraterno consilio*, Bd. 3, 22; S. 292, 8. In þám freóndlican geflíte *in hac amica contentione*, Gr. D. 116, 6.

**freóndlíce.** *Add :*—Ælfríc abbod grét freóndlíce Sigferd, Ælfc. T. Grn. 1, 5. Þá þe Gode híwcúþlícor and freóndlícor þeówiað *hi qui Deo familiarius serviunt*, Gr. D. 165, 1.

**freónd-líþe;** *adj. Gentle with friends* or *relations :*—Gif hé bið on .xxix. nihta ealdne mónan ákenned, sé bið gód and freóndlíþe, Lch. iii. 158, 19. v. E. S. 39, 340.

**freónd-ræden.** *Add :* (1) cf. freónd, (1) :—Hé him getíðað þæs ðe hé bitt, ná for freóndrædene (cf. for þán hé his freónd ys, Lk. 11, 8), Hml. Th. i. 248, 33. (2) cf. freónd, (4) :—Wæs sió fæmne mid hyre fæder willan welegum biwedded : wyrd ne ful cúðe freóndrædenne, hú heó from hogde, Jul. 34. (3) cf. freónd, (5) :—Se geréfa hine ácwællan ne dorste on þæs folces gewytnysse for heora freóndrædene, Hml. S. 2, 301. Þeáh þe hé séce tó godum freóndrædenne, Jul. 220. (4) cf. freónd, (6) :—Freóndrēddene healdan wið þone ł *to keep on good terms with the bishop*, Cht. Th. 141, 6, 9. Hí forlætaþ lufan and sibbe, þæs geférscipes freóndrædenne, Met. 11, 82. Warna þæt þú næfre freóndrædene nyme wið þá landes men *cave ne unquam cum habitatoribus terrae illius jungas amicitias*, Ex. 34, 12. [[v. *N. E. D.* friendrede.]

**freóndscipe.** *Add :* (1) cf. freónd, (1) :—Hé gefyrn tó mé geþeóded wæs híwcúðlíce in manigfealdum freóndscipum *dudum mihi in amicitiis familiariter juncto*, Gr. D. 237, 22. Freóndscipas *amicitias*, Kent. Gl. 601. (2) cf. freónd, (5) :—Manna freóndscipe biþ swíþe hwílwendlic ; for þon úre yldran swultan and swíþe oft ús from wendan, ah sé þe Godes freóndscipe begyteþ, ne þearf sé næfre wénan þ hé him onwended weorþe, Bl. H. 195, 25–28. Þurh þe eorðbúende onfóð freoþo and freóndscipe, Gen. 1760. Git mé freóndscipe cýðað, 2515 : An. 478. (3) cf. freónd, (6) :—Hé gemyndgade Iónas þære fæhðe þe Xersis him tó geworht hæfde . . . Hé bæd hié eác þ hié genunden þæs unárímedlican freóndscipes þe hié hæfdon tó Atheniensum, Ors. 2, 5 ; S. 82, 19. ' Wes ús fæle freónd ' . . . Abraham onfeng freóndscipe be freán hæse, Gen. 2735.

**freónd-spéd.** *Add :*—Bið þæt æghwylcum men sélre þæt hé hine gehealde on his freódóme gesundne, þeáh þe hé his freóndspédum treówige, þænne hé scyle æfter þám bendum þæs freódómes ceápian, Nap. 26.

**freó-ness.** v. frignes (*l.* fríg-nes) *in Dict.*

**freó-riht.** *Add :*—Wæron nú lange freóriht fornumene and ðrælriht generwde *now for long the rights of the free have been taken away and the rights of the thrall have been curtailed*, Wlfst. 158, 15.

**freós (?)**—Gehlódon him tó húðe hordwearda gestreón, feá (feó ?) and freós, Dan. 66.

**freósan.** *Add :*—Hit begann on æfnunge egeslíce freósan, Hml. S. 11, 153.

**freó-sceatt, es ; m.** *Property entirely at the owner's disposal, property of which the owner has absolute possession :*—Ná þá áne þe freó synt, ac gyt má þá þe æhtborene synt and óþera manna freósceattas (freó sceattas ?) and for þám ánum foroft gefreóde *not those only that are free, but still more those that are born chattels and the absolute property of other men, and for the particular purpose are very often freed* ; non solum liberi, sed etiam plerumque et ex conditione servili, sed propter hoc a dominis liberati, R. Ben. 138, 21. [v. *N. E. D.* free, 28 b *at one's own disposal*, e.g. *own disposal*, e. g.]

**freót.** *Add :* (1) *the condition of being free :*—Ælcon men freót þe wíteþeów wære, oððe hé mid his feó gebohte, Cht. Crw. 23, 28. Gif þeów mon wyrce on Sunnandæg bútan his hláfordes hæse, þolie his freótes, Ll. Th. i. 104, 6. Hér geswutelað on ðissere béc ðæt Eádríc hæfð geboht Sægyfu his dohtor æt Ælfsige abbod tó écum freóte and eall hire ofspring, C. D. vi. 209, 10, 14 : 210, 32. (2) *a grant of freedom* (in this sense the word occurs as feminine), *manumission :*—Ælsig þe þá menn bohte hig freóde uppan Petrocys weófede æfre saclés . . . Gif hwá þás freót ábrece, hebbe him wið Críste geméne, Cht. Th. 627, 29.

**freót-gifa.** *Add :* Wrt. Voc. ii. 59, 18.

**freót-gifu.** *Substitute :* freót-gift, e ; *f. Manumission :*—Freótgift (*printed* -gife, but see Angl. viii. 452) *manumissio*, Wrt. Voc. i. 60, 1.

**freop-.** v. friþ- : **freoþa.** *Dele, and see* fultumiend, (3).

**freót-man.** *Add :*—Sceóte man ælmessan be þám þe man þonne tó

þearfe geræde ... hwīlum be teóþunge, hwīlum be mannes efenwihte, hwīlum be freótmen, hwīlum be healffreón, Wlfst. 171, 4. Hē geann Gode his sáwelscættas, þ is .i. hid and .i. pund penega and .vi. and twēntig freótmonna for his sáwle, C. D. B. iii. 652, 18; Shm. 159, 6.

**fretan.** *Add*: (1) *of human beings*:—Freteð *lurcatur* (*gula dulcis fercula victus*, Ald. 204, 24), Wrt. Voc. ii. 96, 43 : 52, 36. (1 a) *figurative*:—Sácerdas þe fretað and forswelgað folces synna *sacerdotes qui comedunt peccata populi*, Ll. Th. ii. 326, 40. Þá þe freotas (*deuorant*) hús widwana, Mk. R. 12, 40. (2) *of animals*:—Đæt ilce đæt se hund áspáw, hē hit eft frit, Past. 419, 30. Fryt *devorat*, Ll. Th. ii. 174, 31. Fretan *lurcare* (*gulosa beluarum ingluvies praedam lurcare* non audens, Ald. 49, 8), Wrt. Voc. ii. 82, 51 : 52, 35. (3) *to destroy* by the action of (*mid*) *animals or things*:—Hié þæt corn fræton mid hirā horsum, Chr. 894; P. 88, n. 4. Đonne hié bióð innan fretene mid đære ádle *dum se ista intrinsecus peste consumunt*, Past. 235, 11. v. ge-fretan; moþ-freten.

**fret-máse, fretnes.** v. frec-máse, frec-nes : **frettan** *gulosa*. v. frec : **frettan** *to consume*. *Add* : v. ge-, of-frettan.

**fricca.** *Add*:—Sē đe đone sácerdhád onfēhð, hē onfēhð friccan (fryccean, *v. l.*) scīre and foreryneles đā hēr iernað beforan kyningum and bodigeað hira færelt ... Gif se sácerd bið ungerád đæs lāreówdōmes ... hwæt mæg hē bodigean má đonne se dumba fryccea *praeconis officium suscipit quisquis ad praedicationem accedit* ... *sacerdos si praedicationis est nescius, quam clamoris vocem daturus est praeco mutus?*, Past. 91, 20–26.

**Fricg,** e ; f. *The name of a Teutonic goddess, the wife of Odin*:—Se deófol hine þám hálgan æteówde on þæra hæþenra goda hīwe ... hwīlon on Mercuries þe men hátað Ôþon, hwīlon on Ueneris ... þe men hátað Fricg, Hml. S. 31, 717. Đone syxtan dæg hī gesetton đære sceamleásan gydenan Uenus geháten and Frycg on Denisc, Sal. K. p. 124, 140. ¶ a weak genitive occurs :—Dæg Friggan *die Ueneris*, Archiv cxx. 297, 33. See also E. S. 39, 341. [*The Scandinavian forms of the names are given*, Ôðinn *and* Frigg, *the English would be* Wôden *and* Frīg, *q. v.*]

**fricgan.** *Add* (?) :—Hié frugan (frūgan ? = frungon *for* frugnon. v. fregnan) ł āhsadun hine *interrogabant eum*, Mt. R. 12, 10.

**frician** (frīcian (?) *the MS. has* frīcudun (fricedan, *v. l.*); *but cf.* (?) frick *to move briskly*, D. D.). *Add*: [Al hit is idel þ me at plege bihalt ... fet oppied ... and shuldres wrenchied, armes and honden frikied, O. E. Hml. ii. 211, 17.]

**friclan.** *Add*:—þæt hē geóce fricle, Hpt. 33, 73, 15. v. *next word*.

**friclo.** *Add*: *eager desire*:—þū þá sóðfæstan · *Supplex roga* · fultumes bidde fricolo (*the first* o *is marked for deletion*) · *Virginem almam*, Dôm. L. 36, 21.

**frico.** *Add*: [*Cf.* Goth. faihu-frikei *covetousness*.] : **fricolo.** v. friclo: **frid-hengest.** *Add*: [*Cf.* (?) *Low Lat.* pare-frīdus < paraverēdus *from which comes* Ger. pferd : O. H. Ger. pfer-frit.] : **frig, frigu** (?). *l.* frīg.

**Frīg,** e ; f. *The name of a Teutonic goddess to whom in the Roman mythology Venus was considered most nearly to correspond. The name occurs only in connexion with the sixth day of the week*, the dies Ueneris, *which is called* Frīge dæg. v. Fricg.

**-frige.** v. ge-frige : **friges.** *l.* frīgea, *and add*: [Goth. frauja. Cf. Icel. freyja.]

**Frīge-æfen.** *Add*:—On đám Frīgeæfen, þæs þe hē on mergen þrowode, manode hē his folgeras, Hml. A. 73, 6. v. Frīge-niht.

**Frīg(e)-dæg.** *Add*:—Langan (-un, MS.) Frīgedæges þrowunge *parasceue passione*, Angl. xiii. 409, 633. Þæs Friándæges (cf. O. Frs. Frigendei) *sexta feria*, R. Ben. I. 43, 12. v. Langa-Frīgedæg.

**frig(e)-nes.** *Add*:—þū ætīctest on þīnre frignysse, hū þá þing man gyldan sceolde *addes etiam, quomodo ea reddere debeant*, Bd. 1, 27; Sch. 67, 18.

**Frīge-niht,** e ; f. *The night between Thursday and Friday*:—On þære Frīgenihte þe ætforan Eástron bið, hæfde úre Hælend swiþe langsume spræce wiþ his leorningcnihtas, Nap. 26. Hig hyra clænnysse healdon æfre Sunnannihte and Frīgenihte, Ll. Th. ii. 190, 19. Hē wæs sume Frīgeniht in ciricean. Þá on þá þriddan tíde đáre nihte ..., Shrn. 113, 4. Ne mæssenihtum ne Frīgenihtum, Wlfst. 305, 24.

**frig-man.** *l.* frīg man. v. freó.

**frignan.** [*The different treatment of the* g *in this word gives rise to a great variety of forms*. (1) *the* g *may be retained, see the forms in* Dict., *to which add* p. pl. [ge-]frungan; pp. [ge-]frognen. (2) *the* g *may be absorbed giving* (a) frīnan; p. frǣn, pl. frūnon; pp. frūnen; *or* (b) frīnan *may be regarded as of the ablaut series* ī, á, i *and have* p. frán, pl. frinon; pp. [be-]frinen. (3) *the* g *may be assimilated and forms as from* frinnan *result, see prs.* frinne, ppr. frinnende; p. pl. frunnon. *Here perhaps belongs the form* frunian, Wrt. Voc. ii. 14, 54.] *Take here the examples given under* frinan (*l.* frīnan). *Add*:—Frīgno *consulo*, Txts. 51, 514. Ic frīne, Wrt. Voc. ii. 14, 63 : *consulo*, i. *requiro vel inquiro*, Wülck. Gl. 209, 30. Frunian (frunnan ?) *consuluerunt*, Wrt. Voc. ii. 14, 54. (1) *to ask, inquire*:—Gif ic ígregno (frǣgno, L.) ne gī

ondsworiað mē *si interrogauero non respondebitis mihi*, Lk. R. 22, 68 : 23, 14. Đeáh đe mon tuwa frigne, gebíd đū mid đære andsware, Past. 385, 12. Wæs hē gemēt frignende, nalles lǣrende, 25. Fraegnende (fregnende, R.), Lk. L. 2, 46. Mē sylfum frīnendum, Bd. 4, 19; Sch. 440, 14. (1 a) *to ask* a question. (a) *where the question is given in a dependent clause*:—þū frugne (frūne, *v. l.*) ... æfter hū fela daga heó mōste in cyrican gangan, Bd. 1, 27; Sch. 78, 6. Hē frægn hwæt þæt swefen bude, Dan. 528 : Fin. 22. Hē frǣn (frægn, *v. l.*) hwæđer þá landleóde crīstene wǣron, Bd. 2, 1; Sch. 109, 19. Huæs sié sunu Crīst fregnende (*interrogans*), Mk. p. 5, 4. Huá his wǣre đe neesta fraignende (*sciscitante*), Lk. p. 6, 19. (β) *where the question is given directly*:—Hié gegrētte sē þe on greóte stōd ... frægu (and) reordade : ' Hwanon cōmon gē ...?,' An. 255 : 556. Hē međelwordum frægn : ' Hwæt syndon gē ...?,' B. 236. Ongan his magu frignan : ' Hū geweard þē þus ...?,' Gū. 983. (γ) *with an acc. pronoun*:—Heó worda gehwæs wiđersæc fremedon ... þæt heó frignan ongan, El. 570. (2) *to ask about, after,* &c. :—Gif þū gehýre ymb þæt hálige treó frōde frignan, El. 443. Be þám frignan, 1068. Ælc ácsiende and frīnende æfter his friénd, Ors. 4, 5 ; S. 166, 12. Frægnende of mæhte his *sciscitantes de potestate ejus*, Lk. p. 10, 6. (3) *to ask, question* a person :—Hwæt mec fregnestū *quid me interrogas?*, Jn. R. 18, 21. Brēgas his frignað bearn monna, Ps. Srt. 10, 5. Frign feder đinne, ii. p. 192, 9. Welle fregna iówih ic worde *interrogabo uos ego unum uerbum*, Lk. R. L. 20, 4. Frignan, Jul. 346 : Gū. 1184. (3 a) *to ask* a person a question :—þæt þū mē frigne (frinne, frīne, *v. ll.*) swá hwæt swá þū wille, Bd. 4, 29; Sch. 528, 17. (3 a a) *where the question is given in a dependent clause* :—Ic þē frigne (ic bidde þ þū secge mē, *v. l.*) hwæþer áht óþres sý, Gr. D. 20, 7. Gif ic hine frigne (frīne, *v. l.*) hwæþer hē wite þe nyte, 262, 19. Frǣng (frægn, *v. l.*) ic ánra gehwilcne hwæþer ..., Bd. 4, 5; Sch. 375, 7. Frægn (frān, *v. l.*), Bt. 3, 1; F. 4, 27. Hit hine frægn (frān, *v. l.*) hū þ gewurde, F. 6, 1. Worde frægn wuldres aldor Cain hwǣr Abel wǣre, Gen. 1002. Hine frugnon (frūnon, *v. l.*) his geféran for hwan hē þis dyde, Bd. 4, 3; Sch. 361, 12. Heó cwæð þæt heó frugne (frūne, frægu, *v. ll.*) hwæt hī sōhton, 3, 8; Sch. 222, 15. Hine frignan (frīnan, *v. l.*) for hwan ..., 4, 22; Sch. 457, 19. Hine frignende (frīnende, *v. l.*) for hwan ..., 2, 6; Sch. 137, 1. Fraignende, Mk. p. 4, 8. (3 a β) *where the question is given directly*. v. (3 b δ) :—Hē frægn hine : ' Hwæt gifest þū me ...?,' Gen. 2173 : 2268: An. 921. Hine frægn se geroefæ cwæþende : ' þu eart cyning Iudēana ?,' Mt. R. 27, 11. Frugnon ł áxsadun hine cwæþende : ' Lāreú ...,' 22, 23. Frugnun, Lk. R. 22, 64. (3 b) *to ask* a person about something. (a) *with gen.* (γ) :—þū mē frignest þæs þe ic ær ǣngum ne wolde melda weorðan, Gu. 1201. Ne frign đú unc nóhtes má, Nar. 32, 5. (β) *with prep.* :—Wē æfter ferscum wætre hié frinon, Nar. 11, 22. Tō fregnanne (frægu-, L.) hine of đissum worde *interrogare eum de hoc uerbo*, Lk. R. 9, 45. (γ) *where* (β) *and* (a) *are combined* :—Symle ymb đæt đe hine tueóde, đonne orn hē inn tō đǣm temple, and frægn đæs Dryhten, Past. 103, 4. (δ) *where* (β) *and* (3 a β) *are combined* :—þá hǣled oretmæcgas æfter æđelum frægn : ' Hwanon ferigeað gē scyldas ...?,' B. 332. (4) *to ask* information of or from a person. (a) *with gen.* :—Gongen hié tō đǣm hálgan gewritum, frīne đára hwæt hié dōn scylen, Past. 103, 10. (β) *with prep.* :—Hē wæs fram him eallum frignende (frīnende, *v. l.*) hwylc him þúhte þeós nīwe lár, Bd. 2, 13; Sch. 164, 7. v. be-frignan.

**frignes** *freedom*. v. frīnes : **frignes** *inquiry*. v. frignes.

**frignung,** e ; f. *Question, inquiry*:—Ac þá word mē secgendum óđru sōcn and frignung (frīninge, áxung, *v. ll.*) on mōd becumen *sed mihi haec dicenti alia suboritur quaestio*, Gr. D. 137, 29. Nâht tō láfe ne wunað þære frignunge and ácsunge be þám wísum de his nihil quaestionis remansit, 323, 23. Tweógan be þissere sōcne and frignunge (*quaestione*), 305, 15. v. be-frignung; frægning.

**friht, freht,** es ; n. *Inquiry about the future, divination. Take here passages under* fyrht *in Dict., and add*: [*Cf.* Icel. frétt *intelligence; inquiry ; inquiry of gods or men about the future*.] v. wamm-freht, *and the following words*.

**frihtrung.** *Add*: frihtung :—Frihtrung. frictrung, frictung *hariolatus*, Txts. 41, 196. Frihtrung, Wrt. Voc. ii. 10, 55.

**frimdig.** *Add*:—Ic eom fyrmdig tō đám hīwum þæt hý hine ceósan, C. D. ii. 114, 18. Hē underfǣng þone cnapan swā swā hē frymdig wæs *he received the boy even as he requested*, Hml. S. 3, 13. Cf. firmettan.

**frisca.** v. frysca : **frist-mearc.** v. first-mearc.

**friþ.** *Add*: (1) *peace* as opposed to strife, discord :—þǣr is frið freóndum bitweón bútan æfestum, ... sib bútan níđe, Cri. 1659. Bisceop sceall saca sehtan and frið wyrcan, Ll. Th. ii. 312, 14. Ne wēnaþ gē þe ic cwōme frið ł sibb (*pacem*) tō sendanne on eorðe; ne cwōm ic frið tō sendanne ac sweord, Mt. R. L. 10, 34. (1 a) *of friendly relations between peoples*:—þá þá Engle and Dene tō friðe and tō freóndscipe fullíce fēngou, Ll. Th. i. 166, 7. (1 b) *absence of dissension* among a people :—Wese áwa frið on Israhēla fælum folce, Ps. Th. 148, 14. Hié on friðe lifdon mid heora aldor, Gen. 19. þæt man frið and freóndscipe rihtlíce healde, Ll. Th. i. 304, 12. (2) *peace, state in which law and order are maintained, absence of disorder and crime*:—þū scealt fēran

and frið lǽdan þǽr sylfǽtan ēðel healdað morðorcræftum *you shall go and introduce law and order among the murderous cannibals*, An. 174. (2 a) in a technical legal sense :—Be fryðe. Eádweard cyning myngode his wytan . . . þ hý smeádon ealle hū heora frið betere beón mæhte þonne hit ǽr þām wæs, Ll. Th. i. 162, 1 : 220, 1 : 242, 12. Ic þancige Gode . . . þæs friðes þe wē nū habbað æt þām þýfðum, 250, 5. Laga tō friðes bōte, 292, 3. Tō ūre ealra friðe, 236, 27 : 238, 8. þ frið swā healdan swā Æðelstān cyng hit gerǽd hæfð, 240, 2. þone frið, 14. Hē folces frið bētte, Chr. 959; P. 114, 20. þ gōde frið þe hē macode on þisan lande, swā þ ān man mihte faran ofer his rīce mid his bōsum full goldes ungederad, 1086; P. 220, 12. (3) *peace* as opposed to war. (a) *agreement settled between two peoples previously at war, peace after war* :—Æt þām hearmum þe gedōn wǽre ǽr þ frið geset wǽre, Ll. Th. i. 288, 2 : 152, 2. Hē frið genam wið hié and hī under þǽm friðe beswāc, Ors. 4, 12; S. 210, 10. Hē wæs winnende oþ hē genōm frið wiþ þæt folc *adeo infeliciter praelia gessit, ut foedus cum Numantinis facere cogeretur*, 5, 2; S. 218, 30. Mon fæstnode ðone frið wið Eást-Engle, Chr. 906; P. 94, 21. (b) *cessation of hostilities* :—Man wið þone here friðes ceápode, Chr. 1004; P. 135, 24. Twā and twēntig þūsend punda mon gesealde þām here of Ænglalande wið friðe, Ll. Th. i. 288, 13. Sió lāf wiþ þone here frið nam, Chr. 867; P. 68, 26 : Ors. 1, 10; S. 46, 8. (c) *abstinence or freedom from attack* :—God lýfde þæt hý him mid hondum hrīnan mōsten and þæt frið wið hý gefreoðad wǽre *God allowed them to lay hands on him and no attack was made on them in return*, Gū. 382. Gíslas syllan friðe tō wedde, Ll. Th. i. 156, 5. Hié micle āþas swōron and þā gōdne frið heóldon, Chr. 877; P. 74, 21. þ hý mōstan þām læppan frið gebicgean, Ll. Th. i. 284, 13. (d) *friendly (instead of hostile) relations* :—Wē cōmon of fyrlenum lande, and wē gewilniað friðes and freóndrǽdene wið eów (*pacem vobiscum facere cupientes*), Jos. 9, 6. On his rīce nid friðe gesittan, Ors. 6, 34; S. 290, 21. (4) *security from molestation* :—Wē gesāwon hys angsumnisse þā hē ūs friðes bæd, and wē him nānes ne tīpedon (*dum deprecaretur nos, et non audivimus*), Gen. 42, 21 : An. 1130: Jul. 320. Hē mid friðe þurh Normandīg faran ne mihte *he could not pass through Normandy unmolested*, Chr. 1094; P. 229, 32: By. 179. þæt hié hine gebröhten of þǽre folcsceare, þæt hé on friðe wǽre, Gen. 1872. Geceás hē Bizantium, tō ðon ðæt him gelīcade þæt hié þǽr mehten betst frið binnan habban *Byzantium aptissimum judicavit, ut receptaculum sibi fieret*, Ors. 3, 7; S. 116, 6. Lǽtað frið āgan gistas mīne (*viris istis nihil mali faciatis*, Gen. 19, 8), Gen. 2471. Hē āh æt gefeohte frið *he shall receive no hurt in battle*, El. 1184. (4 a) *where security is assured by the law or by a person in authority* :—Se cyng hēt beódan, þ ealle . . . eall swā hī friðes weorðe beón woldan, þ hí on hīrede tō tíde wǽron, Chr. 1095; P. 232, 1: Met. 1, 35. Ælc ceápscip frið hæbbe . . . þēh hit unfriðscyp sý, Ll. Th. i. 284, 20 : 286, 5, 8, 10, 12. Sē þe on þām hūse beó hæbbe frið mid þe *qui tecum in domo fuerint, redundabit in caput nostrum, si eos aliquis tetigerit*, Jos. 2, 19. ¶ where the authority is superhuman :—Friðes earnian tō Dryhtne, Reb. 13. Friðes wilnian tō þām golde þe hē him tō gode teóde, Dan. 214. þū (*Noah*) scealt frið habban . . . þonne sweart wæter werodum swelgað, Gen. 1299. (5) *protection*. (a) *by a person* :—Him frið Drihtnes wið gryre aldor gescylde, Dan. 466. Hē mē þone hālgan heáp helpe bidde, friðes and fultomes, Ap. 91. Beornas forhte friðes wilneden, miltsa tō mǽrum (*Domine, salva nos, perimus*, Mt. 8, 25), An. 448. Beþurfon hī þ hī ōleccan þǽm æfter friðe þe māre habbað *alieno praesidio indigentes*, Bt. 26, 2; F. 92, 29. Hié on friðe Drihtnes of gryre treddedon, Dan. 438. Dryhten folcrǽd fremede, swā hē tō friðe hogode (*he was earnest to protect them*), An. 622. On frið Dryhtnes gelædan, 1036. Ic mē frið wille æt Gode gegyrnan . . . mec Dryhtnes hond mundað, Gū. 228. (a a) *protection of subjects by a ruler* :—Eall þeós worold geceás Agustuses frið ; and eallum monnum nānuht swā gōd ne þūhte swā hié tō his hyldo becōme, and þ hié his underþeówas wurden, Ors. 5, 15; S. 250, 16. Hié gecuron his (*Theodosius'*) frið *Romano sese imperio dediderunt*, 6, 35; S. 292, 13. Hē (*Christ*) him frið beóded . . . 'Onföð mínes fæder rīce,' Cri. 1341. (a β) *almost in a personal sense* :—Hié gesōhton Agustus him tō friþe, Ors. 5, 15; S. 250, 14. Seó þeód gesōhte Ecgbryht cyning him tō friþe and tō mundboran, Chr. 823; P. 60, 18. Hē gesōhte Rōmāne him tō friþe, and hié sendon þone consul mid him mid firde, Ors. 5, 7; S. 228, 13. þæt his hergas wǽron mihtigran mannum tō friðe þonne Drihten, Dan. 716. (b) *by a place* :—Hié burga gehwone ābrocen hæfdon þāra þe þām folce tō friðe stōdon, Dan. 64. (b a) in a technical sense of the privilege of a sanctuary :—Be circena friðe. Wē settað æghwelcere cirican þis frið, Ll. Th. 64, 7–9. ¶ figurative :—þonan ǽnig ne mæg firendǽdum fāh frið gewinnan *from hell may no sinner escape to a sanctuary*, Cri. 1001. (6) *terms made with an enemy of the law, inlawing of an outlaw*. Cf. friþ-leás :—Sē þe ūtlages weorc gewyrce, wealde se cyninge þæs friðes (*qui opus utlagii fecerit, ejus revocatio sit in misericordia regis*, Lat. version), Ll. Th. i. 382, 19. v. ciric-, deór-, mæþel-, un-, weorold-friþ.

**frīþ.** *Substitute :* Fair :—Mec (*the cuckoo*) seó friðe mæg (*the bird* 

*that hatches the cuckoo's egg*) fēdde oð þæt ic āweóx *the fair lady* (cf. freólec mæg *used of a woman*) *nurtured me, till I grew up*, Rä. 10, 9. [*Icel.* frīðr *fair, beautiful*.]

**frið-āþ,** es ; *m.* An oath confirming peace made between two hostile powers :—Ðā þet gafol gelēst wæs and þā friðāðas gesworene, þā tōfērde se here, Chr. 1012 ; P. 143, 5.

**frið-bēna** *a criminal who asks for asylum*, v. friþ, (5 b a), *or for reconciliation with the law*, v. friþ, (6).

**frið-bræc.** *Substitute :*—frið-brǣc, -brēc, e ; *f. A breach of the peace concluded between two hostile peoples* (English and Danes) :—Gyf eahta men beón ofslagene, þonne is þ friðbrēc, binnan byrig oþþon būton . . . Be friðbrēce binnan byrig. Gyf hit binnan byrig gedōn bið, seó friðbrǣc, Ll. Th. i. 286, 25–30. [This is part of the arrangement (v. friþ-māl) made by the English with the Danes under Anlaf.]

**frið-candel.** *Add : The light that affords protection and security from molestation*, as evil spirits and influences ceased to operate at sunrise. Cf. for example the Latin hymn with its gloss :—Tungel scīnþ nū nīwe þ hit nyme ǽlc þing derigendlices *sidus refulget jam novum ut tollat omne noxium*, Hy. S. 37, 14.

**frið-geard.** *Add :* (1) *an enclosure where a fugitive was secure from molestation, where he had* friþ (v. friþ, (5 b a)), *an asylum* [v. Grmm. R. A.], Ll. Th. ii. 298. 16. (2) *a place where peace prevails.* v. friþ, (1), Cri. 399. v. friþ-splott.

**frið-gewrit.** *Add :* v. friþ-māl.

**frið-her[e]paþ,** es ; *m. The king's highway, a public road which was under the king's* friþ. [Cf. De pace regia et .iiii. chiminorum vel viarum regalium, Ll. Th. i. 447, 6. Omnes herestrete regis sunt, 519, 11] :—On Wifeles ford; ðonne andlang ðæs friðherpaðes (*Icknield Way?*), C. D. v. 214, 35.

**friþian.** *Add :* (1) *to protect* a person or institution :—Hwā is monna on Angelcynne wuniende þ nyte hū hē (*Eadgar*) Godes rīce, þ is Godes cyricean, fyrþrode and friþode, Lch. iii. 438, 3. (2) *to protect, maintain the sanctity of* a day :—þone heaan dæg-(*Sunday*) healdað and friðiað ealle þā ðe cunnon crīstene þeáwas, Dōm. L. 54, 27. (3) *to protect* an operation, *keep from unfavourable conditions* :—Hēde se scīre healde þ hē friðige and forðige ǽlce (tilþe) þe ðām ðe hit sēlest sý, Angl. ix. 259, 14. (4) *to grant immunity to* a criminal :—Gif Philippus wolde gefæstnian mid āþe þ seó leáse wrǣgistre ne wurde fordǣmed. Ðā swōr Philippus þ hē friðian wolde þā leásan wudewan, Hml. S. 2, 209. (5) *to give asylum to* :—Gif hwā þeóf friðige, Cht. E. 229, 32. v. fyrþran for other examples.

**friþi[g]end,** es ; *m. A protector* :—Hē ys ūre friðigend and ūre gescyldend *adjutor et protector noster est*, Ps. Th. 32, 17. þū eart mīn friðiend and mīn gefultumend and mīn gescyldend *adjutor meus et liberator meus esto*, 39, 21. Uton lufian ūre cyrican, for ðām heó bið ūre friðiend and werigend wið þæt micele fýr on dōmes dæg, Wlfst. 239, 7. v. ge-friþi(g)end.

**friþ-leás.** *Substitute :* Outlawed. Cf. friþ, (6) :—Gif hwā þæne friðleásan man (*hominem pro culpa exiliatum, expulsum quem Angli uocant* friðleásne man, *exlegem*) healde, Ll. Lbmn. 318, 11. [*Icel.* frið-lauss *outlawed*.]

**friþ-mæl, -māl.** *l.* friþ-māl. The word seems Scandinavian. Cf. *Icel.* māl *a stipulation, an agreement ;* frið-māl ; *pl. words of peace ;* friðmælask *to sue for peace*.

**friþ-scip.** *Substitute :* friþ-scip, es ; *n.* A *guard-ship*(?), a ship on the look-out for hostile vessels (?) :—Of manegum landum māre (*more than the trinoda necessitas*) landriht ārīst tō cyniges gebanne, swilce is . . . scorp tō friðscipe and sǽweard, Ll. Th. i. 432, 8. [*Thorpe would read* fird-scipe.] Cf. unfriþ-scip.

**friþ-sōcn.** *Dele* 'A peace-refuge,' *and for the passage substitute* :—Ēhte his ǽlc þāra þe Godes freónd sī, būton þ gewurþe þ hē ætberste, and swā deópe friðsōcne gesēce þ se cyninge him þurh þ feores geunne. *Add :* v. friþ, (4 a), sōcn ; VI.

**friþ-splott.** *Substitute :* A place which is a sanctuary on account of the sacred character superstitiously attributed to it, an asylum :—Wē lǣrað þ preósta gehwilc ǽlcne hǣðendōm ādwǣsce, and forbeóde . . . þā gemearr þe man drīfð on mislicum gewiglungum and on friðsplottum and on ellenum . . . and on stānum, Ll. Th. ii. 248, 1–6. [Cf. þórólfr hafði mikinn ātrūnað ā fjalli þvī . . . er hann kallaði Helgafell . . . ok svā var þar mikil *friðhelgi*, at þar skyldi engu granda, hvarki fē ne mönnum, Landnāma.] v. friþ-geard ; ge-friþian ; I. 4.

**friþ-stōl.** *Add :*—Wē wǣron geladeðe tō ðām hālgan hām and tō ðām cynelican friðstōle þǣr Crīst wunað and rīxað, Wlfst. 265, 18.

**friþ-stōw.** *Add :* (1) in a personal sense, *a refuge.* Hē ys geworden friðstōw (*refugium*) þearfendra, Ps. Th. 9, 9 : 17, 1. Beó mīn friðstōw, and gedō mē hālne *esto mihi in locum refugii, ut salvum me facias*, 30, 3. (2) in a technical sense, *a place of safety for a criminal, an asylum, a sanctuary* :—Hē sceal fleón tō ānra ðāra ðreóra burga ðe tō friðstōwe gesette sint (*the cities of refuge ; civitates, quo possit evadere qui propter homicidium profugus est*, Deut. 19, 3) and libbe, Past. 167, 2.

**friþsum.** *Add :* v. ge-friþsum.

**friþsumian**; *p.* ode *To make peaceable, reconcile* :—Ealle friðsumaþ God (cf.? *per eum reconciliare omnia in ipsum*, Col. 1, 20) on eallum his mhtum, Hpt. 21, 189, 28. Cf. ge-sibsumian.

**friþu.** *Take here* freoþo *in Dict. and add* :—Þu mē wǣre freoða fultumiend *refugium meum es tu*, Ps. Th. 70, 3. v. wīc-freoþu.

**friþu-.** *See the* compounds given under freoþo(-u)-, frioþo-(u)-.

**fro** [= from] :—Fro him *ab eo*, Lk. L. 13, 17.

**frocx.** *Dele, and see* frosc.

**frōd.** *Add:* I. wise. (1) of persons :—Nǣnig þæs frōd leofað þæt his mǣge ǣspringe þurh his ǣgne spēd witan, Sch. 76. Guma gehðum frōd, El. 531. (1 a) *skilled* in a subject :—Fyrngidda frōd, El. 543. (2) of discourse, counsel, &c. :—Frōde geþeahte, Men. 182. Frōde lāre, Fä. 94. Frōdum wordum, Gn. Ex. 1. II. old :—Frōd *grandaevus*, Wrt. Voc. ii. 41, 10. Frōdrae *provectae*, Txts. 84, 758. Frōdre *preuectue*, Wrt. Voc. ii. 68, 38. (1) of persons, animals, or plants :—Hæfde frōd hæle nigon hund wintra and hundseofontig tō, Gen. 1222. Frōd cyning, hār hilderinc, B. 1306. Frōd guma sægde fela geongum, Fä. 53. Draca sceal on hlǣwe frōd, Gn. C. 27. Fugol frōd, geealdad, wintrum gebysgad, Ph. 426. (1 a) with dat. or gen. of noun of time :—Dægrīme frōd, Gen. 2173. Gomol bið snoterost, fyrngeárum frōd, sē þe ǣr fela gebīdeþ, Gn. C. 12. Fēnix byrneð fyrngeárum frōd, Ph. 219. Hæfde v. and syxtig and nigon hund eác nihtgerīmes wine frōd wintres, Gen. 1194. Treów . . . frōd dagum, Rä. 54, 4. (2) of things :—Frōd fyrngeweorc (*a statue*), An. 738: *the universe*, Ph. 84. Frōd fyrngewritu (*the Old Testament*), El. 431.

**frōde**; *adv. Prudently, wisely.* v. feorh-lege.

**frōd-ness.** v. un-frōdness.

**frōf(e)rian, frōfernis.** *Dele, and see* frēfran, frēfer-ness.

**frōfor.** *Add:* [*A weak form occurs in the late* Shrn. 202, 16.] (1) *consolation.* (a) *the action of consoling* :—Þē is nū frōfres māre þearf þonne unrōtnesse *medicinae tempus est, non querelae*, Bt. 3, 3; S. 9, 17. 'Ic eów sende frōfre Gāst' . . . þ gelimplic wæs þ hē his leornerum frōfre sende, Bl. H. 131, 21. Hī ne mihton mid heora frōfre his dreórignysse ādwǣscan, Hml. Th. ii. 134, 19. Ic eów mid wunige forð on frōfre *I will remain on with you consoling you*, Cri. 489 : 1361. Ferðþes frōfre gemētton . . . hǣleð hygegeómre, Gū. 895. (b) *the state of being consoled, alleviation of distress* :—Gē frōfre ne wēnað, þæt gē wræcsīða wyrpe gebīden, Gū. 479 : B. 185: An. 1707. Ic wiðsóc sāwle mīnre frōfre *negavi consolari animam meam*, Ps. Th. 76, 3. (c) *comfort, freedom from distress* :—Hine gē hēr on stariað and in frōfre geseoð frætwum blīcan, Cri. 522. (2) *a consolation, a particular action that consoles, a person, thing or circumstance that affords consolation or comfort* :—Eálā Wīsdōm, þū þe eart sió hēhste frōfer wērigra mōda *summum lassorum solamen animorum*, Bt. 22, 1; F. 76, 9. Sió ān frōfer erminga æfter ðām ermðum þisses līfes, 34, 8; F. 144, 29. Frōfor, Hy. 7, 9: Gū. 1184. Ðū in unrōtnisse frōffer (*solatium*), Rtl. 105, 7. Hē nānre frōfre beinnan þām carcerne ne gemunde, Bt. 1; F. 4, 2. Hē sægde mancynne tō frōfre þ hē sylfa ūs gesēcean wolde, Bl. H. 119, 29. Sē Hālga Gāst wæs . . . þǣm apostolum tō frōfre gehāten, 131, 13: Gen. 955: 1108. Þā gódan God geseoð heóm tō frōfran and tō gefeán and tō āre, Shrn. 202, 16. His swǣsne sunu . . . feóres frōfre, Exod. 404; Cri. 338. Hē frōfre gecwæð . . . hēht his līchoman hāles brūcan, An. 1467. Hē āsende þisne frōfer þus cwæðende : 'Eálā . . . þīne gebedu synd gefyllede . . . þ ge ne beón gewemmede,' Hml. S. 4, 91. Wæs him frōfra mǣst heofonrīces weard, El. 196. (3) *aid, succour* :—Gode þancigende þe him ne forwyrnde frōfres, Ap. Th. 18, 26. Hié him frōfre and fultomes wilnodan, þ hié mōston ðǣra feónda searo ofercuman, Bl. H. 201, 28. Se engel cwōm on fultum and on frōfre, 203, 21 : B. 1273. Þæt he wǣre gemedemod him forgyfan hwylcehugu frōfre (*aliquod solatium*) þǣr tō eardianne . . . and sōna hē gemētte ǣnne beran standan beforan þām durum, Gr. D. 206, 5. Gedō nū frǣmsume frōfre þīne *benigne fac*, Ps. C. 139. Fyrena frōfre, B. 628. Frōfras (*solacia*) him beón gesealde, R. Ben. I. 62, 14: 65, 11. v. ge-, hilde-frōfor.

**frōfor-bōc.** v. frōfer-bōc *in Dict.*

**frōfor-gāst.** *Add* :—Se þridda hād is on þǣre hālgan þrynnysse Hālga Frōforgāst, Hml. A. 1, 13. Fæder and Sunu and Frōfergāst, Wlfst. 73, 5.

**frōfor-lic**; *adj. Consolatory, of consolation* :—Hē cwæð frōferlicum wordum tō ūs eallum : '*Conuertimini, filii, reuertentes,*' Wlfst. 49, 16.

**frōforlīce**; *adv. In a way that consoles or comforts or succours* :—Frōforlī[ce] *inconsolabiliter* (the *in-* is not glossed), An. Ox. 56, 187. Wudewum and steópcildum frōforlīce fylstan tō rihte, Wlfst. 295, 3.

**frōfor-word**, es; *n. A word of consolation, consolatory talk* :—Hē nān frōforword ne onfó ne ne gehýre æt heora ǣniges mūþe *nec sermonem consolationis ex cujuslibet eorum ore percipiat*, Gr. D. 344, 28.

**frōfrung.** *Dele*: frogga. *Add*: v. wǣter-frogga: from. v. fram: from-. v. fram-: frore. *Dele, and see* hilde-frōfor.

**frosc, forsc, frox** (*q. v. in Dict.*), **frocx,** es; *m. A frog* :—Forsc *luscinius,* Wrt. Voc. ii. 113, 31. Frocx, 51, 28. Reguwyrm *lumbricus,* frox *luscinius, ýce rana,* 71, 13-15. Frosc *ranam,* An. Ox. 54, 2. Frox, Bl. Gl. Forsc, Ps. Srt. 77, 45. Forscas *ranas,* 104, 30. ¶ in

local names :—Forscaburna, C. D. iii. 383, 29. Æt Froxafelda, 127, 33. [*v. N. E. D.* frosh. *O. H. Ger.* frosc *rana* : *Gen.* frosch : *Icel.* froskr.]

**frostig.** v. forstig.

**frowe,** an ; *f. A lady* :—Seó frowe þe ūs freán ācende (*the Virgin Mary*), Dōm. L. 291. [From (?) *O. H. Ger.* frouwa *domina, matrona.*] Cf. freó *a lady.*

**frox.** v. frosc.

**frum.** *Add* :—Æt fruman cerre (frumcerre, *v. l.*), Bt. 41, 4; F. 252, 12. [*The passage from* Rtl. 35, 13 *is* :—Frūnies frūmcend *primę originis,* frūnies *glosses* originis, *and* primę *is glossed by* fruncenð.]

**fruma.** *Add:* I. *a beginning.* (1) *the first part or point of a continuous period, action, work, &c.* :—Se dæg wæs fruma þyses iǣnan leóhtes, Bl. H. 133, 10. Ðæs circean þus gecýðe æt fruman (*at the time of its foundation*) seó ilce bōc, 197, 26. Se godspellere sōna on fruman (*in the very first part of his work*) his godspell swā be þǣre Iōhannes gebyrde wrāt, 161, 25. ¶ *the beginning of time* :—Swā God æt fruman getihhod hæfde, Bt. 39, 6; F. 220, 26: 41, 2; F. 246, 17. Hī on fruman tō Godes hīwunga gesceapene wǣron, Bl. H. 61, 7. Þīne welan þe þū (*the Devil*) on fruman begeáte æt þæs ǣrestan mannes unhýrsumnesse, 85, 30. (2) *the first member of a connected series* :—Se fruma wæs þ mon forstæl ǣune wimman æt Īcescā, Cht. Th. 206, 19. Þára manna þe þæt bōcland on fruman (*in the first instance*) gestrindon, Ll. Th. i. 88, 19. (3) *the first stage of a development* :—Þisse ādle fruman mon mæg ý þelīce gelācnian, Lch. ii. 232, 16. II. *source, origin* :—'Dū cennest sunu' . . . Mid þý þe heó gehýrde þone fruman þæs godcundan tūddres, þā cwæþ heó : 'Hū mæg þis þus geweorþan . . .?,' Bl. H. 7, 20. II a. *of a person, source, author* :—Sē sē ðæt wæter ūt forlēte wǣre fruma ðǣre tōwesnesse (*caput jurgiorum*), Past. 279, 13. Dryhten, þū ūs ālēsdest from deáþes fruman, Bl. H. 89, 32. v. weorold-fruma.

**frum-ācenned** *nativity* :—Ðone blindo from frumācennisse *caecum a natiuitate*, Jn. p. 5, 19. Cf. frum-byrd.

**frum-bearn.** *Add:* (1) *a first-born child, the eldest child* :—His wīf sunu on woruld brōhte, se eafora wæs Enoc hāten, freólic frumbearn, Gen. 1189 : 1056. Þām yldestan eaforan, frumbearne, 1215. Hē slōh ǣghwylc frumbearn *percussit omne primogenitum*, Ps. Th. 104, 31. Frumbearna gehwylc, 77, 51 : Exod. 38. Ǣðele frumbearn *primogenita*, 134, 8. ¶ *figurative* :—Banan mancynnes fācnes frumbearn (*the devil*), An. 1296. (2) *one of the first two or three children, an elder child* :—Adames and Euan aforan wǣron freólicu twā frumbearn cenned, Cain and Abel, Gen. 968. Þā yldestan Chus and Cham hātene wǣron, frumbearn Chames, 1618.

**frum-byrd.** *Add* [:—Swā swā Imme mīn mōder on mīnre firmbirde dage tō forme gife it mē gæf, C. D. iv. 216, 2.] Cf. frum-ācenness.

**frum-byrdling.** *l.* -birdling, *and add: A youth, one whose beard has just come* [cf. *Icel.* frum-vaxti *just grown to full strength, in one's prime*] : **frum-cend.** *Dele, and see* frum.

**frum-cenned.** *Dele last passage, and add:* I. *first-born* :—Næs þæt cild for ðī gecweden hire frumcennede cild swilce heó ōðer ācende, ac for ðī þe Crīst is frumcenned of manegum gāstlicum gebrōðrum, Hml. Th. i. 34, 24. Sunu hire frumcende (þone frumkendu, R.) *filium suum primogenitum*, Mt. L. 1, 25. Frumcende (-cennedne, R.), Lk. L. 2, 7. II. *primitive* :—Þā frumcennedan *primitiva*, Wrt. Voc. ii. 68, 72. v. next word.

**frum-cennende** *primitive* :—Frumcennendre (-cynnend-, Hpt. Gl. 448, 27) *primitivae (ecclesiae)*, An. Ox. 1775.

**frum-cirr, -cerr, -cyrr.** *Take here* **frum-cyrr** *and add:* (1) *definite, first time as opposed to second, third, &c.* :—Æt frumcirre . . . æt ōðrum cirre . . . æt þriddan cirre, Ll. Th. i. 214, 4. (2) *indefinite, in the phrase* æt frumcirre *at once* :—Sió gesihð æt fruman cerre (frumcerre, *v. l.*), swā ðā eágan on besióþ, hió ongitaþ ealle ðone ondwlitan þæs līchoman, Bt. 41, 4 ; F. 252, 12.

**frum-dysig,** es ; *n. First folly* :—Þā mōdigan and þā ungehýrsuman sōna on þām frumdysige swinge man, Nap. 26.

**frum-geweorc,** es; *n. A first building* :—Fram Mōyses gebyrdtīde þā forð tō Salamones gebyrde and his mǣran frumgeweorces ðæs temples, Angl. xi. 9, 11. Oð ðæt frumgeweorc ðæs temples (*the building of the first temple*), 4, 22.

**frum-gewrit,** es ; *n. An original writing, an original deed* or *charter* :—Wē wǣron ādīlegode of þām frymþelican frumgewrite þe wē tō heofenum āwritene wǣron, Wlfst. 252, 12. [Cf. *Icel.* frum-brēf *an original deed* ; frum-rit *the original writing* (of MSS.).]

**frum-gifu.** *For* Hpt. 457 *substitute* :—Frumgyfe, wyrþmynte *praerogativam*, An. Ox. 2154.

**frum-grīpa.** *Substitute*: **frum-gripa,** an ; *m. A first-fruit* :—Utan gelǣstan Gode þā gerihta þe him tō gebyrian . . . ūre frumgripan gangendes and weaxendes, Wlfst. 113, 6. v. frum-ripa.

**frum-heowung.** *l.* -hīwung, -heówung, *and for* Cot. 154 *substitute* :—þǣre frumheówunge *plasmatica*, Wrt. Voc. ii. 67, 36.

**frum-ildu**; *f. The first age, youth* :—Fram ðǣre frumildo *a primaevo* (*pubertatis tyrocinio*, Ald. 33, 8), Wrt. Voc. ii. 2, 52. v. frymþ-ild.

**frum-leóht.** *Add*: Btwk. 194, 22: **frum-líc.** *Substitute*: frum-lic *original, primitive.* v. *next word, and* cf. frym-lic.

**frumlíce**; *adv. Originally*; originaliter, An. Ox. 1155.

**frum-lída,** an; *m. A chief sailor, captain of a vessel*:—Se heáhengel Sanctus Michael se æðela nówend and se gleáwa frumlida ... sē ðe his scip mid heofonlicum wælum gesylleð, An. Ox. 32, note.

**frum-meolc, -meoluc.** *Substitute*: *Milk fresh from the cow* (?), *the best milk*:—Frummeoluc *nectar* (*in the same glossary* nectar *is variously rendered by* wín, þone swētan smæc, wiu-gedrinc, hunig oððe mildeáw, *and* nectareus *by* hunigteárlic, *the word, as in later times, seems to have been used vaguely in a favourable sense of* drink), Wrt. Voc. ii. 62, 7.

**frum-mynetslege,** es; *m. A first minting*:—Feówer siðon man áwende mynetísena on his dagum ... and on þám frummynetslæge wǣron twá and sixtig penega gewihte seolfres on ánum penege, and on þǣm æftran em sixtig, and on þǣm þryddan ... and on þám feórþan ... Ðá wæs þæt feoh þ Malchus hæfde þæs forman mynetslæges on Decies naman. Ðonne betweónan Decies frummynetslæges dagum ... and Theodosius tíman ..., Hml. S. 23, 477–485.

**frum-rípa.** *l.* -ripa. *Add*: *The verses on which the passage is based are*:—Decimas tuas et primitias tuas non tardabis reddere; primogenitum filiorum tuorum dabis mihi. De bobus et ovibus similiter facies, Ex. 22, 29–30. v. frum-gripa.

**frum-sceaft,** e; *f. Substitute*: es; *m.* (*where the gender is marked it is masculine.* Cf. *too* þone fruman sceaft (v. frum), geó-sceaft grimne; *and add*: (1) *a first shaping, birth*:—þē wǣre sēlre ... þǣr þu wurde æt frymþe (frumsceafte, *v.l.*) fugel ... þonne þu ǣfre on moldan man gewurde *it had been better for thee ... if thou hadst been born a bird ... than that thou shouldst have been ever a man on earth,* Seel. 79. þá þe hine æt frumsceafte forð onsendon ǣnne ofer ȳðe umbor wesende, B. 45. (1 a) *the first shaping of the world, the creation*:—Tunglu him healdad betwuh sibbe ... swá hí gewenede wuldres ealdor æt frumsceafte (cf. þá ealdan sibbe ðe hí on gesceapne wǣron, Bt. 39, 13; F. 232, 26), Met. 29, 7: Rä. 4, 14: An. 798. Seó forme bóc, Genesis, befēhð þás racu fram frumsceafte, Ælfc. T. Grn. 3, 19. (2) *origin*:—Eálá gē eorþlican men, hwæt gē þeáh magon hwæthwego ongitan swelce eów mǣte be eówrum frumsceafte, þ is God *vos o terrena animalia, tenui licet imagine, vestrum tamen principium somniatis,* Bt. 26, 1; F. 90, 4. (3) *original constitution* or *condition*:—Clǣne wæs þeós eorðe on hyre frumsceafte, ac wē hí habbað syððan áfȳlede, Wlfst. 92, 4. Geworhte hē tȳn engla werod ... on micelre fægernisse, fela þúsenda, on þám frumsceafta þæt hí ... hine wurðedon ealle líchameleáse, leóhte and strange, búton synnum on gesǣlðe libbende, swá wlitiges gecindes swá wē secgan ne magon, Ælfc. T. Grn. 2, 25. [v. *N. E. D.* frumshaft.]

**frum-sceapen.** *Add*: I. *first-formed*:—Se frumsceapena man, Adam, næs gestrȳned ne ácenned, ac God hine gesceóp. Seó óðer gesceapennys wæs swá þæt God gesceóp Euan of hire weres sídan, Hml. Th. ii. 8, 22. Frumsceapena *protoplastus,* i. *primitus plasmatus* i. *Adam,* An. Ox. 687. þæs frumsceapenes *protoplasti,* i. *Ade,* 3884. Tó ðám frumsceapenan wífe Euan, Hml. Th. i. 194, 31. II. *of a document, original*:—Of þám frymþelican (frumsceapenan, *v. l.*) frumgewrite, Wlfst. 252, 12.

**frum-sceat.** *Add*:—Hē ofslóg ǣlcne frumsceat *percussit omne primogenitum,* Ps. Rdr. 104, 36.

**frum-sceppend-sceppend.** *l.* frum-scippend, -scep[p]end, *and add*:—Frumsceppend *auctor,* Rtl. 122, 10.

**frum-slǣp,** es; *m.* (*not f.*) *Add*:—Hē on þǣre ylcan nihte æfter his frumslǣpe clypode, Hml. Th. ii. 26, 5.

**frum-spellung,** e; *f. A first telling, an original story*:—Titelung, frumspellung *recapitulatio* (*the passage glossed is*: Paradisum Cherubin conclusisse *recapitulatio* Geneseos originaliter declarat, Ald. 16, 35), An. Ox. 1153: 2, 31.

**frum-sprǣc.** *l.* -sprǣc, *and add*: *First words of a discourse*:—Seofon hálige men ðǣra naman wē áwriton on ðǣre frumsprǣce heora hálgan ðrowunge, Hml. S. 23, 120.

**frum-talu** *the first statement of a case* (?), cf. talu; V. (*for delata l.* delatio).

**frum-teám,** es; *m. The first teám* (v. teám; II. *in Dict.*).

**frum-tíd,** e; *f. The first part of a period*:—On þǣre frumtíde his inbetȳnednesse *inclusionis suae tempore primo,* Gr. D. 212, 5.

**frum-wæstm.** *Add*:—Of dínum frumwæstmum syle ðearfum, Hml. Th. ii. 102, 10. [Cf. *Icel.* frum-vöxtr *first-fruits.*]

**frum-wífung,** e; *f. First marriage by a man*:—Lǣwede man mót óðre síðe wífian, ac þá canones forbeódaþ þá bletsunga .þǣrtó þe tó frumwífunge gesette sȳn, Ll. Th. ii. 332, 34, 38: Wlfst. 304, 27. [Cf. *Icel.* frum-verr *a first husband.*]

**frum-wilm,** es; *m.* (1) *the first inflammation of disease*:—Æfter ádle welme onweg gewitenre ... þonne of þám frumwelme ..., Lch. ii. 82, 3. (2) *the first fervour* of feeling, &c.:—On þám frumwylme heora gecyrrednesse, R. Ben. 135, 5.

**frymþ.** *Dele* ' es; *m.* ' *and in l.* 15 'Frymþas ... Lye', *and add*:—Frymð *origo,* Wrt. Voc. ii. 64, 73. Frymþum *exordia,* i. *principia,*

145. 75. (1) *the beginning* of something:—From frymþe middangeardes, Chr. 6; P. 6, 1. Frimþe, 616; P. 23, note 4. Frǣmðe, Angl. xi. 4, 16. Fremðe, 5, 10. Hē wolde ðǣre ealdan ǣ ende gesettan, and þysse níwan frymð gesettan, Hml. A. 152, 21. (2) *the beginning.* (a) referring to eternity:—On frymðe wæs word, Hml. Th. i. 40, 8. Tó ðám éðele becuman ðe him on frymðe se heofonlica Fæder gemynte, ii. 218, 18. Þe (*Christ*) rodera weard æt frymðe genóm him tó freóbearne, Cri. 223: 121. (b) referring to time, *the beginning of the world*:—Hē mec worhte æt frymðe, þá hē þisne ymbhwyrft ǣrest sette, Rä. 41, 6. (c) *the beginning of a condition;* æt (on) frymþe *at the outset, at first, in the first instance, to begin with*:—Nó hwæðre Ælmihtig ealra wolde Adam and Euan árna ofteón Fæder æt frymðe, Gen. 954. Þonne hȳ æt frymðe gemētað *at their first meeting,* Cri. 1666. Swylc hē æt frymðe wæs, Ph. 239. Þǣr þu wurde æt frymðe fugel *if thou hadst been born a bird,* Seel. 79. Drihten him tó earde geceás Sione ǣrest æt frymðe *praeelegit Sion in habitationem sibi,* Ps. 131, 14. Þæt byð secga gehwǣm snytru on frymðe *initium sapientiae,* 110, 7. Swá mē on frymðe gelomp yrmðu, Hy. 4, 83. ¶ *in phrases denoting the Deity, the beginning* or *source of all things*:—Fæder frymþa gehwæs, Ph. 197. Frymþa God, Jud. 33. Frymða Waldend, 5. (3) *first produce,* in pl. *first-fruits*:—Be frymþum oþþe offrungum *de primitiis siue oblationibus,* Scint. 165, 17. [v. *N. E. D.* frumth.]

**frymþe-líc.** *Add*: , frymþ-líc *original*:—Frymþlices *originalis,* An. Ox. 5061. In bysene ðǣre frymðlícan (frymþelecan, *v. l.*) cirican *in exemplum primitiuae ecclesiae,* Bd. 4, 23; Sch. 468, 3. Of þám frymþelican (frymþ-, frumsceapenan, *v. l.*) frumgewrite, Wlfst. 252, 12. Fremðlíce originalia, Kent. Gl. 1162.

**frymþ(e)líce**; *adv. Originally*:—Frymſþlíce *originaliter,* An. Ox. 5211.

**frymþ-ild** [e?]; *adj. In its first years, young*:—Of frymſþyldum *a primeuo* (i. *ab ineunte*) (*pubertatis tyrocinio*), An. Ox. 2381. On frymð-yldre *in primeuo* (*rudimento*), Angl. xiii. 34, 185. v. frum-ildu.

**frysca,** an; *m. The name of some bird*:—Frysca *butio* (*butio* is a bittern, but is glossed by *cýta,* Wrt. Voc. i.-29, 32: 63, 17: ii. 11, 35), Wrt. Voc. ii. 102, 34. Cýta, frisca *butium,* 126, 81. [*Butio seems confused with* buteo *a buzzard.*]

**fugel.** *Add*:—Seóþ henne on wætre, ádó þone fugel of, Lch. ii. 336, 13. Ic sende fuhlas wēdende, Wlfst. 231, 12. v. sǣ-fugel.

**fugel-cynn.** *Add*: *a kind* or *species of birds*:—On ðǣre dúne bið þ fugelcynn þe grifus hátte ... On þǣre ylcan stówe byð óðer fugelcynn fēnix hátte *mons ubi est griphus auis ... In eo etiam monte est auis faenix,* Nar. 39, 1–3. On culfran híwe ... On bócum is gerǣdd be ðám fugelcynne þæt his gecynd is swíðe bilewite, Hml. Th. i. 320, 4. Culfran and turtlan ... þás twá fugelcyn ne singað ná, 142, 17. Saga mē hū fela is fleógendra fugelcynna? Ic ðē secge, iiii and fíftig, Sal. K. 190, 18. [*O. H. Ger.* fogal-chunni.]

**fugel-dæg,** es; *m. A ðay on which poultry might be eaten*:—Gif hit fuguldaeg sié. Gif hit þonne festendæg sié, Cht. Th. 460, 20.

**fugelere.** *Add*:—Fugelere *auceps,* Wrt. Voc. ii. 5, 64. Fuglere *aucupis,* 8, 35. [*O. L. Ger.* fugelere: *O. H. Ger.* fogalâri *auceps.* Cf. *Icel.* fuglari.]

**fugeles beán** *vetch*:—Fuglaes beán, fugles beán *vicium,* Txts. 106, 1085. Fugles beáne *viciam, pisas agrestes,* 112, 35.

**fugeles leác** *viumum* (*vicium?* v. *preceding word, and* cf. *O. H. Ger.* fogal-krūt *viciam*).

**fugelian.** *Add*:—Ælcne man lyst, siððan hē ǣnig cotlýf on his hláfordes lǣne getimbred hæfð, þæt hē mōte huntigan and fuglian and fiscian, Solil. H. 2, 10. [*O. H. Ger.* fogalôn.]

**fugel-lím.** *Add*:—Fugellíme *visco,* Wrt. Voc. ii. 81, 56: 94, 34: An. Ox. 3105.

**fugel-net.** *Add*: [cf. panthera *rete aucupale,* Corp. Gl. H. 89, 155]:

**fugelnoþ**; *m? Dele?*: fugeloþ; *Add*: m. [*O. H. Ger.* fogalod *aucupium.*]

**fugel-timber.** *Substitute*: *Bird-material* (v. timber; I), *the young bird* which develops:—Hē (*the Phenix*) ǣrest bið swylce earnes brid, fæger fugeltimber; þonne furðor wridað þæt hē bið wæstmum gelíc ealdum earne, Ph. 236.

**fugel-treós?** *Substitute*: fugel-treów, es; *n. A pole for spreading bird-nets*:—Fugultreó *amites* (*amites perticae aucupales,* Festus), Wrt. Voc. ii. 100, 18. Fugeltrió, 6, 58.

**fugelung, fuglung,** e; *f. Fowling*:—Fuglung *aucupium,* Wrt. Voc. ii. 8, 39.

**fugol** *fugitive.* v. flugol.

**fúht.** *Add*:—Fúhtum *rorante,* Germ. 399, 462. Of fúhtre wætre *ex luto madido,* 390, 97. v. next word.

**fúhtiende.** *Substitute*: fúhtian; *p.* ode *To become moist*:—þá ðá þurh hīwunge beóð swá hole swá hreód ..., and þá ðe fúhtigende beóð on fúlre gálnesse, on swylcum se deófol macað his wununge, Nap. 26. v. fýhtan.

**ful-, -ful.** v. full-, -full.

**fúl;** *adj. Add*:—Fedus, deformis, turpis *vel* fúl, Wrt. Voc. ii. 148,

40. *Feda* vel *polluta* fúl, 44. *þǽȝe* fúlan *obscaene*, 63, 11.   **I.** in a physical sense. (1) *offensive to the senses* :—Lazarus . . . on byrgenne wæs fúl wunigende, Bl. H. 75, 5.   Fúles hlondes *fetentis lotii*, An. Ox. 3273. Mid fúlum adelseáþe *putido latibulo*, 4751.   þ fúle *fetidum*, i. *fetentem*, 2821.   Fúle unclǽnnessa *olidas squalores*, 4454.   Of þára múðe út eóde þ fúluste fýr, þ ic ná árǽfnian ne mihte, Gr. D. 89, 24.   Se líchoma on þone heardestan stenc and on þone fúlostan bið gecyrred, Bl. H. 59, 13. þǽm fúlæstum *putentissimis* (*nidoribus*), Wrt. Voc. ii. 82, 4.   **I a.** of disease :—Fúlre ádle *feda peste*, Txts. 181, 50.   Fúle untrumnyssa *purulentas* (i. *putridas*) *invalitudines*, An. Ox. 1975.   (2) opposed to clean, *dirty, miry, filthy* :—Líchoma horig ł fúl *corpus sordidum*, Hy. S. 26, 26.   Fúl *squalidus* (gloss to *squalida jugera*, Ald. 139, 19), An. Ox. 18 b, 81.   Fúl maal on rægel *stigmentum*, Wrt. Voc. i. 26, 12.   Fúles horewes *squalentis cęni*, An. Ox. 2545.   Fúle *cenulenti*, i. *lutosi*, Wrt. Voc. ii. 130, 76.   Swín þe simle willnaþ licgan on fúlum solum, Bt. 37, 4; F. 192, 26.   Fúle syle *lurida* (i. *caccabata*) *uolutabra*, An. Ox. 4289. Ðet swín . . . bið fúlre ðonne hit ǽr wæs, Past. 421, 3.   (3) opposed to fair of aspect, *dark, ugly* (?), an epithet of the black alder :—Fúlae treó (treá, Ep.) *alneum*, Txts. 39, 117.   Fúle treów, Wrt. Voc. ii. 6, 47. Fúlan beámes rind, Lch. ii. 78, 12. [Cf. *O. H. Ger.* fúl-boum : Ger. faul-baum.]   **II.** figurative. (1) *morally polluted* :—Fúlre gálnysse, fúles forligeres *lupanaris incesti*, An. Ox. 4222.   Gilt sliporne ł fúlne *culpam lubricam*, Hy. S. 15, 38.   Mid fúlustre gewilnunge *turpissimo desiderio*, Angl. xi. 117, 29.   (1 a) *guilty of a charge* :—Be þisum þeófum þe man on hrædinge fúle geáxian ne mæg, and man eft geáxað þe hé fúl bið and scildig, . . . þ menn þe æt ordále fúle weordað, Ll. Th. i. 238, 29–32.   (2) of language :—þíne eáran áwend fram fúlre sprǽce, Wlfst. 246, 7.   (3) *disgraceful, infamous* :—Fúlra *olidarum* .i. *fedorum* (*nuptiarum*, the marriage of Herod with his brother's wife), An. Ox. 1783.   þæs fúlan wuhta þú sceoldest áwurpan of ðínum ríce, Hml. Th. ii. 488, 12.   ¶ *used substantively*, on fúl lecgan, on fúlan lecgan *to bury ignominiously* (of burial in unconsecrated ground, the opposite of *clǽne leger*). v. instances under fúl, e ; f. in Dict. v. un-fúl.

**fúl, es ; n.** *Add* :—Widl and fúl *inluviem*, Wrt. Voc. ii. 44, 53. (1) in a physical sense :—Ne bið áht geméted bútan líg and cyle and láðlic fúl (*foetor*), Dóm. L. 205.   (2) in a figurative sense. *Take here passages under* fúl, es ; *m., and add* :—Að ðæt hé nyste ne fúl ne fácen . . . Nyste ic on þám þingum þe þú ymbe speast fúl ne fácn, Ll. Th. i. 182, 1–3.

**fúl, es ; m.** v. *preceding word* : fúl, e ; f. v. fúl ; *adj.* II. 3. ¶ : fúl-beám. v. fúl ; I. 3.

**fúle ; adv.** *Foully.* (1) in a physical sense :—Lazarus þe læg on byrgene fúle stincende, Hml. Th. i. 496, 28.   Eal se líchoma stincð fúle, Lch. ii. 236, 14.   Hé stanc swá fúle þ man hine ferian ne mihte, Hml. S. 25, 545.   On þá fúle stincendan eá *in foetentem fluvium*, Gr. D. 319, 14.   (2) in a moral sense :—þám forlegene hóringas, Wlfst. 165, 33.   Fúle áfýlede hórcwenan, Ll. Th. i. 172, 21.

**fúle treów.** v. fúl ; I. 3 : **fulgian** *to baptize.* v. fulwian.

**fúlian.** *Add* :—Sealf wiþ þon þ dolh ne fúlige . . . ceów þá rinde on þ dolh, ne fúlaþ hit, Lch. ii. 96, 16, 9.   Fúliendum fexe *squalente capillatura*, An. Ox. 1213.   Fúligendum limum *putrescentibus membris*, Scint. 45, 7.   [*O. H. Ger.* fúlén *tabescere.*]

**fúliend-líc.** v. un-fúliendlíc.

**full.** *Add* : I. *having a receptacle empty.* (1) absolute :—Orcas fulle, Jud. 19.   (2) *with gen.* :—Búc ful wæteres, Hml. Th. ii. 422, 19.   On ceác fulne wínes, Ll. ii. 30, 23.   Twégen fǽtels full ealað oððe wæteres, Ors. 1, 1 ; S. 21, 16.   (3) where a receptacle is used as a measure. v. ceác-, hand-full :—Dó þæs dústes fíf cuculeras fulle, Lch. i. 196, 13.   Drince þreó ful fulle, 88, 13.   (4) *with prep.* :—Hwæt fremað þ þæt ðín cyst stande ful mid gódum, and ðín iugehýd beó ǽmtig ælces gódes ?, Hml. Th. ii. 410, 11.   **II.** *containing abundance of.* (1) of material objects :—Wæs wæter wǽpna ful, Exod. 450.   Béc sint fulle þára bisna, Bt. 29, 1 ; F. 102, 11.   (2) in a non-material sense, *abounding* in, *abundantly characterized* by (cf. adjectives in *-full* formed from nouns). (a) *with gen. sing.* :—Se wer is wísdómes and cræfta full *vir totus ex sapientia virtutibusque factus*, Bt. 10 ; F. 28, 17 : El. 939.   Mæg sigores full, Sancta Maria, Cri. 88.   Tornes fulle, Gú. 176.   Ealre fǽgernesse full, Bl. H. 115, 6.   þá yfelan sint fulle ælces yfeles, Bt. 37, 3 ; F. 190, 18.   Se héhsta gód is ælces gódes fullast, 34, 2 ; F. 136, 13.   (b) *with gen. pl.* :—Weorðmynda full *full of honours*, Cri. 378 : Crä. 24.   Synna and mána full, Bl. H. 75, 7 : 109, 29.   Oferhygda full, Mód. 43.   Cearena full, Cri. 962 : Jul. 618.   Hét leahtra ful tó cwale lǽdan synna leáse, 612.   (c) *with inst.* :—Fíf mægnum full, Sal. 136.   Eáge æfþancum ful, 497.   **III.** *full of food* :—þú wǽre swá gífre swá hund, and þú nǽfre nǽre full þe má þe hell, Wlfst. 241, 7.   **III a.** figurative :—þú git tó full sý þæs þe þé lǽfed is, þ þé for þý wlátige, Bt. 11, 1 ; F. 30, 19.   Hí (*avarice and hell*) habbað unáfylledlíce grǽdignysse þ hí fulle ne beóð nǽfre, Hml. S. 16, 285.   **IV.** *complete, perfect, whole* (said both of material and immaterial things) :—God is þæt fulle gód and þ fullfremede, þ nánes willan wana ne biþ . . . Gif nán wuht wana nǽre, þonne nǽre nán wuht full ; for þý biþ ǽnig full þing þe

sum þing biþ wana, and for þý biþ ǽnig þing wana ðe sum biþ full ; ælc þing biþ fullost on his ágenum earda *omne enim, quod imperfectum esse dicitur, id imminutione perfecti esse perhibetur. Quo fit, ut si in quolibet genere imperfectum quid esse videatur, in eo perfectum quoque aliquid esse necesse sit*, Bt. 34, 1 ; F. 134, 18–24.   (1) of material things :— þ ilce þú miht geþencan be ðám líchoman and be his limum. Gif þára lima hwilc of biþ, ðonne ne biþ hit nó full mon swá hit ǽr wæs, Bt. 37, 3 ; F. 190, 27.   (2) of immaterial things :—Seó fulle gesǽlþ *perfecta felicitas*, Bt. 34. 2 ; F. 134, 32 : 136, 11 : 34, 9 ; F. 146, 21, 27, 28.   Se fulla anweald, 36, 7 ; F. 184, 8.   Gif hwá mid fullan willan forlǽt ælc gód, 36, 6 ; F. 182, 6 : 35, 6 ; F. 170, 19.   Écne anweald and fulle genyht, 33, 3 ; F. 126, 13.   Suá hwá suá hæfð fulle hǽle his líchoman, Past. 251, 3.   Hí wénaþ þ hié mægen habban full gód and fulle gesǽlþa on ðisum andweardum gódum.   Ac þá fullan gesǽlþa and þ héhste gód is God self (*Deum veramque beatitudinem unum atque idem esse monstravimus*), Bt. 34, 7 ; F. 144, 15.   **IV a.** *entitled to all the privileges implied by a designation* :—Eall þeódscipe hine heafde for fullne cyning, Chr. 1013 ; P. 144, 6.   **V.** *complete* in number, quantity, extent, *whole, entire* :—Gif þet fulle mægen þǽre wǽre *if the full strength of the East Angles had been there*, Chr. 1004 ; P. 135, 37.   Erian fulne acer *arare integrum agrum*, Coll. M. 19, 21.   Wæs án gér full þæt seó eorþe wæs cwaciende *per totum fere annum terraemotus fuerunt*, Ors. 2, 6 ; S. 88, 10.   Heó þrím wucum fullum (*tribus septimanis*) ne mihte úte cuman, Bd. 5, 4 ; Sch. 567, 15.   Hé besæt þone castel fulle six wucan, Chr. 1087 ; P. 224, 12.   þes moncwealm wæs on Rómánum full (fulle, Bos. 55, 24) II geár (*per biennium*), Ors. 3, 3 ; S. 102, 9.   [*See* full ; *adv.*]   **V a.** of a council, *where none or few of the members are absent* :—Hér sæt full sinoð æt Cealchýðe, Chr. 785 ; P. 52, 19.   **V b.** *completed, that has reached the limit* :—Fulne ende þínes lífes þú hæfst gelifd *plenam jam etatis finem habes*, Nar. 30, 10.   **VI.** used substantively :—Nǽfre seó fyl be fullum ne weorðe *non usque ad satietatem bibamus*, R. Ben. 65, 2.   Hié ðá béc eallæ be fullan geliornod hæfdon, Past. 5, 20.   v. ofer-, wæter-full.

**full ; adv.** *The two passages given here may be taken under* full ; *see* Gen. 50, 10 : Bd. 2, 14 ; S. 517, 33 *under* full *in Dict., and* full ; V. *above* ; *but see also* ful-líce, (6).   *The forms of adjectives and adverbs given in the Dictionary as compounds with* full- (ful-) *may be taken as adjectives and adverbs qualified by the adverb* full (ful).   Fol *is another form of this adverb*, e. g. fol neáh, Past. 35, 21 : Ors. 1, 10 ; S. 48, 11, 12.

**full a** *cup* with liquor in it.   *Add* :—Bæd hé þone bisceop blætsian his ful ; hé nolde, and se dysiga dranc bútan bletsunge, Hml. S. 12, 70.   Hé gesénode án wínes ful, and onsende sumum were, Shrn. 126, 17.   Dreó full gódes wínes, Lch. i. 196, 13.   [þe ilke þat halt þene nap, he hine drinkeð up ; oder uul me þider fareð . . . þenne þat uul beoð icumen, þenne cusseoð heo þreoien, Laym. 14333–8.]

**-full** *forming nouns.* v. ceác-, hand-full, *and cf.* full ; *adj.* I. 3.

**fulla, an ; m.** *The full, the highest stage reached by anything, the perfection, perfect specimen of a kind or class* :—Hwæt mæg beón wóp oððe sáriguys, gif þær næs se mǽsta ǽgðres ? oþþe hwæt mæg beón geómrung and wánung, gyf þ næs se fulla ǽgðres ?, Hml. S. 23, 104.

**ful-lǽst.** *Add* : v. fylst.

**ful-lǽstan.** *Add* :—þte fullǽste mé *ut adiuuet me*, Lk. R. 10, 40. v. ge-fullǽstan ; fylstan.

**full-berstan** *to be shattered* :—On þyssum þrým stapelum sceall ælc cynestól standan . . . and áwácie heora ænig, sóna se stól scylfð ; and fulberste heora ænig, þonne hrýsð se stól nyðer, Ll. Th. ii. 308, 1 : Wlfst. 267, 18.

**full-bétan.** *Add* :—Oþ þæt þám abbode þince þæt hí fulbét hæbben *usque dum abbas judicaverit satisfactum esse*, R. Ben. 70, 8, 18 : 71, 2.   [*O. H. Ger.* fol-buozen *satisfacere*.]

**full-boren ; adj.** (1) in a physical sense, *fully formed and living at birth* :—Ic gonge mid cwican cilde, nalæs mid cwellendum, mid fulborenum, nalæs mid fǽgan, Lch. iii. 66, 29.   Ðá wíf ðe ðá geeácnodan bearn cennað ðe ðonne git fulborene ne beóð, ne fyllað hié nó mid ðám hús ac byrgenna *conceptas soboles feminae si priusquam plene formentur proferunt, nequaquam domos sed tumulos replent*, Past. 383, 35.   (1 a) figuratively :—Ðonne ðǽm móde sió sóðfǽsðnes on geeácnod bið, ǽr ðǽm ðe hit fulboren sié, Past. 367, 18.   (2) in a legal sense, *of birth that satisfies prescribed conditions, legitimate* :—Mid eahta and feówertig fulborenra þegena (*tainis plene nobilibus*, Lat. vers.), Ll. Th. i. 228, 4. [*O. H. Ger.* ful-boran *legitimus*.]

**full-cúþ.** *Take here* ful-cúþ, *and add : familiar.* Cf. seld-cúþ :—Hé him ealdor gesette ús eallum fulcúðne, Brihtnóð geháten, Cht. Th. 242, 3.   Hig wǽron farende þurh án wésten on hiora fulcúðne weg, Shrn. 37, 33.

**full-dón ; p. -dyde** *To complete, perform* :—Eall þ yfel þ hí ǽr ðan begunnon, hí þ eall syððan fuldydon, Hml. S. 23, 288.   Hí þæt fuldón *hoc perficiunt*, R. Ben. 70, 21.   *Praeteritum imperfectum, þæt is* unfulfremed forðgewiten, swilce þæt ðing beó ongunnen and ne beó fuldón, Ælfc. Gr. Z. 124, 5.   [*O. H. Ger.* fol-tuon *perficere*.]

**full-faran** *to perform a journey* :—For unfriðe man mót freólsǽfenan nýde fulfaran betweónan Eferwíc and six míla gemete, Ll. Th. ii. 298, 26. [*O. H. Ger.* folle-faran *perambulare.*]

**full-fremed**; *adj.* (*ptcpl.*) *Perfect.* (1) *fully trained* or *conversant* :—Heó weóx and weard fulfremed on gódra mægna heányssum, Hml. A. 126, 337 : 122, 187 : Bl. H. 73, 16. Þridde cyn muneca is ánsetlena þe on mynsteres wununge fulfremede sindon (*jam coenobiale conversatione perfecti*), R. Ben. 134, 22. Fulfremedum leornerum, 21, 16. (2) *of complete excellence* :—Wæs hé on gódum for Gode swíþe fulfremed, Bl. H. 217, 10. Gyf þú wylt fullfremed (ful-, *v. l.*) beón *si vis perfectus esse*, Mt. 19, 21 : Hml. Th. i. 62, 3. Tó ðǽm staðole fulfremedes weorces *ad virtutis statum*, Past. 65, 16. Geþyld weorc folfremed hæbbe, þæt gé sýn fulfremede (*perfecti*) and ansunde on nánum ǽteorigende, Scint. 8, 8. Tó gódum fremmingum fulfremedra dǽda, Hml. A. 48, 581. Ne mǽtte ic nó ðín weorc sullfremed (*plena*) beforan mínum Gode, Past. 445, 21. Fulfremed, 22. Ðonne hié ðenceað hú hié selfe scylen fullfremodeste (ful-, *v. l.*) weorðan, 41, 23. (3) *in* grammar applied to a tense which denotes a completed action :—*Praeteritum perfectum* ys forðgewiten fulfremed ... *Praeteritum plusquam perfectum* is forðgewiten máre þonne fulfremed, for ðan ðe hit wæs gefyrn gedón, Ælfc. Gr. Z. 124, 5-9. v. un-fullfremed, full-fremman.

**full-fremedlíc**; *adj. Perfect*:—Fulfremedlicre *apologitica* (as in the glossary the three words which precede *apologitica* and the three that follow it occur in Ald. 38, 23 : 39, 2 : 39, 3 : 40, 30: 40, 32: 40, 37 respectively, it seems certain that *fulfremedlicre* is a gloss to Ald. 40, 11 : *Apologetica* verborum veritate defenditur), Wrt. Voc. ii. 2, 65. On rihtum geleáfan and on fulfremedlícum weorcum þurhwunian, Bl. H. 77, 19. v. next word.

**full-fremedlíce.** *Add:* (1) *completely, entirely, to the full extent* :—Heó him ne geþafode fulfremodlíce on þá eorðan ástreccan, Hml. S. 23 b, 606. Gif wé þá dagas fulfremedlíce for Gode lifgeaþ (*if we live those days entirely for God*), þonne hæbbe wé úre daga þone teóþan dǽl for Gode gedón, Bl. H. 35, 25. Getogen on Hebréiscum gereorde fulfremedlíce, Hml. Th. i. 436, 14 : Bl. H. 217, 4. Hí þ fulfremedlíce oncneówan, 177, 19. Þæt þæt gehwilc on him sylfum be dǽle hæfð, þæt hé hæfð on óðrum werode fulfremodlíce ... Is gehwilc ðǽra weroda þám naman gecíged ðe ðá gife getácnað þe hé fulfremedlícor underféng, Hml. Th. i. 348, 18-31. Fulfremedlícor *plenius* i. *perfectius*, An. Ox. 2375. (2) *of completed action* :—*Tempore praeterito perfecto amaui* ic lufode fulfremedlíce, Ælfc. Gr. Z. 130, 17 : 133, 5.

**full-fremednes.** *Add:* (1) *completeness* :—Sē þe fulfremednesse hálige drohtnunge habban wile, þæt þá synd gesette tó lifes bysene hálegra fædera lára, þára gemen gelǽt maunan tó fulþungenre fulfremednesse, R. Ben. 132, 18-133, 1. Tó ðǽre fremminge on fulfremednysse *to the carrying of them out completely*, Hml. A. 11, 272. (2) *the greatest excellence* :—God is full ǽlcre fullfremednesse, Bt. 34, 3 ; F. 136, 19. Fulfremednesse weg þe wé on féran sceolan, Bl. H. 21, 16. Fulfremednysse *perfectionem*, An. Ox. 1011. v. un-fullfremednes.

**full-fremman (-fremian).** *Add:* (1) *to bring to an end, complete, finish*:—Tó þon þ hé sceolde gegearwian and fulfremman þone wáh mid þám óþrum bróþrum *ut ipse parietem cum fratribus perficeret*, Gr. D. 126, 2. Þá fulfremedan (full-, *v. l.*) weorc *perfecta opera*, R. Ben. 20, 6. (2) *to bring to pass* :—Fulfremet *perficit* (*malum*), Kent. Gl. 581. Þ ðie wé hátaþ Godes foreþonc, þ biþ ðá hwíle þe hit mid him biþ on his móde, ǽr þám þe hit gefremed weorþe ... Ac siþþan hit fullfremed biþ, ðonne hátaþ wé hit wyrd, Bt. 39, 5 ; F. 218, 24. (3) *to do, perform, accomplish* :—Bútan tweón hé fullfremede (ful-, *v. l.*) ðá synne *culpam procul dubio perpetraret*, Past. 264, 4. Yrre ne sceal mon fullfremman (ful-, *v. l.*) *iram non perficere*, R. Ben. 17, 5. Ne gǽld ús nán ðing te fullfremmanne ðá gódan weorc, Past. 445, 30. Swá hwylc gód swá þú beginst, þæt hit þurh Drihten tó fulfremedum ende cuman móte, mid gebede gewilna *quicquid agendum inchoas bonum, ab Domino perfici oratione deposcas*, R. Ben. i, 11. (4) *to perfect, bring to a proper condition* :—Fulfrema (-freme, Ps. Rdr.) stepas míne on síþfætum þínum *perfice gressus meos in semitis tuis*, Ps. L. 16, 5 : 79, 16. v. ge-fullfremman.

**full-fremming.** v. un-fullfremming.

**full-fylgan** *to follow* a teacher ; *persequi* :—Sē forwyrcð hine sylfne sē þe ábrecð Godes bebodu and fulfylgð deófles unlárum, Ll. Th. ii. 330, 29. Hí beóð þæs wel wyrðe, þæt deófol openlíce fandige hwá him fullfyligean wille, Wlfst. 95, 19. [*Cf. O. H. Ger.* folle-folgón.]

**full-gán.** *Add:* (1) *to follow* a profession, *carry on* an office, *apply oneself to*, *practise* a habit :—Sē ðe his woruldlustum eallum fulgǽþ, Bt. 31, 1 ; F. 112, 6. Gif hwá forlǽt ǽlc gód and fulgǽþ þám yfele, 36, 6 ; F. 182, 7. Þ mon fulgá eallum his lustum, 24, 2 ; F. 82, 13. Ne fulgá hé eallunga ðæs líchoman wilnunga *nec totum se ad hoc, quod agit, conferat*, Past. 395, 10. Hí secgaþ þ hí mægen þý éþ hiora wísdóme fulgán and hine gehealdan *sic enim clarius testatiusque sapientiae tractatur officium*, Bt. 39, 2 ; F. 212, 19. Hió hyre firenluste fulgán ne móste bútan manna bysmrunge, Ors. 1, 2 ; S. 30, 33. Þæt hié his giongorscipe fulgán (fyligan, MS.) wolden, Gen. 249. (2) *to give effect*

*to, carry out* :—Sē þe ne hwyrfð his mód æfter ídlum geþóhtum, and him mid weorcum fulgǽð, þeáh hí him on mód cumen, Ps. Th. 23, 4. (3) *to execute* a command, task, &c., *do* a person's will :—Ælc wuht his rihtgesetnesse fuleóde bútan menn ánum, Bt. 5, 3 ; F. 12, 9. Þá on ðǽm tweón þe hié swá ungeorne his willan fulleódon *fastidiose ducem in disponendo bello audientes*, Ors. 3, 11 ; S. 146, 24. Fulgá nú se mete ðǽre wambe willan, and sió wamb ðæs metes, Past. 317, 16. Hí ðínum willan woldon fulgán, Bt. 3, 4 ; F. 6, 24. (4) *with the idea of help, service* :—Sceaft nytte heóld, feðergearwum fús fláne fuleóde *the shaft did its office well, swift-winged helped on the arrow-head*, B. 3119. Ealle þá þe ... hié selfe forworht hæfdon, hié hit eall forgeáfon wið þǽm þe hié him æt þǽm gewinnum fuleódon *dictator homines quicunque sceleribus obnoxii essent, impunitate promissa, militiae mancipavit*, Ors. 4, 9; S. 192, 1. [*O. Sax.* ful-gán: *O. H. Ger.* folle-gán.]

**full-gangan.** *Add:*—Ic ne mót mid mínum ðeáwum mínra ðénunga fulgangan, Bt. 7, 3 ; F. 20, 32. [*O. Sax.* ful-gangan: *O. H. Ger.* folle-gangan.]

**full-gearwian**; *p.* ode. (1) *to complete, finish* :—Þ hé sceolde fullgearwian þone wáh mid þám gebróðrum *ut ipse parietem cum fratribus perficeret*, Gr. D. 126, 2. (2) *to equip fully* :—Án scegð is eall gearo bútan þám hánon, hé hine wolde fulgearwian his hláforde tó gerisnum, Cht. Crw. 23, 9. Oð ðæt gé weorðen fullgearowode mid ðǽm gǽsðlican cræfte ... wé fullgearowode weorðað ... *quoadusque induamini virtute ex alto ... induimur ...*, Past. 385, 4-7.

**full-gedrifen** *crammed full* :—Hé is réðra ðonne eal middangeard, ðeáh hé sý binnan his feówer hwommum fulgedrifen wildeóra, Sal. K. p. 150, 23.

**full-gRówan** *to come to maturity* :—Ðæt hié ne móten fulgrówan (full-, *v. l.*) ne wæstmbǽre weorðan, Past. 67, 23.

**full-healden** *contented* :—*Contentus*, i. *sufficiens* éþhelde *vel* geþæf, fulhealden, Wrt. Voc. ii. 135, 2. [*Cf. O. H. Ger.* folle-haltan.]

**fullian** *to baptize.* v. fullwian.

**fullian** *to fulfil.* *Add:* (1) *to become full, fill up* (intrans.) :—Tó wunde clǽnsunge ... smire þá wunde mid, þonne fullað hió, Lch. ii. 92, 7. (2) *to make full, fill* :—Þá ylcan ungesewenlican gefyllende onstyriað and gyt fulliað þá mænniscan líchaman *ipsa invisibilia implendo movent carnalia corpora*, Gr. D. 270, 16. (3) *to fulfil* an order, *carry out* an injunction :—Ic ðæs forecuaedenan uuord fulliae, C. D. i. 293, 1. [*O. Sax.* fullón *to do a person's will: O. H. Ger.* follón.] v. ge-fullian.

**ful-lic**; *adj. Full.* (1) Cf. full; II :—Seó Níl is ealdor fullicra eá *Nilus est caput fluuiorum*, Nar. 35, 19 note. (2) Cf. full; V :—Fullic þ God behét hé onfehð *he will receive what God promised in full*, Scint. 60, 2. (3) Cf. full; V a :—Hér wæs gefíit and fullic (wæs gefíitfullic, sæt full, *v. ll.*) senoþ, Chr. 785 ; P. 52, note 2. [*v. N. E. D.* fully; *adj.*]

**fūl-lic.** *Add*:—Fúllic *fedus*, Ælfc. Gr. Z. 292, 4. Hit is fúllic þinge and Gode láð, þæt hí ... befýlað hí selfe ... þæt hí farað fram wífe tó wífe, and hí eall swá stunte nýtenu dóð, Wlfst. 305, 7. Ic ne mæg for sceame þá sceandlícan dǽde, þæt ǽnig man sceole etan on gange, swá fúllíce secgan swá hit fúllíc is, E. S. viii. 62, 18.

**fullíce.** *Add:* (1) *in full measure, abundantly* :—Fullíce gebéd satisfactum, R. Ben. I. 78, 13. Hé his Déman ierre fullíce tó him gecígð *plene in se iram judicis provocat*, Past. 39, 9. Hé him fullíce líciaþ, Bt. 35, 6 ; F. 170, 21. Ðínne miltheartnisse fullícor (*plenius*) wé ongéton, Rtl. 34, 32. (1 a) *fully, so as to satisfy* with food :—Fullíce *affatim* (famelicum prophetam *affatim* paverit, Ald. 50, 32), An. Ox. 3686. (2) *in a full manner* or *degree, thoroughly* :—Þ hé fullíce mæg dón *quod plene potest agere*, Scint. 60, 2. Þ hé his ealdan yfelu swá fullíce fullfremme, swá hé hí ǽr dyde, Bt. 35, 6 ; F. 170, 18 : Bl. H. 55, 15. Ne magon ðider fullíce becuman ðá stæpas ðæs weorces ðieder ðe hé wilnað *quo desiderium innititur, illuc gressus operis efficaciter non sequuntur*, Past. 65, 16. (3) *completely* (as opposed to *partially*) :—Cweð man útlaga Rótberd arcb fullíce, Chr. 1052 ; P. 183, 13. Gif hiora anweald biþ fullíce ofer þ folc, Bt. 39, 2 ; F. 212, 20. Þ se dæg mid þǽre nihte fullíce gefrætwod sý mid feówer and twéntig tídum *the full equipment is twenty-four hours*, Angl. viii. 306, 13. Hié heora scriftum fullíce geandettiaþ, Bl. H. 193, 22. Hé fullíce mynster getimbrede *he built a monastery complete in every respect*, 221, 5. Gyf þrǽl þegen fullíce áfylle, Wlfst. 162, 8. Wé magon fullecor (fullícor, *v. l.*) ongietan and tósceádan ðá sprǽce *hanc discretionem plenius agnoscimus*, Past. 115, 6. (4) *fully, without reservation* or *qualification* :—Eal ðeód hine fullíce underféng, Chr. 1013 ; P. 144, note 2. (5) *fully, without defect* :—Ðeáh hé nǽre fullíce after óþerre endebyrdnesse gefulwad, Bl. H. 213, 14. Engle and Dene tó friðe and tó freóndscipe fullíce féngon, Ll. Th. i. 166, 8. (6) *with numerals*. v. full; V :—Wæs án gér fullíce þæt seó eorþe wæs cwaciende *per totum fere annum terraemotus fuerunt*, Ors. 2, 6 ; S. 88, 10. Seofon geár fullíce, Hml. S. 10, 7. Heó twéntig wintra wunode mid hyre were fullíce, Hml. A. 38, 350. Fullíce lxx wintra, Wlfst. 14, 7. Þ hé hæfde fullíce fíf hída ágenes landes, Ll. Th. i. 190, 15. (7) *of completed action* :—*Praeteritum perfectum* ys forðgewiten fulfremed : *steti* ic stód fullíce, Ælfc. Gr. Z. 124, 7. [*O. Sax.* fullíko: *O. H. Ger.* follícho *funditus, largiter.*]

fúl-líce. *Add :* (1) in a physical sense :—Gif heora hwylc fúllíce oððe þe gýmeleáslíce mynstres þing behwyrfe *si quis sordide aut negligenter, res monasterii tractaverit*, R. Ben. 56, 11. Etan fúlíce on gangsetlum, E. S. viii. 62, 13. v. fúl-lic. (2) in a moral sense :—Gýfernys fúllíce (*turpiter*) on gálnysse tólætt, Scint. 106, 13. Fúllícor *turpius*, 98, 1.

full-mægen, es ; *n. Great power, authority* :—Heofonwara fulmægen and heora hláfordes þrym, Wlsft. 186, 14.

fullnes. *Add :*—Fullnis *pleni[tudo]*, Rtl. 111, 28.

fulloc. *Substitute :* ful-loc (ful loc ?), es ; *n. A full, final agreement :*—Wé willað þ . . . getrýwe gewitnes and riht dóm and fulloc (ful loc ?) . . . fæste stande, Ll. Th. ii. 302, 6. v. loc ; II, and cf. Icel. full-mæli *a final, full agreement.*

full-rípod ; *adj. Mature :*—Þeáh hý fulrípode sýn and wel áfandode (*gravissimi et probatissimi senes*), R. Ben. 139, 9.

full-secgan *to give a full account* (of). (1) *intrans. :*—Wé wyllað nú fulsæcgan be ðám wífe, Hml. S. 3, 633. (2) *trans. :*—Hé fulséde his síð him eallum, Hml. S. 4, 284.

full-sleán *to effect the death of* a person, *kill outright :*—Gif Petrus móste þone man fulsleán, þonne ne héte hine Críst ná geswícan þæs weorces, Ll. Th. ii. 386, 30.

full-þungen ; *adj. Fully grown, perfect, complete :*—Tó fulþungenre fulfremednesse *ad celsitudinem perfectionis*, R. Ben. 133, 1.

full-trúwian. *Add* to ful-trúwian in *Dict.:* [*O. H. Ger.* fol-trûen.]

fulluht. v. full-wiht.

full-weaxen ; *adj. Full-grown :*—Hé (*John*) on wéstene wunode oð þæt hé fullweaxen wæs, Hml. Th. ii. 38, 5. Ǽr hira feðra fulweaxene sín, Past. 383, 30.

fullwere, fulwere, es ; *m. A baptist :*—Sée Iôhannes ácennes þæs fulweres, Shrn. 95, 6. Críst onféng fulwihte fram Iôhanne þám fulwere, 48, 25.

fullwian. *Take here* fullian in *Dict.* *and add :*—Ic þe fullwie on mínne Godfæder, Shrn. 106, 13. Ðá ongan hé fullwian ðá óðre cnihtas, 78, 28. [v. *N. E. D.* full to *baptize*. *The word seems a compound of* full *and the verb seen in O. H. Ger.* wîhen *to consecrate.*]

full-wiht. *Take here* fulluht, *and add :* *The word is masc. and fem. as well as neut.* (1) *masc. :*—Sió hreówsung scolde bión ǽr ðém fulwihte. Se fullwuht ðone mon geclénsað, Past. 427, 6. Þurh þæne fulluht, Ll. Lbmn. 413, 22, 36. (2) *fem. :*—Þá þenunge fulwihte (fullwihtes, *v. l.*) *ministerium baptizandi*, Bd. 2, 2 ; Sch. 118, 15. Þám gerýne fulwihte (fulluhte, fulwihtes, *v. ll.*) bæþes, 3, 3 ; Sch. 199, 16 : 1, 27 ; Sch. 71, 14 : 3, 7 ; Sch. 213, 7. Þæt gerýne þære hálgan fulwihte, Bl. H. 213, 10. Fulwihðe untrumes forsittan, Ll. Th. i. 38, 9. (3) *uncertain :*—Hé hine tó fulluhte nam (cf. *eum de lauacro exeuntem suscepit*, Bd. 3, 7. Óswold his onféng, Chr. 635 ; P. 26, 3), Hml. S. 26, 133. ¶ fulwihte *in* noun :—Án is geleáfa, . . . án is fulwihte, Hy. 11, 9. [v. *N. E. D.* fullought.]

fullwihtan (-ian). v. ge-fullwihtan ; fullwihtere.

fullwiht-bæþ. *Substitute for what is given at* fulluht-bæþ : (1) *a font :*—On fulluhtbæþe in *baptisterio*, An. Ox. 4087 : 4360. (2) *baptism :*—þ gerýne onfón fulluhtbæþes *sacri baptismatis sacramenta percipere*, Bd. 1, 27 ; Sch. 76, 6 : Guth. 76, 4.

fullwiht-béna, an ; *m. One who asks for baptism :*—Fulwihtbéna *rogator baptismi*, Wrt. Voc. ii. 132, 59.

fullwiht-ele, es ; *m. Oil used at the rite of baptism :*—Preósta gehwilc ǽgðer hæbbe ge fulluhtele ge seócum smyrels, Ll. Th. ii. 258, 15.

fullwiht-fæder (fulwiht-) *a baptismal father*, expressing the relation of the baptizer to the person baptized :—Kynegils his fulluhtfæder Sée Birine geúþe (cf. Cynegils wæs gefulwad from Birino, Chr. 635), Cht. Th. 115, 31. Marcus wæs mid Petre . . . Petrus wæs his godfæder, and hé lange folgode his fulluhtfæder Petre, Hml. S. 15, 144.

fullwiht-stów. *Take here* fulwiht-stów in *Dict.*, *and add :*—Fulwíhtstówe *baptisterio*, Wrt. Voc. ii. 78, 61 : 11, 72.

fullwiht-þegnung, e ; *f. Baptismal service :*—Ðá twá word *abrenuntio* and *credo* þe man æt fulluhtþenunge on gewunan hæfð, Wlsft. 38, 9.

fullwiht-wæter, es ; *n. Baptismal water :*—þæt tácnode þ ðurh his blód fulwihtwæter gewyrþan sceolde, Nap. 27.

full-wyrcan. *Add :*—Hé fulworhte on Eferwíc þ ǽnlice mynster þe Eádwine begunnon hæfde, Hml. S. 26, 109. Ðér wurdon þá forewearda fullworhte, Chr. 1109 ; P. 242, 14. [*O. H. Ger.* fola-wurchen *consummare.*] v. un-fulworht.

fúlnes. *Add :* (1) in a physical sense :—Fúlnes (fúllness, *v. l.*) *fetor*, Bd. 5, 12 ; Sch. 619, 20. Þá fúlnesse (fúlnessa, *v. l.*) *fetorem*, Sch. 624, 1. Fúlnesse *putores*, Wrt. Voc. ii. 66, 63. (2) in a moral sense :—Fúlnys *obscenitas*, i. *turpitudo*, An. Ox. 3674. Fúlnesse *obscenitatis*, 1727. Fólnesse (but the o is not quite distinct) *turpitudinem*, Kent. Gl. 171.

ful-scrid. v. scrýdan in *Dict.*

fúl-stincende. *Add :*—Ðone fúlstincendan migðan, Lch. i. 284, 9. Þá fúlstincendan eá *foetentem fluuium*, Gr. D. 322, 21.

fultum. *Add :* I. *help, assistance :*—Fultum (fulteám, Erf.) *emolu-*

mentum, Txts. 59, 743. Fultum oððe leán *emolomentum*, Wrt. Voc. ii. 29, 29. Hé fultumes bæd *solatium petivit*, Past. 305, 3. Mundbyrde and fultome *presidio*, Wrt. Voc. ii. 67, 41. Hannibal tó his fultume cóm, Ors. 4, 9 ; S. 190, 6. Fultum *favorem*, Wrt. Voc. ii. 37, 53. Þone fultum and þæt weorc Agustus gebohte mid fela M talentana *Augustus ad reparationem eorum magnam vim pecuniam largitus est*, Ors. 6, 1 ; S. 252, 27. Gif þás fultumas (*remedies*) ne sýn helpe, Lch. ii. 262, 15. II. in a personal sense. (1) of a single person :—Wæs God heora fǽle fæltum (*adjutor*), Ps. Th. 77, 34. Se getreówa fultum him tó cóm, Scs Bartholomeus, Guth. 28, 25. (2) of troops :—Hé férde mid fultume . . . þe lǽs þe hí secgon þæt hí mid hira folce hig sylfe álýsdon and mid heora fultume him gefuhton sige *ne glorietur Israel et dicat : Meis viribus liberatus sum*, Jud. 7, 1, 2 : Hml. S. 18, 327. Mid his miclan fultume *ob magnitudinem virium*, Ors. 4, 1 ; S. 154, 26. Swá clǽne hié námon heora fultum mid him þætte heora proletarii ne móston him beæftan beón, 15. Hé máran fultum and máre mægen. hæfde *plures habebat auxiliarios*, Bd. 3, 14 ; Sch. 254, 14. [v. *N. E. D.* fultum. *From* full *and* teám ; cf. *O. H. Ger.* folla-ziohan *suppetere, fulcire, adjuvare.*] v. ciric-, scrúd-fultum.

fultuma. v. ge-fultuma.

fultuman. *Add :*—Fultumaþ *subpeditat*, Wrt. Voc. ii. 88, 10. Ne fultumað hé nóht tó his hiéremonna niéðdearfe *subditorum necessitatibus minime concurrunt*, Past. 136, 3. Hé tiohchode him tó fultemanne (*ut solatium daret*), 305, 4. Fultemendum *adsessore*, Txts. 42, 95 : Wrt. Voc. ii. 7, 34.

fultumend. *Add :* Fultemend *frutina*, Wrt. Voc. ii. 109, 30. Fultumend, 36, 15 : *fautor*, 95, 66. Fultumiend, An. Ox. 3807. (1) *a helper* of a person (*gen.*) :—Þú eart mín fultumend, Ps. Th. 26, 11. Crístena manna fultumigend, Hml. Th. ii. 304, 4. Þú eart fultumiend þára þe nabbað náwðer ne fæder ne módor *pupillo tu eris adjutor*, 9, 34. (2) *an assistant* to a person (*dat.*) :—þ hé wǽre þe fultumigend, Wlsft. 240, 13. (3) *a helper, promoter* of a thing (*gen.*) :—þu mé wǽre freoða fultumiend *refugium meum es tu*, Ps. Th. 70, 3. Wé sint fultemend eówres gefeán *adjutores sumus gaudii vestri*, Past. 115, 25. þ his geongran wǽron his dǽde fultumiendas (*facti illius adjutores*), Gr. D. 243, 13. (4) *an assistant* to a condition, *one who helps to bring about* a condition :—Hié beóð fultemend tó hiera wǽdle (*adjutores calamitatis extitissent*), Past. 377, 3. v. ge-fultum(i)end.

fulwa, an ; *m. A fuller :*—Hire bróhte Godes engel swylcne gerelan swylcne nǽfre nǽnig fulwa, þæt is nǽnig webwyrhta, þæt mihte dón on eorðan, Shrn. 56, 9. v. web-wyrhta.

fulwere. v. fullwere.

fundian. *Dele* tó-fundian *at end, and add :* I. of movement. (1) of persons, *to go with the object of reaching a person* or *place, direct one's course to* :—Suá mon oft lett fundigendne monnan and his færelt gǽld *velut iter tendentis impediant*, Past. 257, 6. Geseah hé sume sáwle út fundigende of hyre líchaman, Wlsft. 140, 10. (1 a) where the goal is marked by a preposition or adverb :—Sáwul fundaþ of lícfate tó þám longan gefeán, Gú. 1062 : 1238. Sé þe on lagu fundað *he that will go to sea*, Seef. 47. Hí woldon cuman tó sumere þára stówa ðe hí ðonne tó fundiaþ, Bt. 34, 7 ; F. 144, 10. Férde sum ridda . . . and hit lǽdde forð mid him þǽr hé fundode tó, Hml. S. 26, 224. (1 b) with infin. giving purpose :—Wé fundiaþ Higelác sécan, B. 1819. (1 c) where (1 a) and (1 b) are combined :—Hé hider fundaþ on þysne middangeard mancyn sécan, Kr. 103. (1 d) with the idea of hostility :—þ Cnut fundode hiderward and wolde gewinnan þis land, Chr. 1085 ; P. 215, 30. Þurh þone eorl þe mid unfriðe hider tó lande fundode, 1101 ; P. 237, 4. Gegaderade Phtolomeus micle fird ongeán him þá hwíle þe hié tógaðereweard fundedon . . ., Ors. 3, 11 ; S. 146, 5. Tó áwirgenne þæt folc þe fundode wið his *maledic populo huic sedenti contra me*, Num. 22, 6. (2) of things, *to move so as to reach* a point :—Ðæt wæter, ðonne hit bið gepynd, hit uppað and fundað wið ðæs ðe hit ǽr from cóm *illud repetit, unde descendit*, Past. 277, 7. (2 a) of that which injures. Cf. (1 d) :—Cýdde man mé þ ús mára hearm tó fundode þonne ús wel lícode, Cht. E. 230, 1. Swá benne ne burston ne fundian (*not strike inwards?*), Lch. ii. 352, 1. II. of action, purpose, *to strive to attain* an end or object. (1) the end marked by a preposition or adverb :—Twá ðing sindon þe ǽlces monnes ingeþanc tó fundaþ, þ is willa and anweald, Bt. 36, 3 ; F. 176, 6. Þinga gehwilc þiderweard fundað, Met. 13, 14. Hwidre ic þe nú teohhie tó lǽdenne . . . ðider fundian, Bt. 22, 2 ; F. 78, 2. (1 a) with reflex. dat. :—Fundige hé him tó lissa blisse, Sch. 100. (2) with infin. :—Monige . . . witan fundiað, hwylc . . ., Mód. 16. (3) with gerund :—Hié fundiað tó bigietenne, and beóð suíðe gedréfede *cogitationis turbidae aestibus anhelant*, Past. 127, 20. Blódig regn and fýren fundiaþ þás eorþan tó forswylgenne, Bl. H. 93, 3. Sé ðe fundige wíslíce tó sprecanne *cum fortasse sapiens videri desiderat*, Past. 93, 24. Gif mon fundige wið his feónd tó gefeohtanne, Lch. ii. 154, 5. (4) with a clause :—Þá fundiaþ þ hié willon genimon myccle herehýþ, Bl. H. 95, 1. III. in the following passages fundian *is used as the equivalent of* fandian. [*In M. E.* found *is used with the meaning as well of* fandian *as of* fundian. v. *N. E. D.* found] :—Mid orþance þisses

dinges fundian (fandian, fondian, v. ll.), Lch. i. 100, 7. Wē sculon be þæs andgites mæðe fandian (fundigan, v. l.), Bt. 42; S. 147, 15. Fanć-ian (fundian with a over the u, v. l.) þâra þióstra, 36, 3; S. 105, 25. v. ge-fundian.

**fundung.** Add:—Ðis godspel sprecð ymbe ðæs Hælendes fundunge, and hū hē betǣhte ealle ðā geleáfullan his Fæder ǣr ðan ðe hē ūp ástige, Hml. Th. ii. 362, 15. [v. N. E. D. founding.] v. fram-fundung.

**funta** (?) *a spring* (?); the word occurs only in place-names:—Lond æt Cendeles (Ceadeles, C. D. B. iii. 40) funtan, C. D. ii. 293, 20. In loco qui Fobbefunte nominatur, 138, 35. Ðis syndon ðā landgemǣre tō Fobbefunten, iii. 279, 13. Ruris particulam cujus uocabulum est æt Fobbafuntan, 278, 30. Loco qui nuncupatur uocabulo Hamanfunta . . . Ðis synd ðæs landes gemǣre æt Hamanfuntan, 175, 9, 30. Æt Byrh-funtan and æt Hafunt, 203, 31. In illo loco ubi ruricoli uocitant Hamanfunta . . . Ðæs landæs gemǣro æt Hamanfuntan, v. 220, 12, 30. On ðone forde tō Teofunte, iii. 395, 13. In loco qui appellatur be Tefunte, ii. 68, 15. Tō Teofuntinga gemǣre, iii. 414, 14. Cf. also Funt-geal, Funte-mel.

[**funtian.** v. ge-funtian]: **furan.** v. fūrian.

**furh.** Add: *gen.* furh, fūre:—Furh *occa* (v. filging), Wrt. Voc. ii. 62, 63. Andlanges ðǣre fyrh tō ānum anheáfdum . . . ðanon on āne furh an æcer neár ðæm hlince . . . andlanges ānre furh oð hit cymð tō ānum byge; ðanone of ðæm byge forð on āne furh, C. D. v. 153, 23-32. On þā nīwan furh, andlang þǣre furh, C. D. B. ii. 112, 21. Æfter fūran on turfhleó; of turfhleó æfter heáfdan eft andlang fūr . . .; of ðǣre strǣte andlang fūra . . . ā andlang fūran, C. D. iii. 15, 26-31. Andlang fūra on setþorn; . . . of þām heáfodon andlang fūra . . . of hláwe andlang fūre, 436, 14-18. On fyrh *in occa*, Wrt. Voc. ii. 47, 64. Big ðam heáfde tō ðǣre fureh; æfter ðǣre fureh, C. D. iii. 384, 16. Se yrðlincg āmyrð his furuh (furh, v. l.), gif hē lōcað tō lange underbæc, Hml. S. 16, 181. þonne man þā sulh forð drīfe, and þā forman furh on sceóte, Lch. i. 404, 2. Fūra *sulcorum*, An. Ox. 2733. On fūrum *scrobibus*. i. *fossulis, scrobes sunt fosse*, 2018. Furhum *scrobibus*, Txts. 94, 884. Andlang strǣte on ðā deópan fūra, C. D. B. iii. 188, 35. v. ende-, mǣr-, þweorh-, wæter-furh.

**furh** (?) [; *pl.* fyrh], or fyrh (?); *f. A fir, pine*:—Of ðā[m] ellen-stubbe on ðane ōðerne ellenstubbe; ðanone on ðā ealdan fyrh, C. D. vi. 102, 26. On ðā ealdan firh, 97, 24. [Cf. *Icel. fỹri-skōgr a fir-wood.*] v. next word.

**furh-wudu.** For 'Gl. C. . . col. 1' *substitute:*—Furhwudu *pinus*, Wrt. Voc. ii. 117, 36. [O. H. Ger. for(a)ha *picea: Icel.* fura *pinus.*]

**fūrian** *to furrow:*—Þā þā fūrede *cum sulcaret*, An. Ox. 2492. v. ge-fūrian, fỹr(i)an.

**fur-lang.** Add: I. as a lineal measure. (1) originally '*the length of the drive of the plough before it is turned,*' usually 40 rods, *the eighth of a mile*:—Of ðone forda ūp on ðā rīde in furlang wið sūðan ðā cyrican; andlang rīde, C. D. vi. 1, 25. Of ðǣre ealdan dīc on Grinde-wylles lace in furlang, 48, 11. Ðus feor sceal beón þæs cinges grið fram his burhgeate þǣr hē is sittende on feówer healfe his, þ is .iii. mīla and .iii. furlang (*quarentenis*, Lat. vers.) . . ., Ll. Th. i. 224, 9. (2) *translating Latin* stadium:—Furlang *stadium*, Wrt. Voc. i. 38, 9. Wæs seó wīcstōw on lengo .xx. æs furlonga long *castra in longum stadia .xx.*, Nar. 12, 16. II. *an area of land a furrow-long in width* (v. Seebohm, Vill. Comm., pp. 2-4):—Ān furlang hīna herðlandes be-tweónan ðǣre strǣte and ðǣre mædwe, C. D. iii. 18, 28. Oð ðæs furlanges ūpende (cf. at ðas akeres ūpende, 434, 2), 418, 23. On ðæs langan furlanges eástende, vi. 48, 9. Forð bufon scortan hlince æt ðæs furlanges ende, v. 111, 6. Ðweres ofer ān furlang on gerihte on ān ǣlrbed, 153, 35.

**furþor.** Add: (1) local:—Ðā eóde hē furþor oþ hē gemētte ðā graman gydena, Bt. 35, 6; F. 168, 23. (2) *to* or *at a more advanced point of progress*:—Lǣre mon siððan furður on Lǣdengeðióde ðā ðe mon furður lǣran wille, and tō híeran hāde dōn wille, Past. 7, 14; Gū. 1195. His heáh geweorc furður āspyrgan, Sch. 29. (3) of degree or extent, *to a greater degree or extent, more thoroughly or completely*:—Swā hē mā drinceð, swā hyt furður clǣnsað, Lch. i. 352, 25. Hwā mæg ǣfre ōðrum furður freóndscipe gecȳðan, þonne hē his āgen feorh gesylle and ðurh ðæt his freónd wið deáð āhredde (*majorem hac dilectionem nemo habet ut animam suam quis ponat pro amicis suis*, Jn. 15, 13), Wlfst. 111, 4. Oft gē dyslice dǣd gefremedon . . . nǣfre furður þonne nū, El. 388. Þū feónde furður hȳrdes þonne þīnum Scyppende, Cri. 1395: Crä. 34. (4) denoting superiority:—Suā suæ hē on ðyncðum bið furður (-or, v. l.) ðonne ðā ðe sié on his weorcum and ðeáwum suā micle furður *sicut honore ordinis superat, ita morum virtute transcendat*, Past. 81, 24. Hē wolde beón furður on ōðrum earde þonne hē on his āgenum wǣre, Hml. S. 6, 189. Hē wæs furður on hlīsan and on mihte, Hml. Th. i. 478, 27. Se heofenlica cyning is mǣrra and furður tōforan ðām eorðlican cininge, Hex. 38, 5. Hīe sceoldon habban ēce eardungstōwe on ðæs fæder hūse furður ðonne his ǣgnu bearn *in domo Patris aeterna mansione filiis praeferuntur*, Past. 409, 5. (4 a) denoting greater importance or significance, *more*:—Nō þ ān þ hī magon

gesēran beón, ac þy furþor þ (cf. hit is sellicre þæt . . ., Met. 11, 50) heora furþum nān būton ōþrum beón ne mæg, Bt. 21; F. 74, 18. Ic geanbidode oþ ic wiste hwæt þū woldest, and hū þū hit understandan woldest, and eác þy furþor ic tiolode swīþe geornfullīce þ þū hit forstandan mihtest *eum tuae mentis habitum vel exspectavi, vel, quod est verius, ipsa perfeci*, 22, 1; F. 76, 26. Ānra gehwylc hæfð syndrige gyfe fram Gode, sume furðor þonne sume, R. Ben. 64, 10. (5) denoting excess, *beyond, over and above*:—Hī underfōð ǣgðer ge forhæfdnesse þe eaðmōdnesse furður donne hié gehāten *ultra habitum assumunt opera*, Past. 409, 30. (5 a) denoting transgression:—Hē furðor ne gedyrstlæce tō dōnne, þonne him beboden sȳ, R. Ben. 55, 10. (6) denoting increase:—Ic heóld wið ealle hȳnða þines fæder gestreón, and furðor hī geeácnode, Hml. S. 9, 43: Angl. viii. 299, 10. (7) denoting continued action:—Hī hira firene furþur ēhtan *apposuerunt adhuc peccare ei*, Ps. Th. 77, 19 (*or under* (6)). Gif þū furður dearst tō þām ānhagan aldre genēðan, An. 1352. Hē furður gen eorlscipe efnde, B. 3006. Þū scealt furður gen sīðfæt secgan *you shall go on and tell more of your journey*, Jul. 317: 347: Ph. 236: Sat. 225. Heora sicbeámas furþor (*printed* furþon) ne mihton blǣda bringan, Ps. Th. 104, 29. (8) of time, *later*:—Gē sægdon þæt gē cūðon mīne aldorlege, swā mē ǣfre weard oððe ic furður findan sceolde, Dan. 140. Hē furðor cymeð ufor ānre niht ūs tō tūne, Men. 33. Ofer midne winter furður fīf nihtum, 125.

**furþra.** Add: (1) of an animal's foot, *fore*:—Nim þone swȳþran fōt þone furðran *take the right fore-foot* (of a badger), Lch. i. 328, 4. (2) *more excellent*:—Furþra *prestantior*, i. *excellentior*, Germ. 395, 40.

**furþrung.** Dele.

**furþum.** *Take here* **furþan** *in Dict., and add*: I. *even*, intimating that the sentence in which it occurs expresses an extreme case of a more general proposition implied, and generally prefixed to the particular word, phrase, or clause, on which the extreme character of the statement or supposition depends. (1) attached (a) to the subject:—Ge furðon þā sprǣcon þæt ylce þe ic betst trūwode, Ps. Th. 40, 9. Ge furþum seó stōw þe . . . þū cwist þ þīn wrǣcstōw sȳ, heó is þām monnum ēþel þe . . ., Bt. 11, 1; F. 32, 26. Ge furþum manna līchaman forealdiað, Solil. H. 10, 7. (a a) in negative sentences:—Ne weard furðon ān tō lāfe *non remansit ne una quidem*, Ex. 10, 19. Þæt furðon nān tācen . . . næs gesewen, Hml. Th. i. 62, 16. Nō þ ān þ hī magon gesēran beón, ac . . . þ heora furþum nān būton ōþrum beón ne mæg, Bt. 21; F. 74, 18. And furþon litlincgas nellaþ forbīgean me *et nec parvuli nolunt praeterire me*, Coll. M. 29, 1. Hit furðum cēpemen ne gefaraþ, Bt. 18, 2; F. 62, 36. Ne ān furðum ealra wǣre *non est usque ad unum*, Ps. Th. 52, 2, 4. Nǣnig furðum wæs þæt hē eft sīðade hyhta leás, Gū. 895. (b) to the object:—Feáwa . . . cūðen . . . furðum ān ǣrendgewrit of Lǣdene on Englisc āreccean, Past. 3, 15. Þ wē furþum (-on, v. l.) þ eáland gesēcean mihton *si vel ipsam insulam repetere possemus*, Bd. 5, 1; Sch. 552, 5. Bió ðē unīðe tō clipianne, ge furðum ðīna āgna sprǣca *loquere in causa tua vix*, Past. 385, 11. Hē hēt ofsleán ealle þā witan, ge furþon his āgene mōder, and his āgene brōðer; ge furðon his āgen wīf hē ofslōg mid sweorde, Bt. 16, 4; F. 58, 6-8. Ge furðum ðāra scylda ðe openlīce beóð gesewena . . . hié belādian, Past. 241, 1. Hwǣr mæg ic wīsran findan, oððe furðon þinne gelīcan *numquid sapientiorem et consimilem tui invenire potero*?, Gen. 41, 39. (b a) the object of a clause:—Ge furþon, þ wyrse wæs, wē geheórdon þ sum sunu ofslōg his fæder, Bt. 31, 1; F. 112, 14. (b β) in negative sentences:—Ne furþon ān þyrl . . . þū ne miht dōn *nec saltem unum foramen . . . vales facere*, Coll. M. 31, 17: 29, 13: Gen. 14, 23. Ic furðum ānne ānlēpne ne mæg geðencean, Past. 3, 17. Ðā ōðre ne begáð furðum hira ǣgne endebyrd-nesse, 409, 31: 403, 27: Bt. 15; F. 48, 16. Hē furðon orsorh ne brīcð his genihtsumnysse *even his abundance he does not enjoy without anxiety*, Hml. Th. i. 64, 34. Þæs þe ic furðum ǣr ǣfre ǣngum ne wolde monna melda weorðan, Gū. 1201. (c) to word, phrase or clause expressing time, manner, place, &c.:—Þæt ic lufige ge furðum on þeófum (þeawum, MS.) *quas amo etiam in latronibus*, Solil. H. 16, 14. (c a) in negative sentences:—Ne furðum on ðām broce (*etiam in tribulatione positus*) nyle ālǣtan his geornfulnesse, Past. 269, 10. Suā unryht suā wē furðum betwuxn hǣðnum monnum ne hiérdon, 211, 8. Ne lufige ic nānwiht . . . ofer þæt, ne furðum þām gelīce, Solil. H. 25, 18. (d) to a hypothetical clause:—Gif ic ǣnig unriht wið hī gedōn hæbbe, oððe furðum him gulde yfel wið yfle, Ps. Th. 7, 4. Hwæþer hit tōwearde sōð sȳ oððe hwæðer mē on swefne mǣte, Hml. S. 23, 522. (e) to the predicate to emphasize the full extent of the statement:—Wē nyton furðon git hwæt seó offrung beón sceal *praesertim cum ignoremus quid deceat immolari*, Ex. 10, 26: Solil. H. 15, 17. Wē his furðon ne gefrēdað, Past. 139, 20: 241, 22. Wē nōhwæðer ne hit witan nyllað, ne hit bētan nyllað, ne furðum ne rēcað hwæðer wē hit ongieten, 195, 6: Wrt. Voc. i. 86, 74: Solil. H. 66, 14: Met. 8, 32. Hī þæt tōwearde līf ne sōhton, ne þ furþum gelȳfdon þ hit ō wǣre *uitam futuram non quaerentes, siue etiam non esse credentes*, Bd. 3, 30; Sch. 331, 13. And gē furðon ne gelȳfdon Drihtne *et nec sic quidem credidistis Domino*, Deut. 1, 32. Hī nǣron furðan wyrðe þ . . ., Hml. S. 23, 367: Ælfc. Gen. Thw.

2, 9. **II.** *just*, of time. (1) *of an exact point of time* :—Þonne dæg and niht furþum scade, Lch. ii. 346, 13. Þā sunne ūp furðum eóde, Gen. 2539. (2) *where actions are contemporaneous* :—Đā hē furþum on Þ leóht cōm, ðā beseah hē hine underbæc *just as he reached the light he looked back*, Bt. 35, 6; F. 170, 14. Hringīren song ... þā bié tō sele furðum gangan cwōmon *the armour clanged directly they started for the hall*, B. 323. Swā hē furðum oncneów ... hē heora bēne gehýrde, Ps. Th. 105, 33: 138, 11. (3) *where one action takes place soon after another* :—Nim gāte meoluc þonne hió furþum āmolcen sié, Lch. ii. 188, 12. Īsen þonne hit furþum sié of fýre ātogen, 256, 15. Đonne hit furðum ryht andgiet underfangen hæfð *jam aliquid de veritatis intellectu conceperat*, Past. 367, 16, 20. Swā wit furðum sprǽcon *as we were just saying*, B. 1707. Ic þǽr furðum cwōm ... sōna mē ... hē wið his sylfes sunu setl getǽhte *I had only just come, when he placed me by his own son*, 2009. Ic furþum weóld folce *I had just come to the throne*, 465; Gen. 875. Đā cyld þonne hī furþum gān magon ... wilniaþ sumes weorþscipes, Bt. 36, 5; F. 180, 7.

**fús.** *Add*: **I.** *where there is prompt or rapid movement.* (1) *of a person* :—Hē fús gewāt from his āgenum for Isaac lǽdan, Gen. 2869. Þǽr fúse feorran cwōman tō þām ædelinge, Kr. 57. Hē gemētte Hingwar mid eallre his fyrde fúse tō Eádmunde (*hurrying to Edmund*), Hml. S. 32, 96. (2) *of a material object* :—Woruldcandel scān, sigel sūðan fús, B. 1966. Sceaft ... feðergearwum fús, 3119. (3) *of a non-material thing personified* :—Cōm ofer foldan fús sīðian mǽre mergen þridda, Gen. 154. **II.** *ready to go, eager to act* :—Sum munuc ... mid gemáglicum bēnum gewilnode þ hē mōste of ðām munuclife ... Đā ðā hē swā fús wæs (cf. his swiðlíce geornes, Gr. D. 156, 6), Hml. Th. ii. 176, 18. Rād Iulianus mid mycelra fyrdunge swīðe fús tō wīge, Hml. S. 3, 207. Đā wæs here fús forðwegas, Exod. 248. **II a.** *of an animal* :—Se wonna hrefn fús ofer fǽgum, B. 3025. **III.** *where the movement or readiness refers to departure from this world* :—Beórscealca sum fús and fǽge, B. 1241. Fród and fús, El. 1237. Fús sceal fēran, fǽge sweltan, Gn. Ex. 27. Of líce is gǽst swīðe fús, Gū. 1273. Hē his gǽst āgeaf on Godes wǽre, fús on forðweg, Men. 218: Gū. 918. Ic eom sīðes fús ūpeard niman, 1050. Fúsne on forðsíð, 1121. **IV.** *eager for an object* (*gen.*) :—Hýdweard gearo, sē þe ǽr lange tíd leófra manna fús æt færoðe feor wlātode, B. 1916.

**fús**, es; *n. Dele, and see* fús; **IV**: fúse. *Dele.*

**fús-trendel.** *Substitute*: fustran [= ? fýr-stanes]:—Heofonlíces fustran ligette *coelestis foci* (i. *ignis*) *fulmine*, An. Ox. 1428.

**fýhtan**; *p. te To moisten* :—Þeáh þe gewǽtte, fīhte *quamvis umectaretur*, An. Ox. 3470. Fýhtan *umectare*, 7, 14. Fīhten, 658. [*O. L. Ger.* fūhtian *rigare: O. H. Ger.* fūhten.] v. fúht.

**fyhtling.** v. fihtling: **fyht-wíte.** v. fiht-wíte.

**fýlan.** *Add*:—Þā þe mid gehwylcum unþeáwum þā stōwa þe tō Godes þeówdōme gehālgode wǽron fýlað and besmýtað, Ll. Th. ii. 408, 34. Fýlde *effeminavit*, Germ. 393, 190. Hī noldon hī fýlan mid þām fúlan hǽðenscype, Hml. S. 25, 30. Gyf mon mēte þ hē fíled sý, Lch. iii. 174, 31. [*v. N. E. D.* file.]

**fylc.** *l.* fylce: **fylcea.** v. ge-fylcea: **fylcian.** *Add*: v. ge-fylcian: **fyld.** v. fild: **fylde-stól.** v. fild[e]-stól.

**fylgean.** *Add*: **I.** *of movement.* (1) *marking relative position* :—Þ ǽrre folc and þ æfterre ... wē synt þe þǽr æfter fylgeaþ, Bl. H. 81, 33. Seó menigo þe þǽr beforan fērde and seó þe þǽr æfter fylgde, 71, 10. (2) *marking accompaniment* :—Him fylgede mycel manigo þæs folces, Bl. H. 247, 36. Woendun þ hē wǽre hiæ mið fylgende *existimantes illum esse in comitatu*, Lk. R. L. 2, 44. (3) *to follow with intent to reach, to pursue* (lit. or fig.) :—Wē him fleóndum fylgeaþ, Bl. H. 115, 18. Ic gongo and gē fylgas ī soecas mec *ego uado et queritis me*, Jn. R. L. 8, 21. Hwílon stōd þ man sceolde þrywa týman þǽr hit ǽrest befangen wǽre, and syþþan fylgean teáme swā hwǽr swā man tō cende, Ll. Th. i. 288, 30. (4) *to follow a track, proceed along a line marked out* (lit. or fig.) :—Þonne fylge wē Drihtnes swaþe, Bl. H. 75, 13. Ic mōste þīnum swaðum fyligan, Hml. S. 23 b, 710. **II.** *of action or condition.* (1) *with a personal subject.* (a) *to follow another.* (a) *as his disciple* :—Sē þe fylgeþ mē, ne gǽþ hē on þeóstro, Bl. H. 103, 31. Cum and filig mē, Hml. Th. ii. 400, 14. Fylg mec ī soec mec *sequere me*, Lk. L. 5, 27. (β) *as a dependant, retainer* :—'Gif þū feallest tō mē and mē weorþast' ... 'Ic þe ne fylge,' Bl. H. 31, 14. Fíliendne *adherentem*, i. *sequentem*, An. Ox. 3362. ¶ *to follow a person's banner* :—Wē sceolan weorðian þ hālige sigetācen Crīstes rōde and æfter fylgeon, Bl. H. 97, 13. (b) *to follow an example, teaching, &c.* Cf. fylgend-líc :—Hié Drihtnes bysenum ne fylgeað, ac hié fylgaþ deófles lārum, Bl. H. 25, 10. Gif þū filian wilt lārum mīnum, Dōm. L. 32, 67. Fylgean, Bl. H. 219, 30. Đāra apostola gilā? wē ongēton tō fylgenne *apostolorum magisterium cognovimus exequendum*, Rtl. 30, 31. (c) *to follow a profession, devote one's self to, diligently attend to.* Cf. fylgestre :—Sē ðe feld *qui sectatur* (*avaritiam*), Kent. Gl. 536: 679. Þā men þe þyssum uncystum fyligað, Bl. H. 29, 9. Þā þe þyssum sange fylgeaþ, 45, 36. Anna gebedum fyligde (*obsecrationibus seruiens nocte ac die*, Lk. 2, 37), Ll. Th. ii. 324, 8. Hē campdōme fyligde *he followed*

*the profession of arms*, Hml. S. 31, 17. Beó þū eádmód ... and gebedum filige, Dōm. L. 28, 6. Þ wē ne fylgeon unwitweorcum, Bl. H. 111, 2. Fylian *heora bócum* and gebedum georne, Ll. Th. ii. 322, 8. (d) *to attend to* a person medically :—Drince þā hwíle þā hē þurfe; and þǽr sió ādl gesitte, fylge him simle mid tigehorne oþ þ hāl sié, Lch. ii. 120, 16: 118, 16. (e) *to accommodate one's self to the will of another, yield to a thing* : *obsequi* :—Se cleweþa bið suíðe rów, and ðeáhhwæðere gif him mon tō longe fylgð (*lets it have its way*), hē wundað, Past. 71, 20. (f) *to try to gain* :—Hē in þissere byrig fylgeþ þām wraðum þises hwílendlícan lífes mid lǽcecræfte *ipse in hac urbe per medicinae artem temporalis vitae stipendia sectatur*, Gr. D. 344, 10. Soec sibbe and fylg ðā, Ps. Srt. 33, 15. (2) *the subject a thing.* (a) *marking association, accompaniment* :—Ne felhð *non sequetur* (*eum sanitas*), Kent. Gl. 1055. Tantalus on þisse worulde ungemetlíce gīfre wæs and him þār (*in Hades*) þ ilce yfel fyligde (*filgde, v. l.*), Bt. 35, 6; F. 170, 1. Ne forlēton hī nó þ gecyndelíce gód; ac simle him wolde þ fylgean, 27, 3; F. 100, 7. (b) *marking pursuit, attack* :—Feld *persequitur* (*malum peccatores*), Kent. Gl. 462. **III.** *of time.* (1) *to follow, do what has already been done by another* :—Hī ealle becumað tō ðām ēcan lífe, and þū sylf sīðð an him fyligst tō Godes ríce, Hml. S. 6, 334. (2) *to happen* or *come at a later time* :—Þām tācnum sōna fyligde mycel hunger, Chr. 293; P. 57, 1. Fíliendre *æftergencgnesse successurae posteritati*, An. Ox. 2694. v. full-, of-, ofer-fylgan.

**fylgedness.** v. æfter-fylgedness: **fylgend.** *Add*: v. æfter-fylgend.

**fylgend-líc**; *adj. That may be imitated.* Cf. fylgean; **II.** 1 b :—Fyligendlíce *imitabilem*, Angl. xiii. 421, 803.

**fylgend-líce.** v. æfter-fylgendlíce: **fylgend-ness.** v. æfter-fylgendness.

**fylgestre, an**; *f. A female follower.* v. fylgean; **II.** 1 c :—Fíliestrum sectatricibus (*inlaesae uirginitatis*), An. Ox. 1228.

**fylging** *following.* *Add*: v. æfter-fylging: **fylging** *occa.* v. filging.

**fyll, fyllu (-o).** *Add*: **I.** *fill, full supply* of food, &c. :—*Manducat unumquodque animal in mari alterum. Et dicunt quod vii minoribus saturantur maiores, ut* vii fiscas sǽlaes fyllu, sifu sǽlas hronaes fyllu, sifu hronas hualaes fyllu, An. Ox. 54, 1. Dō þ wōs and þā wyrte on wín, drince þonne ... symle ān ful tō fylles (*always one cup as a full dose, v. tō*; **II.** 5), Lch. i. 82, 14. **II.** *with idea of excess, repletion, satiety* :—Fyll and druncennyss *saturitas et ebrietas*, Scint. 106, 4. þæt þǽr nǽfre seó fyl be fullum ne weorðe *ut non usque ad satietatem* (oferfylle, R. Ben. I. 72, 12) *bibamus*, R. Ben. 65, 2. Sió wamb bið āðened mid fylle for gíefernesse *venter ingluvie extendituur*, Past. 311, 12. Fæste hē nū ongeán þ hē ǽr þurh fylle unriht gefremode, Ll. Th. ii. 284, 2. v. ofer-, untíd-, wǽl-fyll(-u, -o).

**fyll** *a fall*, **fyllan** *to fell*. v. fill, fillan.

**fyllan.** *Add*: **I.** *to fill* :—Fylde *farsit*, Wrt. Voc. ii. 97, 12: 37, 46. **I a.** *to fill with.* (1) *with gen.* :—Ne fylð sē his āgen hús gōðra cræfta, Past. 251, 5. (2) *with inst.* :—Wē þín hús ēcum gōdum fyllað, Ps. Th. 64, 1. Fyllað eówre fromcynne foldan sceátas, Gen. 1533. (3) *with prep.* :—Þ leóhtfæt man mid ele fylleþ, Bl. H. 127, 30. Đū fyldest þás eorþan mid mistlícum cynrenum nētena, Bt. 33, 4; F. 132, 25. Hig fyldon hira saccas mid hwǽte, Gen. 42, 25. **II.** *to fulfil* :—Ne cuom ic tō slītenne ah tō fyllenne (gefyllenne, R., *adimplere*), Mt. L. 5, 17. Đā fyllennda willo Godes *implentes voluntatem Dei*, p. 15, 11. v. for-, full-fyllan.

**fylled-líc, -ness, fyllend-líc.** v. ge-fylledlíc, -ness, -fyllendlíc: **fyllere.** v. fæt-fyllere: **fylle-seóc.** v. fille-seóc.

**fylleþ.** (1) *filling, completion.* v. scip-fylleþ. Cf. *O. H. Ger.* fullida *consummatio, supplementum.*] (2) *full moon.* v. fylleþ-flód, winter-fylleþ. [Cf. *Goth.* fullíþ (*g.pl.*) *neomeniae.*]

**fylleþ-flód, es**; *m. n. Spring-tide, high tide at full* (or *new*) *moon* :—Fylledflíod *malina*, Txts. 35, 20. On ǽlcum ānum geáre weaxeð þ flód ðæs sǽs feówer and twēntigum sīða and swā oft wanað. Fylleþflíod bið nemned on Lǽden *malina*, and se nēpflíod *ledo*, Shrn. 63, 30. v. fylleþ.

**fylle-wǽrc.** v. fille-wǽrc.

**fylling, e**; *f.* (1) *filling* of a vessel, &c. :—Mid þǽre cillan fyliinge (cyllfyllinge, *v. l.*), Gr. D. 250, 27. (2) *completion, complement* :—vi fliccen and ōþer vi tō fyllincge, Nap. 55, 33. v. bytt-, cyll-, ge-fylling.

**fyll-nis, -ness.** *Add*: *completeness, abundance* :—On Críste ānum is ealles siges fylnes þurhtogen, Bl. H. 179, 7. Of fyllnisse his alle wē onfēngon uuldor *de plenitudine ejus omnes accepimus gratiam*, Jn. L. R. I, 16. Fylnysse *liberalitat, gratia*, An. Ox. 7, 228. v. ge-fylness.

**fyllung.** v. fylling: **fylmen.** v. filmen: **fylne.** v. fillen: **fyl-nes.** v. fyll-nis.

**fýl-ness.** *Add*:—Hwæt sceoldon þe (*the soul*), þeódeorðan fýlnes, úre ǽlmessan?, Wlfst. 240, 15. Seó fýlnes (*foetor*) þæs stincendan mistes, Gr. D. 319, 11. Mist unārǽfnedlíce fýlnesse and unswētes stences *foetoris intolerabilis nebula*, 318, 28. Fýlnesse *fuliginis*, Wrt. Voc. ii. 34, 41.

**fylst, e**; *f. Substitute*: fylst, es; *m., and add* :—Fylstes mínes

*auxilii mei*, Ps. Rdr. 61, 8. Swegen bæd him fylstes ongeán Magnus, Chr. 1048; P. 167, 13. Gefultuma mē nū ānegra ǽlces ōðres fylstes bedǽled, Hml. S. 23 b, 442. Būtan Godes fylste, 11, 314: 21, 345. Mid freónda fylste, Ll. Th. i. 248, 3. Mid biscopes filste, ii. 290, 3. Hē gehēt þ hē him on fylste beón wolde, Chr. 1050; P. 169, 18. Begīm þū mē tō fylste *in adjutorium meum intende*, R. Ben. 60, 5. Þurh Godes fylst oferwinnan, Hml. S. 16, 378.

**fylsta.** v. ge-fylsta.

**fylstan.** *Add:* (1) absolute:—Fylstende *adstipulans*, Wrt. Voc. ii. 9, 39. (2) with dat. of person helped:—Drihten fylst him ǽfre, Hml. S. 11, 311. Se heáhengel him fylstende stōd, Hml. Th. i. 506, 16. (3) *to help* a person (*dat.*) to (*tō*) something, *to help* to the attainment of an end:—Hwīlon þes middaneard teáh menn fram Gode ... nū hē fylst ūs tō Gode, Hml. S. 28, 172. Þ ǽlc geréfa fylste ōðrum tō ūre ealra frīðe, Ll. Th. i. 236, 27. Ic beóde þ hý fylstan þām biscopum tō Godes gerihtum and tō mīnum kynescipe and tō ealles folces þearfe, Cht. E. 230, 17: Wlfst. 268, 2: 295, 3: Ll. Th. ii. 312, 39. Ðām smeá-wyrhtum hē sceal tō tōlan fylstan, Angl. ix. 263, 17. Fylstan him tō þæs cynges freóndscipe, Chr. 1046; P. 169, 1. (3 a) without dat. of person:—Gē fylstað on unriht wið sceatte and nellað tō rihte *ye help unjustly for a bribe, and will not help* (men) *to get justice*, Wlfst. 46, 27. Tō ciricbōte sceal eall folc fylstan, Ll. Th. i. 410, 12. Gif se landrīca nelle tō steóre filstan, ii. 298, 19: i. 250, 6. Ne scylan hyg ǽnig unriht geþafian ac tō ǽlcan rihte geornlīce fylstan, ii. 310, 19.

**fylstend,** es; *m. A helper:*—God mīn fylstend mīn *Deus meus adiutor meus*, Ps. L. 17, 3: 61, 9. v. ge-fylstend.

**fỹlþ.** *Add:* (1) physical:—Fỹlþ *putor*, i. *fetor*, An. Ox. 3323: *putredo*, Scint. 38, 19. Of fỹlþum and of fenne *sordibus ac luto*, Germ. 388, 12. Horslice fỹlþu *putidos* (*ergastuli*) *squaloris*, An. Ox. 1790. (2) figurative, *moral impurity, foul practice*:—Seó fūle *fornicatio*, seó hātte fỹlðe on Englisc, Wlfst. 249, 8. Fỹlþe (*ab omni spurcitiae*) *sentina*, An. Ox. 666. Tō wiþersacunge fỹlþe *ad apostasiae volutabrum*, 3041. Þās fūlan wuhta þū sceoldest āwurpan of ðīnum rīce, ðý lǽs þe hī mid heora fỹlðe ūs ealle besmīton, Hml. Th. ii. 488, 13. Ic ætwand þæs deófles fỹlðe, Hml. S. 7, 229: 23, 174. Ðā fỹlðe ādōn of þām Godes temple þe Antiochus þǽr ārǽran hēt on hǽðene wīsan, 25, 378. Wið forliger and wið ǽghwilce fỹlðe, Wlfst. 115, 10. Maþelunge fỹlþe *garrulitatis incestum*, An. Ox. 2948. Fỹlþa *spurcalia*, 2060. Hē geclǽnsod hæfde Godes templ fram eallum þām fỹlðum þe hē þǽr ārǽrde, Hml. S. 25, 538. [*O. L. Ger.* fūlitha *putredo*: *O. H. Ger.* fūlida *putredo, putor, spurcitia*.]

**fynde.** *Add:* v. earfoþ-, īþ-, unge-fynde.

**fyndel,** e; *f. A device, invention:*—Tō fyndele *ad inventionem*, Scint. 108, 12. Gyf hī hyra fyndele (*adinuentionem*) þrīstfulle gecuran, Angl. xiii. 369, 54.

**-fyndig.** v. ge-fyndig: **fynegian.** *Add:* v. ge-fynegian: **fynig;** *adj. Add:* [v. *N. E. D.* fenny.]

**fynig,** es; *n. A moist, marshy place:*—Tō ðām ealdan ādfini; of ðām finie, C. D. v. 194, 3. Tō Cleran finie, 195, 10. [Cf. *N. E. D.* finny, finewy.] v. ād-, popul-fynig; fenw.

**fyniht;** *adj. Produced in marshy, fenny places:*—Mettas þe gōd blōd wyrceað, swā swā sint scilfixas finihte, Lch. ii. 244, 25. [Cf. He must abstaine from maryshe fyshes and fennie, *N. E. D. s.v.* fenny.]

**fynt** (?), es; *m. A fount, spring* (?):—Of fintes leáge, Cht. Crw. 7, 41, 54. Cf. funta.

**fỹr.** v. feor.

**fỹr.** *Add:* (1) *fire*:—Ðonne mon beám on wuda forbærne, ... geselle. .ɪx. scill., for þām þe fýr bið þeóf ... sió æx bið melda, nalles þeóf, Ll. Th. i. 128, 19. On þissum geáre atýwde þ wilde fỹr (v. wilde, IV), Chr. 1032; P. 159, 4. Fỹr oððe fýres god *Vulcanus*, Wrt. Voc. ii. 95, 6. Rīcu forheregian swā swā fýres lēg dēð drīgne hǽþfeld, Bt. 16, 1; F. 50, 4. Wolcn on fýres gelīcnesse, Chr. 979; P. 122, 25. Ðā burh hī mid fýre ontendan woldon, 994; P. 129, 1. Þā Walas flugon þā Englas swā fýr, 473; P. 14, 5. Þā lǽgdon hī fýr on *they set fire to the minster*, 1070; P. 205, 23. Hǽðenscipe bið þ man weorðige fýr oþþe flōd, Ll. Th. i. 378, 19. (1 a) *fire* as one of the four elements:—Feówer gesceafta ... feówrþe is fýr ... þ fýr is yfemest ofer eallum þyssum woruldgesceaftum, Bt. 33, 4; F. 128, 30–38. Ūre līchoma wæs gesceapen of feówer gesceaftum, of eorþan and of fýre and of wætere and of lyfte, Bl. H. 35, 13. (1 b) *fire* of hell:—Manna gītsung is swā byrnende swā þ fýr on þǽre helle, Bt. 15; F. 48, 19. On þām ēcan fýre mid deófle, C. D. iv. 52, 9. On ēce fýr sendan, Bl. H. 125, 2. (1 c) in fýre *wesan to be on fire*:—Gelamp hit þ þ hūs eall wæs in fýre *contigit culmen domus subitaneis flammis impleri*, Bd. 3, 10; Sch. 234, 8 note. (2) *a fire, fuel in a state of combustion*:—Fýr *haec pira*, An. Ox. 18 b, 76. Gif fýr sié ontended rýt tō bærnenne, gebēte þone æfwerdelsan sē þ fýr ontent, Ll. Th. i. 50, 27. Nān mann ne cume innon þǽre ciricean siþþan man þ fýr in byrð þe man þ ordāl mid hǽtan sceal, 226, 10. Wǽron þā cnihtas on þ fýr (fēr, v. l.) onsended; þā ne onhrān þ fýr him nō, Mart. H. 24, 3. Hine man on þ fýr wearp, Bt. 7, 3; F. 22, 12. Hē geseah feówer ormǽte fýr ātende ... 'þās

feówer fýr ontendað ealne middaneard,' Hml Th. ii. 338, 7. Geseón on smēðum felda fela fýra byrnan, Ors. 3, 11; S. 142, 15: Nar. 13, 3: 12, 31. (2 a) *a fire on a hearth*:—Fýre (*ante*) *larem*, An. Ox. 4652. Fýrum *laribus*, fýr *larem*, Wrt. Voc. ii. 53, 13, 14. (2 b) *a piece of burning material*:—Fýrum, brandum (*rogi*) *torribus*, i. *ignibus*, An. Ox. 3520. Fýrum āda *globis flammarum*, 3555. (3) *fire from heaven, lightning*:—Hwīlum God sendeþ his engla gāstas, hwīlum hē sendeþ þurh fýres lēg, Bl. H. 203, 15. Sende Drihten fýr of heofenum, 153, 29. (4) *a disease*:—Wylde fýr *erisipilas*, Wrt. Voc. i. 20, 3. v. beácen-, cwic-fýr.

**fyran to go.** Dele.

**fỹran, fỹrian;** *p. de, ede To furrow, cut with a ploughshare* (lit. and fig.):—Fýreð *obliquat* (*ferri stimulus* ... *sulcos obliquat ad instar aratri*, Ald. 263, 12. The passage occurs in a riddle, 'De pugillaribus'), Wrt. Voc. ii. 64, 67. Þ scer tungan ūre fýrian (*printed* scyrian, *but see* An. Ox. 2492 note) nā durre eorþan heortan īremedre *ut uomer linguae nostrae proscindere non audeat terram cordis alieni*, Scint. 124, 5. Ongeán fīrigende hand *manus resulcans, iterum aperiens*, An. Ox. 46, 49. [*O. H. Ger.* fur[h]en *sulcare*.] v. ge-fýran (-ian); -fýrede, fūrian.

**fỹr-bǽr.** Substitute: **fỹr-bǽre;** *adj. Fire-bearing, fiery*:—Fýrbǽrelīga ræscetunga *igniferas fulminum coruscationes*, An. Ox. 4421: 2, 327.

**fỹr-bēta.** *Add:*—Fýrbēta *focarius*, Wrt. Voc. ii. 149, 80.

**fyrclian.** Substitute: v. twi-fyrclede.

**fỹr-crūce,** an; *f. A cooking-vessel, kettle*:—Fýrcrūce *cucuma*, Txts. 55, 621: *cucuma*, i. *cacabus, caldarium*, An. Ox. 44, 1.

**fyrd, fyrd-.** v. fird, fird-: **fyrderung.** Dele, and see fyrþrung: **fyrdinga.** Dele: **fyrdrian.** v. firdian: **fyrd-tiber.** v. fird-tiber: **-fýre** (-i, -o). v. þweorh-furh: **-fỹrede.** v. twi-, þri-fýrede; fýrian.

**fỹren.** *Add:* (1) *composed of fire, made of fire, hring globus ignis* Ors. 5, 10; S. 234, 3. Blōdig regn and fýren, Bl. H. 93, 3. 'Send mē þīnne engel on fýrenum wolcne' ... Fýren wolc[n] āstāh of heofonum, 245, 30. On anlīcnesse fýrenra lēgea, 135, 3. (2) *on fire, flaming, burning.* (Take here fýren cylle, pecelle *in Dict.*):—Gelamp hit þ þ hūs eall wæs innan fýren and ongan semninga byrnan *contigit culmen domus subitaneis flammis impleri*, Bd. 3, 10; Sch. 234, 8. Geteald tō þǽre fýrenan eá and tō þǽm īsenan hōce ... getogen mid þon īsnan hōce on þǽre picenan eá ... hī hine besencton on þā fýrenan eá, Bl. H. 43, 24–30. On þǽre fýrenan helle, 45, 5. Fýrenum ādum *flammiuomis* (i. *ardentibus*) *torribus*, An. Ox. 4024. (3) of a dart, *bearing fire*:—Flugon þā lēgetu swylca fýrene strǽlas ... mid þǽm fýrenum strǽlum ācweald, Bl. H. 203, 9, 28. Hē gedēð his flān fýrena, Ps. Th. 7, 13. (4) *burning, red-hot*:—Hié hine hæfdon geþreátodne mid fýrenum racentum, Bl. H. 43, 31. (5) figurative:—Is þīn āgen sprǽc innan fýren *ignitum eloquium tuum*, Ps. Th. 118, 140: Ps. Srt. 118, 140. [*O. H. Ger.* fiurīn *igneus, ignifer, ignitus*.]

**fỹren-full.** *Add:*—Fýrenfulle *igneum*, Hpt. Gl. 427, 19.

**fỹr-feaxe.** Substitute: **fỹr-feaxen;** *adj. Having locks of flame*:—Se fýrfeaxna [engel *angelus*] *ignicomis* (Ald. 146, 35), Wrt. Voc. ii. 90, 31: 47, 17.

**fỹr-fōda,** an; *m. Fire-food, fuel*:—Fīrfōdan *malleoli*, An. Ox. 7, 88.

**fỹr-gearwunge.** Substitute: **fỹr-gearwung,** e; *f. Preparation with fire, cooking*:—Fýrgearwungum *focularibus* (cf. cocturam aut assaturam alimentorum in focularibus praeparatam, Ald. 51, 33), Wrt. Voc. ii. 34, 34.

**fỹr-gebeorh** (-g), es; *n. A fire-screen*:—Fýrgebeorh, Angl. ix. 265, 1.

**fyrgende.** v. firenian: **fyrh** *a fir* (?). v. furh.

**fỹr-hāt.** *Add:*—Fýrh[āt] *torrida*, An. Ox. 56, 203. [v. *N. E. D.* fire-hot.]

**fỹr-hole.** Dele, and see fýr-þolle: **fyrht** *divination*. v. friht.

**fyrhtan.** *Add;* , fyrhtian. I. *to make afraid*:—Fyrhtaþ, gebrēgþ *consternat*, i. *perterritat*, Wrt. Voc. ii. 133, 66. Þæt hī ne fyrhte þæt gewin ðæs sīðfætes, Bd. 1, 23; Sch. 50, 3. Fyrhtede wērun *conterriti*, Lk. R. 24, 37. II. *to become afraid*. v. Rtl. 102, 21 (*in Dict.*). [*Goth.* faurhtjan *to fear*: *O. Frs.* fruchte: *O. Sax.* forhtian: *O. H. Ger.* furhten.] v. ge-fyrht(i)an.

**fyrhþ,** e; *f.:* fyrhþe, es; *n. A wood, wooded country:*—Ðet firhde bituihn longanleág and ðem sūðtūne, C. D. i. 261, 9. West andlang ðæs fyrhðes, Cht. E. 158, 19. Oþ cincges firhþe, of cincges fyrhþe:—andlang strǽte on geriht oð cincges fyrhþe, C. D. ii. 265, 28–33. Æt ðǽre baran fyrhðe, iii. 130, 31. On ðā ferhðe forwearde, v. 382, 2. ¶ Locis siluaticis ad Fleferth, ii. 160, 9. [v. *N. E. D.* frith.] v. ge-fyrhþe.

**fyrhtnes.** *Add:* v. wæter-fyrhtness.

**fyrhto** (-u). *Add:*—Gif ðū hafast mid þē wulfes hrycghǽr on sīðfæte, būtan fyrhtu þū ðone sīð gefremest, Lch. i. 360, 22. Blindre fyrhto *ceca formidine*, Wrt. Voc. ii. 130, 81. Þe fyrhto þæs tintreglican wītes *de uerrore futuri judicii*, Bd. 4, 24; Sch. 487, 19. Hē mid mycelre fyrhte wæs geslegen, Guth. 88, 18. v. ge-fyrhto.

**fỹr-hús.** Substitute: *a room with a fire*:—Būr *camera*, fýrhús

*caminatum*, Wrt. Voc. i. 58, 7. Fýrhūses (*printed* -hýses) hlĭwing *caumene refugium*, Angl. xiii. 397, 461. [v. *N. E. D.* fire-house.]

fȳrian *to make a furrow*. v. fýran: fyrle. v. firl[u]: fyrlen. v. firlen: fyrm. v. firm: fyrmdig. v. frimdig.

fyrmest; *adj. In* l. 5 *for* Cot. 153 *substitute* Wrt. Voc. ii. 67, 7, *and add*: I. marking order in time:—Hē tō fulluhte heora fyrmest beáh, Hml. S. 10, 150. Seó bōc ys gehāten Genesis, ... for þām þe heó ys firmest bōca, Ælfc. Gen. Thw. 2, 34. II. marking order in rank, importance. (1) of persons:—Maurus wæs fyrmest muneca tō đām mǣran Benedicte, Hml. S. 6, 51. Nembroð fyrmest wæs æt þēre getimbrunge þēre byrig Babilonian *Nemroth condendae Babyloniae auctor exstiterat*, Angl. vii. 40, 380. 'On þām gefērscipe wǣran þā fyrmestan Mellitus, ... Rufianus, Chr. 995; P. 128, 32. (2) of things:—On þām fyrmestum stōwum ealles his anwealdes, Lch. iii. 440, 12. II. marking order in merit, *excellent*:—Hū se lāreów sceal beón on his weorcum fyrest (*praecipuus*). Se lāreów sceal bión on his weorcum heálic (*praecipuus*), Past. 81, 1.

fyrmest; *adv. Add*: I. of position:—Wæs feorhbealu fǣgum, sē þe fyrmest læg, B. 2077. Hē on þām folce fyrmest eóde, By. 323. I a. where position marks importance:—Hī sēcað đæt hié fyrmest hlynigen æt ǣfengiefium, Past. 27, 7. II. of rank:—þā þe under Alexandre fyrmest wǣron, Ors. 3, 11; S. 142, 18. III. marking highest degree of excellence, completeness:—Hū hē Gode fyrmest gecwēman mæge *how he may best please God*, Wlfst. 280, 18. Hū ic Crístendōm ǣfre mihte fyrmest ārǣran, Ll. Lbmn. 269, 12. ¶ swā (forþ, mycel) swā ... fyrmest as (*far, much*) as ... *ever possible*:—Swā swā ic fyrmæst mæg *quantum possum*, Solil. H. 53, 21. Swā swā hē būtan synne fyrmest mæge *in quantum sine peccato valet*, Past. 451, 24. Swā micel swā wē hit fyrmest witon *to the best of our knowledge; in quantum cognitioni hominis conceditur*, Ors. 1, 1; S. 14, 28. Hæfþ hē his sceoppendes onlícnesse swā forþ swā ǣnegu gesceaft fyrmest mæg hiere sceppendes onlícnesse habban *he hath his Creator's image as far as any creature can possibly have its Creator's image*, Bt. 14, 2; F. 44, 28. þ his grið stande swā forð swā hit fyrmest stōd on his yldrena dagum (*as well as ever it stood in his ancestor's days*), Ll. Th. i. 292, 3. Eal ic him gelǣste, swā forð swā uncre wordgecwydu fyrmest wǣron *I have carried out our agreement in every particular*, 182, 12. Man sealde Godwine his eorldōm swā full and swā forð swā hē fyrmest āhte *they gave Godwin his earldom with all the rights and powers that he had ever possessed*, Chr. 1052; P. 180, 30.

fyrmþ. v. firmþ.

fyrn; *adv. Add*:—Fyrn *olim*, Wrt. Voc. ii. 64, 75. Đā đe wǣron forðfērede for hund geárum oððon gyt fyrnor (firnor, *v. l.*), Wlfst. 96, 7.

fyrn-. v. firen-.

fyrn-dagas. *Add*:—Swíðe eald feoh þe man on fyrndagum slōh, Hml. S. 23, 614. v. gēfyrn-dagas.

fyrn-geár. *Add*: [(1) *a past year*. v. Dict.] (2) *the preceding year* (cf. Quam gibod Godes fernun gēre, Hēl. 217):—Gif þū wille witan hū eald se mōna wǣre fyrngeáre on þysne dæg, Lch. iii. 228, 9, 14. [þe lost of uernyere, Ayenb. 92, 4.]

fyrn-geára. *l.* fyrn geára: fyrnhicge. v. firenicge: -fyrn-ness. v. ge-fyrnness.

fȳr-panne. *Add*:—Fýrpannæ (-ponne) *vel* herth *arula*, Txts. 36, 5. Fýrpanne, Wrt. Voc. ii. 6, 35: i. 66, 37. [v. *N. E. D.* fire-pan. *O. L. Ger.* fiur-panna *arula*.]

fȳr-ræce (?), an; *f. An implement for removing ashes from a fire-place*:—Ferrece (=? fýrræce) *vatilla*, Wrt. Voc. i. 287, 7. Cf. fýr-scofl.

fyrs *furze. Add*:—Fyres *ruscus*, Wrt. Voc. i. 285, 48. Fyrrsum *ramnis*, An. Ox. 23, 12.

fȳr-scofl, e; *f. For* Cot. 24 *substitute* Wrt. Voc. ii. 11, 16, *and add*: Cf. glēd-scofl, fýr-ræce.

fyrs-gāra, an; *m. A triangular piece of land covered with furze*:—On đane fyrsgāran, C. D. iv. 8, 35.

fyrsian. v. firsian.

fyrs-íg, e; *f. An island on which furze grows*:—On Beferíge, đonne on Fyrsíge, C. D. v. 300, 17.

fyrs-leáh *a lea on which furze grows*:—Be norðan fýrsleáge, swā of norðenwardre fyrsleáge, C. D. v. 232, 30.

fȳr-smeortende. *Add: smarting like a burn.* The Latin has *ignitos ciniphes.*

fyrsn. v. firsn.

fyrs-penn, es; *m. A pen or fold made of furze* (?):—On fyrspenn; of fyrspenne, Cht. E. 266, 21.

fyrs-rǣw, e; *f. A row or fence of furze*:—On āne firesrēwe, C. D. vi. 230, 30.

fyrs-sceaga (?), an; *m. A furze-thicket* (?):—Onbūtan færsscagan on đā díc đæt hit cymð tō đǣre rōdæ, C. D. iii. 229, 29.

fyrst *a threshold. Dele, and see first:* fyrst *time*. v. first.

fyrst; *adj. For* 'First ... Exod. 399' *substitute*: (1) *first, foremost in position*:—Hē wæs mid þǣm fyrstum mannum on þǣm lande *he*

*was among the first men in the country*, Ors. 1, 1; S. 18, 13. (2) *foremost in virtue or worth, best, of great excellence*:—Hū se lāreów sceal beón on his weorcum fyrest (*praecipuus*). Se lāreów sceal beón on his weorcum heálic (*praecipuus*), Past. 80, 1. Tō þām meðelstede gelǣdde Abraham Isaac ..., fyrst ferhðbana; nō þý fæg[en]ra wæs, wolde líge gesyllan beorna sēlost his swǣsne sunu tō sigetibre *to the meeting-place led Abraham Isaac ..., noble destroyer of life; not the more joyous was he (i. e. he was sorely troubled), to the flames would the best of men give his dear son as a sacrifice*, Exod. 399.

fȳr-stān. *Add*:—Fýrstān, flint *petra focaria*, Wrt. Voc. ii. 68, 8. [v. *N. E. D.* fire-stone.]

fyrstig. *Add*: v. forstig.

fȳr-tang, e; *f. Fire-tongs*:—Hē sceal fela andlōmena tō hūsan habban ... fýrtange, Angl. ix. 263, 9.

-fyrþan. v. ā-fyrþan: fýrþling. v. feórþling.

fȳr-þolle? *Substitute*: fýr-polle, an; *f.* I. *apparatus for cooking, fryingpan* (v. þolle), *oven*:—þū setst hig swā swā ofen (fýrþolle, MS. T.) fýres *pones eos ut clibanum ignis*, Ps. Spl. 20, 9. II. *apparatus for torture*; catasta (Catastae, genus tormenti, i. e. lecti ferrei, quibus impositi martyres, ignis supponebatur, Du Cange):—Hyrdla, fýrþollena *catastarum*, An. Ox. 4485: catastarum, i. eculei, 2, 340.

fyrþran. *Add*:—Fyrþru *proveho*, Wrt. Voc. ii. 118, 31. þū mīnne naman and anwald friþast and fyrþrast, Lch. iii. 436, 27. Hē tō geleáfan gebígde ungerīm folces, and fyrðrode cyrcan, and preóstas gehādode tō đæs Hǣlendes biggengum, Hml. S. 36, 112 : Lch. iii. 438, 3. Mē đincð þæt mē nān þing ne mage þæs āmærran þæt ic hyt ne firðrige and fremme *cum alia nulla re crederem commoveri*, Solil. H. 33, 2. Ne tǣce wē nā ... þæt hē leahtras fyrðrige and weaxan lǣte *non dicimus ut permittat nutriri vitia*, R. Ben. 121, 7. þæt hē Godes cyrcean fyrðrie and frydie, Wlfst. 266, 16. Hē hit forseah, sē þe hit fyrþran sceolde æfter hiera āgnum gewunan, Ors. 4, 12; S. 210, 7. Unriht ālecgan and rihtwīsnysse fyrðrian, Hml. Th. ii. 78, 1: Hml. S. 19, 240. ¶ governing a clause:—Fyrðrige Ōslāc eorl þ þis stande, Ll. Th. i. 278, 5. [*O. H. Ger.* furdren.]

fyrþriend, es; *m. One who promotes, advances, &c., a patron*:—God eallum þām þe wel þencað simle is fultum and firþriend, C. D. B. ii. 389, 17.

fyrþringnes. *Add after* promotio:—Fyrþringnes *exaltatio bonorum*.

fyrþrung. *Add*:—For crístendōmes fyrðrunge, Wlfst. 176, 2. Ic on Rōme be þes pāpan fyrþrunge and leáfe mynster geworhte, Cht. Th. 116, 29. Weder hlūttor gesihð, ceápes ferðrunge hit getācnað, Lch. iii. 198, 17. Buccan gesihð, ferðrunge getācnað, 206, 2. v. scip-fyrþrung.

fyrþung. v. scip-fyrþung.

fȳr-tor. *For* Cot. 93 *substitute*:—*Farus*, beácanstān, *in promontoria rupis posita*, i. fýrtor, Wrt. Voc. ii. 76, 14. *Farus, Grecum est nomen, nam fos, lux, oros autem visio, apud eos nominatur, hinc compositum nomen est fari*, id est fýrtor, 39, 64.

fyrwet. v. firwit: fȳsian. y. físian.

fȳst. *Add*:—Colapsus, i. *colafus*, *pugnus* fýst *vel tarastrus*, Wrt. Voc. ii. 134, 45. Físt [*in* Wülck. Gl. 291, 17 *it is printed* fýsð], i. 64, 74. Gif man ōðerne mid fýste in naso slæhð .iii. scill. gebēte, Ll. Th. i. 16, 17. þanne ic sleá swíðe mid fýste, breóst mīne beáte *ego percutiam pugnis pectora*, Dōm. L. 29 : 160. Ongan heó þerscan heó sylfe mid hire fýste (mid fýstum *v. l.*) ge eác mid hire brādum handum *cum semetipsam alapis pugnisque tunderet*, Gr. D. 68, 28. Gif þū gyrde habban wille, þonne wege þīne fýst swylce þū swingan wille, Tech. ii. 122, 11. Fýstum *pugillis*, i. *colaphis*, An. Ox. 4694.

fȳst-gebeát. *Substitute*: *Hitting with the fist, fisticuffs*:—'Tō gemōtum and tō gecidum and tō íersunga and tō fýstgebeáte gē fæstað' ... đæt fýstgebeát belimpð tō ierre '*in judicia et rixas jejunatis, et percutitis pugnis*,' ... *pugnus pertinet ad iram*, Past. 314, 3-5.

-fȳstlian. v. ge-fýstlian: fýst-slǣgen. *For* Cot. 79 *substitute* Wrt. Voc. ii. 32, 2 : fyþer. v. fiþer.

fyxe, an; *f. A she-fox, vixen*:—Đǣr fyxan díc tō brōce gæð, C. D. ii. 29, 1.

fyxen; *adj.* v. fixen *in Dict., and add*: [*O. H. Ger.* fuhsīn (fell) *vulpinum.*]

# G

gabban, gabbung, gabere. *Dele.*

gabote. *Add*:—Gabutan (gauutan, Corp. Gl. H. 87, 27, *and see note on the word at* p. xlii *where the following Latin glosses are quoted*, 'parapsis, gabata vel catinum' 'pisi, gavata (*v. l.* gabata) vel patina') *parabsides*, Ep. Gl. 18 f, 25. [*O. H. Ger.* gebeta(-ita, -iza) *catinum gavata, vasis.* From Latin.]

gabul-roid. *l.* -rond, *and dele* '*a line ... staff.*'

gád *a goad. Add*:—Gaad *stiga*, Wrt. Voc. ii. 121, 43. Gǎd *cuspis*, 17, 4. Derigendlic bið đē þæt þū spurne ongeán þā gāde (*durum est tibi contra stimulum calcitrare*). Gif se oxa spyrnð ongeán đā gād, hit dereð him sylfum, Hml. Th. i. 390, 9 : 386, 9.

**gaderian.** *Add*: I. *to join, unite*:—Đá hwíle þe sió sáwl and se líchoma gederode beóþ, Bt. 35, 1; F. 156, 4. I a. *of matrimonial union.* v. gaderscipe:—Æt þám giftan mæssepreóst sceal mid Godes bletsunge heora gesomnunge gederian, Ll. Th. i. 256, 7. II. *to bring together* persons:—Gaderiađ eów tó þá þe Godes æ lufiađ, and wrecađ eówer folc on đám fúlum hæđenum *take unto you all those that observe the law, and avenge ye the wrong of your people* (1 Macc. 2, 67), Hml. S. 25, 268. Hé ongan gadrian folc ofer eall his eorldóm, Chr. 1052; P. 175, 8. II a. *used reflexively or intransitively*:—Ær þám þe hé and þæt folc hý gaderade, Ors. 3, 9; Bos. 65, 29. Se cing cóm and men gadorodon ongeán, Chr. 1052; P. 176, 35. III. *to bring together* things, *collect* to one place, *accumulate, amass*:—Hí (*worldly goods*) him þincaþ deóre, for þám þú hí gaderast and heltst on þínum horde . . . þú gæderast máre þonne þú þurfe, Bt. 14, 2; F. 44, 3–8. Biþ hlíseádigra sé đe hit selþ đonne sé þe hit gaderaþ . . . ge eác þá welan beóþ hlíseádigran þonne þonne hié mon selþ þonne hié beón þonne hié mon gadraþ and healt, 13; F. 38, 11–15. Mid đý đe hé sceolde his gestreón tóweorpan, mid đý hé hié gadrađ, Past. 55, 11. Đæt mód gæderađ him selfum tó lofe eall đæt gód . . . *sibi arrogare incipit omne bonum, quod* . . . , 463, 34. Þonne feor and neáh hé (*the Phénix*) þá swētestan somnađ and gædrađ wyrta and wudubléda tó þám eardstede *colligit hinc succos et odores divite silva*, Ph. 193. Hé him of hira ceasterwarena forđrycnesse gestreón gaderiađ, Ll. Lbmn. 475, 27. III a. *of produce, to bring* for storing, *garner*:—Đone hwǽtte geadrias in berern mín *triticum congregate in horreum meum*, Mt. L. 13, 30. Fela tilđa hám gæderian, Angl. ix. 261, 17. III b. *used absolutely*:—Seó grundléase swelgend hǽfđ swíþe manegu wēste holu on tó gadrianne (-enne, *v. l.*), Bt. 7, 4; F. 22, 33. IV. *to gather* fruit, crops, harvest, &c. (lit. and fig.):—Se eorþlica anweald nǽfre ne sǽwþ þá cræftas, ac lisþ and gadraþ unþeáwas, Bt. 27, 1; F. 94, 25. Þonne gē þone coccel gadriađ (geadrias, L.) *colligentes zizania*, Mt. 13, 29. Hí gadriađ (geadriges, L.) of his ríce ealle gedrēfednesse, 41. Wē geadredon đá *colligimus ea*, Mt. L. 13, 28. IV a. *of the action of a net*:—Gelíc ásendum nette on sǽ and of ǽlcum fisccynne gadrigendum (geadrigende, L., *congreganti*), Mt. 13, 47. V. *to gather* literary material, *compile*:—Of đǽre béc þe Bēda gesette and gaderode of manegra wísra lǽreówa bócum, Lch. iii. 232, 4.

**gaderigend-líc.** *For* 'Som. . . . Lye' *substitute*:—*Congregativa* (*adverbia*) syndon gadrigendlíce (gaderigendllíce, *v. l.*), *simul samod*, Ælfc. Gr. Z. 229, 4.

**gader-scype.** *Substitute*: **gader-scipe** (**gæder-**), es; *m. Union, the union of marriage*:—Gæderscipe *jugalitas*, i. *matrimonium*, Hpt. Gl. 438, 36. v. ge-gaderscipe, gaderian; I a.

**gader-tang, gæder-teng.** *l.* -tenge, *and add*: *Contiguous, conjoint, in contact or connexion*:—Gǽdertangne *conjunctim* (-*um*?), Wrt. Voc. ii. 136, 33. (1) *of material things*:—Đá landgemǽro đæsse búrlandes tó Abbendúne, đæt is gadertang on þreó genamod, đæt is Hengestes íg and Seofocanwyrđ and Wíhthám (i. e. *the land lies altogether but it is divided into three parts, each with its own name*), C. D. v. 401, 25. (1 a) *with dat.*:—Se milte biđ emlang and gædertenge þǽre wambe, Lch. ii. 242, 15. Se maga biþ neáh þǽre heortan . . . and geadortenge (*connected with*) þám bræg[en]e, 176, 3. (2) *of non-material things, continuous*:—Sóþe lufe gædertenge hæbbende *caritatem continuam habentes*, Scint. I, 4. Þurh seofen gædertange (*printed* -lange) dagas *per septem continuos dies*, Angl. xiii. 444, 1127.

**gadertangnes.** *Add*:—Hí líchaman fæstena mid gædertangnysse þreágeađ *corpus jejunium continuatione castigant*, Scint. 52, 15.

**gaderung, gæderung.** *Add*: I. *a joining, union.* v. gaderian; I a:—Geadrung *copulam* (the bond of matrimony), Rtl. 109, 19. II. *an assembly.* v. gaderian; II:—Cwæđ hé beforan ealre þǽre gaderunge: 'Gē Tharsysce ceastergewaran . . . ,' Ap. Th. 26, 2. Ætforan þáre engelican gæderunge *ante angelicum consessum*, Au. Ox. 1753. III. *gathering* of herbs:—Wyrta gaderunge mid galdre begán *herbarum collectionem cum incantatione facere*, Ll. Th. ii. 190, 33. III a. *gathering* of crops, fruit, &c. v. gaderian; IV:—Hærfest, bóceras getrahtniađ þæne naman for þǽre rípunge ođđe for þǽre gaderunge, Angl. viii. 312, 27. IV. *a gathering of words, text*:—Geadrung *textu*, Mt. p. 10, 17. v. stán-gaderung.

**gader-wist** *a being together, company. Take here* **gador-wist** *in Dict., and add*:—Gaderwiste *contubernium*, Wrt. Voc. ii. 17, 54. Gadorwiste *contuberniam* (-*um*? *or* -*a*? v. Mk. 6, 39, to which the gloss belongs), 73, 33. v. ge-gaderwist.

**gadinca.** *Substitute*: **gadinca**, an; *m. A wether sheep*:—Gadinca *vel* hnoc *mutinus* (in a list of animals; cf. *mutinae* carnes, eaedem q. vervecinae, Migne), Wrt. Voc. i. 23, 49. Gadinca *mutinus*, ii. 58, 14.

**gád-íren,** es; *n. A goad*:—Hé sceal habban gádíren, Angl. ix. 263, 4. v. gád-ísen.

**gád-ísen.** *Add*: Cf. gád-íren: **gador-wist.** v. gader-wist.

**gædeling.** *For* 'A companion . . . Dan. 422' *substitute*: *A kinsman, relative*:—Geaduling *fratuelis*, Wrt. Voc. ii. 109, 15: *patruelis*, 116,

26. His gædelinges (*uncle's*) gūđgewǽdu, B. 2617. Gewát him se gōda mid his gædelingum, B. 2949. Geþenc . . . hwá þá gyfe sealde gingum gædelingum (*Shadrach, &c.*), Dan. 422.

**gædere.** *Add*: v. ge-gædere: **gæder-lang.** v. gader-tang: **gæfel** *a fork.* v. gafol: **gǽgan, gǽgednes.** v. for-, ofer-gǽgan, -gǽgednes: **gǽging.** v. for-gǽging: **gǽgl-bǽrnes.** v. gagol-bǽrnes: **gǽglisc.** v. gagolisc: **gǽgn-.** v. geán-.

**gægne**; *adv. Concisely, briefly*:—Gǽgne *compendiose, breviter*, Wrt. Voc. ii. 132, 57. [Cf. Icel. gagn-orđr *speaking shortly, to the point.*] v. gēn; *adj.*

**gǽl[e?].** v. gál: **gǽlæþ.** *Dele, and see* ge-lǽd.

**gǽlan.** *Add*: (1) *to delay*:—For đǽm gif ús ne lyst đǽra ǽrrena yfela đe wē ǽr worhton, đonne ne gǽld ús nán đing te fullfremmanne đá gódan weorc đe wē nú wyrcead *nisi enim retro aspicerent, erga coeptum studium nullo torpore languerent*, Past. 445, 29. Đ́ỹ lǽs hine ǽnig wuht gǽlde ungearowes *ut tarditas nulla generetur*, 171, 23. (2) *to dupe*:—Gǽl (*nec*) *lactes* (*quemquam labiis tuis*), Kent. Gl. 942. [By þyse bonke3 þer I con gele, Allit. Pms. 28, 930.] v. tó-gǽlan.

**gǽleþ** *catesta.* v. ge-lǽd.

**gǽling,** e; *f. Delay*:—Geđencan ne con hwæt him losađ on đǽre gǽlinge đc hē đá hwíle ámierred *he cannot consider what loss he suffers in the delay in which he wastes the time*, Past. 39, 1.

**gǽls,** e; *f. Lust, voluptuousness*:—Lícamlicere gǽlse *carnalis luxus*, An. Ox. 611. v. gǽls-líc, *and next word.*

**gǽlsa.** *Add*: lust:—Ǽlc gǽlsa scyldig *scelerata libido*, Dóm. L. 237. Mid sticelum gǽlsan *luxuriae stimulis*, 179. þá þe đá eorđlican grǽdignysse and gǽlsan ungefóhlíce fremmađ *qui luxuria et libidine pascitur et delectatur*, Angl. vii. 26, 252: Wlfst. 166, 29. Ámyrran gemyndum módes gǽlsan, Mód. 11. Gǽlsum *libidinibus*, Scint. 69, 15. *Loca humentia* . . . getǽcniađ þá fúlan gǽlsan, Wlfst. 249, 18. Se clǽna cniht hǽfde oferswíđod woruldlice gǽlsan, Hml. S. 4, 58: Hml. Th. ii. 70, 24. [Cf. A. R. gelsunge *luxury*: O. H. Ger. geilsunga.]

**gǽlsa,** an; *m. A glutton*; fig. *one who is inordinately fond of* a pursuit:—Gif mann biđ ǽkenned on xxvi nihta ealdne mōnan, sē biđ weorces gǽlsa (*he will be a glutton of work*), Lch. iii. 158, 15. [Cf. O. H. Ger. geilisōn *luxuriare*.]

**gǽls-líc**; *adj. Producing wantonness or excess*:—Gǽlslic þing is wín *luxuriosa res est vinum*, Nap. 27. v. gǽls.

**gǽlstre.** v. wyrt-gǽlstre: **gǽlp.** v. gielp: **gǽf-gǽlp.** v. â-gǽlwed [v. N. E. D. gally(-ow)]: **gǽnan.** v. tó-gǽnan: **gǽngang.** v. geán-gang: -**gǽre.** v. æt-gǽre: **gǽrede.** v. twi-gǽrede, gára, gár-æcer.

**gærs.** *Add*: I. *herbage*:—Híg ođđe gærs *foenum*, Wrt. Voc. i. 80, 45: ii. 35, 30. Graes, 108, 48. Grēne gærs *carrassinum* (*carpassinum*? cf. gærs-grēne), 13, 40. On þǽre stōwe wæs mycel gærs (gers, *v. l.*, gærs ł heig, L., hēg ł gers, R. *foenum*), Jn. 6, 10. Grǽse *gramine*, Wrt. Voc. ii. 41, 63. Gers ł hēg londes, Mt. L. 6, 30. Þ gærs (gers, R.), Lk. L. 12, 28. 'Underfō hē gærs.' Basilius underfēng þæt gærs đus cweđende: 'Đū ús sealdest nýtena andlyfene,' Hml. Th. i. 450, 5–8. II. *a herb, plant*:—Mára allum wyrtum ł gærsum (grasum, R.) *majus omnibus holeribus*, Mk. L. 4, 32. III. *the blade of corn*:—Miđ đý gewōx brord ł níwe gers, and wæstm worhte *cum crevisset herba, et fructum fecisset*, Mt. L. 13, 26. Eorđo wæstmas ǽrest gers (*herbam*), æfter đon đone đorn, Mk. R. L. 4, 28. IV. *pasture, grazing*:—Ⅲ. oxnum gers mid cyninges oxnum, C. D. ii. 64, 29. Hiora gemǽnan æceras ođđe gærs, Ll. Th. i. 128, 8: 434, 17. V. *the grass-covered ground*:—Ofer groenum grese (groene gers, L.), Mk. R. 6, 39: Mt. L. 14, 19.

**gærsama.** *Dele second passage.*

**gærs-grēne.** *For* 'gramineus . . . Lye' *substitute*:—Graesgroeni, gresgroeni *carpasini, carpassini*, Txts. 47, 393. Gærsgrēne *carbasini* (v. Ld. Gl. H. carbasini, color gemme, id est uiridis), Wrt. Voc. ii. 128, 55.

**gærs-hoppa** (græs-). *Add*: -hoppe, an; *f.*:—Gærshoppe *locusta*, Wrt. Voc. i. 281, 46: ii. 51, 60. Gershoppe, Ps. Srt. 108, 23. Gereshoppe, 104, 34.

**gærs-irþ,** e; *f. Ploughing done by the gebúr for his lord as an equivalent for an allowance of pasturage*:—Of đám tíman đe man ǽrest eređ of Martinus mæssan se gebúr sceal ǽlcre wucan erian .I. æcer . . . : tōeácan đám .Ⅲ. æceras tó bēne, and .Ⅲ. tó gærsyrđe. Gyf hē máran gærses beđyrfe, đonne earnige đæs swá him man đafige *he must plough two acres in return for the pasturage granted him. If he need more pasturage, he must earn it in such way as may be allowed him*, Ll. Th. i. 434, 17. [Cf. N. E. D. grass-earth.] Cf. gafol-irþ.

**gærs-stapa.** *Add*:—Hyllehama ođđe gærstapa *cicada*, Wrt. Voc. ii. 21, 54. [Cf. O. H. Ger. houui-stapfo *locusta*.]

**gærs-swín.** *Add*: *a swine paid for the privilege of using the lord's woods for the pasturage of swine.* Cf. cap. 49 of Ine's Laws concerning the illegal pasturing of swine, Ll. Th. i. 132, 11.

**gærs-tún.** *Add*:—Gærstún *crovitorium* (cf. *croutura locus septus*, *sepimentum*, Migne), Wrt. Voc. ii. 137, 14. *Pratum quod juxta*

civitatem habetur, quod Saxonice Garstone appellatur . . . This sunꝺe the gemeare thes gerstunlandes, and thære mede, C. D. B. ii. 349, 32–39. Forꝺ tó Ósmundæs garstúnæs hyrnan; ꝺonan forꝺ on bican gerstúnes hyrnan, i. 540, 2–3. On lyngærstún eástewerdne, iii. 55, 16. [v. N. E. D. garston.] v. hors-gærstún.

**gærstún-díc.** *Add :*—On becenes grestúndíc; ꝺet á be díc on Eccen, C. D. v. 330, 35.

**gærsum,** es; *m. n. Substitute :* **gærsuma**(-e), an; *m. (f.) :* **gær-sum,** es; *m. :* e; *f., and add* I. in a collective sense, *treasure :*—Heora gærsama fornéh eall losade, Chr. 1075; P. 209, 38. Gif hé ne sealde þe máre gersuman, 1047; P. 171, 14. Hí budon þám pápan mycelne garsuman and seolfer, Chr. 995; P. 130, 22. Gærsuman, 34. Ealne his gærsuman and his orf, 1078; P. 213, 28. Walþeóf bæd for-gyfenysse and beád gærsuman, 1076; P. 211, 34. II. *an article of value;* in pl. *treasures :*—Hé forleás ægꝺer ge men ge hors and feola his gersuma (unárímede gærsaman, *v. l.*), Chr. 1076; P. 213, 6. Hí be-reáfedan hí æt eallon þan gærsaman þe heó áhte, þá wæron unátellendlice (nam of hire eall þ heó áhte on golde and on seolfre and on unásecgend-licum þingum, *v. l.*), 1043; P. 163, 35. þám (Henry) hé becwæꝺ gersuman unáteallendlice, 1086; P. 219, 14. Hé sceáwode þ mádmehús, and þá gersuman þe his fæder gegaderode; þá wæron unásecgendlice ænie men hú mycel þær wæs gegaderod, on golde and on seolfre, and on faton, and on pællan, and on gimman, and on manige oꝺre deórwurꝺe þingon. Se cyng dælde þá gersuman for his fæder sáule, 1086; P. 222, 14–20. Hé hæfꝺ geinnod þ ær wæs geútod þurh Godes fultum . . . and þurh his gærsuma, Cht. Th. 428, 10. ¶ *The word translates* munus, *though this is used in the sense of office,* service :—Fram ælcere gærsuman woruldlicra brúcunga unmæne *ab omni munere secularium functionum immunes,* C. D. B. i. 154, 15.

**gærs-yrþ.** v. gærs-irþ : **gæst** *a guest.* v. gist : **gǽst** *spirit.* v. gást : **gǽstan.** *Add :* [v. N. E. D. gast.]

**gǽst-lic** (gæst-?); *adj. Terrible, ghastly :*—Ongitan sceal gleáw hæle hú gǽstlic biꝺ, þonne eall þisse worulde wela wéste stondeꝺ, Wand. 73. Cf. (?) gǽstan.

**gǽten.** *Add :* Mid gǽtenum smeruwe, Lch. i. 178, 18. [O. H. Ger. geizín *caprinus.*]

**gaf;** *adj. Dele, and see* gaf-sprǽc : -gaf; *n. See* ge-gaf : **gafelian.** v. gafolian.

**gafeluc.** *Add :*—Gafeluca *iaculo, sagitta,* Hpt.Gl. 432, 44. Gaflucas *catapultas, sagittas,* 405, 53. Gafelucas, arwan *catapultas,* 505, 56. Hí scuton mid gafelucum . . . oꝺ þ hé eall wæs beset mid heora scotungum swilce igles byrsta, Hml. S. 32, 116.

**gafol** *tribute. Add :* (1) in the following glosses :—Gedæbin gebil gedaebeni geabuli *debita pensio,* Txts. 56, 336. *Cesareum tributum, i. regalis* gafol, Wrt. Voc. ii. 131, 3. Gebles (geabules, gaebles) monung *exactio,* Txts. 60, 394. Gafules manung, Wrt. Voc. ii. 30, 10. Gafeles andfengend *numerarii,* 62, 34. Gaebuli, geabuli *aere alieno,* Txts. 42, 115. Gedéfum gafule *debita pensione,* Wrt. Voc. ii. 25, 23. (2) *pay-ment exacted by a stronger from a weaker people, by the conqueror from the conquered :*—On þisum geáre wæs þ gafol gelǽst ofer eall Angelcynn; þ wæs eallæ .lxxii þúsend punda, Chr. 1018; P. 155, 10. Man sceolde gafol gyldon þám flotan . . . Leófsig gesætte þet hí féngon tó gafle . . . and him man geald .xxiii. þúsend punda, 1002; P. 133, 36. Cáseres gæfel, Mt. L. 17, 24. Gæfel (gæfle, R.) onfón *tributum accipere,* 25. Geafel, Mk. L. 12, 14; Lk. L. 20, 22. Gæfelo *tributa,* 23, 2. (2 a) figurative :—Wé wæron gefreoþede feónda gafoles, Bl. H. 105, 23; Wlfst. 251, 16. Se middangeard ús (*devils*) wæs lange ær underþeóded, and ús deáþ mycel gafol geald, Bl. H. 85, 12. (3) *payment exacted by the state, a tax :*—Æt gæflæs monunge *in teloneo,* Mt. R. 9, 9. Gif wilisc man geþeó þ hé hæbbe híwisc landes and mæge cyninges gafo forꝺ bringan (þám cyng gafol gyldan, *v. l.*), Ll. Th. i. 186, 14. Land-ágende men ic lǽrde þ hié heora gafol águldon, Bl. H. 185, 21. (4) *payment exacted by the church :*—Hú hí Godes lage heóldon and Godes gafel lǽstan, Ll. Th. i. 350, 8. (4 a) of payment exacted by the Jewish law :—Þte saldun gæfel (*hostiam*) æfter ꝺætte ácweden wæs in æ Drihtnes, twoege turturas ł twoege birdas culfra, Lk. R. 2, 24. (5) *payment exacted by a lord, e. g. rent by a landlord :*—Gafel *tributis (serviet),* trifetum, Kent. Gl. 426. Se hláford tó his gafole búton wítnunge tó, Ll. Th. i. 270, 19. Gif se hláford wile þ land árǽran tó weorce and tó gafole, 146, 4. Mid ús is geræd þ hé sylle .v. sustras huniges tó gafole, 436, 2. Sum hit is ꝺan scipwealan tó gafole gesett, C. D. iii. 450, 19. (5 a) figurative :—Hwane manaþ God máran gafoles þonne þone biscop, Bl. H. 45, 16. Gif gé gesáwen hwelce mús þæt wǽre hláford ofer óþre mýs and sette him dómas and nídde hié æfter gafole *si inter mures videres unum aliquem jus sibi ac potestatem prae ceteris vendicantem,* Bt. 16, 2 ; F. 52, 3. (6) *a contribution exacted in aid* of the needy, *a rate :*—þæt úre teóþan sceattas sýn earmra manna gafol (*a poor-rate*), Bl. H. 41, 24. Teóþunga gafelu (*tributa*) synd beþurfendra sáwla, Scint. 108, 15. (7) *interest on a loan :*—Hé gýmꝺ grǽdelíce his teolunge, his gafoles, Hml. Th. i. 66, 11. 'Ic wolde mín ágen ofgán mid ꝺám gafole.' God forbeád . . . þæt nán ꝺæra manna þe rihtwís beón wile ne sceal syllan his feoh tó gafole. Ðis gafol . . . nis ná woruldlic, ac is gástlic, ii. 554, 8–12. þ hé his feoh ne his æhta tó nánum unrihtum gafole (*ullo injusto foenore*) ne lǽne ; þ is, þ hé hine máran ne bidde tó ágyfanne þonne hé him ǽr lǽnde, Ll. Th. ii. 194, 16. (8) *a debt* (lit. and fig.), *due, obligation :*—þ wǽre mid gafoles neóde (*necessitate debiti*) sum getreówe wer . . . þ hé wǽre geswænced fram his moniendum fore .xii. scyllingum, Gr. D. 157, 21–33. Sé þe geswænced wæs mid þæs gafoles manunge (*necessitate debiti*), 158, 12. Gemǽnelicum deáþes gafele *generali mortis debito,* An. Ox. 1448. Nán fram þám gefule (*debito*) þeówdómes sí beládud, Angl. xiii. 439. 1057. Þænne gaful gemǽnre týddernysse tó ágyldenne ænig geclypad byþ *cum ad debitum communis fragilitatis exsoluendum quis uocatus fuerit,* 442, 1093. v. æ-gafol(e); *adj.*

**gafol,** e ; *f. A fork. Take here* geafel *in Dict., and add :*—Furca, furcula *diminutive* gæfie, Wrt. Voc. ii. 151, 82. Hé sceal habban . . . race, geafie, Angl. ix. 263, 7. Forcelle gæfie, *dictae quod frumenta celluntur, i. commoventur,* Wrt. Voc. ii. 150, 17. [O. L. Ger. gabala : O. H. Ger. gabala *furca, furcilla.*] v. berigeblæ ; gafol-rand.

**gafol-bere.** *Add :* Cf. bere-gafol.

**gafol-fisc,** es ; *m. Fish paid as toll* or *tribute :*—Ic geann þám munecan tó fódan mín gafolfisc þe mé áríst be sǽlande *concedo maritimos pisces qui mihi contingere debent annualiter per thelonei lucrum,* Cht. Th. 307, 37.

**gafol-freó ;** *adj. Free from tax* or *tribute :*—Ic habbe gifen . . . ꝺat cotlíf ꝺe ic wæs boren inne . . . and áne hýde . . . scotfré and gafolfré, C. D. iv. 215, 33. Gauelfré, 191, 18.

**gafol-geréfa** *a tax-gatherer. Take here* gæfel-geroefa *in Dict., and add :*—Matheus se gæfelgeroefe (*publicanus*), Mt. R. 10, 3.

**gafol-gilda** *one who pays gafol. Add :* (1) v. gafol, (2) :—Hanna mid eallum his folce wearꝺ Rómánum tó gafolgieldum and him ǽlce geáre gesealde twá hund talentana siolfres, Ors. 4, 6 ; S. 170, 26. (2) v. gafol, (7) :—Gafolgilda *fenerator,* Wrt. Voc. ii. 33, 43. v. next word.

**gafol-gildere.** *Add : a debtor.* v. gafol, (8), (7) :—Gif ꝺú wilt þæt þis feoh becume tó ꝺínre sáwle ꝺearfe, tóꝺæl hit ꝺearfum and wanhálum, wydewum and steópbearnum and hafenleásum gafelgyldrum, Hml. Th. ii. 484, 33. Cf. Lk. 7, 41 *under* gafol-gilda.

**gafol-heord.** *Add : a swarm of bees rented from the lord,* the rent (gafol) being paid in honey : **gafol-hwítel.** *l.* -hwítel *a whittle* or *blanket to be paid to the lord as a tax :* **gafolian** (-el-) *to confiscate.* v. ge-gafolian.

**gafol-irþ,** e ; *f. The ploughing by the gebúr and the sowing from his own barn of a certain portion of the lord's land and the reaping and carrying of the crop to the lord's barn by way of rent :*—His (the gebúr) gauolyrde .iii. æceras erige and sáwe of his áganum berne, Ll. Th. i. 434, 18. Cf. þá gerihta þæ ꝺá ceorlas sculan dón tó Hysseburnan . . . .iii. æceras geerian on heora ágenre hwíle and mid heora ágenan sǽde gesáwan, and on heora ágenre hwíle on bærene gebringan, Cht. Th. 144, 28–38.

**gafol-land.** *Add :*—Tó strǽt synd .xii. hída .xxvii. gyrda gafollandes . . . tó Middeltúne .v. hída .xiii. gyrda gafollandes . . . tó cinges túne .v. hída synd .xiii. gyrda gafollandes and .i. hída bufan díc ꝺæt is nú eác gafolland, C. D. iii. 450, 12–18.

**gafol-lic ;** *adj. Connected with tribute* or *taxes :*—Fiscalis reda gebellicu[m] waegnfearu, Wrt. Voc. ii. 108, 63. Fiscalis ræde gafellicum wænfare, 35, 56. Gafollic *fiscale (tributum),* An. Ox. 6, 20.

**gafol-manung,** e ; *f. A demanding of tax* or *tribute, ' the receipt of custom' :*—Sittende tó geafolmonunge *sedentem ad teloneum,* Mk. R. 2, 14.

**gafol-rand,** es ; *m. A pair of compasses :*—Gafelrond (*printed* -rod) *circinnus,* Wrt. Voc. ii. 131, 25. Gabulrond, gabelrend, gabarind *circino,* ferrum duplex, unde pictores faciunt circulos, Txts. 51, 469. Gabulrond *radio,* 93. 1711. Gafolrand *circinnum,* Wrt. Voc. ii. 22, 50. [Gabul-hrand *circino,* Grff. ii. 531.] v. gafol *a fork.*

**gafol-swán.** *Add : a swineherd who had a herd of swine from the lord on condition of paying a certain part of the stock.* Cf. gafol-heord : **gafol-tíning.** *l.* -týning. **gafol-wydu.** *l.* -wudu : **gafol-yrþ.** v. gafol-irþ.

**gaf-sprǽc,** e ; *f. Buffoonery, scurrility :*—Hwǽr biþ his gafsprǽc, and ꝺá ídelan gamenunga, and his ungemetegode hleahter ?, Bas. 50, 28. [v. N. E. D. gaff.] v. ge-gafsprǽc ; gaffetung.

**gagátes.** *l.* gagates *jet, at end for* Lch. iii. *l.* Lch. ii., *and add :*—Hér biꝺ geméted gagates stán ; sé biꝺ swylce blæc gim, gif mon déꝺ on fyr, nǽdran fleógaþ áweg ꝺone stenc *gignit lapidem gagatem ; est nigrogem-meus, et ardens igni admotus incensus serpentes fugat,* Bd. 1, 1 ; Sch. 9, 5. [v. N. E. D. gagate.]

**gagat-stán,** es ; *m. Jet :*—Gagatstán *gagates,* Wrt. Voc. i. 38, 28.

**gagol.** *Add :*—Mid gealge móde oferswíþed *lascivo superatus animo,* Bd. 5, 6 ; Sch. 576, 8. v. gagolisc.

**gagol-bǽre ;** *adj. Lascivious, wanton.* v. next word.

**gagolbǽr-nes.** *Add :*—Gagolbærnesse *lascivia,* Wrt. Voc. ii. 49, 70. Sé ꝺe eall his mód biꝺ áfiogen tó gæglbærnesse *qui totis cogitationibus ad lasciviam defluens,* Past. 73, 11.

**gagolisc, geaglisc, geglesc**; adj. Lascivious, wanton:—Mid geaglisce (gæglisce, geglescum, v. ll.) môde oferswîðed lasciuo superatus animo, Bd. 5, 6; Sch. 576, 8.

**gagul-suillan.** l. gagul suillan, and see swillan in Dict.

**gál**; adj. Add:—Gál, wrǽne petulcus, i. luxuriosus, An. Ox. 3336. Se Iovis weard swá swîðe gál, þæt hê on his ágenre swyster gewîfode, Wlfst. 106, 12. Twá mǽdencild ... þ án sydefull and þ ôðer sceandlic ... þ clǽne herigendlic, þ gále tǽllic, Hml. S. 5, 281. Gálre, wrênre petulantis, An. Ox. 4705. Gálre fluentis, i. lascive, Wrt. Voc. ii. 149, 62. Se ðe behylt wîmman mid gálre gesihðe and fúlum luste, Hml. Th. i. 492, 17. Mid clǽnnysse þæt gále gecynd gewyldan, 360, 2. Helle bryne eów wæs gegearwod for eówer gǽlnesse gǽlra dǽda, Angl. xii. 510, 12. [v. N. E. D. gole.] v. wíf-gal.

**galan.** Add: (1) of human speech, (a) in poetical or passionate expression:—Se geonga ongann geómran stefne gehǽfted for herige hearmleóð galan, An. 1129: 1344. Sorhleóð galan to lament, Kr. 67: Cri. 623. Gehyrde heó hearm galan (tell his woes) helle deófol ... 'Wá mê forworhtum ...,' Jul. 629. (b) in incantation:—Ic galdorwordum gôl, Reim. 24. Þá drýas mid langum onsangum hî gôlon on (hyre on gôlon, v. l.), oð þ se deófol of hire út eóde diutius incantationibus agere malefici moliebantur, ut diabolus exiret, Gr. D. 73, 27. Galdor galende (rumpitur anguis), Wrt. Voc. ii. 86, 66: 19, 6. (2) of the cry of a bird:—Hrefen uppe gôl, El. 52. Siððan þú gehýrde galan geomorne geác on bearwe, Bo. 22. (3) of a trumpet. Cf. singan:—Hié bearhtm ongeáton gúðhorn galan, B. 1432. [v. N. E. D. gale.] v. ge-galan.

**galdere.** For 'Som. Ben. Lye' substitute:—Wyrincgalere ł galdre Marsum, Hpt. Gl. 519, 46. Galdras marsi, An. Ox. 8, 245. Galdra aruspicum, i. magorum, 4068. Galdrum aruspicibus, 4193. Þ eówer nán galdras ne sêce, Hml. S. 17, 78.

**galdor.** Add: (1) a song, poem. Cf. galan, (1 a):—Sié þæs gemyndig sê ðe lufige þisses galdres begang, þæt hê geóce mê fricle, Hpt. 33, 73, 14. (2) an incantation, a charm. Cf. galan, (1 b):—Deóflices galdres necromantiae, i. demonum invocationis, An. Ox. 1927: 2021. Galdres prestigie, 4700. Mid galdre necromantia, 2909: 4055. Ne wyrta gaderunge mid nánum galdre (incantatione) bûtan mid Pater noster, Ll. Th. ii. 192, 1. Antecrîst hæfð mid him drýmen ... and þá ðe cunnan galder ágalan, Wlfst. 194, 18. Þ ic môte þis gealdor tôðum ontýnan, Lch. i. 400, 4. Galdra prestrigiarum, An. Ox. 4056: incantationum, 4477: 4940: cantionum, Wrt. Voc. ii. 128, 14. Ne gîm þú drýcræfta and galdra non declinetis ad magos, nec ab ariolis aliquid sciscitemini, Lev. 19, 31. Þá drýas mid langsumum galdrum (incantationibus) hyre on gôlon, Gr. D. 73, 25. Hǽlðe sêcan æt unálýfedum tilungum, oððe æt wyrigedum galdrum, oþþe æt ǽnigum wiccecræfte, Hml. Th. i. 474, 21. (3) the sound of a trumpet. Cf. galan, (3):—Hié Hygeláces horn and býman gealdor ongeáton, B. 2944. v. sige-, wyrmgaldor.

**galdor-cræft.** Add:—Galdurcreftas bióð ágalene from ðǽm snottran, Ps. Srt. 57, 6. Galdorcræfta aruspicum, Wrt. Voc. ii. 3, 3 a. Sêc lytle stánas on swealwan bridda magan ... hî beóþ gôde wiþ ... yfium gealdorcræftum, Lch. ii. 306, 13. Sê þe galdorcræftas (incantationes) behealdeð, Ll. Th. ii. 154, 29.

**galdor-galend**; es; m. A magician, enchanter:—Galdergalend marsi, Wrt. Voc. ii. 58, 21. v. galan, (1 a).

**galdor-galende.** v. galan, (1 a).

**galdor-galere.** For 'Cot. ... 193' substitute: — Galdorgaleras auruspices, Wrt. Voc. ii. 6, 24. Galdorgalera ariolorum, 5, 17.

**galdor-leoþ.** For Cot. 188 substitute:—Galdorle(ó)dum carminibus, Wrt. Voc. ii. 85, 56.

**galdor-sang**, es; m. An incantation:—Gif hwylc wîf wiccunga begá and þá deóflican galdorsangas (diabolica cantica magica), Ll. Th. ii. 154, 26. Ne wê galdorsangas onginnen, Wlfst. 253, 10.

**galdrygea.** Substitute: galdricge, an; f. One who uses magical formulae, a magician, enchantress:—Galdriggan incantatores, Wrt. Voc. ii. 111, 60. Galdrigean incantationes (-tores?), 45, 61.

**galend.** v. galdor-galend.

**galere.** Add:—Galras marsi, An. Ox. 7, 308. Galra marsorum, 240: 8, 179. v. wirgung-galere.

**gál-freólsas.** For 'Som ... Lye' substitute:—Gálfreólsas lupercalia, An. Ox. 4715. Gálfreólsum lupercalibus, i. idolatriis, 4861.

**gál-full.** For 'Scint. ... 58' substitute:—Gálful þing wîn luxuriosa res uinum, Scint. 105, 5. Gelustfullunge gálfulre mislǽre delectationem libidinose suggestionis, 88, 7. Dohter gálfulle filiam luxuriosam, 177, 2. Mid wordum gálfullum verbis luxuriosis, Angl. xi. 117, 38. Þurh gálfullan spǽce per lascivia joca, Ps. L. fol. 183, 11.

**gálfullíce.** For Scint. 13 substitute:—On geoguþe gálfullíce (luxuriose) lybbende and on ylde forhæbbende, Scint. 70, 8.

**gálian**; p. ode To be licentious (gál):—Sê þe gálað, libbende deád hê ys qui luxuriatur, uiuens mortuus est, Scint. 87, 10. v. á-gálian.

**Gallias (-e).** Add:—On þǽm gefeohte þe hié wið Gallium hæfdon, Ors. 4, 7; S. 184, 11.

**Gallisc.** Add:—þ hié sceolden mid monnum heora godum blôtan, and þ sceolde beón án Gallisc wǽpnedmon and án Gallisc wîfmon, Ors. 4, 7; S. 184, 6. Hiora anlícnessa ne mehton from Galliscum fýre forbærnede weorþan, 2, 8; S. 94, 14.

**galness.** v. on-galness.

**gál-ness.** Add:—Gálnyss gehorwigende libido sordidans, Hy. S. 5, 5. On ðám lǽndenum is getácnad seó fúle gálnes, Ll. Th. ii. 368, 35: Hml. A. 17, 98. Se ôðer leahtor is forligr and ungemetegod gálnyss; sê is geháten fornicatio, Hml. S. 16, 276: Hml. Th. ii. 220, 3. Seó gálnes (luxuria) æt hyre ǽfengereordum sitt, Prud. 40: 41: 43. Fúlre gálnysse lupanaris incesti, An. Ox. 4221. Hwæt getácnað þæs fylmenes ofcyrf bûton gálnysse wanunge?, Hml. Th. i. 94, 33. Swîðor for bearnteáme þonne for gálnysse, ii. 70, 20: Ap. Th. 25, 10: Hml. A. 30, 144. Þú leofast on gálnysse (libidine), Dôm. L. 178. Gálnesse luxu, An. Ox. 8, 362. For eówer gǽlnesse gǽlra dǽda, Angl. xii. 510, 11. Gálnesse petulantiam, Wrt. Voc. ii. 66, 24. Áfyrra fram mê ðá fúlan gálnysse, Bt. 42; F. 260, 9. Sê ðe wile his gálnysse gefyllan swá oft swá hine lyst, Hml. Th. i. 148, 23. [v. N. E. D. goleness.] v. ealu-, weoroldgálness.

**gál-scipe.** Add:—Ðis synt þá îdelnessa þisse worlde ... gálscipe (lascivia), Ll. Th. ii. 174, 33. Se seofoða heáfodgylt ys luxuria, þ ys gálscype, Angl. viii. 337, 4. Byrnendes gálscipes flagrantis furie, Wrt. Voc. ii. 149, 36. Of gálscipe petulantia, An. Ox. 5290. Mid gálscipe (libidine) beón gewemmed, Scint. 89, 3. Scyldað eów wið gálscypas and swîðe georne wið ǽwbrecas, Wlfst. 40, 12. [v. N. E. D. goleship.]

**gálsere.** For Off. Reg. 15 substitute:—Sê ðe wǽre gálsere on fúlan forligere, weorðe sê clǽnsere his ágenre sáwle, Wlfst. 72, 6.

**gál-smerc.** l. -smǽre, R. Ben. 30, 8. Cf. smǽr[e] in Dict.

**galung.** Add: Galunge incantationum, An. Ox. 4940.

**Gal-walas.** Add:—Hê hyne onsende tô Galwala mǽgðe tô þǽre ceastre þe ys nemned Limouex, Shrn. 98, 27.

**gál-wrǽne.** l. gál, wrǽne. v. gál: **gambe.** v. gombe.

**gamel (-ol).** Add: I. of great age. (1) of persons:—Ic eom gomel wintrum, Ps. Th. 70, 16. Gomol bið snoterost, fyrngearum frôd, sê þe ǽr fela gebîdeþ, Gn. C. 11. (2) of things:—Sweord, gomele láfe, B. 2563. II. ancient, of a time long past:—Gomele gefyrn ealra cyninga cyning sægdon tôweard, Cri. 135.

**gamelian**; p. ode To grow old:—Ne gomelað God in gǽste, Gn. Ex. 11. [Cf. Icel. gamlaðr very aged.]

**game-lic.** v. gamen-lic.

**gamen.** Add: (1) amusement, mirth:—Hê sceal þonan geómor hweorfan, þám bið gomenes wana þe þá earfeða dreógeð on sárgum sefan, Gú. 1328. Ðú dwollige leofast swylce þê tô gamenes, Hml. A. 6, 141. Dyde ic mê tô gomene ganetes hleóðor, Seef. 20. Hý sceolon habban him gomen on borde, Gn. Ex. 183. Hê álegde gamen and gleódreám, B. 3021. (2) jest, game (in to make game of):—Ic sceal habban mê ðæt tô gamene subsannabo, Past. 249, 1. Þæt hî him tô gamene gedydon what they made a jest of, Hml. Th. ii. 254, 4. Þæt gê eów tô gamene feónda áfillað swá fela swá gê reccað, Wlfst. 132, 20. (3) a game, pastime:—Sum bið swîðsnel, hafað searolic gomen (dancing and tumbling? cf. sealting), gleódǽda gife for gumþegnum, leóht and leoðuwác, Crä. 82. Gamena augin ludorum gesticulatio, An. Ox. 2871. Sleglicum gamena gamene scenico ludorum joco, 2886. Man geswîce freólsdagum hǽðenra leóþa and deófles gamena, Ll. Th. ii. 248, 12.

**gamenian.** Add:—Gamenian mid cnafan iocari (i. ludere) cum paruulo, Scint. 172, 19. Cúðberhtus arn plegende mid his efenealdun ... Án drywintre cild þone gǽmnigendan Cúðberhtum befrán: 'Tô hwí underþeódst þú ðê þisum ýdelum plegan, Hml. Th. ii. 134, 9.

**gamen-lic (game-)**; adj. (1) exciting mirth, ridiculous. Cf. gamen, (2):—Gamelic, bysmerlic ridiculosum, An. Ox. 2251. Gamelicne, 7, 360. Gamilicne, 8, 351. (2) of a game or pastime. Cf. gamen, (3):—Gamenlicum theatrales, An. Ox. 4369. [O. H. Ger. gaman-lih ridiculus.]

**gamenung.** Add:—Þurh gálnesse gamenunga per lasciuia ioca, Ps. L. fol. 183, 11.

**gamen-wáðu.** l. -wáþ: **gamian, gaming.** Dele.

**gán.** Add: I. of movement, irrespective of the point of departure or destination. (1) to go on foot, walk:—'Ôþer hæíþ his fôta geweald þ hê mæg gán ... ôþer næíþ his fôta geweald þ hê næge gán ... and onginþ creópan ... hwæþer ðára twêgra þincþ þe mihtigra?' Ðá cwæþ ic: 'Sê bið mihtigra sê ðe gǽþ þonne sê þe criépð,' Bt. 36, 4; F. 178, 11-16. Healte gáð claudi ambulant, Mt. 11, 5. Heó sóna árás and eóde (ambulabat), Mk. 5, 42. Hê on þám temple eóde, 11, 27. Eóde Isaac on þám wege deambulabat Isaac per viam, Gen. 24, 62. Drýgum fôtum gán ofer sǽs ýþa, Bl. H. 177, 18. Wê gedóð þæt hí gán ne magon, Hml. Th. ii. 486, 13. Þá cyld þonne hí furþum gán magon, and ðá ealdan ceorlas ðá hwíle þe hí gán magon, Bt. 36, 5; F. 180, 6-8. Þ sê wǽre an feþe mihtigost sê ðe mihte gán ... oþ þisse eorþan ende, 21. (1 a) where work is being done on foot:—Hê on his æcere eóde, and his sulh on handa hæfde, Ors. 2, 6; S. 88, 8. (2) to move along, proceed (irrespective of mode of progression):—Se mann

āna gǽþ ūprihte, Bt. 41, 6; F. 254, 30. Geond ealle eorþan gǽþ heora swēg, Bl. H. 133, 34. Suā suā healt monn oððe untrum, hwīlum hié gǽð, hwīlum hié restað, Past. 67, 11. Ðā eóde hē furþor, Bt. 35, 6; F. 168, 23, 28. Þæt feórðe cyn fyrmest eóde, wōd on wǽgstreám, Exod. 310. Gǽð from geate tō geate ðurh midde ðā ceastre, Past. 383, 2. Þū meahtest þe gān singende þone ealdan cwide, Bt. 14, 3; F. 46, 28. (3) to take a specified course :—Hī gehātað holdlīce, swā hyra hyht ne gǽð, Leás. 14 : Ps. Th. 138, 11. Seó orsorhnes gǽþ scȳrmǽlum, Bt. 20; F. 72, 4. Gǽð on Drihtenes bebodum, Deut. 29, 12. Gif hwā swā dyrstig sȳ þ ongeán Godes lage gā, Cht. E. 230, 20. Ðæt mon wite Godes beboda weg, and ðǽr nylle on gān, Past. 67, 10. (4) to be guided or determined by :—Eall þæs cyninges rǽd eóde be his dihte, Hml. S. 6, 143. (5) to be habitually in a specified condition :—Gǽð gerēfa mín fægen freóbearnum, Gen. 2181. Gǽð gē gewǽpnode, P. 83, 12. (6) of a female, to go with young, be pregnant :—Feówer and twēntig mónða gǽð seó mōdor (the elephant) mid folan, Hml. S. 25, 569. (7) gān forþ, (a) of time, to pass, elapse :—Ðā hwīle ðe hē ǽne betyrnð gǽð forð feówor and twēntig tīda, Hex. 8, 31. (b) of a circumstance, event, to happen, come to pass, take place :—Rǽd forð gǽð, Exod. 525. Gif se hund losige, gā þeós bōt hwæðere forð, Ll. Th. i. 78, 5 : 130, 15. Sceal sōð forð gān wyrd, Gen. 2354. (8) of coinage, &c., to pass, be current :—Gā ān mynet ofer ealne þæs cynges anweald, Ll. Th. i. 268, 27. (9) of a ransom, to be accepted :—Hund-twelftig saltera sealma gǽð for xii mōnþa festen, Lch. iii. 166, 22. (10) of events, to have a specified issue, turn out so and so :—Hē him feala foresǽde swā him syððen an eóde, Shrn. 15, 10, 21 : 16, 24. II. where movement from a place is the primary notion. (1) to move away, depart :—For hwan gǽst þū, and þū forlǽte þā þe þē bǽdon?, Bl. H. 249, 4. Eáde abiit, Mk. R. 6, 46. Hié eódun þonan abierunt, Mt. R. 2, 9. Uton gān heonon, Jn. 14, 31. Him upp gāndum of ðām baðe, Gr. D. 343, 7. (1 a) gān of to relinquish a position, occupation, &c. :—Hē gǽð of his mǽglage þonne hē gebȳhð tō regollage, Ll. Th. i. 348, 2. Ǽðelm eóde of ðām geflīte, Cht. Th. 174, 2. III. where the prominent notion is that of destination or direction. (1) of self-originated motion or action. (a) to take one's way, proceed to a place or person, go into a place, move in a specified direction :—Dol bið sē þe gǽð on deóp wæter, sē þe sund nafað, Sal. 224. Nōe on þā earce eóde, Mt. 24, 38. Eóde eorl tō þām ceorle, By. 132. Deáh hī men oððe hundas wiþ eódon, Bt. 35, 6; F. 168, 3. Gā ðē tō ǽmetthylle, Past. 191, 25. Cōm ðǽr gān in tō mē wīsdōm, Bt. 3, 1; F. 4, 17 : B. 1163. (a a) where the destination is given by a clause :—Hē eóde þæt hē for eaxlum gestōd Denigea freán, B. 358. (b) where the place mentioned is intended to include what is done there :—Gā nū tō setle (go and feast), symbel-wynne dreóh, B. 1782. (c) where the purpose or motive of going (to a place) is indicated (a) by simple infin. :—Eóde Daniel swefen reccan sīnum freán, Dan. 158. Eóde folccwēn tō hire freán sittan, B. 640 : 918. Ðenden hié eódun bycgan, Mt. R. 25, 10. Þonne mon wile slāpan gān, Lch. ii. 228, 5. Ðā cōm in gān ealdor þegna Hrōðgār grētan, B. 1644. (β) by clause :—Gǽð fromlīce þæt gē gūðfreán gylp forbēgan, An. 1334 : 1184. (γ) by a coordinated verb, generally united to go by and :—Gǽð and leornigeað euntes discite, Mt. 9, 13. Gān þā þe þ geat āgan and gebēten, Ll. Th. i. 128, 8. Hȳ gān siþþan and gescyldigen hine, 206, 3. Þ hē eóde preófa sum . . . and þone að syllen, 204, 28. Uton gān and hlāfas bicgan, Mk. 6, 37. ¶ without and :—Þonne gǽð oðer man, seleþ his ceáp fore, Ll. Th. i. 142, 2. (δ) by a substantive (with tō) denoting (or implying) an action to be performed :—Gǽð hē tō medo, B. 603. Eóde hē fǽmnan tō sprǽce hē wæron to have speech with the maiden, Jul. 89. Tō geþæhtunge eódun consilio inito, Mt. R. 27, 7. Gā man tō scrifte, Wlfst. 181, 2. Gā hē eft tō þām ordāle, Ll. Th. i. 294, 17. Tō þisum hūsle tō gānne, Ll. Lbmn. 414, 2. (ε) by a substantive (with on) denoting function in which the subject is to be employed :—Gā seó mǽgð him on borh, Ll. Th. i. 198, 24. (d) to apply to, betake oneself to, with the idea of appeal or surrender :—And swā eágan gǽð earmre þeówenan, þonne heó on hire hlǽfdigean handa lōcað, Ps. Th. 122, 3. On þā rǽdenne þe hē him gā tō honda, Ll. Th. i. 142, 3. (e) to turn to, betake oneself to an occupation, course of action, &c., go to law :—Ne gā þū mid þīuum esne in tō dōme, Ps. Th. 142, 2. (2) of passive movement, change of state, &c. (a) to be carried, moved, impelled to, towards a place, person, &c., into a place or condition, lit. and fig. :—Ðurh ðone æpl ðæs eágan mon mæg geseón, gif him ðæt fleáh on ne gǽð, Past. 69, 18. Gǽð seó sunne on þ tācn Aquarium, Angl. viii. 305, 35. Mín lār in gǽð on þīn ondgit, Bt. 13; F. 36, 33. Sió heáfodpanne gǽþ on riht sōna, Lch. ii. 342, 7. Mín ceáf bið tō þē eóde, Ps. Th. 60, 4. Gān hié ealle on þeówot, Ll. Th. i. 106, 17. Sceolde monig ides bisieude gān on fremdes fǽðm, Gen. 1970. (b) to pass, be paid, be allotted to a person or object :—Gǽð gelīce bōt tō eallum, Ll. Th. i. 98, 16. Gā ǽlc cyric-sceatt intō þām ealdan mynstre, 262, 16. Gā þ bócland þām cyninge tō handa, 420, 11. (c) to be appropriated to a purpose :—Hit riht is þ þriddan dǽl þære teóðunge þe tō cirican gebyrige gā tō ciricbōte, oðer dǽl þām Godes þeówan, þridde Godes þearfum, Ll. Th. i. 342, 8. (d)

to be one of the constituent elements of something, be amongst the conditions requisite for something :—Ne gǽd nā māre tō mētinge būton þæt þū hit geseó and herige, Hml. Th. i. 186, 6. Gif wē willað āreccan ealle ðā gewitnyssa . . ., þonne gǽð þǽr swīðe micel hwīl tō, 18, 11. (e) to amount, be equivalent to :—xv. pund wætres gāþ tō sestre, Lch. ii. 298, 26. (f) to attain, reach, extend :—Se rodor gǽð under ðās eorðan ealswā deóp swā bufan, Hex. 10, 2. On þīs ilcan geáre eóde se sǽster hwǽtes tō .lv. penega and eác furðor, Chr. 1039; P. 161, 28 : 1043; P. 165, 1. IV. of movement towards the speaker, to come :—Se man þe ongeán ūs gǽð homo qui venit in occursum nobis, Gen. 24, 65. Hēr gǽð se swefnigend ecce somniator venit, 37, 19. Gā þē hēr tō mē huc ad me ingredere, Gr. D. 25, 20. Gǽð tō ūs, By. 93. Gā hē hider tō mē, Past. 383, 1. Lǽtan hī hēr beforan ūs forð gān, Hml. S. 23, 681. V. special uses with preps. or adverbs. (1) beforan gān to take precedence of :—Sanctus Iōhannes gǽþ beforan eallum ōþrum wītgan, Bl. H. 167, 22. (2) gān forð mid to produce, come out with :—Ðā þūhte ūs eallum þ Helmstān mōste gān forð mid ðon bōcon, Cht. Th. 170, 17. (3) mid gān to accompany, be with :—Ne eódun hī mid him, Jn. 6, 66. His metecū mōt gān mid hlāfordes oxan . . . gā his metecū mid hlāfordes cū, Ll. Th. i. 438, 16, 20. (4) of gān to be uttered :—Of eallum ðǽm worde þe gǽþ of Godes mūþe, Bl. H. 27, 9. (5) ūp gān to begin, start :—Andlang Cendefer ðǽr hit (the boundary) ǽr ūp eóde, C. D. v. 40, 17. (6) ūt gān. (a) to go to the closet, have an evacuation :—Hwīlum hē oft on dæge ūt gǽð, and þonne lytlum ; hwīlum ǽne, and þonne micel, Lch. ii. 230, 21. Hū man lyste ūt gān, and ne mæg, 164, 17. (b) to leave a permanent habitation or occupation :—.vi. geár þeówige hē, þȳ siofoðan beó hē frióh. Mid swelce hrægle he in eóde, mid swelce gā hē ūt, Ll. Th. i. 46, 4. (c) to proceed to the business of a court :—Þ man habbe gemōt . . ., and gān ūt þā yldestan .xii. þegnas and se gerēfa mid and swerian . . ., Ll. Th. i. 294, 3.

gandra. v. ganra : ganet. v. ganot : ganet-fatu, Wrt. Voc. ii. 56, 59. v. gemet-fæt.

gang. Add : I. going, walking, moving on foot, step. (1) of living beings :—Þǽr nǽfre feóndes ne bið gang on lande, An. 1696. Petrus mid his gange getācnode ǽgðer ge ðā strangan ge ðā unstrangan on Godes folce, Hml. Th. ii. 390, 16. Þurh his fóta gange ambulando, Bd. 4, 3; Sch. 349, 14. Gif ic mīne heorde þrafige on gancge (in ambulando), R. Ben. 120, 20. Tō rāde oþþe tō gange for riding or walking, Ll. Th. i. 232, 15. Wið fóta sāre fram miclum gange, Lch. ii. 68, 16 : 6, 18. Hrædne gang rapidum gressum, An. Ox. 50, 43. Hȳ habbaþ þæs þe leóhtran gang, Lch. i. 342, 12. Wǽron hyra gongas smēðe and gesēfte, Gū. 703. Mid gongum, mid rādum, oþþe mid þȳ þe hine mon bere oþþe on wǽne ferige, Lch. ii. 30, 28. (1 a) the sole of the foot (?) :—Wið fótswylum . . . haran lungen . . . neoþan tō gewriþen, wundorlīce þā gongas beóþ gehǽlede, Lch. i. 342, 19. (1 b) the being habitually in a specified condition. Cf. gan ; I. 5 :—Be sceápes gonge mid his flīese. Sceáp sceal gongan mid his flīese of midne sumor, Ll. Th. i. 146, 9. (2) of things :—Freóbearn wurdon ālǽten līges gauge, Dan. 263. Mid swātes gange with the flow of blood, Kr. 23. Wǽgea gangas þonne sǽstreámas swīðust flōwað elationes maris, Ps. Th. 92, 5. (2 a) of non-material things :—Ǽrmorgenes gancg exitus matutini, Ps. Th. 64, 9. Þē untrymnes ādle gongum (with attacks of disease) bysgade, Gū. 990. II. power of walking or of moving about :—Healte men onfēngon heora gonge, Shrn. 137, 27. Wē gedōð þæt hī gān ne magon . . . Wē forgifað him nū gang, Hml. Th. ii. 486, 15. III. mode of walking, walk, gait :—Eustachius hī behealdende be heora gewunelican gange hī gecnēow, Hml. S. 30, 234. Mid swȳðe sorhleásum and bealdum gange securo gressu ac libero, Gr. D. 319, 17. IV. a walk, journey :—Tō leáne his ganges, Gr. D. 143, 6. Woerig of gonge (geong, L.) fatigatus ex itinere, Jn. R. 4, 6. Gong (geong, L.) dōn iter facere, Lk. R. 13, 22. Geong l fær iter, Lk. L. 10, 33 : Rtl. 176, 23. Þurh þīn sylfes gong tō eorðan, Cri. 254. Forhabban hine wyð micele gangas, Lch. iii. 134, 19. IV a. like colloquial go, time, occasion of going :—Gehwæþerne gang swīgende either time (going and returning) in silence, Lch. ii. 76, 17. V. a way, road, path, passage :—Þā ongunnon hī būton ǽlcere lǽttinge in gangan ; mē þ godcunde mægen þæs ganges bewerede, Hml. S. 23 b, 408. Wæs on gange gifu oft geǽhted, B. 1884. Ic gong tō þām āgan mōste, Jul. 517. Biófoðon unrehte in gongum (geongom, L.) eruut praua in directa, Lk. R. 3, 5. Gongas (geongas, L.) semitas, Mk. R. 1, 3. Geongas, Lk. L. 3, 4. V a. a track :—Lāstas wǽron wīde gesȳne, gang ofer grundas, B. 1404. Uton fēran Grendles māgan gang sceáwigan, 1391. VI. course of time or events :—Eall þæs þe hē in fyrndagum gōdes oððe gāles on his gǽste gehlōd geára gongum, Cri. 1036 : Jul. 693. Hū mæg ic þæt findan, þæt swā fyrn geweard wintra gangum ?, El. 633. Wyrda þæt findan, þæt swā fyrn geweard wintra gangum ?, El. 633. Wyrda gangum, 1256. VII. a stream of words, a narrative :—Þæt hē him on spellum gecȳðde, onwrige worda gongum, hū hē his wīsna trūwade, Gū. 1134. VIII. space traversed by that which moves (swiftly), expanse covered :—Under swegles gang under the canopy of heaven, An. 208 : 455. Wolcna gang the cloud-covered sky, Dan. 624. Tungla gang the firmament of moving stars, Cri. 884. Ofer geofones gong over

*the rolling expanse of ocean*, Ph. 118. Ýða gelaac, wíd gang wætera, Ps. Th. 118, 136. **VIII** a. oxan gang *an ox-gang, a bovate, the eighth part of the carucate*. 'The carucate being the extent of land ploughed by one plough, with its team of eight oxen, an eighth of this was considered as the share of each ox of the team,' *N. E. D.* :—Hé sealde án(e) híde búton ánes oxan gang, C. D. B. iii. 370, 5, 7. Twégra oxena gang, 346, 20. **IX.** *legal process* (? cf. *Dan.* retter-gang *legal procedure, process*) :—Ðus man sceal swerigean ðonne man haið his æhte gebryid, and bringeð hí on gange (cf. Þ orf Þ ic on spece, and Þ ic mid N. befangen hæbbe, 15), Ll. Th. i. 178, 11. **X.** *a company of people (?), a gang.* Cf. beó-gang, genge :—Basilius eóde tó ánes preóstes húse, and hét his gebróðra beón his geféran. Anastasius wæs geháten se mæssepreóst þe se bisceop tó fundode swá færlíce mid gange ... Se bisceop gewende mid his gebróðrum hám, Hml. S. 3, 467. **XI.** *a step, stair* :—Gangas *pulpita* (cf. in pulpito, in gradu ubi lectores legunt, Ld. Gl. H.), Germ. 394, 221. **XII.** *a privy* [v. *N. E. D.* gong] :—Gang *latrina*, Wrt. Voc. i. 82, 12. Ic ne mæg for sceame þá sceandlican dæde, þæt ænig man sceole etan on gange, swá fúllíce secgan swá hit fúllic is, E. S. viii. 62, 18. v. beó-, ciric-, ears-, fald-, forlig-, geán-, hand-, niþer-, ofer-, ráp-, relic-, samod-, set-, sulhgang.

**gangan.** *Take here* geongan, *and add*: **I.** *of movement irrespective of point of departure or destination.* (1) *to go on foot, walk* :—Halto geongeð *claudi ambulant*, Lk. L. 7, 22. Mid fótum gangan, Met. 31, 8. Cóm se Hælend ofer þá sǽ gangende (geongende, L.) *venit ambulans supra mare*, Mt. 14, 25. Árás Þ mægden and geongende (gong-, R.) wæs (*ambulabat*), Mk. L. 5, 42. (1 a) *to go on business* :—Wyrce hé þám hláforde þe him fore ríde oþþe gange, Ll. Th. i. 232, 21. ¶ gangende *pedestrian, foot as opposed to mounted* :—Ðá gangendan mænigeo *pedestres*, Mt. 14, 13. Ægþer ge rídendra ge gangendra here, Ors. 3, 7; S. 112, 6: Chr. 1085; P. 215, 36. Gangendra manna and gehorsedra manna, Hml. S. 25, 556. (2) *to move along, proceed* (irrespective of mode of progression) :—Geseah hé, þá hé bi sesse geóng, máððumsigla fela, B. 2756. Hé on orde geóng, 3125. Gif feórrancumen man búton wege gange (*if he does not travel on the road*), Ll. Th. i. 42, 24. Gif. feorcund mon bútan wege geond wudu gonge, 116, 1. Gangan ofer foldan wang, Men. 113. Þeóf sceal gangan in þýstrum wederum, Gn. C. 42. Gangan forð *to advance*, By. 170. Gangend[e] feða *an army on the march*; agmen, Wrt. Voc. i. 18, 34. ¶ gangende *animate* or *live* as opposed to inanimate objects :—Þíne frumrípan gangendes (gong-, *v. l.*) and weaxendes, Ll. Th. i. 52, 31: Wlfst. 113, 6. Hé sealde him tó bóte gangende feoh, Gen. 2719. (3) *to take a specified course* (lit. or fig.) :—Ic on wegum gange þǽr ic þíne gewitnesse wát, Ps. Th. 118, 14. Ne ic on mægene miclum gange, 130, 2. Gancge, 85, 10. Gang swá, Sat. 701. Gionga in leht mægna *ambulare in luce virtutum*, Rtl. 37, 5. (3 a) where the course is expressed by an adv. acc. :—Ealle þe his gedéfne weg gangað *omnes qui ambulant in viis ejus*, Ps. Th. 127, 1. (4) *to be habitually in a specified condition* :—Neb bið hyre æt nytte, niðerweard gongeð, Rä. 35, 3. Sceáp sceal gongan mid his flíese oð midne sumor, Ll. Th. i. 146, 10. (5) *of coinage, &c., to pass, be current* :—Gange án mynet ofer ealne þæs cynges anweald, Ll. Th. i. 268, 27: 322, 29: Wlfst. 272, 2. (6) *to take place* :—Múða gehwylc mete þearf, mǽl sceolon tídum gongan *every mouth needs meat, meals there must be at proper times*, Gn. Ex. 125. (7) of events, *to have a specified issue* :—Godes spelbodan sægdon ... swá hit nú gongeð, Gú. 13. Long is tó secganne, hú hyre ealdorsceaft æfter gongeð, Rä. 40, 23. **II.** where movement *from* a place is the primary notion. (1) *to depart* :—Geongas *exeunt*, Lk. L. 4, 36. Geong from mé *exi a me*, 5, 8. Þæt hé þone múð ufan mid mettum áfylle, and on óðerne ende him gange þæt meox út fram, E. S. viii. 62, 15. Þú mé ne forléte út gangan mid mínre háþeortan of þisse ceastre, Bl. H. 249, 15. From gonga (geonga, L.) *abire*, Jn. R. 6, 67. Forleorton geonga *dimiserunt*, Mk. L. 12, 3. (1 a) *of death* :—Heora gást gangeð *exiet spiritus ejus*, Ps. Th. 145, 3. Þonne þæs monnes sául út of his líchoman gangeþ, Bl. H. 195, 9. Ic beó gangende of mínum líchoman, 139, 19. Gást gangende *spiritus vadens, et non rediens*, Ps. Th. 77, 39. **III.** where the prominent notion is that of destination or direction. (1) *of self-originated motion or action.* (a) *to take one's way, proceed* to a place or person, *go into a place, move in a specified direction* :—Ic on þín hús gange *introibo in domum tuum*, Ps. Th. 65, 12. 'Hwyder wilt þú gangan.' 'Ic wille gangan tó Róme,' Bl. H. 191, 16. Hwyder magon gyt gangan from mínum willan?, 187, 25. Utan gangan on þissum carcerne, 247, 1. Sum sceal on féðe on feorwegas gongan, Vy. 28. (a a) where the destination is given by a clause :—Ic ána gonge ... þǽr ic sittan mót sumorlangne dæg, Kl. 35. Hé gíong þæt hé bi wealle gesæt on sesse, B. 2715. Hét beornas gangan, þæt hí on þám eásteðe ealle stódon, By. 63. (b) where the place mentioned is intended to include what is done there :—Hió tó setle geóng *she took her place at table*, B. 2019. (c) where the purpose or motive of going (to a place) is indicated (a) by simple infin. :—Ic geongo (gongo, R.) gegeruiga iúh styd, Jn. L. 14, 2. Geát geóng

sóna tó setles neósan, B. 1785. Gé móton gangan Hróðgár geseón, 395. (β) by gerundial infin. :—Ic geongo (gongo, R.) tó cunnanne ða ilca *eo probare illa*, Lk. L. 14, 19. (γ) by a clause :—Utan gangan þæt wé bysmrigen bendum fæstne, An. 1358. (δ) by a co-ordinated verb, generally united to *go* by *and* :—Nú gé raðe gangað and findað ..., El. 372. Gange hé feówra sum tó and oðsace, Ll. Th. i. 286, 17. ¶ without *and* :—Gé nú hraðe gangað, sundor ásécað ..., El. 406. (ε) by a substantive (with *to*) denoting or implying an action to be performed :—Gange ǽlc man þæs tó gewitnesse þe hé durre on þám háligdóme swerian, Ll. Th. i. 292, 13. Gange hé tó þám ordále, 280, 9. Þis folc tó húsle gange, Bl. H. 207, 6. Þ gé tó þýs húsle ne gangen ne tó ðǽm ordále, Rtl. 114, 21. (ζ) by a substantive (with *on*) denoting function in which the subject is to be employed or condition into which he enters :—Gif bescoren man gange him an gestlíðnesse (*go and stop as a guest*), Ll. Th. i. 38, 12. Gangon hí him on borh, 202, 16. (2) *of passive movement, change of condition, &c.* (a) *to be carried, moved, impelled* :—Monnum þyncð þæt sió sunne on mere gange, Met. 28, 38. In gange mín bén on þínre gesihðe, Ps. Th. 118, 170. Gongen hié ealle on þeówot, Ll. Th. i. 106, 17. Þú scealt on eorðan gangan, and eft tó eorðan weorðan, Bl. H. 123, 10. Án steorra sóna tó setle gangende, Chr. 1097; P. 233, 27. (b) *to reach, extend* :—Wintres dæg wíde gangeð, Men. 202. (c) *to pass to a certain condition, become* :—Þú mé scealt edwitt mín of áwyrpan, þæt mé tó incan áhwǽr gangeð, Ps. Th. 118, 39. **IV.** *of movement towards the speaker, to come* :—Gang þú hider in tó mé *huc ad me ingredere*, Gr. D. 25, 21. Gang mé neár hider, Bl. H. 179, 30. Gangaþ nú tó mé on wolcnum, 157, 25. Hét him recene tó ríce þeóden his sunu gangan, Gen. 865. **V.** special use with preps. or adverbs, *út* gangan. (1) *to go to the closet, have an evacuation* :—Hwilum hié wel gelyst út gangan, and him þá byrþenne fram áweorpan, Lch. ii. 230, 23. (2) *to leave a permanent habitation* or *occupation* :—Mid swelce hrægle hé in eóde, mid swelce gange hé út, Ll. Th. i. 46, 4. v. feld-, fot-, gearu-gangende, *and cf.* gán.

**gang-dagas.** *Add: days on which processions were made during which prayers for peace and prosperity were recited.* [Cf. the description of 'lætania majora' :—On ðǽm dæge eall Godes folc mid eáðmódlíce religonge sceal God biddan þ hé him forgefe ðone geár siblíce tíd, and smyltelíco gewidra, and genihtsume wæstmas, and heora líchoman trymnysse, Shrn. 74, 9-12.] :—Se móna on gangdagum ne mæg beón iungra þonne án and twéntig nihta eald, ne yldra þonne nigon and xxtig, Angl. viii. 324, 35. Geseah hé swýþe mycele weorud swylce on gangdagan, Vis. Lfc. 11. Cómon þá scipo tó þám gangdagum (gan-, *v. l.*), Chr. 1016; P. 149, 3. Tó þám gongdagan, 1063; P. 191, 9. Ofer Eástron ymbe gangdagas oþþe ǽr, 892; P. 82, 30. Sé þe stalað ... on Gangdagas ... wé willað ... sié twybóte, Ll. Th. i. 64, 24. Bútan wíte oð Gongdagas, 222, 23. Inne ðá háli wuca æt Gangdagas *in sancta ebdomada rogationum*, C. D. iv. 209, 18. [v. *N. E. D.* gang-days.] v. gang-wuce.

**gange.** v. úp-, wæfer-gange: **gangel.** *Add:* v. neáh-gangel.

**gangel-wæfre.** *Add:* —Gongelwafre *aranea*, Wrt. Voc. ii. 10, 35. Gif hunta gebíte mannan þ swiðre óþre naman gangelwefra, Lch. ii. 14, 20.

**gang-ern.** *Add:* —Gangren *preclauam* (þ *clauū*, MS.), Hpt. 33, 246, 80.

**gange-wifre.** *Add:* —Gongeweafre *aranea*, Ps. Srt. 89, 9. Gongeweafran, 38, 12.

**gang-setl.** *Add: A stool* (of a privy) :—Þás úplendiscan wíf wyllað oft drincan and furþon etan fúllíce on gangsetlum ... hit is bysmor þæt ǽnig man ... þone múð ufan mid mettum áfylle, and on óðerne ende him gange þæt meox út fram, and drince þonne ǽgðer ge þæt ealu ge þone stenc, E. S. viii. 62, 13. v. next word.

**gang-stól**, es; *m. A stool, seat* of a privy :—Beþige mon þone bæcþearm on gongstóle, Lch. ii. 236, 7.

**gang-tún.** *Add: A draught-house* :—Hí worhton ánne gangtún þǽr ðǽr se god Baal ǽr wæs gewurðod (*they brake down the house of Baal, and made it a draught-house*; fecerunt pro æde Baal latrinas, 2 Kings 10, 27), Hml. S. 18, 379.

**gánian.** *Substitute:* —Þeáh þe mé synfulra múðas on gánian *quia os peccatoris super me apertum est*, Ps. Th. 108, 1. Gángende múþe *hiulco rostro*, Wrt. Voc. ii. 79, 34. Gániende *oscitantes*, 65, 1. Gánigende þrotbollan *hiulcas gurguliones*, An. Ox. 8, 190. [v. *N. E. D.* gane. O. H. Ger. geinôn *dehiscere, patescere, oscitare*.] v. á-gánian; gínan, geonian.

**ganot.** *Add:* —Ganot (gonot) *vel* dopaenid *fulix*, Txts. 62, 419: Wrt. Voc. ii. 36, 20. Ganet *cygnus*, Germ. 394, 221. Ganótes *fulice*, Bl. Gl.

**ganra.** *Add:* —Anser [*vel* ganra (*added in another hand*)] hwít gós, Wülck. Gl. 284, 12. Gandra (ganra, *v. l.*) *anser*, Ælfc. Gr. Z. 43, 14. Gif wíf eteð hanan flǽsc oððe ganran, Lch. iii. 144, 24. ¶ in a place-name :—Andlang weges upp on gandran dúne, C. D. v. 166, 6.

**gánung.** *Add: opening of the mouth* in scorn or abuse (? cf. Ps. Th. 108, 1 *under* gánian) :—Gánung *gannatura* (cf. *gannature* bysmires, 85,

67), Wrt. Voc. ii. 70, 30. [Ganynge *oscitatus*, Prompt. Parv. 185 : *hiatus*, Cath. Ang. 149.]

**gapian.** v. ofer-gapian.

**gár.** *Add :* I. *a weapon with a pointed head.* (1) where the use is uncertain :—Gár oft þurhwód fǽges feorhhús, By. 296. Þurh gáres gripe gǽst onsendan (cf. gripon under sceát werun scearpe gáras, Gen. 2064), An. 187. Gáras *spicula*, i. *sagitte*, An. Ox. 2c98. (2) *a weapon that is hurled :*—Gár *jaculum*, Kent. Gl. 965. Oft hé gár forlét, wælspere windan on þá wícingas, By. 321. (3) *a weapon with which a thrust is made :*—Hé mid gáre stang wlancne wícing, By. 138. Mé on beáme beornas sticedon gárum, Sat. 511. (4) either (2) or (3) :—Darod sceal on handa, gár golde fáh, Gn. C. 22. Sceal gár wesan monig mundum bewunden, hæfen on handa, B. 3021. Gáras stódon ætgædere, æscholt ufan grǽg, B. 328. Gáras líxton, El. 23. (5) *an arrow :*—Hyné Hǽdcyn of hornbogan flāne geswencte . . . and his mǽg ofscét blódigan gáre, B. 2440. (6) either (2) or (5) :—Wid flyge gáres, Crä. 66 : B. 1765. On þæt fǽge folc flāna scúras, gáras . . . hetend hildenǽdran þurh fingra geweald ford onsendan, El. 118. II. *the head of a weapon :*—Gár sceal on sceafte, ecg on sweorde and ord spere, Gn. Ex. 203. Feólhearde speru, gegrundene gáras, By. 109. ¶ phrases :—Gylpplega gáres *battle*, Exod. 240. Ford beran gár tó gúde, By. 13. Tógædere gáras beran *to join battle*, 67. Cf. gár-berend. III. fig. of sharp pain (from cold). Cf. spere :—Habbad heó on ǽfyn fýr edneówe ; þonne cymd on úhtan forst fyrnum cald, symble fýr odde gár, Gen. 316. IV. *a wedge-shaped piece of land.* v. gára :—Tó des góres súdende, C. D. v. 40, 13. v. nafo-, tóþ-, wíg-gár. *Also in proper names*, e. g. Eád-gár.

**gára.** *Add :* (1) *a gore* of land ['When a field, the sides of which are straight, but not parallel, is divided into lands, the angular piece at the side is called a gore.' Leicester Gloss. in *N. E. D.*] :—Of dám .iii. æceran tó dám gáran ; of dám gáran tó dám ódran gáran, C. D. iii. 423, 31. Tó dám ealdan gáran, 37, 28. On done scearpan gáran weste-werdne, 279, 22. On done ealdan gáran ; of dám gáran á de heáfdan, 438, 29. Ymbútan ǽnne gáran, 456, 21. On snelles gáron, 97, 32. On done smalan gáre, 10, 28. (2) *a gore* of material, *flap*, *lappet*. Cf. *Prompt. Parv.* goore of a clothe *lacinia* :—Sadol *sella*, felt *mento*, gáran *ulcea*, Wrt. Voc. i. 83, 72. [v. *N. E. D.* gore. O. Frs. gáre *a lappet* : O. H. Ger. gēro : Ger. gehren : Icel. geiri *a triangular strip* : land-geiri *a gore of land*.] v. hút-, fyrs-gára ; *and cf.* gár-æcer.

**gár-æcer**, es ; *m.* A *strip of land tapering at one end*, not having parallel sides like the ordinary acre-strip. v. Seebohm, Vill. Comm., s.v. gored acres :—On ǽnne gáran ; donne of dan gáran on ǽnne gáræcer ; dæt andlanges dǽre fyrh tó ánum andheáfdum . . . dauon west on ǽnne góran ; andlanges dǽre fyrh . . . on áne gáræcer . . . and se gáræcer in on dæt land . . . tó twám gáræcer[um] and dá gáræceras in on dæt land, C. D. v. 153, 19–154, 1.

**gár-clife.** *Add :*—Gárclife *agrimonia*, Wrt. Voc. i. 67, 13.

**gáre**, an ; *f.* A *javelin* (?) :—Ic geann twégra hída þe Eádríc gafelad ælce geáre mid healfum punde and mid ánre gáran, Cht. Th. 517, 18.

**gár-leác.** *Add :*—Gaarleec, gárlęc, -léc *alium*, Txts. 39, 113. Gár-leác, Wrt. Voc. ii. 8, 45.

**gár-secg.** *Add :* I. *ocean*, sea as opposed to land or air :—Sǽ *mare* vel *aequor*, gársecg *oceanus*, Wrt. Voc. i. 41, 64. Folde . . ., gársecg, Gen. 117. Ealne middangeard ymbféran swá gársecg (*oceanus*) beliged, Nar. 20, 15. Swá swá lyft and lagu land ymbclyppad, gársecg embegyrt gumena ríce, Met. 9, 41. Gársecg fandad hwæder ác hæbbe ædele treówe, Rún. 25. Þú gársecges grundas geworhtes, Hy. 10, 7. Gár-secges gǽst (*the whale*), Wal. 29. On gársecge *oceano*, Wrt. Voc. ii. 64, 68. Seó dridde India líd tó dám micclum gársecge . . . hæfd on ódere sídan done grimlican gársecg, Hml. Th. i. 454, 13–15. Hé gesette þone gársecg on his goldhorde, Ps. Th. 32, 6. Þone wídgyllan gársecg, Hml. A. 3, 53 : Ph. 289 : An. 371. II. *a particular part of the general body of water, an ocean :*—Se gársecg þe man hǽt Brittan-isca . . . on ódre healfe þæs gársecges earme is Brittannia, Ors. 1, 1 ; S. 22, 24. Od done gársecg *usque ad oceanum Aethiopicum*, S. 26, 10, 16, 24, 26. v. eást-, súþ-, út-gársecg ; *and* secg sea.

**gár-þrǽc.** *l.* -pracu : **gár-wíga.** *l.* -wiga.

**gás-ríc**, es ; *m.* An *impetuous creature, a furious animal* (used of the whale ; cf. the description in Wal. 5 : Se micla hwæl biþ unwillum oft geméted frécne and ferdgrim faredlácendum) :—Fisc (*a whale*) fiódu ahóf on fergenberig ; warþ gásríc grorn þǽr hé on greút giswom (*the whale was sad at being stranded*), Txts. 127, 6. [*For sense of* gás cf. *Icel.* geisa *to rage*, geisan *impetuosity : for the compound cf. the proper name* Gaisaricus, *and for similar form in the case of a common noun cf.* Germ. wüterich.]

**gást.** *Add :* I. *breath :*—Orop odde gást *flamen*, Wrt. Voc. ii. 37, 12 : An. Ox. 18, 43. II. *spirit, ghost, principle of life :*—Ic eallunga unástyrigendlic bútan gáste lǽg, Hml. S. 23 b, 576. Sóna swá hé þás word gecwæd, hé his gást onsende, Bl. H. 191, 29. Heó ágeaf hire gást, Shrn. 72, 13. III. *spirit* in contrast with body, *the immaterial part of man :*—Seoþþan se líchoma and se gást gedǽlde beóþ, Bl. 111, 30.

Úre gást biþ swíþe wíde farende úrum unwillum, Bt. 34, 11 ; F. 152, 3. Gefeáde gaast (*spiritus*) mín in Gode, Lk. L. 1, 47. Gebyrad þ hig gebiddon on gáste, Jn. 4, 24. Sóþfæste sáwle, gǽst háligne, Chr. 1065 ; P. 193, 21. Eádige beóþ þearfena gástas, Bl. H. 159, 29. Gehiérsume dǽm de úre gǽsta (gásta, *v. l.*) Fæder bid, Past. 255, 8. III a. *a person.* Cf. similar use of *soul :*—Duru sóna onarn þurh handhrine háliges gástes (*at the touch of St. Andrew's hand*), An. 1002 : 1623. Gewít þú mid híwum on þæt hof (*the ark*) gangan, gásta werode, Gen. 1346. Hé þám leódum sende hálige gástas (*the prophets*), þá þám werude wísdóm budon, Dan. 26. III b. *used of spiritual beings :*—God sendeþ his engla gástas tó ǽrendwrecum, Bl. H. 203, 14. III c. *an incorporeal thing* (fire, &c.) :—Líg ealle forswealg, gǽsta gífrost, B. 1123 : Cri. 814. Þec gǽstas hergen, byrnende fýr and beorht sumor, Az. 94. IV. *an incorporeal being, a spirit*, (a) good :—Mid þreáte háligra gásta, Bl. H. 95, 7. Englas beód tó degnunge gǽstum on world sended, 209, 23. (b) bad :—Se forhwyrfda gást, Bl. H. 31, 4. Mid áwyridum gástum *furiis*, i. *malignis spiritibus*, An. Ox. 4666. V. *divine spirit :*—His þegnas wǽron þágyt flǽsclices módes, and nǽron mid gástes mægene getremede, Bl. H. 17, 6. VI. *the soul of a deceased person*, spoken of as inhabiting the unseen world :—Huaet his gástae aefter deóthdaege doemid uueorthae, Txts. 149, 19. Fóe se hláford tó and dá hígon and þæt lond mínum gáste nytt gedóen, C. D. i. 311, 19. Híg samod restad on ǽre byrgenne, and þá gástas samod gefeód on ánum wuldre, Mart. H. 214, 19. v. frófor-, þegnung-gást.

**gást-brúcende** *practising in spirit.* v. gást ; III :—Ealle þá gódnyssa þe hé bebreác, hé wæs gástbrúcende, Hml. S. 23 b, 34.

**gást-cund.** *Add :*—Ic eom andette Gode and menniscum men, gást-cundum lǽce, Angl. xi. 102, 58.

**gástende ?** *l.* ge-áscende ? :—Dá reahte hé [hú] hys mód fór oft gástánde (geáscende ?) and smeágende mislicu and selcúd þing, and ealles swídust ymbe hyne sylfne, . . . and hwilc good him wǽre betst tó dónne, and hwylc yfel betst tó forlétende *volventi mihi multa ac varia mecum diu, ac per multos dies sedulo quaerente memetipsum ac bonum meum, quidve mali evitandum esset*, Solil. H. 3, 1. [This passage seems in part a continuation of the preface, in part translation of the text.]

**gást-gifu**, e ; *f.* A *spiritual gift, spiritual grace :*—Gástgifu vel háligu carismata, dona (cf. charismatum, divinorum donorum, 75, 54), Wrt. Voc. ii. 129, 5. Cf. gást-lic ; III.

**gást-lic.** *Add :* I. *pertaining to the spirit.* v. gást ; III :—Gástlicre úþefnesse *extaseos*, Wrt. Voc. ii. 31, 68. On módes heánnesse, on gástlicre gesihde *in extasi*, 47, 21. Dæg mid glædnise gástlicum (*spiritali*) uē wordia, Rtl. 89, 26. Ealle þæs monnes good ge gást-lice ge líchomlice, Bt. 34, 6 ; F. 140, 31. II. *spiritual* as opposed to bodily, fleshly, physical :—Se gáslica wulf *typicus Benjamin*, An. Ox. 1922. Seó cwén (*the queen of Sheba*) . . . seó gástlice cwén, gástlice geladung, Hml. Th. ii. 588, 1. Hé is se grundweall þǽre gástlican cyrcan, 22. Hí him þá gástlican lác geoffriad on menigfealdum gemetum, 14. Sé forlét his gástlican wǽpna and féng tó his spere and tó his sweorde, Chr. 1056 ; P. 186, 27. II a. of relationship, *spiritual* as opposed to natural :—Godes geladung bewýpd hire gástlican cild, Hml. Th. i. 84, 29. III. *spiritual* as opposed to worldly or profane, divine, heavenly, holy, sacred :—Gástlecum andgite *anagogam* (cf. *anagogen*, i. *superno sensu* úplican ł heofenlicum angite, An. Ox. 184), Wrt. Voc. i. 1, 10 : allegoriam, i. *parabolam*, An. Ox. 182 : 8, 15 b. On gástlicre gesihþe *in oromate* (cf. *in oromate*, i. *uisione superna* on úplicere gesihþe, An. Ox. 404), Wrt. Voc. ii. 43, 60 : 62, 62. Gǽst-licre, 75, 65. Æfter gástlicre gebýcnuncge *tropologiam*, An. Ox. 8, 15 c. Gástlicre geryne *mistico officio*, 2883. Þ gástlice, heofenlice *contemplativam* (*vitam*), andwurdan *practicam*, 2432. Gástlicra sylena ł gyfa *charismatum* i. *donorum* (cf. gást-gifu), 342 : 2863. Náne wuht ongitan dára gástlecena beboda *nequaquam spiritalia praecepta cognoscere*, Past. 27, 1. Mid gástlicum trahtnungum *mysticis* (i. *diuinis*) commentariis, An. Ox. 171. Gástlicum gerecednessum *mysticis* (i. *sanctis*) explanationibus, 1081. Mid gástlicum *praesagis*, 1529. Gáslicum orþangcum *spiritalibus commentis*, 3226. Dá gǽsdlecan (gástlican, *v. l.*) bebodu *spiritalia praecepta*, Past. 29, 21.

**gástlíce.** *Add :* (1) *spiritually* opposed to physically, corporeally :—His micelnesse ne mæg nán monn ámetan ; nis þ deáh nó líchomlíce tó wénanne, ac gástlíce, Bt. 42, 258, 14. Tódál þǽra metta wé ne healdaþ, for þon þe ealle þá gástlíce (*spiritaliter*) wé understandaþ, An. Ox. 40, 27. Gástlíce *typice*, 11, 103. Þǽr dú gemunan woldest hwylcra gebyrda þú wǽre and hwylcra burgwara for worulde, oþþe eft gástlíce hwilces geférscipes dú wǽre on dínum móde, Bt. 5, 1 ; F. 10, 4. (2) *spiritually* opposed to carnally :—Done monn de gǽstlíce (gást-, *v. l.*) liofad *qui spiritaliter vivit*, Past. 61, 7. Þæt dæt gé gǽsdlíce (gást-, *v. l.*) underféngon, gé willad geendigan flǽsclíce *cum spiritu coeperitis, nunc carne consummemini*, 207, 14.

**gát.** *Add :*—Sume bróhton gáte hǽr . . . þæt gáte hǽr getácnode þá stíþan dǽdbóte, Ælfc. Gen. Thw. 3, 31–36. Gáta hús *caprile*, Wrt. Voc. ii. 23, 12. Gáta loc *titule*, 122, 41. Mid gǽtena (gǽtenum, *v. l.*, *with*

*a later gloss* gotene) smerwe, Lch. i. 178, 18. Þá gæt, Wlfst. 288, 4. ¶ *the word occurs in local names*, e. g. Gát-hám, Gáte-hlinc, -wyl, Gáta-ford, -tún, C. D. vi. 290. v. wudu-gát.

**gát-ánstig** (-stíg?) *a goat-path* (-sty?) :—On horsweg; of horswege innan gátánstíge, C. D. B. i. 417, 12. v. stíg, stíga, stig.

**gát-hyrde.** *Add:*—Gáthiorde *caprarius*, Wrt. Voc. ii. 22, 27.

**gauutan.** v. gabote.

**ge.** *Add:* I. connecting two words or clauses, *and* (1) alone :— Mannes heáfod ge þá sculdro magan in, Bl. H. 127, 9. Þræfian mid lufe ge mid láþe, 45, 8. Þæs byscopes líf on bysceopháde ge ær bysceopháde *cujus uiri et in episcopatu et ante episcopatum uita*, Bd. 4, 6 ; Sch. 382, 7. (2) *with* eác :—Hit God wrecende wæs on him selfum . . ., ge eác (*ac*) . . . ealle eorþan wæstmbæro gelytlade, Ors. 2, 1 ; S. 58, 19. Be þisse ondweardan tíde, ge eác be þære tóweardan, Bl. H. 15, 4. (2 a) where the two words (clauses) are connected with others:—Þénode Willferð þone bysceophád on Eoforwícceastre, and eác swylce (*nec non et*) on eallum Norþanhymbrum, ge eác (*sed et*) on Pehtum, Bd. 4, 3 ; Sch. 349, 9. I a. where the second clause gives an extreme case, *even* :— Wé gehiérdon betueoxn eów unryhthæmed, ge suá unryht suá wé furðum betwuxn hæðnum monnum ne hiérdon *auditur inter vos fornicatio, et talis fornicatio qualis nec inter gentes*, Past. 211, 8. Him bið leófre ðæt hé secge . . . ge ðeáh hé nyte hwæt hé sóðes secge, 217, 15. Hé lið inne mónað, ge hwílum twégen (*sometimes even as long as two months*), Ors. 1, 1 ; Swt. 20, 21. Swá þ þá hæðenan ðe raðor gelífdan. Oft ge þúsend manna ætgædere gelífde, Ll. Th. ii. 372, 17. ¶ ge furþum *even* :— Ge furþon *etenim*, Ps. Th. 40, 9. Bió ðe uníðe tó clipianne, ge furðum ðína ágna spræca, Past. 385, 1 : 241, 1. Hé hét ofsleán ealle þá wísestan witan, ge furþon his ágene módor . . . ge furðon his ágen wíf hé ofslóg, Bt. 16, 4 ; F. 58, 6–8 : 31, 1 ; F. 112, 14 : 11, 1 ; F. 32, 26. Wyrta eft onginnað seárian, and swá eall nýtenu and fugelas ; ge furðum manna líchaman forealdiað, Solil. 4, 10, 7. Þæt ic lufige ge furðum on þeófum *quas amo etiam in latronibus*, 16, 13. II. where ge introduces the first word or clause, and is followed by (1) ge as a connective, *both* . . . *and* . . . :—Ge . . . ge *tam* . . . *quam*, An. Ox. 2745 : S, 281. Is micel unrótness ge of ðínum yrre, ge of ðínum gnornunga, Bt. 5, 1 ; F. 10, 24. Ge on lande, ge on óþrum þingum, ge on óþrum gestreónum, Bl. H. 51, 7. Hé ge his þeóde, ge eác þám cynnum Scotta and Pehta, ge mid his lífes bysene, ge mid láre, ge mid ealdorlicnessa ðreá, ge mid árfæstnesse his sylena swíðe brícsade, Bd. 3, 27 ; Sch. 322, 8–16. (1 a) *and* :—Ge hér on worlde, ge eác on þære tóweardan, Bl. H. 53, 20. Ge þ hié him selfum heora synna bebeorgaþ, ge eác óþre syngiende rihtaþ, 63, 24. (2) *and* :—Hí hit eall álugon, ge wed, and eác ápas, Chr. 947 ; P. 112, 25. Hé geleornade ge hwæs hé God bæd and tó him wilnade, and þ he his béne gehýrede wæron *didicerat et quid ille petisset, et quia petita inpetrasset*, Bd. 3, 27 ; Sch. 321, 13.

**ge-.** *Add:* Both ge- and gi- are used in the oldest glossaries : e. g. on p. 48 of O. E. T. nine words with the prefix occur ; in four cases both the Epinal and Erfurt glosses have *gi-*, in one they have *ge-*, in two the Epinal has *ge-* where the Erfurt has *gi-*, and in two the Epinal has *gi-* where the other has *ge-*. In each case the Corpus Gloss. has *ge-*. In this glossary, however, *gi-* is found, e. g. *gi-brec*, 2152, and in later glossaries also, e. g. *gi-mynd*, Wrt. Voc. ii. 53, 73. Besides the forms given may be noted *ga-eádun*, Erf. 75 ; *gy-byrdid*, Ep. 228. In the Durham Ritual the regular form is *gi-*.

**gé.** *Add:*—Gee sint salt eorðes, Mt. L. 5, 13. Gié, 14. Nú gé magan sylfe sóð gecnáwan, An. 1560. Hwí séce gé ymbútan eów þá gesélþa ðe gé oninnan eów (iów, *v. l.*) habbaþ . . . geset?, Bt. 11, 2 ; F. 34, 4. Þonne gé mannes sunu upp áhebbaþ, þonne gecnáwe gé þ ic hit eom, Jn. S, 28. Ne gecure gé mé, 15, 16. Cunne gé (uutas gé, L.) tócnáwan heofones híw, ge ne magon witan þæra tída tácnu, Mt. 16, 3. Ne þurfon gé wénan þ gé þ orceápe sellon, Bl. H. 41, 12. Gehérde gé *audistis*, Mt. L. 5, 21. Ne geseáð gié mec, Jn. L. 16, 16. Geseáð gié *uidetis*, 12, 19. Wite gé hwæt ic eów dyde ?, Jn. 13, 12. Ne cúðu gié (cuðon gé, R.) þte . . . , Lk. L. 2, 49. Huæd gestyredo aro gié (aron gé, R.) ?, 24, 38. Mett habbas gé (gee, R.) ?, Jn. L. 21, 5. Bringaþ gé eówerne teóðan sceat, Bl. H. 39, 26 : 41, 9, 10. Dóeð gié wæstm . . . and nællas ga cuoeða, Mt. L. 3, 8, 9. Nelle gé wénan (nællas gié woenæ, L., ne wénaþ gé, R.), Mt. 5, 17. Habbað gé sealt on ieów (eów, *v. l.*) and sibbe habbaþ betweoh iów, Past. 93, 22. Waa ieów (eów, *v. l.*) welegum, 181, 23. Oninnan eów selfum, Bt. 14, 2 ; F. 44, 16. Iówih (iuih, L.) *vobiscum*, Jn. R. 14, 30. Mid iówh, Mt. L. 26, 11. Iúch *uobis*, Jn. L. 1, 15. Iúh, Mt. L. 3, 11. Iouh (iów, R.), Mk. L. 4, 11. Iucgh, Rtl. 107, 3. Ofer eówic . . . eów *super vos* . . . *vobis*, Ps. Srt. 128, 8 : 113, 14. Mið iówih and in iów *apud vos et in vobis*, Jn. R. 14, 17. Hé iówih (iuih, L.) læreð and gitrióweð iówih (iuh, L.) alle ðá ðe swá hwæt in cwedo iów (iúh, L.) *ille uos docebit et suggeret uobis omnia quaecumque dixero uobis*, 26. Hé foreliórað iówih (eów, R.) *praecedit nos*, Mt. L. 28, 7. Iúc *uos*, Jn. L. 3, 7. Þæt gé healdan eów sylfe (*uosmet*) ænlíce, Coll. M. 35, 37. Gé dóþ eów sylfe wyrsan þonne eówre ágne æhta, Bt. 14, 2 ; F. 44, 36. Eáþmódgiaþ eów sylfe, Bl. H. 99, 3. v. eówer, git.

**geá.** *Take here* iá *in Dict., and add:* I. where a question is answered in the affirmative. (1) where the question is put positively :—Sume *aduerbia* syndon con- vel adfirmatiua . . . mid ðám wé áséðað úre spræce. *Etiam* geá : *manducasti hodie?* æt ðú tódæg? *etiam feci* geá, ic dyde, Ælfc. Gr. Z. 226, 10–13. Hæfst þú ænig gedeorf? *etiam*, ic hæbbe (*etiam, habeo*), Coll. M. 20, 11, 35. Canst þú temian hig? Geá, ic cann, 25, 23. Gelýfst þú þæs . . . ? Geá, ic hys gelífe, Solil. H. 18, 8 : 20, 20. Hweðer þú wille beón blíðe ? Geá lá geá, 34, 11. (2) where the question is put negatively :—Ne canst þú huntian búton nníd nettum? Geá (*etiam*), bútan nettum huntian ic mæg, Coll. M. 21, 23. 'Láruua iúr ne unband cáseres gæfel ?' Cueð : 'Gee (gé, R. *etiam*),' Mt. L. 17, 25. II. where agreement or consent is expressed :—Manige fédaþ þá getemedon ofer sumor. Geá (*etiam*), swá hig dóþ, Coll. M. 26, 17. Mé þincd nú þæt þé þince þæt . . . Geá, swá mé þincd, Solil. H. 20, 9. 'Gif þú þone man tó mé gelædest . . . ic wille gelýfan.' Volosianus hym andswarode, and þus cwæð : 'Geá,' hláford, and gif ic swylcne man geméte, hwylce méde sceal ic hym behátan ?,' Hml. A. 188, 200. Geá lá gé amen, Ps. Rdr. p. 302, 18. III. in the Lind. and Rush. Glosses, and in Rtl. the word is used as an emphatic particle glossing *etiam*, *jam*, and as an alternative for *súþ*, *sóþlíce*, *witodlíce* :—Gée ł éc sóð *etiam*, Mt. p. 12, 15. Gé ł sóð-líce, Mt. L. 11, 9. Geé ł sóðlíce, 12, 8. Wutetlíce ł gé ðeh ðe seel sié *etiamsi oportuerit*, 26, 35. Gée *etiam*, Mt. p. 14, 13 : Rtl. 22, 15. Gee, Mk. L. 13, 22. Gee (gé, R.) ł sóðlíce *iam*, Mk. L. 8, 2. Sóð ł gee, 12, 34. Gee ł uutudlíce, Jn. L. 9, 27. Gee, Jn. L. 14, 19 : 21, 6. Gée (gee, R.), 16, 16 : 19, 33. Gee, 16, 32 : 4, 51. Gee, Mk. L. 15, 44. Gí, Mk. R. 15, 42.

**ge-ábilgan** *to exasperate* :—Geábylgode (*exacerbavit*) Drihten se synfulla, Ps. Spl. 9 second, 4.

**geác.** *Add:*—Gaec, géc *cuculus*, Txts. 55, 618. Geác *geumatrix*, Wrt. Voc. ii. 109, 64 ; *geumatrex*, 40, 69. ¶ Geáces súre :—Géces (geácaes, gécaes) súre *accitalium*, Txts. 37, 58. Geácas súre, Wrt. Voc. ii. 4, 32. Iéces (iáces) súrae *calciculium*, Txts. 47, 380. ¶ In a place-name :—Tó Geáces leá, C. D. v. 342, 24. Geákes leá et óðer Geákes leá, iii. 101, 15. Æt Iáces leá, 125, 9. [The tenth riddle is on the cuckoo.]

**ge-aclian.** l. -áclian.

**ge-ácolmódian** *to terrify, cow* :—Fyrhtaþ, gebrégþ, geácolmódaþ *consternat*, i. *perterritat, contristat, convincat, indomitat*, Wrt. Voc. ii. 133, 67.

**geador.** v. gader- : **geador-tenge.** v. gader-tang.

**ge-æbiligan.** *Add:*—Hwæt sé geearnige þe geæbylið (*scandalizauerit*) énne þára læstena þe on God behycgað, R. Ben. 55, 14. Sé ðe bepæhð ænne Godes þeówena, hé geæbiligð ðone Hláford, Hml. Th. i. 516, 20. Hé ðám fæderum bebeád þæt hí heora bearn ne geæbiligdon (*patres, nolite ad iracundiam provocare filios vestros*, Eph. 6, 4), ii. 324, 26. Byð geæbylged *indignabitur*, Bl. Gl. : Ps. L. 102, 9. Ic hálsige þe þ þú ne beó geæbylged ougén þíne þeówene, Hml. S. 30, 349.

**ge-æcnóslian** *to degenerate* :—Geæcnósliendum *degenerante*, Wrt. Voc. ii. 138, 38.

**ge-æfenian.** *For second passage substitute* :—Geéfenedan deige, Kent. Gl. 186.

**ge-æf(e)st(i)gian** *to be envious* :—Ne gefíolle hé nó on swæ opene scylde ðæt hé his bróður ofslóge, gif hé ær ne geæfstgode (æfstgade, *v. l.*) ðætte his bróður lác wæron ðancweordlícor onfongne ðonne his (*nisi Cain invidisset acceptam fratris hostiam*), Past. 235, 3.

**ge-æhtendlic.** v. ge-eahtendlic.

**ge-ælan** *to burn* :—Geæl cealcstán swíðe, Lch. ii. 98, 13. Geældes heortes hornes ahsan, 120, 26.

**ge-ælfremedan** *to alienate, estrange* :—Þæt heora nán ne beó geæl-fremod fram ðám micclan húse, Hml. Th. i. 350, 4. Ðá hálgan geseóð þá fordónan swá micclum fram him geælfremode swá micclum swá hí beóð fram Drihtne áscofene, Hml. Th. i. 332, 24. Ðonne hí geæmetgade bióð ðæt hié magon bet dón ðonne óðre menn *meliora agere vacantes*, Past. 401, 7. II a. generally reflexive, *to free oneself*. (1) from occupation, (a) absolute, *to be disengaged* :—Geæmetgiað eów and gesióð *vacate et videte*, Ps. Th. 45, 9. (β) with gen. :—Hú hié hié geæmettian (-æmeti-gian, *v. l.*) scoldon ðærra weorca, Past. 131, 5. (γ) with prep. :—Þonne heó mæg hí fram hyre láre geæmtigan, Ap. Th. 22, 12. (2) in order to do something, *to make* or *get time for a purpose, devote oneself to* :—Þ hé hine geæmtogode (-ænitigode, -æmetgode, *v. ll.*) Gode tó þeówianne,

**ge-ælfremede** synt þá synfullan *alienati sunt peccatores*, Ps. L. 57, 4. [*These forms might be from* ge-ælfremian, *but cf.* ælfremed, *and the verbal noun* ælfremedung *alienatio*, Ps. Rdr. 28₅, 14.]

**ge-ælged.** v. ge-telged.

**ge-æmtian.** l. -æmtian, *and add:* I. *to empty, remove the material contained in* something :—Þá eágan wæron út ádýde of þám eáhhringum, and se óðer æppel wæs geæmtigod and se óðer hangode gehál, Hml. S. 21, 280. II. *to free* a person from occupation, *give leisure to* a person for a purpose :—Hé gyrnde þ he wære geæmtigod tó his gebede *vacare oratione concupiscens*, Gr. D. 290, 16.

Gr. D. 52, 8. Hé hine geǽmtigode tó þám weorce, 329, 12. Geǽmtigeað inc tó gebedum, Past. 399, 35. On tídum þám hí geǽmtian [gebrðdru?] rǽding ... þe lǽs þe sí gemét [bróðor] ásolcen, sé geǽmtige *ídelnesse horis quibus vacant fratres lectioni ... ne forte inveniatur frater accidiosus, qui vacet otioso*, R. Ben. I. 83, 7.

**ge-ǽnan** (?) *to unite oneself to, join with* :—Be ðám þingum þe ðú mé ǽr sédest þat þú ... for nánum þingum eft tó gecyrran nolde ... ácsige ic þe hweðer þú áðer oððe for (fór, MS.) heora lufum, oððe for ǽniges þinges lufum hym eft tó geénan (geénan, MS.) wille, Shrn. 184, 11. Cf. ge-áned.

**ge-ænged.** v. ge-engan.

**ge-ǽrendian.** *Add :* **I.** *to do an errand or a business* :—Se man þe bringð médsceat þám geréfan, sé geǽrendað bet (*does his business better*) þonne sé ðe nǽnne ne bringð, Wlfst. 238, 9. Se cing Gode þancode þ hé swá geǽrndod swá ðan ealra leófuste wes, Chr. 995 ; P. 131, 24. **II.** *to obtain by negotiation or intercession.* (1) *for a person* (*dat.*) :—Geǽrendodon mé ðá hiwan ðet þá men móstan on þan londe wunien, Cht. Th. 152, 13. Þá sendon hié Filónem tó þon þ hé him sceolde Gaiuses mildse geǽrendian *Philonem legatum ad Caesarem miserunt*, Ors. 6, 3 ; S. 258, 5. (2) *from* (*æt*) *a person* :—Ic geǽrndede æt Cnute þæt land, Cht. Th. 368, 9. **II a.** *to go to* (*tó*) *a person and obtain for another* (*dat.*), *apply to a person and obtain* :—Englas mé geǽrndodon tó þám Hǽlende, þ ic hí gebicgan móste, Hml. S. 36, 176. Nán man ne mæg him sylfum rihtlíce tó his Drihtne his þearfe geǽrndian bútan ..., Wlfst. 136, 15.

**ge-ǽrnan.** *Add :* *to reach a place by riding* :—Wé settað ǽghwelcere cirican ... þis frið. Gif hié fáh mon geierne oþþe gǽrne (*reach it on foot or on horseback*), Ll. Th. i. 64, 9.

**ge-ǽsce[, an ; f. ?]** *Inquiry* :—Wé witon swíþe lytel þæs þe ǽr ús wæs búton be gemynde and be geáscunge (geáscum, v. l.), Bt. 42 ; F. 256, 26.

**ge-ǽswicod.** *Substitute :* **ge-ǽswician ;** *p.* ode *To offend* (in the Biblical sense) :—Sé ðe geǽswicað ánum ðyssera lyttlinga (*qui scandalizaverit unum de pusillis istis*, Mt. 18, 6), Hml. Th. i. 514, 15. Geáswicað, R. Ben. I. 62, 13. Tó hwý gedréfest þú þíne geþóhtas tó geǽswicianne on mé swylce ic hwylc gást syrwiende gebedu fremme *scandalizabatur in mente putans ne spiritus esset, qui se fingeret orare*, Hml. S. 23 b, 283. Ic swýðe geǽswicod (*ashamed.* Cf. hé wæs myccle scame þrowiende and hé swá scamiende út of ðám temple wépende gewát, 119, 87) eóde út of ðám Drihtnes temple, Hml. A. 122, 170. Sé bið eádig þe on mé ne bið geǽswicod (*scandalizatus*, Mt. 11, 6), Hml. Th. i. 480, 19. Þæt ðá beón getimbrode þurh his behreówsunge ðe ǽr wǽron þurh his mándǽda geǽswicode, 498, 12. Geáswicode, R. Ben. I. 62, 9.

**ge-ǽþan.** **I.** *to make oath concerning, confirm by oath* :—Hé hit mid áðsware geǽðde and geswór, þus cweðende : ' Ic ... geǽðe and swerige þurh þone lifigendan Godes sunu ... þ þás word ... nǽron of nánes mannes handa gehíwode,' Nap. 27. Wé lǽrað þ preóst bísæce ordél ǽfre ne geǽðe (*in cases where the validity of the ordeal was disputed a priest was not to swear to the validity?* The previous canon enjoins that ' ǽnig preóst ne stande on leásre gewitnesse ' ; in the present one the ' bísæce ordél ' may be ordeals which, it was contended, had been conducted improperly (cf. Gif preóst ordǽl misfadige, gebéte þ, Ll. Th. ii. 296, 9), and to the validity of which he was not to swear (falsely)), Ll. Th. ii. 258, 4. **II.** *to administer an oath to, swear a person.* v. ge-ǽðed *in Dict.* [O. H. Ger. ge-eiden *adjurare* ; ge-eidemo *conjurato.*]

**ge-ǽþele.** *Add :* [cf. O. H. Ger. ge-edeli *nobilitas.*]

**ge-ǽt[t]rian** *to poison* (lit. and fig.). *Take here* ge-ǽtred, *and add* :—Ondrǽd þé þone ðrowend þe geǽttrað mid þám tægle ... biþ his hiht geǽttrod mid þæs ðrowendes tægle, Hml. Th. i. 252, 9. Nǽddran fela manna tó deáðe geǽttrodon, ii. 238, 12. Wæs án cnapa geǽttrod þurh nǽddran, 514, 6. þ flæsc wæs geǽttred mid þý werrestan ættre, Shrn. 84, 28. On þá oferhýda þǽre geǽttredan deófies láre, Cht. E. 242, 21. Hé mid geǽttrode fíán hine ofsceótan wolde, ac seó geǽttrode flá wende ongeán, Hml. Th. i. 502, 18. Geǽttrodre *liuida*, Germ. 401, 31. Geǽttrodne hláf, Gr. D. 118, 5. Geǽtredum *infectis*, Wrt. Voc. ii. 43, 62.

**ge-ǽwed.** v. un-geǽwed, *and next word.*

**ge-ǽwnod.** *Add* :—Under Móyses ǽ móste se bisceop habban án geǽwnod (í-ǽwod, v. l.) wíf, Hml. S. 10, 219. Ne hí ne beóþ geǽwnede *neque nubentur*, An. Ox. 1265. Geǽwnedra *conjugatorum*, 1006.

**geafel, es ; m.** *Substitute :* **geafel, e** (*and ?* geafle, an) ; **f.**, *and add* :—Gæfle *furca, furcula diminutive*, Wrt. Voc. ii. 151, 82. Hé sceal habban .. race, geafie, Angl. ix. 263, 7. Gæfle *forcelle*, Wrt. Voc. ii. 150, 17. [O. L. Ger. (fiésc-, mist-) gabala.]

**geafla.** v. gifian : **geaflas.** *For* ' Geaflas ... Cot. 91 ' *substitute* :—Geaflum *faucibus*, Wrt. Voc. ii. 38, 53 : **geafle?** *Dele, and see* geafel *a fork* : **geafol-monung.** v. gafol-manung : **ge-aforud.** l. ge-uferod. In Ps. Spl. 36, 37 *exaltatum* is glossed by geáforadne, but the correct form, geuferudne, occurs in Ps. Rdr. 36, 35.

**ge-ágan** *to possess* :—þæt hí gelýfon tó geágenne þá écan welan, Hml. Th. i. 64, 19.

**ge-ágen.** *Add* :—Æfter ðínum geágenum gewitte, Shrn. 181, 32 : **ge-ágennud.** v. ge-ágnian.

**geagl.** l. geagl, *and add* :—Geágla *mandibularum*, Wrt. Voc. ii. 54, 69 : i. *dentium molarum*, An. Ox. 2444. Eáhla, 2, 83. Geálgan *mandibulas, i. dentes molares*, 1206 : 5015. v. swillan ; II.

**geaglisc.** v. gagolisc.

**ge-ágnian.** *Add :* **I.** *to have as one's own, possess, occupy* :—þín sǽd geágnað (þín ofspring sceal ágan, Gen. 22, 17) his feónda gatu *possidebit semen tuum portas inimicorum*, Hml. Th. ii. 62, 10. On eówerum geðylde gé geáhniað eów (*possidebitis*, Lk. 21, 19) eówere sáwla, 544, 4. Eádige beóð þá líþan, for ðan þe hí þæt land geágniað (*possidebunt*, Mt. 5, 4), i. 550, 19. Bréðer þe Godes ege his sáule geáhnige *cujus animam timor Dei possidet*, R. Ben. 85, 22. Swá swá náht hæbbende and ealle þing geágnigende (*possidentes*, 2 Cor. 6, 10), Hml. Th. i. 550, 7. Geágnode, Ælfc. Gr. Z. 15, 6. **II.** *to get or secure possession of, acquire for a person* (*dat.*) :—Se arcebiscop geáhnode (*acquisivit æternam hereditatem*) Gode and Scé Andrea þá land, Cht. Th. 273, 23. Hé lét þá Godas þeówas þǽra áre brúcan þe him geáhnod wæs, Hml. S. 3, 354. **II a.** *reflexive* :—Cnut geáhnode (-ágenede, v. l.) him þet land, Chr. 1028 ; P. 157, 21. Uton faran and geáhnian ús þæt land, for þan þe wé magon mid mihte hit bigitan, Num. 13, 31. Him ealle þás cynerícu on his ǽnes æht geágnian, Bl. H. 105, 12. On þám setle þe hé him sylfum geágnod hæfde, Nic. 16, 14. **III.** *to adopt a child* :—Tó ðǽm ðæt gé Gode geágenudu (-ágnudu, v. l.) bearn (*adoptionis filii*) beón scielen, Past. 263, 22. **IV.** *to prove one's title to property, secure by shewing title* :—Sé þe yrfe him geágnian wille ... sylle þone áð þ hit on his ǽhte geboren wǽre, Ll. Th. i. 204, 12. Þæt Helmstán móste gán forð mid ðon bócon and geágnigean him ðæt lond, Cht. Th. 170, 18. Þá getǽhte man Wynflǽde þ hió móste hit hyre geáhnian, 288, 36. **V.** *in a bad sense, to usurp* :—Geáhnian *usurpare*, An. Ox. 5, 15. Geáhnode *usurpate*, 5307.

**ge-ágnung, e ; f.** *Acquisition* :—Ðet mæg tó sóðe seggan Ælfsige be ðére geágnunga ðisses landes, C. D. ii. 304, 5.

**geáhpe.** v. geáþ.

**geal-ádl.** *Add* :—Ealládla *melancolias*, An. Ox. 7, 223 : Angl. xiii. 33, 166.

**gealg.** v. gealh.

**gealga.** *Add* :—On gealgan treówe (cf. galga-tré *in Dict.*) *patibulo*, An. Ox. 391. Róde gelgan *gabuli patibulo*, 3089. Þá gefæstnodon hí hine on róde gealgan ... Hé þǽre róde gealgan underféng, Hml. Th. i. 588, 16-19: Bl. H. 27, 28 : 97, 11. On galgan geworhtre *eculei* (cf. *eculei, cruci*, 81, 49), Wrt. Voc. ii. 31, 76. Gealgan *labaro* (Christi), An. Ox. 1860.

**gealga (?), an ; m.** *Sadness, gloom* :—Ðæs sweartan galgan (cf. *the gloss to the same passage in* An. Ox. 2960 :—Sweartes geallan) *melancoliae*, Wrt. Voc. ii. 81, 8 : 56, 72. v. gealh(-g).

**gealgmódlíce (?), gealglíce (?) ; adv.** *Bitterly* :—Gealg[módlíce (?) -líce (?)] *acriter*, Hpt. Gl. 456, 53.

**gealgmódnes (?), gealgnes (?), e ; f.** *Gloominess, sullenness* :—G[e]alh[módnes (?), -nes (?)] *obstinatio*, An. Ox. 56, 157.

**gealg-treów.** *Add* :. *a gallow-tree* (gallows-tree comes in only in the 19th cent. The older form remains in local names e. g. Gallowtree-gate in Leicester) :—Tó ðam galhtreówe on deópan dene, C. D. iii. 439, 12.

**gealla ; I.** *Add* :—Gealla *fel*, Wrt. Voc. i. 65, 53 : 283, 83 : 71, 7 : *melancolia*, ii. 58, 23. Sweartes geallan *melancolię, i. fellis*, An. Ox. 2950. v. eorþ-gealla.

**gealled.** l. geallede : **geallig.** *Dele, and see* gealgmódlíce (?).

**gealpettan ;** *p.* te. **I.** *to devour, eat greedily* [? v. N. E. D. galp *to gape* ; D.D. gaup *to gape, devour*] :—þá ðe hér swíðost galpettað and on unrihttídum on oferfyllo bióð forgriwene, þá bióð þǽr on mǽstum hungre forþrycced *those that here eat most greedily and are steeped in unseasonable excess, they will there be oppressed with grievous hunger*, Nap. 27. **II.** *to speak noisily* [? v. D.D. gaup *loud, noisy talking, chatter.* Cf. O. Sax. galpón :—Ne galpó þu far þínum gebun te swíðo *do not say too much about your gifts*, Hél. 1563]. v. next word.

**gealpettung, e ; f.** *Noisy, boastful talking* :—Þá hé oftost tesoword spræc in his onmédlan gælpettunga (*in his arrogant talking*), þá earnode hé mé þǽre mǽsta[n] gestynþo, Nap. 27. v. preceding word.

**ge-ambehtan, -embeht(i)an** *to minister. Take here* ge-embeht-an *in Dict.*, *and add* :—Gif huá mé embehtes (*ministrat*) ... gif huelc mé geembehtað (*ministrabit*), Jn. R. 12, 26. Geembihtatun *ministraverunt*, Mt. p. 7, 3. Him geembehte ðú *illi servies*, Mt. L. 4, 10. Ne cuóm þte geembehta (giembihte, R.) him ah þte hé geembehtade óðrum, Mk. L. 10, 45.

**geán** *again.* v. gegn : **geán, geána** *still.* v. gén, géna.

**ge-anbídian** (-and-), *and add :* **I.** *absolute, to wait* :—Ic geanbidode oþ ic wiste hwæt þú woldest, Bt. 22, 1 ; F. 7625. þ folc stód geanbidiende, Lk. 23, 35. **II.** *to wait for.* (1) *to wait for the coming or return of a person* (*gen.*) :—Ðá bed heó þá cwelleras ðæt hí hire geanbidedan medmicle hwíle ; þá eóde heó on hire palatium,

Shrn. 75, 24. (2) *to wait for the coming to pass* of something. (a) *with gen.* :—Hē Godes rīces geanbidode, Mk. 15, 43. (b) *with acc.* :—Hē geandbidode ðone frōfer ðe behāten wæs, Hml. Th. i. 136, 1. Hē geanbidude Godes rīce, Lk. 23, 51. (c) *with a clause* :—Hē geanbidað þæt wē tō beteran gecyrren *he waits for our conversion,* R. Ben. 25, 21. III. *to wait* for the settlement of what is uncertain :—Drihten geanbidaþ hwæþer wē mid weorcum his lāre gefyllan willen, R. Ben. 4, 16. Hē geanbidode þǣr hwæðer man him tō būgan wolde, Chr. 1066; P. 200, 8.

ge-anbidung, e; *f. Expectation* :—Drihten mē generede of eallre geanbidunge (*expectatione*) folkes, Gr. D. 107, 25.

geán-bóc; *f. A duplicate charter* :—Geánbóc tō Beonetleáge, C. D. vi. 177, 24. Geánbēc (*printed* Cean-) intō Glēweceaster, iii. 208, 25. Ðás gēnbēc hýrað intō Wincescumbe, 256, 1 : C. D. B. iii. 338, 20.

ge-anbyrdan, -andbyrdan. *Add* :—Geondbyrde, Ll. Th. i. 404, 13 note.

geán-cirr, es; *m. Take here* geán-cyr *in Dict., and add : return* :—Gesǣligum geáncyrre *felici reditu,* Hy. S. 57, 22. Ðone rēdan wiðersacan on his geáncyrre gegladian, Hml. Th. i. 450, 19. Geáncyr *postliminium, reuersionem,* An. Ox. 7, 187.

geán-cwide. v. geagn-, gegn-cwide *in Dict.*

geán-cyme. *Add* :—Him wildeór ne dereþ ne ǣnig yfel geáncyme, Lch. i. 176, 5. Fram geáncyme *ab occursu,* Scint. 188, 6. Þū bewruge mē fram gemētinge (gēncyme, MS. T.) āwyrgedra *protexisti me a conventu malignantium,* Ps. Spl. 63, 2. Gēncymas *adinventiones,* Ps. Rdr. 275, 4.

ge-andetness, e; *f. Confession* :—Giondetnisses *confessionis,* Rtl. 59, 7.

ge-andettan. *Add* : I. *to confess, acknowledge* wrong-doing, weakness, &c. :—Geondeton (*confitentes*) synna hiora, Mt. L. 3, 6. Geandet swā hwætt swā þū þāron wite, Ll. Lbmn. 414, 34. I a. as an ecclesiastical term, *to confess* to a priest. (a) *trans.* :—Þæt hié heora synna cunnon onrihtlīce geandettan, Bl. H. 43, 16. Hit geandettan and bētan, Wlfst. 34, 17. Būton hit ǣr geandet and gebēt wǣre, 25, 15. (β) *reflex.* :—Þǣm mannum þe heora synna and unrihtes geswicaþ, and hié (*or* hié *may refer to* synna) Gode and heora scriftum geandettiaþ, Bl. H. 193, 23. II. *to admit for oneself* an assertion, *concede, allow* :—Ðe ilca geondete lomb niomende synno middangeardes *ipsum fatetur agnum tollentem peccata mundi,* Jn. p. 3, 6. Geondate (giondetted, R.) *confessus est,* Jn. L. 1, 20. Þ ðā ídlo hiá . . . geondetad sint *ut inutiles se . . . fateantur,* Lk. p. 9, 7. III. *to confess, declare one's belief* that :—Gif hwelc hine giondette (geondetate, L.) Crīst *si quis eum confiteretur Christum,* Jn. R. 9, 22. Sē ðe ðe ilca Godes suna bið geondetað *qui eum Dei filium confitetur,* Jn. p. 3, 10. IV. *to confess* a person or thing, *acknowledge as having a certain character, declare one's faith in* :—Mannes geþanc þē geandet, R. Ben. 24, 17. Sē ðe geondetas meh before monnum, Mt. L. 10, 32. Sel folcum crīstinum ðā ðe giondetað (*quae profitentur*) tō ongeattanne, Rtl. 15, 15. V. *to make acknowledgement of a benefit* to a person, *give thanks or praise* :—Ðió giondetade (geondittéd, L.) Drihtne *haec confitebatur Domino,* Lk. R. 2, 38. On niht ārīsan and Drihtne geandettan, R. Ben. 40, 14. v. un-geandett.

ge-andspornan, -spurnan *to offend* :—Gif ēgu ðīn giondspyrned (-spurnað, L.) ðec *si oculus tuus scandalizat te,* Mk. R. 9, 47. Giondspyrnas (-spurnas, L.), 42. Ðis iówih geondspyrnað (ondspyrneð, L.), Jn. R. 6, 61. Giondspurnedon ł geondspurnedo woeron *scandalizabuntur,* Mt. L. 13, 57. Geondspyrne *scandalizet,* Lk. L. R. 17, 2. Ðēh ðe alle ondspyrnendo sié, ic næfra geondspyrnad bióm, Mt. L. 26, 33 : Mk. L. 14, 27, 29. Geondspyrned, 6, 3. Geondspurnad, 4, 17 : Mt. L. 13, 21.

ge-andswarian (-ond-). *Add* : I. *to answer* in words :—Geondsuarede *respondens,* Mt. L. 26, 25 : Lk. L. 7, 43. Geondsuarade (giondsworade, R.), 22, 51 : 14, 5. Geondsuearede, Jn. L. 18, 23. Geondswearade, 2, 19. Geondsuærade, 3, 3. Geonsuarede, Mk. L. 14, 61. Geonsuarede, Mt. L. 27, 12. Geondsuaredon *responderunt,* Lk. L. 20, 7. Geondsuearadun (giondsworadun, R.), Jn. L. 7, 47. Geondsuærende *respondens,* Mt. L. 27, 25. Nis nāht mā þ mæge geandswarian openlīce þām rihte þe þū recest *nihil est quod responderi valent apertae rationi,* Gr. D. 210, 9. II. *to respond* with action :—Ðonne ðæt mennisce mōd Godes glædmōdnesse mid gōdum weorcum ne geandsworað *cum largientem Deum humana mens boni operis responsione non sequitur,* Past. 391, 6.

ge-andweard (?); *adj. Present, in the presence* of a person :—Þás mīne dohtor þe ic beforan ðē, Diana, geandweard (= geandweardod?) hæbbe, Ap. Th. 24, 21. v. next word.

ge-andwerdian. *Add* : -werdian :—Se heáhengel geondweardode (*printed* geong weardode) Marian sáwle beforan Drihtne, Bl. H. 159, 9. Hē . . . hine sylfne beheáfdodne æfter ðon ðridan dæge eft geondweardode (-ne, MS.), 181, 2. Þā þā hē wæs geondweardod and gecýðed Benedicte *praesentatus Benedicto,* Gr. D. 129, 20 note. Swylce hē tō þām egefullan Godes dōme geandweardod (-werded, R. Ben. I. 36, 5) beón scyle *se tremendo judicio Dei representari existimet,* R. Ben. 31, 11.

ge-andwlatod; *adj. Bold-faced* :—Geandwlatade sceamleáste *frontosam inpudentiam,* An. Ox. 8, 365. Geandwlatude, Angl. xiii. 37, 277.

ge-andwyrdan. *Add* : -wordan, -weardan, -wærdan :—Geonduearded *respondens,* Mt. L. 25, 40. Hē giondworde, Mk. R. 12, 34: 14, 61. Gewonduorde (-worde), Mt. L. 20, 22 : 22, 1. Geonduaearde, Mk. L. 6, 37. Geonduærde, Lk. p. 10, 13. Geonduordon *responderunt,* Mt. L. 25, 9. Geondweardon, 21, 27. Geonduærdon, Jn. L. 8, 39. Geonduardon, 7, 52. Gewondueardon, Mt. L. 12, 38. Huæd gié geonduearde (*respondentis*), Lk. L. 12, 11. Geondwearde *respondere,* 14, 6.

geán-dýne; *adj. Steep;* fig. *arduous* (cf. uphill) :—Þis is mid sumum mannum swýþe geándýne þing and earfoðlīce þing *hoc apud nonnullos res ardua est et difficilis,* Ll. Th. ii. 134, 6. Cf. dún, æf-dýne.

geán-gang, es; *m.* I. *a going back, return* :—Gif man mægðman nēde genimeð . . . Gif gángang geweorðeð . . . *if return takes place* (i. e. if the woman goes back to the people she was taken from), Ll. Th. i. 24, 7. II. *a going to meet* :—Gægngð (= -geong?) *obbiatio* (= *obviatio*), Rtl. 195, 25.

ge-angsumian. *Add* :—Þā deóflu ðā sāwle mid ðreátungum geangsumiað, Hml. Th. i. 410, 8. Hungor þæt landfolc micclum geangsumode (cf. genyrwde *coangustabat,* Gr. D. 145, 5), ii. 170, 32. Weard geancsumod se árleása Pascasius . . . wōdlīce geancsumod þ his mágas ne mihton his mōdleáste ácuman, Hml. S. 9, 103, 124. Hē læg geancsumod, orwēne līfes, 21, 114. Geancsumod on mōde, 9, 116. Geangsumod (-anc-, *v. l.*), 25, 224. Heó weard oð deáð on mōde geancsumed . . . and æt Gode ābæd þ heó hire gāst āgeaf, Chr. 1093; P. 228, 13. Hē micclum weard geangsumod, and for his mágum swīðor þonne for him sylfum, Hml. A. 97, 168. Ðæt folc weard geangsumod on mōde for þǣre wæterleáste, 107, 176. Mid ðwyrnyssum geangsumod, Hml. Th. i. 612, 35. Mid synnum geancsumede, 342, 11.

geán-hweorfan. v. ongeán-hweorfende : geán-hworfennis. v. ongeán-hworfennes.

geán-hwyrf (-hwurf), es; *m. Return* :—Geánwurfe *reditu,* An. Ox. 559.

ge-ánlǣcan. *Add* : I. *to unite* one person to another, *unite* persons as associates :—Feówer þeóda hine underfēngon tō hláforde, Peohtas and Bryttas, Scottas and Angli, swā swā God hī geánlǣhte tō ðām, Hml. S. 26, 107. Hē weard geánlǣht mid geleáfan tō ðām hālgan were, 19, 103. Geánlǣht *ascissitur* (*militonum catervis*), An. Ox. 4178. Wǣron þā fyrmestan heáfodmen Hinguar and Hubba, geánlǣhte þurh deófol, Hml. S. 32, 30. I a. *intrans. To join together* in an undertaking :—Geánlǣhtan *conspiraverant,* Wrt. Voc. ii. 134, 11. II. *to get together, collect, assemble* :—Geánlǣhte Lisias fīf and sixtig þūsenda fyrdendra þegena, Hml. S. 25, 362.

ge-anlīcian. *Add* : I. *to make like* :—Se wyrttruma gehwylcne man him geanlīcað, Lch. i. 318, 12. Ic beó geanlīcod (*assimilabor*) niðerstigendum on seáðe, Ps. L. 27, 1. Þe lǣs þe hē sig geanlīcod þām hunde ne adsimuletur cani, Ll. Th. 16, 16. Ic eom yslum and axum geanlīcod (*I am become like dust and ashes,* Job 30, 19), Hml. Th. ii. 456, 13. Is sǣd þ hyre wyrttruma sý geanlīcud þǣre nædran heáfde, Lch. i. 318, 9. Ne mihte seó his swaðu næfre beón þǣm ōðrum flōrum geonlīcod and gelīce gehīwad, Shrn. 80, 35. II. *to act towards* a person as if he were another :—Þ hī sceoldon þone ylcan Ricgan geonlīcian (þ hī . . . geanlīcodon, *v. l.*) þām cynge *ipsum regem esse simulantes* (cf. swilce hē hit sylf wǣre, Hml. Th. ii. 168, 14).

ge-ánlician (?) *to join together* in an undertaking :—Geánlīcude *conspirati* (cf. ge-ánlǣcan ; I a. *But perhaps the form is* geanlīcude. v. Hpt. Gl. 426, 71 *where the Latin is* conspirati, consimilati), An. Ox. 863.

ge-anmētan. *l.* ge-anmēdan [cf. ge-eáþmēdan *for forms of p. tense and pp.*]. v. an-mōd.

geán-nis. *For* Hpt. Gl. 513 *substitute* :—Geánnysse *obuiam* (in sponsi *obuiam* subuolas, Ald. 65), An. Ox. 4610.

geánol (-ul); *adj. In the way, so as to meet* :—Geánulum *obuio,* Germ. 399, 264.

geán-pæþ. v. gegn-pæþ *in Dict.* : geán-ryne. *Add* :—Gēnryne *occursus,* Ps. L. 18, 7. On gegenym *in occursum,* Ps. Srt. 58, 6 : geán-slege. v. gegn-slege *in Dict.*

geán-talu (? *the word in the passage is not feminine*), e ; *f. Gainsaying, contradiction, dispute, objection* :—Gā þā ōþræ v. hīda forð mid . . . mid eallum þingum swā hit þonnæ stænt būtan ǣlcon geántalæ, Cht. Th. 587, 24. Būten alken gēntale, 594, 11. Cf. . . . in vita mea. *Post autem* sine contradictione *reciperent sua,* 600, 31.

geanðe (?) :—Mið ðý wæs Petrus in word from geanðe ł sunduria (*deorsum.* Has the glosser taken *deorsum* = *de adversum* and glossed it by *from* geán, and written both word, ðe = or, and symbol, ł, to connect this gloss with an alternative one, which, however, seems to render *seorsum* (cf. sundrig *seorsum,* 6, 31) ?), Mk. L. 14, 66.

geán-þingian. v. þingian ; IV a : ge-anþracian. v. ge-onþracian.

ge-anwealdian; *p.* ode *To exercise authority, bear rule over* :—Deáð him furðor ne bið rýcsend ł ne gionwældiað (*dominabitur*), Rtl. 26, 33

Sóðfæsto gionuældas folcum *justi dominabuntur populis*, 86, 36. Geanwealdiaþ, Ps. L. 48, 15. Ne on sweorde heora geanwealdedan (*possederunt*) eorðan, 43, 4. Geonwældad (-ed, R.) biðon ł ríxað *dominantur*, Lk. L. 22, 25.

**ge-ánwyrdan;** *p.* de *To be in agreement, conspire* :—Geánlæhtan *vel* geánwyrdan *conspiraverant*, Wrt. Voc. ii. 134, 11. [Cf. *O. Sax.* énwordi *in agreement.*]

**ge-anwyrde.** *Substitute* : **ge-anwyrde** *in the phrase* ge-anwyrde beón. (1) *to profess, declare oneself to be* :—Ic eom geanwyrde monuc *professus sum monachum*, Coll. M. 18, 28. (2) *to make confession of* :—Him man wearp on þ hé wæs þes cynges swica and ealra landleóda, and hé þæs geanwyrde wes (hé was þas gewyrde, *v. l.*), þeáh him þ word of scute his unnþances *debuit esse delator patriae, quod ipse cognovit ita esse, licet verbum illud improviso exprimeret*, Chr. 1055; P. 185, 7.

**geáp, geáp, geápes.** *Take all together under* geáp, *and add* : I. *curved, bent* :—Geáp curfa, Wrt. Voc. ii. 21, 46. Geápum *pandis*, 116, 23 : *curvis*, 21, 16. (1) *of a line* :—Geápum ł gebígedum *pando, curvo* (*arcu*), Hpt. Gl. 405, 69. Geáp, Wrt. Voc. ii. 74, 70. Geápe, 69, 4. On geápum galgan rídan, Vy. 33. In ða geápan linde, C. D. iii. 375, 5. On geápan gáran westeweardne, v. 173, 6. (2) *of a surface.* (a) *vaulted* (of the roof of a house) :—Ræced hlífade geáp and goldfáh *the hall towered up with roof vaulted and gay with gold*, B. 1800. Ruin. 11. Strúdende fýr steápes and geápes forswealh eall *every roof was burnt*, Gen. 2556. Under geápne hróf, B. 836. Þás hofu dreórgad and þæs teáfor geápu (*these vaulted and red-tiled roofs?*), tigelum sceáded hróstbeáges róf, Ruin. 31. (b) *curved* (of a boat). v. sǽ-geáp. (c) *rounded* (of a mountain) :—Munt is hine ymbútan, geáp gylden weal (*or under* (1)?), Sal. 256. (d) *with convex surface* :—Gim sceal on hringe standan steáp and geáp, Gn. C. 23. II. *crafty, clever, astute* :—Geáp *callidus*, Wrt. Voc. i. 85, 37. Sé þe gehealt þreágincga geáp (*astutus*) hé wyrð, Scint. 114, 1. Gép (*astutus*) ealle deð mid geþeahte, 199, 10. Mann gép (*uersutus*) bedíglað ingehýd, 94, 17. Án fox þe is geápest ealra deóra, Shrn. 14, 19. Sé þincð nú wærrest and geápest þe óðerne mæig beswícan, 17, 23. [Ne beo ʒe noht ʒepe (*prudentes*) toʒene ʒiu seluen. Đe man is ʒiep toʒenes him seluen þ is smegh oðer man to bicharren . . . *Estote prudentes sicut serpentes* . . . beoð giepe alse þe neddre, O. E. Hml. ii. 195, 4-16.]

**geáp** *glosses* cornas, Wrt. Voc. i. 287, 39 : ii. 16, 76. [Sievers, Angl. xiii. 325, would read *coruas = curuas*; but the list of words in which the first example occurs contains no other instance of an adjective, and the second example occurs among a group of words very similar to that in which the first is found : so that *cornas* seems meant for a noun. Perhaps geáp might be the same form as in *earn-geáp*; or could it be connected with Icel. *gaupa* a lynx?]

**geápan.** *Dele.*

**geáplíce.** *l.* geáplíce, *and add* : *cleverly, cunningly* :—Geáplíce *callide, ingeniose*, Wrt. Voc. ii. 127, 59 : *procaciter*, Kent. Gl. 804. Þa betealde hé (*Herod*) hine swíðe geáplíce, swá swá hé wæs snotorwyrde, Hml. Th. i. 80, 9. Hig tósceádað þ stæfgefég on þrym wísan geáplíce swíðe, Angl. viii. 313, 17. [Wil he . . . ʒepliche speke, Piers P. 15, 183.]

**geáp-ness,** e; *f. Cleverness, cunning, astuteness* :—Wær geápnes *argumentum* (cf. *argumento* orðonce, gleáwnesse, 2, 11), Wrt. Voc. ii. 125, 1.

**geáp-scipe.** *Add* : *cleverness, astuteness* :—Gépscipe *stropha*, An. Ox. 18 b, 80. Hé ríxade ofer Englæland, and hit mid his geápscipe swá þurhsmeáde, þ næs án híd landes innan Englælande þ hé nyste hwá heó hæfde, Chr. 1086; P. 220, 19. [Swich ʒepship forbeded ðe apostel þere he seið : '*Nolite esse prudentes aput uosmetipsos*' . . . Đe man noted wel his ʒiepship þe birged him seluen wið his agene soule unfreme . . . To swich ʒiepshipe mineʒede hure Helende his apostles, O. E. Hml. ii. 195, 2-10. Heo færden mid ʒeapscipe and mid wisdome, Laym. 2760.]

**gear.** v. mylen-gear.

**geár.** *Add* : (*n.*) *and m.* I. *as a unit of time-measurement.* (1) *in the case of* (approximately) *exact measurement*, the number of years being given :—Þa wæs syxte geár Constantines cáserdómes, El. 7. Ánes geáres cild oððe lamb *anniculus*, Ælfc. Gr. Z. 287, 11. Wé ealne þysne geár lifdon mid úres líchoman willan, Bl. H. 35, 27. Án cométa ofer ealne geár sceán, Hml. iii. 300, 32. Se here þær sæt .i. geár, Chr. 869; P. 70, 4. Þær wæron gehealdene heora líc án geár and seofan mónaþ, Bl. H. 193, 13. Þreó geár, 215, 36. Sume tén geár, Bt. 38, 1; F. 194, 7. Ymb xiii geár, Gen. 2302. (2) *of indefinite periods of time* :—Hé feala geára lifde, Bl. H. 219, 7 : Bt. 18, 3; F. 66, 18. Wintra fela . . . geára mengeo, Gen. 1726. Geára gongum *in the course of time*, Cri. 1036 : Jul. 693. Æfter feáwum geárum, Bl. H. 99, 8. Æfter geárum, El. 1265. Mænig gér, Bt. 29, 1; F. 102, 21 note. (2 a) *the years of a person's life* :—Geáras míne *anni mei*, Ps. Th. 30, 11. Heora dagena tíd . . . and heora geára gancg, Ps. Th. 77, 32. II. *as a chronological unit.* (1) *for the purposes of the calendar* :—Be ðæs geáres tídum. *Annus solaris* hæfð . . . twelf mónðas, and þ gér hæfð nigon þúsend tída and seofon hund tída and syx and syxtig, Angl. viii. 320, 19.

Đære sunnan geár is þ heó beyrne þone miclan circul *zodiacum* and gecume under ælc þæra twelf tácna, Lch. iii. 244, 20. Heóld þæt Ebreisce folc done forman geáres dæg on lenctenlicere emnihte, Hml. Th. i. 100, 1. Tó geáres dæge on *New Year's day*, Chr. 1096; P. 232, 17. Þæs geáres *during the year* 871, 871 ; P. 72, 15. Nú tó geáre *this year*, Angl. viii. 327, 10 : 329, 36. On þæm geáre bið þreó hund daga and fíf and syxtig daga, Bl. H. 35, 22. Is se mæsta dæl ágangen, efne nigon hund wintra and .lxxi. on þýs geáre, 119, 2. Wæs se winter þý geáre grim, 213, 31. Perseus wæs ealne þone geár Rómáne swencende, Ors. 4, 11; S. 208, 13 : 3, 5; S. 106, 10. Þá sylfan tíd síde herigeas habbað foreweard geár, Men. 6. ¶ *used of the time occupied by a revolution of the moon* :—Đæs mónan geár hæfð seofon and twéntig daga and eahta tída. On ðám fyrste hé underyrnð ealle ða twelf tácna þe seó sunne underged twelf mónað . . . þis is þæs mónan geár, ac his mónað is máre, Lch. iii. 246, 24-248, 15. (2) *for the purposes of calculation in dealing with that which recurs regularly* :—Æt gáres cépinge *annuis nundinis*, C. D. iv. 209, 20. Þ feoh þe mon ðám ferdmonnum on geáre sellan sceolde, Bt. 27, 4; F. 100, 14. Him tó móse sceal gegangan geára gehwylce . . . þría þreóténo þúsend, Sal. 288. III. *the year as made up of the seasons* :—Be þæs monnes mihtum sceal mon þá lǽcedómas sellan . . . and hú geáres hit sié (*according to what time of year it may be*), Lch. ii. 238, 22. God biddan þ hé him forgéfe done geár siblice tíd and smyltelíco gewidra and genihtsume wæstmas and heora líchoman trymnysse, Shrn. 74, 11. III a. *especially with reference to the yearly renewal of vegetable life* :—His gesceafta weaxaþ and eft waniaþ . . . hí ælce geáre weorþaþ tó ædsceafte, Bt. 34, 10; F. 150, 16. Brengþ corþe ælcne westm ælce geáre, 39, 13; F. 234, 14. Gif hit gebyrað on geáre (*if it happen some year*) þæt næðer ne byð . . . ne æceren ne bóc ne óðer mæsten, Nap. 10, 28. III b. *the spring season* :—Þæt geár mót brengan blósman, Bt. 7, 3; F. 20, 22. Gér byð gumena hyht, þonne God læted hrúsan syllan beorhte bléda beornum, Rún. 12. Wæs folde geblówen, geácas geár budon, Gú. 716. IV. *with respect to productivity of the ground, a* (*good or bad*) *year* :—Æfter cóm gód gér (geár, *v. l.*) and wæstmberende, Bd. 4, 13; Sch. 419, 12. Hærfest hæleðum bringeð géres wæstmas, Gn. C. 9. V. *the name of the Runic letter g.* See Rún. 12 above. v. gebann-geár.

**geara;** *adv.* v. gearwe.

**geára.** *Take here* geáraʒ, geáro *in Dict., and add* :—Geára oþþe geógára *jam*, Wrt. Voc. ii. 48, 11. Geára gewunan odðe gewunede *obtani*, 65, 3. þæm þe geára ábolgen wæs for manna synnum, Bl. H. 9, 6. Swá swá geára beboden wæs Godes folce, 35, 19 : 93, 29. Sé him wæs geára . . . geþeóded, Guth. 52, 6. Sé wæs geára (gára, *v. l.*) and longe þæm Godes were in wære gedeóded gástlices freóndscipes *iamdudum uiro Dei spiritalis amicitiae foedere copulatus*, Bd. 4, 29; Sch. 527, 16. Ná ealles full geáre (geáro, *v. l.*) *non ante longa tempora*, Gr. D. 228, 5. Þæt wæs geára iú, Kr. 28. Ús geára ær wítgan þe toweardne sægdon, Bl. H. 87, 10 : Met. 20, 52. Þá þe ær wæron Godes þa gecorenan geára on helle, Bl. H. 103, 11 : Ps. Th. 147, 8. Þú gegearwadest geára ærest þæt þú rihte beeúdest *tu parasti aequitatem*, 98, 4 : 121, 2.

**geár-bót,** e; *f. Penance extending over a year* :—Þár mót tó bóte stídlic dædbót . . . sumon geárbóte, sumon má geára, sumon mónðbóte, sumon má geára, Ll. Th. ii. 278, 11.

**gearc** (?); *adj. Ready, active, quick* :—On orde stód Eádweard se langa, gearc (gearo? cf. þá ñotan stódon gearowe, wíges georne, 72. *But see* yark; *adj. in D.D., and* gearcian) and geornful, By. 274.

**gearcian.** *Add* : I. *to prepare, make ready* :—Hé sceolde gearcian and dæftan his weig . . . Hé gearcað þone weig cumendum Gode, Hml. Th. i. 362, 7-11. Ealle míne ðing ic gearcode (*omnia parata*) ; cumað tó þám giftum, 522, 8. Gearcode hé his fare and tó Englelande cóm, Chr. 1091; P. 226, 28. Hí gearcodon hí sylfe tó wíge, Hml. A. 104, 68, 75. Gearciað þá þing þe eów gewunelíce synd tó bebyrigunge, Hml. S. 3, 579. Hé hét gearcian tó heora gyftum mænigfealde mærða, Hml. A. 95, 103. Þysum tó gearcigenne þá reþestan wíta, Hml. S. 24, 21. Éce brynas gearcigendum *eterna incendia preparanti*, Angl. xi. 116, 18. I a. *to dress food, skins, &c.* :—Ic bicge hýda and fell and gearkie (*praeparo*) hig mid cræfte, Coll. M. 27, 29. Gearca ús gereordunge, Hml. Th. i. 60, 18. Bere is swíðe earfode tó gearcigenne, 188, 4. II. *to present, furnish, supply* :—Gearcaþ wæfersýne *prestat spectaculum*, An. Ox. 1225. Wala gearcode *uibices exhibuit*, 4488. Wé ne gearcian *nullatenus prebeamus*, i. *adhibeamus*, 749. Þæt gé án clæne mæden gearcion Críste *virginem castam exhibere Christo*, Hml. A. 30, 140. Tó gearcygenne *adhibenda*, Wülck. Gl. 251, 19. Gearciende *exibens*, An. Ox. 4638.

**gearcung.** *Take here* gærcung *in Dict., and add* :—Gearkinge *lustrationis*, An. Ox. 7, 126. Gearc[inge] *praeparatione*, 3617. Húmeta dorstest ðú gán tó mínre gearcunge (*the feast I have prepared*. Cf. ealle míne ðing ic gearcode ; cumað tó þám giftum, 522, 8) búton gyftlicum reáfe?, Hml. Th. i. 530, 2.

**gearcung-dæg.** *Add* :—Oðrum geáre þe wæs gearcungdæg (*Parasceuen*), Mt. 27, 62. v. geearcung-dæg ; gearwung-dæg.

**geár-cyning** *a king who holds authority only for a year.* For Cot.

48 *substitute* :—Gērcyning oððe heretoga *consul*, geárcyninges *consulis*, Wrt. Voc. ii. 20, 4, 3. Geárcyninges *consulis*, 96, 8. Geárcynges, Germ. 388, 24.

**geard.** *Add* : I. *a fence, hedge* :—His fôt wearð fæst on ānum sāgle þæs geardes (on ānum hegesāhle, *v. l., in sude sepis*), Gr. D. 24, 27. Hē ofer þone geard (hege, *v. l. sepem*) stāh, 23, 26. Hē stāh upp on þone geard (hege, *v. l.*), 24, 20. Hē sette wīngeard, and hege ī geard ymbtȳnde ðane *plantavit vineam, et sepem circumdedit ei*, Mt. R. 21, 33. Gaerdas *crates* (cf. hegas *crates*, Wrt. Voc. ii. 105, 49), Hpt. 33, 250, I. II. *an enclosure* :—Of sealtleáge in ðone hyrstgeard, C. D. iii. 400, 2. ¶ in the following either sense might be taken :—On ðone mōr ; of ðām mōre ondlong geardes on ðæt hlȳpgeat, C. D. iii. 180, 27 : vi. 219, 7. On mǣrgeard ; andlang geardes, iii. 462, 3. Andlang norðgeardes, 399, 31. On ðone æcergeard ; ā be ðǣm gearde, 458, 25. v. æcer-, ealdor- (?), sceadu-, wīte- (?) geard.

**geár-dagas.** *Add* : I. *days, lifetime* :—Heora geárdagum *in their days*, Gen. 1657. II. *days of yore* :—Ān wæs on geárdagum Gode wel gecwēme, Isaias se wītega, Wlfst. 44, 21. Hit gewearð on geárdagum þæt God sylf spæc of Synai munte, 66, 9.

**geár-dagum.** *Dele first passage, and see preceding word* : **geardlic.** *Dele, and see* middangeard-lic.

**geard-steall,** es ; m. *A stack- or cattle-yard* (? cf. garth-stead *a stackyard ; a yard in which cattle are kept*, D. D. : Icel. garð-staðr *a hayyard*) ; *or the site of a fence* (?) :—Ondlang ðæs aldan geardstealles . . . ; and swā æfter ðām hegestealle, C. D. iii. 391, 8.

**geare.** v. gearwe : **-geáre,** *combined with numerals to form adjectives giving age.* v. ofer-, ōþer-, þri-, twēntig-geáre. Cf. -wintre.

**geár-fæc,** es ; n. m. *A year's space* :—Gelôme on geárfæce gearwiað eów tô hûsle, Wlfst. 72, 1.

**ge-arfoþ, ge-arfoðe.** *Dele, and see* earfoþe ; *n.,* earfoþe ; *adj.*

**geár-gemearc.** *Substitute : Measurement of time expressed in years.* Cf. fôt-, mil-gemearc ; geár-gerim :—Mē onsende sigedryhten mīn, siððan ic furðum ongon on þone æfteran ānseld būgan geárgemearces (*directly after I had begun the second year of my inhabiting the hermitage.* In the prose legend the corresponding passage is : Ðan æfteran geáre þe ic þis wēsten eardode, þæt on æfen and on ærnemergen God sylfa þone engcel mīnre frôfre tô mē sende, Guth. 86, 3-5), . . . engel ufancundne, sē mec ēfna gehwām . . . and on morgne gesôhte, Gū. 1215. [*The note given above under* ān-seld *is wrong* (būgan = to dwell), *and* ān-seld *is neuter.*]

**geár-gemynd,** es ; n. *A yearly commemoration on the anniversary of a person's death* :—Ðis is seó caritas þe Baldwine abbod hæfð geunnon his gebrôðrum for Eádwardes sāwle, ƀ is healf pund æt his geárgemynde tô fisce, Nap. 28. Tô mīnon geárgemynde, ib.

**geár-geriht.** *Add* :—þæt wē eal gelǣstan on geárgerihtan þæt ûre yldran hwīlum ǣr Gode behētan ; ðæt is sulhælmessan and Rômpenegas and cyricsceattas and leóhtgescota, Wlfst. 113, 9.

**geár-gerim.** *Substitute : Reckoning by years.* (1) *where duration is measured and the year is taken as the unit.* v. geár ; I :—Bootes cymeð on þone ilcan stede eft ymb þrītig geárgerimes (cf. ymb þrittig wintra, Bt. 39, 3 ; F. 214, 15), Met. 28, 30. Cf. winter-gerim. (2) *in chronological reckoning.* (a) *anno mundi* :—Fram frymðe middaneardes tô ðām flôde, ƀ wæs geárgerimes twā ðusenda wintra and twā hund wintra and twā and feówertyg wintra . . . þonne wæs ealles āurnen geárgerimes fram frymðe middaneardes oþ Cristes ācennednesse fīf ðusend wintra and eahta and twēntig wintra, Angl. xi. 9, 2-16. Gērgerimes, 4, § 3, 2. þā wæs āgan geárgerimes . . . feówer þusend and hundteóntig and þreó and sixtig geára, Wlfst. 15, 1. (b) *in Roman history* :—Ic ymbe Rômāna gewin on þǣm geárrime (-gerime) forð ofer þæt geteled hæbbe (*I have not followed the chronological order, but have anticipated* ; *aliquantum Romanas clades recensendo progressus sum*), Ors. 3, 7 ; S. 110, 12. (c) *anno Domini* :—Kl. Ianuarius gif hē biþ on Sǣternesdæg . . . fȳr rícsaþ on þām geáre gǣrgerimes, E. S. 39, 342. Cf. geárgemearc.

**geár-getal.** l. -getæl, *and add* : I. *a number of years, years of existence.* (1) *age* of a person :—Gif hē bið cealdre gecyndo, þonne cymð seó ādl æfter feówertigum, elcor cymð æfter fīftigum wintra his gǣrgetales, Lch. ii. 284, 22. (2) *age* of the world :—Findan hū micel þæs geárgeteles is āurnen . . . fram frymðe middaneardes tô ðām flôde, Angl. xi. 9, 1. II. *the number of days in a year* (?) :—Dô hē ƀ .vii. geárgetælu beón binnon þrim dagum þus gefadode . . . Nime hē him tô .xii. manna and fæsten .iii. dagas . . . begite septies .cxx. manna ƀ fæstan eác for hine .iii. dagas ; þonne wyrð gefæst swā fæla fæstena swā bið daga on .vii. geárum, Ll. Th. ii. 286, 22. Cf. winter-getæl.

**geár-hwāmlíce** ; adv. *Yearly, annually* :—Sȳ æfre seó ælmesse gelǣst geárhwāmlíce, Cht. Th. 560, 3. Cf. dæg-hwāmlíce.

**ge-ārian.** *Add* : I. *to honour, shew respect to* (acc. or dat. (? v. ârian)) :—Ðæt wē ûre hiéremen swā geārigen, swā wē hié eft geegsian mægen *ne dum praelatus quisque plus se quam decet dejicit, subditorum vitam stringere sub disciplinae vinculo non possit*, Past. 118, 5. II. *to shew mercy to* (dat.). (1) *to do kindness, help* :—Lícige þē nū þæt þū

geárige [mē] *complaceat tibi, ut eripias me*, Ps. Th. 39, 15. Bið hē swīð ryhtlíce mid ðǣm gehīned ðe mon wēnð ðæt mid geárod sié *und nutrita pie creditur, inde justius damnatur*, Past. 391, 8. Ðætte ðonne hira niéhstan ðurh hié beóð gereorde and geárode, ðæt hié selfe ne fæsten ðæs hlāfes ryhtwisnesse *cum per eos carnis subsidiis reficiuntur proximi ipsi remaneant a justitiae pane jejuni*, 137, 24. (2) *to refrain from unkindness, spare* :—Se ilca monegum yfelum wið hine selfne forworhtum ǣr geárode *malis ante noverat pie parcere*, Past. 37, 1. III. *to endow, present* :—Hē wæs geárad mid freóðôme fram his hlāforde *a domino suo libertate donatus est*, Gr. D. 12, 1. Mid welum geweorþod and mid deórwyrþum ǣhtum gegyrewod (geárod, *v.l.*), Bt. 14, 3 ; F. 46, 12. [Cf. O. H. Ger. ge-ēren *honorare* ; ge-ērēt *praeditus*.]

**geár-langes** ; adv. *For a year* :—Hit standan geárlanges *dimitte illam hoc anno* (Lk. 13, 8), Hml. Th. ii. 408, 6. Cf. dæg-langes.

**geárlic.** *Take here* gērlic *in Dict., and add* :—Gērlicae *annua*, Txts. 42, 94. Gērlice, Wrt. Voc. ii. 6, 67. (1) *that occurs yearly* :—Geárlíc freólsdæg *annua festiuitas*, Ælfc. Gr. Z. 287, 12. Ðes freólsdæg is ûs geárlic, ac hē is heofonwarum singallic, Hml. Th. i. 442, 30. þā geárlican gehāt *annua vota*, Wrt. Voc. ii. 5, 55 : 92, 9. (2) *that lasts a year* :—þes geárlica ymbrene ûs gebringð efne nû þā tíd lentenlices fæstenes, Wlfst. 284, 19. (3) *that forms part of a year* :—On ðām dæge wurdon geárlice tída gesette, Hml. Th. i. 100, 3. On eallum geáre sind getealde ðreó hund daga and fīf and sixtig daga ; gif wē teóðiað þās geárlican dagas, 178, 21.

**geárlíce.** *For Cot. substitute* Wrt. Voc. ii. 5, 49.

**geár-market** *a yearly market, fair* :—On ealra þæra manna gewitnesse þe sēceað geármarket (-morkett, C. D. iv. 291, 19) tô Stôwe, Cht. Th. 372, 15. [O. H. Ger. iār-marchit *nundinae* : Ger. jahr-markt *a fair*.]

**gearn.** *Add* :—Gearn *filatum*, Wrt. Voc. ii. 35, 45 : 148, 52 : **gearn-bed.** v. fearn-bedd.

**gearn-winde,** an ; f. *Add* :—Gearnuuinde *reponile*, Wrt. Voc. ii. 119, 12. Gernwinde *conductum*, 16, 33. Hē sceal habban fela towtôla spinle, reól, gearnwindan, Angl. ix. 263, 11. [Cf. reele, garnewyne, clewe *alabrum, iurgillum, glomerus*, Wülck. Gl. 628, 1. A yernwynder or a reel *appendium*, 564, 31. Ȝarnwindel *girgillus*, Prompt. Parv. 536.]

**gearo.** *Add* : I. *in a state of preparation, so as to be capable of immediately performing* (or *becoming the object of*) *such action as is implied or expressed by the context* :—Symle hȳ Gūðlác gearone fundon Gū. 885. Beó gē gearwe (gearua, L., *parati*), Mt. 24, 44. þā þe gearwe wǣrun eódun in, 25, 10 : Bl. H. 125, 12. Côm se cyning mid fulre fyrde þider ǣr hī gearwe wǣron, Chr. 1014 ; P. 145, 19. Sôna þæs þe hié wǣron, swā wǣron þā nicoras gearwe, tôbrúdon hié swā hié þā ôðre ǣr dydon, Nar. 11, 11. Gié wosað gearuu, Lk. 12, 40. Wē beóð eádmôdlíce gearawe, Ll. Th. i. 238, 27. Ælc here hæfð ðȳ læssan cræft ðonne hē cymð, gif hine mon ǣr wāt, ǣr hē cume ; for ðæm hē gesihð ðā gearwe ðe hē wēnde ðæt he sceolde ungearwe findan. Him wǣre iéðre ðæt hē hira ǣr gearwa wēnde ðonne hē hira ungearra wēnde, and hī gearuwe mētte, Past. 433, 27-31. Þ hē ûs gearwe finde, Bl. H. 83, 1. Þ ǽlc man hæbbe symle þā men gearowe þe lǣden þā men þe heora āgen sēcan willen, Ll. Th. i. 162, 23. Ðætte hié swā micle gearran finde se ytemesta dæg, ðonne hē cume, swā hī hēr æmtegran biôð, Past. 401, 6. I a. *dressed, armed.* v. gearwe *clothing, arms* :—Onfundon þæs cyninges þegnas þā unstilnesse, and þā þider urnon swā hwelc swā þonne gearo wearþ, Chr. 755 ; P. 48, 7. Fore him englas stondað gearwe mid gēsta wǣpnum, Gū. 60. II. *ready to do* (dat. infin.). (1) *having all preparations made, having all other business accomplished* :—Eall folc gearu wæs heom on tô fônne, Chr. 1009 ; P. 139, 20. Wē sungon be eallum hālgum . . . æfter þyssum, prím . . . eft wē sungon nôn, and nû wē synd hēr gearuwe gehȳran hwæt þū ûs secge, Coll. M. 34, 1. Hī wǣron gearwe tô fihtan[n]e ongeán þone kāsere, H. R. 3, 9. Beón gearwe mid him silfum and mid wīfe and mid ærfe tô farenne þider ic wille, Ll. Th. i. 220, 6. (2) *willing, not feeling or shewing reluctance* :—Ic eom gearu (-o, L. R.) tô farenne mid þē, ge on cwertern ge on deað, Lk. 22, 33 : An. 72. II a. *with clause* :—Nū ic eom gearo þæt ic gange tô mīnum discipulum, Bl. H. 247, 32 : Jul. 398 : 365 : Rä. 24, 4. III. *with case of a substantive, ready, willing to do, suffer,* &c. :—Ic beó gearo sôna willan þīnes *I am ready to do what you wish*, Jul. 49. III a. *with preps.* (1) tô, in, on, *prepared, inclined or willing to do, suffer, give,* &c. what is indicated by the substantive :—Hē āþas swôr þæt hē gearo (geare, *v.l.*) wǣre mid him selfum, and on (mid, *v.l.*) allum þām þe him lǣstan woldon, tô þæs heres þearfe, Chr. 874 ; P. 72, 32. Gearuw tô reáflâce, Ps. L. 16, 12. Hē sceal geara beón on manegum weorcum tô hlāfordes willan, Ll. Th. i. 436, 3. Sum bið ā wið firenum in gefeoht geara, Crä. 90. Beó þū on sið gearu, Gū. 1148 : El. 222. Sculon ðā hālgan weras stondan gearuwe tô gefeohte wið ðæm fiénd, Past. 433, 16. Ðonne menn gearuwe beóð tô Lífes bebodum, Hml. Th. i. 362, 12. His men beón gearuwe ge tô rīpe ge tô huntoðe, C. D. v. 162, 27. (2) tô. (a) *ready to go to a place* :—Sôna wǣron gearwe hæleð tô þǣre hālgan byrg, Crí. 460. (β) *brought into*

*such a condition as to be immediately liable to*:—Hé wiste þ menn wǽron tó deáþe gearwe; þá gelaþode hé hié tó écean lífe, Bl. H. 103, 7. **IV.** having the quality of being *prepared* or *willing to act when necessary, prompt, quick*:—Gearu *promptus*, Wrt. Voc. i. 55, 41. Ðe gást georo (gearo, R., hrǽd, W. S., *promptus*) is, Mt. L. 26, 41. Se gást is gearu (gearuu, L., georo, R.), Mk. 14, 38. Gearo gúðfreca goldmáðmas heóld, B. 2414. Ic habbe nú ongiten þ ðú eart gearo tó ongitanne míne láre *te ad intelligendum promtissimum esse conspicio*, Bt. 36, 5; F. 178, 30. Gearuum *expeditis*, Wrt. Voc. ii. 107, 67. **V.** of mental power, *characterized by quickness* or *promptness*:—Onstēp mínne hige in gearone rǽd, Hy. 4, 39. **VI.** of action, *characterized by alacrity* or *willingness*:—Heó gearwe (or under **IX.**: or *adv.?*) funde mundbyrd æt þám mǽran þeódne, Jud. 2. **VII.** *in the condition of having been prepared for some purpose*:—þonne þ ordál geara sý, Ll. Th. i. 226, 18. Him wæs gearu sóna þurh streámrǽce strǽt gerýmed, An. 1581. Eów wæs mínes fæder ríce ǽr woruldon gearo, Cri. 1346. þē is súsl weotod gearo tógegnes, Sat. 693. Betst beadorinca wæs on bǽl gearu, B. 1109. Ys mín heorte gearu (gearuw, Ps. L.) ... þæt ic Gode cwēme, Ps. Th. 107, 1. Ne scealt þú forhycgan forgifnesse gearunge tíman *spernere tu noli veniae tibi tempora certa*, Dóm. L. 91: 68. Gē sceolan habban þreó ampullan gearuwe tó þám þrým elum, Ll. Th. ii. 390, 6. þē synt tú gearu, swá líf, swá deáþ, El. 605. Gerewe sint tēlerum ... *parata sunt derisoribus judicia*, Kent. Gl. 720. Habbað word gearu ... eall getrahtod, An. 1360. **VII a.** of food, *dressed, cooked*:—Bere is swíðe earfoðe tó gearcigenne, and þeáhhwæðere sēt ðone monn, þonne hé gearo bið, Hml. Th. i. 188, 5. **VII b.** of ships, *equipped for service*:—Ænne scegð .lxiiii. ǽre, hé is eall gearo bútan þám hánon, Cht. Crw. 23, 8. Man sceolde mid scipfyrde faran ..., ac ðá þá scipu gearwe wǽron ..., Chr. 999; P. 133, 4: El. 227. Rōmāne scipa worhton ... Æfter siextegum daga þæs þe ðæt timber ácorfen wæs, þǽr wǽron xxx and c gearora ge mid mǽste ge mid segle (*centum triginta navium classis deducta in ancoris stetit*), Ors. 4, 6; S. 172, 5. **VIII.** *finished, complete*:—Ðǽm synfullan náuht ne helpað his gódan geðóhtas, for ðǽm ðe hé nǽfð gearone willan untweógende tó ðǽm weorce, ne eft ðǽm ryhtwísan ne deriað his yflan geðóhtas, for ðǽm ðe hé nǽfð gearone willan ðæt wóh tó fulfremmanne *nec malos bona imperfecta adjuvant, nec bonos mala inconsummata condemnant*, Past. 423, 25–28. **IX.** *so placed or constituted as to be immediately available when required* or *wished for, close at hand, within reach, convenient for use*:—Gyt ne cóm mín tíd; eówer tíd is symble gearu (gearua, L., georo, R.), Jn. 7, 6. Bringaþ gē on mín beren eówerne teóðan sceat ... Gedóþ þ eów sý mete gearo on mínum húse *inferte omnem decimam in horreum, et sit cibus in domo mea* (Malachi 3, 10), Bl. H. 39, 28: An. 1537. Gearo sceal gúðbord *ready to hand shall the shield be*, Gn. Ex. 203. Sē þe þæt gelǽsteð, him bið leán gearo, Gen. 435. þǽr is help gearu, milts æt mǽrum manna gehwylcum, An. 909. Næs him ðon gearu tó ásecganne swefen, Dan. 128. Þet hit him georo wǽre swá hwilce dæge swá hí hit habban woldon, Chr. 874; P. 73, 26. On Gode standeð mín geara hǽle, Ps. Th. 61, 7. Hí eódon heom tó heora garwan feorme, Chr. 1006; P. 136, 24. Ðæt hí ealneg hæbben ðá sealfe gearuwe ðe tó ðǽre wunde belimpe, Past. 453, 9. Byð his dǽdbót Gode andfengre, and Godes mildheortnes him micle þe gearwre, Wlfst. 155, 15. Gearuwre, Ll. Th. i. 372, 5. **IX a.** used of a person:—Hé is se góda God and gearu standeð (cf. *God is a very present help*, Ps. 46, 1), Ps. Th. 117, 2. Hé is God mín and gearu Hǽlend, 61, 2. Se geatweard sceal cýtan habban wið þæt geat, þæt þá cuman simle gearone hæbben ... (*ut venientes semper presentem inveniant* ...), R. Ben. 126, 19. Hí hæfdon gearwe (gearuwe, v. l.) māgistras (māgistras gearwe, v. l.) *haberent in promtu magistros*, Bd. 4, 2; Sch. 345, 13.

**gearo**; *adv.* v. gearwe: **gearo-brygd**; *f. l. m.*: **gearod**. *l.* geárod. v. ge-árian.

**gearolíce**. *Add*: geare-, gear-líce *well*. (1) of sight, perception:—þá mihte hé mid þan óþron geseón, and on þám inne hé gearlíce oncneów hwæt þǽr inne wæs, Guth. 98, 5. (2) of knowledge, understanding:—Ic habbe gearolíce (cúðlíce, v. l.) ongyten þte ús is seó mihte ðearf, Gr. D. 1, 3. Gearelíce (gearo-, v. l.) witan þás heregas, Wlfst. 254, 11. Magan wē geseón and oncnáwan and swíþe gearelíce ongeotan, Bl. H. 107, 23.

**gearo-wita**. *Add*:—Swilce sió smeáung and sió gesceádwísnes is tó metanne wiþ þone gearowitan *uti est ad intellectum ratiocinatio*, Bt. F. 224, 4.

**gearo-witol**; *adj. Ready-witted, sagacious*:—Gearwitelum *sagaci*, An. Ox. 56, 108. ¶ the word also glosses *austerus*:—Scrípen ł gearuutol *austerus*, Lk. L. 19, 21. Gearnfull ł gearuutol, 22. [Næs þe king noht so wis, ne swa ȝǽrewitele (warwitele, 2nd MS.), Laym. 1854.]

**gearo-witolness**, e; *f. Sagacity*:—Ongeán þám ingehýde and gearawitolnesse þe of Godes ágene gife cymð, se deófol sǽwð nytennysse, Wlfst. 53, 16.

**gearo-wyrde**; *adj. Having ready utterance*:—Se geonga wæs

geworden gearowyrde (geara-, georo-, v. ll., *loquela promtus*), sē þe ǽr wæs dumb, Bd. 5, 2; Sch. 561, 2.

**ge-eárplættan** *to buffet*:—Se sceocca mē geárplæt (colaphizet, 2 Cor. 12, 7), Hml. Th. i. 474, 13.

**geár-rím**. *Add: reckoning by years*. v. geár-gerím, (2 b).

**geár-torht**. *Substitute: Bright with the beauty of spring* (? v. geár; **III.** 6):—Hé seów sǽda fela, sóhte georne þæt him ... bróhte geártorhte gife grēne folde, Gen. 1561.

**gearu-fang** ?:—Gearufang *proceris*, Wrt. Voc. i. 63, 75. v. feng (2 a).

**geár-wæstm** *yearly fruit*:—þæt heó hæbbe ǽlce gēre ealra geárwæstma þá þrié dǽlas, C. D. ii. 175, 25.

**gearwan-leáf**. v. georman-leáf.

**gearwe**; *adv*. Take here geare, geara, gearo *in Dict., and add*: **I.** with verbs of knowing, *well, certainly, clearly*:—Geare (gere, v. l.) witan, Past. 190, 11. Swíþe geare, Bt. 14, 2; F. 44, 8. Genóg geare, Bl. H. 175, 30. Wē þæs gelēfað and geare witan þ ..., 13, 22. Gere (cf. swutolor witan, 11), Past. 429, 9. Hē geare nyste hwǽr ..., El. 719. Ne ful geare wiste, 860. Geara, Guth. 70, 4: Bt. 35, 6; F. 170, 8. Ne wēne ic his, ac wát geara (geare, v. l.), 38, 6; F. 208, 14. Geare cunnan, Wand. 69: B. 2070: El. 167. Gearwe cunnan, Wand. 71. Gearor witan, Past. 429, 19: Bl. H. 13, 21. Gearwor, Nar. 33, 3. Gearwor, Gr. D. 203, 24. Gearor ongitan, Bl. H. 129, 9. þone cúþon manige úrra cúðra freónda and eallra gearost seó hálige fǽmne *quem nostrorum multi noverunt, et maxime sacra virgo*, Gr. D. 199, 11. **I a.** with verbs of observation, *well*:—Fóre míne and míne gangas þú gearwe átreddest (*investigasti*), and ealle míne wegas wel foresáwe, Ps. Th. 138, 2. Geara ic sceáwade *considerabam*, 141, 4. **II.** *readily, willingly, eagerly*:—Geare andettan, Ps. Th. 146, 7. Geara, 53, 6: 91, 1. Ic on ðē geare hycge *sperabo in te*, 90, 2. þonne wē his geara ēhtan, 70, 10. **III.** *with ready goodwill*. Cf. gearo; **VI.**:—Wesað gē fram Gode geara gebletsade *may you have his ready blessing*, Ps. Th. 113, 23. **IV.** *readily, promptly*. Cf. gearo; **IV.**:—þú mē eart geara andfencgea, Ps. Th. 58, 9, 18. þú mē wǽre geara trymmend, 70, 3. **V.** marking thoroughness, completeness of an action. Cf. gearo; **VIII.**:—Strǽle beóð scearpe ... syððan of glēdon wesað gearwe áhyrded, Ps. Th. 119, 4. Hafa gebrocen glæs geara gegrunden, Lch. ii. 144, 16. Hí Iacób geara ātan *comederunt Jacob*, Ps. Th. 78, 7. þeós eorðe sceal eall ābifigan, ... geara forhtigan (*be thoroughly terrified*), 113, 7. **VI.** *at hand, within reach, near*. Cf. gearo; **IX.**:—Bið ús Godes milts þe gearwur, Ll. Th. i. 424, 23. **VII.** *readily, without difficulty* or *delay*:—Sē ðe him tó ðam hálgan helpe gelífeð, tó Gode gióce, hē þǽr gearo findeð, Vald. 2, 28. Heó gearwe (but see gearo; **VI.**) funde mundbyrd æt ðám mǽran þeódne, Jud. 2.

**gearwe** *dress*. Take here geare *in Dict., and add: gear, goods*(?):—Ealle Rōmāne woldon ymb xii mónað bringan tógædere þone sēlestan dǽl hiora gódra geara (gearwa, v. l.) (heora góda gegearod tó heora geblóte, v. l.), and hiora siþþan fela wucena ætgædere brúcan, Ors. 6, 21; S. 272, 25. v. gold-, mete-gearwe.

**gearwe** *yarrow*. *Add*:—Geruuae, geruȝ millefolium, Txts. 76, 623. Gearuuae, 639. Gearewe, Ælfc. Gr. Z. 311, 1. Seó reáde gearuwe, Lch. iii. 24, 2. Wyl on meolcum þá reádan gearwan, ii. 354, 9.

**ge-árweorþian**. *Add*:—Ðonne ðú geárweorðas *cum* [*de*] *honestaveris*, Kent. Gl. 959. God hí geárwurðað tóforan óðrum mannum on þám ēcan wurðmynte, Hml. A. 22, 192. Giárwyrðigeð (*honorificabit*) ðec sǽwel mín, Rtl. 1, 5. Seó hálige Maria mid hire geneósunge hine geárwurðode, Hml. Th. ii. 512, 18. Heora góda hlísa geárweorþige þá þe hý tó þǽre mæssan þēnunge gecuren, R. Ben. 141, 5.

**gearwian**. *Dele* 'gerwan, ... gierian,' *and add*: **I.** *to make ready*:—Farað and gearwiað (earwiað, v. l.) ús, þ wē úre eástron gewyrcon, Lk. 22, 8. **I a.** *to make ready* to do something:—Huēr wiltu þ wē gearwiga (iarwan, R.) ðē til eottanne eástro?, Mt. L. 26, 17. Hine forcuoede gearuande *se excusare studentes*, Lk. p. 8, 13. **II.** *to make ready*. (1) a thing for use, a place for occupation:—Ic gearuwe byrnende blācern *paravi lucernam*, Ps. Th. 131, 18. Ðe deádum monnum líf gearuwad (gearwað, v. l.) *vitam mortuis praeparans*, Past. 261, 18. Ðá heofonlícan rícu gearwaþ eallum geleáffullum, Bl. H. 31, 6. (1 a) where the purpose for which a thing is prepared is given:—Hē gearwaþ þinne innoð his Suna tó brýdbūre, Bl. H. 9, 9. (2) of ships, *to equip*:—þ man æghwilce geáre sóna æfter Eástron fyrdscipa gearwige, Ll. Th. i. 324, 7. (3) of food or meals, *dress* food, *prepare* a meal:—Martha gearwode þám Hǽlende æfengereordu, Bl. H. 67, 26. Gearwa (gearw, earwa, W. S.) mē ðætte ic giriordige *para quod cenem*, Lk. R. 17, 8. Georwigað (gearuas, L.) ús eóstru þte wē ete, 22, 8. **III.** *to bring to completion* or *maturity*:—Se hāta sumor drýgð and gearwaþ sǽd and blēda, Bt. 39, 13; F. 234, 15. **III a.** *to come to maturity*:—Treówu grēnu wexað and gearwað and rípað, Solil. H. 10, 5. **IV.** *to make ready* a person (1) *to do something*:—Gearwa þē and þú on þone síð fēre, Guth. 86, 26. (2) for an action:—Gearwige hē hine tó húselgange, Ll. Th. i. 322, 7: 310, 7. (3) *to dress, clothe*:—Gearwaþ *uestit*, Mt. R. 6, 30. **V.** *to procure, provide*:—Hit gerewað *parat*

(*cibum*), Kent. Gl. 133. Émetan gearwiað *formicę parant* (*cibum sibi*), 1103. Ðá ðe dú georwades *those things which thou hast provided*, Lk. R. 12, 20. VI. *to do, perform* :—Begæþ, gearwaþ *exercet*, i. *parat*, Wrt. Voc. ii. 144, 64. Hié sculon lätteówdóm gearwian ðám geleáffullum and him sculon fore beón *ut sacrum ducatum praebeant, fidelibus praesunt*, Past. 139, 16. Þegnunge gearwian, Bl. H. 247, 10. VII. *to grant* :—Gearwig ł gionn þte cirica ðín giðii *praesta ut ecclesia tua proficiat*, Rtl. 18, 21. v. full-, ymb-gearwian; girwan.

ge-árwirþan (?) *to honour* :—Biðon geárwyrðed *faenerantur*, Lk. L. 6, 34. v. un-geárwyrd ; ge-árweorþian.

gearwung. *Add*:—Mettes gearwing *Parasceuen* (v. gearwung-dæg), Mt. L. 27, 62. Æfter þæm gearwunga dæge, Mt. R. 27, 62 : Jn. L. 19, 31.

gearwung-dæg, es ; *m. A day of preparation* :—Georwungdæg wæs *parasceue erat*, Jn. R. 19, 31, 42. Fore gearuungdæg (on ðæm dæge gearuadon heora mett tó eástro symble, *note in margin*), Jn. L. 19, 42. Cf. gearcung-dæg.

gearwutol. v. gearo-witol.

ge-ascian. *l.* -áscian, *and add*: I. *to ask* (1) a question of a person :—Hé geáscade (*sciscitabatur*) from him huer Críst ácenned wére, Mt. L. 2, 4. (2) a person a question :—Hé geáscode hiá, ‘Huu feolo láfo habbað gié?,’ Mk. L. 8, 5 : 14, 60 : 15, 2. Geáscadon *interrogabant*, 13, 3. (2 a) *about a matter, inquire into* :—Geáscende (gastánde, MS.) ænd smeágende (*quærerens*) mislicu þing, Solil. H. 3, 1. (2 b) a person *about a matter* :—For hwon wiþsæcst þú þæs þe þú eart geácsod *quare negas quod inquireris?*, Gr. D. 190, 12. II. *to ask for, try to find by inquiry, inquire for* a person :—Se cásere hét geáxian ofer eall sumne æltæwne drý, Hml. S. 14, 49. Wæs Apollonius gesóht and geácsod, ac hé wæs náhwár fundon, Ap. Th. 6, 8. III. *to find out by asking, seek out, discover*. (1) a material object :—Se cásere áxode hine embe his wíf and his suna, hú hé hí geáxode, Hml. S. 30, 398. Ælcne þára þe hió geácsian myhte ... hió tó hyre gespón, Ors. 1, 2 ; S. 30, 30. Hæbbe ic nú forbærned þá ealdan gewritu þe ic geáhsian mihte, Cht. Th. 490, 33. Ealle his sceattas þe hí mihton geáxian, Chr. 1064 ; P. 190, 18. Hí sóna ealle wæron geáscode (*requisiti*), and wæron gelætene, Gr. D. 182, 8. (2) a non-material object :—Sume synna se man wandaþ þ hé hí ásecgge, búton se mæssepreóst hié æt him geácsige, Bl. H. 43, 18. IV. *to get to know* a fact, circumstance, &c., *to learn, hear* :—Mid þý þe (type, MS.) geáscode *cum re*[*s*]*cisset*, Wrt. Voc. ii. 15, 72. Nówiht gedégled þ ne sé geáscad *nihil occultum quod non scietur*, Mt. L. 10, 26. (1) the object a pronoun representing a circumstance given (a) in a preceding clause :—Cóm se þ ... , and þá þe Willelm þ geáxode, Chr. 1071 ; P. 208, 3 : Hml. S. 14, 50. Healde se landhláford þ orf ... oþ þæt se ágenfrígea þ geácsige, Ll. Th. i. 276, 15. (b) in a following clause :—Gif hé þ geácsað, þ hit sóð is, Ll. Th. i. 276, 8. Þá geáscade se cyng þæt, þæt hié út on hergað fóron, Chr. 911 ; P. 96, 10. Ðá þ se hláford geáhsode, þ þ hrýþer swá férde, Bl. H. 199, 9. (2) the object a clause :—Man geáxað þe hé fúl bið, Ll. Th. i. 238, 30. Ic hæbbe geáhsod (-ácsod, *v. l.*) þ úre frið is wyrse gehealden, 220, 1 : 240, 26. (3) with acc. and infin. :—Manig yfel wé geáxiað wæstmian, Bl. H. 109, 1. Wé geáscodon his geceasterwaran beón Godes englas, and wé geácsodon þæra engla geféran beón þá gástas sóðfæstra manna, Wlfst. 2, 1–4. (4) with acc. and complementary (a) adjective :—Be þisum þeófum þe man on hrædinge fúle geáxian ne mæg *of these thieves who cannot at once be shewn on examination to be guilty*, Ll. Th. i. 238, 30. (b) adverb :—Se ealdorman hine ðær geáxode (cf. *pervenit ad aures principis confessorem Christi penes Albanum latere*, Bd. 1, 7), Hml. S. 19, 32. Hí eódon þær hí geáxodon Ulfcytel mid his fyrde, Chr. 1010 ; P. 140, 7. (c) clause :—Þone þe wé geáxian, þ fúl sý, Ll. Th. i. 228, 13. V. *to get information about* a person or thing, *hear of*. (1) *with acc.* :—Wé fram dæge tó óþrum geáxiað ungecynelice deáþas ... and wé gehýrað oft secggan worldrícra manna deáþ ... swá wé eác geáxiað mislice ádla, Bl. H. 107, 25–31. Hét se cásere georne smeágan hwær man æfre þá hálgan geáxian mihte ... Man áxode on porte ... man scrútnode on ælcere stówe þær man hí æfre geáxian cúðe ; ne mihte hí nán man náhwer findan, Hml. S. 23, 264–269. Ne meahte mon búton feáwa ofslagenra geáhsian, Ors. 2, 8 ; S. 94, 12. (2) *with be* :—Wé geácsodon be þám heofonlican éðle, Wlfst. 2, 1. Hé hæfde geáxod be ðæs Hælendes wundrum (cf. Ic hæbbe gehýred be ðé, hú ðú hælst ðá untruman, 90), Hml. S. 24, 86. VI. *to find out* (*the character* or *designs of* ) a person :—Geáscoden *ut caperent* (v. Ut caperent eum in sermone, Mt. 22, 15), Wrt. Voc. ii. 73, 14. VII. *to get to know* (*the nature of*) a thing :—Hwí gé nellon, siþþan gé hiora þeáwas geácsod habben, him onhyrian, Bt. 40, 4 ; F. 240, 3. [*O. H. Ger.* ge-eiscón *rogare, audire, discere, cognoscere, scire*.] v. un-geáxod.

ge-áswician. v. ge-áswician : ge-ásyndrod. *For* R. Ben. interl. 43 *substitute* :—Hé geásindrod fram geférrædene [ealra] reordige ána *sequestratus a consortio omnium reficiat solus*, R. Ben. I. 77, 13.

geat. *Take here* gæt *in Dict., and add* : (1) *the gate* of an enclosure, *the opening in a fence* or *wall to allow passage, and provided with a movable barrier*. (a) the enclosure a field :—Gif ceorlas gærstún hæbben gemænne ... gán þá þe þ geat ágan, Ll. Th. i. 128, 8. (b) where the

enclosure contains a habitation :—Ceorles weorðig sceal beón wintres and sumeres betýned. Gif hé bið untýned and reeð his neáhgebúres ceáp in on his ágen geat, Ll. Th. i. 126, 15. On þære byrig ... hié þá gatu him tó belocen hæfdon, Chr. 755 ; P. 48, 16. Geatu, 901 ; P. 92, 8. Geatu *portas*, Ps. Th. 23, 7. Gæto, Rtl. 18, 40. (b a) the enclosure a city :—Mihton geseón Winceastre leódan here þ hí be hyra gate tó sæ eódon, Chr. 1006 ; P. 137, 11. Binnan þám gatum (*of Derby*), 921 ; P. 101, 30. Hí betýndon þære ceastre gatu, Bl. H. 241, 11. (b β) used figuratively :—Þurh þ nearwe get (geat, *v. l.*, gætt, L. R.), Lk. 13, 24. Helle gatu (geatt, L.), Mt. 16, 18. Gættana *portarum*, Rtl. 59, 21. Neirxna wonges gætto *paradisi portas*, 124, 7. (2) *the gate, doorway of a building* :—Geat *janua*, Wrt. Voc. i. 81, 13. Se wítega geseah án belocen geat on Godes húse (*portam sanctuarii*), and him cwæð tó sum engel : ‘þis geat ne bið nánum menn geopenod, ac se Hælend ána færð inn þurh þæt geat,’ Hml. Th. i. 194, 1–4. Gesomnad tó duru ł tó gæt (geat, R.) *congregata ad januam*, Mk. L. 1, 33. Tó þæs mynstres geate sý geatweard geset ... Se sylfa geatweard sceal cýtan (*cellam*) habban wið þæt geat, R. Ben. 126, 15–19. Beforan gatum forþtiges *pro foribus uestibuli*, An. Ox. 3827. Gesáwon wé in þære byrig and on geaton (*in the doorways*) men ... ðá hié ús gesáwon hié selfe sóna in heora húsum hié miþan, Nor. 10, 16. (3) *a passage between hills* :—Swá Dor scadeþ, Hwítan wylles geat, Chr. 942 ; P. 110, 15. (4) *the barrier which closes the opening* :—Helle geatu and hire þá ærenan scyttelas hé ealle tóbræc, Bl. H. 85, 6. [¶ the word alone or in composition occurs often in the Charters. v. Midd. Flur. s.v.] v. ceaster-, deór-, hlid-, hlíp-, mynster-, port-, stán-, templ-, tyrn-geat.

geátan. *Add*:—Ic hit íete, Chr. 675 ; P. 37, 33. þ hé scolde þ géten mid his writ, P. 35, 33. Hé geátte mannan heora wudas and slætinge, 1087 ; P. 223, 33.

ge-atelod. *l.* ge-atolod, *and for* Cot. 202 *substitute* Wrt. Voc. ii. 76, 28. v. atolian.

geáþ. *Add* (?) :—Ne synt þíne geáhðe áwiht þe þú hér on moldan mannum eówdest, Seel. 74 ; geúþelíce. v. eúþelíce.

ge-atolhíwian *to make hideous, horrible*, &c. :—Geatolhíwaþ *devenustat, deformat*, Wrt. Voc. ii. 139, 52.

geatolic. *Add*: *adorned, splendid*. (1) of persons :—Geatolic gúðcwén golde gehyrsted, El. 331. (2) of things :—Hý sæl timbred, geatolic and goldfáh, ongytan mihton, B. 308. Bil ... wæpna cyst ... gód and geatolic giganta geweorc, 1562.

geatwe. *Add*:—Wyrmas mec ni áuefun, ðá ði goelu godueb geatum fraetuað, Txts. 151, 10.

geat-weard. *Add*:—Be ðæs mynstres geatwearde (*ostiario*). Tó þæs mynstres geate sý geatweard geset ... Se geatweard (*porterius*) sceal cýtan habban wið þæt geat, R. Ben. 126, 14–19. Heó becóm tó þám mynstre ... þá eóde se geatweard tó þám abbode, and cwæð him tó : ‘Fæder, hér is cumen ... ,’ Hml. S. 33, 136. Wæs ðær swiþe egeslic geatweard, ðæs nama sceolde beón Caron, Bt. 35, 6 ; F. 168, 18. [Seo heofenlice iateward, Chr. 656 ; P. 31, 32. v. *N. E. D.* gate-ward.]

ge-bacen. *Add* :—Hláf þe sý mid smeruwe gebacen, Lch. i. 144, 18.

ge-bæc. *Add* : [(1) *what is baked*. v. Dict.] (2) *baking* :—Coquo gebyrað tó gebæce, Ælfc. Gr. Z. 176, 2. [Cf. *Prompt. Parv.* batche or bakynge *pistura*. *Ger.* ge-bäck *baking* ; *batch*.]

ge-bæcu. *Add*: v. bæce.

ge-bédan. *Add*:—þæt hió gebædde *compellere*, Wrt. Voc. ii. 95, 16. Gebéded *actus*, 89, 69 : 5, 50 : *compulsus*, 14, 55. Ðonne sió sául hire unðonces gebædd wierð (*urgetur*) ðæt yfel tó forlætanne, Past. 251, 13. ¶ where the compelling cause is given :—Hé wæs gebædded for neódþearfa swá myccles plyhtes *tanta periculi necessitate compulsus*, Gr. D. 48, 2. Hé wæs mid nýde gebædded and mid his ágnum wíte þ hé ongan swerian þ ... *poena sua exigente compulsus est jurare ...* , 255, 10 : Bl. H. 83, 32.

ge-bælded. v. ge-bildan : ge-bænden. v. ge-bendan : ge-béne. v. gebán.

ge-bæran. *Add* :—Gebæraþ *gestiunt*, Scint. 181, 12. Hé ongan biterlíce wépan ... þá þ his geféra geseah, hé hine ácsade, hwæt him wære, and for hwon hé swá gebærde (*quod intuens comes, quare faceret, inquisivit*), Bd. 4, 25 ; Sch. 498, 8. Hé hreówlíce beforan Gode gebærde, Hml. S. 23, 396. Wæron hié ealle unróte, and sárlíce gebærdon, Bl. H. 225, 14. Wrec ðé gemetlíce, and eác swá gebær (*behave with moderation*), Prov. K. 46. Hé wolde ælcne cuman swiþe árlíce underfón and swiþe swæslíce wiþ gebæran, Bt. 16, 2 ; F. 52, 32. Hú mæg mon earmlícor gebæron þonne mon hine underþeóde his flæsce, 31, 1 ; F. 114, 23. [*O. L. Ger.* gi-bárion.]

ge-bærd-stán. v. ge-bærnan ; I : ge-bære. v. ge-bæru.

ge-bærnan. *Add*: I. *to expose to the action of heat* :—Gebær[n]d stán *calcis vi*[*v*]*a*, Wrt. Voc. i. 38, 27. Gebærnd lím *calcis viva*, ii. 127, 49. II. *of a lamp, to cause to give light* :—Ne ænig dæcele gibérned (-að, L.) *nemo lucernam accendit*, Lk. R. 11, 33. Gebernes, Lk. L. 8, 16. Léht in ús gibern *lucem in nobis accende*, Rtl. 38, 3. II a. *of a fire, to kindle, cause to give heat* :—Fýr ðæt gefe ðín ðyde þte giberne uêre *ignis quem gratia tua fecit accendi*, Rtl. 38,

21. Gibernedum ofne *accensa fornace*, 102, 31.   III. *to consume with heat* :—Ðá halm [hé] geberneð *paleas comburet*, Lk. L. R. 3, 17. Þte úsig ne giberne (*exurat*) lég synna, Rtl. 100, 22. Þ sié gebernedo *ut incendantur*, 145, 14.

ge-bærness, e ; *f. Behaviour, a particular instance of behaviour* :—Gebærnessum *gestu* (sanctum voluit maculoso lædere *gestu*, Ald. 189, 20), Wrt. Voc. ii. 95, 4. v. gebǽru.

gebærn-lím. v. ge-bærnan ; I.

ge-bǽru. *Add*: [The declension and gender of this word are uncertain. In An. 1572: Ph. 125: Wrt. Voc. ii. 91, 59: 40, 28 the forms seem to belong to the declension of feminine nouns which remain unchanged in the singular, and to this declension all the other instances (especially Wrt. Voc. ii. 42, 57) might belong. In Wrt. Voc. ii. 110, 21: Gr. D. 111, 9 the forms are almost certainly plural, and might belong to a neuter singular *ge-bǽre*, to which also might be referred all but the four singular forms given above ; and in favour of the neuter is the Old Saxon gi-bári (an thīnumu gibārea).]   I. in the following glosses :—Gebéro *gestus*, Txts. 65, 957.   Gebéro *habitudo*, Wrt. Voc. ii. 42, 57: *egestus*, 142, 70: *exegestus*, 29, 54. Gebéro, 107, 47. Gebéru *habitudines*, 110, 21. Gebǽrum *gestis* (*gestus*, Wülck. Gl. 412, 8), 40, 27: *gestibus*, 43.   II. *behaviour, demeanour, conduct, bearing, manners* :—Andrea orgete wearð folces gebǽro, An. 1572. Gebǽro *gestu* (strophoso fallere *gestu*, Ald. 157, 18), Wrt. Voc. ii. 91, 59: 40, 28. Hé gefeóll under hine sylfne for his módes wídgálnesse and for his unclǽnnysse gebǽrum (for his unclǽnnysse, *v. l.*) *vagatione mentis et immunditia sub semetipsum cecidit*, Gr. D. 108, 2. Geseah ic týn geonge men . . . genóh pǽslice on líchaman and on gebǽrum, and ful lícwurðe mé þúhte, tó mínes líchaman luste . . . Hí míne unsceamlican gebǽra geseónde mé on heora scip námon tó him, Hml. S. 23 b, 369–378. Þá deófla of þám geswenctum mannum mid wundorlicum gebǽrum (*with wonderful behaviour, behaving in a most extraordinary manner*) wurdon him fram, 31, 1212. Mid cnihtum þe unrǽdlíce férdon on ídelum lustum and wáclicum gebǽrum, Ælfc. T. Grn. 17, 16. Ongeán Godes ege deófol syleð dyrstignesse mid dwǽslicum gebǽrum réceleásum mannum, Wlfst. 59, 20. Wé wéndon þæt þú wǽre godfyrht and hǽfdest gástlice gebǽru, 240, 27. Placidus þágyt heóld his cniht-þeáwas and gebǽru (-o, *v. l.*) *Placidus puerilis adhuc indolis gerebat annos*, Gr. D. 111, 9. Se engel him geheht þ hé wolde geseón heora gebǽro (*see how they behaved*), Bl. H. 203, 1.   III. *movement, gesture, action* :—Gif þú þone mon lácnian wille, þænc his gebǽra, and wite hwilces hádes hé sié ; gif hit biþ wǽpnedman and lócað ŭp . . . gif hit biþ wíf and lócað niþer . . ., Lch. ii. 348, 13–18. Mid eargum gebǽrum bifiend *formidilosis gestibus tremebunda*, An. Ox. 4895 ; Wrt. Voc. ii. 40, 43. Se bera náwiht eówode his rédnesse on his gebǽrum (*motibus*), Gr. D. 206, 8. Gebǽ[ru], dǽde *gestus*, i. *actus*, An. Ox. 2183.   IV. *voice, cry* (? cf. þu (*the owl*) miht mid þine songe afere Alle þat ihereþ þine ibere, O. and N. 222) :—Bið swá fǽger fugles gebǽru . . . wrixleð wóðcræfte wundorlícor, beorhtan reorde, þonne ǽfre byre monnes hýrde under heofonum, Ph. 125.

ge-bǽtan. *Substitute*: (1) *to bridle and saddle* a horse [v. bǽtan] :—Þá wæs Hróðgáre hors gebǽted, B. 1399. (2) fig. *to bridle, curb, restrain* :—Þonne se ælmihtiga þá gewealdeþeru wile onlǽtan þára brídla þe hé gebǽtte mid his ágen weorc (cf. þonne ǽr hé þ gewealdleþer forlǽt þára brídla þe hé þá gesceafta mid gebrídlode hæfþ, Bt. 21 ; F. 74, 32), Met. 11, 76. Hæfð se alwealda ealle gesceafta gebǽt mid his brídle (cf. mid his brídle befangene, Bt. 21 ; F. 74, 6), 11, 23. v. next word.

ge-bǽte, -bǽtel. *Substitute*: *The harness of a horse, bridle and saddle* :—Hé þæt gebǽte (gebǽtel, þæne brídel, *v. ll.*) of áteah *stramine subtracto*, Bd. 3, 9 ; Sch. 230, 4. Hé hét þǽm þearfan þ hors syllan mid þám cynelican gebǽtum (gerǽdum, *v. l.*) *praecepit equum, ita ut erat stratus regaliter pauperi dari*, 3, 14 ; Sch. 257, 14. v. preceding word.

ge-bán, -bǽne, es ; *n. Bones* :—Mid his gebána reliquium (gebǽnum, *v. l.*) *apud mortua sua ossa*, Gr. D. 86, 11. [*O. H. Ger.* gi-beini *ossa*: *Ger.* ge-bein.]

ge-bann. *Add* :—Geban *edictum*, Wrt. Voc. i. 72, 72. (1) *an edict, a decree* of a temporal or spiritual prince ordering the doing of something by those under him :—Óðer is seó gesetnys ðe se cyning býtt ðurh his ealdormenn, óðer bið his ágen gebann on his andweardnysse, Hml. Th. i. 358, 32. Þæs cáseres gebann þe hét ealle middangeard áwrítan, 32, 29. Geban, ii. 500, 3. Of manegum landum máre landriht áríst tó cyniges gebanne, swilce is deúrhege tó cyniges háme . . . and sǽweard . . ., Ll. Th. i. 432, 7. Se cásere sette gebann (*exiit edictum a cesare*, Lk. 2, 1), þæt . . ., Hml. Th. i. 30, 1. Ic sette nú ðis gebann on eallum mínum folce, þæt . . ., ii. 20, 26 : Hml. S. 4, 107. Ðá ǽrendracan budon þám crístenum ðæs cáseres geban, 28, 44. Þá bisceopealdras þ geban setton, þ swá hwá swá wiste hwǽr hé wǽre, þ hé hyt cýdde, Hml. A. 67, 51. Godcundlice bebudan geban *diuina sanctserunt edicta*, i. *decreta*, An. Ox. 1302. Gebannum *edictis*, i. *decretis*, 3037 : 3435. (1 a) *a mandate, an order* sent by a prince to individuals :—Ðá sende Gezabel ánne pistol tó Naboðes néhgebúrum mid þisum gebanne: 'Habbað eów gemót . . .,' Hml. S. 18, 188. (2) *a*

*summons to assemble* :—Bið geban micel and áboden þider eal Adames cnósl *omnes homines cogentur adesse*, Dóm. L. 128 : Wlfst. 137, 24. Tó ðǽm gebanne ðæs tóhopan nán monn mæg cuman *ad unam vocationis spem nequaquam pertingitur*, Past. 345, 19. (3) *a proclamation, manifesto* :—Se cyningc gesette þis geban, þus cweðende :—'Swá hwilc man swá mé Apollonium lifigende tó gebringð, ic him gife fífti punda goldes . . .' Ðá þá þis geban þus geset wæs . . ., Ap. Th. 7, 6–11. [*O. H. Ger.* gi-ban *scitum*.]

ge-bannan. *Add* :—Þá gebeón (geban, *v. l.*) hé his fyrde and micel werod gesamnode *exercitum colligit copiosum*, Bd. 2, 12 ; Sch. 160, 24. [Havestu ibanned ferde, O. and N. 1668. *O. H. Ger.* gi-bannan *to summon* a meeting.]

gebann-geár. v. gebonn-gér *in Dict*.

ge-barian *to bare, take the covering off* :—Gebarudre róde *nudata cruce*, Angl. xiii. 419, 766. [*O. L. Ger.* gi-barón *manifestare*.]

ge-baswian *to dye purple* or *crimson* :—Ðá stánas wǽron gebaswad mid his blóde, Shrn. 74, 32.

ge-bátad. *Substitute*: ge-batian ; *pp.* od *To get better* (of a wound), *be healed*. Gebatad *medullata*, Wrt. Voc. ii. 58, 27. Tó gehwylcum bryce . . ., þonne byþ hyt fæste gebatod, Lch. i. 370, 20. Lege on þæt gebatod sié, ii. 134, 7. Hire wæs micel wund open ðá heó mon on byrgenne dyde, and þá hí mon eft ŭp dyde of þǽre byrgenne ðá wæs hit gebatad, þ þǽr næs bútan seó swaðu on (cf. Wæs seó wund fæstlíce geháled (*curatum*), Bd. 4, 19 ; Sch. 449, 3), Shrn. 95, 2.

ge-baþian ; *p.* ode *To bathe, wash* :—Heora ǽlc án .c. þearfendra manna gebaðige, Cht. Th. 616, 25. Hé næs geefesod, ne eác bescoren oððe gebaðod, Hml. Th. ii. 298, 20. [*O. H. Ger.* gi-badón *luere, abluere*.]

ge-beácn, es ; *n. Signs, movements* intended to express a meaning :—Twégen seólas mid heora fíyse his fét drýgdon, . . . and siððan mid gebeácne his bletsunge bǽdon, Hml. Th. ii. 138, 13.

ge-beácnian. *Dele* -bécnian, -bícnian, *last passage, and bracket, and add*: (1) *to make signs* :—Gebeácnað *annuit* (*oculis*), Kent. Gl. 143 : 328. (2) *to shew by signs, indicate, make known* :—Niht nihte gecýð ł gebeácnaþ wísdóm *nox nocti indicat scientiam*, Ps. L. 18, 3. (3) *to give command by signs* :—Búton hé tó ælcum men mǽge gebeácnian þ hé irne on his willan *nisi ad nutum cuncta suppetant*, Bt. 11, 1 ; F. 32, 20.

ge-beácnung. *Substitute*: The word glosses cathegoria :—Gehíwunge oððe gebeácnunge *cathegorias* (cf. *cathegorias* (= *Aristotelicas categorias*, Ald. 43, 7), i. *nuntiationes* ł *praedicationes* lára, bodunga, An. Ox. 3128), Wrt. Voc. ii. 24, 12. v. ge-bícnung.

ge-beágian. *Dele* -bégian, *and second passage, and add* :—Gebeágað (so *the MS.*) *coronat*, Ps. Spl. C. 102, 4. v. ge-bígan.

ge-beard[e]. v. un-gebeard[e].

ge-bearded[e] ; *adj. Bearded* :—Heó wearð for þǽre mycclan gecynde and hǽte þæs lustes gebeardedu (-berd-, *v. l.*) *calore nimio contra naturam barbas esset habitura*, Gr. D. 279, 14.

ge-bearo (?) ; *n.* (*m.* ?) *A wood* :—On wítan stán on ðæt gebeare norðeweardne (cf. on easteweordne ácbeara, 26), C. D. v. 232, 36.

ge-beát. *Add* :—Hé hét . . . þæt þá cwelleras . . . hine beóton. Hé on ðám gebeáte clypode, Hml. Th. i. 424, 32.

ge-beátan. *Add* : *to pound* :—Genim pipor and gebeát, Lch. ii. 32, 2 : 64, 19 : 72, 2. Gibeátoen, gebeátten, -beáten *battuitum*, Txts. 44, 140. Gebeáten, Wrt. Voc. i. 288, 10 : ii. 11, 63 : *martisa*, 59, 31. Heortes horn tó dúste gebeáten, Lch. i. 334, 11. Gebeáten swíðe smale, 358, 9. Betonican seáw gebeátenre, ii. 30, 3. Nim mucgwyrte gebeátene, i. 380, 21. v. un-gebeáten.

ge-bécan. *Add* :—Ðá gesealde se cyng and gebécte ðæt land Æðelstáne ealdormenn tó hæbbenne and tó syllanne for life and for legere ðám him leófost wǽre. Æfter ðám getídde ðæt Ecgferð gebóhte bóc and land æt Æðelstáne ealdormenn, Cht. E. 202, 22–26. Æðelstán cyning gebécte .xx. hída intó Wigoraceastre, C. D. B. iii. 657, 1. Gebécte intó mynstre and Æþelríce betǽhte, 3 : 7 : 9. Gebécte and intó mynstre Gode tó lofe geúðe, 5. Gebécte and gefreóde and betǽhte Alhwine bisceope, 11. Cf. ge-bócian.

ge-bécn-. v. ge-bícn-.

ge-béd. *l.* -bed, dele II, *where for* gebed *l.* gebod, *and add*: I. *a prayer* to a human being, *request* :—Miltsa mé, abbud, and gefyl nú óþer gebæd mínre béne, Hml. S. 236, 705.   II. *where the person addressed is divine*. (1) *prayer, praying* :—Hús mín hús gebeddes (*orationis*) is, Lk. L. 19, 46. Seó stemn þǽre heortan bið swíðe gedréfed þonne gebede (*in prayer*), Bl. H. 19, 10 : 217, 28. On þára apostola gebede *when the apostles pray*, 141, 3. Þá gebróðor tó gebede hyldon, An. 1029. Hé from gebede swíceð, ne mæg gewunian in gebedstówe, Jul. 373. Hié on gebed feóllon, Gen. 847. (2) *a prayer* :—Críst sylf sang Pater noster ǽrest and þæt gebedd his leorningcnihtum tǽhte ; and on ðám godcundan gebede sýn .VII. gebedu, Wlfst. 20, 16. Gebedo *oramina* (famulus Christi supplex *oramina* fudit), Wrt. Voc. ii. 93, 50 : 64, 47. Gebeodo dína (of gibeodum dínum, R.) *deprecacio tua*, Lk. L. 1, 13. Gebeadum *obsecrationibus*, 2, 37. (2 a) *a single petition* :—

Seofon gebedu (-bēdu, MS.) sint on þām Pater noster. On þām twām formum wordum ne synd nāne gebedu, ac sind herunga ... þæt forme gebed (-bēd, MS.) is, 'Sý ðīn nama gehālgod' ... þæt ōðer gebed (-bēd, MS.) is ..., Hml. Th. i. 262, 21–32. Gebed (-bēd, MS.), 264, 16, 29: 266, 19: 268, 5: 270, 7. Gebedu (-bēdu, MS.), 270, 17, 18, 26. (3) *a prayer* as an act of worship or ritual, *prayer* of the church:— Hē mid micclum wōpe þære byrgenne gebæd worhte mid sealmsange and mid ōþrum gebedum þe tō þære wīsan belumpon, Hml. S. 23 b, 745–7. Se þridda cnapa wacode swīðor for ege þonne for his gebedum, Vis. Lfc. 47. Hē fēng on his gebedo, swā his gewuna wæs, for þær wæs ān forehūs æt þære cyrcan duru, 32. v. æfen-, cnéow-, in-, ūht-, wīg-gebed.

gebed-bygen, e; f. *The buying of prayers, paying for the saying of prayers* :—Gif for godbōtan feohbōt ārīseð .... þ gebyreð rihtlīce ... tō gebedbigene ..., Ll. Th. i. 328, 6.

ge-bedda, ... an; f. *Substitute:* ge-bedda, an; m. [*this is the usual form, but* gebedde *occurs in* C. D. iii. 50, 3. Cf. ge-maca, ge-mæcca *for gender*], *and add:* I. *one who lies in bed with another, a bedfellow.* (1) of a married woman :—Migdonia leng nolde cuman tō hire weres bedde ... Hire wer bæd þ seó cwēn mōste cunnian gif heó mihte hire (*Migdonia's*) mōd gebīgan þ heó (*Migdonia*) his gebedda wære, Hml. S. 36, 303. (2) fig. in connexion with the grave :— Wyrmum tō mete and tō gebeddan weorðan, Wlfst. 240, 22. Þonne ñæsc onginneð hrūsan ceósan tō gebeddan, Rūn. 29. II. *a consort, wife* of a great man :—Leófrīc eorl and his gebedda, C. D. iv. 72, 20. Se cyning and his gebedda and heora sunu, Hml. Th. ii. 476, 4. Abraham and his gebedda, i. 92, 21. Godes ðegen Zacharias, his gebedda (*uxor*, Lk. 1, 5) Elizabeth, 352, 1. Ðæs cāseres gebedda Libia, and his heáhgeréfan wīf Agrippina, 374, 32. Nicostratus mid his wīfe ... Tranquillinus and his gebedda, Hml. S. 5, 131. Se þegn wæs wunigende būtan wīfes neáwiste, for ðan þe his gebedda gefæren wæs of līfe, 6, 132. Mæden swilcere gebyrde þe his (*Ahasuerus*) gebedda wære, Hml. A. 94, 74. Se cāsere and his mānfulla gebedda, Hml. S. 31, 652. Eádleofu his gebedde, C. D. iii. 50, 3. Eádgār cyning þā his gebeddan betæhte, Lch. iii. 440, 15. Gif hē wið þæs cyninges gebeddan (*conjuge*) hæmde, Ll. Th. ii. 188, 25. Tō onfóanne gebeddan ðīn *accipere conjugem tuam*, Mt. L. 1, 20. Gebed, 24. Gebed ł wīf *uxorem*, p. 14, 16. Þā cōm leóf Gode (*Abraham*) idesa lædan, swæse gebeddan, and his suhtrian, wīf on willan, Gen. 1775.

ge-beddian *to make a bed* :—Him wearð gebeddod mid hnescre bedding, Hml. S. 37, 191.

ge-beded, Hpt. Gl. 503, 75. *l.* ge-beden. v. An. Ox. 4152: gebeden *compulsus*, An. Ox. 4580. *l.* (?) ge-béded (= ge-bǽded): gebed-giht. *l.* -gīht, *and add:* Bedgoing. Cf. sunn-gīhte. [Cf. *Goth.* gāhts.]

gebed-hūs. *Add:*—Gebedhūs *oratorium vel oraculum*, Wrt. Voc. i. 58, 64. Be mynstres gebedhūse (*oratorio*). Gebedhūs sý tō þan ānum þe hit gecweden is, þæt is þær þær nān þincg elles geworht ne sý būtan þām ānum weorce ..., þæt is gebedrǽden, R. Ben. 81, 2–5. Ǽghwǽr, ge on weorce, ge on gebedhūse (*oratorio*), gè innan mynstre, ge on wyrtgearde, 31, 5. Cyrice ... is ūs gesceapen tō gebedhūse, uā tō nānum gemōthūse, Wlfst. 232, 24. In þām gebedhūse (*oratorio*) þæs eádigan Laurentius, Gr. D. 40, 30. Gebædhūse, Hml. S. 6, 206. Fela ðeóda synd ... hī ænne God wurðiað, þeáh ðe heora gereord and gebedhūs manega sind, Hml. Th. ii. 582, 6.

ge-bēdian. *Substitute:* ge-bedi(g)an *to worship, pray* :—Hē þōhte þæt hē wolde Rōme gesēcan, and ðā hālgan stōwe ðāra eádigra apostola ... geseón and him þǽr bodigan (gebedigan, gebiddan, gebodian, v. ll.) *Romam uenire ad uidenda atque adoranda beatorum apostolorum ... limina cogitauit*, Bd. 5, 9; Sch. 591, 3.

gebed-mann. *Add:*—Ǽlc riht cynestōl stent on þrym stapelum ... ān is *oratores* ... Oratores sindon gebedmen þe Gode sculan þeówian and dæges and nihtes for ealne þeódscipe þingian georne, Ll. Th. ii. 306, 33: Wlfst. 267, 11.

gebed-rǽden. *Add:* prayers :—Þǽr (on gebedhūse) nān þincg elles geworht ne sý būtan þām ānum weorce þe tō Gode belimpð, þæt is gebedrǽden (þ syndon hālige gebedu, v. l.), R. Ben. 81, 5. Þæt ic dyde for hiora godcundre gebedrǽdenne (*because of their praying for me*), C. D. ii. 111, 10. For hire gebedrǽdenne, iii. 421, 4. Hió mādmas tō Cantwaran cyricean brōhte hire tō gebedrǽdene (*to secure prayers for herself*), Lch. iii. 422, 15: Hml. S. 32, 259. Byst þū on ūre eallra gebedrǽdene *eris in nostris omnium precibus*, Ll. Th. ii. 226, 5. Gemunað mē on eówre gebedrǽdenne *remember me in your prayers*, 332, 13. Ðæt hié mē on heora gebeddrǽdenne hæbben, C. D. v. 333, 9. Ic bidde þē, mīn Drihten, þæt ðū helpe ... ealra þæra þe tō mīnre gebedrǽdene þencað and hyhtað lybbendra and forðgewitenra (*all those, living or departed, that look and hope for my prayers*), Angl. xii. 500, 28. Hē hine sylfne befæste þæs weres gebedrǽddene (-rǽdenne, v. l.) *se viri commendans orationibus*, Gr. D. 39, 13. Þæt hý him tō Gode mid heora gebedrǽdene þingian *ut orent pro ipso*, R. Ben. 70, 12. Hē wylle æfter forðsīðe ... gebedrǽdenne habban, Wlfst. 307, 24. Gebedrǽdene ārǽran *to promote the practice of praying*, Ll. Th. i. 314, 9.

gebed-sealm, es; m. *A precatory psalm, psalm containing a prayer* :—Þām xii. gebedsealmum, Lch. ii. 136, 12. Sing þās gebedsealmas *Miserere mei, Deus*, ..., iii. 12, 7.

gebed-stōw. *Add:*—Ic synful breóst mīne beáte on gebedstōwe, Dōm. L. 30.

gebed-tīd, e; f. *An hour appointed for prayer* :—Hē æt nǽnigre gebedtīde wolde on ðære cyrican wunian ðæt hē mid þǽm ōþrum his gebed gefylde, Shrn. 65, 15. Æt gehwelcre gebedtīde Godes englas cōman and lǽddan hī on ðā lyft, 107, 25. v. morgen-gebedtīd.

ge-bēgan, ge-bēgdnes, ge-bēgendlic, ge-bēldan. v. ge-bīgan, ge-bīgedness, ge-bīgendlic, ge-bildan.

ge-belg. *Add:*—Gif hwām fram his ealdore geboden sý tō ðigene, and hē hit mid gebelge forsace (*and he angrily, resentfully, refuse*), R. Ben. 69, 20. Lā leófan men ... būtan gebelge hlystað (*listen without taking offence*), Wlfst. 178, 30.

ge-belgan. *Add:* I. *with reflex. acc.* :—Ne gebelg þū þē wið mē ... Ne gebelge ic mē nāwiht wið þē, ac fagnige þæs þū cwyst, Solil. H. 35, 6–10. Ðā sǽde heó þ heó nān land hæfde þe him āht tō gebyrede, and gebealh heó (*acc. or nom.? Cf.* III *in Dict.*) swīðe eorlīce wið hire sunu, Cht. Th. 337, 24. Hié hié gebulgon *indignatione permoti*, Ors. 2, 8; S. 92, 11. II. *construction uncertain.* (1) of persons :—Hē wæs swýþe gebolgen for þære smerenesse, Bl. H. 75, 21. Lēt hē ðe breóstum, þā hē gebolgen wæs, word ūt faran, stearcheort styrmde, B. 2550. Hē wearð yrre gebolgen, Jul. 58. Þonne hī weorþaþ gebolgen (gebolgene, Met. 25, 45), ðonne wyrþ þ mōd beswungen mid þām welme þære hātheortnesse, Bt. 37, 1; F. 186, 20. (1 a) of the Deity :—Wearð gebolgen heofones waldend, Gen. 299. (2) of animals :—Eofore cēnra, þonne hē gebolgen bīdsteal giefeð, Rā. 41, 19. Wæs gebolgen beorges hyrde (*the firedrake*), B. 2304. Wyrmas and wildeór ... bitere and gebolgene, 1431. [O. H. Ger. sih gibelgan (zi) *irasci*.]

ge-bēn. *Dele* Ben. Lye, *and add:*—Waciað ... on gebedum, and gif seó cyrce bið geopenad þurh eówre gebēna, habbað hī eów siþþan ǽfre, Hml. S. 3, 331.

ge-bendan *to put in bonds. Add:*—Hiene þā burgleóde gebundon ... Ac hē fealh of þǽm bendum þe hiene mon gebende (*lapsus e vinculis*), Ors. 5, 11; S. 236, 13. Man þā hālgan hæfte and gebende, Hml. S. 23, 105. Gebænde, Wlfst. 14, 6. xı sīðan hund þūsenda hī lǽddon gebende, 296, 26.

ge-bēnlic. *Dele, and see* gyden-lic.

ge-benn. *For* Cot. 79 *substitute* :—Gebennum *edictis*, Wrt. Voc. ii. 33, 12: ge-beod. *Dele, and see* ge-bed.

ge-beódan. *Add:* I. *to order* a person (dat.) to do something :— Hēht hire þā āras gebeódan Constantīnus, þæt hió cirican ... getimbrede, El. 1007. Gif him þæt fæsten swā geboden nǽre, Wlfst. 181, 13. II. *to order to come, summon* :—Ic gefrægn folctogan fyrd gebeódan, Gen. 1961. III. *to proclaim, announce* :—Suā hwǽr geboden bið godspell ðis *ubicumque praedicatum fuerit evangelium istud*, Mk. L. R. 14, 9. III a. *to proclaim as an edict* or *ordinance* :— Gebeád hē sīnum leódum, þæt sē wǽre his aldre scyldig þe þæs onsóce, Dan. 449. Þænne bises gebeoden weorðe, Men. 32. III b. *to give official notice of* :—Hié hine his mǽgum gebeóden (gebodien, v. l.), Ll. Th. i. 64, 19. Hit beó seofon nihtum geboden ǽr gemōt sý *notice of a meeting must be given seven days before it is to be held*, 208, 27. IV. *to offer.* (1) *to offer for acceptance.* (a) of material objects :—Hē Willferð bæd þæt hē him þæs sīðfates lǽtteów wǽre, and him nicel feoh wið þām gebeád (*promissa non parua pecuniarum donatione*), Bd. 4, 5; Sch. 372, 13. Him Hygd gebeád hord and rīce, B. 2369. Hē him æt gebeád, Ph. 401. Ne sceal him mon ānne mete gebeódan, ac missenlice, Lch. ii. 240, 15. (b) of non-material objects. *to offer* a condition, homage, respect, &c. :—Wurþmynt gebeódan, Hml. S. 11, 8. Ūrum Hǽlende hyldo gebeódan, Ps. Th. 94, 1. Gebodenes sinscipes, An. Ox. 3910. Gebodene *oblatam*, 3595. (2) *to give into the power of, commit* :—Gif hē self his wǽpno his gefān ūt rǽcan wille ... hié hine his mǽgum gebeóden (or *under* III?, *the Lat. version has* offeratur, *but* gebodien *is in one MS.*), Ll. Th. i. 64, 19. Geboden tō bǽle, Dan. 414. (3) *to offer to do, do to a person* :—Rihtlaga is þæt man ōðran gebeóde, þæt hē wylle, þæt man him gebeóde, Wlfst. 274, 12. Þæt ūre ǽlc ... nānum ne gebeóde þæt, þæt hē nelle þæt man him gebeóde, Hml. Th. i. 260, 30–32. Hwī wolde gē mē þās þing gebeódan (cf. for hwon wolde gē wiþ mē þus dōn *quare in me facere ista voluistis?*, Gr. D. 105, 19), ii. 158, 25. (4) *to offer, present, cause* to be subject to what is unpleasant :—For þǽm lytlan ege þe him mon gebeád, Ors. 3, 1; S. 94, 27. Ic him Geáta sceal eafoð and ellen gebeódan, B. 603. Þē gūðgewinn gebeoden wyrðeð, An. 219.

ge-beógol, -bugol (-būgol? *but for the vowel cf.* fiugol); adj. *Ready to yield* :—Beó ðū swýðe gebeógul (-bugol, v. l.) mid gebýgedum (-bīg-, v. l.) mōde þīnum wiðerwinnan *esto consentiens adversario tuo cito*, Hml. A. 4, 93. Ūs ne hēt nā se Hǽlend him (*the devil*) beón gebeógole (-bug-, v. l.), 5, 123. v. ge-bygle.

ge-beór. *Add: a guest at a meal* :—Gebeór *convictor, conviva*, Wrt. Voc. ii. 135, 72. Tō lytlum beóde ǽwfæste þearfan Crīst gebeór

(*conuiuam*) beón witan, Scint. 158, 11. Wæs his gewuna þ hé wolde ʼswýþe lytel drincan, þeáh hé mid gebeórum blíðe wære, Vis. Lfc. 24. Se cyning bebeád þám gebeórum eallum þ hí blíþe wæron æt his gebeórscipe, and þ ælc mann drunce þæs deórwurðan wínes be þám þe hé sylf wolde, Hml. A. 92, 20. Gemétte hé gebeóras blíðe æt þám húse, . . . and sæt mid þám gebeórum blissigende samod, Hml. S. 26, 225. Drihten mid sélran wíne þá gebeóras gegladode, Hml. Th. ii. 54, 30.

**ge-beorc.** *Add:*—Of gebeorce hunda and mid stafe hyrdes wulfa wódness tó áflígenne ys *latratu canum baculoque pastoris luporum rabies deterenda est,* Scint. 119, 15. Wiþ hundes gebeorc, Lch. i. 28, 20 note.

**ge-beorg.** *Add:*—Geberg *refugium,* Wrt. Voc. ii. 118, 74. **I.** verbal abstract. (1) *protection, saving* of an object :—Bið sé gebeorges þe bet wyrðe, þe hé for neóde dyde þ þ hé dyde, Ll. Th. i. 412, 13. Gebeorhges, 328, 24. For þæra gebeorge . . . ðe hé habban wyle gehealden and geholpen, Wlfst. 86, 18. Maria wæs Jósepe beweddod for micclum gebeorge (*to secure effectual protection*), Hml. Th. i. 40, 34. On gebeorge beón wudewum *to be protecting widows,* 118, 18. His folce tó gebeorge *for the protection of his people,* Hml. S. 25, 679. Tó gebeorge and tó friðe eallum leódscype, Ll. Th. i. 276, 21. Feóre tó gebeorge *to save his life,* 330, 12. Sendan beágas wið gebeorge *to send treasure in return for safety,* i.e. *to buy off attack,* By. 31. Gebeorh *praesidium* i. *adiutorium* (*Dei laturi*), An. Ox. 2260. Begitað hí ðe máre gebeorh æt Godes dóme, Wlfst. 300, 14 : Ll. Th. ii. 314, 16. Ne bið þér fultum nán þ wið þá biteran þing gebeorh mæge fremman *auxilium nullus rebus praestabit amaris,* Dóm. L. 223 : Wlfst. 139, 14. (2) *saving* from doing wrong(?) :—Besceáwige hé á his ágene týddernesse and þurh þæt gebeorh sý ne forbrýte hé ná þæt tócnysede hreód *let him ever consider his own weakness and by that means let there be protection (let him be saved) from crushing the bruised reed* (the Latin is : Suam fragilitatem semper suspectus sit, memineritque calamum quassatum non conterendum), R. Ben. 121, 5. **II.** that which protects. (1) of persons :—Þú eart mín trymnes and mín gebeorh *fortitudo mea et firmamentum meum es tu,* Ps. Th. 30, 4. Gebeorg *refugium,* Ps. Spl. C. 58, 19. Geácsode se wræcca Sce Gúþláces forðfóre ; for þon hé ána ær þon wæs hys gebeorh and frófor (*his refuge and comfort*), Guth. 94, 4. (2) of places :—Gebeorge *praesidio* (in solo liberae mentis *praesidio* servatur), An. Ox. 5395. (3) of things :—Rand sceal on scylde, fæst fingra gebeorh, Gn. C. 38. [*O. L. Ger.* gi-berg *theca* : *O. H. Ger.* geberg *aerarium.*] v. bán-breóst-, feorh-, fýr-, rand-, sceonc-gebeorh ; gebyrg.

**ge-beorgan.** *Add:* **I.** *to protect.* (1) *to prevent the happening of evil* (*acc.*) *to an object* (*dat.*), *ward off* from :—Ic mé gúðbordes sweng gebearh, Gen. 2694. Ðis is seó líhtingc þe ic wylle eallon folce gebeorgan þe hig ær þyson mid gedrehte wæron *this is the alleviation by which I will protect all the people from those things with which they were before troubled,* Ll. Th. i. 412, 19. [*See also* Ps. Th. 93, 12 : 59, 4 *in Dict.*] (1 a) with dat. of object alone, *to protect, save, guard* :—Þonne gebyrhst (-birhst, *v.l.*) ðú þínre ágenre sáwle, Wlfst. 7, 9. Ðæs líchoman læcas . . . ge ðæm líchoman gebeorgað, ge eác ða mettrymnesse áfiémað, Past. 457, 5. Hé heom ætbærst and him sylfan gebearh þær hé þá mihte, Chr. 1052; P. 178, 30. Þ man þisum earde gebeorgan (-beorhgan, *v.l.*) mihte, ær hé mid ealle fordón wurðe, 1006; P. 137, 20. Hé wile gebeorhgan (-byrgan, -beorgan, -burgan, *v.ll.*) þám þe hym sýn gecorene, Wlfst. 19, 10. Swá man mæg stýran and eác þære sáwle gebeorgan, Ll. Th. i. 394, 16 : Gen. 1838. ¶ in the passive the object of the action is in the dative :—For ðæs láreówes wísdóm unwísum híeremonnum bið geborgen, Past. 29, 6. Him swá geborgen sý heora unwilles, þ heora tó fela ne losien, Ll. Th. i. 274, 4. Gyf hé for slǽwðe his hláfordes forgýmð, ne bið his ágnum wel geborgen, 440, 16 : Dan. 436. (2) *to protect an object* (*acc.*) *from* (*wiþ*) :—Hí wið cyle and wið hæton hí sylfe geburgon, Hml. S. 23, 420. Heó sí geborgen wið ealra bealwa gehwylc, Lch. i. 402, 10. Ne wyrð næfre folces wíse wel geræde, ne wið God well geborgen (*secure from incurring God's anger.* Cf. gebeorglic), on þám earde þe man wóh gestreón lufað, Ll. Th. ii. 312, 28. (2 a) without object, *to protect* from :—Hé mihte wið deáð gebeorgan and deáð forbúgan, Wlfst. 23, 16. (3) combining the construction of (1) and (2) :—Hé wið cwealme gebearh cnihtum (cf. beorgan; **I.** 2 *for dat.*) on ofne lácende líg *he protected the youths from death, in the fiery furnace, kept the leaping flame from them,* Dan. 475.— **II.** *to prevent the doing of ill, guard against.* v. beorgan ; **III.** :—Gebeorh þ hié ungemeltnesse ne þrowian *see that they do nothing to produce indigestion,* Lch. ii. 184, 11. **II a.** *to abstain* from wrong-doing :—Nis on ænigne tíman unriht álýfed, and þeáh man sceal freólstídon . . . geornlicost gebyrgan, Ll. Th. i. 398, 19.

**ge-beorglic.** *Substitute:* Safe, not productive of harm *or* preventive of harm. [*Take here* Coll. M. 24, 21 *under* ge-beorhlic] :—God forgifð ús menigfealde wæstmas, þæra wé sculon brúcan swá ús gebeorhlic (*in such a way as not to harm ourselves*), Hml. S. 11, 357. Gif hwá hæfð his hláforde sáre ábolgen, ne bið him ná gebeorhlic, þæt hé in him ætforan gá, ær hé gebéte ; ne húru ne bið ná gebeorhlic þám þe wið God hæfð forworht hine sylfne . . . , þæt hé tó hrædlíce intó Godes húse

racige, Wlfst. 155, 16–21. Sý on þære bóte swilc forgifnes swilce hit for Gode gebeorglic (-beorh-, *v.l.*) sý (*as that there be no danger of incurring God's anger.* Cf. Ll. Th. ii. 312, 28 *under* gebeorgan ; **I.** 2. *The Lat. version has* remissio uenialis apud Deum) and for weorulde áberendlic, Ll. Th. i. 266, 6. Gefadige man þá steóre swá hit for Gode sý gebeorhlic (*the Lat. versions have* erga Deum clementius, propter Deum parcibilis), 376, 17. Man dóm æfter dæde medemige be mæðe swá for Gode sí gebeorhlic, 318, 6. Ne tæce wé ná mid swá geráðum bysenum and gebeorhlicum lárum, þæt hé leahtras fyrðrige, ac þæt hé snotorlíce hý wanige, R. Ben. 121, 7.

**ge-beorglíce.** v. un-gebeorhlíce : **ge-beorhlic.** v. ge-beorglic.

**ge-beorhtian.** *Dele bracket, and add:*—Ic gebrehtade *clarificaui,* Jn. p. 6, 18. Mec geberhtade *me clarificabit,* Jn. L. 16, 14. Giberhta *declaret,* Rtl. 102, 43. Is geberhtad *declaratur,* 3, 3. ¶ in a physical sense, *to make the sight good* :—Haran geallan wið hunig gemencged . . . þá eágan gebeortigeaþ, Lch. i. 344, 5. [*O. H. Ger.* ge-berahtón *clarificare.*]

**ge-beorhtness,** e ; *f.* Brightness, *splendour* :—Gebrehtnis *clarificationis,* Jn. p. 6, 15. Giberhtnisse, Jn. R. 16, 14.

**ge-beorhtnian** ; *p.* ode To make bright, *splendid, to glorify* :—Ic ðec geberhtnade í wuldrade *ego te clarificaui,* Jn. L. 17, 4. Þte sune ðín ðec geberhtna (berehtnað, R.) *ut filius tuus clarificet te,* 1. Gebrehtnige *clarificare,* p. 6, 17. Geberehtnad (gibrehtnad, R.) *clarificatus,* 13, 31. Gif God geberhtnad (gibertnad, R.) næs in ðǽm, and God geberhtnade (gibertnade, R.) hine, 32. Geberehtnad (giberhtnad, R.), 15, 8. Gibrehtnad (giberhtnad, R.) í giuuldrad uére *clarificaturus esset,* 21, 19.

**ge-beormad** *leavened* ; fermentatus, Mt. R. 13, 33. v. ge-birman.

**ge-beornan.** v. ge-birnan.

**ge-beórscipe.** *Take here* **ge-bǽrscipe, -beárscipe** *in Dict., and add:*—Singal gebiórscipe *iuge conuiuium,* Kent. Gl. 521. Weard seó þénung in geboren and æfter þám cynelíce gebeórscipe, Ap. Th. 14, 15. Se cyning bebeád þám gebeórum, þ hí blíþe wæron æt his gebeórscipe, Hml. A. 92, 21. Se þearfa . . . þe mid þé is tó cumenne tó engla gebeórscipe, 142, 107. Ælc ðæra manna ðe ðæne deófollican unðeáw hæfð, þ hé wile on his gebeórscipe þurh his hálsunge and ðurh his neádunge gedón, þ óðre men nimað máre ðonne hit gemet sý, 145, 22. Dydon hí þá mæstan gebeórscype, Hml. S. 30, 387. Gibeársciopo *continua* (*conuiuia?*), Rtl. 31, 1. In gebeársciopum *in conuiuis,* Lk. L. 20, 46. Ðerh gebeárscipo *per conuiuia,* 9, 14. Swá oft swá gé eów geménelice gebeórscipas gegearwiað, gé ðá fatu ðæs micclan gemetes, ðe þreó men oððe feówer . . . hwílum willes, hwílum geneádode gewuniað of tó drincanne, of eówrum gebeórscipe áwurpað eall swá áttor, Hml. A. 145, 43.

**ge-beorþor.** *Add:*—Þurh þæt gebyrðor (-beorþor, *v.l.*), Wlfst. 251, 14. v. cniht-gebeorþor.

**ge-beót.** *Add:* (1) *a promise to do great things, a boast, boasting :* —Ða bóceras gýmaþ tó gebeótes þæra fíf stafa þe synd vocales gecíged *the grammarians make a boast of taking care of the five letters that are called vowels,* Angl. viii. 327, 35. Ða andwyrde Petrus mid gebeóte : ʼIc ðe næfre ne æswicige . . .ʼ. Se Hælend beseah tó Petre, and hé sóna gemunde his micclan gebeótes, Hml. Th. ii. 246, 1–248, 35. Hé ofwearp Goliam þe mid gebeóte (*with proud challenge*) clypode bysmor Godes folce, Hml. S. 18, 20. (2) *a promise to do hurt, a threat, threatening* :—Hé . . . gebealh hine, and mid gebeóte cwæð : ʼWite ðú þ ðú wurðan scealt . . . ofslagen, Hml. A. 107, 146 : Hml. S. 3, 222. Hé swór þ hé hine wolde fordón. Ða cwæð Georius him tó : ʼIc ne forhtige for ðínum gebeóte,ʼ 14, 101. Hé swór þ hé Godes hús wolde forbærnan . . . Hé eft genam fyrde, wolde his gebeót mid weorcum gefremman, 25, 621. Mid manna blódum þe ic þurh gebeót and þurh hátheortnesse ágeat *with men's blood that I shed through hot words and hot temper,* Angl. xi. 113, 36. Áðwæsc nú ðás gebeót and ðás wópas tóbrec, Shrn. 68, 9.

**ge-beótian.** *Add:*—Ne mæg þ beón leás þ God gebeótode tó þám unrihtwísum mannum *falsum non erit quod minatus est Deus,* Gr. D. 334, 11. Hé geendode þæt he lange tó þæm áwergdum gástum gebeótod hæfde, Bl. H. 83, 26.

**gebeótlic** ; *adj.* Arrogant, *proudly threatening* :—Pharao him filigde mid his gebeótlicum crætum and gilplicum riddum *Pharaoh followed them with a threatening array of chariots and with his braggart knights,* Hml. Th. ii. 194, 22.

**ge-beótung.** *Substitute:* The word glosses *fascinatio,* Wrt. Voc. ii. 38, 46, which may have been understood in the sense of boasting. Cf. *fascinatio* : *laudatio stulta,* Ld. Gl. H. 12, col. 2, or in the sense of threatening. Cf. *fascinatio, inuidia,* Corp. Gl. H. 53, 4.

**ge-beówed.** v. ge-bíwan.

**ge-beran.** *Add:* **I.** *to bear, bring* :—Þ cild Críst wearð geboren ágeán of Egiptan, Chr. 3 ; P. 5, 22. Sió gifu þæs hálegan gerýnes . . . bútan ænigre yldinge is tó berenne (gebeorenne, -anne, *v.ll.*) *sancti mysterii gratia . . . sine ulla dilatione offerenda est,* Bd. 1, 27 ; Sch. 80, 3. Geborenae *exposito,* Txts. 58, 359. Geborene, Wrt. Voc. ii. 29,

61. **II.** *to bear* young. (1) *to carry* in the womb :—þū wuldres þrym bósme gebǣre, Cri. 84. (2) *to bring forth :*—þīn wīf þē gebereþ (*pariet*) sunu, Bl. H. 165, 9. Gif hió cwic bearn gebyreð, Ll. Th. i. 22, 4 : 24, 1. Hē hyre gecýdde þæt heó sceolde geberan (*parere*) Godes sunu . . . þā weard heó on innoðe geeácnod and mid þām cilde weard sōna, and þæt gebær, ðā hit þæs tima wæs, Wlfst. 22, 5–9. Heó ācende hyre suna Gode myd gāste ðe heó myd līchaman on myddangearde gebær, Shrn. 151, 8. Siþþan þū ǣrest geboren wǣre oð þisne dæg *from the very day you were born until this day*, Bt. 8; F. 24, 21. Sōna swā hē ācenned wæs and geboren *at his birth*, Bl. 167, 10. For geborene ge for ungeborene, Ll. Th. i. 152, 6. (2 a) of an animal :—Sylle hē þone dǣl ꝥ hit on his ǣhte geboren wǣre, Ll. Th. i. 204, 14. ¶ geboren *born*. (a) with reference to rank, position, &c. :—Gylde hine man swā hē geboren sý, Ll. Th. i. 174, 15. Þæt þes eorl wǣre geboren betera, B. 1703. Hī cuǣdon þæt hæt rīce tó his honda healdan sceoldon, for þǣm hira nān næs on fædrenhealfe tó geboren, Chr. 887; P. 80, 22. (b) with reference to nationality, relationship :—Hē of hiora (*the Goths'*) lande geboren wæs *he was a native of their country*, Ors. 6, 37; S. 296, 12. His geborena brōþer *frater germanus*, Gr. D. 344, 9. Grǣf geóde strēgan brōðor his geborenum, Seef. 98. Man mót feohtan mid his geborene (-um, *v. l.*) mǣge, Ll. Th. i. 90, 24. Syndon him twēgen beornas geborene brōðorsybbum *he has two brothers*, An. 690. (c) with a complementary noun or adjective:—Hē bið mennisc man geboren, Wlfst. 84, 12. Sum cild sié full hāl geboren, Bt. 38, 5; F. 206, 22. Gif mon sié dumb oþþe deáf geboren, Ll. Th. i. 70, 14. Blindum giborenum (*caeco nato*) ēgo untýndist, Rtl. 101, 38. [*Goth.* ga-bairan : *O. Sax.* gi-beran : *O. H. Ger.* gi-beran.] v. un-geboren.

**ge-bered.** *For first passage substitute* :—*Maceretur autem* gecneden bið *sive* gebered bið, Wrt. Voc. ii. 58, 55. [v. *N. E. D.* berry. Cf. *O. H. Ger.* berien *terere* : *Icel.* berja *to beat, thrash.*]

**ge-berhtan.** v. ge-birhtan : **ge-berhtnian.** v. ge-beorhtnian : **ge-berian.** v. ge-byrian : **ge-bernan.** v. ge-bærnan.

**ge-berst,** es; *n.* *Add* :—þǣra beorga geberst *the bursting asunder of the hills*, Wlfst. 186, 7. Wið ómena geberste, Lch. iii. 42, 29. v. eorþ-geberst.

**ge-berstan** *to burst* :—Hnescað se swile and gebersteþ, Lch. ii. 202, 11. [*O. H. Ger.* ge-brestan *deficere.*]

**ge-bésmed.** *Add : Swelled out by the wind :*—Segelbósmas gebésmed *carbasa sinuata*, Wrt. Voc. ii. 88, 26.

**ge-bétan.** *Add :* **I.** *to make good, cause to flourish :*—Sǣnde ic þā gewideru þe ealle eówre wæstmas and eordlice tilþa fullīce gebétað *dabo uobis pluuiam temporibus suis, et terra gignet germen suum, et pomis arbores replebuntur*, Wlfst. 132, 14. **II.** *to make good* what is defective. (1) *to repair* material objects, *mend :*—þā burg man gebétte and geedneówade þǣr heó ǣr tóbrocen wæs, Chr. 921; P. 103, 6. Þæt se cræftga cume . . . and gebéte, nū gebrosnad is hūs under hrófe, Cri. 13. Hē gefór þā burg and hēt hié gebétan, Chr. 922; P. 104, 2 : 923; P. 104, 10. Ǣlc burh sý gebét .xiiii. niht ofer Gangdagas, Ll. Th. i. 206, 14. (1 a) *to trim* a lamp, *kindle* or *mend* a fire :—Hē gebétte ꝥ leóht *refovebat lumen*, Gr. D. 227, 6. Undergesettum and gebéttum mycclum fýre hē wæs þǣr forbærned *supposito igne concrematus est*, 307, 20. (2) in a medical sense, *to do good to, cure, remedy :*—ꝥ sār hyt wel gebét, Lch. i. 200, 6. Hyt þā deáfan gebéteþ, 362, 22. (3) *to remedy, do away with* an unsatisfactory condition, *mend* matters, *ameliorate :*—Gif ðe wæs gold tó lytel oððe seolfor . . . ic ðæt sóna gebéte, ac ne forlǣt mē, Shrn. 140, 27. þū Hróðgāre wīdcūðne weán gebéttest, B. 1991. Wæs hungor ofer hrūsan; ꝥ heofona weard gebétte, Chr. 975; P. 122, 1 : 1087; P. 223, 23. God ūre yfel gebétte, and cýdde his mihte and his mildheortnysse ðæt hē swā mycel yfel mihte gebétan, Hex. 26, 25–27. ꝥ hē his geféra wǣre tó þām cynge, and his wīsa wið hine gebétte (*would make his relations with the king more satisfactory*), Chr. 1050; P. 169, 31. Gebét ðā weorc ðe deádlicu sint in ðē *confirma cetera, quae moritura erant*, Past. 445, 20. Gebéte hit God, þonne his willa sý, Chr. 1085; P. 217, 22. Gebétan *emendare*, Kent. Gl. 957. Hū ne mæg se cyning þæne tweón eáðe gebétan *cannot the king easily put an end to the doubt?*, Wlfst. 3, 12. Nā geþafian, gif hī hit gebétan magan, ꝥ ǣnig crīsten man óðrum derige tó swýðe, Ll. Th. ii. 312, 39. Hit ne magon þā welan eallunga gebétan, Bt. 26, 2; F. 92, 37. Hæfde Eástdenum leód oncýððe ealle gebétte, inwidsorge, þe hié ǣr drugon, B. 830. (4) *to correct* what is morally or intellectually wrong, *amend, reform.* (a) a person :—Hē mid heardre þreá hī on sprǣc and hī gebétte *aspera illos inuectione corrigebat*, Bd. 3, 5; Sch. 205, 1. Godes hālgan fela wundra worhtan . . . and þurh þæt mænigne man gebétan, Wlfst. 84, 6. Gelǣred preóst ne scǣnde þone sāmlǣredan, ac gebéte hine, gif hē bet cunne, Ll. Th. ii. 246, 19. Þæt ðā wītu þā gebétan þe hī brociaþ, Bt. 39, 11; F. 230, 8. For ðǣre sylfan scame hē beón gebétte (*emendentur*), R. Ben. I. 76, 11. (b) a thing :—On ðǣm earfoðum þā longe ǣr tó yfle gedyde, hē gebétt (-bét, *v. l.*) *in adversis rebus longi temporis admissa terguntur*, Past. 35, 9. Godcunde lāra and wīslice woroldlaga . . . þeóde þeáwas gebétað, Ll. Lbmn. 269, 25. **III.** *to make good, make reparation*

*for, make amends for, atone for.* (1) in a moral or spiritual sense, *to repent of, do penance for* sin :—Mid þǣm sāwlum þe hēr on worlde . . . heora synna geondettaþ and wið Gode gebétaþ, Bl. H. 57, 27. Hē gebétte balanīða hord mid eáðméde higeþance, Ps. C. 151. Gif hī hwæt gesyngodon . . . ꝥ hī hit eft mid hreówsunge gebéton, Bt. 41, 3; F. 248, 14. Hyra unlustas hī sceolan gebétan sylfwylles on þyssum līfe, Hml. Th. i. 148, 27 : ii. 602, 20 : Ors. 2, 1 ; S. 64, 8. Ne þearf þæs nān man wēnan ꝥ his līchama móte oþþe mæge þā synbyrþenna on eorþscrafe gebétan, Bl. H. 109, 31. Synna bewēpan and wið God gebétan, Hml. S. 12, 160. (1 a) in an ecclesiastical sense :—Būton hē wið God gebéte fullīce swā biscop him tǣce, Ll. Th. i. 346, 12 : 246, 7. Gebéte hē ꝥ deópe for Gode, 324, 26. Gebéte hē hit mid godcundre bóte, 328, 2. ' Sýn hý þæs wyrðe þe on þām canone cwæð . . . būton hý gebétan,' 244, 14. Nymðe heó hit hér mid þingonge bóte gebéte, C. D. i. 114, 27. Ā swā mon bið mihtigra . . . swā sceal hē deóppor synna gebétan, Ll. Th. i. 328, 15. ꝥ hē hit swā gebétt hæbbe, swā him his scrift scrife, 212, 22. (2) *to make reparation for* wrong-doing, *give satisfaction for* injury :—Sendon hié ǣrendracan and bǣdon þæt him man gebétte þæt him ðǣr tó ābylgðe gedón wæs *missi legati, ut de illatis quereretur injuriis*, Ors. 4, 1; S. 154, 11. þā Norðhymbra . . . wið Eádréd cyning gebéton þā dǣde, Chr. 948; P. 112, 34. Gān þā . . . and gebéte þām óðrum þone ǣwyrdlan, Ll. Th. i. 128, 8. ꝥ hī mihtan hiora scylda þurh wīte gebétan, Bt. 38, 7; F. 210, 10. (2 a) in a legal sense, *to make reparation for* an offence by undergoing punishment or by paying a fine. (α) where the penalty is not defined :—Gif hwā folces fyrdscip āwyrde, gebéte ꝥ georne, Ll. Th. i. 324, 5. Gebéte ꝥ deópe for worolde, 26. Gebéte hē hit mid woroldcundre steóre, 328, 2. Būton hē wið men þe deóplīcor gebéte, 346, 12. Gebéten þā þone gylt þe hine geféngon, 148, 10. Ǣr hē hæbbe wið þā mǣgðe gebét, 248, 15. (β) where the penalty is a fine, given (β 1) in the dat. (inst.) case :—Gif wið ceorles birelan man geligeð, vi. scillingum gebéte, Ll. Th. i. 6, 14. Seofonfealdre bóte gebéte hē hit, ii. 240, 7. Gebéte hē þæs þeófes were, i. 392, 15. Sē ꝥ gebéte his dryhtne .c. scill., 38, 6. (β 2) with prep. :—Gebéte hē þæs borges bryce mid .v. pundum, Ll. Th. i. 62, 8 : 330, 29. Gebéte ꝥ mid .viii. scitt., 94, 11 : 260, 14. Gebéte hē hit mid eallum þām þe hē āge, 102, 20. Gebéte hē þæt, swā swā hit gelagod is : būnda mid xxx penigan, þrǣl mid his hīde, þegn mid xxx scillingan, Wlfst. 181, 8. Gebéte mid were man wið wīte, Ll. Th. i. 62, 4. Gebéte mid fulre bóte, 330, 26. (β 3) by adverb or phrase :—.ii. bóte gebéte, Ll. Th. i. 4, 2. Gebéte hē ꝥ be þǣm þe seó dǣd sý, swā he were, swā be wīte, 168, 5. Gebéte ꝥ be lahslite, ii. 294, 1. **IV.** *to obtain reparation for, avenge :*—þæt wē on Adame and on his eafrum andan gebétan, Gen. 399. Þæt wē Rómana bismer gewrecan (gebétan, *v. l.*, *here* or (?) *under* I. 3) sceolde *missus pro abolenda macula*, Ors. 5, 2; S. 216, 16. v. un-gebétt.

**ge-bétendness,** e; *f. Emendation, correction :*—Gebétendnysse *emendationem*, An. Ox. 58, 6.

**ge-beterian.** *Add :*—ꝥ wē ūre līf and ūre þeáwas gebeterian, Hml. A. 149, 136. þæt hý for ðǣre scame gebeterede sýn (*emendentur*), R. Ben. 68, 18. [*O. H. Ger.* ge-bezirón.]

**ge-beterung, -betrung** *edification.* *For* Som. Ben. Lye *substitute :* —Wē wyllað sume óðre trimminge gereccan tó eówre gebetrunge, Hml. Th. i. 448, 10. [*O. H. Ger.* ge-bezerunga *aedificatio.*]

**ge-betron** ? :—Preóstas . . . mid heora módes gebetron (*with the superior condition of their mind?* Cf. betera *as substantive?*) witon wel hwæt byð *lamentum*, Angl. viii. 313, 12.

**ge-bícnan, -bícnian.** *Add :* **I.** *to make a significant gesture that gives or asks for information, to point to* an object, *inquire by signs :*— Ān lamb bícnode mid his swýðran fēt, swilce hit þā wæterǣddran geswutelian wolde. Ðā undergeat Clemens þæs lambes gebícnunge and cwæð : ' Geopeniað þās eorðan on þyssere stówe þǣr ðǣr þæt lamb tó gebícnode,' Hml. Th. i. 562, 12. Gebécnade (-ede, R.) ðǣm Petrus *innuit huic Petrus*, Jn. L. 13, 24. Gebécnadon fæder his huoelcne wælde geceiga hine *innuebant patri ejus quem uellet uocari eum*, Lk. L. 1, 62. **I a.** *to command by a nod, to command :*—Būton hē tó ǣlcum men mæge gebécnan ꝥ hē ierne on his willan, Bt. 11, 1 ; F. 32, 20. **II.** *to point out by a sign.* (1) *to indicate* an object by a gesture :—Judam hlāfes mid rǣcing gebécnade *Judam panis porrectione significat*, Jn. p. 7, 3. (2) *to point out* by a written sign :—Gebécnas ꝥ getācnas *significans* (*per minii distinctionem*), Mt. p. 11, 14. **III.** *to mark, note* by help of a sign :—Rīmas ðā ǣr ðū gebécnades (*signaveras*; cf. *quos numeros adnotabis*, 6), Mt. p. 4, 7. **IV.** *to shew figuratively, represent symbolically :*—Hē sceal smeágan embe ꝥ ǣce līf . . . swiðor þonne embe þā eorðlican þing, swā swā his wæstm him gebícnað, Hml. S. 1, 61. Ðegnum ongelīc wīfes . . . inlǣded, ðā ilca from feder tó lufanne gebécnas (*significans*), Jn. p. 7, 16 : 3, 10 : 8, 6. Ðæt cýdde se wītga, ðā hē ðæt openlīce sǣde, ðætte suā geweard, and ðæt gebiecnode, ðæt ðā giet diegle wæs, Past. 331, 5. Nóe getācnode Críst, and þæt flód . . . gebícnode þæt wæter ūres fulluhtes, Hml. Th. ii. 60, 4. Ne fó wē nó on ðā bisna . . . for ðæra leásena spella lufan, ac for ðæm ðe wē wolden mid gebécnan þā sóðfæstnesse, Bt. 35, 6 ; S. 101,

12. Mid þām þe hē cwæþ: 'Uton wircean,' ys seó Ðrinnys gebícnod, Ælfc. Gen. Thw. 3, 15. [*O. Sax.* gi-bóknian: *O. H. Ger.* ge-bouhnen *figurare.*]

ge-bícnend, -bícnī[g]end *glosses* index :—Gebēcnend mīn *index meus,* Ps. Srt. 72, 14. Gebícnigend, Germ. 393, 51. Spǽc ídel ídeles ingehýdes gebícnigend ys *sermo uanus uanae conscientiae index est,* Scint. 204, 2.

ge-bícnendlic, -bícnigendlic. *Add: figurative, allegorical.* Cf. ge-bícnan: IV :—Gebēcnendlicum *allegoriam,* Wrt. Voc. ii. 1, 9.

ge-bícnung. *Add:* (1) v. ge-bícnan; L. (2) cf. ge-bícnan; IV :—Ic ðā stōwe þe se fearr geealgode synderlíce lufige, and ic wolde mid þǽre gebícnunge geswutelian þæt ic eom ðǽre stōwe hyrde, Hml. Th. i. 504, 1.

ge-bídan. *Add:* I. *to remain* in the same place or condition, *continue, abide* :—Gif se āþundena swā āswollen gebít oþ þone fíf and twēntigeþan dæg, Lch. ii. 200, 23. Gebūge hē hengenne and þǽr gebíde oþ þæt hē gā tō Godes ordāle, Ll. Th. i. 396, 28. Betere is tō gebídanne ǽnne dæg mid þe *melior est dies una in atriis tuis,* Ps. Th. 83, 10. II. *to wait with, abide* a person :—Ge ꝥ ābídas (gebiddas, R.) mec *sustinent me,* Mk. L. 8, 2. III. *to last until* a definite time (*gen.*) :—Þū nāst hwæþer ðū mergenes gebítst, Wlfst. 286, 27. Gif ic tō mergen middeges gebíde, Hml. S. 3, 590. Hwæðer ðū merigenes gebíde, Hml. Th. ii. 104, 26. Hwā helpð ūs, þæt wē ǽfenes gebídon? . . . Hwā fylst ūs, þæt wē dæges gebídon? *quis nobis det vesperam?* . . . *quis nobis det mane?,* Deut. 28, 67. Wē nyton, þonne wē tō ūre reste gāð, hwæþer wē mōton eft dæges gebídan (*live to see the morning*), Wlfst. 151, 18: Bl. H. 213, 25. IV. *to wait, abstain from action, remain passive* :—Geofon swaðrode . . . brimrād gebād, An. 1589. IV.a. where the limit of waiting is given :—Hē gebít, oð ðæt ðā yfelan ongitaþ hyra yfel, Bt. 38, 3; F. 202, 14. Hié swā ondrǽdendlíce gebídon þæt se ege ofergongen wæs, and þǽr siþþan wælgrimlíce gefuhton, Ors. 4, 2; S. 160, 31. Gebíd ðū mid ðǽre andsware, oð ðū wite ðæt ðín sprǽc hæbbe ǽgðer ge ord ge ende, Past. 385, 12. Hwæþer ðū þínes āgenes þonces hí forléte, þe þū gebíde hwonne hí þé forlētan, Bt. 8; F. 26, 13. Gebídan, oþ þæt . . . , Wand. 70: El. 865. V. *to await, wait for* a person, time, an event. (1) *with acc.* :—Wræcmon gebād lāstweard, Exod. 137. Þā þe gebiodon lēsing *qui expectabant redemtionem,* Lk. L. 2, 38. (2) *with gen.* :—Hē stille gebād āres sprǽce (*or acc.?*), Gen. 2909. Hwī ne magon gē gebídan gecyndelíces deáðes?, Bt. 39, 1; F. 210, 27: Met. 27, 7. Ic gebídan wille þæs þe mē mín Dryhten dēmeð, Gū. 349: Gn. Ex. 105. (3) *with clause* :—þā ungesǽligan menn ne magon gebídon hwonne hē him tō cume, Bt. 39, 1; F. 212, 2. Gebídan hwæt mē God dēman wille, Sat. 108. Gebídan hwænne þū eft cyme *to await the time of thy return,* An. 399. VI. *to get by waiting* or remaining, *to have, experience* that which befalls. (1) the subject a person :—Hwelcne endedæg mín mōdor oþðe mín geswuster nū gebídan scoldon *quem exitum mater mea sororesque mee habiture sint,* Nar. 31, 20. (1a) *to enjoy* good :—Þonne gebíde wē þe māre gebeorh æt Godes dōme, Ll. Th. ii. 314, 15. Ealra þǽra wynna þe ic on worulde gebād, By. 174. Hé lytle stilnesse gebād, þā hwíle hē ríces weóld, Chr. 1065; P. 195, 26. Ic mē weána ne wēnde bōte gebídan, B. 934. Sē þe āh lífes wyn gebiden in burgum, Seef. 28. (1b) *to endure, undergo, suffer* ill :—Fela ic weána gebād, Fins. 25. Myccle scipbrocu hē gebād, Bl. H. 173, 6. Hē oft gebād geād íserncūre, B. 3116. Mín heorte gebād hearmedwít feala, and yrmðu mænig eác āræfnede, Ps. Th. 68, 21. Hí gebídan myccle earfoðnysse þā hí hāmward fōran, Chr. 1061; P. 189, 36. Yrmða gebídan, Wlfst. 26, 12. Ellen gefremman oðþe endedæg gebídan ꝥ dō or díe, B. 638. Bið geómorlic gomelum ceorle tō gebídanne, þæt his byre ríde giong on galgan, 2445. Ic earfoðwíle þrowode, breóstceare gebiden hæbbe, Seef. 4. (2) the subject a thing :—Þæs tūn gebād æfter geárum swíðe manigne hlāford and swíðe manigne mundboran, Hml. A. 199, 146. Þes wāg gebād . . . ríce after ōðrum, Ruin. 9. Seó herepað æt hilde gebād . . . bite írena, B. 2258. Feala ic (*the cross*) gebiden hæbbe wrāðra wyrda, Kr. 50. VII. *to live through* a period, *live* (many) years :—Mín fæder gebād wintra worn, B. 264. Gif on middan mannum geweorðeð, þæt hí hundeahtatig ylda gebíden, Ps. Th. 89, 11. Hē wintra lyt gebiden hæbbe, B. 1928. Hē fíf and hundteóntig lifde wintra gebídenra, Gen. 1185. VIII. *to reach, arrive* at a time :—Ealle wē scylan ǽnne tíman gebídan, þonne ūs wǽre leófre þonne eall þæt on middanearde is, þǽr wē worhton . . . Godes willan, Wlfst. 208, 30: Ll. Th. i. 370, 18. Ic þæs lífes ne mæg ǽfre tō ealdre ende gebídan, Ph. 562: B. 1386: Gū. 807. Hē hæfde his ende gebídenne on eorðan unswǽslicne, Jud. 64. IX. *to obtain* :—Hí bǽdon þone híred ꝥ Ælfstān mōste beón þæs þriddan peniges wurðe of þǽre tolne . . . ac hý forwyrndon heom ealle tōgædere endemes, ꝥ hē hit nā sceolde nǽfre gebídan (*that he should never obtain the grant?*) . . . Nā gebād Ælfstān nǽfre on nānan ōþre wísan þone þriddan penig, Cht. Th. 340, 32-341, 31.

ge-biddan. *Add:* I. *to ask.* (1) *to ask* for something (*gen.*) :—Ǽr man hæbbe þriwa his rihtes gebeden, Ll. Th. i. 386, 13. (2) *to ask, make request* to a person :—Ne sceal nān faran . . . būton hē gebeden sý, Ll.

Th. ii. 386, 6. Swā swā hē gebeden wæs þurh þā geleásfullan, Ælfc. T. Grn. 12, 35. (3) *to ask* a person for something :—þæt þū ne þurfe mē týðian þæs þe þū gebeden eart, Gr. D. 28, 9. (4) *to ask* for something for a person :—Gebide þē miltsunge, Hml. Th. ii. 414, 12. II. of prayer to an object (person or thing) held sacred. (1) *to pray, say a prayer* :—Andreas þā gebæd, Bl. H. 247, 14. Ðūs gebiddende, 245, 3. (1a) reflexive, *to say one's prayers* :—Hē hine gebæd, Bl. H. 217, 26. Maria hié gebæd tō þǽm gebede þe se engel hire tō cwæþ, 145, 23. Heó gebæd hig tō þām pāpan, Shrn. 150, 4. Gebide þē þriwa eást, Lch. iii. 60, 15. ꝥ hē hine on cirican georne gebidde, Ll. Th. i. 334, 29. Mid þām paternostre hē sceal hine gebiddan, Hml. S. 12, 262. Heó wæs hié gebiddende, Bl. H. 137, 23 : Hml. S. 7, 224. (2) *to pray* to an object :—Andreas gebæd tō Drihtne, Bl. H. 247, 23. Hí gebǽdon tō Drihtne, 239, 1. (2a) reflexive. (a) *with acc.* (*or uncertain*) :—Gebæd ic mē tō him, Bl. H. 191, 15. Uton gebiddan ūs tō ūrum Drihtne, 139, 31. Gehwā sceal hine gebiddan tō his Drihtne ānum (*Dominum Deum tuum adorabis,* Mt. 4, 10), Hml. Th. i. 166, 28. Hē wæs simle hine tō Drihtne gebiddende, Bl. H. 229, 19. (β) *with dat.* :—Menn gebiddaþ him tō þyssum beácne (*the Cross*), Kr. 83. ꝥ hí him tō Gode gebǽdon, Hml. S. 30, 425. (3) *to pray for,* (a) a person :—'Gebide for míne sunu' . . . Se hālga gebæd for þæt seóce cyld, Hml. S. 3, 307-11. Gebide for mē, 23 ᵇ, 718. ꝥ hē for hine gebidde, Bt. proem. 11. (b) a thing :—Gebiddaþ for eówrum synnum *intervenite pro vestris erratibus,* Coll. M. 36, 7. (4) *to pray to, adore, worship* :—Gebiddað hine *adorabunt eum,* Ps. Spl. 44, 13. Se hālga gebæd bilwitne fæder breóstgehygdum, An. 998. Hié God and þone heáhengel gebǽdon, Bl. H. 201, 13. Ðā ongunnan hí . . . deófulgyld weorþian and gebiddan (worþodon and gebǽdon, *v. l.*) *coeperunt adorare simulacra,* Bd. 3, 30; Sch. 331, 17. Ðū, God, āna tō gebiddene, Hml. S. 7, 225. Se Hālga Gāst is . . . gebeden and gewuldrod, Hml. Th. ii. 598, 9. (4a) *to pray to* God for a person :—Gebide nū for mē þone God ðe ðū wurðast, Hml. Th. ii. 312, 12.

ge-bierde. v. ge-birde.

ge-bígan. Take here ge-bégan in *Dict., and add :*—Gebígþ *flectit, curvat, inclinat,* Wrt. Voc. ii. 149, 44. Gebíged *curva,* 23, 47. I. *to cause to move* from a position or direction :—þā þōhton hié ꝥ hié sceoldon of þām muntum hié gebígan mid hiora flāna gescotum, Ors. 6, 36 ; S. 294, 23. II. *to bend, give shape* or direction to an object :—Gebēgð *curvat* (*fornicem*), Kent. Gl. 755. *Circumflexus accentus* gebíged accent, Angl. viii. 333, 26. Gebégdes *adunci,* Wrt. Voc. ii. 9, 60. Gebígdre stíge *flexo tramite, inclinato,* 149, 45. Gebégde *curbo* (*poplite*), 83, 14. Gebíge[n]dne hláf *laganum,* Ex. 29, 23. Gebégdum *aduncis,* Wrt. Voc. ii. 99, 22. IIa. reflex. of a person, *to bow* in reverence :—Hē hine eádmōdlíce gebígde ādūne tō his fōtum, Hml. S. 10, 128. III. *to incline,* turn a person to, *bring to accept* a faith, practice, object of worship, &c. :—Hē þæt hǽðene landfolc tō Crístes geleáfan mid bodunge gebígde, Hml. Th. ii. 164, 20. Hē hine tō fulluhte gebígde . . . ðā gebrōðra ðe hē ǽr tō Gode gebígde, Hml. S. 15, 26, 38. Tō brýdbúres geþeódnesse gebígdan *ad thalami copulam inclinarent,* An. Ox. 3201. Gif hē mihte hí gebígan tō his synscipe, Hml. Th. ii. 476, 21. Gyf þū Godes folc gebígean ne miht tō rihte, Wlfst. 7, 8. Hē wolde gebígan his leóda tō geleáfan and tō þām lifigendan Gode, Hml. S. 26, 46. Hine gebégean tō beteran wege, Chr. 1067; P. 201, 29. IV. *to turn, bring* to a desired condition, *adapt* :—Ūre mōd gebíg, þanc and þeáwas on þín gewil, Hy. 7, 77. Se bisceop ne mihte gebígan his sprǽce tō Norðhymbriscum gereorde swā hraþe, Hml. S. 26, 68. V. *to turn* thought, attention, &c., *bring to consider* :—Hē gebígde his mōd tō untrumra monna diógolnessum, Past. 99, 22. VI. *to bend, subdue, humiliate, subject* :—Wlǽttuncg ānrǽdnesse gebígde *deformatio statum cordis inclinat,* An. Ox. 4469. Englisce menn ꝥ land gebýgdan þan kyninge tō handan, Chr. 1074; P. 209, 20. Þæt hí mē gebýgean of eorðan, Ps. Th. 16, 10. Þū miht león and dracan liste gebýgean *conculcabis leonem et draconem,* 90, 13. Þā þeówas uneáþe ōferwunnene wurdon, and vi m ōfslagen ǽr hié mon gebíggean mehte, Ors. 5, 3; S. 222, 29. Ic eom gebíged (-bígged, *v. l.*) and gehēned *incurvatus sum et humiliatus,* Past. 67, 18. Ic tō nāwihte eom nýde gebíged *ego ad nihilum redactus sum,* Ps. Th. 72, 17. Burga fífe wǽran under Norðmannum nýde gebégde, Chr. 942; P. 110, 20. v. un-gebígan.

ge-bígan, -bégan; p. de To crown :—Hié þā swā sigebeorhte and swā gebégde mid mycelre blisse tō hām fōran, Bl. H. 203, 30. v. beáh, ge-beágian.

ge-bígednes. *Add: curvature* :—Hricges gebígednesse *spinae curvaturam,* An. Ox. 2469: ge-bígendlic. *Add:* v. un-gebígendlic: ge-bihþ. *l.* ge-byhþ.

ge-bild *boldness.* Take here ge-byld in *Dict., and add :*—Uton mid gebylde būgan tō fulluhte, Hml. S. 3, 52. Cwæð Cecilia mid gebylde, 34, 137: Hml. Th. ii. 508, 29. Ic ðās bōc āwende ; nā þurh gebylde mycelre lāre, i. 2, 19.

ge-bild; *adj. Substitute:* ge-bildan, -byldan; *p.* de ; *pp.* -bild, -bilded. I. *to embolden, encourage, give confidence to* [*Take here* ge-byld,

**-bylded** *in Dict.*] :—Mid þȳ mægne hē wæs gebælded (gestrangod, *v. l.*) of ðæs ælmihtigan Godes fultume *qua virtute fretus ex omnipotentis Dei auxilio*, Gr. D. 26, 31. Gebyld *fretus*, i. *fultus*, An. Ox. 126. Gebeld, 2042 : 3682. Gebyld *fretus* .i. *fiduciam habens*, Wrt. Voc. ii. 150, 70. Gebyldum *predito*, An. Ox. 4135. Gebild *freti*, i. *fundi*, 781. **II.** *to cover* (?), *protect* (?), *bind* a book. [v. *N. E. D.* bield *to protect, shelter.* Sc. and North. dial. *to cover, cover over.*] :—Eðilwald ðis bóc ūta giðrȳde and gibelde (-bélde, MS.) suā hē uel cūðæ, Jn. p. 188, 3.

**ge-bilegan.** *Substitute :* ge-bilgan; *p.* de To anger, offend:—Swā swā heó gebylged wǽre heó cwæð *quasi indignata subjunxit*, Bd. 4, 9 ; S. 398, 1. Mid hwylcum sáre gegremed and ābolgen (gebylged, *v.l.*), Gr. D. 207, 25. Gode gebyligdum *Deo offenso*, Scint. 198, 13.

**ge-bind.** *Add :* I. *constipation, costiveness* :—Gebind *tenacitas ventris, tentigo*, Wrt. Voc. ii. 145, 60. Wið stede and for gebinde . . . wið innoþa wrǽce and gif gebind men byþ, Lch. i. 338, 3-9. **II.** as a measure of quantity, *a bind* (v. *N. E. D.* bind (5) : ' A Bind of eels . . . consisted of ten sticks, and every stick of twenty-five eels ') :—Man gelǽste ǽlce geáre . . . þreó gebind ǽles, Cht. Th. 328, 33.

**ge-bindan.** *Dele* II, *and add* :—Geband *devinxit*, Wrt. Voc. ii. 106, 21. Gebindende *astringentes*, 3, 12. **I.** *to bind* with a material band. (1) *to fasten* an inanimate object with a band, clasp, &c., *wrap round* :—Gebindan beám ǽrenum clammum, Dan. 519. Þeóstre hām (*hell*) gebunden fæstum fȳrclommum, Sat. 38. Wæs gebunden since duru ormǽte, Cri. 308. Bil wrǽttum gebunden, B. 1531. Scyld sceal gebunden, Gu. Ex. 94. (2) *to bind* a person as captive or prisoner :—Gif man mannes sume gebindeð, .vi. sciłł. gebéte, Ll. Th. i. 24, 15. Hine man geband . . . and hine lēt ofsleán, Chr. 1049 ; P. 168, 36. Þone ealdor þeóstra hē geband, Bl. H. 85, 5. Hī hine sendon on þæt carcern, and hié gebunden his handa behindan, 241, 28. Gif mon cierliscne mon gebinde unsynnigne, Ll. Th. i. 84, 2. Gif man æt unlagum man gebinde, forgilde be healfan were, 408, 19. Hē hine hēt gebindan and siþþan ofsleán, Bt. 29, 2 ; F. 104, 26. Hē þā gebundenan of carcerne ūt ālǽdde, Bl. H. 239, 34. (2 a) the object abstract :—Ne mæg þ word mon mid sweorde ofsleán, ne mid rāpe gebindan, Bt. 13 ; F. 38, 29. **II.** *to bind.* (1) *to fasten* one object to another :—Hāt hine on rōde gebindan, Bl. H. 189, 34. Þ hweól ðe Ixion wæs tō gebunden, Bt. 35, 6 ; F. 168, 31. Cweornstān gebundene *scopulum* (*collo*) *conexum*, An. Ox. 4458. On ðǽm bearwum sāula hangodan be heora handum gebundne, Bl. H. 209, 36. (2) *to tether* an animal :—Gyt gemētaþ eoselan gebundene, Bl. H. 79, 28. **III.** *to bind* a band :—Is þes wītes clom feste gebunden, Sat. 104. **IV.** of nonmaterial bands. (1) denoting obligation :—Wē beóð mid Gode suā micle suiðor gebundne *tanto apud Dominum obligatiores sumus*, Past. 117, 23. (2) denoting union, connexion :—Fæste gebunden gesiblíce sōfte tōgædere, Met. 20, 67. Word ōðer fand sōðe gebunden *one word followed the other without interruption*, B. 871. (3) denoting restraint, hindrance :—Seó orsorge wyrd gebint ǽlc þāra mōda þe hire brȳcþ, Bt. 20 ; F. 70, 36. Hine gebindaþ þā wōn wilnunga mid heora racentum, 16, 3 ; F. 56, 17. Dū gebunde þ fȳr mid racentum, 33, 4 ; F. 130, 31. Se heáhengel mid þǽre swigunge fæstnunga geband þone fæder, Bl. H. 167, 11. Ðone sunu mid wyriungum gebindan, Hml. Th. ii. 30, 6. Ðæt mōd bið gebunden mid gedrēfednesse, Bt. 6 ; F. 16, 2. Eldo gebunden, B. 2111. Wanhāle, wītum gebunden, An. 580. (3 a) hindrance from a physical cause :—His wíf mid bearne swǽrlíce gebunden gǽð, Hml. Th. ii. 324, 21. (3 b) where the restraint is pleasant, *to captivate* :—Hǽfde hē mē gebunden mid þǽre wynsumnesse his sanges, Bt. 22, 1 ; F. 76, 6. (4) denoting ensnaring (?) :—Arues wēnde þ hē his ríce gemiclian sceolde, þā hē his dohtor Philippuse sealde. Ac hē (*Philip*) hiene on ðǽre wēnunge geband (*got him in his toils thanks to this expectation*), and him ðæt ān genam þæt hē self hǽfde *Aruba, cum per hoc quod societatem Macedonum adfinitate regis paciscebatur, imperium suum se dilataturum putaret, per hoc deceptus amisit*, Ors. 3, 7 ; S. 112, 12.

**ge-bird[e].** **I.** *bearded. Take here* ge-byrd *in Dict.* **II.** *grown up ; pubes* :—Gebierdne, þone æþelan geongan *indolem* (perhaps the passage glossed is: Pulcherrimam pubertatis indolem, Ald. 63, 25), Wrt. Voc. ii. 44, 80. [*O. H. Ger.* gi-parta *pubentes.*] v. un-gebeard[e].

**ge-birgan ;** *p.* de (*a strong form* gebarg *occurs* Jn. L. 2, 9) *To taste. Take here* ge-byrgan (*l.* -byrgan) *in Dict., and add* :—Nǽnig weorona ðāra giberged (gebirgað, L., *gustabit*) feorme míne, Lk. L. 14, 24. Ðā ðe of ðǽre gebirgað *qui ex ea gustaverint*, Rtl. 99, 22. Mid ðȳ gebirigde (inbergde, R.) *cum gustasset*, Mt. L. 27, 34. [Ingeberigde ł ingebarg *gustavit*, Jn. L. 2, 9.] Þ hiá gebirigdon *gustaturos*, Mk. p. 4, 3.

**ge-birhtan.** *Take here* ge-byrhtan *and* ge-brihtan *in Dict., and add :* I. *to make bright* :—Geberhtes *clarificabit*, Jn. L. 16, 14. **II.** *to become bright, to shine* :—Ic āhyrde mīne sunnan, and heó gebyrhteð þonne forbærned heó ealle þīne æceras, Wlfst. 260, 8. [*Goth.* ga-bairhtjan.] Cf. ge-beorhtian.

**ge-birigan.** *Dele, and see* ge-birgan.

**ge-birman** *to ferment. Take here* ge-byrman, *and add* :—Gebirm mid giste, Lch. ii. 96, 21. Cf. ge-beormad.

---

**ge-bisceopian** *to confirm* :—Gif hwā gebisceopige hine tuwa, and hē hit wite *si quis bis confirmatus sit, et hoc sciat*, Ll. Th. ii. 164, 15.

**ge-bisgian.** *l.* ge-bisgian, *take here* ge-bysgian *in Dict., and add* :—Gebysgian *occupare*, Wülck. Gl. 253, 41. Se Hǽlend wæs gebysgod betwux micelre menigu on ānum wēstene, Hml. Th. ii. 384, 17.

**ge-bismerian.** *Add* :—Gif preóst ōðerne forseó oþþe gebismirige mid worde oþþe mid weorce, gebéte þ, Ll. Th. ii. 294, 17. Gebysmerian *ludificare*, Wrt. Voc. ii. 50, 7. Mid forheriunge swā gebismrad swā Babylonia wæs, Ors. 2, 4 ; S. 74, 36. Þū unc hæfst gebysmrod, Guth. 42, 4.

**ge-bismerung**, e ; *f. Mockery, derision, scorn* :—Gebismerung *illusio*, Ps. L. 78, 4. Gebism[r]u[n]gce *ludibrio*, An. Ox. 11, 181. Mīne gebysmerunge *reverentiam meam*, Ps. L. 68, 20. For missenlicum deófoles gebysmerungum *propter illusiones diabolicas*, R. Ben. 83, S.

**ge-bisnian.** *Add :* I. *to set an example, serve as a model* :—Hē þā leóde gebígde tō Godes geleáfan, and him wel gebysnode mid weorcum, Hml. S. 26, 73. Heó hym eallum gebysnode mid gōddre gedrohtnunge tō Godes þeówdōme, 2, 125. Swā swā ūre Hǽlend þurh hine gebysnode (-bisnode, *v.l.*), Hml. A. 45, 529. **II.** *to model, form* in accordance with a model or exemplar :—Swā swā hit āwriten is on þāra apostola drohtnunge, þe þām muneca líf is gebysenod, R. Ben. 57, 7.

**ge-bisnung.** *Add* :—Leóde geneósian, and mid lāre and gebysnunge þæs sōþan geleáfan and mid þweále fulluhtes geclǽnsian, Lch. iii. 434, 1. Beón eádmóde æfter his gebysnunge (-bisnunge, *v.l.*), Hml. A. 10, 258. Hē Crīstes gebysnunge geefenlǽhte, Hml. Th. 34, 15. Eall þ hē gegearwode ūs on gebysnunge gōdes weorces *hoc nobis in exemplum actionis praebuit*, Gr. D. 60, 23. Ic sylf beó andsǽte þurh swylce gebysnunge (*by setting such an example*), Hml. S. 25, 98. Hē sceal Crīste folgian be Crīstes gebysnungum, Hml. A. 18, 109. Hē gecneordlǽhte æfter wīsra lāreówa gebisnungum *in study he followed the example set by wise teachers*, Hml. Th. ii. 118, 19. Gif hine hwā mid tihtinge and gebisnungum gōdra weorca getrymð, i. 306, 12. Drihtnes þeówum gelíc on gebisnungum *Domini ministris par documentis*, Hy. S. 73, 3. Lāre gibisnunga *doctrinae documenta*, 72, 30. Þā gebysnunga his lāre *exempla doctrinae*, Gr. D. 61, 1.

**ge-bit.** *Add* :—Tōða gebitt, Hml. Th. i. 132, 26 : 530, 15. Gebit, 30.

**ge-biterian.** *Add* :—Ðā cempan him budon drincan gebitrodne wīndrenc . . . þes gebiteroda drinc hæfde getācnunge his deáðes biternysse, Hml. Th. ii. 254, 14-19.

**ge-bíwan, -beówan** *To rub, polish* :—Gebeówed *confricatus*, i. *limatus, exprimatus*, Wrt. Voc. ii. 133, 25. v. bíwan.

**ge-blǽcan** *to make pale, disfigure* :—Geblǽcte *exterminavit*, Ps. Spl. C. 79, 14. [Cf. bleichent *exterminant* (gloss on Mt. 6, 16), Gall. 410.]

**ge-blǽdan.** *Add :* v. ættor-geblǽd, Lch. iii. 36, 22.

**ge-blǽdfæst.** *Substitute : Prosperous, flourishing* :—Him on lāste setl wuldorspēdum welig stōdan gifum grōwende on Godes ríce, beorht and geblǽdfæst, Gen. 89.

**ge-blǽdfæstness**, e ; *f. Prosperity, success* :—Ðā gemētte ic sumne man þe mē þrȳ penegas sealde, mid þām ic mē þrȳ hlāfas bohte ; þā ic mē hæfde genōh gehȳðe tō mínes sīðfætes geblǽdfæstnysse (*I had abundantly what was of advantage to the success of my journey.* The Latin has : . . . dicens, Accipe haec nonna. Ego autem accipiens, tres ex eis panes comparavi, et hoc accepi benedictioni mei itineris congruos), Glostr. Frg. 108, 26 (see note, p. 115) ; Hml. S. 23 b, 492.

**ge-bland.** *Add :* v. gicel-gebland.

**ge-blandan.** *Substitute :* ge-blandan ; *pp.* ge-blanden, -blonden [*In the two instances where the past tense occurs the forms are* ge-blond, Wrt. Voc. ii. 94, 16, ge-blondan, An. 33. *Under* blandan *is given* blēnde *as a past subjunctive, but this form might be placed as a present* (*or past*) *under* blandan. v. ge-blendan. Cf. gang *as a past tense of* gangan.] *To mix, blend* :—Geblonden *infectum*, Wrt. Voc. ii. 111, 77. Geblanden, 45, 17 : *confectum*, 14, 49. **I.** *to mix* with :—Is him þæt heáfod hindan grēne, wrǽtlíce wrixled wurman geblonden, Ph. 294. **II.** *to mix* things that should be kept separate :—Ðona geworð ðæt mið ūs giblonden ł gimencged (*mixta*) aron alle, and in Marc moniga Lucas and ēc Matheies, Mt. p. 3, 7. **III.** *to mix, prepare* with (harmful) ingredients :—Hī geblondan drȳas þurh dwolcræft drync unheórne, An. 33. Hié him sealdon āttor drincan þæt mid lybcræfte wæs geblanden, Bl. H. 229, 12. Eów wæs ād inǽled āttre geblonden, Gū. 640. **IV.** *to make turbid, disturb, trouble* :—Scír bið gedrēfed burna geblonden, Met. 5, 19 : An. 424 : Rä. 4, 22. Scūr winde geblanden, Gn. C. 41 : Met. 20, 81. **V.** denoting possession of evil qualities or properties, *to infect, corrupt.* [Cf. *O. Sax.* baluwes giblandan, mid sorogon giblandan.] (1) in a physical sense :—Wæs seó lyft heolfre geblanden, Exod. 476. Oð þæt is þæt, spilde geblonden, āttor, Rä. 24, 8. (2) in a moral sense :—Geblond *infecit* (*corda venenis*), Wrt. Voc. ii. 94, 16. Siofa synnum fāh, sāre geblonden, gefylled mid fācne, Leás. 16. Is þes middangeard māne geblonden, 31. Nīða geblonden (*Holofernes*), Jud. 34. v. ge-blendan.

ge-bláwan. _Add:_—Gebláwen _conflatum_, Wrt. Voc. ii. 133, 18. **I.** _of persons._ (1) _to breathe:_—Eft wē gibláue _respiremus_, Rtl. 43, 29. (2) _to spit:_—Gibleów (gebléuu, L.) _expuens_, Mk. R. 7, 33. (3) _to aspire:_—Gebláwan asspirare, i. _accedere_, _adflare_ (eo vallo muniti, quo grassanti stultitiae _adspirare_ fas non sit, Bt. Bk. I. prosa 3), An. Ox. 34, 4. **II.** _of the wind, to blow:_—Hwona gebláwað wind _unde flavescat ventus?_, Rtl. 192, 33. Geblēwun windas, Mt. L. 7, 25. Geblēuun, 27.

ge-blecte. _Dele, and see_ ge-blǽcan.

ge-blégenad. _Substitute:_ ge-bleg[e]nod _having blains, blistered:_ —Wiþ geblegnadre tungan, Lch. ii. 4, 2. Geblegenadre, 50, 1.

ge-blénd. _Dele, and see_ ge-blendan _to mix._

ge-blendan _to blind. Dele bracket, and add:_—Sume hī wurdon geblende, Chr. 1076; P. 212, 26. v. ge-blindan.

ge-blendan; p. de _To mix:_—Geblende _infecit_, Wrt. Voc. ii. 47, 35. Hī mē geblendon unswētne drync ecedes and geallan, Cri. 1438. [Cf. Ic eom swētra þonne þū beóbreád blende (_this is given in Dict. as p. subj. to_ blandan, _but it may be taken as pres._ (_or past_) _to_ blendan) mid hunige, Rä. 41, 59.] v. ge-blandan.

ge-bleód. _Add:_—Gebliód reáf _stragulam vestem_, Kent. Gl. 1144.

ge-bleoh; _adj._ v. un-gebleoh.

ge-bletsian. _Add:_ **I.** _to hallow, consecrate:_—Fiscas gebledsade (_benedixit_), Mt. L. 14, 19. Hē wæs gebledsod and tō his cinestōle áhofen, Chr. 795; P. 57, 18. Stīgand preóst wæs gebletsod tō biscope tō Eást-Englum, 1042; P. 163, 22. Mid gebletsudum wætere _benedicta aqua_, Angl. xiii. 395, 435. Geblesedum, 413, 685. **I a.** _to make the sign of the cross upon_ an object:—Eallum Crīstenum mannum is beboden þ hī ealne heora līchoman seofon sīþum gebletsian mid Crīstes rōde tācne, Bl. H. 47, 15, 12. Hī ne cunnon ðone geleáfan, ne eác hī gebletsian, Hml. S. 5, 238. **II.** _to call holy, adore:_—þē gebletsige ... weorca gehwilc, Dan. 363. Drihten sī gebletsad, Ps. Th. 65, 18. Gebledsod, An. 540. Sī Godes nama ēcelīce gebletsod, Ll. Th. i. 374, 33. Ðū eart gebletsod God, Ll. Lbmn. 415, 33. **III.** _to prosper, favour, benefit:_—þū gebletsudest bearn Israhēla, Aarones hūs eác gebletsadest _Dominus benedixit domui Israel, benedixit domui Aaron_, Ps. Th. 113, 21. þá gebletsode Metod þá forman twā, Gen. 192. Gebletsige, 1505. Ūs gebletsa, Ps. Th. 66, 1. Gebletsige ūs Drihten, 6. Sī gebletsod (gebloedsad, L.) þ rīce, Mk. 11, 10. Gebledsod, An. 524. Wes þū gebletsod; for þon se wæstm þīnes innoþes is gebletsad, Bl. H. 5, 4. Ealle ūre eorþan wæstmas beóþ gebletsode, 51, 13. v. un-gebletsod.

ge-bletsung, e; _f._ **I.** _consecration._ v. ge-bletsian; **I:**—þá gebletsunge heó þǣr tō on Rōme begeat þám þe þá áre tō Godes þeówdōme ..., Lch. iii. 432, 6. **II.** _blessing._ v. ge-bletsian; **III:**—Hē gibloedsade ūsig in ǽlcum gibloedsunge gǽstlicum _benedixit nos in omni benedictione spiritali_, Rtl. 45, 39.

ge-blindan _to blind._ [_Goth._ ga-blindjan.] v. fore-geblind.

ge-blindfellian; _p._ ede _To blindfold, cover the face_ or _eyes:_—þá cnihtas gefēngon þone Aman and hine geblindfelledon (_operuerunt faciem ejus_), Hml. A. 100, 276. [He þolede þet me hine blindfellede (cf. uelauerunt eum, Lk. 22, 64: blindfolded hym, Tyndale) ... þauh þu ƿine blindfellie on eorðe, A. R. 106. To blyndfeyld, blyndfelle _uelare_, Cath. Angl.]

ge-blinnan. _Add:_—Wē geblunnan _desivimus_, Wrt. Voc. ii. 28, 23. (1) _to cease_ from action that has been continuous:—Hē bideþ þæs ēcan leóhtes, and nō ne geblinneþ, Bl. H. 17, 35. Geblann þ wind _cessavit ventus_, Mt. L. 14, 32: Lk. L. 8, 24. Geblann gespreaca _cessavit loqui_, 5, 4. Mið ðȳ wēre gebiddende þte geblann, 11, 1. (2) that has been recurring or habitual:—Hī nānum dæge ne geblunnon (geswicon, _v. l._) þ hī ne druncon of þám ylcon fate _ut nullo die cessarent bibere ex illo vasculo_, Gr. D. 66, 22.

ge-blissian. _Add:_ **I.** _intrans.:_—Hē geblissað on his heortan _laetabitur corde_, Ex. 4, 14. Ðá geblissiað _qui letantur_, Kent. Gl. 22. Geblissa _letare_, 108. Geblissa þū gōda þeówa _euge bone serve_, Mt. 25, 23. On ēcum gesetednessum heó geblissige (_gaudeat_), Angl. xiii. 381, 231. þ on þīnum ūpstige geblissian þīne gecorenan, Bl. H. 87, 24. **II.** _trans._:—þū þīne fyrde geblissast, Hy. 7, 47. Ealle weorðaþ and fēhþ and geblysaþ (cf. blisung, Ps. Spl. 64, 13) fæder ætsomne _cunctos fovet, implet, honorat_, Dōm. L. 274. Heó fērde hál tō hire fæder and hine geblyssode ... and ealle for hire hǽle blyssodon, Hml. S. 7, 280. Geblisgende _letificantes_, Ps. Rdr. 18, 9.

ge-blissung. _Add:_—Mid mycelre geblissunge _cum magna hilaritate_, Angl. xiii. 367, 28.

ge-blīþe; _adj._ (_or adv._) _Blithe_ (_or blithely_):—Hē swȳþe geblīþe hine hēt gyrwan tō þám manigum þæs heofonlican rīces, Guth. 80, 1.

ge-blīþian _to make glad:_—þū geblīðgodest [mē] on geweorce þīnum _delectasti me in factura tua_, Ps. Rdr. 91, 5. [Cf. _O. H. Ger._ ge-blīden _exhilarare._]

ge-blōdegian. _Add:_—Geblōdegude _cruentabat_, An. Ox. 4251. Ásleah .IIII. scearpan mid brande; geblōdga ðone brand, Lch. iii. 52, 2. Mid wunde hī geblōdigian, Hml. Th. ii. 88, 24. Geblōdgad _cruentata_,

i. _sanguinolenta_, _sanguinata_, _sanguinea_, Wrt. Voc. ii. 137, 19. Þeáh hit beó geblōdegod on sumum lime, E. S. viii. 62, 41: Hml. S. 31, 779. Hī woldon habban þone hālgan Eásterdæg geblōdegodne mid þæs Hǽlendes blōde, Hml. A. 68, 62. þá hors mid þám spurum geblōdgode wǣron, Gr. D. 15, 4.

ge-blōt. _Add:_—Bringan þone sēlestan dǣl hiora gōdra geara tō heora geblōte, Ors. 6, 21; S. 272, 26. Hē wæs blōtende diófolgildum mid monslihtum ... Eów mæg gescomian þæt gē swá heánlic geþōht sceoldon on eów geniman for ānes monnes ege and for ānes monnes geblōte ... Hū heán hē wearþ his geblōta and his diófolgilda þe hē on gelīfde, 6, 37; S. 296, 13–23. Hē hēt dōn tō geblōte ealle þá cuman þe hiene gesōhtan, Ors. 1, 8 tit.; S. 1, 20.

ge-blōwan. _Add:_ ¶ ge-blōwen _blown_ (as in full-_blown_), _blooming, in bloom, that has blossomed._ (1) _lit._ (a) _of plants_:—Ealra beáma beorhtast geblōwen, Ph. 179. Secgeað lǽcas þte geblōwene wyrta þonne sién betste tō wyrcenne tō drencum, Lch. ii. 146, 17. (b) _of a place, blooming_ with plants:—Hī becōmon tō sumum felda fægre geblōwen, Hml. S. 21, 351: Gū. 715. Is þæt æðele lond blōstmum geblōwen, Ph. 21. Haswig feðra (_the Phenix_) grēne eorðan áþȳhð, foldan geblōwene _assueti nemoris dulce cubile fugit_, 155. (2) fig. _flourishing, blooming:_—Hē (_the Phenix_) bið feþrum gefrætwod, swilc hē æt frymðe wæs, beorht geblōwen _reformatur qualis fuit ante figura_, Ph. 240.

ge-blyged. v. un-geblyged.

ge-bōcian. _Add:_—þis is þára twēntiga hīda bōc ... þe Eádrēd cing gebōcode Ōswīge his þegne on ēce yrfe, C. D. iii. 426, 13, 22 (and often). Cf. ge-bēcan.

ge-bod. _Add:_—Mid egeslicum gebode (v. Acts 16, 18: Praecipio tibi in nomine Iesu Christi exire ab ea) _imperio terrente_, An. Ox. 1940. (1) _an edict, order, a mandate_ of temporal or ecclesiastical authority :— Gif hwelc preóst ofer biscopes gebod mǽssige, gilde for þám gebode .xx. ōr, Ll. Th. ii. 290, 17. Hī eów gedwealdon mid þám manigfealdum gebodum, i. 56, 17. Gebodum _edictis_ (_Claudii Caesaris_), An. Ox. 4130. Gebodo _edicta_ (_Diocletiani_), Wrt. Voc. ii. 84, 20: 31, 25. Ælc ... þára þe þá gebodu gehȳrde, Ll. Th. i. 232, 12. (2) _a command, an order_ of the Deity:—Gif þ sōþ is ... hit wæs unnet gebod ... þ God beád, Bt. 41, 3; F. 246, 32. 'þis bebod se Hǽlend ūs sealde ...' 'Gif þis gebod eów wǣre geseald fram eówrum Drihtne ...', Bl. H. 233, 21. Drihten, eall ic hit ǽræfnie for þīnum gebode, 241, 33.

ge-bodian. _Add:_ (1) _to announce_ a fact:—Hī genāmon twēgen cnihtas ... þis wæs gebodod (_nuntiatum_) Furtunato, Gr. D. 80, 11. (2) _to announce_ a person, _give official notice of:_—Gehealde man hine .xxx. nihta, and hine his mǽgum gebodie (cf. hine his freóndum gecȳðe, 16) and his frióndum, Ll. Th. i. 90, 8. Gehealden hī hine .xxx. nihta, and hié hine his mǽgum gebodien (gebeóden, _v. l._), 64, 19.

ge-bogen _occupied_, ge-bōgian. v. ge-būan: ge-bolged. _Dele._

ge-bolstrod _supported on pillows_ or _cushions:_—Gesyttan fægere gebolstrod, Angl. viii. 308, 36.

ge-boned. l. ge-bōned _ornamented._ v. bōn: ge-borhfæstan _to pledge._ For Cot. 107 _substitute:_—Geborhfæstan _intertiare_, Wrt. Voc. ii. 45, 36: ge-bōsmed. _Dele, and see_ ge-bēsmed.

ge-botl, es; _n. A dwelling:_—þá byrig hē geseah eall on ōþre wīsan gewend on ōþre heó ǽr wæs, and þá gebotla (botla, _v. l._) geond þá byrig eall getimbrode on ōþre wīsan on ōþre hī ǽr wǣron, Hml. S. 23, 511.

ge-brádian (?) _to extend:_—Gebrádende (-brǽd- ?) _dilatans_, Ps. Srt. 47, 3. v. ge-brǽdan.

ge-brǽc. _Dele_ '_O. H. Ger._ ka-preh,' _and add:_—Ðá cwōm þǣr semninga swīðe micel wind and gebræc _tum repente euri uentus tanta vis flantis exorta est_, Nar. 22, 27. v. fȳr-gebræc, _and cf._ bræclian.

ge-brǽceo. _Substitute:_ ge-brǽc, e; or ge-brǽceo (-brǽcu); _indecl.; f. Phlegm, rheum, catarrh:_—Gibrēc, gibreec, gebrēc _pituita_, Txts. 86, 775. Gibrēc (ge-) _reuma_, 92, 856: _umecta_, 107, 2152. Gebyraec, 113, 71. Isica tyndri, sicunia (_reuma? pituita_?) gibrēci, reuma streum, 116, 180. Wiþ gebrǣceo (-brǽce, _v. l._) and wiþ nyrwyt, Lch. i. 48, 11, 7. Wið gebrǣceo, 236, 24, 15. Heó gebrǣceo ūt átȳhð, 12. [_O. L. Ger._ gi-braechi _catarrum._] v. hræc-, neb-gebrǽc.

ge-brǽcseóc. _Substitute:_ ge-brǣcseóc (-brǽc- ?); _adj. Talking loudly and foolishly_ (? cf. ge-brǽc), _delirious, mad:_—Sum gebrǣcseóc man (_freneticus quidam_) becōm þider on ǽfenne ... þá on morgenne gehǽlede gewitte árás, Bd. 4, 3; Sch. 365, 17. Gebrǣcsióce (-seóce, 86, 65) _comitiales_ (cf. comitiare, loqui, Corp. Gl. H. 34, 627: _comitiales_, i. garritores_ ylfie _vel_ mōnaþseóce, Wrt. Voc. ii. 132, 25: þá symbelmōnað-lican ádla, 20, 39), Wrt. Voc. ii. 19, 5.

ge-brǽdan. _Add:_ **I.** _to spread out:_—Genim þá leáf, gebrǽd on gærse, Lch. ii. 124, 20. **II.** _to extend, enlarge:_—Hē gebrǣdde his rīce oþ India gemǣro _ad Indiam extendit imperium_, Ors. 5, 2; S. 218, 25. Hié ne mōt heore mearce gebrǣdan ofer þá eorþan, Bt. 21; F. 74, 28. Mid ðǽm bióð synna swīðe gebrǣdda, Past. 30, 14. [_O. H. Ger._ ge-breiten _dilatare._]

ge-brǽdan _to roast. Add:_ (1) _lit.:_—Gif þū finde fisc on ōþrum fisce innan, genim þone and gebrǽd swīþe, Lch. ii. 90, 10. Gebrēded

fiaesc *viscera tosta*, Wrt. Voc. ii. 123, 67. Þæt fiæsc beó gebræd on fýre, Angl. viii. 322, 14, 16. Nān ðing hreáw, ne on wætere gesoden, ac gebræd tô fýre, Hml. Th. ii. 264, 5. Dǣl fisces gebrēdedes (-brēddes, R.), Lk. L. 24, 42. Gebrǣdedne æppel, Lch. ii. 132, 14. Genim gôsa tungan gebrǣdde, 90, 8. Gebrǣdde ǣgru, 100, 11. (2) fig. of fiery trial :—Se gebrǣdda fisc getācnode þone Hǣlend þe wæs on ðǣre earfoðnysse his ðrowunge gebrǣd, 292, 5-7. Hāligne līchaman on weófode rôde gebrǣdne *sacrum corpusculum in ara crucis torridum*, Hy. S. 82, 13. [O. L. Ger. gi-brādan; p. -brēd: O. H. Ger. ge-brātan; p. -briat.]

ge-brǣgden; adj. *Cunning, crafty* :—Gebrægdnes *wærlotes astus*, Wrt. Voc. ii. 9, 33. Hwær côm sē þe þā gebregdnan dômas dēmde, Bl. H. 99, 32. v. brægden.

ge-brǣgdenlīce; adv. *Cunningly* :—Gebregdenlíce *astute*, Ps. Srt. 82, 4.

ge-brǣgdnys. *Dele, and see* ge-brǣgden.

ge-brastl, es; n. *Crackling sound* :—Ne bið þǣr līges gebrasl, ne se lāðlica cyle, Dôm. L. 259 : Wlfst. 139, 29. Þæra līgetta blǣst (gebrastl, *v. l.*), 186, 5. Gebrastles *salis*, Germ. 398, 226.

ge-brec. *Add:* (1) *a breaking.* v. bān-, hlāf-, weall-gebrec. (2) *a crash, noise* :—Gebrec hlūd unmǣte, Cri. 954. Borda gebrec, El. 114. Cirm, swēg, gebrec *fragor*, Wrt. Voc. ii. 36, 13. Gebrece, swoege *fragore*, 33, 79. [O. H. Ger. ge-breh *fragor, crepido.*] v. ge-bræc.

ge-brēc. v. ge-bræc.

ge-brecan. *Add:* —Gebrǣce *elideret*, Wrt. Voc. ii. 33, 9. **I.** lit. *to break.* (1) *without sense of injury* :—Mið ðý onfēng hlāf and gebrǣcg (*fregit*), Lk. L. 22, 19 : 24, 30. Gebrægc, Mk. L. 6, 41. (2) *with sense of injury done.* (a) *to the body* :—Sē ðe faelles ofer stān ðiosne gebrocen (-broken, R.) bið (*confringetur*); ofer ðone fallas gebrecceð (*conteret*) hine, Mt. L. 21, 44. Bān ni gebraecgað gē (*comminuetis*), Jn. L. 19, 36. Him hildegrāp bānhūs gebrǣc, B. 2508. Lēg þæt bānhūs gebrocen hǣfde, 3147 : Ph. 229. Líc sāre gebrocen, bānhūs blôdfāg, An. 1406. Gif þeóh gebrocen weorðe, Ll. Th. i. 18, 13 : 12, 6. Hwæþer hē leuge ǣr āfeolle oððe gebrocen wurde, Lch. ii. 258, 25. Þā gebrocenan bān, Ps. C. 81. (b) *to a thing, to break to pieces, demolish, break up* :—Hē manig templ and deófolgyld gebrǣc and gefylde . . . Hē bæd þ hē ðæt deófolgild gebrǣce and gefylde. Þā hē hit gebrecan ne môste, þā cômon twēgen englas . . . and þ gild gebrǣcan, Bl. H. 221, 2-32. Nô gebrocen weorðeð holt on hīwe, Ph. 80. Wong gebrocen tô beorgum, Ruin. 33. **II.** fig. *to crush, destroy* :—Ic gebreocu hié swē swē dūst *comminuam illos ut pulverem*, Ps. Srt. 17, 43. Hornas synfulra ic gebreocu (*confringam*), 74, 11. Hē on þām folce feóndgyld gebrǣc, Ps. Th. 105, 24. Þāra manna bearn þe ǣr man gebrǣc *elisos*, 145, 7. Hē eall þæt mægn þæs āwyrgedan gāstes on him gebrǣc, Guth. 60, 5. **III.** *intrans. with prep. To break into, interrupt* :—Þ þē ne þūhte tô hefig þ þū ongunne hwæthugu gebrecan in þone wīsdom þǣre gerecenysse *neque pro hac re interrumpere expositionis studium grave videatur*, Gr. D. 7, 34. v. un-gebrocen.

gebrec-drenc. *Substitute: A medicine for the windpipe* :—Gebrecdrenc *arteriaca*, Wrt. Voc. ii. 7, 72.

ge-bredan. *l.* -brēdan, *and see* ge-bregdan.

ge-brēfan; *p.* ed *To state briefly, epitomize* :—Gif hwylcum cnihte lyste mā þinga and deópra gesetnyssa be him witan þonne wē hēr habbað gebrēued, Angl. viii. 308, 11. Nū wē þās þing habbað sceortlīce gebrēued, 322, 22. [O. L. Ger. gi-brēuid *conscriptum* ; O. H. Ger. ge-briefen *aditulare, abbreviare, designare, describere*. Cf. *Icel*. brēfa *to give a brief account of*.]

ge-brēgan. *Add:* —Consternat, i. *perterritat* fyrhtaþ, gebrēgþ, Wrt. Voc. ii. 133, 66. Ðæt leóht côm of heofenum and hine (*St. Paul*) gebrēgde . . . Hē swā gebrēged on eorðan feóll, Past. 443, 19-22. Gebrēged *pertimescens*, Gr. D. 59, 26.

ge-bregd *quick movement.* The Latin original on which is based the passage given under this word is : Non ibi . . . vis furit horrida venti.

ge-bregdan. *Take here* ge-bredan (*l.* -brēdan) *in Dict., dele* II, *and add:* **I.** *to pull out, draw.* (1) *with dat.* (cf. bregdan) :—Hē gebrægd his sweorde, Bl. H. 233, 7. Gif mon beforan ærcebiscepe geféohte oþþe wǣpne gebregde (-brēde, *v. l.*), Ll. Th. i. 70, 19. Gif hē wǣpne gebrēde and nô feohte, 88, 1. (2) *with acc.* :—Petrus hæfde suuord gebrægd hine *Petrus habens gladium eduxit eum*, Jn. L. R. 18, 10. **II.** *to withdraw, take away* :—Nis cūð hū oððe on hwylcere tīde hyre līchama gebrōden wǣre, oððe hwider hē āhafen sý, Hml. Th. i. 440, 19. **III.** *to knot, bind* :—Hē ne geliéfð ðæs grīnes ðe hē mid gebrogden (-brōden) wyrð *quo stranguletur laqueo non agnoscit*, Past. 331, 20. **IV.** *to bring a charge against a person, braid* (in *upbraid*) :—Se deófol wyle wið þīnre sāwle campian and þē ūp gebrēdan ǣlc þæra þinga þe þū wið God āgylte, Wlfst. 249, 3. **V.** *to feign* :—Heó gebrǣd hī seóce (cf. *Icel.* bregða sēr sjukum), Hml. S. 2, 151.

ge-bregdenlīce. v. ge-brǣgdenlīce : ge-brēgdnes. *Dele.*

gebregd-stafas. *Substitute : Cunning skill* :—Ic īglanda eallra hæbbe bôca onbyrged, þurh gebregdstafas lārcræftas onlocen Libia and Grēca I *of the islands all have the books browsed on, and by cunning skill the learning unlocked of Lybians and Greeks*, Sal. 2.

ge-brehtnian. v. ge-beorhtnian : ge-brehtnis. v. ge-beorhtnes.

ge-brēman. *Substitute for the passage* :—Drihten wolde gebrēman and geweorðian þā Iudēiscan æfter þǣre wīsan þe on ðǣre ealdan ǣ beboden wæs, Hml. A. 152, 18. Nônsanges on ðǣre endebyrdnesse sī gebrēmod gebed *none eo ordine celebretur oratio*, R. Ben. I. 47, 11.

ge-brengan. *Add:* **I.** *to bring* to or from a place. (1) *where the object is material* :—Gif gebrenges (*offeres*) ðing ðīn tô wīgbed, Mt. L. 5, 23. Gebrengað t lǣdað hiá *educit eas*, Jn. L. 10, 3. Hié þā scipu binnan Lundenbyrig gebrôhton, Chr. 896; P. 89, 21. Gebrôhtun (*obtulerunt*) him monuo dumbne, Mt. L. 9, 32. Gebreng ðing ðīn, 5, 24. Gebrengað ðæs hiona *auferte ista hinc*, Jn. L. R. 2, 16. Hē ôðer wīf þǣm ôðrum æt hām gebrenge, Ll. Th. i. 10, 8 : 22, 3. Hié þā men gebrengen beforan kyninges gerēfan on folcgemôte, 82, 11. Wolde ic biddan þæt þū ūs gebrôhte ofer hwæles eðel on þǣre mǣgðe, An. 273. Hē bebeád þ mon þone apostol gebrôhte on Bothmose *Apostolus in Patmum relegatus fuit*, Ors. 6, 9; S. 264, 10. Ne mæhtun gebrenga (*offere*) hine him, Mk. L. 2, 4. Gebreingendum t geasfendum, Mt. p. 14, 1. Forstolen þingc under þæs wīfes cǣglocan gebrôht, Ll. Th. i. 418, 20. (2) *where the object is non-material* :—þā niþemestan ic gebrenge æt þām hēhstan and ðā hēhstan æt þām niþemestan, þæt is þ ic gebrenge eáþmôdnesse on heofonum and þā heofonlican gôd æt þām eáþmēdum, Bt. 7, 3; F. 22, 1-3. Hē hǣdene þeáwas innan þysan lande gebrôhte, Chr. 959; P. 115, 11. Ic þē snyttro on gebrôhte, Bt. 7, 3; F. 20, 11. Hē wolde ðǣm fortrūwodum monnum andrysno hālwendes eges on gebrengean, Past. 385, 17. Mið gebrôchtum mæhtum *conlatis uirtutibus*, Lk. p. 6, 1. **I a.** *where the point reached is abstract, as in to bring to justice* :—Se man þane ôðerne æt rihte gebrenge, Ll. Th. i. 34, 2. Hē wæs tô deáðe gebrôht, Hml. S. 25, 725. **I b.** *of legal status* :—Ælc freó man beó on hundrede and on teóðunge gebrôht, Ll. Th. i. 386, 20. **II.** *to bring* to or from a state, condition, action, &c., *cause to be* :—Seó hrædwilnes ðæt môd gebrengð on ðǣm weorce þe hiene ǣr nān willa tô ne spôn *mentem impellit furor, quo non trahit desiderium*, Past. 314, 9. Se āwiergda gǣst ðæt môd gebre[u]gð on manegum unðeáwe *mentem maligni spiritus per innumera vitia seducendo corrumpunt*, 463, 31. Ðā hē on ôþrum hīwe gebrengþ, Bt. 39, 8; F. 224, 10. Þū gebrôhtest his feóndas on blisse *laetificasti inimicos ejus*, Ps. Th. 88, 35. Ne gebrôhte ðe nān ôþer man on þām gedwolan būtan þē sylfum, Bt. 5, 1; F. 5, 36 : Hml. Th. ii. 476, 11. Hī hine on yrre gebrôhtan *in iram concitaverunt Deum*, Ps. Th. 77, 19. Hī þet wærod on fleáme gebrôhtan, Chr. 1006; P. 137, 9. Ic wæs on þām bysmore and on þǣre sceame þe hý mē on gebrôhton, Solil. H. 12, 7. Ðætte hiene sió gewilnung ðǣre gīsernesse of his môdes fæstrǣdnesse ne gebrenge, Past. 316, 7. Hī ðā uncystegan on yfelre hneáwnesse ne gebrengen, 453, 29. **II a.** *with complementary adj.* (*ptcpl.*) :—Hē mæg þone lāðan gāst . . . fleónde gebrengan, Sal. 87 : 147. **III.** *to bring* forth, produce. v. forþ-gebrengan *in Dict.* :—Wæstm gebrôhte t gebrenges *fructum affert*, Mt. L. 13, 23. Þte uæstm gié gebrenge (tôgibrenge, R., *adferatis*), Jn. L. 15, 8. v. ge-bringan.

ge-brengnis *an offering* (?). v. brengnes *in Dict.* In Mk. L. 12, 44 the word glosses *victus*, but the passage refers to an offering.

ge-breówan *to brew* :—Genim alomalt mid ðý wætere, gebreów mid grýt cumb fulne ealað mid ðý wætere, Lch. iii. 28, 8. Ne bið ðǣr nǣnig ealo gebrowen, Ors. 1, 1; S. 20, 19. Ne dranc hē wīnes drenc, ne nānes gemencgedes wǣtan ne gebrowenes, Hml. Th. i. 352, 7.

ge-bridlian. *l.* -brīdlian, *and add:* —Ne gebrīdlode (*frenaret*) hē hī nô mid swā swīðlicre ðreáunga his lāre, Past. 391, 33. Hý sint gebrīdlod (-ð, MS.) mid ðǣm brīdle Godes beboda, Solil. H. 10, 16.

ge-brihtan. v. ge-birhtan.

ge-bringan. *Add:* **I.** *to bring* to or from a place. (1) *where the object is animate* :—Gif mon cierliscne mon on hengenne ālecgge (gebringe, *v. l.*), Ll. Th. i. 84, 4. Gif mon þeóf on carcerne gebringe . . . forgyldan hý hine oþþe hine eft þǣrinne gebringan, 198, 21-26. Þæt man crīstene men on hǣðendôme (*in heathen lands*) ne gebringe, 378, 1. Cuce orf hē on gemǣnre lǣse gebringe, 274, 26. Hē hine sceal æt stæðe underfôn, and eft þǣr gebringan, 354, 25. Hēt hē hine gebringan on carcerne and þǣrinne belūcan, Bt. 1; F. 2, 25. Hēt Eádrēd cyning gebringan Wulstān arcebiscop in Iudanbyrig on þǣm fæstenne, Chr. 952; P. 112, 35. Nimon Sigeferðes lāfe and gebringon binnan Mealdelmes byrig, 1015; P. 146, 3. (1 a) *figurative as regards the place* :—Ðā undrīestan on ðǣm wege gebringan gôdra weorca, Past. 211, 15. Godes þæt hālige folc on rihtne weg gebringan, Hml. S. 23, 363. (2) *where the object is inanimate* :—Hē his sylfes þǣr bān gebringað, Ph. 283 : 271. **I a.** *where the point reached is given by an abstract noun* :—Hū hē þ rīce on rihtwīsra anwald gebringan mihte, Bt. 1; F. 2, 20. Hū hī mihton hine tô deáþe gebringan, Hml. Th. i. 214, 32. **II.** *to bring* to or from a state, condition, action, &c., *cause to be* in such and such a state :—Sió hrædwilnes ðæt môd gebrin[g]ð on ðǣm weorce ðe hine ǣr nān willa tô ne spôn, Past. 215, 9. Seó hālgung deófla on fleáme gebringeð, Ll. Th. i. 360, 32. Mīne sāwle gē on betran gebringað, Gū. 349. Ðætte hine sió gewilnung of his môdes fæsðrǣdnesse ne gebrienge, Past. 317, 7. Mīnes mūðes mē

môdes willa on heáhsælum gebringe *voluntaria oris mei beneplacita fac*, Ps. Th. 118, 108. Hê wæs þencende hû hê his brôðor on þǽm onwalde gebringan mehte, Ors. 6, 36; S. 292, 24. Se cyng sume hêt on hæftneðe gebringan, Chr. 1095; P. 231, 34. v. ge-brengan.

ge-brítan; *p.* te; *pp.* -bríted, -brítt *To pound, bruise, crush.* Take here ge-brytan (*l.* -brýtan) *in Dict., and add :*—Gebrýtte *fricabat*, Wrt. Voc. ii. 37, 39. (1) lit. :—Ðeós wyrt hafað geoluwe blôstman, and gif þú hý betweónan þínum fingrum gebrýtest, þonne hafað heó swæc swylce myrre, Lch. i. 256, 9. Genim . . . gebærned sealt tô swýþe smalan dúste gebrýt, 216, 4. (2) fig. :—God eall heora wǽpn gebrýt *Dominus confringet arma*, Ps. Th. 45, 8. þára synfulra mægen þú gebrýttest *dentes peccatorum conteruisti*, 3, 6. God ealle his fýnd gebrýtte, 46, arg. Gebrýtende gefeoht *conterens bella*, Ps. Rdr. p. 280, 3. Hý wǽron gebrýtte swá hrædlíce swá swá hradu ýst windes scip tôbryceð *in spiritu vehementi conterens naves*, Ps. Th. 47, 6. Eal mín bán synt gebrýtt, 6, 2. [*Some of the passages here given might belong to* ge-bryttan, *q.v.; but see also* brítan.]

ge-britenod. v. ge-brytnian: ge-brittan. v. ge-bryttan.

ge-bríwan; *p.* de *To make into pottage* (v. bríw), *make* (*pottage*) :—Gebríw wel swíþne bríw mid hwǽtemelwe, Lch. ii. 354, 11. Beren breád, clǽne níwe buteran and níwe beren mela oððe grytta tôgædre gebríwed swá côcas cunnon, 220, 11.

ge-broc. *Add :* (1) *a breaking.* v. scip-gebroc. (2) *a fragment :* —þá legde hê beforan heom þone hláf, and þá þá hí wǽron gereordade, hê gesomnode of þám mǽre on þám gebrocum (*fragmentis*) þonne se hláf sylf ǽr wǽre. Eác swylce hê brôhte eft on ôðre dæge þám wyrhtum tô gereordnesse, ac þ þǽr wæs tô láfe of þám gebrocum wæs þá gyt mǽre þonne þá gebrocu ǽr wǽron . . . efne swylce þá gebrocu þæs hláfes þurh þone æt weóxon, Gr. D. 252, 13-23. v. hláf-gebroc. (3) *trouble.* *Take here* ge-brôc (*l.* -broc) *in Dict., and add :*—Gíf hê þá áne untreówþa ne gedyde, from ðæm dæge hê mehte bútan gebroce eallra Cartaina onwald begietan, Ors. 4, 5 ; S. 170, 12.

ge-brocian; *p.* ode; *pp.* od. *Take here* ge-brôcod (*l.* -brocod) *in Dict., and add :* I. *to hurt, injure, break a bone.* Cf. ge-broc, (1), (2) :—Gíf widobáne gebroced weorðeð, Ll. Th. i. 16, 6. II. *to afflict, distress, trouble, vex.* Cf. ge-broc, (3) :—Críst gehǽlde fela þǽra þe unhále wǽron, and Antecríst gebrocað and geuntrumað þá ðe ǽr hále wǽron . . . syððan hê þæne mann gebrocod hæfð, syððan hê mæg dôn, swylce hê hine gehǽle . . . hê gebrocað mænigne man díhlíce and gehǽld eft ætforan mannum, Wlfst. 97, 9-18. þá besæt Scipia hié on hiera fæstenne, and hié tô þon gebrocode (*Numantini fame trucidati*), Ors. 5, 3 ; S. 220, 26. Se líchoma gebrocad wierð mid sumre mettrymnesse . . . ðæt gebrocode flǽsc (*afflicta caro*) gelǽrð ðæt môd . . . gewyrceað ðá wunda on ðǽm gebrocodan (-edan, *v. l.*) môde hreówsunga wunda, Past. 257, 7-24. Án mǽden licgende on paralisyn, lange gebrocod, Hml. S. 26, 214. Gebrocode and eft árétte, Ps. Th. 28, arg. Þeh þe hié swíðe gebrocode wǽren on hiora licgendan feó *cum pudenda penuria esset aerarii*, Ors. 4, 10; S. 196, 17. þone mete dǽle man swá gebrocedum mannum þe swá fæstan ne magon *let the food be distributed to men so afflicted with infirmity as to be unable to fast*, Wlfst. 181, 15. v. un-gebrocod.

ge-brogne. *The gender is uncertain.* v. brogna(-e?): ge-brosn-endlíc. v. un-gebrosnendlíc.

ge-brosnian; *p.* ode; *pp.* od *To decay, become corrupt; of places, to become ruinous.* *Take here* ge-brosnod *in Dict., and add :* (1) in a physical sense :—Ðú ne geðafast þæt mín líchama gebrosnige (*nec dabis sanctum tuum videre corruptionem*, Ps. 16, 10), Hml. Th. ii. 16, 27. Ðonne ðín flǽsc beó gebrosnod, Past. 249, 14 : 251, 9. Míne herewíc syndon gebrosnode and gemolsnode, Bl. H. 113, 26. (2) in a moral sense :—þénas þá on nánre flǽscbesmitennysse beóð gebrosnude *ministros qui in nullo carnis contagio corrumpantur*, Scint. 69, 11. v. un-gebrosnod.

ge-brosnodlíc. *Add : corruptible :*—Ðysse worulde wela is hwýlwendlíc and feallendlíc and gebrosnodlíc, Wlfst. 263, 12. Ic wát þ nán eorðlíc anweald ne nán gebrosnodlíc nys náht bútan his ánes, Angl. xvii. 121, 16. Gebrosnod[líc?] *corruptibilem*, An. Ox. 8, 11.

ge-brosnung. *Add :* (1) in a physical sense :—Geseón forrotodnesse ł gebrosnunge *videre corruptionem*, Ps. L. 15, 10. (2) in a moral sense :—Heó bútan gebrosnunga wæs geeácnod, and on þǽm cnihtgebeorþre heó á clǽne þurhwunode, Bl. H. 3, 17. v. un-gebrosnung.

ge-brot. (1) *a fragment.* See Lk. 9, 17 *in Dict.* (2) *broken material, a collection of fragments.* See Mt. 15 (*not* 16), 37 *in Dict.* [In this passage the A. V. has *broken meat.*] v. corn-gebrot.

ge-brot *a barn-keeper.* Dele.

ge-brôþor. *Add :*—Fratres gebrôþor, *et aliquando* gemǽgas, *aliquando* gelondan, *quas Latini paternitates interpretantur*, Wrt. Voc. ii. 39, 46. Fratres gebrôþru *vel* gela[n]dan *vel siblings*, i. 52, 3. I. *those who have one or both parents the same :*—On Tracia wǽron twêgen cyningas ; þá wǽron gebrôþor (-brôðra, *v. l.*) *fratres duo, Thraciae reges*, Ors. 3, 7; S. 114, 16 : 4, 9; S. 192, 18. þá þe wǽron gebrôðor of fæder and of mêder, 3, 11; S. 152, 35. Gif twêgen gebrôðra wið án

wíf forlicgan, Ll. Th. i. 168, 18. Mid ús wǽrun seofun gebrôðru, Mt. 22, 25. On þone teógeþan dæg bið seofon gebrôðra ðrowung . . . ðá gebrôðor Publius wolde oncerran fram Crístes geleáfan, Shrn. 102, 22-26. Gebrôþra (-e, MS.) wíf *janitrices*, Wrt. Voc. i. 52, 32. Gê sǽdon þæt gê á má gebrôðra hæfdon (*alium habere vos fratrem*), Gen. 43, 6. Swá se hálga wer sǽde þám mǽdene be hire gebrôðrum (cf. hire brôðor Ecgfridus, 146, 13, his (*Ecgfrith's*) cyfesborena brôðor, 148, 17), Hml. Th. ii. 148, 20. Hê geseah twêgen gebrôðra (-u, *v. l.*), Mt. 4, 18. I a. applied to Christians :—Wê habbað ǽnne heofonlicne fæder and áne gástlice môdor, þ is Godes cirice, and þý wê sín gebrôðra, Ll. Th. i. 336, 9. II. *those who are united by a common interest :* —þá arn se eádiga Iôhannes tô eallum þám apostolum and wæs cweðende tô him : 'Bletsiað, gebrôðor þá leófestan, úrne Drihten,' Bl. H. 141, 19. II a. *the members of a religious society :*—Ðá gehyrde hê sumne þára gebrôðra sprecan þæt hê wolde fêran . . . Se brôðor côm eft hám, þá his gebrôðro æt gereorde sǽton, Bd. 3, 2; Sch. 197, 6-18. Ic eóde tô cyrcean and sang mid gebrôþrum, Coll. M. 33, 25 : 35, 25. III. *as a courteous form of address :*—Andreas cwæð : 'Brôðor (*the person addressed is the captain of the boat*), onfôh ús on þ scip' . . . Andreas andswerede : 'Gehýrað, gebrôðor (*the captain and his two companions*),' Bl. H. 233, 7-14. v. wil-gebrôþor.

ge-brúcan. *Add : [in Northern Gospels p.* -brêc, -brǽc; *pl.* -brêcon]. I. *to use food, eat :*—Gíf huá of ðǽm gebrúcceð (*manducauerit*) . . . Gíf huælc gebrúcces (*gibrúches, R.*) . . . Se ðe gebrúccað (-eð, *R.*), Jn. L. 6, 50, 51, 54. Ðá ðe gibrúcað (*utuntur*) of ðǽm (*apples*), Rtl. 99, 4. Gebrǽc *edens*, Lk. p. 11, 13. Brúcende wæs ł gebrǽc *edebat*, Mk. L. 1, 6. Hláfas gebrêc (*comedit*) ðá nêron gelêfed him tô gebrúcanne (*edere*), Mt. L. 12, 4. Gié gebrêcon (*manducastis*) . . . Fadero úsero gebrêicon . . . Aldro iúero gebrêcon, Jn. L. 6, 26, 31, 49. Ðá flêgende gebrêcon (*comederunt*) ðá ilco, Mt. L. 13, 4. þte ðú gebrúcca (*manduces*) eástro, Mk. L. 14, 12. Búta gié gebrúcce, Jn. L. R. 6, 53. þte gebrúcce (*gibrúche, R.*) ðás, Jn. L. 6, 5. þte gebrêce *ut pranderet*, Lk. L. 11, 37. Gebrúcca *manducare*, Lk. L. 22, 15 : Mt. L. 6, 25. þá hláfas wǽron fornumene and gebrocene *panes consumti fuerunt*, Gr. D. 145, 11. II. *to have or possess what gives pleasure, profit, &c., to enjoy :*—Gangað gê and þæs horses mid gôde gebrúcað, forþon ic his þearfe næbbe, Gr. D. 15, 24. Ðú úsig Iôhannes gilêfes symbelcennesse þte uê gibrúca *nos Iohannes concedis natalicia perfrui*, Rtl. 56, 15. Gebro[cen] *fretus*, i. *functus*, An. Ox. 2042. [*Swá* ibrúce *ic mine rice, ne scule gie mine mete ibite*, O. E. Hml. i. 233, 3. *O. H. Ger.* ge-brúhan *uti, fungi*.]

ge-bryce, es; *n. A fragment :*—Gebricu *fragmina*, An. Ox. 11, 140. Gebrycum *fragmine*, i. *particulis*, Wrt. Voc. ii. 150, 32.

ge-brýcgan. *Substitute :* ge-bryccan (?) *to use :*—Gibrycgende *utenda*, Rtl. 97, 33. [For cg = cc cf. ðrycges = ðrycces, 122, 14, *and cf. the whole word with* lífbrycgung, 7, 29. *But perhaps* brycgende = brúcende, *see the forms with cc under* ge-brúcan, *and cf.* (?) ofscýfende *for the mutated vowel.*]

ge-brycgan; *p.* ode; *pp.* od. I. *to bridge a road, cover with planks, stones, &c., so as to make it passable :*—Weard æteówod . . . án weg fram ðám húse þe hé on gewát . . . ástreht oð heofonan. Se weg wæs mid pællum gebricgod, Hml. Th. ii. 186, 34. II. *to bridge a stream.* [Wes Auene stram mid stele ibrugged, Laym. 21276.] v. brycgian.

ge-bryddan. *Add : [O. H. Ger.* ge-brutten *tremefacere, perterrere.*]

ge-brýdian; *p.* od *To marry :*—Wæs ôðres cempan wíf . . . seó wæs án geár gebrýdod and feówer mônað, Shrn. 84, 31. Seó wæs twám werum gebrýdad, and hwæþre heó wæs clǽne fǽmne. Ǽrest heó wæs gebrýdad Tondberhte and æfter þǽm heó wæs seald Ecgferðe tô cwêne, 94, 18-21. [Cf. *O. H. Ger.* ge-brútên *nubere.*]

ge-bryidan. v. brigdan.

ge-brýsan. *Substitute :* ge-brýsan, -brýsian; *p.* de, ede; *pp.* ed. I. *to bruise, crush, pound.* (1) lit. :—þá stánas nales þ án þ hí his limu tôbrǽcon, ac eác swylce mid ealle his bán gebrýsedon (-brýsdon, tôbrýsdon, *v. ll.*) *saxa non solum ejus membra, sed etiam ossa contriverant*, Gr. D. 125, 23. His preósta ǽnne of horse feallende and gebrýsedne (tôbrýsednde, *v. l.*) *clericum suum cadendo contritum*, Bd. 5, 6; Sch. 573, 7. (2) fig. :—þeáh se rihtwísa áfealle, ne wyrð hé gebrýsed, ne his nán bán tôbrocen *cum ceciderit justus, non conturbabitur*, Ps. Th. 36, 23. II. *to season :*—Gebrýsdre (-brydre, MS.) *condito (pulmentario)*, An. Ox. 2, 248. Gebrýsde (-bryrde, MS.), 7, 271. [*The word is glossed by* gestrýdere *in An. Ox. 3754 : all three are glosses on Ald. 51, 31.*]

ge-brýsednes. *For* 'contusio . . . Lye' *substitute :*—Geþræstednes *vel* gebrýsednes, forgnidennes *contritio*, Wrt. Voc. ii. 134, 78.

ge-bryttan. *l.* -brýtan, *and see* ge-brítan.

ge-brytnian; *p.* ode *To distribute, dispense :*—Ðá eorðlican hláfordas sint tô ðǽm gesette ðæt hié ðá endebyrdnesse and ðá ðegnunga hiora hiêrêdum gebrytnige *terrenae domus dominus famulorum ordines ministeriaque dispertiens*, Past. 319, 20.

ge-brytsen *a fragment :*—Twelf wylian fulle þǽra gebrytsena (brytsena, *v. l.*), Mt. 14, 20 : Jn. 6, 13.

ge-brytsnian *to distribute, spend :*—Næfre welan ne beóð bútan synne begytene, ne nán þā eorðlican þing ne mæg bútan synne gebrytsnian, E. S. viii. 473, 33.

ge-bryttan ; *p.* te *To break to pieces, crumble up :*—Gebrytte *frico,* Wrt. Voc. ii. 150, 75. Gif þū finde fisc on ōþrum fisce innan, genim þone and gebræd swīþe, and gebryte on drincan and sele þām seócan drincan, Lch. ii. 90, 10. Heorotes lungena . . . þonne hié ful wel ādrūgode synd, gebryte and gegnîd, and gesomna mid hunige, 216, 9. [*Some of the passages given under* ge-brītan *might belong here.*]

ge-bryttian ; *p.* ode *To dispense, expend :*—Gebryttade *exibuit,* Wrt. Voc. ii. 83, 64 : 31, 22. Wē sculon him gefremman and gebryttian hwylcnehuga dæl þære brōðorlican lufan *debemus ei aliquid caritatis impendere,* Gr. D. 345, 24. Gebryttode *inpensa,* Wrt. Voc. ii. 45, 9.

ge-būan. *Take here* ge-bōgian, -būgian, -bȳa *in Dict., and add :* —*p.* -bȳede ; *pp.* -būd, -bogen. **I.** *intrans. To dwell :*—Gebȳde in ceastra *habitavit in civitate,* Mt. L. 2, 23. Gebȳde (gibȳede, R.), Jn. L. 1, 14. Gewunedon ł gebȳedon ðēr *habitant ibi,* Mt. L. 12, 45.. Gebȳdon (gibȳedun, R.), Lk. L. 11, 26. Ðā āre ðe hē get on gebogen hæfð, C. D. ii. 135, 2. [The Latin of Ors. 1, 10 *in Dict.* is : 1u Cappadociae Pontique ora consederunt.] **I a.** *with reflex. dat. :*—Hæfde hió hire gebōgod on ānan wyrtigan hamme, Hml. S. 30, 312. **II.** *To inhabit* a dwelling, *occupy (and cultivate)* land, *possess :*—Ðā milde gebȳes (*possibeunt*) hlifgiendra eorðo, Mt. L. 5, 4. Swelce gē āne willen gebūgean ealle ðās eorðan *numquid habitabitis soli vos in medio terrae?,* Past. 329, 25. Hié ne dorston forþ bī þære eá siglan for unfriþe, for þēm ðæt land wæs eall gebūn on ōþre healfe þære eás. Ne mētte hē ēr nān gebūn land . . . þā Beormas hæfdon swīþe wel gebūd (-būn, *v. l,*) hira land, Ors. 1, 1 ; S. 17, 22–28. Gebūgan and gesyttan, Angl. viii. 308, 35. Hæfdon Caldēi þā lond gebūn on freódome *Babyloniae proprietas apud Chaldaeos fuit,* 2, 1 ; S. 60, 34. Hī hæfdon eft þā burg gebūne (-bogene, *v. l.*), 3, 1 ; S. 96, 4. Heora ēþel on heofenum sceolde eft gebūen and geseted weorþan mid hālgum sāwlum, Bl. H. 121, 33. Hī habbað nū eit heora eard gebōgod and þā burh Hierusalem, Hml. A. 106, 135.

ge-būgan. *Add :* **I.** *intrans.* (1) *to bow, bend the body :*—Hē hine on cirican gebidde, and tō Godes weófedan gebūge, Ll. Th. i. 334, 30. Se wyrm gebeáh tōsomne. . . . Gewāt gebogen scrīðan, B. 2569. Ābogenre ł ge[bogenre] *curva,* Hpt. Gl. 436, 62. (2) *to bend one's steps, turn, go.* (a) *of persons :*—Gē þearfum forwyrndon þæt hī under eówrum þæce mōsten in gebūgan, Cri. 1505. (β) *of things :*—Þȳ lǣs se āttres ord in gebūge under bānlocan, Cri. 768. (2 a) *of withdrawal, retirement, voluntary or enforced :*—Hē gebeáh binnan twām geárum tō þām ylcan mynstre and munuc weard, Hml. S. 21, 88. Þ muneca gehwylc þe ūte sȳ of mynstre . . . gebūge intō mynstre, Ll. Th. i. 306, 3. Gehādod man . . . borh finde, oþþe on carcerne gebūge, 168, 8. (3) *of adhesion, submission, &c., by a follower, vassal, tenant, worshipper, &c.* (a) *to a person or institution :*—Íc wille beón N. hold and getrīwe . . . and eall þ lǣste þ uncer formǣl wæs, þā ic tō him gebeáh and his willan geceás, Ll. Th. i. 178, 9. Hē gebeh . . . mid lande intō Scē Augustine, and ælce geáre gyld . . . .i. pund tō geswutelunga . . . and æfter his dæge gange þæt land intō Scē Augustine, C. D. ii. 300, 6. Mid þǣm monnum þe him tō gebugon, Chr. 901 ; P. 92, 7. Þ ðū gebūge mid biggengum tō þære gydenan Uesta, Hml. S. 7, 100. Behāt Gode þ ðū tō him gebūge, gif hē þe nū gehelpð, 353 ; Ll. Th. i. 424, 4. Þ Basilia sceolde gebūgan tō ðām cnihte, oþþe man hī tōheówe, Hml. S. 2, 359. Mid þām flotan þe him tō gebogen wæs, Chr. 904 ; P. 93, 24. (b) *to a belief, practice, condition, &c. :*—Mynstermunuc gǣd of his mæglage þonne hē gebȳhð tō regollage, Ll. Th. i. 346, 3. Ælces hādes men gebūgan tō þām rihte þe him tō gebyrige, 304, 24 ; 348, 29 : 378, 12. Fela manna nolde tō godcundre bōte gebūgan, 166, 16. Gif preóst tō rihte gebūgan nelle, ac ongeán biscopes gerǣdnesse widerige, ii. 296, 17. Ǣr hē hæbbe tō ǣlcum rihte gebogen, i. 250, 1. Þǣm gebogenan mǣdene *to the converted maiden,* Hml. S. 2, 88. Seó cwēn and Decius dohtor tō Crīstes geleáfan and tō ðām hālwendum fullohte gebogene wǣron, Hml. Th. i. 434, 10. (4) *of abandonment, defection :*—Ðā Wylisce men syððon hī fram þām cynge gebugon, heom manege ealdras of heom sylfan gecuron, Chr. 1097 ; P. 233, 20. Manīg fram þām eorle gebogen wæs, 1091 ; P. 226, 9. **II.** *trans. To submit to.* Cf. I. 2. :—Gebūge hē hengenne and þær gebīde, Ll. Th. i. 396, 27. Man nolde godcunde bōte gebūgan, 166, 18. Ǣr þām þe hē hæbbe godcunde bōte gebogene, 312, 3. [Goth. ga-biugan *to bend :* O. H. Ger. ge-biugan *curvare.*]

ge-būgian. v. ge-būan : ge-bugol. v. ge-beógol.

ge-būnes (-būnnes?) *habitation :*—Þis is synfulra stōw on tō eardianne and hiera gebūnes. . . . Hyra gebūnes bið mid deóflum. . . . Seó heofonlice gebūnes, Nap. 28.

ge-būr (-bȳr). *Add :* **I.** *glossing Latin words :*—Gibuur *colonus, vicinus,* Txts. 46, 163. Gebūr *colonus,* Wrt. Voc. i. 288, 32. Gebȳr, ii. 17, 6. **II.** *used of others than English :*—Ic wæs gebūr on þām lande þe [hātte] Nisibim, Shrn. 36, 21. Hit gelamp in Samni þ sumes rīces mannes tūn wæs, in ðām his gebūr (*colonus*) hæfde sunu, Gr.

D. 11, 4. Nīwum gebūrum *rudibus (florulentae telluris) colonis,* An. Ox. 11, 87. **III.** *as a technical English term it has much the same meaning as villein.* v. Seebohm, Vill. Comm. s.v. :—Se gebūr sceal his riht dōn (*then follows an account of what the gebūr was bound to do*), C. D. iii. 450, 34. Dudda wæs gebūr intō Hæðfeldan, vi. 211, 28. Brāda hātte wæs gebūr tō Hæðfelda, and Hwīte hātte ðæs Brādan wīf, wæs gebūres dohtor tō Hæðfelda, 212, 15–17. Cynelm hātte Cēnwaldes fæder, wæs gebūr intō Hæðfelda, and Manna hātte Cēnwaldes sunu, sit æt Wādtūne under Eádwolde, 26. An hió ðām hīwum ðāra gebūra ðe on ðām gafollande sittað, and ðēra þeówra manna hió an Eádgyfe, 132, 30. [O. H. Ger. ge-būr, -būro *municeps, incola, vicinus, civis, rusticus.*] v. tūn-gebūr ; ā-būrod.

gebūr-land, es ; *n. Land occupied by gebūras :*—Ðis sindon þā landgemǣro þæs gebūrlandes (þǣsse būrlandes, C. D. v. 401, 34) tō Abbendūne, C. D. B. iii. 201, 14. [For the amount of land held by a *gebūr* see Ll. Th. i. 434, 24, where '*his gyrd landes*' is spoken of. The *gebūrland* at Abingdon is described in the charter as 'aliquam terrae portionem, id est secundum aestimationem xx cassatorum.']

ge-buterod *buttered, dressed with butter :*—Seóþ henne and hocces leáf on wætre, āðo þone fugel of and þā wyrta, sele sūpan þ broð wel gebuterod, Lch. ii. 336, 14.

ge-bycgan. *Add :* **I.** *to buy goods :*—Sē þe hine gebohtte *qui eum emerat,* Bd. 4, 22 ; Sch. 460, 12. **I a.** *to buy as a trader :*—Wilt þū syllan þing cȳpan þīne hēr, ealswā þū hī gebohtest þǣr ? Ic nelle, ac ic wylle heora cȳpan hēr luflicor þonne ic gebicge (*emi*) þær, Coll. M. 27, 15–19. Þte hiá gebohte *ut negotiarentur,* Lk. p. 10, 1. **II.** *of payment by the husband before marriage :*—Gif mon wīf gebycgge, and sió gyft forð ne cume, Ll. Th. i. 122, 5. **III.** *to obtain by payment* a benefit, an advantage, office, &c. (1) *where the payment is material :*—Lundene waru griðede wið þone here and heom frið gebohtan, Chr. 1016 ; P. 153, 9. Eádsige arceb . . . bletsode Sīward tō biscope . . . se arðbiscop wēnde þ hit sum ōðer mann ābiddan wolde oððe gebicgean, 1043 ; P. 164, 5. Hū woldest þū gebycgan, þā þū gesǣlgost wǣre . . . mid hū micelan feó woldest þū þā habban geboht þ þū swutole mihtest tōcnāwan þīne frīnd and þīne fȳnd ? Ic wāt þ þū hit woldest habban mid miclan feó geboht þ þū hī cūþest wel tōscādan, Bt. 20 ; F. 72, 17– 22 : 34, 9 ; F. 146, 12. Gebohtre scīre wītnung *ambitus judicium,* Wrt. Voc. i. 21, 12. (2) *where the payment is non-material :*—Sume gebycgaþ weorþlicne hlīsan ðisses andweardan līfes mid heora āgnum deáþe, Bt. 39, 11 ; F. 228, 27. Mē þincð þ hit hæbbe geboht sume swīþe leáslice mǣrþe, 24, 3 ; F. 82, 25. **IV.** *to pay for work done :*—Þone fultum and þæt weorc Agustus gebohte mid fela M talenta *Augustus ad reparationem magnam vim pecuniae largitus est,* Ors. 6, 1 ; S. 252, 28. **V.** *to secure the services of a person by payment, to hire :*—Nǣnig ūsic mid leáne gebohte *nemo nos conduxit,* Mt. R. 20, 7. **VI.** *to buy those in slavery, to redeem :*—Godwīg hæfð geboht Leófgīfe and hyre ofspring mid healfon punde æt Ælsige tō ēcean freóte, C. D. iv. 271, 16. ¶ gebycgan ūt *to buy out, redeem :*—Ægelsige hæfð geboht Wilsige his sunu ūt æt Ælfsige abbod and æt eallon hīrede tō ēcean freóte, C. D. iv. 271, 4, 10 : 270, 17. **VII.** *to rescue from punishment* by payment. (1) *secular :*—Sē þe fals wyrce þolige þǣra handa þe þ fals mid worhte, and hē hī mid nānum þingum ne gebicge, ne mid golde, ne mid seolfre, Ll. Th. i. 380, 18. (2) *spiritual :*—Þā sāwla þe Crīst mid his āgenum līfe gebohte, Ll. Th. i. 304, 17, 22. **VIII.** *to pay the penalty for.* Cf. ā-bycgan :—Þ hit manige yfele men mid heora feóre gebohtan, Bl. H. 45, 23. Ælc þæra manna þe yt oððe drincð on untīman . . . wīte hē þ his sāwl sceal sārlīce hit gebicgan (-bycgean, *v. l.*), Hml. S. 12, 77. Hē hēt þ hī āwendon his geþanc fram Crīste, and cwæð þ hī sceoldon sylfe hit gebicgan, gif hī ne bīgdon his mōd, 35, 55. **IX.** *to sell* [ = be-bycgan] :—Ðeáh hwā bebyccge (gebicge, *v. l.*) his dohtor on þeówenne, Ll. Th. i. 46, 12.

ge-bygle ; *adj. Submissive :*—Þ hē on Normandig gewunnen hæfde syððon on sibbe and him gebygle wunode, Chr. 1105 ; P. 239, 35. Se cyng him ongeán þā Manige behēt, þe fram þām eorle gebogen wæs, gebygle tō dōnne, and eall þ his fæder þær begeondan hæfde, 1091 ; P. 226, 9.

ge-bygu, e ; *f. A bend :*—Andlang Wilig on hyssa pōl ; ðæt on ðǣre gebyge, C. D. v. 150, 6.

ge-byhte, es ; *n. A bight, bend :*—Andlang dīces oð þæt gebyhte ; of þām gebyhte andlang hagan, C. D. i. 257, 33.

ge-byhþ. *Take here* ge-bihþ *in Dict.* : ge-byld *boldness.* v. ge-bild : ge-byld ; *adj.,* v. ge-bylded. v. ge-bildan : ge-bylgan. v. gebilgan : ge-bȳr. v. ge-būr.

ge-bȳran (?) *to furnish with* gebūras, *colonize :*—Gebȳrdum gemǣre *colono fine,* Wrt. Voc. ii. 134, 26. Cf. ā-būrod.

ge-byrd. *Add : n.* (see Bl. H. 167, 8 : Hml. S. 4, 256 *below*). **I.** *birth.* (1) *bearing of a child* by the mother :—Þū wuldorfæste hlǣfdige þe God æfter flǣsces gebyrde ācendest, Hml. S. 23b, 433. Oft þæt gegongeð þætte wer and wīf in woruld cennað bearn mid gebyrdum, Vy. 3. (2) *of a child, the being born :*—Ǣr þon þe hē þære gesȳnelican gegaderunge menniscre gebyrde onfēnge, Bl. H. 165, 36. Hē on þære

his gebyrde oferswíþde ealle ǽ þisse menniscan gebyrde, 167, 3. Hé latode on þissum líchomlicum gebyrde, 8. Manige on his gebyrd gefeóþ, 165, 10. On þá his gebyrd, 167, 16. Þá Críst cóm on ðás woruld þurh ménnisce gebyrde, Wlfst. 82. 15. (2 a) where the birth is celebrated yearly:—Be þisse hálgan tíde weorþunga . . ., þonne is þ seó foremǽre gebyrd Sancte Iôhannes . . . nǽniges Godes háligra gebyrd . . . ciriecan ne mǽrsiaþ nemþe Crístes sylfes and þyses Iôhannes, Bl. H. 161, 4-11. Hér segð ymb Drihtnes gebyrd . . . þy forma dæg Dryhtnes gebyrde, Lch. iii. 164, 13-28. On þone ilcan dæig Godes circean árworðiad Scã Anastasiam gebird, Shrn. 30, 20. **II.** the origin of a thing:— Gebyrdum cunabulis, An. Ox. 3137. **III.** what is born, offspring, a child:—Þ nǽfre betuh wífa gebyrdum (inter natos mulierum) nǽnig mǽrra geboren wǽre, Bl. H. 161, 23: 167, 18. **IV.** parentage, lineage:—Hé wæs of Dauides mǽgðe and wolde andettan mid Marian hire gebyrde, Hml. Th. i. 30, 9. Tô ǽwisclicum bismer gebyrda ad infame dedecus natalium (i. propinquorum), Hpt. 507, 10. Gebyrda ł freónda natalicium, 37. Gemunan hwylcra gebyrda þú wǽre, Bt. 5, 1; F. 10, 3: R. Ben. 12, 20. Hé befrán hí be hyre gebyrdum, Hml. S. 8, 40. Bisceopas ne beóð nú be gebyrdum gecorene, 10, 228. Hé hine tô ôþrum men híwað, and his gebyrda mid þám bedíglað, Hml. S. 23, 692. **IV a.** where the character (high or low) of birth is marked:— —Wæs se cyning æþelre gebyrde erat rex natu nobilis, Bd. 2, 15; Sch. 175, 10. Wer tor worolde æþelre gebyrde (æþelra gebyrda, v. l.) vir ad saeculum nobilis, 5, 10; Sch. 604, 11. Þá cnihtas lyfedan búton éhtnysse for hyra mycclum gebyrde, Hml. S. 4, 250. Wæs hé for worlde swíþe æþelra gebyrda and gôdra, Bl. H. 211, 19. Þeáh hwá wexe mid micelre æþelcundnesse his gebyrda, Bt. 19; F. 68, 31: Gr. D. 151, 23. Of æþelum gebyrdum ácenned generosis natalibus ortus, An. Ox. 4151: Wrt. Voc. ii. 59, 73: Ap. Th. 20, 2. Hí ne beóð swá æðele on gebyrdum swá hí woldon. Sume beóþ swíðe æþele on heora gebyrdum, Bt. 11, 1; F. 30, 31-33. Hí taliað þe wyrsan for heánon gebyrdan þá þe heora yldran on worolde ne wurdan welige, Ll. Th. i. 334, 2. **IV b.** good birth:—Ic wát þíne æðelborennysse, and ic þé for ðí tihte þ ðú þám godum geoffrige æfter þínre gebyrde, Hml. S. 4, 131. Bebyriað hire (Jezebel) líc for hire gebyrdum (sepelite eam; quia filia regis est, 2 Kings 9, 34), 18, 351. Hwí ofermôdige gé ofer ôþre men for eówrum gebyrdum?, Bt. 30, 2; F. 110, 15. Gebyrdan, Ll. Th. i. 332, 34. Heó ôþerne tealde tôforan his gebyrdum she accounted another of better family than his, Hml. S. 7. 75. **V.** rank, position due to birth:—Se wurðfulla cniht þá brýdlác geforþode, and gefette þ mæden mid woruldlicum wurðmynte swá swá heora gebyrde wǽron (in a manner befitting their rank), Hml. S. 34, 22. Cwæð hé tô þám cynegum: 'Beorgað eówrum gebyrdum, and búgað tô úrum godum,' 24, 33. Eóde swá ábútan be heora gebirdum and be heora geþingþum, Jud. p. 161, 25. **VI.** nature, natural character. v. ge-byrde:— Eall þeós mennisce gebyrd Sancte Iôhanne bedyrned is human frailties were unknown to St. John, Bl. H. 167, 17. Þonne seó wamb bið hátre gebyrdo and gecyndo, Lch. ii. 220, 16. Tô hwon þú sceole for ôwiht þysne man habban, ungelǽredne fiscere þone leásostan, and náwþer ne on worde ne on gebyrdum mid nǽnigre mihte gewelgode (endowed with no natural abilities), Bl. H. 179, 15. **VII.** what happens, fate, lot (cf. (?) Icel. bera (impers.) to befall, happen; at-burðr a chance, haþ):— —Conditio, i. status, procreatio, natura, sors, gescæp, gewyrd, gescæft, gebyrd, Wrt. Voc. ii. 135, 63. **VIII.** continuity (?), uninterrupted order. v. ge-byrdelíce, -byrdlic:—Náh seó môdor geweald, þonne heó magan cenned, bearnes blǽdes, ac sceal on gebyrd faran án æfter ánum the children must in order die one after the other, Sal. 384. Heó wearð beloren bearnum and brôðrum; hié on gebyrd hruron (they fell one after the other) gáre wunde, B. 1074. [These two passages might belong to **VII**.] v. flǽsc-gebyrd.

**ge-byrd** bearded. v. ge-bird[e].

**ge-byrdan** to border, fringe:—Gebyrdid (-ed, v. l.) clabatum, Txts. 50, 228. Clavatum, sutum vel gebyrd, Wrt. Voc. ii. 131, 57. [O. L. Ger. gi-burdid clavatum.] v. be-byrdan, borda.

**gebyrd-boda** (?) one who announces a birth:—Sé onsended wæs · Summo de throno · and þære clǽnan · Clara voce · þe gebyrdboda (þa gebyrd bodede?) · bona voluntate · þ heó sceolde cennan · Christum regem, Dôm. L. 36, 17.

**gebyrd-dæg.** Add: the anniversary of birth:—Se gebyrddæg (natalitius dies) eádigan Procules þæs martires, Gr. D. 61, 27. Ær Eástrum and ær Crístes gebyrddæge (ante dominicum natale), Bd. 4, 30; Sch. 535, 20.

**ge-byrde, -bierde.** Dele -bierde, and add: v. un-gebyrde; gebyrd; **VI:** ge-byrded clavatum. v. ge-byrdan: ge-byrded temeratum. v. un-gebyrded: ge-byrdelíce. Add: v. ge-byrd; **VIII,** and next word.

**ge-byrdlic;** adj. Orderly, harmonious:—þú hý hæfst ealle gesceapene gebyrdlice and gesôme, and tô þám geþwǽre þæt heora nán ne mæg ôðerne mid ælle fordôn dissonantia usque in extremum nulla est, Solil. H. 5, 13.

**gebyrd-tíd.** Add: **I.** the time of a person's birth:—Ymbe nigon hund wintra and nigon and seoxtig ðæs ðe Drihtnes gebyrdtíde wæs,

C. D. iii. 50, 9. Fram gebyrdtíde (-a, An. Ox. 2842) iugeðe ab ipsa cunabulorum temeritudine, Hpt. Gl. 473, 7. Of úres Drihtnes gebyrdtíde tô þám ende, Wlfst. 312, 2. Ðis wæs gedôn ðý geáre ðe wæs ágán fram Crístes gebyrdtíde nigon hund wintra and hundnigontig wintra, C. D. iii. 255, 22. Gebyrdtíde, 256, 18. Fram Abrahames ácennednesse forð oð Môyses gebyrdtídu . . . fram Môyses gebyrdtíde forð tô Salomones gebyrde, Angl. xi. 9, 7-11. **I a.** the day of Christ's birth and the days following up to Twelfth-night (cf. **II a**):—On ðám forman dæge his gebyrdtíde hé weard æteówed þrým hyrdum, Hml. Th. i. 104, 30. Weard hé on þám eahtoðan dæge his gebyrdtíde ymbsniden, 94, 19. **II.** the anniversary of a person's birth, birthday:—XL. nihta ǽr Geólum (middan wintra, úres Dryhtnes gebyrdtíde, v. ll.) xl. diebus ante Natale Domini, Ll. Th. ii. 162, 12. Ær Crístes gebrydtíde, Bd. 4, 30; Sch. 535, 21. Hí hæfdon on ðám tíman micele blisse on heora gebyrdtídum, Hml. Th. i. 480, 29. **II a.** one of the days between Christmas-day and Twelfth-night. [v. **I a,** and cf. Her segð ymb Drihtnes gebyrd ymb þa XII niht his tíde, Lch. iii. 164, 13, and see Hml. Th. i. 94, 19 above.]:—Hé cymð tô ús on þǽre þriddan gebyrtíde, Vis. Lfc. 22.

**gebyrd-tíma, an;** m. Time of birth:—Of þám heregange tô Crístes gebyrdtíman, Wlfst. 312, 2. v. preceding word.

**ge-býred** colonized. v. ge-býran.

**ge-byredlic.** Add:—Gibyredlices oportunitatis, Rtl. 12, 27. v. un-gebyredlic.

**ge-býren.** v. neáh-gebýren.

**ge-byrg** protection:—Beón on gebyrge (eo written over y, v. l.) wude-wum, Wlfst. 119, 4: 209, 1. Cf. ge-beorg.

**ge-býrgan** to taste. l. -byrgan, and see ge-birgan: **ge-byrga.** v. leód-gebyrga: **ge-byrgednes.** The better reading of the passage given in Dict. under ge-byrigednes is ge-byrgednes, Bd. 4, 32; Sch. 546, 3.

**ge-byrgen** tinipa?, Wrt. Voc. i. 288, 69.

**ge-byrgen[n], e; f.** A grave:—Se wífmon, sé hyre bearn áfédan ne mæg, genime heó sylf hyre ágenes cildes gebyrgenne dǽl, wrý on blace wulle and bebicge tô cépemannum, Lch. iii. 68, 5.

**ge-býrian.** l. -byrian, take here ge-berian in Dict., and add: **I.** to happen. (1) where the subject is a noun (or pronoun):—Gif him forðsíð gebyrige, Ll. Th. i. 236, 35: 434, 27. Ælc þing cymþ of sumum ðingum, for ðý hit ne biþ weás gebyred; ac þǽr hit of náuhte ne cóme, þonne wǽre hit weás gebyred, Bt. 40, 5; F. 240, 28-30. (2) with hit as subject, and a clause following the verb:—Gif hit ǽfre gebyreþ þ heó blôdes onbirigð, Bt. 25; F. 88, 11: 38, 4; F. 204, 19: 39, 10; F. 226, 35. Hit oft gebyrað (-eþ, Bt. S. 47, 6) þ . . ., 20; F. 70, 22. (3) without a subject, but with clause following the verb:—Ðonne getíðeþ (gebyreð, v. l.) oft þ hé næfþ ðone anweald, Bt. 33, 2; F. 124, 13. Þǽr oft gebyreþ þ hí weorþaþ bereáfode, 29, 2; F. 104, 16: 39, 10; F. 226, 34: Past. 105, 19. Gif þonne gebyrige þ heora hwilc bige habban wille, Ll. Th. i. 156, 2. **I a.** with dat. of person, to happen to a person:—Swá gebyreþ ǽlcum, Bt. 35, 4; F. 162, 27. Ic eów cýðe hú eówer ǽlcon gebyred, Gen. 49, 1. Oft hwǽm gebyreð ðæt hé hwæt mǽrlices gedeð, Past. 39, 6. Ðǽm forhæbbendum hwílum gebyrede ðæt hié gewíten of hiera geleáfan, 317, 25. **II.** to fall to, be granted, be allotted to a person or object, belong to:—Irnaþ ealle . . . ǽlc wilnaþ . . . þone beág habban, ac ánum hé gebyraþ (-eð, v. l.), Bt. 37, 2; F. 188, 13. Healsfang gebyreð bearnum . . . ne gebyreð nánum mǽge þ feoh búte þám þe sý binnan cneówe, Ll. Th. i. 174, 24-26. Se wer gebirað mágum, and seó cynebôt þám leódum, 190, 8. Feohbôt gebyreð tô gebedbigene, 328, 5. Him gebyrede þ feorh earfoðlíce hardly was life granted him, Hml. S. 12, 64. Wé gebyrian sceolon oðche heofonwarena cyninge oðche hellewítes deóflum æfter úrum forðsíðe, Wlfst. 151, 19: 241, 18. **III.** for a person (dat.) to be concerned with (tô) an object, to have to do with:—Hwæt synd þás? gebyrað him áht tô þé? what are these? have they anything to do with you?; quid sibi volunt isti? et si ad te pertinent?, Gen. 33, 5. Wé sceolon forbúgan þone deóful, for ðan ðe him ne gebyrað náht tô ús, Hml. Th. i. 270, 14. Ne gebyrað him nán þincg ne tô wífe ne tô worldwíge neither wife nor war is any concern of his, Ll. Th. i. 346, 22. Tô woruldgewinne búgan þe him náht tô ne gebyrað (-iað, v. l.), Hml. S. 25, 832. Næs hé æðelboren, ne him náht tô þám cynecynne ne gebyrode he was not of noble birth, and was in no way connected with the royal race, Hml. Th. i. 80, 33. 'Sege mé on hwilcere byrig þú geboren wǽre, oþþe tô hwilce byrig þé tô gebyrige.' Ðá cwæð hé: 'Ic lǽte þ mé tô nánre byrig swá rihte ne gebyrige swá tô þissere byrig' 'tell me in which town you were born, or to which town you belong.' He said: 'I suppose that to no town do I belong with so much right as to this town,' Hml. S. 23, 673-676. **IV.** to belong to, be included in or connected with, to pertain:—Hwílon Wentsǽte hýrdon intô Dúnsǽtan, ac hit gebyreð rihtor intô West-Sexan, Ll. Th. i. 356, 18. Ealle þá þe tô Godes ríce gebyrigað, Hml. Th. i. 236, 30. Þá þing þe swíþost tô Godes lage gebyriað mid rihte, Wlfst. 164, 14. Ne gebyriað þás twégen dǽlas tô ðám cræfte, Ælfc. Gr. Z. 294, 10. Ðá gemetu gebyriað tô leóðcræfte, 295, 19. Ðá ealdras heom cartan fundon and eall þ þǽrtô

gebyrede, Nic. 12, 8. Sȳ hē þæs þeówweorces wyrðe þe þærtó gebyrige, Ll. Th. i. 164, 13 : 330, 27 : 342, 8. Ealle gerihtu ðe him tó gebyrigean, 434, 25.   V. of payment (lit. or fig.), to belong, be due :—Mid ūs is geræd þ hē sylle .v. sustras tó gafole ; on suman landum gebyreð māre gafolræden, Ll. Th. i. 436, 2. On manegum landum gebyreð deópre. swānriht, 14. For þām cynedóme gebirað ōðer swilc tó bóte, 190, 7. Of Dyddanhamme gebyreð micel weorcræden, C. D. iii. 450, 30. Ofer eall ðæt land gebyrað æt gyrde .xii. penegas . . , 24.   V a. with dat. of person to whom a due belongs :—Æt ælcum were gebyreð æfre se ōðer fisc ðām landhláforde, C. D. iii. 450, 26. Æhteswāne gebyreð stīfearh, Ll. Th. i. 436, 22, 26, 33. Him gebyriað .v. æceras tó habbanne, 432, 23. Forgylde þām þe hit gebyrige, 410, 16.   VI. to belong to a person as a duty, be incumbent on, be the duty of, to behove. (1) with noun (or pronoun) as subject :—Bisceope gebyreð ælc rihting . . . Hē sceall gehādode men ǣrest gewissian þ heora ælc wite hwæt him mid rihte gebyrige tó dónne, Ll. Th. ii. 312, 9–12. (2) where the duty is described in a clause following the verb, (a) which has hit as subject :—Hyt gebyrede (oportuit) þæt þū befǣstest mīn feoh myneterum, Mt. 25, 27. (b) which has no subject :—Syþþan gebyreþ þ man sylle . . , Ll. Th. i. 250, 16. Sulhælmessan gebyreð þ man gelǣste, 342, 30 : 352, 16. (2 a) with dat. of person :—Beóceorle gebyreð þ hē sylle . . , Ll. Th. i. 434, 36 : 436, 11. Bisceopum gebyreð þ . . , ii. 316, 11, 22, 26. Gebyrað, 34. Se geleáfa þe ǣghwylcum men gebyreð þ hē wel gehealde, Bl. H. 111, 13.   VII. to belong to a thing, be requisite for proper performance :—Gif hē teám gecenne, and sȳ on ōðre scīre sē þe hē tó tȳmð, hæbbe hē swā langne fyrst swā þærtó gebyrige, Ll. Th. i. 288, 19 : 308, 11. Godes lagum fylge man and lāreówum hlyste, swā þærtó gebyrige, 332, 27. Beón þa heregeata swā hit mǣðlic sȳ. Eorles swā þærtó gebyrige, þ onsyon eahta hors . . , 414, 5.   VIII. to be appropriate, suitable, convenient. (1) in a physical sense :—Ðætte hē ǣghwelcum men finde ðone lǣcedóm ðe him tó gebyrge ut congrua singulorum vulneribus medicamina opponat, Past. 453, 13. (2) in a moral sense, to be seemly :—Nān gebeórscipe ne gebyrað æt līce, ac hālige gebedu þær gebyriað swȳþor, Hml. S. 21, 316. Sē þe þ nelle, þ his hāde gebyrige, Ll. Th. i. 306, 22.

ge-byrigdnes. v. ge-byrgednes : ge-bȳrild. v. neáh-gebȳrild.

ge-byrman. v. ge-birman.

ge-byrst ; adj. Having bristles, bristly :—Gebyrstum setigero (apro), An. Ox. 23, 3.

ge-byrþen, e ; f. What is borne or born, a child :—Þurh þæt gebyrðor (gebyrðene, v. l.) wē wurdon ālȳsede, Wlfst. 251, 14.

ge-bȳsgian. v. ge-bisgian : ge-bȳsnian, -bȳsnung. v. ge-bisnian, -bisnung.

ge-bytlu. For ' indecl. f. A building' substitute pl. n. A group of buildings, a dwelling-place, residence [cf. the plural use of hús in this sense in Icel.], in l. 5 for 580, 32 read 354, 32, and add :—Man bytlode āne gebytlu . . . Hē befrān hwām ðā gebytlu gemynte wǣron, Hml. Th. ii. 354, 32–35. Wǣron þa gebytlu on ðām dæge geworhte, 356, 8. Þis synd gāstlices cræftes tól and gebytla, R. Ben. 19, 3. Se cyng Willelm tó Pentecosten forman sīðe his hīréd innan his nīwan gebyttlan æt Westmynstre heóld (William in the twelfth year of his reign for the first time kept court in the new palace of Westminster, Hen. Hunt.), Chr. 1099 ; P. 234, 34. Ic hire beád gymmas . . . and mǣre gebytlu, Hml. S. 8, 36. Ic ārǣre þā getimbrunge þ hire hróf oferstīhð ealle gebytlu, 36, 72. Miht þū mē ārǣran on Rómānisce wīsan cynelice gebytlu ?, 92. Hē hylt ealle þā gebytlu ðǣre gelaðunge, Hml. Th. i. 580, 21 : 582, 22.

ge-bytlung. Add :—Ne beó wē tó weallum oððe tó wāgum geworhte on þǣre gāstlican gebytlunge, Hml. Th. ii. 582, 14.

ge-cǣlan. In Lk. 16, 24 one MS. has gehǣle, in another this is altered to gecǣle (= gecéle ?. v. ge-célan) : ge-cǣlcian. v. ge-cilcan : ge-cǣnenis. v. ge-cennes : ge-cǣnnan. v. ge-cennan.

ge-camp ; n. (not m.). Add :—Gecampe bello, Wülck. Gl. 248, 13.   I. warfare, battle. (1) literal :—Cempa þe on nānum gecampe nāht ðegenlices ne gefremode, Hml. Th. i. 342, 5. Iulianus wolde neádian preóstas tó woruldlicum gecampe, Hml. S. 25, 834. (2) fig. spiritual warfare :—Hī sceolon mid sige þæs gāstlican gecampes tó him eft gecyrran þe hī tó þām gefeohte āsende, Hml. Th. ii. 402, 14. Gecampes (cenobialis) militig, An. Ox. 4169. Godes fyhtling (St. Paul) sóhte þone feld þæs gecampes (certaminis campum), Gr. D. 110, 15. Muneca cyn þe . . . under abbodes tǣcinge on gecampe wuniaþ (militans sub abbate), R. Ben. 9, 4. Wē magon ðā feóndlican leahtras mid gecampe oferwinnan, gif wē cēnlīce feohtað, Hml. S. 16, 379.   II. a struggle, conflict, contest. (1) physical :—Ús nis nān gecamp ongeán flǣsc and blód non est nobis colluctatio adversus carnem et sanguinem (Eph. 6, 11), Hml. Th. ii. 218, 4. Pleglices gecampes Olimphiaci agonis, An. Ox, 2, 5. Ælc ðǣra þe on gecampe wind (in agone contendit, 1 Cor. 9, 25), forhæfð hine sylfne fram eallum þingum, Hml. Th. ii. 86, 22. (2) non-physical :—Hū micel wǣre þ gecamp (certamen) þe wann on þæs rihtwīsan mannes breóstum, Gr. D. 18, 4. Hē ābād mid his gebróðrum tihtende hī tó ðām tówerdan gecampe (the coming persecu-

tion), Hml. S. 4, 103. Gyt mid gāstlicum gecampe winnað ongeán ðone drȳ, Hml. Th. i. 374, 22. God sette gecamp geleáffullum sāwlum, 64, 19.

ge-campian. Add : (1) to fight a fight :—Gē habbað gecampod gódne campdóm, Hml. S, 34, 262. (2) to get by fighting :—Ne byð nǣfre leán þæs sigores, būton hit sȳ mid gewinne gecampod sine labore certaminis non est palma victoriae, Gr. D. 221, 8. (3) to fight for a person (dat.), serve as a soldier :—Ānum cinge sī gecampod uni regi militatur, R. Ben. 9, 102, 15. [O. H. Ger. kichemfit ist einemu chuninge militatur uni regi.]

ge-canc. For ' Som. . . . 510 ' substitute :—Gecance ludibrio, i. uituperatione, An. Ox. 1473. Mid gecance gannitura, 4504. v. canc.

ge-capitulod furnished with headings to the sections of a book. [O. H. Ger. ge-capitalót titulatus, prenotatus.] v. un-capitulod in Dict.

ge-ceápian. Add : (1) to purchase as a matter of business :—Þæt mon ælcne ceáp mehte be twiefealdan bet geceápian þonne mon ǣr mehte ut duplicia, quam usque ad id fuerant, rerum uenalium pretia statuerentur, Ors. 5, 13 ; S. 248, 2. Godríc begeat þ land . . . hē sealde his sweostor ān marc goldes . . . on geceápodne ceáp . . . þes ceáp wæs geceápod on Wii, Cht. Th. 350, 12–21. (1 a) figurative :—Þás hālgan cȳpan, Petrus and Andreas, mid heora nettum and scipe him þæt éce līf geceápodon, Hml. Th. i. 580, 20. (2) to obtain by payment (material or non-material) :—Wē sint on þǣm friþe geborene þe hié þā uneáðe hiera feorh mid geceápedon, Ors. 5, 1 ; S. 242, 22. Hæfde seó earme wudewe mid ānum feórðlinge þæt éce līf geceápod, Hml. Th. i. 582, 21. Þær is māðma hord grimme gecea[po]d (purchased with Beowulf's life), B. 3012. v. ge-cīpan.

ge-ceasterwaran ; pl. Fellow-citizens :—Mīn se leófesta freónd . . . ic sille eówrum geceasterwarum hundteóntig þūsenda mitta hwǣtes, Ap. Th. 9, 14. Wē geácsodon his geceasterwaran beón Godes englas, Wlfst. 2, 2.

ge-célan. [The passage in I is from Lch. i. 146, 14.] Add :—Ðætte hē gewǣte his ȳtemestan finger on wættre and mid ðǣm gecéle mīne tungan, Past. 309, 7. Gekéle (-céle, v. l.), Gr. D. 304, 18 : 310, 14. Þte geceóla tunga mīn ut refrigeret linguam meam, Lk. L. 16, 24. Þæt hē hys (Dives) þurst myd þī gecélde, Solil. H. 67, 30. Ðæt ic sié gecoeled ut refrigerer, Ps. Srt. 38, 14. [O. H. Ger. ge-kuolen refrigerare.] See ge-cǣlan.

ge-celf. l. (?) ge-celfe, -ci[e]lfe.

ge-cemban to comb :—Ic his heáfod mid gambe gekamde, C. D. iv. 261, 2.

ge-cenenis. Dele, and see ge-cennes.

ge-cennan. Substitute : I. to bring forth, bear children :—Gecennes sunu pariet filium, Mt. L. i. 21, 23. Gecende (peperit) sunu hire frumcende, 25. þ cneúreso gicende quod generatio edidit, Rtl. 108, 29. Of ðaem gecenned ł geboren is Haelend de qua natus est Iesus, Mt. L. 1, 16: Mt. p. 13, 2: p. 14, 1. Gecenned ł ācenned nati, Jn. L. 8, 41. Gecened, 13.   II. to give forth a statement, declare, make known. (1) absolute, to state the conditions of a case :—Ic gecende be ðām ðe ic cūðe ; sē ðe bet cunne gecȳðe his māre I have set forth the state of things as I knew it ; let him that knows it better give it more fully, Angl. ix. 265, 13. (2) with object :—In regula suindrig ān ēghwelc ðā ne habbas in ōðrum gecendon in canone propria unusquisque quae non habentur in aliis ediderunt, Mt. p. 3, 17. (3) with object and complementary adj. :—Ic þe ēcne God gecenne, Hy. 10, 4. (4) to declare a course of action :—Gif hē teám gecenne, and sȳ on ōðre scīre sē þe hē tó tȳmð, Ll. Th. i. 288, 18. (5) to make an (exculpatory) statement about a person :—Gif se bana oðbyrste, feórðe manwyrð hē (the man who allows the escape) tó gedó, and hine gecenne mid gódum ǣwdum þ hē þane banan begeten ne mihte, Ll. Th. i. 28, 2, 8. [Goth. ga-kannjan to make known : O. H. Ger. ge-chennen gignere.]

ge-cennes (?) a calling (?) :—Oð þone dæg his gerecenesse (gecǣnenisse, gecīgednisse, gecīgednesse, v. ll.) of middangearde usque ad diem suae uocationis, Bd. 5, 12 ; Sch. 634, 8.

ge-cennice. l. -cennicge. v. cennicge.

ge-ceorfan. Take here ge-cearfan in Dict., and add : (1) to cut off, cut down :—Trē gecorfen bið ł [man] gecearfas arbor exciditur, Mt. L. 7, 19. Ðió eárlprece ðone Petrus gecurfe (absciderat), Lk. p. 11, 6. Gecearfa abscidi, Mt. p. 14, 15. (2) to behead a person :—Hē gecearf (giceorf, R.) hine decollauit eam, Mk. L. 6, 27.

ge-ceorlian ; p. ode To take a husband, marry :—Wīf ðe tuwa geceorlige mulier quae bis viro nupserit, Ll. Th. ii. 232, 1.

ge-ceósan. Add : I. to choose, select :—Ðā ðe woruldmonnum dynceað dysige, ðā geciésð (-cīst, v. l.) elegit Dryhten, Past. 203, 23. Ofer ealle ōþre ic þā stówe geceás, Bl. H. 201, 9. Geceás hē him þone deáþ, þ him mon ofléte blódes on þām earme, Bt. 29, 2 ; F. 104, 22. Geceós ðē nū fultum, Hml. S. 25, 399. Healde gehwā mid riht his ǣwe . . . būton þ gewurðe þ hī būta geceósan . . . þ hī getwǣman, Ll. Th. ii. 300, 27.   I a. to choose for the service of a person (dat.) :—þā twelf apostolas þām ēcean Gode gecorene wǣron (Deo electi fuerant),

Ll. Lbmn. 413, 13. þā þe Gode gecorene wǣron sōna swā hȳ geborene wǣron, Wlfst. 196, 10. ¶ geceósan tō (1) *to choose* king, bishop, &c., *elect* :—Ic þē gefyrþrede mid mīnum lārum tō þon þ þē mon tō dōmere geceás, Bt. 8 ; F. 24, 30 : Chr. 1041 ; P. 163, 10. Hine geces tō fæder and tō hlāforde Scotta cyning, 924 ; P. 104, 18 : 921 ; P. 103, 19. Se aþþ forðgefaren wæs ; þā geceás hē Æðelsige nunuc þærtō, 1061 ; P. 190, 4. Se fiota eall gecuron Cnut tō cyninge, 1014 ; P. 144, 28. Tō bisceope gecoren *in praesulatum electus*, Bd. 2, 18 ; Sch. 182, 3 : Chr. 830 ; P. 62, 6. Heó wæs gecoren tō mēder hire Scyppende, Bl. H. 13, 14. Gewitnes sȳ geset tō ælcere byrig. Tō ælcere byrig .xxxiii. sȳn gecorene tō gewitnesse, Ll. Th. i. 274, 9. (2) *to elect to an office* :—Þā sylfan him prāfostscīre betǣhtan þe þæne abbod tō abbodhāde gecuran (-cor-, *v. l.*) (*ab eis qui abbatem ordinant*), R. Ben. 124, 17. II. *to accept*. (1) *to accept after deliberation* or *examination*, *approve* a law, regulation, &c., *decide*. (a) of those who make a law :—Þis syndon þā dōmas ðe Ælfrēd cyncg geceás (cf. þā ðe mē ryhteste ðūhton, ic þā hēron gegaderode, and þā ōðre forlēt, 46, 22), Ll. Lbmn. 17, 2. Dis syndon þā dōmas þe Ælfrēd cyncg and Gūðrum cyncg gecuran, Ll. Th. i. 166, 5. Gecuran and gecwǣdon, 7 ; 314, 3. Dis is seó gerǣdnes þe Engla cyng and . . . witan gecuran and gerǣddan, 304, 4. Swā gōde laga swā hȳ betste gecuron, 276, 18. Gebēte þæt swā scīre witan geceósan, Wlfst. 172, 4. Ic hæbbe gecoren and mīne witan hwæt seó steór beón mæge, Ll. Th. i. 276, 30. Sēe Eádweardes mæssedæg witan habbað gecoren þ man freólsian sceal on .xv. kal. Aprilis, 308, 20. Se cyng and his witan habbað gecoren and gecwēden þ . . ., 342, 6. (b) of those subject to a law :—Eádgāres lage þe ealle men habbað gecoren and tō gesworen, Cht. E. 231, 4. Wille ic þ symble mid eów gehealden sȳ þe gē tō friðes bōte gecoren hæfdon, Ll. Th. i. 278, 2. (2) *to accept* a condition :—Hē eall þ lǣste þ uncer formǣl wæs þā ic tō him gebeáh and his willan geceás (*became his vassal*), Ll. Th. i. 178, 9. Wið þām þe heó his (*the suitor's*) willan geceóse *if she decide to marry within the year*, 416, 8. III. *to try* (?) :—On .xxii. and .xxiii. nihta seó mǣtincg bið gecornes and gesiftnes and eall costunge full ; ne bið þ nā gōd swefen (*the dream is full of trial and strife*), Lch. iii. 156, 7.

ge-ceówan. *Add* :—Æscþrotu gecowen on mūþe and āwringen þurh clāð, Lch. ii. 36, 19.

ge-cēpan ; *p.* te *To be on the look-out for* a person (*gen.*) :—Hī nān ōþer ðing nyston, buton þ se cāsere hēte heora gecēpan, Hml. S. 23, 444. v. cēpan ; VII. 1 a.

ge-cerran, -cerring. v. ge-cirran, -cirring.

ge-cīd, es ; *m. n.?* l. *n.*, and add : I. *strife, contention, quarrel* :—Gecīd *lis*, Wrt. Voc. ii. 94, 13 : 50, 28. Gefiit and gecīd *divortium*, 58, 26. Gyf him þince þ hē geseó fela fugla ætsamne, þ byð æfest and gecīd (gefiit and cīd, *v. l.*), Lch. iii. 168, 17. þ byð gecīd wyð his freónd, 172, 31. Gecygde (-ciid, *v. l.*) ond gefiite *litigio, contentioni*, Bd. 1, 14 ; Sch. 38, 24. Hē ongan him symble andswarian mid gecīde (*cum jurgio*), Gr. D. 64, 34. Dā lēgo giciidana (-ara ?) *flammas litium*, Rtl. 167, 18. Tō gemōtum and tō gecīdum (*in rixas*) gē fæstað, Past. 315, 4. Hié styrigað gefiitu and geciid *rixae occasionem commovent*, 293, 21. Ne sceal mon nāne gefiytu ne gecīd ūp āhebban, Ll. Th. ii. 438, 31. Wyrignyssa and gecȳd *maledicta et jurgia*, 224, 31. II. *chiding, reproof* :—Gif hwylcum brēþer byþ gecīd (mid gecīde, *v. l.*) oþþe gestȳred *si quis frater corripitur quolibet modo*, R. Ben. 131, 1. v. next word.

ge-cīdan. I. *to dispute*. v. Dict. II. *to chide, reprove* (with dat.) :—Đurh ðone wītgan wæs gecīd (-cīdd, *v. l.*) hierdum *pastores increpat per prophetam*, Past. 123, 9. Gif hwylcum brēþer for ænigum litlum gylte byþ gecīd oþþe gestȳred fram his abbode *si quis frater pro quavis minima causa ab abbate suo corripitur*, R. Ben. 131, 1.

ge-cīgan. *Dele passage* Ph. 454, *and add* : I. *intrans. To call, cry out, exclaim* :—Gicēgde (geceigede, L.) stefne micler *exclamauit uoce magna*, Lk. R. 1, 42. Geceigdon, ðus cueðende *clamauerunt, dicentes*, Mt. L. 8, 29. Fore fyrhtnise geceigdon, 14, 26. I a. *to call to* a person, *invite* :—Gecīg ðē tō þīnum frȳnd, Ap. Th. 16, 13. Cf. Cēgde heó tō eallum þǣm apostolum on hīre hordcofan *uocauit omnes apostolos in cubiculo suo*, Bl. H. 143, 33. II. *trans. To call* a person, *summon, bid come*, (with acc.) :—Ic gecǣge mīne englas, Bl. H. 183, 4. Geceigdon aldro his *uocauerunt parentes eius*, Jn. L. 9, 18. ' Hāt clypigan ðā apostlas.' Hī wurdon hrædlīce gecīgde, Hml. Th. ii. 488, 23. Wēron geceigd twelfe ðegnas his *conuocatis duodecim discipulis suis*, Mt. L. 10, 1. (β) with dat. :—Geceiged ł geceigide (gicēgde, R.) frióndum and nēhebūrum *conuocat amicos et uicinos*, Lk. L. 15, 6. Hē hēht geceiga ðǣm esnum ł ðā esnas *iussit uocari seruos*, 19, 15. (I a) *to call to* be a guest, *to invite*. (a) with acc. :—Sē ðe ðec and hine geceiged ł geceigide (gicēged, R.), in gelaþode, W. S.) *qui te et illum uocauit*, Lk. L. 14, 9. (β) with dat. :—Mið ðȳ ðū dōest gebǣrscip geceig (gicēg, R.) ðorfendum, unhālum *uoca pauperes, debiles*, Lk. L. 14, 13. (γ) uncertain :—Tō geladðian and gecīgean *adsciscere* (-ier, MS.), Wrt. Voc. ii. 9, 30. Gecīed *asciscebatur*, An. Ox. 2533. (1 b)

to call as a follower, *bid* a person *come to hear, obey*, &c. :—Se mildheorta God tō him þā þe him wurðe beóð gecȳgð, Hml. S. 30, 18. Ic geceide *uocaui*, Kent. Gl. 10. Ne cuōm ic geceige sōðfeaste, Mt. L. 9, 13. Sē ðe ongiete ðæt hē sié geceiged (-cigged, *v. l.*) mid godcundre stemne, Past. 379, 19. Monigo sint geceiged (gecǣged, R.), Mt. L. 20, 16. (1 c) *to call* to a work, duty, &c. :—Ealle tō geþeahte gecīan wē secgat *omnes ad consilium uocari diximus*, R. Ben. I. 17, 17. Habbað eów mid . . . swā fela lǣwedra tō þǣm gecȳdra hȳ hié þ hālige gerȳne ārwurðlīce mid eów brēman mægen, Ll. Th. ii. 404, 28. (1 d) *to call* to a condition, course of life, *bring* to a state :—Hē þ folc . . . tō ðām heofonlican gecīgde and geladðode, Bd. 4, 28 ; Sch. 525, 5. Wē sind āsende tō gecīgenne mancynn fram deáðe tō līfe, nā tō scūfenne fram līfe tō deáðe, Hml. Th. ii. 488, 30. þ Maria sȳ gecēged tō deáþe, Bl. H. 145, 9. Eft gecīged beón tō hlūttornesse geleáfan *ad simplicitatem fidei reuocari*, Bd. 2, 5 ; Sch. 136, 3. (2) *to call* so as to attract attention, *address* a person :—Gecēgde hine stefn of heofenum, Bl. H. 187, 5. Stefn cwæð, ' Cum, Anastasius,' and þā him swā gecīgdum þǣr wǣron eác ōþre vii brōþru be naman gecīgde . . . seó stefn eft gecīgde þone eahtoþan brōður . . . seó gesomnung eall gehȳrde þā stefne, þā næs nǣnig tweó þþ hit neálæhte þāra forðfōre þe þǣr gecīgde wǣron, Gr. D. 52, 22–34. Hē gecīgde þone hālgan man be his naman, and se hālga wer nolde andswarian, 122, 13. Geciwde (=-cīgde?) *compellat. i. alloquitur*, Germ. 397, 400. (3) *to call* as a suppliant, *call on, invoke* :—Hē him Dryhten gecȳgð on fultum, Ph. 454. Ealle þā þe mǣrsiað heora gemynd, and hī gecīgað tō fultume, Hml. S. 30, 470. (3 a) *to invoke* a person's name :—Gif þū on īdelnesse cīgst (gecȳgst, *v. l.*) mīnne noman, Ll. Th. i. 44, 8. (4) *to provoke* :—Gē ȳldran, ne sceolan gē eówru bearn tō yrsunge geciégean, Ll. Th. i. 430, 39. III. *trans. To call, name*. (1) *to call* a person or thing so and so :—Ænne of tuoelfum diúbul geceiges (*appellat*), Jn. p. 5, 3. God gecīgde (*uocauit*) þā drīgnisse eorðan and þǣra wætera gegaderunga hē hēt (*appellauit*) sǣs, Gen. 1, 10. þā gin[g]ran þā yldran ārwurðe hī gecīan *juniores priores suos nonnos uocent*, R. Ben. I. 106, 2. Hē sceolde beón Nazarēnisc gecīged, Hml. Th. i. 88, 26. Bið geceid sunu Godes, Lk. L. 1, 35. Gecēd, Lk. p. 5, 11. Wē beóð Godes hūs gecīgede, Hml. Th. ii. 582, 15. Gecǣgede, Bl. H. 47, 5. (2) *to call* by a name :—Geceige hine noma fadores his *uocant eum nomine patris eius*, Lk. L. 1, 59. Ne ænig is sē ðe geceiged (gicēged, R.) ðisum noma, 61. Se sunu wæs geciged þæs fæder naman, Hml. L. i. 478, 11. Hē ðōran naman wæs gecīged Godwine, Chr. 984 ; P. 124, 4. (3) *to call* a name :—Hiá geceiges noma his . . . *uocabunt nomen ejus Emmanuhel*, Mt. L. 1, 23. Dū gicēg noma his Iōhannes, Lk. R. 1, 13.

ge-cīgednes. *Dele second passage, and add* : I. *a call, summons* :—Seó stefn sume hwīle geswigode tō his gecīgednysse and hine eft genemde, Gr. D. 53, 8. v. ge-cīgan ; II. 2. II. *a name* or *appellation* :—Gecīednysse *uocabulo, i. nomine*, An. Ox. 1503.

ge-cīgnes. *Substitute* : *A call, summons* :—Oð ðæne dæg his gecīgnesse of middangearde *usque ad diem suae uocationis*, Bd. 5, 12 ; Sch. 634, 7. Ofer mīnre gecīgnesse þū gesettest ealle þīne apostlas tō mīnre byrgenne *on the occasion of my call* (*when the time of my death was announced to me*), *thou didst appoint all thy apostles to attend my burial* (cf. Maria . . . þū bist ǣr þrim dagum genumon of þīnum līchoman, and ealle Drihtnes apostolas beóþ sende þē tō bebyrgenne, 137, 24–27), Bl. H. 143, 29.

ge-cīgung, e ; *f. A calling, invocation* :—Bletsien hī hī selfe mid Crīstes rōde tācene þurh gecīginge þǣre hālgan þrynnysse, Nap. 28. Giceigingcum ūsum *invocationibus nostris*, Rtl. 97, 37. v. on-gegung.

ge-cīlcan *to whitewash* :—Gelīco gié sint byrgennum oferhīudum ł ūta gecēlcad *similes estis sepulchris dealbatis*, Mt. L. 23, 27. [O. L. Ger. gi-kelkian.] Cf. nīw-cilct.

gecile. v. gicel : ge-cīpan. *Take here* ge-cēpan *and* ge-cȳpan *in Dict., and add* : [O. H. Ger. ge-kaufen *emere*.]

ge-cīpe ; *adj. For sale* :—Ðǣr (*in the temple*) wǣron gecȳpe hrȳðeru and scēp and culfran. On ðām dagum . . . man offrode hrȳðeru . . . ; ðā tihte seó gītsung þā sācerdas þæt man ðillic orf þǣr tō ceápe hæfde, Hml. Th. i. 406, 17 : 412, 1.

ge-cirpsian *to curl* :—Gecyrpsudum *crispo*, Germ. 394, 284.

ge-cirran. *Take here* ge-cerran, ge-cyrran *in Dict., and add* :
A. *trans*. I. of actual movement. (1) *to turn, turn back, change the direction of motion of*, (a) a living creature :—Isaias wæs āwæg farende, ac God hine gecyrde, Hml. S. 18, 422. Se cyningc hȳ gecyrran wolde eft tō Egyptum, Ors. 1, 7 ; S. 38, 23. (a) *to repulse* an advancing enemy (lit. and fig.) :—Hē ofercuōm ł gecerde (*Iudaeos*) *conuincit*, Mk. p. 4, 19. Men þe þis land bewiston him fyrd ongeán sændon, and hine gecyrdon, Chr. 1091 ; P. 226, 27. Dǣr weard se cyng of France þurh gesmeáh gecyrred, and seó fyrding tēhwearf, 1094 ; P. 229, 29. (b) a thing :—Seó strǣl weard eft gecyrred, and þone mon, þe heó ǣr from sended wæs, sceát, Bl. H. 199, 22. (2) *where motion has been caused, to replace, return* to a former position :—Gecerr (-cer, R.) suord in stōwe his *converte gladium in locum suum*, Mt. L. 26, 52. Hæfde Metod ēgstreám eft gecyrred, Gen. 1415. (3) *to go to* a person, *visit* :

—Mē gedafeniđ þæt ic tō dæg þē gecyrre (*hodie in domo tua oportet me manere*, Lk. 19, 5), Hml. Th. i. 580, 34. Hī eft hine ne gecyrdon, Hml. Th. i. 82, 10. Đā tungelwītegan þone cyning gecyrdon, 108, 28 : 110, 3. Hī noldon đone rēđan cwellere eft gecyrran, 80, 26. (4) *to change the direction of* a body at rest :—Wendaþ mīn heáfod ofdūne ... mīn heáfod sceal beón on eorþan gecyrred, Bl. H. 191, 6.         II. *to cause to feel* or *act, to move* :—Miđ hreáwnisse gecerred *poenitentia motus*, Mt. L. 21, 29. Miđ miltheortnise gecerred *misericordia motus*, Lk. L. 7, 13 : 10, 33 : 15, 20.         III. *to direct the course of action* of a person to or from an object, *induce to adopt* or *abandon* :—Hē hī gecyrde tō Crīstes geleáfan, Chr. 565 ; P. 19, 6. Hē þā munecas on ryht gecierde, þæt hié Eástron on ryht heóldon (gecyrde tō rihtum Eástrum, *v. l.*), 716 ; P. 42, 15. Gecerde *correxit* i. *convertit* (*Romam a funesto ritu*), An. Ox. 2069. Gecærred tō geleáfa Crīstes, Mk. p. 1, 6.         IV. *to direct* to an end, *turn* on an object to be considered :—Oft sió hǣlo đæs līchoman on unđeáwas wearđ gecierred (-cirred, *v. l.*) *plerumque accepta salus carnis per vitia expenditur*, Past. 251, 10. þā þe on heora heortan and on willan on God gecyrred wǣron, Bl. H. 133, 25.         V. *to turn* a person to another. (1) with idea of submission, devotion, *to make a subject* or *an adherent* to :—þone mǣstan dǣl hié geridon and him tō gecirdon (þ folc hym tō gebīgde, *v. l.*), Chr. 878 ; P. 74, 27. Weorđađ monige æfter đæs līchoman scylde tō Gode gecerred, Past. 411, 2. þā sind tō Crīste gecirde, Ll. Th. i. 56, 12. (2) with idea of kindness, favour :—þ hē fædera heortan tō heora bearnum gecyrre (-cerre, L. R.), Lk. 1, 17.         VI. *to turn, change* :—Đā đoht gesēgon gecerde *quae sensum uidebantur mutare*, Mt. p. 2, 17. Geóguđ is gecyrred, El. 1265.         VI a. of moral or spiritual change, as a theological term, *to convert* :—Se gecyrreda sceađa, Hml. Th. ii. 124, 32. Būton gē beón gecyrrede (-cerred, L.) and gewordene swā swā lytlingas, Mt. 18, 3.         VI b. *to turn* into, *convert* :—þ wæter gecerde in wīn *aquam conuertit in uinum*, Jn. p. 3, 11. þyses fýres hǣto sý gecyrred on wǣtne deáw, Hml. S. 30, 441; Guth. 88, 14. Nama wæs gecyrred on þæt betere, El. 1061. Hē biđ gecirred (-cierred, *v. l.*) tō āre, Past. 269, 2. Hī synd gecyrrede tō heora gecynde, Hml. Th. i. 68, 29.         VI c. *to turn* into another language, *translate* :—In Grēcisc sprēc gecerred *in Graecam linguam uersa*, Mt. p. 2, 4.         B. *intrans.* I. of movement (lit. or fig.) (1) *to turn, go, come* :—Ǣlc healde his endebyrdnysse, swā swā hē tō mynstre cōm, swylce ic þus cweđe : ' Gif twēgen on ānum dæge tō mynstre gecyrrađ,' R. Ben. 114, 13. Hī tō đām cilde gecyrdon, Hml. Th. i. 108, 29. þā wīf ealle tōgædere gecirdon *the women all came together*, Ors. 1, 10 ; S. 46, 5. (1 a) *to return* :—Đonne hē gecerres (*reuertatur*) from symblum, Lk. L. 12, 36. Seó sib gecyrđ tō đām bydele, Hml. Th. ii. 534, 13. Hē on hine seolfne gecerde *in se reuersus*, Lk. L. 15, 17. Miđ đý gecerde of londe *regresso de agro*, 17, 7. Hē eft tō Cantwarebiri gecyrde, Chr. 995 ; P. 131, 25. Gecyrde hē ongeán, Hml. Th. i. 60, 6. Hī gecyrdon him hām, ii. 518, 30. Gecyrr hām, i. 60, 17. Gecyr tō Ezechian, Hml. S. 18, 423. Betere đæt hī đone weg ne ongeáten, đonne hī underbæc gecerden ..., Past. 445, 33. Hit wǣre nyttre tō gecyrrenne, Bt. 40, 5 ; F. 240, 20. Gecearredo uēron ł gecerred wæs ēghuelc in hūs hiora, Jn. L. 7, 53. (1 b) *to go* to a person as a guest :—Hē tō menn synfullum gecerde *ad hominem peccatorem divertisset*, Lk. L. 19, 7. (2) of change of attitude, *to turn* :—Đe Hǣlend gecerde *Iesus conuersus*, Mt. L. R. 9, 22. Hē gecerde ymb *conuersus*, Mk. L. R. 8, 33. Gecerdo *conuersi*, Mt. L. 7, 6.         II. *to come to a condition, arrive at* :—Hēr cuōm micel sciphere on West-Wealas, and hié tō ānum gecierdon (*the Danes and Welsh came to an agreement*), Chr. 835 ; P. 62, 16. Drihten wile þ ealle men sýn hāle and gesunde, and tō þon andgite gecyrran, Bl. H. 107, 18. On wrǣđo gecerred wæs *he had gone mad* ; in furorem uersus est, Mk. L. 3, 21.         III. *to turn* (a) *to action, attempt to do, set about, perform* :—Monige men tō dǣdbóte and tō andetnesse gecyrraþ, Bl. H. 65, 7 : 129, 23. Đā yfelan ongitaþ hyra yfel and gecierrađ (-cyrraþ, *v. l.*) tō goode, Bt. 38, 3 ; F. 202, 15. Hié tō þām gecirdon þæt hié wiþ þone here winnende wǣrun *they set about fighting with the Danes*, Chr. 867 ; P. 68, 21. Buton heora hwelc eft tō rihtre bóte gecirre, Bt. 3, 1 ; F. 6, 5 : Ll. Th. i. 196, 3. (b) *from action, to desist* from, *cease to do* :—þ hē fram synnan gecyrre, Ll. Th. i. 326, 8. þeówdōme gecyrrendum *ex seruitio conuertenti*, R. Ben. I. 13, 17. þ wē ealle fram synnum gecyrran þæs þe wē dōn magan, 314, 6. (c) *to turn* from one to another :—Gif hwā wille fram unrihte gecyrran eft tō rihte, Ll. Th. i. 410. 21.         IV. *to turn* to, *give assent to, be favourably disposed* to :—Āhyld mīne heortan þæt ic on þīne gewitnysse gecyrre *inclina cor meum in testimonia tua*, Ps. Th. 118, 36. Wē nellaþ gecyrran tō his onsægednyssum, Hml. S. 28, 50. Hē sende Scottum gewrit þ hī scoldon gecerran tō rihtum Eástrum, Chr. 627 ; P. 25, 29.         V. *to turn for hel[p] to, have recourse to* :—þæt hē gecyrre tō þām sēlran and tō þon sōþon lǣcedōme, Bl. H. 107, 15.         VI. *to turn* to a person, *be favourably disposed to*. (1) *to be gracious* :—Ic tō eów mid siblufan gecyrre, Reb. 8. Ic þe bidde þ þū mē eallunga tō gecyrre, Angl. xii. 512, 35. (2) *to make submission* :—Ǣlc healde his endebyrdnesse swā hē gecyrde ... Gif twēgen on ānum dæge tō Gode

gecyrrađ ..., R. Ben. 115, 10–13.         VII. *to turn, change* :—Se wlite tō ylde gecyrreþ, Bl. H. 59, 7. Gecerređ īsmere on his āgen gecynd, weorþeđ tō wætere, Met. 28, 61.         VII a. of spiritual change, *to be converted* :—Se cining gecerde and wearđ gefullod, Chr. 616 ; P. 23, 24. Hweþer hié gecyrran woldan, oþþe ǣnige dǣdbóte dōn þæs mānes þe hié wiđ heora Dryhten gedydon, Bl. H. 79, 5.

**ge-cirredness.** *Take here* ge-cyrredness *in Dict., and add* : I. *a going to a place, the going* of a monk to a monastery. [Cf. tō mynstre gecyrran, R. Ben. 114, 13.] :—Sȳ swylcera gebyrda oþþe gecyrrednesse swylce hē sȳ (*whatever his birth or the time of his coming to the monastery*), sȳ hē gemedemad on stede swā swā his gecerrednes sȳ, R. Ben. 12, 20–13, 2 : 107, 10–11. Healde hē simle þone styde his gecyrrednesse *locum illum semper attendat quo ingressus est in monasterio*, 113, 5. Ǣlc endebyrdnys on mynstre sceal beón gehealden be heora gecyrrednysse (*according to the date of entrance*), 112, 23.         II. *conversion* :—Ōswold hine tō fulluhte nam, fægen his gecyrrednysse, Hml. S. 26, 133. Se deófol nam graman ongeán þone Godes man for þæs folces gecyrrednysse fram his fūlum biggengum, 29, 185. Geefenslæce hē Paules gecyrrednysse, Hml. Th. i. 56, 24 : 578, 30. Mid sōđre gecyrrednysse Dryhten gesēcan, Hml. A. 53, 82. þeóda gecyrrednesse *gentium conuersionem*, An. Ox. 40, 4.

**ge-cirring,** e; *f.* A *turning* [v. ge-cirran ; A. I. 1 a] :—On gecyrrincge feónd mīnue on bæcling *in conuertendo inimicum meum retrorsum*, Ps. L. 9, 4.

**ge-clǣman.** *Add* : Geclǣmede *inlita*, Germ. 390, 43.

**ge-clǣnian.** *Add* : , ge-clāsnian.         I. *to cleanse* an object from impurity (*gen.* or *prep.*). (1) physical :—Gold womma gehwylces geclǣnsod, El. 1311. Seolfur earđau geclāsnad *argentum terrae purgatum*, Ps. Srt. 11, 7. (2) *to cleanse* from sin, *purify* from evil :—Dryhten geclāsnađ (*mundet*) sāwle his, Ps. Srt. 40, 3. From scyld mīnre geclāsna mec, 50, 4. þ wē ūre mód geclǣnsian from yfelum wordum, Bl. H. 39, 3. Ūre heortan geclǣnsian from ōþrum geþōhtum, 21, 4. Geclǣnsod *lustratus*, Wrt. Voc. ii. 50, 26 : El. 1035 : Ps. C. 74. Wyrđ hē eallra synna geclǣnsod, Past. 413, 31. Fulwihtes geryne wē sȳn geclǣnsude, An. Ox. 40, 18. (3) *to clear, prove innocent* of a charge :—þā witan gerehton þæt heó sceolde hire fæder hand geclǣnsian ... and heó ... geclǣnsude hire fæder þæs ǣgiftes (*she cleared her father of the charge that he had not repaid the money*), Cht. Th. 201, 33–202, 6. Hē hine ǣlces þinges geclǣnsode þe him mann onsǣde, Chr. 1022 ; P. 157, 5. Gif man esne tihte, his dryhten hine his āne ađe geclǣnsie (-clēnsige, 12), Ll. Th. i. 42, 7. Geswicne (geclēnsie, *v. l.*) sē hine, 110, 16 : 112, 3 : 134, 12. Būton hē hine mid fulre lāde wiđ mē geclǣnsian mæge, Cht. E. 231, 2.         II. *to remove impurity* from an object :—Wē oft āgyltađ ; þonne sculon wē on þǣre forhæfdnesse ... þ geclǣnsian, Bl. H. 35, 17.         v. un-geclǣnsod.

**ge-clǣnsung.** *Add* : Giclēnsunge, Rtl. 16, 35.

**ge-clāpian ;** *p.* ode To *clothe*. v. ge-clāded *in Dict.* : ge-cleofian. v. ge-clifian : ge-cleopung. v. ge-clipung : ge-clibs. v. ge-clips.

**ge-clifian.** *Take here* ge-cleofian *in Dict., and add* : (1) *to stick* to (tō *or dat.*) :—Gecleofige tunge mīn gōmum mīnum *adhaereat lingua mea faucibus meis*, Ps. L. 136, 6. Deós wyrt wyle hrædlīce tō đām men geclyfan, Lch. i. 306, 4. Mīn tunge ys gecleofod (*adhaesit*) tō mīnum gōmum, Ps. Th. 21, 13. (1 a) *to stick* together :—Hió gedeþ þ flǣsc tōgædere geclifađ, Lch. i. 134, 13. Þ tōgædere gecligen (-clifian, *v. l.*), 316, 1. (2) *to stick* on :—Geclyfode on eorđan innođ ūre *adhesit in terra uenter noster*, Ps. Rdr. 43, 25. Þ þǣr nǣre nān þing on þǣre stōwe þe se stāntorr on geclyfian mihte (*quo inhaerere potuisset*), Gr. D. 12, 19.

**ge-cliht.** v. ge-clyccan : **ge-clingan.** v. ge-clungen.

**ge-clipian.** *Take here* ge-clypian *in Dict., and add* : I. *intrans.* (1) *to call out, cry, exclaim* :—Gecliopade (*clamavit*) đe Hǣlend stefne micle, Mt. L. 27, 46 : Mk. L. 10, 48. Gecliopade fæder *exclamans pater*, 9, 24 : Lk. L. 4, 33 : 9, 38. (2) *to call* so as to attract attention, *call* to a person :—Đā đe gecliopadon efnum aldum *clamantis coaequalibus*, Mt. L. 11, 16.         II. *trans.* (1) *to announce loudly, declare* :—Đæt hē sumne hearm geswigode đǣr đǣr hē freme gecleopian (-clipian, *v. l.*) meahte, Past. 49, 22. (2) *to call* a person, *bring by calling* :—Gecliopad wæs þ folc (tōgædere geclypedre menegu, W. S.) *conuocata turba*, Mk. L. 8, 34. (3) *to call, name* :—An þǣre stōwe þe ys geclyped (is genemned, *v. l.*) Sælesberi, Chr. 552 ; P. 60, 7. Eádmund ... Irensīd wæs geclypod for his snellscipe, 1057 ; P. 187, 36. Wyrđe þæt ic sē gicliopad ērendwraca *dignus uocari apostolus*, Rtl. 60, 7. Is geclioppad *appellatur*, 43, 37.

**ge-clips** *clamour* :—Geclibs *clamor*, Past. 222, 9. Ne wend þū þe on þæs folces unrǣd ..., on heora sprǣce and geclysp (-clæsp, -clebs, -cleps, *v. ll.*), Ll. Th. i. 54, 7. Geclibs forlǣtan, Past. 222, 13.

**ge-clipung,** e; *f.* A *calling, cry, an appeal* :—Gecleopunga þearfan *deprecationem pauperis*, Ps. L. 21, 25.

**ge-clofa,** an; *m.* A *duplicate charter* :—þysses gewrites geclofan nam Ǣlfhere tō swytelunga, C. D. B. iii. 547, 12. [þisses iwrites icloua (idoua, MS.) is on Cridiamtone mid hure elder boken, Cht. E. 422, 20.]

**ge-clūtod.** *For second passage substitute :*—Gesceód mid geclūtedum (*behammenum, v. l.*) scōn *clavatis calceatus caligis*, Gr. D. 37, 13.

**ge-clyccan ;** *p.* -clyhte ; *pp.* -clyht *To bend, incurve* the hand :—Nā sȳ āstreht hand þīn tō nimene ; heó sȳ tō syllene gecliht *non sit porrecta manus tua ad captandum ; sit ad dandum collecta*, Scint. 99, 2. v. clyccan.

**ge-clyft** *cleft, split* :—Geclyfte *sectilem*, Germ. 393, 152. [Cf. *O. H. Ger.* kluftig *fissilis* : *Ger.* klüftig.]

**ge-clystre, es ;** *n. A bunch of grapes* :—Geclystre *butros*, Wrt. Voc. i. 285, 73 : ii. 11, 31. Geclystre *botyrum*, Ps. Srt. ii. 193, 1. Þ tō lāfe wunodon swȳþe feáwa geclystru þāra wīnbyrgena *ut rari racemi remanerent*, Gr. D. 57, 9. Hē eóde in þone wīngeard and gesomnode þā geclystru þāra byrgena . . . hē hēt hine wringan þā feáwa geclystru þāra byrgena, and hē of đām ylcan geclystrum ūt āþȳde lytelne dǽl wīnes, 58, 9–20.

**ge-cnǽwe.** *Add :* , -cnāwe. **I.** of persons. (1) *acknowledging the accuracy* of a statement :—' Þis gewrit is gefylled.' And hig ealle wǽron þæs gecnāwe, Lk. 4, 22. (2) *acknowledging the justice* of a charge that is or may be made, *making confession* of sin. (a) with gen. :—Nū cȳdde mē man þet Aðelwold and ic sceoldon ofneádian þā bōc . . . Nū ne eom ic nānre neáde gecnǽwe, Cht. Th. 296, 1. Hī feóllon tō his fótum āfyrhte, gecnǽwe heora gyltes (cf. wǽron andettende þ hī gegylt hæfdon *se deliquisse confessi sunt*, Gr. D. 127, 17), Hml. Th. ii. 168, 7. Hī þær wunedon, gecnǽwe heora synna, Hml. A. 102, 15. (b) with clause :—Ic ne eom gecnǽwe þ ic ǽnigean menn geáfe þā sōcne . . . gyf ǽnig mann secge þ ic hig ǽr him geunnan sceolde . . . ; C. D. iv. 222, 27. Hē ođsōc þ hē hit wǽre. Hī þā ongēn hine gecnǽwne gedydon (*made him confess*) . . . þ hē hit wæs, Hml. S. 30, 274. (3) *cognizant* of :—Ðyssa þinga is gecnǽwe ǽlc dohtig man on Kænt, Cht. Th. 313, 18. Se cing cwæđ þ Leófsige and mænige men đǽre spǽce gecnǽwe wǽron, 540, 12. **II.** of things, *acknowledged, recognized* as valid :—Hit wæs gecnǽwe on Sūđ-Seaxan and on West-Seaxan, Cht. Th. 273, 19.

**ge-cnāwan.** *Add :* **I.** *to recognize, identify* an object :—Mid đām þe þ mōd wiþ his bewende, đā gecneów hit swīþe sweotele his āgne mōdor, Bt. 3, 1 ; F. 4, 29. Eft hine gecneów ōđer þīnen, Mk. 14, 69. Beheóld hē hī and gecneów hī be hyre wlite, Hml. S. 30, 363. Hēlias cōm, and hig hyne ne gecneówon (*cognouerunt*), Mt. 17, 12. Þā wurdon hyra eágan geopenude, and hig gecneówon hine, Lk. 24, 31. Heó helode hire nebb, þæt hē hig ne mihte gecnāwan (*ne agnosceretur*), Gen. 38, 15. Gif þū nū sweotole gecnāwan miht đā anlīcnessa þǽre gesǽlþe, đonne is þearf þ ic þe hī selfe getǽce, Bt. 33, 1 ; F. 118, 3. Hī hī gecnāwan mōston, þ hī gebrōđra synd, Hml. S. 30, 377. **II.** *to acknowledge,* (1) a person :—Hē wæs tō cinge ongyten and gehered, ge of cilda mūþe gecnāwen and weorþad, Bl. H. 71, 33. (1 a) where a payment is made as acknowledgement :—Ys đis seó oncnāwennis đe hē hæfđ God mid gecnāwen . . . on circlicum mādmum, Cht. Th. 429, 8. (2) a claim, *to pay by way of acknowledgement.* v. ge-cnāwness :—Man sceal for Godes ege mǽđe on hāde gecnāwan (*pay respect to the clergy*), Ll. Th. i. 362, 5. Gebyređ þ man his geswinces leán gecnāwe on đām endum đe tō efenlǽse licgan, 440, 12. **III.** *to know, be acquainted with* :—Hié hæfdon mīne ǽ, and hī mē ne gecniówon (-cnēwon, *v. l.*) *tenentes legem nescierunt me*, Past. 29, 1. **IV.** *to know, be conversant with* a subject :—Sē þe Godes bebodu ne gecnǽwđ *hic, qui ea quae sunt Domini nescit*, Past. 29, 1. **V.** *to have a clear apprehension* of :—Mon mæg sweotole ongitan, þ ǽlc mon đæs wilnaþ, þ hē mæge þ hēhste gōd begitan, đǽr hī hit gecnāwan mihtan, Bt. 24, 4 ; F. 86, 35. Sió ungleáwnes biþ on þe selfum, þ đū hit ne canst on riht gecnāwan, 39, 40 ; F. 226, 34. **VI.** *to be cognizant of* a fact, *understand* :—Gecnāwađ (cf. understandaþ, 7) þæt sōđ is, đeós woruld is on ofste, Wlfst. 154, 4. Wē habbađ þurh Godes yrre bysmor gelōme, gecnāwe sē đe cunne, 159, 2 : 162, 2. Þær gewitnysse biđ and man gecnāwan can þ hær bregde biđ, Ll. Th. i. 390, 11. Wē on þām gecnāwan magon þ þeós world is scyndende and heononweard, Bl. H. 115, 19. **VI a.** with dependent question :—Swā blinde þ hī on breóstum ne magon gecnāwan (cf. hī nyton, Bt. 32, 3 ; F. 118, 22) hwǽr þā ēcan gōd sindon gehȳdda, Met. 19, 31. **VII.** *to make known, declare* :—Gyf ǽnig mann sȳ þ . . . secge þ ic hig ǽr him geunnan sceolde, ic wylle þ hē cume beforan mē mid his sweotelunge and dōme gecnāwe hwǽr ic hig him ǽr geūđe, C. D. iv. 222, 32. v. un-gecnāwen.

**ge-cnāwness, e ;** *f. An acknowledgement.* v. ge-cnāwan ; **II.** 2 :—Nū dōđ hig æt ǽlcum heorđe tō gecnāwnisse þām canonicon ānne penig tō Eástron ǽlce geáre, Cht. Th. 609, 7. [Cf. þu seist þ on Gode bileuest, and dost cnownesse þ he is þi louerd, O. E. Hml. ii. 25, 4.]

**ge-cneátian ;** *p.* ode *To make clear, explain, investigate* :—Oþ inwyrde swētnesse *ad medullam enucleata* i. *inuestigata (manifestata, aperta*, Hpt. Gl. 410, 30), An. Ox. 176.

**ge-cnedan.** *Add :*—Gecneden *conspersam*, Wrt. Voc. ii. 15, 42. *Malagma, quod sine igne maceretur et comprehendetur ; maceretur autem* gecneden biđ *sive gebered* biđ, 58, 55. Gecnūwa wiđ buteran swīđe wel, lege neahterne swā gecneden, Lch. ii. 94, 7. [*O. H. Ger.* ge-knetan *interere* ; *pp.* ge-knetan *conspersus, defricatus.*]

**ge-cneord.** *Add :*—þ hē folc Drihtne geornfullīce gestrȳnde, and embe þā gestreón swīþe gecneord wǽre, Lch. iii. 434, 10. Būton ōđrum trahtbōcum đe hē mid gecneordum andgite deópđancollīce āsmeáde, Hml. Th. i. 436, 19. Ā swā hē gecneordra swā biđ hē weorđra, Angl. ix. 260, 19.

**ge-cneordlǽcan.** *Add :*—Ic gecnyrdlǽce (-cneord-, -cnerd-, *v. ll.*) *studeo*, Ælfc. Gr. 154, 5. (1) *to study, endeavour earnestly* :—Hycge hē and gecneordlǽce þæt hine mon lufian mǽge swīþor þonne ondrǽdan *studeat plus amari quam timeri*, R. Ben. 121, 11. Gecneordlǽcan *exercere* i. *studere (affectum erga suorum obsequia principum)*, An. Ox. 241. (2) *to study, examine carefully* :—Gecneordlǽcaþ *scrutamini*, An. Ox. 1086. (3) *to study, apply oneself to learning* :—Hē gecneordlǽhte æfter wīsra lāreówa gebisnungum (*he studied according to the examples set by wise teachers*), and gefæstnode his lāre on fæsthafelum gemynde, Hml. Th. ii. 118, 18. Tō þysum twām wīfmannum āwrāt Hieronimus menigfealde trahtbēc, for đan đe hī wǽron swīđe gecneordlǽcende on bōclicum smeágungum, i. 436, 11.

**ge-cneordlīce.** *Add :*—þā hǽđenan mid lācum heora leásra goda gecneordlīce munde bǽdon, Hml. Th. i. 504, 19. Hē Godes beboda gecneordlīce mid weorcum gefylđ, ii. 228, 24. Gecnyrdlīcost *studiosius*, Wülck. Gl. 250, 39.

**ge-cneordnes.** *Add :* (1) *desire, eagerness* :—Hī nǽron mid gecnyrdnysse ǽniges reáflāces getogen, Hml. Th. i. 586, 3. Hī gehȳraþ mid micelre gecneordnesse *audiant incredibili studio*, R. Ben. 138, 4. Gecneordnesse ł geornfulnesse, An. Ox. 295. (2) *diligence, earnest endeavour* :—Þone þe hī lufedon on līfe, þām hī woldon deádum mid menniscre gecneordnysse đenian, Hml. Th. i. 220, 32. On ǽlcum wīghūse wǽron þrittig manna feohtende mid cræfte and mid gecneordnesse farende, Hml. S. 25, 563. Þurh gecnyrdnysse hāligra gebeda, Hml. Th. i. 118, 7 : ii. 124, 26. Æfter nearođancum gecneorþnissa (*studiorum*) heora āgyld him, Ps. Rdr. 27, 4 : 98, 8. Hē forgifđ đā gāstlican geđincđu ǽlcum be his gecneordnyssum, Hml. Th. i. 346, 31. (3) *study, careful examination.* Cf. ge-cneordlǽcan, (2) :—Þyssum gecneordnessum *his argumentis*, i. *studiis*, An. Ox. 2290. Gecneordnessa, smeáunga *argumenta*, 3127. (4) *study* of a scholar :—Leorninghūses gecneor[d]nesse *gymnasii studio*, An. Ox. 3224. (4 a) *a study, a subject studied, an art practised* :—Mē āwehton þā gecneordnessa þe ic gīrstandæg gehȳrde, Ap. Th. 19, 6. Bōclicum lāreówdōmum, gecneordnessum *liberalibus studiis*, i. *exercitiis*, An. Ox. 3100. v. ungecnirdness.

**ge-cneórednis.** *Substitute : Descent, ancestry* :—Būtan gecneórednesse *sine genealogia* (*without descent*, Heb. 7, 3), An. Ox. 5096. v. cneór(e)dness.

**ge-cneórness, e ;** *f. Posterity* :—Gecyneórnessa *posteritatis*, An. Ox. 11, 113. v. cneórnis.

**ge-cneówian.** *Add :*—Se cempa gecneówode tō þām bisceope fulluhtes biddende, Hml. S. 3, 277. Betere is þæt se cāsere, þonne hē tō Rōme becymđ, þæt hē wurpe his cynehelm and gecneówige æt đæs fisceres gemynde, þonne se fiscere cneówige æt þæs cāseres gemynde, Hml. Th. i. 578, 7. Gesinge hē fiftig sealma and gecneówige æt ǽlcon heora ; and gif hē gecneówian ne mǽge, singe hundseofontig sealma *cantet quinquaginta psalmos et inter singulos eorum in genua procumbat ; si in genua procumbere nequit, septuaginta psalmos cantet*, Ll. Th. ii. 134, 37. [Cf. *O. H. Ger.* ge-chniuwen.]

**ge-cnirdness.** v. ge-cneordness : **ge-cnoden.** *l.* -cnōden, *and see* cnōdan.

**ge-cnos, es ;** *n. A knocking together, collision* :—Gecnosu *conlisiones*, Wrt. Voc. ii. 20, 45. v. ge-cnyssan.

**ge-cnucian.** *Add :*—Tabule byþ gecnucod *tabula pulsatur*, Angl. xiii. 402, 536. Tācne gecnucedum *signo pulsato*, 383, 255. Gecnucedre tabulan *pulsata tabula*, 390, 359.

**ge-cnūwian ;** *pp.* -cnūwad, -cnūad *To pound together* :—Genim rūdan and wermōd, gecnūwa and meng wiþ eced and ele, Lch. ii. 18, 6 : 12 : 19. Gecnūa on ceald wæter, 20, 3 : 94, 6 : 322, 26. Finoles wyrttruman gecnūadne, 30, 6.

**ge-cnycc.** v. -cnycc : **ge-cnyccan** (*not* ge-cnyttan).

**ge-cnyccan ;** *p.* -cnyhte ; *pp.* -cnyht *To bind together, connect* :—Unācnycendlicre sibbes bende gicnyhtest *insolubili pacis uinculo nexuisti*, Rtl. 108, 21. Gicnyht tō lufe *nexa fidei*, 109, 41. Gebundeno foet and hond gecnyht (honda gecnyted, R.) *ligatus pedes et manus institis*, Jn. L. 11, 44. v. -cnycc.

**ge-cnyclan** (-ian) ; *p. de, ede ; pp. ed To bend, crook* :—Geniclede carperrabat, Wrt. Voc. ii. 95, 48. Genicelde *carperabat*, 128, 70. Genyclede, genicldae *obuncans* (cf. *obuncabat*, i. *reflectebat* beclypte, gebīgede, An. Ox. 2956), Txts. 81, 1408. Gecnyclede, Wrt. Voc. ii. 63, 18. Geniclede *carperra*, 19, 68.

**ge-cnyllan ;** *pp.* -cnylled *To strike, ring* a bell :—Gecnilledum tācne *pulsato signo*, Angl. xiii. 382, 247. Bellan gecnylledre *campana pulsata*, 384, 274. Gecnyllendum (-edum ?) ōþrum stundum *pulsatis reliquis signis*, 380, 219.

**ge-cnyrdlǽcan.** v. ge-cneordlǽcan.

**ge-cnyssan.** *Add:* I. *to batter, dash* (of sea, tempest, &c.) (lit. or fig.):—Sē gecnyseð ða lytlan his *qui adlidet parvulos suos,* Ps. Srt. 136, 9. Þæt cinene scip gecnysed *rimosa barca (turbine) quassata,* Wrt. Voc. ii. 88, 21. Ic eom gecnyssed (-cnysed, *v. l.*) mid þām stormum þǽre strangan hreóhnesse in þām scipe mines mōdes *in naui mentis tempestatis ualidae procellae illidor,* Gr. D. 5, 19. Ic eom nū swā þ twig þ bið ācorfen of þām treówe, and āworpen on micclum ýstum and ēghwanon gecnissed, Hml. S. 30, 192.    II. *of mental distress:*—Ðū gecnysdydyst mē *allisisti me,* Ps. Spl. C. 101, 11. Hē wæs gecnyssed fram sumum geþancum, Hml. S. 23 b, 48. Gecnysyde *elisos,* Ps. Spl. C. 145, 7. [*O. H. Ger.* ge-knussen *allidere, collidere, quassare.*]

**ge-cnyttan.** *Dele first two and last two passages* (v. ge-cnyccan), *and add:*—Gecnyttan *adnecterent,* Wrt. Voc. ii. 3, 19. Gibundenne foet and honda gecnyted *ligatus pedes et manus institis,* Jn. R. 11, 44. Wǽre gecnyt *nodaretur,* An. Ox. 5005. Gecnytne *conexum,* 7, 306. Gecnyttum *nodatis,* Wrt. Voc. ii. 97, 65.

**ge-cōcnian;** *p.* ode *To season food:*—Gecōcanade cycene *condito culine (pulmentario),* Wrt. Voc. ii. 83, 28. v. cōcnung.

**ge-cōcsian;** *p.* ode *To fry, cook:*—Bān mīna swā swā on cōcerpannan gecōcsoda (*confrixa*) synd, Ps. Rdr. 101, 4. Gecōcsade, Wrt. Voc. ii. 133, 26.

**ge-coecton.** v. ge-cweccan: **ge-cǽlan.** *Dele, and see* ge-cēlan.

**ge-cōlian;** *p.* ode *To cool* (intrans.):—Hrēr tōsomne, lǽt gecōlian, Lch. ii. 354, 13.

**ge-collenferhtan** *to make void:*—Gecollenferhtaþ ł āidliaþ oþ grundweal on hire *exinanite usque ad fundamentum in ea,* Ps. L. 136, 7.

**ge-cope.** *l.* ge-cōp, *and add:*—Þ seó stōw mihte beón gecōp (*aptus*) wyrta on tō settanne, Gr. D. 49, 8. For ðǽm ðonne wē forslāwiað ðone gecōpustan tíman, ðætte wē ðonne ne beóð onǽlde mid ðǽre lustbǽrnesse ūres mōdes *ipsa quippe mentis desidia, dum congruo feruore non accenditur,* Past. 283, 2.

**ge-cōplic;** *adj. Fit, apt, suitable, opportune:*—Genōh gecōplicu wíse hī sylfe gegearwode *occasio apta se praebuit,* Gr. D. 60, 5. Gecōplice word forðstæppan of mūðe þínum þænne þū gecōplicne tíman fintst *oportuna uerba procedant ex ore tuo cum oportunum tempus inueneris,* Scint. 81, 18. v. un-gecōplic.

**ge-cōplice.** *Add:*—Hī nā seó hand and þ gewrit þæs wrítendan swā gecōplíce (cōplíce, *v. l., apte*) ne onfēngce, Gr. D. 9, 19. Þ seó stōw mihte beón gecōplíce wyrta on tō settanne, 49, 8. v. un-gecōplíce.

**ge-cor,** es; *n. Choice, decision:*—Eóuwer gecor. Gif eów huā brocie for eóuuere gecore, Txts. 436, 3–4.

**ge-corded;** *adj. Having a cord* (?):—Hacele geflenod *vel* gecorded *lacerna,* Wrt. Voc. i. 59, 22.

**ge-coren.** *Add:* (1) *distinguished, prominent:*—Hī nǽron for nānum crǽfte gecorene, būton for dyseges folces heringe, Bt. 27, 3; F. 100, 3. (1 a) *distinguished by excellence, excellent, noble:*—Se eádiga wer wæs gecoren man on godcundum dǽdum and ealra gesnyttra goldhord, Guth. 92, 16. Þāra monna mōd þe beóð on heora gecynde gecorene *praestantes natura mentes,* Bt. 18, 1; F. 60, 22. Þā feówer and twēntig gecorenra þe God heriað (cf. *vigintiquattuor seniores cantabant . . . dicentes: 'Dignus es, Domine,'* Rev. 5, 8–9), Ll. Lbmn. 415, 18. Þā æþelan, þā gecorenan *emeritos,* Wrt. Voc. ii. 32, 73. Þæt gecoreneste *lectissima* (*uirgo*), 95, 43 : 52, 66. (2) *approved, held in high esteem:*—Ðysse wyrte syndon twā cynrena . . . ōþer ys tō lǽcedōmum swýþe gecoren, Lch. i. 298, 6. (2 a) *with dat. of person approving:*—Wæs ðæt Gode swíðe gecoren man on his dǽdum, Bl. H. 211, 15. Se sunnandæg is swíðe micelum gecoren eallum Godes gesceaftum, for ðām þe hē wæs ealra daga se ǽresta, and hē bið se nēxta, Wlfst. 209, 31. Heó wǽron þā sēlestan and þā gecorenestan witan ǽgðer ge Gode ge mannum, 214, 4. (3) *beloved; dilectus:*—Eálā ðū mīn gecorena *dilecte mi,* Kent. Gl. 1125. (4) *honourable; probus:*—Gecorenum *probo* (*proco*), Wrt. Voc. ii. 95, 20. Wer gecorenne (-one, -ene, *v. ll.*) on his þeáwum *uirum probum moribus,* Bd. 3, 23; Sch. 299, 9.

**ge-cor-ness.** v. gecoren-ness: **ge-corenlíc.** *For* Cot. 74 *substitute:* Gecorenlíce *eleganti,* Wrt. Voc. ii. 30, 27: **ge-corenlíce.** *For* Cot. 77 *substitute:*—Gecorenlíce ł æþelíce *eleganter,* Wrt. Voc. ii. 31, 71.

**gecoren-ness.** *Take here* ge-corenes *in Dict., and add:*—Seó gecorennys (-corenes, *v. l.*) þǽre gefērrǽdene *electio sociorum,* R. Ben. 112, 7. Be Godes hǽse and gecorennyse, Hml. Th. i. 388, 16. Sē wæs tō cynincge āhafen swýðor for folces gecorennysse þonne ðurh Godes rǽd, Hml. S. 18, 2. Þǽr wǽron bisceopas of gehwilcum burgum tō þǽre gecorennysse, 31, 268. v. tō-gecorenness.

**ge-cost.** *Add:*—Scyttisc gecost gealdor wiþ ǽlcum āttre, Lch. ii. 10, 23. v. un-gecost.

**ge-costian.** *Add:* (1) *to try, prove, test:*—Ðā aelāruuas cunnedon ł gecostadon (*temptantes*) hine, Mk. L. 10, 2. Ðis cwæð ðæt gicostade hine, Jn. R. L. 6, 6. Ēghwelc mið fýre sié gicostad, Mk. R. 9, 49. (1 a) *to try* with inducements to evil, *to tempt:*—Þte hē woere gecostad ł gecunned (*temtaretur*) from diáble, Mt. L. 4, 1. Gecosted (-ad, R.), Lk. L. 4, 2 : Rtl. 91, 7. Gūðlāc gecostad wearð, Gū. 124. (2) *to try, vex, afflict:*—Cnæht mīn mið ysle is gecunned ł gecosted *puer meus*

*male torquetur,* Mt. L. 8, 6. Ðā ðe gecosted wēron (*uexabantur*) from gāstum unclǽnum, Lk. L. 6, 18. (3) *to prove, shew to be good:*—Þte him gicuoeme ðǽm hine gicostade *ut ei placeat cui se probavit,* Rtl. 60, 13. Gicostia and ædeáwa *comprobet ac manifestet,* 100, 28.

**ge-cow,** es; *n. What is chewed, food:*—Eálā, ðū wyrma gecow and wulfes geslit and fugles geter, Nap. 28.

**ge-crammian** *to stuff, cram:*—Wǽran gecrammede *farciuntur, replentur,* An. Ox. 3517. Cf. ge-crimman.

**ge-creópan;** *p.* -creáp, *pl.* -crupon *To creep, crawl.* (1) of a human being:—Hē ne meahte gangan, ac hē gecreáp in þā ciricean *he could not walk, but he crawled into the church,* Shrn. 126, 25. (2) of a reptile:—Gecreáp þǽr inn tō þām hālgan men sum unhýre nǽddre, Gr. D. 211, 13.

**ge-crimman;** *p.* -cramm; *pp.* -crummen *To stuff together, cram full:*—Gecrummen (*printed* -trummen) *confertam* (mensuram bonam confertam), Lk. 6, 38), Wrt. Voc. ii. 17, 59. Gecrum[m]en, 74, 44. [Cf. *O. H. Ger.* ka-chrumman *refertim.*] Cf. ge-crammian.

**ge-crincan.** *Take under* ge-cringan.

**ge-cringan.** *Take here* ge-crincan, *and add:*—Gecrong *occubuit,* Wrt. Voc. ii. 115, 37. Gecrang, 63, 61. Gecrong *oppetere(t),* 93, 16. Gecrang, 64, 45. Gecrunge *succumberet,* 80, 7.

**ge-crístnian.** *Substitute: To administer the rite of* crístnung *to a person. See the passage given under* crístnian; II. [*The passages given under* crístnian; I *and* IV (*l.* III) *should be taken under* II. *In* Bd. 5, 6; Sch. 581, 1–19 *the rite is evidently referred to, as it says:* Hē (*the bishop*) on mīnne andwlitan bleów; *and it was the ritual that* (*in* Sch. 580, 19) *it is said the dull priest could not master. The rite was introductory, and preceded, sometimes by years, that of baptism. The person who had undergone the rite became a Catechumen*], *and add:*—Se bisceop hī gecrístnode, and tǽhte hī þā gerýna þæs hālgan geleáfan, and gefullode hī, Hml. S. 30, 93 : 31, 1036 (v. crístnian). Fleáh hē tō Godes ciricean, and bæd þ hine mon gecrístnode, þ bið seó onginnes and se ǽresta dǽl þǽre hālgan fulwihte, Bl. N. 2, 4. Ðeáh hē þā gyt nǽre fullíce gefulwad, ah hē wæs gecrístnod . . . hweðre hē þæt geryne þǽre fulwihte mid gōdum dǽdum heóld, Bl. H. 213, 15. Martinus nū iu gecrístnod ǽr his fulwihte hē mid þysse hrægle mē gegyrede *Martinus adhuc catechumenus hac me ueste contexit,* Bl. N. 3, 14. Þā þā hē wæs týn wintra, þā wearð hē gecrístnod (cf. þā þā hē wæs eahtatýnewintre, hē wearð gefullod, 90), Hml. S. 31, 23. Am hē tō cyrcan fulluhtes biddenne; and hē wearð þā gecrístnod (cf. gefullod ðā ðā hē on ylde eahtatýne geára wæs, 502, 1), Hml. Th. ii. 498, 30. Cōm ān gecrístnod man . . . ac hē wearð seóc swā þ hē forðférde ungefullod, Hml. S. 31, 207. Gecrístnad *caticizatus,* Wrt. Voc. ii. 84, 56 : 18, 54. Gecrísnod, An. Ox. 4084. Gecrístnodes *catacumini,* 2207. Gecrístnode *catacuminos,* 2881.

**ge-croced.** *Substitute: Saffron-coloured:*—Gecrocedre (gecrogedre, An. Ox. 5206) *croceo,* Hpt. Gl. 524, 37.

**ge-croged.** v. ge-croced: **ge-crumen.** v. ge-crimman.

**ge-crymian, -cryman** *To crumble* bread:—Nim of ðām hālgedan hlāfe þe man hālige on hlāfmæssedæg feówer snǽda and gecryme on þā feówer hyrnan þæs berenes, Lch. iii. 290, 28. [v. *N. E. D.* crim.]

**ge-crympan;** *p.* te *To crimp, curl:*—Gecrymptum *calamistratis,* Wrt. Voc. ii. 21, 73.

**ge-cryppan;** *p.* te *To crook* a finger, *close* the hand :—Genim gecrypte hand fulle, Lch. ii. 276, 13. v. cryppan.

**ge-cuman.** *Add: to move to* an object, *to reach by moving:*—His cræft gecymð on ælcere ædre, Bt. 34, 11 ; F. 152, 1. Ðæt heáfod gecymð on ðǽre eorðan *caput sese ad terram declinat,* Past. 133, 2. Gif cymeð (*uenerit*) on ðā æfterra waccane, and gif on ðā ðirdda wacan gecymeð (*uenerit*), Lk. L. 12, 38. Gecymes, Jn. L. R. 7, 27. Gecymmes, Mk. L. 13, 36. Ðū gecuōme *uenisti,* Jn. L. 2 : 11, 27. Sē ðe gecuōm (*uenerat*) tō ðǽm Hǽlende, 19, 39. Gecōmon, Mt. 20, 9. Gecwōmun, Mt. L. 16, 5. Gecuōmon *conuenerunt,* Rtl. 58, 41. Genim ðē mīnne rǽd and gecum tō ðām apostole, Hml. Th. ii. 414, 12. Oð þ ríc Godes gecyme (*ueniat*), Lk. L. 22, 18. Gecwōme hē cwoðend *uenisse se dicens,* Mt. p. 14, 12. Se feónd sǽde þ hē wolde gecuman mid (féran tō, *v. l.*) þām brōðrum *hostis quod ad fratres pergeret indicavit,* Gr. D. 124, 27. Æt þām weorce gecuman, Hml. Th. ii. 166, 16. Hē férde from Antiochian, forþan þe hē wæs apostol and sceolde gehwǽr gecuman, Hml. S. 10, 13. Gecuma *uenire,* Mt. L. 22, 3. Gecuma tō him *adire ad eum,* Lk. L. 8, 19. Gicyme *peruenire,* Rtl. 56, 37. ¶ *to agree* upon ; *convenire.* v. Ll. Th. i. 30, 20 *under* ge-cwēman, 2. [*Goth.* ga-kwiman *in to arrive at: O. H. Ger.* ge-queman *venire.*]

**ge-cundelic.** *In* Bt. S. 31, 25 *the reading is* gecundlic.

**ge-cunnian.** *Add:* (1) *to try, test:*—Hī gelýfdon him be eallum þām geþeódum, þeáh hī hyra gecunnian ne mihton *crediderunt de omnibus linguis quas probare minime ualebant,* Gr. D. 301, 1. (1 a) *to try maliciously, insidiously, to tempt:*—Gecunnedon of ðǽm gafel *temtantes de tributo,* Mt. p. 19, 4. Gecunnadun, 6. Gecunned *tentatus,* 7. Þte hē woere gecunned from diáble, Mt. L. 4, 1. (2) *to try to know; to*

*inquire* :—Gecunnia and ásca ... huulíc monn sē, Mt. L. 10, 14 margin. (3) *to learn by trial, ascertain, know* :—Onsióne earðes and heofnes wutað gié gecunnia (gicunniga, R., *probare*), ðis tíd ne gecunnað (gicunigas, R., *probatis*) gié, Lk. L. 12, 56. Hē wolde gecunnian (*probare*) þæs þe hē ær gehýrde, Gr. D. 142, 9. Hū þū meaht gecunnian hwæþer hit healsgund sié (cf. healsgundes tācn hwæþer hē hit sié, 44, 7), Lch. ii. 2, 17. (4) *to prove, shew to be right, approve* :—Sié ðā sóð intrahtnung þ ðā apostolas gecunnedun *sit illa uera interpretatio quam apostoli probauerunt*, Mt. p. 2, 6. (5) *to try, attempt* :—Gicunned bið *innitatur*, Rtl. 19, 29. Gecunnate *conati*, Mt. p. 7, 2. Gecunnad, 9. (6) *to try, vex, afflict* :—Cnæht mín mið yfle is gecunned *puer meus male torquetur*, Mt. L. 8, 6. [O. Sax. gi-kunnôn *to learn by experience*.]

**ge-cúþ**; *adj. Known* :—Hine þā monige his gecúðra monna ácsodon, ge æþelcunde ge ōðre *multi uiri noti ac nobiles requirebant*, Gr. D. 22, 14 note.

**ge-cúþlǽcan**; *p.* -lǽhte *To make friends* with, *attach oneself to.* (1) *intrans.* :—Ðā cōm án gecrístnod man and gecúðlǽhte tō Martine, and wunode mid him, Hml. S. 31, 207. (2) *reflex.* :—Paulus hine gecúðlǽhte tō ðām hālgan heápe Crístes hírēdes (cf. *tentabat se jungere discipulis*, Acts 9, 26), Hml. Th. i. 388, 10.

**ge-cwealmbǽran** (-cwylm-) *to torture to death, kill* :—Gecwylmbǽred (-cwelm-, Hpt. Gl. 470, 45) *extorqueretur*, i. *cruciaretur*, An. Ox. 2740. Wē synt gecwylmbērode *mortificamur*, Ps. L. 43, 22.

**ge-cwealmfull** (-cwelm-); *adj. Deadly* :—Cwylmbǽre ł gecwelmfulle *perniciosa, pestifera, mortifera*, Hpt. Gl. 428, 32.

**ge-cweccan.** For *gecwecton read gecoecton, and for* 7 *read* 6. *Add : to shake* :—Gecwehton *uibrato*, Germ. 401, 28. Efne gequoeccad (-gicwæced, R.) bið *conquassabitur*, Lk. L. 20, 18.

**ge-cwed**, es; *n. A declaration, an appointment* :—Gecwed *indictio*, Wrt. Voc. ii. 46, 18.

**gecwed-fæsten**, es; *n. An appointed fast* :—Æfæstenu and gecwedfæstenu ic oft ágǽlde, Angl. xi. 99, 62.

**ge-cwednis.** Dele.

**ge-cwedrǽden.** *Add* :—Cleopode Pompeius him tō ymbe Rōmāna ealde gecwedrǽdenne ... 'Gefēra, gemyne ðæt ðū úre gecwedrǽdenne ne oferbrec[e]' ... þæt wæs seó gecwedrǽden þe Rōmāne geset hæfdon, þ hiora nān ōðerne on þone andwlitan ne slóge, þǽr þær hié æt gefeohtum gemētte, Ors. S. 242, 5-12. Hē oferbræc heora gecwedrǽdenne, þæt wæs þ hié hæfdon gecweden þæt ..., 108, 8. v. ge-cwidrǽden.

**gecwed-stōw**, e; *f. An appointed place* :—Se foresprecena wer tō þǽre gecwedstōwe (*ad certum locum*) wæs gelǽded, Gr. D. 183, 7.

**ge-cwelman** = ge-cwilman : **ge-cwelmbǽran.** v. ge-cwealmbǽran : **ge-cwelmfull.** v. ge-cwealmfull.

**ge-cwēman.** *Add :* (1) *to please, be pleasing to, be agreeable to* :—Ic ðē on hleóðre hearpan gecwēme, Ps. Th. 107, 2. Þū ēce líf eallum dǽlest, swā hēr manna gehwylc Metode gecwēmað, Hy. 10, 58. Ic ne gecwēmde *non placui*, Wrt. Voc. ii. 60, 27. Heora ofspring, þone dǽl ðe him ǽr gecwēmde, Hml. Th. i. 28, 3. (2) *to satisfy, content* by discharge of an obligation or demand :—Micel is þ sācerd āh tō dōnne ... gif hē his Drihtne gecwēmeð mid rihte, Ll. Th. i. 360, 31. Þā þe Gode hýrdan and mid rihte gecwēmdon, Ll. Lbm. 472, 13. Se man þām ōðrum riht gedó, gecwime (= -cwēme? or = -cume?) an feó oþþe an āðe *let the one man do the other right, satisfy him by payment or by giving security on oath* (or *agree upon payment or security*), Ll. Th. i. 30, 20.

**ge-cwēme.** *Add :* I. *pleasing, acceptable* :—Gecwēme ł wynsumlic *votivum, acceptum, desiderativum*, Hpt. Gl. 446, 51. Þām men geþeód mid gecwēmre geférrǽdene on wynsumre drohtnunge, Hml. Th. i. 438, 23. Hafað ðeós wyrt swýþe gecwēme swæc, Lch. i. 264, 19. Gecwēme *beneplacita*, Wrt. Voc. ii. 125, 32. Gecwēme lāc *grata munuscula*, An. Ox. 4502. Gecwǽmest *hindcealf gratissimus hinnulus*, Kent. Gl. 110 : 598. I a. *with dat., agreeable to* :—Gecwēme is him *beneplacitum est ei*, Ps. Rdr. 146, 10. Þurh yfelra manna rǽdas þe him ǽfre gecwēme wǽran, Chr. 1100; P. 235, 22. Ðā ðe gecuoeron (gicwoeme, R.) sint him *quae placita sunt ei*, Jn. L. 8, 29. Gif him þ gecwēmre byð, Ll. Th. i. 489, 14. Þǽm wiþerweardan beóþ þæs mannes synna gecwēmran þonne goldhord, Bl. H. 43, 21. II. *convenient, suitable, fit.* (1) *fit for* (*tō*) a purpose :—Seó wyrt is tō lǽcedómum wel gecwēme, Lch. i. 260, 4. Ðeós wyrt nafað gecwēme sǽd tō lǽcedōme, 292, 21. (2) *fit for the use of* a person (*dat.*) :—Is seó geoluwe swíþost lǽceon gecwēme, Lch. i. 294, 11. ¶ in the following the translation seems inexact :—Mid gecwēmre dugeþgyfe *cum gratuita* (i. *gratis data*) *munificentia*, An. Ox. 2574 : 3065. For his gecwēmum feó *accepto pretio*, Gr. D. 341, 1. v. un-, wel-gecwēme.

**ge-cwēme**; *adv.* (?) *Pleasantly, agreeably* :—Gecwēme *contente* (the Latin, however, is probably gen. fem. Cf. ðǽre gehealdnan *contente*, 79, 41), Wrt. Voc. ii. 20, 20.

**ge-cwēmedlic.** *Substitute* : *Well-pleasing,* and add :—Hit bið swýðe rihtlic líf and Gode gecwēmedlic, Wlfst. 304, 19.

**ge-cwēmednes.** *Add* :—On gecwēmednessum heora *in beneplacitis eorum*, Ps. L. 140, 5. ¶ ānum tō gecwemednesse *to the delight of*

*a person, so as to please a person* :—Heó plegode him eallum tō gecwēmednysse (cf. *cum saltasset et placuisset Herodi simulque recumbentibus*, Mk. 6, 22), Hml. Th. i. 480, 31. Sē ðe leahtras begǽð deófle tō gecwēmednysse, ii. 110, 27 : S. 13, 271.

**ge-cwēmlic.** For *pleased* read *pleasing*, and add : *suitable, fit* :—Gecwēmlíce *congruam*, R. Ben. I. 78, 5.

**ge-cwēmlíce.** *Add* : (1) *agreeably, so as to please, acceptably* :—Wel ðrowað se man and Gode gecwēmlíce, sē ðe wind ongeán leahtras, Hml. Th. i. 164, 20 : Hml. A. 14, 22. Þæt þe gē tō frides bóte gecoren hæfdon mid micclum wísdóme and mē swýðe gecwēmlíce, Ll. Th. i. 278, 3. Hū hē Gode gecwēmlícost mihte lybban, Guth. 30, 15. (2) *so as to satisfy, satisfactorily* :—Ús þ gecwēmelíce cýþað þǽre sōðfæstnesse word *veritatis nobis verba satisfacerent*, Gr. D. 315, 14. (3) *suitably, conveniently, fitly* :—Þeós wíse nū hī sylfe gecwēmlíce gegearwode *occasio apta se praebuit*, Gr. D. 60, 6.

**ge-cwēmnes.** *Add* :—Gode tō gecwēmnysse and earmum and eádigum tō þearfe and tō friðe, Ll. Th. i. 272, 15. Þonne hē sceáwaþ þus eádmódlice geþingunge and gecwēmnesse úres módes wið úre þā nēhstan *dum tale placitum nostrae mentis aspexerit*, Gr. D. 349, 34. On gecwēmnessum heora *in beneplacitis eorum*, Ps. Rdr. 140, 5. v. wel-gecwēmnes.

**ge-cwēmsum.** *Substitute* : *Agreeable, pleasing* :—Ungewemmed, gecwēmsumere *inlibata* (David ... *inlibata* virginitate praeditus), An. Ox. 5000.

**ge-cweþan.** *Add* : I. *to speak* :—Mið ðý yfle hiá gecuoeðas iúh *cum maledixerint vobis*, Mt. L. 5, 11. Mið ðý gecueð *cum dixisset*, Mk. L. 1, 42. Gelíc alle hiá gecuoedon *similiter omnes dicebant*, 14, 31. Þte ne ǽnigum gecuoede, Lk. L. 5, 14. II. *to say.* (1) with noun (pronoun) object :—Þæt þæt ic tō eów gecweðe, þæt ic cweðe tō eallum mannum, Hml. Th. 524, 16. Heora nān nyste hwæt ōðer gecwæð, 472, 28. Þā cwæþ hē : 'Þanc ic dō ...'. Sóna swā hē þæs word gecwæþ, Bl. H. 191, 23-29. Heó word gecweþan ne mihte, Guth. 88, 25. Ðā ðe in ðíostrum gié cuoedon in lēht biðon gecoeden, Lk. L. 12, 3. Gecuoedno (gicuedno, R.), 19, 28. (2) with the words spoken. v. II a :—Gecuoeð : 'Gif gegerelo his ic hrína, ic hāl beóm,' Mk. L, 5, 28. Gecuēdon : 'Huona ðissum snytru ðius ?,' Mt. L. 13, 54. Gecuoeða : 'Huæt is ðes ?,' Lk. L. 7, 49. Hē ne mōste gecweþan : 'Miltsa mē, God,' Bl. H. 43, 31. (3) with a clause. v. II a :—Þā gecwæð se abbod and ealle þā gebrōðra þæt þér ne mihte nā mā muneca wunian, Hml. S. 6, 265. Is gecweden þ hié ealle on yppan wunedon, Bl. H. 133, 26. (4) *to say, tell, give an account of* a circumstance :—Þte ne ǽnigum hiá gecoedon (gicwēde, R.) þte áworden wæs, Lk. L. 8, 56. II a. *to say* something about (*be*) :—Críst be Iōhanne gecwæð þ ... nǽnig mǽrra ... geboren nǽre, Bl. H. 161, 23. Þis næs gecweden be Críste, þ his fót æt stāne oþspurne, 29, 30. Swā hit þe þon gecweden is : 'Se mon þe nū dēmeþ ...,' 95, 35. III. *to declare, announce.* (1) a purpose, intended action :—Gif hē Italiam gesōhte, swā hē gecweden hæfde, Ors. 3, 8 ; S. 122, 29. Hæfde se cyning gecweden gefeoht ongeán ðā Indiscan, Hml. Th. ii. 482, 5. (2) a circumstance, time :—Hē hire hǽle gecwæþ and gehēt *salutem illius dixit*, Gr. D. 29, 33. On þǽre ylcan tíde þe God gecwæð (*praedixerat*), Gen. 21, 2. IV. *to settle.* (1) *to agree upon* a course of action, *arrange, fix* a time :—Hē cwæð tō ðām gebrōðrum þæt hē wolde sylf on ðām dæge ðe hē gecwæð þǽr gecuman (cf. hē heom gehēt þ hē æfter heom cuman wolde, and heom þone dæg geñǽmde, Gr. D. 147, 27) ... þā se hālga wer ne cōm, swā swā hē gecweden hæfde (cf. on þām gesettan dæge and ǽrgenamnedan ne cōm, Gr. D. 148, 27), Hml. Th. ii. 172, 9-21. Hié gecwǽdon folcgefeoht him betweónum, Ors. 5, 7 ; S. 230, 10. Þā gecwǽdon hié þæt hié sume hié beæftan wereden, 20. Gecwǽdan, Chr. 1094 ; P. 229, 6. Hié hæfdon gecweden þæt hié ealle emlíce tengden, Ors. 3, 6 ; S. 108, 9. Hē þā folc gelǽdde þǽr hié tōgædere gecweden hæfdon (*where they had agreed to meet* ; in campum), Ors. 4, 6 ; S. 174, 31. (2) *to settle* a regulation, law, an ordinance :—Ealle hig gecwǽdon þ ne þeówe ne freó ne mōton in þone here faran bútan leáfe, Ll. Th. i. 154, 24. Seó gerǽdnis þe Ælfrēd cyng and Gūðrum cyng gecuran and gecwǽdon, 166, 7 : 314, 4. Seó gerǽdnis þe þā biscopas and gerēfan gecweden habbað, 228, 7. Þ ǽlc ōðrum fylste, swā hit gecweden is, 236, 29. Sig hit swā gecweden ; mid swā hwām swā ic hit mid finde, beó hē mín þeów *fiat juxta vestram sententiam: apud quemcumque fuerit inventum, ipse sit servus meus*, Gen. 44, 10. (2 a) where property is to be disposed of by will :—Ðæt hit nǽnig man nǽfre ne onwende on nāne ōðre wísan bútan swā swā ic hit sylf gecweðe æt ðām nýhstan dæge. Ic ... mid ðisse gewitnesse gecweðe hū ic ymbe mín yrfe wille æfter mínum dæge, C. D. ii. 114, 9-14. (2 b) *to settle* property, *assign to a* person :—Mín yldra fæder hæfde gecweden his land on ðā sperehealfe, C. D. ii. 116, 16. Þām (*traitors*) hié nāne mildheortnesse ne dorston gecweðan (-cwǽd-, *v. l.*), Ll. Th. i. 58, 10. V. *to offer, propose* :—Brutus gecwæð ānwíg wið þone cyning, ac him Tarcuinius ōðerne ðegn ongeán sende, Ors. 2, 3 ; S. 68, 16. VI. *to order* :—Eal ðæt ic gecwæþ þ hē dōn sceolde, eall hē þ dyde, Bl. H. 181, 2. VII. *to give orders* for (*tō*) action :—Iulianus gecwæð tō gefeohte (cf. Iulianus

gegaderode his here, Hml. S. 31, 95), Hml. Th. ii. 502, 4. Hé gecwæð tó gefeohte ongeán Arfaxað *pugnavit contra Arphaxad*, Hml. A. 103, 26. **VIII.** *to call, name,* (1) a person or place:—Leódscipe Madian gecweden, Jud. 6, 1. In þære stówe þe is gecueden Deórham, Chr. 577; P. 18, 31. (2) a name:—His tónama wæs Cambises gecweden, Hml. A. 103, 25. His nama wæs gereht 'Godes strengo.' Wel þæt wæs gecweden, Bl. H. 9, 15. (3) *to call* an object so and so, *say that it is so and so* :—þ byþ rihtlíce gecweden gyldrædene, þ wé þus dón, Cht. Th. 607, 23. Scilla ðet is sæhund gecweden, An. Ox. 26, 61. Þær wǽron háte baðu þe wǽron hálwende gecwedene ádligendum líchaman, Hml. Th. i. 86, 22. (4) *to name, mention, speak of* :—Seó sáuwul oððe þ líf oððe seó edwist synd gecwædene tó hyre sylfra, and þ gemynd oððe þ andgit oþþe seó wylla beóð gecwædene tó sumum þinga edlesendlíce, Hml. S. 1, 117. (5) *to say, use certain words as a true description of an object* :—Næs nánum men forgifen þæt hé móste habban oððe gecweðan his ágen fulluht búton Iōhanne ánum *nobody but John could say that his baptism was his own, could call his baptism his own*, Hml. Th. ii. 48, 3.

**ge-cwician.** *Add* : (1) in a physical sense :—Sume hé gecwicað mid oroðe, Gr. D. 268, 19. (2) in a spiritual sense :—Ðá ðe hé wyl hé gicwicað, in. R. 5, 21. Gecwuca mé æfter ðínum wordum, Dryhten, Past. 465, 29.

**ge-cwicung,** e; *f. Vivifying, quickening* :—þurh þæs líchaman gecwicunge *per vivificationem carnis*, Gr. D. 218, 17.

**ge-cwide.** *Add* : (1) *a condition, an agreement* :—Gecwide *conditio*, Wrt. Voc. i. 20, 54. Ne hé má eft tó him hwearf æfter heora gecwide (-cwyde, *v. l.*) *neque ultra ad eum juxta suum condictum rediit*, Bd. 4, 25; Sch. 496, 10. (2) *a will* :—Ðis is Wulfgates gecwide . . . þ is þonne þ hé geann ǽrest Gode his sáwelscattas . . ., C. D. B. iii. 652, 16. v. word-gecwide.

**ge-cwidrǽden.** *Add* :—Gecwydrǽdden *conspiratio*, An. Ox. 2975. Witan hwæt úre gecwydrǽddene (cf. seó gerǽdnis . . . gecweden, 228, 7), gelǽst sý, Ll. Th. i. 236, 5. v. ge-cweþan; **IV.**

**ge-cwidrǽdness,** e; *f. An agreement, a covenant* :—Hér swutelað seó gecwydrǽdnes ðe . . ., Nap. 28.

**ge-cwildfull;** *adj. Pernicious, deadly* :—Cwylmbǽre, gecwyldfulle *perniciosa*, i. *mortifera*, An. Ox. 920.

**ge-cwilman.** *Take here* ge-cwylman *in Dict., and add* :—Gecwylmdon *secto*, Germ. 400, 524. Heora líchaman sceoldon beón mid mislicum tintregum gecwilmede, Hml. Th. ii. 424, 18.

**ge-cwis.** *For* Cot. 46: Hpt. 519 *substitute* :—Gequis *conspiratio*, An. Ox. 4955. v. fácen-gecwis.

**ge-cwisan;** *p.* de *To crush* :—Sumes þegnes cniht feóll fǽrlíce of his horse . . . and swíðe wearð gecwýsed, þ hí wéndon þ hé þǽrrihte sceolde sweltan, Hml. S. 21, 325.

**ge-cwylmfull.** v. ge-cwealmfull : **ge-cynn.** *The better reading is* ge-cynd. v. Sch. 82, 20.

**ge-cynd.** *Dele* II, *and add* : ge-cyndo(-u); *indecl. f.* : ge-cynd; *f. also has gen.* ge-cynd (Bl. H. 31, 32); *dat.* ge-cynd (Bl. H. 121, 30). **I.** *birth* (?) :—Gecynda *natilicium*, Wrt. Voc. ii. 62, 11. Þú eart sunu and fæder ána ǽgðer; swá is þín æðele gecynd miclum gemǽrsod, Hy. 7, 43. **II.** *a native place* or *position, that to which one has a natural right* :—Brytland him wæs on gewealde . . . Normandíge þ land wæs his gecynde, Chr. 1086; P. 220, 25. Þeáh ðú teó hwelcne bóh of dúne . . . swá þú hine álǽtst, swá sprincþ hé úp, and wrígaþ wið his gecyndes (widu went on gecynde, Met. 13, 55). Swá déð eác seó sunne . . . heó sécþ hire gecynde . . . Swá déþ hit gecseaft, wrígaþ wiþ his gecyndes, and gefagen biþ gif hit ǽfre tó cuman mæg, Bt. 25; F. 88, 22–29: Met. 13, 67. Onhelded wið þæs gecyndes (hire gecynde, Bt. 25; F. 88, 7) þe him cyning engla æt frymðe fæste getióde, 12. Leóht . . . stíged on lenge, clynimad on gecyndo, Sal. 414. **II a.** *natural condition, lot to which one is born* :—Beó gehealden on ðínum gecynde, ðonne hæfst ðú genóh *be content with your lot, then you will have enough*, Prov. K. 50. **III.** *the character* or *quality derived from birth* or *native constitution, natural disposition, nature* :—Seó gesceádwíslice gecynd *rationalis natura*, Past. 349, 25. Wæs úre gecynd geedneówod, Bl. H. 11, 10. Þisses fugles gecynd fela gelíces be Crístes þegnum beácnað, Ph. 387. Hwæt is heora (*the elements*) ǽlces gecynd? Ðæs fýres gecynd is hát and dríe . . . Hwylces gecyndes is seó heofon? Fýres gecynde, Angl. vii. 12, 104–108. On gimma gecynde (*natura*) carbunculus bið diórra ðonne iacintus . . . ðæs ðe sió endebyrdnes and ðæt gecynd (*naturae ordo*) forwiernð ðǽm iacinte, se wlite hit eft geiécð, and ðeáh ðe ðæt gecynd and sió endebyrdnes (*naturalis ordo*) ðæs carbuncules hine úp áhebbe, his blióh hine gescent, Past. 411, 25–32. Sió fordrúgade gecyndo, Lch. ii. 222, 4. Hys gecynde is swíþe hát and slǽpbǽre, i. 284, 22. Þysum wífe wæs inne swýðe fýrenu and hát gecynde (gecynd, *v. l.*) *valde ignea conspersio corporis*) . . . ongunnon lǽcas secgan þ hire wolden beardas weaxan for þǽre hǽte hyre gecyndes . . . heó wearð for þǽre mycclan gecynde and hǽte þæs lustes gebeardedu, Gr. D. 279, 7–14. Þǽre eorðan gecynde (-cynd, *v. l.*) *natura soli illius*, Bd. 4, 28; Sch. 521, 13. Þæt híw úre týddran gecynde,

Bl. H. 29, 4. Ðeáh hí ðæt gód hira gecynde gehál nolden gehealdan *si accepta naturae bona integra servare noluerunt*, Past. 403, 19. Stánas sint stilre gecynde and heardre, Bt. 34, 11; F. 150, 24. Ðeós wyrt is strangre gecynde, Lch. i. 274, 18. Þonne hió bið hátre gecyndo, ii. 220, 16 : 20: 22: 26. Gif hé bið cealdre gecyndo, 284, 20. Heó nán þincg on hire næfd horses gecyndes, Hml. S. 21, 488. Hé bið getiéged tó óðrum monnum mid onlícre gecynde, Past. 111, 20. Him wæs on gecynde þ hé symble wæs reád on his andwlitan *cui ex conspersione semper facies rubere consueverat*, Gr. D. 187, 15. For his gecynde *conspersione*, 17. Gecynde *consparsione*, Wrt. Voc. ii. 86, 14 : 19, 1 : An. Ox. 4648 (the passage is *consparsione ingenitam*). Mid þǽre menniscan gecynd, Bl. H. 121, 30. Be wambe missenlicre gecyndo, Lch. ii. 220, 14. Of flǽsclicum gecynde, Past. 159, 1. Gewend tó ðam hehstan gecynde, þæt is God, Hml. Th. i. 262, 13. Æfter sóðum gecynde þæt wæter is brosniendlic wæta, ii. 270, 5. Hé onféng þá ilcan gecynde, Bl. H. 23, 24. His þá menniscan gecynd, 127, 24. Wæstmas beóð þurh ágne gecynd eft ácende, Ph. 256 : 329. Ásyndrod fram synnum þurh clǽne gecynd, Hy. 9, 11 : 52. Mǽge seó wyrd þe gedón þæt þá þing ðíne ágene sién, þá þe heora ágene gecynd þe gedydon fremde, Bt. 14, 1; F. 40, 32. Hé wæs on ánum háde twégra gecynda, Bl. H. 33, 33. **IV.** *nature* in general, in the abstract, *the established order of things* :—His mód and his andgit ðæt gecynd áscierpð *cujus sensum natura exacuit*, Past. 69, 8. Seó gecynd hit onscunað þæt hié magon weorþan tógædere gemenged, Bt. 16, 3; F. 54, 13. Ic eom nú máre ymbe þ gecynd (*de naturali intentione*) þonne ymbe þone willan . . . þú mihst wena be manegum þingum þ þ gecynd is swíþe micel. . . . Má wilniaþ ðá nétenu ðæs ðe hí wiluiað for gecynde (*ex naturae principiis*) þonne for willan . . . hwílum þæt gecynd (*natura*) ofercymþ þone willan, 34, 11 ; F. 150, 31–152, 12. Hyngran, þyrstan . . . eall þ is of untrumnesse þæs gecyndes (*ex infirmitate naturae est*), Bd. 1, 27 ; Sch. 82, 26. Þára tó feala woroldwuniendra wind wið gecynde, Met. 13, 17. Þá þurh gecynd Críst heriað, Hy. 7, 24. Ealra wihta þára þe æfter gecyndum cenned wǽre, Rä. 40, 15. **V.** *natural state* or *condition* :—Seó sáwl ne mæg forleósan þ líf hire ágenre gecynde, Gr. D. 337, 5. Þæt hí bǽdon þæt ðá gyldenon gyrda eft tó þan ǽrran gecynde áwendon . . . 'Berað ðá gyrda tó wuda . . . hí synd gecyrrede tó heora gecynde, Hml. Th. i. 68, 18–29. Þ wæter, gefylledre ðære ðénunge, hwearf eft tó gecynde (*ad naturam*), Bd. 1, 7 ; Sch. 25, 17. Hwí þ ís weorþe, and eft for þǽre sunna scíman tó his ágnum gecynde weorþe, Bt. 39, 3 ; F. 216, 1 : Met. 28, 62. Hí mé onhwyrfdon of þǽre gecynde þe ic ǽr cwic beheóld, Rä. 72, 4. **VI.** *a natural quality, property,* or *characteristic* :—Úðwitan secgað þætte án gecynd ǽlcre sáwle yrsung wǽre, óðer wilnung, is seó þridde gecynd þǽm twǽm betere sió gesceádwísnes, Met. 20, 184–188. Is þæt micel gecynd þínes gódes . . . for þon hit is eall án . . . þú and þæt þín gód, 26 : Bt. 33, 4 ; F. 128, 14. Is þ formicel gecynd þ úrum líchoman cymð eall his mægen of ðám mete þe wé þicgað, and ðeáh færð se mete út þurh ðone líchoman, 34, 11 ; F. 150, 34. Þú man worhtest and him . . . sealdest word and gewitt and wæstma gecynd (*the property of growth*), Hy. 9, 56. Úpwitan secgaþ þ sió sáwul hæbbe ðrió gecynd ; án ðára gecynda is þ heó biþ wilnigende . . . twá ðára gecyndu (-a ?) habbaþ nétenu, Bt. 33, 4 ; F. 132, 3–5. **VII.** *gender, sex* :—Nim of eallum clǽnum nítenum seofen and seofen ǽgðres gecyndes (*masculum et feminam*), Gen. 7, 2 : 3. **VII a.** *sexual organs.* v. gecynd-lim :—Wépen, gecynd *veretrum*, Wrt. Voc. i. 44, 58. Swá hwylc man swá on gecynde (*in genitalibus*) óðerne wanhálne dó, Ll. Th. ii. 148,17. Hié beheledon heora fæderes gecynd (cf. gesceapu, 22) *operuerunt uerenda patris sui*, Gen. 9, 23. Inádle on wífes gecyndon and on fótum, Lch. ii. 176, 1. **VII b.** =mónaþ-gecynd :—Þú scealt simle þám wífe . . . drenc sellan on þá ilcan tíd þe hire sió gecynd æt wǽre, Lch. ii. 330, 24. **VIII.** *the manner* or *way natural* or *proper to any one, mode of action* :—Ðeáh hire biþ forwierned hire gecyndes ðurh þæs monnes willan, Bt. 34, 11 ; F. 152, 13. Lamb spǽcan on mennisc gecynde, Mart. H. 2, 19. Hé (*the whale*) hafað óðre gecynd . . . se mereweard múð ontýneð . . ., Wal. 49. **IX.** *character as determining the class to which a thing belongs, generic nature* or *quality* :—Se abbod cwæð on his gedwilde þ úres Drihtenes líchama and his godcundnes wǽre ánes gecyndes, Ll. Th. ii. 374, 25. Sceáwa þǽr nú dúst, and drýge bán, þǽr þǽr þú ǽr gesáwe æfter flǽsclicre gecynde fægre leomu on tó seónne, Bl. H. 113, 22. **X.** *a race, a natural group of animals* or *plants having a common origin* :—Seó mennisce gecynd mæg mid rihte þǽm Scyppende lof secgean, Bl. H. 123, 3. Manna gecynd, El. 735. Nán gesceaft (gecynd, *v. l.*) . . . búton mon, Bt. 35, 4 ; F. 160, 24. Nis nænigu gecynd cwiclífigende, ne fugol ne fisc . . ., Sal. 419. Þone feónd þisse menniscan gecynd, Bl. H. 31, 32. Þá hálgan setl gefylde mid þǽre menniscan gecynde, 121, 35 : Past. 411, 32. Tó wlitegum engla gecynde, Hml. Th. i. 12, 14. Þú . . . ealle gesceafta tósyndrodest on manega, sealdest ǽlce gecynd ágene wísan, Hy. 7, 66. Ne forseoh þú nǽfre þíne gecynd *carnem tuam ne despexeris* (Is. 58, 7), Bl. H. 37, 22. God geswác his weorces swá þæt hé ná má gecynda siððan ne gesceóp, ac swá þeáh hé gemenigfylt dæghwomlíce þá ylcan gecynd, Hml. Th. ii. 206, 10–12. **XI.** a

*family, a tribe, nation* :—Gecynda *nationum*, Ps. Rdr. 286, 7. **XI a.**
*descendants, progeny* :—Wulfsie Wotringabyras innon ðæt gecynde
*cuidam Wulfsio dederunt Wotryngebyri, sibi et suae progeniei in
hæreditatem futuram* (vi. 54, 25), C. D. ii. 381, 13 : 14 : 15 :
18. **XII.** *a class distinguished by common attributes, genus, sort* :
—Woruldmonna seó unclǽne gecynd, Cri. 1017. Nán ðing ðæs
gecyndes, Hml. Th. ii. 370, 5. Eorðan gecynda, Cri. 1181. v. eald-,
inwit-, médren-, mónaþ-, sundor-gecynd.

**gecynd-bóc.** *Add* :—Gecyndbóca gerecednesse (*juxta*) *Geneseos
relatum*, An. Ox. 50 : 1154.

**ge-cynde** *nature*. v. ge-cynd.

**ge-cynde**; *adj. Add* : *natural, native*. (1) *that is in accordance
with nature* or *the usual course of things* :—Gecynde riht *jus naturale*,
Wrt. Voc. ii. 49, 6. Þone deáþ þe eallum monnum gecynde is, Bt. 39,
10 ; F. 228, 9. Sé ús gesette . . . sibbe gecynde (cf. se ilca gesette . . .
gecyndelice sibbe eallum his gesceaftum, Bt. 21 ; F. 74, 1), Met. 11, 14.
(2) *implanted by nature, innate, inherent* :—Gecynde *insitum*, Wrt. Voc.
ii. 43, 55. Wrænnes bið ælcum men gecynde, Bt. 34, 11 ; F. 152, 12.
Salomon þeáh swýðe wel, eal swá him gecynde wæs, Wlfst. 277, 17,
Him wæs gecynde þ hé symble wæs reád on his andwlitan *cui ex conspersione semper facies rubere consueverat*, Gr. D. 187, 15. Swá déð se
gecynda cræft ælcum men *agit cujusque rei natura quod proprium est*, Bt.
16, 3 ; F. 54, 32. (3) *naturally pertaining* to, or *associated with,
proper* :—Nis hit nó þe gecynde þte þú hí áge . . . ac þá heofencundan
þing þe sint gecynde, Bt. 14, 1 ; F. 40, 33. Tól tó swelcum cræfte
swelce þú cunne þ ðé is gecynde, and þ þe is riht tó habbenne, F. 42, 7.
Þám treówum ðe him gecynde biþ úpheáh tó standanne. . . . Hió cymþ
swá úp swá hire yfemest gecynde bið *she mounts as high as ever it is
natural for her to go*, 25 ; F. 88, 21–28 : Met. 13, 63. (4) *belonging
to one by birth, descent,* or *inheritance* :—Ús is from úrum ærestan mǽge
gecynde ðæt wé ælc yfel on ðrió wísan ðurhtión, Past. 417, 20. Him
wæs bǽm on þám leódscipe lond gecynde, B. 2197. Hé sǽde þ Móyses
wǽre þæs Jósepes sunu ; þ him wǽran fram hym drýcræftas gecynde
(*paternae scientiae haereditas*), Ors. 1, 4 ; S. 34, 14. (4 a) *native*
(country, language) :—Ágen *vel* gecynde sprǽc *idioma, proprietas linguae*,
Wrt. Voc. i. 55, 46. Gecynde under scada *patrias sub umbras*, An. Ox.
32, 4. (5) *rightful* (lord) :—Hí cwǽdon þ him nán leófre hláford nǽre
þonne heora gecynde (-a, *v. l.*) hláford, Chr. 1014 ; P. 145, 3. v. un-
gecynde.

**ge-cyndelic.** *Add* : *kindly, native*. (1) *that is according to natural
laws, in agreement with nature* :—Æt fruman wæs gehealden seó gecyndelice ǽ (*lex bonae naturae*), swá þ nán óðrum ne derode ; eft þeós
ǽ (*naturalis lex*) becóm tó gýmeleáste, Angl. vii. 8, 70 : Hml. S. 11,
348. Hwí ne magon gé gebídan gecyndelices deádes?, Bt. 39, 1 ; F.
210, 27. Hé gesette gecyndelice sibbe eallum his gesceaftum, 21 ; F.
74, 1. (2) *implanted by nature, innate, inherent* :—Gecyndelic *naturalis
(curiositas)*, An. Ox. 4, 1. Gecyndelicere *genuini*, 5092. Gecyndelicre
*natiua (uenustate)*, 7, 364 : 8, 357. Of gecyndelicre tyndran *de ingenito
fomite*, Wrt. Voc. ii. 139, 64. Ne wát þ gé wénaþ þ gé nán gecyndelic
gód ne gesǽlþa on innan eów selfum nabbaþ *itane nullum est proprium
vobis atque insitum bonum?*, Bt. 14, 2 ; F. 44, 16. (3) *naturally
belonging* to, *proper* :—Þám fódre þe him (*animals*) gecyndelic biþ, Bt.
14, 2 ; F. 44. 24. (4) *native* (land) :—In ðǽre gecyndelice *in genetali*
(*solo*), Wrt. Voc. ii. 80, 34 : 46, 64. (5) *generative, of generation*.
v. ge-cynd ; **VII a,** gecynd-lim :—Seó gecyndelice hǽtu . . . gestilleþ on
þé, Bl. H. 7, 27. Gif man gekyndelice lim áwyrdeð, Ll. Th. i. 18, 10.
Gif wíf of ðám gecyndelican limon þone fléwsan þæs wǽtan þoligen, Lch.
i. 308, 1 : 64, 21. ¶ *used substantively* :—Gyf wíf cennan ne
mæge, nime þysse wyrte wós mid wulle, dó on þá gecyndelican, 266, 9.
v. un-gecyndelic.

**ge-cyndelíce.** *Add* : (1) *in accordance with nature*. v. gecyndelic, (1) :—Ðá getreówan freónd God gecyndelíce gesceóp tó ge-
mágum, Bt. 24, 3 ; F. 82, 31. (2) *inherently, by natural disposition*.
v. ge-cyndelic, (2) :—Críst is good gecyndelíce, Hml. Th. i. 238, 17.
Þurh þ hé ealle þinc . . . búton ǽnigum geswince swilce gekyndelíce of
gewunan (swylce gecyndelíce and gewunlíce, R. Ben. 32, 1) gehealde *per
quam universa . . . absque ullo labore velut naturaliter ex consuetudine
incipiet custodire*, R. Ben. I. 36, 15. v. un-gecyndelice.

**gecynde-sprǽc.** *Dele, and see* ge-cynde, (4 a).

**gecynd-lim.** *Add* : *sexual organs*. v. ge-cynd ; **VII a.** (1) *of
a male, genitalia* :—Gecindlimu *genitalia*, Wrt. Voc. i. 44, 59. Lust
gecyndlima *uoluptas genitalium*, Scint. 106, 9 : Lch. i. 370, 3. On
gecyndlimum minum, Angl. xi. 117, 25. Hé him ealle þá gecyndlimu
of ácearf, Gr. D. 26, 27. Nim heortes gecyndlimu (-leomo, *v. l.*), Lch.
i. 336, 20. (2) *of a female, vulva, uterus* :—Of méddernum rife,
gecyndlime *de uulua*, An. Ox. 1496. Fram gecyndlime *a uulua, ab
utero*, Ps. L. 57, 4. (3) *as a symbol of indecency* :—Gecyndlim *dedecus,
turpitudinem*, Germ. 390, 120.

**ge-cyndnes.** *Add* :—Gecyndnesse *nationis*, Ps. Rdr. 286, 7. Ge-
cyndnessa ꝥ wæstmas heora *nascentiæ eorum*, 289, 22.

**ge-cyndo(-u).** v. ge-cynd.

**ge-cynehelmian** *to crown* :—Beón gecynehelmod *coronari*, Scint. 11,
6. Úre mægen byþ gecynehelmud *nostra uirtus coronabitur*, 209, 6.

**ge-cýpan.** v. ge-cípan : **ge-cýpe.** v. ge-cîpe : **ge-cypsed.** v.
ge-cyspan.

**ge-cyrnod** ; *adj. Jagged, having grainlike excrescences* :—Wiþ
scurfedum nægle ; nim gecyrnadne sticcan, sete on þone nægl wið þá
wearta, Lch. ii. 150, 4. Gecyrnode cambas *serratas cristas* (of a cock),
An. Ox. 26, 15.

**ge-cyrnlad.** *Add* :—Gecyrnlude appla *mala granata*, An. Ox. 3841.
Gecyrnlode, 2, 258.

**ge-cyrpsian.** v. ge-cirpsian : **ge-cyrran.** v. ge-cirran.

**ge-cyrtan** ; *p.* te ; *pp.* cyrt *To shorten, cut off* :—Gecyrte *truncas*,
Germ. 400, 139. [*O. H. Ger.* uuerdent gecurzite (*breuiabuntur*) thie
taga.]

**ge-cyrtenlǽcan** ; *p.* -lǽhte *To make sweet* :—Gecertenlǽhte *indul-
cauit* (the Latin is : Mellitus versuum epigrammatibus *inculcauit*),
An. Ox. 5408.

**ge-cyspyd.** *Substitute* : **ge-cyspan, -cypsan** ; *p.* te ; *pp.* -cyspt,
-cysped *To fetter* :—Beóþ gecyspte *conpediuntur*, Wrt. Voc. ii. 22, 26.
Gecyspedra (-cypsed-, Ps. Spl.) *compeditorum*, Ps. Rdr. 78, 11. Drihten
tólýseþ gecyspede (-cypsede, Ps. Spl.), 145, 7. Ðá gecypsedan, Hml. Th.
ii. 414, 23.

**ge-cyssan.** *Add* :—Hé gecyste þone man þe wæs egeslíce hreóf, Shrn.
147, 6. Þte gecyste hine *ut oscularetur eum*, Lk. L. R. 22, 47. [*O. H.
Ger.* ge-kussen.]

**ge-cýþan.** *Add* : **I.** *to make known* by words. (1) *to give information of, tell, give notice of, report* :—Ic þe gecýþe for þon þe manega
tintrega hié þé on bringað, Bl. H. 237, 4. Mid þyssum wordum hé
gecýþde þ hé wolde beón swyltende, 75, 32. Þú gecýð . . . ne mæg
ofer þæt Ebréa þeód . . . ríce healdan, El. 446. Giefe . . . þe mé álýfed
nis tó gecýðenne cwicra ǽngum, Gú. 1223. Þis wæs þám kyninge sóna
tó Normandíe gecýðed (-cýdd, *v. l.*), Chr. 1076 ; P. 211, 20. Him wæs
gecýðd þ Wyllelm wolde hider, 1066 ; P. 197, 15. Higeláce wæs síð
Beówulfes gecýðed, B. 1971 : 2324. ¶ *with complementary
adjective* :—Se cyng wæs deád gekýd *the king was reported dead*, Chr.
1093 ; P. 227, 20. (1 a) *of official notice, to report,* (a) *a matter* :—
His scrift hit gecýðe þám biscope, hweðer hé tó þǽre bóte cirran wolde,
Ll. Th. i. 212, 23. (β) *an object, to give notice of the place or condition of* an object :—Gif þé become óðres monnes giémeleás fioh on
hand, gecýð (-cýðe, *v. l.*) hit him, Ll. Th. i. 54, 10. Gif hé wille his
wǽpen sellan, hine mon gehealde, and hine his freóndum gecýðe (cf.
hine his mǽgum gebodie, 8), 90, 16. (2) *to bear witness, testify*. v.
ge-cýþednes :—Þte [hé] gicýðed him *ut testetur illis*, Lk. R. 16, 28.
Is gecýðed *testatur*, Jn. p. 1, 7 : p. 6, 19. (2 a) *with complementary
adj.* :—Sóð þæt gecýðed mænig (*many a man will testify that it is true*)
. . . , þæt þæt geweorðeð . . . , An. 1437. (3) *of a formal statement, to
declare* :—Gecýþe seó gewitnysse þ on Godes helde, þ heó him on sóðre
gewitnysse sý, Ll. Th. i. 388, 22. Gif mon þæs ofslægenan weres bidde,
hé mót gecýðan þ hé hine for þeóf ofslóge, . . . Gif hé hit dierneð, Ll.
Th. i. 116, 4. (3 a) *of a statement by one in authority, to announce,
proclaim, declare,* (a) *with acc.* :—God his miltse onwreáh, and his
mǽgsibbe gecýðde, Bl. H. 107, 3. Gehát him þurh hálig word God
self gecýðde, Gen. 1797. ¶ *with complement* :—Þú eart cynebearn
gecýðed cwycum and deádum, Hy. 7, 117 : El. 816. (b) *with clause* :
Ic Æðelstáne cyning eallum mínum geréfum . . . gecýðe . . . þ ic wille
. . . , Ll. Th. i. 196, 35. Þú (*God*) mé gecýðdest þæt þú mundbora
mínum wǽre, Hö. 74. Him (*David*) gecýðan Waldendes dóm, Ps. C.
18. 'Secgge ic (*St. Michael*) . . .' Ðá þ wæs þus gesprecen and gecýðed,
Bl. H. 201, 10. Him Drihten þ gecýþed hæfde ; 225, 3 : Dan. 113.
(4) *to make an object known, tell* its character :—Gecýþe ús þone weg,
Bl. H. 233, 20. Hé (*John*) hine (*Christ*) ǽr monnum gecýðan and
gesecgan teolode, ǽr þon þe hé sylfa lifde, 165, 31. (5) *to describe,
relate, give an account of* :—Ic þé mæg yfla gehwylces ór gecýðe oð
ende forð, Jul. 353. Ðás circean þus æteówde ond gecýþde seó ilce bóc,
Bl. H. 197, 25. Se ðe bet cunne gecýðe his mǽre, Angl. ix. 265, 14.
Nǽnig óðrum mæg wlite and wísan wordum gecýðan, Rä. 81, 7. Mid
giddum gecýþan hú wundorlíce Drihten welt eallra gesceafta, Bt. 25 ; F.
88, 2. (6) *to make known* what is asked about, *tell* in answer to
a question :—Búton þú mé sóð gecýðe, El. 690. Þæt hí mé þinga
gehwylc gecýðan þe ic him tó séce, 409. (6 a) *with an indirect
question* :—Gecýþe ús hwylce gemete þú cóme, Bl. H. 141, 20. Þ þú
mé gecýðe hwæt þes þegn sý, Jul. 279. Þæt hæt him on spellum
gecýðde hú hé his wísna trúwade, Gú. 1133. Gecýðan hwá teóde
eorðan, An. 79 : El. 861. Ofost is sélest tó gecýðanne hwanan eówre
cyme syndon, B. 257. Hwæt eów sélest ðynce tó gecýðanne, gif þeós
cwén úsic frigneð, El. 533. (7) *to confess* :—Æghwilc crísten man . . .
gewunige gelómlíce tó scrifte, and unforwandodlíce his synna gecýþe,
Ll. Th. i. 310, 6. **II.** *to make known by action, shew* kindness, &c.,
*display*. (1) *to perform an action* :—Hé feala tácna gecýðde, An. 711.
Manigfeald wundor . . . wǽrcn and gyt beóð æteówed and gecýðed,
Bl. H. 209, 16. (1 a) *with dat. of person seeing the action* :—Hé

mannum gecýþde on þás ondweardan tíd ealle þá þing þe æfre ǽr from
wītgum gewītgode wǽron be his þrowunga and be his ǽriste, Bl. H. 83,
27. Hé wundra feala weorodum gecýðde, An. 564. Him gecýðde
cyning ælmihtig wundor for weorodum, El. 866. (1 b) with preposition
marking the object affected by the action :—Him Crist fore woruldlicra
mā wundra gecýðde, Gú. 374. Þancas secggan ealra his geofena, and
ealra his miltsa and fremsumnessa, þe hé wiþ ūs æfre gecýþde, Bl. H. 115,
24. (2) *to shew* kindness, favour, *display* power, &c. :—Drihten nolde
his þá myclan miht gecýþan, Bl. H. 33, 18. (2 a) with dat. of person :
—Godes mōdor on þám hire mildheortnisse þǽre burhware gecýðde, Chr.
994; P. 129, 4. Hé wolde ūs his miltse gecýþon, Bl. H. 39, 23.
Gecýðan, An. 289. Þū mē hafast sybbe gecýðed, 358. (2 b) with
preposition marking the object affected :—Hé ealle eáþmódnesse and eal
geþyld and ealle mildheortnisse wiþ mancynn gecýþde, Bl. H. 123, 31.
Þū miltse on ūs gecýð, Cri. 157. Þū miht þíne mihte gecýþan on þínre
þeówan, Bl. H. 157, 3. Hié gecýðdon hwelce hláfordhyldo hī þóhton tō
gecýþanne on hiora ealdhláfordes bearnum, Ors. 6, 37; S. 296, 4. (3)
*to make to know* a feeling, *cause* a feeling :—Gecýþ nū middangearde
blisse (*make the world to know joy*), þ on þínum ūpstige geblissian ealle
þíne gecorenan, Bl. H. 87, 24. III. *to shew, prove* :—Gecýðde
*probavit*, Wrt. Voc. ii. 66, 74. Gecýðde *contestans*, Lk. p. 2, 14. (1)
*to establish practically the truth of* a statement, (a) where the statement
is contained in a preceding clause :—Leóht hafað ... Crīstes gecyndo;
hit þæt gecýðeð ful oft, Sal. 409. Þū eart milde ...; þæt þū gecýðdest,
þá þū..., Hö. 79 : Hy. 9, 16. Hé tō gewinne on þ mynster eóde ;
and þ sylfe mid dǽdum gecýðde (*quod ipsum facto monstrauit*), Bd. 4,
3; Sch. 353, 20: Exod. 406. Wæs hé... monad, swā þ sōna æfter
gecýþed wæs (*ut mox patuit*), Bd. 5, 6; Sch. 580, 4. (b) the statement
a dependent clause following :—Þonne gecýþe ic þ ic wāt ǽr hwæt hé
þenceþ, Bl. H. 181, 10. Ic gecýþe þ ic eom ðǽre stōwe hyrde, 201, 7.
Heó hire self gecýþ þ heó nānwuht ne biþ, Bt. 20 ; F. 70, 24. Hié
gecýðað on heora endunge þ hié nāwþer ne bióð, 16, 3 ; F. 56, 26.
Mid þǽre bysene hé gecýþde þ sōðfæste men habbaþ mid him þeófas,
Bl. H. 75, 27 : An. 700. Būton ic openlíce gecýþe þ ic God sý,
Bl. H. 181, 36. Hé wolde mannum gecýþan þ se āwyrgda gást æfestgaþ
..., 29, 21. On þǽm wæs gecýþed þæt hé wæs on ānum hāde twēgra
gecynda, 33, 32 : 35, 3 : Bt. 14, 2 ; F. 44, 35 : An. 90. (b a) where
the clause is in apposition to a noun or pronoun :—Hió hit gecýþ self
mid hire hwurfulnesse, þæt hió biþ swíþe wancol, Bt. 20 ; F. 70, 34.
Hé þæt gecýðde, þæt hé cræft hæfde, Sat. 200. Sōð is gecýðed, ...,
þæt þū wið waldend wǽre heólde, Exod. 419 : B. 700. ¶ of legal
procedure, *to prove* a point by performing the prescribed formalities :—
Gekýþe hé in wiófode ... þ wæs ðe ilca undeornunga ... gebohte ...
gif hé þ ne mæge gecýþan mid rihtre canne ..., Ll. Th. i. 34, 8–12.
Gecýðe hé be wīte þ hé ne gewita ne gestala nǽre, 118, 14 : 132, 15.
Mót hé gecýþan ... þ hé him nān ōðer ne sealde būton þ ilce, 150, 8.
Ðet se biscop ond ðā hīgen mōsten mid ðǽre gecýðan ðet hit suā wǽre
ārǽden on Æðelbaldes dæge, C. D. i. 279, 7. (2) *to prove the existence
of* something experimentally :—On heora wandlunga hié gecýþdon heora
fæstrǽdnesse, Bt. 7, 2 ; F. 16, 32. (3) *to prove by argument, by speech :*
—Æteáude ł gecýðde in godspell þ wæs ðe ilca ungewæmmed *manifestans
in euangelio quod erat ipse incorruptibilis*, Jn. p. 1, 5. Nū þe is genóh
openlíce gecýþed þætte nān þára gōda þin nis, Bt. 14, 2 ; F. 42,
28. IV. *to make known the position of* an object, *enable to find,
shew* :—Sæge ūs hwæðer ðú hér wīte ǽnigne ælþeódigne þe hātte
Placidas ... gif ðū hine ūs gecýþest, wē þe willað syllan mēde, Hml. S.
30, 253. Þæt þē gecýðe cyning ælmihtig hord under hrūsan, El.
1091. ¶ used intrans. *to appear*. Cf. æt-íwan :—Andrea, arís,
and gecýð (*St. Andrew had been invisible*) him, þæt hié ongieton mín
mægen on þē wesan *Andrew, arise and shew (thyself) to them, that they
may know my power is in thee*, Bl. H. 241, 14. IV a. *to make
known the character of* something, *enable to understand* :—Nū mæg sōð
hit sylf gecýþan, Bl. H. 187, 16. IV b. *to reveal, disclose* :—Hé
wilnodū þ God gecýþde þ mannum bemiðen wæs and bediglde, Bl. H.
199, 32. Þonne bið gecýðed hwā unclǽnnisse līf ālīfde, Dōm. 62. V.
*to make known, famous, to celebrate* :—Heó meotod sceolde cennan ...
swā hit gecýðed weard geond middangeard, Men. 52. Þ wæs foremǣre man
for Gode, and his gōd wæs swíðe gecýðed, Bl. H. 217, 3. Æfter þǽre
gecýþdan ǽriste, 133, 14. His hālines and wundor wǽron manigfealde
gecýðde geond ðis ēgland, Chr. 641 ; P. 27, 25. v. un-gecýð.

**ge-cýþedness**, e ; f. *Testimony* :—Gecýþednesse *testimonium*, Ps. L.
121, 4.

**ge-cýðelíc.** Dele.

**ge-cýþlǽcan**; p. lǽhte *To become known* :—Heó gecýþlǽchte *innotescat*, An. Ox. 2, 312. Gecýþlǽce, 8, 234.

**ge-cýþnes.** Add : (1) *witness, testimony* :—Gewitnes *vel* gecýðnes
*testimonium*, Wrt. Voc. i. 47, 27. Þone āworpenne hāliges gewrites
gecýþnesse (*testificatione*) hī oncnāwaþ, An. Ox. 40, 7. Hī cýþdon þ
mid leáre gecýþnesse, Bl. H. 173, 35. (2) of the scriptures, *testament* :
—Gecýþnesse *instrumenti* (*ueteris propheta*), An. Ox. 1765. Þis fæsten
wæs āsteald on ðǽre ealdan gecýðnysse, Hml. Th. ii. 100, 2 : Wlfst.

285, 16. Witan hwæt sý betwux ðām twām gecýðnessum ; ðǽre ealdan
ǽ ǽr Crīstes tōcyme and þǽre nīwan gecýðnesse under Crīstes gife, Ll.
Th. ii. 368, 10–12. Gecýþnessa *testamentorum* (*duorum*), An. Ox.
1547.

**ge-dæf**, Wülck. Gl. 257, 30. v. ge-þæf.

**ge-dæftan.** Add :—Ðonne sió ungedæftnes hit ne cann eft gedæftan
*si habere importunitas opportunitatem nescit*, Past. 97, 19. Hé hēt þá
gedæftan þ deófles templ, Hml. S. 4, 369.

**ge-dæft[e]líce.** Add : (1) *gently, mildly* :—Gif hé hit gedæftelíce
āsægð *si molestias tranquille lingua diceret*, Past. 273, 20. (2) *in
a fitting manner, suitably* :—Secge him mon suíðe gedæftelíce for his
āgnum scyldum *modis congruentibus de proprio reatu feriendi sunt*, Past.
185, 12. His līchama on ðǽre cyricean norðportice gedæftelíce (-dæft-
líce, *v. l.*) wæs bebyrged *in porticu aquilonali decenter sepultum est*, Bd. 2,
3; Sch. 124, 16. v. un-gedæft[e]líce.

**ge-dæftness.** v. un-gedæftness.

**ge-dæft[u]** ; f. *Gentleness, meekness* :—Gāð tō þæs wyrtgeardes geate
and mid gedæftum (*tranquille*) biddaþ and mid bletsunge nimaþ, Gr. D.
202, 12. v. ge-dæfte ; adj.

**ge-dǽlan.** I. *to divide* a whole into parts. (1) of a material whole.
(a) where the parts are no longer in contact :—Stānas uneáþe tōsomne
cumaþ, gif hī gedǽlede (tōdǽlde, *v. l.*) weorþaþ, Bt. 34, 11 ; F. 150, 25.
(b) where the parts remain in contact, *to mark the limits of the parts*.
Cf. VI a :—Is se finta fægre gedǽled, sum brūn, sum basu, sum splottum
beseted, Ph. 295. (2) of a non-material whole, *to distinguish the
component parts of* :—For þám þ hēhste gód wǽre mistlic and on swā
manigfeald gedǽled, þ hit nān mon ne mæg eall habban, Bt. 34, 9 ; F. 146,
17. II. *to dissolve* union, *part* company :—Þeáh his líc and gǽst
hyra somwiste gedǽlden, Gú. 942. Þū freóde scealt gedǽlan, ālǽtan
lufau mīne, Cri. 166. Síð wæs gedǽled, Exod. 207. III. *to
separate* (1) two or more objects :—God leóht and þýstro gedǽlde
*divisit lucem a tenebris* (Gen. 1, 4), Cri. 228. Hié heápum tōhlódon
hleóðrum gedǽlde, Gen. 1693. (2) *to part* man and wife :—Hé gedǽlde
wíf and wǣpned, Gen. 27, 44. Wit beótedan þæt unc ne gedǽle nemne
deáð āna ōwiht elles, Kl. 22. (3) *to separate* one object from another :
—Hé gedǽlde þæt leóht fram þām þeóstrum, Gen. 1, 4. Hé mynte þæt
hé gedǽlde ānra gehwylces líf wið líce, B. 731. Hé sceolde gedǽlan
feorh wið flǣsce, Ap. 36. Hé wilnode þæt hé wurde gedǽled wið hý
and wið heora yfelnesse, Ps. Th. 41, arg. III a. used reflexively.
(1) *to part from* one another :—Gif wit unc gedǽlað, Rä. 82, 7. Þeáh
seó sāwl and se līchama hý gedǽlan, Solil. H. 66, 6. (2) of married
people :—Hié be him lifgendum hié gedǽldun, Chr. 718 ; P. 42, 20.
Wer and wíf ðā ðe on hǣmede geþeódde wǣron ... mid hyra bēgra
geþafunge hī hig gedǽlon (*separentur*), Ll. Th. ii. 150, 30. (3) *to
separate* oneself from (α) a material object :—Ic mē ondrǣde þæt ic mē
scyle gedǽlan wið mīne freónd, oððe hī wið mē, Solil. H. 33, 11. (β)
from a non-material object, *to cease to do* :—Nó hé hine wið monna
miltse gedǽlde, ac gesynta bæd sāwla gehwylcre, Gú. 302. III b.
*to form a dividing line between* objects :—Hǣfde wederwolcen wīdum
fǣðmum eorðan and ūprodor efne gedǽled, Exod. 76. IV. intrans.
*To separate.* (1) *to go away from one another, part* :—Ðǣr nǽfre leófe
ne gedǽlað, ne lāðe ne gemētað, Wlfst. 204, 24. Mē gedǽlað, sibbe
tōslītað sinhīwan tū (*body and soul*), Jul. 697. Syððan hié gedǽldon
(or under V a?), An. 5. (2) of a whole, *to separate into parts, split
up* :—Hé gehēht ðæt meniga þ hé gedǽlde (*should separate into
companies* ; discumberet) ofer eorðu, Mt. L. 15, 35. V. *to share.*
(1) *to divide* into parts and take them, *divide* an inheritance, spoil, &c. :
—Oft weorðlic reáf men gedǽlað *dividere spolia*, Ps. Th. 67, 12. Þte
hé gidǽle mec mið þ erfe *ut diuidat hereditatem mecum*, Lk. R. L. 12,
13. Sceal yrfe gedǽled deádes monnes, Gn. Ex. 80. Habbað emne
gedǽled dæg and nihte sunne and mōna, Met. 29, 35. (1 a) of the
partition and occupation of land :—Þý geáre Healfdene Norþanhymbra
lond gedǽlde, Chr. 876 ; P. 74, 12. Gefōr se here on Miercna lond,
and hit gedǽldon sum, and sum Ceólwulfe saldon, 877 ; P. 74,
22. ¶ of the diversity existing among the earth's inhabitants :—Is
þes middangeard dālum gedǽled *there is great diversity among those
who live on the earth*, Gú. 25. (2) *to get advantage from, have a share
in* :—Gifstōl sceal gegierwed stondan, gif hine guman gedǽlen (*if men
have their part in it*, i. e. *get gifts from the king?*), Gn. Ex. 69.
Gedǽlan Dryhtnes þecelan, Sal. 418. (3) *to get, enjoy* :—Ðý lǽs ðā
īdlo gidǽle ne *uanitates* (*h*)*auriat*, Rtl. 162, 32. Ealle his ǣhta ríce
rēðemann gedǽle *scrutetur foenerator omnem substantiam ejus*, Ps. Th.
108, 11. V a. intrans. *To make a division of work* :—Syððan hié
gedǽldon (or under IV. 1), swā him Dryhten hlyt getǣhte *after they* (the
apostles) *had apportioned the work among themselves, as the Lord himself
had shewn the portion of each to be*, An. 5. VI. *to distribute.*
(1) *to scatter* objects :—Þá freátorhtestan tunglan [wurdon] gedǽlede
*limpida lumina spargerentur*, An. Ox. 1686. (2) *to spend* :—Ne þurfon
wē nā tō ūrum mǣgum ... ðencean tō ðām swyþe, þæt him man ǣfter
his forðsíþe tō ðām micel fore gedǽle, þæt hit hine fram wītan ālýsan,
Wlfst. 306, 5. Þ þ ofer byð ic hohgie swā ǣndebyrdlíce gedǽlan swā ic

ændebyrdlícost mæg *divitias, si prouenerint, sapientissime atque cautissime administrandas esse,* Solil. H. 35, 19. Áspendre, gedǽledre *erogate,* i. *dispensate,* An. Ox. 1841. Þǽre gedǽledan *eroganté,* Wrt. Voc. ii. 33, 3. (3) of almsgiving:—Hé his ǽhta þearfendum gedǽled *dedit pauperibus,* Ps. Th. 111, 8. Þone þriddan dǽl hé þearfum gedǽlde (*distribuit*), Bd. 5, 12; Sch. 614, 13. Sié þæt feóh gedǽled þearfum, Ll. Th. i. 198, 12. Donne ðú ealle gedǽlde hæfst, þonne bist ðú ðe self wǽdla, Bt. 13; F. 38, 35. (4) *to give as a person's share, hand over, give:*—Sumne se hára wulf deáðe gedǽled, Wand. 83. Hié þín feorh ne magon deáðe gedǽlan, An. 957: 1219. (5) of the dispensations of Providence, *to allot, assign, grant:*—Hé gedǽleð, sé þe áh dómes geweald, missenlíce leóda leoðocræftas londbúendum, Crä. 27. Dreámas hé gedǽlde, Sat. 19. Swá beóð módsefan dálum gedǽled, Mód. 22. Á þe bið gedǽled, ... wunað wísdom in, Fä. 48. For hwám næron eorðwelan ealle gedǽled leódum gelíce?, Sal. 342. (6) *to utter* words. Cf. tó-dǽlan; XI:—Mín gehát þæt míne weleras ǽr wíse gedǽldan, Ps. Th. 65, 12. VI a. *to diffuse, spread:*—Ðerh gedǽlde *perfudit,* Mt. p. 20, 2. v. efen-gedǽlan; ge-dál.

ge-dǽle (?), es; *n.* *A portion* of common land. v. gedál-land:—Úp be hagan oð ða gedéla, C. D. v. 381, 26. Cf. ge-dál.

ge-dǽledlíce. For *separatim* Cot. 201 *substitute*: sequestratim, Wrt. Voc. ii. 75, 45. ge-dǽman. *Dele, and see* ge-clǽman.

ge-dafen. *Take here* ge-defen *in Dict., and add:*—Gedaebeni (-debin, Erf.) geabuli *debita pensio,* Txts. 57, 648. Gedafene gaful, Wrt. Voc. ii. 139, 70. Swá hit gedafene is, Bl. H. 115, 15. Gedafenre *oportuno,* Bl. Gl. Gedafenum *debitis,* Wrt. Voc. ii. 28, 36.

ge-dafen, es; *n.* (or ge-dafenu; *f.?*) *What is due* or *fitting:*—Þá wæs þær ylding þǽre tíde þe man sceolde þá lícþegnunge and þá gedafenu þǽre byrgene gefyllan and gyldan *cum mora esset temporis ad explendum debitum sepulturae,* Gr. D. 84, 5. Ágylde se wer þám wífe hire gedafenu (*debitum*), 218, 5. Cf. ge-défe; *n.*

ge-dafenian. *Add:*—Gedafenaþ *conuenit,* Wülck. Gl. 252, 15. (1) the subject a noun. (a) with dat. or uncertain:—Rehtwíse gedeofenað efenherenis *rectis decet conlaudatio,* Ps. Srt. 32, 1. Ðé gedeafenað ymen, 64, 2.... Húse ðínum gedeafineað (*decent*) ða hálgan, 92, 5. Gedafenie[n]dre beclýsinge *competenti clausula,* An. Ox. 5356. (b) with infin. or clause :—Swylces módes wer má gedafonade (-dafen-, *v. l.*) beón tó bysceope gehálgad (þ hé wǽre tó bisceope gehálgod, *v. l.*) þonne hé cyning wǽre *a man of such a disposition was more suited to be consecrated a bishop than to be a king; talis animi uirum episcopum magis quam regem ordinari deceret,* Bd. 4, 11; Sch. 404, 2. (2) the subject a pronoun. (a) with an infin. :—Hú hit gedafenige on his gesihðe beón *qualiter oporteat in conspectu ejus esse,* R. Ben. I. 52, 17. (b) with a clause in apposition :—Wel þ gedafenaþ þ hé eorþan ástige, Bl. H. 13, 19: Cri. 551. Wel þ gedafenode þ Dryhten swá dyde, Bl. H. 67, 12: 77, 12. (3) without a subject. (a) alone :—Godes laga healdan swá swá his háde gedafenað, Ll. Th. i. 346, 24. Dó hire swá dohtrum gedafenað *faciet illi juxta morem filiorum,* Ll. Lbmn. 30, 6 note. (b) with a clause :—Mé gedafenaþ þæt ic nú tódæg þe gecyrre, Hml. Th. i. 580, 33: Bl. H. 227, 13: 55, 4: 149, 11. Us gedafanað þ ..., Bd. 4, 3; Sch. 362, 15. (c) with infin. :—Þá án þá þe tó ǽfæstnesse belumpon, and his þá ǽfestan tungan gedafenode (-deofanode, *v. l.*) singan *ea tantummodo, quae ad religionem pertinent, religiosam ejus linguam decebant,* Bd. 4, 24; Sch. 482, 9. (d) with gerundial infin. :—Swá ǽnigan crístenan mæn ne gedafenað tó dónne, Ll. Th. i. 316, 11. Hú monnum gedafonode (-dafen-, *v. l.*) on hiera beddum tó dónne, Past. 99, 20.

ge-dafenigendlic, -dafniendlic; *adj. Suitable, convenient* :—Gedafniendlic *conueniens,* An. Ox. 1126. Gedafniendlíce *conuenientia,* 3891. Mid gebedum gedafnigendlicum (*competentibus*), Angl. xiii. 419, 772. v. un-gedafniendlic.

ge-dafenigendlíce. *Substitute* : *Suitably, agreeably* :—Gedafsenigendlíce *consequenter,* Scint. 9, 4 : *conpetenter,* 158, 6.

ge-dafenlic. *Add:*—Wæs þ eác gedafenlic (-dafen-, *v. l.*) þætte þæt swefen gefylled wǽre *oportebat impleri somnium,* Bd. 4, 23; Sch. 472, 19. Gedoefenlic is *oportet,* Jn. p. 4, 1. Wæs gidæfendlic *oportebat,* Jn. R. 4, 4. Hit is nú swýþe gedafenlic tíma, þæt wé ús sylfe clǽnsian, Wlfst. 103, 17. Mid gedafenlíce *conpetenti,* Wrt. Voc. ii. 24, 70. Of gedafenlicum rǽdelse *congrua conjectura,* An. Ox. 7, 84. Mid gedafenlicum (-dafenlíce, -defenlíce, *v. ll.*) ege *debito cum timore,* Bd. 4, 3; Sch. 362, 18. Wé willað ymbe þás emnihte sprecan on gedefenlíce stówe, Lch. iii. 240, 2. Hit wæs healdende swýðe gedafenlíce ylde on his þeáwum, Gr. D. 95, 1. Weorþiaþ God mid gedafenlícum þingum, Bl. H. 41, 9. v. un-gedafenlic.

ge-dafenlíce. *Add:*—Sé þe gedafenlíce and endebyrdlíce tó cymð *qui ad regimen ordinate peruenerit,* Past. 75, 1. Swýðe gedafenlíce (-dafíce, Hpt. Gl. 415, 52) *non inconuenienter,* i. *non incongrue,* An. Ox. 389. Gedafenlíce forgifene *conuenienter* (printed -es) *nuptae,* Wrt. Voc. ii. 135, 47. Hé ðone hálgan grétte, biddende þæt hé him dægwistes gedafenlíce tíðode *he greeted the saint, asking that he would furnish him suitably with provisions,* Hml. Th. ii. 134, 30. v. un-gedafenlíce.

ge-dafenlicness. *Add:*—Gesetton ða hálgan fæderas þ wé fæston mid geráde, and ælce dæg eton mid gedafenlicnysse, swá þ úre líchama álefed ne wurðe, Hml. S. 13, 103.

ge-daflíc. *l.* ge-daflíce, *and see* ge-dafenlíce : ge-dafniendlic. v. ge-dafenigendlic.

ge-dál. *Add* : I. *division, separation.* Cf. ge-dǽlan; I. 1 :—On ǽgðre healfe þæs scipes wæs regnes storm, and in þ ilce scip nán regnes dropa ne gefeóll ... þis wundor þæs regnes gedáles (*hoc quod de diuisa pluuia factum miraculum*), Gr. D. 196, 14. II. *dissolution, destruction.* Cf. ge-dǽlan; II :—Of ðám dǽle heora tóworpnysse and gedáles *ex parte suae destructionis,* Gr. D. 205, 6. Deáþa gedál dreógan tó ðie, Gú. 206. Ymb gedál sacan middangeardes, Gn. Ex. 28. III. *parting, separation* of two or more objects. Cf. gedǽlan; III, IV :—Ne bið leófra gedál, ne láþra gesamnung, Bl. H. 65, 20. Críst leng wið him líchomlíce wunian nolde ... him ne wæs nǽnig earfoþe þæt líchomlíce gedál (*that bodily parting*), 135, 31. Earmlic gedál líces and sáwle, Wlfst. 187, 15. Se Hǽlend ús helpe gefremede þurh his líces gedál (*the parting of the body from the soul, death*), Ph. 651. IV. *a dividing* of property, *sharing.* Cf. ge-dǽlan; V :—Þá dǽldon þá cwelleras þǽra martyra wǽpna and gewǽda ... Æfter ðám gedále ..., Hml. S. 28, 87. Ic gean mínum wífe and mínre dehter healfes þæs landes æt Cunningtúne tó gedále (*to divide between them*), búton þám feówer hýdon ðe ic Æðelríce and Ælfwolde gean ... And ic gean Ælfmǽre and his breðer þára twégra landa tó gedále ... And ic gean mínum þrým bróðrum tó gedále þæs landes æt Trostingtúne, búton þám ðe ic gean Ælfwolde ðæs ðe Æðelríc hæfde, Cht. Th. 597, 14–598, 4 : Gen. 1400. His hírédcnihton eallon v. pund tó gedále (*to be divided amongst them*), ælcon þe þám þe his mǽð wǽre, Cht. Crw. 23, 26. V. *a distributing, spending, giving.* Cf. gedǽlan; VI :—Gedál *dispensatio,* Wrt. Voc. ii. 140, 65. Gedále *expenso,* 145, 45. Ðý lǽs hié for ðæm gedále ðæs feós wilnigen ðisses lǽnan lífes ... Ðonne hé his ælmessan dǽld, Past. 323, 12. Gif hé ǽr ðæm gedále cann gemetgian hwæt hine anhagie tó sellanne, 341, 12. Hé ða láre him forgeaf þæt hí hí dǽldon eallum ðeódum, Be ðám gedále cwæð sum wítega, Hml. Th. ii. 400, 23. VI. *a share, portion, part* :—On þǽre tócnáwnesse ǽgðre gedáles (dǽles, *v. l.*) *in qua cognitione utriusque partis,* Gr. D. 311, 11. VII. *difference* :—Micel gedál is on wæpnedes and wífes and cildes líchoman, and on þám mægene þæs dæghwámlican wyrhtan and þæs ídlan ..., Lch. ii. 84, 15. Eálá, þú man, hwæt dést þú þ þu ne sý þám dumban nytene gelíc? Geþenc hú micel gedál God betweox ús gesceóp, Ll. Th. ii. 394, 29. Ðæt sceal geþencan sé þe bið manna sáwla lǽce ... þ gedál and þ gesceád, hú hé mannum heora dǽla gescrífe, and hí þeáhhwæðere ne fordéme ne hig ormóde ne gedó *he must consider the difference between suitable shrift and one that condemns the penitent or makes him desperate,* 260, 13. v. ge-dǽle.

gedál-land. *Add* : *Dole-land, common land in which various persons have portions indicated by land-marks.* v. Seebohm, Vill. Comm. c. iv :—Ðás nigon hída licggeað ongemang óðran gedállande, feldlǽs gemǽne and mǽda gemáne and yrðland gemǽne, C. D. vi. 39, 9. Cf. dál-mǽd.

gedál-líc. v. un-gedállic.

ge-deád *dead* :—Dohter mín gedeád is *filia mea defuncta est,* Mt. L. 9, 18.

ge-deágian *to dye, colour* :—Gedeágod *colorata,* Wrt. Voc. ii. 19, 14.

ge-deápian. v. ge-deópian : ge-deáðian. *For* ge-déðan *substitute* ge-díþan.

ge-deáw; *adj. Bedewed, wet with dew* :—On morgenne þonne sió wyrt gedeáw sié, Lch. ii. 92, 15. Wildre rúdan gedeáwre, 26, 10.

ge-deccan *to cover. Substitute* ge-décan *to smear.* v. décan.

ge-défe. *Add* : I. *suitable, fitting, seemly* :—Hé má lufedon dióra drohtað, swá hit gedéfe ne wæs, Met. 26, 92. Tó forðspównesse gedéfore heánesse *ad profectum debiti culminis,* Bd. 2, 4; Sch. 127, 5. Gedéfum gafule *debita pensione,* Wrt. Voc. ii. 25, 22. Gedéfum *debitis, congruis,* 139, 72. II. of persons. (1) *righteous, good* :—Ædele lǽreów, árfæst and gedéfe, Hml. Th. i. 596, 32. Manige hálge and gedéfe wítgan wǽran ǽr Sancte Iôhanne, Bl. H. 161, 12. Hié bútú wǽron swíþe gedéfe beforan Gode *erant justi ambo ante Deum* (Lk. 1, 6), 30. Wuna mid ús, þæt þu ús gedéfra[n] gedó, for þon þe we níwe syndon tó þissum geleáfan gedón, 247, 34. (2) *staid, sober* :—Sé wæs wintrum geong and on his þeáwum eald and gedéfe *aetate juuenis, sed moribus grandaeuus,* Gr. D. 219, 3. Of gesægne swíðe gedéfra and getreówra háda *personarum grauium atque fidelium relatione,* 278, 23. (3) *quiet, meek, gentle* :—On gedéfre heortan *corde quieto,* Wülck. Gl. 252, 29. Behealde ic tó þám eádmódan and tó þám gedéfan (*quietum*), Scint. 18, 8. His gást wunað ofer ðone eádmódan and ofer þone gedéfan, Hml. A. 40, 394. Gedéfe mód *tranquillam mentem,* Wülck. Gl. 252, 20. Þá gedéfan *quietos,* Hy. S. 3, 23. III. of things. (1) *quiet* :—On tídum gedéfum *horis quietis,* Hy. S. 4, 30. (2) In the metrical Psalms it is used as a favourable epithet of indefinite meaning :—Ealle þe ... his gedéfne weg lustum gangað *omnes ... qui ambulant in*

*viis ejus*, Ps. Th. 127, 1. Dyde gedēfe mægen Dryhtnes swӯđre *dextera Domini fecit virtutem*, 117, 36. Mîue gedēfe word *verba mea*, 140, 8: 145, 6. v. lǽr-(?), un-gedēfe.

**ge-dēfe (?)**, es; *n.*: **ge-dēfu (?)**; *f. What is seemly; seemliness*, Gn. Ex. 189. [v. list.] Cf. ge-dafen; *n.*

**ge-dēfedlic.** *See next word.*

**ge-dēfelic.** *Add:*—Swӯđe gedēfelice eldo, Gr. D. 95, 1. Mid gedēfelicre (-dēfedlicre, *v. l.*) ārwyrđnesse *dignae uenerationis gratia*, Bd. 4, 30; Sch. 534, 5. v. ge-dafenlic.

**ge-dēfelīce.** *Add:*—Hē his bisceophād gedēfelīce for Gode geheóld, Bl. H. 219, 31. Hū mæg ic đē āna gedēfelīce deáđþēnunga gegearwian?, Nap. 16, 35. v. un-gedēfelīce.

**ge-dēfnes.** *Add:*—Lǽt mē mid gedēfnysse mīne dagas geendian, Angl. xii. 499, 7.

**ge-dēglic.** v. ge-dīglic: **ge-dela.** v. ge-dǽle.

**ge-delf.** *Add:* (1) *digging, act of digging*:—Sum underdealf þā duru mid spade . . . leát tō gedelfe, Hml. S. 32, 212. 'Geopeniađ þās eorđan on þyssere stōwe' . . . Æt đam forman gedelfe swēgde ūt ormǽte wyllspring, Hml. Th. i. 562, 14. v. marnstān-, ymb-gedelf. (2) *an excavation, a ditch, quarry, hole.* v. leád-, stān-gedelf.

**ge-delfan.** *Add:* (1) *intrans. To dig*:—Hē gedalf in eorđo *fodit in terra*, Mt. L. 25, 18. Þā hē hæfde gedolfen twēntig fōta on đǽre eorđan, H. R. 13, 14. (2) *trans. To dig a hole*:—In đǽm gedolfene byrgenne his stōue *in defossum sepulturae suae locum*, Jn. p. 2, 1. [þenne hē haueđ ene put idoluen þonne ualleđ he þermne, O. E. Hml. i. 49, 28.]

**ge-dēman.** *Dele second passage, and add:* **I.** *to judge.* (1) *absolute*:—Gié æfter līchoma gedoemas (*iudicatis*) . . . Đǽh ic gedoemo (*iudico*), dôm mīn sōđ is, Jn. L. 8, 15, 16. Nellađ gié gedoema, Lk. L. 6, 37. (2) *to judge a person*, (a) *with dat. (or uncertain)*:—Swā hē gedēmđ ūs swā wē hēr dēmađ þām þe wē on eorđan dōm ofer āgan, Ll. Th. ii. 314, 13. Se dēma sē þe ōđrum on wōh gedēme, i. 266, 15. (b) *with acc.*:—Hē gedoemed hine *ille iudicabit eum*, Jn. L. R. 12, 48. Þte [hē] gedoemde middangeard, 3, 17. Gidoema cuico and deádo *judicare uiuos et mortuos*, Rtl. 120, 37. Gif đā twelf mǽgđa āna beóđ gedēmede æt đām micelum dōme, Hml. Th. i. 396, 3. (3) *where the matter of judgement is given*:—Hwæt from iów solfum ne gidoemađ đætie sōđfæst is?, Lk. R. L. 12, 57. Gidoem þte sōđ is, Rtl. 102, 17. (3 a) *with cognate accusative*:—Of þissum ānum dōme mon mæg geþencean þ hē æghwylcne dōm on riht gedēmeđ, Ll. Th. i. 56, 30. Sōđfæstne dōm gedoemađ, Jn. R. L. 7, 24. Him ne biđ nān dōm gedēmed, Hml. Th. i. 396, 19: Dan. 655. Mid þӯ ic geseó mīnne dōm gedēmedne beón *cum uiderim iudicium meum iam esse completum*, Bd. 5, 14; Sch. 646, 3. (4) *to adjudge* reward, punishment, &c., *assign*:—God þām nāne mildheortnesse ne gedēmde þe hine oferhogodon, ne Crīst þām nāne ne gedēmde þe hyne sealde tō deáđe, Ll. Th. i. 58, 10–12. León hwelpas sēcađ þæt him grǽdigum æt God gedēme, Ps. Th. 103, 20. (5) *to settle, decide, decree*:—Wiþersacana [dofunga] wiþsacan [fædera] laga āwritenum gesettnessum gedēmdan *apocrifarum deliramenta abdicare patrum scita scriptis decretalibus sancxerunt*, An. Ox. 1967. Þonne wæs gedēmed þæt hī ealle sceoldon singan *cum esset decretum ut omnes cantare deberent*, Bd. 4, 24; Sch. 482, 16. Leng feorg gehealdan þonne him gedēmed wæs, Gū. 1032. **I a.** *of unfavourable judgement, to condemn, censure*:—Gedēmađ and tǽlađ *obtuperabitis* (l. (?) vituperabitis*). Cf. tǽldon *uituperauerunt*, Mk. 7, 2), Wrt. Voc. ii. 63, 63. Gif him man gedēme, gilde twifealdon, Ex. 22, 9. Wīf from fordoemendum gedoemede *mulierem accusatoribus condemnatam*, Jn. p. 5, 9. **I b.** *to execute judgement* on a person, *carry out a sentence*:—þe þū mīne ēhtend for mē ealle gedēme *quando facies de persequentibus me judicium?*, Ps. Th. 118, 84. **II.** *to deem, suppose*:—Nelleđ gē gedoema forđon ic cuōm tō sendenne sibbe *nolite arbitrari quia uenerim mittere pacem*, Mt. L. 10, 34. Gedoemendo wēron þ . . . arbitrati sunt quod . . . , 20, 10.

**ge-deóful-geld.** *Dele.*

**ge-deón**; *p.* de *To suck*:—Đā breósto đā đū gediides *ubera quae suxisti*, Lk. L. 11, 27. v. deón.

**ge-deópian**; *p.* ode *To become deep*:—Gideápadon niólnisso *preruperunt abyssi*, Rtl. 81, 24. [Cf. þe dic wes idoluen and ideoped, Laym. 15473. *Goth.* ga-diupjan *to dig deep*.] v. deópian.

**ge-deorf.** (1) *labour, toil, work*:—Gif gedeorf (*labor*) ođþe sumerhǽte hwylces eácan (*an increase of food*) behōfige, R. Ben. 64, 17. Of folclicum gedeorfe *ex plebeio labore*, 138, 22. On sceortum gedeorfe *labore breui*, Wülck. Gl. 256, 27. Woldon hremmas hine bereáfian æt his gedeorfum . . . Đā hremmas flugon . . . , and se hālga his geswinces breác, Hml. Th. ii. 144, 13–20. (2) *trouble, laborious effort, difficulty*:—'Micel gedeorf biđ mē þæt ic mīne feónd lufige.' Ne wiđcweđe wē þæt hit micel gedeorf ne sӯ; ac gif hit is hefigtӯme . . . , Hml. Th. i. 56, 1–4. Þæt hӯ þe glædlicor būtan gedeorfe and miclum geswince heora gebrōđrum đēnien *ut sine murmuratione et graui labore seruiant fratribus suis*, R. Ben. 59, 15. Epactas . . . būtan gedeorfe wē magon gecӯđan heora ūpspring, Lch. iii. 282, 3. (3) *trouble, tribulation,*

*affliction*:—On gedeorfe *in tribulatione*, Ps. L. 4, 2. Gedeorf mîn *laborem meum*, 24, 18. Gedeorfu heortan mînre *tribulationes cordis mei*, Ps. Rdr. 24, 17.

**ge-deorfan.** *Substitute:* **I.** *to labour, do hard work*:—Oxanhyrde, hwæt wyrcst þū? Eálā, hlāford mîn, micel ic gedeorfe (*laboro*), Coll. M. 20, 25. **II.** *to perish, be destroyed, be wrecked* (lit. or fig.). (a) *of a person*:—Gedurfan *naufragauerunt* (*duae faeminae a fide*), Wrt. Voc. ii. 85, 60: 60, 68. Đā hī oninnan þǽm sǽfærelde wǽron, þā gedu[r]fon (*a letter is erased before the* f) hî ealle and ādruncen *obruta est et interfecta universa Aegypti multitudo*, Ors. 1, 7; S. 38, 33. Heora scipa gedearf (r *erased*); gedraf, *v. l.*) cc and xxx *Romana classis infando naufragio eversa est; nam de trecentis navibus ducentae et viginti perierunt*, 4, 6; S. 176, 19. Hiora scipa gedurfon L and C *centum quinquaginta naves onerarias perdiderunt*, 28. [Ha beon þurh me idoruen, Marh. 16, 1. He was idoruen in alle hio ođre wittes, A. R. 106. Þu bodest cwalm of orve oþer þat londfolc wurþ idorve, O. and N. 1158.] v. ge-dirfan.

**gedeorf-leás.** *Substitute: Without trouble, prosperous*:—Gedeorfleásum *prospero*, Germ. 402, 59.

**ge-deorfsum** *grievous.* *Add:*—Đis wæs swīđe gedyrfsum geár hēr on lande þurh wæstma forwordenessa and þurh þā mænigfealde gyld, Chr. 1105; P. 240, 4.

**ge-derednes**, e; *f. Injury, hurt*:—Wiđ gehwylce gederednyssa, Lch. i. 322, 1.

**ge-derian.** *Add:* (1) *absolute*:—Hē gelǽrđ þæt hē swicollīce hīwige . . . , and under þām leáslican hīwe swiđost gederige, Wlfst. 53, 27. Gederod *lessus*, Wülck. Gl. 257, 27. Đǽm gederedum *lesis*, Wrt. Voc. ii. 53, 31. (2) *with dat.*:—Sē đe heom gederige mid worde ođđe weorce, Ll. Th. ii. 240, 6. Gif hit gewierđe þ man gehādedum oþþe ælþeódigum gederode (-ede, *v. l.*), i. 192, 18. Nān mon ne mæg þām gesceádwīsan mōde gederian, Bt. 16, 2; F. 52, 17. v. un-gedered.

**ge-dēpan.** v. ge-dīpan.

**ge-dīcan** *to make a dīc*:—On đā dīc đe hē gedīcte, C. D. iii. 367, 6.

**ge-dīfan**; *pp.* ed *To plunge, immerse*:—Rammes wul on wætere gedӯfed and æfter þām on ele, Lch. i. 356, 12. v. dīfan.

**ge-dīgan.** *Add:* **I.** *to escape* danger. (1) *used absolutely*:—Seó wiht (*a steer*), gif hió gedӯgeđ, dūna briceđ, gif hē tōbirsteđ, bindeđ cwice (cf. *the Latin riddle*: Si vixero, rumpere colles incipiam, vivos moriens aut alligo multos, Prehn, p. 212), Rä. 39, 6. (2) *with acc.* (a) *to come successfully out of* conflict:—On swā hwylcum gefeohte swā đu bist [đū bist] sigefæst, and þū þ gedīgest, gif þū đone fōt mid þe hafast, Lch. i. 328, 7. (b) *to escape from* danger, harm, &c.:—Feá þæt gedӯgađ þāra þe gerǽcađ rynegiestes wǽpen, Rä. 4, 57. Ic þæt unsōfte ealdre gedīgde, B. 1655. Gefeónde þ hē þone deáđ gedīgde (*evaserit*), Gr. D. 203, 14. Se brōþer gedīgde þ *wîte frater evasit supplicium*, 346, 6. Hē geortrȳwde hweþer hē mihte gedīgean (*evadere*) swā myccle frēcnesse þāra ӯþa, 34. Þū þæs dēman scealt yrre gedӯgan, Jul. 257. (b a) *of things*:—Nǽnig mōste heora hrōrra hrīm æpla gedīgean *occidit moros eorum in pruina*, Ps. Th. 77, 47. (c) *to escape from* an enemy:—Þone feónd, þām hē wæs geseald, hē þone nā ne gedӯgde *eum hostem, cui traditus fuerat, non evasit*, Gr. D. 327, 18. (d) *to recover from* illness:—Būtan þā āne þe hӯ þā slitnesse gedīgean mǽgen *iis tantummodo exceptis, quae a tali laceratione convalescere possint*, Ll. Th. ii. 166, 25. **II.** *to benefit, profit.* v. dīgan:—Gyf hyt hwā gedō, ne gedīge hit him nǽfre, Lch. i. 384, 11.

**ge-dīglan, -dīglian.** *Take here* **ge-dīéglan, -dīhligean** *in Dict., and add:* **I.** *to hide, conceal*:—Hē hit gediégleđ (*abscondit*), Past. 451, 16. Đā đe oninnan him gedīglađ and gehӯdađ (*occultant*) đā godcundan lāre, 379, 4. Wîf his gedēgelde (*occultabat*) hiá, Lk. L. 1, 24. Biđ gedēgled *contexitur*, Mt. p. 9, 10. **II.** *to lie hid*:—Ne gedēgelde *non latuit*, Lk. L. 8, 47. v. dīglan.

**ge-dīglic.** *adj. Hidden, secret*:—Ofgestīgnisse g[e]dēglice *descensionis occultae*, Mt. p. 8, 4.

**ge-dihtan.** *Add:* (1) *to direct, order, give direction* to a person (*dat.*):—Wīse menn hit āfunden þurh þone hālgan wīsdōm, swā heom God gedihte, Lch. iii. 154, 7. Ān scyp þe Godd sylf gedihte Nōe tō wyrcanne, Wlfst. 10, 10. (1 a) *with acc. of direction, to give a direction*:—Hē gedihte þisne cwyde . . . 'Nimađ þisne scyldigan . . .' þā tugon hī þone halgan wer, swā hē him gediht hæfde, Hml. S. 14, 151–159. (2) *to direct* what is to be written or spoken, *dictate* a letter, speech, &c.:—Seó ealde gesetnys đe hē þurh Mōysen gedihte, Hml. Th. ii. 56, 16. Þæt gewrit āwrāt Godes ængel, swā swā seó hālige þrynnys hit gedihte, Wlfst. 292, 21. Đā āwrāt se earming mid his āgenre handa, swā swā se deófol him gedihte þone pistol, Hml. S. 3, 383. (3) *to appoint, ordain*:—Ymbrenfæstena healde man rihte, swā swā Scs Gregorius Angelcynne hit gedihte, Wlfst. 272, 18: Ll. Th. i. 320, 21. Dǽdbōta sind gedihte on mislice wīsan, iii. 280, 3. (4) *to order, manage, rule*:—þæt heáfod gewissađ þām ōđrum limum, swā swā þæt mōd gediht đā getōhtas, Hml. Th. i. 612, 14. (4 a) *of the divine ordering*:—God is swā mihtig, þæt hē ealle đing gediht and gefadaþ būtan geswince, Hml. Th. i. 470, 24: Hml. A. 24, 15: Lch. iii. 278

14. (5) *to compose* a letter, verse, &c. :—Ærendgewrit þe on þyson and-gite wæs gediht, Hml. S. 23, 792. Þás vers mid gyldenum stafum áwritene þus wæron on his spræce gedihte, Angl. viii. 325, 48. (5 a) *to draw up* regulations, laws, &c. :—Ðás týn beboda God sylf gedihte and áwrat, Wlfst. 66, 21. Án þára geræðnessa þe Engla cyning gedihte mid his witena geþeahte, Ll. Th. i. 340, 4. (6) *to construct, make* :—Se Fæder gedihte ealle gesceafta þurh his Wísdóm, and se Wísdóm is his Sunu, Hml. Th. ii. 206, 16. God gesceóp man on ðám sixtan dæge, ðá ðá hé gesceafta gedihte, 260, 22. (7) *to perform, do* :—þá ealle þás ðincg þurh Godes fadunge þus wurdon gedihte, Hml. S. 23, 347. (8) *to arrange* :—God þás þingc swá gescifte, and mid his fadunge gedihte, þ heora nán gefélan ne mihte, Hml. S. 23, 257. Hú hé þurh gesihðe gedihte þá mynstertimbrunge *de fabrica monasterii per visionem ab eo disposita*, Gr. D. 147, 11. Þæs mynstres getimbrunga gedihtan, Hml. Th. ii. 172, 11. Hé sceall ládunge gedihtan þ ænig man óðrum ænig wóh beódan ne mæge, Ll. Th. ii. 312, 16. Gedihtere endebyrdnesse sealmsangas *disposito ordine psalmodie*, R. Ben. I. 51, 4. Siþbóc gedihte *itinerarium digestum (decem voluminibus)*, An. Ox. 2024. Gedihte *digesta* (antiquarum arcam legum ab illo mirabiliter *digesta*), 147 : 2175. (9) *to deck, adorn* :—Gediht *vel* gesiwad hrægel *aucupicta vel frigia vestis*, Wrt. Voc. i. 40, 18.

ge-dihtnian; *p.* ode *To dispose, order, arrange; disponere* :—Gediht-nað *disponat (cor hominis viam suam)*, Kent. Gl. 551. Ðæt God swá gedihtnað (geændebyrdeð, *v. l.*) of þære micelan gedihtnunge (-stihtunge, *v. l.*) his ærfæstnysse *quod Deus ex magnae pietatis dispensatione disponit*, Gr. D. 146, 28. þ God ær ealre worulde gedihtnode (geteohhode, *v. l.*) him tó forgifenne *quod eis Deus ante secula disposuit donare*, 54, 26.

ge-dihtnung *a dispensation, disposing*, Gr. D. 146, 28. *See preceding word.*

ge-dilgian. *l.* ge-dílgian, *and add*: II. *intrans. To perish* :—Gyf þú ænig ðing ðisse stale wite, þonne gedýlegie ðín heorte, Ll. Lbmn. 415, 25.

ge-dingan (?) *to press, throw oneself with force* :—Gedind *appetit*, Kent. Gl. 1155. [Cf. *Mid. E.* ding *to throw oneself with force, dash, press, drive*.]

ge-dípan *to baptize* :—Gedéped *baptizatus*, Mt. R. 3, 16. [*O. Sax.* gi-dôpian : *O. H. Ger.* ge-toufet *baptizatus*.]

ge-díran. *Take here* ge-dýran *in Dict.* : ge-direlan, Wrt. Voc. ii. 27, 62. *l.* ge-girelan.

ge-dirfan; *pp.* ed. I. *to cause to labour.* Cf. ge-deorfan ; I :—Ic beó sóðlíce gedyrfe[d?] on bebodum þínum *ego autem exercebor in mandatis tuis*, Ps. L. 118, 78. II. *to endanger, imperil.* Cf. ge-deorfan ; V :—Cild bið on wætere gedyrfed; gif hé ætwint, langlífe hé bið, Lch. iii. 184, 4 : 188, 4. Gedyrfed *jactata*, Germ. 402, 46. Betere ys þæt for manegra hælþe án beó genyþerud, þænne þurh ánes leáfe manega beóð gedyrfede (*periclitentur*), Scint. 115, 20. Scypu beóð gedyrfed (*per[i]clitantur*) on wídsæ, Archiv cxx. 297, 19.

ge-dirnan. *Take here* ge-diernan, ge-dyrnan *in Dict., and add*: I. *trans. To hide* :—Gedyrned *oppilatum (silentio)*, Wrt. Voc. ii. 78, 74 : 64, 23. II. *intrans. To hide oneself, lie hid* :—Ge-diernan *dilituisse* (Apollonius *delituisse* fertur haud procul a delubro), Wrt. Voc. ii. 83, 9 : 26, 61. ge-dyrnan, 140, 40.

ge-dírsian. *Take here* ge-dýrsian *in Dict., and add*: [*O. H. Ger.* tiurisôn *glorificare*; ni was noh thanne gidiurisôt *nondum fuerat glorificatus*.]

ge-dípan, -dépan; *pp.* ed. I. *to put to death, kill* :—Mid deáðe gedéðed sé *morte moriatur*, Mk. L. R. 7, 10. Of hwælcum deáðe uére sweltende † gedéðed *qua morte esset moriturus*, Jn. L. 12, 33. Þte hiá woere gedéðed † gecuelledo *ut interficerentur*, Lk. L. R. 23, 32. II. *to mortify* (in the theological sense) :—Þte úsig ágéfe Gode gidéðed líchome (*mortificatos carne*), Rtl. 21, 32. Gidéðod, 25, 43. [*O. H. Ger.* ge-tôden.] Cf. dídan.

ge-dof (?), es ; *n. Absurdity, stupidity, nonsense* :—Gedofu, gefleard delaramenta, i. errores, An. Ox. 418. [*See note there in which Napier rejects* ge-dofu *in favour of* gedofunge. v. dofung.]

ge-dofung. *See preceding word.*

ge-dohtra; *pl.* (dual?) [*Two*] *daughters* :—Heora (*Jupiter and Juno*) gedohtra wæron Minerua and Uenus (cf. heora twá dohtra wæron Minerua and Uenus, Wlfst. 106, 15), Sal. K. p. 121, 33.

ge-dón. *Add*: I. *to put.* (1) lit. *to place* in or on a material object, *give position or direction to* :—Hé þone hláf tóbræc on twá, and hine gedyde on his twá sléfan, Bl. H. 181, 16. God feorh in gedyde, Gen. 184. Heó hyre bán on níwe þrúh ásette and on cyricean gedyde, (*ossa eius in locello nouo posita in ecclesiam transferri*), Bd. 4, 19 ; Sch. 445, 4. Hí his líc gedydon on þrúh, Bl. H. 191, 33. Hié ciricean áræðon . . . and þær gedydon twá weófedu in, 205, 15. Gedó forð beácen þín, El. 784. Hé mec þær oninnan . . . gedón wolde, B. 2090. Reádes goldes swá micel ðær is tó gedón[g], C. D. vi. 132, 22. (1 a) = á-dón (?) *to put away, remove* :—Gedóð (cf. ádóþ, Ps. Rdr. 23, 7, 9) eówre geatu *tollite portas vestras*, Ps. Th. 23, 9. In v. 7 tollite is translated by un-dód. (2) fig. (a) *to put* from (*fram*), *put out of one's*

power :—Ðá mé fram fleám gedydan *periit fuga a me*, Ps. Th. 141, 5. (b) *to put* or *bring* into a position or relation :—Sóna þæs folces þone mæstan dæl hé ðæm cyninge on onwald gedyde *exercitum statim Cyro tradit*, Ors. 1, 12 ; S. 52, 28. Þe læs man eft twæme· þ man ær tósomne gedydon (*joined in matrimony*), Ll. Th. i. 256, 11. Philippus hæfde ealle Crécas on his geweald gedón, Ors. 3, 7 ; S. 118, 27. (c) *to bring* a person to or out of a condition :—Hé hié tó eáþmódre hérsum-nesse gedyde, Chr. 828 ; P. 62, 4. Hí Læcedemonie mæst ealle áwéstan, and tó þon gedydon þ hí hí selfe léton for heáne *Spartani ultima prope-modum desperatione tabuerunt*, Ors. 3, 1 ; S. 98, 22. Drihten mæg úre fýnd gedón tó náhte *Deus ad nihilum deducet tribulantes nos*, Ps. Th. 59, fýnd gedón tó náhte *Deus ad nihilum deducet tribulantes nos*, Ps. Th. 59, Bl. H. 69, 7. 11. Tó hwon sceolde þeós smyrenes beón tó lore gedón ?, Bl. H. 69, 7. Tó náuhte gedóne, Bt. 37, 3 ; F. 190, 19. Uncúð bið þé tó hwan þé þín Drihten gedón wille, Dóm. L. 32, 60 : Seef. 43. Hé hæfð gedón út his twégen suna *he has redeemed his two sons from slavery*, C. D. vi. 209, 23. ¶ tó deáþe gedón *to put to death* :—His slagan þe hine tó deáðe gedydon, Hml. Th. i. 300, 14. Hú hí mihton hine tó deáðe gedydon, 26, 22. (c a) *to put* a thing to a use :—Tó hwan hió þá næglas gedón, 26, 22. II. *to apply money, expend* :—Gif sélost gedón meahte, El. 1159. II. *to apply money, expend* :—Gif wé þá dagas fulfremedlíce for Gode lifgeaþ, þonne hæbbe wé úre daga þone teóþan dæl for Gode gedón . . . Nú is þearf þ wé þone teóþan dæl for Gode gedón, Bl. H. 35, 24–28. III. *to impart* to a person. (1) *to bestow, confer* a material object :—Him Rómáne gedydan ænne gyld-enan scield *cui a senatu clypeus aureus decretus est*, Ors. 6, 25 ; S. 276, 14. (2) *to cause by one's action* a person (*dat.*) *to have* a faculty :—Sé gedyde blindum men gesihðe, dumbum men spræce, Shrn. 82, 34. Sé gedyde blindum men gesihðe, 85, 24. (3) *to bring* some affecting quality or condition to a person. (a) the object a noun (pronoun), *to do* a person good, harm, &c. :—þ þú sý gemyndig hwæt mín fæder þé gedyde, Bl. H. 151, 24. Ðá ilcan þe ðé gedydon þás gnornunga, Bt. 7, 2 ; F. 18, 10. Máran hearm and yfel þonne hí ǽfre wéndon þ heom ǽnig burhwaru gedón sceolde, Chr. 994 ; P. 129, 3. Mé láðes wiht gedón, Gú. 285. Ðæs ðe ðín niéhsta ðé wiðerweardes gedón hæbbe, Past. 349, 11. Fremena þara ic þe gedón hæbbe, Gen. 2820. Ælc þæra þinga þe him gedón oððe gecwéden wære, Chr. 1014 ; P. 145, 8. (b) the object a clause :—Wénst þú mæge seó wyrd þe gedón þæt þá þing ðíne ágene sién . . . Bt. 14, 1 ; F. 40, 31. Nán mon ne mæg þám móde gedón þ hit ne sié þ þ hit biþ, 16, 2 ; F. 52, 17. III a. *to shew* mercy, *do* honour, justice, &c. :—Hé him deádum lytle mildheortnesse gedyde, Ors. 3, 9 ; S. 128, 15. God gedyde his miltsunge on Rómánum, 6, 38 ; S. 296, 28. Se man þám óðrum riht gedó, Ll. Th. i. 30, 20. Heora nǽnig him tó cerran nolde, ne him nǽnig[r]e dón gedyde, Bl. H. 213, 35. IV. *to do* (with object denoting action). (1) the object a noun (pronoun) :—Hwæt gódes ic gedó *quid boni faciam ?*, Mt. L. 19, 16. Gif hwá hwæt ungewealdes gedéð, Ll. Th. i. 412, 15 : 16. Drihten onféhþ lustfullíce eallum ðǽm gódum þe ǽnig man gedéþ his þǽm níehstan, Bl. H. 37, 25. Hé eall gedéð, swá his willa byð, Ps. Th. 113, 11. Eall þæt wé tó góde gedóð . . . eall þæt wé tó yfele gedóð and gefremmað, Wlfst. 233, 7–9. Ðæt hé tó góde gedyde (*anteacta bona*), he forliesð, Past. 35, 8 : Chr. 81 ; P. 8, 8. Þá hond þe tó yfle gedyde, hé gebétt, Past. 35, 8 : Chr. 81 ; P. 8, 8. þára árfæstra dǽda þe hé gedyde, Bl. H. 213, 27 : Hml. S. 27, 134. Hé gedyde sweotol tácn (*docuit*) . . . mid þǽm þe hé hét crístenra monna éhtan. Ors. 6, 22 ; S. 274, 6. þ ðú gedó hér swilc tácn . . . þ ðis wæter ðisne man ne onfó, Ll. Lbmn. 415, 29. Gif hit þeów man gedó, Ll. Th. i. 172, 7. þ hé ǽnig þára góda forylde þe hé þonne þý dæge gedón mihte, Bl. H. 213, 24. Gif hié þis gedón magan, 183, 6 : An. 342. þæt wæs gedón, Wlfst. 210, 5. Mæhto ðá ðe ðerh honda hs biðon gedóen (*efficiuntur*), Mk. L. R. 6, 2. (1 a) the object a clause, *to achieve, bring to pass* that :—þú nǽfre gedést þæt þú mec ácyrre from Crístes lofe, Jul. 138. Drihten gedéð þæt hé firenfulra geþancas tóweorpeð, Ps. Th. 128, 3 : 129, 3. Se yfla willa gedéð þæt hé gedréfð . . . (cf. se yfela willa gedréfð . . .), Bt. 31, 2 ; F. 112, 24), Met. 18, 1. Gedóð þ gé mé geunnon mínes ágenes, Ll. Lbmn. 148, 8. Drihten wyle gedón þæt hé áhweorfe hæítnéð, Ps. Th. 125, 1. (2) *to do* good, evil, right, wrong, *act* rightly, &c. :—þonne hié láð gedóð, Gen. 624. Mycel yfel beforan þé ic gedyde, Bl. H. 87, 30. Nǽsð hé riht gedón, Gen. 360. (3) *to commit* sin, crime, &c. :—Gif fríman edorbrecðe gedéð, Ll. Th. i. 8, 15. Dǽdbóte dón þæs mycclan yfeles and mánes þe hié wið heora Drihten gedydon, Bl. H. 79, 6. Ðá gedónan synna, Past. 257, 21. Ǽr gedénra, Cri. 1266. ¶ pp. gedón *finished, completed, brought to a conclusion.* (1) of action :—Hit wæs elles feáwum mannum cúð ǽr hit gedón wæs, Chr. 1043 ; P. 164, 3. Ðissum þus gedóne, 1086 ; P. 218, 35 : 222, 13 : 1090 ; P. 225, 15. (2) of time :—þǽm gedónum *qua peracta (intercapedine)*, An. Ox. 3402. IV a. with noun of action as object, *to make* attack, move, excuse, &c. :—Eolxsecg wundað beorna gehwylcne þe him ǽnigne onfeng gedéð, Rún. 15. Gif ic on helle gedó hwyrft ǽnigne *si descendero in infernum*, Ps. Th. 138, 6. Hí nǽnige láde gedón ne magon, Bl. H. 57, 20. V. *to make, bring about* a state, condition, *cause to be* as the result of action. (1) with noun object :—Heó (*the Nile*) gedéð mid þǽm flóde swíþe þicce eorþwæstmas, Ors. 1, 1 ; S. 12,

36. Hē gedyde fela martyra *plurimos ad coronam martyris sublimavit*, 6, 33; S. 288, 19. (2) with clause:—Ic gedō *þ* eówru wíf beóđ wydewan, Ll. Th. i. 52, 19. Ic gedóm *þ* git beóþan monna fisceres *faciam uos· fieri piscatores hominum*, Mt. R. 4, 19. Gedyde ic þæt þū hæfdest mægwlite mē gelícne, Cri. 1383. Gedóþ *þ* eów sȳ mete gearo, Bl. H. 39, 28. Gedón đætte hiera Drihten lícige đǽm folce *to bring it about that their Lord may be pleasing to the people*, Past. 147, 7. Ic wille gedón *þ* ǽlc man sȳ folcrihtes wyrđe *I will have it that every man be entitled to folkright*, Ll. Th. i. 164, 20. Hē gedyde þæt Antonius his freónd weorđ, Ors. 5, 13; S. 244, 28: 6, 18; S. 272, 1. (3) with noun (pronoun), and complementary (a) adjective:—Đā tunglu þū gedēst þē gehȳrsume, Bt. 4; F. 6, 32. Hē hine fracodne gedéđ, Hml. Th. ii. 320, 22: Hml. S. 23 b, 390. Þā smalan wyrmas þone man deádne gedóđ, Bt. 16, 2; F. 52, 12. Hē hié gedyde lípran, Ors. 5, 12; S. 244, 15. Đȳ lǽs sió ánfealdnes hine tō ungeornfulne gedoo (-dō, *v. l.*), Past. 239, 2. Gedó, 453, 23: Ll. Th. i. 48, 25: 108, 2: 136, 7. Hine mōton his mǽgas unscyldigne gedón (unsyngian, *v. l.*), 116, 8. Hē bæd þæt hē wǽre Crísten gedón, Chr. 167; P. 8, 19. (b) participle:—Hē ús gedyde dǽlnimende þæs heofonlícan ríces, Bl. H. 11, 1. Hȳ gedydon đæt cild sprecende, Shrn. 142, 22. (c) phrase:—Erre mōde git mē gedydon *ye made me of angry heart*, Bl. H. 189, 25. (4) with complementary adjective and clause:—Hié cūđ gedydon þæt hié him þæt gold tō gode noldon, Dan. 196. (5) *to endow with qualities or properties*:—Gif hwā gewilnigeđ tō gewitane hū gedón mann hē wæs *if any one wants to know what sort of man he was*, Chr. 1086; P. 219, 16. **V** a. *to make, produce, do one thing from another*:—Gedón *ductum* (Ambrosius . . . nomen Ambrosiae de nectare *ductum*, Ald. 154, 5), Wrt. Voc. ii. 91, 26. **V** b. *to make, conclude a treaty of peace*:—Hē gedyde þone yfelan friþ on Numantium *infamia de foedere apud Numantiam pacto*, Ors. 5, 3; S. 220, 19. **VI.** gedón tō *to make, cause to become, cause to take the character of.* (1) of persons:—Þā ōđre þeóde hē tō gafolgieldum gedyde *caeteras urbes vectigales fecit*, Ors. 3, 9; S. 124, 7. Hē monege gedyde tō martyrum *plurimos ad coronas Christi de suis cruciatibus misit*, 6, 22; S. 274, 5. Hié nánne mon geweligian ne magon, būton hié ōþerne gedón tō wǽdlan, Bt. 13; F. 40, 1. Hē nolde hí tō flȳmum gedón, Ps. Th. 77, 27. (2) of things:—Wē hine willađ ácwellan and ús tō mete gedón, Bl. H. 231, 15. Þúsend daga biđ gedón tō ánum sunnandæge, Wlfst. 210, 5. **VII.** *to make, cause* a person *to do something.* (1) with a clause:—Đǽre scame ic gedoo đæt đū forgietsđ, Past. 207, 11. Þū gedēst þæt hī þe geseóþ, Bt. 33, 4; F. 132, 35: Met. 20, 272. Hē gedyde þæt Octauianus sealde his swostor Antoniuse, Ors. 5, 13; S. 244, 28. His þegnas lǽddon him tō þone eosol and gedydon *þ* hē þǽr on gesittan mihte *adduxerunt asinam . . . et eum desuper sedere fecerunt* (Mt. 21, 7), Bl. H. 71, 6. Gedō þū *þ* eall cynn cweþe . . . , 159, 5. (2) with acc. and infin., whose logical subject is the preceding acc.:—Matheum hē gedyde gangan, Bl. H. 239, 16. (3) with acc. and clause, whose subject is the pronoun representing the preceding acc.:—Þā sunnan þū gedēst *þ* heó þā þeóstre ádwǽscþ, Bt. 4; F. 6, 33. Wundrum lytel mæg gedón þone man . . . *þ* hē wēnþ . . . , 11, 1; F. 32, 21. (4) with infin. alone, its subject being omitted:—Ic ofsleá and lífgan gedóm *ego occidam et vivere faciam*, Ps. Srt. ii. 196, 11. **VIII.** *intrans.* (1) *to act*:—Agathocles gedyde untreówlíce wiđ hiene, Ors. 4, 5; S. 170, 9. Æfter þǽm þe Lisimachus hæfde swā wiđ his sunu gedón, 3, 11; S. 152, 12. (2) *to do, fare*:—Lā wel gedó þē, góda man, Hml. S. 23, 546. **IX.** as a substitute for a verb just used:—Æghwilc unriht áweorpe man . . . þæs þe man gedón mæge, Ll. Th. i. 310, 11. *v.* ǽr-, wel-gedón.

**ge-drǽfan, -drǽfnes.** *v.* ge-drēfan, -drēfnes.

**ge-dræg, -dreag.** *Substitute:* What is drawn together (v. dragan; II), *a concourse, an assembly.* (1) of living beings:—Deófla gedræg sécan, B. 756. (1 a) *a noisy assembly, the tumult made by such an assembly*:—Þǽr biđ cirm and cwicra gewin, gehreów and hlúd wóp . . . earmlíc ælda gedreag, Cri. 1000. Þǽr wæs wóp gehȳred, earmlíc ylda gedræg, An. 1557. Þǽr wæs cirm micel geond Mermedonia mánfulra hlóđ, íordénera gedræg, 43. (2) of things. (a) material:—Ofer deóp gedreag *over the deep tumult of the waves*, Rä. 7, 10. (b) non-material:—Sinsorgna gedreag, Kl. 45.

**ge-dragan** *to draw, drag*:—Gedrah þū þin swurd, Hml. A. 178, 305. Wæs gedragen *traheretur*, An. Ox. 4467. ¶ Wíf điu blódes flóuing geđolade † gedróg (*patiebatur*), Mt. L. 9, 20. *Here the form belongs to gedragan, but the meaning points to gedreógan; perhaps gedreóg should be read.*

**ge-dreccan.** *Add:*—Gedrehte *contractos, strictos*, Germ. 401, 14. **I.** the object a person. (1) the subject a person. (a) *to vex, afflict*:—Þā heáfodmen fyrde sendon, and mænig man mid þām swíđe gedrehtan, Chr. 1096; P. 233, 8. Hine deófol mid his lymum wylle gedreccan, Angl. viii. 324, 19. (b) *to vex, annoy, provoke*:—Hí þone ǽđelan wer oft gedrehton (*ad iracundiam provocabant*), Hml. Th. ii. 174, 9. (2) the subject a thing:—*þ* gyld gedrehte ealle Engla þeóde, Chr. 1052; P. 173, 20. Hunger þisne eard swíđe gedrehte, 1096; P.

233, 5. Arn egeslíc wæter . . . Hē mid þām gedræht wæs, Vis. Lfc. 4, 6. Manege scíran wurdon þǽrle gedrehte þurh þone weall þe hí worhton *the building of the wall proved very burdensome*, Chr. 1097; P. 234, 6. Hȳ wērge wǽtan bǽdan drynces gedreahte *tormented by thirst and weary they begged for a drink of water*, Cri. 1509. **II.** the object a thing, *to injure, destroy*:—*þ* heriendlíc [lof] hē gedrehte *ut favorabile* [*viri Dei*] [*praeconium*] *elideret* i. *frangeret*, An. Ox. 2779.

**ge-dreccednes.** *Add:* ge-drecednes. (1) *tribulation, trouble*:—Earfođlíc is tō átellanne seó gedrecednes . . . and *þ* geswinc . . . þe eall Engla here dreáh, Chr. 1056; P. 186, 32. Gyt weorþeđ mǽre . . . wracu and gedrecednes, Wlfst. 91, 7. Đā sǽde hē þæt swilce earíođnessa and swylce gedrecednessa sculan geweorđan swilce nǽfre ǽr ne gewurdan (*erit tribulatio magna qualis non fuit ab initio mundi usque modo*, Mt. 24, 21), 81, 3. Gedrecednessum (gedrecenyssum, Hpt. Gl. 409, 61) *afflictionibus*, i. *tribulationibus*, An. Ox. 149. (2) *physical ill-treatment, torture*:—Grimlíc gedrecednys (gedrecenys, Hpt. Gl. 499, 24) *atrox uexatio*, i. *punitio* (*lictorum*), An. Ox. 3948. (3) *trouble in a medical sense*:—Wiþ geswel and wiđ fótádle and wiđ gehwylce gedrecednessa, Lch. i. 322, 1.

**ge-drecenes.** *See preceding word.*

**ge-drēfan.** *Add:*—Gedrēfaþ *perturbant*, Wülck. Gl. 252, 7. **I.** in a physical sense, *to disturb, move violently, stir up, trouble* water, make *turbid*:—Se súþerna wind miclum storme gedrēfeþ þā sǽ *mare volvens turbidus auster*, Bt. 6; F. 14, 24: Met. 5, 8. Se gást hine gedrēfde (-droefde, L. R.) *spiritus conturbauit eum*, Mk. 9, 20. Wæter stód dreórig and gedrēfed, B. 1417. Þā gedrēfed wearđ, onhrēred hwælmere, An. 369. Grund is onhrēred, deópe gedrēfed (*stirred to its depths*), 394: 1531. **II.** *to trouble, perturb, disturb the proper operation or condition of*:—Se yfela willa unrihthǽmedes gedrēfđ fulneáh ǽlces libbendes mannes mōd (*the corresponding metre* (18, 3) has gedrǽfd; *as the Latin is* 'omnis voluptas stimulis agit fruenteis,' *perhaps here the verb is* ge-drǽfan *to drive; but see next passage, and* ge-drēfednes), Bt. 31, 2; F. 112, 25. Sió wōde þrág þǽre wrǽnnesse gedrēfþ (gedrǽfþ, Met. 25, 42) hiora mōd *libido versat avidis corda venenis*, 37, 1; F. 186, 18. Þā mistas þe *þ* mōd gedrēfaþ *perturbationum caligo verum confundit intuitum*, 5; F. 14, 17. Þín mōdgeþonc gedrēfan, Met. 5, 23. Seó stemn þǽre heortan biđ swíþe gedrēfed on þām gebede, Bl. H. 19, 10. Weard seó ǽđele gedryht gedrēfed þurh þæs deófles gehygdo, Sal. 457. **III.** *to trouble, cause an unfavourable condition in.* (1) with personal subject. (a) *to afflict, vex, annoy, treat ill*:—Eorđan đū gedrēfdest (gedrōfdes, Ps. Srt.); hǽl hyre wunde, Ps. Th. 59, 2. Tōgeánes đām þe mē gedrǽfdon (*adversus eos qui tribulant me*, Ps. Th. 22, 6), Hml. Th. ii. 114, 28. Ne aenig monn gedroefađ gié *neminem concutiatis*, Lk. L. R. 3, 14. (b) *to cause sorrow, anxiety, fear* &c. *in* a person:—For hwȳ eart þū unrót, mín sáwl, and hwȳ gedrēfst þū (gedroefes đū, Ps. Srt.) mē ?, Ps. Th. 41, 13. Hē his geférscipe swíþe gedrēfde . . . Hié swíþe forhte cwǽdon, Bl. H. 85, 6. Đonne hē ongiett đæt hē his hiéremonna mōd suíđur gedrēfed hæfđ đonne hē scolde *cum subditorum mentem plus quam debuit percussisse considerat*, Past. 165, 21. (2) with non-personal subject expressing (a) affliction, hurtful action:—Se gást sceal sécan helle grund, dǽdum gedrēfed, Seel. 105. Swā hí swíþor bióþ ásyndrode fram Gode, swā hí swíþor bióþ gedrēfde and geswencte, ǽgđer ge on mōde ge on líchoman, Bt. 39, 7; F. 224, 1. (b) an untoward circumstance, an event or act of doubtful import:—Þā wearđ heó on his sprǽce gedrēfed (gedroefad, L. *turbata*), Lk. 1, 29. Þā Herōdes *þ* gehȳrde, þá wearþ hē gedrēfed, Mt. 2, 3. Ic eam deópe gedrēfed, for þon ic worn worda hæbbe gehȳred, Cri. 168. Wurdon hiora wíf gedrēfed *horum uxores viduitate permotae*, Ors. 1, 10; S. 44, 30. Đás þing geseónde hē wearđ gedrēfed, Chr. 1087; P. 223, 16. Đā hí gesáwon þæt hí wurdon þā gedrēfede (-droefed, L., -drȳfed, R.), Mt. 14, 26: Bl. H. 17, 2. (c) fear, anxiety, sorrow, &c.:—Mē bróga þín gedrēfde, Ps. Th. 87, 16. Ys mē heorte gedrēfed, and mē fealleđ on fyrhtu deáđes, 54, 4: 56, 4: Jn. 14, 1: Bl. H. 135, 25. Ic wæs mid sorgum gedrēfed, Kr. 20: Jud. 88: Bt. 1; F. 4, 1. Mid unsibsumnise gedroefedo uoeron *anxietate turbatis*, Jn. p. 6, 1. Gedrēfde, Ps. Th. 67, 5. Gedrēfede, 63, 8: 106, 26. [Ne beođ heo neuer idreaued mid winde ne mid reine, O. E. Hml. i. 193, 58. *O. Sax.* gi-drōbian: *O. H. Ger.* ge-truoben con-, per-turbare, confundere, terrere.]

**ge-drēfedlíc.** *Substitute:* of darkness, thick, dense:—Þȳsþernes swā gedrēfedlíc þæt hit man gefélan mihte *tenebrae crassitudine palpabiles*, Ors. 1, 7; S. 38, 14. *v.* ge-drēfan; I.

**ge-drēfednes.** *Add:* **I.** disquiet, disorder:—Gedrēfednes *conturbatio* (*in fructibus impii*), Kent. Gl. 510. **II.** disquiet of mind, perturbation:—Đone gást sió gedrēfednes út ádrífđ *spiritum perturbatio ejicit*, Past. 220, 12. Seó gedrēfednes mæg *þ* mōd onstyrian *ea perturbationum valentia est, ut movere loco hominem possit*, Bt. 5, 3; F. 12, 24. Þā þeóstro þinre gedrēfednesse, 6; F. 14, 30. Gedrēfednesse, 5, 3; S. 13, 1. Þæt mōd biđ gebunden mid gedrēfednesse *nubila mens est, vinctaque frenis*, 6; F. 16, 2. Mid his mōdes gedrēfednesse and

bisgunga, 35, 1; F. 156, 12. Forlǽtan ǽlce þára gedréfednessa *pertur-batione depulsa*, 36, 1; F. 172, 34. **III.** *tribulation, trouble, anxiety, distress:*—Gedréfednesse *tribulationum*, Wülck. Gl. 251, 40. Be gedréfednysse *de tribulatione*, Scint. 160, 13. Syle ús fultum on úre gedréfednisse (*tribulatione*), Ælfc. T. Grn. 11, 40. 'þú mé hæfst ǽretne on ðám tweón and on þǽre gedréfednesse þe ic ǽr on wæs be þám freódóme. Ac ic eom nú get on micle máran gedréfednesse geun-rótsod, fulneáh oþ ormódnesse.' Ða cwæþ hé: 'Hwæt is sió micle unrótnes?,' Bt. 41, 2; F. 246, 11–15. Se gefeá weard swíþe raðe on heora móde tó gedréfednesse (gedréfednesse, Bos. 70, 11) gecierred, Ors. 3, 10; S. 138, 24. Swá orsorg þ ic náne gedréfednesse næfde, Bt. 26, 1; F. 90, 26. Gedréfednyssum *tribulationibus*, Bl. Gl.

**ge-dréfnes.** *Add:* **I.** in a physical sense, *disturbance, tempest:*—On þǽre hreóhnesse, gedréfnesse *ea tempestate*, i. *ea turbine*, An. Ox. 2420. **II.** *disturbance of mind, perturbation, confusion:*—Bið se módsefa gebunden mid gedréfnesse, Met. 5, 40. Gedrǽfnesse, 22, 61. Gedroefnisse *confusionem*, Ps. Srt. 68, 20. v. folc-gedréfnes, *and preceding word.*

**ge-drehtlíce.** v. un-gedrehtlíce.

**ge-drehtness,** e; f. *Affliction, contrition:*—Hé on swá micelre þrǽstnesse (gedrehtnessum, *v. l.*) and forhæfednesse módes and líchaman áheardode *in tanta mentis et corporis contritione duravit*, Bd. 5, 12; Sch. 615, 3.

**ge-dréme.** v. ge-dríme.

**ge-drencan.** *Add:* **I.** *to cause to drink, supply a person with drink:*—Wætre snytres gidrenceð hine Drihten *aqua sapientiae potabit illum Dominus*, Rtl. 46, 11. Gidrencde, 84, 33. **I a.** *to supply an object with moisture, saturate:*—Gedrenctest *inebriasti* (*terram*), Bl. Gl. **II.** *to plunge into a liquid, soak:*—Gedrengcet héd *subjactum corium*, Angl. viii. 451 (omitted in Wülck. Gl. 165, 6). **III.** *to plunge, sink* (trans.), *drown:*—Of gedrenced sié in grund sǽes *demer-gatur in profundum maris*, Mt. L. 18, 6. [*Goth.* ga-draggkjan ποτίζειν : *O. H. Ger.* ge-trenchen *potare, ebriare, aquare*.]

**ge-dreog** *and* **ge-dreóg.** *Substitute:* **ge-dreóg,** es; *n.* **I.** *a dressing, something used in preparing material for use:*—Ða hremmas bróhton ðám láreówe lác tó médes swínes rysl his scón tó gedreóge (*the passage in Bede's life of Cuthbert is :* Corvi digna munera ferunt, dimidiam axungiam porcinam ; quam vir fratribus . . . ad ungendas caligas praebere solebat, c. 20), Hml. Th. ii. 144, 29. **II.** *seemly, orderly behaviour, gravity:*—Se munuc eádmódlíce mid gedreóge sprece *monachus humiliter cum gravitate loquatur*, R. Ben. I. 35, 10. Þæt mid heálicum gedreóge and gemetgunge árwurðlícor beó *quod cum summa gravitate et mode-ratione honestissime fiat*, 75, 10. Mid ofoste sí becumen ; mid gedreóge þeáhhwæðere þ ne gehigeleás méte tender *cum festinatione curratur : cum gravitate tamen, ut non scurilitas inveniat fomitem*, 17. Ofer ealle his gód hé hine tó ealdre for his gedreóge (cf. hé on rihtne tíman hwǽte gedǽlde his efendeówum, 4) gesette, R. Ben. 123, 6. **III.** tó gedreóge gán *ad necessaria naturae exire*, R. Ben. 32, 22. v. next word.

**ge-dreóg** (-dreóh); *adj.* **I.** *suitable, fit, meet:*—Cneówien him on gedreógre stówe (*in loco congruo*). An gedreóhre stówe. Hí sceolon an gedreógum húse (*in competenti hospitali*) ælmesmanna fét þweán, Nap. 29. **II.** *quiet, orderly.* (1) of persons, *serious in behaviour ;* gravis. Cf. ge-dreóg; *n.*; **II.** (*Take here* ge-dreóh *in Dict.*) (2) of animals, *gentle, tame :* mitis—Hé áwrát Crístes róde tácen on þæs horses heáfde and ealle his rédnysse áwende on geþwǽrnysse, swá þæt hit wæs stillre and gedreóhre (*mitior*) þonne hit wǽre ǽr þǽre wódnysse, Gr. D. 78, 12. [Ða bead se cyningc his cnihtes þ hé ealle wǽron swíðe gedrioge. Þa þa menn on heora bedde wǽron and hit swíðe gedrih wæs, Nap. 29. Cf. Lomb is drih þing and milde *agnus est animal mansuetum*, O. E. Hml. ii. 49, 9. Maide dreiȝ and wel itaucht, 256, 34.]

**ge-dreógan.** *Substitute:* (1) *to do, accomplish :*—Hé wyrs ágylt and máran demm gedríhð (-drígð, *v. l.*) him selfum mid ðǽm lote, Past. 347, 18. Wel hym þæs geweorkes . . . gif hé ealteáwne ende gedreógeð, Hy. 2, 13. (2) *to suffer :*—Wíf ðíu blódes flówing geðolade þ gedróg (-dreóg?) *mulier quae sanguinis fluxum patiebatur*, Mt. L. 9, 20. (3) *to live through, spend* time, life, &c. [v. *N. E. D.* dree, (5)]:—Wisse hé gearwe þæt hé dæghwíla gedrogen hæfde, eorðan wynne, B. 2726.

**ge-dreóglǽcan ;** *p.* -lǽhte *To make seemly, set in order :*—Menn dæftað heora hús and wel gedreóglǽcað, gif hí sumne freónd onfón willað tó him, þæt nán undæslicnys him ne ðurfe derian, Hml. Th. ii. 316, 7. Hé cwæð þ hé wolde gedreóhlǽcan his hámas, Hml. S. 6, 121. Hé hét gedreóhlǽcan þæs deófles templ, 18, 371.

**ge-dreóhlíce.** *Substitute:* **ge-dreóglíce** (-dreóh-); *adv.* **I.** *in an orderly manner :*—Gif man wǽpn gedreóhlíce (*the Latin versions have* discrete ; in aliquo secreto loco ; pacifice) lecge þǽr hig stille mihton beón, gif hí móston, Ll. Th. i. 418, 6. [**II.** *in a seemly manner, respect-fully :*—Hire tó leát Malcus swá dreóhlíce, Hml. A. 178, 311.]

**ge-dreópan ;** *p.* -dreáp *To drop :*—Lǽt gedreópan on þá eágan ǽnne dropan, Lch. ii. 34, 25. [*O. H. Ger.* ge-triufan *stillare*.]

**ge-dreósan.** *Add:* **I.** *to fall.* (1) of mere change of position :—

þæt se wítes bona in helle grund gedreóse, Cri. 265. (2) with idea of destruction. (a) of persons, *to fall* in battle :—Æt hilde gedreás sec[g] æfter óðrum, Val. 1, 4. (b) of material, *to fall from decay :*—Þes wág . . . gedreás, Ruin. 11. Scúrbeorge gedrorene, 5. **II.** *to fall, perish.* (1) of persons, *to die :*—Mægen eall gedreás, þá hé gedrencte dugoð Egypta, Exod. 499. (2) of material things :—Mín líchoma gedreósan sceal, swá þeós eorðe eall, Gú. 343. Míne welan þe ic hæfde syndon ealle gewitene and gedrorene, Bl. H. 113, 25. (3) of non-material things, *to fail, come to an end :*—Bléda gedreósað, wynna gewítað, Rún. 29: Reim. 55. Ne lǽt ðín ellen gedreósan, Val. 1, 7. Gedroren is þeós duguð eal, dreámas sind gewitene, Seef. 86. Dagas míne gedroren syndan sméce gelíce *defecerunt sicut fumus dies mei*, Ps. Th. 101, 3.

**ge-drep.** *Add:* [Cf. *Icel.* drep *a blow.*]

**ge-drepan** *to strike, smite :*—Hé wæs gedrepen (gegripen, *v.l.*) and geþreád fram þám unclǽnan gástum and gefeóll tó þæs deácones fótum *immundo spiritu correptus ad pedes diaconi corruit*, Gr. D. 294, 1. [*O. H. Ger.* ge-trefan *con-, percutere, tangere.*]

**ge-drettan.** *Add:* Cf. (?) ofer-drettan.

**ge-drif,** e ; *f.* . . . . Rush. 1, 31. *Substitute:* **ge-drif** *fever :*—Hál from ridesohte ł gedrif, Mk. R. 1, 31. Wið gedrif, nim snǽgl, and áfeorma hine, and nim þ clǽne fám ; mengc wiþ wífes meolc, syle þicgan, Lch. iii. 70, 3.

**ge-drif,** -drif (?). *l.* ge-drif.

**ge-drif** *a driving.* *Substitute:* A *drive, a tract through which some-thing drives or moves (rapidly) :*—God hig (*the apostate angels*) tódǽlde on þrí dǽlas ; ǽnne dǽl hé ásette on ðæs lyftes gedríf, óðerne dǽl on ðás wæteres gedríf, þriddan dǽl on helle neowelnisse, Sal. K. p. 186, 21–23.

**ge-drífan.** *Substitute:* *To drive,* (1) *to force a living creature to move :*—Gif ic in Belzebub fordrífo dióules, suno iúera in huǽm hiú gedrífes (*eiciunt*)?, Mt. L. 12, 27. Hé gedrifen wæs (*agebatur*) from dióulæ on woesternum, Lk. L. 8, 29. Suna ríces biðon gedrifen (*eicientur*) in ðyóstrum, Mt. L. 8, 12. (2) *to impel matter by physical force, to carry along* (of wind or water) :—þ scipp gedrifen wæs (*jactabatur*) from ýðum, Mt. 14, 24. Ælc ceápscip frið hæbbe . . . gyf hit undrifen bið. And þéh hit gedriuen beó, and hit ætfieó tó hwilcre friðbyrig . . ., habban þá men frið, Ll. Th. i. 286, 1. (3) *to force matter into something, cram,* v. full-gedrifen. (4) *to carry out, effect, drive a bargain :*—Hé hreówlíce his ceáp gedrifan hæfde, Hml. S. 23, 585. [*O. H. Ger.* ge-tríban *agere, adigere, com-, im-pellere.*]

**ge-drígan.** v. ge-drýgan.

**ge-dríhþ.** *Substitute:* *Gravity* or *seemliness of behaviour ;* in pl. *sober conduct.* v. ge-dreóg :—Wisdóm and weorðscipe gedæfenað biscopa háde, and gedríhða gerísað þám þe heom fyliað (cf. oportet . . . diaconos pudicos esse, non bilingues, non multo vino deditos, 1 Tim. 3, 8), Ll. Th. ii. 318, 42: 314, 34.

**ge-dríhþ,** e ; *f. Action, proceeding, doing.* v. ge-dreógan :—Ne hí þǽr (*at a church*) ǽnig unnit inne ne geþafian, ne ídele spǽce, ne ídele dǽde, ne unnit gedrinc (gedríhþa, *v. l.*), Ll. Th. ii. 250, 7.

**ge-dríman ;** de *To modulate, make harmonious :*—Gedrýmyd *modu-lata*, Germ. 390, 35. Mid gedrémedum cwyde *non dissona sententia*, An. Ox. 4628.

**ge-dríme** *musical, melodious, harmonious.* Take here **ge-dréme,** -drýme *in Dict., and add :*—Stefn gedrýme (-dréme, *v. l.*) *vox canora*, Hy. S. 2, 28. Mid gedrémum swége *eque sonore*, Wrt. Voc. ii. 143, 68. Mid gedrémre swinsunge, [gedré]mum sange *consona melodia*, An. Ox. 4911. Gedrémere, 2593. Mid gedrémere stefne *canora voce*, 2603. Ná mid gedrémum cwyde *dissona sententia*, Hpt. Gl. 513, 49. Mid gedrýmum stefnum *melodis vocibus*, Hy. S. 115, 29. v. dreám.

**ge-drinc,** -drync, es ; *n. Substitute: Drinking.* (1) with the idea of quenching thirst :—Gif hé hyne sylfne mid þǽm ǽspryngum Godes worda gelecð, and his mód mid þǽre swétnesse þæs gástlican gedrinces gefylleð, hé seleð þæs þonne dryncan his þyrstendum móde, Ll. Th. ii. 430, 6. (2) with the idea of feasting :—Ealle þá hwíle þe þæt líc bið inne þǽr sceal beón gedrync and plega . . . his feoh þæt tó láfe bið æfter þǽm gedrynce and þǽm plegan, Ors. 1, 1 ; S. 20, 25–28. Mislice blissa hié hæfdon on hiora gedrynce, Bl. H. 99, 22. (3) with the idea of excess :—Him wæs gecynde þ hé symble wæs reád on his andwlitan. Se cyning wénde þ hit for singalum gedrynce wǽre (*assiduae potationis esse credidit*), Gr. D. 187, 17. Gif hé þurh gedrinc man ácwelle *si ex ebrietate hominem occiderit*, Ll. Th. ii. 230, 28. Man æt ciricwæccan swíðe gedreóh sí, and ǽnig gedrinc . . . þǽr ne dreóge, 250, 12. Secgas mǽnað meodogláes gedrinc, Vy. 57. v. ofer-, wín-gedrinc.

**ge-drinca,** an ; *m. One who drinks with another, one who sits at table with another, a guest, companion.* Cf. ge-beór :—Danihel weard þæs cyninges gedrinca, Nap. 29. [Cf. *O. H. Ger.* trinco *potator*.]

**ge-drincan.** *Add:* **I.** *absolute.* (1) *to take liquid as nourishment* or *to quench thirst :*—Þá hé þone mete bróhte, hé bróhte him eác wín. Þá hé hæfde gedruncn (*quo hausto*), Gen. 27, 25. (2) *to drink intoxicating liquor convivially* or *for pleasure :*—Is tó wyrnanne bearn-eácnum wífe þ hió áht sealtes ete . . . oþþe beór drince, ne swínes flǽsc ete . . ., ne druncen gedrince (*get drunk*), Lch. ii. 330, 8. **II.** *trans.*

(1) *to imbibe* a liquid:—Hē þone unlybban ealne gedranc, Hml. Th. i. 72, 25. Ðæs wōses geswēttes mid hunige gedrinc bollan fulne, Lch. ii. 30, 25. (2) *to swallow the contents* of a vessel:—Hē sende him glæsfat full wīnes, and þ se bysceop gebletsade. Sōna swā hē hit gedruncen hæfde *misit ei calicem uini benedictum ab episcopo; quem ut bibit*, Bd. 5, 5; Sch. 572, 8. III. *to absorb:*—In gedrincaþ *combiberint, contraxerint*, Germ. 391, 18. [Goth. ga-driggkjan: O. Sax. gi-drinkan: O. H. Ger. ge-trinchen.]

ge-drípan. *Take here* ge-drypan (*l.* -drýpan) *in Dict., and add:*—(1) *to cause to fall in drops:*—Þæt Lazarus mid hys fingre hym gedrípte weteris on þā tungan, Solil. H. 67, 29. Gyf þē gedrýptes wīnes lyste, þonne dō þū mid þīnum scytefingre . . . swycle þu tæppian wille, and wænd þīnne scytefingre ādūne and twængc hine mid þīnum twām fingrum, swylce þū of sumne dropan strícan wylle, Techm. ii. 125, 17. (2) *to wet with drops, moisten:*—Of gedrýpydre cláþ weocan *linteolo ebrio* (i. *madido*), Germ. 391, col. 2, 18.

ge-drítan; *p.* -drāt; *pp.* -driten *To drop excrement:*—Nim þæt græs þær hund gedríteþ, Lch. i. 364, 9. [*v. N. E. D.* drite: *Icel.* dríta *cacare.*]

ge-drōf. *Add:*—Gedrōfum *palustri*, Germ. 399, 453. [*The Latin original of Past.* 54, 1 is in *lutosa aqua.*]

ge-drōfednys. *Dele:* ge-drōfenlíc. v. ge-drorenlic.

ge-drohtnian *to live* a life [:—Stídlíce hē his líf ādreáh . . . Mid þan þe hē þuss lange gedrohtned hæfde . . . , Shrn. 13, 26.]

ge-drohtnung, e; *f. Living, course of life:*—Heó hym eallum gebysnode mid gōddre gedrohtnunge tō Godes þeówdōme, Hml. S. 2, 126.

ge-dropa *a kind of date* (cf. *drop* as the name of a kind of plum):—Gedropa *nicolaum*, An. Ox. 474.

ge-drorenlic; *adj. Perishable, transitory, frail:*—Drihten, þū wāst þ ic eom gedrorenlic dūst, Nap. 29. Þeós world is eall forwordenlic and gedrorenlic (*printed* gedrofenlic, *but see* ge-hrorenlic) and gebrosnodlic and feallendlic, Bl. H. 115, 3.

ge-drugian. *l.* -drūgian, *and add:*—Gedrūgde (ādrūgade, R.) *aruit*, Mt. L. 21, 20. Gedrūgad wæs ēsprynge blōdes *siccatus est fons sanguinis*, Mk. L. R. 5, 29.

ge-druncnian. *Add:* *to get drunk:*—Nā þæt ān of wīne gedruncnode menn *non solum ex uino inebriantur homines*, Scint. 107, 4. [*Icel.* drukna *to be drowned.*]

ge-drycnan; *pp.* ed *To dry up, emaciate* with disease:—Ān wind cōm, and se wōl mid þǣm winde. Þes moncwealm wæs . . . ofer ealle menn gelíce, þēh þe sume deáde wǣron, sume uneáþe gedrycnede *aura corrumpens generali cunctos tabe confecit; ut etiam quos non egit in mortem turpi macie exinanitos adflictosque dimiserit*, Ors. 3, 3; S. 102, 10. [*O. H. Ger.* ge-truchinit *exsiccatum, siccatum:* O. Sax. druknian *to dry.*]

ge-drygan. *l.* -drýgan, *and add:*—Þæt wíf foet his mid hērum heáfdes hiræ gedrýgde (*tergebat*), Lk. L. 7, 38. Nim þysse wyrte wyrttruman, and gedríge hine, Lch. i. 102, 8. Genim þās wyrte . . . , and gedríge (-drigge, *v. l.*) hý, 146, 1.

ge-dryht. *Add:* (1) *a band, company; of large numbers, a host:*—Sōðfæste (*the righteous at the day of judgement*), eádigra gedryht, El. 1290: Ph. 635. Gǣsta gedryht Hǣlend hergað, 615. Seó ǣðele gedryht *the host of heaven*, Sal. 456. Mid þā leóhtan gedryht, wuldres āras, El. 737. Sōhte ic þā wloncan gedryht Wiðmyrginga, Víd. 118. Þā geseah ic þā gedriht (þege driht, MS.) in gedwolan lifgan, Israēla cyn unriht dōn, Dan. 22. Ofer ealle æðelinga gedriht (cf. Sodomware . . . corðrum miclum, 2451), Gen. 2462. (2) *a band of followers, retinue, company* of retainers:—Ic and mínra eorla gedryht (cf. hē fíftēna sum sundwudu sōhte, 207), B. 431. Ic sǣbāt gesæt mid mínra secga gedriht, 633. Hrōðgar sæt mid his eorla gedriht, 357: 118: 62. Sibbe gedriht, 387: 729. Se brego mǣra (*Christ*) his þegua gedryht (*the disciples*) gelaðade, leóf weorud, Cri. 457. Wile mid his engla gedryht Meotod on gemōt cuman, 942. Gē geseoð Dryhten faran . . . mid þās engla gedryht, 515. (3) *a host of warriors:*—Seó eorla gedriht (*the Israelites marching through the Red Sea*) ānes mōdes, Exod. 304. Wǣron hwate weras gearwe tō gūðe . . . , fōr folca gedryht, El. 27. v. hí-, sib-, wil-gedryht.

ge-dryhtu. *Substitute:* ge-dryht, e; *f.* [es; *n.?*]; *pl.* ge-dryhtu *What is suffered, fortune, fate* (cf. dreógan):—Gedrihtu *elementa*, i. *fortune* ł *sidera* (the passage is: Cum figura mundi in ictu evanuerit, et enormia creaturarum *elementa* in melius commutata claruerint, Ald. 32, 34. For *sidera* as an alternative to *elementa*, cf. *elementa* sol et luna et reliqui planetae, Migne. Gedrihtu seems a rendering of *fortune*, cf. *fortunae* gewyrdes, 2628), An. Ox. 2371: 7, 145. Gedryhtu, 8, 119: Angl. xiii. 32, 110.

ge-dryncness, e; *f. Immersion, dipping:*—Mid ðǣre hálgan rōde gedryncnysse Iordanem oþhrínan, Hml. S. 23 b, 723. Cf. drynctun *under* drencan; I.

ge-drypan. *l.* -drýpan, *and see* ge-drípan.

ge-drysnan. *Add:*—Gidrysne ðis āttor *extingue hoc virus*, Rtl.

125, 35. Gidrysne ðā lēgo geciida *extingue flammas litium*, 164, 18. Synna lēgo gidrysne (*extinguere*), 64, 10. Sē gidrysnad *extinguitur*, 125, 29. Sune selenis gedrysned ł geendod *filio proditionis extincto*, Lk. p. 3, 4. Lēhtfato ūsræ gedrysned biðon (*extinguuntur*), Mt. L. 25, 8.

ge-dūfan. *Add:* (1) lit. :—Gif hit (*the ordeal*) sý wæter, þ hē gedúfe ōðre healfe elne on þām rāpe, Ll. Th. i. 212, 2. (2) fig. *to plunge into sin*, &c. :—Swā hit him āliéfedlicre ðyncð, swā hē ðǣr diópor on gedýfð *quod licitum suspicatur, in hoc multiplicius mergitur*, Past. 427, 27. Ðā ðe gehealdað wið ðā lytlan scylda, and hwílum gedúfað on ðǣm miclan (*aliquando in gravibus demerguntur*), 437, 33 : 439, 8. [*For the passage from Ors.* 1, 7 *see* ge-deorfan.]

ge-durran *to dare:*—Nænig mon gidarste hine gifregna *nemo audebat eum interrogare*, Mk. R. L. 12, 34: Jn. L. 21, 12. [*Goth.* ga-daursan: O. Sax. gi-durran: O. H. Ger. ge-turren.]

ge-durstignes. v. ge-dyrstignes: ge-dwǣlan. Dele, *and see* ge-dwelian, -dwellan.

ge-dwǣscan; *p.* te. (1) *to extinguish* what is burning:—Þone wlacan smocan wāces flǣsces wætere gedwǣscan *lini tepidos undis exstinguere fumos*, Dōm. L. 52. (2) *to efface, do away with:*—Swylas gedwǣscean *to do away with swellings*, Lch. i. 372, 2.

ge-dwǣs-mann, es; *m. A silly, foolish person:*—Secgað sume gedwǣsmenn þæt sum orfcyn sý þe man bletsigan ne sceole, and cweðað þæt hī þurh bletsunge misfarað and ðurh wyrigunge geðeóð, Hml. Th. i. 100, 29. Ús sceamað tō secgenne ealle ðā sceandlican wiglunga þe gedwǣsmenn (sotmen, *v. l.*) gedrífað . . . þonne hī hwæt onginnað, Hml. S. 17, 101.

ge-dwalian. v. ge-dwolian.

ge-dwelian. *Add:* I. *intrans. To go astray, err, make mistake* with gen. of matter mistaken :—Ægðer þāra ic wōt. Ne mæg nān man þæs gedwæligan *aeque novi. Nam in utroque nihil fallor*, Solil. H. 21, 11. II. *trans. To lead astray.* (1) in a physical sense :—Hí hine geseón ne mihton, and hý swā mid blindnysse wurdon gedwelede (-dwealde, *v. l.*) þ hí eft of þām mynstre ídelhende hwurfon (*sic sua caecitate frustrati a monasterio sunt vacui regressi*), Gr. D. 16, 26. (2) in a mental or moral sense :—þ dysig ðe ðā earman men gedwelaþ and ālǣt of þām rihtan wege *quae miseros tramite devios abducit ignorantia*, Bt. 32, 3; F. 118, 7. Antecríst eal mancyn gedrecð and gedwelaþ, Wlfst. 101, 9. Þæt mōd biþ mid ymbhogum gedwelod (-dweald, *v. l.*) tō þām þ hit ne mæg āredian tō Gode, Bt. 24, 4; F. 84, 33.

ge-dwellan. *Add:* I. *trans. To lead astray.* (1) in a physical sense (v. ge-dwelian; II. 1). (2) in a mental or moral sense. (a) the object a person :—Ðæt hē gewundige ðā heortan ðāra gehírendra . . . , ðæt is ðæt hē hié gedweled *ne erroris vulnere audientium corda feriantur*, Past. 93, 20. Mon ðā heortan and ðæt angiet gedweled, 95, 20. Gedwæled (v. ge-dwelian; II. 2 first passage), Met. 19, 3. Hié hiora hiéremonna mōd gedwellað, Past. 369, 18. Hē gedwealde mænigne man, Wlfst. 11, 2. Hí folc swýðe gedwealdon, 100, 22. Hié eów tō swíðe gedwealdon mid þǣm manigfealdum gebodum (*turbaverunt vos verbis*, Acts 15, 24), Ll. Th. i. 56, 17. Manna mōd syndon āþýstrode and ādysgode and gedwealde þæt hí ǣfre sceolon lǣtan þæt deófol hig gedwellan, Wlfst. 185, 11–14. Gedweald, Bt. 24, 4; F. 84, 33 (v. ge-dwelian; II. 2 at end). Lēton gedwealde men swylce hē Godes sylfes sunu wǣre, Wlfst. 99, 7. (a a) with gen. of matter in respect to which there is error :—Ús se feónd ne gedwelle þæs rihtan geleáfan, Wlfst. 253, 2. Se cwide is on mínum mōde swā fæst þ his mē nān man gedwellan ne mæg (*sine ambiguitate cognosco*), Bt. 33, 3; F. 126, 18. (b) the object a thing, *to confuse, obscure, give a wrong idea of:*—Hígiað ealle mægene ðæt hié ðæt gedwellen ðæt ōðre menn rihtlíce ongieten habbað *student summopere ab aliis recte intellecta destruere*, Past. 365, 23. Hí forþon tiliað þ hí gōd dōn þe hí willað gedwellan þā gife ōðera manna weorces (*ut gratiam alienae operationis obnubilent*), Gr. D. 76, 26. II. *intrans. To err:*—Sē ðe gedweled *qui erraverit*, Kent. Gl. 784.

ge-dwild, -dwyld. *Add:* I. in a physical sense, *wandering:*—Ilias þ beóð gewyn, and Odissia beóð gedwyld (cf. the opening of the Odyssey, 'Sing of the man who wandered much . . . and saw the cities of many men'), swā Omērus on þǣre bēc recð, Angl. viii. 330, 46. II. *error, a being astray:*—þā mynstermenn noldon for menniscum gedwylde (cf. Bd. 3, 11) þone sanct (*Oswald*) underfōn, Hml. S. 26, 179. Ābrōdenum gedwilde *sussurrone* (for the meaning given to this word, cf. *susurronis* desiges, 998) *subtracto*, Kent. Gl. 996. Gedwyldum *erratibus, erroribus*, Wrt. Voc. ii. 144, 18. II a. in an ecclesiastical or theological sense, *false opinion, heresy; superstition, false religion:*—Āsprang on Godes folce mycel gedwyld . . . on ðām tíman þe ðā bisceopas sceoldan Godes þ hálige folc on rihtne weg gebringan, hí swíðost ælces gedweldes tiledon, and ælc gedwyld hí upp ārǣrdon, Hml. S. 23, 353–364. Gedwyldes *superstitionis*, An. Ox. 4429. Gedwylde *superstitione*, 4021. Secgað sume þā Denisce men on heora gedwylde þæt sē Iouis wǣre, þe hý Þōr hātað, Mercuries sunu, þe hí Ōðon namiað, Wlfst. 107, 9: 106, 22. Sum bisceop gelýfde þām

hîwere and hine tô him gebæd, and hê wearð for þām gedwylde ādrǣfed of his anwealde, Hml. S. 31, 839. Heó mid Arrianiscum gedwylde dweligende lyfode, 653. Nestorius cwæð þ on Crîste wǣron twēgen hādas, and hî his gedwild ādwǣscton, Ll. Th. ii. 374, 19. Hit getācnað gydwyldu (*hereses*) ārîsende, Archiv cxx. 50, 23. **III.** *deception, a leading astray.* v. ge-dwyldlic:—Bāal næfde nāne gōdnesse, ac wæs gramlic deófol mid gedwylde āfunden (*was found to be a cruel devil able to deceive* (?)), Hml. S. 18, 48. Antecrîst wile āmyrran mid his gedwylde eall þæt se sōða Crîst ǣr bodade and gesette tô rihte, Wlfst. 195, 17. Ðonne tweónað sela manna . . . for ðām micclum and mænigfealdum gedwyldum þe hî geseoð and gehýrað, hwæðer hê sý se sōða Godes sunu oððe nā ne sý, 196, 13. v. mis-gedwild.

**gedwild-æfterfylgung**, e; *f. A following after error, heresy:*— Kyre *vel* gedweldæfterfelgung (*printed* gedweloæfterfelgund) *heresis*, Wrt. Voc. i. 16, 55.

**ge-dwyldlic**; *adj. That leads astray, deceptive, false.* v. ge-dwild; III:—Antecrîst wind ongeán Godes gecorenan . . . mid gedwyldlicum scîncræftum . . . ; ætforan þām hê wyrcð mænigfealde wundra þæt hê þurh þæt hy tô gedwolan āwende, Wlfst. 196, 18–197, 5.

**gedwild-mann**, es; *m. A heretic:*—Þā gedwyldmen man hæt on Grēcisc Nictales (= *Nyctages*, haeretici qui superfluas existimabant sacras vigilias), Nap. 60, 21. Cf. gedwol-mann.

**ge-dwimere.** *Dele, and see next word.*

**ge-dwimor.** *Add:* I. *an illusion* produced by diabolic agency, *apparition:*—Gedwimore *fantasmate*, An. Ox. 4059. Feor āweg gewîtan swefna and nihta gedwymeru (*fantasmata*), Hy. S. 11, 31. Tunglera gedwimeru *Chaldeorum fantasmata*, An. Ox. 3269. **II.** *delusion, deception:*—Sume swefna beóð of deófle tô sumum swicdôme . . . ac his gedwimor ne mæg derian þām gódum, Hml. S. 21, 408. Gedwimeres (-dwomeres, Hpt. Gl. 514, 72) *nebulonis* (atrum *nebulonis* phantasma, Ald. 66, 31. *For the sense in which* nebulonis *seems to be taken here* cf. nebulonis heówunga, leásunge, 2238), An. Ox. 4695. **II a.** *a delusion, that which* (*by diabolic power*) *gives a false idea, deceit:*—Ne gýman gē galdra . . . ne weordian gē wyllas ne ǣnige wudutreówu, for ðām æghwylce îdele syndon deófles gedwimeru, Wlfst. 40, 16. Hig worhton sela gedwimera on anlîcnessum, 11, 5. Se deófol wyrcð þonne wundra þurh his scîncræft mid leásum gedwimorum, Hml. S. 35, 351. Sum gedwola mid manegum gedwimorum þæt land-folc bedyfrode lange, 31, 834. Hê (*St. Martin*) geseah gelôme þā deóflu mid mislicum gedwymorum (cf. þā deófla mid heora searocræftum him (*St. Martin*) cômon gelôme tô, Hml. S. 31, 706) . . . hê næs bepæht ðurh heora leásungum, Hml. Th. ii. 512, 21. **II b.** *a delusion, a false idea entertained, error:*—Wæs ān hālig stôw swýðe gewurðod . . . swilce ðǣr martyres lāgon . . . Martinus ne gelýfde þām leásum gedwimore (cf. mid heálicum gedwylde, Hml. Th. ii. 506, 27), Hml. S. 31, 346. **II c.** *a practice that deludes:*—Gedwimere *necromantia*, An. Ox. 4701.

**ge-dwimorlic**; *adj. Illusory, existing only apparently:*—Hû Benedictus ādwæscte þ gedwimorlice fýr . . . Geseah hê þ þ fýr wæs gebúht on þāra brōðra eágum . . . Hê . . . þā brōðru þe hê gemætte mid þām gedwimorlicum fýre bepǣhte ongeán gecîgde *de phantastico incendio* . . . *Ignem in oculis fratrum esse considerans* . . . *eos, quos phantastico reperit igne deludi, revocavit*, Gr. D. 123, 16–124, 11. Him gedúht swylce . . . seó kycene forburne; ac hit . . . wæs þæs deófles dydrung . . . Ðā gebrōðra wǣron mid ðām gedwymorlicum fýre gebysgode, Hml. Th. ii. 166, 4–11.

**ge-dwimorlîce.** *Add: in appearance only, not really:*—Weard ān mǣden forbróden (*changed to a mare*) þurh drýmanna dydrung, ge-dwimorlîce swā ðeáh . . . Macharius cwæð: 'Ic geseó þis mǣden on menniscum gecynde, and heó nis nā āwend swā swā gē wēnað . . . ac on eówrum gesihðum hit is swā gehîwod, Hml. S. 21, 474. v. un-gedwimorlîce.

**ge-dwînan.** *Add:*—Þonne deriende gedwînað heonone þysse worulde gefeán, gewîtað mid ealle, þonne druncennes gedwîneð mid wistum *noxia tunc hujus cessabunt gaudia saeli, ebrietas, epulae*, Dôm. L. 231, 233. Gedwān *disparuit .i. evanuit*, Wrt. Voc. ii. 141, 18 : 27, 34.

**ge-dwol**; *adj. Heretical:*—Arrianus se gedwola bisceop, Gr. D. 234, 10, 21 : 235, 1. v. gedwol-bisceop.

**ge-dwola** *error. Add:* I. *error, wrong conduct:*—Gedwolum *erratis*, An. Ox. 43, 8. Hê geseah þ eal manna cynn on missenlicum gedwolum from heora Scyppende gewitene wǣron, Bl. H. 103, 5. **II.** *a practice that deceives, leads into error.* Cf. gedwol-cræft:—þā þe galdorcræftas and gedwolan begangaþ and mid þǣm unwære men bewîcaþ and ādwellaþ, Bl. H. 61, 23. **III.** *erroneous opinion or doctrine:* —Wiðerweardra gedwola *apocryphorum naenias*, Mt. p. 10, 9. v. scîn-gedwola.

**ge-dwola** *one who errs. Add:* I. *one who acts wrongly, a wicked person:*—'Wā ðām ðe talað yfel tô gôde, and gôd tô yfele . . . Swilce gerihtwîsiað þone ārleásan for sceattum' . . . Eft cwæð Salomon be swilcum gedwolum: 'Hî (*impii*) blissiað on yfelnesse,' Hml. Th. ii. 322, 20. **II.** *one who errs from imperfect knowledge:*—Geleáfan

ungelǣredes folces and gedwolena *fidem indocti vulgi ac neofitorum*, Angl. xiii. 421, 803. **III.** *one who errs in matters of doctrine, a heretic:*—Arrianus wæs se mǣsta gedwola þe of mancynne cōme, Ll. Th. ii. 374, 1 : Hml. A. 59, 196. Olimpius wæs eác gedwola on ûres Drihtnes geleáfan (*in respect to his belief in our Lord*), 204. Sê þe him (*the apostles and wise teachers*) wiðcwyð and heora gesetnessum, hê byð gedwola, 22, 199 : Hml. S. 1, 19. Valens wæs on Crîste gefullod, ac hê ne cûþe his geleáfan, ac folgode gedwylde . . . Se gedwola, 3, 299. Nestorum þone gedwolan þe cwæð þ on Crîste wǣron twēgen hādas, Ll. Th. ii. 374, 18. þ hālige godspell hæfð oferswîðod swylcera ge-dwolena andgit, Hml. S. 1, 8. **IV.** *one who wanders in his mind, a frantic person:*—Ged(w)olan *lymphaticus*, An. Ox. 11, 176.

**gedwol-bisceop**, es; *m. A heretical bishop:*—Arrianus se gedwol-biscop þāra ungeleáffullra Langbeardna, Gr. D. 234, 10, 21 : 235, 1. Gecyrdum þām gedwolbiscope, 238, 20. Se fæder sǣnde þone gedwol-biscop, 11 : 15.

**ge-dwolen.** *Add: wanting in understanding, foolish:*—Gedwolenum *vecordi*, Kent. Gl. 308.

**gedwol-fǣr**, es ; *n. or -faru*, e; *f. A going astray:*—Gewǣcede on gedwolfǣre *defectos in abductione*, Ps. Rdr. p. 291, 30.

**gedwol-godas.** *Substitute:* **gedwol-god**, es; *m. n. A false god:*—Ðes gedwolgod (*Mercury*) . . . is Oðon gehāten on Denisce wîsan, Wlfst. 107, 6. Lāc tô weorðunge þissum gedwolgode (*Mars*), 106, 30. On hæþenum þeódum ne dear man forhealdan lytel ne mycel þæs þe gelagod is tô gedwolgoda weorðunge . . . ne dear man gewanian . . . ænig þǣra þinga þe gedwolgodan gebrôht bið, 157, 12, 7.

**ge-dwolian.** *Add:* -dwalian. I. *to go astray, wander from the path.* (1) lit. :—Gif gedwalige (-duologia, L., *erraverit*) ān ðāra scîpa . . . hê gāð soece þætte gedwalode (-duolade, L., *erravit*) . . . hê māre gefeáþ be þǣm þonne be þǣm . . . þe ne gedwaladan (*erraverunt*), Mt. R. 18, 12–13. Gif mon on his wege biþ gedwolod, Lch. ii. 290, 17. (2) fig. :—Ne eart þû ealles of þām earde ādrifen, þeáh þû ðǣr ne gedwolode *tu a patria non quidem pulsus es sed aberrasti*, Bt. 5, 1 ; F. 8, 36. **II.** *to err*, Bl. H. 87, 30 : Mk. R. 12, 27. v. Dict.

**ge-dwollîce** ; *adv. In error, erringly:*—Hî worhton wôlîce and ge-dwollîce him hæþene godas, and þone sôþan God forsāwon, Wlfst. 105, 9.

**ge-dwolma**, an ; *m. Chaos:*—Gedwolman *chaos*, Wrt. Voc. ii. 21, 63.

**gedwol-mann.** *Add: one who is in error,* (1) *a mistaken person, one who acts under a misapprehension :*—Fæder, . . . forgif ðâs ðæde þisum gedwolmannum, for ðan ðe hî nyton hwæt hî nû dôð, Hml. Th. ii. 256, 8. (2) *one who holds erroneous opinions in matters of faith,* (a) *an opponent of Christianity :*—Andeteras (*confessores*) Crîstes naman mid sôðum geleáfan andetton bealdlîce betwux gedwolmannum, Hml. Th. ii. 558, 24. (b) *an unorthodox person, a heretic, schismatic :*—Ðā gedwol-menn (*haeretici*) mid wôre lāre ofsleáð ðæt môd geleáffullra monna, Past. 367, 15 : 369, 17. Of ðām gedwylde þe gedwolmen setton be hyre ācennednysse, Hml. A. 24, 6 : Hml. S. 1, 5. Ðā gedwolmen þe dwelodon þone cāsere, 3, 312. Hê folgode gedwylde þurh gedwolmanna tihtinge, 296. Gedwolmanna *scismaticorum* i. *hereticorum*, An. Ox. 417: Hpt. 474, 49. Hê wolde sweltan for rihte ǣr ðām þe hê forsuwode þone sôðan gelýfan betwux þām gedwolmannum þe hine drehton, Hml. S. 3, 669.

**gedwol-sprǣc**, e ; *f. Heretical speech, heresy:*—Twēgen ðǣr wǣron bisceophādes men þe ælces yfeles heáfodhebban wǣron . . . hî Godes gelaðunge drehton and mid heora gedwolsprǣce eall folc āmyrdon, Hml. S. 23, 369.

**ge-dwolsum.** *Substitute: Misleading:*—Æfre sê þe āwent of Ledene on Englisc, ǣfre hê sceal gefadian hit swā þ þ Englisc hæbbe his āgene wîsan; elles hit biþ swîþe gedwolsum tô rǣdenne þām þe þæs Ledenes wîsan ne can, Ælfc. Gen. Thw. 4, 10.

**gedwol-þing**, es ; *n.* I. *a false thing:*—Hý forgýmdon heora Drihten, and wurðedon þurh deófles lāre mistlice gedwolþing, and worhton fela gedwimera on anlîcnessum, Wlfst. 11, 4. **II.** (*magical*) *delusion, sorcery:*—Balzaman smyring wiþ scînlāce and wiþ eallum gedwolþinge, Lch. ii. 288, 14. Wið ælces cynnes gedwolþing, 290, 16.

**ge-dwomer, ge-dýfan.** v. ge-dwimor, ge-dîfan.

**ge-dyn** ; *m. l.* **-dyne**; *n., and add:*—Hit anginne eal ætgidre brastligan, and ðā hameras beátan and for eallum ðysan gedene ne mæg sió sāwle hî gerestan, Sal. K. p. 85, 21.

**ge-dyngan** *to dung, manure. Substitute:*—Seó eá þæt land midde-weard oferfleów mid fôtes þicce flôde, and hit þonne mid ðām gedynged weard *fluvius per plana diffusus augmentis ubertatis inpendebatur*, Ors. 1, 3 ; S. 32, 7. Gedyngde æceras *ceratos agros*, Wrt. Voc. ii. 130, 22.

**ge-dyppan.** *Dele, and see* ge-dîpan: **ge-dýran.** v. ge-dîran.

**ge-dýre.** *l.* **-dyre** ; *n. :*—On heora gedyrum and oferslegum, Hml. Th. i. 310, 29 : 40, 12. On ægðrum gedyrum and on þām oferslege, Angl. viii. 322, 12. ¶ *as a part used for the whole, a door :*—Wurdon gemētte ætforan heora gedyrum twā hund mittan meluwes on fætelsum *ducenti farinae modii ante fores cellae* (ætforan ðæs mynstres geate, Gr. D. 145, 26) *inventi sunt*, Hml. Th. ii. 172, 4.

**ge-dyrfan.** v. ge-dirfan: **ge-dyrfsum.** v. ge-deorfsum: **ge-dȳrsian.** v. ge-dīrsian: **ge-dyrst.** *l.* (?) ge-dyrft. Cf. ge-deorfan.

**ge-dyrstig.** *Substitute: Bold, daring:*—Gedyrstig (-durst-, Erf.) *ausus*, Txts. 43, 245: Wrt. Voc. ii. 7, 44. (1) in a favourable sense, *having courage, confidence:*—Ne gidyrstig wæs ǣnig hine gefregna *neque ausus fuit quisquam eum interrogare*, Mt. L. 22, 46. Be þǣre wīsan þe ic nǣfre ǣr næs gedyrstig þē tō āxianne, Guth. 84, 20. Ne mæg þǣr ǣni man be āgnum gewyrhtum gedyrstig wesan dēman gehende *nullus ibi meritis confidit judice praesens*, Dōm. L. 170. Saga hū þū gedyrstig þurh deóp gehygd wurde þus wīgþrīst ofer eall wīfa cyn, þæt þū mec gebunde, Jul. 431. (2) in an unfavourable sense, *presumptuous, audacious:*—Gif hē tō þan gedyrstig wǣre ꝥ hē þæt ābrǣce, C. D. ii. 131, 18. Swā wē magon betst ðā gedyrstigan (*protervos*) gelǣran, Past. 209, 15. [*O. H. Ger.* ge-turstig *ausus, audax.*]

**ge-dyrstigan.** *l.* -dyrstigian, *and add:*—Gif for micelre ārweorðnesse hwylc man ne gedyrstgað (-dyrstigaþ, -drystigað, þyrstgað, *v. ll.*, *praesumit*) onfoon, Bd. 1, 27; Sch. 83, 22. For hwon gedyrstigodest (-dyrstgadest, *v. l.*, *praesumsisti*) þū ꝥ þū stalodest?, Gr. D. 25, 7. ꝥ wīf wel gedyrstgade (*praesumsit*), Bd. 1, 27; Sch. 83, 8. Þām þe gedyrstgoden ꝥ . . ., 5, 21; Sch. 677, 19. [*O. H. Ger.* ge-turstigōn *usurpare.*]

**ge-dyrstignes.** *Substitute:* **I.** *presumption, audacity:*—Ðȳ lǣs sió gedyrstignes his mōdes hine tō upp āhebbe *ne mentem praesumtio spiritus levet*, Past. 79, 17. Sȳ forboden on mynstre ǣlcere gedyrstignesse (*praesumtionis*) intinga, R. Ben. 129, 13. Hié nō sceolon ābūgan þurh ǣnige gedyrstignesse *ne temere declinetur a quoquam*, 15, 21. Gif hwylc þurh gedyrstignesse . . . *qui praesumpserit* . . ., 130, 4. Þurh þā gedyrstignesse (-durst-, Ll. Th. i. 270, 24) þe folces men wiðhæfton þǣre gelōmlican myngunge, Ll. Lbmn. 206, 22. ꝥ gē gehȳrdon þā oferhygdlican gedyrstignesse þæs elreordgan kyninges, Nar. 19, 11. ꝥ hē heora oferhȳd tōweorpe and gedyrstignesse (-þyrstignesse, *v. l.*) drēfe *ut superbiam eorum dissipet et conturbet audaciam*, Bd. 4, 3; Sch. 362, 8. **II.** *a bold undertaking:*—Gedyrstignessum *ausis*, Wrt. Voc. ii. 9, 32.

**ge-dyrstlǣcan.** *Add: to presume.* (1) absolute:—*Audeo* ic dearr, *audens* gedyrstlǣcende, *ausus* gedyrstlǣht, *ausurus* sē ðe gedyrstlǣcð, Ælfc. Gr. Z. 247, 3–5. (2) with an object:—Gif wē mid rīcan mannan hwæt embe ūre neóde manian willað, þæt wē ne gedyrstlǣcað (*praesumimus*) būtan mid micelre eáðmōdnesse, R. Ben. 45, 16. Gif hwā hit būtan his leáfe gedyrstlǣce, 79, 19. Ne hȳ nān þing ne gedyrstlǣcen, ne nǣnne ontige on þām mynstre būtan þǣre mæssan ānre, 140, 9. (3) with a clause:—Gif hwylc brōðor būton his abbodes hǣse gedyrstlǣcð ꝥ hē nime . . ., R. Ben. 50, 10. Hū gedyrstlǣhtest þū ꝥ þū þus oft stalodest?, Gr. D. 25, 7. Þū nǣfre ne gedyrstlǣc ꝥ þū . . . geneálǣce, 135, 8. Hwā dear nū gedyrstlǣcan ꝥ hē derige þām folce?, Hml. A. 101, 306. (3 a) where the extent of presumption is defined by the clause:—ꝥ hē nā ne gedyrstlǣhte tō þām ꝥ hē þone Godes þeów ǣnig þing hrepode, Gr. D. 38, 32. (4) with dat. infin.:—Þæt nān ne gedyrstlǣce his āgenne rǣd tō bewerigenne, R. Ben. 15, 12: 55, 10: 56, 17. (5) with a preposition:—'Ūre Fæder . . .' Ne gedyrstlǣce nān man be mǣgðhāde būtan sōðre lufe, Hml. Th. i. 54, 10. (6) with a reflexive dative:—For hwig gedyrstlǣhtest þū þē ꝥ ðū ꝥ geþanc āsendest?, Nic. 17, 6.

**ge-dyrstlǣcing,** e; *f. Boldness:*—Mid gedyrstlǣcinge his (bylde þǣre, *v. l.*) hīwcūðnysse *ausu familiaritatis*, Gr. D. 71, 18.

**ge-dyrstlic;** *adj. Bold, audacious, presumptuous:*—Þæt wīf wel gedyrstlice dǣde dyde þæt heó Drihtnes hrægle gehrān *bene praesumsit quae uestimentum Domini tetigit*, Bd. 1, 27; Sch. 83, 9.

**ge-dyrstnes,** e; *f. Presumption:*—Gif hwā þis ofergȳme þurh ǣnige gedyrstnesse, R. Ben. 129, 9. v. ge-dyrstigness.

**ge-dysig.** *Dele.*

**ge-dysigian** *to be foolish:*—Dweledon (dwoliað, C., gedisegan, T.) heortan *errant corde*, Ps. Spl. 94, 9. v. next word.

**ge-dysigend** *one acting foolishly:*—From dearflicum ⁊ from gidyssgindum unwīsum *a praesumtoribus imperitis*, Mt. p. 2, 1.

**ge-eácnian.** *Add:* **I.** *to make greater, add to, increase, augment:*—Hē his synna geeácnað, Hml. S. 16, 292. Wē geeácniað heora werod, Hml. Th. i. 214, 23. Hī mid ðām geeácniað yfelnysse him sylfum, Hml. S. 13, 298. Ic heóld þīnes fæder gestreón, and furðor hī geeácnode, 9, 43. Hē ðæs dæges leóht geeácnode mid ðām scīnendum tunglum, Hex. 6, 31. Ic wylle mīne bernu geeácnian (*horrea mea majora faciam*, Lk. 12, 18), Wlfst. 286, 19. Hī ne sceolon heora bodunge ālecgan, ac swīðor geeácnian, Hml. Th. ii. 232, 15: Chr. 1067; P. 201, 28: Geieácnian, Cht. Th. 125, 18. Wē sceolan geeácnian ūs þā ēcean spēda, Hml. S. 12, 269. Geeácnude weldǣda *macta merita*, An. Ox. 3542. **II.** *to add:*—Þā sōna geeácnode (geēcte, *v. l.*) hē þǣr tō 'þīnes mūðes,' Gr. D. 139, 8. ꝥ hē geeácnige āne elne tō hys anlīcnesse *adicere ad staturam suam cubitum unum*, Mt. 6, 27. Ealle þās þing eów beóð þǣr tō geeácnode *haec omnia adicientur vobis*, 33. **III.** *to become* or *to make pregnant:*—Þonne hraþe geeácnað heó, Lch. i. 346, 7. Wīf tō geeácnigenne *to make a woman pregnant*, 4. Ǣr ðon þe heó geeácnad wǣre *before she conceived*, Shrn. 47, 29. Eua cende hire bearn on sāre, for þon þe heó on synnum geeácnod wæs . . . Maria fǣmne cende, for ðon heó wæs fǣmne geeácnod, Bl. H. 3, 13–17, 18, 22. Heó geeácnod wæs of þǣm Hālgan Gāste, 11, 14. Þæt wīf mid bearne geeácnod wæs, Guth. 8, 12. **IV.** *to conceive* a child:—Geeácnaþ *concipit*, Wrt. Voc. ii. 136, 22. Ān mǣden sceal geeácnian (*concipiet*) and ācennan sunu, Hml. Th. ii. 14, 2. Geēcnande *concipiens*, Lk. L. 1, 31. Geēcnad wēre *conciperetur*, 2, 21. Sē þe wæs geeácnod of þām Hālgan Gāste *qui conceptus est de Spiritu Sancto*, Ps. L. fol. 199, 5. Þonne him sió sōðfæsðnes on geeácnod bið, ǣr ðǣm ðe hit fullboren sié, Past. 367, 17. Hwæðer hē wite þe nyte, hwænne hē geeácnod (-ēc-, *v. l.*) wǣre, Gr. D. 262, 19. On synne hē bið geeácnod, Bl. H. 59, 34. Geeácnud (*regenerantis gratiae vulva*) *conceptus*, An. Ox. 3134. **V.** *to bring forth:*—Ic wæs geeácnad *ego parturiebar*, Kent. Gl. 267.

**ge-eácnung.** *Add:* **I.** *conceiving, conception.* (1) in active sense:—Þā æfter þan wǣron gefylde nigan mōnað hire geeácnunge, þā cende Anna hyre dohtor, Hml. As. 125, 282. ꝥ hē bodige hire geeácnunge, Bl. H. 143, 24. (2) in passive sense:—Scī Iohannis geeácnung, Shrn. 133, 26. **II.** *what is conceived:*—Hyre geeácnung (*or* **I.** 1?) is of ðām Hālgan Gāste (*quod in ea natum est de Spiritu Sancto est*, Mt. 1, 20), Hml. As. 135, 630. Wīf seó þe tō ǣwyrpe gedō hire geeácnunga on hyre hryfe *mulier quae utero conceptum excusserit*, Ll. Th. ii. 154, 15. **III.** *parturition, birth:*—Swilc gedafenað geeácnung *talis decet partus Deum*, Hy. S. 43, 32. Wið ꝥ wīf hrædlīce cenne . . . Sōna swā eall seó geeácnung gedōn beó, Lch. i. 218, 23. Geeácnungum *partubus*, An. Ox. 3136. **IV.** *what is born:*—Þū Alȳsend . . . geeácnung mǣdenes *Redemptor* . . . *partus virginis*, Hy. S. 41, 34.

**ge-eádgian.** *Add:*—Þū ge(e)ádgast *beabis, beatum facis*, Wrt. Voc. ii. 125, 28.

**ge-eádmōd-, -mēd-.** v. ge-eáþmōd-, -mēd-: **ge-eahtedlic, -eahtendlic.** v. un-geeahtedlic, -geeahtendlic.

**ge-eahtian.** *Add:*—Geahtige mon ðone ceáp, syle þone teóþan pænig for Gode, Lch. iii. 56, 12. v. un-geeahtedlic.

**ge-ealdian.** *Add:*—ꝥte hiá lifiā and gialdia *ut vivent et senescant*, Rtl. 111, 14.

**ge-ealgian.** *Add:*—Hē ūres Drihtnes heorde gealgað (ealgað, *v. l.*) R. Ben. 122, 2. Ðā stōwe þe se fearr geealgode, Hml. Th. i. 502, 33. Þæt hē ōþerne mid ǣnigum anginne geealgige (*defendere*), R. Ben. 129, 6.

**ge-eardian.** *Add:*—Þū geeardast on heom *habitabis in eis*, Ps. L. 5, 12.

**ge-earnian.** *Add:* **I.** *to deserve, merit.* (1) *with acc.:*—Hē him sylfum rēþne dōm geearnaþ and begyteþ, Bl. H. 95, 34. Gefeán . . . þe þū ǣr on worlde mid geleáfan tō mē . . . geearnodest, 63, 29. Nis nān tweó ꝥ hē forgifnesse syllan nelle þām þe hié geearnian willaþ, 65, 9. (2) *with clause:*—Ic þē lǣre þæt þū hospcwide ne fremme, . . . þonne þū gearnest ꝥ þē bið ēce līf seald, El. 526. Þīne heortan tō rǣde gecyr and geearna ꝥ þīne bēna sȳn Gode andfenge, Bl. H. 113, 27. Geearnian wē ꝥ ūre se ȳtmesta dæg sȳ engla gefeá, 101, 34. ꝥ gē mid eówrum ǣhtum geearnian ꝥ gē þone ēcan gefeán begytan mōtan, 53, 29. Ǣghwylc man sceal on worlde geearnian ꝥ him ꝥ gōd mōre tō ēcum mēdum gegangan, 101, 17. Gehearnian, Angl. xii. 514, 28. (3) *absolute:*—Swā hē hēr geearnað, Kr. 109. Swā hī geearnedan, Ps. Th. 78, 13. For þā ōðre swā hȳ geearnian, Ll. Th. i. 222, 21. Swā wīte swā wuldor swē wē nū geearnian willaþ, Bl. H. 23, 7. **I a.** *to deserve of* (*tō*) a person. (1) *with acc.:*—Tō ðǣm ðe þone ēcean ēðel mid mōde and mid mægene tō Gode geearniað, Bl. H. 209, 25. (2) *with gen.:*—Gif ic tō þisum þe mē swencað þæs geearnod hæbbe, Ps. Th. 7, 3. (3) absolute:—Him swā leánian swā hē hire tō geearnud hæfde, Cht. Th. 202, 22. Mid wyrsan leáne þonne hē tō him geearnod hæfde, Ors. 5, 4; S. 224, 33. **II.** *to earn, gain by labour, acquire:*—Þonne geearnige wē ūs heofena rīce, Angl. xii. 514, 33. Þurh ꝥ hē geearnode him þā gife Hāliges Gāstes, Bl. H. 113, 32. ꝥ man mid māndǣdum him sylfum geearnige edwīt . . . mid gōdum dǣdum geearnige him þā ēcean ræste, 101, 24–26. Folgere gebyreð ꝥ hē on twelf mōnðum .II. æceras geearnige (*habeat*) . . . gyf hē māre geearnian mæig (*deservit*) him bið sylfum fremu, Ll. Th. i. 438, 4–7. ꝥ wē þurh ꝥ gegearnian ūra synna forlǣtnesse, Bl. H. 35, 36. Ðā wolde hē geearnian him hereword (*adquirere sibi laudem*), Chr. 1009; P. 138, note 9. Fram Gode nā mæg gegearnian (*mereri*) ꝥ hē bitt, Scint. 45, 2. Geearnian, Bl. H. 25, 22: 17, 21. On þisse sceortan tīde geearnian ēce ræste, 83, 2: 111, 3. Hē gǣþ . . . Drihtne tō geearnienne medome folc, 165, 15. ꝥ wǣron geearnode *ut* (*praemia*) *promerentur*, An. Ox. 5421. v. ge-arnian *in Dict.*

**ge-earnung.** *Add:* **I.** *merit, desert:*—Swungen oþ ꝥ hē swylte, swā his geearnung wæs, Bl. H. 193, 4. Geearnuncg, Ps. Th. 57, 6. Be geearnunga ānra gehwelcre *according to the merit of each one*, Met. 20, 228. His geearnunga þǣr wǣron oft beorhte gecȳþed, Shrn. 52, 11. Æfter heora geearnunga anddyfene, R. Ben. 13, 7. Þurh Ōswaldes geearnungum, Hml. S. 26, 39, 108. Se līchoma bið þonne undeáþlic . . . sceal þeáh beón gelīc his geearnungum (*its condition will be in accordance with its deserts*), Bl. H. 21, 32. Ðā habbað swīðe misleca geearnunga, Past. 95, 8. Þurh Scē Ælfēges hālgan gegearnunga, Chr. 1023; P. 156, 28. **II.** *action that deserves gratitude:*—Gif hī þā geearnunga ealle

gemundon þe hē him tō duguðe gedōn hæfde, By. 196. v. eft-ge-earnung; ge-arnung.

**ge-eárplættan**; *p.* te *To box the ears, buffet* :—Se sceocca mē geárplætt (*angelus Satanae me colaphizet*, 2 Cor. 12, 7), Hml. Th. i. 474, 13. v. plættan.

**ge-earwian.** v. ge-gearwian.

**ge-eástrian;** *p.* ode *To put after Easter* :—Fram *septuagesima* oð fíftēne niht beón geeástrode (*until fifteen days after Easter*; cf. fram *septuagesima* oð fíftēne niht ofer Eástran, 118, 1), Wlfst. 208, 24.

**ge-eáþmēdan.** *Add:* , -eáþmēdian; *p.* ede. **I.** (1) the object a person. (a) *to humiliate* :—Þā eágan þāra ofermōdena þū geeáðmētst (*humiliabis*), Ps. Th. 17, 26. Geeádmētst, Hml. A. 107, 166. Þisne geeáðmēddeþ (*humiliat*) and þysne āhefþ, Ps. Spl. 74, 7. Þū woldest ūs geeáðmēdan, Ps. Th. 43, 20. Ælc þe hine āhefþ sceal beón geeáðmēt, Hml. A. 114, 408. (b) *to make submissive, subject, subdue* :—Ðā þeóde þe wið ūs ārisan hē wolde geeáðmēdigan, Hml. A. 126, 318. Gecir tō þínre hlæfdian and beó geeáðmēt under hire handa (*humiliare sub manu illius*), Gen. 16, 9. Hig wurdon geeáðmētte under heora handum (*humiliati sunt sub manibus eorum*, Ps. Th. 105, 31), Ælfc. T. Grn. 11, 35. (2) the object a high place, *to lower* :—Ælc dūn bið geeáðmēt, Hml. Th. i. 360, 33. **II.** where inferiority is acknowledged. (1) reflexive. (a) where an attitude that expresses humility is taken :—Seó leó āleát mid þām heáfde and feóll tō his fótum and geeáðmēdde hī tō him, Hml. S. 30, 418. (b) where worship is paid :—Tiberius hyne sylfne geeáðmēdde, Hml. A. 192, 319. Þā seó hālignes hym wæs tō bróht, þā feóll hē nyðer ástreht and myd ryhtum geleáfan hyne þærtó geeáðmēdde, 189, 247. Ne geeáðmēde þū þe tō hira unrihtum godum *noli adorare deum alienum*, Ex. 34, 14. Gif ǽnig man geeáðmēde hine tō sunnan and tō mōnan *adoret solem et lunam*, Deut. 17, 3. (c) where submission is made :—Geeáðmēdaþ eów sylfe tō Godes willan, Hml. A. 165, 23. Þ folc ne sceal forhycgan þ hī tō him (*the clergy*) hī geeáþmēdon, Bl. H. 47, 30. (2) where the reflexive pronoun is omitted. (a) cf. I a :—Hig feóllon on þā eorðan and geeáðmeddon wið hine *adoraverunt proni in terram*, Gen. 43, 26. (b) cf. 1 b :—Āgit mē þone dryhten þe ðū tō geeáðmēddest, Hml. A. 189, 243. (c) cf. 1 c :—Geeáðmēt *cedit*, An. Ox. 1005. **III.** *to worship, adore.* (1) *with acc.* :—Hig geeáðmēdað hira hearga *adorant simulacra eorum*, Ex. 34, 15. Hī geeáðmēdedon ealle þā fǽtten eorðan *adoraverunt omnes pingues terrae*, Ps. L. 21, 30. Ic hyne wylle geeáðmēdan, Hml. A. 189, 244 : 191, 313. (2) *with dat.* :—Ic hym geeáðmēdan wylle and hym þeówian, Hml. A. 190, 265. **IV.** with the idea of condescension. (1) of human beings :—Tō ðon þaeti for mínum synnum hī (*the clergy of Worcester*) heó geeáðmēdden þaette heó wǽren þingeras wið Drihten, C. D. i. 114, 17. (2) of the Deity or angels :—Críst hine tō þon geeáþmēdeþ þ . . ., Bl. H. 5, 14. Ic mē tō þām geeáðmētte, þ ic eów mid eáðmódnysse þēnade, Hml. A. 159, 183. Geeáðmēdde, 151, 8. Geeáþmēdde, Bl. H. 11, 33. Hē (*St. Michael*) hine geeáðmēdde þ . . ., 197, 14. Drihten hine geeáðmēdde swā steórrēðra, 235, 23. v. eáþ-mēdan (-ian).

**ge-eáþmēdian.** *See preceding word.*

**ge-eáþmōd(i)gian, -mōdi(g)an.** *Add:* —God hine geeáðmódað (*-æád-, v. l.*) þ hē gehýreð þára bēne *exaudire preces dignatur Deus*, Gr. D. 70, 17. Críst giéðmódade (*humiliavit*) hine seolfne, Rtl. 21, 26. Ðē ðe hine suelc lytel cild geeðmódade (*humiliaverit*), Mt. p. 18, 5. v. eáþmōd(i)gian.

**ge-eáþmōdlíce (-eád-).** *Dele, and see* eáþmódlíce.

**ge-eáwan.** *Add:* —Þā wǽron geeáwde swǽ hit āwriten is ðæt hié wǽron ymb eall ūtan mid eágum besett, Past. 194, 18. v. ge-eówan, -íwan.

**ge-eblícadun.** v. ge-efenlícad : **ge-ebolsian.** v. ge-eofulsian.

**ge-ecgan;** *p.* -egede *To harrow* :—Se lyðra þe ǽgðer ge sǽwð ge lasor ge coccul on manna æceron, and syððan hit grynlíce geegð mid sace and wrace, Angl. viii. 300, 25. v. ecgan.

**ge-ecgode (-ede);** *adj. Edged, provided with an edge* :—Tōbrocene tigelan scearpe geecgode, Hml. S. 37, 179.

**ge-ēcnian.** v. ge-eácnian : **ge-edcēgan.** *l.* -cígan.

**ge-edcenned.** *Substitute:* ge-edcennan; *p.* de *To regenerate* :—Þurh þæne fulluht þe se mæssepreóst eów of geedcende *per illud baptismum, quo uos sacerdos regenerauit*, Ll. Lbmn. 413, 41. Geedcenned of wætere and of hāligum gāste *renatus ex aqua et spiritu*, Jn. 3, 5. His gecoren-an beóð geedcennede on fulluhte, Hml. Th. ii. 524, 31. Geedcynnede of þām Hālgan Gāste *renati Sancto Spiritu*, Hy. S. 43, 15 : Hml. Th. i. 394, 26 : 566, 24.

**ge-edcwician.** *Add:* (1) *to come to life again* after death :—Hē ne geedcucað ǽr ðām gemǽnum ǽriste, ac hē is tō ēcum wítum geniðerod, Hml. Th. i. 382, 2. Hē clypode: 'Thabita, ārīs,' and heó þǽrrihte geedcucode, Hml. S. 10, 71. Gewát hē of worulde . . . hē wearð geedcucod. Þā clypode se geedcucoda, 36, 131. Dóndum þām geedcukedan dǽdbóte, Gr. D. 90, 4. Mid geedcucedre *rediuiua* (*sospitate*), An. Ox. 4338. (2) *to recover consciousness, feeling* :—Raþe wund geedcucað (*reuiuescit*) gif raþor lācnung byð gegearwud, Scint.

45, 8. Hē læg dumb swā oð deáþ beswungen . . . hē þā geedcucode, Hml. S. 25, 794.

**ge-edfreólsian;** *p.* ode *To re-enfranchise, to restore to freedom* :—Þis is ealra þāra landa freóls þe Eádgār cyning geedfreólsade Wulfríce his þegene on ēce yrfe (cf. ego, Eádgār, . . . cuidam ministro . . . Wulfríc . . . rura, que ei . . . interdicta fuerant, perpetualiter restituo, aeternam libertatem concedens, 360, 13-17), C. D. ii. 361, 27.

**ge-edhiwod.** *Substitute:* ge-edhíwian; *p.* ode *To give another shape to* :—Nelle gē beón geedhíwode þissere worulde ac beóð geedhíwode on níwnysse andgytes eówres *nolite conformari huic saeculo, sed reformamini in nouitate sensus uestri*, Scint. 58, 3, 4.

**ge-edhyrt.** *Substitute:* ge-edhirtan; *p.* te *To refresh, reanimate* :—Geedhyrte *recreata, refota, refecta*, Germ. 390, 173.

**ge-edlǽcan.** *Dele* 'Geedlǽcend . . . 484,' *and add:* **I.** *trans. To repeat* :—Þū mīnne teónan geedlǽcst, Hml. S. 8, 73. Þā þe he beweóp geedlǽcð *haec quae fleuerat repetit*, Scint. 45, 17. Geedlǽhð, Hml. Th. ii. 380, 13, 14. Gehyðlēct, Kent. Gl. 602. Geedlǽcð *iterat*, 988. Þā ylcan lāre þe hē him ǽr tǽhte hē eft geedlǽhte, Hml. Th. i. 28, 7. Hē eft geedlǽhte his word, Ælfc. T. Grn. 17, 3. Nā geedlǽc þū (*iteres*) word mānfull, Scint. 79, 10. Ne geedlǽce hē hig eft nā *ne repetat illa postea*, Ll. Th. ii. 136, 15 : Hml. Th. ii. 288, 24. Mon sceal þā sylfan sealmas ǽlce niht geedlǽcan, R. Ben. 44, 5. Geydlǽcan, Hpt. 31, 13, 317. Þæt fers sý geedlǽht, R. Ben. 60, 6. Wund geedlǽht *uulnus iteratum*, Scint. 48, 18. Sealmas beón geedleehte (*repetantur*), R. Ben. I. 51, 3. **I a.** *with dat.* :—Se man ðe wile his synna . . . gebētan, þonne mōt hē geornlíce warnian þ hē eft ðām yfelum dǽdum ne geedlǽce, Hml. Th. ii. 602, 24 : Hml. S. 12, 161. **II.** *intrans.* (1) *to repeat, recur* :—Ðǽs āteorigendlícan woruld þe tyrnð on seofon dagum, and hī symle geedlǽcað (*the days always recur*), Hml. Th. ii. 214, 30. Geedlǽcend(e) twyfealdnys *iterata dupplicatio*, Angl. viii. 331, 23. (2) *to persist in a statement* :—Nis þær ðæs geáres ord, ne eác on ðisum dæge, . . . þeáh ðe ūre gerímbēc on þissere stōwe geedlǽcon, Hml. Th. i. 98, 29.

**ge-edlǽsian.** *Add:* v. ge-edlesende.

**ge-edleánend, es;** *m. A rewarder, remunerator* :—Rehtwís geedleánend *justus remunerator es*, Txts. 420, 28.

**ge-edleánian;** *p.* ode *To reward, requite, repay* :—Ic gedleániu (*retribuam*) dōm feóndum, Ps. Srt. ii. p. 196, 23. Geedleánas *retribues*, 130, 2. Hē āgelt þ geedleánaþ mē *retribuet mihi*, Ps. L. 17, 25. Geedleánades *retribuisti*, Ps. Srt. ii. 191, 42. Geedleánedun *retribuebant*, 34, 12. Geedleániendum *repensanda*, i. *retribuenda*, An. Ox. 1519.

**ge-edleánung, e;** *f. Retribution, requital* :—In geedleánunge *in retribuendo*, Ps. Srt. 54, 21.

**ge-edlesende (?);** *adj.* (*ptcpl.*) *Reciprocal* :—Geedlæsend tale *reciproca* (i. *iterata*) *disputatio*, An. Ox. 3205. Seó geedlǽsend *reciproca* (*ferocitas*), 3538. On geedlǽsendum *in reciprocis* (i. *iteratis*) (*conflictibus*), 3216. v. ge-edlǽsian in Dict.

**ge-edlian.** *Dele.*

**ge-edníwian, -níwan.** *Add:* (1) *to renew* what is weakened, *restore to efficiency* :—Ðæt gōde mōd, ðe sió hǽlo ful oft āweg ādríefð, ðæt gemynd ðǽre medtrymnesse geedníwað (-níwað, *v. l.*) (*reformat*), Past. 255, 17. Þū mē geedníwodest mín ríce *tu restituisti mihi haereditatem meam*, Ps. Th. 15, 5. Tō þām ǽrrum antimbre geedníwude (*fragmina*) *in pristinum statum reformavit* (i. *innouauit*), An. Ox. 1832. Críst ūs geedníwode tō his gelícnisse, Ælfc. T. Grn. 3, 34. God wolde þurh hine geedníwigian ðisne ealdne middangeard, Hml. S. 22, 12. Wæs ūre gecynd geedneówod, Bl. H. 11, 10. Þonne wesaþ þíne handa geedneówode, 153, 12. Swā oft swā hī beóð mē āsægde, hī beóð mē geedníwde *mihi quoties narratur, innouatur*, Gr. D. 255, 28. (2) *to restore* a disused practice :—Se cāsere Godes cyrcan gegódode . . . and Godes lof geedníwode, Hml. S. 27, 135. (3) *to renew* an action, *do again* what has been done before, *repeat* :—Se man þe æfter his dǽdbóte his mānfullan dǽda geedníwað, Hml. S. 12, 162. Wē geedníwiað and gemyndigað ðǽre scylde ðe ūre ieldesta mǽg ūs on forworhte *parentis primi lapsus iteratur*, Past. 313, 14. Geedníwa *instaura*, Wrt. Voc. ii. 46, 20. [O. H. Ger. ge-niuwōn *reformare, reparare*.]

**ge-edníwung, e;** *f. Renewal, restoration* :—Ǽr þǽre gyfte and geedníwunge (*restitutionem*) þāra líchamana on dōmes dæge, Gr. D. 295, 11.

**ge-edstaþelian (-stálian).** *Add:* to re-establish. **I.** *to restore to well-being.* (1) physical. (a) of persons :—Þū hǽlde geedstaðelast, Hml. Th. i. 466, 8. Hē tō þām geedstaþoledan (*the man restored to health*) cwæð, Hml. A. 198, 119. (b) of things, *to repair, make sound again* :—Geedstaþeles *suscitabis* (i. *instaurabis hanc veteranam civitatem et pene mortuam in juvenculam*, An. Ox. 2137. 'Geedstaðela þās tōcwýsedan gymstānas' . . . Ðā wurdon ðā gymstānas ansunde, Hml. Th. i. 62, 12. Þū ðe geedstaþolo[dest ?] (*restitues*) yrfeweardnysse míne mē, Ps. L. 15, 5. (2) moral or spiritual :—Þū geedstaðelodest ðisne tōbrocenan middangeard, Hml. Th. i. 62, 11. Sceoldon ealle heofenlíce ðing and eorðlíce beón geedstaðelode on Críste, 214, 25. **II.** *to restore, renew* what has been exhausted, *to rebuild*

a ruin :—þā hālgan mynstru . . . tōrorene geendstālude (*restauravit*), Angl. xiii. 366, 15. Ðurh hine (*Noah*) wearð mancynn geedstaþelod, Hml. S. 16, 24.    **III.** *to repeat, establish for a second time :—* Geetstaþoliat *instaurant* (*hostes superati bellum*), An. Ox. 11, 80. Hē (*Antichrist*) geedstaðelað nīwe tempel þǣr þǣr Salamon hæfde ǣr ārǣred þæt mǣre tempel, Wlfst. 195, 4.

**ge-edstaþeliend,** es ; *m. One who re-establishes, restores, repairs :—* Geedstaþeliend ealles manncynnes *reparator humani generis*, Angl. xi. 112, 3.

**ge-edstaþelung,** e ; *f. Restoration, repair, renewal :—*Flǣscæt þām untrumum for geedstaþelunge (*reparatione*) sȳ geðafod, R. Ben. 61, 2. Þæt teóðe werod forweard. þā wæs mancynn gesceapen tō geedstaðe-lunge (*to supply the loss*) ðæs forlorenan heápes, Hml. Th. i. 342, 25.

**ge-edþrāwen.** For ' Som.' *substitute :—* Mid geedþrāwenum twīne *cum bisso retorto*, An. Ox. 1062.

**ge-edwistian.** *Add :—*Ic ne beó geedwistod ł ic ne gemǣnsumige mid gecorenum heora *non communicabo cum electis eorum*, Ps. L. 140, 5.

**ge-edwyrpan.** *l.* -wirpan, *and add :—*Sōna swā hȳ geedwyrpte (-ede, *v. l.*) beóð and gestrangode *ubi meliorati fuerint*, R. Ben. 61, 2.

**ge-edyppol ;** *adj. That should be brought up again for examination :* —Geedyppole *recensendos*, Germ. 396, 280. Cf. yppan, yppe.

**ge-efenlǣcan.** *Add :* **I.** *to imitate.* (1) *of a person,* (a) *with the object a person.* (α) *with acc. To act as another has done :—*þā þe þwyrlīce dōð, deófiu hī geefenlǣceað (*demones imitantur*), Scint. 53, 16 : 84, 11. Ne geeuenlǣc þū wyrcende unrihtwīsnesse, Ps. L. 36, 1. Þæt þā unandgytfullan hine geefenlǣcen, R. Ben. 11, 17. Þæt wē hine efenlǣcende mid geþylde earfeþa þolien, 6, 1 : Lch. iii. 440, 18. (β) *with dat. :—*Se man þe deófle geefenlǣcð, sē bið deófles bearn, Hml. i. 260, 12. Hē geeuenlǣcð Gode, ii. 228, 3. Hī ne geefenlǣcað nā Abrahame, Hml. A. 35, 266, 269 : 46, 538. Hyre geeuenlǣhton hyre cnihtas, Hml. S. 2, 101. Þīnum Drihtne geefenlǣc, 21, 371. Wē sceolon geefenlǣcan þysum hyrdum, and wuldrian ūrne Drihten, Hml. Th. i. 44, 1. (γ) *absolute :—*Nelle þū geeuenlǣcan mid þām āwyrgedum *noli emulari in malignantibus*, Ps. L. 36, 1. Earfoþe tō geefenlǣc-enne, R. Ben. 138, 27. (b) *the object the conduct of a person, to do what another has done :—*Hē Crīstes gebysnunge ārfæstlīce geefenlǣhte, Hml. Th. ii. 34, 16. Ne ðū ne geefenlǣc *nec imiteris* (*vias ejus*), Kent. Gl. 59. Se abbod geefenlǣce þā bysene þæs ārfæstan hyrdes *pastoris boni pium imitetur exemplum*, R. Ben. 51, 16. (c) *to act in accordance with a rule followed by another :—*Hī geefenlǣcað þone cwide þe Drihten be him sylfum cwæþ *hi illam domini imitantur sententiam*, R. Ben. 20, 14. Þæt hē mid dǣdum ūres Drihtnes stefne geefenlǣce þe þus be him sylfum cwyð, 26, 6. (2) *of a thing, to be like, resemble :—*Ðeós wyrt is gecweden *iris illyrica* of ðǣre misenlicnysse hyre blōstmena, for þȳ þe is geðūht þ heó þone heofonlican bogan mid hyre bleó geefen-lǣce, Lch. i. 284, 15.    **II.** *to put on a level with, compare :—*Geefenlǣhte *compensat*, Germ. 399, 298. Geeuenlǣhte *coaptat*, i. *equiparat*, An. Ox. 50, 28. Þām ne mæg nān dǣdbēta beón geefenlǣht, for ðan ðe hī sind rihtwīse and behreówsigende, Hml. Th. i. 342, 12.

**ge-efenlǣcestre.** For ' Scint. 13, Lye' *substitute :—* Lang clǣnnyss æfter synne geefenlǣcestre (*imitatrix*) ys mǣdenhādes, Scint. 71, 11.

**ge-efenlǣcung.** *Add :—*Hit is gewunelic on hālgum gewritum þæt gehwam bið fæder genamod be his geefenlǣcunge (*according to whom he imitates*) ; gif hē geeuenlǣcð Gode on gōdum weorcum hē bið Godes bearn gecīged ; gif hē geeuenlǣcð deófle . . . hē bið deófles bearn, Hml. Th. ii. 228, 2. Deófles bearn, nā þurh gecynd . . ., ac ðurh þā geefen-lǣcunge, i. 260, 14.

**ge-efenlīc.** For ' Bd. 4, 29 ; . . . Ca' *substitute :—*þ hē swā geefenlīca wǣre (hī swā geefenlīco wǣron, *v. l.*) mid þā gyfe his þingeres *aequatus gratia suo intercessori*, Bd. 4, 29 ; Sch. 531, 8.

**ge-efenlīcad.** *Substitute :* **ge-efenlīcian ;** *p.* ode, (1) *to make even, adjust :—*Geeblīcadum *quadrare*, Wrt. Voc. ii. 118, 53. (2) *to make equal* or *like, liken :—*Hwelc bið geefenlīcad (*aequabitur*) Dryhtne ?, Ps. Srt. 88, 7 : Bd. 4, 29 ; Sch. 531, 8. *Comparatus*, i. *assimilatus* geefen-līcad, Wrt. Voc. ii. 132, 76.

**ge-efesian.** *Add :—*Seó fǣmne cwæð þ heó wolde hī sylfe bedīglian . . . and for ðȳ underfǣnge þā gyrlan wǣrlices hādes and wurde geefsod (-efesod, *v. l.*), Hml. S. 2, 232.

**ge-efnettan.** v. ge-emnettan.

**ge-efstan.** *l.* -efestan, -efstan, *and add :* (1) *to get by hastening :—*Geonet oððe geefest *preoccupetur* (v. (?) Ald. 17, 37), Wrt. Voc. ii. 65, 78. (2) *to strive after :—*þ ān wæs swīðost fram heom eallum geefst, þ heora ǣlc wǣre on līchaman deád and on gāste libbende *the one most earnest endeavour of all was to be dead in the body and living in the spirit*, Hml. S. 23 b, 90.

**ge-eftgadrian.** *See next word.*

**ge-eftgian** *to repeat :—*þā þā hē þis gelōmlīce sprǣc mid geeftgodre (geeftgadrode, *v. l.*) sprǣce *cum hoc iterata crebro voce repeteret*, Gr. D. 277, 1.

**ge-egesian.** *Add :—*Ðās hǣðenan . . . mid fyrhte geegsa (-egesa),

---

Hml. S. 25, 372. Se wēna ðāra tōweardena yfela hié geegesige *cum suspecta mala contristant*, Past. 395, 2. Ðæt wē ūre hiéremenn suā geārige suā wē hié eft geegesian (-egsian, *v. l.*) mæge *ut praelatus subditorum vitam stringere sub disciplinae vinculo possit*, 119, 5. Þæt þāra ōþra gehwylc þurh þæt geegesad sȳ *ut ceteri metum habeant*, R. Ben. 129, 19. Geegsod, Hml. S. 21, 74.

**ge-eggian.** *Add :* [*Icel.* eggja. v. *N. E. D.* egg.]

**ge-eglan.** *Add :—*Hȳ mon band on wilde featras and ðā hyre ne geegledon, Shrn. 133, 12.

**ge-ēhtan ;** *p.* te.    **I.** *to follow, persecute :—*Geoehtas *persequentur*, Mt. L. 10, 23. Gē biðon gewoehtat ł geaehtas īuih, 23, 34. Gif mec geoehton . . . īuih hiá geoehtað, Jn. L. 15, 20. Geoehtadon *perseque-bantur*, 5, 16. Geoehton *persecuti sunt*, Mt. L. 5, 12. Gioehtende am *persecutus sum*, Rtl. 60, 7.    **II.** *to get by pursuit.* (1) *of conquest, to gain a country :—*Claudius cōm tō Brytlande and geeóde mycel dǣl ēglandes, and eác þ ēgeland of Orcanie hē geēhte tō Rōmānan anwealde, Chr. 46 ; P. 7, 29. (2) *to purchase :—*Mid wāclicum wurðe Godes rīce bið geboht, and deórwurðe hit is tō geāgenne. Se ceáp ne mæg wið nānum sceatte beón geēht, Hml. Th. i. 582, 27.

**ge-ehtedlic.** v. ge-eahtedlic.

**ge-elþeódian ;** *p.* ode *To alienate, derange* the mind :—Druncennyss mōd geelþeódað *ebrietas mentem alienat*, Scint. 106, 18.

**ge-embehtan.** v. ge-ambehtan.

**ge-emnettan.** *Add :* **I.** *trans.* (1) *to make level :—*Geemnettende *complanans*, Wrt. Voc. ii. 133, 7. (2) *to make equal :—*Beóð ealle þā fers geemnytte þā nanum getele, Ælfc. Gr. Z. 296, 2. (3) *to equal :—*Þæt hē micelnysse synna mæge geemnyttan (*exaequare*) mid genihtsum-nysse mægena, Scint. 43, 13. (4) *to adjust, square :—*Him bið hefig-tȳme geðuht ðæt hī heora þeáwas be his regole geemnetton, Hml. Th. i. 524, 18.    **II.** *intrans.* To *square, agree, suit :—*Geemuettan and geþæslǣccan *quadrare et congruere*, An. Ox. 4262.

**ge-ēnan.** v. ge-ǣnan : **ge-encgd.** v. ge-engian : **ge-ende.** *Dele.*

**ge-endebredian.** v. ge-endebyrdan.

**ge-endebrednian.** *Add :—*Geendebrednade *ordinavit*, Mt. p. 3, 1.

**ge-endebyrdan (-ian).** *Add :* (1) *to assign its proper place to an object, place in order, place :—*Se Hǣlend geendebyrde þone unspēdigan fiscere ætforan ðām rīcan cásere, Hml. Th. i. 578, 9. Þeáh ðe hē endenēxt on Godes rīce sȳ geendebyrd, ii. 82, 2. Paulus is geendebyrd tō Petre, 522, 2. Seó bōc hātte Liber Ruth and heó is geendebyrd on ūre bibliothēcan, Ælfc. T. Grn. 6, 33 : 10, 41 : 11, 3. Wē beóð geendebyrde tō heora weredum æfter ūrum geearnungum, Hml. Th. i. 344, 17. (2) *to ordain.* (a) *with object a person, to appoint to a position, office :—*Ic eam geendebyrd *ordinata sum*, Kent. Gl. 259. Drihten wæs ǣr eallum worldum geteód and geendebyrd, Bl. H. 31, 22. Þurh þæs geendebyrdan prófostes misfadunge *per ordinationem prepositi*, R. Ben. 124, 4. (β) *with object a thing :—*Ūs næfre swylc ege ne wearþ ǣr tō helle geendebyrded, Bl. H. 85, 14. (3) *to arrange* the parts of a whole, *put in order, dispose :—*Ic geendebyrde *dispono*, Wrt. Voc. ii. 141, 44. Augustinus geendebyrde ðās word þus *Augustine put these words in this order*, Hml. Th. ii. 362, 23. Þā capitulas æfter ðǣre forespræce geendebyrdian *to put an index after the preface*, 2, 19. Giendebredado *ordinata*, Rtl. 109, 25. (3 a) *of orderly narrative, to set forth in order, narrate :—*Ðæt godspel geendebyrt þā eahta eádignyssa, Hml. Th. i. 548, 9. Wē willað āne feáwa cwydas on ðissere bēc geendebyrdian, ii. 520, 6. Heora ðrowung is gehwǣr on Engliscum gereorde fullīce geendebyrd, i. 370, 24. Geendebyrded, Nar. 3, 16. Geendebyrdre *digesto* (*libello*), An. Ox. 5412. Geendebyrd *digestum* (*libelli textum*), 529. Geendbyrde *digesta*, i. *ordinata, composita, enarrata*, Wrt. Voc. ii. 140, 23 : Hml. Th. i. 554, 9.

**ge-endebyrdlíce ;** *adv. In due order :—*Hē sǣde ðæs cildes mōdig-nysse geendebyrdlíce (cf. hē þæt eall þurh endebyrdnesse āsægde *per ordi-nem narravit*, Gr. D. 144, 26), Hml. Th. ii. 170, 30.

**ge-endian.** *Add :* **I.** *trans.* (1) *where the subject of the verb ceases to do something, to bring to an end, to come to an end of :—*þā se Hǣlend þās word geendode, Mt. 7, 28. Þā se Hǣlend geendode þās bigspel, 13, 53. Wē mōton nū geendian þyses godspelles race, Hml. A. 71, 160. Ðiós rēdo geendad bið (*finitur*) on stōne ðēr cuuoeð, Lk. p. 11, 16. Ðæt is tō tācne ðæt mon endebyrdlíce ðone biscepdōm healde, ðæt hē hine on gōdum weorcum geendige, Past. 53, 23. Geendede *transacto* (*officio*), An. Ox. 2144. ¶ lif geendian *to die :—*Ǣghwylc þāra manna þe his līf geendað on þyssum, Bl. H. 37, 4 : 61, 2. Ðā ðe hira līf on firenluste geendigað (-endiað, *v. l.*), Past. 251, 7. Hē fægere ende his līf betȳnde and geendade *pulchro uitam suam fine conclusit*, Bd. 4, 24 ; Sch. 488, 8 : Hml. Th. i. 544, 31. (2) *with the idea of extinction, destruction, to put an end to, make an end of, consume, finish :—*Æfter ðon alle geendade *postquam omnia consummasset*, Lk. L. 15, 14. God gemynte his yfelnysse tō geendigenne, Hml. Th. i. 414, 6. Hē is tōweard þās world tō geendenne, Bl. H. 81, 36. (2 a) *to kill* a person, *destroy* life :—Ðonne se deáð ūre andwerde līf geendað, Hml. Th. ii. 526, 24. Philippus wearð geendod (cf. Philippus on galgan āhangen wæs, Ap. 41), Ælfc. T. Grn. 15, 28. His līf weard geendod,

Bl. H. 113, 8. Sune selenis geendad *filio proditionis extincto*, Lk. p. 3, 4. Hí næron geendode ðurh openne martirdóm, Hml. Th. ii. 544, 29. (3) with the idea of completion, accomplishment. (a) *to finish* (α) a concrete object :—Membrað angan timbran Babylonia . . . , and Samer-amis hié geendade. Ors. 2, 4; S. 74, 11. Torr getimbra . . . gif hæfeð tó geendanne (*ad perficiendum*) . . . ne mæhte geendiga (*perficere*), Lk. L. R. 14, 28, 29. (β) an abstract object (a case, work, course, &c.) :—Ðætte ic geendigo (*perficiam*) uoerc his, Jn. L. 4, 34. Hí ne geendiað ná þá spæce ær heora seód bið áfylled *they will not finish the case till their purse be filled*, Ll. Lbmn. 475, 42. Ic geendode (*consummaui*) þ weorc þ þú mé sealdest tó dónne, Jn. 17, 4. Erning giendade *cursum consummaui*, Rtl. 60, 19. Geendadon alle æfter ae Drihtnes, Lk. L. 2, 39. Þte ic geendia ðá uerca, Jn. L. 5, 36. (b) *to accomplish, perform, effect* a purpose :—Gemyne þú hwæt þú ámeldod-est, hwæt ðú geændadest, Lch. iii. 34, 7. Hé geendode þæt hé gebeótod hæfde . . . eall hé þ gefylde, Bl. H. 83, 25. Derneleger geendade *adulterium committit*, Mk. L. 10, 11. In huelc mæht wundra geendade t dyde (*patraret*), Mt. p. 18, 19. Þær wæs swiþe ryht dóm geendad *a very just sentence was there carried out*, Ors. 6, 34; S. 292, 2. þ ungeháten is sceal beón geendod, Bl. H. 189, 27. Fulwuiht ic hafo . . . oðð ðá hwíl geendad sié, Lk. L. R. 12, 50. Geendad biðon alle ðá ðe áwriteno sindon, 18, 31. Ealle ðing wæron geendode þ þ hálige geurit wære gefylled, Jn. 19, 28. (c) *to make perfect, perfect* :—Geendades lof *perfecisti laudem*, Mt. L. 21, 16. Giendig geongo míno *perfici gressus meos*, Rtl. 167, 1. þ hí sýn geendode on án, Jn. 17, 23. (d) *to fulfil* :—Wítgiung geendad *prophetia completa*, Mt. p. 16, 15. þ were geendad (*adimpleretur*) þ gecueden wæs, Mt. L. 8, 17. (e) *to fill* :—Of onwrihnisse geendad *revelatione saturatus*, Mt. p. 9, 6. Geendad wéron ðá færmo *impletae sunt nubtiae*, Mt. L. 22, 10. (f) of time :—Æfter ðon geendad wéron dagas æhto *postquam consummati sunt dies octo*, Lk. L. R. 2, 21 : 4, 2. Geendade, 2, 43. II. intrans. To come to an end :—Biddon wé Drihten þæs leóhtes þe næfre ne geendað, Bl. H. 21, 13. ¶ of persons, *to die* :—Þá þe wel geendiað, Hml. Th. ii. 526, 21. Ðá Eádréd geendude, Cht. Th. 203, 11 : Hml. S. 6, 350 : 25, 155. Gif hé on þám unrihte geendige . . . Gif hí on þám geendian, Ll. Th. ii. 300, 18, 21. Lét ús þurh þis fýr geendian, Hml. S. 30, 433 : Hml. Th. i. 414, 8. His twá dohtra gewiton fægre geendode (*having made a fair end*), ii. 298, 10. [O. L. Ger. gi-endiōn : O. H. Ger. ge-entōn *consummare, finire, obire*.] v. un-geendod.

ge-endigendlic. v. un-geendigendlic : ge-endodlic *finite*. v. un-gendodlic *in Dict.*: ge-endstálian. v. ge-edstaþelian.

ge-endung. Add : I. local. (1) *an extreme part* :—Seó sunne undergæð þære eorðan geendunge *the sun goes below the horizon*, Lch. iii. 260, 7. (2) *a termination* of a word :—Seó forme *declinatio* hæfð *tres terminationes*, þæt synd ðreó geendunga, Ælfc. Gr. Z. 24, 4: 26, 12. (3) *a concluding passage* :—Seó geendung ús sæde þ þá Iudéiscan þóhton þ hí Críst ofslógon, Hml. A. 71, 161. II. temporal, *a final period* :—Wé sind ðá ðe worulda geendunga on becómon *in quos fines saeculorum deveunerunt*, Hml. Th. ii. 372, 10. III. cessation, termination :—þ æþele líf búton geendunge, Bl. H. 65, 18. Geseah hé genealæcan his lifes geendunge, Hml. S. 26, 156. III a. *ending of life, death* :—Hé ábád þæs óðres geendunge, Hml. Th. ii. 152, 18. On ðam endlyftan geáre his geendunge *in the eleventh year since his death*, 31. Se sunu sceolde són to þám háde æfter his fæder geendunge, Hml. S. 10, 221 : 18, 435. Æfter úre geendunge, 28, 152 : Shrn. 97, 30. þæt hí on eówrum geendungum (*cum defeceritis*) onfón eów intó écum eardungstówum, Hml. Th. i. 334, 28. III b. *ending of existence, end* of the world :—Þás ðing sceolon ærest cuman, ac ne bið swá ðeáh þærrihte seó geendung (*finis*), Hml. Th. ii. 538, 3. On ðissere worulde geendunge, 300, 9 : Hml. A. 165, 23 : 23, 221. Úres Drihtnes apostolas áhsadan hine sylfne ymbe þisre worulde geendunge, Wlfst. 81, 2. Oþ þá geendunga þisse worlde, Bl. H. 157, 30. [O. H. Ger. ge-entunga *definitio*.]

ge-engan ; p. de To constrain, distress, vex, trouble :—[Ic eom] genirwed and geenged *afficior*, Wrt. Voc. ii. 10, 49. Geencgdu *anxia*, 9, 35. [Goth. ga-aggwjan *to distress*: O. H. Ger. ge-engen.]

ge-eofulsian ; p. ode To blaspheme :—Gieofulsadan (gebolsade, L.) *blasphemaba[n]t*, Lk. R. 23, 39. Geebalsadon, Mt. L. 27, 39. Gieofulsadun (geebolsadon L.), Mk. R. 15, 29.

ge-eówan (-ian). Add :—Ic, Ælfréd, eallum mínum witum þás (dómas) geeówde, Ll. Th. i. 58, 29. Geówige hé him þá stówe, Angl. xiii. 427, 895. Hwelce hí hié innan geeówigen Gode, Past. 273, 5. Is þé nú genóg openlíce geeówad þára leásena gesælþa anlícnes, Bt. 24, 3; F. 84, 19. v. ge-íwan.

ge-erian. Add :—Gif mon geþingað gyrde landes and geered, Ll. Th. i. 146, 3. On þæt geræd þe hé ælce geáre of þám lande geerige twégen æceras and þæron his circsceat gesáwe, C. D. ii. 398, 20. .III. æceras geerian on heora ágenre hwíle and mid heora ágenan sæda gesáwan, iv. 306, 27.

ge-etan. Add :—Swá hwá swá of ðám hláfe geett (*manducat*), Hml.

Th. ii. 202, 6. Heó genam of ðæs treówes wæstme and geæt, and sealde hire were and hé geæt, i. 18, 9. Hé geæt þone forbodenan æppel, ii. 240, 21. Hwí eódest þú tó þám hæðenum and on heora húse geæte?, Hml. S. 10, 175. Gé giëtun (*manducastis*) of ðæm hláfum, Jn. R. 6, 26. Fædero úsero geëton, Jn. L. 6, 31 : Mt. L. 14, 20. Of ðám treówe Adam sceolde geetan on ende *of that tree Adam was to have eaten in the end*, Hex. 24, 19. Þeós wyrt fremaþ wel geeten (-an, *v. l.*) and tó þám nafolan gewriþen, Lch. i. 204, 27. [O. H. Ger. ge-ezzan.]

ge-éþian; p. ode To breathe. (1) lit.:—Bewreów ðone man þ se ne mæge út náhwær, bútan hé mæge geéþian, Lch. ii. 338, 19. (2) fig. :—Wé magon witan þ þonne se gást wile hé geéðað tó þæs mannes móde *sciendum est quia quando vult spiritus aspirat*, Gr. D. 146, 14.

ge-éþrian. v. ge-íþrian : gefa. v. gifa.

gefá. Add : (1) in a general sense, *a foe* :—Sé ðe wæs cyrican éhtere . . . , þonne onscunode heó hine swylce hé wære hire gefá, Wlfst. 237, 27. (2) in a legal sense, *one who is party to a blood-feud* (a) as pursuer :—Gif þeów wealh Engliscne monnan ofslihð . . . héden his þá gefán, Ll. Th. i. 150, 1. Gif hé self his wæpno his gefán út ræcan wille, 64, 18. (b) as pursued :—Be fæhðum. Wé beódað, se mon, sé þe his gefán hámsittendne wite, þ hé ne feohte ær þám þe hé him ryhtes bidde, Ll. Th. i. 90, 2. þ naðor ne hý ne wé ne underfón óðres þeóf ne óðres gefán, 288, 5.

ge-fadian. Add :—Ic gefadige *dispono*, Wrt. Voc. ii. 141, 44. (1) *to arrange, set in order* material objects :—Án geteld (*the tabernacle*) mid wunderlicum dihte gefadod, Hml. Th. ii. 198, 23. Hé gefadod hæfde eall his werod swá his þeáw wæs, Hml. S. 30, 305. (1 a) *to ornament, adorn* :—Ðis weorc wæs gefadod mid deórwurðum stánum and reádum golde, Hml. Th. ii. 578, 14. (2) *to dispose of property* :—Þú hæfst þ feoh mid þé, gefada embe lóca hú þú wylle, Hml. S. 3, 285. (3) *to order* conduct, action, life, *manage* a matter :—Yfele þú gefadast þinne ræd, Hml. S. 3, 303. Gif hé his weorc mid wísdóme gefadað, I, 235. Þæt gehíwode yfel deúfol sylf gefadad and gehýwað tó þám þæt hit ðincð gód, Wlfst. 54, 9. þ is se wísdóm þ man his dæda gefadige tó his Drihtnes willan, Hml. S. 13, 326. Hé ealle þing swá gefadige þæt þá sáwla gehealdene sýn, R. Ben. 66, 2. Swylc notu on mynstre sý gefadod and geendebyrd, 125, 9. (3 a) *to arrange* the order of procedure :—Þus gefadodre endebyrdnesse þæs dæglican sealmsanges, R. Ben. 44, 9. (4) of the ordering by superhuman power. (a) in natural phenomena :—Godes miht gefadað ealle gewederu, Lch. iii. 278, 13. (b) in regard to living beings :—Drihten, úrne forðsíð gefada, Hml. Th. i. 414, 33. Eówer síð ne bið ná swá swá wé wéndon, ac wyrð elles gefadod and on óðre stówe, Hml. S. 6, 86. Ealle ðá gerýnu Crístes menniscnysse wæron gefadode þurh mihte þæs Hálgan Gástes, Hml. Th. ii. 280, 3.

ge-fadung. Add :—Se hláford sceal beón líðe þám goodum and egefull þám dysegum . . . elles ne bið his gefadung ne fæst ne langsum, O. E. Hml. i. 301, 15. Wé gelýfaþ þæt mid þisse gefadungce ægðres weorces tíma mæge beón geendebyrd *hac dispositione credimus utraque tempora ordinari*, R. Ben. 73, 7. Æfter þæra hundseofontigra gefadunge *according to the Septuagint*, Angl. viii. 336, 10. On Godes wordes gefadunge *in uerbi dispensatione*, vii. 10, 93. Ne dó hé nán þing ongeán þæs abbodes willan and gefadunge (*ordinationem*), R. Ben. 125, 19. Þá wíslican gefadunge þe geset is be incúþra ðinga endebyrdnesse, Lch. iii. 440, 25.

ge-fæd; n.? Decorum, discretion. Dele ?, for 'Th. i.' l. Th. ii., and add : v. un-gefæd.

ge-fæd; adj. Discreet, well-regulated. Add :—Sé hæfð módes strencðe þe on gódum gelimpum ne forlæt his ánrædnesse, ac bið aa gefæd on æghwylce wísan, swá þæt hé ne bið ne on gefeán tó fægen ne on weán tó ormód, Wlfst. 51, 24.

ge-fædera. For 'godfather,' l. 2 substitute 'gossip.' v. next word.

ge-fædere. Add : (1) of the relation between sponsor and parent or between sponsors ; commater :—Hé gean Ælf(þ)ríð, ðæs cyninges wífæ, his gefæderan, Cht. Th. 527, 14. Ne gewífige hé on his gefæderan (*commatrem*), Ll. Th. i. 364, 25 : Wlfst. 271, 12. (2) of the relation between sponsor and child, *a godmother*; matrina :—Gif hwylc man wífige on his gefæderan (*matrinam*), Ll. Th. ii. 188, 17.

ge-fæderen ; adj. Having the same father :—Þá þríe gebróðor næron ná Philippuse gemédren, ac wæron gefæderen (gefædred, Bos. 60, 19), Ors. 3, 7; S. 114, 14. v. ge-médren.

ge-fædlic ; adj. Suitable, proper :—Wé habbað medomlíce þás þing gehrepod ; hit þingð ús gefædlic þ wé rúmlícor þás gerénu átrahtnion, Angl. viii. 324, 6 : 337, 6 : Wlfst. 245, 19.

ge-fædlíce. Add :—Blíþlíce and gefædlíce *blande et quiete*, Germ. 395, 63. Miht ðú ásmeágan hú gefædlíce (*in how orderly a manner*) seó sunne gesíhð on þám dægmæle, eall swylce sum getýd wer sitte and sum metervers mid his feðere áwríte, Angl. viii. 317, 21.

ge-fædred. Substitute : v. ge-fæderen : ge-fædrian. Dele.

ge-fæge (?), adj. Cheerful, genial (?) :—Freóudum gefægra, B. 913. v. ge-feón, *and for form cf.* (?) ge-sprǽce.

ge-fægen. Add :—Hé sceolde beón ðære sprǽce swá micle gefægenra

suā him māre đearf wæs, and đæs đe gefægenra đe hē him suā eáđmódlīce and suā ārlīce tō spræc, Past. 305, 6-8.

**ge-fægerian.** _Add:_—Fægere se æđela kyning David þis hīw gefægerode þus bȳmendre stefne hleóđriende, Angl. viii. 331, 12.

**ge-fægerness,** e; _f. Beauty_:—Hester wæs swīđe wlitig on wundorlicre gefægernysse, Hml. A. 95, 97.

**ge-fægnian.** _Add:_ (1) _with gen._:—Heó þæs gefægnode þ heó hæfde ealles þæs geáres bigleofan, Gr. D. 69, 13. (2) _with prep._:—Hē gefægnode for þæs feóndes deáþe, Gr. D. 120, 8.

**ge-fægnung.** _Add:_—Gefægnunge _exultationis_, Scint. 65, 5. On gefægenunga _in exultatione_, Bl. Gl.

**ge-fælan.** _Dele, and see_ ge-fillan: **ge-fæll.** v. ge-fill: **ge-fællnis.** v. ge-fillness.

**ge-fælsian.** _l._ -fǽlsian, _and add_:—Gefǽlsode _expiavit_, Wrt. Voc. ii. 83, 76 : 31, 24.

**ge-fær.** _Add_:—On gefere _in profectione_, Bl. Gl. Đ þára Israhēla bearna gefǽre of Egyptum, Angl. xi. 9, 8. v. scip-gefær.

**ge-fǽrede** _larvatos_, An. Ox. 2, 405. [_For_ (?) [un-]gefǽr[g]rede; v. ǽ-fǽgred.]

**ge-fǽstan** _to place._ _Substitute:_ ge-fǽstan; _p._ te. I. _to make fast, make steadfast, confirm_:—Wē wurđiađ þone gefǽstan heáp Godes cýđera _we honour the steadfast band of God's martyrs_, Hml. Th. i. 542, 23. II. _to commit, entrust_:—Hē ágæf ł gefæste đā đǽm londbīgencgum _locavit vineam agricolis_, Mk. L. 12, 1. [_Goth._ ga-fastan _to hold fast_: _O. H. Ger._ ge-festen _firmare, comprobare, mancipare._] v. ge-feastian _in Dict._

**ge-fǽstan** _to fast._ _Add:_ (1) _in a general sense, to abstain from food_:—Mid đȳ gefǽste _cum jejunasset_, Mt. L. 4, 2. Gefaested _macilentus_, Wrt. Voc. ii. 113, 70. Gefǽsted, 55, 59. (2) _to fast as discipline._ (a) _absolute_:—Mid đȳ gié gefǽstas _cum jejunatis_, Mt. L. 6, 16. Gefǽstad _jejunabunt_, Lk. L. 5, 35. Gefǽsdon _jejunabant_, Mt. L. 9, 15. Gefǽsta _jejunare_, Lk. L. 5, 34. (b) _with cognate accusative_:—Se man þe þis gefǽst, Lch. iii. 228, 23. Þā þe Sunnandæges freóls heóldan and heora lencten wel gefǽsten, Wlfst. 244, 19. Þæt þū þīn lengten rihtlīce gehealde and dæghwāmlīce tō ānes mǽles þæt fæsten gefǽste, 247, 34. Þæt hī þæt fæsten þe lustlīcor gefǽstan, 181, 20. Đǽre nihte þe hié þæt fæsten gefǽst hæfdon, Bl. H. 205, 34. Þonne wyrđ gefǽst swā fæla fæstena swā biđ daga on .vii. geárum, Ll. Th. ii. 286, 26.

**ge-fǽstlīce;** _adv._ (1) _with certainty_:—Ic his nāt nǽht gefǽstlīce _nihil abs te dictum est quod me scire audeam dicere_, Solil. H. 32, 9. (2) _firmly, with constancy_:—Gelýf gefǽstlīce Gode _constanter Deo crede_, 53, 12.

**ge-fæstnian.** _Add:_ I. _where motion is prevented._ (1) _to fix._ (a) _to make motionless that which can move_:—Hē sealte ȳþa gefæstnade, Ps. Th. 77, 15. (b) _to place firmly that which can be moved_:—Betwux ūs and eów is gefæstnod (gefæstnad _firmatum_, Lk. L. 16, 26) micel đrosm, Hml. Th. i. 332, 17. Næs nā þæs stronglīc stān gefæstnod, Sat. 517. Weax melted gif hit byđ neáh fýre gefæstnod, Ps. Th. 57, 7. (c) _to fasten on or to something_ (lit. or fig.) :—Fram eallum þām wītum þe đū on mīnum līce gefæstnodest (_hast inflicted_), Hml. S. 8, 160. Hē gefæstnode heora fēt tō eorđan, Hml. Th. ii. 508, 17. Hié mē on beorg āsetton, gefæstnodon mē (_the cross_) þǽr feóndas, Kr. 33. Đæt hī hiora tōhopan gefæstnigen tō đǽm ēcum gōdum _ut spem in bonis perennibus figant_, Past. 393, 31. Hē lēt his līchoman on rōde mid næglum gefæstnian, Bl. H. 85, 2. Gefæstnod nadaretur, Wrt. Voc. ii. 62, 12. Weard hē gefæstnod be þǽre swīþran handa tō þǽre bǽre, 151, 18. Rōde gefæstnad, Cri. 1448. Gefæstnodon sceare and cultre mid þǽre sýl _confirmato vomere et cultro aratro_, Coll. M. 19, 19. Gefæsnode _fixas_ (turmas quasi radicitus _fixas_ . . . immobiles manere fecit, Ald. 52, 6), An. Ox. 3777. (d) _to fasten with a bond, fetter_:—Nǽfre hié se feónd feterum gefæstnađ, Sal. 70. Đā đe racentēg gifæstnigađ _quos catena constringit_, Rtl. 40, 23. Hē þē gefæstnode clommum, An. 1380. Hī woldan mīne fōtas gefæstnian, Ps. Th. 139, 5. Hē liged on carcerne clommum gefæstnad, Cri. 735. (2) _to imprison_:—Se cyng genam Roger eorl and gefestnode hine (sette on prisun, _v. l._), Chr. 1075; P. 211, 14. II. _to make firm, establish_:—Wæs getrymed _vel_ gestaþolad _vel_ gefæstnad _firmaretur_, i. consolidat, Wrt. Voc. ii. 148, 67. (1) _to make firm_ what is constructed:—Hē gefæstnude foldan stađelas _fundavit terram super stabilitatem ejus_, Ps. Th. 103, 6. Hē rodor āhōf and gefæstnode folmum sīnum, An. 522. Þæt gē eówer hūs gefæstnige, Jul. 649. Wæs folde gefæstnad, Jul. 499. (2) _to confirm_ an agreement, a compact, _ratify_ a treaty, an arrangement, &c., _establish_ (friendly) relations:—Cnut cyngc friđ and freóndscipe betweox Denum and Englum fullīce gefæstnode, Ll. Lbmn. 278, 7. Man fullne freóndscipe gefæstnode mid worde and mid wædde, Chr. 1014; P. 145, 11. Hēr gefestnode Eádward cyng friđ wiđ Eást-Engla here, 906; P. 95, 1. Hī mid wedde and mid āþum fryþ gefæstnodon, 926; P. 107, 24. Seó gerǽdnys þe mīne witan gerǽddon, and nū mid wedde gefæstnodon, Ll. Th. i. 272, 4. Swā hit gecweden is and mid weddum gefæstnad, 236, 30, 33. Þ friđ þ . . . ealle gecweden habbađ and mid āđum gefæstnod (-feost-, _v. l._), 152, 4. Hæfdon Eoforwīcingas hire gehāten, and sume

on wedde geseald, sume mid āþum gefæstnod, þ hī on hyre rǽdenne beón woldon, Chr. 918; P. 105, 24. (3) _to confirm_ the condition of an object, _make stable, constant, establish_:—Hē đeignas gefæstnigeđ _discipulos confirmat_, Mt. p. 16, 6. Gefæstnađe, Lk. p. 11, 13. Gehȳr þis herespel and þīnne hyge gefæstna, Sch. 37. Rīce is þīn rǽde gefæstnod, Ps. Th. 144, 13. Þte ryhte cynedōmas þurh ūre folc gefæstnode and getrymede wǽron, Ll. Th. i. 102, 9. (4) _to settle, determine, fix_ a plan, course, &c. :—Þā gefæstnode hē þisne rǽd wiđ þæt werod . . . Đā đā hī ealle hæfdon þisne rǽd betwux him gefæstnod, Hml. Th. i. 10, 26-29. Hē gewunode on þām gesettum tīdum þæs dæges þone ryne his sīđfætes gefæstnian, Hml. S. 23 b, 164. (5) _to confirm, corroborate_ a statement:—Ofer đone ungeleáffulle wrǽđđo geunia gefæstnađ _super incredulum iram manere confirmat_, Jn. p. 4, 3 : Lk. p. 7, 19. Dōm his sōđ uoere gefæstnade _iudicium suum uerum esse confirmans_, Jn. p. 5, 11. Gefæstnade _testatur_, p. 4, 13. Ágann Landfranc atȳwian mid openum gesceáde þ hē mid rihte crafede . . . and mid strangan cwydan þ ylce gefæstnode, Chr. 1070; P. 206, 14. (6) _of steady action_:—Woruldlufe đe on gedwyldum hwyrftlađ, and nǽnne stæpe on Godes wege ne gefæstnađ (_does not take one firm step on the road to God_), Hml. Th. i. 514, 22. III. _to make safe, to secure._ (1) _to secure against attack, fortify_:—Hē þæt eálond begyrde and gefæstnade mid dīce, Bd. 1, 5 ; Sch. 17, 20. Hī gefæstnadon þ byrgenn _munierunt sepulchrum_, Mt. L. 27, 66. Gefeastnodon, p. 20, 3. Gifæstnade mid fultumum _munita praesidiis_, Rtl. 63, 8. Geofonhūsa mǽst innan and ūtan eorđan līme gefæstnod wiđ flōde, Gen. 1323. Hū gefæstnad sȳ ferđ innanweard, wiđsteall geworht, Jul. 400. Wē on þǽre wīcstōwe gesundlīce wīcodon, and ic hæfde mid fæstene gefæstnad þ ūs deór ne sceđđan meahten, Nar. 21, 31. (2) _to prevent encroachment on, to make one's own_:—Tō hwon heólde þū hit þē ānum . . . þæt mihte manegum genihtsumian ? unyđe þe wæs þæt þū hit eall ne mihtest gefæstnian ne mid inseglum beclȳsan, Wlfst. 259, 20. (3) _to commit, entrust._ Cf. be-fæstan :—Gifæstna _accommoda_, Rtl. 105, 37. Gifæstnian _commendet_, 63, 1. [_O. H. Ger._ ge-festinōn _adfirmare, adstringere, confirmare._] v. ge-festnian _in Dict._

**ge-fætan.** _l._ -fǽtan, _and add_ : To lay as a burden, _impose_ :—Tō hwan wyllađ wē on ūs ālecgan and gefætan þā byrþene þe wē ārǽfnan ne magon _quid nobis onera vultis imponere, quae non possumus portare ?_, Gr. D. 165, 27. v. fǽtan.

**ge-fætnian.** _l._ -fǽtnian, _and dele_ ' v. fǽtnian.'

**ge-fǽttian.** _Substitute:_ ge-fǽttian; _p._ ode _To become fat_ or _to make fat_:—Offrung rihtwīses gefǽttađ weófud _oblatio justi inpinguat altare_, Scint. 166, 12. Gemyndig sié Dryhten . . . and onsegdnisse đīne gefaettie (_pinguefiat_), Ps. Srt. 19, 4. Gefǽttod is _incrassatus est_, gefǽttod _inpinguatus_ (Deut. 32, 15), Ps. L. fol. 192, 15.

**ge-fagen.** _Add:_ v. ge-feón.

**ge-fāgod;** _adj._ (_ptcpl._) _Of varied colour, coloured_ (of dress):—Godweb mid golde gefāgod, Bl. H. 113, 20. Mid deórwyrþum reáfum and gefāgedum ne beóþ hȳ gescrȳdde _pretiosis vel coloratis vestibus non induantur_, R. Ben. 137, 8. v. fāgian, fāgness, fāgung.

**ge-fāh, gefāhmon.** _Substitute:_ ge-fāh; _adj. Exposed to the hostility of a slain man's friends because of the murder, at feud_:—Be manslihte . . . Gif of þǽre ōđre mǽgđe hwā wrace dō on ǽnigum ōđrum men būtan on þām rihthanddǽdan, sȳ hē gefāh wiđ þone cyning and wiđ ealle his frȳnd, Ll. Th. i. 248, 12. [_O. H. Ger._ ge-fēh _feidosus, odiosus._] v. fāh, ge-fā.

**ge-fana.** _Dele._

**ge-fandod.** _Substitute:_ ge-fandian; _p._ ode _To try._ (1) _to examine, explore_:—Hē þæt sōna onfand þæt hæfde gumena sum goldes gefandod, heáhgestreóna _he soon found that some man had ransacked the treasure_, B. 2301. (2) _to try_ whether. Cf. fandian (2):—Þæt hié mōsten gefandian hweđer hié heora medsēlđa oferswīþan mehte. Ors. 4, 4; S. 164, 28. (3) _to experience, taste._ Cf. fandian (4):—Sē đe ūs oferdrencđ mid đæs ēcan līfes līđe, hē gefandode geallan biternesse đā hine đyrstte _aeterna nos dulcedine inebrians in siti sua fellis amaritudinem accipit_, Past. 261, 15. Đā đe gefandod habbađ đāra flǽsclicra synna, đā đe đæs nōht ne cunnon _peccata carnis experta, eorum expertes_, 403, 7. Þonne se ān hafađ þurh deáđes nȳd dǽda gefondad, B. 2454. v. ungefandod.

**ge-fandung,** e ; _f. Trial_:—On nǽnre gefandunge (fandunge, _v. l._), R. Ben. 107, 9 note.

**ge-fang** a _joint, clamp._ v. riht-gefang, _and next word._

**ge-fangian;** _p._ ode _To fasten together with joints_ or _clamps, join together_:—Ic ongeat đæt đes middangeard wæs of swīđe manegum and mistlicum đingum gegadered, and swīþe fæste tōsomne gelīmed and gefangod, Bt. 35, 2 ; F. 156, 35. [Cf. _O. H. Ger._ -fangōn.] v. preceding word.

**ge-faran.** _Add:_ I. _intrans._ (1) _of motion._ (a) _to travel, journey_:—Þegen þe mid his ǽrende gefōre tō cinge, Ll. Th. i. 192, 2. Hē walde gefara (_exire_) in Galilēam, Jn. L. 11, 43. Se feónd þe on đā frēcnan fyrd gefaren hæfde, Gen. 689. Hūshleów dǽle man gefarenum, Wlfst. 74, 4. (b) _of a military expedition, to march_:—Hē on Ahtēne

mid firde gefór, Ors. 3, 7; S. 118, 21. Hē gefór mid fierde on Perse *expeditione in Persas facta*, 6, 14; S. 272, 2. Gefór se here on Miercna lond, Chr. 877; P. 74, 22: Dan. 44. Þā hē þǣr tō gefaren wæs, Chr. 894; P. 87, 6: Gen. 2052. Oð þæt folc getrume gefaren hæfdon tōsomne sūðan and norðan, 1987. (2) of that which affects the mind, *to come :*—Him an gefór swīdlic wāfung, Hml. S. 23 b, 691. (3) *to depart, die :* gefaren *defunct :*—Swā þeáh hē gefór on þǣre mettrymnesse *ipse autem, cruciatus non sustinens, vim vitae suae adtulit*, Ors. 6, 30; S. 282, 21. Gif hwā gefare (*mortuus fuerit*) . . . ðām gefarenan brēðer (*defuncto fratri*), Past. 43, 12, 14. Būtan his man raþor tilige, hē biþ ymb þreó niht gefaren, Lch. ii. 46, 19. Hió wæs gefaren *exanimis inventa est*, Ors. 5, 13; S. 246, 35. Gefærenne man, gāstleásne, El. 872. (4) of affairs, circumstances, condition, *to go* well or ill :—Heora wīse on nænne sæl wel ne gefór, nāþer ne innan from him selfum, ne ūtan fram ōþrum folcum *nulla unquam tempora vel foris prospera vel domi quieta duxerunt*, Ors. 4, 4; S. 164, 13. Ðā ðā Dunecan þis eall gehȳrde þus gefaran, Chr. 1093; P. 228, 19: 1066; P. 197, 25. Hū hit gefaran wæs, 995; P. 130, 31. (5) *to fare, get on, succeed :*—Earme gefæreð hē, gif þurh his hnescnysse seó heord forwurð, Ll. Th. ii. 326, 22. Wel lā, mīn Drihten, hwæt ic hēr nū hreówlīce hæbbe gefaren *alas, my Lord! ah! now have I miserably failed by coming here*, Hml. S. 23, 575. **II.** *trans.* To get by going, go and get. (1) *to get to, reach* a place :—Gefærd *adit*, Wülck. Gl. 254, 18. On Indeas, þā nān man mid gefeohte gefór būton Alexander *Indis bellum intulit : quo praeter illam et Alexandrum nullus intravit*, Ors. 1, 2; S. 30, 20. Godes rīce gefaran, Hml. Th. i. 94, 3. Þæt hē swā wuldorfulle leóde geneósian and gefaran wolde, Lch. iii. 434, 1, 5. Decius fērde intō Constantinopolim, . . . and of ðǣre hē fór into Cartagine, and ðānon intō Efese. Ðā hē ðā þreó burga gefaren hæfde, ðā hēt [hē] gelangian him tō ealle ðā burhwara tōgædere (*getting to these towns he in every case summoned the townspeople*), Hml. S. 23, 19. (2) *to save by going :*—Gif hē þissa ǣnig āleóge, nāhwār hē eft his feorh gefare (*he shall not again save his life by going to any asylum*), Ll. Th. i. 332, 24. (3) *to march and occupy* a place, *conquer* persons, *gain* a victory :—Gif ic eft gefare swelcne sige æt Rōmanum *si iterum eodem modo vicero*, Ors. 4, 1; S. 156, 31. Hē sige gefór, Hml. S. 25, 721. Þā fór hē þonan tō Snotingahām and gefór þā burg, Chr. 922; P. 104. 2. Oð þæt heó gefóran (or (1) ?) folc Khananēa, Ps. Th. 104, 23. Hē hēt ōþre fierd gefaran Mameceaster and hié gemannian, Chr. 923; P. 104, 9. (4) *to accomplish* a journey, expedition, *complete* a course :—Se þridda steorra (*Mars*) gefærd his ryne binnan twelf wintrum, Angl. viii. 320, 43. Hē þæt færelt gefór and weorþlicne sige hæfde *feliciter confecit bellum*, Ors. 3, 10; S. 140, 3. (5) *to carry out, execute, manage to do :*—Þ gē nǣfre gedōn ne magon . . . ; hit furðum cēpemen ne gefarað *you will never be able to do that . . . , even merchants cannot manage it*, Bt. 18, 2 ; F. 64, 1. Ðā wyrmas scluncon wundorlīce, wǣron him þā breóst ūp gewende . . . and ā swā hié hit gefóran (*all the while they were executing this movement*) mid þǣm scillum ðā eorðan sliton, Nar. 14, 10. Gegaderode micel folc hit . . . of þām niehstum burgum, þe hit ðā gefaran mehte, Chr. 921; P. 102, 5. Stefnode man Godwine eorle and Harolde eorle tō þon gemōte swā raðe swā hī hit gefaran mihton (*as quickly as they could manage it*), 1048; P. 174, 25. (6) *to get as one's lot or fate, to experience :*—Ðeáh ūra heorda hwylc ān sceáp forgȳme, wē willað þ þe hit forgylde ; hwæt gefarað þonne æt Godes egeslican dōme þā hyrdas þe ne cunnon gehealdan þā godcundan heorda, Ll. Th. ii. 326, 25 : Wlfst. 276, 3. Hwā mæg ðonne ǣhta oððe anwaldes wilnian būtan plió, nū sē swelc plioh ðǣron gefór, sē ðe his nō ne wilnode *quis ergo opes, quis potestatem quaerat innoxie, si et illi extiterunt noxia, qui haec habuit non quaeria ?*, Past. 393, 9. Uton spirian be bōcan hwæt þā gefóran, þā þe God lufedon, and hwæt þā gefóran, ðā þe God grǣmedon, Wlfst. 130, 11–13. Gā hē tō corsnǣde and þǣr þonne æt gefare þ þ God wille (rǣde, l. 29), Ll. Th. i. 344, 23: 362, 20, 26. Gif wē āht gefaran scylan, Wlfst. 121, 14: 282, 10. Bid æt Gode gelang eal hwæt wē gefaran scylan, 122, 9. Se cāsere is nū gyt smeágende hwæt wē gefaran habban (*what has happened to us*), Hml. S. 23, 452. Weard þ wæder swiðe strang, þ þā racentan ne mihton gewitan hwet Godwine eorl gefaren hæfde, Chr. 1052; P. 177, 18. ¶ gefaren *experienced :*—Sē wæs wīde gefaren and gelǣred *he was of wide experience and learning; uir per omnia doctissimus*, Bd. pref. ; Sch. 2, 15. [*O. Sax.* gi-faran *to go* : *O. H. Ger.* ge-faran *conficere, obire.*]

**ge-feá.** *Add: d.* gefeán, gefeáne ; *d. pl.* gefeán, gefeánum. (1) *joy :*—Mid mycle gefeán gewuldrad, Bl. H. 139, 1. Ðām unblīðum sint tō cȳdanne ðā gefeán (*laeta*) ðe him gehātene sindon, Past. 187, 16. Þēh þe hē ūte wǣre belocen fram neorcxnawanges gefeán (*gaudiis*), gemunde þā ylcan gefeán, for þon þe hē ǣr heora breác, Gr. D. 261, 3–6. Ēcum gefeánum wilfægene *sempiternis gaudiis compotes*, Hy. S. 123, 9. Tō gehȳranne þā gefeán (*gaudia*) þæs heofonlīcan rīces, Bd. 4, 2 ; Sch. 345, 9. (1 a) with cause of joy in gen. :—Næs hié þǣre fulle gefeán hæfdon, B. 562. Ic þæs ealles mæg gefeán habban, 2740. Hæbbe þæs gefeán folca ǣghwylc, þæs þe þū hī on rihtum rǣdum dēmest, Ps. Th. 66, 4. (2) *joyous action :*—Gefeá *tripudium*, Wrt. Voc. i. 51,

Gefeáne *tripudio*, i. *gaudio*, Hpt. Gl. 404, 52. [*O. H. Ger.* ge-feho *gaudium.*] v. un-gefeá ; ge-feón.

**ge-feáge.** v. ge-feógan, gefeón.

**ge-fealdan.** *Add :* (1) *to wrap up, roll up :*—Ðæt yfelwillende mōd gefielt hit self twyfeald oninnan him selfum, and sió twyfealdnes ðæs yfian willan hiene selfne twyfealdne gefielt oninnan him selfum *malitiosae mentis duplicitas sese intra se colligit*, Past. 242, 6–9. Hē gefielt his mōd mid wōre twiefealdnesse *ad semetipsa duplicitatis perversitate corda replicuntur*, 245, 15. Ān clīwen suiðe nearwe gefealden (*involutum*), 241, 24. Gefalden bōc *volumen*, Mt. p. 1, 7. Ne bið gifalden *non flectetur*, Rtl. 84, 33. (1 a) *to involve, implicate :*—Nǣnig man compigende Gode gifalde hine (*inplicat se*) gimōtum woruldlicum, Rtl. 60, 11. (2) *to roll about :*—Hē gefeald hine *uolutabatur*, Mk. R. 9, 20. [*O. H. Ger.* ge-faldan *complicare, convolvere.*] Cf. gefildan.

**gefeá-lic.** *Add :*—Gyf him þince þ hē mid cyninge sprece, him cumeð gefeálic gifu tō and gōd, Lch. iii. 172, 3. Fæger and gefeálig fugles tācen, Ph. 510.

**ge-feálíce ;** *adv.* *Joyously, in joy :*—Þæt wē ealle mōtan on þās hālgan tīde ǣghwæðer ge for Gode and for worolde þȳ gefeálícor and þe blīþelícor lifian, Wlfst. 284, 16.

**ge-feall ;** *n.* A falling, fall :*—Tungla gefeall, Wlfst. 186, 3. [v. Cht. Crw. p. 116.] v. stān-, wæter-gefeall ; ge-fill.

**ge-feallan.** *Add: I. intrans.* (1) *to fall* from a higher to a lower position :—Ofer þeáre þe hē gefylþ *super quem ceciderit*, An. Ox. 61, 28. Þā tō heofonum āstīgað, nyðer gefeallað under neowulne grund (*descendunt usque ad abyssos*), Ps. Th. 106, 25 : Cri. 1532. Hie hine forlētan and hē gefeól on þone stocc, Bl. H. 189, 1. Gefeáll regn *descendit pluvia*, Mt. L. 7, 25. Ealle þā yldestan witan gefeóllan of ānre upflóran, būtan se hālga Dūnstān āna ætstōd uppon ānum beáme, Chr. 978 ; P. 123, 2. Se heofon biþ gefeallen æt þǣm feówer endum middangeardes, Bl. H. 93, 5. Gefeallen snāw, Ps. Th. 148, 8. (2) *to fall* from an erect position. (a) of living things :—Āslād and gefióll *labat*, Wrt. Voc. ii. 50, 62. Gefeóll *procumberet*, 66, 9. Hē gefeáll onufa suira his, Lk. L. 15, 20. Gefeól se rīca on his reste middan, Jud. 67. Hē gefeóll tō foldan, 280. (a a) *to stumble, fall* into or over :—Ēghuoelc sē ðe gefalled onufa ðæm stāne, Lk. L. R. 20, 18. Gif gefallas scīp in seáð, Mt. L. 12, 11. Hī on ðone seáð gefeóllan, Ps. Th. 56, 8. (a β) *to fall* in reverence :—þ wīf forhtade . . . and gifeól (gefeáll, L.) bifora him, Mk. R. 5, 33. Þ wīf gifeóll bifora fōtum his, Lk. R. 8, 47. Hē gifeóll on onsiōne, 17, 16. (a γ) *to fall* dead or wounded, *fall* in battle :—Gefallas hiá in mūðe suordes, Lk. L. 21, 24. Micel wæl gefeóll, Chr. 943 ; P. 111, 12 : 1004 ; P. 135, 36. Þær on greót gefeóll se hȳhsta dǣl, Jud. 308. Hwæt wæs on maurime . . . daredlācendra deádra gefeallen, El. 651. (b) of material objects, buildings, &c. :—Þonne gefeallaþ ealle deófolgyld, Bl. H. 93, 16. Þæt hūs nō gefeóll (-feáll, L.), Mt. R. 7, 25, 27 : Lk. L. 6, 49. (3) *to fall.* (a) of persons, *to perish, be ruined :*—Se līchoma lǣne gedreóseð, fǣge gefealled, B. 1755. Gē sweltað . . . swā ealdormann ān gefealled *vos moriemini . . . , sicut unus de principibus cadetis*, Ps. Th. 81, 7. Leáf fealewiað, fealláð on eorðan, . . . swā gefeallað þā þe firena lǣstað, Sal. 315. (b) of things, *to decline, decay, fail :*—Mycel yfel weaxeþ on þīnum rīce, gif þū lǣtest leng þysne drȳ rīxian, . . . and þīn rīce for his lārum gefealleþ, Bl. H. 181, 34. Eáðor is . . . ðon ān merce gefalla, Lk. L. 16, 17. (4) *to fall* to doing something, *to fall* a-doing, *busy one's self* at something, *apply with energy* to :—Hē ofdūne āstāh and gefeóll on þæs ceorles clyppinge *concitus descendit, atque in ejusdem rustici amplexum ruit*, Gr. D. 47, 1 [ : Ap. Th. 16, 23. v. Dict.]. (5) of that which (violently) affects the mind :—Ondo gefeóll (gifeól, R.) ofer hine *timor irruit super eum*, Lk. L. 1, 12. Hē fond his mondryhten ādlwērigne ; him þæt in gefeól hefig æt heortan, Gū. 981. **II. trans.** (1) *to reach by falling, to fall* and *reach, fall* to :—Hē meregrund gefeóll, B. 2100. Hē hreás on hrūsan . . . hē eorðan gefeóll, 2834. Lagu land gefeól (*of the water of the Red Sea when it fell upon the Egyptians trying to follow in the track of the Israelites*), Exod. 482 : 491. (2) *to cause by falling :*—Hit is on leóðum gesungen hwelcne demm hié Rōmanum gefeóllan (*quantam reipublicae orbitatem occasu suo intulerit Fabiorum familia*), Ors. 2, 4 ; S. 72, 11. [*O. H. Ger.* gi-fallan.]

**ge-fearh-sugu.** *l.* ge-fearh sugu, *and add :*—Gefearh sugu *forda*, Wrt. Voc. ii. 36, 60.

**ge-feaxe.** *l.* (?) ge-feax, *and add :* [*O. H. Ger.* ge-fahs *comatus.*] Cf. ge-hǣre.

**ge-feccan.** *Substitute :* ge-feccan, -fecgan *to fetch.* (1) *to go in quest of and bring back.* (a) the object a person :—Hē him hēt tō wīfe gefeccan Cleopatron *Cleopatram sibi occurrere imperavit*, Ors. 5, 13 ; S. 246, 1 : Hml. S. 8, 9. Hēht Neron Petrus and Paulus tō þissum wæferseónum gefeccean, Bl. H. 187, 15. Gefæccan, Hml. S. 2, 197. Hē mæg þā sāwle of sinnihte gefeccan, Sal. 69. (b) the object a thing :—Hāt unmǣlne mon gefeccean healfne sester yrnendes wæteres, Lch. iii. 10, 31. (2) *to go and get* what one seeks, *obtain, get :*—Hē wolde

gefeccan þā lytlan and gebringan ūp tō his rīce, Hml. Th. i. 138, 5. Nān Crīsten mann ne sceal his hǣle gefeccan būton æt ðām Scyppende, 470, 20. Swā þā sculon þe hiora ǣfengifl on helle gefeccean sculon *tamquam apud inferos coenaturi*, Ors. 2, 5; S. 86, 2. Hē wolde þæs beornes beágas gefecgan, By. 160. v. ge-fetian.

**ge-fecgan.** *See preceding word.*

**ge-fēdan.** *Add:* (1) *to give food to :*—Lēt ǣrist þ ðū gefoeda (gifoede, R.) ðā suno *sine prius saturari filios*, Mk. L. 7, 27. Þte gefoede ðā bergas *ut pasceret porcos*, Lk. L. 15, 15. Ofætum wǣre gefēd *holusculis uesceretur*, An. Ox. 3753. Gefoeded, Mt. L. 8, 30. (1 a) *to suckle* an infant :—Ðā breósto ðā ðe ne gefoedon *ubera quae non lactauerunt*, Lk. L. 23, 29. (2) *to bring up :*—Tō Nazareth ðēr wæs gefoeded (*nutritus*), Lk. L. R. 4, 16. (3) *to bring forth :*—Heora āgen gereorde þā ðe hié on gefēded wǣron *linguam propriam in qua nati sunt*, Bd. 4, 2; Sch. 345, 1.

**ge-fēg.** *Add:* (1) of material objects :—*Commisura, s. dicitur tabularum conjunctio* gefēg, cimbing, Wrt. Voc. ii. 132, 10. Gefēge *compage*, An. Ox. 4440. Gefēg *compagines, i. conjunctiones, juncturae*, Wrt. Voc. ii. 132, 69. Of gefēgum *liniamentis* (i. *coniunctionibus*) *corporalibus*, An. Ox. 3412. (2) of non-material objects :—þæt ōðer hīw ys gecīged *zeuma*, þ ys gefeig on Englisc; þis gefēg ys swýðe gelōme on hālgum gewritum, Angl. viii. 331, 9. God gesette twēgen sunnstedas and hē geendebyrde þā twelf mōnðas on twām emnihtum . . . hē eác mid his āgenre mihte geglengde þ gēr mid feówrum gesceaftum, swā þis gefeig ætȳwð eallum þe hyt sceáwiað (*he adorned the year with four seasons, as this framework of the solstices and the equinoxes* (? cf. ge-fēgedness) *shews to all that observe it*, 229, 20. v. riht-, stæf-gefēg.

**ge-fēgan.** *Add:*—Gefēgað *conpingite*, Wrt. Voc. ii. 15, 43. (1) of construction, *to join* the parts of a structure, *construct, compact :*—þæt fær (*the ark*) wið ȳða gewyrc, gefēg fæste, Gen. 1310. Gefēgde *compacta, i. conjuncta* (*delubra*), An. Ox. 2254. (1 a) of the structure of words or sentences :—Gif se nama bið gefēged of twām ansundum dǣlum, *if the noun be compounded of two complete parts*, Ælfc. Gr. Z. 88, 4. Feáwa *coniunctiones* beóð gefēgede, 266, 10. Mid meterlicum fōtum gefēgede *pedibus poeticis compactas, i. coniunctas*, An. Ox. 202. (2) *to attach, join :*—Is se scyld ufan frætwum gefēged ofer þæs fugles bæc, Ph. 309. (2 a) figurative :—Þte hiá ðīnum gifoega hiá ł ætfēla hiá bodum *ut tuis inhaerent preceptis*, Rtl. 90, 22. Hē wæs gefēged mid ðǣre lufan Godes and monna ǣgðer ge tō ðām hiēhstum ðingum ge tō ðām nyðemestum *compage caritatis summis simul et infimis junctus*, Past. 99, 25. (3) *to join* in friendship, *unite :*—þæt gecynd gefēhþ and gelīmþ ðā friénd tōgædere mid untōdǣledlicre lufe, Bt. 24, 3; F. 84, 1. (4) *to constrain, confine :*—Gefēged *arta*, Wrt. Voc. ii. 9, 65. þætte fira gehwylc on his hringe bið fæste gefēged, Wal. 41. (5) *to square, adapt :*—Gefēgan *quadrare*, Wrt. Voc. ii. 85, 21. Ðā stānas wǣron suā wel gefēgede and suā emne gesnidene and gesmēðde, ǣr hié mon tō ðǣm stede brōhte ðe hié on standan scoldon, Past. 253, 14. [*O. H. Gen.* gefuogen *conjungere, copulare, conglutinare, coaptare.*]

**ge-fēgednes.** *Add:* (1) *figure, shape :*—*Figura* is gecweden on Englisc hīw oððe gefēgednyss, Ælfc. Gr. Z. 105, 20. (2) *a conjunction :*—*Polysindeton* ys þæt gebed þe byð mid manegum gefēgednyssum gefrætwod, Angl. viii. 332, 28.

**ge-fēging.** *Add:*—Gefē(g)incga *compages*, Wrt. Voc. i. 42, 66.

**ge-fēgness.** *Add:*—Gefoegnisse, gifoegnissae, gefēgnessi *sarta tecta*, Txts. 95, 1765. [*O. H. Ger.* ge-fuognissa *nexus.*]

**ge-fēlan.** *Add:* (1) *to feel an object, perceive by the sense of touch :*—Ne mihte nān man þ swȳn geseón, and swā þēh hī hit mihton gefēlan Gr. D. 226, 6. (2) *to know by sense of touch or organic sensation* (with clause or acc. and infin.) :—Ðā gefēlde hē þ se deáda man his leoma ealle āstyrede, Bl. H. 217, 30. Gefēldon hī ān swȳn yrnan hider and þider betwyh heora fōtum, Gr. D. 236, 1. Heora nān gefēlan ne mihte hū hī gewurdon on slǣpe, Hml. S. 23, 257. (3) *to feel* pain, *be conscious of a* sensation :—Ne gefēlest (-fēlst, *v. l.*) þū gewin on þīnum fōtum, Gr. D. 330, 6. Ne hī swōl gefēlaþ on magan, ii. 194, 12. Hwylc wundor is þēh þe þā sāwla magan gefēlan þā līchamlican tintregan?, Gr. D. 305, 12. [*O. Sax.* gi-fōlian : *O. H. Ger.* ge-fuolen *sentire, palpare.*] v. un-gefēled.

**ge-fēle** ; *adj. Sensitive :*—Wiþ þǣre gefēlan heardnesse þǣre lifre, Lch. ii. 160, 28 : 206, 13. On þām monnum þe habbaþ swīðe gefēlne magan, 176, 8. v. un-gefēle.

**ge-fēlgan.** v. ge-feólan : **ge-fellan** *to fell.* v. ge-fillan.

**ge-fēlness** *sensitiveness, sensation. Add :*—Gif þ līc tō þon swiþe ādeádige þ þær gefēlnes on ne sȳ, Lch. ii. 8, 14 : 82, 26. Welmes hǣto mid gefēlnesse . . . āheardung þæs magan mid gefēlnesse and mid sāre . . . heardung þǣre lifre būtan gefēlnesse and būtan sāre, 198, 11-14. Þone dǣl þe git hwilcehwega gefēlnesse hæbbe, 84, 1.

**ge-feógan** ; *p.* -feóde *To hate :*—Gefiáð *odit*, Jn. L. 7, 7 : 12, 25. Sē ðe mec gefīið fæder mīn gefīið ł gefiáð, 15, 23. Gefēð íowih mid-dengeord, Jn. R. 15, 19. Gifiáðun (gefiádon, L.) *oderunt*, 24. Gifióge *odisse*, 7, 7.

**ge-feoht.** *Add :*—Gefeoht *bellum* vel *pugna*, Wrt. Voc. i. 84, 15.

(1) *fighting*, (a) in a military sense, *war :*—Gefeohtes bodan *praefeciales*, Wrt. Voc. i. 36, 7. Gefeohtes *duelli*, ii. 96, 27 : 27, 28. Hī cōmon fǣrlīce mid gefeohte tō Judan *they suddenly attacked Judas*, Hml. S. 25, 653 : 670. Þā nān man mid gefeohte ne gefōr, Ors. 1, 2; S. 30, 20. Mid gefeohte sēcan, 3, 1; S. 98, 11. Mid gefeohte cnyssan, S. 96, 8. Ymb gefeoht sprecan, Met. 8, 32. (a a) *rendering the personification* Mars :—Wīg oððe gefeoht *Mavors*, Wrt. Voc. ii. 55, 37. Gefeoht *Martem*, 94, 18 : 96, 23 : 57, 14. (b) *fighting* between two or more persons :—Be preósta gefeohte. Gif preóst ōðerne man ofsleá *of fighting by priests. If a priest slay a man*, Ll. Th. i. 74, 18. Be gefeohte. Gif hwā gefeohte on cyninges hūse . . . Gif hwā on mynstre gefeohte . . . And þeah hit sié on middum felda gefohten, 106, 1-10. (2) *a fight, combat, battle, war.* (a) military, between opposing forces :—Næs nā mid Rōmānum ǣr ne siþþan swā heard gefeoht (*pugna*) swā þǣr wæs, Ors. 5, 7; S. 230, 13. On þǣre frymþe þæs gefeohtes, Bl. H. 203, 5. Se eádiga Michael þǣr wæs tōweard him tō fultome ðā hwīle ðe hié æt þǣm gefeohte wǣron, 205, 3. Æfter þissum gefeohte, Chr. 871; P. 72, 5. On folces gefeohte *in bello publico*, Ll. Th. ii. 150, 32 : 386, 16. Ne gehērde nōn mon ymbe nān gefeoht sprecan, Bt. 15; F. 48, 15. Ungelimplico gefeoht, Bl. H. 107, 28. Gefeoht *bella*, Wülck. Gl. 255, 6. Synd feówer cynna gefeoht *iustum, iniustum, ciuile, plusquam ciuile. Iustum bellum* is rihtlic gefeoht wið ða rēðan flotmenu, Hml. S. 25, 705. (b) *a fight* between two or more persons :—Gif man beforan æðelinge gefeoht āginneð, mid .CL. scillinga gebēte, Ll. Th. i. 332, 3. Mē egleð swȳðe and ūs eallum þā unrihtlican and mænigfealdan gefeoht þe betwux ūs sylfum syndan; þonne cwǣde wē : Gif hwā ǣnigne man ofsleá . . ., Ll. Th. i. 246, 24. Be gefeohtum, 106, 1 note. Sē þe gefeohtu gesihð, blisse hit openað, Lch. iii. 200, 7. (3) figurative, *conflict, struggle* for victory :—Gefeoht *commissio, conflictus*, Wrt. Voc. ii. 132, 22. Gefeohte *conflictu* (*vitiorum*), 77, 1. Sē ðe gifehtað in gefeht *qui certat in agone*, Rtl. 60, 15. Iornia wē forārǣden ūs gifeht *curramus propositum nobis certamen*, 27, 29. Gifeht gāstlices wōghfulnisse *impugnatione spiritalis nequitiae*, 121, 9. Bið ā wið firenum in gefeoht gearo, Crä. 90. [*O. H. Ger.* ge-feht *pugna, praelium, bellum, certamen.*] v. flet-, folc-, in-, on-, scip-, sige-, þurh-, ūt-, weorold-gefeoht, *and* gefeaht *in Dict.*

**ge-feohtan.** *Add :* I. *intrans.* (1) in a military sense. v. gefeoht, (2 a) :—Hēr gefeaht Ecgbryht cyning wiþ .xxxv. sciphlæsta, Chr. 833; P. 62, 10. Æþelwulf him wið gefeaht . . . Æþerēd cyning and Ælfrēd his brōþur wiþ þone here gefuhton, 871; P. 70, 13-16. Antigones and Perðica . . . woldon him betweónan gefeohtan *bellum inter Antigonum et Perdiccam oritur*, Ors. 3, 11; S. 144, 34. Hié hiene sendon on Perse wið hié tō gefeohtanne, 3, 1; S. 96, 12. (1 a) *of fighting* between champions :—Dauid wolde wiþ Goliaþ gefeohtan, Bl. H. 31, 17. (1 b) with cognate object (v. ān-wīg) :—Hēr Cēnwalh gefeaht wiþ Walas and hié gefliémde; þis wæs gefohten siþþan hē of Eást-Englum cōm, Chr. 958; P. 32, 4. Þæs geáres wurdon .viiii. folcgefeoht gefohten wiþ þone here, 871; P. 72, 12. (2) *to fight* in a quarrel. v. gefeoht, (2 b) :—Gif hwā gefeohteð on cirican oþþon on cynges hūse . . . And gif hwā gefeohteð on mynstre, Ll. Th. i. 330, 23, 26. Gif mon beforan cyninges ealdormen on gemōte gefeohte, 86, 14. Gif hwā in cyninges healle gefeohte, oþþe his wǣpn gebrēde, 66, 8 : 70, 18. Gif hwā on cierlisces monnes flette gefeohte, mid syx sciłł. gebēte þām ceorle. Gif hē wǣpne gebrēde and nō feohte, sié be healfum þām, 86, 21. Gif mǣgleás mon gefeohte and mon ofsleá, 78, 20. (3) fig. *to struggle, strive* for supremacy :—Efne þǣm gelícost swylce ðā gesceafta (*wind and flame*) twā him betweónan gefeohtan sceoldan, Bl. H. 221, 15. II. *trans.* (1) *to gain by fighting :*—Ðǣm folce ðe on clǣnum felda weordlicne sige gefeohtað *his qui per fortitudinem in campo victores sunt*, Past. 227, 25. Þone sige þe hē on Persia ðeóda gefeaht, Hml. S. 30, 153. Hié getrūwedon þæt hié mid hiera cræftum sceolden sige gefeohtan, Ors. 2, 4; S. 72, 17 : 2, 5; S. 82, 26. (2) *to maintain* a charge *by fighting :*—Þǣr beteáh Gosfrei Bainard Willelm of Ou þ hē heafde gebeón on þes cynges swicdōm, and hit him on gefeaht, and hine on orreste ofercōm, Chr. 1096; P. 232, 20. [*O. H. Ger.* ge-fehtan *congredi.*]

**ge-feohtsumness,** e; *f. Joyousness, gladsomeness :*—God ūs lǣrað līþnesse and gefeohtsumnesse, diófol ūs lǣrað yrre and unrōtnesse, Nap. 30, 1. v. ge-feón.

**ge-feolan.** l. ge-feólan; *p.* -fealh, *pl.* fulgon. *Take here passage given under* ge-felgan, *and add :* I. *to press* into. (1) *to make one's way* into a place, *get and remain in :*—Wæs þǣr neáh Apollines templ; þā gefealh hē þǣr in and þǣr þā niht gewunode *juxta Apollinis templum fuit, ibique se ad manendum contulit*, Gr. D. 189, 1. Ðā ward his leóhtbora āfyrht swȳðe, and gefeall him on ānan heale and slǣp *his lightbearer became very frightened, and got in a corner and went to sleep*, Vis. Lfc. 36. (2) *to enter* the mind :—Hū se ealda feónd on symbel gefēled ūrum geþōhtum mid his searwum *antiquus hostis quam insidiis nostris cogitationibus insistat*, Gr. D. 222, 6. II. *to stick to.* (1) *to continue* instant in, *pursue unremittingly :*—Swā mycele mā hē gefealh mid geornnysse þām gebedum *tanto annisu precibus incubuit*, Gr. D. 74, 17 : 125, 29 : 247, 26. Hē gefealh his wæcce *instans vigiliis*, 170, 30. Hē

gefealh singallíce his þegnungum and hýrnessum *ejus obsequiis sedule atque incessanter adhaerebat*, 299, 29. (2) *to adhere* to a person, an opinion :—Þá þe Gode gefeólað mid éstfullum móde *qui devota mente Deo adhaerent*, Gr. D. 161, 17. For þon þe ic gefealh and gewunode in Laurenties worde and wæs wið Simmache *quia in parte Laurentii contra Symmachum sensi*, 330, 8. [*Goth.* ga-filhan *to hide : O. H. Ger.* gi-felhan.]

ge-feón *to rejoice. Add :* (1) absolute :—Ic gefeoge *gaudebo*, Ps. Rdr. 74, 10. Alle gefióð (gefeagaþ, Ps. L.) *omnes exultabunt*, Ps. Srt. 5, 12. Gefiáð (gefeogaþ, Ps. L.) bán, 50, 10. Gefeádon (giseádun, R.) ł gefeánde *gaudentes*, Lk. L. 19, 37 : Jn. L. 20, 20. Gefæg wel (geblissa, W. S.) *euge*, Lk. L. 19, 17. Gefeagaþ *exultate*, Ps. L. 2, 11. Gefeogað *gaudete*, gefeogiað *jubilate*, Bl. Gl. Heó wæs swíþe gefeónde and swíðe blissigende, Bl. H. 139, 7. Gefeánde, Gr. D. 69, 17. Gefeónde móde *gaudente animâ*, Bd. 4, 24 ; Sch. 489, 15. Gié bidon gifeád *gauderetis*, Jn. L. 14, 28. (2) where the cause or occasion of rejoicing is given, (a) in *gen. :*—Seó módor þæs gefeah þ . . . , Gr. D. 69, 13 note. Þæt míne fýnd ne gefeón mínes ungelimpes *ut non supergaudeant mihi inimici mei*, Ps. Th. 34, 23. (b) in *dat. (inst.) :*—Seó wamb gefihð drium mettum . . . gefihð wætum mettum, Lch. ii. 220, 18, 21. Hé nihtweorce gefeah, ellenmærðum, B. 827. Hí gefégon burhweardes cyme, An. 659. (c) *with prep. :*—Fore ðissum gefiht (*exultavit*) tunge mín, Ps. Srt. 15, 9. Ðæt mód gefihð on his yfelum, Past. 417, 2. Gefehð (gefyhð, *v. l.*), Mart. H. 84, 3. (On þám ic) gefag (*in quo*) conplacui, Wrt. Voc. ii. 71, 68. Se his gingra gefeah for þæs feóndes deáþe, Gr. D. 120, 8 note. Gefeáde (Gefiehde, Ps. Rdr.), Ps. L. 15, 9. Ealle men on þ 'gefégon, hwylc wundur geworden wæs, Bd. 4, 3 ; Sch. 366, 4. Þ þú gefeó in þæm fromscipe mínes lífes, Nar. 32, 30. Ne wæs hé forlǽten þ hé ofer him deádum gefége, Bd. 1, 7 ; Sch. 26, 3. Þæt nǽfre míne fýnd ne gefǽgen æfter mé *ne quando supergaudeant in me inimici mei*, Ps. Th. 37, 16. Ofer hine deádne gefeón *super eum mortuum gaudere*, Gr. D. 294, 21. Of noma mið áwrittne gefeá *de nominum scriotione gaudere*, Lk. p. 6, 17. His mód wæs gefeónde on Drihten, Bl. H. 227, 9. On óðres góde gefeónde, 75, 20. Gefeónde for ðære andsware, 207, 8 : Past. 213, 13. (d) *by gerundial infin. :*—Gefaeh swæ swæ gigent tó earnenne on weg, Ps. Srt. 18, 6. [*O. H. Ger.* ge-fehan *gaudere*.] v. efen-gefeón ; ge-fægen.

ge-feón ; *p.* -feóde *To gain* (v. feoh) :—Gif middangeard eall gestríóna ł gefeáge *si mundum universum lucretur*, Mt. L. 16, 26. v. be-feón.

ge-feónd *an enemy* :—Þeáh hié ǽr longe gefiénd wǽren, Ors. 3, 7 ; S. 118, 13. v. ge-fýnd *in Dict.*

ge-feormian. *Take* III *separate from* I *and* II, *and to these add :* I. *to entertain* as a guest. v. feormian ; II :—Se Godes wer þe Quadragesimus þǽr gefeormode (-ferm-, *v. l.*) *vir Dei qui receptus hospitio fuerat*, Gr. D. 215, 25. II. *to entertain* as an obligation, v. feormian ; V :—Hé þére cirican láforde geselle éghwelce gére ðrittig scillinga and hine áne niht gefeormige, Cht. Th. 105, 9 : Chr. 852 ; P. 65, 28. III. *to feast.* v. feormian ; VI :—Herôdes his witan gefeormode *Herodes cenam fecit principibus*, Hml. Th. i. 480, 28. Hé ælce dæge symblede and mid micelre wiste wæs gefeormod *epulabatur quotidie splendide*, Past. 337, 25.

ge-feormian *to cleanse. Add :*—Sácerd sé þe þurh unsýfre sprǽce hine besmíted, and ne gefeormige (*mundet*) hine, Ll. Th. ii. 138, 5.

ge-feorrian. v. ge-fearrian *in Dict. :* ge-fer. v. ge-fær : ge-fér. *l.* ge-fére, *q. v.*

ge-féra. *Add :*—Gefêra *collega*, Wrt. Voc. ii. 23, 68. (1) *a companion, associate :*—Hé dyde suá suá ofermód gefêra déð, Past. 305, 6. Wineleás mon genimed him wulfas tó gefêran . . . ful oft hine se gefêra slíteþ, Gn. Ex. 148. Hwæt cunnon þás þíne gefêran (*socii*)?, Coll. M. 19, 1 : 31, 21. Hé gegæderaþ fríind and gefêran þ hié getreówlíce heora sibbe and heora freóndrǽdenne healdaþ *hic fidis sua dictat jura sodalibus*, Bt. 21 ; F. 74, 38. (2) *an associate in work, partner, assistant :*—Hæfst þú (*the ploughman*) ǽnigne gefêran (*socium*)? Ic hæbbe sumne cnapan, Coll. M. 19, 25. Zebedeis sunu wǽron Simones gefêran (gefoero, L., *socii*), Lk. 5, 10. Hig bícnodon hyra gefêran (*sociis*) þe on óðrum scipe wǽron, 7 : Coll. M. 24, 31. (2 a) *an associate in office, a colleague :*—Silla se consul, Pompeiuses gefêra, Ors. 5, 10 ; S. 234, 25. (2 b) of things :—Swá nú fýr déþ and wæter . . . and manega óþra gesceafta . . . þætte nó þ án þ hí magon gefêran beón . . . , Bt. 21 ; F. 74, 17 : Met. 11, 50. (3) *an associate in the execution of a plan, a confederate :*—Hé nolde meldian on his gefêran þe mid him sieredon ymbe þone cyning . . . se cyning hine hét secgan hwæt his gefêran wǽron, Bt. 16, 2 ; F. 52, 20–24. Gif hwá ǽnigum preóste ǽnig wóh beóde, beón ealle gefêran ymbe þ bóte, and beón swá swá áwriten is, 'quasi cor unum et anima una,' Ll. Th. ii. 290, 3. (4) *one of a society or profession :*—Ðá Apostolas and þá eldran bróðor eów cýðað þ wé geáscodon þ úre gefêran sume (*quidam ex nobis*) tó eów cómon, Ll. Th. i. 56, 14. (4 a) *one of the clergy :*—Gif hit ǽnig preóst elles gedó, þolige his wurðscipes and gefêrena freóndscipes, Ll. Th. ii. 290, 10. Gif gehádod man sí mǽgleás, ládige mid gefêran, i. 344, 28. (4 b) *a comrade, brother in arms :*—Æðeríc, æðele gefêra, By. 280. Se man þe ætfleó fram his hláforde oþþe fram his gefêran for his yrhðe, sý hit

on scypfyrde, sý hit on landfyrde, Ll. Th. i. 420, 8. Hár hilderinc bæd gangan forð góde gefêran, By. 170 : 229. (4 c) *a fellow-servant :*—Ðǽm gefero *conservo*, Mt. p. 18, 8. (5) *an associate* from local connexion, *a fellow-citizen, neighbour :*—Gif þú fioh tó borge selle þínum gefêran þe mid þé eardian wille, Ll. Th. i. 52, 21. Sé þe freóndleásan and feorrancumenan wyrsan dóm démeð þonne his gefêran, hé dereð him sylfum, 398, 1. Þ hé sié his gefêrum his gefêrena weorþost *reverendi civibus suis esse nituntur*, Bt. 24, 2 ; F. 82, 6. Gif hwá nylle rídan mid his gefêran, Ll. Th. i. 210, 1. (6) *one that has the same condition* or *experience as another, a companion* in, *sharer :*—Gefêra *particeps*, Germ. 400, 573. (6 a) where the common experience is given, (α) by a case :—Neód is þæt hí beón efenhlyttan þæs edleánes, þonne hí wǽron gefêran ðære ðrowunge, Hml. Th. i. 84, 20. (β) with preposition :—Ǽfre seó sǽ and se móna beóð gefêran on wæstme and on wanunge, Lch. iii. 268, 13. (7) *a consort :*—Ic Aelfréd aldormon and Werburg mín gefêra, Txts. 175, 4. (8) *a follower, adherent, one of a retinue :*—Þá dyde Eustatius on his byrnan and his gefêran ealle, Chr. 1048 ; P. 170, 20. Gefeóran, 173, 1. Mid his (*Romulus*) híwunge and his gefêrena, Ors. 2, 2 ; S. 64, 24. Colman mid his gefêrum fór tó his cýððe, Chr. 664 ; P. 34, 4. Se feónd mid his gefêrum feóllon, Gen. 306. Ic gean healfes þæs stódes mínum gefêran þe mid mé rídað, Cht. Th. 598, 14. Hé Godrum miclum and his gefêran mid feó weorðude, Chr. 878 ; P. 76, 20. (8 a) fig. :—Sió gítsung ðe Sanctus Paulus cuæð ðæt wǽre hearga gefêra *avaritia quae est idolorum servitus*, Past. 157, 6. Sió óðru gesǽlð is leás and beswícþ ealle hire gefêran, Bt. 20 ; F. 70, 34. v. camp-, eald-gefêra.

ge-fêran. *Add :* I. *intrans.* (1) *to go :*—Gefoerde *abiit*, Mk. L. 8, 13 ; *ambulans*, Mt. L. 4, 18 : *egressus*, 18, 28 : *exiebat*, 3, 5 : *migravit*, 19, 1 : *procedens*, 4, 21 : *progressus*, 26, 39 : *secessit*, 12, 15 : *transiit*, 11, 1. Gefoerdon *irent*, Lk. L. 8, 31. Ne durran wé for his onsýne gefêran, Jul. 331. Gefoera *exire*, Jn. R. 1, 43. Gefoerende wæs *profectus est*, Mt. L. 25, 15. (1 a) fig. :—Þæt ic on þínre gewitnysse wel gefêre *converti pedes meos in testimonia tua*, Ps. Th. 118, 59. (2) *to depart* this life, *die :*—Þá þe of middangearde wǽron tó gefêranne (geleóranne, *v. l.*) . . . heó gefêrde (geleórde, *v. l.*) *qui de mundo essent rapiendi*, . . . *transierat*, Bd. 4, 19 ; Sch. 444, 7, 15. (3) *to fare :*—Habbað wé ealle for þínum leásungum lyðre gefêred, Sat. 62. (4) of events, *to go, to come to pass, happen :*—Eall swá hit æt þám ende eall gefêrde *just as it in the end all happened*, Chr. 1066 ; P. 200, 6. II. *trans.* (1) *to go, make a journey :*—Hé uneáþe þone síð gefêrde, Guth. 68, 5. Þá hí hæfdon heora síðfæt gefêredne *peracto itinere*, Bd. 4, 25 ; Sch. 497, 18. (2) *to travel* a road, *traverse* a surface (land, sea) :—Þone gársecg nǽnig mon mid scipe gefêran ne meahte, Nar. 20, 18 : Bt. 18, 2 ; F. 62, 9 note. Ealde staðolas (*the bottom of the Red Sea*) ic ǽr ne gefrægn men gefêran, Exod. 286. (3) *to traverse* a (great or small) distance :—Sume lǽsse gelíðað, oððe micle máre gefêrað, Met. 28, 23. Þ nǽre mára weg þonne meahte on týn dagum gefêran, Nar. 25, 3. Hit næs micel tó gefêranne, 26, 3. (4) *to gain, attain :*—Hé sige gefêrde on manegum gefeohtum, Hml. S. 25, 730. (4 a) with clause :—Hafast þú gefêred þæt þám folcum sceal sacu restan, B. 1855. (5) *to bring about, effect :*—Bíówulfe wearð dryhtmáðma dǽl deáðe forgolden, hæfde æghwæðre (*for Beowulf and the fire-drake*) ende gefêred lǽnan lífes, B. 2844. Þegn folgade, and micel hæfde gefêred, Rä. 38, 4. (6) *to meet with, experience, get* as one's fate or *lot :*—Gé weorn gefêrað earfoðsíða, An. 677. Ic nyste hwæt mín fæder gefêrde *I knew not my father's fate*, Hml. S. 30, 334. Hí hine áxodon þe his wífe and his cildan hwæt hí gefêrdon, 276. Hí þær ǽfre yfel gefêrdon, Chr. 1009 ; P. 139, 27. III. *with causative force, to cause to move, to bring, bear.* [v. *O. Sax.* gi-fôrian *to bring : O. H. Ger.* gi-fuoren *ferre, vehere.*] :—Gefoerdun ł bröhtun *afferebant*, Mk. R. 1, 32. v. un-gefêred.

ge-fêre, *es ; m. A companion :*—Be Aþelbaldes gefêre . . . Aþelbaldes gefêre, þæs nama wæs Ecga, wæs fram þám áwyrgedan gáste unstille, Guth. 60, 9–13. Be Aþelbaldes gefêre . . . cóm Æþelbaldes gefêra þæs nama wæs Ova, 66, 20. Gefêre *comitem*, Wrt. Voc. ii. 23, 42.

ge-fêre, *es ; n. Take here passages under* ge-fêr *in Dict., and add :*—Gegilda . . . his gegilde eft mid eahta pundum gebycge, oþþe hé þolie ǽ gefêres and freóndscipes, Cht. Th. 612, 9. Feáwa witena þæs gefêres (on ðám gefêrscipe, *v. l.*) *pars quamvis parva congregationis*, R. Ben. 117, 20 : 46, 2. Be ealles gefêres endebyrdnesse *de ordine quo congregatur*, 113, 20. Gelaðige se abbod eal þæt gefêre (*omnem congregationem*), 15, 5, 2, 8.

ge-fêre ; *adj. Add :* v. un-gefêre.

ge-fêred ; *adj.* (*ptcpl.*) *Associated, banded together :*—Gefêred *sociata, cuneata*, Wrt. Voc. ii. 137, 30.

ge-fêrendlic. v. un-gefêrendlic.

ge-ferian. *Add :*—Geferedon *afferebant*, Mk. L. 1, 32. Gefere lædde mannan on swíðe fæstne cleofan, Lch. ii. 280, 10. Hám gefêrian, bringan tó bolde, Sat. 148. Hé wæs gefered *excipitur*, An. Ox. 4698. Geferod *vectus*, Wülck. Gl. 254, 10. Gefered wæs heáfod his in disc *allatum est caput ejus in disco*, Mt. L. 14, 11. Geferedne *delatum*, Wrt. Voc. ii. 80, 75. Gefæredne, 26, 50.

**ge-férlǽcan.** *Add*: I. *trans.*:—Geférlǽhton *consocierunt, conjunxerunt*, Wrt. Voc. ii. 134, 21. Geférlǽht *sociata*, 132, 33. (1) of relation between persons:—Stuntne mid witum nā geférlǽc *fatuum cum sapientibus non socies*, Scint. 97, 18. Hyra nān wið cuman (cumena, *v. l.*) hine geférlǽce *hospitibus* . . . *non societur*, R. Ben. 87, 1. Beón geférlǽht *sociari* (*choro*), R. Ben. I. 77, 5 : 90, 9. Geférlǽht *glomeratus, junctus*, An. Ox. 7, 48. Ic eom þysum mǽdenum geférlǽht, Hml. S. 7, 256. Hī wǽron geférlǽhte on fǽstum geleáfan, 28, 20. Beón on sóðre sibbe geférlǽhte, R. Ben. 82, 6. (2) of relation between things:—His līchama is mīnum geférlǽht, Hml. S. 7, 47. Se óðer eáca bið sīf ablativum geférlǽht, Ælfc. Gr. Z. 107, 18. Gyf hig beóð frumcennede *genitivi*, þonne magon hig beón geférlǽhte eallum casum, 104, 8. Weleras geférlǽhte *labia sociata* (*corde*), Kent. Gl. 1003. II. *intrans.* (1) of relation between person and thing:—Ne geférlǽcð *nec sociabitur* (*eis afflictio*), Kent. Gl. 337. (2) of relation between things: —Hærfest and geþungen yld geférlǽcað *autumn and mature age may be classed together*, Angl. viii. 299, 27.

**ge-férlic**; *adj. Social; gregalis*, Germ. 399, 391. v. un-geférlic, un-geférlíce.

**ge-férlíplíce**; *adv. Sociably*:—Heom bām wæs forgifen þ hī moston on ānre eardungstówe geférlíðlíce (-líðlíce, *v. l.*, *socialiter*) lifian ; þām eác gelamp þ hī samod geférlíðlíce (-líðlíce, *v. l.*) férdon of līchoman, Gr. D. 313, 23–25.

**ge-férne.** v. un-geférne.

**ge-férness** (?), e ; *f. Going*:—For þon þe mycelre tīde ǽr þǽre hālignesse hūs geclǽnsod beón sceolde and seó gastlīþnes þæs Crīstes wīsceáweres gebúend wæs þæs Crīstes engles and seó heall þæs hālgan gāstes *mundabatur enim longo tempore sacrificii domus, sanctitatis hospitium, metatum* (*meatum, v. l.*) *metatoris Christi, angeli domicilium* (v. Archiv cxxii, p. 248), Bl. H. 163, 10–13. The original is so imperfectly reproduced by the translation, that it is difficult to connect the several corresponding parts, and to understand what the translation means. To *hospitium* corresponds (though it does not properly translate it) *gastlīþnes*; perhaps to *meatum* (not *metatum*) corresponds *gifernes* = (?) *ge-férnes*. Though *ge-férnes* does not occur elsewhere, yet on the analogy of *ge-leórnes transitus, ge-leóran transire*, it might serve as a gloss to *meatus* alongside *ge-féran meare*. *Gi-* for *ge-* is not used in Bl. H., but *gy-* occurs once, in *gy-fylnes*, 145, 16. Mr. Bradley suggests the emendation *seó gisternes gebúennes* as translating *domicilium*. Dr. Max Förster suggests *gife[n]nes*. v. Archiv cxxii, p. 248.

**ge-férrǽden.** *Add*: I. abstract. (1) of persons:—*Socius sacra, societas* geférrǽden, Ælfc. Gr. Z. 17, 13. Geþeódlícre geférrǽdenne *contubernali sodalitate*, Wrt. Voc. ii. 135, 22 : An. Ox. 2532. Geférrǽddene *consortio, contubernio*. 2148. Geférrǽdena, Hml. S. 3, 395. Ðæt hē hiene from hiera geférrǽdenne ne ðióde *quia se minime a proximorum societate disjungit*, Past. 349, 5 : 113, 13. Hē forsieh ða geférrǽddene (-rǽdenne, *v. l.*) óðerra engla and hira līf *socialem angelorum vitam despiciens*, 111, 23. Geféra, geféra, gemyne þ ðū úre geférrǽddene tō longe ne oferbrec, Ors. 5, 12 ; S. 242, 7. Forspennendlice geférrǽdenne *inlecebrosa consortia*, An. Ox. 223. Tō horena geférrǽdenum *ad meretricum contubernia*, 3330. ¶ on sumes geférrǽdenne beón (habban) *to be (have as) a person's companion, associate*, &c. :—þ hē sceolde woroldlicum wǽpnum onsón and on cininges ðegna geférrǽdenne beón, Bl. H. 213, 3 : 211, 23. Hwelc is wyrsa wōl oððe ǽngum men māre daru þonne hē hæbbe on his geférrǽdenne and on his nēweste feónd on freóndes anlícnesse *quae pestis efficacior ad nocendum quam familiaris inimicus?*, Bt. 29, 2 ; F. 106, 14. þ hwā wolde on þǽre geférrǽdenne beón þe hē wǽre, and þ lufian þ hē lufode, Ll. Th. i. 162, 5. (2) of things :—Hū ne wāst þū þ hit nis nāuht gewunelic þ ǽnig wiþerweard ðing beón gemenged wiþ óðrum wiþerweardum, oððe ǽnige geférrǽdenne wið habban *neque enim sibi solent adversa sociari*, Bt. 16, 3 ; F. 54, 13. Ða gesceafta forlǽtaþ heora geférrǽdenne (*sociam fidem*), 21 ; F. 74, 35. II. concrete, *a society of persons* : —Gif hit mycel geférrǽden (*congregatio*) is, sȳn hȳ mid antefene gesungene, R. Ben. 41, 7, 8. Samnig eeal geférrǽden tō þǽre rǽdincge, 67, 5. On ǽghwilcan mynstre singe eal geférrǽden ǽtgædere heora saltere, Wlfst. 181, 21. Ælfwíg abbud and eall seó geférrǽden on Baðan, C. D. iv. 171, 28. Geférrǽdene, inhírede *clientela*, An. Ox. 2809. II a. of animals :—Ða fuglas ðe ānes cynnes beóð seldon willað forlǽtan hiera geférrǽdenne (*sese deserunt*), Past. 349, 22.

**ge-férscipe.** *Add*: I. abstract. (1) of persons :—Ðæt hié ne sceolden forhyggean ðone geférscipe ðāra synfulra, Past. 103, 15. Hē hine on úrne geférscipe ðurh flǽsces gecynd gemengde *sese nobis per naturae nostrae consortium junxit*, 167, 23. (2) of animals or things :—Sum fearhryþer þæs ōþræs ceápes geférscipe oferhogode, Bl. H. 199, 4. Se yfela willa næfþ nǽnne geférscipe wiþ þā gesǽlþa *ad beatitudinem probra non veniunt*, Bt. 36, 7 ; F. 184, 31. II. concrete. (1) *a collection of persons*. (a) in a general sense, *a company* :—Weard eall se geférscipe (*Ulysses' companions*) forhwerfed tō deórcynnum, Bt. 38, 1 ; F. 196, 2. On þes arcðes gewitnesse and on ealles þæs geférscipes þe him mid wæs, Chr. 1022 ; P. 157, 7. þ þǽr mihten men gyrnan þāra

úplicra burhwara and þæs ēcean geférscipes, Bl. H. 197, 17. Betwuxn his engla geférscipe *inter angelorum choros*, Past. 261, 12. Deóffelicum geférscipe *demonico globo*, Wrt. Voc. ii. 138, 65. Gif gē mē (*the cook*) ūt ādrífaþ fram eówrum geférscipe (*collegio*), Coll. M. 29, 9. (b) in special senses. (a) *a society* of ecclesiastics :—þeáh feáwa witena on þām geférscipe beón, R. Ben. 116, 19. Hādbót . . . ān dǽl þām biscope, óðer þām wībede and þridde geférscipe, Ll. Th. ii. 242, 18. (β) *an association, a guild* :—Scute ǽlc man swā pænig, swā healfne, be þæs geférscipes mǽnio, Ll. Th. i. 234, 10. Ān gildscipe is gegaderod on Wudeburglande, and . . . habað underfangen þone ilcan geférscipe on bróðorrǽdenne, Cht. Th. 609, 3. (γ) *a profession, order* :—Cyning sceal hæbban gebedmen and fyrdmen and weorcmen . . . Ðæt is eác his andweorc þ hē habban sceal . . . þām þrím geférscipum bīwiste . . . gehwæt þæs þe þā þríe geférscipas behófiaþ, Bt. 17 ; F. 58, 33–60, 5. (δ) *a class, social order* :—þǽr ðū gemunan woldest hwylcra gebyrda þū wǽre and hwylcra burgwara for worulde, oþþe ett gāstlíce hwilces geférscipes ðū wǽre on ðínum móde, Bt. 5, 1 ; F. 10, 4. (ε) *a retinue, court ; comitatus* :—Cōm hē mid þā cwēne . . . hē wæs hyre þéna and hyre húses and hyre geférscypes oferealdormon *erat primus ministrorum et princeps domus eius*, Bd. 4, 3 ; Sch. 353, 2. Cyningas bióþ úton ymbstandende mid miclon geférscipe hiora þegna, Bt. 37, 1 ; F. 186, 4. Hē þone ealdor ealra þeóstra geband, and ealne his geférscipe gedréfde, Bl. H. 85, 6. (2) *a company of animals* :—Ða fuglas ðe ānes cynnes bióð seldon willað forlǽtan hiora geférscipe (*sese deserunt*), Past. 348, 22.

**ge-féstr[i]an** *to nourish* :—Wæs geféstred *uesceretur*, An. Ox. 5035. Wǽre geféd, þ hē wæs gefést[r]ud *uesceretur*, i. *reficeret*, 3053.

**ge-fetelsod;** *adj.* (*ptcpl.*). *Substitute* : *Belted, provided with a belt*: —Twā sweord gefetelsode, C. D. ii. 380, 28. v. fetelsod.

**ge-féðe.** *Dele*: ge-feþeran. *Add* : v. un-gefeþered.

**ge-feþrian;** *p.* ode *To load* :—Gefeðrige hē hys wǽnas mid fegrum gerdum, Solil. H. 1, 11. [Iueððred, þet is icharged, A. R. 204.] v. fóþer.

**ge-fetian.** *Add*: I. *to go in quest of and bring back*. (1) the object a person :—Se cniht gefette þ mǽden mid woruldlicum wurðmynte, Hml. S. 34, 21. Amilcor wæs of Sicilium him tō fultume gefett *accitum ex Sicilia Amilcarem*, Ors. 4, 6 ; S. 174, 20. Gefetodne *accitum*, Wrt. Voc. ii. 4, 35. Gefetodnae, gefetatnae, gefeotodne *accetum*, Txts. 42, 105. Gefetadne *arceri* (*jubet Augustus vatem*), Wrt. Voc. ii. 92, 34 : 3, 78. Wurdon gefætte ætforan þām dēman þā crīstenan, Hml. S. 2, 197. (2) the object a thing :—Hī ofer six mīla him wæter on heora exlum gefetton, Hml. Th. i. 562, 4. II. *to go and get* what one seeks, *get, obtain*. (1) with concrete object :—Crīst sitt on heofonum mid þām hālgum þe hē on ðisum lífe gefette, Hml. Th. i. 248, 24 : ii. 368, 33. On þisum geáre Ælfsere gefette þes cyninges līchaman æt Wærham, and geferode hine tō Scæftesbyrig, Chr. 980 ; P. 123, 37. Hī gefetedon his sáule and mid him genāmon and hwurfon tō þām heofonlícan ríce *adsumta secum anima ejus, ad caelestia regna redierunt*, Bd. 4, 3 ; Sch. 364, 19. þȳ lǽs hys cnihtas cōmon and þone līchaman gefetton *ne forte veniant discipuli ejus et furentur eum* (Mt. 27, 64), Hml. As. 183, 61. (2) with abstract object. (a) a noun :—Æt þǽra byrgenan . . . manege gefettan līchamlíce hǽle, Wlfst. 4, 11. (b) a clause :—Blinde gefettan þæt hȳ lōcedan brāde, Wlfst. 5, 1. v. ge-feccan.

**ge-fic.** *Add*:—Ðonne se abbod and se prǽfost ungerāde beóð, ǽgðer ge hyra āgne sáula þurh þās frēcenesse losiað, and eác swylce þāra þe him underþeódde synd, þonne hý sume mid geficum wið þone āone þeódað and leúsettaþ, sume wið þone óþerne *dum contraria sibi invicem abbas prepositusque sentiunt, et ipsorum necesse est animas periclitari, et hi qui sub ipsis sunt, dum adulantur partibus, eunt in perditionem*, R. Ben. 125, 2. v. ficol, fician, fācen.

**ge-figo(-u);** *pl. n. A disease with fig-shaped swellings* :—Wiþ þeorāādle on eágum þe mon gefigo hæt, on Lǽden hātte *cimosis* (=σύκωσις), . . . Eft wið gefigon, Lch. ii. 38, 5–8. Wið gefigom, 2, 10.

**ge-fildan;** *p.* de *To fold up* :—Gefyldende *inplicans, ligans*, Hpt. Gl. 406, 33. v. ge-fealdan.

**ge-filde.** *Add*: [O. H. Ger. gi-fildi *campus*; *pl. campestria* : Ger. ge-filde.]

**ge-fill** *a fall* :—Getimbro temples foresægde ðā gefaello *aedificationes templi praenuntiat ruituras*, Mk. p. 5, 7.

**ge-fillan;** *p.* de. *Take here passages given under* ge-fyllan *to fell, and add* : *To cause to fall*. I. *to fell*. (1) *to strike down a living creature* :— Feónd gefyldan, . . . and hī hyne ābroten hæfdon, sibǽðelingas, B. 2706. Gif hē man tō deáðe gefylle, Ll. Th. i. 170, 10. Ealle ic mihte feóndas gefyllan, hwæðre ic fæste stód, Kr. 38. Ne weard wæl māre folces gefylled sweordes ecgum, Chr. 937 ; P. 110, 1. (1 a) fig. :—Hē ūp āhóf hond his ofer hié ðæt hé gefælde hie (*ut prosterneret eos*), Ps. Srt. 105, 26. (2) *to cut down* wood :—þā hēt ic of þæm wudo þe þǽr gefylled wæs, þ mon fȳr onǽlde, Nar. 12, 28. II. *to strike down* with disease, *destroy* :— Hæfde hē gefylled frumbearna fela, Exod. 38. III. *to overthrow* in argument, *confute* :—Gefælde *destruxit* (*temtantes*), Mt. p. 19, 6. IV.

*to let fall, drop* (trans.) :—Ofer ðone se stán bið gifælled *supra quem lapis ceciderit*, Lk. R. L. 20, 1S. **V.** *to cause to cease, put an end to* :—Þæt Pater Noster morðor gefylled, ádwæsced deófles fýr, Sal. 41. Gefiit gefælde, Lk. p. 11, 4. Gifælle ðæs líchomes untrymnisse *prosternere istam corporis infirmitatem*, Rtl. 115, 11.

**ge-fillness**, e ; *f. Ruin, overthrow* :—Æfter gefaellnisse Babilones *after the overthrow which led to the captivity in Babylon* ; post transmigrationem Babylonis, Mt. L. 1, 12. On gefælnise (gæfelnisse, R.) monigra *in ruinam multorum*, Lk. L. 2, 34.

**ge-fínd** *enemies. Take here* ge-fýnd *in Dict., and add* :—Þá sendon tó Læcedemonium and bædon þ hié gefriénd wurden, þeh hié ǽr longe gefiénd wæren *Lacedaemonios quondam hostes, tunc socios adsciscunt*, Ors. 3, 7 ; S. 118, 13. Gefýnd (*inimici*) úre synt déman, Cant. M. ad fol. 31.

**ge-findan.** *Add :* (1) *to come upon, meet with.* v. findan ; **I.** 1 :—Hé gefand (*invenit*) énne of efneðegnum, Mt. L. 18, 28. Hí inneádon hús gefundun (*invenerunt*) ðone cnæht, 2, 11. (2) *to find.* v. findan ; **I.** 2 :—Wecg in múðe fisces gefundon (*inventum*), Mt. p. 18, 3. (3) *to find* on trial. v. findan ; **I.** 6 :—Hit búta wæstm gefunden bið *sine fructu efficitur*, Mt. L. 13, 22. (4) *to find* by search :—Gefundena rímas *repertis numeris*, Mt. p. 4, 7. (4 a) *to recover* what is hidden away or lost. v. findan ; **II.** 1 a :—Gif losað cásering . . . Mið ðý gefindes, Lk. L. 15, 9. Hí synd nú on díglon behýdde þ hí nán man ne mæg náhwær gefindan, Hml. S. 23, 291. (5) *to determine, provide.* v. findan ; **II.** 9 :—Éac is gefunden . . . gielde þone wer bútan wíte, Ll. Th. i. 84, 12. Nú hæbbe ic gefunden mid þæm witum . . . þ þá ealle beón gearwe, 220, 4.

**ge-findig, -finegod.** *l.* ge-fyndig, -fynegod.

**ge-firenian.** *Add :*—Sé ðe willende on slǽpe gefyrenað (*peccaverit*), Ll. Th. ii. 138, 10.

**ge-fiscian** ; *p.* ode *To fish* (trans.), *to fish for, catch* or *try to catch* fish :—Críst dyde þæt hí mid his heofonlican láre manna sáwla gefixodon . . . be ðám cwæð se wítega : 'Ic ásende míne fisceras, and hí gefixiað hí' (*ego mittam piscatores, et piscabuntur eos*, Jer. 16, 16), Hml. Th. i. 576, 22-27.

**ge-fiþerhamod.** *Add :* v. fiþer-hama.

**ge-fiþerian.** *Add :* Gefiþerede *pennata*, Ps. L. 77, 27 : Bl. Gl. Gefiðeradra *pennatorum*, Kent. Gl. 2.

**ge-flǽschamod.** *Add :*—Geflǽschamod *incarnatum*, An. Ox. 944. v. flǽschama ; ge-flǽscod.

**ge-flǽscness.** *Add :*—Ic hálsie ðé þurh úres Drihtnes geflǽscnysse, Ll. Lbmn. 415, 11.

**ge-flǽscod** ; *adj.* (*ptcpl.*) *Incarnate* :—Þurh þ geflǽscode Godes word, Hml. S. 23 b, 597.

**ge-fleard.** *Add : mad, wicked folly* :—Ælce onscununge gefleardes hatað God *omne exsecramentum erroris odit Deus*, Scint. 66, 17. Micle betere is ælcum crístenum men þæt hé náne wæccan æt cyrican næbbe, þonne hé þær wacyge mid ǽnigan gefleardæ, Wlfst. 279, 13. Beón hí (*bishops*) á ymbe wísdóm, and æghwylc gefleard unwyrð lǽtan, Ll. Th. ii. 316, 27. Hig prútlíce gýmað þæs miotacismus gefleard, Angl. viii. 313, 25. Gedwolmanna gefleard *schismaticorum deliramenta*, An. Ox. 418.

**ge-flenod** (-flén-?) ? :—Hacele geflenod *lacerna*, Wrt. Voc. i. 59, 22.

**ge-fleógan.** *Add :*—His gást sceolde gefleógan tó heofena heáhnysse, Shrn. 112, 11. Se earn on ðám ófre gesæt, mid fisce geflogen, þone hé ðǽrrihte geféng, Hml. Th. ii. 140, 3.

**ge-fleón.** *Add :* [(1) *to flee.*] (2) *to fly* :—Ne mæg úre sáwul gefleón tó heofonan ríce, búton heó hæbbe fiðera þ ǽre sóðan lufe, Hml. Th. ii. 318, 26. v. ge-flygena.

**ge-flíman.** *Take here* ge-flǽman, -fléman, -flíéman, -flýman *in Dict., and add :* (1) *to put to flight* a defeated enemy :—Þá Gotan hié mid gefeohte gefliémdon *victo exercitu*, Ors. 6, 34 ; S. 290, 25. Hé gefeaht wiþ Gotan and gefliémed weard, and bedrifen on ánne tún, S. 292, 1. Grendel wérigmód on weg þanon . . . fǽge and gefiýmed feórlástas bær, B. 846. (1 a) of spiritual foes :—Þú scealt wið feónda gehwæne healdan sáuwle þíne ; á hí winnað . . . þú miht hý gefliýman, Dóm. L. 32, 67. Geflémede sié diúblas *fugantur demones*, Rtl. 145, 14. (2) *to put to flight, chase* an animal :—Hédstapa hundum geswenced, heorot . . . feorran gefliýmed, B. 1370. (3) *to drive away* inanimate objects :—Hé hafaþ ealle þíne þeóstro mid his beorhtnesse gefliémed, Bl. H. 85, 22.

**ge-flíme.** v. ge-flíme *in Dict.*: ge-flíít vannus. *Dele.*

**ge-flíít.** *l.* -flit, *and add* :—Geflit *capistrinum*, Wrt. Voc. ii. 103, 33 : *capestrinum*, 13, 60. Compung and gefiit *concertatio*, 20, 40. Gefiit and gecíd *divortium*, 28, 26. *Cavillum, cavillatio* bismrung, gefiit *convitium*, 129, 68. Gefiite *divortio*, 28, 14. (1) *strife, contention* in the abstract :—Nis þér (*heaven*) ege, ne gefiit, ne yrre, ne nænig wiþerweardnes, Bl. H. 25, 31. Oferhýdo ond gefiite and æfeste *animositati, contentioni, inuidiae*, Bd. 1, 14 ; Sch. 38, 24. Gefeoht þe of gefiite cymð betwux ceastergewarum *bellum ciuile*, Hml. S. 25, 711. (2) *a dispute, contest, difference.* (a) in an unfavourable sense :—Gefiit *tumultus*, Mt. L. 27, 24. Gefiitt (gifiit, R.) áuorden uæs bituih Iudéum *dissensio facta est inter Iudaeos*, Jn. 10, 19. Gefiitt *schisma*, 9, 16. Lætað áweg ealle

saca and ælc gefiitt, and gehealdað þás tíd mid sibbe and mid sóðre lufe, Hml. Th. i. 180, 1. Ðonne betweoxn eów bið yfel anda and gefiitu (*contentio*), Past. 345, 14. Hié styrigað gefiitu (-flietu, *v. l.*) and geciid *rixae occasionem commovent*, 293, 20. Geseah hé ðá mǽstan gefiitu (-fleoto, *v. l.*) and gewinn þára werigra gásta *uidit . . . maxima inalig norum spirituum certamina*, Bd. 3, 19 ;. Sch. 278, 7. (b) where there is no ill-will :—Þæt Herebald fram ðám gefiite (*certamine*) [*a race*] hine áhebbe, Bd. 5, 6 ; Sch. 575, 16. (3) in a military sense :—Hié woldon . . . gefeohtan . . . and monig ígland áwéstan on ðæm gefiite, Ors. 3, 11 ; S. 144, 30. On þére tíde wǽron Iudan on miclum gefiite and on micelre unsibbe wið þá landleóde *adversus incolas Iudaei atrocissima bella gesserunt*, 6, 10 ; S. 266, 1. Hié micel gefiit hæfdon *in arma surgentes*, 6, 34 ; S. 290, 24. (4) *a contest with words, dispute, disputation, argument* :—Áworden wæs gefiit (gifiitt, R., *contentio*) bituih him huelc hiora geseen woere mára, Lk. L. 22, 24. Þ gefiit, p. 11, 3. Gefiites, tale *disputationis*, i. *certationis*, An. Ox. 2267. On gefiite *certamine* (v. Ald. 151, 35), Wrt. Voc. ii. 91, 8 : 19, 31. Gefiit *conflictum* (*contra certantes arte magistros*), 91, 6. Æfter þyssum wǽron manegu gefiitu, Bl. H. 187, 7. Gefiitum *conflictibus* (*disputans*), Wrt. Voc. ii. 81, 25 : 18, 27. (5) in a legal sense, *a dispute that is to be settled by a judge, a contested case* :—Higa eóde of ðám gefiite (cf. Higa wolde him oðflitan ðæt lond, 169, 23), Cht. Th. 174, 2. Hwí biþ elles ælce dæg swelc seófung and swelce gefiitu and gemót and dómas *unde forenses querimoniae*?, Bt. 26, 2 ; F. 92, 16. Gefiitum *negotiis*, An. Ox. 5391. Ðæt hé gesette óðre for hine tó démenne betweox ðæm folce ymbe hira gefiita (-o, *v. l.*) *ut pro se alios adjurgia dirimenda constituat*, Past. 131, 16. (5 a) figurative :—In þám freóndlican gefiite (*contentione*) þére wrixiendlican eádmódnesse þér eóde tó genóh rihtwís déma, þ wæs se cniht þe wæs átogen of þám wætre, Gr. D. 116, 6. ¶ tó gefiites :—Tó gefiites *certatim*, i. *strenue*, An. Ox. 106 : 2232. Ælc óþrum tó gefiites (*certatim*), hú hé swýðust mæge, hýrsumige, R. Ben. 132, 2. Tó gefiites hé swincað on weorce *certatim in opere laborantes*, 136, 15. v. fyrn-, samod-, weorold-gefiit.

**ge-flíítan.** *Add :*—Hié (*S. Peter and S. Paul*) wiþ Simone þæm drý fǽstlíce gefiiton and gewunnon, Bl. H. 173, 2. Seó mǽtingc bið gecornes and gefiitnes (*disputed matter*) and eall costunge full, Lch. iii. 156, 7. [*O. H. Ger.* ge-flízan.]

**gefiit-ful.** *l.* -flit-, *and add* :—Gefiitful *peruicax*, i. *contunax*, ł *superbus*, An. Ox. 4094. Ðá gesibsuman menn sind Godes bearn gecígede, and witodlíce ðá gefiitfullan sind deófles lyma, Hml. Th. i. 604, 34.

**gefiitful-ness**, e ; *f. Contentiousness, quarrelsomeness* :—Míne synna þe ic . . . gefremede . . . on hatunge and on gefiitfulnesse, Angl. xi. 102, 84.

**gefiit-georn.** *Add :*—Gif hira hwylc gefiitgeorn (*contentiosus*) bið, R. Ben. 130, 20. Ne ænig man ne sý tó sacfull ne ealles tó gefiitgeorn, Wlfst. 70, 19 : Lch. iii. 428, 34. Beón úre fét gesceóde mid þære sybbe bodunge, and úre stafas sýn on úrum handum tó sleánne þá wyrmas . . . Hwæt synt þá wyrmas búton lýðre men and gefiitgeorne, Angl. viii. 323, 31.

**gefiit-glíw**, es ; *n. Jeering, mockery* :—Gefiitglíwe (*printed* -slit-) *cavillatione* (cf. *cavillatio* bismrung, gefiit *convitium*, 129, 68), Wrt. Voc. ii. 85, 65 : 18, 65.

**gefiit-mǽlum.** *Add :*—Gehírsumnesse him sylf gefiitmǽlum (*certatim*) hí beódan, R. Ben. I. 117, 8.

**ge-flog**, es ; *n. Infectious disease* :—Þ nǽfre for gefioge feorh hé gesealde, syþðan him mon mægðan tó mete gegyrede,. Lch. iii. 34, 9. Cf. on-fsiyge.

**ge-flogena.** v. wuldor-gefiogena.

**ge-flówan.** *Add :* From gifǽue *affluit*, Rtl. 81, 12.

**ge-fnésan** ; *p.* -fnæs, *and add* :—Ad sternutationem. Þis þá tylung tó þan manne þe wel gefnesan ne mæge, Lch. iii. 100, 9.

**ge-fóg.** *Add :*—Gefóg *commissuram*, Wrt. Voc. ii. 72, 37 : 17, 44. þára gefóga *compaginum*, Lch. i. lxxii, 9. Gefógum *compaginum, conjunctionum*, Wrt. Voc. ii. 132, 72. v. stán-gefóg, *and cf.* ge-fég.

**ge-fóg**, es ; *n. Fitness* :—Gedó on þ fæt þe þú hit mæge on mid gefóge geseóþan *put it into a vessel in which you can suitably seethe it*, Lch. ii. 28, 16. v. un-gefóg, *and next word.*

**ge-fóg** ; *adj. Fit, suitable* :—Be þæs monnes mihtum sceal mon þá lǽcedómas sellan þe þonne gefóge synd heáfde and heortan, Lch. ii. 238, 21. v. un-gefóg, *and preceding word.*

**ge-fóge.** v. un-gefóge : ge-fóglic. [*O. H. Ger.* ge-fuoglîh *aptus.*] v. un-gefóglic : ge-fóglíce. v. un-gefóglíce.

**gefóg-stán**, es ; *m. A stone hewn so as to be ready for use in building* :—Wé scylen beón on ðisse ældeódignesse útane beheáwene mid swingellan, tó ðæm ðæt wé eft sién geteald and geféged tó ðæm gefógstánum on ðære Godes ceastre bútan ðám hiéwete ælcre suingean *nunc foris per flagella tundimur, ut intus in templum Dei postmodum sine disciplinae percussione disponamur*, Past. 253, 19. v. stán-gefóg.

**ge-folc.** *Dele :* gefole. *l.* ge-fol.

**ge-folgian** ; *p.* ode *To reach, attain* :—Ðonne hé him ǽr tíde tó tióð

ðæt hí ne magon ne ne cunnon, ðonne is him tó ondrǽdanne ðæt him weorðe tó lore ðæt hié tó ryhtre tíde gefolgian meahton *ne cum arripiunt intempestive quod non valent, perdant quod implere quandoque tempestive potuissent*, Past. 383, 27.

**ge-fón.** *Add:* I. *trans. To take, catch.* (1) *To catch* animals, fish, &c. :—Hwylce wildeór swýþost geféhst þú? Ic gefeó heortas, Coll. M. 21, 29. Mænige gefóþ (*capiunt*) hwælas, 25, 1. Hú geféncge hú hig? Heortas ic gefénge (-fengc? *cepi*) on nettum and bár ic ofslóh, 22, 9–11. Þá fixas þe gē geféngon (*prendistis*), Jn. 21, 10. Gefóh fox, Lch. ii. 104, 12. Þē gehuntian and gefón mid þám nettum mínre mildheortnysse, Hml. S. 30, 49. (1 a) fig. *to catch, entrap* a person :—Þte hiá geféngo, (gefinge, R.) hine in word *ut caperent eum in sermone*, Mt. L. 22, 15. (2) *to take hold of, take;* of vigorous or hasty action, *to seize, grasp* :—Gif ic míne fíðeru gefó *si sumsero pennas meas*, Ps. Th. 138, 7. Ic on ofoste geféng micle mid mundum mægenbyrðenne hordgestreóna, hider út ætbǽr cyninge mínum, B. 3090. Hē geféng fetelhilt hreóh and heorogrim, 1563. Hond rond geféng, 2609. Hiá geféngon lēhtfat *acceptis lampadibus*, Mt. L. 25, 3. (2 a) with abstract object :—Þū hafast unbiþyrfe ofer witena dóm wísan gefongen, Jul. 98. Þis is ealdordóm uncres gewinnes on fruman gefongen (v. ealdordóm ; IV), Jul. 191. (2 b) with the idea of violence, *to seize* a person :—Hē geféng slǽpende rinc, B. 740. Ðá óðero geféngon (*tenuerunt*) ðegnas his and ofslógun, Mt. L. 22, 6. Geféngon ï wæs gefóen hine *apprehensum eum*, 21, 39. Mið ðý gefóen wēron ðegnas his *apprehensis servis ejus*, 21, 35. (2 b β) *to seize* in a struggle :—Gráp þá tōgeánes, gúðrinc geféng atolan clommum, B. 1501. Geféng be eaxle Gúðgeáta leód Grendles módor, 1537. (2 c) in a legal sense, *to arrest, apprehend, take* :—Ðe aldormonn and embehtmenn geféngon (giféngun, R.) ðone Hǽlend *tribunus et ministri comprehenderunt Iesum*, Jn. L. 18, 12. Gif hwa on cyninges healle gefeohte . . . and hine man gefó, Ll. Th. i. 66, 9. Bebudan Rómáne þæt mon Hannibal gefénge, Ors. 4, 11 ; S. 204, 26. Þte geféngo (gifēngun, R., *apprachendant*) hine, Jn. 11, 57. Þá smeádon hí þ hí geféngon hine *quaerebant eum tenere*, Mk. 12, 12. Swá swá tó ánum sceaðan gē férdon mid swurdon mē gefón (tō gefóanne, L., *comprehendere*), 14, 48. (2 d) *to take in war, capture* :—Hē geeóde Agrientum þa burg, and geféng (*cepit*) Hannonam heora lǽtteów, Ors. 4, 10 ; S. 196, 33. Hē gefeaht wiþ .vii. sciphlǽstas, and hiera án geféng, and þa óþru gefliémde, Chr. 875 ; P. 74, 6. Hí .ix. scipu geféngun, 851 ; P. 64, 15 : 897 ; P. 90, 26. Hí geféngun Praen and gebundenne hine on Mierce lǽddon, 796 ; P. 56, 8. Þær weard Orithia gefangen (*capta*), Ors. 1, 10 ; S. 48, 1 : 4, 11 ; S. 208, 18. Þær wæs Hasterbal ofslagen . . . and vm his heres gefangen, 4, 10 ; S. 198, 29 : 4, 11 ; S. 204, 18. Se here gewende tó scipon mid þám þingum þe hí gefangen hæfdon, Chr. 1016 ; P. 153, 7. Fela wurdon ofslægen and eác gefangene, 1079 ; P. 214, 30. (3) *to receive, accept* :—Hié geféngon mearde hiora *receperunt mercedem suam*, Mt. L. 6, 2. Mið ðý geféngon *accipientes*, 20, 11. Hiá gefóen hæfdon feh *accepta pecunia*, 28, 15. (4) *to get, obtain, gain, take* courage (*with inst.*) :—Sárge gē ne sóhton, ne him swǽslic word frófre gesprǽcon, þæt hý þý freóran hyge móde geféngen, Cri. 1513. (5) *to take, bring, carry* :—Gefēng (*assumpsit*) hine dióbul in hálig ceastra, Mt. L. 4, 5. II. *intrans. To lay hold* :—Gif mon on cirliscre fǽmnan breóst gefó, Ll. Th. i. 68, 14. Gif hwa on nunnan hrægl oþþe on hire breóst bútan hire leáfe gefó, 72, 9. II a. fig. *to put one's hand* to a matter, *make attempt* at :—Hē hæfde ful oft ǽr on gearnan, C. D. ii. 113, 12. [*Goth.* ga-fáhan : *O. Sax. O. H. Ger.* gi-fáhan.]

**ge-forewyrdan, -wordan.** *Take here* ge-forword *in Dict., and add : To settle* the terms of an agreement, *agree* :—Nū wille ic ðæt heora cwide stande swá swá hit geforewird wes on gódre manna gewitnesse, C. D. iv. 201, 4. Standan ðá forword ðe ǽr wið ðæne arcebiscop geforwyrd wǽran, iii. 352, 5. v. fore-word.

**ge-forþian.** *Add:* I. *to put forth, proffer, present, contribute* :—Hē ongan smeágan hwæt him sǽlost tó geforðienne of his cynelicum mádmum Gode tó lofe and him silfum tó ēcere þearfe, C. D. B. ii. 389, 13. [Cf. Forþe we him ure rihte bileue and luue for gersum *proferamus ei de cordis nostri thesauro fidei sensum*, O. E. Hml. 43, 11.] II. *to forward, prosper, promote the well-being of* :—Hē hí geforðode on tægerum þeáwum, Hml. A. 94, 83. His engel geforðige ðē and þíne fare gewissige, Hml. S. 22, 29. Hú hē yrðe mæge fyrme geforðian, Angl. ix. 261, 5. III. *to carry out, accomplish, perform* :—Se cniht þá brýdlác geforþode, Hml. S. 34, 21. Þ hē under him ðane hálgan regol geforðian æfter mynsterlicum þeáwe *that he might carry out the holy rule according to monastic custom*, Cht. Th. 242, 5. Dauid hit hæfde gemynt ǽr tó dónne, ac hē ne geforðede hit ná, ac hit weard þurh his sunu geforðad, Wlfst. 277, 26. Sē þe þis forsitte and hit geforðian nylle, Ll. Th. i. 284, 4 : ii. 288, 22 : Chr. 1097 ; P. 233, 24. 'Man ofsleá Amanes mágas.' Þis weard geforþod, Hml. A. 101, 312. On þone seofoðan dæg ðú gerestest. Þá wæs geforðad ðín fægere weorc, Btwk. 198, 8.

**ge-forweorþan.** *Dele* :—Gefótcypstra *compeditorum*, Ps. L. 101, 21 : ge-forword. v. ge-forewyrdan.

**ge-frǽge ; adj.** *Add* :—Gefrǽge *audita*, Wrt. Voc. ii. 6, 12. Eálá, mín Drihten, þæt þú eart ælmihtig, micel, módilic, mǽrþum gefrǽge and

wundorlic (cf. hú micel and hú wunderlic þú eart, Bt. 33, 4 ; F. 128, 4), Met. 20, 2. Rómwara betest, monna módwelegost, mǽrðum gefrǽgost, Past. 9, 12. v. un-gefrǽge.

**ge-frǽgelic, -frǽg(e)líce.** v. un-gefrǽgelic, -gefrǽglíce : gefrǽgen. v. ge-fricgan.

**ge-frǽgnan.** *For strong forms see* frignan, *and to weak forms from* ge-frægn(i)an *add* :—Gefraignas *interrogauerit*, Lk. L. 19, 31. Gefraignde *interrogavit*, 15, 26 : 23, 9. Gefraignades *interrogabant*, Mt. L. 12, 10. Gefrægndon *interrogauerunt*, Mk. L. 4, 10. Gefregndon, 1, 27.

**ge-frætewian.** *Add : to equip, dress, attire* :—Wē úrne líchoman gefrætwiað, Bl. H. 99, 7. Gefratwode *conficit*, Germ. 401, 122. On swylcum heówe swá hié ǽr hié sylfe gefrætwodan, Bl. H. 95, 19. On his lífes þeáwum hē wæs swíþe gefrætwod, Hml. S. 23 b, 20. Mid golde and seolfre gefrætwod, Bl. H. 127, 8. Þ se dæg fullíce gefrætwod sý (*be equipped*) mid feówer and twēntig tídum, Angl. viii. 306, 13. Onginneþ seó feórþe bóc gefrætwedu and áwritenu mid wíslicum wordum and on gesprǽcum witena, gr. D. 259, 22. Gefrætwadne *compturum*, Wrt. Voc. ii. 95, 29. Þær sǽton six árwurðlíce menn, swíðe wurðlíce gefrætwad, Vis. Lfc. 19. v. un-, ymb-gefrætwod.

**ge-frætwung, e ; f.** *Ornament, adornment* :—Gefratewung reáfa *ornatus uestium*, Scint. 144, 13. Gefratewunga líchamena *ornamenta corporum*, 18. G[e]fratewun[ga] *ornamentorum*, An. Ox. 4819.

**ge-frásian.** *Add* :—Gefrásende wēron in huelc mæht wuudra dyde, of fuluiht gefrásas *interrogantes in qua potestate mira patraret, de baptismo Iohannis interrogat*, Mt. p. 18, 19–19, 1.

**ge-frécnod.** *Substitute :* ge-frécnian ; *p.* ode. I. *to endanger, imperil* :—Gif hí on sǽ oððe on lande gefrécnode beón, Hml. S. 30, 436. II. *to make or become fierce* :—Hyra aldor máne gemenged, móde gefrécnod (cf. hē wæs rēðe and rǽdleás, 177), Dan. 184.

**ge-frēdan.** *Add :* (1) *absolute, To have sensation* :—Seó sáwul is *sensus, þ* is andgit oððe félnyss, þonne heó gefrét, Hml. S. 1, 184. (2) *to be sensible of* an object that touches the body :—Se lǽce wile ðæt se untruma his lǽceseax gefréde, ǽr hē hit geseó, Past. 187, 10 : 331, 21. Gefrédan hiere feónda speru, 277, 23. Ðon má ðe mon his feax mæg gefrédan bútan ðám felle, 139, 21. Sē þe bær líc gefréddan wolde, hē hyt scolde myd barum handum gefrédan, Solil. H. 43, 14. (2 a) *to feel* a blow, heat, cold, &c. :—Ðú þás dyntas náht ne gefrétst, Hml. S. 4, 147. Hē þæs fýres bryne gefrédde him onbútan, 31, 884. (3) *to be sensible* of an action (*gen.*) :—Ðæt feax grēwð ofer ðǽm brægene and his (*the growing*) mon ðeáh ne gefréd (-frēt, *v. l.*) *capilli super cerebrum insensibiliter oriuntur*) . . . Suá giémeleáslíce oft sceacað úre geðóhtas from ús, ðæt wē his (*the careless escape of the thoughts*) furðum ne gefrédað (*quasi nobis non sentientibus procedunt*), Past. 139, 16–20. (4) of the sense of taste :—Ðý lǽs hē ðá bieternesse ðǽre wyrte gefréde, Past. 303, 15. (5) *to be sensible of* a state or condition :—Hē swilces nán þing ofer þ on him sylfum ne gefrédde (ongæt, *v. l.*), Gr. D. 102, 4. Him bið ðæt sár ðe gefrédre, gif sió wund bið tó ungemetlíce fæste gewriðen *ita ut gravius scissuram sentiat, si hanc immoderatius ligamenta constringant*, Past. 123, 19. (a) *with acc. and complement, to feel* a thing so and so :—Hē hine selfne untrumran gefréd on his líchoman, Past. 407, 25. (b) *with clause* :—Þær þær hit gefrét þ hit hraþost weaxan mæg, Bt. 34, 10 ; F. 148, 21. Ðonne gefréd (-frēt, *v. l.*) hē ǽresð hwelc heó tó habbanne wæs, Past. 249, 7. Ðæt hit ongieton and gefréden ðæt hié suá micle má beóð Godes bearn, 251, 21.

**ge-frédelíce.** v. un-gefrédelíce.

**ge-frédmǽlum.** *Substitute : Gradually, little by little, imperceptibly* :—Gefrédmǽlum, stundmǽlum *sensim, paulatim*, Hpt. Gl. 482, 50.

**ge-fréfran.** *Take here* ge-fréfrian, *and add* :—God sylf gefréfrað ús, Hml. S. 25, 123 : Hml. Th. i. 550, 30. Þú mē gefréfrodest (-adest, *v. l.*) *consolatus es me*, R. Ben. 60, 2. Hē þone nacodan mid náhte ne gefréfrode, Hml. Th. ii. 500, 25. Ðá earman men gefréfra mid þínum gódum, i. 180, 6. Gifroefrað gié bituiën *consolamini invicem*, Rtl. 28, 41. Þæs cildes dreórignysse gefréfrian, ii. 134, 19 : i. 338, 1. Hē wæs gefréfred *solatur*, An. Ox. 2279.

**ge-fréogan.** v. ge-friguan.

**ge-fremdian** *to make an alien of* a person, *excommunicate* :—Gefremdiga *anathematizare*, Mk. L. 14, 17. [*O. H. Ger.* ge-fremiden *abalienare, privari* ; gefremidôt *anathema sit*.]

**ge-fremednes.** *Substitute* þ þá word sóþe wēron seó gefremednes (*effectus*) Stephanes deáðes, Gr. D. 318, 15.

**ge-fremian, ge-fremman.** *Take these together, and add :* I. *intrans. To get good, profit* :—Náht ne gefremaþ feónd on him *nihil proficiet inimicus in eo*, Ps. L. 88, 23. II. *trans.* (1) *to advance, further, promote* :—Gefremið, gifraemith, gifremit *provehit*, Txts. 89, 1629. Hine God ofer ealle men forð gefremede, B. 1718. Gifremid, -fraemid *provecta*, Txts. 84, 759. Gefremed, Wrt. Voc. ii. 68, 39. (2) *to effect, accomplish, commit* a crime :—Ic þonne gefremme þæs monnes neáðþearfnesse, Shrn. 77, 8. Eall þú gefremest *tu perfecisti eam*, Ps. Th. 67, 10. Gefremeþ *committat*, Wrt. Voc. ii. 132, 37 : *efficit*, i. *perficit*, 142, 58. Hí gylt gefremmað, Ps. C. 14. Gefremode *transegit* (*anachoreseos*

*vitam*), An. Ox. 2518. Þæt gefremede Diulius þæt þ angin weard tîdlîce þurhtogen *quod Diulius celeriter inplevit*, Ors. 4, 6; S. 172, 2. Gefreme *perfice*, Ps. Srt. 16, 5. Gefrem *exerce*, Germ. 401, 65. Hê wolde his gebeót mid weorcum gefremman, Hml. S. 25, 621 : Crü. 62. Hwæt sêlest wære tô gefremmanne, B. 174. Gefremed *commissum*, Wrt. Voc. ii. 14, 52 : *expedita*, 145, 38. Ðâ hwîle þe hit biþ on his môde, ǽr þâm þe hit gefremed weorþe, Bt. 39, 5; F. 218, 23. Weard seó menniscnys þurh þone micclan willan gefremmed, Hml. Th. i. 196, 25. Of gefremedre genihtsumnysse *de congesta* (*virtutum*) *copia*, An. Ox. 3344. Þâ gefremedon *commissa*, Wrt. Voc. ii. 23, 37. (2 a) as a verb of incomplete predication :—Ús þis se æðeling ýdre gefremede, Cri. 627. Þæt hê crîsten wære gefremed *ut Christianus efficeretur*, Bd. 1, 4; Sch. 16, 19. ¶ ge-fremed *perfect* :—Ic wille beón gefremed in lîtlum weorce, Shrn. 35, 20. v. ǽr-, riht-, un-gefremed.

ge-fremming, e; *f.* I. *furtherance, a making effectual* :—Godes miht him wæs mid tô gefremminge heora bodunga *God's power was with them to make their preaching effectual*, Hml. Th. i. 310, 16. II. *operation, effect* :—Syle drincan .ix. dagas, þu wundrasð ðǽre gefremmincge, Lch. i. 110, 22. Gefremminge, 290, 13. Þæt hê ne geortrûwige on bênum gefremmincge *ut non desperet precibus effectum*, Scint. 33, 9. II a. *accomplishment, fulfilment of a dream* :—Swefen næsð gefremincge, Lch. iii. 184, 15. Gefremminge, 186, 4. Gefreminge, 12. v. on-gefremming.

ge-fremðian. v. ge-fremdian.

ge-freógan. *Add* : I. *to free*. (1) *to free* from slavery :—Eádgyfu gefreóde Æþelgyfe, Wuncildes wîf, on feówer wegas on middes sumeres mæsseæfen, Cht. E. 256, 3 : 255, 18, 31. Florus his menn gefreóde ætforan ðâm weófode, Hml. S. 6, 239. Marh gefreóde Leðelt and ealle hire teám on his ǽgen reliquias, and hê hié hêt lǽdan tô mynstere and gefreógian on Petrocys reliquias, Cht. Th. 626, 36. Gefreód hêr on tûne, 626, 25. Gefreód *manumissus*, Wrt. Voc. i. 60, 4 : ii. 59, 17. Þâ þe æhtborene synt and for þâm ânum gefreóde, R. Ben. 138, 21. Hêr geswutelað on ðisse Crîstes bêc ðæt Ælfric Scot and Ægelric Scot synt gefreód for Ælfsiges abbodes sâwle tô êcan freóte, C. D. vi. 209, 13 : 211, 2. Uê nænigum ne gehêrdon ǽfre, huu ðû cueðes, 'Gê biðon gefriód (-frióðe, R.),' Jn. L. 8, 33. (1 a) figuratively :—Gif sunu iów gefrióð (-friáð, L.), sóðlîce frió gé bióðon, Jn. R. 8, 36. Gefriáð, 32. (2) *to free* from bonds, prison, captivity, &c., *liberate, release* :—Cwôm engel Godes and þæt fŷr tôsceáf, gefreóde fâcnes clæne (*Juliana*), Jul. 565. Se cyng lædde fyrde intô Wealan and þǽr gefreóde fela hund manna, Chr. 1081; P. 214, 13. Gefreóge (-friged, L.) hine gif hê wile *liberet eum si vult eum*, Mt. R. 27, 43. Hwæþer cume Elias and gefreóge (cyme gefriéga) hine *an veniat Helias liberans eum*, 49. Of seáðe gefreód *de puteo liberatum*, Lk. p. 8, 9. (2 a) figuratively :—Seó wiðerwearde wyrd onbint and gefreóð ǽlc þâra þe hió tô geþiéð, Bt. 20; F. 72, 2. (3) *to free* from obligation, work, &c. :—Gefreód *feriatus*, Wrt. Voc. ii. 33, 55. Þeówe men þâ ðrig dagas beón weorces gefreóde, Wlfst. 181, 19 : 171, 20. (4) *to free* from tribute, penalty, &c. :—Suâ micle mâ wê ûre hiéremenn gefreógað (-eað, *v. l.*) æfter ðâm godcundan dôme, suâ wê hêr hiera synna wrecað suîðor, Past. 117, 25. Se pâpa Marinus gefreóde Ongelcynnes scôle be Ælfrêdes bêne, Chr. 885; P. 80, 5. (4 a) *to free* land from taxes or services :—Eall ðæt land sŷ êcelîce gefreód ealra þeówdôma, C. D. vi. 202, 18. Leáfa gebohte . . . ðis land mið ðŷ friáðôme ðe hit hêr gefriád wæs, C. D. B. ii. 154, 18. (5) *to free* from evil, trouble, &c. :—Gefrîg ûsich from yfle, Mt. L. 6, 13. Gifriáðo from allum yflum, Rtl. 17, 31. (5 a) *to free* from a person who troubles :—From dióble gefriáð bið *a daemonio liberatur*, Mk. p. 4, 7. Mið ðŷ ðû gást mið wiðerworde ðînum, sel geornlîce þte ðû sê gefreód from him, Lk. L. 12, 58. II. *to love, embrace* :—Gefrîgode hiá *complexans eos*, Mk. L. 10, 16.

ge-freógend, -frîgend, es; *m. A liberator* :—Gefrîgend (gefreógynd, Ps. Spl. C.) *liberator*, Ps. Srt. 17, 49, 3 : 39, 18.

ge-freólíc; *adj. Free, ready, willing* :—God ðû ðe ûs tô gimêrsanne eástorlíc hâlgo girŷno gifriólíco gidôhtas (*liberiores animos*) giûðes, Rtl. 32, 9.

ge-freólsian. *Add* : I. *to free*. (1) *to free* from obligation, labour, &c. :—Gefreólsod *feriatus*, An. Ox. 1012. (2) *to free* from (secular) claims, *to consecrate* :—Gefreólsod *consecratur*, An. Ox. 1493. (3) *to free* from an unpleasant condition (e. g. doubt) :—Þû mê hærst gefreólsod (-frŷlsod, *v. l.*) þǽre tweóunge mînes môdes, Bt. 41, 3; F. 248, 25. II. *to celebrate* a festival :—Is heó wel wyrðe þæt hire âcennednys ârwurðlíce gefreólsod sŷ, Hml. Th. i. 354, 23.

ge-freósan; *p. pl.* -fruron *To freeze* :—Gefruron swâ swâ weallas wæteru, gefruron ŷþa on middele sǽs *gelauerunt tamquam muros aquae, gelauerunt fluctus in medio maris*, Ps. Rdr. 281, 8.

ge-freoþian. v. ge-friþian.

ge-frett. *Substitute* : ge-fretan; *p.* -fræt, *pl.* -frǽton; *pp.* -freten *To devour, consume* :—Sê ðe gefrett feh his *qui deuorauit substantiam suam*, Lk. L. 15, 30. Flêgendo gefrêten þ *uolucres comederunt illud*, 8, 5. Gefreaten bið ł gespilled bið *demolitur*, Mt. L. 6, 19.

ge-frettan; *p.* te *To devour* :—Tô flêgendum ðâ ðe gefrettað ðâ *ad volatilia quae comedunt messes*, Rtl. 147, 9.

ge-frícgan *to ask*. *Add* :—Gefraigende Drihtne *interrogante Domino*, Mt. p. 17, 16 : ge-friéga. v. ge-freógan : ge-frígian. v. ge-freógan.

ge-frignan. *Take here* ge-frinan (*l.* -frînan) *in Dict., and add* pp. -frognen. I. *to ask, question*. (1) absolute :—Ic fora iúih gefregno *ego coram uobis interrogans*, Lk. L. 23, 14. Ðâ uuðuuto gefrugnon *conquirentes*) mið him, Mk. L. R. 9, 14. (1 a) *to ask* a question, the question given in a dependent clause :—Se geroefa gefraign huoeðer ł gif monn Galilesca woere *Pilatus interrogauit si homo Galilaeus esset*, Lk. L. 23, 6. Mið him efne gefrugnon (giffrugnun, R.) huæd hit wêre, Mk. L. 9, 10. Gefraigende Drihtne huæs sunu wêre Crîst, Mt. p. 19, 8. (2) *to ask* about, after, &c. :—Gefrægn ðone weligo from lîf êce *interrogans diues de uita aeterna*, Lk. p. 9, 16. (2 a) where (2) and (1 a) are combined :—Gifraigað of sedum aldum, huoelc sié woeg gôd, Rtl. 36, 13. (3) *to ask. question* a person :—Huæd mec gefraignes ðû ? Gefregn ðâ *quid me interrogas* ? *Interroga* me, Jn. L. 18, 21. Hine gefraignas (-frægnas, R.), 9, 23. Ne nêddarf is þte huælc ðec gefraigna (gifregne, R., *interroget*), 16, 30. Hine þ hiá gefrugno (-un, R.) *eum interrogare*, Mk. L. 9, 32. Hine forðor gefregna (*interrogare*), Mt. 22, 46. (3 a) *to ask* a person a question :—Ne darstun hine gifregna (-frægne, L.) æuiht, Lk. R. 20, 40. (3 a α) the question given in a dependent clause :—Hê gefrægn hine gif ł huoeðer huoelchuoego gesêge, Mk. L. R. 8, 23. Gefraegn, 15, 44. Gefraign, 12, 28. Gefrugnon hine ðegnas his huæt . . ., Lk. L. 8, 9. Gifrǽgnun, Jn. R. 9, 15. Gefrognen wæs hwenne cymeð rîce Godes, Lk. R. L. 17, 20 : Jn. p. 5, 12. (3 a β) the question given directly :—Gifrǽgn (-fregn, L.) hine : 'Hwæt ðê noma is,' Mk. R. 5, 9. Gefraign hine se Hǽlend cuoeð : 'Huæd ðê noma is,' Lk. L. 8, 30 : 23, 3. Gefraegn, Mk. L. 15, 4. Gefrugnon hine ðâ ðreátas cuoedendo : 'Huæd wê dôað,' Lk. L. R. 3, 10. Nǽnig mon ne gifregno (gefregne, L.) mec : 'Hwider gongestû,' Jn. R. 16, 5. Gefrægnende wæs, Mk. L. 14, 61. (3 b) *to ask* a person about something :—Ðe biscop gefraign (-frægn, R.) ðone Hǽlend of his ðegnum and ymb his lâre, Jn. L. 18, 19. Ðegnas his of ðǽm ilca gefrugnon hine, Mk. 10, 10. (4) *to ask information about* a subject :—Gefregna *inquisita*, Mk. p. 2, 4. (4 a) *to ask* a person (*acc.*) *for information about* a subject :—Gefrugnun hine ðegnas his bissen *interrogabant eum discipuli ejus parabolam*, Mk. L. 7, 17. (4 b) *to ask* of a person :—Gefrægn ðâ tîd from ðæm, Jn. 4, 53. II. *to learn by inquiry*. (1) *with acc.* :—Ic þæt wundor gefrægn, Rä. 48, 2. Hié wuldor gesâwon, swâ hæleð gefrûnon, Exod. 388. Medoærn micel gewyrcean, þonne yldo bearn ǽfre gefrûnon, B. 70. (2) *with acc. and infin.* :—Ic þæt wîf gefrægu cŷðan môdes sorge, Gen. 2242 : Sal. 179. Hî gûðcyning gefrûnon hringas dǽlan, B. 1969. (2 a) *with acc. and complementary ptcpl.* :—Se sêlesta þâra þe wê ǽfre gefrûnen âcennedne, Gû. 1334. Þâra þinga þe hêr þeóda cynn gefrugnen æt fruman geworden under wolcnum, Cri. 225.

ge-frînd *friends*. *Take here* ge-frŷnd *in Dict., and add* :—Ne furþon þætte þâ wolden gefriénd beón þe wǽron gebrôðor of fæder and of mêder, Ors. 3, 11; S. 152, 34. Hî wurdon ðâ gefrŷnd for ðǽre dǽde, swâ swâ hî nǽron nǽfre ǽr on lîfe, Hml. Th. ii. 252, 3. v. ge-fînd.

ge-friþian. *Take here* ge-freoþian *in Dict., and add* : I. *to protect, shelter*. (1) *to defend* from harm, *guard* from injury :—Þû gehǽlst ûs and gefreoðast (*custodies*) fram heora yfle, Ps. Th. 11, 8. Gif hê for slǽwðe his hlâfordes forgŷmð, ne bið his âgnum wel geborgen; gif hê eal wel gefriðað þe hê healdan sceal, ðonne bið he leánes weorðe, Ll. Th. i. 440, 17. Hine gefriðede (-frið-, *v. l.*) sió lufu and se geleáfa *quem fides et caritas abscondit*, Past. 167, 25. Hî gemêtton þǽr âne ǽrene anlícnysse þe se deófol gefriðode, Hml. Th. ii. 166, 2. Gescylded and gefreoðod (-friðedu, *v. l.*) fram þâm gyftum *defensa*, Gr. D. 199, 17. Hys yrþ sî gefriþod wiþ ealra feónda gehwæne, and heó sî geborgen wið ealra bealwa gehwylc, Lch. i. 402, 9. (2) *to preserve* game :—Forgâ ǽlc man mînne huntnoð, lôc hwǽr ic hit gefriðod wille habban, Ll. Th. i. 420, 26. (3) *to shelter* a place from weather :—On gefriþedum (*opacis*) stôwum, Lch. i. 70, 3. (4) *to protect* from a feeling of (superstitious) reverence, where sanctity is attributed to a place or object. v. friþ-geard, -splott :—Wæs ân pîntreów wið þ templ gefriðed, swîðe hâlig geteald on þâ hǽþenan wîsan, Hml. S. 31, 390. II. *to save, rescue* :—Hê bið gefriðod from his âgnum costungum *eripitur a sua tentatione*, Past. 107, 2. Onlŷsde and gefreoðode *absoluti*, Gr. D. 344, 1.

ge-friþiend, es; *m. A protector* :—Beó mîn gefriðiend *esto mihi in protectorem*, Ps. Th. 30, 3. Hê is gefriþiend ǽlces þâra þe him tô hopað, 17, 29.

ge-frôfor *consolation* :—Dînes gifrôfoð *tuae consolationis*, Rtl. 18, 35. Gifrôfrum *consolationibus*, 39, 15.

ge-frohtian. *Dele* : ge-frŷnd. v. ge-frînd.

ge-fullfremman (-freman) *to accomplish, complete, perpetrate* :—Gefulfreme þ *perfice illud*, Scint. 201, 5. Þ hê gefulfremige þâ gôd þe hê beginne, Hml. A. 150, 154. Synn byþ gefullfremmed (*perpetratur*), Scint. 228, 10.

ge-fullian *to become full*. *Add* : v. un-gefullod.

ge-fullian. *l.* ge-fulwian, *take here* ge-fulwian *in Dict., and add* :—Sôna ðæs þe hiene mon gefulwade (gefullade, hê gefullwad wǽre,

*v. ll.*) . . . fram Sergio hē gefulwad (gefullad, *v. l.*) wæs, Bd. 5, 7 ; Sch. 583, 15-24. Hē tó gefulliane (-enne, *v. l.*) cóm tó Rōme, Sch. 582, 14. Ǽr heó gefullud wǽre, Shrn. 31, 2. Dóð ǽrest hreówsunga, and weorðað siððan gefullwade, Past. 443, 16. v. un-gefullod.

**ge-fullwihtan(-ian)** *to baptize :*—Scs Augustinus gefulwihte Æþelbryht Cantwara cyning, Lch. iii. 422, 5. Hēr wæs Crīst gefulluhtud, Chr. 30 ; P. 6, 8.

**ge-fultuma.** *Add :* Ps. Spl. 26, 15. Cf. ge-fylsta.

**ge-fultuman.** *Add :*—Gefultumaþ *suppeditent,* i. *subministrent,* An. Ox. 16, 91. De is gefultumad *qui adjuvatur,* Kent. Gl. 657. (1) *to help :*—Gode gefultumiendum, Chr. 797 ; P. 57, 31. (2) *to help* an object (*dat.*) :—Wē gefultumað ūrum ondgite, Past. 69, 13. (3) *to help* to something, *help in getting :*—Ne gefultumað hē nāwuht tó his hiéremonna niédþearfe *subditorum necessitatibus minime concurrunt,* Past. 137, 2. (3 a) *to help* a person (*dat.*) to get something :—Ðone ðe him tó eallum gefultemað, Past. 387, 11. þ heó him gefultumode tó his āgenum feore *rogavit pro anima sua,* Hml. A. 100, 273. Hí bǽdon hine þæt hē him tó heora ealdrihtum gefultumede, Bt. 1 ; F. 2, 24. Ealra þāra þinga þe mē Crīst tó gefultumian wyle, Cht. Crw. 22, 3. ¶ the object to be got expressed by a clause :—Bǽd Burgrēd Æþelwulf þæt hē him gefultumade þæt him Norþ-Walas gehiérsumode, Chr. 853 ; P. 64, 25. (3 b) *to help* a person (*dat.*) to do something :—Hí bǽdon þæt hié him gefultumadon þæt hié wiþ þone here gefuhton, Chr. 868 ; P. 68, 32. Sió hering ūs gefultume ðæt wē hié wiðermōde ne gedón, mid ðǽre tælinge, Past. 213, 1.

**ge-fultumend.** *Add :*—Gefultumend æt ǽlcere ðearfe *adjutor in opportunitatibus,* Ps. Th. 9, 10 : 39, 21. Gefultumigend, Ps. L. 77, 35 : *fautor,* Wrt. Voc. ii. 34, 36.

[**ge-fundian** *to direct one's course* to a place :—Se[ó] stōw þǽr þū tó gefundest, Nar. 48, 6.]

[**ge-funtian** *to baptize :*—Sē þe gelýfd and is gefunted (*baptizatus*), Mk. 16, 16 (12th cent. MS.).]

**ge-fūrian** *to furrow :*—Gefūrede *sulcate,* An. Ox. 4323. Cf. ge-fýr(i)an.

**ge-fýlan.** *Add :*—Ǽlc hine sylfne on līchaman and on sāwle mid þām hǽþengylde earmlīce gefýlde, Hml. S. 23, 31. Ic þē wille biddan þ deóflu . . . mīnne clǽn[n]e līchaman ne gefýlan, Hml. A. 172, 65. Speccan blǽccan gefýlede (*saecularis*) *scoriae atramento foedatos,* An. Ox. 653.

**ge-fylce.** *Dele* Nar. 19, 22 *at end, and add :*—Gefylce *communipulares, commilitones, socii,* Wrt. Voc. ii. 132, 51 : An. Ox. 859. Harold cyningc and Tostig eorl and heora gefylce wǽron āfaren of scipe, Chr. 1066 ; P. 198, 19. Fram gefylce *a manipulo,* An. Ox. 2555 : *manipulo, caterua, legione,* 3688. Se mōdiga deófol mid his gefilce wyle wið þīnre sāwle campian, Wlfst. 242, 9. Hē sende hí mid gefylce tó Judēiscum folce . . . Hí begunnon tó feohtenne on twām gefylcum ; . . . him æfter eóde þ óðer gefylce, Hml. S. 25, 652-670. *Castra, oppida herewīc vel* gefylco, Wrt. Voc. ii. 129, 37. Martinus campdóme fyligde betwux lārlicum gefylcum (*trained bands*), Hml. S. 31, 17. *See next word.*

**ge-fylcea** (?), an ; *m. An ally* (?) :—Of þǽm teóndscipe þe ūs ǽr betweónum wæs þ Porrus se kyning seoðþan wæs mē freónd and eallum Grēca herige, and mīn gefēra and gefylcea (*my comrade and ally; or* ? gefylcea *gen. pl., my comrade and (my) troops* : the Latin is : Factus amicus ex hoste Macedonibus), Nar. 19, 22. [Cf. *Icel.* fylkir *the ruler of a fylki* ; poet, *a king.*]

**ge-fylced.** *Substitute :* ge-fylcian ; *pp.* ed *To array troops, set in order for fighting :*—Wyllelm him cóm ongeán on unwǽr ǽr his folc gefylced wǽre, Chr. 1066 ; P. 199, 29.

**ge-fylgan.** *Add : to obtain* (with dat.) :—' Gif monn mīnne noman nemneð in ǽnigre frēcennisse . . . , ðonne gefylge sē ðīure mildheortnesse.' Ðā cóm stefn of heofenum . . . ' Swā hwelc swā . . . mīnne naman þurh þē gecēgð, ic hine gehēre,' Shrn. 73, 7.

**ge-fyllan** *to fill* with (*gen. dat.* (*inst.*) or *with preps.*). v. ge-sellan, -fillan *in Dict., and add :* (1) *to fill* a place, vessel, &c. :—Ic gefelle *repleam* (*thesauros eorum*), Kent. Gl. 253. Mon þæt lāmfæt leádes gefylde, Jul. 578. Bið eal þes ginna grund glēda gefylled, Dōm. 12. Oþ þæt se wīda ceafl gefylled bið, Wal. 60. Gefellede innoþas *impleta viscera,* Hy. S. 96, 30. Þā leóhtfatu beóð simle mid ele gefylde, Bl. H. 127, 34. Tǽnelum gefyldum *fiscillis refertis,* Wrt. Voc. ii. 79, 71 : *farsis,* 37, 47. (I a) fig. :—Wē sceolon ūre heortan gefyllan mid þǽre swētnesse godcundra beboda, Bl. H. 37, 8. Beóð gefylde mid gefeán mūdas ūre, Ps. Th. 125, 2. (2) *to provide abundantly,* cf. (3). (a) the object a person, *to fill* with food (lit. or fig.) :—Þū gefylde mē Godes līchoman, gāstes dryncæs, Seel. 144. Þæt hē þæs earman līchoman gefylle, Bl. H. 37, 29. þ wē gefyllon þæs þearfan wambe mid ūrum gōdum, 39, 29. Þæt fremde ne sceoldan beón gefyllede (gefylde, *v. l.*) ūres mægenes, Past. 251, 1. (b) the object a place, *to store, stock abundantly* (lit. or fig.) :—Eorðan þū gefyllest wæstmum *terram inebriasti,* Ps. Th. 64, 9. Gefylleþ Drihten eówer beren mid genihtsumnesse, Bl. H. 41, 11. Gefylled wearð eall þes middangeard monna bearnum, Gen. 1553. Eorðe and eall þæt heó mid gefyld is *terra et plenitudo ejus,*

Ps. Th. 23, 1. Ðā ciricean stōdon māðma and bōca gefyldæ (-a, *v. l.*), Past. 5, 10. (c) where a quality, attribute, &c. is produced in a high degree. (a) the object a person :—Ælces gōdes þeáwas hē gefyllþ ðone ðe hine lufað, Bt. 27, 2 ; F. 98, 2. Hē wæs swīþe gefylled mid unþeáwum, Ors. 6, 3 ; S. 256, 23 : Leás. 17. Gefylled full mid gyfe *referta plena gratia,* Hy. S. 112, 11. Heó gefylled wæs wīsdōmes gife, El. 1143. (β) the object a thing :—Hū manegra yfela ðā welan sint gefylde, Bt. 32, 1 ; F. 114, 6. (d) where a feeling is excited in a high degree, *to fill* with joy, &c. (a) the object a person :—Eom ic mid lufan Dryhtnes gefylled, Gū. 625. Ic eom gefylled mid broce and mid iermdum, Past. 253, 8. Wē syndon gefyllede mid ealre eáþmōdnesse, Bl. H. 153, 31. (β) the object a place :—Se burgstede wæs blissum gefylled, Gū. 1291. (3) *to occupy entirely.* (a) a space (lit. or fig.) :—Ælce stōwe hē gefylþ, Bl. H. 19, 26. Gærstapan gefyllað (*implebunt*) þīne hūs, Ex. 10, 6. þ hūs wæs Hāliges Gāstes gefylled. Se swēg gefylde þ hūs, se Hálga Gāst gefylde þā apostolas, Bl. H. 133, 20-22. Unrōtnyss gefylde eówre heortan, Jn. 16, 6. Cóm micel werod gāsta and þis hūs innan of mǽstan dǽle sittende gefylde (-fylldon, *v. l.*), Bd. 5, 13 ; Sch. 638, 19. Wǽron his eágan gefyllede mid teárum, Bl. H. 187, 36. (b) of time :—þās twelf tācna synd swā brāde, þ hī gefyllað twā tīda mid hyra ūpgange, Lch. iii. 246, 7. (4) *to satisfy,* (a) a (hungry, needy) person :—Hē þā hungrian mid gōdum gefylled (*satiavit*), Ps. Th. 106, 8 : Bl. H. 5, 9. Þæt wē gefyllan swā mycele mænegu *ut saturemus turbam tantam,* Mt. 15, 33. þās woruldsǽlþa ne magon ðone earman gefyllan, for þam þe hē simle wilnað hwæshwugu þæs þe hē næft, Bt. 11, 1 ; F. 34, 1. Bið gefyld sāwl mīn, Cant. M. 9. (b) a thing :—þū gefyllest fægrum blǽdum treówa *satiabuntur omnia ligna silvarum,* Ps. Th. 103, 26. Of wæstmum weorca þīnra eall eorðan cīð ufan bið gefylled (*satiabitur*), 12. (5) *to fulfil, accomplish, complete, finish* a work :—Saturnus gefyld his ryne oþ þrittig geára fyrste, Scrd. 18, 32, 33, 34. God gefylde on ðām seofoðan dæge his weorc, Hex. 20, 9. Sē ðe ā þenced þæt hē his lust on ðon gefylle *qui implevit desiderium suum ex ipsis,* Ps. Th. 126, 6. Sē ðe wile his gālnysse gefyllan swā oft swā hine lyst, Hml. Th. i. 148, 23. Ic wæs sended tō þǽm þ ic sceolde gefyllan mīne þrowunge, Bl. H. 155, 25. Gif hió bið gefelled (*desiderium*) *si complebitur,* Kent. Gl. 457. Gefylledum ryne *consummato curriculo,* An. Ox. 2146. (5 a) *to fulfil* a desire, promise, *perform* a duty, *execute* an order, *judgement* :—Gif wē gefyllað wunigendes þēnunge *si compleamus habitatoris officium,* R. Ben. I. 5, 11. Hē gefylde his behāt, Hml. Th. ii. 284, 16 : Ps. Th. 110, 4. Hē Godes hǽse gefylde, Scrd. 23, 5. Hē eal þ se arð at him crafede eádmēdlīce gefylde, Chr. 1070 ; P. 206, 18. Ǽr þan mē gefylle Wealdend willan mīnne, El. 1084. Ðā ofergesettan ōðerra monna giémenne gefyllen, Past. 191, 22. þā ǽ gefyllan *legem adimplere,* Mt. 5, 17. Hwæþer wē mid weorcum his lāre gefyllan willen, R. Ben. 4, 17. Hí fērdon tó gefyllenne his beboda, Hml. S. 28, 58. Hæfde hē eall gefylled, swā him seó æðele bebeád, wīfes willan, El. 1131. Gefylledre wilsumnesse *deuotione completa,* Bd. 1, 7 ; Sch. 25, 14. Ic þīne dōmas wāt gefylde, Ps. Th. 118, 164. (5 b) *to fulfil* what has been foretold or symbolized. v. ge-fylledness, (3) :—Ealle þā þing þe ǽfre ǽr from wītgum gewītgode wǽron . . . eal hē þ gefylde, Bl. H. 83, 30 : An. Ox. 40, 13. Þæt seó wītegung wǽre gefylled, Hml. Th. i. 80, 3 : Cri. 213. Ðā wæs gefylled þ ǽr gecweden wæs, Bl. H. 69, 24. Hē hæfde gefylled swā ǽr biforan sungon wītgena word, Cri. 468. Gefyld, Chr. 607 ; P. 22, 5. Ealle þās dǽda and mǽrsunga þā tōwearde wǽron gebýcnunga wē oncnāwaþ wesan gefyllede *omnia haec facta et caelebrationes quae futura erant indicia cognoscimus esse completa,* An. Ox. 40, 13. (5 c) *to make complete, complete* what has been imperfect, *fill up* :—Ðā ðe hira līf on firenluste geendigað, ne gefyllað hié gōdra rīm ac āwiergedra gǽsta, Past. 251, 7. His tīddæge rīm wæs gefylled, Gen. 1166. (5 d) of time, *to complete* a period :—þā wǽron gefylde dagas on rīme, An. 1697. Ðā ðā III winter gefylled wǽron æfter Pendan slege *tribus annis post occisionem Pendan,* Bd. 3, 24 : Sch. 314, 15. [*Goth.* ga-fulljan : *O. H. Ger.* ge-fullen *ex-, im-, re-plere.*] v. un-gefylled.

**ge-fylledlic.** v. un-gefylledlic.

**ge-fylledness.** *Add :* (1) *fullness, that which fills.* v. ge-fyllan (2 b) :—Eorðe and eall hire gefyllednys, Hml. Th. i. 172, 9. (2) *performance.* v. ge-fyllan, (5 a) :—Mid gefyllednesse gōdre þēnunge *si compleamus officium,* R. Ben. 4, 24. (3) *fulfilment.* v. ge-fyllan, (5 b) :—Seó nīwe gecýþnis wæs gefyllednys ealra þǽra þinga þe seó ealde gecýþnis getācnode tōwearde tō Crīste, Ælfc. Gen. Thw. 2, 14. (4) *fullness* of time. v. ge-fyllan, (5 d) :—þā þā ðāra tīda gefyllednys cōm *ubi venit plenitudo temporis,* Hml. Th. i. 194, 16.

**ge-fyllendlic.** *Add : that may be completed :*—Gefyllendlicre eldo *consummabilis aevi,* Wrt. Voc. ii. 134, 7. v. un-gefyllendlic.

**ge-fylling,** e ; *f. Completion :*—Ealre gefyllinge ł ǽlcre geændunge ic geseah ende *omnis consummationis vidi finem,* Ps. L. 118, 96.

**gefylling-tíd,** e ; *f. A time that completes, that forms the concluding part of a series :*—Gefyllingtíd *completorium* (the last canonical hour, which completed the religious services of the day), Wrt. Voc. ii. 133, 3.

**ge-fylnes.** *Add:*—Gefyllnisse *consummationis*, Ps. Srt. 58, 14. Gefylnesse *supplemento*, Wrt. Voc. ii. 77, 9.

**ge-fylst.** *Dele.*

**ge-fylsta.** *Add:*—Þæt se mæra engel (*Michael*) beó Crístenra manná gefylsta on eorðan and þingere on heofonum, Hml. Th. i. 518, 32. Wē sind Godes gefylstan *we are labourers together with God:* Dei sumus adjutores, 8, 8: Hml. S. 11, 309. Hí tó Antecríste búgað and weorþað his gefylstan eallum heora mihtum, Wlfst. 93, 10.

**ge-fylstan.** *Add:*—Him gefylste God tó māran āre, Ors. 6, 33; S. 288, 8. Hí him gefylstan þ hié eft tó hiora āgnum becōman, 4, 3; S. 162, 20.

**ge-fylstend**, es; *m. A helper:*—Gefylstend *adjutor*, Ps. Rdr. 17, 3: 26, 9.

**ge-fýnd.** v. ge-fínd: **ge-fynegian.** v. ge-finegod *in Dict.*

**ge-fýran(-ian)** *to furrow:*—Gefýrede *sulcatas*, An. Ox. 2, 319. v. fýran(-ian), ge-fúrian.

**ge-fyrht.** *Substitute:* ge-fyrhtan, -fyrhtian; *p.* te, ode; -fyrht, -fyrhted (-od). I. *to make afraid.* Take here instances under ge-fyrhtian *in Dict., and add:*—Ic wæs swíðe gefyrhted and gebrēged (*perterritus*), Bd. 5, 12; Sch. 617, 18. Gefyrhtedo wēron *conterriti*, Lk. L. 24, 37. II. *to be afraid (of), fear:*—Þte ælc man ondrēde and gefyrhtiga nome Drihtnes *ut omnis homo timeat et contremescat nomen Domini*, Rtl. 101, 1. [O. H. Ger. ge-furhten *terrere*.]

**ge-fyrhþe**, es; *n. Wood, wooded country:*—On accan gefyrhðe; of ðan gefyrhðe on ford, C. D. v. 376, 11. v. fyrhþ.

**ge-fyrhto;** *p. l.* ge-fyrhto (-u); *indecl.;* [ge-fyrht, e]; *f., dele passage from Bl. H. (for which see* ge-wyrht*), and add:*—Se cwylra mid gefyrhto genam his swurd and hire heáfod of āslōh, Nar. 48, 22.

**ge-fyrn** *long ago.* *Add:*—Gefyrn ær jam [*pridem ?*], An. Ox. 56, 93. (1) in contrast with '*just now,*' where a comparatively short period may be in question:—Hē gefyrn smeáde hwær hí bigleofan biddan sceoldon, ða ða hí ða fare fērdon būton wiste, Hml. Th. ii. 138, 32. *Praeteritum plusquamperfectum* is forðgewiten māre þonne fulfremed, for ðan ðe hit wæs gefyrn gedōn : steteram ic stōd gefyrn, Ælfc. Gr. Z. 124, 9. (1 a) in reference to a previous part of a treatise or discourse:—Deós Anna þe wē gefyrn ær embe sprǽcon, Hml. Th. i. 148, 10: Bt. 33, 4; F. 130, 24. Ic ðe sǽde gefyrn ær on ðisse ilcan bēc, 35, 3; F. 158, 32. Ær gefyrn, 36, 7; F. 182, 29. Gefirn ǽr, Solil. H. 54, 1. (2) of a period considerable, (a) in respect to a person's life:—Hē wiste his geendunge gefyrn ær hē fērde fram ðissum lífe, Hml. Th. ii. 516, 1. Hū gefyrn hē gelýfde, 310, 15. Gefirn (*quatuordecim fere anni*), Solil. H. 35, 12. Þis þ ic gefyrnost gemunan mæg, Hml. S. 30, 322. (b) in respect to all past time :—Gefyrn *antiquitus*, Wrt. Voc. ii. 85, 18. Ephese hātte þeós burh, and heó wel gefyrn swā gehāten wæs, Hml. S. 23, 550. Ús þe gefyrn on deápes dymnysse sǽton, Nic. 12, 36 : Cri. 63. Se ealda cuide þe mon gefyrn cwæþ, Bt. 14, 2; F. 44, 12. God behēt gefyrn worulde Abrahame, Hml. Th. ii. 12, 23. Hē wæs gefyrn worulde, and swíþe fela geara synd nū āgāne syððan hē gewāt of þysan lífe, Hml. S. 23, 727. Swā Sedulus iú gefyrn giddode, Angl. viii. 332, 16. v. un-gefyrn.

**gefyrn-dagas;** *pl. m. Days of old, old times:*—Þus ealde penegas þe on gefyrndagum (gefirndagum, *v. l.*) geslægene wæron on yldrena tíman, Hml. S. 23, 588. [*Laym.* ine ivurndaȝen.]

**gefyrn-gewiten;** *adj. Long-past:*—On ðām gefyrngewitenan tíman, Hml. S. 23, 8.

**ge-fyrnness**, e; *f. Antiquity:*—Be gefyrnysse hāligra wæccena *de uigiliarum antiquitate.* . . . Be dægredsanges gefyrnysse and ealderlicnysse, Nap. 30.

**ge-fyrþran.** *Add:* -fyrþrian. I. *trans. To advance, promote the interests of, support, help on:*—Ic þe gefyrþrede mid mínum lārum tó þon þ þē mon tó dōmere geceás *thanks to my instructions you were advanced to a judgeship*, Bt. 8; F. 24, 29. Datius wæs gefyrðrod mid trymnesse rihtes geleáfan, Gr. D. 184, 15. Gefyrþredo *fulta*, Wrt. Voc. ii. 34, 52. Gefyrþrede *freti*, 33, 47. I a. *to help by giving, to endow, enrich :*—Eádgār cynincg þone crístendóm gefyrðrode, and fela munuclífa ārǣrde, Hml. S. 21, 446. Ðone freóls hí gefriðodon and gefyrðredon, þeáh hē on gewrite ne stóde, Cht. Th. 115, 35. Hē ðisne freóls ǽfre gefyrþrian wolde, 116, 19. Hí sind mid gifum and gestreónum gefyrþrode, Bt. 3, 4; F. 6, 27. II. *intrans.* [v. N. E. D. *to further (intrans.)*] *to get on, be enriched:*—Gefyrðro (gifyrdro) *ditor*, Txts. 57, 678: Wrt. Voc. ii. 25, 50. [O. L. Ger. gi-furthren *promovere*.]

**ge-fýsan.** *Add: to impel, incite, make eager:*—Ne leng bídan wolde wyrm, ac mid bǽle fór fýre gefýsed *no longer would the dragon bide, but fared forth furious with fire and flame*, B. 2309. Heorte gefýsed sæcce tó sēceanne *a heart fiercely stirred strife to seek*, 2561. Wiga gūðe gefýsed *a warrior burning for battle*, 630. Sorgende folc, hearde gefýsed (*sternly urged on*), Cri. 891. Beornþreát monig farað ofestum gefýsde *many a man marches on, hastening and hurrying*, Pa. 52. Swā lagu tōglídeð, flōdas gefýsde (*wind-driven waves*), El. 1270.

**ge-fystlian.** *l.* -fýstlian *and for* '*pugnis* . . . Scint. 2' *substitute:*

—Gif syngiende gefýstlude gē forþyldiaþ *si peccantes colafizati suffertis*, Scint. 7, 14. [*Cf. O. H. Ger.* ge-fūstōn *colaphizare*.]

**ge-gada.** *Add: a colleague, confederate, consort:*—Gegada *complex*, Wrt. Voc. i. 86, 34. Him niman ōðerne gegagan (-gadan ?) *alium sibi conjugem sumere*, Ll. Th. ii. 152, 35. Gegadan *collegam*, Germ. 399, 299 : *alumni*, 398, 137. Hē læg swā deád . . . ða wendon his gegadan þ hē wǽre gebysgod . . ., Hml. S. 7, 174. Cóm þæs gerēfan suna mid his sceandlicum gegadum, 163 : 19, 40. Seó myltestre began faran tó hire gegadan, Hml. A. 195, 21. Hēt se cāsere his gegadan tó faran and beódon þām crístenum þ hí cōmon him tó, Hml. S. 28, 41. [O. Sax. gi-gado. Cf. O. H. Ger. ge-gat *conjunctus:* Ger. gatten *to join:* gatte *consort*.]

**ge-gadere.** v. ge-gædere.

**ge-gaderedness**, e; *f. A gathering* of diseased matter :—Wið gehwylce gegæderednyssæ, Lch. i. 322, 1 note.

**ge-gaderian.** *Add:* I. *to join together:*—Tó geseteto ł gegeadrad *adpositos*, Mt. p. 12, 4. (2) *to unite* the parts which form a whole :—Ðū gegæderast ða hiofonlican sāwla and ða eorþlican líchoman, Bt. 33, 4; F. 132, 22. Oðer biþ se mon, . . . oðer his gódnes, ða gegædraþ God and eft ætgædre gehelt, 34, 3; F. 136, 33. Hē gegaderode ða sāula and ðone líchoman, 30, 2 ; F. 110, 12. Ða iif ðing, ðonne hí ealle gegaderode beóð, ðonne biþ þ God . . . Ðonne ða fíf þing . . . ealle gegadorade beóþ, ðonne beóþ hit eall ān ðing, Bt. 33, 2 ; F. 122, 14-18. Þá gōd ealle gegæderode biúþ swelce hí sién tó ānum wecge gegoten . . . tó ānum gōde gegaderod, 34, 9 ; F. 146, 20-22. Gegaderude, 37, 2 ; F. 190, 3. (3) *to put together* what is made up of parts, *compose, join together* what is broken :—Of Críste tó God endebrednis gegeadred bið (*contexitur*), Lk. p. 4, 10. Gif þū ǽnne stān tóclifst, ne wyrþ hē nǽfre gegaderod swā hē ǽr wæs, Bt. 34, 11 ; F. 150, 26. Ðes middangeard wæs of mistlicum ðingum gegaderod, and swíþe fæste tōsomne gelímed ; nǽren hí gegaderode and gerādode swā wiþerwearda gesceafta, ðonne ne wurdon hē ne geworhte ne gegaderode, 35, 2 ; F. 156, 33-37. Manega naman beóð gegaderode of myslicum swēge and getācniað ān þing, Angl. viii. 332, 6. Gegædradon *conpactis*, Wrt. Voc. ii. 104, 43. (3 a) in reference to the union of marriage cf. (4 b) :—Þte God gegeadrad (efnegigedrað, R.) *quod Deus junxit*, Mk. L. 10, 9. Gegadrade (-gead-, L.) *conjunxit*, Mt. R. 19, 6. (4) *to join together* persons (a) as friends:—Hē gegæderaþ frínd and gefēran þ hié heora sibbe healdaþ, Bt. 21 ; F. 74, 38. (b) in marriage. Cf. (3 a) :—Gif hí on rihtgesincipe gegaderode sýn *si legitimo matrimonio conjungantur*, Ll. Th. ii. 232, 6. ¶ used intransitively :—Gif hí ǽne tōgāð, hí sceolon eft gegadrian, oððe siððan wunian symle būton hæmede, Hml. Th. ii. 324, 2. (5) *to join* one person to another as an associate, colleague, adherent :—Ðū úsic tó Gode gegadrades ðorh flǽsces gemǣnnisse *nos Deo conjungeres per carnis contubernium*, Ps. Srt. ii. p. 203, 3. Ðū ðǽm Paul' tó bodianne wuldur ðín gigeadriga gimeodumad arð *illi* (Peter) *Paulum ad predicandam gloriam tuam sociare dignatus es*, Rtl. 58, 39. Gegaderade *adsciti*, Wrt. Voc. i. 287, 77 : ii. 5, 27. Wǽron gegæderede *adglomerantur* (*orthodoxorum phalangibus*), Hpt. Gl. 488, 44. (6) *to come to* a conclusion, *give adhesion to* a proposition :—Forlǽte hē unnytte ymbhogan . . . , and gegæderige (cf. gesamnige his ingeþonc, Met. 22, 10) tó þām ānum, and gesecge his āgnum mōde, þ hit mæg findan oninnan him selfum ealle ða gōd þe hit úte sēcþ, Bt. 35, 1 ; F. 154, 23. II. *to bring together* persons, *to collect* an army, *fleet*, &c., *assemble* a council:—Hē gegaderode wyrhtan gehwanon, Hml. S. 6, 157. Gegaderade sió lāf of Eást-Englum micelne here, Chr. 894 ; P. 88, 3. Hē eft gegaderode ōþerne here him tó, Hml. S. 25, 483. Man fyrde ongeán hí gegaderode, Chr. 998 ; P. 131, 14. Man gegaderode þā scipu tó Ludenbyrig, 992 ; P. 127, 9. Hié fierd gegadorode, 867 ; P. 68, 22. Ðā biscopas somnung gegeadredon (*concilium colligunt*), Jn. p. 6, 10. Fird gegadrian (-gader-, *v. l.*), Chr. 905 ; P. 94, 1. Fultum gegaderian, 1016; P. 147, 8. Mid þau scipan ðe hē gegaderian nihte, 1001 ; P. 132, 12. Hér wæs sinoð gegaderod, 788 ; P. 55, 13. Tóforan þām concilium þe þær gegadered was, 1070; P. 206, 15. Se cyng hǽfde gegadrod (-gaderod, *v. l.*) sum hund scipa, 911 ; P. 96, 6. Hí woldon faran tó heora cynehlāforde and tó þām witan þe mid him gegaderode wǽron, 1048 ; P. 174, 6 : 894 ; P. 87, 19. II a. reflexive, *to come together, assemble :*—Ær þám þe hē and þæt folc hié ðær gegaderede, Ors. 3, 9; S. 126, 29. Eft gegadorode micel here hine of Eást-Englum, Chr. 921 ; P. 101, 23. Þā Wylisce menn hí gegaderodon, and wið þā Frencisce . . . gewinn úp āhófon, 1094 ; P. 230, 1 : 1093 ; P. 228, 26. II b. intransitive :—Gegadrode ón hlóþ (gegaderodan án hlōð, *v. l.*) wícenga and gesæt æt Fullanhamme, Chr. 879 ; P. 76, 23. Micel hearm gedón wæs . . . oð þ folc gegaderede . . . hí gegaderodan ealle on Gleáwcesterscíre æt Langa treó, mycel fyrd and unārímedlic, 1052 ; P. 175, 4-11. II b a. *to agree :*—Gegadriges ł efnesæcgas fēwero *concordant quattuor*, Mt. p. 3, 13. III. *to bring together* things (material or non-material), *collect :*—Seó sēleste gesælþ þe þā óþra gesælþa ealle oninnan him gegaderaþ, Bt. 24, 1 ; F. 80, 20. Hí gegaderiað monifeald dysig, 3, 1 ; F. 6, 4. Hē gegaderode ðæra gymstāna bricas, Hml. Th. i. 62, 9. Ic þe wolde gegæderigan

manigu spell and manega bisna *crebras coacervabo rationes*, Bt. 36, 3 ; F. 178, 31. **III** a. *to accumulate, amass* wealth, &c. :—Hé hordað, and nát hwám hé hit gegaderað (*congregat*), Hml. Th. i. 66, 5. Eallne þone welan ðe hí gegaderigaþ, Bt. 11, 1 ; F. 32, 6. Þ hé gegaderige ungerím þissa welena, 26, 3 ; F. 94, 13. Þeáh hí gegaderigen ealle þás andweardan gód, 32, 2 ; F. 118, 2. Hié woldon ormǽte feoh gegaderian, 24, 2 ; F. 82, 17. Eall þás gód gegaderian tógædre, 24, 4 ; F. 86, 3. Mid gegaderodum hefe lyffetunge ofðriccan, Hml. Th. i. 494, 4. **IV.** *to gather* fruit, crops, &c. :—Gegeadredon þ unwæstm *colligentes zizania*, Mt. L. 13, 29. Sint gegaderade *collecta sunt* (*foena*), Kent. Gl. 1040. **IV** a. figurative :—Se eorþlica anweald nǽfre ne sǽwþ þá cræftas, ac lisþ and gadraþ unþeáwas, and þonne [hé] hí gegadrad hæfþ, þonne eówaþ hé hí, Bt. 27, 1 ; F. 94, 26.

**ge-gaderscipe.** For ' Hpt. . . . 416' *substitute* :—Gegæderscype *jugalitas*, i. *matrimonium*, An. Ox. 1360 : 1373. Gegæderscipes *conjugii*, 221. Ǽwlices gegæderscipes *legitime jugalitatis*, 583 : 5030.

**ge-gaderung.** *Add* : **I.** *a joining together, union, a joint, bond; what results from joining.* (1) in the following glosses :—Gegederung *conpagem*, Wrt. Voc. ii. 104, 80. Gegæderong, 15, 10. *Compagem, juncturam vel* gegaderung, 132, 70. Gegaderunga *copulas*, 23, 59. (2) *a joining together to form a whole* :—Ǽr þon þe hé þǽre gerýnelican gegaderinge menniscre gebyrde onfénge *before he received the mysterious joining together and compacting of the body* (cf. Eph. 4, 16) *that precedes the birth of man*, Bl. H. 165, 35. (3) *a whole formed by joining* :—Hwæþer þ þynce unweorþ seó gegaderung ðára þreóra þinga, ðonne þá þreó biþ tó ánum gedón, Bt. 33, 1 ; F. 120, 29. (4) *what joins, a bond* :—Hí beóð álýsde fram þǽre gegaderunge heora líchaman *a carnis suae copula solvantur*, Gr. D. 277, 14. (5) *the union* of persons in friendship, marriage, &c. :—Hú gerád hiora gegaderung wæs . . . hǽmedes þe þæs gǽstes, Hml. A. 200, 161. Gyftlicere gegæderunge *nuptialis copule*, An. Ox. 4402. Heálice gegaderunga (*legitima conjugia*) ne mót mon gesceádan bútan bêgea geðafunga, Ll. Th. ii. 152, 33. **II.** *a gathering together* of people, *a congregation, an assembly, a synagogue* :—Gegaderung *congregatio, concio*, Wrt. Voc. i. 50, 29 : *sinagoga*, 16, 53. Sume naman synd *collectiva . . . congregatio* gegaderung, Ælfc. Gr. Z. 13, 12. Seó gegaderung (*consilium*) þára áwyrgedra mé ofsǽton, Ps. Th. 21, 14. Gegæderunga *congregationis*, R. Ben. I. 107, 2. Fram gegaderunga mycelre *a concilio multo*, Ps. Spl. 39, 14. On swylcere gegaderunge (*the feast of Ahasuerus*), Hml. A. 93, 45. **III.** *a collection of material, accumulation.* (1) as a verbal noun :—Hí nyton nán ôþer gód ðonne eallra ðára deúrwyrðestena ðinga gegaderunga tó heora anwealde, Bt. 24, 4 ; F. 86, 5. (2) *collected material* :—Þúsendfealdre gegaderuncge *millena congerie* (i. *cumulo*), An. Ox. 435. Gegæderunge, hýpe *congerie* (*prunarum*), 4780. On reáde gegæderunge (hýpan) *in rubicundas* (*gemmarum*) *congeries* (i. *congregationes*), 1822. (2 a) in a medical sense, *a collection of diseased matter* :—Gyf þǽr hwylc gegaderung biþ, heó þá áfeormaþ, Lch. i. 228, 22. Wið ealle gegaderunga þæs yfelan wǽtan of þám líchoman, 236, 18. Wið cyrnlu and wið ealle yfele gegaderunga, 300, 1. Wið gehwylce gegaderunga, 322, 1 note.

**ge-gaderwist,** e ; *f. A being together* :—Gegadorwist *contubernium*, Wrt. Voc. i. 52, 37. v. gader-wist.

**gegader-wyrhtan ;** *pl. m. Workmen gathered together from all parts* :—Ongunnon of ðám gegaderwyrhtum (cf. hé gegaderode swiðe góde wyrhtan gehwanon, 157) tǽlan ðone hálgan, Hml. S. 6, 186.

**ge-gæde.** *Dele.*

**ge-gædere** (-gad-) ; *adv. Together* :—Hí ealle gegadere wundrodon, Hml. S. 30, 385.

**ge-gælen.** v. ge-galan : **ge-gæncg.** v. ge-genge.

**ge-gaf ;** *adj. The passage given here belongs to* gegaf-sprǽce, *q. v., but perhaps the adjective* ge-gaf *may be inferred from the compound* gegaf-sprǽce *along with the noun* ge-gaf ; cf. ídel-sprǽce, yfel-sprǽce. Cf. *too* gegaf-sprǽc *and* dol-sprǽc.

**ge-gaf** *buffoonery, scurrility* :—Ne geríseþ ǽnig unnytt ǽfre mid bisceopum, ne doll ne dysig . . . ne cildsung on ǽnig gegaf on ǽnig wísan, ne æt hám, ne on síðe, ne on ǽnigre stôwe, Ll. Th. ii. 314, 32.

**ge-gafelian, ge-gafelod.** *Substitute* : **ge-gafolian ;** *p.* ode *To seize as tax or tribute, confiscate* :—Wǽre gegafelod *infiscaretur* (ne ab Imperatoribus locuples gazarum opulentia *infiscaretur*, Ald. 43, 23), Wrt. Voc. ii. 81, 68 : 46, 69. Beón gegavalad *proscriberentur* (ne possessiones earum fiscali jure *proscriberentur*, Ald. 69, 6), Hpt. Gl. 517, 59.

**gegaf-sprǽc** *buffoonery.* *Add* :—Sume menn drincað æt deádra manna líce ofer ealle þá niht and gremiað God mid heora gegafsprǽce, Hml. S. 21, 315. Hí willað wacian and wôdlíce drincan binnan Godes húse and mid gegafsprǽcum Godes hús gefýlan, 13, 78. Gegafsprǽce and ídele word and þá word þe leahter ástyrien on eallum stôwum wé forbeúdaþ *scurrilitates vel verba otiosa et risum moventia in omnibus locis dampnamus*, R. Ben. 22, 4.

**gegaf-sprǽce ;** *adj. Given to buffoonery, scurrilous* :—Hé wæs gegaf-

sprǽce (cf. nunquam se ad sanctae conversationis habitum venire, jurando, irascendo, deridendo testabatur, Gr. D. bk. 4, c. 38), Hml. Th. i. 534, 2.

**ge-galan ;** *p.* -gól ; *pp.* -galen, -gælen *To enchant;* incantare :—Gegaelen *incaniata*, Wrt. Voc. ii. 111, 59. Gegælen (*printed* -grelen, *but see* Wülck. Gl. 422, 24), 45, 60. Beóþ gegalene fram wísum, Ps. Spl. 57, 5.

**ge-gán.** *Add* : **A.** *of movement.* **I.** *movement irrespective of the point of departure or destination.* (1) *to go on foot, walk* :—Gif hwelc gigæs (gegaas, L.) on dæg *si quis ambulauerit in die*, Jn. R. 11, 9. Arás þ mægden and geeóde (*ambulabat*), Mk. L. 5, 42. Mið ðý geeóde in temple, 11, 27. Halto geeádon, Mt. L. 15, 31. (2) *to take a specified course* (lit. or fig.) :—In bebodum mínum gigieð (-gǽð ?) *in praeceptis meis ambulauerit*, Rtl. 10, 10. (3) *of time, to pass, elapse* :—Mið ðý geeóde þ sunnedæg *cum transisset sabbatum*, Mk. L. R. 16, 1. (4) *of an event, to happen, come to pass* :—Þá þæt geeóde þæt se wer wearð wíne druncen, Gen. 1562. Þæt geeóde ufaran dógrum, B. 2200. **II.** *where movement from* a place is the primary notion. (1) *to depart* :—Ðá geeóde ðona ðe Hǽlend *transeunte inde Iesu*, Mt. L. 9, 27. Geeóde *abiit*, 13, 25. Mið ðý se unclǽne gaast geeóde from ðæm menn, Lk. L. 11, 24. Mið ðý forleortan hine geeódon (gieðdun, R.) *relicto eo abierunt*, Mk. L. 12, 12. Geeádon, Mt. L. 2, 9 : 22, 22. (1 a) *to depart* from this world, *pass away* :—Ne bið geeád ðiús cnēwureso *non praeteribit haec generatio*, Mt. L. 24, 34. **III.** *where the prominent notion* is that of direction or destination. (1) *of self-originated motion or action.* (a) *to proceed* to a place or person, *go into a place* :—Gif on lond ðú gegaas *si in uicum introieris*, Mk. L. 8, 26. Geeóde *adgrederetur* (*lupanar*), Wrt. Voc. ii. 85, 30. Geeódun, gihiódum, geeádun *adgrediuntur*, Txts. 39, 78. Geeódon, Wrt. Voc. ii. 4, 44. Hiá geeádon in bergum *illi abierunt in porcos*, Mt. L. 8, 32. Þ hiá gegǽ in ceastra *euntes in castella*, 14, 15. Þte geeádon in ðá ceastra, Lk. L. 9, 12. (b) *where the purpose or motive of going* (to a place) is indicated, (a) by simple infin. :—Geeóde on mór gebidda, Mk. L. 6, 46. (β) by gerundial infin. :—Mið ðý geeódon tó bycganne *dum irent emere*, Mt. L. 25, 10. (γ) by a substantive (with *tó*) denoting or implying an action to be performed :—Tó ðæhtunge ðonne geeódon *consilio inito*, Mt. L. 27, 7. (δ) by a substantive (with *on*) denoting function in which the subject is to be employed :—Ðú eart on borg gegán ðínum friénd, Past. 192, 18. (2) *of passive movement* (lit. or fig.). (a) *to be allotted* or *assigned* to a person :—Ne gegǽð him þær nǽnig fæsten *non opus erit eis jejunare*, Ll. Th. ii. 144, 17. An fæsten gegǽð wudewan and fǽmnan ; mǽre gegǽð wífe þám þe wer hafað *unum jejunium competit viduae et puellae; majus competit mulieri virum habenti*, 156, 9, 10. (b) *to happen* to a person, *come upon* :—God ánawát hwæt his deádan gegǽð *quid mortuis suis eveniat*, Ll. Th. ii. 166, 19. Him swá geeóde swá swá Aidanus him bæd, Hml. S. 26, 102. Geióde, Ps. C. 13. For þan ðæs wíte on eówre handa geeóde, Ps. Th. 57, 2. (c) *to contribute* to a result :—Ic ágælde þæt tó mínre sáwle frætwum belumpe, and mé tó éces lífes earnunge gegán sceolde, Angl. xi. 98, 30. **IV.** special uses with preps. or adverbs, út gegán *to go to the closet, have an evacuation* :—Gif mon ne mæge út gegán, Lch. ii. 276, 12. **B.** with the idea of attainment, *to get by going.* **I.** *to get* a material object. (a) *to get by allotment* :—In þǽm dǽle þe hé mid tán geeóde, Bl. H. 121, 9. (b) *to acquire* (a) by peaceful action :—Eádnóð gebeád þæt land ealre ðǽre mǽgðe hwæðer hit ǽnig swá (*by taking orders*) gegán wolde, Cht. Th. 167, 31. (β) by force, *to conquer* a place, *take* a town, *win* spoil :—Hé geeóde (*expugnavit*) þá burh, Jos. 10, 35 : Ors. 4, 10 ; S. 196, 33. Eádmund geeóde eal Norþhymbra land him tó gewealdan, Chr. 944 ; P. 110, 30. Þá Deniscan þæt lond all geeódon, 870 ; P. 70, 8. Þæs þe his cyn ǽrest West-Seaxna lond on Wealum geódon, P. 4, 21. Hié siþþan geeódon Europe and Asiam þone mǽstan dǽl *cum Europae maximam partem domuissent, Asiae vero aliquantis civitatibus captis*, Ors. 1, 10 ; S. 48, 18. Hig geeódun his land and ealle his burga . . . þǽre wíc hig geeódon *tulit Israel omnes civitates ejus . . . cujus viculos ceperant*, Num. 21, 25, 32. Eal (*all the spoil*) þæt þá þeódguman geeódon, Jud. 332. Gegáð þá buruh and forbernað hí sóna *cum ceperitis civitatem, succendite eam*, Jos. 8, 7. God him (*William the Conqueror*) geúðe þ hé móste Engleland gegán, Chr. 1086 ; P. 219, 25 : 1066 ; P. 196, 5. Swá earme wíf hæfdon gegán þone cræftgestan dǽl and þá hwatestan men ealles þises middangeardes, Ors. 1, 10 ; S. 48, 5. **II.** *to get* to a position or point. (1) *to get* to a person (*dat.*), *get into the keeping* or *power of* :—Wé gelýfað þ hé gegáð Gode, búton hé þe swíðor forscyldgod wǽre, Hml. Th. ii. 462, 22. Hí beóð ðurh gódre fremminge Gode betǽhte, and gé sylfe him gegáð þurh gódum geearnungum, 554, 24. Ǽlc man, sé ðe wile Gode gegán, sceal gelýfan on ðá Hálgan Ðrynnysse, 604, 23. Mín Drihten, ne lǽt mé deóflum gegán, Angl. xii. 502, 20. (2) local, *to get* to a place or position :—Se maga geonga under his mǽges scyld geeóde *the youth got under his kinsman's shield*, B. 2676. Hí síð drugon, geeódon tó þæs þe eorla hleó . . . gefrúnon hringas dǽlan, 1967. Hí forð onetton, oð hié gegán hæfdon tó þám wealgeate, Jud. 140 : 219. Hié tógædre gegán

hæfdon, B. 2630. Þa hî swâ feor gegân hæfdon swâ hî þâ woldon, Chr. 1010; P. 141, 7. Tôsomne gegânre *coeunte, conglutinato*, An. Ox. 48, 4. (3) of time, *to get* to a specified point :—Oð ðæt wintra rîm gegæð in þâ geoguðe, Gû. 470. (3 a) *to come, arrive* :—Oð þæt seó tîd cymeð, gegæð gearrîmum, þæt þâ leomu geloden weorðað, Vy. 5. (4) *to get* to a stage, *come* to a specified point :—Gif hit þonne tô bôte gegâ, Ll. Th. i. 340, 16 : 360, 3. **III.** *to get something done.* (1) *to do, perform* :—Hê hit eall his fôtum geeóde *he did all his travelling on foot*; pedum incessu vectus, Bd. 3, 5 ; S. 203, 5. Eall þæt ic æfre tô unnytte . . . nîd hondum gefênge oððe fôtum geeóde (*all that I have gone and done*), Angl. xi. 98, 44 : 101, 46. Ic þîne bebodu wolde gegân, Ps. Th. 118, 40. (Cf. v. 78.) (2) *to bring about a result by walking* :—Oððe hê gegæð on þâm dæge þæt hê sý wêrig *or he gets on that day tired with walking*, Wlfst. 212, 29. **IV.** *to act upon by going*, used of a plough in movement which is thus preparing the land for cultivation :—Ârise seó æcerteóðung â be þâm þe seó sulh þone teóðan æcer gegâ *even as the tenth acre is ploughed*, Ll. Th. i. 342, 11 : Wlfst. 208, 6 note. v. fore-, full-gegân.

**ge-gang,** es; *m. Chance, hap, event* :—Gegong *casus*, Wrt. Voc. ii. 21, 66. Gegang *eventus*, 30, 40. Wyrde oððe gegonges *fati*, 33, 65. Be wyrde oððe geionge *de fatu*, 27, 60. Gegong *casum*, 22, 9. Gegongum *casibus*, 19, 63 : 94, 79. v. winter-gegang.

**ge-gangan.** Add : **A.** of movement. **I.** movement irrespective of the point of departure or destination. (1) *to go* on foot, *walk* :—Gif huoelc gegeongað (*ambulauerit*) on næht, Jn. L. 11, 10. (2) of an event, *to happen, come to pass* :—Gif þæt geganged, þæt þê gâr nimeð, B. 1846. Hû geganged þæt gôde oððe yfie ?, Sal. 362. **II.** where movement *from* a place is the primary notion, *to depart* :—Gegangende *cesuram*, Wrt. Voc. ii. 14. 18. Gegandende, 103, 59. **III.** where the prominent notion is that of direction or destination. (1) of self-originated motion or action. (a) *to proceed* to a place or person, *go into* a place :—Þeáh ic on mînes hûses hyld gegange, Ps. Th. 131, 3. Gif in lond ðû gegonges *si in uicum introieris*, Mk. 8, 26. Tô hwon wê gigonge (gegeonge, L.) *ad quem ibimus* ?, Jn R. 6, 68. Gegeonga in bergum *ire in porcos*, Mk. p. 3, 6 : Mk. L. 9, 43. (b) where the purpose of going (to a place) is indicated by a substantive (with *tó*) denoting or implying an action to be performed :—Tô rûne gegangan, Jud. 54. Hié tô hûsle gegangen hæfdon, Bl. H. 209, 6. (2) of passive movement (lit. or fig.). (a) *to be allotted* to a person :—Him tô môse sceal gegangan geâra gehwylce þriâ þreóténo þûsend gerîmes, Sal. 288. (b) *to happen* to a person (*dat.*), *befall* :—Geganged þâm mannum . . . þæt heó ealle forbeornað, Wlfst. 206, 30 : Vy. 10, 1. þ þæm biscopum . . . gelîce gegange þæm biscope þe Paulus geseah, Bl. H. 45, 4 : þâ wæs gegongen guman . . . þ hê geseah . . ., B. 2821. (c) *to contribute* to a result :—þ him þ gôd môte tô êcum mêdum gegangan, Bl. H. 101, 18. **B.** with the idea of attainment, *to get by going.* **I.** *to get by force* :—Sê þe hine gefô and gegange *he that seizes and secures him*, Ll. Th. i. 42, 17. Wê witan ôþer îgland . . . wê eów fultumiað þ gê hit magon gegangan, Chr. P. p. 3, 13. Ne sceole gê swâ sôfte sinc gegangan, By. 59. **II.** *to get to* a position or point. (1) *to get to* a person, *get into the protection or power* of a person :—þæt hê Gode gegange (cf. ge-gân ; B. II. 1), Lch. iii. 442, 7. (2) local, *to get to* or at a place or position :—Of hwylcere wîsan þâm môde hit gegange þæs slæpendan, Bd. 1, 27 ; Sch. 94, 4. Gegangendo *coituras*, Wrt. Voc. ii. 15, 11 : 104, 81. Gegangende, 136, 42. (3) of time, *to come, arrive* (cf. ge-gân ; B. II. 3 a) :—His aldres wæs ende gegongen, B. 822. Wæs endedæg gôdum gegongen, 3036. **III.** *to act upon by going* (cf. ge-gân ; IV) :—Swâ hit seó sulh gegange, Ll. Th. i. 262, 9. [*Goth.* ga-gaggan : O. Sax. O. H. Ger. gi-gangan.]

**ge-gearcian.** Add : **I.** *to make ready* :—Ic eów betæcð mycele healle gedæfte, gegearwiað (gegearuað, L., gegeorwigað, R.) ðâra, Lk. 22, 8. **II.** *to make ready* something for use, enjoyment, &c. :

Næfre þû wîta þæs fela gegearwast, Jul. 177. Þîne hæle þû geearwodest (gigeorwades, R.), Lk. 2, 31. þæt hê him stôwe gegearwade þæt hê restan mihte *ut sibi locum quiescendi praepararet*, Bd. 4, 24 ; Sch. 489, 7. Gegearuadon (-georwadan, R.) wyrta gemong, Lk. R. 23, 56. Gegearawa *prepara*, Kent. Gl. 939. Gegearwiað Drihtnes weg *parate viam Domini*, Mt. 3, 3. Þâ mærða þe God hæfð gegearwod þâm þe his willan gewyrcað, Wlfst. 167, 9. ¶ where the purpose for which preparation is made is given :—Þone sêlestan dæl hiora gôda gegearod tô heora geblôte, Ors. 6, 21 ; S. 272, 25. **II a.** of food, meals, &c. :—Gê eów gemænelice gebeórscipas gegearwiað, Hml. A. 145, 43. Ic gegearwode (geiarwad, R.) mîne feorme, Mt. 22, 4. Hig gegearwodon him Easterþenunga, 26, 19. Ær se mete gegearwod wære, Ors. 1, 7 ; S 36, 28. **III.** *to bring to completion, make, form* :—Ðâ hê gegearwade *quando praeparabit* (*coelos*), Kent. Gl. 269. Þte wîsfæst folc Crîste gigearwade *ut perfectam plebem Christo praepararet*, Rtl. 76, 17. Fulfremed folc gegearwian (gigeorwiga, R.), Lk. 1, 17. Tô þon þ hê sceolde gegearwian and fulfremman þone wâh *ut parietem perficeret*, Gr. D. 126, 2. Is gegearwod *paratur* (*in imbri vehementi fames*), Kent. Gl. 1043. **III a.** *to bring to be* of a certain character :—Heó efenwyrðe hî on eallum þingum þâm bysceope gegearwade *condignam se in omnibus episcopo praebuit*, Bd. 4, 6 ; Sch. 384, 6. **III b.** *to establish* procedure :—Þû gegearwadest þæt þû recene, God, rihte beeódest *thou dost establish equity*; tu parasti equitatem, Ps. Th. 98, 4. **IV.** *to dress, equip, arm* :—Gegearuas *vestit*, Mt. L. 6, 30. Ðâ cempo gegearwodon hine mið fellereáde hrægle *milites induunt eum purpura*, Mk. L. 15, 17, 20. Ne Salomon suâ gegearued wæs (*coopertus est*), Mt. L. 6, 29. Gæst gegearwd (cf. un-gegearwod), Gû. 662. Wæron secgas sôna gegearwod wæpnum tô wigge, El. 47. **IV a.** of the trappings of a horse :—Hors is gegearwad *equus paratur* (*ad diem belli*), Kent. Gl. 807. **V.** *to provide, procure, furnish* :—Weolan gegearwað *divitias parat* (*manus fortium*), Kent. Gl. 321. Gegearwiað *praeparant* (*misericordia et veritas bona*), 492. Hwæs beóð þâ ðing þe ðû gegearwudest *whose shall those things be, which thou hast provided* ?, Lk. 12, 20. Hê lîfes bysene on him sylfum gegearowode *exemplum uiuendi exhibens*, Bd. 4, 23 ; Sch. 470, 21. Þâra gôda brûcan þe Engle gewunnan and gegearwedon, 4, 4 ; Sch. 369, 14. Gegearwiende *exibentes*, Wrt. Voc. ii. 33, 19. Sý him eallum þæslic wyrðment gegearwod *omnibus congruus honor exibeatur*, R. Ben. 81, 21. Gegearewod, 83, 17. Gegearwedum *adibitis*, 3, 32. Nis ænig monna môde þæs cræftig þæt hî (cræftas) ânum ealle weorðen gegearwade, Crä. 100. **VI.** *to do, perform* :—Þâ rihtwîsan men gegearwiað þâ wundru *miracula exhibent*, Gr. D. 161, 26. Is cûð þæt hwîlum þâs wundru hî dôð (gegearwiað, v. l.) of heora mihte, hwilum eác gegearwiað of heora bene *constat quod aliquando haec ex potestate, aliquando vero exhibent ex postulatione*, 162, 5. Þis wundor gedôn and gegearwian *hoc miraculam exhibere*, 166, 18. Ân lufu is þe þû miht mê gegearwian *there is one kindness that you may do me*; unum est quod mihi impendere beneficium potes, 182, 6. Hié sculon lædteówdôm geearwian, Past. 138, 17. **VII.** *to make easy to do* :—Mê þæt mægen þe ær þæs inganges duru bewerede æfter þan þone ingang þæs sîðfætes gegearwode, Hml. S. 23 b, 464. v. un-gegearwod.

**ge-gearwung.** Add : **I.** *preparation* :—Þâ wæs se dæg parasceue, þ is gegearwunge (-earwunge, v. l.), Lk. 23, 54. **II.** *doing, working*. Cf. ge-gearwian ; VI, V :—Tô gegearwunga his *ad operationem suam*, Bl. Gl. For gegearwunge þære sôðan lufe *pro caritatis exhibitione*, Gr. D. 39, 22.

**ge-gearwungness.** Either ge-gearwung or (?) ge-gearwness (cf. hirwness *for form*) should be read. In l. 2 for praeparatio substitute praeparationem.

**ge-gegnian.** Add :—Sôðfæstnis gigegnað him suoelce môder ârwyrðe *justitia obviabit illi quasi mater honorificata*, Rtl. 45, 23. [Cf. O. H. Ger. gaganen *obviare, occurrere* : Icel. gegna *to meet, encounter*.]

**ge-gehâwian.** v. ge-hâwian : **ge-gehold.** v. ge-healdan : **ge-gêman.** v. ge-gîman : **gegendan** ?:—Ðâ gegendan (gengendan ?) *arsantes*, Wrt. Voc. ii. 9, 51.

**ge-geng,** e; *f. A body of fellow-travellers, a company* :—Seó sæ âdrencte Pharaonem and ealle his gegenge . . . Crîst deófol silfne besencte and ealle his gegenge, Btwk. 196, 4, 8. v. ge-genge ; *n.*

**ge-genga,** an; *m. A fellow-traveller, companion* :—Gegenga *conviator*, Wrt. Voc. ii. 135, 71. Gegenta *pedissequis, conviator*, Txts. 114, 85. þæt êce fýr wæs deófle gegearwod and his gegengum (-gengum, -gængum, geferum, v. ll.) eallum, Wlfst. 184, 18.

**ge-genge,** es; *n. A company* :—Hê þæne þeódfeónd on helle grund besencte mid eallum þâm gegenge þe him ær fyligde, Wlfst. 86, 21. Hê wæs on ðâm gegængcge þâr man Crîst bænde, Ll. Th. ii. 386, 23. v. ge-geng; *f.*

**ge-genge;** *adj. Convenient, suitable, agreeable* :—Unc wearð God yrre for þon wit him noldon hnîgan mid heáfdum . . . : ac unc gegenge ne wæs þæt wit him on þegnscipe þeówian wolden, Gen. 743.

**ge-gengedness.** v. æfter-gegengedness.

**ge-geótan.** Add : **I.** *to pour* a liquid :—Yfel wæte bið gegoten on

þ lim, Lch. ii. 284, 28.    **II.** *to pour molten metal, found, cast:*—þū gegute *fundasti*, Ps. Spl. T. 88, 12. Hig habbað him gegoten ān gylden cealf *fecerunt sibi vitulum conflatilem*, Ex. 32, S. Gegoten *conflatilis*, Wrt. Voc. i. 34, 16: *fusile*, Wülck. Gl. 245, 22. þā gód ealle gegaderode biúþ swelce hī sién tō ānum wecge gegoten, Bt. 34, 9; F. 146, 20. Ælc calic gegoten beó þe man hūsl on hālgige, and on treówenum ne hālgige man ænig, Ll. Th. ii. 252, 21: Sal. 31. [*O. H. Ger.* ge-giozan *conflare, effundere*.]

**ge-gerela.** v. ge-girela: **ge-gerwan.** v. ge-girwan: **ge-giddian.** *Take here* ge-gyddian *in Dict.*

**ge-gifan** *to give.* (1) *to deliver, hand over:*—þā þām Godes mæn his āgen hors gegifen (āgifen, *v. l.*) wæs *cum servo Dei caballus suus redditur*, Gr. D. 16, 1. (2) *to give* as a present:—Hig noldon him āgyfan nān þingc þæs þe se cyng heom gegyfen (geunnen, *v. l.*) hæfde, Chr. 1049; P. 168, 19. Hē hæfð gegyfen þæ gegyldhealle, Cht. Th. 605, 6. Eall þā woruldgód þā þe him gegyfene (-gyfne, gifene, *v. ll.*) wǽron *cuncta quae sibi donabantur*, Bd. 3, 5; Sch. 202, 19. (3) *to give* in marriage:—Hē Crīsten wīf hæfde him gegyfen (him wæs forgifen, *v. l.*), Bd. 1, 25; Sch. 53, 7.

**ge-gifod.** *Add:* [*O. H. Ger.* habet si imo gegebōt.]

**ge-gilda.** *Add:*—Syndon ðis ðā forword þe . . . þā gegyldan gecoren habbað . . . æt ælcon gegyldan ǽnne peningc . . . æt twām gegyldum ǽnne brādne hlāf . . . sceóte ælc gegylda ǽnne gyldsester fulne clǽnes hwǽtes, Cht. Th. 605, 17–606, 8. Gif hwilc gegilda forþfǽre, gebrynge hine eal se gildscipe þǽr hē tō wilnie, 610, 35. [The word occurs often in these documents.]

**ge-gildan.** *Take here* ge-gyldan *in Dict., and add:*—Him man geald (gegeald, *v. l.* v. p. 295) .xxiii. þūsend punda, Chr. 1002; P. 133, 37. Gegylde hē ān pund, Cht. Th. 611, 16. Bīde mon mid þǽre wīterǽdenne oþ þæt se wer gegolden sié, Ll. Th. i. 148, 4.

**ge-gilde,** es; *n. Membership in a guild:*—Gif gegilda his gegildan ofstleá, bere sylf wiþ māgas þ hē brǽc, and his gegilde eft mid eahta pundum gebycge, oþþe hē þolie ā geséres and freóndscipes, Cht. Th. 612, 7.

**ge-gildscipe.** *Take here* ge-gyldscipe *in Dict.*

**ge-gíman.** *Take here* ge-géman *in Dict., and add:* (1) *to take care with, correct:*—Gegēmes *corrigens*, Mt. p. 12, 13. (2) *to take care of medically, cure:*—Alle in untrymnisse gegēmde *cunctos infirmitate curavit*, Mk. p. 2, 13: Lk. p. 6, 9: p. 8, 9. Monigo gegēmed woeron *multi curantur*, p. 4, 19.

**ge-gimmod.** *Take here* ge-gymmod *in Dict.*

**ge-girela,** an; *m.:* **ge-girelu,** e; *pl. n.* -girele (-a); *gen.* -girela; *f. Take here* ge-gerela *in Dict., and add:* (1) in a collective sense, *apparel, clothing, raiment:*—Of þām unmetta and þām ungemetlican gegerelan . . . onwǽcnaþ sió wōde þrāg þǽre wrǽnnesse, Bt. 37, 1; F. 186, 16. Gegyrwað þone līchaman mid nīwum hræglum and gegyrelan (-gyrlan, *v. l.*) *noua indumenta corpori circumdate*, Bd. 4, 30; Sch. 536, 19. In gegerelan bigyldum ymbswapen *in vestitu deaurato circumamicta*, Ps. Srt. 44, 10. Heó him æteówde ealne hire gegyrelan (*omnem indumentum*) þe heó wolde æt hire byrgenne habban, Bl. H. 143, 35. Hē nāht elles nǽfde būton his ānfealdne gegyrelan (*nothing but the clothes he was wearing*), ah eall þ hē māre hæfde, eal hē þ ǽr . . . for Gode gesealde. 215, 4, 10. (2) *a garment, an article of clothing:*—Gegerla *vel* godweb (cf. goduuebbe *toga*, 122, 55) *fasces*, Wrt. Voc. ii. 146, 52. Scrūd ł gegyrlu *vestimentum*, Ps. L. 101, 27. Gegyrlu ł wǽfels *amictus*, 103, 6. Hloðan, gegirelan *liniamento*, Wrt. Voc. ii. 50, 4. Gegyrlan gegyred (*regali*) *fasce togatus*, 94, 82: 37, 41. Hē hine on ðæs þearfan gegyrelan æteówde, Bl. H. 215, 29. Gegerelo (-u, R.) aldum *uestimento ueteri*, Mk. L. 2, 21. Gegearuad huíte gegerela (-gerla, R.) *indutus ueste alba*, Lk. L. 23, 11. Gigerila *indumentum*, Rtl. 103, 22. Gegirelan *cieclades*, Wrt. Voc. ii. 19, 72. Hwǽr beóþ þā glengeas and þā mycclan gegyrelan þe hē þone līchoman mid frætwode?, Bl. H. 111, 36. þā gegyrelan and þā hrægel *indumenta*, Bd. 4, 31; Sch. 543, 18. Gif þū wēnst þte wundorlice gegerela hwelc weordmynd sié, þonne telle ic þā weorþmynd þām gegyrelan þe hié worhte *pulcrum variis fulgere vestibus putas? . . . ingenium mirabor artificis*, Bt. 14, 1; F. 42, 18. Mid þǽre gehrinennesse þāra ylcra gegyrela (-gyrelena, -gyrlena, *v. ll.*). Bd. 4, 19; Sch. 450, 15. Gegerelan *amiculis*, hrægle *amiculo*, Wrt. Voc. ii. 5, 20. In huítum gegerelum *in albis*, Jn. L. 20, 12. Gigerlu *uestimenta*, Mk. R. 11, 7. Gigerela *stolas*, Rtl. 48, 1. (2 a) *an ornament that is worn:*—Gegirelan *discriminalia*, Wrt. Voc. ii. 27, 62. (3) *a banner.* Cf. gūþ-fana:—Gegyrele *labara* (*labarum signum ex panno aut serico confectum*), Wrt. Voc. ii. 52, 9. v. bisceop-, diácon-, earm-, feoht-, munuc-, sceanc-gegirela.

**ge-girelian** *to clothe.* v. ge-gerelad *in Dict.*

**ge-girelic** (?); *adj. Pertaining to clothes:*—Gegerelican *amiculis* (cf. gegerelan *amiculis*, 5, 20), Wrt. Voc. ii. 82, 80.

**ge-girnan.** *Take here* ge-gyrnan *in Dict., and add:*—Gegernð *desiderat*, Kent. Gl. 798. Gegyrnende, wilniende *competentes*, An. Ox. 2882.

**ge-girnendlic;** *adj. Desirable:*—Gegyrnendlice *desiderabilia*, Ps. Rdr. 18, 11.

---

**ge-girnung,** e; *f. A desire, request:*—Ðis ys Ælfgyfæ gegurning tō hīræ cinehlāfordæ . . . heó hyne bitt for Godæs lufun þæt heó mōte beón hyre cwydes wyrðæ, Cht. Th. 552, 27.

**ge-girwan.** *Take here* ge-gerwan, ge-gyrian *in Dict., and add:* **I.** *to prepare* an object for use:—Hē hēt him ȳðlidan gegyrwan, B. 199. Ic geongo gegeruiga (*parare*) iúh styd, Jn. L. 14, 2. Gegaerwendne *conparantem*, Wrt. Voc. ii. 104, 47. Bið foldan dǽl fægre gegierwed . . . corfen, sworfen, Rä. 29, 1. Alle gegerwad *omnia parata*, Mt. L. 22, 4. **I a.** *to prepare* food, *dress, cook:*—Haran sina gegyre and him syle þicgan, Lch. i. 344, 15. Man ne mihte nānne mete gegyrwan, Ors. 1, 7; S. 36, 27. Sunu þǽm fæder tō mete gegierwan, 1, 12; S. 52, 24. **II.** *to dress:*—Gegeruuid *preatextatus*, Wrt. Voc. ii. 117, 78. Gegirwed, 68, 34. (1) *to clothe* with or in a garment (*lit. or fig.*):—Gegereð hine āwergednisse *induit se maledictione*, Ps. Srt. 108, 18. Ic gegerede mec mid hēran, 34, 13. Hē gegyrede hine (mid, *v. l.*) his munucgegyrelan *ipsius habitu indutus*, Bd. 1, 7; Sch. 20, 23. Gigeride, Rtl. 45, 29: 79, 7. Hiá gegeredon (*induerunt*) hine mið his gewēdum, Mt. L. 27, 31. Mid fellum gegerwed *pellibus uestitus*, Nar. 27, 1. Gegered, Ps. Srt. 131, 9. Gegyrlan gegyred *fasce togatus*, Wrt. Voc. ii. 94, 83. Synd hī on sōðfæstnesse gegierede *induantur justitia*, Ps. Th. 131, 9. (2) *to put on* a garment:—Dryhten wlite gegereð (*decorem induit*), gegereð Dryhten strengu, Ps. Srt. 92, 1. Wlite ðū gegeredest, 103, 1. (3) *to clothe* with armour, *arm:*—Hēt ic ælcne mon hine mid his wǽpnun gegerwan and faran forð *jussi ut armati agmen sequerentur*, Nar. 9, 26. Wǽpnum hié gegyrwan *to arm themselves*, 10, 28. Mid wǽpnum gegered *armis indutus*, 9, 28. Hē hine tō gūðe gegyred hæfde, B. 1472. Mid heregeatwum gegyrede, Bl. H. 221, 29. (3 a) where an object is personified:—Ic (*a sword*) eom . . . fægere gegyrwed, byrne is mīn bleófāg, Rä. 21, 2. **III.** *to ornament, adorn:*—Mid since gegyrwed, Kr. 23. Gegyred mid golde, 16. Golde gegerede and gimcynnum, Met. 25, 6. **IV.** *to equip, furnish, supply:*—Seó wiht wæs wundrun gegierwed, hæfde feówere fét under wombe, Rä. 37, 2: 68, 2: 30, 3: Sch. 61. **V.** *to direct:*—v. ge-girwung. (Cf. *Icel.* göra *to send, dispatch*):—Lǽd ðíne willas gind ðín lond, and gegier (-gierwe, *v. l.*) ðæt hié iernen bi herestrǽtum *deriventur fontes tui foras*, Past. 373, 5. Seó genihtsumnes þæs wæteres byð ǽrest gesomnod in wīdum seáðe, oþ þ æt nēxtan hit byð gegæred (-ger-, *v. l.*) in myccle cá *aquarum abundantia in extenso prius lacu colligitur, ad postremum vero in amnem derivatur*, Gr. D. 98, 17. þ wæter is gegyred tō þām neoðerum stōwum fram þām cnolle þæs muntes *ut aqua ab illo montis cacumine usque ad inferiora derivetur*, 113, 13. **VI.** *to present, give:*—þā māðmas ic þē bringan wylle, ēstum gegyrwan, B. 2149. [*O. H. Ger.* ge-garewen.]

**ge-girwung,** e; *f. Direction:*—Gegiringe mīne ðū āsmeádest *directionem meam inuestigasti*, Ps. Rdr. 138, 3. v. ge-girwan.

**ge-giscan;** *p.* te, de *To stop up, close:*—Gegiscte (gigiscdæ, Ep.; gescdae, Erf., gigisdae, Ld.) *oppilauit, clausit*, Txts. 83, 1447. Gegiscde, betȳnde *oppilauit*, Wrt. Voc. ii. 65, 18.

**ge-gītsian** *to covet and get, to get by unscrupulous means, extort:*—Hié wilniað ðæt hié gegītsien æt ðæm ungetȳdum folce wīsdōmes naman *ut apud imperitum vulgus scientiae sibi nomen extorqueant*, Past. 365, 22.

**ge-giwian, -giowian.** *Add:*—Suā huæd ðū gegiuað (giowas, R.) *quaecumque poposceris*, Jn. L. 11, 22. Gigiuað *exposcit*, Rtl. 103, 42. Gié gegiuað *petieritis*, Jn. p. 7, 6. Gegiuað (giowigas, R.), Jn. L. 14, 14: 16, 23. Gegiuas *expetunt*, Mt. p. 13, 9. Gé gegiuuedes *petisses*, Jn. L. 4, 10. Gegiuade gié (giowadun, R.) *petistis*, 16, 24. Hiá gegiuudon (gegiowadun, R.), Mk. 15, 6. Gigiuia *appetat*, Rtl. 77, 5: 105, 5. Gigiuiga hiá *postulent*, 48, 38. Gegiuad *expetita*, 122, 5.

**ge-gladian.** *Add:* **I.** *trans.* (1) *to make glad, gladden.* (a) of a physical effect, (α) of cheerful appearance:—Gegladað *exilaret* (cor gaudens *exhilarat* faciem), Kent. Gl. 516. (β) of the reviving effects of a medicine:—Hyt þone innoð wið þæs geallan tōgotennysse gegladað, Lch. i. 270, 5. (2) of a mental effect:—Ðū ūsig gigladas *nos laetificas*, Rtl. 31, 32. Giglædas, 21. Ne þǽr ārfæstnes sib ne hopa ne swige gegladað *nec pax nec pietas immo spes nulla quietis flentibus arrident*, Dōm. L. 220. Hé his folc gegladode *dedit requiem universis provinciis*, Hml. A. 95, 107. Gegladiga *laetificet*, Rtl. 18, 15. Ic beó gegladod *exhilaror*, Wrt. Voc. ii. 145, 3. (2) *to please:*—Sē sē þe dēð þæt his þearfa beóð, sē gegladað God; and sē þe dēð ænig unnyt, . . . hē ābelhð his Drihtne, Wlfst. 279, 1. Gif hī mid gōdum weorcum hine gegladiað, Ælfc. T. Grn. 6, 16. þ hig God gegladige, Ll. Th. ii. 256, 8. (3) *to make propitious, propitiate:*—Se cāsere . . . offrigende his lāc his ārleásum godum wolde hī gegladian . . . þ hī him fylstan sceoldon, Hml. S. 28, 38. (4) *to appease, reconcile, make gentle* what is hard. (a) the object a person:—Hē mid gebedum gegladað God, Hml. S. 3, 562. Gegladode *demulcet*, An. Ox. 2, 137. þ hī þone rēðan cāsere mid sceattum gegladodon, Hml. S. 3, 231. Gegladedon *repropitiarent, i. mitigarent*, An. Ox. 4724: 2, 374. Gegladudon *reconciliarent*, 7, 328. ¶ *to reconcile* to (*dat.*):—þæt hē him God gegladode, Hml. Th. ii. 30, 33. (b) the object a feeling (anger, &c.):—Gegladað *placabit* (*indignationem*),

Kent. Gl. 559. Hē wolde hyra rēðnysse gegladian (gelīdian, *v.l.*) *studuit eorum asperitatem placare,* Gr. D. 80, 16. **II.** *intrans. To be glad, rejoice:*—Gegladade ł glæd uæs *gauisus est,* Jn. L. 8, 56. Gigladia cirica ðīn *laetatur aecclesia tua,* Rtl. 72, 14. Gigladia uē *gaudeamus,* 38, 29: *letamur,* 49, 20. Rihtwīse gegladian on blisse *justi delectentur in laetitia,* Ps. Spl. 67, 3.

**ge-glādung,** e ; *f. A delighting, delectation :*—Gegladunga *delectationes,* Scint. 210, 4.

**ge-glædness,** e ; *f. Gladness, joy :*—Giglædnisso *gaudia,* Rtl. 31, 23.

**ge-glengan.** **Add:** (1) *to set in order, arrange :*—Ealle geglengende *cuncta conponens,* Kent. Gl. 277. Geglengede *composita,* 570. Geglengedu, Wrt. Voc. ii. 23, 44. (2) *to adorn, ornament :*—Mid leóðe geglengan, Angl. viii. 301, 46 : 326, 2. Geglenged *ornata,* An. Ox. 4393: *compta,* 8, 324 : *comptus,* i. *ornatus,* Wrt. Voc. ii. 132, 82. Seó heorte bið geglenced þurh Godes neósunge, Hml. Th. ii. 316, 6. Būtan geglengcedre *sine pompulenta,* An. Ox. 3729. Þā geglengdan *falerata,* i. *comta,* 539. Þā geglengedan, Wrt. Voc. ii. 33, 41. Geglencdum *gemmatis,* i. *pictis,* 128 : *pompis,* 23, 25.

**ge-glengendlic.** *Substitute :* **ge-glengendlīce ;** *adv. Delicately, elegantly :*—Geglencendlīce glencan *delicate* (i. *pompose*) *componere,* An. Ox. 1202.

**ge-glófed** *gloved :*—Ic nāt hū þū hym onfōn mage mid geglófedum handum ; ðū scealt dōn bær līc ongeán, Solil. H. 42, 11.

**gegn, gēn ;** *adj.* Take here gēn in *Dict., and add :* cf. gægne, gegnum : **gegn-.** v. geán-: **gegnian.** v. ge-gegnian.

**ge-gnīdan.** **Add :**—Gegniden *dilitum,* Wrt. Voc. ii. 140, 38. Gegnidenan *attrite,* 81, 3 : 5, 12. [*O. H. Ger.* ge-gnitan *defricatus.*]

**gegninga.** *Substitute : Directly, straightway,* (1) *of motion, without deviating :*—Hȳ gongað gegnunga tō Hierusalem, Gū. 785. (2) *of time, at once :*—Embe hand, hrædlīce sōna þærrigte, gēnunga *jam jam, cito,* Germ. 388, 73. Sē þe gelīð, raðe hē styrið oððe gēnunge hē ārīseð, Lch. iii. 188, 21. Þæt hié gegnunga gyldon sceolde *that they should at once sacrifice,* Dan. 212. Þær þū gegninga gūðe findest, An. 1351: 1356. Geagnunga, El. 673. (3) *without intermediate agency :*—Hwā meahte mē swylc gewit gifan, gif hit gegnunga God ne onsende?, Gen. 672. Þæt hit geguunga from Gode cōme, 683. (4) *directly to an end, without modification, completely, simply :*—þæt mæg secgan sē þe wyle sōð sprecan, þæt se mondryhten, sē eów geaf eóredgeatwe . . . gēnunga gūðgewædu forwurpe (*that he simply threw away the weapons he gave you*), B. 2871. [*O. Sax.* gegnungo.]

**gegnum.** **Add :** *directly, straight on.* v. gegn ; *adj.*

**ge-gnysan.** *Dele, and see* ge-cnyssan.

**ge-gōdian.** **Add : I.** *to furnish with, present :*—Gegōdod *donatus,* Hml. Th. ii. 468, 14. (1) *to furnish with a material object :*—Syfiincge gegōded (-rod-, MS.) *pulmentario potiretur,* An. Ox. 3757. Gegōd[ode] *ineptam* (*cirris crispantibus*), 4647. (1 a) *to endow with property, enrich :*—Se bisceop nȳdde þæt folc þæt hī ðone ðriddan dæl þæs feós underfēngon, and hē mid þām twām dælum þæt mynster gegōdode, Hml. Th. i. 452, 23 : Hml. S. 6, 147. Se cāsere Godes cyrcan gegōdode, 27, 134. Hī þā crīstenan gegōdodon, 2, 267. Gegōdigende mænige *locupletantes multos,* Scint. 178, 7. (2) *to endow with non-material objects :*—Getincnesse gegōdod *facundia fretus,* An. Ox. 311. Gegōdedum *praedito,* i. *ditato* (*facundia dictandi*), 911. Galdre gegōdedum *necromantia freto,* 4133. Gegōdedne *fortunatum,* 2561. Þā synd gegōdede *potiuntur* (*puritatis palma*), 1743. Mynegunge gegōdude *monitu freti,* Angl. xiii. 375, 142. **II.** *to do good physically :*—Genim þā ylcan wyrte and syle þigccean ; heó gegōdað, Lch. i. 72, 15. **III.** *to make* (*morally*) *good, improve :*—Þ seó stōw þurh hine gegōdod and geriht wære, R. Ben. 108, 12. **IV.** *to increase the dignity of, enhance :*—Ne byð seó þēnung þæs nā þe wyrse. Ne eft nis ænig swā mære . . . þæt ador ðæra þēnunga gegōdian oððon gemycclian mæge, Wlfst. 34, 11.

**ge-gōdud.** *See preceding word :* **ge-gong.** v. ge-gang.

**ge-got,** es ; *n. A shedding of tears :*—On willsumnesse gebeda and on teára gegote *in orationis et lacrimarum deuotione,* Bd. 4, 30 ; Sch. 536, 1.

**ge-grāpian.** **Add :** *to lay hold of with the hand ; to reach :*—Seó clæne beó oft wīde and sīde blōsman gegrēt . . . and hig grimme windas gemētað, and þā wreccan geswencað, þ heó earfoðlīce cýððe gegrāpað (*that hardly can she reach home*), Angl. viii. 324, 15. Gegrāpade *contractavit,* i. *palpavit,* Wrt. Voc. ii. 135, 28.

**ge-greátian ;** *p. ode To become thick* or *stout :*—Gegreátod *incrassatus,* Ps. L. fol. 192, 15.

**ge-grelen,** Wrt. Voc. ii. 45, 60. v. ge-galan.

**ge-gremian.** **Add : I.** *of a physical effect :*—Wiþ þon þe men mete untela melte . . . gegremme mid wyrtdrence þ hē spīwe, Lch. ii. 226, 7. **II.** *of a mental effect :*—Gigremid, gigremit *irritatus in rixam,* Txts. 68, 515. Gigraemid, gigremid *lacessitus,* 74, 593. Gegremed, Wrt. Voc. ii. 50, 51. (1) *to irritate a person :*—Se man þe æfter dædbōte his mānfullan dæda geednīwað, sē gegremað God, Hml. Th. ii. 602, 25 : S. 12, 163. Hī gegremedon þe *irritauerunt te,* Ps. L. 5, 11. Gegræmedon, Wlfst. 166, 19. Gelōme wē habbað gehrepod ymbe þæs

mōnan ryne, and wē wēnað þ wē gegremion iunge men, Angl. viii. 328, 13. Se wīsa ne wilnað nā tō hrædlīce ðære wræce, ðeáh hē gegremed sié *sapiens laesus in praesens se ulcisci non desiderat,* Past. 220, 15. Hē geseah þæt hē wæs bepæht, and weard þearle gegremod, Hml. Th. i. 80, 14 : 512, 14. (2) *to irritate* an animal :—Hī gebundon þone bysceop on sumne fearr, and þone gegremedon þ hē hleóp on unsmēðe eorðan, Shrn. 152, 1.

**ge-grētan.** **Add : I.** *to approach, visit :*—Seó beó blōsman gegrēt, Angl viii. 324, 13. Man cyrican gegrēte mid leóhte and lācum, Wlfst. 73, 20. Þ hī Godes cirican gridian and fridian, and mid leóhte and lācum hī gelōme gegrētan, Ll. Th. i. 326, 17. Gōdum gegrētan, B. 1861. **II.** *to assail :*—Mec longeðas lyt gegrētað, Gū. 287. **III.** *to afflict, visit* with displeasure, &c. :—Seó æ ne gegrēt þone rihtwīsan mid nānum yfele, ac heó·gewītnað þā unrihtwīsan, Hml. S. 17, 19. Þte ðū mec ne gegroeta ł ne pīnia *ne me torqueas,* Lk. L. 8, 28. **IV.** *to address, accost, salute :*—Wīsdom mīn mōd mid his wordum gegrētte, Bt. 3, 1 ; F. 4, 18 : B. 1979. Hē gegrētte hindeman sīðe swæse gesīðas, 2516 : Fä. 15. Nō hē mid hearme gæst gegrētte, æc cwæð þæt wilcuman Wedera leóde fōron, B. 1893. Gegrētte *salutavit,* Lk. L. R: 1, 40. Hyt gerīst þ wē þā *regulares feriarum* mid leóðe gegrētun, Angl. viii. 302, 6. Gegroeta *salutare,* Mk. L. 12, 38. Gegroetæ, 15, 18. Gegroeted wæs *salutatur,* Lk. p. 3, 15. Gegrēttre rōde *salutata cruce,* Angl. xiii. 21, 779. [*O. H. Ger.* ge-gruozen *movere, compellere.*] v. un-gegrēt.

**ge-grētlic ;** *adj. Of greeting, recommendatory :*—Stafum gegrētlicum *litteris commendaciis,* R. Ben. I. 103, 6.

**ge-grinan.** v. ge-grīnian.

**ge-grindan.** **Add :**—Tuu wīf gegrundon on coernæ *duae molentes in mola,* Mt. L. 24, 41. Gegrunden *fressa,* i. *molita, fracta, divisa,* Wrt. Voc. ii. 150, 68. *Faba fresa* gegrunden beán s. *dicta quia molata est,* 146, 62 : 39, 68. xxvii piporcorn[a] gegrundenra, Lch. iii. 48, 10.

**ge-grīnian ;** *p. ode To ensnare :*—Gegrīnað, gefēhþ *inlaqueat,* Germ. 390, 41. Ðū eart gegrīnad *inlaqueatus es,* Kent. Gl. 122. Nis preóstes cwēne ænig ōðer þing būtan deófles grīn, and sē þe mid þām gegrīnod byð . . . , hē byð þurh deófol gefangen, Ll. Th. ii. 336, 26.

**ge-grip.** **Add :**—Gegrip *corruptionem* (correptionem *seems to have been read*), Ps. Spl. T. 15, 10. v. ge-gripennis.

**ge-grīpan.** **Add : I.** *to lay hold of* (1) a material object, *to take with the hand, grasp :*—Hē wæpn gegrāp mid tō campienne, Bl. H. 167, 1. Se Hēlend āþenede hond his and gegrāp hine (*apprehendit eum*), Mt. R. 14, 31. Ealle þā apostolas hié gegrīpan on hire middel, Bl. H. 141, 29. Ic wille gegrīpan þ palmtwig, and hit tō eorþan āfyllan, 151, 15. Nim swā mycel swā þū mid þrīm fingron gegrīpan mæge, Lch. i. 230, 11. Mið ðȳ gegripen (-grippen, L.) wæs hond his *praehensa manu ejus,* Mk. R. 1, 31. Gegripen *adprehensum,* Kent. Gl. 192. (1 a) *to seize with an implement :*—Fȳrene tangan him on handa hié hæfdon, and . . . hié mē mid þæm gegrīpan woldon, Bd. 5, 12 ; Sch. 621, 15. (2) a non-material object :—Hié gegrīpað (*arripiunt*) ðone cwide ðæs apostoles hiora gītsunge tō fultome, Past. 53, 3. **II.** *to get possession of, obtain, acquire :*—Gegrīp *arripe* (*prudentiam*), Kent. Gl. 64. Underfōð ł gegrīpað steóre ł lāre *apprehendite disciplinam,* Ps. L. 2, 12. Suæ iornað gié þte gié gigrīpa (*conprehendatis*), Rtl. 5, 37. **III.** with idea of violence, constraint :—Gegrīpe *capiat, retineat,* Wrt. Voc. ii. 128, 48. (1) *to seize* a person, *take* captive, *apprehend* a criminal. (a) the subject a person :—Sē ðe swā hwēr hine gegrīpes (*adpraehenderit*), hē bītes, Mk. R. L. 9, 18. Hē hyne gegrāp *arripiebat illum,* Lk. 8, 29. Gāst gigrāp (*apprehendit*) hine, Lk. R. 9, 39. Gigriopun Símōn, 22, 26. Hwonne hī mē gegrīpan and tō helle locum gelædan, Bd. 5, 13 ; Sch. 640, 16. Hē mē swā lādode þ hié mē ne gegripon, Bl. H. 151, 27. Sendun ðā aldormen embihtmenn þte hiæ gegripe (-grioppo, L.) hine, Jn. R. 7, 32. Sōhtun hine tō gigrīpanne, 30, 44. Hē wæs gegripen (*correptus*) fram þām unclænum gāstum, Gr. D. 294, 1. (b) the subject an animal :—Ān leó gegrāp mē·and arn tō wuda, Hml. S. 30, 331. (c) the subject a thing :—Sió wilnung ðæs īdlan gielpes gegrīpð ðæt mōd, Past. 373, 20. Gegrīpeð, 143, 5. Þām þe se æfterra deáþ gegrīpð, Bt. 19 ; F. 70, 18. Gegrīpað *capiunt* (*impium iniquitates suae*), Kent. Gl. 116. Ðā gegrāp hine swīðlic ege, Hml. S. 23 b, 212 : 460. Gegripun ł gehæfton *comprehenderunt,* Ps. L. 39, 13. Þte ðīostro iúih ne gegrīpa (*compraehendat*), Jn. L. 12, 35. Ðe lēs ðū sió gegripen hiora onwaldum *ne capiaris nutibus illius,* Kent. Gl. 161. (2) *to seize* a thing, *take with violence* as a robber :—Gegrīpeð *diri*[*pi*]*et* (v. Mt. 12, 29), Wrt. Voc. ii. 72, 58 : 26, 33. Ðonne hē gegrīp[ð] *cum rapuerit,* Kent. Gl. 705. Ne bið gegripen *non rapitur,* 71. (3) *to take, catch* game :—Wildeór gegrīpan, Hml. S. 23 b, 735. v. ge-grippan.

**ge-gripenis.** **Add :**—On gegripnesse (-grīp-?) *in corruptionem,* Ps. Spl. T. 29, 11. v. ge-grip.

**ge-grippan ;** *p. de.* **I.** *to lay hold of, obtain, acquire :*—Folc ðīn frōfro līfes deádlīces onfōe, and ēco gifeá gigrippa (*comprehendat*), Rtl. 39, 27 : 63, 20. Gigrippe sōðfæstnesse *adprehendet justitiam,* 45, 23. **II.** *to seize :*—Gāst gegrippde hine, Lk. L. 9, 39. Gegrippedon, 23, 26. Sumo ualdon gegrioppa hine, Jn. L. 7, 44. Soecendo hine tō gegriopann[e], Jn. p. 5, 5. v. ge-græppian in *Dict.*

**ge-grówan.** *Add:* **I.** *to grow together, unite by growing:*—Swá fæste his heáfod wæs gegrówen tó ðám líchaman, swylce hit næfre of ácorfen nære *ita caput ejus unitum fuerat corpori, ac si nequaquam fuisset abscissum,* Gr. D. 198, 28. **II.** *of soil, to produce, bear:*—Se æcer syððan gegreów .c. sída sēlor þonne hē ǽr dyde, Shrn. 137, 25. Swá se fiicbeám ofersceadað ðæt lond ðæt hit under him ne mæg gegrówan, Past. 337, 11.

**ge-grunded.** *Dele.*

**ge-grundstaþelian;** *p.* ode *To found, build on a firm foundation:*—Hí ne magon áfyllan mín fæstræde geþanc þe is gegrundstaþelod, Hml. S. 8, 21.

**ge-gyld.** *Add:*—Mid þám fægerum stafum gegylde, Guth. 4, 2. .11. gegylde weófodsceátas, Cht. Th. 244, 18.

**ge-gylden;** *adj. Golden:*—Ðá gegyldnan *aurea,* Wrt. Voc. ii. 3, 69.

**ge-gyltan.** *Add:*—Hē gegylte on neorxnawonge, Angl. xi. 1, 15. Ic eom ondetta synne þe hie on gegyltan, 98, 21.

**ge-gymian, -gymm(i)an** *to pierce, cut into the flesh:*—Gif man sié gegymed, and þū hine gelácnian scyle . . . þ dolh rēt mid ealdan spice, Lch. ii. 352, 18-354, 5: 304, 12. Gif man gegemed weorðeð, .xxx. sciłł. gebēte, Ll. Th. i. 18, 8. v. gymian.

**ge-gyrd.** v. forþ-gegyrd.

**ge-gyrdan.** *Add:*—Gegyrded (-að, R.) hine *praecingit se,* Lk. L. 12, 37. Ðū waldes ðec gigyrde *cingebas te,* Jn. L. 21, 18. Gegyrded *praecinctus,* 13, 5. *Luna* beón gegyrd (*cingi*), Lch. iii. 206, 19.

**ge-gyrian.** v. ge-girwan: **ge-gyrnan.** v. ge-giman.

**ge-habban.** *Add:*—Gehæbbende *cohercens,* Wrt. Voc. ii. 21, 74. **I.** *to have, possess* (of relative position):—Gif hié (þíne menn) yfele sint, ðonne sint hié þē pleólicran gehæfd þonne genæfd, Bt. 14, 1; F. 42, 22. **II.** *to retain, detain, keep* (1) a person (a) in a place:—Hē hí hwylcehwugu dagas mid him gehæfde *eos aliquot diebus secum retinuit,* Bd. 5, 10; Sch. 601, 9. Hē þone ǽrendracan on ðám mynstre sume hwíle gehæfde (*detinuit*), Gr. D. 39, 25. Hē wæs gehæfd (-hæfed, *v. l.*) *retentus,* Bd. 5, 10; Sch. 597, 14: 5, 19; Sch. 658, 18. Petrus wæs gehæfd on ðám cwearterne, Hml. Th. ii. 380, 31. (b) in a state or position:—þám þe se æfterra deáð gegrípð and on écnesse gehæfð, Bt. 19; S. 47, 2. Sió ungelícnes hira geearnunga híe tiēlð sume behindan sume, and hira scylda hí ðær gehabbað, Past. 107, 20. (2) a thing. (a) material:—Ne mæg ðæt scip nó stille gestondan, būton hit ankor gehæbbe, Past. 445, 13. Wiþ ðon þe man ne mæge his mete gehabban, and hē spíwe, Lch. i. 76, 20: ii. 190, 8. (b) non-material:—Ðára synna gē gihabbað *quorum peccata retinueritis,* Jn. L. 20, 23. Ne mæg hē þá swētnesse þisse worulde nó gehabban, gif heó hine fleón onginþ, Bt. 11, 1; F. 32, 36. **III.** *to restrain:*—Hē hine gehæfde (*restringeret*) fram æghwylcum unnyttum worde, Gr. D. 11, 8. Ðæt gē eów gehæbben sume hwíle, Past. 99, 15. **IV.** *to contain, have involved:*—Gif þ lange swá biþ, þonne gehæfþ hit on uneþelícne wæterbollan *if that is so for long, then it has a dropsy hard to cure involved in it,* Lch. ii. 204, 13. **V.** *to have room or capacity for, to allow, suffer:*—þæt heora land ne wǽre tó þæs mycel, þ hí mihton twá þeóde gehabban (on gehabban, *v. l.*) *quia non ambos eos caperet insula,* Bd. 1, 1; Sch. 11, 10. **VI.** *to uphold, maintain, preserve:*—Hē his ríce mid micelre uniéðnesse gehæfde, Ors. 6, 24; S. 276, 2. Ne ic máran getilige tó haldænne þonne ic . . . þá men on gehabban and gehealdan mage þe ic forðian sceal, Solil. H. 35, 18. þyssera hyrda gemynd is gehæfd be-eástan Bethleem áne míle, Hml. Th. i. 42, 34. **VII.** *to have, experience, be subject to:*—On þám heofenlicum ēðele nis nán niht gehæfd, Lch. iii. 240, 12. **VIII.** *to hold, keep* in some relation to oneself:—Būton se hláford hine wille on borh gehabban, Ll. Th. i. 228, 28. **IX.** *to have in the mind, hold, entertain* a feeling, &c.:—Fácn ne sceal mon on heortan gehabban *dolum in corde non tenere,* R. Ben. 17, 7. **IX a.** *to exhibit* (a feeling, &c.) *in action:*—Gif hié ðá hálwendan forhæfdnesse gehabban ne mægen *if they cannot be continent,* Past. 401, 32. **X.** *to hold, consider as:*—Hē for his lifes geearnunga wæs gehæfd (and ongyten, *v. l., habebatur*) micelre hálinesse man, Gr. D. 26, 6. þæs emnihtes dæg ys gehæfd, swá swá Bēda tǽcð, þæs on ðám feórðan dæge, Lch. iii. 240, 5. Nis se Fæder gehæfd gemǽnelíce Fæder from ðám Suna and þám Hálgan Gáste, *Trin.* i. 498, 29 : 32. Gehæfd swilce hálig stów, ii. 506, 26. Gehæfde *habebatur* (*celebris*), An. Ox. 3606. Hē befrán ðone pápan hwæt hí wǽron gehæfde (*what they were considered to be*). þá sǽde se biscop þæt hí sóðlíce wǽron hálige mæssepreóstas, Hml. Th. ii. 310, 12. **XI.** *to hold, carry on, engage in:*—Hí geðasfedon þæt ðær cýping binnan gehæfd wæs, Hml. Th. i. 406, 6. **XI a.** *to carry on* an institution :—Basilius tó þære byrig ferde on þæra wæs gehæfd þ foresæde mynster, Hml. S. 3, 325. **XII.** *to treat* well or ill:—Hē fram him fremsumlíce wæs onfangen and micle tíd mid him well gehæfd (-hæfed, *v. l.*) wæs (*habitus est*), Bd. 4, 1; Sch. 340, 16. **XII a.** of the effect of natural causes, e.g. sickness:—Heó wiste þ þ folc swá yfle wæs gehæfd mid scearpum hungre for heora synnum, Hml. A. 110, 249. þ þū síðige tó mē and míne untrumnysse gehǽle, for ðan þe ic eom yfele gehæfd, Hml. S. 24, 98.

*intrans. To have* at (wiþ), *to attack:*—Drihten hig gehyrde, þæt hig gehæfdon (-hæfton, Thw.) wið hine, þæt hig feóllon on þám gefeohte ætforan Israhēla bearnum *Domini sententia fuerat, ut indurarentur corda eorum et pugnarent contra Israel et caderent,* Jos. 11, 20.

**ge-hæccod.** *Dele.*

**ge-háda.** *Add:*—Beó þæslic wurðmynt gegearwod þám rihtgelýfedum úrum gehádum (*domesticis fidei*), R. Ben. 82, 1.

**ge-hádian.** *Add:*—Fram þám biscopum oþþe abbodum þe þone abbod gehádodun, R. Ben. 124, 11. Gesette hē þæne and gehádige tó ðám dihte abbodhádes, 119, 11. Gif hwylc abbod mæssepreóstes behófige, geceóse hē of his ágenum gefērum þe þæs hádes wyrðe sý, and hine gehádian lǽte, 111, 19.

**ge-hádod.** *Add:*—Ne úre ǽnig his líf ne fadode swá swá hē scolde, ne gehádode regollíce ne lǽwede lahlíce, Wlfst. 160, 1 : Bl. H. 43, 7. v. un-gehádod.

**ge-hæc.** v. mearh-gehæcc.

**ge-hæcca, an;** *m. A sausage:*—Gehæcca *farcimen,* Wrt. Voc. ii. 39, 77. v. mearh-hæccel.

**ge-hæft, es;** *m. A captive:*—Ðæt ðá bendas sumes gehæftes (*captiui*) tólýsende wǽron, Bd. 4, 22; Sch. 454, 9. v. hæft a captive; ge-hæft; *adj.*

**ge-hæft, e;** *f. A taking captive:*—Sē þe ne sealde ús on gehæfte ł tó fængce tóðum heora *qui non dedit nos in captionem dentibus eorum,* Ps. L. 123, 6.

**ge-hæft;** *adj. Add:*—Gif wífe hæftnýd gelympe, gif se wer onfó óðrum wífe and þ gehæfte (*captiva*) ymbe .v. winter cume, Ll. Th. ii. 152, 6. Ðæt dumbe and ðæt gehæfte neát *subjugale mutum,* Past. 257, 11. Hē mót gehæftne man álýsan, Wlfst. 294, 32.

**ge-hæftan.** *Add: To prevent free movement or action.* **I.** *to restrict, restrain, confine:*—Ðonne monn ðæt mód gehæft *cum cogitatio per custodiam restringitur,* Past. 273, 17. Hié nellað hié gehæftan and gepyndan hiora mód, swelce mon deópne pool gewerige, ac hē lǽt his mód tóflówan . . . and ne gehæft hit ná mid ðám gesuincium gódra weorca *se ad superiora stringendo non dirigit, neglectam se expandit, et studiorum sublimium vigore non constringitur,* 283, 13-16. Sume weriað wísdómes streám, welerum gehæftað, ðæt hē út ne tóflóweð, 469, 3. **II.** *to bind, fetter* (1) with material bonds:—Se geonga . . . gehæfted (cf. fetorwrásnum fæst, 1109), An. 1129. (2) with non-material bonds:—Sē þe gehæft sié mid ðære unnyttan lufe þisse middangeardes *capti, quos ligat improbis catenis terrenis habitans libido mentis,* Bt. 34, 8; F. 144, 24. Gehefted, Met. 21, 5. Sefa . . . unrótnesse geræped, hearde gehæfted, 25, 49. Hē ealle gesceafta hæfð geheaþorade and gehæfte mid his unanbindendlicum racentum *stringat ligans irresoluto singula nexu,* Bt. 25; F. 88, 5. **III.** *to fasten* one thing to another:—Síhhemes mód wæs gehæft tó Dinan *conglutinata est anima ejus cum ea,* Past. 415, 25. **IV.** *to seize, arrest, capture.* (1) the subject a person:—Swá hraðe swá hí becumað tó ðyssere byrig gehæftað hí, Hml. Th. ii. 494, 12. Se dēma hēt gehæftan Crisantum and Darian, Hml. S. 35, 136. Wæs sum wyln gehæft tó swinglum, 21, 166. (2) the subject a (non-material) thing:—Gehæfton mē unrihtwísnyssa míne *comprehenderunt me iniquitates meae,* Ps. L. 39, 13. Geheft *captus* (*propriis sermonibus*), Kent. Gl. 123. Meteleás . . . hungre gehæfted, El. 613. Hī mǽndon meteleáste, hungre gehæfte, An. 1160. **V.** *to take captive, make prisoner:*—Seó ungeðwǽrnes þá mægnu syrwde and gehæfte *discordia virtutibus insidiatur et capitur,* Prud. 78 a. Wæs seó burhwaru mǽst ofslegen and gehæft, Chr. 980; P. 124, 8. Ic geseó óðre æ . . . wiþfeohtende þære æ mínes módes and gehæftedne (*captiuum*) mē is lǽdende. Hū gif hē gehæfted (*captiuus*) wæs, Bd. 1, 27; Sch. 98, 6-11. Gehæftum heora feóndum *captis hostibus,* 5, 12; Sch. 620, 7. Hí weorþaþ geræpte mid þǽre unrótnesse and swá gehæfte *moeror captos fatigat,* Bt. 37, 1; F. 186, 22. **VI.** *to put into the power of another, bring into bondage, enslave.* (1) lit.:—Genam se sciphláford mē neádinga . . . and hē mē gehæfte on his ēðle, Hml. S. 30, 358. (2) fig.:—Ðý lǽs hē sié gehæft mid ðám úterran ne exteriorbus deditus, Past. 127, 14. Gehæft *mancipatus,* An. Ox. 1164: 2352: 779. **VII.** *to confine* to a place or locality, *imprison:*—Seó stów þe þū nú on gehæft eart . . ., heó is þám monnum ēþel þe þǽr on geborene wǽran, Bt. 11, 1; F. 32, 27. Loce gehæft *clustello continetur,* An. Ox. 5397. Gehæftad wæs diwl in helle *damptnatus est diabolus in infernum,* Rtl. 197, 25.

**ge-hæftednis.** *Add: a taking; deception; captio:*—Geheftednis ðá gedægladon gegrípeð hié *captio quam occultaverunt adpraehendat eos,* Ps. Srt. 34, 8.

**ge-hæftfæst.** *Dele.*

**ge-hæftn(i)an.** *Add:*—þū bist mid deófles anwealde gehæftned *juri diaboli mancipaberis,* Gr. D. 135, 16. Ealle þe þǽr gehæftnede wǽron *captivi omnes,* 292, 18. Fram deófle hí beóð hæfde and gehæftnede *a diabolo captivi tenentur,* 336, 18. þám gehæftnedum mannum *captivis,* 293, 3.

**ge-hæftnídan** *to make captive, seize:*—þū bist mid deófles anwealde gehæftniéded (-hæfdnēded, *v. l.*) *juri diaboli mancipaberis,* Gr. D. 135, 15.

**ge-hæftnys.** *Add:*—Gehæftnesse ł hæftnunge *captivitatem*, Ps. L. 125, 1.

**gehæft-world.** *Substitute:* **gehæft-weorold**, e; *f. A world of captivity* or *bondage, the world before redemption through Christ :*—Eálá Maria, eall þeós gehæftworld bídeþ þínre geþafunga; for þon þe God þe hafaþ tó gísle on middangearde geseted, and Adames gylt þurh þe sceal beón geþingod . . . þurh þe sceal beón se ingang eft geopenod, Bl. H. 9, 4. [Cf. Hig (*the devils at the Harrowing of Hell*) wǽron clypigende . . . 'Eall eorþan myddaneard ús wæs symble underþeód oð nú . . . Hwæt eart þú þe ús wylt áteón ealle þá þe wé gefyrn on bendum heóldon,' Nic. 16, 15-35.]

**ge-hæg,** es; *n. A hay, an enclosed piece of land, a meadow :*—Oxena gehæg and án mylen, C. D. iv. 77, 28. Grēnes gehæges *vernantis prati* An. Ox. 551. Of gehæge *ex* (*sacrorum voluminum*) *prato*, 1422. Ic āna sæt innan bearwe, mid helme beþeht, holte tōmiddes; þǽr þá wæterburnan urnon onmiddan gehæge, Dōm. L. 4. Oð gāta gehægge, C. D. iii. 429, 14. Horsa gehæg, 373, 18. ¶ in place-names :—Trium possessionem terrarum . . . concedo . . . ; tertia seorsum sita usitato uocabulo Æt Oxangehæge (*Oxhey*) nominatur, Ch. Crw. 24, 14 : 25, 50 : 27, 109. Modicam telluris portionem, trium scilicet aratrorum, ubi nominatur aet Brōmgehaege, C. D. i. 216, 22. Brōmgeheg, 190, 1. v. wudu-gehæg.

**ge-hægan.** v. ge-hnǽgan : **ge-hæge.** *l.* ge-hæg, *q. v.*

**gehæg-holt** *a copse in an enclosure* (?), *a copse where there is pasture* (?) :—Ðis synt ðá denbǽra ðe tó ðissum londe belimpað . . . gehægholt, C. D. ii. 195, 16.

**ge-hǽlan.** *Add:* I. *to heal, cure.* (1) *to heal* a person (a) who is sick in body or mind :—Antecríst geuntrumað þá ðe ǽr hále wǽron ; and hé nǽnne gehǽlan ne mæg, būton hé hine ǽrest áwyrde. Ac syððan hé þæne mann gebrocod hæfð, syðþan hé mæg dōn swylce hé hine gehǽle . . . hé gebrocað mænigne man díhlíce, and gehǽlð eft ætforan mannum, Wlfst. 97, 10-18. Ic wāt míne sáule synnum forwundod, gehǽl þú hý, Hy. 1, 4. Þone blindan þe on líchoman wæs gehǽled ge eác on mōde, Bl. H. 21, 10. Hé gehǽledum (gehǽlde, *v. l.*) gewitte (*sanato sensu*) árás, Bd. 4, 3; Sch. 366, 1. Manige men on feforádle þurh þyses wǽtan onbyrignesse wurdan gehǽlde, 209, 12. Wǽron gehǽlede þrý fōtádlige men þurh þone cýðere, Hml. Th. ii. 26, 19. (a a) *to heal* from, *cure* of a disease (*prep.* or *gen.*) :—Hé sumne mann gehǽlde fram þām micclan fōtádle, Hml. S. 24, 162. Hé monge gehǽlde hefigra wíta, þe hine ádle gebundne gesōhtun, Gū. 857. Heó weard þurh þ fram þæs blōdes flēusan gehǽled, Hml. A. 187, 178. (b) *to relieve* of anxiety, *restore* to peace of mind :—Is mín mōd gehǽled, hyge vmb heortan gerūme, Gen. 758. (2) *to heal* a disease, wound, &c. (a) physical :—Þū gehǽldest míne ádla, Bl. H. 89, 3. Lǽcecynn þe mid wyrtum wunde gehǽlde, Rä. 6, 12. Monige ádle þurh þ beóð gehǽlde, Bl. H. 127, 13 : 209, 14. (b) of mental distress, *to relieve, remove* anxiety, &c.:—Hé mé sára gehwylc gehǽlde, hygesorge, Gū. 1219. God mæg gehǽlan hygesorge heortan mínre, Cri. 174. II. *to make safe, save* a person :—Hé þearsigendra sáwla gehǽleð *animas pauperum salvas faciet*, Ps. Th. 71, 13. Sió Segor gehǽlde Loth fleóndne. Swā ðéð sió Segor ðæs medemestan lífes : ðá ðe hire tó befleóð hió gehéalð, Past. 399, 15. Cōm ic þ ic gehǽle (*saluificem*) middaneard, Jn. 12, 47. Þ middaneard sý gehǽled (*saluetur*) þurh hine, 3, 17. Gehǽled bið *saluabitur*, Jn. L. 10, 9 : Chr. 1067; P. 202, 14. Þurh hire beorþor sceolde beón gehǽled eall wífa cynn and wera, Bl. H. 5, 23. Þá hálgan ǽr Crístes cyme . . . wurdan mid his ǽriste gehǽlede, 81, 32. Mannes Sunu cōm tó gehǽlenne (*salvare*) þ forweard, Mt. 18, 11. Feáwa synt þe synt gehǽlede (*saluantur*), Lk. 13, 23. II a. *to save* from something :—Gehǽl mé of ðisse tíde *saluifica me ex hora hac*, Jn. 12, 27. Mid blōðhreówes weres bealuwe gehǽle *de viris sanguinum salva me*, Ps. Th. 58, 2. III. *to hail, salute* :—Hé þone cniht gehǽlde (-hálette, *v. l.*) and him bebeád *puero resalutato praecepit*, Gr. D. 36, 27. [Goth. ga-hailjan *to heal* : O. Sax. gi-hélian *to heal* ; *to save* : O. H. Ger. gi-heilen *sanare* ; *salvare*.] v. ge-hǽled.

**ge-hǽle** ; *adj. Safe, secure* :—Hé gehǽle gedéð rihte heortan *salvos facit rectos corde*, Ps. Spl. 7, 11. v. hǽle ; ge-hál.

**ge-hǽled.** *Substitute: safe, salutary* :—Hí þōhtan þ him wíslicra and gehǽledra wǽre þ hí hám cirdon, ðonne hí þá elreordian þeóde geférdan . . . ; and þis gemǽnelíce him tó rǽde curon *redire domum potius quam barbaram gentem adire cogitabunt, et hoc esse tutius communi consilio decernebant*, Bd. 1, 23 ; Sch. 49, 4. Hí tó rǽde fundon mid gemǽnre gedeahte, þæt him sélre and gehǽledre wǽre (*quia satius esset*) þæt hí ealle hwurfon tó heora ēðle, 2, 5 ; Sch. 135, 10. v. ge-hǽlan ; II.

**ge-hǽledlic.** v. un-gehǽledlic.

**ge-hǽledness,** e ; *f. Healing* :—Lácnunge and gehǽlednesse *curationis*, Gr. D. 247, 11.

**ge-hǽlendlic.** v. un-gehǽlendlic.

**ge-hǽman.** *Add:* (1) in a good sense, *to marry* :—Gehǽmed *nupta*, An. Ox. 1176. (2) in a bad sense, *to have illicit intercourse* :—Uenus wæs swá fúl and swá fracod on gálnysse, þæt hyre ágen bróðor

wið hý gehǽmde, Wlfst. 107, 16. Þ man wið swustor gehǽme, Ll. Th. i. 404, 27. v. un-gehǽmed.

**ge-hǽme** (?) ; *adj. With which one is at home, familiar, to which one is accustomed :*—Mé is swíðe gehǽme *saepe mihi usu uenit*, Solil. H. 32, 24.

**ge-hǽplic** ; *adj. Convenient, orderly :*—Gihaeplicae (-e) *conpar*, Txts. 48, 205. Gehaeplice *ordinatus*, 83, 1462. Gehǽplice *conpar*, Wrt. Voc. ii. 14, 70.

**ge-hǽplicness,** e ; *f. Fitness, opportunity :*—On geheplicnissum *in oportunitatibus*, Txts. 122, 6.

**ge-hǽre.** *l.* (?) ge-hǽr. Cf. ge-feaxe.

**ge-hǽt.** *Substitute:* **ge-hǽtan** ; *p.* te To heat. (1) physical :—Genim senepes sǽd . . . and xx piporcorna, gesamna eall mid ecede, gehǽt on wætere, Lch. ii. 24, 17. Gehǽt ceald wæter mid hátan íserne, 100, 20. Gegníd mid wíne, and gehǽtte, 214, 21. Þ sý gehǽt būtan smíce, i. 120, 8. Wear fulne gehǽttes wínes, ii. 214, 12. On gehǽttum wíne, i. 368, 3. Háte stánas wel gehǽtte, ii. 68, 5. (2) of passion, emotion, &c. :—Gehǽt wæs heorte mín *concaluit cor meum*, Ps. L. 38, 4.

**ge-hǽtan** *to promise.* Dele.

**ge-hagian.** *Substitute: v. impers.* (1) *with acc. of person.* (a) *to be convenient* or *suitable for* a person to have or do (*tó*) something :—Mid swelcan yrfe swelcan hí ðenne tó gehagað *cum tali pecunia quae tunc competens erit*, C. D. v. 137, 15. (b) *to be within the means* or *power of* a person :—Swá hwylc mínra fædrenmǽga swá ðæt sió, ðæt hine tó ðan gehagige, ðæt hé ðá ōðora lond begeotan mǽge and wille, ðonne gebycge hé ðá lond, C. D. ii. 120, 26. Utan álýsan gehǽfte, gif ús tó ðám gehagie, Wlfst. 119, 9. (2) *with dat. To be within the means* or *power* of a person :—Dōn heora ælmessan swá forð swá hám fyrmest gehagie, Hml. A. 141, 75 : 143, 129. Cf. on-hagian.

**ge-hál.** *Add:* I. *whole, unbroken :*—Se tægel sceolde beón gehál on þām nýtene æt þǽre offrunge, Ælfc. Gen. Thw. 3, 39. Gif mon ōðrum rib ofsleá binnan gehálre hýde, Ll. Th. i. 98, 11. II. *entire, sound, in good condition, uninjured :*—Hire líchama wæs gefunden eal gehál, Chr. 798 ; P. 56, 33. Þǽre kicenan getimbrung stód gehál and gesund (*sanum*), Gr. D. 124, 14. Ðǽra steorrena nán ne fylð of ðám rodere ðá hwíle ðe ðeós woruld wunað swá gehál, Hex. 14, 3. Scearp sweord ðá wunde tōsceát, and gǽð gehálre ecgge forð, Past. 453, 17. II a. of abstract objects :—Ðeáh hí ðæt gōd hira gecynde gehál nolden gehealdan, ðæt hí hit hūru tōbrocen gebéten *si accepta naturae bona integra servare noluerunt, saltem scissa resarciunt*, Past. 403, 19. III. *complete, with no part wanting :*—Ðæs mōnan trendel is symle gehál and ansund, Lch. iii. 242, 4. Þ weorc stód gehál, Hml. S. 31, 1235. Ne bæd hé nō ðæt hé hine fortýnde mid gehále wáge, ac hé bæd dura tó, Past. 275, 23. Brōhte him se hræfn gehálne hláf, Shrn. 50, 14. Gehál beren eár, Lch. ii. 54, 11. IV. *undivided, not in pieces :*—Ælc þára wuhta ðe him beón þencþ, þ hit þencþ ætgædere beón, gehál, undǽled, Bt. 34, 12 ; F. 152, 27. Wyrc swá hit man gehál forswelgan mæge, Lch. i. 354, 6. V. *healthy :*—Hé (a leper) weard hál and cōm tó Martine mid gehálre hýde, Hml. S. 31, 568. VI. *safe :*—Sé ðe gehálne (*salvum*) gedó, Ps. Spl. 7, 2. [Goth. ga-hails.]

**ge-hala,** an ; *m. One who shares another's secrets, a confidant :*—Gehala *vel* gerúna *sinmistes vel consecretalis*, Wrt. Voc. i. 18, 18. Sege ús nū þ sōðe būton ǽlcon leáse, and wé beóð þíne gehalan and þíne midspecan, ne wé nellað þ ámeldian, ac hit eall stille lǽtan, þ hit nán man ne þearf geáxian būton ús sylfum, Hml. S. 23, 590. v. helan.

**ge-hálettan ;** *p.* te *To salute, greet :*—Hé gehálette þone cniht and him þus bebeád *puero resalutato praecepit*, Gr. D. 36, 27. Þá Langbearde hé grétte and gehálette *Langobardos salutavit*, 250, 18.

**ge-hálgegend.** *l.* ge-hálgigend.

**ge-hálgian.** *Take here* ge-heálgian *in Dict., and add :* I. *to make holy, sanctify, purify :*—Fore him ic gihalgo (*sanctifico*) mec solfne þ sint and hé gihálgade (*sanctificati*) in sōðfæstnisse, Jn. R. 17, 19. Þæt templ þ gold gehálgað (*sanctificat*), Mt. 23, 17 : 19. Ðone ðe fæder gehálgade *quem pater sanctificauit*, Jn. R. L. 10, 36. Gehálga hig tó dæg *sanctifica illos hodie*, Ex. 19, 10. Hí wurdon gebígede tó Crístes geleáfan and mid fulluhte gehálgode (*or under* II?), Hml. Th. i. 72, 8. Wítgan mid Háliges Gástes geofum onlýhte and gehálgode, Bl. H. 161, 14. Gihálgado *sanctificati*, Rtl. 99, 4. II. *to consecrate, set apart* (a person or thing) *as sacred to God, dedicate to religious use, bless* (a thing) *so as to be under divine protection :*—Gode gehálgað *consecratum*, Wrt. Voc. i. 28, 46. Ic ðá ciricean geworhte and ic hié gehálgode, Bl. H. 207, 2. Ðū frumcendo ðrowerena in Stefanes blóde gihaelgadest (*dedicasti*), Rtl. 44, 34. Cirican þe biscep gehálgode, Ll. Th. i. 64, 8. God þone seofeðan dæg gehálgode, Ex. 20, 11. Hié ciricean ǽrðon and þá gehálgodan on S. Petres naman, Bl. H. 205, 14 : 15. Gibloedsia and gihálgia ðás giscæft, Rtl. 115, 16. Gihálgiga, 103, 42. Biscope is forbod preóst tó gehálgenne férunga, Mt. L. 10, 14 note. Scolastica wæs fram cildháde Gode gehálgod, Hml. Th. ii. 182, 23. Binnan gehálgodum líctúne licgan, Ll. Th. i. 212, 20. Gehálgodne *initiatum*, Wrt. Voc. ii. 45, 70. II a. *to consecrate* to an office :—Sende

Æþelwulf cyning Ælfréd his sunu tô Rôme. Þá wæs domne Leo pápa, and hé hiene tô cyninge gehálgode, Chr. 853; P. 64, 30. Hér hæt Ecgferð gehálgian Cúðberht tô biscope, and Theodorus hine gehálgode tô biscope tô Hagustaldeshâm, 685; P. 39, 16. Forlêt se cyng þá hlæfdian, seó wæs gehálgod him tô cwêne, 1048; P. 176, 7. Agustinus wæs gehálgod ærcebisceop *Augustinus archiepiscopus ordinatus est*, Bd. 1, 27; Sch. 60, 10. Mid þæm mannum þe beóþ Críste tô brýdum gehálgode, Bl. H. 61, 15. Wearþ þæt ríce tôdæled on .v., and .v. kyningas tô gehálgode, Chr. 887; P. 80, 20. III. *to honour as holy, reverence:*—Sî þín nama gehálgod, Mt. 6, 9. Se gehálgoda Hælend, Cri. 435. IV. *to keep holy* a day:—Gehálga þone reste-dæg, Ex. 20, 8. [*O. H. Ger.* ge-heiligôn *sanctificare, sacrare, initiare.*] v. un-gehálgod.

ge-hálian; *p.* ode. I. *to heal:*—Wæs seó wund gehálod *uulnus curatum*, Bd. 4, 19; Sch. 449, 3: Hml. S. 32, 178: Lch. ii. 66, 24. II. *to save:*—Cuôm sunu monnes geháliga (*salvare*) gelosade, Mt. L. 18, 11.

ge-hálsian. *Add: to make a solemn appeal to:*—Þá áxode hine se ealdorbiscop and mid áðe gehálsode, þæt hé openlíce sæde gif hé Godes sunu wære (*princeps sacerdotum ait:* 'Adjuro te per Deum vivum, ut dicas nobis si tu es Christus filius Dei, Mt. 26, 63), Hml. Th. ii. 248, 17. Hálsunge gehálsod *exorcismo, i. adjuratione catacizatus,*' An. Ox. 4084. Gehálscd *interpellata, .i. obsecrata,* 4147.

ge-hámettan. *Substitute:* To domicile, settle in a fixed residence and so bring within reach of the law:—Wê cwædon þe þæm hláford-leásum mannum þe man nân ryht æt begytan ne mæg, þ man beóde þære mægðe þ hí hine tô folcryhte gehámetten, and him hláford finden, Ll. Th. i. 200, 7.

ge-hammen; *adj. Clouted, patched:*—Gescód mid gehammenum scôn *clavatis calceatus caligis,* Gr. D. 37, 13.

ge-handlian; *p.* ode To handle, treat a subject:—Ús þingð beheflic þ wé on þisre stôwe ymbe þane *saltus lunae* wurdliun and hine gehandlion, Angl. viii. 308, 16.

ge-hange *inclined, disposed*(?) :—Líf wæs mín longe leódum in gemonge, tírum getonge, teala gehonge, Reim. 42.

ge-hargian *to hang* (intrans.), *be suspended:*—þ hé gehongiga *ut suspendatur,* Mt. L. 18, 6.

ge-happian = (?) ge-heápian, *q. v.*

ge-hát. *Add:* I. *a promise:*—'Ic eów freoþige ...' Him þá wæs þæt heofenlice gehát, Bl. H. 135, 27. Eal þín gehát þe þú mé gehét, 143, 28. Ne hopa ðú tô swíðe tô ðâm ðe ðê man geháte; ðær lyt geháta bið, ðær bið lyt lygena (*where there are few promises, there are few lies*), Prov. K. 7. Þá leásan men treówa gehátað fægerum wordum ..., habbað on gehátum hunigsmæccas, Leás. 28. I a. *what is promised, a promised good:*—Ic sendo gihát (*promissum*) fædres mínes in iówih, Lk. R. 24, 49. Hé bád sóðra geháta, hwonne him Freá reste ágeáfe, Gen. 1425: Cri. 541: Gú. 913. II. *a promise to a deity, a vow*—Gehát oððe wirgnes *devotatio,* Wrt. Voc. ii. 26, 2: i. 29, 1. Minutia hæfde geháten heora gydenne Dianan þæt heó wolde hiere líf on fæmnháde álibban ... Heó hiere gehát áleág, Ors. 3, 6; S. 108, 19. Þá geárlican gehát *annua vota,* Wrt. Voc. ii. 5, 55. Þá ælmessan þe Ælfréd cing gehét ... hí (*the English*) swýðe bêntigde wæron æfter þám gehátum, Chr. 883; P. 79, 9. Ðú forgeldes Drihtne giháta aðas ðíne (*vota juramenta tua*), Mt. L. 5, 33. Gehát, Ps. Th. 65, 13. III. *a promise to do something required, a stipulation:*—Gehát *stipulatio,* Wrt. Voc. i. 20, 55. v. feoh-, fore-gehát.

ge-hata. *Substitute:* A rival, an opponent:—Gehata *emulus,* Wrt. Voc. ii. 30, 20.

ge-hátan. *Add:* I. *to order, command:*—Gehátes *jubet,* Mt. p. 14, 13. Mid ðý gehét ł gehátend wæs *cum jussisset,* Mt. L. 14, 19. (1) *to give orders* to a person:—In mæhte geháteð gástum unclænum in potestate imperat spiritibus immundis, Lk. L. 4, 36. (2) *to command, order* something. (a) with simple direct object:—Ðing þ gehét Môyses *munus quod praecepit Moses,* Mt. L. 8, 4. For ðon dyde ðá ðe him geháten hæfde ł gehét (*imperauerat*), Lk. L. 17, 9. (b) the order contained in a clause:—Gehét (*praecepit*) ðegnum his þ nænigum menn cuæðas, Mt. L. 16, 20: Mk. L. 9, 9: *imperat,* Mk. p. 3, 20. Wê gehéhtan ðæt ..., Mt. p. 2, 17. Þte gehát (*jubeat*) Drihten ne yfel ... gewyrce, Rtl. 146, 33. Þte ne gehéhte (*imperaret*) him þte ... gefoerdon hiá, Lk. L. 8, 31. (c) with acc. and infin., the noun in acc. being subject to the infin. verb:—Gehét ðá ðegnas ástíge in scipp *jussit discipulos ascendere in naviculam,* Mt. L. 14, 22. (cc) with infin. alone:—Gehét gán ofer streám *jussit ire trans fretum,* Mt. L. 8, 18. (d) with acc. and dat. infin. cf. (e):—Ðá fíondas gehéht tô lufianne *inimicos praecepit diligendos,* Mt. p. 14, 18. (e) with infin. and acc., which is object to infin. cf. (d):—Hine (*Uriah*) gehéht David ofslaa, Mt. L. 1, 6 note. Wecg gesealla gehéht, Mt. p. 18, 3. Gehát gehalda byrgenn, Mt. L. 27, 64. II. *to bid come, summon, call:*—Gif cyning his leóde tô him geháteð, Ll. Th. i. 2, 8. Se cyning him tô gehét (-héht, *v. l.*) Cedd *clamavit ad se Cedd,* Bd. 3, 22; Sch. 293, 12. Hé him tô gehét monigne læce, Ors. 6, 30; S. 282, 18. Mið ðý ge-

hátne uêron ðeignas his *convocatis discipulis suis,* Jn. p. 1, 14. II a. *to invite* to a feast:—In ðæm særnum ðér hé seolf uæs geháten (*inuitatus*), Jn. p. 3, 11. Tô gereordum wêron geháten *ad nuptias invitatis.* Mt. p. 19, 4. III. *to call.* (1) *to apply an epithet to* a person or thing, *call* so and so:—Ðæccile líchomas êgo gehéht *lucernam corporis oculum appellans,* Mt. p. 15, 2. For hwý God is geháten sió hêhste êcnes, Bt. 42; F. 256, 23: 34, 2; F. 136, 7. Hí bióþ yfele gehátene, 37, 4; F. 192, 11. (2) *to call* by a name, *name:*—On þone stede þe is geháten Certices óra, Chr. 495; P. 15, 19. Boetius wæs ôþre naman geháten Seuerinus, Bt. 21; F. 76, 4. Þriddan naman hé wæs geháten Cicero, 41, 3; F. 246, 27. IV. *to promise.* (1) *to engage to give or bestow* (a) a material object (a) *with acc.* :—Þú ús mycel herereáf gehéte, Bl. H. 85, 20. Hé gehét þe folcstede, Gen. 2201. For hwâm wæs elles Canonea land Israhéla folce geháten, búton for ðæm ðe ðæt folc nolde geliéfan ðeáh him mon feorrland on fierste gehéte, gif him sóna ne sealde sum on neáweste sê him ðæt máre gehét?, Past. 389, 31-35. Hié him sendon âne tunecan, þá þe hié tô gehéton, Ors. 5, 10; S. 234, 24. Gehátten bið ł geháteð is *pollicetur,* Mt. p. 2, 14. (β) *with gen.* :—Hé him gehét leána, B. 2989. (b) a non-material object (a) *with acc.* :—Hé his ondueardnisse gehéht ł gehátes *suam praesentiam pollicetur,* Mt. p. 20, 8. Ús Meotod máre gód geháteð, Az. 90. Hí gehátaþ þá sóþan gesélþa, Bt. 26, 1; F. 90, 17: 16: 92, 11: 32, 2; F. 118, 1. Hí treówa gehátað, Leás. 25. Þære láre þe ðú mé ær gehéte, Bt. 40, 5; F. 240, 12: 3, 4; F. 6, 19. Hé gehét Rômánum his freóndscipe, 1; F. 2, 8: Jul. 639. Líf gehét (*promittit*) êce, Mt. p. 18, 12. ¶ with complementary adjective : Hé him sige tôweardne gehéht, Bl. H. 201, 33. (β) *with gen.* :—Swá hwæs swá his irsung willaþ, þonne gehét him þæs (cf. þ eall gehæt, Met. 25, 52) his réccelést, Bt. 37, 1; F. 186, 24. (2) *to undertake to do* (or *refrain from*) an action. (a) with simple object :—Micel is þ þú gehætst, and ic ne tweóge ðæt ðú hit mæge geléstan, Bt. 36, 3; F. 174, 31. Hé ryht gehét, Ps. Rdr. 14, 4. Ongan hé hine biddan þ hé hine gemundbyrde ... ðá gehét hé him þ, Bt. 35, 6; F. 168, 22: By. 289. Hé him gehét his æriste, Bl. H. 17, 3. (b) with clause :—Ic árás swá ic gehét þ ic dón wolde, Bl. H. 183, 29. Gehét, Bt. 33, 3; F. 126, 7. Þú mé gehéte þ þú hit woldest mé getæcan, F. 126, 10. Hé gehét ðæt hé swá dón wolde, Past. 307, 11. Gehátend wæs hir þ sealla walde *pollicitus est ei dare,* Mt. L. 14, 7. Hæfdon hí hire geháten þ hí on hyre rædenne beón woldon, Chr. 918; P. 105, 24. (c) combining (a) and (b) :—Ic þæt geháte þæt ic heonon nelle fleón, By. 246. Þú him þæt gehéte ... þæt þú heora fromcyn ícan wolde, Dan. 316: An. 1420. (d) with dat. infin. :—Hé englas gehét wiþ mé tô sendenne, Bl. H. 181, 26. (3) *to undertake that* something *shall* (or *shall not*) *be done* by another. (a) with simple object :—Hé him ðæs Hálgan Gástes cyme tôweardne gehét, Bl. H. 117, 14. Abrahame wæs geháten Cristes cyme, Ors. 6, 1; S. 252, 30. (b) with clause :—Hé gehét þæt hý ealdrihta ælces môsten wyrðe gewunigon, Met. 1, 35. Hié him gehéton þæt hiera kyning fulwihte onfón wolde, Chr. 878; P. 76, 14. (c) combining (a) and (b) :—Ic hit þe geháte, nó heó on helm losað, B. 1392. Ic hit þe gehát, þæt þú môst sorhleás swefan, 1671. (4) *to promise* to a deity, *to vow :*—Þá ælmessan þe Ælfréd cing gehét, Chr. 883; P. 19, 7. Hié gehéton æt heargtrafum wígweorðunga, B. 175. Heó hæfde geháten heora gydenne Dianan þæt heó wolde hiere líf on fæmnháde álibban, Ors. 3, 6; S. 108, 16. (5) *to promise* evil, *threaten with* something. (a) with direct object :—Ælc yfel man him gehét, Chr. 1036; P. 160, 4. Hé wean oft gehét, B. 2937. Him hí ermðu gehéton, Gú. 418. (b) with clause :—Hym Godes andsacan swíðe gehéton þæt hé deáða gedál dreógan sceolde, Gú. 205: 542. (c) combining (a) and (b) :—Þú þæt gehátest, þæt þú hám on ús gegán wille, Gú. 242. (6) with cognate accusative, *to make* a promise, *vow* a vow :—Sê ðe gehát gehét, Past. 403, 3. Ic (*David*) gehát gehét *David votum vovit,* Ps. Th. 131, 2. Eal þín gehát þe þú mé gehéte, Bl. H. 143, 29. (7) *to promise* a person, *to betroth* :—Sió geháten wæs geong suna Frôdan, B. 2024. (8) *absolute, to make a promise or vow:*—Hí gehátað holdlíce, swá hyra hyht ne gæð, Leás. 14. Gehéht *spopondit,* Lk. L. R. 22, 6. Þæt man gylde and gehéte, Ps. Th. 64, 1. God hæfð swíðe wel geháten Israhéla folce, Past. 304, 12. V. *to assert confidently :*—Þú gehéte þæt þec hálig gæst wið earfeðum eaðe gescilde, Gú. 427. Ic gehátan dear þæt þú þær treówe findest, Bo. 10. v. fore-gehátan; un-gehátan.

ge-háthéortan. *See next word.*

ge-háthirtan, -heortan; *pp.* -háthirt (-hyrt, -heort). I. *to make angry, anger :*—Se hláford gehátthyrt (*iratus*) cwæð tô his ðeówan, Hml. Th. ii. 374, 25. Se hálga wer weard gehátthyrt ðurh his unstæð-dignysse, 176, 18: Hml. S. 8, 112: 22, 220. Philippus swíðe gehátt-heort hét hí gefæccan, 2, 191. Wæs gehátheort *inflammatur,* An. Ox. 4009. Gehátthord *furibundus, i. iratus,* 3019. I a. *reflexive, to become angry* (v. háthirtan):—Se Godes wiðersaca hine ðá gehátthyrte *he worked himself into a fury,* Hml. Th. i. 450, 9. II. *to be angry:*—Ðá ðe on cildum mid ungesceáde gehátheortað (*exarserint*), R. Ben. 130, 7.

**ge-háthyrt, ge-háthyrtan.** *See preceding word.*

**ge-hatian**; *pp.* od *To hate* :—Gehatud *exosa,* An. Ox. 4923.

**gehát-land.** *Add* :—Geléddum his folce tô þám gehátlande *perducto ad terram repromissionis populo,* Gr. D. 204, 12.

**ge-háwian.** *Add* : I. *to notice, observe* an object :—Ælc man ðára þe ǽágan heft ǽrest háwað þæs ðe hê geséon wolde oð ðone first þe hê hyt geháwað. Þonne hê hyt geháwad heaft, ðonne gesyhð hê hit, Solil. H. 27, 7. þæt ic þê geháwian mæge *ut aspiciam te,* 11, 18. Ðreó þing sint neódbehéfe ðám eágan élcere sáwle : án is þæt hál sién ; óðer þæt heó háwien ðes þe heó geséon wolden ; þridde þæt hí magen geséon þæt þæt hí geháwian *tria ad animam pertinent, ut sana sit, ut aspiciat, ut videat,* 30, 5. II. *to notice* a circumstance, action, &c. :—þá þá hí náht ne geháwedon *cum illi ex olivis oleum defluere non cernerent,* Gr. D. 250, 25.

**ge-heád.** v. ge-heán.

**ge-heáfdod**; *adj. Having a head* :—Geheáfdod hringce *Samothracius,* Wrt. Voc. i. 40, 60. v. un-geheáfdod.

**ge-heald, -hæld.** *Substitute* : **ge-heald,** es ; *n.* I. *observation, marking, noticing* :—Rîce Godes ne mið gehald tô cymende *regnum Dei non cum obseruatione uenturum,* Lk. p. 9, 10. II. *the obseruance* of something prescribed, *holding, keeping* :—Gewrit be gehealde rihtra Eástrana, Bd. 5, 21 ; Sch. 678, 20. Betwyh gehald (*obseruantiam*) regollices þeódscipes, 5, 23 ; Sch. 695, 7. III. *a watch, guard* :—Sete swǽse geheald mûðe mînum *pone custodiam ori meo,* Ps. Th. 140, 4. Gehald, Rtl. 179, 9. Giheaeld, 180, 12. IV. *protection, shelter* :—Ælfgár gesóhte Griffines geheald, Chr. 1055 ; P. 187, 2. IV a. in a personal sense, *a protector, guardian* :—Fràncena kyning and Wyllelm eorl sceoldon beón his geheald, Chr. 1071 ; P. 206, 23. þæt mynster beó þám bisceope underþeód, and hê beó þertô gehald and mund, Cht. Th. 391, 17. [Hwan hit sniuþ ... þar in ich habbe god ihold, O. and N. 621.] Cf. ge-hild.

**ge-heald** ; *cpve.* -healdra, -hildra (-hæld-, -hyld-); *adj. Safe. Take here* **ge-hyldra** in *Dict.,* and add :—þæt him wíslicre and gehaldre (*tutius*) wǽre, Bd. 1, 23 ; Sch. 49, 4. þæt him gehealdre (gehǽledre, *v. l.*) wǽre *quia satius esset,* 2, 5 ; Sch. 135, 10. On gehældran (gehealdenre, *v. l.*) stôwe, 2, 2 ; Sch. 120, 13. v. ge-hildelic.

**ge-healdan.** *Add* : I. *to hold, keep, take care* or *charge of* (1) a person :—þeódnes bearn sceolde folc gehealdan, B. 911. (2) a flock (*lit. or fig.*) :—Seó heord þe hê tô Godes handa gehealdan sceall, Ll. Th. ii. 312, 26. (3) a thing :—Hê onsende sînra þegna worn ... þæt him ... geheólde éðne éðel æfter Ebréum, Dan. 77. Hê sealde his sweord ombihtþegne, and gehealdan hêt hildegeatwe, B. 674. Selle hê his wǽpn and his ǽhta his freóndum tô gehealdanne, Ll. Th. i. 60, 8. Tô gehealdenne *recondenda* (*defruta apothecis*), Wrt. Voc. ii. 79, 78. Biþ hit him tôgeánes gehealden on þám heofonlican goldhorde, Bl. H. 53, 14. þér wǽron gehealdene heora lîc án geár and seofon mônaþ, 193, 13 : Bd. 3, 11 ; Sch. 237, 16. II. *to guard, preserve, protect, save* (1) a person :—Dryhten gehilt (*servabit*) his háligra fêt, Past. 65, 11. Heora earmas hý ne geheóldon *brachium eorum non salvabit eos,* Ps. Th. 43, 4. Gehealde þê Drihten *Dominus custodit te,* 120, 5 : Ll. Th. i. 424, 26 : Bl. H. 135, 26. Wela þe ne mæg hine selfne gehealdan ne his hláford *potentia quae ne ad conservationem sui satis efficax inveniur,* Bt. 29, 1 ; F. 102, 15. Heó lufode þeóstro for hire synnum and heó wæs á þeh gehealden fram hire synnum, Bl. H. 147, 26. Swá hwá swá wile gehealden beón *quicumque vult salvus esse,* Ath. Crd. 1. Hî beóþ þonne wiþ God gehealdene *they will be safe as regards God,* Bl. H. 658, 11. (2) a thing or place :—Hafa nú and gehald húsa sélest, B. 658. Gehealdenum *salua* (*lintre*), An. Ox. 640. Gehealdenre myrcelse *saluo signaculo,* 4033. On gehealdenre stôwe *in tutiore loco,* Bd. 2, 2 ; Sch. 120, 14. His bán þér nú gehaldene syndon (*seruantur*), 3, 11 ; Sch. 235, 18. (2 a) the object non-material :—Strengðe gehealdan, Solil. H. 37, 10. Gehealdenre clǽnnysse, Hml. A. 19, 125. II a. *to guard* against, *protect* from :—Hê hí wið feóndum geheóld *protector eorum est,* Ps. Th. 113, 18 : B. 3003. þê gehealde Drihten wið þ yfela gehwám *custodiat animam tuam Dominus,* Ps. Th. 120, 6. Gif hî hî sylfe willon wiþ Godes erre gehealdan, Bl. H. 47, 26. III. *to hold, keep from getting away, detain* :—Hwæt wǽron þá wýf ... for hwylcon þyngon ne geheólde gê hig?, Nic. 7, 33. Forfôh þone frætgan and fæste gehealdan, Jul. 284. Gehealde hê his gefán .vii. niht inne, Ll. Th. i. 90, 5, 7. Gif hê self his wǽpno his gefán ût rǽcan wille, gehealden hî hine .xxx. nihta, 64, 18. Alle sôðfæste ðá ðe ðér on styde gihalden wæs (*detinebantur*), Rtl. 101, 20. IV. *to hold, support with the hand* :—Mimming gehealdan, Val. 1, 4. IV a. *fig. to support, maintain, uphold* :—Gyf hwá riht forbúge and ût hleápe, forgylde þ ángylde sê þe hine tô ðám hearme geheóld (cf. qui aliquem manu tenebit et firmabit ad dampnum faciendum, 252, 26), Ll. Th. i. 260, 8. V. *to have as* one's *own, be in possession of, have the enjoyment* or *use of* :—Sê þe Waldendes hyldo gehealdeð, B. 2293. Rîce hê geheóld fîftig wintru, 2208 : Sat. 347. Ne geeódon úre foregengan ná ðás eorðan mid sweorda ecgum, ne hý mid þý ne geheóldou *non in gladio suo possidebunt terram,* Ps. Th. 43, 4. Welan þicgan ... forð gehealdan, Vy.

63. VI. *to keep, retain, not to lose* :—Wiþ þám ðe hê þone welan begite and gehealde, Bt. 33, 2 ; F. 124, 2. Beþearf ælc mon fultumes ... þ hê mæge gehealdan his welan, 26, 2 ; F. 92, 20 : 33, 2 ; F. 124, 6. In fǽgum feorg gehealdan, Gú. 1031 : B. 2856. Hê caraσ þæt his feoh gehealden sý, Hml. Th. i. 66, 10. Bið sum corn sǽdes gehealden on þére sáwle sôðfæstnesse, Met. 22, 37. VI a. *to retain in the mind, remember* :—Gehýr gyt sum bigspell, and gehald þá wel þe ic þê ǽr sǽde, Bt. 37, 3 ; F. 190, 21. Is þîn gemind swá mihtig þæt hit mage eall gehealdan (-en, MS.) þæt þú geðencst, Solil. H. 4, 1. VI b. with complement, *to keep* in a specified place or condition :—Seó geheóld *conseruauit* (*virginitatis stolam inviolabilem*), An. Ox. 4385. þæt þú mýnne lýcuman gehealde hálne, Solil. H. 13, 17. Geheólde, Jul. 31. Ðeáh hí ðæt gód hira gecynde gehál nolden gehealdan *si accepta naturae bona integra servare noluerunt,* Past. 403, 19 : Cri. 300. þú hæfst git gesund gehealden eall, Bt. 10 ; F. 28, 9 : Ph. 45. Hwî is Enoh swá lange cucu gehealden *quare Enoc tanto tempore servabatur a morte?,* Angl. vii. 10, 85. VI c. *to hold, oblige to adhere* to :—Finde him ælc man þ hê borh hæbbe, and se borh hine þonne tô ælcon rihte gelǽde and gehealde, Ll. Th. i. 268, 8 : 280, 8 : 386, 25. VI d. reflex. *to conduct* oneself :—Ælc wydewe þe hî sylfe mid riht gehealde, Ll. Th. i. 310, 1. VII. *to keep in existence* or *operation, maintain* a quality, state, &c., *exercise* an action :—þá hwíle þe Agustus þá eáðmétto wiþ God geheóld þe hê angunnen hæfde, Ors. 6, 1 ; S. 254, 7. Hiora þegnunga and geférscipe fæste gehealdan, Met. 11, 47. VIII. *to keep inviolate, observe* a law, faith, &c. :—Sê byð gesǽlig þe þone dôm gehylt, Ll. Th. i. 370, 27. Gif wê hit þus gehealdað, 242, 11. Gif gê gehealdað hálige láre, Exod. 560. Ic þæt á geheóld þæt ic þîne bebodu geheólde, Ps. Th. 118, 100. Hê fulwihte onféng and þæt forð geheóld, El. 192. Gê geheóldon þæt eów se hálga beád, An. 346. þæt hié heora fulwihthádas gehealdan, Bl. H. 109, 26. þæt hî Godes ǽwe on riht geheóldan, 45, 26. Ægðer ge tô gehérenne ge tô gehealdanne, Bt. 22, 1 ; F. 76, 21. Æt fruman wæs gehealden seó gecyndelice ǽ *in hominibus primus lex bonae naturae servabatur,* Angl. vii. 8, 69. Úre frið is wyrse gehealden þonne mê lyste, Ll. Th. i. 220, 3 : 250, 7. þ symble mid eów gehealden sý þe gê tô frídes bôte gecoren hæfdon, 278, 2. Ealles folces ǽw and dômas þus sién gehealdene, 102, 16. IX. *to hold back, restrain* from action :—Gif hrýðera hwelc sié þe hegas brece and gá in gehwǽr, and sê hit nolde gehealdan, sê þe hit áge, Ll. Th. i. 128, 13. Beón ealle fæstende and fram heora wîfe gehealdene, 226, 20. IX a. reflex. *to restrain oneself* from (*wið dat. acc.*), *refrain* :—Monige bioð ðára ðe hié gehealdað wið unryhthǽmed *multi sunt qui scelera carnis deserunt,* Past. 399, 7. Ðá ðe hî gehealdað wið ðá lytlan scylda *qui minimas cavent noxas,* 437, 2. Hê hine wíð eallum þám heálicum synnum geheóld, Bl. H. 213, 5. Hî wênað ðæt hî of hira ǽgnum mægene hî hæbben gehealden wið ðá lytlan scylda, Past. 439, 13. X. *to keep within bounds, prevent excess; gehealden modest; continent, chaste* :—Mid þám wunode án mǽden mǽrlîce drohtnigende geond feówertig geára sec fægre gehealden, Hml. S. 3, 469. Hyge sceal gehealden, hond gewealdan, Gn. Ex. 122. XI. *to content, satisfy, pay* :—Hê of his ágenum þone gehealde þe þ orf áge, Ll. Th. i. 354, 8. Gehealde man of mínan golde Ælfríc and Godwine æt swá myclan swá mîn brôðer wát ðæt ic heom mid rihte tô geuldende áh, C. D. iii. 363, 26. Án pund penega hê lǽnde Túne and his geswysternon; gehealdon hî hine, Cht. Crw. 23, 21. Wênstú, gif hwá óðrum hwæt gieldan sceal, hwæðer hê hine mid ðý gehealdan mæge ðæt hê him náuht máre on ne nime, ne ðæt ne gielde ðæt hê ǽr nam *nec debitor absolutus est, quia alia non multiplicat, nisi et illa, quae ligaverat, solvat,* Past. 425, 2. Ðǽre gehealdnan *contente,* Wrt. Voc. ii. 79, 41. XI a. gehealden on *satisfied with, not desiring more* than (v. ge-healden in *Dict.*) :—Beó lá nú on þysum gehealden, Hml. S. 23 b, 384. Seó gîtsung ne cann gemet, ne nǽfre ne biþ gehealden on þére nídþearfe, ac wilnaþ simle máran þonne hê þurfe *avaritiae nihil satis est,* Bt. 26, 2 ; F. 94, 6. þ hê þone ád funde ... þe se onspeca on gehealden wǽre, Ll. Th. i. 158, 20. þá dyde hió swá hió dorste aþe gebiorgan, þá næs hê þá gyt on þám gehealden, bútan hió sceolde swerian þ his ǽhta þér ealle wǽron, Cht. Th. 290, 2. Ðá hǽþenan noldon beón gehealdene on swá feáwum godum, Wlfst. 105, 32. Se apostol manode ðá medeman þæt hî beón gehealdene on heora bigleofan and scrúde (*habentes alimenta, et quibus tegamur, his contenti sumus,* 1 Tim. 6, 8), Hml. Th. ii. 328, 14 : Bl. H. 185, 17. XII. *to withhold from present use, reserve, lay up* :—Úre Drihten længest geheóld Philisteás *Dominus Philisthaeos diutius reservavit,* Gr. D. 204, 10. Ðá ongeat Martinus þæt Drihten him þone þearfan geheóld, þæt hê him miltsian sceolde, Bl. H. 215, 1. Se wurðmynt wæs þises dæges mǽrðe gehealden, Hml. Th. i. 36, 18. Bið gehealden *custoditur* (*justo substantia peccatoris*), Kent. Gl. 465. XIII. *to hide, not to divulge, keep* a secret :—Hê geheóld and gehæl þá deógolnysse mid him, Gr. D. 98, 20. XIV. *to hold* a faith, opinion, &c., *accept as true* :—þis is se rihta geleáfa þe ǽghwylcum men gebyreð þ hê wel gehealde and gelǽste, Bl. H. 111, 13. XV. *to keep in proper order* :—Ne mæg hê bútan þisum þás tôl gehealdan, Bt. 17 ; F. 60, 6. XVI. *to provide for*

*the sustenance of, support* :—Ne ic māran getilige tó haldænne, þonne ic genetlíce bî beón mage, and þá men on gehabban and gehealdan þe ic forðian sceal, Solil. H. 35, 18.

**ge-healden.** v. ge-healdan; **XI, XI a.**

**ge-healden[n]**, e; *f. Holding, keeping* of a festival :—Be gehealdenne rihtra Eástrena *in obseruatione Paschae*, Bd. 5, 21; Sch. 676, 17.

**ge-healdend**, es; *m. One who keeps* or *saves, who does not spend* :—Mǽden . . . geswincful, gehealdend *a maiden . . . laborious, that takes care of her money*, Lch. iii. 192, 23.

**ge-healdendlic (?)**; *adj. That is to be kept* :—þá gehealdennelicun (gehealdendlican? The word glosses *custodienda*, and its form seems to be due to a confusion of the gerundial *tó gehealdenne* = *custodiendus* with an adjective like *lufigendlic* = *amandus*) and þá gelóhgenlican, R. Ben. I. 63, 5.

**geheald-fæst**; *adj. Safe, secure* :—Byrne sió gehealdfæste *lurica tutissima*, Lch. i. lxxi, 2. Gehealdfæstesðe, lxxiv, 11.

**ge-healdnys.** *Add:* [*O. H. Ger.* ge-haltnissa *pudicitia, salus.*]

**ge-healdsum.** *Substitute:* **I.** *that takes care of, is protective of* :—Gif hé bið ákenned on .xxiiii. nihta, sé bið geswincfull on his lífe. Gif hé bið on .xxv. nihta, sé bið gehealtsum his lífes, Lch. iii. 158, 14. **II.** *that is careful of property, saving, not given to spending, frugal* :—Ðy lǽs se hneáwa and se gítsigenda fægnige ðæs ðætte menn wênen ðæt hé sié gehealdsum on ðǽm ðe hé healdan scyle oðde dǽlan *ne cor tenacia occupet, et parcum se videri in dispensationibus exultet*, Past. 149, 18. **III.** *exercising restraint, modest, virtuous, sober* :—Wíf hálig and gehealdsum *mulier sancta et pudorata*, Scint. 225, 16. þá wǽron hálige bisceopas gehealtsume (-heald-, *v. l.*) on þeáwum (cf. 1 Tim. 3, 2: Tit. 1, 8). **III a.** *continent* :—Gehęald[sume] *caelibes*, An. Ox. 665. **IV.** *safe, inviolate* :—For gehealdsumere side[ful-nesse] *pro pudicitia conseruanda*, An. Ox. 2666. Gehealtsumestre *integerrime (virtutis)*, 4511. v. un-gehealdsum.

**ge-healdsumlíce.** v. un-gehealdsumlíce.

**ge-healdsumnes.** *Add:* **I.** *moral restraint, modesty, sobriety.* v. ge-healdsum; **III** :—Gehealdsumnyss *inpuderatio*, Scint. 225, 16. **I a.** *abstinence, refraining* from :—Uton wē yfel forlǽtan and eft ne geedlǽcan, þæt wē móton Gode gedéon þurh gódre gehaltsumnysse, Hml. Th. ii. 380, 19. þá láreówas swincað swiðor þonne ðá lǽwedan on heora gehealdsumnysse þe hí healdan sceolon, Hml. A. 57, 165 : Hml. S. 2, 311. Gif wē þá heáfodleahtras forseóþ þurh gehealtsumnysse (-heald-), 25, 699. **I b.** *continence, chastity* :—Gehealdsumnesse *castitatis*, An. Ox. 354 : *castimoniae*, 1121 : 1777: *celibatus*, 1395. **II.** *observance, keeping* of a law, festival, &c. :—Fædera lára gēmen and gehealdsumnes *patrum doctrinarum observatio*, R. Ben. 133, 1 : R. Ben. I. 118, 1. Mid gýmene and gehealdsumnesse gódra dǽda *observantia bonorum actuum*, 3, 10. Mid gehealdsumnesse þæs regoles, 16, 6. þurh gehaltsumnysse Godes beboda, Hml. Th. ii. 280, 32. Se Sæternes-dæg wæs gehálgod mid micelre gehealdsumnysse, 208, 1. Lænctenfæstenes gehealdsumnesse *quadragesime observationem*, R. Ben. I. 84, 9. **III.** *preservation, maintenance* :—For sóðere sibbe gehealdsumnesse (*conservatione*), R. Ben. 5, 14. Tó gehealdsumnesse gemǽnre sibbe and sóþre lufe *propter pacis karitatisque custodiam*, 125, 5. **IV.** *charge, custody* :—Ðá þá hé heóld þá gehealdsumnysse regollices lífes *cum regularis vitae custodiam teneret*, Gr. D. 104, 3. v. un-ge-healdsumnes.

**ge-heálgian.** *In* l. 4 *for* 13 *read* 12 : **ge-healtsumnys.** v. ge-healdsumnes.

**ge-heán, -hín** (ȳ, ié), **-hígan (?)**; *pp.* -heád, -hýd, -híged. **I.** *in a physical sense, to elevate, raise high* :—Gehýdne *porrectam* (*in edito turrem*), An. Ox. 8, 237. Gehígde *edita*, i. *alta*, Wülck. Gl. 226, 8. **II.** *to exalt* :—Ðá wæs Bryten swíde geheád in miclum wuldre Godes geleáfan and andetnesse *denique etiam Brittaniam tum plurima confessionis Deo deuotae gloria sublimauit*, Bd. 1, 6; Sch. 19, 4. Swá micelum swá ǽnig má woruldlices wyrðscypes wyrðnysse byð gehýd (*sublimatur*), Scint. 181, 16. Geuferod, gehéd þurh lǽrewlicum basincge *fretus*, i. *functus magistri melote*, An. Ox. 1470. [*Laym.* ihæȝed : *A. R.* iheied : *Marh.* iheiet: *O. H. Ger.* ge-hóhen *exaltare*.] v. heán.

**ge-heáne.** *Dele; the MS. of* Rtl. 42, 40 *has* gihére.

**ge-heápod.** *Substitute:* p. ode *To heap together, pile up* :—Geheápodan *coacervassent*, Wrt. Voc. ii. 15, 12. **I.** *to heap up* material (used figuratively) :—Ðæt se gítsere him on geheápige ðá byrdenne eorðlicra ǽhta *avaro . . . terrena lucra cum pondere peccati cumulare*, Past. 329, 20. Gód gemet and full, geheápod *mensuram bonam confertam et coagitatam*, Lk. 6, 38 : Wrt. Voc. ii. 133, 13. **II.** *to accumulate, get a large amount of* :—Geheápað *coacervat* (*divitias usuris*), Kent. Gl. 1045. Gihappia (= ? giheápie) *accumulet*, Rtl. 85, 29. Geheápod *concinnatas* (cf. concinnatus (i. multiplicatus) factiones (i. falsitates), Ald. 38, 15), *congregatas*, Wrt. Voc. ii. 136, 20. **III.** *to gather together* (?), *assemble* (v. heáp *a number of people*) :—Geheápod, Bl. H. 175, 17. [*O. H. Ger.* ge-houfón *accumulare*.]

**ge-heaþorian.** *Take here* **ge-haþrian** *in Dict., and add* :—Efne-

gehaðrigas (-að, R.) ðec *coangustabunt te*, Lk. L. 19, 43. Hæfð geheaðærod heofonríces weard ealle gesceafta, Met. 11, 31.

**ge-heáw.** *Add:*—þær bið eágna wóp and tóða geheáw, Hml. A. 168, 128.

**ge-heáwan.** *Add:*—Geheapen (-heáwen?), Ruin. 12. [*O. H. Ger.* ge-houwan *fodere, concidere.*]

**ge-hebban.** *Add:*—Áhefað bēcon, gihebbað (*exaltate*) stefne, Rtl. 18, 38.

**ge-hédan;** **I.** *For* 'to hide, conceal' *substitute to keep, store up* (cf. hédd-ern). **II.** *For* 'to acquire, . . . seize' *substitute to take charge* or *possession of, to take, have. In* Met. 27, 15 gehende *is to be read rather than* gehéde. v. ge-hendan. *Dele* v. ge-hýdan.

**ge-hefed** *weighted, weighed down* with a burden :—Hefe gehefedum *mole grauatis*, Wülck. Gl. 251, 16.

**ge-hefeldian** *to fix the weft* or *woof* :—Forcorfen is swylce fram wefendum wífe líf mín þá gyt þe ic wæs gehefaldad *praecisa est uelut a tenente uita mea dum adhuc ordirer*, Cant. Ez. 12. Gehefeldad, Ps. Srt. ii. 184, 34: An. Ox. 3731.

**ge-hefigian.** *Add:* **I.** *to make of serious import* :—Ðonne hié willað him selfum ðæt yfel ðæt hié ðurhtugon tó suíde gelíhtan ðæt hié ðonne ondrǽden for ðæs láreówes ðreáunga ðæt hié hit him gehefegien (-hefgien, *v. l.*) *cum sibi quis malum, quod perpetravit, laeuigat, hoc contra se grauiter ex corripientis asperitate pertimescat*, Past. 159, 21. **II.** *to make dull, make slow of understanding* :—Eálá gē ungewitfullan Galatæ, hwá gehefegode (-hefgade, *v. l.*) eów O insensati Galatae, quis uos fascinauit?, Past. 207, 15. Behealdað eów ðæt gē ne gehefegien eówre heortan mid oferǽte and oferdrynce, 129, 19. **III.** *to make oppressive* :—Gehefegad is ofer mē hond ðín *grauata est super me manus tua*, Ps. Srt. 31, 4. **IV.** *to make oppressed, weigh down, burden, afflict* :—Ðæt is ðonne ðæt mon gadrige ðæt ðicke fenn on hine and hine mid ðý gehefegige *auaro contra se densum lutum aggrauare est . . .*, Past. 329, 20. Gihefgindum diáb' heorte *ingrassante diabolico corde*, Rtl. 102, 39. Þeáh þæt mód nú myd þæt byrðene þæs líchaman gehefegod sió, Solil. H. 63, 22. **V.** *to make heavy* with weariness, sleep, &c. :—Móyses handa wǽron mycclum gehefegode, Hml. S. 13, 23. Him wǽron gehefgode ðá eágan of ðám menigfealdum teárum, 23, 249. Gehefegode *grauati*, Mt. 26, 43.

**ge-hégan.** *Add:* [*O. Frs.* heya *to hold a meeting.*]

**ge-hegian;** *p.* ode *To hedge, fence* :—Gehega þíne eáran mid þornigum hege *sepi aures tuas spinis*, Wlfst. 246, 8.

**ge-helan.** *Add:* **I.** *trans. To conceal* :—Hé geheóld and gehæl þá deógolnysse mid him *secretum tenuit desiderium*, Gr. D. 98, 20. Hyra willa bið þ hí beón geholene *latere in uoluntate habent*, 61, 4. **II.** *intrans. To hide, conceal oneself* :—Hé ne maehte gehæla *non potuit latere*, Mk. L. R. 7, 24.

**ge-helmian.** *Add:*—Gehelmad *cristata*, Wrt. Voc. ii. 21, 11. [*O. H. Ger.* ge-helmót (-it) *galeatus.*] Cf. ge-hilmed.

**ge-helpan.** *Add:*—Gehelpan *subuenire*, An. Ox. 57, 4. Geholpene *fotam*, Wrt. Voc. ii. 34, 46. **I.** *to add one's own action* or *effort to that of another, further the action* or *purpose of* :—Gif God þē nū gehelpð, and þú hæfst sige, Hml. S. 7, 354. Gehelp ðínum mágum ðe ðá mánfullan besittað, 25, 400. Cuoeð hir þte fultume í gehelpe (*adiuuet*) mec, Lk. L. 10, 40. Hiá bēcnadon ðæm foerum þte gecuómon and gehulpo hiá, 5, 7. **II.** *to relieve the wants* or *necessities* of a person, *to succour* :—Sceal se ríca dǽlan his byrðene wið þone ðearfan, þonne hē . . . ðám þearfan gehelpð, Hml. Th. i. 254, 33. Ofþryhtum þe gehealp, Hml. S. 30, 6. Forgif him fultum and heora gehelp, 440. Gihelp úser *adiuva nos*, Mk. R. 9, 22. Hē bæd þone Ælmihtigan þ hē þám menn (*with broken limbs*) geheolpe, Hml. S. 21, 330. Gehulpe, Hex. 22, 17. Hié þær wurdon mid hungre ácwealde, þær heora þá ne gehulpe þá þær æt hám wǽron, Ors. 2, 6; S. 88, 5. Hē wolde tó helle gecuman tó gehelpen[n]e Adames, Hml. S. 24, 179. þám eádmódum gehelpende (*consulens*, i. *succurrens*), An. Ox. 4123. **III.** *to benefit, do good to, be of use* or *service to.* (1) the object a person :—Ne ðē nán scíncræft ne gehelppe tógeánes ðisum Godes dóme, Ll. Lbmn. 415, 26. Hié ðára diégelnesse bet trúwigen ðonne ðǽre hú hié óðerra monna mǽst gehelpen. Se áncenneda Godes sunu wæs férende ðæt hē úre gehulpe *utilitati ceterorum secretum praeponit suum, quando ipse Summi Patris unigenitus, ut multis prodesset, egressus est*, Past. 47, 1–4. Se lǽce, ðonne hē ðǽm siócan ne trúwað, and wēnð ðæt his gehelpan ne mæge, 391, 24, 26. Ðǽm mæg beón suíðe raðe geholpen from his láreówe *quibus citius a praedicante succurritur*, 225, 22. (2) the object a disastrous thing, *to lessen the evils of* :—Hú heora godas þurh heora blótunge þæs monncwealmes gehulpon, Ors. 3, 3; S. 102, 16. **III a.** *abs.* or *intrans. To be of use* or *service, avail* :—Megene ne gehelpaþ *uires non suppetunt*, Kent. Gl. 931. Ne ǽniht gehalp *nec quicquam profecerat*, Mk. L. R. 5, 26.

**ge-héme.** v. ge-hǽme : **ge-hén.** v. ge-híne : **ge-hénan.** v. ge-hínan.

**ge-hendan.** *Add: to grasp, seize, catch* :—Nyle deáð ǽnig swæð ǽfre forlǽtan, ǽr hē gehende (? gehede, MS., *the prose corresponding to*

*the passage is:*—Ǽr hē gefēhþ þ þ hē æfter spyreð, Bt. 39, 1; F. 212,
1) ðæt hē æfter spyrede, Met. 27, 15. Hig beóþ gelæhte ꝥ gehende
on heora mōdignysse *comprehendantur in superbia sua*, Ps. L. 58, 13.
[*Icel.* henda *to catch.* Cf. *Goth.* fra-hinþan *to take captive.*]

**ge-hende;** *adj.* *Add:* I. local:—Ne mæg þær ǽni man gedyrstig
wesan dēman gehende *nullus ibi confidit judice praesens*, Dōm. L. 170.
Sume naman syndon . . . stōwlice . . . *propinquus* gehende, Ælfc. Gr. Z.
14, 20. Gehendes *proxime*, Germ. 388, 54. Fērde hē tō gehendum
burgum, Ælfc. T. Grn. 16, 32. Land ðæ him gehændre beó and behēfe
*terra quae eis vicinior sit vel utilior*, Cht. Th. 493, 20. Him tō
geneálǽhton his discipuli þ hī gehendran wǣron līchamlīce, þā þe mid
mōde his bebodum geneálǽhton, Hml. Th. i. 548, 26. II. temporal:—
Ūre hǣl is gehendre þonne wē gelýfdon, Hml. Th. i. 602, 1, 21. III.
of order or degree:—Cherubim sind āfyllede mid gewitte swā miccle
swīðor swā hī gehendran beóð heora Scyppende ðurh wurðscipe heora
geearnunga, Hml. Th. i. 344, 4. IV. of association, intimacy, &c.:
—þā him hē dyde gehende *ea sibi fecit socia*, Scint. 104, 5. þ heora
stefn sý Gode gehendre (*vicinior*) þonne him syluum, Nap. 30. [*O. H.
Ger.* ge-henti.]

**ge-hende;** *adv.* *Add:*—Sume adverbia syndon frumcennede . . .
*prope* gehende is frumcenned, and *propius* gehendor cymð of ðām, Ælfc.
Gr. Z. 232, 11. I. local:—Hai þe þær gehende wæs, Jos. 7,
2. II. temporal:—Ne bið seó geendung þyssere worulde nā gyt,
ðeáh ðe heó gehende sý, Hml. Th. ii. 342, 21. Swā hwylc Sunnandæg swā þær byð gehendost, Angl. viii. 329, 12. III. of scrutiny,
*closely*:—Bēda and Rabanus þe wel gehende an āsmeádun ymbe þisum
cræfte, Angl. viii. 308, 13. IV. of kinship, association, &c.:—Se
Hǣlend bodade sibbe ūs ðe feorran wǣron, and sibbe þām ðe gehende
wǣron (*iis, qui prope*, Eph. 2, 17), Hml. Th. i. 106, 17. v. ful-, un-
gehende.

**ge-hende;** *prep.* *Add:* I. local:—Wæs gehæfd gehende ðære byrig
swilce hālig stōw, Hml. Th. ii. 506, 26. Hē becōm tō ānre birig
gehende Ephesan, Ælfc. T. Grn. 16, 32. Seó rǣding cwyð wel gehende
þām ende, Angl. viii. 323, 32. þā Judēiscan de on Crīst gelýfdon
wǣron him gehendor stōwlice, Hml. Th. i. 106, 19. Seraphim sind
Godes neáwiste gehendost, 346, 24. Se mōna yrnð ealra tungla
niðemest and ðære eorðan gehendost, Lch. iii. 248, 10. II.
temporal:—Deáðe gehende *in articulo mortis*, Dōm. L. 59. Manna
gehwylc ǽfre him gehende endedæges wēne, Ll. Th. i. 374, 17; Wlfst.
75, 8. Ūs þincð þæt hit sý þām tīman swýðe gehende, 79, 12. III.
marking kinship, association, &c.:—þā Judēiscan ðe on Crīst gelýfdon
wǣron him gehendor ðurh cýððe þ̄ære ealdan ǽ, Hml. Th. i. 106, 19.

**ge-hendnys.** *Add:* I. in a local sense. (1) *nearness, neighbourhood*:—Gif hwā feorran cōme and wolde his lāc Gode offrian, ðæt hē on
gehendnysse (*at hand*) tō bicgenne gearu hæfde, Hml. Th. i. 406, 23.
Hēr on gehendnysse syndon [þā] þe þīne deórlingas beón sceoldon, Hml.
S. 23, 147. (2) *what is at hand*:—Hergiendum gehwylce gehendnysse
bereáfiendum *grassatoribus obuia queque uastantibus*, An. Ox. 2713. II.
of kinship, *relationship, propinquity*:—Gehendnys *propinquitas*, An.
Ox. 4180. v. un-gehendnyss.

**ge-heold.** v. ge-hild: **ge-heorcnian.** *Take here* ge-hercnian
*in Dict.*: **ge-heordnes.** v. ge-hirdnes.

**ge-heort.** *Add:*—þ hī hī gereordodon, and þ hī wurdon þe geheort-
ran wið þām āwyrgedan strangan and þone ealdan wiðerwinnan, Hml. S.
23, 241. v. un-geheort.

**ge-heortlīce;** *adv.* *Vigorously, thoroughly* (?):—þā sōna æfter þisre
stefne geheortlīce him wǣron þā limu cwiciende and fægre (*the Latin is*:
Post quam vocem *paulatim recalescentibus membris*), Gr. D. 317, 16.

**ge-heplicnes.** v. ge-hæplicnes: **geher.** *Dele*: **ge-hēran.** v. ge-
hīran.

**ge-hergian.** *Add:* I. intrans. (or abs.) *To harry, ravage*:—Gehergeode Wulfhere oþ Æscesdūne, Chr. 661; P. 32, 12. Hannibal sende
sciphere on Rôme and þær ungemetlīce gehergeodon *classis Punica in
Italiam transiit, ejusque plurimas partes longe lateque vastavit*, Ors. 4,
6; S. 180, 4. I a. *with on, to make predatory attacks upon*:—Se
here oft gehergode on Pehtas and on Strætlæd-Wealas, Chr. 875; P. 75,
2. On Wiht gehergade Wulfhere and gesalde Wihtwaran tō Æþelwalde,
661; P. 32, 14. II. trans. (1) *to overrun with an army, ravage,
lay waste* a country:—Hē gehergode þ land, Hml. S. 27, 25. His scipu
gehergodon Mænīge, Chr. 1000; P. 133, 15. Hit gewearð . . . þ þā
hǣðenan leóda þ land gehergoden, Hml. S. 27, 21. (1 a) *to pillage*
a town:—Hēr wæs Wecedport gehergod, Chr. 988; P. 125, 22. Hēr
wæs Gypeswīc gehergod, 991; P. 127, 1. (2) *to harass by attack or
exaction after conquest*:—Hī wurdon gehergode and gehýnde eahtatýne
geár under heora handa *afflicti sunt et oppressi per annos decem et octo*,
Jud. 10, 8. (3) *to make captive in war, carry off as spoil*:—Seó fird
gehergade swīðe micel on þǣm norðhere ǽgðer ge on mannum ge on
gehwelces cynnes yrfe (*the English took much spoil from the northern
army both in men and in cattle of every kind*, Chr. 910; P. 94, 29. þ
mīn weorod . . . and eal mīn her[e] goldes and eorcnanstana (-e, MS.)
þ hié gehergad and genumen hæfdon micel gemet mid him wǣgon *milites*

*omnes auri ex rapina margaritarumque non paruam secum praedam
ueherent*, Nar. 6, 32. Hī nāmon menn and swā hwæt swā hī findan
mihtan, and gewendon him tō Baldewines land, and sealdon þær þet hī
gehergod hæfdon, Chr. 1046; P. 167, 1. Ealle þā men þe hié gehergead hæfden, Ors. 4, 6; S. 178, 13. Gif hwylc mǽden beweddod bið,
and under þām bið gehergod (*in captivitatem ducta*), Ll. Th. ii. 186,
27: Ælfc. T. Grn. 9, 36. Hié wǣron gehergeode and of hiera earde
ālǽdde, Past. 267, 14. Gehergode, Gr. D. 182, 7. (3 a) *to lead
captive* to a place:—Hē wæs gehergod tō Sirian lande, Ælfc. T. Grn.
11, 6. ¶ gehergod *captive*:—Hæftlingc oððe gehergod *captivus*,
Ælfc. Gr. 179, 4. Se heáfodman þæs gehergodan folces, Ælfc. T. Grn.
9, 41. Hē sealde þæt feoh for gehergodum mannum, and þā þe on
hæftnēdum wǣron, Hml. S. 31, 1292. Álese hī æt ōðrum mannum
heora þeówan and hūru earme gehergode men, Ll. Th. ii. 282, 15.
Swilce hit gehergode hæftlingas wǣron *quasi captivus gladio*, Gen. 31,
26. (4) *to carry off by force*:—Deófol gehergad þā synfullan, and
gehæfte tō þære hellican byrig gelǽt, Hml. Th. ii. 66, 33. Crīst tō helle
fērde and ðær of gehergode eal þæt hē wolde, Wlfst. 126, 13. [*O. H.
Ger.* ge-heriōn *vastare*.]

**ge-hērian.** *l.* -herian, *and add:*—Se Drihten on engla endebyrdnesse
wæs gehered. þā hē wæs ācenned, þā cleopodan hié: 'Wuldor sý Gode
. . .,' Bl. H. 93, 8. Heó bið gehered mid Gode, for þon þe hire bið
mycel wuldor gegearwod, 145, 10. Hē (*St. John*) mid þære sōþfæstnesse
stefne gehiered wæs and geweorþod (cf. sē sceal beón gehered ofor ealle
þeóda and geweorþod, 71, 16. Gehered . . . and weorþad, 33), 165, 1.
Seó wyrt is gehered (-od, *v. l.*) on þām muntlandum þe man Cilicia and
Pisidia nemneþ (*the kind that grows in Cilicia and Pisidia is spoken
very highly of*), Lch. i. 160, 15. Nān mon ne biþ mid rihte for ōþres
gōde nō ðý mǽrra ne nō ðý geheredra, Bt. 30, 1; F. 108, 27.

**ge-herigendlic;** *adj. Praiseworthy*:—Samod geherigendlīcne (=?
samod- ꝥ ge-herigendlīcne. Cf. samod-herung *conlaudatio*) *conlaudabilem*, Hy. S. 109, 19.

**ge-herlicnes,** Bl. Gl. *l.* ge-heplicnes, *and see* ge-hæplicnes: **ge-
hīgan** (?) *to elevate.* v. ge-heán: **ge-hild** *a secret place. In* Ps. Spl.
T. 16, 13 *perhaps* ge-hīddum *should be read for* gehildum. Cf. gehýddum *abditis*, Wrt. Voc. ii. 98, 34: 4, 17.

**ge-hild,** es; *n.*; -hildo (-u); *f.* I. *a watch, guard*:—Gē habbað
gehæld (*custodiam*); gǣþ and haldeþ swā gē cunnun, Mt. R. L. 27, 65.
Gesett gehæld mūðe mīnum, Rtl. 182, 16. Ne mihte ic gangan tō
eástdǣlum for Rômwarena cempena neáhhergunge and for [Persisc]ra
gehældum, Hml. A. 200, 174. I a. *a watch, period during
which watch is kept*:—Swē swē gehaeld (*custodia*) in naeht, Ps.
Srt. 89, 4. From gehæld morgenlicum, Rtl. 181, 1. II. *a taking
care* to prevent hurt, *watchful care*:—þā þā hē wæs geswænced mid
þæs līchaman swinglan hē hæfde symble ðære heortan frōfre þurh þā
gehyldu (-hældu, *v. l.*) þæs Hālgan Gāstes (*per Sancti Spiritus custodiam*),
Gr. D. 275, 1. III. *keeping, preserving, preservation* from injury
or destruction:—þ hié for his gehylde (-hælde, *v. l.*) Gode heora bēne
geóten *qui pro eius custodia Deo preces fundant*, Bd. 1, 27; Sch. 73, 14.
Hē ǽr Gode fylgan nolde ꝥn gehælde (on gehyldo, *v. l.*) þæs biscopes
līfes *Deum sequi prius in custodienda vita episcopi noluit*, Gr. D. 195,
12. Þte of ðǽm tōweardum uē hæbbe gihæld ut *de futuris malis
nostris habeamus custodiam*, Rtl. 123, 31. III a. *a place for
keeping in safety*:—Settun swē swē æppeltūn gehaeld *posuerunt Hierusalem velut pomorum custodiam*, Ps. Srt. 78, 1. IV. *defence* from
attack; *a defence*:—Hē ne bið belocen mid nānum gehieldum nānes
fæstenes *nulla munitione custodiae circumcludit*, Past. 277, 18. V.
*keeping* what is prescribed, *observance* of a festival:—Be gehylde rihtra
Eástrana *in obseruatione Paschae*, Bd. 5, 21; Sch. 676, 18. V a.
*an observance*:—In gehaeldum ðīnum bieóde *in observationibus tuis
exercebor*, Ps. Srt. 76, 13. VI. *keeping* of a law, faith, obligation,
&c.:—For gehylde Crīstes beboda *propter obseruantiam mandatorum
Christi*, 3, 22; Sch. 298, 3. Hē mǣgena gehyld (-heold, -hæld, *v. l.*)
and swīþust sibbe and Godes lufan lǣrde *virtutum, sed maxime pacis et
caritatis, custodiam docuit*, 4, 23; Sch. 468, 1. Regollices þeódscipes
gehyld (-heold, -hæled) *custodiam disciplinae regularis*, 4, 27; Sch.
516, 21. v. ge-heald.

**ge-hildan** *to incline.* *Take here* **ge-hyldan** *in Dict., and add:*—
Mid þý þe hē þā flascan gehylde *cum flasconem inclinasset*, Gr. D. 142,
12. [*O. H. Ger.* ge-helden *inclinare*.] v. heald; *adj.*

**ge-hildelic;** *adj. Safe* (cf. ge-hild; III):—Se weg is mycele gesundlicra, and þ is myccle gehyldelicre līf *tutior est via*, Gr. D. 348, 10. v.
ge-heald; *adj.*

**ge-hildness.** *Take here* **ge-hyldness** *in Dict.*: **ge-hildra.** v. geheald.

**ge-hilmed;** *adj.* I. *having a helmet, helmed*:—Gehylmed *galeatum*,
Wrt. Voc. ii. 41, 9. II. *having foliage* (v. helm; II):—þǣm
gehilmdum grǣfum *frondosis dumis*, Wrt. Voc. ii. 93, 75: 37, 36.
[*O. H. Ger.* ge-hilmit *frutectum*; ge-hilmi *fruteca*.] Cf. ge-helmian.

**ge-hilt.** *Substitute* **ge-hilte;** *pl.* (*used like pl. of* hilt *with singular
meaning*) -hiltu: **ge-hīn.** v. ge-heán.

**ge-hínan.** *Add*: **I.** *to make humble* (heán), *to humble, humiliate* :—Sume hē gehýneð, sume āhefeð *hunc humiliat, et hunc exaltat*, Ps. Th. 74, 7. Áhafen ic wæs and gehýned *exaltatus autem humiliatus sum*, 87, 15. Þā þā seó sāwl on līchoman wæs gehæfd and gehýned (geeáðmódad, *v. l.*, humiliata), Gr. D. 173, 22. **I a.** *to humble* an enemy, *defeat, subject* :—Hē þone ealdor ealra þeóstra geband and gehýnde, Bl. H. 85, 6. Hē eów gehýnde and in hæft bidrāf, Gū. 569. Hwearf þā tō helle, þā hē gehēned wæs, Godes andsaca, Sat. 190. Nū sind gehýnde and gehæfte in helle grund deóña cempan, Cri. 562. **II.** *to treat with contempt, despise* :—Hē gehēued ðone ðe mec sende *spernit eum qui me misit*, Lk. L. 10, 16. Ne magon hī þonne gehýnan heofon cyninges bebod, Cri. 1525. Hē gihēned bið *contempnatur*, Mk. R. L. 9, 12. **II a.** *to treat with dishonour, to degrade, dismiss from office* :—Geheende *exauctoravit*, Wrt. Voc. ii. 107, 60. Gehēnde *deordinavit*, i. *exauctoravit*, 139, 77. Gehiénde *exactoravit*, 29, 67. Gehēned *exactoratus*, 70, 9. **III.** *to oppress, afflict, reduce to misery* :—Þæt gehýreð God, and hī gehýneð eác *God shall hear, and afflict them* (A. V.), Ps. Th. 54, 19. Ne gehēne (gehýn, *v. l.*) þū hine mid þý eácan *non eum usuris opprimes*, Ll. Th. i. 52, 23. Hē sette him weorca mægestras þæt hig gehýndon mid hefigum byrðenum *ut affligerent eos oneribus*, Ex. I, 11. Is wēn þæt heó mec eft wille earmne gehýnan yflum yrmðum, swā heó mec ǽr dyde (cf. þone heó gebond and mid wītum swong, 613), Jul. 633. Hungre gehýned, El. 720. Ic ǽr hyhtful geweard and nū gehýned éom, gōda geásne, 923. Gehiéned, Past. 66, 19. Gehēned, Ps. Th. 118, 67. Beón hig gehínede and gefyllon þā weorc *opprimantur operibus et expleant ea*, Ex. 5, 9. Tō mænige wǽron foryrmde and gehýnede, Wlfst. 158, 29. **IV.** *to condemn* :—Cwoen sūðerne gihēned (*condemnavit*) hiá, Lk. R. L. 11, 31. Gehǽnas, Jn. L. 8, 10. Hiá gehēnað ðā ilca *condemnabunt illam*, Lk. L. 11, 32. Alle geniðrad-on ł gehēndon (*condemnaverunt*) hine, Mk. L. R. 14, 64. Gehēned bið *condemnabitur*, 16, 16. Ne bið hē for giémelēste gehiéned *ne damnari ex negligentia debeat*, Past. 165, 7. Bið hē swiðe ryhtlíce mid ðǽm gehíned ðe mon wēnð ðæt mid geárod sié *unde nutrita pie creditur, inde justius damnatur*, 391, 7. Gange hē of dōme gehýned *cum judicatur, exeat condemnatus*, Ps. Th. 108, 6. Hē hafaþ ealle scyldige fordēmde and gehýnde, Bl. H. 87, 2. **V.** *to accuse* :—Ðá ðe ðec gehēnað *qui te accusant*, Jn. L. R. 8, 10. Gehēndon (*accusabant*) hine ðā hēhsácerdas, Mk. L. R. 15, 3 : Lk. L. 23, 10. Þte heá gehēndon (*accusarent*) hine, Lk. L. R. 11, 54. Gehǽne (gihēna, R.) *accusare*, Jn. L. 8, 6. [*Goth.* ga-haunjan *humiliare: O. H. Ger.* ge-hônen *humiliare, dehonestare, illudere, confundere, foedare*.]

**ge-híne ;** *adj.* *Mean, poor, frail* :—Ðā gehēno *kaduca*, Rtl. 189, 31. v. heán.

**ge-hindred ... *impeditus*. Substitute : ge-hindrian ;** *pp.* -hindrod (-ed) *To hinder, impede, check*, and add :—Þ hī for þām gylte gehindrode wǽron þe hī þone Godes wer ǽr on wege his horses bereáfedon *quia ex culpa quam servo Dei in via fecerant, illa sui itineris dispendia tolerabant*, Gr. D. 15, 13. [*O. H. Ger.* ge-hintarôn (-iren).]

**ge-hípan** *to heap together*. *Take here* ge-hýpan *in Dict.*, *and cf.* ge-heápian.

**ge-híran.** *Take here* ge-heóran, -hióran *in Dict.*, *and add* : **I.** *intrans.* *To hear, perceive sound* :—Eáran ge habbað, and ne gehýrað (-hērað, L.), Mk. 8, 18. Gif se hlyst oðstande, þ hē ne mæge gehiéran, Ll. Th. i. 92, 24. Sume magon gesíon, sume magon gehíran (-hýron, *v. l.*), Bt. 41, 5 ; F. 252, 23. **I a.** *said of the ear* :—Gif óðer eáre nāwiht gehēreð, Ll. Th. i. 14, 5. **II.** *trans.* *To hear* sound or that which causes sound, *to have cognizance of by means of the ear.* (1) *the object a noun (pronoun)* :—Þīne stefne ic gehiére, Bl. H. 241, 6. Hē nān óðer þingc on gewitnysse ne cýþe būtan þ ān þ hē geseah oþþe gehýrde, Ll. Th. i. 274, 18. Gif hwā hreám gehýre and hine forsitte, 392, 17. Of heofonan gehýrdne (*auditium*) þū worhtest dōm, Ps. L. 75, 9. (2) *the object a clause* :—Gehýrstū hwæt Símón cwiþ ?, Bl. H. 183, 8. Heó gehýrde hū se feónd and se freónd geflitu rǽrdon, El. 953. Mihte man gehēran þæt hý wæs tóða geheáw, Sat. 338. **II a.** *said of the ear* :—Ðā eáran ongitaþ þ hī gehióraþ, Bt. 41, 4 ; F. 252, 8. **III.** *with object followed by* (1) *an infinitive* :—Hē gehýrde myccle menigo him beforan fēran, Bl. H. 15, 16. Hē gehýrde þone blindan cleopian, 19, 18. Gif þē þæt gelimpe þæt þū gehýre ymb þæt hālige treó frōde frignan, El. 442. (2) *a pres. ptcple.* :—Ne gehýrdest þū Drihten cweþende, for þon ic eów sende, Bl. H. 237, 28. Þǽr mon mæg sorgende folc gehýran ... cearum cwíðende, Cri. 891. (3) *with past ptcple.* :—Heó gehýrde þone helle sceaðan oferswíðedne (-ende, MS.), El. 957. (4) *with a clause* :—Hwæþer þ āuht sié þ wē oft gehióraþ þ men cweþaþ be sumum þingum þ hit scyle weás gebyrian *whether there is anything in what we often hear men say of some things, that a thing happens by chance*, Bt. 40, 5 ; F. 240, 14. (Or *under* IX. 3 b :—*We are often told that things happen by chance*.) **III a.** *with ellipsis of object before infin.* :—Gif sum dysig man þǽs bōc rǽt oþþe rǽdan gehýrþ, Ælfc. Gen. Thw. 1, 15. Wē gehēraþ hwílum secgan þ ..., Bt. 41, 2 ; F. 246, 16. Þū gehýrdest oft reccan on ealdum spellum, 35, 4 ; F. 162, 5. Wē nū gehýrdon þis godspel beforan

ūs rǽdan, Bl. H. 15, 30. Þonne wē gehýron Godes bēc ūs beforan reccean and rǽdan, and godspell secggean, and his wuldorþrymmas mannum cýþan, 111, 16. **IV.** *to exercise the sense of hearing intentionally, to give ear, hearken, listen.* (1) *intrans.* :—Gehýre sē þe wille, Exod. 7. v. ge-hírend. ¶ *with interjectional force* :—Gehēres thū *heus!*, Wrt. Voc. ii. 110, 26. Gehýrsþū, 42, 63. Gehýrstū betsta cāsere, gif þū wilt, þū miht ongyton þ ..., Bl. H. 183, 10 : 85, 18. (2) *trans.* *To listen* (*attentively*) *to* (a) *a person* :—Gehýr mē, Bl. H. 175, 11. Críst him tō cwæð : 'Gehýre mē,' 231, 27. Hēr is mín leófa Sunu ... ; gehýrað (-hērað, R., -hēras, L.) hyne, Mt. 17, 5. Gif þū wilt gehýran þone apostol, ne swyltst þū on ēcnesse, Hml. S. 36, 358. (b) *speech, sound.* (α) *the object a noun* (pronoun) :—Ðā gehērde hē swíþe geþyldelíce þæs wīsan monnes word sume hwīle, Bt. 18, 4 ; F. 66, 33. Gehēr ān spell, 37, 1 ; F. 186, 1 : Met. 25, 1. Gehýr, Sch. 37. Heó wolde gehýran his word and his lāre, Bl. H. 67, 28. Nis hit nō þ ān þ hī nyllaþ þisse race gelēfan, ac hī hit nellaþ furþum gehíran, Bt. 38, 5 ; F. 204, 25. Hig þisne egeslican cwide gehýran sculon, Ll. Th. ii. 396, 21. (β) *the object a clause* :—Geheór (-hēr, *v. l.*) geþyldelíce hwæt ic nū sprecan wille, Bt. 35, 5 ; F. 166, 21. Gehērað hwæt se lāreów sægde, Bl. H. 39, 10. Gehērað hū se godspellere sægde be þisse tīde, 15, 3. **V.** *to hear* a religious service, *hear* mass :—Þā þe heora cyrican forlǽtaþ, and forhycggaþ þā Godes dreámas tō gehērenne, Bl. H. 41, 36. **VI.** *to hear judicially, to try* :—Georne gehýreð heofoncyninga hýhst hæleða dǽde, Dōm. 107. Þonne wile Dryhten sylf dǽda gehýran hæleða gehwylces, Seel. 91. **VII.** *to listen to with compliance, hear* a suppliant or a supplication. (1) *the object a person* :—Hió cleopiað tō mē and ic gehiére hié, Ll. Th. i. 52, 18, 27, þū gehýrdest þone hālgan wer, þā þū geýwdest þām eorle bān Jósephes, El. 785. 'Wuna mid ūs ...' Hē hié þā nolde gehiéran, ac hié forlēt, Bl. H. 247, 35. (2) *the object a thing* :—Hié hrýmað tō mē and ic gehíre hira hreám, Ex. 22, 23. Heora bēna hē gehýreð, Bl. H. 107, 21. Gehýr míne stefne, 89, 13. Críst cwæþ þ hē nelle gehýran þæs gímeleásan mannes gebedrǽdene, 57, 4. Hē clypað tō Gode and his stemne (stemn ?) ne bið gehýred. Āhyld ðīn eáre tō ðæs wǽdlan bēne, þæt God eft ðíne stemne gehýre, Hml. Th. ii. 102, 19. Heora bēna wǽron æt Gode gehýrede, Bl. H. 201, 34. **VIII.** *with dat., to listen to* one who commands, *to obey.* (1) *a person* :—Uindas and saes gehēras (-hēraþ, R.) him *venti et mare oboediunt ei*, Mt. L. 8, 27. Gif hié mē oð ðæt on ryht gehiérad ... on mínum geongum māgum swelce mē betst gehiérað, C. D. ii. 176, 1-4 : 175, 35. Ou ðā hand ðe hire ǽfre betst gehýre on uncer bēga cynne, vi. 138, 27. (2) *a command* :—Gehēr þū Meotodes rǽdum ... Lǽt of þínum staðole strēamas weallan, An. 1500. **VIII a.** *to serve, minister to* :—Gif huā mē gehēres *si quis mihi ministrat*, Jn. L. 12, 26. Hiá gehērde him *ministrabat eis*, Mt. L. 8, 15. Wífo monigo gehērdon him, 27, 55. Ne ǽnig esne mæg tuæm hláferdum gehēra (*seruire*), Lk. L. 16, 13. **IX.** *to learn by hearing, hear of, be informed of, be told.* (1) *the object a noun* :—Ic nǽfre ne geseah ne gehýrde nǽnne wísne mon þe mā wolde bión earm ðonne welig, Bt. 39, 2 ; F. 212, 16. Ǽlc man ... þāra þe þā gebodu gehýrde, L! Th. i. 232, 12. Diórwyrþra hrægla hī ne girndan ... ne hió nānwuht ne gehērdon ... ne gehērde nān mon þā get nānne sciphere, ne furþon ymbe nān gefeoht sprecan, Bt. 15 ; F. 48, 5-15. Hū mihte þæt gewyrðan þæt hý ne gehýrde Hælendes miht ?, An. 574. Þǽr bið gehýred ... þín micele miht, Hy. 7, 32. (2) *the object a clause* :—Wē gehýrað þ Drihten forseah þone welan þisse worlde, Bl. H. 23, 29 : 25, 21. Wē nū gehýrað hwǽr ūs hearnstafas onwōcan, Gen. 939. Gehýrde ic þæt Eádweard ānne slōge, By. 117. þū nū gehýrdest hū hit beón mæg, Bl. H. 7, 34. Gehýron wē nū tō hwylcum gemete heó sang, 5, 6. Þū miht gehýran hū ūs wuldres weard dǽdum lufode, An. 595 : 812 : El. 511 : Kr. 78. On þæs engles wordum wæs gehýred þ þurh hire beorþor sceolde beón gehǽled eall wīfa cynn, Bl. H. 5, 22. (3) *the object a pronoun* (a) *representing the statement in a preceding clause* :—Se gerēfa weard wið hine forwrēged swylce hē his gōd forspilde ... 'Hwí gehýre ic þis be þē ?,' Lk. 16, 2. Fērde Malcolm ... Ðā þā se cyng þis gehýrde, Chr. 1091 ; P. 226, 28. 'Ic wolde þ þū leornodest hū þū mihtest becuman tō ðām sóþum gesǽlþum ...' 'Mē lyste nū þ geheóran' (-hēran, *v. l.*), Bt. 33, 3 ; F. 126, 31. (b) *with a succeeding clause in apposition* :—Þā hit se Allwalda eall gehýrde, þæt his engyl ongan ofermēde āhebban, Gen. 292 : 2385. On morgenne gehiérdon þæt þæs cyninges þegnas ... þæt se cyning ofslægen wæs, Chr. 755 ; P. 48, 11. (v. III. 4.) (c) *with a relative clause* :—Þæt ōðre gehýron be mē þæt, þæt ic wilnige, swā swā hý ǽr gehýrdon þæt, þæt ic nolde, Ps. Th. 50, 9. **X.** *intrans.* *To be informed about* :—Ðā gehýrde þe þā bam wundrum þe Basilius worhte, Hml. S. 3, 496. [*Goth.* ga-hausjan : *O. Sax.* gi-hôrian : *O. H. Ger.* ge-hōren *audire, exaudire, parere, obedire*.] v. un-gehíred.

**ge-hirdan ;** *p.* de. **I.** *in a physical sense, to harden, temper* metal :—Hē (*the goldsmith*) gehýrdað and gehyrsteð wel, Vv. 74. Gesmyrede and gehyrde *lita* (cf. ātre gemǽled *lita* (*veneno spicula*), 96, 69, *and see* āhyrded, B. 1460), Wrt. Voc. ii. 51, 49. **II.** *in a moral sense.* (1) *to inspire with fortitude, strengthen, confirm* :—Se gefeá ðāra hesfon-

licena gôda hî gehierde (*roborat*) wið ðæm brocum, Past. 393, 35. (2) *to harden, make obdurate* :—Drihten hig gehyrde *Domini sententia fuerat ut indurarentur corda eorum*, Jos. 11, 20. [*Goth.* ga-hardjan : *O. H. Ger.* ge-harten *obfirmare*.]

**ge-hirdness**, e ; *f. Keeping guard, watchful care.* Take here ge-heordnes, ge-hyrdnes *in Dict., and add* :—On hû mycelre Godes gehyrdnysse beóð þá þe cunnon hý sylfe forseón on þysum lífe *in quanta custodia sunt qui in hac vita seipsos despicere noverunt*, Gr. D. 39, 29.

**ge-híredlic** ; *adj. That is heard, audible* :—Lá hwá sprecð myhta Drihtnes gehêredlice dô ealle herunga hine *quis loquetur potentias Domini ? auditas faciet omnes laudes eius?*, Ps. L. 105, 2. v. ge-hírendlic.

**ge-hírend**, es ; *m. A hearer* :—Sió stefn ðæs láriówes ðurhfærð ðá heortan ðæs gehírendes (-hiér-, *v. l.*) *pastoris vox auditorum cor penetrat*, Past. 81, 9. Ðá heortan ðára gehírendra (-hiér-, *v. l.*) *audientium corda*, 93, 20. Áweccan þ môd þára gehêrendra, Bt. 34, 4 ; F. 138, 30. þ hit wurde tô nytte ðám gehêrendum, 35, 5 ; F. 166, 17. Hê geseah ðá his gehýrend (*suos auditores*) þone Eástordæg onfôn, Bd. 5, 22 ; Sch. 685, 3.

**ge-hírendlic** ; *adj. To be heard, audible* :—Tô gehýrendlicere stemne *ad audiendam uocem*, Ælfc. Gr. Z. 152, 6. Gehêrendlice (*auditam*) dô mê mildheortnesse ðíne, Ps. L. 142, 8. v. ge-híredlic.

**ge-hírness.** Take here ge-hýrnes *in Dict., and add* : (1) *the sense of hearing* :—Sefa *sensus*, gesihþ *visus*, gehírnes *auditus*, Wrt. Voc. i. 282, 30 : ii. 7, 77. Gehêrnes, Bt. 41, 4 ; F. 252, 6. Healte men onfêngon heora gonge, and deáfe gehýrnesse, Shrn. 137, 28. (2) *hearing, listening* :—Manige men þá word lustlíce gehýraþ : . . seó gehýrnes and seó geornnes ne bið nyt on þæm ungelýfdum mannum, Bl. H. 55, 31. Ontýn eárna hleóþor þ mín gehêrnes hehtful weorðe, Ps. C. 78. Syle mínre gehýmesse gefeán, þæt ic gehýre þæt ic wylle *auditui meo dabis gaudium et laetitiam*, Ps. Th. 50, 9. Ic forhtige for þissere gehýrnesse *auditu paveo*, Gr. D. 212, 3. Eall his lof mægen leóde gehýran, and his gehýrnesse hêr oncnáwan *quis auditas faciet omnes laudes ejus?*, Ps. Th. 105, 2. [*O. H. Ger.* ge-hôrnesse *auditus*.]

**ge-hírstan** *to fry.* Take here ge-hyrstan *in Dict., and add* : (1) lit. :—Bærned *vel* gehyrsted *frigi*, Wrt. Voc. ii. 150, 77 : 36, 42. Gáte blædre áhyrste, sele etan, sume swá gehyrste gegnídaþ tô dúste, Lch. ii. 88, 26. Haran sina gedrýgede and mid sealte gebrædde and gehyrste, i. 344, 13. (2) figurative :—Hwæt is ðinga þe ðæs láreówes môd swíður gehierste and gegremige ðonne se anda ðe for ryhtwísuesse bið úp áhafen *quid vero acrius doctoris mentem quam zelus Dei frigit et excruciat?*, Past. 164, 2.

**ge-hírsum.** Take here ge-hýrsum *in Dict., and add* : (1) *obedient* :—Hê weard gehýrsum tô þí þæt hê willes deáð þrowade *factus obediens usque ad mortem*, R. Ben. 26, 15 : 126, 8. Ne sié his giémen nó ðý læsse ymb þá gehiérsuman (-hír-, *v. l.*), Past. 74, 15. (2) *obedient to* (a) *a person* :—Ðá tunglu þú gedêst þe gehýrsume, Bt. 4 ; F. 6, 32. (b) *a law, command,* &c. :—Hié wæron þære godcundan æ swíþe gehýrsume, Bl. H. 163, 3. v. un-gehírsum.

**ge-hírsumian.** Take here ge-hýrsumian *in Dict., and add* : I. *to obey* (1) *a person* :—Gif hí gehírsumedon heora Scippende on riht, Ælfc. T. Grn. 3, 7. Ús ne hêt ná se Hælend him gehýrsumian ús tô forwyrde, Hml. A. 5, 124. Þá búrþênas ábudon þære cwêne þæs cyninges hæse, ac heó hit forsôc and nolde gehýrsumian him tô his willan, 93, 43 : Ll. Th. i. 194, 19. (2) *a command, law,* &c. :—Gehýrsumie *pareat*, i. *obediat* (*praecepto*), An. Ox. 296. Hí hine hálsedon þ hê gehýrsumode þæs engles wordum, Hml. A. 124, 263. Gif gê willað mínum bebodum gehýrsumian, Hml. Th. i. 86, 34. II. *to obey a master, serve, be a servant to* :—Þte hwæd úsum gihêrsumiað hêrnise *ut quid nostro ministratur officio*, Rtl. 106, 22. God sylf behêt his hálgum þênum þe on clænum mægðháde him gehýrsumiað on his heofenlican húse, Hml. A. 41, 424. Ðê úe gihêrsumiga *tibi famulemur*, 15, 32. Gehýrsumiendre í þeówiendre *uernacula*, i. *famulante*, An. Ox. 288. v. un-gehírsumod.

**ge-hírsumnes.** Take here ge-hýrsumnes *in Dict., and add* : (1) *obedience* :—Getíðige ús God þ wê magon eów secgan his láre, and eów gehýrsumnysse þ gê ðá láre ðwendon tô weorcum, Hml. A. 12, 310. Hwæðer hê carfull sig tô godcundum weorcum and tô gehýrsumnysse si *solicitus est ad opus Dei, ad obedientiam*, R. Ben. 96, 17. (2) *as a technical term, the order given to a monk by his abbot* : (*obedientia quidquid ab abbate monachis injungitur*, Migne) :—Gif þú tô hwilcere gehírsumnesse scapulares beþurfe, Tech. ii. 127, 18. v. un-gehírsumness.

**ge-hírtan.** Take here ge-hyrtan *in Dict., and add* :—Gehyrt vel gehlýwþ *focilat*, i. *reficit*, Wrt. Voc. ii. 149, 82. Gehyrte *foverat*, 150, 12. I. *the object a person.* (1) *to encourage, revive the spirits, animate* :—Hê wolde gehyrtan ðá þe se cásere ácwealde . . . þá geseah hê hú sume þá crístenan woldon áwácian for ðám wítum and gehyrte heora môd, Hml. S. 5, 19-23. Godes engel hine gereordode and mid his ræde gehyrte, 22, 139. Þá gehyrte hê his geféran mid wordum, 25, 335. Ond þá mid þý þe þ mín werod gehyrted and gestilled wæs *quae res quum anime quietiorem fecisset exercitum*, Nar. 8, 17. (1 a) reflex. *to recover from grief, fear,* &c. :—Heó on eorðan feóll and mid mycelre

hefignysse gefylled weard þæt heó word gecweþan ne mihte. Mid þan heó eft hig gehyrte, Guth. 88, 25. (2) *to restore the mental power of* :—Gewitleáse gehyrtende *inerguminos*, i. *amentes refocilando*, i. *confortando*, An. Ox. 3059. II. *the object a thing.* (1) *to revive, refresh* :—Se regn þe fullíce mihte þá eorðan wel gehyrtan *pluvia quae plene terram satiare potuisset*, Gr. D. 210, 21. (2) *to cherish, shelter* :—Gehertan *fouere* (*exigua tuguria*), An. Ox. 11, 14.

**ge-hírung.** Take here ge-hêring *in Dict.*

**ge-hírwan.** Take here ge-hyrwan *in Dict., and add* : *to speak ill of, blaspheme, dishonour* :—Hê Godes mihte gehyrwde þus cweðende (cf. *sermones quibus blasphemaverunt me*, 2 Kings, 19, 6), Hml. Th. i. 568, 7. Aldormen sácerda geherdun (gehêndon, L.) hine *principes sacerdotum accusantes eum*, Lk. R. 23, 10. Nalles hige gehyrdon (= ? gehyrwdon) háliges láre, Exod. 307. On ðá tíid ðe se biscephád swá gehiered (gehêned, *v. l.*) suá huelc swá hine underfêng, hê underfêng martyrdóm. On ðá tíid wæs tô herigeanne ðæt mon wilnode biscephádes, Past. 53, 18. Þus gerád gôd beón gehyrwed *huiuscemodi dehonestari* (i. *deturpari*), Hpt. Gl. 420, 26. On gemænum naman muneca ingehýd byð gehyrewed *sub generali nomine monachorum proposito blasphematur*, R. Ben. 136, 5.

**ge-hiscan.** v. ge-hyscan : **ge-híwad.** v. ge-híwian ; VI. 1.

**ge-híwcúplician** ; *p.* ode *To make familiar to* :—For ðí is eallum geleáffullum mannum tô wacienne, for ðan ðe seó êstfulnys þære wæccan is gehíwcúplicud eallum hálgum, Nap. 30.

**ge-híwendlic** ; *adj. Figurative* :—Ðæm gehiówendlican *allegoriam* (cf. (*secundum*) *allegoriam* gástlicum angite, An. Ox. 182), Wrt. Voc. ii. 9, 6. v. ge-híwian ; V.

**ge-híwian.** *l.* -híwian, *and add* :—Gehiówiaþ *fingunt*, Wrt. Voc. ii. 38, 19. Gehíwian *inficere*, 47, 49. I. *to form, fashion* :—Ic eom sê þe man of eorðan gehíwode, Hml. S. 30, 63. Sê gehiéwade (*finxit*) heortan heara, Ps. Srt. 32, 15. Seó sáwul ealle líchamlicra þinga híw mæg on hyre sylfre gehíwian, and swá gehíwode on hyre môde gehealdan, i. 1, 225. Blôdig wolcen on mistlíce beámas wæs gehíwod, Chr. 979 ; P. 122, 26. Þás twelf tácna sind swá gehíwode on ðám heofenlicum roderum, and synd swá bráde þ hí gefyllað twá tída mid hyra úpgange, Lch. iii. 246, 6. Þára treówa æcyrfe on fatu gehíwad (-e, -heówad, *v. ll.*) wæron (*formarentur*), Bd. 3, 22 ; Sch. 291, 6. II. *to alter the form of, transform* :—Drihten hine sylfne tô men gehíwode, Wlfst. 144, 31. II a. *to alter the appearance of, make to look like* :—Þá gehíwode hê hine sylfne tô sumum ælþeódigum men *peregrinum quempiam se simulans*, Gr. D. 75. 4. Hê is gehíwod tô crístenum men, and is earm hæðengylda, Hml. Th. i. 102, 16. Seó gýtsung gehíwod wæs weordlíce on gegyrelan *avaritia transformatur in habitum honestum*, Prud. 61. III. *to make an object appear other than it really is* :—Deófol gemacað þæt sume men beóð swá gehíwode líceteras swylce hý Godes ege habban, and bið eal heora ingeþanc mid fracode áfylled. Nis nán wyrse yfel . . . þonne þæt gehíwode yfel (*evil that is made to appear good*), for ðam deófol sylf hit gefadað and gehíwað tô þám þæt þæt þincð ærest gôd þe wyrð yfel on ende, Wlfst. 54, 4-11. IV. *to assume an appearance or character not belonging to one, to feign* :—Mid gehýwedre hálignysse, Hml. Th. i. 406, 11. Gehíwedre ceápe *dissimulato negotio*, An. Ox. 4837. V. *of representation by a material or verbal figure.* Cf. ge-híwendlic, ge-híwung :—Wel geheówede Dauid þ, þá hê wolde wiþ Goliaþ gefeohtan, Bl. H. 31, 16. Þruh þá is gehíwot *per quem* (*gastrimargia*) *figuratur*, An. Ox. 11, 101. Gehíwudre spræce tropologiam, 8, 15 c. Swá micel is betwux þære gehíwodan anlícnysse and ðám sôðan ðinge so *much difference is there between the image made to represent a thing and the real thing*, Hml. Th. ii. 240, 16. VI. *to paint* :—Gezabel gehíwode hire eágan mid rude *Jesabel depinxit oculos suos stibio* (2 Kings 9, 30), Hml. S. 18, 342. Gehíuadne *purpuratum*, Lk. p. 9, 2. (2) *of natural complexion.* Cf. ge-híwlæcan ; II :—Benedictus wæs blíðe on andwlitan, mid hwítum hærum, fægere gehíwod (*with a fresh complexion*), Hml. Th. ii. 186, 20. v. un-gehíwod.

**ge-híwian** *to marry.* Add : [*O. Sax.* gi-híwian : *O. H. Ger.* ge-híwen *nubere*.]

**ge-híwlæcan** ; *p.* -læhte. I. *to form, fashion, shape* :—And eác manna wynsumlíc wlita æfter his ágenan anlícnessan gehýwlæhte, Nap. 30. II. *to colour.* Cf. ge-híwian ; VI. 2 :—Heó ágyfð þ gecyndelíce híw, and hê byð gehýwlæht swylce hê of swíðe háton bæþ: eóde, Lch. i. 262, 14.

**ge-híwodlíce** ; *adv. Formally, apparently* :—Ealle naman mæst teóð genitivum : *amicus illius* his freónd . . . Hí magon eác sume beón geðeódde dativo gehíwodlíce : *amicus illi est* hê is him freónd . . . Sume nimað accussatiuum gehíwodlíce : *exosus bella* onscuniende gefeoht, Ælfc. Gr. Z. 250, 13-251, 1.

**ge-híwung.** Add : *an image, figure.* v. ge-híwian ; V :—Leásæ gehíwunga *falsa imagine*, Wrt. Voc. ii. 147, 1. VI gemetum þá geheówunge swefna gehrínað þæs mannes môd *sex modis tangunt animum imagines somniorum*, Gr. D. 339, 2. Gehíwunge oððe gebeácnunge *cathegorias*, Wrt. Voc. ii. 24, 12.

**ge-hladan.** _Add:_ I. _to heap up, load:_—Gehladen _fertum_ (omitted at Wrt. Voc. ii. 147, 76), Wülck. Gl. 237, 2: _faltum_ (cf. _faltum_ embhêped, 146, 75), Wrt. Voc. ii. 37, 61. Gehlæden _onustus_, 63, 59. Gehladenum _onustis_, 79, 72. Gehla[dene] _referta_, i. _repleta_, An. Ox. 466. II. _to draw water:_—Gange mædenman tô wylle þe rihte eást yrne, and gehlade âne cuppan fulle forð mid ðâm streáme, Lch. iii. 74, 14. [_O. H. Ger._ ge-hladan _onerare, augere_; ge-ladan _gravidus_.]

**ge-hlæg.** _l._ -hlæg, _and add:_—Oft wê gewuniað þ wê þâm woruldmannum hwæthugu mid sprecað for gehlæge, and þâ ylcan spræce wê nimað lustlîce, þeáh þe heó sî ûs unwyrðelîce and unrihtlic tô sprecane _dum plerumque eis ad quaedam loquenda condescendimus, paulisper assueti, hanc ipsam locutionem quae nobis indigna est, etiam delectabiliter tenemus_, Gr. D. 209, 21.

**ge-hlænian.** _Add:_—Gehlænian _macerare_, Wrt. Voc. ii. 96, 34: 57, 16. Gehlænedum _macilento_, 54, 61.

**ge-hlænsian**; _p._ ode _To make lean:_—Gewiss ys þæt þurh forhæfednysse flæsc sî gehlænsud (_maceretur_), Scint. 53, 8. Gehlænsedum _macilento_, i. _tenuato_, An. Ox. 2123.

**ge-hlæstan.** _Add:_—Hê hêt his scip mid hwæte gehlæstan, and mid micclum gewihte goldes and seolfes, and mid reáfum, Ap. Th. 6, 3.

**ge-hleápan.** _Add:_ to _jump_ (fig.):—Æfter þissum hig gehleápað on metaplasmum, Angl. viii. 313, 28.

**ge-hlencan**; _pp._ ed _To twist, bend_ (?):—Gif men sió heáfodpanne beó gehlenced, âlege þone man ûpweard, drîf .ii. stacan æt þâm eaxlum, lege þonne bred þweóres ofer þâ fêt, sleah þonne þriwa on mid slegebytle; hió gæþ on riht sôna, Lch. ii. 342, 4: 302, 29. [Cf. _M. H. Ger._ lenken _to turn, bend_.]

**ge-hleótan.** _Add:_ I. _trans._ (1) _to obtain by lot:_—þâ hluton þâ consulas hwelc hiera ærest þæt gewinn underfênge. þâ gehleát hit Quintus Flaminius _bellum ... quod Quinctius Flaminius sortitus_, Ors. 4, 11; S. 202, 34. (2) _to have allotted, obtain, get:_—Mildheortnyss fram midþoligende fremedre yrmþe nama(n) gehlêt _misericordia a compatiendo aliene miserie nomen sortita est_, Scint. 147, 4. Hê gehleát _sortitur_, i. _adipiscitur_, An. Ox. 3619. Hê gehieóte âmânsumunge wrace _sortiatur excommunicationis vindictam_, R. Ben. I. 57, 15. Gehleóte hê þâ genyþerunge þe Scarioth geearnude, C. D. B. i. 156, 4. (3) _to allot, assign_ as a person's share, _give:_—Hît wæs gehloten tô Jósepes bearna lande _fuit in possessionem filiorum Joseph_, Jos. 24, 32. [Nas hit noht swâ iloten, Laym. 7819. þu art ilote to him, H. M. 11, 13.] II. _intrans. To be allotted._ [Cf. _Icel._ hljótask _to be allotted, fall by lot_]:—Hié sendon hlot him betweónum, hwider hyra gehwylc faran scolde tô læranne. Se eádiga Matheus gehleát tô Marmadonia (cf. þâm (_Matthew_) God hlŷt geteóde ût on þæt îgland, An. 14), Bl. H. 229, 6. [Him scal ileoten bitterest alre baluwen, Laym. 31306.]

**ge-hleóþ.** _l._ -hleóþor. v. un-gehleóþor, ofer-hleóþor: **ge-hleow**; _adj. l._ -hleów.

**ge-hleówan.** v. ge-hlîwan: **ge-hlette.** v. ge-hlytta: **ge-hlidad**; _part. Substitute:_ **ge-hlidian**; _p._ ode _To cover with a lid_ (gehleodad _is a v.l. to_ gehlidad, Bd. Sch. 445, 21). [þes put he hat þat heo beo euer ilided and iwrien, A. R. 58.] Cf. un-hlidian.

**ge-hlihhan**; _p._ -hlôh, _pl._ -hlôgun _To laugh at, deride:_—Hiá gehiôgan hine _deridebant eum_, Mt. L. 9, 24.

**ge-hlinian, -hleonian**; _p._ ode. I. _of a person, to recline, rest, sit at table:_—Sê ðe gehlinað (-hlionað, R.) ... sê ðe gehrestað (gihlionað, R.) _qui recumbit ... qui recumbit_, Lk. L. 22, 27. Gehlionade _discubuit_, 7, 36: _recubuit_, 11, 37. Gehlionade ł geræste _recumbens_, Mt. p. 8, 17. Gesætt ł gehlinade _discubuit_, Lk. L. 22, 14. Gelionede (-hlionade, R.) _accumberet_, Mk. L. 2, 15. Ðâ ðe gelionodon ł gehlionade wêron _qui recumbebant_, Mt. L. 14, 9. Gehlinig _recumbe_, Lk. L. 17, 7. II. _of things, to rest, lie:_—Ðâm godwebbe ðióstro ne magon cxxtigum mîla neáh gehleonian _darkness cannot lie within a hundred and twenty miles of that curtain_, Sal. K. 152, 20. [_O. H. Ger._ ge-hlinôn _recumbere_.]

**ge-hlinung**, e; _f. Resting, reclining:_—Gihlionunga, Lk. R. 17, 7.

**ge-hlîta**, an; _m. A consort, fellow:_—For gehlŷtum ðînum _prae consortibus tuis_, Ps. Spl. C. 44, 9. Cf. efen-hlîte, ge-hlytta.

**ge-hlîwan, -hleówan**; _p._ de _To shelter, cherish, refresh:_—Gehyrt _vel_ gehlŷwð _focilat_, i. _reficit_, Wrt. Voc. ii. 149, 82. Fovet, i. _nutrit, pascit vel_ gehlŷwð, 150, 9. Gehlîwan _fovere_, i. _alere, auxiliari_, 11. I. _in a physical sense._ (1) _to warm:_—Plûmfeþera hnescnyss geonglice lima nâ gehlŷwe (_printed_ gehylpe) _plumarum mollities iuuenilia membra non foueat_, Scint. 144, 5. Of flŷsum mînra sceápa wêron gehlŷwde (_calefacti_, Job 31, 20) ðearfena sîdan, Hml. Th. ii. 448, 18. Gehlŷde, Job Thw. 165, 2. (2) _to refresh:_—Spîw and hit gehlŷwð (_refrigerabit_) þê and þû nâ tô gelæd lîchaman ðînum untrumnysse, Scint. 170, 6. II. _in a spiritual sense:_—Sê þe gehŷrsumað fæder, hê gehlŷwð (_refrigerabit_) mæder, Scint. 174, 3. Gesihþe gehleówende hê þurhteó þ heó ne îdelnysse hlade _visum fovendo contegat ne vanitates hauriat_, Hy. S. 9, 14. Fruman gecyrredra geswæsum gehlŷwende ł gehyrtende (_refouenda_) synd gemetum, Scint. 61, 10.

**ge-hlîwung.** v. geteld-gehlîwung.

**ge-hlot.** _Add:_ _allotment, determination, settlement._ Cf. ge-hleótan;

I. 3:—Sweotollîce ûs gedyde tô witanne Alexander hwelce þâ hæðnan godas sindon tô weorþianne, þ hit swîþor is of þâra biscepa gehlote (_from what the priests determine shall be said_) and of heora âgenre gewyrde þ þ hié secgað þonne of þâra goda mihte _Alexander nobis prodidit, diis ipsis mutis et surdis, in potestate antistitis quid velit fingere_, Ors. 3, 9; S. 126, 33.

**ge-hlôw.** _Dele_, -hleów, _and add:_ _bleating:_—Se feónd ongan onhyrgian ... hrŷðra gehlôwe (_balatus pecorum_), Gr. D. 185, 3. Gehlôw _mugitum_, An. Ox. 1465. Weard hê geþreád fram þâm âwyrgdan gâste ... and ongan beón swîðe geswænced mid gehlôwum (_balatibus_), Gr. D. 223, 8.

**ge-hlŷd** _covered._ v. ge-hlîwan.

**ge-hlŷd.** _Add:_ I. _sound made by the voice, a cry:_—Gif se sâcerd bið ungerâd ðæs lâreówdômes, hwæt forstent his gehlŷd _sacerdos si praedicationis est nescius, quam clamoris vocem daturus est praeco mutus?_, Past. 91, 25. I a. _in an unfavourable sense._ (1) _clamour, noise, din:_—Weard micel gehlŷd hlihhendra deófla, Hml. S. 31, 810. Simpronius mid swîðlicum gehlŷde hêt hî gefeccan, 7, 81. Hê clypode mid gehlŷde, 36, 362. Mid wêdendum and egislicum gehlŷde _bachanti et furibundo strepitu_ (i. _clamore_), An. Ox. 3811. (2) _excessive speech, garrulity:_—Wordig gehlŷd _uerbosa garrulitas_, An. Ox. 1417: 1612. (3) _of inopportune speech:_—Ræde hê swâ, þæt hê ôþre mid gehlŷde ne geunstille, R. Ben. 73, 14. (4) _violent speech, outcry:_—Betere wê âhreddon ûs sylfe of ðissere burhware gehlŷde, Hml. S. 23, 202: 22, 187. Ðâ hæðenan clypodon mid gehlŷde ... 'Beó se ârleása ofslagen,' 22, 160: 23, 612. Grymetende mid gehlŷde, 7, 242. II. _noise made by people in excited action, tumult, disturbance, din_ of business:—Swêgende gehlŷd gedrêfde _tumultuans_ (_secularium_) _strepitus obturbabat_, An. Ox. 5432. Ðâ bróðru þâ mid gehlŷde wurpon wæter on þ fŷr swylce hit tô âdwæscenne _cum jaciendo aquam, et ignem quasi extinguendo perstreperent_, Gr. D. 123, 29. Hê mid his âþenedre honda gestilleþ þâ gerûxl and þ gehlŷd eallra manna _extensa manu omnium tumultus sedat_, 265, 13. II a. _a tumult, uproar, disturbance:_—Næs nâ on freólsdæge þe læs þæs folces gehlŷd wurde _non in die festo ne forte tumultus fieret populi_, Mk. 14, 2. III. _the noise made by an animal:_—Eosola gehlŷd _ruditus asinorum_, Gr. D. 185, 3. IV. _the noise made with things:_—Ðâ gehŷrde hê gelŷd þâm gelîcost swylce þæra muneca setl færlîce feóllon ealle tôgedere, and wæs æfre swâ leng swâ hlúddre. Ðâ æfter langum fyrste geswâc þ gehlŷd, Vis. Lfc. 47-50. On þære ylcan nihte wæs geworden mycel gehlŷd (_strepitus_) on þâm hrôfe þære cirican, efne swylce hwylc man urne þær geond dwoliende. Ðâ âweóx and bræclade mâra swêg ... swylce eall seó cyrice wære ... tôworpen fram þâm grundweallum, Gr. D. 236, 10.

**ge-hlyst**, es; _n. Substitute:_ **ge-hlyst**, e; _f. Hearing:_—Þæs þe hî âgyltan þâr oþþe þurh oþþe þurh gehlyste æniges yfeles þinges, oþþe þurh îdele spræce, R. Ben. 128, 2.

**ge-hlystan.** _Add:_ I. _to listen to_ (gen. dat.):—Ðâ gecorenan menn giornfulle bioð his worda tô gehlystanne, Past. 381, 19. II. _to obey:_—Gehlystað _obaudite_, Bl. Gl.

**ge-hlyste**; _adj. Audible:_—þ heora stefn sŷ Gode gehendre and gehlystre þonne him syluum _ut vox vicinior sit Deo quam sibi_, Nap. 30.

**ge-hlystfull.** _Add:_—Beó þû bêntŷþe ł gehlystfull _depraecabilis esto_, Ps. L. 89, 13.

**ge-hlyta.** v. ge-hlîta.

**ge-hlytta**, an; _m._ I. _a partner, fellow:_—For gehlyttum _prae consortibus_ (_tuis_), Ps. Rdr. 44, 8. II. _one chosen by lot:_—Betweox midde gehlyttan _inter medios cleros_, Ps. Rdr. 67, 14. Cf. efen-hlŷta.

**ge-hlytto.** _Add:_ I. _a lot;_ sors:—Gehlytte (_printed_ -slytte) sors, Rtl. 191, 39. Gehlette _sorte_, An. Ox. 11, 110. II. _fellowship:_—Gihlytto _consortium_, Rtl. 95, 35: 97, 8. Ðînra hehstaldra gihlytto, 105, 21. Nængo gihlytto trióleásra _nulla consortia perfidorum_, 59, 21. Ærestes gilytto _resurrectionis consortia_, 22, 40. v. tô-gehlytto.

**ge-hlyttrod.** _Substitute:_ **ge-hlŷttr(i)an**; _p._ (e)de, ode _To make clear, clarify, purify:_—Genim wîn and fearres geallan ..., gemeng wiþ þŷ leáce, dô on ærfæt, læt standan nigon niht, âwring þurh cláþ, and gehlŷttre wel, Lch. ii. 34, 7. Gehlŷttrod wîn _meracum vinum_, Wrt. Voc. i. 27, 61. [_O. H. Ger._ ge-hlûteren _defecare_.]

**ge-hlŷwan.** v. ge-hlîwan.

**ge-hnæcan.** _Add:_—Þeós wyrt ealde wunda gehæleþ and eác hyre dûst wexende flæsc wel gehnæceþ, Lch. i. 292, 19. (In one MS. the vowel of each verb has an accent.) Gehnæcþ (= ? -hnægþ. Cf. hlihcaþ (= hlihgaþ), 391, 17) _deprimit_, Germ. 401, 117. [Cf. _O. H. Ger._ ge-[h]nicchen; _p._ [h]nicta _conterere, atterere: Icel._ hnekkja _to check, thwart_.]

**ge-hnægan.** _Add:_—Gehnægith _sternit_, Wrt. Voc. ii. 121, 35. Full oft hit ðæs deófles dugoð gehnægeð, Sal. 399 (2nd ed.). Gehnæcþ (= ? -hnægþ, _see_ ge-hnæcan) _deprimit_, Germ. 401, 117. Sê þe hine âhæfaþ, hê bið genægeþ; and sê þe hine genægeþ (_humiliaverit_), hê bið âhæfen, Mt. R. 23, 12. Ic eom gesæged and gehnæged and swîðe geeáðmed _incurvatus sum et humiliatus sum usquequaque_, Ps. Th. 37, 8. Hiora rîce wæs gehnæged _inclinata sunt regna_, 45, 5. Fleáh fæge

gást, folc wæs geh[n]ǽged, Exod. 169. [*Goth.* ga-hnaiwjan *to humble:* O. H. Ger. ge-hneigen *inclinare, subjugare.*]

**ge-hnǽstan**; *p.* te *To come into conflict with, contend:*—Sē þe mec fēhð ongeán and wið mægenþisan mínre genǽsteð, Rä. 28, 10. v. ge-hnǽst.

**ge-hnesctun.** *Substitute:* ge-hnescan, -hnescian; *p.* -hnescte, -hnescode *To make nesh.* **I.** in a physical sense. (1) *to soften hard material:*—þ hearde hyt gelīðigað and gehnesceaþ, Lch. i. 368, 2. Gehnescige mon mid þȳ þ forsetene yfel ... hē þone forheardodan swile gehnesce ... wirð se swile swā heard swā stān, and ne mæg hine mon gehnescian, ii. 212, 15-22. Hū mon mæg gehnescan þā heardnesse, 168, 8. Oþ þ ðā corn þurh ðone wǽtan gehnehsode sȳn, i. 92, 14. Wurdon þā gyrda gehnexode swilce hit fæðera wǽron, Hml. S. 35, 190. (1 a) figurative:—Ðǽr wǽron gehnescode hiera breóst ... beóð hira breóst gehnescod *ibi subacta sunt ubera earum ... ubera subiguntur,* Past. 403, 34-405, 2. (2) *to alleviate, relieve* pain:—Oft hearda wunda beóð mid liðum beðengum gehnescode and gehǽlede *plerumque dura vulnera per lenia fomenta mollescunt,* Past. 183, 21. **II.** *to make gentle* or *tender.* (1) of persons:—Genehxa þā heardheortnysse mínre þǽre stǽnenan heortan, Angl. xii. 500, 14. Ðæt mon ðā heardan heortan gehnescige, Past. 154, 3. (2) of speech:—Gehnistun word heora *mollierunt sermones suos,* Ps. Srt. 54, 22. Genexode synt his sprǽcu *molliti sunt sermones eius,* Ps. L. 54, 22. **III.** *to weaken, enfeeble.* (1) *to relax the vigour of:*—Ðonne mon lǽt tōslūpan ðone ege and ðā lāre suīður ðonne hit ðearf sié for wācmōdnesse, ðonne wierð gehnescad ðonone sió ðreáung ðæs anwaldes, Past. 289, 3. (2) *to cause to be yielding* (cf. hnesce tō lustum, Hml. Th. ii. 220, 4):—Ðing ðe heora hláford þurh oferflówednysse tō unlustum gehnexað, Hml. Th. ii. 92, 19. Óðre mid lyffetungum tō leahtrum gehnexian, Hml. S. 16, 174.

**ge-hnígan.** *Add:* [*O. Sax.* gi-hnígan *to bend, bow:* O. H. Ger. ge-hnígan.]

**ge-hnigian** *to cause to bend;* reflex. *to bow:*—Ne geþrístlǽce hē þ hē hine tō Godes weófode gehnigie *non audeat se ad altare Dei inclinare,* Ll. Th. ii. 176, 3.

**ge-hnycned** *drawn(?), pinched* (?):—Eþung bið sārlic, gehnycned neb, Lch. ii. 258, 17. [Cf. (?) *Icel.* hnykkja *to pull.*]

**ge-hnyscan.** *Add:*—On þone þe se stān falleþ, gehnyscet (*conteret*) hine.

**ge-hnyssan** (?) *to afflict:*—Se gehnysta gást, hiorte geclānsod and geeádmēded *spiritus contribulatus, cor contritum et humiliatum,* Ps. C. 127. Cf. hnossian. [*But* gehnyst *might belong to* ge-hnyscan. Cf. ge-hnistun *under* ge-hnescan; V. 2.]

**ge-hnyst.** *See preceding word.*

**ge-hoferod.** *Add:*—Wæs sum earm ceorl egeslíce gehoferod, and ðearle gebíged þurh ðone brādan hofor, Hml. S. 21, 95.

**ge-hófod;** *adj. Hoofed, having a hoof:*—þā þe synd gehófode on horses gelícnysse wǽron unclǽne, Hml. S. 25, 44.

**ge-hogian;** *p.* ode; *pp.* od. **I.** *to resolve, determine.* (1) with infin.:—þū gehogodest sæcce sēcean ofer sealt wæter, B. 1988. (2) with clause:—Hæfde hē gehogod, þæt hē gedǽde, swā hine Drihten hēt, Gen. 2892. (3) with pronoun and clause in apposition:—þā ic ǽrest hyt gehogede, þæt ic hine tō swíþe ne lufige, Solil. H. 35, 14. Hē þæt on his mōde gehogode (-hogod, *v. l.*) and geteód hæfde (*decreuerat*), þæt hē wolde his þeóde fordón, Bd. 3, 24; Sch. 307, 6. Gē þæt gehogodon, þæt gē on fāra folc feorh gelǽddon, An. 429. (3 a) with pron., relative clause, and clause in apposition:—Đā þæt gebogode Mēda aldor, þæt ǽr man ne ongan, þæt hē Babilone ābrecan wolde, Dan. 687. **II.** *to look for, hope for:*—Israhēla hūs on Drihten helpe gehogedan *Domus Israel speravit in Domino,* Ps. Th. 113, 18. **III.** *to conceive:*—Beón gehoged *conici,* i. *intelligi,* An. Ox. 2688. v. ge-hycgan.

**ge-hogod;** *adj. Having* (such and such) *thoughts:*—Gefeorma mīne sāwle, fæder moncynnes, hædre gehogode (*having anxious thoughts*) hǽl, ēce God ... Ic ymb sāwle eom forht, Hy. 4, 62. Cf. ge-hugod.

**ge-hola.** *Add:*—Wē beóð þíne geholan, and ealne wæg þíne midsprecan, ne wē nellað ðē ámeldian, ac hit eall stille lǽtan, Hml. S. 23, 590.

**ge-holian** *to get:*—Ðætte ðonne hié wēnen ðæt hié ðone gilp and ðæt lof begieten hæbben ðæt hié ǽr wilnodon, ðæt hié ðonne hæbben mid ðȳ scame geholode *ut unde adepta gloria creditur, inde utilis subsequatur confusio,* Past. 209, 19. [*O. H. Ger.* ge-holōn, -halōn *adipisci, obtinere.* O. Sax. gi-halōn *to gain, obtain.*]

**ge-holian;** *p.* ode *To hollow out:*—Geholedum (*gescafenum*) telgrum cauatis corticibus, An. Ox. 255: 11, 15: deasceato, i. *dolato,* Germ. 395, 381. [*O. L. Ger.* ge-[h]olade *exesa* (*antra*): O. H. Ger. geholōt *cauatus.*]

**ge-hōn, -hongian.** *Substitute:* **ge-hōn** *to hang* (trans.). **I.** *to fasten* to an object above:—Genim þās wyrte, and gehōh hȳ tō ðǽre hýse, Lch. i. 98, 1. **II.** *to fasten* to a cross, *crucify:*—Gehēngon hine *crucifixerunt eum,* Mt. L. 27, 36. Þte hiá gehēngon ł mæhton āhōa hine, Mk. L. 15, 20. Mæhte ic hafo gehōa ðec ł ðec tō hōanne, Jn. L. 19, 10. Þte hē sē gehōen ł āhongen, Mt. L. 26, 2: Mk. L. 15, 15. **III.** *to hang* with, *decorate* with that which is suspended:—

Wudu bið blēdum gehongen *lucus frondis honore viret,* Ph. 38. Sindon þā bearwas blēdum gehongene, wlitigum wæstmum *genus arboreum procero stipite surgens,* 71.

**ge-hopian;** *p.* ode *To hope:*—Ic gehopige on hine *sperabo in eum,* Ps. L. 90, 2. Gehopud *speratus,* Scint. 27, 14: 172, 1.

**ge-hopp,** es; *n. A little bag, a seed-vessel* of a plant, *a pod.* Cf. codd:—Gehopp *folliculum,* Wrt. Voc. ii. 36, 40. [Cf. *N. E. D.* hoppe *the seed-vessel of flax.*] v. hoppe.

**ge-horian, ge-hornian.** v. ge-horwian: ge-hornung. *Dele.*

**ge-horsod** (ge-horsian). *Add:* **I.** *provided with* or *possessed of a horse:*—Hē sceal beón gehorsad þ hē mǽge tō hláfordes seáme þ syllan *equum habeat quem ad summagium domini sui prestare possit,* Ll. Th. i. 436, 6. Hē sceal beón gehorsad tō hláfordes neóde *equum habeat in opus domini sui,* 436, 18. **II.** *mounted* (of cavalry):—On his fēðehere wǽron XXXII M, and þæs gehorsedan fífte healf M, Ors. 3, 9; S. 124, 12. XM gehorsedra and eahtatig M fēþena, S. 126, 3: 3, 10; S. 138, 17. Hundteóntig þūsenda gangendra manna and twēntig þūsenda gehorsedra manna, Hml. S. 25, 557. þ ǽlc man hæbbe æt þǽre syhl wel gehorsede men *omnis homo habeat duos homines cum bonis equis de omni caruca,* Ll. Th. i. 208, 13.

**ge-horwian, -horgian, -horian;** *p.* ode. **I.** *to defile.* (1) with material filth, *to spit upon:*—Ongunnun summe efne-gespitta ł gehorogæ (*conspuere*) hine, Mk. L. 14, 65. Gehorǽd bið (*conspuetur*), Lk. L. 18, 32. [Cf. Gē mid horu speówdon on his andwlitan, El. 297.] (2) with moral impurity:—Gálnyss gehorwigende *libido sordidans,* Hy. S. 5, 5. Gif gē mid synnum gehorgode beóð, Nap. 30. **II.** *to disgrace, treat shamefully:*—Ðene hiá mid sceófmum (*scomum,* R.) miclum gehoruadon (*Skeat prints* gehornadon, *but Cook in his Glossary to the Durham Book gives* gehoruadon) *illum contumeliis affecerunt,* Mk. L. 12, 4. v. horh, horu.

**ge-hradian.** *Substitute:* **I.** *trans.* (1) *to cause a thing to be done rapidly:*—Hē sóna getimbrian hēt mǽrlic mynster on þreóra geára fæce. þæt wile þincan ungeleáflic eallum þǽm þe þā stówe on uferum tídum geseóð and þis ne gemunaþ. Hē þ ilce mynster þus gehradod hēt Sēā Marian gehálgian, Lch. iii. 438, 16. (2) *to cause to attain an end quickly, to prosper* a person or undertaking:—God hī sóna gehradode, swā þ hī þǽr gemētton āne mǽre þrūh, Hml. S. 20, 78. Heora síðfæt wæs from Drihtne sylfum gehradad and gefyrðrad *a Domino suum iter erat prosperatum,* Bd. 4, 19; Sch. 446, 2. **II.** *intrans.* **To come quickly, happen quickly:*—Sóna wōl ealra māna somod gehradode *luxuriam continuo omnium lues scelerum comitari adcelerauit,* Bd. 1, 14; Sch. 38, 18.

**ge-hradige,** Angl. viii. 303, 27. v. ge-rādian: **ge-hrado.** v. wægn-gehrado: **ge-hrǽcan.** l. -hræccan (= -reccan): **ge-hrǽdnys.** *Dele* v. ge-hwǽdnes: **ge-hrēman.** v. ge-hríman.

**ge-hremmed.** *Substitute:* **ge-hremman**; *p.* -hremde; *pp.* -hremmed *To hinder, impede.* (1) *to prevent the free action of:*—Dóð hūru þæt hī ne magon ūre tunga gehremman, ne ūs ālēfian, Hml. Th. ii. 488, 5. þ se brōðor ðe hine synderlíce gebiddan wyle tō Gode, þ hē ne beó gehremmed oððe gelett (*impediatur*) þurh (mid, *v. l.*) ǽniges ōðres onhrópe ... þe lǽs ðe þā gehremmede beón (*impedimentum patiantur*) þe ðā gebedu lufiað, R. Ben. 80, 7-15. (2) *to prevent the right action of, be a stumbling-block to:*—þe lǽs te gehremde (gelette) ne (*castos*) *offenderet,* An. Ox. 3675. þ ús deófol ne mæge mid syngrínum tō swíðe gehremman, Btwk. 196, 20. (3) *to prevent from reaching* an object, *keep* from:—Ús nān þinge on worulde fram Gode ne gehremme, Hml. S. 23, 207. þ heora mōd fram Drihtne ne sȳ gehremmed *mens impediri non possit,* R. Ben. 137, 14.

**ge-hreódan.** v. ge-hroden.

**ge-hreósan.** *Add:* **I.** *to fall* from an upright position, *fall to the ground;* of a structure, *to fall in ruins:*—Monige weallas mid seofon and fíftegum torran gehruron and geseóllan (*conruerunt*), Bd. 1, 13; Sch. 37, 13. Seó eorðe wæs āstyred and on manegum stówum gehroren (-hropen, Th.) *revelata sunt fundamenta orbis terrarum,* Ps. Th. 17, 15. **I a.** *to fall* in battle:—þ mīne fȳnd on mínre gesihþe feallan and gereósan (*corruant*) swā swā gereás (*corruit*) Golias ætforan Dauides ansȳne, and swā swā gereás and wearþ besenct Faraones folc on þǽre reádan sǽ ... and swā swā geriás Amaleh ætforan Móissu ... Swā feallan and gereósan (*cadant*) mīne fȳnd under mínum fótum, C. D. B. ii. 333, 7-12. **II.** *to fall* from a prosperous condition:—Feallan hī ł gehreósan hī (*decidant*), Ps. L. 5, 11. Đā wæs gehroren sió ūpāhæfenes Paules, ... and æfter ðǽm hryre hē ongan timbran eáðmódnysse elationis ejus fabrica tota corruerat, et post ruinam suam humilis aedificari requirebat,* Past. 443, 29. **III.** *to fall* from a higher to a lower level, *fall headlong:*—Oft ðonne se hirde gǽd on frēcne wegas, sió hiord gehríst *cum pastor per abrupta graditur, ad praecipitium grex sequatur,* Past. 31, 1. Dryhten forlēt hine (*Lucifer*) of dūne gehreósan, Sal. 458. **III a.** of strong emotion, e.g. fear, *to fall* upon:—Gehreás ł onsæt egsa ofer hig *incubuit timor super eos,* Ps. L. 104, 38. **IV.** *to rush* upon, *move with violence:*—On gehreósan *ingruere,* Wrt. Voc. ii. 43, 73. **IV a.** of inconsiderate action:—

Ðonne ðæt ierre hæfð anwald ðæs monnes, ðonne gehrīsð (-hríesð, *v. l.*) hē on sume scylde, Past. 288, 9.

**ge-hreóðan.** *l.* -hreódan.

**ge-hreówan.** *Substitute :* **ge-hreówan ;** *p.* -hreáw, -hreów. **I.** *to cause sorrow to, grieve* a persoɔ (*acc.*). (1) the subject a noun :—Mec þīn weá æt heortan gehreáw, Cri. 1494. Mec his bysgu gehreáw, Gū. 686. (2) without subject :—Gehrēues mec *paenitet me*, Lk. L. 17, 4. **II.** *to cause sorrow, repentance, or regret* to a person (*dat.*). (1) the subject a noun :—Ne selle mon tō fela . . . ðý læs hwā him self weorðe tō wædlan, and him ðonne gehreówe sió ælmesse, Past. 325, 8. (2) the subject a pronoun representing a circumstance already mentioned :—Satanus swearte geþōhte þæt hē wolde on heofonum hēhseld wyrcan . . . Him þæt eft gehreáw, Sat. 374. Ne wilnað nā se wīsa tō hrædlīce ðære wræce, ðeáh hē gegremed sié, ac wýscð ðæt hit (*the wrongdoing*) him (*the wrongdoer*) gehreówe, ðæt hē (*the wise man*) hit mæge siððan forgifan, Past. 220, 16. Þec gelegdon on bend hæðene . . . Him þæt gehreówan mæg, þonne heó endestæf gesceáwiað, Sat. 540. (3) without subject and followed by a clause giving reason for regret :—Þā gehreów hym þ hyne æfre swā on hys geþōhte getweóde, Shrn. 155, 18. [*O. H. Ger.* ge-[h]riuwan.]

**ge-hreówness** *penitence, repentance.* v. ge-hreónis *in Dict.*

**ge-hreówsian ;** *p.* ode *To repent :*—þ hiæ gihreówsadun (-hreáw-, L.) *paeniterent*, Lk. R. 10, 13.

**ge-hrepod.** *Substitute :* **ge-hrepian ;** *p.* ode *To touch :*—*Tactus* gehrepod is participium ; and *tactus* hrepung is nama, Ælfc. Gr. Z. 255, 3. (1) *to touch* with the hand :—Gehrepa hire byrigene, and þū bist sōna hāl, Hml. S. 9, 19. (2) *to touch, cause emotion* in a person :—Hē wæs gehrepod (*tactus*) mid heortan sārnisse wiðinnan, Gen. 6, 6. (3) *to treat* a subject ; *to treat of* (*ymbe*) a subject. v. hrepian :—Nū hæbbe wē be dæle gehrepod ymbe his sīð, Angl. viii. 306, 48. v. un-gehrepod.

**ge-hrēran.** *Add :* **I.** *to stir together, mix up* material :—Gehrēr twā ægru on hātum wætere, Lch. ii. 76, 28. Dō mēle fulne buteran on, and gehrēre tōgædere, 86, 18. **II.** of the operation of natural forces, *to set in violent motion :*—Þurh winda gryre wolcn wæs gehrēred, Dōm. L. 8. [*O. Sax.* gi-hrōrid (mōd, hugi): *O. H. Ger.* ge-hruoren *movere, commovere.*]

**ge-hrero.** v. ge-hror.

**ge-hresp,** es ; *n. Plundering :*—Þurh hæðenra manna gehresp and gestrodu, Nap. 30. *See next word.*

**ge-hrespan.** *Add : to plunder.* [Cf. *O. H. Ger.* hrespan *vellere.*] : **ge-hrifnan.** *l.* -hrifian.

**ge-hrídrian** (?) *to sift, winnow :*—Ic sweóp ł gehrudrede ( = (?) -hriid-rede, -hrídrede) mīnne gāst *scobebam spiritum meum*, Ps. L. 76, 7. [Cf. *other versions of the passage :*—Ic windwode on mē gāst mīnne *uentilabam in me spiritum meum*, Ps. Rdr. Srt.]

**ge-hrifnian ;** *p.* ode *To be gorged* (? cf. hrif) :—Alexandres æfterfolgeras xiiii geár þisne middangeard tótugon and tótæron þæm gelícost þonne seó leó bringð his hungregum hwelpum hwæt tō étanne : hié ðonne gecýðað on ðæm æte hwelc heora mæst mæg gehrifnian. Swā dyde Ptholomeus þā hē tōgædere gesweóp ealle Ægyptum and Arabia *principes ejus xiiii annis orbem dilaniaverunt, et veluti opimam praedam a leone prostratam avidi discerpsere catuli. Itaque Ptolemaeo Aegyptus Arabiaeque pars sorte provenit*, Ors. 3, 11 ; S. 142, 26.

**ge-hrīman.** *Take here* ge-hrēman *in Dict.:* **ge-hrimpan.** v. rimpan *in Dict. for examples.*

**ge-hrīnan.** *Add :* [*weak forms*, ge-hrīnde, -hrīnade, *occur in Northern Gospels*] :—Gehrīnan *contingere*, Wrt. Voc. ii. 22, 16. **I.** *to touch* with some part of the body :—Se hróf wæs þ man mid his handa neálíce gerǣcean mihte, in sumre stōwe hē wæs þ man mid his handa neálíce gerǣcean mihte, in sumre eáþelíce mid heáfde gehrīnan, Bl. H. 207, 23. (1) *with dat.* :—Wīf ðió gehrīned him *mulier quae tangit eum*, Lk. L. 7, 39. Gié ānum fingre ne gehrīnað ðæm hondhæfum (*sarcinas*), 11, 46. Hē gehrān him (*eos*), Mt. L. 17, 7. Hió gihrān wēdum his, Mk. R. 5, 27. Hiá gibēdun hine þte giwēdun his gihrinon (-hrinon, L.), and swā oftor gihrionun him hāle giwurdun, 6, 56. Þte hē gihrine ðǣm *ut tangeret eos*, 10, 13. Þ hiæ him gihrionun, 3, 10. (2) *with acc.* :—Ic þone ðerscwold gehrān, Hml. S. 23 b, 413. Hē gehrān hond his *tetigit manum ejus*, Mt. L. 8, 15 : Lk. L. 5, 13 : 8, 45. Gehrine *tetigerit*, 8, 47. Þ hē hiæ gehrine (gehrīnade, L.) *ut eos tangeret*, Lk. R. 18, 15. Þte hine gehrīnde *ut illum tangeret*, Mk. L. 8, 22. Þte hine hié gehrīndon ł hrīna mæhtes, 3, 10. Þ wlōh wēdes his gehrīne mōston, Mt. L. 14, 36 : Jn. L. 20, 17. Hine tō gehrīnanne, Lk. L. 6, 19. Suá huæd ðǣm gihrīned bið *quicquid eo tactum fuerit*, Rtl. 121, 7. **II.** *to have intercourse with.* Cf. wīf-gehrine :—Sē ðe gihrīneð portcuoene *qui adheret meretrici*, Rtl. 106, 30. v. un-gehrinen.

**ge-hrine,** es ; *m. Touch* ; *tactus*, Wrt. Voc. i. 64, 21 (Wülck. Gl. 290, 2 *gives* æthrine). v. wīf-gehriue.

**ge-hrine** *ornament.* v. ge-rēne.

**ge-hringan, -ian ;** *p.* (o)de ; *pp.* ed, od *To ring :*—Sý gehringed þonne seó eahteoðe tíd bið healf āgan, R. Ben. 73, 14. Sē gehringed (*pulsetur*) belle, Angl. xlii. 380, 212. Beóþ gehringde (*pulsantur*)

ealle bēcnu, 428, 902. Gehrinde, 401, 525. Gehringede, 402, 537. Gehringode, 530.

**ge-hrinian** *to touch.* v. ge-hrīnan.

**ge-hríran ;** *p.* de *To cause to fall to the ground* (v. ge-hreósan ; I), *to overthrow, demolish* a building :—Gehriéred *diruta* (*sacella*), Wrt. Voc. ii. 79, 59.

**ge-hrisian** *to shake together :*—Gehrysed *coagitatum*, Wrt. Voc. ii. 74, 45 : 17, 60.

**ge-hroden ;** *pp.* of ge-hreódan.

**ge-hróp,** es ; *n. A cry :*—Mīn gehróp (*clamor meus*) cōm beforan his ansýne, and eác on his eáran hit eóde, Ps. Th. 17, 6. Ongyt mīne stemne and mīn gehróp *intellige clamorem meum*, 5, 1.

**ge-hropen,** Ps. Th. 17, 15. v. ge-hreósan ; I.

**ge-hror.** *Add :*—Mancwealm and ādla and gehrora (-o, -hrero, *v. ll.*) þære þeóde *pestilentia et exterminium gentis*, Bd. 1, 14 ; Sch. 37, 25.

**ge-hrorenlic ;** *adj. Perishable, transitory :*—Þeós woruld is eall forwordenlic and gehrorenlic and gebrosnodlic and feallendlic, and eall þeós woruld is gewitenlic, Nap. 30. Sē ðe þæt þenceð þæt hē of þysse gehrorenlican worulde þone heofonlican ríce begite, ib.

**ge-hrudrian.** v. ge-hrídrian : **ge-hrumpen.** v. rimpan.

**ge-hruxl.** *Substitute :* **ge-hrūxl,** es ; *n. Noise, tumult :*—Ðā brōðru mid gehlýde wurpon wæter on þ fýr . . . þā wearð se Drihtnes wer mid þām ylcan gehrūxle (-rūxle, *v. l.*) (*eodem tumultu*) āstyrod, and þyder becōm, Gr. D. 124, 3. Geswenced mid þām gerūxlum and uneðnessum sumra woruldlicra ymbhogena *quorundam secularium tumultibus depressus*, 3, 4. Hē mid his āþenedre handa gestilleþ þā gerūxl and þ gehlýd eallra manna *extensa manu omnium tumultus sedat*, 265, 13. Gehrūxlu *tumultus*, i. *seditiones*, Germ. 392, 24. Wǣpna gerūxlu *armorum strepitus*, E. S. xxxix. 344.

**ge-hū.** *Substitute : In every way, in all sorts of ways :*—Ðeáh þe seó sǣ sý gebýged gehū (*is bent in all sorts of ways*), heó wunað swā ðeáh on ðære eorðan bōsme binnan hyre gemǣrum, Hex. 10, 30. God hit gewræc, þ hī swultan gehū (*they died by all manner of deaths*), S. 13, 232. God gemyltsode mancynne gehū, 284. Hē is gecweden hlāf þurh getācnunge, and lamb, and eác and gehū elles (*in every other way he is called, it is typically*), Hml. Th. ii. 268, 17.

**ge-hūfod ;** *adj. Provided with* a hūfe (*q. v.*) :—Gehūfud *vittatus*, Germ. 397, 525. v. hūfian.

**ge-hugod.** *Add :* [*O. Sax.* gi-hugid *minded, disposed.*]

**ge-huntian.** *Add :*—Ic cōm þ ic mē þē ætýwde þurh þysne heort, and for hine þē gehuntian and gefōn mid þām nettum mínre mildheortnysse, Hml. S. 30, 49.

**ge-hūsa** a *domestic, one of a household. Add :*—Sý wyrðment gegearewod . . . þām rihtgelýfedum ūrum gehūsum *honor exibeatur domesticis fidei*, R. Ben. 83, 1. Hiore gehūsan *domesticis suis*, Kent. Gl. 1138. Gehūse his *domesticos ejus*, Mt. L. 10, 25. [*O. H. Ger.* ge-hūsa *vernacula.*] v. neáh-gehūsa.

**ge-hūslian.** *Add : to administer the eucharist* to a person (*acc.*) :—Basilius gehūslode þone cnapan, Hml. S. 3, 459. Þænne hī beóþ gehūslude *dum communicantur*, Angl. xiii. 425, 860. Þā cild man bere tō mæssan, þ hyg beón gehūslode, Ll. Th. ii. 392, 13.

**ge-hūsscipe.** *Add :*—Gehūscipe (*domus*) Israēla folces . . . gehūscipes Aarones . . . gehūscipe Lefes, Ps. Srt. 134, 19, 20. Gehūscipe (v. Txts. 327), 97, 3. Forget gehūsscipe (v. Txts. 250) feadur ðínes, 44, 11.

**ge-hwá.** **A.** as noun. **I.** *every one* (*thing*), *each one.* (1) *alone :*—Healde gehwā mid riht his ǣwe, Ll. Th. ii. 300, 26. Gearwige tō hūslgange oft and gelōme gehwā hine sylfne, i. 310, 8 : 322, 8 : 424, 19. Þīne dōmas rǣcað efne gehwām, ǣghwylcum men āgen gewyrhta, Hy. 7, 15 : Rä. 12, 8. Þæt wē magon gefrēdan hwæt bið heard, hwæt huesce, . . . and swā gehwæt, Hml. Th. ii. 372, 33. (1 a) *as antecedent :*—Hý gebētton gehwæt þe tōbrocen wæs of þām, Ll. Th. ii. 356, 7. (2) *with gen. pl. of* (a) a *noun :*—Hē bebeád þ monna gehwā him hām fērde *singulos domum redire praecepit*, Bd. 3, 14 ; Sch. 254, 19. Æðelinga wyn and eorla gehwæs wyn and weorðmynd, Rūn. 27. Fæder frymða gehwæs, Ph. 197 : Cri. 47. Þū wyrda gehwǣre sōð oncnāwest, An. 630. Freá folca gehwæs, Dan. 401. Gōda gehwæs, An. 338 : Jul. 323. In daga gehwām, Dan. 287. Wið nīða gehwām, Ph. 451. On healfa gehwām, Exod. 209 : An. 121. Of ædra gehwǣre, Gen. 1374. In mǣgða gehwǣre, B. 25. On healfa gehwore (-hwone ?), Cri. 928 : Ph. 336. Mēca gehwane, B. 2685. On tída gehwone, Gen. 2305. Burga gehwone, Dan. 63. Ymb healfa gehwone, Cri. 61. (aa) *with* gen. of a noun of multitude :—Gumcynnes gehwone, B. 2765. (ab) *where emphasis is given by the use of* eall *qualifying the noun :*—Æt ealra manna gehwæs mūðes reorde, Seel. 93. On ealra londa gehwām, Rä. 34, 13. Ealra feónda gehwane, Sal. 147. Gehwone, 97. (b) *an adj. or ptcpl. used substantively :*—Cyning clǣnra gehwæs, Cri. 703 : An. 914. Eádigra gehwām . . . lifgendra gehwām, Exod. 4, 6. Hē geaf blisse gehwǣm ēgbūendra, Chr. 995 ; P. 122, 1. Wiþ lāþra gehwæne, 937 ; P. 106, 17. Wið gesibbra gehwone, Mōd. 69 : Ph. 606. (c) *a þ ānra gehwām* (cf. ǣlcum men, Bt. 15 ; F. 48, 3) genōh þūhte, Met. 8, 6. (ca) *where the phrase governs a genitive :*—Bióð ānra gehwæs monna

módsefan áwegede, Met. 7, 23. Ánra gehwǽm eorðbúendra, 12, 18. On ánra gehwám æðeles cynnes, Exod. 227. Gumena gehwǽne þyssa burhleóda, Jud. 186. (cb) with demonstrative :—Is þára ánra gehwám orgeate tácen, Sch. 8. (d) pronoun :—Him on scínað ǽrgewyrhtu, on sylfra gehwám, Cri. 1242. **II.** *any one* (*thing*). (1) alone :—Búton gehwá beó geedcenned of wætere and of þám Hálgan Gáste, ne mæg hé faran in tó heofenan ríce *nisi quis renatus fuerit ex aqua et spiritu, non potest introire in regnum Dei*, Hml. Th. i. 94, 10. Þone mete þe gehwá brúcan wolde, gif him þæt fæsten swá geboden nǽre, Wlfst. 181, 12. Þonne hé sǽde gehwæt (mé hwæt rehte, *v. l.*) be ealdra manna dǽdum, Gr. D. 86, 22. Hé (*the interjection*) getácnað hwílon ðæs módes blisse, hwílon sárnysse, hwílon wundrunge and gehwæt, Ælfc. Gr. Z. 278, 6. (1 a) as antecedent :—Ic gehwám wille þǽrtó tǽcan þe hine his lyst má tó witanne, Ors. 3, 3 ; S. 102, 24. (2) with gen. :—For gehwæt heardes oððe hnesces . . . þæs ðe mé innan oððe útan gebyrede, Angl. xi. 98, 52. Scealt þú georne geþolian gehwæt þæs þe tó heora þénungum belimpþ *aequo animo toleres oportet quidquid intra fortunae aream geritur*, Bt. 7, 2 ; F. 18, 25. Wǽpnu and mete and ealo and cláþas and gehwæt þæs þe þá þré geférscipas behófiaþ, 17 ; F. 60, 5. Nis hit nán wundor ðeáh hwá wéne þ swylces gehwæt (hwæt, *v. l.*) unmyndlinga gebyrige, Bt. 39, 2 ; F. 214, 9. **III.** *some one* (*thing*) :—Oft gehwá gesihð fægre stafas áwritene, þonne heraɖ hé ðone wríteere, Hml. Th. i. 186, 2. Þ is lǽsse, þ man wíte gehwæt hwylces, þonne þ sý, þ his man wíte and eác bodie, Gr. D. 138, 2. **B.** as adjective, *every* :—Ríces gehwæs, Dan. 114. Be naman gehwám, 424. Gange of dóme gehwám deópe gehýned *cum judicatur, exeat condemnatus*, Ps. Th. 108, 6. On mǽgðe gehwǽre, Fä. 74. In ceastre gehwǽre, El. 973. On stówe gehwáre, Cri. 490 : Ph. 206. Tó yfele gehwám scearpe, Ps. Th. 56, 5. Æt leóhte gehwám, 62, 1.

**ge-hwǽde.** *Add* :—Gehwǽde *modicus*, Ælfc. Gr. Z. 29, 9 : *exiguus*, Wrt. Voc. i. 51, 19. **I.** applied to material objects. (1) of size :— Fram dúne gehwǽdre *a monte modico*, Ps. L. 41, 7. Bát gehwǽdne *lembum exiguum*, Wülck. Gl. 254, 26. Ðeós wyrt hafað gehwǽdne wyrttruman, Lch. i. 260, 5. Þú gesáwe gehwǽde mot . . . and ne gesáwe þone mǽstan cyp, R. Ben. 12, 3. Hæbben hý scapulare, þæt is gehwǽde cugelan and slýfleáse, 89, 13. Mid hangiendre hande dó hé swilce hé gehwǽde bellan cnyllan wille, Tech. ii. 118, 7. Fulle of gehwǽdum leáfum and langum and scearpum and fǽttum, Lch. i. 258, 2. Heó hafað blóstman and sǽd swýþe gehwǽde, 250, 21. Hafað seó lǽsse smæle leáf and gehwǽde, and seó óðer hafað máran leáf and fǽtte, 264, 18. (1 a) *little, young* :—Se Hǽlend him tó clypode sum gehwǽde cild (*parvulum*), Hml. Th. i. 510, 25. (2) of quantity :—Áfedde seó wudewe þone wítegan mid ðám lytlan melewe and þám gehwǽdan ele, Hml. S. 18, 66. **II.** applied to non-material things. (1) of time :— Ic eom gehwǽde tíd (*modicum*) mid eów, Jn. 13, 33. (2) of sound :— Áweht tó his stefne þeáh þe heó gehwǽde (*modica*) wǽre, Gr. D. 85, 9. **III.** of quality, degree, significance, &c. :—Forhæfednys swá spærlic l gehwǽde *parsimonia tam frugalis*, An. Ox. 3749. Gehwǽdum *mediocri* (*ingenio*), 4048. For ǽnigum gehwǽdum (*minima*) intinga geþread, R. Ben. I. 116, 10 : R. Ben. 131, 4. Gehwǽde *minusculum* (*opusculum*), An. Ox. 5422. Gedǽf on gehwǽdum (*printed* -whǽdum) *contentus modicis*, Wülck. Gl. 257, 31. Gehwǽdeste *gracillima*, i. *humillima* l *minima* (*fragilitas*), An. Ox. 710. **IV.** the neuter used adverbially :—Gehwǽde hneppast *paululum dormitabis*, Kent. Gl. 135 : *modicum*, 946. v. un-gehwǽde.

**ge-hwǽdnes.** *Add* : **I.** *smallness* of size or extent, *slenderness* :— Ísen úre sáwle náteshwon byð gelǽdd tó gehwǽdnysse scerpnysse (*ad subtilitatem*, i. *exilitatem acuminis*), Scint. 150, 4. **II.** *fewness* of number :—On gehwǽdnesse *in paucitate* (*plebis*), Kent. Gl. 494. Gehwǽdnesse *paucitatem* (*dierum*), Bl. Gl. **III.** *poorness, meanness* of condition, *mediocrity* :—Gehwǽdnys, medemlicnys *mediocritas*, i. *paruitas*, An. Ox. 2596.

**ge-hwǽmlic.** *Add* : v. dæg-gehwǽmlic : **ge-hwǽmlíce.** v. dæggehwámlíce.

**gehwǽr.** *Add* : **I.** *everywhere*. (1) where there is motion, (a) all over an area, throughout a space :—Heora fýnd férdon freólíce gehwǽr swá þicce swá gærstapan *ipsi veniebant et instar locustarum universa complebant*, Jud. 6, 5. Gehwár ábútan woffiende *circumquaque debachantes*, An. Ox. 3775. Þearfe bringeð Maius micle geond menigeo gehwár, Men. 79. (b) to every place :—Hé férde fram Antiochian, for þan þe hé wæs apostol, and sceolde gehwǽr gecuman and Crístendóm árǽran (cf. dixit eis: ‘euntes in mundum universum praedicate euangelium,’ Mk. 16, 15), Hml. S. 10, 13. (2) where there is doing or being, (a) all over a limited area :—Wæs micel hearm gedón gehwǽr be þǽm sǽriman, Chr. 981 ; P. 124, 12. Gewaer *parumper* (the passage in which the word occurs is :—Interea Brittania cessatum quidem est *parumper* ab externis bellis, Bd. 1, 22. The glosser seems to have read this as meaning that *everywhere* war with outsiders had ceased), Txts. 182, 84. (b) at every place where a certain condition is possible :— Gehwǽr sácerdas and mæssepreóstas betwih wíbedum wǽron slægene *passim sacerdotes inter altaria trucidabantur*, Bd. 1, 15 ; Sch. 43, 15. (c) denoting frequent occurrence, *in very many places* :—Gehwár

(-hwǽr, *v. l.*) *passim*, Ælfc. Gr. Z. 236, 14. Þ man swá geongne man cwealde . . . swá hé geáxod hæfde þe man gehwǽr (*ubique*) dyde, Ll. Th. i. 240, 26. Óðre béc man hæfð wíde gehwǽr on crístendóme Críste tó lofe, Ælfc. T. Grn. 19, 39. (cc) of statements in books :— Hit is áwriten on Crístes béc, and gehwǽr on óþrum bócum, Hml. Th. i. 136, 24. (d) *in every instance* :—Hé þ in scopgereorde mid þá mǽstan swétnesse geglencde, and in Englisc gereorde wel gehwǽr forðbróhte, Bd. 4, 24 ; Sch. 481, 12. **II.** indefinite. (1) *anywhere* without restriction, *anywhere one pleases*. (a) of motion :—Gif hrýðera hwelc sié þe hegas brece and gá in gehwǽr (*quolibet*), Ll. Th. i. 128, 12. (b) of position :—Þá welmas þá þe beóþ gehwǽr geond þone líchoman, Lch. ii. 204, 14. (2) *somewhere* :—Wæs eác eorðstyrung on manegum stówum on Wygracestre and on Wíc and on Deórbý and elles gehwǽr (*in some other places*) and eác þ wilde fýr on Deórbýscíre micel yfel dyde and gehwǽr elles, Chr. 1049 ; P. 167, 24-27.

**ge-hwǽre** *concors*. v. ge-þwǽre.

**ge-hwǽþer.** *Add* : *Each of two*. **I.** used substantively. (1) alone. (a) *each* of two objects :—Gesíðcund man . . . ceorlisc man . . . gehwæðer þ hǽmed forlǽte, Ll. Th. i. 38, 7. (b) *each* of two circumstances, conditions, &c. (a) the circumstances already stated :—Ne meahte seó weáláf wíge forstandan gestrión ; sealdon unwillum éðelweardas ádas. Wæs gehwæðeres wá, Met. 1, 25. (β) the circumstances following :—Him wæs gehwæðres wá, ge . . . , ge . . . , El. 628. Dó þonne gehwæþer, ge on ðá wunde lege, and eác drinc swýþe þearle, Lch. i. 78, 9. (2) governing a genitive :—An wíg gearwe ge æt hám ge on herge, ge gehwæðer þára efne swylce mǽla swylce hira mandryhtne þearf gesǽlde, B. 1248. Ic gemyndige þ mǽran Raab and Babilonis, þæt gehwæðer (*printed* -whæðer), Ps. Th. 86, 2. Hé bêgea gehwæðeres *memor ero Rahab et Babylonis*, Ps. Th. 86, 2. Hé sealde hiora gehwæðrum, B. 2994. (3) used reciprocally :—Hygeláce wæs nefa hold, and gehwæðer óðrum hróðra gemyndig, B. 2171. ¶ *passing into a conjunction*. v. ǽgþer :—Seó wyrt deáh gehwæþer ge þæs mannes sáwle ge his líchoman, Lch. i. 70, 3. Gehweþer ge his ágen geweorc ge on his naman gehálgod, Bl. H. 197, 6. **II.** adjectival :— Gehwæðeres *promiscui*, Wrt. Voc. ii. 66, 58. Æt gehweðerum múðe, Ll. Th. i. 96, 11. Wearþ micel wælsliht on gehwæþere hond, Chr. 871 ; P. 72, 2 : By. 112. **III.** adverbial, *in each case*. Cf. I. ¶ :— Þǽre eorðan on nánre ne mót se rodor neár þonne on óðre stówe gestæppan, stríceð ymbútan ufane and neoðane efenneáh gehwæðer (*equally near both above and below*; cf. se rodor is þére eorþan emneáh ge ufan ge neoþon, Bt. 33, 4 ; F. 130, 23), Met. 20, 141. [*O. H. Ger.* ge-hwedar *uterque*.]

**ge-hwæðeres.** *Dele.*

**ge-hwætness,** e ; *f. Quickness, rapid movement* :—Atomes . . . rímcræftige men óðerwhile hátað for his gehwætnysse *momentum* (cf. *Momentum* . . . hé ys gecweden for þǽra tungla hwætnysse *momentum*, 6), Angl. viii. 318, 37.

**ge-hwanon.** *Add* :—Hé gegaderode góde wyrhtan gehwanon, Hml. S. 6, 157. Ðá hǽðenan him cómon tó gehwanon, 25, 395. Geseah ic leóht gehwanon mé ymbútan scínende *I saw light that came from all sides shining about me*, 23 b, 550.

**ge-hwearf, -hwerf.** *Add* :—Ðis is biscopes gehwearf and ðára hígna ðára londa æt Beórhám . . . (cf. in the charter so endorsed : Placuit archiepiscopo ejusque familia . . . aliquam vicissitudinem terrarum inter se habere), C. D. B. i. 526, 19. Wes ðises gehwerfes tó gewitnesse *hic sunt testes hujus commutationis*, C. D. vi. 207, 21, 26. Æðeluuold biscop sealde mé tó gehwerfe (*mutuaui*) ðone hám Heartingas wið ðám mynsterlande, iii. 60, 30. Geseoh, ic þe sylle þysne man tó gehwarfe for hine *ecce, hunc hominem pro eo vicarium praebeo*, Gr. D. 180, 20 : 181, 28. v. land-gehwearf.

**ge-hwearfnes** (-hwerf-), e ; *f. Conversion* :—Scē Paules gehwerfnes tó Críste, Shrn. 58, 26. Sé ðe nú giet on synnum is, nǽsð hé nó forlǽten ðone trúwan his gehwearfnesse (*conversionis*) ; ac sé sé ðe æfter his gehwerfnesse (*post conversionem*) tó lange wlæc bið, ðonne lytlað him se tóhopa, Past. 447, 12-15.

**ge-hweled.** *Substitute* : **ge-hwelian** ; *pp.* ed *To inflame with foul matter* :—Sió díegle wund bið sárre ðonne sió opene, for ðám ðæt worsm ðæt ðérinne gehweled bið, gif hit bið út forlǽten, ðonne bið sió wund geopenod tó hǽlo ðæs sáres *vulnera clausa plus cruciant. Nam cum putredo, quae interius fervet, ejicitur, ad salutem dolor aperitur*, Past. 273, 22. Siþþan þ geswel biþ gehweled and tóbyrst, Lch. ii. 208, 4. Hit ðæt gehwelede on ðæm óðrum geopenað and út forlǽt, ðæt hit wierð ðonon gehǽled *doloris fervor vulnere aperto temperatur*, Past. 275, 5.

**ge-hwemman** ; *p.* ed *To slope* :—Næs þæt hús æfter manna gewunan getimbrod, ac mid mislicum torrum gehwemmed (*the walls were not smooth and vertical but of varying inclination on account of projecting rocks*) tó gelícnysse sumes scræfes, Hml. Th. i. 508, 17. Cf. hwem-dragen.

**ge-hweorf,** es ; *n. A turning* :—On ðone lið þéra eaxla betweox gesculdrum biþ micel ece and on þám gehweorfe þára bána on þám sweoran, Lch. ii. 242, 13.

**ge-hweorfan.** *Add* : **I.** trans. (1) *to turn, direct* :—Gif hié ðá

trumnesse ðǽre Godes giefe him tô unnyte gehweorfað *si acceptae incolumitatis gratiam ad usum nequitiae inclinent*, Past. 247, 8. (2) *to overturn* :—Hê gehwerf[d] *subvertit* (*insidias impiorum*), Kent. Gl. 315. Âhwerfdon *vel* gehwurfan *evertere*, Wrt. Voc. ii. 144, 28. (3) *to exchange*. Cf. ge-hwearf :—Hió becwið him hyre goldfâgan treówenan cuppan, þæt hê îce his beáh mid þâm golde, oþþe hî mon æt him gehweorfe mid .xvi. mancussum reádes goldes, Cht. Th. 536, 20. II. *intrans*. (1) *to return* (a) to a place :—Hê gehwearf þonan tô his âgnum, Chr. 584; P. 294, 6. Hig gehwurfon (*regressi sunt*) on Hierusalem, Lk. 24, 52. Of þâm æcere gehworfenum *regresso de agro*, 17, 7. (b) to a position, condition, &c. :—þ hê geearnode, þ hê eft gehwurfe tô his fæder gife and freóndscipe, Gr. D. 238, 13. (2) of action, *to turn* (a) to a person :—Gehweorfen tô mê þâ þe hyldu tô dê âhtan *convertantur ad me qui timent te*, Ps. Th. 118, 79. (b) to action : —Ðæt hê gehweorfe tô hreówsunga *ad poenitentiae lamenta conversus*, Past. 167, 18. (3) of happening. (a) *to be transferred, pass* to :—Asiria anwald gehwearf on Mêdas *Arbatus regni summam ad Medos transtulit*, Ors. 2, 1; S. 60, 17: 1, 8; S. 42, 6. (b) *to turn back, be averted* :—Gesecge man hwǽr ǽnig gewin ǽr þæm crîstendôme swâ gehwurfe, gif hit ongunnen wǽre *qui praeteritis temporibus de compressione bellorum simile probarit exemplum*, Ors. 6, 4; S. 260, 7. [*O. H. Ger*. ge-hwerban *conuerti*.] v. ge-hwirfan.

**ge-hwerf, ge-hwerfness.** v. ge-hwearf, ge-hwearfness : **ge-hwerft.** v. ge-hwyrft.

**ge-hwider.** *Add* : I. where there is motion, *to every place, to all parts, in all directions*. (1) used generally :—Hê ðanon eóde gehwyder (-hwider, on gehwylce healfe, *v.ll.*) ymb þâ stôwa, and þǽr godcunde lâre bodode *inde ad praedicandum circumquaque exire consueverat*, Bd. 3, 17; Sch. 267, 17. Sende man hý gehwider, Ll. Th. i. 278, 9. Hê têrde geond fela burga gehwider, Hml. S. 29, 102. þǽre burge ceasterware þe ǽr gehwider tôdrifene wǽron *cives urbis illius qui quolibet dispersi essent*, Gr. D. 198, 15. (2) limited by an implied condition :—Hê hæfde ǽnne lâtteów þe hine lǽdde gehwider (*wherever he went*), Hml. S. 21, 203. þâ férdon ætforan him gehwyder, 16, 148. II. where influence is exerted :—Hî mid þý þrymme þreátiað gehwider ymbsittenda ôþra þeóda (cf. hî þreátiaþ eall moncynn, Bt. 37, 1; F. 186, 6), Met. 25, 13. III. of position, *on all sides, in every direction* :—Seó bôc fram monigum oft gehwider ymb âwriten wæs *a multis sunt circumquaque transcripta*, Bd. 4, 18; Sch. 437, 16.

**ge-hwilc.** *Add* : I. *each, every*; in pl. *all*. (1) as noun. (a) alone : —Gif man in mannes tûn ǽrest geirneð, .vi. scillingum gebête; sê þe æfter irneð .iiii. scillingas; siþþan gehwylc scilling, Ll. Th. i. 6, 17. Gehwilc, 16, 4. Æt þâm feówer tôðum fyrestum, æt gehwylcum .vi. scillingas, 16, 2. Hió forlêt sêcan gehwylcne âgenne eard, El. 598. Sete tâcn on gehwilcne wǽpnedcynnes, Gen. 2311. Gif hit sié binnan wǽdum, gehwilc .xx. scætta gebête, 18, 5 : 14, 13. (aa) as antecedent :—Hê hêht þæt segn wegan gehwilcne þe his hîna wæs wǽpnedcynnes, Gen. 2371. (b) in agreement with *ân* :—Ânum gehwilcum is hǽl gehendre, Hml. Th. i. 602, 21. God ǽnne gehwilcne þurh his Gâst geneósað, ii. 316, 11. (c) with *ânra* :—Ânra gehwelc wênde, Ors. 3, 7; S. 114, 35. þæt ânra gehwylc cræft his begange *ut unusquisque artem suam exerceat*, Coll. M. 31, 31. Underfêhð ânra gehwilc be ðâm ðe hê geearnode, Hml. Th. i. 602, 28. Gehwylc, Bl. H. 11, 18 : 107, 12. þæt hê gedǽlde ânra gehwylces lîf wið lîce, B. 732. For ânra gehwylcum onsundrum, Seel. 97. (c 1) with a noun in agreement with *ânra* :—þ ânra manna gehwylc sceáwige hine sylfne, Bl. H. 57, 33. Ânra manna gehwylcne ic myngie, 107, 10. (c 2) with a genitive governed by *ânra gehwilc* :—Ânra gehwylc þâra apostola biþ geseted tô his synderlicre stôwe, Bl. H. 143, 22. Sceal ûre ânra gehwylc beran his dǽda, 63, 29 : Sal. 355. Ânra gehwilcum ymbstandendra folces Sodoma, Gen. 2488. þâ frægn ic ânra gehwylcne heora *interrogavi unumquemque eorum*, Bd. 4, 5; Sch. 375, 8. ¶ as antecedent :—Stôd egesa ânra gehwylcum þâra þe of wealle wôp gehýrdon, B. 784. (c 3) reciprocal :—Framige ânra gehwylc ôþron on cræfte hys, Coll. M. 31, 25. (d) with gen. pl. :—þâra gehwelc wê willað sié twybôte, Ll. Th. i. 64, 24 : Rä. 71, 5. Hwider hyra gehwylc faran scolde, Bl. H. 229, 5. Gehwylc hiora *each of the two*, B. 1166. þê firina gehwilc âbûgeð, Cri. 56. Monna gehwylc geceósan môt, 589. Wana wilna gehwilces, Gen. 2272. Benumen leáfa gehwelces, Met. 4, 24. Æfter ýsta gehwelcre (cf. æfter eallum þâm ýstum, Bt. 34, 8; F. 144, 28), 21, 15. Âscyred scylda gehwelcre, El. 1313. Hê wæs witena gehwilcum (cf. ælcum witum, Bt. 28; F. 100, 27) lâð, Met. 15, 5. þæt man lǽte manna gehwylcne, ge earmne ge eádigne, folcrihtes wyrðe, Ll. Th. i. 316, 27. Hê dêmeð leán þeóda gehwylcre, Cri. 848 : B. 805. Nihta gehwylcere, Ps. Th. 104, 34. Daga gehwylce, Bl. H. 59, 26 : Kr. 136 : B. 2450 : Sal. 551. Gehwelce, Met. 13, 21. Gehwilce, 1, 54 : Gen. 848. þinga gehwylce, Hy. 4, 12. Nihta gehwylcere, Ps. Th. 133, 3. (d 1) with *ealra* qualifying gen. pl. :—þǽr habbað heó on ǽfyn . . ., ealra feónda gehwilc, fýr edneówe, Gen. 314. Alra tâcna gehwylc, El. 645. Ymb ealra landa gehwylc, Gn. C. 46. (d 2) with gen. governed by noun in gen. pl. :—þegna gehwylc þînra leóda, B. 1673. Monna

gehwilc þǽre cneórisse, Gen. 2317. Wihta gehwilce deóra and fugla deáðlêg nimeð, Cri. 982. (d 3) as antecedent :—Monna gehwilc þe wið his waldend winnan ongynneð, Gen. 297. Secgan Dryhtne þonc duguða gehwylcre þe ûs simle gefremede, Cri. 601. þæt is heálic rǽd monna gehwylcum þe gemynd hafað, 431. Secga gehwylcum þâra þe on swylc staráð, B. 996 : An. 1154. þǽr is âr gelang fira gehwylcum þâm þe hié findan cann, 982. Dôma gehwilcne þâra þe him Drihten bebeád, Exod. 520. ¶ with verb in plural :—Mîn êhtan ongunnon ealdurmonna gehwylc *principes persecuti sunt me*, Ps. Th. 118, 161. Swâ hêr manna gehwylc Metode gecwêmað, Hy. 10, 58. (dd) *every kind* of :—Open êce scræf yfela gehwylces, Exod. 537. Torn þolode wine Scyldinga, weána gehwelcne, B. 148. Sǽda gehwilc on bearm scipes beornas feredon, Exod. 374. (2) as adjective. (a) alone :—þæt gehwilc sprǽc hæbbe ândagan, Ll. Th. i. 158, 7. Ðæt môd gehwelces monnes, Past. 255, 15. Gehwylces hâdes men, Bl. H. 47, 34. Wiðerweardnes wuhte gehwelcre, Met. 11, 78. Tô gehwylcere byrig, Ll. Th. i. 194, 3. Gif man þeóh þurhstingð, stice gehwilce .vi. scillingas, 18, 16. Unfâcne seó gehwilce *with sterling money all of it*, 10, 5. Gehwilce morgene, Lch. ii. 108, 2. Æt þâm neglum gehwylcum scilling, Ll. Th. i. 16, 14. On gehwylcum heora mǽgðum *in suis quique prouinciis*, Bd. pref.; Sch. 6, 4. On gehwylcum burgum blissoden þâ Crîstenan, Hml. S. 2, 278. Of gehwilcum stôwum wýdan and sýdan gegaderod, C. D. B. ii. 389, 22. Geond gehwylce weras *uiritim*, Ælfc. Gr. Z. 232, 17. Gehwylce wǽpenleáse *inermes quosque, i. universos*, An. Ox. 724. (aa) as antecedent :—Ðâs leásan spell lǽraþ gehwelcne man þâra þe wilnaþ helle þióstra tô fliónne, Bt. 35, 6; F. 170, 16. Wið gehwylce yfelu þe on þâm innoðe dereð, Lch. i. 280, 18. (b) with qualifying words :—Gehwilc ôðer tild, Angl. ix. 259, 12. Ânes gehwylces mannes dǽda, Wlfst. 244, 21. Ânes gehwylces geleáffulles mannes môd, Hml. Th. i. 412, 24. Ânum gehwilcum gelýfedum men wæs Crîstes tôcyme ǽgðer ge hryre ge ǽrist, 144, 26. Tô ânum gehwylcum menn, ii. 76, 13. Gehwylce ǽnlîpige on heora burgum be him sylfum cendon, i. 34, 4 : ii. 124, 9. Æt þâm ôðrum tâum gehwilcum healf gelde . . . æt þâm ôðrum gehwilcum, Ll. Th. i. 20, 3, 6. Of syndrigum gehwylcum cyricum (cyriceum gehwylcum, *v. l.*) *ex singulis quibusque ecclesiis*, Bd. 1, 27; Sch. 65, 15. Syndrige stôwe gehwylce *singula quaeque loca*, 5, 11; Sch. 607, 4. (c) with *ânra* :—Ðeáh ðe ânra gehwylc gâst hæbbe synderlîce .xii. feðerhoman, and ânra gehwylc federhoma hæbbe .xii. windas, and ânra gehwilc wind twelf sigefæstnissa, Sal. K. 152, 1-3. Folc ânra gehwylc, Cri. 1026. (d) with *mǽstra* :—Æt mǽstra gehwilcere misdǽde, Ll. Th. i. 58, 6. ¶ *of every kind* :—Be gehwelces ceápes ângelde, Ll. Th. i. 138, 9. Hê sceal beón, swâ ic ǽr be beócere cwæð (beóceorl sceal geara beón on manegum weorcum, 3), oftrǽde tô gehwilcon weorce, Ll. Th. i. 436, 18. Wǽron hyra tungan getale teóuan gehwylcre, Ps. Th. 56, 5. Hwî God geðafian wolde þæt þâ hǽðenan his hâlgan mid gehwilcum tiutregum âcwellan môston, Hml. Th. i. 566, 30. On ðǽre stôwe beóð gehǽlede gehwilce untrume, Hml. S. 4, 125. Se Hǽlend sǽde gelômlîce bigspel be gehwilcum ðingum, ii. 562, 11. II. *some, certain, many*. (1) as noun :—Ðâ gehýrdon gehwilce on lîfe hâlige englas singan on his forðsîðe, Hml. Th. ii. 518, 8. (2) as adjective. (a) alone :—Cwǽdon gehwylce lâreówas þæt . . ., Hml. Th. i. 440, 21 : 468, 5. Gehwylce gôde mæn (*boni quique*) ûs wǽron wiðtogone, Gr. D. 256, 21. þâ bugon gehwylce æðelborene menn tô Maures mynstre . . . oð þ þǽr gadorod wæs hundteóntig muneca and feówertig ealles, Hml. S. 6, 260. Nû smeádon gehwilce men oft, and gyt gelôme smeágað, Hml. Th. ii. 268, 7. Gehwilce geleáffulle ðe Gode gecwêmað, 556, 5. Gehwilce strongeste *fortissimi quique*, Kent. Gl. 224. Hê sǽde his gesîhðe Ælfride and gehwilcum eáwfæstum mannum (cf. quae uiderat idem uir . . . referre uolebat illis solummodo, qui . . . profectum pietatis ex eius uerbis haurire uolebant, Bd. 5, 12; Sch. 630), Hml. Th. ii. 350, 3. Âcsode hê hine be gehwilcum þingum *he asked him about several things*, Guth. 80, 11. (b) with *ôþer* :—On ðyssere geférrǽdene wǽron Petrus and Iôhannes . . ., and gehwilce ôðre . . . Eal seó menigu wæs ân hund manna and twêntig, Hml. Th. i. 296, 16 : 38, 10 : Hml. S. 29, 92 : Ælfc. Gr. Z. 293, 16. Dûnstân . . . and Aþelwold, and ôðre gehwylce, 21, 459 : Hml. A. 22, 211. (bb) *of some* (*other*) *kind* :—Fleán and ôðre gehwilce wyrmas, Hex. 14, 31. (c) correlative, *some* . . . *some* (*others*) :—Gehwylce gebrôðra . . ne beóð swâ carfulle . . . and gehwilce ôðre beóð mid sârnysse onbryrde, Hml. Th. i. 340, 23-28. (d) gehwilc . . . ôþer *some* . . . *other* :—þonne gehwilce synfulle menn ôðre heora gelîcan . . geôlǽcað, Hml. Th. i. 494, 2. III. *any*. (1) as noun :—Gif hrýðera gehwylc (hwelc, *v. l.*) sié þe hegas brece, Ll. Th. i. 128, 12. Gif mînra geréfena hwylc (gehwylce, *v. l.*) þis dôn nylle, 212, 27. (2) as adjective :—þonne þ môd byð tôdǽled tô manegum þingum, þonne byð hit þe lǽsse tô gehwilcum ânum synderlicum þinge : and swâ mycele swýðor hit byð undercropen on gehwilcum ânum þinge, swâ micele swâ hit byð wîddor âbysgod on manegum þingum *cum animus dividitur ad multa, fit minor ad singula : tantoque ei in una qualibet re subripitur quanto latius in multis occupatur*, Gr. D. 41, 9-17. [*O. Sax*. gi-hwilîk : *O. H. Ger*. gehwelîh *omnis, quivis*.] v. dæg-gehwilc.

**ge-hwilcness**, e; *f. Quality:*—For gehwilcnysse leahtres *pro qualitate criminis*, Hy. S. 36, 28. Æfter stówa gehwylcnysse *secundum locorum qualitatem*, R. Ben. I. 91, 10. Būtan þissum þingum . . . synt geswutelunga and gehwylcnyssa, Angl. viii. 299, 23. v. hwilc-ness.

**ge-hwirfan, -hweorfan.** *Take here* ge-hwyrfan *in Dict., and add:*—I. *trans.* (1) *to cause to go, to transfer* from one place to another:—Hé hine āscéd of ðæm worldríce and hine gehwirfde (-hwyrfde, *v. l.*) tó ungesceádwísum neátum, Past. 38, 23. Gehwyrfede *translati* (*de mundi calamitate*), An. Ox. 978. (2) *to transfer possession of* from one to another, *bring into the power of.* Cf. ge-hweorfan; II. 3 a:—Se hālga stede wæs gehwyrfed ðam cyninge tó handa *locus regali fisco subditus erat*, C. D. iii. 63, 28. (2 a) *to bring to acknowledge* another faith:—þ hí hine fram heora godum ācyrdon, aud tó þære níwan æfæstnesse þæs crīstenan geleáfan gehwyrfde (*transferrent*), Bd. 5, 10; Sch. 602, 6. (3) *to cause to act, turn* to action. Cf. ge-hweorfan; II. 2 b:—Ðæt gedreátade mód bið suíðe raðe gehwierfed tó fióunga *correpti mens repente ad odium proruit*, Past. 167, 13. (4) *to cause to return.* (a) *of material objects, to replace, restore:*—Gehuerf (*converte*) suord ðín in stówe his, Mt. L. 26, 52. His gesceafta ne mótou tóslūpan, ac bið gehwerfde eft tó þám ilcan ryne þe hié ǽr urnon, Bt. 21; F. 74, 11. (b) *of non-material objects, to bring back* to doing or being, *to recall:*—Sió medtrymnes ðæt mód gehwierfð gehwelces monnes hine selfne tó ongietanne *molestia corporalis ad cognitionem sui mentem revocat*, Past. 255, 15. (5) *to change, alter, put one thing for another:*—Ðā ðā from bócerum ł geēcad ł gihwerfde arun ł ymbcerred wē boetas *ea quae a librariis aut addita sunt aut mutata corrigimus*, Mt. p. 2, 2. (6) *to turn to (into), bring* an object to a different condition, *reduce to, convert* into:—þás getimbro fýr fornimeð aud on axan gehwirfeð (-hweorfað, -hwyrfað, *v. ll.*) *haec aedificia ignis absumens in cinerem convertet*, Bd. 4, 25; Sch. 498, 12. Tó náhte hé gehwyrfde *ad nihilum redigit Israel*, Ps. L. 77, 59. Ðætte hié ðone hālwendan drync ðæs wīnes ne gehwierfen (-hwyrfen, *v. l.*) him selfum tó ǽttre *quia saluberrimum vini potum in veneni sibi pocula vertunt*, Past. 364, 9. Ic eom tó náhte gehwyrfd *ego ad nihilum redactus sum*, Ps. L. 72, 22. Oft se oferǽt wierð gehwierted tó fierenluste *plerumque edacitas usque ad luxuriam pertrahit*, Past. 309, 14. Hié wurdon gehwierfde inne on ðám ofne tó āre *in fornace in aes versi sunt*, 267, 20. (7) *to give a different form to* the expression of thought, *to turn* into prose or verse, *translate* from one language to another:—Paulinus bóc of metergeweorce on geráde sprǽce ic gehwyrfde (-hwirfde, *v. l., transtuli*), Bd. 5, 23; Sch. 698, 9. þæt hé in swinsunge leóðsonges þæt gehwyrfde *hunc in modulationem carminis transferre*, 4, 24; Sch. 485, 17. Seó bóc wæs yfele of Grēcisce on Lēden gehwyrfed (*translatam*), Bd. 5, 23; Sch. 698, 12. Ðā ðā of flítendum trachterum yfle geworht ł gihuersde arun *ea quae a vitiosis interpretibus edita sunt*, Mt. p. 2, 1. (8) *to change the conduct of* a person, *cause to act in a manner contrary* to previous action:—Hū feala þū ætýwdest mē gedréfednessa, gehwyrfd and þū gelíffæstest [mē] *quantas ostendisti mihi tribulationes, et conversus uiuificasti me*, Ps. L. 70, 20. (8 a) *to change the belief, opinions, &c.,* of a person, *to convert:*—Oft gebyreð ðæt ðā bióð mid líðelicre race gehwirfde (-hwyrfde, *v. l.*), and eft ðā medwísan oft mid bisenum gehwirfde (-hwyrde, *v. l.*) *illos plerumque ratiocinationis argumenta, istos nonnunquam melius exempla convertunt*, Past. 204, 2. Sé gehuerfde *convertantur*, Mt. L. 13, 15. Gehwerfed, Mk. L. R. 4, 12. (9) *to change for the worse, pervert, corrupt:*—þa cóm semninga grim wól ofer ðā gehwyrfdon módes menn (gehweorfdan menn módes, *v. l.*) *interea subito corruptae mentis homines acerba pestis corripuit*, Bd. 1, 14; Sch. 39, 2. (10) *to change one thing for another, exchange.* (a) with gen., *to make exchange of:*—Hí ealra þinga gehwyrfdon ge on cucan ceápe ge on óðrum, C. D. v. 378, 20. Hí gehwyrfdon landa wið Ælfwine *commutationem terrarum fecerunt contra Ælfwinum*, v. 207, 7. Be þon þe nān mon gehwyrfe yrfes būtan gewitnesse, Ll. Lmbn. 156, 1. (b) *with dat., to make exchange with:*—Oft se welega and se wǽdla habbað gehwierfed (-hweorfed, *v.l.*) hiera ðeáwum *plerumque personarum ordinem permutat qualitas morum*, Past. 183, 10. Hié ðém landum iehwerfed hefdan, C. D. ii. 66, 21. (c) with acc., *to exchange:*—Wulfríc hit siððan æt him gehwyrfde mid ðám ðe him gecwémre wæs, C. D. iii. 291, 21. II. *intrans. To return* to a place, occupation, &c.:—Heó nele swā beón gefréfrod, þæt hí eft tó woruldicum gecampe gehwyrfon, Hml. Th. i. 84, 30. Farende and nā gehwyrfende *uadens et non rediens*, Ps. L. 77, 39. [*O. Sax.* gi-hwerbian: *O. H. Ger.* ge-hwerben *convertere.*]

**ge-hwirfedness**, e; *f.* I. *inclination* (? cf. ge-hweorfan; I):—þone bryne þære flǽsclican gehwyrfednysse, Hml. S. 23 b, 523. II. *conversion:*—Seó sóðe gehwyrfednes (*conversio*) mæg beón on þære ýtemestan tíde, Ll. Th. ii. 172, 31. Ðás herigendlicestan gehwyrfednysse ǽgðer ge dǽda þe þeáwa . . . þæs ārwurðan Egyptiscan Marian, Hml. S. 23 b, 1. v. ge-hwyrfedness *in Dict.*

**ge-hwirfness**, e; *f.* I. *return.* v. ge-hwirfan; I. 4:—Hé wítegode on þám sealme be þæs folces gehwyrfnesse of heora hæftnýde, Ps. Th. 24, arg. II. *conversion;* in a special sense, *the adoption of the*

*monastic life:*—Ðæt munucas āwunien in þære hýrsumnesse þe hié Gode gehéhton in þá tíd heora gehwyrfnesse (-hwyrfe-, *v.l., conuersionis*), Bd. 4, 5; Sch. 377, 5.

**ge-hwitan**; *p.* te; *pp.* [-hwitt], -hwited: -hwitian; *p.* ode; *pp.* od *To whiten:*—Gihúidadon hiá *dealbaverunt eas*, Rtl. 48, 1. Ic beó gehwítad *dealbabor*, Wrt. Voc. ii. 139, 83. Gehwíted (-hwítad, Srt.), Ps. L. 50, 9. Hig beóð gehwítode (-hwítte, Srt.) *dealbabuntur*, 67, 15. [*Goth.* ga-hweitjan: *O. H. Ger.* ge-hwîzit *dealbatus.*]

**ge-hwyrft**, es; *m. A revolution:*—On geáres gehwyrftum *in anniversariis*, Angl. xiii. 446, 1158. v. wundor-gehwyrft.

**ge-hwyrftness**, e; *f. Return:*—Hé wítegode . . . be his āgenre gehwyrftnesse (-hwyrfnesse? v. ge-hwirfness) of his wræcsíðe, Ps. Th. 22, arg.

**ge-hwyrftnian.** *The reading of the earlier MS. is* ge-hrifnian, *q.v.*

**ge-hycgan.** *Add:* (1) *to think of, consider.* (a) with acc.:—þ ic on mínum móde betwih þás eorðlican gedréfednesse hwílum gehicge þá heofonlican þing, Gr. D. 1, 20. (b) *with clause:*—Sceáwa nū and gehige hū heora sāwla lifgiað *pensa eorum animae qualiter vivunt*, Gr. D. 271, 13. (2) *to think, conceive, have an idea of:*—Ne mæg ic þæt gehicgan, hū ic in þǽm becwóm, Sat. 179. (3) *to resolve, determine:*—For þon scyle mon gehycgan þæt hé Meotude hýre, Sch. 98. v. gehogian.

**ge-hycglic.** v. ge-hygdlic: **ge-hýd** *exalted.* v. ge-heán.

**ge-hýd** *provided with skin:*—On þám syxtan mónþe hé (*the foetus*) byþ gehýd, Nar. 50, 5.

**ge-hýdan.** *Dele* ge-hédan, *and to* I. *add:*—*Condit*, i. *abscondit, reservat vel* selt *vel* gehýt, Wrt. Voc. ii. 135, 56. Gehýdde *occulit*, 65, 23. Gehýddum *abditis*, 98, 34. (1) *to hide, put out of sight, bury* in the ground:—Dæriste þ wíf gehýdeð (*abscondit*) in meolo mitto, Lk. L. R. 13, 21. Ic gehýdde (*abscondi*) cræft ðín on eorðo, Mt. L. 25, 25. Gehýdde ł ðegelde, 13, 33. (2) *to hide* an object in order that it may not be found:—Strión monn gehýdde, Mt. L. 13, 44. Þám þe unrihte inne gehýdde wrǽte under wealle, B. 3059. (3) *to hide* in order to shield:—Gewint se iil tó ánum cliéwene, and tíhð his fét suā hé inmest mæg, and gehýt his heáfod (*caput abscondit*), Past. 241, 12. Hié biddaþ þ seó eorþe hié forswelge and gehýde . . . hié cweþaþ tó þǽm dúnum: 'Feallaþ ofer ús, and ús bewreóþ and gehýdad,' Bl. H. 93, 27–33. (4) *reflex.:*—Se Hǽlend becierde hié and gehýdde hiene *Jesus fugit in montem ipse solus*, Past. 33, 15: Jn. L. 12, 36. (5) *to keep* a matter *from the knowledge of others:*—Ðū gehýddest (*abscondisti*) ðás from snottrum and ædeáuades ðā ðám lytlum, Lk. L. 10, 21. Ne is gehýded þte ne oncnáuen bið, 8, 17: 12, 2: 19, 42. Nǽnig is gehýded (*occultum*) þ ne sé gewitten, Mt. L. 10, 26. Hié ðeahtigað on hiera módes rinde monig gód weorc tó wyrcanne, ac on ðám piðan bið óðer gehýded (*aliud in imis intentio supprimit*), Past. 55, 23. Hé þá oðéwde openlíce þ hé ǽr diégellíce gehýd hæfde, Ors. 6, 34; S. 288, 32. (6) *to hide* from sight, *prevent from being seen, cover up:*—Ne mæg burug gehýda ofer mór geseted, Mt. L. 5, 14. Ongunnun sume gehýda (*uelare*) onsióne his, Mk. L. 14, 65. Þeós lǽne gesceaft longe stóde heolstre gehýded, Hy. 11, 13. (6 a) fig.:—þá dysegan sint swā blinde, þæt hí ne magon oncnáwan hwær þá ēcan gód sindon gehýdde, Met. 19, 32. [*The passage given under* II *may belong to* I. *The Latin of* Ps. Th. 55, 6 *is:* Inhabitabunt et abscondent ipsi calcaneum meum observabunt, *which is translated:* Oneardiað þá þe swā þenceað þæt heó gehýden hælun míne. Gehýden *may refer to* abscondent. *For passage under* III *see next word.*]

**ge-hýdan** *to fasten with a cable made of hide* (? cf. þæt gafol bið . . . on þám sciprápum þe beóð of hwæles hýde geworht, Ors. 1, 1; S. 18, 18):—Wēnað wǽglíðende þæt hý on eálond sum eágum wlíten, and þonne gehýdad heáhstefn scipu tó þám unlonde (*the whale*) oncyrrápum . . . and þonne in þæt églond úp gewítað (cf. an ealond he (*the sailors*) wenen it (*the whale*) is, . . . sipes on festen and alle up gangen, Misc. 17, 533), Wal. 13.

**ge-hýdness.** v. ge-hýpness.

**ge-hygd.** *Add:*—Gehygde glidderre *sensu lubrico*, Ps. Srt. ii. 202, 17. Ūrum gehygdum *nostris sensibus*, 201, 3. Mé þinceþ þ iu þám gehigdum þyses hālgan weres wǽre Heliseus gāst *ego sancti viri praecordiis Elisaei spiritum video inesse*, Gr. D. 130, 9. v. mis-gehygd.

**ge-hygdlic**; *adj. Considerable* (?):—Seó syn þære gýmingce ymb his gehygdlicu (-hycglice, *v.l.*) þingc and spéde *peccatum curae rei familiaris*, Gr. D. 328, 16. [*O. H. Ger.* ge-huctlîh *memorabilis.*]

**ge-hyhtan.** *Add:* I. *to hope.* (1) *intrans.* (a) *to hope, trust* in:—Wē gehyhtað on þé, Ps. Th. 32, 18. Gehihtaþ ł hopiaþ, Ps. L. 32, 22. On þone gé gehyhtað (gihyhtas, R.), Jn. 5, 45. þá þe on þé gehihtað, Hml. S. 30, 236: Gr. D. 70, 19. þá þe gehihtiaþ on his mildheortnysse *qui sperant super misericordia eius*, Ps. L. 32, 18. Beóð gehyrte and gehihtað on God, Hml. S. 25, 257. Gihyhte in nome Drihtnes *speret in nomine Domini*, Rtl. 19, 27. (b) *to look with hope to*:—Tó hwám mæg ic heononforð gehyhtan (-hyltan, MS.)?, Hml. S. 33, 273. (2) *trans. To hope for, hope to get.* (a) with acc.:—Ðæt þ ic gehihte, þ ic hæbbe nū, Hml. S. 7, 235. þ wē gehihtan sceolon þá māran gód þurh

þā lytlan, Gr. D. 70, 23. (b) with clause, *to hope* that :—Þ gōd þe gehwylc man gehyhteþ Þ sȳ gedōn for hine, Gr. D. 348, 11. Hē gehyhte þæt him God sealde his gewinnes frōfre, Guth. 94, 7. Wē gihyhton dætte hē wēre eftlēsing Israēles, Lk. R. L. 24, 21. (bb) *to look* to a person *with hope* that :—Basilius gehihte tō him and gewilnode Þ hē hine befæste Æquitio *Basilius petit ab eo ut eum Equitio committeret*, Gr. D. 27, 23. II. *to look forward with hope, to rejoice* :—Gehiht *exultat*, i. *gaudet, laetatur, gloriatur*, Wrt. Voc. ii. 146, 28.

ge-hyhtendlic; *adj. To be hoped for* :—Paulus cwæð Þ se geleáfa wēre gehyhtendlicra þinga spēd *est fides sperandarum substantia rerum*, Gr. D. 269, 13.

ge-hyhtlic. *Dele.*

ge-hylced; *adj. Bent*; of legs, *bandy* :—Gehylcedom *diuaricatis* (*cruribus*), Germ. 398, 252.

ge-hyld. v. ge-hild: ge-hyldan *to forbear*. v. ge-ildan: ge-hyldan *to bend*. v. ge-hildan: ge-hyldelic. v. ge-hildelic: ge-hyldig. v. ge-þyldig: ge-hyldra. v. ge-heald: ge-hylmed. v. ge-hilmed: ge-hȳn. v. ge-heán: ge-hȳnan. v. ge-hínan.

ge-hyngr(i)an. *Add : To make hungry* (used impersonally) :—Mid ðȳ hine gehyngerde *cum esurisset*, Lk. L. 6, 2. Gewyncerde *esuriit*, Mk. L. 11, 12. Syllan mete þām gehingredum, Wlfst. 119, 7: 209, 4.

ge-hȳpan. v. ge-hípan: ge-hȳran. v. ge-híran.

ge-hȳran. *Add* : , -hȳrian :—Gehȳrud *conductus*, Germ. 394, 193.

ge-hyrdan. v. ge-hirdan: ge-hyrdnes. v. ge-hirdness: ge-hȳrend. v. ge-hírend.

ge-hyrned. *Add* :—Nædre gehyrnedu, Wrt. Voc. ii. 16, 2.

ge-hȳrnes. v. ge-hírness.

ge-hyrst. For second passage substitute :—*Faleras vel* gehyrste, Wrt. Voc. ii. 147, 4.

ge-hyrstan *to adorn. Add :*—Gehyrsteþ *comit*, Wrt. Voc. ii. 25, 1. Hríme gehyrsted, hagolscúrum geond middangeard Martius rēðe, Men. 35. Gehyrste *falerato* (Ald. 2, 32), Wrt. Voc. ii. 75, 1 : 36, 73 : *falerato*, i. *ornato*, 146, 72. Gehyrsti *falerata*, 108, 35. þā biōð gehyrste mid heregeatwum hildetorhtum, sweordum swíðe geglengde, Met. 25, 8. Swegle gehyrste, Cri. 393.

ge-hyrstan *to fry*. v. ge-hirstan.

ge-hyrstan *to murmur. Add* : [From ge-hwistran? : for hy- = hwy-(-i) cf. ymb-hyrft = ymb-hwyrft, Mt. L. p. 1, 2 ; for metathesis cf. (?) gyrstan = gestran-. *The word might then be compared with* whistren *to whisper, and with* hwæstrian, *q. v.*]

ge-hȳrsum. v. ge-hírsum: ge-hyrtan. v. ge-hirtan.

ge-hȳrung, e ; *f. Hiring* :—Gehȳrung *conductio*, Wrt. Voc. ii. 135, 70.

ge-hyrwan. v. ge-hirwan.

ge-hyscan. *Add :*—Drihten gehyscd hine *Dominus irridebit eum*, Ps. L. 36, 13.

ge-hyspan. *Add* : (1) *to insult, mock* :—Gehypste Dryhten se synfulla *exacerbavit Dominum peccator*, Ps. L. 9, 25. Gecance gehispende *ludibrio insultantem*, An. Ox. 1474. (2) *to reproach, upbraid* :—Se wer þe wæs Gode gehálgod gehyspte Arrianum þone gedwolbiscop swā swā hit gebyrede (*exprobravit ut debuit*), Gr. D. 238, 15.

ge-hȳþan *to plunder, spoil* :—Hungor hē (*the Pater Noster*) gehíded (áhȳþeþ, *v. l.* [*under* á-hȳþan *this passage is wrongly translated*]), helle gestrúded *hunger it harries, hell lays waste*, Sal. 73.

ge-hȳþe; *adj. Convenient, suitable* :—Ic nāht gehȳdes hæbbe þis weorc tō begangenne, Hml. S. 23 b, 783. Ic mē hæfde genóh gehȳþe tō mínes sídfætes geblædfæstnysse, 492. (v. ge-blædfæstness.) Híwcūþ, gehȳþe *domestica*, i. *congruentia*, An. Ox. 4183 : 2, 294.

ge-hȳðegod. v. ge-hȳþigian.

ge-hȳþelic (-hȳþ-); *adj. Convenient, opportune* :—Gehȳþlic, þæslic *vel* gescrǽpe *commodus*, i. *honestus, congruus, utilis*, Wrt. Voc. ii. 131, 81. Gehȳþelic wǽta *liquor oportunus*, i. *conueniens*, An. Ox. 2755. On tíde gehȳþelicre *in tempore opportuno*, Ps. Spl. 31, 7 : Bl. Gl. Gehȳðlic, Ps. Spl. T. 144, 16.

ge-hȳþelíce (-hȳþ-); *adv. Conveniently, suitably* :—Æfter þām beó him gegearwod gehȳðlíce eal mennislic fremfulnes *post hec omnis ei exhibeatur humanitas*, R. Ben. 83, 18. Gehȳþlícor *commodius, congruentius*, Wrt. Voc. ii. 132, 3.

ge-hȳþelicness (*printed* ge-lisþelicnis) *glosses* opportunitas, Ps. Spl. T. 9, 9. *See also* Nap. 81.

ge-hȳþig; *adj. Convenient, suitable, agreeable*. v. next word.

ge-hȳþigian *to make suitable, free from restraint or distress* :—Fruman gecyrredra geswǽsum gehȳðiggende synd gemetum *primordia conuersorum blandis refovenda sunt modis*, Scint. 61, 10. Gehȳþegode *expedita*, Germ. 391, 31.

ge-hȳþness(-hȳð-), e ; *f.* I. *commodity, convenience, advantage* :—Ðȳ lǽs hié gedwelle sió gehȳdnes and ðā getǽsu ðe hié on ðǽm wege habbað *ne subsidia itineris in obstacula perventionis vertant*, Past. 387, 13. þæt þū hwylce þénunga mínon lytlan líchoman tō gehȳdnysse gegear-

wige, Hml. S. 23 b, 252. II. *glossing* opportunitas :—Gehȳdnis *oportunitatem*, Wrt. Voc. ii. 115, 56. On gehȳþnesse *in opportunitatibus*, Ps. Spl. T. 9 second, 1. v. on-gehȳþness.

ge-hȳþþu(-o), *indecl. f. Commodity, suitable provision* :—Ic mē þrȳ hláfas gebohte : ic mē hæfde genóh gehȳððo tō mínes sídfætes geblædfæstnysse, Hml. S. 23 b, 492. (v. ge-blædfæstness.)

ge-hȳwian. v. ge-híwian.

ge-ícan. *Add* : *pp.* -íht. I. *to add*. (1) with the idea of supplementing or completing, *to put* to something already placed. (a) of a material object :—Ofgif þǽre eorðan Þ hire is, and Þ dūst tō þām dūste geíc, Hml. S. 23 b, 751. Genim þās wyrte wel gepunude . . . geȳc þonne þǽrtō sumne dǽl l.uniges, Lch. i. 312, 11. (b) *to associate* one person with another :—Fylstende and geécende *adstipulans*, Wrt. Voc. ii. 9, 39. (c) of non-material objects :—þā geécte hē þǽrtō Þ word ' þines mūðes,' Gr. D. 139, 10. þā geíchte (-ȳhte, *v. l.* -ecde, L., -ecte, R.) hē (*adiciens*) sum bigspell, Lk. 19, 11. Tō wæccenne foresǽgde . . . , geécte bisin (*subjiciens parabolam*), Mt. p. 19, 16. Tō gécde *addens*, Jn. p. 5, 13. Stonde Þ ic and míne witan tō mínra yldrena dómum geȳhton, Ll. Th. i. 272, 32. Ne geéc ðū *ne addas* (*quidquam verbis illius*), Kent. Gl. 1074. Sí geǽht *addetur*, 296. Geéced (-ad) *addita*, Mt. p. 2, 13, 2. (2) with the idea of increase, augmentation, *to provide more, give in addition* :—Tō geécað *addunt* (*divitiae plurimos amicos*), Kent. Gl. 667. Hē geíhte þā teáras þām teárum, Hml. S. 23 b, 200. Hē tō geécde óðerne esne, Lk. L. 20, 11, 12. Geéce tō leng his elne ān, 12, 25. (3) of numerical calculation :—Geȳc twelf þǽrtō, Angl. viii. 301, 20. (4) *to grant* (*additional*) good to a person :—Tō geécð *addet* (*labiis ejus gratiam*), Kent. Gl. 569. Gesald bið l geéced (-íct, W. S.) bið íowh *adicietur uobis*, Mk. L. R. 4, 24. Ðās ealle geéced bioð eów, Mt. R. 6, 33. Geíhte (geéced, L.), Lk. 12, 31. II. *to add to* (1) by way of supplement or completion. Cf. I. 1 :—Swíðe wel hē hit geiécte (-ícte, *v. l.*) mid ðissum, þā hē cwæð . . . *apte subjungitur* . . . , Past. 161, 18. þā witan þā syþþan wēron oft Þ seolfe geníwodon and mid góde gehíhtan, Ll. Th. i. 166, 9. Hē cwæð Þ hē ne cóme nó þæs bebodu tō brecanne, ac mid eallum gódum tō geécanne (cf. *non veni solvere legem sed adimplere*, Mt. 5, 17), 56, 2. þonne deáh þis wiþ hunige geȳced, Lch. ii. 252, 15. (2) *to increase, augment, enlarge*. Cf. I. 2 :—Hē geiécð (-ícð, *v. l.*) ðā ídelnesse ðe hē of áceorfan sceolde, Past. 93, 21 : 411, 30. Se mónð þe byð embolismus . . . geícð Þ gēr Þ þæs geáres beóð þreóttȳne mónðas, Angl. viii. 309, 32. Hē Rómāna bismer on þǽm færelte geiécte swíþor turpiorem ipse auxit infamiam, Ors. 5, 2 ; S. 216, 16. Octauianus gerȳmde Rómāna ríce . . . and wæs for ðí Augustus gecíged, þæt is, ' geȳcende his ríce.' Se nama gedafenað . . . Críste . . . sē ðe his heofonlice ríce geȳhte, Hml. Th. i. 32, 18–22. Geíc (-ec, L. R.) úrne geleáfan *adauge nobis fidem*, Lk. 17, 5. Gif hwā . . . þās úre gyfe geieácnian wille oððe gemonifældan, geiéce him God eal gód bēr on worlde, Cht. Th. 125, 19. Þ hē geéce *ut augeat*, Kent. Gl. 833. Geíht *auctus*, Wülck. Gl. 251, 2. God hæfð geéced mínne ege, Bt. 39, 2 ; F. 212, 33. Gehíhte *macta*, An. Ox. 4, 64. (3) *to furnish, endow*. Cf. I. 4, *and see* eácen :—þonne bið geȳced and geedníwad moncyn þurh Meotud (cf. Sceal þonne ānra gehwylc . . . leoðum onfón and líchoman, edgeong wesan, 1030–3), Cri. 1040. v. má-geéct, tō-geíht.

ge-ícendlic. *Dele* tō-geícendlic: ge-ídlian. *Add :*—Giídlage *evacuare*, Rtl. 103, 5: ge-iermed. v. ge-irman: ge-iéwan. v. ge-íwan.

ge-íht; *adj. Yoked together* :—On twā geiht *biiugus*, on ðreó geiht *triiugus*, Ælfc. Gr. Z. 289, 2. [Cf. *O. H. Ger.* ge-ioht *jugalis*; viórjuchig *quadrijugus*.]

ge-íhtness. v. tō-geíhtness.

ge-ilca *same* :—Eall þe geilcan gerihta . . . eall þæ geylcan gerihta (cf. þā ilcan 11, þe ilcan 14), Cht. Th. 433, 25, 36.

ge-ildan *to delay, defer, put off* :—Gehylde *distulit*, Ps. Spl. 77, 15. Þe bið geeld *qui differtur*, Kent. Gl. 443. Wæs geelded *protelaretur*, Wrt. Voc. ii. 67, 43. Geylded *tricabatur*, 88, 17. Geyld *dilatum*, 140, 34.

ge-illerocaþ. *Substitute:* ge-illerocad *surfeited with wine* :—Geillerocad (geillerocað, Ps. Spl. C. 77, 71) from wíne *crapulatus a vino*, Ps. Srt. 77, 65. Oferfylled, geilleroccad *crapulatus*, i. *subito inebriatus*, Wrt. Voc. ii. 136, 57.

ge-impian; *p. od To engraft*; fig. *to introduce into, mingle in* :—Ðonne hwelc æfter hálgum hāde hine selfne fæstlíce geimpað on eorðlicum weorcum *cum quilibet post sanctitatis habitum terrenis se actibus inserit*, Past. 133, 25. Lóca nū hū se hálega wer sē ðe suā fæstlíce geimpod wæs tō ðǽm hefenlicum dígolnessum *ecce jam coelestibus secretis inseritur*, 99, 18. v. impian.

ge-inbryrdan *to cause remorse* to a person :—Ne geinbryrde sind *nec compuncti sunt*, Ps. Srt. 34, 16.

ge-inbúan *to inhabit* :—In Jacob giinbȳa *in Jacob inhabita*, Rtl. 65, 17.

ge-incígan *to invoke* :—On dægi ðonne giincége (*invocavi*) ðec, Rtl. 20, 29.

**ge-indrencan** *to intoxicate :*—Bióð geindrencte *inebriabuntur,* Ps. Srt. 35, 9.

**ge-inlîhtan** (-ian); *p.* -lîhte, -lîhtade *To illuminate :*—Giinlîht *accende,* Rtl. 3, 15. Giinlîhte *inlumina,* 13 : *inlustra,* 46, 14. Giinlîhta *inlumina,* 37, 17. Giinlîchta *inlustra,* 99, 37. Giinlîhta *inluminet,* 37, 21. Giinlîhtado *inluminata,* 46, 16.

**ge-innian.** *Add :* (1) *to put into a place.* (a) *to restore* property to rightful ownership :—Gyf hwá genyrwe ðæt ic ... on éce yrfe geseald hæbbe, Drihten his andweald genyðrige ... nymðe hé ... geinnige ðæt hé on úrum Drihtne gereáfod, C. D. v. 331, 8. Hér swuteláð hwæt Leófric hæfð gedón intó Sancte Petres minstre ... Ðæt is ðæt hé hæfð geinnod ðæt ær geútod wæs, iv. 274, 21. (b) *to restore* a person to a position :—On Wódnesdæg bisceopas ásceádað ... út of cyrican ... ða ðe ... hý sylfe forgyltan ; and eft on Ðunresdæg ... hý geinniað intó cyrican þá þe ... heora synna bétað, Wlfst. 104, 13. Stande hé þær úte ... oð þæt hé mid hreówsunge geinnige hine sylfne ... intó Godes húse, 155, 24. Wé nýdað út þá forsyngodan of Godes cyrican, oð þæt hí mid dædbóte hí sylfe geinnian, tó þám þæt wé hý þyder in eft lædan durran, 154, 29. (2) *to supply the place of* what is taken, *replace, fill up* a deficiency :—Hé him gá tó honda oþþæt hé his ceáp him geinnian mæge, Ll. Th. i. 142, 4. Ðú geswóre Apollonio þ þú woldest him geinnian swá hwæt swá seó sæ him ætbræd, Ap. Th. 23, 7. Wé sceolon mid gebedum and lofsangum ús geinnian swá hwæt swá wé ... hwónlícor gefyldon, Hml. Th. i. 548, 1. (3) *to make up for,* repair a fault :—Nú sceole wé úre gýmeleáste geinnian, Hml. Th. i. 180, 18. Hí willað geinnian ða æftran hínðe mid þám uferan gestreónum, 340, 32. (4) *to lodge* (v. *inn a lodging*) :—Þæs cynges cniht hæfde geinnod þone godspellere æt his húse, Hml. Th. ii. 474, 15. Hé ácwealde Castolum þe hæfde geinnod ealle þás hálgan, Hml. S. 5, 385. [*O. H. Ger.* diu geinnóton mih in dia *ecclesiam.*]

**ge-inníwian** *to renew :*—Giinníwado *innovati,* Rtl. 33, 36.

**ge-inseglian.** *Add :*—Hé þæt fæt myd hys hringe geinseglode, Hml. A. 190, 253. Hí ða ðrúh geinnseglodon (*signantes lapidem,* Mt. 27, 66), Hml. Th. ii. 262, 11. Seó teág wæs geinsæglod mid twám sylfrenan insæglan, Hml. S. 23, 756. Geinseigled *armatam,* i. *signatam,* An. Ox. 752.

**ge-insettan** *to institute :*—Geinsetet aron *instituuntur,* Jn. p. 1, 10.

**ge-ionge.** v. ge-gang.

**ge-irfeweardian.** *Take here* **ge-erfeweardian** *in Dict., and add :*—Cynren his geyrfeweardað (*hereditabit*) land, Ps. L. 24, 13. Geyrfweardiað *hereditabant,* 36, 11.

**ge-irgan.** *Add :*—Wyrð þurh Godes mihte sóna deófol swýðe geyrged, Wlfst. 33, 20.

**ge-irman.** *Add :* I. *to make wretched, afflict.* (1) the object a person :—Genæt, geyrmþ *conterat,* Wrt. Voc. ii. 135, 5. Gé beóð gesealde feóndum tó gewealde, ða eów geyrmað and swíðe geswencað, Wlfst. 133, 9. Þæt wíf hire ágenne teám mid wyriunge geyrmde, Hml. Th. ii. 34, 31. Ða underðiéddan mon sceal læran ðæt hié elles ne sién genæt ne geirmed (-iermed, *v. l.*) *subditos non subjectio conterat,* Past. 189, 16. Ealle ða gódan færlíce geyrmde hreówlíce wurdon, Hml. S. 23, 24. Hí beóð geyrmde ðurh unwíse cyning on manegum gelimpum, Hml. Th. ii. 320, 3. (2) the object a thing :—Byð his eard geyrmed ægðer ge on heregunge ge on hungre ..., O. E. Hml. i. 303, 14. II. *to make poor :*—Geyrmde *exsumptuavit, pauperavit,* Wrt. Voc. ii. 146, 37. [Cf. *O. Sax.* gi-armód (*applied to* Lazarus).] v. irman.

**ge-irnan.** *Take here* **ge-yrnan** *in Dict., and add :* A. *intrans.* I. *to run, run about :*—Giiorniað *discurrent,* Rtl. 86, 36. Geurnun (*currebant*) tuége ætgædre, Jn. L. R. 20, 4. Ia. of the movement of a vessel :—Scipu frécedlíce geyrnað *ships have perilous runs* (*naues perclitantur in pelago,* 297, 20), Archiv cxx. 298, 6. II. *to run to and reach.* (1) *to run* to a person :—Gesæh ðone Hælend fearre tó gearn (*cucurrit*) and worðade hine, Mk. L. R. 5, 6. Giarn and cuóm tó Simon Petre, Jn. L. R. 20, 2. All folc geuurnon groeton hine *omnis populus ... accurrentes salutabant eum,* Mk. L. 9, 15. (1a) *to run and meet* a person who approaches :—Gearn *occurrens,* Mk. p. 4, 6 : Jn. p. 6, 12. Iu ðær stówe ðér gearn him (giarn tó tó him, R.) Martha *in illo loco ubi occurrerat ei Martha,* Jn. L. 11, 30. Geurnon him tuoege *occurrerunt ei duo,* Mt. L. 8, 28. Giurnon (gwurnun, L.) tógægnes him, Jn. R. 4, 51. Brydgume cymende giiorne (*occurrere*), Rtl. 106, 10. (1b) with the idea of attack :—Gelamp sume síðe, ðær hé sum gild bræc, þ þær gearn mycel menigeo tó him ... and ealle swíðe erre wæron (cf. sáh him on þ cyrlisce folc swýðe wédende, Hml. S. 31, 462), Bl. H. 223, 5. (2) *to run* to a place :—Georn xvi-wintre mæden tó ðære bære, seó wæs blind ácenned, and heó meahte sóna geseón, Shrn. 140, 1. Tó ðær byrgenne gearn (*currens*) and geseah þe áworden wæs, Lk. p. 11, 9 : Lk. L. R. 24, 12. (2a) where violent entry is made :—Gif man in mannes tún ærest geirneð .vi. scillingum gebéte ; sé þe æfter irneð, .iii. scillingas, Ll. Th. i. 6, 16. Cf. gegangeð, 10, 3. III. *to run* and do something :—Giarn (geharn, L.) án and gefylde copp mið æcede, Mk. R. 15, 36. IV. *to run together, coagulate :*—Ne læt geyrnan þ æg ... dó of þ mon gegnídan ne mæge, þ bið geurnen, Lch.

---

ii. 272, 16–22. Snáw cymð of ðám þynnum wætan þe ... byð gefroren ær þan hé tó dropum geurnen sý, iii. 278, 25. V. *of action, to run into, fall* into :—Hé in nænigre leásunge synne ne georn *nec falsitatis incurrebat peccatum,* Gr. D. 22, 30. VI. *of mental process, to occur to the mind :*—Swá hwæt swá þe on mód geurne *quidquid animo occurrit,* Gr. D. 147, 9. B. *trans.* I. *to run* a course, *run through, over* a space :—Þes circul (*the zodiac*) ys tódæled on twelf, and seó sunne geyrnð þás twelf fætu binnan .xii. mónðum, Angl. viii. 298, 16. Saturnus geyrnð his ryne binnan þrittigum wintrum, 320, 40 : 42 : 45. Tó geyrnanne weg *ad currendam uiam,* Ps. L. 18, 6. II. *to run and reach* a place (of shelter) :—Gif cirican fáh mon geierne, Ll. Th. i. 64, 9 : 90, 9. Gif hwá sié deáðes scyldig, and hé cirican geierne, hæbbe his feorh ... Gif hwá his hýde forwyrce, and cirican geierne, sié him sió swingelle forgifen, 104, 13–16. III. *to run and obtain, obtain by running :*—Gif forworht man friðstól geséce, and þurh þ feorh geyrne, Ll. Th. i. 332, 17. Náhwár hé eft his feorh gefare ne geyrne, 24. v. ge-rinnan.

**ge-irsian.** *Take here* **ge-eorsian, -yrsian** *in Dict., and add :*—God, ðú ðe sóðlíce giiorses (*irasceris*), Rtl. 40, 23. Hwæt þá Datianus deófollíce geyrsode ongeán ðone hálgan wer, Hml. S. 14, 23. Læt þíne godas geyrsian, gif hí áht magon, 7, 113.

**ge-isned** ; *adj. Furnished with iron :*—Geîsnedum *ferrato* (*clypeo*), An. Ox. 4232.

**ge-îþan.** *Take here* **ge-éðan** *in Dict., and add : to be gentle.* v. eáþe, (2) :—Ic þe bidde þ þú árîse, and wit þonne bégen biddan þ God þysum wífe geýþe (gemiltsige, *v. l.*), Gr. D. 216, 2. *See next word.*

**ge-îþrian.** (1) *to become easier, suffer less, get better :*—Seóc raþe geéðrað, Lch. iii. 196, 16. (2) *to make easier, make less laborious :*—þ God for his mildheortnesse eów geéðrað þ gewinn swá earfoþlíces weges, Gr. D. 113, 8.

**ge-îw(i)an.** *Take here* **ge-ýwan** *in Dict., and add :*—Hé hí gehýt ... and eft geéwð, Bt. 39, 8 ; S. 131, 7. Gehíwygiende *meditata* (*meditari indicare, significare,* Migne), Germ. 390, 98. Ðá wæron geiéwde, Past. 195, 18. v. ge-eáwan, -eówan.

**ge-lácian.** *Add : to accompany with gifts :*—Crístes móder, Godes beboda gemyndig, eóde tó Godes húse mid láce, and gebröhte þæt cild þe heó ácende gelácod (*she brought the child and gifts along with it* ; cf. hí sceoldon bringan ánes geáres lamb mid heora cylde Gode tó láce, and áine culfran, 140, 1) tó þám Godes temple, Hml. Th. i. 134, 27.

**ge-lácnian.** *Add :* -lécnian (*in Northern Gospels*) :—Hé gelécnade ða unhále *curavit languidos,* Mt. L. 14, 14. Geleicnade, 12, 22. Gelécnige *curare,* 17, 16. Gelécnæge ł wosa gelécned, Lk. L. 8, 43. Gif mon þá greátan sinwe forsleá, gif hié mon gelácman mæge þ hié hál sié, Ll. Th. i. 100, 4. Gelácnod *curaretur,* i. *sanaretur,* An. Ox. 2076. Fotus, i. *nutritus, refectus, recreatus, calefactus vel* gelácnod, Wrt. Voc. ii. 149, 78.

**ge-lád.** *Add : a lode, water-course :*—Vicum qui nu[ncupatur] Æt Euulangeládæ, C. D. B. i. 297, 10. Æt Eánflæde geláde, C. D. v. 402, 2. Norð út onefen þæt gelád, and swá eástweardes þæt hit cymeð eft widnioðan þæt gelád on Sæferne, ii. 150, 12–14. v. wæter-gelád.

**ge-ládian.** *Add :* (1) *to make lád* (q. v.) :—Gif hé ládian wille, geládige be dæde mæðe, swá mid þrifealdre, swá mid ánfealdre láde, Ll. Th. i. 346, 14. Ælc þe gewita oþþe gewyrhta sí þær útlendisc man inlendiscan derie, geládie þære midwiste þ þes orfes weorðe, 354, 29. Búton hé on húsle geládian móte, 362, 21. (2) generally reflexive, *to clear oneself :*—Ne beó þám þeófe ná þe geþingodre, oþþe hine þe þæm geládie, Ll. Th. i. 198, 20. (a) where the degree of *lád* is given :—Gif hié mon teó, geládie hí be sixtegum hída, Ll. Th. i. 68, 19. Be his ágnum were geládige hé hine, 120, 18. Gylde hé, oþþe hine be fullan geládige, 392, 19. Gyf hine man teó þ hé hine út sceóte, geládige hine swá hit on lande stande, 260, 9. (b) *to clear oneself of a charge* of cognizance, connivence, &c. (*gen.*) :—Gyf se landman æniges fácnes gewita sý, þonne sý hé wítes scyldig, búton hé hine þære gewitnesse geládie, Ll. Th. i. 354, 27. (c) *to clear oneself by shewing* that one had no cognizance of a matter, did not connive at (*clause with* þæt) :—Gif hé nyte hwá hit stæle, geládige hine selfne þ hé þær nán fácn ne gefremede, Ll. Th. i. 50, 31. Búton hé hine geládige þ hé hine fléma nyste, 382, 22. Búton hé hine geládige þ hé ná bet ne cúðe, 384, 15. Ðolien ealles þæs hý ágon, gif hí wóh tæcen, oþþe geládian hí þ hí bet cúðon, 354, 11. (d) where (a) and (b) are combined. v. (1) :—Sé ne cúðon, 354, 11. (d) where (a) and (b) are combined. v. (1) :—Sé þe diernum geþingum betygen sié, geládie (geclænsie, geswicne, *v. ll.*) hine be .cxx. hída þára geþinga, Ll. Th. i. 134, 12. (e) where (a) and (c) are combined :—Gebéte hé þæs þeófes were þám hláme mid fullan áðe geládige þ hé him nán fácn mid nyste, Ll. Th. i. 392, 16. v. un-geládod.

**ge-læca**(-ea), an ; *m. A competitor :*—Gelæcea *emula,* Germ. 391, 27.

**ge-læcan** *to compete :*—Gelæcende *emula,* Germ. 391, 27.

**ge-læccan.** *Add :*—Ic gelæcce *arripio,* Ælfc. Gr. Z. 275, 12. I. without sense of violence. (1) *to take, take hold of, catch :*—Þá árás hé and gelæhte hine be þám swuran, and cyste and clypte, Hml. S. 30,

335. (2) *to take, catch* fish, &c. :—On ðām ærran fixnoðe wurdon swā fela gelæhte þæt þæt net tōbærst ... On ðām æftran fixnoðe wurdon gelæhte micele and manega fixas, and þæt net āþolode, Hml. Th. ii. 290, 16–21. (3) *to take, pick up* food :—Þā hwelpas gelæccað þā cruman (*catelli edunt de micis*, Mt. 15, 27), Hml. Th. ii. 50, 31. (4) *to take* as a possession, *get, receive* :—Judas ðā gelæhte þæs Appollonies swurd ... and hē wann mid þām on ælcum gefeohte, Hml. S. 25, 295. Ðū and Æðelmær swylcera gewrita mē bǣdon, and of handum gelæhton, p. 4, 39. Hū hī mihton ðām cāsere gecwēman þ hī sumne scætt æt him gelæhton, 23, 55. Ne mihte hyra ælc ānne bitan of ðām gelæccan (*non sufficiant ut unusquisque modicum quid accipiat*, Jn. 6, 7), Hml. Th. i. 182, 11. (5) *to take* a person preparatory to action, *to take* and do something :—Gelahte hine of ðǣm folce sundurlīce, Mk. L. 7, 33. Gelæhte hine Petrus ongann gedrēadtaige hine, 8, 32. Se Hǣlend gelahte cnæht sette hine nēh him, Lk. L. 9, 47. Gehlahte, 14, 4. Gelahte se groefa ðone Hǣlend and geswanng, Jn. L. R. 19, 1. II. with the idea of violence or haste. (1) *to take* a person, *seize, apprehend, capture* :—Nǣnig moun hine gelahte (*apprehendit*), Jn. L. R. 8, 20. Embehtmenn gefēngon ł gelahton (*comprehenderunt*) ðone Hǣlend, 18, 12. Hī ūs gegripon ł gelahton him *nos diripiebant sibi*, Ps. L. 43, 11. Þæt folc his cēpte and hine gelæhton, Hml. Th. ii. 506, 7. Hē wolde Wulnoð gelæccan cucene oððe deádne *take him alive or dead*, Chr. 1009; P. 138, note 9. Osréd gelæht wæs and ofslagen, 792; P. 55, 29. Daniel se wītega weard gelæht, Ælfc. T. Grn. 9, 38. Wurdon sume his men gelæhte of Frencyscan mannan, Chr. 1075; P. 210, 15. (1 a) *to seize* with an implement :—Hī woldon mē gelæccan mid heora tangum, Hml. Th. ii. 350, 34. (2) *to take* from, *rescue* :—Dauid gelæhte þæt scēp of ðām deórum, Ælfc. T. Grn. 7, 24. (3) *to lay hold of* a person who struggles :—Hē feóll tō þǣre eorðan mid egeslicum anginne, and hine gelæhton ðe ðār nēh wǣron, Chr. 1042; P. 162, 14. (4) of an animal, *to take, seize* :—Cymð se yfela and gelæhð (*rapit*) hit, Hml. Th. ii. 90, 24. Ān wulf gelæhte mīnne bróðor, Hml. S. 30, 330. Gelæcce (*rapiat*) swā swā leó, Ps. L. 7, 3. (5) *to seize, lay hands on; snatch up* :—Gelæhton þā weardmenn his wealdleðer fæste, þæt hē mid fleáme ne burste, Ælfc. T. Grn. 18, 14. Gif hwilc man þ wǣpn gelæcce and hwylcne hearm þǣr mid gewyrce, Ll. Th. i. 418, 8. Ne nān ne gedyrstlǣce þæt hē fǣrlīce bōc gelæcce (*arripiat*), and þær būtan foresceáwunge onginne tō rǣdenne, R. Ben. 62, 5. (6) *to obtain by force* :—Hē gelæcð ðurh strece þæt heofenlice rīce, Hml. Th. i. 360, 9. (7) *to take, carry off* :—Hē fela goldhordas forð mid him gelæhte, Hml. S. 25, 11. (8) of disease, feeling, &c., *to seize, catch* :—Hine gelæhte wundrung, Hml. S. 23, 501. Hine gelæhte unāsecgendlic ādl, Hml. Th. i. 86, 3. Of gyrninge gālscipe gelæht *cupiditatis petulantia captus*, An. Ox. 5291. (9) *to catch* a disease :—þæt bærnet þe hē gelæhte æt ðām unrihtwisum were, Hml. Th. ii. 346, 25.

ge-læccendlic. v. un-gelæccendlic.

ge-lǣdan. *Add*: I. where there is movement. (1) where the movement of the object is not the act of the subject, *to lead, bring, conduct*. (a) the subject a person :—Ic þē ūt gelædde of Ægypta londe, Ll. Th. i. 44, 4. Ðrió cnæhtas of ofone ðū gilæddest (*eduxisti*), Rtl. 101, 36. Hē ūs of hæftum hām gelædde, Sat. 553. Hē hine gelædde ealle þā gemǣru, Cht. Th. 140, 21. Se cyng geleádde ealle his sciphere tō Lægeceastre, Chr. 972; P. 119, 9. Hié micle fierd tō Reádingum gelǣddon, 871; P. 70, 15. Þonne gemēte gyt eoselan gesǣlede and hire folan; onsǣlaþ hié and tō mē gelǣdaþ, Bl. H. 69, 36. Hē beforan þone cyning gelǣd wæs, Bt. 16, 2; F. 52, 23. Ðā wǣron hié gelǣdde fram his gesyhþe, Bl. H. 189, 36. (b) the subject a thing :—Folc wæs on lande; hæfde wuldres beám werud gelǣded, Exod. 567. (2) where the movement of the object is the act of the subject, *to bring* in the hands or in a receptacle, *carry, bear* :—Ic Dauides horn deórne bringe, forð gelǣde *producam cornu Dauid*, Ps. Th. 131, 18. Hwylce þinc gelǣdst (*adducis*) þū ūs?, Coll. M. 27, 5. Hē (*Noah*) gelǣdde ofer lagustreámas māðmhorda mǣst (*the contents of the ark*), Exod. 367. Gē mec ūp gelǣddon, þ ic of lyfte londa getimbru geseón meahte, Gū. 455. Onfōh ūs mid eów on þ scip, and gelǣdaþ ūs on þā ceastre, Bl. H. 233, 8. Hēr wæs Sēē Oswaldes līc gelǣded (-lǣdd, *v. l.*) of Beardanigge on Myrce, Chr. 909; P. 94, 31. Geleád, 1076; P. 213, 2. Wæs māðma fela of feorwegum gelǣded, B. 37. Wæs Gūðlāces gǣst gelǣded on ūpweg, englas feredon, Gū. 1279. (2 a) where the object is part of the subject :—Sē ðe unscyldig in ðǣs wætre hond gisendes, hāl hiá gilǣde (*educat*), Rtl. 102, 37. II. *to bring* to a position, condition, &c. (1) the subject a person :—Hē hine gelǣdeþ on ēce forwyrd, Bl. H. 25, 14. Ūs tō hǣlo hýðe gelǣdde Godes gǣstsunu, Cri. 860. Hē hine tō folcryhte gelǣde, Ll. Th. i. 204, 7 : 284, 1. Þ hē ūs gelǣde on þone gefeán his wuldres, Bl. H. 55, 29. Þ hē ūre sáula gelǣde on gefeán, 211, 8. Tō deáðe hié þē willaþ gelǣdan, ac hī ne magon, 237, 7. Hié wǣron fram synnum ālēsde, and tō þǣm ēcean life gelǣdde, 135, 5. (2) the subject a thing :—Hiera hāþeornes hié on færspild gelǣd (-lǣt, *v. l.*), Past. 295, 20. Seó forhæfdnes hine geclænsaþ and gelǣdeþ tō forgifnesse, Bl. H. 37, 15. III. where the object is non-material. (1) *to bring* to the notice or knowledge of a person, *bring* evidence, proof, &c. :—Hē gelædde ðone āð be fullan, Cht. Th. 171, 21. Þ hē gelædde ungeligne gewitnesse þæs, Ll. Th. i. 158, 19. Godwine hæfð gelǣd fulle lāde æt ðan unrihtwīfe ðe Leófgār bisceop hyne tihte, Cht. Th. 373, 31. (2) *to bring* what affects or acts upon a person :—Ic brógan tō lāðne gelǣde þām þe ic līfes ofonn, Jul. 377. Tō Gūðlāces gāste hý gelǣddun frāsunga fela, Gū. 159. Þā sweartan helle healdan sceolde sē þe be his heortan wuht lāðes gelǣde, Gen. 531. (2 a) *to bring* to a thing :—Swā is lār and ār tō spōwendre sprǣce gelǣded, Gū. 593. [*O. H. Ger.* ge-leiten con-, de-, e-, *in-ducere*.]

ge-lǣdenlic. *l.* ge-lǣdendlic, *and add* :—On bȳman gelǣdendlicum *in tubis ductilibus*, Ps. L. 97, 6 : Ps. Rdr. 97, 6.

ge-lǣfa *leave*. v. ge-leáfa.

ge-lǣfan *to leave*. *Add*: I. *to leave* :—Somnias ðā ðe hiá gelǣfdon ðā screádunga *colligite quae superauerunt fragmentorum*, Jn. L. 6, 12. Ginómun ðæt gilǣfed (ofer gelǣfed, L.) wæs ł þ tō lāfe wæs of ðæm screádungum *sustulerunt quod superauerat de fragmentis*, Mk. R. 8, 8. II. *to be left, remain* :—Genumen wæs þte gehlaefde *sublatum est quod superfuit*, Lk. L. 9, 17. Ðā ðe gelǣfdon [ł] uēron tō lāfe *quae superfuerunt*, Jn. L. 6, 13.

ge-lǣmed. v. ge-lemian.

ge-lǣnan *to grant* for a time, *lend, lease* land :—Wē habbað ... gelǣned heom ðæt land of ðǣre strǣt ðe ūre wæs heore hūs on tō rȳmende, ðā hwīle ðe hī libbeð ... and æfter heore dǣie hī gyfeð heore hūs and heore land and ūre Crīste and Sancte Petre, C. D. vi. 209, 28–210, 7. Gelēned feoh *vel* on borh geseald *res credita*, Wrt. Voc. i. 20, 70. Wēnst ðū þ hī (*earthly goods*) ā þe deórwyrþran seón þe hī tō þīnre note gelǣnde wǣron, Bt. 14, 2 ; F. 44, 2.

ge-lǣnde. v. ge-lendan : ge-lǣnged. v. ge-lengan.

ge-lǣr. *Add* : (1) in a physical sense :—Gif hwā ofer gemet þigþ mete, þæs mon tilað þe eáþelīcor þe mon raþor gedō þ hē spīwe and gelǣr sié, Lch. ii. 240, 18. Þonne se geohsa of þǣre īdlan wambe cymð and of þǣre gelǣran, 62, 1. Þonne findest þū þā blǣdran gelǣre, 250, 21. (2) figurative, *empty-handed* :—Nānne forlǣt þū gelǣrne fram þē, E. S. viii. 474, 52. [Nim ane gelare pina hnutte, Lch. iii. 92, 17. Þa þa water wel al ilædden and þe put was ilær, Laym. 15961. þe clerkes adde the stretes sone iler, R. Glouc. 541, 15.]

ge-lǣran. *Add*: I. *to teach*. (1) with acc. of person :—Seó wiþerwearde wyrd gebēt and gelǣred ælcne þāra þe hió hī tō geþiét, Bt. 20 ; F. 70, 35. Mē gelǣr *doce me*, Ps. Ben. 24, 4. Swā wē magon betst ðā gedyrstigan gelǣran, Past. 209, 15. Ic wēnde þ ic þe gió gelǣred hæfde þ þū hī oncnāwan cūþest, Bt. 7, 1 ; F. 16, 19. Wē sceolan beón gelǣrede mid þysse bysene, Bl. H. 19, 14. (2) with acc. of person and acc. of thing :—Mē þīnra stīga stapas gelǣr, Ps. Ben. 24, 6. ¶ rǣd gelǣran *to give counsel* :—Ne meahton wē gelǣran leófne þeóden rǣd ǣnigne þæt hē ne grētte goldweard þone *we could not give the dear prince any counsel that would prevent him attacking the dragon*, B. 3079. Ne mæg þec sellan rǣd mon gelǣran, Gū. 250. (3) with acc. of person and prep., *to bring* to something *by teaching*, *to instruct* in :—Ðæt gebrocode flǣsc gelǣrd ðæt ūpāhæfene mōd tō ryhttre eáðmódnesse, Past. 257, 14. Heó gelǣrde hyre suna tō Godes geleáfan, Shrn. 151, 6. Hē þysne wer on Godes þeówdōm getýde and gelǣrde, Bl. H. 217, 5. Wæs his fæder gelǣred in þā gerýno Crīstes geleáfan *pater eius sacramentis Christianae fidei imbutus est*, Bd. 2, 15 ; Sch. 174, 14. I a. *to teach* as a master, *educate*. (1) with acc. of person :—Ic þē getýdde and gelǣrde, Bt. 7, 3 ; F. 20, 10. Se fæder gelǣrde þ mǣden mid hālgum gewritum ... and mid ealhum woruldlicum wīsdōme, Hml. S. 33, 26. Ne eart þū se mon þe on mīnre scole wǣre āfēd and gelǣred, Bt. 3, 1 ; F. 4, 19. Hē wæs on Rōme gelǣred, Chr. 565; P. 19, 13. Philippus þā hē cniht wæs ... mid Paminunde gelǣred weard *Philippus apud Epaminondam ... eruditus est*, Ors. 3, 7 ; S. 110, 23. (2) with acc. of person and of thing :—Ic ðē geongne gelǣrde snytro, Bt. 8 ; F. 24, 28. II. *to train* an animal or bird :—Wildu hors mid gierdum fullīce gelǣran and ðā temian, Past. 303, 12. Se wælisca heafoc weorðeð tō hagostealdes honda gelǣred, Vy. 92. III. *to persuade* a person (1) to do something. (a) with clause :—Ic gelǣrde Simon þæt hē sacan ongon wið Crīstes þegnas, Jul. 297. Heó gelǣrde þone cyning þæt hē Cassander upp āhōf, Ors. 3, 11 ; S. 148, 4. Wearþ Simon āwent wiþ ðām apostolum and gelǣred þ hē feala yfla sægde (cf. Jul. 297 *ante*), Bl. H. 173, 20. (b) with pronoun and clause in apposition :—Mē þæt gelǣrdon leóde mīne ... þæt ic þē sōhte, B. 415. (2) to accept a doctrine, counsel, &c. :—Gelǣrde unc se atola ... þæt wit blǣd āhton, Sat. 413.

ge-lǣred. *Add*: I. of persons. (1) *instructed, skilled, wise* :—Gelǣred oferswīþestre *docta victrix*, Wrt. Voc. ii. 141, 68. Sē ðe gemetegað ... gelǣred [is] *qui moderatur [sermones suos], doctus [et prudens est]*, Kent. Gl. 622. Hond bið gelǣred, wīs and gewealden ... sele āsettan, Crä. 45. Ofer gelǣredne *super eruditum (semita vitae)*, Kent. Gl. 534. (2) *learned, erudite* :—Uncūð hū longe swā gelǣrede biscepas sién, Past. 9, 4. þæs hālgan weres and þæs gelǣredestan Bonefatius *uiri sanctissimi ac doctissimi Bonifatii*, Bd. 5, 19 ; S. 660, 8. Paminunde, þǣm gelǣredestan philosophe (*summo philosopho*), Ors. 3,

7 ; S. 110, 21 : 6, 18 ; S. 270, 27. **II.** of things. (1) of thought, action, &c., *displaying skill, wisdom*, &c. :—Gelæreddum gedancum *eruditis cogitationibus*, Kent. Gl. 240. (2) *connected with or resulting from learning, learned* :—Gelærede áþrotu *docta fastigia* (l. *fastidia*), Wrt. Voc. ii. 141, 69. v. ær-, un-, wel-gelæred.

**ge-læredlíce.** v. un-gelæredlíce.

**ge-lærednes.** *Add* : *erudition* :—Ásprang hire hlísa and wísdóm and gelærednys geond ealle þá ceastre, Hml. S. 33, 29. v. un-gelæredness.

**ge-léstan.** *Add* : **I.** *to do, perform.* (1) the object denoting action :—Ic wolde ymbe þone lǽcedóm ļāra þīnra lāra hwēne māre gehŷran . . . and ðē swīþe georne bidde þ þū hī mē gelǽste, Bt. 22, 1 ; F. 76, 21. Tó gesetton dæge gelǽste hē þ hē ǽr sceolde, Ll. Th. i. 260, 15. Hī nellað þone sang gelǽstan, Hml. S. 21, 244. Gif hwā geniéd sié tó hlāfordsearwe, þ is þonne ryhtre tó āléoganne þonne tó gelǽstanne, Ll. Th. i. 60, 6. þ gehwilc sprǣc hæbbe āndagan hwænne heó gelǽst sŷ, 158, 8. (2) *to do habitually, practise* :—Se mon þe þā sōþfæstnesse mid his mūþe sprecþ, and hié on his heortan geþencþ, and hē hī fullíce gelǽsteþ, Bl. H. 55, 16. Se geleáfa þe ǽghwylcum men gebyreð þ hē gelǽste, 111, 13. þæt hié lufan Dryhtnes, and sybbe sylfra betweónum, freóndrǣdenne gelǽston, El. 1208. (3) *to do something to a person, bring* some affecting condition upon :—Ic þe sceal mīne gelǽstan freóde, B. 1706 : Hy. 10, 40. **II.** *to carry out* what has been previously declared or arranged, *to execute* (1) an intention, a plan, &c. :—Heó þencende wæs hū heó hit gewrecan mehte ; and þ eác mid dǣdum gelǽste, Ors. 2, 4 ; S. 76, 25. Hēton him secgan, þ him leófre wǣre tó feohtanne þonne gafol tó gieldanne. Hié þæt gelǽstan swā, I, 10 ; S. 44, 14. Sceótend þōhton Italia ealle gegongan ; hī gelǽstan swā, Met. 1, 13. Eall þæt wæs gelǽsted, Bl. H. 105, 13. (2) a promise, pledge, vow, &c. :—Hē gehēt and gelǽste swā, B. 2990. þonne þū behát behǣtst, ne wanda þū þæt þū hit ne gelǽste ; Deut. 23, 21. þ hē gelǽste eów þæt hē mid ǽðe swōr, 29, 12 : Ll. Th. i. 82, 6. þās andweardan gōd ne magon gelǽstan heora lufiendum þ hī him gehātaþ, Bt. 32, 2 ; F. 116, 34 : 40, 5 ; F. 240, 16 : Exod. 557. Gē murciað nū for þǣm þe monega folc . . . noldon eów gelǽstan þæt hié eówre behēton ; and nellað gelǽstan hū lāð eów selfum wæs tó gelǽstanne eówre āþas þǣm þe ofer eów anwald hæfdon, Ors. 3, 8 ; S. 122, 14–17. (3) an agreement, a compact, &c. :—þā gewearð hī him betweónum . . . Hī þ swā gelǽston, Ors. 6, 30 ; S. 280, 22. þæt ic monnum þās wǣre gelǽste, Gen. 1542. Ðās gewrioto and ðās word haldan and gelǽstan, C. D. ii. 121, 31. Witan hwæt ūre gecwydrǣddene gelǽst sŷ, Ll. Th. i. 236, 5. (4) a threat, boast, &c. :—Ðā gebeótode Cirus ðæt . . . Hē þ mid dǣdum gelǽste, Ors. 2, 4 ; S. 74, 1. Hæfde Eást-Denum leód gilp gelǽsted, B. 829. **III.** *to carry out* an order, wish, &c. :—' þū þæs cyninges bebod begange' . . . þæt eall gelǽste Elene, El. 1197. Mid eallum þām þe Drihtnes bebodu willaþ gelǽstan, Bl. H. 53, 32. Hæbbe ic þīne willan gelǽst, Gen. 727 : Hy. 6, 10. **III a.** *to perform* what is enjoined by law. (1) secular :—Him (*Edward*) þūhte þ hit mæctor gelǽst wǣre þonne hit scolde, þ hē ǣr beboden hæfde, Ll. Th. i. 162, 3. Wē beódad . . . Gif wē hit eall þus gelǽstan willað, 238, 19. (2) religious or ecclesiastical :—Gif munuc þ gelǽste, Ll. Th. i. 306, 10. Hī hogedon georne þæt ǽ Godes ealle gelǽste, Dan. 219. **IV.** *to discharge* an obligation, *pay* a due, debt, tax, penalty, &c. :—Gif geneátmanna hwilc his hlāfordes gafol him tó þǣm rihtāndagan ne gelǽst, Ll. Th. i. 270, 17. Ne þearf ic N. sceatt ne scilling . . . ac eal ic him gelǽste þ þ ic him scolde, 182, 10. Neádwīsnesse gelǽste *debitum soluit*, An. Ox. 2397. Gelǽste exsoluit (*mortis uindictam*), 4327 : 3818. þæt hē Godes gerihta gelǽste, Wlfst. 157, 12. Gelǽste hē Gode his teóðunga, Ll. Th. i. 272, 1. Gelǽste man sulhælmessan þonne .xv. niht beón ouufan Eástran, 262, 17. Sáulsceat man gelǽste æt openum grǣfe, 308, 4, 6. Gelǽste ǽlc wuduwe þā heregeata binnan twelf mónðum, 416, 16. Gelǽste *persolueret*, An. Ox. 1991. þis ðe gelǽsten ðe on ðissem gewrite binemned is ðǣm hīgum . . . and hió forgīfeð fīftēne pund for ðŷ ðe mon ðās feorme ðŷ soel gelǽste, C. D. i. 312, 13–18. Hē ne mihte þ gafol ālecgan þe heó gelǽstan sceolde, Hml. S. 3, 181. Sceóte ǽlc gegylda ǽnne gyldsester . . . and þ beó gelǽst binnan twām dagum . . . and se wudu beó gelǽst binnan ðrým dagum, Cht. Th. 606, 6–13 : Ll. Th. i. 232, 7 : 262, 20. **IV a.** *to give* what has been promised :—þæt ūre rīce beó ūs gelǽst, swā swā Críst ūs behēt þæt hē wolde ūs ēce rīce forgyfan, Hml. Th. i. 264, 2. **V.** *to accompany* :—Tó gelǽstunne *comitauere*, Wrt. Voc. ii. 105, 19. Tó gelǽstanne, 15, 24. (1) the subject a person, *to follow*, stick by a person. (a) *with dat.* :—Tó ðǣre heofenlican Hierusalem ūs gebrincð se Hǣlend, gif wē him gelǽstað, Hml. Th. i. 210, 25. Hwylc hira sēlost gelǽste hlāforde æt hilde, An. 411. Mid him sylfum and mid eallum þām þe him gelǽstan wolden, Chr. 874 ; P. 73, 28 : 920 ; P. 100, 19. (b) *with acc.* (cf. 2 b) :—þæt hine on ylde gewunigen wilgesīðas, leóde gelǽsten, B. 24. (2) the subject a thing. (a) in a local sense, *to be present with, not to leave* :—Symle him gelǽste þæt swearte tācn on dæg and þæt fŷrene on niht *numquam defuit columna nubis per diem nec columna ignis per noctem*, Ex. 13, 22. (b) of that which is carried by a person :—þis sweord mec oft gelǽste,

B. 2500. **VI.** *not to fail, to last* :—Ic lecge þā grundweallas þe gelǽstað ǽfre, Hml. S. 36, 67. Gelǽstendum lífe *comite vita, sospite vita*, Wrt. Voc. ii. 132, 20. **VI a.** *not to fail* a person (*dat.*) :—Him micele āgenre is þ him ǽfre on ēcnesse gelǽst, Ll. Th. i. 272, 12. **VI b.** with idea of sufficiency :—Daga gehwylce hī heom þ wīn tó bryce hæfdon, and hit heom gelǽste *they used the wine every day, and it lasted them* (to the end of the journey), Gr. D. 66, 20. Fæste hē .ii. dagas tógædere, gif him mægen gelǽste, Lch. ii. 218, 2. þeós andwearde tíd þyses dæges ne mæg ūs genihtsumian ne gelǽstan tó þysum bysenum *the time would not last us out for these examples*, Gr. D. 91, 25. þes pallium þe ic werige wyle mē gelǽstan, Hml. S. 36, 160. [*Goth.* ga-laistjan *to follow* : *O. Sax.* gi-lēstian *to perform* : *O. H. Ger.* ge-lēsten *efficere, reddere* (*votum*).]

**ge-léstfullian** *to prove by witness* :—Ic gelǽstfullige *contestabor*, Ps. L. 80, 9.

**ge-læswian.** *l.* -lǽswian, and add : *to pasture, feed cattle* :—Ic gilēse ꞇcíp mīno *ego pascam* (printed *þarcam*, but see Ezech. 34, 15) *oves meas*, Rtl. 10, 3. Ðā ðe gelēsuadon *qui pascebant*, Lk. L. 8, 34. þe gelēsuade ᵹ gefoede ðā bergas *ut pasceret porcos*, 15, 15. Hū is nū gelǣswod seó heord Crīstes gesamnunga, Hml. S. 23 b, 254.

**ge-lǽt.** v. wæter-gelǽt.

**ge-lǽtan.** *Add* : **I.** *to leave, allow to have, grant* :—Ic eaforan þīnum spēdum wille stēpan and him sōðe tó mōdes wǣre mīne gelǽtan, (gelǽstan ? v. 1542), Gen. 2366. For gebētendnysse tó fyrstan synt gelǣtene (*nobis*) *propter emendationem* (*malorum hujus uite dies*) *ad inducias relaxantur* (R. Ben. l. 5, 6), An. Ox. 58, 8. **I a.** *to let* land, &c. :—Ælfwīg hæfð gelǣten tó Stīgande .xxx. hŷda landes wið .x. marcan goldes and wið .xx. pundon seolfres, C. D. iv. 171, 28. **II.** *to cause to move, bring.* Cf. ge-lǣte :—Gif hió (*the wound*) swīþor unsŷfre weorþe, clǣnsa mid hunige and gelǣt eft tógædere, Lch. ii. 210, 2. **II a.** of the movement of a ship [cf. Icel. lāta til lands, at landi *to stand towards land*], *to stand, shape a course* :—Gelíce þām þe on lēfan scipe neáh lande gelǣtaþ (*like those that in a crazy vessel shape a course near land, have nearly made the land*), and hit þonne se storm ūt ādrīfeð swā feorr þ hŷ æt nēcstan ne magon nān land geseón, Gr. D. 5, 25. **III.** *to put* into a position, *commit, entrust* :—On treówe gelǣton *fidei commissum*, Wrt. Voc. ii. 148, 76. [*O. H. Ger.* ge-lāzan *adnuere, praestare, largiri, cedere.*]

**ge-lǽte.** *Substitute* : *A place where roads meet, where one road opens into another.* Cf. ge-lǣtan ; **II** :—Biuium twēgra wega gelǣte, *trijuium* þreóra wega gelǣtu, *competum* fela gelǣtu, Ælfc. Gr. Z. 31, 5–7. In twēga wega gelǣte *in bino* (= biuio, Mk. 11, 4), Wrt. Voc. ii. 73, 40 : *in biuio*, 46, 47. þæt wīf æt þǣra wega gelǣte (*in bivio*) sæt, Gen. 38, 21. Twēgra wega gelǣtu *biuium*, þreóra *triuium*, Ælfc. Gr. Z. 288, 9. þā belocenan wega gelǣta *conpeta clausa*, Wrt. Voc. ii. 19, 56. *Competalia* æt þām wega gelǣtum wǣran, Wrt. Voc. ii. 86, 28 : 19, 2. þā hǣðenan æt wega gelǣtum him lāc offrodon, Wlfst. 107, 4. Gif wīfman hire cild æt wega gelǣton (*ad compita viarum*) þurh þā eorðan tīhð, Ll. Th. ii. 210, 18 : Hml. S. 17, 148. Gað tó wega gelǣtum (gelǣta, L.) *ite ad exitus viarum*, Mt. 22, 9 : Wrt. Voc. ii. 73, 13 : 9, 2. Gilētum, Rtl. 107, 35. Æt woegena gelǣtum *in biuio*, Mk. L. R. 11, 4. Andlang strǣte oþ þǣra strǣta gelǣto, C. D. iii. 436, 22. [*O. H. Ger.* ge-lāz *commissura, conjunctura, exitus* (*viarum*).] v. þeóh-, weg-gelǣte.

**ge-lǽððe** :—Tó Indeum aldre gelǣððe Bartholameus, Ap. 43. *In the second edition of Grein's Bibliothek the reading of the MS. is taken to be* gelǣdde. *Perhaps* genēðde *should be substituted ; the phrase* aldre genēðde *occurs in* ll. 17, 50, *and the construction with* tó *is found in* An. 1353 :—Tó þām ānhagan aldre genēðan.

**ge-lafian.** *Add* : [*O. L. Ger.* gi-labōn : *O. H. Ger.* ge-labōn *fovere, refocilare, reficere.*]

**ge-lagian.** *Add* : **I.** of general regulations, *to fix by law, establish as law* :—Iulius se cāsere þisne bissextum gelagode on þǣre stōwe þe wē nū hine healdað, Angl. viii. 306, 40. Be þǣre steóre þe Eádgār gelagede, Wlfst. 272, 8. Gif hē his ælmessan rihtlíce ne gelǣste, swā swā hit gelagod sŷ, 172, 4. Gebēte hē þæt, swā swā hit gelagod is, 181, 8. Heora yldran heom tealdan hū hit was gelagod syððan Scs. Ags. tó þisan lande cōm, Chr. 995 ; P. 128, 26. **II.** of a regulation that affects a single person, *to fix, appoint* :—Se kyngc Wyllelm hine underfēngc, and hē wæs þǣr on his hīrēde, and tóc swilce gerihta swā he him gelagade, Chr. 1075 ; P. 210, 28.

**ge-lagu.** *Substitute* : ge-lǽg, es ; *n. A lay, layer, material spread out, a stretch* of water :—Ofer holma gelagu, Seef. 64. [Cf. *Icel.* lág *a layer.*] Cf. licgan.

**gelan** (?) *to pour.* v. tó-gelan.

**ge-landa.** *Take here* ge-londa *in Dict.*, and add :—*Contribulus*, i. *ciues, consanguineus mǣg*, gelanda, Wrt. Voc. ii. 134, 76. Fratres gebrōþor, *et aliquando* gemǣgas, *aliquando* gelondan, *quas Latini paternitates interpretantur*, 39, 47. *Fratres* gebrōþru *vel* gelo[n]dan *vel* siblingas, i. 52, 3. [*O. L. Ger.* ge-landan *fratres de patre nati.*]

**ge-landian.** *Substitute* : ge-landod ; *adj.* (*ptcpl.*) *Landed, pos-*

*sessed of land:*—Se geréfa ... gesylle mē .cxx. sciłł., and be healfum þām ǽlc mīnra þegna þe gelandod sȳ, Ll. Th. i. 240, 20.

**ge-lang.** *Add:* I. of an object, *to be got, coming* (1) from (*æt*) a person on whose good will the grant or possession of the object depends, where the recipient of the object depends upon the person for it. (a) the object material:—Hī setton him ǽnne wicnere getréowne ... æt þām wæs gelang eall heora fóda (*they depended upon him for all their food*), Hml. S. 23, 218. (b) the object non-material:—Ǽt þe is ūre lȳf gelang *salus nostra in manu tua est*, Gen. 47. 25. Biđ æt Gode ánum gelang eal, hwæt wē gefaran scylon, Wlfst. 122, 8. Is seó bót gelong eal æt þē ánum, Cri. 152. Is eal æt þē lissa gelong, B. 2150. (2) from or in a place (*hwǽr, þǽr*). (a) the object material:—Eáþe wē magon geséon on ōþre healfe ūrra feónda hwǽr se drinca is gelang ... ac ... wē him ne magon būton gefeohte tō cuman *aquam quidem in conspectu esse respondit, sed eam ferro vindicandam*, Ors. 5, 8; S. 232, 10. (b) the object non-material:—Þǽr is ár gelang fīra gehwilcum þām þe hié findan cann, An. 981: Jul. 645: Seef. 121. II. of a circumstance, event. (1) *dependent* upon (*on*), *attributable, owing* to a person:—Gif þū wēnst þ hit on þē gelɔng sȳ þā woruldsǽlþa on þē swā onwenda sint, Bt. 7, 2; F. 16, 29. Gif hit deád weorđe būtan fulluhte, and hit on preóste gelang sȳ, Wlfst. 120, 10. (2) *consequent upon, resulting* from, *attributable* to a cause:—Hié hæfdon longsum gefeoht ǽr þāra folca āþor fluge. Þæt wæs swīþost on đǽm gelong, þæt Hasterbal swā late fleáh for þon þe hē elpendas mid him hæfde *diu incertus belli eventus fuit, elephantis maxime Romanam infestantibus aciem*, Ors. 4, 10; S. 198, 26. Frægn Scipia hiene an hwȳ hit gelang wǽre þ Numentię swā rade āhnescaden (*qua ope res Numantina fuisset eversa*), 5, 3; S. 222, 15. v. ge-lenge.

**ge-langian.** *Add:* I. *to call, summon.* (1) absolute:—*Cieo* and *cio* ic gelangige odđe geladige, Ælfc. Gr. 220, 11. (2) *to send* for a person, *call* a meeting:—Ic áxie þone intingan hwī þū mē gelangodest *interrogo quam ob causam accessistis me*, Hml. S. 10, 135. Gelangige (*convocet*) se abbod ealle gegæderunge, R. Ben. I. 17, 12. Hēt se bisceop hī gelangian, Hml. S. 2, 74: 23, 761: 34, 204. (3) *to send for* a person to come to another. (a) *with dat.*:—Gelangiađ hē đone martyr Mercurium, Hml. Th. i. 450, 31. (b) *with* tō, (a) *preceding the dat.*:—Gelanga hine tō þē *accessi eum*, Hml. S. 10, 142. Hī gelangigan hider tō þām bisceope, 23, 680. Hē hēt gelangian đā preóstas tō his andwerdnysse, Hml. Th. ii. 310, 11. (β) *following the dat.*:—Gelangode hē him tō his ercediácon, Hml. S. 31, 1387. Hē hēt him gelangian þā gelȳfedan men tō, 3, 94. Hē hēt gelangian him tō ealle đā burhwara tōgædere, 23, 20. II. *to get hold of*:—Gif hit þeóf beó, and gif hē hine binnan twelf mōnđum gelangian mæge, āgife hine tō rihte, Ll. Th. i. 268, 11. [*O. H. Ger.* ge-langōn *to attain.*] v. ge-lengan.

**ge-lást.** *Substitute:* I. *performance, act of performing*:—Þæt hē ūs þurh his gife gefultumige tō gelǽste his geboda, R. Ben. 5, 4. II. *a performance, what is performed* as an obligation, *a vow.* Cf. ge-lǽstan; II. 2:—Þē biđ ágolden gelást *tibi reddetur uotum*, Ps. Rdr. 64, 2: Bl. Gl. Ic āgylde þē gelást mīne *reddam tibi uota mea*, Ps. Rdr. 65, 13. III. *what is paid* as a due, *a (fixed) contribution.* Cf. ge-lǽstan, IV:—Þ ǽlc gelást forđcume þāra þe wē ealle gecweden habbađ ... be .xxx. pæn. oþþe be ānum hrȳđere, Ll. Th. i. 232, 5. Wē cwǽdon þ ūre ǽlc scute .iiii. pæng ... Wē tellan .x. menn tōgædere, and se yldesta bewiste þā nigene tō ǽlcum gelǽste þāra þe wē ealle ge-cwǽdon, 220, 15–23. [Cf. *O. Sax.* gi-lēsti *a deed.*]

**ge-lástfull.** *Substitute: Helpful, aiding, assisting, doing service* to. Cf. ge-lǽstan; V:—Þæt ǽlc man wǽre ōđrum gelástfull (*alii coadjutor*, Lat. vers.) ge æt spore ge æt midrāde, Ll. Th. i. 232, 11. Gegaderade Cassander fird. Þā Olimpias þæt geáscade, þæt þæs folces wæs swā fela tō him gecirred, þā ne getriéwde hió þæt hiere wolde se ōđer dǽl gelástful beón, ac hió fleáh tō đǽm fæstenne *audito aduentu Cassandri, Olympias, diffisa Macedonibus, in urbem concedit*, Ors. 3, 11; S. 148, 18.

**ge-laþian.** *Add:* I. *to call, summon.* (1) construction uncertain:—Gelađade *adhibuit*, Wrt. Voc. ii. 99, 40. Geladode, 4, 49. (2) *to summon* a person, *call together* people:—Gelađige (*convocet*) se abbod eal þæt gefēre, R. Ben. 15, 5. Geladian *arcessire (pedissequas)*, Wrt. Voc. ii. 86, 9. Gelaþgan *adsciscere (turmas)*, 94, 21. Wǽre gelaþod *adsciceretur*, i. *aduocaretur*, An. Ox. 4088. (3) *to summon* to:—Tō geladian *adsciscere*, Wrt. Voc. ii. 9, 30. (a) *to a person*:—Gif hwa geuntrumod beó, þæt hē gelaþige him his sācerd tō *si quis infirmatus sit, ut uocet ad se sacerdotem suum*, Ll. Th. ii. 178, 24. (b) *to a place*:—Se Hǽlend hine on đām dæge tō heofonum gelađod hæfde, Hml. Th. i. 74, 23. (c) *to a condition or action*:—Þā gelaþode hē hié tō ēcean līfe, Bl. H. 103, 7. Hē wolde deófol gelaþian tō campe wiþ hine, 29, 20. (4) *to summon* for a purpose:—Hē hæfde þā þing gefyllede þe hē fore gelađod wæs, Ælfc. T. Grn. 17, 37. II. *to call for the performance of, demand*:—Sylfiicre lu[fe and nā] gelađedre *ultroneo affectu [et non] acticio*, i. *inuito* [*famulamine*], An. Ox. 56, 111. III. *to take into* one's house (?). Cf. (?) *Goth.* ga-laþon *to take in* a stranger:—Ne mæg nān wīf hire bōndan forbeódan þ hē ne mōte intō his cotan gelōgian (ge-lađyan, *v. l.*) þ þ hē wille, Ll. Th. i. 418, 24. [*Goth.* ga-laþōn *to call, invite, entertain: O. H. Ger.* ge-ladōn *vocare, invitare.*] v. un-gelaþod.

**ge-laþung.** *Add:* I. *a calling, summoning*:—Seó godcunde geladung *euocatio diuina*, R. Ben. 23, 14. II. *those who are called, a church;* ecclesia. (1) *the whole body of Christians on earth, the church*:—Ealle Godes cyrcan synd tō ānre getealde, and seó is seó geladung þe wē embe sprecađ ... Nū syndon ealle Crīstene men ānum naman gehātene, ... seó hālige geladung þe gelȳfđ nū on God, Hml. A. 29, 115–123. Crīst ūs circean ārǽrde, þe is his geladung, Ælfc. T. Grn. 8, 2. (2) *a particular part of the general body, a church*:—Đæt Crīstes geladung, đe đā git was nīwe on Engla lande, nǽre būtan ārbiscope, Chr 616; P. 22, 35. On þǽra gewitnysse þe þū (*the bishop*) wissian scealt on þissere geladunge, Ælfc. T. Grn. 17, 37. (3) *the assembly of saints in heaven*:—Hī ǽfre wuniađ on đǽre ēcan geladunge, Hml. A. 29, 120.

**ge-latian;** *p.* ode. I. *to grow torpid*:—Gilattia *torpescit*, Rtl. 125. 27. II. *to be slow* about a matter (*gen.*), *be dilatory*:—Smeáge gehwā georne hine sylfne, and þæs nā ne gelatige ealles tō lange, Wlfst. 165, 24.

**ge-latu** (?) *a hindrance*:—Gilatto⁹ *impedimenta*, Rtl. 96, 11.

**ge-laured.** *Substitute: Mixed with the juice or blossom of laurel*:—Dō spātl tō and gelauredne ele, þ is laures seáw odđe blōstman gemenged, Lch. ii. 226, 2.

**geldan;** *pp.* geald. v. ā-geldan.

**gelde.** *Substitute: Geld* (v. *N. E. D.* s.v.), *barren, unproductive*:—*Effeta,* i. *sine foetu, debilis, priuata, sine fructu, vel gelde, uacuata, ineruata, sterilis, stulta,* Wülck. Gl. 226, 22. *Effeta* [nā?] berende biđ odđe gelde odđe āfyldum, 394, 26. [*O. H. Ger.* galt: *Ger.* gelt *not giving milk: Icel.* geldr.]

**ge-leáf** *leave:*—Geleáf *licentia,* Scint. 165, 4. Nime hē leáfe (geleáfe, *v. l.*), Ll. Th. i. 386, 16. Cf. ge-leáfa.

**ge-leáf;** *adj. Having belief.* v. un-geleáf.

**ge-leáf;** *adj. Leafy:*—Geleáf hrīs *frondes,* Wrt. Voc. ii. 39, 69. *Frondes,* s. *dicuntur virgultae vel umbras* geleáf rīs *vel* bogas, 151, 7. [*O. H. Ger.* ge-loub *virens, frondens.*]

**ge-leáfa,** an; *m. Leave:*—Be þes cynges gelǽfan (leáfe, lǽfe, *v. ll.*), Chr. 1043; P. 165, 10. [God yaf yleaue þe dyeulen, Ayenb. 50, 16.]

**ge-leáfa.** *Add:* I. *the mental action, condition,* or *habit of trusting to a person* or thing, *trust, faith:*—Þīn āgen geleáfa þe hæfþ gehǽledne *fides tua te saluum fecit,* Bl. H. 15, 27 : Mk. 10, 51: Lk. 18, 41. Þīn geleáfa (*belief in thee*) on ūrum mōde þurhwunige, Hy. 6, 8. Þone gefeán þe þū mid geleáfan tō mē geearnodest, Bl. H. 63, 28. Heó āhte trumne geleáfan tō þǽm Ælmihtigan, Jud. 6: 345. Hē getrymede heora geleáfan, Bl. H. 17, 8. Gif wē willaþ on Drihten gelȳfan ... wē sceolon þone geleáfan mid gōdum dǽdum gefyllan, 23; 10. Ne hī on gewitnesse hæfdon on hiora fyrhđe fæstne geleáfan *nec fides habita est illis in testamento ejus,* Ps. Th. 77, 36. Þ hī rihtne geleáfan habban on þone sōđan God, Ll. Th. i. 326, 12 : 372, 33. Beran in breóstum beorhtne geleáfan, Gū. 770. I a. *belief in God, Christian faith:*—Hē lǽrde þā leóde on geleáfan weg, An. 1682. Þām þe ic līfes ofonn, leóhtes geleáfan, Jul. 378. Hē hī tō geleáfan onbryrde, Bl. H. 107, 2. Leóde lǽran þ hī lifgen on geleáfan, Dōm. 49. II. *mental acceptance of a statement* or *fact:*—Hē wæs þurh þæs mæsse-preóstes lāre on fullum geleáfan heofonrīces *de vitae aeternitate securus,* Ors. 6, 34; S. 290, 12. Hȳ him sylfum sēllan þūhton þonne Crīst; gelugon hȳ him æt þām geleáfan, Hy. 4, 56. Þā men þā þe Godes rīces geleáfan habbađ *the men who believe in God's kingdom,* Bl. H. 55, 17 : 77, 4. Heó geleáfan nōm þæt hī þā bysene from Gode brungen hæfde, Gen. 650. III. *what is believed, the proposition* or *set of propositions held true; the doctrines of a religious system:*—Geleáfa se geleáffulla þes is þ ... ✝ *Fides catholica haec est ut ...,* Ath. Crd. 3. Ān is geleáfa, ān is fulwiht, ān fæder ēce, Hy. 11, 8. Þæs geleáfiican geleáfan *catholice fidei,* Wrt. Voc. ii. 129, 56. Ne gelȳfe ic nō þ hit ge-weorþan mihte ... and ic nō ne wearþ of þām sōþan geleáfan *nec umquam fuerit dies, qui me ab hac sententiae ueritate depellat,* Bt. 5, 3; F. 12, 6. Hē wolde þone Xpes geleáfan (-lǽfan, *v. l.*) geryhtan, Chr. 680; P. 38, 9. Monega þeóda Crīstes geleáfan (*the Christian religion*) onfēngon, Ll. Th. i. 58, 1 : El. 491. Þ hē cunne rihtne geleáfan understandan, Ll. Th. i. 372, 23. Bodiađ beorhtne geleáfan *preach the gospel,* Cri. 483. IV. *a formal statement* of doctrines believed, *a creed:*—Hēr is geleáfa and gebed ... Pater Noster on Englisc ... Se lǽssa crēda, Hml. Th. ii. 596, 1–11. v. un-geleáfa.

**ge-leáfful.** *Add:* I. *having faith,* or *trust:*—Hē wæs Gode geleáffull on his heortan, Shrn. 76, 21. II. *having the Christian faith, Christian:*—Blissian nū eall geleáffull folc, for þon þe for ūs Crīstes blōd wæs āgoten, Bl. H. 91, 7. Godes đeówas hī wurđiađ on geleáffulre geladunge, Hml. Th. ii. 560, 2. Of geleáffullan cynne heó wæs āsprungen, Chr. 1067; P. 201, 8. Þ wīf biđ gehālgad þurh geleáffulne wer, 15. Se eosel þe Crīst on sittan wolde tācnaþ þ geleáffulle folc Judēa (*those of the Jews that believed on him*), Bl. H. 79, 30. Ealle geleáffulle men *all Christians,* 35, 9. II a. used substantively in pl., *believers, Christians, the faithful:*—On þǽre gesihđe wesađ ealle geleáffulle, Bl. H. 13, 28 : 81, 16. Mid geleáffullum hē gefylde þysne middangeard, 11, 8. Heó brōhte eallum geleáffullum ēce hǽlo, 5, 30. Ōþrum geleáffullum

teala dôn, 75, 18. **III.** *catholic, orthodox* :—Geleáfful *catholicus, rectus*, Wrt. Voc. ii. 129, 54. þone geleáffullan geleáfan *catholicam fidem*, Ath. Crd. 1. Seó emniht is on .xii.ᵐᵃ kl. April., swā swā þā geleáffullan rǽderas (*orthodox scholars*) hit gesetton, Lch. iii. 256, 21. Geleáfulra *catholicorum* (*patrum*), An. Ox. 172. Geleáf[ulra] *orthodoxorum*, 4574. **IV.** *of the church*; substantively in pl., *ecclesiastics* :—Ofermódinesse geleáf[ulra] *insolentiam ecclesiasticorum*, An. Ox. 5302. v. riht-, un-geleáffull.

**ge-leáffullic.** v. un-geleáffullic.

**ge-leáffullíce ; adv. I.** *confidently* :—Geleáfullíce *fidenter*, An. Ox. 1335. **II.** *in accordance with faith, faithfully* :—Woerc geleáffullíce uē biseno niomað *opus fideliter imitemur*, Rtl. 62, 23. **III.** *in accordance with the Christian faith* :—Þū eart gelǽred geleáffullíce, Hml. S. 29, 130. v. un-geleáffullíce.

**ge-leáffulnes.** *Add* : v. un-geleáffulnes.

**geleáf-hlystend.** *Substitute* : *One who is being instructed in the faith before baptism, a catechumen, a candidate for baptism* :—Geleáfhlystendes *catacumini*, i. *audientis*, An. Ox. 2207. Geleáfhlystende *competentes* (= baptismi candidati, qui baptismum postulabant, Migne), An. Ox. 7, 202 : 8, 158. Geleáfhlystendra *competentium* (v. Angl. xv. 206), Angl. xiii. 31, 103. Geleáflystendra, An. Ox. 2, 69. Geleáfhlestendra *catechumenorum, auditorum*, Hpt. Gl. 458, 7. v. leáf-hlystend.

**ge-leáfleás.** *Add* :—Nis nán þincg swá láð þám geleáfleásum deófle swá þ hine man gebidde bealdlíce tô Gode, Hml. S. 13, 50. Ic eom begoten mid deáwe . . . and þá geleáfleásan forswǽlede, 7, 231.

**ge-leáfleásness,** e ; *f. Incredulity, want of belief* :—On þám dæge wæs þæra Judéiscra manna geleáfleásnys gewiten fram mannum and riht geleáfa ásprang onmang Godes geladunge, Wlfst. 294, 2.

**ge-leáfleást.** *Add* :—From þǽm þystrum heora geleáfleáste genereð, Lch. iii. 432, 25. Hē wæs þæra hǽþen[r]a láreów on heora geleáfleáste, Hml. S. 29, 7, 84. Seó burhwaru (*of Jerusalem*) forférde for hyre geleáfleáste, Hml. A. 46, 549. For heora geleáfleáste þá þá hí wurðodon hǽþængyld, 102, 5. Ádrǽfde þín lár þá geleáfleáste from mē, Hml. S. 5, 110. Lāriówas ūt gewitun of Angla lande for þǽre geleáfléste þe him þá onsǽge gewearþ, Cht. Crw. 19, 7. Nele ūre heofonlica Fæder ūs syllan þæs deófles geleáflǽste, gif wē hine biddaþ þæt hē ūs sylle sóðne geleáfan, Hml. Th. i. 252, 29.

**ge-leáflic.** *Add* : **I.** *credible, probable* :—Hit is swíðe geleáflic þæt hē hyre miceles ðinges tīðian wylle, Hml. Th. i. 454, 1. Augustinus sǽde þæt ân þing wǽre ungeleáflic . . . For ðyssere twýnunge nolde wē hreppan his ðrowunge. Heó is swāðeáh eall full geleáflic, būton ðām ānum þe Augustinus wiðsæcd, ii. 520, 11–19. **II.** *catholic* :—Þæs geleáflícan geleáfan *catholice fidei*, Wrt. Voc. ii. 129, 56. [*O. H. Ger.* ge-louplîh *credibilis, probabilis* : *Ger.* glaublich.] v. eall-, un-geleáflic.

**ge-leáflíce ; adv. I.** *credibly, in a manner that commands* or *allows belief* :—Hī heofenan ríce mid Hǽlende ástigon swā swā wíse lāreówas geleáflíce secgað (*as we are credibly informed by learned doctors*), Hml. Th. ii. 258, 29. Ús is tô witonne þætte þ wæs geleáflíce gestihtod þæt Jóseph fôr tô Bethlem fram Galilea *we are to know that without doubt it was ordained that Joseph went to Bethlehem from Galilee*, Nap. 81. **II.** *in accordance with Christian belief.* v. riht-geleáflíce. [*O. H. Ger.* ge-louplícho *credibiliter*.]

**ge-leáfnes-word.** v. leáfnes-word.

**ge-leáfsum.** *Add* :—Þá hālwendan men and þá geleáfsuman þá þe tô ūrum Drihtne cóman þá hē tô heofonum ástígan wolde, Bl. H. 117, 9. ¶ tô geleáfsuman so *as to produce belief* :—Uneáðe mæg mon tô geleáfsuman gesecgan swā monigfeald yfel *in tanta malorum multitudine difficillima dicta fides*, Ors. 3, 9 ; S. 128, 20. Cymð se lytega sǽtere and āteleð him eall ðæt hē ǽr tô góde gedyde, and gerzcd him ðonne tô geleáfsuman (*tells him and gets him to believe*) ðæt hē sié so gesǽlgosta on eallum cræftum, Past. 463, 13. v. un-geleáfsum.

**ge-leáfsumness.** v. un-geleáfsumness.

**ge-leahtrian.** *Add* : **I.** *to reproach, blame, upbraid* :—Hē gehyspte Arrianum . . . and hine geleahtrode, swā swā hit gebyrede *Arriano exprobravit ut debuit*, Gr. D. 238, 15. Hē wæs geleahtrod from Gode *increpatur a Domino*, Past. 355, 1. Gelaechtrad (*printed* gelaechtnad, Wrt. Voc. ii. 110, 45 : Txts. 69, 1029) *hoctatus* (*hortatus*, Wrt.), Wülck. Gl. 26, 38 *and* Corp. Gl. H. 63, 141. Geleahtrod, Wrt. Voc. ii. 43, 9. Sió geleahtrad *notetur*, 61, 28. Geleahtrode sýn míne fýnd *confundantur inimici mei*, Ps. Th. 34, 4. **II.** *to vitiate, corrupt* :—Gif hine mon leahtorfulne ongit . . . him mon secge þæt hē þanon gewíte, þe lǽs þe hē mid his yrmðe ôþre geleahtrige (*ne eius miseria alii vitientur*), R. Ben. 109, 20. Geleahtrod mid heáfodlicum gyltum *vitiatus capitalibus criminibus*, Ll. Th. ii. 196, 16.

**ge-leánian.** *Add* : **I.** *to repay* a debt, loan, &c. :—Ic wille, gif ic ǽnigum menn ǽnig feoh unleánod hæbbe, þæt míne māgas þæt hām geleánian, Cht. Th. 491, 6. **II.** *to recompense, remunerate* :—Byð geleánod *remunerari*, An. Ox. 42, 1. (1) *to give remuneration for* well-doing (*acc.*) *to a* person (*dat.*) :—Drihten ealle þá gód mannum geleánað mid twyfealdre méde éces lífes, Bl. H. 101, 23. (2) *to give recompense* for loss, suffering, &c. (*gen.*) :—þá þá seó tíd neálǽhte þ

him sceolde beón geleánod his swā mycelre þrowunge and geþylde *cum tempus esset, ut tanta ejus patientia remunerari debuisset*, Gr. D. 282, 5. (3) *to repay, requite* injury, wrong-doing, &c. :—Him ofðyncð ðæt hē hit suā geðyldelíce forbær ðæt hē ðæt bismer ne forgeald, and ðencð ðæs tīman hwonne hē hit wyrs geleánian mæge *ut . . . se non reddidisse contumelias doleat, et deteriora rependere, si occasio praebeatur, quaerat*, Past. 227, 23. [*O. Sax.* gi-lônôn : *O. H. Ger.* ge-lônôn *retribuere, remunerare, recompensare.*]

**ge-leást.** Dele.

**ge-leccan.** *Dele last passage, and add* : **I.** *to moisten, irrigate* land :—Geleht eorðe *irrigata terra*, Scint. 50, 14. Geleht lyftum, Met. 20, 98. **II.** *to moisten the lips of* a person, *give drink to* a person :—Gif hē hyne sylfne mid þǽm ǽspryngum Godes worda gelecð, and his mód mid þǽre swētnysse þæs gāstlican gedrinces gefylled, hē seleð þæs þonne dryncan his þyrstendum móde, Ll. Th. ii. 430, 5.

**ge-lecg.** v. lim-gelecg.

**ge-lecgan.** *Add* : **I.** *with a material object.* (1) *to lay, place* :—Gyf þysse wyrte sǽd man ofer þá scorpiones gelegð, Lch. i. 248, 23. Noldon hî þæt feoh gelecgan on heora fǽtelsum, Hml. Th. ii. 250, 17. Hē wæs on ðissere beðunge geléd, i. 86, 24. On scríne geléd *in sarcofago delatum*, An. Ox. 2905. Gelegdum *jactatis*, Wrt. Voc. ii. 48, 44. (2) *to settle the regulations concerning* an object, *determine by law the character of* :—Se wudu is gemǽne swā hē on ældum tímum gelægd wæs *sylva, sicut antiquis temporibus lege cautum erat, est communis*, C. D. iv. 202, 13. **II.** *with a non-material object, to lay* a command, task, &c., upon a person :—' Ābeódað míne ǽrende tô ðām gemóte . . . and cýðað hwæm ic mínes landes geunnen hæbbe ' . . . Heó ridon tô ðām gemóte and cýðdon . . . hwæt heó on heom geléd hæfde, C. D. iv. 55, 9. [*Goth.* ga-lagjan *to lay, lay up*: *O. H. Ger.* ge-leggen *ponere, mittere, dis-, re-ponere*.]

**ge-léd, -loed, -leód, gloed** *glosses* catasta (*catasta instrumentum torquendi, genus lecti ferrei, quo, impositis Christianis, ignis supponebatur*, Migne) :—Catasta, *genus supplicii vel woepe, eculeo simile, nomen ludi vel* geléd, *quadrupalim*, Wrt. Voc. ii. 129, 45. Geloed (gloed, Ep., geleód, Erf.) *catasta*, Txts. 47, 363. ¶ the same obscure word seems intended in the following two (not independent) glosses :—Gæleð *catesta*, Wrt. Voc. i. 288, 24 : ii. 17, 5. Of the five forms which here gloss *catasta* the only one to which a meaning may easily be given is *gloed*, which elsewhere translates *carbo*. This form might apply to the fire used in the form of torture denoted by *catasta*. There seems no root with which to connect *-lôd-*, mutated forms of which would appear as *-loed-, -léd, -leód-* (?), and *gæled* looks like a gloss to *cantat.*

**ge-léf (?)** *weak* :—Geleófe yldo *aetate provectae*, Bd. 3, 8 ; Sch. 222, 1.

**ge-léfed.** *Add* : **I.** *weakened, injured, infirm* :—Gif nýten byð deád oððe gelewed *si jumentum mortuum fuerit aut debilitatum*, Ex. 22, 10, 14. Oð þ se dǽl þæs líchoman þe ádeádode wæs and gelewed tô þǽre ǽrran hǽlo becume, Lch. ii. 284, 18. Hē gehǽlde mistlíce gebrocode men, blinde and deáfe and dumbe and mistlíce gelewede, Wlfst. 99, 4. Hēr syndan þurh synleáwa sāre gelewede tô manege, 165, 26. **II.** *of age, advanced. Take here* gelýfed *in Dict., and add* :—Þára ðe gelýfdre yldo. (geleófe yldo, *v. l.*) wǽron earum quae aetate provectae erant, Bd. 3, 8 ; Sch. 222, 1. Gelýfdre yldo *provectioris aetatis*, 4, 24 ; Sch. 482, 12. [*O. Sax.* gi-lêbôd (*of Lazarus* 'ulceribus plenus.')] v. ā-léfian, *and cf.* -lǽw, -lǽweo.

**ge-léfen.** v. ge-lífen : **ge-legen.** v. smeá-gelegen : **ge-lêgeo.** v. ge-lêgu.

**geleger-gild** *glosses* Lupercalia :—Gelegergield *Lupercalia*, Wrt. Voc. ii. 53, 2. Cf. gál-freóls.

**ge-legerod** *confined to bed by sickness* :—Hē on ðám lande ðā gelegered weard, Hml. Th. ii. 152, 23. Binnon feówertig geára fæce næs nán man gelegerod on eallum ðām folce, 196, 13.

**geleger-scipe.** v. dirne-gelegerscipe.

**ge-légu (?), -legu (?)** *a tract of land.* Cf. (?) leáh(-g). *In the following compounds* :—Confiniae terrae, ab australi plaga Uuisleág . . . a septemtrionale Meósgelégeo (-leg-?), C. D. B. i. 266, 26. On marge wei and Grimgelæge, C. D. v. 136, 2. Wið rāhgelæga, iii. 391, 32.

**ge-lemian** *to cripple, disable.* v. ge-lǽmed *in Dict.* : **ge-land.** *See next word.*

**ge-lenda.** *Substitute* : *One rich in landed estates* :—Gelenda, landspēdig *locuples* i. *dives*, An. Ox. 3154. v. ge-lend *in Dict.*

**ge-lendan.** *Add* : **I.** *to go to* land from the water, *to land* :—Hí oferreówon ðone brym and gelendon on ðám lande þe is gehāten Gerasenorum (*enauigauerunt ad regionem Gerasenorum . . . et cum egressus esset ad terram*, Lk. 8, 26–27), Hml. Th. ii. 378, 24. **II.** *to go, proceed.* (1) *of persons* :—Conon gelende tô Ahtēna *Conon Athenas pergit*, Ors. 3, 1 ; S. 98, 23. Hē þôhte þæt hē on þā burgware on ungearwe becôme ; ac hit him weard ǽror cūþ . . . þā gelende hē tô ānre ôþerre byrig (*castellum quoddam occupat*), 4, 5 ; S. 166, 33. Gecwǽdon þæt þá hām gelendon *eos Spartam remittunt*, 1, 14 ; S. 56, 25. (2) *of things*. (a) *material* :—Nis nán tô þæs lytel ǽwelm þ hē þá sǣ ne gesêce, and eft of þére sǣ gelent in on þā eorþan *there is no*

*spring so small that it do not make its way to the sea, and again from the sea it goes into the earth,* Bt. 24, 1; F. 80, 25. Ðæt scip . . . būton ðā rōwend hit teón, sceal fleótan mid ðý streáme : ne mæg hit nō stille gestandan, būton . . . mon mid rōðrum ongeán tió ; elles hit gelent mid ðý streáme, Past. 445, 13. (b) non-material :—Ic wolde witan hwæðer (= hwider ?) þū wēne þæt se wīsdōm þonne gelænde, oððe seó clēnnes, . . . ðonne se man gewīte, oððe hwanon heó ǽr cumen, oððe hwǽr hý sīen, Solil. H. 51, 6.

**ge-lengan** *to call for :*—Gelængdum dǽdum *pervocatis actibus,* Hy. S. 90, 9. v. ge-langian.

**ge-lengan** *to lengthen. Add : I. to extend, increase the amount of :*—Ne durre wē ðās bóc nā miccle swīðor gelengan, Hml. Th. ii. 520, 4. Wē willað þysne cwyde gelencgan, Hml. S. 24, 81. Æfter þæs gyltes gemete sceal beón gelencged (-lengen, *v. l.*) þǽre āmānsumunge gemet *secundum modum culpe excommunicationis debet extendi mensura,* R. Ben. 48, 15. **II.** *to prolong* an action, state, condition, &c. :—Munecas þǽre tīde lof mid kyrriole gewurðiað ; hwæt hig oft þ lof gelengað, Angl. viii. 320, 7. Hī gelencgdon ðā gebedu, Hml. S. 9, 22. Þæt hé his gebed gelenge (his gebed beó gelend *oratio pretendatur*), R. Ben. I. 53, 12), R. Ben. 46, 2. Þ hé his līf gelengde, Hml. S. 3, 599. Swylce hī magon heora līf gelengan, Hml. Th. i. 100, 21. Gelenced *proteletur (disputatio nequaquam ulterius),* An. Ox. 5355. Elðeódignys mīn gelængd is *incolatus meus prolongatus est,* Ps. L. 119, 5. Gelengedre letanian *prolongata letania,* Angl. xiii. 405, 580. **III.** *to protract, perform slowly, draw out :*—Se sealm sý gecweden būtan antefene, and hē sý on swēge gelencged hwæthwāra *psalmus dicatur sine antiphona subtrahendo (=protrahendo) modice,* R. Ben. 37, 8. **IV.** *to defer :*—Hopa þe byð gelencged geswenced sāwle *spes quae differtur affligit animam,* Scint. 130, 9. Remmingce wæs gelengced (*debita vicissitudo, quasi quodam dilationis) obstaculo, tricabatur* (i. *tardebatur*), An. Ox. 5451. [*O. H. Ger.* ge-lengen *extendere, protendere, protrahere.*]

**ge-lenge.** *Add :*—Wel is eác tō warnianne þ man wite þ hý (*the bride and bridegroom) þurh mǽgsibbe tō gelænge ne beón,* Ll. Th. i. 256, 10. [*Cf. O. H. Ger.* ge-lang *affinis ;* ge-lengida *affinitas.*] v. līc-gelenge (?).

**ge-leóf ;** *adj. Dear, affectionate, loving* one another :—Mid geleófre fērrǽdene *contubernali sodalitate,* Hpt. Gl. 461, 66. On þǽre fīftan cneórysse geleófe men hig mōton gesamnigan *in quinto propinquitatis gradu licet caris hominibus in matrimonium ire,* Ll. Th. ii. 152, 23. [Þar two ileove in one bedde liggeþ iclupt, O. and N. 1047. *O. H. Ger.* ge-liob *loving* one another.]

**ge-leóf** *weak.* v. ge-lēf : ge-leófan. v. ge-līfan : ge-leofian. v. ge-libban : **ge-leógan.** *Add :* cf. ā-leógan.

**ge-leóhtan** *to provide light* (?) :—Ic geann ðæs landes æt Rægene . . . ðām bisceope tō geleóhtenne *I grant the land at Rayne to the bishop for the provision of lights for the church* (cf. leóht-, weax-gescot), C. D. iii. 305, 4.

**ge-leoran.** *l.* -leóran, *and add : I. of persons, to pass away from this life. die :*—Ne gelióreð (*transibit*) cneóreso ðiós oð ðæt alle ðās geworðe, Mk. L. R. 13, 30. Gelióreð *praeteribit,* Lk. L. R. 21, 32. Geliórade *obiit,* Lk. p. 2, 4. Ðý dæge ðe se abbod geleórde, Shrn. 65, 21. Gif hē giliórde (geliórade, L.) *si obisset,* Mk. R. 15, 44. **II.** *of things.* (1) *to pass from the body :*—Þ se drænc sý ðe ǽr geleóred, Lch. iii. 20, 3. (2) *to pass away, cease :*—Oþ þ seó ýst forð geleóred *until the storm passes,* Shrn. 81, 27. (3) *to pass away, cease to exist, come to nothing :*—Heofon and eorðo geliórað (*transibunt*), wordo mīne ne gelióreð (*praeteribunt*), Mt. L. 24, 35. Gilióred (geliórad, L.) bioðon *transibunt,* Lk. R. 21, 32. Gehlióred, Mk. L. 13, 31. v. fore-geleóran, forþ-geleóred.

**ge-leórednes.** *Add : I. a passing from one place to another, a migration.* v. Dict. **II.** *a passing from one state to another, ecstasy, transport of a vision.*—On ūplicere gesihþe geleórednesse *in oromate extaseos (raptus),* An. Ox. 405. Geleórednesse *oromate,* i. *in visione somni,* 2278. **III.** *a passing from this world, departure, decease :*—Se dæg wæs tō becumen hire geleórednysse, Hml. S. 33, 285. **III a.** *the anniversary of a person's death :*—On ðone .viii.an dæg þæs mōnþes byþ þæs bisceopes geleórudnes Sēi Audomari, Shrn. 127, 20. v. forþ-geleóredness.

**ge-leórendlic.** *For Rtl. 28, I substitute :*—Ðisses woruldes giliórendlices *hujus seculi transeuntis,* Rtl. 18, 1.

**ge-leórnes.** *Add :* (1) *departure, decease :*—Gefylled woeron dagas geliórnises his (*assumtionis eius*), Lk. L. 9, 51. Ðe doeg geliórnisse his *diem recessus sui,* Jn. p. 1, 14. Æfter giliórnise ūsra *post obitum nostrum,* Rtl. 124, 7 : Shrn. 50, 2. Æfter forðsīþe and æfter geleórnesse þāra twēgra *post decessum duorum,* Gr. D. 192, 8. Ðæs giliórnise (*depositionem*) wē gimērsia, Rtl. 89, 14. Giliórnise hiora *exitus illorum,* 86, 16. (2) *the anniversary of a person's death :*—On ðone nygeðan dæg ðæs mōnðes bið Sēe Pegean geleórnes, Shrn. 48, 38 : 51, 28 : 52, 15, and often.

**ge-leornian.** *Dele ‘ inquire,’ and last passage. Add : I. to acquire*

*knowledge of* a subject *by study, thought, instruction,* &c. :—þ sē ne durre beón wīsdōmes lāreów ōðres mannes, sē þe hine ǽr him sylfum ne geleornað, Gr. D. 12, 27. Hē fram Godes ængle þ bebod underfēng and þurh nǽnigne menniscne man ne geleornode *mandatum ab angelo didicit, quod per hominem non cognovit,* 13, 24. Bonifatius lāreówdōme hē geleornode Crīstes feówer bēc, and getæl rihtra Eástrena, and monige ōðre, ðā de belumpon tō ciriclicum þeódscipum, ðe hē on his ðeódscype geleornian ne mihte, Bd. 5, 19 ; Sch. 660, 11–17. Ðā bóc wendan on Englisc . . . swǽ swǽ ic hié geliornode æt Plegmunde mīnum ærcebiscepe . . . Sidðan ic hié geliornod hæfde, swǽ swǽ ic hié forstōd . . . ic hié on Englisc āwende, Past. 7, 18–25. Leorniaþ wīsdōm, and þonne gē hine geleornod hæbben, ne forhogiaþ hine, Bt. 16, 1 ; F. 50, 26. Him sealde Iustinus āne Crīstene bóc . . . Siþþan hē þā geleornod hæfde, Ors. 6, 12 ; S. 266, 22. Þā hē þās bóc hæfde geleornode, Bt. proem. ; F. viii. 8. **II.** *to acquire skill in the doing of* something *by study, thought, instruction,* &c., *to learn* to do. (1) *with acc.* :—Se deófol cann eall þæt yfel and ealle þā drýcræftas þe ǽfre ǽnig ǽfre geleornode, Wlfst. 101, 3. (2) *with clause :*—Sē sit on wōlberendum setle, sē ðe gesceádwīslīce tōcnāwan con gōd and yfel, and ðeáh geleornað ðæt hē dēð ðæt yfel *in cathedra pestilentiae sedere sed ex ratione mala discernere, et tamen ex deliberatione perpetrare,* Past. 435, 23. þā geleornedon his byrelas him betweónum hū hié him mehten þ līf oþþringan, and him gesealdon ātor drincan : þā forlēt hē his līf *Alexander, cum ministri insidiis venenum potasset, interiit,* Ors. 3, 9 ; S. 136, 14. Hē geleornige ðæt hē selle Gode his āgne breósð, Past. 81, 25. Geleornigen ðā bearn ðæt hī hīeren hira ieldrum, 191, 1, 4. **III.** *intrans. To acquire knowledge of a subject, receive instruction :*—Ēghwelc sē ðe gehērde from feder and geliornade, Jn. L. R. 6, 45. Huu ðes stafas wāt, mid ðý ne geliornade, 7, 15. **III a.** *to get instruction from a book, to read :*—Ðā geleornas *legentes,* Mt. p. 13, 8. **IV.** *to get knowledge of* a fact, *be informed of, become acquainted with :*—Geliornigen ðā blīðan on ðǽre ðreáunga ðæt hié him ondrǽden, and gehiéren ðā unblīðan ðā leán ðæs gefeán ðe hié tō hopiað *discant laeti ex minarum asperitate, quod timeant ; audiant tristes praemiorum gaudia, de quibus praesumant,* Past. 187, 17. **V.** *to learn* from a book, *read :*—Tō eácan þan [þe hē] sylf geleorned hæfde on bōcan, Chr. 995 ; P. 128, 24. Ne ðis geleornadon þte dyde Dauid *nec hoc legistis quod fecit Dauid?,* Lk. L. 6, 3. [*O. H. Ger.* ge-lernen(-en).]

**ge-leoþewǽcan.** v. ge-liþewǽcan : **ge-leoþian.** v. ge-liþian.

**ge-les.** *Add :*—Þis gewin and þyssum gelic (þis gelis ? cf. 5, 7 ; Sch. 585, 1 *where gelice and geliese are two readings*), þeós gēmen þē wæs, and þis þū hyrde dydest *hic labor, hoc studium, haec tibi cura, hoc pastor agebas,* Bd. 2, 1 ; Sch. 108, 14. Hē barn in gelise (*studio*) ǽwfæstes līfes, 4, 27 ; Sch. 511, 11. Tō ǽfestnesse geliese, 5, 7 ; Sch. 585, 1. Gesǽligum gelesum ābysegad *studiis occupatus felicibus,* 5, 19 ; Sch. 660, 21. Betwyx geleso (-leoso, *v. l.*) þǽre godcundan leornunge, 3, 13 ; Sch. 249, 11.

**ge-lēsan.** *Dele second passage (v. ge-lǽswian), and see* ge-līsan : **ge-leswian.** v. ge-lǽswian : **ge-leðran.** v. ge-liþran.

**ge-lettan.** *Add : I. to hinder* a person from going where he intends, *to stop :*—Hē wolde tō his mēder . . . ac Godwine hine gelette, Chr. 1036 ; P. 158, 22. Flōdwylm ne mæg manna ǽnigne ofer Meotudes ēst gelettan, An. 518. Hē weard þurh weder gelet, Chr. 1097 ; P. 233, 17. Hē him swā gelettum and swā genýddum hwæthugu getǽse gedyde *ei commodum coacto renitentique dedit,* Gr. D. 39, 26. Se cyng geáxode þ his feónd gelætte wǽron, and ne mihten nā geforðian heora fare, Chr. 1085 ; P. 216, 7. **I a.** *to hinder* a person from a journey (*gen.*) :—Ne gelette ūs þæs sīðes se feónd, Wlfst. 252, 16. **I b.** *the object a personification :*—Forþum oð oreldo gōd weorc hine (*death*) hwīlum gelettað, Bt. 41, 2 ; S. 142, 19. **II.** *to hinder* a person from acting, *impede :*—Ðonne ðæt flǽsc bið gelett (-let, *v. l.*) mid sumum broce, Past. 257, 1. **II a.** *to keep* a person from doing something (*gen.*) :—Hit hine ðāra synna gelett ðe hē dōn wolde, Past. 257, 22. Hine ne meahte Meotudes willan longað gelettan, Gū. 330. **III.** *to hinder* a person from progressing or developing :—Hý bodedon on Rōme Crīstendōm, ac se deófles man hý gedrehte and þæt folc gelette wundorlīce swýðe, Wlfst. 98, 18. **IV.** *to hinder the movement* of a material object :—Þā slōh se cwellere mid þām swurde hire tō, ac seó hālige þrynnys þ swurd gelette, Hml. S. 12, 223. **V.** *to hinder, impede* action, movement, &c. :—Gelet *tricaverit* (si lethi somnus palpebrarum convolatus non *tricauerit*), An. Ox. 8, 414. Gelettan *praepedire (integritatis castimoniam),* 3949. Þæt deófol wyle ǽlces mannes geþanc, gyf hē mæg, swýðe gelettan, Wlfst. 101, 15. Ic nolde þurh gielpcwide gǽstes mīnes frōfre gelettan, Gū. 1210. Ne dorston þā gelettan leng wuldorcyninges word *they durst not longer delay to carry out God's command,* An. 801. Hys sýðfæt wæs geletted, Shrn. 98, 30. **V a.** *to prove a stumbling-block to, to offend :*—Gelette *offenderet* (ne pudibunda nuditas castos *offenderet* obtutus), An. Ox. 3675. [Goth. ga-latjan : *O. Sax.* gi-lettian : *O. H. Ger.* ge-lezzen *retardare.*]

**ge-lēwan.** *Dele, and see* ge-lēfed.

**ge-libban, -lifian, -leofian**; *p.* -lifde, -lifode (-leof-) *To live.* **I.** *to be alive* :—Mid ðӯ gehērdon þte gelifde and gesēne wǣre, Mk. L. 16, 11. **II.** *to pass life* under specified conditions :—Sume on hǣðenscipe gelifdon, Ll. Th. ii. 366, 13. Gif swā biþ geleofad *si sic vivitur*, Ps. L. 185 a, 16. **III.** *to escape spiritual death* :—Ðis dô þte ðū gelifige, Lk. L. 10, 28. **IV.** *trans.* (1) *to have as part of one's life, to experience* :—Ne ondrǣd ðū ðē deáð tô swīðe ; ne geleofað man nǣht miriges ðā hwīle ðe mon deáð ondrǣt *life hath no mirth while death is feared*, Prov. K. 16. (2) *to get by living, to live to do* :—Hē cyng beón sceolde, gif hē hit gelifode *he should have been king, if he had lived to do it*, Chr. 1093; P. 228, 11. Fulne ende þīnes lîfes þū hæfst gelifd *plenam etatis finem habes*, Nar. 30, 11. [*O. H. Ger.* ge-lebēn *to experience, live to see.* Cf. *Ger.* er-leben.]

**ge-líc, es ; n. Substitute :** **I.** *what is like* :—' Ic nāt nānwiht Godes gelîces (*Deo simile*)' . . . ' Ic wondrie þīn, hwī þū secge þæt þū Gode nāwiht gelīces nyte (*nihil te nosse Deo simile*)' . . . Gyf ic wiht him gelīces wiste, ic wolde þat lufian, Solil. H. 15, 13–19. Næfð hē nāht men gelīces *de homine nihil habet*, Gr. D. 46, 28. Næfdon hī māre monnum gelīces ðonne ingeþonc, Met. 26, 93. Nānne mon ne lyst nānes ðinges būton goodes, oððe hwætshwegu ðæs þe goode gelíc biþ. Maniges þinges hī wilniaþ þe full gôd ne biþ, ac hit hæfþ ðeáh hwæthwegu gelīces goode, Bt. 34, 7 ; F. 142, 33. Þisses fugles gecynd fela gelīces beácnað, Ph. 387. **II.** *a similitude, parable* :—Þ gelíc getimbrendes torres gesceáded *similitudinem aedificandae turris exponit*, Lk. p. 8, 14.

**ge-líc. Add :** **I.** *like* some other object. (1) with dat. of object :—Þū eart mihtig Drihten, nis þē ealra gelíc āhwǣr on spēdum *quis similis tibi? potens es, Domine*, Ps. Th. 88, 7. Ic ne geseah ǣnigne mann þē gelícne steóran, An. 494. Ic mæg on ūrum tîdum gelíc anginn þǣm gesecgan *ego poteram similia in diebus nostris narrare*, Ors. 3, 2 ; S. 100, 20. Winde gelícra þonne gemetfæstum monnum, Bt. 37, 4 ; F. 192, 23. Wildiórum gelícran ðonne monnum, 38, 5 ; F. 208, 1. Hwām beón ðäs ðyllecan gelíccran (-lícran, *v. l.*) ðonne ðǣm folce ðe . . . ,' Past. 227, 24. Is seó eággebyrd hîwe stāne gelícast, Ph. 302. Funde hē ôþerne þurh eall þing him þone gelícestan (swīþe gelícne, *v. l.*), Bd. 4, 22 ; Sch. 457, 6. Swā swā geonge men magon gelícoste beón ealdum monnum, Bt. 10 ; F. 28, 33. (2) without dative, the object already indicated or implied :—Gelíc ī ilca gecuēdon *eadem dixerint*, Mt. p. 11, 1, 18. Of þām gelícestan gesceáde *simillima collatione*, An. Ox. 248. (3) with dat. instead of elliptical possessive :—Gedyde ic þæt þū hæfdest mǣgwlite mē gelícne, Cri. 1384. **II.** *like* some other action or condition. (1) with dat. of pronoun and clause stating the action, &c. Cf. *like* as in later times. v. ge-líce :—Hit bið gelíc þām swylce hit swā sӯ . . . bið gelíc þām swylce sunne sӯ āþystrad *it will be just as if it really is so . . . it will be as if the sun is darkened*, Wlfst. 93, 1–5. Seó wíse is gelícost þon þ hit ne byð nyt, þēh þe gebeden sӯ for deófle, Gr. D. 336, 10. Nū is þon gelícost swā wē on laguflôde liðan, Cri. 851. Is þon gelícost swā hē on landsceape stille standan, An. 501. Hwæþer seó sibb sié þǣm gelícost þe mon nime ǣnne eles dropan . . . , Ors. 4, 7 ; S. 182, 23. Is þ endeleás wundor, ðäm gelícost þe on sumes cyninges hîrēde sién gyldenu fatu forsewen and treówenu mon weorþige, Bt. 36, 1 ; F. 172, 18 : Wlfst. 3, 14. Bið þ gelícost þon þe hig æteówen þone staðol hyra geleáfan, Ll. Th. ii. 426, 1. (2) without dat. Cf. L. I :—Dôn dǣdbôte for heáfodlicum gyltum geár oððe twā on hläfe and on wætere, and þe þām lǣssum gyltum wucan oððe mônoð eall be gelícon (*similiter*), Ll. Th. ii. 134, 5. (3) with *swā, swā gelíc* = such :—Anlíce beóð swā þā beón berað būtū ætsomne . . . Swā beóð gelíce þā leásan men, Leás. 24. (4) correlative clauses :—Þyslic mē is gesewen ðis andwearde lîf manna . . . swā gelíc, swā ðū æt swǣsendum sitte . . . , Bd. 2, 13 ; Sch. 165, 17. **III.** used of two or more objects, *like* one another, as predicate, *alike* :—Ealle men hæfdon gelícne fruman *omnem hominum genus simili surgit ab ortu*, Bt. 30, 2 ; F. 110, 7. Gesihþ and gehērnes and gefrēdnes ongitaþ ðone líchoman, and þeáh ne ongitaþ hī hine gelíce, 41, 4 ; F. 252, 8. Ne mæg nān monn habban gelíc lof on ǣlcum londe, for þon þe on ǣlcum lande ne lícaþ þ on ôþrum lícaþ, 18, 2 ; F. 64, 25. Ðā gelícan habbað heóm gelíc, Solil. H. 65, 24. Ne beóð þā leán gelíc, Mód. 76. Se maga and se unmaga ne beóð nā gelíce, ne ne magon nā gelíce byrðene āhebban, Ll. Th. i. 328, 16. Monnes líchoman limu beóþ hwæthwegu tôdǣled ; ac þǣra lima gecynd is þ hie gewyrcaþ ǣnne líchoman, and ðeáh ne beóþ eallunga gelíce, Bt. 34, 6 ; F. 142, 17. Ealle gesceafta þū gesceópe him gelíce (*like one another*), and eác on sumum þingum ungelíce, 33, 4 ; F. 128, 26. Didymus, þ ys gelícust on ūre geþeóde *Didymus (twin), that is just alike in our speech*, Jn. 20, 24 : 21, 2. **IV.** *of like amount, degree,* &c., *equal.* v. ge-líca ; II :—Gelíc *compar*, Ælfc. Gr. Z. 43, 2. (1) *equal* to another (*dat.*) :—Wēnan þ ǣnig þing wǣre betere ðonne God, oþþe him gelíc (cf. nān wuht nis betere ðonne hē, ne emngôd him, 18, 7), Bt. 34, 3 ; F. 136, 30. Se Hālga Gāst is ðām Fæder and ðām Suna gelíc and efenēce, Hml. Th. i. 280, 15. Hē hine sylfne dyde Gode gelícne (*aequalem*), Jn. 5, 18. Hig sint englum gelíce (*aequales*), Lk. 20, 36. Þū dydest hig gelíce (*pares*) ûs, Mt. 20,

**12.** (1 a) object stated in a clause :—Gif hit geweorded þ man unwilles ǣnig þing misdêd, nā bið þ nā gelíc þām þe sylfwilles misdêd (*the two faults are not equal in turpitude*), Ll. Th. i. 328, 22. (2) of several things, *equal* to one another, *the same in each case.* (a) of objects :—Gif hwā ôðres godsunu sleá, sié sió mǣgbôt and sió manbôt gelíc, Ll. Th. i. 150, 14. Mæssepreóstes āð and woruldþegenes is geteald efendӯre (bið gelíc gedêmed, *v. l.*), 182, 15. Ne sîn ealle circan nā gelícre mǣðe wyrðe, 340, 26. Nabbaþ ealle gesceádwîse gesceafta gelícne frӯdôm *libertatem non in omnibus aequam esse constituo*, Bt. 40, 7 ; F. 242, 21 : Solil. H. 65, 25, 21, 22. Cyning and arcebiscop āgan gelícne and efendӯrne mundbryce, Ll. Th. i. 330, 17. Gelíc heá onfeingon mearde *parem acceperunt mercedem*, Mt. p. 18, 13. Manigu wîtu wǣron māran þonne ôðru ; nū sint ealle gelíce, 68, 7. Þ þās Godes gerihta standan ǣghwǣr gelíce, 272, 14. Gehwǣr hit is hefigre, gehwǣr eác leóhtre, for ðām ealle landsida ne sӯn gelíce (*equalia*, Lat. vers.), 434. 31. (b) of actions, conditions, &c., stated in clauses, *equal* (in badness) :—Ne bið nā gelíc þ man wið swustor gehǣme and hit wǣre feorsibb, Ll. Th. i. 404, 27. Gif hwā hwæt ungewealdes gedêþ, ne bið þ eallunga nā gelíc þe hit gewealdes gedêð, 412, 15. (c) with irregular construction :—Gif monnes tunge bið of heáfde ôðres monnes dǣdum gedôn, þ bið gelíc and eágan bôt (*the compensation for*) *pulling out a man's tongue and the compensation for destroying an eye are equal*, Ll. Th. i. 94, 21. (d) *at an equal height, on a level* :—Gif se ord sié ufor þonne hindeweard sceaft, gif hié sién bū gelíc, Ll. Th. i. 84, 18. Gelícere heolre *equa bilance*, An. Ox. 4601. (3) of a comparison, *between equal things, fair* :—' Hwæþer ðära twêgra (*a walker and a crawler*) þincþ þe mihtigra?' Ðā cwæþ ic : 'Nis þ gelíc ; sē biþ mihtigra sē ðe gǣþ, þonne sē þe crӯpþ, Bt. 36, 4 ; F. 178, 15. **V.** *befitting, suitable.* v. ge-líclíc :—Gelíc his geearnungum, Bl. H. 21, 32. Hū ne miht þū gesión þ ǣlc wyrt and ǣlc wudu wile weaxan on þǣm lande sélost þe him betst gerîst. . . . Ælces landes gecynd is þ hit him gelíce wyrta and gelícne wudu tӯdrige *herbas atque arbores intueris sibi convenientibus innasci locis . . . dat cuique natura quod convenit*, Bt. 34, 4 ; F. 148, 19–29. **VI.** *likely, probable* :—Mē gelícost þincð þætte ealle witen eorðbüende þoncolmôde, þæt hî þǣr ne sint, Met. 19, 12. v. an- (on-), un-gelíc.

**ge-líca. Add :** **I.** *the like* of another (*gen. or possessive pronoun*), *one that has the same characteristics as another.* (1) of persons :—Hwæt wǣron hī būton fearra gelícan, þā ðā hī heora fӯnd mid horne líchamlícere mihte potedon?, Hml. Th. i. 522, 24. Sindon hiora gelícan forgitene, Met. 10, 59. Habban þíne ǣhta þíne gelícan, Hml. S. 2, 176. Tô Ðeódríce and tô Nerône and tô manegum heora gelícum, Bt. 16, 1 ; F. 50, 1. (1 a) *the like* of a person, *such a person as* (depreciatory) :—Hwylc eom ic, þ ic ǣfre þus his gelícan (þyslicum men, *v. l.*) þeówie *quis sum ego, ut isti serviam?*, Gr. D. 144, 10. (2) of things :—Nið . . . stala . . . gälscipe . . . and fela ôþre þyssa gelícan (*multae aliae harum similes*), Ll. Th. ii. 174, 35. **II.** *an equal, a peer.* Cf. ge-líc ; IV :—Hit is ungecyndelicu ofermôdgung ðæt se monn wilnige ðæt hine his gelíca ondrǣde *contra naturam est superbire ab aequali velle timeri*, Past. 109, 12. Nis nān wîshādes mann hire gelíca, Hml. Th. ii. 10, 12. Nān mihtigra þe nis, ne nān þîn gelíca, Bt. 33, 4 ; F. 128, 11, 19. Hē næfð nǣnne rícran, ne furþum nǣnne gelícan, 42 ; F. 258, 5. Þæt hié (*the Romans*) swā heáne hié geþôhten þæt hî (*the Carthaginians*) heora (*the Romans*) gelícan wurden, Ors. 4, 6 ; S. 178, 18. Lādige hē hine mid .xi. his gelícena, Ll. Th. i. 154, 8. Hē mǣðe cann on mannum, ge on his gelícum ge on lǣssum mannum, Wlfst. 58, 4. v. efen-, un-gelíca.

**ge-lícan** *to liken.* v. ge-lícian *to make like.*

**gelíc-bisen** *a copy, an imitation ; in a personal sense, an imitator* :—Of his gelícbisene *ex ejus imitatione*, Rtl. 50, 4. Hiora gelícbisin, 91, 37. Gimaco ī gilícbiseno Godes *imitatores Dei*, 12, 11.

**ge-líccettan.** v. ge-lícettan.

**ge-líccian** *to lick* :—Ðā hundas his wunda gelíccedon, Hml. Th. i. 330, 22. [*O. H. Ger.* ge-lecchôn *lambere.*]

**gelíce. Add :** **I.** *in like manner, similarly* :—Eft gelíce *ibidentidem*, Wrt. Voc. ii. 47, 50. (1) with dat. (a) of a noun, *in the manner of, in the same way as, as in the case of* :—Sôðfæste men sunnan gelíce in heora fæder ríce scînað (*justi fulgebunt sicut sol in regno patris sui*, Mt. 13, 43), Sat. 307 : Ph. 601. Hié scînað englum gelíce, El. 1320. Heofon bū āðenedest hӯde gelíce *extendens coelum sicut pellem*, Th. 103, 3 ; 101, 3. Kyningas beóð eallum mannum gelíce ácende, and ôðrum mannum gelíce sweltað, Solil. H. 59, 21–23. Hē mæg streámas gefeterian, þæt þū mid fôte miht on treddian eorðan gelíce, Ps. Th. 65, 5. Seó sāwl færð hweóle gelícost, Met. 20, 217. (b) with pronoun (þām), *like that, similarly* :—Gelíc þon *similiter*, Mt. p. 17, 6 : p. 20, 4. Gelíce þām Ænglisc sceal Wyliscan rihte wyrcean, Ll. Th. i. 356, 15. Genim ðäs wyrte þe man *rutam* and þām gelíce (*with nearly the same form*) ôðrum naman rūdan nemneþ, Lch. i. 198, 20 : 234, 11. Genim þäs wyrte þe man *coliandrum* and ôþrum naman þām gelíce cellendre nemneð, 218, 16 : 176, 18 : 220, 9 : 226, 20 : 230, 3 : 236, 11. (2) with *swā* :—Swā gelíce *similiter*, Ps. L. 67, 7. Hē ne dyde þæslíce ī

swā gelíce ǽlcere þeóde *non fecit taliter omni nationi*, 147, 20. Swā gelíce bið þám gódum and ðám yfelum, Bt. 36, 4; F. 178, 19 : Chr. 1067; P. 202, 15. Swae gelíc *similiter*, Mt. p. 11, 1. Þ mónan triów gelíce swá on niht dyde, Nar. 27, 18. **II.** *in like degree, equally* :—Gelíce *pariter*, Wrt. Voc. ii. 116, 49. (1) with adj. or adv. (word or phrase) :—Hí sindon ealle gelíce mihtige, Hml. Th. ii. 42, 25. Simle hé biþ gelíce manþwǽre, Bt. 42; F. 258, 9. Ǽgþres gelíce micel be gewihte, Lch. i. 208, 4 : ii. 124, 17. Gelíce lang, iii. 258, 1. Hí syndon Gode gelíce leófe, Wlfst. 300, 5. Wintres and sumeres wuda bið gelíce blédum gehongen, Ph. 37. Nǽðer ne hí þeder gelíce eáðe cumað, ne hí þér gelíce eáðe ne beóð, Solil. H. 44, 11. Þes moncwealm wæs ofer ealle menn gelíce *aura generali cunctos tabe confecit*, Ors. 3; S. 102, 9. (1 a) *equally* with another :—Gelíce *aeque* (*ut collega edoctus*), An. Ox. 2303. His sáwl bið gelíce (*aeque*) clǽne, ealsuá þ cild bið, Ll. Th. ii. 178, 32. (2) with a verb :—Næs his hergiung on þá fremdan ána, ac hé gelíce slóg þá þe him wǽron mid farende *nec minor ejus in suos crudelitas, quam in hostem rabies fuit*, Ors. 3, 9; S. 130, 20. Þá folc feóllon on ǽgðere healfe gelíce *pari pugna discessum est*, 4, 10; S. 198, 5. Se deáð þone rícan gelíce and þone heánan forswelgþ, Bt. 19; F. 68, 33. Se Hálga Gást gǽð of ðám Fæder and of ðǽm Suna gelíce, Hml. Th. i. 280, 17 : 406, 29. Þér gǽð gelíce bót tó eallum *compensation is made to the same amount in all the cases*, Ll. Th. i. 98, 16. Ealle cyrcan godcundlíce habban hálgunge gelíce, 340, 27. For hwám nǽron eorðwelan ealle gedǽled leódum gelíce ?, Sal. 343. (2 a) with a dative :—Ne lufige ic nánwiht þisses andweardes lífes ofer þæt, ne forþum þám gelíce, Solil. H. 25, 18. **III.** with pronominal forms and clauses, equivalent to the later *like as* with the clauses introduced by these two words, *in the same way as;* in hypothetical clauses, *just as if* :—Wé gelíce sceolon leánum hleótan, swá wé weorcum blódun, Cri. 783. Cnuca mid smerwe þám gelíce þe ðú clyþan wyrce, Lch. i. 108, 10 : 144, 18. Hé dyde gelíce þon swylce hé slépe, Gr. D. 85, 7. Beóð þínes wífes welan gelíce swá on wíngearde weaxen berigean *uxor tua sicut vitis abundans*, Ps. Th. 127, 3. Hé spræc gelícost ðæm ðe hit hwelchwugu syn wǽre, Past. 397, 28 : Ors. 5, 1; S. 214, 4. Hé fór tó ánre byrg gelícost þǽm þe hé hié ábrecan þóhte, 5, 7; S. 230, 1 : 6, 31; S. 286, 15 : 6, 36; S. 294, 11. Wé synd þám gelícost gescapene on þissum worulde þe sum cyning háte sum forworht wíf on carcern dón . . ., Wlfst. 2, 18. Efne þǽm gelícost swylce . . ., Bl. H. 221, 14. **III a.** with ellipsis of verb in the clause :—Deáð hit lufade þér gelíce swilce lífes ingang *mortem videlicet ut ingressum vitae amabat*, Gr. D. 4, 27. Dropeteð blód swá þon gelícost þe tóbrocen fæt, Lch. ii. 230, 25. **III b.** gelíce and (with a clause), *in the same way as* :—Gelíce and mon mǽd máwe, hié wǽron þá burg hergende and sleánde, Ors. 2, 8; S. 92, 15. (v. and; **IV.**) [*O. Sax.* gi-líko : *O. H. Ger.* ge-líhho.] v. on-, un-gelíce.

**ge-lícettan;** *p.* te. **I.** *to imitate* :—Gelíccetton *simulare* (*gestit simulare sui perpendicula patris*, Ald. 158, 4), Wrt. Voc. ii. 91, 66. **II.** *to make a thing appear like something better than it is, to give an appearance of goodness to* a thing :—Ðonne hwá on ðá leásunga beséhð, ðonne ne mæg hé of, ac sceal ðonne niéde ðencean hú hé hié gelícettan mæge, Past. 239, 13. Oft ungemetlico forgifnes bið gelícet, ðæt mon wéned ðæt hit sié mildheortnes, ond oft ungemetlicu irsung bið gelícet, ðæt menn wénað þæt hit sié ryhtwíslic anda *saepe inordinata remissio pietas creditur, et effrenata ira spiritalis zeli virtus aestimatur*, Past. 149, 9–11. **II a.** *to make to appear like to* (tó) :—Sceal se reccere witan ðæt ðá undeáwas beóð oft gelíccette (-lícette, *v. l.*) tó gódum ðeáwum and tó mægenum ðurh leásunga *scire rector debeat, quod plerumque vitia virtutes se esse mentiuntur*, Past. 149, 3. **III.** *to act as if doing what is not really done, to pretend* :—Ðeáð ðe gód ðiégellíce dóð, and swá ðeáh on sumum weorcum gelíccetað ðæt hí openlíce yfel dón *qui bona occulte faciunt, et tamen quibusdam factis publice de se mala opinari permittunt*, Past. 449, 21. **IV.** *to obtain by false pretences* :—Ðæt hié gegítsien and gelícetten æt ðǽm ungetýdum folce wísdómes naman *ut apud imperitum vulgus scientiae sibi nomen extorqueant*, Past. 365, 22.

**ge-lícgan.** *Add:* **I.** of living creatures. (1) *to be in a prostrate* or *recumbent position* :—Hé gelæg (*jacebat*) tó dura his, Lk. L. 16, 20. In ðæm gelæg menigo micelo, in. L. R. 5, 3. (2) *to assume a prostrate* or *recumbent position* :—Benedictus eóde tó ðæs cnapan líce, and ðǽr on uppon gelæg, Hml. Th. ii. 182, 15. (3) *to lie sick, be confined to bed* :—Hé gefeóll of ánre stægere and for ðý gelæg (*eccidit per cancellos coenaculi sui, et aegrotavit*, 2 Kings 1, 2), Hml. S. 18, 232. Gelegen wæs swǽr Sýmónes febrende wæs *decumbebat socrus Simonis febricitans*, Mk. L. R. 1, 30. (4) *to lie with a person, have sexual intercourse with* :—Gif man wið cyninges mægdenman geliged, Ll. Th. i. 6, 4, 11, 13 : 10, 6. Gif man his esnes cwynan geliged, 24, 9. Gif óðer mon mid hire gelǽge ǽr, 68, 17. **II.** of inanimate things. (1) material, *to rest in a horizontal position on a surface* :—Þæs hálgan weres líc on þám ceosole gelæg, Hml. S. 37, 271. (2) non-material, *to be appointed* (cf. what *lies* before a person = what is to happen to him) :—Gif ðæt God geteód habbe, ond mé ðæt on láne gelíð ðæt gesibbra ærfeweard

fordcymeð, C. D. ii. 121, 26. **III.** of land, *to pertain, appertain to* :—Mid eallum ðám túnum ðe him tó gelicgað *cum uillulis omnibus ad se rite pertinentibus*, C. D. iii. 350, 6. **IV.** *to be overcome with fear* :—Mið ðý ðóhte gelegeno (gelegne, R.) woeron *dum mente consternatae essent*, Lk. L. 24, 4. [*O. Sax.* gi-liggian: *O. H. Ger.* ge-ligen, -likken.] v. tó-gelicgende.

**gelíc-gemaca.** *Dele.* v. ge-líc; **IV.** *and* ge-maca.

**ge-lícian;** *p.* ode. **I.** *to make like* or *to be like.* (1) *to imitate.* Cf. ge-líc; **I** :—Tó gelícanne *ad imitandum*, Rtl. 22, 36. Haedno forebeádend gelícad *gentiles prohibens imitandos*, Mk. p. 4, 15. (2) *to liken, compare.* Cf. ge-líc; **IV** :—Geefned bið ł gelíced bið *assimilabitur*, Mt. L. 7, 24. [*Goth.* ga-leikón (*with or without* sik) *to be like, imitate; to liken, compare* : *O. H. Ger.* ge-líhhen *assimilare.*] **II.** *to like* (v. *N. E. D.* like *to seem, look like*), *seem likely.* Cf. ge-líc; **VI** :—Þá geceás hé him áne burg wið þone sǽ, Bizantium wæs háteno, tó ðon þæt him gelícade þ hié þer mehten betst frið binnan habban, and eác þ hié þér gehendaste wǽren on gehwelc lond þonan tó winnanne *maritimam urbem, Byzantium, aptissimam judicavit, ut receptaculum sibi terra marique fieret*, Ors. 3, 7; S. 116, 6.

**ge-lícian** *to please.* *Add:* **I.** with a subject expressed. (1) a person :—Gelícað (*quasi pater in filio*) *complacet* (*sibi*), Kent. Gl. 40. Móna se þreótteóþa . . . cild ácenned . . . ofermód, him sylfum gelícigende, Lch. iii. 190, 14. Mǽden scamfæst, clǽne, wǽrum gelíc(i)gende, 192, 3. (2) a thing :—Him wel gelícode his wurðfulniss, Ælfc. T. Grn. 2, 34. Him gelícade hire þeáwas, Chr. 1067; P. 201, 32. Áscian Italie hiera ágene londleóde hú him þá tída gelícoden, Ors. 5, 1; S. 214, 12. **II.** with indefinite *hit* or without subject expressed :—On þám mé wel gelícað *in quo mihi bene complacuit*, Mt. 17, 5. On þám wel gelícode mínre sáwle, 12, 18 : Bl. H. 29, 28. Woldon hí innian hí þær heom sylfum gelícode, Chr. 1048; P. 172, 21. Hit beforan þe swá gelícode *sic placuit ante te*, Lk. 10, 21. Gif man wíf weddian wille, and hit swá hire and freóndan gelícige, Ll. Th. i. 254, 3. **III.** *to seem good* :—Ús eallum gelícode þá, þ wé sendon Paulus and Barnaban, Ll. Th. i. 56, 19. [*Goth.* ga-leikan : *O. H. Ger.* ge-líhhen *placere, com-placere.*] v. wel-gelícod.

**ge-líclic.** *Add:* Gelíclic *apta*, An. Ox. 4271. v. un-gelíclic; ge-líc; **V.**

**ge-líclíce.** *Add:* v. un-gelíclíce.

**ge-lícnes.** *Add:* **I.** *the quality of being like* or *equal* :—Swá micel gelícnys is on ðyssere Hálgan Ðrynnysse, þæt se Fæder nis ná máre þonne se Sunu on ðære godcundnysse, ne se Sunu nis ná máre þonne se Hálga Gást ; ne nán heora án nis ná lǽsse þonne eall seó Ðrynnys, Hml. Th. i. 282, 32. **II.** *that which resembles an object, a like shape, a semblance* :—Ne wæs þæt ná fugul ána, ac þǽr wæs ǽghwylces ánra gelícnes horses and monnes, hundes and fugles, and eác wífes wlite, Rä. 37, 10. Þú (the dead body) lámes gelícnes, Seel. 19. Hé gestrínde sunu tó his gelícnesse and anlícnysse *genuit ad imaginem et similitudinem suam*, Gen. 5, 3. Tó Godes gelícnisse *ad similitudinem Dei*, **I.** Tó gilícnesse Goddes *ad imaginem Dei*, Rtl. 109, 11. Mid forewittigere gelícnysse *presago* (*vituli*) *simulacro*, An. Ox. 1969. Wolcen on fýres gelícnysse, Chr. 979; P. 122, 25. His eágan wendon on gelícnysse sweltendra manna, Hml. Th. i. 86, 25. ¶ *of likeness in action, on* (þǽre, þá) gelícnesse *after the manner of, in like manner* as :—On gelícnesse *ad instar*, Wrt. Voc. ii. 9, 49. Se wǽta cymþ tó þám tóþan on þǽre gelícnesse þe hyt of húse dropað on stán, Lch. iii. 104, 10. Þ hí . . . yrre fram him ácyrde on þá gelícnesse Niniuítwarona (*instar Nineuitarum*), Bd. 4, 25; Sch. 493, 4. Wel þ gedafenode þ Drihten swá dyde on þá gelícnesse, Bl. H. 67, 12. Efne þǽm gelícost swylce (on ðá gelícnesse swá, Bl. N.) ðá gesceafta him betweónan gefeohtan sceoldan, 221, 14. **II a.** *form, shape, figure* :—Gelícnysse *linia-mento* [this gloss seems to shew that in Wrt. Voc. ii. 79, 47–48, *liniamento* limgelecg, *afflatus* eácen *vel* gelícnes, gelícnes belongs to *liniamento*. The mistake is repeated in Wrt. Voc. ii. 5, 6], An. Ox. 2510 : 8, 131. Æteówed wæs in óðre gelícnisse (on ðórum híwe, W. S.) *ostensus est in alia effigiae*, Mk. R. L. 16, 12. **III.** *the representation of an object, an image, a copy* :—Hwæs gelícnis his þæt *cujus est imago haec ?*, Mt. R. L. 22, 20 : Mk. L. R. 12, 16. Gelícnes *iconisma* (*regale compto stemmate depictum*), Wrt. Voc. ii. 88, 45 : 47, 14. Æples gelícnes on þǽre ascan bið geméted, Ph. 230. Ic hêt wircan þǽr of ánes celfes gelícnysse, Ex. 32, 24. Gelícnessa *signa* (cuncti velut aenea *signa* rigebant), Wrt. Voc. ii. 94, 10. **IV.** *an example, a parable* :—Gelícnesse *paradigmate* (cf. *paradigma* bíspel, bysene, 66, 3), Wrt. Voc. ii. 96, 81. In gelícnessum *in parabulis*, 73, 25. v. an-(on-), un-gelícnes.

**ge-lícung.** *Substitute: Pleasing, pleasure* :—Þ him mon mettas gife . . . swá swá beóþ æppla . . . and hláf gedón on ceald weter oþþe on hát be þǽre gelícunge þæs magan (*according as one or other is agreeable to the stomach*), Lch. ii. 176, 19.

**ge-lícweorþ[e],** -wirþe, -wyrþe ; *adj.* *Pleasing, agreeable to* :—Enoch wæs Gode gelícwurðe, Hml. S. 16, 17. Ðonne mæg hé eówian ðǽr Gode swíðe gelícweorðe (lícwyrðe, *v. l.*) forhæfdnesse, Past. 315, 19. v. wel-gelícwirþe.

ge-lícweorþness (-wirþ-). v. wel-gelícwirþness.

ge-lífan. *Take here* ge-léfan *in Dict., and add*: I. *absolute, to exercise faith*:—Ne ondrǽd þú ðe, gelýf (geléf, L., giléfes, R.) for án, Mk. 5, 36. 'Gif þú gelýfan (geléfe, L. R.) miht, ealle þing synd gelýfedum (ðǽm geléfes *credenti*, L. R.) mihtlíce'... Hé cwæð: 'Ic gelýfe (-léfo, L. R.),' 9, 23-24. Þ ðú mæge þý bet gelýfan, Bt. 36, 3; F. 176, 4. I a. *to hold the true faith, be converted to Christianity*:—Bodiað godspel... sé ðe gelýfð and bið gefullod, sé bið gehealden, Hml. Th. i. 300, 28. Þǽr gelífde ǽrest sum ríce man mid ealre his duguðe (cf. praefectum ciuitatis cum domo sua conuertit ad Dominum, Bd. 2, 16), Chr. 627; P. 25, 23. Þá wigan ne gelýfdon *the men were heathens*, Dan. 58. II. *with preps*. (1) *to believe in* (on) (a) a person, (a) *with acc*.:—Wé geleófað on Drihten, Bl. H. 247, 3. God biþ milde þǽm monnum þe on hine geléfaþ, 47, 33. Manige sculon geleófan on mínne naman, 237, 14. (β) *with dat*.:—Þæt gé geleófon on mínum Drihtne, Bl. H. 247, 22. (b) a thing:—Hé in his meahte gelýfeð, Seef. 108. On mínne geleáfan geleófan, Bl. H. 249, 11. ¶ *where the article of belief or trust is given*:—Ic on God gelýfe, þæt mínre sprǽce spéd folgie, Ps. Th. 55, 4. Ic gelýfe on þé, þæt þú eart se éca kyning, Hy. 3, 37. Ic þæt gelýfe in líffruman, þæt hé mec nǽfre wille ánforlǽtan, Gú. 609. (2) *to believe in the existence of*:—Wé sceolan geléfan on þ éce líf and on þ heofonlíce ríce, Bl. H. 111, 11. (3) *to trust to, look with confidence or hope to* (cf. hopian tó):—Wé ealle tó þe án gelýfað, Hö. 69. Þá cyrcan þe gé tó gelýfað, Wlfst. 232, 16. ¶ *where the subject of trust or hope is given*, (a) *by a noun or pronoun*. Cf. V. 2:—Ic helpe tó þé gelýfe *ad te confugi*, Ps. Th. 142, 10. Gif wé ús tó þám hálgan helpe geléfað, Sat. 291. Hé him tó anwaldan áre gelýfde, frófre and fultum, B. 1272: 909. Ne sceolde þe nán man swelces tó geléfan, Bt. 5, 1; F. 10, 3. (b) *by a clause*:—Gelýfe ic tó Gode, þ úre frið bið betera, Ll. Th. i. 242, 11. Gelýfe ic tó eów, þ gé willan fylstan, 250, 5. Ic gelýfe tó þé, þæt þú mé nǽfre wille ánforlǽtan, An. 1286. Nú is tó gelýfenne tó ðan leófan Gode, þ hí blission mid Xpe, Chr. 1036; P. 158, 36. (4) *to trust to the doing or being of something, expect confidently*:—Ic gelýfe tó lífe æfter deaðe, and ic gelýfe tó árisenne on dómes dæge, and eal þis ic gelýfe þurh Godes mægen and miltse tó geweorðonne, Ll. Th. ii. 262, 14-17. (5) *to consider as* (tó), *think a thing so and so*:—Ðá lytlan synna mon ne geléfð tó nánre synne *minor culpa quasi nulla creditur*, Past. 437, 26. Þéh hí sýn þæs morþres scyldige, hí hit him tó nánre synne ne gelýfaþ, Bl. H. 65, 11. III. *with gen. to believe in the existence or reality of an object, in the actual occurrence of an event or condition, in the genuineness of a document*. (1) *with noun*:—Lisse ic gelýfe leahtra gehwylces, Hy. 10, 54. Hé ne geliéfð ðæs grínes ðe hé mid gebrogden wyrð, ǽr ðon hé hit gefréde, Past. 331, 20. Sé þe wénþ þ þis sóþ ne sié, ðonne ne geléþ hé nánes sóþes, Bt. 36, 3; F. 178, 7. Wé þe gelýfað Crístes ǽristes, Hml. Th. i. 222, 2. Þá þe sóþes gelýfað and georne þæt smeágeað, Wlfst. 4, 8. Ðá Saducie andsacedon ðǽre ǽriste æfter deaðe, and ðá Fariséos geliéfdon ðǽre ǽriste, Past. 362, 6. Búton tweón hí geliéfen ðára leána, 407, 29. Ðætte hié ðý fæstlícor geliéfden ðára écena ðinga *ut ad aeternorum fidem certius roboretur*, 389, 36. Hí noldon æt fruman gelýfan his ǽristes of deaðe, ðá ðá hit him gecýdd wæs, Hml. Th. i. 300, 25: Bl. H. 111, 9. Gif gé nellað geléfan þæs ǽrendgewrites, Wlfst. 214, 20. (2) *with pronoun*:—Ne swylt nán þára þe gelýfð on mé; gelýfst þú ðyses (*credis hoc*)?, Jn. 11, 26. Ic hæbbe eów áreht rihtne geleáfan; sé ðe hine áht þisses tweóð and his gelýfan nele... and sé ðe... his ealles gelýfð, þæs ðe ic rehte þæt ðurh God geweard..., Wlfst. 28, 12-16. Ðá scamleásan nyton ðæt hié untela dóð,... and ðeáh hit mon him secgge, hié his ne geliéfað, Past. 206, 2. Gif hié þæs ne geliéfen *if they will not admit that*, Ors. 5, 1; S. 214, 11. Ic ðé wolde get reccan sume race, ac ic wát þ þis folc his nyle geléfan (*ne illud quidem acquiescent*), Bt. 38, 6; F. 208, 5. (2 a) *with pronoun and clause in apposition*:—Ðæs ic geléfe, þþe ǽlc unriht wítnung sié þæs yfel þe hit déð, Bt. 38, 6; F. 208, 20. Gelýfst þú þæs, þæt ic þé mæge dón gewisran be Gode...?' Geá, ic hys gelífe, Solil. H. 18, 6. IV. *with dat*. (1) *to believe a person when making a statement*:—Gyf hé Israhéla cyning sý, gá nú nyþer of ðǽre róde, and wé gelýfað hym (*credimus ei*), Mt. 27, 42. Hé lícette þ hé sceolde bión se héhsta God, and þ dysige folc him gelýfde, Bt. 38, 1; F. 194, 14: Met. 26, 40. Iôhannes cóm on rihtwísnesse wege, and gé ne gelýfdon him, Mt. 21, 32. Gif hié him ne geléfað, ǽscian Ispánie, Ors. 5, 1; S. 214, 14. Hæbbe man gewitnesse ungeligenra manna þe man gelýfan mæge, Ll. Th. i. 158, 12. (1 a) *where statement to be believed is given*, (a) *directly in a clause*:—Gelýf mé þ seó tíd cymð..., Jn. 4, 21. Geliéf mé, nú ic hit ðé secge, næfst ðú ðær náuht æt..., Bt. 14, 2; F. 44, 6. (β) *indirectly by a pronoun in gen*.:—Se deófles man gealp þæt hé Godes bearn wǽre, and þæt folc him tó swýðe þæs gelýfde, Wlfst. 99, 18. (2) *to believe on a person, give credence to the claims made by or for a person*:—Sēs Adrian geseah hú ánrǽde þá crístenan men wǽron; þá gelýfde hé Críste, Shrn. 59, 26. (3) *to believe a statement, accept as true*:—Þá menn ðe þysum leásungum geléfdon, Bt. 38, 1; F. 196, 8. Wit þæs áwærgdan wordum gelýfdon, Sat. 416. Ne

gelýfdon menn lárum sínum, An. 814. Hí ne woldon wordum Drihtnes gelýfan, Ps. Th. 77, 24. Gehýr monig spel, wite ðeáh hwylcum ðú gelýfan scyle, Prov. K. 72. (4) *to believe in something, accept as genuine*:—Hí noldan his wundrum wel gelýfan *non crediderunt in mirabilibus ejus*, Ps. Th. 77, 31. Nô hwæðere þæt Daniel gedón mihte, þæt hé wolde Metodes mihte gelýfan, Dan. 169. (5) *to trust to*:—Þær gelýfan sceal Dryhtnes dóme sé þe hine deád nimeð, B. 440. V. *with acc*. (1) *to believe*:—Wé gelýfað eall þæt ðæt wé witon, Solil. H. 18, 9. (1 a) *with acc. and clause in apposition*:—Heó sóð ne gelýfde, þæt þǽre sprǽce spéd folgie, Gen. 2383. (2) *to expect confidently for one-self, feel sure of*. Cf. II. 3. ¶:—Ne hé him fultum þǽr fæstne gelýfde, Ps. Th. 51, 6. Ðé wæs þeós hwearfung betere, for þám þæt þú þé betre ne geléfde, Bt. 7, 3; F. 22, 25. VI. *with clause*:—Þú geleófst þ seó wyrd... þás woruld wendan ne mæge, Bt. 5, 3; F. 14, 10. Sceolon gelýfan eorlas hwæt mín æðelo sién, An. 734. ¶ *with passive construction*:—Gif Agustinus is milde and eaðmódre heortan, þonne is hé gelýfed þ hé Crístes geoc bere *si Augustinus mitis est et humilis corde credibile est, quia iugum Christi portet*, Bd. 2, 2; Sch. 117, 3.

ge-lífan *to grant, allow. Take here* ge-léfan, ge-lýfan *in Dict., and add*: I. *to grant something to a person* (*dat*.):—Gilébdae (-lép-) borg *verecundiae concesserim vadimonium*, Txts. 106, 1089. Hé hafað ús gelýfed burh and beágas, Exod. 555. Ágefeno i gileéfeno wópum *indulta fletibus*, Rtl. 40, 5. II. *to grant, allow something to be done*:—Mæht dónde ne geléfes forbeádes *uirtutem facientes non sinit prohiberi*, Mk. p. 4, 9. (1) *with infin*.:—Hé ne walde geléfa ðerh-delfa hús his *non sineret perfodi domum suam*, Mt. L. 24, 43. Is geléfed on symbeldæge gelécnia *licet sabbato curare?*, Lk. L. R. 14, 3. (2) *with gerundial infin*.:—Is geléfed tó seallane geafel?, Mk. L. R. 12, 14: Lk. L. R. 13, 14. (3) *with clause*:—Gileéf þte úsig ne giberne lêg *concede ut nos non exurat flamma*, Rtl. 100, 22. On ðæm dagum is geléfed tó wyrcanne i þ gié wyrce, Lk. L. 13, 14. III. *to allow a person* (*dat*.) *to do something, allow something to be done by a person* (*dat*.). (1) *with infin*.:—Geléf mé geonga *permitte mihi ire*, Lk. L. 9, 59. Þte geléfde him ingeonga, 8, 32. Geléfde him fara *dimitteret*, Mt. L. 14, 22. Gif is geléfed were þ wíf forleta, Mk. L. 10, 2. (2) *with gerundial infin*.:—Ðá néron geléfed (-léfed, R.) him tó gebrúcanne *quos non licebat ei edere*, Mt. L. 12, 4. Ne is giléfed ðe tó habbanne láfe bróðer ðínes, Mk. R. L. 6, 18: Lk. L. 6, 4. (3) *with clause*:—Ne is geléfed ðé þ ðú geniomæ beer ðín, Jn. 5, 10. III a. *to give permission to a person* (*dat*.):—Bédon hine ðá gaastas... and geléfde him (*concessit eis*), Mk. L. R. 5, 13: Lk. L. 8, 32. III b. *absolute, to give permission*:—Hé bædd ðone gröefa þte genôme líchoma: and geléfde ðe groefa, Jn. L. R. 19, 38. IV. *to allow a person* (*acc*.) *to do something*:—Ne geléfde ðá gesprecca *non sinebat ea* (*daemonia*) *loqui*, Lk. L. 4, 41: p. 5, 20. Ðá... gibblinna giléf *quos... cessare concede*, Rtl. 16, 27. v. un-geléfed.

ge-lífan *to make dear* (leóf). *Take here* ge-lýfan *in Dict., and add*: [*O. H. Ger.* ge-liuben *commendare*:—Sih Abraham Druhtine giliubta.]

ge-lífed. *Take here* ge-lýfed *in Dict., and add: endowed with belief, believing*:—Se gelýfeda ætwint ðám frecednyssum ðæra deóflicra costnunga, Hml. Th. i. 368, 32. Hwônlíce gelýfede menn *men of little faith*, 566, 28. ¶ *believing on*, (1) *with acc.*, cf. ge-lífan; II. 1 a a:—Sum man... swíðe gelýfed on þone lyfiendan God, Ælfc. T. Grn. 11, 5. Sum mæden... on ðone Hælend gelýfed, Hml. S. 7, 7. Cômon his ágene landleóde gelýfede (-leóf-, *v. l.*) on God, 14, 172. (2) *with dat.*, cf. ge-lífan; II. 1 a β:—Sume sædon þ hí wæran on Críste gelýfede, Hml. S. 2, 303. v. riht-, un-gelífed; cf. be-lífed.

ge-lífed *allowed, lawful*. v. un-gelífed, *and next word*.

ge-lífedlic. *Take here* ge-lýfedlic *in Dict., and add*:—Gileéfedlicum geadrunge *legitima societate*, Rtl. 110, 18.

ge-lífedlic; *adj. Credible*. v. un-gelífedlic.

ge-lífedlíce; *adv. With confidence in a person, trustfully, in good faith*:—Mardonius hiene wæs georne lǽrende þæt hé hámweard fóre... Xersis swíþe geliéfedlíce his þegne gehiérde, and þonan áfór *regem Mardonius adgreditur, suadens regem in regnum redire oportere... Probato consilio... rex Abydum proficisitur*, Ors. 2, 5; S. 84, 1. Hé his ǽrenddracan onsende, and him secgan hét þ hé geornor wolde sibbe wið hiene þonne gewinn. Se ealdormon geliéfedlíce mid sibbe þára ǽrenda anféng, 3, 1; S. 96, 19.

ge-lífedlíce; *adv. Lawfully*:—Búton gileófað i (gileofadlíce?) gifehte *nisi legitime certauerit*, Rtl. 60, 15. v. lífedlic.

ge-lífen; *adj. Having permission, excused*:—Hæfe mec gileéfenne (-léfen, L.) *habe me excusatum*, Lk. R. 14, 19. v. ge-lífenscipe.

ge-lífen; *adj. Having belief or faith, believing, faithful*. [*Goth.* ga-laubeins *fidelis*.] v. un-gelífen, ge-lífenness.

ge-lífend. v. un-gelífend: ge-lífende. v. riht-, un-gelífeude: ge-lífendlic. v. un-gelífendlic: ge-lífenness. v. un-gelífenness, ge-lífen: ge-lífenscipe. *Take here* ge-léfenscipe *in Dict., and add*: v. ge-lífen *excused*.

ge-líffæstan, -fæstian; *p.* -fæste, -fæstade; *pp.* -fæst, -fæsted. I.

*to make alive.* (1) of physical life:—Se Fæder āwecð þā deádan and gelíffæst, Jn. 5, 21. Þurh þone gāst syndon gelíffæste ealle þā gesceafta þe se Fæder gesceóp, Hml. A. 2, 20. (2) of spiritual life:—þū gelíffæst mē *viuificabis me*, Ps. L. 137, 7: 142, 11. Swā hwylc swā his sāwle forspilþ, sē hig gelíffæstað, Lk. (W. S., L., R.) 17, 33. þū gelíffæstodest mē, Ps. L. 118, 93. Ðe ilca sâuel his gelíffæstade, Rtl. 10, 24. Gelíffæsta mē, Ps. L. 118, 25. Gilíffæsted gāste *vivificatos spiritu*, Rtl. 21, 34. II. *to keep alive:*—Drihten hine gehylt, and hine gelíffæst, and gedéð hine gesǣligne on eorðan, Ps. Th. 40, 2. III. *to make active, quicken:*—Sōna seó unwæstmfæstnes fram him fleáh, and sōna heora ylda gelíffæsted wæs and geleáfa, and seó clǣnnes onfeng, Bl. H. 163, 18. IV. *to endow with active properties:*—Ic wæs gemedemod gebiddan þā gerýnu þǣre deórwurðan and þǣre gelíffæstan rōde, Hml. S. 23 b, 467.

ge-líffæstnian; *p.* ode *To make alive, quicken:*—þū gelíffæstnast mē *viuificabis me*, Ps. Rdr. 142, 11.

ge-lifian. v. ge-libban: ge-lígenod. v. ge-lygenian.

ge-liger. *l.* -ligere (-ligre), *and add:*—Geligere *adulterium*, Wrt. Voc. ii. 7, 76. Ic eom ondetta sodomiscre synne þe hié on gegyltan, þæt is geligre, Angl. xi. 98, 21. Geligeres *prostibuli* (v. forlig-gang), Wrt. Voc. ii. 65, 77. Þurh þ grimme bismergleów þæs mānfullan geligeres, Hml. S. 23 b, 451. Diernes gelíres scyldig *adulterinae cogitationis reus*, Past. 143, 2. Ealra þāra Rōmāna wīf þe hē mehte, hē tō geligre geniédde, Ors. 2, 2 ; S. 66, 29. Sameramis . . . mid ungemetlicre wrǣnnesse manigfeald geligre fremmende wæs . . . æt nēhstan hyre āgene sunu hió genam hyre tō geligere . . . hió gesette . . . þæt nān forbyrd nǣre æt geligere betwuh nánre sibbe *haec, libidine ardens, . . . inter incessabilia stupra . . . tandem filio inceste cognito . . . praecepit ut inter parentes et filios . . . de conjugiis adpetendis . . . liberum fieret*, 1, 2 ; S. 30, 26–35. Geligra wītnung *incerta* (*incesti?*) *judicium*, Wrt. Voc. ii. 49, 29. Þ gē forberen . . . from dernum geligerum (*ut abstineatis vos ab . . . fornicatione*, Acts 15, 29), Ll. Th. i. 56, 26. v. dirne-geligere.

ge-ligernes. *Substitute for second line:*—Ælcne þāra þe hió geácsian myhte þæt kynekynnes wæs, hió tō hyre gespōn for hyre geligernesse, and syððan hió hý ealle beswác tō deáðe *cum omnes, quos regie arcessitos, meretricie habitos, concubitu oblectasset, occideret*, Ors. 1, 2 ; S. 30, 31. Wearð Alexander ofslagen from his āgenne mēder, þeh heó hiere ōþerne sunu eác ǣr ofslōge, for hiere geligernesse *Alexandro scelere matris occiso, quamvis ea, jam commisso adulterio et altero filio interfecto, generi nuptias mariti morte pepigisset*, 3, 7 ; S. 110, 26. Cf. for-legen[n]es.

ge-lignian. v. ge-lygenian: ge-ligre. v. ge-ligere.

ge-líhtan *to lighten:* ge-líhtan *to alight. Substitute:* ge-líhtan; *p.* te. I. *to make light.* (1) *to mitigate, make less painful or severe.* (a) *to assuage* physical pain:—Wið þæs cwiðan sāre and wið þone hǣtan, genim þás wyrte . . . heó hyne (*if hyne refers to cwiðan the passage belongs to* (2)) gelíhteð, Lch. i. 294, 13. Ic mínne buruh gelēhte (cf. lēhtan, 8, 28), Nar. 12, 11. þā heardnysse mínes gewinnes mid heofonlican sprǣcum hē gelíhte (*printed* -hihte) *duritiam laboris mei coelestibus oraculis sublevabat*, Guth. Gr. 165, 87. (b) *to mitigate* a penalty:—Mid ānne mæssan man mæg ālýsan .xii. daga fæsten, and mid .x. mæssan man mæg gelíhtan .iiii. mōnða fæsten, and mid .xxx. mæssan man mæg gelíhtan .xii. mōnða fæsten (cf. Cantatio unius missae pro tribus diebus, . . . duodecim missae pro mense . . ., 62, 6–8), Ll. Th. ii. 286, 6–9. Ðus mæg mihtig man and freóndspēdig his dǣdbōte mid freónda fultume gelíutan, 14. (2) *to relieve* a person of pain, inconvenience, &c.:—þā woldon þā preóstas þ hē lǣge on ōðre sídan, and gelíhte hine swā, Hml. S. 31, 1360. Ðonne gehefegað ðone hund ðæt ilce ðæt hine ǣr gelíhte *canis, unde levigatus fuerat, rursus oneratur*, Past. 419, 30. þæt þā munecas hwæthwara furþor restan þonne healfe niht, þæt seó dæges þigen tōferd sý on þǣre nihtelican reste, and seó hǣte þǣre þigene oferslegen, and se maga gelýht *ut modice amplius de media nocte pausentur, etiam digesti surgant,* R. Ben. 32, 15. *Digesti*, i. *sereni, levi* gelíhte, Wrt. Voc. ii. 140, 20 (v. preceding passage). (3) *to make light of, undervalue:*—Ðonne hié willað him sylfum ðæt yfel ðæt hié ðurhtugon tō suíðe gelíhtan *cum sibi quis malum, quod perpetravit, laevigat*, Past. 159, 20. II. *to become light, be mitigated:*—Wundorlíce hraðe þ sār gelýhteð þæs þe gelǣrede lǣceas secgeað, Lch. iii. 48, 24. III. *of motion.* (1) *to alight:*—Gelíhte *dissiluit, descendit*, Wrt. Voc. ii. 141, 7. Hē gelíhte of his horse *descendit*, Gr. D. 18, 22. Him cōm rídende tō sum ridda . . . þā gelíhte se cuma, Hml. Th. ii. 134, 34. Hí ridon tō þǣre eá, and þǣr gelíhton sōna for ðām langsuman færelde, Hml. S. 28, 34. (2) *to descend* from a higher to a lower place (v. *N. E. D.* light; 7):—Cōm þegen Hǣlendes hām tō helle . . . segde ús þætte seolfa God wolde helwarum hām gelíhtan. Ārās þā ānra gehwylc . . . wǣron ealle þæs fægen, þæt Drihten wolde him tō helpe hām gesécan, Sat. 426–436. (3) *to come* to a place, *approach* (v. *N. E. D.* light; 10 b):—Sē þe þeóf wrecan wille and ǣhlíp gewyrce oþþe on strǣte tō gelíhte, Ll. Th. i. 230, 11. Sōna þæs þe hē gelýhte (-líhte, *v. l.*, neálǣhte, *v. l.*) tō þām hearge, þā sceát hē mid his spere *mox ut adpropiabat ad fanum, injecta in eo lancea*, Bd. 2, 13 ; Sch. 169, 1. [*O. H. Ger.* ge-líhten *lenire.*]

ge-líhtan. *Add:* I. *to make light, give light to. Take here* ge-lýhtan *in Dict.* II. *to be* or *become light, to shine :*—Gilēhta *luceat*, Rtl. 37, 29 : 173, 41.

ge-líman. *Add:* -limian:—Hē (*the conjunction*) gelímað þā word, Ælfc. Gr. Z. 258, 12. Gelímed *conglutinata*, Wrt. Voc. ii. 104, 69 : 133, 36. Tōsomne gelímed *glutinatum*, 40, 26. Fugellíme gelímedne *visco glutinatam*, 81, 57 : An. Ox. 3016. Gelímedre *conglutinatae*, 9, 6. [*O. H. Ger.* ge-límen *conglutinare : Icel.* líma *to glue.*]

ge-limp. *Add:* I. *what happens:*—Gelimp *casus*, Wrt. Voc. ii. 18, 56 : *eventus*, 30, 40. Gelimpa *eventuum*, 31, 72. Gewyrdelicum gelimpe *fortuitu casu*, An. Ox. 3793. Mid gesǣligum gelimpum *fortuitis casibus*, 4186. II. *what happens in the case of a person, lot, hap, fortune :*—þ endenēcste gelimp *suprema sors*, An. Ox. 1835. Hē on earfoðnyssum bið gedyldig and on gōdum gelinipum (*in prosperity*) ne forlǣt his ānrǣdnesse, Wlfst. 51, 23 : Hml. S. 1, 221. II a. *good fortune, success :*—Wē sceolon ǣigðer ge on gelimpe ge on ungelimpe cweðan : ' Ic herige mínne Drihten,' Hml. Th. i. 252, 12 : Hml. S. 16, 251. Hē wæs suíðe ūpāhafen on his mōde for his anwalde and for his gelimpe *successu suae potestatis elevatus*, Past. 39, 14. II b. *misfortune, mishap, hard lot, ill case :*—Sý hē gelícum gelimpe āmānsumad, and on gelícre wrace dǣdbēte *similem sortiatur excommunicationis vindictam*, R. Ben. 50, 13. þǣr eardode sum man Garganus gehāten : of his gelimpe (*he was accidentally shot*) wearð seó dūn swā gecíged, Hml. Th. i. 502, 11. Hē þā hire ārehte ealle his gelymp, and æt þǣre sprǣcan ende him feóllon teáras of ðām eágum, Ap. Th. 15, 26. III. *what happens in the case of a thing, event, outcome :*—Gelimp wīsan *euentum* (i. *quod euenit*) *rei* (*praestolante*), An. Ox. 2165. IV. *in a technical sense, accident :*—*Pronomen* hæfð syx *accidentia*, þæt synd syx gelimp, Ælfc. Gr. Z. 92, 8 : 242, 15. v. mis-, un-, weás-gelimp.

ge-limpan. *Add:* I. *to happen.* (1) construction uncertain :—Gelamp *obtigit*, Wrt. Voc. ii. 65, 2 : *contigit*, i. *accidit, evenit*, 135, 12 : *attigisset*, 88, 23. Geward ł gelump *accidit*, Mt. p. 3, 7. (2) the subject a noun (pronoun), *to take place, be done* or *made :*—Þý ǣrestan dæge gelimpeð mycel gnornung, Bl. H. 91, 30. Monigfealde wundra gelimpað, Bd. 1, 7 ; Sch. 27, 13. On eallum ðæm tācnum þe þǣr gelimpað (-eð, MS.), Bl. H. 201, 8. Eft gelamp ōþer wundor, 219, 6. Reówlic þing þǣr gelamp, Chr. 1083 ; P. 215, 7. Ríces gehwæs rēðe sceolde gelimpan . . . ende, Dan. 114. (3) the subject a pronoun, (a) used indefinitely :—Hū emnlíce hit gelomp ymb ðās heáfodrícu, Ors. 2, 1 ; S. 62, 11. Drihten cwæþ : ' . . . Ealle þás getimbro beóþ tōworpene . . .' Swā swā hit seoþþan gelamp, Bl. H. 79, 2 : El. 1155. Swā hit ǣfre gelim[pe] *amen*, An. Ox. 56, 104. (b) referring to an occurrence already stated :—Hēr Eádgār wæs tō cyninge gehālgod . . . þǣr wæs preósta heáp gegaderod . . . ðā þā ðis gelamp, Chr. 973 ; P. 118, 21. Cirus ealle Babylonia āwēste, and ealle Asirie on Persa anwald gedyde. þæt þā swā gelomp, ðætte . . ., Ors. 2, 1 ; S. 62, 4. þæt wundra sum þūhte, þæt hē mā wolde earme gǣstas hrínan lǣtan, and þæt hwæðre gelomp, Gū. 491. Gif mon beforan ærcebiscepe gefeohte oþþe wæpne gebregde . . . Gif beforan ōðrum biscepe þis gelimpe, Ll. Th. i. 70, 20 : 332, 5. Gif þises hwæt gelimpe, 86, 18. (c) representing a clause that follows the verb:—Gif þ gelimpeþ, þ hē hit eft spíwende ānforlǣteþ, Bl. H. 57, 7. Þonne gelimpeþ þ æfter feáwum dagum . . . þ se líchoma byð freten, 99, 7. Hit gelomp þ se ārwyrða wer on nearanesse becōm, Bt. 1 ; F. 2, 26 : Sat. 534 : 569 : El. 271. Ðā gelamp hit þet se cyng forðférde, Chr. 1016 ; P. 148, 15. Hit gelamp þte ān hearpere wæs, Bt. 35, 6 ; F. 166, 27. þā gelamp þ, þ ealle men onscunodan þone drý, Bl. H. 173, 31. Wē swylc ne gefrugnan gelimpan, þæt þū . . ., Cri. 79. (4) where the subject is not expressed:—Ābeád weroda ealdor : ' Nū sié geworden leóht . . .' and þā sóna gelomp, þā hit swā sceolde, leóma leóhtade, Cri. 233. (4 a) where the verb is followed by a substantive clause:—Gelamp þ him ansende sāwla Neriend wītgan, Ps. C. 16 : Sat. 478. Gelomp þ ān swíþe wīs mon ongan fandigan . . ., Bt. 18, 4 ; F. 66, 27. II. *with dat.* of person affected by an event, action, &c., *to happen* to a person, *to come upon, befall.* (1) the subject a noun :—Mycel egsa gelimpeþ eallum gesceaftum, Bl. H. 91, 18. Mē gelomp yrmðu, Hy. 4, 83. Mē gelamp sorg, Jul. 442. Hū mycel yfel þē gelamp, Bl. H. 31, 13. Him wirse gelamp, Sat. 24, 175. Hire se willa gelamp, þæt heó on ǣnigne eorl gelýðe frōfre, B. 626 : El. 963. Gif him þyslicu þearf gelumpe, B. 2637. Ðā ðingo him gelimpa scealde *quae ei euentura*, Mk. L. 10, 32. (1 a) where the noun denotes the form of words in which the event is described, e. g. a sentence, curse, &c. :—þis is se cwyde þæs godcundlican dōmes . . . ' Sē ðe deirað, derige hē gyt swýðor . . .' þes cwyde gelamp Herōde, Hml. Th. i. 484, 19. þām gelamp seó āwyrigung . . . ' Wā þām þe wītegað . . .,' Hml. S. 15, 115. (2) the subject a pronoun. (a) indefinite :—Anbídende hwæt him gelimpan scolde, Hml. S. 7, 20. (b) referring to a condition, an occurrence already stated :—Sē ðe hālig is, beó hē gyt swýðor gehālgod.' þis gelamp þām fulluhtere, Hml. Th. i. 484, 22. Huu miceles tídes is of ðon ðis him gelamp, Mk. L. 9, 21. Gif æðelborenran wífmen þis

gelimpe, Ll. Th. i. 70, 2. Gif syxhvndum þissa hwæđer gelimpe, 88, 3. (c) representing a clause that follows the verb :—þ oft manegum mannum gelimpeþ . . . þ heora heortan beóđ gemanode, Bl. H. 129, 6. (3) where the subject is not expressed :—Đa yfelan habbaþ gesǣlþa, and him gelimpþ oft æfter hiora águum willan, Bt. 39, 2 ; F. 214, 5. Sum sáre angeald ǽfenræste, swá him ful oft gelamp, B. 1252. Hé geseah hú þǽre þeóde scolde gelimpan, Wlfst. 44, 26. Mē tó dæg swá wunderlíce is gelumpen, Hml. S. 23, 742. Swá is þissum nū móde gelumpen, Met. 3, 7. (3 a) where the verb is followed by a substantive clause :—Oft swiþe manegum men gelimpeþ þ hé hine wiđ þás world gedǽleþ, Bl. H. 125, 10. Þonne hwylcum men gelimpeþ þ his fæder gefærþ, 131, 24. Þá gelamp him þ his líf weard geendod, 113, 7. Him on fyrste gelomp . . . þæt hit weard gearo, B. 76. III. of things, (1) to be made, be produced :—Mænifealde leán gelumpon copiosa emolumenta prouenerunt, An. Ox. 2636 : Wrt. Voc. ii. 79, 68 : 66, 33. (2) to fall to, belong to, be assigned to :—Pronomen hæfđ syx accidentia, þæt synd gelimp. Him gelimpþ species . . ., Ælfc. Gr. Z. 92, 8 : 119, 12. Tíd gelimpđ worde tempus accidit uerbo, 123, 12 : 268, 10. Þreó đing gelimpađ þisum dǣle tria accidunt coniunctioni, 258, 14. Sume naman synd accidentia þe gelimpađ ánum gehwylcum, 12, 13. Him swá fela gereorda gelamp swá đǣra wyrhtena wæs, Wlfst. 105, 5. IV. to turn out, have as an issue :—Wēndun gē þæt gē Scyppende sceoldan gelíce wesan ; eów þǣr wyrs gelomp it turned out worse for you, Gū. 637. Hē lyt ongeat þæt him on his inne swá earme gelamp, Gen. 1567. IV a. with complement, to turn out so and so :—Hit mē wyrse gelomp, Sat. 125. Him þǣr sár gelamp æfst, Gen. 28. V. to turn to, come to a state, condition, &c. :—Gelimpeđ iúh on cýđnise continget uobis in testimonium, Lk. L. R. 21, 13. Gif gē gelýfaþ þ eów þ tó góde gelimpe, Bl. H. 41, 17. Tó hwylcum ende wēnest þú þæt seó mettrumnys wylle gelimpan ?, Guth. 80, 21. VI. to fall in with, be suitable to :—Gelimpan quadrare, An. Ox. 4262. Forgylde hē þ ángylde, and þ wíte swá tó þám ángylde gelimpan wylle, Ll. Th. i. 66, 3. [Laym. A. R. i-lomp ; p. ; þa wes hit ilumpen (bivalle, 2nd MS.), Laym. 7195. O. H. Ger. ge-limphan conuenire, condecere, oportere, competere.]

ge-limpfull. Add : convenient.

gelimplǽcan to become fitted :—Gelimplǽcan coaptari, An. Ox. 80.

gelimplic. Add : I. that happens or befalls :—Gelimplíce fatali, Wrt. Voc. ii. 38, 4. Gilimplicum gimaerende successibus determinans, Rtl. 164, 38. I a. in grammar translating accidens. v. ge-limp. IV :—Sume naman synd accidentia, þæt synd gelimplice, þe gelimpađ ánum gehwylcum, Ælfc. Gr. Z. 12, 13. Word hæfđ seofon gelimplice đing uerbum habet septem accidentia, 119, 12. II. fitting, suitable, convenient, apt. (1) of persons, competent, fit :—Gif se yrđlincg behylt underbæc gelóme, ne biđ hé gelimplic tilia, Hml. S. 16, 179. Stýran þǣre nytennysse þurh mynegunge gelimplices lǣreówes, Hml. Th. ii. 134, 6. (2) of things :—Þá gelimplican congrua, i. conuenientia, Wrt. Voc. ii. 133, 38. Gelimplíce daele conpetentes portiunculas, 104, 78 : 132, 65. (a) of material things :—Þá gebrōhte se biscop ealle þá hálgan bán on gelimplicum scrýnum, Hml. S. 11, 275. (b) of non-material things :—Agustinus líchaman hē þǣr gesette mid gelimplicre áre, Shrn. 122, 28. Mid gelimplicre endebyrdnesse weorþian, Bl. H. 207, 33. Wē willađ nū sume eów geopenian, and sume eft on gelimplicere tíde, Hml. Th. ii. 200, 6. Gelimplicum horis competentibus, Bd. 2, 12 ; Sch. 162, 2. (3) with a clause :—þ gelimplic wæs, þ hē his leornerum frófre sende, Bl. H. 131, 22 : 133, 24. III. fitted for, adapted to :—Ælc byđ gelimplic tó his lífes tilunge, Hex. 16, 4. Þú ealle lima mē gescéope tó menniscum bricum gemǣte and gelimplice (apta), Angl. xi. 112, 18. [O. H. Ger. ge-limphlíh competens.] v. un-gelimplic.

ge-limplíce. Substitute : I. in a physical sense, fitly, so as to fit :—Hí gemētton áne mǣre brúh . . . and þ hlyd đǣrtó gelimplíce gefēged, Hml. S. 20, 82. II. so as to meet the requirements of a case, suitably, fitly :—þ þínes lífes lofu singan wē, heortan unclǣnre wom þú gelimplíce (apte) tólēs, Hy. S. 72, 22. þ wē on đysse æfterfylgendan béc gerisenlícur and gelimplícur secgađ id libro sequente dicetur, Bd. 3, 29 ; Sch. 330, 5. Be đám is gelimplícor þonne mǣre tó reccenne þonne nū sý, Hml. Th. i. 216, 34. III. rightly, properly (of arrangement or order) :—Þæt hié oncnēwen hū gelimplíce úre God on þǣm ǣrran tídum þá rícu sette ut intelligant unum Deum disposuisse tempora, Ors. 2, 1 ; S. 64, 1. Aduerbia beóđ gelimplícor geendebyrde, gif hí standađ on foreweardan on đǣre sprǣce, Ælfc. Gr. Z. 241, 9. IV. in a becoming manner :—Hí gelimplíce heora yldran wǣron gehýrsume, Hml. A. 129, 439. V. rightly, properly, in accordance with the actual state of the case :—Gelimplíce hē ús lǣrde and monade hú wē ús gebiddan sceoldan, and hwæđere cwæþ : ' Éower Fæder wát hwæs eów þearf biþ ǣr gē hine biddan' quite properly he taught us and admonished how we should pray, and yet said, ' Your Father knows what you need before you ask him,' Bl. H. 19, 35. Sē biđ gelimplíce Godes gifu gecíged þe đurh góde geearnunga Godes gife begyt, Hml. Th. i. 586, 25. Be đám is gyt gelimplíce gecweden . . ., ii. 80, 28. [O. H. Ger. ge-limpflícho consequenter, congruenter, competenter.] v. un-gelimplíce.

ge-limplicness, e ; f. Opportunity, occasion :—Fultum in gelimplicnissum adjutor in oportunitatibus, Ps. Srt. 9, 10.

ge-limpwíse. Dele. l. gelimp, wíse : ge-lióma. Dele.

ge-lísan ; p. de. I. to loosen, relax, weaken the connexion of the parts of an object, crush ; v. ge-lýsan in Dict. II. to redeem, release :—Gilēsdes úsig redemisti nos, Rtl. 29, 19. Eft gilēsdest, 102, 25. Gilēseno aron gié redemti estis, 24, 38. [Goth. ga-lausjan.]

ge-lisfullíce (?) ; adv. Eagerly, zealously, earnestly :—Nán þínra þegna neódlícor ne gelistfullícor (-lisfullícor ? v. ge-les ; ge-lustfullícor, v. l.) hine geþeódde on úra goda begangum þonne ic nullus tuorum studiosius quam ego culturae deorum nostrorum se subdidit, Bd. 2, 13 ; Sch. 164, 21.

ge-lísian. The original Latin is : Qui modica spernit, paulatim decidit.

ge-lísnes redemption. v. ge-lésness in Dict. : ge-lispelicnis. Dele, and see ge-hýþelicnes.

ge-líþan. Add : I. of journeying (by water), to come to land, arrive, reach port :—Geláþ adtigisset (portum attigit, Ald. 80, 5), Wrt. Voc. ii. 88, 23. Gelidun adplicuerunt (v. Mk. 6, 53), 73, 34. Hý tó lande geliden hæfdon, Jul. 677. II. to go, pass away :—Synt lífwynne geliden, El. 1269. v. ge-lýđen in Dict.

ge-líþewácian ; p. ode. I. to render gentle, soften a person :—Hié wǣron tó sybbe geliđewácede and gefeohtan ne meahton they were brought to the gentleness of peace and could not fight, Nap. 15, 28. II. to mitigate, soften the rigour of misery, pain, &c. :—Geliđewáca þisne unliđan cyle, Hml. S. 11, 192. See next word.

ge-líþewǣcan. l. ge-líþewǣcan (-leoþe-), and add : I. to make pliant or flexible, restore the activity of :—Of slǣpe geliđewǣhtum liđum wē árísađ somno refectis artubus surgimus, Hy. S. 14, 20. I a. to refresh, revive :—Geliþewǣc ús þínum bēnum releva nos tuis precibus, Hy. S. 129, 8. II. to mitigate, soften the rigour or severity of, calm the violence of :—Hē sceal forberan rēđra manna angin, þæt hē đurh his liđnesse heora graman geliđewǣce, Hml. Th. ii. 532, 11. Tó geliþewǣcan (-liođe-, Hpt. Gl. 455, 1) wōdnesse ad sedandam uesaniam, An. Ox. 2056. Scúrum geliþewǣhte (incendia) imbribus sopita, i. mitigata, 4031. III. to make to suit a purpose, adapt (?) :—Hē geliþewǣhte tó geleáfan heora wurđfullan templ .he adapted their magnificent temples to the service of the Christian faith, Hml. S. 31, 482. IV. to become pliant :—Geliþewǣhte lentesceret, An. Ox. 3108. V. to become gentle :—Geleoþewǣcan mitescere (cruenta severitas mitescere non novit, Ald. 68, 11), An. Ox. 4791. v. leoþuwác, and previous word.

ge-líþian, -leoþian ; p. ode To unloose, relax, release :—Hē his sylfes wyllan geleođode (-liđode, v. l.) in him sylfum þǣre blisse geweald sponte sibi laetitiae frena laxabat, Gr. D. 203, 26. Þæt wē hwílon úre mód geliđian (-leođigen, v. l.) . . . betweoh þás eorđlican carfulnysse, 1, 9. Mæg se biscop þæs mannes syngrína þurh Godes þafunge þe swýđor geliđian þe þus wile georne helpan him sylfan, Wlfst. 155, 26. Seó hálige sáwl wæs álýsed and geleođod of þám líchaman sancta illa anima carne soluta est, Gr. D. 282, 17. Seó geleođode syn þǣre unhýrsumnesse weard him tó deáđe in þám wege peccatum inobedientiae in ipsa fuerit morte laxatum, 294, 26. Hē swá swýđe gebunden geare ongeat and georwēnde þ him nǣfre ofer þ ne mihte beón geleođad constrictus nimis relaxari se jam posse desperabat, 326, 12.

ge-líþian. Take here Shrn. 130, 5 and Past. 159, 3 in Dict., and add:—Þæt yrre wēdendra gelíþige ut iram saeuientium mitiget, Scint. 121, 1. Đæt hé ryhtlíce and stíđlíce wrecan sceolde, đæt hé đæt ne forielde . . . đætte tó ungemetlíce ne sié geliđod đǣm scyldgan ne hoc, quod agi recte ac graviter potuit, immature praeveniens laeviget, Past. 151, 2.

ge-líþigian. Take here all passages except Shrn. 130, 5 and Past. 159, 3 under ge-líþian in Dict., and add : I. to render a person gentle, mollify, appease :—Hē þone geyrsodon cásere geliđgode, Hml. S. 3, 194. Hine geliđegode seó árfæste behreówsung þǣre mildheortnysse pectus pietas vicit, Gr. D. 18, 20. Biđ geliđgod lenietur (princeps), Kent. Gl. 964. II. to make a person glad (?) :—Þú geliþegodest delectasti, Ps. Spl. 91, 4. III. to mitigate pain, &c., soften asperity, &c. :—Hyt þone wlættan þæs magan gelíþigaþ, Lch. i. 204, 21. Hyt geliþegaþ þone gicþan, 25. Is swíđe micel niédđearf đæt mon mid micelre gemetgunge swelcra scylda đreáunga geliđigie and gemetgige necesse est, ut magno moderamine ipsa delicti correptio temperetur, Past. 158, 3.

ge-líþran (-lēþ-) to make frothy, to lather :—Gníd swíđe oþ þ eall gelēþred sié, Lch. ii. 18, 20 : iii. 2, 3.

gella. v. stán-gella.

gellan. Add :—Hwínende fleág giellende gár on grome þeóde, Vid. 128. Hý gyllende gáras sændan, Lch. iii. 52, 23.

gellet. Add : [From Latin ? Cf. O. H. Ger. glosses gebita (v. gabote) galletum, catinum, vasis. See also N. E. D. gallon] : gelm. v. gilm : gelo. v. geolo.

ge-loccian ; p. ode. Substitute : To allure, entice, win over by gentle means :—Olehte, i. geloccade delinuit, Wrt. Voc. ii. 138, 50. Hē

hī swā unrōte ōleccende tō him geloccode *tristem blanditiis delinivit*, Past. 415, 18. Ne hine ne geloccige nān ōliccung tō hiere willan *non blanda usque ad voluptatem demulceant*, 83, 18. [*O. H. Ger.* ge-locchōn *mulcere: Icel.* lokka *to allure: O. L. Ger.* loccōn *allicere, attrahere, mulcere.*]

ge-lōcian. *Add:*—Đū gelōcas ł g[e]siist *tu videris*, Mt. L. 27, 4.

ge-loda *a brother.* v. ge-landa: ge-lodr. *In* l. 3 *read* gelodr.

gelod-wyrt. *Add:*—Gelodwyrt *eptafylon*, Wrt. Voc. ii. 29, 11: 107, 1, 29.

ge-loed. v. ge-lēd.

ge-lofian; *p.* ode *To put a price upon, value, appraise:*—Næfð Godes rīce nānes wurðes lofunge, ac bið gelofod be ðæs mannes hæfene. Heofenan rīce wæs ālǣten þisum gebrōðrum for heora nette and scipe, and ðām rīcan Zachēo tō healfum dǣle his ǣhta, Hml. Th. i. 580, 21: 582, 28.

gelōgend-lic; *adj. Disposable, that is to be laid in order:*—þā gelōhgenlican *recolligenda*, R. Ben. I. 63, 5.

ge-logian. *l.* -lōgian, *and add:* I. *to put together.* (1) *to join:*—Gelōgod and gefēged *compositus*, Germ. 391, 188. (2) *to collect, bring together:*—þ eall middaneard, swylce under ānum sunnan leóman gelōgod (*gegaderod, v. l., collectus*), wǣre beforan his eágan gelǣded, Gr. D. 171, 11. (3) *to put together* property, *accumulate, lay up:*—Mā swā hī hyra forspillan forgyfende þænne fremede gesettan gelōgiende *malunt se suum perdere largiendo quam aliena restituere conponendo*, Scint. 158, 9. (4) *to put together* ingredients, *season* food (?):—*Condio* ic gelōgige oððe sylte (*condo* ic gescyppe is ðǣre ðriddan), Ælfc. Gr. Z. 192, 12. II. *to place in order, order, arrange, dispose.* (1) the object material:—Hī gelōgodon ðā untruman be ðǣre strǣt þǣr Petrus forð eóde, Hml. Th. i. 316, 14. (2) the object non-material:—Drihtnes ðrowunge wē willað eów secgan . . . nā swā ðeáh tō langsumlīce, gif wē hit swā gelōgian magon, Hml. Th. ii. 240, 31. His līf wæs þus gelōgod; ðā þā hē twelf wintra wæs betǣht Benedicte, and hē wunode mid him twēntig wintra, and on his āgenum mynstre em feówertig geára, Hml. S. 6, 357. (2 a) of language, *to write in good style:*—*Scemata* sind mislīce hīw and fǣgernyssa on Lēdensprǣce, hū heó betst gelōgod beó, Ælfc. Gr. Z. 295, 5. Sindon twā bēc gesette on endebyrdnisse tō Salomones bōcum, swilce hē hig gedihte; for þǣre gelícnisse his gelōgodan sprǣce (*on account of the likeness to his style*) . . ., Ælfc. T. Grn. 8, 42. III. *to place, settle, fix* an object (1) in the place it is to occupy. (a) the object a person. (a) of permanent occupation:—God hine gelōgode in paradýso, Wlfst. 153, 19. Hē gelōgode on heofena rīce engla weredu, 306, 22: Hml. Th. i. 440, 24. þām preóstum þe hē þǣr gelōgode, Ælfc. T. Grn. 16, 38. On þā gerād þ hē nǣfre eft Englisce ne Frencisce in tō þām lande (*Scotland*) ne gelōgige, Chr. 1093; P. 228, 29. Þæt þæt mōd blissige hit beón gelōgod leohte *ut mens gaudeat se collocari lumine*, Hy. S. 24, 3. God eów ne forlǣt, oð þ gē gelōgode beón, Hml. S. 6, 88. (β) of temporary occupation, reflex. *to take up one's quarters:*—Þā gelōgode Benedictus hine sylfne on sumes stýpeles ūpflōra *in turris superioribus se Benedictus collocavit*, Gr. D. 170, 13. (ββ) of animals:—Hwelpas leóna on heora cleofum beóþ gelōgode (*collocabuntur*), Ps. L. 103, 22. (γ) where the purpose of placing is given:—God gelōgode cherubim tō gehealdenne þone weg þe lið tō lífes treówe, Angl. vii. 30, 285. (b) the object a thing:—Đā sǣ hē gelōgode swā swā heó ligið git widinnan ðā eorðan, Hex. 10, 28. Binnan him (*the firmament*) is gelōgod eall ðes middaneard, 8, 28. (2) in the position or condition in which it is to be. (a) where the object is personal:—Hē minne fæder gelōgode on þǣm heáhfædera getele, Hml. S. 2, 421. Gefylde ǣr for hlāfum hig gelōgodon *repleti prius pro panibus se locauerunt*, Cant. An. 5. þ hē gelōgie (*collocet*) hine mid ealderum folces his, Ps. L. 112, 8. Gedafenað þ hī heora heortan wyrtruman on ðām lifiicum wylle, ðæt is God, gelōgian, Hml. Th. ii. 402, 12. Seó geleáffulle gelaðung is gelōgod on Crīste, Hml. S. 15, 123. Hē understōd on hwilcum gedeorfum þis mennisce līf is gelōgod, Hml. Th. ii. 82, 34: 370, 23. (b) the object a thing:—Rōmāne þone bissextum gelōgodon on Februario, Angl. viii. 306, 7. IV. *to place* an object for safe keeping, storage, carriage, &c., *put, bring, deposit.* (1) a material object:—Gif preóst on circan ungedafenlice þingc gelōgige, Ll. Th. ii. 294, 12. Hýse gelōgige *gurgustio recondat* (*alimoniam*), An. Ox. 308. Ne mæg nān wíf hire bōndan forbeódan þ hē ne mōte in tō his cotan gelōgian þ þ hē wille, Ll. Th. i. 418, 24. Hī wendan on ānum scipe mid swā miclum gǣrsuman swā hī mihton þǣr on mǣst gelōgian tō ælcum mannum, Chr. 1052; P. 176, 19. Gelōgodne *receptum*, Germ. 400, 522. (1 a) *to place* a body, bones, &c., in a coffin or tomb, *bury* in a church:—Gelōgode his bān ferode tō Wintanceastre and mid wurðmynte gelōgode binnan ealdan mynstre, Hml. S. 26, 142. Gebrōhte se bisceop ealle þā bān on gelimplicum scrýnum, and gelōgode hī ūp on cyrcan, 11, 275. Men his līchaman binnon ðām temple wurðfullīce gelōgodon, Hml. Th. i. 452, 28. His innoð tōfleów, nāteshwōn gelōgod on nānre byrgene, ii. 250, 26. His bān wurdon gebrōhte tō Alexandria, and þǣr gelōgode, i. 486, 16. (2) a non-material object:—Hester . . . hæfð āne bōc . . . for þan

þe Godes lof ys gelōgod þǣr on, Ælfc. T. Grn. 11, 13. Se ðe hæfð ðā sōðan lufe, hē hylt ealle gewritu ðe sind gelōgode on langsumum cwydum, Hml. Th. ii. 314, 16. V. *to fill* a place with occupants, *to occupy, garrison* a fortress:—Wyrðe is seó stōw þ hī man gelōgige mid clǣnum Godes þeówum, Hml. S. 32, 256. Godes rīce bið gelōgod mid engla weredum and geðungenum mannum, Hml. Th. i. 344, 11. Se stede ne worðe gelōged mid ōðres hādes mannum þanne mid munecum, Cht. Th. 348, 6. VI. *to settle* what is disturbed or disordered. (1) of material things:—Nim mucgwyrte gebeátene and wið ele gemenged; gelōgode smyre mid, Lch. i. 380, 22. (2) of non-material things:—Gesibsume sind ðā on him sylfum ðe ealle heora mōdes styrunga mid gesceáde gelōgiað, Hml. Th. i. 552, 24. Ic þā myclan hearmas þe ūs tō fundedon swā gelōgod hæbbe, þ wē ne þurfon þanon nēnes hearmes ūs āsittan, Cht. E. 230, 9. VII. *to arrange* a course of action, *order* one's conversation, *regulate:*—Hē his līf gelōgað mid wīsdōme, Wlfst. 52, 24. þ ðū gelōgie þīn līf on eádmōdnysse, Hml. A. 10, 263. þ ūre līf beó swā gelōgod þ ūre ende geendige on God, Hml. S. 16, 6. VIII. *to dispose* a person to act:—Crīst gelōgode his apostolas and ealle his gecorenan, þæt hī fērdon sylfwilles, Hml. Th. ii. 526, 13. v. ge-lōgung.

ge-lōgod. v. ge-lōgian; II. 2 a.

ge-lōgung, e; *f. Order, arrangement:*—þǣre gelōgunge þ dægrædsangum geendedum sōna beón gecwedene twēgen sealmas *eo ordine ut matutinis finitis mox dicantur duo psalmi*, Angl. xiii. 407, 599.

ge-lōm; *adj. Frequent:*—Hī worhton āne cyrcan þām hālgan, for þan þe gelōme (*or adv. ?*) wundra wurdon æt his byrgene, Hml. S. 32, 172. þā wunda þe þā hǣþenan mid gelōmum scotungum on his līce macodon, 182. Hē mid gelōmum siccetungum mǣnde, 31, 1019.

ge-lōman. *Substitute:* ge-lōma, an; *m.* I. *a tool, an implement, utensil:*—Gelōma *utensile*, Wrt. Voc. ii. 124, 24. Næs nǣnig wēn þæs gelōman (*a wood-bill*) . . . Se hālga man āgeaf þām Gotan þone gelōman, and cwæð: 'Lōca nū! hēr is þīn gelōma,' Gr. D. 114, 1–18. Hē hēt weorpan īserne gelōman in þæs mynstres wyrtgeard, þa īserngelōman gewunelice naman wē hātaþ spadan and spitelas, 201, 19. II. in a collective sense, *furniture:*—Gelōma *suppellex* (*cuncta culinae suppellex*, Ald. 66, 15), Wrt. Voc. ii. 86, 17. v. īren-, īsern-gelōma; cf. andlōman.

ge-lōme. *Add:*—Gelōme *crebrius*, Wrt. Voc. ii. 15, 64. Þider gelōme (*frequenter*) se Hǣlend cwōm, Jn. R. 18, 2. Gyrdelse ðe hine man gelōme gyrt *zona qua semper praecingitur*, Ps. Th. 108, 19. Gelōme ic eów sǣde, Hml. Th. ii. 72, 24: i. 566, 34. Þider þū fundadest longe and gelōme, Cri. 1672. Swā hē geornor and gelōmor Godes hūs sēce, Wlfst. 155, 8. ¶ combined with oft:—Sind freólsbrices wīde geworhte oft and gelōme, Wlfst. 164, 9: Gen. 1670: Bl. H. 209, 14. Wē gehýrað oft secggan gelōme worldrīcra manna deáþ, 107, 29.

ge-lōmlǣcan. *Substitute:* I. *to be or to become frequent, happen frequently:*—Þonne middangeardes wīta gelōmlǣcað, Hml. Th. i. 612, 7. Efne ðā fǣrlīce æteówdon gelōmlǣcende līgas sweartes fýres *ecce subito apparent crebri flammarum tetrarum globi* (Bd. Sch. 617), ii. 350, 19. Þes middangeard is mid ylde ofsett swylce mid gelōmlǣcendum hefigtýmnyssum tō deáðe geðreád, 614, 21: 578, 34. II. *to do frequently, repeat:*—Gelōmlǣcþ *iterat, repetit*, Wrt. Voc. ii. 150, 63. Gelōmlǣcende *iteranda*, An. Ox. 3824. II a. *to denote frequent action:*—Sume word synd gecwedene *frequentativa*, þæt synd gelōmlǣcende, for ðan ðe hī getācniað gelōmlǣcunge, Ælfc. Gr. Z. 213, 7. III. *to frequent, visit frequently:*—Gelōmlǣcþ *frequentat, visitat*, Wrt. Voc. ii. 150, 63. IV. *to visit in large numbers, celebrate* a festival:—Gelōmlǣc *celebres, frequentes*, Hpt. 31, 8, 134. For symbelnysse gelōmlǣcende *pro festivitate frequentanda*, An. Ox. 3824.

ge-lōmlǣcing. *Substitute:* I. *a frequent doing, repeated action.* v. ge-lōmlǣcan; II a. II. translating *frequentia:*—Hī mōdes mid ecge andwerdnysse Godes and engla gefērrǣdenne gelōmlǣcinge (*frequentiam*) besceáwiað, Scint. 62, 16.

ge-lōmlǣcnys. *Substitute: A numerous assembly:*—Gesettað dæg symbel on gelōmlǣcnessum *constituite diem sollemnem in confrequentationibus*, Ps. Rdr. 117, 27. On gelōmlǣcnyssum *in condensis*, Ps. Spl. 117, 26. v. ge-lōmlǣcan; IV; gelōmlicnes.

ge-lōmlic. *Add:*—Mid gelōmlice *crebra*, Wrt. Voc. ii. 23, 34. I. *that is done or happens often, frequent, constant:*—Gelōmlic þ wæs . . . þ . . . *it often happened . . . that . . .*, Bi. H. 223, 17. Gelōmlic gibed *continua oratio*, Rtl. 74, 22. Folces men wiðhæfton þǣre gelōmlican mynegunge, Ll. Th. i. 270, 25. Hē hié frēfrede for þǣre gelōmlican sorge, Bl. H. 135, 23. Gilōmlica *fultumo continuata praesidia*, Rtl. 64, 31. II. *that is at a place often or that does something often, constant, assiduous:*—Gelōmlic *frequens, celer, assiduus*, Wrt. Voc. ii. 150, 66. Gelōmlic lǣce *frequens hyrudo, sanguisuga assidua*, Hpt. 31, 12, 272. III. *numerous, many:*—Gelōmlice (gelōmelicere, Hpt. Gl. 458, 76) *æxa crebri bipennes*, An. Ox. 2, 70. Gelōmlican *frequentes, densos, multos*, Wrt. Voc. ii. 150,

67.       **IV.** *frequented, attended by many:*—Gilōmlíca symbeltído *frequentata sollennitas*, Rtl. 67, 3.

**ge-lómlíce.** *Add:* **I.** *of action, frequently, constantly:*—Wē myne-giað ǣlcne getreówfulne man, þ hē gelōmlíce lufige cumlíðnysse and nānum cuman ne forbeóde þ hē ne mōte on his hūse gerestan, Hml. A. 147, 82. Gē gelōmlíce winnað, and ā embe þ sorgiað, þ wē ūrne líchoman gefyllan, Bl. H. 99, 6. Soeca uē gilōmlíce *frequentemus*, Rtl. 80, 26. Gelōmlíce, Ll. Th. i. 358, 13. Drihten gecígde hine sylfne mannes bearn gelōmlícor ðonne Godes bearn, Hml. Th. i. 610, 28. **II.** *of condition, frequently, in many places, in many instances:*—Gelōmlíce ðā stānas swā of ōðrum clife stæðhlýplíce ūt sceoredon, Bl. H. 207, 19.

**ge-lómlícness,** e; *f.* **I.** *frequency, repetition.* v. ge-lómlíc; **I:**—*Repetitio* on Englisc gelōmlícnys, Angl. viii. 331, 27. **II.** *a numerous assembly.* v. ge-lómlíc; **III, IV,** ge-lōmlǣcness:—In gelōmlícnissum *in confrequentationibus*, Ps. Srt. 117, 27.

**ge-lómrǽd[e];** *adj. Frequent:*—Úre hālige fæderes mid gelōm-rǣdre menunge ūs gemenegið *nos sancti patres frequentativis orationibus admonent*, Cht. Th. 316, 27.

**ge-londa.** v. ge-landa.

**ge-lósian.** *l.* -losian, *and add:* **I.** *intrans. To be lost, perish:*—Gif ic forlēto hiá fæstende in hūs hiora, hiá gelosað (gíloesigas, R., *deficient*) on woeg, Mk. L. 8, 3. Sunu mín gelosade (*perierat*) and gemoeted is, Lk. L. 15, 24. **II.** *trans.* (1) *to lose:*—Sē ðe gelosas sāul his fore mec, infindes hiá *qui perdiderit animam suam propter me, inveniet eam*, Mt. L. 16, 25. (2) *to destroy:*—Sōhton hine gelosage ł tō spillanne *quaerebant eum perdere*, Jn. L. 10, 59.

**gelostr.** v. geolstor: **ge-loten.** v. ge-lútan: **gelp-ness.** v. gilp-ness: **gelu.** v. geolo.

**ge-lūcan.** *Add:* **I.** *to close* what is open:—Hyt þā wunda āclǣnsað and ðā dolh gelýcð, Lch. i. 108, 22. **II.** *to lock, fasten with a bolt,* &c.:—Gelocen boge *an arblast* (v. arblast), *a crossbow*; balista, Wrt. Voc. i. 35, 56.

**ge-lufian.** *Add:* **I.** *to love.* (1) *to feel affection for* a person:—Gif gié gelufas mec *si diligitis me*, Jn. L. 14, 15 : 28. Đū lufades hiá suæ mec gelufades, Jn. L. R. 17, 23 : 24. Suæ gelufade mec se faeder ic lufade iuih, 15, 9. Đone ðe Haelend gelufade (*amavit*), Mt. p. 8, 16. Đæt hē sí gelufod (-ad, L., R.) *ut diligatur*, Mk. 12, 32. Gelufodes *dilecti*, Ps. L. 67, 13. (2) *to feel desire for* a thing, *like:*—Gelufadan menn ðíostro, *dilexerunt homines tenebras*, Jn. L. 3, 19. Gelufadon uuldor monnes, Jn. L. R. 12, 43. **II.** *to shew affection* by gesture, *to caress:*—þ hē gelufude mid his brādre hand þā nunnan and ofer þā sculdru geþaccode *ut in terga sanctimonialis feminae blandiens alapam daret*, Gr. D. 189, 22.

**ge-luggian.** *Dele.*

[**ge-lumpenlic**; *adj.* **I.** *occasional, accidental:*—þā ōðre brōðru tō cirican gewitene wēron fore sumum gelumpenlicum intingan, Angl. x. 143, 82. **II.** *opportune, suitable:*—Hē in gelumpenlicum stōwum biscopas hālgede, Angl. x. 141, 17. *From a twelfth-century MS.* v. ge-limplic.]

**ge-lustfull;** *adj. Welcome:*—Gelustfullesta *desiderantissimus*, i. *qui desideratur*, Wrt. Voc. ii. 139, 25.

**ge-lustfullian.** *Add:* **I.** *to delight* (intrans.), *to take pleasure:*—Gemyndig ic wæs Godes and ic gelustfullode (*delectatus sum*), Ps. L. 76, 4. Ne sceal man unālýfedlíce gelustfullian *non concupiscere*, R. Ben. 16, 19. **I a.** *to delight* in, *rejoice* over:—Hió gelustfullað ofor hālwendan hire, Ps. L. 34, 9. Wēstensetlan on wēstenes wununge gelustfulliað, R. Ben. 134, 16. Ne gelustfulla ðu *ne delecteris* (*in semitis impiorum*), Kent. Gl. 68 : 112. **II.** *to give delight to, delight* (with dat.):—Đā gelustfullode ðām cyninge heora clǣne líf and heora wynsume behāt (*rex ipse delectatus uita mundissima et promissis eorum suauissimis*, Bd. 1, 26), Hml. Th. ii. 130, 9. **II a.** *used impersonally:*—Sume word synd gecwedene inpersonalia . . . *iuuat* gelustfullað, Ælfc. Gr. Z. 206, 6. Mē gelustfullað *libet mihi*, 207, 5. **II a.** with infin.:—Ús gelustfullað þyssera rynela angir preóstum ætýwan, Angl. viii. 302, 32. **II a β.** with dat. infin.:—Ús gelustfullað gyt furður tō sprecenne be him, Hml. Th. i. 360, 29. **III.** *to delight* a person (acc.):—þu ne gelustfulladest fýnd míne *nec delectasti inimicos meos*, Ps. L. 29, 2. þu gelustfullodest [mē] on þínum weorce *delectasti me in factura tua*, 91, 5. Ic wes gelustfullad *delectabar*, Kent. Gl. 278. þā rihtwísan beóð gewistfullode and beóð gelustfullode, Ps. L. 67, 4. **III a.** *where the cause of,* or *occasion for, delight* is given:—Ic wæs gelustfullod mínre hæftnýde, Hml. A. 202, 245. Ne wēne ic nā þ þes wer wǣre gelustfullod on (mid, *v. l.*) ārfæstnysse weorce (mōde, *v. l.*), ac on (mid, *v. l.*) þæs bisceopes tǣlinge *hunc virum non pietatis opere delectatum aestimo, sed episcopi derogatione*, Gr. D. 76, 16. **IV.** *construction uncertain.*—Gelus-fullað *delectat* (*animam*), Kent. Gl. 458. ¶ in the following passage the constructions of **I a** and **II a a** seem confused:—Ic gewilnode þæs wínes on þǣm ic ǣr gelustfullode tō oferdruncennysse brūcan, Hml. S. 23 b, 534.

**ge-lustfulling.** *Substitute:* **ge-lustfullung,** e; *f.* **I.** *a taking pleasure, delight.* v. ge-lustfullian; **I:**—Nān gelustfullung flǣsces, nān lust yfel *nulla delectatio carnis, nulla voluptas mala*, Scint. 3, 9. On gewilnunge and ungelustfullunge (on gelustfullunge?) unclǣnre *in concupiscentia et in delectatione inmunda*, Angl. xi. 116, 12. Nā mid ege helle, ac mid Cristes lufan and gelustfullunge mihta *non timore gehennae, sed amore Christi et delectatione virtutum*, R. Ben. I. 36, 17. On gewilnungum and gelustfullungum flǣsces *delectationibus carnis*, Scint. 2, 16. **II.** *a giving pleasure.* v. ge-lustfullian; **II, III:**—Gelustfullung mid sange *delectatio carmine* (but the Latin is: *Delectatum crimine*, Ald. 78, 4), An. Ox. 5377. **III.** *pleasantness, delight, pleasure:*—Hí ondrǣdað þolian [for] gelustfullunge middaneardes *timent carere oblectamento mundi*, Scint. 63, 4. Hē forhæfde hine sylfne fram gelustfullunge þysses lífes, Shrn. 12, 22. **IV.** *pleasure as a personification:*—Seó gelustfullung (*voluptas*) gewundedum fótum þurh þā þornas fleáh, Prud. 53. **V.** *that which produces pleasure, an object* or *source of delight, a delight:*—Mid gelustfullunga (or *under* **III**) oblectamento (*theoricae vitae satiantur*), An. Ox. 14, 34. Genih-sumre wenne gelustfullunge *opulenti luxus oblectamenta*, 11, 46. þurh gelustfullunga ídelra bigspella *per oblectamenta inanium fabularum*, Scint. 221, 16. þū onfēhst þára ēcra gōda gelustfullunga, Hml. S. 30, 245.

**ge-lustian;** *p.* ode *To take pleasure* in:—Ne gelusta þū síþfatum ārleásra *ne delecteris semitis impiorum*, Scint. 186, 5. [*Cf. Goth.* lustōn *to desire* : *O. H. Ger.* lustōn *delectari, desiderare*.] v. ge-lystan.

**ge-lútan.** *Add:* **I.** *of movement.* (1) *intrans. To bend the body:*—þā lōcode hē þær geloten and gebíged in þone ofn *in clibanum incurvatus aspexit*, Gr. D. 251, 26. (2) *trans. To bend the head, place on a couch, recline:*—Sunu mannes ne hæfis huěr heáfud gehlūtes ł gebēges (*reclinet*), Mt. L. 8, 20 : p. 15, 16. **II.** *of the day, to decline, approach an end:*—Ofernōn oððe geloten dæg *suprema* (cf. suprema, quando sol suppremit, Corp. Gl. H. 112, 654; *and:*—þeáh seó sunne ofer midne dæg lúte tō þǣre eorþan, Bt. 25; F. 88, 25), Wrt. Voc. i. 53, 14.

**ge-lútian.** *l.* -lutian : **ge-lýf-.** v. ge-líf-: **ge-lýfed** *weakened.* v. ge-léfed: **ge-lygen** *false.* v. un-gelygen.

**ge-lyg(e)nian;** *p.* ode; *pp.* od *To charge with falsehood:*—Đā ne gecneów se portgerēfa þára namena nān ðing þe hē·uamode, ac hē sóna gelignode hine, and cwæð : ' Nū þurh þínre leásan tale ic ongyten hæbbe þ þū eart ān forswíðe leás mon,' Hml. S. 23, 686. Gif hé wolde gefæstnian mid āþe, þ seó leáse wrǣgistre ne wurde fordǣmed. Đā swōr hē þ hē friðian wolde þa leásan wudewan, ðeáh þe heó gelignod wurðe, 2, 210. Gif hwā furðon ǣnne man hatað, swā hwæt swā hē tō gōde gedēð, eal hē hit forlýst; for ðan ðe se apostol Paulus ne bið gelignod (*will not be charged with lying*) þe cwæð : ' þeáh ic āspende ealle míne ǣhta . . . gif ic næbbe ðā sōðan lufe, ne fremað hit mē nān ðing,' Hml. Th. i. 52, 34–54, 5.

**ge-lýhtan.** v. ge-líhtan: **ge-lymp-.** v. ge-limp-.

**ge-lynd.** *Add:* ge-lyndo(-u); *f.:* ge-lynde, es; *n. Grease;* arvina:—Gelynd *adeps*, Wrt. Voc. ii. 10, 27. Gelynde *arvina*, i. 283, 36. Wið ǣlcum sāre, gemylted leōn gelynde, Lch. i. 366, 1. Foxes gelyndes dǣl, ii. 308, 1. Mid gelynde *adipe*, Ex. 29, 22 : Lch. i. 328, 8. Hundes gelynde . . . mid ealdum ele gemylt, 362, 21. Nim fearres gelyndo and beran smeru and weax, ii. 48, 5. Genim henne gelyndo, 310, 3.

**ge-lýsan.** v. ge-lísan: **ge-lýsednes.** *Dele.*

**ge-lystan.** *Add:* **I.** *with acc. of person,* and (1) *gen. of thing desired:*—Hý gelyst ǣlces ýdeles, R. Ben. 136, 22. þā mē gelyste þǣre deóglan stōwe þe ic ǣr on wæs in mynstre; seó is þǣre gnornunge freónd *secretum locum petii amicum moeroris*, Gr. D. 3, 10. Geseah heó ǣnne leahtric and bý gelyste þæs lactucam *conspiciens concupivit*, 30, 33. (2) *with infin. of action a person desires to do:*—Hwílum hié wel gelyst ūt gangan and him þā byrþenne fram āweorpan, Lch. ii. 230, 23. **II.** *with dat. of person (and infin.):*—Hē hæfde hí þā hwíle þe him geliste, Chr. 1046; P. 164, 30. v. ge-lustan.

**ge-lytfullíce.** *Add:* [ge-lystfullíce?]

**ge-lytlian.** *Add:*—Gewanude *vel* gelytlade *deminute*, Wrt. Voc. ii. 138, 67. **I.** *trans.* (1) *to make less than something else:*—þū gelitludest hine lythwōn lǣs fram englum *minuisti eum paulo minus ab angelis*, Ps. L. 8, 6. (2) *to make less than before, to diminish, lessen,* (a) *with regard to number, size,* &c.:—Nýtenu heora hē ne gelitlode *iumenta eorum non minorauit*, Ps. L. 106, 38. Seó sunne wæs swelce heó wǣre eall gelytladu *solis orbis minui visus est*, Ors. 4, 8; S. 188, 22. Líg byð gelytlud, āteorigendum holte *flamma minuitur, deficiente silva*, Scint. 56, 19. (b) *in respect to quality, degree,* &c.:—Suā beóð monige lǣcedōmas ðe sume āðle gelytliað and sume gestrongiað; suā eác hlāf ðe strongra monna mægen gemiclað, hé gelytlað cilda *medicamentum, quod hunc morbum imminuit, alteri vires jungit; et panis, qui vitam fortium roborat, parvulorum necat*, Past. 173, 22–175, 1. (c) *in respect to extent:*—Sōðfæstnes ys swýðe gelytlod *diminutae sunt veritates*, Ps. Th. 11, 1. (3) *to belittle, depreciate, make out* a person

*to be inferior to the character claimed for him:*—Hē wolde gelitlian þone lifigendan Drihten, and sǽde þ hē nǽre on sōðre godcundnesse his fæder gelīca, ac wǽre lǽsse on mihte, Ll. Th. ii. 374, I. **II.** *intrans. To become little, decrease, run short:*—Gelytlade ðára farmana wīn *defecit nubtiarum uinum,* Jn. p. I, 9.

**ge-lytlung,** e; *f. Diminution, failure, lack:*—Metta gelytlung forscrincan dēð gewilnunga yfele *escarum indigentia marcescere facit desideria mala,* Scint. 57, I.

**ge-maad.** v. ge-mád.

**ge-maca.** *Add:* **I.** *an equal, a fellow, companion* (1) of persons: —*Inpar* ungemaca; *dispar* ungelīc; *compar* gelīc, gemaca; *separ* āsyndrod gemaca, Ælfc. Gr. Z. 43, .1–3. Fædores gimaca *Patris compar,* Rtl. 165, 11. Gimacca (*or under* ge-mæcca?), 164, 3. Wolde gē nū ðæt gē næfden nánne gemacan or ðýs gemǽnan middan-gearde *habere in communi mundo consortes minime potestis?,* Past. 331, 2. Wosað gié gimaco Godes *estote imitatores Dei,* Rtl. 12, 11. (2) of things :—Ic gean þes beáhges gemacan þe man sealde mīnum hláforde, Cht. Th. 524, 28. **II.** *a mate.* (1) of persons, *one of a married pair,* (a) *either husband or wife* [cf. ge-bedda *which is used of a husband,* Hml. Th. i. 134, 20]:—*Hic et haec conjunx* þes and þeós gemaca, Ælfc. Gr. 73, 12. Wudewan hád is þ man wunige on clǽnnysse ... æfter his gemacan, ǽgðer ge weras ge wīf, Hml. A. 20, 155. (b) *a husband:*—Wīf sceolde syððan mid Godes bletsunge geneálǽcan hyre gemacan, Hml. Th. i. 134, 23. (c) *a wife:*—Sume þá apostolas hæfdon him gemacan, Hml. A. 14, 34. (2) of animals, *one of a pair:*—Ádruncon ealle cwice wihta būton ehta mannum ... and ælces cynnes twá gemacan, Wlfst. 206, 27. v. hand-, land-, un-gemaca.

**ge-macian.** *Substitute:* **I.** *to make, fashion, construct* a material object :—Hē þám gemǽron castelas lēt gemakian, Chr. 1097 ; P. 233, 25. Gē ne sceolon beón rance mid hringgum'geglengede, ne eówer reáf ne beó tō ranclīce gemacod, ne eft tō wáclīce, Ll. Th. ii. 358, 6. **II.** *to produce by action, bring about* a condition of things, *make peace,* &c. :—Hī þæra cinga sehte swá gemacedon, þ se cyng Melcolm tō ūran cynge cōm, and his man weard, Chr. 1091 ; P. 227, 2. **II a.** *with dat.* of person affected by feeling produced :—Eác is hearm Gode módsorg gemacod, Gen. 755. **III.** *to use:*—Sæ ælmihtiga wyrhta geworhte on anginne ealne middaneard on his mycclum cræfte, ac hē sylf wæs ǽfre unbegunnen scyppend, sē ðe swá mihtiglīce gemacode swylcne cræft, Hex. 4, 4. **IV.** *to cause to be.* (1) with adj. complement :—Þá sind sōðe welan, and heora lufigendne gemaciað weligne ēcelīce, Hml. Th. ii. 88, 29. (2) with subst. complement :—Þone hē ǽr ēhtende martyr gemacode, Hml. Th. ii. 82, 24. (3) with *tō* and dat. :—Gif hē him þæt mǽden mihte gemacian tō wīfe, Hml. S. 3, 366. **V.** with dependent clause, *to cause* that, *bring about* that :—Hē on lāreówes onlīcnesse ðā ðēnenga ðæs ealdordōmes gecierð tō hláforddōme, and gemacað ðæt his ege and his onwald wierð tō gewunan *ex simulatione disciplinae ministerium regiminis vertit in usum dominationis,* Past. 121, 25. Hē gemacode þæt fýr cōme ufan swilce of heofenum, Hml. Th. i. 6, 11. Hī gemacodon þæt him cōmon tō creópende fela næddran, ii. 488, 20 : Chr. 1075 ; P. 211, 9 : Hml. S. 31, 498. Gemaca þ ðá wīf gecyrran sylfwilles tō ūs, 36, 373. Gē habbað ūs gedōn láðe Pharaone and eallum his folce, and gemacod þæt hig wyllað ūs mid hyra swurdum ofsleán *foetere fecistis odorem nostrum coram Pharaone et servis ejus, et praebuistis ei gladium ut occideret nos,* Ex. 5, 21. **V a.** *to arrange* with a person that something shall be done :—Hire wer gemacode wið þone cyning þ man sette on cweartern þone apostol, Hml. S. 36, 275. [O. Sax. gi-makōn : O. H. Ger. ge-mahhôn.]

**ge-macian;** *p.* ode *To make equal* or *like* (v. ge-mæc, ge-maca), *liken, compare.* (Cf. ge-līcian ; I. 2) :—Gemacade ł gemacað *comparat,* Lk. p. 5, 13. [O. H. Ger. ge-mahhôn *comparare, aequiparare.*]

**ge-mád;** *adj. Foolish, senseless, mad:*—Gemaad *vecors,* Wrt. Voc. ii. 123, 36. Gemád *fatue* (Qui dixerit, 'Fatue,' Mt. 5, 22), 72, 8. [O. Sax. gi-mēd *foolish:* O. H. Ger. ge-meit *stultus, baridus, stolidus.*] v. ge-mǽdan.

**ge-mæc, -mæcc, -mæce.** *Add:*—Gemæc *compar germane, similis fratri,* Wrt. Voc. ii. 132, 75. Of ðǽre wīsan mæg beón ongyten, þ heora bēgra geearnung wæs gemæce (mæcc? ; -mæc, *v. l.*) qua ex re colligitur, quia utrorumque par fuerat meritum, Gr. D. 313, 23. v. un-gemæc[c], *and next word.*

**ge-mæcca.** *Take here* ge-mecca *in Dict., and add:* **I.** *an equal, a like, fellow :*—Fædor gimacca (*but see* ge-maca; I. 1) *Patris compar,* Rtl. 164, 3. Þonne hī gegadriaþ þá gelícan tō heora gemæccum in þám gelícum tintregum, and þá oferhýdigan mid þám oferhígdum ... *cum pares paribus in tormentis similibus sociant, ut superbi cum superbis ...,* Gr. D. 316, 4. **II.** *a match, one suited to another.* v. ge-mæc :— Gyrnde hē him his gemæccan tō nýmanne *adoptata sibi coaetanea virgine,* Guth. Gr. 104, 7. **III.** *a married* (or *betrothed*) *person.* (1) of a man or woman :—Gemæcga *conjunx,* Wrt. Voc. i. 50, 8. (2) of a woman :—His fæder wæs on hǽðenscipe wunigende, and his gemæcca samod, Hml. Th. ii. 498, 26 : Hml. S. 3, 470. Ic eom Arcestrate þín gemæcca, Ap. Th. 25, 8. Ic bæd his dohtor mē tō gemæccan, be þǽre

ic mæg secgan þ heó his ágen gemæcca wǽre, 9, 3–5. For hwan nelt þū (*Joachim*) hám gehweorfan tō þínum gemæccan ?, Hml. A. 122, 165. Nelle þū ondrǽdan Marian þíne gemæccan (*conjugem*) tō onfônne, Mt. 1, 20. God him swylce gemæccean forgeaf, Chr. 1067 ; P. 201, 33. þ ic mōte þíne þeówene míne gemeccan geseón, Hml. S. 30, 237. Hī him tō nimað mæged tō gemæccum mínra feónda, Gen. 1259. **III a.** in pl. *man and wife:*—Gemæccan *conjuges,* Wrt. Voc. ii. 52, 33. Tū beóð gemæccan, Gn. Ex. 23. v. efen-, riht-gemæcca.

**ge-mæclic.** *Add:*—Gemæclic *conjugalis,* Wrt. Voc. ii. 136, 32. Þá þe gálnysse flaesces mid gemæclicum (*coniugali*) wyrþscype gewríþað, Scint. 182, 16. [Ge]mæclican anten[dnyssa] *tedas iugales,* An. Ox. 18, 27.

**ge-mǽd.** *Dele, and see next word.*

**ge-mǽdan.** *Add: pp.* ge-mǽd. **I.** *to make insane:*—Gemǽd amens (puer ... vertitur in rabiem fraudatus mente sagaci, bacchatur ... amens, Ald. 176, 17), Wrt. Voc. ii. 94, 4 : 5, 59. **II.** *to make foolish:*—Gemǽdid *ineptus,* Wrt. Voc. ii. 111, 70. Gemaeded *vanus,* 123, 13. Gemǽdedne *vecordem* (*juvenem,* Prov. 7, 7), 87, 51. v. ge-mád (*not* ge-mǽd).

**ge-mǽdla** *chatter.* v. ge-maðel. *Substitute:* **ge-mǽdla** *fury, madness ; vecordia.* v. ge-mád.

**ge-mǽg,** es. *Substitute:* **ge-mǽgas, -mágas;** *pl. Take here* ge-mágas in *Dict., and* add:—*Fratres* gebrōþor, *et aliquando* gemǽgas, Wrt. Voc. ii. 39, 46. v. sib-gemágas. Cf. ge-mǽgþ.

**ge-mǽgenod.** *The original Latin is:* Postquam Caedualla regno potitus est.

**ge-mǽgfast.** *Dele.*

**ge-mǽgþ** *power. Substitute:* **ge-mǽgþ, -mǽhþ,** e ; *f. Greed, importunate desire:*—Ðū wāst þ mē nǽfre seó gītsung and seó gemǽgþ ðisses eorðlican anwealdes for wel ne lícode, ne ic ealles for swíþe ne girnde þisses eorþlican ríces *scis ipsa minimum nobis ambitionem mortalium rerum fuisse dominatam,* Bt. 17 ; F. 58, 23. *Take here* ge-mǽhþ in *Dict.*

**ge-mǽgþ.** *Substitute: A collection of kinsmen, a family:*—Seó dǽd ... þætte ealre worolde swelce sibbe bringan mehte, þte twá þeóda ǽr habban ne mehton, ne ðætte lǽsse wæs, twá gemǽgþa *omnibus gentibus unam fuisse voluntatem inservire paci ; quod prius ne una quidem civitas, unusve populus civium, vel, quod majus est, una domus fratrum habere potuisset,* Ors. 3, 5 ; S. 108, 2. Cf. ge-mǽgas.

**ge-mǽhþ.** v. ge-mǽgþ *greed:* **ge-mǽl.** *See next word.*

**ge-mǽlan** *to stain, smear. Add:*—Átre gemǽled *lita* (*spicula veneno*), Wrt. Voc. ii. 96, 69 : 52, 69. [O. H. Ger. ge-meilen *polluere.*] v. mál.

**ge-mǽnan.** **I.** *to mean, signify. Take here* ge-mǽnan ; I. *in Dict., and* add:—Nū behealde wē ðá næddran ... Hwæt gemǽnð þæt ?, Hml. Th. ii. 238, 32. Petrus smeáde hwæt his gesihð gemǽnde, Hml. S. 10, 109. **II.** *to have in mind. Take here* ge-mǽnan ; **IV.** in *Dict.* v. mǽnan *to mean.*

**ge-mǽnan.** **I.** *to tell, say, mention* a matter :—Þēh eów lytles hwæt swelcra gebroca on becume, þonne gemǽnað gē hit tō (v. tō ; I. 5 f 1 þǽm wyrrestan tídum, and magon hié hreówlīce wēpan *if some little of such troubles come on you, then you talk of it as the worst times, and can bewail them miserably ; injurias, quibus aliquando vescantur, relatu tristiori deplorant,* Ors. 3, 7 ; S. 120, 5. Þæt þǽr ǽnig mon wordum ne worcum wǽre ne brǽce, ne þurh inwitsearo ǽfre gemǽnden, þeáh hié hire beággyfan banan folgedon (*though they were following the slayer of their lord, this was not to be mentioned with the malicious intent of provoking quarrels*), B. 1101. **II.** *to speak* a language :—Hwílum ic onhyrge gūðfugles hleóðor, hwílum glidan reorde mūðe gemǽne (cf. hē that word gisprak, gimёnda mid is mūðu, Hēl. 830) *sometimes I imitate the voice of the eagle, sometimes I speak the kite's language with my mouth,* Rä. 25, 6. v. mǽnan *to tell, relate.*

**ge-mǽnan** *to lament, complain.* **I.** *trans. To complain of, have as a grievance:*—Gif þū gemune þ þín brōðer oðde freónd áht ungeþwǽrlices wið þe gemǽne *si recordatus fueris quia frater tuus habet aliquid adversum te,* Gr. D. 349, 24. **II.** *to lament, mourn. Take here* ge-mǽnan ; **III.** in *Dict., and* add:—Ðá ðe gemǽnas *qui lugent,* Mt. L. 5, 5. Ne gemǽnde ge *non planxistis,* 11, 17. Gemǽnde *vapulabit,* Lk. L. 12, 47. v. mǽnan *to lament.*

**ge-mǽne.** *Dele last passage, and* add: **I.** *that is held in joint possession :*—Se wuda gemǽne þe intō loceres leáge hýrð oð ðæs cinges inwuda, and hēr is se wuda ðe intō tūneweorde hýrð, C. D. B. iii. 189, I. Ǽgðer ge etelond ge eyrðlond ge eác wudoland all hit is gemǽne þára fíf and tuёntig hída, C. D. ii. 95, 15. Ðás nigon hído licggeað on gemang ōðran gedállange, feldlǽs gemǽne and mǽda gemǽne and yrðland gemǽne, vi. 39, 8–10. Tō gemǽnan hylle, v. 100, 21. On ðan gemǽnan lande gebyrað ðártō fíf and sixti æccera, 326, 33. Gif orf ungecýd on gemǽnre lǽse wunað, Ll. Th. i. 276, 1 : 438, 14. On þane gemǽnan gáran, C. D. v. 78, 9. **I a.** *that is shared* between persons (*dat.*) :—Þolige hē healfes weres, and þ sý gemǽne hláforde and bisceope, Ll. Th. i. 398, 6. Þ sí gemǽne Crīste and cyninge, 344, 4 :

348, 2c. þā woruldbōte hig gesetton gemǣne Crīste and cynge, 166, 17. Unc sceal sweord and helm, byrne and byrduscrūd bām gemǣne (be used to defend both of us), B. 2660. **I a a.** that is enjoyed in common :—þā þe āscyrede sȳn fram þām gemǣnan gereorde privati a mense participatione, R. Ben. 49, 4. **I b.** where the same circumstance, condition, &c., is found in two or more cases :—þæt nū bletsung mōt bǣm gemǣne werum and wīfum, Cri. 100. Se mægdhād is gemǣne ægþrum cnihtum and mǣdenum, Hml. A. 33, 224. **I c.** of the properties of things :—Swā hwā swā ðone gemǣnan gōd eallra gōda forlǣt, Bt. 36, 6 ; F. 182, 9. **I d.** of abstract objects, belonging to or concerning equally :—Sȳ þes rǣd gemǣne eallum leódscipe, ægðer ge Anglum ge Denum ge Bryttum, Ll. Th. i. 272, 33 : 276, 21 : 278, 4. ¶ habban (āgan) gemǣne, beón ānum āwiht gemǣnes to have in common. (1) where all parties form the subject of the verb. (a) with a material object, to take an equal share of something, to have between them :—Hæbben hī him þ weorð gemǣne (dividunt pretium, Ex. 21, 35), 50, 11. Be þan þe ceorlas habbað land gemǣne and gærstūnas. Gif ceorlas gærstūn hæbben gemǣnne (-mǣne, v. l.), oþþe ōðer gedālland, tō tȳnanne, 128, 4-6. (a a) of the relation of parents and children :—Be ðon ðe ryhtgesamhīwan bearn hæbben . . . Gif ceorl and his wīf bearn hæbben gemǣne, Ll. Th. i. 126, 3. (b) with a non-material object. (a) of joint action, to share action, responsibility, &c. :—Habban þā geréfscypas bēgen þā fullan spǣce gemǣne, Ll. Th. i. 236, 25. Wē hæfdon ūs ealle þā āscean gemǣne, 230, 18. (β) of sameness of properties :—þæt āne lufe ealle gesceafta hæbben gemǣne (est cunctis communis amor), þæt hī þiówien swilcum þiódguman, Met. 22, 93. (2) habban gemǣne wiþ, mid to have in common with others. (a) with a material object, to take an equal share of something with another :—Tō healfum fō se cyng, tō healfum se geférscipe. Gif hit bōcland sȳ, þonne āh se landhlāford þone healfan dǣl wið þone geférscipe gemǣne the landlord and the fellowship have the half between them, Ll. Th. i. 228, 20. (b) with a non-material object, (a) to have a matter between oneself and another, have a matter to settle with another :—Sē þe oferhogie þ hē heom hlyste, hæbbe him gemǣne þ wið God sylfne (it is a matter to be settled between himself and God), Ll. Th. i. 332, 31. Á swā hē gecneordra swā bið hē weordra, gif hē wið witan hafoð his wīsan gemǣne if he has to do with a wise man, Angl. ix. 260, 21. (β) to have in company with, have the same as another :—Þis leóht wē habbaþ wið nȳtenu gemǣne, ac þæt leóht wē sceolan sēcan þ wē mōton habban mid englum gemǣne, Bl. H. 21, 13-15. (c) without object, to have to do with :—Þū scealt understandan þæt þū hæfst wið strangne gemǣne, Wlfst. 250, 2. Sē ðe þis āwendan wyle, hæbbe him wið Gode gemǣne on þām micclan dōme, C. D. iv. 277, 29. (3) beón ānum āwiht gemǣnes to have anything to do with :—Nāwiht þē siæ on þām sōþfæste gemǣnes nihil tibi et justo illi, Mt. R. 27, 19. **II.** belonging to everybody :—Hū mihtest þū sittan on middum gemǣnum rīce, þ þū ne sceoldest þ ilce geþolian þ ōðre men, Bt. 7, 3 ; F. 22, 17. Ðiós eorðe eallum mannum bringð gemǣnne fōster, Past. 335, 11. **II a.** in an ecclesiastical sense, catholic :—Geleáfa se gemǣna fides catholica, Ath. Crd. 42. **III.** that stands in the same relation to two or more objects, common as in common enemy :—Him bið wind gemǣne, Gn. Ex. 54. Mehten hié heora gemǣnan fiénd him from ādōn, Ors. 3, 7 ; S. 118, 15. **III a.** of the relation of a child to its parents :—Mīn wīf and uncer gemǣne bearn, Cht. Th. 480, 22. **IV.** denoting joint action or agreement :—Mid gemǣnre geþeahte communi consilio, Bd. 2, 5 ; Sch. 135, 9. Gif man āsylled bið on gemǣnum weorce. Gif mon ōðerne æt gemǣnan weorce offelle, Ll. Th. i. 70, 9. On gemeánre dǣde þonne man bið nýdwyrhta, 412, 12. Hié þrȳ cwǣdon þurh gemǣne word with united voice they spoke, Dan. 362 : Gen. 2474. **V.** denoting association (cf. ge-māna), acting or being together with others. (1) local. Cf. hand-gemǣne :—Hȳ ealle gemǣnum handum on ānum wǣpne (with their hands placed together on one weapon) þām sēmende syllan . ., 174, 21. Freá engla hēht wesan wæter gemǣne, þā nū under roderum heora ryne healdað (dixit Deus : 'Congregentur aquae quae sub coelo sunt,' Gen. 1, 9), Gen. 158. (2) denoting companionship, collaboration, &c. Bǣm inc (God and Christ) is gemǣne Heáhgǣst, Cri. 357. Ealle forgielden þone wer gemǣnum hondum (jointly), Ll. Th. i. 80, 17. **VI.** that passes or subsists between, mutual, reciprocal. (1) of material things :—þām folcum sceal . . . sacu restan, . . . wesan māðmas gemǣne, manig ōðerne gōdum gegrētan, B. 1860. (2) of non-material things :—Sib wæs gemǣne bām . . . ǣghwæðer ōðerne earme beþehte, An. 1015. Unc gemǣne ne sceal elles āwiht nymðe lufu langsumu, Gen. 1904. Beó eallum crīstenum mannum sibb and sōm gemǣne, and ǣlc sacu tōtwǣmed, Ll. Th. i. 320, 28 : 370, 10. Unriht is tō wīde mannum gemǣne, Wlfst. 159, 23. Tūddor bið gemǣne incrum orlegnið, Gen. 914. Ðone ealdan teónan gewrecan þe him on ǣrdagum gemǣne wæs, Ors. 3, 1 ; S. 98, 10. Ne sig þē and þisum ryhtwȳsan men nān þyng gemǣne let there be nothing between you and this righteous man; nihil tibi et justo illi (Mt. 27, 19), Nic. 3, 11. Wæs unefen racu unc gemǣne, Cri. 1460. Gemǣne on eów sylfum sōþe lufe hæbbende mutuam in vobismet ipsis caritatem habentes, Sci. 1, 3. Oft wǣron teónan weredum gemǣne (facta est rixa inter

pastores gregum Abram et Lot, Gen. 13, 7), Gen. 1897. **VII.** belonging to a community, public :—Tō ūre gemǣne þearfe, Ll. Th. i. 230, 15 : 232, 2. Æt ūrum gemǣnum sprǣce, 5. Of ūrum gemǣnum feó, 234, 28. **VIII.** free to be used by all, general, public :—Gemǣne metern coenaculum, Wrt. Voc. i. 58, 50. **IX.** inferior in degree, minor, used of the ecclesiastical orders below the sub-deacon (earlier the deacon); from the sub-deacon upwards the orders were 'sacri ordines' :—Gif hwylc lǣwede man hine forswerige . . . fæste .iiii. geár. Gif hē bið gemǣnes hādes man (si sit clericus), fæste .v. geár, subdiácon .vi. geár . . . bisceop .xii., Ll. Th. ii. 192, 7. Mid gemǣnes hādes mannum cum clericis, 196, 20. Wīsman gehādod gemǣnes hādes mulier ordinata clericali ordine, 186, 31. Gemǣnes hādes preóstum is ālȳfed, æfter ðæs hālgan Gregorius tǣcinge (v. Bd. 1, 27 ; Sch. 63, 3-5 : Preóstas and Godes þeówas būtan hālgum hādum gesette clerici extra sacros ordines constituti), þæt hī sȳferlīce sinscipes brūcon. Witodlīce ðām ōðrum þe æt Godes weófode þēniað, þæt is mæssepreóstum and diáconum, is forboden ǣlc hǣmed, Hml. Th. ii. 94, 25. v. hand-gemǣne.

**ge-mǣnelic.** Add : **I.** that belongs to or concerns all human beings :—On hālgum bōcum is se gemǣnelica deáð slǣpe wiðmeten . . . ealle mōton slāpan on ðām gemǣnelicum deáðe, Hml. Th. ii. 566, 27-34. Se gemǣnelica deáð þæs mannes līchaman tō deáðe gebringð . . . Ne mæg nān man ætberstan þām gemǣnelican deáðe, ðe eallum mannum becymð, Hml. A. 54, 97-106. Gemǣnelicum gafole generali (mortis) debito, An. Ox. 1447. **II.** denoting co-operation, association :—[Ge]mǣnlicere [ge]férrǣdene contuberniali sodalitate, An. Ox. 2353. Swā oft swā gē eów gemǣnelice gebeórscipas gegearwiað, Hml. A. 145, 43. **III.** belonging to a community, public, general :—þæt eal folc fæste tō gemǣnelicre dǣdbōte, Wlfst. 180, 23. Swā swā man gerǣde for gemǣnelicre neóde, Ll. Th. i. 324, 1 : 382, 2. **IV.** ordinary :—Sume menn dyslīce fæstað ofer heora mihte on gemǣnelicum lenctene (in Lent, which being of ordinary occurrence, did not call for excess in fasting?), Hml. S. 13, 94. **V.** of persons, common, without special rank :—Embe þyssera ancersetlena, and eác gemǣnelicra muneca drohtnunge, Hml. Th. i. 546, 1. **VI.** not ceremonially clean :—Gemǣnelicum (communibus) mið hondum, þ is unðuegenum, Mk. L. 7, 2. [O. H. Ger. ge-meinlîh communis.]

**ge-mǣnelîce.** Add : -mǣnlîce. **I.** in common, in joint possession :—God eallum mancinne forgeaf him gemǣnlîce fisccinn and fugelcinn and þā feówerfētan deór, Ælfc. T. Grn. 4, 41. þ feoh hī mid heom tō þām scræfe gemǣnelîce hæfdon, Hml. S. 23, 213. þ hī ealle habbon heofonan rīce him gemǣnelîce him sylfum tō mēde, Hml. A. 45, 519. **II.** where there is participation in attributes, characteristics, &c., in common with others :—Mǣdenu magon beón Crīstes mōdru. Eall Crīstes geladung is Crīstes mōdor . . . , Maria is mōdor līchamlîce and mōdor gāstlîce, līchamlîce heó āna and gāstlîce gemǣnelîce (Mary alone is according to the flesh Christ's mother, but in a spiritual sense she shares the title with others), Hml. A. 33, 214-223. **III.** jointly, together. (1) where persons act together :—Hī ealle gemǣnelîce him hȳren cuncti obediant, R. Ben. 15, 15 : Hml. A. 179, 341 : Bd. 1, 23 ; Sch. 49, 11. Hē gemǣnlîce (-mǣne-, v. l.) ðancað non occurrit, ut simul omnes dicant versum, R. Ben. 69, 10. (2) where persons are affected together :—Ic nū þās þing wrīte tō þe gemǣnelice and tō mīnre mēder and mīnum geswustrum, Nar. 3, 7. (3) where things are done together :—Seó hēs and þā fulfremedan weorc gemǣnelîce (communiter) būtū þā þing beóð gefyllede, R. Ben. 7. **IV.** in general, without exception :—Ealle gē geleáffulle men synt tō myngienne gemǣnlîce, from þon lǣston oð þone mǣstan, Ll. Th. ii. 418, 26. Drihten þe ūs ealle gemǣnelîce (pariter) tō ēcum līfe gelǣde, R. Ben. 132, 9. Hē ðis bōc āurāt Gode and Sancte Cūðberhte and allum ðǣm hālgum gimǣnelîce, ðā ðe in eólonde sint, Jn. L. p. 188, 2. **V.** mutually :—þā ōþre heom gemǣnelîce betwyh on þisse þēnunge þeówian ceteri sibi invicem serviant, R. Ben. 59, 4. Gebiddað eów gemǣnelîce orate pro invicem, Scint. 30, 12 : 37, 6 : 64, 16. [O. H. Ger. gemeinlîhha communiter, consonanter, generaliter.]

**ge-mǣnelicness,** e ; f. Generality :—Wīdgil gemǣnelicnes passiua (plurimorum) generalitas, (specialis singulorum proprietas), An. Ox. 5385 : 8, 400.

**ge-mǣnigfealdian,** -fildan. v. ge-manigfealdian, -fildan.

**ge-mǣnnes.** Add :—**I.** joint tenancy of property :—Duobus carris dabo licentiam silfam ad illas secundum antiquam consuetudinem et constitutionem in aestate perferendam in commune silfa quod nos Saxonicae in gemēnnisse dicimus, C. D. ii. 1, 27. **II.** joint occupancy of a place, fellowship of those who together occupy a place :—Sȳ hē āscyred fram beódes gemǣnnesse privatur a mense participatione, R. Ben. 49, 2. þæt wē his rīces gemǣnnesse mid him āgan mōten ut regni ejus mereamur esse consortes, 6, 2. **III.** fellowship, communion with people :—Ne bið hē nā wyrðe ǣnigre gemǣnnysse (communione) mid eáwfæstum mannum, Ll. Th. ii. 174, 36. **IV.** sharing, imparting :—Weldǣde and gemǣnnysse (communionis) nelle gē forgytan, Scint. 165, 18. **V.** common, general, (in) common, (in) general. Cf. gemǣnelîce ; **IV :**

Gif in gemǽnnisse alle God gebédon *si in commune omnes Deum deprecarentur*, Mt. p. 9, 5.

ge-mǽnscipe. *Add*: I. *communion of persons*:—Hé bið gemǽnscipe ðǽre hálgan gelaðunge geférlǽht, Hml. Th. i. 494, 18. II. *union of parts*:—Þæt þin sáwl and þin líchama tóðǽlað heora gemǽnscype, Wlfst. 248, 23. III. *community of goods, possession in common*:—Gif hý þonne hwæt syllan willan, sellan hí þæt þǽre hálgan stówe tó rihtum gemǽnscipe, R. Ben. 103, 20.

ge-mǽnsumian. *Substitute*: ge-mǽnsumian, -mǽnsuman; *p.* ode, ede. I. *to make one's own common to others, to impart, communicate.* (1) *trans.*:—Seó þeód þone wísdóm Angelfolce cýðde and gemǽnsumode (-ede, *v.l.*) *gens illa scientiam populis Anglorum communicare curavit*, Bd. 5, 22; Sch. 682, 13. Gé wilniað ús þá þing gemǽnsumian (-suman, *v. l.*) (*communicare*), I, 25; Sch. 55, 7. (1 a) *to administer* the Eucharist:—Húsel þ genihtsumige tó gemǽnsumigenne eallum *eucharistia quae sufficit ad communicandum cunctis*, Angl. xiii. 415, 708. (2) *intrans.*:—Neódum háligra gemǽnsumigende *necessitatibus sanctorum communicantes*, Scint. 147, 13. (2 a) of speech, *to talk to*:—Ná gemǽnsuma þu menu ungelǽredum *non communices homini indocto*; jest not with a rude man (Ecclus. 8, 4), Scint. 97, 8. II. *to join with others in taking, to partake, communicate* (in an ecclesiastical sense), with gen.:—Ic on þǽre cyrcan þæs Drihtlican líchaman and his blódes gemǽnsumode, Hml. S. 23 b, 627. Gemǽnsumeden heó þæs líchaman úres Drihtnes, 113. Gemǽnsumigende gerýnæ[s] *communicans sacramentum* (*Dominicum*), An. Ox. 2140. III. *to make a union between, unite, join, associate* (trans.):—Ic mé gemǽnsumode þám liffǽstan gerýnum úres Drihtnes, Hml. S. 23 b, 503. III a. of matrimonial union, *to unite in marriage, to marry.* Cf. ge-mǽnung:—Ne hiá biðon gemǽnsumad, i. ne ceorl hæfis wífes gemána, ne wíf hæfis ceorles *neque nubentur*, Mk. L. R. 12, 25. IV. *to have fellowship with, associate* (intrans.), *have to do with*:—Ic ne gemǽnsumige mid gecorenum heora *non communicabo cum electis eorum*, Ps. L. 140, 4. Sé þe gemǽnsumað mid ofermódigum *qui communicauerit cum superbo*, Scint. 83, 5. V. *to defile*:—Þás yfelu gemǽnsumiað (*communicant*, i. *contaminant*) mann, Scint. 102, 17. [*O. H. Ger.* ge-meinsamón *communicare, participare.*] v. mǽnsumian.

ge-mǽnsumnes. *Add*: *fellowship*:—Bi gemǽnsumnissæ *super communicatione* (*vestra in evangelio Christi*, Phil. I, 5), An. Ox. 62, 2. Ðerh gimǽnsumnisse hálgana *per communionem sanctorum*, Rtl. 113, 26.

ge-mǽnsumung. *Substitute*: *Administration* of the Eucharist. v. ge-mǽnsumian; I. 1 a:—On þǽre mæssan gemǽnsumung ys gearwud *in qua missa communicatio prebetur*, Angl. xiii. 414, 706. Æfter gemǽnsumunge ł húselgange *post communionem*, R. Ben. I. 69, 6. v. mǽnsumung.

ge-mǽnung, e; *f.* *Union* in marriage, *nuptials*:—Fǽmnan beóð hyre on fultume oð þone dæg eówra gemǽnunga, Hml. A. 132, 538. Tó hwan forhǽle ðu ús þíne gemǽnunge swá clǽnre fǽmnan, 135, 650. Cf. ge-mǽnsumian; III a.

ge-mǽran *to fix limits.* v. ge-mǽrian.

ge-mǽran *to divulge. Add*:—Wæs þis geworden on Beornica mǽgðe, and feor and wíde gemǽred (*longe lateque diffamatum*), Bd. 5, 14; Sch. 647, 16. [*O. L. Ger.* gi-mârian *manifestare.*]

ge-mǽre. *Add*: ge-mǽru(-o), e (or *indecl.?*); *f. A border, margin, coast*:—Tó ðǽm gemǽrum *ad oras*, Wrt. Voc. ii. 10, 52. I. in the case of a country or district. (1) *frontier, border*, (by the sea) *coast*:—Þá brycge þe æt þǽm gemǽre wæs, Ors. 2, 5; S. 78, 15. Þá hié tó ðǽm gemǽre cómon mid hiera firde, þá hæfdon hié hiera clúsan belocene *Athenienses angustias Thermopylarum occupavere*, 3, 7; S. 112, 34. Néh Sumersǽton gemǽre (-mǽran, *v. l.*) and Dæfenascíre, Chr. 1052; P. 179, 9. ¶ binnan gemǽre (gemǽrum) *within a country*:—Siþþan hé binnan ðǽm gemǽre wǽre, Ors. 2, 4; S. 76, 10. Gif hwá binnan þám gemǽrum úres ríces reáflác dó, Ll. Th. i. 108, 8. (1 a) with reference to English political divisions. Cf. *border* used in connexion with England and Scotland. (a) *the border* between Northumbria and Mercia:—Súðmǽgðe oð gemǽre Humbre streámes Myrcna cyninge on hýrnesse underðeódde wǽron *prouincias australes ad confinium usque Hymbrae fluminis Merciorum regi subiectae sunt*, Bd. 5, 23; Sch. 691, 6. Hé wæs sumes mynstres (*Wearmouth*) abbod be-norðan gemǽre (*in Northumbria*), Shrn. 134. 13. His líchoma rested be-norðan gemǽre in ðám mynstre Lastinga eá, 142, 21 (cf. be-súðan sǽ *across the channel, in France*, 145, 17). Hér Ósréd Norðanhymbra cining wǽrð ofslagen be-súðan gemǽre (*in Mercia*), Chr. 716; P. 43, 9. (*For the construction in these passages*, cf.: Naðer be-norðan mearce, ne be-súðan, Ll. Th. i. 232, 18.) (β) *the Welsh border*:—Hé be þám gemǽron castelas lét gemakian, Chr. 1097; P. 233, 25. (2) *a border district;* in pl. *borders, territories*:—Gebýrdum gemǽre *colono fine*, Wrt. Voc. ii. 134, 26. In gemǽra ł in tún *in villam*, Mt. L. 26, 36. On Bethleem and on eallum hire gemǽrum (-moerum, R., *finibus*), Mt. 2, 16: Hml. Th. i. 80, 16: Mt. L. R. 4, 13. Þ hé férde fram heora gemǽrum (-mérum, R.), Mt. 8, 34: Mk. 5, 17; 7, 31. Of þám Chanáeiscum gemǽrum, Mt. 15, 22: Hml. Th. ii. 110, 8. In gemǽrum *in fines*, Mt. L. 15, 39. Garganus seó dún stent on Campania landes gemǽron

(gemǽro, Bl. H. 197, 19) wið þá sǽ Adriaticum, Hml. Th. i. 502, 5. Sum cwén, Saba gehǽten, cóm fram ðám súðernum gemǽrum tó Salamone, ii. 584, 9. In londum ł gemǽrum *in vicis*, Mt. L. 6, 2. In gemǽro *in fines* (*Iudaea*), 19, 1: Mk. 7, 31. In ða nǽsta gemǽro (gimǽru, R.) and londo *in proximas uillas et uicos*, 6, 36. Hwæt is þes þe þus unforht gǽþ on úre gemǽro?, Bl. H. 85, 15. (3) *with idea of remoteness, an extremity, end,* (*uttermost*) *part* of earth or heavens:—Fram gemǽre eorðan *ab extremo terrae*, Ps. Rdr. 134, 7. God gewealt gemeára eorðan (*finium terrae*), Ps. L. 58, 14. Heó cóm fram landes gemǽrum (gemǽrum eorðo, L., ende eorðe, R.) *venit a finibus terrae*, Mt. 12, 42. Gemǽrum (endum, W. S.), Lk. L. R. 11, 31: Bd. 5, 7; Sch. 584, 14. Æt þám ýtmestan eorþan gemǽrum, Bl. H. 119, 25. Æt þá ytmestan gemǽro *in fines orbis terrae* (Ps. 19, 4), 133, 35. Oð heofona gemǽru(-o) *usque ad terminos coelorum*, Mt. W. S. L. R. 24. 31. II. in the case of landed property, *a boundary*:—Mǽd pratum, gemǽre (*n. sing.* or ? *pl. f.*) *fines, hafudland limites*, Wrt. Voc. i. 38, 1–3. Lið ðæt gemǽre on gerihte of foxhylle ..., C. D. ii. 249, 34. Þæs hagan gemǽre ... lið úp of þǽm forda ..., C. D. B. ii. 305, 22. Andlang ðæs gemǽrhagan ... andlang gemǽres, C. D. vi. 9, 5: 234, 20, 21, 23. Andlang gemǽres on hæselburh ... of ðám forda á be gemǽre, iii. 438, 13–16, 17, 18, 21. Be gerihtum gemǽre, 404, 29. On feówer gemǽre, 397, 3. On fíf gemǽre, vi. 226. Ðis syndon ðæs londes gemǽro tó Abbandúne, 5. Gemǽra gedál *finium regundorum actio*, Wrt. Voc. ii. 39, 30: 148, 61. Hé hine gelǽdde ealle þá gemǽru, swá hé him of þám ealdan bócum rǽdde, C. D. v. 140, 32. Ne oferstepe ðú ealde gemǽro *ne transgrediaris terminos antiquos*, Kent. Gl. 854. ¶ In composition with words denoting objects that help to form a boundary:—On gemǽrbeorg and of gemǽrbeorge, C. D. B. ii. 140, 26. On gemǽrbeorgas, C. D. iii. 403, 29. On ðone gemǽrhagan, ðanon andlang ðæs hagan, v. 70, 22. Andlang ðæs gemǽrhagan, vi. 9, 4. Ollonc ðæs gemǽreheges, 234, 11. Ǽrest on ðá gemǽrlace; andlang lace, 8, 26. On gemǽrstán; ðonne of gemǽrstáne, iii. 403, 29. Be rihtre mearce tó ðǽt gemǽrðornan, 404, 32. On ðæt gemǽrtreów, 342, 30. Andlang gemǽrweges, 383, 28. Innan ðone gemǽrwyl; andlang streámes, 193, 9. III. in other local connexions:—Gif þú scyle áceorfan unhál lim of hálum líce þonne ne ceorf þú þ on þám gemǽre þæs hálan líces ac micle swíþor ceorf on þ hále líc, Lch. ii. 84, 28. Hé cóm on þ gemǽre leóhtes and þeóstro *noctis prope terminos*, Bt. 35, 6; F. 170, 13. IV. *a line* (lit. or fig.) *that cannot* or *should not be passed, a bound, limit*:—Ðá bebeád se biscop: 'Ásettað mé ongeán þysum fýre' ... Se líg æt þám gemǽre (*illo termino*) þæs biscopes (*the bound made by the bishop's person*) wearð gecyrred, Gr. D. 48, 9. Wit habbað oferhleóðred (-leóred?) þ gemǽre uncres leóhtes (*but the Latin is:* excede terminos luci nostri), Nar. 32, 7. Hé gesette ðǽre sǽ gemǽru (cf. circumdabat mari terminum suum, Prov. 8, 29), þ heó náteshwón ne mót middaneard ofergán, Hml. Th. ii. 378, 22. Gewisse healdende gemǽru (*limites*), Hy. S. 35, 15. V. of time, a *predetermined date, a term; terminus.* (v. Angl. viii. 324, 45–325, 12):—þ hé gýme æfter .xii. Kl. Apr. hwǽr beó se móna feówertyne nihta eald, and wite eác þ hé byð þ gemǽre þæs termenes pasche, Angl. viii. 322, 34. Gif þú wille witan þ gemǽre *terminum septuagesimalis* ... þonne on þám teóðan stent se termen, þ gemǽre, Lch. iii. 226, 29–228, 3. On ðám dæge bið seó eásterlíce gemǽru þe wé hátað *terminus*, 244, 13. VI. *a termination, ending.* Cf. ge-mǽrung:—Sé þænne hæfið gemǽre (*terminum*) gálnysse þænne lífes, Scint. 87, 1. Ðec léhtes ǽr gemǽre wé bidde *te lucis ante terminum poscimus*, Rtl. 180, 6. v. eást-, eorþ-, land-, norþ-, norþwest-, sǽ-, súþ-, út-gemǽre; mǽre.

ge-mǽrian; *p.* ode *To fix the bounds of*:—Hé hine gelǽdde ealle ðá gemǽru, swá hé him of ðám aldan bócum rǽdde, hú hit ǽr Æðelbald cyning gemǽrude and gesalde, C. D. v. 140, 33. Léhtes singal tído gelimplicum gimaerende *lucis diurna tempora successibus determinans*, Rtl. 164, 38. Þú hæfst ægþer gedón ge ðá gesceafta gemǽrsode (-mǽrode? : *the corresponding metre has:* Ðú þǽm gesceaftum mearce gesettest, Met. 20, 89) betwux him ge eác gemengde, Bt. 33, 4; F. 130, 1. v. ge-mǽre.

ge-mǽrsian. *Add*: I. *to make known* or *famous, spread the fame* of a person:—Ðá ilco gemǽrsadon (*diffamaverunt*) hine in alle eorðe ðý, Mt. L. 9, 31. Ðes gemǽrsad wæs mid hine *hic diffamatus est apud illum*, Lk. L. 16, 1. II. *to noise abroad, make widely known* a matter, *spread the fame of*:—Gimǽrsia *praedicare*, Rtl. 30, 37. Ríc Godes gemǽrsad bið ł áboden bið (*euangelizatur*), Lk. L. 16, 16. Gemǽrsad (*divulgatum*) is word ðis, Mt. p. 20, 5. Wæron gemǽrsad mérsong of him in all stówe ðæs londes, Lk. L. 4, 37. Wéron gemǽrsad alle worda ðás, 1, 65. III. *to celebrate* a fast, festival, rite, &c., *perform with due honour*:—Þte ðis fæstin oestlicre hérnise wé gimǽrsia, Rtl. 9, 31. Færma drihtenlico gemǽrsad aron *coenae dominicae celebrantur*, Lk. p. 11, 3. ¶ The word glosses *uapulare* in Lk. p. 7, 19:—Esne ... huónum gemǽrsia gefæstnað *seruum ... paucis uapulare confirmat*. In the text, Lk. 12, 47, *uapulabit* is glossed gesuuincgde ł gemǽnde.

ge-mǽrsian *to fix the bounds of.* v. ge-mǽrian.

ge-mærung, e; f. A termination, ending, finishing:—On gemærunge (cf. geendunge, Ps. Srt. ii. p. 191, 15) in consummatione, Ps. Rdr. 285, 19. v. ge-mære; VI.

ge-mæssian. Add :—Sanctus Paulus hæfeð nū gemæssad, and bletsað nū þis folc, Vis. Lfc. 17.

ge-mæstan. Add: To feed with mast, fatten animals:—þonne hig gemæstað referunt dum corpora (glandiferis fagis), An. Ox. 23, 27. ' Ic ofslōh . . . mīne gemæstan fugelas (altilia)' . . . þā gemæstan fugelas getācniað þā hālgan lāreówas . . . þā sind gemæste mid gife þæs Hālgan Gāstes . . . Sē ðe mid fōdan þære ūplican lufe bið gefylled, hē bið swilce hē sig mid rūmlicum mettum gemæst. Mid þyssere fætnysse wolde se sealmwyrhta beón gemæst, ðā ðā hē cwæð, ‘Beó mīn sawul gefylled swā swā mid rysle and ungele,’ Hml. Th. i. 522, 6-35. Tō bulluce gemæstum ad uitulum saginatum, Scint. 169, 15. Gemæstra swīna, An. Ox. 23, 27.

ge-mæte. Substitute: I. meet, of suitable dimensions, made to fit (with dat.):—Heó ðone clāð hire on ādyde, and wæs swīðe gemæte hire micelnysse (it was a very excellent fit), Hml. S. 7, 157. Seó ðrūh wæs geworht hire swā gemæte swylce heó hyre sylfre swā gesceapen wære, and æt hire heáfde wæs āheáwen se stān gemæte þām heáfde (ita aptum (gemæte, Bd. Sch. 451, 14) corpori uirginis sarcofagum inuentum est, ac si ei specialiter praeparatum fuisset, et locus quoque capitis seorsum fabrefactus ad mensuram capitis illius aptissime figuratus apparuit, Bd. 4, 19), 20, 102-6. Besceáwige se abbod þæra reáfa gemet, þæt hý ne synd tō scorte, ac gemæte þām þe hyra notiað (uestimenta utentibus ea mensurata), R. Ben. 89, 19. II. meet, suitable for a purpose, fitted, apt:—Gemæte gewrixl apta uicissitudo, An. Ox. 4271. Lima menniscum brycum gemæte þū sealdest mē membra humanis usibus apta dedisti, Angl. xi. 116, 15. Lima tō menniscum bricum gemæte, 112, 18. [He wes of his speche ælche monne imete, Laym. 6584. O. H. Ger. ge-māzi aequalis.] v. un-gemæte.

ge-mæte; adv. v. un-gemæte: ge-mætgan. Dele, and see ge-huūægan: ge-mæðian. Add: v. mæþian: ge-māg. v. ge-māh: ge-māgas. v. ge-mægas.

ge-māh. Add :—Unsæle, gemāh inprobus, Wrt. Voc. ii. 45, 16. Gemāh inproba, 46, 54. Gemāh vel bald frontuosus, 151, 26. Se gemā inportunus, 43, 71. Gemāh scīnhīw fīðð pervicax monstrum (the devil) fugit, Hy. S. 142, 12. Ys hatigendlic sē þe gemāh ys tō specenne est odibilis qui procax (i. stultus vel luxuriosus) est ad loquendum; by much babbling he becometh hateful (Ecclus. 20, 5), Scint. 79, 15. (Seó) scamleáse, gemāh (in Proverbiis mulier illa) procax [cf. gemāgum (-māghum?) andwlitan procaci vultu (Prov. 7, 13), Kent. Gl. 193], An. Ox. 5277. (Seó) gemāge inportunus i. ferus, inmitis (cupidus, improbus, Hpt. 425, 59) (gastrimargiae draco), 811. Tō gemāgum ad inportunum, i. ad inonestum (praelium), 807. Welerum gemāgum labris procacibus (i. uerbosis ł inpudentibus, 7, 107), 1939. Wið ðæm gemāum contra inprobos (v. Bd. 1, 14: Ut ueniret contra inprobos malum), Txts. 181, 38.

ge-māh (?) evil :—Gemāh inperbitas (=? gemāhnes (q. v.) inprobitas), Wrt. Voc. ii. 48, 57.

ge-māhlic. Take here ge-māglic in Dict., and add: , ge-mālic :— Tō ðæm gemālecan ad inportunum (cf. An. Ox. 807 under ge-māh), Wrt. Voc. ii. 2, 1. I. shameless, impudent :—For þan wē nellan nān gȳmeleás yrfe forgyldan, būton hit forstolen sȳ ; mænige men specað gemāhlice sprǣce (many men make most impudent claims for compensation. The Latin version has ‘fraudulentas locutiones’), Ll. Th. i. 238, 11. II. wanton :—Hié him andwyrdon þ hit gemālic wære and unryhtlic (that it would be a wanton outrage) þæt swā oferwlenced cyning sceolde winnan on swā earm folc responderunt, stolide opulentissimum regem adversus inopes sumsisse bellum, Ors. 1, 10; S. 44, 11. III. of supplication, importunate :—(I) in a good sense, persistent, pertinacious :—Se mildheorta God wile þæt wē mid gemāglicum bēnum his mildheortnesse ofgān, Hml. Th. ii. 126, 5. (2) in a bad sense :—Hē fylgede þām hālgan were mid gemāglicum bedum (gemālicum bēnum, v. l. importunis precibus), Gr. D. 156, 2 : Hml. Th. ii. 176, 15.

ge-māhlīce. Add : -māglice, -mālice :—Gemālīce importune, Wrt. Voc. ii. 85, 44. I. impudently :—Gemāhlīce (-māglīce, Hpt. Gl. 475, 39) prociter, i. inpudenter, An. Ox. 2945. II. pertly, saucily :—þæt hī nā gedyrstlǣcan gemāhlīce (procaciter) bewerian þ heom gesawen bið, R. Ben. I. 18, 2. III. importunately, pertinaciously :—Gemāh[līce] pertinaciter (perseverare in precibus), An. Ox. 3391 ; perseveranter, Hpt. Gl. 486, 4. Hē bæd gemāhlīce Paulum þ hē hine gehēlde, Hml. S. 29, 53. þā þearfan swýðe gemāhlīce (importune) bædon þ se biscop him sum þing syllan sceolde, Gr. D. 63, 30. Sum fugel swīþe gemāglice (importune) gefeól on þæs hālgan mannes andwlitan, 100, 20.

ge-māhlicnes. Substitute : Importunity, inconvenience :—Ðȳ lǣs ðurh ðā wilnunga ðissa eorðcundlicra ðinga ðæt mōd ādīstrige se forhwierfda gewuna gemālicnesse ne mentem per terrenarum rerum cupidinem importunitas pulvereae cogitationis obscuret, Past. 79, 19. In gemālicnissum in oportunitatibus, Ps. Srt. 9, 22.

ge-māhnes. Add: , boldness :—Gemāh inperbitas (=? gemāhnes improbitas), Wrt. Voc. ii. 48, 57. Gemāgnesse inprovitatem (v. Lk. 11, 8), 74, 48. Gemāhgnesse (printed -mang-), 46, 55. þā unfordyttan (ānwillan) gemāgnysse obstinatam inportunitatem i. garrulitatem, An. Ox. 3614.

ge-māleca. v. ge-māhlic : ge-mālīce. v. ge-māhlīce : ge-malmægen. Dele : ge-man the hollow of the hand. Dele, and see ge-māna.

ge-māna. Add :—Gemānan consortio, Wrt. Voc. ii. 23, 31 : commertio, 24, 6. Tō þǣm gemānan ad copulam, 17. On þǣm gemānum in consortio, 44, 78. I. a sharing, partaking in common :—Him se pāpa Petrus tō naman sceóp, þæt hē þām aldre þāra apostola his naman gemānan (nominis ipsius consortio) geðeóded wære, Bd. 5, 7 ; Sch. 584, 16. II. what is held in common, common property :— Ðiós eorðe eallum monnum is tō gemānan geseald . . . Sē ðonne unryhtlīce talað, sē þe talað ðæt hé sié unscyldig, gif hē ðā gōd, þe ūs God tō gemānan sealde, him synderlīce āgnað cunctis hominibus terra communis est . . . Incassum ergo se innocentes putant, qui commune Dei munus sibi privatum vindicant, Past. 334, 9-13. Wit uncerne dǣl oððæstan uncrum mǣge, on þā gerǣdene ðe hē hit eft gedyde unc gewylde . . . ; and hē swā dyde, ge ðæt yrfe, ge ðæt hē mid uncre gemānan begeat, and ðæt hē sylf gestrýnde, C. D. ii. 113, 2-8. Ðæs ðe hē on uncrum gemānan gebruce, 13. Ic ann ðæs landæs Alfwerdæ . . . and Ælfwaræ him tō gemānan, iii. 360, 30. Eallum mīnum hīredwīfmannum tō gemānum, 295, 4. III. fellowship, association, society, intercourse :—Hī āwo tō ealdre engla gemānan brūcað, Cri. 1646. Wē biddað ðæt wit mōten bión on ðǣm gemānon ðe ðaer Godes ðiówas siondan, C. D. i. 292, 28. Hē nāh æfter forðsīðe crīstenra manna gemānan he cannot be buried with Christians, Ll. Th. i. 372, 34. III a. of spiritual fellowship :—Fram gemānan wiþersacedan a (Christi) consortio apostatauerant, An. Ox. 4491. III b. of marriage, sexual intercourse :— Sincipes gemāna[n?] iugalitatis consortia (acc.) i. contubernia, An. Ox. 3912. þ lust uīfes gemāna uolunt[at]em nubere, Jn. p. 1, 3. Tō werlicum gemānan ad maritale consortium, i. matrimonium, An. Ox. 4076: 1549: Wrt. Voc. ii. 77, 69 (printed geman). Tō samwiste gemānan ad copulae consortium, An. Ox. 3379. Hǣmedscipes gemānan hymenei commercio, 3220. Wæs hió ungederod fram þæs hǣðenan gemānan (cf. 218-220), Hml. S. 30, 314. Heó nāhte þurh hǣmedþing weres gemānan, Wlfst. 15, 16. þurh hǣmedþing wīfes gemānan, Ll. Th. i. 306, 19. Ne ceorl hæfis wīfes gemāna, ne wīf hæfis ceorles on ǣrist, Mk. Rbc. 12, 25. Gemānan contubernia (nuptiarum), An. Ox. 1784. IV. a fellowship, society, company of persons, community :— Gemāna societas, contubernia, Wrt. Voc. ii. 135, 18. Gemānan gedāl communi dividendo actio, 133, 1. Sý hē āworpen of gehādodra gemānan, Ll. Th. i. 346, 10 : 362, 31 : ii. 296, 19. Tō gemānum (tō geferrædenum) horena ad contuberia meretricum, An. Ox. 3330. Gemānan fleónde contubernia, i. consortia (mortalium) subterfugiens, 3702. V. fellowship, communion in a theological sense :—Wē gelýfað þæt hāliga gemāna sý: hālige men habbað gemānan hēr on līfe on gōdum dǣdum, and hý habbað gemānan on þǣm tōweardan þurh ðā edleán þe heom þonne God gyfð, Wlfst. 24, 12-16. Ciriclicæs gemānan þolian, Ll. Th. i. 38, 3. Of ciriecan gemānan āscāden, 36, 19. God hine āwende of ealra crīstenra gemānan, C. D. vi. 149, 30. VI. partaking of the Eucharist, communion; the Eucharist :—Ne gewiton þā nunnan of þēre cyrican betwyh þām þe bescyrede wæron þæs godcundan gemānan, for þon þe hī onfēngon þone gemānan fram Drihtne þurh þone Drihtnes þeówan dum inter eos qui communione privati sunt, minime recederent, communionem a Domino per servum Domini recepissent, Gr. D. 153, 13-16. þām se Godes wer sealde mid āgenre hand þone gemānan (hūsl, v. l.) ūres Drihtnes līchaman, þ is þ hūsl, 155, 3. v. bed-, cifes-, ciric-, hǣmed-, rest-, wīf-gemāna.

ge-mane. Add: ge-man (?). The reading of another MS. is gemonu. v. Angl. i. 334. The Latin is: Homines quorum capita capita leonum.

ge-mang. Dele last two passages, and add: I. mixing, combining, coagulating :—Gemang coagolatio, Wrt. Voc. ii. 133, 14: concretio, i. coagolatio, 136, 26: confectio, Hpt. Gl. 449, 61. Ðǣm lāreówe is tō mengenne ðā liðnesse wið ðā rēðnesse, and of þæm gemange (-monnge, v. l.) wyrce gemetgunge miscenda est lenitas cum severitate ; faciendum quoddam ex utroque temperamentum, Past. 125, 14. II. a mixture :—Oxumelli, eceddrinc, ecedes and huniges and wæteres gemang, Lch. ii. 284, 33. Man nime āne cuppan huniges and healfe cuppan spices, and mængc on gemang þ hunig and þ spic tōgædere, iii. 76, 5. Ofer allo gimongo wyrtana ł wyrteno gimonge super omnia aromata, Rtl. 3, 40. III. a mixing with people, intercourse, commerce (of sexual intercourse) :—Flǣsclicum gemange carnali commercio, Wrt. Voc. ii. 128, 73. Gesēgon uncre hlāfordas þ wit lufedan unc betweónan ; þā hió unc bæddan tō gemangum, Hml. A. 204, 309. IV. a collection of objects, throng, crowd (I) of persons :—Berað linde forð in sceaðena gemong, Jud. 193. Hī herepað worhton þurh lāðra gemong, 304. (1 a) an assembly for business, a meeting :—Hē wæs gōd wer and ryhtwýs, and wæs nǣfre hys wylles þær man þone Hǣlend wrēgdon on

nānum gemange (cf. *hic non consenserat concilio* (gìsomnunge, R., somnung, L.) *et actibus eorum*, Lk. 23, 51), Nic. 6, 8. (2) of things :— þǣr þā wæterburnan swēgdon and urnon onmiddan gehǣge . . . eác þǣr wynwyrta weóxon and bleówon innon þām gemonge (*among the streams*) on ǣnlicum wonge (*the passage seems to be based on :* Inter florigeras fecundi cespitis herbas, Dóm. L. 6. ¶ on (in) gemange (*following a dative*) *among* (used still in poetry after the noun) :—Wiht wæs nó werum on gemonge, Rā. 32, 4 : 11. Bið āweaxen wyrtum in gemonge fugel *alitur mediis in odoribus ales*, Ph. 265. Mágum in gemonge, Jul. 528. v. æg-, blód-, worms-, wyrt-gemang.

ge-mang, es ; *n.* *A business ;* negotium :—Geendedum þysum gást-licre áseormunge gemange *finito hoc spiritualis purgaminis negotio*, Angl. xiii. 387, 312. Ne mæg ic āna eówre gemang ācuman *non valeo solus negotia vestra sustinere*, Deut. 1, 12. v. mangian.

ge-mang *among*. *Add :* I. of the relation of a thing (or things) to surrounding objects with which it is grouped :—Gif hē his ǣhta bere geman[g] þāra unfriðmanna ǣhta intó hūse, Ll. Th. i. 286, 11. II. of the relation of a thing (or things) to the whole surrounding group or composite substance :—Hié gemong þǣre heringe þyllica bismra on hié selfe ásǣdon, Ors. 4, 4 ; S. 164, 4. III. of the relation of anything in a local group to the other members of the group, although these do not actually surround it :—Zosimus hine sylfne tó fulfremednysse āþenede gemang þām emnwyrhtum, Hml. S. 23 b, 97. Nalles nā ðæt ān ðæt hē gód doo gemang (-mong, *v. l.*) óðrum monnum, Past. 81, 22. IV. of the relation of a thing to others in the same nominal or logical group :—Gemong þǣm óþrum monegum wundrum *inter multa prodigia*, Ors. 4, 3 ; S. 162, 5. V. of the relation of a fact or event to the circumstances during which it happens, *during, in the course of* :—Gemong þǣm gewinnum (*in eo bello*) hē forlēt his xv. suna, Ors. 3, 11 ; S. 152, 25 : 150, 8. Þunor ofslóg fela þúsend monna gemong þǣm gefeohte, 6, 13 ; S. 268, 17 : 2, 2 ; S. 66, 1. Gemang þǣm gefeán hié hié selfe oferdrencton, 5, 3 ; S. 222, 5. Ic arn symle þā āxunga þǣre æscan tó wriðende, and gemang þám (*while so doing*) ðæs dæges síðfæt gefylde, Hml. S. 23 b, 496. ¶ Gemang þām þe :—Gemong þǣm þe (*while*) Pirrus wið Rómāna winnende wæs, Ors. 4, 1 ; S. 160, 6. v. on-gemang.

ge-mangcennys. *Substitute :* ge-mangenness, e ; *f.* *A mixing, preparation* of material :—Gemangcennys ł mencingc *confectio*, Hpt. Gl. 450, 29. v. ge-mangness.

ge-mangian. *For* 'to traffic, trade' *substitute* 'to gain by traffic.'

ge-mangnys. *Add :*—Slāwyrmes gemangnys *spalangii* (*pestifera*) *confectio*, An. Ox. 1857. Gemang[nys] *confusio*, 18, 12. v. ge-mangenness.

ge-manian. *Dele first passage, and add :* I. *to bring to mind* what ought to be done, *urge* a person to do something :—Sticelse ābryðnesse gemanod ł getiht *stimulo conpunctionis instigatus*, i. *praemonitus*, An. Ox. 602. Gemanad *compulsa*, 4366. II. *to bring to mind* what should not be forgotten, *remind, admonish :*—þonne hié þ eall gemunan and þurh þ leóht gemanode beóþ, Bl. H. 129, 21, 8. Ælfwine cwæð . . . 'Gemunað þā mǣla . . .' Offa gemǣlde . . . 'Hwæt! þū Ælfwine hafast ealle gemanode þegenas tó þearfe,' By. 231. III. *to advise, instruct :*—Hiú gemonade from móder hire cweð *illa, praemonita a matre sua, inquit*, Mt. R. 14, 8. IV. *to demand of* a person (*acc.*) what is due (*gen.*) :—Ne þurfon wē nā þæs wēnan, þæt úre Drihten ūs nelle þǣra leána gemanian, þe hē ūs hēr on eorðan forgyfen hafað, Wlfst. 148, 16 : 261, 18. IV a. *to make demand* for a debt, *to dun :*— Sum hafenleás man sceolde āgyldan healf pund ānum men and wæs oft gemanod for ðǣre lǣne, Hml. Th. ii. 176, 35. [*O. Sax.* gi-manón : *O. H. Ger.* ge-manón *memorare, admonere, commonere.*]

ge-manigfealdian ; *p.* ode. *Take here* ge-mænigfealdian, -monigfealdian *in Dict., and add :* I. *trans.* *To multiply.* (1) *to make numerous :*—Þū gemanigfealdodest þíne mildheortnesse *multiplicasti misericordias tuas*, Ps. Th. 35, 7. Þū gemanigfealdodest þíne wundru *multa fecisti tu mirabilia tua*, 39, 5. Hý wǣran gemanigfealdode (*multiplicati*) ofer ðā gerím, 6 : 14 : 24, 17 : 37, 19. Þā earfoðu mínre heortan synd tóbrǣd and gemanigfealdod *tribulationes cordis mei dilatatae sunt*, 24, 15. (2) *to increase the quantity of, enlarge.* (a) the object material :—God ðū ðe cirica ðín níuo symle [ac]endnise ðū gimonigfaldast *Deus, qui ecclesiam tuam novo semper foetu multiplicasti*, Rtl. 30, 15. Hē his cyrican timbrede, and wundorlícum weorcum gebrǣdde and gemonigfealdode (*ampliauit*), Bd. 5, 20 ; Sch. 674, 10. (b) the object non-material :—Gemycla nū and gemonigfealda þā hǣlo ðæs cynges *magnificans salutare regis ipsius*, Ps. Th. 17, 48. Heora unmiht and heora untrymð is gemanifealdod, 15, 3. Þeáh gemanigfealdod sý þæt wuldor his hūses, 48, 16. Ðæt him scylen hiera wísdóm bión geiéced and gemanigfaldod (-faldod, *v. l*) (*multiplicari*), Past. 381, 2. Ðætte wǣre gemanigfaldod hreám, 427, 33. (3) *to add :*—Hē tó geíhte þā teáras þām teárum, and gemænigfealdode þā sworetunga þām siccetungum, Hml. S. 23 b, 201. (4) *to reward :*—Ondetnisse Petres heofna mið cægum gemonigfalded wæs *confessio Petri coelorum clavibus muneratur*, Mt. p. 17, 17. II. *intrans.* *To abound, become much :*— Mæhtig is God ǣlc gefe gimonigfaldiga gidóa *potens est Deus omnem*

---

*gratiam abundare facere*, Rtl. 13, 14. [*O. H. Ger.* ge-managfaltón *multiplicare, crebrescere.*] See next word.

ge-manigfildan, -fealdan ; *p.* de. *Take here* ge-mænigfyldan *in Dict., and add : To multiply.* (1) *to make numerous :*—Þū woldest mínne ofspring gemenigfyldan swā sǣceosol þe nān man ātellan ne mæg, Gen. 32, 12. Þū woldest his cynn gemenigfealdan swā steorran beóð on heofenum *multiplicabo semen tuum sicut stellas coeli*, Ex. 32, 13. Israēla folc weóx swilce hig of eorðan spryttende wǣron gemænigfylde *quasi germinantes multiplicati sunt*, 1, 7 : Scint. 176, 6. (1 a) of repeated action :—Sē ðe lufað sunu his, hē gemænigfylt (*assiduat*) him swingla, Scint. 176, 9. (2) *to increase the quantity of, enlarge, extend.* (a) the object material :—Hē his cyrícean wundorlícum weorcum gebrǣdde and gemonigfylde (*ampliauit*), Bd. 5, 20 ; Sch. 674, 10. Þ gemænigfyldan *ut cumularent*, An. Ox. 8, 226. Gemænifyldon, 7, 296. (a a) fig. :—Gemenigfylde God Jafeth *dilatet Deus Japheth*, Gen. 9, 27. Hē gemētte fela gemænigfylde (-men-, -fealde, *v. ll.*) on geleáfan and on Godes gife ðeónde, Hml. S. 15, 41. (b) the object non-material :—Þū gemænigfyldest þíne mǣrsunge, Ps. L. 70, 21. [*For*] gemænigfyldre ofermódnesse *propter publicatam insolentiam*, An. Ox. 8, 389. Gemæniflydre, 7, 380. (3) as an arithmetical term :—Gemænigfyld þā þreó þurh feówer, þriwa feówer beóð twelf, Angl. viii. 328, 20. Nymað týn and gemænigfyld þ getæl feówer síðon ; feówer síðon týn beóð feówertig, 25.

ge-manna. v. ge-men.

ge-mannþwǣrian ; *p.* ode *To make gentle :*—Ðætte hié gemonn-ðwǣrige (-man-, *v. l.*) sió lufu hiora niéhstena *ut ex proximi amore man-suescunt*, Past. 363, 21.

ge-mārian ; *p.* ode *To make greater* (māra), *enlarge, increase :*— Leahter swígende byð gemārud *crimen tacendo ampliatur*, Scint. 40, 16. [*O. H. Ger.* ge-mērón *augere, amplificare.*]

ge-martyrian. *Add :* (1) *to put to death because of religious belief :*— Hī heafdon þone arcð. mid him oð þone tíman þe hī hine gemartyredon (cf. God swutelað þæs hālgan martires mihtæ, 1012 ; P. 143, 4), Chr. 1011 ; P. 142, 11. Se cāsere hió hēht gemartyrian, Shrn. 72, 13. Enoh and Elias þurh þone þeódfeónd gemartrode (-martirode, *v. l.*) weorðaþ, þe God sylfa fela hund wintra geheóld, Wlfst. 85, 19. (2) *to put to a cruel death*, slay an innocent person :—Ongan Þunor þone cyning biddan þ hē móste þā æþelingas dearnunga ācwellan . . . hē dyde swā hē ǣr gyrnende wæs, and hē hī on niht gemartirode innan ðæs cyninges heáhsetle, Lch. iii. 424, 29. On þysum geáre wearð Eádweard cyning gemartyrad (ofslegen, *v. l.*), Chr. 978 ; P. 122, 16. (3) *to inflict suffering on, torture :*—þā clǣnan þe dæghwāmlíce campiað . . . wið unlustas . . . Hī beóð Crístes martyras þurh ðā munuclícan drohtnunge, nā ǣne gemartirode, ac oft dígollíce, Hml. A. 36, 295. [*O. H. Ger.* ge-martirót *passus.*]

ge-maðel. *l.* (?) ge-mæþel : ge-meagende, Hy. S. 108, 33. *l.* ge-metgende : ge-meaht. v. un-gemeaht : ge-mearc. *Add :* v. eág-gemearc.

ge-mearcian. *Add :*—Smāt, gemaercode *inpingit*, Wrt. Voc. ii. 111, 57. Gemearcode *inpingit* vel *signat*, 45, 59. I. *to fix by marks, mark out* a site, way (*lit. or fig.*), *fix the boundaries of, plan :*—þǣre ilcan niht þe mon on dæg hæfde þā burg mid stacum gemearcod, swā swā hié hié þā wyrcean woldon, wulfas ātugon þā stacan úp *cum mensores ad limitandum Carthaginensem agrum missi, stipites, terminorum indices fixos, nocte a lupis revulsos reperissent*, Ors. 5, 5 ; S. 226, 18. Hē hæfð gemearcod ǣnne middangeard, Gen. 395. Þū hæfst yfele gemearcod uncer sylfra síð, 791. I a. *to measure.* Cf. míl-gemearc :—þæt þanon wǣre tó helle duru hund þúsenda míla gemearcodes, Sat. 724. II. *to make a mark on :*—Hū Martirius gemearcode þone hláf, Gr. D. 86, 12. Ongæt hē þ se hláf næs nā gemearcod (*signatus*) . . . se hláf wæs gemēted gemearcod mid Crístes róde tācne, 87, 7-23. Cain gewāt mordre gemearcod (cf. Posuit Dominus Cain signum, Gen. 4, 15) mandreám fleón, B. 1264. II a. *to mark* a place so as to know it again :—Hē þǣr tācen āsette and þā stówe gemearcode *posito ibi signo*, Bd. 3, 9 ; Sch. 231, 6. II b. *to mark* an object so that it may serve as an index. *Take here* ge-mearcod *in Dict., and add :*— Tó ðǣre gemearcodan æfsan, of ðǣre gemearcodan æfsan, C. D. B. ii. 358, 30. Andlang mærce tó ðāra apoldre, þonon tó ðām gemearceden stocce, iii. 188, 36. III. *to form by marks, describe* a circle, *portray, design :*—Hī ymb hine gemearcodon (*designaverunt*) ānne hring on ðǣre eorðan, Gr. D. 196, 27. Hē geseah þ hālwænde tācen Crístes róde on myceles líohtes brihtnesse ongeán him geset and gemearcod, H. R. 3, 23. Ic geann Eádríce ðæs swurdes ðe seó hand is on gemearcod, C. D. iii. 363, 21. IV. *to mark, seal :*—Gemearcod *signatus* (*fons*), An. Ox. 3899. V. *to make with the hand* the sign of the cross on :—Se apostol his eágan gemearcode mid þǣre hālgan róde, Hml. S. 29, 55. VI. *to assign, appoint :*—Ne weard wyrse dǣd monnum ge-mearcod, Gen. 595. Nis unc sceattes wiht tó mete gemearcod, 814. VII. *to indicate in writing, note, record :*—þā hī þis gehȳrdon, hī writon þone deg and gemearcodon ymbhigdiglíce *quod illi audientes, sollicite conscripserunt diem*, Gr. D. 306, 13. Wæs on þǣm

scennum þurh rūnstafas rihte gemearcod, geseted and gesǣd, hwām þ sweord geworht wǣre, B. 1695. Tō þeossum hālgum þe heora gemynd hēr on gemearcude siendon, Gr. D. 2, 12. [*O. Sax.* gi-markōn *to design, determine; to note: O. H. Ger.* ge-marchōn *constituere, decernere, terminare.*]

**ge-mearcod.** v. ge-mearcian; **II b**: **ge-mearcund.** *l.* ge-mearcung.

**ge-meargian**; *pp.* od *To fill with marrow; medullare*:—Onsægdnessa gemeargode (*medullata*) ic offrige þē, Ps. L. 65, 15.

**ge-mearr.** [*The Latin of* Past. 401, 20 *is*: Quem igitur caelibem curarum secularium impedimentum praepedit.] *For* Gl. Prud. 662 *substitute* Germ. 397, 496, *and add*: *futility, vanity*:—Nā on gemear þū gesettest suna manna *non uane constituisti filios hominum*, Ps. Rdr. 88, 48. [Cf. mirran; **II**, *and O. H. Ger.* ki-merrit *irritum*; far-marrit *irritum, sine effectu.*]

**ge-mearr**; *adj. The other reading in the passage is*: Gif ēnig yfelra manna wǣre.

**ge-mec.** *Dele.* v. Bt. S. 24, 9: **ge-mēd.** *Dele.*

**ge-mēde.** *Substitute*: **ge-mēde,** es; *pl.* (*used sometimes with singular meaning*) -mēdu; *n. That which is agreeable* to one (*gen.*) or *in conformity with one's will, pleasure*:—Būtan sum heora freónda þā land furþor, on þæs arcebisceopes gemēde (*as may be agreeable to the archbishop*), ofgān mage, Cht. Th. 355, 23. [Gif āni land sȳ out of þan bissoprīche gedōn, ich wille þ hit cume in ongeán, ōđer þ man hit ofgō on hise gemōđ swō man wiđ him bet finde mage *si quid inde fuerit sublatum, volumus quod revocetur, vel quod aliter ei satisfaciat*, 387, 23.] Se cyng gebēcte þ land Æđelstāne . . . Æfter þām getīdde þ Ecgferđ gebohte bōc and land æt Æđelstāne on cynges gewitnesse and his witena, swā his gemēdo wǣron [*as was agreeable to the king*, i.e. *the king was satisfied with the transaction*), 208, 9. Eádgār cyning beád ǣlcon his þegna þe ēnig land on þan lande hafde, þ hī hit ofeódon be þes biscopes gemēdon (*in conformity with the bishop's will*) ođđe hit āgēfon, 295, 12. Đǣr þā eádigan fundon mid ealra gemēdum (*to the satisfaction of all*) þās dōmas, Ll. Th. i. 36, 12. Nō hēr cūđlīcor cuman ongunnon lindhæbbende; ne gē leáfnesword gūđfremmendra gearwe ne wisson, māga gemēdu (*what their pleasure might be*), B. 247. [Themu manne te gimōdea *for the satisfaction of the man*, Hēl. 3207. *O. H. Ger.* ge-muati *what is agreeable.*] *See next word.*

**ge-mēde.** *Add*: (1) of persons:—Hī ōđer twēga ođđe wīf habbađ him gemæc, ođđe him gemēde nabbađ, Bt. 11, 1; S. 24, 9. (2) of things, *that satisfies requirements, adequate, suitable*:—Heó hit Ōsulfe on ǣht gesealde wiđ gemēdan feó (*the land was sold for a fair price*, or (?) *a price that had been agreed on*), Cht. Th. 170, 21. [Rtl. 50, 6 *might be taken under previous word.*]

**ge-medemian.** *Add*: **I.** *to make mean* (v. medume; **I**), *humble, bring to low estate*:—Se myccla mægenþrym . . . þurh þone man gemedemod wæs mannum tō helpe *the great majesty* (*of Christ*) *through incarnation was brought to low estate for the help of men*, Bl. H. 179, 9. **I a.** used reflexively, *to condescend, deign.* (1) with clause:—Ūre Drihten hine gemedemode, þ hē ūs sealde þā wæstmas, Bl. H. 39, 17. Drihten hine sylfne gemedemode, þæt hē tō woruldlicum giftum gelađod cōm, Hml. Th. ii. 54, 7: i. 56, 28. Wē biddaþ þē þ þū gemedemige þē, þ þū cume, Nic. 10, 9. Þ đū gemedemige þē sylfne, þ þū sīđige tō mē, Hml. S. 24, 97. (2) with *tō*:—Đā đā se Hǣlend man beón wolde, đā gemedemode hē hine sylfne tō deáđe āgenes willan, Hml. Th. i. 224, 22. (3) combining (2) and (1):—Hē wolde menniscnesse underfōn, and tō đan hine sylfne gemedemian, þæt hē wolde beón geboren sōđ man, Wlfst. 194, 3. **II.** without personal object, *to condescend, deign, vouchsafe.* (1) with infin.:—God sē þe gemedemađ (*dignatus est*) eall syllan, teóþunge fram ūs gemedemađ (*dignatur*) ongeán biddan, Scint. 108, 19–109, 1. Þ goldhord þe þū mē sylfum gemedemodest æteówan, Hml. S. 23 b, 738. Đone deáđ þe se Hǣlend gemedemode for mannum þrowian, Hml. Th. i. 50, 7. Þ þū lytles hwæthwegu gemedemige underfōn, Hml. S. 23 b, 712. Gimeoduma đū girihte *digneris dirigere*, Rtl. 171, 3. Đióstro gimetdomia đū *tenebras* (*auferre*) *digneris*, 38, 27. Gibloedsia gimeodomia *benedicere dignare*, 95, 8. Gimeodumia, 170, 21. (2) with clause:—Crīst gimeodumode þte fulwad wēre *Christus dignatus est baptizari*, Rtl. 114, 30. **III.** in the following the construction seems determined by a misunderstanding of the Latin *dignari*, which is taken to be passive. (1) with infin.:—Ūsig eft giboeta gimeadumad arđ *nos instaurare dignatus es*, Rtl. 23, 9. Gimoedumad, 36, 37. Þone se Hǣlend wæs gemedemod tō his mildheortnysse gecīgan, Hml. S. 30, 353. (2) with gerundial infin.:—Drihten, beó þū gemedemad mē tō gehēranne, Shr. 104, 22. **IV.** *to make fit, order, regulate*:—Swā gemedemod mid dæg þæt gewyrdan ealle þing *sic temperatur, ut cum luce fiant omnia*, R. Ben. I. 74, 4. Sȳ gemedemud ǣt metes *sit temperatus cibus escae*, Scint. 50, 14. **V.** *to deem worthy to be* in a state, position, &c. Cf. Hml. Th. i. 424, 15:—Hié cwǣdon, '*Deo gratias*, for đon wē wǣron tō dæge ealle on ānnesse gemedemode.' For đon is se cwide gefylled, '*Ecce quam bonum habitare fratres in unum*,' Bl. H. 139, 26. **VI.** *to estimate, measure, fix the degree* or *worth of*:—Besceáwige hē ā þone steal his gecyrrednesse and hine be þām gemedemige būtan hine mon for đām sācerdhāde furđor forlǣte *illum locum attendat quando ingressus est in monasterio, non illum qui ei pro reuerentia sacerdotii concessus est*, R. Ben. 107, 11. Sȳ hē gemedemed on stede and on setle, swā swā his gecerrednes sȳ, 13, 1. **VI a.** furþor gemedemian *to honour, advance in dignity*:—Gif hit swā getīmige þæt se abbod and seó gecorenes þǣre geferrǣdenne hine for his līfes gearnunge weorđian wile and furđor gemedemian *si forte electio congregationis et voluntas abbatis pro vite merito eum promovere voluerit*, 113, 8. Gif se æþelborena mid godcundum cræfte þone unæþelborenan oferþȳhđ, sȳ hē gemedemad furđur be his gearnungum þonne se unæþelborena, 12, 16. Furđor beón gemedemod *in majori loco stabiliri*, 110, 7. [Cf. *O. H. Ger.* ge-metamēn *moderare.*]

**ge-mēder.** *Dele*: **ge-medmicel.** *This should be taken under* **ge-medummicel, -medemmicel.** v. medum-micel: **ge-mēdness.** v. un-gemēdness.

**ge-mēdred.** *Substitute*: *Having the same mother*:—Wē habbađ ealdne fæder, and hē hæfđ mid him ūrne gingstan brōđor . . . and his gemēdryda brōđor (*uterinus frater*) wæs deád, Gen. 44, 20. Jōsep geseah his gemēdrydan brōđor Benjamin, 43, 29. Gemēdred, Ors. 3, 7; Bos. 60, 19. v. ge-mēdren.

**ge-mēdren**; *adj. Having the same mother, born of the same mother*:—Þā þrié gebrōđor nǣron nā Philippuse gemēdren (ge-mēdred, Bos. 60, 19), ac wǣron gefæderen *fratres patri ex noverca genitos*, Ors. 3, 7; S. 114, 13.

**ge-mēdrian.** *Dele*: **ge-mēdryd.** v. ge-mēdred: **ge-medum-micel.** *Take here passage under* **ge-medmicel** *in Dict.* v. medum-micel.

**ge-meldian.** *Add*:—Ǣne ic God spræcan gehȳrde, and þæt treówe ongeat tīdum gemeldad *semel locutus est Deus, duo haec audivi*, Ps. Th. 61, 11. [*O. H. Ger.* ge-meldōn *prodere, deferre.*]

**gēme-.** v. gīme-.

**ge-melcan**; *p.* -mealc; *pp.* -molcen *To get by milking, draw milk* from an animal:—Āþwer buteran þe sié gemolcen of ānes bleós nȳtne, Lch. ii. 112, 25. [*O. H. Ger.* ge-melchan *emulgere.*]

**ge-meltan.** *Add*: **I.** *to melt* (intrans.):—Mīn heorte is gemolten swā þæt weax *factum est cor meum tamquam cera liquescens*, Ps. Th. 21, 12. Gemolten *liquefacta*, Bl. Gl. **II.** *to digest* (intrans.):—Tācn ādeádodes magan, hū þ ne gemylt þ hē þigeþ, Lch. ii. 158, 15: 186, 21. v. ge-miltan.

**ge-meltan** *to melt* (trans.). v. ge-miltan: **ge-meltness.** v. un-gemeltness: **ge-men.** *Add*: [Cf. (?) *O. H. Ger.* ge-manna *viritim.*]

**ge-mengan.** *Add*:—Gemenge *confici*, Wrt. Voc. ii. 15, 1. Gemængan, 104, 77. Gemenged *infectus*, 110, 68. Gemengde *infici*, 45, 53. Gemengde, gimaengdae, gimengdæ, Txts. 71, 1104. **A.** *trans.* **I.** *to mix* (1) two or more substances:—Þū þǣm gesceaftum mearce gesettest and hī gemengdest eác, Met. 20, 89. Þū hæfst þā gesceafta gemengde, Bt. 33, 4; F. 130, 2. (1 *a*) of non-material objects, *to combine, associate*:—Gif đā đweoran and đā unryhtwīsan hiera yfel mid sibbe gefæstnigađ and tōsomne gemengađ (-eađ, *v. l.*) *si perversorum nequitia in pace jungitur*, Past. 361, 12. (2) one or more substances with other(s). (*a*) with prep. (*wiþ, mid*):—Gif þū hī wiþ fȳr ne gemengdest, Bt. 33, 4; F. 130, 11. Hiora blōd hē gemengde mid āsægdnisum hiora, Lk. L. R. 13, 1. Genim wīn and fearres geallan, gemeng wiþ þȳ leáce, Lch. ii. 34, 5. Wīn wiđ geallan gemenged (wiđ gallan gemænged, R., miđ galla gemenceđ, L.), Mt. 27, 34. Þeáh hit wiđ ealla sié gemenged weoruldgesceafta, Met. 20, 128. His līchama wæs gemengeđ mid þǣre eorþan, Bl. H. 241, 26. Loccas mid þisse eorđan synd gemengde, 243, 35. (*b*) with case:—Hrīm and snāw hagle gemenged, Wand. 48. (2 *a*) of non-material objects:—Hlehter sāre byđ gemincged *risus dolori miscebitur*, Scint. 171, 11. **II.** *to prepare by putting various ingredients together, mix* medicine, drink, &c.:—Hió gemende *miscuit* (*vinum*), Kent. Gl. 286. Gemenced ǣg (cf. ǣg-gemang) *ocastrum*, Wrt. Voc. i. 290, 46. Ne dranc hē wīnes drenc, ne nānes gemencgedes wǣtan, Hml. Th. i. 352, 6. **II a.** *to mix and* so *lessen the strength of* (fig.):—Eardlicum gifremnissum gimengadum *terrenis affectibus mitigatis*, Rtl. 18, 17. **III.** *to unite so as to form a whole*:—Þū gegæderast đā hiofonlican sāwla and đā eorþlican līchoman and hī on đisse worulde gemengest, Bt. 33, 4; F. 132, 24. Þū gemengest þā heofoncundan hider on eorđan sāwla wiđ līce; siđđan wuniađ þis eorđlice and þæt ēce samod, Met. 20, 234. **IV.** *to unite* persons to others in dealings or intercourse, *join, associate*:—Ic mē tō middes heora gemengde and him tō cwæđ: 'Nimađ mē on eówer færeld,' Hml. S. 23 b, 373. Ic mē tō þām ingangendum gemengde, 458. **IV a.** of sexual intercourse. v. ge-mengness, -mengedness:—Gif hié tō ungemetlīce hié gemengađ on đǣm hǣmede *cum immoderatae admixtioni servientes*, Past. 397, 11. **V.** *to disturb, throw into confusion, mix up.* (1) the object material:—Oft smylte sǣ sūþerne wind gedrēfeđ, þonne hié gemengađ micla ȳsta, onhrērađ hronmere *si mare volvens turbidus Auster misceat aestum*, Met. 5, 9. Se sūþerna wind miclum storme gedrēfeþ þā sǣ . . . heó þonne gemenged wyrþ mid đām

ýþum, Bt. 6; F. 14, 25. Wæs on blóde brim weallende, ýða geswing eal gemenged, B. 848: 1593. (2) the object non-material :—Ðæs cyninges ríce ge foreweard ge forðgang swá monigum styrenessum wiðerweardra þinga ýðiað and gemengde syndon, þ þ mon nū gyt gewitan ne mæg, hwæt be þissum man wrítan mæg, Bd. 5, 23; Sch. 689, 2. **VI.** *to mix up, fail to distinguish, confound, confuse* :—Ne gemengende (*confundentes*) hādas ne edwiste tótwæmende, Ath. Crd. 4. Ðæt gimencged (*mixta*) aron alle, and in Marc moniga Lucas and ēc Matheies, Mt. p. 3, 7. **VII.** *to infect* with moral evil :—Swá hyra aldor dyde māne gemenged. Dan. 184. Synfulle beóð māne gemengde, El. 1296. **B.** *intrans*. To mix, be mixed, unite to :—Ðætte sió mennisce ðlicung for nānum freóndscipe ðærtō ne gemenge (-mencge, v. l.) ut nihil se ei humanitatis admisceat in hoc, Past. 78, 9. Þ gecynd nyle næfre nānwuht wiþerweardes lǽtan gemengan, for þām heora ǽgþer onscunað óþer agit cujusque rei natura quod proprium est, nec contrariarum rerum miscetur effectibus, et ultro, quae sunt adversa, depellit, Bt. 16, 3; F. 54. 36.

**ge-menged.** *Add :* (1) *mixed, composite, not simple* :—Lyft is gemenged . . . nis þæt nān wundor, þæt hió sié wearm and ceald, Met. 20, 79. (2) *in which distinction is not made* :—Gemenged *promiscuum*, An. Ox. 3854. Sum cyn is gecweden *epicena*, þæt is on Lēden *promiscua* and on Englisc gemenged *hic corvus* ðes hremn swá hwæðer swá hit byð swá hē, swá heó, Ælfc. Gr. Z. 19, 11. v. blód-gemenged.

**ge-mengedlic**; *adj. Mixed together* :—Gemengetlic (gimengidlicę, Ep., gimaengidlicæ, Erf. *permixtum*. Perhaps *permixtim* should be read, and the English words would then be adverbs) *permixtum*, Txts. 85, 1542.

**ge-mengedlíce**; *adv. Confusedly*. See preceding word.

**ge-mengednys.** *Add :*—Nis nā gerunnen tōgædere seó godcundnys and seó menniscnys, ac seó godcundnys is ymbscrýd mid þære menniscnysse, swā þæt þær nys nāðor gemencgednys ne tōdāl, Hml. Th. ii. 8, 7.

**ge-mengness.** *Take here the instances given under* **ge-mengednys**, *and add: sexual intercourse, copulation.* v. ge-mengan; IV a :—Hié gewemmað ðone āliéfedan gesinscipe mid ðære unliéfedan gemengnesse *in ipso conjugio jura transcendunt*, Past. 397, 14. Gif bróðor mid brēðer hæme þurh his líchaman gemengnysse (*per copulationem corporis*), Ll. Th. ii. 230, 10. v. wyrt-gemengness.

**ge-mengung.** *For* ' *mixtura*, Cot. 35 ' *substitute* :—Gemengiunge (gimaengiungiae, Ep., gemengiungae, Erf.) *confusione*, Txts. 53, 522. Gemengunge, Wrt. Voc. ii. 14, 68.

**ge-menigfealdan.** v. ge-manigfildan.

**ge-meode** *glosses* dignatus :—Ðū hiów líchoman genioman gemeode (gemeodemad? v. ge-medemian; *but see next word*) ðū wēre *tu formam corporis adsumere dignatus es*, Ps. Srt. ii. p. 202, 38.

**ge-meodniss.** *Add :*—Ymb gemeodnissum (-meodomnissum? v. medumness; *but see preceding word*) Rōmānisca *de dignitatibus Romanorum*.

**ge-merce.** v. ge-mirce.

**ge-merian**; *p.* ed *To purify* :—Man nime āne cuppan gemeredes huniges and healfe cuppan clǽnes gemyltes spices, Lch. iii. 76, 4. Wring þurh clāð on gemered hunig, 12, 16. Cf. ā-merian.

**ge-met.** *Add :* I. *measure, measurement, determination of amount* :—Be þæs scriftes dihte and be his sylfes gemete gebyreð þ ðā nýdþeówan hlāferdum wyrcan, Ll. Th. ii. 314, 3. **II.** *size or quantity determined by measurement, dimensions* :—God is būtan gemete, for ðy ðe hē is ǽghwǽr. Hē is būtan gete . . . Hē is būtan hefe . . . Hē ealle gesceafta gelōgode on ðām ðrim ðingum, þæt is, on gemete, and on getele, and on hefe, Hml. Th. i. 286, 10–15 : ii. 586, 32. Gehīwad tō þām gemete (*ad mensuram*) hyre heáfdes, Bd. 4, 19; Sch. 451, 20. Ælc wæs on twēgra sestra gemete *capientes singuli metretas binas*, Jn. 2, 6. Ptolomeus wrāt ealles þises middangeardes gemet on ānre bēc, Bt. 18, 1; F. 62, 7. **II a.** fig. :—On gimett ældes gifylnisse *in mensuram aetatis plenitudinis*, Rtl. 83, 17. **II b.** (*good, short*) *measure* :—Gōd gemet (*mensuram*) hig syllað on eówerne bearm, þām sylfan gemete þe gē metað eów byð gemeten, Lk. 6, 38. **III.** *a measure, an instrument for measuring* :—False gewihta and wōge gemeta, Ll. Th. i. 310, 13. (1) *a vessel* :—Ēghuæic ān wæs tuisestre gemet, Jn. L. 2, 6 *margin*. (2) *a line* :—Ne beó ǽnig metegyrd lengre þonne óðer, ac be þæs scriftes gemete ealle gescyfte, and ælc gemet on his scriftscíre and ǽghwylc gewihte beó be his dihte gescyft swíþe rihte, Ll. Th. ii. 314, 5–8. **IV.** *a system or standard of measuring* :—Gange ān gemet and ān gewihte swilce man on Lundenbyrig and on Wintanceastre healde, Ll. Th. i. 270, 1. **V.** *a rule, pattern* :—Gemetum *normulis* (cf. *normulis*, i. *regulis* bysnum, An. Ox. 180 (gloss to Ald. 4, 29)), Wrt. Voc. ii. 62, 9. **VI.** *what is meet or adequate, due amount or degree* :—Gif him þegniað mæged and mæcgas mid gemete (*fitly, adequately*) ryhte, fēdað hine fægre, Rä. 51, 7. Þē gemete (cf. ungemet; II a) monige þeówiað, Gū. 472. Gif þū ðæt gemet habban wille and ðā nýdþearfe witan wille *si quod naturae satis est replere indigentiam velis*, Bt. 14, 1; F. 42, 5. Hwæt magon wē dōn, gyf þū

nāst þæt gemet? Þū sceoldest witan hwænne þē genōh þūhte, Solil. H. 15, 8. [*Perhaps here might be taken the passages given at* **gemet**; *adj.*] **VII.** *measure* as opposed to excess, *extent not to be exceeded*. *limit.* (1) *of* space :—Merestreáma gemeotu, An. 454. (2) *of amount* :—Þý weorðað on foldan swá fela fira cynnes; ne sý þæs magutimbres gemet ofer eorþan, gif hī ne wanige sē þæs woruld teóde, Gn. Ex. 33. (3) *of degree* :—Hē hæfde eádmōdnysse ofer mennisc gemett, Hml. S. 31, 46. Gýtsung gemet nāt *auaritia modum ignorat*, Scint. 99, 5. Seó gítsung ne cann gemet *avaritiae nihil satis est*, Bd. 26, 2; F. 94, 6. Þū woldest gemetigan mýnne wōp, and ic ongyte nān gemet mýnra yrmða *modum vis habere lacrymas meas, cum miseriae meae modum non videam*, Solil. H. 48, 23. ¶ *in prepositional phrases* :—Þæs ne wēndon ǽr witan Scyldinga þæt hit ā mid gemete (*by fair means? using only natural strength*) manna ǽnig tōbrecan meahte, nymðe líges fǽðm swulge, B. 779. Hwelc fremu is ðē þ þæt þū wilnige þissa gesǽlþa ofer gemet (*beyond measure*), Bt. 14, 1; F. 42, 9. Gif þū ofer gemet (*to excess*) itst, 14. Hē wæs ofer eall gemett stearc, Chr. 1086; P. 219,23. **VII a.** *measure* in Biblical phrases :—Ne sylþ God þone gāst be gemete (tō gemet *ad mensuram*, L.), Jn. 3, 34. Gē gefyllaþ gemet (-mett, L.) fædera eówra, Mt. R. 23, 32. **VII b.** in reference to speech that is regulated by measure, *metre* :—Metra, þæt is on Englisc gemetu. Ðā gemetu gebyriað tō Lēdenum leóðcræfte, Ælfc. Gr. Z. 295, 18. **VIII.** *measure, amount* of something granted :—Ānum ēghuoelc sald is gefe æfter gimett giselenisse Crīstes *unicuique data est gratia secundum mensuram donationis Christi*, Rtl. 83, 1. **IX.** *a person's gemet, what is suited to his condition, capacity* or *power, a person's post or place* :—Drihten his ðǽm hālgum sægde, þ heora gemet nǽre, þ hié þ wiston, hwonne hē ðisse worlde ende gesettan wolde (*non est vestrum nosse tempora*, Acts 1, 7), Bl. H. 119, 8. Næs his gemet, þ hē hine costode *it was not for him to tempt him*, 29, 34. Mīn gemet is, þ . . ., 187, 17. Ǽghwylces mennisces monnes gemet is, þ . . ., 163, 35 : 205, 23. Mā þonne ǽniges monnes gemet sý, þ hié āríman mǽge *more than is within any man's power to count*, 63, 1. Māran þinges þonne ǽnges mannes gemet wǽre hēr on eorðan, þ hit witan mihte, 117, 21. Nis mīn gemet swilcum cilde tō onfōnne, Hml. A. 132, 520. Lufian wē ūrne Sceppend æfter ūrum gemete, Bl. H. 5, 35: 73, 28. Ofer mīn gemet, An. 1482. **X.** *manner, way, wise, mode; modus* :—On wunderlicum gemete, wīse *mirum in modum*, An. Ox. 1252: Lch. i. 90, 25. Þýs gemete *hoc modo*, Bd. 5, 12; Sch. 615, 11. On þī gemete swilc man næddran fleó, Hml. S. 23 b, 318: Bl. H. 123, 24. Tō hwylcum gemete, 5, 7. Gecýþe ūs hwylce gemete þū cōme, 141, 20. Nānum gemete *nullo modo*, Gr. D. 155, 30. Ealle gemette *omnimodo*, 256, 24. Mid suman gemete, wīsan *quodammodo*, An. Ox. 1230 Tō suman gemete, 1076. On manegum gemetum geneósað God manna sāwla; hwiltīdum mid lāre, hwīlon mid wundrum, Hml. Th. i. 410, 26. Ōþrum gemetum, Bl. H. 209, 13. Wundorlicum gemetum *mirum in modum*, Bd. 4, 19; Sch. 449, 4.

**ge-met**; *adj. Perhaps in the passages given here* gemet *is a noun used predicatively.* v. ge-met; VI.

**ge-metan.** *Add :* I. *to measure, determine size, quantity,* &c. :—Þē is behēfe þing, ārwurða cleric, þ þū gemete on getæl, Angl. viii. 303, 26. Of mīnum āgenum gōde āgifan þā teóðunga . . . swā man rihtost mage oþþe gemetan, oþþe getellan, oþþe āwegan, Ll. Th. i. 194, 8. **I a.** with dimensions as object :—Beó þær gemeten nygon fēt, Ll. Th. i. 226, 12. **II.** *to apportion by measure* :—Gemet þte metende gié bidon eft gemeten iúh bið, Lk. L. 6, 38. [*Goth.* ga-mitan: O. H. Ger. gemezzon.]

**ge-metan** *to paint.* l. ge-mētan, *and add* :—Gemēt (gemýt, Hpt. Gl. 525, 3) *picta* (*vestis*), An. Ox. 5236. Þonne man on brede hine beón gemētne gesihð *when a man in a dream sees himself painted on a board*, Lch. iii. 206, 18. Gemētum tepedum *tapetibus pictis*, Kent. Gl. 200.

**ge-mētan.** *Add :* A. *to meet.* I. *trans.* (1) *to meet with, come upon* or *across, fall in with* :—Ðā eóde hē furþor, oþ hē gemētte ðā graman gydena, Bt. 35, 6; F. 168, 24. Se here ætbærst . . . and gemētte se here ðā scipu of Eást-Englum, Chr. 992; P. 127, 17. Þā hī hāmweard wǽron . . . þa gemētton hī sciphere wīcinga, 885; P. 79, 22. (2) *to meet* that which is moving in an opposite direction :—Hig grimme windas gemētað and þā wreccan geswencað, Angl. viii. 324, 14. Hiene gemētte ān mon, þa hē for from þære byrig, Ors. 6, 31; S. 286, 14. (2 a) *with acc. and infin.* :—Þā gemētte hē mycele fyrde cuman ūp of sǽ, 982 ; P. 124, 25. (3) *to meet, encounter* an enemy :—Fauius gemētte Galba cyning *Fabius regi Arvernorum occurrit*, Ors. 5, 6; S. 228, 2. Ridon .ii. eorlas ūp. Þā gemētte hié Æþelwulf on Englafelda and him þær wiþ gefeaht, Chr. 871; P. 70, 12. Se here wolde faran on hergaþ . . . þā gemētton þā men hié of Hereforda, 918; P. 98, 17. Sōna swā hī cōmon on Stūre mūðan gemētton hī .xvi. scipa wīcinga, 885; P. 79, 19. (3 a) *with reflex. pron.* used reciprocally :—Næs long tō þon þæt hié āglǽcean hý eft gemētton, B. 2592. (3 b) *to encounter* hostility, opposition, &c., *meet* attack :—Hī sǽdon þ hī nǽfre wyrsan handplegan on Angelcynne ne gemētton þonne Ulfcytel him tō brōhte, Chr. 1004; P. 136, note 1. (4) *to come into association with*; with reflex. pron. used

reciprocally, *to come together :—*Ægþer hiora (se wela and se anweald) biþ ðý forcúþra, gif hí hí gemétaþ, Bt. 27, 2 ; F. 98, 16. **II.** *intrans.* (1) of two or more persons, *to meet, come together, come into one another's company :—*Ðær leófe ne tódǽlað, ne láðe ne gemétað, Wlfst. 190, 2 : 204. 24. Þonne hý (*or acc.* cf. I. 4) æt frymðe gemétað, engel and seó eádge sáwl, Cri. 1666. (2) *to meet* in battle :— Þ hiora nán óðerne on þone andwlitan ne slóge, þǽr þǽr hié æt gefeohtum gemétte, Ors. 5, 12 ; S. 242, 12. **B. to find. I.** without idea of premeditation, search or effort. (1) *to meet with, come upon, come across.* (a) with simple object :—Gleómen simle sumne gemétað gydda gleáwne, Víd. 138. Hé gemétte swíþe manig folc, Bl. H. 141, 32. Gemoette *inuenit*, Mt. R. 18, 28. Ðeáh nú (þú?) on londe león geméte, wynsume wiht wel ætemede, (þe) hire mágister miclum lufige, Met. 13, 18. Hwæt is þæt, bróþor? hú eart þú hér gemét? *how come you to be found here ?*, Bl. H. 237, 26. (a a) *to find* that to which one is directed :—Gang tó ðæs sǽs waroðe, and þú þǽr gemétst scip, Bl. H. 231, 30. Gangað . . . and gé þǽr gemétað fictreów, 239, 6 : 147, 30. (a β) *to find* in records :—Þá þe ic gemétte áwþer oþþe on Ines dæge oþþe on Offan, . . . þá þe mé ryhtoste þúhton, ic þá hér on gegaderode, Ll. Th. i. 58, 23. (b) *with obj. and infin.* :—Ðá hé hié gemétte swá wandrian, Past. 415, 23. Hé hine gemétte sittan on scridwǽne, Bt. 27, 1 ; F. 96, 1. Cómon hí tó sǽ and þǽr gemétton scip standan, Hml. S. 30, 164 ; Bl. H. 237, 18 : Añ. 1063. (c) *with obj. and complement :—* Ðæt mód ðæt se dióful gemét on unnyttum sorgum, Past. 415, 24. Gif hé geméteð óðerne æt his ǽwum wífe, Ll. Th. i. 90, 25. Gif heó man ǽfre eft on earde geméte, 220, 10. Be feorrancumenum men bútan wege gemétton, 114, 13. (2) *to come upon* what has been hidden or not previously observed :—Hé hét delfan ða eorðan, and hí gemétton áne ǽrene anlícnysse, Hml. Th. ii. 166, 2. Seó ilce bóc seó on þǽre ciricean funden wæs and geméted, Bl. H. 197, 27. (3) *to meet with, get, obtain, experience* (a) something advantageous, *to find* favour, &c. :—Framunge þú gemést *profectum inuenies,* Scint. 219, 3. Þú gemétest gife beforan Gode, Bl. H. 7, 18. Gemét *repperiet (bona),* Kent. Gl. 565. Þǽr wé sib and lufu gemétað, Hy. 7, 30. For þý sint góde men góde ðe hí gód gemétað . . . Ðá gódan begitaþ þ gód þ hí willniaþ . . . Ðá yfelan nǽron ná yfele, gif hí geméttan þ gód þ hí willniaþ, ac for þý hí sint yfele þe hí hit ne gemétaþ *certum est adeptione boni bonos fieri . . . adipiscuntur boni quod appetunt . . . mali vero si adipiscerentur, quod appetunt bonum, mali esse non possent,* Bt. 36, 3 ; F. 176, 28–178, 2. Hí æt him helpe gemétton, Gú. 894. Ðæt hé geméte forgiefnesse, Past. 165, 22. Reste gemétan, Bd. 5, 12 ; Sch. 616, 17. (b) something disadvantageous :—Hine bismriende hié cwǽdon : 'Hwæt is þæt þú hér gemétest?' *what luck have you had here ?*, Bl. H. 243, 8. Hé sceolde þæt ilce mǽnan, and eác þæt ylce gemétan, Ps. Th. 37, arg. Nis þǽr ǽnig sár geméted, ne ádl, ne ece, Bl. H. 25, 30. (4) *to discover on inspection* or *consideration* :—Wé ne gemétað náne geswutelunge on bócum, hwí þes dæg tó geáres anginne geteald sý, Hml. Th. i. 98, 18. Þá swaðo ðe on ðǽm marmanstáne geméted wǽron, Bl. H. 207, 13 : Ph. 231. (4 a) *with obj. and infin.* :—Hé hine geneósian wolde: þá gemétte hé hine hleonian on þám hale his cyrcan, Guth. 82, 21. Hié gemétton hæle bídan, An. 143. (4 b) *with obj. and complement.* (a) a noun :—Þæt heáfod wæg geméted scépes heáfod, Bl. H. 183, 22. (β) an adj. or ptcpl. :—Ic nǽfre þé ǽr gemétte þus méðne, Gú. 988. Gemétte hé his geþoftan slǽpende, Bd. 3, 27 ; Sch. 320, 21 : Bl. H. 145, 6. Hé gemétte þá wríteras wrítende, Gr. D. 35, 33. Hweðer hé cwicne gemétte Wedra þeóden, B. 2785. Hié gemétton þæs carcernes duru opene . . . Hié cwǽdon : 'Þin carcern open wé gemétton, and nǽnige wé þǽr gemétton, Bl. H. 239, 24–28. (γ) a phrase :—Gemétte hié ealle þá apostolas embe þǽre eádigan Marian ræste, Bl. H. 147, 4. (5) *to find by experience* or *trial* :—Ne wæs his drohtoð þǽr swylce hé ǽr gemétte, B. 757. 'Ic eom Drihtnes þeówen . . .' þǽr wæs fæger eádmódnes geméted on þǽre fǽmnan, Bl. H. 9, 22 : Gú. 502. (5 a) *with complement* :—Ne onscunige ic nó þæs neoþeran stówe, gif ic þe gerádne geméte, Bt. 5, 1 ; F. 10, 16 : 27, 2 ; F. 96, 28. Þ wé úrne Déman mildne geméton, Bl. H. 97, 3. Þ on ús ne sý geméted nǽnigu stów ǽmetig gástlicra mægena, 97, 3. (5 b) *to find out* in misdoing :—Sé þe on hláfordsearwe gemét sý, Ll. Th. i. 268, 23. **II.** with the idea of search or effort. (1) *to discover by searching :—*Gif ic mínum eágum unne slǽpes . . . oþ þæt ic geméte (-moete, Ps. Srt.) stówe Drihtne gecorene, Ps. Th. 131, 5. Ic sóhte and ne gemoette, Ps. Srt. 68, 21. Hí sóhton þ forwlencte hrýþær. Ðá gemétte hé hit æt néhstan, Bl. H. 199, 14. Þǽr sió ród geméted wæs, El. 1013. Ic sóhte hine and ne wes gemóted stów his, Ps. Srt. 36, 36. (1 a) *with obj. and infin.* :—Hé ðone fearr gehwǽr sóhte, and æt néxtan hine gemétte standan uppon ðám cnolle, Hml. Th. i. 502, 14. (2) *to find out, ascertain* by mental effort :—Áfunde, gemét *experiretur* (ut nutum supernae majestatis argumentis evidentibus *experiretur,* Ald. 46, 34), An. Ox. 3401. (3) *to procure* for a person :—Ic mé deórne scealc gemétte, Ps. Th. 88, 17. [*Goth.* ga-mótjan.] v. ge-mittan.

**gemete.** *Dele, and see* ge-met; VI, ge-métan; B. I. 1 : ge-méted. *Dele:* ge-métednes. *Add:—*On gemétednessum *in adin-*

*uentionibus,* Ps. L. 105, 29. Gemétednesse *adinuentiones,* 98, 28 : **ge-metelic.** v. gemetlic.

**ge-métend, es ; m.** *One who finds out, an inventor, a discoverer :—*Onfindend and gemétend *inuentor,* Germ. 391, 1.

**ge-metfæst.** *Add: keeping due measure.* (1) *moderate in expenditure, not extravagant, frugal.* Cf. ge-metgung ; **I a :—**Gemetfæst *frugi, parcus uti,* Wrt. Voc. ii. 151, 32. (2) *not yielding to anger* or *impatience, meek, gentle :—*In geþylde inægene gemetfæst *patientiae uirtute modestus,* Bd. 4, 28 ; Sch. 525, 14. Hé wæs líðe and gemetfæst on his worde, and hé wæs geþyldig and eádmód *erat colloquio blandus, temperantia modestus,* Guth. Gr. 111, 82. Hé wæs swíðe geþyldig and eádmód and gemetfæst on eallum his lífe, Bl. H. 213, 8. (2 a) as an epithet of a quality :—Embe his efencempan hé hæfde micele lufe and gemetfæst gedyld and sóðe eádmódnysse, Hml. S. 31, 45. (3) *not overbearing, kind :—*Hé wæs árfæst and gemetfæst and mildheort on his dǽdum, Bl. H. 217, 8. Wer milde and gemetfæst, Gú. 1080. Hé hæfð sundorgecynd milde gemetfæst. Hé is monþwǽre, nele láðes wiht ængum gezǽnan, Pa. 31. (4) *sober, discreet, honest, orderly.* v. gemetfæstnys, (2), ge-metlǽcan :—Æfæstes lífes and gemetfæstes abbod *religiosae ac modestae uitae abbas,* Bd. 5, 12 ; Sch. 631, 23. Fela sceal tó holdan hámes geréfan and tó gemetfæstan manna hyrde, Angl. ix. 265, 11. Þám ungestæþþegan þú miht secgan þ hé biþ unstillum fugelum gelícra ðonne gemetfæstum monnum *inconstans studia permutat ? nihil ab avibus differt,* Bt. 37, 4 ; F. 192, 24. Se wísdóm gedéþ his lufiendas wíse and wǽre and gemetfæste, 27, 2 ; F. 98, 1. v. ungemetfæst.

**ge-metfæstan.** *Take here* ge-mǽtfæstan, ge-metfestan *in Dict.*

**ge-metfæstlic ; adj.** *Moderate, gentle :—*Mid gemetfæstlicre þreáunge *modesta increpatione,* Gr. D. 145, 17. v. un-gemetfæstlic.

**ge-metfæstlíce.** *Add: gently, meekly :—*Drihten þ ongeat, þ se deófol þone Iudas lǽrde þ hé hine belǽwde. Ac þ hé þeáhhwæþere gedyldelíce ábær and gemetfæstlíce scírde, Hml. A. 154, 68. Críst ealle þás þing for mancynnes lufan mildheortlíce ábær and gemetfæstlíce árǽfnede, 163, 270. v. ge-metfæst, (2).

**ge-metfæstnys.** *Add:* (1) *meekness, gentleness.* v. ge-metfæst. (2) :—Petrus tihte geleáffulle wíf tó eádmódnysse and gemetfæstnysse (cf. *the ornament of a meek and quiet spirit ;* quieti et modesti spiritus, 1 Pet. 3, 4), Hml. Th. i. 98, 3. (2) *sobriety, discretion.* v. ge-metfæst, (4) :—Þæt sý mid micelre gestæþðignesse and gemetfæstnesse *cum omni gravitate et modestia,* R. Ben. 47, 14. Ðæt sý mid micelre gemetfæstnesse and gestæþþignesse gedón *ipsum cum summa gravitate et moderatione honestissime fiat,* 67, 14. (3) *moderation* in food, *temperance :—*Gang hé tó his gereorde and mid micelre sýfernysse and gemetfæstnysse his góda brúce, and ná mid nánre oferfylle ne mid oferdrince, Hml. A. 144, 16. v. un-gemetfæstnes.

**gemet-fæt.** *Add:—*Gemetfatu *metretas* (v. Jn. 2, 6), Wrt. Voc. ii. 74, 9 : 56, 59 (*printed* ganetfatu).

**ge-metgian.** *Add:* **I.** *to set a measure* or *limit* to something to prevent excess. (1) the object personal :—For ðǽm ðæt gé eówer mód gemetgien on ðǽm níðe *ut in increpationis zelo se spiritus temperet,* Past. 159, 15. (2) the object a thing :—Sé ðe gemetgað *qui moderatur (sermones suos),* Kent. Gl. 621. Gif hí þone midmestan weg áredian willaþ, þonne scylan hí selfe him selfum gemetgian þá winsuman wyrde ; þonne gemetgaþ him God þá réþan wyrde, Bt. 40, 3 ; F. 238, 23–26. Ðǽr ðǽr ðú neóde irsian scyle, gemetiga ðæt ðeáh, Prov. K. 24. Micel niédðearf is ðæt mon mid micelre gemetgunge ðreáunga gelíðige and gemetgie *necesse est ut magno moderamine correptio temperetur,* Past. 159, 4. *Temperantia,* þ is gemetgung, mid þǽre sceall seó sáwul ealle þing gemætgian, þ hit tó swíþe ne sý, ne tó hwónlíce, Hml. S. 1, 161. Þ man sí gesceádwís and gemetigian cunne ge his sprǽce ge his swígan, Prov. K. 2. Faestene gemetegude (*moderata*) scylon beón . . . for þí gehwǽde and gemetegud (*temperatus*) mete flǽsce and sáwle nytlic ys, Sciut. 51, 9–11. Beóð on twá healfa þǽre hǽtan twégen dǽlas gemetegode (*the temperate zones*), náðor ne tó háte ne tó cealde . . . Beóð twégen dǽlas on twá healfa þám gemetegodum dǽlum (-e, *v. l.*) . . . cealde, Lch. iii. 260, 23–262, 2. **II.** *to mitigate* what is excessive, *allay, moderate :—*Ðú gimetgadest (*mitigasti*) légo fýra, Rtl. 100, 20. Þú woldest gemetigan mýnne wóp *modum vis habere lacrymas meas,* Solil. H. 48, 22. **II a.** *to modify by mixing, temper, prepare :—* Drync mínne mid wópe ic gemetgade (*temperabam*), Ps. Srt. 101, 10. Þ ýþ lígas gemetegie *ut unda flammas temperet,* Hy. S. 17, 14. Þǽrtó hé sceal beón snoter, þæt hé . . . gemetgige þá snotornysse mid þǽre strengðe, Wlfst. 247, 20. Þeós wyrt wið óman fremaþ on þás ylcan wísan gemetegud, Lch. i. 304, 24. Uætro wíne gimetgado *aquas vino temperatas,* Rtl. 114, 36. **III.** *to manage properly, regulate, order, dispose :—*Rícsend mæhtig gimetgað giscæfta wrixla gimetgiende *temperat rerum vices,* Rtl. 164, 12. Hé gesceafta gesceapen hæfð, and þám ǽallum stiórað and hí ǽalle gemetgað, Solil. H. 59, 18. Fægere hé gemetegode þǽra namena gelícnyssa, Angl. viii. 332, 3. Ðæt sió hering getrymme and gemetgige ðæs wácmódan mód wið ða tælinge, Past. 213, 2. Hé sceal gemetgian swá cræftelíce his stemne *tanta arte vox tem-*

*peranda est*, 453, 12. Rixiende and gemetgende (*moderans*) worulda ealle, Hy. S. 108, 33. Gimetgende *frenans*, Rtl. 162, 26. Hió bióð gemetgode *temperantur* (*sortes a Domino*), Kent. Gl. 586. **IV.** *to fix the measure* or *amount of* :—For ðære rihtwísnesse hē gereceð ðæs gyltes bóte, and for ðære mildheortnesse hē gemetgað þære scylde wíte, Ll. Lbmn. 474, 11. Gif hē cann gemetgian hwæt hine anhagige tó sellanne, hwæt hē healdan scyle *si bene jus possidendi disponatur*, Past. 341, 12. Godes gecorenra wuldor is gemetgod be heora geearnungum, Hml. Th. i. 446, 9. v. un-gemetgod.

**ge-metgiend**, es; *m. One who regulates, disposes.* v. ge-metgian; **III** :—Drihten, þū eart mín sceapen[d] and mín gemetgyend *Lord, thou hast created me and dost order my life*, Solil. H. 11, 6.

**ge-metgung.** *Add:* **I.** *moderation, temperance.* v. ge-metgian; **I** :—*Temperantia*, þ is gemetegung ... witodlíce gemetegung is eallra mægena módor, Hml. S. 1, 161: Wlfst. 247, 15. Sam hī þyrfon, sam hī ne þurfon, hī willaþ þeáh. Hwǽr is ðonne seó gemetgung ?, Bt. 26, 2; F. 92, 31. **I a.** *moderation in expenditure, frugality.* Cf. ge-metfǽst, (1) :—Spærnysse, gemetgunge *frugalitatis*, An. Ox. 2122. **II.** *management, regulation.* v. ge-metgian; **III** :—Ðæt mon mid micelre gemetgunge ðreáunga gemetgie *ut magno moderamine correptio temperetur*, Past. 159, 3. Gemetegunge *moderamen* (*imperii eidem regendum commisit*), An. Ox. 4996. **II a.** *a regulation, an arrangement* :—Ðæt wæs wunderlicu gemetgung ðætte ðā ðā hē him selfum wæs lytel geðúht, ðā wæs hē Gode micel geðúht *miro autem modo cum apud se parvulus, apud Deum magnus apparuit*, Past. 113, 16. God dælþ manega and mistlice gemetgunga eallum his gesceaftum and welt eallra *multiplicem rebus gerendis modum statuit*, Bt. 39, 5; F. 218, 20. Sió wyrd dælþ eallum gesceaftum andwlitan and stówa and tída and gemetgunga *fatum singula digerit in motum, locis, formis, ac temporibus distributa*, F. 218, 33. **III.** *fixing of measure or amount, measuring.* v. ge-metgian; **IV** :—Hine God gesette tó ðǽm ðæt hē gemetlíce gedǽle ðone hwǽte. Ðurh ðā gemetgunge ðæs hwǽtes is getácnod gemetlico word *per mensuram tritici exprimitur modus verbi*, Past. 459, 13. v. un-gemetgung.

**ge-mēting.** *Add:* **I.** *meeting.* v. ge-mētan; **A.** (1) *the coming together* of two or more persons :—On gemētinge *in conveniendo*, Bl. Gl. Æt gemētinge, Ll. Th. ii. 424, 30. Hē hī tó him genam and clypte, and hī ealle þancunge dydon for heora gemētinge, Hml. S. 30, 384. (1 a) *a hostile meeting* :—Heora gemētting wæs æt Trefia, Ors. 4, 8; S. 186, 31. Gemēti[n]g, 5, 7; S. 228, 24. Somnite æt ōþran gefeohte mid māran fultume tó Rōmāna gemētinge cōman, 3, 8; S. 120, 25. Hē hié mid þǽm ilcan wrence beswác þe hē æt heora ǽrran gemētingge dyde, 4, 9; S. 188, 33. (2) *an assembly, a body of persons who have come together* :—Ælc gemētinc *omnis conventus* (*plebis*), Bl. Gl. Hāligra heáh gemētincg *consilium sanctorum*, Ps. Th. 88, 6. Hwylce word hē gehŷrde be him sprecan in gemētinge (*conventu*) þāra æwyrgedra gāsta, Gr. D. 190, 18. Eft bihald ofer ðás gimoetinge (*conventionem*), and ðīn bloedsunge ofer hiá (*eos*) ðerhdǽl, Rtl. 110, 32. Þā gemētinga and gesomnunga hwíttra monna *albatorum hominum conventicula*, Gr. D. 319, 1. Gemētincga *conventicula, conventus*, Wrt. Voc. ii. 135, 46. Ðæt ieldesðe setl on gemētengum (*conventibus*) hī sēcað, Past. 27, 8. **II.** *an invention.* v. ge-mētan; **B** :—Gemētinga *adinuentionum*, An. Ox. 2, 437. **III.** *a convention, an agreement* :—Þŷ lǽs þe Godes þeów æniges teónan óht ongeáte for þissere gemētingce (*gemitting, v. l.*) *ex conventione eadem*, the agreement that he should be brought to Rome), Gr. D. 35, 27. v. ge-mitting.

**ge-metlǽcan.** *For the passage substitute* :—Ðeáh wē nū ofer úre mǽð ðencen and smeágen, ðæt wē dōd for Gode; ðonne wē hit eft gemetlǽcað, ðonne dōð wē ðæt for eów *sive mente excedimus, Deo ; sive sobrii sumus, vobis*, Past. 101, 12.

**ge-metlic.** *Add:* (1) *pertaining to measuring* (?) :—Gemetlic *funalis* (cf. metrāp *for connexion of a rope with measuring*), Wrt. Voc. ii. 151, 57. (2) *measurable*—Gemetelice (*mensurabiles*) þū āsettest dagas míne, Ps. L. 38, 6. (3) *meet, suitable, fit* :—þ hē ne wilnige wynsumran wyrde ðonne hit gemetlic sié, Bt. 40, 3; F. 238, 21. (4) *meeting the requirements of a case, sufficient* :—Philippuses yfel mehte þēh þā giet be sumum dǽle gemetlic þyncan, ǽr Alexander tó ríce fēng *sufficerent ista ad exemplum miseriarum insinuata memoriae nostrae gesta per Philippum, etiamsi Alexander ei non successisset in regnum*, Ors. 3, 7; S. 120, 16. (5) *keeping due measure, not excessive* :—Ðurh ðā gemetgunge ðæs hwǽtes is getácnod gemetlico word (*modus verbi*), ðŷ lǽs hira mon mā geóte on ðæt undíope mód ðonne hit behabban mæge, Past. 459, 13. (6) *gentle, mild.* v. ge-metfǽst, (3) :—Ðǽm scamleásan ne wyrð nō gestíered būtan miclum ðreán ; ðā scamfǽstan beóð oft mid gemetlicre lāre gebetrode *impudentes ab impudentiae vitio non nisi increpatio dura compescit ; verecundos plerumque ad melius exhortatio modesta componit*, Past. 205, 23. (7) *sober, discreet.* v. ge-metfǽst, (4) :—Hæle sceal wísfæst and gemetlic, módes snottor, gleáw in gebygdum, georn wísdómes, Fä. 87. Lǽrd ūs Godes engel stilnesse and gemetlice sprǽce ... Lǽrd ūs se deófol unstillnesse and ungemetlice hleahtras and unnytte sprǽce, Wlfst. 233, 13–18. v. un-gemetlic.

**ge-metlíce.** *Substitute:* (1) *in due measure* or *amount* :—Ðæt hē him tó tíde gemetlíce gedǽle ðone hwǽte *ut det illis in tempore tritici mensuram*, Past. 459, 12. (1 a) *in time, early* :—Sī gedón [nōn] gemetlícor *agatur nona temperius*, R. Ben. I. 81, 18. (2) *in a fitting manner, meetly, suitably* :—Ðonne ðā lāreówas ongietað ðæt hī gemetlíce and medomlíce (*modis congruentibus*) lǽrað, Past. 461, 30. (3) *moderately, in moderation, temperately.* (a) of a person's action :—Wrec ðē gemetlíce, Prov. K. 46. Ðǽr ðē āuht tweóge, lofa ðæt gemetlíce, 62 : 70 : Solil. H. 48, 19. Hē beór ne drince, and gemetlíce wín and eala, Lch. ii. 88, 11. Ne gēmdon hié nānes fyrenlustes, būton swíþe gemetlíce þā gecynd beeódan ; ealne weg hī æton ǽne on dæg, Bt. 15 ; F. 48, 7. Ne ic māran getilige tó haldænne, þonne ic gemetlíce bī beón mage (*nec aliud quidquam praeter necessarium victum*), Solil. H. 35, 17. Gemetlícost, Met. 8, 16. (b) of the operation of things (disease, &c.) :—Hē wæs lícumlíce untrymnesse þrycced, hwæþere tó ðon gemetlíce (*adeo moderate*) þ hē ealle þā tíd mihte ge sprecan ge gongan, Bd. 4, 24 ; Sch. 488, 14. (4) *regularly, in due order.* Cf. ge-metgian; **III** :—Nǽron nō swā gewislíce, ne swā endebyrdlíce, ne swā gemetlíce hiora stede and hiora ryne funden on hiora stōwum and on hiora tíðum *non tam certus naturae ordo procederet, nec tam dispositos motus, locis, temporibus explicaret*, Bt. 35, 2 ; F. 158, 3. [*O. H. Ger.* ge-mezlīhho *commode.*] v. un-gemetlíce.

**ge-metlicung.** *Substitute: A making* gemetlic, *securing the proper condition* of something :—Tó wambe gemetlicunge, Lch. ii. 230, 6 : 164, 3. [Cf. *O. H. Ger.* ge-mezlībhen *temperare*.]

**ge-mētnes.** *Add:*—On ðone þryddan dæg þæs mōnþes byþ mǽrsod Sēē Stephanes líchoman gemētnes, Shrn. 113, 2.

**ge-metness.** v. un-, wiþ-gemetness.

**ge-mettan.** *Substitute:* ge-metta, an; *m. One that eats with another, a guest*, and add :—Maximus geladede for oft þone ārwurðan wer . . . þ hē wǽre his gemetta; þā forhæfde hē hine ǽfre fram his gebeórscipe, cwæð þ hē ne mihte his gemetta beón þe ānne cāsere ofslōh and ōþerne āflŷmde, Hml. S. 31, 610–615. [*O. H. Ger.* ge-mazzo *conviva.*]

**ge-miclian.** *Add:* **I.** *to enlarge, extend, increase.* (1) the object material :—Næfdon hī nān wín būton on ānum gewealdenum butruce. Maurus bletsode þ wín, and cwæð þ God mihte gemycclian þone wǽtan, Hml. S. 6, 277. (2) the object non-material :—Hláf, ðe strongra monna mægen gemiclað, hē gelytlað cilda *panis, qui vitam fortium roborat, parvulorum necat*, Past. 175, 1. Hié wēndon þ hié mehten þ yfel mid þǽm gestillan, and þā diófla hit mid ðǽm gemicledan, Ors. 4, 4 ; S. 164, 20. Gemycla and gemonigfealda þā hǽlo þæs cynges *magnificans salutare regis ipsius*, Ps. Th. 17, 48. Hē wēnde þ hē his ríce gemiclian sceolde *imperium suum se dilataturum putaret*, Ors. 3, 7 ; S. 112, 11. Gemicelgende *magnificans*, Ps. Rdr. 17, 51. **II.** *to make great, noble, excellent, powerful, increase the power, worth, dignity of.* (1) the object personal :—Þū þīn folc gemicladest, and him sealdest geniht eallra gōda, Ps. Th. 4, 8. Hī gemiclade mihtig Drihten ... gemicla ðē, Drihten, þæt þū wundur wyrce, 125, 3. Þū eart gemiclod (meahtum mǽre, Ps. Th. 103, 1) *magnificatus es*, Bl. Gl. On ðǽm naman Drihtnes wē sŷn gemyclade, Ps. Th. 19, 5. (2) the object a thing :—Twā ðing syndon swā mycele and swā mǽre, þæt ǽfre ǽnig man ne mæg ðæron ǽnig ðing āwyrdan ne gewanian ... ne eft nis ǽnig swā mǽre ... þæt āðor ðæra þēnunga gegōdian oððon gemycclian mæge, Wlfst. 34, 3–11. Hū gemiclode (micle, Ps. Th. 91, 4, micel, 103, 23 : micellíce, Ps. Srt.) þíne weorc *quam magnificata opera tua*, Bl. Gl. **III.** *to magnify, glorify, extol.* (1) the object personal :—Hē lǽrde in somnungum hiora and gemiclad (gemǽrsod, W. S.) wæs (*magnificabatur*) from allum, Lk. L. 4, 15. (1 a) the object the Deity :—Ic gemiclie *magnificabo* (*Deum in laude*), Bl. Gl. Gemicliað *magnificate* (*Deum*), Bl. Gl. (2) the object a thing :—Mægen bið gemiclad, meaht gesweotlad, wlite bið geweorðad, Rä. 81, 18. [*Goth.* ga-mikiljan.]

**ge-miclung.** *Add:* **I.** *greatness* :—Gemiclung ⁊ mǽrð þín *magnificentia tua*, Ps. Rdr. 8, 2. Þín mǽrsunge ⁊ gemiclunga *magnitudinem tuam*, Ps. L. 70, 8. **II.** *a great thing, great deed* :—Þū worhtest mǽrþa ⁊ gemiclunga *fecisti magnalia*, Ps. L., Ps. Rdr. 70, 19.

**ge-midleahtrian;** *p. ode To reproach* :—Þe lǽs hē āfyrre þē gyfe and hē (þē ?) sī gemidleahtrud *ne forte auferat tibi gratiam, et convitietur tibi*, Scint. 200, 6.

**ge-midlian.** *l.* -mídlian, *and add:* (1) *to bridle* (fig.), *restrain* :—Sē þe gelustfullunge gemídlað (*refrenat*), Scint. 88, 7. Manige ge mídliað hiera gíefernesse and ātemiað hira líchoman *carnem gulae refrenatione edomant*, Past. 345, 23. Swā horsum mídlu synd on tó asettenne swā heortan úre mid þeartne synd tó gemídligenne (*frenanda*), Scint. 55, 12. Beón gemídlad *frenarier* (*refrenari ?*), Wrt. Voc. ii. 150, 49. (2) *to muzzle a dog* :—*Canes muti non valentes latrare*; eal swilce hē cwǽde, þæt gemídlede hundas ne beorcað tó nāhte. Dumbe beóð þā bydelas and tó fæste gemídlede, þe for ege oððe lufe wandiað Godes rih tó sprecanne, Wlfst. 191, 2–6. v. un-gemídlod.

**ge-midlige.** *Dele.*

**ge-midsípian** *to accompany* :—Gemidsípegad *vel* gefēriæht *comitata* i. *sociata*, Wrt. Voc. ii. 132, 32.

**ge-mígan.** *Add:*—Gif se útgang forseten sié oððe gemígan ne mæge, Lch. ii. 260, 10.

**ge-mildian** *to make gentle, calm;* mitigare :—On styrenisse ýða ðú gemildgas (*mitigas*), Ps. Srt. 88, 10. Ðæt ðú gemildgie *ut mitiges,* 93, 13.

**ge-mildscad.** *Dele, and see* ge-milscod : **ge-milds-.** v. ge-milts-.

**ge-milscod** (-ad, -ed) ; *adj.* (*ptcpl.*) *Sweetened with honey* :—Gemilscod wín *melicratum,* gemilscad wæter *mulsurum;* Wrt. Voc. ii. 59, 32, 33. Gewyrce him gemilscade drincan, þ is micel dæl bewylledes wæteres on huniges godum dæle, Lch. ii. 202, 26. Drince *mulsa,* þ is gemilscede drincan, 11. v. milisc, miliscian.

**ge-miltan.** *Take here* ge-mieltan, -myltan *in Dict., and add* **ge-meltan.** (1) *to melt, liquefy* :—Gemaelteð (gemelteð, Ps. Rdr., gemyltet, Bl. Gl.) *liquefaciet,* Ps. Srt. 147, 18. Hé ádrígþ þá wætan, and wirð se swile swá heard swá stán, and ne mæg hine mon gemeltan ne gehnescian, Lch. ii. 212, 22. Gemaelted (*liquefacta*) is eorðe, Ps. Srt. 74, 4. Healfe cuppan clænes gemyltes spices, Lch. iii. 76, 5. On gemelt weax gedón, ii. 72, 7. (2) *to digest* :—Heald geonce þ se mete sí gemylt, Lch. ii. 284, 3. Sele him þá mettas þa þe ne sién tó raðe gemelte, 196, 16. (3) *to weaken, abate* :—Se gesíð hét sendan on fýr Agapan and Chonie, and þá þ fýr wæs gemelted (*had burnt itself out*), þá wæron ða fæmnan tó Críste geléored, and þá líchoman wæron swá gesunde þ him næs forbærned ne feax ne hrægl, Shrn. 69, 33. v. ungemilt.

**ge-miltsian.** *Add:* I. *to take pity on* :—Gemiltsige *miserescat,* Wrt. Voc. ii. 57, 26. (1) *the object a person.* (a) *with dat.* :—Þám ábryrdum hé gemilseþ *contritis* (*corde*) *miserescit,* An. Ox. 4124. Drihten him gemiltsode (-mildsode, *v. l.*), Hml. S. 13, 266. Hé gemilsade him *misertus est eis,* Mt. L. 9, 36. ¶ *in the passive the object of pity is in the dative* :—Næfre ne wurde syððan mancynne gemiltsod, ðe má ðe ðám deóflum is, Hml. Th. i. 112, 18. (b) *with gen.* :—Gemiltsa mín *miserere mei,* Ps. L. 50, 1 : Ps. Rdr. 56, 1. God smeáde hú hé mihte his and ealles mancynnes gemiltsian, Hml. Th. i. 18, 35. (2) *the object a thing, to pardon, be lenient to* sin :—Ðú gemildsast synne mínre *propitiaberis peccato meo,* Ps. Rdr. 24, 11. II. *to make mild* :—Gemiltsa þín mód mé tó góde, sile þíne áre þínum earminge, Hy. 2, 2.

**ge-miltsiend.** *Add:*—Gemiltsiend *miserator,* Ps. Rdr. 85, 15 : 111, 4. Gemildsiend, 110, 4.

**ge-miltsung.** *Add:*—Gemiltsunga *propitiatio,* Ps. L. 129, 4. Lýs þíne synna mid ælmessum on þearfena gemiltsunge *peccata tua eleemosynis redime, et iniquitates tuas misericordiis pauperum* (Dan. 4, 24), Ll. Th. ii. 434, 25. Gemun gemildsunga (*miserationum*) þínra, Ps. L. 24, 6.

**ge-mimor.** *Add: fixed in the memory, got by heart, thoroughly known.* See next word.

**ge-mimorlíce.** *Add:*—Capitul gemimorlíce tó rec[c]anne (*printed secanne, but v.* reccanne, 39, 6 : 48, 2) *lectio memoriter recitanda,* R. Ben. I. 44, 4.

**ge-mind.** *Dele bracket at end:* **ge-mindbliðe.** *Dele.*

**ge-minsian ;** *p. ode* **To lessen, impair the credit of :**—Heó goda meaht forhogde and mec swíðast geminsaþe, Jul. 621. Ne mæg ænig man Godes mihta ne his mærða geminsian ne ænig ðing áwyrdan, Wlfst. 35, 3.

**ge-mirce, es ; *n.*** I. *a limit, boundary* :—þú const þá gecynd mínes módes mec á gewunelíce healdon þ gemerce (v. Angl. i. 508) sóðes and rihtes *naturam animi mei non ignoras, solere me terminum equitatis custodire,* Nar. 2, 23. II. *a mark, sign* :—Gimerco (gemerca, L.) ðás gifylgeð *signa haec sequentur,* Mk. R. 16, 17. v. fen-, land-gemirce.

**ge-mircian (-merc-).** *Take here* ge-mercian *in Dict., and add:* I. *to fix by marks, determine* :—Fore gemercade ⁊ getǽhte *praefigit,* Mt. p. 15, 7. II. *to mark out, distinguish by a mark, designate* :—Téno of tal ðé mercas ic gemercade *decem numero tibi titulos designavi,* Mt. p. 11, 3. Hé seolf of inwritting gemercad bið *ipse ex inscribtione signatur,* 4, 5. III. *to signify, express* :—Gemercade *significans,* Lk. p. 2, 7. IV. *tò form by marks, portray* :—Gemercade *compingens* (as if from *pingere* to paint ?), Mt. p. 1, 18. V. *to mark, put a mark on.* (1) *to make the sign of the cross on* :—Ðerh ástrogdnise ðisses wætres gibloedsades and saltes on ðinum nome gimercado (*significatas*), Rtl. 117, 12. (2) *to seal* (lit. or fig.) :—Sé ðe onféd his cýðnisse his gimercade (*hath set to his seal,* A. V.; *signauit*) for ðon God sóðfæst is, Jn. R. L. 3, 33. Ðiosne gimercade Drihten, 6, 27. Gemercadon ðone stán *signantes lapidem,* Mt. p. 20, 4. VI. *to appoint* :—Æfter ðás of-gemercade (*designavit*) Drihten óðoro hundseofontig tuoege, Lk. L. R. 10, 1.

**ge-mircung.** *Take here* ge-mercung *in Dict.*

**ge-mirran ; *p.* de.** I. *to hinder, obstruct the proper action or operation of.* (1) *the object personal* :—Synt gemyrde múðas ealle þá unriht sprecað *obstructum est os loquentium iniqua,* Ps. Th. 62, 9. (2) *the object a thing* :—Tó huon eorðo gemerras *why cumbereth* (*occupat*) *it the ground ?*, Lk. L. 13, 7. II. *to obstruct right conduct in a person, lead astray, deceive* :—Mód gemyrred in synna seáð, Jul. 412.

Unwíslicum gémnisum besuicceno ⁊ gemerredo *stultis sollicitudinibus seducti,* Lk. p. 2, 11. Gé synd searowum beswicene, oððe sél nyton, móde gemyrde, An. 747. [*Goth.* ga-marzjan *scandalizare : O. H. Ger.* ge-merren *im-, prae-pedire, retardare, frustrare.*]

**ge-miscan, -myscan** *to injure, offend* :—Gemyscan *deformare* (illustrem Christi famulam sermone procaci *deformare* studet, Ald. 188, 13), An. Ox. 17, 47. v. miscan.

**ge-mittan.** *Add:* I. *to meet.* (1) *to meet that which is coming in an opposite direction* :—Hine gemitte án man, þá hé fór fram þære byrig, Ors. 6, 31 ; Bos. 128, 34. (2) *to meet, encounter an enemy* :—Þá gemytton [þá men] hý of Hereforda and of Gleáweceastre, and him wið gefuhton, Chr. 915 ; P. 99, 17. (2 a) *to meet attack, encounter hostility* :—Hí sǽdon þ hý nǽfre wyrsan handplegan on Angelcynne ne gemitton þonne Ulfcytel him tó bróhte, Chr. 1004 ; P. 136, note 1. (3) *to come into association with, into the company of* :—þá hié gemitton weorces wísan, Gen. 1687. (3 a) *with reflex. pron. used reciprocally* :—þonne wé ús gemittað on þám mǽstan dæge, Dóm. 104. II. *to find.* (1) *with no idea of search, premeditation or effort.* (a) *to come upon, come across, meet with* :—Gefoerde gefánd ⁊ gemitte (*invenit*) ǽnne of efneðegnum his, Mt. L. 18, 28. Mið ðý untýnde þ bóc, gemitte tó stówe ðér áwritten wæs, Lk. L. R. 4, 17. Ðá hé cóm ongeán ðæm herge, þá gemitte hé þér swelcne feld swá him ǽr on swefne ætýwed wæs, Shrn. 70, 16. þá eóde þ folc on þá sǽ and hig gemytton þér stǽnen hús, 150, 22. (a a) *with obj. and infin.* :—Hié æt burhgeate beorn gemitton sylfne sittan, Gen. 2426. (a β) *with obj. and complement* :—Ðiosne woe gemitton (*inuenimus*) undercerrende cynn úserne, Lk. L. R. 23, 2. (b) *to find* on inspection or consideration :—Nóht ic gemitto indinges in ðissum menn, Lk. L. 23, 4. Næneht inding deáðæs ic gemitte (*inueni*) in him, Lk. L. R. 23, 22. þá hí þér tó cómon, ða ne gemitton hí þér nænigne bryne, Shrn. 73, 38. þá gemittan hié on þǽm marmanstáne swylce mannes swaðu, Bl. H. 203, 34. (b a) *with obj. and complement* :—Mið ðý cymeð gimittes (gemitteð, L.) iówih slépende, Mk. R. 13, 36. Gimitte ⁊ fand þ mægden licgende, 7, 30. Gemittæ, Mk. L. 14, 37. Men gemitton hire líchoman gesunde æfter þám fýre, Shrn. 115, 15. II. *to find after search or effort* :—Hé cuóm gif huæt gemitte on ðæm, Mk. L. R. 11, 13. Soecað gié mið ðý gimitta mæge, Rtl. 10, 26. Soeca . . . gimitta, 14, 16. v. ge-métan.

**ge-mitting.** *Add: a convention.* v. ge-méting ; III. **gemme.** *Dele :* **gém-nis.** v. gím-ness.

**ge-mód, es ; *n.* The mind, heart** :—Se háta maga þurst þrowað and nearonesse and geswógunga and gemódes tweónunge (cf. þám men bið þurst getenge and nearones and geswógunga and módes tweónung, 194, 3), Lch. ii. 160, 6. Ne mid swiðran his nele brýsan wanhydig gemód wealdend engla, Dóm. L. 50.

**ge-mód.** *Add: in agreement with others.* (1) *peaceable, not at variance* :—On óðre wísan mon sceal manian ðá ungemódan, on óðre ðá gemódan (*pacati,* cf. ða geðwǽran, ða gesibsuman *used to translate the same* pacati, 345, 4, 6), Past. 177, 10. (2) *united, having the same purpose* :—Gemóda *conjuratus,* i. *concordatus, consentiens,* Wrt. Voc. ii. 136, 31. Gimódae, gemóde *conjurati,* Txts. 48, 201. Gemóde, Wrt. Voc. ii. 14, 66. Ðá his folgeras swá hié unwiðerweardran and gemódran beóð, swá hié fæstor tósomne beóð gefégde tó gódra monna hiénðe *sequentes illius, quo nulla inter se discordiae adversitate divisi sunt, eo in bonorum gravius nece glomerantur,* Past. 361, 20. v. un-gemód.

**ge-módigness.** v. un-gemódigness : **ge-módness.** v. un-gemódness.

**ge-módod.** *Add:*—Gezabel wæs hetelíce gemódod (*bloody-minded*) ; seó tihte hyre wer tó ælcere wælhreównysse, Hml. S. 18, 50.

**ge-módsum ; *adj. In agreement, in accord* :**—For ðon swá micle swá hié gemódsumeran (-sumran, *v. l.*) bióð betwux him, swá hié beóð bealdran ðá gódan tó swenceanne *quia, quo sibi in malitia congruunt, eo se robustius bonorum afflictionibus illidunt,* Past. 361, 13. [*O. H. Ger.* ge-mótsam *commodus.*]

**ge-módsumian, ge-módsumnes.** *The Latin originals are:* perversorum amicitiis vita nostra concordat ; testatur quod cum malis concordiam non teneret.

**ge-molsnian.** *For* Solil. 2 *substitute* :—þeáh se líchama wære gemolsnod, wæs seó sáwl simle lybbende, Solil. H. 10, 12.

**ge-mót.** *Add:* Gemóte *conuentione,* Wrt. Voc. ii. 17, 50. Gemót *consessus,* ii. 133, 57. I. *with the idea of two parties coming face to face.* (1) *a meeting with others for consultation, discussion, &c.* :—Heródes gewende tó Cesaream, and ðær hæfde gemót wið Tyrum and Sidoniscum. Mid þám ðe hé módode, Hml. Th. ii. 382, 29. Hé hét gelangian him tó ealle ðá burhwara tógædere, cwæð þ hé gemót wið hí habban wolde, Hml. S. 23, 21. (2) *a hostile meeting, an encounter* :—Wénde ic þæt þú þý wærra weorðan sceolde wið sóðfæstum swylces gemótes, þe þé oft wiðstód, Jul. 426. Oft ic wíg seó . . . ic á bídan sceal láðran gemótes, Rä. 6, 10. Nænig man compigende Gode gifalde hine gimótum woruldlicum *nemo militans Deo inplicat se negotiis* (negotium *praelium,* Migne) *secularibus,* Rtl. 60, 11. II. *a gathering or assembly of a number of people for some purpose.* (1) *in a general sense* :—Heáfædra

fela swylce eác hæleða gemót, wîtgena weorod, wîfmanna þreát, Hö. 47. Gemôte *concessum* (ante angelicum coelestis theatri *consessum*, Ald. 24, 10), Wrt. Voc. ii. 78, 22. Hê gecwæð þ hí cômon ealle tô ânum gemôte, þ hê mihte him secgan hwæt him tô dônne wǽre, Hml. S. 36, 205 : An. 650. Hí longe (long, *v. l.*) gemót ymb þæt hæfdon, hwæðer hit tácnade þe sibbe þe unsibbe, Ors. 5, 5 ; S. 226, 20. (2) in more special senses. (a) *a deliberative assembly, a council :*—Hê biþ gemôte (*consilio*) scyldig, Mt. R. 5, 22 : Wrt. Voc. ii. 72, 7 : 17, 45. Hié sellaþ eówic on gemôtum (*conciliis*), Mt. R. L. 10, 17. (b) *an ecclesiastical council, a synod :*—[Tô sinoþ]licum gemôte *ad synodale concilium*, An. Ox. 2093. Hê gesomnade bisceopa gemôt and synoð ætgædere mid monigum mâgistrum cyrícean, Bd. 4, 5 ; Sch. 372, 20. (c) *a religious assembly, congregation :*—Ne âhýdde ic nâ þíne mild-heortnesse on myclum gemôtum (*a synagoga multa*), Ps. Th. 39, 11. (d) *a judicial assembly, a court :*—Hê eóde in þæt dômern ðǽr ðǽr Caluisianus wæs in miclum gemôte . . . þâ yrsode se dêma, Shrn. 116, 32. 'Habbað eów gemôt, and tômiddes settað Nabod, biddað leáse gewitan þ hí hine forsecgan . . . þâ heáfodmenn budon him tô gemôte, Hml. S. 18, 189–195. ¶ of the last judgement :—Mægna cyning on gemôt cymeð þrymma mǽste, Cri. 833. Monge beóð on gemôt lǽded sýra cynnes: wíle fæder engla seonoð gehêgan, dêman mid ryhte, Ph. 491. (e) *a popular assembly for voting :*—Genoot *contio, convocatio populi*, Txts. 53, 584. (3) used to denote the meetings in England at which legal, administrative, and other business was done. (a) where the meeting was of national importance :—Hér wæs þ myccle gemôt æt Kyrtlingtûne, Chr. 977 ; P. 122, 8. On þissum geáre wæs þ mycele gemôt (*a grand council of Danes and English*, William of Malmesbury) on Oxonaforda, 1015 ; P. 145, 20. þ gemôt æt Brômdûne, Ll. Th. i. 280, 11. Wæs sionoðlic gemôt on ðǽre mǽran stôwe ðe mon hâted Clofeshoas, and ðǽr se cyning ond his biscopas ond his aldormenn ond alle ðâ wioton ðisse ðióde ðǽr gesomnade wǽron, Cht. Th. 70, 10. Gerǽdde se cyng and his witan þ man sceolde habban ealra gewitena gemôt on Lundene . . . and stefnode man Godwine tô þon gemôte, Chr. 1048 ; P. 174, 20–25 ; Ll. Th. i. 238, 36. Geðenc nû hweðer âwiht mani mann cynges hâm sêce þér þær hê on tûne byð, oððe hys gemôt, oððe hys fird ; oððe hweðer ðê ðince þæt hí æalle on ânne weig þeder cumen, Solil. H. 44, 3. Ofer þis gemôt (cf. 36, 4–14), Ll. Th. i. 38, 4. On þâm gemôtan þeáh wurðan on namcûðan stôwan, 348, 17. (b) where the meeting concerned a locality (hundred, borough, &c.) :—Gecýðe in gemôtes (cf. folcgemote, 12) gewitnesse cyninges geréfan, Ll. Th. i. 82, 16. On folces gemôte, 76, 5. Gif mon beforan cyninges ealdormen on gemôte gefeohte, 86, 13. Ic wille þ ǽlc man sý griðes wyrðe tô gemôte and fram gemôte, 422, 5. Ic wille þ ǽlc geréfa hæbbe gemôt â ymbe feówer wucan, 164, 20. Sêce man hundredes gemôt, 386, 1. On þâm meðelstede þâ hê gemôt hæfde, By. 199. Hí Sunnandæges folciscra gemôta (cf. folcgemôta, 320, 12) geswícan, Ll. Th. i. 326, 21. (c) *a meeting for settling cases, court :*—Wæs se þ Walchere ofslagen æt ânum gemôte (*the meeting was to decide whether Liulf had been slain by the bishop's orders.* v. Flor. Worcester), Chr. 1080 ; P. 214, 9. Ðæt nân scýrgeréfe oððe môtgeréfe ðar habban ǽne sôcne oððe gemôt (*placitum*) bûton ðes abbudes hǽse, C. D. iv. 200, 10. Ranulf his capellan ealle his (*the king's*) gemôt ofer eall Engleland dráf Ranulf *carried on all the law-courts over all England*, Chr. 1099 ; P. 235, 1. (4) *a place where a meeting is held :*—On gemôte *in foro*, Mt. R. 23, 7 : Germ. 400, 14. III. of inanimate objects, *meeting, junction.* v. ge-mittung :—On wega gemôtum *in competis*, Wrt. Voc. ii. 46, 12. v. ceápung-, gûþ-, hand-, torn-gemôt.

**gemôt-beorg**, es ; *m. A hill where a 'gemót' is held :*—Ǽrast on æscwoldes hlâw ; ðonne on gemôtbiorh, C. D. ii. 195, 10. Ou æscstede ; ðanon on ðæne gemôtbeorh, v. 82, 20.

**gemôt-hûs**, es ; *n. A house where a 'gemót' is held :*—Curia, i. *domus concilii, conventus* gemôthûs vel [gemôt]stôw *congregatio*, Wrt. Voc. ii. 137, 51. Cyrice is ûs gesceapen tô gebedhûse, nâ tô nânum gemôthûse, bûtan ymbe þæt heofoncunde ríce and lâre, Wlfst. 233, 1 : 303, 2. Forð on pâpan holt sûðweardne ; þonne on ðæt gemôthûs (*to the manere ; ad manerium*, later translations), C. D. B. ii. 246, 2. v. môt-hûs.

**ge-môtian** ; *p.* ode. I. *to talk* about ; ge-môtian ymb (be) *to discuss :*—Ûs þingð genôh þ wê ymbe þæs bissextus wurðscipe habbað þus gemôtod, and ymbe his geréna manega þing gehrepod, Angl. viii. 308, 9. Wê habbað be þâm bissextum gemôtud, and be Ianuarium manega þing gehrepode, 309, 23. II. *to attain by argument or discussion, to discuss to purpose :*—Leóf, hwonne bið ângu spǽc geendedu, gif mon ne mæg nôwðer ne mid wed ne mid âða geendigan ? oððe gif mon ælcne dôm wile onwendan ðe Ælfrêd cing gesette, hwonne habbe wê gemôtad ? *Sir, when will any suit be ended, if it can be ended neither with pledge nor with oath ? or if people want to upset every law that king Alfred made, when have our meetings and discussions been to any purpose ?*, Cht. Th. 172, 4–10.

**gemôt-leáh** ; *gen.* -leáge ; *f. A field where a 'gemót' is held :*—Tô gemôtleáge eástewearde, C. D. vi. 94, 10. In gemôtleáge, v. 103, 29.

**gemôt-mann**, es ; *m.* I. *one who addresses a meeting, an orator.* Cf. môtian ; II, môtere :—Gemôtman *contionator*, Wrt. Voc. i. 73, 24. Gemôtmanna *contionatorum* (*qui pro rostris in edito stantes popularibus catervis contionantur*, Ald. 32, 7), Wrt. Voc. ii. 79, 16 : 18, 18. II. *a member of a council, a counsellor.* v. ge-môt; II. 2 a :—Gemôtman *decurio* [cf. decurio, consiliarius (=Mk. 15, 43 : Joseph nobilis decurio *an honourable counsellor*, A. V.), Wrt. Voc. ii. 73, 34]; Ælfc. Gr. Z. 35, 5. III. *an auditor of accounts in a market* (?), cf. ceápung-gemôt :—Môtstôw *forus*, gemôtman logotheta (logotheta, *qui rationes accepti et depensi expendit ac discutit*, Migne), intinga *negotium*, cýpingc *negotiatio*, Wrt. Voc. i. 47, 22–25.

**gemôt-stôw.** *Add :* (1) *a place of assembly :*—Gemôtstôw *concilia-bulum*, Wrt. Voc. i. 49, 36. In gemôtstôwum *pro rostris* (see second passage under gemôt-mann ; I), Wrt. Vcc. ii. 79, 19 : An. Ox. 2322 : Hpt. Gl. 460, 76. *See first passage under* gemôt-hûs. (2) *a place where a law-court is held :*—Hê hæfde âne gemôtstôwe gecweden ymb sume neódþearfe þæs mynstres *erat pro utilitate monasterii causa constituta*, Gr. D. 21, 1. v. môt-stôw.

**gem-stân.** v. gim-stân.

**ge-munan.** Take here ge-monan, ge-mynan *in Dict., and add :*—Þû ge-manst, -munst, hê ge-manþ, -muneþ, -myneþ, *pl.* ge-munon (-an) ; þ. ge-mýste (cf. *O. Sax.* far-munsta) :—Ne sint gemunene *non recorden-tur* (either the verb is taken to be passive or *gemunende* should be read), Kent. Gl. 1131. I. *to retain in mind, recall to mind, recollect, bear in mind.* (1) with acc. :—Ic geman mín âgen dysig, Bt. 35, 2 ; F. 156, 27. Hié gemunan (-on, *v. l.*) ðone tôhopan, and forgietað hira demm, Past. 345, 1. Ic ðis eall gemunde, 5, 8. Ðǽr þu nû gemundest ðâ word þe ic þé sǽde, Bt. 35, 2 ; F. 156, 21. þâ gemunde (-mýste L.) Petrus word þas Hǽlend *recordatus est Petrus verbi Jesu*, Mt. R. 26, 75. (2) with gen. :—Ic ne gemune nânre his synna, Hml. S. 12, 156. Ðæs bismeres ðû ne gemansð, Past. 207, 12. Wíf . . . ne gemynes ðæs hesígnise *non meminit pressurae*, Jn. L. 16, 21. Ne gê eft gemynas síf hlâfana, Mt. L. 16, 9. Ðínra synna ne weorðe ic gemunende, ac gemun ðû hiora, Past. 413, 22. (3) with clause :—Gif þû gemanst þæt brôþor þín hæfð ǽnig þincg ongeán þé, Scint. 23, 14. Gemunst, Bt. 36, 3 ; F. 176, 22. Gemunst (-manst, *v. l.*) ðû þ wit ǽr sprǽcon, 38, 3 ; F. 200, 11. Mín môd gemanð hû (gemyneð hwilc, *v. l.*) hit ǽr wæs, Gr. D. 4, 11 ; 6, 8. Swâ mycel swâ nân man ne gemunet þ hit ǽfre ǽror dyde, Chr. 1099 ; P. 235, 7. Gemunde ic hû ic geseah . . hû ðâ ciricean stôdon bôca gefyldæ, Past. 5, 8. Ðætte ðæt môd . . gemyne of ðǽm suingum tô hwǽm eal monncynn gesceapen is, 255, 18. Ðæt hí gemunen ðæt hié . . . bióð gesomnode, 397, 8. Seldon hié willað gemunan hû micel hié nimað, 343, 16. (4) where (1) and (3) are combined :—þ is þ ic gefyrnost gemunan mæg, þ mín fæder wæs cempena ealdorman *the earliest thing that I can remember is that my father was a captain*, Hml. S. 30, 322. I a. *to bear in mind, no to forget to do :*—Gefêra, gemyne þ ðû úre gecwedrǽdenne tô longe ne oferbrec, Ors. 5, 12 ; S. 242, 7. Gemunon wê symle þ wê þâ gôc dôn þe ûs Godes bêc lǽraþ, Bl. H. 73, 26. þ hê oft hæbbe on gemynde þ mannum is mǽst þearf tô gemunenne, þ is þ hí rihtne geleáfan habban and þ hí rihtne crístendôm healdan, Ll. Th. i. 326, 11. II. *to re-member (and pray for)* (1) *the living :*—Gemune þû mê earminge or þínum gebedum, Hml. A. 178, 311. (2) *the dead :*—On ðâ geráð ðe he gemunen hí and Ôsmôdes sáulæ tô his gemunde dege *ea ratione ut memore sint ejus et animae Osmodi ad anniversarium ejus*, Cht. Th. 493, 10. III. *to bear in mind as worth considering, mind, think of :*—Ðâ cwǽdon hí þ, þ hí þæs ne gemundon þonne mâ þe heora geséran Chr. 755 ; P. 49, 23. IV. *to record, make mention of.* Hê gemanþ *memoratur*, i. *dicitur*, An. Ox. 1598. Gemunað *memorant* Wrt. Voc. ii. 55, 34. Nú ic þyses Alexandres gemyndgade, ic wille þæ mâran Alexandres gemunende beón, Ox. 3, 7 ; S. 110, 11. Is ge munen, gesǽd *memoratur*, An. Ox. 1514 : 2814. Gereht, gemunen 2206. V. absolute, *to exercise the faculty of memory :*—Seó sâwu þurh þæt gemynd gemanð, Hml. Th. i. 288, 28. Seó sâwul is *memoria* þæt is gemynd, þonne heó gemanð, Hml. S. 1, 186. Gemynen (*remini scentur*) alle gemǽru eorðan, Ps. Srt. 21, 28. VI. *to exercise th mind* (?), *meditate, consider.* v. Ps. Spl. 62, 7 *in Dict.* :—Rǽswodan spǽcan, wǽran gemunende *comminiscuntur* (cf. comminiscuntur, pro tractabantur i meditabuntur, An. Ox. 7, 209), Wrt. Voc. ii. 24, 2. VII. *to put in mind, remind* a person of something, *charg with :*—Ic gemunde þê fâcnes, þér nân næs, Hml. A. 135, 641. v munan.

**ge-mund.** *Dele.*

**ge-mundbyrdan.** *Add :*—Placidas gemundbyrde þâ ðe fordêmdœ wǽron, Hml. S. 30, 6.

**ge-mundian.** *Add :*—Philippus þâ crístenan gemundode, Hml. S. 2, 283. Gemunda (*fove*) þâ biddendan, Hy. S. 3, 31. Gebide for mœ and for mîne ungesǽlignysse gemunde, Hml. S. 23 b, 719. Fultumes biddende æt Gode, þ hê hí gemundian sceolde, 25, 337. [*O. H. Ger* ge-muntôn.]

**ge-munecod.** v. un-gemunecod : **gêmung.** v. gîmung.

**ge-muning**, e; *f. Remembrance, recollection :*—Synna gemuni[n]cge *peccaminum recordationem*, Angl. xiii. 378, 191.

**ge-mynd.** *Add :* **I.** *the faculty of memory :*—Seó sáwul is *memoria*, þ is gemynd, þonne heó gemanð, Hml. S. 1, 185. Gé hwæthwega godcundlíces on eówerne sáule habbaþ, þæt is andgit and gemynd and se gesceádwísa willa, Bt. 14, 2; F. 44, 25. Æghwilc ungemyndig hine sceolde eft gewendan in tó sínum módes gemynde *quod quisque discit, immemor recordatur*, Met. 22, 58. **II.** *the state of being remembered :*—Hé gemynd dyde mǽrra wundra *memoriam fecit mirabilium suorum ;* he hath made his wonderful works to be remembered (A. V.), Ps. Th. 110, 3. **II a.** in phrases. (1) on gemynd *so as to preserve the remembrance :*—Byð gesǽd on hyre gemynd þæt heó þiss dyde, Mt. 26, 13 : Mk. L. R. 14, 9. Þis wæs gedón on mín gemynd, Bl. H. 69, 20. Gé monigfeald on gemynd witon, alra tácna gehwilc *you know everything that can keep alive the memory* (of the Trojan War), El. 644. (2) (*to be in*) *mind :*—Byð on éceum gemynde æghwylc, Ps. Th. 111, 6 : Rtl. 177, 35. Seó gesihð him wæs on swá micelre gemynde *the vision was so well remembered by him,* Shrn. 51, 33. (2 a) *the state of being remembered and considered.* Cf. **VIII.**—Wæs him on gemynde (cf. hé ongeat, Bt. 1 ; F. 2, 14) yfel and edwít, þæt him kyningas cýðdon, Met. 1, 54. Hire wæs Godes egsa mára in gemyndum þonne eall þæt máððum-gesteald, Jul. 36 : Gú. 139 : Bo. 30. (3) (*to have, bear, &c. in*) *mind.* Cf. **VIII** :—'Gemunst þú þ ic þé ǽr sǽde.' 'Þ ic hæbbe genóg fæste on gemynde,' Bt. 36, 3 ; F. 176, 24. Þ hé oft hæbbe on gemynde þ mannum is mǽst þearf oftast tó gemunenne, Ll. Th. i. 326, 10. Æghwylc þára is wyrðe synderlíce in gemyndum tó habbanne *sunt digna memorie singula*, Angl. iv. 140, 22. Lǽt þé on gemyndum (*remember*), hú mé bysmredon weras, An. 962. (4) (*to come to (into), occur to*) *mind :*—Mé arn tó gemynde oft, Ll. Lbmn. 269, 16. Hwílum án, hwílum óðru cymð tó gemynde, Past. 413, 30. Mé cóm oft on gemynd, 3, 2. Þæt unriht on gemynd cume *in memoriam redeat iniquitas*, Ps. Th. 108, 14. Gode nó syððan hié in gemynd cumað, El. 1303. (5) (*to bring, call to*) *mind :*—Him in gemynd his Dryhtnes naman dumba bróhte, Rä. 60, 7. (5 a) (*to take to (into), fix in*) *mind :*—Ðeáh ealra þǽra worda hí wǽron forgytene, námon him þá gedwollnen ǽnlípige tó gemynde *though they did not remember all those words, the heretics kept in mind single ones*, Hml. S. 23, 390. Ic nam mé tó gemynde þá gewritu and þá word þe se arceb mé fram þám pápan bróhte, Cht. E. 229, 23. Þára manna gehwám þe on gemynd nime . . ., El. 1233. (6) (*out of*) *mind :*—Ne cumon eów þás word of gemynde wá lange swá gé lybbon *ne obliviscaris verborum quae viderunt oculi tui, et ne excidant de corde tuo cunctis diebus vitae tuae*, Deut. 4, 9. Wé lǽtað hit of gemynde swilce hit nǽfre ne gewurde, Hml. S. 23, 278. **III.** *memory of many persons :*—Hé folces frið bétte swiðost þára cyninga þe ǽr him gewurde be manna gemynde, Chr. 959 ; P. 114, 22. **III a.** *the length of time over which the recollection of a number of persons extends,* (*within living*) *memory :*—Sume ǽr, sume síð, sume in úsra tída gemyndum, Gú. 849. **IV.** *that which is remembered, the account of events so far as they are recollected :*—Eal þæt gemynd þe tó cýðanne wǽron *memoria digna* (the Latin seems misunderstood as *memoria* is ablative), Bd. prep. ; Sch. 3, 3. **IV a.** *that which is remembered of a person or thing, memory, remembrance, recollection of.* (1) with gen. :—Ðæt góde mód ðe sió hǽlo áweg ádriéfð þæt gemynd ðǽre medtrymnesse (*infirmitatis memoria*) geedníewað, Past. 255, 17 : 463, 16. Onbryrded mid gemynde his synna *conpunctus memoria peccatorum suorum*, Bd. 3, 27 ; Sch. 319, 17. Hæfde ic þáget hwæthwega gemynd on mínum móde þǽre unrótnesse þe ic ǽr hæfde *ego nondum penitus insiti moeroris oblitus*, Bt. 36, 1 ; F. 170, 26. (2) with clause :—Ná hí gemynd hæfdan hit his hand werede *non sunt recordati manum ejus, qua die liberavit eos*, Ps. Th. 77, 42. **IV b.** *recollection perpetuated among men,* (*blessed*) *memory :*—Gemynd ðín ðorhwunað in weoruld weorulde *memoriale tuum permanet in saeculum saeculi*, Ps. Srt. 101, 13 : 134, 13. Heora gemynd wunaþ, Bl. H. 171, 32. Gimynd (*memoria*) míno in gecneóreso woruldo, Rtl. 3, 34. Ic gedó þæt hira gemynd geswícð of eallum mannum, Deut. 32, 26. Ðǽre eádegan gemynde wer *reverendae memoriae vir*, Past. 173, 16. Ic ádílige Amaleches gemynd, Ex. 17, 14 : Chr. 979 ; P. 123, 20. Martira gemynd áreccan, Men. 69. **V.** *something which serves to commemorate, a commemoration, memorial.* (1) a material object :—Betere is þæt se cásere . . . gecneówige æt ðæs fisceres gemynde, þonne se fiscere cneówige æt ðá cáseres gemynde, Hml. Th. i. 578, 5-8. Tó þám gemynde (*a memorial church*) þæs hálgan Stephanes, ii. 26, 27. Ðá stánas beóð hér tó gemynde (*ad monumentum*) Israéla bearnum, Jos. 4, 7 : Bl. H. 189, 15. Wrít þis on béc tó gemynde *scribe hoc ob monumentum in libro*, Ex. 17, 14. Forlǽt hí his fét þær on þá eorþan besincan mannum tó écre gemynde, Bl. H. 127, 22. Wegan máððum tó gemyndum, B. 3016. Dryhtne in gemyndum, Gú. 186. Gé frætwaþ gemynde sóðfestra *ornatis monumenta justorum*, Mt. R. 23, 29. (2) a non-material object :—Þæt ys mín nama and þæt ys mín gemynd (*memoriale*), Ex. 3, 15. Nú is seó mæsse þe man mæssað gemynd his þrowunge, Ll. Th. ii. 376, 13. **V a.** *with reference to the dead.* (1) *com-*

*memoration service :*—On ðæt gerád þ mín gemynd mid him þý fæstlícor sió, and hió ǽlce gére gemyndgien ðá tíde mínes forðsíðes, C. D. v. 186, 6. Tó his gemunde dege *ad anniversarium ejus*, Cht. Th. 493, 13. On þá gerád þe man [his] gemynd æfter his dege tó þǽre hálgan stówe dó in Wintanceastre, 158, 15. Tó tídsongum mín gemund dón, 159, 9. (2) *annual commemoration of a saint :*—On ðone fíf and twéntegðan dæg ðæs móndes bið Scē Urbanes gemynd, Shrn. 86, 9. Gemin[d] dóþ þǽre hálgon Margaretan *memoriam beatissime Margaretae facite* (Hml. A. 220, 426), Nar. 49, 16. **VI.** *what puts in mind, a reminder, warning :*—Magon wé ús þis (the case just told) tó gemyndum habban, and þás bysene on úrum heortum staþelian, þ wé ne sceolan lufian worlde glengas tó swiþe, Bl. H. 113, 34. Þæt mæg æghwylcum nien tó gemyndum módsnottera, Seel. 128. **VII.** *mention, record :*—Ðrǽles gódes and yfles gemynd áworden *serui boni malique mentione facta*, Lk. p. 7, 18. Him on gómum bið Godes gemynd *exaltationes Dei in faucibus eorum*, Ps. Th. 149, 6. Ic syngode mid gemynde þæs fácnes, þǽr nán næs, Hml. A. 135, 640. Gemind *mentionem*, i. *memoriam*, An. Ox. 4350. Mid þám cnihte þæs gemynd ic ǽr bufan dyde *cum puerulo, cujus superius memoriam feci*, Gr. D. 112, 27. **VIII.** *the action or state of thinking about, minding, heeding something, thought of* (*gen.*) :—Mága gemynd mód geondhweorfeð, Wand. 51. Hí unwǽre men áweniaþ from Godes gemynde, Bl. H. 61, 25. His gást áhwearf in Godes gemynd, Dan. 630 : Cri. 1537. Ic þín gemynd on módsefan begange *memor fui tui*, Ps. Th. 62, 6. Sé þe forhogaþ þ hé Godes bebodu healde oþþe ǽnig gemynd hæbbe Drihtnes eáþmódnesse, Bl. H. 83, 16 : Fä. 63. Drihten sylle þé gemynd his beboda, Angl. xii. 516, 3 : Hy. 4, 22. **IX.** *mind, purpose :*—Næs him nilde gemynd on módsefan, and hé þearfendra éhte *non est recordatus facere misericordiam, et persecutus est hominem pauperem*, Ps. Th. 108, 16. **IX a.** gemynd(e) habban *to have a mind, be disposed, desire :*—Þá þe þæs gemynde mycle habbað, þæt heó his word efnan *memoria retinentes mandata ejus, ut faciant ea*, Ps. Th. 102, 17. **X.** *the moral tendency, moral character :*—Sceal on leóht cuman sínra weorca wlite and worda gemynd and heortan gehygd fore heofona cyning, Cri. 1038. **XI.** *mind, consciousness, intellect :*—On ferhðcofan fæste genearwod, móde and gemynde, þæt hé mægða síð wíne druncen gewitan ne meahte, Gen. 2604. On gemynd drepen *stupefied*, 1571. Monna gehwylcum þe gemynd hafað, Cri. 431. Hý láre bǽron in his módes gemynd, Gú. 89. Hé sealde him snyttru on sefan gehygdum, mægenfæste gemynd, 445 : El. 1248. Þurh gemynda spéd, worde and gewitte, wíse þance, Gen. 1957. **XI a.** in a personal sense :—Críst eardað on þǽre deue eádmódnesse and on þám gemynde wísdómes (*in the person who has wisdom in his mind?*), for þám simle se wísa mon eall his líf lǽt orsorh, Bt. 12 ; F. 36, 23. **XII.** *the healthy state of the mental faculties,* (*sound*) *mind.* v. ge-myndleás :—Ne lǽt hé búton swilce hé of his gemynde wǽre, Hml. S. 23, 634. Hé wæs onwended of his sylfes gemyndum, Gr. D. 260, 11. **XII a.** *waking* or *normal consciousness :*—Gimynde biniming *lithargiam*, Wrt. Voc. ii. 53, 73. Se áwyrgeda gást swá swíþe hine drehte þæt hé his sylfes nǽnig gemynd ne hæfde *ab immundi spiritus violentia grassabatur, ita ut, quid esset, vel quo sederet, vel quid parabat facere, nesciret*, Guth. Gr. 148, 4. v. efen-, fyrn-, gást-, geár-, in-, mis-, mód-, un-, úp-gemynd.

**gemynd-beniming.** *Dele, and see* ge-mynd ; **XII a.**

**gemynd-blíþe** ; *adj. Happy from what one recollects* (?), *having happy memories* (?). The word, however, glosses *memoriale* :—Gemyndblíþe *memoriale*, Ps. Spl. T. 101, 13.

**gemynd-dæg.** *Add : the anniversary of a person's death :*—Scs Gregorius gemynddæg (*March* 12. Cf. On ðone twelftan dæg ðæs móndes (*March*) bið Scē Gregories geleórnes, Shrn. 62, 18), Ll. Th. i. 92, 5.

**gemynd-drepen.** *Dele, and see* ge-mynd ; **XI.**

**ge-mynde** ; *adj. Mindful :*—Sécende blód heora gemynde hé is *requirens sanguinem eorum recordata est*, Ps. L. 9, 13. Elenan wæs mód gemynde ymb þá mǽran wyrd, El. 1064. v. in-gemynde.

**ge-myndelic.** *Add :* **I.** *that deserves to be remembered, memorable :*—Him gelamp swýðe gemyndelic (*valde memorabilis*) wíse, Gr. D. 227, 3. Gehýr þú þás race be þám apostole and swíðe gemyndelíc eallum geleáffullum, Ælfc. T. Grn. 16, 13. **II.** *that brings to mind, admonitory, hortatory.* v. ge-myndiglic :—Ðes cwyde mæg beón swýðe gemyndelic eallum þám þe . . . Godes folce riht bodian sculon, Wlfst. 283, 7. Gemindelic gehádedum mannum, 304, 2. Gemyndelice *exortatoria*, Wrt. Voc. ii. 145, 74. **III.** *that preserves the memory of something :*—Gemyndelic *memoriale*, Bl. Gl. Eówres gemyndelican memoriale, Wrt. Voc. ii. 54, 31. Þá þrúh on gemyndelicre stówe hí gesetton *sarcophagum in memoriale quoddam posuit*, Guth. Gr. 169, 159.

**ge-myndelíce.** *Add : by heart :*—Gemyndelíce *memoriter*, Wrt. Voc. ii. 145, 74. Sý án ǽnlýpig rǽdincg gerǽd gemyndelíce bútan béc (*memoriter*), R. Ben. 34, 12. Gemyndelíce bútan béc gecweden, 38, 10. Gemyndelíce bútan béc gesǽd *ex corde recitatus*, 34, 1. Sý gecweden án rǽding gemyndelíce bútan béc, 36, 20.

**ge-myndelicnes (ge-mynd-)** *memory, remembrance:*—Gemynde-licnes *memoriale (tuum)*, Ps. Rdr. 134, 13. Gemyndlicnes, 103, 13.
**gemynd-full.** *Take here* ge-mendful *in Dict.*
**ge-myndig.** *Add:* I. *having remembrance of.* (1) without construction:—Hē gecostad weard in gemyndigra monna tīdum (*in the times of men who can remember the events;* cf. mīne dihteras . . . mihton gemunan . . . þā wundru þisses eādigan weres (*Guthlac*), Guth. Gr. 103, 48), Gū. 125. (2) with gen.:—Guma gidda gemyndig, sē þe ealdgesegena worn gemunde, B. 868. Drihten is swíþe gemyndig ealra þāra gifena þe hē ūs tō lǽteþ, and wē eall āgyldan sceolan þ hē ūs sealde, Bl. H. 51, 23 : 215, 24. (3) with clause :—Þū sý gemyndig hwæt mín fæder þē dyde, Bl. H. 151, 24. Þæt ne sý gemyndig monna ǽnig hū Israhēla naman ǽnig nemne *non memorabitur nomen Israel amplius*, Ps. Th. 82, 4. I a. *where special conditions are implied.* (a) *with gen.:*—Gif hwilc mon sié on ondyrstlecum wīsum, and hē sý mínes naman gemyndig (*remembers my name and calls upon it*), Drihten, gefrida dū hine, Shrn. 101, 31. Hē wæs þǽra worda gemyndig . . . and his folc lǽdde, Ps. Th. 104, 37. Beó geofena gemyndig *remember to give*, B. 1173 : Gen. 2163. Hē wæs gemyndig ealre his mildheortnesse, Bl. H. 159, 21. (β) *with dat. infin.:*—Hē is swýþe gemyndig heora blōd tō wrecanne *requirens sanguinem eorum memoratus est*, Ps. Th. 9, 12. (2) *where gratitude is implied:*—Hý nā synd gemyndige handa his *non sunt recordati manus eius*, Ps. Rdr. 77, 42 : Bl. Gl. (3) *where warning is to be taken:*—Beód gemyndige Lothes wīfes, Lk. 17, 32. (4) *where kindness, compassion, &c., is implied:*—Hit beón mæg þ hē wǽre gemyndig manna týddernesse, Bl. H. 197, 13. Wes þū mín gemyndig, 147, 36. Wes þū gemyndig manna bearna, Ps. Th. 73, 17. (4 a) *having remembrance and making mention of* in prayer :—Swā hwæt swā þū bǽde, eall hit biþ gehēred, and swā hwæt swā þū wǽre gemyndig, þ forgifeþ þē God *quidquid petisti, exauditae sunt deprecationes tuae, et quod memorata nunc es, hoc tibi datum est* (Hml. A. 219, 375), Nar. 47, 25. (5) *where hostility is implied.* (a) *with gen.:*—Mīn unwīsdōmes ne wes þū gemyndig, Bl. H. 89, 11. (β) *with clause:*—Wes gemyndig þ bē unwīse edwīta fela oft āsprǽcon, Ps. Th. 73, 21. II. *deserving of remembrance, memorable.* Cf. ge-mynd; IV :—Se gemyndiga pāpa *papa memoratus*, Bd. 5, 7; Sch. 584, 9. III. *deserving of commemoration.* Cf. ge-mynd; V:—Se dæg bid gemyndig Godes dēowum de dā hālgan āsende tō ēcere myrhde *the day of a saint's death is the one for God's servants to take as his commemoration day*, Hml. Th. i. 354, 7. IV. *mindful of.* (1) *having the thoughts engaged upon.* Cf. ge-mynd; VIII. (2) *with gen.:*—Sē þe nū biþ gemyndig Drihtnes þrowunge and his ǽriste ealle mōde . . . sē þe forhogaþ þ hē ǽnig gemynd hæbbe Drihtnes eáp-mōdnesse, Bl. H. 83, 13. Swā cwæd eardstapa earfeda gemyndig, Wand. 6. Wē sceolan beón gemyndige Godes beboda and ūre sāwle þearfe, Bl. H. 25, 26. (b) *with dat.:*—Gemyndig winemǽga hryre, Wand. 6. (c) *with prep.:*—Gemyndig ymb þæt mǽre treó, El. 213. (d) *absolute:*—Rincas rǽdfæste . . . ā fricgende . . . , ā gemyndge mǽst monna wiston, Sch. 16. (2) *mindful of and doing* what is fit :—Se hālga ongan āra gemyndig sprecan fægre, Gen. 1899. Hē fremede swā him se ēca bebeád . . . wǽre gemyndig (*carrying out the compact*), 2372. Wealhþeów cynna gemyndig grētte guman on healle, B. 613 : 2171. Hē ārās elnes gemyndig, Gū. 1268 : Jul. 601. (3) *mindful of a command, counsel, &c., obedient to, acting in accordance with.* (a) *with gen.:*—Him þā fēran gewāt fæder ælmihtiges lāre gemyndig, Gen. 1780 : 1943. Wæs heó gemyndig Dryhtnes willan, Jul. 601. Hē reordode rǽda gemyndig, Exod. 548. Hē sprǽc snytra gemyndig, Gen. 2463. Hié wǽron gemyndige ealra Godes beboda, and þǽre godcundan ǽ swíþe gehýrsume *erant justi ante Deum incedentes in omnibus mandatis et justificationibus Domini* (Lk. 1, 6), Bl. H. 163, 2. Sýn wē gemyndige þæs þe ūs Críst bebeád on þyssum godspelle, 39, 14. (b) *with dat.:*—Godes gifu ūs gewissad tō his willan, gif wē gemyndige beód Crīstes bebodum and dǽra apostola lāre, Hml. Th. i. 312, 34. (4) *mindful of the welfare of* a person :—Þū on heáhsetle sitest gāsta gemyndig, Hy. 8, 31. (5) *careful, anxious* about something, *solicitous.* (a) *with gen.:*—Martha, wes þū behýdig and gemyndig Marian þinga, Bl. H. 67, 33. Wē sceolon nū beón gemyndige ūre sāula þearfe, 101, 16. (b) *without construction:*—'Ic þē bidde þæt þū mē behýdigne and sorhfulne be þisse wīsan ne lǽte' . . . Hē cwæd : 'Mín bearn, nelt þū beón gemyndig' *adjuro te, ne me sollicitum de hac re dimittas . . . Ait : Fili mi, de hac re sollicitare noli*, Guth. 165, 80. (6) *mindful* of what one purposes to do, *intent* on. Cf. ge-mynd; IX, IX a.:—Eft wæs ānrǽd, nalas elnes læt, mærda gemyndig mǽg Hygelāces, B. 1530. Fýrdraca fǽhda gemyndig rǽsde on þone rōfan, 2689. Bealuwa gemyndig, 2082 : Gū. 417. V. *having mind, having great intellectual power*, cf. ge-mynd ; XI :—Eálā Gabrihel! hū þū eart gleáw and scearp, milde and gemyndig, wīs on þīnum gewitte and on þīnum worde snottor, Hö. 77. v. efen-, eft-, un-gemyndig.
**ge-myndig,** es; *n. Memory* of a person. v. ge-mynd; IV a :—Ic wilnode . . . æfter mīnum līfe þām monnum tō lǽfanne þe æfter mē wǽren mīn gemyndig (gemynd, *v. l.*) on gōdum weorcum, Bt. 17; F. 60, 16.

**ge-mynd[i]gian.** *Add:* I. *to recall the memory* of (*gen.*) :—Wē geednīwiad and gemyndgiad dǽre scylde de ūre ieldesta mæg ūs on forworhte *parentis primi lapsus iteratur*, Past. 313, 15. II. *to remember:*—Symble bid gemyndgad morna gehwylce eaforan ellorsīd, B. 2450. II a. *to remember with kindness, compassion, &c.* :—Ūre eádmēdu Drihten gemyndgade *in humilitate nostra memor fuit nostri Dominus*, Ps. Th. 135, 24. III. *to remind* a person of something :—Sió godcunde gemetgung his unmehta done man gemyndgad *superna moderatio infirmitatis memoriam ad mentem revocat*, Past. 465, 32. Dæt his lāreów hine suíde lythwōn gemyndgige his undeáwa *quod eis doctor mala sua saltem leniter ad memoriam reducit*, 207, 4. IV. *to preserve the memory of, commemorate:*—Hió ǽlce gēre gemyndgien dā tīde mīnes fordsīdes, C. D. v. 186, 8. V. *to make mention of.* (1) with gen. :—Nū ic þyses Alexandres gemyndgade *Alexandri istius mentione commonitus*, Ors. 3, 7 ; S. 110, 9. (2) with acc. :—Dió cuoen suddǽles gemyndgade *reginam austri commemorat*, Lk. p. 7, 8. Gemyndged is *memoratur*, p. 3, 13. VI. *to think of:*—Ic on mōde gemyndgade hū mē ǽrran dagas ālumpan, metegade on mōde þīne mǽran weorc, and ymbe þīne handgeweorc hogode *memor fui dierum antiquorum, meditatus sum in operibus tuis, in factis manuum tuarum meditabar*, Ps. Th. 142, 5. v. eft-gemynd(i)gian.
**ge-myndiglic;** *adj. That brings to mind, that serves to warn, admonitory:*—Des cwyde mæg beón swýde gemyndiglic eallum þām þe tō þām gesette sýn, þæt hī Godes folce riht bodian sculon, Wlfst. 7, 3. v. ge-myndelic; II.
**ge-myndiglicnes.** *Take here* ge-mindiglicnes *in Dict., and add:* v. ge-myndelicnes.
**ge-mynd[i]gung,** e ; *f. A memorial, monument:*—Hē þǽr his selfes longe gemyndgunge (-mynegunge, Bos. 54, 14) gedyde *magnum monumentum in reparatione ejus operatus est*, Ors. 3, 1 ; S. 98, 25.
**ge-myndleás.** *Add:*—Gemyndleás *amens vel demens*, Wrt. Voc. i. 75, 55. Gemyndlǽs *freneticus*, An. Ox. 11, 177. v. ge-mynd ; XII.
**ge-myndlicnes.** v. ge-myndelicnes.
**ge-myndlīst,** e ; *f. Madness, senselessness :*—Þola þū naman gemyndlǽste (-lýste, Hpt. 31, 7, 111) *careas nomine limphatici* (i. *dementis*), Lch. i. lx, 8.
**gemynd-stōw.** *Add:* a *tomb :*—On gemyndstōwum *in monumentis*, Ps. Rdr. 87, 6.
**gemynd-wirþe ;** *adj. Worthy to be had in remembrance.* (1) of persons:—Wē witon manige foremǽre and gemyndwyrþe weras forþgewitene þe swíþe feáwa manna ā ongit, Bt. 19; F. 70, 12. (2) of things, *worthy of record:*—Hē mē ealle dā þe gemyndwurde wǽron onsende *ea mihi, quae memoria digna uidebantur, transmisit*, Bd. pref. ; Sch. 3, 3.
**ge-myne.** *Add:* cf. ge-mun.
**ge-mynegian.** *Add:* I. *to make mention of :*—Māre ic þyses gemyngade þonne ic his mid ealle āsǽde *ut commemorata sint haec magis quam explicata*, Ors. 3, 2 ; S. 100, 26. Dā hē gemynegode (-myngode, *v. l.*) þǽra eádigra martyra *cum beatorum martyrum mentionem faceret*, Bd. 1, 7 ; Sch. 19, 14. Se gemyngode pāpa *papa memoratus*, Sch. 584, 9. II. *to remind* of a duty, *admonish :*—Wē synd gemynegode (-myngode, *v. l.*) þurh dysses dæges wurdmynt . . . eów nū tō secgenne sum ding be hyre, Hml. A. 24, 1. Tō þan þ wē beón gemyngode (-myngode, *v. l.*) þ wē ūre mōd on ælcere gedrēfednysse tō Gode āwendon, Angl. vii. 38, 358.
**ge-mynegung.** v. ge-mynd[i]gung: **ge-mynig.** v. eft-gemyndig.
**ge-myntan.** *Add:* (1) *to mean, purpose, design :*—Dā forlēt hē, swā hē gemynte gefyrn, þone woruldlican campdōm, Hml. S. 31, 131. Hē rād þyder hē ǽr gemynt hæfde *ad hospitium, quo proposuerat, accessit*, Bd. 3, 9 ; Sch. 231, 9. God fērde ford, swā hē gemynt hæfde, Gen. 18, 33. (1 a) with case:—þā gemunde hē hwæt hē ǽr be dan cilde gemynte *he remembered what his intentions about the child had been*, Hml. Th. i. 80, 12. (1 b) with clause :—God gemynte þ he wolde þurh þ wæter þā synne ādīlegian *praedestinavit Deus in aquis abluere peccatum*, Angl. vii. 6, 55. (1 c) with dat. infin. :—Hē ārǽrde þæt tempel þe his fæder gemynte tō ārǽrenne, Hml. Th. ii. 578, 9. Hē gemynte þā mādmas tō genimenne, Hml. S. 25, 769. (1 d) construction uncertain :—Gemynte *decreuit* (*contemnere*), An. Ox. 2699. (2) *to destine* a thing for a person. (a) with dat. of person :—Ic stihte † ic gemynte gekýþnysse mīnum gecorenum *disposui testamentum electis meis*, Ps. L. 88, 4. Hē sceal þæt wīte dolian de hē de gemynte, Hml. Th. i. 372, 16. Tō dām edele becuman de him se heofenlica Fæder gemynte, ii. 218, 19. Heom þā wīta gemynte wǽron, Hml. S. 23, 112. (b) with prep. *tó :*—þ hē gemente tō Abrahame *quod disposuit ad Abraham*, Ps. L. 104, 9. (3) *to destine* a person to (*tó*) a condition, fate, &c. :—Gif hē hine ǽr tō munuchāde gemynte *si prius se monachismo addixisset*, Ll. Th. ii. 142, 10. (4) construction uncertain :—Dæt gemynte irre *molitam iram*, Wrt. Voc. ii. 58, 37.
**ge-myrran.** v. ge-mirran: **ge-myscan.** v. ge-miscan: **ge-mýste.** v. ge-munan.
**ge-mýþ.** *Substitute:* ge-mýþ, e ; *f.* (?): ge-mýþe, es ; *n.* [The

form and gender of the word are not quite certaiu. A dat. sing. fem.
occurs once, but it is in a rather late charter with corrupt forms; all
other instances are in dat. pl. Corresponding forms in other languages
are neuter, so probably the English.] *A mouth* of a river, valley, *opening* of one road into another, of an enclosure. (1) where one stream
joins another:—Of Temede gemýðan; andlang Temede in wynnabæces
gemýðan... in Temede múðan (cf. of Temede streáme in wynnabæce
... in Temede streám, 386, 8–19) *de Tamede* múðan *recto cursu in os
wynnabæce ... transit in ore Temede*, C. D. iii. 382, 4–24. Æfter
ðam bróce ðæt hit cymð tó ðam gemýðan, 389, 35: of ðam gemýðan,
424, 23. Andlang bróces tó ðæs cinges gemýðan; of ðam gemýðan
west be bróce, 407, 10. Tó ðæm gemýðan, and æfter streáme, Cht.
Crw. 20, 33. On forde ætgénon gemýðan, C. D. iii. 435, 22. On
ðam gemiddum andlang ðære wealdíc ... æft tó gemiðum, v. 346, 20–
30. On ðam gemýðum; west andlang Beaddingaburnan, vi. 214, 13.
Andlang bróces on ðā mýðy; of ðás gemýðon, iii. 48, 26. (2) where
a river flows into the sea:—Æt ðám gemýðum (-myndum, *v. l.*) Tíne
streámes *juxta ostium Tini fluminis*, Bd. 5, 6; Sch. 573, 18. (3)
where one road opens into another:—Forð on ðā denu tó ðæra wega
gemýðan, C. D. iii. 409, 7. (4) *the mouth of a valley* (?); *cf. Icel.*
dals-mynni:—Of Dellen norð intó ðære gemýðe; eást intó hafegeæte,
C. D. iv. 157, 10. Ymbe cráwan hyll útan ðæt hit cymeð tó ðam gemýðum; ðæt úp be ðam gemǽnan lande in hæðbeorh, iii. 391, 29. (5)
*opening of an enclosure* (?):—Andlang hagan tó hagena gemýðum; of
ðen gemýðun on Techanstedes hagan, C. D. v. 336, 25. [*O. L. Ger.*
gi-múþi: *O. H. Ger.* ge-mundi: *Icel.* mynni.]

**gén**; *adv.* *Add*:—ðæs gén tó tácne is (is git tó tácne, *v.l.*) *denique*,
Bd. 2, 6; Sch. 138, 14. And gén (gyt, *v.l.*) sóðre ðæt ic Drihtnes
wordum sprece *immo ut uerbis Domini loquar*, 4, 23; Sch. 476, 13.

**géna.** *Take here* **geána,** **geóna** *in Dict.,* and *add*:—In Ongel-
cyrícean, on ðære þu ána nú géna (gyt, gyta, *v. ll.*) eart bysceop geméted *in Anglorum ecclesia, in qua adhuc solus tu episcopus inueniris*,
Bd. 1, 27; Sch. 73, 3. Geóna (geáne, L., wé gyt, W. S.) feówer
mónoðas sindum *athuc quatuor menses sunt*, Jn. R. 4, 35. Geóna (ðā
geáne, L., þá gyt, W. S.) hine sprecende, Lk. R. 8, 49. Mið ðý ðā
geáne (*adhuc*) synfullo wé woeron, Rtl. 22, 9. Ne ðā geána (ne gyt,
W. S.) *nondum*, Mt. L. 16, 9. Wið geána *usque modo*, 24, 21. Wið
ðā geána *usque athuc*, Jn. L. 2, 10.

**ge-nǽgan.** *Add*: I. *to approach* a person with (1) a material
object:—Wiste genǽgdon módige mete þegnas (*food was brought*),
Exod. 130. (2) with non-material object. (a) *to address* with words,
El. 385 (v. Dict.). (b) *to attack, assault* with ill-feeling, &c.:—Ic (*a
sword*) mé wénan ne þearf ðæt mé bearn wræce, gif mé gromra hwylc
gúðe genǽged (gehnǽged? v. ge-hnǽgan), Rä. 21, 19. Wé þec níða
genǽgað, Gú. 261. Hearde genearwod, níða genǽged, B. 1439. (b a)
of the attacks of illness, trouble, &c.:—Hú geward þe þus, fæder, ferð
gebysgod, nearwe genǽged?, Gú. 986. [*In the last passage in Dict. for
Cri.* 1126 *read* Gú. 1126.]

**ge-nǽgled.** *Substitute:* **ge-nǽglian;** *p.* ede, ode. I. *to nail,
attach* one object to another *by nails*:—Hiá gelǽddon hine þ hiá on róde
genǽglede *duxerunt eum ut crucifigerent*, Mt. L. 27, 31. Sié áhóen í
fæste genǽglad on róde *crucifigatur*, 22. Genǽgled, 26. Genǽglod,
Hml. Th. i. 82, 25. II. *to fasten together by nails, construct by
means of nails.* v. nǽglian:—Scip sceal genǽgled, scyld gebunden, Gn.
Ex. 94. [*O. H. Ger.* ge-nagalit, -negelit *infixus, clauatus*.]

**ge-néman;** *p.* de *To take away by force*:—Hé hét þriddan dǽl
ágifan þám mannum þe hé hit ær on genǽmde, Guth. 14, 11. Þone
mǽstan dǽl ðínra ǽhta þú onfehst þá ðe on þe genémde (*genumene,
v. l.*) wǽron *maximam possessionem tuarum, quae tibi ablatae sunt,
portionem recipies*, Bd. 5, 19; Sch. 671, 6. Cf. ge-niman.

**ge-nǽmnian.** v. ge-nemnan: **ge-nǽstan.** v. ge-hnǽstan.

**ge-nǽstan.** *Add: to destroy, corrupt*:—Ic genæto *conficiam*, i. *con-
fundam*, Wrt. Voc. ii. 133, 30. Genǽt, geyrmþ, forbrýt, tóbrecþ
*conterat*, 135. 5. Wyrð ðæt mód besuicen and genǽt (-nǽtt, *v.l.*) mid
ðæra ólicunga ðe him underðiédde beóð *seductus ab his, quae infra
suppetunt*, Past. 111, 6.

**ge-namian.** *Add*: I. *to give a name* to an object, *call* so and so
(proper or common noun):—Ætforan ðám cásere, Aurelianus genamod,
Hml. Th. ii. 308, 3. Wé habbað áne gástlice módor, seó is *ecclesia*
genamod, Wlfst. 67, 14. Ðæt land is on þreó genamod, ðæt is Hengest-
esíg and Seofocanwyrð and Wihthám *the land is divided into three
parts named respectively* ..., C. D. v. 401, 25. Fæder and Sunu and
Hálig Gást ne magon beón tógædere genamode (*cannot be included under
one name*), Hml. Th. ii. 282, 20: 606, 23. Biscop Grécisc is noma
woerces ... ofer, insceáwre; for ðon biscopas oferinsceáwras genomado
bíðon *aepiscopus Graecum est nomen operis* ... *epis super, scopus inspector; ideo episcopi superinspectores nominantur*, Rtl. 194, 25. I a.
*to call* by a name:—Ðú sunu ðínne tuoelf nomun genomadest *Filium
tuum xii. nominibus nominasti*, Rtl. 145, 12. II. where a
descriptive epithet is applied to an object, *to speak of as* (*tó*):—Eal seó
gelaðung ðe stent on mǽdenum and on cnapum, on ceorlum and on

wífum, eal heó is genamod tó ánum mǽdene, swá swá Paulus cwæð ...
'*uirginem castam exhibere,*' Hml. Th. ii. 566, 12. III. *to
mention by name, mention*:—Hit is gecweden þæt se ealda Israhel oferwann seofon ðeóda, eahteoðe wæs Pharao, ac hí oferwunnon micle má
þonne ðær genamode wǽron, Hml. Th. ii. 218, 26. IV. *to
assign* something to a person:—ðæs hé eftleán wile ealles genomian,
Cri. 1101. Hit is gewunelic on hálgum gewritum þæt gehwám bið
fæder genamod be his efenlǽcunge: gif hé geeuenlǽcð Gode ..., hé bið
Godes bearn gecíged, Hml. Th. ii. 228, 2. V. *to nominate,
appoint* a person to a particular work:—Hé his cempan tó ðam slege
genamode, Hml. Th. i. 88, 3. Þæra cempena suna wurdon genamode
tó ðam ylcan campdóme þe heora fæderas on wǽron, Hml. S. 31, 32.
Hé hit mid gewitnysse bohte ðára manna þe tó gewitnysse genamode
synt, Ll. Th. i. 276, 7.

**ge-namne.** *Substitute:* **ge-namn;** *adj. Having the same name*:—
Ic seah rǽpingas (*the two buckets of a draw-well*) on ræced fergan under
hróf sales hearde twégen: þá wǽron genamne, nearwe bendum gefeterade
fæste tógædere, Rä. 53, 3. [Cf. *O. H. Ger.*:—Sint kenammin, i.
*habent kelíchen namen.*]

**génan** (?) *to drive.* v. gínan: **ge-nápan.** *This word, as regards
form and meaning, is uncertain*: **gén-bóc.** v. geán-bóc: **gén-cwide.**
v. geán-cwide, *where add*:—Géncwides *capitula*, R. Ben. I. 49, 9:
**gén-cyme.** v. geán-cyme.

**gén-dele** (**geán-**); *adj. Steep*:—Géndeles *ardui*, Hpt. Gl. 416,
18. Cf. of-dæl, -dæle, geán-dýne.

**gendnes** (?):—Ongeánwurde í gendnyssa (=gehendnyssa? v. ge-
hendnys; I. 2; or = geánnyssa? v. geán-nis) *obuia*, Hpt. Gl. 499, 66.
**ge-neádian.** *Add*: I. construction uncertain:—Geneádode *coegit*,
An. Ox. 1941. Hé wæs geneádod *cogeretur*, i. *compelleretur*, 1846.
Geneádod *coacta*, 4365. Beón geneádode *compellantur*, 1257. II.
absolute:—Geneádod bryce *debitus usus*, Wrt. Voc. ii. 139, 74. Ge-
neáded *inuitus*, An. Ox. 2541. III. *to compel, force* (1) to (*tó*)
an action:—Hé bebeád his cempum þ hí ðā crístenan cynegas tó þære
offrunga geneádodon mid wítum, Hml. S. 24, 44. (2) *to do* (*clause
with þæt*):—Hé mid Iulianes wérinysse weard geneádod þ hé þá niht on
his mynstre gewunode, Gr. D. 38, 25. v. ge-nídan.

**ge-neah.** *Dele* '*f* [?],' *and in bracket l.* gi-nógi.

**ge-neah.** *Substitute:* **ge-neah,** *pl.* -nugon; *p.* -nohte. I.
impersonal, *it suffices* a person, *a person has enough, abounds* in:—Wé
eáðe magon úpcund ríce forð gestígan, gif ús on ferðe geneah, and wé
willað healdan heofoncyninges bibod, Sch. 35. [Cf. *O. H. Ger.* ganah
inan *abundabit* (Mt. 13, 12, *where the Rushworth Gloss. has* genyht-
sumað).] II. with subject. (1) *to suffice, have sufficient power
sumað).]* to do something:—Nǽnig mennisc tunge ne geneah þæs ácendan engles
godcund mægen tó gesecgenne, Bl. H. 165, 5. (2) *to have abundance
of* (?):—Gifstól sceal gegierwed stondan, hwonne hine guman gedǽlen.
Gífre bið se þám golde onféhð, guma (guman? v. I) þæs on heáhsetle
geneah, Gn. Ex. 70. [*Goth.* ga-nah *sufficit*: *O. H. Ger.* genah. Cf.
ge-nyhtsumian.]

**ge-neah, -neh;** *adv. Take here* ge-neh *in Dict.*:

**ge-neahhe.** *Add*: I. *abundantly, sufficiently*:—Ic sylle geneahhe
heora hungrium hláf tó fylle *pauperes ejus saturabo panibus*, Ps. Th. 131,
16. I a. in a vague sense as intensive, *enough* (cf. *assez in
French*), *fully, quite, very* (*much*). (1) with adj. or adv.:—Is mín
feorh tó helldore hylded geneahhe *my life is quite turned down to the
gate of hell; vita mea in inferno appropinquauit*, Ps. Th. 87, 3. Hí
ús wiðerwearde wǽron geneahhe *they were adverse enough to us*, 123, 3:
El. 1065. Swég úp ástág níwe geneahhe (*new enough*, i. e. that had not
been heard before, for Grendel had never been attacked in the hall), B.
783. Hé hǽðengield gesóhte neóde geneahhe (*very diligently*), Jul. 24.
Georne sécan nearwe geneahhe, El. 1158. (2) with verb:—Þoune mé
costunga cnysdon geneahhe *dum tribularer*, Ps. Th. 119, 1. Hé þeóstra
þegnas ... nýd onsette and geneahhe bibeád (*straitly charged them*),
Gú. 669. Hreósað geneahhe tóbrocene burgweallas *the ruined city walls
fall to the ground*, Cri. 977. II. *often, frequently*:—þá henna hire
áfyrrde án fox, sé cóm geneahhe (-neahche, *v.l.*) næht feorran (þá henna
gelómlíce áweg bær án fox cumende of þám neáhlande, *v. l.*), Gr. D. 69,
28. Se deácon hæfde him tó þeáwe þ hé cóm geneahhe tó Benedicte,
and hé geneahhe (gelómlíce, *v. l.*) geneósode (*frequentabat*) his
mynstres, 170, 1–4. Hé geneahhe férde tó heora húse, 154, 12: Angl.
xi. 99, 70: Sal. 378. Heó cyrreð geneahhe, oft and gelóme, Rä. 43,
10: 9, 2: Deór. 32. Is úre sáwl swíðe gefylled mid edwíte oft and
geneahhe, and ús oferhýdige forseóð oft and gelóme, Ps. Th. 122, 5.
Sendan swíðe geneahhe ofer waðema gebind wérigne sefan, Wand. 56.
þæt þám be his líf cúðon ... þig geneahhor his lífes tó gemyndum cóme,
Guth. Gr. 103, 1. III. *constantly, assiduously, persistently*:—
Hine þá se Godes wer geneahhe (-nehhe, *v. l.*) þreáde and gelómlíce
mynegode *cum eum vir Dei assidue corriperet et frequenter admoneret*,
Gr. D. 155, 27. Béc syndon bréme, geneahhe geweotede weotedan willan
þám þe wiht hycgeð, Sal. 237. Hé manode geneahhe bencsittende, Jud.
26. Hí him on healfa gehwone ymbútan farað ... geneahhe, Cri. 930.

Ic þin sóð weorc sēce geneahhe *justificationes tuas exquisivi*, Ps. Th. 118, 94 : 141, 2. Lócað geneahhe fram þām unlǣdan hláford *the lord persistently turns his face from the wretched man*, Sal. 381. Hē ne wandode, ac fýsde forð flāna genehe *he flinched not, but kept the shafts flying*, By. 269. Ic Drihten sōhte swýðe geneahhe *Deum exquisivi*, Ps. Th. 76, 2 : 85, 13. Singað him sealmas swīðe geneahhe, 146, 1. Swā hwylc mon swā þis godspell hæbbe on his gewealde, þæt hē hit cýðe Godes folce swýðe genehhe, Wlfst. 213, 28.

**ge-neahhelíce**; *adv. Constantly, perpetually* :—Þ wæs eallra mǣst þǣr getácnod genehhelíce, Þ God worhte þurh his gegyrelan *illud tamen est praecipuum, quod Deus per vestimentum illius assidue dignabatur operari*, Gr. D. 210, 14.

**ge-neahhie.** *Take here* ge-nehige (*l.* ge-nehge) *in Dict., and add* :—Sceolon wē nū gemunan ūre nýdþearfe, and genehge þencean emb ūre sāula þearfe, Bl. H. 101, 32. *v.* ungemet-geneahhie.

**ge-neahlíce**; *adv. Take here* ge-nehlíce *in Dict., and add* : I. *constantly, assiduously* :—Mid þý se Godes wer hine geneahlíce (*assidue*) ðreátode and gelōmlíce lǣrde, Gr. D. 155, 27.    II. *constantly, usually* :—Hē hine sylfne ungyrede, and þ reáf þe he genehlíce on him hæfde, hē hit slēfde on þone man *exuens se luterio melotinae, in quo ille orare solebat, ipsum circumdedit*, Guth. Gr. 153, 21.

**ge-neálǣcan.** *Add* : I. *to move nearer to an object, get near.* (1) absolute :—Ðā þā se cyng mid his fyrde geneálǣhte, Chr. 1091 ; P. 226, 37. Stód se Hǣlend and hēt hine lǣdan tō him. þā hē geneálǣhte (geneólcode, L., geneálocode, R., *appropinquasset*) hē āhsude hine, Lk. 18, 40. (2) with dative :—Mid ðý þ fýr him geneálǣhte *cum ignes adpropinquassent*, Bd. 3, 19 ; Sch. 279, 10. þā hē geneálǣhte (geneólecte, L.) þǣre ceastre gate, Lk. 7, 12. (3) with prep. :—Hī geneálǣcton oþ tō gatum deáþes, Ps. L. 106, 18.    II. *to come or go to a person or place.* (1) absolute :—Geneálǣhton (geneólǣcadon, L., gangende tō him, R.) his leorningcnihtas *accedentes discipuli*, Mt. 13, 10. Geneálǣhtun (geneólēcton, L., cumende, R.), 14, 12. Genēlēcdon (tō gangende, R.), Mt. L. 15, 12. Geneólēcdon (tō gineólicadun, R., tō cōmon, W. S.) *accesserunt*, Mk. L. 6, 35. Geneálǣc and gecoffra þīne lāc, Hml. S. 14, 34. Geneólēcende (heom tō gangende, R.) *accedens*, Mt. 28, 18. Geneálǣcende (cwōm ł geneólēcde, L., cōm ł geneólēcade, R.), Mk. 1, 31. (2) with dat. :—Hē sylfwilles tō ðrowienne middanearde geneálǣhte *he voluntarily came to earth to suffer*, Hml. Th. i. 82, 28. Geneálǣhte (geneólēcade ł tō cuōm, L.) him ān hundredes ealdor *accessit ad eum centurio*, Mt. 8, 5. Geneálǣhte (geneálācde, L., cumende, R.) him ān bōcere *accedens unus scriba*, 19. Mid ðý þe hī eft geneálǣcton (-neólēcton, *v. l.*) þām fýre, ðā tōdǣlde se engel ðone lēg þæs fýres, Bd. 3, 19 ; Sch. 280, 13. Hē ne dorste his neáwiste geneálǣcan *he durst not come into his neighbourhood*, Hml. Th. i. 88, 21. (3) with prep. *tó*, (a) where *tó* precedes dat. :—Hē geneólēcde (gangande, R.) tō ðǣm forðmest *accedens ad primum*, Mt. L. 21, 28. Geneálēcde, 30. Ðā geneálǣhte (genēlēcde, L., cumende, R.) Petrus tō him, Mt. 18, 21. Geneálǣhton (geneólēcedon, L., eódun, R.) his leorningcnihtas tō him, 5, 1. Geneálēcdon (eódun, R.) tō him, Mt. L. 15, 1. Tō þisum hūsle tō gānne ne tō þisum weófude tō geneálǣcenne, Ll. Lbmn. 414, 2. Genēleccende (geneólācede, L., *accedens*) tō him se costere, Mt. R. 4, 3. (b) where dat. precedes *tó* :—Him tō geneálǣhte Ruben, and cwæð him tō, Hml. A. 119, 80. Hē hym tō geneálǣhte and hine gefullode, 184, 85 : 182, 48. Him tō geneálǣhtan his hyrdas ... ac āhōfen hine ūp, 123, 227. Ðā geneálǣhton (genēlēcdon, L., eódun, R.) hī him tō, Mt. 17, 19 : Lk. 8, 24. Him þā geneálǣhton (gecneólēcdon, L., gineólicadun, R.) tō Iacobus and Iōhannes, Mk. 10, 35. (4) with adverbs :—Þyder þeóf ne geneálǣcð (geneólēced, L., gineólicað, R., *appropiat*), Lk. 12, 33. Hié selfe sǣdon þæt hié ǣr flugon ær hié tōgædere geneálǣcten *ipse rex ante se victum quam congressum fuisse prodiderit*, Ors. 4, 6 ; S. 170, 25.    II a. *to come or go to doing or suffering* :—Oð ðæt se tíma cōm þ hē sylfwilles þām deáðe geneálǣhte, Hml. A. 72, 172.    III. *of lines or surfaces, to approach* :—Ðeáh se rodor þǣre eorðan nāwer ne geneálǣce, on ǣlcere stōwe hē is hire emnneáh, Bt. 33, 4 ; F. 130, 22.    IV. *to come near a person, come into personal relations with* :—Hē ālýsð sāwle mīne from þām þā þe geneálǣciaþ mē, Ps. L. 54, 19. Tō nā geneálǣc tō Drihtne mid twy-fealdre heortan *ne accesseris ad Dominum duplici corde*, Scint. 65, 15.    IV a. *the subject a thing* :—Geneálǣcige gebed mīn on gesiþe þīnre, Ps. L. 118, 169.    IV b. *of the relation between married people* :—Forlēteð monn fæder his and mōder and geneólēces (gineólicas, R., *adhaerebit*) tō wīfe his, Mk. 10, 7.    IV bb. *of sexual intercourse* :—Sceolde heó forhabban ... fram hire gebeddan ; ... and syþþan mid Godes bletsunge geneálǣcan hyre gemacan, Hml. Th. i. 134, 23.    V. *of time or events.* (1) *to draw nigh* :—Godes ríce geneálǣcð (geneólācað, L., tō gineólicað, R.), Lk. 10, 11. Hyre tōworpennes geneálǣcð (geneólēcað, L., gineólicað, R.), 21, 20 : 28. Tīd geneálǣcð, 8 : Mt. 26, 45. Geneálǣhte freólsdæg, Lk. 22, 1. Geneólēcde eástro, Jn. p. 4, 14. Geneólicde, 3, 12. þā hǣþenan geneálǣhton tō Oswolde. þā geseah hē geneálēcan his lífes geendunge, Hml. S. 26, 157. (I a) *used impersonally* :—Þā þā hit geneálǣhte þ hē

his lufe geswutelode, Hml. A. 73, 3.    Þā hit geneálǣhte þ hig sceoldan fēran, 201, 212. Gineólicod wæs eóstrum, Jn. R. 2, 13. (2) *to come, happen* :—Mid ðý dæg maccalic gecuōm ł geneólēcde (gineólicade, R.) *cum dies opportunus accidisset*, Mk. L. 6, 21.    VI. *to come near in character* :—Sē ðe on muneclicere drohtnunge gyrnð ðæra ðinga ðe hē on woruldlicere drohtnunge næfde, būton twýn him geneálǣhð se hreófia Giezi, and þæt þæt hē on líchaman geðrowade, þæt ðrowað þes on his sāwle, Hml. Th. i. 400, 3.    VII. *to come near in feeling, opinion, &c., consent to, agree to.* Cf. ge-nēhwian ; II :—Gē geneólēcað woercum fadora iúera *consentitis operibus patrum vestrorum*, Lk. L. R. 11, 48. Hī mid mōde his bebodum geneálǣhton, Hml. Th. i. 548, 27.

**ge-neán.** *Substitute : To get near.* (1) *to approach* :—Swipu ne geneálǣcþ ł ne geneáhaþ (*appropinquabit*) þīnum getelde, Ps. L. 90, 10. (2) *to be attached to, fixed to.* Cf. ge-neálǣcan ; IV b :—Ðā sōðfæstnesse ðīnes trumlícor gineá ðū dóst lāre *eos veritatis tuae firmius inherere facias documento*, Rtl. 34, 28. [O. H. Ger. ge-nāhēn sih *to approach*.] *v.* ge-nēhwian.

**ge-nearwian.** *Add* :—Biþ þ sār on ðā swiðran sídan on þā scare and þā wambe swíþe genearwod, Lch. ii. 232, 4.

**ge-neát.** *Add* : I. *one who enjoys* (*v.* neótan) *with another, one who belongs to the household* or *following* (*comitatus*) *of a superior* :—Genaeot *inquilinis* (cf. *inquilinus* inbūend, 134, 24), Wrt. Voc. ii. 111, 53. Geneát, 45, 57.    I a. *where the superior is a king, prince, or great man*, cf. beód-, heorþ-geneát, geneát-scolu :—Bigstandaþ mē (*Satan*) strange geneátas, Gen. 284. Geneátum *parisitis* (Dulcitius, Dioclesiani Satrapa, a propriis *parasitis* et domesticis clientibus non agnoscitur, Ald. 66, 23), Wrt. Voc. ii. 66, 62.    II. *as a technical English term.* (1) *one of a king's household* or *retinue.* Cf. I a :—Cyninges geneát, gif his wer bið twelf hund sciłł., Ll. Th. i. 114, 10. þær weard ofslægen Lucumon cynges gerēfa ... and Æðelferð cynges geneát, Chr. 897 ; P. 91, 10. (2) *one of a private person's household.* Cf. I :—Gif þīn geneát stalie and losie þē, Ll. Th. i. 116, 10. (3) *a tenant holding by service* (*and rent*) *to the lord* :—Se geneát sceal wyrcan swā on lande swā of lande, hweðer swā him man být, C. D. iii. 450, 31. Geneátes riht. Geneátriht is mistlic be ðām ðe on lande stænt. On sumon hē sceal landgafol syllan ..., Ll. Th. i. 432, 11. Hē hēht his geneát, Ecglāf hātte, rīdan mid ceastersētna preóste, Wulfhūn hātte, and hē hine gelǣdde ealle ðā gemǣra ... and se ceastersētna preóst hit gerād and se Æðelwaldes geneát mid hine ... Ðus him gewīsede se Æðelwaldes mon ðā gemǣru, C. D. v. 140, 30–141, 30.    III. *used of a thing which is an adjunct of another* (?), *the boat belonging to a larger vessel* (?) :—*Fasellus vel* geneát, *i. genus holeris*, Wrt. Voc. ii. 146, 54. [O. L. Ger. ge-nōt :—Thuner and Uuōden ... ende allum thēm unholdum the hira genōtas sint, Heyne 88, 7 : O. H. Ger. ge-nōz *socius, sodalis, contubernalis, cliens*.]

**geneát-riht.** *Add* : Ll. Th. i. 432, 12.

**ge-neát-scolu.** *Substitute* : geneát-scolu, e ; *f. A band of retainers* (*v.* ge-neát ; I a) :—Swylt ealle fornōm secga hlōðe and hine sylfne (*Heliseus, who is described as æðeles cynnes ríce gerēfa*, 18) mid ... hý helle sōhton. Ne þorftan þā þegnas in þām þýstran hām, seó geneátscolu ... tō þām frumgāre ... wēnan, þæt hý in wīnsele beágas þēgon, Jul. 675–687.

**ge-nec.** *Dele* : ge-nēdan. *v.* ge-nīdan.

**ge-nefa.** *Substitute* : (1) *a nephew* :—Gaius his nefa (genefa, *v. l.*) fōr on Sirie *Caium, nepotem suum, Augustus ad ordinandam Syriae prouinciam misit*, Ors. 6, 1 ; S. 254, 11. Hē gefeaht wið Pompeiuses nefan (genefon, *v. l., nepotes*), 5, 12 ; S. 244, 6. (2) *the son of a cousin* :—Adrianus, Traianuses nefa (genefa, *v. l.*) *Hadrianus, consobrini Trajani filius*, 6, 11 ; S. 266, 6.

**ge-neh.** *Dele, and see* ge-neahhie : **ge-nehlíce.** *v.* ge-neahlíce. **ge-nēhlíce.** *Dele, and see* ge-neahlíce ; II.

**ge-nēhwian.** *Add* : I. *to approach, draw near* :—Tō geneólēcde ł gehnēhwade (*adpropinquavit*) ríc heofna, Mt. L. 10, 7.    II. *to consent.* Cf. ge-neálǣcan ; VII :—Ðes ne efne-genēhuade (-ginēhwadæ, R.) tō dēdum hiora *hic non consenserat actibus eorum*, Lk. 23, 51. *v.* ge-neán.

**ge-nemnan.** *Add* : I. *to give as a name to an object.* (1) *a proper name of* (a) *a person* :—Monno ... wæs genemned *hominem Matthaeum nomine*, Mt. L. 9, 9. Wes heora heratoga Reóda gehāten, from þām heó sind genemnode Dæl Reódi, Chr. P. 5, 2. þus hié wǣron genemnode, Dubslane and Maccbethu, 891 ; P. 82, 26. (b) *a place* :—On þā burh þe ys genemned (*dicitur*) Effrem, Jn. 11, 54. On þām staþe þe is genemned Ypwines fleót, Chr. 449 ; P. 12, 7 : 552 ; P. 16, 25 : 926 P. 107, 24. (c) *with a cognate accusative* :—Þū his naman hǣlend ge-nemnest, Lk. 1, 31. Genemne ðū noma is haelend *vocabis nomen ejus Iesum*, Mt. L. i. 21. (2) *a class name* :—Ðeáh þū ealle gesceafta āne naman genemde, ealle þū nemdest tōgædere and hēte woruld *though thou gavest each element a separate name, thou didst name them collectively and call them world*, Bt. 33, 4 ; F. 128, 27. Leóht wæs þurh Drihtnes word dæg genemned, Gen. 130.    II. *where a title or descriptive term is used, to call.* (1) *of a person* :—Ðā apostolas

genemde *quos apostolos nominavit*, Lk. L. 6, 13. Genemna laruas *vocare Rabbi*, Mt. L. 23, 7. Þ biđ hálig Godes sunu genemned, Bl. H. 7, 24. Sê þe heora cyning mid rihte genemned wǽre, 177, 12. Þā syndan huntigystran genemde, Nar. 38, 3. (2) of a thing :—Ic forlēto đā boec đā from Lucianus and Hesichio genemnedo *praetermitto eos codices quos a Luciano et Hesychio nuncupatos*, Mt. p. 2, 10. (2 a) of the title of a book :—Đā bóc đe is genemned on Englisc Hierdebóc, Past. 7, 19. **II a.** *to call* so and so, *say that* a person or thing *is* so and so :—Ðeignas salt eorđu genemde *discipulos sal terrae appellans*, Mt. p. 14, 11. Ic genemned eam nihthrefne gelíc, Ps. Th. 101, 5. **II b.** genemnan tô *to speak of as* :—Heó hie sylfe tô đeówene genemde (cf. Ic eom Drihtnes þeówen, 20), Bl. H. 9, 24. Oft biđ on hālgum gewrietum genemned midfeorh (-feorwe, MS.) tô gioguđhāde *in sacro eloquio aliquando adolescentia juventus vocatur*, Past. 385, 31. Godes gelađung is genemned tô ānum mǽdene, Hml. Th. ii. 10, 20. Hē wæs syđđan eall genemned tô Sunnandæge ođ đæs Mônandæges lihtincge, Wlfst. 210, 3. **III.** *to mention by name* (person or thing) :—Æđelwald . . . and Óscytel, and swiđe monige eác him þe wē nū genemnan ne magon, Chr. 905; P. 94, 15. Hāligne Gāst . . . Fæder ođđe Freóbearn. Ne sint þæt þreó Godes þriwa genemned, Hy. 10, 44. Man sceal habban wǽngewǽdu . . . , and fela đinga đe ic nū genǽmnian ne can, Angl. ix. 264, 6. **III a.** *to mention* :—Þāra on hāde sint syx genemned, El. 741. **IV.** *to name* in an appeal for help, *to invoke* :—Þā genemde þǽra scypmanna ān Sēs Martynus and hyne bæd hylpes. Þā stylde se storm sôna, Shrn. 147, 8. [*In* Bt. 33, 4; F. 128, 31, 35 *probably for* genemned *should be read* gemenged *as in the corresponding* Met. 20, 66, 79.] [*O. H. Ger.* ge-nemnen, -nennen.] v. ǽr-genemned.
**ge-nemnendlic.** v. un-genemnendlic: **genende**, Wrt. Voc. ii. 9, 34. v. ge-nîdan.
**ge-neódian**; *vb. impers.* *To be need* (1) of something for a person :—Gyf þe smælre candelle geneódige, Tech. ii. 120, 20. Ðonne þe martirlogium geneódie, 121, 1. (2) that something be done :—Gyf þ geneódige (gif gebyrige þ for neóde, *v. l.*) þ ūre ǽnig tô ôđrum fǽce mid yrfe, Ll. Th. i. 156, 10.
**ge-neórþ**; *adj. Content* :—Geneórđ (ginehord, Erf. Gl.) *contentus* (perhaps the gloss belongs to the passage from R. Ben. given under *eáþhylde*. v. Ld. Gl. H. *contentus* in Index), Txts. 53, 544.
**ge-neósian.** *Add* : **I.** *to visit* a person, *come for the sake of intercourse* :—Hē geneósode đā buruhware đurh his menniscnysse, Hml. Th. i. 404, 21. Hē wolde hellwara geneósian, 480, 26. Hē wolde þone hālgan geneósian and wiþ gesprecan *veniebat ad verbocinium beati viri*, Guth. Gr. 153, 2. **I a.** *to visit* the sick :—Heó untrume menn mihte gehǽlan, swā hwylcne swā heó geneósode licgende on sāre, Hml. S. 2, 130. ' Ic wæs geuntrumod, and gē mē geneósodon (*visitastis*, Mt. 25, 36)' . . . 'Hwænne gesāwe wē đe untrumne, and wē đē geneósodon (*venimus ad te*, Mt. 25, 39)?,' Hml. Th. ii. 108, 7–13. Utan seóce geneósian, Wlfst. 119, 9 : Guth. Gr. 163, 49. **I b.** *to come in a vision to* :—Þās geneósode se hǽlend, and hēt hî gān tô þām cwearterne, Hml. S. 4, 231. **I c.** where the divine power operates upon a person :—On manegum gemetum geneósađ God manna sāwla; hwîltîdum mid lāre, hwîlon mid untrumnyssum, Hml. Th. i. 410, 26. God þā geneósode (*visitavit*) Sarran, and gefylde hys word, Gen. 21, 1. Hig cwǽdon þ God hys folc geneósude, Lk. 7, 16. þ seó upplice gifu hine geneósode, Gr. D. 38, 7. Hē wearđ geneósod þurh God, and se hālga gāst hēt hine faran tô Alexandria byrig, Hml. S. 15, 11. **II.** *to visit* a place or thing, *come for the sake of doing* :—Hē geneósode Benedictes mynster gelômlîce *ejus monasterium frequentabat*, Gr. D. 170, 1. Ūre Dryhten đysne middangeard þurh sôđe menniscnysse geneósode, Hml. Th. i. 56, 29. Send þinne engel on fýrenum wolcne, þæt þā embgange ealle þás ceastre þæt ne magen geneósian for þǽm fýre, Bl. H. 245, 30. Geneó[sian] *adisse*, i. *uisitasse* (*paradisi delitiis*), An. Ox. 1954. Brǽdnysse geneósod (*heremi*) *uastitatem adgressus*, i. *uisitatus*, 3637. ¶ *with gen.* :—Hē geneahhe geneósode his mynstres *ejus monasterium frequentabat*, Gr. D. 170, 3.
**ge-neósung.** *Add* : **I.** *visitation, making of a visit.* (1) *visiting* a person :—Him tô becôm for geneósunge þingon Seruandus *Seruandus ad eum visitationis gratia convenerat*, Gr. D. 169, 27. Leahter gālnysse on geneósunge (*uisitatione*) wîfa byđ ācenned, Scint. 89, 15. (1 a) *visiting* a sick person :—Hē wearđ fǽrlîce dumb, and his wîf āsende tô þām bisceope and bæd his geneósunge, Hml. S. 22, 74. (1 b) *a visitation* of God. v. ge-neósian; **I c** :—God cwæđ þæt hē wolde his folc gesēcan mid hāligre geneósunge, Hml. A. 126, 316. On manegum gemetum geneósađ God manna sāwla . . . ac gif heó đās geneósunga forgýmeleásađ, Hml. Th. i. 410, 28. **II.** *a being visited* :—Ðū ne oncneówe đone tîman đînre geneósunge, Hml. Th. i. 404, 21.
**ge-ner.** *Add* : (1) *refuge, safety, asylum* :—Sý þū mē on hūse generes *esto mihi in domum refugii*, Ps. L. 30, 3. Hý sceoldon fægnian, þonne hý on genere wǽron, Ps. Th. 39, arg. Betere wē faran ūs intô þām mycclan scræfe . . . and đǽr wē magon on genere wunian, Hml. S. 23, 204. Gif . . . hî manna ǽnig on genere heólde, 50. Gehwā sôhte gener (or (2)) đǽr hē ǽnig findan mihte, 231. (2) *a place of safety,*

*a refuge, an asylum* :—Hiera wíf ācsedon . . . hwider hié fleón woldon ; þæt hié ôđer gener nǽfden, būton hié on heora wîsa hríf gewiton *uxores quaerentes num in uteros uxorum vellent refugere*, Ors. 1, 12 ; S. 54, 4. Hē his wunda gewrāđ, and wolde him sum gener sēcan, Hml. Th. ii. 356, 28. (2 a) used of a person :—Geworden is Drihten gener (*refugium*) đearfena, Ps. Spl. 9, 9. Gener ł frôfor mín, 58, 19.
**ge-nerenes.** *Add* :—Lôca tô mînre generennesse *ad defensionem meam adspice*, Ps. Th. 21, 17. Hý ongunnon biddan þæs cnihtes generenesse *coeperunt pro ereptione illius orare*, Gr. D. 325, 7.
**ge-nerian.** *Add* : **I.** where evil is being experienced, *to take out of an unfavourable position, to deliver* :—Mid hine ic eam in geswince, ic genergu hine, Ps. Srt. 90, 15. Ðec miđ am, þte ic genere (*eruam*) đec, Rtl. 55, 14. **I a.** marking position from which there is delivery (a) by preps. :—Þonne genyreþ God eów of eallum deófles costungum, Bl. H. 99, 3. Nū þū generedest mîne (*Eve's*) sáule of þǽre neoþeran helle, 89, 27. Hē þæs ôþres sáule of wîtum generede and of tintregum ālēsde, 113, 33. Hē þā hālgan sāuwla þonon ālǽdde, and hié generede of deófles anwalde, 67, 19 : Dan. 448. Genere mē of þysses deáþes bendum, Bl. H. 89, 23. Nis sē þe generge (*eripiat*) of hondum mínum, Txts. 413, 77. Hwylc manna is þæt fram helle locum his sāwle generige (*eruet*)?, Ps. Th. 88, 41. Þte ginerede (*eriperet*) ūsig of ondueardum worulde wôgsum, Rtl. 27, 17. Seó heofonlice cwēn wearđ tôdæg generod fram đyssere mānfullan worulde, Hml. Th. i. 446, 16. Of deófles nýdgewalde genered, Cri. 1451. Hē hî gelǽdde of leođobendum . . . generede fram nîđe, An. 1039. (β) by gen. :—Ingange mín bēn on þinre gesihđe symble æt þearfe ; dô þæt đū mē generige nîđa gehwylces (*eripe me*), Ps. Th. 118, 170, 169. Wǽron ūre sāwla nîþa generede *anima nostra sicut passer erepta est de laqueo venantium*, 123, 6. **I b.** *to cure* of disease :—Hē eów fram blindnesse bôte gefremede, and fram unclǽnum generede deófla gāstum, El. 301. Generad *fotus* (cf. *fotus* gelācnod, Wrt. Voc. ii. 149, 77), An. Ox. 18 b, 31. **II.** where evil threatens, *to put in safety, prevent harm to* :—Cirica đîn from ellwara đū gineredes fryhte gættana *aecclesiam tuam ab infernorum eruis terrore portarum*, Rtl. 59, 19. Genere mē (*eripe me*) fram nîþe nāhtfremmendra, Ps. Th. 58, 2. **III.** *to protect* against :—Nǽfre þū mē wiđ swā heardum helle wîtum ne generedest, Seel. 48. Wuldres God hié generede wiþ þām nîđhete, Dan. 279. Ālýs mē and genere wiđ lagustreámum, Ps. Th. 143, 8. Hæfde hē sele Hrôđgāres genered wiđ nîđe, B. 827. **IV.** where II and III are combined :—Genere mē wiđ nîþe fram yfelum menn *eripe me ab homine malo*, Ps. Th. 139, 1. **V.** *to prevent from getting harm, hold back* from hurt. (1) with prep. :—Hî Gode þonciađ . . . þæt hē hý generede from nîđcwale and eác forgeaf ēce dreámas, Cri. 1258. Biddan wē ūrne Drihten þ hē ūs generige from þon ēcan cwealme, and ūs gelǽde on þone gefeán his wuldres, Bl. H. 25, 28. Hē wolde ūs from ēcum wîtum generian, and ūs gelǽdan on þā ēcean eádignesse, 97, 18. (2) with gen. :—Nǽfre þū mec swā heardra helle wîta ne generedest, Seel. 48. **VI.** *to keep from destruction, preserve, save* life :—Hē his feorh generede, þeáh hē wæs oft gewundad, Chr. 755 ; P. 48, 29 : Dan. 234. Hē mîne leóde generede, and mē tîr forgeaf, El. 163. Sume wíg fornam, sume aldor generedon, 132. Đǽr ic mæg mín feorh on generian *salvabor in ea*, Past. 399, 23 : Ors. 2, 5 ; S. 84, 16. Weard mycel wæl geslegen, and se đæl þe þǽr āweg côm wurdon on fleáme generede, Chr. 894 ; P. 88, 1. **VI a.** *to save* a person in respect to his life (*dat.*) :—Ælmǽr þe se arcđ ǽr generede his lîfe (æt his lîfe, *v. l.*), Chr. 1011 ; P. 141, 26. Blîđe wǽron eorlas . . . aldre generede, Dan. 259. [*Goth.* ga-nasjan : *O. Sax.* gi-nerian : *O. H. Ger.* ge-nerien *liberare, reparare, servare, salvum facere*.]
**gener-stede**, es ; *m. An asylum* :—Friđhūs *vel* generstede *asylum*, Wrt. Voc. i. 59, 2.
**ge-nesan.** *Add* : **I.** *to escape from* an evil in which one is involved. (1) *absolute* :—þæt ealde wundor þǽra þreóra cnihta þe āworpene wǽron in þone byrnende ofen, and swā þeáh ungederede genǽson *antiquum trium puerorum miraculum, qui projecti in ignibus laesi non sunt*, Gr. D. 219, 19. (2) *with acc.* :—Þā men uneáđe þone ciele genǽson *magnus hominum numerus frigoris acerbitate perierunt*, Ors. 4, 8 ; S. 188, 2. Þū đysne nîđ genesan môte, Lch. iii. 52, 17. **II.** *to avoid* an evil in which one might become involved :—þ wē þurh þ ǽlmessan þā ēcan tintrega magon genesan, Ll. Th. ii. 394, 22. Cf. ge-nerian.
**ge-nēþan.** *Add* : **I.** where something perilous or of doubtful issue is undertaken. (1) *to venture to go* :—Se wyrm genēđeđ tô, Seel. 119. Hē genēđde ofer þone munt, Ors. 4, 8 ; S. 188, 3. Thomas þríste genēđde on Indéa ôđre dǽlas, Ap. 50. (1 a) with dat. (inst.) of life imperilled :—Hē in Achagia aldre genēđde, Ap. 17. Hē mec heálsode þæt ic on holma geþring ealdre genēđde, B. 2133. Hē selfa ne dorste under ýđa gewin aldre genēđan, 1469. Gif þū furđur dearst tô þām ānhagan aldre genēđan, An. 1353. (2) *to venture on* an action. (a) *with acc.* :—Merecondel (*the sun*) uncūđne weg nihtes genēđeđ, Met. 13, 59. Ic under wætere weorc genēđde, B. 1656. Ic genēđde fela gūđa, 2511. Wē frēcne genēđdon eafođ uncūđes, 959. (b) *with clause* :—Ne dorste hē genēđan þæt hē hié mid firde gesôre, Ors. 1, 10 ; S. 48, 31.

(3) *combining* (1) *and* (2 b) :—Hē genēdde under ǣnne elpent þæt hē hiene on þone nafelan ofstang, Ors. 4, 1 ; S. 156, 10. **II.** of presumptuous conduct, *to presume to do.* (a) with acc. :—For þon þe hē wolde ofer his āgen mægn āht swylces genēþan (gedyrstlǣcean, *v. l.*) *quia ultra vires volunt quidquam praesumere*, Gr. D. 73, 4. (b) with clause :—Ne genēð (gedyrstlǣc, *v. l.*, *praesumas*) þ þū gā tō þām hālgan hāde, Gr. D. 135, 9. Þ gē ne genēdon þ gē þis hūsl dicgon, Ll. Lbmn. 415, 6. (bb) where the clause marks the degree of presumption :—þ hē nō genēdde tō þon þ hē āht grētte þone Godes þeówan *ne servum Dei contingere auderet*, Gr. D. 38, 32. (c) with infin. :—þ sē ne durre (genēðe, *v. l.*) beón wīsdomes lāreów *ut praeesse non audeat*, Gr. D. 12, 26. (d) with prep. :—Mē forgif þ ic nǣfre unmedeme ne untrum tō þīnum līchoman and tō þīnum blóde ne genēþe (*presume to take the Sacrament*), Angl. xii. 507, 6. [O. H. Ger. ge-nenden *audere*.]

ge-nettian *to entangle in a net* :—Genetted *inretita*, An. Ox. 4596. [Cf. O. H. Ger. bi-nezzōn *inretire*.]

geng *a privy. l.* genge, *q.v.* : -geng *practice.* v. bī-geng: -geng *company.* v. ge-geng: -genga. v. æfter-, ān-, bī-, fore-, fræt-, ge-, in-, mān-, nīd-, niht-, ofer-, sǣ-, sceadu-, sundor-, weald-, wer-genga.

gengan *Add* :—Novb and Decb mid seofon rihtingum glǣdlīce gengað, Angl. viii. 302, 8. Man gengde geond eall ābūtan þone portweall, Hml. S. 23, 267. For him Jordanen gengde on hinder *Jordanis conversus est retrorsus*, Ps. Th. 113, 3. Fengel geatolic gen[g]de, B. 1401. Nā him strēamas gewættan fót, þā hī on Jordane gengdan æfter *abierunt in sicco flumina*, Ps. Th. 104, 36. Giestas gengdon, Reim. 11. [Forð gengden (geinde, 2nd MS.) þa quenen 3eoud wudes, Laym. 12865. Þe hare gengþ a wey ward, O. and N. 376. *Goth.* gaggida *abiit*.] v. tō-gengan.

genge, an; *f.* A *privy, drain* ; *latrina* :—Genge *latrina*, Wrt. Voc. ii. 112, 15 : 52, 15 : 71, 8. Gengan *latrine* (ilia Arii in *latrinae* cuniculum defluxerant, Ald. 39, 7), 80, 65. Gengena *latrinarum* (*spurca purgamenta*, Ald. 54, 30), 84, 9 : 52, 39. Cf. gang ; **XII.**

genge ; *f.* A *gang.* *Substitute* : genge, es ; *n.* A *band, company, troops* :—Heora āgene menn wolden hergon þone mynstre, þ wæs Hereward and his genge, Chr. 1070; P. 205, 11. Hē sende æfter Leófrīce eorle and æfter Sīwarde eorle and bæd heora gencges. Hī him tō cōmon mid medemum fultume, 1052; P. 175, 17. Se cining sende Ealdred mid genge, P. 176, 13. Hē gewende tō Brytlande and begeat him þǣr micel genge, 1055; P. 185, 38. [Hī flemden þe king and sloghen suithe micel of his genge, Chr. 1138; P. 266, 7. *In Layamon* genge *is used of military forces as in the Chronicle* :—Nis þe (Hengest) non neod to bringen mid þe muchel genge, 15025. He sende æfter genge, 28803. He somnede genge and wolde mid fehte faren, 29330. Arthur com mid mucle his genge (alle his folke, 2nd MS.), 23850. *The word occurs often in the Ormulum, mostly in a general sense*, e.g. þatt all þatt geuge (*folk*) mihhte lefenn uppo Criste, 6956. þeȝȝre (*angels'*) genge sholide ben wiþþ gode sawless ekedd, 3918. Miccle mare genge off Lerninngcnihhtess, 19566 : *but also of a military host* :—Faraoness genge, 14851. v. *N. E. D.* ging.] v. ge-genge, *and* cf. gang ; **X.**

genge ; *adj. Add* : *in season* :—Ðonne sceadd genge (*not sceaddgenge under which the passage is given in Dict.*) sȳ *when shad is in season*, Cht. Th. 544, 28. [Snou and haȝel heom is genge, O. and N. 1002. v. *N. E. D.* genge ; *Icel.* gengr *able to walk; passable; of money, good, current.*] v. for-, forþ-, ge-, tīd-, un-, ūþ-genge.

-genge ; *f.* v. bī-, niht-genge: -genge ; *n.* v. bī-geuge: -gengel. v. æfter-, fore-gengel: -gengere. v. bī-gengere: -gengestre. v. bī-gengestre.

gēn-gewrit (*should be entered under* geán-gewrit) *glosses* descriptio (*rescriptio seems to have been read*), An. Ox. 8 b, 2.

-gengness. v. æfter-gengness: ge-niclede. v. ge-cnyclan(-ian).

ge-nīdan. *Take here* ge-nēdan, ge-nȳdan *in Dict., and add* :—Geþreátod and genīded *invitus*, genīddan *invitant* (cf. genēded *invitatus*, Lk. L. R. 14, 8), Wrt. Voc. ii. 44, 59, 60. Genēded *actus*, genēdde (*printed* -nende) *acta*, 9, 22, 34. Genīdedu *coacta*, 24, 48. **I.** of movement, *to force* to or from a position or place :—Genēd, þā genumenan *abrepta*, i. *sublata*, Wrt. Voc. ii. 143, 75. (1) a person :—Hē geniédde eft þā Seaxan tō hiera āgnum lande, Ors. 6, 33; S. 288, 21. Nearwe genȳddon on norðwegas, Exod. 68. (2) a thing :—Hē slóh hildebille þæt hyt on heafolon stód nīde genȳded, B. 2680. **II.** *to force a person into or out of a condition or relation* :—Hē ealle Crēcas on his geweald geniédde, Ors. 3, 9; S. 122, 33. Hē hié geniédde eft tō Rōmāna onwalde, 6, 26 ; S. 276, 22. Sermende geniéddon Dati from Rōmāna onwalde, 6, 24; S. 276, 5. Hē hæfde ealle Asiam on his geweald genȳd, 1, 2; S. 28, 29. Oft ðæs lāriówdómes ðegnung bið untǣlwierðlīce gewilnad, and untǣlwyrðlīce monige bióð tō geniédde (-nīdde, *v.l.*) (*ad hoc nonnulli laudabiliter coacti pertrahuntur*), Past. 11, 9. **II a.** *to force a person to assume the position or character of.* (1) with prep. :—Hē him tō gafolgieldum hié geniédde, Ors. 3, 9; S. 130, 34. (2) with clause :—Hē geniédde Arhalaus þ hē wæs his underþeów, 5, 11 ; S. 238, 1. **III.** *to force a person to bodily or mental action.* (1) bodily :—Hē hié tō geligre geniédde, Ors. 3, 9; S. 132, 7.

Gif þeów mon þeówne tō nēdhǣmde genēde, Ll. Th. i. 78, 14. Gif hine mon tō genēdan scyle, 60, 13. Gif hwā tō hwæðrum þissa (āð and wed) geniéd sié, 60, 4. Ne bið hē tō nānum weorce genēded, Bt. 42 ; F. 258, 11. (2) mental :—Hē geniét ðone dēman tō irre, Past. 93, 10. Se dēma bið geniéded (-nīded, *v.l.*) tō ðǣm ierre, 39, 10. **IV.** *to force* a person to do something. (1) absolute :—Genēt *compulit* (*laborare*), Kent. Gl. 572. Genēdod *invitus* (*uerum bonum nemo perdit inuitus*), Wlck. Gl. 252, 35. Mid ðǣre lustfullnesse wē bióð genēdode *delectatione vincimur*, Past. 417, 30. Nȳde genȳdde, B. 1005. (2) with clause :—Sió ungeðyld geniét ðone monnan ðæt hē geopenað all his ingeðonc, Past. 220, 11. Hē geniédde þā cyningas þæt hié sealdon hiera suna tō gīslum, Ors. 4, 11 ; S. 204, 3. Ealle Asiam hié geniéddon þ hié him gafol guldon *perdomitam Asiam vectigalem fecere*, 1, 10 ; S. 44, 18. Ealle þā burgware ne mehton hiene ǣnne geniéddan þ hé him on hand gān wolde, 3, 9; S. 134, 17. Hē bið geniéd mid ðǣm folgoðe ðæt hē sceal heálīce sprecan *loci sui necessitate exigitur summa dicere*, Past. 81, 5. Hē wæs genȳded (*coactus*) fram wērignysse his geféran þ hē wunode þā niht on his mynstre, Gr. D. 38, 24. Hié weorðað geniédde mid hiera ūpāhæfenesse ðæt hié ðā tǣlað, Past. 302, 11. (3) with infin. :—Genēded is from allum āwrīta *coactus est ab omnibus scribere*, Mt. p. 9, 1. (4) with dat. infin. :—Genēd in tō gonganne *compelle intrare*, Lk. R. L. 14, 23. Hié weorðen geniédde hiera undeáwas tō herianne, Past. 302, 19. (5) with prep. governing a pronoun (cf. **III.**), and clause (cf. (2) above) :—Ungecyndelic is ǣlcre wuhte þ hit wilnige frēcennesse ðeáh deápes, ac þeáh manig þing bið tō þǣm genēd þ hit willnaþ ðara ǣgþres, Bt. 34, 11 ; F. 152, 9. **V.** *to force a condition on a person* :—Nele God habban genȳdne þeówdóm, Hml. Th. ii. 490, 15. **VI.** *intrans.* (?) *To force one's way to*(?) :—Se wyrm genȳdde tō mē, Seel. 119. [O. H. Ger. ge-nōten *cogere, impellere, exigere, subigere, angariare*.] v. un-genīd ; ge-neádian.

ge-nīdedlic. *Take here* ge-nēdedlic *in Dict., and add* : genȳdenlic *is the form in one MS.*, Bd. Sch. 59, 15 : ge-nīdmāgas. *Take here* ge-nȳdmāgas *in Dict., and add* : v. nīd-mæg: ge-nīhe ; *adj. Near. Take here* ge-nȳh *in Dict.* : ge-niht. v. ge-nyht.

ge-nihtian ; *p.* ode *To become night, grow dark* :—Þā geþȳstrode hit and efne fæstlīce genihtode (*tenebrae factae sunt*, Mt. 27, 45) ofer eallne middangeard, Nap. 31.

ge-niman. *Add* : **I.** *to take, move an object in the hand from its place, to pick up* what lies on a surface, *pull off* what is fixed, *pluck* fruit :—Hē āwearp his reáf . . . hē eft his reáf genam, Hml. Th. ii. 242, 26. Hē genam þone calic, Mt. 26, 27. Hē genōm (*sustulit*) beer his, Jn. L. 5, 9. Genam hē his bogan and hine gebende, Bl. H. 199, 17: Jud. 77. Hē wand him ymbūtan þone beám, genam þǣr þæs ofætes, Gen. 493. Hē genam his sciccels þe hē him on hæfde, Bl. H. 215, 6. Huu monig mondo ðara screáðunga fulle gié genōmon (*sustulistis*), Mk. L. R. 8, 19. Genōman, Gū. 673. Fīfo īdlo genōmun lehtfato (*acceptis lampadibus*), Mt. L. 25, 3. Genōmon l āhōfon stānas Judēas, Jn. L. R. 10, 31. Genōmon (*acceperunt*) tuicg, 12, 13. Genim (*tolle*) bedd þīn, Mt. R. L. 9, 6. Genim (*erue*) ēgo ðīn and worp from ðē, Mt. L. 5, 29. Genioma ðā ehera *vellere spicas*, 12, 1. Genimænde *accipiens*, Mt. R. 25, 3. Genimmende, Mt. L. 26, 27. **I a.** *to take* for a special purpose, *provide oneself with* :—Maria genam ān pund smerenesse, and smerede þæs Hǣlendes fēt, Bl. H. 69, 1. Corn senepes þ genōm (genimede, R.) monn geseáw *granum sinapis quod accipiens homo seminavit*, Mt. L. 13, 31. Genōmon hreád and slógun heáfud his, Mt. L. R. 27, 30. Genim elehtran, Lch. ii. 142, 7 (and often). Cwæþ se wrītere þ Maria genāme ān pund smyrenesse, Bl. H. 73, 17. **I b.** *to take* a person to direct his proceedings :—Genim ðone cnæht and mōder his, and flēh, Mt. L. R. 2, 13. **I c.** with abstract object, *to take up* a practice :—Gif hē unriht hǣmed genime, Ll. Th. i. 38, 5. **II.** *to lay hold of, put the hand on, hold* with the hand an object :—þū mīne hand genáme *tenuisti manum meam*, Ps. Th. 72, 19. Hē þone cniht genam fæste mid folmum, Exod. 406. Se smið eóde tō his byrgene and genam āne hringan . . . Hē teáh ðā þ īsen ūp of ðām stāne, Hml. S. 21, 63. Hǣlend geðenede hond genōm (*apprehendit*) hine, Mt. L. 14, 31: Bl. H. 245, 13. ¶ geniman *to take by* :—Genam Martinus hine be his handa, Bl. H. 219, 19. Hē hine be healse genam, B. 1872. **II a.** *to hold* with the mind :—Genim nū fæste þ þ ic spreke *fixum tene quod loquor*, Gr. D. 172, 30. **II b.** fig. (1) *to retain* :—Ðāra synna þe nimað genumeno (*retenta*) sint, Jn. L. 20, 23. (2) *to restrain* (?) :—Sió ābisgung hine scofett hidres ðædres . . . ac him bið ðearf ðæt hē hine genime simle be ðǣre leornunge hāligra gewrita, Past. 169, 15. **III.** with the idea of force, hostility, treachery, *to take, seize, lay hands on, catch.* (1) of the action of persons :—Heó þæt deófol genōm, Jul. 288. Hié hine genāmon and his eágan ūt āstungan, Bl. H. 229, 15. Þȳ lǣs hī ūs eft genimon and on tintregu ūs on gebringan, 229, 10. Hié sōhton hine þæt hié hine genāmon, 241, 12. Þte hine genōmo (ginōme, R.) *ut raperent eum*, Jn. L. 6, 15. Þ hiá ðone Hǣlend mið inwite genōme (*tenerent*) Mt. L. 26, 4. (1 a) fig. *to catch tripping* :—Þte hiá genōmo hine in word *ut caperent eum in sermone*, Mt. L. 22, 15 : Mk. L. R. 12, 13 : Lk. L.

20, 20. (2) of the action of disease:—Heó genummen wæs miclum feberādlum *tenebatur magnis febribus*, Lk. L. 4, 38. (3) of deleterious influence on material, *to taint* (?):—Wið genumenum mete (cf. gif mete sȳ āwyrd, 14), genim elehtran, lege under weófod, sing nigon mæssan ofer, þ̄ sceal wiþ genumenum mete; lege under þ̄ fæt þe þū wille on melcan, Lch. ii. 142, 7-9. **IV.** *to take away, get hold of and carry off, remove*:—þ unberende treó hē genimes, Jn. L. 15, 2 margin. Gif ðū genōme (*sustulisti*) hine, Jn. L. R. 20, 15. Genōmon (dydon āweg, W. S.) ðone stān *tulerunt lapidem*, R. 11, 41: 20, 13: Mt. L. R. 14, 12. Genōme *tolleret*, Mk. L. R. 15, 24: Jn. L. R. 19, 38. Brengan blōsman and eft geniman, Bt. 7, 3; F. 20, 22. Genioma (tō genimanne, R.) *tollere*, Mt. L. 24, 17. Genumen bið *auferetur*, 9, 15. Uēre genumeno (ginumune, R.) *tollerentur*, Jn. L. 12, 31. **IV a.** where the place is given from which the object is taken:—þā genam (*tulit*) hē ān ribb of his sīdan, Gen. 2, 21. Ne biddo ic þte ðū genimme (*tollas*) hiá of middangeorde, Jn. L. 17, 15. þū bist genumen of þīnum līchoman, Bl. H. 137, 26. **V.** with idea of violence or wrong-doing, *to carry off* another's possession, *to take* spoil, *steal, abduct* a woman:—Gif man inne feoh genimeð, Ll. Th. i. 10, 1. Gif man widuwan genimeð, 20, 13. Gif man mægðman nēde genimeð, 24, 3. Alexander genōm þæs cyninges wīf (*raptus Helenae*), Ors. 1, 11; S. 50, 7. Ic gefrægn hord reāfian ānne mannan ... segn genōm, B. 2776. þæt wīf þæt hē hæfde ǣr genumen būtan cynges leáfe, Chr. 901; P. 92, 13. Se ðe nȳde genumene mete (*cibum furatum*) þicge, Ll. Th. ii. 218, 27. þā genumenan *abrepta, sublata*, Wrt. Voc. ii. 143, 76. Genumenum *demptis*, 93, 61. **V a.** *to deprive of* power:—Cymað Rōmānisce and giniomað ūserne stōwe and cynn, Jn. R. L. 11, 48. **V b.** *to rob* a house:—Hūs ðæs genimeð *domum illius diripiat*, Mt. L. 12, 29. **V c.** where the person is given from whom an object is taken:—Gif Drihten on þē genimþ þā nigan dǣlas, Bl. H. 51, 2. Genimeþ, 53, 4. þū genāme brȳde æt beorne, Gen. 2637. Hē him ðæt an genam þæt hē self hæfde, Ors. 3, 7; S. 112, 12. þæt seó wyrd þē on geniman ne mihte, Bt. 11, 2; F. 34, 14. His cræft mon ne mæg on him geniman, 19; F. 70, 3. Of genimma ł from genimma *diripere*, Mt. L. 12, 29. Wulfgeate wæs eall his ār on genumen, Chr. 1006; P. 136, n. 5. Hié mīnne naman habbaþ on mē genumen, Bt. 7, 3; F. 20, 29. Ælc bit ðæs reāfiāces ðe him on genumen biþ, 26, 2; F. 92, 17. Hit wæs mid unrihte him of genumen, Chr. 1072; P. 208, 19. þ hæfis genumen bið from him, Mt. L. 13, 12. þīne ǣhta þe on ðē genumene wǣron (*ablatae sunt*), Bd. 5, 19; Sch. 671, 6. **V cc.** of the action of things:—Ald clāð genimes (*tollit*) fyllnisse his from wēde, Mt. L. 9, 16. Eall ðā sceard ðe seó sǣ him on genumen hæfþ, Bt. 18, 1; F. 62, 13. **V d.** used of the operation of things:—Niht ne genimeð þurh þȳstru þæs heofonlican leóhtes scīman *non nulla rapit splendorem lucis amoenae* (Dōm. L. 25, 128), Wlfst. 139, 25. **VI.** *to take* to oneself, *take possession of*:—Ic wyrpe þā unclǣnan ūt and genime (*sumo*) mē clǣne tō mete, Coll. M. 23, 17. Max mīne on eá ic wyrpe and spyrtan, and swā hwæt swā hig gehæftaþ ic genime, 13. Mē þū mid wuldres welan genāme *cum gloria sumsisti me*, Ps. Th. 72, 19. þā aldursācerdas genōman (geniomende, L.) ðā scillingas, Mt. R. 27, 6. Ginumni *adepto*, Txts. 42, 100. Genumene *ademptam*, Wrt. Voc. ii. 85, 2. **VI a.** *to occupy* a place:—Weg þe hī eardunge on genāman, Ps. Th. 106, 3. þǣr hié fæstlīce eard genāmon, Gen. 1654. **VI aa.** of things:—Eall þ his (the *habitable part of the earth*) fennas and mōras genumen habbað, Bt. 18, 1; F. 62, 14. **VII.** *to take* a part of a whole, *derive* from a source:—þeós bið gecīged fǣmne, for þām þe heó ys of were genumen, Gen. 2, 23. Hē genam on eallum dǣl ǣhtum sīnum, Gen. 1498. **VIII.** *to take, obtain by effort.* (1) *to catch* fish, &c.:—Bringað of ðǣm fiscum ðā ilco gē ginōmun (*prendistis*), Jn. L. R. 21, 10. On gefeng fiscana ðone genōmon (*ceperant*), Lk. L. 5, 9. (2) *to take* in war, *capture*:—Hē gefeaht wiþ feówer sciphlæstas Deniscra monna, and þāra scipa tū genam, 882; P. 78, 1. Se cyng þone castel gewann and þæs eorles men genam, Chr. 1094; P. 229, 14. Hī þǣr genāman inne ealle þā gehādode menn and weras and wīf, 1011; P. 141, 29. Hī gefuhton and unārīmedlice herereáf, 473; P. 14, 3. Hié genāmon Wihte eáland and ofslōgon feala men, 527; P. 16, 6. Genumenan werede *capta manu*, An. Ox. 46, 17. (2 a) fig.:—Rīc heofna hiá geniomes, Mt. L. 11, 12. **IX.** where movement (lit. or fig.) is induced, *to take* a person, *get* a person *to move, bring*:—Nǣnig men ne mæg cuma tō mē, būta fæder ginioma (genimmǣ, L. *traxerit*) hine, Jn. R. 6, 44. **IX a.** *to take* a living creature with oneself:—ðe Hǣlend genōm (*assumsit*) ðā ðegnas dēglīce, Mt. L. R. 20, 17: Mk. L. R. 5, 40. Hǣlend genam his twelf þegnas sundor of þǣm weorode, Bl. H. 15, 6. ðæt deófol genam mid him ōþre seofon deóflo, 243, 4. þū seofone genim on þæt sundreced tūdra gehwilces, Gen. 1335. ðȳ lǣs genime ðec mid doema ł gelǣdæ ðec tō dōme *ne forte trahat te apud judicem*, Lk. L. R. 12, 58. **IX b.** *to take* an object that does not move itself, *bear, carry, bring*:—Fīfo īdlo ne genōmun oele mið him, Mt. L. R. 25, 3. ðā genāman men þone stoc on weg, Bl. H. 189, 14. Genimaþ (cf. gelǣdan hēt līfes brytta, An. 823) Andreas and his discipuli and āsettað hié beforan

Mermedonia ceastre, 235, 14. Ne is gelēfed ðē þ ðū genioma (ginime, R., bere, W. S.) beer ðīn, Jn. L. 5, 10. þte ginōme (bǣre, W. S.) rōde his, Mk. R. L. 15, 21. Ne ǣniht gelǣdde ł genōmo, Mk. L. 6, 8. **IX bb.** the object abstract:—þā menniscan gecynd þe hē genam tō his godcundnesse, Bl. H. 115, 32. **X.** *to take, get control of* an object and do something with it (cf. the later *to take and do*):—ðā genam hine se āwyrgda gāst, and hē hine lǣdde on þā hālgan ceastre, Bl. H. 27, 10. þone rom hē genam, and hine on ād āhōf, Gen. 29, 29. Hī genāman þæs folces hundteóntig þūsenda, and mid him gelǣddon, H. 79, 20. Genōmon līchoma and biuundun hine, Jn. L. R. 19, 40. **XI.** *to take, accept, adopt* as (*tó*):—Wineleás mon genimeð him wulfas tō gefēran, Gn. Ex. 147. Ic ðē giungne mē tō bearne genōm, Bt. 8; F. 24, 24. þē rodera weard genōm him tō freóbearne, Cri. 223. Hió þone ǣnne genam tō gīsle, El. 599. **XII.** *to receive, get, obtain* what is handed over or paid:—Ic wæs syfanwintre þā mec sinca baldor æt mīnum fæder genam, B. 2429. Hē gesalde him hine ... Genōmun ðone Hǣlend, Jn. L. R. 19, 16. Gif hwā hine geniman (*receive and protect*) wille, Ll. Th. i. 230, 5. Genime hē vi. sciłł. weorð wed, 132, 13. Hit hæfþ genumen (gewunnen, *v. l.*) þæs folces ōlecunga, Bt. 24, 3; F. 82, 24. **XIII.** *to receive* a person who offers himself:—Genōmun (*exceperunt*) hine ðā Galilesce menn mið ðȳ alle gesēgen ðā ðe geuorhte, Jn. L. R. 4, 45. **XIV.** *to receive* an impression, *get* a feeling excited, *take* pleasure, a dislike, &c.:—Hē genōm him tō wildeórum wynne, Gū. 713. Genam Saul micelne nīð tō Dauide, Hml. Th. ii. 64, 16. Hié him æfest tō genāman, Bl. H. 7, 11. Genāman him æfest tō þā ealdormen, 177, 20. Wē ne sceolon geniman nāne lustfullunge tō ðǣre tihtinge, Hml. Th. i. 174, 32. Næfst þū tō ǣnegum andan genumen, Met. 20, 36. **XV.** *to take* into or with the mind. (1) *to understand*:—Sē ðe mæge genioma geniomiss *qui potest capere capiat*, Mt. L. 19, 12. (2) *to learn* (cf. Icel. *nema* to learn):—Hē lāra wel genōm, C. D. B. ii. 376, 15. (3) *to take* into one's head to do something:—Heó on mōd genam þæt heó his lārum hȳrde, Gen. 710. (4) *to get* an idea:—Eów Rōmāne mæg gescomian þ gē swā heánlic geþōht sceoldon on eów geniman ... þ gē sǣdon þ þā hǣðnan tīda wǣron beteran þonne þā crīstnan, Ors. 6, 37; S. 296, 17. **XVI.** *to contain*:—Fatto sex niomende ł genōmon (ginim, R.) syndrige sestras tuoege *hydriae sex capientes singuli metretas binas*, Jn. L. 2, 6. **XVII.** friþ (wǣre) geniman wiþ (*acc.* or *dat.*) *to make peace* (*a treaty*) *with*:—Hē frið genam wið hié *Lusitanos in deditionem recepit*, Ors. 4, 12; S. 210, 9. Wǣre genōman *foedus fecerunt*, Wrt. Voc. ii. 39, 25. Hæþen here genāmon (genam, *v. l.*) friþ wiþ Cantwarum, Chr. 865; P. 68, 8. Mon sceolde frið wið hī geniman, 1002; P. 133. 32. **XVII a.** treówa geniman tō *to give one's word to* (cf. *take* = give):—For þām treówum þe þū genumen hæfdest tō Abrahame, Dan. 313. **XVIII.** *intrans.* *To go* (cf. *take* = go in M. E.):—þā gesāwon hié þ se eádiga Michael genam and þā slōg on þæs hūses duru, Bl. H. 141, 29. ðā genāmon þā Walas and ādrifon sumre eá ford ealne mid scearpum pīlum innan þām wetere (the passage in Bede from which this is derived is: In ulteriore ripa Cassobellauno duce immensa hostium multitudo consederat, ripamque fluminis ac pene totum sub aqua vadum acutissimis sudibus praestruxerat, Chr. P. 5, 10. [Goth. ga-niman *to take, take with one; receive; conceive; learn*: O. Sax. gi-niman: O. H. Ger. ge-neman *auferre, rapere, recipere*.] v. æt-genumen; ge-nǣman.

**ge-nip.** *Add*: **I.** *a cloud, an accumulation of vapour.* (1) *a cloud in the sky*:—Wolcnu ł genipu *nubes*, Ps. L. 17, 13. Winterbiter weder and wolcna genipu, Az. 105. (1 a) *a storm-cloud*:—Gyf strongra storm and genip swīþor þreáde *si procella fortior aut nimbus perurgeret*, Bd. 4, 3; Sch. 361, 3. þā wæs swȳðe mycel genip geworden in þām wolcnum, and unmǣte rēnas rīndon *collecto in nubibus aere immensa nimis pluvia erupit*, Gr. D. 196, 1. (2) *a cloud resting on the earth*:—þicce genip (*nubes densissima*) oferwrēh þone munt, Ex. 19, 16. Mid þȳstro genipum þæs muntes cnoll eal oferswōgen wæs, Bl. H. 203, 8. Mid þeósterlicum genipu oferhongen, Hml. Th. i. 504, 30. **II.** *darkness, obscurity.* (1) of night; in pl. *shades* of night:—þrang þȳstre genip, þām þe hē sceóp nihte naman, Gen. 139. Dagas forð scridun, nihthelma genipu, Gū. 943. þurh nihta genipu hī neósan cwōman, 321. Ne se mōna næfð nānre mihte wiht þ hē þǣre nihte genipu mǣge fleógan *pallida nocturnam nec praestat luna lucernam*, Dōm. L. 110. Tīr ā byð on fǣrelde ofer nihta genipu, Rūn. 17. (1 a) of the darkness to which the sun seems to sink:—Fǣreð sunne in þæt wonne genip under wætra geþring, Sch. 79. (2) of a place without light:—In þissum neowlan genipe (Hell), Sat. 102. Fyrgenstreám under næssa genipu niðer gewīteð *the stream plunges into dark depths*, B. 1360. **III.** fig. *darkness* of trouble:—Gewītað ðā genipu ūre dreórignysse, Hml. Th. i. 614, 29. **IV.** of dim sight:—Wið eágena þȳstru and genipe, Lch. i. 366, 13.

**ge-nīpan.** For '**II.** *to rise as a cloud* ... Exod. 454' substitute:—Him ongēn genāp atol ȳða gewealc: ne þǣr ǣnig becwōm herges tō hāme *the horrid waves grew dark as they rolled on to meet them; not one of that host got back to his home*, Exod. 454. Werð genipen *stetit*

i. *inhorruit* (nimbosisque polus *stetit* imbribus), An. Ox. 34, 2. *Add:*
**II.** *to make dark* (?) :—Þǽr niht ne genípð (genímð ? v. ge-niman ; Vd) nǽfre þeóstra þæs heofenlícan leóhtes scíman, Dóm. L. 253.

**genip-full**; *adj. Cloudy* :—Winter genipful *hiems caliginosa*, Archiv cxx. 297, 39.

**ge-nirwan (-ian).** *Take here* ge-nyrwian *in Dict., and add* :—Genyrwiaþ *coangustant, arctant*, Wrt. Voc. ii. 133, 15.     **I.** of space-relations. (1) *to make narrow, contract* :—Se arc wæs swá genyrwed þ hé wæs mid ánre fæðme belocen ufewerd *area collecta in cacumen angustum, ita ut cubitus sit longitudinis et latitudinis*, Angl. vii. 34, 325. (1 a) with idea of pressure :—Ne generewe [ofer mé] pytt his múþ *neque urgeat super me puteus os suum*, Ps. L. 68, 16. (2) *to press into a small space, crowd.* (a) *to crowd* a person, *give little space to* :—Se Godes sunu wæs on his gesthúse genyrwed, þæt hé ús rúme wununge on heofonan ríce forgife, Hml. Th. i. 36, 1. (b) *to crowd* a place, *put too many people into* :—For ðæs folces geðryle wæs þæt gesthús ðearle genyrwed, Hml. Th. i. 34, 34.     **II.** of extent or amount, *to diminish, reduce, curtail* :—Gyf hwá genyrwe ðæt ic Gode geseald hæbbe, C. D. v. 331, 5. Wǽron ðrǽlriht generwde and ælmesriht gewanode, Wlfst. 158, 15.     **III.** *to oppress, afflict, trouble* in body or mind : —Hé genyrwde ðá crístenan, Hml. S. 29, 191. Seó wédl þæra andlyfna genyrwde ealle *omnes alimentorum indigentia coangustabat*, Gr. D. 145, 6. Geswencedæ t genyrwiende hig *coartans eos*, Ps. L. 34, 5. Genirwed and geenged *afficiar*, Wrt. Voc. ii. 10, 49. þ wǽre genyrwed meteléste *angeretur* (i. *stringeretur*) *cibi inopia*, An. Ox. 4851. Genierwed on his móde *anxie afflictus corde*, Past. 231, 21. Ne sprǽc hé hit nó for ðý ðe his mód áuht genierwed wǽre mid ðære uncúðe ðæs síðfætes *neque Moysi mentem ignorantia itineris angustabat*, 304, 17. Gif hý for þysum gylte genyrwode (*afflicti*) wurðað, Ll. Th. ii. 164, 28. Cf. ge-nearwian.

**ge-niþerian.** *Add:* **I.** *to bring down, cast down, degrade, humiliate* (1) a person or place occupying an exalted position :—Oft ðis andwearde líf úp áhefeð ðá yfelan, ac se tócyme ðære écan eádignesse hié geniðrað, Past. 389, 27. Hierusalem áhéned bið t gehníðrad bið (*calcabitur*) from hǽdnum, Lk. L. 21, 24. (1 a) used of a thing :—Gif *h* byð gesett þǽr hé standan ne mæg, þonne sceal man hine þus genyðerian, Angl. viii. 333, 39. (2) a person who exalts himself :—Ðú hié geniðrades, ðá hí hí selfe úp áhófon *dejecisti eos, dum allevarentur*, Past. 391, 9. For ðæm wlite ðínra cræfta ðú wurde úp áhæfen, and ðonan ðú wyrst geniðrad *ex virtutum decore te elevas, ipsa tua pulchritudine impelleris, ut cadas*, 463, 22. Éghuelc se ðe hine áhebbað gehniðrad bið (*humiliabitur*), Lk. L. 14, 11. (2 a) the pride of a person :—Hú God þá mǽstan ofermétto geniðerade, Ors. 2, 5 ; S. 84, 12.     **II.** *to condemn* :—Nǽllað gié gehniðra (*condemnare*) þte gié ne sé gehniðrad, Lk. L. 6, 37. Beón genyðered *condemnari*, An. Ox. 2916. Wæs geneþorod *damnatur*, 3769. Manega unrihtlíce fram yfium dēmum genyþrode wǽron, Hml. S. 30, 8.     **II a.** *to condemn* to a punishment :—Híg genyðeriað (geniðredon, L.) hyne tó deáðe *condemnabunt eum morte*, Mt. 20, 18. Hí hine deáþe genyþeriað (geniðriað tó deáðe, L. R.) *damnabunt eum morte*, Mk. 10, 33.     **II b.** *to pass sentence* (?) :—þ ic on gefealle on þone genyðredan (-endan?) cwyde þæs sláwan þeówes (þeawas, MS.) *that I fall under the sentence passed on the slothful servant*, Hml. S. 23 b, 14.     **III.** *to accuse* :—Mið ðý (wæs) gewroeged t geniðrad (*accusaretur*), Mt. L. 27, 12. [*O. H. Ger.* genidaren *prosternere, dejicere, humiliare, condemnare.*]

**ge-niþerigendlic**; *adj. Worthy of condemnation* :—Manega genyþerigendlíce wiþerwyrde ágyltan beóð gesewene *multa damnabilia reprobi commissse uidentur*, Scint. 162, 18.

**ge-niþerung.** *Add:* **I.** *humiliation* :—Ne áwend þú mannan tó geniþerunge (-nyðerunga, Ps. Spl.) *ne auertas hominem in humilitatem*, Ps. L. 89, 3.     **II.** *condemnation* :—þǽre sáwle is micel genyðrung þ mon þá wuldorfæstan Godes weorc bediglige, Hml. S. 23 b, 11.

**ge-níþla.** *Add:* v. ferhþ-geníþla.

**ge-níwian.** *Add:* **I.** *to renovate, restore* what has decayed or been injured. (1) the object material :—Eft geníuað wæs hond his *restituta est manus ejus*, Lk. L. 6, 10. Eal bið geníwad feðerhoma, swá hé æt frymðe wæs, Ph. 279. Hé (*the Phenix*) forð wunað wæstmum geníwad, ealles edgiong, 580. Hrægl bið geníwad, Rä. 14, 9. (2) the object non-material :—Eft geníues *restituens*, Mt. p. 13, 4. Hé eft geníweges alle *restituet omnia*, Mt. L. 17, 11. Gást rehtne geníowa, Ps. Srt. 50, 11 : Ps. C. 93. Ðá eftácennednisses hérnise giníwe gimeodumad arð *quos regenerationis misterio innovare dignatus es*, Rtl. 35, 17. Wǽron ǽrendræcan gesend tó Englalande tó geníweanne ðone geleáuan ðá Scs Gregorius ús sende, Chr. 785 ; P. 54, 12. Bið geníwad feorh, Ph. 279.     **II.** *to renew* what has ceased to operate :—Hyht wæs geníwad, Cri. 529 : An. 1012 : Jul. 607 : Gú. 926 : Kr. 148 : Jud. 98. Sorg bið geníwad, Wand. 50 : B. 1322. Cearo bið geníwad, Wand. 55 : B. 1303. þá se wyrm onwóc, wróht wæs geníwad, 2287.     **II a.** *to repeat* :—Giníwia *frequentare*, Rtl. 9, 13. [*O. H. Ger.* ge-niwôn *renovare.*]

**gēn-lǽd.** v. lad ; **II.**

**gennelung.** *l.* ge-miclung.

**ge-nóg**; *adj. Add:* **I.** in agreement with a noun, which it generally follows :—Ne bið ðær nǽnig ealo gebrowen, ac þær bið medo genóh, Ors. 1, 1 ; S. 20, 19. Hond gemunde fǽhðo genóge, B. 2489. Hé cúðe sóð genóg, Gú. 266. Gefæstnodon mé feóndas genóge, Kr. 33. þ hé næbbe sǽlþa genóge, Bt. 14, 2 ; F. 44, 19 : 11, 1 ; F. 32, 8. Ic eów wísige þæt gé genóge neón sceáwiað beágas and brád gold, B. 3104.     **II.** as predicate :—'Hér synt twá swurd.' Hé cwæð : ' þ ys genóh (-nóg, R., *sat est*),' Lk. 22, 38. Genóg is ús *sufficit nobis*, Jn. L. R. 14, 8. Genóh is, Kent. Gl. 1088. Genóh bið munece twá tunican *sufficit monacho duos tonicas*, R. Ben. I. 92, 8. Genóh byð þám leorningcnihte þæt hé sý swylce hys láreów, Mt. 10, 25. Ælcum men þúhte genóg on þǽre eorþan wæstmum, Bt. 15 ; F. 48, 3. Genóh, Met. 8, 7. Him ðǽr genóg ðyncð, Past. 449, 14.     **III.** used absolutely in singular :—þá þurfon swíþe lytles þe máran ne willniaþ þonne genóges, Bt. 14, 2 ; F. 44, 14. Hió gehǽt him ǽghwæs genóg (-nóh, *v.l.*), Past. 71, 23. Gelde swá hé genóh áge (*the MS. has* hâge *with* gono *written above it*) *let him pay as he may have enough* i. e. *as much as his means allow*, Ll. Th. i. 30, 2. ¶ habban genóg *to have enough* :—þe lǽs þe wé and gé nabbon genóh *ne forte non sufficiat nobis et vobis*, Mt. 25, 9 : Jn. 14, 8 : Hml. Th. i. 182, 19. þ hié ǽghweþer ge þám þearfan hrægl syllan mihtan, ge hwæþre him sylfum genóg hæfdon, Bl. H. 215, 14. Hé hæfþ ǽlces gódes genóh, Bt. 10 ; F. 28, 14 : Bo. 34.

**ge-nóg**; *adv. Add:* **I.** with verb, *abundantly, sufficiently* :—Geseah ic balzamum þæs betstan stences genóh of þǽm treówum út wealian *video opobalsamum cum optimo odore omnibus undique arborum ramis habundantissime manans*, Nar. 27, 22. Genóg fremmað *sufficit*, Rtl. 191, 37.     **II.** with adj. or adv. as an intensive, *enough, very*, (1) with adj. :—Genóh mánfulne gylt *satis* (i. *valde*) *probrosum facinus*, An. Ox. 2782. Genóh sutel *satis euidens*, 4538. For þon þe genóh gecóplicu wíse hí sylfe gegearwode *quia occasio apta se praebuit*, Gr. D. 60, 4. Geonge men genóh þæslice on líchaman, Hml. S. 23 b, 370. Hé is genóg orsorg (*quite secure*) ǽlces eorþlices eges, Bt. 10 ; F. 28, 17. Hit genóh ǽmettig læg and genóg wéste and ge his náne note ne hæfdon, Ors. 1, 10 ; S. 48, 24. (2) with adv. :—þ wé genóg raðe tó þǽm becwóman, Nar. 11, 27. Bebinde genóh wearme, Lch. ii. 270, 9. Ic ongite genóh sweotule þ . . ., Bt. 7, 1 ; F. 16, 10. þú wást genóg geare ðæt þú mé oferswíðan ne miht *thou knowest very well that thou canst not overcome me*, Bl. H. 175, 30.

**ge-nógan.** *Substitute:* ge-nógian (?) *to abound* [ :—Inóget *habundat* Nap. 81.] [Cf. *O. H. Ger.* ge-nógen *sufficere.*]

**ge-notian.** *Add:* —Genotad *functus, usus*, Wrt. Voc. ii. 152, 19.

**ge-notian** *to note, mark* :—Of oferwritenum ðás in foruuard fore genotad infundes *ex superscriptionibus quas in fronte notatas invenies*, Mt. p. 12, 2.

**ge-nugan.** v. ge-neah : **genung.** v. ginung : **gēnunga.** v. gegn-inga : **ge-nycled.** v. ge-cnyclan (-ian): **ge-nýdan.** v. ge-nídan : **ge-nýdenlic.** v. ge-nídedlic : **ge-nýd-magas.** v. ge-nídmǽgas : **ge-nýh.** v. ge-níhe.

**ge-nyht.** *Add:* **I.** *sufficiency* :—Ðæm ðegnum is beboden ðæt hié him ðæt tó genyhte dón ðæt hié him sellen *servants are bidden to be satisfied with what is given them*, Past. 321, 2.     **II.** *abundance, plenty, opulence* :—For ðære genyhte ðæs flówendan welan hé blissað *rerum affluentium abundantiam exultat*, Past. 55, 8. Geniheðe *opulentia*, Angl. xiii. 35, 199. Ginyhþ *largitate*, Rtl. 98, 3? þú wunast on þǽre héhstan genyhte *ubi summa plenitudo*, Solil. H. 9, 9. Gebeorh bringeð tó genihte wæstme *montem uberem*, Ps. Th. 67, 15, 16 : 91, 13. Hé sende on heora múþas mete tó genihte *misit saturitatem in animas eorum*, 105, 13. Gé geniht (*abundantiam*) águn, Ps. Th. 121, 6. þá miclan geniht þínre wéðnesse, 144, 7. Hé can weána lyt, and hæfð byrga geniht, Run. 8. Hé sylð goldes and seolfres genyhða, Wlfst. 196, 21. Sellan éce mǽrþa and fulie genyht, Bt. 33, 3 ; F. 126, 13.

**genyht-full.** *For* Lye *substitute* :—Genyhtfullum (genyctfullum, Ep. Erf.) *profusis*, Txts. 89, 1627.

**ge-nyhtlíce.** *For* Cot. 6 *substitute* :—Genycthlíce *abunde*, Wrt. Voc. ii. 98, 17. Genihtlíce (*printed* -riht-), 4, 14. [*O. H. Ger.* ge-nuhtlhho *sufficienter, largiter.*]

**ge-nyhtsum.** *Add:* **I.** *abundant, plenteous, being in great quantity* :—Cóm reng micel and genyhtsum *descendit pluuia copiosa*, Bd. 4, 13 ; Sch. 419, 10. Eówer lufu is suíðe genyhtsumu *caritas vestra abundat*, Past. 213, 12. Wæs gold swá genihtsum and seolfor swá stánas ofer eorðan, Angl. xi. 8, 27. Syb genihtsum *abundantia pacis*, Ps. Th. 71, 7. [Genihtsum *affatim*, Wrt. Voc. ii. 2, 25. v. ge-nyhtsumlíce.] Genih-sumre wennę *opulenti luxus*, An. Ox. 11, 44. Of genihtsumum edhwyrfte *exuberante reditu*, 8, 67. Of genihtsumere *sumtuosa, copiosa* (*alimonia*), 1840. Genihtsume *fertilem* (*praedam*), 110. þá genihtsumestan *uberrimam* (*facunditam*), 113. þá genihtsummestan áfundennessa *uberrima experimenta*, 81. ¶ beón (wesan) genyhtsum *to be abundance* :—On þínum torrum wese genihtsum *fiat abundantia in turribus tuis*, Ps. Th. 121, 7. Bið on þínes húses hwommum genihtsum

*abundans in lateribus domus tuae*, 127, 3. **II.** *abounding in, having in large quantity :*—Genihtsumnes (genihtsumnes?) þæs yfeles *copia*, Wrt. Voc. ii. 22, 18. Is þīn milde mōd genihtsum *tu copiosus misericordia*, Ps. Th. 85, 4. Þæt hē dō his đéowan rīce for worulde, genihtsume on welan, Hml. Th. i. 64, 17. Mid þǽm genihtsumestan *opimis*, Wrt. Voc. ii. 64, 60. **III.** *giving or providing in abundance :*—Bloedsunga ginyhtsum ondǽlend *benedictionum largus infusor*, Rtl. 103, 38. Bringđ folcum genihtsum Blōtmōnađ eádignesse, Men. 194. Heora sceáp wǽrun swīþe genihtsum *oves eorum abundantes*, Ps. Th. 143, 17.

**ge-nyhtsumian.** *Add :* **I.** *to abound, have abundance :*—Ǽlc þǽra đe hæfđ, him biđ māre geseald, and hē genihtsumađ (*abundabit*), Hml. Th. ii. 556, 12. Genyhtsumaþ (hē hæfđ genōh, W. S.), Mt. R. 25, 29 : 13, 12. Þǽm hæbbendum mon sceal āgyfan and hī genyhtsumiađ, Ll. Th. i. 196, 23. **I a.** *to abound in, have abundance of.* (1) the subject a person :—Þā men goldes genihtsumiađ *auro habundant*, Nar. 31, 5. Þā canonicas þe on þǽm gyltum genihtsumedon, Lch. iii. 440, 12. (2) the subject a thing :—Þīne wīnwringan genihsumiađ *torcularia tua redundabunt* (*vino*), Kent. Gl. 36. Ǽghwæþer ge seó sǽ ge heora eá fiscum genihtsumade (*piscibus abundabant*), Bd. 4, 13 ; Sch. 420, 8. **II.** *to be abundant :*—Þonne ungerīme bysna mænifealdlīce genihtsumiaþ *cum innumera exempla affatim exuberent*, An. Ox. 1690. Genihtsumiendum geánwurfe *exuberante reditu*, 558. **III.** *to be sufficient, suffice :*—Þ genihtsumaþ þ þū dydest, Nar. 44, 6. Ic hæbbe āne burh þe unc bām genihtsumađ, Hml. S. 24, 101. Tuu hund penninga ne genyhtsumiađ (*sufficiunt*) him, Jn. L. R. 6, 7. Him mæg heora āgen lār genihtsumian, Hml. Th. ii. 594, 18. **III a.** *used impersonally :*—Þī lǽs đe hit ne genihtsumige ūs and eów *ne forte non sufficiat nobis et vobis*, Hml. Th. ii. 570, 13. ¶ *with clause following :*—Him genihtsumađ þ wē hī lufian, Hml. S. 16, 264. Wē gelyfađ þæt ǽnlīpugum munecum genihtsumige þæt hē hæbbe cugelan and syric, R. Ben. 89, 21. **IV.** *to have enough of, be satisfied with :*—Næs ic nā genihtsumigende on þām geongum, ac ic eác swylce manega ælđeódige besmāt, Hml. S. 23 b, 395. [*O. H. Ger.* ge-nuhtsamón *abundare, sufficere, locupletare.*] v. ofer-genyhtsumian.

**ge-nyhtsuming(-ung),** e ; *f. Abundance :*—On genihđsumunge *in habundantia*, Ps. Rdr. 77, 25.

**ge-nyhtsumlīce.** *Add :* **I.** *abundantly :*—Genihtsumlīce *affatim*, Wrt. Voc. ii. 3, 26. [Genihtsum *affatim*, 2, 25. *Perhaps the gloss belongs to the passage given under* ge-nyhtsumian ; **II,** *and* ge-nihtsumlīce *should be read ; or possibly (?) the word intended to be glossed is* exuberent, *and* ge-nihtsumiađ *should be read.*] Þǽr fleów wæter genihtsumlīce *egressae sunt aquae largissimae*, Num. 20, 11. **II.** *sufficiently :*—Beón þǽr bed genihtsumlīce (*sufficienter*) ofersprǽdde, R. Ben. 85, 22 : R. Ben. I. 90, 7.

**ge-nyhtsumnes.** *Add :*—Genyhtsumnes *ubertas*, Wrt. Voc. i. 53, 47. **I.** *a large amount, an ample supply :*—Ginyhtsumnise (*printed* genyhtsume) lēcedōme *abundantia remediorum*, Rtl. 40, 29. Of gefremedre genihtsumnysse *de congesta* (*virtutum*) *copia*, An. Ox. 3345. Fæsten for hwǽtes genihtsumnesse, ōđerne for wīnes, þriddan for eles, Shrn. 138, 13. **II.** *a condition of plenty :*—Wē sindon cumen tō þǽm gōdan tīdun . . . and tō đǽre genihtsumnisse þe hié fore gielpađ, Ors. 4, 7 ; S. 182, 15. **III.** *a sufficiency, sufficient supply :*—Sum him mid bær þæs līchaman genihtsumnysse, Hml. S. 23 b, 127.

**ge-nyrwian.** v. ge-nirwan.

**geó.** *Add :*—Geó, gefyrn *quondam*, Wülck. Gl. 254, 4. Þǽm englum gelīc þe geó Gode wiþsōcan, Bl. H. 49, 7. Geó (gió, ió, iú, *v. ll.*) on ealddagum *a temporibus antiquis*, Bd. 4, 27 ; Sch. 517, 5. Giú on Nōes dagum . . . giú (gió, *v. l.*) on Torcwines dagum, Bt. 16, 1 ; F. 50, 6-8. Đāra wiotona đe giú wǽron giond Angelcynn, Past. 5, 19. Iú (gió, *v. l.*), 3, 3. Iú (ió, *v. l.*), 216, 24. Iú, fyrn *olim*, Wrt. Voc. ii. 64, 75. Ic wæs iú in heofnum hālig ængel, Sat. 81 : Seel. 61. Ne aron nū cyningas swylce iú wǽron, Seef. 83 : B. 2459. Đǽr đā cnihtas iú ǽr eardodon, Hml. Th. i. 62, 25 : 318, 14 : Bt. 16, 1 ; F. 48, 35. Wē iú hæfdon ǽrror wlite, Sat. 151. Iú . . ., ǽr þan . . ., Kr. 17. ¶ geára geó (iú) *long ago.* v. geó-geára :—Þæt wæs geára iú . . . þætte mid englum oferhygd āstāg, Mōd. 57 : Sch. 11 : Wand. 22 : Gū. 11 : Kr. 28. ¶ þā (nū) geó *already :*—Hwylce geđincđe hē hæfde ætforan Gode đā giú on his cildhāde, Hml. Th. ii. 154, 26. Swā fulfremedlīce hē drohtnode on anginne his gecyrrednysse swā þæt hē mihte đā gyú beón geteald on fulfremedra hālgena getele, 120, 4. Sprǽc hē swelce hit đā giet nyste đæt hié hit him đā ió (iú, *v. l.*) ondrēdon, Past. 213, 24. Staþol wæs iú þā, Rä. 70, 2. God nū iú rīxađ on him, Hml. Th. i. 520, 23. His brýdbedd mē is geara nū iú mid dreámum, Hml. S. 7, 43. [*In the following passage, if* geó *be the true form, the word is used of the future, but perhaps instead of* geó weorþeđ *should be read* geweorþeđ :—Ic eów secge þ þ geo weorþeđ, þ ealle þās getimbro beóþ tōworpene, Bl. H. 77, 35.]

**geoc.** *Take here* iuc *in Dict., and add :* **I.** *a* (*material*) *yoke.* (1) *for animals :*—Scear *vomer*, culter *cultor*, geoc *jugum*, Wrt. Voc. i. 74, 74. (2) *a collar to secure prisoners :*—Boia (boia *torques vinctorum*, Migne), *arcus vel* geoc, boias sweorcopsas, Wrt. Voc. ii. 126, 42, 43.

Hié mon on geocum and on racentum beforan hiera triumphan drifon (*but the Latin is :* Catenatis, sub jugum missis), Ors. 5, 1 ; S. 214, 16. **II.** *a* (*non-material*) *yoke.* (1) of that which unites people :—Sié in đǽr[e] iwocc lufes and sibbes *sit in ea jugum dilectionis et pacis*, Rtl. 109, 33. (2) of that which represses or oppresses :—Hié under đǽm geoke (gioke, *v. l.*) his hlāforddōmes đurhwunigen, Past. 197, 8. Hī onbugon tō þām wynsuman iuce wuldres cyninges, Hml. S. 29, 178. Hū hefig geoc hē beslēpte on ealle þā þe on his tīdum libbende wǽron, Bt. 16, 4 ; F. 58, 16. Eálā ofermōdan! hwī gē wilnigen þ gē underlūtan mid eówrum swiran þ deáþlice geoc, 19 ; F. 68, 27. **III.** *a measure of land, as much land as could be ploughed in a day by a yoke of oxen* (?). The word is given as Kentish in the D. D., and the charter from which the following passage is taken is Kentish. Cf. geoc-led :—Đonne đes londes xvi gioc ǽrđelondes and medwe all on ǽce ǽrfe tō brūcanne, C. D. i. 316, 25. v. under-geoc.

**geóc.** *Add :* **I.** *help in danger or difficulty :*—Þæt ic þē tō geóce gārholt bere, B. 1834. Ne mæg þǽre sāwle þe biđ synna ful gold tō geóce, Seef. 101. Đē wearđ māđma cyst (*a sword*) gifeđe tō eóce unc, Vald. 1, 25. Geóce gelyfde brega Beorhtdena, B. 608. Byrne ne meahte gārwigan geóce gefremman, 2674. Gearo wæs sē him geóce gefremede . . . heora feorh generede metodes weard, Dan. 233. **I a.** *the divine help asked in prayer :*—Ic đē georne gebide gēce and miltse, Txts. 174, 1. Hū sceal mīn cuman gǽst tō geóce, nemne ic Gode sylle hýrsume hige, Gū. 338. Hē geóce fricle, Hpt. 33, 71, 10. Þāra þe geóce tō him sēceđ, An. 1154. Sē đe him tō đǽm hālgan helpe gelīfeđ, tō Gode gióce, Vald. 2, 28. **II.** *consolation in sorrow or trouble, comfort :*—Flǽsc þæt seó fǽmne gebær geómrum tō geóce, Cri. 124. Frōfre gǽst in Gūđlāces geóce gewunade, Gū. 108. Gehātan geómrum gǽste geóce ođđe frōfre, Seel. 108.

**geoc-boga.** *Take here* iuc-boga *in Dict., and add :*—Geocboga *jungula*, Wrt. Voc. ii. 98, 21.

**geocian ;** *p.* ode *To join, yoke :*—Ic geocige (iucige, *v. l.*) jungo, Ælfc. Gr. Z. 174, 1. v. ge-iukod *in Dict., and* un-geocian.

**geoc-led, -let, -leta** *a yokelet* (*an old Kentish name for a small farm,* D.D.) :—*Mediam partem unius mansiunculae, id est* ān geocled *ubi* ecgheannglond *appellatur*, Txts. 455, 4. Ān ioclet, C. D. i. 249, 20. *In loco ubi ab indegenis ab occidente* Kasingburnan *appellatur demediam partem unius mansiunculae, id est* ān ioclet, 250, 15. Ān iocled, 239, 18. Ān swulung and ān iocleta, ii. 102, 21.

**geócor.** *For passage from Beowulf substitute :*—þæt [he, MS.] wæs geócor sīđ þæt se hearmscađa tō Heorute āteah, B. 76, 5. *Add :*—Ne hē sorge wæg, geócorne sefan, dreórigne hyge, Gū. 1111.

**geocsa.** v. gesca.

**geoc-sticca, -stecca,** an ; *m. A yoke-stick.* (Later a yoke-stick is 'a yoke for carrying pails.' v. D.D.) *Take here* iuc-sticca *in Dict., and add :*—Geocstecca *obicula*, Wrt. Voc. ii. 115, 33. Geocsticca, 63, 29.

**geocsung.** v. giscung : **geoc-tíma.** *Take here* iuc-tēma *in Dict. :* **geó-dǽd.** *Take here* iú-dǽd *in Dict., and add :* cf. ǽr-dǽd.

**geó-dæg** *a former day, day of old :*—Þū gehyrdest þætte giódagum gelomp, Bt. 18, 4 ; F. 66, 27. Iúdagum Rōmāni gehālgedon on þissa tungla gemynde heora dagas, Ängl. viii. 321, 4. Iúdagum se biscop Theophilus wrāt ǽnne pistol, 322, 45. *See* geó *in Dict., and cf.* ǽr-dæg.

**ge-oferian.** v. ge-uferian.

**ge-offrian.** *Add :* **I.** *to sacrifice, immolate :*—Offrunga þǽre ealdan ǽwe wē nā ne geoffriaþ (*immolamus*), An. Ox. 40, 20. Hē funde him ānne ram Gode tō geoffrigenne, Prud. 1 b. Eástrun ūre geoffrud (*immolatus*) is, An. Ox. 40, 30. **II.** *to devote to the service of a divinity.* (1) *the object a thing :*—Hē wurđlic lāc geoffrode tō ūres Drihtenes byrgene, þ wæs ān gylden calic, Chr. 1058 ; P. 189, 19. Hē geoffrode his lāc þām almihtigan Gode, Hml. S. 25, 794. (2) *the object a person :*—Anna geoffrode Gode Samuhel, Hml. A. 34, 260. Gif hwylc rīce mon his bearn Gode on mynstre geoffrian wile, R. Ben. 103, 11.

**geofola.** v. gifla.

**geofon.** *Add :* **I.** *ocean, sea, flood :*—Ic gewīte sēcan gārsecges grund ; gifen biđ gewrēged, Rä. 3, 3. Gārsecg, geofon geótende, An. 393. Geofon (*the Red Sea*), Exod. 447. On geofones stađe, 580. Ymb geofenes stæđ gearwe stōdon sǽmearas, El. 227. Ofer geofenes stream *across the sea*, 1201. Hwā āspyred đæt deófol of geofones holte, Sal. K. 146, 27. Þā bāt glideđ on geofone, An. 498. Storm oft hreóh gebringeđ, geofen in grimmum sǽlum, Gn. Ex. 52. **II.** *a flood, deluge :*—Flōd ofslōh, gifen (*Noah's flood*) geótende, giganta cyn, B. 1690. Geofon (*the water that had poured from the pillar*) swađrode, An. 1587 : 1626. Duguđ wearđ āfyrhted þurh þæs flōdes fǽr . . . geonge on geofene gūđrǽs fornam, 1533. [*O. Sax.* geƀan.]

**geó-geára.** [Perhaps this should be taken as two words. v. An. 1388 :—Sē þe þā fǽhđo iú wiđ God *geára* grimme gefremede.] *Add :*—Geára ođđe geógeára *jam*, Wrt. Voc. ii. 48, 11. Geógeára (iú-, -ieára, *v. ll.*) geworht *antiquitus facta*, Bd. 1, 26 ; Sch. 57, 20. Geógeára (iú-,

v. l.) jamdudum, 4, 4; Sch. 370, 23. Bryten wæs Iúgeára (originally higeára) Albion háten Brittania cui quondam Albion nomen fuit, 1, 1; Sch. 7, 6. Geógeára on ealdum spellum, Bt. 31, 1; F. 112, 15. Iúgēre ealdum wítum, Exod. 33. v. ær-geára.

**geógelere.** Substitute: A magician:—Fela þinga dydan þá geógeleras on Egypta land þurh drýcræft, Wlfst. 98, 9. Drýas, iúgeleras marsi, An. Ox. 4476. Iúgelera aruspicum, 4020: magorum, i. ariolorum, 4069: 4089.

**geóguþ.** l. geoguþ, and add: I. youth as a period or stage of existence:—Gód sceal wið yfele, geogoð sceal wið ylde sacan, Gn. C. 52. Ðínre giogeðe adulescentiae tuæ, Kent. Gl. 109. Ðære scame ðe ðú on iuguðe worhte confusionis adolescentiae tuae, Past. 207, 11. On geoguðe his earfoðsíð forspildan, on yldo eft eádig weorðan, Vy. 58: Wand. 35. On ælde ꝛ on giogeðe, Ps. C. 142. luguðe (tenerrima) aetatula (infantis), An. Ox. 7, 198. Fram gebyrdtída iungan iugeðe ab cunabulorum teneritudine, 2843. Tó láre befæst sóna fram iugoðe, Hml. S. 6, 2. Fram mínre gugoðe a iuuentute mea, Ps. L. 70, 5. God scóp geoguðe and gumena dreám ... Wintra rím gegæð in þá geoguðe, Gú. 466-470. I a. youth as the season of strength:—Bið geenidówad swē swē am guguð (juuentus) ðín, Ps. Srt. 102, 5. Gigoð, Rtl. 169, 39. Þær is geogoð búton ylde, Bl. H. 65, 17. Ongan eldo gebunden gomel guðwiga geoguðe cwíðan, hilde strengo, B. 2112. I b. youth as a period of immaturity:—Ðá ðe unmedome bióð tó ðære láre oððe for giogúðe oððe for unwísdóme, Past. 375, 19. Þá þe for geoguðe gyt ne mihton breóstnet werian, Exod. 235. Ic wæs on geoguðe, grame mē forhogedon adolescentior ego sum et contemtus, Ps. Th. 118, 141: El. 638. Ne forsió nán mon ðíne gioguðe (adolescentiam), Past. 385, 30. II. youthful qualities or nature:—Geogoðe indolis (ut puer indolis librorum disceret artes, Ald. 166, 33), Wrt. Voc. ii. 92, 70: 80, 68. Giogúðe indolem (pubertatis), 85, 68. III. the young. (1) of persons:—Seó iuguð þe be þám wege wæs ácenned populus qui natus est in deserto, Jos. 5, 5. Sió geogoð (cf. geonge gúðræs fornam, 1533) áràs, An. 1636. Þeós fægre geogað forwurðan sceall, Hml. S. 4, 311. Seó yld hí gebæd, and seó iuguð wrát, Hml. Th. ii. 506, 21. Sécan hwilc þære geogoðe gleáwost wære, Dan. 81. Wē lærað þ preóstas geoguðe geornlíce læran, Ll. Th. ii. 254, 25. Þá ealdan sceal earmlíce licgan æt hám hungre ácwolcne, and man sceal þá geoguðe geómorlíce lædan gehæft ... of heora ēðle, Wlfst. 295, 17. (1 a) of persons in a subordinate position:—Ymbeóde ides Helminga duguðe and geogoðe dæl æghwylcne, B. 621. (1 b) a person's young ones, children:—Nóe mid bearnum under bord gestáh gleáw mid geogoðe (Noah went in, and his sons, and his sons' wives, Gen. 7, 7), Gen. 1370. Hē geogoðe strýnde, suna and dohtra, 1152. Hē þá geogoðe wile árum healdan ... mid góde gyldan wille uncran eaferan, B. 1181. (2) of animals:—Sý ælcere geoguðe teóðrung gelæst be Pentecosten, Ll. Th. i. 262, 20: 306, 31: Wlfst. 116, 2. .i. lamb of geáres geogeðe, Ll. Th. i. 438, 23. .i. ticcen of geáres geogoðe, 28. (3) of plants:—Swá swá nýwlicra elebergena ꝛ guogað elebeáma sicut nouelle oliuarum, Ps. L. 127, 3. v. cild-, cniht-, magu-geoguþ.

**geoguþ-cnósl.** Before Ic bíde add:—þær ic (a badger) wíc búge, bold mid bearnum.

**geoguþ-hád.** Add: juventa, adolescentia, pueritia, anni juveniles:—Iuguþhád juventa, Wrt. Voc. ii. 47, 73. Þá scylda mínes iugoðhádes (juventutis), Ps. Th. 24, 6. Gigoðhádes, Rtl. 167, 31. From gigoð-háde mínum, Mk. R. 10, 20. Gigoðháda, Lk. R. 18, 21. In geogoð-háde þæs líchaman costung wealleþ, and þonne fram þám fiftigoðan geáre cólað seó hæte, Gr. D. 102, 21. Sē wæs þá gyt on his geogoðháde (in annis juvenilibus), 298, 25. Blíðsa, cniht on ðínum gioguðháde laetare, juvenis, in adolescentia tua, Past. 385, 34. On giohðháde, Kent. Gl. 1096. Fram geoguðháde a pueritia, Scint. 189, 17. Of eorðscræfe ærist fremman, gáste onfón geoguðháde to arise from the grave, become alive and young, An. 783. þe hwíle þe hit on cnihtháde biþ, and swá forþ eallne giogoþhád, Bt. 38, 5; F. 206, 24.

**geoguþhádnes.** Add:—Seó stów on þære þe þú þ fægereste werod on geogeðhádnesse (geoguð-, v.l.) gesáwe scínan locus iste in quo pulcherrimam hanc iuuentutem fulgere conspicis, Bt. 5, 12; Sch. 627, 19.

**geoguþ-lust.** Take here geoguþ-lust in Dict.

**geoguþ-myru.** Substitute: geoguþ-miru (-myru); gen. -miru, -mirwe; f. The tenderness of youth (?):—Ic þá wihte (a young bull) geseah wæpnedcynnes geoguðmyrwe grædig (hungry with the hunger of a young creature. Cf. grædig applied to the hungry young of animals in Ps. Th. 103, 21:—León hwelpas sécað þæt him grædigum æt God gedéme), Rä. 39, 2. [For second part of the compound cf. O. H. Ger. marawī, muruwī teneritudo.]

**geohhol, gehhol, gehol, geól;** n. pl. (cf. Icel.). Take here geól in Dict., and add:—Þý twelftan dæge ofer geohhel (geohol, ge(o)h(o)l (the o's above the line), geochol, v. ll.) epifaniae, Bd. 4, 19; Sch. 443, 9. On Gehhol (Geól, Geohhol, v. ll.), Ll. Th. i. 64, 23. On Gehhol (-el, v.l.), 92, 3. .xl. nihta ær geólum (middan wintra, úres Dryhtnes gebyrdtíde, v. ll.) xl. diebus ante Natale Domini, ii. 162, 12. [Bugge connects the word (primitive form jehuela) with Latin joculus.]

**geohhol-dæg.** Take here Geóhel-dæg (l. geohel-) in Dict., and add:—Se ærysta dæg in natale domini, ðæt is ærysta geohheldæg, Shrn. 144, 17. [In ane ȝeoldæie (holy day, 2nd MS.), Laym. 22737. þe þrittennde daȝȝ fra ȝoldaȝȝ, Orm. 11063. Cf. Icel. jóla-dagr.]

**geohhol-mónaþ**, es; m. December:—Iúlmónaþ Decembris, Chr. P. 280, margin. [Icel. jól-mánuðr.] v. geóla.

**geohsa.** v. gesca.

**geoht,** es; n. Substitute: A yoke of oxen, a pair of horses:—Se ceorl sē þe hæfð óðres geoht (oxan, v.l.) áhýrod, Ll. Th. i. 140, 8. Iuht subiugales, uiles æquos (indomitos bigarum subiugales, Ald. 30, 12), An. Ox. 7, 135: uiles æquas, Angl. xv. 205, 101. [Cf. O. H. Ger. alle kiioht omnes jugales (currum).] v. hýr-geoht.

**geó-hwílum** formerly, of old:—Þeáh ic geóhwílum gecóplíce funde, ic nú misfó, Bt. 2; F. 4, 8. Cf. ær-hwílum.

**geól.** v. geohhol: **geola.** v. geolo.

**Geóla.** Take here Iúla in Dict., and add:—Ianuarius, þ is on úre gedeóde se æftera Geóla; þ bið se æresta geáres mónað mid Rómwarum and mid ús, Shrn. 47, 15. Ianuarius ... on Englisc se æfterra Geóla, Lch. ii. 214, 20.

**ge-ólæcan.** v. ge-óleccan: **geole.** v. geolo.

**ge-óleccan, -lécan.** Substitute: I. to caress, treat with gentleness:—God hwílon ús geólæht, and hwílon eác beswingð, Hml. Th. ii. 330, 2. II. to flatter:—Þonne synfulle menn óðre heora gelícan mid derigendlicere herunge geólæcað, Hml. Th. i. 494, 4. III. of things, to charm, allure:—Geólæhte, gladode demulcet (blandimentorum lenitas), An. Ox. 3004. Swylce ðá woruldsælþa wæron ðá hí ðe mæst geólectan talis erat fortuna, cum blandiebatur, Bt. 7, 1; S. 15, 28.

**geolhstor.** v. geolstor.

**geolo(-u);** gen. geolwes; n. I. a yellow colour:—Gelu, gelo crocus, Txts. 50, 242. Geolo, Wrt. Voc. i. 288, 47. Geolu, i. 17, 13: 137, 9. II. yellow material, yolk of an egg:—Dó on hunig æges geola, Lch. ii. 130, 12. [Cf. O. H. Ger. gelo aurugo.] v. æger-geolu.

**geolo;** adj. Add: The word glosses aureus, croceus, flaveus, flavus, fulvus, gilvus, luteus, libosus, melinus, rubens, rubeus, rubicundus, succinaceus, venetus, lutei ·coloris:—Gelu, geolu flavum, Txts. 62, 432: gilvus, 64, 458. Geolu, geholu venetum, 104, 1064. Geolu fulvus vel flavus, Wrt. Voc. i. 77, 1: flabum, ii. 35, 67: melinum, 59, 36: melinum vel croceum, 12, 23: succinaceus vel croceus vel flavus, 46, 52: lutei coloris, ii. 137, 9: croceus, i. rubicundus, rubeus, 10: fuluum, flavum, splendidum, nigrum, Wülck. Gl. 245, 35. Giolu aureus, Wrt. Voc. ii. 10, 30. Geola swylce twymylte wex fex flaua cesaries, An. Ox. 4462: Wrt. Voc. ii. 149, 19. Geolwum croceo, An. Ox. 50, 10. Gioluwre crocea, Wrt. Voc. ii. 17, 14. Genim geoluwne stán, Lch. i. 374, 14. Goelu godueb, Txts. 151, 10. Geolewra flauentium, i. rubentium (fauorum), An. Ox. 1667. Geolewum andweorcum fuluis metallis, Wülck. Gl. 245, 36. Geolwum oððe deorcum fulvis, Wrt. Voc. ii. 34, 64. Þá geolwan groceos (croceos Titan radios diffundit, Ald. 165), 92, 59. Ðá giolwan libosas, 52, 61. [In the following instances the glosses seem to refer to other words than those given :—þám geolwum lutea (Aurora in fulvis ... lutea bigis; the gloss applies to fulvis), Wrt. Voc. ii. 93, 56: lautea, 52, 60. Geole fiys setosa vellera; the gloss seems determined by a later line, Croceo mutavit vellera luto, Ald. 75. Cf. the erroneous gloss to this line in Wrt. Voc. ii. 87, 31 crocea þá geolwan.] ¶ used substantively (cf. preceding word):—Genim æges þ geoluwe, Lch. ii. 22, 19. ¶ seó geolwe ádl jaundice:—Wiþ þære geolwan ádle, Lch. ii. 106, 14: 172, 24: 294, 6. Of gealádle sió biþ of þære geolwan, 106, 14.

**geolo-ádl.** Dele, and see preceding word: **geolo-blác.** Dele, and see geolwe.

**geolo-hwít.** Add: White with a tinge of yellow:—Geoluhwít gilvus, Wrt. Voc. i. 46, 44. Gioluhwít, ii. 42, 12.

**geolo-reád.** Add: red with a tinge of yellow:—þæt giolureáde lutea, Wrt. Voc. ii. 53, 8. Þá giolureádan crocata, 20, 19. v. geolwe.

**geolstor, gelostr, gillister,** es; n.: **geolstor,** e; **gillistre,** an; f. Take here geolhstor in Dict., and add:—Gelostr supuratio, Wrt. Voc. ii. 121, 74. Geolstor tabo, i. sanie, An. Ox. 2, 228. Þonne yrnð þ gillister út, Lch. ii. 24, 18. Weaxeð sió yfele gillestre and þ yfele blód, 148, 6. Hreófligum wyrmse (geolstre) elephantino tabo, i. sanie, An. Ox. 3585. Geol(s)ter uirus (acc.), 4855. Wyrms, geolstre uirus (atrum ueneni uirus infundentia), 4991. Lǣte flówan of þám nebbe þá gillistran, Lch. ii. 18, 17. Þá gilstre, iii. 2, 13. Swiling wið gillistrum tó heáfdes hǣlo, ii. 2, 3. [O. L. Ger. gillistra; f. gillistr; n.]

**geolstrig.** Substitute: I. poisonous:—Mánfulra ættrig ꝛ geolstri wyrta sæp dirorum uirulentus, i. uenenatus graminum suc(c)us, An. Ox. 1849. II. full of corrupt matter, purulent:—Geolstri purulentus, An. Ox. 2, 403. Mid geolstrigum wundum purulentis uulneribus, 5361. Iulstrie purulentas, 4, 30: 7, 111.

**geolwe, geole;** adv. With a yellow tinge:—Se andwlita biþ geolwe blác (cf. hire andwlita biþ reáde wan, 19) the face is pale with a tinge of yellow (sallow), Lch. ii. 348, 16. Geole reád vel geole crog flavum, i. fulvum, rubeum, Wrt. Voc. ii. 149, 15.

**geolwian**; *p.* ode *To become yellow* or *ruddy* :—Nā beheald þū wīn þænne hit geoluwað (*flauescit*), Scint. 105, 7. Geolwaþ, Wrt. Voc. ii. 149, 18. Þā geolewedan (gegeolewedan, An. Ox. 108) *crocata*, Hpt. Gl. 408, 57.

**geómær**, *l.?* geon-cær = geán-cir, *q. v.* :—Gāst gangende, næs se geomær eft *spiritus vadens et non rediens*, Ps. Th. 77, 39.

**geó-man**. *Take here* iú-man *in Dict., and add* :—Swā geómen cwædon, Lch. iii. 430, 32.

**geómor**. *Add* : I. *of persons, feeling sad* :—Hige geómor, swýðe mid sorgum gedrēfed, Jud. 87. Him wæs geómor sefa, . . . hyge murnende, Cri. 499. Geómor sefa, murnende mōd, B. 49. Geómor sefa, hyge gnornende, Gū. 1181. Sefa geómor, mōd morgenseóc, Hy. 4, 94. Hē geómor wearð, sārig for his synnum, Dōm. 87. Ic þis giedd wrece bi mē ful geómorre, Kl. 1. **I a.** *sad of soul, at heart* :—Hē mōdes geómor meregrund gefeóll, B. 2100. **I b.** *with cause of sadness given in gen. or inst.* :—Geómor gūdæda, Ph. 556. Reónigmōde . . . gehðum geómre, El. 322. **II.** *expressing sadness, melancholy* :—Hē ongann geómran stefne hearmleóð galan, An. 1128 : Met. 1, 84. [*Perhaps the passage under* geómor-gid (geómor gid?) *might be taken here.*] **III.** *having a cheerless sound or appearance* :—Þeós geómre lyft *triste coelum*, Exod. 430. Geác monað geómran reorde, Seef. 53. **IV.** *of a season in which sadness is experienced* :—In þā geómran tīd (*the last day*), Ph. 517.

**geómore, geómre**; *adv. Sadly, mournfully* :—Weard undyrne cūð, gyddum geómore, þætte Grendel wan wið Hróðgār, B. 151. Þær wæs tōða geheáw hlūde and geómre, Sat. 340.

**geómor-gid**. v. geómor; II.

**geómor-lic**. *Substitute* : I. *causing sorrow, miserable, grievous, sad* :—Bið geómorlic gomelum ceorle tō gebīdanne, þæt his byre rīde giong on galgan, B. 2444. Mid þæm þe þā burgware swā geómorlic angin hæfdon *non secus ac si capta esset, turbata civitas fuit*, Ors. 4, 5 ; S. 166, 15. **II.** *expressing sorrow, mournful, sad* :—Ðā ongan ic heófonde forðbringan þā geómorlican siccetunga, Hml. S. 23 b, 429. [*O. Sax.* jāmar-līk : *O. H. Ger.* jāmar-līh.]

**geómorlíce**. *Add* : I. *in a way that causes sorrow, miserably* :—Man sceal þā geoguðe geómorlíce lædan gehæft, heánlíce mid heardum bendum, Wlfst. 295, 17. **II.** *in a way that expresses sorrow, lamentably, mournfully* :—Tō Gode gebiddende and tō him heora neóde geómorlíce mænende, Hml. S. 23, 141. [*O. H. Ger.* jāmarlīhho luctuose.]

**geómor-mōd**. *Add* : I. *of persons*. (1) *sad-hearted, sad of soul, sorrowful* :—Þā wearð Esau swīðe sārig and geómormōd (*consternatus*), Gen. 27, 34. Cain gewāt gongan geómormōd, wineleás wrecca, Gen. 1050. Ic teáras sceal geótan geómormōd, Cri. 173. Geómormōd, . . . earg and unrōt, 1407 : Hy. 10, 29. Ā scyle geong mon wesan geómor-mōd, heard heortan geþoht, swylce habban sceal blīþe gebǣro *if a young man must ever be sad of soul, brave heart's thought, also cheery bearing must he have*, Kl. 42. Geómormōdes drūsende hyge, Gū. 1033. Gewitan him (*the apostles after the ascension*) gongan . . . geómormōde, Cri. 535 : An. 406. (2) *gloomy from a sense of evil fortune or danger* :—Eald æscwiga, sē þe eall geman gārcwealm gumena (him bið grim sefa), onginneð geómormōd geongum cempan . . . higes cunnian, B. 2044. Þām folce geómormōdum (*the people threatened by Holofernes' army*), Jud. 144. **II.** *of birds* :—Fugelas cyrrað from þām gūþfrecan geómormōde eft tō earde, Ph. 353.

**geómor-ness**, e; *f. Sadness, trouble* :—Gedrēfednes t̄ geómornes *tribulatio*, Ps. L. 118, 143.

**geómre**. v. geómore.

**geómrian**. *Add* :—Þū geómrast for þām þe heó onhwyrfed is, Bt. 1 ; F. 16, 9. Ðū giómras gemas, Kent. Gl. 94. Hē swýþe weóp and geómrian ongan *flens et gemens*, Guth. Gr. 162, 33. Gēmerian and wēpan *gemere et flere*, Scint. 34, 3. Ðā ic þā ðis leóþ geómriende āsungen hæfde *haec dum querimoniam lacrymabilem styli officio designaverem*, Bt. 3, 1 ; F. 4, 16. Ǣfre ic wurde syððan geómriende *deducetis canos meos cum dolore ad inferos*, Gen. 42, 38. Geómriende *ejulantes*, Mk. 5, 38. ¶ geómrian tō *to sigh for, long for* :—Hī geómriað tō ðām upplican, Hml. Th. i. 520, 23. [*Gullen þa helmes, ჳeoumiereden eorles*, Laym. 23492. *O. H. Ger.* āmarōn : *Ger.* jammern.] v. ā-, begeómrian ; gīmran.

**geómrung**. *Add* :—Geómrung *gemitus*, Wrt. Voc. ii. 42, 11. Mid geómrunge and mid wōpe (*vel gemitu vel fletu*) hī getācniaþ heora mōdes lufe, R. Ben. 138, 5. Hē for þæs Mōdes geómrunge (geómrunga, v. l.) næs nāuht gedrēfed *nihil meis questibus mota*, Bt. 5, 1 ; F. 8, 26.

**geon**; *pron. Yon, that* :—Arīs and gong tō geonre byrg *surgens ingredere civitatem* (Acts 9, 6), Past. 443, 25. [*Goth.* jains: *O. H. Ger.* jenēr : *Icel.* enn.] See next word.

**geonan**. v. be-geonan : ge-onbyrded. v. un-geonbyrded.

**geond**. *Add* : **gend** (v. geond-geótan), **gind, giend, gynd**. A. *with acc.* **I.** *where position is marked.* (1) *distribution of objects* (a) *over a surface* :—Ealle hī lāgon slæpende geond þā eordan *they all lay about on the ground sleeping*, Hml. S. 23, 260. Mid gymstānum gefrætewod geond eall *adorned all over with jewels*, 36, 140. (b) *within an area* :—Þær sint swīðe micle meras geond þā mōras *there are very large lakes among the moors*, Ors. 1, 1 ; S. 19, 5. Gind þæt lond tōbrǣd, 4, 8 ; S. 188, 12. Weras geond þā wīnburg, An. 1639. Ūre bisceopas geond eal Rōmāna rīce *our bishops throughout the Roman empire*, Bl. H. 187, 3. Secgað ðǣm welegum gind ðisne middangeard, Past. 181, 14. Geond ealne middaneard, Hy. 3, 12. Monge sindon geond middangeard hādas under heofonum, Gū. 1. Heá beorgas geond sīdne grund *the high hills throughout the wide world*, Gen. 1388. Ealle ðā reliquias ðe gind ealne middangeard sindon, Rtl. 114, 18. Ætter burgum geond Bryten innan, Gū. 855. (bb) *among a people* :—Þām snoterestum geond Iudēas, El. 278. (c) *within a space* :—Þā cynn þe flōd wecceð geond hronrāde, Gen. 205. (cc) *a room, hall, &c.* :—Ealle geond windsele, Sat. 386. Geond þæt sīde sel *throughout the spacious hall*, An. 763. Hringdene geond þæt sæld swæfon *they slept all about the hall*, B. 1280. Ne gōd hafoc geond sæl swingeð *no hawk has its perch in the hall*, 2264. (2) *diffusion of an object throughout a space* :—Eówerne naman tōbrǣdan geond ealine eorþan, Bt. 18, 2 ; F. 64, 5 : Vid. 99. Þǣr wæs cirm micel geond Mermedonia, An. 42. Wynn geond wuldres þrym, Cri. 71. Cōm micel hǣte giend Rōmāne, Ors. 2, 6 ; S. 88, 15. (3) *distribution to or diffusion through many places* :—Hē þæt wīn tōdǣlde geond ealle þā kyfa and geond ealle þā fatu, Gr. D. 58, 22–24. Drihten eów tōdrīfð geond ealle þā þeóda (*in omnes gentes*), Deut. 4, 27. Wæs geond werþeóde Waldendes wracu wīde gefrǣge, Edg. 53. Wæs ūre līf geond londa fela fracuð, Az. 23. Seó treów geond bilwitra breóst ārīseð, Gn. Ex. 161. (3 a) *where a like circumstance occurs at different places* :—Beóð eorþan styrunga geond stōwa (*per loca*), Lk. 21, 11. (4) *distribution among other objects, between* :—Geseah ic wīngeard, and þā twigo his hongodon geond þā columnan *vineam inter columnas pendentem miratus sum*, Nar. 4, 29. **II.** *where there is movement.* (1) *of a body* (a) *on a surface, across, over, about* :—Manig wyht is mistlīce fērende geond (geon, v. l.) eorþan *quam variis terras animalia permeant figuris*, Bt. 41, 6 ; F. 254, 24. Fleógan crupon geond eall þā limu, Ors. 1, 7 ; S. 38, 3. Fērdon folctogan feorran and neán geond wīdwegas, B. 840. Swā wē on laguflōde ofer cald wæter ceólum līðan, geond sīdne sǣ sundhengestum flōdwudu fergen, Cri. 853 : Gen. 1331. (b) *within an area, through, about* a country (or people) :—Hī ealle heora līfdæde geond missenlīce þeóda (*per diversas prouincias*) farað, R. Ben. 9, 21 : Sat. 270. Hē sum his folc sende gind þæt lond tō herigenne, Ors. 4, 8 ; S. 188, 10. Þ hrýþer geond þ wēsten fērde, Bl. H. 199, 10 : 12. Þā heáfodleásan man hēngc on ðā portweallas . . . flugon hrócas and hremmas geond þā portweallas and tōslíton ðā hālgan Godes dýrlingas, Hml. S. 23, 79. (c) *within a space, through, about, in* :—Heó hwearf geond þæt reced, B. 1981. Hē hwearf geond þone wudu, Bl. H. 199, 13 : Ll. Th. i. 114, 15. Hié hine tugon geond þǣre ceastre innan, Bl. H. 241, 25. (cc) *within a medium* (earth, water, air) :—Hornfisc glád geond gārsecg, An. 371. Git geseóþ hine geond heofenas fēran, Bl. H. 187, 34. Heofonfuglas lācende geond lyft farað, Az. 144 : El. 734. (2) *where there is motion of a fluid, growth of a plant* (lit. or fig.). (a) *through an area* :—Lǣd ðīne willas gind ðīn lond, Past. 373, 5. Rǣhton wīde geond werþeóda wrōhtes telgan, Gen. 991. (b) *through a medium* :—Se ǣwelm biþ smūgende geond þā eorðan, Bt. 24, 1 ; F. 80, 26. (3) *where there is movement to every part of an object, throughout.* (a) *the subject material* :—Hē ūs fēran hēt geond ginne grund: 'Farað geond ealle eorðan sceátas, bodiað geleáfan ofer foldan fæðm' (*euntes in mundum uniuersum praedicate euangelium*, Mk. 16, 15), An. 329–336 : Cri. 481. His apostolas tōfērdon geond þisne middaneard, Hml. S. 36, 15. Hundes fleógan cōmon geond eall þæt mancyn, Ors. 1, 7 ; S. 38, 2. Man gengde geond eall ābutan þone portweall, Hml. S. 23, 267 : 355. (b) *the subject non-material* :—Geond ealle eorþan gǣþ heora swēg *in omnem terram exiuit sonus eorum*, Bl. H. 133, 34. Wordhleóðor āstāg geond heáhræced, An. 709. Wæs geond þā werþeóde lǣded morgenspel, El. 969. (4) *where there is movement to many places* :—Gā geond þās wegas and hegas *exi in uias et sepes*, Lk. 14, 23. Heó wǣded geond weallas, Rä. 35, 5. **III.** *marking the locality to which sight is directed*, (*to look*) *through, over* :—Sioh geond þās sīdan gesceaft, Cri. 59. Hē lōcade geond þæt lāðe scræf mid ēgum, Sat. 727. **IV.** *marking the locality of action or condition.* (1) *in or on a place, throughout* :—Wē weorðiað wīde geond eorðan heáhengles tīd, Men. 176. Geond woruld innan, Cri. 469. Bodað geond ealne middangeard *praedicatum in toto mundo* (Mt. 26, 13), Bl. H. 69, 19 : 121, 3. Geond þā burh bodað beorne manegum, An. 1122. Cūð is wīde geond middangeard þ . . ., Gū. 508. Þ wē ūre gesibsumnesse healdon gynd ealne mīnne anweald, Ll. Th. i. 246, 23 : 270, 10. (2) *among* people :—Ic geond þeóde (*inter gentes*) sealmas singe, Ps. Th. 56, 11 : Men. 127. Geond ealle þeóda, Hy. 9, 2. Geond hæleða bearn, Men. 121. Sēcan geond Israēla earme lāfe, Dan. 80. **V.** *of time, during, through, for* :—Geond fīf mōnþas, Hml. S. 21, 145. Geond nigon geára fec, 157 : 3, 469. Geond ealra worulda woruld, Sat. 224. Gynd ǣnlípie dagas *per singulos dies*, Ps. L. Lnd. p. 248, 15. Þurh dæg t iand dæg *per diem*, Ps. L. 12, 2 :

21, 3. **B.** with dat. **I.** local, *about in*. (1) of rest :—Hí geond missenlicra monna húsum wuniað *they live about in different people's houses*; *per diversorum cellas hospitantur*, R. Ben. 9, 23. (2) of motion :—Hí férdon wórigende geond eallum Rómániscum ymbhwyrfte, Hml. Th. ii. 30, 28. **II.** of time, *through* :—Geond þá (= þám or? þane) ylcan tíman *per idem tempus*, An. Ox. 397.

**geond**; *adv. Add* : **I.** marking position, *yonder, away there* :—Hér hí synd full gehende geond on Célian dúne *here they are quite close away there on the Celian hill*, Hml. S. 23, 305. Hí synd hér geond on þám scræfe æt Célian dúne, 734. Gyf Wealh Englis(c)ne man ofsleá, ne þearf hé hine hider ofer (*over here*) búton be healfan were gyldan, ne Ænglisc Wyli[s]cne geon[d] ofer (*away over there*), Ll. Th. i. 354, 20. **II.** where there is motion, *thither, over there* :—Þanon ealle wé flugon geond tó þære dúne *thence we all fled over there to the hill*, Hml. S. 23, 740. Uton þyder geond gán *let us go over there to the place*, 748 : 321. Bræd þ heáfod hider and geond, Lch. ii. 38, 4. **II a.** with a verb of looking :—Ic lócade hider and geond (*huc illucque*), Bd. 5, 12 ; Sch. 622, 2.

**geondan.** *Add*: v. wiþ-geondan.

**geond-bláwan** *to breathe upon*; afflare :—Gindbleáw *afflarat*, Germ. 397, 494. Geondbláwen *afflatus* (*coelesti spiraculo*), An. Ox. 49.

**geond-drencan** *to saturate with liquor* :—Ginddrencað *inebriant*, Kent. Gl. 111.

**geond-faran.** *Add*: **I.** *to traverse, pass through* :—Gindfærð *pertransit*, Ps. L. 38, 7. Þá þe iandfarað (*perambulant*) paðas sǽ, 8, 9. *Sideralis* se circul hátte, for þan þá tunglan hine geondfarað, Angl. viii. 317, 35. **II.** *to penetrate, permeate*. Cf. þurh-faran :—Wæs þ hús eall gefylled and geondfæren (? *printed* -tæren) mid stence *fragrantia aspersa est*, Gr. D. 286, 25.

**geond-felan.** *Substitute*: **geond-feólan**; *pp.* -fólen *To permeate, fill throughout* :—Þæt wítehus . . . deóp, dreáma leás . . . geondfólen fýre, réce and reáde lége *a dungeon horrible on all sides round as one great furnace flamed*, Gen. 43.

**geond-féran.** *Add* :—Geondfér[dest] *circuisti* (*limina*), An. Ox. 2129. Genférde *penetrauit, circuiuit*, 3945. Ic ðá wynstran dǽlas Indie wolde geondféran *sinistram partem Indie sectari institui*, Nar. 20, 20. Geondférende *lustraturus*, Wrt. Voc. ii. 53, 54.

**geond-flówende** *reciprocus*, An. Ox. 2363. v. ongeán-flówende.

**geond-gangan** *to go through* or *about, perambulate* :—Beón gesette án oðþe twégen ealde witan þe þæt mynster geondgangen and þæs gýman *deputetur unus aut duo seniores qui circumeant monasterium*, R. Ben. 74, 15. Geondgongendra (-gang-, Ps. L.) *perambulantium*, Ps. Srt. 67, 22.

**geond-geótan.** *Add* :—*Fusi*, i. dispersi, confusi vel gendgotene, Wrt. Voc. ii. 152, 8. **I.** *to cover by pouring, overspread* with a liquid :—þ man ealle þá bydenu mid pice geondgute *omnia dolia pice superfusa*, Gr. D. 57, 30. Hé wæs geondgoten mid þæs swátes dropum *he was bathed in perspiration*, Hml. S. 23 b, 233. Þá weard heó eall mid teárum geondgoten *she was bathed in tears*, 33, 234. **I a.** fig. *to cover* with confusion, &c. :—Þú gendgute hine mid gescændnysse *perfudisti eum confusione*, Ps. L. 88, 46. Mid ádle geondgoten, Bd. 4, 31 ; Sch. 543, 4. Geondgotene synt þíne weleras mid Godes gyfe *diffusa est gratia in labiis tuis*, Ps. Th. 44, 3. **II.** *to spread* (1) a liquid (*lit. or fig.*) over a surface :—Gindgoten is gife on welerum þínum, Ps. L. 44, 3. (2) objects *about* or *over* a surface :—Geondgeótað (gend-, Hpt. Gl. 408, 19) *diffundunt* (*densos exercitos per campos*), An. Ox. 91. **II a.** *to spread* (intrans.) *over* :—Sped geondgýt (gend-, Hpt. Gl. 447, 24) *glaucoma suffundit*, An. Ox. 1729. **III.** *to spread* (trans.) *through* a space, *pour into* (lit. or fig.), *infuse* :—Monna inngeðonc giendgeótan (gind-, *v. l.*) and gewæterian *interiora infundere*, Past. 137, 10. Þ of þám ilcan wíne wǽron gesewene uneáðe ealle þá fatu geondgotene *ut ex eodem vino omnia vascula vix infusa viderentur*, Gr. D. 58, 27. **III a.** *to saturate, soak* with :—Grytte geondgotene mid wíne, Lch. ii. 200, 9. **III b.** *to spread* (intrans.) *through, pour through* :—Sió blódsceáwung geondgét ealne þone líchoman, Lch. ii. 222, 9.

**geond-hirdan**; *pp.* ed *To harden thoroughly, temper thoroughly* :—Seó fían ðe sý fram hundtwelftigum hyrdenna geondhyrded, Sal. K. p. 150, 28.

**geond-innan.** *l.* geond innan. v. geond.

**geond-irnan.** *Take here* **geond-yrnan** *in Dict., and add*: **I.** of motion, *to run through* or *over* :—Ær þon þá yfelan wǽtan þá limo geondyrnen, Lch. ii. 228, 16. Þ se seáw mæge þ heáfod geondyrnan, 18, 15. **II.** of mental action, *to run over* a subject :—Geondyrnan (*percurrere*) þá þing þe syndon ongunnene be his lífe, Gr. D. 103, 10.

**geond-leccing**, e ; *f. Moistening* :—Gyndleccincg ofeweard underfehð sáwl þænne heó hí sylfe on teárum heofenríces mid gewilnunge geswencþ ; gyndleccing neaþewerd onfehð þænne helle súslu wépende ondræt *inriguum superius accipit anima, cum sese in lacrimis caelestis regni desiderio affligit ; inriguum inferius accipit, cum inferni supplicia flendo pertimescit*, Scint. 27, 5–9.

**geond-leóhtend**, es ; *m. One who gives light over* or *through*; the word, however, is used to gloss *perlustrator* : O Thoma Christi *perlustrator* (geondleóhtend) lateris, Hy. S. 128, 12.

**geond-líhtan.** *Add* :—Ðæt Godes leóhtfæt gindsécð and gindliéht (geondlíht, *v. l.*) ealle ðá diógolnesse ðære wambe, Past. 259, 10. Þær becóm seó beorhtnys . . . þ wé ealle eondlýhte wǽron . . . þær wæs fǽringa geworden on ansýne swylce þær gylden sunna onǽled wǽre, and ofer ús ealle eondlýhte, Nic. 12, 20–23.

**geond-récan** *to smoke thoroughly, fill with smoke* :—Þonne hé restan wille, hæbbe gléda þærinne, lege stor on þá gléda, and réc hine mid þ hé swǽte, and þ hús geondréc, Lch. ii. 348, 6.

**geond-sceáwian.** *Add* :—Ic seó ꝼ geondsceáwige *perspexero*, Ps. L. 118, 6.

**geond-scínan.** *Add* :—Hwý scíneð seó sunne swá reáde on morgene? For ðám hire twýnað hwæðer heó mæg ðe ne mæg ðisne middangeard geondscínan, Sal. K. 192, 2. Ðone ðe ðone folgað ðurh ðá sunnan goodes weorces giendscínan (geond-, *v. l.*) wille, Past. 337, 17.

**geond-scríþan**; *p.* -scráþ *To go through* or *about, traverse* :—On þisre endebyrdnysse geondscríð se circul his ryne, Angl. viii. 302, 16. Se móna gelóme geondscríð þæne circul þe hátte *zodiacus*, 320, 37. *Zodiacus* ys se circul genemned þe þá twelf tácna geondscríðað, 317, 33. Eall þis lyft ys full hellicra deófla, þá geondscríðað ealne middangeard, Wlfst. 250, 3.

**geond-scríþing**, e ; *f. A going about* :—Mid flugelum færeldum ꝼ geondscríðincgum *fugitiuis discursibus*, An. Ox. 263.

**geond-sécan.** *Add*: *to investigate* :—Ðæt Godes leóhtfæt gindsécð (geond-, *v. l.*) ealle ðá diógolnesse ðære wambe *lucerna Domini investigat omnia secreta ventris*, Past. 259, 10.

**geond-smeágan.** *Substitute*: *To search through, investigate, examine thoroughly* :—Þ wé geondsmeáge ðá dígolnesse úre heortan *discussis penetralibus cordis nostri*, Bd. 4, 3 ; Sch. 363, 1. Geondsmeád *enucleata*, Wrt. Voc. ii. 107, 25. *In the Corpus Gloss. the entry immediately preceding that just given is, '*enixe, omnibus uirtutibus nitit*,' v. Corp. Gl. H. 48, 211. This explains the mistake in Wrt. Voc. ii. 29, 36 *enixe* geondsmeád oððe geornlíce; geondsmeád belongs to enucleata, which has been omitted, while geornlíce renders enixe. [The two glossaries, it will be seen on comparison, appear closely connected at the parts cited.]*

**geond-sprengan.** *Substitute*: *To scatter over* or *through* :—Se áwyrgeda gást his heortan and 'geþanc mid his searwes ǽttre geondspre(n)gde and mengde *cujus praecordia malignus spiritus ingressus pestiferis vanae gloriae fastibus illum inflare coepit*, Guth. Gr. 137, 6. Mec (*a book*) fugles wyn (*a pen*) geond[sprengde] speddropum (*ink*), Rä. 27, 8. Bysn godcundre rihtwísnesse leornincgcnihta[s] geþancum geondsprenced (-sprecend, MS.) [sí] *fermentum divine justitiae in discipulorum mentibus conspergatur*, R. Ben. I, 12, 1.

**geond-springan** *to spread about, be diffused* :—Gewîdmǽrsede, geondsprang (gendspranc, Hpt. Gl. 473, 2) *percrebruit* (*gloria ejus per totius mundi cardines*), An. Ox. 2840.

**geond-stredan.** *Substitute*: **geond-stregdan, -strédan**; *p.* stregde, -strédde ; *pp.* -stregd, -stréd *To strew about, scatter about* or *over* :—Ic geondstregde (-stréde, *v. l.*) spargo, Ælfc. Gr. Z. 172, 8. **I.** *to strew* something *about* or *over* :—Genipu swá swá axan hé geondstrǽt (*spargit*), Ps. L. 147, 16. Þæsma godcundre rihtwísnesse on his underþeóddera módum sý geondstregd (*conspergatur*), R. Ben. 10, 19. Þ sǽd . . . gindstréd oððe onǽled, Lch. i. 252, 10 : 264, 22. **I a.** *to scatter, disperse* :—On ðeódum þú gindstrǽcdest (*dispersisti*) ús, Ps. L. 43, 12. **II.** *to strew* an object with something, *sprinkle over* with water, &c. :—Ic giondstreíde *aspersi* (*cubile meum myrrha*), Kent. Gl. 201. Geondstrégde *condivit, salivit*, Wrt. Voc. ii. 135, 58. Mæssepreóst hig geondstregde (*aspergat*) mid háligwætere, Ll. Th. ii. 234, 22. Geondstréd mid swǽcce þæs écan lífes, Hml. Th. ii. 536, 18. **II a.** *to overspread* :—Eorendel geondstrét heofon *aurora spargit polum*, Hy. S. 30, 2.

**geond-swógan** (?) *to rush through* or *over* a surface, *invade* a country : —Þætte nán bisceop ðres bissceopscíre gynswóge (= gynd-? or in-? *other readings give* on-, in-) *ut nullus episcoporum parrochiam alterius inuadat*, Bd. 4, 5 ; Sch. 376, 10. Cf. þurh-swógan.

**geond-tæren.** v. geond-faran ; II.

**geond-wadan** *to go through* a subject, *make oneself acquainted with, study* :—Ryhtspell monig Gregorius gleáwmód gindwód ðurh sefan snyttro, Past. 9, 10.

**geond-wlitan.** *Add* :—Hé his ágen weorc eall geondwlíteþ (*cuncta tuetur*) endemes þurhsyhð ealle gesceafta (cf. hé geseóþ and þurhseóþ ealle his gesceafta ǽndemest, Bt. 41, 1 ; F. 244, 11), Met. 30, 15.

**geond-yrnan.** v. geond-irnan.

**ge-onet, ge-ónétan** (?). *Substitute*: **ge-ónettan**; *p.* te *To get by hastening, seize, occupy* :—Tó huon eorðo giónetað *quid terram occupat*, Lk. L. R. 13, 7. Geónette (geom-, MS.) *occupavit* (cf. ónete *occupavit*, 712), Txts. 82, 717. Geónet *preoccupetur* (v. ge-efstan), Wrt. Voc. ii. 65, 78. Geónet spéd *substantia festinata*, Kent. Gl. 440.

**geong** *a course.* v. gang.

**geong** *sighs.* For geong another MS. has guornung, *which seems the right reading.* Perhaps geong *has come from the error of a copyist whose eye was caught by* forðgeonge *that follows almost immediately?*

**geong.** *Add:* I. *of age.* (1) applied to persons :—Geong *puber,* Wrt. Voc. ii. 92, 72. Iung *adultus,* 3, 71. Hē wæs wintrum geong and on his þeáwum eald, Gr. D. 219, 3. Gewiton ealdgesīðas swylce geong manig, B. 854. Ongit, guma genga, El. 464. Cwæð Salomon tō iongum monnum : ' Ðū gionga (*adolescens*),' Past. 385, 10. (1 a) translating words that express the characteristics of youth :—þ iunge tenerrima (*virgo*), Ań. Ox. 4119. Swā swā beardleás, swylce geongum hægstealde *ut effebo hircitallo,* i. *sine barba,* 3476. Iunge (beardleás) heápas *inuestes* (i. *sine barba*) *cateruas,* 2876. (2) applied to personal attributes, *youthful* :—Iunges cildhādes *rudis infantiae,* Ań. Ox. 2275. Fram þære sylfan iungan mearunesse *ab ipsa rudi* (*cunabulorum*) *teneritudine,* 1491. Gebyrdtīda iungan iugeþe (*ab ipsa*) *cunabulorum teneritudine,* 2843. Swā swā se geongeste æþeles iuguþhādes wrennesse *quasi tenerrima nobilis infantię lasciuia,* 1093. (3) applied to things, *fresh, young, new* :—Iungum wyrtūna ofætum *recentibus* (i. *nouis*) *hortorum holusculis,* Ań. Ox. 3750. II. *in reference to a change of condition, new, recent* :—Iungum *neutericis,* i. *nouellis* (*catholicae fidei sectatoribus*), Ań. Ox. 1673. III. *marking order in time, in superlative, last* (cf. *Ger. der jüngste tag*) :—þæt wæs þám gomelan gingæste word ǽr hē bǽl cure . . . him of hreðre gewāt sāwol, B. 2817. IV. *marking rank, degree.* v. gingra :—Hē gesette under him gingran cāsere, Ors. 6, 30 ; S. 278, 21. Ūre Āliésend hine gemedomode tō biónne betwiux ðǽm lǽsdum and ðǽm gingestum monnum, Past. 301, 14. v. sām-geong, *and next word.*

**geonga,** an ; *m. A young man* :—Eálā geonga (*adolescens*), ðē ic secge āris, Lk. 7, 14. Geongan *effebi,* Wrt. Voc. ii. 92, 55. Iunglingas ł iungan and fǽmnan *iuuenes et virgines,* Ps. L. 148, 12.

**geong-lǽcan** *to grow up, become adult* :—Iunglǣhte *adholesceret,* Ań. Ox. 4361.

**geong-lic.** *Take here* iung-lic *in Dict., and add* :—For geonglices (geonlices, *v. l.*) mǣdenes plegan, Mart. H. 156, 18. Iunglices cildhādes *nascentis infantie,* Ań. Ox. 966. On iunglicere *in tenero,* i. *inuenili,* 3360. Hē fēng tō rīce on iunglicre ylde, Hml. S. 18, 459. Geonglica lima *iuuenilia membra,* Scint. 144, 4. ¶ *used substantively, a young person, a juvenile* :—Understand þū geonglic þ ic wyð þē nu gerīmige, Angl. viii. 307, 39.

**geonglicnes.** *Add* :—þænne forman synd geoguðe oððe geonglicnysse ūre tīda *cum prima sunt adolescentiae uel iuuentutis nostrae tempora,* Scint. 124, 3.

**geongling.** *Take here* iungling *in Dict., and add* :—Iunglingc eam ic *adolescentulus sum ego,* Ps. L. 118, 141. Iunglingc, Gen. 4, 23. Iunglingc *pubescentem,* Ań. Ox. 3608. Cnihtas, geonglingas *puberes,* Wrt. Voc. ii. 66, 12. Gunglingas *iuuenes,* Ps. L. 77, 63 : 148, 12 : *iuuenculos,* Angl. xiii. 374, 121. Be þám men þe hine mid geonglingum (*juvenibus*) besmīteð, Ll. Th. ii. 180, 10.

**geongra.** v. gingra : **geonian.** v. ginian : **geon-lic.** v. geong-lic.

**ge-onlīcan ;** *p.* -līcte, -līhte *To make like ; reflex. with* tō, *to pretend to be* :—Hē geonlīcte (-līhte, *v. l.*) hine sylfne tō sumum ælþeódigum men *peregrinum quempiam esse se simulans,* Gr. D. 75, 4.

**geonre ;** *adv.* Dele, *and see* geon : **ge-onrettæ.** v. ge-orrettan : **geonung.** v. ginung.

**ge-onþracian** (-an-) *to be afraid of* :—Geanðracige *horrescat,* Wülck. Gl. 251, 24.

**geópan.** The subject of the riddle is a bow, the poison it first takes in, then spits out, is the arrow.

**ge-openian.** *Add:* A. *trans.* I. *to open* a door, gate, &c., *so as to admit of passage* :—Gatu heofonan hē geopnode (*aperuit*), Ps. L. 77, 23. Se preóst nolde undón þā duru mid cǽge, ac se bisceop hī geopenade mid his worde, Hml. S. 3, 485. Geopena ongeán mē līfes geat, Hml. Th. i. 76, 3. II. *to open* a box, &c., *an enclosed space, render passage possible into* an enclosed place :—Ic geopnige mīnne mūþ, Ps. L. 77, 2. Heofonan mid worde þū geopenast, Hy. S. 106, 3. Hī geopenodon heora hordfæt, Hml. Th. i. 78, 27. Geopenigende neorxnewange *reserans paradysum,* Hy. S. 83, 11. Sié þára manna gehwǽm geopenad engla rīce, El. 1231. Hē betȳnde his eágan þe lǣs þā cwelleras gesāwon þ his eágan geopenode wǣron, Bl. H. 231, 13. II a. *figurative* :—His heortan dīegelnesse hit geopenað, and þæs ōþres heortan belocene hit þurhfærþ, Bt. 13 ; F. 38, 26. Þám bið wīte geopenad *he will go into torment,* An. 891. III. *to open, spread out* :—þu openast handa þīne, Ps. L. 144, 16. IV. *to make an opening in, cut* or *break into* :—Hē mid swere his sīdan geopenode, Hml. Th. ii. 260, 11. Geopnadon *patefacientes,* Mk. L. 2, 4. V. *to open* a way, *make clear* a passage :—Hē him duru ontȳneð, ingong geopenað, Gū. 966. Geopenige ūre sárnys ūs inßer sōðre gecyrrednysse, Hml. Th. ii. 124, 6. Bið se torr þyrel, ingong geopenad, Jul. 403. VI. *to uncover, disclose to view, shew.* See B. I. :—þā geopenedan *publicatam* (*protervorum insolentiam*), Wrt. Voc. ii. 87, 74.

VII. *to lay bare* *to the mind, disclose, reveal, declare, make known.* (1) the object a noun or pronoun :—Heó onwrīhð hire ǽwelm, þonne heó geopenaþ hiore ðeáwas (*cum mores profitetur*), Bt. 20 ; F. 70, 25. Heó þá mōd þē geopenaþ ðīnra getreówra freónda *amicorum tibi fidelium mentes detexit,* F. 72, 13. Word geopenað ælces monnes geþanc and his þeáwas, ðeáh hī hwīlum behelie, Prov. K. 58. Hē þá word geopenade þe englas ne dorston, Hml. S. 15, 165. Hē þ (*a plot*) þē geopenode, Hml. A. 98, 221. Nys nán dīhle þing þæt ne wurðe geopenod *nihil est occultum quod non scietur,* Mt. 10, 26. [Nán þing] oferwrigen þ ne beó geopenad [*nihil*] *opertum quod non reuelabitur,* An. Ox. 61, 11. (2) the object a clause :—Hió him geopenaþ hū tiédre þæs andweardan gesǽlþa sint, Bt. 20 ; F. 72, 3. Drihten sylf geopenað ūs þæt þæt sǣd is Godes word . . . þone sǣdere hē belǽfde ūs tō sécenne, Hml. Th. ii. 90, 6. Seó ætȳwnes heofonlices wundres geopenade (-opnode, *v. l.*) hū ārwyrþlīce hī wǣron tō onfónne *miraculi caelestis ostensio, quam reuerenter eae suscipiendae essent, patefecit,* Bd. 3, 11 ; Sch. 237, 4. VII a. *to open* one's heart, *disclose* one's thoughts, designs, &c. :—Hē his geðanc geopenode, and ofer eall clypode, Hml. S. 23, 320. Þæt se man geþeó on þǣre sandunge, and his ingehȳd beó geopenod, Scrd. 23, 2. VII b. *to make known, declare, spread the knowledge of* :—Gewurðe þīn willa geopenod geond ealle world, Hy. 7, 36. VIII. *to make clear, explain, expound* :—God geopenade Abrahame hwæt hē mid þære sprǽce mǣnde, Gen. 18, 20. Ūs biscopum gedafenað þ wē þá godcundan lāre . . . eów preóstum geopenan on Engliscum gereorde, for ðám þe gē ealle ne cunnon þ Lǣden understandan, Ll. Th. ii. 364, 9. Wē willað nū mid scortre trahtnunge þás rǣdinge oferyrnan and geopenian, gif heó hwæt dīgles on hyre hæbbende sȳ, Hml. Th. i. 388, 30 : Angl. viii. 335, 35. Fela wē habbað gesett ymbe þissum þingum, and gyt ūs gelustfullað þás þing tō geopenianne, 312, 41. IX. *to proclaim* :—Sī þē wuldor and lof wīde geopenod geond ealle þeóda, Hy. 9, 1. B. *intrans.* I. *to become disclosed, come into sight* :—Ic þē, weroda waldend, . . . biddan wille, þæt mē þæt goldhord, gásta scippend, geopenie (*or* = þu geopenie? *and to be taken under* A. VI), þæt yldum wæs lange behȳded, El. 792. II. *to give explanations* about a subject :—Ymbe þises bissextus gefyllednysse wē willað rūmlīcor iungum cnihtum geopenian, Angl. viii. 306, 15.

**ge-openung,** e ; *f. Opening* :—In þám dæge ūs byð æteówed seó geopenung (-opnung, *v. l.*) heofena, Wlfst. 186, 1.

**ge-orettan.** v. ge-orrettan.

**georman-leáf.** *Substitute:* georman-leáf (geormant-, geormen-), es ; *n. Mallow* :—Geormantlāb *malva,* Txts. 78, 656. Geormenleáf *malua herratice,* Wrt. Voc. i. 69, 15 : *malua erratica,* Lch. iii. 303, 22. Geormenletic (-leáf?) *malva,* Wrt. Voc. i. 31, 41. Genim geormenleáf, Lch. ii. 148, 8 : 68, 12. Lege on geormenleáf, 108, 18. Nim geormenleáf niþeweard, 80, 9. Geormanleáfa *maluarum,* An. Ox. 97. Geormenleáfa, Wrt. Voc. ii. 75, 23. [Eormeleáfes sǣd, Lch. iii. 134, 2. Geormaleáf, i. 380, 26.]

**geormen-letic.** *See preceding word.*

**georn.** *Add:* I. *eager for, desirous* of something. (1) with gen. (a) of that which is to be done or to happen :—Ne beó nǣnig man nīþa tō georn, Bl. H. 109, 28. Mánbealwes georn, Dan. 45. Is nū fūs þider gǣst sīðes georn, Gū. 1018 : 1241 : Bo. 41 : B. 2783. Wæs þǣre wīsfægra guma georn on mōde, Jul. 39. Ic wæs symles willan þīnes georn on mōde *I was ever eager in my heart to do thy will,* An. 66 : Gū. 839 : El. 268. (b) of that which is to be got :—Ne sceal hē beón tō georn deádra manna feós, Bl. H. 43, 12. Goddreáma georn gǣst, Gū. 1273. Weorðmynda georn, Met. 1, 51. Dōmes georn, An. 961 : Rä. 32, 16. Earn ǣtes georn, Jud. 210. (2) with dat. :—Ic eom sīdes fūs . . . edleánan ( = -um ; *or* edleána? *under* I. 1 b) georn, Gū. 1051. (3) with clause, *eager to do* :—Sceolan wē beón geornran þ wē Godes bebodu healdan, þonne wē ūrne teónan gewrecan, Bl. H. 33, 23. II. *diligent, zealous* :—Mē mīne ágen word sōcon, and wiðer mē wǣran georne, Ps. Th. 55, 5. II a. *diligent* about something (*but see* georne, (2)) :—Hū giorne (georne, *v. l.*) hié wǣron ǣgðer ge ymb lāre ge ymb liornunga, ge ymb ealle ðá ðiówotdōmas ðe hié Gode dōn scoldon, P. 3, 9. v. ciric-, druncen-, ēst-, feoh-, feþe-, firenlust-, fiīt-, forþ-, friþ-, gefiit-, gilp-, of-, teóþung-, unhearm-, weax-, wōh-, wrōhtgeorn.

**geornan.** v. girnan, geornian.

**georne.** *Add:* (1) *where an effort has to be made, with a will, in earnest* :—Nō ic him þæs georne ætfealh, B. 968. Geóca ūs georne, Az. 12. (2) *where a duty or business has to be done, diligently* :—Ic offylgde from fruma alle georne (*diligenter*), Lk. L. R. 1, 3. Diófolgield georne ǣghwylce geáre, þ is sulhælmessan .xv. niht on ufan Eástran . . . , Ll. Th. i. 306, 30 : i. 168, 26. Yrðe georne forðian, Angl. ix. 261, 21. Æghwilc unriht āwurpe man georne of þisan earde, Ll. Th. i. 322, 12. Gȳme hē his crīstendōmes georne, 310, 5 : 304, 6. Æghwilc crīsten man unrihtǣmed georne forbūge, 306, 24. Beorge man georne þ man þá sāwla ne forfare, 304, 16. Godes cyrican georne sécan, Bl. H. 47, 28. Ūre synna bētan georne, Wlfst. 266, 7. Beó man georne ymbe

friðes bôte, Ll. Th. i. 310, 22 : 278, 13 : ii. 290, 2. Swā hē geornor and gelômor Godes hûs sêce, Wlfst. 155, 8. Godes grið is ealra griða geornost tô healdanne, Ll. Th. i. 330, 3 : 358, 18. Man āwyrtwalige æghwylc unriht swā man geornost mæge, 376, 9 : 310, 26. Hē sceal beón ymbe sôme swā hē geornost mæg, ii. 312, 13. (3) where pains are taken to produce completeness, *carefully* :—Friþaþ and fyrþraþ swiþe georne *elaborat*, Bt. 34, 10 ; F. 148, 30. Hē gyrede hine georne mid gæstlicum wæpnum, Gū. 148. (4) where there is a strong desire to attain an end or to produce an effect, *earnestly, pressingly* (of a request, inquiry, injunction, &c.) :—Georne gefraignede *sciscitabatur*, Mt. L. 2, 4. Georne geliornade *diligenter didicit*, Mt. L. R. 2, 7. Biddan wē georne ūrne Drihten, Bl. H. 25, 27 : Ors. 4, 10 ; S. 196, 13. Loth him georne beád reste and gereorda (*he pressed upon them*), Gen. 19, 3), Gen. 2440. Crîstene men wē lærad swîðe georne þ . . ., Ll. Th. i. 372, 15 : Ors. 2, 5 ; S. 82, 28. For eal crîsten folc þingian georne, ii. 240, 4. Hē mā cēgde and geornor bæd, Bl. H. 19, 12. (5) of thinking, examining, observing, listening, &c., *carefully, attentively* :—Maria georne (giorne, L.) sceówade in ða byrgene *Maria prospexit in monumentum*, Jn. R. 20, 11. Behealdað nū georne, Bl. H. 99, 18. Þ hē his āgene dēda georne smeáge, 109, 12 : Ll. Th. i. 380, 13 : 382, 5. Hē sceal snotorlîce smeágean and georne ðurhsmūgan ealle ða ðing, Angl. ix. 259, 21. Geþence hē swîðe georne, Ll. Th. i. 376, 18. Wē ūs sylfe geðencean and gemunon þonne geornost, þonne wē gehŷron Godes bēc rædan, Bl. H. 111, 16. (6) *gladly, willingly* :—Baloham ful georne fēran wolde ðær hine mon bæd, ac his êstfulnesse witteáh se esol *Balaam pervenire ad propositum tendit, sed ejus votum animal praepedit*, Past. 255, 22. Gife ic hit þē georne, Gen. 679. Dô hē swā him þearf is, gebûge georne intô mynstre, Ll. Th. i. 306, 3. Wē willað georne lufian and healdan *gaudenter amplectimur*, 440, 22. Ne hē him Godes fyrhtu georne ondrædað *they are not willing to feel the fear of God*, Ps. Th. 54, 20. Hē geornor wolde sibbe þonne gewinn, Ors. 3, 1 ; S. 96, 18. (6 a) of the course of events, *happily, prosperously* :—Hit āgann mid heom gôdian georne *they began to have uninterrupted prosperity*, Wlfst. 14, 14. (7) *eagerly, zealously* :—Frŷnd synd hié mîne georne, Gen. 287. (8) of the passage of time, *rapidly* :—Hit tô ðam dôme nū georne neálæcð *it rapidly approaches the day of judgement*, Wlfst. 18, 14, 17. (9) with verbs of knowing, believing, &c., *well, thoroughly* :— Hē wiste ful georne *optime noverat*, Gen. 39, 3. Wē witan ful georne, Wlfst. 157, 7. Mage wē wēnan oþþe georne witan, Ll. Th. i. 238, 23. Þone þe rædgeþeaht georne cûðe, El. 1163. Ongitan giorne, Met. 29, 3. Hî þæt ongeáton and georne gesāwon, By. 84. Gereccan swā georne þone dǣl swā hē gearo stondeð, Dôm. 32. Wē georne gelŷfað, Cri. 753 : Ps. Th. 55, 4. Hē georne trūwode metodes hyldo, B. 669. Þ wē þe geornor witon, Bl. H. 15, 31 : Ll. Th. ii. 312, 25. Geornor ongietan, Ors. 2, 1 ; S. 60, 9. Þā dihteras þe his lîf geornost cûðon, Guth. 4, 24. Hē getrūwode on îdel gylp ealra geornost, Ps. Th. 51, 6. (10) *completely, entirely* :—Him gāst weorðeð georne āfyrred, Ps. Th. 103, 27. [*O. Sax. O. H. Ger.* gerno.] v. for-, un-georne.

**geornes.** v. georn-ness.

**georneste** ; *adj. Substitute :* georneste ; *adv. Earnestly* ; serio, Wrt. Voc. ii. 80, 73. v. eorneste ; *adv.*

**georn-full.** *Add :* I. *diligent, active, earnest* :—Geornfull þēn *sedulus minister*, Hy. S. 70, 25. Geornfull hālsung *intenta supplicatio*, 19, 13. Geornfull *gimnicus*, An. Ox. 18 b, 43. Þ þū mid ealles môdes geornfullan ingeþance higie, þ þū mæge becuman tô þām gesælþum, Bt. 22, 2 ; F. 78, 18. Hē cwædon þ wē genôg raðe tô þæm mere becwôman, gif wē geornfulle wæron, Nar. 11, 28 : Met. 19, 27. II. *desirous, eager* :—Geornful *cupidus* (*castitatis amator*), An. Ox. 363. (1) *desirous* of (*gen.*), *eager* for :—Rômāne wæron þæs færeltes geornfulle, Ors. 4, 10 ; S. 196, 17. Geornfulle beón Godes miltsa, Bl. H. 109, 9. (2) *desirous* to do. (a) with dat. infin. :—Þū sædest þ þū swîþe geornfull wǣre hit tô gehŷranne, Bt. 22, 2 ; F. 78, 4. Ðæt bið ðæt mon his stemne gehiére þonne ðā gecorenan men giornfulle bióð his worda tô gehlystanne *cujus vocem amicos auscultare est electos quosque verbum praedicationis illius desiderare*, Past. 381, 18. (b) with clause :—Wæs hē sôna geornfull þ hē wolde diégellîce þone crîstendôm onwendan *christianam religionem arte potius quam pestilens insectatus*, Ors. 6, 31 ; S. 286, 2. Martha wæs geornful þæt heó þon Hǣlende tô gecwēmnesse þegnode, Bl. H. 67, 28. II a. *desirous to possess, avaricious, hard* :—Ðū wistes þ ic gearnfull (georn-, R.) monn am, nimmes þ ic ne gesett *sciebas quod ego austerus homo sum, tollens quod non posui*, Lk. L. 19, 22. III. *anxious, solicitous about.* (1) with prep. :—Hē wæs geornful ymb Drihtnes lāre, Bl. H. 217, 9. Ðæt hié ymb hié selfe swā geornfulle sién ðæt hié tô slāwlîce ðæra ne giémen þe him befæste sién *ut sic in propria sollicitudine ferveant, ut a commissorum custodia minime torpescant*, Past. 190, 23. Huæd of ôðrum geornfullo (*solliciti*) gié sînt, Lk. L. 12, 26. (2) with clause :—Nallað gié gearnfulle (*solliciti*) wosa huu gié geonuearde, Lk. L. 12, 11. Geornfullo, Lk. L. R. 12, 22.

**geornful-lic** ; *adj. Careful, zealous, assiduous* :—Ðā ic ðǣre heortan heardnesse mid geornfullicre fandunge and āscunge and ðreáunge tôslāt

---

*cum cordis duritia vel studiosis percunctationibus vel maturis correptionibus scinditur*, Past. 155, 4.

**geornfullîce.** *Add :* (1) where a great effort is made, *eagerly, earnestly.* Cf. georne, (1) :—Geornfullîce hogiendum *enixe nitentibus*, An. Ox. 4373. (2) *diligently.* Cf. georne, (2) :—Ealle þās þēnunge begān and geornfullîce (*diligenter*) wyrcean, R. Ben. 19, 11. Þ wē swîþe geornfullîce ûs geþŷdon tô ûrum gebedum, Bl. H. 133, 7. Þ hē swā þæslic folc Drihtne geornfullîce gestrŷnde, Lch. iii. 434, 9. (3) *carefully, attentively.* Cf. georne, (5) :—Spyriende geornfullîcor *scrutando enixius* (*rimaretur*), An. Ox. 3104. (4) *willingly.* Cf. georne, (6) :—Geornfullîcor *libentius*, An. Ox. 281. (5) *well.* Cf. georne, (9) :—Geornfullîce *sollerter* (*nosse*), An. Ox. 855.

**geornfulnes.** *Add :* (1) *eagerness.* (a) *desire to have* :—Þæs êcean lîfes hē sceal mid ealre geornfulnesse (*concupiscentia*) girnan, R. Ben. 17, 22. (b) *desire to do* :—Þæt gefeoht wæs gedôn mid micelre geornfullnesse of þæm folcum bǣm *ingentibus utrimque animis pugna committitur*, Ors. 3, 9 ; S. 126, 2 : 5, 11 ; S. 236, 20. (2) *earnestness.* Cf. georne, (4) :—Mid micelre geornfulnesse æt Gode biddan forgifennesse ealra gylta, Hml. A. 142, 114. (3) *diligence, studious care* :—Fyrewittre carfulnysse geornfulnes *curiosae sollicitudinis sollertia*, An. Ox. 907. Geornfulnes *diligentia* i. *cura*, 1328. Geornfulnysse *curiositate*, 143 : *intentione*, 165 : *studio*, 295 : *industriam*, 43 : *operam, studium*, 57, 11.

**geornian** ; *p.* ode. (1) *to desire, ask for* :—Gedô þ gē georniað þāra þinga þe gē mē rihtlic begytan mæg . . . Gif ic eów ealla eówra þinga geunne on þā gerāde þe gē mē mîne georniað (*exoptetis*), Ll. Th. i. 196, 29–32. Þ hē on þā wîsan hire geornige þ hē hŷ healdan wille swā wær his wîf sceal, 254, 6. (2) *to beg* :—Hē gesaet æt woeg giornade *sedebat juxta uiam mendicans*, Mk. L. 10, 46. (3) *to entreat earnestly* :—Cwôm tô him licðrower giornede hine *uenit ad eum leprosus depraecans eum*, Mk. L. 1, 40. v. girnan.

**georn-lic.** *Add : earnest* :—Hwæþere for his geornlicum bēnum þ hē him fultum sôhte *ne tamen obnixe petenti nil ferret auxilii*, Bd. 3, 7 ; Sch. 218, 5.

**geornlîce.** *Add :*—Geornlîce *anxie*, Wrt. Voc. ii. 8, 60 : *enixe*, 29, 36 : *examusim*, 30, 6 : 107, 73 : *obnixe*, 115, 20 : 65, 30. Geornlîcor *enixius*, 32, 60. Geor[n]lî[cor] *sollertius*, An. Ox. 56, 132. Geornlîcost *instantissime*, Kent. Gl. 1159. (1) *with a will, with all one's power, vigorously.* Cf. georne, (1) :—Him se gŷsel ongan geornlîce fylstan, By. 265. Heó geornlîce mîne sāwle swŷðe onbîgdon, Ps. Th. 56, 7. Hî geornlîce Godes costadan *they did all they could to tempt God*, 77, 20. (2) *diligently.* Cf. georne, (2) :—Hié geornlîce heora gebedum ætfulgon, Bl. H. 201, 18. Synna geornlîce bētan, Ll. Th. i. 310, 6. Tô Godes weófedan geornlîce gebûgan, 334, 30. Dôn geornlîce þancas, Bl. H. 39, 13. Geornlîce earnian, þegnian, wyrcan, Wlfst. 180, 20 : Gen. 585 : Az. 109. Nis on ǣnigne tîman unriht ālŷfed, and þeáh man sceal freólstîdan geornlîcost beorgan, Ll. Th. i. 398, 18. Gŷm þū þæs earmestan geornlîcost, Wlfst. 250, 7. (3) *earnestly, urgently.* Cf. georne, (4) :— Sceolan wē geornlîce biddan, Bl. H. 19, 15 : Ll. Lbmn. 415, 28 : Cri. 262. Ic wille geornlîce tô Gode cleopian, Bt. 3, 4 ; F. 6, 27. Geornlîce lǣran, Ll. Th. i. 314, 4. Loth hig laðode geornlîce *compulit illos*, Gen. 19, 3. Geornlîce sêc þ þū sôð wite, Cri. 440. For eal crîsten folc þingian geornlîce, Ll. Th. i. 332, 29. Wæs him beboden geornlîcor þ . . ., Bl. H. 215, 17. (4) *carefully, attentively, intently.* Cf. georne, (5) :—Ûs is suiðe geornlîce tô gehiéranne *solerter audiendum est*, Past. 315, 23 : Bl. H. 55, 6. Seó môdor sæt geornlîce hlystende hire tale, Hml. S. 30, 320. Wuton wē þ geornlîce gemunan, Bl. H. 125, 3. Smeáge man geornlîce *diligentissime perscrutantes*, Deut. 19, 18. Geþencean wē geornlîce, Bl. H. 37, 2 : 115, 5. Ongon ic geornlîcor þā stôwe sceáwigan, Nar. 27, 19. (5) *willingly, gladly* ; cpve. *rather.* Cf. georne, (6) :—Sel geornlîce þte ðū se gefreód *give willingly* (?) *that you may be freed* (but the Latin is : Da operam liberari), Lk. L. R. 12, 58. Sē þe wile geornlîce þone Godes cwide singan, Sal. 84. Geornlîcor *propensius* (*laudari censeo*), An. Ox. 591 : Wrt. Voc. ii. 65, 67. (6) with verbs of knowing, understanding, *well.* Cf. georne, (9) :—Georlîce *diligenter* (*agnosce*), Kent. Gl. 1037. Geornlîce ongitan, Bl. H. 203, 25 : 205, 2. [*O. H. Ger.* gernlîhho *diligenter, libenter.*]

**georn-ness.** *Take here* geornes *in Dict., and add :* (1) *diligence, assiduity* :—Geornes *industria*, Wrt. Voc. ii. 111, 23. Seó gehŷrnes and seó geornnes ne bið nyt on þǣm ungelŷfdum mannum (cf. hū nyt bið þǣm men þēh hē geornlîce gehŷre, 4), Bl. H. 55, 31. ¶ of geornnesse *on purpose* :—Gif hwā of geornnesse and gewealdes ofsleá his þone nēhstan *si quis per industriam occiderit proximum suum*, Ll. Th. i. 46, 26. (1 a) *ill-timed assiduity, importunity* :—Hē fylgede þām hālgan were mid gemāglicum bedum . . . Se ārwyrða fæder wæs geswænced mid unluste his swiðlican geornnesse (*nimietatis ejus taedio affectus*), Gr. D. 156, 6. Fore giornisse his ārîseð *propter inprobitatem eius surget*, Lk. L. R. 11, 8. (2) *desire* for something :—Giornisse lofes mennisces *appetitio laudis humanae*, Mt. p. 14, 19. v. feoh-, firwet-, lust-, sib-, wîf-, yfel-geornness ; girn-ness.

**geornung.** v. girning : **geornustlíce.** v. eornostlíce : **georran.**
v. girran.

**ge-orrettan, -onrettan, -órettan** *to disgrace, put to shame* :—
Georrettan *infamare*, Wrt. Voc. ii. 92, 34 : 47, 26. Ealle beóđ geórette,
eác gescende *confundantur*, Ps. Th. 82, 13. Elle genóman æsnas his and
geonrettæ ofslógun *reliqui tenuerunt servos eius et contumelia adfectos
occiderunt*, Mt. R. 22, 6.

**georsod.** *Dele* : **georstan-dæg.** v. gistran-dæg : **georsten-lic.**
v. gistern-lic.

**georstu** *Oh* :—Georstu Dryhten gefreá sáwle míne *O Domine libera
animam meam*, Ps. Srt. 114, 4 : 115, 16 : 117, 25. [*From* (?) gehéres
þú. Cf. gehéresthū *heus*, Wrt. Voc. ii. 110, 26 ; *and for a similar
interjectional use cf.* sehđe *ecce*, Ps. Srt. 32, 18 ; 38, 6.]

**ge-ortríwan, -treówan** ; *p. de.* *Take here* ge-ortréwan *in Dict.,
and add* : I. *to despair of.* (1) *with gen.* Cf. I a :—Ne þú tó wáclíce
geortreówe æniges gódes *spemque fugato nes dolor adsit*, Met. 5, 35.
(2) *with prep.* :—Hé næfre ne geortreówe be Godes mildse *de Dei
misericordia nunquam desperare*, R. Ben. 19, 2. Þá đe ne lǽtađ ge-
ortréwan (-treówan, *v. l.*) be þýs andweardan lífe *quae nec praesentis
solamen temporis abesse patiantur*, Bt. 10 ; S. 23, 7. Ne sceolon wé
næfre geortrýwan be Godes mildheortnesse, Ll. Th. ii. 400, 1. (3)
*with clause* :—Sé đe tó lange wúnađ on đæm wlacum treówum, hé
geortreówđ đæt hé æfre mæge on welme weordan (*calore desperato*),
Past. 447, 9. (4) *absolute, to despair* :—Hé geortríewđ *in desperatione
est*, Past. 447, 11. I a. *reflex. to cause* (*oneself*) *to despair.*
Cf. I. 1 :—þæt đú þe ne geortrýwe nánes gódes, Bt. 6 ; F. 14,
35. II. *to doubt, distrust.* (1) *to doubt the possibility of, be
uncertain about something,* (a) *with acc.* :—Þonne bið ús gesewen þæt ús
ǽr gesǽd wæs, þeáh þe wé hit nú geortrýwan (-trúwian, *v. l.*), for đý
wé hit geseón ne magon, Wlfst. 3, 18. (aa) *with acc. and clause in
apposition* :—Nis þ tó geortrýwanne (-enne, *v. l.*), þ on úre yldo þ beón
mihte *nec diffidendum est nostra aetate fieri potuisse*, Bd. 4, 19 ; Sch.
441, 7. (b) *with clause* :—Hé geortreóweđ hweþer hí sóđe sýn, for
þon þe hé næfre ne cúþe þurh gewisse áfandunge . . . hí geortreówdon
hwæđer hí sóđe wǽron þe næron *quia per experimentum non novit,
veraciter esse diffidat* . . . *diffidunt an vera sint*, Gr. D. 261, 18–22.
(2) *not to trust* in something :—Sý þu næfre swá synful þæt þu æfre
geortrýwe on Godes mildheortnysse, Angl. xii. 517, 26. (3) *not to
trust* to a person (*dat.*) *for doing something* (*clause*) :—Ne geortríewe
(-trúwige, Bos. 48, 45) ic ná Gode þæt hé ús ne mæge gescildan *I trust
to God that he can preserve us*, Ors. 2, 5 ; S. 86, 4.

**ge-ortrúwian.** *Add* : I. *to despair of.* (1) *with gen.* :—Geseah
hé þ án leó genóm þ cild . . . hé đá wæs geortrúwod þæs cildes, Hml. S.
30, 178. (2) *with prep.* :—Be Godes mildheortnesse geortrúwian *de
Dei misericordia desperare*, R. Ben. I. 22, 11. I a. *reflex. to cause*
(*oneself*) *to despair, to despair* :—Ne geortrúwige nán man hine sylfne
for his synna micelnysse, Hml. Th. ii. 124, 30. ¶ ge-ortrúwod
*desperate* :—Hwilc ánwilnys and geortrúwad wylla, Hml. S. 4,
310. II. *to make doubtful about* :—Nolde God þ hí wǽron
geortrúweda þám wéne þæra ælmæssena *ut non de eleemosynarum
aestimatione fallerentur*, Gr. D. 331, 28. II a. *to doubt.* v.
ge-ortríwan ; II. 1 a, II. 3.

**ge-orwénan.** *Add* : (1) *absolute* :—Gif đu georwénst *si despera-
veris*, Kent. Gl. 925. Ne georwén đu *ne desperis*, 702. (2) *to despair
of.* (a) *with acc.* :—Nán georwénan scyl forgyfenysse *nullus desperare
debet ueniam*, Scint. 48, 6. (b) *with* (*negative*) *clause* :—Đá þe hé
georwénde þ him næfre ofer þ ne mihte beón geleođad *cum relaxari se
jam posse desperaret*, Gr. D. 326, 11. (c) *to despair of a person* (*acc.*)
in respect to some particular (*clause*) :—þ sculdt wæs georwéned fram
þám lǽcum þ hé æfre trum wurde *a medicis desperatus*, Gr. D. 338, 29.
(3) *to despair of* (*be*) :—Ne scealt þu ná georwénan be þíra synna
forgyfenesse, Archiv cxxii. 257, 20.

**ge-orwirþan** ; *p. de To dishonour, defame, traduce* :—Georuuierdid
*traductus*, Txts. 100, 990. Georwyrđed *traducta*, Wrt. Voc. ii. 85, 14.

**ge-orwirþe** ; *adj. Dishonoured, traduced* :—Georuuyrde *traductus*,
Wrt. Voc. ii. 122, 59.

**ge-orwyrþed.** v. ge-orwirþan : **geó-sceaft** *is masc., not fem.* Cf.
frum-sceaft : **geosterlíc.** *Dele* : **geostra.** v. gister-dæg, gistran-æfen,
-dæg, -niht : **geót.** v. blód-geót.

**geótan.** *Add* : I. *trans.* (1) *to pour, cause to flow.* (a) *the
object a liquid or powder* :—*Aquarius,* þ is sé þe wæter gýt (geót, *v. l.*),
Lch. iii. 246, 5. Hé geát on græswong háligra blód, Jul. 6. Hí mid
spere of mínre sídan swát út guton, Cri. 1449. Geót ou bollan, Lch. ii.
50, 12. Geót on múđ þ ilce dúst, 140, 2. (aa) *to shed tears* :—Ealle
teáras guton *omnes lacrimas fundunt*, Bd. 4, 28 ; Sch. 523, 7. (b) *with
a non-material object* :—Sió slǽwđ giétt slǽp on đone monnan *pigredo
immittit soporem*, Past. 283, 6. Hí gártorn geótađ gífrum deófle, Sal.
145. (2) *to pour away, squander* :—þæt hé ne ágále gæstes þearfe, ne
on gylp geóte, Cri. 818. (3) *to found, cast, make with molten metal* :—
Wurdon tóbrocene þára hǽþenra goda anlícnyssa þurh þæra manna
handa þe hí macodon and guton, Hml. S. 29, 181. II. *intrans.*

(1) *to pour* with a liquid :—Hí teárum geótađ, Cri. 1567. (2) *to pour,
flow, gush,* (a) *of the* (*violent*) *motion of a liquid* (lit. *or* fig.) :—Léton
geótan háte streámas, Ruin. 43. Geótende stréam unrihtwísnessa mé
gedréfdon *torrentes iniquitatis conturbaverunt me*, Ps. Th. 17, 4. Flód
ofslóh, gifen geótende, giganta cyn, B. 1690. Geótende gegrind grund
eall forswealg, An. 1592. (b) *of the motion of many bodies* :—Þá
gǽstas on ælce healfe in guton *subeuntibus ab undique illis*, Guth. Gr. 127,
109. (c) *of a non-material object,* e. g. speech :—Geótende gielp
*boasting that pours forth in floods*, Fä. 41. v. geond-, in-, of-geótan ;
blód-, teár-geótende.

**geótend,** es ; *m.* I. *one who pours or sheds.* v. blód-geótend. II.
*an artery* :—Geótend, sinewind *arteriae* (printed *anteriae*), Wrt. Voc.
ii. 8, 29. *See next word.*

**geótend-æder,** e ; *f. An artery* :—Gif þu geótendædre ne mæge
áwríþan, genim þ selfe blód þe ofyrnđ, gebærn on hátum stáne, and
gegníd tó dúste, lege on þá ædre þ dúst, and áwríđ swíđe, Lch. ii. 148,
16 : 16, 7. *See preceding word.*

**geótend-lic** (?) ; *adj. Molten* :—Geotenlic (geótendlic (?), gegotenlic
(? v. ge-geótan ; II ; *and cf. O. H. Ger.* ki-cozzanlíh *fusorius*), goten-
lic (?)) *fusilis*, Germ. 394, 284.

**geótere.** *Add* : [ʒeetere *conflator*, Wick. Jer. 6, 29. Belle-ʒeter
*campanarius*, Prompt. 30.]

**ge-óþer** (?) *other* :—His cnihtas and ealle đe geóđre híredmen, C. D.
vi. 155, 9.

**geóting** *pouring* ; *founding.* [*Prompt.* ʒetinge *fusio* : *Wick.* ʒeting
*conflatio.*] v. in-geóting.

**geów.** v. gíw : **ge-owedan.** *Dele* : **geówian,** Angl. xiii. 427, 894.
v. eówan : **geoxa.** v. gesca : **geoxung.** v. giscung : **gep.** *l.* gép. v.
gcáp : **ge-palmtwígod.** *l.* -twigod : **ge-picod.** v. pician.

**ge-píled** ; *adj. Provided with spikes* :—'Æteówiađ his gesihđum eal
þæt wíta tól.' Þá wurdon forđ áborene ísene clútas . . . and leádene
swipa and óđre gepílede swipa, Hml. Th. i. 424, 20. Mid gepíledum
swipun swingende, 426, 22 : 432, 14. v. píl.

**ge-pílian** *to beat in a mortar* :—Swilce hít on pílan gepílod wǽre
*quasi pilo tusum*, Ex. 16, 14.

**ge-pilod** *piled up. Dele, and see preceding word.*

**ge-píned.** *Substitute* : **ge-pínian** ; *p.* ode *To torment, punish* :—
[Đá þá leásen gewíten hí swíđe gepínedon, Hml. A. 174, 161. Hé heom
ætealde of þan Nazarenísscen kinge, hwu hé gepíned wæs, 194, 38.]
Gepínodes *semustulati*, Germ. 397, 348. Hulco wéro đrouendo hreáferas
suá geearnadon þte hiá wére gepíned scearplice *qualia sint passuri raptores
sic maerentur puniri tenaces*, Lk. p. 9, 4.

**ge-piporian.** v. piporian.

**ge-plantian** *to plant.* *Take here* ge-plantod *in Dict., and add* :—
Đæt đú getimbre and geplantige *ut aedifices et plantes*, Past. 441, 32.
Treów þe geplantod is *lignum quod plantatum est*, Ps. L. 1, 3.
[*O. H. Ger.* ge-pfianzôn *propagare.*]

**ge-platod** *beaten into thin plates* :—Geplatod *obrizum*, An. Ox. 11, 61.
v. platian.

**ge-pós.** *l.* -pos, *and add* :—Swá byđ se ealda man ceald and snoflig ;
flegmata þ byđ hráca ođđe geposu, deriađ þám ealdan, Angl. viii. 299, 36.

**ge-prician** ; *p.* ode. I. *to prick, stimulate* :—Hé nys gepricud
(*stimulatus*) on unrótnysse gyltes, Scint. 79, 8. II. *to mark with
dots* :—Seó forme ábēcēđ ys bútan pricon, and seó óđer ys gepricod on
þá swýđran healfe, and seó þrydde on þá wynstran healfe, Angl. viii. 332,
43. III. *to note* :—Se lust ys tó witanne swá wé hér bufan gepric-
odon hwǽr se forma mónđ cume tó mankynne, Angl. viii. 324, 21.

**ge-punian.** *Add* :—Gepuna đá wyrte tósomne, Lch. i. 374, 7.
Genim þás wyrte on mortere wel gepunode, 312, 11. Gepunede beáne
*fabe frese vel pilate*, Wrt. Voc. i. 21, 26.

**ge-racent[t]eágian, -racodteágian** ; *pp.* od *To chain, put in
chains* :—Hé weard geracenteágod [and] betǽht tó þám gewinne (cf. hé
wearđ gelǽht tó þám gecampe, and on racenteágum gelǽd, Hml. Th.
ii. 500, 8), Hml. S. 31, 35. Geracodteágodum earnum *catenatis lacertis*,
Wrt. Voc. ii. 129, 47.

**ge-rád.** *Add* : [*The word seems to be feminine sometimes,* e. g. on
hwylcre gerád, Gr. D. 172, 29 ; *so that in the phrase* on þá gerád þæt,
*it may perhaps be, at least sometimes, rather fem. sing. than neut. pl.*
Cf. ge-sceaft *for declension.*] I. *understanding, discernment* :—
Hlystađ georne and nytađ ná đe máre, lóciađ bráde and nán þing gecnáwađ
mid ænigean geráde, þæs đe eów þearf sý, Wlfst. 47, 14. Þ sceolon
preóstas witan mid fullum geráde (cf. witan mid wísdóme, 305, 8), Angl.
viii. 312, 13. Þ se sceáwre wite mid fullum geráde þe þis gewrit áspyrađ,
331, 1. Ic myugige þæne þe þis wilnađ mid geráde áspyrian, 299, 3. Findan
mid geráde, 332, 46. II. *reason, sense, discretion* :—Hú gerádes
mæg se biscep brúcan đære hirdelican áre, gif hé self drohtađ on đám
eorđlicum tielongum *qua mente animarum praesul honore pastorali utitur,
si in terrenis negotiis ipse versatur*, Past. 133, 3. Gesetton đá hálgan
fæderas þ wé fæston mid geráde, Hml. S. 13, 102. Đá réceleásan menu
þe bútan geráde lybbađ, and on eallum þingum wadađ ou heora ágenum
willan, 17, 238. Ánfealde wíse on fullan geráde, Ll. Th. ii. 318,

39.    **III.** *condition, order of things, mode:*—Ic ne can hwilcere ændebyrdnesse and on hwylcre (hwylc, *v. l.*) gerád þ beón mæg, þ eall middaneard sȳ gesewen fram ánum mæn *non conjicere scio quonam ordine fieri potest, ut mundus omnis ab homine uno videatur*, Gr. D. 172, 29. Ic wolde þ mē wǽre gecȳþed on hwilc gerád (*quo ordine*) þ mihte beón þ . . . , 149, 25. Wē wyllað ámearkian þǽra twelf mónða naman, and gecȳðan eall þ gerád þ heora gehwylcum folgað, Angl. viii. 305, 28. Stande on þæt ilice gerád on ēcnesse swā hwæt swā Crīste geseald biþ on cyricena ǽhtum, Lch. iii. 444, 10.    **IV.** *condition settled between persons, understanding arrived at by persons, stipulation:*—Eádmund lēt eal Cumbraland tō Malculme on þ gerád þ hē wǽre his midwyrhta, Chr. 945 ; P. 110, 34 : 1091 ; P. 226, 4. Ealle þā men þe hié on ðeówdōme hæfdon hié gefreódon, on þæt gerád þæt hē him áðas swóran þ . . . , Ors. 4, 9 ; S. 190, 31. Þā Pyhtas heom ábǽdon wíf æt Scottum, on þā gerád (þ forewyrd, *v. l.*) þ . . . , Chr. P. 3, 16. Hī wurdon sehte on þā gerád þ hē nǽfre eft Englisce ne Frencisce intō þām lande ne gelógige, 1093 ; P. 228, 28.    **IV a.** *a condition on which depends the performance of something, upon which a grant or the like is consequent:*—Ic wille eówres geunnan eów on þā gerád (geráde, 196, 32) þe gē mē geunnan mínes, Ll. Th. i. 198, 1. Þ hē hine on þá gerád (geráde, *v. l.*) feormige þ hē hine tō folcryhte gelǽde, gif hé gylt gewyrce, 204, 7. Þ þá ealle beón gearwe . . . tō farenne þider ic wille . . . on þá gerád (geráde þe, *v. l.*) hȳ nǽfre eft on eard ne cuman, 220, 8. Þ se hláford hine oþþe þá mágas on þ ilce gerád út niman þe man þá menn út nimð þe æt ordále fūle weorðað, 238, 31.    **V.** *design, intention, (in) order (that):*—On þá gerád *ea intentione*, Wrt. Voc. ii. 142, 20 : Wülck. Gl. 87, 1. Marius bæd þæt him mon sealde þone seofoþan consulatum and eác þæt gewin . . . Þá Silla geácsade on hwelc gerád Marius cōm tō Rōme *Marius . . . adfectavit septimum consulatum, et bellum suscipere Mithridaticum, quo Sulla cognito*, Ors. 5, 11 ; S. 236, 8. Þ man ágife þá ciricsceattas and þá sáwlsceattas tō þām stōwum þe hit mid riht tō gebyrige . . . on þá gerád þ (*in order that*) þá his brúcan æt þám háligan stōwum þe heora cirican begán willað, Ll. Th. i. 196, 10.    v. un-gerád.

**ge-rád;** *adj.*    *Add:* **I.** *skilled, instructed:*—Wíte þú, geráda preóst, Angl. viii. 330, 17. On ðám heofonlican lífe beóð ealle ful wíse, and on gástlicre láre full geráde, Hml. Th. i. 270, 33.    **II.** *well arranged, ordered, disposed, adapted:*—Ne mæg nán mon on þisse andweardan lífe eallunga gerád beón wiþ his wyrd *nemo facile cum fortunae suae conditione concordat*, Bt. 11, 1 ; F. 32, 11. Seó tunge þe hæfde getinge sprǽce and geráde, Wlfst. 148, 1.    **III.** *constituted, of such and such a kind:*—Sió áheardung is on twā wísan gerád *the hardening is of two kinds*, Lch. ii. 204, 6.    ¶ *with adverbs.* (1) hū gerád *of what kind*; qualis:—Ic mæg ongitan hū gerád þises mannes líf ys, Guth. 72, 2. Ongan ic ácsian hū gerád hiora gegaderung wæs . . . hǽmedes, þe þæs gástes, Hml. A. 200, 160. (2) swā gerád *such*; talis, hujusmodi, istiusmodi, illiusmodi:—Swā gerád *istiusmodi*, Ælfc. Gr. 74, 10. Hit is sum swā gerád þ his nis náu neódþearf, Bt. 41, 3 ; F. 250, 3. Be swā gerádes monnes slege. Gif mon swā geráde mon ofsleá, Ll. Th. i. 80, 1–2. For swā gerádum gylte *pro tali culpa*, R. Ben. 71, 9. Se crístena and se góda Theodorus . . . God gescifte ǽnne swā geráde mann (*a good Christian*) . . . se ilca góda mann . . . , Hml. S. 23, 410–417. Swā geráde mánswican, Wlfst. 55, 6. Sume yfele menn swā geráde beóð *perversi quique tales sunt*, Past. 363, 14. Suā suā managra cynna wyrta and grasa beóð gerád, 173, 20. Mid swā gerádan dǽdan, Wlfst. 55, 4. Swā geráde wyrta, Lch. ii. 280, 19. Swā geráde (*hujusmodi*) ælmyssan dǽlan, Ll. Th. ii. 222, 8. (3) þus gerád *of this kind* ; hujus(ce)modi, talis :—Þus gerád *huiusmodi*, ðus gerád man *huiusmodi homo*, ðus geráde men *huiusmodi homines*, Ælfc. Gr. Z. 74, 8. Him þúhte þ þus gerád ungelimp . . . geearnod wǽre, Ll. Th. i. 270, 11. Þus gerádes mannes *huiusmodi hominis*, Ælfc. Gr. Z. 74, 8, 18. Þus ger- ráddre (-ráddere, 11, 12) besceúwunge *huiuscemodi contemplationis*, An. Ox. 243 : 998. Þus gerád gód *huiuscemodi*, i. *tale bonum*, 588. Fæstenu, ælmyssan and óþre þus geráde (*huiusmodi*), Scint. 52, 9. Þus gerádra mihta *huiuscemodi*, i. *talium miraculorum*, An. Ox. 3062. Mid þus gerádum (*huiusmodi*) gerýnum, 40, 12 : Mk. 9, 37.    v. of-gerád ; ge-rǽde.

**ge-rádegian.**    *Add:* , -rádigian *to arrange* a matter :—Ðis ðe ic tō sibbe and tō gesehtnesse betweoh þám mynstre gerádigod (þe radi god, MS.) hæbbe (cf. *the title of the charter*: De aquis et molendinis constitutio regis Eadgari), C. D. B. iii. 417, 5.

**ge-rádelíce.** v. ge-rádlíce: **ge-radian** (= ge-hradian), R. Ben. 73, 14.

**ge-rádian.**    *Add:* **I.** *to reckon* (?) :—Þe is behéfe þing þ þú gemete on getæl, þ ys swylce ic þus hyt gehrádige (? *or* gehradige *do it quickly*. v. ge-hradian), Angl. viii. 303, 27.    **II.** *to prepare* :—Se mæssepreóst sceal cild fullian, swā raðe swā man raðost mæge hí gerádian tō fulluhte, Ll. Th. ii. 384, 27.

**ge-rádlic ;** *adj. Reasonable, proper, appropriate :*—Nú wē ealles ymbe þás þing geornlíce smeágeað, . . . wel gerádlic hyt eác þingð ús þ wē hēr tō gecnytton þá epactas . . Nú hit geríst þ wē þissa epacta ápinsiun, Angl. viii. 300, 44. Nú wē sprǽce habbað ymbe þone bissextum, hyt byð gerádlic þ wē ápinsiun his sīð, 305, 46. Nú habbe wē be dǽle gehrepod ymbe his sīð, nú þingð ūs þ hyt sȳ swȳðe gerádlic þ wē gecȳðon . . . , 307, 1.

**ge-rádlíce ;** *adv. Intelligently, clearly :*—Genōh gerádlíce (-ráde-, *v. l.*) ic wát *plane scio*, Gr. D. 91, 5. Ic swā gerádelíce ne can *nec conjicere scio*, 172, 28. Þá epactas þe wíse preóstas oft ymbe gerádlíce wurdliað, Angl. viii. 300, 45. Wē habbað ymbe þǽre sunnan ryne manega þing gerádlíce átrahtnod, 308, 15. Cf. ge-rǽdelíce.

**ge-rádnes.**    *The word is not found in the printed vocabularies.*

**ge-radod.** *Substitute* (?): ge-rádod ; *adj. Intelligent, reasonable :*—Móna se syx and twēntigoða, cild ácenned gemindig, mǽden gerádod, Lch. iii. 196, 7.

**ge-rádscipe.**    *Add:* *intelligence, understanding :*—Nis ǽnig man þætte þæs gerádscipes swā bereáfod sié, þæt hē andsware ǽnige ne cunne findan on ferhðe, gif hé frugnen bið, Met. 22, 50.

**ge-rǽc.** v. ge-rec.

**ge-rǽcan.**    *Dele passage from* Met. 5, 31, *and add :* **I.** *trans.* (1) *to stretch out, extend* the hand, &c. :—Petre hond ðú geráhtest (*porrexisti*), Rtl. 101, 42. Geráhte (*extendens*) hond in ðegum, Mt. L. 12, 49 : 14, 31 : Mk. L. R. 1, 41. Swíðre giræc *dexteram extende*, Rtl. 14, 38. Hē ne mihte his handa tō his múðe gerǽcan, Hml. Th. ii. 96, 23. (1 a) *with immaterial object, to present* a case, claim, &c. :—Hē móste mid his foráðe his hláford ǽspelian æt mistlican neódan, and his onspǽce gerǽcan mid rihte, Ll. Th. i. 192, 3. (1 b) *construction uncertain* :—Gerǽcean *pretendere*, Wrt. Voc. ii. 67, 52. (2) *to hold out* something *and give it* to a person, *hand* to a person :—Hē onfēng hláfe and bræc and giráhte him, Lk. R. L. 24, 33. (2 a) *with immaterial object, to give, yield, grant* :—Hē clǽne girȳno ús smyltnisse giræce (*tribuat*), Rtl. 31, 30. (3) *to succeed in touching* by stretching the hand or some other part of the body :—Se hróf hæfde mislice heáhnysse ; on sumere stōwe hine man mihte mid heáfde gerǽcan, on sumere mid handa earfoðlíce, Hml. Th. i. 508, 19. On sumre stōwe se hróf wæs þ man mid his handa neálíce gerǽcean mihte, in sumre eáþelíce mid heáfde-gehrínan, Bl. H. 207, 22. Him wæs gesewen þ hē meahte mid his handum gerǽcean heofenes tungol, Shrn. 111, 29. (3 a) *to obtain by effort* :—Of þyssere ylcan byrig mangunge ic mē þ feoh gerǽhte, Hml. S. 23, 670. Hit biþ geornlic þæt mon heardlíce gníde þone hnescestan mealmstán æfter þǽm þ hē þence þone soelestan hwetstán on tō gerǽceanne *it is desirable that very soft stone be rubbed hard, if it is thought that the best whetstone is to be obtained from it*, Ors. 4, 13 ; S. 212, 29. (3 b) *to obtain by seizing, get at* :—Hē on þá burg fǽrende wæs, and hié geráhte *iter fecit, cepitque urbem*, Ors. 2, 4 ; S. 74, 6. Hié wurdon swíþe meteleáse . . . þon hie hié ne meahton nánne mete gerǽcan, Chr. 918 ; P. 100, 1. (3 c) *to take* from (*on*) a person :—Hē on þám fǽrsceaðan feorh gerǽhte, By. 142. Hié lange wǽron þæt dreógende ǽr heora áðer mehte on ōþrum sige gerǽcan, ǽr Alexander late unweorðlicne sige geráhte *diu anceps pugna tandem tristem pene victoriam Macedonibus dedit*, Ors. 3, 9 ; S. 134, 8 : 3, 1 ; S. 96, 33. (4) *to succeed in touching* with a weapon, *to strike, wound* :—Ic áglǽcan orde gerǽhte, hildebille, B. 556. Hē mid orde ánne gerǽhte flotan, By. 226. Sē þe his þeóden þearle gerǽhte, 158. v. ge-reccan ; **VI.** (5) *to come to, arrive at* a place, object, &c. :—Swā wíde swā þá wítelác geráhton rúm land wera, Gen. 2555. Ðá þe cyricean gerǽcean magon, Ll. Th. ii. 420, 12. (5 a) *with a personal object, to get at* for hostile or friendly intercourse :—Hē mehte ǽgherne (here) gerǽcan, gif hié ǽnigne feld sécan wolden, Chr. 894 ; P. 84, 26. Bútan hē þone bisceop gerǽcean (*adire*) ne mæge, Ll. Th. ii. 170, 21. Gif hē bisceop gerǽcan ne mæge *si ad episcopum pervenire nequeat*, 176, 33.    **II.** *intrans.* (1) *to stretch out, extend* a certain distance :—Hyre leóman ne magon tō þám lande gerǽcan, Lch. iii. 260, 11. (2) *to move, go* :—Ic þurh hylles hróf gerǽce, Rä. 16, 27.    **III.** *construction uncertain :*—Gerǽhte *transit*, An. Ox. 46, 12.

**ge-rǽd** *elegans.* v. ge-rǽde.

**ge-rǽdan** *to advise,* ge-rǽdan *to arrange.* [*These two verbs seem to have coalesced* (v. rǽdan), *and are taken together.*] *Add:* **I.** *to advise, suggest :*—Hē him tō gefeccean hēt his witan, þ hí him gerǽddon hwæt him þe ðám sélost ðúhte, tō dōn[n]e wǽre, Lch. iii. 426, 12. God him (*Decius*) ðis geþanc on móde ásende . . . and Decius lēt him tō rǽde þ hē hit gerǽdde (*what God had suggested to him*), Hml. S. 23, 320.    **II.** *to arrange, dispose :*—Þá þe gerǽdaþ heora heortan fullfremedlíce fram ǽlcum synlustum þæs líchaman *qui perfecte cor ab omni delectatione carnis excutiunt*, Gr. D. 323, 4. Geraedit *degesto* (cf. *degesta*, i. *disposita*, 138, 34 : *digesta*, i. *ordinata*, 140, 22), Wrt. Voc. ii. 106, 31. Gerǽded, 25, 38. Gerǽdde *concin[n]atas* (*factiones*), An. Ox. 4, 44. Þá gerǽddan *adoptivas*, 9, 17.    **II a.** *to dress, equip, harness.* v. ge-rǽdod.    **III.** *to determine* a condition, *decide, settle* a course of action :—Ic fare swā hwider swā þú mē tō mundbyrdnesse gerēdst, Hml. S. 23 b, 454. Mon gefæstnode þone frið . . . , swā swā Eádweard gerǽdde, Chr. 906 ; P. 94, 22. Man geald gafol Deniscan mannum, 991 ; P. 127, 3. Man gerǽdde þ man hine lǽdde nō Ēligbyrig, 1036 ; P. 160, 5 : 161, 2. Ðá gerǽddan

þá witan þ man æfter þám cyninge sende, 1014; P. 145, 1. Geræddon, Lch. iii. 426, 13. Gyf man þæt geræde, gold and glencga álecge man þá hwíle, Wlfst. 170, 7. Dô man út his eágan . . . oþþe hine hættian, swá hwilc þissa swá mon þonne geræde, Ll. Th. i. 394, 15. On þám fyrste þe witan geræden, 176, 1. Geræd *destinatum*, Germ. 397, 429. Hí ræddon swá þ hí woldon þone cyng gesettan út of þám cynedóme, and hit weard sóna gecýdd þám cynge hú hit wæs geræd, Chr. 1075; P. 211, 2. Næs nán máre unræd geréd (-ræd, *v. l.*) þonne sé wæs, 1016; P. 151, 4. Mid ús is geræd þ hé sylle .v. sustras huniges tô gafole, Ll. Th. i. 436, 1. **III a.** *to decide* a (doubtful) point, *come to the conclusion* that:—Ðá geræddon witan þ hit betere wære þ man týmde þær hit ærest befangen wære, Ll. Th. i. 290, 1. **III b.** *to determine* legal ordinances, official regulations, &c., *ordain* ; instituere :—Ðis man gerædde ðá se micela here côm tô lande, Wlfst. 180, 18. Ðis is seó gerædnes þe Eádgár cyng mid his witena geþeahte gerædde, Ll. Th. i. 262, 1: 358, 5. Seó gerædnes þe míne witan geræddon (cf. instituerunt, 336, 15), 272, 3: 350, 6: 168, 15: Angl. ix. 259, 6. Gerædde man friðlice steóra folce tô þearfe, Ll. Th. i. 304, 20: 324, 1: Wlfst. 170, 19. Witan habbad gerædd, þ . . ., Ll. Th. i. 224, 24. Þá laga þe Æðelréd cyng and his witan geræddon habbad, 291, 1. **IV.** *to consult the good of, provide for*:—Geræddan *consulebant* (v. (?) succesurae posteritati *consulebant*, Ald. 36, 36), Wrt. Voc. ii. 23, 79. Hú ic mihte þearflícast mé sylfum gerædan for Gode and for worolde, Ll. Lbmn. 269, 17. **V.** *to read* :—Ðá gerédes *legentes*, Mt. p. 13, 8. Bið geréded *legitur*, Lk. p. 11, 16, 17. *See next two words.*

**ge-ræde**; es; *n.* *Add: The word seems used only in the pl.,* gerædu(-a). *An ornament, trapping.* (1) for a person :—Wé lærad þ man geswîce higeleásra gewæda and dislicra geræda, Ll. Th. ii. 248, 16. (2) for a horse :—Æfteráp *postela*, gerædu *falere*, brídel *frenum*, Wrt. Voc. i. 84, 5-7. Geræda *effipia*, Hpt. 31, 7, 85: *effipiam*, 6, 82. Þæt hors mid ðám cynelicum gerædum þe him on stódou *equum, ita ut erat stratus regaliter*, Bd. 3, 14; Sch. 257, 15: By. 190. Módigne stédan mid gyldenum gerædum gefreatewodne, Hml. Th. i. 210, 15. Rídende on horsum mid gyldenum gerædum, Hml. S. 25, 491. Ic bicge hýda and fell, and gearkie hig, and wyrce of him . . . brídelþwancgas and geræda (*frenos et phaleras*), Coll. M. 27, 35. [Cf. Icel. reiði *harness* of a horse.] v. segl-geræde.

**ge-ræde**, es; *n. Counsel, design, device* :—Þær þá æðelestan hæleða gerædum hýdde wæron, þurh nearusearwe, næglas on eordan, El. 1108. Forþsnoterne hæleða gerædum (cf. rædum *snottor*, wîs on gewitte, An. 469), 1054. [*O. Sax.* gi-rádi *advantage*: *O. H. Ger.* ge-ráti *consilium, consolatio*. Cf. *Icel.* rædi *rule, management.*] v. ge-rædan.

**ge-ræde**; *adj. Add: I.* *skilled, instructed, advised* :—Be gerædre *consulta*, An. Ox. 8, 130. Tô þig þ ðá óþre ðe gerædran beón and ðe beteran (gelærede sýn and gebeterade, *v. l.*) ðurh his gódan gebysnunga *ut eius exemplo alii erudiantur*, R. Ben. 108, 24. **II.** *arranged, disposed properly :—Ne wyrd næfre folces wíse wel geræde on þám earde þe man wôh gestreón lufað *a people's condition will never be well ordered in the land where wrongful gain is loved*, Ll. Th. ii. 312, 28. Gerædre *eliganti*, Wrt. Voc. ii. 33, 22. **III.** *simple, plain;* of language, *prose :—Ærest eroico metro, and æfter fæce gerædum (-e, *v. l.*) worde (*plano sermone*), Bd. 5, 23; Sch. 698, 18. v. un-geræd; ge-rád; *adj. and sbst.*

**ge-ræded.** v. ge-rædod.

**ge-rædelíce**; *adv. Clearly, completely :—Ic bidde þ mé þis gerædelícor (-réde-, *v. l.*) sý gerihted (fullícor getrahtnod, *v. l.*) *hoc planius* (*plenius, v. l.*) *exponi postulo*, Gr. D. 102, 19. v. un-gerædelíce; ge-rádlíce.

**ge-rædian.** v. ge-rædian.

**ge-ræding.** *Substitute: Counselling* :—Geræding *consulta* (cf. rædas consulta, 79, 46: 94, 7), Wrt. Voc. ii. 24, 45.

**ge-rædnes.** *Add: I. determination, decision, definition.* Cf. gerædan; **III a** :—Þú mid þus mycelre tódælednesse and gerædnesse tósceádest manna gástas and nýtena . . . Salomon gedyde ofer eall gemænelíce þás gerædnesse mid þysum wordum *spiritus hominum atque jumentorum tanta distinctione discernis . . . quibus verbis generalem definitionem subinfert*, Gr. D. 264, 13-22. Þone æftran cwide hé spræc of fullum gesceáde and gerædnesse *hoc ex rationis definitione subjunxit*, 266, 10. **II.** *an ordinance, official enactment.* (1) of the secular authority (king and witan). v. ge-rædan; **III b.** (a) of a collection of regulations :—Æðelstanes cyninges gerædnes (*the decrees of the council of Greatanlea*), Ll. Th. i. 194, 1. Eádmundes cyninges ásetnysse (gerædnes, *v. l.*), 244, 1. Seó gerædnys þe míne witan æt Anðeferan gerædon, 272, 2. Ðis is seó gerædnes þe Engla cyng and ægðer ge gehádode ge læwede witan gecuran and gerædedan, 304, 3. Ðis is seó gerædnys þe Cnut cyninge mid his witena geþeahte gerædde, 358, 3. Ðis is seó woruldcunde gerædnes, 376, 4. Ðis is seó gerædnes þe Angelcynnes witan and Wealhþeóde rædboran betweox Dúnsætan gesetton, 352, 1. Ðis is seó gerædnyss hú mon ðæt hundred haldan sceal, 258, 2. Sé þe of þissa gerædnesse gá, 214, 3. Ðis is án þára gerædnessa þe Engla cyning gedihte mid his witena geþeahte, 340, 4. (b) of a single regula-

tion :—Úres hláfordes gerædnes and his witena is þ . . ., 304, 14, 18, 21: 306, 1. Be witena gerædnessan. Ðis sindon þá gerædnessa þe Engla rædgifan gecuran . . . And witena gerædnes is þ . . ., 314, 2-13: 20. Æðelstánes geræd[d]nesse, 198, 14. (2) of ecclesiastical authority :—Gif preóst tô rihte gebúgan nelle, ac ongeán biscopes gerædnesse wiðerige, Ll. Th. ii. 296, 18. **III.** *a legal agreement* embodied in a charter:—God þá gehealde for bæm lífum þe uune þ þeós geræduis stondon môte in ecnesse, C. D. ii. 132, 19. Þás gerædnesse eali se hióréd mid Crístes róde tácne gefæstnodon, 150, 33. God þone gehealde þe þás úre sylena and úre gerædnyssa healdan wylle, Cht. E. 242, 19. v. un-, weorold-gerædness.

**ge-rædod** (-ed). *Add: Falerato vel fictitio*, i. *ornato* gerædod, gehyrste, Wrt. Voc. ii. 146, 71. Gerædedum *falerato*, An. Ox. 7. Gerædedum (= gerédedum; *this and the preceding one are glosses on* Ald. 2, 32), 3, 4. Feówer hors, twá gerædede (cf. *in the article on heriots*: Feówer hors, twá gesadelode, Ll. Th. i. 414, 10), C. D. ii. 380, 27. Hú hit gewurþan mihte þ englas sceoldon rídan on gerædedum horsum (v. geræde), Hml. S. 25, 509.

**ge-ræf.** *Add: As* á-ráfian = *dissolvere*, á-ræfan = *expedire*. ge-ræf weorþan on hine, *applied to the crime, would mean that the person referred to could not free or clear himself of the charge. The Old Latin version renders* geresp (*v. l.* geræf) weorðe by firmetur.

**ge-ræfnian**; *p.* ode *To suffer* :—Hé sorgode má þe þám þe þá synne fremede, þonne be him sylfum þe þone æfwyrdlan geræfnode (*tolerabat*), Gr. D. 291, 10. v. á-ræfnian.

**ge-ræft.** *Dele, and see next word.*

**ge-ræpan.** *Substitute: To fasten with a rope, bind, chain* :—Geræped *inretita* (*tenacissimis vinculis*), An. Ox. 4596. Hé hafad ealla gesceafta geræped (cf. hé hí hæfd gehæfte, Bt. 25; F. 88, 5) mid his racentum *ligans singula nexu*, Met. 13, 8. Him þinced þæt hé sié racentan geræped *videbit intus arctas dominos ferre catenas*, 25, 37. Him wyrd sefa . . . unrótnesse geræped (-ræpeð, MS.), hearde gehæfted (cf. hí weorþaþ geræpte (printed -ræfte) mid þære unrótnesse and swá gehæfte, Bt. 37, 1; F. 186, 21) *moeror captos fatigat*, 25, 48.

**ge-ræsan.** *Substitute: To rush.* (1) of impetuous movement, *to press, force one's way* :—Mid ðý ðá menigo gerædson (*inruerent*) on him, Lk. L. 5, 1. (2) of violent action, *to attack, assault* :—Priscus gerásde on þá fæmnan in crístenmonna midle, swá wulf gerásed on sceáp on miclum éwede, Mart. H. 170, 26. Swá hwylce swá þ hors on geræsan mihte, hit bát and hira lima tôtær *quoscumque potuisset invadere, eorum membra morsibus dilaniaret*, Gr. D. 78, 3. (2 a) of fighting :—Næfre mon þon wurdlícor wígsíd áteáh, þára þe wid swá miclum mægne geræsde, Gen. 2095. Hé wid áttorsceaðan orede geræsde, B. 2839. Þá hí tôgedore gerædson, þá man ofslóh ðes cáseres geréfan, Chr. P. 5, 9. (3) of rash, inconsiderate conduct :—Be þám men þe hæfd his rihtæwe, and geræst on ælþeódigum wífmen (*ad mulierem peregrinam se convertit*), Ll. Th. ii. 180, 16. Gif gehádod mæden tô hæmedþinge geræst (*ad fornicationem se convertat*), 28: 29. Gif hwylc mædenman þurh deófles costnunga on hæmedþing geræse (*se ad fornicationem convertat*), 188, 11.

**ge-ræstan.** v. ge-restan: **ge-ræþle**, an; *n. A harness. l.* geræþlan; *pl. Harness* of a horse.

**ge-ræwe** in the phrase on geræwe *in a row* :—Hí ealle on geræwe sæton, Hml. S. 23, 779. Of ðám alre tô ðám twám wycan standad on geréwe swá ðæt gemére gæd, C. D. iii. 424, 8.

**ge-ræwen.** *Substitute: Having rows or strips* :—Geræwen hrægel *segmentata vestis* (cf. golde siowode *segmentata* (fulgebat veste virago, Ald. 195, 18), ii. 95, 49), Wrt. Voc. i. 40, 10.

**ge-ræwod** (-ud); *adj.* (*ptcpl.*) Of troops, *drawn up in line* :—Geræwud (printed -rærud) féða *acies*, Wrt. Voc. i. 18, 26.

**ge-rafende, -rawende.** *Dele, and see ge-ráwan.*

**ge-rár**, es; *n. The roar* of a wild animal :—Náht ôþres ne gehýrde bútan leóna grymetunge and wulfa gerár, Shrn. 50, 10.

**ge-ráwan** *to make a row* or line :—Geráwende *infindens* (*labara per terram trudito dextra, quatuor infindens directo tramite sulcos*, Ald. 153, 33), Wrt. Voc. ii. 91, 24: 47, 22.

**gerd.** v. gird.

**ge-reáfian.** *Add: I. to take with violence, rob* something :—Hié gereáfiad suá heáne láriówdôm suiðor ðonne hine geearnien *culmen regiminis rapiunt potius quam assequuntur*, Past. 27, 19. Þú hit ná hú elles begitan ne miht, búton þú hit forstele oððe gereáfige, Bt. 32, 1; F. 114, 8. Gehreáfian (*diripiunt*) ældeódige geswinc his, Ps. L. 108, 11. Ðá ðe hiora ágnu ðing sellað, and ðá ðe wilniað ôðerra monna gereáfigan (-reáfian, *v. l.*) *qui sua distribuunt, et qui rapiunt aliena*, Past. 319, 13. I a. *to rob* from (on) a person :—Nymðe hé geinnige ðæt hé on úrum Drihtne gereáfað, C. D. v. 331, 9. **II.** *to strip* an object of a covering, clothing, &c. :—Gehreáfadon hine ðæs fellereádes *exuerunt illum purpura*, Mk. L. 15, 20. Mid ðý gehreáfod hús wæs *nudato tecto*, Lk. p. 4, 20. [*O. H. Ger.* ge-roubôn *vastare*.]

**ge-reáfian**; *p.* ode *To robe, provide with vestments* :—Gé preóstas sculon beón gebôcode and gereáfode swá swá eówrum háde gebirad, Ll. Th. ii. 382, 36.

ge-rec. *Add*: *and* gerecu, e ; *f.* (*see* Bt. 5, 3 ; F. 14, 3). **I.** *rule, government*:—Micelne fultum gereces (*maximum regendi auxilium*) heó on him gemëtte, Bd. 4, 26 ; Sch. 508, 19. Hē seofontīne winter on bisceoplicum gerece fore wæs *decem ac septem annos eidem prouinciae pontificali regimine praeesset*, 2, 15 ; Sch. 177, 6. Heó onfēng þām gerece þæs mynstres, 4, 6 ; Sch. 384, 2 : 5, 20 ; Sch. 673, 23. On his mynstre þe hē hæfde under gerece Cūðbaldes þæs abbudes, 5, 19 ; Sch. 672, 16. Þū nystest mid hwilcan (hwelcere, *v.l.*) gerece God wylt þisse worulde *quibus gubernaculis mundus regatur oblitus es*, Bt. 5, 3 ; F. 14, 3. Mid þām ilcan gerece is gereaht gewrixle þæs flōdes and þæs ebban *pelagus regens*, 21 ; F. 74, 29. **I a.** *a rule, decree*:—Gerec decretum, Germ. 398. 49. **II.** *an orderly condition, a quiet time* [cf. *O. H. Ger.* in allen ge-rechen sīn *florere*]:—Gefylsta on gerecum *adiutor in oportunitatibus*, Ps. Rdr. 9, 10 : 22 : Ps. Spl. 9 second, I. Geræcum, 9, 9. [*The Latin word seems to have been misunderstood in a favourable sense*, cf. gefultumend æt ælcere ðearfe, Ps. Th. 9, 10, *and see* un-gerec.] **III.** *an explanation, exposition, account*:—Be emnihte æfter Anatalius gerece (race, *v.l.*) āne bōc *de aequinoctio iuxta Anatolium una epistola*, Bd. 5, 23 ; Sch. 698, 2. v. in-, un-gerec.

ge-rec *a tumult*. In Mt. L. 27, 24 gerec *seems a mistake for* un-gerec (*q.v.*): *the Rushworth Gloss has* un-gerec (*printed* -reo).

ge-rec *a pinnace* (?):—Gerec *liburnices*, Wrt. Voc. ii. 112, 67 : 50, 79.

ge-reca. *Dele, and see* heáh-gerëfa.

ge-recan ; *p.* -ræc *To move, come, go*:—Tôsomne geræc (*printed* -ræt) *congelaverat*, Wrt. Voc. ii. 133, 37. Þ blôd tôsamne geræc, Bl. H. 183, 25. v. recan.

ge-rēcan *to smoke, fumigate*:—Dô glēda an glēdfæt, and lege þā wyrta on ; gerēc þone man mid þām wyrtum, Lch. ii. 346, 4. Gyf hyt bið mid gerēced, i. 356, 14. [*O. H. Ger.* ge-rouhen *libare aromatibus*.]

ge-reccan. *Add*: **I.** *to extend*:—Gereceþ *extendit*, Wrt. Voc. ii. 140, 49. **II.** *to offer, give*. v. reccan ; **II**:—Wē gereccað lofu ūrum Sceppende *referamus laudes creatori nostro*, R. Ben. I. 46, 11. Heáhsittendum þancas gereccean hȳ nā yldon *celsithrono grates referre non distulerunt*, Angl. xiii. 368, 39. **III.** *to tell, say*. (1) *to state a fact*:—Ic þē gerecce swīþe hraþe þ ðū ongitst þ hē biþ for lytlum þingum oft gedrēfed, Bt. 11. 1 ; F. 32, 17. Hē geræcð him tô geleáfsuman (*see* ge-leáfsum) ðæt hē sié se gesælgosta, Past. 463, 13. Gerecce man hū manega þāra sién, Ll. Th. i. 82, 12. Hī synden gerehte *allocuntur*, An. Ox. 2287. (2) *to relate, narrate, record*:—Historia, þæt is gerecednyss ; mid þǣre man āwrīt and gerehð (-recþ, *v.l.*) þā ðing þe wǣron gedône on ealdum dagum, Ælfc. Gr. 296, 9. Āwrāt oððe gerehte *digessit*, Wrt. Voc. ii. 27, 11 : *narrat, exponit*, An. Ox. 1555. Gerecce *expediet*, Wrt. Voc. ii. 145, 39. Gereccan *expedire*, i. *narrare*, 33. Nū wylle wē sum ðing scortlīce eów be him gereccan, Hml. Th. ii. 118, 3. Heofona heáhðu gereccan, Dôm. 31. Is gereht *memoratur*, An. Ox. 1986 : 2206. Hit is gereht on ðyssere pistolrǣdinge hū se Hālga Gāst cóm, Hml. Th. i. 314, 1. Gerehtum *digessit* (*l.* *digestis*. v. Ald. 201, 1), Wrt. Voc. ii. 96, 21. (3) *to pronounce judgement, declare the law, decree, decide, order, direct* what should be done :—Ǣrest for ðǣre rihtwīsnesse hē (*the judge*) gereceð (*dicat*, Lat. vers.) ðæs gyltes bôte, Ll. Lbmn. 474, 9. Ðā geræhte Uulfrēd ond alle ðā wiotan ðet se biscop ond ðā hīgen môsten mid āðe gecýðan, C. D. i. 279, 5. Þonne setton wē þ hē hit ne môste sellan . . . and þ þonne on cyninges gewitnesse gerecce beforan his mǣgum, Ll. Th. i. 88, 21. Ne wandiað for nānum þingum folcriht tô geregceanne ( = segceanne ?, -reccanne, *v.l.*); and þ gehwilc sprǣc hæbbe āndagan hwænne heó gelǣst sy, þ gē þonne gereccan, 158, 6–8. Bēte swā him dōmeras gereccen (*quantum arbitri judicaverint*, Ex. 21, 22), 48, 18. Geselle him mon .c. sciłł. tô bôte, būton him witan māre gereccan, 100, 14. Is ciépemonnum gereht . . . , 82, 10. Ðonne wille wē cweðan ðæt hē sié genóg ryhtlīce his brôðor deáðes scyldig . . . Nū ðonne nū ðā līchomlican lǣcas ðus scyldige gerehte (-reahte, *v.l.*) sint, Past. 377, 22. (4) gereccan (on *or dat. of person*) *to charge (with)*. Cf. secgan on :—Gif hit man him on gerecce mid sôðe, Ll. Th. i. 222, 4. Se man ðe ðis forsitte . . . and him mon eft þ ilce gerecce, 258, 15. (5) *to explain, expound*:—Race geswuteliaþ . . . sutelīcor gerehte [*haec non modo x*] *collationes* [*patrum*] *propalabunt* ; [*verum etiam Gregorius per allegoriam*] *clarius elimavit*, i. *exudavit, elicuit*, An. Ox. 916. Sē gerehte *elimauit, manifestavit* (*itinerarium Petri decem voluminibus digestum*), 2026. Þā dīglan gerehte trahte *clancula elicuit commentis*, Wrt. Voc. ii. 94, 30. Gerǣhte, 31, 57. Gerece *dissere* (*nobis parabolam*, Mt. 13, 36), 72, 64 : 26, 34. Ic wolde get þ þū mē hwæthwegu openlīcor gereahte (-rehtest, *v.l.*, *edisseras*) be mīn môd swīþost gedrēfed biþ, Bt. 39, 4 ; F. 216, 10. (5 a) *to interpret, translate*:— Se cyning gerehte his witan on heora āgenum gereorde þæs bisceopes bodunge (cf. se cyning his ealdormannum wæs walhstod (*interpres*) geworden, Bd. 3, 3 ; Sch. 200, 17), Hml. S. 26, 65. His nama wæs gereht 'Godes strengo,' Bl. 9, 14 ; 81, 1. (6) *to shew, prove*:—Ǣr wē þe hæfdon þ gereaht þ God wǣre þurh hine selfne good (*Deus ipsum*

esse bonum monstratus est*) . . . Ic nysse hwæt se fruma wǣre . . . þā gerehtest þū mē þ hit wæs God. Ðā nysse ic eft ymb þone ende, ǣr þū mē eft gereahtes þ ðæt wǣre eác God. Ðā sǣde ic þē þ ic nysse hū hē ealra þāra gesceafta wiōlde ; ac þū hit mē hæfst nū swīðe sweotole gereht, Bt. 35, 3 ; S. 97, 6–24. Ic wēne þæt hit sié nū þearf þ ic þē gerecce hwǣr þ hēhste gôd is *nunc demonstrandum reor, quonam haec perfectio constituta est*, 34, 1 ; F. 134, 3 : 35, 5 ; F. 166, 4. 'Ic ne mæg nān ôþer geþencan, būton hit weás swā gebyrige, būton ðū mē get þy gesceádlīcor ôþer gerecce.' Ðā andswarode hē : 'Nis hit nān wundor ðeáh hwā wēne þ swylces hwæt unmyndlinga gebyrige þonne hē ne can ongitan and gereccan for hwī God swylc geþafað' *nisi causa deprehendatur, quid est quod a fortuitis casibus differre videatur?* *Nec mirum, inquit, si quid ordinis ignorata ratione temerarium credatur*, 39, 2 ; F. 214, 6–10. Gerecce hē *demonstret, ostendat*, 38, 2 ; F. 198, 24. Ic wolde þ þū mē gereahte hū . . . *vellem has ipsas audire rationes*, 38, 6 ; F. 208, 7. Eal þ þū gereccan miht (*monstraveris*) þ þīnes āgnes wǣre, 7, 3 ; F. 20, 8 : 13. Hē sceal beforan ðǣm ðearlwīsan Dēman mid gereclicre race gereccean ðæt hē ðæt ilce self dyde þe hē ôðre men lǣrde *apud districtum judicem cogitur tanta in opere exsolvere, quanta eum constat aliis voce praecepisse*, Past. 192, 15. Ic þe hæfde gereaht be monegum tācnum *te persuasum permultis demonstrationibus scio*, Bt. 11, 2 ; S. 26, 10. Ǣr wē þe hæfdon þ gereaht (-reaht, *v.l.*) þ God wǣre þurh hine selfne gôd *Deum beatitudinem ipsam esse concessimus*, 35, 3 ; F. 158, 21. Swā mihtigne swā wē hine gereahtne habbað *eum potentissimum concessimus*, 35, 4 ; S. 98, 16. Untweólicere ealdorlicnesse is gesēþed ł gereht *indubitata auctoritate asstipulatur*, i. *creditur*, An. Ox. 217. (7) gereccan tô *to reckon as, to make to stand for*:—Uton gereccan þone anweald and þ geniht, dôn þǣr weorþscipe tô, and gereccan þonne þā þreó tô ānum *addemus sufficientiae potentiaeque reverentiam, ut haec tria unum esse judicemus*, Bt. 33, 1 ; F. 120, 27. Is siô nosu gereaht tô gesceádwīsnesse *per nasum discretio exprimitur*, Past. 65, 21. **IV.** *to guide, direct, govern*. (1) *to direct, regulate* the movements of material objects :—Mid þām ilcan gerece is gereaht swīþe anlīc gewrixle þæs flōdes and ðæs ebban, Bt. 21 ; F. 74, 29. Sint gereahte diri(g)*antur* (*deriventur* fontes tui foras, Prov. 5, 16), Kent. Gl. 103. (1 a) *to send in a straight line* ; gangan gereht *to go direct*:—Gang nū tô þīnum mynstre mid Godes sibbe gereht, Hml. S. 23 b, 706. (1 b) *to direct the course of* a non-material object, *bring* into a condition (cf. *O. H. Ger.* ge-recchen *revehere*):—Eall Italia rīce hē in anwald gerehton, Bt. 1 ; F. 2, 5. (2) *to direct* a person in his actions, &c.:—[Drihten] gerecht [mē] *Dominus regit me*, Ps. Rdr. 22, 1. Hē gerecþ (*diriget*) biliwite, 24, 9. Gerecð, Kent. Gl. 346. Gereceþ *dirigit*, i. *regit*, ic wæs gereaht *dirigebar*, Wrt. Voc. ii. 140, 49, 50. Gerece mē on sôþfæstnisse þīnre, Ps. Rdr. 24, 5 : Ps. Ben. 24, 4 : Ps. Th. 89, 18. Biôð gereahte *reguntur* (*sapientia*), Kent. Gl. 439. (2 a) *to instruct*:—Ic þē mæg gereccan be sumere bisne þ þū miht ongiton þ . . . , Bt. 27, 3 ; F. 98, 17. (3) *to direct* the actions, &c., of a person :—Weorc handa ūrra gerece (gehræce, Ps. L.) *opera manuum nostrarum dirige*, Ps. Rdr. 89, 17. Ic wilnode andweorces þone anweald mid tô gereccenne, Bt. 17 ; F. 60, 8. Ðonne biþ ðæt rīce wel gereht (-reaht, *v.l.*), ðonne sē ðe ðǣr fore bið suiðor wilnað ðæt hē rīcsige ofer monna unðeáwas ðonne ofer ôðre gôde menn *summus locus bene regitur, cum is, qui praeest vitiis potius quam fratribus dominatur*, Past. 117, 10. Ic þæs wīsce þæt wegas mīne on ðīnum willan weorþan gereahte *utinam dirigantur viae meae*, Ps. Th. 118, 5. Gerǣhte, Gū. 740. (3 a) *to correct*:—Gerecð *corrigit* (qui rectus est *corrigit* viam suam), Kent. Gl. 806. (4) *to direct* words to a person, *address*:—Ðone cwide Paulus gereahte eft tô biscepum, Past. 104, 9. (5) *to rule* as a lord :—Hāl dô folc þīn, and gerece (*rege*) hý, Ps. Rdr. 27, 9. **V.** *to assign*:—Man hine āðýmde ðā, and man gerehte Ǣðelrēde cyninge ðæt land and ǣhta, C. D. iii. 291, 18. Hī an ðāra xv hīda ðæ hire hlāford hire lǣfde, and him man on āgene þæt gereahte *ipsa concedit xv hidas quas ei uir suus reliquit, et pro qua ei pretium datum fuit*, v. 137, 11. Ðūs wǣron ðā land . . . ðām cinge Eádgār gereht on Lundenbyrig . . . Man gerehte on cinges þēningmanna gemôte ðǣre stôwe and ðām biscope ðā forstolenan bēcc, vi. 80, 11–21. **V a.** *to appoint*?:—Gesette, gerehte *praeposuit* (*omnibus generalium virtutum gradibus* . . . speciale virginitatis privilegium *praeposuit*, Ald. 6, 23), An. Ox. 344. **VI.** *to reprove, reproach*:—Heó mec swā torne tǣle gerahte, Jul. 73. Hē þā hālgan weras hospe gerahte, 300. Mē sôðfæst symble gerecce, and mildheorte môde þreáge *corripiet me justus in misericordia, et increpabit me*, Ps. Th. 140, 7. Hī hrædlīce, æfter þǣm þe þā wīf hié swā scondlīce gerǣht hæfdon, gewendon, Ors. 1, 12 ; S. 54, 5. [*Passages* 1, 2, *and* 4 *might be taken under* ge-rǣcan ; **I.** 4.] [Nu ich habbe þe iraht hu he hauede þene nome icaht, Laym. 10842. *O. H. Ger.* ge-recchen *ex-, distendere, porrigere, expedire, enarrare, explanare, interpretare, revehere, perficere*.] v. ungereccan.

ge-recednes. v. ge-reccednes: ge-reccelic. v. ge-reclic.

ge-recednes (-recced-). *Add*: **I.** *history*:—Historia, þæt is gerecednyss (-recced-, *v.l.*) ; mid þǣre man āwrīt and gerehð þā ðing and þā dǣda þe wǣron gedône on ealdum dagum and ūs dyrne wǣron,

Ælfc. Gr. Z. 296, 8. [Æfter] gerecednesse, gástlicum angite . . . *secundum historiam, allegoriam* . . ., An. Ox. 181. **I a.** *a history, story, narrative :*—Hér onginneð seó gerecednes be Antioche . . . and be Apollonige, Ap. Th. 1, 1. Þære ærran gerecednyssa *prioris instrumenti ;* the Old Testament, An. Ox. 1676. Fiþerdæledre gerecednysse (*the gospels*), 1796. Cyrclicere gerecednysse *ecclesiasticæ historiae,* 2273. Mid witiendlicere gerecednysse *prophetica relatione,* 1585 : 3142. Of gereccednysse (spelle, *v. l., relatione*) Honorates, Gr. D. 134, 13. On ðære ealdon gerecceduysse *in the Old Testament,* Hml. Th. ii. 60, 8. Gecyndbóca gerecednesse *geneseos relatum* i. *relationem,* An. Ox. 51. Wē ne wrítað nā māre būton þā nacedan gerecednisse, Ælfc. T. Grn. 23, 4. Swā swā gē rædað on eówrum gerecednyssum, Hml. S. 5, 177. **II.** *explanation, exposition, interpretation :*—Hē sylð his gife ðam ðe hē wile . . . sumum men hē forgifð gereccednysse mislicra sprǽca (*alii datur interpretatio sermonum,* 1 Cor. 12, 10), Hml. Th. i. 322, 29. **II a.** *an explanation :*—Gerecednessum *explanationibus,* An. Ox. 1082. **III.** *direction :*—On gerecednesse heortan *in directione cordis,* Ps. Rdr. 118, 7.

**ge-receness, e ; f. I.** *telling, narration :*—Ne magon hý ðære tungan gerecnisse áspyrian *they cannot follow what the tongue says,* Sal. K. p. 150, 4. **II.** *interpretation, explanation :*—Tó mægwlite gáslicre (-a, *v. l.*) gerecenesse (-a, *v. l.*) *ad formam interpretationis,* Bd. 5, 23 ; Sch. 696, 4. **III.** *proof, testimony.* Cf. ge-reccan ; III. 6 :—Gerecenesse *congerie* (v. (?) testimoniorum *congerie,* Ald. 7, 36 ; *but see* ge-recenness), Wrt. Voc. ii. 23, 26. **IV.** *direction ; correctio, directio.* v. ge-reccan ; **IV** :—Gerecenes setles his *correctio sedis eius,* Ps. Vos. Srt. 96, 2. On gerecenesse heortan *in directione cordis,* 118, 7. Mīne gerecenesse *directionem meam,* 138, 3. **V.** *going, departure* (?). v. reccan ; III :—Oð þone dæg his gerecenesse (*or* gerec(n)nesse ?. v. ge-recenness) *of middangearde usque ad diem suae uocationis,* Bd. 5, 12 ; Sch. 634, 8.

**ge-recenian.** *Add :* *to arrange, set in order :*—Þá hē hæfde ealle his fare gerecenod (-reconod, *v. l.*), Chr. 1052 ; P. 180, 15. Gerecanade *condito,* Wrt. Voc. ii. 18, 45. [*O. H. Ger.* ge-rehhanón *parare* (*viam*), *disponere.*]

**ge-recenness** (?), e ; f. **I.** *a coming together* (?) :—Gerecenesse *congerie* (cf. *congerie* ge-gæderuncge, An. Ox. 435), Wrt. Voc. ii. 23, 26. **II.** *a going, departure* (cf. ge-witenness). v. ge-receness ; **V.** v. ge-recan.

**ge-reclic** (-recce-) ; *adj. That affords proof* or *explanation.* v. ge-rec ; III : *or orderly.* v. ge-rec, II, un-gerec :—Hē sceal beforan ðæm ðearlwísan Dēman mid gereclicre (-recce-) race gereccean ðæt hē ðæt ilce self dyde þe hē óðre men lǽrde *apud districtum judicem cogitur tanta in opere exsolvere, quanta eum constat aliis voce praecepisse,* Past. 192, 15. *See next word.*

**ge-reclíce.** *Substitute : In an orderly manner.* (1) of movement, *smoothly, quietly :*—Æspringe ūt áwealleð of clife . . . and gereclíce rihte flóweð, Met. 5, 14. Ofer rodorum gereclíce feðerum lácan (*to fly smoothly*), 24, 8. (2) of action :—Hē eallum gereclíce racað and eáðelíce hit eall set *regit cuncta fortiter suaviterque disponat,* Bt. 35, 4 ; F. 162, 1. v. un-gereclíce.

**ge-recness.** v. ge-receness : **ge-reca.** v. ge-rec.

**ge-redian. I.** *to reach, get at :*—Sceal him mon . . . blód lætan on þám swíþran earme on þære niþerran ædre. Gif þá mon ne mæge eáþe geredian, þonne sceal mon on þære middelædre blód lǽtan, Lch. ii. 210, 10. **II.** *to carry out, effect, do :*—Ne sēc ðú þurh hlytas hū ðē geweorðan scyle . . . ; eáðe gerædað God ðæt hē wile be ðē, ðeáh hē hit ðē ǽr ne secge, Prov. K. 32. **III.** *to find out, hit upon :*—Sē hæfð gódne rǽd þe him geredað ǽfre hwæt him tó dónne sý and hwæt tó forlætenne, Wlfst. 57, 15. Gerædað, 51, 19. v. á-redian.

**ge-réfa.** *Add :* **I.** in Latin-English glossaries :—Geroefa *commentariensis,* Wrt. Voc. ii. 104, 63. Geréfa, i. 18, 43 : 60, 31 : *curator,* 57, 39 : *prepositus,* 72, 67 : *preses,* ii. 66, 51 : *coors* (cf. *coors* þreát (a gloss to Jn. 18, 12 *cohors* et *tribunus ; so that perhaps it is* tribunus *not* coors *to which* geréfa *belongs*), 21, 28. Geroefan *proceres,* 118, 32 : *censores,* 103, 57. Geréfan, 14, 17 : *exactores,* 32, 45 : *functi,* 39, 43. Geréfena *comitum,* 22, 2. **II.** rendering Latin titles of non-English officials. v. geréf-mann :—Jósep wæs geréfa (*decurio*), Lk. 23, 50. Hē wæs ðæs geréfan sunu *cujusdam curialis* (cf. *decuriales* burhgeréfa, Wrt. Voc. i. 18, 42) *filius,* Gr. D. 125, 8. Sæge Stephane þám geréfan *dic Stephano optioni* (*optio est qui militaris ducis vices agit, vel qui centurioni adjutor datur*), Gr. D. 314, 5. Man ofslóh ðæs Cǽseres geréfan, sē wæs Labienus geháten (cf. *Labienus tribunus occisus est,* Bd. 1, 2), Chr. P. 5, 9. Geréfan *presides* (ad *presides* (tó dēmum, W.S.) ducimini, Mt. 10, 18), Wrt. Voc. ii. 72, 46. Geréfan (*publicani*) and synfulle men geneálǽhton ðám Hǽlende, Hml. Th. i. 338, 9. Hē heóld in þisse ylcan byrig geréfena stówe and scíre *in hac urbe locum Praefectorum servans,* Gr. D. 340, 32. **III.** *a bailiff, steward.* (1) English :—Be gesceádwísan geréfan. Gescádwís geréfa sceal . . . (*the duties of the reeve are then given*), Angl. ix. 259, 3. Þæs biscopes geréfa, Ll. Th. i. 342, 16 : 262, 24. Gif man biscopes esne tihte, cǽnne hine an geréfan hand ; oþþe

hine geréfa clēnsie, oþþe selle tó swinganne, 42, 4. Þone Frenciscan ceorl þe seó hlǽfdige heafde hire gesett tó geréfan, Chr. 1003 ; P. 135, 6. Gif gesíðcund man fare, þonne mót hē habban his geréfan mid him and his smið, Ll. Th. i. 144, 3 : 280, 14. Nys nánum mæssepreóste álýfed, ne diácone, þ hí geréfan (*praefecti*) beón, ne wícneras (*procuratores*), ii. 198, 21. (2) not English :—Damascus wæs Abrahames geréfan (*procuratoris*) sunu, Angl. vii. 44, 425. Hē (*Abraham*) clipode him tó his yldestan geréfan (*seruum seniorem domus suae*) þe ealle his þing bewiste, Gen. 24, 2. þā sǽde se wíngeardes hláford hys geréfan (*giroefæ,* L., geroefa, R., *procuratori*), Mt. 20, 8 : Wrt. Voc. ii. 73, 4. **IV.** *a public* or *royal official.* (1) English or general :—Ic, Abba, geroefa, C. D. i. 310, 3 : 311, 27. Cuðmon .iii. scipu, and se geréfa þér tó rád, and hié wolde drífan tó þæs cyninges tūne, Chr. 787 ; P. 54, 4. Hē ne róhte hū swíðe synlíce þá geréfan hit begeáton of earme mannon, ne hū manige unlaga hí dydon, 1086 : P. 218, 17. Hí genáman þone arcð Ælfeáh and Ælfword þæs cynges geréfan, 1011 ; P. 141, 27. (1 a) where the district in which the reeve's authority is exercised is given :—Æthelnóth se geréfa tó Eastorēge (cf. ego Cuðredus rex Cantuariorum . . . dabo Aeðelnoðo prefecto meo fidelissimo in provinciae Cantiae, 233, 28), C. D. i. 234, 25. On þýs geáre gefór Ælfréd wæs æt Baðum geréfa, Chr. 906 ; P. 94, 21. (1 b) where the function is given :—On helle beóþ yfele geréfan þá þe nū on wóh dēmaþ . . . Be þǽm dēmum Críst sylf wæs sprecende . . . Se yfela dēma onfēhþ feó, Bl. H. 61, 25–31. (2) foreign :—Se árleása geréfa (*he is called* se ealderman þára sácerda, 153, 1), Bl. H. 151, 13. (2 a) where the district is given :—Tarquinius ðære burge geréfa, Shrn. 120, 12. Þære ceastre geréfa, 123, 24. v. æf-, burg-, feoh-, folc-, gafol-, heáh-, híréd-, mót-, port-, tūn-, trehing-, under-, wægn-, weard-, weorc-, wíc-geréfa. See Andrews's *Old English Manor,* s. v.

**geréf-ærn.** *Add :* [See Ald. 62 : Cujus pater (Urbanus) in palatio magistri militum officio fungens.]

**geréf-land.** *Substitute : Land held by a reeve :*—Þá mǽde þa gebyrað tó ðam geréflande, C. D. B. i. 544, 1. [Cf. Pro iiijor acris que vocantur Refìond (*quoted from* N. E. D. *q. v.*).] v. sundor-geréfland, *and see* geréf-mǽd.

**geréf-lang** (?). *Substitute : One who serves under a reeve* (?), *that belongs to the reeve's staff* (?) :—Ðá geréflanges of Christes circean underfón ðá gerihte *ministri aecclesiae Christi rectitudines accipiant,* C. D. iv. 24, 3. Cf. (?) lenge, lengan ; *O. H. Ger.* ge-lang *affinis.*

**geréf-mǽd.** *Substitute : Meadow-land held by a reeve :*—vi æcras mǽde on ðá geréfmǽde (*joining on to the reeve's meadow-land* ?), C. D. iii. 53, 2. [Cf. Et prepositus habebit j pratum quod appellatur Refmede (*quoted from* N. E. D.).] v. geréf-land.

**geréf-mann, es ; m.** *The word is used to translate Latin forms elsewhere translated by* ge-réfa. v. ge-réfa ; II :—Sum geréfman *quidam curialis,* Gr. D. 308, 13. Sum man háten Stephanus, sē wæs on getale þára geréfmanna (*in numero optio fuit*) . . . 'Sæge Stephane þám geréfan (*dic Stephano optioni*)' . . . 'Ic eom onsænded tó Stephanes hūse þæs geréfan (*ad Stephanum optionem*),' 314, 1–14.

**geréf-scipe.** *Add :* **I.** *consulate.* v. ge-réfa ; I, II :—Geréfscipe *consulatus,* Wrt. Voc. ii. 18, 19 : 79, 40. [Cf. Maxence steorede þe refschipe in Rome *Rome Maxentium Augustum nuncupauerunt,* Kath. 11. Under Maximien hehest i Rome, þ is heh reue . . . ant se riche refschipe to rihten, Jul. 9, 11.] **II.** *stewardship, office of bailiff.* v. ge-réfa ; **III :**—Ne mót mid rihte nán preóst beón worldstrútere on geréfscipe (cf. 198, 21), Ll. Th. ii. 386, 8. **III.** *reeveship.* v. ge-réfa ; **IV :**—Gif man spor gespirige of scýre on óðre . . . habban þá geréfscypas bēgen þá spǽce gemǽne, Ll. Th. i. 236, 24.

**geréf-scir** or -scire. *Substitute :* **geréf-scír, e ; -scíre, an ; f. I.** *office of* ge-réfa. v. ge-réfa ; I, II :—Geréfscíre *praefecturae* (*dignitas*), An. Ox. 1382. Hē is nū geréfscíre healdende in Rómebyrig *in Romana civitate locum praefectorum servans,* Gr. D. 193, 9. **II.** *stewardship.* v. ge-réfa ; III :—Hē is tó ágeldenne gescád his geréfscíran (*uillicationis*), R. Ben. L. 107, 16. Groefscíre, Lk. L. 16, 2. From ðǽm groefscíre, 4. Mín hláford míne geréfscíre (þ groefscíre, L.) fram mē nymð, Lk. 16, 3.

**ge-regne, -réne, es ; n.** *Take here* ge-rēn *in Dict., and add :* **I.** *a structure, building :*—Gesih ðás miclo gehríno ł glencas (getimbrunga, W.S.) *uide has magnas aedificationes,* Mk. L. 13, 2. **I a.** *edification :*—Gód word tó gehrīne *bonus sermo ad edificationem,* Rtl. 12, 27. **II.** *an instrument :*—In aldum gehrīne *in ueteri instrumento,* Mt. p. 2, 11. **III.** *an ornament :*—Hæled gierede mec (*a book*) mid golde ; for þon mē glíwedon wrætlic weorc smiða. Nū þá gereno and se reáda telg wíde (beóð) mǽre, Rä. 27, 15 (v. Jn. p. 188, 4 *infra*). Ðære hálegestan hálignesse gimmas on ðǽm gerēnum ðæs biscepes gierelan *sanctuarii lapides in ornamento Pontificis,* Past. 135, 12. Billfrið gismioðade ðá gihrīno ðá ðe útan on sint, and hit (*the book*) gihrīnade. mið gold and mið gimmum, Jn. p. 188, 4 (v. Rä. 27, 15 *supra*). Tó middangeardes gihrīna *ad mundi ornatum,* Rtl. 108, 29. Wē hig willað mid trahtnunge geglengan and heora gerēna gecýðan, Angl. viii. 326, 2. *See next word.*

**ge-regnian.** *Add*: I. *to put in order, garnish, trim*:—Hī gehrīndon (*ornauerunt*) lēhtfato hiora, Mt. L. 25, 7. Hūs mið bēsmum geclǣnsad and gehrīnæd *domum scopis mundatam et ornatam*, 12, 44. II. *to prepare, dress* material. v. ge-regnung:—Gecnūwa þā wyrta, gemeng wið buteran and on þā ilcan wīsan gerēna þe ic ǽr cwæþ, Lch. ii. 94, 27. Gehīwian, geregnian *inficere* (cf. ? *vellera succo inficere*, Ald. 75, 17). Gerēnodne senep, Lch. ii. 184, 8. Genim hrȳþeren fǣsc gesoden on ecede and mid ele gerēnod mid sealte, 186, 18. Swā gerēnode, 62, 7. III. *to arrange, contrive, plan*:—Wīf, gif heó mid hwylcum cræfte hire hǣmed gerēnad *mulier, si aliquo molinine, fornicationem suam peregerit*, Ll. Th. ii. 156, 8. Þæs geregnedan *concinnati* (cf. ? *concinnati facinoris*, Ald. 38, 27), Wrt. Voc. ii. 23, 80. Geregnodae *mendacio conposito*, Txts. 76, 618. Gerēnode, Wrt. Voc. ii. 55, 63. IV. *to ornament, adorn*:—Gē gehrīnas (*ornatis*) byrgenna sōðfæstra, Mt. L. 23, 29. Hē hit (*a book*) gihrīnade mið golde and mid gimmum, Jn. p. 188, 4. Dæt hrægl . . . scolde beón . . . gerēnod mid golde, Past. 83, 24. Gerēnod cæppe *penula*, Wrt. Voc. i. 25, 55. Geafum gehrīned (*ornatum*), Lk. L. 21, 5. Þte þū sié gihrīnad *exornari*, Rtl. 105, 19. Ic ann Ǽdelwerdæ ānæs gerēnodæs drincæhornæs, C. D. iii. 361, 8. Sittan on gerēnedum scridwǣne *in curuli sedere*, Bt. 27, 1 ; F. 96, 1. Ne mē nā ne lyst heáhsetla mid golde and mid gimmum gerēnedra, 5, 1 ; F. 10, 17. Ǽteówigende him þā gerēnodan tunecan, Hml. S. 10, 66. Dās fato cræfte gihrīnado hǣdenra giclǣnsiga *haec vascula, arte fabricata gentilium. emundare*, Rtl. 97, 27. v. un-geregnod, ymb-gerēnod.

**ge-regnong.** *Substitute*: **ge-regnung**, e ; *f. A preparation of drugs*, &c. :—Geregnong *confectio* (cf. *robetae et spalangii confectio confectio*, Ald. 25, 16). [*The gloss to this passage in* Wrt. Voc. ii. 78, 45 *is* gereohnung (*l.* geregnung? *or* gereónung? v. gereónian)], Wrt. Voc. ii. 18, 12. v. ge-regnian ; II.

**gerela.** v. girela : ge-rēn. *l.* ge-rēne, *and see* ge-regne.

**ge-rendrian** *to strip off* bark, *peel*:—Gerendra elnrinde and āwyl swīðe, Lch. ii. 66, 24. Cf. be-rindran.

**ge-rēne** *ornament*. v. ge-regne.

**ge-rennan** ; *p.* -renned *To coagulate* (trans.) :—Þā meolc geren mid cȳslybbe, Lch. iii. 18, 11. Dūn gerenned *mons coagulatus*, Ps. Cant. 67, 16. [*O. H. Ger.* ge-rennen ; *pp.* ge-rant, -rennit *coagulare*.]

**ge-reócan** *to smoke* (trans.), *fumigate, steam* :—Wyrc beþinge . . . hæt stānas swīþe hāte . . . hē sitte on stōle ofer þǣre beþinge þ heó hine mǣge tela gereócan, Lch. ii. 340, 8.

**ge-reohnung.** v. ge-regnung.

**ge-reónian.** *Add*:—Unrihtwīsnessa eówre handa gereóniaþ *iniustitias manus uestrae concinnant*, Ps. L. 57, 3. Fācna bepǣcunge gereónedan strofas *factione concinnabant*, An. Ox. 2899. Gereónedes *concinnati* (*facinoris*), 2823 : 2918. Gereónude *conspirati*, 863. Þā gereónedan leásunga *concinnatas factiones*, 2802.

**ge-reónung.** *Substitute for second passage* :—Swicful feónda gereónung *fraudulenta emulorum factio*, An. Ox. 2243. v. ge-regnung.

**ge-reord** *speech*. *Add*: [*The word seems feminine in* Bd. 1, 23 ; Sch. 49, 8.] I. *voice, language, speech, words* :—Ne mage wē āwrītan ealle his wundra on ðisum scortan cwyde mid cūðum gereorde, Hml. Th. ii. 514, 30. Word mīn onfōh . . . ; ongit mīne clypunga cūðum gereorde *verba mea percipe ; intellige clamorem meum*, Ps. Ben. 5, 1. I a. *the voice* of a trumpet, *notes* of a horn :—On gehreorde t on stefne bēman *in uoce tubae*, Ps. L. 46, 6. Þonne ic (*a horn*) winde sceal swelgan of sumes bōsme, hwīlum ic gereordum rincas laðige tō wīne, hwīlum sceal stefne mīnre flȳman feóndsceaðan *when I must swallow wind from somebody's lungs, sometimes with my notes I summon men to the feast, sometimes with my voice I put foes to flight*, Rä. 15, 16. II. *a language, tongue* :—Þurh þ gereord (*Hebrew*) þe ǣrest cōm on middanearde, Angl. vii. 40, 387. Þā eallreordan þeóde, þāra ðe hī furðon þā gereorde (*furðum* gereord, *v. l.*) ne cūðan *barbaram gentem, cuius ne linguam quidem nossent*, Bd. 1, 23 ; Sch. 49, 8. In Englisc gereorde (on Englisce reorde, *v. l.*), 4, 24 ; Sch. 481, 12. Heora ælc oncneów his āgen gereord, Hml. Th. i. 314, 15. Wǣron swā fela gereord swā ðǣr manna wǣron, 22, 23 : 318, 22 : ii. 582, 5 : Angl. vii. 40, 382. On þām dæge wurdon tōdǣlede manna gereordu ; and ǣr wæs eall woruld sprecende on ān gereord, and nū synd gereord twā and hundseofontig, Wlfst. 211, 17-20. Swā micel ungewiss on þeóda gereordum, Ors. 3, 9 : S. 136, 24. Hī cūðon ealle woruldlice gereord, Hml. Th. i. 298, 7 : ii. 202, 20 : Ll. Th. ii. 370, 27. v. Lǣden-, scop-gereord.

**ge-reord** *food*. *Add*: [*n.*] *and* f.? *See first passage under* II. *food, meat* :—Beren hlāf wæs his gereorde, Shrn. 110, 6. Be abbodes beódes gereorde. Ðæs abbodes mȳse sceal ā beón gemǣne þearfum of *the food at the abbot's table. The abbot's table must ever be shared by the needy*, R. Ben. 93, 2. Him wæs hlāf ān tō gereordum and wæter tō drynce *of solid foods he ate only bread and had only water to drink*, 100, 28. I a. *in pl. a meal, feast* :—Hē him tō rǣde genōm þæt hē hié ealle tō gereordum (*filiae nuptiis*) tō him gehēte, Ors. 4, 5 ; S. 166, 27. Hē fōddor bigeð, æfter ðām gereordum ræste sēceð, Pa. 36. Gyf hig hwylc hȳrēdes fæder tō hūse gelaðige, sē þe wyle . . . æt him onfōn þā gereord gāstlicre lāre, and him syllan līchamlice gereordo, Ll. Th. ii.

410, 21-25. ¶ æt gereorde (-um) *at meat, at table* :—Sæt hē mid ðām cynincge æt gereorde, Chr. 1053 ; P. 182, 20. Hlengendes æt gereordum (ligendes æt geriordum, L.) *recumbentis*, Mt. R. 26, 7. II. *a meal, feast, refection* :—Oð ðæt þ gereord (oð þæt gereord, ðā gereorde, *v. ll.*) gefylled wæs *usque ad prandium completum*, Bd. 5, 4 ; Sch. 569, 15. Þæs hālgan gereordes *of the Lord's supper*, Hml. S. 23 b, 621. Be gereordes tīdum *quibus horis reficiunt fratres*, R. Ben. 65, 12. His gereordes þigene hē āna underfō æfter gebrōðra gereorde *refectionem cibi post fratrum refectionem solus accipiat*, 49, 7. Martha gelaðode hine tō hire gereorde, Hml. Th. ii. 438, 11. His metes gereord hē āna underfō *cibi refectionem solus percipiat*, R. Ben. 50, 3. Hē gearcode him gereord *fecit convivium*, Gen. 19, 3. v. ǣfen-, beód-, cyning-, nōn-, symbel-, undern-gereord[e].

**ge-reord** ; *adj. Having a language.* v. un-gereord.

**ge-reordan.** *Add*: I. *absolute, to take food for refreshment, take refreshment, eat, feast* :—Hī sǣton þ hig gemǣnelīce gereordodan, Hml. S. 23, 243. Gehriordig *epulare*, Lk. 12, 19. Gif þā gebrōþru on middæg gereorden, gereorde (-reordige, *v. l.*) hē on nōn *si fratres reficiant sexta hora, ille frater nona*, R. Ben. 49, 8. Tō middæges hī gereordian (*reficiant*), tō ǣfenne hī gereordian (*cenent*) . . . hī gereordian (*prandeant*), R. Ben. I. 73, 4-9. Þæt hig habbon him tō gereordienne *ut habeant ad vescendum*, Gen. 1, 30. Æfter þām ætgædere gereordende, Hml. S. 23 b, 115. II. *with object, to refresh* a person with food :—Ōþerne þū gereordst *alium reficis*, Scint. 160, 8. Is hit cyn þ gē þone nid eówrum gāstlicum lārum gereordian þe eów mid his woroldlicum gōdum gereordað, Ll. Th. ii. 410, 27. Hū heó mihte þurh Godes lāre hire sāwle gereordigan, Hml. Th. ii. 440, 19. Ic beó gereordod *uescor*, An. Ox. 56, 348. Gereordede *saginantur, i. pascuntur, nutriuntur*, 993. Ðonne hiera niéhstan ðurh hié beóð gereorde (*reficiuntur*) ðæt hié selfe ne fæsten, Past. 137, 24. Hié næfre ne beóð gereorde mid gōdum weorcum, 283, 12. II a. *reflexive, to refresh oneself, take food* :—Hē gereordode hine æfter his ǣriste, Hml. Th. i. 296, 24. Hē gelōme æt heora hūse hine gereorde, ii. 438, 19. Þenunge hē þider brōhte þ hī be dǣle hī gereordodon, Hml. S. 23, 240. Arīs and gereorda þe (*surge et comede panem*, 1 Kings 21, 7), 18, 185. Gifernys bið þæt se man ǣr tīman hine gereordige, Hml. Th. ii. 218, 29. v. ǣfen-gereordian, un-gereordod.

**gereord-dæg,** es ; *m. A day on which a meal* or *feast is celebrated* :—On þām mōnðe þe Aprilis [hātte], þǣre nigeðan nihte, on þām drihtenlican gereorddæge (*on Holy Thursday.* Cf. tō þon hālgan ǣfenne þæs hālgan gereordes, þ is tō þām hālgon þurresdæg, 621), and æfter þām hūslgange, Hml. S. 23 b, 753.

**ge-reordedlic, -reordlic.** v. un-gereordedlic.

**gereord-gleáwness,** e ; *f. Skill with the voice* :—Singað him on gehreordgleáwnesse *psallite ei in uociferatione ;* play skilfully with a loud noise (A. V.), Ps. L. 32, 3.

**ge-reordig-hūs.** *Dele, and see* gereording-hūs.

**ge-reording.** *Add*: I. *the taking* or *the giving of refreshment* :—Ðæs mōdes gereordung is betere þonne ðǣre wambe *it is better to refresh the mind than the belly*, Hml. Th. ii. 440, 19. Hē sæt tō þām cāsere and hī swȳðe blȳðe wǣron for Martines gereordunge (*because Martin feasted with them*), Hml. S. 31, 630. Tō þæs līchamon gereordunge (þone līchaman mid tō gereordianne, *v. l.*) *ad reficiendum corpus*, Gr. D. 129, 6. II. *a meal, refection* :—Gereordunga *prandii*, R. Ben. I. 73, 9. Gereordunge æfter gereordunge āna hē under[fō] *refectionem cibi post fratrum refectionem solus accipiat*, 56, 12. Hē mē gesyllde mid nīwre gereordunge *nova refectione me satiat*, Gr. D. 86, 23. Þ wē mōton becuman tō his gereordunge, Hml. A. 10, 247 : Hml. S. 31, 625. Metes gereordung (*cibi refectionem*) āna hē underfō, R. Ben. I. 57, 7.

**gereording-hūs,** es ; *n. A refectory* :—Gereordunghūs *refectorium*, Wrt. Voc. i. 82, 18.

**gereording-tīd,** e ; *f. Meal-time* :—Hē cōm symle tō his gereordungtīde (*ad horam refectionis illius*), Gr. D. 118, 12 : 145, 13.

**ge-reordness.** *Substitute*: I. *refection, refreshment, the taking* or *giving of food* :—Wæter gereordunge *aquam refectionis*, Ps. L. 22, 2. On þā tīde his gereordnysse *ad horam refectionis illius*, Gr. D. 118, 13 : 145, 14. Hē hī in gelaðode tō gereordnesse, 252, 12, 16. Hē brōhte mē hlāf tō gereordnesse, 347, 32. Wīn tō his heortan gereordnysse, Ll. Th. ii. 438, 17. Genihtsumlic wæstm ðā willnodon gereordnesse (*refectionem*) gegearowode, Bd. 4, 28 ; Sch. 521, 23. II. *a refection, food* :—Hē mē gereordode mid nīwre gereordnysse, Gr. D. 86, 24. III. *the condition of having been fed* :—Gereordnisse *saturitatem*, Ps. Srt. 105, 15.

**ge-resp.** *Substitute*: *Proved* against (*on*) a person :—Gif mon folcleásunge gewyrce, and hió on hine geresp (ge-ræf, *v. l.*) weorðe, Ll. Th. i. 80, 21. v. ræpsan.

**ge-rest.** *Add*:—Mið ðȳ uēre cynig in his gireste *dum esset rex in accubitu suo*, Rtl. 4, 11. v. wind-gerest?

**ge-resta.** *Add*: m. [cf. ge-bedda, ge-maca, -mæcca] :—Tācnað þ dēmena and gerestena cwealm, Lch. iii. 168, 6.

**ge-restan.** *Add:* -ræstan. I. *intrans.* (1) *to repose on a couch,
lie down :—*Ic neapiu and gerestu *obdormiam et requiescam,* Ps. Srt. 4, 9.
Sē đe gehrestađ *qui recumbit,* Lk. L. 22, 27. Monige synnfulle gereston
(-ræston, L., *discumbebant*), Mk. R. 2, 15. Geræstun, Mt. L. 9, 10. Þ
hē ne mæge þonne hē cymeþ tō his wīfe hyre mid gerestan, Lch. i. 364,
3. (1 a) *to rest in the grave, lie buried :—*Marcus gerested Alexandrea,
Rtl. 195, 33: 196, 9, *and often.* Gerestes, 196, 13. Lucas gereste in
þǣr byrig *Lucas requievit Bochtia,* 196, 1, *and often.* (1 b) *of animals,
to lie on the ground :—*Ic scīp mīno giresta dōm *ego oves meas accubare
faciam,* Rtl. 10, 3. (2) *to desist or refrain from exertion :—*Ic fiigu
and gerestu, Ps. Srt. 54, 7. (2 a) *of things, to cease, not be active :—*
Gerestađ *conquiescunt* (*jurgia*), Kent. Gl. 997. (3) *to be at ease,
remain undisturbed, dwell :—*Hwelc eardađ in selegescote đīnum, ođđe
hwelc gerested in munte đīnum?, Ps. Srt. 14, 1. Monige cymas and
gehrestas (wuniađ, W. S.) miđ Abraham in rīc heofna, Mt. L. 8, 11.
Hierusalem . . . in þē sāwle sōđfæstra simle gerestađ, Cri. 53. Flēgende
heofnes girestun (gehræston, L.) on telgum his, Lk. 13, 19. On sibbe
gerestian hē gewunađ, Scint. 11, 19. (4) *of position, to rest on :—*þā
se gāst gereste on him, hig wītegodon, Num. 11, 25. (5) *to lie or lean
upon, support oneself on :—*Đe ofer brēst Drihtnes geræste, Mt. p. 8, 17.
Gireste (giræsti, L.), Jn. R. 21, 20. (6) *to remain confident :—*Flēsc
mīn gerested in hyhte, Ps. Srt. 15, 9. II. *reflexive, to rest oneself.*
(1) *to repose in sleep :—*Gedō þæt ic mōte slāpan and mē gerestan, Ps.
Th. 4, 9. (1 a) *of the sleep of death, to die, fall on sleep :—*Hēr Iohs
hine gereste in Effesia (cf. hē (*John*) eōde cucu and gesund intō his
byrgene, Hml. Th. i. 74, 25), Chr. 100; P. 9, 13. (2) *to refresh by
resting :—*Gān wē sēcan ūre gesthūs þ wē magon ūs gerestan, Ap. Th.
18, 16. (3) *where labour is desisted or refrained from :—*Ōđer, resten-
dæg . . . is þæt ēce līf, . . . on þām wē ūs gerestađ ēcelīce, Hml. Th. ii.
208, 6. Hē hine gereste on þone seofođan dæg, Ll. Th. i. 44, 13.
(3 a) *to desist from exertion, labour, &c.* (*gen.*) :—Hié heora gefeohta
hié gerestan, þēh hié þæs hungres and þæs moncwealmes ne mehte
*cessatum est a praeliis, cessatum tamen a mortibus non est,* Ors. 2, 4; S.
70, 9. (4) *to be at ease, remain quiet, dwell, lodge :—*Hwā eardađ on
þīnum temple, ođđe hwā mōt hine gerestan on þǣm hālgan munte?, Ps.
Th. 14, 1. 'Hæt him findan hwǣr hē hine mæge wurđlīcost gerestan
(*where he may lodge most honourably*),' . . . Apollonius onfēng þǣre
wununge đe hym betǣht wæs, Ap. Th. 18, 22–25. (4 a) *with
adverbial complement :—*Đonne gerest đæt mōd hit orsorglīce on đǣre
fortrūwunga *mens in sui confidentia secura requiescit,* Past. 463,
10. III. *trans.* (1) *to give rest to a person, cause to cease or
refrain from work :—*Gerested *feriatus,* Wrt. Voc., ii. 108, 41. Gerested,
33, 56. Gerestad *feriatus, pausatus, quietus,* 148, 3. (2) *to lodge.*
Cf. II. 4 :—Gyf man mēte þ hē weorđlīce gerestod sió, gōd þ byđ, Lch.
iii. 174, 32. [*O. H. Ger.* ge-resten *requiescere, cessare, pausare.*]

**ge-rēþre;** *adj. Constant :—*Hē biđ simle ryhtes gedeahtes gedafa, for
đǣm hē biđ suīđe arod and suīđe gerēđre on ryhtum weorcum *dum rectis
persuasionibus acquiescit, constanter se in bono opere dirigit,* Past. 306, 15.

**ge-rēþru.** *Add:* Oars for rowing *or steering, tackle of a ship :—*
Geroeđro, giroeđro, geroedra *aplustra,* Txts. 41, 178. Gerēđru, Wrt.
Voc. i. 63, 68. Gerēþro, ii. 10, 57. Gerēđro, 7, 5. þā hwīle þe þā
rōwendas þæs scipes gegearwodon ōþre gerēđru *dum nautae navis armamenta repararent,* Gr. D. 306, 4. [See note on Chr. 891 in Chr. P. ii.
103–5.] v. web-gerēþru.

**ge-rēþru?** v. ge-rīþre : **gēr-hwamlīce.** v. geár-hwāmlīce : **gerian.**
v. girwan : **ge-ricsian.** *Take here* ge-rīxian *in Dict.*

**ge-rid** meat, food(?). v. bed-gerid, *which may mean the food laid up
by the ants in the ant-hill :—*Eall seó lustfulnes and swētnes þæs līchaman
weorđeþ tō wyrma geride *dulcedo illius vermes* (Job 24, 20 where the
A. V. has, 'the worm shall feed sweetly on him'), Gr. D. 323, 3.

**ge-rid,** es; *n. Riding :—Equitatus* ferdwerod *vel* eóred, gerid, *i.
equitatio,* Wrt. Voc. ii. 143, 73.

**ge-rid** fever, inflammation (?). v. þeór-gerid.

**ge-rīdan.** *Add:* I. *to ride with others :—*Nū ic þǣr IIII men sende
(cf. nonne tres viros *misimus in medium ignis* ?, Dan. 3, 24) tō sīđe, nales
mē sylfa gerād, Az. 175. Gif þonne nelle hwā ge[rī]dan (rīdan, tō
rīdan, *v. ll.*) mid his geférum, Ll. Lbmn. 160, 16. II. *to traverse
by riding, ride over, ride along the boundaries of land :—*Đā ic sylf
gerād, C. D. v. 331, 1. Đus se preóst hit gerād and se geneát mid
hine (cf. hē hēht his geneát rīdan mid preóste, and hē hine đā gelǣdde
ealle đā gemǣru, 140, 30), 141, 24. Heó ealle þā þā landgemǣre
geridan, eal swā heó man on fruman þām bisceope lǣdde, iv. 235,
3. III. *to obtain by riding, ride and get, take possession of :—*
Đā gerād Æđelwald þone hām æt Winburnan būtan đæs cyninges leáfe
. . . and hæfde ealle đā geatu forworht, Chr. 901; P. 92, 3. III a.
*tō handa geridan to bring into a person's power or possession :—*Ic wille
đæt man it geride mē tō handa, C. D. iv. 222, 6. Hī sǣdon þām kinge
þ hē hæfde swýđe āgylt wiđ Crīst þ hē ǣfre sceolde niman ǣnig þing of
xp̄es cyrc̄ . . . , sǣdon þām kinge embe Sandwīc þ hit wæs him tō handa
geriden . . . Se king . . . swōr þ hit nǣfre næs nā his rǣd nā his dǣd þ
man sceolde Sandwīc dōn ūt of xp̄es cyrc̄, 57, 9–17.

**ge-rīd-men.** *Dele.*

**ge-rif** *a seizing. Substitute:* **ge-rif,** es; *n. A string* of things,
*a number of things strung together* (v. *N.E.D.* and *D.D.* riff, reeve
*a string* or *rope of onions*) :—Ān gerif fisca *una serta,* Wrt. Voc. i. 54,
40. Ān gerif fisca ođđe ān snǣs fisca ođđe ōđra þinga, 64, 9. [*Cf.
Icel.* rifa *to tack together.*]

**ge-rīf,** es; *n. A garment :—*Fōtsīd gerīf *limus* (limus *vestis quae ad
pedes producitur,* Isidor, v. Nap. 25), Wrt. Voc. i. 16, 45.

**ge-rīflod;** *adj. Wrinkled :—*Geryflodre *rugoso* (*cortice tectus*), An.
Ox. 26, 24. v. rīfelede.

**ge-rignan, -rīnan** *to rain on, wet with rain :—*Biđ gerīned *conpluitur,*
Wrt. Voc. ii. 22, 30.

**ge-riht.** *Add:* I. *where direction is marked, a straight line.* [The
phrase on *gerihte* (*geriht*) occurs often in the charters which give the
boundaries of land, and corresponds to various Latin phrases, e. g. *per
rectitudinem uiae,* C. D. v. 279, 1, 7 : *directe,* iii. 374, 10, 13 : *in directum,* 376, 16 : *recto cursu, itinere,* 381, 20, 30 : *recta semita, via,* 32 :
386, 23 : *rectissima tramite,* 388, 2] :—Ymb ūre landgemǣra ūp on
Temese . . . þonne on gerihte tō Bedanforda, Ll. Th. i. 152, 10. On
gerihte â be đan heáfdan, C. D. iii. 394, 32. Of đām beorge forđ on
geriht on đæt sīc, 38, 32. Dol him ne ondrǣdeđ þā deáđsperu, swylteđ
hwæđre gif him Meotud on geryhtu lǣteđ strǣle fleógan, Rä. 4, 55. II.
*a rule, canon :—*Gerihte *canone* i. *regula,* An. Ox. 3984. II a. *a direction, ordinance, precept :—*Swā miclan swā hē (*the provost*) furđur on
weorđmynte forlǣten biđ, swā miclan hē sceal geornlīcor Godes gerihta
healdan and regules beboda *quanto prelatus est ceteris tanto eum oportet
sollicitus observare precepta regule,* R. Ben. 125, 21. III. *justice
(in to bring to justice) :—*Ǣlc sý on borge gebrōht, and gehealde se borh
hine and gelǣde tō ǣlcon gerihte (rihte, *v. l.*), Ll. Th. i. 388, 1. IV.
in pl., *rights of a person, service, payment, &c. that a person is entitled
to, secular or ecclesiastical dues :—*Ǣhte swāne . . . gebyređ stīfearh . . .
and elles đā gerihtu đe đeówan men tō gebyriađ, Ll. Th. i. 436, 23.
Hēr swutulađ hwylce gerihta langon in tō Tāntūne . . . Đæt is of đam
lande æt Nigon hīdum . . . cirhsceattas, . . . heorđpenegas, . . . hāmsōcn
. . . Dunna . . . geaf tō gerihton .v. circsceattas . . . and of eáforda đā
ilcan gerihtu . . . Ealdred . . . dyde đe ilcan gerihta đæ man dyde of
Nigon hīdon . . . of Lidigerde .i. circsceatt and eall đe geilcan gerihta đe
man dyde of Baggabeorge . . . eall đæ geylcan gerihta đe man dēđ of
Cedenon, C. D. iv. 233, 3–34. Þ gē ne gearnian deáđ . . . mid ǣnigum
oftige Godes gerihta, ac ǣgđer ge earm ge eádig . . . gelǣste Gode his
teóđunga, Ll. Th. i. 270, 1. Nān mæssepreóst nānne mon . . . of ōđre
preóstscyre lǣre þ mon . . . him heora teóđunge syllan and þā geryhtu
þe hig þām ōþrum syllan sceoldan, ii. 410, 33. Gelǣstan Gode þā gerihtu
þe him tō gebyrian, þæt is se teóđa dǣl ealra þǣra đinga þe hē ūs tō forlǣten hæfđ, and ūre frumgripan gangendes and weaxendes, Wlfst. 113, 3.
Se scādwīs gerēfa sceal ǣgđer witan ge hlāfordes landriht ge folces gerihtu,
Angl. ix. 259, 5. V. *service, payment, &c. due from a person,
duties, obligations :—*Gebūres gerihte. Gebūrgerihta sýn mislice, gehwār
hý sýn hefige, gehwār eác medeme. On sumen lande is þ hē sceal wyrcan
tō wicweorce . . . forđige hē ofer þ geár ealle gerihtu đe him tō ge-
byrgean, Ll. Th. i. 434, 3–26. Landlaga sýn mistlice swā ic ǣr sǣde ;
ne sette wē na đās gerihtu ofer ealle đeóda, 440, 20. VI. *a rite,
office of the church :—*Ne sylle him nān preóst hūsl, ne nān þǣra gerihta
þe Crīstenum men gebyređ (*neque ullum eorum rituum qui Christianum
hominem decent*), Ll. Th. ii. 184, 23 : i. 406, 17. Heó gecóm tō đǣra
hālgena byrgenum and þǣr wunade of þæt Sixtus . . . biscop gehādode
đe mihte behwyrfan đā hālgan martiras mid gāstlicum sangum and Godes
gerihtum, Hml. Th. ii. 312, 31. Dō se sacerd him forgifennysse and his
gerihto *sacerdos ei remissionem det, et ritus ejus exsequatur,* Ll. Th. ii.
172, 20. þā smyrenysse begytan and þā gerihto þe þǣr tō gebyrgeađ
ǣlc þǣra manna þe đās gerihto hæfđ, his sāwl biđ clǣne, 178, 32–34.
Ǣlc sacerd sceal cunnan his gerihto (*officia;* cf. đā lāre þe tō his hālgan
hāde belimpđ, 200, 10), 196, 6. Ic eóde tō Godes đēnunge, and þæt
folc gebletsode, and him Godes gerihtu dyde, Hml. Th. ii. 32, 12. Ulf
đ ne cūđe dōn his gerihta (-e, *v. l.*) swā wel swā hē sceolde *nescivit
ministerium suum,* Chr. 1047; P. 171, 15. Ne nǣnne man man ne lǣte
unbisceopod tō lange, þe lǣste him forđsīđ getímige, and hē nǣbbe þā
gerihtu þe him tō gebyredon, Wlfst. 300, 28 : Hml. Th. ii. 142, 9.
Wurdon gelōme þā mǣdenu and se biscop on sundersprǣce gebysgode . . .
and hæfdon heora gerihtu mid þām biscope, Hml. S. i. 2, 342. VII.
*right, lawful procedure :—*Gif hwā būton gerihtum hit ābrecan wille
God hine tō rihtere bōte gecerre, C. D. iii. 5, 19. v. burg-, folc-, gebūr-,
port-geriht.

**ge-rihtan.** *Add:* I. *to right, set in order, make clear :—*Gerihte
*elimavit* (*itinerarium Petri decem voluminibus digestum luce clarius elimavit,* Ald. 27, 21. Cf. elimavit, interpretavit (haec Gregorius per allegoriam luce clarius elimavit, Ald. 13, 31), 76, 82), Wrt. Voc. ii. 29, 26.
Gerīæhte (gerihte?, gereahte (? cf. An. Ox. 2026 where the gloss is *elimauit, manifestauit* sē gerehte)), 78, 64. Bēda betwyx þām ōđrum þingum
þe hē beorhtlīce gedihte þás þing hē tō gerihte, and mid leóđlicum metre
be þām mōnđum þus giddode, Angl. viii. 301, 34. II. *to direct.*

(1) *to address* words to a person:—Ðone cwide Paulus geryhte tô biscepum, Past. 105, 8. (2) *to keep in right order, regulate the actions of*:—Girihte (*dirigere*) and gihálga and gihalda heorta and lícoma úsra, Rtl. 171, 3. Bêda cwæð ꝥ Ian. and October wæron mid twâm bendum gerihte, ꝥ ys ꝥ hig habbað twâ rihtinga, Angl. viii. 301, 48. (3) *to cause to move straight* to a point (*lit.* or *fig.*):—Girihte mec in sôðfæstnisse ðíne, Rtl. 167, 23. (4) *to regulate the course of, guide, instruct*:—Hié eówra sâwla mâ forhwerfdon þonne hié gerihton, Ll. Th. i. 56, 18. Geriht (*dirige*) mînne weg (se weg ys mín weorc), Ps. Th. 5, 8. Æfter þâm þe hê sylf geriht weard, Lch. iii. 440, 1. Ðâs bêc hê sceal nêde habban, gif hê wyle þâm folce æfter rihte wísigan, ... and beó hê æt þâm wær ꝥ hí beón wel gerihte, Ll. Th. ii. 350, 18. (5) *to order to be given, assign*:—Wíse worldwitan Críste and cyninge gerihtan þâ bôte, Ll. Th. i. 348, 15. **III.** *to correct.* (1) a person. (a) *to reform, amend*:—Ðonne ic man geryhtan ne mæg and hine geléran *quos corrigere nequeo*, Past. 153, 11. Ðâ suelcan wê magon ealra betest geryhtan mid ðý ꝥ wê hié forbúgen *quos melius corrigimus, si declinamus*, 293, 22. Gif hê þurh ðâ swingella ne bið geriht *si nec correxit opera sua*, R. Ben. 52, 8. (a a) used intransitively for reflexive:—Gif hê þurh þreále nele gerihtan, R. Ben. 126, 5. (b) *to rebuke*:—Mid ðý gerihte (-rihðe, L.) *cum corriperetur*, Lk. R. 3, 19. (2) *error*. (a) a mistake, a scribal error:—Ic bidde, gif hwá þâs bôc âwrítan wylle, þæt hé hig gerihte wel be þære bysne; ... mycel yfel dêð se unwrítere, gif hê nele hys wôh gerihtan, Ælfc. T. Grn. 24, 30–34: 21, 40: Hml. Th. i. 8, 11: Hml. S. p. 6, 75. Girihte *emendare*, Mt. p. 2, 12. Geboetað ł girihtad *emendata*, 15. Girihtæ *emenda*, 1. an erroneous practice:—Besmeáge hê his heorde, for þon þær synd sume wísan tô gerihtenne and tô gebêtenne, Hml. S. 23 b, 634. [O. H. Ger. ge-rihten *ordinare, dirigere, apponere, corrigere.*] v. un-geriht.

**ge-rihtlæcan.** *Add*: pp. -læced. **I.** *to make straight* (lit. or fig.):—Hê (*John*) Crístes wegas gerihtlæhte mid wordum, Hml. S. 16, 96. Sceal gehwâ gerihtlæcan þæt þæt hê ær tô wôge gebígde, Hml. Th. i. 8, 14. *Via iustorum recta facta est*, þæt is þæra rihtwísra wæg is gerihtlæced, Hml. S. 2, 61. **II.** *to direct.* (1) *to cause to move in a certain direction* (*lit.* or *fig.*), *to an end or purpose*:—Is ôðer wiðerwinna ðe ús wyle gerihtlæcan fram úrum unðeáwum ... þæt is Godes word þe ús gewissian sceal, Hml. A. 5, 125. Gyf ðæron gerihtlæhte (*dirigantur*) wegas míne tô gehealdenne rihtwísnessa, Ps. L. 118, 5. (2) *to regulate the course of, guide, instruct* a person, *advise*:—Hí heora lífes ðeáwas æfter Godes bebodum gerihtlæcað, Hml. Th. i. 536, 24. Weorc úra handa gerihtlæc (*dirige*) ofer ús, Ps. L. 89, 17. Þæt wê úre ðeáwas be his bebodum gerihtlæcon, Hml. Th. i. 578, 32. Gif ðú nelt gerihtlæcan þone unrihtwísan wer and him sylfum secgan his unrihtwísnesse (*si non annunciaveris impio, neque locutus fueris ut avertatur a via sua impia*, Ezechiel 3, 18), Hml. A. 12, 300. Sê þe behýd scylda his nâ byð gerihtlæht, Scint. 37, 7. Hú hê his âgen líf gerihtlæcan mid rihtre æfestnesse, Lch. iii. 438, 30. **III.** *to correct.* (1) a person, *to reform, amend*:—God gerihtlæcð ðâ synfullan and hylt ðâ gôdan, Hml. S. 21, 93. Lâr þín gestýrde ł gerihtlæhte (*correxit*) mê, Ps. L. 17, 36. Þâ hwíle þe wê magon ús gerihtlæcan, Hml. A. 8, 194: Hml. Th. ii. 572, 11. Gyf hê ðurh mynegunge nele beón gerihtlæht *ammonitus si non correxerit*, R. Ben. 112, 14. Se cyning weard gerihtlæht þurh þære cwêne geleáfan, Hml. A. 101, 323. Ðeáh ðe se stunta beó gemynegod, hê ne byð gerihtlæht (*non emendetur*), Ælfc. Gr. Z. 264, 5. Ne bið se stunta mid wordum gerihtlæced, Hml. Th. ii. 352, 15. Mid langsumum broce hê weard gerihtlæced, i. 536, 2. Wê ne synd þurh his swingla gerihtlæhte, 580, 4. (2) *error*:—Hê sylf gerihtlæce his dæda and þeáwas tô his Drihtnes willan, Hml. S. 21, 49. Gif hwylc brôðor ... nelle his þeáwas gerihtlæcan (*non emendaverit*), R. Ben. 52, 6. Hí noldon heora synna gerihtlæcan, Hml. Th. ii. 352, 22. (3) used absolutely:—Gif hê þurh mynegunge gerihtlæcan nelle, R. Ben. 113, 14.

**ge-rihtreccan.** *Substitute*: To shew rightly, demonstrate. v. reccan; III. 6:—Ic þe meg secgan þæt ic eom seó gesceádwísnes ðínes môdes, þe ðe wið sprecð, and ic eom seó racu ðe mê onhagað ðê tô gerihtreccenne (*the demonstration that it is in my power to give you*), þæt þú gesyhst myd þínes môdes eágan God swâ sweotole swâ þú nú gesyhst myd ðæs lícuman æágan ðâ sunnan *promittit ratio quae tecum loquitur, ita se demonstraturam Deum tuae menti, ut oculis sol demonstratur*, Solil. H. 26, 5–9.

**ge-rihtwísian.** *Add*:—Gerihtwísiendre *justificante*, Wülck. Gl. 251, 35. **I.** *to maintain the righteousness* of a person:—Gê eów sylfe beforan mannum gerihtwísiaþ, Lk. 16, 15. **II.** *to exculpate*, in theology *to declare* or *make free from the penalty of sin*:—Andetnys gerihtwísað, andetnys synne forgyfednysse sylð, Scint. 40, 13. Ðâ ðe God gerihtwísode on ðyssere worulde, Hml. A. 45, 516. Mid ânre clypunge weard þæs synfulla gerihtwísad, Hml. Th. ii. 430, 1. Sê þe behýt his leahtras, ne bið hê gerihtwísad, Angl. xii. 513, 16. **III.** *to shew* an action, statement, &c. *to be right, defend as right*:—Swâ hwæt swâ ðú cwist oþþe dêst, ic hit gerihtwísige, Hml. Th. i. 380, 4. Eall ic gerihtwísige ꝥ þú cwist, Bl. H. 185, 35.

**ge-rihtwísung**, e; f. *Justification*:—Gerehtwisunge míne *justificationes meas*, Ps. Srt. 88, 32.

**ge-rím.** *Add*: **I.** *number, measurement that determines how many*:—Of geríme geteald (beón) *laterculo dinumerari*, An. Ox. 3227. Þâ hig wæron on gehríme scortum *cum essent numero brevi*, Ps. L. 104, 12. Heora tel oferstíhð sandceosles gerím, Hml. Th. i. 536, 35. ¶ gerímes *in number*:—Hê giémde hwæt hê hæfde monna gerímes, and ne nôm nâne ware húlíce hié wæron, Ors. 5, 4; S. 224, 21. Se tíma wæs standende twâ þúsend wintra and twâ hund and twâ and feówertig geára gerímes, Angl. viii. 336, 2. **I a.** in phrases denoting that objects cannot be counted:—Hý wæron gemanigfealdode ofer ælc gerím (*super numerum*), Ps. Th. 39, 6. **II.** *reckoning, computation* of time. v. gerím-cræft:—Þâ Egyptiscan ðeóda ongunnon heora geáres getel on hærfeste. Nú ongind úre gerím on ðysum dæge, Hml. Th. i. 98, 24. Gyf þú nelt hine tellan tô þâm mônan ... þonne âwægst þú þone eásterlican regol and ælces níwes mônan gerím, Lch. iii. 264, 17. **II a.** *a calendar, numeral*:—Mæssepreóst sceal habban ... sangbôc and handbôc, gerím (gerímbôc ? *q. v.*) and pastoralem, Ll. Th. ii. 350, 14. **III.** *a number, class of objects*:—Þâ beóð on hæðenra manna geríme *cum gentilibus adnumerandi sunt*, Ll. Th. ii. 154, 30. Seó forme âbecêdê on þâm geríme ys bútan pricon, Angl. viii. 322, 42. Forgif mê ꝥ ic môte on þâm geríme beón þe ðú þá fore gebædæ, Angl. xii. 508, 10. **IV.** *a period of a certain number of days* (?):—Wê sceolan under þæm feówerteóþan geríme (*Lent*) syllan þone teóþan dæl úre worldspêda, Bl. H. 35, 18.

**ge-rím;** adj. v. un-gerím.

**ge-ríman.** *Add*:—Ealswâ feala mærþa ic geríme (*numerabo*), An. Ox. 4762. Ic geríme hí *dinumerabo eos*, Ps. L. 138, 18. Hí gerímdon (*dinumerauerunt*) ealle bân míne, 21, 18. Wê sceolon geríman úre misdæda, Hml. Th. ii. 430, 7. Seó ungemetlice mengeo þæs folces wæs þâ iéðre tô oferwinnanne þone heó ûs sié nú tô gerímanne, Ors. 2, 5; S. 80, 12. Is gerímed *supputatur*, An. Ox. 3832. [O. H. Ger. gerímen *numerare*.]

**gerím-bôc** *a numeral, calendar*, &c. v. ge-rím; II, II a:—Sume úre ðéningbêc onginnað on Adventum Domini; nis ðeáh þær for ðý ðæs geáres ord, ne eác on ðysum dæge nis mid nânum gesceáde, þeáh ðe úre gerímbêc on þissere stôwe geedlæcon, Hml. Th. i. 98, 28.

**ge-rímcræft.** *Substitute*: gerím-cræft, es; m. The science of number, arithmetic:—Gerímcræft *arithmeticam*, An. Ox. 7, 390. ¶ the word almost always occurs in reference to calculation connected with the calendar. Cf. ge-rím; II, II a:—Hêr onginð gerímcræft æfter Ledenwarum ... and Engliscum þeódum, Angl. viii. 298, 1. Bêda cwæð on þære bôc þe hê gesette be gerímcræfte and hig *de temporibus* genemde, 308, 38. Þâ Egiptiscan þe sêlost cunnon on gerímcræfte tealdon ꝥ seó lenctenlice emniht is on duodecima kl. April., Lch. iii. 256, 7. Wíse Rômâne gesetton on gerímcræfte þæt næfre ær xi. kl. Aprelis Eástortíd gewurðan sceal, 226, 8: Hex. 8, 5. Swâ swâ láreówas secgað on gerýmcræfte, 12, 23. Wê cweðaþ on gerímcræfte Cathedra Sancti Petri seofon nihton ær þâm mônðe þe wê Martius hâtað, Hml. S. 10, 1. Wê gesetton on þissum enchiridion ... manega þing ymbe gerímcræft, Angl. viii. 321, 34.

**ge-rímed.** v. un-gerímed: **ge-rímedlic.** v. un-gerímedlic.

**ge-rímian;** p. ode To calculate, compute:—Understand þú ꝥ ic wyð þê nú gerímige *understand the computation that I am making with you*, Angl. viii. 307, 40.

**ge-rímlic.** v. un-gerímlic: **ge-rínan** to rain on. v. ge-rignan: **ge-rínan** to touch. *The passage should be given under* ge-hrínan: **ge-rinelic.** v. ge-rýnelic: *nauum* gerinen (l. germen, v. Corp. Gl. H.), Txts. 35, 24.

**ge-rinnan.** *Add*: **I.** of persons, *to come together, congregate.* Cf. Goth. ga-rinnan *convenire, congregare*:—Ealle weorðaþ Fæder ætsomne ... and on heofonsetle heán gerinnað his sunu blíðe *the Father honours all together ... and in high heaven his sons assemble glad* (the Latin is: Cunctos (Deus) honorat ... collocat Altithrono laetosque in sede polorum), Dôm. L. 276. **II.** of material, *to coagulate, condense* (intrans.), *get mingled*:—Gerunnen *concretum*, Wrt. Voc. ii. 105, 36: 15, 34: *concreta*, i. *commixta, conjuncta, coadunata*, 136, 24. Gerunnenes *refrigerati*, Germ. 398, 143. **II a.** figurative:—On ânum æge þæt hwíte ne bið gemenged tô ðâm geolcan, and bið hwæðere ân æg. Nis eác Crístes godcundnys gerunnen tô ðære menniscnysse, ac hê þurhwunað þeáh on ânum hâde untôtwæmed, Hml. Th. i. 40, 29.

**ge-rinning**, e; f. Coagulation, thickening:—Wið þâ gerynnincge þæs wormses ym(b) ðâ breóst ... syle þicgean ...; þâ breóst beóð âfeormude, Lch. i. 292, 8.

**ge-ríp.** *Add*: **I.** *harvest, gathering of grain*, &c.:—Fela landa wuniað gyt on hæðenscipe and úres Hælendes geríp mænigfeald is on mancynne, Hml. S. 29, 128. Æfter heora gerípe (*printed* gerepe, Lch. iii. 252, 23) gæð seó eá upp, and oferflêt eal þæt Egyptisce land, Scrd. 27, 1. **II.** *what is reaped, corn*:—Hê lædde hâm tô his byrene ꝥ âsnidene geríp (*messem*) þe hê ær mid his handa geseów, Gr. D. 290, 20. Heora æceras ær wæron âþroxene ær ænig ryftere ꝥ geríp (*the MS.*

*has the accent*) gaderode, Hml. S. 31, 1218. Ic sende iów giríp (girípa? *the Latin is* metere) þte gē ne wunnun, Jn. R. 4, 38. *See next word.*

**ge-rípan.** *Add:*—Gehrioppa *metere,* Jn. L. 4, 38.

**ge-rípan** *to rob, spoil:*—Hús ðæs gehrýpes *domum illius diripiat,* Mt. L. 12, 29.

**ge-rípian.** *Add:* I. *of vegetables, to get ripe:*—Hēt hē him bringan bere tō sǣde . . . Hit weóx . . . and wel gerípode, Hml. Th. ii. 144, 13. II. *of non-material objects, to get mature:*—Se mynstres hordere sī . . . wīs, on gerípedum þeáwum (*maturis moribus,* R. Ben. 54, 8: R. Ben. I. 61, 5. [*O. H. Ger.* gerífén (-ōn) *maturescere.*] v. un-gerípod.

**ge-rís** *rage:*—Gerís *rabies,* Wrt. Voc. ii. 118, 66. v. rīsan.

**ge-rísan** *to be fitting.* [*In line* 11 *l.* gerise beþ.] *Add:* I. *with noun subject:*—Þænne dreám gerist, Men. 58. Fǣmne æt hyre bordan gerísed, Gn. Ex. 64: 67. I a. *with dat. of object:*—Ðē gerist māra campdōm, Hml. Th. i. 418, 8. Ðǣm alde ne gehrísed (*conuenit*) þ ēsceapa, Lk. L. 5, 36. II. *with pronoun subject.* (1) *referring to preceding statement:*—Wīde is geweorðod, swā þæt wel gerist, hāligra tīd, Men. 120. (2) *representing a following clause:*—Wel þ gerás þ heó wǣre eáðmōd, Bl. H. 13, 16. Rihte hit gerist þæt hine ealle riht-willende herian *rectos decet collaudatio,* Ps. Th. 32, 1. II a. *with indefinite* hit *as subject:*—Swā swā hit wel swā ārwyrðum bisceope gerás *iuxta uenerationem tanto pontifice dignam,* Bd. 3, 17; Sch. 268, 23. Swā hit ús eallon gerise, Ll. Th. i. 238, 17. III. *with no subject expressed:*—Hī hine weorþodan, swā cinige geríseþ, Bl. H. 69, 32. Gā þ land . . . swā gegódod swā heom bām gerísan mage, C. D. iv. 86, 15. III a. *where a clause follows the verb:*—Suelcum ingedcone gerist (*congruens*) ðæt hē . . . wið ða scíre ne winne, Past. 61, 10. Gerist þ him mon lytlum ða mettas selle, þā þe late melten, Lch. ii. 176, 22. Wel þē gerísed þæt þū sié heáfod, Cri. 3. III b. *with infin.:*—Sileð bodo ðæm gerises bodage *dat praecepta quibus debeant praedicare,* Lk. p. 6, 14. Gehrísed (girísed, R.) mē geonga, Lk. L. 13, 33: 17, 25. III bb. *with acc. and infin.:*—Ðās gerás geðrouia Críst *haec oportuit pati Christum,* Lk. L. R. 24, 26. III c. *with gerundial infin.:*—Ðā ðe gehrísed tō cuoeðanne *quae oporteat dicere,* Lk. L. 12, 12. Gerísed tō wyrcanne, 13, 14. Gerás tō wyrcanne, 11, 42. [*O. Sax.* gi-rísan: *O. H. Ger.* ge-rísan *decere, convenire, congruere.*] v. un-gerísan.

**ge-rísan** *to rise together:*—Gif gē girioson (*consurrexistis*) mid Críste Rtl. 25, 1.

**ge-risene.** [*In line* 4 *l.* Bd. 1, 26.] *Add:*—Sēc man ymbe mínre sáwle þearfe swā hit beón mæge, and swā hit eác gerysne sý, C. D. ii. 117, 2. Ne wēre girisen ł reht tō unbindanne *non oportuit solui,* Lk. R. 13, 16. Æfter gerisenre (-rys-, *v. l.*) āre his lífes and hāda *iuxta honorem et uita et gradu eius condignum,* Bd. 4, 26; Sch. 508, 10. Hē sóna þāra gerisne andsware onsende *nec mora, congrua quaesitui responsa recepit,* 1, 27; Sch. 61, 1. Þā gerisnan *ratam* (*rata et grata holocaus-tomata,* Ald. 72, 29. Cf. rata, perfecta, Corp. Gl. H. 101, 14), Wrt. Voc. ii. 87, 9. Ðā giriseno wræccum *digna plagis,* Lk. R. 12, 48. v. sácerd-, un-gerisene.

**ge-risene**; *n. Add:* I. *honourable conduct, dignity:*—Alfwold Eást-Engla kyning, mid rihte and mid gerisenum ríce healdend (*rite regimina regens*), Guth. Gr. 101, 4. II. *honour shewn to a person:*—Þ hē (*the new bishop*) mōte beón þæra þinga wyrþe þe oþre beforan wǣron, Dúnstān and mænig oþer, þ þes mōte beón eall swā rihta and gerysna wyrðe, Cht. E. 232, 22. Ænne scegð . . . hē wolde ful gearwian his hláforde tō gerisnum, Cht. Crw. 23, 9. v. un-, weorold-gerisene.

**ge-risenlic.** *Add:* I. *meet, fitting, proper as a matter of duty:*—þ þes mōte beón eall swā rihta wyrðe, þ inc byð bām þearflic for Gode and eác gerysenlic for worolde, Cht. E. 232, 23. þ ēgo lǣred blíðe wēre gerisnelic *oculum docet simplicem esse debere,* Lk. p. 7, 10, 17. Ne wēre gerisnelic ł reht tō unbindanne *non oportuit solui,* Lk. L. 13, 16. Gehrisnelic woere gefeáge *oportebat gaudere,* 15, 32. II. *suitable, suited to one's needs:*—Gif þeós nīwe lār ōwiht cuðlicre and gerisenlicre brenge *si haec noua doctrina certius aliquid attulit,* Bd. 2, 13; Sch. 166, 8. III. *deserving honour, honest, creditable:*—Ðonne mon hwæt ryhtlices and gerisenlices geðencð *quando qua justa, qua honesta cogitan-tur,* Past. 155, 24. Ðeáh ðe ful monige mid gerisenlicum weorcum (*honesta actione*) ārísen from eorðan, 157, 8. v. un-gerisenlic.

**ge-risenlíce.** *Add:* I. *suitably, appropriately:*—Hwā mæg þā nú, þe ic beeóde, gerisenlícor tōweorpan þonne ic sylfa *quis ea, quae colui, aptius quam ipse destruam?,* Bd. 2, 13; Sch. 168, 3. Hwilc biscop . . . gehālgad wǣre, þ wē on ðysse æfterfylgendan bēc gerisenlícur (-rysen-, *v. l.*) and gelimplícur secgað *quis . . . dedicatus sit antistes libro sequente oportunius dicetur,* 3, 29; Sch. 330, 4. Tō swylcre tíde swylce heom eallum þince ðæt hī best and gerisenlícost hī forðbringan magon, C. D. iii. 295, 10. II. *honourably.* (1) *in a way that deserves honour, creditably:*—þ ic unfracodlíce and gerisenlíce mihte steóran þone anweald þe mē befæst wæs, Bt. 17; F. 58, 27. (2) *in a way that shews honour or respect:*—Þæs bisceopes bān . . ., swā swā hit wel swā ārwyrðum bisceope gerás, gerisenlíce gehealdene wǣron *ossa eius . . .*

*iuxta uenerationem tanto pontifice dignam condita sunt,* Bd. 3, 17; Sch. 268, 24. v. un-gerisenlíce.

**ge-risennes.** *Substitute: Congruity, suitability:*—Gerisnessa *con-gruentia,* Wrt. Voc. ii. 24, 37.

**ge-rislic.** *Substitute: In agreement with, similar:*—Wæs hē geris-licre (gelícre, *v. l.*) willsumnesse mōdes þām cyninge *pari ductus deuotione mentis,* Bd. 5, 19; Sch. 653, 19. v. ge-risenlic.

**ge-risnian.** *Add:*—Gerisnian *convenire,* Wrt. Voc. ii. 15, 65. Gerisniende *congruentes,* 24, 46.

**ge-rípe,** es; *n. A small stream, rivulet:*—Of deópan cumbe on cwenena brōce; of cwenena brōce úp be ðām geríðe (geride, C. D. B. iii. 37, 24; *but see on* ðā (= ðā) eá, 27, wid (= wid, 29) tō ðām beorgan, C. D. iii. 430, 1.

**ge-rípre,** es; *n.?:*—Of ðām gāran in on ða ýfre; of ðære ýfre, in on ða gareðru; of ðām gereðran, C. D. iii. 279, 24. Of ðæm crundele on ða lytla hwītan gerýðra beneaðan ýfre on ðane þorn, 415, 32.

**gér-líc.** v. geár-líc: **gernan.** v. girnan: **ge-rod.** v. web-gerod: **ge-ródfæstnod.** v. rōd-fæstnian.

**ge-roscian** (-rōscian?); *pp.* od *To dry by heat:*—Geroscod *parsus* (l. *passus*), Wrt. Voc. i. 288, 60. Geroscade *pasceos* (l. *passos*), ii. 116, 31. v. ge-rōstian.

**ge-rōsod.** *Substitute:* (1) *flavoured with rose-leaves:*—Dō hwōn gerōsodes eles tō, Lch. ii. 40, 4. Mucgwyrte seáw wiþ gerōsodne ele gemenged, 68, 10. (2) *rose-scented:*—On gerōsedne brǣd *in rosatum odorem,* An. Ox. 3278. Gerōsodne, 2, 185.

**ge-rōstod.** v. rōstian; ge-roscian.

**ge-rótsian.** *Substitute: To gladden, delight:*—Se ilca lust ðe hine geunrótsað on ðære dégelnesse his mōdes hine eft gerótsat, gif hē him wiðstent, Past. 417, 9. Girótsiað *contristant,* Rtl. 56, 20. (*Either* ge-unrótsiað *or* un-gerótsiad *should be read.*) v. un-gerótsod.

**ge-rōwan.** I. *to row, sail:*—Hrōwundum ł mið ðý gehrówun *nauigantibus,* Lk. L. 8, 23. II. *to reach by rowing* (*sailing,* &c.), *sail to a place:*—Ðona gehrēwun *enauigauerunt,* Lk. L. 8, 26. III. *to traverse in a vessel, row along* a boundary:*—Ðā ic sylf stundum gerád, stundum gereów, C. D. v. 331, 2.

**gerst.** Dele.

**ge-rúm;** *adj. Ample, far-reaching, unrestricted.* v. rúm; VI:—Syndon þíne willan rihte and gerúme, Dan. 291. [*Ger.* ge-raum.]

**ge-rúme;** *adj. Substitute:* **ge-rúme;** *adv. Without the pressure of care.* v. rúme; III:—Is mín mōd gehǣled, hyge ymb heortan gerúme (*thought has free play round my heart*), Gen. 759.

**ge-rúmlíce;** *adv. With large limit of space:*—þā wæs eáðfynde þe him elles hwǣr gerúmlícor ræste [sōhte] . . . heóld hyne syððan fyr sē þǣm feónde ætwand *then was easily found who elsewhere for himself with larger limit of space looked for a bed,* i. e. *who would not sleep in the hall . . . : kept himself after further away who the foe fled from,* B. 139.

**v. ge-hrimpan: ge-runn.** [Cf. *O. H. Ger.* ge-runnida *concretum, coagula.*] v. cýs-gerunn: **ge-rúxl.** v. ge-hrúxl: **gerwan.** v. girwan.

**ge-ryd.** *For second passage see* girwan; I; *for first passage substi-tute:* **ge-rýdan** (-ryddan?, v. ā-ryddan); *pp.* -rýd *To clear* land:—Ic ongyte þæt þā worlde lustas ne sint eallunga āwyrtwalode of ðínum mōde þeáh se grāf geryd sí *though the stumps have not been rooted out entirely, the trees have been cut down and cleared away,* Solil. H. 39, 5. [*O. H. Ger.* riuten *evertere* (*nemora*). Cf. *Icel.* ryðja *to clear* land.] v. un-gerýde.

**ge-rýde;** *adj. Smooth, easy, pleasant:*—þā unc gerýde wæs, Rä. 64, 15. v. un-gerýde.

**ge-rýdelic.** v. un-gerýdelic: **ge-rýdelíce.** v. un-gerýdelíce: **ge-rýdness.** v. un-gerýdness.

**ge-rýman.** *Add:* I. *to make roomy.* (1) *to enlarge so as to occupy a greater space:*—Hē his ēdel gerýmde, Hml. S. 25, 283. Hié út hiora ēðel gerýmdon, Past. 3, 8. þonne sió wund sié clǣne, gerýme þ þ þyrel tō nearo ne sié, Lch. ii. 208, 24. (2) *to extend so as to include a greater space:*—Hié woldon gerýman (*dilatare*) hiora landgemǣru, Past. 366, 4. II. *to remove obstruction from* (1) *so as to allow passage, clear a way, passage,* &c.:—þu him weg gerýmdest on þǣre reádan sǣ, Hml. S. 11, 184. Hié gerýmdon þone úpgang and geworhtan, Bl. H. 201, 17. Hē hæfð ús gerýmed rihtne weg tō ēcan lífe, Wlfst. 18, 6. Hē hæfð gerýmed rihtwīsum mannum infær tō his ríce, Hml. Th. i. 28, 12. Ic wæs þǣr inne, þā mē gerýmed wæs . . . sið ālýfed inn under eorðweall, B. 3088. (2) *so as to allow occupation, to clear* a space:—Tō þǣre hýde . . ., þā ús gerýmde rodera Waldend, Cri. 866. Hié him flet ge-rýmdon, healle and heáhsetl, B. 1086. Ðām hālgum gāste byð eardung-stōw on þām menn gerýmed, Wlfst. 34, 3. Hig noldon þ útlendiscum þeódum wǣre þes eard þurh þ þe swíðor gerýmed, þe hí heom sylfe ǣlc ōðerne forfóre, Chr. 1052; P. 180, 25: Met. 1, 19. þē (*Noah after the Deluge*) is ēðelstōl eft gerýmed, Gen. 1485: B. 1975. Wæs benc gerýmed, 492. Eów is gerýmed, gāð ricene tō ús *cleared is the ground for you, come to us quickly,* By. 93. (2 a) *where the obstruction, person*

or thing, removes itself, *to leave clear*, of persons, *to evacuate* :—Seó sǽ ût flówende him gerȳmde þreora mîla [fæc?] drîes færeldes, Hml. Th. i. 564, 18. Hî flugon and þæt îgland eallunge gerȳmdon ðǽm æðelan cempan, ii. 142, 33. (3) so as to allow access, *to clear the way to* :— Gife unscynde mægencyning ontȳnde, tîdum gerȳmde, El. 1249. (4) so as to allow free action, *to give free course to* :—Hê his godcundnesse mid sôþum wîsum gerȳmeþ *he gives free play to his divine powers*, Bl. H. 179, 24. Metod môd gerȳmde, Exod. 479. (4 a) the object a moving thing, *to clear a course for* :—þá ongunnon hî on ôðre stôwe gerȳman þá eá *fluvium per loca alia derivare conati sunt*, Gr. D. 192, 22. (4 b) the object an action, *to make the way clear for, give opportunity for* :— Ne gladige hê on þæt, swilce him gerȳmed sȳ and antimber geseald, þæt hê God bereáfige, Lch. iii. 442, 36. þá him gerȳmed weard þæt hié wælstôwe wealdan môston, B. 2983. III. *to clear away an obstruction* :—Swá hwæt swá þæne migdan gelet, hyt gerȳmd and ford gelǽdeþ, Lch. i. 90, 27. Wegas syndon drȳge, holm gerȳmed, Exod. 284. IV. intrans. *To make* or *leave the way clear* to (tó) a place, condition, object, *make way* for a person :—Hê ôðrum gerȳmeð wyrmum tô wiste *he leaves the way clear for other worms to get food*, Seel. 123. Árîse se gingra and þám yldran tô setle gerȳme *minor surgat et det majori locum sedendi*, R. Ben. 116, 5. God ûs gerȳme tô ðǽre êcan myrhðe, Wlfst. 80, 7. þæt him Dryhten þurh deáðes cwealm tô hyra earfeða ende gerȳme *that for them the Lord by death's pang clear the way to the end of their troubles*, Gû. 196.

ge-rȳne. Add : I. *what is kept from observation* or *knowlèdge, a secret, mystery* :—Gerȳna vel dîgla *sacramentum* vel *mysterium*, Wrt. Voc. i. 47, 26. Dyrne gerȳna *abdita* (*secretorum*) *arcana* (*produntur*), An. Ox. 4216. For foresmeá[gende] gerȳna dîgla *ob indaganda secretorum archana*, 1505. Ðys syndon þá hálgan gerȳnu þe þá twêgen wîtegan gesáwon and gehȳrdon, Nic. 19, 5 : 11, 29. II. *what is beyond mere human comprehension, a mystery*. (1) of speech (prophecy, allegory, &c.) :—Wê nestan ǽr hwæt se blinda wæs; nû wê magon ongytan hwæt þ gerȳne tâcnaþ, Bl. H. 17, 14. Gerȳna *oracula*, An. Ox. 2535. (2) of actions, events, &c. :—Se Hǽlend his þegnum sǽde his þrowunga... hié ne mihton þá word ongeotan þæs heofonlican gerȳnes, Bl. H. 17, 9. III. *what is beyond ordinary knowledge, an obscure subject* :— Wê tôdǽlað þá dagas þæs geáres þurh seofon, and swá wê becumað tô þám andgite swá myceles gerênes (*y is written over the second* e), Angl. viii. 302, 39. Bissextus ... wê wyllað nû ymbe his gerȳnu smeágan, 305, 41. Iungum cnihtum geopenian þ hig ôðrum gecȳðon þe his gerêna ne cunnon, 306, 17. IV. *a mystic meaning* :—Hê (*Felix*) ealle þá ðeóde æfter þám gerȳne (-um, *v. l.*) his noman (*iuxta sui nominis sacramentum*) fram wôhnesse álȳsde, Bd. 2, 15; Sch. 176, 22. V. in a theological sense, *a religious rite, sacrament of the church* :—On þǽre cyricean biþ sungen þ hálige gerȳne, Bl. H. 77, 16. þám gerȳne onfôn fullwihtes baþes, Bd. 1, 27; Sch. 76, 6. Gerȳne *sacramento*, i. *misterio* (*baptismatis*), An. Ox. 2074. Gemǽnsumiende gerȳnæ *communicans sacramentum* (*Dominicum*), 2141. Hê sealde hi[m] þ hálige gerȳne Crîstes lîchaman and blôdes, Hml. S. 30, 97. Clǽne girȳne *sacrificium*, Rtl. 109, 21. Ðá gerȳnu (-o, *v. l.*) þæs heofonlican cyninges *sacramenta caelestis regis*, Bd. 2, 9; Sch. 143, 17 : Hml. S. 23 b, 112. Gerȳnum *sacramentis* (*missarum*), An. Ox. 2875. Gerȳna *sacramenta* (*catholicae fidei*), 3218. V a. *the consecrated elements of the eucharist* :—Hê hî gesmyrode mid gehálgudum ele, and eác gehúslode mid þæs Hǽlendes gerȳnum, Hml. S. 3, 80. v. ge-rȳno, gerȳnu.

ge-rȳnelic. Add : I. *secret* :—Eall swá seó gerȳnlice sôðfæstnys cwyð *sicut arcana justitia dicet*, Ll. Th. ii. 168, 5. Ǽr þon þe hê þǽre gerȳnelican gegaderunge menniscre gebyrde onfênge *before he was formed in the secrecy of his mother's womb*, Bl. H. 165, 35. II. *mystic, allegorical, figurative* :—þ swîðe wel in þám hálgan stǽre mid gerȳnelicre gesǽgene (*figurata narratione*) is áwriten, Gr. D. 245, 15. Gerȳnelice smeáunge *typicum* (i. *mysticum*) *scrutinium*, An. Ox. 1083. III. *pertaining to a sacrament*. v. ge-rȳne. V:—Hê þigde þá gerȳnu ... and þá wæs singende þá gerȳnelican sangas his sealma (*mysticos psalmorum cantus*), Gr. D. 275, 13. ¶ The following gloss seems erroneous :—*Secundis* i. *serenis* (has *secretis* been read ?) gesundfullum, gerȳnelicum, An. Ox. 2581.

ge-rȳnelîce. Add : I. *in secret, mysteriously* :—Eal þæt se sácerd dêð þurh ðá hálgan þênunge gesewenlîce, eal hit fulfremeð se hálga gást gerȳnelîce, Wlfst. 36, 9. II. *mystically* :—Gerȳnelîce *mystice*, Wrt. Voc. ii. 55, 84. Swá swá hit hêr mid sumum wordum gerȳnelîce gereht is, Gr. D. 246, 16. Ðis wed wê healdað gerȳnelîce, Hml. Th. ii. 272, 7. Gerȳ[nelîce] *tropice*, i. *tipice*, An. Ox. 5088.

ge-rynning. v. ge-rinning.

ge-rȳnu. Add : gen. e (?). I. *a secret, secret counsel* :— Nyte gê ðá micclan deópnysse Godes gerȳnu (cf. Godes dîgelan dômas, 3)?, Hml. Th. ii. 340, 8. II. *a mystery* :—For ðî is þæt hálige húsel geháten gerȳnu, for ðan ðe ôðer ðing is ðǽron gesewen, and ôðer ðing undergyten, Hml. Th. ii. 270, 27. II a. *mystery, mysterious matter* :—Þis godspel is mid menigfealdre mihte þǽre heofenlican gerȳnu áfylled, Hml. Th. i. 90, 10. III. *a*

*religious rite, sacrament* :—Gâstlicere gerȳne *mistico* (*baptismatis*) *officio*, An. Ox. 2884. Hê þigde þá gerȳnu (*sacramentum*) þæs drihtenlican lîchaman and blôdes, Gr. D. 275, 12. III a. *the consecrated elements of the Eucharist* :—Sacerdas cômon and hî gehûsloden mid hâligre gerȳnu, Hml. S. 9, 148.

ge-rȳþre. v. ge-rîþre.

ge-saca. Add : *One who is in conflict with another*. (1) in a general sense, *an opponent, adversary* :—þ sum wer wunne on þǽre hefigestan hatunge his gesacan (*adversarii sui*), Gr. D. 158, 26. (2) where a case is tried, *an accuser* :—Him wæs leáf seald þæt hê môste him scyldan on andweardnesse his gesacena (-ona, *v. l.*) (*praesentibus accusatoribus*) ... wæs cȳðed þæt hys wrêgend and his gesacan (*accusatores eius*) leáse wið hine syredon, Bd. 5, 19; Sch. 668, 1–2. [Cf. ga-sachio in Salic law, Grm. R. A. 855.]

ge-sacan. *In the passage* ge-sêcan *seems a necessary emendation :* ge-sacu. *Against the emendation* ge-saca *it may be noted that the other nouns in the passage, beginning,* 'Nô hine wiht dweleð,' *represent things* (âdl, yldo, inwitsorh), *and a noun of the same kind seems more suitable than one denoting a person. If* eówan *could here be intransitive, like the compound* æt-eówan, gesacu *and* ecghete *would be parallel.*

ge-sadelod. Add :—Se nacoda assa bið mid reáfum gesadelod, Hml. Th. i. 210, 30. v. ge-rǽdod.

ge-sadian. Add : [O. H. Ger. ge-satôn *satiare, saturare*] : ge-sêccan *disserere*. v. ge-secgan.

ge-sǽgdnis. Substitute : ge-sǽgednes, e; f. I. *a sacrifice, an offering* (especially of the Eucharist) :—Wê sceolon Gode âsecgan þá dæghwámlîcan onsægdnesse his lîchaman and blôdes. Þeós gesægdnes gehǽleð þá sáwle *debemus Deo quotidianas carnis ejus et sanguinis hostias immolare. Haec victima animam salvat*, Gr. D. 348, 18. *Nolite dare sanctum canibus*, þ is ðȳ hálga gesægdnisse æt hundum nêre gesald, þ is unwyrðum monnum, Mt. L. 7,.6 mgn. II. *a mystery of religion* :— Iúh gesald is þ gê witte clǽno rȳno ł gesægdnisse ł diópnise (*mysteria*) rîces heofna, Mt. L. 13, 11. v. on-sægdnes.

ge-sǽlan *to bind*. Add : I. *to bind* a living creature. (1) with a material bond :—Satan læg sîmon gesǽled (cf. rîded racentan sâl, 372), Gen. 765. (2) *to restrain, confine* with non-material bonds :—Sûsle gesǽled, ... wîtum gebunden, Jud. 114. II. *to bind* a thing, *put a cord, chain,* &c., *round an object, to secure by binding* :—Hê hêt gebindan beám ǽrenum clammum and îsernum and gesǽledne in sûsl dôn (*clamavit:* '*Germen radicum alligetur vinculo ferreo et aereo,*' Dan. 4, 12), Dan. 521. þér wæs helm monig ..., earmbeága fela searwum gesǽled (*ingeniously strung together ?*), B. 2764.

ge-sǽlan. Add : I. of a person, *to succeed* in a purpose, *bring about something*. Take here ge-sǽlan *to be successful* (in Dict.). II. of a concrete thing, *to be brought about, be made, come into existence* :—Hî wênað þ þ ealdgesceaft ǽfre ne wênað, þ hit weás côme, nîwan gesǽlde (cf. wênaþ þ þ ne sié eald gesceaft, ac sié weás geworden nîwane, Bt. 39, 3; F. 216, 4), Met. 28, 73. III. *of non-material things, events, circumstances,* &c. (1) the subject a noun, *to befall, happen, come to pass* :—Siððan him gesǽlde sigorworca hrêð, Exod. 316. Swylce mǽla swylce hira mandryhtne þearf gesǽlde, B. 1250. (1 a) a pronoun representing a preceding circumstance :—þæt ne geweorðe þ þyllic gȳmelêst gelimpe. Sȳ georne bewarnod þæt hit ná ne gesǽle (*proveniat*). Gif hit gelimpe (*contigerit*), R. Ben. 36, 6. (2) the circumstance, &c., given in a following clause, *to happen* that. (a) the subject a pronoun in apposition to the clause :—Oft þæt gesǽleð, þæt wê brecað ofer bædweg, An. 511. Gif þæt gesêle, þæt mîn cynn gewîte, Cht. Th. 472, 4. (b) the subject a more or less indefinite *hit* :—Hit oft gesǽled þ ..., Nar. 7, 25. Hit gesǽlde (cf. hit gebyrede, Bt. 38, 1; F. 194, 2) gió on sume tîde, þæt Aulixes hæfde cynerîcu twá, Met. 26, 4: 9, 23. Hit mæg eáðe gesǽlan, ðæt hié ðá ôðre tǽlen, Past. 333, 20: 427, 24. (c) the subject not expressed :—Swá gesǽlde þæt wê wada cunnedon, An. 438: 661. IV. referring to the course of events. (1) the subject the indefinite *hit* = matters, things :—Gif hit þonne hwæt elles gesǽlde *if then matters turned out somewhat differently*, Cht. Th. 166, 20. (2) the subject not expressed :—Hwîlum ûs on ȳdum earfoðlîce gesǽled *at times things go hard with us at sea*, An. 515.

ge-sǽlan *to succeed*. See preceding word: ge-sǽlge. For Cot. 89 substitute Wrt. Voc. ii. 37, 63. (Gesǽlge might be adjective, fauste *being* = faustae. Cf. *for the termination* (-e = ae) attrite gegnidenan, 5, 12. v. also 5, 3.)

ge-sǽlþ. Add : -sǽligþ. (Cf. mirigþ *and* mirig) *happiness*. [Uniseli bið þe ʒitsere þe þurh his iselhðe leosað, O. E. Hml. i. 109, 30. Iseluhðe, A. R. 382.] v. un-gesǽlþ.

ge-sǽlig, es; m. *One who carries a standard*. [*The gloss in which the word occurs is:* Wîcbora, gesǽli *signifer*, i. *qui signum fert*, An. Ox. 3808. *The passage glossed is:* Signifer duelli fertur ... *Napier suggests that* gesǽd, *rather than* ge-sǽli *should be read, and that the gloss belongs to* fertur. Cf. fertur sǽd, An. Ox. 4, 2.]

ge-sǽlig. Add : I. *happening by chance, fortuitous* :—Mid gesǽligum gelimpum *fortuitis casibus*, An. Ox. 4185. II. *happy, favoured by*

*lot, position,* or *other external circumstance, fortunate :*—Tô hwon sceoldan mîne frîénd seggan þæt ic gesælig mon wǽre? Hû mæg sê beón gesælig sê þe on ðâm gesælþum ðurhwunian ne môt? *quid me felicem jactastis amici?*, Bt. 2; F. 4, 14. Hû gesælig seó forme eld wæs *felix nimium prior aetas,* 15; F. 48, 2. Se singala ege ne lǽt nônne mon gesælinne (*felicem*) beón ... Ic wundrige hwî men ... wênen þte þis andwearde lîf mæge þone monnan dôn gesæligne ..., þonne hit hine ne mæg æfter þŷs lîfe earmne gedôn, 11, 2; S. 26, 6–17 : 14, 1; F. 42, 21. Dôn swâ gesæligne þ hê nânes þinges mâran ne þyrfe, 26, 1; S. 58, 17. Sume hê bereáfaþ hiora welan (*weal;* quosdam remordet) swîþe hraþe þæs ðe hî ǽrest gesælige weorþaþ, 39, 11; F. 218, 22. Gesǽlie, 5, 13; S. 13, 21 : 36, 2; S. 104. Gesælige hî (*the Innocents*) wurdon geborene þæt hî môston for his intingan deáð þrowian, Hml. Th. i. 84, 1. Gif nû hwâ cwiþ þ sê seó gesælig, sê ðe his woruldlustum fulgæþ, hwî nyle hê cweþan eác þ ðâ nŷtenu seón gesælige (-sælegu, *v. l. beatae*), Bt. 31, 1; F. 112, 6. þâ yfelan bioþ micle gesæligran ðe on ðisse worulde habbaþ micelre weán *feliciores esse improbas supplicia luentes,* 38, 3; F. 200, 2. Getǽc mê sumne mann þâra þe ðê gesælegost þince, 11, 1; F. 32, 16 : 20; S. 48, 12; 26, 1; S. 58, 26. Se gesælgesta, 8; S. 24, 26. þone ealra gesælgostan mon hêr on worulde, 11, 1; S. 24, 25. **II a.** *having a fortune, wealthy :*—Hê gewât ǽhte lǽdan ... golde and seolfre swîðfeorm and gesælig, Gen. 1770. **II b.** *favoured* in respect to mental or moral endowments, *happy* in disposition, &c. :—Ðæt hê sié se gesælgosta on eallum cræftum ofer ealle ôðre men *quasi prae ceteris praepollens,* Past. 463, 13. **III.** *happy* in respect to moral or spiritual well-being, *blessed* :—Sê he gôd biþ, sê biþ gesælig, and sê ðe gesælig biþ, sê biþ eádig, Bt. 36, 6; F. 182, 12 : Bl. H. 101, 5. Nôe wæs gôd, nergende leóf, swîðe gesælig, Gen. 1286. Se feónd and se freónd ... synnig and gesælig, El. 956. Ðû miht ongitan þ ǽlc gôd man biþ eádig, and þ ealle gesælige men beóþ Godas *bonos omnes, eo ipso quod boni sunt, fieri beatos liquet; sed qui beati sunt, deos esse convenit,* Bt. 37, 2; F. 190, 6. **III a.** *of the happiness of heaven* :—In lifgendra londes wynne hê gesælig eardaþ, Cri. 438 : 1461. Mid his hâlgum on ðâm êcan êðle wê syððan gesælige rîxiað, ælces yfeles orsorge, Hml. Th. ii. 222, 26. **IV.** *happy, characterized by good fortune, favourable, propitious :*—Gesælig wæs heora âcennednys, for ðan ðe hî gemêtton þæt êce lîf on instæpe þæs andweardes lîfes, Hml. Th. i. 84, 6. Gesælige synde[r]gife *felix priuilegium,* An. Ox. 2588. Gesæligum (*propter*) *secundos* (*eventus*), 4549. Gesæligum edhwyrftum *felici reditu,* Wrt. Voc. ii. 148, 30. v. un-, weorold-gesælig.

**ge-sælige;** *adv. Happily.* v. ge-sælge.

**ge-sæliglic.** *Add :* **I.** *happy* from one's lot. Cf. ge-sælig; **II :**—Gesett hæfde hê hié swâ gesæliglîce, Gen. 252. **II.** *of things, happy, characterized by good fortune.* Cf. ge-sælig; **IV :**—Bið hyra meaht and gefeá swîðe gesæliglic sǽwlum tô gielde, Cri. 1079. Hû gesæliglica tîda ðâ wǽron giond Angelcynn, Past. 3, 4.

**ge-sæliglîce.** *Add :*—Nǽron hî (*the Innocents*) gerîpode tô slege, ac hî gesæliglîce þeáh swulton tô lîfe, Hml. Th. i. 84, 6 : Bl. H. 171, 11. þâ hê þâm biscope þâ fremdan hǽlo forgeaf, þâ becôm hê gesæliglîce tô his âgenre hǽle, Gr. D. 190, 30. v. un-gesæliglîce.

**ge-sælignes.** *Add :* **I.** *hap, fortune.* v. ge-sælig; **I :**—Wǽgendre gesælignesse *fallentis fortunae,* Wrt. Voc. ii. 146, 73. Gesælinesse *fatu,* An. Ox. 2627. Hwæt wilnast þû þonne þ þu hæbbe æt swelcre gesælignesse? *quid autem tanto fortunae strepitu desiderastis?*, Bt. 14, 2; F. 44, 5. **I a.** *a hap, fortune, an event :*—Gesundfullum gesælinessum *secundis successibus,* An. Ox. 2582 : *prosperis successibus,* i. *fortunis,* 3995 : 4260. **II.** *happiness, good fortune, happy estate.* v. ge-sælig; **II.** (1) *of persons :*—Ðyncð him ðæt hié wiellen âcuelan for ðære medtrymnesse ðæs ôðres gesælignesse (*felicitatis*), Past. 231, 21. Ðâ sceáwede ic mîne gesælinesse (*felicitatem*) and mîn wuldor and þæ ... gesælignisse mînes lîfes, Nar. 7, 21. (2) *of things, favourable condition, richness of soil :*—þâ gesælignesse þære eorðan *fertilissimarum regionum felicitatem,* Nar. 5, 23. **III.** *blessedness, beatitude.* v. ge-sælig; **III :**—Ðû sǽdest þ Godes gôdness and his gesælignes and hê self þæt þ wǽre eall ân *ipsam boni formam, Dei, ac beatitudinis loquebaris esse substantiam,* Bt. 35, 5; F. 164, 24. **IV.** *a happiness, what is characterized by good fortune, a favourable condition or circumstance.* v. ge-sælig; **IV :**—On eallum þisum lîchamlicum gesælignessum, Bt. 24, 3; F. 84, 10. v. un-gesæligness; ge-sælþ.

**ge-sællic.** *Add :*—Gesælicum gelimpum *fortuitis casibus,* Hpt. Gl. 504, 53. v. ge-sælig; I.

**ge-sællîce.** *Add :*—Gesælîcor *salubrius,* R. Ben. I. 18, 5. v. ungesællîce.

**ge-sælness,** e; *f. A hap, chance, event :*—Gesælnessum *successibus,* Hpt. Gl. 500, 21 : 506, 10. v. ge-sæligness; I a.

**ge-sæltan.** v. ge-siltan.

**ge-sælþ.** *Add :*—sælþu(-o). **I.** *a hap, fortune, an event :*—Of gesundfullum gesælþum *secundis,* i. *prosperis successibus,* i. *fortunis,* An. Ox. 3633. **II.** *happiness, good fortune,* (a) *favourable condition :*—Micel gesæld bið þê, þæt ðû on ðînre gesælðe ne forfare, Hml.

Th. ii. 392, 33. Ðonne hié gesióð ðâra ôðerra gesælðo (-a, *v. l.*) eáciende *dum augmenta alienae prosperitatis aspiciunt,* Past. 230, 19. Sume bioð tô ungemetlîce blîðe for sumum gesælðum, 455, 8. **III.** *happiness, blessedness.* Cf. ge-sælig; **III :**—Hæfde God þæs mannes sâwle gegôdod ... mid undeáðlicnysse and mid gesælðe ... wê forluron þâ gesælðe ûre sâwle, Hml. Th. i. 20, 1–3. **III a.** *the happiness of* heaven :—On Crîstes rîce is êce gesæld and eádignys, Hml. Th. i. 460, 18. Englas on gesælðe libbende, Ælfc. T. Grn. 2, 26. Gif hié geðenceað ðâra gesælða ðe him ungeendode becuman sculon *si attendatur felicitas, quae sine transitu attingitur,* Past. 407, 30. v. un-, weorold-, ge-sælþ.

**ge-sǽte,** es; *n. An ambush, a snare :*—Alles næhtes gisêto *totius noctis insidias,* Rtl. 37, 19. Cf. sǽt.

**ge-sǽtnian.** *Take here ge-setnian (l. -sêtnian) in Dict.*

**ge-sǽwe (?);** *adj. That may be seen, visible, apparent :*—Swâ swâ þeós gesêwe (gesewene?) sunne ûres lîchaman ǽágan onleóht, swâ onlîht se wîsdôm ûres môdes ǽágan, Solil. H. 44, 24.

**ge-sǽwness (?),** e; *f. The surface of the sea :*—Geséunes *aquor,* Wrt. Voc. ii. 8, 33. [Cf. (?) O. H. Ger. sêwen *stagnare.*]

**ge-sagian.** v. ge-secgan : ge-sagu. *Add :* þte hiá geendebrednadon ðæt gesaga *ordinare narrationem :* gesagun. *Add :*—Ðâ gisagune (cf. ge-segen : Icel. sǫgn; or *l.* ge-sagunc (=ung)). *See preceding word :* ge-sahte. v. ge-sêcan.

**ge-samhîwan.** *Add :* Ðâ gesomhîwan (*conjuges*) ... ðæt môd ðâra crîstenra gesamhîwena (*conjugum*), Past. 395, 31, 3. v. riht-gesamhîwan.

**ge-samnian.** *Add :* **I.** *to collect, get together.* (1) the object living creatures, *to assemble* for a common purpose :—Hê gesomnade alle ðâ aldormenn biscopa, Mt. L. 2, 4. Ðâ hêt heó gesomnian ealle þâ gelǽredestan menn, Bd. 4, 24; Sch. 485, 3. Ðider gesomnad biðon (*congregabuntur*) ðâ earnas, Mt. L. 24, 28. On þære stôwe wê wǽron gesamnode, Bl. H. 141, 27. Hié þyder in wǽron tô ðǽm lofsangum gesamnode, 207, 36 : 67, 21. (2) the object things. (a) material :—Gesomnadon *collegerunt,* Jn. L. R. 6, 13. Rômâne gesomnodon al þâ goldhord þe on Bretene wǽron, Chr. 418; P. 10, 17. þ unmǽte gestreón oþþe eal se wela þe hî dæghwâmlice gesamnodan *all the wealth that daily they amassed,* Bl. H. 92, 29. *Malagma, quod ... comprehendetur ... comprehendatur* in heáp bið gesamnod, Wrt. Voc. ii. 58, 57. Ic (*rain*) eom ... wedre gesomnad, Rä. 31, 2. (aa) *to collect* what is growing, *gather* fruit, corn, &c. :—Gesomnas (*gisomnigað, R.*) uæstem *congregat fructum,* Jn. L. 4, 36 : *colligent,* 15, 6. Ne of ðornum gesomnað (*colligunt*) fîcbeám, Lk. L. 6, 44. Gesomnigæþ (*colligite*) þâ weód ... hwǽte gesomnigaþ (*congregate*) in berern mîne, Mt. L. 13, 30. Ûre wæstmas gesamnian *to get in our harvest,* Bl. H. 39, 12. Gesomnad biðon ðâ unwæstma *colliguntur zizania,* Mt. L. R. 13, 14. (b) non-material. (a) *to accumulate* crimes, *heap up* damnation :—Hæfdon hié wrôhtgetême wið God gesomnod, Gen. 46. (β) *to concentrate* thought :—Gesamnige hê, swâ hê swîðost mæge, ealle tô þâm ânum his ingeþonc, Met. 22, 11. **II.** *to form by collecting, to collect* an army, a crowd, *assemble* a council :—Eádmund cyning gesomnode micelne sinoð tô Lundenbyrig, Ll. Th. i. 244, 2 : Chr. 673; P. 35, 22. þâ gesomnode man fyrde, 1001; P. 133, 21. Ær sió fierd gesamnod wǽre, 894; P. 84, 35. þær wæs gesamnod geþeahtendlic ymcyme, Ll. Th. i. 36, 7. þǽr witena bið worn gesamnod, Sal. 400. **III.** used reflexively, *to assemble, come together, meet.* Cf. ge-samnung; **II :**—Ðâ gesomnodon wê ûs ymb þ, Ll. Th. i. 56, 18. Æþelstân cyning and Sihtrîc Norðhymbra cyng heó gesamnodon æt Tameweorðige, Chr. 925; P. 105, 19. **III a.** used intransitively :—Tô þære ylcan stôwe ealle gesomniað (*congregantur*), Ll. Th. ii. 178, 8. Gesomnedon *glomerarentur* (*plures*), Wrt. Voc. ii. 83, 44. Farisêos gesomnadun (*conuenerunt*) in ân, Mt. R. L. 22, 34 : Mt. L. 27, 62. Gesomnadun tô him ǽghwonan, Mk. L. R. 1, 45. **IV.** *to join* one thing to another, *join* things together so as to form a whole :—Wel þê gerîsed, þæt þû heáfod sié healle mǽrre and gesomnige sîde weallas fæste gefôge, Cri. 5. þ sum anweald ... his swâ gesomnige (*conjunxerit*) swâ hê þone ûrne dêþ, Bt. 34, 3; F. 138, 1. **IV a.** *of the union* of body and soul :—Sâwl and lîchoma ... wunedon ætsomne ... se ælmihtiga hî ǽror gesomnade, Met. 20, 246. Beóð þonne (*the day of judgement*) gegædrad gǽst and bânsele, gesomnad tô þâm sîde, Dôm. 103. þæs dæges sâwla and lîchaman beóð gesamnode, Angl. viii. 336, 31. **IV b.** *of the union of marriage :*—Ne synt hig twêgen, ac ân flǽsc. Ne getwǽme nân man þâ þe God gesomnode (*conjunxit*), Mt. 19, 6. þte hiá mið woere hire gisomnia ðû gimeodomiga *ut eam cum uiro suo copulare digneris,* Rtl. 108, 42. Ðâ gesinhîwan ... bioð gesomnode (*conjuncti*) ðæt ..., Past. 397, 9. **IV bb.** used reflexively, *to marry :*—Gif wer and wîf hý gesomnien (*in matrimonio se conjunxerit*), Ll. Th. ii. 146, 36. Gif þeówa and þeówen hig gesamnigon (*se conjunxerint*), 150, 15. Geleófe men hig môton gesamnigan (*in matrimonium ire*), 152, 24. **V.** *to form by union of elements, make by joining :*—þæt mon eúðe tôslîted, þætte nǽfre gesomnod wæs, Rä. 1, 18. **V a.** *of the marriage union :*—Hê gesamnað sinscipas

clǽnlice lufe *conjugii sacrum castis nectit amoribus*, Met. 11, 91. Þæt God gesamnode (*junxit*), ne syndrige þ nán man, Mk. 10, 9. Tógædere gesamnod *nodatur*, i. *ligatur* (*licitis connubii nexibus*), An. Ox. 1403. **VI.** used reflexively, *to join together* for a common purpose, *to associate* for common action :—Hié móton hié gesomnian, gif hié willað, tó þám were. Gif hí hié gesamnian nellen, gielde sê þæs wǽpnes onláh þæs weres þriddan dǽl *they may join together, if they like, to pay the 'wer'. If they do not like, let him who lent the weapon pay a third of the 'wer'*, Ll. Th. i. 74, 4-6. [*O. H. Ger.* ge-samanôn *colligere, congregare, cumulare, glomerare*.]

**ge-samnung.** *Add* : **I.** *a collection of objects whether permanently or temporarily associated.* (1) *an assembly of persons, congregation, company* :—Eal sió gesomnung (-sam-, *v. l.*) ðǽre hálgan ciricean *cuncta congregatio ecclesiae*, Past. 367, 6. Heó hine geþeódde tó gesomnunge (-sam-, *v. l.*) þára Godes þeówa *illum fratrum cohorti adsociauit*, Bd. 4, 24; Sch. 486, 9. Mid þǽm ieldestum witum and eác micelre gesomnunge Godes þeówa, Ll. Th. i. 102, 6. Untódǽledlicre gesomnunge *inseparabili* (*angelicae sodalitatis*) *collegio*, i. *congregatione*, An. Ox. 1027. Hê underféng ðá hálgan gesomnunga (-sam-, *v. l.*) tó ymbhweorfanne *susceptae ecclesiae colonus*, Past. 293, 3. (1 a) as verbal noun (?), *assembling* :—þæt wê sendan and wilnian fultum be swá manegum mannum swá ús cinelic þince . . . , þ þám forworhtum mannum beó þe mára ege for úre gesomnunge (or *under* (1) ), Ll. Th. i. 236, 17. (2) *of things.* (a) material, *a heap, mass* :—Gesomnung *congeries* (*gemmarum*), Wrt. Voc. ii. 78, 38. Gesamnunge, 18, 11 : Mt. p. 4, 3. (b) non-material, *a great number, multitude* :—Be gesomnungum *de congestu* (*de congesta virtutum copia*, Ald. 45, 34), Wrt. Voc. ii. 82, 24 : 26, 53. **III.** *a coming together, meeting.* v. ge-samnian; **III** :—Ne bið leófra gedál, ne láþra gesamnung, *friends will not part, foes will not meet*, Bl. H. 65, 20. **IV.** *union, junction.* v. ge-samnian; **IV** :—Godes circe þurh gesomninga sóðes and ryhtes beorhte blíceð, Cri. 700. **IV a.** *the union of marriage.* v. ge-samnian :—þǽre gesomnunge *copulae* (cf. *carnalis copulae*, Ald. 22, 22 : or 46, 23 : 61, 27), Wrt. Voc. ii. 23, 55. In þǽre ǽrestan geþeódnysse weres and wífes preóste gedafenað þ hê mæssan singe and ðá gesamnunga (*conjugium*) bletsige, Ll. Th. ii. 154, 20. Æt þám giftan sceal mæssepreóst beon; sê sceal mid Godes bletsunge heora gesomnunge gederian, p. 256, 7. [*O. H. Ger.* ge-samnung *collectio, concio, congregatio.*] v. bóc-, heáh-, preóst-gesamnung.

**ge-samodlǽcan.** *Add* : Gesomodlǽcð *conlocet* : ge-sanco. l. ge-scinco, q. v.

**ge-sár,** es ; *n. Pain, soreness* :—Wið þára gewealda gesár oððe geswell, Lch. i. 94, 22.

**ge-sárgian.** *Add : to wound.* (1) of physical injury :—Wið liþa sáre, gyf hý of hwylcum belimpe gesárgude beoð *if they are injured by any accident*, Lch. i. 312, 2. Wǽron hié (*the Danes*) tó þǽm gesárgode, þæt hié ne mehton Súð-Seaxna lond útan berówan, Chr. 897; P. 91, 14. (2) of spiritual injury :—Synnum gesárgod, Seel. 67. [*O. H. Ger.* ge-sêragôt *vulneratus.*]

**ge-sáwan.** *Add : p.* -seów (-seáw, -seáwde *in Lindisfarne Gospels*). **I.** *to sow seed, a plant* :—Nó þú gód sǽd geseówe (-seáw, L.) *nonne bonum semen seminasti ?*, Mt. R. 13, 27. Þte ðú ne gesáudes, Lk. L. 19, 22. Geseáw *seminavit*, ofergeseáw ł geseáwde siðe *superseminavit zizania*, Mt. L. 13, 24, 25 : 31. Mið ðý giseów (geseáw, L.) *dum seminat*, Mk. R. 4, 4. Þ ðú ne gesǽwe (gesáudesd, L.) *quod non seminasti*, Lk. R. 19, 21. Sêdo geseáwun, Mt. p. 8, 19. Gesáwe *seminare*, Mt. L. 13, 3. Gesáwen *seminatum*, 19. Þá þe gesáwene (-sáuen, L.) synt, Mk. 4, 20. Gesáwena plantan *plantaria*, Wrt. Voc. i. 39, 13. figurative :—*to sow* error, &c. :—þ deófol his falses tó fela ongemang ne gesáwe, Ll. Th. ii. 312, 27. **II.** *to sow land* :—Gesáwen æcer *vel* land *seges*, Wrt. Voc. i. 53, 55.

**ge-sáweled.** *Add :* -sáwlod *endowed with life* :—Ér þám þe hit (*utero conceptus*) gesáwlod wǽre *antequam animatus fuit*, Ll. Th. ii. 154, 17.

**ge-sáwenlic** (-saw-?); *adj. Visible* :—Hit is earfoðrecce hwæt hê gesáwenlicra (-sew-, *v. l.*) wundra geworhte, Wlfst. 22, 14. Cf. ge-sewenlic.

**ge-sáwenlíce** (-saw-?); *adv. Visibly* :—Eal þæt se sácerd dêð þurh þá hálgan þénunge gesáwenlíce (-sew-, *v. l.*), eal hit fulfremeð se hálga gást gerýnelíce, Wlfst. 36, 8. v. ge-sewenlíce.

**gesca, geocsa, geohsa, geoxa, gihsa,** an ; *m.* **I.** *hiccough or sobbing* :—Gesca, iesca *singultus*, Txts. 97, 1865. Gescea *singultum*, Wrt. Voc. i. 289, 35. **II.** *yox* (v. D. D. *s. v.*), *hiccough* :—Gesca *tentigo* (cf. *extentio*, i. *tenacitas ventris*, *tentigo*, Wrt. Voc. ii. 145, 59), Txts. 101, 1996. Hwonan se micla geoxa cume, oþþe hú his mon tilian scule . . . þonne forstent se geohsa, Lch. ii. 60, 17-23 : 25 : 28 : 62, 1, 9. þám monnum þe for fylle gihsa slihð *for the men that hiccough attacks on account of repletion*, 60, 24. Sicetit *vel* gesca slǽet *singultat*, Txts. 97, 1857. Sele him wiþ geohsan ceald wæter and eced drincan, Lch. ii. 62, 13. **III.** *sobbing* :—Mê þiós siccetung hafað ágǽled, þes geocsa (cf. ic nú wêpende and gisciende . . . misfó, Bt. 2 ; F. 4, 8), Met. 2, 5. v. giscian.

**ge-scád-.** v. ge-sceád-.

**ge-scádwyrt.** *Substitute* gescád-wyrt, e ; *f. The name of some plant* :—Gescádwyrt (giscáduuyrt, Ep., gescanuuyrt, Erf.) *talumbus*, Txts. 101, 1979. Gescáduyrt *berbescum*, Lch. iii. 300, col. 2. Gescádwyrt nioþowearde, ii. 274, 18. v. ge-scaldwyrt.

**ge-scǽnan** *to shatter. Add* :—Gescǽneð hié *comminuet eas*, Ps. Vos. 28, 6.

**ge-scǽnan** (*causative to* ge-scínan) *to cause to shine, make bright* :—Git his sweord scíneð swíðe gescǽned, and ofer ðá byrgenna blícað ðá hieltas, Sal. 222. [*O. H. Ger.* ge-skeinan *notum facere.*]

**ge-scǽnctest.** v. ge-scencan : **ge-scǽned.** v. ge-scǽnan : **ge-scǽned** *conlisio*. See next word.

**ge-scǽnedness,** e ; *f. A dashing together* :—Gecnosu oððe gescǽned[nessa] *conlisiones*, Wrt. Voc. ii. 20, 45. Gescǽningnessa (-scǽnednessa ? : -scǽninga, -scǽnnessa ?) *conlisiones*, 24, 74.

**ge-scǽning, ge-scǽnness.** *See preceding word* : ge-scafan. v. ge-sceafan : ge-scaldwyrt. *Add* : v. gescád-wyrt : gescan. v. ge-giscan : ge-scandene. v. ge-scendan : ge-scandlic. v. ge-sceadlic : ge-scapen. v. ge-sceapen : gescea. v. gesca.

**ge-sceád.** *Add* : **I.** *a division, part* :—Nime hió hire þriddan sceat (gesceád), þæne þriddan dǽl þǽre ǽhta, *v. ll.*), Ll. Th. i. 138, 19. **I a.** *a division* into parts, *classification* under heads :—Þis ys þ gesceád þára lácnunge, Lch. iii. 138, 25. **II.** *distinction* between things :—Wæs heora ǽghwæþer Heáwold nemned. Wæs þis gesceád (*distinctio*) . . . óþer wæs cweden se bleaca Heáwold, óþer se hwíta, Bd. 5, 10 ; Sch. 599, 18. Gif seó *declinatio* sceal tósceádan . . . ; ac þæt ne byð nán gesceád, Ælfc. Gr. Z. 112, 2. þrý eácan synd . . . for gesceáde oððe for fægernysse, 107, 4. Ic þá geþeóde tó micclan gesceáde telede *I reckoned the language* (of a book translated into English) *distinguished the book in a very important respect from the original* (the book's being translated made a great difference), Lch. iii. 442, 4. Hê can him gesceád betweox sóðe and unsóðe, Wlfst. 51, 28. 'Gif hê is milde . . . Gif hê is unmilde . . .' Cwǽdon hí : 'Be hwon magon wê þis gesceád witon ?' '*si mitis est . . . sin autem inmitis . . .*' Aiebant : '*Unde hoc dinoscere ualemus ?*,' Bd. 2, 2 ; Sch. 117, 9. Hý mihton georne tócnáwan, gif hí cúðon þæt gesceád, Wlfst. 105, 22. **III.** *discernment, recognition of the characteristics of something* ; gesceád witan, cunnan *to have accurate knowledge* of, gesceád gecýþan *to give exact knowledge* of :—Be hwám magan wê þises gesceád witan ? *unde hoc dinoscere ualemus ?*, Bd. 2, 2 ; Sch. 117, 9. þæt hê his crístendómes gesceád wite, and þæt hê cunne rihtne geleáfan rihtlíce understandan, Wlfst. 20, 8. þ hí cunnon heora crístendómes and heora fulluhtes gesceád witan, Ll. Th. ii. 330, 25. þæt hý heora fulluhtes gesceád witan . . . for ðám se man þe ne can þæs gesceád . . . , Wlfst. 123, 9-11. Hêr mæg geseón ǽlc man þe telcræftas ǽnig gesceád can . . . þ hit is máre þonne 372 wintra syððan ðyllic feoh wæs fǽrende on eorðan, Hml. S. 23, 699. Ic wêne, lá úplendisca preóst, þ þú nyte hwæt beó *atomos*, ac ic wylle þe þises wordes gesceád gecýþan, Angl. viii. 318, 15. **IV.** *discretion, discrimination* :—Gesceádes *discretionis*, An. Ox. 1756. Mid þám gemetgunge þæs gesceádes, Bd. 3, 5 ; Sch. 208, 3. Man sceal mǽðe on háde gecnáwan mid gesceáde, Ll. Th. i. 362, 5. Ælc þe gesceád wite (*omnis qui discrecionis particeps est*), hliste him georne, 424, 19 : Bd. 3, 5 ; Sch. 207, 20. **V.** *reason, reasoning faculty, understanding* :—Gesceád is ðǽre sáwle forgifen tó stýrenne hire ágen líf, Hml. S. 1, 107. Hwæl . . . and ylp . . . mannes gesceád hí mæg gewyldan, Hml. S. 25, 573. Ðonne hí mid fulle gesceáde ongietað ðæt ðæt wæs leás and ídelnes ðæt hí ǽr heóldon *cum certo judicio deprehenderint falsa se vacue tenuisse*, Past. 441, 18. Hyt him swá gedihte mid fulre mihte sê ðe mid eallum gesceáde þá þing gegaderode, Angl. viii. 312, 12. Nán nýten næfde nán gesceád ne sáwle bútan hê (*Adam*) ána *inter omnia animantia terrae nullum rationale inveniebatur nisi ille solus*, Angl. vii. 22, 212. **VI.** *reasonable conduct, rational plan* :—þ man ne sceal fandian Godes, þá hwíle þe hê mæg mid ǽnigum gesceáde him sylfum gebeorgan *homo non debet tentare Deum, quando habet quid faciat ex rationabili concilio*, Angl. vii. 42, 405. **VII.** *order, disposition, method* :—Tíd, endebrednisse, tal, gesceád, oððæ reihtniss (*dispositio, vel ratio*), Mt. p. 13, 1. þám Iudeíscum ðe Godes ǽ cúðon, and ðám hǽðenum þe þæs godcundan gesceádes nyston, Hml. Th. i. 106, 4. Wercendes Godes gesceád *operantis Dei dispositionem*, Mt. p. 13, 11. Gesceád *tenorem*, i. *ordinem* (*dictandi*), An. Ox. 7, 396. **VIII.** *way, manner* :—Tó suman gesceáde *quodammodo*, i. *quadam ratione*, An. Ox. 941. **IX.** *art, science* :—*Nota*, þæt is mearcung. þǽra mearcunga sind manega . . . ǽgðer ge on sangbócum ge on leóðcræfte ge on gehwylcum gesceáde, Ælfc. Gr. Z. 291, 12. **X.** *reason, ground* :—*Ethimologia*, þæt is namena ordfruma and gesceád (-scád, *v. l.*), hwí hí swá gehátene sind, Ælfc. Gr. 293, 6. Ic secge nú þ ic ǽr forsuwade for þám ungewunan woroldlices gesceádes (*on account of the unusual character of the physical reason*), Angl. vii. 12, 115. Búton hê hit for hwylcum gesceáde dô *nisi aliqua rationabilis causa existat*, R. Ben. 12, 14. For sóþes wísdómes gesceáde, 10. For ðám gesceáde, þæt hí nǽron gelíce . . . , Ælfc. Gr. Z. 26, 9 : 96, 4. Se móna went ǽfre þone hricg tó þǽre sunnan weard . . . Cweðað sume menn, þe þis gesceád ne cunnon, þ se móna hine wende be þan þe

hit wedrian sceal, Lch. iii. 268, 1.    **XI. an account.** (1) ordered speech :—Geþeahtung, gesceád vel racu conlatio, Wrt. Voc. ii. 134, 44. Getincnes, gescád oratio, An. Ox. 319. Gesceáde collatione, 249. Ealles þyses gesceád gē magon būton tweón gelýfan the account of all this you may believe without hesitation, Hml. S. 23, 734. Gesceád oracula (apostolorum), An. Ox. 7, 358. (2) reckoning, calculation :—þá gelǽredan hine healdað þe þisum foresǽdan gesceáde (cf. geteald, 4 : 6), Lch. iii. 266, 12.    ¶ gesceád ágildan to render an account :—Se ríca sceal ealra ðǽra góda þe him God álǽnde ágyldan gesceád, hū hē ðā átuge, Hml. Th. i. 274, 3. Ágildan gesceád for þínre sáwle, Ælfc. T. Grn. 18, 26. Ágyldan Gode full gesceád for ūrum dǽdum, Angl. viii. 336, 37.    **XII. argument, reasoning :**—Clemens þām hǽðenum leódum gelícode, for ðan ðe hē mid hospe heora godas ne gebysmrode, ac mid bóclicum gesceáde him geswutelode hwæt hī wǽron, Hml. Th. i. 558, 14.    v. tungol-, un-gesceád.

**ge-sceád ; adj.    I. reasonable, discreet, prudent :**—Hí setton him ǽnne wícnere getreówne and swíðe gesceádne, Hml. S. 23, 217. þá ne beóð nā wíse ne gesceáde þe Gode nellað hýran, Ll. Th. i. 334, 5. [Ger. ge-scheit.] v. un-gesceád.    **II. calculated, fixed** (? cf. ge-sceád ; XI. 2) :—Gesceád ratum, Kent. Gl. 1164.

**ge-sceádan. Add : I. to separate.** (1) of material objects. (a) to form a line of separation between :—Pirifiát and scipfliót, ðā gesceádað þæt land westan and eástan, C. D. ii. 86, 26. (b) to arrange :—Gesceáden gisomnung distincta congeries, Mt. p. 4, 3. (c) to scatter, shed :—Genim þás wyrte tó dūste gecnucode, gesceád (-scád, v. l.) tó ðām sáre, Lch. i. 290, 12. (2) of non-material objects. (a) to distinguish :—Đū ðe dæg gisceádas (discernis) from næhte, dēdo ūssa from ðióstra gisceád (distingue) miste, Rtl. 36, 29. (b) to deprive of :—Hígo ðīn ælcum mægne gisceádest familiam tuam omni virtute destitui[s], Rtl. 31, 15.    **II.** of mental operations. (1) to expound :—þ gelíc gesceáded similitudinem exponit, Lk. p. 8, 15. (2) to write out a narrative :—Godspel wēre gesceáden euangelium describturum, Lk. p. 3, 11. (3) to decree :—Gescádað decernunt, Kent. Gl. 246. v. tó-gesceádan.

**ge-sceáden.** Dele, and see ge-sceád ; V.

**ge-sceádenlíce (-scád-) ; adv. Severally :**—Gescádenlíce separatim (quomodo virginitas, castitas, jugalitas tripertitis gradibus separatim differant), Wrt. Voc. ii. 77, 48.

**ge-sceádlic ; adj. Shady. Cf. sceadu ; IV :**—Of gesceadlicum scenico (scenico i. umbroso pleglicum, of gescandlicum (but cf. scenam, i. umbram sceade, 65), Hpt. Gl. 474, 7), An. Ox. 2, 115.

**ge-sceádlic ; adj.    I. reasonable, suitable :**—Gyf þing gesceádlic swá gyrnþ si res rationabilis ita exigerit, Angl. xiii. 374, 130. Ðæt áhrērede mód mid ðǽre gesceádlican andsuare bið getǽsed commotae mentes responsorum ratione tanguntur, Past. 297, 17.    **II. rational, based on reason** or argument :—Is þis wundorlic and winsum and gesceádlic (gesceádwíslic, v. l.) spell pulcrum hoc atque pretiosum, sive πόρισμα, sive corollarium vocari mavis, Bt. 34, 5 ; F. 140, 10. v. ungesceádlic, and next word.

**ge-sceádlíce. Add : I. reasonably, in reason, fitly :**—Drihten, forgyf mē þæt ic þe cunne rihtæ and gescǽdlíce biddan (ut bene te rogem), Solil. H. 4, 22. Ful gesceádlíce ðū mē andswarast and ful rihte optime omnino, 39, 3 : 47, 3. Gif hē gesceádlíce (-sceáde-, v. l.) mid eáðmódnesse hwilcu þing tǽle si qua rationabiliter cum humilitate reprehendit, R. Ben. 109, 8. Be ðām is suíðe gesceádlíce (apte) gecueden, Past. 171, 17. Ðū mid geþeahte þínum wyrcest þæt ðū þǽm gesceaftum swá gesceádlíce mearce gesettest, Met. 20, 88.    **II. discreetly, with discrimination :**—Wē scylon gesceádlíce (-scáde-, v. l.) tódǽlan ylde and geogoðe, Ll. Th. i. 412, 9. Gescádlíce, 328, 18.    **III. rationally, in accordance with reason :**—Ic þe náuht ne dwelode, ac sǽde ðē swíþe lang spell swíþe gesceádlíce be Gode, Bt. 35, 5 ; F. 166, 2. v. un-gesceádlíce.

**ge-sceádness, e ; f. A decree** (? cf. ge-sceádan ; II. 3), decision (?) :—Wē þæs nāne bysne nabbað, ne on bóca gesceádnyssum (in auctoritate scripturarum), ne on hāligra fædera hǽsum, Nap. 32, 1.

**ge-sceádwís. Add : I. exercising discernment, intelligent, discerning :**—Ælc gesceádwís man mæg witan þ hig beóþ full earme, Bt. 29, 2 ; F. 104, 11 : 27, 1 ; F. 96, 6 : 28 ; F. 100, 30. Gescēdwíse (-sceád-, v. l.) menn ne magon ongietan ðæt hit belimpe tó nytwyrðlicre ðearfe, Past. 281, 11. Se engel hine cýdde þām gesceádwísum Iudēiscum ðe Godes ǽ cūðon, Hml. Th. i. 106, 2.    ¶ applied to superhuman beings :—Ðonne se gesceádwísa God hwæt wyrcþ þæs ðe wē ne wēnaþ cum ab sciente geritur, quod stupeant ignorantes, Bt. 39, 10 ; F. 226, 24. Se gesceádwísa engel, Hml. Th. i. 106, 1.    **II. acting with judgement, discreet, sagacious, prudent :**—Gesceádwís discretus, i. modestus, Wrt. Voc. ii. 141, 17. Hū se lǽreów sceal bión gesceádwís (discretus) on his swígean, Past. 89, 3 : 151, 5. Is sió lytle nosu ðæt mon ne sié gescádwís (-sceád-, v. l.) parvo naso est qui ad tenendam mensurum discretionis idoneus non est, 65, 20. þ man sí gesceádwís and gemetigian cunne ge his sprēce ge his swígan, Prov. K. 2. Hē befrán his gefēran rǽdes, and cwæð tó his gesceádwísan brēðer, Hml. S. 25, 398 : Angl. ix. 259, 1. Feáwa sient tó þām gesceádwíse, gif hē

wyrð on ungeþylde, þ hē ne wilnige þ his sǽlþa weorþan onwende, Bt. 11, 1 ; F. 32, 32.    **III. endowed with reason** or intelligence, rational, intelligent :—Man ... godcundlíce gesceádwís divinum merito rationis animal, Bt. 14, 2 ; F. 44, 18. Sió sáwul biþ gesceádwís, 33, 4 ; F. 132, 5. Nis nān gesceádwís gesceaft þ nǽbbe freódóm neque fuerit ulla rationalis natura, quin eidem libertas adsit arbitrii, 40, 7 ; F. 242, 16 : 36, 7 ; F. 182, 7. Ic wāt þ ic on libbendum men and on gesceádwísum eom esse me scio rationale animal, 5, 3 ; F. 12, 27. þām gesceádwísan móde libero animo, 16, 2 ; F. 52, 17. Hwæt willaþ wē cweþan, gif ðā gesceádwísan nillaþ spyrian æfter wísdóme, 36, 6 ; F. 180, 36.    v. un-gesceádwís.

**ge-sceádwíslic. Substitute :**—Discretum, detractum vel gesceádwíslic, Wrt. Voc. ii. 141, 12.    **I. endowed with reason, rational :**—þǽre sáwle gecynd is ðryfeald ... þridde dǽl is gesceádwíslic, Hml. S. 1, 97. On eówerre sáule is andgit and gemynd and se gesceádwíslica willa, Bt. 14, 2 ; F. 44, 25.    **II. based on reason** or argument :—Ic eom geþafa ðæs þe ðū segst, for þām þe ðū hit hæfst gesēþed mid gesceádwíslicre race assentior, cuncta enim firmissimis nexa rationibus constant, Bt. 34, 9 ; F. 146, 8. v. ge-sceádlic ; II.    **III. in accordance with reason, reasonable :**—Gif sum gesceádwíslic (rationabilis) intinga wunige, R. Ben. I. 14, 1. Gesceádwíslicre mynegunge rationabili monitu, Angl. xiii. 447, 1167. v. un-gesceádwíslic.

**ge-sceádwíslíce. Add : I. distinctly, clearly :**—þæt ic wille gescádwíslecor gesecgean, þæt hit mon geornor ongietan mæge quod utrum ita sit, apertissime expedire curabo, Ors. 2, 1 ; S. 60, 9.    **II. discreetly, prudently, sagaciously :**—Gif hē self wēnð ðæt hē sié wís and gesceádwíslíce (-sceád-, v. l.) ryhtwís si candorem sibi justititae seu sapientiae tribuit, Past. 69, 23.    **III. reasonably, in accordance with reason :**—Gif hwylc bróðor unsceádelíce hwæs bidde, hē gesceádwíslíce (rationabiliter) his yfelan bēne forwyrne, R. Ben. 54, 15 : R. Ben. I. 61, 12 : 102, 1 : Bt. 13 ; F. 38, 3.    **III a. fittingly, agreeably** (?) :—Ðá se wísdóm ðis leóð swíþe lustbǽrlíce and gesceádwíslíce āsungen hæfde haec cum philosophia leniter suaviterque cecinisset, Bt. 36, 1 ; F. 170, 25.    **IV. in a way that depends upon reasoning, that affords proof, rationally :**—Eall ðis þu gerehtest tó sóþe swíþe gesceádwíslíce būton ælcre leásre rǽdelsan haec nullis extrinsecus sumtis, sed altero ex altero fidem trahente, insitis domesticisque probationibus explicabas, Bt. 35, 5 ; F. 164, 31. v. un-gesceádwíslíce.

**ge-sceádwísnes. Add : Discretio, i. divisio gesceádwísnes,** Wrt. Voc. ii. 141, 16.    **I. discretion, prudence :**—Be þæs mæssepreóstes gesceádwísnysse de presbyteri prudentia, Ll. Th. ii. 128, 10. Hē munuclíce leofode betwux ðám lǽwedum folce mid mycelre gesceádwísnysse, Hml. S. 26, 82.    **II. discrimination :**—On eallum mannum behofað gesceádwýsnysse, þeáh ðe hī gelíce fyrene fremmen erga omnes homines discrimine opus est, etsi similia crimina committant, Ll. Th. ii. 132, 29.    **III. a reckoning :**—Hēr æfter synt āmearkode þā feówer gesceádwýsnyssa ymbe þæne forman mónoð, and ymbe þæne termen, and ymbe þæne Eásterdæg and þæs dæges mónan, Angl. viii. 324, 28.    **IV. reason, the reasoning faculty :**—Ūs segð ælc gesceádwísnes þ God sié þ hēhste gód bonum esse Deum ratio demonstrat, Bt. 34, 2 ; F. 136, 4. Ðá men habbaþ eall þ wē ǽr ymbe sprǽcon, and eác tó eácon ðæt micle gife gesceádwísnesse, 41, 5 ; F. 252, 29 : 18, 4 ; F. 66, 24. Sē þe gesceádwísnesse hæfð, sē mæg dēman and tósceádan hwæt hē wilnian sceal and hwæt hē onscunian sceal quod ratione uti naturaliter potest, id habet judicium, quo quodque discernat ; per se igitur fugienda optandave dignoscit, 40, 7 ; F. 242, 17 : 13 ; F. 40, 7. Ðū ūs sealdest gesceádwísnesse þæt wē magon tósceádan good and yfel, Solil. H. 7, 13.    ¶ as a personification :—Ðá cwæþ seó Gesceádwísnes, Bt. 5, 3 ; F. 12, 1.    **V. a reason, an argument :**—Lóca nū hwæþer ðū wille þ wit spyrigen æfter ǽnigre gesceádwísnesse furþor, nū wit þ āfunden habbaþ þ wit ǽr sóhton sed visne rationes ipsas invicem collidamus?, Bt. 35, 5 ; F. 162, 31. v. un-gesceádwísness.

**ge-sceafan. Add :**—Hornes sceafoþan swiþe smale gesceaf, Lch. ii. 132, 11. Gif hē þæs stānes gesceafenes hwilcne dǽl on wǽtan onfēhð, 298, 6. Hýfa gescafenum getreagede telgrum tuguria cauatis consuta corticibus, An. Ox. 255. [O. H. Ger. ge-scaban radere, abradere.]

**ge-sceaft. Add : a masc. pl. ge-sceaftas occurs.    I. what is created.** (1) all created things, creation :—Twā ðing syndon : ān is Scyppend, óðer is gesceaft ... þæt is gesceaft, þæt se sóða Scyppend gesceóp. þæt sind ǽrest heofonas, and englas ..., and syððan þeós eorðe ... and sǽ ... Nū ealle ðás ðing synd mid ānum naman genemnode gesceaft, Hml. Th. i. 276, 8–14. (1 a) creation in respect to this world only, the (created) world :—Gif se man gesihð Godes leóht, þonne bið þæt gesceaft swíðe nearu geðúht, Hml. Th. ii. 186, 7. Swylce gedrēfednessa swylce ne gewurdon of frymðe þǽre gesceafte (cf. of middangeardes fruman, Mt. 24, 21) þe Gód gesceóp (ab initio creaturae quam condidit Deus), Mk. 13, 19. Ealre eorþcundre gesceafte totius terrestris creaturae (possessor (Adam)), An. Ox. 692. (2) with collective force, creation, created objects of a particular kind. (a) of rational creatures :—' Bodiað eallum gesceafte' ; ac mid þām naman is se mann āna getācnod, Hml. Th. i. 302, 12. Bodiað godspell ealre gesceafte,

Mk. 16, 15. Ús gedafenað tó dónne dugeðe menniscum gesceafte (*to all men*), Hml. Th. ii. 318, 17. (b) of other things:—Hwí eów þince þǽre ungesceádwísan gesceafte gód betere þonne eówer ágen gód, Bt. 13; F. 40, 5. Ðæt hé anweald hæbbe ... ofer eallum gesceafte (cf. hé sig ... ofer ealle gesceafta *praesit ... universae terrae*, Gen. 1, 26), Hex. 18, 17. (3) *a created thing, a creature:*—Nis nán þing on gesceaftum him bedíglod, Hml. Th. i. 334, 14. (3 a) of rational beings:—Se deófol wyrð áfýmed fram þǽre menniscan gesceafte, þe ǽr ðurh Adam forworht wæs, and ðám hálgum gáste byð eardungstów on þám menn gerýmed, Wlfst. 34, 1. Forhtiaþ ealle gesceafta, ge heofonware ge eorþware, Bl. H. 11, 4. Eallum wísfæstum gesceaftum ecne dóm gesetton, 121, 20. (3 b) of other things:—Gif hwá his wæccan æt ǽnigum wylle hæbbe, oððe æt ǽnigre óðre gesceafte (*creaturam*), Ll. Th. ii. 210, 12. Þára gimma oððe ǽniges þára deádlicena ðinga ðe gesceádwísnesse næþ ... þeáh hié Godes gesceafta sién, Bt. 13; F. 40, 9. Stánas sind gesceafta, Hml. Th. i. 302, 13. Manna líchaman forealdiað swá swá óðre gescæaftas ealdiað, Solil. H. 10, 8: 9, 12. Ðurh ðá gesceaftu ðe hé gesceóp, Hex. 10, 13: Bt. 39, 13; F. 234, 22, 24. (4) *one of the four elements:*—Þ unandgytfulle gesceaft þæs wætres *elementum irrationabile*, Gr. D. 194, 7: 91, 11. Hit of ungelícre gesceafte (*from water, not fire*) gewurde, 220, 2: Angl. vii. 48, 456. *De elementis.* Ðeós lyft ys án ðæra feówer gesceafta, þe ǽlc líchamlic ðing on wunað. Feówer gesceafta synd ... *aer, ignis, terra, aqua,* Lch. iii. 272, 11–15: Bt. 33, 4; F. 130, 20. Swylce ðá gesceafta (se lég and se wind) him betweónan gefeohtan sceoldan, Bl. H. 221, 14. Úre líchoma wæs gesceapen of feówer gesceaftum, 35, 12. II. *what is shaped, arranged, ordered:*—*Conditio, i. status, procreatio, natura, sors, regula, lex, rectitudo gescæp, gewyrd, gescæft, gebyrd,* Wrt. Voc. ii. 135, 63. (1) *the external condition, state, position of an object:*—Nǽnig eft cymeð hider þæt mannum secge, hwylc sý meotodes gesceaft (*what heaven is like*), sigefolca gesetu, þær hé sylfa wunað, Gn. C. 65. Hé gelógode on þǽre heofonlican gesceafte, þæt is on heofona ríce, engla weredu, Wlfst. 8, 1. (2) *the internal condition, nature, constitution of an object:*—Sió geðyld is gesett tó hierde úrre gesceafte *custodem conditionis nostrae patientiam esse Dominus monstravit,* Past. 220, 4. On ðæs líchoman gesceafte wé underféngon ealle ðá ðénunga ðe wé nú ðíówiað *in corporis positione accipimus quod in actione servemus,* 233, 9. Ne mæg mín líchoman wið þás lǽnan gesceaft deáð gedǽlan (*my body cannot separate death from this frail condition natural to it*) ac hé gedreósan sceal, Gú. 342. Heó sægde ymb hyre sylfre gesceaft: 'Is mín módor cynnes þæs deórestan,' Rä. 34, 8. On ríhtne (-re?) gesceaft, Dan. 366. Hé (*God*) mid his ágenre mihte geglengde þ gér mid feówrum gesceaftum (*the four seasons*), Angl. viii. 299, 19. (2 a) of physical condition, *sex:*—In gescæf[te] téderlicum *in sexu fragili,* Rtl. 51, 7. Gesceafta ne beóð for nánum óðran þinge ástealde bútan for bearnteáme ánum, Hml. A. 20, 160. (3) *what is shaped as a person's lot, lot, fate, condition of life:*—For hwám winneð þis wæter ..., dreógeð deóp gesceaft (*drees a hard weird*), Sal. 393: 248. Forgietan him þára geócran gesceafta, Gn. Ex. 182. (4) *a condition imposed by providence, order of providence:*—Ðá ðe him underðiédde beóð ðurh Godes gesceafte *eos quos per conditionem tenet subditos,* Past. 201, 18. Heofontorht swegl gescynded in gesceaft Godes (*in accordance with God's order*) under foldan fæðm, Sch. 74. (5) *ordered course of events:*—Wyrda gesceaft, Dan. 132: Wand. 107. [*O. H. Ger.* ge-skaft *forma, figmentum, conditio.*] v. eald-, wæter-gesceaft, *and* cf. ge-sceap, ge-sceapennys.

**ge-sceamian.** *Add:* I. *to be ashamed, feel shame:*—Gesceomadon (giscomadun, R.) *uerebuntur,* Lk. L. 20, 13. I a. *with gen. of cause:*—Ic yfeldǽda gescomede, Jul. 713. Þæt hý ǽlces unryhtes gescomedon, Cri. 1303. II. *used impersonally, to cause shame to* (*dat.*), *shame a person* (*acc.*). (1) *with acc.:*—Eówerne andwlitan ná ne gescamað *vultus vestri non erubescent,* Ps. Th. 35, 5. Nabbe gé nánne gemánan wið hine, for ðám ðætte hine gesceamige (*ut confundatur*), Past. 357, 6. Hine sceal on dómes dæg gesceamian, Wlfst. 238, 12. (1 a) *with gen. of cause:*—Hié hira selfra gesceamige *erubescant,* Past. 333, 22. (2) *with dat.:*—Gesceamian ... swá þám men dyde, Wlfst. 238, 14. (2 a) *with gen. of cause:*—Þ him gesceamige heora unrihtes, Ll. Th. ii. 364, 22.

**ge-sceand;** *adj. Ashamed.* [*Perhaps such an adjective may be inferred from* gesceandnes (*q. v.*). Cf. *O. H. Ger.* scant *ashamed,* un-scant *unashamed.*]

**ge-sceandness.** *Add:*—*Shame:*—Þ þú mé ne genýde tó áreccenne míne gesceandnysse (-scynd-, *v. l.*), Hml. S. 23 b, 361. [*See preceding word; but* ge-sceandness *may be a verbal noun connected with* ge-scendan; *for the unmutated, as well as the mutated, form in such a noun see* leáfness, líf-ness.]

**ge-sceánon.** *l.* ge-sceánan.

**ge-sceap.** *Add:* I. *birth, creation:*—Cennung, gescæp *concretio,* Wrt. Voc. ii. 136, 26. v. cenning. II. *what is created.* (1) *creation, created things:*—Ic þec biddan wille þurh þæt æðele gesceap þe þú, fæder engla, on fruman settest, Jul. 273. (2) *a creature:*—On ðám

æfteran dæge God gesceóp ðá gesceapu ðe ðisne heofon healdað, Sal. K. p. 178, 16. III. *what is shaped, ordered:*—*Conditio, natura, sors, regula, lex, rectitudo gescæp, gewyrd, gescæft, gebyrd,* Wrt. Voc. i. 135, 63. (1) *of material things, shape, form:*—Hí beóð oð ðene nafolan on menniscum gesceape *usque ad umbilicum hominis speciem habent,* Nar. 36, 19. Adam ... God gehíwad hæfde tó mænniscum gesceape, on þrytiges wintres ylde, Angl. xi. 2, 26. Nípende niht, scaduhelma gesceapu scríðan cwóman, B. 650. (2) *nature, natural condition:*—Án þára nunnena wæs swýþe fægru æfter þæs líchaman gesceape *una virginum juxta carnis hujus putredinem speciosa videbatur,* Gr. D. 28, 26. Wixþ se milte ofer gesceap, Lch. ii. 242, 28. On gesceap *naturally,* Rä. 39, 4. Ǽr gé sceonde wið gesceapu fremman *ere ye commit shameful sin against the laws of nature,* Gen. 2469. (3) *lot, fate, appointed condition of life, destiny:*—[Hé] heóld on heáh gesceap *he fulfilled a high destiny,* B. 3084. Ic (*a cuckoo*) under sceáte, swá mín gesceapu wæron, ungesibbum weard eácen gæste, Rä. 10, 7. Swá scríðende gesceapum (*fortuitu* v. wyrd-gesceap) hweorfað gleómen, Víd. 135. Dryhten scyred and scrífeð and gesceapo healdeð (*governs the destinies of men*), Vy. 66: Gen. 2827. Gesceapu dreógeð *fulfils its destinies,* Ph. 210: Rä. 69, 4. (4) *a condition imposed by providence, order of providence:*—Swá gesceapu wæron werum and wífum, Gen. 1573. Bídan selfes gesceapu heofoncyninges, 842. (5) *ordered course of events:*—Wyrda gesceapu, Rä. 40, 24. IV. *shaping, forming:*—On gesceape *in* (*rerum visibilium*) *plastica,* An. Ox. 8, 346. V. *privy part:*—Þæs fylmenes ofcyrf on ðám gesceape, Hml. Th. i. 94, 33. [Cf. *Icel.* skap *state, condition;* sköp; *pl. fate, destiny:* sköp-in (*with article*) *the genitals.*] v. wyrd-gesceap. Cf. ge-sceaft, ge-sceapennys.

**ge-sceapen.** *Add:* v. un-gesceapen, ge-sceapennys, ge-scippan.

**ge-sceapennys.** *Add:* I. *creation:*—Mennisc gesceapennys is on feówer wíson. Adam næs gestrýned ne ácenned, ac God hine gesceóp. Seó óðer gesceapennys wæs swá þæt God gesceóp Euan of hire weres sídan. Ne sind þás twá gesceapennyssa nánum óðrum gelíce. Seó ðridde gesceapennys is þæt men beóð gestrýnede þurh wer and þurh wíf. Seó feórðe gesceapennys wæs swá þæt Críst weard ácenned of mǽdene bútan were, Hml. Th. ii. 8, 22–30. Genesis ne spricð ná be þǽra engla gesceapenisse, Ælfc. T. Grn. 23, 8. God gesceóp æt fruman twégen men and hé geswác ðá þǽra gesceapennyssa, Hml. Th. ii. 206, 22. II. *disposition, ordering* of events:—Nán yfel þing næs on þám englum, ne nán yfel ne cóm þurh Godes gesceapennisse, Ælfc. T. Grn. 2, 28.

**ge-sceaplíce.** *Add:* [Cf. *Icel.* skapligr *suitable, meet;* skapliga *fitly.*]

**ge-scearfan.** *Substitute:* ge-scearfian; *p.* ode *To cut up, cut to shreds:*—Gescearfa þás wyrta on gód eala, Lch. ii. 324, 22: 334, 7. Gescearfa ðú *succides,* Lk. L. 13, 9.

**ge-scearian.** *Add: to grant, allot, assign:*—Ðýs twéntigum hídum, ðá ic rúmódlíce gescarode ... Gyf hwá genyrwe ðæt ic Gode on éce yrfe gesæld hæbbe, C. D. v. 331, 2. [Cf. *O. H. Ger.* [harm-]scarôn.] v. ge-scirian.

**ge-sceaþian.** *Add: to do harm:*—Deófol bið á ymbe þæt án, hú hé on manna sáwlum gescaðian mæge, Wlfst. 191, 11.

**ge-sceatt.** v. scír-gesceatt.

**ge-sceatwyrpan;** *p.* te *To betroth:*—Gesceatwyrpe *despondi,* Wrt. Voc. ii. 25, 72. [*The O. H. Ger.* scaz-wurf (v. Grmn. R. A. 332) *manumissio seems to shew that the word is connected with* sceatt *not* sceát, *though the phrase in* sceátt álecgan (v. sceát; IV) *desponsare might seem to point to* sceát.] Cf. be-sceatwyrpan.

**ge-sceáwian.** *Add:* I. *to see, behold, perceive:*—Þte hérnise clǽnum gesceáwiga wé ymbseáne *ut misterium puro cernamus intuitu,* Rtl. 35, 37. Þ hire hálga symbelcen[nisse] gisceáwia ué (*conspiciamus*) ðá éce, 80, 26. Næs hé goldhwæte gearwor hæfde ágendes ést ǽr gesceáwod *he had never before seen more clearly the Lord's munificence, i. e. he had never had such good fortune as had befallen him in the acquisition of the dragon's hoard,* B. 3075. II. *to look on with favour, regard:*—Éce God, symbeltíde dæges ðisses mildelíce gisceáwia (*intuere*), Rtl. 77, 11. III. *to look at with care, consider.* (1) *of material objects, to examine, reconnoitre:*—Hæfdic þæs kyninges wíc and his fæstenu gesceáwod, Nar. 19, 14. (2) *to consider* a subject, circumstance, condition or things:—Gesceáwa þonne þú þá strangan lǽcedómas dó hwilc þ mægen sié and sió gecynd þæs líchoman, Lch. ii. 84, 10, 23. Asca ... huulíc monn sé, is lár gesceáwig, Mt. L. 10, 14 note. Gesceáwiað eów selfe *considerans te ipsum,* Past. 159, 11. Gif hé hæbbe ealle on fóðre tó ágifanne, gesceáwige mon, ágife ealle *if he have to pay all in fodder, let the matter be looked into, let him pay all,* Ll. Th. i. 140, 9. Úton wé gesceáwian þá heálican gewyrhto Sancte Jóhannes, Bl. H. 167, 4. [*O. H. Ger.* ge-scouwôn *videre, respicere, speculari, considerare.*]

**ge-sceáwung,** e; *f. Observation:*—On mínre ágenre gesceáwunge, Hml. S. 23 b, 695. v. fore-gesceáwung.

**ge-sceldod.** v. ge-scildod.

**ge-scencan;** *p.* te *To give to drink:*—Þú gescænctest mid wíne

onbryrdnesse *potasti nos uino compunctionis*, Ps. L. 59, 5. Wín gescenct *uinum potatum*, Scint. 105, 16.

**ge-scendan.** *Add* :—Þá gescendan *confusam*, Wrt. Voc. ii. 24, 33. I. *to disfigure, spoil, injure, mar, defile, corrupt.* (1) physical :—Ðeáh ðe ðæt gecynd ðæs carbuncules hine úp áhebbe, his blioh hine gescent *quem naturalis ordo praetulerat, coloris qualitas foedat*, Past. 411, 32. Gescendende (printed -scand-, Wrt. Voc. ii. 28, 55) *deturpans* (dira cutis callositas elephantino tabo *deturpans*, Ald. 49, 16), Wülck. Gl. 390, 40. Gif mon óðrum þá geweald forsleá uppe on þám sweoran, and forwundie tó þám swíðe þ hé náge þæra geweald, and hwæðere lifie swá gescended (*contumeliatus*), Ll. Th. i. 100, 12. (2) non-physical:—Sió gesceádwísnes hié selfe gescind (-scent, *v. l.*) mid ðære ungemetgodan smeáunge *actionis suae rectitudinem confundit*, Past. 67, 8. Gescient (-scent, *v. l.*) hé ðá gódan weorc ðe hé ær on stillum móde ðurhteáh *siqua a se tranquilla mente fuerant bene gesta confundit*, 215, 16. Ðæt hé ðæt good ðære mildheortnesse ne ðyrfe gesciendan (-scendan, *v. l.*) mid gidsunge, 341, 14. Ne ús ne gedafenað þæt wé úrne líchaman, ðe Gode is gehálgod . . ., mid unþæslicum plegan and higeleáste gescyndan, Hml. Th. i. 482, 10. Ne wilnige sé ná beón ðingere for óðerra scylde, sé ðe bið mid his ágenum gescinded (*quem crimen depravat proprium*), Past. 63, 21. Se láriów bið gescinded (-scend-, *v. l.*) mid ðære ofersprǽce *rectorem loquacitas inquinat*, 95, 21. II. *to discomfit, defeat utterly*:—Xersis wæs þá æt þwám cirrum on ðæm londe swá gescend (-scynd, *v. l.*) *Xerxes, bis victus in terra*, Ors. 2, 5; S. 82, 6. Gescende *prostrati*, Wülck. Gl. 245, 23. III. *to confound, abash, bring to shame* :—God mundað þá stówe, and þá slihð and gescynt þe þær sceadian willað, Hml. S. 25, 805. Ne ondrǽd ðú ðé, for ðæm ðú ne weordest gescended (*non confunderis*), Past. 181, 10. Hé ongiet hine selfne ofercymenne and gesciendne (-scendne, *v. l.*) *sine bravio remaneat*, 229, 21. Ðá mód ðe Dryhtne ungeféru sint weorðað gesciende (-scended, *v. l.*) (*damnabuntur*), 245, 24. On helle beóð symle gescynde ðá ðe hire tó cumað, Hml. Th. ii. 66, 23. III a. *to confound* in argument, *confute* :—Oferstǽlþ, gescent *confutat*, i. *confundit, convincit*, Wrt. Voc. ii. 133, 45. Gescende *confundit* (*Pharisaeos*), Lk. p. 8, 10. ðæt eallum ðisum gefiitum wæs ðæra deófla gefeoht swíðe stiðlic . . . ðæt þæt ðurh Godes dóm ðá wiðerwinnan wurdon gescynde, Hml. Th. ii. 340, 31. III b. *to put to shame, make to appear despicable* :—Bið gescend, forhoged *confunditur* (non furva mergulae factura confundit), An. Ox. 520. III c. *to bring to act shamefully* :—Hwá bið gesciended (-scend-, *v. l.*) ðæt ic eác ðæs ne scamige *quis scandalizatur, et ego non uror ?*, Past. 101, 4. IV. *to confound, confuse, disturb, throw into disorder* :—His mód and his andgit ðæt gecynd áscirpð, and hé hit self gescient mid his ungewunan *cujus sensum natura exacuit, sed conversationis pravitas confundit*, Past. 69, 9. Ðý lǽs his sprǽc gescynde (-scende, *v. l.*) ðá ánmódnesse ðæra ðe ðærtó hlystað *ne ejus eloquio audientium unitas confundatur*, 93, 25. Sió tunge bið gesciended (*confunditur*) on ðám láriówdóme, ðonne hió óðer lǽrð, óðer hió liornode, 27, 11. V. *to blame, rebuke* :—Se earma úpáhafena sié mid his wordum geðreátod and gescended, ðonne hé ongiet ðæt hine ne magon his iermða geðreátigean and geeáðmédan *tanto districtius in paupere elationem feriat, quanto eam nec illata paupertas inclinat*, Past. 183, 14. [*O. H. Ger.* ge-scenten *infamare, confundere.*] v. un-gescended.

**ge-scendnys.** *Add*:—Gescyndnes *confusio*, Ps. L. 68, 8. Mid gescændnysse, 88, 46 : 68, 20. v. ge-scændnes.

**ge-scendþ**, e; *f. Confusion* :—Sién oferwrigen gescendðe (gescentðe, Ps. Vos.) *operiantur confusione*, Ps. Srt. 108, 29.

**ge-sceód.** v. ge-scógan: **ge-sceón** *to happen*. *Add*: [Cf. *O. H. Ger.* ge-scehan ; *p.* -scah *accidere, contingere*.]

**ge-sceorf.** *Substitute: Irritation of the stomach* :—Be wambe coþum . . . Gif hire bið oninnan wund, þonne biþ þær sár and beótunga and gesceorf, Lch. ii. 220, 4: 228, 25. Sceal him mon sellan hát wæter drincan, þonne stild þ gesceorf, 240, 23. Þis deáh eác þám þe þ gesceorf ðrowiað, 176, 22. v. sceorfan.

**ge-sceorpan.** *Add*: v. sceorpan : **ge-sceot, ge-sceót** (*l.* -sceot). v. ge-scot : **ge-sceót** *ready*. v. sceót.

**ge-sceótan.** *Add*: I. *trans.* (1) *to shoot* an arrow, *hurl* a spear, &c. :—Ær þær wǽre ǽnig spere gescoten, Chr. 1055 ; P. 186, 5. Arewan, gauelucas wǽron gescotene *catapultae diriguntur*, i. *misse sunt*, An. Ox. 4240. (2) *to assign to a position, allot* to a place :—Þás Godes ðegnas þe . . . sind godas getealde, hwider gescýt [man] heora endebyrdnesse (*to which band is their order assigned*), búton tó ðám werode ðe sind hláfordscipas gecwedene ?, Hml. Th. i. 346, 5. (3) *to form with sloping sides that tend to meet and so make an angle* (? v. sceát, -scíte) :—Se arc wæs fyðerscýte, and . . . wæs fram nyðeweardan óð ufeweardan swá tógædere gescoten (gestoten ?, getogen, *v. l.*) and swá genyrwed þ hé wæs mid ánre fǽðme belocen ufewerd *arca habuit quatuor angulos ex imo assurgentes, et iisdem paulatim usque ad summum in angustum attractis in spatium unius cubiti fuit collecta*, Angl. vii. 34, 365. II. *intrans.* (1) *to fall, happen, occur* :—Gyf se terminus becymð on ðone Sunnandæg . . . Gyf se terminus gescýt on sumon dæge þǽre wucan, Lch. ii. 244, 16. (2) *to fall to the share of, be allotted to* :—Ealle þá ðing

þe ús gesceótað of úres geáres teolunge, Hml. Th. i. 178, 28. Heora ǽlcum gesceát án pund goldes, ii. 494, 5. Weald þeáh eówer eard ús gesceóte (*nobis sorte debetur*), Jos. 9, 7.

**ge-sceppan.** v. ge-scippan.

**ge-sceran.** *Substitute:* I. *to shear.* (1) *to cut the hair off* the head :—Heáfod him beón gescoren hearm getácnað, Lch. iii. 200, 21. Gesce(o)rene *rasam*, An. Ox. 56, 12. (2) *to cut the wool off* sheep :—Sceáp gesihð gescorene hýnðe getácnað, Lch. iii. 208, 26. II. *to cut through.* (1) of a person's action :—Hé him on heáfde helm gescer, þæt hé blóde fáh búgan sceolde, B. 2973. (2) of the operation of a weapon :—Seó ecg geswác þeódne æt þearfe ; þolode ǽr fela handgemóta, helm oft gescær, B. 1526. [*O. H. Ger.* ge-sceran *radere, resecare*.]

**ge-scére.** v. secg-gescére : **ge-scerian.** v. ge-scirian : **ge-scerpan.** v. ge-scirpan : **ge-scert.** v. ge-scyrtan.

**ge-sceþþan.** *Add*:—Nóht iúh gesceðeð (gisceðð̣as, R.) *nihil uobis nocebit*, Lk. L. 10, 19. Heó gúðrinc gesfeng . . . nó þý ær in gescód hálan líce ; hring útan ymbbearh þæt heó þone fyrdhom þurhfón ne mihte *she clutched the warrior . . . none the more did she do hurt within to his body ; the mail without protected, so that she might not pierce the corslet*, B. 1502. Bill ǽr gescód . . . þám þara máðma mundbora wæs, 2777. Forð gewát Cham of líce, þá him cwealm gescód (*when mortal sickness wrought him hurt*), Gen. 1623 : Dan. 668. Him wlenco gesceód *pride proved his destruction*, 678. Hé eów gesceód, þá hé áferede of fæstenne mancynnes má þonne gemet *when he did you grievous harm, when he carried off more men than was meet*, An. 1178. Þú þæt gehéte . . . þæt ús heterófra hild ne gesceóde, 1422. Ne biþ hire (*the stomach*) gesceded fram cealdum mettum, Lch. ii. 220, 25. ¶ where the particular, in respect to which injury is done, is marked :—Hié fela folca feore gesceódon, Dan. 15. Ær him fǽr Godes þurh egesan gryre aldre gesceóde, 593. v. un-gescepþed.

**ge-sciftan.** I. *to divide into shares* among people. *Take here* gescyftan *in Dict*. II. *to assign, appoint, ordain* :—Is lencten ús eallum tó dǽdbóte gescyft, þæt wé on þám fæce . . . wið God gebétan . . ., Wlfst. 102, 17. Stów gecwéme gebróþrum sí ámearcud (*designetur*) . . . þæt hús ealswá wé sǽdan gescifte (*designatam*), Angl. xiii. 397, 464. Syndon eahta heálice mægnu þurh Godes mihte mannum gescyfte, Wlfst. 68, 19. II a. *to appoint* a person to a position, office, &c. :—God gescifte ǽnne swá gerádne mann þe áhte geweald ealles ðæs splottes *God appointed a man of this kind to be the owner of all the plot*, Hml. S. 23, 414. Beón gescyfte (*ordinentur*) gebróþru, þá tó sealmsange geǽmtian, Angl. xiii. 444, 1121. Gescifte, 422, 815. Sýn twégen tó þám sylfan gescyfte (*destinati*), 410, 640. III. *to arrange, regulate* :—God sylf ðás þingc swá gescifte and mid his fadunge gedihte, Hml. S. 23, 256. Hú bisceophádas wurdan ǽrest ástealde and be Godes dihte mannum gescyfte, Wlfst. 176, 7. II a. *to regulate* a measure, weight, &c. :—Ne beó ǽnig metegyrd lengre þonne óðer, ac be þæs scriftes gemete ealle gescyfte, and ǽlc gemet and ǽghwilc gewihte beó be his dihte gescyft swíðe rihte, Ll. Th. ii. 314, 5–8.

**ge-scild.** *Add* : Gescyld *refugium*, Ps. Spl. T. 17, 1.

**ge-scildan.** *Add* : (1) *to defend, save* :—Ne geortríewe ic ná Gode þæt hé ús ne mæge gescildan tó beteran tídun *ut se ad meliora tempora reservarent*, Ors. 2, 5 ; S. 86, 4. God mec mæg eáðe gescyldan, Gú. 213. Hió mægen ne hæfde hié tó gescildanne, Ors. 4, 6 ; S. 174, 12. Gescyldendum *defensante*, Wrt. Voc. ii. 27, 49. Ðonne ðæt líf ðæs líchoman bið gescilded (-scielded, *v. l.*, *protegitur*), Past. 141, 7. Seó burg wearð gescilded *praesentem perditionem Deus avertit*, Ors. 3, 2 ; S. 100, 23. Wæs gesceld *defenditur*, i. *custodiebatur*, An. Ox. 2960. (2) *to defend* against, *protect, preserve* from. (a) *with* fram :—Hé bið gescylded fram (wið, *v. l.*) ǽghwylcum nǽddercynne, Lch. i. 198, 7. Mid gebedum fram deáþe gescilded (-scylded, *v. l.*) *orationibus a morte servatus*, Bd. 3, 23 ; Sch. 305, 2. Gescilded fram ðære tíde his deáþes *ab articulo mortis retentus*, 3, 30 ; Sch. 331, 20. (b) *with* wiþ, and (a) *dat.* :—Hé ús gescildað wið earfharum, Cri. 761. Þæt þec hálig gǽst wið earfeðum gescilde, Gú. 428. (β) *acc.* :—Hé hine wið ðæt fýr gescilde *ab ignibus defenditur*, Past. 399, 20. Þ úre Hǽlend þé wið ealle fýnd gescylde, Hml. S. 23, 837 : Bl. H. 19, 16.

**ge-scildend.** *Add* : *a defender, saviour* :—Þú eart mín friðiend and mín gefultumend and mín gescyldend *adjutor meus et liberator meus es tu*, Ps. Th. 39, 21. Gescyldend *ultorem*, Ps. Spl. 8, 3 : *defensorem*, Ps. Rdr. 8, 3. Gescyldendas *protectores*, p. 291, 38.

**ge-scildnes.** *Add* :—Gescyldnys *tutela*, i. *defensio*, An. Ox. 3556. Ǽfre se deófol winð nú ongeán úrne geleáfan ; ac seó gescyldnys is æt úrum Fæder gelang, Hml. Th. i. 252, 3. Hí bǽdon Godes gescyldnysse wið þone Syriscan here, Hml. A. 107, 70. Gescyldnesse *tutamini*, i. *protectioni*, An. Ox. 394 : *clypeo*, 2100 : *defensaculo*, 2390 : *defensionem*, i. *gubernationem*, 2795. For gescildnesse (-scield-, *v. l.*) his heorde *pro defensione gregis*, Past. 89, 23. Hé him þone rén tó gescildnesse onsende, Ors. 4, 10 ; S. 194, 30. His sáwle tó gescyldnesse, Chr. 959 ; P. 115, 16.

**ge-scildod** *provided with a shield.* *Take here* **ge-sceldod** *in Dict.,* *and add:*—*Scutum* scyld, *scutatus* gescyldod, Ælfc. Gr. Z. 256, 15.

**ge-scīnan.** *Add:* I. *to shine:*—Eft gesceán onsióne his *resplenduit facies ejus,* Mt. L. 17, 2. Gewoedo his huît swîðe gesceán (giscionun, R.) *uestitus eius albus refulgens,* Lk. L. 9, 29. II. *to shine on:*—Swâ se fiicbeám ofersceadað ðæt lond ðæt hit under him ne mæg gegrôwan, for ðæm hit sió sunne ne môt gescînan, Past. 337, 12. [*O. Sax.* gi-skînan *to shine : O. H. Ger.* ge-scînan.]

**ge-scincio.** *Add:*—Gescincio *exugia* (cf. *exugia* gihsinga ł micgern, 30, 13), Wrt. Voc. ii. 108, 3. Gescinco *exigia,* 30, 51 : 287, 35 (*printed* gesanco).

**ge-scipe,** es; *m.* (?) *Shape* (?), *condition, nature* (?), cf. ge-sceap; III. 1, III. 2 :—Se wyrm gebeáh snûde tôsomne . . . Gewât þa byrnende gebogen scrîðan, tô gescipe (*according to its shape? after the manner of reptiles?*) scyndan, B. 2570.

**ge-scippan.** *Take here* **ge-sceppan** *in Dict.,* *and add:* I. *to create, form.* (1) of the operation of divine power :—God gesceóp æt fruman twēgen men, and hē geswâc ðâ ðæra gesceapennyssa . . . ac . . . hē gescypð ælces mannes lîchaman on his môðer innoðe, and him sâwle siððan on besett. Ne beóð ðâ sâwla nâhwâr ær ðan wunigende, ac se ælmihtiga wyrhta hî gescypð ælce dæge, swâ swâ hē dêð þâ lichaman, Hml. Th. ii. 206, 21–27. Of frymðe þære gesceafte þe God gesceóp (giscóp, R., *condidit*), Mk. 13, 19. Smiðode oððe gescóp *cudaret* (*summus princeps,* Ald. 156, 22), Wrt. Voc. ii. 19, 36. Gesceapen *cretus* (cf. ácenned *cretus,* 24), 21, 30. Tô þære ilcan eorþan þe se lîchoma ær of gesceapen wæs, Bl. H. 21, 29. Úre lîchoma wæs gesceapen of feówer gesceaftum, 35, 12. Gescapene (-scepen, Ps. V.) hý syndon *creata sunt,* Ps. Rdr. 148, 5. Þa sibbe ðe þa tunglu on gesceapne wæron, Bt. 39, 13 ; F. 232, 26. (1 a) where the character, condition, &c. assigned at creation are given. Cf. ge-sceap; III. 2. (a) *with complementary adj.* :—Þ wē ûrne lîchoman and ûre sáule swâ unwemme him âgeofan, swâ hē hié ær gesceóp, Bl. H. 103, 22. (β) *with* tô :—God gesceóp tô mæran engle þone þe nû is deófol ; ac God ne gesceóp hine nâ tô deófle, Hml. Th. i. 12, 19. Þære gecynde ðe heó tô gesceapen wæs, Bt. 25 ; F. 88, 7. Ðâs eorþlican wæstmas sint gesceapene nêtenum tô andliefene, and þâ woruldwelan synt gesceapene tô biswice þâm monnum þe beóð neátenum gelîce, 14, 1; F. 42, 1–3. (2) where the subject of the verb is a man :—Hwæþer þû fægerra blôstmæna fægnige swelce þû hié gescôpe, Bt. 14, 1 ; F. 40, 25. Þû hit ne gescéópe, 14, 2 ; F. 42, 35. II. *to shape, give a particular form to.* Cf. ge-sceap; III. 1 :—Godes gâst fêrde ofer þâ wæteru tô gescyppenne and tô geliffæstenne þ ungehîwode antimber (*ad formandam et vivificandam informem materiam*), Angl. vii. 16, 155. Hwanon wæs Adames nama gesceapen ? Fram iiii steorrum, Sal. K. 178, 32. Strîc on twâ healfa þînes fêt þâm gemete þe hî gesceapene beóð, Tech. ii. 126, 10. II a. *to shape* after or according to (*tô*) a pattern :—Wē sint gesceapene æfter ðære biesene ûres Scippendes . . . sê ðe tô Godes bisene gesceapen is (*ad Dei imaginem conditus*), Past. 249, 22. Hî on fruman tô Godes hîwunga gesceapene wæron, Bl. H. 61, 7. ¶ naman gescippan *to name* a person (*dat.*) :—Hit wæs gewunelic þæt þâ mâgas sceolden þâm cilde naman gescyppan on ðâm eahtoðan dæge, ac hî ne dorston nænne ôðerne naman Crîste gescyppan þonne se heáhengel him gesette, Hml. Th. i. 94, 22–26. III. of the ordering by Providence, *to ordain, appoint, destine.* Cf. ge-sceap; III. 3. (1) *to destine* a person to (*tô*) a condition, lot, &c. :—Ðætte ðæt môd gemyne of ðæm suingum ðe ðæt flæsc ðolað tô hwæm eal monncyn gesceapen is *ut animus cui sit conditioni subditus, ex percussa, quam sustinet, carne memoretur,* Past. 255, 19. Þa sâr and þâ brocu þe se man tô gesceapen is, Bl. H. 59, 34. Wâ biþ þæm mannum þe ne ongytaþ þisse worlde yrmþa, þe hié tô gesceapene beóþ . . . ne hié ongytaþ þæt hî gesceapene wæron tô þon êcan lîfe, næs nâ tô þon êcan deáþe, 61, 2–8. ¶ of human ordering? :—Hē (*Ptolemy*) tôgædere gesceóp (-sweów, -sweóp, *v. l.*) ealle Egyptum and Arabia *he ordered all Egypt and Arabia should be united?* (the Latin is : Ptolemaeo Aegyptus Arabiaeque pars sorte provenit), Ors. 3, 11 ; S. 142, 27. (2) *to ordain* a condition for a person :—Næs him gesceapen fram Gode . . . þæt hē sceolde Godes bebod tôbrecan, Hml. Th. i. 18, 28. Gif þ sôþ is þ hit him swâ gesceapen wæs, þ hî ne môston elles dôn, Bt. 41, 2 ; F. 246, 20. Gif þ sôð beón mæg, þ him swâ gesceapen wæs, Hml. S. 17, 234. [*Goth.* ga-skapjan: *O. Sax.* gi-skôp; *p.:* *O. H. Ger.* ge-scafan, -sceffan *creare, condere, formare.*]

**ge-scippend.** *Take here* **ge-sceppend** *in Dict.,* *and add:*—Mid mêder ealra gescippendes, Nar. 48, 3.

**ge-scīran.** *l.* ge-scîran, *and add:*—Ne mæht ðû gescîra (*uilicare*).

**ge-scirian.** *Take here* **ge-scerian** *in Dict.,* *and add :* *To separate, remove* from :—Ðâ him ðæt lið gescîred (-sciered, *v. l.*) wæs *digesto vino,* Past. 295, 7. Gescerede *degesta,* i. *disposita,* Wrt. Voc. ii. 138, 35. [*O. H. Ger.* ge-scerian *privare, impendere.*] Cf. ge-scearian.

**ge-scirdan** (?) *to injure, ruin* :—þâ côm atol æglæca morðres mânfreá myrce gescyrded (*ruined by black crime?*), cf. ic eom synnum forwundod, Sat. 131 : or (?) *evil* (*for myrce as epithet of the devil* cf.

mirki mênskaðo, Hel. 1062), *ruined*) deófol deáðreów duguðum bereáfod, An. 1315. v. scirdan.

**ge-scirpan** *to sharpen.* *Take here* **ge-scerpan** *in Dict.,* *and add :* I. *to make more active, strengthen.* (1) of sight (lit. or fig.) :—Þîn þ lîchamlice eáge ne gesyhð âht lîchamlices, bûton hit gescyrpe (*acueret*) þâ þing tô geseónne seó unlîchamlice wîse, Gr. D. 269, 21. Bûton hî sýn gescyrpte þurh þâ ungesewenlican, 270, 2. (2) the object a person :—Ic þurh þâ mynegunge and lufe gescyrped (getrymmed, *v. l.*) on mînum môde, Gr. D. 1, 18. II. *in grammar,* ge-scirpt *acute :*—*Acutus accentus,* þæt ys gescyrpt accent, Angl. viii. 333, 25. [*O. L. Ger.* gi-skerpian.]

**ge-scirpan** *to dress.* *Take here* **ge-scerpan** *in Dict.,* *and add :* I. *to dress, clothe.* (1) of people :—Þâ árâs hē sylf and hine gescyrpte *surrexit, vestimento se induit,* Gr. D. 297, 12. Þeáh wê ûs gescirpen mid þý reádestan godwebbe, Wlfst. 262, 21. In ðâm godwebcynne bið S. Mihhael gescyrped on dômes dæg, Sal. K. p. 152, 22. (2) of things, *to cover* as with a garment :—þ treów biþ ûton gescyrped (-scerped, *v. l.*) mid þære rinde, Bt. 34, 10 ; F. 150, 7. II. *to equip, provide with necessaries for a journey* :—Þâ sende hē hine tô Rôme and hine þider well gescyrpte (*cunctis, quae necessitas poscebat itineris, largiter subministratis*); and hine hêt, þonne hē eft tô his êðle hweorfan wolde, þ hē tô him côme. þ hē hine wel hâm gescyrpte, Bd. 5, 19 ; Sch. 659, 20–25. Man beád þ man sceolde twêgen cempan gescyrpan tô þære fyrde, Hml. S. 30, 298.

**ge-scirpendlīce;** *adv. So as to fit :*—Seó heáfodstôw gescyrpendlîce gehîwod ætýwde tô þâm gemete hyre heáfdes *locus capitis ad mensuram capitis illius aptissime figuratus apparuit,* Bd. 4, 19; Sch. 451, 19.

**ge-scōgan, -sceón** *to shoe, put on shoes, furnish with shoes;* calciare :—Gisceó ðec sceohðongum ðînum *calciate caligas tuas,* Rtl. 58, 11. Côm se Godes wer gescôd (-sceód) mid gehammenum scôn, Gr. D. 37, 12. Gescôd, Lch. iii. 200, 22, 23. ‘Sceógeað eówre fêtt’ . . . ðonne hæbbe wē bêgen fêtt gescôge, Past. 44, 10–13. Beón ûre fêt gesceóde, Angl. viii. 323, 28. [*O. H. Ger.* ge-scuoht *calciatus.*]

**ge-scola** *a fellow-debtor.* *Add :*—Gescolan *condebitores,* Wrt. Voc. ii. 105, 23.

**ge-scola** (-scôla ?), an ; *m. A fellow-scholar :*—Gescola *condiscipulus,* i. *consolaris,* An. Ox. 2271.

**ge-scola,** an ; *m. One of the same troop* (scolu), *companion, comrade :*—þæt wæs gegearwod fram fruman þisses middaneardes deóflum and his gescolum (cf. Mt. 25, 41), An. Ox. 2271, note.

**ge-scortian.** *Take here* **ge-sceortian** *in Dict.*

**ge-scot.** *Take here* **ge-sceot** *in Dict., and add:* I. *a weapon shot or hurled, an arrow, a dart, spear, javelin :*—Gesceot *cateia,* i. *telum,* Wrt. Voc. i. 34, 30. Ânes cynnes gesceot *clava* vel *cateia* vel *teutona,* 35, 44. Gif hit wære êsa gescot oððe ylfa gescot oððe hægtessan gescot, nû ic wille ðîn helpan. Þis ðe tô bôte êsa gescotes, Lch. iii. 54, 9–15. Gescotum *calamis, sagittis,* Germ. 392, 52. Ðâ dîglan gescotu (*jacula*) ðæs sweocolan feóndes, Past. 431, 5 : Ps. Vos. 54, 22. I a. *collective, missile weapons :*—Gesceot *pila,* Wrt. Voc. i. 35, 45. Swâ hié on hîran stede gestondað, swâ him mâre gescot and mâ flâna hiera feónda tô cymð (*eo crebrioribus sagittis insidiatoris impetuntur*), Past. 407, 22. II. *a shot, shooting or hurling of a missile :*—Mid îdelum gescotum *iactibus uacuis,* An. Ox. 49, 2. Þâ þôhton hié þ hié sceoldan ærest of þæm muntum hié gebîgan mid hiora flâna gescotum, Ors. 6, 36 ; S. 294, 23. Ge mid scotum (gesceotum, *v. l.*), ge mid stâna torfungum, ge mid eallum heora wîgcræftum, 3, 9 ; S. 134. 15. II a. *rapid movement* of a missile, *flight* of an arrow :—Þâ wæmna flugon mid swiftum gesceote on heora fînd, Jud. Thw. 162, 8. III. *a part* of a building shut off from the rest, *chancel :*—Gesceot *cancella,* Wrt. Voc. ii. 128, 8. Ðâ stôd his franca binnan þâm gesceote, Hml. S. 3, 267. Heó þæt gesceot hrepode, Hml. Th. ii. 32, 28. IV. *a shot, scot, contribution :*—Gif hwylc monn þone ândagan oferhebbe æt his gescote, bête be twifealdum, Cht. Th. 614, 23. [*O. H. Ger.* ge-scoz *missile, jaculum : Ger.* ge-schoss.] v. fleax-, leóht-, mealt-, melo-, sâwel-, weax-gescot.

**ge-scota,** an ; *m. A fellow-soldier, comrade :*—Gescota *commanipularius,* Wrt. Voc. ii. 104, 82. Incempa *vel* gescota *commanipularius, collega, miles,* 132, 49.

**gescot-feoht.** *Add :*—Æt gescotfeohta, Ps. Th. 75, 3.

**ge-scræf,** es ; *n. A den :*—Gê dydon hit tô gescræfe (*speluncam*) scaþena, Mt. R. 21, 13.

**ge-screncan.** *Add : To trip up* (fig.), *cause to fall, throw down :*—Hē ðurh ealle uncysta ðâ môd gescrencð *per universa vitia animum supplantat,* Past. 73, 2. Gescrenctes (*supplantasti*), Ps. Srt. 17, 40. Gescrenc hié *supplanta eos,* 16, 14. Ðâ ðôhtun gescrencan gongas mîne, 139, 5. Ðâ sâwle mid sumre leásunge gescræncan and beswîcan *animam ex aliqua falsitate laqueare,* Gr. D. 339, 23. Ne bioð gescrencte (*supplantabuntur*) gongas his, Ps. Srt. 36, 31.

**ge-scrence;** *adj. Withered, dry :*—Hē hæfde hond gescrengce ł drýge *habebat manum aridam,* Lk. L. 6, 8. Cf. mis-scrence.

**ge-screncednes.** *Add :*—Gescrencednisse *supplantationem,* Ps. Srt 40, 10: ge-screope. v. *next word.*

**ge-scrépe, -scroepe, -scrǽpe, -screópe;** *adj. Fit, suitable, adapted :*—Hit is gescrǽpe (scroepe, *v. l.*) on lǽswe sceápa *alendis apta pecoribus,* Bd. 1, 1; Sch. 8, 8. Gescroepe (-scrópe, *v. l.*) ærneweg *via apta currui equorum,* 5, 6; Sch. 575, 1. Seó þrúh wæs swá gescreópe (-scrǽpe, *v. l.*) þǽre fǽmnan líchaman geméted *ita aptum corpori uirginis sarcofagum inuentum est,* 4, 19; Sch. 451, 14. Gehýþlic, þæslic *vel* gescrǽpe *commodus,* i. *congruus, utilis, aptus,* Wrt. Voc. ii. 131, 81. Netto menniscum giwunu giscroepo wilde deáro tó onfóanne *retes humano usui aptus bestias ad capiendas,* Rtl. 117, 14. v. un-gescrépe; *adj.*

**ge-scrépe, es;** *n. An advantage :*—Lǽn, gescrǽpe *commodum, lucrum, utile,* Wrt. Voc. ii. 132, 1. Fela óþerra gescrépa (-screópa, *v. l.*) hé ongeat heofonlíce him forgyfen wesan *alia commoda caelitus sibi fuisse donata intellexit,* Bd. 4, 22; Sch. 461, 17. v. un-gescrépe; *n.*

**ge-scrépelíce.** *Add :*—Gescrépelíce (-scrópelíce, *v. l.*), Bd. 4, 19; Sch. 451, 19.

**ge-scrépness, e;** *f. Advantage, commodity :*—Gescroepnis conpe[n]dium, Wrt. Voc. ii. 105, 14. v. un-gescrépness.

**ge-scríf.** *Substitute: What is prescribed, decreed, or appointed.* (1) *a judgement, edict :*—Þæt gescríf *censuram,* Wrt. Voc. ii. 24, 61. Gebennum oððe gescrifum *edictis* (cf. *edictis,* i. *decretis* gebannum, An. Ox. 3037 (Ald. 41, 27)), 33, 12. (2) *a prescribed practice, rite, ceremony :*—Gescrifu, dómas *ceremonias* (cf. *gentilitatis cerimonias* hǽþenscipes bígengeas, An. Ox. 2624 (Ald. 35, 36)), Wrt. Voc. ii. 23, 54. [Cf. *O. L. Ger.* ge-scríf: *O. H. Ger.* ge-scrip *scriptura.*]

**ge-scrífan.** *Add:* **I.** *to decree, appoint something to a person.* (1) *of the dealings of Providence:*—Hé (*St. Andrew*) Marmedonia mǽgðe hæfde gesóhte . . . þám hé (*the MS. has* hé) (*the Deity*) him fóre gescráf (cf. þú scealt þá fóre geféran, 216) *he had reached the tribe of Mermedonians . . . to them the Lord had appointed him a journey,* An. 848. Gewát hé féran, swá him Scyppend wera gescrifen hæfde, 788. (2) *of the orders of secular or ecclesiastical law:*—Symble se man þám óðrum byrigean gesette, and þám riht áwyrce þe tó hiom Cantwara déman gescrifen, Ll. Th. i. 30, 14. **II.** *to order, bind a person to do or suffer something, compel, subject:*—Ne þearf man ná fæsten fram Eástran oð Pentecosten, búton hwá gescrifen sig, oþþe hé elles fæsten wylie, Ll. Th. i. 368, 28. Gescriuene, geþrǽste, geþreáde *addicti* (uiolentis naturae legibus *addicti,* Ald. 20, 30), An. Ox. 1452. **III.** *to shrive a person:*—Eów gebyrað þ gé beón gescrifene on ðissere wucan, oððe húru on ðǽre óðre, Hml. S. 12, 291.

**ge-scrincan.** *Add: To contract* (intrans.) :—Gif sino gescrince . . . monegum men gescrincað his fét tó his homme, Lch. ii. 68, 1–2. Hond gescruncan (*arida*), Lk. L. 6, 6. Þ wíf gescryncan áhóf *mulierem curuatum erigens,* p. 8, 4. Þá gescruncenan and þá þynhlǽnan *marcida,* Wrt. Voc. ii. 57, 22. Gif sinwe sién gescruncene, Lch. ii. 328, 7.

**ge-scroepe.** v. ge-scrépe: **ge-scróp.** v. un-gescróp: **ge-scropenys.** *Dele.*

**ge-scrýdan.** *Dele last passage for which see* ge-scirdan, *and add: To clothe* a person with (*mid*) a garment :—Hé hine gescrýdde mid his byrnan, Hml. S. 25, 279; Hml. A. 130, 479. Hí mid hǽran hí gescrýddon tó líce, Hml. S. 12, 36. Gescrýd *circumamicta,* An. Ox. 1024. Seó slápolnys byð gescrýdd mid tætticum *dormitatio vestietur pannis,* Hml. A. 9, 237. Mid hǽran gescrýd tó hire líce, 108, 207. Gescríd mid goldum and mid gimmum, Chr. 1086; P. 219, 9. Hé gelǽdde Mardocheum mǽrlíce gescrýdne, Hml. A. 99, 241.

**ge-scúfan; p. -sceáf; pp. -scofen, -scyfen. I.** *to cause movement,* with idea of violence, *to eject, expel:*—Gescyfen diúbol *ejecto daemone,* Mt. p. 16, 4. **II.** *to cause action, to impel, drive:*—Ðá ðe unmedome bióð tó ðǽre láre, and ðeáh for hiora hrǽdwilnesse beóð tó gescofene *quos a praedicatione imperfectio prohibet, et tamen praecipitatio impellit,* Past. 375, 20.

**ge-sculdre.** v. gescyldru: **ge-scunian, -scynian.** (1) *to detest.* v. scunian; **III.** (2) *to fear,* Rtl. 32, 9.

**ge-scý.** *Take here* ge-scóe *in Dict., and add:*—Ðwongas giscóes his *corrigiam calciamentorum eius,* Lk. R. 3, 16. Mid gescý níwum (ealdum) beón gescód *calciamento nouo (ueteri) calciari,* Lch. iii. 200, 22, 23. Þám se cyning sealde his ágen gescý (*calceamenta sua*), Gr. D. 130, 33. Gescóe mín *calciamentum meum,* Ps. Srt. 59, 10: 107, 10. 'Ne bere gé mid eów . . . gescý (*calciamenta*)' . . . Hwæt mǽnað þá gescý?, Hml. Th. ii. 522, 19–25. Gescý *calceos,* Wrt. Voc. ii. 127, 46. Ic bicge hýda and fell . . . and wyrce of him gescý (*calceamenta*) mistlíces cynnes, Coll. M. 27, 31. Giscóe, Lk. R. 10, 4. Gesceóe, Mt. L. 3, 11.

**ge-scýfan.** *Dele, and see* ge-scúfan: **ge-scýftan.** v. ge-sciftan: **ge-scýgean.** v. -scígan: **ge-scýld(i)an.** v. scyldan: **ge-scýldod.** v. ge-scildod.

**ge-scyldru.** *Take here* ge-sculdre *in Dict., and add: The shoulder-blades:*—Mid gescyldrum his *scapulis suis,* Ps. Srt. 90, 4. On ðone lið þæra eaxla betweox gesculdrum, Lch. ii. 242, 12. Ofer gescyldru *super scapulas,* Ps. Srt. ii. p. 192, 33. v. middel-gescyldru.

**ge-scynian.** v. ge-scunian: **ge-scyrdan.** v. ge-scirdan: **ge-scyrian.** v. ge-scirian: **ge-scyrpendlíce.** v. ge-scirpendlíce.

**ge-scyrtan.** *Add :*—Gescyrdte *breuiauit,* Mk. L. 13, 20. Þín líf ne gescyrt, Hml. S. 37, 149. Mid fiffétedum ł gescertum *brachicatalectico,* An. Ox. 130. Gescyrted biðon *breuiabuntur,* Mt. L. 24, 22.

**gese.** v. gise: **ge-sealfian.** v. sealfian.

**ge-seáw.** *Add: Full of moisture, soaked :*—Nim þæs eceddrences swá mycel swá þe þince, dó rǽdic on þ seáw þæs drinces, lǽt beón nihterne on, syle on morgenne . . . þæne rǽdic swá geseáwne tó þicganne, Lch. ii. 286, 12. [Cf. *Icel.* söggr *dank, wet.*]

**ge-sécan.** *Add:* **I.** *to seek.* (1) *to look for* an object whose position is not known, *try to find:*—Ðene ðú gesóhtes rím *illum quem quaerebas nunerum,* Mt. p. 4, 4. Fram ðreátum gesóht wæs *a turbis quaesitus,* Jn. p. 4, 17. (2) *to try to get:*—Ðe wiðerworda gisóhte (gesóhta, L., gesóhte, Wrt. Voc. ii. 74, 2) iówih *Satanas expetiuit uos,* Lk. R. 22, 31. Gesóhte rest *quaerens requiem,* Mt. L. 12, 43. Gesóhton leás witnessa *quaerebant falsum testimonium,* 26, 59. Gesécæn hí him sǽmend, Ll. Th. i. 30, 18. Sceal fǽmne hire freónd gesécean, Gn. C. 44. Gié nǽllað gesoeca hwæd gié geete, Lk. L. R. 12, 29. (2 a) *to ask for* as a favour or a right, *to make a claim in respect to:*—Geséce se æbǽre þeóf þ þ hé geséce . . . and sé þe ofer þis stalige, geséce þ hé geséce *perquirat abere þeof quicquid perquirat . . . qui deinceps furabitur, querat quicquid querat,* Ll. Th. i. 390, 27–392, 2: 268, 22–23. Þæs ne sý nán forgifnes, gesécen þ hí gesécen, 276, 3. Þ ealra wítegena blód sý gesóht (*inquiratur*) . . . swá bið gesóht (*requiretur*) fram þisse cneórysse, Lk. ii. 50, 51. Ðǽm micel gesald wæs, micel bið gesóht from him, Lk. L. R. 12, 48. (3) *to try to do, attempt, endeavour:*—Hiá gesóhton ðec tó gestánane *quaerebant te lapidare,* Jn. L. 11, 8. (4) *to try to learn by asking, to question:*—Ðá uuðuuto gefrugnun ł gesóhton mið him *scribas conquirentes cum illis,* Mk. L. 9, 14. **II.** with idea of movement, *to go or come to:*—Ðú gesécst *adibis,* Wrt. Voc. ii. 3, 33. Gesécan *adire,* 2, 55. (1) *to go to a person* (a) *for residence or intercourse:*—Ic for láre intingan eów hér gesóhte, Hml. S. 23 b, 71. Þá gesóhtan hié hine and him þæt wundor sægdon, Bl. H. 199, 28. Hé ús wile on ðómes dæg gesécan, 123, 33. Godes Sunu hié hæfde gesóht, 13, 3. (b) *in order to help:*—Gesóhte *uisitauit,* Lk. L. R. 1, 68. Hé ús gesóhte hider on middangeard, Bl. H. 129, 11: 11, 34. Ús gesécean mid lufan, 119, 30. (c) *in order to hurt, with hostile intent, to attack:*—Hanna hiene æt þæm fæstenne gesóhte mid xx m, Ors. 4, 5; S. 168, 30. Þá gesóhton hié hié mid firde *patriam bello cinxerunt,* 4, 9; S. 164, 29. Be ðon ðe mon óðerne on ciricean geséce . . . Gif . . . hine man þǽr séce oþþe yflige, Ll. Th. i. 248, 14. Þæt hé hine wolde mid fyrde tó gefeohte gesécan *bellum indicens,* Bd. 2, 12; Sch. 153, 18. Sé þe þ nolde, þæt hié wolden þá mid gefeohte gesécan *denuntians contradictorem pacis bello impetendum,* Ors. 3, 1; S. 94, 25. (d) *for help or protection, to apply to, appeal to:*—Nǽnig næs tó ðæs untrum ðe hine gesóhte, þ hé sóna hǽlo ne onféng, Bl. H. 223, 24. Gesóhton þá hláfordas Rómane (*Romam deferuntur*), and hí him gefylstan, Ors. 4, 3; S. 162, 20. Gif landleás man his mágas geséce, Ll. Th. i. 204, 6. Gif hwilc þeóf gesóhte þone cing . . . þ hé hæbbe nigon nihta fyrst, 222, 26: 230, 7. Hé wolde gesécan helle goda . . . and biddan þ hí him ágeáfan eft his wíf, Bt. 35, 6; F. 168, 13. Ic þe (*God*) gesóht hæbbe *ad te mihi redeundum esse sentio,* Solil. H. 12, 10. (dd) *where the object sought is given:*—Seó þeód gesóhte Ecgbryht him tó friþe and tó mundboran, Chr. 823; P. 60, 18. Germanie gesóhton Agustus ungeniédde him tó friþe, Ors. 5, 15; S. 250, 14. Ne geséce nán man þone cyng for nánre sprǽce, Ll. Th. i. 266, 9. Lǽrde hé his sunu þæt hé him ongeán fóre, and hiene him tó friþe gesóhte, Ors. 5, 12; S. 242, 32. (e) *to go to* one who is before, *to follow:*—'Ne mægo ðe nú fylge ł soeca (*sequi*), ðú gesoecas (*sequeris*) æfter ðon.' For huon ne mægo ic ðec gesoeca (gisoecan, R., *sequi*), Jn. L. 13, 36–37. Gesoec (gisoecas, R.) mec *sequere me,* 21, 19. Mec gesoeca *me sequatur,* 12, 26. (2) *to go to a place,* for residence, doing business, intercourse:—Þǽr wunian mót sé þa stówe geséceþ, Bl. H. 105, 2. Þone innoþ geceás and gesóhte úre Drihten, 11, 21. Hé férde mid swá mycclan here swá nǽfre ǽr þis land ne gesóhte, Chr. 1085; P. 215, 37. Þá wǽron þá ǽrestan scipu Deniscra monna þe Angelcynnes lond gesóhton, 787; P. 54, 7. Nis þ nǽnig man þ þurfe þone deópan grund þæs hátan léges gesécan, Bl. H. 103, 16. (aa) *to attend* a meeting, ceremony, &c.:—Nán man swá dyrstig ne sý, þ hé áðor oððe cýpinge wyrce, oððe ǽnig mót geséce, Cht. E. 231, 22. Gá (se tihtbysiga man) tó þám ordále. And gif se ágena frigea nelle þ ordál gesécean, Ll. Th. i. 294, 19. (a β) *of animals or moving things:*—Nis nán tó þæs lytel ǽwelm þ hé þa sǽ ne geséce, Bt. 24, 1; F. 80, 25. Ðá sægde se bisceop þ . . . ne fugel ne wildeór ne nǽnig ǽtern wyrm þǽr dorste gesécean (*adire*) ðá hálgan gemǽro, Nar. 28, 7. (b) *for protection, security, help:*—Swá swá on his freólstíde his byrgene geséhð, hé gewent gesundful ongeán, Hml. Th. i. 564, 33. Ðá gesahte (-sóhte?) hé ðínes fæder líc, Cht. Th. 173₂ 7. Gif hé friðstówe geséce, 14, 46, 25: 340, 10: 332, 16. Gif þára mynsterháma hwelcne for hwelcre sclyde geséce, 60, 24. Gif hwelc mon cirican geséce, 64, 20. (c) *to reach* a position of rest, *arrive at, get as far as:*—Þá scipu tóscuton and hé ðone grund gesóhte mid horse mid ealle *he went to the bottom horse and all,* Hml. Th. ii. 304, 28. Hí

wǣron sōna deáde swā hí eorðan gesōhtan (solo adlidebantur), Bd. I, 12; Sch. 35, 4. Gif hí Cwicchelmes hlǣwe gesōhton þet hí nǣfre tō sǣ gān ne sceoldan, Chr. 1006; P. 137, 6. Oð ðæt seó ex sý gesōht, Lch. iii. 2, 11. (cc) of motion in ships, to reach land :—Sōna swā ðæt forme scip land gesōhte (came to anchor) . . . þā cōm se cyning self mid his scipe, and land gesōhte (landed), Ors. 4, 5; S. 166, 9–16. Hié ne dorston þæt land nāwer gesēcan on þā healfe they durst not land anywhere on that side, Chr. 918; P. 98, 26. III. to get by seeking. (1) Cf. I. 2 :—Libras tuoege tēno libras gesōhte mna tua decem mnas adquisivit, Lk. L. R. 19, 16. (2) Cf. I. 2 a :—þ hí nǣfre feorh ne gesēcean . . . þ hé nǣfre þ feorh ne gesēce nunquam sibi uitam adquirant . . . numquam sibi uitam impetret, Ll. Th. i. 392, 1–3. þ hí nǣfre feorh ne gesēcen, būton se cyningc him feorhgeneres unne, 268, 24. (3) Cf. I. 4 :—Æfter tíd þ gesōhte from drýum secundum tempus quod exquisierat a Magis, Mt. L. 2, 16.

ge-seccan. Dele, and see ge-sēcan ; I. 2 : ge-sēcednes. Dele.

ge-secgan. Take here forms under ge-sagian, and add : I. with acc. (1) where the object denotes a collection of words, to say words, tell a tale, give a list, account, &c. :—Herenisse hiora gisæcge ðió cirica laudem eorum pronunciet ecclesia, Rtl. 61, 26. Gesǣd prolatum (quod cum calumniae gannitura prolatum), An. Ox. 4505. Ondetnis lofes hælendes gesægd is (v. Mt. 11, 25) confessio laudis Iesu refertur, Mt. p. 16, 11. Gesægd is foresægdnisse explicit praefatio, 12, 6. Cynnresuo feórtig tuā endebrednise gesaegd is (v. Mt. 1, 1–17) generationum quadraginta duarum ordo narratur, 13, 15. Gesaegd aron heáfudwearda ðara rēda exbliciunt cabitula lectionum, 20, 9. (2) where the object denotes what is spoken about. (a) to give an account of, speak of, tell, narrate :—Ic nū his dǣda gesugian scyle, oþ ic Rōmāna gesecge, Ors. 3, 17; S. 120, 18. Đā ðing ðā gehērde æfter lufu wundara gesaegde ea quae audierat juxta fidem gestorum narravit, Mt. p. 8, 12. Nænigum menn ðū gecuoeðe ðis þ gesæge (dixeris), Mk. L. 8, 26. Sanctus Iōhannes lífes weorþunga gesecgan, Bl. H. 163, 36. Uneáðe mæg mon tō geleáfsuman gesecgan swā monigfeald yfel in tanta malorum multitudine difficillima dictis fides, Ors. 3, 9; S. 128, 20. þ mæste wæl on hæðene here þe wē ǣfre gesecgan hērdon, Chr. 851; P. 65, 16. Nǣnig mennisc tunge ne geneah þæs engles mægen tō gesecgenne, Bl. H. 165, 6. Tō gesecganne, Angl. ix. 265, 4. Bið gesægd þti ðiós dyde, Mt. L. 26, 13. Hwī wæs þæra engla synne forsuwod on þǣre bēc Genesis, and þæs mannes wæs gesǣd (patefactum) ?, Angl. vii. 4, 27. (b) to give notice of, make known, announce :—Hē gesæged (cýð, W. S.) alle adnuntiabit omnia, Jn. L. R. 4, 25 : Jn. L. 16, 14. Đā ðe tōwearde aron hē gesæges iúh, 16, 13. Đā hiorda gesægidon (nuntiaverunt) alle, Mt. L. 8, 33. Gisægi (annuncia) folce mīnum hēhsynna hiara, Rtl. 5, 16. Hē hine monnum gecýþan and gesecgan teolode, Bl. H. 165, 31. Đā hērde Ægelríc þet gesecgon, Chr. 1070; P. 207, 26. (c) to speak of, expound, discuss :—Bisen gesægde ł getrahtade parabolam exponit, Mt. p. 17, 3. Syndriga stōwa gewutta ðū mæht and mid sōðe gesæcca propria loca scire possis ac vere disserere, 11, 2. Ic gehēre hwæt þū woldest witan, ac ic hyt ne mæg myd feáwum wordum gesecgan, Solil. H. 64, 23. (3) the subject a pronoun referring to a clause :—þ gesægd, þ hē wēre gewis his sylfes fordfōre, Bd. 4, 24; Sch. 491, 19. (4) where the verb is of incomplete predication :—Hē þone Hǣlend on þysne middangeard cumende gesecgean wolde, Bl. H. 165, 35. Wēron gesægd sum ōðero ofslægeno nuntiatis quibusdam occisis, Lk. p. 8, 1. II. where the object is a clause, to say, tell, declare :—Stefn þte hē wēre clioppendes in uoestern gesaeged vocem esse clamantis in deserto enuntiat, Jn. p. 3, 6. Gesege hwæþer þ betere þince, hwæþer þe . . . , þe . . . , Bt. 8; F. 26, 10. Gesecge hē his mōde, þ hit mæg findan . . . , 35, 1; F. 154, 23. Ic ðē mæg mid feáwum wordum gesecgan hū manegra yfela ðā welan sint gefylde, 32, 1; F. 114, 6. Mē ðincð þæt þū hæbbe genōh sweotole gesǣd, þæt ǣlces mannes sāwl nū sí and ā beó, Solil. H. 63, 29. Him wæs gesǣd, þ Willelm eorll wolde hider cuman, Chr. 1066; P. 196, 4. II a. in the passive with an infinitive complementary to the subject :—Hē is gesǣd memoratur (hoc fecisse), An. Ox. 3873 : 1514 Heó wæs gesǣd narretur (superstitionis contemptrix extitisse), 4432. Gesǣde memorantur, i. dicuntur, 1610. III. used absolutely :—Lōca þ ðū ǣnigum menn gesæcga vide nemini dixeris, Mt. L. 8, 4. Bebeád þte ne ǣnigum men hiá ne gesægde, Mk. L. R. 7, 36. Miððý uæs ongeten gehäten is ðegnum gesaeccanne quo cognito iubetur discipulis nuntiare, Jn. p. 8, 4. III a. with prep. to speak, tell about :—Hió ne cuðon gesecgan be þām sigebeácne, El. 165. Scortlíce ic hæbbe nū gesǣd ymb þā þrie dǣlas þises middangeardes breviter tripartiti orbis divisiones dedi, Ors. 1, 1; S. 10, 3. Hwæðer ðē nū sí genōh sweotole gesǣd be þam wísdome, Solil. H. 66, 2. [O. Sax. gi-seggian : O. H. Ger. ge-sagēn, -segen dicere, de-, pro-, re-ferre, exponere, digerere, memorare.] v. fore-gesægd.

ge-sedian. l. ge-sēdan or ge-seddan. v. sēdan.

ge-segen. Add : -sewen, -sawen, -seagon. I. saying, narrating :—Gesǣgene dictu, Wrt. Voc. ii. 28, 47. Betwyh þā his gesawene (-seagone, v. l.) inter dicendum, Bd. 3, 19; Sch. 282, 8. II. what is said, either in speech or writing, a narrative, relation :—Ús gedafenaþ

þ wē gehýron þā word hāligra gewreota . . . Manige men beóþ þe þā word þǣre hāligan gesægene lustlíce gehýraþ, Bl. H. 55, 4–26. Gesegene, 9. þ in þām hālgan stǣre mid gerýnelicre gesægene (-segne, v. l.) is āwriten and þus gecweden quod in sacra historia figurata narratione describitur, quae ait, Gr. D. 245, 15. Ic geleornode æt gesægene (relatione) ārwyrðra witena þ þ ic secge, 9, 20. Gesægne narratione, 215, 6. Hē cwæð, swā seó ilce wíse manigum men cūð wæs be his sage (gesagone, v. l.) aiebat, sicut res eadem multis innotuit, 318, 27. Þurh hāligra bōca gesægene (rēdinge, v. l.) gehýred, 1, 4. Gesægenum assertionibus, Wrt. Voc. ii. 2, 31. Hū mæg ic forlǣtan þæt ðæt ic can, and lufian þæt ðet mē uncūð is būton be gesegenum?, Solil. H. 23, 10: 69, 28. Þurh swylcra manna gesewenàn gefàn, 60, 14. Mid gesegenum þāra fremdra tǣlnesse, Guth. Gr. 102, 32. Ne gelýfde ic ǣniges monnes gesegenum swā fela wundorlicra þinga non crediderim cuiquam esse tot prodigia, Nar. 2, 10. v. eald-gesegen.

ge-seglian. Add : v. ge-siglan.

ge-segness, e ; f. Saying, expressing :—Beforan gesegnesse lícwurðe beyond expression pleasing, Hml. S. 23 b, 73.

ge-segnian. Add : (1) to make the sign of the cross upon anything in token of blessing or consecration, cross :—Hē him gebæd and hine gesegnode (-sēnode, v. l.) mid Crīstes rōde tācne signans se signo sanctae crucis, Bd. 4, 24; Sch. 491, 3. Gisægna hine consigna eum, Rtl. 120, 7. Men gesēgon cuman fægre hand of heofonum and gesegnian þæs hūses duru, Shrn. 71, 7. Hí gesāwon þ hē wæs gemearcod mid þý gerýne Crīstes rōde tācnes, þā cwǣdon hí : 'Þis is ǣmtig fæt and gesegnod (signatum),' Gr. D. 190, 3. (2) without reference to the cross, to dedicate, offer :—Swā hwylc man swā feóndum gesēnodne (immolatum) mete þicged, Ll. Th. ii. 156, 17. [O. H. Ger. ge-seganōn benedicere.] v. un-gesegnod.

ge-sehtlian. Add : v. ge-sæhtlian.

ge-sehtness. Add : agreement, concord, peace :—Ic forgife sibbe and gesehtnysse eów þ gē būtan ōgan eówres eardes brūcan dabo vobis pacem et absque pavore habitabitis in terra vestra (Lev. 26, 6), Hml. S. 13, 160.

ge-selda. Add : [Cf. O. H. Ger. ge-sello collega, sodalis.]

ge-selen[n], e ; f. A gift, contribution, tribute :—Cunnende of gyld ðæs cǣseres geselenne temtantes de reddendo caesaris trižuto, Mk. p. 5, 1.

ge-sellan. Add : I. to give as a present to a person, confer gratuitously the ownership of. (1) with dat. of person :—Ic eówrum cynne Khananēa land on āgene æht gesylle (dabo), Ps. Th. 104, 10. He geselleð gōdo biddendum hine, Mt. L. 7, 11. Gesilið, Lk. L. 11, 22 : 14, 16. Cēnwalh gesalde Cūþrēde iii. þūsendo londes, Chr. 648; P. 28, 1. Æghwylcum drihten māððum gesealde, B. 1052. Æghwæt þæs þe him ænig mon for Godes noman geselle, Ll. Th. i. 92, 11. Ðiós eorðe eallum mannum is tō gemānan geseald, Past. 335, 10: 337, 3. (2) without dat. :—Eal hē þ ǣr for Gode gesealde, Bl. H. 215, 5. Gif gē gelýfað þ eów þ tō gōde gelimpe þ gē hēr syllaþ, þonne biþ hit eów nyt geseald (it will be given to your advantage), 41, 18. Is ǣlc feoh betere geseald þonne gehealden, Bt. 13 ; F. 38, 20. II. of the Deity, to grant, bestow a faculty, power, advantage, &c. :—Ðū gesealde him mæht, Jn. L. 17, 2. Nyle se Waldend ǣngum ānum ealle gesyllan gǣstes snyttru, Cri. 683. Sē þe hit begyteð, þon bið ēce eádignes geseald, Bl. H. 97, 30. II a. with infin. (or gerund) :—Drihten, tídlices lífes ðǣm gisel sibb gifeáia Domine, temporalis vitae eos tribue pace gaudere, Rtl. 73, 26. Iúh gesald is tō uutanne vobis datum est nosse, Mt. L. 13, 11. II b. with clause :—Ðū ūsig hālgawara earnunga gisaldest þte giwordia nos sanctorum merita tribuisti venerari, Rtl. 73, 30. Iúh gesald is þ gē witte, Mt. L. 13, 11. III. to deliver, hand to a person :—Gefered wæs heáfod his in disc and gesald wæs ðer mǣdne, Mt. L. 14, 11. III a. to give meat or drink, a cup containing drink :—Suā huā drinca geseleð iuh quisquis potum dederit uobis, Mk. L. R. 9, 41. Heó ful gesealde ēðelwearde, B. 615. Líchoma his ūs gesealla tō eattanne, Jn. L. 6, 52. III b. to give to eat or drink (infin.) :—Ðū gesealdes mē eatta . . . gesaldon mē dringe, Mt. L. 25, 35. IV. to hand over. (1) to give into the keeping of, commit, entrust :—Fíf cræft mē gesaldes (tradidisti), Mt. L. 25, 20. Gesaldest, 22. Hē gesalde Wihtwaran Æþelwalde Sūþ-Seaxna cyninge, Chr. 661; P. 32, 15. Eást-Engle hæfdon Ælfrēde foregīsla .vi. geseald, Chr. 894; P. 84, 19. Tō gísle gesalde, 1093; P. 228, 20. Ealle þing mē synt gesealde (tradita) fram mīnum Fæder, Mt. 11, 27. (1 a) of lending :—Gif þū fioh tō borge gesylle (mutuam dederis) þīnum geféran, Ll. Th. i. 52, 21. Gelēned feoh vel on borh geseald res credita, Wrt. Voc. i. 20, 70. (1 b) to give a pledge, guarantee, security :—Gif hwā ōðerne godborges oncunne, ard tión wille þ hē hwelcne ne gelǣste þāra þe hē him gesealde, Ll. Th. i. 82, 6. Symble se man þām ōðrum byrigean geselle, 30, 13. Wed gesyllan, El. 1284. Ðonne hafas ðū ðín wed geseald defixisti apud extraneum manum tuam, Past. 193, 4. Siþþan hē him byrigan gesealde hæbbe, Ll. Th. i. 30, 17. (1 c) to hand on information :—þte hiá geendebrednadon ðæt gesaga . . . suǣ gesaldon (betæhtun, W. S. tradiderunt) ūs ðā ðe gesēgon, Lk. L. R. 1, 2 : Mt. p. 7, 3. (2)

*to give* in marriage :—Gesaldon *nubtum tradentes*, Mt. L. 24, 38. (3) *to hand over, deliver* to a hostile power (person or thing). (a) *with dat.* :—Hé his geár geseleð wælhreówum *annis suos crudeli tradit*, Past. 249, 24. Ðe doema gesellæs ðeh ðǽm ðegne, Mt. L. 5, 25. God wylme gesealde Sodoman, Gen. 1925. Ðá aldormenn gesaldon ðec mé, Jn. L. 18, 35. Nalde ué gesealla hine ðé, 30. Fýre gesyllan, Gen. 2506 : Exod. 400. Hé biþ geseald hæþnum mannum, Bl. H. 15, 9 : Lk. 18, 32. Gesald, Lk. L. R. 18, 32. Hié mé habbað gesealdne heora wlencum, Bt. 7, 3 ; F. 20, 30. (b) *with prep.* :—Hiá gesellas (*tradent*) iúih in gemótum, Mt. L. 10, 17. Geseles iúih in costuncge, 24, 9. Hé hí on hæftnýd gesealde, Ps. Th. 77, 61. Ðý lǽs gesellæ ðec ðe fýónd tó dóme, Mt. L. 5, 25. In bælblyse gesyllan *to commit to the flames*, Exod. 400. Tó deáðe gesyllan *morti tradere*, Ps. Th. 117, 18 : Mt. L. 10, 21. (c) *with dat. and prep.* :—Gif þú þé selfne tó anwealde þám woruldsǽlþum gesealdest, Bt. 7, 2 ; F. 18, 34. (4) *to hand over treacherously, betray* :—Án of iúih geselleð (belǽwð, W. S., *tradet*) meh, Jn. L. 13, 21. Menigo bituih geseallas (belǽwað, W. S.), Mt. L. 24, 10. Þ Ióhannes gesald (belǽwed, W. S.) wǽre, 4, 12. Sunu monnes gesald bið (*tradendus est*) in hond monna, 17, 22. Geseald, Bl. H. 73, 1. (5) *to dedicate* to God, *consecrate* :—Hé his blǽd Gode ealne gesealde, Gú. 74. Gehét se cining Pauline þ hé wolde his dohtor gesyllan Gode (cf. filiam suam Christo consecrandam Paulino adsignauit, Bd. 2, 9), Chr. 626 ; P. 25, 11. V. *to give in exchange.* (1) *to sell* for (*wiþ*) a price :—Hé gesealde wiþ feó heofenes Hláford, Bl. H. 69, 13. Ealle (*bishoprics and abbeys*) hé wið feó gesealde, Chr. 1100 ; P. 235, 27. Godes cyrcean wið feó gesyllan, 1093 ; P. 227, 24. (2) *to sell at* (tó) a (certain) price :—Þ hié man gesealde tó þrím hunde penega, Bl. H. 75, 22 ; Mk. 14, 5. Ðis mihte beón geseald tó myclum wurðe, Mt. 26 ; 9. (3) *to sell* :—Hý hine gesealdan cípemonnum *eum mercatoribus vendiderunt*, Ors. 1, 5 ; S. 34, 2. Ic ne mæg swá fela gefón swá fela swá ic mæg gesyllan (*vendere*), Coll. M. 23, 29. (4) *to give in payment* :—Hé geselþ eallne ðone welan æfter ðám anwealde, bútan hé hine mid lǽssan begitan mæge, Bt. 33, 2 ; F. 124, 10. Twá and twéntig þúsend punda goldes and seolfres mon gesealde þám here of Ængla lande wið friðe, Ll. Th. i. 288, 12. Hiá gesealdon hiá in lond lámwrihtæs *dederunt eos in agrum figuli*, Mt. L. 27, 10. lx. sciłł. gesellan wið his feóre, Ll. Th. i. 148, 16. Hé cwæþ þ hé eall þ ᵹód þ hé mihte for méde þislicre fremsumnesse gesyllan wolde, Bd. 2, 12 ; Sch. 157, 4. VI. *to give* what may be demanded, *pay* tribute, tax, fine, compensation, &c. :—Cantware geþingodan wiþ Ine and him gesaldon .xxx. m̃., for þon hié ǽr Mul forbærndon, Chr. 694 ; P. 40, 12. Gif se oxa þeów ofstinge, geselle þám hláforde .xxx. sciłł., Ll. Th. i. 50, 4. Se hláford þe ryhtes wyrne . . . gesylle þám cynge .cxx. sciłł., 200, 16 : 340, 12. Gesylle hé þone þriddan dǽl his ágenre teóðunge intó his cyrican, 366, 24. Geselle hé .cxx. sciłł. tó wíte, 86, 5 : 104, 3 : 106, 7 : 200, 3. Geselle hé him .xxx. sciłł. tó bóte, 96, 18 : 266, 15. Gesyllan bí þám cynge .cxx. sciłł., and forgyldan þone wer his mágum, 202, 15. Mót hé gesellan byrnan and sweord on þ wergild, 136, 14. Penningslæht gesella ðæm cáseri *censum dare cæsari*, Mt. L. 22, 17. VII. *to give up, surrender, lose* :—Þær hé his feorh gesealde, Chr. 855 ; P. 66, 18 : Gen. 1739. Manig man his feorh for cyle gesealde, Bl. H. 213, 32. Hé þám folce feorg gesealde, Ap. 58. VIII. where the object denotes action regarded as given by the agent and received by the person affected, *to give* help, protection, &c. :—Ic þé míne wǽre gesylle, Gen. 1329. Embehtsumnise hé geselle Gode *obsequium se praestare Deo*, Jn. L. 16, 2. IX. *to give forth, give* (as in *give* tongue), *make a sound* :—Ǽr ðon se hona stefne gesella (*uocem dederit*), Mk. L. R. 14, 30. X. *to put forth* in words, *give evidence, answer,* &c. :—Cýðnisse in godspell gesileð *testimonium in euangelio datur*, Jn. p. 1, 4. Þte ondsuære wé gesellæ *ut responsum demus*, Jn. L. R. 1, 22. Eást-Engle hæfdon Ælfréde áþas geseald, Chr. 894 ; P. 84, 19. XI. *to offer, present* for consideration, *shew* :—Bécon gesalde *signum daret*, Jn. p. 3, 13. XII. *to assign, appoint* to an office, for a purpose :—Him man berigean geselle his feoh tó healdenne, Ll. Th. i. 30, 5. Ðá hálgan gewritu sint ús tó leóhtfatum gesald, ðæt wé mægen geseón hwæt wé dón scylen *Scriptura sacra quasi quaedam nobis lucerna sit posita*, Past. 365, 14. XII a. *to allot, assign* a share, reward :—Sé þe hine gefó and gegange healfne hine áge ; gif hine man cwelle, geselle heom man lxx. sciłł., Ll. Th. i. 42, 18. Him wæs leán geseald setl on swegle, Gú. 756. XIII. *to cause to have.* (1) *to cause to receive* a benefit, injury :—Þær is sigorspéd geseald, þám þe séceð tó him, An. 911 : 646. (2) *to produce* in a person or thing a state, feeling, &c. :—Ic eów geselle ðá ðurhwuniendan sibbe, Past. 351, 13. Sib gesealla him *pacem dare eis*, Jn. p. 7, 8. Gesealla hlíf middangearde *dare uitam mundo*, p. 4, 18. (3) *to endow with* a quality, faculty, &c. :—Him freá gesealde wǽpna geweald, Exod. 20. Him wæs gǽst geseald, Dan. 533. Ic on þé oncnáwe wísdómes gewit geseald, An. 646. [*Goth.* ga-saljan *to offer, sacrifice ; O. Sax.* gi-selliau *to hand over, deliver.*]

**ge-seltan.** v. ge-siltan : **ge-sēm.** See next word.

**ge-sēman.** Substitute : I. the object a person. (1) *to reconcile* adversaries :—Læt inc gesēman ǽr ðú ðín lác bringe *vade prius recon-*

*ciliari fratri tuo*, Past. 349, 12. Hié bǽdan Philippus þæt hé heora ládteów wǽre wið Focenses, and . . . þæt hé . . . oþþe hié gesémde, oþþe him gefultumade þ hí hié oferwinnan mehten (*vel differri bellum, vel auferri*) . . . Hé him gehét þ hé hié geséman wolde (*pacem promisit*), Ors. 3, 7 ; S. 114, 21–28. Wearð þ mǽste gewinn . . . hié mid nánum þinge ne mehton gesémede weorþan, 2, 2 ; S. 64, 34. Hí gesémede beón ne mihtan . . . Hí mid mycelon unsehte tócyrdon, Chr. 1094 ; P. 229, 7–12. (2) *to end dispute between* persons by giving judgement upon their claims, *to arbitrate between* :—Wǽron twégen cyningas ymb þ ríce winnende . . . þá sendan hié tó Philippuse and bǽdon þæt hé hié ymb þæt ríce gesémde *cum Philippum duo reges de regni terminis ambigentes judicem praeoptavissent*, Ors. 3, 7 ; S. 114, 18. Ic inc gesēman ne mæg *I cannot judge between you*, Bl. H. 181, 8. Ús sceal ord and ecg geséman, By. 60. Wé beóð ætforan Gode gesémde *before God shall the case between us be decided*, Hml. Th. ii. 338, 1 : Bl. H. 183, 13. (2 a) of legal decision :—Se cyning bæd and hét þ hí scioldon Wynflǽde and Leófwine swá rihtlíce geséman swá him ǽfre rihtlícost þúhte (*the case between Wynflæd and Leofwine was to be settled with absolute justice*), Cht. Th. 288, 30. (3) *to settle the doubts of* :—Mé fyrwet bræc . . . ǽr þon mé geunne éce dryhten þæt mé gesēme snoterra mon, Sal. 251. II. the object a thing, *to settle* a dispute, *make up* a quarrel :—þéh heora gewinn þá gesémed wǽre, Ors. 1, 12 ; S. 52, 25. II a. of a legal settlement, *to give judgement in* a suit, *make award in as arbitrator* :—Gif man óðerne tihte . . . gesécæn hiom sǽmend . . . siþþan sió sace gesémed sió an seofan nihtum se man þám óðrum riht gedó . . . gif hé þonne þ nylle gelde þonne .c. búton aðe siþþan áne neaht ofer þ gesēm hié *if a man bring a charge against another . . . let them get them an arbitrator . . . within seven days of the award being made it must be carried out. If the party concerned refuse to do this he must pay a hundred as fine, without the option of an oath ; then one day after this payment the case may be settled*, Ll. Th. i. 30, 17–32, 3. [The passage is somewhat obscure. *Hié* might be acc. f. sing. or pl. ; in the translation just attempted it has been taken as the former, and as referring to *sacu* ; so that the meaning of the latter part of the regulation is taken to be that a party to a suit, who failed to carry out the arbitrator's award, would be liable to a payment of a hundred, and only when this payment had been made would he be able to get a legal settlement of the case.]

**gesen,** i(e)sen, i(e)send, isern, eosen *entrails ; exta* :—Gesen *exta*, i. *intestina*, Wrt. Voc. ii. 145, 28. Iesen *exta*, 107, 68. Isen, 30, 1. Iesendne, isend, 91, 38. Iesende *extis*, 96, 45. Iesende oððe innelfe, 31, 67. Gebégdum isernum *tortuosis intestinis*, Lch. i. lxxii, 8. Eosenum, lxxiv, 31. [Cf. (?) *ising* a sausage, Halliw. Dict.]

**ge-sendan.** Add : I. the object a living creature. (1) *to cause to go* on an errand, for a purpose, to a place, *dispatch* :—Ðú mec gesendes, Jn. L. 17, 8. Ne gesende God sunu his in middangeard þte gedoemde middangeard, 3, 17. Bisin fadores in wīngeard suna ðæs gesendnes (*mittentis*), Mt. p. 19, 1. Wǽren ǽrendracen gesend of Róme tó Ængla lande, Chr. 785 ; P. 55, 3. Wéron gesendene hergas his *missis exercitibus suis*, Mt. L. 22, 7. In cummenum foreonfoeng, in missis embichta *in venientibus praesumtio, in missis obsequium*, p. 8, 2. (2) with a sense of compulsion or violence, *to send* to prison, into exile, &c. :—Mæht gesenda ł tó gesendanne in tintergo, Lk. L. 12, 5. Hé gesendad wæs in carcerne, 23, 25. Gesendet, Jn. L. 3, 24. II. where the object is not a living creature, *to cause to be conveyed* :—Rehtlic wǽre ðec gesende strión mín mynetrum, Mt. L. 25, 27. III. *to communicate motion to* an object, *move* to a place of rest, *put, lay.* (1) the object material :—Helpend ne hafo ic þte gesende (dō, W.S.) mec in þ fiscpól, Jn. L. 5, 7. Gif ðes monn hond his in ðisum wætre gisende, Rtl. 102, 7 : 100, 39. (2) the object non-material :—Mið diúl gesende in heorta þte salde hine, Jn. L. R. 13, 2. IV. with a stronger sense of motion, *to cast, throw* :—Hí gesendon nett in sǽ, Mt. L. 4, 18. Ðá yfio hí út gesendon (áwurpon, W.S.), 13, 48. Ðá ðe gesendon ðingo hiora . . . *qui mittebant munera sua in gazophilacium*, Lk. L. R. 22, 1. On sǽ gesended (beworpen, W.S.), Mk. L. R. 9, 42. V. *to send forth, emit* sound, *utter* a word :—Ðás ásægdniso tó eáre rúmmódnise ic gisendo (*emitio*), Rtl. 125, 7. Mið ðý gesende stefne micla *emissa uoce magna*, Mk. L. 15, 37. Gesended ne þ áne word *emissum non solum uerbum*, Mk. p. 1, 10. VI. the object not expressed, *to send* a *messenger* or a *message* :—Gié gesendon tó Ióhanne and cýðnise getrymede, Jn. L. 5, 33. Hí gesendon in alle lond ðǽm, Mt. L. 14, 35. [*Goth.* ga-sandjan : *O. H. Ger.* ge-senten.]

**ge-sēne.** v. ge-síne : **ge-seócled.** v. ge-síclian.

**ge-seón.** [For first two lines substitute: ge-seón, -sión, ic -seó, -sió, -sié, þú -sihst, -siehst, -syhst, -syxt, hé -sihþ, -siehð, -seohþ, -syhþ, -seóþ, pl. -seóþ, -sióþ ; p. ic, hé -seah, -seh, þú -sáwe, -sége, pl. -sáwon, -sēgon, -seágon, -sǽgon ; imp. -seoh, -seah, pl. -seóþ ; subj. prs. ic -seó, -sió, -sié ; p. -sáwe, -sége ; pp. -sewen, -seowen, -segen, -seogen, -sawen (-sáw-?). *Northern and Mercian forms :* ge-seá, -seán, -sión, ic -seóm, -sióm, -siúm, þú -siist, -síst, -seás, hé -siið, -siis, -síþ, -sís ; pl. -seáþ, -siáþ, -seás ; p. ic, hé -sæh, -sægh, -seh, þú -sége, pl. -sēgon, -ságon ; imp. -sæh, -sægh, -seh, -sech, -sih, pl. -seaeþ, -siáþ ; subj. prs. -sē, -see, -sié, -sii,

*pl.* sēn; *p.* -sēge; *part. prs.* -siónde, -siénde, -sēende, -segende; *pp.* -segen, -segn, -séen *To see.*] *Add:*—Þū gesēge *crevisti*, geseah *crevit*, Wrt. Voc. ii. 20, 54, 55. **I.** *to have the faculty of vision, to exercise that faculty.* (1) literal:—Ne gesyhþ sē nǣfre *he will remain blind for ever*, Bl. H. 153, 22. Hē sóna geseh *he at once recovered his sight*, 15, 27. Lāreów, þ ic geseó (gesii, L., gisié, R.) *Lord, that I might receive my sight* (A.V.), Mk. 10, 51. Hī his eágan āstungon . . . eft Gode fultomiendum hē meahte geseón, Chr. 797; P. 56, 12. Beóð onforan eágan, ne magon geseón, Ps. Th. 113, 13. Mihte hē mid þan ōþron eágan geseón, Guth. 98, 4. (2) figurative:— Ðū gesiist (-sihst, R.) geworpe ðone mot, Mt. L. 7, 5. Fader ðīn gesiið (-syhð, W.S., -sīð, R.) in dēgelnisse, 6, 4. Ne sciolon geseá (ne geseóþ, W.S., R.), 13, 13. **II.** *trans. To see* a material object. (1) *with acc.*:—Ic gesié heofonas *videbo caelos*, Ps. Srt. 8, 4. Gif þū gesyxt (-sihst, *v.l.*) wulfes spor ǣr þonne hyne, Lch. i. 360, 19. Ðū gesīst, Mt. p. 12, 4. Þ folc wundrað þæs þe hit seldost gesiehð, Bt. 39, 3; S. 126, 22. Geseohð, 41, 1; S. 141, 18. Ic þē mīnum eágum geseah, Gen. 820. Mon gewundodne monn ne geseah, Bt. 15; F. 48, 16. Hig gesāwon (-sēgon, -seágon, *v.ll.*) ǣnne weg, Mart. H. 44, 18. Gesǣgon, El. 68. (1 a) where the subject is inanimate:—Þē gesāwon ýþa, Ps. Th. 76, 13. (1 b) where seeing implies life:—Hī sunnan ne geseóð syððan ǣfre, Ps. Th. 57, 7. (1 c) irregular constructions:—Hē geseah swā swā scīnende sunne *he saw what looked like sunshine, it seemed to him as if the sun were shining*, Hml. S. 23 b, 741. Þǣr gelāðe mid him leng ne mihton geseón tōsomne (*they could not keep in sight of one another?*); sīð wæs gedǣled, Exod. 207. ¶ the past participle is used to form the passive, but also as an adj. governing dat. of person. (a) as passive or uncertain:—Wunderleca nǣdran wǣron gesewene (-seogene, *v.l.*) on Sūþ-Seaxna londe, Chr. 773; P. 50, 22. (b) as adj., *visible to*:—Þonne biþ ūs gesawen (-sewen, *v.l.*) þæt ūs ǣr gesǣd wæs, Wlfst. 3, 17. Ing wæs ǣrest mid Eást-Denum gesewen secgum, Rūn. 22. (2) *with acc. and infin.*:—Þū gesihst weallas blīcan, Sal. 234. Hē freán gesihð faran, Cri. 925. Mon geseah hine hreófe clǣnsian, Bl. H. 177, 15. Þǣr hē þæt wīf geseah stondan, Gen. 547: Hō. 50. Geseah hē rinca manige swefan, B. 728. Swā ic ǣfre ne geseah ǣnigne mann þē gelīcne steóran, An. 493. Hē hine geseah on singalum gebedum beón ābysgadne, Bd. 1, 7; Sch. 20, 2. (3) with acc. and complementary adj. (ptcpl.) in nom. or acc.:—Ic þē geseah murciende, Bt. 5, 1; F. 8, 28. Gē geseóð grōwende eorþan wæstmas, Bl. H. 59, 2. Hī geseóð egefulne þone ðe hī eádmōdne forhygedon, Hml. Th. i. 300, 19. Hyne nān man yrre (yrne?) geseah ne ungeornfulne tó Crīstes þeówdōme, Guth. 92, 23: Gū. 1026. Mon geseah hine blinde onlýhtende, Bl. H. 177, 15. Hē geseah Sīmón fleógendne, 189, 1. Wē gesēgon windas and wǣgas forhte gewordne, An. 455. Dō þū ðā lǣcedōmas swilce þū þā līchoman gesié, Lch. ii. 84, 15. Þæt hē geseó his wīf and his bearn sweltende, Bt. 10; F. 28, 39. Þ hī gesāwon mannes blōd āgoten, Ors. 1, 2; S. 30, 9. Hī gefēgon þæs þe hī hyne gesundne geseón mōston, B. 1628: 1998. Wǣron geseowene (-sawenæ, *v.l.*) fýrene dracan on þām lyfte fleógende, Chr. 793; P. 55, 34. (3 a) with complementary phrase:—Hē geseah þone hālgan wer swā unrōtes mōdes, Guth. 80, 14. (4) with infin. and its object:—Ic lāfe geseah mīnum hlāforde beran, Rä. 57, 10. Heó geseh niman hyre cild, Hml. Th. i. 146, 10. (5) the object a clause:—Ic mæg heonon geseón hwǣr hē sylf siteð, Gen. 666. **III.** the object an event, action, a condition, &c., where visible effects are produced in a material body, *to see, be witness of.* (1) *with acc.* (noun, or pronoun referring to a noun or to a clause):—Þæt synfull gesyhð, Ps. Th. 111, 9. Þte gesiis (gisæh, R., geseah, W.S.), þ getrymed *quod vidit, hoc testatur*, Jn. L. 3, 32. Þāra rícra manna unþeáws manige men geseóþ, Bt. 27, 1; F. 94, 27. Hī ofsleáþ þā āwergdan . . . þonne geseóþ ealle gesceafta ūres Drihtnes mihte, þeáh hié nū mennisce men oncnāwan nellan, Bl. H. 95, 9. Ic gesæh unrehtwīsnisse in cestre, Ps. Srt. 54, 10. Þū gesēge fyrenfulra wīte, Ps. Th. 90, 8. Þæt folc þis wundor geseah, Bl. H. 15, 29. Sīmón wearþ fǣringa geong cniht, and sóna eft eald man . . . þā Nerón þ geseah, Bl. H. 175, 6. Hī mīn sylfes weorc gesāwon mid eágum, Ps. Th. 94, 9. Geseágon, Cri. 1154. Hī þ oncnāwan ne mihton þ hié þǣr geseágon, Bl. H. 105, 29. Gesāwun (gesēgon ⁊ gesēende, L., gesǣgon, R.), Mt. 26, 8. Þā hig gesāwon (geseénde, L., gesēgun, R.) þā eorþbifunge, 27, 54. Geseón morðorbealo māga, B. 1078. Sibbe synfulra gesíende, Ps. Srt. 72, 3. Him þæt wundra mǣst gesewen þūhte *it seemed to him the greatest wonder seen*, Gū. 1101. (2) *with a clause*:—Sē ðe mon gesihð ðæt stronglic weorc wyrcð, Bt. 16, 3; F. 54, 28. Geseó wē þæt oft gelimpþ þ . . ., Bl. H. 125, 9. Hié geseóð hū God þā stōwe weorþaþ, 129, 25. Fyrd geseah hū hlifedon seglas, Exod. 88. Hē geseah þæt gē . . . wīte legdon, Gū. 684. Wē gesāwon þæt . . ., Dan. 474. Eágan mīne gesāwon hū ýða gelaac . . . ganged, Ps. Th. 118, 136. **IV.** where a fact (stated in a clause) is realized by means of the eyes, *to know from ocular evidence*:—Ic geseó þ þās brōþor synd geswencede, Bl. H. 233, 25. Ic on his gearwan geseó þæt hē is ǣrendsecg, Gen. 657. Ðū gesyhst þæt ic swā dyde, Ps. Th. 58, 4. Gerēfa mīn . . . geseóð þæt mē of brýde bearn ne wōcon, Gen. 2184. Wē gesióð þætte

heofonsteorran ealle efenbeorhte ne scīnað, Met. 20, 231. Hē geseah þ hié nǣnige bōte dōn noldan, Bl. H. 79, 7. Eówer fela geseah þæt wē þrý sendon, Dan. 412. Sóna gesāwon ceorlas þæt wæs brim blóde fāh, B. 1591. Dryhten forðlōcað ofer bearn monna þæt hē gesié hwæðer sié ongietende oððe soecende God, Ps. Vos. 13, 2. Ne magon gē gesión þ hē spyraþ æfter fuglum?, Bl. H. 210, 28. Geseón, Gen. 611. Hē mæg geseón, þonne hē on þæt sinc starað, þæt ic gódne funde beága bryttan, B. 1485. Magon wē geseón and oncnāwan and swīþe gearelīce ongeotan þ þisses middangeardes ende swīþe neáh is, Bl. H. 107, 22. Hē wæs geseónde þæt seó bǣr wæs gesigefæsted, 151, 8. **V.** *to turn the eyes* or *mind to* an object, *look at, observe, notice, regard.* (1) physical (or figurative):—Tō hwī gesihst þū (gesiistū, L., gesihstū, R.) þ mot on þīnes brōðor eágan, and þū ne gesyhst (geseǣs, R.) þone beám on þīnum āgenum eágan?, Mt. 7, 3. Ǣghwilc þāra þe gesiþh (gesīs, L.) wīf tó gītsanne, Mt. R. 5, 28. Rǣre ūp þīn heáfod and geseoh þis þ Sīmón dēþ, Bl. H. 187, 35: 241, 32. Ácer ēgan mīn ðæt hié ne geseón īdelnisse, Ps. Srt. 118, 37. Hē biþ þām yflum egeslic tó geseónne *he will be awful for the evil to look at*, Cri. 920. (2) mental :—Dryhten gesyhð þā eádmēdu *Dominus humilia respicit*, Ps. Th. 112, 5. Mīn eádmēdu geseah *vide humilitatem meam*, 118, 153. Smeá and geseoh (gesægh, L., gesih, R.) *scrutare et vide*, Jn. 7, 52. Geseoh, An. 1283. Gesæh (lóca, W.S.) in hū miclum ðeh āhēnas, Mk. L. R. 15, 4. Geseóð hū cyme weorc Drihten worhte, Ps. Th. 65, 4. Gesegende (-sēende, R., lōciende, W.S.) ne sciolon geseá, Mt. L. 13, 13. Wæs hē mid þǣre godcundan gife gesewen (-sawen, *v.l.*) and gemildsod *diuina gratia respectus*, Bd. 1, 7; Sch. 20, 5. **VI.** *to see* a person or place. (1) *to visit, have personal communication with* a person:—Eft ic eów geseó (gesiúm ⁊ gesié, L., gesióm, R.), Jn. 16, 22. Hī God geseóð (geseás, L.), Mt. 5, 8: Bl. H. 13, 27. Ic wāt hē mē bebeád, þā ic hine nēhst geseah, Gen. 536. Hē mæg geseón sweglcyning, 2658: Ph. 675. Nū gē mōton gangan Hrōðgār geseón, B. 396. (2) *to visit, go to* a place:—Þæt ic līf æfter ōðrum geseó and gesēce *that I go to another world after this one*; Hy. 4, 31. Gewiton him þā wīgend wīca neósian, Frysland geseón, B. 1126. **VII.** *to see* with the mind's eye:—Gif hwelc mon mæge gesión ðā birhtu þæs heofonlican leóhtes mid hlūttrum eágum his Mōdes *hanc quisquis poterit notare lucem*, Bt. 34, 8; F. 146, 2. (1) *to see, observe, notice,* (a) *with acc.*:—On him Dryhten gesihð firenbealu, Cri. 1275. Sum spearca sōþfæstnesse ðāra þe ðe wit ǣr ne gesāwon, Bt. 35, 5; F. 164, 3. Geseón on him selfum synne genóge, Cri. 1265: 1314. Wēnaþ þā dysigan þ ǣlc mon sié blind swā hī sint, and þ nān mon ne mæge seón (gesión, *v. l.*) þ hī gesión ne magon, Bt. 38, 5; F. 206, 21. Þæs ðe mē gepūht is and ic gesewen hæbbe *ut ego mihi videor perspexisse*, Bd. 1, 25; Sch. 55, 5. (b) *with acc. and infin.*:—Gesihð hē þā dōmas wonian, Gū. 27. (2) *to see, learn by examination* or *inquiry, find out*:—Geseoh gif ic on swiculne weg eóde, Ps. Th. 138, 21. Þæt ic gesē willan Dryhtnes, Ps. Srt. 26, 4. Hē heora þearfe forgeaf, oð þæt hwā gesǣwe hwæt hē him dōn wolde, Bd. 1, 25; Sch. 53, 3. (2 a) *to read in a narrative*:—Þā geseah ic þā gedriht in gedwolan lifgan, Dan. 22. (3) *to come to know, have certain knowledge of*:—Hēr wearð Eádwine cining ofslagan . . . and hī fordydan eall Norðhymbra land. Þā þ Paulinus geseah, Chr. 633; P. 25, 33–37. Þās þing geseónde, 1087; P. 223, 15. (4) *to know by clear evidence* a fact (stated in a clause):—Ic geseóm (gisióm, R., mē þyncð, W.S.) þte ðū arð uītga, Jn. 4, 19. Ic geseó þ ðē is nū frófre māre ðearf þonne unrōtnesse, Bt. 3; F. 6, 15. Hē geseah (-sægh, L.) þ hē wæs āwǣged, Mt. R. 2, 16: Gen. 1270. Geseóð þæt ic āna eom, Deut. 32, 39. Gesiáð, Ps. Srt. ii. p. 196, 7. Wē woldun þū gesāwe þæt . . ., Gū. 439. Geseón hwæðer him mon sōð þe lyge sagað, Cri. 1307. ¶ in the passive, *to seem*; *videri*:—Þæs þe mē gepūht and gesewen is, Bd. 1, 25; Sch. 55, 4. Þæt hē þām cūðum and þām uncūþum wæs gelīce gesegen *ita ut extra humanam naturam notis ignotisque esse videretur*, Guth. Gr. 170, 177: 163, 40. Huæt ðē gesegen is (þincþ, W.S., ðynceð, R.) *quid tibi videtur?*, Mt. L. 17, 25. Þ gesēen bið hæfis *quod videtur habere*, 25, 29. Þā þe hiora andlyfene needþearflico gesawen wǣron (videbantur), Bd. 1, 26; Sch. 57, 4. **VIII.** *to experience, meet with, feel*:—'Ic sende tó þē Andreas, and hē þē ūt ālǣt.' Swā mē Drihten tó cwæþ, ic gesié (*I experience just what the Lord said I should*), Bl. H. 237, 36. For hwon wāst þū weán, gesyhst sorge?, Gen. 877. Geseóð sorga mǣste synfan men sārigferðe, Cri. 1082. Blǣdes and blisse þe hý geseóð, 1257. Wǣre hié fundon, wuldor gesāwon, hālige heáhtreówe, Exod. 387. Hī bōte gesāwon, 582. Ðū gesee ðā gōd sind, Ps. Srt. 127, 5. Geseán gebrosnunge *videre corruptionem*, 15, 10. Gesián dægas gōde, 33, 10. Swegldreámas geseón, Cri. 1349. **IX.** *intrans. To look on*:—Þā mē on fægere geseóð *videbunt me*, Ps. Th. 118, 74. Þǣr hī on gesāwon ealle *in conspectu omnium*, 105, 35. Geseoh on mē *respice in me*, 68, 16. Hē wæs geseónde on norðanweardne þisne middangeard, Bl. H. 209, 30. **X.** *to take care* that something (or is or is not) done :—Gesih (warna, W.S.) ðū þ nǣnigum menn ðu coeðe, Mk. L. R. 1, 44. Lóca ⁊ geseh (gesech, R.), Mt. L. 8, 4. Geseáð (geseaeþ, R., warniaþ, W.S.) þte nān nyte *videte ne quis sciat*, 9, 30. Geseóð gē þ hē ǣrest

cymeð *procurate ut ipse prior adueniat*, Bd. 2, 2; Sch. 117, 10. **XI.** *to regard* as, *look upon* as :—Ne hí for āwyht eorþan cyste þā sēlestan geseón woldan *et pro nihilo habuerunt terram desiderabilem*, Ps. Th. 105, 20. [*Goth.* ga-saihwan : *O. Sax.* gi-sehan : *O. H. Ger.* ge-sehan.] v. un-geseónde, un-gesewen, -gesawen.

**ge-seóþan;** *p.* -seáþ; *pp.* -soden *To cook in a liquid, seethe, boil.* [*Take here* ge-soden *in Dict.*] :—Gedō on ceác fulne wīnes and geseóþ . . . þonne hió gesoden sié, Lch. ii. 30, 23. Gāð and geseóðað (*coquite*) ūra wyrhtena sufl, Gr. D. 201, 24. Genim þás ylcan wyrte, seóð on ele, and syððan þū hý gesoden hæbbe tōgædere gedōn, i. 142, 17. Gesoden wyrtmete *fordalium*, Wrt. Voc. ii. 38, 56 : 150, 2. Foxes lungen on hāttre æscan gesoden, Lch. i. 340, 5. Swīðe fæste gesoden ægra sþþe gebrædde, ii. 194, 5. Selle him flǣsc etan smælra fugla gesodenra and gebrǣdra, 182, 13. v. un-gesoden.

**ge-seówan, -síwan, -seowian** *to sew. Take here* ge-siwed *in Dict., and add :*—Geseówe mid seolce, Lch. ii. 358, 25. Gesióuuid, -siówid, -síuuid *sarcinatum*, Txts. 95, 1763. Gesiówed *consutum*, Wrt. Voc. ii. 104, 39. Gesiúwid *netum*, 114, 66. Gesīwid *consutum*, 23, 20. Gesíuuid, An. Ox. 53, 32. Gesēwed (? *printed* geseped) is *sarcidis* (=? *sarcitus*. Cf. *sarcitum, consutum*, Corp. Gl. H. 104, 32), Wrt. Voc. i. 288, 51. Gesíuwide *adsutae*, Wrt. Voc. ii. 99, 19. Gesīwede, 3, 67. Geseówede, An. Ox. 5334. Geseowade *consuta*, 56, 31.

**ge-seped.** *See preceding word :* ge-serwan. v. ge-sirwan : **ge-set,** *es* ; *n. See* ge-sǣte.

**ge-sete.** *l.* ge-set, *and add :* the word seems to occur only in the plural :—Hwǣr cwōm māððumgyfa? hwǣr cwōm symbla gesetu? hwǣr sindon seledreámas? *what has become of the giver of treasure? What has become of the houses of feasting? Where are the joys of the banqueting-hall?*, Wand. 93. Hwylc sý Meotodes gesceaft sigefolca geseta, þǣr hē sylfa wunað, Gn. C. 66. Tō heallicum geseton *ad palatinas aulas*, An. Ox. 2997 : 7, 215. Yldran ūsse (*Adam and Eve*) sōhton sorgfulran gesetu, Ph. 417. Hæleða ēðel, leóða gesetu, An. 1261. v. fyrn-, sǣ-geset(u).

**ge-setednes, ge-setenes.** v. ge-setnes.

**ge-setenness, e;** *f. Sitting :*—Gesetenisse mīne *sessionem meam*, Ps. Srt. 138, 2. v. ge-sittan; *pp.* -seten.

**ge-sēðan.** *Add :*—Ic gesēþe *vel* āfæstnie *confirmo*, i. *astruo*, Wrt. Voc. ii. 133, 28. Gesēþ *conprobat*, 10. **I.** *to declare true, state as a fact, assert, affirm :*—Hē geworhte twā mycle leóhtfatu swā Genesis gesēð, Angl. viii. 299, 14. Gesēðað *contendunt*, i. *dicunt* (eundem in sarcofago vitaliter quiescere *contendunt*, Ald. 25, 26), An. Ox. 7, 100. Wē magon þ tō sōðe gesēðan, þ hyt swā wæs, for ðon wē habbað trume gewitnysse, Angl. viii. 307, 3. Ús gedafenað þæt wē hit wēnon swīðor þonne wē unrǣdlíce hit gesēðan, Hml. Th. i. 440, 31. Ealdorlícnesse is gesēþed *auctoritate asstipulatur* i *adfirmatur*, An. Ox. 217. **II.** *to shew by evidence the truth* of a statement, *to prove :*—Mid āfundennyssum wē gesēþaþ *experimentis* i. *argumentis astipulabimur*, An. Ox. 3897. Hē gesēðde þæt heora (*the Jews*) fordfæderas Godes frýnd gecīgede wǣron, Hml. Th. i. 558, 20. Gif þū gesēþan miht þ ǣnig deáþlic man swelces hwæt āgnes ǣhte *si cujusquam mortalium proprium quid horum esse monstraveris*, Bt. 7, 3; F. 20, 7. Dū hit hæfst gesēþed mid gesceádwīslicre race *cuncta firmissimis nexa rationibus constant*, 34, 9; F. 146, 7. **II a.** where a forecast is proved correct by the event :—þæs gehātes and þæs wītedómes sōð se afterfylgenda becyme þāra wīsena gesēðde and getrymede (*astruxit*), Bd. 4, 29; Sch. 530, 13. Wyrd wæs geworden, swefn gesēðed, Dan. 654. **III.** *to attest, bear witness to* what one has seen or knows :—Þysse wyrte onfundelnysse manega ealdras gesēðað, Lch. i. 140, 10. Gesēþendum (*ipso*) *adtestante*, An. Ox. 1326. v. ge-sōþian.

**ge-sēþend, es;** *m. One who asserts* or *affirms :*—Gesēþend *conuntiator*, i. *adsertor*, Wrt. Voc. ii. 136, 43 : *firmator*, i. *adsertor*, 148, 65.

**ge-sēþness, e;** *f. Assertion, affirmation :*—þæt hē geseah hē gesōðode þurh his gesēðnysse, þeáh þe hý sume noldon his lāre underfōn ne his gesēðnysse, Nap. 32.

**ge-sēþung.** *Add :*—Gesēþungum *assertionibus*, i. *adfirmationibus*, An. Ox. 2067.

**ge-setl.** *Add : a seated assembly :*—Ætforan gesetle (-sytle, Hpt. Gl. 447, 65) *ante consessum*, An. Ox. 1753.

**ge-setla, an;** *m. One who sits with another :*—Gesetlan *sessorem*, An. Ox. 56, 20. Ðās ðīne gesǣtlan (*these that sit with thee*) synd mīne gebrōðra, Hml. S. 2, 237. Gif gegilda myd þǣm ete . . . þe his gegildan stlōg . . . gilde ān pund, būtun hē ætsacan mæge mid his twām gesetlun þ hē hine nyste, Cht. Th. 612, 16 : 23. [*O. H. Ger.* ge-sedalo *accubitor.*]

**ge-setnes.** *Take here* ge-setednes *in Dict., and add :* [ge-setednes, ge-set[t]nes *and* ge-setenes *might be taken separately, the former being connected with the past part., the latter with the infin., of* ge-settan; *cf.* ge-sealdnes, ge-selenes, ge-sellan.] **I.** *position* in reference to two or more objects :—Ic hæbbe ān weorc mē tō gewissunge æfter steorrena

gesetnyssum swā swā hī standað on heofonum, Hml. S. 5, 262. Hī cwædon þæt ælc man beó ācenned be steorrena gesetnessum, and þurh heora ymbryna him wyrd gelimpe, Hml. Th. i. 110, 7. **II.** *combination, composition.* (1) *putting together of material, construction :*—Ǣr middaneardes gesetnysse (*constitutione*), Hml. A. 70, 126. (1 a) *a medical preparation* (?) ; compositio :—Genim þás ylcan wyrte gecnucude, lege tō þām sāre . . . eác ūre ealdras cwǣdon þ ðeós gesetednys heálicost is, Lch. i. 176, 10. (2) *putting together of words.* (a) *a compound :*—þā synd on Grēcisc *kakosyntheton, vitiosa compositio*, gecwedene, and synt lyðre gesetnyssa, swylce ic þus cwede *bonumaurum*, þonne ic hyt sceolde þus tōdǣlan *bonum aurum*, Angl. viii. 313, 26. (b) *composition :*—Barbarismum hig on heora gesetnyssa forbūgað, Angl. viii. 313, 18. (c) *a composition, writing, work, narrative, treatise :*—Hēr is seó gesetenis Alexandres epistoles, Nar. 1, 1. Gesetnys, racu *textus* (*libelli Eugeniae*), An. Ox. 4242. Gesettnesse *textu*, 3448. Ne secge wē nān þincg nīwes on þissere gesetnysse (cf. on þyssere bēc þǣra hālgena þrowunga, 36), Hml. S. p. 4, 46. On þǣre gesetnysse be worulde frymðe, Angl. viii. 307, 5. Be þǣre gesetnysse of ðām gedwylde, Hml. A. 24, 5. Wē geendiað þus ðās gesetnysse (*homily*), Hml. S. 15, 226 : Hml. A. 44, 511. Þā wīsan lāreówas āwriton þe þǣre clǣnnysse mycele bēc on manegum gesetnyssum, 22, 197 : 198. ¶ of the scriptures. (1) *the Old Testament :*—Seó bōc (*Ezra*) ys geendebyrd on þissere gesetnysse, Ælfc. T. Grn. 10, 41 : 11, 3. (2) *the New Testament :*—Hē (*Matthew*) ys se forma godspellere on þǣre gesetnyse, Ælfc. T. Grn. 12, 32 : 14, 15. (3) *of the several books of the bible :*—Isaias on his gesetnysse, Hml. A. 21, 188 : Ælfc. T. Grn. 9, 8. Daniel on his gesetnisse, 45. Heó on ðæra wītegena gesetnysse rædde, Hml. Th. i. 42, 20. Of Mathees gesetnysse ge of Lucas, ii. 468, 13. Hē (*St. John*) āwrāt on wundorlicre gesetnysse, Hml. S. 15, 163. Ongann hē þā godspellican gesetnysse, ðus cweðende, Hml. Th. i. 358, 14: 300, 21. Heora (*the Sibyls'*) bēc ne synd nā on ūre gesetnissum on þǣre biblioþecan, Ælfc. T. Grn. 10, 35. Feówer godspelleras āwriton his ðrowunga on feower gesetnyssum, Hml. Th. i. 216, 19. **III.** *size, extent :*—Gesetnes *statura*, An. Ox. 5311. Hē (*Ezechiel*) āwrāt āne bōc, micele on gesetnisse, swīðe deóp on andgite, Ælfc. T. Grn. 9, 39. Twelf wītegan (*the minor prophets*) . . . twelf bēc āwriton be sumum dǣle lǣssan on gesetnysse, micele on andgitte, 10, 9. **IV.** *arrangement, scheme, figure* of speech :—Gesetnisse *dispositionis*, Lk. p. 2, 8. Æfter þissum hig gehleapað on metaplasmum, þ ys þ hig gewurdiað heora spǣce, and heora meterversa gesetnyssa and cyrtenlice scemata (*vel figure*) *lexeos* and *dianoeas* āscrutniað, *lexeos* beóð ðæra worda gesetnyssa and *dianoeas* byð þ andgit, Angl. viii. 313, 28–31. **V.** *an established practice, course, institution, institute :*—In reogolum cyriclicre gesetnesse se behýdegæsta *in ecclesiastica institutionis regulis sollertissimus*, Bd. 5, 20; Sch. 675, 17. Cēpan his mǣles and mid gesceáde his gesetnysse healdan, Hml. S. 16, 319. Þāra þeóda sint swīþe ungelíca and heora gesetnessa swīþe mislica *diversarum gentium mores inter se atque instituta discordant*, Bt. 18, 2; F. 64, 22. Gesettnessa, An. Ox. 247. Monig nytlieo ðing cyriclicra gesetnessa *multa ecclesiae institutis utilia*, Bd. 5, 20; Sch. 676, 1. Man ārǣrde cyrcan . . . and mynsterlice gesetnyssa, Hml. S. 26, 86. **VI.** *an ordinance, a law, decree, statute :*—Decretum, i. *institutum, positum, consilium, placitum* geþōht *statutum laga, diffinitum* gesetnes *judicium*, Wrt. Voc. ii. 137, 80. (1) *an ordinance* of the civil or the ecclesiastical authority, *a law human or divine :*—Folcrǣdenne *sive* ealles folces gesetnes *lex*, Wrt. Voc. ii. 53, 80. Medríc(r)a gesetnysse *plebiscita*, riccra gesetnes *senatus consultum*, kyninga gesetnysse *constitutio*, i. 20, 65–67. Seó ealde gesetness *the Mosaic law*, Jud. 15; Thw. p. 159, 29. Godcundre gesettnesse *divinae sanctionis* (*praecepta*), An. Ox. 1629. For þǣre gesetnysse þe nān mann ne mōste tō þām hāde becuman būton of Aarones cynne, Hml. A. 16, 77. Æfter Godes gesetnysse, 19, 139: 20, 151. Ðā beóð scyldige ðe ðā gesetnysse (*the injunction as to fasting*) tōbrecaþ þǣre hālgan gelaðunge, Hml. Th. ii. 330, 35. Hwæne þū forsāwe and hwæs (*God's*) gesetnysse (*of the Mosaic law*), Ælfc. T. Grn. 20, 15. þ ealle gebugon tō his hǣdenscipe and tō his gesetnyssum, Hml. S. 25, 17: 11, 24. Tō Godes gesetnyssum, Hml. A. 6, 131. Gesetnessum *sanctionibus* (*decalogi*), An. Ox. 842. Āwritenum gesetnessum *scriptis decretalibus*, i. *statutis*, 1966. Gesettnessa *statuta* (*apostolica*), 5143. Gesetednessa, Hpt. Gl. 523, 27. Ealle þā gesetnessa þe tō hearde wǣron hē gedyde līþran, Ors. 5, 12; S. 244, 14. Rihtra dōma gesetenesse (-setnesse, *v. l.*) *decreta iudiciorum*, Bl. Gl. Swylce hē ne cunne Crīstes gesetnyssa. Mōyses ūs lǣrde on his gesetnissum, Ælfc. T. Grn. 20, 9: gesetnyssa. Hml. A. 8, 198. (2) *a settlement, an order with respect to property,* in pl. *a will :*—Heáhgerēfan gesetnysse *legatum testamentum*, Wrt. Voc. i. 20, 38. Ic ðās gesettnesse sette gehweder ge for hīgna lufon ge ðeára sáula ðe hær beforan hiora namon āuuritene siondon . . . þis is gesetnes Ōsulfes and Bearnðrýðe, Txts. 444, 42–45. (3) *an ordinance handed down to successive generations, a tradition :*—Hwylc gesetnes (-setnes, *v. l.*) tō fylgeanne sý *quae sequenda traditio*, Bd. 2, 2; Sch. 114, 10. Æfter gesetnisse ældra *juxta traditionem seniorum*, Mk. L. R. 7, 5. Æfter gesetnisse (*lage*, W.S.), Mt. R. 15, 2. Hī heora seolfra þeáwas and

gesetnesse (-setenesse, *v. l.*) betran dydon *suas traditiones praeferrent*, Bd. 2, 2; Sch. 113, 21 : 116, 13. (4) *a natural law, order of providence :*—Þá wildan deór be úres Drihtnes gesetnysse syndon mannum underþeódde, Hml. A. 64, 290. Hé hæfð heora mearce gesette ... Mid þám ilcan gerece is gereaht swíðe anlíc gewrixle þæs flódes and þæs ebban. Þá gesetennesse (gesetennes þa, MS.) hé lǽt standan þá hwíle þe hé wile, Bt. 21; S. 49, 26. (5) *an order, a regulation :*—Þá byrlas scencton be þæs cyninges gesetnysse (*sicut rex statuerat*), Hml. A. 93, 26. (6) *instruction, what instructs :*—Gesetnysse *instrumenti, quod instruit*, An. Ox. 1765 : 1675. Gesettnysse, 437. Hé férde tó gesetednysse and lǽre þæs gástlican lífes *ad institutionem spiritalis vitae pergeret*, Gr. D. 150, 22. (7) *a purpose :*—Gisetnise *proposito*, Rtl. 103, 30. Gisetnisse *propositum*, 104, 4. v. folc-, riht-gesetness.

ge-setnian. *l.* ge-sétnian, -sǽtnian.

ge-settan. Add : [*The participle of ge-sittan seems used in* Lk. p. 9, 6 :—Geseteno *posita*; *and in* Lk. L. 22, 41 :—Gesetnum *positis*.] I. *to set, put, place, lay :*—Ðá gesettan *inditas*, Wrt. Voc. ii. 111, 38; 48, 82. (1) *to move a material object to a position of rest :*—Geseton him þ ród *imposuerunt illi crucem*, Lk. L. 23, 26. Þ hond him gesette hé (*imponeret*), Mt. L. 19, 13. Þte hiá gesetta (*ponerent*) before hiá, Mk. L. R. 6, 41. Gisette (gesete, L.), Lk. R. 9, 16. Acas tó wyrtrumma geseted (*posita*), Mt. L. 3, 10. Þte ðæccilla under mitta geseted (giseted, R.) bið (*ponatur*), Mk. L. 4, 21. Hé gesæh ðá hrægla gesettedo, Lk. L. 24, 12. Gisetedo (gesattedo, L.), Jn. R. 20, 6. (1 a) *of burial :*—Sum bysceop on ðá cyrcan þone lýchaman gesette, Shrn. 152, 6. Þ hié woldon his bán on níwe cyste gedón and on þǽre ylcan stówe bufan eorðan gesettan and gestaþolian (*locarent*), Bd. 4, 30; Sch. 534, 6. Biheóldun hwér wére giseted (gesettet, L.), Mk. 15, 47. Gesetted, Jn. L. 19, 41. (1 b) *to lay up, store :*—Ðú hæfes monig góda gisetedo, Lk. R. 12, 19. (1 c) *with idea of violence :*—Hé gesette hine on fetera, Hml. S. 21, 415. (2) *to put in position, fix in place, plant* a tree :—God ealle tungla geset *dedit sidera coelo*, Bt. 30, 2; F. 110, 12. Þu sǽ gesettest *tu confirmasti mare*, Ps. Th. 73, 13 : Cri. 1165. Steorran hé geworhte, and gesette (*posuit*) on þǽre heofenan, Gen. 1, 17 : Hml. Th. i. 100, 9. Twégen beámas God handum gesette, Gen. 463. Tree hæfde sum man geseted, Lk. L. 13, 6. Wræðstuðu þám wáge tó wreþe geseted, Bd. 3, 17; Sch. 269, 23. (3) *of a building, town, &c., to set, situate, place, found :*—Hé gesette ðá grundas ofer carr ... þ hús gesettet (*fundata*) wæs onufa carr, Lk. L. 6, 48. Burug ofer mór geseted, Mt. L. 5, 14 : Bl. H. 197, 21. Is seó ciricc geseted on þǽm cnolle, 17. Þaet mynster is geseted in Huicca maegðe, C. D. i. 114, 14. (4) *to place, determine the position* (lit. or fig.) *in a series of objects :*—Gesette *praeposuit* (*omnibus virtutum gradibus in catalogo*), An. Ox. 344. In endebrednise forðmest geseted is *Mattheus in ordine primus ponitur*, Mt. p. 12, 8. (5) *fig. to put in a certain relation, subject to* a condition :—Ealle hé hí oððe wið feó gesealde, oððe on his ágenre hand heóld and tó gafle gesette, Chr. 1100; P. 235, 28. I a. *where the object is non-material :*—Sunes noma ðǽm feder eftginíwes í gesetes *filii nomen patri restituens*, Mt. p. 13, 4. Þú on ús sáwle gesettest, Met. 20, 177. Hé þá þing stafum áwrát and on béc gesette *ea litteris mandando*, Bd. 4, 18; Sch. 437, 13. Bíspell gesætte *parabolam exponit*, Mk. p. 3, 4. Hí gesettan (*added*) tó godcundan rihtlagan worldlaga, Ll. Th. i. 334, 22. Geseton alle ðáðe gehérdon in heorta hiora, Lk. L. i. 66. Gesetted *ponite*, 21, 14. Þisse worlde ende gesettan, Bl. H. 117, 28 : Gú. 995. His sáuel þ hé walde gesete *suam animam positurum*, Jn. p. 6, 3. Wæs on þǽm scennum þurh rúnstafas geseted (*placed on record*) hwám þæt sweord geworht wǽre, B. 1696. Hé tó heófenum lócade þyder his módgeþanc á geseted wæs, Bl. H. 227, 17. Þá gesælþa þe gé oninnon eów habbaþ geset, Bt. 11, 2; F. 34, 5. Hé hæfþ heora mearce swá gesette, 21; F. 74, 27. II. *to cause a person to take a position.* (1) *local,* (a) *to post, station :*—Þone foregengan hé wið ealdorgewinnum gesette, Gú. 506. Hé gesette twá folc diegellíce on twá healfa his, Ors. 4, 6; S. 174, 32. Þá foreweardas wǽron feor ðǽm fæstenne gesette, 4, 10; S. 200, 12. (b) *to place, settle* permanently :—Se bisceop þær gesette góde sangeras, Bl. H. 207, 31. On þǽm londe hé heora fela gesette (*habitare praecepit*), Ors. 3, 5; S. 104, 26. Hié hiene þǽr gesetton, 5, 2; S. 218, 28. (bb) figuratively :—Wé under gyfe gesette *nos sub gratia positi*, An. Ox. 40, 10. (2) *of official position, office, duty, to place in a position of authority :*—Ofer eall þ hé áh hé hyne gesett (-setteþ, R., *constituet*), Mt. 24, 47. Geset (settes, L., -setes, R.), Lk. 12, 42. Hié gesetton Hannonan ofer hiora scipa *Annonem navali prelio praefecerunt*, Ors. 4, 6; S. 172, 12. (2 a) gesettan tó, (a) *to make king, &c., appoint :*—Hé gesette his sunu tó cininge, Ælfc. T. Grn. 7, 28 : Chr. 1097; P. 235, 15. Hé hié tó gafolgieldum gesette *he made them tributaries*, Ors. 4, 6; S. 176, 22. Gesete him synfulle tó ealdrum *constitue super eum peccatorem*, Ps. Th. 108, 5. (β) *to appoint to* a title, *give the title of :*—Hé gesette Eugenium tó þǽm ríces noman þ hé casere wǽre *legit hominem cui titulum imperatoris inponeret*, Ors. 6, 36; S. 294, 12. (γ) *to set* to the doing of something. (γ 1) with noun implying action :—Þú gesettest þíne apostolas tó mínre byrgenne, Bl. H. 143, 29. Mec gesette Críst tó compe, Rä. 7, 1.

Hé gesette Theodosius him tó fultume, Ors. 6, 35; S. 292, 6. Hé gesette his sunu tó þám onwalde *filium suum caesarem legit*, 6, 22; S. 274, 5. Ilirice gesetton Ueteromonem tó hiora anwealde *Vetranionem imperatorem sibi creaverunt*, 6, 31; S. 284, 19. (γ 2) with gerund :—Hé gesette heáfodmenn tó gehealdenne þ folc, Hml. S. 25, 403. (γ 3) with pronoun and clause :—Hé wæs tó ðon geset þæt hé sceolde stúpian ... *officii sortitus, ut acclinis* ..., Ors. 6, 23; S. 274, 24. (2 b) with clause giving the office :—Hiene mon gesette þæt hé wæs hiérra þonne consul *dictator creatus*, Ors. 5, 12; S. 242, 28. Punice gesetton Hannibalem þæt hé mid scipum wunne *Hannibalem a Carthaginibus classi praepositus*, 4, 6; S. 172, 25. (2 c) with complementary noun :—Hé weard geset cumena ðén, Hml. Th. ii. 136, 23. (2 d) *to put* into, or out of an office, state, &c. :—Hí rǽddon swá þ hí woldon þone cyng gesettan út of Englelandes cynedóme *they decided to depose the king*, Chr. 1075; P. 210, 12. Hé gesette on sácerdhád Iudas, El. 1055. Wæs eft geseted in aldordóm Babilone weard *he was restored to power*, Dan. 641. (2 e) *to cause to assume an attitude of mind*, as in *to set* a person against :—Hé wæs on fóre geseted, Hml. S. 23 b, 156. Wæs se fruma fæstlic geseted wið synnum, Gú. 746. III. *to assign* something to a person, *allot, appoint.* (1) *of human agency :*—Gesettan *destinare* (*hoc opusculum vobis*), An. Ox. 5427. Ne dó gé náht máre þonne þ eów geset (-seted, R., -setted, L., *constitutum*) is, Lk. 3, 13. (2) *of the Deity :*—Ælcum ðú gesettest his ágene sunderstówe, Bt. 33, 4; F. 128, 30 : Hy. 7, 21. Hé gesette unáwendedlicne sido and þeáwas eallum his gesceaftum, 21; F. 72, 32 : Met. 11, 21 : Az. 115 : Gen. 1684. God þæt wíte tó wrece gesette, Sat. 494. Hé wile eallum wísfæstum gesceaftum ecn[e] dóm gesetton, Bl. H. 121, 20. Of ðám ryne þe him geset is, Bt. 21; F. 74, 5 : 21 : Met. 11, 56. Geseted, Sat. 678. Hú þæs gástes síð æfter swyltcwale geseted wurde, An. 156. IV. *to occupy.* (1) land for cultivation :—.xii. hída gesettes landes, Ll. Th. i. 144, 6 : 9. (1 a) *to occupy* with cultivators :—Hé gesett (-seteþ, R.) hys wíngeard myd óðrum tilion, Mt. 21, 41. Hú þis land wǽre gesett oððe mid hwylcon mannum, Chr. 1085; P. 216, 16. (1 b) *to plant :*—Nóe yrðling began tó wircenne þæt land and gesette (*plantavit*) wíneard, Gen. 9, 10: Mt. L. 21, 33. Gesetton *plantabant*, Lk. R. 17, 28. (2) *to occupy* with inhabitants :—Hí gesetton Sennar leófum mannum, Gen. 1655. Gesettan heofena ríce mid hlúttrum sáwlum, 396 : 364. Sceal fromcynne folde þíne geseted wurðan, 2205. Þæt eorðe and úproder and síd wæter geseted wurde woruldgesceafte, 100. (2 a) *to occupy* a conquered land or place :—Ðý ilcan geáre gesette Ælfréd cyning Lundenburg, Chr. 886; P. 80, 10. Se here ... geridan Westseaxna land and gesetton, 878; P. 75, 26. Gesettan on hyra sylfra dóm wuldres wynlond, Mód. 64. (2 aa) *to occupy* with people :—Hé ealle þá londbígengan wolde út ámæran, and his (mid his, *v. l.*) ágenra leóda mannum gesettan, Bd. 4, 16; Sch. 425, 5. (2 b) *to garrison :*—Bútan þám castelan ðe wǽron gesætte mid þæs cynges manna, Chr. 1100; P. 236, 33. (3) *to possess :*—Þu gesettyst *possedisti*, Ps. Spl. C. 138, 12. Þæt hí hálignesse Godes gestríon *haereditate possideamus nobis sanctuarium Dei*, Ps. Th. 82, 9. (4) *of material, to occupy* space :—Þæs dæges godspel is eal mǽst mid háligra manna naman geset, Hml. Th. ii. 466, 23. V. *to decree, ordain :*—Wé gesettað *sancimus*, An. Ox. 419. Gesettan *sancxerunt*, 1967 : 5138. (1) with a clause :—Hió gesette (*praecepit*) þæt nán forbyrd nǽre æt geligere betwuh nánre sibbe, Ors. 1, 2; S. 30, 34. Se cyng gesette (*instituit*) þ se Englisca lǽdige hine mid írene, Ll. Th. i. 489, 20. Hié gesetton þ ..., 58, 5. Rómane hæfdon níwlíce gesett þæt þá móston ǽgþer habban ge feorh ge freódóm, Ors. 4, 10; S. 202, 27. (1 a) with pronoun and clause in apposition :—Hié þ gesetton, þ hé ... swungen wǽre ..., Bl. H. 193, 3. (2) with noun :—Hié orr seonoðum monegra misdǽda bóte gesetton, Ll. Th. i. 58, 15 : 166, 13. Seó gerǽdnes þe hí gesetton, 352, 2. Ealle ðá ðing be Godes mynstran ðá wǽron gesett be Wihtgáres dæge, Chr. 796; P. 56, 29. Ðá se seonoð geset (-seted, *v. l.*) wæs *quod cum esset statutum*, Bd. 2, 2; Sch. 116, 3. ¶ of divine decrees :—Hé ús gesette þ wé hine biddan sceoldan, Bl. H. 21, 3. Dómas swá hié God gesette, 81, 5 : Gú. 29. Godcundlice þus gesettan geban *diuina taliter sancserunt edicta*, i. *decreta*, An. Ox. 1301. Riht gesettan *legem promulgare*, 1305. VI. *to settle, fix.* (1) *to fix* an amount :—Hí þæt feoh gesetton on ðrittig scillingum, Hml. Th. ii. 242, 18. Hí þ gyld gesettan wið þone here, Chr. 1016; P. 152, 27. (2) *to fix* a time, *fix the date of :*—Þá tíde þá þe Fæder gesette, Bl. H. 117, 24. Gesetton hálige fæderas þá tíd þæs fæstenes foran tó Crístes þrowunga, 27, 24. Gesetton cyricena aldoras þ fæsten foran tó his þrowunga, 35, 6. Tó gesetton dæge gelǽste hé þ hé ǽr sceolde, Ll. Th. i. 260, 14. Hé hiora (*Easter*) gesetton tíde nyste *canonicum eius tempus ignorans*, Bd. 3, 17; Sch. 272, 3. (3) *to settle* a plan, *determine* to do :—Þá gesetton hí fæstlíce fore unmǽtnesse þæs gewinnes þ hí forléte þá getimbro *statuerunt ob nimietatem laboris structuram relinquere*, Bd. 3, 8; Sch. 225, 20. VII. *to put together, compose, constitute :*—Gesette *condidit*, Wrt. Voc. ii. 104, 36. Gesettan *conderunt*, 16, 7. *Edite*, i. *renate, renouate, reparate, constitute vel gesettaþ*, Wülck. Gl. 226, 10. (1) *to form, construct, create, make.* (a) *of material things :*—Oft wíc beóþ on manegum stówum medmyccle gesette

*often villages are in many places made small*, Bl. H. 77, 24. (b) of non-material things :—Þæt hē (*Joseph*) his ealdormen ealle lǣrde, swā hē his sylfes mōd geseted hæfde *ut erudiret principes suos sicut seipsum*, Ps. Th. 104, 18. ¶ of the operations of the Deity :—On ðām feórðan dæge gesette se Ælmihtiga ealle tungla, Hml. Th. i. 100, 9. Ealle gesceafte hē gesette on siex dagum, Gū. 22. Hē ealle gesceafta gesette (cf. gelōgode, 286, 13) on ðrīm ðingum, ꝥ is on gemete and on getele and on hefe, Hml. Th. i. 102, 33 : Angl. viii. 299, 13. Ær middaneard gesett wæs *ante constitutionem mundi*, Jn. 17, 24. Gesett hæfde hē hié swā gesǣliglice, Gen. 252. (I a) to compound a draught :— Hē wæs lǣcecræftig ; hē gesette gōdne morgendrænc wið eallum untrumnessum, Lch. iii. 70, 17. (I b) *to form, make up the requisite number for, complete* :—Hī gesetton þā gifta endemes (*impletae sunt nuptiae discumbentium*, Mt. 22, 10), Hml. Th. i. 526, 13. (I c) *to create* an officer :—Gesetton Rōmāne II cāseras *duo Imperatores creati sunt*, Ors. 6, 23 ; S. 274, 17. (2) *to compose* a quarrel, *settle* a difference, suit, &c. :—Hē mid þý wífe wælfǣhða dǣl sæcca gesette, B. 2029. (3) *to make peace, war* :—Hē grið wið hī gesætte, Chr. 1002 ; P. 133, 35. Būtan þū ǣr wið hī geþingige, sibbe gesette, Jul. 200. Huælc cynig bið fǣrende tō gesettanne feht (*committere bellum*), Lk. L. 14, 31. (4) *to put in order, arrange, adorn* :—þū tída fram middaneardes fruman oþ ðone ende endebyrdlíce gesettest *tempus ab aevo ire jubes*, Bt. 33, 4 ; F. 128, 7. þā gesettan *ordinatissimam*, Wrt. Voc. ii. 115, 65 : 65, 29. Wǣrun heora dohtru deóre gesette (cf. geglengde, Ps. Srt.) *filiae eorum compositae*, Ps. Th. 143, 15. (5) *to compose, write* a book, narrative, poem, &c. :—Se saltere ys ān bōc þe hē (*David*) gesette, Ælfc. T. Grn. 7, 27 : 10, 45. Marcus leornode of Petres bodunge hū hē ðā bōc (*the gospel*) gesette . . . Lucas ðā godspel āwrāt . . . and *Actus Apostolorum* eác hē gesette, Hml. S. 15, 148, 155. Fela bēc hē gesette be ðām sōðan geleáfan, 29, 87. Hē cýdde . . . hū hē weard gehǣled . . . and Landferd hit gesette on Lǣden, 21, 402. Gesette *edidit* (*opusculum*), An. Ox. 11, 171 : 2316. þæt heó gesette *ut conponat* (*carmen*), 904. Ic gesett hæbbe of þisum feówer bōcum (*the gospels*) wel feówertig lārspella on Englisc, Ælfc. T. Grn. 13, 45. VIII. *intrans.* (I) of living creatures, *to place oneself, settle* :—Se hālega gǣst on tungena onlícnesse gesette ofer ðā apostolas *super pastores primos in linguarum specie Spiritus sanctus insedit*, Past. 93, 1. Heó (*the dove*) gesette swīðe wērig on treówes telgum, Gen. 1469. (2) of water, *to settle, subside* :— Se flōd gesette, Wlfst. 10, 15. [*Goth.* ga-satjan : *O. Sax.* gi-settian : *O. H. Ger.* ge-sezzen.] v. fore-gesettan ; riht-, ymb-gesett.

**ge-settendlic ;** *adj.* *Canonical* :—Mid sange gesettendlices rynes *cum decantatione canonici cursus*, Angl. xiii. 390, 362. Cf. ge-settan ; VI 2.

**ge-séuling.** *Dele* : ge-séunes. v. ge-sǣwness.

**ge-sewenlic.** *Add* :—Hī gesáwon þæt se heofonlica mete wæs gesewenlic, Hml. Th. ii. 274, 29. Cempa eordlic ongeán feónd gesewenlicne (*uisibilem*) fǣrd tō gefeohte, Scint. 61, 4. v. un-gesewenlic, gesāwenlic.

**ge-sewenlíce.** *Add* : *evidently* :—Hwæt hē geþwǣrige gesewenlíce hē nāt *quid consentiat* [*e*]*videnter ignorat*, Scint. 229, 5. v. un-geswenlíce, ge-sáwenlíce.

**ge-sib.** *Add* : I. as adjective :—Gesib *vel* cūþ *cognata*, i. *conjuncta, propinqua*, Wrt. Voc. ii. 133, 33. Of gesibbum *de consanguineo*, 138, 9. (I) applied to persons :—þeáh ðe se sanct wǣre gesib him for worulde, Hml. S. 21, 87. Þǣre gesibban *consanguine* [the Latin is *consanguinei* (*fratris*)], Wrt. Voc. ii. 90, 49 : 19, 26. Gesibbum *contribuli* (*populo*), An. Ox. 3989. Gesybbum, 2, 280. In ðǣm gesibban *in tribuli*, Wrt. Voc. ii. 84, 32 : 46, 77. Gesibbe *contribuli*, 14, 48. (The first three out of the last five glosses refer to Ald. 55, 35, so probably do the last two.) þā cwæd se cāsere ðæt hī wǣron gesibbe, and for ði heó sprǣce þillice word him fore, Hml. Th. ii. 310, 9. Freóndum swǣsum and gesibbum, Gen. 1612. Hāt hine selfne oþþe swā gesibne swā hē gesibbost hæbbe, Lch. i. 350, 18. ¶ where marriage is in question :—Oda arcebiscop tōtwǣmde Eádwī cyning and Ælgyfe, for þǣm þe hī wǣron tō gesybbe, Chr. 958 ; P. 113, 25. Be gebrōþrum, hū gesibbe wíf hig habban mōton *de fratribus, quam prope cognatas uxores habere possint*, Ll. Th. ii. 130, 8. (2) applied to a condition :—Þǣre gesibban *cognate* (*propinquitatis*), Wrt. Voc. ii. 80, 27. Gesibbre mǣgrǣdene *propinquæ necessitudinis*, An. Ox. 2810. II. as substantive :—Angeán gesybne his *aduersus proximum suum*, Ps. Rdr. 100, 5. Ne eart þū þon leófra mēder ne fæder, ne nǣnigum gesybban (nǣngum gesibbra, *v.l.*), þonne se swearta hrefn, Seel. 54. Hē bebeád ꝥ ǣlc mǣgþ ymbe geáres ryne tōgædere cōme þæt ǣlc man þý gearor wiste hwǣr hē gesibbe hæfde, Ors. 5, 14 ; S. 248, 17. v. un-gesibb.

**ge-sibbian.** *Add* : I. *to reconcile* those who are at variance :— Sibba þā cídenda[n] men and þū hié gesibbast *try to reconcile disputants and you will reconcile them*, Lch. iii. 176, 26. On ðisum wræcfullum lífe wē sceolon ðā ungeðwǣran gesibbian, Hml. Th. ii. 442, 15. II. *to ally, confederate* those who are not acting together :—Críst for ðī āstāh of heofenum tō ðisum middanearde þæt hē wolde mancynn gesibbian and geðwǣrlǣcan tō þām heofenlicum werode, swā swā Paulus cwæd : 'Se

---

is ūre sib, sē ðe dyde ǣgðer tō ānum ' (v. Eph. 2, 12–14), þæt is engla werod and mancynn tō ānum werode, Hml. Th. ii. 580, 2. Gesybbode *confederantur*, Germ. 397, 437. Tōscereð gesibbade *separat federatos*, Kent. Gl. 604.

**ge-sibling.** *Add* :—Gesiblingas *abnepotes*, Germ. 393, 179. Wǣron þā gesyblingas (*the descendants of Noah*) þus tōdǣlde, Angl. xi. 3, 64. Ǣt hwām nimað eordlíce cynegas gafol, æt heora gesiblingum oþþe æt ælfremedum (*a filiis suis an ab alienis*, Mt. 17, 25), Hml. Th. i. 510, 33. Gesiblingum *contribulium, amicorum*, An. Ox. 3, 3. Mǣglicum l̄ gesibli(n)gum *contribulibus*, i. *parentibus*, Hpt. Gl. 403, 18.

**ge-sibness.** *For Lye substitute* :—Gesibnesse *adfinitate*, Wrt. Voc. ii. 4, 53.

**ge-sibsum.** *Add* : I. *peaceable, pacific, not disposed to quarrel* :—Þ se man hæbbe ðā sōðan lufe on his mōde . . . and beó gesibsum, geðyldig, and ðolmōd, Hml. S. 17, 55. Se gesibsuma lǣfð symle yrfeweard æfter him *sunt reliquiae homini pacifico*, Ps. Th. 36, 36. Hié wǣron swā geþwǣre and swā gesibsume þæt hié ealle forgeáfon þǣm cāsere þā fǣhðe, Ors. 6, 4 ; S. 258, 27. Gesibsume *pacatos*, Wrt. Voc. ii. 68, 76. II. *at peace, not in conflict* :—þeóda him betweónum būton þeówdōme gesibbsume wǣron *nations were at peace with one another without one being the slaves of the other*, Ors. 1, 10 ; S. 50, 1. III. *that brings about peace* :—Gesibsuma God gemetgaþ ealla gesceafta and geþwǣraþ þā hē betwuh him winnaþ *haec concordia temperat aequis elementa modis . . . pugnantia*, Bt. 39, 13 ; F. 234, 9. v. un-gesibsum.

**ge-sibsumian.** *Add* : I. *to become gesibsum, come to an agreement, be reconciled* :—Gang ǣr and gesybsuma wið þinne brōðer *vade prius reconciliari fratri tuo*, Mt. 5, 24. Gā ǣr gesibbsumian breþer þínum, *reconciliari fratri tuo*, Mt. 5, 24. Gā ǣr gesibbsumian breþer þínum, Scint. 23, 16. II. *to make gesibsum, bring to an agreement, reconcile, conciliate* :—Sē þe brōþer his lator gesibsumað God him lator *reconciliat Deum sibi tardius placat*, geglađaþ *qui fratrem sibi tardius reconciliat Deum sibi tardius placat*, Scint. 25, 7. Nā gesibsumað God mænigfeald gebedes spǣc *non conciliat Deum multiplex orationis sermo*, 25, 13. Lōca hwylc crísten man sý ungesibsum, man āh on þām dæge hine tō gesibsumianne, Wlfst. 295, 5. Hēr cýð on ðysum gewrite hū Godwine and Leófwine wurdon gesybsumode ymbe ðæt land, C. D. iv. 266, 10.

**ge-sibsumlíce.** *Add* :—Heó begeat on hire geweald . . . gesybsumlíce (*contrast the capture of Derby*, P. 101, 29) þā burh æt Ligraceastre, Chr. 918 ; P. 105, 22.

**ge-sibsumnes.** *Add* :—Of þǣre offrunga þe man for gesibsumnysse offrað *de pacificorum hostiis*, Lev. 7, 32. Þ wē ūre gesibsumnesse and geþwǣrnesse fæstlícost ūs betweónan healdon, Ll. Th. i. 246, 22. v. un-gesibsumness.

**ge-sícan** *to wean.* *Substitute* : ge-sícan ; *p.* -sícte, -síhte ; *pp.* -síced *To cause to suck, suckle* :—Eádige sind ðā breóst þe swylce gesíhton (cf. *ubera quae lactauerunt*, Lk. 23, 29), Hml. Th. i. 84, 16. Gesíced *that has been suckled, weaned* ; *ablactatus*, Ps. Spl. 130, 4.

**ge-síclian.** *Take here* ge-séclod *in Dict., and add* :—Godwine gesíclode . . . and eft gewyrpte, Chr. 1052 ; P. 182, 13. Sē þe unendebyrdlíce mægenu gegrípan hogað, raþe hē byð gesíclud (*periclitatur*), Scint. 101, 15. Hē weard gesícelod, Hml. S. 7, 65. Weard his hors gesíclod (-sícclod, *v.l.*) and sōna feóll (v. Bd. 3, 9 ; Sch. 229, 18–), 26, 205. Wæs se king þā binnan Oxnaforde swýþe geseócled, C. D. iv. 57, 4.

**ge-sída.** *Substitute* : ge-sidu(-a) ; *pl. n.* Appurtenances, apparatus. v. heort-, sulh-gesidu ; ge-sidian.

**ge-sídu** (?) ; *pl.* The sides of an object :—On gesíðum hūsys þínys *in lateribus domus tue*, Ps. Cam. 127, 3.

**ge-sidian** ; *p.* ode *To arrange, determine* :—Ðonne þū setrǣgel habban wille, þonne plice þū ðíne āgene gewéda mid twām fingrum, tōspréd þíne twā handa and wege hī swylce þū setl gesydian wille, Tech. ii. 122, 19. *See other examples under* sydung *in Dict.*

**ge-sidu.** v. ge-sída.

**ge-siftan.** *Dele the passage, and add* :—Genim grēne rūdan leáf, scearfa smale and cnuca swíðe, and beren meala gesift dō þǣrtō, Lch. iii. 8, 15. Þæt folc nam gesyft melu (*conspersam farinam*), Ex. 12, 34.

**ge-sígan.** *Add* : I. *to sink* or *fall back* :—Gesāh *relabitur*, Germ. 401, 12. II. *of the depression of a surface, to sink* :—þý lǣs þider in ysel þohha gesíge, Lch. ii. 208, 18. III. *of the movement of a fluid, to run into or out of* :—Gyf wæter on eáran swýþe gesigen (-siged, *v.l.*) sý, Lch. i. 34, 6 : 188, 6. IV. *to sink, subside* (?) :—Heán sceal gehnígan, ādl gesígan, Gn. Ex. 118. [*O. H. Ger.* ge-sígan *to sink, fall.*]

**ge-sigefæstan.** *Add* :—Se eádiga wer swā gesigefæstod (-ed, *v.l.*) weard (*percepto ubique certandi bravio*) þæt hē þā bysmornysse forhogode heora costunga, Guth. Gr. 127, 4. Gesigfæstad *coronatus*, Rtl. 48, 36 : 60, 15. ¶ Gesigefæsted *crowned with victory, triumphant* :—Hē (*Christ after the harrowing of hell*) wolde gesigefæsted eft sídian tō þǣm líchoman, Shrn. 68, 19. Hē cōm hām symle gesund and gesygefæsted, 96, 25.

**ge-sigfæstnian.** *For* 'crown' *read* 'be crowned,' *and for* 'Mt. Kmb.,' 'Jn. Skt.' *read* 'Mt. p.,' 'Jn. p.'

ge-siglan; *p. de* To *sail, accomplish a journey by sailing :*—Hé siglde be lande swā swā hé meahte on feówer dagum gesiglan, Ors. 1, 1; S. 17, 17: 20: 13. v. ge-seglian.

ge-siht. *Add :* I. *faculty of seeing :*—Gesihð *visus*, hlyst *auditus*, Wrt. Voc. i. 42, 54. Blind sceal his eágna þolian, oftigen bið him torhtre gesihðe, Gn. Ex. 40. Blindum gesihðo *caecis uisum*, Lk. L. 4, 18. I a. *the exercising of the faculty, a seeing :*—'Hié God geseóð.' On þære gesihðe wesað ealle geleáffulle, Bl. H. 13, 27. II. *sight* (lit. or fig.) *of a person or object.* (1) *where the person sees.* (a) with gen. of person :—On wera gesiehðe, An. 620. Tó gesyþþe *ad* (*regis*) *presentiam*, An. Ox. 3015. Fore gesigðe his *ante conspectum suum*, Lk. L. 9, 52. Fram Nerónes gesyhþe, Bl. H. 189, 36. Hí ne mōston cuman on his eágon gesihðe, Chr. 1048; P. 174, 10. Hié gestódon on gesihþe þæs eádigan Andreas, Bl. H. 243, 6. (b) with dat. :—Hí nā heom God setton on gesyhðe *non proposuerunt Deum ante conspectum suum*, Ps. Th. 53, 3. Him wæs ān on gesyhðe engel, Dan. 273. Cain gewāt gongan Gode of gesyhðe, Gen. 1050. (c) with other constructions :—Hí āsetton on gesyhðe sigebeámas þrý fore Elenan cneó, El. 847. (2) *where the person or object is seen :*—Æt þære gesyhðe þæs sigebeámes, El. 965. Hwilce þū gesihðe hæfst cræfta, Gen. 617. Hé hié gelædeþ on sibbe gesyhþe, Bl. H. 79, 34. III. *eyes together with the faculty of sight :* visus, oculi :—Wé ūsse gesyhðe (ūre gesyhðe, *v. l.*) upp āhófon *uisum leuabimus*, Bd. 5, 1; Sch. 552, 13. Hé ne mihte bedydrian Martines gesihðe, Hml. S. 31, 824. Þ næron gewemmede Martines gesihþa on ōðra manna deáðe, 127. Þ ic þíne anlícnysse sceáwige mid swā mænigfealdum besmitenum gesihþum (*with eyes in so many ways defiled*), 23 b, 435. Godes gesyhða behealdað ægðer ge góde ge yfele *oculi Domini speculantur bonos et malos*, R. Ben. 25, 13. God ðā hæðenan ðeóda ætforan heora gesihðum ādwæscte, Hml. Th. i. 46, 20. Gesiþþe *uisus* (*mortalium uisus aufugiunt*), An. Ox. 3170. IV. *a looking at, look :*—Gesihð *obtutus*, Wrt. Voc. ii. 62, 42. Gesihþum *obtutibus*, An. Ox. 406. V. *what is seen, a sight.* (1) seen with the bodily eyes :—Æfter ðære angelica gesihða (*uisionem*), Jn. p. 8, 3. Cyning wæs þý blíþra . . . þurh þā sægeran gesyhð (*the cross seen in the sky*), El. 98. Nænigum men gié cueðe ðone gesihða, Mt. L. 17, 9. (2) seen in sleep or in ecstasy, *a vision :*—Gesihð and wītegunga beóð gefyllede *impleatur uisio et prophetia*, Hml. Th. ii. 14, 15. Wæs S. Michael þæm bisceope on gesihþe æteówed, Bl. H. 205, 35. On úplicere gesihþe geleórednesse *in oromate* (i. *uisione superna*) *extaseos*, An. Ox. 404. Gesiþþe *in uisione*, i. *in somno*, 2107. Þā hé slép, þā geseah hé Críst . . . Ðā hé þā gesihþe geseah (*quo uisu*), Bl. H. 215, 31. Ic þe hāte þæt þū þās gesyhðe secge mannum, Kr. 96. ᵥ v. lim-, sib-gesihþ.

ge-sihþnes *a vision :*—Forma gesihðnis *prima uisio*, Mt. p. 9, 9.

ge-siltan; *p. te; pp. -silted, -silt* To *salt.* *Take here* ge-sylt *in Dict., and add :*—Fleót þ fām of, geselt swíþe wel, Lch. ii. 96, 9. Nim þreó snǣda buteran, gemenge wið hwǣten mela, and gesylte, 152, 18. Netle gesoden on wætre and geselt, 228, 3. Sié gesælt *sallietur*, Mk. L. 9, 49. Gesælted bið *salietur*, Mt. L. 5, 13. v. un-gesilt.

ge-síman. *Take here* ge-sýman *in Dict., and add :*—Gýmena hefum hé bið gesýmed (*adgrauatur*), Scint. 181, 17. Se sceaða wæs on róde scyldig and mānfull, mid undǣdum eall gesýmed, Dōm. L. 58. Gesýmedum (-sém-, Hpt. Gl. 468, 26) *honustis*, An. Ox. 2644.

ge-sincan. *Add :* [*Goth.* ga-siggkwan: *O. H. Ger.* ge-sinchan.]

ge-síne. *Take here* ge-sýne *in Dict., and add :* I. *of material objects, visible, to be seen :*—Þ mon þære cyrcean flór emlíce gewyrce, þ þær nān byrgen gesýne ne sý, Ll. Th. ii. 408, 13. Gesēne wēre hine cuæð *uidendum se dicit*, Jn. p. 7, 14. Ceastra beóð feorran gesýne, Gn. C. 1. II. *of non-material objects, when visible results are produced, to be seen, evident,* (1) with noun :—Wæs wælræs wera wíde gesýne, B. 2947. Syndon þíne mihta ofer middangeard gesýne, Hy. 9, 50. Unrím wundra gesýnra, Men. 129. (2) with clause :—Þā wæs gesýne þæt se síð ne þāh, B. 3058. III. *to be perceived by the mind, evident, manifest :*—For þan is gesýne, cūð, oncnāwen, þæt þū cyninges eart þegen . . . for þan þe sóna sæholm oncneów, An. 526: 549: El. 144. Nū is gesēne þæt þū eart sylfa God, Sat. 441: 230. Hit is on ūs eallum swutol and gesēne (-syne, *v. l.*) þæt wē ǣr þysan oftor brǣcan þonne wē bēttan, Wlfst. 159, 5. Mið ðý uæs áuorden cuðlíce gesēne þte . . . *quo facto cognoscitur quod . . .*, Jn. p. 3, 11. ¶ in the Lindisfarne and Rushworth glosses the word is used to translate *videri*, (1) as passive of *videre :*—þte gesēne wēre from hiá *quia uisus esset ab ea*, Mk. L. R. 16, 11. Gesēne hine *uiso eo*, Mt. L. 8, 34: Lk. L. 10, 31. Gesēne ðone Hælend, Lk. L. R. 23, 8. Gisēne, Jn. L. 20, 20. Þ gié sē gesēno (-seánæ, R.) from him *ut uideamini ab eis*, Mt. L. 6, 1. Gesēne (-sǣnæ, R.), 5: 23, 5. Woeron gesēne *uisi*, Lk. L. R. 9, 31. (2) with the meaning *to seem, appear* (translating also *parere, apparere*). (a) *to seem to the eye :*—Þ ðū ne sē gesēne monnum fæstende *ne uidearis hominibus jejunans*, Mt. L. R. 6, 18. Þ hiá sē gesēne (-seánæ, R.) *ut apareant*, 16. Ðā ðe biðon gesēne (*parent*) monnum wlittig, Mt. L. 23, 27. (b) *to seem to the mind :*—Huæt iúh is gesēne *quid uobis uidetur?*, Mt. L. 18, 12: 21, 28. Gē gesēne bið monnum sóðfæste

*paretis hominibus justi*, 23, 28. Gesēne woeron suā fromdóen wordo ðās uisa sunt sicut deleramentum uerba ista, Lk. L. R. 24, 11: Rtl. 86, 14. v. forþ-, íþ-, un-gesíne.

ge-síne; *adv. Manifestly, clearly, openly :*—Cuoeð him se Hælend eáunge ꝉ gesēne, Latzar þte deád is *dixit eis Jesus manifeste, Lazarus mortuus est*, Jn. L. 11, 14.

ge-sínelic. *Take here* ge-sēnelic *in Dict.*

ge-sínelíce; *adv. Visibly :*—Hé þ tācen þære bærnnesse gesýnelíce (-sēne-, *v. l.*) eallum mannum on his sculdre bær *signum incendii uisibile cunctis in humero portauit*, Bd. 3, 19; Sch. 281, 14. Gisēnelíce is gibisnendo *visibiliter est informanda*, Rtl. 103, 30.

ge-singalian. *Add :*—Ic gesingalade *continui*, Ps. Srt. 88, 51. Gesingalie *continuet*, Germ. 388, 37. Gesingalede *continuati*, Ps. Srt. 140, 6.

ge-singallícode. *Substitute :* ge-singallícian; *p. ode* To *continue, perpetuate :*—Gesingallícode *continuati*, Ps. Vos. 140, 6. See *preceding word.*

ge-singan. *Add :* I. *to make a sound.* (1) *of persons, to play* an instrument :—Wē gesungun iúh mið hwistlum *cantauimus nobis tibiis*, Lk. L. 7, 32. (2) *of a bird* (*cock*), *to crow :*—Gisingeð ðe hona *cantabit gallus*, Jn. R. L. 13, 38. Ðe hona gisang, 18, 27: Mk. R. L. 14, 68: Lk. R. L. 22, 60. Hona gesang ꝉ gecrāwæ (creów, R.), Mt. L. 26, 74. Aer ðon se hona gesinga (gisunge, R.), Mk. L. 14, 72. II. (1) *to sing praise, glory, &c., to a person, repeat words which express :*—Ðæm wē gesinga wuldur *ipsi cantantes gloriam*, Rtl. 163, 15. (2) *to recite, repeat* forms used in religious services (prayer, psalm, mass) :—Sē þe Pater noster inweardlíce gesingð, Ll. Th. i. 372, 29. Ān mæssepreóst him mæssan gesang, Hml. S. 4, 230. Gā eft tó ciricean, gesing .xii. mæssan ofer þām wyrtum, Lch. ii. 356, 9. Ðās fíf salmas gesing (*decanta*), Rtl. 183, 29. Gesinge (*cantet*) hé fíftig sealma on cyricean oðða on ōþre dígolre stówe, Ll. Th. ii. 134, 11. Þ ælc gegilda gesinge ān fíftig oþþe begite gesungen, i. 236, 37. Mið ðý ward gebed gesungen *facta oratione*, Jn. p. 2, 2. Þā seó cyrice gehālgad wæs and se bisceop mæssan gesungene hæfde, Bd. 5, 4; Sch. 567, 21. III. *to celebrate in words :*—Sculan wē martira gemynd . . . wrecan wordum forð, wisse gesingan, Men. 70. [*O. H. Ger.* ge-singan *canere, psallere.*]

ge-sinhíwan. *Add :*—Gesinhígum, Bd. 1, 27; Sch. 80, 11: 4, 5; Sch. 379, 1. *See next word.*

ge-sinhíwen; *adj. Married :*—Ne mótan gesynnhíwenu on ānum bedde cuman, Wlfst. 305, 28. Þonne wēnað uncre hláfordas þ wē sýn swā swā gesinhína, Hml. A. 204, 300 (=Shrn. 40, 20, *given in Dict. under* ge-sinhíwan).

ge-sinlíce. *Substitute :* I. *continually, very often :*—Þes regul ic wille þæt gesinlíce (*sepius*) sié gesǣd, R. Ben. 127, 9. Hé breác gesinlíce Dūnstānes rǣdes, Lch. iii. 440, 4. II. *diligently :*—Hé georne behogige and gesinlíce (georne, *v. l.*) gíme hwæþre . . . *curiose intendat et sollicitus sit . . .*, R. Ben. 97, 14.

ge-sinscipe. *Add :*—Gesinscipe *conjugium vel matrimonium*, Wrt. Voc. i. 50, 10: *connubium*, 52, 36. Samwista gesinscypes (-syn-, Hpt. Gl. 520, 56) *copula matrimonii*, An. Ox. 5002. Gif hwylc geong man hæmeðþing gewyrce būtan rihtum gesinscipe (*legitimo conjugio*), Ll. Th. ii. 164, 23. Tó gesinscipum *ad* (*nuptiarum*) *commercia*, An. Ox. 3593. Ðā ðe hyre girndon tó rihtum gesynscipum, Ap. Th. 3, 8. Gewilnede gesinscipes (-sen-, Hpt. Gl. 506, 49) *optata connubia*, An. Ox. 4288.

ge-sinscippan *to marry :*—Tó gerihtanne þone gemānan gesinsceppendra (-sienscyp-, *v. l.*) *ad disponendum cubile conjugatorum*, Gr. D. 218, 4.

ge-sirwan. *Add :*—Gesyrewude (-serwade, Hpt. Gl. 459, 45) *hastati*, i. *armati*, An. Ox. 2258. Gesyrewede (-serwede, Hpt. Gl. 495, 45) *armatas*, i. *instructas*, 3794.

ge-síþ. *Add :* ge-síþe [?; *pl.* ge-síþþas (v. Gen. 2067: 1908), *a ja-stem with long root-syllable treated as if the syllable were short?* For the stem cf. *Goth.* ga-sinþjan, *d. pl., O. Sax.* te gisíðea (*also* te gisíða).] I. *one who goes with another* (*v. síþ*), *a companion :*—Swā swā hé wēre gesíð (*comes*) lícumlicre gegaderunge, Bd. 2, 9; Sch. 145, 9. I a. *a comrade in arms :*—Stópon secgas and gesíðas, Jud. 201. II. *an attendant :*—Hé (*St. Martin*) wæs betǣht tó þām gewinne mid ānum his þeówan þe his gesíðe (gesíða, *v. l.*) wæs (cf. Ænne cniht hé hæfde tó his ðenungum forð, Hml. Th. ii. 500, 8), Hml. S. 31, 37. III. *a follower, retainer* of a great man, king, &c. :—Geneátum, gesíþum (*printed* -soþum) *parasitis* (cf. parasitis, ministris (= Ald. 53, 12), 83, 50), Wrt. Voc. ii. 66, 62. Higelác þǣr æt hām wunade selfa mid gesíðum, B. 1924. Dióre gecēpte drihten Crēca Troia burh tilum gesíðum, Met. 26, 20. Gegrētte Beówulf hindeman síðe swǣse gesíðas, B. 2578. ¶ where the prince was not of this world :—Þegnas heredon Fæder frumsceafta; hé him þæs, leófum gesíðum, leán æfter geaf, Cri. 453. Hé (*Lucifer*) cwæð þæt hé mid his gesíðum wolde hýðan heofona ríce, Sal. 453. III a. *a person of rank, one considerable from his connexion with a prince, from an official position :*—Wæs sumes gesíðes (*comitis cuiusdam*) tūn nóht feor ūrum mynstre, Bd. 5, 4; Sch. 567, 8. Gesíðas *optimates*, Wrt. Voc. ii. 115, 17. IV.

a person in an official position:—Sisinnius se gesíð (comes Sisinnius, Ald. 67, 8), Shrn. 69, 32. Se hǽðna Ægypta gesíð, 84, 26. Gesíðas satrape, Wrt. Voc. ii. 95, 21. [O. H. Ger. ge-sint comes.] v. dryht-, eald-, folc-, samod-, weá-, wil-, wyn-gesíþ, and next two words.

ge-síþ. Add: [The word seems to be a ja- stem, like the O. Sax. gisíði, but to be treated as if the root-syllable were short. Cf. ge-síþþas in the preceding word.] A body of followers, retinue:—Hé earfoða dreág, hǽfde him tó gesíðe sorge and longað, wintercealde wrǽce, Deór. 3.

ge-síþa, an; m. I. a companion:—Gesíþa comeans, socius, Wrt. Voc. ii. 132, 47. Getreów gesíþa fida comes, 148, 73. Gesíþan comite, Angl. xiii. 369, 59. Gesíþan comitem (i. socium) (angelicae castitatis), An. Ox. 1185. Gesíðan on gangum comites gressibus), Hy. Srt. 38, 27. Gesíþum comitibus (castae sodalitatis), An. Ox. 4283. II. a comrade in arms:—Gesíþan manipulares (i. socii) (coelestis militiae), An. Ox. 4732. III. an attendant. v. gesíþ; II. IV. a follower, retainer:—þegn, gesíþa cliens, i. socius, Wrt. Voc. ii. 131, 70. [Goth. ga-sinþa: O. H. Ger. ge-sindo.] v. mid-, weg-gesíþa, and two preceding words.

ge-síþcund. Add: I. in a general sense, gentle by birth, gentle in contrast with simple:—Gif his sunu and his sunu sunu þ geþeóð þ hí swá micel laudes habban, siþþan bið se ofsprinc gesíðcundes cynnes be twám þúsendum, Ll. Th. i. 188, 11. Drihten on dreó tówearp þá cneordnysse, þæt wæs wælisc (servile) and on cyrlisc cynn (simple) and on gesýðcund cynn (gentle), Angl. xi. 3, 63. II. of the gesíþ class:—Gif gesíðcund mon (cf. se gesíð, 5) þingað wið cyning . . . oþþe wið his hláford for þeówe oþþe for frige, Ll. Th. i. 134, 2. Ánes gesíðcundes mannes wíf coniugem comitis, Bd. 5, 4; Sch. 567, 2.

ge-síþian to go:—Tó eallum bebodum þínum ic wæs gesíðod ad omnia mandata tua dirigebar, Ps. L. 118, 128.

ge-síþman. In the bracket in l. 2 read gesíðman, and add: The word seems to have the same meaning as gesíþ. I. v. ge-síþ; III a:—Ánes gesíðmannes (cf. sumes gesíðes, l. 8: it is the same person in each case) wíf coniugem comitis, Bd. 5, 4; Sch. 567, 1. II. v. ge-síþ; IV:—Gesíþmen satrape, An. Ox. 874. v. ge-síþwíf.

ge-síþrǽdenn, e; f. Company:—Comitatus, consecutus vel gesíþrǽden, Wrt. Voc. ii. 132, 18.

ge-síþwíf. Add:—Hé sǽde þ þǽr wǽre sum æþele gesíðwíf (matrona quaedam nobilis), Gr. D. 71, 30.

ge-sittan. Dele last citation, and add: A. intrans. I. where change of position is made. (1) of persons, to sit. (a) after standing, to sit down, take a seat:—Gangende se Hǽlend of húse gesæt (-sætt, v. l.) bi sǽe, Mt. R. 13, 1: Sat. 470. Féða eal gesæt, B. 1424. Gesæt þá wið sylfne sé þá sæcce genæs, mǽg wið mǽge, 1977. Gesǽdt, Mk. L. 16, 19. Geséton (gisittende, R.) sedentes, Mt. L. 13, 48. Wyrcas ðætte ða menn gisitte (-a, L.) facite homines discumbere, Jn. R. 6, 10. Hí gedydon þ hé þær on (on the ass) gesittan mihte, Bl. H. 71, 7. (b) after lying, to assume a sitting posture, sit up:—Heó beseah tó Petre and gesæt (-set, v. l.) hire upp (viso Petro resedit, Acts 9, 40), Hml. S. 10, 72. (2) of things, to come to rest, rest:—Fór fámig scip (the ark) .L. and .c. nihta . . . þá on dúnum gesæt holmærna mǽst, Gen. 1421. II. where posture is given, to be seated:—Hire sweostor gesæt big Hǽlendes fótum, Bl. H. 67, 26. Petrus gesæt úta, Mt. L. 26, 69: Jn. L. 9, 8. Cued ðæt gesitta suno mínne . . ., Mt. L. 20, 21. II a. where purpose of sitting is indicated, to sit at meat, in council:—Monig oft gesæt ríce tó rúne, B. 171. Hé gesæt him sundor æt rúne, Wand. 111. Gesæt tó symble Caldéa cyning, Dan. 701. Syððan wé tó symble geseten hæfdon, B. 2104. II b. figurative:—Ofer stól geséton wuðuto super cathedram Mosi sederunt scribae, Mt. L. 23, 2. III. to settle. (1) of persons. (a) of individuals, to dwell, reside:—Hé fór tó Róme and þǽr gesæt (wunode eal tó his lífes ende, v. l.), Chr. 874; P. 72, 27. Hé forlét þá burg þe hé on geseten wæs, Ors. 6, 30; S. 282, 8. (b) of a body of people. (a) of permanent occupation, to settle, live in a country:—Sume þá Gotan fóron on Ispanie and þǽr gesǽton, Ors. 6, 38; S. 298, 7. Hié wilnedon tó him þ hié mósten on his ríce mid friðe gesittan, 6, 34; S. 290, 21. Hé heora fela gesette wið þone sǽ, and hié þǽr gesetene sint giet oð þisne dæg quos ibi usque in hodiernum diem consistere opinio est, 3, 5; S. 104, 27. (β) of temporary occupation, to stay, have one's quarters:—Hǽðene men on Tenet ofer winter gesǽton, Chr. 851; P. 65, 10. (2) of (non-material) things, to settle, have its seat:—Þǽr sió ádl gesitte, Lch. ii. 120, 16. Gif se uíc weorðe on mannes setle geseten, iii. 30, 16. IV. with the idea of oppression, to fall upon, come upon:—þæt hé mid welerum geworht habbað, him þæt ilce sceal on gesittan labor labiorum ipsorum operiet eos, Ps. Th. i. 139, 7. V. to relinquish work, retire from office; residere:—Hér Danihel gesæt on Wintanceastre, and Húnferþ féng tó biscdóme, Chr. 744; P. 46, 2. Cynewulf ð gesæt in Lindisfarna ee, 779; P. 53, 23. B. trans. I. to sit a seat (as in to sit a horse), sit on:—Ic sǽbát gesæt, B. 633. I a. figurative as in to sit on the throne:—þíne suna gesittað þ cynesetl filii tui sedebunt super thronum, Hml. S. 18, 384. Hé mid sige gesæt siððan his cynestól, Hml. Th. ii. 306, 1. þ ǽlc oþer ð scolde beón munechádes mann þe þone arðstól gesǽte, Chr.

995; P. 129, 26. II. to preside over (?):—Hér gesæt (sette, v. l. Gesette, rather than gesæt, might be expected here, either in the sense 'ordained,' cf. ge-settan; V. 2, or in the sense 'convened,' cf. ge-setl: but see sittan; IV) þeodorius senoþ on Hǽþfelda, Chr. 680; P. 38, 8. III. to occupy, take possession of, possess:—Gesittende possessurae, Wrt. Voc. ii. 67, 20. (1) to possess territory:—Sǽd his erfweardnesse gesiteð eorðan semen eius hereditabit possidebit terram, Ps. Vos. 24, 13. þǽr hí yrfestól gesittað haereditatem acquirent eam, Ps. Th. 68, 37. Ða reáferas Godes ríce ne gesittað (possidebunt), Past. 401, 30. Gesittað (possidete) ríce þte eów geiarwad wæs, Mt. R. 25, 34. (1 a) of conquered territory:—Hié gesittað land Cananéa, Exod. 442. Hé búde on Eást-Englum, oð þ lond ǽrest gesæt, Chr. 890; P. 82, 11. Hié geridon Wesseaxna lond and gesǽton, 878; P. 74, 26. þá súððǽlas þyses eálondes hí him gesǽton and geáhnodon australes sibi partes insulae uindicarunt, Bd. 1, 1; Sch. 10, 17. (2) to occupy, possess a dwelling-place:—Hý fela setla gesǽton, Gú. 115. Nǽfdon on þám lande sǽlða gesetena, Gen. 785. (2 a) of violent occupation:—Gé gesittað sigeríce beórselas beorna, Exod. 562. (3) to possess a thing:—Hé líf ǽce gesitteþ vitam aeternam possidebit, Mt. R. 19, 29. Háligra sáwla gesittaþ Dryhtnes dreámas, Gú. 93. IV. to occupy, live in:—Hé ána gesæt dýgle stówe, Gú. 129. Hé feára sum mearclond gesæt, 145. [Goth. ga-sitan: O. Sax. gi-sittian: O. H. Ger. ge-sizzen sedere, residere: possidere.]

ge-siwed. v. ge-seowian: ge-slǽcce, Ps. Srt. 7, 3. v. ge-lǽccan; II. 4.

ge-slǽpan. Add:—Mið ðý geslépdon ł geslépæ waldon cum dormirent, Mt. L. 13, 25.

ge-sleán. Add: I. to strike with a material object:—' Gif woe geslás ł huoeðer móto wé geslaa in suorde (gislá mid sworde, R.).' And geslóg án of ðǽm esne aldormonnes ' si percutimus in gladio.' Et percussit unus ex illis seruum principis, Lk. L. 22, 49, 50. Hé geslóg breóst his, 18, 13. Mið ðý gislóg síde Petres, Rtl. 58, 7. Mið fýstum hine geslaa ł geðearsca colaphis eum caedere, Mk. L. 14, 65. I a. figuratively:—Hé hine mid hý worde geslóg (perculit), Past. 115, 15. Ðæt hí beóð mid strengran cwide ðæs dómes geslægene ut eos durior sententia feriat, 433, 35. II. to strike with a stamp, hammer, &c., to coin money, forge implements:—Feoh þe wæs geslagen on Decius cáseres tíman, Hml. S. 23, 659. Penegas on gefyrndagum geslægene, 588: Gen. 583 (in Dict.). III. to strike (and break) an object against something:—Fela henne ǽgru gesleá on án fæt break many hen's eggs into a vessel, Lch. ii. 264, 24. Picge hé geseáw broþu . . . and geslegen ǽgru and breád gebrocen on hát wæter, 5. IV. to strike and kill, slay:—Tó acuoellanne ł gesleá ǽnig interficere quemquam, Jn. L. 18, 31. þte wére geslægen occidi, Lk. L. R. 22, 7. Geslaegen, Mt. p. 17, 8. V. to gain by striking (fighting):—Hí týr geslógon æt sæcce, Ædelst. 4. V a. to bring about by fighting, make slaughter:—Geslóh þín fæder fǽhðe mǽste, wearþ hé Heaþolāfe tó handbonan mid Wilfingum . . . Siþþan þá fǽhðe feó þingode, sende ic Wylfingum ealde mádmas, B. 459-472. þára folca ǽgðer on ðōerum micel wæl geslógan, Ors. 3, 1; S. 98, 6. VI. of an adder, to sting:—Fram nǽdran geslegene a serpente percussi, Bd. 1, 1; Sch. 13, 7. VII. to drive, fix a peg, stake, &c., pitch a tent:—Gif hé hæbbe geteld geslagen, Ll. Th. i. 286, 9. VIII. where an impression is produced on the mind, or a condition of mind or body is brought about:—Ðá geslóh hine sóna se snáwhwíta hreófla, Hml. A. 58, 186. Heó wearð mid hreóflan (-um, v. l.) geslagen, 177. Oft weorðað men áfǽrde . . . ðonne ðæt geslægene mód (percula mens) gesihð . . ., Past. 441, 25. Hí swýðe mid þǽre fyrhte wǽron geslegene, Guth. 92, 1. [O. H. Ger. ge-slahan percutere, caedere, figere.]

ge-slífed, ge-sliht. Take here respectively ge-sléfed, ge-slyht in Dict.

ge-slit. Add: I. a bite, sting of a snake:—Ðyssera nǽddrena geslit eów mihte tó deáðe gebringan, Hml. Th. ii. 490, 4. Gehǽlede fram ðǽra nǽddrena geslite, 240, 12. Weard án cnapa þurh nǽddran geslit neálíce ádýd . . . Hé sette his finger on þá wunda þe se wurm tóslát, Hml. S. 31, 951. II. what is bitten:—Eálá, ðú wyrma gecow and wulfes geslit, Nap. 28, 29.

geslit-glíw, es; n. Jeering, bitter jesting:—Geslitglíwe cavillatione (cum cachinnanti cavillatione flagitans, Ald. 63, 11), Wrt. Voc. ii. 85, 65: 18, 65. Cf. slítan; VII: but see geslit-glíw.

ge-smacian; p. ode To pat, caress, soothe:—Gesmacode demulcet, pro demulcebat (mentem . . . nec blandimentorum lenitas demulcet), An. Ox. 3004.

ge-smæccan to taste:—Ic gesmæcce sapio, Ælfc. Gr. Z. 221, 9. v. ge-smecgan.

ge-smeágan. Add:—Gesmǽgeð retractat, An. Ox. 50, 54. Hiá gesmeáwdon (cogitabant) bituih him, Mt. L. 16, 7. Gesmeáudon (gismeádun, R.), Lk. L. 20, 5. Gesmeáge cogitare, 5, 21. Beón gesmeád conici, i. intelligi, An. Ox. 2688.

ge-smeágung, e; f. Inquiry, consideration:—Gesmeángum, spyrungum, áxungum adinventionum, An. Ox. 5214.

ge-smeáh. Add: v. smeáh: ge-smecgan. Add: v. ge-smæccan.

**ge-sméþan.** *Add:* I. *to smooth* what is rough to the touch, *polish* :—Ðā stānas on ðæm temple wæron swā emne gesnidene and gesméðde, Past. 253, 14. II. *to remove irritating properties* in food. v. smēþe; V:—Meoluc mid hunige gesmēþed, Lch. ii. 222, 13. *See next word.*

**ge-sméþian;** *p.* ode *To make smooth, remove inequalities from a surface* (lit. or fig.), *level* an inequality :—Þonne ic fram fyrde gecyrre ic tōwurpe ðās burh and hī gesmēðige, Hml. Th. i. 450, 10. Clincig gesmēþiende sīþfæt *asperum planes iter*, Hy. S. 104, 35. Wōhnyssa beóð gerihte and scearpnyssa gesmēðode, Hml. Th. i. 360, 34.

**ge-smicerad.** *Substitute* : ge-smicerian; *pp.* od *To make elegant* (smicer) :—Gesmicerade *fabrefactis* (pulcherrima membrorum liniamenta *fabrefactis* vultibus decorare, Ald. 81, 8), Wrt. Voc. ii. 88, 44 : 37, 24. [*O. H. Ger.* ka-smechrōt *expolitus*.]

**ge-smirian.** *l.* ge-smirwan. *Take here* ge-smyrian *in Dict.*, *and add* :—Gesmirwid *delibutus*, Wrt. Voc. ii. 106, 37. Gesmired *dilibatus*, 70, 5. Gesmyred *delibatus*, 26, 27. Gesmirede and gehyrde *lita*, 51, 49. I. *to smear* with grease :—Mycgerne gesmired *seuo madefactus* (*fomes*), An. Ox. 2764. II. *to anoint* as part of the ritual of consecration to an office :—Ic ðē tō cynincge gesmyrode, Hml. S. 18, 321. Bið gesmyrod ealra hālgena Hālga (*ungatur Sanctus sanctorum*, Dan. 9, 24) ... On ælcere hādunge ... æfre sē ðe ðær gehādod bið, hē bið gesmyrod mid gehālgodum ele ... Nū is Críst gesmyrod, nā mid eorðlicum ele, ac mid gife ðæs Hālgan Gāstes, Hml. Th. ii. 14, 15-30. [*O. H. Ger.* ge-smiret *impinguatus*.]

**ge-smiten.** *Substitute* : ge-smītan; *pp.* -smiten *To smear, daub* :—Gāte fiǽsc gebærned tō āhsan mid wætere on gesmiten, Lch. ii. 72, 9. Blōd gesmiten on þæs seócan mannes wambe, 236, 17. [*Goth.* ga-smeitan *linere: O. H. Ger.* ge-smizen *litus*.]

**ge-smiþian.** *Add: to make skilfully* :—Billfrið se oncræ hē gesmioðade ðā gihrīno ðā ðe ūtan on sint *Billfrið the anchorite made the ornaments that are on the cover of the book*, Jn. p. 188, 4. Heofonan rīces cǽig nis gylden, ne sylfren ne of nānum antimbre gesmiðod, Hml. Th. i. 368, 35. *Fabrefactum*, i. *ornate compositum vel ornamentum vel* gesmiðodum, Wrt. Voc. ii. 146, 58.

**ge-smittian;** *p.* od *To smudge, smear with dirt, befoul* :—Gesmittad *cacabatus*, An. Ox. 7, 323 : 8, 282.

**ge-smyltan.** *Add: to calm* :—Þeós wyrt āwendeþ hagoles hreóhnysse, and gyf þū hȳ on scyp āhēhst, tō þām wundorlic heó is, þ heó ǽlce hreóhnysse gesmylteþ, Lch. i. 308, 17.

**ge-smyrian.** v. ge-smirwan: **ge-snǽdan.** v. snǽdan; I. *in Dict.:* **ge-sneorcan.** v. sneorcan *in Dict.*

**ge-snid.** *Add:* I. *cutting* by a surgeon, *cutting* with a lancet. Cf. snīþan; II:—Beóð oft ðā wunda mid ele gehǽlda, ðā ðe mon mid gesnide (*incisione*) gebētan ne meahte, Past. 271, 2. II. *killing.* Cf. snīþan; IV:—Swā swā sceáp tō gesnide, R. Ben. 27, 10.

**ge-snīþan.** *Add:* I. *to cut into slices, cut up* :—Nim niþeweardne eolenan, gesnīþ on hunig, ete swā manige snæda swā hē mæge, Lch. ii. 358, 20. II. *to cut, hew* stone :—Gesniden *dolatum*, Wrt. Voc. ii. 106, 60 : 25, 64. Ðā stānas wæron emne gesnidene, Past. 253, 14. III. *to cut grass or corn* (? v. snīþan; VII) :—Hēht him þte gesnīða gedydon (þ hiᵹ gesnide, R.) alle ofer groene gers *praecepit illis ut accumbere facerent omnes super uiride faenum* (is it possible that the translator thought that the order was to cut the grass?), Mk. L. 6, 39. [*O. H. Ger.* ge-snīdan *dolare, putare, concidere*.]

**ge-snīðan** *to lie down. See* preceding word: **ge-snīþung.** *Dele:* **ge-snot.** *Add:* Lch. ii. 4, 13.

**ge-soc;** *n.* (not *m.?*). *Add: sucking* :—Āgyld þū mē mid biternesse leán, swā swā mōdor dēþ hyre bearne, þonne hió hit fram hire breósta gesoce weneþ *sicut ablactatus est super matrem suam, ita retribues in animam meam*, R. Ben. 22, 21.

**ge-sod;** *n. Add:* I. *cooking, boiling* :—Gesod *cocturam* (*alimentorum*), An. Ox. 3759. II. metaph. *trial* as by fire. v. seóþan; II:—Ic hié wolde geclǽnsian mid ðǽm gesode ðæs broces *purgare eos per ignem tribulationis volui*, Past. 267, 19. [*O. H. Ger.* ge-sot *coctio*.]

**ge-soden.** v. ge-seóþan.

**ge-sōm.** *Add: Crist* cwæð on his godspelle þ nān cynerīce ne stent nāne hwīle ansund, gif hī gesōme ne beóð (*if the people are not united.* Cf. Si regnum in se diuidatur non potest stare regnum, Mk. 3, 24), Hml. S. 13, 238. Beóð swīðe gesōme *ne irascamini*, Gen. 45, 24. v. ungesōm.

**ge-sōð.** v. ge-sīþ; III.

**ge-sōþian.** *Add:* I. *to prove the truth* of a statement, charge, &c. :—Gif hē gewyrce þ man hine āfylle þurh þ þe hē ongeán riht geanbyrde, gif man þ gesōðige (gesōðian mæge, *v. l.*), licge ægilde, Ll. Th. i. 404, 13. I a. gesōþian on ānum *to convict a person* of something. Cf. *Icel.* sanna ā einum :—Gif se Englisca beclypað Frenciscne mid ūtlagan þingan, and wille hit on him gesōþian (*super eum inueritare*), Ll. Th. i. 489, 23. Gif hit him on gesōðod weorðe, 324, 18. II. *to attest, bear witness to* :—þæt hē geseah hē gesōðode eác þurh his gesēðnysse, Nap. 32, 3. v. ge-sēþan.

**ge-sotig.** *Dele.* v. grotig: **ge-spænning.** *Dele, but* cf. for-spennan, -spenning: **ge-spǽtan.** v. spǽtan; II. *in Dict.:* ge-span *a tamarisk tree. Dele, and see* ge-span *a clasp.*

**ge-span** *suggestion. Add* :—Ūs is gecynde ðæt wē ælc yfel on ðriō wīsan ðurhtión, ðurh gespan (*suggestione*) ... Ðæt gespan bið ðurh dióful ... Ðā wæs Adam ðurh gespan ðǽre næddran oferswīðed ... On ðǽm gespane wē magon ongietan ðā synne, Past. 417, 19-30.

**ge-span[n].** *Add:* I. *a yoke* :—Hié nān gespann ðæs flǽslican gesinscipes ne gebiégð *eos nequaquam jugum copulae carnalis inclinat*, Past. 401, 3. II. *a clasp, buckle* :—Gespan, gespon *murica, aureum in tunica*, Txts. 76, 624 : *mauria de auro facta in tonica*, 113, 78 : Wrt. Voc. ii. 55, 78. [*O. H. Ger.* ge-spann *spinter, murica, minor murenula*.]

**ge-spanan.** *Add* :—On gespanest *inlicias*, Wrt. Voc. ii. 45, 15. I. *in a good sense* :—Ðæt hē ðā medwīsan tō māran angienne mid ðǽre liðelican bisnunga gespōne *quatenus hebetes ad majora conscendere imitatio blanda suaderet*, Past. 205, 18. II. *in a bad or an indifferent sense* :—Hē gespan him tō ealle Kentingas, Chr. 1052 ; P. 178, 24. [*O. Sax.* ge-spanan : *O. H. Ger.* ge-spanan *illicere, persuadere, hortare.*]

**ge-spannan.** *Add* :—Ðā ðe bióð gesponnene tō gesinscipe *qui carnali copulae inhaerent*, Past. 399, 2.

**ge-sparian.** *Add: to save, not to use.* v. sparian; II :—Swā hwæt swā hȳ gespariaþ on heora forhæfednesse and swā hwæt swā tōforan þām neádbehēfum belifen byð on heora mægenes tilunge *quidquid necessarium victui superest ex operibus manuum et epularum restrictione*, R. Ben. 138, 15.

**ge-spēdan.** *Add* :—Gespēd ł gesundful sīðfæt hē dēþ ūs *prosperum iter faciet nobis*, Ps. L. 67, 20. Seó hǽl wearð gespēd on Iudan handum, Hml. S. 25, 286.

**ge-spēdsumian.** *Add* :—Gespēdsumede *prosperabantur*, An. Ox. 3630.

**ge-spelia.** *Add:* -speliga *a vicar* :—Crīstes gespelia hē (*the abbot*) is and his note and spelinge on mynstre healt *abba Christi agere vices in monasterio creditur*, R. Ben. 10, 11. Þ hē (*the king*) sȳ on ware and on wearde Crīstes gespeliga, Ll. Th. ii. 304, 24. Hē (*Gregory*) Sanctum Agustinum him tō gespelian funde *he provided St. Augustine as a substitute for himself*, Lch. iii. 434, 7. Nū syndan biscopas Petres gespelian, Wlfst. 177, 18. Hālige lāreówas Drihtnes gespelian sind, Hml. Th. ii. 320, 27.

**ge-speornan.** v. ge-spornan.

**ge-spillan.** *Add: to waste* :—Hē gispilde (*dissipauit*) feh his, Lk. L. 15, 13 : 16, 1. Bið gespilled *demolitur*, Mt. L. 6, 19.

**ge-spinnan** *to spin* :—Gespunnen *netum*, An. Ox. 3738. [*O. H. Ger.* ge-spunnan *tortum, retortum.*]

**ge-spittan.** *Add* :—Efne-gespitta (gispita, R.) *conspuere*, Mk. L. 14, 65 : **ge-splottod** *spotted.* v. splott; II.

**ge-spornan.** *Take here* ge-speornan *in Dict., and add* : I. *to tread upon, light upon* :—Ðæt ðeófol on ðā eorðan gewīteð, and þanon helle wēsten gespyrreð (-spyrneð ?), Sal. K. p. 148, 31. II. *to strike against, beat upon* (of the wind) :—Windas bleówan and þæt hūs swīðlice gespurnun (*impegerunt in domum illam*), R. Ben. 4, 13.

**ge-spōwan.** *Add* :—God þē gemiclað þ þē forþ gespēwð þ þū dōn wilt, H. Z. 21, 189, 13.

**ge-sprǽc.** *Add:* [ge-sprǽc, ge-sprǽce (v. god-gesprǽce), ge-sprec, ge-spræc (? cf. ge-sprǽcan = ge-sprecan, *and* cf. gebrec *and* ge-bræc). These forms are taken together as they cannot always be distinguished with certainty either by form or by meaning; where the quantity of the vowel is uncertain it is left unmarked.] I. *speech, talking* :—Gearowyrde on gesprǽce (-sprece, *v. l.*) *loquella promtus*, Bd. 5, 2 ; Sch. 561, 3. Ðæt is best ... þ man ... gemetigian cunne ge his sprēce ge his swīgan, and wite hwonne hē gesprēce hæbbe (*when he have occasion for speaking*), and hwanne him geanswaræd sī, Prov. K. 2. II. *a speech, language* :—Hē andwyrde þām ælreordan gesprece (-sprǽce, *v. l.*) in eadem barbara (Bulgarica) *locutione respondit*, Gr. D. 300, 24. Ne sind gespreocu (*loquellae*), Ps. Srt. 18, 4. III. *what is said, a speech, saying, an oracle, words* :—Gesprec Drylhtnes *eloquium Domini*, Ps. Srt. Vos. 104, 19 : 118, 50 : *eloquia*, 11, 7. Gecȳþed mid ealdorlicnesse þæs hālgan gespreces (þǽre hālgan sprǽce, *v. l.*) *auctoritate sacri eloquii*, Gr. D. 323, 13. After gesprece ðīnum *secundum eloquium tuum*, Ps. Srt. 118, 41. Gesprec ðīn (ðīne gesprecu, Ps. Vos.) ne heóldun *eloquia tua non custodierunt*, 158 : 162. Gespreocu (gesprec, Ps. Vos.) Dryhtnes *eloquia Domini*, Ps. Srt. 17, 31. Gespreocu (gesprecu, Ps. Vos.), 118, 103. Gespreco *oracula*, Wrt. Voc. ii. 62, 43. Þæs þe ūs cȳþað þā hālgan gesprǽcu (-sprecu, *v. l.*) *quod sacra testantur eloquia*, Gr. D. 294, 21 : Hml. S. 23 b, 92. Gesprǽca *uerborum*, i. *sermonum*, An. Ox. 2, 169. On þæs hālgan gewrites gesprecum (*eloquiis*), Gr. D. 138, 35. In mīnre heortan ic gehȳdde þīne gesprǽcu (gesprecu, Ps. Vos., gespreocu, Ps. Srt., spǽca, Ps. L. 118, 11), Ll. Th. ii. 402, 38. IV. *a speaking to or with, colloquy, dialogue, conversation* :—Mē simle is swȳþe leóf ealldra manna gesprǽc (sprǽc, gesprǽca, *v. ll.*) *mihi senum*

*collocutio·esse semper amabilis solet*, Gr. D. 79, 18. Seó þridde bóc Sancte Gregorius gespræces (-spreces, *v. l.*) and Petres *liber tertius dialogorum Gregorii*, 259, 21. In þám gespræce þǽre hálignysse *in sacris colloquiis*, 167, 9. Ic wæs mid his gesprece (-spræce, spræce, *v. ll., allocutione*) geréted, Bd. 5, 1 ; Sch. 551, 6 : *conloquio*, 3, 22 ; Sch. 293, 23. Mid his wýtum gesprec (spræce, gespræce (Bd. S.), *v. ll.*) and geþeaht habban *habito cum sapientibus consilio*, Bd. 2, 13 ; Sch. 163, 23. Hig on manegum gespræcum heora gástlic líf smeádon, Guth. 52, 6. On gespræcum (-sprecum, *v.l.*) *in dialogues*, Gr. D. 259, 22. Hí betwyh heom þá hálgan gespræcu (-sprecu, *v. l.*) spræcon *inter sacra colloquia*, 167, 11. Gesprecu (sprǽcu, *v.l.*), 168, 17. [Cf. *O. H. Ger.* gesprāhhi[n] *oraculum*.] v. god-gespræce, -gesprec.

**ge-sprec.** *See preceding word.*

**ge-spreca.** *Add:*—Abraham wæs Godes gespreca (cf. æfter ðǽre spræce se Ælmihtiga úp gewende (Gen. 17, 22), 92, 8), Hml. Th. i. 90, 19. Móyses wæs Godes sylfes gespeca (-spreca, *v.l.*) (cf. Drihten spræc wið Móises swá man spricð wið his freónd, Ex. 33, 11), Wlfst. 13, 5.

**ge-sprecan.** *Add:* I. absolute, *to speak.* (1) *to have the faculty of speech, not to be dumb*:—Dumbo dyde þte hiá gesprecas *mutos fecit loqui*, Mk. L. 7, 37. Gebrōht wæs him dumb, and geleicnade hine suæ þ hē gespræc, Mt. L. 12, 22. Ðreátas gesēgon monigo gesprēcon, 15, 31. (1 a) *to exercise the faculty of speech, not to be silent*:—Ne gelēfde ðā gespreca *non sinebat ea loqui*, Lk. L. 4, 41. (2) *to talk, converse*:—Mið ðȳ gespræcc (wē gisprēcun, R.) *in woege dum loqueretur in uia*, Lk. L. 24, 32. (2 a) *to talk with, converse together*:—Gesprēcon betuién him *conloquebantur ad inuicem*, Jn. L. R. 11, 56. Efne gesprēcon, Lk. L. 4, 36. Ðā hiordas gisprecun (*loquebantur*) bitwih him, Lk. R. L. 2, 15. Mið him gesprēcon, Mt. L. 17, 3 : Lk. L. 9, 30. (2 b) *to speak about*:—Nǽnig eáuunge gespræc of him, Jn. L. R. 7, 13. Þá þá hí umbe óþer þing gesprecon hæfdon, Chr. 1070; P. 206, 9. (2 c) *to speak to or with some one about something*:—Tó faeder of brehtnise his gespræc, Jn. p. 7, 18. Ðá ilco gesprēcon him bituih of ðǽm allum, Lk. L. R. 24, 14. (3) *of public speaking*:—Mið ðȳ gespræc, Lk. L. 11, 37. Hē lǽrde ðā menigo, þte geblann gespreaca, 5, 4. II. with cognate object. (1) *a noun denoting speech or a pronoun referring to a statement, to speak words, &c., say*:—Word Godes gispreces (*loquitur*), Jn. R. L. 3, 34. Word hē gespræcc, Mk. L. 8, 32. Gespræc Beówulf gylpworda sum, B. 675. Hiera sundorsprǽce þe hié gesprǽcan *the colloquy they were to have*, Ors. 4, 10 ; S. 202, 13. Ðā ðe gespreccenda woeron ðā wītgo, Lk. L. 24, 25. Siððan he hit gesprecen hæfð, Past. 81, 7 : Ors. 2, 8 ; S. 92, 8. Ðā ðis gesprecen wæs, Bt. 18, 1 ; F. 60, 18. (1 a) *to speak to a person*:—Fela Daniel tó his drihtne gespræc sóðra worda, Dan. 594. Hwæt gespræcc him, Jn. L. 10, 6. (1 b) *to speak of*:—Monigo of his micelnise gespræc, Lk. p. 5, 12. (2) *where the object denotes the matter expressed in the words spoken*:—Þ uē uuton uē gesprecas (-spreocas, R.), Jn. L. 3, 11. (3) *where the object is that which is spoken about, to speak about*:—Þá wǽre and þá winetreówe þe git on ǽrdagum oft gesprǽcon, Bo. 52. (4) *the object a clause*:—Wæs gesprecen ðurh Salomonn bi ðǽm Wísdóme ðæt se Wísdóm wille sóna fleón ðone þe hine fíiéhð, Past. 247, 16. Þá hē hæfde gespecen þat hē wolde, Chr. 1048 ; P. 173, note 1. III. with a personal object. (1) *to speak to a person, accost*:—Ic gesprece sumne mann *adorior*, Ælfc. Gr. Z. 219, 1. Tó þám burnan þe wytt unc ǽrest gesprǽcon, Hml. S. 23 b, 707. (2) *of more or less formal speech, to address*:—Hē árás and þá gebróðru gespræc (cf. him tó spræc *fratres allocutus est*, Gr. D. 105, 16) : 'Gebróðru, miltsige eów God ...,' Hml. Th. ii. 158, 24 : 474, 26. Heó gespæc deór *alloquitur bestiam*, An. Ox. 4899. Hē cwæð þ hí Críst gesprǽce þysum godspellicum wordum : 'Ne háte ic eów nǽ þeówan ...,' Hml. S. 2, 86. Gesprecendum *contionante*, An. Ox. 3459. (3) *to speak in reproof, exhortation, &c.*:—Þá lufode hē hine, and gelóme hine gespræc tihtende tó geleáfan, Hml. S. 3, 573. Se hálga wer hine eft gespræc and git þryddan síðe, and swýðe hine þreáde, 21, 59. Þá englas þá hwíle Heliodorum gesprecon, sǽdon þ hē sceolde Onian mycclum þancian, 25, 789. (4) *to speak with, have an interview with*:—Hí áxodon hwæðer Petrus þǽr wununge hæfde, woldon hine gesprǽcan, Hml. S. 10, 112. Hē hēt him tó gelangian þá deófolgildan ... wolde hí gesprecan, 18, 370. Ðeós tíd cymð ymbe twelf mónað, þ ǽlc man sceal his scrift gesprecan (*confessarium suum alloqui*), Ll. Th. ii. 224, 33. IV. *to agree, settle*:—Þá gesprǽcon hié him betweónum þæt hié wolden anwendan ealle þá gesetnessa, Ors. 6, 10 ; S. 264, 19. Hí tó fullan friðe gesprǽcon þ hig ealle mid him súð faran woldon, Chr. 1066 ; P. 197, 31. Tostig eorl him cóm tó mid eallum þám þe hē begiten hæfde, eall swá hȳ ǽr gesprecen hæfdon, P. 196, 26. [*O. Sax.* gi-sprekan : *O. H. Ger.* gi-sprehhan *loqui, dicere, alloqui, compellare, convenire, constituere*.]

**ge-sprecen** *what is said.* v. god-gesprecen.

**ge-sprengan.** *Add:*—Pealman beón gesprengede (-spring-, MS.) mid geblesudum wætere *palmae aspergantur benedicta aqua*, Angl. xiii. 409, 622. [*O. H. Ger.* ge-sprengen *spargere, conspergere*.]

**ge-spring.** *Dele.*

**ge-springan.** *Substitute* : *To spring.* I. *to burst forth*, of a fluid *to spirt out*, of sparks, drops, &c. (lit. or fig.), *to fly*:—Þæt blód gesprang, B. 1667. Of þám wrōhtdropan wíde gesprungon, Gn. Ex. 196. II. *of energetic speech, to burst forth* in words :—In ðæt mearda of heofne cwōm loceted ł gesprang (cf. gesprintan) : 'In fruma waes word' *in illud prooemium e coelo veniens eructavit* : 'In principio erat verbum,' Mt. p. 9, 7. III. *to grow* as a plant (*lit. or fig.*) :—Sigemunde gesprong æfter deáð dæge dōm unlytel, B. 884. IV. *of fame, report, &c., to spread, be diffused*:—Gesprang mērsung his in alle Syria *abiit opinio ejus in totam Syriam*, Mt. L. 4, 24. Gesprang (*processit*) mērðu (*rumor*) his in al16 lond, Mk. L. 1, 28. V. *to reach by spreading, spread and reach* (fig.) :—Wídgongel wíf word gespringeð (cf. word) ; II. 4 and 5 *for the occurrence of word as the subject of* springan) ; hǽleð hȳ hospe mǽnað *rumour reaches a rambling woman* : (i. e. she gets talked about) *men make a mock of her*, Gn. Ex. 65. VI. *with a causative force, to send forth* a stream :—Cirica ... fēwor streámas neirxna wonga ongelíc gespranc (cf. ge-sprintan) *ecclessia ... quattuor flumina paradisi instar eructans*, Mt. p. 8, 5. [*O. H. Ger.* gespringan *exsilire*.]

**ge-sprintan** ; *p.* -sprant, *pl.* -sprunton *To burst forth* (? cf. *Icel.* spretta ; *p.* spratt, of water, *to burst out, spirt out. The word, however, seems used with causative force. Cf.* ge-springan ; VI), *to send forth* words. Cf. ge-springan ; II :—In foresaga rocgetede ł gisprunt word *Johannes in prochemio eructavit uerbum*, Jn. p. 187, 26.

**ge-sprucg.** *Dele, and see* ge-stric : ge-spryng. v. will-gespryng : **ge-spyrreþ.** v. ge-spornan : **gest.** v. gist : **ge-staþeled.** v. ge-staþelian ; III.

**ge-stǽlan.** *l.* -stǽlan, *dele first passage, in last for* leágung *l.* leásung, *and add* : *to bring home to a person a charge, liability, &c., to prove something to have been committed by, or to be due from, a person* :—Gif mon on sōlces gemóte cyninges gerēfan geyppe eofot (þeófðe, *v.l.*), and his eft geswícan wille, gestǽle on ryhtran hand (*let him make the charge good upon one who more justly may be charged* ; *pertrahat hoc ad rectiorem manum*, Old Lat. vers.), Ll. Th. i. 76, 6. Heó þá fǽhðe wræc þe þú Grendel cwealdest ... heó wolde hyre mǽg wrecan ge feor hafað fǽhðe gestǽled (*to the full has she made good her charge of slaying*), B. 1340. v. ge-stǽl.

**ge-stǽn.** *l.* -stǽn.

**ge-stǽnan.** *Add:* I. *to cast stones at*:—Hiá soecað ðec tó gestǽnane, Jn. L. 11, 8. Áne hē wæs gestǽned oð deáð, Hml. Th. i. 392, 3. II. *to set with precious stones*:—Mid gimcynnum gestǽned, Wlfst. 263, 4. [*O. H. Ger.* ge-steinen *lapidibus ornare* ; ge-steinōn *lapidare*.]

**ge-stǽppan.** *Add*: -p. stōp ; *pp.* -stapen. I. *of living creatures*:—For hwí gesteppe ic ł gā ic *quare incedo*, Ps. L. 41, 10. Þá gestóp hē tó ánes wealles byge, Ors. 3, 9 ; S. 134, 19. Tó ðē gistepe uē *ad te gradiamur*, Rtl. 51, 9. I a. *with cognate acc., to step a step, take a step*:—Ǽlc þæra stæpa and fótlǽsta þe wē tó cyricean weard gestæppað, Wlfst. 302, 27. I b. *where fōt is subject*:—Symble wæs drýge folde swá his fót gestóp, An. 1584. II. *of inanimate objects*:—Se rodor þǽre eorþan on nánre ne mót neár þonne on óðre stōwe gestæppan (cf. ðeáh se rodor þǽre eorþan náwer ne geneálǽce, Bt. 33, 4 ; F. 130, 22), Met. 20, 140.

**ge-stæddig.** *Add: grave, staid*:—Gestæþþig, ánrǽde *constans, stabilis*, Wrt. Voc. ii. 133, 69 ; *gravis*, 41, 74. Hē wæs gestæddig on lēce, Hml. S. 31, 296. v. un-gestæþþig.

**ge-stæþþiglíce.** v. un-gestæþþiglíce.

**ge-stæddignes.** *Add: staidness*:—Gesete, Dryhten, hirde mínum mūðe and ðá duru gestæddignesse (*ostium circumstantiae*), Past. 275, 22. Seó rípung his gestæþþignesse sȳ swylc þæt hine ne worian lyste *cuius maturitas eum non sinat vagari*, R. Ben. 126, 17. Mid gestæþþignesse clypian *cum gravitate loqui*, 30, 13. Gehwylc tó ðám Godes weorce efste—þæt þonne sȳ mid mycelre gestæþþignesse, 47, 14 : 67, 15. Mid gestæþignesse and nó mid higeleáste, 68, 2. v. un-gestæþþigness.

**ge-stál** *an obstacle.* *Substitute*: ge-stǽl, es ; *n.* I. *a charge, an accusation*:—In þám dæge (*doomsday*) ús byð æteówed ... se rēða wealdend and se rihta dōm, úre fyrena edwit and þǽra feónda gestǽl, Wlfst. 186, 17. Gestálum *objectionibus* (for meaning of *objectio* cf. ea quae *tibi obiciuntur* ab his *what these witness against thee*, Mk. 14, 60), Wrt. Voc. ii. 115, 30 : 63, 27. II. *recrimination* (?):—Pascasius on þám geflite þe geworden wæs weaxendum þám gestǽle geleáffula wera ymb Simmachim and Laurentium geceás Laurentium *Paschasius in ea contentione quae inardescente zelo fidelium inter Symmachum atque Laurentium facta est Laurentium elegit*, Gr. D. 329, 15. v. ge-stǽlan.

**ge-stala.** *For* 'A thief' *substitute* : *One who thieves with another, an accomplice in theft.*

**ge-stalian** *to steal.* *Add*:—Þæs ylcan his fæder eágum hē gestalode þá tíd *ejusdem patris sui oculis furabatur horas*, Gr. D. 98, 28. **ge-stǽlian** (*from* ge-staþelian) *to found*:—Munucregol ... þe Eádgár kyning hēt þone biscop gestǽlian (-staþelian, *v.l.*), Chr. 975 ; P.

121, 32.   ¶ Gestaþelode *is given as a variant of* gestalode *furabatur,* Gr. D. 98, 28.

**ge-standan.** *Add:* **A. intrans.**  **I.** of attitude, *to stand, hold oneself erect:*—Âlêdon hié þær limwêrigne, gestódon him æt his líces heáfdum, Kr. 63. Ðá ðe ne magon uncwaciende gestondan on emnum felda, Past. 41, 7. Ðá ðe beóð mid hira ágnum byrðennum ofðrycte ðæt hié ne magon gestondan, 51, 24. Ne mihte hê on fótum leng fæste gestandan, By. 171.  **I a.** where something is to be done by the person while standing :—Gestód se Hǽlend and cliopade, Jn. L. 7, 37. Petrus gestód and uærmde hine, 18, 25.  **II.** of situation or position, *to be placed, be* (cf. use of forms from Lat. *stare* in Romance languages).  (1) of living creatures :—Middum iówre gistód ðone gê iów ne cunnun, Jn. R. L. 1, 26 : 35. Gestód Judas mið ðǽm, 18, 5. Ðe ðreátt ðe gistód ofer sǽ, 6, 22. Maria gestód æt ðǽm byrgenne uoepende, mið ðý gewǽp gebêg hiá seolfe, Jn. L. 20, 11. Móder his and bróðero gestódon úta, Mt. L. 12, 46. Gestódon alle mêgas his farra, Lk. L. R. 23, 49. Þonne gê beforan kyningum gestondan, Bl. H. 171, 17. Mannes swaðu þon gelícost þe þær sum mon gestóde, 203, 36. Ân treów þ mæge .xxx. swína under gestandan, Ll. Th. i. 130, 3.  (1 a) *to stand after moving, station oneself, take one's stand :*—Arn hê sóna on þ hús, and ðá gestód ongeán þæm lêge, Bl. H. 221, 11. Gestáh hê steápe dúne þæt hê on hrófe gestód heán landes, Gen. 2898 : 2575.  (1 a a) of a thing personified :—Ic wilnige ðætte ðeós sprǽc stigge . . . suǽ suǽ on sume hlǽdre . . . oð ðæt hió fæstlíce gestonde on ðǽm solore ðæs módes, Past. 23, 18.  (2) of things. (a) material, *to be stationed,* after movement, *become stationary :*—Stearra mið ðý cuóm gestód ofer, Mt. L. 2, 9.  (b) non-material, *to have place :*—Æfter þære menigeo mínra sára þe mê ær on ferðe fæste gestódan *secundum multitudinem dolorum meorum in corde meo,* Ps. Th. 93, 18.  **III.** of condition, *to be so and so.*  (1) with complementary noun as in *to stand* a friend to a person :—Drihten him fultum gestandeð and him scyldend byð *Dominus adjutor eorum et protector eorum est,* Ps. Th. 113, 20. Hê him fultum gestód, 19. Ealle þe ehtend him ær gestódan *omnes qui eos ceperunt,* 105, 35.  (2) with complementary adj. (ptcpl.) :—Þú hire on hæle hold gestóde, Ps. Ben. 34, 3. Gestód þ folc básnende, Lk. L. 23, 35.  (3) with phrase or oblique case of noun :—Þú mê on fultum fæste gestóde *fuisti adjutor meus,* Ps. Th. 62, 6. Gestód Rômeburg xii winter mid miclum welum *Rome was very prosperous for twelve years,* Ors. 6, 1 ; S. 254, 6. Þá him wyrrest on feóndscipe gestódon *qui oderunt eos,* 105, 30. Ðonne gê gestondan on êhtnessum, Bl. H. 171, 17. Nú seó heora iugoð and seó midfyrhtnes bútan ǽgwylcum leahtre gestanden (*exstitit*), 163, 4. Nalæs þ ân þ heó þǽm andweardum lífes bysene gestóde (*uitae exemplo extitit*), Bd. 4, 23 ; Sch. 472, 13.  **IV.** to be fixed as a law regulation, &c. :—Swá hit on ælddagum gestód, C. D. iii. 272, 33.  **V.** *to remain undisturbed :*—Lêton hí hine âne hwíle âbídan and gestandan *sistere illum paullisper fecerunt,* Guth. Gr. 129, 153.  **VI.** *to cease to move, stop, stand still :*—Se Hǽlend gehýrde þone blindan cleopian, and hê sóna gestód, Bl. H. 19, 18.  **VII.** *to remain stationary :*—Þ þæt hnesce wæter hæbbe flór on þære fæstan eorðan, for þám þe hit ne mæg on him selfum gestandan, Bt. 33, 4 ; F. 130, 5.  **VIII.** *to last, not come to an end :*—Se líchama gestandeþ and þurhwunað in þám ungeænedlican wíte *caro semper subsistit,* Gr. D. 264, 6. Babylonia gestód tuwa seofon hund wintra on hiere onwealde, Ors. 6, 1 ; S. 252, 6.  **IX.** *not to fall, be upheld :*—Tó ðǽm ðæt hí sién ârǽrde and gestonden on ryhtum weorce, Past. 443, 35. Hú mæg gestonde ríc his?, Mt. L. 12, 26 : Mk. L. R. 3, 26.  **X.** *to curdle, congeal* (cf. *Ger.* ge-stehen *to curdle*) :—Hrêr swíðe tó þ gestanden sié, Lch. ii. 94, 9 : 21.  **B. trans.**  **I.** *to cause to stand, place, bring :*—Gif hê þurh myngunge gerihtlǽcan nele, sý hê on þæs bisceopes gewitnesse gestanden (hit stande on ðæs bisceopes dôme, *v. l.* *episcopus adhibeatur in testimonium*), R. Ben. 113, 15.  **II.** *to attend* a service :—Gestande hê him mæssan þæra þreóra daga ǽlcne, Ll. Th. i. 210, 29 : 334. 34 : Wlfst. 103, 3. His mæssan gestandan and gehýran, 302, 22 : Hml. A. 141, 73. Hyra mæssan gestandan *missae suae adesse,* Ll. Th. ii. 190, 14. Hê ne mihte his tídsangas gestandan mid his gebróðrum, Hml. Th. ii. 160, 20.  **III.** *to attack, assail, seize.*  (1) of living creatures :—Ðá ná gestód hê ná ǽlcne onsundran, ac heora ǽlces sweordfætelsas hê hêt forceorfan and hí mid bendum hêt gewríðan, and cwæþ tó heom eallum : '. . . oð þæt ic eft eów gestænde, and ic ðonne wið eów stíðlícor áginne, Hml. S. 23, 177–183. Gestódon hine hundas hetelíce, 12, 52.  (1 a) *to attack* with words, *to reprove, blame :*—Gif þú ne gestenst þone unrihtwísan and hine ne manast (*si non annunciaveris impio, neque locutus fueris,* Ezechiel 3, 18), Hml. Th. i. 6, 24. Þonne se lároéw gestent sumne unrihtwísne, and hine manað tó rihtwísnysse, ii. 374, 13. Þá gestódon his frýnd his fæder and cwǽdon : 'Tó plihte þínes heáfdes bodað þes þín cnapa,' Hml. S. 35, 31.  (2) of rough weather :—Þæt treów . . . þonne semninga storm gestænded and se stranga wind, Wlfst. 262, 7.  (3) of disease :—Sê þe hine ádl gestandeð, Lch. iii. 182, 5 *and often.* Micel manncwealm becóm . . . and ǽrest ðone pápan gestód, Hml. Th. ii. 122, 17. Gestanden mid hefigre untrumnesse *percussa febribus,* Bd. 4, 23 ; Sch. 474, 15. Gehrinen and

gestanden mid untrymnesse *tactus infirmitate,* 5, 13 ; Sch. 636, 5. Âdle gestonden (forgripen, *v. l.*) *langore correptus,* 5, 7 ; Sch. 584, 3 : 3, 19 ; Sch. 283, 12. Heó wearð gestanden on þá breóst mid cancre *cancri ulcere in mamilla percussa est,* Gr. D. 279, 26.  (4) of that which affects the mind (temptation, astonishment, &c.) :—Hine þær gelæhte syllic wundrung, and on þære gesihðe hine gestód wundorlic wafung, Hml. S. 23, 502.

**ge-stapan.** *Dele, and see* ge-stæppan.

**ge-staþelfæstan.** *Add:* -fæstian.  **I.** of a material object, *to fix firmly :*—Neówe plant gestaðolfæstode (gesteaðulfestad, Ps. Srt.) *novella stabilita,* Ps. Vos. 143, 12.  **II.** of a person. (1) *to fix in a position to be occupied :*—Munuc gestaþolfæstan mæg abbod on máran þænne in eóde stede-*monachum stabilire potest abbas in maiori quam ingreditur loco,* R. Ben. I. 103, 2.  (2) *to fix* in condition so that there is no falling away :—God þá nigon engla werod gestaþelfæste swá þæt hí nǽfre ne mihton fram his willan gebúgan, Hml. Th. i. 6, 8. Drihten gestaþolfæstige þê on his willan tó eallum gódum weorcum, Angl. xii. 516, 5.  **III.** of non-material objects, *to make effectual :*—Geðaeht ðæt hié ne maehtun gesteaðulfestian (-staþolfæston, Spl.) *consilia quae non potuerunt stabilire,* Ps. Srt. 20, 12.

**ge-staþelian.** *Add:*—Gestaþelaþ *fundat, edificat, construat, consolidat,* gestaþelad *fundatum, consolidatum,* Wrt. Voc. ii. 152, 14, 17.  **I.** *to fix in a position or place, place permanently, set.* (1) the object a living creature :—Ðæt hê gesteaðelie (*collocet*) hine mid aldermonnum, Ps. Srt. 112, 8. Hê gesæt Godfæder on þá swíþran healfe . . . hê symle þær gestaþelod wæs, Bl. H. 91, 6.  **I a.** of residence, *to settle, lodge :*—Hwelpas leóna . . . in bedcleofum heara hié gesteaðeliað (*se conlocabunt*), Ps. Srt. 103, 22. Benedictus gestaþolode (gelógode, *v. l.*) hine sylfne (*se collocavit*) in þǽm uferan dælum þæs torres and Servandus gestaþelode (gereste, *v. l.*) hine (*se collocavit*) in þám neoðeran dælum, Gr. D. 170, 16–20. Getimbrede hê þær mynster and munecas þær gestaðolade (*collocavit*), Bd. 4, 4 ; Sch. 368, 20. Hê þær þá Engliscean men gesette and gestaþelade *Anglos ibidem locavit,* Sch. 370, 14.  **I a a.** figurative :—Gesteaðelode (*collocavit*) mê in dégulmessum *he hath made me to dwell in darkness* (A. V.), Ps. Srt. 142, 3.  (2) *to fix* residence :—Sê ðe gestaðelað his den *qui collocat cubile suum (in petra),* Kent. Gl. 1106.  (3) the object a non-material thing :—Þá ingehýd heora heortan fæstlíce on þone heofonlican hyht gestaþelodon, Bl. H. 135, 30. Ic gesette míne hyht on þec þæt hió fæstlíce stonde gestaðeled, Hy. 4, 38. Þæt sí þín nama in úrum ferhðlocan feste gestaðelod, 6, 5. Hió tó Gode hæfde freóndrædenne fæste gestaðelad, Jul. 107.  **II.** *to build :*—Beóð him of þám wyrtum wíc gestaðelad in wuldres byrig, Ph. 474. Paules mynster forbarn and þý ilcan geáre wearð eft gestaþelad, Chr. 962 ; P. 114, 7.  **III.** *to found* a town, institution, &c. :—Heó gestaðelode ðæt fæmna mynster þ is nemned on Bercingum, Shrn. 138, 1. Ðis is seó freólsbóc tó ðan mynstre . . . swá swá hit Wulfríc gestaðelode for hine and for his yldrena sáwle, C. D. vi. 149, 37. For mínra yldrena sáwlan ðe ðone bisceopstól gestaþeloden (*statuerunt*), iv. 197, 14. Næfre syðþan heó (*London*) gestaþeled (-stabeled, MS.) wæs, Chr. 1077 ; P. 213, 11.  **III a.** of a condition :—Æfter þám líge líf bið gestaðelad, Dóm. 118.  **IV.** of the operations of the Deity :—Ðú gestaþoladest eorþan . . . þ heó ne helt on náne healfe, Bt. 33, 4 ; F. 130, 35. Drihten snytro gisette earðe, gistaðelade (*stabilivit*) heofnas, Rt. 81, 22 : Kent. Gl. 44.  **V.** *to make firm, establish, regulate :*—Hê mynster getimbrede, and hit mid ǽfæstum þeáwum gesette and gestaþolode *fecit monasterium, et religiosis moribus instituit,* Bd. 3, 23 ; Sch. 302, 22.  **VI.** *to establish* a practice, procedure, &c., *settle* a plan, course of action :—Ic þinne síþfæt gestaðelode and getrymede, Bl. H. 231, 28. Drihten eallum geleáfullum monnum heora gong gestaþelade tó lífes wege, 17, 19. Ic oncneów of cýðnissum ðínum, forðon in êcnisse ðú gesteaðulades (*fundasti*) ðá, Ps. Srt. 118, 152.  **VII.** *to make firm.* (1) in a physical sense, *to cause not to be relaxed :*—Þá sóna wæron gestaðelode and gehælde ealle þá leomu and þá seonu in hire líchaman *omnes in ejus corpore nervi ac membra solidata sunt,* Gr. D. 228, 26.  (2) *to make steadfast or stable :*—Gif heora móder wǽre swá riht and swá gestaðelod and swá geendebyrd swá swá þá óþre gesceafta sindon, Bt. 21 ; F. 76, 1. Sín gestaðelade *stabilientur* (*viae tuae*), Kent. Gl. 80 : Ps. Th. 138, 20. (3) *to make effectual, carry into effect :*—Geþeahta þá þe hí ne mihton gestaðelian (*stabilire*), Ps. L. 20, 12.  **VIII.** *to strengthen* a town with troops, *garrison :*—Fór Eádweard cyning tó Mældúne and getimbrede þá burg and gestaðelode ær hê þonon fóre (*King Edward went as far as Maldon, and rebuilt the town, placing a guard of soldiers in it before he left it,* Flor. Worc.), Chr. 920 ; P. 100, 16.  **IX.** *to restore* what has fallen (lit. or fig.) or been lost :—Swá hwæt swá ðú on sǽ forlure, ic ðe þ on lande gestaðelige *whatever you have lost at sea, that I will make good to you on land,* Ap. Th. 19, 14. Gyf hê þe gehýrð, þú gestaðelast friónda bróðor, Mt. 18, 15.

**ge-staþeliend,** es ; *m.* One who establishes :—Andig gestaþeliend (níwiend) *zelotypus (sanctimoniae) informator,* i. *plasmator,* An. Ox. 365.

**ge-staþolfæstnian.** Add: I. to establish, secure from disturbance :—Ðe ilca ðerhgiendiga and gitrymma and gistaðolfæstniga ðæm wuldor and onwæld ipse perficiet et confirmabit solidabitque ipsi gloriam et imperium, Rtl. 22, 5. II. to make effectual, carry into effect :—Geþeahta þa þe hí ne mihton gestaþolfæstnian consilia quae non potuerunt stabilire, Ps. L. 20, 12.

**ge-staþolung.** Add: placing, ordering :—Gestaþelung collocatio, Wrt. Voc. ii. 134, 32. Ælc endebyrdnes on mynstre sceal beón gehealden . . . be þæs abbodes gestaþelunge (ut abbas constituerit), R. Ben. 113, 23.

**ge-steal.** Add: [þan tóþa þa tunga tó spæce gesteal ys the tongue with the teeth is the apparatus for speech (?), Lch. iii. 102, 27.]

**ge-stealla.** Place before ge-stealla, and add: v. æht-, feoh-, fiet-, in-, mádum-, þrýþ-, wil-, wuldor-gesteald.

**ge-stealla.** Add: [O. H. Ger. [nót-]gestalla.]

**ge-stédhors.** l. Bd. 2, 13, and add: (gestédd-, stód-hors, v. ll.)

**ge-stedigian;** p. od To bring to a standstill :—Férde se hálga wer . . . þa gehýrde hé feorran færlíce hreám wépendre meniu, and hé weard þá gestedegod befrínende georne hwæt þ færlíces wære, Hml. S. 31, 242.

**ge-stefnan.** Add: to reciprocate, alternate :—Gistaebnendrae, gestaefnendre reciprocato, Txts. 92, 864. v. stefnan.

**ge-stefnan** (-ian) to provide with a border or fringe :—Mid godewebbum gestefnede sericis clauatg, An. Ox. 5323. Gestefnode, 7, 374 : 8, 376. v. stefnan (-ian).

**ge-stefnian** to summon, call on a person to act :—Hié gestefniað him betweónum wið ðæm unclænum gástum they (the angels) call on one another to fight against the unclean spirits, Verc. Först. 125, 7.

**ge-stellan.** v. ge-stillan.

**ge-stenc.** For gistencs l. gistences, and add :—In gestenc in odore, Rtl. 12, 15.

**ge-stence.** Add :—Heó hafað trumne wyrtruman and swýþe gestencne (-stæncne, v. l.), Lch. i. 284, 19.

**ge-steóran.** v. ge-stíran: **ge-stépan.** l. -stípan (v. stípan), and add after Ohtheres in l. 5 wigum and wæpnum: **ge-stéped.** v. stépan in Dict.: **ge-steppan.** v. ge-stæppan: **ge-stice.** v. stice; II. in Dict.

**ge-stician, -sticcian.** l. -sticcan, and add :—Sume hig wæron myd sperum gesticode, Hml. A. 186, 164.

**ge-stígan.** Add: A. intrans. I. to move upwards, ascend, come or go up. (1) in a physical sense :—Ðene fisc sé ðe ærist gestíge (ascenderit), Mt. L. 17, 27. (1 a) of motion on the ground :—Gestág in mór ascendit in montem, Mk. L. 5, 1. (1 b) of motion on to an object rising from the ground :—Gestáh hé on gealgan heáhne, Kr. 40. (1 c) to go on to a ship :—Ic on ceól gestáh, An. 901. Gestág in scipp ascendens in nauiculam, Mt. L. 9, 1. Hé (Noah) under bord gestáh, Gen. 1369. (2) in a moral sense, to rise to higher things :—Him is micle iédre tó gestíeganne (-stíg-, v. l.) on ðone ryhtan wísdóm, Past. 203, 17. II. to descend. (1) of motion on earth :—Oðer before mec gestíged (descendit), Jn. L. 5, 7. Críst áðúne gestág in ðæm gedolfene byrgenne, Jn. p. 2, 1. Of gestág of mór discendisset de monte, Mt. L. 8, 1. (2) of motion from heaven to earth :—Ic sylf gestág in mōdor, Cri. 1419. B. trans. I. to mount, ascend. (1) in a physical sense, (a) of motion on the ground :—Hé biorg gestáh, Gú. 146. (b) of motion on to an object rising from the ground :—Sum mæg heáhne beám gestígan, Cri. 679. (bb) to mount a throne, couch, &c. :—Heó hyre cynesetl gestíhð, Angl. viii. 324, 15. Sarrah beddrecte gestáh, Gen. 2715. Reste gestígan, 2228. (c) to go on board :—Hé bát gestág, Gú. 1302. Scealtú ceól gestígan, An. 222. (2) of spirits, to mount to a position in heaven, rise to heaven :—Him þa sóðfæstan on þá swiðran hond mid rodera weard reste gestígað, Sat. 612. Hé þá éican gefeán and þá heofonlícan eádignesse gestáhg (-stáh, v. l.) and gesóhte aeterna gaudia petiuit, Bd. 4. 3; Sch. 359, 16. Dryhten wile úp heonan eard gestígan, Cri. 514: 630. Cwicra gehwylc . . . þara þe wile heofona heáhðu gestígan, Dóm. 97. Úpcund ríce gestígan, Sch. 35. II. to descend to, reach by descending :—Ne se steorra (Ursa) gestígan wile westdæl wolcna ; ealle stiorran sígað æfter sunnan under eorþan grund, hé ána stent Ursa nunquam occiduo lata profundo, cetera cernens sidera mergi, cupit oceano tingere flammas, Met. 29, 12. III. to reach, attain a lofty position :—Nænig þæs swíðe in þeóde þrym þisses lífes forð gestíged none amongst men attains such a pitch of earthly glory, Crä. 20.

**ge-stígness.** v. of-gestígness.

**ge-stihtian, -stihtan.** Add: I. to decide, determine :—Gestihtigan decernere, Wrt. Voc. ii. 27, 70. Ne cwæð hé hit ná gestihtiende ac þýwende (non decernendo, sed minando), Gr. D. 151, 7. II. to dispose, arrange. (1) to arrange people :—Hé gestihte his werod swá hit gewunelic wæs, Hml. S. 30, 26. (2) to arrange a matter. (a) with noun or pronoun :—Hit geweard swá hit God gestihtade þ . . . , Ors. 6, 21 ; S. 272, 20. Cýðnisse gestihtadun testamentum disposuerunt, Ps. Srt. 82, 6. Se abbud eal gestyhtige and gesette þæt him gemæne bið, R. Ben. 15, 18. (a a) to arrange for or with a person :—Ic gestihtade cýðnisse gecorenum mínum, Ps. Srt. 88, 4. Ðú gestihtades him yfel, 72, 18 : 83, 7. Ðæt

(testamentum) gestihtade tó Abraham, 104, 9. (b) with infin., to arrange to do :—On ancerlífes drohtnunge hé gestihtode his líf geendian in anchoretica conuersatione uitam finire disposuit, Bd. 3, 19 ; Sch. 283, 1.

**ge-stihtung.** Add :—Ðæt wille ic gecýþan, þæt þá rícu of nánes monnes mihtum swá gecræftgode ne wurdon, ne for nánre wyrde, buton from Godes gestihtunge ut omnia haec Dei judiciis disposita, non autem humanis uiribus, aut incertis casibus accidisse perdoceam, Ors. 2, 1 ; S. 60, 24 : 62, 11. Seó leó heóld þæt cild ungederod æfter Godes gestihtunge, Hml. S. 30, 183. Cunnan hwylce wæren Godes gestihtunge (þá þing þe syndon Godes gestihtungo, v. l.) nosse quae Dei sunt, Gr. D. 137, 8.

**ge-stillan, -stellan, -styllan;** p. ed. Take here ge-styllan in Dict., and add: To reach by leaping (v. stellan to leap), to assail, attack (of disease) :—Hé wæs gestelled (correptus) mid feferádle, Gr. D. 276, 13. Gestelled and gedreád, 286, 16 : 288, 8. Gestelled (percussus) mid mettrumnesse, 284, 1. Drepen and gestelled, 298, 27 : 300, 6. Gestilled (-stelled, v. l.), 289, 12.

**ge-stillan.** Add: A. intrans. To be or become still, cease from :—Ic gestille vel áblinne cessam, desistam, cessavero, Wrt. Voc. ii. 131, 4. I. of persons or things. (1) not to be moving :—Eorðe cwæcede and gestilde (quievit), Ps. Srt. Vos. 75, 9. Hí náuþer ne gestillan ne móton ne eác swiþor styrian, Bt. 21 ; F. 74, 7. (2) not to be active :—Swá styrigende is seó sáwul þ heó furðon on slæpe ne gestylþ, Hml. S. 1, 132. II. with respect to sound, to be silent, not to sound :—Ne gestilde næfre stefen cearciendes wænes, Lch. iii. 430, 33. III. of violent action, pain, passion, &c., to stop, subside, be allayed, be restrained :—Syððan gestilde se flód and gecyrde fram þám cyriclande se a terris ecclesiae fluminis aqua compescuit, Gr. D. 194, 3 : An. 532. Eall hellwara wítu gestildon þá hwíle ðe hé hearpode, Bt. 35, 6 ; F. 170, 4. B. trans. I. to cause to be still, stop :—Gestillende conpescens, Wrt. Voc. ii. 14, 47. (1) to prevent motion :—Ðára unstillena gesceafta styring ne mæg nó weorþan gestilled, Bt. 21 ; F. 74, 4. (2) to stop action :—Hé ðá ealdan onsægednyssa ealle gestilde, Hml. Th. ii. 210, 15. Hí woldon þá wíta gestillan, Hml. S. 5, 39. Þæt gewinn weard sume hwíle gestilled, Ors. 3, 5 ; S. 106, 5. (3) to stop an agent, restrain from doing something. (a) with acc. :—Menn woldon sceáwian . . . ac God hí gestilde, Hml. S. 32, 243. For þí . . . þæt hé ús fram middangeardes lufe gestilde, Hml. Th. i. 608, 11. Hé næfre byþ gestilled fram unrihtwísra wrace ab iniquorum ultione non sedatur, Gr. D. 335, 15. Þú ne beó gestild ne compescaris, Ps. L. 82, 2. Gestilled, Sal. 117. Ne magon þá unstillan woruldgesceafta weorþan gestilde, Met. 11, 19. (b) with dat. :—Godes engel gestillde ðæm horsum, Shrn. 72, 3. II. in reference to sound. (1) to prevent a sound :—Hí willað gestillan his stemne, Hml. Th. i. 156, 17. (2) to silence a person :—Þæt folc hine wolde gestyllan. Hé hrýmde ðæs ðe swíðor, Hml. Th. i. 156, 19. III. to allay, mitigate :—Gestilde mitigaret, Wrt. Voc. ii. 58, 51. (1) to assuage, abate heat :—Gestilde sedans (torrida cum gelidis sedans incendia flabris, Ald. 146, 36), Wrt. Voc. ii. 90, 32. (2) to allay anger, passion, &c. :—Gestildes eorre ðín mitigasti iram tuam, Ps. Srt. 84, 4. Hiora gítsunge gestillan, Past. 341, 17. Æghwylc mennisc leahter on his cennendum gestilled wæs, Bl. H. 163, 16. (3) to calm excited persons :—Se eorl sylf earfoðlíce gestylde þ folc, Chr. 1052 ; P. 180, 10. [O. Sax. gi-stillian to still: a tempest : O. H. Ger. ge-stillen sedare, compescere, mitigare.]

**gestinc.** v. gisting.

**ge-stincan.** Add :—Wé oft gestincað mid úrum nosum ðæt wé mid úrum eágum gesión ne magon rem, quam oculis non cernimus, plerumque odore praevidemus, Past. 433, 20. Hí tugon heom tó and gestuncon þá swétnesse þæs wundorlícan stences suauitate mirifici odoris trahebant, Gr. D. 236, 25. Swylce wé . . . gestincen (odoramus) þá æppla . . . þéh hé hí ne cúðe gestincan (odorare), 256, 18. Heó cwæð þ heó næfre ær náht swilces ne gestunce, S. 4, 349. [O. H. Ger. ge-stinchan to perceive by smell.]

**ge-stingan;** pp. -stungen To stab, pierce by thrusting :—Hé wæs mid spere on hys sýdan gestungen, Ll. Th. ii. 416, 31. Ahsa hwæþer hé æfre wære slegen on þá sídan oððe gestungen, Lch. ii. 258, 24.

**ge-stíran.** Take here ge-steóran, -stíóran, -stiéran, -stýran in Dict., and add: I. to guide, direct (1) a person :—Meaht þú Adame gestýran . . . and hé þínum wordum getrýwð, Gen. 568. Hígo ðín rúmlíce bihalda . . . þte beodum sié gistéored familiam tuam propitius intuere . . . ut precibus gubernetur, Rtl. 59, 27. (2) an action :—Dédo úsra gerihta and gestióra ðú actus nostros dirigas et gubernas, Rtl. 174. 35. II. to restrain (1) a person (dat.) from action (gen. or clause) by (mid. or inst.) certain means. (a) with dat. of person only :—Forstond þú mec and gestýr him (devils), Hy. 4, 58. (b) with dat. of person and means used :—Gif him Scipia ne gestírde . . . mid þém þ hé his sweord gebræd, Ors. 4, 9 ; S. 190, 21. Mid þém him wæs swíþost gestiéred þæt him mon gehét fulwiht, 6, 33 ; S. 288, 24. Ðém scamleásan ne wyrð nó gestiéred bútan micelre tælinge impudentes impudentiae vitio non nisi increpatio dura compesci, Past. 205, 22. (c) with gen. of action and means :—Ðætte hié mid hiora onwalde gestiéren

(-stīran, *v. l.*) ðāra scylda, Past. 116, 14. Hié monegra unðeáwa gestiéran (-stīran, *v. l.*) meahton mid hiora lārum, 44, 23. (d) with dat. of person, and (α) gen. of action :—Gyf heó hym hyra reáflāces ne gestȳrað *si non eos a rapacitaie cohibeant*, Ll. Lbmn. 475, 32. Ne wolde þæt wuldres dēma geþafian, ac hē him þæs þinges gestȳrde, Jud. 60. Þǣm Gotan þæs gewinnes gestiéran, Ors. 6, 37; S. 296, 11. Hē him his unðeáwa ðonces gestiéran (-stīran, *v. l.*) ne meahte, Past. 35, 19. Gestīran ðǣre wilnunge ðǣm unmedemum, 40, 4. Gesteóran, Bt. 16, 4; F. 58, 15: Ll. Th. i. 220, 20. Gif þū þām sinfullan nelt synna gestȳran and unriht forbeódan, Wlfst. 177, 5. Swā wyrð gestiéred ðǣm gītsere ðæs reáflāces *occasio rapiendi subtrahitur*, Past. 341, 11. (β) with clause :—Burgendum hē gestiérde þ̄ hié on Gallie ne wunnon, Ors. 6, 33; S. 288, 23. Þ̄ ðā wītu gestīrden oþrum þ̄ hí swā dōn ne dorsten, Bt. 39, 11; F. 230, 7. (e) with dat. of person, gen. of action, and means :—Mid ðȳ gestiérde ðǣm wītgan his dyslicre wilnunge *prohibuit prophetae insipientiam*, Past. 257, 12. Þætte him his feónd mæge swā eáþe gewinnes mid wordum gestiéran, Ors. 3, 1; S. 94, 32. (2) a thing in its operation. (a) with dat. :—Gif gītsunga ne bið gestiéred, hió wile weahsan mid ungemete *avaritia, si in parvis non compescitur, sine mensura dilatatur*, Past. 71, 16. Þā monegan (yfelu) þe hié wēndou þæt hié mid hiera deófolgildum gestiéred hæfden, Ors. 5, 2; S. 218, 4. (b) with acc. :—Unwoeder sǣs mid word gestiórde *tempestatem maris uerbo compescit*, Lk. p. 5, 19. Þurh ūs scylen bión hiora scylda gestiéred mid cræfte, Past. 117, 20. (3) *to keep* from a state or condition, *remove* from :—Nis hit him nó swā longe ālēfed swā þē ðyncð, ac ðū miht ongitan þ̄ him biþ swīþe hrædlīce gestióred (-stȳred, *v. l.*) hiora orsorgnesse *si id ipsum quod eis licere creditur auferatur*, Bt. 38, 2; F. 196, 23. **III.** *to reprove, rebuke* :—Gistiórende (-ande, L.) wæs ðǣm gāste *comminatus est spiritui*, Mk. R. 9, 25. Sȳ him āne gestȳred and eft and þriddan sīðe *correptus semel et iterum atque tertio*, R. Ben. 46, 18. Sȳ him gestȳred *corripiatur*, 130, 20. Gif hwylcum brēþer for ǣnigum gylte byþ gecíd oþþe gestȳred (*corripitur*), 131, 2. [O. H. Ger. ge-stiuren *sublevare, sustentare*.]

**ge-stīþian.** *Add :* To make firm, stiffen :—Wē hiera mōdes meruwenesse gestīðigen mid ðǣm ðæt hié gehiéren ðæt wē hié herigen *eorum teneritudinem laus audita nutriat*, Past. 210, 18.

**gest-lið.** *l.* -līþe, *and see* gist-līþe: **ge-stoten.** *v.* ge-sceótan; **I.** 3: **gestran.** *v.* gistran.

**ge-strangian.** *Add:* **A.** *trans.* **I.** *to strengthen* a person. (1) in respect to bodily health :—Wundorlīce þeós wyrt gestrangað, Lch. i. 134, 5. Hȳ (*certain herbs*) tō mete geþigede mycelon ðone līchaman gestrangiað, 320, 20. Gif hē on fefore sȳ, syle drincan on wearmum wætere; mycelon hē byþ gebēt and gestrangod, 214, 12. Ðū bist gestrangod *foueris*, Kent. Gl. 114. (2) in respect of mental, spiritual, &c., condition :—Ealle þā þe mē ǣfre yfel cwǣdon gestranga tō þīnum willan, Angl. xii. 501, 6. Gestrangiað eówere heortan and eówer mōd *confortetur cor vestrum*, Ps. Th. 30, 28. God ūs gestrangige and getrymme tō ūre āgenre þearfe, Wlfst. 306, 13. Ðæt hié hera mōd mid gestæððignesse gestrongien *ut mentem gravitate roborent*, Past. 307, 20. Sié gestrongod heorte ðīn, Ps. Vos. 26, 14. (3) *to make powerful.* (a) of ability to resist attack :—Gestrangað þē God ongeán þīne fȳnd, Angl. xii. 517, 25. Þæt mægen þæra synfulra byð forbrocen, ac Drihten gestrangað (*confirmat*) þā rihtwīsan, Ps. Th. 36, 16. Þū gestrangod *roborabitur* (*homo ex impietate*), Kent. Gl. 393. Oþ þæt þū gestrangie heora mōd on mīnne geleáfan, Bl. H. 249, 9. Þā þeóda wǣron tō swīðe gestrongode, þ̄ hié mon leng ne mehte mid geseohtum oferswīþan, Ors. 6, 35; S. 292, 8. (b) of ability to act :—þū gestrangodes þīne handa ofer mē, Ps. Th. 37, 2. Hē þē and ūs gestrangige, and ūs gerecce þā weorc tō begangenne þe him līcige, Hml. S. 23 b, 75. Þā þe feódon mē gestrongade wǣron ofer mē, Ps. Vos. 17, 18. **II.** *to strengthen* a thing. (1) *to restore* health :—Begȳmed, gestranged *fotam*, i. *confortatam* (*medicamine ualetudinem*), An. Ox. 4353. (2) *to strengthen, fortify* a place :—Ðā hē gestrangade *quando vallabat* (*gyro abyssos*), Kent. Gl. 272. (3) *to make powerful in operation* :—Lǣcedōmas ðe sume ðāle gelytliað, and sume gestrongiað *medicamentum quod hunc morbum imminuit, alteri vires jungit*, Past. 173, 23. (4) *to establish, strengthen* purpose, faith, &c. :—Sint gestrangade *roborantur* (*cogitationes consiliis*), Kent. Gl. 747. **B.** *intrans. To become strong* :—þȳfð *gestrangað theft is committed with increasing frequency*, Lch. iii. 186, 22. Cf. gestrengan.

**ge-streágung.** *Substitute :* ge-strangung, e; *f. Strengthening, invigoration :*—Gestra[n]gunge *uegetatione*, i. *stabilitate* i *confortatione* (*membrorum*), An. Ox. 1445.

**ge-streáwian.** *v.* ge-strewian.

**ge-streccan.** *Substitute for passage :*—Bet him gestreht and wel ges[t]reht gesihð beorhtnysse getācnað *lectum sibi stratum et bene stratum uiderit, claritatem significat*.

**ge-stredd.** *See next word.*

**ge-stregdan, -strēdan;** *pp.* strogden *and* -stregd(ed), -strēd(ed) (v. stregdan). **I.** *to strew, scatter :*—Tuiggo hiá ge[s]trēdon

(strǣgdun, R.) i legdon on weg *ramos sternebant in via*, Mt. L. 21, 8. Þā gestrōdnan *vel* tōstencte *dispersae*, i. *distribute*, Wrt. Voc. ii. 140, 70. Reste mid wyrtgemengnessum gestrēded, Wlfst. 263, 6. **II.** in special senses. (1) *to strew* with seasoning, *to season :*—Mid sealte beón gestrēdd *sale esse conditum*, Scint. 97, 12. Gestrȳddre *condito*, An. Ox. 3754. (2) *to make a bed :*—Hē wolde þ̄ him wǣre þǣr gestrēd neáh þǣre byrgenne *stratum fieri sibi juxta sepulcrum voluit*, Gr. D. 257, 22.

**ge-strengan.** *Add :*—Gestrengid (-strenigd, MS.) *formata*, i. *facta*, An. Ox. 46, 8.

**ge-streón.** *Add:* **I.** as verbal abstract. (1) *getting* by effort, *gaining, acquiring* by dealing, *traffic, commerce :*—Gestrión *commercium*, Wrt. Voc. ii. 104, 41. Gestreón *negotium*, Hpt. Gl. 469, 5. Mangung, gestreón *mercimonium, commercium*, An. Ox. 4007. Seó gesomnung þāra deórwyrþra gimma oþþe þ̄ unmǣte gestreón goldes and seolfres, Bl. H. 99, 28. Of eorþlicum cȳpinga gestreóne *de terreno nundinarum mercati*, An. Ox. 2656. Mid mangunge, gestreóne *commercio*, 3064. Ne mage gē Gode ðeówian and eóweres feós gestreóne, Hml. Th. ii. 460, 31. (1 a) of getting by violence, *rapine, robbery :*—Wæs hē hogiende tō gestreóne (reáflāce, *v. l.*) manna ǣhta *in rapinam rerum inhians*, Gr. D. 162, 32. (2) *begetting* of children, *procreation, production :*—Genitiuus is gestrȳnendlic: mid þām casu byð geswutelod ǣlces ðinges gestreón, Ælfc. Gr. Z. 22, 13. Ðā ðe for bearnes gestreóne hǣmed begáð, Hml. Th. i. 148, 22: ii. 94, 3: 590, 23. For bearna gestreóne, Solil. H. 36, 8. **II.** of material or non-material objects, *what is got* by effort, *gain, profit, advantage, acquisition :*—Ðincþ þē þ̄ lytel gestreón . . . þætte þeós wiþerweardnes . . . þā mōd þē geopenaþ ðīnra getreówra freónda, Bt. 20; F. 72, 11. Manigra folca gestreónes hié wieóldon *labores populorum possederunt*, Past. 391, 4. Gestreó[ne] *questu*, An. Ox. 8, 69. Gestrión *lucrum*, Kent. Gl. 431. Þā unrihtwīsan dēman him of hira ceasterwarena forþrycnesse gestreón gaderiað, Ll. Lbmn. 475, 23. Hē sēcð ðisses middangeardes gestreón (*lucrum*) . . . Hē scolde his gestreón (*lucra*) tōweorpan, Past. 55, 9–11. Gestreón *emolumenta*, i. *lucra*, An. Ox. 557 : Wrt. Voc. ii. 32, 70. Gestreónu *lucra*, Scint. 76, 12. Hē wilniað ðisses middangeardes gestreóna, Past. 331, 21. Godes ðonces, nals nā for fraceðlecum gestreónum (*turpis lucri gratia*), 137, 21. Of unryhtum gestreónum and of mānðǣdum, 343, 4: Bl. H. 25, 6. Āgife hē Drihtne þone teóþan dǣl for his ðǣm eorþlicum gestreónum, 49, 30: 51, 8. Gestreónum *compendiis*, Wrt. Voc. ii. 15, 61. Oðer ondrēd ðæt hē forlure sprecende ðā gestrión ðe hē on ðǣre swīgan geðencan meahte *iste ne tacitae contemplationis lucra loquens perderet*, Past. 49, 20. **III.** *interest, usury, revenue :*—Of gestrióne *fenore*, Kent. Gl. 1046. Gestreón *reditus* (pl.), An. Ox. 4832. **IV.** *possession, property, wealth :*—Gestrión *patrimonium*, Wrt. Voc. ii. 115, 78. Ðā ðe hira āgen nyllað sellan . . . geðencen ðæt ðiós eorðe, ðe him ðæt gestreón of cōm . . . , Past. 335, 10. Monegum men genihtsumað þisse worlde gestreón æt his ende, Bl. H. 97, 25. Gestreónes, yrfes *patrimonii*, An. Ox. 3151. Welan, fæderes gestreónes, 3604. Þ̄ hē of his yldrena gestreóne hine sylfne fercian mōte, Hml. S. 23, 597. Hē æfter him tō eallum his gestreónum fēng *haereditatem ejus adsumsit*, Ors. 5, 13; S. 244, 23. **IV a.** of costly things, as collective, *treasures, wealth, treasure.* Cf. ge-streónfull: **I.** 2 :—Hē begeat Alexandriam, and mid hiere gestreóne hē gewelgade Rōmeburg *Alexandria potitus est, et Roma opibus ejus aucta est*, Ors. 5, 13; S. 246, 36. Earme synt þises middangeardes gestreón . . . Hwǣr synt þā welegan þisse weorolde? hwǣr is nū heora gold? Wālā þ̄ for swā medmiclum gestreóne hī synt lǣdde tō swā heardum tyntergum, Ll. Th. ii. 396, 25–31. Gold and godweb, Iōsephes gestreón, Exod. 587 : B. 2037. Gestrión (gistrión goldes, R.) *thesaurum*, Mk. L. 10, 21. Þāra gestreóna *gazarum*, Wrt. Voc. ii. 40, 42. Nǣnig man on worlde tō ðæs mycelne welan nafað, ne tō ðon mōdelico gestreón, Bl. H. 111, 24. Ædelinga gestreón, frætwe and fǣt gold, B. 1920: 3167. Gestrión, Met. 1, 23. Þās lǣnan gestreón, īdle ǣhtwelan, Ap. 83. Gestrióna *thesauros*, Mt. L. 6, 19. Gestreóno (-e, R.) *pecunias*, Mk. L. 10, 23. v. ǣht-, ǣr-, bearn-, bōc-, botl-, dryht-, eald-, eorl-, fæder-, feoh-, folc-, fyrn-, heáh-, hord-, horn-, lang-, māðm-, sinc-, þeód-, un-, unriht-, weorold-, wōhgestreón.

**ge-streónan.** *v.* ge-strínan: **ge-streónd.** *v.* ge-strínd: **ge-streónendlic.** *v.* ge-strínendlic.

**ge-streónfull.** *Substitute :* **I.** of things. (1) *profitable, advantageous.* v. ge-streón; **I.** :—Hī wilniaþ þā heafene þysse gestreónfullan wǣdle *exigunt sumptum lucrosae egestatis*, R. Ben. 136, 1. (2) *costly, precious.* Cf. ge-streón; **IV a.** :—Mid gestreónfullum bīleofena fōdan *sumptuosa pabulorum alimonia*, An. Ox. 1570. On gestreónfulre spēdinesse *sumptuosa opulentia*, 3603. Gestreónfulle gewistfullunga *sumptuosas opulentias*, 1930. **II.** of persons, *that has received much gain* (?), *highly favoured* (?) :—His (*our heavenly Father's*) þā leófan and þā gestreónfullan bearn, Bl. H. 131, 27.

**ge-strewian.** *Take here* ge-streáwian *in Dict., and add :*—Reste mid goldleáfum gestrewed, Wlfst. 263, 6. [Goth. ga-straujan: O. H. Ger. ge-streuuen *sternere*.]

**ge-stric.** For *m.*? l. *n.*, for the translation substitute *leonem infestare uiderit, inimici seditionem significat,* and add:—Wíf tôspræddum loccum hine gesihð gestric (spriicg, MS. v. Archiv cxxv. 61, 5) getácnað *mulierem sparsis crinibus se uiderit, seditionem significat,* Lch. iii. 208, 11.

**ge-strícan;** *pp.* -stricen. **I.** *to stroke, smooth with the hand :*— Pyles tácen is þæt þu mid þínum scytefingre sume feþer tácnum gestríce on þýne winstran hand innewearde and lege tô þínum eáron *the sign for a cushion is that with your forefinger you make as if you were smoothing a feather into the flat of your left hand and lay your hand to your ear,* Tech. ii. 126, 7. **II.** *to form with a stroke of a pen :*—Quincunx . . . beóð þus gehíwod. Triens . . . beóð þus mid feðere gestricene. Quadras . . . beóð þus ámearcod, Angl. viii. 334, 41–44.

**ge-strínan.** *Take here* ge-streónan, -strýnan *in Dict., and add :* -strínian; *pp.* od. **I.** *to acquire, get by effort :*—Ðá ðe willað sellan ðæt hí gestrínað (-striénað, *v. l.*) *qui sua tribuunt,* Past. 335, 3. Dúne þá þe beget í gestreónde (*adquisiuit*) his swýðre, Ps. L. 77, 54. Ðeáh hié hit hrædlíce ætsomne ne gestríendon (*quidquid eorum nequitia nec simul nec repente congregauit*), hié hit ðeáh swíðe hrædlíce ætsomne forluron, Past. 333, 18. Ðá ðe witan willað hwæt hié sellað, and nyllað wietan mid hwelcum woo hié hit gestriéndon *qui quanta largiuntur aspiciunt, sed quantum rapiunt non perpendunt,* 343, 23. Gestríon adquire (*prudentiam*), Kent. Gl. 63. Þ [man] þære flæscun geweorð on fisce gestriéne *let the worth of the meat be got in fish,* Cht. Th. 159, 1. Gestrîned *adquisita,* Wrt. Voc. ii. 2, 58. **I a.** *to get as advantage or profit, gain :*—Þu gestreónest bróðer ðîn *lucratus eris fratrem tuum,* Mt. R. 18, 15. Hê monncynnes mæst gestriénde (-strýnde, *v. l.*) rodra wearde, Past. 9, 11. Hê gestriónde (gestriónende wæs, L.) ôþre fêfe, Mt. R. 25, 16. Gestreónde, 17. Hwæt helpeð menn ðeáh þe hê middengeard ealne gestreóne (-stríona, L.) *quod prodest homini si mundum universum lucretur,* 16, 26. Gestriéne, Past. 331, 11. Wênþ þ hit hæbbe sum heálic gôd gestrýned *videntur quandam claritudinem comparare,* Bt. 24, 3; F. 82, 23. Þínum gewritum sáwle beóþ gestrínode (*lucrantur*), Hy. S. 73, 15. ¶ In Mt. L. 21, 41 the word glosses *locare* (which is confused with *lucrari?*). **II.** *to lay up treasure :*—Sê ðe gistríneð (-að, L.) *qui thesaurizat,* Lk. R. 12, 21. Gistriónde *thesaurizauit,* Rtl. 45, 33. Nællas gié gestriónaige (=? gestreóna í gestriónige) *nolite thesaurizare,* Mt. L. 6, 19. **III.** *to get children, beget :*—Cende í gestriónde *genuit,* Mt. L. 1, 2. Hê bearn gestrínde be his gebeddan, Ælfc. T. Grn. 3, 21. Gestriéne, Past. 43, 14. Gestríne, 42, 13. Gestrénen *procreare,* i. *generare,* An. Ox. 3387. Tô gestriénanne, Past. 399, 4. Ælcon men þe on þysan lífe byð gestreóned, Hml. S. 23, 597. Strong gestrýned, Seel. 45. Þeáh manige bearn beóþ gestrýned, Bt. 31, 1; F. 112, 9. [*O. H. Ger.* ge-striunen; *p. ita lucrari.*]

**ge-strínd,** e; *f.* **I.** *gain :*—Gestreónde *questu,* Wrt. Voc. ii. 76, 12. **II.** *progeny.* v. ge-streónan; **III** :—Sôð gistrýnd *progeniem,* Rtl. 29, 28. [*O. H. Ger.* ge-striunida *lucrum.*]

**ge-strínend,** es; *m. One who acquires* or *gains :*—Gestriónend ðú bist bróðeres ðínes *lucratus eris fratrem tuum,* Mt. L. 18, 15. Gestreónendra *adquisitorum,* An. Ox. 796.

**ge-strínendlic.** *Take here* ge-strýnendlic *in Dict., and add : to be begotten :*—Mid gestrênendlicere stofne *progenie propaganda,* An. Ox. 1665. Gestrýnendlicra yrfwerda *liberorum procreandorum,* i. *filiorum generandorum,* 1402.

**ge-strínian.** v. ge-strínan.

**ge-strod.** For the two separated forms substitute : **ge-strod,** es; *n.* **I.** *confiscation :*—Gestrod *proscriptionem* (cf. fordêminge, rýpincge æhta *proscriptionem,* i. *fraudationem rerum,* i. *possessionum,* An. Ox. 3149: in both cases Ald. 43, 19 is glossed), Wrt. Voc. ii. 81, 67. **II.** *robbery, rapine :*—Scottas ne sætincge ne gestrodu (-a, *v. l.*) wið Angeldeóde syrwaþ *Scotti nil contra gentem Anglorum insidiarum moliuntur aut fraudium,* Bd. 5, 23; Sch. 692, 11. In gestrodu nyllað gewillian *in rapinas nolite concupiscere,* Ps. Srt. Vos. 61, 11. Syndan cyrican bereáfode þurh hæðenra manna gestrodu, Verc. Först. 164, 12. **III.** *spoil, booty, ill-gotten gain. See passage in Dict. under* ge-strod *plunder.* v. unriht-gestrod; ge-strúdan, ge-strúd.

**ge-strúd,** es; *n. Robbery, rapine :*—Wæs hê onbærned mid þære hæte his gítsunge and higiende tô gestrúde (gestreóne, reáflâce, *v. ll.*) manna æhta *suae auaritiae aestu succensus, in rapinam rerum inhians,* Gr. D. 162, 32. v. ge-strúdan; ge-strod.

**ge-strúdan.** *Add :*—Gestreád *conroderet* (Attila adeo intolerabilis reipublicae remansit hostis, ut totam pene Europam excisis inuasisque ciuitatibus atque castellis *conroderet,* Bd. 1, 13), Txts. 180, 26. v. ungestroden; ge-strýdan.

**ge-strúdian;** *p.* ode *To commit rapine, prey on :*—Þá bióð þǽr on mǽstre nearonesse forþylmed þá þe hér hiora líchaman mid mæstum unrihtum byldað and þ on ôðrum mannum mid wô gestrúdiaþ, Nap. 32. *See next word.*

**ge-strýdan;** *p.* dè *To rob* something from a person (*dat.*) :—Gif man ôðrum men æht gestrýde *si quis alium bonis spoliauerit,* Ll. Th. ii. 238, 4. [*O. H. Ger.* ge-strúten *exterminare.*] *See preceding words.*

**ge-strýnan.** v. ge-strínan : **ge-strýnd.** v. ge-strínd.

**ge-strynge.** *Substitute :* ge-strynge (?), es; *m. A struggler, wrestler :*—Gestrynga, plegstôwa *palestrarum* (cf. palestrarum, luctantium, Ld. Gl. H. 41, 45), Wrt. Voc. ii. 66, 50.

**ge-stun.** *Substitute :* **I.** *a deafening noise, crash :*—þæt swînlice gestun *porcinus* (*paganorum*) *strepitus,* Wrt. Voc. ii. 85, 31. Gestunum *fragoribus* (*fratoribus,* MS.), 150, 41. **II.** *a storm, tempest, hurricane :*—þæt gestun and se storm and seó stronge lyft brecað bráde gesceaft *hurricane and storm and tempest break up the wide world,* Cri. 991. Dol swylteð, gif him Meotud þurh regn ufan of gestune lǽteð strǽle fleógan, Rä. 4, 56. þurh gestun *per turbinem,* Wrt. Voc. ii. 68, 73. *See next word.*

**ge-stund.** The Latin original is : Ita immensis vagitibus horrescere audiebantur, ut totam pene a coelo in terra intercapidinem clangisonis boatibus impleverunt.

**ge-styllan** *to spring.* v. ge-stillan.

**ge-styntan;** *p.* te *To make blunt, to check :*—Gestint *retundit,* i. *coercet,* Germ. 392, 94. *See next word.*

**ge-stynþo** [=ge-styntþo?]; *f. Coercion, repression* (?) :—þá hê oftost tesoword sprǽc in his onmêdlan gǽlpettunga, þá earnode hê mê þǽre mǽsta[n] gestynþo and þára mǽstan benda, Nap. 32. *See preceding word.*

**ge-stýran.** v. ge-stíran.

**ge-styrian.** *Dele second passage* (v. ge-stíran; **II.** 3), *and add :* **I.** *to disturb the stability of* a material object :—Se streám ne mæhte ðæt hûs gestyurige (*movere*), Lk. L. 6, 48. Mið ðý gestyred bið þ wæter *cum turbata fuerit aqua,* Jn. L. R. 5, 7. **II.** *to disturb the mind* of a person :—Gaast gestyrede í gedroefde (*conturbauit*) hine, Mk. L. 9, 20. Gestyred wæs (*commota est*) all ðíu ceaster, Mt. L. 21, 10. Mið miltheortnisse gestyred wæs (*motus est*), Lk. L. 15, 20. Gestyred wæs (*turbatus est*), and ondo gefeóll ofer hine, Lk. L. R. 1, 12. Wæs hê semninga mid unrôtnesse gestyred *subita arreptus moestitia,* Guth. Gr. 170, 4.

**ge-suirfed.** *Dele :* ge-sumgdon, Mt. L. 21, 8. v. ge-swingan.

**ge-sund.** *Add :* **I.** *sound, without flaw* or *defect.* (1) of persons, *in good health :*—Sum môder bær hire sámcuce cild . . hê cwæð þæt hire cild gesund beón sceolde, Hml. Th. ii. 150, 19. Hê eóde cucu and gesund intô his byrgene, i. 74, 25. Ne swelte ic mid sáre, ac ic gesund lifige, Ps. Th. 117, 17: Bl. H. 245, 14. Hê is git hál and gesund *viget incolumis,* Bt. 10; F. 28, 14: Wrt. Voc. i. 46, 5. Hê hine hálne and gesundne æteówde, Bl. H. 177, 27. Þær wê gesunde sǽl weardodon, B. 2075. (1 a) of spiritual health :—Wile fæder eahtan hû gesunde suna sáwle bringen, Cri. 1075. (2) of things :—Swá swá sió nafu bið gesund . . . Se wǽn biþ micle leng gesund þe lǽs biþ tôdǽled from þǽre eaxe, Bt. 39, 7; F. 222, 26–29. Hí eallne his líchaman gemêtton onwealhne and gesundne *inuenerunt corpus totum integrum,* Bd. 4, 30; Sch. 534, 18. Heora reáf wǽron ealle gesunde, Hml. S. 23, 438. **II.** *where injury is avoided, uninjured.* (1) of persons :—His gebedu ádwæscton þone líg, and hê belâf gesund, Hml. S. 29, 251: Jul. 584. Ne sý him bánes bryce . . . ac gê hine gesundne ásettað, Gú. 673. Gesun[de] úp ástandan synd rǽdde *sospites* (*e thermis*) *emersisse leguntur,* An. Ox. 4783. (2) of things. (a) material :—Seó studu gesund and ungehrinen from þám fýre ástôd *posta tuta ab ignibus et intacta remansit,* Bd. 3, 10; Sch. 234, 14. Gif sweordhwíta wǽpn tô feormunge onfô, oððe smið monnes andweorc, hit hǽl gesund begen ágifan swá hit hwæðer hiora ǽr onfênge, Ll. Th. i. 74, 10. (b) non-material :—þæt ic þín sôðfæst word gesund môte healdan, Ps. Th. 118, 20. Þú hæfst gesund gehealden eall þ deórwyrþoste þætte þú þe besorgast hæfde *si quod in omni fortunae tuae censu pretiosissimum possidebas, id tibi diuinitus illaesum atque inuiolatam seruatur,* Bt. 10; F. 28, 9. **III.** *where danger is escaped, safe.* (1) of persons :—þ hê hine gemundbyrde þá hwíle ðe hê þǽr wǽre, and hine gesundne eft þanon bróhte, Bt. 35, 6; F. 168, 22. Gehealde hine .xxx. nihta gesundne, Ll. Th. i. 90, 8. þæt hié hiæ gesunde burgen *subtrahentes se pugnae,* Ors. 2, 5; S. 80, 23. Þancigende his gescyldnysse hí ealle gesunde cômon eft tô heora earde, Hml. S. 25, 453. Stôpon úp weras of wǽge and hyra wicg gesund, Rä. 23, 21. (2) of things. (a) *that escapes danger :*—Gesund *salua* (*reuerentia*), An. Ox. 5269. (b) *that averts danger* (?) :—Mid gesund *cum tuta* [v. (?) cum tuta pelta, Ald. 11, 28], Wrt. Voc. ii. 23, 32. **IV.** of a condition, *free from evil, misery,* &c., *prosperous, happy :*—Gesundne síð secgas áseten hæfdon, El. 997 : 1005. Hí gesittað him on gesundum þingum, Gn. Ex. 57. Gesundra *dexterior,* Wrt. Voc. ii. 28, 22. Hit oft gesǽleð on þǽm sêlran þingum and on þǽm gesundrum (*in secundis rebus*), Nar. 7, 26. **IV a.** in valedictory expressions :—Heó rǽhte hire handa him tô and hêt hine gesund faran (*she bade him farewell*), Ap. Th. 27, 2. Farað nú gesunde and gesǽlige becumað, Hml. S. 6, 89. Hê háteð hý gesunde faran, Cri. 1342.

**ge-sundelic.** v. ge-sundiglic.

**ge-sundful.** *Add :* **I.** of living things, *in good health.* Cf. ge-sund; **I** :—Þǽm cilde wæs sôna bet. Þá cwǽdon þá gedwolmen . . . þ

his sunu wǽre gesundful þurh hí, Hml. S. 3, 315. Hé gesundful síðode on fótum, sé ðe on bǽre þider geboren wæs, Hml. Th. ii. 150, 14 : 136, 5. Ysle gesundfullum *asello sospite*, i. *sano*, An. Ox. 3664. (2) of things. Cf. ge-sund; I. 2 :—His swiðre hand is gesundful oð þis, Hml. S. 26, 103. **II.** *prosperous, happy*. Cf. ge-sund; **IV** :—Hwíl-tídum þeós weorold is gesundful, hwílon heó is mid mislicum þingum gemenged, Hml. Th. i. 182, 34. Ðurh cyningces wísdóm folc wyrð gesǽlig, gesundful, sigefæst, Ll. Th. ii. 306, 5. Gesundfullum gesǽli-nessum *secundis successibus*, An. Ox. 2581 : 3632 : *prosperis* (i. *lętis*) *successibus*, 3994.

**ge-sundfullian.** *Add* :—Mislimp hé gesundfullige tearte *casus secundet asperos*, Hy. S. 16, 5. Gesundfullod hiht *secunda spes*, 28, 5.

**ge-sundfullíce.** *Add* :—Hit is Godes wunder þæt þysum cild-geongum cyningce þus gesundfullíce eallu þing underþeódde synt on his cynelicum anwealde, Lch. iii. 436, 9.

**ge-sundfulnes.** *Dele last passage, and add* : I. *good health* :—Gesuntfulnessa *incolomitati* (*pristinae valetudinem restituit*), An. Ox. 11, 147. Is on líchaman se lǽssa man betere mid gesundfulnysse þonne se unhála beó and hæbbe Golian mycelnysse, Hml. A. 40, 410. **II.** *good fortune, prosperity, happiness of condition* :—þæt hé óðres mannes ungelimp besǽrgie and on his gesundfulnysse fægnige, Hml. i. 584, 6. Ne breác Heródes his cyneríces mid langsumere gesundfulnysse (*with lasting prosperity*), ac búton yldinge him becóm seó godcundlice wracu þe hine mid menigfealdre yrmðe fordyde, 84, 34 : Lch. iii. 440, 7 : Ll. Th. i. 256, 8. On ðǽm gesundfulnessum (*in prosperis*) ... on ðǽm earfeðum (*in adversis*) ... on ðǽre gesundfulnesse (*in prosperis*) mon forgiett his selfes, Past. 35, 4-7. God wíle foresceáwian úre gesundful-nysse, Hml. S. 13, 137 : Lch. iii. 440, 17. For nánum ungelimpum, ne eft on nánum gesundfulnyssum, Hml. Th. ii. 92, 29 : 31. **II a.** *abundance* :—Of gesundfulnesse *saturitate*, Kent. Gl. 34.

**ge-sundig.** *Add* : v. ge-syndig.

**ge-sundiglic** ; *adj. Prosperous, favouring* :—Gesundiglíce windas *secundi venti*, Bd. 5, 1 ; Sch. 553, 13. Gesundelican *secundis*, Wrt. Voc. ii. 79, 65. v. ge-syndiglic.

**ge-sundlic** ; *adj.* I. *healthy* :—Gesceáwa ælce dæge þ þín útgong and micge sié gesundlic, Lch. ii. 226, 20. **II.** *safe*. Cf. ge-sund; **III** :—Se weg is mycele gesundlicra *tutior est via*, Gr. D. 348, 10. **III.** *prosperous* :—On þám gesundlicum þingum *in prosperity*, Bd. 4, 23 ; Sch. 475, 10. v. ge-syndlic.

**ge-sundlíce.** *Add* : I. *safely* :—Sió nafu fǽrþ néhst ðǽre eaxe, forþý hió fǽrþ gesundlícost, Bt. 39, 7 ; F. 222, 22. **II.** *prosper-ously, happily* :—Hé þæs ríces twislunge eft tó ánnesse bróhte, and swá gesundlíce ealles weóld, þæt þá þe his yldran gemundon þearle swíþe wundredon, Lch. iii. 436, 4. v. un-gesundlíce.

**ge-sundrian.** *Add* : [*O. H. Ger.* ge-suntarón.] v. ge-syndrian.

**ge-súpan.** *Add* : [*a wk. past* súpede *occurs in* Mk. p. 4, 3 : *see passage in Dict. under* ge-suppan] :—Mið ðý gebirigde ł geseáp (*gustasset*) nalde drinca, Mt. L. 27, 34.

**ge-suppan** = ge-súpan.

**ge-swǽccan.** I. *to smell.* v. swecc ; II :—Hý mid nosan ne magon náht geswæccan bútan unstences ormǽtnesse *foetor ingenti complet putredine nares*, Dóm. L. 206. Nosa hí habbað and ne gestincað (geswæccað, *v. l.*), Ps. Cam. 113, 6. **II.** *to taste.* v. swecc ; I :—Ic geswæcce *sapio*, Ælfc. Gr. Z. 221, 9.

**ge-swǽlan.** *l.* ge-swǽlan : **ge-swǽpa.** v. swǽpa *in Dict., and cf.* ge-swope : **ge-swǽre** *affliction. Dele. The form in* Rtl. 41, 37 *is* gisuoenc : **ge-swǽre.** *In bracket* l. ge-swár, *and dele* ' ge-swǽre, *subst.* ; *and* ' : ge-swǽred. v. swǽran *in Dict.*

**ge-swǽs.** *Add* :—Geswǽse *blandum*, Wülck. Gl. 257, 8. I. *of persons, kind, charitable, loving* :—Hé wæs swíðe geswǽs eallum swinc-endum, and on mislicum yrmðum mannum geheólp (cf. hé swincendum fylste, Hml. S. 31, 53), Hml. Th. ii. 500, 16. God cymð ungesewenlíce tó geswǽsre heortan þe gehýrsum bið his hǽsum (cf. Lufa ðínne Drihten ... Lufa ðínne néxtan, 314, 6-9) mid weorce, 316, 4. **II.** *of things, kind, pleasant, alluring, agreeable, persuasive* :—Wolde se heofenlica lǽce mid geswǽsum bigspelle þæt geswell heora heortan gelácnian, Hml. Th. i. 338, 22. Se biscop ðá ungeðwǽran preóstas on sibbe gebróhte mid geswǽsre láre, ii. 516, 16. Ne hlyste gé heora geswǽsan lyffetunge, 404, 29. Eádmódnysse cýðan mid geswǽsre ðénunge, 242, 33. Þá gewylnunga þisse worulde synt swíðe swicole, þeáh þe hí geswǽse beón, Hml. S. 2, 165. Ðæt hé wiðsóce þám geswǽsum lustum, 5, 315 : 35, 132 : Hml. A. 15, 59. Hæfde Ióhannes hire (*Mary*) gýmene mid geswǽsum ðénungum, Hml. Th. ii. 256, 30. Geswǽsum gemetum *blandis modis*, Scint. 61, 10. Hé mid geswǽsum wordum ólehte þám mǽdene, Hml. S. 7, 83.

**ge-swǽse** ; *adv. Pleasantly* ; blandide, Wrt. Voc. ii. 127, 5.

**ge-swǽslic** ; *adj. Pleasant, alluring* :—Ðæt hé wiðsóce þám ge-swǽslicum lustum, Hml. S. 5, 315.

**ge-swǽslíce** ; *adv. Kindly, lovingly* :—Þá besárgode hé ðǽre sorh-fullan méder, and geswǽslíce hire sunu cyste, Hml. Th. ii. 150, 18.

**ge-swǽsnes.** *Add* :—Seó gálnys bepǽcð ðá mihta mid hyre geswǽs-nyssum (*blandimentis*), Prud. 43 b. Mæncgende ógum geswǽsnyssa (*blandimenta*), R. Ben. I. 14, 15. Geswǽsnusse *blandimenta*, i. *oblecta-menta*, An. Ox. 607.

**ge-swǽsscipe**, es ; *m. Friendship, loving companionship* :—þær is geswǽsscipe (cf. geþoftscipe, Wlfst. 265, 9) engla and geférrǽden apostola, Nap. 32.

**ge-swǽtan.** *Add* : I. *to forge together* (?), *weld* (cf. *O. H. Ger.* ge-sweizen *frigere* : *Ger.* schweissen *to forge together*) :—Gisuêtit *ferru-minatus*, Goetz ii. 579, 58. (*See Angl.* xx. 395.) **II.** *to cause to labour* (?). v. swǽtan ; I a :—Yrfewyrdnysse þíne geswǽtton (*perhaps only an error for* geswǽncton ; Ps. Srt. *has* geswecton) *haereditatem tuam uexauerunt*, Ps. Cam. 93, 5.

**ge-swápan** ; *p.* -sweóp *To sweep together, take possession of, get into one's power* :—Ptholomeus tógædere gesweóp ealle Egypt and Arabia *Ptolemaeo Aegyptus Arabiaeque pars sorte provenit*, Ors. 3, 11 ; S. 142, 27.

**ge-swát** ; *adj.* v. -swát *in Dict.*

**ge-sweartian** *to blacken* :—Gesweartode *denigratos*, An. Ox. 4669. [*O. H. Ger.* ge-swarzón *infuscare*.]

**ge-swebban** ; *p.* -swefde, -swefede : -swefian ; *p.* ode. *Take here* ge-swefian *in Dict., and add* : I. *of living things, to send to sleep, lull* :—Ðá drýmen hæfdon him mid twégen ormǽte dracan ; ac se apostol þá dracan geswefode, Hml. Th. ii. 474, 7. Geswefed *sopitus* (*somno*), An. Ox. 4975. Þá weardmenn wǽron ǽr geswefode, Hml. S. 11, 200. I a. *of the sleep of death, to cause to die, deprive of life* :—Críst wæs mid deáðe geswefod on þǽre róde *Christus in cruce dormivit*, Ang. vii. 22, 215. Þis mǽden inne læg on deáðe ge-swefod. **II.** *of things, to calm, quiet* :—Gelíþewǽhte, geswefede *sopita*, i. *mitigata* (*incendia*), An. Ox. 4031.

**ge-sweccan.** v. ge-swæccan : **ge-swefian.** v. ge-swebban : ge-swefnian. v. swefnan : I. *in Dict.*

**ge-swêge** ; *adj. Harmonious, sonorous, concordant* :—Geswêge *con-sona*, Wrt. Voc. ii. 134, 23. Of geswêgum dréme *consona armonia* (*psallentes*), An. Ox. 7, 173. Of geswêgre *canora* (*voce concrepans*), 175. Mid geswêgre singan stæfne *sonora psallant uoce*, Angl. xiii. 410, 641. His mǽdenu mé singað mid geswêgum stemnum, Hml. S. 7, 44. v. un-geswêge.

**ge-swegra**, an ; *m. A cousin* :—Geswegran *consobrini*, i. *ex sorore et fratre vel ex duabus sororibus*, Wrt. Voc. ii. 134, 18. v. ge-swigra, ge-sweór.

**ge-swel.** *Add* :—Ân geswel (-swell, *v. l.*) weóx mycel under þám cynnbáne *tumorem maximum sub maxilla habebat*, Hml. S. 20, 51. Atelicum geswelle *informi tumore*, Hpt. 33, 238, 13. Wearð Cúðberhtes cneów mid heardum geswelle álêfed, Hml. Th. ii. 134, 24. Se lǽce sceolde ásceótan þ geswell (*incidere tumorem*, Bd. 4, 19), Hml. S. 30, 63. v. fót-, in-geswell.

**ge-swelg**, es ; *n. A gulf, whirlpool, an abyss* :—Betwyx sandhriccan (and) geswelge swyliendes *inter Scyllam et barathrum uoraginis*, An. Ox. 635. Grutte, on geswelge *in uoraginem*, 701. Geswelgum *carybdibus*, i. *uoraginibus*, 4620.

**ge-swelge.** *See preceding word* : ge-swelgend. *Add* :—Ge-swel[g]inde *voragine*, Hpt. Gl. 507, 58. v. swelgend.

**ge-swellan** *to swell* :—Biþ gehwæþer geswollen, Lch. ii. 46, 9. Gif se geswollena mon on þǽre lifre swá áswollen gebít, 200, 22. Wiþ geswollenum sáre, 202, 5. [*O. H. Ger.* ge-swellan *tumere, tumefieri*.]

**ge-sweltan.** *Add* : [*weak forms occur in Lindisfarne gospels*] :—Ðaeh becyme mec þ ic efne-gesuelta ðê *etsi oportuerit me commori tibi*, Mk. L. 14, 31. Se Hǽlend ásuelte (*expirauit*) ... Gesæh ðe aldormon þte suá clioppende gesuelte (*expirasset*), 15, 39. Gesuelta *mori*, Jn. L. 4, 47 : 18, 14. Ic sóna wæs geswolten and mín gewit and ealle míne styrennesse forleás mox uelut emoriens sensum penitus motumque omnem perdidi, Bd. 5, 6 ; Sch. 577, 8.

**ge-swenc.** *Add* : *trial, affliction* :—In gesuoencge *in temtationem*, Lk. L. 22, 46. Gisuoenc (*printed* gisuoere) *afflictionem*, Rtl. 41, 37.

**ge-swencan.** *Add* :—Geswenced *fessa*, Wrt. Voc. ii. 38, 73. I. the subject a person. (1) *to cause distress, fatigue, &c., by labour, or any injury to the body* :—Hyne Hǽðcyn fláne geswencte *Hæðcyn troubled him sore with his shot*, B. 2438. Úre fæder biddeð þ gé eów on þone weg ne geswencean *rogat pater noster ne fatigati debeatis*, Gr. D. 39, 16. Mid úra wǽpna byrþenum swíðe geswencte *onere armorum con-fecti*, Nar. 12, 1. (2) *where there is distress, suffering, &c., from hard treatment, to afflict* :—Ne geswenð *non affliget* (*Dominus fame animam justi*), Kent. Gl. 314. (2 a) *of disciplinary treatment* :—þ hé blíþe þæs earman líchoman gefylle on þon þe hé hine sylfne geswence, Bl. H. 37, 30. (3) *where distress is caused by ill-treatment, to ill-treat, harass, punish, torture* :—þá gingran þá yldran mid deáþe geswencaþ, Bl. H. 171, 23. He his þeówas mid teónan geswencton and ofslógon *servos ejus contumelia adfectos occiderunt*, Mt. 22, 6. Hié monege cyningas geswencton, tó þon þ hié eall gesealdon ... wiþ hiera earman lífe *inquietudo bellorum qua illi* (*reges*) *adtriti sunt*, Ors. 5, 1 ; S. 214, 19.

Hié magon ða gódan swá micle swíður geswencean swá hié hiora ánmódlícor éhtað *bonos deterius deprimunt, quos et unanimiter persequuntur,* Past. 361, 24. Hé began tó sleánne his wítneras þ hí swíðor sceolde þone hálgan geswæncan, Hml. S. 37, 116. Heó wæs swíðe geswenced (*vexatus*), Gr. D. 72, 30. Gé bióðun giswenced *uapulabitis,* Mk. R. 13, 9. **I a.** the agent an animal:—Hædstapa hundum geswenced, heorot, B. 1368. **II.** where distress is caused by (unfavourable) circumstance. (1) of bodily distress from disease, famine, &c.:—Tóbláwennys his innoð geswencte, Hml. Th. i. 86, 13. Gif hwelc folc bið mid huugre geswenced *si populos fames attereret,* Past. 377, 8. Mid sáre geswenced, mid mislicum ecum, Bl. H. 59, 7 : 227, 8. Ádle gebysgad, sárum geswenced, Gú. 1110. Ðá ðe gesuoenced woere ꝥ wéron gesuoencde (geswæncte, R.) ádlum *qui uexabantur languoribus,* Mk. L. 1, 34. Wæs sió ofermycelo héto . . . men wéron miclum geswencte, Ors. 1, 7 ; S. 40, 4. Þás bróþor synd geswencede of ðisse sæwe hreónesse, Bl. H. 233, 26. (1 a) where the distress is disciplinary :—Ðonne ðæt flæsc bið gesuenced ðurh færhæfdnesse *cum per abstinentiam caro fatigatur,* Past. 87, 24. Ðonne se líchoma bið mid fæstenne gesuenced (*atteritur*), 315, 6. (2) of distress of mind (and body):—Geswenð *affligit* (*animam spes, quae differtur*), Kent. Gl. 444. Gecostod and geswenced *probatus,* Guth. 12, 7. Sé ðe bið mid his ágnum scyldum geswenced *quem crimen depravat proprium,* Past. 62, 21. Suá hé mildheortlícor bið gesuenced (*fatigatur*) mid óðerra monna costungum, 107, 3. Mid woruldsorgum geswenced, Bt. 3, 1 ; F. 4, 21. Sorgum geswenced, An 116 : Met. 3, 8. Bióð hié on hira móde gesuenced for ðæm æmtan ipsa sua quiete fatigantur, Past. 127, 24. Hí bióþ gedréfde and geswencte ægþer ge on móde ge on líchoman, Bt. 39, 7 ; F. 224, 1. Ué biðon gisuencdo úsum ondspyrnissum *fatigamur nostris offensis,* Rtl. 42, 25. (3) of distress from adversity, from want or loss of means :—Bit geswenced *affligitur* (*malo qui fidem facit pro extraneo*), Kent. Gl. 363. Is geswenced of hénðe *afflictus est damno,* 810. Gif freóndleás man swá geswenced weorðe þurh freóndleáste þ hé borh næbbe, Ll. Th. i. 396, 26. Ðý læs hí weorþan wyrsan gif hí ástyrede bióþ and geswenced (-swencte, *v. l.*) *quem deteriorem facere possit adversitas,* Bt. 39, 10 ; F. 228, 6. **III.** where both subject and object are things :—Bið heard winter and yfel lencten and eorþan wæstmas swíþe geswencte *the fruits of the earth will have a very hard time,* Archiv cxx. 298, 10.

**ge-swencedlic.** v. un-geswencedlic.

**ge-swencednes.** *Add :*—þá weard hé geneádod þ hé on his ágenre geswencednysse (-swænced-, -swencend-, *v. ll.*) oncneówe hwæt hé sylf wæs *compulsus est cognoscere in sua vexatione quid esset,* Gr. D. 73, 5 : 11. Fram geswincednesse (*the vowel of the second syllable is not clear, it may be y*) *a tribulatione,* Ps. L. 106, 39.

**ge-swencness,** e ; *f.* *Labour, hardship, trouble, distress :*—Ús wæs swælc geswencnis mid deórum becymen *tantus oriebatur tumultus,* Nar. 14, 30. Ne spræce hé . . . be Lazares geswencnesse (*contritione*), þá þá hé cwæð þ hé onféncge manige yfel on his lífe, Gr. D. 310, 27. For þám þingum swá monigra geswencnissa þ wé ealle þá niht férdon mid þurste gewæcte, Nar. 11, 29. Swá monigra geswencnissa and earfeðo, 14, 23.

**ge-sweór,** es ; *m.* A cousin:—Gesweóras *consobrini,* Wrt. Voc. ii. 134, 19. v. ge-swegra.

**ge-sweorc.** *Add :*—Geswerc (*nebulam*) swé swé eascan strigdeð, Ps. Srt. 147, 16. Mycel swég cymþ and gesweorc, Verc. Först. 132, 3.

**ge-sweorcan.** *Add :* **I.** of physical darkness :—Bið úpheofon sweart and gesworcen *tristius coelum tenebris obducitur atris,* Dóm. L. 105: Wlfst. 137, 9. **II.** of dark passions. (1) sadness :—Ic geþencan ne mæg for hwan módsefa mín ne gesweorce, Wand. 59. (2) fear:—Wé férað gesworcene mid ege and mid fyrhðu, Verc. Först. 147, 18. (3) anger :—Weard gecýðd þám cyninge embe Iudan sige, and hé geswearc on móde (*when king Antiochus heard these things, he was full of indignation,* 1 Macc. iii. 27), Hml. S. 25, 329. **III.** of mental darkness, *to become unconscious, lose perceptive power* (?) :—Ic geswearc swá swá deád from heortan *excidi tamquam mortuus a corde,* Ps. Vos. 30, 13.

**ge-sweordod ;** *adj.* *Provided with a sword :*—Gesweordod (-swurd-, -swyrd-, *v. ll.*) *gladiatus,* Ælfc. Gr. Z. 257, 1. Þá cwómon twégen englas gescildode and gesweordode, Nap. 32.

**ge-sweorf,** es ; *n.* *Add :*—Geswearfes of seolfre syx pænega gewæge, Lch. i. 336, 8. Gesweorf *ferruginem,* i. *rasura ferri,* Wrt. Voc. ii. 147, 65 : *ferrugine,* 35, 32.

**ge-sweorfan.** For 'Glos. . . . 19' *substitute* Germ. 391, 41, *and add :*—Gesuirbet *elimat,* Wrt. Voc. ii. 107, 16. Geswyrfeþ, 29, 25. [*O. H. Ger.* gi-suorban *detersa.*]

**ge-sweostor.** *Add :*—Twá gesweostor, Bd. 1, 27; Sch. 68, 3. Ealle hálige men beóð his gebróðru and gesweostru, Hml. Th. i. 260, 34. Mín gesweuster *sorores mee,* Nar. 31, 20. Eal crísten folc heó lufode, and sæde þæt hý wæron hire geswustra, Wlfst. 237, 19. Maria and Martha wæron twá geswystru, Hml. Th. i. 130, 4. Lazares geswustru, ii. 438, 16. Hé hæfde twá gesweostor him tó wífum, Ors. 6, 16; S. 270, 17.

**ge-sweostren ;** *adj.* *Of sisters :*—Geswusterenu bearn *sobrini,* Wrt. Voc. i. 52, 6. ¶ *as* pl. substantive. (1) *cousins* on the mother's side :—Gesweosternu *consobrini ex duabus sororibus,* Wrt. Voc. ii. 134, 19. Gesustrenu *consobrini,* i. 52, 5. (2) *sisters :*—Twégra bróþor oþþe twégra gesweosterna (swustra, gesweostra, *v. ll.*) sunu and dohtor *duorum fratrum vel duarum sororum filius et filia,* Bd. 1, 27; Sch. 69, 3. Sceolden hí bión swelce hí wæren geswysterna (-swystrena, *v. l.*) bearn, for ðæm þe hé sceolde beón heofones sunu and hí eorþan, Bt. 35, 4 ; S. 98, 32. Be þám men þe wífað on twám geswystrenum (*qui duas sorores in matrimonium ducit*), oððe wíf nimð bróður æfter óðrum, Ll. Th. ii. 180, 18. Án pund penega hé lænde Túne and his geswysternon, Cht. Crw. 23, 20. [Cf. *O. L. Ger.* ge-sustruon *sisters,* Kl. Nom. Stam. § 68.]

**ge-sweotulian.** *Add :* **I.** *to shew* a material object to a person :—Ic ne mæg mé þé geswutelian . . . for þon ic eom wífhádes mann and wæfelsum bereáfod, Hml. S. 23 b, 205. **II.** *to manifest, make known, reveal.* (1) the object a person :—Ic geswutelige (*manifestabo*) him mé sylfne . . . þú wylt þé sylfne geswuteligan ús, Jn. 14, 21, 22. On þysum dæge Críst wæs geswutelod þám þrým cyningum . . . hé weard on þysum dæge middangearde geswutelod, Hml. Th. i. 104, 19–23. (2) the object a thing :—Hié gereccað ðis andwearde líf fleónde and ðæt tówearde gesueotoligeað (-sweotuliað, *v. l.*) *dum fugitiva esse praesentia indicant, quae sunt futura manifestant,* Past. 91, 7. Se Hælend geswutelode him (*St. John*) þá tóweardan onwrigenysse, Hml. Th. i. 58, 33. (2 a) where concealment is desired, *to discover, make evident :*—Wé cwædon be þám mannum þe mánsworan wæran, gif þ geswutelod wære, Ll. Th. i. 160, 20. Fácn geswuteled *strofam propalatam,* An. Ox. 3653. **III.** *to shew, prove, demonstrate* by action :—Ic gesweotelige ꝥ ic geséðe þé God þín ic eam *testificabor tibi Deus tuus ego sum,* Ps. L. 49, 7. Abraham geswutelode mid þære dæde þ man ne sceal fandian Godes *ostenditur in isto ejus facto quod homo non debet tentare Dominum,* Angl. vii. 42, 404. þ wé mid þám geswutelian þ wé gemyndige beón þære myclan mildheortnysse, Btwk. 216, 18. Oferfundennessum geswutelian *experimentis comprobasse,* An. Ox. 544. **IV.** *to make clear* what is obscure, what is imperfectly understood, *to explain :*—Gesutulað *explicabit,* Germ. 392, 23. Geswuteliaþ *propalabunt* (si vestra solertia plenius animaduerti (*undergytene*) maluerit, collationes . . . *propalabunt*), An. Ox. 912. Hé geswutelede *explanat* (*arborem congrua interpretationis conjectura*), 1562. Þæt ic geswu[telige] *ut pandam,* 5059. Geswitlenede *explanans,* 11, 59. Weard micel wundor on heofonum gesewen, swelce eal se hefon birnende wære. Þæt tácen weard on Rómánum swíþe gesweotolad mid þæm miclan wólbryne monncwealmes *Romae . . . gravis pestilentia . . . incanduit, ut merito praecedente prodigio coelum ardere visum sit, quando caput gentium tanto morborum igne flagravit,* Ors. 2, 6 ; S. 86, 24. **V.** *to shew* by signs, figuratively, symbolically, *indicate, signify.* Cf. ge-sweotulung ; I :—Gamena augin ealderdóm geswutelaþ (*cum pueriles*) *ludorum gesticulatio* (*pontificalem futuri praesulis*) *auctoritatem portenderit,* An. Ox. 2874. Mid þissum wordum se wítega gesweotolað (*ostendit*) þ . . ., R. Ben. 21, 13. Seó godcundlice wracu hine mid menigfealdre yrmðe fordyde, and eác geswutelode on hwilcum súslum hé móste ecelíce cwylmian, Hml. Th. i. 86, 2. Ðæt hé geswutolade mid þám deádum fellum þ hí wæron deádlice *ut eos mortales fuisse insinuaret,* Angl. vii. 30, 284. Geswutelian *designasse* (per allegoriam Hiericho typum mundi *designasse*), An. Ox. 5137. Gesweoteliende *signantem,* i. *demonstrantem* (statuam regnorum saecula signantem), 1545. Þurh þá sylfan offrunga Crístes þrowunge geswytelude wé oncnáwaþ *per eadem sacrificia Xpi passionem insinuatam cognoscimus,* 40, 23. Hér is geswutelod úre sylfra forwyrd, tóweard getácnod, Jud. 285. **VI.** *to make a clear statement of, declare :*—þám crédan sceal ælc crísten man geswutelian rihtne geleáfan, Ll. Th. i. 372, 26. Geswu[teliende] heófun[ge] *depromens querimoniam,* An. Ox. 3365. Hér is geswutelod on þisum gewrite hú Eádgár cyngc wæs smeágende hwæt tó bóte mihte, Ll. Th. i. 270, 8.

**ge-sweotulung.** *Take here* ge-swutelung *in Dict., and add :* **I.** *a shewing by signs or symbols, indication, signifying.* v. ge-sweotulian ; V :—Wé streowiað axan uppan úre heáfda tó geswutelunge þ wé sculon úre synna behreówsian, Hml. S. 12, 39. **II.** *a declaration.* v. ge-sweotulian ; VI :—Geswute[lunge] *titulo* (pro christianae religionis *titulo* eas accusantes), An. Ox. 4840.

**gesweotulung-dæg** *Epiphany :*—Ðes dæg is geháten *Epiphania Domini,* þæt is Godes gesweotulungdæg, Hml. Th. i. 104, 19.

**ge-swerian.** *Add :* **I.** *absolute, to use an oath in confirmation of a statement, promise,* &c. :—Forebeádas næfræ gesueriga *prohibens omnino jurare,* Mt. p. 14, 17. On án gesworene *conspirati,* Wrt. Voc. ii. 20, 22. **I a.** *to swear* by:—Suá huelc gesuerias ðerh ðone tempel, Mt. L. 23, 16. **II.** with cognate object, *to swear* an oath :—Hwæt mænde se áð swá gesworen?, Hml. Th. ii. 234, 31. Ðá þet gasol gelést wæs and þá friðáðas gesworene, Chr. 1012; P. 143, 5. Fore áðum giswornum (*gesuoerenum,* L.) *propter iusiurandum,* Mk. R. 6, 26. **III.** with clause containing statement of that which is

confirmed by oath, *to swear* that . . . :—Hē ongann gesuoeria þte ic nāt, Mk. 14, 71. Hié gesworen hæfdon đæt hié ōþer forleósan woldon, Ors. 2, 3; S. 68, 27. **III. a.** *to swear* by . . . that . . . :—Hē him geswōr on his goda noman þæt hē ǣgþer wolde . . . , Ors. 4, 6; S. 178, 9. **IV.** combining II and III, *to swear* an oath that . . . :—Āđ þte giswōr ł þte gisworen biđ tō Abrahame þte būta ondo . . . hēre wē him, Lk. R. L. 1, 73. Hié āđas geswōran þ hié nǣfre noldon æt hām cuman . . . , Ors. 1, 14; S. 56, 19. Hié him betweónum āþas geswōran þ . . . , 2, 4; S. 70, 15. **V.** *to confirm by oath, swear to an agreement* :—Đās forewarde geswōran .xii. þa betste of þes cynges healfe and .xii. of þes eorles, Chr. 1091; P. 226, 17. Þær seó forewearde ǣr wæs gewroht and eác gesworen, 1094; P. 228, 37. **VI.** *to swear a person, swear in, administer an oath* to a person who is promising to discharge an obligation :—Hē wæs of his earde ādrifen, and đēh wæs tō cinge gesworen *he had been sworn in as king*, Chr. 1041; P. 162, 10. [*O. Sax.* gi-swerian *to swear* an oath : *O. H. Ger.* ge-swerien, -swerren *jurare, conjurare.*]

**ge-swētan.** *Add :*—Se lǣce, đonne hē bietre wyrta dēđ tō hwelcum drence, hē hié gesuēt mid hunige, Past. 303, 13. Geswētte *dulcavit*, Wrt. Voc. ii. 28, 35 : *indulcavit*, 45, 24. Geswēt *condies*, 16, 11. Geswēt mid hunige, Lch. ii. 20, 6. Geswēt wīn *dulcis sapa*, An. Ox. 5492. Geswētt, 2, 494. Medo geswēt *vel* weall *defrutum*, i. *vinum*, Wrt. Voc. ii. 138, 24. Geswēttes ealoþ, Cht. Th. 158, 23. Geswēttum *lento defruto*, Wrt. Voc. ii. 52, 70. Æfter þon sealte mettas mid ecede geswēte, Lch. ii. 184, 8. [*O. H. Ger.* ge-sōzen *indulcare, condire.*]

**ge-sweđerian.** *Take here* ge-swiđrian *in Dict., and add :*—þ fullfremede mōd geswyđrode (-swiđrade, *v. l.*) ymbe hine fram þǣre heánnesse þāra oferhygda *erga illum illa mens effera ab elationis fastu detumuit*, Gr. D. 188, 3. *For additional examples see* sweđrian *in Dict.* : ge-sweđrung. *v.* ge-swæđrung, sweđrung *in Dict., and add :*—[Gyf on Tīwes deg þunried, þonne tācned þ westmas geswid[r]unge (cf. *tonitruum in iii.ª feria, fructus terre periclitabunt*, Archiv cxx. 47, 8), Lch. iii. 168, 2.]

**ge-swētleht.** *l.* -lǣht, *and add :*—Onsægdnissa geswētlǣhta, Ps. Rdr. 65, 15.

**ge-swic.** *Add :* **I.** *an offence :*—Tō geswicum *ad scandala*, Wrt. Voc. ii. 97, 4. **II.** *cessation :*—Sȳ hē betāht Satane intō helle grunde and đǣr ā cwylmie mid Godes wiđsacum būte geswice, C. D. iv. 107, 17. *v.* ge-swicu.

**ge-swícan.** *Add :* **I.** *to cease, stop.* (1) absolute :—Ne geswíced *non tricaverit* (tricare *cessare*, Migne), Wrt. Voc. ii. 60, 1. (a) *to cease from proceeding, to retire, retreat :*—Gecier lā and gesuíc, ne folga mē *recede, noli me persequi*, Past. 295, 15. (b) *to cease* from action, (ill-) *doing, desist :*—Būton hē eft self gesuíce, Past. 191, 9. Būton hē eft geswíce and winne wiþ þā unþeáwas, Bt. 36, 6; F. 182, 4. Man forgā þýsđe be eallum þām þe he āge. And sē þe be wītum geswícan nylle, Ll. Th. i. 210, 4. (c) *to give up* a condition, *withdraw* from a position :—Nān man on his godsibbe ne wiñge, and gif hit hwā gedō, nǣbbe hē Godes mildse būtan hē geswíce, Ll. Th. ii. 300, 17. (2) with gen., (a) of persons. (a) *to cease* from doing :—Gif hē đǣre hnappunge ne geswícđ, Past. 194, 11. Hē geswác đæs dihtes, Hex. 20, 14. Man mānfulra dǣda geswíce, Ll. Th. i. 378, 6. Gif wē wilnigon đæt hié đæs wōs geswícen, Past. 367, 23 : 304, 5. Hié noldon þæs weallgebreces geswícan, Ors. 3, 9; S. 134, 30 : 4, 9; S. 192, 33. Hē wāt þ hē untela dēđ, and nele đeáh þæs geswícan, Bt. 39, 12; F. 232, 1 : Ll. Th. i. 306, 19. Gif hē đonne giét geswícen næsđ his āgenra unđeáwa *si ergo adhuc in ejus corpore passiones vivunt*, Past. 59, 24. (β) *to withdraw* from a course of action :—Gif mon on folces gemōte cyninges gerēfan geyppe eofot, and his riht geswícan wille, gestǣle on ryhtran hand gif hē mæge, Ll. Th. i. 76, 6. (b) of things, *to cease* from moving :—Wiđ þāra sina bifunge . . . hý geswícađ þǣre bifunge, Lch. i. 106, 2. (3) with dat. infin. *to cease* to do :—Ne geswícaþ non *desinunt (faciem humectare)*, An. Ox. 659. Đā ungesewenlícan fýnd ne geswícađ nǣfre wiþ đē tō campienne, Hex. 34, 26. Ne hié ne geswác đā gesceafta tō edníwigenne, 20, 13. Ne geswác hē tō manienne his gingran *nec discipulos suos admonere cessabat*, Gr. D. 27, 3. (4) with clause :—Hí nyllađ geswícan (cf. ne magon forlǣtan *non desistunt*, 7) đæt hí ōđre men ne reáfigen *sua tribuentes aliena rapiunt*, Past. 335, 4. **II.** *to omit* to do an act that should be regularly repeated, *fail to do :*—þ hí nānum dæge ne geswícon þ wín tō drincene, Gr. D. 66, 22. **III.** *to abstain* from again doing. (1) absolute :—Hē hit georne gebēte, and syđđan geswíce, Hml. Th. i. 268, 21. Gā seó mǣgđ him on borh þ hē ǣfre geswíce, Ll. Th. i. 198, 24. (2) with gen. :—þ hē ǣfre swylces geswíce, 202, 17. þ hē þanan forđ ǣfre swilces geswíce, 346, 14. Cýpinga and folcgemōta and huntađfara and woroldlicra weorca on þām hālgan dæge geswíce man georne, 320, 12 : 308, 11. þ hí sunnandæges cýpinga geswícan, 326, 21. Mon sceal īdelra worda geswícan, R. Ben. 21, 15. **IV.** *to fail.* (1) of persons. (a) *to fail in* duty, loyalty, &c., to a person, *betray, desert, revolt* from :—Ealle Italiam geswicon Rōmānum and tō Hannibale gecirdon *omnis Italia ad Annibalem, desperata Romani status reparatione, defecit*, Ors. 4, 9; S. 192, 3.

Strange geneátas, þa ne willađ mē æt þām strīđe geswícan, Gen. 284. Hē underþiédde Rōmānum eall þa folc þe him nīwlíce geswicen hæfdon *Germaniam in pristinum statum reduxit : trans Danubium multas gentes subegit*, Ors. 6, 10; S. 264, 26. þā þegenas heom geswicon hæfdon, Chr. 1067; P. 201, 8. (b) *to fail* to do, *not to succeed :*—Heó ne geswāc *non cessit (ad capessendam passionis palmam)*, An. Ox. 4096. (2) of things, *to prove ineffective :*—Gūđbill geswāc æt nīđe, B. 2584. **V.** *to become feeble, faint, fail ;* deficere. (1) of persons :—Girísed symle gebidda and ne geswíca (*deficere*), Lk. R. L. 18, 1. (2) of things :—Blēda gedreósađ, wynna gewītađ, wǣra geswícađ, Rūn. 29. Geswicen *euanuerunt*, An. Ox. 3980. Geswícan *mitescere*, 3852. Hē hire swingele behēt gif heó suwian nolde. Heó cwǣđ : 'þæs lifigendan Godes word ne magon geswícan, ne forsuwode beón,' Hml. S. 9, 71. **VI.** *to deceive, seduce :*—Giseás gē đætte nǣnig iōw giswíce (*seducat*) . . . monige hiá giswícas (*seducent*), Mk. R. L. 13, 5, 6. Gesuíca (forlǣre, R., beswíce, W. S.) *seducat*, Mt. L. 24, 4. Tō giswícanne đā gicornu *ad seducendos electos*, Mk. R. L. 13, 22. [*O. Sax.* gi-swīkan *to betray* a person, a trust : *O. H. Ger.* ge-swīhan *cessare, discedere, relinquere, mentiri, deficere.*]

**ge-swícendlíce.** *v.* un-geswícendlíce.

**ge-swícennes.** *Add :* **I.** *cessation* from doing, *a leaving off* of a practice. *v.* ge-swícan ; **I** :—Behāte hē ǣrest bōte and geswicenesse ealra þǣra unþeáwa þe hē fore ādrǣfed wæs, R. Ben. 53, 10. Hē synna forgyfđ þām đe mid dǣdbōte dōđ geswicennysse, Hml. A. 1, 17. þone bisceop hē geteohhade mid teónan tō forseónne. Hē behēt þā geswicennysse þām bisceope, Hml. S. 31, 678. Seó sōđe behreówsung and dǣdbōt mid geswicennyssum yfeles ūs āþwyhđ, 12, 144. **II.** *abstaining* from doing again what has been given up. *v.* ge-swícan ; **III** :—Gif hē āgylte, hē hit georne gebēte and syđđan geswíce ; for đi ne biđ nān bōt nāht būton þǣr beó geswicenes, Hml. Th. i. 268, 22.

**ge-swicneful.** *Dele, and see* ge-swincful : **ge-swicte.** *v.* ge-swingan.

**ge-swicu** (? i-stem, *fem.*, cf. Sievers' Grammatik, § 268), e ; *f. Cessation :*—Witun þā đe đyllicne gylt þurhteóđ, and nāne geswice dōn nell[ađ], Hml. A. 148, 123 note. *v.* ge-swicu.

**ge-swícung.** *For* 'R. . . . Angl.' *substitute :*—Būton geswícincge *sine intermissione*, Angl. xiii. 372, 103.

**ge-swiđung.** *v.* ge-sweđrung.

**ge-swigan ;** *p.* de. **I.** *intrans. To be silent.* (1) *to cease speaking :*—Hē ongann cliopia . . . Mid đý gewearp woedo his geswígde (giswígende, R., *exiliens :* the glosser seems to have connected the word with *silere*) cuōm tō him, Mk. 10, 47-50. Ne mæghton word his getēla and gesuígdon (*tacuerunt*), Lk. L. 22, 26. (2) *not to break silence, to keep silent.* *v.* ge-swígung :—Gif đās gesuígas, stānas clioppogađ, Lk. L. 19, 40. (2 a) *to keep silent* when questioned :—Đæ hēhsācerd geáscade đone Hǣlend . . . hē gesuígde (*tacebat*), and nōht geonsuarede, Mk. L. 14, 61. 'Lā freónd, huu inneádes . . . ?' Hē gesuígde (*obmutuit*), Mt. L. 22, 12. Gefraignende Drihtne . . . gesuígdon, Mt. p. 19, 9. Geswígdon eall þā deófolgyld, Shrn. 151, 33. (2 b) *to be (almost) incapable of speech, be greatly astonished :*—Gestylton ł gesuígdon (*stupebant*) alle đā menigo and cwēdon, Mt. L. 22, 23. **II.** *trans.* (1) *to make silent, silence ;* pp. ge-swiged *tacitus* :—Aldum geswíga đā tunga *senis mutare* (as if connected with *mutus*, cf. l. 9) *linguam*, Mt. p. 1, 5. Singed ođ þæt seó sunne sǣged weorđed; þonne hlyst gefēđ . . . fugol biđ geswíged, Ph. 145. (2) *not to mention :*—Huelchwoego tō ēccanne, geswíga, gegēma *aliquid addere, mutare* (cf. **II.** 1), *corrigere*, Mt. p. 1, 9. Đæs noma geswíged is *cuius nōmen tacetur*, Lk. p. 11, 10.

**ge-swígian** (*l.* ge-swigian, -swugian ; *and for* Mt. L. 22, 12 : 12, 23 : Shrn. 151, 33 : Ph. 145 *see* ge-swígan). *Add :* **I.** *intrans. To be silent.* (1) *to cease speaking, keep silence after speaking :*—Đā geswígode (*oōticuit*) se Wīsdōm āne lytle hwīle, Bt. 7, 1; F. 16, 5. Đā đis gesprecen wæs, þā geswígode (-sugode, *v. l.*) þ Mōd, 18, 1; F. 60, 18. Geswugode, 24, 1; F. 80, 5. Gesweogode (-swugode, *v. l.*), 39, 2; F. 212, 10. Geđreádon hine þte gesuígode, hē micle māra cliopade, Lk. L. 18, 39. Sē gemetgađ irre, sē đe đone disigan hætt geswugian *qui imponit stulto silentium iras mitigat*, Past. 279, 19. (2) *not to break silence, keep silent, hold one's peace :*—Gesugiađ hié for ege *reticent ex timore*, Past. 302, 3. þa geswugode ic (*obmutui*) and ne ondyde nā mīnne mūđ, Ps. Th. 38, 11. þā þū swā wel geswugodes and swā lustlíce gehērdest mīne lāre *cum verba nostra tacitus attentusque rapiebas*, Bt. 22, 1; F. 76, 23. Ācsode hine hwæþer him þūhte þ hē ūþwita wǣre . . . ' Ic wolde cweþan þ þū ūþwita wǣre, gif þū geswugian (-sugian, *v. l.*) mihtest,' 18, 4; F. 68, 4. **II.** *trans.* (1) with gen. *to refrain from the saying of something :*—Þæt hē sceolan īdelra worda geswigian *a malis verbis debet tacere*, R. Ben. 21, 14. (2) with acc. *To cause by being silent :*—Ōđer ondrēd đæt hē ongeáte on his swýgean đæt hē sumne hearm geswigode (-swugade, *v. l.*) đǣr đǣr hē freme gecleopian meahte, gif hē ymb đæt geornlíce swunce *ille ne damna studiosi operis tacendo sentiret*, Past. 49, 21. (3) *to silence* (?) :—Beón gesuwod *tacere*, R. Ben. I. 26, 3.

**ge-swigra, -swirga, -swiria,** an ; *m. A cousin :*—Geswiria ođđe

swustur sunu *consobrinus*, Wrt. Voc. ii. 14, 73. Gesuigran, gesuirgion, gisuirgian *consobrinus*, Txts. 53, 530. Cf. ge-swegra [ge-swegra *and* ge-swigra *seem* an-*stem and* jan-*stem of same root. See* Kl. Nom. Stam. § 14].

ge-swígung, e; *f. Silence, refraining from speech.* v. ge-swígan; I. 2:—Gegearwien wē ūra sáula clǣnnesse mid geþyldmōdnesse and geswígunge ðonne ūs man on ðweorh tō sprece, Nap. 33, 13.

ge-swimman; *pp.* -swummen *To swim* :—þā hié hæfdon feórðan dǣl þǣre eá geswummen *jam quartam fluminis partem natauerant*, Nar. 10, 31.

ge-swin. *Add:* v. swin[n].

ge-swinc. *Take here* ge-swincg *in Dict., and add:* I. with respect to action, *labour* of body or mind, *toil, hard work* :—Ðǣr wæs suíðe suíðlic gesuinc, and ðǣr wæs micel swát ágoten *multo labore sudatum est*, Past. 269, 12. Hū hefig ðæt twiefalde gesuinc (*duplicitatis labor*) bið . . . óðer is ðára gesuinca (geswinga, v. l.) ðæt hí simle sēceað endeléase lādunga . . . Hē gewērgað his heortan mid ðý geswince . . . 'Ðæt gesuinc (*labor*) hira ágenra welena hié gedrycð', Past. 239, 4-15. Ys þ fordyslic geswinc þ gē winnaþ tō ðon þ gē wilniaþ eówerne hlísan tō gebrǣdanne, Bt. 18, 1; F. 62, 17. Ne forlǣte hē þa ǣscan . . . and wē þonne him his geswinces geþanceden, Ll. Th. i. 234, 27. On ídelan geswince, Bt. 19; F. 68, 27. Oferfohten būtan ǣlcum geswince, Past. 279, 2. Ic nát hū nyt ic beó, būtan þæt ic mín geswinc ámirre, Ors. 4, 13; S. 212, 26. þ is sió án ǣst eallra ūrra geswinca *haec requies laborum*, Bt. 34, 8; F. 144, 27. Mid ðǣm gesuincium (-swincum, v. l.) gōðra weorca *studiorum sublinium vigore*, Past. 283, 16. On dyslicum gesuincum *stulto labore*, 131, 14. Geswinceum, Gr. D. 6, 30. Ge-swincum, Hml. Th. ii. 82, 23. I a. of agricultural labour :—Hē ða eorðan áseów . . . Hē his geswinces breác, Hml. Th. ii. 144, 23. Hǣig-werde gebyreð þ man his geswinces leán gecnāwe, Ll. Th. i. 440, 12. Bydele gebyreð sum landstycce for his geswince, 8. II. with respect to suffering, *travail, trouble, hardship, tribulation* :—Ðyncð him gesuinc ðæt hē bið būtan woroldgesuincium *laborem deputant, si in terrenis negotiis non laborant*, Past. 129, 1. Ne beheóld hit nán þing seó scipfyrding būton folces geswinc, feós spilling, and heora feónda forðbylding, Chr. 999; P. 133, 10. Hē geendode his dagas æfter mycclum geswince and earfoðnissum his lífes, 1016; P. 148, 17: Bl. H. 59, 25. Ēþelíce būton ǣlcum geswince, Bt. 35, 4; F. 162, 2. þæt hí leornigen ðone cræft geþylde on þám langan geswince, 39, 11; F. 228, 26. Men heafdon mycel geswinc þæs geáres, Chr. 1085; P. 216, 4. Gif hié geðenceað ðára gesǣlða ðe him ungeendode æfter ðǣm geswince becuman sculon, ðonne ðyncað him ðý leóhtran ða geswinc ðe ofergán sculon (*leve fit quod transeundo laboratur*), Past. 407, 31. Se wind strongra geswinca oððe se rēn ungemetlices ymbhogan, Bt. 12; F. 36, 18. On ðǣm gesuincium (-swincum, v. l.) *in tribulatione*, Past. 267, 22. On ðǣm gesuincum *in adversis*, 35, 7. Efnðrowiende on hira gesuincum *sympathetic in their troubles*, 97, 21. II a. of physical weariness :—Hæbbe hē þás wyrte mid him, ðonne ne ongyt hē ná micel tō geswynce (-swince, v. l.) þæs síðes, Lch. i. 106, 7. v. weorold-geswinc.

ge-swincan. I. *to labour, toil* :—Ic wundrige hwí swá mænige wíse men swá swíþe geswuncen mid ðǣre sprǣce and swá litel gewis funden, Bt. 41, 4; F. 250, 20. II. *to labour* under, *be afflicted with* :—þonne se ufera dǣl þæs líchoman on ǣnigum sáre oððe on earfeþum geswince, Lch. i. 332, 9. v. un-geswuncen.

ge-swincfull. *Substitute:* I. of persons. (1) *laborious, industrious.* v. ge-swinc :—Mǣden scamfæst, geswincful, clǣne, Lch. iii. 192, 2-23. þæs hādes men þe hwýlum wǣron geswincfulleste on godcundan þeówdōme, þa ne swincaþ á swíðe ymbe ǣnige þearfe, Ll. Th. ii. 322, 20. (2) *full of trouble, that has to contend with difficulties, that endures hardships.* Cf. ge-swinc; III :—Cild ácenned gímeleás, ge-swincful (*or under* (3)?) on forman ylde (cf. hē bið þrowere, 156, 27 : *both passages refer to one born on the tenth day of the moon*), Lch. iii. 188, 19. Hē bið geswincfull (*or under* (1)?) on his lífe (cf. cild ácenned (*on the* 24th *day*) winnende, 194, 27), 158, 13. (3) *causing trouble, troublesome* :—Gif hié yfele sint ðonne sint hié þe pleólicran and geswincfulran (*Fox prints* geswincnefulran, *but Sedgefield gives only* ge-swincfulran) gehǣfd þonne genǣfd si *vitiosi moribus sunt, perniciosa domus sarcina*, Bt. 14, 1; F. 42, 22 note. II. of action. (1) *that involves labour, laborious, toilsome, difficult* :—Hit bið swíðe geswincful ðæt mon ǣlcne mon scyle onsundrum lǣran, hit is ðeáh earfoðre ealle ætsomne tō lǣranne *cum valde laboriosum sit unumquemque instruere, longe tamen laboriosius est auditores innumeros uno eodemque tempore instruere*, Past. 453, 10. Geswincfulnyss nys menn forlǣtan his, ac swýþe geswincful ys forlǣtan hine sylfne *laboriosum non est homini relinquere sua, sed valde laboriosum est relinquere semetipsum*, Scint. 60, 12. Geswincfulles gewinnes *laboriosi certaminis*, An. Ox. 1115. (2) *that requires effort, energy, &c., active* (not contemplative) :—Ðás twá geswustru hæfdon getácnunge ðises andweardan lífes and ðæs ēcan . . . Ǣgðer líf is herigendlic, ac þæt án is swá ðeáh geswincful, Hml. Th. ii. 442, 34. Geswincfulre *practicae*, i. *actualis* (*conversationis*), geswincful

---

*actualem*, An. Ox. 994, 996. III. of condition, *in which trouble is experienced, of great distress* :—Cūð is gehwilcum menn þæt þis líf is geswincful and on swáte wunað, Hml. S. 34, 142. [Ðis wæs swíðe geswincfull geár and byrstfull on eorðwæstman, Chr. 1116; P. 246, 33.] v. ofer-geswincfull.

ge-swincfulnys. *Add: Labour, difficulty, trouble* :—Geswincful-nyss nys menn forlǣtan his *it is no trouble to a man to leave his things*, Scint. 60, 11. v. ge-swincfull; II. 1.

ge-swinclic; *adj. That requires labour, laborious, hard* (of work) :—Bebeád Drihten eów þæt gē healdan þone Sunnandæg fram ǣlcum geswinclicum worce (*non facies omne opus in eo*), Wlfst. 294, 18.

ge-swincness, e; *f. Tribulation, trouble, trial* :—On mínre geswinc-nysse (*tribulatione*) ic þē tō clypige, Guth. 28, 23. Sē þe manigfealdlíce geswincnysse and earfoðnysse dreógeð *qui suffert temptationem*, 12, 6. Geswincnyssa ł gedrēfednyssa *tribulationes*, Ps. L. 24, 17. Of eallum geswincnyssum, 22.

ge-swing. *Add: swing.* v. hand-, sweord-geswing.

ge-swingan. *In last passage l.* ge-swingdon, *and add:* [*weak forms occur in* Lind.] :—Geswuing *uapulabit*, Lk. L. 12, 48. Æfter ðon gesuinged hiá (geswungen bið, R.) *postquam flagellauerint*, 18, 33. Gesuuingde (giswicte (= -swencte? cf. ge-swencan; L. 3; *or* -swingde?), R.) *vapulabit*, 12, 47. Geswungen *flagellato*, Kent. Gl. 713: *tortus*, An. Ox. 46, 48: *cesum*, i. *percussum*, 10.

ge-swip *a scourge.* Dele: ge-swip *cunning.* Dele, *and see next word.*

ge-swipor (-er); *adj. Cunning, crafty* :—Hē geswiperum (-swippre, v. l.) mūðe (*ore astuto*) wrehte, Bd. 2, 9; Sch. 146, 24. [Cf. O. H. Ger. swephar, swef(f)ar(i) *astutus, callidus.*]

ge-swipore; *adv. Cunningly, craftily* :—Hí fácen geswipere syredan *astute cogitauerunt consilium*, Ps. Th. 82, 3. [Cf. O. H. Ger. swepharo.]

ge-swiporlíce. *Add: The MS. has* geswiworlice. [Cf. O. H. Ger. swepharlíh *pernix.*]

ge-swipornes. *Add:* —On unnytte geswipurnesse, Verc. Först. 89, 7. Gesweopornessa *versutias* (v. Mk. 12, 15), Wrt. Voc. ii. 73, 47.

ge-swiria. v. ge-swigra : ge-swíþfrom. *See* swíþ-from *in Dict.:* ge-swíðrian. v. ge-swedrian.

ge-swíþrian *to be or become strong* :—Bliss engla sangum geswíþerod, Verc. Först. 135, 29.

ge-swōgen. *Add:* —Hē nē gýmde nánes lenctenes fæstenes, ac began tō etenne; hē feóll þá æt þǣre forman snǣde under becc geswōgen, Hml. S. 12, 63. þ hié sýn sóna geswōgene, gif hié þone mete næbben, Lch. ii. 196, 10. v. swōgan *in Dict.*

ge-swōgung. *Add:* —þám men bið þurst getenge and nearones and geswōgunga, Lch. ii. 194, 3: 160, 6. Se mon geswōgunga þrowað and mōdes geswǣðrunga, 206, 9. Hí heortcoþe wyrceað and angnessa and geswōwunga, 176, 13.

ge-swope (?, -swōpe?) *sweepings, rubbish* :—Gaesuope *peripsima*, Txts. 111, 15. Gisupop (= suopo? *the vowel being replaced by the consonant following it in the alphabet, a not unfrequent device, and o put for p to avoid three consecutive p's*) *peripsima superhabundans, purgamenta*, Hpt. 33, 250, 15. [Cf. O. H. Ger. ga-sopho *peripsima*, ga-sopha *quisquiliae, purgamenta.*] v. ge-swǣpa.

ge-swurdod. v. ge-sweordod: ge-swutelian. v. ge-sweotulian.

ge-swyrf. *Add:* —Geswyrfes of seolfre syx peninga gewǣge, Lch. i. 336, 8. v. ge-sweorf.

ge-swyrfan. *Dele, and see* ge-sweorfan: ge-swystra. *Dele first passage, and see* ge-sweostren: ge-swystren. v. ge-sweostren: ge-swydrian. v. ge-swedrian: ge-sýcan. v. ge-sícan: ge-syd. v. -syd *in Dict.*: ge-sydian. v. ge-sidian: ge-syfled hláf. v. syfian *in Dict.*: ge-syfl-melu. *Dele, and see* ge-siftan: ge-syft. v. ge-siftan.

ge-sylhþ *a plough.* *Substitute: a team* (of oxen) *for a plough* :—Ágife hē þ land þám hírēde mid swá myclum swá se hírēd him on hand sette; þ synd .xii. þeówe men, and .ii. gesylhðe oxan, and .i. hund sceápa, Cht. Th. 435, 6. [Cf. Hē geann án sylhðe oxna, Cht. Crw. 23, 4. *Here* (*unless* ánre *might be read for* án?) sylhðe *seems to be neuter* (*an* ioja-*stem*, v. Kl. Nom. Stam. § 70), *and to be similar in form and meaning to* M. H. Ger. pfluogide *a pair of plough-oxen : but* gesylhðe *above with plural in* e *seems to be feminine:* oxan *seems to be an instance of a gen. pl. in* an *instead of* (e)na.]

ge-sylt. v. ge-siltan: ge-sýman. v. ge-síman.

ge-syndgian *to prosper* (trans.) :—þá ongeáton hí þæt heora síðfæt wæs fram Gode gehradod and gesyndgad *intelligentes a Domino suum iter esse prosperatum.* Bd. 4, 19; Sch. 446, 2. *See next word.*

ge-syndig; *adj. Fair, favourable* :—Tō þon þæt gesyndge windas ūs æt lande gebrōhte *adeo ut secundi nos uenti ad terram comitarentur*, Bd. 5, 1; Sch. 553, 13. v. ge-sundig.

ge-syndiglic; *adj. Prosperous* :—On gesyndelecum þingum *in prosperity*, Bd. 4, 23; Sch. 475, 10. v. ge-sundiglic.

ge-syndrian. *For* 'R. Ben. . . . Lye' *substitute:* R. Ben. I. 56, 9, *and add:* —On eallum stōwum yld ná sí gesindrod (*discernatur*) on endebyrdnesse, 105, 6. Swā swā án man bið man ðá hwíle ðe sió sáwl

and se líchoma biþ ætsomne, þonne hí þonne gesindrede bióþ, ðonne ne
bið hē þ þ hē ǽr wæs, Bt. 37, 3; F. 190, 25.  v. ge-sundrian.

ge-sýne.  v. ge-síne.

ge-syngian.  *Add*: I. *to act wrongly, make a mistake*:—Leófa
dohtor, þū gesingodest mid þ̄y þe þū woldest witan his naman and his
gelimp, Ap. Th. 16, 2.  II. *of moral wrongdoing, to sin*. (1)
intrans. (a) *absolute*:—Ðonne hē of yfelum willan ne gesyngað, Past.
157, 25.  Ne wēnde Ezechias þæt hē gesyngode, 38, 3.  Ðæt hē gemēte
forgiefnesse ðæs ðe hē ðurh ðā geornfulnesse his andan gesyngade *ut
veniam obtineat, ex eo quod per zeli ejus studium peccat*, 165, 23.  Ǽr
ðǽm ðe hē gesyngige, 407, 4.  Hí on hira inngeðonce ongieten ðæt hié
gesyngoden, 417, 35.  Hié suuncon ymb ðæt hū hié meahton gesynglan,
239, 21.  (b) *to sin* in respect to a particular matter :—Hū suiðe hē on
ðām gesyngað, Past. 39, 2.  Ðæt hē self suiður on ðǽm ne gesyngige,
149, 23.  God forlēt ðæt mōd his gecorenra gesyngian on sumum lytlum
ðingum, 467, 11.  (c) *to sin against*:—þē ānum ic gesyngade, Bl. H.
87, 29.  Gif seofo síða gesynngiga (gesyngað, R.) in ðec *si septies
peccauerit in te*, Lk. L. 17, 4.  ¶ *of one special form of sin* :—Hē
gesyngias *moechatur*, Mt. L. 19, 9.  Ne gesynnge ðū *non moechaberis*,
5, 27.  Gesyngege *moechari*, 32.  (2) trans. *to commit* a sin :—Hē
teohhode gif hī hwæt gesyngodon (-en, *v. l.*) on þām frýdôme þ hī hit
eft on ðām freódóme gebēton, Bt. 41, 3; F. 248, 13.

ge-synlíce.  v. ge-sinlíce.

ge-syntlǽcan *to prosper*:—Well gesyntlǽcan *bene prosperare*, Ps.
Rdr. 117, 25.

ge-synto.  *Add*: I. *of physical soundness*. (1) *of persons* :—Ic
wēne þ hē wǽre biddende ðā upplican ārfæstnesse mīnra gesynta *pro
mea, ut reor, sospitate supernae pietati supplicans*, Bd. 5, 6; Sch. 578,
23.  (2) *of things* :—Hē þone tōbrocenan calic þǽre ǽrran gesynto eft
āgeaf *fractum calicem pristinae incolumitati restituit*, Gr. D. 50,
2.  II. *of favourable condition* :—Eála sē bið ofersǽlig sē þe mid
gesyntum swylce cwyldas and wítu mæg wel forbūgon *felix o nimium qui
illas effugiet poenarum prospere clades*, Dóm. L. 248.  [O. H. Ger. ge-
suntida *sanitas, prosperitas*.]

ge-syrwan.  v. ge-sirwan: **get, geta.** *l.* gēt, gēta.  v. gít, gíta:
**ge-taccod.**  v. ge-þaccian.

ge-tácnian.  *Add*: I. *to mark*. (1) *make a mark* on a material
object :—Getácnod *clavato, signato*, Wrt. Voc. ii. 131, 58.  On þǽre
stówe wæs getácnod swilce fordrūwod burna *in the place were marks as
of a dried-up burn*, Hml. S. 23 b, 196.  (2) *to mark* by assigning a
special condition :—Þēh þe ǽgher þissa burga þurh Godes díegelnessa
þus getácnod wurde *quamvis in tantum arcanis statutis inter utramque
urbem convenientiae totius ordo servatus sit*, Ors. 2, 1; S. 62, 25.
(3) *to mark* as witness, *set to one's seal* :—Hié tácen secgende wǽron
þā þe Drihten sylf getácnode, Bl. H. 161, 21.  II. *to indicate,
shew, make known*. (1) the subject a person (or not expressed). (a)
*with acc.* :—Þæt Octavianus sweotole getácnode . . . hē self sǽde þæt seó
dǽd his nǽre, Ors. 3, 5; S. 106, 30.  On þē wrāt God . . . and ryhte
ǽ getácnode on týn wordum, An. 1514.  Hē sylf ǽlce tíd getácnige
(*nuntiet*), R. Ben. 72, 12.  (b) *with clause* :—On ðǽm twǽm wordum
hē ūs getácnode for hwelcum ðingum wē sceolden ūre gódan weorc helan
and for hwelcum wē hī sceolden cýðan *qualiter videnda essent vel
qualiter non videnda ex sententiarum fine monstravit*, Past. 451, 10.
Getácna mē þǽr sēlast sý sáwle mínre . . . , Hy. 4, 9.  Ðeáh hit on
sumum ðingum getácnad sié ðæt hē hwelc wundor wyrcean mæge, Past.
119, 9.  On þǽm burgum wæs getácnad þæt Críst is eádmódegra help
*probans Deum solum esse conservatorem humilium*, Ors. 3, 2; S. 100,
24.  Getácnod, 3, 5; S. 106, 26.  (c) *intrans.* :—On þǽm ǽrrum
gewritum ic þē cýþde and getácnode be þǽre āsprungnisse sunnan and
mônan *prioribus litteris significaueram de solis luneque eclipsi*, Nar. 3,
12.  (2) the subject a thing :—Tal getácnas (*significans*) tó chwǽm of
tēnum mercum tal oncnáwes, Mt. p. 11, 14.  Gif þǽr beóð seofon ealra,
þonne getácniað hig þ se termen byð on Sæternes dæg, Angl. viii. 326,
26.  *Adverbia temporalia* synd ðā ðe tída getácniað, Ælfc. Gr. Z. 223,
17 *and often.*  ¶ where what is future is indicated :—Ge dóm ágon
. . . swā eów getácnod hafað Dryhten þurh míne hand, Jud. 197.  Hér
is geswutelod ūre forwyrd, tōweard getácnod þæt þǽre tíde ys neáh ge-
þrungen þe wē sculon æt sæcce forweorþan, 286.  III. *to signify*.
(1) *of words, to mean* :—*Significatio* ys getácnung, hwæt þæt word
getácnige, Ælfc. Gr. Z. 120, 1.  Hwæt is getácnod on þām worde þe
God cwæð: ' Þū scealt deáðe sweltan'?  Se twyfealda deáð wæs mid
þǽm getácnad *quid significat in eo quod dixit: 'Morte morieris'?
Duplicem mortem designat*, Angl. vii. 22, 196–199.  (2) *to express a
meaning by means of a figure, express symbolically* :—Ðā niétenu
getácnigeað (-tácnað, *v. l.*) ðonne mon hwæt ryhtlices geðencð, ðonne
ne ligeð hé is sóð cyning, Hml. Th. i. 116, 9.  Ðæt gold getácnode
þ hē is sóð cyning, Hml. Th. i. 116, 9.  Ðæt ūs getácnode Loth swíðe
wel on him selfum, ðā hē fleáh ðā biernendan ceastre.  Mid ðǽm ðe
hē fleáh ðā birnendan Sodoman, hē getácnode ðæt wē sculon fleón ðone
unliéfedan bryne ūres líchoman *quod bene Loth in semetipso exprimit, qui
ardentem Sodomam fugit . . . Ardentem Sodomam fugere est illicita*

*carnis incendia declinare*, 397, 32–36.  Seó nîwe gecýþnis is gefyllednis
ealra þǽra þinga þe seó ealde gecýþnis getácnode tówearde be Críste,
Ælfc. Gen. Thw. 2, 15.  Cwæþ se godspellere, ' Hǽlend cóm syx dagum
ǽr eástrum tó Bethania ' : on þon is getácnod þ hē cóm on þǽre syxtan
ylde on þysne middangeard, Bl. H. 71, 25: Past. 83, 25.  (2 a) *to
express the character of* an object by transferring a significant name :—
Galað is on Englisc gewitnesse heáp . . . Ðý is swíðe ryhte getácnod (*non
incongrue exprimitur*) ðurh Galates naman sió hálige gesomnung, Past.
367, 7.  (3) *to be the figurative representative of, be the symbol of* :—
Se gefarena brôðor getácnað Críst.  Hē . . . cuæð: ' Cýðað mínum
brôðrum ' *frater defunctus ille est, qui . . . dixit: ' Dicite fratribus
meis*,' Past. 43, 18.  Sió hreófl getácnað þæt wôhhǽmed *per scabiem
luxuria designatur*, 71, 4.  Hwæt getácnað ðæs sácerdes hrægl
būton ryht weorc *vestimenta sacerdotis quid aliud quam recta opera
debemus accipere ?*, 93, 12.  Sió niht getácnað ðā ðístro ðǽre blindnesse
ūrre tídernesse *per noctem exprimitur caecitas nostrae infirmitatis*, 433,
13.  þ fictreów . . . getácnaþ þā synfullan . . . , Bl. H. 71, 35.  Lazarus
getácnaþ þysne middangeard, 75, 5.  Getácnaþ *praefigurat*, An. Ox.
2510.  Hwæt getácniað ðā twelf oxan būtan ðā endebyrdnessa ðǽra
biscopa *quid duodecim bobus, nisi pastorum ordo, designatur ?*, Past. 105,
5: Bl. H. 73, 8: 121, 24.  Getácnaþ, Past. 155, 14.  Getác[nigend]
obumbrans, Hpt. Gl. 525, 59.  Þurh þæt lamb he wæs getácnud (*figura-
batur*), An. Ox. 40, 31.  (4) *to indicate figuratively* what is future,
betoken, portend, be a prognostic of :—Ic getácnie *portendo*, An. Ox.
18 b, 69.  Fugelas on swefenum se beóð gesyhð and mid him winneð saca
sume hit getácnað, Lch. iii. 198, 7 *and often*.  Getácnude *portenderat*,
An. Ox. 1794: *praefigurat*, 3715.  Þæt wæs sweotole getácnad, þā hē
cniht wæs . . . mon geseah ymbe þā sunnan swelce ān gylden hring, and
weóll ðā on wille ele.  On þǽm hringe wæs getácnad þæt . . . , and se ele
getácnade miltsunge eallum moncynne, Ors. 5, 14; S. 248, 6–13.
Getácnod *praesignabatur*, An. Ox. 5057.  [Cf. *Goth*. ga-taiknjan *to
give a sign, warn*: O. H. Ger. ge-zeihhanôn *signare, designare, demonstrare, significare*.]

ge-tácniendlic.  *Add*: I. *to be shewn, to be indicated* :—Be ge-
tácniendlicum tídum Godes weorces *de significanda hora operis Dei*, R.
Ben. 72, 9.  II. *symbolical* :—Hí getácnigendlice lác offrodon.  Þæt
gold getácnode þæt hē is sóð cyning, Hml. Th. i. 116, 8.

ge-tácnigendlíce; *adv. Figuratively, symbolically*:—Þæt wíf cwæð
. . . ' þā hwelpas etað of ðām crumon þe feallað of heora hláfordes
mýsan.'  Swíðe getácnigendlíce spræc þis wíf.  Seó mýse is seó bóclice
lár . . . æfter gǽstlicum andgite þā hwelpas etað ðā cruman, Hml. Th. ii.
114, 23–29.

ge-tácnung.  *Add*: I. *a sign, mark*. (1) *a mark* made on an
object :—Bóceras habbað on heora cræfte tácna . . . and mē þingð
wynsumlic þ ic þǽra preósta notas þām bócerum gekýðe þe lǽs þe hig
witan þ þā rímcræftige we:as sýn būtan cræftigum getácnungum, Angl.
viii. 333, 19.  (2) *a significant gesture, sign* of feeling made by a
person :—Þæt nǽfre nānre céorunge yfelnes on āhwylcum worde oðþe
getácnunge (*in aliquo qualicumque verbo vel significatione*) geswutelod
wurðe, R. Ben. 58, 9.  (3) *a signal* :—Þæt sý mid sumere getácnunge
gebeden and nā mid menniscre stefne *sonitu cujuscumque signi potius petatur
quam voce*, R. Ben. 62, 16.  (4) *a warning signal, notice of danger* :—
þū forgǽfe ondrǽdendum þē getácnunge (*significationem*), þ hig fleón,
Ps. L. 59, 6.  II. *figurative representation* :—Getácnung *prae-
figuratio*, An. Ox. 1802 : Ælfc. T. Grn. 11, 11.  Hē hēt wurpan þæt
net on ðā swiðran healfe for ðǽre getácnunge.  Seó swíðre healf
getácnað ðā gódan, Hml. Th. ii. 290, 11.  Þæt getel ðǽra fixa hæfð
māran getácnunge ðonne ge understandan magon *the number of the fishes
represents figuratively more than you can understand*, 292, 3.  Þū
miht sceáwian þā getácnunga þæt Adam getácnude, Ælfc. T. Grn. 3,
32.  Getácnunge *typum*, i. *figuram*, An. Ox. 213: 5136.  Seó bóce ys,
. . . mid deópum andgitte on díglum getácnungum, Ælfc. T. Grn. 10,
42.  III. *of words, signification* :—*Significatio* ys getácnung,
hwæt þæt word getácnige, Ælfc. Gr. Z. 120, 1 : 223, 1, 16.  Hwílon
hē (*the preposition*) geeácnað and gefylð þǽra worda andgit þe hē tó
cymð, and hwílon hē áwent heora getácnunge and hwílon wanað, 268,
2.  Wæs seó ealde ǽ swíðe earfoðe tó understondenne; ac þonne wē
cumað tó ðām smedman, þæt is tó ðǽre getácnunge, þonne gereordað
heó ūre mód, Hml. Th. i. 188, 8.

ge-tǽcan.  *Add*: p. -tǽhte *To shew*.  I. *to present to the mind
for consideration* :—Getǽc mē nū sumne mann þāra þe ðē gesǽlegost
þince, Bt. 11, 1; F. 32, 15.  II. *to give a knowledge of* an
object :—Gif þū gecnāwan miht ðā anlícnessa þǽre sóþan gesǽlþe, þonne
sippan is þearf þ ic þē hí selfe getǽce (-tǽce, *v. l.*) (*ordo est deinceps,
quae sit vera monstrare*), Bt. 33, 1; F. 120, 1.  Ic sceal be sumere
bisene sume anlícnesse þǽre wísan þē getǽcan, oþ þ þ hig cúþre sié
*quae tibi caussa notior est, eam prius designare verbis atque informare
conabor*, 22, 2; F. 78, 14.  Ðū mē gehēte lytle ǽr þ þū hí woldest mē
getǽcan *eam tu paullo ante monstrasti*, 33, 3; F. 126, 10.  Ic hit þē
wille getǽcan *hoc verissima ratione patefaciam*, 34, 9; F. 146, 13.
Ðǽr ic hæbbe getǽht hwelc hierde bión sceal *monstrare qualis esse*

*debeat Pastor*, Past. 467, 20. **III.** *to shew* an object to a person so that the object may be attained by the person, *to shew* a way, place, &c. (1) lit.:—Hē mē wið his sunu setl getǣhte, B. 2013. Him freá engla wíc getǣhte, Gen. 2837. Gūðlác bæd þæt hē him þā stōwe getǣhte *Guthlacus illum locum sibi monstrari a narrante efflagitat*, Guth. Gr. 114, 22. (2) fig.:—Getǣc mē þone weg, Bt. 36, 3; F. 174, 32. Ic ðē wille getǣcan ðone weg þe ðē gelǣt tō þǣre heofenlican byrig *viam tibi, quae te domum revehat, ostendam*, 36, 1; F. 172, 28: 40, 5; F. 240, 17. **IV.** *to shew* a person the direction that must be taken, the direction being marked by a preposition, *to send:*—Nān man ne getǣce his getibtledan man fram him, Ll. Th. i. 210, 23. **IVa.** *to assign* a person to a position:—His fæder hine strýnð be his āgenre freódehter, and hē bið his mōder twām sibbum getǣht (*he is assigned to two of his mother's relationships*), þæt hē bið ǣgðer ge sunu ge brōðer, Wlfst. 193, 7. **V.** *to shew* the course that must be followed, *to direct, appoint, prescribe, enjoin, impose.* (1) absolute:—Gebēte hē swā bisceop getǣce, Ll. Th. i. 168, 18 : ii. 300, 17. Bēte swā him dōmeras getǣcan *quantum arbitri judicaverint*, 48, 18. (2) with acc. :—Smyltnisse gesette t getǣhte *silentium imposuisset Saducaeis*, Mt. L. 22, 34. Smeágean mid hwylcere fulfremednysse se dǣdbēta getǣht hæbbe þ him getǣht wæs (*id quod ei praescriptum erat*), Ll. Th. ii. 178, 13. (3) with clause :—Hē him getǣhte hwæt hī on ðǣm dōn sceolden, hwæt ne scolden *quid facere, quidve non facere deberet, indixit*, Past. 405, 29. Þā getǣhte man Wynflǣde þ hió mōste hit hyre geāhnian, Cht. Th. 288, 34. Hālig hundum ne is sellennde fore-gemercade t getǣhte *sanctum canibus non dandum praefigit*, Mt. p. 15, 7. **Va.** *to warn:*—Ðe angel fore-gelǣrde t foregetǣhte *angelo praemonente*, Mt. p. 14, 2. **VI.** *to teach :*—'Ic wolde þ þu leornodest hū þū mihtest becuman tō ðām sōþum gesǣlþum.' Ðā cwæþ ic : 'Hū ne gehēte þū mē gefyrn ǣr þ þū hit woldest mē getǣcan,' Bt. 33, 3; F. 126, 31. **VIa.** *to persuade:* cf. lǣtan :—Wē getǣceþ (lǣrað, W. S.) him *suadebimus ei*, Mt. R. 28, 14. **VII.** *to shew* in action, *give effect to :*—On hundrede wē wyllaþ þ mon folcriht getǣce æt ǣlcere spǣce, Ll. Th. i. 260, 12.

**ge-tǣl.** *Add:* **I.** *the precise sum* of any collection of individual objects:—Wæs gemenigfylld þæt getel crīstenra manna, Hml. Th. i. 44, 21. Symle bið hāligra manna getel geeácnod ... Nis þæt getel Godes gecorenra lytel, 536, 24–26. Þæt getel ðæra fixa hæfð mǣran getācnunge ðonne gē understandan magon, ii. 292, 3. Þurh þ ungerímedlic getell þāra mǣrra cýðra, Ll. Lbmn. 413, 15. Getæl t gerīm (getel, Ps. Spl., getell, Ps. L.) daga mīnra *numerum dierum meorum*, Ps. Rdr. 38, 5. Þ getæl þāra stafena wē þencað tō cýðanne, Angl. viii. 335, 40.] **II.** *a particular sum of units*, of a kind determined by the context :—Æfter þām þūsende bið se deófol unbunden. Nū is þæt þūsendfeald getæl āgān, Wlfst. 243, 24. Fulfremedum þreófealdum getæle *perfecto trino numero*, Hy. S. 60, 29. Þæs mōnan swiftnes āwyrpð ūt ǣnne dæg and āne niht of ðām getæle (-tele) hys rynes ǣfre ymbe neogontȳne gēar (*a day has to be deducted from the number of days in a lunation every nineteen years*; cf. binnan nigontȳne wintrum wurde ān dæg gelytlod of þæs mōnan ylde, Angl. viii. 308, 27), Lch. iii. 264, 22. Ān þūsend ... twā þūsend and swā forð tō ǣlcum getele (-tǣle, *v. l.*), Ælfc. Gr. Z. 282, 12. **III.** *a sum* or *total of abstract units :*—þæt twelffealde getel getācnode þ twelf apostolas, Hml. Th. i. 190, 11. Syxtigfeald getel (-tell, -tæl, *v. ll.*) *sexagenarius* ... þūsendfeald getel (-tæl, *v. l.*), millenarius, Ælfc. Gr. Z. 285, 5-10. Hundfeald getel is fulfremed, Hml. Th. i. 338, 27. þūsend getel bið fulfremed, and ne āstīhð nān getel ofer þæt. Mid þām getele bið getācnod seó fulfremednys ..., 188, 34-190, 1. Hylt Godes gelaðung þis hundseofontigfealde getel. ii. 86, 2. **IIIa.** *a word that denotes a number, a cardinal numeral :*—Adverbia cumað of ǣlcum getele, Ælfc. Gr. Z. 285, 13. **IV.** *the full number* of a collection of objects. (1) where inclusion in the collection is marked:—Hē mihte beón geteald on fulfremedra hālgena getele, Hml. Th. ii. 120, 5. Seó bōc ys geteald tō þisum getele ... Hester seó cwēn hæfð eác āne bōc on þisum getele, Ælfc. T. Grn. 11, 10-13. (2) *the class* or *category* of :—Getæl *catalogus*, Wrt. Voc. ii. 15, 39. On getæle *in catalogo* (*in catalogo* charismatum enumerantur, Ald. 6, 22), 43, 61. Mōdignys ys endenēxt gesett on getele ðæra heáfodleahtra, Hml. Th. ii. 222, 3. **Va.** (large, small, &c.) *collection* or *company* of persons or things:—Cōm þæt mycele sǣflōd ... and ādrencte manncynnes unārīmædlice geteall (-tel, -tæl, *v. ll.*), Chr. 1014; P. 145, 29. **VI.** *a certain company* of persons, *collection* of things, not precisely reckoned :—*In centuriis seniorum et juniorum divisus; centurias* getalu *sive* heápas *dictae*, Wrt. Voc. ii. 49, 34. **VII.** *number* in the abstract :—God ealle gesceafta gelōgode on gemete, and on getele and on hefe, Hml. Th. i. 286, 14. Hē ealle gesceafta gesette on ðrīm ðingum : *in mensura, et pondere, et numero*, þæt is on gemete, and on hefe, and on getele, ii. 586, 32. *Numeralia* syndon ðā ðe getācniað getel (-tæl, *v. l.*), Ælfc. Gr. Z. 232, 6 : 280, 18. **VIIa.** in phrases denoting that objects have not been, or cannot be, counted :—Ymbsealdon mē yfiu þāra nis getell (*quorum non est numerus*), Ps. L. 39, 13: 146, 5. God is būtan getele,

for ðon ðe hē is ǣfre, Hml. Th. i. 286, 11. **VIII.** *a calculated space* of time :—Twā hundredum and seofen and sixtigum fiftȳne geáres getel *olimpiade ducentesima sexagesima septima*, An. Ox. 3036. þæt nǣfre ǣr .xi. kl. Aprelis, ne nāht æfter .vii. kl. Mī. eástortīd gewurðan sceal. Ac on þison getele, lōc hwǣr hit þonne tō gegā, healde hit mon þǣr mid rihte, Lch. iii. 226, 10. Getalum *laterculis* (pentecoste septenis hebdomadarum curriculis calculatur sicut Iubileus septenis annorum *laterculis* supputatur, Ald. 53, 7), Wrt. Voc. ii. 50, 29. **IX.** *in* grammar, *number, property in words of* denoting that one, two, *or more objects are spoken of* :—Sum getel (-tæl, *v. l.*) bið ǣfre menigfeald: *singuli homines* ǣnlīpige men ... Gyt ðǣr is ōðer getel (-tæl, *v. l.*) æfter ðisum: *singularis* ānfeald, Ælfc. Gr. Z. 284, 5-17. Gýt synd manega getel (-tæl, *v. l.*) on mislicum getācnungum: *simplum* be ānfealdum, 286, 16. **X.** *of speech, rhythm* :—Rīma getæl *rithmus* (cf. rithmus, numerus, 7, 274), Corp. Gl. H. 103, 179. Cf. rīmgetæl. **XI.** *computation, reckoning* :—Getæl *conputatio*, Wrt. Voc. ii. 15, 38. Getæl *calculus*, An. Ox. 21, 8. Geteles *supputationis, i. computationis*, 1535. On getales rīme, Sal. 38. Of getele *calculo*, An. Ox. 3229. Ne magon wē þā tīde be getale healdan dagena rīmes, Men. 63. Þā stafas þe preóstas on heora getæle habbað, Angl. viii. 335, 39. Is þæt þūsendfeald getæl āgān æfter mennisclicum getæle, Wlfst. 243, 24. Be ealdum getele wǣron þa āgāne ðreó hund geára, Hml. S. 23, 486. Ān eórod is gecweden on ðām ealdan getele six ðūsend manna and six hund and six and syxtig, 28, 12. Nǣron nāne tīda on þām geárlican getæle ǣr ðām God gesceóp ðā tunglan tō geárlicum tīdum, Hex. 12, 21. Syððan lēt gān þ getæl swā wē nū cwǣdon *then let the counting go on as we have just said*, Angl. viii. 326, 30. Þā ealdan Rōmāne ongunnon þæs geáres ymbryne on ðysum dæge ... þā Egyptiscan ðeóda ongunnon heora geáres getel on hærfeste ... Rihtlīcost bið geðūht þæt þæs geáres anginn sý gehæfd on þām dæge þe þæt Ebrēisce folc heora geáres getel onginnað, Hml. Th. i. 98, 19-33. **XII.** *recounting, telling of :*—Æfter getal tuoentig fēuer aldra *post expositionem viginti quattuor seniorum*, Mt. p. 10, 1. v. geár-, heáfod-, mīl-, sealm-, seofon-, þūsend-, un-getæl (-tel).

**ge-tæl;** *adj.* Take here what is given in Dict. under **ge-tal**, *and add :* Having mastery of :—Getælne *competem* (l. competem). v. dialecticae artis *competem*, Ald. 46, 8), Wrt. Voc. ii. 82, 27.

**ge-tǣlan.** *Add:* **I.** *to blame, reprehend, condemn.* (1) the object a person :—Cuēn sūðdǣles ārīses in dōm mid cneórisso ðas and getēleð (*condemnabit*) ðā, Mt. L. 12, 42. Getēleð (*condemnabunt*), 41. Getēldon hine tō deáðe *condemnabunt eum morte*, 20, 18. Þte hine ginōmun t giteldun on wordum *ut eum caperent in uerbo*, Mk. R. L. 12, 13. þ heora mōd hæfde hwæthugu þæs þe hit mihte hit sylf big getǣlan *ut eorum animus habeat unde se ipse reprehendat*, Gr. D. 204, 3. Sē ðe ōðerne tǣlan wille ... beðence hē hwæðer hine ne mæge ǣnig man getǣlan, Wlfst. 233, 23. Se weliga ðe on ðǣm godspelle getǣld is ... nis hit nō gesǣd þæt hē for ðý getǣled wǣre ðý hē ōðre menn reáfode *neque dives in evangelio ... aliena rapuisse perhibetur*, Past. 337, 23-339, 2. (2) the object a thing :—Ðā ūpāhafenesse hē getǣlde (*reprehendit*), Past. 39, 21. Ic nāt hū ic mæge heora dysig swā swīþe getǣlan swā ic wolde *quid dignum stolidis mentibus imprecer*?, Bt. 32, 3; F. 118, 27. Ðæt wæs getǣled ðurh ðone mūð ðære Sōðfæstnesse *quod ore Veritatis increpatur*, Past. 439, 27. **II.** *to contemn, despise, mock :*—Dý lǣs ðu gitēla *ne despicias*, Rtl. 43, 13. Getēled bið *contempnatur*, Mk. L. 9, 12 : *inludetur*, Lk. L. 18, 32. **III.** *to maltreat, vex, abuse, entreat spitefully :*—Þte ne gitēled mec ne suggillet me, Lk. R. L. 18, 5. Swā þte hiā him bitwih gitēldun *ita ut se inuicem conculcarent*, 12, 1. Mid fræceðo geyfled t getēled *contumelia adfectus*, Mt. L. 22, 6.

**getǣl-circul,** es; *m.* A cycle *for computation :*—Se niganteóða getælcircul *circulus decennovenalis* ; the Metonic cycle, Wrt. Voc. ii. 131, 34.

**getǣl-cræft,** es; *m.* Arithmetic :—Getælcræ[ft] *arithmetica*, An. Ox. 3117.

**getǣl-fers,** es; *n. Verse that depends on the number of feet :*—Mid getelferse t syxfētum *catalectico uersu*, An. Ox. 127.

**ge-tǣlfull;** *adj. Numerous :*—Getellfull (getellfullnyss?) on ān gegæderud ȳþigende gefremþ genihtsumnysse *numerositas in unum coacta exundantem efficit copiam*, Scint. 231, 10.

**ge-tǣlged.** v. ge-telged.

**getǣl-sum;** *adj. Harmonious, rhythmic :*—On ge[tæ]lsumum leóðe *carmine rithmico*, i. numerali, An. Ox. 390. v. tælsum.

**getǣl-wís;** *adj. Skilled in computation :*—Compos ... *prudens vel* getælwīs, Wülck. Gl. 207, 40. Þæs geáres dagas þe getelwīse witan nemniað *solaris annus*, Angl. viii. 316, 45.

**ge-tǣsan.** *Add:* fig. *to touch, affect the mind :*—Ðæt āhrēred mōd, ðonne hit ongiet ðæt him mon birgð mid ðære gesceádlican andsuare, hit bið getǣsed on ðæt ingeðonc *commotae mentes, dum et parci sibi sentiunt, et tamen responsorum ratione in intimis tanguntur*, Past. 297, 18.

**ge-tǣse,** es; *n. Add :*—Commodum nyt and getǣse and bryce, Wrt.

Voc. ii. 24, 63. Ðȳ lǽs hié gedwelle sió gehȳdnes and þá getǽsu ðe hié on ðǽm wege habbað . . . Eác hí sint tó monienne ðætte hié nó ne geliéfen ðætte ðá willan and ðá getǽsu ðe him on disse worulde becumað sién leán *ne subsidia itineris in obstacula perventionis vertant* . . . *Admonendi itaque sunt, ut quaeque in hoc mundo consequuntur non praemia credant*, Past. 387, 13–18. v. un-getǽse; ge-tǽsu.

ge-tǽse; *adj. Dele bracket at end, and add :*—Hió bið eádgum leóf, earmum getǽse, Rä. 81, 22. Hé him geneádodon and gelettum gedyde sume getǽse hȳðde his geswinces *ei laboris sui commodum coacto renitentique dedit*, Gr. D. 39, 27. Ne mæg se man him nánre mild-heortnesse wēnan, sē þe nū forleósað þá getǽsan tíde þǽre dǽdbóte, Archiv cxxii. 259, 45. [His sweord þe him wes itase (þat he louede swiþe, 2nd MS.), Laym. 6502.] v. un-getǽse.

ge-tǽslíce; *adv. Easily, agreeably, conveniently :*—Hé ús selð his oele, ðonne hé úre líf líðelíce and getǽslíce fered *oleum suum nobis tribuit, cum vitam nostram blanda lenitate disponit*, Past. 368, 12. v. un-getǽslíce.

ge-tǽsnes. *Substitute :* I. *fitness, convenience* for a purpose :—Habban ealle fultum and frófor be þǽre gefērrǽdenne micelnesse and be þǽre stówe staðole and getǽsnesse *habeant omnes solacia secundum modum congregationis aut positionem loci*, R. Ben. 59, 1.     II. *advantage, profit :*—Sió getǽsnes *commodities*, Wrt. Voc. ii. 23, 27. Getǽsnes *conpendio*, 24, 23. v. un-getǽsnes.

ge-tǽsu; *indecl. or gen. e ; f. Commodity, profit, advantage :*—Tó þon þæt hé him swá gelettum and swá genȳddum forgeáfe and gedyde hwæthugu getǽse (-tǽsu, *v. l.*) his gewinnes *ei laboris sui commodum coacto renitentique dedit*, Gr. D. 39, 28. v. ge-tǽse; *n*. and *adj.*

ge-tal; *adj. See* ge-tæl.

ge-talian. *Add : to account, consider to be* so and so :—Hé bið untwȳlíce mynetcȳpa getalod, Hml. Th. i. 412, 16.

getan. *Dele, and see* gítan.

ge-tang; *adj. In juxtaposition, close to* an object :—Sió filmen . . . is on óðre healfe brád, ge hríned ðǽre sídan, on óðre is ðám innoðe getang, Lch. ii. 242, 21. Seó geogað ná getang licge (getanglíce ne licge, *v. l.*), ac sió yld þá geogoðe tólicge *adolescentiores fratres juxta se non habeant lecta, sed permixti cum senioribus*, R. Ben. 47, 15. v. ge-tenge.

ge-tange ; *adv. Near to, in connexion with :*—Líf wæs mín longe leódum in gemonge, tírum getonge *long was my life among men, always glorious*, Reim. 42.

ge-tanglíce; *adv.* v. ge-tang.

ge-tanned. *Add :*—Getannod *medicatum* vel *confestum* (omitted after Wrt. Voc. i. 47, 33, see) Angl. viii. 451.

ge-targed. *Add :*—Getargede *scutati*, An. Ox. 2259.

ge-tawa; *pl. f. Substitute :* ge-tawu(-a), -teá; *pl. n. Implements, apparatus :*—Gif mannes getawa (*instrumenta genitalia*) beóþ sáre, Lch. ii. 70, 7. Ðis syndon þá wǽpena þe deófol mid oferswíðed bið ; þ is ofthrǽdlíce rǽdinga háligra bóca and gelómlíce gebedu. Ðis syndan þá getawa þe mon mæg heofona ríce mid begytan, Ll. Th. ii. 404, 3. [Cf. *O. H. Ger.* gi-zauua *suppellex.*] v. gúþ-, lǽce-, scip-, wíg-getawu(-a); geatwe.

ge-tawian. *Add :* I. *to dress, prepare* material :—Wulfes flǽsc wel getawod (*conditam*) and gesoden, Lch. i. 360, 14. Ðá þæt land ðá getawod wæs *dum praeparata terra*, Bd. 4, 28; Sch. 521, 3.     II. *to treat* a person (ill), *bring* or *put* to shame. (1) of personal action :—Sume wurdon getawod tó scande *some were shamefully entreated*, Chr. 1076; P. 212, 28. (2) of the operation of disease :—Án man wæs yfele getawod, and hine æt se cancor, Hml. S. 6, 284. v. ge-teágan.

-gete. v. be-, eáþ-gete.

ge-teágan. *Add :*—Him mon selle leóhte wyrtdrencas swilce swá bið wel geteád alwe, Lch. ii. 226, 14.

ge-teáma. v. ge-tíma: ge-tel. v. ge-tæl: ge-télan. v. ge-tǽlan.

ge-teld. *Add :*—Geteld *tentorium*, Wrt. Voc. ii. 122, 16. Geteldu ł eardungstówa *tabernacula*, Ps. L. 82, 7. Þíne geteld, 83, 2. On middum þǽm úrum wícum and betwih þǽm geteldum *inter ipsa tentoria in media castrorum parte*, Nar. 12, 25.     ¶ geteld sleán *to pitch a tent :*—Man slóh án geteld ofer þá bán, Hml. S. 26, 180. Gif hé his scip uppe getogen hæbbe oþþon hulc geworhtne oþþon geteld geslagen, Ll. Th. i. 286, 9. Wolde Petrus sleán ðreó geteld (cf. *si vis, faciam tria tabernacula*, Mt. 17, 4), Hml. Th. ii. 242, 8.     ¶ the necessity for tents when travelling in England is suggested by the following :—Ælfwold biscop geann þám æþelinge twēgra getelda, and Ælfwolde munuce ánes horses and ánes geteldes, Cht. Crw. 23, 10–12. Ælfríc arcebiscep cwæð intó sancte Albæne his geteld, C. D. iii. 352, 14. Hió becwið Ælfwolde hyre reáde geteld, vi. 132, 12. Cf. Ælfríc biscop I biquæðe míne teld and mín bedreáf ðat ic best hauede ūt on mí fare mid mē, iv. 302, 27. [*O. H. Ger.* ge-zelt *tentorium, tabernaculum, papillio.*] v. gang-geteld.

geteld-gehlíwung, e; *f. Shelter afforded by a tent :*—Hyt wæs wundorlic Moyses geteldgehlíwung, Angl. viii. 308, 34.

---

ge-telged. v. telgan *in Dict., and add :*—Ge[t]ælged *colerata*, Wrt. Voc. ii. 87, 20.

ge-tellan. *Add :* I. of speech, *to tell.* (1) *to relate, give an account of, state :*—Geteled is ðæhtung ðǽra Iudēa *refertur consilium Iudaeorum*, Mt. p. 20, 1 : Lk. p. 4, 12. Ic ymbe Rōmāna gewin on þǽm geárríme forð ofer þ geteled hæbbe *Romanas clades recensendo progressus sum*, Ors. 3, 7 ; S. 110, 12. Ðærbufan is geteald hwelc hē beón sceal, gif hē untælwierðe bið *cum virtutum necessaria subsequenter enumerat, quae sit irreprehensibilitas ipsa manifestat*, Past. 53, 10. (2) *to enumerate :*—Winterfeorm, Eásterfeorm . . . and fela ðinga ðe ic getellan ne mæig, Ll. Th. i. 440, 28. Impian, beána sáwan, . . . wyrtūn plantian, and fela ðinga ic eal geteallan ne mæig, Angl. ix. 262, 13. (3) *to discuss, dispute.* Cf. talu ; II :—Bituih him geteledon huā woere hiora mǽra *inter se disputauerint quis esset illorum maior*, Mk. L. 9, 34.     II. of number, *to count.* (1) *to determine the number of a* collection of objects, *compute the amount of :*—Getelles *computat* (*sumtus*), Lk. L. R. 14, 28. Swá man rihtost mage oþþe gemetan oþþe getellan oþþe áwegan, Ll. Th. i. 194, 8. Geteald *dinumerari*, An. Ox. 3228 : *calculatur*, i. *numeratur*, 3830. Getealde *calculantur, numerantur*, 1537. Geteledra tȳn þúsendo *decem milia*, Ps. Th. 90, 7. Wē gesēgon eówic standan twelfe getealde (*twelve in number*), An. 885. (1 a) getellan wiþ *to compare* one amount *with* another :—Gif þú getælest (-tel-, *v. l.*) ðá hwíle þisses andweardan lífes wið ðæs ungeendodan lífes hwíla, hwæt bið hit þonne ? *quod si ad aeternitatis infinita spatia pertractes, quid habes?*, Bt. 18, 3 ; F. 66, 4. (2) *to reckon, fix* as the number which completes a whole :—Hwí is ðis fæsten þus geteald þurh feówertig daga ? On eallum geáre sind getealde ðreó hund daga and fíf and sixtig daga, Hml. Th. i. 178, 19–21. On ðám geáre synd getealde twelf mōnðas and twá and fíftig wucena, Lch. iii. 246, 11. (3) *to reckon, estimate, consider.* (a) where the amount of an object is given as so and so :—Ealne þone eard Asiam, sē is geteald tó healfan dǽle middaneardes, Hml. Th. i. 68, 35. (b) where a total which is formed by two or more objects is given as so and so :—Wæs geteald ǽfen and merigen tó ánum dæge *evening and morning were reckoned a day*, Lch. iii. 232, 11.     III. *to consider :*—Hwæt is bearn mannes þet þú getelest (*reputas*) hine?, Ps. L. 143, 3. (1) with an object having a noun, adjective, or phrase in apposition, *to consider, account* a thing such and such. (a) noun :—Giteled wæs scendung giliórnise hiora *existimata est afflictio exitus illorum*, Rtl. 86, 16. Geteled bið wer snotre *shall be considered a wise man*(?) ; *assimilabitur viro sapienti*, Mt. L. 7, 24. Hū unlíht Abraham beón clǽne þ hē nǽre forligr geteald *quomodo defenditur Abraham adulterii reus non esse?*, Angl. vii. 46, 440. Hrȳðeres belle . . . is melda geteald, Ll. Th. i. 260, 17 : 340, 14. Heó weard heálic gyden geteald, Wlfst. 106, 14. (b) adj. :—Hé is geteald árwurðost ealra þǽra goda, Wlfst. 106, 10 : Chr. 1086; P. 221, 29. Hé bið scyldig geteald *poenae reus addicitur*, Past. 459, 27. Bið geteald *reputabitur* (*stultus, si tacuerit, sapiens*), Kent. Gl. 625. Mæsse-preóstes áð and woruldþegenes is geteald efendȳre, Ll. Th. i. 182, 15. Get(e)alde *putabantur* i. *existimabantur* (*pudicitia praediti*), An. Ox. 1733. (c) phrase :—þæt hé sȳ tóforan óðrum mannum þurh his glencge geteald, Hml. Th. i. 328, 30. (2) with object and prepositional phrase, *to consider* as, in the character of :—Seó oferflównes hyre ne mæg on synne geteled beón *ei superfluitas in culpam non ualet reputari*, Bd. 1, 27; Sch. 81, 17. Ðás men wǽron getealde for ðá mǽrostan godas, Wlfst. 106, 16. (3) with a clause :—Gitelede hine gisihðe gesēge *estimabat se visum videre*, Rtl. 58, 15. Geteledon symbel ne woeron wyrðe *studentes cena non fuerint digni*, Lk. p. 8, 13.     IV. *to assign.* (1) *to assign* something to a person, *ascribe, impute :*—Wer þǽm ne geteleð (*imputauit*) Dryhten synne, Ps. Vos. 31, 2. Man geteald him (*Oswold*) þ nigonðe geár (*ut idem annus Osualdi regno adsignaretur*, Bd. 3, 1), Chr. 633; P. 27, 6. (2) *to assign* a person or thing. (1) to a duty, position, &c., *to depute, delegate* ; cf. *to be told off* for a duty :—Getealde *delegavit*, Wrt. Voc. ii. 26, 4. Hé getiðode and getealde þá bróðru tó þám mynstre and him ealdor gesette *consentiens deputatis fratribus patrem constituit*, Gr. D. 147, 21. Ic eom hér geteald and geseted æfter mínum ænde *hic post mortem deputatus sum*, 343, 26. Getealdne *deputatam* (-*um*? cf. pini stipitem paganorum ceremoniis *deputatum*, Ald. 30, 32), Wrt. Voc. ii. 28, 48. þá unrihtwísan men beóð getealde tó þám ēcan wíte *iniqui aeterno supplicio deputati*, Gr. D. 335, 17 : 336, 11, 14. On þára manna gewitnesse þe him tó gewitnesse getealde syndon, Ll. Th. i. 162, 13. (b) to a class or category :—Suiðe ryhte sē bið geteald tó ðæm líceterum *inter hypocritas jure deputatur*, Past. 121, 23. Tó ðám ðæt wē sién geteald and gefēged tó ðæm gefōgstánum on ðǽre Godes ceastre *ut intus in templum Dei disponamur*, 253, 19. Sind getealde *deputa[n]tur* (*secundo eunuchorum gradui*), An. Ox. 1624.     V. *to number, include* in a class :—Hē mid unrihtwísum geteald (-teled, L. R.) wæs *cum iniustis deputatus est*, Lk. 22, 37 : *reputatus*, Mk. 15, 28.     V a. getellan tó *to consider of the same class with, as the equal of* another ; *annumerare :*—Ðes is úre God, and nis nán óðer geteald tó him, Hml. Th. ii. 12, 30. [*O. Sax.* gi-tellian : *O. H. Ger.* ge-zellen *calculare*,

*numerare, con-, de-numerare, censere, recensere, com-, de-, im-, re-putare.*]

**ge-téman, ge-téme.** v. ge-tíman, ge-tíme : **ge-temesed.** *Add :* v. temesian.

**ge-temian.** *Add :* I. *to tame.* v. tam :—Ylpas getemode and tó wíge gewenode, Hml. S. 25, 558. II. [as causative to a verb corresponding to *O. H. Ger.* ge-zeman ; *p.* -zam *convenire decere*] *to cause to be fitting, to allow* (?) :—Dú ne mihtest getemian þ míre andetnysse leóht-fæt sceolde ácwyncan, Hml. S. 23, 810. [*Goth.* ga-tamjan *to tame* : *O. H. Ger.* ge-zemmen *domare*.] v. un-getemed.

**ge-temprian.** *Add :* I. *to temper, prepare* material :—On þá onlícnesse geworht þe senop bið getemprod tó inwísan, Lch. ii. 184, 22. II. fig. *to prepare, adapt* :—Ge tó gódum ge tó yfelum getempera heortan þíne *et ad bona et ad mala tempera cor tuum*, Scint. 172, 15.

**ge-temprung.** v. un-getemprung.

**ge-tengan.** *Add :* I. *intrans. To hurry* :—Hé mid fleáme tó wuda getengde, Hml. Th. i. 384, 8. II. *reflex. To press, apply oneself to* ; *incumbere* :—Ongan Dryhtnes ǽ georne cýðan, and hine sylfne getengde in Godes þeówdóm, æscróf unsláw, El. 200.

**ge-tenge.** *Take here* ge-tænge *in Dict., and add :* I. *of local relations, close against.* (1) *lying on or by, in contact with* :—Eall líchoma eorþan getenge (cf. sume licgaþ mid eallon líchoman on eorþan, Bt. 41, 6 ; F. 254, 25) *alia extento sint corpore, pulveremque verrunt*, Met. 31, 7. Þonne ic (*a swan*) getenge ne beóm flóde and foldan, Rä. 8, 8. Ic (*the furrow made by a ship*) . . . ánum getenge liðendum wuda líce míne, 11, 4. Mec (*an oyster*) ýða wrugon eorðan getenge, 76, 2 : 7, 3. (2) where an object stands by another :—Þára óðrum (one of the buckets of a draw-well) wæs án getenge wále, Rä. 53, 5. Treów wæs getenge, 57, 9. (3) where an object is placed at, or reaches to, a height :—Hægles scúr heofone getenge, Gen. 808. Wuldorgimm wloncum (wolcnum?) getenge, Rä. 81, 20. Beorc byð . . . heáh on helme . . . lyfte getenge (with its top close against the sky), Rún. 18. Eorþan cyningas . . . on heáhsetlum hrófe getenge (cf. on þám héhstan heáhsetlum, Bt. 37, 1 ; F. 186, 2) *quos vides sedere celsos solii culmine reges*, Met. 25, 5. II. *of the effects or operations of disease, distress, &c., attacking, oppressing* :—Gif men sý sogoþa getenge (-tænge, -tæncge, *v. ll.*), Lch. i. 196, 16. Þonne hé bið mid ómum geswenced, þám men bið þurst getenge and nearones, ii. 194, 2 : 13 : 118, 10. Gif men unlust sié getenge, 150, 17 : 152, 12. Him biþ his feorhádl getenge *his last illness will have attacked him*, 320, 20. For ðǽm þurste he getenge wæs eallum mínum herige and þǽm nýtenum *quadrupedalia et exercitus sitiebant*, Nar. 8, 24. Þe is swíþe micel unrótness getenge *plurimus tibi affectuum tumultus incubuit*, Bt. 5, 1 ; F. 10, 24. Nis þé nán unáberendlic broc getenge *nec tibi nimium tempestas incubuit*, 10 ; F. 30, 5. Þám werigan wearð wracu getenge *vengeance came upon him*, Sat. 711. Swá fela áwyrigedra gásta wǽron ðǽm ǽnum men getenge (cf. intrauerunt daemonia multa in eum, Lk. 8, 30), Hml. Th. ii. 378, 30.

**getenys.** *Dele :* ge-teogo (-tigu). v. egeþ-getigu, sulh-geteoga : **ge-teóh.** *Dele second passage.*

**ge-teohhian.** *Add :* -teochian, -teohchian. I. *to consider* :—Hé geteohode *ratus est* (quem dignissimum *ratus est*, Ald. 64, 3), An. Ox. 7, 312. Geteohchode, 8, 251. II. *to determine, destine, appoint* :—Hié geteochodon *adposuerunt*, Ps. Rdr. 77, 17. Geteohige *adponat*, 9, 39. Wé gehéraþ hwílum secgan þ hit scyle eall swá geweorþan swá God æt fruman getiohhod hæfde, Bt. 41, 2 ; F. 246, 17. (1) *to destine something for or to a person* :—Ðá leán ðe him God getiohchod hæfð, Past. 387, 18. Þæt héhste gód is nánum men getiohhod, ac is eallum monnum *ipsum bonum veluti praemium commune propositum*, Bt. 37, 2 ; F. 188, 15. Drihten áfyrreð þæt ríce fram him and hæfð þé gemynt and geteohhod, Guth. 78, 8. (2) *to destine a person to a place, condition, &c., assign* :—Hié mé habbað gesealdne heora wlencum and getehhod tó heora leásum welum, Bt. 7, 3 ; F. 20, 30. Wá byð ðám þe þǽr (hell) bið geteohhod, Wlfst. 146, 11. Wæs ic geteohhod (-tihad, *v. l.*) in þás wítelican stówe *in hoc poenali loco deputatus sum*, Gr. D. 330, 7. Geteohhod on þá hellewítu, Verc. Först. 116, 10. III. *to determine, intend, resolve* to do :—Geteohhade *conaverit*, Wrt. Voc. ii. 136, 45. Geteohode *deliberaret* (*virginale munus occultare*), An. Ox. 4213 : 8, 288. Geteohhode, 2, 302. Ic swór swá swá ic getiohhod hæfde ðæt ic wolde gehealdan ðíne dómas *juravi, et statui custodire judicia tua*, Past. 465, 24. (1) with acc. :—Gif hé þ þurhtió þ hé getiohhod (-tiohhad, *v. l.*) hæfþ, Bt. 34, 7 ; F. 144, 4. (2) with clause :—Hé geteohhade þ hé mé má þinga gerehte *studebat alia narrare*, Gr. D. 83, 10. Hé getihhade þ hé þás woruld forhogode, Angl. v. 143, 86. Ðá hé getiohchod ðæt hé his ondettan sceolde, Past. 419, 9. (3) with gerundial infin. :—Ic geteohhode mín líf on mægðháde tó geendigenne, Hml. Th. i. 198, 26. Þone hé ǽr geteohhode mid teónan tó forseónne, Hml. S. 31, 677. Gif hé ðǽm gehiérsuman mannum næfde geteohchad (-tiohhad, *v. l.*) his éðel tó sellanne *nisi correctis haereditatem dare disponeret*, Past. 251,

23. Gif hí God næfde on ēcnesse getiochod tó gehǽlanne *nisi salvandos in perpetuum cerneret*, 391, 32. Ðæt ilce ðæt hé getiohchod hæfde tó biddanne *hoc quod petere se promittebat*, 419, 12.

**ge-teohhung,** e ; *f. Determination, ordinance* :—Hé wiste þ hit æfter his geteohhunge ágan sceolde, Hml. A. 154, 69.

**ge-teón.** v. níþ-, un-geteón.

**ge-teón.** *Add :* I. *to draw together* :—Gewyrce and tó getió *con-trahat*, Wrt. Voc. ii. 21, 43. II. (1) with idea of horizontal movement, *to draw along, pull, drag* :—Óðri ðegnas on scip cuómon and drógon ł getugun ðára fisca segni, Jn. L. 21, 8. Ic wæs getogen þurh þisse ceastre lanum, Bl. H. 243, 29. Ic wæs getogen tó tintregum, 243. Wæs getogen, gedragen *traheretur* (*per publicum*), An. Ox. 4467. (2) where there is movement from within or from without, *to draw a sword, haul a net* :—Hé his byrnsweord getýhþ, Bl. H. 109, 34. Hé geteáh his seax, 215, 5. Giteh *educens*, Mk. R. 14, 47. Geteóh þín sweord *effunde frameam*, Ps. Th. 34, 3. Ne maehton þ nett geteá (*trahere*), Jn. L. R. 21, 6. Þ hé wǽre getogen mid þon ísnan hóce on þǽre picenan eá, Bl. H. 43, 25. Getogone sueorde *stricta macera*, Wrt. Voc. ii. 121, 33. (3) where the movement is up or down, *to heave a sigh* :—Getogene siccetunga *ducta suspiria*, An. Ox. 4531. III. *to bring, lead* :—Heora ǽgþer þ mǽste folc ongeán óþerne geteáh, Ors. 2, 7 ; S. 90, 17. IV. *in various figurative senses.* (1) *to bring up, educate, instruct* :—Ðínne diácon ðe ðú getuge, Hml. Th. i. 418, 4. Críst þá apostolas mid sóðre láre geteáh, and eallum ðeódum tó láreówum gesette, i. 542, 6. Ungetogene menn geceás Drihten him tó leorning-cnihtum, and hí swá geteáh þæt heora lár oferstáh ealne woruldwísdóm, 576, 30. Hé (*St. Paul*) wæs from cildháde on ðǽre ealdan ǽ getogen, 384, 26 : 428, 23. Getogen on Hebréiscum gereorde, 436, 13. Marcus wæs mid Petre getogen on láre, Hml. S. 15, 142. Sum mǽden on cræftum getogen, 35, 79. Tó wircemne godeweb swá swá hí wǽron getogene, Ælfc. T. Grn. 21, 21. In stafas and on leornunge getogen *litteris edoctus*, Guth. Gr. 111, 92. (2) *to bring to, lead.* (a) *to bring a person to action or condition* :—Seó wiþerweardnes oft ealle þá þe hiere underþeódde bióþ neódinga getíhþ tó þám sóþum gesælþum (*ad vera bona retrahit*), Bt. 20 ; F. 72, 10. Seó ofersylf þæs líchoman getýhþ þone mon tó synnum, and seó forhæfdnes hine gelædeþ tó forgifnesse, Bl. H. 37, 14. Hé Peohta ðeóde him tó hýrnesse geteáh, Bd. 3, 24 ; Sch. 313, 22. Deáðberende gyfl þá sinhíwan tó swylte geteáh, Gú. 823. Hé wæs getogen tó ðære godcundan sceáwunga *in contemplationem rapitur*, Past. 101, 25. Ic eom getogen tó fremdum þeáwum, Bt. 7, 3 ; F. 20, 25. Hé wæs getogen tó háþeortnesse *ad iracundiam trahitur*, Gr. D. 63, 8. (b) *to bring something on a person* :—Ðæt geswinc hié him selfe hiera ágnes gewealdes him on getióð, Past. 238, 5. Ðá iersigendan him tó getióð ðæt ðætte hié eáðe bútan bión meahton *iracundi, quae tolerentur, important*, 293, 18. (3) *to draw to, attract, allure* :—Deófol hié getýhþ tó eallum uncystum, Bl. H. 25, 11. Sume ic geteáh, tó gefliote fremede, þæt . . . , Jul. 483. Hwæþer nú gimma wlite eówre eágon tó him getió *an gemmarum fulgor oculos trahit ?*, Bt. 13 ; F. 40, 2. His hiéremenn geteón tó beteron *subditos ad meliora pertrahere*, Past. 81, 16. Hí næron mid gecnyrdnysse ǽniges reáfláces getogene tó ðám ðe hí widútan sceáwodon, Hml. Th. i. 586, 3. (4) *to draw to oneself, take* into one's possession or control, *attach* to oneself :—Hé him geteáh tó micelne monfultum, Ors. 5, 2 ; S. 216, 8. Him geteáh Antonius tó gewealdon ealle Asiam, 5, 13 ; S. 244, 31. Hé sealde him wóste land þæt hí mid táne getugan rihte worte *divisit eis terram in funiculo distributionis*, Ps. Th. 77, 55. Uesoges wolde him tó geteón þone suððǽl, p. 1, 24. Tó geteón *usurpare, i. uindicare* (*monarchiam*), An. Ox. 675. Hú dear ǽnig lǽwede man him tó geteón Crístes wican ? Ne furðon nán gehádod man ne sceal him tó geteón þæt hé Críst spelige búton . . . , Hml. Th. ii. 592, 27–29. Getión, Bt. 38, 1 ; F. 196, 15. (5) *to bring forth, produce* :—Forþ getíhþ *producit, i. ostendit*, An. Ox. 228. (6) *to draw together, unite* :—Hé þá twá mægða on án folc geteáh *unum compaginatae in populum*, Bd. 3, 6 ; Sch. 211, 9. Hé wæs híwcúðlíce tó mé geþeóded and getogen *familiariter obstrictus*, Gr. D. 3, 28. (7) *to draw together, constrain, restrain* :—Geteh *constringe*, Ps. Srt. 31, 9. Mid his brídle befangene and getogene, Bt. 21 ; F. 74, 6. (8) *to draw* into a course of action, *draw on* to do something :—Þá getugon Somnite him on fultum Pirrusan, Ors. 3, 5 ; S. 106, 3. Hé wolde hí him on fultum geteón for heora wígcræfte, 3, 7 ; S. 112, 3. V. *intrans.* (1) *to contend, dispute* :—Sé ðe in erning gifistað ł giteð *qui in agone contendit*, Rtl. 5, 39. Ge-cídon ł getugon *litigabant*, Jn. L. R. 6, 52. (2) *to pull together, agree* (?) :—Getugun ł flioton *conspiraverant*, Jn. L. R. 9, 22. v. ge-togen.

**ge-teón ;** *p.* -teóde. *Add :* I. *to do, effect, cause* :—Heora feorh generede Metodes weard . . . , hálige him þǽr help geteóde, Dan. 236. Hé wolde guman findan þone þe him on sweofote sáre geteóde, B. 2295. II. *to determine* a course of action :—Hé þ on his móde gehogod and geteód hæfde, þ hé wolde ealle his þeóde fordón *totam eius gentem delere decreuerat*, Bd. 3, 24 ; Sch. 307, 7. III. *of the decrees of Providence.* (1) *to determine* to do :—Drihten geteód hæfde

þ hē þon biddendan ēce līf forgeáfe, Bl. H. 19, 35. (2) *to appoint* a course of action, lot, condition to a person, *determine* an event:—Unc sceal weorðan swā unc wyrd geteóð Metod manna gehwæs, B. 2526. Þām (*St. Matthew*) God hlýt geteóde ūt on þæt īgland, An. 14. Gif ðæt God geteód habbe, ond mē þæt on lǣne gelīð, þet gesibbra ærfeweard forþcymeð wēpnedhādes, Cht. Th. 483, 15. Earm bið sē þe sceal āna lifgan, wineleás wunian, hafað him wyrd geteód, Gn. Ex. 174. (3) *to appoint* a person or thing to a course, &c., *destine*:—Wið þæs gecyndes þe hī Fæder æt frymðe fæste getióde (cf. þāre gecynde ðe ǣlc gesceaft tō gesceapen wæs, Bt. 25; F. 88, 7), Met. 13, 13. Gif ōþer nýten wǣre geteód tō þon ēcan līfe, Bl. H. 29, 5. Þā āne men habbaþ Crīst on heora heortan þe geteóde beóþ tō þon ēcan līfe, 75, 35. Þæt wē ne weorðan geteódde (-teohhode, *v. l.*) on þā hellewītu, Verc. Först. 116, 10. (3 a) where the course, &c., is not given:—Sē þe wæs ǣr eallum worldum geteód and geendebyrd, Bl. H. 31, 22. Cf. ge-tīung.

**ge-teorian.** *l.* ge-teórian, *and add*: I. of persons, *to be exhausted, be fatigued.* (1) of bodily weariness:—Gif mon fram longum wege geteórod sié, Lch. ii. 150, 19. Mē genihtsumiað þās tintrega, for þon ic eom geteórod . . . þū wāst þā menniscan týddernysse, Bl. H. 243, 27. (2) of mental weariness:—Nis hit nān wundor ðeáh þū getiórie (-týrige, *v. l.*) *verendum est, ne deviis fatigatus* . . ., Bt. 40, 5; F. 240, 23. (2 a) *to grow weary* of doing, *cease from weariness* to do:—Ic þe bidde þ þū ne geteórige for mē gebiddan, Hml. S. 23 b, 320. II. of things, *to be used up, come to an end, fail.* (1) material:—Þā hyra feoh geteórode *cum defecisset emptoribus pretium*, Gen. 47, 15. Þā þ wīn geteórude *deficiente uino*, Jn. 2, 3. (2) non-material:—Him nǣfre seó langung ne geteórode, Bl. H. 113, 14. Ān weorc hē hæfde . . . nǣfre geteórod *one work he had that never failed*, Hml. S. 23 b, 35. v. un-geteórod.

**ge-teórigendlic**; *adj. Defective, imperfect*:—Swā hwylc swā tīdlice and geteórigendlíce fyligð *quisquis temporalia ac defectiva sequitur*, Scint. 181, 4. v. un-geteórigendlíce.

**ge-teórigendlíce.** v. un-geteórigendlíce.

**ge-teórodness, e**; *f. Exhaustion*:—Hēr seó gýtsung wundrede hyre geteórodnesse (*but the Latin is*: Avaritia stupefacta fatescit), Prud. 66 a.

**ge-teórung.** *Add:*—Geteórung *defectio*, Wrt. Voc. ii. 138, 21: Lch. iii. 212, 10.

**ge-teóþian.** *Add:*—Hē wolde his irfe geteóðian, Past. 101, 17.

**ge-teóung** *contraction.* v. ge-tēung: **ge-teóung** *arrangement.* v. ge-tīung.

**ge-ter** *a tearing. Substitute*: I. *what is torn*:—Eálā, ðū wulfes geslit and fugles geter, Nap. 28, 29. II. *a tearing apart*:—Geter *dilaceratio* (*crudelis membrorum*), An. Ox. 3946. III. *dissension, discord*:—Dissentio, discordia *vel* geter, Wrt. Voc. ii. 141, 4. Hīwcūðlic geter *domestica scissura*, 70. Estus, inquietudo *vel* geter, 144. 23. Seó mēting bið geteres ful and geflites and costunge, ne bið þæt gōd swefen, E. S. 39, 347.

**ge-tete.** *Dele.*

**ge-tēþed**; *adj. Provided with teeth, toothed*:—Heardum tōðum and miclum hit wæs gegyred and getēþed *duris munitum dentibus*, Nar. 21, 1.

**ge-þaccian**; *p.* ode. I. *to strike gently* with the open hand, *pat, clap*:—Hē lufode mid his brādre handa þā nunnan and ofer þa sculdru geþaccode *in terga sanctimonialis feminae blandiens alapam dabat*, Gr. D. 189, 22. II. *to soothe by patting* (?), *tame*:—Getaccodon (-þaccodon?) *edomitis*, Germ. 402, 63.

**ge-þæf.** *Add*: (1) *not wishing for change*:—Ēþhelde *vel* geþæf *contentus*, Wrt. Voc. ii. 135, 2. Gif munuc eáðhylde biþ and geþæf, þeáh hine man wācne talige *si omni uilitate contentus sit monachus*, R. Ben. 29, 3. (2) *not wishing change* in something. (a) of men:—Hū hē his āgene unðeáwas ongietan wille and hira geþæf bión (cf. (?) gerest ðæt mōd hit orsorglīce on ðǣre fortrūwunga, 463, 10 : *both passages refer to the same subject*) *how he will recognize his own faults, and yet wish for no change in them* (? the Latin is : Infirmitatem suam quotidie quanta consideratione cognoscat), Past. 23, 22. (b) construction uncertain:—And geþæf and hē bið on gewunan . . . geþeef is þ þ þ hē gemēt and *contentus fuerit consuetudine loci quam invenerit* . . . *contentus est quod invenerit*, R. Ben. I. 101, 14–17. Gehýrsumiendre geþæfe (-þafe, Hpt. Gl. 413, 18) stilnesse *uernacula contentae quiete*, An. Ox. 289. v. ge-þafa.

**ge-þǣnan**; *p.* de *To moisten*:—Ādrīg tō dūste, geþǣn mid hunige, Lch. ii. 144, 1. Sōna wæs seald se regn, sē þe fullice mihte þā eorðan wel geþǣnan *repente pluvia tribuebatur, quae plene terram satiare potuisset*, Gr. D. 210, 21. Tō þām þ þurh þā tōflōwennysse þæs streámes beón geþǣnede (-þēn-, *v. l.*) þā inngeþancas geleáffulra breósta, 94, 22. v. þān, *and cf.* ge-þawenian.

**ge-þæslǣcan.** *Add:*—Geþæslǣcþ *coaptat*, i. *conjungat*, Wrt. Voc. ii. 133, 11. Geþæslǣcaþ *congruant*, 40: *congruunt*, An. Ox. 5175. Hine sylfne on eallon þingan hē gehīwige and hē geþæslǣce *se omnibus conformet et aptet*, R. Ben. I. 16, 6. Geþæslǣcan *congruere*, An. Ox. 4263.

**ge-þæslic.** *Add:*—Geþæslice *congruentia*, i. *conuenientia*, An. Ox. 3891. v. un-geþæslic.

**ge-þafa.** *Add*: [The word, which occurs only as predicate of the verbs *beón, weorþan*, seems at least generally to be an adjective; in some instances it appears indeclinable, see the last three passages, and cf. similar adjectival forms in Icelandic.]   I. where there is consent to an action or a condition, acquiescence in an arrangement. (1) with gen. :—Hē cwæð ðæs ðe hē gebruce, æfter his dæge hē nānum menn sēl ne ūðe ðonne mē : and ic ðæs ðā wæs wel geþafa, C. D. ii. 113, 15. Mid þý wit ðæt uneðelíce þurhtugon þæt hē ðæs geþafa beón wolde *cum hoc difficulter inpetraremus*, Bd. 5, 4; Sch. 568, 19. Hī nyllað geðáfan beón ōðerra monna geðeahtes *alienis consiliis non acquiescunt*, Past. 305, 15. (2) with gen. and clause :—Gif his wolde mīnra þegna hwilc geþafa wurdan þæt hē ūp heonon mihte cuman, Gen. 414. (3) with dat. :—Þone þe byð heora leahtrum geþafa *vitiis suis consentientem personam*, R. Ben. 118, 7.   II. where the correctness of a statement is admitted. (1) with gen. :—Ðises ic eom ealles geþafa, Bt. 32, 2 ; F. 122, 20. Hī ealne þone bryce uppon þone cyng tealdon, ac hē nolde þæs geþafa beón, Chr. 1094; P. 229, 9. (2) with clause:—Hē geþafa beón nolde þæt hē untela dyde, Ps. Th. 9, 35. Eall moncyn is ānmōdlíce geþafa þ God is fruma ealra gōda *Deum rerum omnium principem bonum esse communis humanorum conceptio probat animorum*, Bt. 34, 2 ; F. 136, 1. Wē sceolon beón geþafan (geþafa, *v. l.*) þ se God sié eallra ðinga betst *hunc esse rerum omnium praecellentissimam confitemur*, 34, 3 ; F. 136, 31. (3) with dat. :—Þā hī Agustines lārum ne his bēnum geþafa beón woldon *cum neque precibus neque hortamentis Augustini adsensum praebere uoluissent*, Bd. 2, 2 ; Sch. 113, 21. v. ge-þæf.

**ge-þafian.** *Add*: -þeafian. I. *to permit*:—Ne cweðo ic nō ðæt bebeódende, ac lǣrende and geðafigende *hoc autem dico secundum indulgentiam, non secundum imperium*, Past. 397, 28. (1) with acc. :—Ðone gedwolan ðe hē stíeran sceolde hē oft tō suīðe geðafað, Past. 143, 11. Ðonne God hwæt wyrcþ oþþe geþafaþ, Bt. 39, 10 ; F. 226, 25. Hē geþafað þā dyrnan geþingo, Ll. Th. i. 240, 16. Būte hit God wille oððe geþafige, Bt. 41, 2 ; F. 244, 19. Wē nellað geþafian þ unriht, Ll. Th. i. 388, 4 : ii. 312, 17. Hwīlum sint tō geðafianne (-enne, *v. l.*) ðæs eorðlican tielunga, Past. 135, 21. (1 a) with dat. of person :—Nā ðā āne ðe yfel dōþ, ac ǣlc þāra þe hit ðām dōndum geðafiað, Ll. Lbmn. 475, 37. Ðā hē him geðafode ðone gielp, ðā forbeád hē him ðæt yfel, Past. 459, 1. Swā gōde laga swā . . . ic heom ā geþafode and geþafian wille, Ll. Th. i. 276, 18. Nele him mon nǣnne teám geðafian, 260, 2. Ne sý him gemǣne þigen geþafod, R. Ben. 69, 13. (1 b) with complementary participle :—Hē geðafode ðā scylde unwītnode, Past. 123, 6. (2) with clause :—Hwīlum hē geþafaþ þ þā gōdan habbaþ unsǣlþa, Bt. 39, 2 ; F. 214, 3 : Bl. 45, 19. Þ hī ne geþafian, gyf his waldan magan, þ þær ǣnig unriht ūp āspringe, Ll. Th. ii. 312, 36 : 39. Geþafian þ men forwyrcean hī sylfe, 30. (2 a) with dat. of person :—Geðafað him mon ðæt hē hiene restð, Past. 142, 20. Hē him ne geðafað ðæt . . ., 419, 3 : 4. Hē his suna geþafode þæt hē læg mid Lucrettie, Ors. 2, 2 ; S. 54, 20. Þ hié þǣm ne geþafian þ hié heora līf on wōh lifgean, Bl. H. 45, 11. (3) with infin. and dat. :—Nāðer ne hié selfe on ryhtne weg gān noldon, ne ōðrum geðafigean, Past. 59, 21. (4) with acc. of pronoun representing clause or phrase :—Ðǣm hié geðafigað ðyllic, Past. 143, 22. Gif hit tō bōte gegā, and se cyng þ geþafige, þonne bēte man, Ll. Th. i. 340, 16. Gif hē þā hand lēsan wille, and him mon þ geþafian wille, 66, 5. (5) construction uncertain :—Bēten hī swā swā man geðafige, Ll. Th. i. 168, 20. Būtan hē hine æt þām cynge gebicge swā swā hē him geþafian wille, 266, 19.   II. *to permit* what is displeasing to oneself, *suffer.* (1) with acc. :—Hē ne can ongitan tor hwī God swylc geþafaþ, Bt. 39, 2 ; F. 214, 10. Hē gedwolan wiðsōc and þone ne geðafode, Bd. 5, 21 ; Sch. 676, 17. Gif yfel þeáh bión scyle, and hē hit geþafian wile, Bt. 36, 1 ; F. 172, 6. (2) with acc. of pronoun representing a clause or phrase :—Þā hī (*Rome*) hiere āgen ealdormonn and Gotona cyning hiere anwaldes beniman woldon, hit God ne geþafode, Ors. 2, 1 ; S. 62, 29. Swā swā hit God æt fruman wisse and ðeáh geþafode, Past. 443, 9. Hē þōhte idese besmītan : ne wolde þæt wuldres dēma geþafigan, Jud. 60. III. *to permit* something (troublesome) to be done to oneself, *to submit to, suffer.* Cf. ge-þafung; II. (1) with acc. :—Ic mid eáðmēdum eall geþafige *humiliter sentiebam*, Ps. Th. 130, 3. Hwæt ōðre men him forberað and geðafiað *what other men put up with and submit to from them*, Past. 397, 5. Hē suīgende geðafode swingellan *tacitus flagella toleravit*, 261, 11. Ðā hālgan menn geðafedon bismer *sancti ludibria experti*, 205, 11 : Hml. S. 23, 88. Ðæt hē suingellan geðafige *ut flagella toleret*, Past. 261, 20. Þ hē þæt ilce yfel ne geþafige ōþrum monnum þe hē ǣr ōþrum dyde *that he may not submit to the same evil from others, that he before did to others*, Bt. 16, 2 : F. 54, 6. Nið geðafian, Dan. 633. Ic geþafian sceal his dōm and him wesan underþýded, Gū. 572. (2) with clause :—Hē geðafode ðæt hine mon mid fýste slōg . . . þ geðafode ðæt him mon sette ðyrnenne beág on ðæt heáfud *colaphos pertulit . . . spinis caput supponere non recusavit*, Past. 261, 12–14. Ðæt hē him nylle geðafigean ðæt hē hine snīðe, 185, 26 : 187, 8. (3) with acc. of pronoun repre-

senting a clause:—Ðæt hié ongieten ðæt hié mon tǣle, and ðæt eáð-
módlíce geðafigen *deprehendi se cognoscunt et perpeti*, Past. 151, 15.
Hǣfton hí hine. Gif hé nylle hit geþafian, Ll. Th. i. 210, 8. **IV.**
*to consent, assent.* (1) *to consent to a person, be in agreement* with:—
Hé him lustlíce geþafode *cui cum ille libenter adquiesceret*, Bd. 3, 23;
Sch. 302, 16. Ðæt hié ne gedeafien wiðerbrocum *ne consentiant
adversariis*, Ps. Srt. ii. p. 194, 37. Sió geþafigende *assentatrix*, Wrt.
Voc. ii. 88, 5. (1 a) *to consent* to action:—Gif hit swá getímað þæt eal
geferrǣden þone tó abbode gecӯst þe hyra leahtrum geþeafige (-þaf-, *v. l.*)
*si omnis congregatio vitiis suis consentientem personam elegerit*, R. Ben.
119, 7. (2) *to assent to a request* (*dat.*), *acquiesce* in a plan, an opinion,
&c.:—Ne hió ne geþafod ǣniges bēnum *nec adquiescet cuiusquam
precibus*, Kent. Gl. 174. Hé his bēnum geþafode *qui precibus eius
adnuens*, Bd. 3, 7; Sch. 215, 19. Þā geþafode hē heora geþeahte
*adnuit consilio eorum*, 4, 30; Sch. 534, 11. Hé his willan and his
heofonlicum lustum geþafade (*adnuit*), 5, 19; Sch. 655, 17. Mid þӯ hé
nā his bēnum geþafian nolde *cum rex nullatenus precibus illius assensum
praeberet*, 3, 24; Sch. 307, 5. (3) *to admit the justice* of reproof,
advice, &c., *attend* to:—Sē ðe geðafeð *qui adquiescit* (*increpationibus*),
Kent. Gl. 542. Ne gedeafede *non adquievit*, 96. Ic þú Agustinus lārum
ne his bēnum ne his þreám geþafigean woldon *cum neque precibus, neque
hortamentis, neque increpationibus Augustini adsensum praebere uoluissent*, Bd. 2, 2; Sch. 113, 20. (3 a) *to attend* to a person:—Sē ðe
gedeafeð *qui adquiescit* (*arguenti*), Kent. Gl. 455. Ne wænd þú þē nó
... on þæs unwísestan lāre, ne him ne geþafa, Ll. Th. i. 54, 8. (4) *to
consent to* action or condition to which one is invited or called, *make
oneself a party to*. (a) with acc.:—Se gǣst bið oferwunnen mid ðǣre
lustfulnesse, ðæt hē hit gedafað ... Eue hí underðiódde mid lustfulnesse
swā swā líchoma. Ðā wæs Adam ... ðurh Euan lustbǣrnesse oferswíðed,
ðæt hē gedeafode ðā synne *spiritus victus delectatione consentit* ... *Eva
quasi caro delectationi subdidit, Adam delectatione superatus assensit*,
Past. 417, 24-29: 18. Leáses monnes dómas ne geþafa þū, Ll. Th. i.
54, 4. Sē ofer þ̄ lāde geþafie oþþe sē þe hӯ sylle, Ll. Th. i. 298, 7.
Ðæt byð se mǣsta wurðscipe, ðæt mon cunne riht gecnāwan, and hit
ðonne wylle geþafian, Prov. K. 9. Hē gedeafigende folgað ðǣre costunga,
Past. 417, 11. Bæd hé þā cempan þ̄ hí onféngon gereorde mid him;
geþafode þ̄ óþer, óðer ðām wiþsóc, Shrn. 129, 32. (b) with clause:—
Ðā geþafedon hí þæt hí him wíf sealdon *uxores dare consenserunt*, Bd. 1,
1; Sch. 11, 26. (c) absolute, *to consent*:—Ægðer ge he wolde ge hē
nolde, and ðeáh for eáðmódnesse gedeafode *nolunt et obedivit*, Past. 51,
10. (5) *to consent to* action under compulsion:—Ðone nӯdde Decius
deófolgeld tó begangenne. Þā hé þæt ne geþafode ..., Shrn. 128, 17.

**ge-þafung.** *Add:* -þeafung. **I.** *permission:*—Ne hē nān þing
næbbe būtan þæs abbodes sylene and geþafunge *ne quicquam liceat habere
quod abbas non dederit aut non permiserit*, R. Ben. 57, 5. Būton se
abbod him geþafunge (*permissionem*) sylle, 69, 6. **II.** *submission
to action, toleration.* Cf. ge-þafian; **III.**:—*Verbum* is word, and word
getācnað weorc oððe ðrowunge oþþe geþafunge ... þrowung byð þonne
ðū cwyst, *verberor* ic eom beswungen ... Geþafung byþ ðonne ðū cwyst,
*amor* ic eom gelufod, Ælfc. Gr. Z. 9, 2-7. **III.** *consent:*—Ús is
gecynde ðæt wē ǣlc yfel on ðrió wísan ðurhtíon: ðurh gespan and ðurh
lustfulnesse and ðurh gedeafunga (*consensu*) ... Sió geðafung bið ðurhtogen ðurh ðone gǣst ... mid ðǣre gedeafunge wē bióð gebundne, Past.
417, 19-31. Mid ðǣre gedeafunga ðæs unryhtes *consentiendo perversis*,
351, 21. Mid geþafunge Crístes geleáfan *cunctis adnuentibus fidei*, Bd.
3, 22; Sch. 292, 15. Swā hwæt swā hӯ būtan his leáfe dóþ and his
geþafunge *quod sine patris spiritalis fiat voluntate*, R. Ben. 77, 4: 3.
Wē þā gedeafunga þæs dryncces dóð *consentiamus ut ... bibamus*, 65,
1. ¶ on geþafunge gān *to consent*:—Gif hé on geþafunge gǣð *si
consenserit*, R. Ben. 103, 3: 119, 15.

**ge-þanc.** *Add:*—Gedeanc *cogitatio*, Wrt. Voc. i. 42, 37. Mód *vel*
geþanc *animus*, 33. Geþancge *cogitatione*, An. Ox. 56, 3. **I.** *a
thought, what a person thinks:*—Ne wyrð ðǣr bedíglod þæt dígleste
geþanc þe ǣnig mon ǣfre geþóhte, Wlfst. 25, 14. Healde hē hine ðæt
hine his āgen geþanc ne biswíce *ne se imago cogitationis illudet*, Past.
57, 22. Þā þóhte ic þæt ..., ac mín lātteów andwyrde þǣrrihte mínum
geðance, Hml. Th. ii. 350, 14. Worda and dǣda, þeáwa and geþonca,
Cri. 1584: El. 1286. Gif hié synna fremmað þeáwum and geþancum,
Gen. 2413: El. 312. Ic þæt ne forhycge heortan geþoncum, Ph. 552:
Gū. 1227. Þā móðwatan on geþancum, Dan. 358. Hí mid geþoncum
(*thoughtfully, wisely*) þeóden heredon, Az. 68. God gesyhþ ǣlces
monnes geþanc and his word, and his dǣda tóscǣt, Bt. 40, 7; F. 242,
32. Geþancu (*cogitationes*) horige gebed mid fæstene út ānӯtt, Scint.
36, 12. **II.** *a thought, purpose, intention:*—Hwilcan geþance
mæg ǣnig man ǣfre geþencan on his móde þ̄ hē tó sācerdan heáfod
āhylde ... and sóna hit siþþan scyrde, Ll. Th. i. 334, 32: 28. God
geseah his gedeanc, þæt hé ne ēhte geleáffulra manna ðurh andan, Hml.
Th. i. 390, 5. Hē hæfde gód geþanc, By. 13. Beóð tóstencte geþancu
(*cogitationes*) þǣr þǣr nys geþeaht *without counsel purposes are dis-
appointed* (A. V. Prov. 15, 22), Scint. 199, 11: (A. V. Prov. 20, 18),
13. Gedeancas, Ps. Th. 91, 4. **III.** *a device, design, what is*

thought out:—Þæt hié lāð Gode þurh þæs wrāðan geþanc weorðan
sceoldon, Gen. 631. Þurh dyrne geþanc *by dark design*, 532. Gelēr-
eddum gedeancum *eruditis cogitationibus;* of witty inventions, (A. V.),
Kent. Gl. 240. Leáse on geþoncum, Cri. 1120. Drihten firenfullra
fǣcne gedeancas tóweorpeð, Ps. Th. 128, 3. **IV.** *thought, faculty
or act of thinking, mind:*—Wác bið þæt gedeanc on crístenum men, gyf
hē ne cann understandan þurh rihtne geleáfan þæne þe hine gesceóp,
Wlfst. 20, 9. Weard him hӯrra hyge and on heortan geþanc māran
módsefan þonne gemet wǣre, Dan. 491. Gleáw geþances, 743. Nis
mē on geþance *vel* on móde *non mihi est cordi*, Wrt. Voc. i. 54, 47.
Gif hē ǣr on ðæs ofermódan engles wísan innan his gedeance (*ingeðonce,
v. l.*) of Godes gesiehðe ne āfeólle *nisi more superbientis angeli a conspectu conditoris prius intus aversione mentis caderet*, Past. 359, 1.
Gehwā on geþance healde, Ll. Th. i. 424, 20. Þríste on geþance, An.
237: El. 267. Gleáw in geþance, 807. Þā þe þurh ānfeald geþanc
God lufiað, Wlfst. 24, 12. Hæbban fæstrǣde geþanc tó úrum Drihtne,
101, 23: Hml. S. 8, 20. Þurh gleáwne geþanc hē ǣrest hearpan hlyn
āwehte, Gen. 1078: Dan. 536. Wec þú clǣne hiortan in mē, mód-
swíðne geþanc, Ps. C. 89. Blinde on geþoncum, Cri. 1127. ¶ in
adverbial phrases. Cf. Romance adverbs from Lat. *mente:*—Folc
Drihten herað holdlice, hróre geþance, Ps. Th. 101, 16. Ic þē
andette holde geþance, 118, 7. Ic þæt wēnde þríste geþonce, Jul.
358. **IV a.** *thought, thinking* about something:—Þǣr nǣfre
unnytte sprǣce nǣron, ne geþanc goldes and seolfres, Hml. S. 23 b, 88.
[*O. H. Ger.* ge-danc *cogitatio, intentio, sollertia, intellectus, anima.*]
v. breóst-, in-, mód-, un-geþanc.

**ge-þancfull.** v. un-geþancfull.
**ge-þancian.** **I.** *to express in words* or *have in mind feelings of
gratitude:*—Efne-geðoncadon *congratulabantur*, Lk. L. R. 1, 58.
Efne-geðoncaiges (geðongias, R.) *congratulamini*, 15, 6. Efne-geðon-
gigas (giðonccigas, R.), 9. **II.** *to express gratitude by action,
shew gratitude, reward:*—Rómáne him geþancodon ealles his geswinces
mid wyrsan leáne þonne hē tó him geearnod hæfde, Ors. 5, 4; S. 224,
32. [*O. H. Ger.* ge-dankón.]

**ge-þancmetian.** *Add:* v. þanc-metung: **ge-þancod.** v. riht-
geþancod.

**ge-þancol.** *Add:* (1) *mindful:*—Hē þurh þæs gehātes myngunge
swíþe geþancol on anginne his ríces began þā stówe tó fyrþrienne, eal
swā hé ǣr behēt on his cildgeogoðe, Lch. iii. 438, 8. (2) with gen.,
*mindful* of something:—Hí nā synd gemyndige ł geþancule handa his
*non sunt recordati manus eius*, Ps. Rdr. 77, 42. Utan beón geþancole
úre āgenre þearfe, Wlfst. 127, 27.

**ge-þang.** *Add:* Cf. ge-þungen: **ge-þawenian.** *Add:* Cf. ge-
þeánan.

**ge-þeaht.** *Add:* m. (e. g. geþeahtas, Gr. D. 137, 20), f. (e. g. mid
bróþorlicre geþeahte, Bd. 3, 22; Sch. 292, 8), n. (e. g. ðæt ryhte
gedeaht, Past. 287, 14). **I.** *consultation, deliberation* by many:—
Beóð tóstencte geþancu þǣr þǣr nys geþeaht (*consilium*); þǣr þǣr manega
synd geþeahteras beóð getrymmede, Scint. 199, 12. Ic gehӯrde ... mid
þec þegn æt geþeahte, Gū. 1189. Hafa ðú mid þone bysceop sprǣce and
geþeahte hwæt tó dónne sié, Bd. 1, 27; Sch. 74, 12. Hē hæfde
geþeaht mid his witum and freóndum *facto cum suis consilio*, 3, 22;
Sch. 292, 12: 4, 1; Sch. 336, 16. Hæfde se cyng mycel geþeaht and
swíðe deópe sprǣce wið his witan, Chr. 1085; P. 216, 15. Geþancu
mid geþeahtum beóð gestrangude, Scint. 199, 13. Þā þe ongynnað
gesibbe geþeahtu *qui ineunt pacis consilia*, 9. Gedeaht, Kent. Gl.
421. **I a.** *consideration, deliberation* by an individual:—' Ne doo
ðú nānwuht būtan gedeahte (*sine consilio*) ... lǣt simle gān ðín eágean
beforan ðínum fótum.' Ðonne stæppað ðā eágan beforan ðǣm fótum
ðonne ðæt ryhte and ðæt gesceádwíslice gedeaht (*recta consilia*) gǣð
beforan weorcum. Ac sē ðe āgímeleásað ðæt hē ðence ..., Past. 287,
11-15. Sē sit on wóles setle, sē ðe yfel wyrcð mid gedeahte (*ex
judicio*), 435, 22. **II.** *advice, direction:*—Manege ic āwearp mid
mínra witena geþeahte, Ll. Th. i. 58, 20: 246, 20. Seó gerǣdnes þe
Eádgár cyng mid his witena geþeahte gerǣdde, 262, 3: 340, 5. Ic
Æðelstán mid geþeahte Wulfhelmes arceb. and mínra óðera biscopa,
194, 2. Mid geþeahte and mid lāre Cēnrēdes mínes fæder and Heddes
mínes biscepes ..., 102, 2. Be bisceopes geþeahte, iii. 300, 28. Bēte
hē be his scriftes geþeahte, i. 374, 8. Ǣnig man ... ciricþēn ne útige
būton biscopes geþehte, 306, 29. Óswió Sigebyrhte mid freóndlicre
geþeahte (*consilio*), oft tó sprǣc, Bd. 3, 22; Sch. 292, 8. Wē niagon
eów syllan hālwende geþeahte (*consilium*), 1, 1; Sch. 11, 12. Him se
bisceop hālwendlice gedeaht forðbróhte and hié lǣrede þ̄ ..., Bl. H.
205, 18: Ps. Th. 106, 10. Byþ hǣl þǣr þǣr fela geþeahtu synd,·Scint.
199, 15. Ic ne gӯmde þín nytlicra geþeahta mínra freónda, Nar. 6,
26. Sē þe wís ys, hē gehӯrð geþeahtu, Scint. 199, 8. **III.**
*wisdom, prudence, discretion:*—Geþeaht geheald þē (*discretion shall
preserve thee*, Prov. 2, 11), Scint. 199, 5: 16. Gēþ ealle dēð mid
geþeahte (*every prudent man dealeth with knowledge*, Prov. 13, 16),
199, 11: 10. Mid geþeahte and mid andgite (Bt. 33, 4; F. 132, 8:
Met. 20, 200. Gehealt lage and geþeaht (*keep sound wisdom and*

*discretion*, Prov. 3, 21), Scint. 199, 6. Þurh snyttro geþeaht, El. 1060. Mē rúmran geþeaht wísdóm onwreáh, 1241. **IV. *purpose, design, device, plan:*—**Geþeaht, orþanc, searwu *molimen*, An. Ox. 123. Gif ys of mannum geþeaht þis oððe weorc, Scint. 199, 3. Hié gesetton þ hē ... swungen wǣre oþþæt hē swylte ... Sóna swá him þ geþeaht tó cóm, Bl. H. 193, 5. Þú wēndest þ þiós slíþne wyrd þás woruld wende bútan Godes geþeahte *has fortunarum vices existimas sine rectore fluitare*, Bt. 5, 3; F. 14, 5: 5, 1; F. 8, 32. Þiós wandriende wyrd færþ æfter his foreþonce and æfter his geþeahte, swá swá hē tiohhaþ þ hit sié, 39, 6; F. 220, 7. Hwæþer þú on ǣngum geþeahte swá twió-rǣde sié þ ðē helpe hwæþer hit gewyrþe þe hit nó ne gewyrþe, 41, 3; F. 250, 8. Fróde geþeahte *with prudent purpose*, Men. 182. Swá geendode se wita (*Ahitophel*) his wælhreówe geþeaht, sē þe wolde berǣdan his rihtwísan hláford, Hml. S. 19, 213: Hml. Th. i. 82, 31. Manna wísdóm and rǣdas syndon náhtlíce ongeán Godes geþeaht, Chr. 979; P. 123, 33. Þurh eówer geþeaht *as the result of your design*, Past. 443, 8. Geþeahtu árleásra fácenfulle, Scint. 138, 7. Þám apostole þá Godes geþeahtas wǣron onwrigene, Gr. D. 137, 20. Þurh geðeaht *designedly; per consilia*, Past. 435, 26. Hí geþóhtun geþeahta þá þe hí ne mihton gestaþolfæstnian *they imagined a mischievous device, which they are not able to perform* (A. V.), Ps. L. 20, 12. Drihten tóstencð geþeahtas ðeóda ... Geþeaht Drihtnes on ēcnysse wunað, 32, 10-11. **V. *a council, deliberative assembly:*—**Þú bist gewuldrad þ bið wísra geðeaht and háligra geþēincg, Ps. Th. 88, 6. Se bisceopsinoð þæs Niceniscan geþeahtes, Angl. xi. 8, 1. [Tó sinoþ]licum gemóte ꝥ geþehte *ad synodale concilium*, An. Ox. 2093. v. un-geþeaht.

**ge-þeahtendlíce.** v. un-geþeahtendlíce.

**ge-þeahtere.** *Add:*—Hwilc wæs his geþeahtere (*consiliarius*)?, Gr. D. 136, 22. Geþeahteras *consiliarii*, Scint. 199, 12. Dauid sang þisne sealm be his unscyldinesse wið his sunu and wið his geþeahteras þe hine on wóh lǣrdan, Ps. Th. 25, arg. ¶ rendering the Latin *consul:*—Hwæt wille wē cweþan be þínum twám sunum, þá sint ealdormen and geþeahteras *quid dicam liberos consulares?*, Bt. 10; F. 28, 31.

**ge-þeahtian.** *Add:*—Gif tuoege from iúih efne-geðeaehtas ꝥ biðon ymb án *si duo ex vobis consenserint*, Mt. L. 18, 19.

**ge-þeahtung.** *Add:*—Conlatio, i. conductio, comparatio, conciliatio, i. datio, contentio geþeahtung, gesceád *vel* racu, Wrt. Voc. ii. 134. 43. Þá þing þe beóð on Godes geþeahtunge (*design*, cf. ge-þeaht; IV) (þá þe beóð Godes geþeahtunge, v. l.) *quae Dei sunt*, Gr. D. 137, 4.

**ge-þearfan** *to be need:*—Ne myr ðú eal ðæt ðú hæbbe, ðý lǣs ðē geðearfe tó óðres mannes ǣhtum *do not waste all you have, lest there be need to you of another man's property*, Prov. K. 73. v. þearfan.

**ge-þeáwe;** *adj. In accordance with habit, customary:*—Sume dæge sænde se hálga wer þæra muneca sumne, swá him geþeáwe (-þýwe, v. l.) wæs *quadam die misit ex more*, Gr. D. 142, 33. v. un-geþeáwe, ge-þíwe.

**ge-þeáwfæst.** v. un-geþeáwfæst.

**ge-þeáwian;** *pp.* od *To form the habits* or *character of* a person, *educate:*—Fæderas ic (*St. Paul*) manode þæt hí mid steóre Godes eges heora cild geðeáwodon (cf. *patres, educate filios vestros in disciplina et correptione Domini*, Eph. 6, 4), Hml. Th. i. 378, 23. ¶ ge-þeáwod. (1) *accustomed* to a usage, practice, &c.:—Þá Iudéiscan wǣron swá geðeáwode þæt hí setton wæterfatu on flóra æt heora gebeórscipum ... þá wǣron gesette for ðǣm ðeáwe six stǣnene wæterfatu, Hml. Th. ii. 56, 32. (2) *of such and such manners, character, behaviour, habits*, &c.:—Heó (*Esther*) wæs wíslíce geþeáwod *she was of prudent behaviour*, Hml. A. 95, 99. Ðás eahta eádignyssa (*the beatitudes*) synd eów mǣdenum tó lufigenne þ gē wíslíce lybbon and wel geþeáwode (*virtuous*) beón ... ne nán undeáw æfre on eów ne ríxige, 47, 574.

**ge-þegnian.** *Add:*—Is áwriten ðætte Dauid suiðlíce hreówsade ðæt hē him (*Saul*) suá ungeriesenlíce geðēnigan (-ðēnian, v. l.) sceolde, Past. 199, 18.

**ge-þegnsum, -þensum.** *Take here* ge-þēnsum *in Dict., and add:* (1) of persons:—Godes ege myndgað þæt mon þearfum and elþeódegum monnum geþēnsum sý, R. Ben. 85, 6. Malchus se geþēnsuma (cf. Malchus heora ðēnigmann þá ðēnunga heom geornlíce þēnode, 239), Hml. S. 23, 4. (2) of things:—Geþēnsume scúras *coloni nimbi*, i. *manna pluviae famulantes*, Wrt. Voc. ii. 134, 28.

**ge-þencan.** *Add:* **I. *to think, deliberate, take counsel or thought:*—**Huælc geðences (*cogitans*) mæge atēce tó lícnesse his elne ēnne?, Mt. L. 6, 27. Hiá geðóhtun betuih him, Mt. L. 21, 25: Mk. L. 8, 16. Geðóhton þte hine spildon *cogitauerunt ut interficerent eum*, Jn. L. 11, 53: 12, 10. **II. *to think* a thought:—**Secge hē mē, gif hē god sý, hwæt hē sí geþóht oþþe gecweden oþþe gedón, Bl. H. 179, 34. Þonne hē dēþ þ hē geþóht hafaþ, þonne gecýþe ic þ ic wát ǣr hwæt hē þenceþ, 181, 9. **II a. *where the object of the verb is the matter of the thought:*—**Se mon sē þá sóþfæstnesse mid his múþe sprecþ and hié on his heortan geþencþ, Bl. H. 55, 15. For ðǣm ðe swíðe fela unálēfedes wē oft geðenceað *quia illicita animum multa pulsarent*, Past. 425, 9. **III. *to suppose, hold as an opinion* or *a belief.* (1) with

*clause:*—Gē nó ne geðóhton on eówerre heortan ðæt ic suugode, suelce ic hit ne gesáwe, Past. 151, 21. Geðence hē ðæt hē bið self gelíc ðám ilcan monnum *aequalem se ipsis fratribus agnoscat*, 117, 15. ¶ Wē magon geþencan þ hit biþ deáþes ylding swíþor þonne lífes, Bl. H. 59, 32. Swá þeáh is tó geþencenne þ þá fíf þing ... þeáh hí tónemde beón mid wordum, þ hit is eall án ðing, Bt. 33, 1; F. 122, 9. þ is micel syn tó geþencenne be Gode þ ǣnig gód sié búton on him, 34, 3; F. 138, 5. (2) with acc. and complementary adj.:—þæt hiora gerisna nǣre þæt hié swá heáne hié geþóhten þæt hí heora gelícan wurden, Ors. 4, 6; S. 178, 17. þá consulas noldon hié selfe swá earge geþencan, 4, 10; S. 194, 15. **IV. *to employ the mind* on a subject, *think of* or *on, consider.* (1) with acc.:—þæt wē magon ongietan, gif wē geðenceað ðá twēgen wítgan *quod cognoscimus, si duorum prophetantium facta pensamus*, Past. 49, 2. Ðonne hié geðenceað ðá ryhtan lufe *dum eorum cor in pacis internae cognitione suspenditur*, 363, 12. Geðenc ðone brídel ðínre mettrymnesse swíðe geornlíce, 467, 2: Dan. 420. þæt hē his sáwle síð geþence, Seel. 2. Hē sceal hine selfne geðencan and ongietan *ad semetipsum redeat*, Past. 461, 27: Bl. H. 95, 24. Is ðeós bisen tó geþencenne, Bt. 23; F. 78, 24. (2) with gen.:—Gif hié geðenceað ðǣra gesǣlða sí *attendatur felicitas*, Past. 407, 30. Hē geþóhte his misdǣda, Ors. 6, 34; S. 290, 26. Þonne ic his geþencean sceal, 3, 12; S. 142, 13. Ne sculon hí geðencean hiera ealdordómes *non in se potestatem debent ordinis pensare*, Past. 107, 24: Gr. D. 3, 15. (3) with prep.:—Be þissum þingum geþenc, Bl. H. 41, 1. Sceolon wē gemunan úre nýdþearfe and geþencean embe úre sáula þearfe, 101, 32. (4) with an indirect interrogative clause:—Lyt þú geþóhtes (gemundest, v. l.) tó hwan þínre sáwle þing siððan wurde, Seel. 19. Hē geðóhte hú hē wolde ðæt mon him miltsode, Past. 101, 10. Geðenc nú hwæt þínes ágnes seó, Bt. 13; F. 38, 1: Past. 467, 1: 5, 5. Geðenceað hwelces wítes gē wēnen ðǣm, 329, 12. Geðence gē hwæt gē sien, 159, 14. Hié sculon geðencean hú gelíce hié beóð óðrum monnum on hira gecynde *debent aequalitatem pensare conditionis*, 109, 1. Gemunan and geþencan hú ..., Bl. H. 55, 12. Gehýran and geþencean hwæt hē dyde, and mid hwý hē ús freó gedyde, 83, 31. **V. *to think* of something, where it is implied that effect will be given to the thought, *to determine, resolve, intend, purpose, mean:*—Geþóhte deliberaret (quamvis auctor integritatis virginale munus occultare deliberaret, Ald. 59, 12), Wrt. Voc. ii. 85, 13. (1) with acc.:—Hē forgitt swíðe hræðe ðæt hē ǣr ǣfæstlíces geðóhte *obliviscitur libenter quidquid religiose cogitavit*, Past. 57, 8. Rómáne hæfdon swíþor fleám geþóht þonne gefeoht, Ors. 4, 1; S. 158, 24. (2) with infin.:—Ic geþóhte ádrífan of selde, Sat. 187. (3) with clause:—Satanus swearte geþóhte þæt hē wolde on heofonum hēhseld wyrcan, Sat. 371. Geþence hē þ hē nánum men ne dēme þ hē nolde þ hé him dēmde, Ll. Th. i. 56, 31. Geþencean wē geornlíce þ wē ús healdan wið leahtras, Bl. H. 37, 2: Past. 363, 12. Hwilcan geþance mæg ǣnig man geþencan on his móde þ hē tó sácerdan heáfod áhylde, Ll. Th. i. 334, 32: Bl. H. 51, 27. Hí hæfdon geþóht þæt hié sceoldon Italiam forlǣtan, and hié þæt swá gelǣsten, gif him Scipia ne getýrde, Ors. 4, 9; S. 190, 19. (4) with a preposition determining direction of intended motion:—Ealne þone here hē hēt þonan wendan þe hē ǣr tó geþóht hæfde, Ors. 4, 10; S. 202, 8. **VI. *to form an idea in the mind, conceive:*—**Geþóhte hē in his móde nytte geþeahte *concepit utillimum mente consilium*, Bd. 4, 31; Sch. 541, 12. Ne mæg ic nǣfre geþencan ... hwonon him ǣnig unrótnes cuman sceolde, Bt. 33, 1; F. 122, 8. Ic geþencan ne mæg for hwan módsefa mín ne gesweorce, Wand. 58. **VI a. *to form an idea of, have a conception of:*—**Swá mycel ungelimp swá man náht ǣdelíce geþencan ne mæg, Chr. 1085; P. 217, 20. **VII. *to effect by thinking, think out, devise, design:*—**Þú ealle gód mid þínes ánes geþeahte geþóhtest and geworhtest ... swá swá þú self geþóhtest þ geworhtest þisne middangeard, Bt. 33, 4; F. 128, 19-24. Gif úre hláford ús ǣnigne eácan geþæncean mæge tó úrum friðgildum, Ll. Th. i. 238, 16. Man ne mihte geþeoncean ne ásmǣgian hú man of earde hí gebringon sceolde, Chr. 1006; P. 137, 15. Fácen on heortan geþencendra yfelu, Scint. 138, 8. Sió syn ðe longe ǣr geðóht bið *exquisita per studium peccata*, Past. 435, 28. **VIII. *to perceive after consideration, learn:*—**Gē magon eáþe geþencan, gif gē hit georne ymbe smeágan willaþ and æfter styrian, þ nánre wuhte líchoma ne beoð tēderra þonne þæs monnes *quid, si corpus spectes, imbecillius homine reperire queas*, Bt. 16, 2; F. 52, 7. Of þissum ánum dóme mon mæg geþenceau, þ hē ǣghwelcne on riht gedēme, Ll. Th. i. 56, 29. **IX. *to remember* a person or thing.** (1) with gen.:—Gē ne geþenceað þæra fíf hláfa *non recordamini quinque panum*, Mt. 16, 9. (2) with acc.:—Nis nán swá eald man þe þíne mágas nú mage geþencan, Hml. S. 23, 709. Wē ne magon swá þeáh ealle naman áwrítan ne furþor geþencan, Wrt. Voc. i. 85, 74. **IX a.** with the implication that conduct will be influenced by remembrance:—Gif ic þē ne geþence þonne mē bet bið, ic wísce þ ic eft forlidennesse gefare, Ap. Th. 12, 9. Geþence hē word and wedd þe hē Gode betǣhte, Ll. Th. i. 306, 5. **X. *to bear in mind* a fact (that should influence conduct or opinion) stated in a clause:—For hwon ne geþóhtest þú þ hit is eal Godes?, Bl. H. 51, 1. Geþencaþ eác þ on ðisum pearroce búgiaþ swíþe manega ðeóda *adde*

*quod hoc ipsum septum plures incolunt nationes*, Bt. 18, 2; F. 62, 27: Bl. H. 99, 6. Geþencean wē þæt, 23, 18: 29, 4. Geþencan wē hū Drihten cwæð, 'Eádige...,' 25, 19: Ll. Th. i. 196, 1. Is tō geðencanne ðæt... *notandum quod...*, Past. 53, 17. Is tō geðencanne ðætte... *considerandum est quod*...302, 20. Gif ægðer bið unwís, ðonne is tō geðencanne hwæt Crísð cuæð...'Gif se blinda ðone blindan lǽt...,' 29, 6. **X a.** with pronoun and clause in apposition:—þ ús is tō geþencenne, þ úre Drihten...fæstte...Ús is þonne nēðþearf þ wē fæston, Bl. H. 27, 28. **XI.** *to keep in mind* what is to be done, *take care* that:—Is tō geðencenne ðæt wē tō ungemetlíce ðā eáðmódnesse ne healden, ðý lǽs se anweald áslacie ðæs recendómes *intuendum est, ne, dum immoderatius custoditur virtus humilitatis, solvantur jura regiminis*, Past. 119, 3. **XII.** *to think for* þyncan:— Huæt ðe gesegen is ł ðē geðence (ðynceþ, R., þincþ, W.S.) *quid tibi videtur*, Mt. L. 17, 25: 22, 17, 42. [O. Sax. gi-thenkian *to think, devise: O. H. Ger.* ge-denchen *concipere, proponere*.]

**ge-þenian.** *Add:*, -þennan :—'Geðen hond ðín.' And geðenede 'extende manum tuam.' *Et extendit*, Mt. L. 12, 13. Geþen[ed] *deductum*, An. Ox. 28, 12. [O. H. Ger. ge-dennen *extendere*.]

**ge-þenian.** v. ge-þegnian: **ge-þensum.** v. ge-þegnsum.

**ge-þeód,** e; *f.* **a** *people* :—Duguðe (*angels*) and geþeóde (*men, peoples*), Adam ǽrest and þ ǽðela cyn, engla ordfruman (*the princes of the angels*), þ þe eft forward, Sat. 19. v. in-geþeóde.

**ge-þeód,** e; *f.* **Fellowship, association** :—Geþeóde *conabuli* (*contubernii*?? cf. *contubernalis* geþeódlíc, 135, 21), Wrt. Voc. ii. 136, 46. Ne sceal hē ágan nāne geþeóde nāðer ne wið þæt mynster ne wið þā geférrǽdene *non debet sociari corpori monasterii*, R. Ben. 109, 17.

**ge-þeódan.** *Add:* , -þiódan, -þiédan, -þídan, -þýdan :—Geþeóded *conexa*, Wrt. Voc. ii. 21, 71. Geþeód *textum*, Germ. 399, 302. **A. trans.** **I.** of local relations. (1) *to bring into contact*. (a) *to join together* several things :—Geþeóddum þínum þrím fingrum hryse þíne hand, Tech. ii. 124, 3. (b) *to apply* one thing to another :—Ne hē ne geðíod *nec applicat* (*ad os suum manum suam*), Kent. Gl. 712. Geþiudde *adplicuit* (cf. tō dyde *adplicuit* (*flammas*), 85, 59), Wrt. Voc. ii. 99, 41. Geþídde, 4, 50. Tō geþeód *applica* (*ignes, saxa*), An. Ox. 4761. (bb) used reflexively, *to come up to an object, arrive at* :—Ic mē eft tō þære dura geðeódde, Hml. S. 23 b, 462. (c) of situation, *to be contiguous* :—Eást-Seaxe syndon Temese streáme tōsceádne fram Centlande and tō eástsǽ geðeódde (*orientali mari contigui*), Bd. 2, 3; Sch. 122, 16. (d) *to join together* people, *unite in one company* :—Aldermen tōsomne geþeóde singendum *principes conjuncti psallentibus*, Ps. Srt. 67, 26. (2) *to join together* so as to form a whole :—Geþíod *concinnat*, Kent. Gl. 419. (3) *to join* so as to form an integral part of a whole, *to insert* into. Cf. **VI** :—Þā sume wē gēmdon geþeódan in þis úre ciriclice stǽr *e quibus nos aliqua historiae nostrae ecclesiasticae inserere curauimus*, Bd. 4, 7; Sch. 385, 2. **II.** *to join* action :— Wæs geþeóded and ongunnen hefig gewin and micel gefeoht betweoh hine and Æþelréde *conserto graui proelio inter ipsum et Aedilredum*, Bd. 4, 21; Sch. 452, 18. Geþeódre ðæde *conjuncto actu*, Wrt. Voc. ii. 136, 37. **III.** *to serve as a link between* :—Seó miht geswutelað hwæt þes dǽl (*the conjunction*) mǽge fremman, for ðan ðe hē hwílon geþeót óðre dǽlas and hwílon tōscæt, Ælfc. Gr. Z. 258, 18. **IV.** *to join, attach* one person to another. (1) as adherent, follower, &c. :— Ǽghwilc hine sylfne tō Gode geðeóde, Hml. S. 23 b, 147. Ic mē sáwle míne tō Gode hæfde georne geðeóded *Deo subdita erit anima mea*, Ps. Th. 61, 5. (2) as a fellow, friend, &c. :—Áwende móde hē hine geðíédde (-ðídde, *v.l.*) tō feldgongendum deórum *hunc agri bestiis mutata mente conjunxit*, Past. 39, 23. Heora nān hine eft tō his geférum ne geþeódde, Hml. S. 23 b, 135. Ðæt hē hiene selfne geðeóde (-ðíode, *v.l.*) tō eallum his hiéremonnum, tō ǽghwelcum be his andefne *ut ad sua singulis congruat*, 175, 3. Swā swā gē eów innan ne geðíeden tō ðǽm áwiergedum gǽstum *te immundis spiritibus non conjungas*, 375, 6. Ǽnig him gebróðra on ǽnigre nā sí geþeód geférrǽdene *nullus ei fratrum in ullo jungatur consortio*, R. Ben. I. 57, 2. Hý geþeóde geþeódscipum on gemang betwyx heáhfæderas and hálige wítegan *vaticidis juncti patriarchis atque prophetis*, Dôm. L. 282. (2 a) *to join* as man and wife :—Hē silfa wæs mid þām fúlestan horwe þártó (*to his daughter*) geþeód, Ap. Th. 24, 15. Wæs geþeód *foederatur* (*Bersabae inlegitimo jugalitatis vinculo*), An. Ox. 5031. Geþeód *foederatorum*, i. *copulatorum* (*nexibus jugalitatis*), 340. (3) as a protector, supporter, &c. :—Seó wiþerwearde wyrd gebēt and gelǽred ǽlcne þára ðe hió hí tō geþiét, Bt. 20; F. 70, 36. **V.** *to attach* a person to a non-material object, *to join* as adherent, follower, &c. :—Geðeód hine tō clǽnnysse þínes geleáfan, Hml. S. 7, 329. Hē wilnode singallíce hine geðiédan (-ðídan, *v.l.*) tō ðǽre lufan his Scippendes *amori conditoris sedulo inhaerere desiderans*, Past. 49, 16. Hí wilniað oþþe him sélfe rícsian oþþe hí tō ðára rícena freóndscipe geþeódan *hi vel regnare ipsi volunt, vel regnantibus adhaerere conantur*, Bt. 24, 2; F. 82, 9. (2) as a fellow, associate, &c. :—Ðonne wē ús unwǽrlíce geðiédað tō yfelra monna freóndscipe *cum incaute malorum amicitiis jungimur*, Past. 353, 23. Suā micle suā wē ús swíður geðiédað and gemódsumiað tō ðæra

yfelena freóndscipe, ðætte wē swā micle fier beóð ðæm hiéhstan ryhte áðiédde *ab illo, qui summe rectus est, eo ipso jam discrepat, quo perversorum amicitiis vita nostra congruat*, 355, 7. Dauid, ðā hē hine eallunga geðiédde tō ðæm geðoftscipe ðǽre incundan sibbe David, *dum totum se ad foedera pacis internae constringeret*, 353, 3. (3) as protector, helper, &c. :—Ðonne sió lufu for mildheortnesse hié geðiéd (-ðiét, *v. l.*) tō his níhstena ðearfe *cum caritas ad ima proximorum se misericorditer attrahit*, Past. 103, 17. **VI.** geþeódan in *to involve in*. Cf. **I.** 3:— þ hí ne dorston hí gemængan and geþýdan in þā scylde þære gýtsunge *ut istos avaritiae tanta damnatio misceri in culpa prohiberet*, Gr. D. 345, 4. **VII.** *to apply, employ for a purpose* :—Wē ne geþeódan *nullatenus adhibeamus* (*scapularum terga pro scutorum umbonibus*), An. Ox. 749. Geþeóddum searaþancum *adhibitis argumentis*, 4071. **B. intrans.** **I.** of local relations. (1) *to cleave to, remain in contact* with :—Geþeóde tunge mín gómum mínum *adhaereat lingua mea faucibus meis*, Ps. L. 136, 6. (1 a) of non-material objects :—Geþeóde *heresceret* (*ut quicquid scrutando rimaretur... intra sagacis animi conclave radicatum haeresceret*, Ald. 43, 1), An. Ox. 3112. (2) of constant attendance in a place :—[Cwear]tenys þrexwoldum tō geþeódde *lautomie liminibus herescit*, An. Ox. 4641. Tō geþeódenne *adherentem* (*ecclesiae liminibus*), 3362. **II.** *to attach oneself* to a person. (1) *to be an adherent, a follower* of :—Hit is áwriten þ sē þe geþeóded tō (*fylged, v. l.*) Drihtne, þonne byð án gāst his and Drihtnes *scriptum est, 'Qui adhaeret Domino, unus spiritus est*,' Gr. D. 136, 13 : 17. Swā swā englas on heofonum þē geðhýrsumiað and mid eallum gemete tō ðē geðeóðað, swā menn þe on eorðan sind, beón hí ðinum willan geþhýrsume and tō ðē mid ealre geornfulnysse geðeódan, Hml. Th. i. 264, 18-22. Sió leáse gesæþ tíhþ þ þe hiere tó geþeódaþ, Bt. 20; F. 72, 7. Geðeódde sum hǽðen wer him (*St. Martin*) tó, Hml. Th. ii. 504, 22. Þā unscæðþigan geðeóddon (*adheserunt*) mē, Ps. L. 24, 21. (2) *to be a helper, protector*, &c. :—Seó wiðerwearde wyrd gefreóþ ǽlc þára þe hió tó geþiéd (-ðiét, S. 47, 24), Bt. 20; F. 72, 3. **III.** *to adhere* to a condition, action, &c. :—Bys[num] tō geþeóddon *exemplis herescunt*, An. Ox. 4916. Hē tō geþeóde *adhaerescat*, 2355. **IV.** of things :—Geþeódeþ þē setl unrihtwísnesse *adheret tibi sedes iniquitatis*, Ps. L. 93, 20. Þingc unriht ne geþeódde (*adhęsit*) mē, 100, 4. v. tó-, un-geþeóde, under-geþeóded.

**ge-þeóde.** *Add:*—Wæs ic ungleáw þæs geþeódes þára Indiscra worda, Nar. 29, 15. Sió ǽ wæs ǽrest on Ebréisc geðiode funden, Past. 7, 1. Ðæt wē sumæ bēc on ðæt geðíode (-ðeóde, *v. l.*) wenden ðe wē ealle gecnáwan mægen, 8. Se þridda dǽl gesæt æt his byrgenne betweoh þā men þe heora geþeóde (geþeódo, *v. l.*) ne cúðon, Mart. H. 180, 2. From wiðcwedenisse geðiéda (*linguarum*), Ps. Srt. 30, 21. ¶ *tongue* as distinguishing nationality (cf. Out of every kindred, and *tongue*, and people, and nation, Rev. 5, 9) :—Þæt is mid Estum þeáw þæt þǽr sceal ǽlces geðeódes man beón forbærned, Ors. 1, 1; S. 21, 11. v. Lǽden-geþeóde.

**ge-þeódlǽcan;** *p.* -lǽhte *To adhere, cleave* to :—Ðā rihtan geðeóðlǽhtun mē *recti adheserunt mihi*, Ps. L. 24, 21.

**ge-þeódlíc;** *adj.* Of comrades, social :—Geþeódlícre geférrǽdenne *contubernali sodalitate*, Wrt. Voc. ii. 135, 21.

**ge-þeódnes.** *Add:* **I.** *a connexion* :—Líchamlicere geþeódnesse lustum *carnalis copulę* (i. *coniunctionis*) *uoluptatibus*, An. Ox. 1605. Tō brýdbúres geþeódnesse, 3200. **II.** *company, society* :—Ic wille habban his dohtra tō mínre geðeódnysse, Hml. S. 7, 311. **II a.** *a company, society, fellowship* :—Geférrǽdene, geþeódnysse *clientela*, An. Ox. 2809.

**ge-þeódrǽden.** *Add:* **I.** *a joining together* :—Fingra geþeódrǽdene *digitorum coniunctione*, Scint. 69, 19. **II.** *communion, fellowship, association, society, company* :—Ne nān bróðer óðerne mid his geþeódrǽdenne ne lette, R. Ben. 74, 23. Hí manna geþeódrǽdenne forsáwan *hominum consortia reliquerunt*, 134, 21. Nān bróðor him nāne geþeódrǽdene tō nǽbbe *nullus ei fratrum in ullo jungatur consortio*, 49, 16. Gif hwylc bróðor gedyrstlǽcð þ hē ǽnige geþeódrǽdenne nime wið þone ámánsumedan sí *quis frater presumperit fratri excommunicato se jungere*, 50, 11.

**ge-þeódsumnes.** *Add:*—Geðiódsumnisse tō ðæm fíonde on woeg foresæged *consentiendum aduersario in uia pronuntiat*, Lk. p. 8, 1.

**ge-þeón.** *Take here the passages given under* ge-þíhan *and* ge-þingan (v. þeón), *and add*: hē -þíhþ; *p.* -þáh, -þong (Gr. D. 225, 21); *pp.* -þigen, -þungen :—Geþíhþ, oferstíhþ *excedit, superat*, Wrt. Voc. ii. 145, 71. **I.** of persons in respect to physical or moral growth, *to material or spiritual progress*. (1) absolute, *to profit, be successful* :—þ sē geðeó, sē ðe hit gehýre, Bd. pref., Sch. 2, 4. Nôht gewæxe ł geðii se fíond in ðǽm *nihil proficiet inimicus in eis*, Rtl. 179, 5. Suelce wē máran ðearfe hæbben ðæt hié geðeón ðonne hié selfe sí *profectum eorum nobis potius quam illis profuturum dicamus*, Past. 304, 3. Þæt se eorðlica man sceolde geþeón and geearnian mid eáðmódnysse þā wununga on heofena ríce, Hml. Th. i. 12, 26. Sel ús hiora bissene giðíá *da nobis eorum imitatione proficere*, Rtl. 62, 16. Ðeáh hí on ðǽre winstran handa bión gedigene, hí beóð mid ðǽre swíðran tóbrocene *etsi in sinistra*

*ejus proficiunt, dextera franguntur*, Past. 389, 25.    ¶ ge-þigen, -þogen ; *pp.*    (a) *of physical growth, grown up, adult :*—Geþo[gen] *adultus*, An. Ox. 18 b, 5.  Geþogenne *adultum*, 3607.    (b) *successful, prosperous :*—Befæste hē his sunu tō lāre . . . for ðām þe on ðām dagum ne mihte nān man beón geþogen (*a man could not get on*), būton hē hǣþene bēc hæfde geleornod and þā cræftas cūþe þe kāseras þā lufodon, Hml. S. 35, 10.    (c) *of highly developed powers :*—Ðā ðe ðonne giēt tō ðǣm gewintrede ne beóð ne geðiegene (-þigene, *v. l.*) (cf. ðā ðe unmedome bióð tō ðǣre lāre oððe for gioguðe oððe for unwīsdōme *quos a praedicatione imperfectio vel aetas prohibet*, 19), Past. 375, 15.  Hālige menn . . . wundorlīce geþogene . . . wē . . . ne magon ðā þing gefyllan þe hī gefremodon, Hml. S. 12, 280.    (2) *where that in which growth takes place is stated :*—Heó on þā kynewīsan geþēh, eall swā hire gecynde wæs, Chr. 1067 ; P. 202, 18.  On Godes lāre geþogen, Ælfc. T. Grn. 12, 34.  On ðeáwum geþogen tō Godes þēnungum *by moral excellence fit for God's services*, Ll. Th. ii. 380, 27.    (3) *where that in relation to which growth takes place is stated :*—Is se man betera, gif hē Gode geðīhð (*if he advances spiritually so as to gain the favour of God*), þonne ealle ðā nȳtenu sindon, Hml. Th. i. 16, 14.  Se mǣsta ðǣl þæra manna þe Gode geðeóð, þurh clǣnnysse hī geðeóð, ii. 22, 15.  Micel menigu geðeáh Gode of Iudēiscre ðeóde, 376, 9.  Þā gecorenan ðe Gode geþugon ðurh martyrdōm, i. 444, 16.  Se bið gesǣlig . . . þe mæg . . . his þeódne geþeón, and þonne mōt habban heofonrīce *felix . . . qui . . . conjunctus Christo coelestia regna tenebit*, Dōm. L. 251.    (4) *where the extent to which growth takes place is stated.*    (a) *with prep. :*—Geðīcð se æðeling tō heálicum cynesetle *the prince is promoted to a lofty throne*, Hml. Th. i. 110, 27.  Oþ þ hē geþeáh (geþong, *v. l.*) tō ārwyrþum þeáwum *usque ad reverendos provexit mores*, Gr. D. 225, 21.  Hē þǣr geþēh tō gōdon men *he there developed into a good man*, Chr. 1057 ; P. 188, 11.  Gif hē beó tō þām gewelegod þ hē hȳred āge . . . Gif hē ne geþeó būton tō healfre hīde (*if his property does not exceed half a hide*), Ll. Th. i. 188, 1.  Sē ðe eornost næfð, earfoðlīce hē sceal ǣfre geþeón tō ǣnigre geðingðe *hardly shall he ever be advanced to any dignity*, Hml. A. 48, 584.    (b) *with clause :*—Hē æfter fæce geðeáh (-þāh, *v. l.*) þæt hine man tō mæssepreóste hālgode *postmodum ad ordinem presbyterii promotus est*, Bd. 3, 23; Sch. 305, 13: Ll. Th. i. 182, 16.  Gif leornere wǣre þ þurh lāre geþuge þ hē hād hæfde, 192, 12.  Geþeón þæt hē wese þrīsthycgende *to succeed in being daring*, Gn. Ex. 50: Gn. C. 44.    II. *of things.*    (1) *to flourish.*    (a) *of plants :*—His wæstmas genihtsumlīce geþugon (*uberes fructus ager attulit*, Lk. 12, 16), Wlfst. 286, 16.    (b) *fig.*—Sē þe his þeódenstōl geþeón wile, Vīd. 13.    (2) *to be profitable to :*—Him seó dǣd ne geþeáh *the deed did not profit him*, Sat. 576.  Þte ūs fæsten giðii (*proficiat*), Rtl. 14, 26.  Giðii (*prosit*) ūs gibed, 70, 7.    II a. *of persons, to be produced in abundance.*  Cf. II. 1 a :—Of ðām mynstre geðugon ædele biscopas þurh Martines lāre gehwilcum leódum *there was an ample crop of noble bishops from the monastery through Martin's teaching for every people*, Hml. Th. ii. 506, 24.  [*Goth.* ga-þeihan : *O. Sax.* gi-þīhan : *O. H. Ger.* ge-dīhan *augeri, proficere, procedere, excrescere.*]

ge-þeón *to press.*  v. ge-þeówan.

ge-þeón *to receive, take, get :*—Sceal wīf geþeón lof mid hyre leódum, leóhtmōd wesan, rūne healdan, rūmheort beón *a lady must have the praise of her people, must be cheery, keep counsel, be liberal*, Gn. Ex. 85.  Ann ic his mīnra swæstarsuna swælcum se hit geðián wile, C. D. i. 311, 15.  Cf. ge-þicgan.

ge-þeóstrian, -þiéstrian, -þīstrian *to darken.  Take here ge-þióstrian in Dict., and add :*—Ðā mōd ðe nān sceadu geðiéstrað ðǣre twiefealdnesse, Past. 243, 23.  Sunna ofer geðióstrad bið *sol obscurabitur*, Mt. L. 24, 29.  v. fore-geþióstrod.

ge-þeówan *to press.  Take here ge-þéwan, -þíwan, -þȳwan, -þeón, -þȳan, -þȳn in Dict., and add :* I. *physical, to press.*    (1) *to put pressure on an object at rest :*—Se scamull him wæs geworden eall swā geþȳwed weax *scamnum illud factum est tanquam cera*, Angl. xvii. 114, 7.    (1 a) *to press into a particular shape :*—Gæten smeoro geþȳd tō poslum, Lch. i. 354, 9.    (2) *to produce by pressure the shape of something, make impress of, stamp :*—Swilce mannes fōtlāsta fæstlīce on ðām stāne geðȳde (cf. swā hié on wexe wǣron āðȳde, Bl. H. 205, 1), Hml. Th. i. 506, 12.    (3) *to cause to move by pressure, to thrust :*—Geþȳdum *adacto*, i. *coacto* (ense capulo tenus per utraque latera *adacto*, Ald. 70, 24), An. Ox. 4946.  Tō geþȳdum, 2, 411.    II. *to compel, force a person to do something :*—Ðā clericas þe Ceólnoð þǣr sette far swylcre neóde geðȳ[ed] (*compulsus*) swā wē seggan wyllað, Chr. 870; P: 283, 29.    III. *to oppress, subjugate :*—Geðēdum *subjugatis*, Wrt. Voc. ii. 121, 69.  [*Goth.* ga-þiwan ; *p.* -þiwaida *to pierce.*]

ge-þeówian *Add :*, -þȳwian.    I. *to serve :*—Is ānum Drihtne geþeówad and gehȳrsumod *uni domino servitur*, R. Ben. 111, 2.  II. *to reduce to servitude :*—Ne ǣnig man ōðerne on unriht ne geþeówige, Wlfst. 70, 6.  Halwun freóde Hægelflǣde hire wimman . . . Crīst him wurðe wrāð þe hī hǣfre geþȳwie, Cht. E. 253, 17.  Wæs se ðeódscipe (*the Jews*) geðeówod under heora feónda gewealde, Wlfst. 14, 8.  Man freóge on ǣlcum tūna ǣlne (ǣlcne ?) wītæþeównæ mann ðæ undær hiræ

geðeówuð wæs, C. D. iii. 360, 7.  [*Goth.* ga-þiwan ; *p.* -þiwaida *to enslave.*]

ge-þeówrǣden (?) *fellowship, association :*—Ne sceal hē habban nāne geþeówrǣden (-þeódrædenę ?: ge-þeóde, *v. l.*) nāðor ne wið þ mynster ne wið þā geferrǣdene *non debet sociari corpori monasterii*, R. Ben. 108, 18.

ge-þersc, es ; *n.  Beating, whipping, flogging :*—Þā þā onsittendas þāra horsa mid langum geþersce (*diu caedendo*) hyra hors geswencton, Gr. D. 15, 11.  Þā gelæhte hē þone fōtscamul and beót Libertinum on þ heáfod . . . Ðā þā hē swā swīðe mid geþersce mistucod (swa swīþe geswungen *vehementer caesus*) wæs, 20, 33.  [*O. H. Ger.* ge-dresc *tritura.*]

ge-þerscan. *Add :*—Ðone geðuurscon *hunc caedentes*, Lk. L. 20, 11.  Geðorscen *caesum*, 10.

ge-þēwan.  v. ge-þeówan: ge-þián.  v. ge-þeón.

ge-þicfyldan. *Substitute:* ge-þicfildan *to make thick :*—Geþycfyldan *densere*, Germ. 401, 21.  v. þic-feald.

ge-þicgan.  [The strong and weak forms may be taken under one head.] *Add : to take and keep as one's own, receive :*—Gyf hine mǣte þ hē hebbe gyldene beág, þ byð þ hē geþihð heálicne ealdordōm, Lch. iii. 170, 23.  Hē landriht geþah *he became entitled to the same rights as a native of the country in which he had settled, became naturalized*, Exod. 354.    II. *to take* food :—Lima wyrm frīteð . . . and þā wist geþygeð, Reim. 76.  Þā blǣda . . . þe ic (*Adam*) þē on teónan geþah *the fruit that in contempt of thee I ate*, Gen. 885.  Þeós wyrt fremað gecnucud and on wine geþiged, Lch. i. 210, 22: 282, 6.  For mete geþiged *taken as food*, 300, 11.  Se geþigeda mete, ii. 186, 21.  Fornam Crīstes godcundlice miht ðone geðigedan mete, Hml. Th. i. 296, 29.  Hȳ tō mete geþigede ðone līchaman gestrangiað, Lch. i. 320, 19.  Fram mettum mid gemete geþigdum, Lch. ii. 220, 26.    II a. *to take and drink from* a cup :—Cwēn ful gesealde ēðelwearde . . . Hē on lust geþeah symbel and seleful (*he ate and drank*), B. 618.  Cf. ge-þeón *to take.*

ge-þiéstrian.  v. ge-þeóstrian: ge-þīhan.  v. ge-þeón.

ge-þind, es ; *n.  A swelling :*—Leoþusār *vel* geþind (= leoþugeþind ?) *condolomata articula* (*condoloma* dicitur de tuberculis ex inflammatione natis circum anum ; *condolomatus* condolomate laborans, Migne), Wrt. Voc. ii. 135, 68.  Wið liþa sāre (*ad condilomata*) and wið geþind, Lch. i. 150, 1.

ge-þinde *rivals.  Dele, and see* ge-þyngþu : ge-þing. *l.* ge-þinge, *q.v.* : ge-þingan *to thrive.*  v. ge-þeón.

ge-þingan *to determine.  Add :* [a strong *pp.* seems to occur in Gr. D. 206, 15.]    I. *to appoint* to an office :—Hraðe sōna wæs æfter mundgripe mēce geþinged þæt hit sceáden mǣl scȳran mōste, cwealmbealu cȳðan, B. 1938.    II. *to assign* an office to a person :—Seó heordelice gȳming tō þām beran wæs geþungen (*for a similar incorrect formation by analogy cf.* (?) ge-þong = ge-þeáh.  v. ge-þeón ; I. 4 a) *injungebatur urso cura pastoralis*, Gr. D. 206, 15.    III. *to fix a time :*—Se kalendus cymeð geþincged on þām ylcan dæge ūs tō tūne, Men. 7.  Þæs ymbe þreó niht . . . þætte hālig mōnð hæleðum geþinged fēred tō folce, 164.  v. un-geþinged.

ge-þinge, es ; *n.  Take here the passages given under* ge-þing, *and add :* I. *an agreement* between persons, *compact :*—Ðis is geðinge Eádwaldes and Cyneðrȳðe ymbe ðet lond, C. D. i. 295, 32.  Ðis sindan geðinga Ealhburge and Eádwealdes et ðǣm londe, 296, 31.  [Ð]is earan Cwǣnðrȳðe geðincgo and biscopes and þeára þegna on Cantwara byrg, C. D. B. i. 533, 2.  Abban . . . geðinga tō krīstes cirican, Txts. 449, 71.  Ðis sint Ecgberhtes geðingeo and Æðeluulfes uuið arcebiscep, 436, 14.  Gethingio *aparitio*, Wrt. Voc. ii. 100, 52.  Geþingio *aparatio*, 4, 70.    II. *an arrangement, a satisfaction of claims :*—Geðynge *expiando*, Rtl. 23, 20.  Ne seleð Gode geðinge his *non dabit Deo placationem suam*, Ps. Srt. 48, 8.    II a. *as a legal term :*—Be diernum geðinge.  Sē þe diernum geþingum betygen sié, geswicne hine þāra geþingea, Ll. Th. i. 134, 11-13.  Gif hē geþafað ðā dyrnan geþingo, 240, 16.    III. *intercession, mediation :*—Þes broþer getogen wæs of þisum leóhte mid geþingum (þingungum, *v. l.*, *intercessionibus*) þæs hālgan weres, Gr. D. 54, 6.  Sē wæs wið his feóndum gescilded, sē þe þā anlīcnesse tō geþingum (-þingunge, *v. l.*) sōhte, Mart. H. 60, 24.  Gif hē wolde geþingum þinne naman, 68, 12.  Hē wæs ābysgod mid his bēnum ymb þæs diácones geþingu tō Gode *Germanus se in precibus constrinxit*, 330, 13.    IV. *arrangement, determination* of course to be followed :—Onbīdan worda geþinges *to await the determination made after speech*, B. 398.  Bīdan beorna geþinges *to wait for the determination arrived at by warriors*, El. 253.    V. *a condition* appointed to a person, *a circumstance* determined by providence :—Wēne ic tō þē wyrsan geþingea, B. 525.  Þearlra geþinga, An. 1600.  Ædeles geþingu, þæt of his cynne cenned sceolde weorðan wuldres God, 757.  Hē him wītgode wyrda geþingu *he should foretell to him what was appointed to happen*, Dan. 545.  [*O. H. Ger.* ge-dingi *pactum, placitum, conditio.*]

ge-þingelic. *Dele.*

ge-þingian. *Add :* I. *to try to get favourable terms* for a person,

*intercede, mediate*. (1) absolute:—Gehwylces mannes dǽda clypiað tó Gode and gewrēgað oþþe geþingiað, Scrd. 20, 38. (2) *to intercede for a person*:—Gif hwelc monn cymð, and bitt ūrne hwelcne ðæt wē hine lǽden tó sumum rīcum menn, and him geðingien *si quis veniat, ut pro se ad intercedendum nos apud potentem quempiam virum ducat*, Past. 63, 2. (3) *to intercede for a person to or with another*:—Se lāreów bið unscyldig, gif hē þæt folc mid lāre gewissað and him wið God geðingað, Hml. Th. i. 240, 11. *Oratores* synd þā ðe ūs tó Gode geðingiað, Hml. S. 25, 816. Crīstes leorningcnihtas . . . ðám wīfe tó him geðingodon, Hml. Th. ii. 112, 15. þæt heó ūs geðingige tó hyre āgenum suna, i. 204, 29. Geþingie, Wlfst. 299, 24. (4) *to intercede for something from a person*:—Hys frȳnd bǽdon Onian þ hē his līfe geðingode æt Gode, Hml. S. 25, 784. II. *to obtain favour by intercession, intercede successfully for a person*:—Fram ūrum æfterran mǽge ðe ūs eft geðingode, Past. 313, 17. Ne mǽg eal middaneard ānum ðǽra geðingian þe Críst þus tó cweð, 'Discedite a me, maledicti,' Hml. Th. ii. 572, 27: 528, 14. Hé nāt hwæðer him selfum geðingod bið *utrum sibi sit placatus ignorat*, Past. 63, 10. III. *to obtain by intercession*:—Geþingedon *repropitiarent* (*deorum favorem*), An. Ox. 4724. IV. *to make terms, settle*. (1) absolute:—Geðingadon *paciscitur*, Wrt. Voc. ii. 116, 54. Hēr Cynegils and Cuichelm gefuhtun wiþ Pendan, and geþingodan þā, Chr. 628; P. 24, 18. Swā hé þonne geþingian mæge, Ll. Th. i. 142, 3. (2) *to settle* a claim, dispute, &c.:—Būtan hī hit ofgān tó rihtan gafole, swā swā hyt hȳ geðingian magan, Cht. Th. 478, 22. (3) *to atone for wrong-doing*:—Adames gylt þurh þē sceal beón geþingod, Bl. H. 9, 6. (4) *to settle the terms of an agreement, agree* to do:—Geþingodon *pacti sunt* (*pecuniam illi dare*, Lk. 22, 5), Wrt. Voc. ii. 73, 73. (5) *to lay down the conditions for a person to attain an object*:—Ic bidde þ þū mē geþingie hū ic wurðe his biggenga *I pray that thou lay down for me the conditions how I may become his worshipper*, Hml. S. 35, 205. (6) *to settle with a person, come to terms, be reconciled*:—Hēr Cantware geþingodan wiþ Ine, and him gesaldon .xxx. m̄., Chr. 694; P. 40, 12. Gif hē wið ðone ōðerne geðingian wile, Past. 425, 1. (7) *to make terms for a person with another, settle claims brought against a person*:—Ne beó þām þeófe nā þe geþingoð-e *none the more is the case against the thief settled for him*, Ll. Th. i. 198, 19. (8) *to arrange a matter for a person with another*:—Goda gesōhte þone kynincg, and bæd þ hē him geþingude wiþ Eádgifu his bōca edgift *regem requisivit Godo, ut pro eo me* (Eadgiua) *rogaret quatinus ei redderem libros terrarum suarum*, Cht. Th. 202, 32. (9) *to accept* offered terms (?):—Hiera se æþeling gehwelcum feoh and feorh gebeád, and hiera nænig hit geþingian (geþicgean, onfón, *v. ll.*) nolde, Chr. 755; P. 294, 26. [*O. H. Ger.* ge-dingôn *pacisci, fedus pangere, convenire*.]

**ge-þingio.** v. ge-þinge.

**geþing-sceat.** *Substitute*: *Money paid to a person in order that terms may be granted by him, price paid for favourable terms*:—'Hē ne sealde Gode nānne mētsceat for his sāule, ne nǽnne geðingsceat wið his miltse.' Ðæt is se mēdsceat wið his sāule '*non dabit Deo propitiationem suam, nec pretium redemptionis animae suae.*' *Pretium redemptionis dare est*, Past. 339, 10.

**geþing-stów,** e; f. *A place of assembly*:—Geþincstōwe *conciliabulum*, Hpt. Gl. 403, 39.

**ge-þingþ,** e; f. I. *intercession*. v. ge-þingian; I:—Tó þan þ hē ābǽde him þā helpe þæs hālgan mannes þingunga (geðingða, *v. l.*) *intercessionis ejus opem impetravit*, Gr. D. 77, 24. II. *making of terms, agreement, composition*. v. ge-þingian; IV:—Be diernum geðinge (dyrnunge þincðe, *v. l.*). Sē þe diernum geþingum (geþingðum, *v. l.*) betygen sié, Ll. Th. i. 134, 11–12. III. *a court where claims are settled* (?):—þ grið þ se ealdorman on fíf burhga geþincðe sylle, bēte man þ mid .xii. hund, and þ grið þ man sylled on burhge-þincþe, bēte man þ mid .vi. hund., Ll. Th. i. 292, 5–8.

**ge-þingþu;** I. v. ge-þyncþu: ge-þingþu; II. v. ge-þingþ; III. **ge-þingung.** *Add*:—Sē wæs wið his feóndum gescilded, sē þe þā anlícneste tó geþingunge sōhte, Mart. H. 60, 24.

**ge-þinnian.** v. ge-þynnian: **ge-þinþenes.** v. ge-þungennes: **ge-þióstrian.** v. ge-þeóstrian: **ge-þíwan.** v. ge-þeówan.

**ge-þíwe.** *Take here* ge-þýwe *in Dict., and add*:—Sume dæge sǽnde se hālga wer þǽra muneca sumne, swā him geþýwe wæs *quadam die misit ex more*, Gr. D. 142, 31. v. ge-þeáwe.

**ge-þofta.** *Add*: of equals, *a fellow, an associate, ally*; of inferiors, *a follower, client*:—Geþofta (gidopta, Ép.), gidogta, Erf.) *contubernalis*, Txts. 51, 503. Geþofta colifeste (=*collibertus*), Wrt. Voc. ii. 98, 3: *cliens*, 17, 41: *contubernalis*, i. *domesticus*, *comes*, *conviva*, *assecla*, 135, 20. God hine (*Abraham*) geceás him tó geþoftan (cf. Abraham amicus Dei appellatus est, James 2, 23), Hml. Th. i. 46, 12. Cassander sende his fultum tó Lisimache his geþoftan (the Latin is: Cassander Lysimachum cum ingenti manu pro se sociis in auxilium misit), Ors. 3, 11; S. 150, 15. Hē āspon DC monna tó him his geþoftena (the Latin is: Quingentos societate invitatos), 5, 2; S. 218, 11. Manege geþoftan ic hæbbe, gyf hī mē hwæt secgað þæt hī selfe gesēwen oððe gehýrdon, ic

hys gelýfe eall swā wel swā ic hit self gesēwe oððe gehýrde, Solil. H. 60, 33. v. treów-, wil-geþofta; þoft.

**ge-þofta** (?), an; *m. Fellowship, society*:—Sinscipes (sein-, MS.) geþoften (cf. gemǽna contubernia, societas, Wrt. Voc. ii. 135, 18), samwistu matrimonii contubernia, An. Ox. 414. Cf. brý-tofta (= brýd-þofta).

**ge-þoftian.** *Substitute*: *To make a league or alliance with, league, ally* oneself. (1) *to league together*, with reflex. dat. or acc.:—Seleucus and Demetrias hí (him, Bos. 75, 14) tógædere geþoftedan *Seleucus Demetrio jungitur*, Ors. 3, 11; S. 150, 29. (2) *to league with* (*wiþ*) a person:—Cassander geþoftade wið Ptholomeus and wið Lisimachus and wið Seleucus, and hié ealle winnende wǽron wið Antigones *Ptolomaeus et Cassander, inita cum Lysimacho et Seleuco societate, bellum instruunt*, S. 148, 34. (2a) with reflex. dat.:—Geoweorþa geþoftade him wiþ Bohan *Iugurtha societatem cum Boccho fecit*, 5, 7; S. 230, 8.

**ge-þoftrǽden[n].** *Add*:—Be þám ðe gehādod man geþoftrǽdene nimð wið wífman *de eo quod ordinatus homo in consortium cum muliere intret*, Ll. Th. ii. 196, 1. Geþoftr[ǽdena?] or geþofts[cipas? v. geþoftscipe] contubernia, Hpt. Gl. 416, 28.

**ge-þoftscipe.** *Add*: league, alliance, and substitute for passages:—þǽr is geþoftscipe engla and geférrǽden apostola, Wlfst. 265, 9. Ðý lǽs hē sié innan āsliten from ðǽm geðoftscipe ðæs incundan Dēman *ne interni foederis discussione feriantur*, Past. 351, 24. Ðā hē ðone geðiédde tó ðám geðoftscipe ðǽre incundan sibbe *dum se ad foedera pacis internae constringeret*, 353, 3. Geþoftsc[ipas (or -e)] contubernia (*feminarum*), Angl. 32, 510.

**ge-þóht.** *Add*: I. *a thought, what a person thinks, an idea, opinion*:—Ðā ðe oser ōðre bióð, giémen hié . . . ðý lǽs ðæt geðóht hine ofersuīðe, Past. 119, 16. For hwý bið se ryhtwísa gecostod mid yfle geðóhte, and ne bið gewemmed, būton for ðý ðe ðæm ryhtwísan ne deriað his yflan geðóhtas, for ðǽm ðe hé næfð gearone willan ðæt wóh tó fulfremmanne, 423, 23–28. Swā heánlic geþóht geniman, þ gé sǽdon þ þā hǽðnan tīda wǽron beteran þonne þā crístnan, Ors. 6, 37; S. 296, 17. Ne bescȳt se deófol nǽfre swā yfel geþóht intó þám men, Angl. vii. 28, 260. Suā giémeleáslíce oft sceacað ūre geðóhtas (*cogitationes*) from ūs, Past. 139, 20. Hiora geðóhtas beóð āweallene on hiora mōde, 271, 15: Seef. 34. Druncne geþóhtas, Dan. 18. Mid hǽtum his geþohta, Bd. 2, 12; Sch. 155, 11: Bl. H. 19, 15. Manna geþóhtas nænig mon ne wāt, 181, 11. Ic geseah ðā innemestan geðóhtas, Past. 155, 7. Hē ongiet his āgne unnytte ðeáwas and geðóhtas, 259, 14: Dōm. 36: Sat. 206: 488: Crä. 22. Heortan geþóhtas, Cri. 1048. God gesyhþ ǽlces monnes geþóht and his word and his dǽda tōscæt, Bt. 40, 7; F. 242, 32. II. *thought, intention, purpose*:—Hé gehýrde on Beówulfe fæstrǽdne geþóht, B. 610. God gewræc on þǽm ārleásan men his ārleáse geþóht, Ors. 6, 31; S. 286, 14. Geðóhtas heortan his (geþóht his mōdes, Ps. Th.) *cogitationes cordis ejus*, Ps. L. 32, 11. Hī smēþe sprǽce habbað and in gāstcofan grimme geþóhtas, Leás. 13. III. *what is thought out, a device, design*:—Geþóht (*molimina*) mentis, An. Ox. 26, 4. Forweorðað ealle þā geþóhtas þe hí þóhtan ǽr *peribunt omnes cogitationes eorum*, Ps. Th. 145, 3. IV. *what is determined after thought, a determination, decree*:—Decretum, i. institutum, positum, consilium, placitum geþóht, statutum laga, diffinitum gesetnes *judicium*, Wrt. Voc. ii. 137, 79. Geðóht *decreta*, 106, 32. Geþóht, 25, 39. V. *counsel, deliberation*. Cf. ge-þeaht; I:—Hé hæfde geþóht mid his witum and freóndum *facto cum suis consilio*, Bd. 3, 22; Sch. 292, 13: 4, 1; Sch. 336, 15. Hé āwyrpð smeáunga ł geþohta (*cogitationes*) folca, Ps. L. 32, 10. þā geþóhtas, Ps. Th. 32, 9. VI. *counsel, direction, advice*. Cf. ge-þeaht; II:—Hē ūs sealde hǽlwendne geþóht and heofonlíce bebodu, Bl. H. 11, 35. VII. *thought, the faculty of thinking* or *the exercise of that faculty, mind*:—Hyge Evan, wīfes wāc geþóht, Gen. 649. Is se sylfa geþóht (*ipsa cogitatio*) tó āsmeágeanne, Bd. 1, 27; Sch. 95, 16. Hāles giðóhtes *sanae mentis*, Mk. R. 5, 15. Of alle geðóhte (*mente*) ðīnum, 12, 30. On geðohte besmiten, Sch. 93, 16. Hē hine oðfloh innan his geðóhte eallum ōðrum monnum *cunctis in cogitatione se praetulit*, Past. 39, 15. On his geþóhte tó mōdig, Bl. H. 109, 27. Eóde se Wisdóm neár mīnum hreówsiendan geþóhte, Bt. 3, 1; F. 426: Wand. 88. Wē āgyltaþ þurh feówer þing, þurh geþóht and þurh word and þurh weorc and þurh willan, Bl. H. 35, 14. Tó ðǽm ðætte ðū mæge ðín geðóht gehealdan *ut custodias cogitationes*, Past. 273, 10. Mēdsceattas āblændað wísra monna geþóht *munera excaecant prudentes*, Ll. Th. i. 54, 18. þám þe hafað wísne geþóht, Cri. 922. Sumum hē syled milde heortan, þeáwfæstne geþóht, Crä. 109: Sal. 239: Fä. 44. VIII. *mind* (with reference to purpose, intention):—Ic ne mētte wíf þrīstran geþóhtes, Jul. 550. Hió wyrpð on ðæt geðóht hwæthugu tó bigietenne *adipiscenda quaeque cogitationi objicit*, Past. 71, 22. Hī habbað wísne geþóht fūsne on forðweg, Gú. 772. Wē geáscodon Eormanríces wylfenne geþóht, Deór. 22. Ðū ūs tó gimǽrsanne eástorlíc hālgo girýno gifríólico giðóhtas giwðes *nobis ad celebrandum paschale sacramentum liberiores animos praestitisti*, Rtl. 32, 9. IX. *conscience*. v. in-geþóht. v. in-, weorold-geþóht.

**ge-þōhtung,** e; f. _Counsel_:—Þū scealt gedeón be þisse geþōhtunge, Hpt. 21, 189, 8. Cf. ge-þeahtung.

**ge-þolian.** _Add:_ I. _to suffer_ what is evil, _be subjected to._ (1) of persons:—Sāules his loswist gedolas _animae suae detrimentum patiatur_, Mt. L. 16, 26. Đā đe oehtnisse gedolas fore sōđfæstnisse, 5, 10. Blōdes flōuing gedolade, 9, 20. Hē earfeđu geþolade, lādlicne deáđ, Cri. 1173. Hleór geþolade árleásra spātl, 1435. Torn geþolode wine Scyldinga, B. 147. Þām þe teónan geþoledan _injuriam patientibus_, Ps. Th. 145, 6. Hū mihtest þū sittan on middum gemænum rīce þ þū ne sceoldest þ ilce geþolian þ ōđre men?, Bt. 7, 3; F. 22, 18: 31, 1; F. 110, 26. Ādreógan wīte, wræc geþolian, Cri. 1515. Feolo gedolega _multa pati_, Mt. L. 16, 21. Gedoliga (giđoelge, R.), Mk. 8, 31. Gedolia † gedrowia, Lk. L. 9, 22. (2) of things:—Rīc heofna mægen gedolas _regnum coelorum vim patitur_, Mt. L. 11, 12. II. _to suffer_ what is salutary, _undergo_ treatment:—Feolo gedolade _fuerat multa perpesa_, Mk. L. 5, 26. III. _to bear evil, be patient under, submit to_:—Ic þæt sār for þē þurh eáđmēdu eall geþolade, hosp and hearmcwide, Cri. 1443. Tō đǣm đæt hié gehealden đā strenge đǣre gedylde . . . gedencen hié nū monig yfel ūre Dryhten gedolode (_pertulit_), Past. 261, 4. Geþola þeóda þreá, nis seó þrāh micel þæt þē hí swencan mōtan, An. 107. Ne mæg hē nō ryhtlīce gedyld lǣran, būton hē self gedyldelīce ōđerra monna tiónan gedolige (_tolerare_), Past. 217, 4. Đæt hié lustlīce đæt geswinc đǣra costunga forsión and gedolien, 407, 29. Flītera fācna hē geþolede _scismaticorum strofas pertulerit_, An. Ox. 2897. Đonne đæs sellendan mōd ne cann đā wǣdelnesse gedolian _cum dantis mens ferre inopiam nescit_, Past. 325, 15. Þý eþ geþolian swā hwæt earfoþnessa swā ūs on becōme, Bt. 10; F. 30, 12: 7, 2; F. 18, 25. Nis mē earfeđe tō geþolianne þeódnes willan, Gū. 1039. IV. _to tolerate_ what is not approved, _bear_ what is not pleasing, _endure_ a condition:—Hē earfođlīce geþolode þæt hē dōgora gehwām dreám gehýrde hlūdne in healle, B. 87. Hē ne mæg gedolian đæt hine menn forsión _despectionem ferre non potest_, Past. 217, 10. Se eorl nolde yrhđo geþolian, By. 6. Þæt wæs Satane sār tō geþolienne þæt hē þā menigeo geseah hweorfan fram helltrafum, An. 1691. V. _to suffer_ the doing or happening of something, _allow_ to take place:—Unāscendedo uosa gidolađes _inlesos esse patiaris_, Rtl. 114, 7. Ne giđole đu from đǣr unāþīnedlīce þte sié āboren _nec patiaris ab illa inpune bajulari_, 113, 36. VI. _intrans. To remain, stop, wait, continue._ (1) of persons:—Gedoligas (giđoeligas, R., gebīdađ, W.S.) hēr _sustinete hic_, Mk. L. 14, 34. (2) of things, _to stick, cleave_:—Cembe heó hyre feax; þ þær on þām cambe geþolige, gesomnige (cf. þ feax þe on þām cambe cleofige, somnige, 21) _let her comb her hair; the hair that sticks in the comb let her collect_, Lch. i. 332, 14. [Goth. ga-þulan: O. Sax. githolōn.]

**ge-þot** (?), es; n.: **ge-þota** (?), an; m. _A shout, howl_:—Geonung, geþota (_pl. n.?_ or _sing. m.?_), rārung _barritus_, Wrt. Voc. ii. 125, 19. [Cf. _Icel._ upp-þot _a great stir_; þytr _a sound_.] v. þeótan.

**ge-þracen.** _Substitute: Strong, hardy, enduring_:—Geþracen hors _mannus vel brunnicus_ (brunicus _equus tolutarius_, Isidore), Wrt. Voc. i. 17, 22. [Cf. _Icel._ þrekinn _enduring_; modern, _stout of frame_.] v. þracu.

**ge-þræc.** _Dele_ geþrec _clangor_, and add: _a collection of objects pressed together, a throng_:—Synna gehwǣr selfum æt eágan firendēda geþrec (_the throng of my misdeeds_) beforan standeþ _delictum meum coram me est semper_, Ps. C. 44. Geþræce _apparatu_ (duces, quibus Cerethi et Pelethi cum horrendo belli _apparatu_ mancipantur, Ald. 12, 1), An. Ox. 778. Geþrece, 7, 59: 8, 87: Wrt. Voc. ii. 76, 53. Fyrdungce, geþræce (Scythica gens cum infinito duelli _apparatu_ proficiscens, Ald. 64, 10), An. Ox. 4560: Wrt. Voc. ii. 85, 72: Hpt. Gl. 512, 9. Geþrece, An. Ox. 7, 313: 8, 252. Geþrec _apparatum_, Wrt. Voc. ii. 100, 53. Ne þurh þreáta geþræcu (đerih đreá[t]un giđraec, _v. l._ Txts. 151, 6) þrēd mē ne hlimmeđ _nor through thick-coming torments_ (? the processes to which the thread is subjected in weaving: cf. the original riddle of Aldhelm 'DE lorica,' Nec radiis carpor, duro nec pectine pulsor) _does the thread resound with me_ (nec garrula fila resultant, Ald. 257), Rä. 36, 6. v. searu-, wǣpen-geþræc.

**ge-þræstan.** _Add:_—Geþræste _attrivit_, Wrt. Voc. ii. 6, 11: contrivit, 134, 80. I. _to crush_ material, _break to pieces, smash._ v. ge-þræstedness: I.:—Mid þý fylle đæs wāges forþryccende hē geþræste (tōcwýsde, _v. l._) ænne þāra muneca _parietem evertit, atque unum monachum opprimens ruina contrivit_, Gr. D. 125, 6. Gedræste geatu đā ǣrenan, Ps. Vos. 106, 16. Đā heán muntas beóđ genehhe mid heofenfýre geþræste, Wlfst. 262, 15. II. _to destroy_:—Ealle trymenesse hlāfes gedræste, Ps. Vos. 104, 16. III. _to vex, distress, afflict._ (1) the body:—Þā āsweóll him se līchama . . . sārlīce hē wæs mid þām sāre geswenced . . . þā sǣde hē him þone intingan þurh hwæt hē ǣrest swā geþræst wǣre (_causam vexationis suae narrabat_), Guth. Gr. 153, 18. Ic wæs swīđe geþræst for þyses wēstenes wæter wǣdlnesse, Hml. S. 23 b, 537. (2) the mind:—Gif þū gesihst ēhtere þīnne þearle wēdende, wite þū þæt fram ātendendum his deófle byþ geþræst (_ab accensore suo demone_ (_p_)_urguetur_), Scint. 208, 4. IV. _to constrain, bind, confine_:—Geþræst artatur, i. constringitur, An. Ox.

2121. Sī geþræst, gehæft _mancipatur_, i. _retinetur_, 1164; mancipatur, i. _commendetur_, 2352. Gescriuene, geþræste _addicti_ (geþrēsde _adducti_, Hpt. Gl. 440, 37), 1452. Geþræste _artabantur_, 4876.

**ge-þræstedness,** e; f. _Crushed condition_:—Geþræstednes _vel_ gebrýsednes, forgnidennes _contritio_, Wrt. Voc. ii. 134, 78. I. _of material._ v. ge-þræstan; I :—Geunrōtsode for geþræstednysse (tōcwysednysse, _v. l._) þæs brōđres _contristati contritione fratris_, Gr. D. 125, 12. II. of the mind, _contrition_:—In ūre heortan geþræstednesse _in cordis contritione_, Gr. D. 349, 2. v. ge-þræstnes _in Dict._

**ge-þræstnes.** _Dele_: ge-þræstnes. _Add:_ v. ge-þræstedness: geþrāfod. _See next word._

**ge-þrafian;** _p._ ode _To press, urge, compel_:—Hē cwæđ þ sume dæge wǣre mid gafoles neáde geþrafod (genēded, _v. l._) sum geleáffull wer _quia die quodam fidelis vir quidam necessitate debiti compulsus_, Gr. D. 157, 22.

**ge-þrafu** (?), e; f.: -þræf (?), es; n. _Pressure_(?), _compulsion_; _rebuke_ (?):—Hwæt sceal him þæt genumene, þ hē eft mid geþrafe sceal āgildan? _what good to him is that which he takes and has to repay under compulsion?_, Nap. 33.

**ge-þrang.** _Add:_ v. folc-geþrang.

**ge-þrāwan.** _Add:_—Hwīte twīne geþrāwen _bisso retorto_, Wrt. Voc. ii. 77, 22. Gedrāune _retorto_, 119, 7. Geþrāwenum _tortis (cincinnorum crinibus)_, An. Ox. 1198. v. ge-edþrāwen.

**ge-þreágan,** -þreán, and (?) -þreáwian (v. ge-þrēwud [ē = eá. Cf. brēd = breád, 72] _incita_ (=incitata (?)), Germ. 390, 82 (_but with the remark_ 'b aus þ'). _Add:_ I. _to rebuke, reprove_:—Gedrād đā ǣlāruas _increpat Pharisaeos_, Lk. p. 9, 1. Gedreáde him se Hælend _increpauit illi Iesus_, Lk. L. 4, 35. Hē gedreáde (giđreóde, R.) hiá _increpans illos_, 9, 21. Geþreáte, Mt. L. 17, 18. Đīn āgen þwyrnes þē sceal geþregean _arguet te malitia tua_, Wlfst. 49, 12. Beón gedreáde _increpare_, An. Ox. 5349. II. _to chastise, chasten, correct_:—Sceal đǣr bión gierd. Đæt is đæt hē gedreáge his hiéremenn . . . Gif đǣr sié gierd mid tō đreágeanne _est virga districtionis_ . . . _Si est virga districtionis, quae feriat_, Past. 124, 22. Đætte eft sién hira scylđa gedreáde mid đām đæt wē hié tǣlen _culpa increpata castigat_, 211, 20. Hý þý hýhstan beóđ þrymme geþreáde, Gū. 45. III. _to trouble, afflict._ (1) a person, (a) in the body:—Heó wæs mid feferādle geþreád (_febre correpta_), Gr. D. 286, 16: 288, 8. Synt geþreáde (_wearied_) þegnas mīne . . . duguđ is geswenced, mōdigra mægen miclum gebysgod, An. 391. (b) in mind:—Forht . . . egesan geþreád, Gen. 2668. Abraham egsan geþreádne, 1865. (2) of things, _to injure_:—Þā heán muntas beóđ genehhe mid heofenfýre geþreáde, Wlfst. 262, 15. IV. _to press, constrain_:—Gedreáte (_coegit_) đegnas his āstīge đæt scip, Mk. R. 6, 45. Geþreád _castigata_ (_sermonum severitate_), An. Ox. 4013. Geþreáde _addicti_, 1452. [O. Sax. gi-þrōōn: O. H. Ger. ge-drouwen.]

**ge-þreát** _violence_:—Heó wearđ geleaht and tō þām hǣđenan temple getogen mid gedreáte þ heó þǣre gydenan Diane godes wurđmynt gebude (cf. se gerēfa hī nīdde þ heó Crīste wiđsōce, Shrn. 31, 18), Hml. S. 2, 384. Þā þe fæste heora geleáfan on God hæfdon, and for nānes mannes gedreáte heora Drihtne wiđsacan noldon, 23, 70. v. þreát; ge-þrīt.

**ge-þreátian.** _Add:_ I. _to press, oppress, afflict_:—Þæs middaneard is for miclum geswenct and mid manegum earfođnyssum yfele geþreátod, Hml. S. 28, 166. Þeód wæs oflysted metes . . . hungre wǣron þearle geþreátod, An. 1117. II. _to press, urge, force_ to do something:—Suā chuā đec genēdes † gedreátas (_angariaberit_) mīle straedena, Mt. L. 5, 41. Geþreátod and genīded _invitus_, Wrt. Voc. ii. 44, 59. (1) with prep. _to force_ to (_tō_) an action:—Đonne ūs se deáđ tō forđsīđe gedreátađ, Hml. Th. i. 414, 21. Gif mon ceorles mennen tō nēdhǣmde geþreáteđ, Ll. Th. i. 78, 12. Gif mon wīfmon tō niédhǣmde geþreátige, 18. Þæt hī đā crīstenan tō heora mānfullum offrungum gedreátodon, Hml. S. 4, 34, 5. (2) with clause:—Nǣfre þū geþreátast þīnum beótum, ne wīta þæs fela gegearwast, þæt ic þeódscype þīnne lufie, Jul. 176. III. _to repress._ (1) the object a person, _restrain, correct_:—Þone earman ne magon his iermđa gedreátigan and geeáđmēdan _pauperis elationem nec illata dignatus inclinat_, Past. 183, 15. Đā đe beóđ swā āheardode on unryhtwīsnesse đæt hī mon ne mæg mid nānre đreáunge gedreátian (cf. mid nānre swingellan gebētan _neque per flagella corrigere_, 9) _qui flagella contemnunt_, 263, 5. Swelce sió gedyld hæbbe đæt mōd gedreátod and gecæfstrod _quando auimum patientia intra se frenare compellit_, 218, 22. (2) the object a thing:—Swā se lēg weard gedreátod þurh Sanctes Martines gebedu þ hē nænigum ōđrum ærne scepþan ne mihte, Bl. H. 221, 15. Wæteregesa sceal geþýd and geþreátod liþra wyrđan, An. 436. IV. _to rebuke, reprove_:—Gedreátas † forcýđas _increpat_, Mt. p. 19, 11: _arguit_, 12. Giđreátađ, Jn. R. 8, 46. Gedreádas, Lk. p. 6, 15. Gedreádade _increpauit_, Mt. L. 8, 26: 20, 31. Gedreátadon, 19, 13. Giđreáta (gedreát, L.) _increpa_, Lk. R. 19, 39. Gedreátaige _increpare_, Mk. L. 8, 32. Đæt se earma ūpāhafena sié mid his wordum gedreátod and gescended _ut in paupere elationem feriat_, Past. 183, 14. Gedreátad _increpata_, Lk. p. 6, 9. Bið gedreátad _arguitur_, Mk. p. 4, 2. ¶ strong

forms of the participle occur in the Lindisfarne Gospels:—Wēron geðreátne, Mt. L. 20, 31. Wēron geðreáten *increpantur*, Mk. p. 3, 15. Geðreátnum *increpatis*, 2, 17.

**ge-þreodian**; *p.* ode *To determine, resolve:*—Forneáh hē geþreodode þ hē forlēt (þōhte tō forlǣtenne, *v. l.*) þ wēsten *ut pene deserere eremum deliberaret*, Gr. D. 101, 7.

**ge-þrēte.** v. ge-þrít: **ge-þrēwud.** v. ge-þreágean.

**ge-þring, -þryng.** Add:—Ðǣr (*in hell*) is ealra yrmða gehwylc and ealra deófla geþring (-þryngc, *v. l.*), Wlfst. 94, 4. Geðring (-þringc, -þringc, *v. ll.*), 114, 6. Ic mē ongan mǣncgan tō ōþrum, þ ic wolde inn geþringan . . . Mín líchama wæs swíðe geswenced for þām nýde þæs geþringes, Hml. S. 23 b, 421. Ealle ðā gehýrdon þe ðǣr æt wǣron . . . on ðām egeslican geþryngce ðā man þā martyras cwylmde, 23, 92. [*Cf. O. H. Ger.* ge-drengi *a crowd, press : Ger.* ge-dränge.] v. heáh-geþring.

**ge-þringan.** *Add:* I. *intrans. To press, force one's way:*—Ic wolde on sume wīsan inn geþringan, Hml. S. 23 b, 412. II. *trans. To exert pressure on an object.* (1) lit.:—Ðā menigo ðec geðringað *turbae te comprimunt*, Lk. L. R. 8, 45. (2) *to use violence with a person, oppress, conquer a people or country:*—Gotan þreáte geþrungon þeódland monig, Met. 1, 3. (2 a) *to force, gain by force* from (on) a person:—Mæg ic þis setl on eów bútan earfeðum āna geþringan (-dringan, MS.), Gū. 216. [*O. Sax.* ge-þringan.]

**ge-þrístian.** *Add:*—Gif morðwyrhtan . . . tō þām geþrístian þ hí on þæs cyninges neáweste gewunian, Ll. Th. i. 324, 12.

**ge-þrístlǣcan.** *Dele* '*to excite*,' *and last passage, and add:*—Wē geþrístlǣcton *presumsimus*, Wrt. Voc. ii. 67, 42. (1) *with infin.:*—Hē nāht geþrýstlǣhte specan, Hml. S. 236, 277. Nāteshwōn lǣran geþrístlǣc *nequaquam docere presumas*, Scint. 126, 14. Ic ne dorste geðrístlǣcan þāra mínra āwuht feala on gewrit settan, Ll. Th. i. 58, 21. Geðrístlǣcende āht secgan, Hml. S. 23 b, 645. (2) *with dat. infin.:*—þ þū nā geþrístlǣce . . . tō gānne, Ll. Lbmn. 414, 1. Nān man ne geþrístlǣce ǣnigne deófles bígencg tō dōnne, Hml. A. 143, 122. (3) *with clause:*—þ þū nā geþrístlǣce þ þū þises húsles onbyrige, Ll. Lbmn. 413, 24. Nǣfre ic ne míne lāstweardas geðrístlaecen þat heó hit on-wenden, C. D. i. 114, 22. Hū hē dorste geþrístlǣcean (for hwon hē geþrýsstlǣhte, *v. l.*) þ hē hēte þone Godes wer swencean, 39, 9. Sceal nān mon geþrístlǣcan (*presumat*) þat hē sprǣce, R. Ben. 16, 2.

**ge-þrístlǣcing**, e; *f.* Presumption:—Þæt nā geþanc geþrístlǣcing gāstes upp āhebbe *ne mentem praesumtio spiritus leuet*, Scint. 122, 18: Verc. Först. 164.

**ge-þrít(?)**, -þrēt (*an* i-*stem noun?*) *clamour of a host, threatening noise:*—[Tō?] geþrēte [*ad?*] *clangorem* (cf. ? *cum ad stridulae buccinae sonum Gothorumque clangorem . . . Roma contremuit*, Ald. 65, 16), Wrt. Voc. ii. 24, 55.

**ge-þrofen, ge-þroren.** v. ge-þweran.

**ge-þrowian.** *Add:* I. *absolute, to suffer;* in a special sense, *to suffer martyrdom, die:*—Ðonne forwyrð ðín bróður, for ðone Críst geðrowade (*propter quem Christus mortuus est*), Past. 451, 34; Jul. 448. Geðrouende hine foresǣgde *passurum se praenuntians*, Mt. p. 17, 17. Geðrowod under ðām Pontiscan Pilate, on rōde āhangen, Hml. Th. ii. 596, 15. ¶ geþrowod *crucified:*—Ðone geðrowodan Críst, Hml. Th. ii. 292, 13. II. *with acc.* (1) *to suffer* what is painful:—Hē geðrowade martyrdom, Shrn. 71, 31. Geþrowade lífes lātteow lāðlic wīte, El. 519. Feolo geðrouia (giðrowiga, R.) *multa pati*, Lk. L. 17, 25. Geðroued in líchoma alle *passus in carne omnia*, Mt. p. 13, 2. (2) *to suffer for, atone for, expiate:*—Gif wē ðās gyltas sylfwilles on andwerdam lífe ne gebētað, wē sceolon neádunge on þām wítniendlicum fýre hī geðrowian, Hml. Th. ii. 590, 31. III. *to sympathize;* conpati:—Sē ðe ne mǣgi giðrouia untrymnissum ūsum *qui non possit conpati infirmitatibus nostris*, Rtl. 91, 5. III a. *to sympathize with, be patient or in harmony* with(?):—Ǣlc gesceaft is sibsumlíce gesceapen mid þínum bebode, swā þ heora nān ōþres mearce ne ofereóde, and se cyle geþrowode wiþ ðā hǣto and þ wǣt wiþ ðām drýgum *tu numeris elementa ligas, ut frigora flammis, arida conveniant liquidis*, Bt. 33, 4 ; F. 128, 33. (v. ge-þweorod.)

**ge-þryccan.** *Substitute:* *p.* -þrycte, -þryhte; *pp.* -þrycced, -þryced, -þryct. I. *to press:*—Ðā hand geðrycð (*premit*) sió incunde lufu, Past. 389, 13. II. *to press down, oppress, depress:*—Ðæt gesuinc hira āgenra welera hīe geðrycð *labor labiorum ipsorum operiet*, Past. 239, 15. Ðætte ðæt lof hié tō ðǣm getrymede ðætte sió monung hié eft ne geðrycte *quatenus eorum mentem, ne admonitio subjuncta concuteret laus praemissa solidaret*, Past. 268, 22. Sē ðe bið geðryced mid ðǣre hefignesse his synna *qui peccati sui pondere premitur*, 268, 9. Ðæt hié sién innan geðryccede (-ðrycte, *v. l.*) mid eádmōdnesse *interius deprimantur*, 119, 15. III. *to repress, compress, restrain:*—Ðone fiónd úserne geðrycg *hostem nostrum comprime*, Rtl. 180, 18. Hié hié selfe niédað tō healdonne ungemetlíce swiggean and for ðǣm bióð swíðe geðrycte *illos violenta custodia indiscreti silentii angustat*, Past. 270, 17. Ðā eádmōdan bióð oft geðrycte mid ðǣre synne ðæs eges, ðonne hié ne durron unðeáwas tǣlan *humiles, ut perversa non increpent, sub specie humilitatis premit culpa formidinis*, 302, 7. IV.

*to express:*—Wē geðryhton (*printed* -dryhton) ł wē āuritton *expressimus*, Mt. p. 3, 2.

**ge-þrýde.** v. ge-þrýn.

**ge-þryle.** *Substitute:* **ge-þrýl**, es ; *n. A press, crowd:*—For ðæs folces geðrýle wæs þæt gesthūs ðearle genyrwed, Hml. Th. i. 34, 34. Onmang ðām mycclan geðrýle and on ðām egeslican geþryngce, Hml. S. 23, 92. v. ge-þrýn, *and cf.* þweál, þweán *for similar relation between noun and verb.*

**ge-þrýn**; *p.* -þrýde. I. *to bind:*—Se líchoma lið on eorðan īsne genearwod and mid racentunge geðrýd and mid bendum gebunden and mid fetrum gefæstnod, Nap. 64, 7. I a. *to bind a book:*—Eðiluald ðis bōc ūta giðrýde . . . and Billfrið gismioðade ðā gihrīno ðā ðe ūtan on sint and hit gihrīnade mid golde (cf. *the riddle on a book :* Mec (*the parchment*) wrāh hæleð hleóbordum, hýde beþenede, gierede mec mid golde; for þon mē glíwedon wrætlic weorc smiða, Rä. 27, 11-14). II. *to repress, restrain:*—Nā for þī rihtlíce synna geþrīð, forgyfenysse wē ortrūwian *neque quia Deus juste peccata distringit, ueniam desperemus*, Scint. 130, 16. III. *to express:*—Geðrýde ł āurāt *expressit*, Mt. p. 3, 6.

**ge-þryng.** v. ge-þring.

**ge-þryscan.** *Add:*—'Ðæt geswinc hiera āgenra welora hié geðryscð (-ðrycð, *v. l.*)' . . . Se feónd ðæt mōd mid grimmum edleáne geðryscð (*premit*), Past. 238, 15-17. Ðætte sió unliéfde byrðen ðissa eorðlicena sorga hí ne geðrysce (*premat*), 401, 6. Geðrysced (-ðryced, *v. l.*) mid ðære hefignesse his synna, 269, 9.

**ge-þrýpfullian**; *p.* ode *To exalt, elevate:*—Nā geþrýdfullud synd eágan míne *non elati sunt oculi mei*, Ps. Rdr. 130, 1.

**ge-þrýþian.** *Substitute:*—**ge-þrýþed**; *adj. Endowed with power* (þrýþ), *powerful, mighty:*—Deáþ nimeþ wiga wælgifre, wǣpnum geþrýþed, ealdor ānra gehwæs, Ph. 486.

**ge-þúf.** *Substitute:*—*Growing luxuriously, leafy, bushy:*—Fǣste geþúf *luxoriante*, Wrt. Voc. ii. 52, 28. I. *of trees, having foliage, of plants, having leaves, leafy, bushy:*—Geþúf fícbeám *frondea ficus*, i. *frondosa*, Wrt. Voc. ii. 151, 15. Geþú[f] *uirescens* (*ramosa fronde*), An. Ox. 2628. Geþúfe beámas *frondea robora*, Wrt. Voc. ii. 151, 12. Þā geþúfan *frondea*, 9. Geþúfum grǣfum *frondosis* (i. *ramosis*) *dumis*, 21. Hyre stela byð mid geþúfum bōgum, Lch. i. 248, 18. II. *of leaves, growing thickly together, bushy:*—Ðeós wyrt hafað lange leáf and geþúfe, Lch. i. 248, 17. Gehwǣde leáf and geþúfe, 256, 5. Heó hafaþ leáf swylce wulfes camb, ac hí beóþ mearwran and hwítran and geþúfran, 278, 15.

**ge-þuhsod.** v. ge-þuxian.

**ge-þun.** *Add:*—Geþun *clangor*, Wrt. Voc. ii. 23, 57. Dyne, geþun, cyrm *clangor, tubarum sonus vel vox tubae*, 131, 52. Dyne *vel* geþun *crepaculum, sonum*, 136, 13.

**ge-þungen.** *Add:* I. in respect to age, *advanced, mature:*—Geþungen yld and swýðe eald yld . . . hærfest and geþungen yld gefērlǣcað, and winter and yld āteoriað, Angl. viii. 299, 25-27. Swylce hit cild wǣre . . . swylce hē medemre ylde man wǣre, and ōðre hwíle swylce hē eald geþungen man wǣre, Wlfst. 99, 15. Cildhād gewīt tō cnihthāde, and cnihthād tō geðungenum wæstme, Hml. Th. i. 490, 3. Þysum cild-geongum cyningce . . . lis foregengan þe geþungene wǣron on yld, Lch. iii. 436, 10. Wē myngiað geþungene and iunge, Angl. viii. 308, 5. II. *deserving;* emeritus:—Geþungen *emeritus*, i. *veteranus miles, prefectus*, Wrt. Voc. ii. 143, 28. Geþungenan cempan *emeritos* (i. *eximios*) *milites*, An. Ox. 892. III. *eminent, distinguished.* (1) *by rank:*—Hē ealdordōm onfēhð . . . geþungen on þeóde, Ph. 160. On ealdormonnes hūse oððe on ōðres geþungenes witan, Ll. Th. i. 106, 6. Biddende his þingunge tō ānum geþungenum ealdormen, Hml. S. 3, 171. Biscepa and ōðerra geþungenra witena, Ll. Th. i. 58, 5. Ercebiscop mid manegum ōðrum geðungenum witum, Hml. Th. ii. 148, 3. Be abbodum and ōðrum geþungenum, R. Ben. 105, 12. Ne mæg se man mōdigan on geðincðum, for ðan þe fela synd geþungenran, Hml. S. 16, 372. (2) *by good qualities, excellent:*—Þú eart beforan Drihtne geþungen, Hml. S. 23 b, 236 note. Þǣr (*in heaven*) is geþungen þegnweorud, Cri. 751. Geþungene (*eminent for scholarship*) preóstas, Angl. viii. 305, 8. Æfter geðungenra lāreówa trahtnungum, Hml. Th. ii. 2, 8: Hml. S. 3, 151. þ hí beón þe geþungenran on þære fandunge, 542, 502. (2 a) *of things:*—Ic hæbbe þe oferþogen on geþungenre lāre, Hml. S. 3, 209. IV. *developed so as to be fit for, fitted:*—Þā þe tō ciriclicum hāde geþungene wǣron *qui ecclesiasticum gradum apte subirent*, Bd. 4, 23; Sch. 469, 1. v. heáh-, un-geþungen.

**ge-þungenlíce.** *Add:*—Geþungenlíce (*printed* geþunglíce, Wrt. Voc. ii. 143, 26) *emature*, Wülck. Gl. 227, 43.

**ge-þungennes.** *Add:* I. *maturity.* v. ge-þungen; I:—Þæs geþungennes hine ne geþafige worian *cuius maturitas eum non sinat vagari*, R. Ben. I. 112, 6. II. *growth, progress, advancement:*—Of geþungenysse *processu . . . conuersationis* (v. R. Ben. I. 6, 8), An. Ox. 57, 1. III. *eminence, distinction.* (1) in regard to rank. v. ge-þungen; III a:—Twelffeald geþungennes *duodenus apex*, Wrt. Voc. ii. 142, 14. *Fastus, elatio vel* geþungennes, 146, 40. (2) in regard to

good qualities, *excellence, nobility, dignity.* v. ge-þungen ; **III b** :—
Weorþscipe *vel* geþungennes *dignitas,* i. *honestas, excellentia, fastigium,*
Wrt. Voc. ii. 140, 25. Geþun[gennes] *sublimitas (virginitatis),* An. Ox.
8, 74. Geþungenesse *fastigium,* i. *summitatem (perfectionis),* 1706.
[Gemyndige swā heálicre geþinþenesse (geþungenesse ? geþincþe ?)
eówres hādes, Ll. Th. ii. 402, 24.] (2 a) *virtue, chastity* :—þ hig witon
þ sió geþungennes ne mæg næfre wesan besmitan, Hml. A. 207, 424 :
203, 284. Biddende mē þ ic forléte mīne geþungenesse, 200, 171.

**ge-þunrian** ; *p.* ode *To thunder* :—Gif on Frīgedæg geþunrad, þonne
getācnað þ nýtena cwealm. Gif on Sæternesdæg geðunrad, þ tācnað
dēmena cwealm, Archiv cxx. 46, 9-11.

**ge-þuren.** v. ge-þweran.

**ge-þuxian, -þuhsian** ; *p.* ode *To grow dark, get obscured by clouds* :—
Bið eac ūpheofon sweart and gesworcen, swīþe geþuxsað (and swīþe ge-
þuhsod, Wlfst. 137, 9), deorc and dimhīw *tristius et coelum tenebris
obducitur atris,* Dōm. L. 105.

**ge-þwǽnan.** *Add* : Sió mildheortnes ðæs lāreówes geðwǽnd and
gelecð (*rigat*) ðā breóst ðæs gehiérendes, Past. 137, 8. Ðonne se lāreów
drincð of ðǽm wielme his āgnes pyttes, ðonne hē bið self geðwǽned and
wel gedrenced mid his āgenum wordum *bibit praedicator sui fluenta putei,
si sui irrigatione verbi infunditur,* 373, 10. Swā ðæt ǽghwelces
mannes mōd swā micle oftor wǽre geðwǽned mid hreówsunge teárum *ut
uniuscujusque mens tantum poenitendo compunctionis suae bibat lacrymas,*
413, 12.

**ge-þwǽran.** v. ge-þwǽrian.

**ge-þwǽre.** *Add* : **I.** *in agreement.* (1) of living creatures or things
personified. (a) of many, *in agreement, at peace with one another* :—
Ealle crīstene men sceoldon beón swā geþwǽre swilce hit ān man wǽre,
Hml. Th. i. 272, 24. Þǽr beóð geþwǽre sāwul and līchama, þe nū on
ðisum līfe him betweónan winnað, 11. Manega gesceafta beóþ swā
geþwǽra þte nō þ ān þ hī magon gefēran beón, ac heora furþum nān
būton ōþrum beón ne mæg, Bt. 21 ; F. 74, 17. þū hæfst ǽlle gesceapene gesōme and tō þām geþwǽre þæt heora nān ne mæg ōðerne mid
ǽlle fordōn *dissonantia usque in extremum nulla est,* Solil. H. 5, 14.
Habbað ǽðele tungol emne gedǽled dæg and nihte, sunne and mōna swīðe
geþwǽre, Met. 29, 37. (a a) *in agreement with (dat.)* :—Hié wilniað
ðæt wē him geðwǽre sién, Past. 255, 1. (b) of a company :—Be gehwǽre brōðræddene *de concordi sodalitate (apium),* An. Ox. 231. (c) of
a single person :—For ðām singalan ege ne mæg hē nō weorþan geþwǽre
on him selfum, Bt. 39, 12 ; F. 232, 3. (2) of things :—Heó hæfð
twā ðing, clǽnnysse and mōdignysse, þe ne magon beón geþwǽre on
hāligre þeáwfæstnysse, Hml. A. 40, 404. **II.** *peaceable, peaceably
disposed, gentle.* (1) of living things :—Oft wíf hine (*a dog*) wrīð ; hē
him wel hēred, þeówað him geþwǽre, Rä. 51, 6. Ðætte on ōðre wīsan
sint tō manianne ðā geðwǽran (*pacati* ; cf. gesibsuman, 6), Past. 345, 4.
Hié wǽron swā geþwǽre and swā gesibsume þ hié ealle forgeáfon þǽm
cāsere þā fǽhðe þe his mǽg hæfde wið hié ǽr geworht, Ors. 6, 4 ; S. 258,
26. (2) of things, *at peace, at rest* :—Streámas eft stille weorðað, ýða
geþwǽre, Rä. 3, 15. v. un-geþwǽre.

**ge-þwǽrian.** *Add* :—Geþwǽrie *respiret (conspiret?),* Germ. 398,
140. **I.** *trans. To reconcile* :—Geþwǽre þē wið hine *reconcilia te ei,*
Ll. Th. ii. 194, 2. Ǽr þām ðe hē hine sylfne geþwǽrige (*reconciliaverit*)
wið his nēhstan, 192, 30. **II.** *intrans. To be in agreement* :—
Geþwǽrie *vel* samod orþie *conspiret,* i. *consentiet,* Wrt. Voc. ii. 134, 13.
Samod geþwǽrende *concordantes,* 24, 8. (1) of persons. (a) *to agree
together* :—Þā ne mihte hī betwyh him sylfne geðwǽrian and geweorþan *cum
invicem concordare non possent,* Bd. 4, 4 ; Sch. 369, 5. Gegadan *vel*
geþwǽriende *complices, conspirantes,* Wrt. Voc. i. 50, 12. (b) *to agree
with another in act or thought* :—Hē bæd hié þ hī on ánnesse sibbe and
in gehylde rihtra eástrena geðwǽrede (-þwǽredon, -hwǽredon, *v. ll.*) mid
þā Crīstes cyricean *obsecrans eos unitatem pacis et catholicae obseruationis
cum ea ecclesia Christi tenere,* Bd. 2, 4 ; Sch. 128, 2. Geþwǽriende
(-hwǽriende, 5376) *assentatrix (lingua),* An. Ox. 2, 461. (c) *where
a person agrees with, consents to, a thing* :—Gif þū geþwǽre nā geþwǽrast
*si cogitationi non consenseris,* Scint. 141, 12. þām eáðmōdum þe mid
heora līfes ðeáwum Crīstes bebodum geþwǽriað, Hml. Th. i. 514, 6.
Gif þū þārtō geþwǽrudest, Ll. Lbmn. 414, 4. Þā men þe þās stale ge-
fremoden and þe þǽrto geþwǽrodon, 438, 9. Se byþ beswicen hwæt hē
geþwǽrige gesewenlīce hē nāt *qui seducitur quid consentiat [e]uidenter
ignorat,* Scint. 229, 5. (2) of things. (a) *to agree together* :—On
þǽre samodgeþwǽriendan gesihðe and onsægdnesse *concordante simul
visione et sacrificio,* Gr. D. 346, 5. (b) *to agree with another.* (a) with
dat. :—Iōhannes stefn geþwǽreþ (-þweorað, *v. l.*) þām ylcan andgyte
*Iohannis vox in aestimatione ista concordat,* Gr. D. 332, 21. Ge-
þwǽraþ (-þwǽriaþ, *v. l.*) þǽre onwrigenesse and þǽre gesegene þæs
brōðor . . . þæt word Ecgbryhtes *conuenit reuelationi et relationi fratris
. . . sermo Ecgbercti,* Bd. 4, 3 ; Sch. 363, 6. (β) with prep. :—His līfes
clǽnnys geþwǽrode (-ede, -hwǽrede, *v. ll.*) mid þām bīgenge his
bodunge *concordabat vitae munditia cum studio praedicationis,* Gr. D.
33, 22. þæt ūre mōd geþwǽrige mid þæs mūðes clypunge *ut mens
nostra concordet voci nostrae,* R. Ben. 45, 11. v. un-geþwǽrian.

**ge-þwǽrlǽcan.** *Add* : **I.** *trans. To reconcile, unite* :—Hē wolde
mancynn gesibbian and geðwǽrlǽcan tō þām heofenlicum werode, swā
swā Paulus cwæð : 'Ipse est pax nostra, qui fecit utraque unum,' Hml.
Th. ii. 580, 2. **II.** *intrans.* (1) of persons or things personified.
(a) *to agree, come to terms with an opponent, be reconciled* with :—Hē
geðwǽrlǽhte wið Pilate (cf. facti sunt amici Herodes et Pilatus, Lk. 23,
12), Hml. Th. ii. 384, 2. Godes word is ūre wiðerwinna . . . wē sceolon
geðwǽrlǽcan wið þ word, Hml. A. 8, 193 : 9, 214. (b) *to agree
together, be companions, act in concert* :—Seó sǽ and se mōna geþwǽrlǽcað heom betweónan, ǽfre hig beóð gefēran on wæstme and on
wanunge, Angl. viii. 327, 25. (c) *to agree with another, be a companion, accomplice of, consent to the plans of* :—Gif þē fēdan synfulle, nā
geðwǽrlǽce him (*non adquiescas eis*), Scint. 191, 10. Ne ðū manslagum
ne geðwǽrlǽce . . . ne yfeldǽdum ne geðwǽrlǽce, Hml. S. 21, 360, 361.
(d) *to agree in a proceeding, consent to, be a party to* :—Ne gebyrað . . .
þ hī geþwǽrlǽcan sceolon on ǽniges mannes deáðe, Hml. S. 32, 223.
(e) *to agree in, or with an opinion* :—Þisum andgite geðwǽrlǽcð Danihel
on his wītegunge, Hml. Th. i. 518, 15. On ðisum andgite geðwǽr-
lǽhð Matheus, 616, 8. Ealle þā geleáffullan fæderas geþwǽrlǽhton on
þām ānum þ God gescypð ǽlces mannes sāwle, Hml. S. 1, 85. (f) *to
act in accordance with, suitably to a condition, adapt oneself* :—þū swīðost geþwǽrlǽcst mīnes sylfes gewilnunge *you act exactly as I desire,*
Hml. S. 37, 108. Þ hāliggewrit wyle tō ūre sprǽce geþwǽrlǽcan (-lǽtan,
MS., -lēcan, -þwērlǽcan, *v. ll.*) and on ūre wīsan ūs tō sprecð *utitur
Scriptura Sancta usitatis nobis verbis, ut coaptet se nostrae parvitati,*
Angl. vii. 34, 320. (2) of things. (a) *to agree together, have the same
characteristics* :—Lengtentīma and cildiugoð geþwǽrlǽcað, and cnihtiugoð and sumor beóð gelīce, and hærfest and geþungen yld gefērlǽcað,
Angl. viii. 299, 26. (b) *to agree with another.* His līfes clǽnnys geðwǽrlǽhte mid þām bīgenge his bodunge *concordabat vitae munditia cum
studio praedicationis,* Gr. D. 33, 22. (c) *to be suited, be adapted to* :—
Gehwǽrlǽcan *congruant (gymnicorum exempla congruant* ad comparationem, Ald. 3, 23), An. Ox. 66.

**ge-þwǽrlic** ; *adj. Concordant, agreeing, harmonious* :—Ne cymð
nāht ungelīc trymnes upp, ac swīþe geþwǽrlicu of ðǽre gemynde gōdra
mægena *non dispar aedificatio oritur ex memoria virtutum,* Gr. D. 8, 3.
Be geþwǽrlicre *de concordi,* Wrt. Voc. ii. 138, 8. v. un-geþwǽrlic.

**ge-þwǽrlīce.** *Add* : **I.** *in agreement, with one accord.* (1) of
persons :—Hī heom betweónan rǽddon and þus geþwǽrlīce cwǽdon :
'Betere wē āhreddon ūs sylfe,' Hml. S. 23, 201. (2) of things :—Nū
sprecð geþwǽrlīce (*concorditer*) mid þỹ mægne þāra wundra seó rihtwīsnes
þāra worda, Gr. D. 154, 6. **II.** *gently* :—Hē geþwǽrlīce mid
Godes ege andswarige *cum omni mansuetudine timoris Dei reddat responsum,* R. Ben. 126, 22. v. un-geþwǽrlīce.

**ge-þwǽrnes.** *Add* :—**I.** *concord, peace* :—Ǽlc ðāra ðe hine āscādan
wille from ðǽre geðwǽrnesse, hē wile forlǽtan ðǽre lufan grēnnisse and
forseárian on ðǽre ungeðwǽrnesse *omnes, qui per discordiam separantur
a viriditate dilectionis, arefiunt,* Past. 359, 14. Gesibsumnesse and geþwǽrnesse ūs betweónan healdan, Ll. Th. i. 246, 22. Hē him eápmēdo
budon and geþwǽrnesse, Chr. 827 ; P. 60, 34. **II.** *gentleness* :—
Underfō hē þā geboda his tǽcendes mid ealre geþwǽrnesse and mid micelre
eáðmōdnesse (*cum omni mansuetudine et obedientia*), R. Ben. 128, 12.
Of irsunge wyxt seofung, and of ðǽre geþwǽrnesse lufu, Prov. K. 23. v.
un-geþwǽrness.

**ge-þwǽrung,** e ; *f. Consent* :—Mid geþwǽrunge geþances *consensione
mentis,* Scint. 228, 12.

**ge-þweán.** *Add* :—Ðū mē geðoas (*altered from* geðuoas) foet, Jn. L.
13, 6. Ic geðuóg laui, 14. Heáfod mīn ne geðuóge ðū, Lk. l.. 7, 46.
Geðuóh *lauit,* Jn. p. 7, 1. Geþoa *lauare,* Jn. L. 13, 5.

**ge-þwe(o)orness,** *depravity* ; *pravitas,* Verc. Först. 145, 5.

**ge-þweorod (-þweór- ?** *according to the metre the syllable is long*) :
—þeáh ānra hwilc sié gebunden gesiblīce tōgædre, þte heora ǽnig ōðres
ne dorste mearce ofergangan, ac geþweorod sint ðegnas tōgædre, cele
wið hǽto, hǽt wið drȳgum ; winnað þweore *tu numeris elementa ligas,
ut frigora flammis, arida conveniant liquidis ( for the prose rendering of
this see* ge-þrowian ; **III a**), Met. 20, 72. [*In both the metre and the
prose* ge-þwǽrian *might have been expected to render* convenire ; *but for
form see* ge-þweoraþ *under* ge-þwǽrian ; **II. 2 b**.]

**ge-þweran.** *Add* :—Fela henne ǽgru gesleá on ān fæt, geþwere þonne
and þicge, and gemenge ǽr wið flétan, Lch. ii. 264, 25. Geþworen
(*printed* -þroren) flŷte *lectidiclatum,* Wrt. Voc. ii. 50, 72 : *lactudiclum,*
52, 6. Githuornae flēti, geþuorne flēte *lectidiclatum,* Txts. 74, 605.

**ge-þwerian.** *Dele, and see two preceding words.*

**ge-þwinglod.** *Add* :—A form þwingel, connected with a verb
þwingan (= O. H. Ger. dwingan *stringere,* O. Sax. bi-þwingan), *and
having suffix* -el *denoting an implement, might be inferred with meaning* 'band' (cf. þwang) ; *then* ge-þwinglod *might mean* 'provided with a
þwingel,' 'bound up.'

**ge-þȳan.** v. ge-þeówan : **ge-þȳdon.** v. ge-þeódan : **ge-þȳlan.** *Dele.*
**ge-þȳld,** e ; *f.* Take here ge-þuild *in Dict.,* and add : es ; *n.* : ge-
þyldo (-u) ; *f. indecl.* (1) ge-þyld ; *f.* :—Sió geðyld, Past. 218, 22. For

ðám dóme his geðylde, 27, 21. Þ mægn þǽre geþylde, Gr. D. 20, 16. Wundorlicre geþylde man, 283, 18. Tó ðǽre geðylde, Past. 222, 8. Ðá geðyld ðe is módur ealra mægena, 215, 19 : 222, 25 : 219, 13. Ðá geðylde ðe is módur ealra mægena, 214, 19 : 217, 18 : 219, 10 : Gr. D. 289, 27. (2) ge-þyld; n.:—Ðæt geðyld, Past. 219, 6. Seó gedréfednys wyrcð geðyld, and þ geðyld áfandunge, Hml. Th. i. 554, 26. Ne sealde hé ús náne bysne his geðyldes, 226, 12 : R. Ben. 135, 8 ; Guth. 50, 26 : Gr. D. 20, 16. On eówrum geðylde, Past. 218, 24 : Lk. 21, 19: Hml. Th. ii. 544, 4 : Hml. A. 21, 176. Hé eal geðyld gecýþðe, Bl. H. 123, 3 a. (3) ge-þyldo (-u) ; f. :—Wundorlicre geðyldo man, Gr. D. 283, 18. Mid his þǽre godcundan geðyldo, 326, 18. Þurh þá geþyldo, 289, 27. Hé lufade þá geþyldo, 290, 15. (4) uncertain forms :—Ne gé þæt geþyldum (patiently) þicgan woldan, ac mec yrringa úp gelǽddon, Gú. 454 : 886. Hé him þá geþyldu (-þylda, v. l.) forgife, Gr. D. 274, 15. Hé lufode þá geþyldu, 290, 15. v. ofer-, un-geþyld.

ge-þyldan (?) ; p. -de to bear patiently, consent to do, tolerate :—Geþylde (geþylde[gode]?) consentiret, i. succumberet (nisi ethnicorum ritu thurificare consentiret, Ald.), An. Ox. 3238. [O. H. Ger. dulten tolerare, sustinere, subire; gedulten pati.] Cf. for-þyldian.

ge-þyldelíce. v. ge-þyldiglíce.

ge-þyldig. Add:—Ic wolde cweþan þ þú uþwita wǽre, gif þú geþyldig wǽre, Bt. 18, 4 ; F. 68, 4. Hé wæs swíðe geþyldig and eáðmód, Bl. H. 213, 7 : Hml. Th. i. 472, 7. Giðyldig, Rtl. 102, 15. Gehyldig, Ps. Spl. 7, 12. Ne hié þám geþyldegum simble ne wuniaþ, Bt. 11, 1 ; F. 34, 2. Se Wísdóm gedéþ his lufiendas geþyldige, 27, 2 ; F. 98, 2. v. un-geþyldig.

ge-þyldigian. Add: I. trans. To bear with patience, tolerate, endure :—Wé magon ongietan mid hú micle irre Dryhten geðyldegað ða ælmessan ðe him man of reáflúce bringþ hoc sacrificium quanta ira aspiciatur, Past. 343, 13. Ðonne meaht ðú ðý wyrs geðyldgian óðres monnes yfel pejus tibi sit aliena prava tolerare, 225, 14. II. intrans. To be patient, have patience :—Ðá ábǽdan hý úneáðe þæt mon geðyldgode sume hwíle, Wlfst. 100, 8. Bisceopum gebyrað, gyf ǽnig óðrum ábelge, þ man geþyldige oð geférena sóme, Ll. Th. ii. 316, 34. v. ge-þyldan.

ge-þyldiglic. Take here ge-þyldelic in Dict., and see next word.

ge-þyldiglíce. Add:—Hé ðá swingle forbǽr swýðe geþyldiglíce (-þylde-, v. l.), Hml. S. 19, 78 : Gr. D. 108, 32. Geðyldelíce, Past. 217, 4 : Hml. Th. i. 176, 11 : Wlfst. 7, 11 : R. Ben. 17, 12 : 28, 9 : Bt. 18, 4 ; F. 66, 34. Geðyldilíce (but geþyldelíce, S. 25, 4), 11, 1 ; F. 32, 32. v. un-geþyldiglíce.

ge-þyldmód ; adj. Of a patient spirit, patient :—Sé þe wǽre weámód, weorðe sé geþyldmód, Wlfst. 72, 7.

ge-þyldmódness, e ; f. Patience :—Gegearwien wé úra sáula clǽnnesse mid lufan and geþyldmódnesse, Nap. 33.

ge-þyldo(-u). v. ge-þyld.

ge-þylmǽdan. Substitute : ge-þylman ; pp. ed To overwhelm :—Hí geþylmede í gewriþene synt ipsi obligati (cf. obligata, oblita, Corp. Gl. H. 84, 4 a) sunt, Ps. L. 19, 9. Cf. for-þylman.

ge-þylmódness. v. ge-þyldmódness : ge-þýn. v. ge-þeówan.

ge-þyncan. Add: I. to seem, appear :—Him ǽr geþúhte þæt him nán sǽ wiþhabban ne mehte, Ors. 2, 5 ; S. 84, 12. Him rǽdlecre geþuhte þ hé frið genǽme, 3, 1 ; S. 96, 15. ¶ geþúht béon, wesan videri. (1) where the subject of the verb is given and a complementary adj. :—Hé him selfum wæs lytel geþúht, Past. 113, 16, 17, 18. Se leóma wæs swíðe lang geþúht, Chr. 1097 ; P. 233, 29 : Rún. 21. Þeáh ðá gecorenan Godes cempan sind feáwa geðúhte, Hml. Th. ii. 82, 12. (2) the subject of the verb not expressed. (a) with infin. and its subject :—Mé ys geþúht Godes þeówdóm betweoh þás cræftas ealdorscype healdan, Coll. M. 30, 15. Hwilce þé [ys] geþúht betwux woruldcræftas healdan ealdordóm quales tibi videtur inter seculares artes retinere primatum?, 23 : 11. (b) with clause :—Him wæs sóðre geþúht þæt hit engles word wǽre, Gú. 1096. II. to seem good or fit :—Hí ealle sealdon þone dǽl heora spéda þe him geðúhte, Hml. Th. i. 582, 19. Godwine fór upp, and Harold, and heora lið swá mycel swá heom geþúhte, Chr. 1052 ; P. 180, 28. [O. H. Ger. ge-dunchen videri.]

ge-þyncþ(u). Take here ge-þingþu ; I. in Dict., and add: I. thriving, prosperous condition. (1) in temporal matters, dignity, honour :—Ne mæg se mann módigan on geðincðum (-ðinðum, v. l.) for ðan þe fela synd geþungenran, Hml. S. 16, 372. Án woruldcynincg ne mæg beón wurðful cynincg búton hé hæbbe þá geþincðe þe him gebyriað, p. 6, 61. Hé swanc for heofonan ríce swíþor þonne hé hogode hú hé geheólde on worulde þá hwílwendlican geþincðu (-ðinccða, v. l.), þe hé hwónlíce lufode, 26, 113. (2) in spiritual matters, virtue, excellence :—Þá clǽnheortan þeónde beóð on hálgan geþincgum, Hml. A. 23, 223. For hyre micclum geðingðum, 25, 31. Ne derode Ióbe náht þæs deófles costnung, ac fremode, for ðan ðe hé wæs fulfremedre on geþincðum and Gode neár æfter ðæs sceoccan éhtnysse, Hml. Th. ii. 450, 2. Þám hálgum mannum þe þurh miccle geðincða Gode geþungon, i. 540, 16. II. advanced position. (1) of per-

sons, rank, status, degree :—Leáfhlestendra geþincþe catacuminorum gradu, i. ordine, An. Ox. 2191. On heálicere démendre geþinhþe in alto tribunalis culmine, 3456. Geþinþe apice (Pontificatus praeditus), 5078. Þá unrihtwísan déman behealdaþ þá geðuncþo ðæs mannes, Ll. Lbmn. 476, 26. Ðæt hé ongite for hwæs geðyncðum ðæt folc sié genemned heord sub cujus aestimatione populus grex vocatur, Past. 75, 7. Swǽ swǽ hé on geðyncðum bið furðor ðonne óðre sicut honore ordinis superat, 80, 23. Hit wæs hwílum þ leód and lagu fór be geþincðum, Ll. Th. i. 190, 12. Swá man hwílum bið mihtigra for worulde, oþþon þurh geþingða heárra on háde, 328, 14. On ðæm dóme ðæs ryhtwísan Déman onwent sió geearnung ðone hád and ðá geðyncðo in examine recti judicis muta merita ordinum qualitas actionum, Past. 411, 25. (1 a) of a thing personified :—Þes dǽl (the participle) næfð nǽnne stede of him selfum, ac byð of worde ácenned, and becymð syþþan tó his ágenre geþingðe (-þincþe, v. l.), Ælfc. Gr. Z. 244, 18. (2) of things, degree, grade :—Geþincþa graduum, An. Ox. 1404. (3) high degree of moral excellence :—Héhnysse, geþinþe fastigio (edito Virginitatis fastigio sublimati, Ald. 13, 36), An. Ox. 930. Geþinþe proposito, i. gradu (in summo Virginitatis proposito, Ald. 14, 23), 968. Gif heálicere eáðmódnesse wé wyllað geþincðe hreppan si summe humilitatis volumus culmen adtingere, R. Ben. I. 27, 13. v. leód-, weorold-geþincþ[u].

ge-þynd. v. ge-þind : ge-þynge, es ; n. Substitute ge-þyng[o] ; f., and add: rank, condition :—Missenlicrǽ yldo and getincge (-tinge, v. l. = -þyn(c)ge (?) men homines condicionis diuersae et aetatis, Bd. 1, 7 ; Sch. 23, 27.

ge-þynge, Rtl. 23, 20. v. ge-þinge ; II: ge-þyngþ[u]. v. geþyncþ[u].

ge-þynnian. Add: I. to make or to become thin (of a person):—Hé ne oncneów hí ná, for þám heó wæs swíðe geþynnod, Hml. S. 33, 236. II. to lessen, diminish, wither :—Smyre mid gáte geallan, ealle þá nebcorn hé áclǽnsað and ealne þone wom hé geðynnað, Lch. i. 348, 26. Geþynnige marceat, extenuetur, Germ. 388, 76. III. to weaken :—Geðynnade (adtenuati) synd égan mín, Ps. Srt. ii. p. 185, 5. v. þynnian.

ge-þyre. v. un-geþyre: ge-þýwan. v. ge-þeówan : ge-þýwe. v. geþiwe : ge-þýwian. v. ge-þeówian.

ge-tídan. Add:—Æfter þám getídde þ Ecgferð gebohte bóc and land æt Ædelstáne, Cht. Th. 208, 5.

ge-tídran (-ian) ; pp. -ed, -od To make or to become weak :—Sceall nýde þlícumlíce fæt beón getýdrod (infirmetur), Gr. D. 227, 27. v. tídrian.

ge-tígan. Add: To bind one thing to another, tie up; alligare. (1) literal :—Þá folan hý gesǽlað (getígað, v. l.) ǽr hý ofer þá eá faran foetus trans flumen alligatos relinquunt, Nar. 35, 11. Hé getígde his hors ðǽr binnon, Hml. Th. ii. 136, 15. Hé getígde ǽnne ormǽtne ryððan innan ðám geate, i. 372, 33. Getígað ǽnne ancran tó his swuran, i. 564, 7. Ðæt esulcweorn tó ðǽm suíran wǽre getíged (-tigged, v. l., suspendatur), Past. 31, 18. Gé gemétað getígedne (alligatum) assan, Hml. Th. i. 206, 10. Getígede (-tiggede, v. l.) assene, Mt. 21, 2. (2) figurative :—Wite hé þæt hé mid þæs regoles bendum is getíged sciens se sub lege regule constitutim, R. Ben. 99, 12. Hé bið getíeged (-tíged v. l.) tó óðrum monnum mid onlícre gecynde aequa ceteris naturae conditione constringitur, Past. 111, 19. Ðá hádas ðǽre hálgan endebyrdnesse beóð getígede (-tígde, v. l.) tó eorðlicum tielengum personae sacrorum ordinum terrenis negotiis inhaerent, 135, 15.

ge-tigu. v. ge-teogo : ge-tihtan. v. ge-tyhtan : ge-tíhtlod. l. getihtlod.

ge-tílian. Add: I. to gain, get by labour :—Ic geann ðæs landes ... nid ealre tylðe swá ðǽrtó getilod bið I grant the land ... with all the produce got from its cultivation, C. D. iii. 294, 8. Sceal gehwá him æteówian hwæt hé mid ðám punde geteolod hæfð, Hml. Th. ii. 558, 10. II. to attend to, treat, cure (with gen.):—Sceal se gesceádwísa lǽce lǽtan ǽr weaxan ðone lǽssan and tilian ðæs máran ... búton hé bégra ætgæddre getilian mæge, Past. 457, 15. Getilian ðæs unryhthǽmdes, 24.

ge-tillan. Add:—Weras blóda ná healfe getillað dagas hyra uiri sanguinum non dimidiabunt dies suos, Ps. Rdr. 54, 24. Getill tange (Job 1, 11), Hml. Th. ii. 448, 32. v. tillan in Dict. for other examples.

ge-tilþ. Add:—Getilþum (iuxta) mercimoniam, i. lucrum, An. Ox. 1408.

ge-tíma a warranter. Take here ge-teáma, ge-týma in Dict., and see teám ; III : ge-tíman to vouch to warranty. Take here ge-téman in Dict., and see tíman ; II : ge-tíman to happen. v. ge-tímian.

getimber-hálgung, e ; f. The feast of tabernacles :—Getimberhálgung scenophegia (cf. scenophegia getimbra hálgung vel geteldwurþung, Wrt. Voc. i. 16, 50), An. Ox. 56, 287.

ge-timbernes. Add:—Getimbernesse aedificia, Verc. Först. 124, 2.

ge-timbran. Add:—Getimberdon aedificabant, Lk. L. 17, 38. (1) to construct a building :—Hé getimberde hús his on sonde aedificavit domum suam supra arenam, Mt. L. 7, 26. Hé getimberde torr, 21, 33. Tor of mycclum beámum getimbrian, Bl. H. 183, 3. (1 a) used of the operations of the Deity :—Hé getimbrode ðá heálican heofenan and ealne middaneard, Hml. Th. ii. 586, 29. (2) to

*build* a town. (à) *to found* :—On middeweardum hire ríce hió getimbrede Babylonia þá burg (*Babylonem condidit*), Ors. 2, 1 ; S. 62, 15. Hié getimbredon Effesum þá burg and monege óðere *cum Ephesum aliasque urbes condidissent*, 1, 10 ; S. 46, 18. Romus and Romulus Rómeburg getimbredon, 2, 1 ; S. 60, 21. Æfter þæm þe Rómeburg getimbred wæs *anno ab Urbe condita*, 2, 3 ; S. 68, 4 (*and often*) : Chr. 409 ; P. 11, 18. (b) *to rebuild, restore* :—Hié (*Rome*) eft Agustus bet getimbrede þonne hió æfre ær wære, Ors. 6, 1 ; S. 252, 25. Gewearð þá senatos þæt mon eft sceolde getimbran Cartainam *Carthago restitui jussa*, 5, 5 ; S. 226, 16. (c) in the Chronicle the word seems to imply fortification :—Hé getimbrade Bebbanburh ; sý wæs ærost mid hegge betíned and þær æfter mid wealle, Chr. 547 ; P. 17, 20. Man þá burh worhte and getimbrede (getrymode, *v. l.*) æt Withám, 913 ; P. 96, 25. Hé hét gefaran þá burg æt Tofeceastre and hié getimbran (cf. mon worhte þá burg æt Tofeceastre mid stánwealle, 102, 29), 921 ; P. 101, 2. Hér on þison geáre wæs Wærincwíc getimbrod, 915 ; P. 99, 9. (3) used figuratively :—Sé ðe þyllic weorc getimbrað on Godes geladunge, Hml. S. 590, 1. ' Ic hæbbe ðé gesetne ðæt ðú tóweorpe and getimbre.' For ðæm búton hé ðæt wóh ær tówurpe ne meahte hé nóht nytwyrðlíce ðæt ryht getimbran, Past. 441, 30–34.    II. *to use as building material* :—Swá hwá swá getimbrað ofer ðisum grundwealle gold oððe seolfor *si quia superaedificat super fundamentum hoc aurum, argentum*, Hml. Th. ii. 588, 23 : 590, 9.    III. *to edify, instruct* :—Þ hé sumne fæder funde þe hine on sumum þingum getimbrede ðæs ðe hé sylf ær ne cúðe, Hml. S. 23 b, 158. Ne mæg ænig mann óþerne getimbran búton hé hine sylfne gelómlíce behealde, 77. Ic wolde eów áne race gereccan, seó mæig eówer mód getimbrian, gif gé mid gýmene hí gehýran wyllað, Hml. Th. i. 412, 36. [*Goth.* ga-timrjan : *O. H. Ger.* ge-zimbrôn *constituere, aedificare.*]   v. ofer-getimbran ; heáh-getimbred.

**ge-timbru.** *Substitute* : ge-timbre, es ; *n.* : ge-timbru (-o) ; *f., g. pl.* ge-timbrema (cf. ge-tíme).    I. *a building, fabric* :—Þ æteówde Þ eall Þ getimbre þære cycenan (*omne coquinae aedificium*) sceolde beón forburnen, Gr. D. 123, 29. Hergiendum getimbres tempel *laudantibus aedificium templi*, Lk. p. 10, 13. Eallre þære cyricean and þám óþrum getimbre, Bd. 3, 17 ; Sch. 269, 17. Þurhwuniendum eallum þám getimbre þæs hámes *perdurante tota domus fabrica*, Gr. D. 119, 27. Swá swá spearwa on getimbre (*aedificio*), Ps. Vos. 101, 8. Swá swá hýg getimbrena ł þæcena *sicut foenum tectorum*, Ps. L. 128, 6. Getimbra *aedificiorum*, Ps. Rdr. Ps. Vos. 128, 6. Eal þás getimbro (-u, *v. l.*) . . . néh is Þ hí ealle fýr fornimeð, Bd. 4, 25 ; Sch. 498, 9. Getimbro (-u, R.) temples *aedificationes templi*, Mt. L. 24, 1 : Mk. p. 5, 6.    II. *building, construction* :—Be þæs temples getimbro *de aedificatione templi*, Bd. S. 23 ; Sch. 696, 16. Þá bróþor óþerra weorca swíðor gýmdon and þysse cyricean getimbro forlēton. Gesetton hí fore unmætnesse þæs gewinnes Þ hí eallinga forlēte þá getimbro þysse cyricean *fratribus alia magis curantibus, intermissum est hoc aedificium . . . Statuerunt ob nimietatem laboris huius structuram ecclesiae funditus relinquere*, Bd. 3, 8 ; Sch. 225, 16–226, 2.   v. heáh-, stán-getimbre.

**ge-timbrung.** *Add* : I. *building, constructing* (lit. or fig.) :—Paulus spræc be ðære getimbrunge þære geleáffullan geladunge. Hé cwæð, ' Ne mæg nán man lecgan óþerne grundweall . . .,' Hml. Th. ii. 588, 17. Þá stánas bæron tó þæs húses getimbrunge (*ad aedificationem domus*) ge ealde men ge geonga, Gr. D. 321, 22. Ealle ðás getimbringe hé geendode binnon ðrim geárum, Hml. Th. ii. 498, 1.    II. *a building, structure, fabric* :—Þære kicenan getimbrung (hús, *v. l.*) *coquinae aedificium*, Gr. D. 124, 13 : 123, 27. Gif hwæs getimbrung ðurhwunað and ðám fýre wiðstent, Hml. Th. ii. 588, 28. Be þæra enta getimbrunge *about the tower of Babel*, 198, 17. On getimbringce *in domicilio*, Ps. L. 101, 7. Árærde getimbrunge *editam structuram*, An. Ox. 410 b. Þysse burge getimbrunge (*aedificia*), Gr. D. 134, 9.    III. *edification, instruction* :—Tó hyra gástlican getimbrunge *pro aedificatione*, R. Ben. 62, 21. Ymbe þære sáule getimbrunge, 21, 18. Getimbrunge *definitionem* (v. (?) plurimum differt inter ambiguas Pharisaeorum traditiones et elucubratram sacrae Scripturae *definitionem*, Ald. 73, 16), Wrt. Voc. ii. 28, 65. Hwæt is hit elles búton getimbrunga and tól háligra manna *quid aliud sunt nisi instituta virtutum ?*, R. Ben. 133, 9.

**ge-tíme,** es ; *n.* [ge-tímu ; *f.* (?) ; *pl.* ge-tímena ; *gen.* ge-tímena. Cf. ge-tímbre.] *A yoke* of oxen :—Ic bohte án getýme (getýmðe, *v. l.*) oxena *jugum boum emi*, Lk. 14, 19. ' Ic bohte fíf getýme oxena . . .' Ðá fíf getýma getácniað ðá fíf andgitu . . . þás andgitu sind rihtlíce wiðmetene fíf getýmum oxena, Hml. Th. ii. 372, 23–24. Twēgra getýmæna læse and týn cúna, C. D. B. i. 544, 2. Fíf hund getýmu, Hml. Th. ii. 446, 13. Fíf hund getýme oxena, . . . þúsend getýme oxena, 458, 16, 18.   v. wroht-getíme.

**ge-tímian.** *Add* : I. with noun or pronoun as subject :—Þis ylce getímað on sumum stówum stówum, Lch. iii. 258, 17. Þá getímode micel hafenleást on Benedictes mynstre, Hml. Th. ii. 170, 32. Gyf Þ getímie, Þ is eallum mannum gemæne, Þ se abbud gewíte of þissum lífe, C. D. B. i. 155, 32. Hé wiste Þ hit (*the betrayal by Judas*) æfter his geteohhunge ágán (getímian, *v. l.*) sceolde, Hml. A. 154, 69.   I a. with

dat. of object affected :—Oft getímað yfelum teala, Hml. Th. i. 332, 15. Gif ús ungelimpas on æhtum getímiað, ii. 328, 27. Him forðsíð getímode, 546, 21. Nis mē nán þing Þ mē on mínum lífe getímode, Hml. S. 37, 107. Þeáh ús ungelimp on æhtum getíme (-tímie, -tímige. *v. ll.*), 13, 287. Þe læste him forðsíð getímige, Wlfst. 300, 28.    II. with indefinite *hit* :—Hit getímað hwíltídum Þ his trendel underscýt þære sunnan, Lch. iii. 242, 18. Gif hit swá getímað, hē sceal his ágen líf syllan for ðæs folces hreddinge, Hml. Th. i. 240, 13. Gif hit swá getímað Þ . . ., R. Ben. 119, 5. Þá getímode hit . . . and Ethna úp ábleów, Hml. S. 8, 221.    III. where no subject is expressed :—Hē began tó reccenne hū him on ráde getímode, Hml. S. 26, 215. Gesáwon hí hú þám ánum getímode, 11, 163. Getímode his wífe wyrs ðonne hē beðorfte, Hml. Th. ii. 142, 2. Getímige ðám óðrum swá him getímige, 36, 4.

**ge-tímu** (-e ?).   v. un-getímu : ge-ting.   v. ge-þyncg(o) : **ge-ting.** v. ge-tyng : **ge-tín.**   v. un-getímu.

**ge-tintregian ;** *p.* ode *To torment* : — Eów ðær (*hell*) deófol getintregað, Hml. Th. i. 266, 35. Hí ðone feórðan getintregodon, Hml. S. 25, 143. Hí ætforan mannum getintregode wæron, Hml. Th. i. 544, 4.

**ge-tirgan, -tirigan ;** *p.* de ; *pp.* ed.    I. *to vex, provoke* :—For ðan þe ðú mē getyrgdest *quia egisti, ut me ad iracundiam provocares*, Hml. S. 18, 212. Weard seó módor biterlíce gegremod fram hire ánum cilde . . ., wolde ðone sunu þe hí getirigde mid wyriungum gebindan, Hml. Th. ii. 20. 6. Sume ðá hæðenan wurdon mid andan getyrigde, i. 562, 29.    II. *to vex, afflict, oppress* :—Getyrged *pertritus*, Wrt. Voc. ii. 69, 14. Getyrge[d], 68, 58.

**ge-tirwan** *to bring to the consistency of tar* :—Scearfa eall Þ smera on pannan, swá micel swá þú sealfe haban wille and þú getyrwan mæge, Lch. iii. 14, 17.

**ge-titelian.** *Add* : I. *to assign.* (1) a person to an office, *nominate* :—Ymbe náne worldbysgunge ábysgode, búton mid þære þe hig tó getitolode beóð (*nisi illos cui nominati sunt*), Ll. Th. ii. 198, 22. (2) something to a person, *ascribe.*   v. *Dict.*    II. *to place a mark above* a letter or syllable :—Þes que is sceort mid þrým stafum gewriten oððe getitelod (*is written with three letters* (que) *or with a mark* q̃), Ælfc. Gr. Z. 265, 8. Án getitelod Ī, getácnað án þúsend, and twēyen ías getitelode, ĪĪ, getácniað twá þúsend, 282, 10–12.

**ge-tíþian.** *Add* :—Ic getíðige *praesto*, Ælfc. Gr. 139, 11.    I. *to grant* a request. (1) absolute, *to consent to a request* (with dat. of person asking) :—Þ hē unc getíðade (-tigðade, *v. l.*), and on þæs gesíðes huus ineóde, Bd. 5, 4 ; Sch. 568, 14. Hié bædon Þ . . Sume him getygðedon, Ors. 3, 7 ; S. 118, 16. God þē getíþige and þíne bēne gehýre, Angl. xii. 515, 13. (2) with gen. of request and dat. of person :—Gif wē þæs biddað þe ús tó écere hælþe fremiað, ús getíðað þæs se heofenlica Fæder, Hml. Th. ii. 528, 20. Hié hine bædon Þ . . .; and hē him þæs getygðade, Ors. 3, 1 ; S. 98, 20. Hē him þære bēne getygðade, 4, 10 ; S. 200, 32. Hié him þæs getygðedon, 2, 2 ; S. 64, 30 : 3, 10 ; S. 140, 18. Ic bidde Þ þú mē ánre lytelre bēne getýðige, Hml. S. 23 b, 712. Him þæs getygðian, Ors. 3, 11 ; S. 146, 31. Him næs getíðod ðære lytlan lisse, Hml. Th. i. 330, 29. Him næs þære bēne getíðod, ii. 528, 6. (3) with dat. of request :—Hē bæd ðá heáfodmenn Þ hí his bēnum getíþodon, Hml. S. 26, 49. (4) with clause and dat. of person :—Getíða mē synfullum Þ ic áteó þás hringan, Hml. S. 21, 66. Getíðige ús God Þ wē magon eów secgan his láre, Hml. A. 12, 309.    II. *to grant, bestow* (with acc. of object granted and dat. of person) :—Crístes deáð getíðað ús þæt éce líf, Hml. Th. ii. 240, 20. Ðær getíðað Drihten micele weldæd geleáffullum mannum, 298, 11. Þisne anweald hē forgeaf Petre . . . þone ylcan andweald hæfð se Ælmihtiga getíðod biscopum, i. 370, 4–13. Críst hæfð micel getíþod eów, Hml. S. 36, 167.

**ge-tíung,** e ; *f. An agreement, arrangement* :—Getíunge, gitíungi, get[o]ing (o *doubtful*) *apparitione* (-*atione*), Txts. 41, 185. Cf. ge-teón ; *wk.* ; ge-þinge ; v.

**ge-toge.** *l.* ge-tog, -toh, *and add* : I. *a contraction, drawing together* :—Wið þá cynelican ádle þe man auriginem nemneð, Þ ys on úre geþeóde þæra syna getoh and fóta geswel, Lch. i. 190, 15. Wið sina getoge, iii. 70, 26. Fore syna getoge, 110, 25.    II. *that with which one draws, a trace* :—Þá múlas þe Þ cræt tugon áfyrhte tómengdon þá getogu, Þ hí teón ne mihton, Hml. S. 31, 973. [Cf. *O. H. Ger.* pi-zog *retinaculum*.]

**ge-togen** *drawn.* *Substitute* : ge-togen ; *adj.* (*ptcpl.*) *Educated* :—Swá getogen man and geþungen láreow, Hml. Th. ii. 122, 13.   v. ungetogen, ge-teón ;   III. 1.

**ge-tónamian.**   v. tó-namian in *Dict.* : ge-togennes. *Dele* : ge-torfian.   *Add* : v. ge-tyrfan.

**ge-tot.** *Add* :—Tó geflītes hý fæstaþ and þæt dígle þing beón sceolde tó sige, þæt is tó bodunge and tó getotes gylpe, gewyrcað *solent certare jejuniis, ut rem secreti victoriae faciant*, R. Ben. 136, 22. Þæt nán þing flǽsclices beforan Gode mid getote ne bógie *ut non glorietur omnis caro coram Deo*, 139, 2. Se mæssepreóst áxað þriddan síðe, ' Wiðsæcst ðú eallum deófles getotum ?,' Hml. Th. ii. 52, 7.   v. tot.

**ge-trahtian.** *Add* : I. *to treat a subject, discuss* :—Hwæt on weg gié getrahtade (gitrachtade, R.) *quid in uia tractabatis ?*, Mt. L. 9, 33.

Getrahtadon *tractassent*, Mk. p. 4, 8. **II.** *to expound, explain* :—Bisen getrahtade *deignum parabolam exponit discipulis*, Mt. p. 17, 3. Đerh Dauið cymendum getrahtade *per Dauid uenientibus interpretabat*, Lk. p. 3, 2. **III.** *to interpret* words, *translate* :—Emmanuhel, đæt is getrahtet (gereht, R., W.S. *interpretatum*), mið ūs God, Mt. L. 1, 23. Đis is ebrisc word þ is getrahtad in Latin *talitha cumi, quod est interpraetatum* ..., Mk. L. R. 5, 41 : Jn. L. R. 1, 42. Getrahted (-ad, R.), Mk. L. 15, 22 : 34. Getrachtad (-trahtad, R.), Jn. L. 1, 41. Getractat (-trach(t)ad, R.), 9, 7. Getrahtado *interpretati*, Rtl. 193, 31. [*O. H. Ger.* ge-drahtōn, -trahtōn *tractare.*]

ge-trahtnian. *Take here the first two passages under* ge-trahtian *in Dict., and add* :—Manega men wēnað þ þes middaneard scule standan on six þūsend wintrum, for đan þe God gescōp ealle þiug binnan six dagum ; ac þæt getæl wise witan on ōðre wīsan getrahtnedon, Wlfst. 244, 4. Ic bidde þ mē þis sȳ fullīcor getrahtnod (-rihted, -recced, *v. ll.*) *hoc plenius exponi postulo*, Gr. D. 102, 21.

ge-treágian *to sew together* :—Hȳfa geholedum getreágede telgrum *tuguria cauatis consuta corticibus*, An. Ox. 256. *In a note to this gloss is cited* :—þ getreágode hrægl, Archiv lxxxiv. 16, 224.

ge-tred, es ; *n.* **I.** *a crowding together, an assembly* of people :—Getred *constipatio*, i. *conventio hominum* (cf. constipatio, conuentio hominum, Corp. Gl. H. 34, 576), Wrt. Voc. ii. 133, 60. **II.** *a treading down.* v. wīn-getred.

ge-tregian. *Substitute : To fear, have a horror of* :—þū ne getregedest mædenes innoþ *non horruisti uirginis uterum*, Angl. ii. 358, 8.

ge-treminc. *l.* -tremminc, *and see* ge-trymming.

ge-treów *faith, fidelity* :—Gif þē þurh getreówa findan þā þe findan, forgef mē þone cræft, Angl. xii. 512, 7.

ge-treów ; *adj.* [*Besides this unmutated* a-stem, *a mutated* a-stem, (ió, ié, ī, ȳ) *and a mixed form* ge-treówe *occur : the* eó-*forms are taken here, the mutated forms under* ge-trīwe.] **I.** *true, trustworthy, honest.* (1) of persons :—Getreów *gesiþa fida comes*, Wrt. Voc. ii. 148, 73. Hwā wēnstu đæt sié tō đæm getreúw (*fidelis*) brytnere ?, Past. 459, 11. Getreówe, Hml. A. 55, 124. Getreúwe (*fidelis*) on eallum wordum his, Ps. L. 144, 13. Gif hē him getreówe ne sȳ *if one party is not trusted by the other*, Ll. Lbmn. 37, 25. Se getreówa man sceal syllan his gōd on þā tīd þe hine sylfne sēlest lyste his brūcan, Bl. H. 101, 19. Đæs getreówan freóndes, Bt. 24, 3 ; F. 82, 34. Ælc freó man hæbbe getreówne borh, Ll. Th. i. 280, 7. Gif þegen hæbbe getreówne man tō foraðe for hine, 388, 16. Getreówe friénd, Bt. 20 ; F. 72, 24. Þā getreówan freónd, 24, 3 ; F. 82, 27. Þīnra getreówra freónda, 20 ; F. 72. 14. Nime se hlāford twēgen getreówe þegenas, Ll. Th. i. 280, 12. Getreówe borgas, 21. Nimað hī heora men mid him, and lǣtaþ þīne feáwan getreówan mid þē, Bt. 20 ; F. 72, 17. Þā Dænescan þe wæs ærur geteald eallra folca getreowast, Chr. 1086 ; P. 221, 29. Tō đæm getreówestan mundboran, Bl. H. 201, 27. (2) of things :—Mid fulre gewitnesse and getreówre, Ll. Th. i. 240, 9. Getreówum *fidis* (*discipulus fidis devotus passibus*, Ald. 150, 32), Wrt. Voc. ii. 90, 75. **II.** *true to a person, loyal, faithful* :—Dauid ymb his getreówne đegn sierede *David devotum militem extinxit*, Past. 37, 8 : 393, 8. Uton beón ā ūrum hlāforde holde and getreówe, Ll. Th. i. 372, 8. Þā þe þām cynge getreówe wæron and eallum his folce, Chr. 1052 ; P. 182, 4. Syndon feáwa þe þǣm deádan getreúwe weorþon, Bl. H. 53, 2. Hié ne beóþ nānum men getreúwe, Bt. 7, 1 ; F. 16, 17. [*O. H. Ger.* ge-triu.]

ge-treówfæst ; *adj.* True, *trustworthy, faithful* :—Hī getreówfæste wæron, dydon swā hī ær gemynton, Hml. S. 23, 340. Geinsæglod mid twām sylfrenan insæglan þe þā twægen getreówfæste menn þærinne lēdon, 757.

ge-treówfull. *Add: faithful, holding the true faith* :—On middele getreówfulre gesomnunge *in medio ecclesie*, Ps. Rdr. 21, 23. Þā getreówfullan for Godes ege ealle līfes wiðerweardnesse forþyldigian scylun *fideles pro Domino universa contraria sustinere debent*, R. Ben. 27, 7. Sǣd getreówfulra *semen Iacob*, Ps. Rdr. 21, 24. Đā getreówfullan Israhēl, 13, 7.

ge-treówfullīce. *Add* :—Eal seó geleáffulle gelaðung getreówfullīce be hire singð, Hml. Th. i. 546, 15.

ge-treówfulness, e ; *f.* Faithfulness :—Sǣd ealre getreówfulnisse *semen Israhel*, Ps. Rdr. 21, 25.

ge-treówian. *Take here* ge-trȳwian *in Dict., and add* : **I.** *to trust* :—Uē getríuadon *confidemus*, Rtl. 7, 7. (1) with dat., *to trust to* :—Wē nytan nānum ōðrum þingum tō getreówiganne, Ll. Th. i. 220, 16. (2) with prep. *to trust in* :—þ hī getreówoden (hē getreówode, *v. l.*) on Godes fultum, Bd. 1, 23 ; Sch. 50, 2. **II.** *to make or to become true* to another, *to confederate* :—Getriúwad *foederatus*, Wrt. Voc. ii. 108, 43. Getreúuade *foederatos*, 109, 1. **III.** *to prove true or honest, clear from a charge* of falseness :—Getrȳwige hine fācnes sē þe hine fēde, Ll. Th. i. 72, 5.

ge-treówleás. *Add:* **I.** *perfidious* :—Hē wæs getreówleáses mōdes wer *perfidae mentis fuit*, Gr. D. 130, 27. Mid þām getreówleásan deófle þe hī tihte tō đam swicdome, Hml. S. 19, 232. **II.** *not holding the true faith, infidel* :—Gif se getreówleása gewīte *infidelis si discedit* (1 Cor. 7, 15), R. Ben. 53, 3. Þā gemynd þāra getreówleásra (-trȳw-, *v. l.*)

---

cyninga *regum perfidorum memoria*, Bd. 3, 1 ; Sch. 193, 9. Þīne godas syndon getreówleásera manna handgeweorc, Hml. S. 14, 21.

ge-treówlic. *Add:* [*O. H. Ger.* ge-triuuelīh *fidelis.*]

ge-treówlīce. *Add:* **I.** *truly, honestly.* v. ge-treów ; **I** :—Hē getreówlīce (-trȳw-, *v. l.*) gelȳfde þ hē mihte gefultumed beón *se ipsum fideliter credidit iuuari*, Bd. 3, 23 ; Sch. 299, 17. Þā đe hira bebodu getreówlīce gefyllað, Hml. A. 147, 79. Hē gegæderaþ gesēran þ hié getreówlīce heora sibbe healdaþ *hic fidis sua dictat jura sodalibus*, Bt. 21 ; F. 74, 39. Heó nolde þā bēc āgifan ær heó wyste hū getríwlīce hē āt landum healdan wolde (*quam fidem de beneficio tenere vellet*), Cht. Th. 202, 26. Getrēwlīce ic dōm in hine *fiducialiter agam in eo*, Ps. Srt. 11, 6. Gitrīwalīce *fideliter*, Rtl. 30, 19. Gitrowalīce, 24, 15. **II.** *faithfully, loyally.* v. ge-treów ; **II** :—Leóf cynehlāford, ne cōm him nān þing tō þance þ hē swā getreówlīce þ þē geopenode *pro hac fide nihil mercedis accepit*, Hml. A. 98, 221. Hlāfordas ic lǣrde þ hié getreówlīce Gode hȳrdon swā heora hlāfordum, Bl. H. 185, 28. **III.** *confidently* :—Getreówlīce *fidenter*, Wrt. Voc. ii. 33, 66. Getriúulīce *confidenter* (*ambulat*), Kent. Gl. 326. [*O. H. Ger.* ge-triulīhho.]

ge-treówness. v. un-getreówness.

ge-treówsian. *Add:* **I.** *to pledge oneself, engage* :—Him cōmon ongeán vi cyningas and ealle wið hine getreówsodon þ hī woldon efenwyrhtan beón on sǣ and on lande, Chr. 972 ; Th. i. 225, 17. **I a.** with reflex. pron. :—Ealle Norðhymbra witan wið þone cyning hī getreówsoden, and binnan litlan fæce hit eall ālugon, 947 ; P. 112, 24. **II.** *to prove true, clear of a charge of fulseness* :—Hē be his hlāfordes were hine getreówsie (-trīw-, *v. l.*), Ll. Th. i. 64, 5.

ge-treówþ. *Add:* **I.** *truth, faithfulness, honesty.* v. ge-treów ; **I** :—Freónda gehwilc mid rihtan getrȳwðan ōðerne lufige, Ll. Th. i. 350, 13. Gif hē hit mid getrȳwðan geearnod, 440, 3. **II.** *loyalty* :—Ānum cynehlāforde holdlīce hȳran, and georne hine healdan mid rihtan getrȳwðan, Ll. Th. i. 314, 12. **III.** *a troth, pledge, covenant, an engagement.* v. ge-treówian ; **II** :—Hēr Norðhymbra ālugon hira getreówaða, Chr. 941 ; P. 111, 9. [*O. H. Ger.* ge-triuuida *confidentia.*] v. un-getreówþ.

ge-tricce *content. After* stōwe *insert* þeáwum, *and for* '61, Lye' *substitute* 109, 7.

ge-tridwet ? :—Getridwet spere *hasta*, Wrt. Voc. i. 35, 40.

ge-trifulian. *Add* :—Getrifula on eced, Lch. ii. 20, 17. Getrifula smale, 90, 27. Rūde getrifeladu mid sealte, 26, 1. Wildre rūdan getrifuladre seáw, 10. Mid cellendre getrifuladre, 82, 7.

ge-trīwan. *Take here* ge-treówan *and* ge-trȳwan *in Dict., and add* : **I.** *to trust.* Tō getrīwenne *comprehendenda*, Wülck. Gl. 251, 37. (1) absolute :—Cōm stefn ufane cwæðende, 'Getrȳw, Eustachi,' Hml. S. 30, 241. Getríue (-treuwe, R.), dohter *confide, filia*, Mt. L. 9, 22. Getrēuað (gitriówað R.) *confidente*, Jn. L. 16, 33. Getrȳwan *fidere*, Wrt. Voc. ii. 33, 67. (2) with dat. *to trust* to a person or thing :—Ic getrȳwe Drihten *in Domino confido*, Ps. Th. 10, 1. Gif hē (*one to whom property had been entrusted, and who had lost it*) gewitnesse hæbbe, and hē (*the owner of the property*) him (*the loser*) ne getríewe, swerige hē (*the loser*) þonne (cf. Ex. 22, 10–11), Ll. Th. i. 52, 4. (2 a) *to trust* a person *to do something* :—Him þā from bugan þe hié bēst getriéwdon þ him sceolde sige gefeohtan, Ors. 2, 5 ; S. 82, 25. (3) with acc., *to trust* a person or thing :—Ic þīne sōðfæstnysse getríewe, Ps. Th. 118, 15. (4) with preps., *to trust in, rely on, be confident* about :—In đē ic getreówu, Ps. Srt. 24, 2. In đē getreóweð sāwul mīn, 56, 2. Getrēweð in God *confidet in Deo*, Mt. L. 27, 43. Þā þe on Drihten getreówað *qui confidunt in Domino*, Ps. Th. 124, 1. Đā đe getreówað in megne heara, Ps. Srt. 48, 7. In đæm gē getreówðun, ii. p. 195, 41. Getreóudon, Lk. L. 18, 9. Israhēlas on Drihten getreówen *speret Israel in Domino*, Ps. Th. 129, 6. Þæt hī getrīwdon (hē getreówde, *v. l.*) on Godes fultum, Bd. 1, 23 ; Sch. 50, 2. Hē geleornode þ hē getreówde mā be his lāreówes mægne þonne be his āgnum *plus didicerat de magistri, quam de sua virtute confidere*, Gr. D. 19, 9. Getreówan in mon, Ps. Srt. 117, 8. Getriówende *confidenti* (*in stultitia sua*), Kent. Gl. 608. (5) with clause :—Ne getríewde hió þæt hiere wolde se ōðer dǣl gelǣstfull beón, Ors. 3, 11 ; S. 148, 17. **II.** *to make true to another, confederate* :—Getreówde, getrēude *foederatus*, Wrt. Voc. ii. 35, 25. Getrēwde *foederatas*, 39, 6. Gitreeudae, getr[ē]udæ, Txts. 62, 436. **III.** *to prove oneself true, clear* oneself of a charge :—Hē be his hlāfordes were hine getriówe, Ll. Th. i. 64, 5. Getrȳwe hē hine be þām wīte, 84, 15. **IV.** *to give confidence to* a person, *persuade* :—Đā ældra getreudon đæm folcum þ hiá bēdon *seniores persuaserunt populis ut peterent Barabban*, Mt. 27, 20.

ge-trīwe. *Take here* ge-trȳwe *in Dict., and add* :—Getrȳwe *fida*, Wrt. Voc. ii. 35, 38. **I.** *trustworthy, honest.* (1) of persons :—Getriówe *fidelis*, Kent. Gl. 360. Gitrīwa *fida*, Rtl. 109, 33. Būton hē hæbbe đæs teóðiugmannes gewitnysse, and sē sȳ wel getrȳwe, Ll. Th. i. 260, 1. Hē tō ælcan teáme hæbbe getrȳwne borh, 290, 7 : 388, 16. Syxa sum ... þe getrȳwe sȳn, 252, 12. Nime se hlāford twēgen getrȳwe men, 396, 2 : 394, 8. Đā getrīwan friénd, Bt. 24, 3 ; F. 82, 27. (2) of things. (a) material, *genuine* :—Þǣre getrȳwan elesealfe *nardi pistici*, Wrt. Voc. ii. 60, 71. (b) non-material :—Getrȳwe gewitnes, Ll. Th. i. 290, 19 : ii. 302, 6. Getrȳwes ingehīdes *fidi prepositi*, Wrt. Voc. ii. 148, 72. Getrī-

wan *fida* (*pollicitatione*), An. Ox. 9, 7. Ne beó ǽnig man ǽniges teámes wyrðe būton hē getrȳwe gewitnysse hæbbe, Ll. Th. i. 388, 21. **II.** *true* to a person or thing, *loyal, faithful :*—Ic eom getrȳwe (*fidelis*) hláforde mīnon, Coll. M. 20, 19. Ic wille beón N. hold and getrīwe, Ll. Th. i. 178, 4. Uton beón ā ūrum hláforde holde and getrȳwe, 372, 8. Þā āne þe him getrīewe wǽron, Ors. 3, 7 ; S. 114, 1. Þā þing ne sint getrēwe tō habbenne ... Nū ðū hié æfter þīnum willan þē getrēwe habban ne miht, Bt. 7, 2 ; F. 18, 15-19. Gitrīuao uosa lārum *fideles esse doctrinis*, Rtl. 124, 27. **III.** *trusting* to :—Cirica ðīn ðroures dīnes gitrīua fultumum *ecclesia tua martyris tui confisa suffragiis*, Rtl. 67, 15 : 72, 16. [*O. Sax.* gi-triwi: *O. H. Ger.* ge-triuui.]

**ge-trudend.** *Dele, and see* strūdend : **ge-trūgung.** v. ge-trūwung.

**ge-trum.** *Add :*—Getrum *nodus*, Wrt. Voc. ii. 62, 33.

**ge-trumian.** *Add :* (1) *intrans. :*—Þū getrumast *convalescas*, Wrt. Voc. ii. 15, 75. Hē þǽre ealdan untrumnesse getrumad wæs *uterno infirmitatis discusso*, Bd. 5, 5 ; Sch. 572, 10. (2) *reflex. :*—Þā getrumade ic mē and gestrangad wæs *convalui*, 5, 6 ; Sch. 581, 11.

**ge-trummen,** Wrt. Voc. ii. 17, 59. v. ge-crimman : **ge-trūwa.** *Add :* See next word.

**ge-trūwad** (-od) ; *adj. Inspired with confidence :*—Gebyld, getrūwad *fretus, i. fiduciam habens*, Wrt. Voc. ii. 150, 71. v. ge-trūwa ; ge-trūwian ; VI.

**ge-trūwian, -trȳgian.** *Add :* I. *absolute :*—Getrūwiað *confidete*, Jn. 16, 33. **II.** *with dat., to trust to :*—Se gelǽreda him ne getrūwað on ðǽre hreón sǽ, Past. 59, 2. Hē getrūwode ðæs mægene ðe hit him bebéad, 51, 16. Him nān folc ne getrūwade, Ors. 4, 12 ; S. 210, 12 : 5, 7 ; S. 230, 7. Ne getrūa ðū *ne innitaris* (*prudentiae tuae*), Kent. Gl. 30. Wē nytan nānum ōðrum þingum tō getrūwianne, Ll. Th. i. 220, 16. **II a.** *to trust* something to a person :—Ðe Hǽlend ne gitrȳgade hine solfne him *non credebat semetipsum eis*, Jn. R. 2, 24. **II b.** *to trust* to a person for something (clause with *þæt*), Gen. 248 (*in Dict.*). **III.** *with gen., to trust* in or to something, B. 2322 (*in Dict.*). **IV.** *with preps.* (be, on, in), *to be confident* about, *trust* in, *rely* on :—Hē getrūwode be his lǽreowes mægene swȳðor þonne be his āgenum mægene *plus didicerat de magistri, quam de sua virtute confidere*, Gr. D. 19, 8. Hē getrūwode on his snotornesse and on ðā bōclican lāre, Ap. Th. 3, 24. **V.** *with clause, to trust* that :— Þā ne getrūwade se eahteþa dǽl þára legian þæt Rōmāne Pirruse wiðstondan mehte *octava legio, diffidens Romanae spei*, Ors. 4, 1 ; S. 160, 8. Hié getrūwedon þ hié mid hiera cræftum sceoldon sige gefeohtan, 2, 4 ; S. 72, 16. Hié getrūwedon þæt hié ofer þǽm īse faran mehten, 4, 11 ; S. 208, 2. **VI.** *to inspire with confidence, persuade.* v. ge-trūwad, ge-trīwan ; IV :—Þā þæt gesāwon þā Egypte, hȳ ðā getrymedon hyra dryas, and getrūwedon mid hyra drȳcræftum þæt hī on ðone ilcan weg fēran meahton *when the Egyptians saw that, their magicians encouraged them, and made them believe with their magic arts that they would be able to go by the same way*, Ors. 1, 7 ; S. 38, 31. **VII.** *to clear from a charge.* Cf. ge-treówian ; III, ge-trīwan ; III :—Sē þe ōðres mannes man underfō þe hé for his yfele him fram dō, and him [hine?] getrūwian ne mæge his yfeles ... Gif se hláford þonne wille þone man mid wōh fordōn ... gif hē lādlēas beó *if A receive B's man, C, that B has turned away for his (C's) ill-doing, and to B C cannot clear himself of the charge of ill-doing. ... But if B wants wrongfully to ruin C ... and if C be innocent*, Ll. Th. i. 220, 19-24. [*Goth.* ga-trauan : *O. Sax.* gi-trūon, -trūōian : *O. H. Ger.* ge-trūen, -trūōn.]

**ge-trūwung.** *Add :* , -trūgung :—Getrūgung, Ps. Srt. 88, 19.

**ge-trymednesse,** e ; *f. A support* :—Getrymednyss (*firmamentum*) mīn and gener mīn beó ðū, Ps. Spl. C. 70, 4. Ealle getrymednesse hláfes hē forgnād, Ps. L. 104, 16.

**ge-trymman.** *Add :* I. *of persons or things, to make strong ; to fortify* against attack (lit. or fig.) :—Man þā burh worhte and getrymode æt Witanhām, Chr. 913; P. 97, 33. Hē his forðfōre getrymede mid onfangennesse þæs dryhtenlican līchaman *obitum suum dominici corporis perceptione munivit*, Bd. 4, 3 ; Sch. 359, 8. Ðætte hié heora heortan getrymigen (-trymmen, *v. l.*) æfter ðæs miclan sige *ut cor post victoriam muniant*, Past. 229, 4. Ic wolde getrymman *munimus*, 41, 4. Ðæt hé beó getrymed and gefrætwod wið ǽlce frēcenesse mid ðysum mægenum *ut contra adversa virtutum ornamento muniatur*, 83, 10 : Bl. H. 225, 33. Gitrymmed wið ðone fíond monnes *offirmatum adversus inimicum hominis*, Rtl. 113, 28. Ǽlce getrymedne (*munitam*) burh þū gebīge tō mē, Hml. A. 103, 49. Þ from (*ab*) wiðirweardnissum uē sié gitrymmed (*muniamur*) in līchome, Rtl. 16, 7. Getrymmedo wið (*contra*), 7, 9. **II.** *to make strong in health, restore to health :*—Hē þǽre ealdan untrumnesse getrymd wæs *uterno infirmitatis discusso*, Bd. 5, 5 ; Sch. 572, 11. **II a.** *reflexive, to get strong, recover health :*—Þā getrȳmede ic mē and gestrangod wæs *conualui*, 5, 6 ; Sch. 581, 11. ¶ *used figuratively :*—Hē hine getrymige and gefylle mid ðǽm ūplican tōhopan *supernae spei refectione convalescat*, Past. 395, 6. **III.** *of non-material objects, to establish, make effective, make valid, confirm :*—Hié hira āgen unryht willað getrymman *student sua perversa roborare*, Past. 367, 2. Getrymman *stabilire* (cogitaverunt

consilium quod non potuerunt *stabilire*, Ald. 60, 33), An. Ox. 4329. **III a.** *of formal regulations, laws, &c. :*—Hē sette synoð, and getrymde and gefæstnode ealle ðā ðing be Godes mynstran ðā wǽron gesett be Wihtgāres dæge, Chr. 796 ; P. 56, 27. Þte ryhte cynedōmas þurh ūre folc gefæstnode and getrymede wǽron, Ll. Th. i. 102, 10. **IV.** *of mental or moral strength, to give strength to* mind or heart, *establish, confirm* faith, *&c. :*—Ðroure ðīn mægne stydfæstnise in ðrouenge gitrymmedest *martyrem tuum virtute constantiae in passione roborasti*, Rtl. 50, 4. Drihten getrymmede (*confortavit*) mec, 60, 25 : Lk. L. (gitrymede, R., gestrangode, W. S.), 22, 43. His geleáfa hine getrymde (-trymede, *v. l.*) *his faith gave him courage*, Hml. S. 26, 15. Hē getrymede heora geleáfan, Bl. H. 17, 8. Heora cyning mid þǽm scopleóðe heora mōd getrymede, Ors. 1, 14 ; S. 58, 1. Getrym (*confirma*) brōðro ðīno, Lk. p. 11, 4. Getrymed (-tryme, R.), Lk. L. 22, 32. Ðæt sió hering getrymme ðæs wācmōdan monnes mōd wið ðā tǽlinge, Past. 213, 2. Ðætte ðæt lof hié getrymede *quatenus eorum mentem laus solidaret*, 22. Getrymian *roborare*, 385, 1. Wē sculon ūre mōd getrymman wið ðisses middangeardes ōliecunga *ut contra favores mundi mentem erigant*, 387, 20. Wolde hē heora geleáfan gestrangian and getrymman mid wundrum, Hml. Th. i. 154, 1. Nǽron hié mid þon godcundan gǽste getrymede, Bl. H. 117, 15 : 121, 7. **V.** *to exhort, encourage, comfort :*—Wē gitrymmeð íuih *ortamur* vos, Rtl. 11, 23. Ōðre gitrymede (getrummade, L.) *alia exortans*, Lk. R. 3, 18. Hē hī mid þǽm gewritum tihte and getrymde tō līfes wege, Hml. Th. i. 388, 27. Hȳ (*the Egyptians*) ðā getrymedon hyra dryas, and getrūwedon mid hyra drȳcræftum þ hī on ðone ilcan weg fēran meahtan, Ors. 1, 7 ; S. 38, 30. Getrymed bið *cohortatur*, Lk. p. 4, 7 : *exortatur*, Jn. p. 7, 4. **VI.** *to establish* a point by evidence, authoritative statement, proof, &c. (1) *to testify, attest :*—Monige wērun ðā ðe godspellas āwritton ðe godspellere getrymmeð (*testatur*) cwoeðende, Mt. p. 7, 1. Getrymes, 15, 8. Getrymeð, Jn. p. 7, 9 : Jn. L. 3, 32. Wē gitrymmað (getrymes, L.) *testamur*, Jn. R. 3, 11. Gē gitrymmað (getrymeð, L.) *testificamini*, Lk. R. 11, 48. Getrymde *testatur*, Lk. p. 6, 13. Getrymed wæs *protestatus*, Jn. L. R. ¬13, 21. (2) *to affirm, confirm :*—Tō lufanne ðone nēsto mid ae getrymmas *amandum proximum lege firmans*, Mt. p. 14, 18. Ērist mið cȳðnise getrymað (*confirmat*), Lk. p. 10, 10 : Th. p. 4, 3. Sum getrymede (-ide, R.) *quidam affirmabat*, Lk. L. 22, 59. Hē wolde þone cwide getrymman on þǽre godcundan dǽde, Bl. H. 215, 27. **VI a.** *cȳþnesse getrymman to bear witness :*—Ic cȳðnisse gitrymmo *testimonium perhibeo*, Jn. R. L. 8, 14. Getrymo, Jn. L. 8, 18. Ðū getrymes, 13. Getrymes *perhibet*, 18. Getrymmes (-trymeð, R.), i, 15. Getrymmeð, 21, 24. Gié getrymies (-trymmas, R.) *perhibetis*, 15, 27. Ic getrymede, 1, 34. Ðū getrymedis, 3, 26. Getrymme (-tryme, R.) *perhibe*, 18, 23. **VII.** *to make* a matter *sure, to engage, promise :*—Ic getrymme *stipulor*, An. Ox. 18 a, 84. **VIII.** *to trim, set in firm order, array* troops :—Getremmað *instruunt* (*certamina*), Hpt. Gl. 425, 57. 'Getrymmiað eów wið ðā burg' ... Suǽ suǽ se here sceolde bión getrymed onbūtan Hierusalem, suǽ sculon beón getrymed ðā word ðæs sācerdes ymbūtan ðæt mōd his hiéremonna, Past. 161, 19-25. Hē hēt þæt hī āne tīd ofer undern hī getrymedon ongeán heora fȳnd, Hml. Th. i. 504, 24. Getrymed fēða *cuneus*, Wülck. Gl. 216, 12. Getrimmed, Wrt. Voc. i. 18, 31. Mið þǽm þe hī hié getrymed hæfdon *cum directa utraque acies constitisset*, Ors. 4, 2 ; S. 160, 28. **IX.** *of fixity of position or purpose :*—Ic þinne sīþfæt gestaðelode and getrymede *I have fixed and settled thy journey*, Bl. H. 231, 28. Hē getrymede (*firmavit*) hys ansȳne þ hé fērde tō Hierusalem *he steadfastly set his face to go to Jerusalem*, Lk. 9, 51. Eal swā hraðe swā hē cōm tō Cantuareberi and hē warð getremmed on his arcestōle, Chr. 870 ; P. 283, 26. **IX a.** *of the position conferred by creation :*—Hæfde se Ēalwalda engelcynna þurh handmægen tēne getrymede (cf. *the prose versions*)—Geworhte hē þurh his wīsdom tȳn engla werod, Ælfc. T. Grn. 2, 23. Hē gesceóp tȳn engla werod, Hml. Th. i. 10, 12), Gen. 248.

**ge-trymming, -tryming,** e ; *f. Protection, confirming, establishing :*—Getremminc *munimentum*, Kent. Gl. 405. Tō getrymmincge eóweres geleáfan, Hml. Th. ii. 378, 9. Getremincgum *sanccionibus*, An. Ox. 11, 109.

**ge-trymnes.** *Add : encouragement, comfort :*—Þurh brōðra getrymnesse (*solacio*), R. Ben. 9, 7.

**ge-trȳwan.** v. ge-trīwan : **ge-trȳwe.** v. ge-trīwe.

**ge-tucian** *to torment,* **ge-tucian** *to adorn. Substitute :* **ge-tūcian** ; *p. ode.* **I.** *to work* metal (?) :—Ðær stent cwēn þē on þā swȳðran hand mid golde getūcode (*after* hand *on* girelan *might have been expected rendering* in vestitu, *and then* mid golde getūcode (inst.) *would* = deaurato) and mid ǽlcere mislicre fægernysse gegyred *adstitit regina a dextris tuis in vestitu deaurato circumamicta varietate*, Ps. Th. 44, 11. **II.** *to treat* a person ill, *maltreat, afflict, inflict injury on.* (1) *of the effects of disease or accident :*—Se heáhgerēfa wæs eall swā yfele getūcod swā Tranquillinus wæs ǽr (cf. Tranquillinus wæs geuntrumed þurh þā mycclan fōtādle, 136), Hml. S. 5, 162. Ic ungewealdes ætspearn æt ānum fōtsceamole, and ic þā weard þus getūcod

(geslægen, v. l.) in scabello impegi, atque hoc pertuli, Gr. D. 22, 23. (2) of punishment for wrong-doing :—Sum man wæs betogen þ hē wǣre on stale ... hī dydon him ūt þā ēagan. Hē cwæð þ hē wurde wōlīce swā getūcod, Hml. S. 21, 276. Swilce hē for his synnum swā getūcod wǣre, Hml. Th. ii. 454, 17. (3) of malicious ill-treatment, persecution, &c. :—Hē Godes þā gecorenan wītnode and hī on yrmðum getintregode, and hī buton gewande getūcude (the MS. has the accent) eall swā hē wolde, Hml. S. 23, 15. Man hī tō eallre yrmðe getūcode, and heora lima man ealle tōbrǣd ǣlc fram ōðrum, 71.

ge-tunecod; adj. Provided with a tunic, dressed in a tunic :—Getunecude togatos, Germ. 393, 155.

ge-twǣfan; Add: (1) to prevent a person (acc.) from action (gen.) :—God eáðe mæg þone dolsceaðan dǣda getwǣfan, B. 479. Nō þǣr wǣgflotan wind sīðes getwǣfde, 1908. (2) to deprive a person (acc.) of something (gen.), B. 1433 (in Dict.). (3) to take something (acc.) from a person (dat.) :—Þý lǣs him wēstengryre ferhð getwǣfde, Exod. 119. (4) with acc. only, to end a dispute. Cf. ge-twǣman (3) :—Ic þæt unsōfte ealdre gedīgde ... ætrihte wæs gūð getwǣfde nymðe mec God scylde I hardly escaped it with life ... almost was battle ended, unless God had protected me, B. 1658.

ge-twǣman. Add: (1) intrans. (recip.) To separate :—Healde gehwā his ǣwe ... būton þ gewurðe þ hī būta geceósan þ hī getwǣman, Ll. Th. ii. 300, 28. (2) to separate one thing from another. (a) with gen., to prevent from action. v. ge-twǣfan, (1). Mē Hagenan hand getwǣmde fēðewigges, Vald. 2, 16. (b) with prep. :—Gif ūre māgas willað ūs getwǣman (-wēman, v. l.) fram Crīste, Hex. 40, 29. Swā þ ūre Drihten wurde getwǣmed (-twēmed, v. l.) fram his heofonlican fæder, Hml. A. 59, 198. (3) to end a dispute, settle a case. v. ge-twǣfan, (4) :—Cnut frið and freóndscipe betweox Denum and Englum fullīce gefæstnode and heora ǣrran saca ealle getwǣmde, Ll. Lbmn. 278, 9. Beó eallum crīstenum mannum sib and sōm gemǣne, and ǣlc sacu getwǣmed, Wlfst. 118, 3.

ge-twancg. Substitute ge-twanc collusion, deception :—Getwance colludio (cf. colludio, fraude, deceptione, Wrt. Voc. ii. 77, 65), An. Ox. 1517. (In both cases the passage glossed is Ald. 21, 22.) [Cf. Prompt. Parv. twynkyn conniveo.]

ge-tweó. Add :—þ ic wite būton getweón þ, þ mē þincð þ ic wite, Solil. H. 21, 4.

ge-tweógan. Add: I. to doubt. (1) where there is imperfect knowledge. (a) impersonal construction :—Swā hwylc swā hine sylfne getweóge be his fulluhte quicunque dubitat de baptismo suo, Ll. Th. ii. 236, 37. (b) with subject :—Gesēgon hine worðadun. Sume ðon getwiedon videntes eum adoraverunt. Quidam autem dubitaverunt, Mt. L. 28, 17. (2) where there is want of faith, confidence, &c. (a) with impersonal construction :—þā hī men neálǣhtan, þā getweóde hié hwæðer hié wið him mæhten cum desistendum certamine propter metum periculi arbitrarentur, Ors. 1, 14 ; S. 56, 31. (b) with subject :—Him ne getweóde treów in breóstum the confidence within him never wavered, Gū. 515. Suā h[w]ā sē ðe cuoeðas ... and ne getuīga in his hearte ah gelēfe quicumque dixerit ... et non haesitauerit in corde suo sed crediderit, Mk. L. 11, 23. II. to hesitate to act :—Crīst ne getuīeda hondum þ woere sald scyldigra Christus non dubitavit manibus tradi nocentium, Rtl. 24, 9. þeáh mē hēte God on flōd faran nǣre hē þæs deóp þæt his ō mīu mōd getweóde though God should bid me go into the water, the water would not be so deep that my heart would hesitate about it (i. e. going into the water), ac ic tō þām grunde gēnge, Gen. 833. [O. Sax. gi-twehōn : O. H. Ger. ge-zwehōn.]

ge-tweógendlīce. v. un-getweógendlīce.

ge-twifealdad. l. ge-twifealdian; pp. ad To double, and add :—Daga gehwylce ūs getwifealdað þes middangeard manegu sār hic mundus tot nobis quotidie dolores ingeminat, Gr. D. 259, 1. [O. H. Ger. ge-zwifaltōt geminatus.]

ge-twifyldan. l. ge-twifildan, and add :—Getwyfylden ingeminent, Wrt. Voc. ii. 44, 22. Mīn sār is getwyfyld, Hml. S. 33, 269. þǣr bið getwifeld quo bimetur (duplicetur), Hpt. 31, 16, 443. Getwifeld duplicata, Hy. S. 104, 25. þā fīf pund hē brōhte his hlāforde getwyfylde, Hml. Th. ii. 554, 32.

ge-twin. Add: -twinn :—Hý beóð þurh āne idese ācende twēgen getwinnas, Sal. 364. In ðǣre cirican þe hý nemnað Scs geminos, æt ðām hālgum getwinnum, Shrn. 134, 23. v. lif-getwinnan, and next word.

ge-twinn; adj. I. twin; geminus, gemellus :—Getuin gemellus, Wrt. Voc. ii. 98, 11. Getwinre edwiste gemine substantiae, Hy. S. 44, 13. Getwinnum gemina, Hpt. Gl. 407, 5. Getwinre mænifyld gemina, i. dupla praeditus (gratia), An. Ox. 1459. Getwinne lǣcedōm gemellam anodiam (ἀνωδυνίαν), Hpt. 31, 5, 46. Getwinnum sangum geminis concentibus, An. Ox. 2605 : 4166 : Wrt. Voc. ii. 32, 21. þæt getwinne mage habban oxan ut geminos possit habere boves, Wülck. Gl. 254, 7. II. as numeral; bini, duo :—Ǣnlīpige singuli, getwinne bini, Ælfc. Gr. 2, 13, 14. Sum getel bið ǣfre menigfeald ... bini getwynne oððe twām and twām, 284, 6. Eálā gē elebeamas (printed -es) getwinne olive bine, Hy. S. 106, 13. Getwinnum [geminis, i.] duobus, An. Ox. 4166.

ge-twinness, e; f. Pairing, joining of two identical things, in grammar, repetition of a word :—Epizeuxis, on lýden super-conjunctio, on englisc getwynnys, þonne man cwyð twā gelīce word on ānum verse, swā swā ys þis consolamini, consolamini, Angl. viii. 331, 35.

ge-twis. Substitute : Having the same parents :—Getwise germani, i. fratres, An. Ox. 3012. See next word.

ge-twisa. Add :—Getwisan germanas (the gloss seems to belong to geminos : the passage is ' geminos germano foedere atres,' Ald. 160, 9), Wrt. Voc. ii. 92, 6 : 41, 42. Getwysan gemellos, 92, 60. Getwisan, 41, 43. Rebecca ācende twēgen getwysan, Hml. Th. i. 110, 21. His wīf wearð mid getwysan (-tweosan, v. l., 12th cent.), Hml. A. 38, 338.

ge-tȳan. v. ge-tȳn.

ge-tȳd. Add: -tydd :—Swylce sum getȳd wer sum metervers mid his feþere āwrīte, Angl. viii. 317, 22. On hwylcere yldo oððe hū getȳd (quomodo edoctus) se man beó, Ll. Th. ii. 156, 19. Se getȳda lǣce ðæs heofonlican lǣcedōmes, ðæt wæs Sc. Paulus peritus medicinae coelestis Apostolus, Past. 397, 15. þæt getydde imbuta, Wülck. Gl. 250, 15. Heó wæs getyddre on þǣre Godes ǣ, Hml. A. 127, 359. On Godes ǣ seó getȳdeste fǣmne, 135, 655. Bēda, gumena se getyddusta, Angl. viii. 301, 47 : 319, 46. Getiddusta, 308, 37. Getyddestum peritissimo, doctissimo, Hpt. Gl. 405, 2. v. ge-tȳn.

ge-tȳdan to instruct. v. ge-tȳn: ge-tȳdan to happen. v. ge-tīdan : ge-tydd. v. ge-tȳd.

ge-tyhtan. Take here ge-tihtan in Dict., and add: I. to allure, attract ; illicere :—Getihte illexit, Wrt. Voc. ii. 47, 36. Getyhted inle[c]tus, 80, 77 : 46, 67. Getyhtid, gitychtid, getyctid inlectus, Txts. 71, 1094. þæs rihtwisan weres līf þurh þā rǣdinge hāligra bōca tō Gode bið getyhted, Ll. Th. ii. 402, 36. II. to urge, instigate :—Gemanod ł getiht instigatus, i. praemonitus, An. Ox. 602. III. to train, educate :—ðǣre getyhtan exercitatae, Wrt. Voc. ii. 108, 7 : 30, 15. þæge getihtan, 144, 68.

ge-tȳhtlod. v. ge-tihtlod: ge-tȳma. v. ge-tīma: ge-tȳme. v. ge-tīme.

ge-tȳn. Take here ge-tȳan and ge-tȳdan in Dict., and add: þ. -tȳde, -tydde ; pp. -tȳd, -tydd :—Tō þǣm þ hē ūs getȳde tō eádmōdnysse wege ut nos ad viam humilitatis instrueret, Gr. D. 59, 30. Ðeáh hine ðā brocu getȳn and gelǣren, Past. 35, 12. Wæs se blaca Heáwold mā on wīsdōme hāligra gewrita getȳd Niger Heauuald magis sacrarum litterarum erat scientia institutus, Bd. S. 10 ; Sch. 600, 3. Galdre getȳdum necromantia freto, An. Ox. 4133. Hié an ānum híerede wǣron āfēdde and getȳde, Ors. 3, 11 ; S. 152, 29. þā scolieras þe on mynstre synd getydde þisra þinga gȳmon, Angl. viii. 335, 43. v. ge-tȳd.

ge-tȳnan. Add: to fence, enclose land :—Gif ceorlas gærstūn hæbben tō tȳnanne and hæbben sume getȳned hiora dǣl ... þām þe hiora dǣl getȳnedne hæbben, Ll. Th. i. 128, 5-9. [O. H. Ger. ki-zūnit consepta.]

getyng-cræft, es ; m. Rhetoric [v. ge-tynge; I. 3; but the word is put as a gloss to mechanica] :—Getincgcræft mechanica, Hpt. Gl. 479, 50.

ge-tynge. Take here ge-tinge in Dict., and add: I. in a good sense :—Getinge dissertas, Wrt. Voc. ii. 28, 24. (1) of persons, skilful with the tongue, elegant in speech, eloquent, witty :—Getincge facetus i. facundus (poeta), An. Ox. 13. Dumbra manna tungan beóð swīðe getinge aperta erit lingua mutorum (Isaiah 35, 6), Hml. Th. ii. 16, 19. Ne weorþeð on worulde ǣnig wordsnotera ne on wordum getingra þonne Antecrīst on worulde ǣnig wordsnotera ne on wordum getingra þonne Antecrīst wyrðeþ, Wlfst. 54, 21. Hē wæs se getingesta wer erat vir eloquentissimus, Gr. D. 180, 9. (2) of speech :—Getinge lepida (sermonum series), Wrt. Voc. ii. 85, 84 : 52, 40. þǣre getyngan lepida (libelli textum lepida urbanitatis facundia digestum, Ald. 80, 32), 88, 38 : 50, 43. Mid getincgere urbana (verborum facundia fretus), An. Ox. 1501. Getyngere urbano (libello), 4, 88. Seó tunge þe ǣr hæfde getinge sprǣce, Wlfst. 148, 1. (3) in a technical sense, rhetorical ; used substantively, a rhetorician :—Getincum (tingcum, Hpt. Gl. 460, 41) lārum rhetoricis disciplinis, An. Ox. 2304. Getincne rhetoricę artis participem, 3357. Getincgum rhetoribus, 3096. ¶ in a list of the arts mechanica is glossed by getingce cræ[ft] which would be more appropriate as a gloss to rhetorica (v. ge-tynglic), An. Ox. 3122. (4) skilful. v. ge-tyngnes ; III :—þā forewittigan ł getincge glǣw[nesse] sagacissimam, i. peritissimam industriam (animi exercere), An. Ox. 70. [II. in a bad sense, speaking much, talkative; linguosus. v. Dict.] v. un-getynge.

ge-tynge ; adv. Courteously :—Getincge affabiliter, An. Ox. 2853.

ge-tynglic. v. ge-tynglic: ge-tyngful. v. un-getyngful.

ge-tynglic (-tynge-); adj. I. elegant of speech :—Mid ðām getingelicum (printed getingetinc) urbene (the Latin is: Quis valet urbanus laudes sermone polito fari, Ald. 165, 14), Wrt. Voc. ii. 92, 58. II. rhetorical :—Getinclices [cræftes] rhetoricae [artis], An. Ox. 3357. þǣm getingelicum rethoricis, Wrt. Voc. ii. 93, 24.

ge-tynglice (-tynge-). Take here ge-tingelice in Dict., and add :—Getyngelīce eloquenter, Wrt. Voc. ii. 143, 24. Mænifealdlīce, getingcelīce affatim (cum innumera beatae virginitatis exempla affatim exuberent), An. Ox. 1689.

ge-tyngnes. Take here ge-tingnes in Dict., and add: I. skill in speaking. v. ge-tynge; I :—Getingnes eloquentia, peritia, Wrt. Voc. ii.

143, 23. Getingnesse *facundia*, 34, 16. Meterlicere getincnesse gegódod *metrica facundia* (i. *eloquentia*) *fretus*, An. Ox. 125. Getincnesse *urbanitate*, i. *disertitudine* (*verborum praeditus*), 2297. Hē ūs selð micle getyngnesse and wlitige spræce ymb sōðfæstnesse tō cȳðanne *nobis luce veritatis plena eloquia subministrat*, Past. 369, 14. Hī eallra gereorda getingnesse hæfdon *they had skill to speak in all tongues*, Btwk. 214, 32. Þurh getingnesse *per facundiam*, Ll. Lbmn. 414, 12. **II.** *elegance* of speech. v. ge-tynge; **I.** 2 :—Mid þæslicere race getinnysse (getignysse, Hpt. Gl. 528, 4) *eleganti prosę sententia* (i. *peritia*), An. Ox. 5403. **III.** *skill*. v. ge-tynge; **I.** 4 :—Getydde on bōclicum cræfte hig witon mid getingnysse heora mōdes þ þ rihtmeterfers sceal habban feówer and twēntig tīman, Angl. viii. 314, 10. For ðæra bōcra getingnyssum, 300, 3. **III a.** *skilful words, wise sayings* :—Ræde hē þæs eádigan weres getingnyssa, Bēdan, Angl. 308, 12. **IV.** *set speech*. Cf. ge-tynge : **I.** 3 :—Getincnes *oratio*, An. Ox. 319.

**ge-tyrfan**; *p.* de *To assail with missiles* (lit. or fig.), *to attack, assault* :—Man gecýdde þ seó nunne wære getyrfed mid ormætum feforādlum *nuntiatum est quod sanctimonialis illa immensis febribus aestuaret*, Gr. D. 29, 9. Cf. ge-torfian.

**ge-tyrfian.** *l.* ge-tyrfan, *and see preceding word* : **ge-tyrgan, -tyrigan.** v. ge-tirgan : **ge-tyrian,** *l.* ge-tȳrian, *and see* ge-teórian : **ge-tyrwan.** v. ge-tirwan.

**ge-uferian.** *Add* : **I.** *to elevate, exalt.* (1) of local relations :—Heálicum bīgelsum geufered *celsis fornicibus sublimatus*, An. Ox. 513. (2) of sound, *to raise the voice* :—Se stunta on hlehtre his stefne geuferað *stultus in risu exaltat vocem suam*, R. Ben. 30, 10. (3) of rank, position :—God hī (*Mary*) ofer engla weredum geufrode, Hml. Th. i. 440, 10. Þone (*Haman*) geuferode (*exaltavit*) se cyning ofer ealle his þegnas, Hml. A. 96, 128 : 101, 325. Mardochēus micclum wæs gewurðod and swíðe geuferod *sublimitas qua exaltavit Mardochaeum scripta est*, 321. Geufered *fretus* (*sceptris imperialibus*), An. Ox. 398. Geuferod, 1470. (3 a) used of a place :—Gesundfullum gesælinessum geoffred (u *is written over* o) (*Syracusae*) *prosperis successibus sublimatur*, An. Ox. 3996. (4) of moral excellence :—On heálicere hēhnysse geufere[de] *edito* (*virginitatis*) *fastigio sublimati*, An. Ox. 931. **II.** *to put off, defer* :—Oft ðā ðwyran dēman for heora gītsunge þone dōm geuferiað and ne geendiað nā þá spæce ær heora seód bið āfylled, Ll. Lbmn. 475, 41. Wæs þæs cnihtes deáð twā niht geuferod ofer þ *per biduum mors eius dilata est*, Gr. D. 301, 2. Gif wē fæstað and þ underngereord tō þám æfengifle healdað, þonne ne bið þ nān fæsten, ac bið seó metetíd geuferad and bið þ æfengyfel getwifealdad, Ll. Th. ii. 436, 30. [*O. H. Ger.* ge-obarón *differre*.] Cf. ge-yferian.

**ge-unárian.** *Add* :—Saul hine bealg wið Samuel . . . ; and ðā hē him from wolde, ðā gefēng hē hine, and tōslāt his hrægl, and hine geunárode, Past. 35, 20. Hēt hē hig (*Eulalia*) nacode geunárian, Shrn. 154, 6.

**ge-unblissian** *to make unhappy, distress* :—Se bisceop wearð geunblissod for þám blódes gyte, Nap. 22, 25.

**ge-unclǽnsian.** *Add* : *to defile* :—Ne geunclǽnsað (*coinquinat*) ðæt nō ðone mon ðæt on his mūð gǽð, ac ðæt ðæt of his mūðe gǽð, ðæt hine geunclǽnsað, Past. 317, 14.

**ge-underþeódan** *to subject* :—Gif hē wǽre neádunga Gode geunderþeód (*subjectus*), Angl. vii. 4, 39.

**ge-unfæstnian.** v. un-fæstnian.

**ge-unhǽlan** *to weaken* :—Faestene gemetegude scylon beón þ hī nā þearle geunhǽlan (*debilitent*) maga[n], Scint. 51, 10.

**ge-unmihtan**; *pp.* -miht *To deprive of strength* :—His gefēran feóllon geunmihte, Hml. S. 25, 771. [Cf. *O. H. Ger.* ge-unmahtēn *languere*.]

**ge-unnan.** *Add* : (1) absolute, *to grant a request, consent* :—Geunnendre mēder (geundremedre, MS.) *matre consentiente*, An. Ox. 4000. (2) with gen. or uncertain. v. (3 ¶):—Hē geann þæs landes in tō þám mynstre, Cht. Crw. 23, 1. Forgefnise ðū giunna *veniam prebes*, Rtl. 18, 7. Hē him ǽgþres geúþe, Ors. 2, 1; S. 64, 12. Geunn ūs tō þissum dæge dæghwāmlices fóstres, Wlfst. 125, 11. Gionn ūs helpe *praesta nobis auxilium*, Rtl. 16, 29. Forgif mē, swegles ealdor, sigor . . . , geunne mē mínra gesynta, Jud. 90. Ic áh þearfe þæt þū mínum gǽste gódes geunne, By. 176. Symbelnis ūs giwnne (*prestet*) fremnise, Rtl. 68, 1. Hī bǽdon Sabini þte hī him geúðen hiora dohtra him tō wífum tō habbanne, Ors. 2, 2; S. 64, 26. Ic wille eówres geunnan eów, on þá gerād þe mē geunnan mínes, Ll. Th. i. 196, 18 : 330, 12. (2 a) with gen. of pron. representing a clause. Cf. (4):—Crístes gespelian þe crístendóm and cynedóm healdaþ þá hwíle þe þæs God geann, Ll. Th. i. 350, 4. Hī bǽdon þ hī móston habbon Morkere heom tō eorle, and se cyng þæs geúðe, Chr. 1064; P. 192, 2. (3) with acc. :—Ic geann him vi mǽran . . . and þá hors, C. D. B. iii. 653, 7. Hē geann Gode his sawelscættas . . . hē geann ānes geáres gafol his monnum . . . hē geann his hláforde .ii. hors and .ii. sweord and .iiii. scyldas . . . and his ann his wífe þæs landes, 652, 16-30. Gewunna ł sella (*exhibebit*) mē mǽ ðon tuelf hergas engla, Mt. L. 26, 53. God hæfð geunnen ðone wurðmynt his gecorenum, Hml. Th. i. 366, 16. Hī habbað geunnen twā land in tō

ðære hálgan stówe, C. D. iv. 72, 20. (3 a) with pron. representing a clause :—Ðis him giwnna (*hoc ei prestare*), þte nǽngo woerding ædeáua, Rtl. 102, 9. ¶ gen. or acc. comes to be used indifferently in the same document, even in the same line :—Ānes hīwscipes hē geann and ān sylhðe oxna ; and hē geann his hláforde twēgen helmas . . . and Ordulfe twēgra bóca . . . and Wulfgāre twēgra wáhryfta and þreó byrnan, and Godríce twēgra byrnena, Cht. Crw. 23, 4-16. (4) with adv. :—Áhte hē .vii. nihta grið, būtan man leng geunnan wolde, Ll. Th. i. 330, 16. (5) with clause :—Gionn (*praesta*) þte ðerh hine wē giearnigo, Rtl. 2, 19 : 3, 7 : 16, 11. Cwæð þæt him geúðe God þæt hī ætsomne síðian móston, Hml. Th. ii. 152, 15.

**ge-unrǽtan.** *Add* :—Míne þearfan þē mildheortnesse bǽdon, and þū hý forhogedest and geunrǣttest, Wlfst. 258, 7. Hī wurdon ealle geunrǽtte (*contristati*), Gr. D. 125, 8.

**ge-unrótian**; *p.* ode *To sadden, grieve* :—Beó se man ongeán gelǽd for mínum leófan Iuliane, nelle ic hine geunrótian on ǽnigum þincge, Hml. S. 4, 295.

**ge-unrótsian.** *Add* : **I.** *trans.* *To trouble, grieve, disquiet* :—þū geunrótsast mē *contristas me*, Gr. D. 38, 19. Swá dætte se ilca lust ðe hine geunrótsað hine eft gerótsat *ut contristet quod libet, et libeat quod contristet*, Past. 417, 8. Hē his gebrōðru ne geunrótsige, R. Ben. 54, 13, 14. Hē hī liðelíce ólehte ðá ðá hē hī geunrótsod hæfde *tristem blanditiis delinivit*, Past. 415, 30. Sárnys ðē hrepode, and ðū eart geunrótsod (*conturbatus es*), Hml. Th. ii. 454, 19 : Bt. 16, 4 ; F. 58, 8 : 41, 2 ; F. 246, 14. Ðē þ gedrēfed and geunrótsad hæfþ, F. 28, 4 : Ps. Th. 9, 21. Ðý lǽs hī scylen selfe beón biddende and for ðý weorðen geunrótsode *ne petentes noxie crucient*, Past. 321, 20. Se middangeord bið glædde, gié biðon geunrótsade (*contristabimini*), Jn. L. 16, 20 : Hml. A. 74, 24. Geswencte and geunrótsode, Gr. D. 125, 10. Hī beóþ mid wǽdle and mid hēnþe ofþrycte and geunrótsode, Bt. 11, 1 ; F. 32, 1. **II.** *intrans.* *To be troubled* :—Tristitia . . . þ is worulde unrótnyss, þonne se man geunrótsoð ealles tō swýðe for his ǽhta lyre . . . Óðer unrótnyss is hálwende, þ is þ se man for his synnum geunrótsige, Hml. S. 16, 289-294. Se unrihtwísa berýpð óðre and blissað ; eft, gif se þearfa hine mid ǽlmessan, þonne geunrótsað hē, Hml. Th. ii. 102, 16. Hē geunrótsode *turbatus est*, 244, 1. Giunrótsode Petrus *contristatus est Petrus*, Jn. L. 21, 17. Þæt hē nǽfre þurh úre yfelan dǽda ne geunrótsige *ut non debeat de malis actibus nostris contristari*, R. Ben. 1, 14. Þæt nǽnig sý gedrēfed ne geunrotsige (*contristetur*), 55, 20 : 58, 1. Þæt hý ne geunrótsigen *ut non scandalizentur*, 55, 12.

**ge-unstillan**; *p.* de *To disturb, disquiet* :—þá scínlác þe him ǽr ætýwdon, ne geunstillað hý hine, Lch. i. 360, 15. Rǽde hē swá þæt hē óþre mid gehlýde ne geunstille (*inquietet*), R. Ben. 73, 14. Se abbod ne geunstille ne ne gedrēfe þá heorde *abbas non conturbet gregem*, 113, 23. Ne hē ne beó unstill and fǽcne, for ðám á byð geunstilled (-od, *v. l.*) and restleás þe mid ðám unþeáwum beléd byð *non sit zelotipus et nimis suspiciosus, quia nunquam requiescit*, 120, 14. Þ ða gebroðra ne beón geunstilde *ut non inquietent fratres*, 84, 8.

**ge-unstillian.** *See preceding word*.

**ge-unþwǽrian.** *Add* :—Geunþwǽrað *dissentit*, Wrt. Voc. ii. 28, 71. Áht þæs þe geunþwǽrige fram þæs incundan regoles smeáðancolnesse *quidquid ab aeternae regulae subtilitate discordat*, Gr. D. 336, 27.

**ge-untreówsian.** *Add* :—Beóð manega geuntrýwsode, Mt. 24, 10.

**ge-untrum** (?) *sick, ill* :—Fíf and twēntig manna myslíce geuntrume (-trumede ? v. ge-untrumian ; **I** a), Hml. S. 21, 187.

**ge-untrumian.** *Add* : **I.** *trans.* *To weaken* :—Hwá bið geuntrumod ðæt ic ne sié eác geuntrumod *quis infirmatur, et ego non infirmor* ?, Past. 101, 3. Ic hopige tō Drihtne, and ic ne weorðe geuntrumod, Ps. Th. 25, 1. Geuntrumod wæs mín mægen, 30, 12. **I a.** of bodily weakness, ill-health :—Antecríst gebrocað and geuntrumað þá þe ǽr hále wǽron, Wlfst. 97, 11. Gif hyra hwylc geuntrumad biþ þæt hē ciricean gegán ne mæge, R. Ben. 140, 19. Weard hē geuntrumod and gewát tō heofenan ríce, Hml. Th. ii. 348, 4. Yfele geuntrumed and orwēna lífes, Hml. S. 3, 300. Geuntrumed þurh þá mycclan fótādle, 5, 136. **II.** *intrans.* *To become weak* :—Míne eágan ádlodon ł geuntrumedon *oculi mei languerunt*, Ps. L. 87, 10.

**ge-unwendness.** *In the passage read* geunwendnes *for* ungewendnes.

**ge-unweorþian** (-wurþ-) *to dishonour* :—Hī befýlað fracodlíce hī selfe and eác geunwurðiað, Wlfst. 305, 11. Þ hē God ne geunwurðige tō wíte him sylfum, Ll. Th. ii. 357, 43. Se crístendóm weorð geunwurðod syððan, Hml. S. 19, 149. Gē beóð geunwurðode and eác gewítnode, 11, 95.

**ge-unwlitigian** *to destroy the beauty of, disfigure* :—Se teter ðæt lim geunwlitigað *impetigo membrorum decorem foedat*, Past. 71, 18. Geunwlitigad *foedatus, deturpatus*, Wrt. Voc. ii. 148, 41.

**ge-urnen**; *adj.* (*ptcpl.*) *Coagulated* :—þá þiccan geuruenon wǽtan, Lch. ii. 194, 19. v. ge-irnan ; **IV.**

**ge-útian.** *Add* :—Geútad, āfýmed *exiliata*, An. Ox. 4849.

**ge-útlagian.** *Add* :—Se pápa is geútlagod and líð him on dígelan for his crístendóme, Hml. S. 34, 131.

**ge-wácian.** *Add* :—Ealle þá getimbru þissere burge wē geseóð mid

langre ealdunge gewācode *hujus urbis aedificia longo senio lassata videmus*, Gr. D. 134, 11. *The Latin of* Ors. 3, 4 *is :* Nisi otio torpuisset. [O. H. Ger. ge-weichen *infirmari.*]

**ge-wǣcan.** *Add : pp. -wǣced :*—Gehuaeh (-wǣhþ?) *adfligit*, Wrt. Voc. ii. 99, 36. Gewǣce *fatigat*, 147, 27. Gewǣcte *infecta*, 47, 70. Gewēhtum *fessis*, Wülck. Gl. 254, 16. I. of the effects on living creatures. (1) physical, (a) *to weary, exhaust* with labour, travel, &c. :—Đā seó lǣtre tíd hí gangende gewǣhte *cum eos tardior hora fatigaret*, Gr. D. 129, 2. Hē wæs swíðe gewǣced ǣgðer ge mid fæstene ge on þām langan geswince, Hml. S. 23 b, 769. Gif wē lange standað, wē beóð gewǣhte, Hml. Th. i. 488, 35. (b) of the effect of disease, age, wounds, famine, &c. :—Hungre ic gewǣce *fame conficiam*, An. Ox. 2441. Gif man on huntuþe rān mid flāne gewǣceþ, Lch. i. 166, 25. Ic for yldum gewǣht eom, þ ic delfan ne mæg, Hml. S. 23 b, 782. Nis hǣlo on flǣsce míne. Gewǣht (*afflictus*) ic eom, Ps. Spl. 37, 8. Wið þæt hwā mid cyle gewǣht (-wēht, *v. l.*) sý, Lch. i. 114, 23. Mid miclum sārum gewǣced *tanto dolore adfectus*, Bd. 4, 11 ; Sch. 405, 14. Ongan hē sworettan swā swā eallunga gewǣced, on þām oreðe belocen, Hml. S. 23 b, 234. Hỹ synt mid untrumnyssum gewǣhte, Hml. A. 146, 57. Wǣron hié mid metelíeste gewǣhte, Chr. 894 ; P. 295, 2. (c) of the effect of ill-treatment :—Hí eów tó deáðe gewǣcað *morte vos adficient*, Hml. Th. ii. 542, 17. Sume hí þā bydelas mid teónan gewǣhton and ofslógon *servos contumelia adfectos occiderunt*, i. 524, 22. Ic ðē hāte gewǣhtne on þǣre róde āfæstnian, 590, 12. Wē synd ealne dæg tó deáþe gewǣhte *morte afficimur tota die*, R. Ben. 27, 9. (2) non-physical :—Ne ðū ðē ǣfre ne lǣt wlenca gewǣcan, Met. 5, 31. Mōd mid horuwe gewǣht *mens sorde saucia*, Hy. S. 37, 12. Wæs gewǣht *afficitur* (*acri angore*), An. Ox. 4011. Ne ðū beó gewǣht þonne hē ðē þreáð *neque fatigeris dum ab eo argueris*, Hml. Th. ii. 328, 22. þæt bearn ne wurdon gewǣhte ðurh wācmódnysse (*that children should not get spoiled by the weakness of parents*) . . Cildra behófiað swíðlícere steóre, 324, 26–34. Gewǣcede *defectos*, Ps. Rdr. 291, 36. II. of things :—Sōna hit ðone dropan gewǣceð *it soon reduces the drop*, 162, 8. Gewǣht *fessa*, i. *fatigata* (*fragilitas moribundae carnis*), An. Ox. 1276 : *labefacta* (*severitas*), 4790. Mid gewǣhtum *obliqua* (*invidia*), 5350. [O. H. Ger. ge-weichen *emollire, enervare, curvare, frangere.*]

**ge-wǣccan.** *Add :*—Hē ðǣm doruorde bebeád þte gewǣhte *ianitori praecipiat ut uigilet*, Mk. L. 13, 34.

**ge-wǣd,** es ; *n. A ford :*—Willelm cyng lǣdde scipfyrde and landfyrde tó Scotlande . . . and his landfyrde æt þām Gewǣde (*the Forth*) inn lǣdde (fērde inn ofer þ Wǣd, *v. l.*), Chr. 1072 ; P. 208, 14. Þis sy[ndon ðā landgemǣro] tó miclan grāfe on Tenet . . . andlang eá on middel gewæd and þonan west on Seolcingfleót, C. D.B. ii. 519, 14. Geuueada *vada brevia*, Wrt. Voc. ii. 123, 17. v. wæd.

**ge-wǣdan.** v. ge-wǣdian.

**ge-wǣde.** *Add :* I. *what is worn by a person.* (1) in a collective sense, *clothing, raiment, clothes :*—Gewoedo his huít swíðe gesceán *uestitus eius albus refulgens*, Lk. L. 9, 29. Of gewēdo huæt gēmende aro gē *de uestimento quid sollicti estis?*, Mt. L. 6, 28. Giwēde *uestimenta*, Lk. R. 23, 34. (2) *a garment :*—Þte fasne gewoede his (fæse giwēdum his, R.) gehrinon *ut fimbriam uestimenti eius tangerent*, Mk. L. 6, 56. On gewedo ald *in uestimentum uetus*, Lk. L. 5, 36. Giwedu his hwítu gescionum, Lk. R. 9, 29. Wē lǣrað þ man geswíce higeleásra gewǣda, Ll. Th. ii. 248, 15. Hí gegearwadon hine mid gewoedum (-wēdum, R.) his, Mk. L. 15, 20 : Lk. L. 7, 25. Gewoedo *uestimenta*, 23, 34. (2 a) *the garment* of a soldier, cf. gūþ-gewǣde :—Uil mec (*a coat of mail*) hātan mith heliðum hyhtlic giuæde, Txts. 151, 12. Dǣldon þā cwelleras þǣra martyra wǣpna and gewǣda . . heora gehwilc hæfde þæs mannes gewǣda þe hē ācwealde, Hml. S. 28, 83–86. (2 b) used of grave-clothes :—þā gewǣda þe heó bewunden wæs mid (cf. ealle þā scýtan (*linteamina*) þe se líchama mid bewunden wæs, Bd. 4, 19 ; Sch. 449, 8), Hml. S. 20, 94. (2 c) *figurative :*—Đās gewǣdu āwrāt se apostol . . . ' Ymbscrýdað eów mid mildheortnysse . . . and mid geðylde,' Hml. Th. i. 60 b, 12. II. *the sails of a ship.* v. ge-wǣdian ; III : wǣde, II :—Of þām scipe wǣron þā naglas forlorene and þā gewǣdu wǣron ūt on þā āworpene *ex navi clavi perditi, vela in undis projecta*, Gr. D. 248, 24. v. breóst-, cyne-, eorl-, fōt-, gūþ-, heáfod-, hrægel-, wægn-, winter-gewǣde.

**ge-wǣdian.** *Add : -wǣdan :*—To *wrap up :*—Ðæt on gewuæð *quod inolcuerit?* (=involucerit? cf. *involucrum* gewynd, Wrt. Voc. i. 41, 25), Angl. xi. 171, 9. I. *to clothe,* (1) a person :—Gwēdon hine tunuc *induerunt eum tunicam*, Mt. L. 27, 28. Gewoedeað hine *induite illum*, Lk. L. 15, 22. Gewēded *uestitus*, 8, 35. Hỹ gewǣdode (*vestiti*) resten, R. Ben. 47, 9. (2) a thing :—Gif gers God swæ geuoedes (*vestit*), Mt. L. 6, 30. II. *to dress* a house, *adorn with hangings, tapestry,* &c. : vestire (= *aulaeis ornare*, Migne) :—Mid ðām geleáfan hē gefrætewad and gewǣdað his hūs, þæt is, þæt hē gegearwað his heortan Gode on tó wunianne, Wlfst. 35, 1. III. *to furnish* a ship with sails. v. ge-wǣde ; II :—Hí þ scip genāmon eall gewǣpnod and gewǣdod, Chr. 992 ; P. 127, 19. [O. H. Ger. ge-wāten, wlenca wātōn *vestire.*]

**ge-wǣgan ;** I. *Add :*—Gewǣged *confectus*, Wrt. Voc. ii. 14, 50.

Hié sint tó manienne ðæt hí baldlíce getrūwien ðæt hí ðā forgiefnesse habbað for ðǣre hreówsunga ðe hí wilniað, ðỹ lǣs hí tó ungemetlíce sién gewǣgde mid ðǣre hreówsunga *admonendi sunt, ut de misericordia, quam postulant, praesumant, ne vi immoderatae afflictionis intereant*, Past. 415, 1. [Siak . . . te wundron giwēgid sick . . . *marvellously afflicted*, Hél. 2327. O. H. Ger. ge-weigit *fatigatus, affectus.*] **ge-wǣgan ;** II. *Add after* mæg : wyrd under heofonum, ac hit þus gelimpan sceal, *and after* Dōm. 115 : cf. ge-wǣgnian.

**ge-wǣge.** *Substitute : Weight.* (1) *determination of amount by weighing :*—In swā hwelce giwēge (on suā huælc gewǣge, L.) giwegen gī bióðon eft giwegen bið iów *in qua mensura mensi fueritis remetietur uobis*, Mk. R. 4, 24. Genim ðū betonican þǣre wyrte twā trymessan gewǣge (*by weight*), Lch. i. 76, 11 : 17 : 22 : 78, 8 : 13. (2) *an amount determined by weighing.* (a) indefinite :—Gewoege ł gemet gōd hiá sellað *mensuram bonam dabunt*, Lk. L. 6, 38. (b) a definite amount :—Genim ðū huniges ānre yndsan gewǣge (cf. genim huniges āne yndsan, 17) *take an ounce weight of honey*, Lch. i. 76, 11. Genim þǣre wyrte twēgra trymesa gewǣge, 78, 24 : 180, 27. Genim týn penega gewǣge, 116, 5 : iii. 46, 11. Betonican swilce ānes peninges gewǣge, ii. 108, 4. Cnuca tó dūste ānre tremese gewihte (gewǣge, *v. l.*), i. 110, 9. [O. H. Ger. ge-wāgi *stater, talentum, mina.*] v. sinc-gewǣge.

**ge-wǣgnian.** I. *to condemn :*—Nelle wē nā þ man gewǣgnige subdiácon . . . ne rǣdere . . . būtan . . . mid vii tungon. And ne mæg man nānne diácon gewǣgnian būtan .xxxvi. sum *nolumus ut subdiaconus . . . vel lector a quopiam damnetur, nisi in .vii. linguis. Nec potest diaconus ullus damnari, nisi in .xxxvi.*, Ll. Th. ii. 168, 2–7 : Nap. 33, 18–22. Be þām þ man nānne preóst mid eáðelicum þingum ne mage gewǣgnian, 24. II. *to deceive, frustrate :*—Gewǣgnian *frustrari*, Wrt. Voc. ii. 34, 25. v. ge-wǣgan.

**ge-wǣpne,** es ; *n. Armour, weapons, arms :*—Hē tóbricð gewǣpnu *confringet arma*, Ps. L. 45, 10. [O.H. Ger. ge-wāfani *armatura, arma.*]

**ge-wǣpnian.** *Add :* I. of persons. (1) of military weapons :—Hē hine gescrýdde mid his byrnan, and hine ealne gewǣpnode, Hml. S. 25, 280. Swā gewǣpned wer *quasi vir armatus*, Kent. Gl. 139. On ðǣre fyrde wǣron feówertig þūsenda swýðe gewǣpnode, Homl. S. 25, 333. Myd seofen þūsend gewǣpnodra manna, Hml. A. 184, 92. (2) of spiritual weapons :—Gié ðǣm ilca smeawnge iúih giwoepnigað *vos eadem cogitatione armamini*, Rtl. 21, 38. II. of animals. (1) of military equipment :—Cumað mycele deór : hí beóð gewǣpnode on ðā wísan þe man hors gewǣpnað, þonne man tó wíge þencð, Wlfst. 200, 11. (2) of natural means of attack or defence :—Hæfde þ deór þríe hornas on foranheáfde, and mid þǣm hornum wæs egeslíce gewǣpnod *bestia tribus armata in fronte cornibus*, Nar. 15, 14. III. of things. (1) material :—Hí þ scip genāmon eall gewǣpnod, Chr. 992 ; P. 127, 19. (2) non-material :—Gewoepnadum mægne *armata virtute*, Rtl. 145, 28. [O. H. Ger. ge-wāfnōt *armatus.*] v. full-, un-gewǣpnod.

**ge-wǣpnung,** e ; *f. Armour, arms.* (1) military. v. ge-wǣpnian ; I. 1 :—Cōm Mercurius mid his gewǣpnunge and weard āsend tó þæs cāseres slæge, Hml. S. 3, 251. Hē fērde mid þām cempum būton gewǣpnunge, 31, 41. Hē næfde nāht būtan his gewǣdum and his gewǣpnunge, 67. (2) spiritual. v. ge-wǣpnian ; I. 2 :—Feohtan mid Godes gewǣpnunge ongeán ðone ungesewenlican feónd, Hml. Th. ii. 402, 18.

**ge-wǣr.** *Substitute : ge-wǣr in the phrase* gewær (*indecl.* cf. wurðan thes firiho barn giwar, Hél. 3641. Uuir knadon geuuar uuorden sín, Notker 38, 9) *weorþan to become aware of* (*gen.*) :—þā fundon hí ðǣre flocrāde þ rād ūt wið Lígtūnes ; and þā wurdon þā landleóde his gewær (*the natives became aware of it*), Chr. 914 ; P. 99, 5. Feórde se eorl tówardes Tīnemūðan, ac þā þe innan þām castele wǣron his gewær wurdon (*became aware of it*, i. e. the earl's march), 1095 ; P. 231, 13.

**ge-wǣred** *confederated, allied :*—Gewǣred *federatus*, i. *coniunctus* vel *pacificatus, amicus*, Wülck. Gl. 238, 9. v. wǣr.

**ge-wǣrlǣcan.** *Substitute : To warn :*—Cain wiste his fæder for-gǣgednysse, and næs þurh þ gewǣrlǣht, ac þǣr tó eácan his āgenne bróðor ācwealde *Cain sciebat damnationem praevaricationis primae, et non timuit originali peccato fratricidii superaddere scelus*, Angl. vii. 32, 303.

**ge-wǣscan.** v. ge-wascan.

**ge-wǣstmbǣrian** *to be fruitful ;* fecundare, multiplicare, Wrt. Voc. ii. 148, 48.

**ge-wǣtan.** *Substitute : To wet, moisten :*—Geuuēted *madefacta*, Wrt. Voc. ii. 113, 73. Gehwēted *madefactum*, 58, 49. (1) the subject a person :—Foxes sina genim and on hunige gewǣt, Lch. i. 340, 17. Gedō on scearp eced, gewǣte swíðe, ii. 192, 19. Onsend Ladzarus ðætte hē gewǣte (*intingat*) his ýtemestan finger on wættre, Past. 309, 6. Stingendum niggan gewǣtte *putenti lotio umectaretur*, An. Ox. 3470. (2) the subject the moisture :—Se ele feóll ofer þa brerdas þǣre bydene and gewǣtte (*inundabat*) þone flór, Gr. D. 160, 13. Streámas . . . nā him gewǣttan fōt þā hí on Iordane gengdan æfter *abierunt in sicco flumina*, Ps. Th. 104, 36. Strengas gurron, wǣdo gewǣtte, An. 375.

**ge-wǣterian.** *Add :* (1) *to supply animals with water*, Coll. M. 20, 31 (*in Dict.*). (2) *to water plants* (lit. or fig.) :—Ðonne grēwð ðæt

sǽd ðára worda ðonne sió mildheortnes ðæs láreówes geðwǽnð ðá breóst ðæs hiérendes. For ðǽm is niéddearf ðǽm reccere ðæt hé mæge óðerra monna inngeðonc giendgeótan and gewæterian (*infundere*), Past. 137, 10. (3) *to water* land:—Ásende Drihten rénscúras and gewæterode þá eorðan, Hml. S. 14, 177. (4) *to pour water on* material:—Hé hét gewæterian ealne þone wudu *ait*: '*Fundite super ligna*,' Hml. S. 18, 125.

ge-wǽxen. v. ge-weaxan: ge-wahsan. v. ge-wascan: ge-walcud. v. ge-wealcian: ge-wana, an; *m. A lack*. Substitute: ge-wana; *adj. Lacking.* v. wana; *adj.* I.

ge-wand, es; *n.* I. *a turning aside, shrinking, hesitation*:— Hé Godes þá gecorenan búton gewande getúcude eall swá hé wolde, Hml. S. 23, 15. Hí búton gewande sóna in tó þám ciningce eódon, 142. Ic eów bidde þ gé búton gewande dón swá ic eów bebeode, 161. II. *fear* of a person:—þæt hý for ðǽre sceame and for gewande þára þe him on lóciað gebeterede sýn *ut visi ab omnibus vel pro ipsa verecundia sua emendentur*, R. Ben. 68, 18. v. wandian.

ge-wane, An. Ox. 5047. v. ge-wanian: ge-wanhálian. v. wan-hálian.

ge-wanian. *Add*:—Gewonede *dempsit*, Wrt. Voc. ii. 27, 54. Gewanude *vel* gelytlade *deminute*, 138, 67. (1) the object material:— Geónet spéd bið gewanad *substantia festinata minuetur*, Kent. Gl. 441. Gewane[dum] locca fexe *dempta cincinnorum cesarie*, An. Ox. 5047. Gewanedum *dempta*, Wrt. Voc. ii. 27, 55. (2) the object non-material. (a) *to lessen* in extent, degree:—Hié sint tó manianne ðæt hié nó hiera fæsten ne gewanigen *admonendi sunt, ut abstinentiam suam sine imminutione custodiant*, Past. 315, 9. Hit dered ðæt sió sibb ne sié gewanod betwux ðǽm yfelum *est noxium, si unitas non desit malis*, 361, 10. Hé wénþ þæt his gesǽlþa sién oþþe suíþe gewanode oððe mid ealle forlorene, Bt. 11, 1; F. 32, 23. (b) *to lessen* in worth, *make inferior, degrade, depreciate*:—Ðonne gewaniað hié ðone hád and gewemmað *superioris loci meritum diminuunt*, Past. 413, 2. Se æht ðára gódra weorca, ðe hé ǽr beeóde, bið gewanod *aestimatio anteacta minuitur*, 133, 23; Bt. 13; F. 38, 28: 35, 4; F. 162, 29. Gewanedum *effeta* (*voluntate*), An. Ox. 8, 280. (3) of wrongful diminution by encroachment, infringement, &c., or by withholding what should be given:—Ic geeácnode tó ðǽre ǽrran sylene ... nán ðæra cyninga þe cumað æfter mé mid unrihte ðiss ne áwende oððe gewanige, C. D. iii. 61, 25. Gyf hé ðisne mínne sundorfreóls gewanige oððe gelytlige *si quis hoc nostrum privilegium minuent vel dempserit*, 350, 16. Wé forhealdað ǽghwǽr Godes gerihta, and ne dear man gewanian on hǽðenum þeódum ǽnig þæra þinga þe gedwolgodon tó lácum betǽht bið, Wlfst. 157, 15.

ge-wara. v. ceaster-gewara: ge-wardod. *Dele, and see* ge-warenian: ge-ware. v. ceaster-geware.

ge-warenian. *Take here* ge-warnian, ge-wearnian *in Dict., and add:* I. *to warn* a person, *put on guard*:—Críst gewarnode his apostolas þysum wordum: '*Vigilate* ...,' Hml. A. 49, 4. Hét hé áwritan hú hine gewarnode Mardocheus, 95, 125. þ hé sí gewarnod fram him *ut videatur ab ipso*, R. Ben. I. 76, 7. Ðurh þæt wyrð mǽst manna beswicen þe hý ne beóð swá wel gewarnode ǽr swá hý beðorfton. Lá! hwæt is se man on lífe búton ... hé ǽr gewarnod þe bet sý, þæt hé þonne ðurh deófol beswicen ne wyrðe, Wlfst. 101, 16-21. I a. *to warn* a person against something:—Folc wið synna gewarnian, Ll. Th. ii. 326, 42. II. used reflexively, *to be on one's guard, take heed*:— Hí swícað þám preóste búton hé hine gewarnige, Angl. viii. 333, 2. Ic eów warnige ... þ gé eów gewarnion, and geornlíce gýmon hwǽr se móna beó, 329, 20. II a. *to be on one's guard* against something:— Ælc gleáw mód hit gewarenaþ wiþ heora þreáunga, Bt. 7, 2; F. 18, 24. Hé on ðæt lond faran wolde. ac hié þá landleóde wið þ gewarnedon, and him mid firde angeán fóran, Ors. 3, 7; S. 116, 21. III. *to ward off* something:—Fultum tó gewearnienne and tó wiðscúfanne swá réþre hergunge *praesidium ad euitandas uel repellendas tam feras inruptiones*, Bd. 1, 14; Sch. 39, 18.

ge-warian. *Substitute*: I. *to warn, put on guard*:—Bisceopas þe godcunde heorde gewarian and bewerian scylan mid wislican láran, Ll. Th. ii. 310, 30: 326, 17. Búton hé ǽr gewarad (gewarnod, *v. l.*) sý, Wlfst. 101, 20: 273, 20. II. *to protect*. Cf. ge-werian:—Wara gewarod *tutela protectum*, An. Ox. 2616.

ge-warnian. v. ge-warenian: ge-waru. v. ceaster-gewaru.

ge-wascan. *Add*:—Genim þás wyrte ... and gewæsc hý wel mid ecede, Lch. i. 104, 2. Mid wætere gewæsc, 204, 19. Niman hí him bréc of hrægelhús; eft swá hý hám cumen, betæcan him gewoxene (-wahsene, *v. l.*) *femuralia de vestiario accipiant; revertentes lota ibi restituant*, R. Ben. 91, 10.

ge-wealc. *Add*:—þ gewealc þára ýða hwaðerode mid windum, Ap. Th. 11, 1. [Cf. *Icel.* válk *rolling, tossing; worry*.] v. ráp-gewealc (?).

ge-wealcan. *Add*: I. *to roll together, press together*:—Heorotes horn gebærned tó ahsan, gegniden on mortere, and þonne ásift and mid hunige gewealcen tó snǽdum, Lch. ii. 238, 2. [*O. H. Ger.* ge-walchen *concretus*: cf. walchare *compressor*.] II. *to pass*:—Gewealcon *emensus* (cf. *emenso* oferférde, áurnenum, Wrt. Voc. ii. 29, 33, 34), Germ. 400, 471.

ge-wealcian; *pp.* od *To curl* with a curling-iron:—Gewalcudum *calamistratis*, An. Ox. 26, 69. v. wealc-spinel.

ge-weald. *Add: The plural is sometimes used with force of singular.* I. *power*. (1) *control* over that which is moved. v. wealdan; I:—Hé næiþ his fóta geweald þ hé mæge gán, Bt. 36, 4; F. 178, 13. (2) *control* in respect to movement, action, &c., over that which moves itself (a person, an emotion, &c. v. wealdan; II):—Ic onbúgan ne mót of þæs gewealde þe mé wegas tǽcneð, Rä. 4, 16. Cuiht oð þ hé sig .xv. winter eald sig hé on his fæder gewealdum (*in potestate sit patris sui*), Ll. Th. ii. 152, 13. ¶ with gen. of person controlled:—Hí þæt wín drincende wǽron, oð hí heora selfra lytel geweald hæfdon, Ors. 2, 4; S. 76, 18. Gif þá gesǽlþa þurh hié selfe heora selfra geweald áhton, Bt. 16, 3; F. 56, 9. (2 a) where control is against the will of the controlled: e. g. *slavery*:—Hwilc gefreólseþ þé nú of úrum gewealde?, Bl. H. 243, 9. Hér is fǽmne (*Hagar*) on gewealde (cf. Sarai hæfde áne þínene, Gen. 16, 1), Gen. 2227. Hí héton lǽdan út weras tó gewealde, 2457. Earme men gesealde fremdum tó gewealde, Wlfst. 158, 13. Hé hié mid hungre on his geweald geniédde, Ors. 4, 10; S. 196, 26. Hé wæs on þǽre cwéne gewealdum, El. 610. Hí (*devils*) habbaþ manega sáula on heora gewaldum, Bl. H. 47, 7. ¶ with gen. of person controlled:—Hé (*David*) his (*Saul*) wel geweald áhte, Past. 37, 5. (3) *power* of protection:—Sé þe Godes útlagan ofer þone ándagan þe se cyngc sette hæbbe on gewealde, Ll. Th. i. 350, 2. Hé him ágeaf wíf tó gewealde, Gen. 1867. Hæfde Gúðláces gǽst in gewealdum módig mundbora, Gú. 666. (4) *power* of one in authority, *rule, dominion, sway.* v. wealdan; III:—þám is wuldor and geðweald, Bl. H. 249, 23. Ealra heáhfædera mægen hé (*St. John*) oferstigeþ on þæm apostolican gewealde, 167, 24. Brytland him wæs on gewealde, Chr. 1086; P. 220, 22. Hé gerád eal Norþhymbra land him tó gewealde, 946; P. 112, 4. Hé Maníge on his geweald gesætte, 1099; P. 235, 3. Sé þe dómes geweald áge *the judge*, Ll. Th. i. 376, 18: Kr. 107. Eádmund cyning geeóde eal Norþhymbra land him tó gewealdan (-wealde, *v. l.*), 944; P. 110, 31. þá dyde hé him þá rícu tó gewealdon, Ors. 3, 7; S. 114, 29. Seó circe bád under hǽðenra hyrda gewealdum, Cri. 705. ¶ with gen. of what is ruled:—Tó þám ðe ðænne áh mynstres geweald, Cht. E. 236, 5. (4 a) *a dominion*—þ eall crísten folc mínra gewealda sóðe sibbe healde, Ll. Lbmn. 216, 1. (5) *power* over a thing, place, *possession, command, mastery.* v. wealdan; IV:—Hé þá clúsan on his geweald hæfde *angustias occupatas emuniit*, Ors. 3, 7; S. 114, 28. Inc sceal sealt wæter wunian on gewealde, Gen. 199. þ weorþ on úrum gewealde habban, Bl. H. 101, 10. Hit his yldran lǽfdan þám tó gewealde þe hý wel uðan, Ll. Th. i. 184, 3. Agan heofon tó gewalde *to have heaven at command*, Sat. 415. Here bróhte Israéla gestreón in his ǽhte geweald, Dan. 757. ¶ with gen. of thing, place:—Sum man áhte geweald ealles ðæs splottes, Hml. S. 23, 415. þá Deniscan áhton wælstówe geweald, Chr. 837; P. 62, 32. þæt hié ánforléten heofonríces geweald, Gen. 694. Nóe and his suna landes geweald áhtan, Wlfst. 10, 16. (6) *power* to determine what one does (of intentional or voluntary action. v. gewealdes; I: wealdan; V):— þ hit nǽfre næs náðer ne his gewile ne his geweald *it was neither his desire nor his intention*, Ll. Th. i. 418, 12. Hé bið swylc monnes geweald *that is not within a man's power to determine*, Vy. 14. Gif hine mon tió gewealdes on þǽre dǽde *if he be accused of intention in the deed*, Ll. Th. i. 84, 15. Ðonne hí forlétað hiora willes and hiora gewealdes ðá gód ðe hí getióhchod æfdon tó dónne, Past. 445, 6. Ðæt gesuinc hié him selfe ðurh hira ágena scylda hira ágnes gewealdes him on getióð, 239, 5. (7) *power* to determine what another does (where another's action is dependent upon oneself. v. ge-wealdes; II):—Ic bidde nú, gif hwá þás bóc áwritan wylle, þ hé hig gerihte wel be þǽre bysne; for þan þe ic náh geweald (*I cannot help it*) þeáh þe hig hwá tó woge bringe þurh leáse wríteras, Ælfc. Gen. Thw. 4, 28. Nú gé habbað gehýred hwæt eów tó dónne is ... gif gé of þysum dóð wé nagon geweald, Ll. Th. ii. 362, 19. (7 a) with clause:—Ælc tiónd áge geweald swá hwæþer hé wille swá wæter swá ísen *it depends upon the accuser whether the ordeal be by water or iron*, Ll. Th. i. 296, 3. (8) *power* that brings something to pass, is the cause or source of something. v. wealdan; VI:—Hwæþer hit nú ðínes gewealdes sié þ se hærfest sié swá welig on wæstmum *et an tua in aestivos fructus intumescit ubertas*, Bt. 14, 1; F. 40, 27. Gif se anweald his ágenes gewealdes gód wǽre, 16, 3; F. 54, 23. For hwý ætwíte gé eówerre wyrde þ hió nán geweald náh, 39, 1; F. 210, 26. Hit gesǽleþ ... hwílum þurh wífes geweald, hwílum þurh weres, Bl. H. 195, 5. (9) *power* to do. v. wealdan; VII:—Ic hæbbe geweald micel tó gyrwanne gódlecran stól, Gen. 280. Hetend hildenǽdran þurh fingra geweald forð onsendan, El. 120. II. *an implement that controls* (lit. or fig.), *a bridle*:—On gewealde ceacan heora gewríð *in camo maxillas eorum constringe*, Ps. Srt. 31, 12. Hé his sylfes willan gelíðode in him sylfum þǽre blisse geweald *sponte sibi laetitiae frena laxabat*, Gr. D. 203, 26. III. *covering, protection* (?):—Tó ofsettenne giuæld heáfdes *ad deponendam comam capitis*, Rtl. 96, 5: 30. Nacode swá hé hí ǽrest gemétte búton gewealdan þæs tóslítenan rægeles þe hé hire ǽr tó wearp, Hml. S. 23 b, 792. IV. *take here* ge-weald *pudenda, in Dict., and add:*—Geweald *inguen*,

Germ. 389, 81. Hē mid þām horne hine þȳde on þ geweald, Hml. S. 31, 787. Wið þǣra gewealda gesār, Lch. i. 94, 22. Þ geswell þāra gewalda, 24. Smyre þā geweald mid þām lǣcedōme, 312, 13. v. þeóh-, un-geweald.

**ge-wealdan.** Add : I. to control the movement of a material object, wield a weapon :—Heora nān ne mehte nānes wǣpnes gewealdan, Ors. 4, 10; S. 194, 19. II. to control movement, action, manage to do some movement or action. (1) with gen. :—Ne mæg ūre sāwul gefleón . . . ðe mā ðe ǣnig fugel his flyhtes gewylt, gif his ōðer fiðere forod bið, Hml. Th. ii. 318, 28. Meaht þū meðelcwidum worda gewealdan ?, Gū. 989. (2) with dat. (inst.) :—Swā hē late meahte oreðe gewealdan, 1199. III. to control, have power over a person :—Betra bið sē þe his āgen mōd ofercymð and gewilt (melior est qui dominatur animo suo) . . sió gesceádwīsnes hæfð ofercumen ðæt mōd and gewield, Past. 218, 15–21. Wið feóndseócum men, þonne deófol þone monnan innan gewealde mid ādle when a devil possesses a man, Lch. ii. 136, 25. III a. where the subject is a passion :—Gif hē yrre ne lǣteð ǣfre gewealdan if he never lets anger have the mastery, Fä. 83. IV. of official authority :—Ð&as gewældes ðǣm hi dominantur eis, Mk. L. R. 10, 42. Hē rīces geweóld, Hml. S. 26, 46. [Goth. ga-waldan : O. Sax. gi-waldan.]

**ge-wealden.** In l. 12 for Lchdm. iii. 362, col. I substitute Hml. S. 6, 275, and add :—Hié gewealdenne here ou Umbre sendon an hergiunge quibusdam suis ad populandos agros in Umbriam praemissis, Ors. 3, 10; S. 138, 7. v. un-gewealden.

**ge-wealdes.** I. of deliberate, voluntary action, intentionally, of one's own accord :—Hȳ fūl ne friðian willes ne gewealdes, Ll. Th. i. 162, 26. Nǣfre willes ne gewealdes ōwiht dōn, 178, 6. Nā gelīc þām þe willes and gewealdes misdēð, 328, 22. Gif hwā hwæt ungewealdes gedēð, ne bið þ eallunga nā gelīc þe hit gewealdes gedēð, 412, 15. Gif hwā of giernesse and gewealdes ofsleá his þone nēhstan þurh searwa si quis per industriam occiderit proximum suum et per insidias, 46, 26. II. where what happens is the result of one's action :—Gif him ðonne gewealdes gebyrige oððe ungewealdes (whether he is responsible or not for what happens), Past. 199, 22. v. un-gewealdes.

**geweald-leþer.** Add :—Gewaldleðrum habenis, Wrt. Voc. ii. 110, 24. Gewealdleþerum, 42, 60. Hē welt þām gewealdleþerum ealle gesceaftu rerum regens flectit habenas, Bt. 39, 13; F. 234, 22. Gewelt-leþrum, Met. 29, 77. Þā gewealdleþeru onlǣtan þāra brīdla frena remittere, 11, 75.

**ge-weallan.** Substitute : I. of liquids, to boil :—Ofer ðās giscæft wætres ðió from fȳre giualla (fervescere) bið gesēne, Rtl. 101, 26. II. fig. to be fervent :—Giualla in Godes lufu ferveat in caritate, Rtl. 105, 3.

**ge-weardian.** v. ge-wardod.

**ge-wearmian.** Add :—Gewearmode intepuit, incaluit, Germ. 401, 25. Nǣfre hē his þā wǣtan hrægl and þā cealdan āsettan wolde oððæt hī of his seolfes līchaman gewearmedon (calefierent) and ādrūgedon, Bd. 5, 12; Sch. 633, 6. Tō þæs eald þe hē ne mihte gewearmigan būton æt fȳre, Nar. 18, 15.

**ge-wearnian.** v. ge-warenian.

**ge-weaxan.** Add : I. to grow, be produced. (1) of animals or plants :—Eall se dǣl sē þe þæs treówes on twelf mōnþum geweaxeþ (-wexð, v. l.), Bt. 34, 10; F. 150, 1. Swā hwā swā gebyrgde þæs on þām beáme geweóx, Gen. 483 : Rä. 78, 6. Ealles ðæs ðe him on heora ceápe geweaxe (cf. ealra þīnra wæsma, Deut. 14, 22), Ll. Th. ii. 432, 29. Weard hrædlīce micel mennisc geweaxen, Hml. Th. i. 20, 21. Alle ðā ðe gewæxen sint mē omnia quae nata sunt mihi, Lk. L. 12, 42. (2) of other things. (a) material :—Wolceno blōstme giwēxon nubes rore concrescunt, Rtl. 81, 24. (b) non-material :—Ne gewexþ (-wyxþ, v. l.) him nān weorþscipe on þǣm no honour accrues to them in that, Bt. 35, 4; F. 162, 28. Hyt gelimpeð ǣfre binnan feówer geára fæce þ ān dæg and ān niht gewixst, Angl. viii. 306, 12. Ungemetlíc cele geweóx on þone ǣfen frigus ingens uespertino accrescebat tempore, Nar. 23, 11. Micil in ūrum bōcum dwola gewǣxe magnus in nostris codicibus error inolevit, Mt. p. 3, 4. II. of growth in animals or plants, to grow, grow up :—Cirus, mid ðon þe hē geweóx, mox ut adolevit, Ors. 1, 12; S. 52, 17. Se cnæht geweóx puer crescebat, Lk. L. R. 1, 80. Ne geweóx hē him tō willan, B. 1711. Mið ðȳ gewōx cum crevisset herba, Mt. L. 13, 26. Gewōx ł gewæxe creverit, 32. Se beám geweóx heáh tō heofenum, Dan. 563. Beó weodewe oð þæt mīn sunu geweaxe (crescat), Gen. 38, 11. Him (a tree) on æðele bið þæt hit on holte hȳhst geweaxe, Met. 13, 52. Gewæxe crescere, Mt. L. 13, 30 : Mk. p. 3, 5. Geweaxen adultus, Wrt. Voc. ii. 90, 39 : 3, 21 : 6, 29. Hē lætt hī (children) habban āgenne cyre, þonne hī geweaxne beóð, Hml. Th. i. 20, 19. III. to grow, increase, wax :—Seó geogoð geweóx, magodriht micel, B. 66. Þte gemonigfaldade ł gewōxe him quod abundabat illis, Mk. L. 12, 44. IV. to prosper, flourish, make progress, grow in grace, &c. :—Se Hǣlend geweóx mið snytro Iesus proficiebat sapientia, Lk. L. R. 2, 52. Gedoefenlic is þte gewōx (crescere), Jn. p. 4, I. Fore gewōxun proficiunt, Mt. p. 9, 18. Tō uæstm giuæxe sáula ad fructum proficiat animorum, Rtl. 9, 9. Nōht geuæxe ł geðii (proficiet) se fiónd in ðǣm, 179, 5. Gūð sceal in eorle geweaxan, and

wīf geþeón mid hyre leódum, Gn. Ex. 85. Heofenlicere cystinesse dugeþgyfe gewexen cnæplingc supernae liberalitatis munificentia mactus puer, An. Ox. 2578. IVa. to flourish for a person, be advantageous to :—Suā huæt from mē ðē gewæxe (giwexe, R.) quodcumque ex me tibi profuerit, Mk. L. 7, 11. [O. H. Ger. ge-wahsan crescere, adolere, exolere.] v. eft-, in-, un-gewēaxen.

**ge-weaxness,** e; f. Increase; interest on money, usury :—Se slāwa þeów þone onfangenau talent from his hlāforde būtan geweaxnysse (cf. mid þām gafole cum usura, Mt. 25, 27; mid gestreóne cum usuris, Lk. 19, 23) āhȳdde on eorþan, Hml. S. 23 b, 15.

**ge-weccan.** I. to rouse from sleep :—In scip slēpende from frohtendum gewaehten wæs in nave dormiens a periclitantibus excitatus, Mt. p. 15, 18. I a. to rouse from the sleep of death, raise the dead :—Foerende ðā deáda gewæcca dohter uadens mortuam suscitare filiam :— Mk. p. 3, 7. Geweht þ mǣden suscitans puellam, Mt. p. 16, 3. II. to excite, stir up :—Ðā biscopas gewehtun (-wæhton, L.) ðone ðreót pontifices concitauerunt turbam, Mk. R. 15, 11.

**ge-wēd.** Add : foolishness; dementia :—Eálā ungesǣligra Iūdēa bewēpendlic gewēd O infelicium Iudeorum deflenda dementia, An. Ox. 40, 1. Menn unwislīce dōð þā þe dwollīce plegað æt deádra manna līce, . . . þonne hī sceoldon swȳðor besārgian þone deádan and biddan for his sāwle būtan gewēde, Hml. S. 21, 312.

**ge-wēd** obliquus. v. ge-wēn : ge-weddian to weed. Dele.

**ge-weddian** to betroth. Add :—Geweddade subarravit (nuptiali dote), Wrt. Voc. ii. 85, 71 : (cum dote fidei), 95, 2. Ðā geweddodan fǣmnan hire yldran ne mōton syllan ōðrum men puellam desponsatam non licet parentibus suis dare alteri viro, Ll. Th. ii. 146, 20.

**ge-weder.** Dele -wider, -wyder, and add : v. un-geweder, ge-widere; ge-wedfæstan. v. wed-fæstan in Dict. : ge-wef. v. ge-wefe.

**ge-wefan.** Add :—Ic wefe texo, gewefen texta, Wülck. Gl. 188, 9. I. literal :—Þicce gewefen hrægl pavidensis vestis, þenne gewefen hrægl levidensis, Wrt. Voc. i. 40, 11, 12. Cyrtel giwefen (geuoefen, L.) ðerh alle tunica contexta per totum, Jn. R. 19, 23. Web rislum and pihtine wæs gewefen peplum radiis et pectine tenebatur, An. Ox. 3742. Mid gewefenum wǣfelsa consuta plecta, 2391. Gewefene contexta (serta), 3935. II. figurative :—Ic (the creation) eall ymbwinde gewefen wundorcræfte, Rä. 41, 85. Of Crīste wið tō God endebrednis gegeadred bið ł gewefen a Christo usque ad Deum ordo contexitur, Lk. p. 4, 10. [O. H. Ger. ge-weban texere, con-, in-texere.] v. gold-gewefen.

**ge-wefe.** Substitute : ge-wef, es ; n. I. what is woven, a web :—Wāgryfta gewef curtinarum textura, Wrt. Voc. ii. 77, 12. II. text ?, context :—Actiuum opus . . . , enarratiuum . . . Gyt ys þridde cynn þǣre rake . . . commune . . . Sē þe wylle ymbe þæs gerīmes deópnyssa spyrian, þonne mæg hē gemētan þisra þreóra cynna rake on þām gewefe þ wē willað þ se sceáwre wite mid fullum gerāde þe þis gewrit āspyrað þ on þām bōccræfte sela hīw synt āmearcode, Angl. viii. 330, 35–331, 2. [O. H. Ger. ge-web textura.]

**ge-wegan.** Add :—I. to bear, have a feeling. v. wegan ; IV. 3 :— Hē wynne gewigeð, Reim. 76. II. to weigh. (1) to weigh in a balance, measure by weight :—In swā hwelce giwēge giwegen gī bióðon eft giwegen bið iów in qua mensura mensi fueritis remetietur uobis, Mk. R. 4, 24. (2) to weigh, be of a certain weight :—þ man myclade þ ordālȳsen þ hit gewege (gewǣge, v. l.) þrȳ pund, Ll. Th. i. 224, 14. Drince on wætere betonican dustes þ ænne pening gewege, Lch. ii. 134, 26 : 18, 4. Nime betonican þ wille þrȳ penegas gewegan, 150, 18. (3) of a weight, to be the equivalent in weight of a certain amount :— Genim betonican swilce swā .III. penegas gewegen, Lch. ii. 52, 13. Swilce swā twēgen penegas gewegen, 64, 17. Swilc swā þrȳ penegas gewegen, 7. [Goth. ga-wigans coagitatus : O. H. Ger. ge-wegan librare, ponderare, appendere ; ge-wegan ; pp. coagitatus.]

**ge-wēlan.** v. ge-wilwan : ge-weldan. v. ge-wildan.

**ge-welgian.** Add :—Gewelegade donat, Wrt. Voc. ii. 141, 72. Ge-welegodum a predito, 2, 3. I. to become rich :—Ellenrōf ūp āstondeð, þrymme gewelgað (becomes enriched with glory, becomes glorious), Pa. 41. II. to make rich. (1) of material wealth. (a) the object a person. (a) to bestow wealth on another :—Ðet ic geweolegie ut ditem (diligentes me), Kent. Gl. 252. God ne hēt ūs gewelegian þā hæbbendan, Wlfst. 287, 24. (β) to make oneself rich :—Gif hē beó gewelegod tō þām þ (gif hē geþeó þ, v. l.) hē āge .v. hȳda landes, Ll. Th. i. 188, 19 : 186, 18. Ne bið geweolegad non ditabitur, Kent. Gl. 789. Þ dū sió geweolugad ut diteris, 861. (γ) the subject the material wealth :—þā welan þisses middangeardes nānne mon geweligian ne magon, Bt. 13 ; F. 38, 37. (b) the object a thing :—Eorðan geweolgian terram locupletare, Ps. Srt. 64, 10. (2) of non-material wealth :—Sió gewelegodest mid þīnum tōcyme, Bl. H. 89, 32. Ungeendedum edleáni[ende] forebeácnum wæs gewelgod infinitis remuneratore prodigiis donatur, An. Ox. 2551. Gewelgode prosperabantur, 3630. Þā sāwla þe beóð gewelgode mid gōdum geearnuncgum, Ps. Th. 44, 13. Æt þām sācergewelgode mid wundorlicre dum . . . , þā wǣron geweolgade (-welgode, v. l.) mid wundorlicre sōðfæstnesse and bilwitnesse a sacerdotibus mira veritate et simplicitate praeditis, Gr. D. 250, 6.

**ge-welhwǽr.** *Add:*—þæs hádes men þe hwỹlum wǽron nyttoste . . . , þá syndon nú unnyttaste gewelhwǽr, Ll. Th. ii. 322, 22.

**ge-welhwilc.** *Add:*—On corne and on flexe and on gewelhwylcon wæstme, Wlfst. 310, 23.

**ge-wḗman.** *Add:*—Fylstende and geḗcende and gewḗmende *adstipulans,* Wrt. Voc. ii. 9, 40. **I.** *to allure* to (1) what is right, desirable :—Oft mon sceal ðone welegan ofermódan tó him loccian mid liðelicre ólicunga, for ðǽm ðæt hḗ hine tó ryhte geweeme (-wḗme, *v. l.*) *nonnunquam superbus dives exhortationis blandimento placandus est,* Past. 183, 20. His þeáwas tó Godes willan gewḗman, R. Ben. 99, 20. His leóda tó Gode gewḗman, Hml. S. 26, 51. Tó þan sóþan geleáfan gewǽmed, Lch. iii. 442, 6. (2) what is wrong, undesirable :—Hwí woldest þú ámyrran mín áncennedan sunu þurh þínne drýcræft and tó þínum Crīste gewḗman, Hml. S. 4, 199. **II.** *to allure* from (1) what is right, desirable :—Gif úre mágas willað ús gewḗman fram Crīste, Hex. 40, 29. Gehwylce men þe hē mihte hē ongan gewḗman (lǽran, *v. l.*) fram his neósunge, Gr. D. 117, 11. (2) what is wrong, undesirable :—Hē wæs biddende þ beó Chrisantum gewḗmde fram Crīste mid sprǽce, Hml. S. 35, 86. Gif þú wille þínne sunu gewḗman fram Crīste, 40.

**ge-wemman.** *Add:*—Gewemmed *infractus,* Wrt. Voc. ii. 48, 80. Gewemde *infecta,* 47, 60. **I.** *physical, to disfigure, mar, blemish :*—Gelícost ðǽm ðe hē gewemme ealne ðone líchoman *quasi totum corpus exasperat,* Past. 73, 1. Næs hyra wlite gewemmed, Dan. 437. **I a.** *to destroy :*—‘Anlícnes, sǽnd mycel wæter . . . swá þæt sién gewemmede ealle þá on þisse ceastre syndon’ (cf. þæt þú on þis folc forð onsende wæter tó wera cwealme, An. 1509) . . . sió onlícnes sendde mycel wæter swá sealt, and hit æt manna líchaman and hit ácwealde heora bearn, Bl. H. 245, 22. **II.** *to impair, diminish :*—Gif ǽnig wylle þás úre sylena gewemman and gewonian on ǽnigum þingum, Cht. E. 242, 21. His miht bið á ēce, his rīce ne bið gewemmed, Bl. H. 31, 27. **III.** *to impair the quality of, corrupt, degrade, profane,* (1) the object personal :—Ðæt mód bið gewemmed mid ðæs anwaldes heánesse *animus potentiae fastigio corrumpitur,* Past. 113, 20 : 313, 25. (2) the object a thing :—Gewaniað hié ðone hád and gewemmað *superioris loci meritum diminuunt,* Past. 413, 2. Þú gewemdest his hálignesse *profanasti sanctitatem ejus,* Ps. Th. 88, 32. Ðý lǽs ðá smyltnesse ðæs dómes gewemme se dierna ǽfst *ne tranquillitatem judicii latens invidia maculet,* Past. 79, 13. Ðý lǽs ðá rúmmódnessa sió unrótnes gewemme *ne largitatem tristitia corrumpat,* 323, 10. Ðonne sió hálignes monnes lífes bið mid eordlícum weorcum gewemmed (*polluitur*), 133, 22. **IV.** *to pollute, defile,* (1) the object personal :—Ðæt gecyndelíce gewitt bið gewemmed mid ðǽm ðe hit cnyssað on unrihta wilnunga *naturales sensus pulsantis concupiscentiae corruptione vitiantur,* Past. 405, 6. For hwý bið se ryhtwísa gecostod mid yfle geðóhte, and ne bið ðeáh gewemed mid ðǽre scylde *tentatur, et tamen eum culpa non inquinat,* 423, 24. (2) the object a thing :—Þú cennest and þínne mægþhád nó ne gewemmest, Bt. H. 9, 1. Heora yrmð áfeormað þæt þæt seó gehwǽde oferflówendnys gewemð, Hml. Th. i. 332, 14. Hié gewemmað ðone áliéfdan gesinscipe mid ðǽre unliéfedan gemengnesse *pulchram copulae speciem admixtis voluptatibus foedant,* Past. 397, 13. Of gewemmedum racum *probrosis factionibus,* An. Ox. 2, 119. **IV a.** *of improper sexual intercourse.* v. ge-wemmend :—Gewemde *incestans (germani thalamum),* Wrt. Voc. ii. 90, 50. Nán man mé gewemde, ac Crist geheóld míne clǽnnysse, Hml. S. 30, 359. Gif hwá þæs cyninges brýde gewemde, Hml. Th. ii. 476, 28. Gewemmendes forligres *maculantis prostibuli,* An. Ox. 4964. [*O. H. Ger.* ge-wemmen *polluere, corrumpere.*] v. un-gewemmed.

**ge-wemmedlic;** *adj. Corruptible:*—His líc weard . . . eft ymbe feówer geár ansund búton gewemmedlicre brosnunge (búton womme gebrosnunge *sine macula corruptionis,* Bd. 3, 19 ; Sch. 284, 3) on óðre stówe bebyríged, Hml. Th. ii. 348, 8. v. un-gewemmedlic.

**ge-wemmedlíce.** *Take here* ge-wemmodlíce *in Dict., and add* v. un-gewemmedlíce.

**ge-wemmedness.** *Add :* **I.** *physical, impurity:*—Ðá ðe Crīste folgiað on hwītum gyrlum ; and hī standað ætforan his drymme bútan ǽlcere gewemmednysse, Hml. Th. i. 90, 2. **I a.** *corruption, decay, death :*—Gewemmednysse *corruptionis,* i. *mortis,* An. Ox. 3999. Hē búton ǽlcere gewemmednysse wuldrað mid Gode . . . him nán þing wiðinnan ne eglað ǽnigre brosnunge oððe gewǽcednysse, Hml. Th. ii. 552, 24. **II.** *moral, corruption, pollution, impurity :*—Gewemmednysse *corruptionis (humanae spurcitiis carens),* An. Ox. 3712. Mid þon gewunon þǽre gewemmednesse synna and mána full, Bl. H. 75, 6. **II a.** *of improper sexual intercourse :*—Geheald þás þíne þínena wið ǽlcere gewemmednysse, Hml. Th. ii. 478, 10. **II b.** *an impure action :*—Hī férdon on heora ídelum lustum and on gewemmednyssum, Ælfc. T. Grn. 17, 15. v. un-gewemmedness.

**ge-wemmend,** es ; *m. An adulterer, a fornicator.* v. ge-wemman ; **IV a** :—Gewemmend and forligend *mechus,* Wrt. Voc. ii. 57, 58.

**ge-wemmendlic;** *adj. Corrupting, polluting :*—Mid gewemmendlicum hīwungum *commentis lenocinnantibus,* i. *maculantibus (illectus),* An. Ox. 2912.

**ge-wemming.** *Add :*—Náht framað fǽmnhád líchaman þár byð geworht gewemmincg (*corruptio*) módes, Scint. 69, 8. Gewemmincge *lenocinii (spurca ludibria),* An. Ox. 2, 318. Cwelmbęre gewemmincce ęttre *pestiferum praeuaricationis uirus,* 11, 84.

**ge-wemness.** v. ungewemness : **ge-wḗn** *hope.* *Dele.*

**ge-wḗn.** þ. -wḗde ; þþ. -wḗd *To make crooked* (wóh) :—*Depravat,* i. *maculat, confundit vel* geweþ *flectat,* Wrt. Voc. ii. 138, 82. Ðone hió gewḗde *obuncabat* (quem nefandis ulnarum gremiis procax *obuncabat,* Ald. 40, 11. Cf. *obuncabat,* i. *reflectebat* beclypte, gebīgede, An. Ox. 2956), Angl. xiii. 33, 155. Gewḗd *obliquus,* Lch. i. lxi, 7 ; Hpt. 31, 9, 168.

**ge-wḗnan.** *Add :* **I.** *to think, suppose :*—Nallað giwoena þte ic forhyccende sié iówih *nolite putare quia ego accusaturus sim uos,* Jn. R. 5, 45. Gewḗnede forþrǽste *putabantur obtruncata,* An. Ox. 803. **II.** *to think probable, expect :*—Ne þ gewoene þ mǽge styrnisse giworða *that a tumult need not be expected* ; ne forte tumultus fieret, Mk. R. 14, 2. **III.** *to hope for :*—þá hwíle ðe ðǽr bið gewḗned ǽnig behreówsung, Hml. Th. ii. 340, 6. [*Goth.* ga-wḗnjan *aestimare : O. H. Ger.* ge-wánen *putare.*] v. un-gewḗned.

**ge-wend.** *l.* ge-wind ; *q. v.*

**ge-wendan.** *Add :* **I.** *trans.* To cause to move, turn :—Geuuendit *transferit,* Wrt. Voc. ii. 122, 72. (1) *to give a certain direction or position to :*—Stande hē on ðám stede þe se abbod swá gēmeleásum monnum tó stealle on sundrum betǽht hæfð, swá þæt hē sý gewend fram þám abbode and fram eallum his gefērum (but the Latin is : Stet in loco quem talibus neglegentibus seorsum constituerit abba, ut *videatur* (glossed by *si gewarnod,* R. Ben. I. 76, 7) ab ipso vel ab omnibus. Cf. ge-wand *for another possible meaning of* gewend *in this passage*), R. Ben. 68, 12. (2) *to bring* to a condition :—Hē Lazarum tó lífe gewende, Hml. S. 23, 432. Gewended tó wuldre, El. 1047. (3) *to turn* from one condition to another :—Middangeard in ðíostrum giwoendad is *mundus in tenebris conversus est,* Rtl. 123, 37. (3 a) of the ripening of grain, fruit, &c. (or under **III,** as *to turn* is used now of grain) :—Wurdon eorðwæstmas eall tó medemlíce gewende, Chr. 1095 ; P. 232, 14. On Ianuarii mónðe gyf hit þunred, hit bodeþ tóweard mycele windes and wel gewænde eorðe wæstme . . . wæstmas wel gewænde . . . wæstme wel gewænde, Angl. x. 185, 5, 8, 12. Hit bið windig læinten and ealle wæstmes yfeles gewænde, xl. 369, 16. (3 b) *to turn* from one language to another, *translate :*—Hē þás bóc hæfde of Lǽdene tó Engliscum spelle gewende, Bt. prooem. ; F. viii. 9. **II.** *reflex. to turn* oneself :—Ne gewend þú þē nó on þæs folces unrǽd *nec plurimorum acquiesce sententiae,* Ll. Th. i. 54, 6. **III.** *intrans.* (1) *of motion.* (a) *to come, go,* the direction or destination being determined by adv. or prep. phrase, (a) where the subject (material or non-material) acts :—Sibb iuer tó iuh eft gewoendas (*reuertatur*), Mt. L. 10, 13. Se here gewende ábuton (eástweard, eft úp on Eást-Seaxan, geond þ land), Chr. 1009 ; P. 139, 14 : 998 ; P. 131, 12 : 1016 ; P. 151, 6 : 1001 ; P. 133, 19. Se cyning gewende ofer æt Brentforda, 1016 ; P. 150, 7. Hē út gewende, 1009 ; P. 138, 17. Heó gewende ongeán . . . seó þe þider gelǽd wæs, Hml. Th. ii. 24, 15. Eft gewende *rediit,* Mt. p. 17, 1. Eft gewoende *recessit,* Mt. L. 2, 14. Gewoende ðona *secessit,* 22 : 4, 12. Gewend tógeánes Amalek, Hml. S. 13, 7. Gif hwá of fyrde gewende, Ll. Th. i. 310, 28. Þæt hē gewende wið Iulianes, Hml. Th. i. 450, 32. Beád mann þ ǽlc mann ȝe feor wǽre forð gewende, Chr. 1016 ; P. 147, 6. Gif hit Crist ús ne behéte, and for ði tó middanearde gewende, Hml. Th. ii. 412, 13. Seó unfriðflota wæs gewend tó Ricardes ríce, Chr. 1000 ; P. 133, 16. ¶ with reflex. dat. :—Hī gewendon heom tó ðám cynge, Chr. 1046 ; P. 169, 2. (β) where the subject is acted on :—Hī of eorðan cómon, and eft tó dúste gewendað, Hml. S. 12, 20. His sáwul gewende tó helle, Hml. Th. i. 20, 10. Oð þæt þú eft gewende tó þǽre ylcan eorþan þe þú of cóme, Hml. S. 12, 24. (b) *to return.* (a) the subject active :—An gewoende *unus reuertitur,* Lk. p. 9, 9. ¶ with reflex. dat. :—Hī gewendon him hám *they returned home,* Hml. S. 25, 439. (β) the subject passive :—Þú tó dúste gewendst, Hml. S. 12, 26. Oþ þæt þú gewende tó eorþan of þǽre þe þú genumen wǽre, Gen. 3, 19. (c) *to turn round :*—Ðý lǽs gewoende (*conversi*) tóslítas iúh, Mt. L. 7, 6. (2) of action, *to turn* to a subject, *turn* to a person :—Hē gewende tó Gode mid eallre heortan, Hml. S. 26, 266. Buton hī tó rihte gewendan, Ll. Th. i. 348, 30. Ðis folc nis nó gewend tó ðǽm ðe hié swingð, Past. 267, 6. Gewoendet tó ðē, Lk. L. 17, 4. (3) of condition :—On hine seolfne gewoende in *se reuersus,* Lk. L. 17, 4. Ðæt ðæt mód ne gewende on selflíce and on ofermētto *that the mind may not come to be proud,* Past. 147, 2. (4) *to change* into :—Hú sió ádl gewent on wæterbollan, Lch. ii. 168, 2. [*Goth.* ga-wandjan : *O. Sax.* giwendian : *O. H. Ger.* ge-wenten.]

**ge-wendedlic, -wendendlic.** v. ungewendendlic : **ge-wḗne.** *Dele,* and see ge-wḗnan ; **II.**

**ge-wenge.** *Add :*—Þonne þú geslegen sié on án gewenge, wænd þ óðer tó, R. Ben. 28, 1. v. wang.

**ge-wenian.** *Take here* ge-wǽnian *in Dict., and add :* **I.** *to accustom, train, make habitual to :*—Tunglu him healdað betwuh sibbe singale, dydon swá lange, swá hí gewenede wuldres ealdor æt frum-

sceafte (cf. healdaþ þá tunglu þá ealdan sibbe ðe hí on gesceapne wǽron, Bt. 39, 13; F. 232, 26), Met. 29, 6. **I a.** *to train to do something* :—Martinus wæs gewenod tó wǽpnum fram cildháde, Hml. S. 31, 16. Ylpas getemode and tó wíge gewenode mid wundorlicum cræfte, 25, 559. **I b.** with complementary adjective, *to make tame* :—Wudufuglas wel átemede þeáh heora láreówas him biódan þá ilcan mettas ðe hí ǽr tame mid gewenedon (*with which they made them tame*. Cf. þone ilcan mete þe se láreów hí ǽror mid tame getéde, Met. 13, 44), Bt. 25; F. 88, 18. **II.** *to draw, attract to or from.* v. ge-wenian; II. *in Dict.*, and wenian; II.

**ge-weorc.** *Add :* **I.** *operative action, operation.* v. weall-geweorc, (2). **II.** *working.* (1) *making* of material objects :—Hé þær hræde geweorce (*citato opere*) of treówe cyricean getimbrede, Bd. 2, 14; Sch. 170, 9. (1 a) with gen. of object :—*Figmenta*, i. *plasmatio hominum* (cf. De figmento : de plasmatione hominis, Ld. Gl. H. 36, 164) geweorc, Wrt. Voc. ii. 35, 47. Geweorce (*in rerum visibilium*) plastica, An. Ox. 5222. Fram þæs temples geweorce tó Cristes ðrowunge *from the building of the temple to the crucifixion*, Angl. xi. 9, 31. Fram fremðe middangeardes oð Róme burhge geweorc, Angl. xi. 5, 19. Oþ þæs temples geweorc, 9, 17. (2) *doing* of operations :—Sé þe Drihtne hýreð and hys willan wyrceð : wel him þæs geweorkes, Hy. 2, 11. Þurh his wundra geweorc *through his doing miracles*, Gú. 500. v. frum-geweorc. **III.** *in a collective sense, work, doings* :—Woldon þá gigántas tóbrecan ðone heofon under him (*Jove*). Ðá sceolde hé sende lýgetu and windas and tówyrpan eall hira geweorc mid *lacessenteis coelum gigantes benigna fortitudo deposuit*, Bt. 35, 4; F. 162, 14. **IV.** *work, labour, any form of long-sustained or habitual activity* :—Gýme gafolswán þ hé æfter sticunge his slyhtswýn wel behweorfe, sæncge, ðonne bið hé ful wel gewyrces wyrðe, Ll. Th. i. 436, 17. Hwanon fiscere ancgel . . .? nis hit of mínon geweorce?, Coll. M. 30, 35. Þ hí férdon on þæt geweorc þæs Godes wordes, Bd. 1, 23; Sch. 50, 1. v. æfen-, brycg-, ealu-, fæsten-, land-, stán-, sulh-, tigel- (1), timber-, weall- (1), web-geweorc. **IV a.** a particular case of labour, *labour* for a particular object :—Þis is þære bricce geweorc on Hrouecæstre *this is the work that has to be done on the bridge at Rochester*, C. D. B. iii. 659, 1. v. tigel-geweorc (2). **IV b.** *workmanship* :—Ðær wæs cyrice geworht and getimbrad wundorlices geweorces (*mirandi operis*), Bd. 1, 7; Sch. 27, 7. Án gylden calic swíðe wundorlices geweorces, Chr. 1058; P. 189, 20. **V.** *a work, deed, action.* v. gúþ-, níþ-, undern-, wuldor-, wundor-geweorc. **VI.** *a work, what is made* :—Weblic gewurc *textrinum opus*, Hpt. Gl. 431, 4. Þá micclan mǽrða, þ syndan ðá geweorc þe Alexander hét gewyrcean *magna insignia que Alexander operari jusserat*, Nar. 33, 20. v. græft-, heáh-, ofer-geweorc. **VI a.** *a* (person's) *work* (with gen. of agent or tool) :—Beaduscrúda betst, Wélandes geweorc, B. 455 : Vald. 1, 2. Godes geweorc, Gen. 604. Enta geweorc, Wand. 87 : Gn. C. 2. Giganta geweorc, B. 1562. Wundorsmiða geweorc, 1681. Carcernes duru, homra geweorc, Jul. 237. Eall his ágen geweorc Drihten bletsige *benedicite Dominum omnia opera ejus*, Ps. Th. 102, 21. His ciricean, his ágen geweorc (cf. hé hié mid his sylfes handum geworhte, 14), Bl. H. 197, 7. v. ǽr-, eald-, fyrn-, hand-geweorc. **VI b.** of buildings :—Hí cwǽdan þ þ templ wǽre þrymlic geweorc, Bl. H. 77, 32. Wiðinnan þám níwan geweorce, Hml. S. 21, 23. Ceastra, . . . weallstána geweorc, Gn. C. 3. v. súþ-, templ-, treów-geweorc. **VI c.** *what is wrought, material prepared by labour* :—Templ of ísernum geweorcum and of ǽrenum geworht *templum aereo et ferreo opere constructum*, Nar. 37, 23. v. ál-, ár-, feþer-, fián-, gold-, stán-geweorc.

**geweorc-líc**; adj. *Of work* :—Weblic, geweorclic *textrinum*, An. Ox. 1042. v. ge-weorc; VI.

**ge-weornian**; p. ode *To wither away, dry up* :—Eall þ mænnisce cyn forslagen geweornode *humanum genus succism aruit*, Gr. D. 258, 13.

**ge-weorodlǽcan** *to sweeten* :—On welerum his býð geweredlǽhþ feónd *in labiis suis indulcatur inimicus*, Scint. 196, 5.

**ge-weorp.** *Dele* 'A throwing, . . . dashing,' and for first passage substitute :—Him þá beorna breogo, þær hé on bolcan sæt, ofer waroða geweorp wið þingode *with him (Andrew) the prince of men, from his seat on the gangway*, across the sands held parley (the boat was close to land, cf. in ceól stigon ellenrófe, 349, so that the words spoken passed over the beach, not over water), An. 306. [*O. H. Ger.* ge-werf *collecta, conlatio.*] v. sand-geweorp.

**ge-weorpan.** *Add :* **I.** *to throw, cast* :—Mann hæfð inngang swá micelre brǽdo swá man mæg mid líþeran geweorpan *habet ingressum amplitudinis quasi iactus fundae*, Bd. 4, 13; Sch. 421, 16. **I a.** where the direction or end of throwing is marked :—Hé beheóld huu ðe here giwarp ðæt mæslen on gazophilacium, and monige weolge giwurpun feolu *aspiciebat quomodo turba iactaret aes in gazophilacium, et multi diuites iactabant multa*, Mk. R. 12, 41. Þte sé geworpen in sǽ *proiciatur in mare*, Lk. L. R. 17, 2. Þ salt bið geworpen út *mittatur foras*, Mt. L. 5, 13. Geworpene *iactari* (*in ardentes thermarum vapores*), An. Ox. 4781. **II.** where a change of position is caused by force, *to cast*

in or out :—Gewarpp ða bibyccenda *ejicit vendentes*, Mt. p. 18, 17. Of ðær gewarp (*eiecerat*) seofa diówles, Mk. L. R. 16, 9. Hine gewurpon ł fordrifon búta ðæm wíngeard, Mt. L. 21, 39. Gif égo ðín geondspornað ðec geworp (*eice*) hine, Mk. L. R. 9, 47. Ðú gesiist geworpe ðone mot, Mt. L. 7, 5. Geworpa diówblas, Lk. L. R. 11, 18. **III.** where an object is moved to a position of rest, *to lay* :—Hæsdon mid him dumbo, blindo . . . and geworpen (*lægdun, R., projecerunt*) hiá tó sótum his, Mt. L. 15, 30. Honda geworpun (*injecerunt*) on ðone Hǽlend, 26, 50. **IV.** *to reach by throwing, throw and catch* :—Se lytega feónd ðæs ǽrestan monnes mód gewearp mid synne gríne *hostis callidus primi hominis sensum in peccati laqueo strinxit*, Past. 309, 18. [*Goth.* ga-wairpan : *O. H. Ger.* ge-werfan.]

**ge-weorþan.** *Add :* **I.** *absolute.* (1) *to come to be* :—Þurh þá fonthálgunge þær gewyrð sóna Godes midwist, Wlfst. 36, 2. Stefn mín gehéred and bið ł geuordes (*fiet*) án plette, Jn. L. 10, 16. Sóðfæstnise ðerh ðone Hǽlend geuærð (*is geworden, W. S., facta est*), 1, 17. Þá gesceafta ne gewurdon ðurh hí sylfe, ac hí geworhte God, Hex. 20, 28. Cwæð hé : 'Geweorðe leóht'; and leóht wæs þærrihte geworden, Lch. iii. 232, 8. Swiðost þára cyninga þe ǽr him gewurde, Chr. 959; P. 114, 21. (2) *to be made*, where an object (material or non-material) results from a person's action :—Mycel wæl gewearð, Chr. 592; P. 21, 10. Symbel geuard (*wæs gemacud, W. S.*) *cena facta*, Jn. L. 13, 2. Gesomnung geweard (*gewordene gecwydrǽdene, W. S.*) *conuentione facta*, Mt. L. 20, 2. Búta him geuorden is (*næs geworht, W. S.*) nóht, Jn. L. 1, 3. Middangeard ðerh hine geuorden (*geworht, W. S.*) uæs, 10. Gebed apostolum gewordne *oratione apostolis facta*, Lk. p. 3, 4. (3) *to come to pass.* (a) of an event, occurrence, action, *to happen, take place, be done.* (a) the subject a noun (pronoun) :—Gif gængang geweorðeð, Ll. Th. i. 24, 7. Swylce þing gewurðaþ for folces synna, Chr. 1086; P. 218, 6. Þá gewearð þæt þridde gewinn Rómana and Cartaina *tertium Punicum bellum exortum est*, Ors. 4, 13; S. 210, 15 : p. 5, 2. Ðis all geweard, Mt. L. 1, 22. Gewearþ mycelu eorþstyrung, Bl. H. 193, 10. Monega wundor gewurdon, Ors. 4, 8; S. 188, 21 : Mt. L. R. 27, 54. Ðý lǽs ungerecc geworde, Mt. L. 26, 5. Undernam Godwine swýðe þ on his eorldóme sceolde swilc geweorðan, Chr. 1052; P. 175, 8. Tó þám mǽsten swicdóme þe ǽfre mihte gewurðan, 1086; P. 221, 31. Þis wæs geworden (-wurden, *v. l.*) on Ciruses dæge *haec temporibus Cyri gesta sunt*, Ors. 4, 4; S. 166, 3. Fela þinga þe on ðám geáre gewordene wǽron, P. 221, 27 : Bd. pref.; Sch. 4, 15. Hé gesihð úre weorc ǽr hí gewordene sién, oððe furðum geþóht, Bt. 41, 4; S. 145, 14. Gewoerden, Mt. L. 11, 21. Geuordeno (giwordne, R.), Jn. L. 3, 21. Gewordene *exerceri*, An. Ox. 40. (aa) with indefinite, *hit* :—Man cýdde Haralde hú hit wæs þær gedón and geworden, Chr. 1066; P. 197, 14. (β) with noun as subject and clause in apposition :—Seó wyrd geweorþan sceal, þ se Scyppend gesittan wile on his dómsetle, Bl. H. 83, 10. (β a) with þæt as subject, and clause in apposition :—Þ geweorþeþ on dómes dæge, þ hé cymeþ tó démenne, Bl. H. 11, 2. (β β) with *hit* as subject, and a clause in apposition :—Gif hit ǽfre gewirð, swá hit swíþe seldon gewyrð, þæt se anweald and se weorðscipe become tó gódum men, Bt. 16, 1; S. 35, 7. Hit gewearð þæt ðám wísan men cóm tó lofe þ se cyning him tiohhode tó wíte, 16, 2; S. 36, 24. ¶ where a clause may be inferred :—Gif hit gewurðan mæg (cf. gif hyt beón mæge *si possibile est*, Mt. 26, 39), áfyrsa þisne calic fram mé, Hml. Th. 544, 16. (γ) with clause only :—Wæs geworden þ Hǽlend geneálæhte Gericho, Bl. H. 15, 15 : Past. 91, 26 : 99, 6. ¶ where the object affected by what happens is given. (1) with dat. *to happen* to :—Geweorðe (-wurþe, *v. l.*) mé æfter þínum worde, Lk. 1, 38 : Bl. H. 9, 20. (2) with prep. *to be done* about (be) :—Hwæt gewyrð be ús? *quid erit nobis?*, Hml. A. 15, 41. Oð ðæt ic wite hwæt God wille, hwæt ge mé geweorðe (-wurðe, *v. l.*) *donec sciam quid de me fieri uelit Deus*, Bd. 5, 19; Sch. 670, 14. (b) where a time or season is reached :—Gewearð efern *facto vespere*, Mt. L. 16, 2 : Mk. L. 1, 32. Morgen gewearð *mane facto*, Mt. L. 27, 1. Gewearð sunnadoeg (gewordenum restedæge, *W. S.*), Mk. L. R. 6, 2 : Lk. L. (*W. S.*), 4, 42. (4) *to come to be possessed* by a person (*dat.*), *fall* to, *come* to. (a) the subject material :—Hé begeat mid his smꜵwrencan . . . æt Steorran . . . þ him gewearð se þridda penig of þære tolne on Sandwíc, C. D. iv. 56, 30. (b) the subject non-material :—Seó hreówsung þe him þá gewearð the *repentance they had come to feel*, Ors. 1, 7; S. 38, 21. Hú mihte ǽfre englum mára gefeá and geofu and blis geweorþan, oþþe mannum mára weorðmynd þonne him on þyssum dæge gewearþ?, Bl. H. 123, 13–15. Þær wæs blis nicel eallum geworden, Chr. 973; P. 118, 10. **II.** *to become, be made.* (1) with predicative substantive :—Gié geuordas ł gié bidon míno ðegnas *efficiamini mei discipuli*, Jn. L. R. 15, 8. Hé Godes þeówa gástlic fæder gewearð, Bl. H. 217, 12. For þon gebode gewurdon fela martyra on x wintra firste *per decem annos caedibus martyrum incessabiliter acta est*, Ors. 6, 30; S. 280, 19. Him wǽre betere þæt hé ǽfre on worulde man ne gewurde, þonne hé gewearð, Hml. S. 26, 10. Geseoh þínne líchaman and loccas þínes heáfdes, hwæt hié syndon gewordene, Bl. H. 245, 7. (2) with predicative adjective :—Hé him grim geweorþeþ, Bl. H. 25, 13. Þ cúþ gewearþ, 121, 4. Hí hále gewurdon

*salui fiebant*, Mk. L. R. 6, 56. Hié bleádran gewurdon, Ors. 2, 5; S. 84, 22. Þurh hwæt seó sául eádegust gewurde, Bl. H. 159, 28. (2 a) with phrase:—Búta gié gewordce suæ lytlo (beón gewordene swá swá lytlingas, W.S.) *nisi efficiamini sicut paruoli*, Mt. 18, 3. (3) with adverb:—Mid þan hé þá wæs forhtlíce geworden for þære gesihþ *cum a visione terreretur*, Guth. Gr. 171, 21. III. with prepositions. (1) geweorþan of. (a) *to be made from, be produced from* :—Þæs wínes þe of þám wætere geworden wæs *aquam uinum factum*, Jn. 2, 9. (b) *to be produced or caused by* :—Þá þe secgað þæt þá anwaldas sién of wyrda mægenum geweordene, Ors. 2, 1; S. 62, 10. (2) geweorþan on. (a) *to get into a state* of being, or feeling, *become* the adjective connected with the noun :—Hí gewurdon on ðære séftnysse, Hml. S. 23, 261. (b) *to get into a state* of action, *fall* to :—Hí gewurdon on slǽp, Hml. S. 23, 257. (3) geweorþan tó. (a) of change in condition, *to become, turn to* :—Ðæs líchaman wlite gewyrðeð tó dúste, Hex. 50, 17. Cweð þ þás stánas tó hláfe geweorðon (tó hláfum sié gewordeno, L.) *dic ut lapides isti panes fiant*, Mt. 4, 3. Geweorðan, Bl. H. 27, 8. Tó eorðan wé sculan ealle geweorðan, Wlfst. 108, 9. Þ wæter tó uíne geworden *aquam uinum factum*, Jn. L. R. 2, 9. Is eal þín blis tó unrótnesse geworden, Bl. H. 85, 33. Heora líchoman beóþ tó dúste gewordne, 101, 2. (b) of the state to which things come, of the event of matters, *to become, come to* :—Uton geþencan tó hwám þá gewurdan þe beforan ús wǽron, and tó hwám wé gewurðan sceolon, Wlfst. 136, 9-11. Gehwá understande hwanan hé sylf cóm, and hwæt hé is, and tó hwám hé geweorðan sceal (*what he must come to*), 108, 7. (c) where a character or function is taken, *to become, turn, turn to* :—Hý gewurdan of englum tó deóflum gewordene, Wlfst. 8, 8. (d) where a result is brought about, *to become, prove a source of, be* :—Geweorðe heó tó woruldscame hire sylfre, Ll. Th. i. 406, 7. Hé þóhte þ seó ylce molde tó lǽcedóme and tó hǽlo untrumra manna geweorðan mihte *cogitans quod futurum erat, quia ad medellam infirmantium idem puluis proficeret*, Bd. 3, 10; Sch. 233, 12. (e) *to be brought to* :—Swelce sió burg wǽre ðurh ðæs sǽs stemne tó scame geworden *quasi per vocem maris ad verecundiam Sidon adducitur*, Past. 409, 35. IV. expressing movement :—Þá geweard se abb æt mid micelan fultume, and lét delfon án mycel gedelf *then the abbot came on the scene with a great force, and had a great trench dug*, C. D. iv. 58, 4. Þæt gé forlǽtan þá unnyttan sprǽca gewurðan and þá unnyttan geþancas of eówrum heortum (*that ye dismiss useless words and thoughts from your hearts*), þonne gé cumað intó Godes cyrican, Wlfst. 232, 17. Beóþ þeóstra forþ gewordene ofor ealre world, Bl. H. 93, 18. V. *to agree with*; convenire. (1) impersonal with acc. of person, *to fall in with the views of, be agreeable to, suit, seem fit, please*. (a) where action or condition pleases a person, (a) cf. (2 b a), the action not stated :—Hé déþ swá swá hine silfne gewyrþ *he does as pleases him*, Ælfc. Gen. Thw. 4, 19. Hú þone cumbolwigan wið þá mægð hæfde geworden *how pleased the warrior had been with the maid*, Jud. 260. (β) the action stated in a following clause, cf. (2 b β):—Þá geweard þone weregan þæt hé costode cyning alwihta *then it pleased the accursed one to tempt the lord of all*, Sat. 669. Ðá geweard hine ðæt hé gecierde inn tó ðæm scræfe *he found it convenient to turn into the cave*, Past. 197, 14. (γ) with gen. pronoun representing a following clause :—Hú geweard þé þæs, þæt þú sæbeorgas sécan woldes máðmum bedæled? *how could it seem fit to you to come to the coast without money?*, An. 307. Gif þæs geweorðe gesíðcundne mannan, þ hé unrihthǽmed genime *if it please a ' gesithcund' man to take to adultery*, Ll. Th. i. 38, 4. Hafað þæs geworden wine Scyldinga, þæt hé mid þý wífe wælfǽhða dǽl gesette, B. 2026. (b) where two or more persons agree to a course of action, *to be agreed, decided, settled by* persons. Cf. (2 c) (α) with clause :—Þá geweard þá senatos þæt mon eft sceolde getimbran Cartainam *Carthago restitui jussa est*, Ors. 5, 5; S. 226, 16: Sat. 256. Rómane hæfde geweordcn hwǽne ǽr þæt hé on Asiam faran sceolde *cum in Macedoniam jam deputatus esset*, Ors. 4, 12; S. 208, 28. ¶ hí geweorþan him betweónum *to be settled by persons among themselves* :—Geweard þá senatos him betweónum þæt mon ealle Cartaina tówurpe *cum senatus delendam Carthaginem censuisset*, Ors. 4, 13; S. 210, 15. Hié ealle geweard him betweónum þæt hié wolden Rómánum geswícan *cum defectionem meditarentur*, 5, 10; S. 234, 13. Þá geweard hí him betweónum þæt hié woldon þá purpuran álecgan *Diocletianus ab invito exegit Maximiliano, ut simul purpuram deponerent*, 6, 30; S. 280, 20. (β) with infinitive :—Ne meahte hié gewurðan weall timbran (*no plan could be settled because of the confusion of tongues*), Gen. 1691. (γ) with gen. of matter agreed about :—Þá hié nánre sibbe ne geweard *infecto pacis negotio*, Ors. 4, 11; S. 204, 34. Ic þé bæd þæt þú léte Súð-Dene sylfe geweorþan gúðe wið Grendel *I prayed you to let the South Danes themselves settle their quarrel with Grendel*, B. 1996. Swíðe hrædlíce þæs ðe hí þæs geworden hæfde *very soon after they had made that agreement*, Chr. 918; P. 105, 26. (c) where there is agreement as to a fact :—Þá þæs monige geweard þæt hine seó brimwylf ábroten hæfde *many agreed that the she-sea wolf had destroyed him*, B. 1596. (2) with dat. (or uncertain) of person. (a) with noun subject :—Ne sǽde ic eów þ

eówrum þeáwum and mínum ne mihte án wíse gewurðan (geþwǽrigan, *v. l.*)? *numquid non prius dixi vobis, quia vestris ac meis moribus minime conveniret?*, Gr. D. 105, 21. (b) impersonal. (a) cf. (1 a a) above :—Se hálega gást hí tódǽlþ be þám þe him gewyrð (*as it ples hym*), Angl. xi. 108, 13 : Hml. Th. i. 322, 30 : 418, 15. (β) with clause, cf. (1 a β) above :—Nú geweard ús þ wé þás bóc gedihton, Hml. S. p. 4, 43 : Ll. Th. ii. 414, 22. (c) where two or more persons (things) agree to a course of action, cf. (1 b). (a) action or condition not stated :—Ðám luste and geswencednysse náht eáðe on ánum tíman ne gewyrð, Hml. Th. ii. 92, 21. Heó hæfde þone sceatt, swá swá him geweard *data illi pecunia, quam promiserant*, Jud. 16, 21. Swá swá mé and eallan þeódscype geweard, C. D. V. 113, 31. Þ eówrum þeáwum and mínum ne mihte ætgædere gewurðan, Gr. D. 105, 21 (v. 2 a above): Hml. Th. ii. 158, 26. (β) with clause :—Þá geweard him betweónan þæt hí þá flaxan gehýddon *facto consilio flasculas absconderunt*, Guth. Gr. 151, 3 : Hml. S. 11, 139 : 12, 232. (γ) with gen. and clause :—Geweard him and þám folce ánes, þ hí hine horsian sceoldan, Chr. 1014 ; P. 145, 16. Him geweard ánes, gif ænig leódscipe wæs ungewylde þan Cásere, þonne send hé him tó swá fela eóroda, Jud. Thw. 161, 35. VI. as auxiliary, with participles. (1) of transitive verbs, *to become, get, be* :—Ðǽr gewyrð ðurh Godes mihte tóscáden þæt wered on twá, Wlfst. 26, 1. Sió stefn geweard gehéred of heofenum, An. 167. Hú geweard þé þus, fæder, ferð gebysgad?, Gú. 984. Gewyrðe his nama ádílgad *deleatur nomen ejus*, Ps. Th. 108, 13. Foretácna mǽst þára þe gewurde monnum oðýwed, Cri. 894. Cearu wæs geníwod geworden, B. 1304. Syndon hí gewordene tólýsde, Ps. Th. 72, 15. (2) of intransitive verbs, *to be, have* :—Þanon ætorcyn ǽrest gewurdon onwæcned, Sal. 219. [*O. Sax. gi-werðan : O. H. Ger. ge-werdan.*]

**ge-weorþian.** Add : I. *to make worthy, give worth to* :—Gé beóþ on gedwolan þonne gé wénaþ þ ænig mæg mid frǽmdum welum beón geweorþod. Gif hwá biþ mid hwelcum welum geweorþod . . . hú ne belimpþ se weorþscipe tó þám þe hine geweorðað, Bt. 14, 3. II. *to make worthy of something, entitle* a person to :—Biþ hé þæs ðegnes rihtes geweorþod (þegenrihtes wyrþe, *v. l.*), Ll. Lbmn. 465, 12. III. *to hold in honour, esteem, venerate* :—Hé weard wíde swíðe geweorðad, for ðám þe hé weorðode Godes naman georne, Chr. 959; P. 115, 2. Offa wæs geofum and gúðum wíde geweorðod *Offa was for liberality and bravery far and wide held in honour*, B. 1959. Þín dóm wunað wíde geweorðad, Cri. 407 : Ap. 15. IV. *to shew honour to, treat with reverence or respect* :—Se engel (*the angel in the fiery furnace*) hæfde on þám wundre gewurþod þe þá gewyrhto áhton, Dan. 444. IV a. in reference to subjects divine or sacred. (1) of honour shewn to a divinity, *to worship, adore* :—Aldro úso in móre ðisum geworðadun (*adorarunt*) and gié cuæðas þte in Hierusolymis . . . geuorðage (*adorare*) gedæfnad is . . . Gié geuorðias (*adoratis*) þ gié nutton . . . Gaast is God and ðá ðe geuorðias (*adorant*) hine . . ., Jn. L. 4, 20-24. Árísað aldormenn and giworðigað (*princes also shall worship*, Is. 49, 7), Rtl. 55, 39. Aldormonn án geneólécde and geworðade hine, Mt. L. 9, 18. Geworðade, 15, 25. Niðer gefeállon geworðadun hine *procidentes adoraverunt eum*, 2, 11 : 14, 33 : Lk. L. 24, 52. God ðinne geworða ðú, Mt. L. 4, 10. Þú gewurþod eart on heofonríce, Hy. 7, 59. (2) of reverence shewn to holy persons or seasons, *to celebrate, commemorate* :—Ðú ðe úsig allra apostola earnunga under ánum gisaldest mérsunge þte ué geworðadon ł giworðia *qui nos omnium apostolorum merita sub una tribuisti celebritate venerari*, Rtl. 124, 32. Byð tíd geweorðad Barðolomeus, Men. 154. V. *to honour* in words, *speak in honour of, celebrate, praise, glorify* :—Geworðade God *glorificabat Deum*, Lk. L. 13, 13. Gehered ofor ealle þeóda and geworðad of cilda múðe (cf. *ex ore infantium perfecisti laudem*, Mt. 21, 16), Bl. H. 71, 17. Hé mid þære sóþfæstnesse stefne gehiered wæs and geweorþod, 165, 1. Wé þé heriað, swá þú eart geworðod á on worlda ford, Hy. 7, 123. VI. *to honour* by granting what is of worth, *put in an honourable position or condition* :—Ús geweorðade Godes gǽstsunu and ús giefe sealde, uppe mid englum éce staðelas, Cri. 659. Hé þone healsbeáh Hygde gesealde . . . hyre wæs æfter beáhþege breóst geweorðod, B. 2176. Wǽrþu gewurðod for þæs eágum þe þé æsca tír forgeaf (cf. *benedictus Abram Deo excelso*, Gen. 14, 19), Gen. 2107. Þurh þone tócyme wé wǽron geweorþode and gewelgade and geárode, Bl. H. 105, 24 : 171, 32. VI a. *to honour* with something (*inst. or mid.*). (1) *to honour* a person by the grant of something (material or non-material) of worth, *enrich, endue* :—Sancta Marian þú mid heofonlicum wuldre geweorþodest, Bl. H. 89, 18. Hé his folc golde and seolfre geweorþade, Ps. Th. 104, 32. Giworðadun hine mid giwēdum his *induerunt eum uestimentis suis*, Mk. R. 15, 20. Geweorðad *donatur* (*virgo peplis donatur dominicis*, Ald. 60, 20), Wrt. Voc. ii. 85, 29. Monige siendum mid miclum giefum monegra cræfta and mægeue geweorðode *sunt nonnulli, qui eximia virtutum dona percipiunt*, Past. 41, 12. Monige men sindon þe bióð geweorðod (geweorðode, *v. l.*) mid miclum Godes gifum (*magnis muneribus ditati*), 44, 15. ¶ geweorþod *adorned* with, *decorated* with, *endowed* with, *made splendid by* :—Sum bróðor mid godcundre gyfe gemǽred and geweorþad (-wurðod, *v. l.*) *frater quidam diuina gratia insignis*, Bd. 4, 24; Sch. 481, 2.

Sit se heofonlica dēma on his heáhsettle helme gewurþod, Wlfst. 137, 17. Secg ... wǽpnum geweorðad, B. 250. Adam stóp, gáste geweorðad, Gen. 1137. Sweót ... sigore geweorðod, Jud. 299. Æðele eorlgebyrdum, welum geweorðad, Met. 10, 28. Geweorþad *fretus* (cf. (?) meterlicere getincnesse gegódod (*fretus*), An. Ox. 126), Wrt. Voc. ii. 23, 32. (2) *to adorn, decorate,* (α) an animal :—Mearh ... midlum geweorðod, El. 1193. (β) a thing :—Oft þá þeódwitan þus heora meteruers gewurðiað, Angl. viii. 332, 16 : 313, 29. Sadol ... since gewurðad, B. 1038. Geweorðad, 1450. Ælfheres láf ... golde geweorðod, Vald. 2, 18. Wuldres treów wǽdum geweorðod, ... gegyred mid golde, Kr. 15. Salem stód weallum geweorðod, Dan. 41. (3) *to honour* a place or season :—Seó stów is mid manegum godcundum wuldrum swíþe heálíce geweorþod, Bl. H. 125, 18 : 197, 12. Þes dæg is geweorþod mid manegum godcundum geofum, 133, 2. [*O. Sax.* gi-werðôn *to honour, esteem: O. H. Ger.* ge-werdôn *appretiare, dignari;* ge-werdôt *praeditus.*]

**ge-wépan.** *Add:* I. *intrans. To weep:*—Hé giweóp (-weæp, L.) ofer ða cæstre *flevit super ciuitatem,* Lk. R. 19, 41. Gewæp, Lk. p. 10, 4 : Jn. L. 20, 11. Gewaepon *flebant,* Lk. L. 8, 52. II. *trans. To weep over, lament* :—Hwæt dést þú, lá flǽsc, hwæt dreógest þú nú, hwæt miht þú on þá tíd þearfe gewépan? *quid, caro, quid facies, illa quid flebilis hora?,* Dôm. L. 176.

**ge-werdan.** v. ge-wirdan : **ge-weredlǽht.** v. ge-weorodlǽcan.

**ge-wérgian.** *Add* :—Geweárgode *lassauerat,* An. Ox. 49, 1. (1) of bodily weariness :—Ne hors ne hé sylf gewérgod wæs, Hml. S. 30, 35 : 31, 1418. (2) of mental or spiritual weariness :—Hé gewérgað his heortan suíðe hearde mid ðý gesuince *duro cor labore fatigatur,* Past. 239, 13. Geþanc metta on ídelnysse gewérgud (*lassata*) ne forspild gebedes strencðe, Scint. 50, 11. v. un-gewérigod.

**ge-werian** *to clothe. Add: to stock* land. *Take here the passages from the charters given in the Dict. under* ge-werian; I. *to defend.* [Cf. vestire *colere agrum,* Migne.]

**ge-werian** *to defend. Substitute:* I. *to dam, prevent water from flowing from.* v. werian ; I a :—Swelce mon deópne pool gewerige, Past. 283, 14. Suíðe deóp pól wǽre gewered, 279, 15. II. *to defend at law, disprove claims made in court upon property.* v. werian ; III b :—Qui terram lite tutam praestiterit, eandem possidetor. Sé þe land gewerod hæbbe be scíre gewitnesse hæbbe hé unbesacen on dæge and æfter dæge tó syllenne and tó gifenne þám þe him leófast sý, Ll. Th. i. 420, 18–22.

**ge-werian ;** *p.* ede *To come to an agreement, make a treaty* :—Nalæs æfter micelre tíde þ hí geweredon (waredon, v. l.) wið him and heora wǽpen hwyrfdon wið heora gefaran *non multo post, iuncto cum his foedere, in socios arma uerterit,* Bd. 1, 15 ; Sch. 40, 6. Hí ðá geweredon tó sumre tíde wið Pehtum *tum inito ad tempus foedere cum Pictis,* Sch. 42, 21.

**ge-wesan.** *Add:* cf. ymb : I. 3 d ; ge-wesness.

**ge-wésan.** *Add:* I. *to steep, soak* :—Genim þás ylcan wyrte, and gecnúwa hý mid smeruwe, and gewæsc (-wés, v. l.) mid ecede, Lch. i. 104, 2 : 204, 19. Genim þás wyrte and rosan wós on wíne gewésed, 214, 1. Mid ecede gewésede, 200, 9. II. *to dye* :—Flýs deáge gewésan *uellera fuco inficere,* An. Ox. 5196.

**ge-wesness,** e ; *f. Controversy, dissension* :—Þá sóhte Colmanus tó þisse gewesnisse and þisse unsibbe lǽcedôm *quaesiuit Colmanus huic dissensioni remedium,* Bd. 4, 4 ; Sch. 369, 17. Cf. ge-wesan.

**ge-wép.** v. ge-wén : **ge-wícan.** *Add:* [O. H. Ger. ge-wíchan *cedere, dis-, re-cedere, deficere.*]

**ge-wícnian ;** *p.* ode *To discharge an office* (wíce), *do service, be steward* (wícnere) :—Twá mynecena wǽron ... þám gewícnode sum eáwfæst man on woruldcarum (*duae sanctimoniales feminae ... quibus quidam religiosus vir ad exterioris vitae usum praebebat obsequium,* Gr. D. ii. c. 23), Hml. Th. ii. 174, 6.

**gewidagur?** :—Gewidagur (gewindagas??) gedón *to cause troublous times* (?) (the Latin form glossed is *derare*), Wrt. Voc. ii. 139, 7.

**ge-wíde.** *See* wíde ; II *in Dict.*

**ge-wíder.** *l.* ge-widere, *and in l.* 3 *for* gewidor abidon *l.* gewidora bidon. *Add:* The word seems to occur only in pl. :—Sumor æfter cymeð, wearm gewideru, Met. 11, 61. Of untídlican gewideran, þæt is, of wǽtum sumerum and of drýgum wintrum *temporum turbata temperies, hoc est, aut siccitas hiemis, aut humor aestatis,* Ors. 3, 3 ; S. 102, 5. Sænde ic þá gewidoru þá ealle eówre wæstmas gebétað, Wlfst. 132, 13. Bringð sumor tó túne wearme gewideru, Men. 90.

**ge-widerian** *to be* (*fair*) *weather* :—On lǽngtene beána sáwan, wíngeard settan, ... and raðe æfter ðám, gif hit mót gewiderian, mederan settan, líusêd sáwan, Angl. ix. 262, 9. v. wederian.

**ge-widerung.** v. un-gewiderung.

**ge-widlian.** *l.* -wídlian, *and add: to profane, pollute* :—Nóht is búta monnum þæt mæge hine gewídliga (*coinquinare*), ah ðá ðe of menn forcumas, ðá sindun ðá ðe giwídligas (gewídlas, L.) (*communicant*) ðone monn, Mk. R. 7, 15. Giwídligas (-egas, L.), 20. Gewídlian *profanare,* Wrt. Voc. ii. 66, 47. Þte hiá nére giwídlad (-æd, L.) *ut non*

*contaminaretur,* Jn. R. 18, 28. Mánfulles, gewídledre *fanatice* (*superstitionis*), An. Ox. 4428. Ic míne ciricean oft sóhte mid gewídlode líchoman and mid unclǽne gegierelan, Angl. xi. 99, 82.

**ge-widmǽran** (-ian) ; *p.* de, ode ; *pp.* ed, od. I. *to spread the fame of, celebrate* :—Þæs hálinysse hlísa hine sylfne gewídmǽrode (-mǽrsode, *v. l.*) feorr and wíde *cujus sanctitatis opinio sese ad notitiam hominum longe lateque tetenderat,* Gr. D. 44, 2. Hí þanon gangende gewídmǽrodon (*diffamaverunt,* v. Mt. 9, 31 (*the passage quoted*), *where the word is translated* gewídmǽrsudun. *To the same passage belongs the* gloss gewídmǽrdan (gewídmǽrsan, 26, 32) *diffamaverunt,* Wrt. Voc. ii. 72, 41) hine geond eal þ land, 60, 11. II. *to spread the knowledge of* a circumstance, *report widely* :—Wæs gewídmǽred (-mǽrsod, *v. l.*) þ hé betwih gebedes word his líf geendade *uulgatum est quod inter uerba orationis uitam finierit,* Bd. 3, 12 ; Sch. 245, 11.

**ge-widmǽrsian.** *Add:* I. *trans.* (1) *to spread the fame of a* person :—His nama wearð gewídmǽrsod wíde geond þæt land *nomen ejus uulgatum est in omni terra,* Jos. 6, 27. (2) *to spread the knowledge* of a fact, event, &c., *to publish, promulgate* :—Ðá hyrdas þá heofenlican gesíhðe gewídmǽrsodon, Hml. Th. i. 36, 13. Riht gewídmǽrsion *legem promulgare,* An. Ox. 1305. (3) *to make known* what is unfavourable or should be concealed :—Mid andetnesse suman gástlicum bréðer þe ... his sáule wundela gehǽlan cunne and hí gewídmǽrsian (*publicare*) nelle, R. Ben. 72, 7. Ofermódnesse gewídmǽrsodre *insolentiam traductam,* An. Ox. 8, 391. II. *intrans. To become widely known, be celebrated* :—Wíde springaþ, gewídmǽrsiaþ *crebrescunt* (*catholicorum laudes*), An. Ox. 2769. Lá hú ne gewídmǽrsude *nonne percrebruit* (*Anthonius*), 2374 : 2840. Cnæplingc ofer eal gewídmǽrsude (*cum*) *puer late crebresceret,* 2585. *See preceding word for other examples.*

**ge-wif** *a disease of the eye.* In l. 3 *l.* 292 *for* 290.

**ge-wife** *fate. Substitute:* ge-wif, es ; *n. Fortune, fate* :—Gewife wyrde *fato fortune* (*gentilitas, quae vitam veritatis expertem fato fortunae et genesi gubernari juxta Mathematicorum constellationem arbitratur,* Ald. 35, 36), Wrt. Voc. ii. 79, 60, 61. Gewife *fato,* gewife *fortune,* 37, 7, 8. Gewife *fortune* (the word seems glossed as dative, but is genitive, the passage being : Ipsos fortunae casibus oppressos, Ald. 42, 5), wyrdum *cassibus,* 81, 44, 45. Gewif, wyrd *furtunum, fatum,* Wülck. Gl. 245, 44. Him Dryhten forgeaf wígspéda gewiofu, B. 697. Cf. wefan ; II : ge-wefan ; II.

**ge-wífian.** *Substitute:* (1) absolute, *to marry, take a wife* :—Æfter heora gewunan hé gewífode, Hml. A. 95, 105. Hé sǽde þ hé gewiiað hæfde *se uxoreo uinculo conligatum fuisse respondit,* Bd. 4, 22 ; Sch. 456, 3. Manige habbaþ genóg geselilíce gewífod *ille nuptiis felix,* Bt. 11, 1 ; F. 32, 5. (2) *with on* (*with dat.*), *to marry* a person :—Hé on his ágenre swyster gewífode, Wlfst. 106, 13. Gewífede, Sal. K. p. 121, 30. Hé gewífode on ðæs cyninges dehter, Hml. Th. i. 478, 23. Ne on gehálgodre nunnan ... ǽnig crísten man ne gewífige ǽfre, Ll. Th. i. 318, 18 : Cht. E. 231, 14. Gif hwá his rihtæwe forlǽte, and on óðran wífe gewífige, Ll. Th. ii. 300, 24. Þæt cniht þurhwunige on his cnihtháde oð þæt hé on rihtre æwe gewífige, Wlfst. 304, 21. Þ ǽnig crísten mann binnan .vi. manna sibfæce on his ágenan cynne ǽfre ne gewífie, Ll. Th. i. 364, 23 : 318, 13. (2 a) with reflex. dat. :—Hí gewífodon him on þám hǽðenum mǽdenum *duxerunt uxores filias eorum,* Jud. 3, 6.

**gewif-sǽlig ;** *adj. Fortunate* :—Gewifsǽli *furtunatus,* þone gewifsǽligan (*but* gewilsǽligan *according to* Wülcker's *reading, see* Wülck. Gl. 406, 2) *fortunatum,* Wrt. Voc. ii. 37, 6, 5. v. ge-wilsǽlig.

**ge-wiht.** *Add:* I. *measurement by weighing* :—Ealra þyssa wyrta gelíce fela be gewihte, Lch. i. 148, 23. II. *an amount determined by weighing* :—Côm Nichodemus mid gemengedre sealfe of myrran and alwan, manegra punda gewyht (*uenit Nicodemus ferens mixturam murrae et aloes quasi libras centum,* Jn. 19, 39), Hml. Th. ii. 260, 35. His scip gehlæston mid micclum gewihte goldes and seolfres, Ap. Th. 6, 3. Twǽgra bêha on twæra punda gewihte, Cht. Th. 522, 22. Gedríge hine, cnuca ðonne tó dúste ánre tremese gewihte, Lch. i. 110, 9. Genim þysse wyrte twégea trymesa gewihte and twégen scenceas wínes, 130, 18. Genim of ægþerre handa þreóra penega gewihte, 246, 24 : 136, 15. Genim ... æscþrote ænne wrid, and ánre yutsan gewihte geswyrfes of seolfre, 216, 11. Genim swýþe smæl dúst, ánes scillinges gewihte, 240, 11. Ánes pundes gewihte eles and twégea ytnsa, 118, 19. ¶ in the following passage the construction seems unusual :—Sý ánes pundes gewihte hláf tó eallum dæge *panis libera una propensa sufficiat in die,* R. Ben. 63, 14. II a. figurative :—Gif hé gewihte besceáwað on edleáne *si pondus considerat in retributione,* Scint. 10, 14. III. *a definite amount used as a measure* :—Gewihte emne ys willa his *pondus aequum uoluntas eius,* Scint. 110, 13. Ǽghwylc gewihte beó be his dihte gescyft swíðe rihte, Ll. Th. ii. 314, 8. Ne sceall hé geþafian fals gewihte, 312, 18. Hé þone regol þe hé mid his handum áwrát betǽhte Maure mid him tó hæbbenne, and heora hláfes gewiht and heora wínes gemett, Hml. S. 6, 291. Unrihte gemeta and wóge gewihta áweorpe man georne, Wlfst. 70, 3. IV. *a system or standard of measurement by weighing* :—Gange án gemet and án

gewihte swilce man on Lundenbyrig and on Wintanceastre healde, Ll. Th. i. 270, 2. v. leád-, seolfor-gewiht(e).

**ge-wil.** Add:—Hí fyligeað heora luste and ídelum gewille, Wlfst. 52, 15. Hí ongunnon godspel tó wrítenne bútan þæs Hælendes wissunge, and be heora gewille (*according to their own will*) sǽdon swá swá him gebúhte, Hml. S. 15, 114. Wé becumað genýdde tó ðære sprǽce for gewille þára woruldháda (*to please the laity*) *ad hanc locutionem velut ex condescensione ducti venimus inviti*, Gr. D. 209, 24. Se æþeling ǽgðer hæfde, ge his plegan ge his gewill *he was amused and at the same time did what he wanted*, Ors. 1, 12; S. 54, 27. Hé genam þ wíf ofer þes cynges willan (gewil, *v. l.*), Chr. 1015; P. 146, 5. Þá þe nellað þæra þinga géman þe man heom bodað, ac willað forð on wóh and gewill dráfan *those who will not heed what is told them, but will persist in error and do what they wish*, Wlfst. 304, 13. Gif hé him God ne ondræt swiðor micle þonne his sylfes gewil, Dóm. L. 30, 39. Þínre unrihtgítsunga gewill tó fulfremmanne, Bt. 7, 5; F. 24, 16. ¶ on gewill *as is desired* by a person, (1) with gen. of person:—Hé sǽde hú hé him an his gewill ondwyrdan (*how he wished him to answer*) þæs hé hiene áscade *monuit quid sibi tamquam consulenti responderi velut*, Ors. 3, 9; S. 126, 29. Hé hét sumne biscep secgan on his gewill *Alexander ordered a certain bishop to say what he* (Alexander) *wanted him to say, as to who his father was*, S. 3, 13; 1, 12; S. 56, 1. Ealle þá worold on hiora ágen gewill onwendende *upsetting all the world at their own sweet will*, 1, 10; S. 48, 10. Hé ðá tíd his lífes on gewil (-will, *v. l.*) ðára áwierdena gǽsta gehwierfð *vitae suae tempora malignorum spirituum voluptatibus administrat*, Past. 249, 23. Ná on ðwyrra manna gewill (-wil, *v. l.*) *prohibere pravorum prevalere consensum*, R. Ben. 118, 13. (2) with dat. of person:—þone þe byð heora leahtrum geþafa and him on gewill gangce *consentientem personam*, R. Ben. 118, 7. Hwí þú wolde þæt sió wyrd on gewill wendan sceolde yfium monnum *why thou wouldst that things should happen as evil men would have them*, Met. 4, 34. v. unriht-gewil[l]; gewilles; un-gewil[l]; *adj.*

**gewil-bod,** es; *n.* *The announcement of a person's will*:—Ne dear ic for Godes ege sóðes geswugian … for ðám se bydel þe ne bodað ná his hláfordes gewilboda (*the messenger that does not give the message that tells his lord's will*), hé mæg him wénan hefelices leánes, Wlfst. 177, 24. Se bydel þe forsweogað his hláfordes gewilboda, 191, 22.

**ge-wilc,** es; *n.* *The rolling of waves*:—Gewylc ýþa sǽs þú líðgast *motum fluctuum maris tu mitigas*, Ps. Rdr. Spl. 88, 10. v. ge-wealc.

**ge-wild, -weold.** Substitute: ge-wild *power, control, in the phrase* ánum tó gewildum gedón *to get into one's power, subdue, subjugate*:—Æfter þǽm þe Alexander hæfde ealle Indie him tó gewildon gedón *perdomita Alexander India*, Ors. 3, 9; S. 132, 9. Siþþan hé þá burg hæfde him tó gewildum gedón, S. 134, 32. Hé him Siuos and Iersomas tó gewildum gedyde *Gessonas Sibosque oppressit*, S. 134, 4. Þæt hié mehton ǽgðer ge þone cyning ge þá cuéne him tó gewildum gedón, 3, 11; S. 148, 9. Cómon hí tó heora ágenum scipum, and þá óþre hindan offóran, and hié ealle him tó gewildum gedydan bútan v. *classem hostiliter invaserunt, quinque tantum navibus per fugam elapsis*, 4, 1; S. 154, 6. v. ge-weald.

**ge-wildan.** Take here **ge-wyldan** in Dict., in which dele passage from Nar. 2, 1, and add:—Domo ic gewylde oððe temige, Ælfc. Gr. Z. 213, 14. Gewylt, temaþ *domat, superat*, Wrt. Voc. ii. 141, 73. I. where active resistance has to be overcome, *to subdue, subject.* (1) by physical force:—Griffus … is swá mycel þæt hé gewylt hors and men, Wrt. Voc. i. 78, 2. Hé bútan wǽpnum gewylde ðá león, Hml. S. 18, 15. (1 a) of conquest by war:—Hé mid his scylde þá burg ne gewylt *non occupabit civitatem clypeus* (Is. 37, 33), Hml. Th. i. 568, 32. Ic gewyllde and oferwann fela ðeóda, 7. Ealle þá cyngas þe on þyssum íglande wǽron hé gewylde, Chr. 926; P. 107, 21: Hml. S. 25, 412. Hé wolde mid wǽpnum gewyldan þá Iudéiscan, 484. Gewyldan mid wíge þá leóda, 28, 3. Wæs hé strang on gefeohte, swá þ þá hǽþenan wǽron fram him swíðe gewylde, 30, 16. ¶ of the Harrowing of Hell:—Se Álýsend cóm þe ðone ealdan deófol gewylde and his gecorenan tó heofenan ríce gelǽdde, Hml. Th. i. 94, 8: 172, 7: Wlfst. 23, 10. (2) by peaceful means:—Bútan gefeohte eal hé gewilde þet hé sylf wolde, Chr. 959; P. 114, 26. (3) figuratively of moral conquest:—Strongra bið sé … þe his ágen mód ofercymð and gewilt ðonne sé þe fæste burg ábrycð. For ðǽm bið se sige micle mára … for ðǽm sió gesceádwísnes hæfð ofercumen ðæt mód and gewield, swelce hé self hæbbe hiene selfne gewildne *melior est qui dominatur animo suo expugnatore urbium … Valde autem victoria major est … quia ipse a se animus superatur, et semetipsum sibimetipsi subjicit*, Past. 218, 16–21. Sé ðe his mód gewylt … Máre sige bið þæt se man hine sylfne ðurh geþyld gewylde, Hml. Th. ii. 544, 9–11. II. *to control, restrain, keep from excess*, (1) of action or movement in persons or things:—þú gewyldst mihta sǽ *tu dominaris potestatis maris*, Ps. L. 88, 10. Gif hé gewelt sí *conpresserit* (labia sua), Kent. Gl. 626. Gewyldende *refrenantes*, i. *prohibentes* (*corporeos gestus*), An. Ox. 2189. Gewyldum *compresso* (*superna potestate incendio*), 4, 63. (2) of conduct, (a) in persons:—Ic þá ic lufige ic gewilde *ego quos amo castigo*, Scint. 160, 15. Man tó

hwón gewilde and stírde þám ðe syngodon, Wlfst. 168, 2. On sumne sǽl gewyld þe sylfne fram unrihtwisnysse *aliquando ab iniquitate compescere*, Gr. D. 132, 28. Hé hæfde ǽnne ofermódne cniht … þone (þám, *v. l.*) hé sylf uneáðe mihte gewyldan (-wealdan, *v. l.*) *superbum puerum habuit cui vix poterat vel ipse dominari*, 36, 7. God mihte hine (*Pharaoh*) mid wildum berum and leónum gewyldan, Hml. Th. ii. 192, 25. Geweldan *cohibere* (*spiritum suum*), Kent. Gl. 976. Hé sí gewyld *refrenetur* (*duro disciplina pedagogio*), An. Ox. 1100. Gewylde *castigati*, Scint. 163, 14. (b) in animals, *to tame*:—Ylp is eallra nýtena mǽst, ac swaþeáh mannes gesceád hí mæg gewyldan, Hml. S. 25, 573. III. *to subdue, reduce* or *destroy the strength of, weaken*, (1) a person:—Ic ábǽd æt Críste þ ðis cwealmbǽra fýr mé ne gewylde, Hml. S. 9, 121. Gif ic beó gebunden … sóna ic beó gewyld *infirmus ero*), Jud. 16, 7. (2) a thing:—Ðeós wyrt ǽlc yfel blód gewyldeþ, Lch. i. 236, 13. Is ðodes mǽrð þe ealle þás wíta gewylde, Hml. S. 35, 197. IV. *to get into one's power so as to prevent escape, seize, secure*:—Gewylde (-wilde, *v. l.*) man hine swaðor man mæge swá cucenne swá deádne, Ll. Th. i. 268, 17. Gewilde, 168, 22. Hé hý gewyldan meahte, nǽre þ hí on neht út ne ætburston of þære byrig, Chr. 943; P. 111, 16. Ágifan þá mágas hine swá gewyld swá hine ǽr út æt þám ordále námon *let the kinsmen give him up as safely secured as he was when they took him from the ordeal*, Ll. Th. i. 230, 2. Hé bið mid ðám deófellicum bendum gewyld, and tó tintregum gelǽdd, Hml. Th. ii. 402, 19. Gewyld *mancipari*, An. Ox. 2681. V. *to force, compel submission to* (tó) an action or a condition, *reduce to subjection, slavery, &c.*:—Hé him tó þeówdóme gewylde ealle Ispanie, Ors. 5, 4; S. 224, 31. Hí gewyldon hí tó þære ylcan stíðnysse *they subjected themselves to the same austerity*, Hml. S. 31, 336. Seó sáwl is ðæs flǽsces hlǽfdige, and hire gedafnað þ heó simle gewylde ðá wylne, þ is þ flǽsc tó hyre hǽsum … gif þ flǽsc sceal gewyldan þone gást tó his lustum, 17, 8–14. Gewilde man hine tó rihte mid steóre, Ll. Th. i. 344, 3. Gewilde man hí tó rihte þances oþþe unþances, 348, 28. For neóde gewildan tó rihte, 16. Hé hit ne mæge tó his willan geweldan, Past. 118, 17. v. un-gewild, and *next word.*

**ge-wilde** subject. Take here **ge-wylde** in Dict., *and add*: Perhaps the three passages, Ors. 3, 9; S. 132, 22: Guth. 56, 23: Ps. Th. 59, 7, *at the end of* **ge-wyldan** *in Dict. might be taken here.*

**ge-wilde;** *adj. Powerful*:—þ se man beó geðyldig and lǽte ǽfre his gewitt gewyldre þonne his yrre, Hml. S. 16, 336. v. wilde.

**ge-wildelic.** v. un-gewildelic.

**ge-wildend,** es; *m.* *A tamer, subduer, subjugator*:—Gewyldend *perdomitor*, Germ. 391, 12.

**ge-wilian** to ge-wilwan: ge-will. v. ge-wil.

**ge-willan** to boil. Take here **ge-wyllan** in Dict., *and add*:—Of geweldum wíne *ex passo*, i. *ex calefacto vino*, Wrt. Voc. ii. 145, 26.

**ge-willes.** v. un-gewilles.

**ge-willian;** *p.* ode To desire:—Gewillað *cupiet*, Ps. Srt. 36, 23: *desiderat*, 41, 2. Ic gewillade *desiderabam*, 118, 131. Gewillade cyning hiów ðín *concupivit rex speciem tuam*, 44, 12: 83, 3: 118, 20. Wyrte þe hé ǽr mid stale gewilnode (-willade, *v. l.*), Gr. D. 25, 16. Gewillian *desiderare*, Ps. Srt. 118, 20.

**ge-willsum.** v. ge-wilsum.

**ge-willung,** e; *f.* Desire:—Gewilladun gewillunge *concupierunt concupiscentias*, Ps. Srt. 105, 14.

**ge-wilness,** e; *f.* Will, desire:—Fram willan i gewilnessa (*voluntate*) welera his, Ps. L. 20, 3.

**ge-wilnian.** Dele first passage, *and add*: in a bad sense, *to covet*:—Ic gewilnie *glisco*, An. Ox. 18 b, 39. I. *to desire* an object (the source from which marked by tó). (1) with acc. or uncertain:—Sé ðe biscephád gewilnað (*desiderat*), gód weorc hé gewilnað, Past. 52, 25. Gewilne *expetit* (= gewilnode *expetivit*, v. Lk. 22, 31), Wrt. Voc. ii. 74, 2: 30, 68. Wyrte þe hé ǽr mid stale gewilnode (*appetebat* [*auferre*]), Gr. D. 25, 16. Ðæs láriówdómes ðegnung bið untǽlwierðlíce gewilnad *praedicationis officium nonnulli laudabiliter appetunt*, Past. 11, 9. Gewilnede gesinscipas *obtata conubia*, An. Ox. 4287. (2) with gen.:—Bilewite cild ne gewilnað wlitiges wífes, Hml. Th. i. 512, 13. Manegra wíta hié gewildnodon wið ðan éce lífe *multos scimus beatitudinis fructum suppliciis quaesisse*, Bt. 11, 2; F. 36, 4. Ne gewilna (*concupisces*) þú þines néhstan ierfes mid unrihte, Ll. Th. i. 44, 21. (3) with dat.:—Sé ðe biscepháde gewilnað, Past. 53, 8. (4) with clause:—Hé gewilnode tó Gode þ hé hine ne lǽte lybban náne hwíle æfter his leófan fæder, Chr. 1038; P. 161, 31. II. *to desire* to do. (1) with infin.:—Ðá fǽmnan þe gewilniað (-wuniað, *v. l.*) onfón galdorcræftigan, Ll. Th. i. 52, 9. Þá gewilniað heora sáwla sellan, 56, 20. (2) with dat. infin.:—Þá wyrta þe hé ǽr mid stale gewilnode tó ætbrédanne (*appetebat auferre*), Gr. D. 25, 16. Hé þ gefremede mán gewilnade tó bedíglianne, Ap. Th. 2, 6. Manega wítegan gewilnudon (gewilnadon, L., *cupierunt*) þá þing tó geseónne, Mt. 13, 17. III. *to desire to go* to (tó), lit. or fig., (1) to a person:—We witon þæt ðú gewilnast tó ðám wuldorfullan Drihtne, Hml. Th. ii. 516, 22. Þú gewilnast tó Críste, Hml. S. 31, 1338. (2) to a place, position, condition, &c.:—Þá þe hé (*St. Martin*) wæs twelf

wintra hē gewilnode tō wēstene (cf. smeágende hū hē (*St. Martin*) on wēstene wunian mihte, Hml. Th. ii. 500, 2), and hē hit eác gefremode gif hē þā ylde hæfde, Hml. S. 31, 26. Hē gewilnode *anhelat* (*ad summum virginitatis fastigium*), An. Ox. 2, 230.

**ge-wilnigendlic.** *Add* : I. *desirable* :—All gewilnien[d]lic *omne desirabile*, Kent. Gl. 238. Gewilniendlic goldhord *thesaurus desiderabilis*, 791. Gewilnigendlic, Hml. Th. i. 116, 34. Gewilniendlice ofor gold *desiderabilia super aurum*, Ps. L. 18, 11. II. *concupiscent, libidinous* :—Ūs is beboden . . . fortredan ðā gewilnigendlice lustas, Hml. Th. ii. 398, 29. III. *capable of desire* :—Uþwytan sæcgað þ þære sāwle gecynd is ðryfeald. Ān dǣl is on hire gewylnigendlic, Hml. S. 1, 97.

**ge-wilnung.** *Add* :—I. *desire to obtain.* (1) in a favourable or indifferent sense :—Gif hē hit herede, eft hē stiérde ðære gewilnunge *laudans desiderium in pavorem vertit quod laudavit*, Past. 53, 9. Mid gewilnungum stefne wē singaþ *votis voce psallimus*, Hy. S. 114, 36. ¶ *desire for a person, love* :—Gewilnunge (*infimi*, i. *terreni*) *amoris*, An. Ox. 1184. (1 a) with gen. of what is desired :—Hē for ðære gewilnunge swelcra weorca biscopdōm ne sēcð *episcopatum non appetit per hunc boni operis ministerium*, Past. 55, 1. Mid ðære gewilnunge ðāra ungesewenlicra ðinga *invisibilia appetendo*, 98, 3. Gewilnunge, for begeate *obtentu*, i. *ob desiderio* (*castitatis*), An. Ox. 2698. Hē micele gewilnunge hæfde Crīstes tōcymes, Hml. Th. i. 136, 9. (1 b) where the desire is expressed in a clause :—Hē þæt gewinn swīþost dyde for þære gewilnunge þe hē wolde hī him on fultum geteón, Ors. 3, 7 ; S. 112, 2. (2) in an unfavourable sense :—Sē bið hoferede, sē ðe sió byrðen ofðrycð ðisse eorðlican gewilnunge (*terrenae sollicitudinis*), Past. 67, 13. Oferswīðde mid sumre unryhte gewilnunge *repentina concupiscentia superati*, 21, 8. Mid hira āgenre gewilnunge onbærnede *sua cupidine accensi*, 27, 18. On ðǣm eorðlicum gewilnungum *terrenis desideriis*, 155, 23. ¶ *desire for the pleasures of sense, lust.* (a) *greediness for food* :—Suā hē sceal etan ðætte hine sió gewilnung ðære gifernesse of his mōdes fæsðrǣdnesse ne gebrienge *ne illos appetitus gulae a mentis statu dejiciat*, Past. 317, 6. Gewilnunga birgena *sepulchra concupiscentiae*, Num. 11, 34. Ðā niétenu for ðære gewilnunge hiera giéfernesse (*appetitu gulae*) simle lōcigeað tō ðære eorðan, Past. 155, 19. (β) *sexual lust.* v. 2 a ¶ β. (2 a) with gen. of what is desired :—Gewilnunge *appetitu* (*pretiosarum vestium*), An. Ox. 5158. Mid ungemǣtlicre gewilnunge anwaldes *dominationis libidine*, Ors. 1, 2 ; S. 28, 27. For ðære gewilnunga woroldgielpes and giétsunga *per ambitum quasi per gulae desiderium*, Past. 157, 2. Mid ungerisenlicum gewilnungum ðissa worolddinga *ambitione inhonesta*, 157, 9. ¶ *greed, lust.* v. 2 ¶. (a) with reference to food :—Se feónd ðæs ǣrestan monnes mōd ontŷnde on ðæs ǣples gewilnunge *hostis primi hominis sensum in concupiscentia pomi aperuit*, Past. 309, 17. (β) of sexual lust :—For ðære sceamleáslecan gewilnunge his wīfes *in appetitu foeminae*, 35, 24. II. *desire to act.* (1) in a good sense :—Georn[fulnysse], gewilnunge *intentione*, i. *desiderio*, An. Ox. 2526. (2) in an unfavourable sense :—Gewilnung, styrung *gestus* (*interioris hominis sanaretur*), An. Ox. 2077. Nā mid gewilnedre (-fylledre ?) gewilnunge *nequaquam effecta voluntate*, 4678. Tolcetunge gewilnunge *titillationum*, i. *stimulorum luxuriae gestus* (*corporeos*), 2183. III. *a desired object, an object of desire* :—Eálā þū Hǣlend ūre ālŷsednyss, lufu and gewilnung (*desiderium*), Hy. S. 83, 33. v. unriht-gewilnung.

**ge-wilsǣlig** (?) ; *adj. Fortunate* :—Ðone gewilsǣligan (-wif-, ? v. gewif-sǣlig) *fortunatum*, Wrt. Voc. ii. 79, 50.

**ge-wilsum.** *Take here* ge-willsum *in Dict., and add* : *voluntary* :—Gewilsuman *spontaneum*, An. Ox. 11, 29. *See next word.*

**ge-wilsumlic** ; *adj. Voluntary, willing* :—Gewynsumlice (-wyl- ?) *ultroneum*, i. *spontaneum*, An. Ox. 235. Gewil[sumlice], 8, 21. [It is the same passage (Ald. 5, 15) that is glossed in both.]

**ge-wilsumness**, e ; *f. A free-will offering* :—Gewilsumnessa mūðes mīnes *voluntaria oris mei*, Ps. L. 118, 108.

**ge-wiltan** ; *p.* te *To roll. Take here* ge-wæltan *in Dict.*

**ge-wilwan** (-ian), **-wylian.** I. *to roll* :—Hē hine sylfne nacodne āwearp and wylede (wylewede, *v. l.*) on þæra þorna ordum, and wæs þær gewylwed (welwed, *v. l.*) lange *nudum se in spinarum aculeis projecit, ibique diu volutatus*, Gr. D. 101, 13, 18. II. *to roll together, band together* :—Hī drīfað þa drāfe crīstena manna fram sǣ tō sǣ ūt ðurh þæs þeóde gewylede (-wil-, -wel-, *v. ll.*) tōgædere, Wlfst. 163, 6. v. wilwan.

**ge-win.** *Add* :—I. *conflict, contest, struggle.* (1) of physical effort, (a) in competition. v. gewin-stōw, *and* cf. (2 a) :—Ðæs pleglican gewinnes *Olimpiaci agonis*, Wrt. Voc. ii. 74, 57 : 4, 62. (b) of hostile conflict, (a) *a fight, battle*, cf. (2 b) :—Of anwīgum *vel* gewinnum *congressibus*, i. *pugnis*, Wrt. Voc. ii. 133, 42. Geedcwicede gewin *rediuiua certamina*, An. Ox. 11, 81. (β) *a war*, cf. (2 c) :—Þis wæs geworden ǣr ðæt gewinn cōme ðurh Hengest and Horsa þe hýndon ðā Bryttas, Hml. S. 19, 147. Þæt gewinn þæt his fæder āstealde *bellum a patre susceptum*, Ors. 2, 5 ; S. 78, 31. Þā gewin wǣron grimlicran þonne hý nū sŷn, 1, 2 ; S. 30, 23. Manega bismerlica gewin gefremede, 1, 8 ; S.

42, 9. Þā folc him betweónum ful x winter þā gewin wraciende (wrecende, *v. l.*) wǣron, 1, 11 ; S. 50, 21. (γ) *war*, cf. (2 d) :—Gōdne hlīsan ǣgþer ge on sibbe ge on gewinne, Bt. 24, 2 ; F. 82, 11. Hē gewinn upp āhōf wið Athenienses *in Athenienses impetum fecit atque arma direxit*, Ors. 2, 5 ; S. 78, 21 : Bt. 1, 1 ; F. 2, 2. Gewinn, Chr. 1094 ; P. 230, 3. Hē him onbeád gewinn *bellum Caesari denuntiavit*, Ors. 5, 13 ; S. 246, 1. (δ) *warfare, fighting*, cf. (2 d) :—Secgan be þære micelnisse ūres gewinnes and compes *gloriam militiae nostrae asserere*, Nar. 2, 28. Þ hī him andlīsene and āre forgeáfon for heora gewinne *ut militantibus debita stipendia conferrent*, Bd. 1, 15 ; Sch. 41, 13. Hié þōhton þæt hié sceoldon mid gewinne þæs landes māre gerǣcan, Chr. 921 ; P. 101, 18. (c) of the action of natural forces :—Hwī ne wundraþ hī þæs gewinnes sǣ and winda and ŷþa and landes, Bt. 39, 3 ; F. 214, 34. (2) figurative. v. (4) : cf. (1 a) :—Geswincfulles gewinnes sigeleán *laboriosi certaminis* (i. *luctaminis*) *palma*, An. Ox. 1116. On gewinne *in conflictu* (*octo principalium vitiorum ultima ponitur*), 4, 17. Þylce nabbað mēde, for þī þe hī næfdon geswinces gewinnu ; þā sōðlíce geanbidað wyrðscype on þām beóð geswincfulle gewinnu (*certamina*), Scint. 70, 11-13. (b) cf. (1 b a) :—Nīwe campas and gewin (*certamina*) þæs ealdan feóndes ongǣn þone Godes þeów, Gr. D. 122, 22. (c) cf. (1 b β) :—For þǣm gewinne þe hē (*the evil judge*) wiþ God wan, Bl. H. 63, 3. (d) cf. (1 b γ) :—Mannes līf is campdōm . . . , for ðan þe ǣlc ðæra ðe Gode geþīhð bið on gewinne wið ðone deófol, Hml. Th. ii. 454, 29. (e) cf. (1 b δ) :—[Mynster]lices gecampes gewin *cenobialis militie tyrocinium*, An. Ox. 4170. Gewinnes *militiae* (*spiritalis bellatores*), 3026. (3) *a conflict with words, contention, dispute* :—Gewin *concertatio* (*prolixa sermonum*), An. Ox. 3204. Gewinnum *conflictibus* (*reciprocis disputans*), 3000. Hē geseah ðā geflitu and gewinn (*certamina*) þāra werigra gāsta. Þā fliton hī him on and mid gelōmlicum oncunningum tiledon þ . . . , Bd. 3, 19 ; Sch. 278, 7. (4) of spiritual or mental struggles. v. (2) :—Hē weard mid grimmum gewinne his līchaman lustes geswǣnced *hunc acri certamine carnis incentiva fatigabant*, Gr. D. 26, 17. II. *labour.* (1) *strenuous effort, hard work* :—Him nænig gewin tō heard ne þūhte, þæs þe hē heora sāulum tō hǣle gewinnan mihte, Bl. H. 227, 3. For hwan gǣst þū swā būton wæstme þīnes gewinnes ?, 249, 5. Gif ic sié þīnum folce nēðþearflíc tō hæbbenne, þonne ne widsace ic þǣm gewinne, 225, 27. Hafa þū æt þīnum gewinne þæt þū mæge *get what you can from your labour*, Wlfst. 259, 24. Gē geseóþ nū mīonra gewinna wæstm gefullian, Bl. H. 191, 23. God nolde hī ābysgian mid þām gewinnum (geswinceum, *v. l.*) þises middaneardes *eos Deus noluit hujus mundi laboribus occupari*, Gr. D. 6, 34. (2) *painful effort, toilsome work* :—Þ hī ne āfyrhte þ gewin ðæs sīðfætes (ne forhtigean þæs gewinnes ne ðæs sīþfætes, *v. l.*) *labor uos itineris non deterreat*, Bd. 1, 23 ; Sch. 50, 4. On gewinne and on swāte hē leofaþ, Bl. H. 59, 36. (3) *physical pain, distress* :—Ne biþ þær sār ne gewinn, Bl. H. 103, 35. His hýd is bryce hundum wið wōles gewinne on tō dōnne. Hafa þære hýde fellsticceo on þīnum sceón, ne gefēlest þū gewin on þīnum fōtum, Lch. i. 330, 3-6. Git ðū scealt fela gewinn habban on ðīnum martyrdōme, Hml. Th. i. 426, 18. (4) *mental distress, trouble.* v. gewin-tīd, -woruld :—Hē gehyhte þæt him God sealde his gewinnes frōfre *sperans in Domino daturum sibi refocillationem aliquam laboris sui*, Guth. Gr. 171, 7. Mīnes gewinnes ende *the end of my troubled life*, 139, 21. v. ær-, eald-, folc-, fyrn-, gār-, gāst-, gūþ-, hand-, in-, leód-, on-, stream-, waroþ-, weorold-, wōl-, ŷþ-gewin.

**ge-wind.** *Substitute* :—I. *what has a curved* or *spiral shape.* (1) *a winding ascent.* Cf. windan ; I. 2 *and* 3 :—Gewind *circuitus ascensus*, Wrt. Voc. i. 37, 4. Gewend *coclea* (cf. coclea, ascensus, quia circuit), Corp. Gl. H. 34, 623. (2) *a tendril of a vine.* Cf. windan ; II. 4 :—Wīngearda gewind *capreoli* (cf. capreoli vel cincinni wīngearda hōcas þe hī mid bindað þæt him nēhst bið, 38, 59), Wrt. Voc. i. 39, 10. II. *what is woven.* Cf. windan ; II. 3, windung :—Mid gewefenum wǣfelsa, gewynde *consuta* (*palmarum*) *plecta*, i. *cratere*, An. Ox. 2392. Gewinde, 2, 79. Gewind *plectas*, Wrt. Voc. ii. 68, 71. III. *what winds round* or *envelops* (as in *winding*-sheet) :—Gewynd *involucrum*, Wrt. Voc. i. 41, 25. v. loc-, þearm-gewind.

**ge-windan.** *Add* : I. *intrans.* (1) of movement, (a) by living things, *to roll together, roll up* :—Se iil . . . sōna suā hiene mon gefēhð, suā gewint hē tō ānum cliéwene *ericius . . . mox ut apprehensus fuerit, semetipsum in sphaeram colligit*, Past. 241, 11. (b) by inanimate things :—Gewand him ūt eall his innewearde, Hml. Th. i. 290, 19. (2) of action, *to go about a matter, act* in reference to :—' Wāst þū hū ic gewand ymbe Creosos þearfe, þā þā hine Cirus forbærnan wolde.' Þā hine man on þ fýr wearp, þā ālýsde ic hine mid heofonlicon rēne, Bt. 7, 3 ; F. 22, 10. II. *trans. To roll back, unroll* :—Wyllene wearp of clīwene gewundene *lanea stamina ex glomere revoluta*, An. Ox. 459. [*Goth.* du-gawindan sik gawaurkjam *implicare se negotiis* : *O. H. Ger.* ge-wintan colligere, torquere, volvere.]

**ge-windla.** v. hring-gewindla.

**ge-winful.** *Add* : I. *laborious, troublesome.* v. ge-win ; II. 2 :—Þām brōþrum wæs swýðe gewinnful and uneáðe niþer tō āstīgenne tō þām wæterseáðe *valde erat fratribus laboriosum ad lacum descendere*,

Gr. D. 112, 17. Ic wolde þ hyra læs wære gewinfulra *utinam minus fuissent laboriosa*, Nar. 2, 29. Hí ne mihton swá gewinnfullicum (gewinesfullicum, *v. l.*) fyrdum (*tam laboriosis expeditionibus*) swencte beón, Bd. 1, 12; Sch. 33, 17. **II.** *full of trouble*. v. ge-win; **II.** 4:—Þis líf is lænlic and hit is gewinful, Ll. Th. ii. 400, 15.

**ge-winfullic.** *Add:*—Swíðe gewinnfullic (*laboriosum*) þ is þ man on symbel hine behealde wiþ þæs feóndes searwe, Gr. D. 222, 7.

**ge-winfullíce.** *Add:*—Æfter þon þe þú swá earfoðlíce and gewin-fullíce gelýfdest *postquam laboriose credidisti*, Gr. D. 305, 16.

**ge-winna.** *Add:*—**I.** of persons, (1) *an enemy, opponent*:—Sé bið Godes gewinna sé ðe wilnað ðæt hé hæbbe ða weorðunga ðe God habban sceolde *hostis Redemtoris est, qui ejus vice ab ecclesia amari concupiscit*, Past. 141, 21. Feónda gewinna (*Guthlac*) Gú. 934. Gé gehýrað hæleða gewinnan, sé þyssum herige mæst hearma gefremede, þæt is Andreas, An. 1199. Helle dióful . . . gecwæd 'Sleað synnigne ofer seolfes múð folces gewinnan' (*St. Andrew*), 1303. Sáwla gewinnan (*the devil*), Jul. 555. (2) *a rival, competitor*:—Gewinna *emulus*, Wrt. Voc. ii. 143, 45. **II.** of things that have opposite qualities, *a contrary*:—Gód and yfel bióþ simle gewinnan *bonum malumque contraria sunt*, Bt. 36, 3; F. 174, 36. v. eald-, ealdor-, láþ-, mód-gewinna.

**ge-winnan.** *Dele in Dict. first two passages under I, and the fourth under II (v. IV below), and add:* **I.** *intrans. To strive, contend, fight*:—Gewon *conflixit*, i. *certavit*, Wrt. Voc. ii. 133, 23. (1) of hostile action against a person:—Gúðlác ána gewon, Gú. 421. (2) *to make war, war, fight*:—Hé heardlíce gewon wiþ Æþelbald cyning, Chr. 741; P. 44, 23. Wénde man þæt þæt gewin geendad wære, þá þá wæron gefeallen þe þær mæst gewunnen *ducibus occisis finita bella videbantur*, Ors. 3, 11; S. 148, 27. Æfter þæm gewunnon Demetrias and Lisimachus *Lysimachus adversus Demetrium pugnavit*, S. 152, 1. **II.** *trans. To get by effort* what is striven for. (1) of peaceful effort:—Him bið leán gearo þæs wé magon fremena gewinnan *reward shall await him from any good we may gain*, Gen. 437. His hyldo is unc betere tó gewinnanne þonne his wiðermēdo, 660. Hí wilniað welan and æhta and weorðscipes (-as?) tó gewinnanne *opes, honores ambiant*, Met. 19, 44. Wénþ þ hit hæbbe sum heálic gód gestrýned ðonne hit hæfþ gewunnen þæs folces ólecunga *favor popularis, quae videtur quandam claritudinem comparare*, Bt. 24, 3; F. 82, 24. (2) of violence:—Hwá mid orde ærost mihte on fægean men feorh gewinnan, By. 125. (2 a) *to get by fighting*, (a) *to conquer* a people or country, *overcome* enemies:—Alexander gewonn ealle Mandos and ealle Ircaniam . . . Æfter þæm wonn Alexander wið Parthim, and hé hié neáh ealle fordyde ær hé hié gewinnan mehte . . . and hé gewonn Drancas þ folc *Alexander Hyrcanos et Mardos subegit . . . Post haec Parthorum pugnam adgressus: quos delevit propemodum antequam vicit. Inde Drangas subegit*, Ors. 3, 9; S. 130, 8–15. Hér cóm Willelm and gewann Ænglaland, Chr. 1066; P. 196, 1. Gewin I oferwin (*expugna*) þá onwinnende mé, Ps. L. 34, 1. Folc þe ær nán folc ne mehte mid gefeohte gewinnan, Ors. 3, 7; S. 112, 31. Þeód wæs gewunnen wintra mænigo *the people was in subjection many years*, Met. 1, 28. Hí þ land hæfdon gewunnen, Bt. 33, 1; F. 194, 9. (β) *to take* a town, castle, &c. :—Hé þá burg gewann *urbem expugnavit et cepit*, Ors. 3, 7; S. 112, 16: 3, 9; S. 136, 2. Hér Regnold cyng gewan Eoferwíc, Chr. 923; P. 105, 1. Hí þá castelas gewunnan, 1069; P. 203, 4. (γ) *to take* things as spoils of war :—Þá men of Hæstingaceastre gewunnon his twá scypa, Chr. 1050; P. 170, 6. Hí þone castel tóbræcon and unárímendlíce gærsuman þærinne gewunnan, 1069; P. 204, 19. (δ) where the object is non-material, *to gain* victory, dominion, power, &c. :—Se woruldcempa gecyrð, syððan hé sige gewinð, hám tó his wífe, Hex. 36, 17. Hí gewunnon þær sige, Hml. S. 26, 26. Julius se Cásere Brettas mid gefeohte cnysede and hié oferswíþde, and swá þeáh ne meahte þær ríce gewinnan, Chr. P. p. 4, 25. **III.** *to get as result of action* what is not desired:—Hete hæfde hé æt his hearran gewunnen, Gen. 301: Sat. 719. **IV.** *to perform with effort, undergo* labour. Cf. winnan; **B.** II:—Him wæs manna lufu tó ðæs mycel þ him nænig gewin tó lang ne tó heard ne þúhte þæs þe hé heora sáulum tó hæle and tó ræde gewinnan mihte *in him was the love of men so great that none of the labour seemed to him too long or too hard that he could do for the good of their souls*, Bl. H. 227, 4.

**gewin-stów.** *Add:* v. ge-win; **I.** 1 a:—Gewinstówe *scammatis*, Wrt. Voc. ii. 74, 67. On gewinstówe *scammate* (cum mundi *scammate* certant, Ald. 190, 23), 95, 9.

**gewin-tíd**, e; *f. A time of distress, troublous time*, v. gewin; **II.** 4:—Oþ þæs gewintíde Langbeardna *ad haec Longobardorum tempora*, Gr. D. 210, 15.

**ge-wintred.** *Add:*—Gewintred *senex*, Ors. 6, 31; S. 284, 22. Wæs geworden þ Jóseph wæs geháten sum gewintrod man, eóde þyder mid iungum mannum, Hml. A. 130, 65. Ðá ðe tó ðæm gewintrede ne beóð ne geðiegene (cf. ðá ðe unmedome bióð tó ðære láre oððe for gioguðe oððe for unwísdóme, 19), Past. 375, 15.

**ge-wirce.** v. ge-wyrce.

**ge-wirdan** *to injure, spoil. Take here* ge-wyrdan *in Dict., and add:*—Eác hylpð gif mon mid eástnûm onbærnedum þá meoluc gewyrð

(*turns the milk*), Lch. ii. 218, 24. Ðý læs hié mid ðý tóle ðæt hále líc gewierden ðe hié sceoldon mid ðæt unhále áweg aceorfan *dum per hoc in se sana perimunt, per quod salubriter abscindere sauciata debuerunt*, Past. 365, 12. Sió scearpnes bið gewird (-wierd, *v. l.*) ðæs æpples *acies pupillae vitiatur*, 69, 3. Gif meoloc sié gewerd (cf. áwyrd, 340, 23), Lch. ii. 312, 27. v. un-gewirded.

**ge-wirde.** v. ge-wirþe: **ge-wirdlian.** *Take here* ge-wyrdlian *in Dict., and add:* (ge-ǽwerdledan, *v. l.*).

**ge-wirman.** *Take here* ge-wyrman *in Dict., and add:*—Seó bródige henn tósprǽt hyre fyðera and þá briddas gewyrmð, Angl. viii. 309, 26. Gewyrmede *fotam*, Wrt. Voc. ii. 34, 46. [*O. H. Ger.* ge-wermen.]

**ge-wirpan.** *Take here* ge-wyrpan *in Dict., and add:* (1) *intrans.*:—Gif hé biþ on xxx nihte ealdne mónan gestanden, uneáðe hé gewyrpð, and þeáh áríseþ, Lch. iii. 182, 26: 188, 11. Geuaerpte *convaluit*, Wrt. Voc. ii. 105, 17. Gewyrpte, 15, 22: 135, 41. Se mæssepreóst sealde þám ádligan of tó súpenne and hé sóna gewyrpte, and syððan leofode lange, Hml. S. 26, 265. Swelce hié lǽgen on longre mettrymnesse and hié ðeáh gewierpten *similes iis quos irruens gravis languor a vita non subtrahit*, Past. 228, 2. Weard him ðá geðúht swilce heó gewurpan (áwyrpan, *v. l.*) mihte, ac heó gewát of worulde, Hml. S. 20, 65. (2) *reflex.*:—Næs hé fæge þá gýt, ac hé hyne gewyrpte, þeáh þe him wund hrine, B. 2976. (2 a) *to recover* from sickness:—Hé hine þære seócnysse gewyrpte, Hml. S. 23 b, 656.

**ge-wirpan** *to estimate. Take here* ge-wyrpan *in Dict.*

**ge-wirþe**, es; *n. Amount* of so much. *Take here* ge-wyrþe *in Dict., and add:*—Hé gesealde twégra æcera gewirde landes *concessit duo iugera ruris*, C. D. vi. 207, 16. Heó on hire múð sende þreóra corna gewyrde, Hml. S. 23 b, 716.

**ge-wis.** *Add:*—**I.** of persons or personal attributes. (1) *certain, not having doubt*:—Se mǽsta dǽl monna ne sécþ on þ him forgifen is, þ is gesceádwísnes (*ratio*), ne þ ne sécþ þ him ofer is, þ is þ englas habbaþ and wíse men, þ is gewis andget (*intelligentia*). . . . Gif wé hæfdon ǽnigne dǽl untweógendes andgites swá swá englas habbaþ, Bt. 41, 5; F. 254, 5. Wé hine wurdiaþ mid gewissum geleáfan, Wlfst. 105, 29. Englas habbaþ gewis andgit, Bt. 41, 5; F. 252, 30, 20. Þæt gé beón gewisse ðonne úre týddernys his worda getácnunga eów geopenað, Hml. Th. ii. 88, 17. (1 a) *certain* of (*gen.*):—Him for án þúhte þ hé þæs gewiss wære, þ hé ǽlcne man gecneówe *the only thing he seemed certain of was, that he knew everybody*, Hml. S. 23, 631. (1 b) *certain*, about (be):—'Ic wolde witan swá be Gode . . . þæt mé nán þing meahte on nánum tweónunga gebringan.' 'Gelýfst þú þæs þæt ic þé mæge dón gewisran be Gode þonne þú nú eart ðe ðám mónan?,' Solil. H. 18, 6. (2) *having knowledge*:—Gewis *docta*, An. Ox. 46, 7. (2 a) *having knowledge* of (*gen.*), *cognizant* of, *acquainted* with :—Ic eom gewis þínra mægena, Lch. i. 326, 4. Wé syndon gewisse þínes lífes and þínes geleáfan trumnesse wé witon *nos experti sumus te, et fidei tuae valitudinem comperimus*, Guth. Gr. 123, 9. Ofáxa ðæs ðe þú mæge . . . and dó ús gewisse þæs þe þú ofáxie, Hml. S. 23, 466. (3) *sure, trusty, that may be relied on*:—Hé heom gesette gewisne fæder (him ealdor gesette, *v. l.*) *fratribus patrem constituit*, Gr. D., 147, 24. Stiéran mon sceal strongum móde and þæt on staðelum healdan and gewis werun (*to be relied on by men?*), Seef. 110. **II.** of things. (1) *certain, that does not admit of doubt, manifest, clear*:—Evidens, i. *manifestus, patens, perspicuus, certum* sweotol, gewis, Wrt. Voc. ii. 144, 35. Þonne gewis is *cum constet*, i. *certum est*, An. Ox. 555. Hwet man gewiss wiste, Solil. H. 20, 10: 27, 2: 30, 2. Sume ðing sind gecwedene be Críste þurh getácnunge, sume ðurh gewissum ðinge. Sóð þing is and gewiss þæt Críst wæs of mædene ácenned, Hml. Th. ii. 268, 12–14. Gewissum clypunga ágnungum *certis uocabulorum proprietatibus*, An. Ox. 877. Nis nánwuht wynsumre ne gewisre ðonne þ þing þ þis spell ymbe is, Bt. 34, 5; F. 140, 12. (2) *sure, unfailing*:—Gewiss *rata* (*recompensatio*), An. Ox. 4, 93. On wege þær is gewis mægen *in via virtutis suae*, Ps. Th. 101, 21. God ne behét nánum elciendum gewis líf oþ mergen, Hml. S. 12, 166. Gewissum, Hml. Th. ii. 602, 29. Þē sind geheáldene ðíne mēda gewisse (*or adv.?*), ii. 516, 24. Swefne sint gewisse, Lch. iii. 186, 19, 27. Gif hí nyston heom tóweard þ gewisse líf þára sáwla (*certiorem animarum vitam*), Gr. D. 271, 4. (3) *free from error, unerring*:—Gewisse dægmǽl ús swá tǽcað, Lch. iii. 252, 22. (4) of a course, *undeviating, direct*:—Hé mid micclan gefeán tó scipe gewænde and mid gewisse seglunge binnon ánum dæge cóm tó Antiochian, Ap. Th. 6, 27. In þǽre stówe fram þám nyþeran dǽle in tó þám uferan wæs samodgang þurh gewisne úpstige (trum stǽger mid gewissum stapum *v. l.*) *quo in loco inferiora superioribus pervius continuabat ascensus*, Gr. D. 170, 24. (5) ? :—Momentum ys gewyss (*under* III ?) stów þǽre sunnan on heofenum. Þonne hé byð feówertig síðon gegaderod, þonne gefylleð hē áne tíd; and hé ys gewiss for þǽra tungla hwætnysse *momentum*, þæt ys styrung *a motu siderum*, Angl. viii. 318, 4. **III.** (a) *certain* (*thing*), *some* : quidam:—Pilatus cwæþ: 'Myd gewyssum gesceáde (v. ge-sceád; VIII) yrn and clypa hyder tó mē þone þe ys Ihs genemned,' Nic. 2, 6. On gewissum tídum (cf. hwíltídum, R. Ben. 73, 5, 6) *certis temporibus*, R. Ben. I. 81, 8, 9. Of gewissum intingan

(cf. for heora leahtrum oððe for háliges lífes geearnunge, R. Ben. 115, 9–10) *certis ex causis*, 105, 9. **IV.** *used substantively in the phrase* tó gewissum *certainly* :—Tó gewissan *presertim*, i. *scilicet*, An. Ox. 1882. **IV a.** of knowledge (to know) *for certain, with certainty, without any doubt* :—Wite gehwá tó gewissan, þæt . . . , Hml. Th. i. 96, 3 : Hml. S. 13, 136. Ic nát tó gewissan hwǽr hé wunað nú, 21, 31. v. un-gewis, *and next word.*

ge-wis, -wiss, es; *n.* **I.** *what is certain.* (1) *certain information* :— Ðá úþwitan þe sǽdon þæt nǽfre nánwiht gewisses nǽre búton twæónunga, Solil. H. 20, 22. Ne mæg ic nán gewis bringan tó mínum geférum, Hml. S. 23, 577. Hé áxode þæs martyres naman . . . ac heora nán nyste nán gewis be þám (cf. nyste heora nán his naman tó secgenne, Hml. Th. ii. 506, 30), Hml. S. 31, 349. Mænige wíse men swíþe swuncen mid ðǽre sprǽce and litel gewis (or *adj.?*) funden, Bt. 41, 4 ; F. 250, 20 (2) *a record giving exact information, certificate* (?) :—Hæbbe se abbod á mid him gewrit ealra þǽra ǽhta ; þonne seó notu on gebróðra gewrixle bið, sý þæt gewis á mid þám abbode, þæt hé wite hwæt betǽht sý and hwæt underfangen *ex quibus abbas brevem teneat, ut dum sibi in ipsa assignata fratres vicissim succedunt sciat quid dat et quid recipit*, R. Ben. 56, 9. **II.** *certainty.* (1) *of knowledge, belief, trust* :—Miccle gewisse *very certainly*, Men. 124. (1 a) mid gewisse *with certainty, without doubt* :—Wé witan mid gewisse þæt hit neálǽcð, Wlfst. 90, 4 : R. Ben. 128, 17. Hwæs gehwá gelýfan sceolde mid gewisse, Hml. S. 23, 406. Mid gewisse trúwiende, 23 b, 777 note. (1 b) tó gewisse *certainly, as a certainty* :—Án þing ic eów secge tó gewisse, Wlfst. 89, 21. Wé nyton tó nánum gewisse hwænne Críst ús wile habban tó him, Hml. A. 55, 121. (2) *of occurrence*, mid gewisse *with certainty, without fail* :—Bissextus ǽfre binnan þám feórþan geáre cymð mid gewisse, Angl. viii. 312, 11. (3) *certainty in action, where a definite course is followed* :—Swá hé six and twéntig daga þ færeld þurhteáh, swilce hé tó sumum menn mid gewisse (*with definite aim*) fóre (*as if he were going to meet some one particular person*), Hml. S. 23 b, 160. (4) *used with indefinite sense*, mid gewisse *certainly, indeed.* Cf. witodlíce, sóþlíce :—Mid gewisse se foresǽda bisceop . . . angan . . . tó befrínenne, Lch. iii. 432, 26. v. un-gewiss.

ge-wisfullíce. *Substitute: Knowingly, with knowledge.* v. ge-wis ; **I.** 2 :—Hé him þá gewát swíþe gewisfullíce (-wiss-, *v. l.*) swilce hé unwís wǽre *recessit igitur scienter nescius*, Gr. D. 95, 31.

ge-wísian. *Add:* **I.** *to shew, point out something* (acc.) *to a person* (dat.) :—Ðus him gewísede se Æðelwaldes mon ðá gemǽru, C. D. v. 141, 29. Þ hió swá myceles his onfón sceolde swá seó hind hire gewísede, Lch. iii. 426, 29. **II.** *to direct a person.* (1) *with acc.* :— Þæt wé ús sylfe ge þá þe wé wísian sceolan swá gewísian swá swá úre ealra þearf sý, Ll. Th. ii. 332, 24. (1 a) *to direct a person to* (tó) *something* :—Þ gesceád hí gewýsigen sceall tó weldǽdum, Hml. S. 1, 148. (2) *with dat.* (and object to (tó) *which*) :—Þá láreówas mid þám cwydum Godes folce gewísiað tó Crístes geleáfan, Hml. Th. i. 214, 1. [*O. Sax.* gi-wísan (*with dat. pers., acc. thing*).]

ge-wislic ; *adj. Certain, that gives certainty* :—Þ wé gelýfdon þá þe wé núgý ne magon mid gewislicre fandunge witan *quatenus crederemus quae adhuc scire per experimentum non possumus*, Gr. D. 261, 28. v. un-gewislic.

ge-wislíce. *Add:* **I.** *where there is certainty as to a fact, certainly, without doubt, unquestionably* :—Hé swór þ þá wǽpnu wǽron gewyslíce þær on æfen, Hml. S. 3, 259. Þ án ús is gewislíce andweard þte þonne biþ, Bt. 42 ; F. 256, 26. ' Ic wolde witan . . . hwæþer þú wisse búton tweón . . . ' ' Ic gewislíce wite,' Solil. H. 56, 4 : 57, 10 : 60, 1. Wé gewislíce witon . . . *there is no doubt that we know* . . . , Bt. 11, 2 ; F. 36, 2. Gif on heortan wé biddan clǽnre gewislíce (*certe*) þú scealt tó beháte, Hy. S. 68, 7. [Giwislíca se Apollon ǽrest hé gemetta meþodicam, Lch. iii. 82, 9.] **II.** *where there is certainty in respect to what is to happen, without fail, surely* :—Gif ðú hæíst ǽnigne feónd, send þone tó þám feó, and hé bið gewislíce dead (*he shall surely die*), Hml. S. 25, 803. **III.** *of the action of things, with certainty, with unfailing regularity* :—Nǽron nó swá gewislíce ne swá endebyrdlíce hiora stede and hiora ryne funden on hiora stówum and on hiora tídum *non tam certus naturae ordo procederet, nec tam dispositos motus locis, temporibus explicaret*, Bt. 35, 2 ; F. 158, 3. **IV.** *knowingly, accurately, in a way that shews knowledge* :—For þon se Drihtnes wer swíðe gewislíce démde be ǽfweardum mannum *cum vir Domini tam scienter de absentibus judicaret*, Gr. D. 231, 3. Heó fram frymðe gewislíce þurh þone Hálgan Gást ealle þing ymbe Crístes menniscnysse geleornode, Hml. Th. i. 440, 2. **V.** *in a way that imparts knowledge, so as to give information, clearly, explicitly* :—Gif hit gylt nǽre, þonne ne geswutulode þæt hálige godspel swá gewislíce be ðám rícan þæt hé wǽre mid purpuran and mid godewebbe, geglencged, Hml. Th. i. 328, 26. Sege mé gewislícor þæt ic hit mæge understandan *tell me more clearly, that I may understand it*, Ap. Th. 15, 24. Wé wyllað nú secgan be ðisum eallum gewislícor, Ælfc. Gr. Z. 242, 19 : 21, 15. **VI.** *clearly, of mental perception* :—Gyf ic gewislíce ongæáte, Solil. H. 41, 3. Him þúhte on healfslǽpendon . . lichaman, ná eallinga swylce on swefne,

ac gýt gewisslícor, þ hé sceolde néde ofer áne swíðe smale bricge, Vis. Lfc. 4. **VII.** *with vague sense* :—Sume (*adverbs*) synd con- *vel adfirmativa . . . scilicet* and *udelicet* gewislíce, Ælfc. Gr. 227, 1. Gewislíce *utique*, Ps. Srt. 50, 18 : 54, 13. Hwylc tácn sette God . . . ? Þæt tácn gewistlíce (*ipsum videlicet signum*) þ hé útlaga leofode, Angl. vii. 32, 306. Gewislíce *scilicet*, R. Ben. I. 51, 8. [*O. H. Ger.* gewislícho *specialiter, firmiter, indubitato* : *Ger.* ge-wisslich.]

ge-wislíce (?) *sagaciously* :—þá gelǽredus[tan] lǽce[as] gewíslíce (*both i's are accented*) smeádon, Lch. iii. 82, 3. v. wíslíce.

ge-wísness, e ; *f. Teaching* :—Be lǽcecræftes gewísnesse *peri didaxeon*, Lch. iii. 82, 2.

ge-wisse ; *adv. Certainly* :—Hé sylf wiste gewissast be ðám, Hml. S. 21, 110. [*O. H. Ger.* gewisso *certe* : *Ger.* ge-wiss.]

ge-wissend. *Dele, and see next word.*

ge-wissian. *Add:* **I.** *to direct.* (1) the subject a person (human or divine), (a) *to direct a person in his actions, a thing in its movements,* (*a*) with dat. or uncertain :—On þám bócum þe Móyses áwrát swá swá him gewissode God, Ælfc. T. Grn. 5, 37. Hé ástealde þe stíðan drohtnunge swá swá Críst him gewissode, Hml. S. 16, 100 : 22, 5. Þ þú mé gewissige bet þonne ic áwyrhte tó þé, Bt. 42 ; F. 260, 5. Sé ús gewissige á on ðysse worulde, and tó þám écan lífe gelǽde, Hml. S. 17, 268. (β) with acc. :—Mód hé begéme and hé gewissige *mentem gubernet et regat*, Hy. S. 16, 9. (γ) *to direct to an end* :—Hé his híwrǽdene tó ðám ylcan gewissode, Hml. Th. ii. 348, 17. Gewissa mé tó ðínum willan and tó mínre sáwle þearfe bet þonne ic sylf cunne, Bt. 42 ; F. 260, 6. ¶ *of authoritative direction by a ruler, teacher, &c.* (a) *absolute* :—Swá ic bufan gewissode *sicut supra taxavimus*, R. Ben. 44, 2. Sé ðe underséhð sáwla tó gewissianne *qui suscipit animas regendas*, R. Ben. I. 16, 17, 22. (β) with dat. or uncertain :—God his weorce gewissað oð ðisse weorulde geendunge *est gubernator in totius mundi naturis*, Angl. vii. 4, 24. Hé mid þǽm pallium þær mæssode swá se pápa him gewissode, Chr. 1022 ; P. 157, 2. Swá ealde úðwitan ús gewissedon, Angl. viii. 333, 5. (γ) with acc. :—Nihte and dæg þú gewissast (*regis*), Hy. S. 6, 4. Embhwerft þú gewissast *orbem regis*, 26, 4 : 91, 21. Se láreów bið unsceldig, gif hé þæt folc mid láre gewissað, Hml. Th. i. 240, 11. Bisceop sceall gehádode men ǽrest gewissian, þ heora ǽlc wite hwæt him mid rihte gebyrige tó dónne, Ll. Th. ii. 312, 10. Þryfealdne gewissigendne cræft *trinam regentem machinam*, Hy. S. 75, 1. (b) *to direct the course, way, &c., of a person* :—Þenc ǽfre embe God on eallum ðínum wegum and hé sylf gewissað wel þíne fare *in omnibus viis tuis cogita illum, et ipse diriget gressus tuos* (Prov. 3, 6), Hml. S. 13, 321. Ásende Críst his engel mid þé, se forðige ðé and þíne fare gewissige, 22, 29. God, gewissa úre dǽda, Hml. Th. ii. 598, 16. Hí eódon tó scipe mid him and bǽdon God þ hé his weg gewissode, 15, 19. (c) *to appoint a time* :—Tó þám ylcan ándagan þe hé him gewissode, Hml. A. 97, 167. (2) the subject a thing :—Hú man mæg þone weg gefaran þe gewissað tó Gode, Ælfc. T. Grn. 7, 39. **II.** *to give information about, inform a person of something* :—Heó him cúðlíce ealle þing ymbe Crístes menniscnysse gewissode, Hml. Th. i. 440, 1. Ic wolde georne æt ðé gewitan þissere byrig rihtnaman, gif þú mé woldest gewissigan *I should like to know from you the proper name of this town, if you would inform me*, Hml. S. 23, 548.

ge-wissung. *Add:* **I.** *a becoming certain, certainty* :—Ealle ðás foresǽdan ðing sind mid micelre gewissunge getrymde þurh ðisne æfterfyligendan cwyde, Hml. Th. i. 614, 31. **II.** *information.* v. gewissian ; II :—Nis geræd on nánre béc nán swutelre gewissung be hire geendunge, Hml. Th. i. 440, 11.

ge-wistfullian. *Add:* **I.** *intrans.* :—Gewistfulla *epulare*, Wlfst. 286, 22. **II.** *trans.* (?) :—Þá rihtwísan beóð gewistfullode *justi epulentur*, Ps. L. 67, 4.

ge-wistfulligend, es ; *m. One that feasts* :—Swég gewistfulgend[es] *sonus epulantis*, Ps. Rdr. 41, 5. v. wistfulligend.

* ge-wistfullung, e ; *f. Feasting, a feast, delightful thing* :—Sanda gewistfullunga (*opulentas*) *ferculorum dilicias*, An. Ox. 1632. Gestreónfulle gewistfullunge *sumptuosas opulentias* (has *epulent-* been read ?), 1931.

ge-wit. *Add:* **I.** *sense, perception* :—Homo man, anima sáwl, animus mód, spiritus gást, sensus gewit, intellectus, andgit, cogitatio geðanc, corpus lichama, Wrt. Voc. i. 42, 31–38. Ðæt gecyndelice gewit *naturales sensus*, Past. 405, 4. Mé þincð nú þæt þú ne trúwie þám úttram gewitte, náðer ne þám eágum, . . . ne ðám hrínunge *respuis in hac causa testimonium sensuum*, Solil. H. 18, 11. Ic mín gewit and ealle míne styrenesse forleás *sensum motunque omnem perdidi*, Bd. 5, 6 ; Sch. 577, 9. **I a.** *a sense, one of the senses* :—Woldest þú þinne cniht mid þám úttram gewit[t]um cunnan? *familiarem tuum sensu vis nosse?*, Solil. H. 18, 18, 20. **I b.** *what is felt, a sense, feeling.* v. witan ; **III** :—þurh wrǽð gewitt, Lch. 459. **II.** *condition of being wise or sensible, good sense, understanding.* v. witan ; **II** :—Sýn gecorene of ðám sylfum gebróðrum þá ðe gódes gewittes (gewitnes, *v. l.* : the 13th cent. MS. has gódes gewitnesse) sýn and háligre drohtnunge (*boni testimonii et sancte conversationis*), R. Ben. 46, 9. Ðæt gé nó tó

hrædlíce ne sién ástyrede from gewitte *ut non cito moveamini a vestro sensu*, Past. 213, 16. Læran sceal mon geóngne monnan . . . sylle him wist and wǽdo oð þæt hine mon on gewitte álǽde, Gn. Ex. 48. **III.** *the faculty of knowing*, (1) in rational beings *the intellectual part of man, intellect :*—Ne séce ic nó hér þá béc, ac þ ðæt þá béc forstent, ðæt is þín gewit (*tuae mentis sedem requiro*), Bt. 5, 1 ; S. 11, 30. Ælc wiste his gewit swá swá hé ǽr wiste ; þ gewit wæs swíþe sorgiende for þám ermþum ðe hí drógan *sola mens stabilis, super monstra, quae patitur, gemit*, 38, 1 ; F. 196, 6. Ic gehére þæt mín gewit is ǽce. Ac mé lyst gýt witan be ðám gewitte þæt ic ǽr ácsode (cf. hweðer ðú ǽfter ðæs líchaman gedále and þǽre sáwle máre wisse þonne ðú nú wást þe lǽsse, 59, 6), hweðer hyt ǽfter ðæs líchaman gedále and þǽre sáwle weóxe þe wanede . . . Ic wát nú þæt þæt lýf á byð and þæt gewit, ac ic ondréde þæt hyt beó on þǽre weorulde swá hyt hér byð on cildum. Ne wéne ic ná þæt þæt lýf þǽr beó bútan gewitte þe má þe hyt hér byð on cildum, Solil. H. 64, 11–20 : 66, 7. Ic niéhst ácsode be mínum gewitte, 65, 4 : 33, 17 : 38, 7. Ic þín gewit mid ealle ne forlét, Bt. 5, 3 ; F. 14, 8. Þu man geworhtest, and him sealdest word and gewitt (*speech and reason*), Hy. 9, 56. Swelce snytro swylce manegum óþrum ieldran gewittum oftogen is, Bt. 8 ; F. 24, 28. (1 a) *an intellectual faculty :*—Woldest þú þínne cniht cunnan mid þám inran gewit[t]um ? *familiarem tuum intellectu vis nosse*, Solil. H. 18, 19. (2) in animals :—Úre gesceádwísnes is betere þonne nýtena andgit sié, oððe þæs gewittes ǽnig dǽl ðe him forgifen is, Bt. 41, 5 ; F. 254, 13. **IV.** in a less definite sense, *the mind :*—Gleáwhýdig Judas (him wæs weallende gewitt (-wilt, MS.) þurh witan snytro) þæt word gecwæð wísdómes ful, El. 938. Nó hé on gewitte blon þæs þe hé ǽr ongann, þæt hé Dryhten herede, An. 1267. Hé on gewitte oncneów þæt . . ., 672 : 770. Wís on þínum gewitte, Hö. 78 : Crä. 13 : An. 470. On gewitte wác, 212. Wísan gewitte, 552. Hé wédde on gewitte, Jul. 597. Onwend þec in gewitte, 144. þæt þæt gewit ne mæg mód onwendan monna ǽnig mid drýcræftum *nec potentia gramina corda vertere non valent*, Met. 26, 100: An. 35. Þurh wís gewit, Cri. 1193. Þurh fród gewit, 1178. Hí deorc gewit hæfdon on hreðre, 640. þæt týddre gewitt, 29. **V.** *right* or *sound mind* (out of one's) *mind, wits :*—Gif hwylc man of his gewitte feóle *si homo quis mente sua excederit*, Ll. Th. ii. 236, 29. Gif mon of his gewitte weorðe, Lch. ii. 288, 20. þ hé hæbbe his gewit *that he have his wits about him*, Ll. Th. ii. 352, 31. Ne wénþ ðæs nán mon ðe his gewit hæfð *nisi qui insaniat, nemo id putat*, Bt. 36, 7 ; F. 184, 3. þ þú forlure þín gewitt, Hml. S. 36, 311. **VI.** *knowledge, prudence, wit, skill :*—þæt þú gewittes ne wást bútan wildeóra þeáw, Dan. 572. þá yldu þurh gewittes wylm wendan tó lífe, Ph. 191. Worde and gewitte, wíse þance, Gen. 1958. mid gewitte gemunan Meotudes láre, Cri. 1200. Ic on þe sylfum oncnáwe wísdómes gewit, An. 645. Hí náhton foreþances, wísdómes gewitt, El. 357 : 1191. **VII.** *conscience :*—Þonne gé ofsleáð hira untruman gewit *percutientes conscientiam eorum infirmam*, Past. 451, 36. v. fer[h]þ-, riht-, un-, unriht-gewitt.

**ge-wita.** Add : **I.** *a witness ; testis.* (1) *one that is present when anything is done, an eye-witness :*—Ðá díeglan yfel habbað écne gewutan on ðæm godcundan Déman *occulta mala sua divinis judiciis anteponunt*, Past. 449, 1. Hwylcre geearnunge hé hæfed wǽre mid þone inlican gewitan *cuius meriti apud infernum testem habitus sit*, Bd. 5, 6 ; Sch. 574, 4. (1 a) *a witness* of something :—Ic (St. Peter), Crístes ðrowunge gewita (-wiota, *v. l.*), Past. 137, 17. þá wolde hé begytan him sylfum sumne gewitan swá myccles wundres *tanti sibi testem volens adhibere miraculi*, Gr. D. 171, 24. þæs ǽghwylc heáhgeréfa wæs gewita on Iudéum þ Ebréa God cóme hider ; and mon geseah . . ., Bl. H. 177, 14. (2) *one that attests :*—Ne beó gé nǽfre on nánre leásre gewitnysse, for þon se leása gewita ne bið hé nǽfre ungewítnod, Ll. Th. ii. 422, 38. Leáse gewitan stældon on mé, Ps. Th. 34, 12. Gelýf hys hálgum, for ðám hí wéron swíðe unleáse gewitan, Solil. H. 63, 35. (2 a) *with gen.* of that which is attested :—Hé cwæþ þ hé wǽre se cúþesta gewita (*testis certissimus*) hyre clǽnnesse, Bd. 4, 19 ; Sch. 440, 19. (2 b) *a witness* for a person, *a* (person's) *witness :*—Hé swór God him tó gewitan, Hml. S. 23 b, 271. Gé beóþ míne gewitan *eritis mihi testes*, Bl. H. 119, 24. (2 a b) *a witness of something for a person :*—Hwæs sceoldan hié úrum Drihtne gewitan beón ?, Bl. H. 119, 26. ¶ *uninflected ?* :—þyses ealles hié sceoldon Drihtne gewita beón, Bl. H. 121, 3. (2 c) *with clause, a witness that . . . :*—Gé sint ealle míne gewitan (-witan, *v. l.*) ðæt ic eom unscildig *contestor vos, quia mundus sum*, Past. 379, 13. (3) *one that proves by example :*—Ic bið him self gewita (him selfum gewiota, *v. l.*) ðæt hé wilnað him selfum gielpes *ipse sibi testis est, quia gloriam quaerit*, Past. 55, 2. Gewuta (-wiota, *v. l.*), 145, 13. **II.** *one having knowledge in common with another ; conscius.* (1) *one cognizant* of a matter (gen.) :—Hálge wítgan . . . mid Háliges Gástes geonlum onlýhte . . . wǽron gewitan ealra Gódes dégolra dóma, Bl. H. 161, 16. (1 a) *one who through confession had knowledge* of something :—Sé þe bið manna sáwla lǽce and heora dǽda gewita, Ll. Th. ii. 260, 13. (2) *a confidant, counsellor, colleague* (cf. conscius, socius, collega, Corp. Gl. H. 35, 695) :—Bisceopum gebyreð þ symle mid heom wunian wel geþungene witan þ hí wið rǽdan magan . . . and þ heora gewitan beón, Ll. Th. ii.

316, 24. (2 a) *a colleague, an associate :*—Wildeóra gewita (*Nebuchadnezzar*), Dan. 624. (3) *one having knowledge of crime, an accessory, accomplice* (cf. conpliciis, consciis, Corp. Gl. H. 36, 707) :—Hé gecýðe . . . þ hé ne gewita ne gestala nǽre (*that he neither knew of, nor took part in, the theft*), Ll. Th. i. 118, 15. Næs ic æt rǽde ne æt dǽde, ne gewita ne gewyrhta, þér man mid unrihte N. orf ætferede, 180, 1. (3 a) *with gen.* of crime :—X. wintre cniht mæg bión þiéfðe gewita, Ll. Th. i. 106, 18. Gif huoelc stale ðis ðerhendeda ł ðerhendadon giwuta uæs *si qui furtum hoc perpetravit, aut perpetrati conscius fuit*, Rtl. 113, 34. (3 b) *with gen.* of criminal :—Úre geréfena swylc þe þǽra þeófa gewita wǽre, Ll. Th. i. 220, 24. þ hé nelle þeóf beón ne þeófes gewita, 388, 7. (3 b a) where the crime is denoted by prep. :—Se hláford þe his þeówan æt þýfðe gewita sý, Ll. Th. i. 200, 20. **III.** *one who is conscious* of something :—Hé cwæð þ hé nǽre ná gewita (hé sylfa nǽre nǽnig gewita, *v. l.*) þæs mægenes þe hé nytende worhte *discedat se conscium in illa virtute non esse, quam nesciens fecisset*, Gr. D. 116, 4. **III a.** *with reflex pron. :*—þ mód him selfum gewita biþ Godes willan *mens sibi conscia*, Bt. 18, 4 ; F. 68, 18. **IV.** *for* wita :—Ealra gewitena gemót, Chr. 1048 ; P. 174, 21.

**ge-witan.** Add : **I.** *to know, have knowledge of :*—Mid ðý gewit ðu *cum scieris*, Mt. p. 4, 6. 'Ðone uoeg gié uuton' . . . 'Huu mago ué þ weg gewuta ?' '*uiam scitis*' . . . '*Quomodo possumus uiam scire ?*', Jn. L. R. 14, 5. **II.** *to know, get knowledge of, learn.* (1) absolute :—Ne walde ǽnig gewuta *nec uolebat quemquam scire*, Mk. L. R. 9, 30. (2) *with acc.* :—Nǽnig siððan wera gewiste þǽre wihte síð, Rä. 30, 14. Hé hopode þ hé þý æfterfyligendan geáre þ gewiste, Hml. S. 23 b, 728. Ic wolde æt ðé gewitan þissere byrig rihtnaman, 23, 547. Hine gewuta (*scire*) ðú mæht of oferwritenum, Mt. p. 12, 2. Gewite, p. 4, 1. Gewutta, p. 11, 1. (3) *with clause :*—þ gié gewitte for ðon sunu monnes hæfes mæht *ut sciatis quoniam filius hominis habet potestatem*, Mt. L. 9, 6. þ hé ásende sumne mann and gewiste (*agnosceret*) and him eft gecýðde hwæt wǽre geworden be Germane, Gr. D. 172, 8. Sum ríce man wolde gewitan æt ðám Hǽlende hú hé mihte habban heofenan ríces myrhðe, Hex. 54, 23. (4) *with acc.* and clause :—þ hé þ sceolde geornlíce gewitan and geleornian hwilces geleáfan Angelcynnes cyrice wǽre *ut, cuius esset fidei Anglorum ecclesia, diligenter ediscere*, Bd. 4, 18 ; Sch. 438, 1. **III.** *to know, be conscious of, learn by the senses :*—þæt hé mægða síð wíne druncen gewitan ne meahte, Gen. 2605. þæs þe ic gewitan mihte *from what I could see ; ut dinoscere potui*, Bd. 5, 12 ; Sch. 620, 15. Eió wolde gewitan (*dignoscere*) mid hire eárum æt his nosþyrlum hweþer ǽnig líflic oroð him inne wǽre, 276, 16.

**ge-wítan ;** p. -wát, pl. -witon. *For* ge-wítan ; **I.** *substitute : To see after, take care of.* (1) with acc. :—Gewíte and beseoh wíngeard þisne vide et visita vineam istam, Ps. Th. 79, 14. (2) *with clause :*—Gewíte þǽre cirican ealdor þ him mon on þám fierste mete ne selle, Ll. Th. i. 64, 16. v. wítan ; **I.**

**ge-wítan** *to go away, depart.* *To* ge-wítan ; **II.** *in Dict.*, *add :*—Geuuíto *facesso*, An. Ox. 53, 25. Gewát *cessit*, An. Ox. 3203. Geuuát[u] *concessit*, Wrt. Voc. ii. 105, 21. *Excidit, cecidit vel* gewát, 145, 9. Gewítendi *decidens*, 106, 11. **I.** *of living things.* (1) *of actual movement :*—Worpende ðá scillingas in temple gewát (*recessit*), Mt. L. R. 27, 5. Férdan, áweg gewítan *abscedunt*, An. Ox. 3590. Mid þý hié þá fyr gewítene wǽron *longius subeuntibus* ðis, Bd. 5, 12 ; Sch. 620, 21. (1 a) where beginning, direction, or end of movement is marked, (a) by prep. or adv. :—Se earn úp gewít bufan þá wolcnu, Bt. 7, 3 ; F. 22, 5. Hié niðer mid gewítan in midde þá neowolnesse *descenderunt in medium baratri*, Bd. 5, 12 ; Sch. 620, 19. Gewite of gecyndlime *procederes* (i. exires) *de uulua*, An. Ox. 1495. (β) by dat. :—Heó (*Hagar*) gewát engles lárum hire hláfordum (cf. Cwæð se engel hyre tó : 'Gecir tó þínre hlǽfdian,' Gen. 16, 9), Gen. 2294. (1 b) where the movement is compulsory, as in banishment, escape, flight :—Gif bana of lande gewíteð, þá mágas healfne leód forgelden, Ll. Th. i. 8, 7. Mé bǽdon and lǽrdon Rómane, þ ic gewát heonon onweg *pressed by the prayers and persuasions of the Romans I fled hence*, Bl. H. 191, 14. Ealdbriht wrecca gewát on Súð-Seaxe . . . Ine gefeaht wið Súð-Seaxum and ofslóh Ealdberht þe hé ǽr út fiémde, Chr. 722 ; P. 43, 25. Hé (*Joseph*) gewát Ægypti *recessit in Ægyptum*, Mt. R. 2, 14 : Wrt. ii. 71, 56. þæt hí gewiton on þǽre and wurdon tó hundum, An. Ox. 26, 61. Petrus eówode þǽm hundum þone hláf, and hié sóna onweg gewitan and náhwǽr ne æteówdon (*they fled at once and were seen no more*), Bl. H. 181, 23. Gewítað (*recedite*) from mé gé unryhtwyrhtan, Past. 27, 23. Ælþeódige mæn, gif hió hiora hǽmed rihtan nyllað, of lande mid hiora ǽhtum and mid synnum gewíten, Ll. Th. i. 38, 2 : 406, 22. Of earde gewítan, 378, 12. Hiera wíf ácsedon . . . hwider hié fleón woldon ; þæt hié óðer gener nǽfden, búton hié on heora wífa hrif gewiton *quaerentes, num in uteros suorum vellent refugere*, Ors. 1, 12 ; S. 54, 4. (1 c) with the idea of abandonment :—Se here forlét þæt geweorc, and þý ilcan sumere ofer sǽ gewiton, Chr. 885 ; P. 78, 5. Þonon (*from heaven*) úre Drihten nǽfre onweg gewiten næs þurh his þá écan godcundnesse, Bl. H. 127, 24. (2) *to depart from this world, die.* v. ge-witenes :—Wé gewítað *occidimus*, i. *deficimus*, Wülck. Gl. 256, 19. Hreás, gewát *occubuit* (*machera crudeliter*

percussus *occubuit*, Ald. 49, 14), An. Ox. 3582. Heó wearð gewundod, ac heó ne gewât swâ þeáh, Hml. S. 9, 128 : 25, 160. Þâ feol hê âdûne and gewât *cecidit et expiravit*, Hml. Th. i. 316, 29, 34. And ðonne se wer gewîte *and then the husband die*, Ll. Th. i. 126, 2 : Solil. H. 52, 8. Gewitte, 10. Gefyrn forþ gewitene *long since dead*, Bt. 19 ; F. 70, 9, 12. (2 a) *to depart* from life, this world, &c. :—Hê gewât of þysan lîfe, Hml. S. 23, 728. Hî of þisse worlde gewiton, Bl. H. 95, 17. Gif hwâ cwydeleás of þyssum lîfe gewîte *if any one die intestate*, Ll. Th. i. 412, 27. Of mînum lîchoman gewîtan, Bl. H. 139, 13. Of lîchoman gewîten, 149, 31. Of lîfe gewiten, Ap. Th. 1, 8. (3) of action. (a) *to depart from a person, abandon, cease from intercourse with* :—Ðû wâst þæt se æca þe nâht fram ne gewŷt, bûton þû fram hym gewîte, Solil. H. 25, 3. Þâ frŷnd gewîtaþ mid þâm welan, Bt. 29, 2 ; F. 106, 9. Wê biddaþ þ þû fram ûs ne gewîte, Bl. H. 145, 18. Hê geseah þ eal manna cynn from heora Scyppende gewîtene wǽron, 103, 5. (b) *to desist from doing* :— Hê gewât from þǽre dûstsceáwunga, Bl. H. 113, 29. (bb) *to desist, withdraw from doing what ought to be done, fall away, decline* :—Gif hwylc gôd man from gôde gewîte, ne biþ hê þon mâ fullîce gôd, Bt. 37, 3 ; F. 190, 28. Ðæt hî nǽfre ne gewîten (-wiét-, v. l.) from þǽre geornfulnesse ðǽre rǽdinge hâligra gewrita *ut a sacrae lectionis studio non recedant*, Past. 171, 20. Ðæt hwîlum gebyrede ðæt hié gewieten (-wit-, v. l.) of hiera geleáfan *discedant quidam a fide*, 317, 25. (4) of condition, *to get* into a condition, attain to what is wished, *fall* into evil :—Ðŷ lǽs hié weorðen ûp âhæfene and on ofermêtto gewîten (-wiét-, v. l.) *ne per elationis impulsum in profundiora mergantur*, Past. 197, 3. Getǽc mê sumne mann þâra þe ðê gesǽlegost þince and on his selfwille sŷ swîþost gewiten, Bt. 11, 1 ; F. 32, 17. II. of things. (1) where there is motion :—Þ fŷr ûp gewit *ignis surgit in altum*, Bt. 39, 13 ; F. 234, 12. Ðonne ðâ twigo forburston, þonne gewitan þâ sáula niðer þâ þe on ðǽm twigum hangodan, Bl. H. 211, 4. (2) *to pass* from a condition or position :—Ðæs lîchoman deáð is þonne seó sáwul him of gewît *corporis mors est dum corpus deseritur ab anima*, Angl. vi. 22, 202. Ðæt sió sib of eówre heortan ne gewîte (*discedat*), Past. 357, 11, 2. Ealle oþre gesceafta âswindaþ for cyle gif hit (*fire*) eallunga from gewîte, Bt. 33, 4 ; F. 130, 35. (3) *to pass* from possession or control ; gewîtan fram *to leave, desert* :—Þonne þâ woruldsǽlþa him fram gewîtaþ, Bt. 8 ; F. 26, 10 : Bl. H. 21, 12. Seó beholene ondweardnes ne gewât from ûs, 77, 2. Ðâ wendon mê þâ woruldsǽlþa heora bæc tô and mê mid ealle from gewitan, Bt. 2 ; F. 4, 13. (4) *to pass away, come to an end, perish* ; v. ge-wîtendlic :—Ǽr þâm þe gewîte (*transeat*) gewîteþ, Wrt. Voc. ii. 72, 4) heofon and eorþe, ân .i. oððe ân prica ne gewît (*praeteribit*) fram þǽre ǽ, .Mt. 5, 18 : Bl. H. 91, 21, 22. Se lîchoma ealdaþ and his fægernes gewîteþ, 57, 30, 14 : 59, 6. Swâ hwæt swâ heó (*an adder*) gesyhð, hyt forscrincd and gewîteþ, Lch. i. 242, 4. God nâne gesceafta ne forlêt eallunga gewîtan swâ þæt hî tô nâwihte weorðe . . . Nân gesceaft swâ clêne onwæg ne gewît, þæt hê eft ne cume, ne swâ clǽne ne forwyrð, þæt hê tô hwan hwugu ne weorðe. Ac hwî wênst þû þonne, nû þâ wâcestan gesceafta eallunga ne gewîtað, þæt seóleste gescaft myd ealle gewîte ?, Solil. H. 62, 26-63, 3. Þ hâlige sǽd on him gedwân and gewât, Bl. H. 55, 30. Þâ ealdan forþ gewitun *uetera transierunt*, An. Ox. 40, 35. Hû êce is ðæt ðæt hié wilniað, and hû gewîtende ðæt is ðæt hié onscuniað (*quam transitoria, quae contemnunt*), Past. 299, 8. Swâ swâ gewîtende smŷc *ut fumus euanescens*, An. Ox. 4062. Þis andwearde lîf is heard and gewîtende and swîðe geswincfull, Verc. Först 165. Eall þ is from heora eágum gewiten, Bl. H. 99, 19. Mîne welan syudon ealle gewitene and gehrorene, 113, 25. v. forþ-gewîtan, -gewiten.

**ge-wîte** *departure*. v. onweg-gewîte.

**ge-wîte, es ; n.** *Punishment, torment* :—Þæt hê him âsecge on hwilcum gewîte ic eom, Solil. H. 68, 5.

**ge-wîtendlic.** In l. 6 l. gewîtendlicum, *and add* : -witenlic *perishable*. v. ge-wîtan ; II. 4 :—Gewîtendlicum lîfe *sole uolubili, presenti uita*, Germ. 388, 3. Gewîtendlic *deciduam*, Wrt. Voc. ii. 28, 19. Hohfulnesse be þingum gewîtendlicum *sollicitudinem de rebus transitoriis*, R. Ben. I. 16, 10. Gewîtendlice *caducis*, Angl. xiii. 440, 1073. Gewitenlice *transitorias*, Kent. Gl. 1180. Ne bidde wê nâ leáse welan and gewitenlice wurðmyntas, Hml. Th. i. 158, 26. Heó oferwinð þâ gewîtendlican geswinc, Hml. A. 77, 102. v. un-gewîtendlic.

**ge-wîtenlic.** v. ge-wîtendlic.

**ge-wîtennes.** *Add* : *departure from this life ; death* (v. ge-wîtan ; I. 2) ; *the anniversary of a person's death* :—On þone endlyftan dæg þæs mônþes byð Sci. Martines gewytennys, Shrn. 146, 32. v. âweg-, forþ-, onweg-gewîtennes.

**ge-witfæst.** *Add* : The Latin is : *Nullus vexatus sine salute* : **ge-witfæstness.** v. un-gewitfæstness : **ge-witfull.** v. un-gewitfull : **ge-witfulness.** v. un-gewitfulness : **ge-wiðerworded** = ge-wiþerweardod. v. wiþer-weardian : **ge-wiþelode.** v. ge-wiþelian.

**ge-wîtigian.** *Add* : (1) *to declare, make known* :—Ðerh ðæra tâceno ædeáwnise mid ðŷ geuîtgade Crîst *per signorum experimenta promens Christum*, Jn. p. 2, 1. Ân gadered wer þ is ded for þ ðæm folce gewîtgade *unum debere mori pro populo prophetizat*, 6, 11. Gewîtga (*prophetiza*) huælc is se ðe ðec slôg, Lk. L. 22, 64 : Mk. L. 14, 65. (2)

*to predict* :—Fader his gefylled wæs hâlge gaaste and gewîtgade (*prophetauit*), Lk. L. R. 1, 67 : Jn. 11, 51. Allæ wîtgo gewîtgedon, Mt. L. 11, 13. Swâ hwæt swâ wæs gewîtgud Xps gefylde, An. Ox. 40, 13. Þâ ðâ se Symeon hæfde gewîtegod þâs wîtegunge be Crîste, Hml. Th. i. 146, 21.

**ge-witleás.** *Add* :—Gewitleása *freneticus*, i. *demoniaticus, insanus*, Wrt. Voc. ii. 150, 51. . I. *out of one's mind, mad*. v. ge-wit ; V :— Ic wênde þ heó gewitleás wǽre (cf. þû forlure þîn gewitt, 311), Hml. S. 36, 352. Lǽg ðǽr sum man on his môde gefangen mid ungewittignesse ; þone swylcne seócne lǽcas nemniað gewitleásne *quidam mente captus jacebat, quem medici phreneticum appellant*, Gr. D. 247, 14. I a. of demoniacal possession :—Þisne (cyricweard) in geeóde se wrǽcenda gâst . . . þâ ongan se deófol þurh ðæs gewitleásan cyricweardes mûð clypian, Gr. D. 200, 20. Gewitleáse, deófolseóce *inerguminos*, i. *amentes*, An. Ox. 3057. II. *foolish, senseless*. Cf. ge-wit ; II, VI. (1) of persons :—Gyf hwylc gewytleás man wênð þ hê hine sylfne geworhte, Hml. S. 1, 67. (2) of actions :—God wolde gewîtnian ðâ Niniuitiscan for heora gewitleásum dǽdum, Hml. S. 13, 274.

**ge-witleást.** *Add* : I. cf. ge-witleás ; I a :—Wið gewitleáste, þ is wið deófulseócnesse, Lch. i. 248, 3. II. 1. cf. ge-witleás ; II. 1 :— His wîfes gewitleást (cf. þu sprǽce swâ swâ ân stunt wîf, 452, 31), Hml. Th. ii. 456, 4. Gewitleást *vechordia*, Hy. S. 9, 20. Þæs cáseres (*Domitian*) witan hine ofslôgon for his wælhreównysse and his gewittleáste, Ælfc. T. Grn. 16, 26. Hwîlon God gewîtnaþ ðæs mannes gewitleáste, Hml. A. 62, 258. II. 2. cf. ge-witleás ; II. 2 :—Hê ne beseah on leásum gewitlŷstum *non respexit in insanias falsas*, Ps. L. 39, 5.

**ge-witlic.** v. un-gewitlic.

**gewit-loca.** *Add* :—Gif þu âwyrtwalast of gewitlocan (cf. of ðînum môde, Bt. 23 ; F. 78, 33) leása gesǽlþa, Met. 12, 26. Þone wîsan on gewitlocan scamian (cf. hine scamian, Bt. 19 ; F. 68, 23), 10, 12. Sume ðone wæterscipe weriað on gewitlocan, wîsdômes stream, Past. 469, 2. Ic ondette mîne synna for ealne mînne lîchoman . . . word and gewitlocan, Angl. xi. 98, 51.

**ge-witnes.** *Add* : I. *witness*. Cf. ge-wita ; I ; ge-witscipe. (1) *personal observation, presence* of witnesses :—Sê þe yrfe bycge on gewitnesse, Ll. Th. i. 212, 12. Bûton hê hæbbe gewitnesse, 282, 26. (1 a) with gen. of person :—þæt hê him sealde wið feoh þæt scræf on hyra gewitnysse (*coram vobis*), Gen. 23, 9. Ðeáh hit nân mon nyte, swâðeáh hit bið beforan monnum gedôn, emne swelce hit sié on ealra ðâra gewitnesse gedôn . . . *nullus fortasse videt, et hoc tamen coram hominibus fecit ; quia tot testes in bono opere secum duxit . . .*, Past. 451, 21. Hê hine geclǽnsode on þes arcêbes gewitnesse (*teste arepa*), Chr. 1022 ; P. 157, 6 : Ll. Th. i. 162, 13 : 198, 13. Cŷþe hê on hwæs gewitnysse hê þone ceáp gebohte, 274, 22. In gemôtes gewitnesse, 82, 16. Ælc mon mid heora gewitnysse bicge, 274, 12 : 276, 6. Nân man hwyrfe nânes yrfes bûton þæs gerêfan gewitnesse . . . , 204, 18. Under þæs bisceopes gewitnesse *under the bishop's supervision*, 198, 10. Hæbbe hê þæs portgerêfan gewitnesse, 158, 11. Man hæbbe getreówe gewitnesse feówer manna, 390, 4, 6. (2) *the practice of having witnesses present at a transaction, the service as a witness in such cases* :—Landcôp and lahcôp and witword and gewitnes, þ þ stande, Ll. Th. i. 294, 1 : ii. 302, 6. Ic wille þ gewitnes sŷ geset tô ælcere byrig . . . Tô ælcere byrig .xxxiii. sŷn gecorene tô gewitnesse . . . Heora ælc þonne hine man ǽrest tô gewitnysse gecŷsd sylle âð . . . sŷn on ælcum ceápe twêgen oþþe þrŷ tô gewitnysse, 274, 6-19. Mid gewitnysse þâra manna þe tô gewitnysse genamode synt, 276, 7. (3) *testimony, attestation*. Cf. ge-wita ; I. 2 :—Galað is on Englisc gewitnesse heáp. Eal sió gesomnung ðære hâlgan ciricean ðurh ondetnesse hielt ðâ gewitnesse ðǽre sôðfæsðnesse *Galaad acervus testimonii interpretatur. Cuncta congregatio ecclesiae per confessionem servit testimonio veritatis*, Past. 367, 5-7. Oxanhyrde môt lǽswian .ii. oxan on gemǽnre lǽse be his ealdormannes gewitnesse (*per testimonium aldremanni sui*), Ll. Th. i. 438, 14. Þ hŷ rihte dômas dêman be ðǽre þ. gewitnesse, Cht. E. 230, 30 : Wlfst. 181, 7. On his nêhebûra gewitnesse, Ll. Th. i. 238, 3. Sê þe land gewerod hæbbe be scîre gewitnesse, 420, 20. Gange ælc man þæs tô gewitnesse þe he ðurre on þâm hâligdôme swerian, 292, 14. Hiê bǽdon þæt hê on þǽre gewitnesse (cf. ge-wita ; I. 2 c) wǽre þæt þæt rîce emne gedǽled wǽre *they asked him to be witness that the kingdom was evenly divided*, Ors. 3, 7 ; S. 114, 18. Hê hæfð ðæs gewitnesse ðe hê cwêman ðencð ðæt hê hit for Gode dyde, Past. 451, 17. Gif hê lâðleás beó sêce swylcne hlâford on þâ gewitnesse swylcne hê wille *si culpa careat, perquirat sibi dominum in testimonio quem voluerit*, Ll. Th. i. 220, 25. Bûton hê hæbbe ðæs hundredes manna gewitnyssa, 258, 22. (4) *oral or written evidence, (false) witness* :—Be wôhre gewitnesse. Gif man âfinde þ heora ǽnig on wôhre gewitnesse wǽre, þ nǽfre his gewitnes eft nâht ne forstande, Ll. Th. i. 204, 22-4. Getrŷwe gewitnes *trustworthy evidence*, 290, 19. Ic hêr on sôðre gewitnesse stande . . . swâ ic mid mînum êagum oferseah and mînum earum oferhŷrde þ þ ic him mid sæcge, 180, 28 : 276, 33. Nân ôðer þingc on gewitnysse ne cŷþe bûtan þ ân þ hê geseah oþþe gehŷrde, 274, 17. Gif mæssepreóst stande on leásre gewitnesse oþþe on mǽnan âðe, 346, 8 : 398, 11 : 388,

23. Ne sǽge þú leáse gewitnesse, 44, 20. Náne gewitnesse hé hit on riht týmde, 158, 16. Búton hé gewitnesse hæbbe þ æfter him ne saga þú, 54, 4. Þ hé hæfde ungeligene gewitnesse þæs þ hit swá gód wǽre, 232, 26. Be ðám ðe hiora gewitnessa beforan bisc̄. áleógað. Gif hwá beforan biscepe his gewitnesse and his wed áleóge, 110, 9–12. False gewihta ... and leáse gewitnessa, 310, 13. (4a) *a testament :*—Ðǽre níwa gewitnesse *noui testamenti*, Mt. L. R. 26, 28. (5) with a personal sense, *a witness ;* testis : or with collective force, *witnesses ;* testes. (a) *one who is present at a transaction.* Cf. ge-wita; I. 1:—On þára manna gewitnesse þe him tó gewitnesse getealde syndon (*qui testes adnumerati sunt ei*), Ll. Th. i. 162, 13: 34, 4. Ðis syndon ðǽra manna naman ðe ðises tó gewitnesse wǽron, Cht. Th. 541, 1. Ðá god ðe hí openlíce dóð beóð swelce hí sién bútan gewitnesse, for ðǽm hí næbbað éce gewitnesse ; ac hí habbað éce gewitnesse ðára yfela ðe hí diégellíce dóð *sine teste est bonum, quod publice faciunt, et non sine aeterno teste, quod latentes delinquunt*, Past. 449, 2–4. (b) *one who bears witness.* Cf. ge-wita; I. 2:—Leás gewitnes *testis mendax (peribit),* Kent. Gl. 801. Gif þǽr bið gewrit oþþe gewitnes (*scriptum testamenti et testes*), Ll. Th. i. 88, 18. Gecýþe seó gewitnysse sý *inuenerit hoc ipsi testes in fide Domini, quod ei in uero testimonio sint,* 388, 22. Mid gewitnysse *cum testibus,* 290, 10: 489, 11. Forþ brengende leáse gewitnesse *proferentem (mendacia) testem fallacem,* Kent. Gl. 153. Cuðmun twoege leáse gewitneso (*testes*), Mt. L. R. 26, 60. Þ gewitnessa ne móston standan, þeáh hí fulgetreówe wǽron, and hí swá sǽdan swá hí tó woldon swerian, Ll. Lbmn. 244, 30. **II.** *knowledge, cognizance.* (1) cf. ge-wita; II. 1:—Dó hé þ mid þæs ealdormonnes gewitnysse, Ll. Th. i. 86, 3 : 282, 18. (2) cf. ge-wita; II. 3:—Gif þeówmon wyrce on Sunnandæg be his hláfordes hǽse. ... Gif se þeówa bútan his gewitnesse wyrce, Ll. Th. i. 104, 4. Gyf se landman ǽniges fácnes gewita sý, þonne sý hé wítes scyldig, búton hé hine þǽre gewitnesse geládie, 354, 27. Gif hwá stalie swá his wíf nyte and his bearn. ... Gif hé stalie on gewitnesse ealles his hírédes, 106, 16. Scyld on gewyrhtum oððe on gewitnesse, Rtl. 114, 23. (3) *knowledge confined to oneself.* Cf. ge-wita; III a:—Swá hwylc man swá mid his gewitnysse hine ðóne síþe fullað *quicunque sciens* (cf. *non ignoranter,* 45, 5) *secunda vice baptizatus sit,* Ll. Th. ii.144, 21. [O. H. Ger. ge-wiznesse *testimonium, testamentum.*] v. in-gewitnes.

**ge-wítnian.** *Add :* I. *to punish* a person :—Gewítnodum *multato (pestilente),* Kent. Gl. 774. Ðé þincþ þ þá orsorgran bióð gesǽligran ðonne þá gewítnodan, Bt. 38, 4; F. 204, 21. **I a.** where cause is given, *to punish* for something :—Wæs sum leódscipe þe God wolde gewítnian for heora gewítleásum dǽdum, Hml. S. 13, 274. Gode ic hæbbe ábolgen ; for þon ic þus bittre weard gewítnad, Hy. 4, 79. Þá þe gewítnode beóð for hiora scyldum, Ps. Th. 44, 16 : Bt. 39, 11; F. 230, 6. **I b.** where mode of punishment is given. (a) with noun :—Wommum gewítnad, B. 3073. Mid deáðe gewítnedra *morti punitorum,* Ps. Vos. 78, 11. (β) in a clause :—God gewítnode ealle his wimmen, swa þæt heora nán ne mihte habban ǽnig cild, Gen. 20, 18. **II.** *to punish, chastise* a fault :—Ne cann Drihten leahtras, ac hé gewítnað leahtras, Hml. Th. ii. 574, 4. Bið gewí[t]nod *multabitur,* An. Ox. 7, 71. **II a.** where mode of punishment is given :—Uton mid wópe gewítnian þæt þæt wé mánfullíce ádrugon, Hml. Th. ii. 124, 22. [O. Sax. gi-wítnôn : O. H. Ger. ge-wízinôn *mulctare, torquere, affligere.*] v. un-gewítnod.

**ge-witod** *certainly* :—Hwylces leánes hý hym wénan magon, and eác wénan ne þurfon, ac witod witan, Ll. Th. ii. 336, 16. v. witod; II.

**ge-witscipe.** For '*A testimony* ... S. 492, 5, 6' *substitute :* Witness-ship. Cf. ge-wita; I. (1) *the condition of being witness of a transaction* :—Sculun of Gallia ríce cuman þá þe æt bysceopes hálgunge on ge-witscype standan (*qui in ordinatione episcopi testes adsistant*), Bd. 1, 27; Sch. 73, 9. (2) *witness, personal observation, presence* of witnesses. Cf. ge-witnes; I n a :—Ne sceal bisscopa hálgung on óþre wísan wesan nemne on gesomnunge and on gewitscype þreóra oððe feówer bisscopa *episcoporum ordinatio sine adgregatis tribus uel quattuor episcopis fieri non debet,* Bd. 1, 27; Sch. 73, 12.

**gewit-seóc.** *Add :* possessed :—Þǽre gewitseócan *inerguminum,* Wrt. Voc. ii. 45, 7. Gif þú wilt lácnian gewitseócne man, Lch. ii. 334, 19. Forhtodon þá deófla on gewitseócum mannum, for ðan ðe hí wiston his tócyme, and þá deófolseócan sóna forhtigende wǽron, Hml. S. 31, 1201.

**ge-wittig.** *Add :* I. *in full possession of one's senses.* Cf. ge-wit; I :—Hé cwico wæs þá géna, wís and gewittig, B. 3094. **II.** *having intelligence, having discretion* :—Þ cild þe læg on cradele ... þá gýtseras lǽten efen scyldig and hit gewittig wǽre, Ll. Th. i. 420, 2. **III.** in (one's) *right mind.* V :—Þær beóð deófolseóce gewittige, Hml. Th. i. 564, 35. Þá wódan þ̄ær beóð gewittige, Hml. S. 29, 338. v. riht-, un-gewittig.

**ge-wittiglíce ;** *adv. Rationally, sensibly, sanely* :—'Ádumba, ðú unclǽna deófol, and gewít of ðám men.' And ðǽrrihte weard se mann geclǽnsod fram ðám fúlan gáste, and gewittiglíce sprǽc, Hml. Th. i. 458, 6. v. un-gewittiglíce.

**ge-wittignes.** v. un-gewittignes.

**ge-wlǽtan.** *Add :*—Gewlǽtte *fedatos (saecularis scoriae atramento),* An. Ox. 4, 13 : Angl. xiii. 28, 26.

**ge-wleccan, -wlecian.** *Dele* -wlecian, *and add :* pp. -wlæcced :—Genim beolonan seáw, gewlece, and þonne on eáre gedrýp, Lch. ii. 40, 13 : 46, 30. Him mon on eáre drýpe gewlæccedne ele, 22, 8. Genim þás wyrte ... on ele gewlæhte (-wlehte, *v. l.*), i. 212, 5. Meng wiþ wífes meoluc and huniges dropan and wínes gewleht tósamne, ii. 42, 5.

**ge-wlitegian.** *Add :*—Gewlitegaþ *comat,* Wrt. Voc. ii. 151, 14. (1) physical, (a) *to give (beautiful) form to* :—Ðá gesceafta hé þwáraþ and gewlitegaþ, hwílum eft unwlitegaþ and on óþrum híwe gebrengþ *elementa in se inuicem temperat, et alterna commutatione transformat,* Bt. 39, 8; F. 224, 9. (b) *to decorate, ornament* with :—Hé mid þám hræglum þus gewlitegod wæs gangende in þ mynster, Gr. D. 131, 21. (2) non-physical :—Beón gewlitegod *decorari (meritorum Margaritis),* An. Ox. 1197. Gewlitegod *decoretur,* i. *ornetur (mandatorum varietate),* 1020. Ðæt tácnað ðætte eal ðá gód and ðá mægenu beón gewlitegode niid ðǽre lufan Godes and monna *ut omnia virtutum bona ex caritate decorentur,* Past. 87, 4. v. ungewlitegian.

**ge-wlitig.** v. un-gewlitig : **ge-wló.** *Add :* -wlóh. v. an-wlóh ; wlóh. **ge-worht** *disposed, constituted.* v. ge-wyrcan ; V.

**ge-wosa, -wesa.** *Dele* -wesa, *and for* 32, 32 : 74, 35 *substitute :* Þte ðas giwosa uê lifiga *ut illius conversatione vivamus,* 32, 32. Þte ðá wé wordiga giuossa? (= giuossana ?) symle uê ðerhfylga bisine *ut quos veneramur, conversationis semper sequamur exemplo,* 74, 35. ge-wesan.

**ge-wrǽht.** v. wreccan (?) *in Dict.*

**ge-wrǽstan.** *Substitute :* To twist together, *bind together* :—Gewrǽstan, gecnyttan *adneterent,* Wrt. Voc. ii. 3, 19.

**ge-wrǽðan.** *Add :* to attack, *molest.* [The Latin of Lch. iii. 212, 4 is :—Ursum ad se infestare viderit.]:—Gif hí hwylc man gefón wille, þonne gewrǽðað hý sóna grimlíce ongén (*they resist savagely*). The Latin is : Si quis eos (*certain animals*) uoluerit apprehendere, corpora sua inarmant, Nar. 34, 7.

**ge-wraxl** (?) *wrestling* :—Gewrixl (-wraxl ?) *palestrum,* An. Ox. 18 b, 68.

**ge-wrecan.** In l. 9 *before* 84 *insert* Ps. Th., *and add :* I. *to carry out, execute.* v. wrecan ; I. d :—Þonne byð þ þæt hé on his feóndum his willan gewryhð (þú ofercymst ealle þíne fynd, *v. l.*), Lch. iii. 176, 10. Þá hié besǽtan þá burg Mæsiane, and ðdas geswóran þ hié nǽfre noldon æt hám cuman ǽr hié þæt gewrecen hæfden *cum se sacramentis obstrinxissent, domum, nisi Messena expugnata, nunquam esse redituros,* Ors. 1, 14; S. 56, 20. **II.** *to wreak, give effect to* anger, &c. :—Hé dreáme benam his feónd ... and his torn gewræc on gesacum, Gen. 58. **III.** *to punish,* with acc. (or clause) of fault and (1) person governed by *on* :—God ofermétto gewræc on þém folce, Ors. 6, 2; S. 256, 5 : B. 107. Tó þon þæt hé an him gewrǽce þæt hié þá slógon *hoc facinus puniendum consuli jussum est,* 4, 1; S. 160, 12. Þá de him biora yfel ryhtlíce on gewrecen wǽre *justa ultione puniti,* Bt. 38, 4; F. 204, 19. (2) with dat. of person :—Hé þæt unfægere wera cneórissum gewrecan þóhte, Gen. 1274. Þéh hit eallum þǽm folcum swá swíþe gewrecen ne wurde, Ors. 6, 2; S. 256, 7. **IV.** where hurt is done in retribution of injury. (1) absolute, *to take vengeance* :—Hé gewræc sȳððan cealdum cearsíðum, B. 2395. (2) *to take vengeance for, avenge* a person :—Wíf hyre bearn gewræc, B. 2121. Hé hyne sylfne gewræc, 2875. Hé þóhte þ hé his fæder and his fæderan-gewrǽce, Ors. 4, 10; S. 196, 15. Þæt hié heora hláford gewrǽcen, 3, 9; S. 134, 30. Hú hé his hláford gewrecan mehte, 6, 36; S. 292, 24: By. 208. (3) *to avenge* a wrong :—Beón geornran þ wé Godes bebodu healdan þonne wé úrue teónan gewrecan, Bl. H. 33, 24. Gewrǽce, Ors. 3, 7; S. 112, 36. Gewrǽcen, 1, 11; S. 50, 12. Hé sécð and smeáð hú hí hit gewrecan mǽge *argumenta ultionis inquirunt,* Past. 225, 21 : Bl. H. 33, 27 : Chr. 921; P. 102, 20. Seó fǽhð geweard gewrecen wrádlíce, B. 3062. (3 a) *to avenge* a wrong on some one :—Hié ondrédon ... þæt hié on him gewrǽcen þá teówan *timentes ne exsules ultionem meditarentur,* Ors. 3, 11; S. 144, 17. Hié treówa sealdon þæt hié his torn mid him gewrǽcon on feóndum, Gen. 2038. ¶ of the action of the Deity :—Þú heora æt þancan ealle gewrǽce *vindicans in omnia studia eorum,* Ps. Th. 98, 9. Gewrec nú, Dryhten, ... þæt mé ys þus torne on móde, Jud. 92. Se synfulla bysmrað Drihten ... hé ne geðencð þæt God hit mæg gewrecan, Ps. Th. 9, 23. [Goth. ga-wrikan : O. H. Ger. ge-rehhan *vindicare, ulcisci.*]

**ge-wreccan** (?). v. wreccan (?).

**ge-wrégan** *to accuse.* *Add* -wrêhte :—Gewrégan *insimulare,* Wrt. Voc. ii. 44, 73. (1) *to accuse* a person :—Þá þe hé wæs gewroeged from aldursácerdum *cum accusaretur a principibus sacerdotum,* Mt. R. L. 27, 12. (2) *to accuse* to somebody :—Clemens weard gewrêht tó ðám cásere for ðám micclan crístendóme þe hé árǽrde, Hml. Th. i. 560, 16. (3) *to accuse* of something :—Hé gewrégde his bróðru tó hira fæder þǽre mǽstan wróhte *accusavit fratres suos apud patrem crimine,* Gen. 37, 2.

**ge-wreón** *to cover, clothe* :—Hwæt drincaþ wé, oþþe hú beóþ wé gewrigene (*operiemur*) ?, Mt. R. 6, 31.

**ge-wrid.** *Substitute the two following words :*

**ge-wrid,** es; *n. A thicket, shrubbery, grove.* v. wrídan :—Gewrid *frutecta,* Wrt. Voc. ii. 38, 25. Betwyx þá fenlican gewrido þæs wídgillan wéstenes hé ána ongan eardian *inter umbrosa solitudinis nemora solus habitare coepit,* Guth. Gr. 115, 53. Hí hine lǽddon betwux þá þiccan gewrido (-u, *v. l.*) þára brémela *eum inter densissima veprium vimina trahebant,* 129, 147. v. treów-gewrid.

**ge-wrid,** es; *n. What is wrapped about an object, a covering, husk.* v. wríþan; II : ge-wríþan; I :—Gewrid *glumula* (cf. eára scalu *spicarum glumula,* An. Ox. 1412), Wrt. Voc. ii. 40, 23.

**ge-wridian,** *l.* -wrídian : ge-wriht. v. ge-wyrht.

**ge-wrinclod[e].** *Add : having an indented outline, serrated* :—Gewrinclode *serrata,* Germ. 398, 217.

**ge-wring** (-wryng?). *Add :*—Stór þe bið of gewringe *stacten,* Wrt. Voc. i. 20, 28.

**ge-wringan.** *Add : I. to squeeze out* moisture :—Celeþonian seáw oþþe þára blóstmena gewring and gemeng wið hunig, Lch. ii. 30, 12. Ðysse wyrte wós wel gewrungen, i. 274, 18. II. *to squeeze together, press* into a shape :—Hé mæg ealla gesceafta on his ðære swíðran hand on ánes weaxæpples onlícnisse geðýn and gewringan, Sal. K. p. 150, 34.

**ge-wrisce,** Hpt. Gl. 412, 66. v. ge-wrixl.

**ge-writ.** *Add :* [*a wk. gen.* gewritena *occurs,* Ælfc. T. Grn. 1, 16] :—Gewrit *caraxatio,* Wrt. Voc. i. 46, 63 : *scriptura,* 75, 8. I. *writing.* (1) *written language :*—Gewrite *grammate* (facundo *grammate,* Ald. 195, 22), Wrt. Voc. ii. 41, 47. Bringað hý Gode on gewrite ealle þæt wé gedóð, Wlfst. 233, 7. Hí þurh ærendrakan and þurh gewrite atíwdon hwí hí ðær beón ne mihton, Chr. 1074; P. 204, 6. Hé áwrát þára muneca regol mid heálicum gewrite and mid torhtum wordum *scripsit monachorum regulam, discretione praecipuum, sermone luculentam,* Gr. D. 175, 3. Monige cúðon Englisc gewrit árǽdan, Past. 7, 17. On gewrit settan *to put into writing,* Ll. Th. i. 58, 22. (2) *a number of written characters :*—Þis mon sceal wrítan on húsldisce . . . + + + A + C D + . . . In principio . . . sunt. Þweah þonne þ gewrit mid hálig-wætre of ðám disce on þone drenc, Lch. ii. 136, 3–9. II. *a writing.* (1) *a written statement, passage from a book :*—Þ heáflíce gewrit weard fordílegod, and se sárlíca cwide eft oncerred . . . ' *Terra es tu . . . ,*' Bl. H. 123, 6. Æftera gewrit wítgiunges *secundum scripturam prophetiae* (Zech. 9, 9), Mt. p. 18, 16. (2) *of official, formal documents.* (a) *of law or jurisprudence :*—Gif þér bið gewrit oþþe gewitnes *si scriptum intersit testamenti et testes,* Ll. Th. i. 88, 18. Wilhelm cyng grét ealla þá þe þys gewrit tó cymð ofer eall Engla-land, 489, 2. Beháten gewrit *pollicita rescripsio,* An. Ox. 5455. Hér geswutelað on þison gewrite hú Æðelréd kyning geúðe þ Æðeríces cwyde standan móste, Cht. Th. 539, 31 : Ll. Th. i. 270, 8. Gewrit *cautionem* (Lk. 16, 6), Wrt. Voc. ii. 73, 63 : 103, 29 : 17, 55. Ðissa gewrita syndon þreó, Cht. Th. 541, 22. Mid gewritum *testamento,* Ors. 5, 13; S. 244, 23. Áht þæs þe on úrum gewritum stent *anything in our* (Athelstan's) *regulations,* Ll. Th. i. 236, 32 : 240, 18. Wríte man manega gewrita be þissum, Ll. Th. i. 278, 8. (b) *a list or catalogue :*—Hæbbe se abbod gewrit (*brevem*) ealra þára ǽhta, R. Ben. 56, 7. (c) *a letter :*—Cartena, gewrita *scedarum,* An. Ox. 2308. Sigewulf hine befrán gelóme feorran mid gewritum be gehwylcum cnottum, Angl. vii. 2, 13. Þá gewritu and þá word þe se arceb mé fram þám pápan bróhte, Cht. E. 229, 23. (d) *text of an agreement :*—Þære sinoðlican dǽde þysses gemetes gewrit is *cuius synodicae actionis huiusmodi textus est,* Bd. 4, 5 ; Sch. 373, 8. (3) *of literary writing, a book, treatise :*—Gewrites *fa[s]it,* Wrt. Voc. ii. 88, 82 : 37, 25. Þú bǽde mé oft Engliscra gewritena, Ælfc. T. Grn. 1, 16. Gewrita *litterarum,* An. Ox. 2008. Ic geseah mycel gedwyld on manegum Engliscum bócum þe ungelǽrede menn tó micclum wísdóme tealdan . . ., and mé ofhreów þæt hí næfdon þá godspellican láre on heora gewritum, Hml. Th. i. 2, 23. ¶ *books dealing with a subject under notice :*—Þæs ðe gewritu secgað, Chr. 973; P. 118, 19. Gif ǽnig mon sié þe on gewritun findan mæge þæt Ianas dura belocen wurde, Ors. 3, 5; S. 106, 8. (3 a) *of the books of the Bible ; as in holy writ.* (a) *of the canonical books, the Scriptures :*—On hálgum gewrietum *in sacro eloquio,* Past. 385, 31. On gewritum (-wurittum, L.) *in scribturis,* Mt. 21, 42. Gé nyton þá hálgan gewritu (giwriotu, R., gewuritto, L.) *non scientes scripturas,* Mk. 12, 24. Ðá gewuriotto, Mt. L. 22, 29. Ðá gewriotu (gewriotto, L.), Lk. R. 24, 32. (β) *of the Apocrypha :*—Tweónendlicra gewrita *Apocrifarum,* An. Ox. 5103. v. fríþ-, frum-, geán- (gēn-), rǽden-gewrit ; dirn-gewritu.

**ge-wrítan** *to write together the names of things to be granted and make the grant, to make a grant in writing.* Cf. gewrit-rǽden :—Nú gewríte ic hire ðæt ðreóra hída lond, C. D. ii. 100, 12. Ðis earon þára manna noman þe gewritene earon from Bynsingtúne in þ bisceopríce tó Uueogornacestre mid heora teáme and mid þý túdre þe from him cume á on éce yrfewardnesse (cf. *sex homines, qui prius pertinebant ad villam regiam in Beonsincgtune, cum omni prole et stirpe eorum, ad eandem conscripsimus ecclesiam, ut semper ad terram ecclesie pertineant,* 133, 25–30), Cht. Th. 134, I. v. un-gewriten.

**ge-wrítere.** v. ǽ-gewrítere.

**ge-wriþ** (?), es ; *n. A strap, thong :*—Lancea wígár, amentum we-

---

gures geriðspere (*l.* (?) wígāres-gewrið (v. Angl. viii. 451), spere[gewrið]), Wrt. Voc. i. 35, 47.

**ge-wríþan.** *Add :*—Gewriðen *religatus* vel *vinculatus,* Wrt. Voc. i. 51, 43. I. *to wrap up* an object with a covering :—Þá brǽd se sceocca hine sylfne tó menn, gewráð his sceancan, Hml. S. 11, 223. I a. *of medical treatment, to bind up, bandage* a limb, wound, &c. :—Se foreda sconca bið gewriðen mid ðǽm bende, suá beóð ðá synna mid láreówdóme gebundne. Sióǽwund wile tóberan, gif hió ne bið gewriðen mid wrǽde . . . Sió wund bið ðæs ðe wierse, gif hió bið unwǽrlíce gewriðen, and bið ðæt sár ðé gefrédre gif sió wund bið tó fæste gewriðen. Suá ðearf ðæt se láreów ðára synna wunde gemetlíce gewríðe *fracturam ligamen adstringit; cum culpam disciplina deprimit . . . saepe deterius frangitur, cum fractura incaute colligatur, ita ut gravius scissuram sentiat, si hanc immoderatius ligamenta constringant. Unde necesse est ut cum peccati vulnus restringitur . . . ,* Past. 123, 13–21. II. *to bind* one object to another. (1) *of material* objects :—Þá deóflu gewriðon his handa tó his hricge, Hml. Th. ii. 416, 9. Dó on ánne clǽnne clǽð, and gewríðe onbútan þæs mannes swyran, Lch. i. 160, 23. Ðá hét he gewríðan ðone pápan and ðone óðerne preóst tó his hricge hindan, Hml. Th. ii. 310, 30. Tó gehwylcum bryce, hundes brægen áléd on wulle and þ tóbrocene tó gewriþen, 370, 19. (2) *of non-material objects, to connect :*—Of þissum fíf vocales wyrcað preóstas heóm ánne circul. Ðér tó hig gewriðað þæne nymendan déf, Angl. viii. 313, 10. (3) *figurative, of adhesion or attachment, to bind.* (a) *the object* to a person, where obligation is accepted :—Munecas tó him cómon, þ hí tó his bysne and tó his lárum hí gewriðon, and tó þære onhýringe his forhæfednysse hí underðeóddon, Hml. S. 23 b, 31. (b) *a thing, where disregard is prevented :*—Gewríð *liga (praecepta in corde tuo),* Kent. Gl. 156. III. *to fasten* to or on a band, rope, &c. :—Hé lét ofdúne þone hláf mid langum rápe gewriðenne *panem in longissimo fune religatum deponebat,* Gr. D. 99, 4. IV. *to fasten* a band :—Heó ænne wernægel . . . becnytte tó ánum hringe mid hire snóde. . . . Ðá geseah heó licgan ðone hring . . . mid snóde mid ealle . . . þá wénde heó þæt . . . seó snód tóslupe ; ac heó áfunde þá snóde mid eallum cnottum swá fæste gewriðen swá heó ǽr wæs, Hml. Th. ii. 28, 27. V. *to bind together, draw together :*—Tólýs sace bendas, gewríþ sibbe wǽre *dissolve litis vincula, asstringe pacis federa,* Hy. S. 29, 3. Wé willað þá stafas onsundron gewriðan *we will group those letters together separately,* Angl. viii. 335, 38. [Twælf swine mid wiðen ywriðen al togadere, Laym. 25974.] VI. *with idea of compulsion.* (1) *the subject* a person, *to bind with bonds :*—Ic eom gebunden mid fýrenum racenteágum fram Crístes englum . . . ; hé úrne ealdor myd fýrenum bendum gewráð, Hml. Th. i. 462, 13. ' Godes engel ús gewráð ' . . . ' Unbinde eów Godes engel, swá þæt gé faron tó Hermogenem and hine gewriðene hider gebringan,' ii. 416, 3–8. Hé gewráð fela manna, and on racenteágum gebróhte tó þære byrig, Hml. S. 31, 1144. In brídelse cécan heara gewríþ (*constringe*), Ps. Srt. 31, 9. Mid bendum fæste gewríðan, Hml. S. 23, 179. Man sceall þé fæste gewriðan ǽgder ge handa ge fét, 713. Ðes deófol is gebunden . . . , and ic dó þæt hé ándet þæt hé is gewriðen, Hml. Th. i. 462, 1. (2) *the subject* a bond :—Tóslít bendas þá gewriðað mé *rumpe uincula quae stringunt me,* Ps. L. fol. 142, 9. Hé bið gewriðen *constringitur (funibus peccatorum suorum),* Kent. Gl. 117. VII. *to prevent the action, movement, &c., of* something, *to check, restrain.* (1) *physical :*—Dó gelómlíce on þá næsþyrlu ; wundorlíce heó þ blód of ðám næsþyrlum gewríð, Lch. i. 198, 22. Hý þæs líchaman swát gewríðað, 322, 9. (2) *of human action or conduct :*—Gyf gewríð *si coagmentat ((constringit, v. l.) crimina uirtus),* Hpt. 31, 18, 491. Wé sceolon gewríðan and gewyldan þá gálnysse, Hml. A. 17, 99. Hí gewriþene synt and hí hruron *ipsi obligati sunt et ceciderunt,* Ps. L. 19, 9. VIII. *to bind* a person, *render obliged.* v. ge-wriþen :—Gewríð *obligat (se in futurum),* Kent. Gl. 447. IX. *to vex, torment :*—Gewríðað seó *vexant pupillas,* Hpt. 31, 10, 183. Hé hét hí gewríðan on ðám breóste mid þære hencgene, Hml. S. 8, 122. [*O. H. Ger.* ge-rídan *contorquere.*] v. hand-gewriþen ; ge-wriþen.

**ge-wriþelian** (?) ; *p.* ode *To bind together :*—[Lilian] reádum gew[r]iðelode rosbeddum [*lilia*] *purpureis conexa rosetis,* An. Ox. 23, 7. [*O. H. Ger.* ge-ridilón vel ge-wittón *discriminare (crinem)*.] Cf. wríþels.

**ge-wriþen ;** *adj.* (*ptcpl.*) *Bound, obliged, under obligation to do :*—Swá micele beón eádmódra gehwylc scyl of gyfe swá micele hyne gewriþenra (*obligatiorem*) beón besceáwað on ágyldendum gesceáde, Scint. 155, 7. Gewriþenre, 21, 2. v. ge-wríþan ; VIII.

**ge-wriþenness,** e ; *f. Binding, condition of being bound up :*—Þér byð þearf tó fæstere gewriðennysse *there will be need for firmer binding,* Lch. i. 370, 20.

**ge-wríþing,** e ; *f. Binding :*—Þænne hé unrihtlíce fǽrunga byþ gewriþen þæne gewríþincge his dóm of ðþrum gylte geearnige *cum iniuste forsitan ligatur, ipsam obligationis suæ sententiam ex alia culpa mereatur,* Scint. 202, 13.

**gewriþ-spere.** v. ge-wriþ.

**gewrit-rǽden[n],** e ; *f. An agreement made in writing, a charter*

*conveying property* (? cf. ge-wrītan):—*Cyrographum,* i. *conscriptio hominis vel manualis scriptio* gewritræden *vel* ágnung, Wrt. Voc. ii. 137, 69. Cf. gecwid-ræden.

**ge-wrixl.** *Add:* **I.** *change from one thing to another* :—Gemǽte gewrixl *apta uicissitudo* (quamvis credatur : '*Insurrexerunt* . . .' . . . apta uicissitudo sequatur : '*Credo* . . .,' Ald. 59, 34), An. Ox. 4272. **I a.** *change* of condition :—*þ* is gewrixles dæg líchaman and sáwla, Verc. Först. 130, 12. **I b.** of change that repeats itself, *regular alternation:*—Gewrixle þæs flódes and þæs ebban, Bt. 21; F. 74, 29. Þú recst þæt geár þurh þæt gewrixle þára feówer týda (*veris, aestatis, autumni et hiemis successionibus*), Solil. H. 9, 18. Hwílum eágan wépað for þæs ofnes bryne . . . hwílum þá tép for miclum cyle gryrrað : þis atule gewrixl earmsceape men wendað þǽrinne (*his miseris uicibus miseri voluuntur*), Dóm. L. 196: Wlfst. 138, 30. **II.** *where one thing is given for another, exchange, what is given in exchange as payment :*—Gewrixle *commutatio* (v. Mt. 16, 26), Wrt. Voc. ii. 72, 72 : 17, 48. Þára hída bóc þe Eádréd gebócode Wulfríce wiþ þæs landes gewrixle þe is æt Pendyfig, C. D. B. iii. 31, 1. Þæt wē magon him gewrixl ágyldan . . . ongeán ealle þá gód þe hé ús forgyfen hæfð, Wlfst. 145, 7. **II a.** *what is given in requital.* v. ge-wrixlian; **II** :—Lénd [Driht]ne . . . his gewric[s]l *feneratur Domino* (*qui miseretur pauperis ; et] vicissitudinem suam [reddet ei*], Kent. Gl. 701. **III.** *of interchange, where wrongful change of places occurs, confusion, disturbance :*—Gewrixl *comotio,* Wrt. Voc. ii. 132, 8. Mistlice wīta cumaþ tó ðám gódum swá hí tó þám yfelum sceoldon, and ðá gód þe sceoldon bión edleán gódum monnum cumaþ tó yflum monnum, for þǽm ic wolde witan æt þé hú þé lícode þ gewrixle (*quaeque tam injustae confusionis ratio videatur, ex te scire desidero*), Bt. 39, 2; F. 212, 31. **IV.** *of reciprocal action, commerce, intercourse.* (1) *friendly* :—Gyfte gewrixle *hymenei commercio,* An. Ox. 7, 236. (2) *hostile :*—Edlǽcendum gewrixlum gewǽht *reciprocis uicibus labefacta,* An. Ox. 4788. **V.** *place, office :*—Hláforddómes gewrixle *consulatus uice,* An. Ox. 272. Gewrixla, 11, 20. Gewrisce, Hpt. Gl. 412, 66. **V a.** *office* discharged by a substitute or successor, *stead.* (*a*) of persons :—Hē genam þone hnæp æt þám cnihte, and mid his handa for gewrixle þæs cnihtes hē þám biscope þone drync sealde *calicem abstulit, eumque per se episcopo vice pueri praebunt,* Gr. D. 186, 8. Gelíce þá biscopas syndan on gewrixle þára apostola on þáre háligra gesomnunge, swá syndan þá mǽssepreóstas on þám gewrixle Crīstes þegna, Ll. Th. ii. 402, 19–22. Þæs gewrixle (*vicem*) begytað nú gebindende and eft onlýsende þá þe nymað þá stówe þæs hálgan reccendōmes, Gr. D. 153, 24. (*β*) of things. v. gewrixl ; **II** :—Hæfdon hí gehálgode tablu on weófedes gewrixle *habentes tabulam altaris uice dedicatam,* Bd. 5, 10; Sch. 601, 19. Eal tungla leóht áspringeþ ; and seóród úres Drihtnes bið árǽred on þ gewrixle þára tungla, Bl. H. 91, 24.

**ge-wrixl** ; *adj. Substitute :* **I.** *alternate.* v. gewrixl(e) ; **I a** :—Gewrixlum sīþum *alternis uicibus,* An. Ox. 7, 216 : 8, 163. Stemnum (v. stefn *a turn*) gewrixlum, 3001. v. ge-wrixlic. **II.** *vicarious.* v. ge-wrixl(e) ; **V a, b** :—Mid ge-wrix[l]ere (gewrislre, Hpt. Gl. 460, 51) *vicaria* (*litterarum relatione*), An. Ox. 2310.

**ge-wrixl palaestrum.** v. ge-wráxl.

**gewrixlian.** *Substitute :* **I.** *to change.* Cf. ge-wrixl ; **I.** (1) *to alter the character of :*—Ðǽm ána ðá ðóht gesēgon geuixla gēmendum *his tantum quae sensum videbantur mutare correctis,* Mt. p. 2, 17. (2) *to transfer the possession of :*—Nis ná álýfed þ þæs mynstres hláford sylle þǽre cyrcean land tó óþre cyrcean ; gif hē þonne hwylc land wylle gewrixlian (*commutare*), dō hē þ mid geþeahte bēgra þǽra híréda, Ll. Th. ii. 236, 17. **II.** *where there is exchange in the form of requital for what is done.* Cf. gewrixl ; **II, II a.** (1) *to give in requital :*—Hē forgeaf ēce dreámas, bið him heofonríce ágiefen ; swá sceal gewrixled þám þe wel heóldon Meotudes willan, Cri. 1261. (2) *to get in requital :*—Ne hē ne giéme hwelce hylde hē mid ðǽre ælmessan ge-wriexle (-wrixle, v. l.) *ne impensae gratiae vicissitudinem requirant,* Past. 323, 18. Fýnd ongeáton þæt hié hæfdon gewrixled wīta unrīm þurh heora miclan mōd, Gen. 335.

**ge-wrix[l]lic** ; *adj. Alternate :*—Gewrixlicum stempnum *alternis vicibus,* An. Ox. 2, 135. v. ge-wrixl ; *adj.* **I.**

**ge-wrixlung, e** ; *f. Changing* from one thing to another. v. ge-wrixl ; **I** :—Þrý mōnðas wyrcað þryfeald[e ?] gewrixlunge þǽra feówer tīman . . . þ ǽlc heora hæfð þrý mōnðas *three changes of season,* spring to summer, summer to autumn, autumn to winter, occur at intervals of three months, . . . so that each season has three months, Angl. viii. 319, 5.

**ge-wryndan.** v. ge-gryndan.

**ge-wuldorbeágian.** *Add:*—Se geleáfa æfter gewunnenum sige gewuldorbeágað (*coronat*) ðá mihta, Prud. 10 b. Cynehelmas óþre gewuldorbeágiað *serta alios coronant,* Hy. S. 104, 23. Gewuldorbeágod on wurþmente *decoratus honore,* 47, 16. Þ hē wǽre áfandod and gerihtwīsod and gewuldorbeágod *ut probaretur, justificaretur, coronaretur,* Angl. vii. 52, 498. Gewuldorbeágode *laureati,* Hy. S. 105, 34 : Hml. S. 11, 128.

**ge-wuldorfullian** ; *p.* ode *To glorify :*—Ðá ðe God geclypode tō

þám clǽnan lífe, and ðá ðe hē gewuldorfullode tō þám ēcan wurðmynte, Hml. A. 45, 517. On ðám bið mīn fæder gewuldorfullod þ gē micelne wæstm forþberon, 48, 587.

**ge-wuldrian.** *Add:* **I.** *to glorify.* (1) *to glorify* God. (a) *to ascribe glory to :*—Hē gewuldrade (*glorificauit*) God, Lk. L. R. 23, 47. Ðū bist gewuldrad, God *Deus, qui glorificatur,* Ps. Th. 88, 6. (b) *to advance the glory of* God *by action :*—Hē bēcnade of huelcum deáðe giuuldrad uēre God *significans qua morte clarificaturus esset Deum,* Jn. L. 21, 49. (2) *to make glorious, bestow glory upon :*—Þū hine ge-wuldrast *gloria coronasti eum,* Ps. Th. 8, 6. Gewuldrad is se heánra hád, Cri. 98. Se Hǽlend næs þá gýt gewuldrud (-uuldrad, L., -wuldrad, R.) *Iesus nondum fuerat glorificatus,* Jn. 7, 39. Þ Godes sunu sī ge-wuldrod (-uuldred, L., -wuldrad, R.) þurh hyne, 11, 4 : 14, 13. Seó cyrice on sundorweorþunge þurh godcundra mægen gewuldrad stondeþ, Bl. H. 197, 10. **II.** *to glory in :*—Gewuldriaþ (*gloriabuntur*) on þē ealle þá þe lufiaþ þinne noman, Ps. L. 5, 12.

**ge-wun.** *For the passages substitute :*—Micel gedāl is on þám mægene þæs þe sié gewun (-win, MS.) þrowungum and þæs þe sié ungewuna swelcum þingum, Lch. ii. 84, 19. Gewune . . . geþǽfe stilnesse hī wuniað *assuete [delitiis et] contentae quiete commorantur,* An. Ox. 287. Gyf lytlan gewune beóð, geswinc hit ná byð, for þi þe of gewunan hit cōm *si paulatim adsueti fiant, labor non erit, quia ex usu uenit,* Scint. 64, 1. Ðeós wyrt is tō þám herigindlic þ hý man wið gewune drenceas gemencgeað, Lch. i. 172, 6.

**ge-wuna.** *Add:*—Gewuna *usus,* Wrt. Voc. i. 54, 68. **I.** *referring to living creatures.* (1) *habitual action, wont, custom, habit :*—Hī ǽghwǽr hergodon and bærndon swá heora gewuna wæs, Chr. 1009; P. 139, 16 : 1016; P. 150, 17. Þ mē þincþ wiþerweard þing ælces monnes gewunan, Bt. 26, 2 ; F. 92, 25. Gif him ǽnig wuht bið wið his gewunan, 11, 1 ; F. 32, 19. Hē dyde æfter his gewunan, Chr. 1085 ; P. 217, 9. Hý dydon heora gewuna (-wunan, *v. l.* v. p. 295), 1006; P. 137, 2. Ealle gesceafta mótan heora gewunan bewitigan būtan mē ánum. Ic eom be-numen mīnra þeáwa and eom getogen tō fremdum þeáwum, Bt. 7, 3 ; F. 20, 24. ¶ on gewunan bringan, habban ; tō gewunan niman *to make a practice of, to be in the habit of using* or *doing :*—Nū þincð heom þis syllic tō gehýranne, for þám þe hig habbað heora yrmðe swá on ge-wunan gebrōht, Wlfst. 269, 28. Ðá twá word, *abrenunteo* and *credo,* þe man æt fulluhtþēnunge on gewunan hæfð, 38, 9. We willað þ munecas regollícor libban þonne hī ǽr þisan on gewunan hæfdon, Ll. Th. i. 346, 28. Ðá lytlan synna mon ne gelēfð tō nánre synne, ac nimð hí tō gewunan *minor culpa dum quasi nulla creditur, in usu retinetur,* Past. 437, 27. (2) *habitual action in a specified connexion, practice of, habit* of :—Se forhwierfeda gewuna gemālicnesse, Past. 79, 19. Ðisse eorðlican drohtunge gewuna *humanae conversationis usus,* 169, 7. (3) *a (person's) habitual action, a habit, custom :*—Ic wát þ nán gewuna ne mæg nánum men beón onwended, þ þæt mōd ne sié þe sumum dǽle onstyred *omnis subita mutatio rerum non sine quodam quasi fluctu contingit animorum,* Bt. 7, 1 ; F. 16, 23. Hē eóde on þá gesamnunge æfter his gewunan (*geuna,* L., *consuetudinem*), Lk. 4, 16 : 22, 39. (3 a) *a custom of a number of people, a general practice :*—[Fæderli]ces gewunan *paternae traditionis (regulam servasse describuntur),* An. Ox. 1627. (3 b) *the habit of a class, manner :*—On eargra cempena gewunan *timidorum more militum,* An. Ox. 740. (4) *custom, usage* in official matters :—Hit is eówor gewuna (-uunæ, L., *consuetudo*) þ ic forgyfe eów ánne mann on eástron, Jn. 18, 39. (5) *custom* in ceremonial, ritual :—Of hǽþenum gewunan *apostatico ritu (turificare),* An. Ox. 4920. Man hine ðǽr gehádede efter þan ealdan gewunan, Chr. 1070 ; P. 204, 9. Æfter heora gewunon hié God gebǽdon, Bl. H. 201, 12. (6) *systematic arrangement, system, method :*—Rōmānisce leóde ongynnað heora geár æfter hæðenum gewunan, Lch. iii. 246, 16. **II.** *referring to things, wont, usual character* of a thing :—Wæs þ hús hwemdragen, nalas æfter gewunan mennisces weorces þ þá wágas wǽron rihte, Bl. H. 207, 18. Ongeán gewunan *contra (creaturae) ritum,* An. Ox. 1820. v. Easter-, níd-, un-, weorold-gewuna.

**ge-wuna** ; *adj. Dele last reference, and add :* **I.** of persons (or things personified), *accustomed, used :*—Ic mē, swá swá ic gewuna wæs, tō middes heora gemengde, Hml. S. 23 b, 372. Hý nán licgende feoh ne mētton, swá hý ǽr gewuna (bewuna, *v. l.,* cf. 16, *where Thorpe prints* gewuna) wǽron, Ors. 3, 7 ; Bos. 61, 31. **I a.** *accustomed* to, with dat. or dat. infin. :—Sincalda sǽ . . . æflāstum gewuna, Exod. 473. Seó gyfu ne bið oncnáwen of þǽre medemnesse, ac gewuna is hī tō getácnigenne of þǽre sáwle dǽdum, Hml. S. 23 b, 241. Forgeafa gewuna wæs him ǽnne of ðǽm gebundenum *dimittere solebat illis unum ex uinctis,* Mk. L. R. 15, 6. Ne oferfar þá Iordanen, swá swá gewuna synt of eówrum mynstrum tō farenne, Hml. S. 23 b, 614. **II.** of things, *customary, usual :*—Geweard se micla moncwealm on Rōme ; ná swá hit gewuna (or *substantive ?*) is, of untīdlican gewideran *ingens Romam pestilentia corripuit ; non, ut adsolet, temporum turbata temperies,* Ors. 3, 2 ; S. 102, 5. ¶ the word seems declined in :—*Obtani* geára gewunan oððe gewunede, Wrt. Voc. ii. 65, 3. v. un-gewuna, be-wuna.

**ge-wundian.** *Add:* **I.** *to cause bodily injury :*—Wið sárum and

gewundedum fótum, Lch. i. 358, 8. Ðæt hié mid dǽm ísene hié selfe tó feore ne gewundigen, Past. 365, 11. **I** a. in cases of fighting or assault. (a) physical :—Sē þe ofslehð man binnan ciricwāgum, hē bið feorhscyldig and sē þe gewundað, sē bið handscyldig, Ll. Th. i. 332, 8. Hē ūt rǽsde on hine, and hine miclum gewundode, Chr. 755; P. 48, 4. Þā burhmen ofslógon .xix. menn on ōðre healfe, and gewundoden þ hī nystan hū fela, 1048; P. 173, 5. Ðone geuundadon *illum uulnerantes*, Lk. L. R. 20, 12. Gif hē wīgie and man gewundie, Ll. Th. i. 170, 9. Gewundige 202, 21 : 404, 8. Gif man ōðerne gewundige, for þæs blōdes gyte fæste .xl. nihta, ii. 148, 24 : 294, 6. Hē hæfde Poros monegum wundum gewundodne, Ors. 3, 9 ; S. 132, 22 : Bt. 15 ; F. 48, 16. ¶ where the place of the wound is given :—Gif man bið on hrif (hrife, *v. l.*), wund (gewunded, *v.l.*), Ll. Th. i. 96,10. On þā herðan wund (gewunded, *v.l.*), 25. On (þā) eaxle gewunded, 94, 22. (β) of spiritual warfare :—Se lytega feónd swā micle iédlicor ðæt mód gewundað swā hē hit ongiet nacodre ðǽre byrnan wærscipes, Past. 431, 10. **I** b. of the action of animals :—Gif oxa ōðres monnes oxan gewundige, Ll. Th. i. 50, 9 : 78, 9. **II.** of a surgical operation (lit. or fig.) :—Him is micel ðearf ðæt hē hine selfne gewundige . . . ðætte ðǽr ðǽr hē ōðerra monna wunda lācnað, hē self ne weorðe aðunden, Past. 461, 31. **III.** of other than bodily injury or pain, *to wound* with non-material instruments. (1) the subject a person :—Ðonne of ðǽre ðreátunga gǽð tó stiðlico word, and mid ðǽm his freónd gewundað, ðonne hē hine on unrótnesse gebringð, Past. 167, 10. For ðǽre eáðmódnesse ðe wē ūre mód mid gewundiað, 467, 10. Hié gewundiað hiera mód mid ðǽm weorcum ðisses flǽsclican lífes, 69, 4. Is wēn ðæt hē gewundige ðā heortan ðǽm gehīrendra mid ðǽre wunde *ne vulnere audientium corda feriantur*, 93, 19. (2) the subject a thing :—Hié nǽnigo firen ne gewundode, Bl. H. 161, 33. Gif sió scyld ne gewundode ðæt mód, Past. 311, 23. Ðæt mód ðætte sió ūpāhæfenes and ðā ofermétto gewundedon, 425, 19.

**ge-wundrian** ; *p.* ode To *make wonderful* :—Gewundra *mirifica*, Ps. Th. 16, 7. Gewundrud *mirificatus*, Ps. Rdr. 138, 14.

**ge-wunelic.** *Add* :—Gewunelic weorc *consuetam opem*, gewunelican *consuetudinariis*, Wrt. Voc. ii. 134, 5, 6. **I.** *usual, of frequent occurrence* :—Þā unlaga þe ǽr þisan wǽran tó gewunelice, Ll. Th. i. 312, 14. **II.** *in accordance with practice.* (1) of a person, *habitual* :—Þā trymede hē hine mid his þā gewunelican ārfæstnysse, Hml. A. 157, 129. (2) of a class :—Hit is swīðe gewunelic ðætte dōmeras and ríce menn on setelum sitten *cathedra judicis esse vel praesidentis solet*, Past. 435, 20. Hit wæs gewunelic on ðám tīman þæt ðā ðe woldon woruldwīsdóm gecneordlīce leornian, þæt hī behwyrfdon heora āre on gymstánum, Hml. Th. i. 60, 26. (3) *in accordance with a general practice* :—Ond monnum bið ðonne gewunelic ðæt hī līðað ðonne on sǽs bryme, Shrn. 88, 1. Þæt sȳ undeóror geseald þonne hit woruldmannum gewunelic sȳ, R. Ben. 95, 17. **III.** *in accordance with the natural order of things* :—Hit nis nāuht gecynde ne nāuht gewunelic þ ǽnig wiþerweard þing bión gemenged wiþ ōðrum wiþerweardum oþþe ǽnige gefærrædenne wið habban *neque sibi solent adversa sociari*, Bt. 16, 3 ; F. 54, 11. Hē gehylt þā gewunelican (-wun-, *v. l.*) gód hālige drohtnunge, R. Ben. 32, 2. **IV.** *ordinary, having the characteristics of the class to which a thing belongs, common* :—Godes wolcn wæs fȳren geðúht on nihtlicere tíde, and on gewunelices wolcnes hīwe on dæge, Hml. Th. ii. 196, 8. Becōmon ðicce ðeóstru ofer Egypta lande, swā þæt heora nān binnon ðrím dagum ōðerne ne geseah, and on Israhēla ðeóde wǽron gewunelice dagas, 194, 6. **V.** *customary, in accordance with fixed custom.* Cf. ge-wuna ; **I.** 4, 5 :—Hit wæs þā gewunelic þ man gesette on cranice ǽlc þǽra dǽda þe gedón wæs mid him, Hml. A. 95, 122. Twēgen sealmas æfter gewunelicum þeáwe (*secundum consuetudinem*), R. Ben. 37, 11 ; *more solita*, 61, 4. Tó heora þǽm gewunelican þeówdóme *ad solitum pensum*, 76, 13. Mid gewunelican cantican *cum canticis consuetudinariis*, 44, 20. Hē wolde offrian æfter Mōyses ǽ þā gewunelican lāc, Hml. A. 58, 184. **VI.** *accustomed to, in the habit of making use of* :—Þā cwōmon þǽr scorpiones swā hié ǽr gewunelice wǽron þæs wætersciepes *scorpiones consuetam petentes aquationem*, Nar. 13, 11. **VII.** to *which one is accustomed.* (1) *habitually used, wonted* :—Hié þā gewunelican fixas ūp tugon and þā tǽron *solitos pisces consumabant*, Nar. 16, 19. (2) *adapted to* :—Ælc wyrt and ǽlc wudu wile weaxan on þǽm lande sēlost ðe him betst gerīst and him gecynde biþ and gewunelic (*sibi convenientibus innasci locis*), Bt. 34, 10 ; F. 148, 21. v. un-gewunelic.

**ge-wunelíce.** *Add* : **I.** *usually, generally.* Cf. ge-wunelic ; **I** :—Man þā bēc rǽt on circan swīðe gewunelíce, Ælfc. T. Grn. 9, 1. On eallum limum ac gewunelícost on þám handum, Hml. S. 1, 200. **II.** *where a practice is made of doing something, as a matter of habit or custom* :—Ðā seó tíd middæges tó becōm, þā oðstód[hē] . . . and hine gewunelíce gebæd, for þan þe hē gewunode on þám gesettum tídum . . . gebiddan, Hml. S. 23 b, 162. Hē beginð tó healdenne swylce gecyndelíce and gewunlíce (-wune, *v. l.*) *velut naturaliter ex consuetudine incipit custodire*, R. Ben. 32, 1. Hī syððan gewunelíce þider sōhton *afterwards they made a practice of visiting the place* (but see Bl. H. 201, 12 under ge-wuna ; I. 5), Hml. Th. i. 504, 6. **II** a. *with constant practice, assiduously* :—Ðā ðe giwunlíce God heriað *qui assidue Deum laudant*,

---

Rtl. 113, 8. **III.** *usually, in ordinary circumstances* :—Syricas beteran þonne þā þe hȳ gewunelíce weriað *tonice solito quas habent meliores*, R. Ben. 91, 11 : An. Ox. 2765. **IV.** *in accordance with fixed custom, properly, regularly.* v. ge-wunelic ; **V** :—Gewunelíce *rite (et regulariter congruere)*, An. Ox. 5145. v. un-gewunelice.

**ge-wunian.** *Add* : **A.** *intrans.* **I.** *to remain.* (1) of persons. (a) *to remain* as resident, visitor, &c., *live, dwell, stay, tarry, abide.* (α) in a place :—Hē gewunade ł gebýde (*habitavit*) in Capharnaum, Mt. L. 4, 13. Hē gewunade on mōre *morabatur in monte*, Lk. L. R. 21, 37. Huǽr gewunade *ubi maneret*, Jn. L. 1, 39. Gewunedon ł gebȳedon ðǽr *habitant ibi*, Mt. L. 12, 45. Gebēdon hine þte ðǽr geuunade (*maneret*), and uunade ðǽr tuoege dagas, Jn. L. R. 4, 40. Hī ne mihton ealle ætgædere gewunian þǽr, Chr. P. 3, 9. Þ heó sylfe magan þe oftor on mynstrum tǽste gewunian and regolíce libban, Ll. Th. i. 348, 2. Hē ne mihte on hūse gewunian ac on byrgenum *neque in domo manebat sed in monumentis*, Lk. 8, 27. Tó dæge in hūs ðīn gedæfned is mē gewunia (*manere*), Lk. L. 19, 5. Sceoldon his þegnas þǽr gewunian atolan ēðles, Sat. 326. ¶ figurative :—Ælc þára ástynt þe on ðē (*God*) gewunað *Deus, in quo manere, consistere est*, Solil. H. 6, 21. (β) with a person :—Gewunade Maria mid hiá suælce mōnaðum ðriim *mansit Maria cum illa quasi mensibus tribus*, Lk. 1, 56. Hē ðǽr gewunade mið ðǽm *illic morabatur cum eis*, Jn. L. 3, 22. Mið hine gewunadun (*mansuerunt*) on dæge ðǽm, Jn. R. L. 1, 39. (b) *to keep one's position* :—Ān æfter ānum fromfoerdun and giwunade (*remansit*) ðe Hǽlend āna, Jn. R. L. 8, 9. (c) denoting continuance, permanence, *to continue.* (α) continuance of position, *to keep on in the same place, not to depart* from a person or place :—Gōst þte giwunað iówih mid in ēcnisse, Jn. R. 14, 16. Hwona þte gehērde, ðonne giwunade (*mansit*) in ðǽr ilca stówwe, Jn. R. L. 11, 6. Gif ǽnig āmānsumad man on þæs cynges neáweste gewunige, Ll. Th. i. 312, 2. Gif morðwyrhtan . . . tó þám geþrīstian þ hī on þæs cyninges neáweste gewunian, 324, 13. Se consul wēnde þ hē būton sorge mehte on þǽm wintersetle gewunian þe hē þā on wæs, Ors. 4, 8 ; S. 188, 5 : Jul. 375. His þegnas hine ne mihton leng mid gewunian, Bt. 38, 1 ; F. 194, 26. (β) continuance of condition, existence :—Fore ðon þ deáðe biðon forbodeno giuunia *idcirco quod morte prohiberentur permanere* (Heb. 7, 24), Rtl. 90, 28. Ic hine willo giwuniga (geuuni ł þte hē gewuniga *manere*, L.) oð ðæt ic cymo, Jn. R. 21, 22. (γ) of action, conduct :—Gif gié gewunas in uorde mínum, ðeignas mína gié biðon, Jn. L. 8, 31. Hē in his gebede gewunade, Gr. D. 16, 21. Frōfre gǽst in Gūðlāces geóce gewunade, Gú. 108. (2) of animals or things (material or non-material). (a) *to occupy* a position temporarily or permanently, *rest, lie* :—Gif uorda mīna in iúch hiá gewunias (*manserint*), Jn. L. 15, 7. Ic gesæh ðone gāst ādūne stígende suælce culfræ and gewunede ofer hine, Jn. L. R. 1, 32. Hafuc sceal on glófe gewunian *the place for the hawk is the (falconer's) glove*, Gn. C. 18. (b) *to remain, not to be removed, be left* :—þte ne geuunadon (*remanerent*) on rōða ðā ¯ichomo, Jn. L. R. 19, 31. Ðā æfterra gewuna wē ondetað ðæt hē wēron *reliqua manere pateremur ut fuerant*, Mt. p. 2, 18. (c) *where continuance is marked.* (α) where position is maintained :—Gif se brīw and se drenc inne gewuniað, Lch. ii. 320, 18. Wið þon þe him mete under ne gewunige *if his food will not keep down*, 190, 1. Suǽ ðió palmtreó ne mæge gebrenge wæstem būta geuuniga in wīngearde, suǽ ne gié būta in mec gié gewunige, Jn. L. 15, 4. Ne mæg him mete under gewunian, Lch. ii. 198, 23 : 158, 26. (β) of continued existence :—Eáða mæhte ðætte hiá gewunadon wið ðiósne ondueard dæge, Mt. L. 11, 23. Urǽdðo geunia getrymeð, Jn. p. 4, 3. Þā gesǽlda ne magon simle gewunigen, Met. 2, 19. **II.** *to be or become accustomed, be wont, to accustom oneself* :—Ic gewunige *soleo*, Ælfc. Gr. Z. 204, 11. *Soleo* ic gewunige, . . . *solitus* gewunod tó sumum ðincge, *soliturus* sē ðe sceal beón gewunod, 247, 5–7 : Hml. Th. ii. 278, 29. Gewunade *adsuetae*, Wrt. Voc. ii. 9, 8. Geára gewunan oððe gewunede *obtani*, 65, 4. (1) with *tó* and noun (pronoun) of accustomed action, *to be in the habit of, get into the habit of, get used to* :—Hē bið on oferméttu āwended and gewunað tó ðǽm gielpe *cor in elationem usu gloriae permutatur*, P. 35, 13. Hit gewunað tó ðǽm synnum . . . hit orsorglíce gewunode tó ðǽm lytlum *mens assueta malis . . . in minimis didicit non temendo peccare*, 437, 29–31. Hȳ eal ōðer specað and ōðer hīwiað . . . þā beóð rihtlíceteras þe tó ðǽm gewuniað, Wlfst. 54, 15. Geswícað eówra misdǽda and gewuniað tó gódan blǽdum *quiescite agere perverse, discite benefacere*, 48, 21. Æghwylc crísten man gewunige tó scrifte, Ll. Th. i. 310, 5 ; 322, 5 : Past. 61, 20. Ne gewunigen gē tó oferetolnisse *non ambulemus in commessationibus*, 317, 18. Ne hē ne mæge fullíce gewunian tó gódum weorcum *nec ad usum boni operis valet assurgere*, 73, 14. Hē hæfð tó gódum weorce gewunad, 65, 15. (2) with dat. infin. :—Gewuniað þā sȳfre Godes þegnas mid mōde and stefne God tó wurðian, Angl. viii. 319, 32. His mōdor gewunode tó fēdenne henna *gallinas nutrire consueverat*, Gr. D. 69, 25. (3) with infin. :—Ðā fǽmnan þe gewuniað onfōn wiccan, Ll. Th. i. 52, 9. Hē gewunode on þám gesettum tídum þone ryne his sīðfætes gefæstnian, Hml. S. 23 b, 162. (4) with clause :—Gewunode ān þeóf þ hē stāh ofer þone hege *fur consueverat per sepem ascendere*, Gr. D. 23, 22 : 68, 15 : 69, 24. Ge-

wunade se geroefæ þe hē forlēte ǽnne gebundenne *consueverat praeses dimittere unum vinctum*, Mt. R. 27, 15. **B.** *trans.* (The transitive character of the following is doubtful. In Angl. xii. 516, 25, where, if the passage is correct, the verb is certainly transitive, a word perhaps is omitted.) *To cause to remain, give a permanent position to, fix, settle.* **I.** *of living creatures :*—Wǽron on þǽm ylcan ȳglande twēgen hréfnas gewunode *there were two ravens that lived on that same island* (but the Latin is : Erant in supradicta insula duo *alites corvi. Aliti* seems to have been read ?), Guth. Gr. 142, 23. Hér is nēdran swēg, wyrmas gewunade *adders have their home here*, Sat. 103. **II.** *of things :*—Yrre ne scealt þū tō lange on þīnre heortan gewunian (*perhaps lǽtan should be supplied*) *thou shalt not too long give place to anger in thine heart*, Angl. 516, 25. Gif ðeór sȳ gewunad (cf. geseten, 16 *for an intransitive participle*) in ānre stōwe, Lch. iii. 30, 6. Gif men synd wænnas gewunod on þ heáfod foran, 46, 21.

**ge-wuni[g]endlic.** v. un-gewuni[g]endlic : **ge-wurms.** *Dele.* v. ge-wyrms: **ge-wuxsað.** v. ge-þuxian.

**ge-wylc.** v. ge-wilc : **ge-wyldan.** v. ge-wildan : **ge-wylde.** v. ge-wilde : **ge-wyldend.** v. ge-wildend : **ge-wildor.** *Dele :* gewylian. v. ge-wilwan : **ge-wyllan.** v. ge-willan : **ge-wylwed.** v. ge-wilwan : **ge-wynd.** v. ge-wind : ge-wynelic. v. un-gewynelic.

**ge-wynsumian.** *Substitute :* **I.** *intrans. To be glad, to exult, rejoice :*—Giwynsumiað unbyergo *exultant solitudines*, Rtl. 1, 17. Sibb Cristes giwynsumiga (*exultet*) in heartum iúrum, 13, 37. **II.** *trans.* (1) *to make pleasing :*—Hig mid þǽre tungan clypole þæne swēg gewynsumiað, Angl. viii. 313, 15. (2) *to make glad, to rejoice :*—Sē þe ārwurþað fæder hē bȳð gewynsumud on bearnum *qui honorat patrem iocundabitur in filiis*, Scint. 174, 1.

**ge-wynsumlic.** *Substitute :*—Gewynsumlice (-wil-? v. ge-wilsumlic) lufe *ultroneum affectum*, Hpt. Gl. 412, 4. Gewinsumlice ł gecwēme *acceptum, desiderativum*, 446, 51.

**ge-wyrcan.** *Add :*—Geworhte *effecit*, i. *perfecit, fecit*, Wrt. Voc. ii. 142, 49. Gewyrce and tō getió *contrahat*, 21, 42. Tō gewyrcenne að *conficiendo*, 6, 31. Gewarht *conderetur*, 105, 13. Geworht, 15, 17. Bið geworht *confici*, 23, 17. Geworht weorc *instructum*, 49, 23. Geworht, i. 21, 38. **I.** *to work* (trans., as in *wrought* iron), *labour a subject, expend labour upon* material to prepare it for a purpose, *adorn* with :—Geworht land *novalis ager*, Wrt. Voc. i. 37, 53. Þæs tempeies segl wundorbleóm geworht, Cri. 1140. Geworhtne *ornatum*, i. *compositum* (diadema gemmis purpureis *ornatum*, Ald. 28, 32), An. Ox. 2120. Mē ne lyst mid glase geworhtra wâga *non requiro comptos vitro parietes*, Bt. 5, 1 ; F. 10, 16. **II.** *to make.* (1) the subject a person, (a) *to form* an object out of material :—Hē gewyrceð helm oððe hupseax, Crä. 63. Gewyrcean wīgbord, B. 2337. Geworht *confecta* (ornamentorum gloria ex ferri instrumentis *confecta*, Ald. 8, 24), Wrt. Voc. ii. 23, 28. Orþoncum geworht, Rä. 69, 3. Hwæþer þū swelces âuht wyrcan mæge oððe geworhtes habbe, Bt. 14, 1 ; F. 40, 26. (aa) where the material is stated :—Ðæt hrægl scolde bión geworht of purpuran, Past. 83, 22. Geworht of ðǽm treówe sethim, 171, 7. Of grēnum âre geworht, Bl. H. 127, 7. Beág of þornum geworht, Cri. 1446. Of, mid feówerfealdum cynne geworhte (*statuam*) *quaterno* (*metallorum*) *genere fabrefactam*, i. *formatam*, An. Ox. 1544. Mon hǽt Corrinthisce fatu ealle þe þǽr of geworhte wǽron, Ors. 5, 2 ; S. 216, 4. (b) *to form* from material, *prepare* from ingredients :—Weolocas of þâm bið geworht (-worhgt, *v. l.*) se weolocreáda tælhg *cocleae, quibus tinctura coccinei coloris conficitur*, Bd. 1, 1 ; Sch. 8, 21. Þeós smerenes wæs geworht of ehtatēne cynna wyrtum, Bl. H. 73, 20. (c) *of the operation of the Deity :*—God Ælmihtig ūs ealle geworhte, Ll. Th. i. 370, 27. Geweorhte, Ps. L. 94, 6. Dryhten ūs of dūste geworhte, Sal. 336. Þīne handa mē geworhtan and geheówodan, Bl. H. 87, 32. Adam wæs of eorðan geworht, Gen. 365. (c) *to build, construct :*—Þæs wyrhtan þe hié (a *church*) his hand geworhte, Bl. H. 205, 12. Hié weófod wlitelíce geworhtan and gegyredon, 6. Þæt hié him tō mǽrðe burh geworhte, Gen. 1666. Tempel mǽst þára þe manna bearn folmum geworhte, Exod. 396. Hlǽw gewyrcean, B. 2802. Gewyrcean tor of treówum and of mycclum beámum, Bl. H. 187, 12. *Agger* eorðbyre *vel* geworht strǽt *strata* vel *delapidata*, Wrt. Voc. i. 37, 33. (ca) of building for defence :—Gewrohte hē weall mid turfum (cf. uallum, quo ad repellendam uim hostium castra muniuntur, fit de cespitibus, Bd. 1, 5), Chr. 189 ; P. 9, 28. Hé geworhte þá burga on ǽgþere healfe eás, 918 ; P. 100, 5. Hé casteles gewrohte, 1086 ; P. 220, 23. Hé hēt gewyrcan þá burg and gesettan and gemannian, 923 ; P. 104, 7. (d) *to work* on material, *make* a mark on, a hole in :—Nǽfre man þǽre moldan tō þæs feale ne nimeþ, þ mon ǽfre þurh þ mæge â þȳ mâran dǽl on þǽm stōplum gewercean (*make a larger cavity in the foot-prints*), Bl. H. 127, 18. (2) the subject a thing. (a) a plant, *to produce* by natural growth, *make* (as in to *make* wood) :—Ēghwelc treó gōd wæstmas gōda gewyrces (bereþ ł wyrceþ, R., *facit*).... Ne mæg trēuo gōd wæstma yfle gewyrca (beoran ł wyrcende R., *facere*), ne trē yfle gōda wæstma gewyrce (beoran, R.), Mt. L. 7, 17, 18. (b) *the constituent parts of a whole :*—Twēgen minuta and healf gewyrcað ǽnne prican, feówer prica gewyrceað âne tíd, Angl. viii. 318, 45. Þára lima

gecynd is þ hī gewercað ǽnne líchoman, Bt. 34, 6 ; S. 87, 24. **III.** of mental work that finds expression in words, *to make* a book, poem, a law, stipulation :—Hē godspell Ebriscum stafum geworhte *evangelium Hebraici litteris edidit*, Mt. p. 2, 8 : 8, 8. Be ðǽm ymene þe wē be hire geworhton, Bd. 4, 19 ; Sch. 439, 15. Þá ǽ þe heora aldoras ǽr geworhton, Ll. Th. i. 26, 6. Nīwe werc gewyrce of alde *novum opus facere ex veteri*, Mt. p. 1, 1. Fæstnunga from lárwum geworht *monumenta ab auctoribus edita*, 7, 5. Gelǽstan eall þet hī on forewarde hæfdon ǽr geworht *to carry out all the stipulations previously made in the agreement*, Chr. 1094; P. 228, 34. **IV.** where a person is brought to a (mental) condition by the efforts of another, *to make* a convert, friend, &c. :—Gē ymbhurfon sǽ and drȳgi þ gié gedóe ēnne ...; and mid ðȳ bið geworht *circuitis mare et aridam ut faciatis unum proselytum; et cum fuerit factus*, Mt. L. 23, 15. His geworhtne wine *the man he had made his friend*, Seef. 115. **V.** of mental or moral constitution, *to dispose, constitute :*—Yrtacus, yfele geworht man, Hml. Th. ii. 476, 18. Ne geseah hine nân man ... mislíce geworhtne (*of variable disposition*), ac on ānre ānrǽdnysse ǽfre wunigende, Hml. S. 31, 307. Men beóð geworhte wōlíce him betwȳnan, Hml. S. 13, 295. Æfter him ríxodon manega cyningas mislíce geworhte, 18, 38 : 386. Ic þá leóde wât ge wið feónd ge wið freónd fæste geworhte (*steadfastly minded towards foe or friend*), B. 1864. **VI.** *to do, make, cause* an effect by effort, *bring about* a result :—Gielde hē swâ wer swâ wunde swâ hē gewyrce *he must pay for death or wound according to the result of his act*, Ll. Th. i. 90, 20. (1) with noun as object :—Gif hē losuest his gewyrcað *si detrimentum sui faciat*, Lk. L. 9, 25. Sē þe þone hearm geworhte, Ll. Th. i. 418, 9. Hē mæg ondrǽdan ðæt hē for his ǽgnum scyldum mâre ierre gewyrce, Past. 63, 11. Þī lǽs unholdan wunde gewyrcen, Cri. 763. Þ þá cyningas heom betweónan seht geworhtan, Chr. 1016 ; P. 152, 24. Ende gewyrcan, Leás. 47. Ne mihton hī âwiht æt mē ǽfre gewyrcean, Ps. Th. 128, 1. (2) the object a clause :—Þ hiá sē gewyrces suno Goddes *esse facit filios Dei*, Jn. p. 3, 3. Gif hē gewyrce þ hine man âsylle, Ll. Th. i. 170, 11 : 404, 12. (3) with pronoun in apposition to clause :—Hū geworhte ic þæt, ... þæt ic þē ongitan ne meahte ?, An. 922. **VII.** *to do* a deed, *perform* an action, *commit* a crime, an offence, *perpetrate.* (1) absolute :—Bēma singan swâ lēgeras gewyrcas (*faciunt*), Mt. L. 6, 2. Swâ hī geworhtan, Cri. 1234. Gewyrca *operari*, Ll. 9, 4. (2) with object :—Ic feóndrǽs gefremede, sǽhðe geworhte, Gen. 900. B. 1577. Hē bēcena geworhte (dyde, W. S.), Jn. L. R. 12, 37 : Bl. H. 219, 3. Hē manslyht geworhte, Mk. 15, 7. Sē þe þ weorc geworhte, Ll. Th. i. 418, 13. Habban leán þe wē on lífe geworhtan, 370, 21. Ðá scylda ðe hié wið hiene geworhton, Past. 343, 18. Gif hē mânweorc gewyrce, Ll. Th. i. 400, 14 : 404, 16 : 312, 8 : 204, 8 : 80, 20 : 230, 10. Þte ic geuyrco uoerca his *operari opera eius*, Jn. L. 9, 4. Þte wē giwyrce werc Godes, Jn. R. L. 6, 28. Hié woldon þæt hié on elþeódigum æt geworhton *they meant to make a meal on the strangers*, An. 1075. Ic mæg mid handum fela wundra gewyrcean, Gen. 280. Mæht salde him dōm gewyrca (þ hē mōste dēman, W. S.), Jn. L. R. 5, 27. Hrēunisse gewyrce *penitentiam agere*, Mt. p. 14, 7. Siþþan wē hit hâtaþ wyrd, syððan hit geworht biþ, Bt. 39, 6 ; F. 220, 10. Culpan womma geworhtra, Cri. 179. Þá geworhtan synna andettan, Bl. H. 25, 18. ¶ the subject an animal :—Gif se hund mâ misdǽda gewyrce, Ll. Th. i. 78, 6. **VIII.** *to do* what is desired or bidden, *execute* an order :—Ic þæt hogode, þæt ic eówra leóda willan geworhte, B. 635. Ūres hláfordes wurðscipe rǽran and his willan gewyrcan, Ll. Th. i. 370, 9. Uillo his geuyrca (dón, W. S.) *uoluntatem ejus facere*, Jn. L. 7, 17 : Hy. 3, 52. **IX.** *to celebrate* a festival :—Doeg ðe symbei mid ðȳ geworht wæs, Jn. L. 7, 14. **X.** *to bring to* a condition, *cause to* assume a character, *turn to, subject* to action. (1) the object a person :—Ic gewirce eów tō wǽdlan *visitabo vos in egestate*, Lev. 26, 16. Hē geworhte his gefēran tō wealdgengum, Ælfc. T. Grn. 17, 31. Þte giworhte hine tō cynige (tō cynge dón, W. S.) *ut facerent eum regem*, Jn. R. L. 6, 15. Mid ðȳ tō cyninge hine uallað dóa ł gewyrca *cum regem eum uellent facere*, Jn. p. 4, 15. Hē wæs tō manegum wītum geworht *cum virum suppliciis se tyrannus adacturum putaret*, Bt. 16, 2 ; F. 52, 20. (2) the object a thing :—Hē geworhte þás bōc tō leóþe *he made a metrical version of this book*, Bt. proem.; F. viii, 9. Wēsten hē geworhte on wídne mere, Ps. Th. 106, 34. Tō ânum geworhta *made into one;* ad unum congestos, Mt. p. 10, 15. **XI.** with complementary words, noun or adj., *to make* an object so and so. (1) *to form* an object with certain characteristics :—His Scyppend hine swilcne geworhte, Angl. vii. 22, 209. Þū þæt fær gewyrc fíftiges wíd elngemeta, Gen. 1307. Ic þē swâ sciénne gesceapen hæfde, wynlíce geworht, Cri. 1388. Ænne hæfde hē swâ swiðne geworhtne, Gen. 252. Deádra manna byrgenna bioð oft swiðe wlitige geworhte, Past. 449, 7. (2) *to cause* an object *to become* so and so, *to change* so as to have certain characteristics :—Hâl hē gewyrcas folc his from synna hiora, Mt. L. 1, 21. Gié geworhton hiá cofa ðeáfana, Mk. L. R. 11, 17. Nallað gē giwærcan (g[e]wyrce, L.) hús fædres mínes hús cēpinge, Jn. R. 2, 16. Ne mæhtū ǽnne hér huít geuirce ł blæc, Mt. L. R. 5, 36. Sáuel his hâl gewyrca, Lk. L. 9, 24. Þū hæfst þē wið Drihten dȳrne geworhtne, Gen. 507. **XII.** *to*

*get by working, deserve* :—Se gâst nimeð æt Gode swâ wîte swâ wuldor swâ him on worulde þæt eorðfæt ǽr geworhte *the Spirit receives from God pain or paradise according to what the body has earned for it by its deeds on earth,* Seel. 8. (1) with noun object, *to deserve good or ill, to incur a penalty* :—Beó se cyng ǽlces þæra wîta wyrðe þe þâ men gewyrcen *the king shall be entitled to every one of the penalties that those men incur by their acts,* Ll. Th. i. 282, 17. Nû hæbbe ic þîne hyldo geworhte and þinne willan gelǽst, Gen. 727 : 505. (2) with clause :— Sceal gleáw guma gôde gewircean . . . þæt hine on ylde gewunigen wilgesîðas, B. 20. Earm bið sê þe wile firenum gewyrcan, þæt hê fâh scyle *from his Scyppende âscyred weorðan,* Cri. 1617. Hê forsôc þone triumphan . . . and seáde þæt hié hæfden bet gewyrht þæt him mon mid heáfe ongeán côme þonne mid triumphan *triumphum suscipere recusavit, quia tantis detrimentis luctus potius debebatur,* Ors. 2, 4 ; S. 70, 20. (3) with pronoun representing a clause :—Ûs ongeán cymað þûsend engla, gif wê þider môton and þæt on eorðan ǽr gewyrcað, Sat. 303. (4) with infin. (?), *to succeed* in doing :—þæt hê gewyrce, ǽr hê on weg scyle, fremman on foldan wið feónda nîð, Seef. 74. [*Goth.* ga-waurkjan : *O. H. Ger.* gewurchen, -wirchen : *O. Sax.* gi-wirkian.] v. un-geworht.

ge-wyrce, es ; *n.* I. *work, forming.* v. ge-wyrcan ; II. 1, ¶ :— Gewyrce *plastica* (in rerum visibilium *plastica,* Ald. 75, 34), Wrt. Voc. ii. 87, 35. II. *what is got by work, profit, perquisite.* v. gewyrcan ; XII :—Æhteswân gebyreð stîfearh, and his gewirce ðonne hê spic behworfen hæfð, Ll. Th. i. 436, 23. Gýme swân þ hé æfter sticunge his slyhtswŷn wel behweorse, sæncge ; ðonne bið hé ful wel gewyrces wyrðe, 17. [The nature of the perquisite may be illustrated from later documents. The swineherd of Glastonbury Abbey received as perquisite one sucking-pig a year, the entrails of the best pig, and the tails of all the others which were slaughtered in the Abbey. v. Andrews's Old English Manor, p. 211 note.] [*Goth.* ga-waurki *negotium; quaestus, lucrum: O. H. Ger.* ge-wurchi *operatio, textus* : cf. *Icel.* yrki *work: O. Sax.* gi-wirki.]

ge-wyrd *fate.* Add ; es ; *n.* :—*Conditio,* i. *status, natura, sors, regula, lex gescæp, gewyrd, gescæft, gebyrd,* Wrt. Voc. ii. 135, 62. [*In view of the Latin words* (regula, lex) *in this gloss perhaps the passage* Men. 66, *given in Dict. under* gewyrde, *should be taken here. See, too,* VII *below.*] I. *fortune* :—Gewyrdes *fortunae,* An. Ox. 2628. II. *one of the Fates* :—Gewyrda *Parcarum,* An. Ox. 5480. III. *what happens, an event.* Cf. ge-weorþan ; I. 3 :—Hér sagað ymb ðâs mǽran gewyrd þe tô þyssum dæge geweard, þætte ælmihtig Dryhten sylfa on þâs world âcenned wæs . . . Be þysse gewyrde þe wê tôdæg weordiað ealle Godes hâlige sǽdon, Verc. Först. 96, 3–11. Gewyrde (*secundum*) *historiam,* An. Ox. 8, 15 a (v. ge-wyrdelic ; II, gewyrd-wrîtere). Gewyrda *fata,* i. *fortuna, eventus,* Wrt. Voc. ii. 147, 28. Cf. Gewyrd *fatus, ta, tum* (ut rerum tibi *fata* latentia solvant, Ald. 153, 9), An. Ox. 18 b, 32. IV. *what is made, an effect.* Cf. ge-weorþan ; I. 2 :— Gewyrde *effectitus* (*operum*), An. Ox. 11, 124. V. *what happens to a person or thing, a condition assigned by fate* :—Fore giwyrd lîchomes foerde wê ongeton *from the condition of mortality imposed upon the flesh we know she has departed ;* quam pro conditione carnis migrasse cognovimus, Rtl. 66, 37. Gewyrdum *fatis* (cf. gewyrd[um] *fatis* (si hoc carneum animae ergastulum ante fatis crudescentibus non *obierit,* Ald. 80, 17), An. Ox. 5479), Wrt. Voc. ii. 147, 26. VI. *what pleases a person, what seems fit, pleasure.* v. ge-weorþan ; V. 1 a [cf. ? *O. H. Ger.* gewurt *oblectatio, delectatio*] :—Hit is of heora âgenre gewyrde þ þ hié secgað *what they say is of their own good pleasure,* Ors. 3, 9 ; S. 126, 33. VII. *what is agreed upon, a condition, stipulation.* v. ge-weorþan ; V. 1 b :—*Conditio* gecwide *vel* gewyrd (*or perhaps to be taken under* gewyrd *speech* ?) *stipulatio* gehât, Wrt. Voc. i. 20, 54.

ge-wyrd *copiousness of speech, verbosity* :—Gewyrd, maþelung *verbositas,* An. Ox. 1419. [*Take here* Shrn. 35, 22 *given in Dict. under* ge-wyrde *and cf. the Goth. and O. H. Ger. forms there given.*]

ge-wyrdan *to injure.* v. ge-wirdan : ge-wyrde *amount.* v. gewirþe : ge-wyrde *speech.* v. ge-wyrd *verbosity, and first passage under* ge-wyrd *fate.*

ge-wyrde ; *adj.* *In agreement* with (gen. cf. (?) ge-weorþan (with gen.) ; V. 1 a γ, b γ, c γ, 2 c γ), *making acknowledgement of* :—Him man wearp uppan þ hê scolde beón ðes cinges swica and hê was ðas gewyrde (*he was in agreement with this,* i. e. he admitted the charge. The Latin version is : Debuit esse delator patriae, quod ipse cognouit ita esse), Chr. 1055 ; P. 184, note 4. v. ge-anwyrde.

ge-wyrdelic. Add : I. *fortuitous* :—Gewyrdelicum gelimpe *fortuitu casu,* An. Ox. 3792. Þâ gewyrdelican âwendennessa *fortuitas permutationes,* 190. II. *of narrative, recording events, historical.* v. gewyrd ; III :—Fram gewyrdelicere race *ab istorica relatione,* An. Ox. 3028. Hyra ôðer âwrât þâs gewyrdelican race, Hml. S. 6, 366.

ge-wyrdelîce. *Substitute: Historically, as if recording events* :— Gewyrdelîce *historialiter* (sententia historialiter quadrare videatur, quamvis secundum anagogen vaticinia credatur, Ald. 59, 29), An. Ox. 4261. Isaias wîtegode be Crîste swîðe gewislîce, swilce hê godspellere wǽre, swîðe gewyrdelîce (*as if recording actual events*), Ælfc. T. Grn. 9, 8. *See preceding word.*

ge-wyrdelîce ; *adv.* *Eloquently* (see next word) ; *with careful attention to words* (?) :—Snodorlîce, þæt is gewyrdelîce *sagaciter, prudenter* (gramaticorum regulas . . . *sagaciter* inquirendo, Ald. 5, 2), Hpt. Gl. 411, 24. Gewyrde[lîce] *uerbatim,* andgytful[lîce] *sensatim,* An. Ox. 56, 120.

ge-wyrdelicness, e ; *f.* *Eloquence* :—Gewyrdelicnesse *facundia,* Angl. xiii. 38, 321.

ge-wyrdigness, e ; *f.* *Eloquence, elegance of speech* :—Gewyrdignysse (-wyrdinesse, An. Ox. 5488 ; -wurðugnysse, 2, 492) *urbanitatis,* Hpt. Gl. 529, 52. Gewyrdi[g?]nesse *facundia,* An. Ox. 8 b, 10.

ge-wyrdlian. v. ge-wirdlian.

ge-wyrd-wrîtere, es ; *m.* *A historiographer* :—Stærwrîtere ł gewyrd-[wrîtere] *istoriographus,* An. Ox. 60, 1. v. wyrd-wrîtere.

ge-wyrht. Add : ge-wyrhtu(-o) ; *f.* I. *a work* :—Dô â þætte duge. Deág þin gewyrhtu ; God þe bið symle gôda gehwylces freá and fultum feónd þâm ôðrum wyrsan gewyrhta *do ever what may profit. Your work will avail ; God will always be a lord to help you in everything good, while he will be a foe to others whose works are worse,* Fä. 4–7. *Reddet Deus unicunque secundum opera sua* : þæt is on ûre geþeóde : hê forgylt ânra gehwylcum æfter his âgenum gewyrhtum, Wlfst. 184, 9. Gif gê scyld on eów witen ðæs ðe eów man tihð oððe on gewyrhtum oððe on gewitnesse *if you know yourselves guilty as principals or as accessories,* Rtl. 114, 23. Be folcleásunge gewyrhtum. Gif mon folcleásunge gewyrce *de publico mendacio conficto. Si quis publicum mendacium confingat,* Ll. Th. i. 80, 19. Cwiðende cwicra gewyrhtu *mourning the deeds done in the flesh,* Cri. 892. II. *desert, merit* :—Æghwæðer ânfealde gewyrht wiged *each gets just what he deserves,* Cri. 1578. þ þe bære (þære, MS.) cennendra gewyrhtum (-fyrhtum, MS.) þæs bearnes weorþe ongyten wǽre *ut ex generantium meritis dignitas germinis nosceretur,* Bl. H. 163, 27. Næs ǽnig mann swâ niðre þæt hê on ân ne sceolde tô helle swâ hê forðfaren wæs ; and þær wæs ǽrest for Adames gewyrhtum, Wlfst. 16, 15. þâ þe be gewyrhtum (-gewyrhte, *v. l.*) âwyrgede wǽron *qui merito maledicebantur,* Bd. 4, 26 ; Sch. 505, 7. Ic âreose be gewyrhtum *decidam merito,* Ps. Spl. 7, 4. þǽr leán cumað werum bi gewyrhtum worda and ðǽda *these rewards will come to men according to their deserts for words and deeds,* Cri. 1368. Geweorhtum, Met. 27, 27. Hî þæs deórau hâm wilniað bi gewyrhtum (*as it deserves*), Gû. 41. Gief hwâ bûton gewrihtum (*without just cause*) hit âbrecan wille, C. D. iii. 180, 22 : 262, 15. ¶ gewyrht(o) âgan *to deserve* (good or ill) :—Hê þone gylt gebête swâ wer swâ wîte, swâ hê gewyrht âge, Ll. Th. i. 66, 13. Hê mé sié ârfæstra þoune ic wið hine gewyrht âge *may he be more merciful to me than my conduct towards him deserves,* Angl. xi. 99, 91. þone ic wið hine geworht âge, 102, 75. Hê hæfde gewurðod þe þâ gewyrhto âhton (*those who deserved it*), Dan. 444. v. ǽr-, eald-, fyrn-, un-gewyrht.

ge-wyrhta. Add :—Ne gê beón gewitan ne gewyrhtan ǽniges morðres ne manslihtes, Wlfst. 40, 7.

ge-wyrman. v. ge-wirman.

ge-wyrms ; *adj.* *Full of matter, purulent* :—Wiþ þǽre lifre wunde þoune se swyle gewyrms tôbyrst, Lch. ii. 160, 23. Gewyrmsum (-wyrmð, MS.) *purulentis* (*vulneribus*), Wrt. Voc. ii. 87, 78. *See next word.*

ge-wyrmsed, -wyrsmed ; *adj.* *Suppurated, purulent* :—Gewyrmsed *saporatus,* Wrt. Voc. i. 289, 20. Lǽcedômas wiþ þǽre lifre wunde þoune se swile gewyrsmed tôbyrst, Lch. ii. 202, 14. Wiþ innan gewyrsmedum geswelle, 6, 27 : 72, 21.

ge-wyrp. *l.* -wyrpe, *and add :* [cf. *O. H. Ger.* sant-wurfi.] v. land-, sand-gewyrpe.

ge-wyrpan. v. ge-wirpan : ge-wyrsmed. v. ge-wyrmsed.

gewyrt-box, es ; *m.* *A scent-box, smelling-box* :—Gewyrtboxas oþþe stencfatu *olfactariola,* An. Ox. 8, 299.

ge-wyrþan *to estimate.* v. ge-wirþan : ge-wyrþe *amount.* v. ge-wirþe.

ge-wyrtrumian. *Substitute:* ge-wyrttrumian ; *p.* ode. I. *to root, fix firmly, establish* :—Gewyrttrumod *radicatum,* i. *fundatum,* An. Ox. 2, 153. Gewyrdtrumed, 3111. þæt gê beón on sôðre lufe gewyrtrumode (*in charitate radicati et fundati,* Eph. 3, 17), Hml. Th. ii. 408, 19. II. *to root up* :—Ic gewyrtrumade *eradicavi,* Rtl. 65, 25.

ge-wyrtûn. *l.* gewyrt-tûn, *and for* Jn. Skt. Lind. *substitute* Jn. R.

ge-wŷscan. Add : (1) *to wish for, desire* :—Gewîscod mid gewillnungum ealra þinga dæg *optatus votis omnium dies,* Hy. S. 89, 2. Gewîscodne geseón mid eágan Crîst *optatum videre lumine Christum,* 54, 31. Gewîscodum *optatis,* i. *desideratis,* An. Ox. 806. (2) *to wish for* something (*gen.*) for a person (*dat.*) :—Agathes him andwyrde : 'Beó þin wîf swylc swâ Uenus . . . and beó ðê swylc swâ Iouis' . . . 'Gif hî sôðe godas synd, gôdes ic þe gewîsce (*if they are true gods I am wishing you something good*) . . . Hât hî swâye fele þ gif ðû hwylcne wyrige, þ ðu gewîsce him ðæs þ his lîf beó gelîc þînum lâðum godum, Hml. S. 8, 65–81. [*O. H. Ger.* gi-wunsken *optare.*]

ge-wŷscedness. *For* R. Ben. . . . Lye *substitute* :—Gê underfêngon gâst gewŷscednysse *accepistis spiritum adoptionis* (*filiorum*), R. Ben. I. 11, 14. v. ge-wŷscing.

ge-wŷscendlic. *Add:* I. *desirable* :—Gewîscendlicum *obtabili,* Angl.

xiii. 373, 109. **II.** *adoptive, made by adoption* :—Gewīscendlice *adoptivas* (*filias*), Hpt. Gl. 404, 58. [**III.** as a grammatical term, *optative.* See Dict.]

**ge-wȳscing.** *Substitute:*—Gē onfēncgon gāst gewȳscincge (*adoptionis*) bearna, Scint. 64, 13. Gewīscinge, R. Ben. 10, 14.

**ge-yferian** *to exalt* :—Drihten geyferað (*sublimabit*) horn Xrīstes his, Ps. L. fol. 186 b, 4. v. ge-uferian.

**ge-yflian.** *Add* : **I.** *to injure* (physically) :—Sē þe man ofslehð binnan ciricderum, sylle þǣre cirican .cxx. sciłł. . . . Sē þe cwicne on þǣre mundbyrde geyfelige (*he who in a church injures a man without killing him*), sylle .xxx. sciłł., Ll. Th. i. 332, 11. **II.** used impersonally. (1) with dat. of person who falls sick :—Him geyfelode þǣr hē mid þām cynge sæt *he was taken ill while sitting with the king*, Chr. 1053 ; P. 185, 13 : 1086 ; P. 218, 37. (2) with acc. of person :—Nam hē his feorme on Wuldahām, and on þām ōðran wolde, ac hine geyflade (*sed infirmatus est*), Cht. Th. 272, 29 (*the Latin version is* 275, 9). ⸿

**ge-yldan.** v. ge-ildan.

**ge-yppan.** *Add* :—Geyppe *depromo*, i. *ostendo, profero, protulero, exposuero*, Wülck. Gl. 219, 23. Wæs geypt *ederetur, nasceretur*, i. *proferetur*, Wrt. Voc. ii. 142, 31. Geypped *exortatus*, 145, 73. **I.** *to bring into view, display* :—Þeáh hē (*May*) wynsumlīce blōwe and blǣdnyssa fǣgere geyppe, Angl. viii. 311, 2. Geypped wæs æðelinga wynn (*St. Andrew*), and hié andweardne eágum meahton gesión sigerōfne, An. 1225. **II.** *to bring into notice, bring to the knowledge of people* :—S. Anastasius þe Scs Basilius geypte, Ll. Th. ii. 344, 31. Wīde byð eorlum geypped æðelinges deað, Men. 157. **II a.** of legal notice, *to lay an information* of a crime :—Gif mon on, folces gemōte cyninges gerēfan geyppe eofot and his eft geswīcan wille, gestǣle on ryhtran hand, gif hē mǣge *if a man in the folkmoot give to the king's reeve notice of a crime* (*done to him by another*), *and afterwards wish to abandon the charge against the other, he shall bring his charge against one who with more justice may be considered the criminal, if he can*, Ll. Th. i. 76, 6. **III.** *to utter, declare* by speech :—Ic geyppe deiglo *eructabo abscondita*, Mt. L. 13, 35. Se dysega ungeðyldega all his ingeðonc hē geypt *totum spiritum suum profert stultus*, Past. 220, 10. Þās word Zosimus mid teárum geypte, Hml. S. 23 b, 195. Hē þās word geypte, Angl. viii. 325, 47. Gesǣd, geypped wæs *prolatum*, i. *narratum est*, An. Ox. 4505. **IV.** *to manifest, prove the existence of by effects* :—Þte in līchome his ðīn mæht sié giypped (*manifestata*), Rtl. 102, 43. **V.** where concealment is desired, *to reveal, expose, betray*. (1) in a bad sense :—Fram leásum āþume geypt *a pellaci genero proditus* i. *propalatus*, An. Ox. 2379. (2) where evil is exposed :—Hē his fæder uncysta nā ne geypte (āmeldode, *v. l.*) *non patris prodebat vitium*, Gr. D. 22, 28. Geypte *prodidit* (*omnem concinnati sceleris scenam prodidit*, Ald. 39, 33), An. Ox. 2921. Hit þurh ǣnne þeówne mon geypped wearð *existente quadam ancilla indice*, Ors. 3, 6 ; S. 108, 31. Eall heora sprǣc wearð geypped and gewȳdmǣrsod, Nic. 8, 25.

**ge-yrfeweardian**. v. ge-irfeweardian : **ge-yrfian**. *l.* ge-irfian : **ge-yrgan**. v. ge-irgan : **ge-yrman**. v. ge-irman : **ge-yrnan**. v. ge-irnan : **ge-yrsian**. v. ge-irsian : **ge-ȳwan**. v. ge-īwan : **gib**. v. gif :

**giccan.** *Add* : [O. L. Ger. jukkian *pruire*.] v. gicce, gicenes, gicþa.

**gicce**, an ; *f. Itch* :—Gyccas *prorigo, urigo cutis*, Txts. 113, 82. [C. M. ȝicche.] v. giccan.

**giccig.** *Substitute : Itchy, irritating* (of skin diseases) :—Þā giccigan untrumnysse *purulentas valetudines*, Hpt. Gl. 453, 8.

**gicel.** *Dele* īs *at end, and add* : , gicele, an ; *f. Ickle* (v. N. E. D. s. v.) :—Gecilae *stiria*, Wrt. Voc. ii. 121, 26. Gecele, i. 289, 33. Þǣr synt tō sorge ætsomne gemenged se þrosma līg and se þrece gicela *frigora mista simul ferventibus algida flammis*, Dōm. L. 191. Se þrosmiga līg and se þrece gycela, Wlfst. 138, 26. [O. H. Ger. kichilla *stiria*.]

**gicel-gebland**, es ; *n. A hailstorm* :—Bletsiað gicelgebland and snāw Drihten *benedicite pruina et niues Dominum*, Ps. Rdr. 293, 70. Cf. snāw-gebland.

**gicelig.** *For* Hpt. . . . 465 *substitute* :—Gicelig *glacialis* (*murus*), An. Ox. 2497. Þā giceligan heáhtorra bearewæs *glaciales alpium saltus*, 2034. Gycelie (gylicie, MS.), 7, 122.

**gicel-stān.** *Add* : Ps. Rdr. 147, 17. Gycelstān, Ps. L. 147, 17.

**gice-ness**, e ; *f. Itching, irritation of the skin* :—Gicenes *prurigo*, Wrt. Voc. ii. 68, 43. Gycenis, gycinis *prurigo*, Txts. 89, 1658. v. giccan.

**gicer, gycer**, es ; *n. A measure of land, an acre* :—Iugeres gycer *unius die opus aratoris*, Ld. Gl. H. p. 34, 75. [Cf. O. H. Ger. iuchart *jugerum*.] Cf. geoc.

**gicþa**, itch. *Add* :—Se giecða bið suīðe unsār, Past. 71, 18. Wiþ wambe gicþan, Lch. ii. 240, 5. Wið wambe gicþum, 166, 7. Gihðum, i. 374, 2. [Þat bearninde ȝecðe (ȝeohðe, *v. l.*) of þ licomliche lust, H. M. 9, 29.]

**gicþa** hiccup. In Lch. ii. 4, 27 *perhaps* gicþan *is a mistake. In the article to which the passage refers the disease spoken of is called* geoxa.

**gid.** *Add* : **I.** *of metrical composition, a poem, song* :—Gyd *carmen*, Wrt. Voc. ii. 143, 18. Leóð wæs āsungen, gleómannes gyd, B. 1160. Sē þe lufige þysses giddes (*the poem on the Apostles*) begang, Ap. 89. Bidde ic monna gehwone þe þis gied (*the poem on St. Juliana*) rǣde, Jul. 719. Hē gyd wreceð, sārigne sang, B. 2446. Gleómen simle gemētað gydda gleáwne (*a connoisseur of songs, one who can appreciate the poet's verses*), Vīd. 139. Ongan hē singan and þus cwæþ : ' Ic wille mid giddum (*in verse*) gecȳþau . . . ,' Bt. 25 ; F. 88, 2. Ides geómrode giddum *the lady chanted a dirge*, B. 1118. **II.** of formal speech :—Gedd *eologium*, Wrt. Voc. ii. 70, 9. Gyd *elogium, verbum*, 143, 18. Geddi *elogio*, 107, 9. Gidde, 29, 20. Spǣce, gydde, An. Ox. 23, 15. Gydde, grētinge, 3182. *Elogio*, i. *dicto* ł gydde, 5, 27. Unhlīsfullum bīwyrda gydde *infami proverbiorum elogio*, 5233. Gidde, Wrt. Voc. ii. 87, 41 : 19, 17. Wes þū giedda wīs, . . . worda hyrde *be wise of speech, keep watch on your words*, Fä. 41. (1) *a maxim, sentence, proverb, wise speech* :—Gydda *proverbiorum*, Wrt. Voc. ii. 87, 42. Gleáwe men sceolon gieddum wrixlan, Gn. Ex. 4. (2) *of didactic speech* :—þū þē lǣr be þon, gumcyste ongit. Ic þis gid be þē āwræc *I have told this tale for your instruction*, B. 1723. (3) *of eloquent, oratorical speech* :—Oft ic wōdboran wordleána sum āgiefe æfter giedde, Rä. 78, 10. For eorlum ān reordode gidda gearosnotor (cf. giddum gearosnotter, 586. Wordcræftes wīs, 592) . . . wordes cræftig, El. 418. Sum bið wōðbora, giedda giffæst, Crä. 36. (4) *of figurative speech* :—Bī þon giedd āwræc Iōb, . . . Hǣlend lofede . . . and hine fugel nemde, Cri. 633. (5) *of prophecy* :—Gydde *uaticinium*, An. Ox. 3708. [Heo biheold ȝuere ænne burinæsse, and hire ȝeddes (wordes, 2nd MS.) sǣide ȝeomere stefne, Laym. 25853.] v. cwide-, fore-, fyrn-, geómor-, sōþ-, word-gid.

**giddian.** *Take here* geddian *in Dict., and add* :—Se wīsdōm geoddode þus, ēcte þæt spell mid leóðe, Bt. 12 ; S. 26, 22. Ongon hē gieddigan and þus singinde cwæð, 32, 3 ; S. 73, 22. Ongan heó of ðām Daviticum sealmum gyddian and þus cwedan, Lch. iii. 428, 17. Se sealmsceop be ðām gyddigende sang, Hml. Th. i. 410, 16. [þe king þus ȝeddien agon (þes word saide, 2nd MS.), Laym. 21429.]

**gidding.** *Dele first and last passages, take here* gedding *in Dict., and add* : **I.** *of metrical composition* :—Bēda þises hālgan līf ǣgðer ge æfter ānfealdre gereccednysse ge æfter leoðlicere gyddunge āwrāt *Bede wrote St. Cuthbert's life both in prose and in verse*, Hml. Th. ii. 134, 1. **II.** *of formal or serious speech.* (1) *a dark saying, riddle, an enigma* :—Geddunga *enigmata*, Wrt. Voc. ii. 32, 54. (2) *of figurative speech, a similitude, parable* :—Gicwæð hē ðās geddunga, onlīcnesse ł bisene *dicebat hanc similitudinem*, Lk. R. 13, 6. Geddunge *parabolam*, 15, 3 : 19, 11. Geddong, Lk. p. 10, 7. Getdung, 7, 3. (Parabola *is often glossed by* geddung *in the Lindisfarne and Rushworth versions of St. Luke's Gospel.*) (3) *of prophetic or divine speech* :—Drihten, . . . giðæht ðīn ald geddung sōð sié *Domine, . . . consilium tuum antiquum verum fiat*, Rtl. 1, 9. Gyddunge gerȳna (*futura propheticae*) *diuinationis oracula*, An. Ox. 2534 : 2, 97. Ðurh Crīstes ðrowunge wurdon ðæra wītgena gyddunga gefyllede, Hml. Th. ii. 372, 13. Gehȳrað wītedōm, lōbes gieddinga, Ph. 549. v. leóþ-gidding.

**gidig**. v. gydig : **gīdsian**. v. gītsian : **gief**. v. gif : **giem**. v. gim : **giend**. v. geond :

**gierende** *taxauerat*, Wrt. Voc. ii. 122, 6. Perhaps the passage to which this gloss belongs is Ald. 27, 14 : Sibi usurpans tantopere taxauerat. other glosses to which are, *taxauerat*, i. *iudicauerat* hē dēmde, An. Ox. 2014: *usurpans* geauligende, 7, 118 ; *taxauerat*, i. *iudicauerat, posse-derat* hē dēmde, Hpt. Gl. 454, 3. As in the Corpus Glossary the *gi-*form of the prefix is very rare (*gi-brec*, Wrt. Voc. ii. 124, 6, is the single instance, unless *gierende* be another), and as there is no other instance of *ǣrendan* (the verb is always *ǣrendian*) perhaps *gierende* is incorrect. If, however, it is correct, it seems to be nearer in meaning to *usurpans* than to *taxauerat*.

**gierstan-dæg**. v. gistran-dæg : **gierwan**. v. girwan : **giest**. v. gist.

**gif**, e ; *f. Substitute* gif, es ; *n., and add* :—Mid þām godcundan gyfe gesawen *diuina gratia respectus*, Bd. 1, 7 ; Sch. 20, 6. v. eard-gif.

**gif.** *Add* : Conj. *introducing a conditional clause. The indicative after gif implies the certain occurrence of a circumstance, the reality of a state, &c., spoken of in the clause, admits the truth of the statement contained in the clause.* Gyf þū wylt, þū miht (Mt. 8, 2) ; *here it is implied that the person addressed is actually willing or can.* Hū magon wē . . . gif þū his ne meaht ōr āreccan? (Dan. 133) ; *here the inability on the part of the person addressed to give any account of the matter is taken as certain.* Gif gē mē lufiað, healdað mīne beboda *you do love me, so keep my commandments. The difference between the indicative and subjunctive after gif may be illustrated by the following passages* :—Gif cyning æt mannes hām drincæð and þær man lyswæs hwæt gedō, Ll. Th. i. 4, 1-2 ; *here the entertainment of the king is an event sure to take place, so* drincæð *is indicative; but the wrong-doing is quite uncertain, so* gedō *is subjunctive.* (See also 2, 8–9.) Gif man frīgne mannan ofsleahð, 4, 6 ; *but* gif *in cyninges tūne man mannan ofsleá*, 4, 4 : *for homicide was a certainty, but that it should take place in a king's town was not so.* Cf. *too* gif frīg man frēum stelð, 6, 2, *with* gif frīg man cyninge stele, 4, 3. *Perhaps the different renderings of the same Latin words are intended to mark a*

*change in the speaker's mind, when in* Mt. 4, 3 si filius Dei es *is trans-lated* gyf þū Godes sunu sȳ, *while in* v. 6 *the rendering is* gyf þū Godes sunu eart. *But sometimes the distinction seems not very clearly marked.* Cf. *with* Ll. Th. i. 4, 1–2 (v. supra): Gif mon hafað spere ofer eaxle and hine mon on āsnāseð . . . Gif beforan eágum āsnāse, 84, 12–14: *here on* āsnāse (*like* gedō) *might have been expected.* Cf. *too*, gif mec deað nimeð, B. 447, *with* gif mec hilde nime, 452, *the reference is to the same peril in each: and* gif gē syndon þegnas . . . , An. 344, *with* gif þū þegn sié . . . , 417, *the evidence of thaneship is the same in both cases.* Gif ceorl būton wífes wīsdóme deófium gelde . . . Ll. Th. i. 40, 4–6. Agif . . . ; gif þū . . . aldres rēce . . . þū sweltan scealt . . . , gif þū wyrnest, Gen. 2654–2660: *here the certainty seems to belong rather to* rēce *than to* wyrnest. *See also in* Mk. L. 12, 19: gef brōðer deað sié I bið (*mortuus fuerit*). **I.** the conditional clause in the indic., and (1) present or future tense. (a) the principal clause present or future *if, when* :—Ealle þās ic sylle þē, gyf þū feallende tō mē geeádmētst (*adora-veris*), Mt. 4, 9: Bl. H. 27, 18 : 13, 9 : Jul. 169 : Jn. 8, 52 : 14, 14 : Gen. 2315 : Exod. 560 : 13, 1182. Gyf hē þē gehȳrð (*audierit*), þū gestaðelast þínne brōðor, Mt. 18, 15. Gif wē willaþ nū on Drihten gelȳfan, þonne beó wē sittende be þǣm wege, Bl. H. 23, 7 : Bt. 3, 4 ; F. 6, 16 : Sat. 251 : Gen. 559 : 2521 : Sch. 35. Him (*the blind man*) bið mycel daru, gif hē hit geseón ne mæg, Bl. H. 21, 8. þū ne bist unscyldig wið mē, gif þū on ídelnesse cýst mīnne noman (cf. *nec habebit in-sontem Dominus eum, qui assumpserit nomen Domini frustra*, Ex. 20, 7), Ll. Th. i. 44, 8 : Cri. 1310 : Mód. 45 : An. 1570 : 1614. Meaht þū Adame gestȳran, gif þū his willan hæfst, Gen. 569 : 570 : 578 : Cri. 781 : B. 1185 : 1822. Gyf gē þā lufiað (*diligatis*) þe eów lufiað (*diligunt*), hwylce mēde habbað gē ?, Mt. 5, 46 : 47. Hū mæg ænig man ryht-wíslíce ācsigan, gif hē nān grot rihtwísnesse on him næfþ?, Bt. 35, 1 ; F. 156, 6 : 7, 2 ; F. 18, 6 : Met. 22, 46. Gief (gif, v. l.) wē ðonne habbað suā micle sorge . . . , ðonne hæbbe wē bēgen fēt gescóde untǣllíce, Past. 45, 10. Gif (gife, L.) þín eáge bið mānfull, eal þín líchama byð þýsterfull, Mt. 6, 23 : Lk. 12, 45. (a a) where the condition depends upon what is implied in the principal clause :—þū gehǣtst . . . ēce líf, gif wē sóð and ryht symle gelǣstað *thy promise is that we shall have eternal life, if we ever do truth and right*, Hy. 7, 75. (b) the principal clause imperative :—Gyf þín brōðor syngað (syngige, R. L., *peccauerit*) wið þē, gā and stýr him, Mt. 18, 15 : 16 : 17. Gif gē Abrahames bearn synt, wyrceað Abrahames weorc, Jn. 8, 39. Gif gē mē lufiað (*diligitis*), healdað mīne beboda, 14, 15. Gif man wið cyninges mægdenman geligeð, .L. scillinga gebēte, Ll. Th. i. 6, 4 (*and often*). (c) where the clause on which the condition depends is dependent :—ðæt wē gedōn, swā wē eáðe magon, gif wē ða stilnesse habbað, Past. 7, 9. (d) the princi-pal clause past :—Gif hī nu gōde sint, þonne wǣron hī swā gesceapene, Bt. 14, 2 ; F. 42, 36. (2) in the past tense, and the principal clause (pres. or fut.) indic. or imper. :—Gif ic þwōh eówre fēt, gē sceolon þweán eówer ǣlc ōðres fēt, Jn. 13, 14. Gif þū . . . gesealdest, hit is riht, Bt. 7, 2 ; F. 18, 33. Nǣnig mon ne sceal gēman his gesibbes, gif hē hine ǣrost āgǣlde Godes þeówdómes, Bl. H. 23, 17. Gif ic dyde ðis . . . gif ic āgald ðǣm geldendum . . . , ic gefallu, Ps. Srt. 7, 4–5. **II.** the conditional clause in the subjunctive, and (1) present tense. (a) the princi-pal clause imperative :—Gif þū sié Godes sunu, cweþ þ þā stānas tō hlāfum geweorþan, Bl. H. 27, 7 : 12. Be ðon gif mon ōðres godsunu ofsleá. Gif hwā ōðres sunu sleá . . . , sié sió mǣgbót and sió manbót gelíc, Ll. Th. i. 150, 11–14 (*and often*). Gif þe þæt gelimpe . . . þonne þū gecȳð, El. 441. Gib Eádwald leng lifige . . . geselle et ðǣm londe .x. ðūsenda, C. D. i. 256, 5. Gief hwā hit ābrecan wille, hæbbe him wið God gemǣne, iii. 180, 22. (b) the principal clause indic. (pres. or fut.) :—Gif hwylc gōd man from gōde gewíte, ðonne ne bið hē þe mā fullíce gōd, Bt. 37, 3 ; F. 190, 28. Gif hit eówer ǣnig mæge gewendan, . . . sóna hié him þe lāðran beóð, Gen. 427. (c) where the clause on which the condition depends is dependent, and (a) present :—Āhycgan, þæt wē on Adame, gif wē mægen, . . . andan gebētan, Gen. 398. (β) past with pres. or fut. sense :—God hæfde getiohhod . . . gif hī ðone frýdom teala gehealdan, þ hē hī wolde weorþian, Bt. 41, 3 ; F. 248, 10. (d) where the condition does not apply directly to the principal clause, but must be inferred :—Gif þū ða nýdþearfe witan wille, þonne is þæt mete and drync and clāþas *if you want to know what is needful,* [*I will tell you;*] *it is meat and drink and clothes*, Bt. 14, 1 ; F. 42, 4. (2) past tense with future sense, and principal clause in indic. (pres. or fut.) :—Gif ic sóð sprǣce, þonne sceal heó sweltan, Cri. 190. **III.** with both clauses in subjunctive, (1) with conditional clause in past subjunctive with present or future sense :—Swā þæt hē mehte ǣgþerre gerǣcan, gif hié ǣnigne feld sēcan wolden, Chr. 894 ; P. 84, 26. Gif God wǣre ðín fæder, witodlíce gē lufedon mē si *Deus pater uester esset, diligeretis utique me*, Jn. 8, 42. Gif se weorþscipe þām welan gecynde wǣre . . . oþþe eft se wela þæs welegan āgen wǣre, þonne ne mihte hē hine forlǣtan, Bt. 27, 3 ; F. 98, 24. Eálā þte ðis moncyn wǣre gesǣlig, gif heora mōd wǣre riht, 21 ; F. 74, 40. Gif eall þisses middaneardes wela cōme tō ānum men, hū ne wǣron þonne ealle ōþre men wǣdlan?, 13 ; F. 38, 20. Hū wolde þē nu lícian, gif hwilc cyning wǣre . . . ?, 41, 1 ; F. 244, 24 : 27.

(2) conditional clause in plupert. subj. with past sense :—Gif þū wǣre hēr, nǣre mín brōðor deád si *fuisses hic, frater meus non fuisset mortuus*, Jn. 11, 21 : 32. Gif þ deófol hine ne gesāwe on ūre gecynde, ne costode hē hine . . . Gif hē nǣre sōþ God, nā him englas ne þegnodon, Bl. H. 33, 35–35, 2 : 29, 4 : Hex. 22, 27 : Gen. 643 : 787 : B. 592 : El. 777 : Bt. 7, 2 ; F. 18, 11 : 40, 6 ; F. 242, 7. Gif hié þā blōtan mehten, hié woldon secgean þæt him hiera godas gehulpan *quam si aruspices celebrassent, diis gloriam vindicassent*, Ors. 5, 2 ; S. 218, 5. **¶** with the present tense in the clause on which the conditional depends :—Hē teohhode gif hī hwæt gesyngoden, þ hī hit eft gebēton, Bt. 41, 3 ; F. 248, 14. **IV.** implying that an unfavourable point is conceded, *even if, suppose* or *granted that* :—Hwider hweorfað wē, . . . gif wē swīcað þē? *suppose we do leave you, where shall we go?*, An. 407. Ac is wunder mycel, . . . gif þū hit sylfa wāst *it is a great wonder, even if it is granted that you know it yourself*, Hy. 3, 20. **V.** the conditional clause alone used as an exclamation :—Eálā gif þū wistest on þyssum þínum dæge þe ðē tō sybbe synt, Lk. 19, 42. Eálā gif ic hæfde þíne synna āna, Hml. S. 3, 521. **VI.** introducing a noun-clause depending on verbs of know-ing, learning, doubting, &c., *whether* :—Gefrægn hine gif I huoeðer (*si*) huoelchuoego gesēge, Mk. L. 8, 23. Huoeðer I gif *si*, Lk. L. 23, 6. Man ne gehȳrde gif ǣnig scyphere wǣre būton āgenre leóde, Hml. S. 21, 448. Secgaþ gif gē willað þām cāsere gehȳrsumian, 9, 226. þū scealt cȳðan, gif þū his ondgitan ǣnige hæbbe, An. 1523. Geseoh gif ic on unrihte eóde, Ps. Th. 138, 21. Ic wille fundigan, gif hié synna fremmað Gen. 2412.

**gifa.** *Add:* = **gefa** :—Hē cuæð ðætte ðone gladan giefan (*datorem*) God lufode, Past. 323, 12. v. ælmes-, freóls-, freót-, leán-, rūm-gifa.

**gifan.** *Add:* —Doto, -as, dono *vel* gifu, Wrt. Voc. ii. 142, 1. Geben (gibaen, Ep. Gl.) waes *inpendebatur*, Txts. 71, 1086. **I.** *to give* a thing as a present :—Se wela þe se cyning gifþ his deórlingum, Bt. 29, 1 ; F. 102, 3. þū sealdest mē wilna geniht. For þan þū ne þearft sceamian . . . þæs þū mē geáfe, Seel. 149. Hē geaf mē sinc and symbel, B. 2431 : 2173. Nān man ne sylle nān hors ofer sǣ, būtan hē hit gifan wille, Ll. Th. i. 208, 19. Geafendum mið ðingum *oblatis muneribus*, Mt. p. 14, 1. **II.** *to grant, confer* an honour, a privilege, office, favour, &c. :—Se anweald þe hē gifþ his deórlingum, Bt. 29, 1 ; F. 102, 3. Gif man his mæn freóls gefe, Ll. Th. i. 38, 15. Þingie hē on þām ceápgilde . . . nāht on þām wíte, būtan hit sē gifan wille þe hit tō gebyrige, 210, 18. Hē scolde heom ðone pallium gifan, Chr. 995 ; P. 130, 34. **II a.** *to give* credit, confidence, affection, &c. :—Þæs cyninges geferrǣden þe hē gifþ his deórlingum, Bt. 29, 1 ; F. 102, 3. Gif bisenum lufu is tó gefanne si *exemplaribus fides est adhibita*, Mt. p. 1, 12. **III.** of superhuman power. Cf. gifeþe :—þū, Drihten, forgeáfe þām sāwlum eard on hiofonum and him þǣr gifst weorþlice gifa, Bt. 33, 4 ; F. 132, 19. Be ðæs andgites mǣðe ðe God ūs gifþ, 42 ; F. 256, 4. God dóm gifeð gumena gehwylcum, An. 1153. Giefeð, Cri. 674 : Crä. 112. Of þām ǣhtum þe ic eów on eorðan geaf, Cri. 1502 : 1382. Drihten þām werude geaf mōd and mihte, Dan. 13. Dryhten hyre weorðmynde geaf, Jud. 343 : An. 317 : El. 365. Hwæt hæfst ðū æt þām gifum þe ðū cwist þ seó wyrd eów gife ?, Bt. 13 ; F. 38, 5. Him weorðeð blǣd gifen, Cri. 878. Gyfen, B. 64. **III a.** used in the expression of a wish :—Se ælmihtiga God him gife wurðscipe, Chr. 1085 ; P. 217, 13. Þē Meotud wist gife, An. 388. **III b.** used absolutely :—Ðæt is his weorþscipe þ hē swā gifol is, and swā rūmedlíce gifð, Bt. 38, 3 ; F. 202, 14. Simle hē biþ gifende, and ne wanaþ his nǣfre nāuht, 42 ; F. 258, 5. **¶** *to give* to do something, *grant* :—Heó wæs gelǣded, gifendum Drihtne and scyldendum, tō ðam munuchāde, Gr. D. 199, 18. **IV.** *to assign the future ownership of* property, *be-queath* :—Sē þe land gewerod hæbbe . . . , hæbbe hē unbesacen on dæge and æfter dæge tō syllenne and tō gifenne þām þe him leófast sȳ, Ll. Th. i. 420, 22. **V.** *to give in marriage* :—Geaf Æþelwulf cyning his dohtor Burgrēde, Chr. 853 ; P. 66, 2. þā þā heó befleáh þām gesettan gyfte . . . in þām hī man gifan wolde *dum constitutis jam nuptiis . . . fugisset*, Gr. D. 199, 16. **VI.** *to deliver,* hand *to a person;* *to give* food :—þā wæs gylden hylt gamelum rince on hand gyfen, B. 1678. Gif man his heówum in fæsten flǣsc gefe, Ll. Th. i. 40, 9. **VII.** *to give* into the hands of, *hand over* to possess or to keep, *consign, commit, entrust* :—Hī (hine) lēton holm beran, geáfon on gārsecg, B. 49. Āgife (gyfe, v. l.) man þām āgenfrigean his āgen, Ll. Th. i. 390, 7. þeáh him eall sié þes middangeard on ǣht gifen, Met. 16, 10. **VIII.** *to give* in discharge of obligation, *pay* :—Him eallum wile Drihten dædleán gyfan, Exod. 263. **IX.** *to give* to a superior, *pay* a tax, due (religious or secular), *make* an offering :—Gef ðing þ bebeád Móyses *offer munus quod praecepit Moses*, Mt. L. 8, 4 : Mk. L. 1, 44. Gif se Frǣncisca byð ofercuman, hē gyfe þām cynge .III. pund, Ll. Th. i. 489, 17. Ðing tō geafanne *munus offerendum*, Mt. p. 14, 13. **X.** *to give up* to, *devote, consign* :—Ic hí ne sparige, ac on spild giefe, Jul. 85. Hī Waldend giefeð feóndum in forwyrd, Cri. 1614. **XI.** where the object is a trans-active act considered as given by the agent and received by the person or thing affected :—þonne swīað hē and hlyst gefeð, Ph. 143. Eów miltse giefeð fæder ælmihtig, Jul. 657. Him se hæle geaf giestlíðnysse, Gen.

2445. Gif bescoren man gange him an giestliðnesse, gefe him man ænes, Ll. Th. i. 38, 13. Hé uoenas geafa embehtsumnise † hérnisse hine hé gefe Gode *arbitretur obsequium se praestare Deo*, Jn. L. R. 16, 2. **XII.** *to offer, present* to the action of another :—Hé beald in gebede bidsteall gifed fæste on fédan, Jul. 388. Giefed, Rä. 41, 19. Gif huá dec slâes in suídra ceica din gef ( *praebe* ) him dý ódera, Mt. L. 5, 39. **XIII.** *to offer* for observation, *set forth* a statement for consideration :—Tó geafanne mid efennisse *adhibita comparatione*, Mt. p. 15, 12. **XIV.** *to allot, assign* :—Þær ys âu tó lâfe, gif þæne Aprili, Angl. viii. 303, 38 : 43. **XV.** *to cause to have* or *receive*. (1) the subject a person :— Brego engla geaf eft blisse gehwæm égbûendra þurh eordan westm, Chr. 975 ; P. 122, 1. (2) of things, *to be productive of* :—Ælcum men his âgen gód gitþ good edleán, Bt. 37, 2 ; F. 188, 27. Dâ cwæþ hé : ' Wênst þû hwæþer ænig þissa andweardana gooda þé mæge sellan fulle gesélþa ?' Dâ answarode ic : 'Nât ic nânwuht . . . þe swelc gifan mæge,' 33, 3 ; F. 126, 23. **XVI.** *to allow to have, not to withhold, to release* :—Is giwuna iów þte énne ic gefe † forléte (*dimittam*) iów in eóstro, wallad gé fordon þ ic gefe (*dimittam*) cynig Iudéa ?, Jn. R. L. 18, 39. v. ge-, on-gifan ; for-gifen.

**gife.** v. gifu : **gifedness.** v. for-gifedness : **gifelness.** v. gifolness.

**gifend, gefend** (*q. v. in Dict.*), es; *m.* **I.** *a giver* :—Apollonius mangeres naman genam mâ þonne gisendes, Ap. Th. 10, 8. **I a.** applied to the Deity. v. gifan ; **III** :—Drihten þe is ealra gereorda gifend, R. Ben. 69, 11. **II.** *one that is in the habit of giving, a liberal person* :—Gifend *largus*, Wrt. Voc. ii. 151, 30. [*Icel.* gefendr ; *pl. givers.*] v. for-gifend.

**gifend-lic.** v. for-gifendlic : **gifenlic, -líce.** v. for-gifenlic, -líce.

**giferlíce.** *Add* :—Gýferlíce *pertinaciter*, i. *insuperabiliter* (instrumenta bellica *pertinaciter* portantes, Ald. 11, 29), An. Ox. 766.

**gifer-nes.** *Add* : **I.** *greediness* for food, *gluttony* :—Gísernes *gastrimargia*, Wrt. Voc. ii. 40, 16. Gýfernes *vel* ofersfil, i. 27, 21. (1) of persons :—Syndon eahta heáfodleahtras . . . Ân is gecwæden *gula*, þ is gýfernyss on Englisc ; seó déd þ man yt ær tíman and drincd, odde hé tó micel nimd on æte odde on wæte, Hml. S. 16, 268. Suá oft suá wé úre hand dód tó úrum múde for giéfernesse ofergemet *per immoderatum usum dum manus ad cibum tenditur*, Past. 313, 14. Tantalus de on þisse worulde ungemetlíce gífre wæs, and him þær (*in hell*) þ ilce yfel fyligde þæs gífernesse, Bt. 35, 6 ; F. 170, 1. ' On giéfernesse (*ingluvie*) dû rícsasd ofer dâ menniscan heortan.' For dæm dæm de on giéfernesse ongietene (*gulae deditos*) beód, wile folgian firenlust . . . Sió wamb bid ádened mid fylle for giéfernesse (*venter ingluvie extenditur*), Past. 311, 2–12. Gísernesse *ingluviem* (*ventris*), Wrt. Voc. ii. 96, 39. Manega mettas gegladiad gýfernysse (*gulam*), Scint. 57, 4. Ic andette gísernesse ætes and drences, ge ær tíde ge ofer tíde. Ic andette ælce gítsunga and æfest, Ll. Th. ii. 262, 25. (2) of animals :—Heora (*animals'*) willa tó nânum óþrum þingum nis áþenod bûton tó gísernesse and tó wrænnesse *quarum omnis ad explendam corporalem lacunam festinat intentio*, Bt. 31, 1 ; F. 112, 8. Fræcum innoþes gýfernesse (*draco boves*) *gulosa ventris ingluvie* (*voraciter glutire solebat*), An. Ox. 2445. **II.** *greed* of money, *cupidity, covetousness, avarice* :—Gísernesse *philargiria* [cf. gítsunge *philargiria* (the third of the deadly sins, Ald. 206, 31), 96, 67], Wrt. Voc. ii. 66, 29 : 50, 20. Deófíce déda . . . on stalan and on strúdungan, on gítsungan and on gísernessan, Ll. Th. i. 310, 17. Ne gé ne beón gewyrhtan stala ne strúdunga, ac strýnad mid rihte. Scyldad eów wid gítsunga and wid gísornessa . . . Scyldad eów wid gálscipas . . ., and wid oferfylle beorgad eów, Wlfst. 40, 6–13. ¶ *In* Bl. H. 163, 12 gísernes *seems an error. See* ge-férnes.

**gifes** *in the phrase* tó gifes. v. gifu : **gifestre.** v. for-gifestre.

**gifeþe**; *adj. Add* :—Gif hit gifeþe is *huius si potis est*, Germ. 402, 84. (1) where what is granted is expressed by a noun :—Eów ys tír gifede, Jud. 157 : Vald. 1, 25. Gyfede, B. 819. (2) the grant given by a clause :—Mé gyfede weard þæt ic áglæcan geræhte, B. 555. Cf. gifan ; **III.**

**gif-fæst.** For Cot. 57 *substitute* :—Giffæst ( *printed* giffæt, *but see* Wülck. Gl. 382, 30) *capax*, Wrt. Voc. ii. 24, 10.

**gif-heal.** *Add* : Cf. Hé healreced hâtan wolde gewyrcean . . . and þær on innan eall gedælan . . . swylc him God sealde, B. 68–72.

**gifian.** *Take here* geafian, geofian *in Dict., and add* :—God mænigfealdlícor gifad mannum þonne hé seó gebeden, Hml. S. 23 b, 617. [*O. Sax.* gebón, gebóian : *O. H. Ger.* gebón, gebén.] v. â-, ge-gifian.

**gifig** (?); *adj. Possessing as the result of gift* or *grant* :—Gifine *compotem*, Angl. xi. 171, 7 (v. note there in which the word is compared with *Goth.* gabeigs : *Icel.* gǫfugr). [Gifig (*and* gifan) *may be compared with* tíþe (*and* tíþian).]

**gifl.** *Add* : v. undern-gifl.

**gifla** (geofola), an ; *m. A small piece of food, a mouthful* :—Geofola *buccila*, Wrt. Voc. ii. 126, 67. v. gifl.

**Gifle** (-as ?); *pl. The people of a district in England* :—Gifla landes is þrýu hund hýda, C. D. B. i. 414, 22.

**gifnes.** *Add* :—Gefnise ûs geræc *veniam nobis tribue*, Rtl. 82, 7.

**gifol.** *Add* : **I.** *liberal, munificent* :—Ne beó gé ódrum monnum suá

gifole (giofole, *v. l.*) dæt hit weorde eów selfum tó gesuince *non ut aliis sit remissio, vobis autem tribulatio, vestra abundantia illorum inopiam suppleat*, Past. 325, 9. Hié wilniad dæt hié gifule (giofole, *v. l.*) dyncen *munifici videri appetunt*, 339, 25. **II.** *gracious* :—Gefol wíf *mulier gratiosa*, Kent. Gl. 366. [*Icel.* gjöfull *munificent.*] v. rûm-gifol.

**gifol-ness**, e ; *f. Liberality, munificence* :—Sint tó manienne dâ de mildheortlíce sellad . . . dý læs sió gídsung dæs lænan lofes ádwæsce dæt leóht dære giofolnesse, odde eft sió giofolness sié gemenged wid unrótnesse, odde eft for dæm giefum his mód fægnige *ne dationis lumen laudis transitoriae appetitio extinguat ; ne oblatum munus conjuncta tristitia obsideat ; ne in oblato munere animus hilarescat*, Past. 321, 22 Gifelnesse *munificentia, largitate*, Hpt. Gl. 466, 57. v. rûmgifolnes.

**gifre.** *Add* :—Ic wât eardfæstne ânne standan, deáfne dumban, sé oft swilged gifrum lâcum (*the subject of the riddle is a bookcase, the* gifre lâc *are books*), Rä. 50, 3. *In* Rä. 27 *a book is the subject.*

**gifre.** *Add* :—Dâ gifran *avida*, Wrt. Voc. ii. 1, 4. **I.** *greedy of food*. (1) of persons :—Gífre *ambro*, Wrt. Voc. ii. 96, 49. Gífre, grædig *consumptor*, i. *devorator*, *gluto*, 134, 1. Etol, gífre *edax*, i. *vorax, vorator*, 142, 29. Dâ gífran *gulae dediti*, Past. 308, 15. (1 a) as an epithet of the mouth, lips, &c. :—Smærum gífrum (grífrum, MS.) *buccis ambronibus*, i. *cupidis* † *auidis*, An. Ox. 698. Gífrum, 5, 19. (1 b) of an action or quality displaying greediness :—Mid gíferre *gulosa* (*fraude*, Ald. 204, 31), Wrt. Voc. ii. 40, 29. (2) of animals :—Swá swá fleógende fugel, donne hé gífre (*avidus*) bid, hé gesihd dæt æs, and donne for dæm luste dæs metes hé forgiet dæt grín, Past. 331, 17. Dæs gífran dopfugeles *voracis mer[g]ule*, Wrt. Voc. ii. 76, 6. Þé sculon moldwyrmas ceówan . . . swearte wihta gífre and grædige, Seel. 74. (2 a) of a quality :—Of gífre frecinesse *gulosa ingluvie*, An. Ox. 4, 37. **II.** *of destructive things, devouring* flame, &c. :—Þeáh gé mínne flæschoman forgrípen gífran lége, Gú. 346. Rícels gífre gléda bærnad, Ps. Th. 140, 2. **III.** *greedy of prey* or *booty, rapacious, ravenous*. (1) of a person :—Ne bid nân heretoga swá gífre on fræmdra manna yrfe swá se unrihtwísa déma byþ on his hýremanna, Ll. Lbmn. 475, 18. His (*Grendel's*) módor gífre and galgmód gegán wolde sorhfulne síd, B. 1277. Gífrum deófle, Sal. 145. Hí (*the fallen angels*) gedúfan sceoldun in þone deópan wælm . . . grædige and gífre, Sat. 32. (1 a) of feeling or action :—Wé þurh gífre mód beswican ûs sylfe, Hö. 95. Deád hine ræsed on gífrum grápum, Gú. 969. (2) of a place that receives many victims :—Helle grædige and gífre, Gen. 793. **IV.** *greedy of money, covetous* :—Gífre bid sé þâm golde onféhd, Gn. Ex. 70. **V.** *in a good sense, eagerly desirous for* (*gen.*) :—Ic wolde ymbe þone læcedóm þára dínra lâra hwéne mâre gehýran . . . Ic heora eom swíþe gífre ægþer ge tó gehérenne ge eác tó gehealdanne *remedia . . . audiendi avidus vehementer efflagito*, Bt. 22, 1 ; F. 76, 20. v. feoh-, heoru-, ofer-, orleg-, wæl-gífre.

**gift.** *Add* : es; *n.* (*m.?* Cf. ærist *for gender*). **I.** *a giving, restoring* :—Hwæþer magon rihtwísra manna sáwla beón onfangene in heofonas ær þære gyfte and geedníwunge þára líchamana on dómes dæge (*ante restitutionem corporum*), Gr. D. 295, 11. v. æ-, ed-, freót, hláford-, ræd-gift. **II.** *a gift* :—Dæt is cyninges andweorc . . . gifta (gifa, *v. l. For the need, in the case of a king, of having gifts to give, see* B. 1719–23) and wæpnu . . . and gehwæt þæs þe þâ þríe geférscipas behófiaþ, Bt. 17 ; F. 60, 4. v. feoh-, hand-gift. **III.** *the giving of a woman in marriage, marriage*. v. gífan ; **V.** [*The word is generally in the plural. Cf.* nuptiae.] (1) *entrance into wedlock, the ceremony* or *procedure by which two persons are made man and wife, nuptials* :—Drihten wolde geswutelian þæt dâ giftu beód herigendlice de for bearnteáme beód gefremode swídor þonne for gálnysse, Hml. Th. ii. 54. 10. Þâ wurdon gearcode þâ gyftu æfter gewunan, and hí cóman on ânum bedde tósomne, Hml. S. 4, 27. Gifta, 7, 312. Æfter gástlicum andgite Drihten cóm tó giftum on dissum middanearde, for dan de hé dâ hâlgan geladunge him tó brýde geceás . . . Críst is se brýdguma, Hml. Th. ii. 54, 11–16. (1 a) *the marriage ceremony with attendant festivities* :—Sum cyning worhte his suna gyfte, Hml. Th. i. 520, 6. Drihten hine sylfne gemedemode þ hé tó woruldlicum giftum geladod cóm, Hml. Th. ii. 54, 8. He sceal foresceáwian þâm mædene gyfta, reáf and hire mægdhádes wurd. Gif hé þâs þreó þing ne déd *providebit puellae nuptias et vestimenta et pretium pudicitiae non negabit. Si tria ista non fecerit*, Ex. 21, 11. Hé dô hiere gyfta, Ll. Th. i. 46, 17. (2) *a particular matrimonial alliance* :—Be don de mon wíf bycgge and donne sió gift tóstande, Ll. Th. i. 122, 4. Þâ þâ heó besleah þâm gesettan gyfte (gyfe, *v. l.*) tó Godes cyrican (*dum constitutis jam nuptiis in ecclesiam fugisset*) . . . gefreodod fram þâm gyftum heó wæs gelæded tó dâm munuchâde, Gr. D. 199, 14–19. (3) *the married state, matrimony, wedlock* :— Gyftu (*this should be gen. sing., but perhaps is pl.; the form in* Hpt. Gl. 520, 57 *is* gifta) bende wære gecnyt *conubii* i. *nuptie nexu nodaretur*, An. Ox. 5003. Gyfte (hæmedscipes, Hpt. Gl. 482, 7) gewrixle *hymenei commercio*, 7, 235. Swá hwylc sé de hafad mannan odde wíf giste (geþeódne ? cf. Wer and wíf on hæmede geþeódde *vir et mulier in matrimonio conjuncti*, 27. Or is giste *pp.* of giftan ?) unâlífedlice swá þeah *quicunque virum aut mulierem habuerit illicite matrimonio conjunctum*, Ll. Th. ii. 150, 24. Hit is scandlic dæt forworode men gifta

wilnian, ðonne gifta ne sind gesette for nānum ðinge būton for bearn-teáme, Hml. Th. ii. 94, 12. Heáp mægdhādes manna on clǽnnysse þurh-wunigende forlǽtenum gistum, i. 546, 23. Tô gyftum *ad* (*thalami*) *tedas*, An. Ox. 2, 199. Gyftu, 3377. Gyfta, hǽmeda *hymeneos*, 1781 : Wrt. Voc. ii. 43, 13. v. brýd-, wíf-gifta.

**giftan** (?) *to marry.* See Ll. Th. ii. 150, 24 *under* gift; III. 3. [*Icel.* giptask *to marry.*]

**gift-búr.** *Add :*—Se quadrans forðstæpð wel orglíce swylce hwylc cyng of his giftbúre stæppe geglenged, Angl. viii. 299, 1. Of gyftbúre ðe *thalamo*, Ps. Rdr. 18, 6.

**gifte-líc.** v. gift-líc.

**gift-feorm,** e; *f. A wedding-feast :*—Be þām þ preóstas ne beón æt giftfeormum, Nap. 33.

**gift-líc.** *Add : .* gifte-líc :—Gyftlicere gegæderunge *nuptialis copule*, An. Ox. 4401. Giftlicum wedde *nuptiali dote*, 11, 158. Giftlican *sponsali* (*peplo*), 5244. Heó bicóm tô giftelicre yldo *she came to mar-riageable age*, Ap. Th. 1, 10. Þá giftelican *nuptiales*, Wrt. Voc. ii. 59, 60. Tô gyftlicum *ad nuptiales* (*copulas*), An. Ox. 3612. Giftlíce rǽdas *sponsalia decreta*, 1122.

**gifu.** *Take here* **geafu** *in Dict., and add : acc.* gife, gifu : gife, an (?); *f. A gift :*—Gifu *donum, datum vel donatum*, Wrt. Voc. i. 28, 57. Twifealdre gife *bino munere*, ii. 126, 26. *Beneficium* freme, i. *donum* gife, 125, 29. **I.** *a giving, bestowal :*—*Datívus* is forgyfendlíc : mid ðǽm casu byð geswutelod ælces ðinges gifu, Ælfc. Gr. Z. 22, 17. Gefe ðoncungo gidóe wē *gratias agimus*, Rtl. 36, 33. **I a.** *a giving by the Deity :*—Hē hié onlýhte mid his þæs Hālgan Gāstes gife, Bl. H. 145, 7. Gefe gefes *donatione gratie*, Rtl. 52, 10. **I b.** *as a legal term, gift, transfer of property :*—Hláfordes gifu þe hē on riht āge tô gifanne, Ll. Th. i. 292, 16. Riht gifu, 422, 1 : ii. 302, 7. **I c.** *a giving in marriage, a wedding.* v. gift ; III. 2. **II.** *habitual giving, munificence, liberality.* Cf. gifan ; III b :—Hwæt wille wē cweþan be þínum twām sunum, þā sint ealdormenn and geþeahteras : on þām is swiotol sió gifu and ealla þā duguða heora fæder and heora eldran fæder, swā swā geonge men magon gelícoste beón ealdum monnum *quid dicam liberos consulares, quorum jam, ut in id aetatis pueris, vel paterni, vel aviti specimen elucet ingenii?*, Bt. 10 ; F. 28, 32. Gyfe *munificentia*, i. *liberalitas*, An. Ox. 2293. Duguþgyfe, gife, cystinysse *munificentiam, liberalitatem*, 1183. **III.** *what is given, a gift.* (1) *the giver a person.* (a) *a present :*—Gifu *zenia*, Wrt. Voc. i. 21, 53. Hig worhton him āne anlícnesse . . . and þāron þus āwriton : ‘Ðás gifu sealde seó ceasterwaru Apollonio,’ Ap. Th. 10, 14. Þ is heora bíwist . . . gifa and wǽpnu and mete . . . , Bt. F. 60, 4. Gyfe, lāc *munuscula* (*fructuum*), An. Ox. 4503. Se pāpa sende him micla gifa, Chr. 885 ; P. 80, 7. Hī geáfon him myccla geofa, 1075 ; P. 209, 30. (b) *a gift to a divinity, an offering, a sacrifice :*—Sē þe áð sellaþ in þǽre geofu (gefo, L., offrunge, W. S., *dono*). . . . Hwæþer māre is geofu (gefe, L.) oþþe wíbed þte hālgaþ ðā geofu (þ gefe, L.) ?, Mt. R. 23, 18, 19. Corban þ is on úre geðeóde gyfu (geafa, L., gefe, R.), Mk. 7, 11. Críste mon bróhte gold tô gefe, Shrn. 48, 19. Mildheortnisse ic willo and nis geafo (*sacrificium*), Mt. L. 9, 13. Þte saldon geafa (offrunge, W. S.) *ut darent hostiam*, Lk. L. 2, 24. Geafa *oblationem*, Rtl. 12, 15. Hālige gife *donaria sancta*, i. *sacrificia*, Wrt. Voc. ii. 141, 79. Þancwurþe gife *grata libamina*, i. *hostia* (*oblaturos*), An. Ox. 367. Gebróhton him geafa (lāc, R., W. S., *munera*), Mt. L. 2, 11. (b b) *a gift to a temple :*—Templ geglenged mid gódum gifum (geafum, L., geofum, R., *donis*), Lk. 21, 5. (c) *a gift to a woman at marriage, a dowry* (For an instance of such a gift see Cht. Th. 312) :—*Dos, dotalis*, i. wed, gifu *vel fædrenfeoh*, Wrt. Voc. ii. 141, 80. Gife *dote*, 71. Brýdlicere gyfe *nuptiali dote*, An. Ox. 4552. (d) *what is given to obtain favour or to avoid injury, in a bad sense, a bribe :*—Gefe tóbrēt *donum* (*hominis*) *dilatat* (*viam regis*), Kent. Gl. 647. Manega giofa (*zelus viri non suscipiet pro redemptione*) *dona plurima*, 175. (2) *the giver a superhuman power.* (a) *a material or non-material good regarded as granted by a higher power :*—Wē wæron ætende grimlíce ǽr wē mihton þās gerína áspyrian, ac ús cóm hræðlíce fultum, wē gelýfað of heofenum, swā hit ræd ys, þ ælc æðele gife nyðer āstíhð fram þām fæder ealra leóhta, Angl. viii. 313, 2. Ðá mettas ðe God gesceóp tô etanne monnum ðǽm ðe Gode ðonciað mid goodum weorcum his giefa (gifa, *v. l.*), Past. 319, 3 : 331, 8. Úre Drihten is gemyndig ealra þāra gifena þe hē ús tô lǽteþ, Bl. H. 51, 24. Geofena, 103, 26. Hwæt hæfst ðū æt þām gifum þe ðū cwist þ seó wyrd eów gife, Bt. 13 ; F. 38, 4. ¶ *the giver a personification :*—Þu miht þæs habban þanc þ þū mínra (*Wisdom's*) gifa wel brúce . . . Hæbbe ic þē benumen þínra gifena þāra þe þē from mē cómon ?, Bt. 7, 3 ; F. 20, 12-15. (b) *a spiritual benefit :*—Þes dæg is geweorþod mid manegum godcundum geofum, næs þǽra gifena lǽs þonne Drihtnes ǽrist, and eác þonne seó gifu þæs Hālgan Gāstes, Bl. H. 133, 2-4. Deós geofu þurh Drihtnes miht on heora heortan álegd wes, 137, 3. Þ is micel gifo þ hē gebít oð ðæt ðā yfelan ongitaþ hyra yfel, Bt. 38, 3 ; F. 202, 14. Gif þū wistest Godes gyfe (geafa, L., *donum*) . . . þū bæde hine þ hē sealde þe lífes wæter, Jn. 4, 10. Ealra þāra gifa þe hē middangearde

forgeaf þurh his tôcyme, Bl. H. 31, 29. (c) *a power or quality miracu-lously bestowed, a Christian virtue emanating from the Holy Ghost :*—Wæs sum bróðor þām godcundlíce forgifen wæs seó gyfu tô singanne, Bd. 4, 24 ; Sch. 480, 19. Gyfe *munus* (*virginale*), An. Ox. 4210. On béc gāstlicra sylena ł gyfa *in catalogo charismatum*, 342. Gifena, Wrt. Voc. ii. 80, 67. Witgan . . . mid Hāliges Gāstes geofum gehālgode, Bl. H. 161, 14. . . . Gifum, 165, 21. (d) *a natural ability or faculty :*—Ælc cræft hæfþ his sundorgife, and þá gife hē forgifþ ælcum ðāra ðe hine lufað, Bt. 27, 2 ; F. 96, 31. Ðá men habbaþ eall þ wē ǽr ymbe sprǽc-on, and eác tô eácan ðǽm micle gife gesceádwísnesse, 41, 5 ; F. 252, 29. **IV.** *grace, favour :*—Oest, gifu *gratia*, Wrt. Voc. ii. 40, 5. Gefo *carissi*, 70, 37. (1) *grace, benevolent regard of the Deity :*—Hú mihte ǽfre englum māra gefeá and geofu and blis geweorþan ?, Bl. H. 123, 14. Mid Godes geafa *Deo donante*, Jn. p. 187, 13. Þú gemétst gife (gyfe, *v. l.* gratiam) myd Gode, Lk. 1, 30 : Bl. H. 7, 18. Þurh Godes gife, 121, 10. Him ealle þá tôweardan þing þurh Godes gife wǽron gecýdde, Guth. 44, 25. (2) *an exceptional favour, privilege, pre-rogative :*—Synderlic gifa *prerogatiua*, An. Ox. 2572. (3) *in a theo-logical sense.* (a) *grace in contrast with law :*—Ǽ wæs geseald þurh Móysen, and gyfu (gefo, L., geofo, R., *gratia*) is geworden þurh Hǽlend Críst, Jn. 1, 17. Wē under gyfe gesette *nos sub gratia positi*, An. Ox. 40, 9. On níwre geleáfan gyfe wē gangaþ *in noua fidei gratia ambu-lamus*, 25. (b) *grace, the divine influence which operates in men to sanctify and to inspire with virtuous impulses :*—Þ him wǽre from Dryhtne sylfum heofonlíc gyfo (gifu, geofu, gyfu, *v. ll.*) forgyfen *caelestem ei a Domino concessam esse gratiam*, Bd. 4, 24 ; Sch. 485, 12. Seó geofu wæs bróht for þǽre synne þæs ǽrestan wífes. . . . Heó wæs mid gife ge-fylled, and seó synn wæs áðílegod, Bl. H. 5, 4. Wæs his heorte innan þurh Godes gifu onbryrdod, þæt hē wǽstenes gewilnode, Guth. 18, 24. (b b) *the divine grace considered as a permanent force :*—Þ cild weóx and Godes gyfu (geafa, L., gefe, R.) wæs on him *puer crescebat et gratia Dei erat in eo*, Lk. 2, 40. Ðū eart Drihtnes gife full, Bl. H. 141, 3. Hál wes ðū mid gyfe gefylled, Lk. 1, 28. Mid godcundre gyfe gemǽred, Bd. 4, 24 ; Sch. 481, 1. (4) *favour, clemency, remission of a penalty :*—Beó hē his inganges scyldig, and þǽr ne beó nán gyfu, Cht. Th. 606, 22. ¶ gifum, tô gifes *gratis :*—Gifum *gratis*, Ps. Rdr. 34, 8. Tô gifes *gratis*, An. Ox. 3069. v. ælmes-, duguþ-, eard- (?), gāst-, un-, weorold-gifu.

**gifung.** *Add :* v. for-gifung : **gíg.** v. gíw.

**gigant.** *l.* gígant, *and add :*—Swā se hyhtenda gígant (Is. 18, 6), Bl. H. 9, 34. Gígent, Ps. Srt. 18, 6 : 32, 16. Scoldon gígantas bión eorþan suna. . . . Ðá sceolde ðām gígantum oþfincan þ . . . hwylc dysig Nefrod se gígant worhte, Bt. 35, 4 ; F. 162, 8-17. Gód and geafolic gíganta geweorc, B. 1562 : 1690.

**gígant-mæcg.** *Substitute : One of the race of the giants, a giant :*—Gígantmæcgas Gode unleófe, micle mánsceaðan Metode lāðe (cf. *Gigantes erant super terram*, Gen. 6, 4), Gen. 1268.

**gígoþ.** v. geoguþ : **gi-hríno.** v. ge-rēne : **gíhsa.** v. gesca : **gíhsinga,** Wrt. Voc. ii. 30, 13. v. ge-scinco : **gíht, gíhte.** v. gebed-gíht, sunn-gíhte : **gíhþig.** *Dele, and see* gydig.

**gild.** *Add :* **I.** *payment.* (1) *of purchase or barter :*—Hwælc seleþ monn geld for ferh his *quam dabit homo commutationem pro anima sua?*, Mt. R. 16, 26. (2) *pay of troops :*—Eádwerd cing scylode .ix. scypa of māle . . . and belifon .v. scypa bæftan ; and se cing heom behét .xii. mónað gyld, Chr. 1049 ; P. 171, 29. (3) *with idea of compul-sion, payment exacted* (a) *by the State, a tax :*—Álede Eádweard cyng þ heregyld . . . þ gyld gedrehte ealle Engla þeóde . . . þ wæs ǽfre ætforan ðātum gyldum þe man geald, Chr. 1052 ; P. 173, 18-22. Þe cyng behét heom þā betsta laga . . . and ælc unriht geold hē forbeád, 1087 ; P. 223, 32. (b) *by the law as compensation or indemnity for loss :*—Nordleóda cynges gild is .xxx. þúsend þrymsa, fiftene þúsend þrymsa bið þæs wergildes, .xv. þúsend þæs cynedómes, Ll. Th. i. 186, 2. Deáh æt stæltyhtlan lād teorie . . . gylde ángyldes þ hē mid beléd wæs. Ðæs óðres gyldes nán þing, ne þæs wítes þe mā, 354, 16. Gif mon wíf mid bearne ofsleá . . . forgielde þone wífman fullan gielde, and þ bearn healfan gelde, 66, 24-68, 2. Ne forlǽte hē þá æscan . . . oþ þæt wē tô þām gilde cuman, 234, 27. Gylde hē þ yrfe, oþþe . . . underwed lecge . . . and þæs on .ix. nihton þ wed undó mid rihtan gylde, 352, 10. Þ man gulde þ ceápgild, and swinge hine man þriwa, oþþe þ óðer gild (gylde, *v. l.*) sealde, 208, 23. Gif wē þonne gyld árǽrdon, 234, 5. (c) *by a superior foreign power, tribute :*—Cunnende of gyld (cf. gild-selen) [ð]æs cæseres geselenne *temtantes de reddendo caesari tributo*, Mk. p. 4, 20. **II.** *that which takes the place of something lost :*—Seth wæs Abeles gield on woruldríce, Gen. 1109. On wráðra gield, 101. **III.** *in a religious sense.* (1) *what is offered.* (a) *concrete, an offering, a sacri-fice :*—Hié Drihtne lāc bróhton ; brego engla beseah on Abeles gield eágum sínum, Gen. 977. Hē þæt gyld (cf. lāc, 1497) on þanc ágífen hæfde, 1506. Gód *hostiae, sacrificia*, Wülck. Gl. 202, 27. (b) *abstract, worship, rite, service, sacrifice :*—Æt ðām gilde *Lupere*[*a*]*lia*, Wrt. Voc. ii. 86, 27. Gield *cultum*, 90, 27. Gild, 19, 24. Geld *ceremoniae*, i. 28, 54 : *ceremoniae*, i. *ritus sacrificandi, religiones, sacrificia*, Wülck. Gl. 202, 27. Þá þe æt þǽm geldum þǽr wæs swín and sceáp and fear

suovetaurili(a), Wrt. Voc. ii. 31, 33 : 86, 33. Hwæðer þā landleóde crīstene wǣron ðe hí on hǣðenra gildum (in hǣðennesse gedwolum, v. l.) lifdon (paganis erroribus essent inplicati), Bd. 2, 1 ; Sch. 109, 22. Gield sacra (Deorum destruxit), Wrt. Voc. ii. 90, 7. (2) a divinity, heathen deity :—Behātað þæt gē wyllað þām deófolgyldum wiðsacan, and þone sóðan God wurðian. . . . 'Beó Godes grama ofer ūs, gif wē ǣfre tō hǣðenum gylde būgað,' Hml. Th. ii. 488, 7. Gield numina, Wrt. Voc. ii. 86, 34 : 92, 80. Gild, 60, 70. (2 a) an idol :—Gield dilubra, Wrt. Voc. ii. 94, 34 : 27, 23. Hē þā īdlan gild bræc, Bl. H. 223, 18, 1. IV. a guild. v. ge-gild:—Hēr is on þis gewrite siú geswitelung þǣre gerǣdnisse þe þiús gefērrǣden gerǣd hæfþ on þegna gilde on Grantebrycge, Cht. Th. 610, 29. Se gylda þe óðerne misgrēt innan gylde, 606, 23. v. blóstm-, bróþor-, ceáp-, cyne-, ge-, geleger-, here-, hýd-, hýþ-, īdel-, nīd-, niht-, scip-gild.

gilda. Add : I. one who pays. Cf. gildan ; I. v. gafol-, nīd-gilda. I a. one who receives pay. v. hȳre-, mēd-gilda. II. one who does worship, sacrifice, &c. Cf. gildan ; IV. v. deófol-, hǣþen-gilda. III. a member of a guild:—Gif hwylcum gildan þearf sí his geférena fultumes, and hit gecȳd wyrþe þæs gildan nīhtstan geféran, būtun se gilda sylf neáh sí. . . . Gif hwā gyldan ofstleá . . . wrece eal gildscipe þone gildan. . . . Gif ǣnig gilda hwilcne man ofstleá, Cht. Th. 611, 11–28. þæs ofslegenan gegildan (gyldan, v. l.) the slain man's guild-brothers, Ll. Th. i. 116, 6 : 112, 8. v. un-gilda.

gildan. Add : I. to pay. (1) to discharge an obligation, debt, &c.:—Wið hē gulde þ scyld donec redderet debitum, Mt. L. 18, 30 : 34. (1 a) with dat. of person paid :—Ryhtlícor wē magon cweðan ðæt wē him gielden scylde ðonne wē him mildheortnesse dón, Past. 335, 19. (1 b) used absolutely :—Ne hæfde hona gulde, Mt. L. 18, 25. Huona guldon, Lk. L. 7, 42. (2) to pay an impost (tax, tribute, &c.) :—þ him leófre wǣre tō feohtanne þonne gafol tō gieldanne, Ors. 1, 10 ; S. 44, 14. (2 a) with dat. of person paid :—Sió wiht (a ship) werum gielded gaful geára gehwām, Rä. 33, 11. Ús deáþ mycel gafol geald, Bl. H. 85, 12. Man geald ǣrest gafol Deniscan mannum, Chr. 991 ; P. 127, 3. Geldas ðā ðe sint cæseres ðǣm cāsere, Mk. L. R. 12, 17. Hié genieddon þ hié him gafol guldon, Ors. 1, 10 ; S. 14, 19. Man sceolde gafol gyldon þām flotan, Chr. 1002 ; P. 133, 32. þā norðmonnum niéde sceoldon gombon gieldan and gafol sellan, Gen. 1978. Gyldan, B. 11. (3) to pay a legal exaction (wergild, wíte, &c.) :—Mana þone þæs ángyldes ; gif hē nǣbbe, gyld (gild, v. l.) þū þ ángylde, Ll. Th. i. 116, 11. Gielde hē ful wíte, 128, 18. Gylde hē lahslit mid Deniscum, wíte mid Englum, 170, 1 : 172, 1 : 384, 20. Gilde hē þæs cynges oferhýrnesse . . . Gif hē ryht wyrcan nylle, ne þā oferhýrnesse syllan . . . , 208, 26. Gielden his mǣgas þone wer, 148, 18. þ man gulde þ ceápgild, 208, 22. þ hē þeófgyld ne gulde, 280, 13 : 294, 23. (3 a) with dat. of person paid :—Gilde se borh þām teónde his ceápgyld, Ll. Th. i. 282, 3 : 390, 23 : 354, 31 : 396, 2. (3 b) used absolutely :—Sí þreóra ān . . . wergild . . . And beó þǣra þreóra swylc hit beó, gilde hē . . . , Ll. Th. i. 332, 19. Swā forð þ ful golden sý, 174, 29. (4) where the object of the verb is (a) that which is used to pay with, to pay cash, &c. :—Ðæt hē him gielde gód weorc for ðǣre giefe ðe hē him ǣr sealde, Past. 339, 11. (b) the amount paid :—Hē ǣlce geáre gyld .i. pund tō geswutelunga, C. D. ii. 300, 8. Seó burhwaru on Lundene guldon .xi. þúsend punda, Chr. 1018 ; P. 155, 12. Gesylle (v. l. gylde) hē .xxx. sciłł., Ll. Th. i. 204, 20 : 208, 11. Gilde hē landrícan .xx. ðran, 294, 17 : 296, 2. Æt þām óðrum tāum healf gelde, 20, 3. Se cyning hēt gyldan þām here .xxi. þúsend punda, Chr. 1014 ; P. 145, 25. 'Huu micel āht ðū tō geldanne hláferde mínum ?' Hē cuoeð : 'Hundteántih ombras oeles,' Lk. L. 16, 5. (bb) to repay an amount taken or borrowed :—Wēnstú gif hwā ðrum hwæt gieldan sceal, hwæðer hē hine mid ðý gehealdan mǣge ðæt hē him nāuht māre on ne nime, ne ðæt ne gielde ðæt hē ǣr nam ?, Past. 425, 1–3. Tuoege scyldgo (debitores) woeron sume ríce menn (feneratori), ān āhte tō geldanne penningas fíf hund, óðer fífteih, Lk. L. 7, 41. (5) the manner or extent of payment given by an adverb (word, phrase, or clause) :—Gif man mannan ofsleá, āgene scætte and unfācne feó gelde, Ll. Th. i. 10, 5. Ǣlc tihtbysig man gange tō þryfealdan ordāle, oþþe gilde feówergilde, 294, 10. Gilde hē .iii. gylde, 15. Ðā hwíle ðe hié peningas hæbben mid tō gieldanne, Past. 327, 18. II. with the idea of recompense, retribution. (a) to give reward, give as retribution :—Sē þe eft gyldeð þā þū him ǣr forgeáfe, and ús eallum gesealdest qui retribuet tibi retributionem tuam quam tu retribuisti nobis, Ps. Th. 136, 8. Hē him dǣda leán gieldeð, Gú. 95. Ceig ðā wercmenn, and geld him meard, Mt. L. 20, 8. Bið golden retribuetur (ei juxta opera manunm suarum), Kent. Gl. 410 : retribuentur (justis bona), 463. (b) used absolutely, to reward, requite, give reward to (dat.) :—þū mínre sāwle gyldest retribues in anima mea, Ps. Th. 130, 4. Gyld oferhýdigum, swā hí ǣr grame worhton, 93, 2. Drihten wile ǣghwylcum ānum men gyldan and leánigean æfter his sylfes weorcum and dǣdum, Bl. H. 123, 34 : Ps. Th. 102, 10. (bb) where the means of reward are given, to reward with (mid) :—Hē þē mid wíte gieldeð, swilce þām óðrum mid eádwelan, Fä. 19. Hē mid góde gyldan wille uncran eaferan, B. 1184. III. to pay for. (1) with idea of gratitude, to repay,

make grateful return for a benefit to a person (dat.) :—Swā gē weorðmyndu Dryhtne gieldað, Gú. 435. Geald þone gūðræs Geáta dryhten Iofore and Wulfe mid ofermāðmum, B. 2991. Swētne medo Hnæfe guldon his hægstealdas, Fin. 40. Mē leánum míne gife gyldan, Gen. 413 : B. 2636. (1 a) with clause :—Gyld mē mid hyldo, þæt ic þe hneáw ne wæs, Gen. 2823. þē wile gāsta weard lissum gyldan, þæt þē wæs leófra his sibb . . . , 2920. (1 b) of ungrateful return for a benefit :—Woldon hié þæt feorhleán fācne gyldan, Exod. 150. (2) with idea of reprisal, to repay an injury, take vengeance for :—Hē nǣnigum yfel wiþ yfele geald, Bl. H. 223, 33. Ne geald hē yfel yfele, El. 493. Him þæt swíðe geald fædera Lothes, Gen. 2079. Folc Ebrēa guldon hyra fyrngeflitu fāgum swyrdum, Jud. 263. Gif hý him ne meahte māran sārum gyldan gyrnwrǣce, Gú. 405. (2 a) with clause :—Gyldað mid gyrne, þæt heó ūssa goda meaht forhogde, Jul. 619. (3) with idea of compensation, reparation, &c. (a) to pay for property lost or wrongly held, an object improperly treated, a person improperly entertained :—Ǣghwilcre sprǣce þe māre sý þonne .iiii. mancussas . . . gif hē ne dyrre (hine lādian), gylde, Bl. H. 223, 33. hé (the subject of the suit) þrygilde, Ll. Th. i. 154, 11. Gylde þ hē mid beléd wæs (what he was charged with stealing), 354, 15. Sceáp sceal gongan mid his fliése oð midne sumor, oþþe gilde þ fliése mid twām pænirgum, 146, 11. Gylde þ yrfe (stolen cattle), 352, 7. Sē þe óðres mannes man underfó . . . gylde hine þǣm þe hē ǣr folgode, and gesylle þām cynge .cxx. scił., 220, 21 : 122, 1. Gif ic gesealde land (land which ought to have gone in the male line) ǣnigre wíðhanda, þonne forgyldan míne mǣgas . . . For ðon ic cweþe þ hí hit gyldan . . . , Cht. Th. 491, 21–29. Gif mon ǣfelle on wuda wel monega treówu . . . forgielde .iii. treówu ǣlc mid .xxx. scił. . . . Ne þearf hē hiora mā geldan, Ll. Th. i. 128, 22. Be ǣlces nýtenes weorðe gif hí losiað. Hors mon sceal gyldan mid .xxx. scił. . . . Ungesawene þing mon mót mid gelde gewyrdan, and syþþan be þām gyldan, 356, 1–7. (b) to pay for a criminal :—Gif hē (an accused person) þ ordāl forfieó, gilde se borh hine be his were, Ll. Th. i. 296, 5. (c) to pay wergild for a slain person :—Gif wíteþeów hine forstalie, hō hine mon and ne gylde his hlāforde. Gif hine mon ofsleá, ne gylde hine mon his mǣgum, Ll. Th. i. 118, 6–8. Gielde hē hine þriddan dǣle . . . healfne dǣl hine gilde . . . ealne hē hine gylde, 120, 12–15. Gif Ænglisc man Deniscne ofsleá, gylde hine mid .xxx. pundum, 286, 21 : 24. Gif man ofslægen weorðe, gylde hine man swā hē geboren sý, 174, 15. Ne þearf hē hine būton be healfan were gyldan . . . healf wer ætfeald, 354, 19. (cc) where the object is omitted :—Gif mannes esne eorlcundne mannan ofslæhð, þane þe sió (v. se ; I. 1 g), þreóm hundum scił. gylde (he shall be paid for with three hundred shillings) ; se āgend þone banan āgefe and dó þǣr þrió manwyrð tó. Gif se bana oðbyrste, feorðe manwyrð hē tó gedó . . . Gif mannes esne frígne mannan ofslæhð, þane þe sié, hund scillinga gelde ; se āgend þone banan āgefe and óðer manwyrð þǣr tó. Gif bana oðbyrste, twām manwyrðum hine man forgelde, Ll. Th. i. 26, 8–28, 8. [From these passages the manwyrð seems to have been 100s., as the payment for any eorlcund man is spoken of both as 300s. and as þrió manwyrþ, that for any free man as 100s. or as a manwyrð ; in either case if the slayer could not be given up an additional manwyrþ had to be paid, making in the one case four, in the other two manwyrþ.] IV. of religious practice. v. gild ; III. (1) with object, to pay a vow, pay homage to a divinity :—On mē synd, God, þæt ic þē min gehāt on herenesse, hyldo gilde in me sunt, Deus, vota tua, quae reddam, laudationes tibi, Ps. Th. 55, 10. þte ic gelde oest níin, Rtl. 169, 7. (1 a) absolute :—Gehātað Drihtne, and him hraðe gyldað, Ps. Th. 75, 8. þē gedafenað, Drihten, þæt þē man on Sion herige and on Hierusalem gylde and gehāte (tibi reddetur votum in Hierusalem), 64, 1. (2) without object, to worship, sacrifice to :—Gif ceorl būton wífes wísdóme deófium gelde . . . Gif būtwū deófium geldað . . . Gif þeúw deófium geldaþ (-eþ ?), Ll. Th. i. 40, 4–7. Hit āwriten is be Salamone, hū hē . . . āfióll, emne oð þæt hē dióðium ongan gieldan Salamon usque ad idolatriam cecidisse describitur, Past. 393, 15. Hē eorlum onmǣdle . . . þæt hié gegnunga gyldan sceolde, Dan. 212. Lupercalibus þǣm gildendum. Luperci vocantur illi sacerdotes qui ministrant deo qui vocatur Pan, Wrt. Voc. ii. 86, 54 : 52, 40. v. ed-gildan.

gild-dæg, es ; m. A day for a religious ceremony. v. gildan ; IV, gild ; III :—Gelddagas (geldagas, Wrt. Voc. i. 16, 54), þæt sind hālige cerimonia vel orgia, Wülck. Gl. 107, 22. Cf. freóls-dæg.

-gilde, es ; n. v. ge-, þegen-gilde : -gilde ; adj. v. ǣ-, ander-, or-, un-, unander-gilde.

-gilde in composition with numerals, forming noun, adj., or adv. v. ān-, endleofan-, feówer-, nigon-, six-, twelf-, twi-, þri-gilde [Icel. -gildr.]

gildend. v. ed-gildend : gildere. [O. H. Ger. ant-geltāri restitutor.] v. gafol-gildere.

gild-scipe. Add :—On Wudeburge lande is eác ān óðer gildscipe gegaderod Críste and Sēe Petre . . . And þis sind þára manna nama[n], Cht. Th. 609, 24. Gif hwilc gilda forþfære, gebrynge hine eal se gildscipe þǣr hē tō wilnie . . . Wrece eal gildscipe þone gildan, 611, 2, 25. Of Alwines gildscipe . . . Of þām gildscipe on Lēge, 610, 1, 9. v. ge-gildscipe.

gild-selenn, e ; f. Tribute :—Gecunnedon of ðǣm gaefel i gyldselenna

cǽseres tō seallanne *temtantes de tributo Caesaris dando*, Mt. p. 19, 5. v. gild ; I. 3 a.

**-gill(e).** v. wid-gil(l), -gille : **gillister, gillistre.** v. geolstor.

**gilm.** *Take here* gelm *in Dict., and add : a wk. pl. occurs :*—Genim þǽre ilcan wyrte gōdne gelm, Lch. ii. 30, 23 : 60, 5. Gylma *manipulorum*, An. Ox. 5252. Gilmum *fasciculis*, 7, 270. Gylmas *manipulos*, i. *fasces*, 3431. Gilman, 2366.

**gilp** *powder*. *For* Cot. 181 *substitute :*—Gilp *scobem* (the passage is : Cuspide vexilli *scrobem* sulcare, Ald. 153, 31), Wrt. Voc. ii. 91, 23.

**gilp.** *Add : n.* (1) *pride, arrogance, vainglory :*—Fastus, elatio vel gebungennes *vel* gelp *vel* arrogantia, Wrt. Voc. ii. 146, 41. þ mycele gylp and seó unrihtgitsung . . . þ is eal mycel synn beforan Gode, Bl. H. 53, 21. Hī flugon forhtigende . . . gylp weard gnornra, Exod. 454. Hié gylp beswāc, wīndruncen gewit, Dan. 752. Þý lǽs him gilp scedde, odde fore þǽre mǽrde mōd āstīge, Crä. 100 : Cri. 684. Gylpes *ostentationis* (*indicium*), Wrt. Voc. ii. 87, 22 : 64, 38. Gilpes *arrogantiae*. 2, 9. Tōþundenes gylpes *tumentis iactantie*, An. Ox. 5374. Gesticced mid dǽre scylde gielpes (gilpes, *v. l.*) *arrogantiae culpa transfixus*, Past. 217, 6. Hē monna cynne gielpes stýred, Crä. 105. Hē in gylpe wæs, Dan. 636. Se āwiergda gǽst hit lǽrd done gielp, Past. 463, 30. Hē āgeát gylp wera, Exod. 514. Gylp forbēgan, An. 1335. Hæfdon hié gielp micel, Gen. 25. Hē on gylp āstāg *he became proud*, Met. 9, 46. Gyddigan þurh gylp micel, Dan. 599 : 695. (v. īdel ; III.) (2) *action that shows pride, ostentation :*—Ne sylþ hē hit ūs tō þon þ wē hit hýdon oþþe tō gylpe syllan, Bl. H. 53, 17. Nō þæt þīn aldor ǽfre wolde Godes goldfatu in gylp beran, ne þý hrador hrēmde, Dan. 755. Þæt hē ne āgǽle gǽstes þearfe ne on gylp geóte, Cri. 818. (3) *where pride finds expression in words, boasting :*—Hwǽr beóþ þā ungemetlican hleahtras and se leása gylp and ealle þā īdlan word, Bl. H. 53, 18. Ic gehýre enlogālra gylp, yfele sprǽce werod habban, Gen. 2408. Ic eom on mōde from, þæt ic wid þone gūdflogan gylp ofersitte, B. 2528. (3 a) *a particular instance of boasting, a boast, vaunt, promise to do great things :*—Ic wāt hwæt se Rōmāna gelp swíþost is, for þon þe hié monega folc oferwunnan, and monege cyningas beforan hiera triumphan drīfon, Ors. 5, 1 ; S. 214, 1. 'Þū (*Babylon*) eart mīn seó mǽre burh þe ic geworhte . . .' For þǽm gylpe hé forfangen weard, Dan. 613. Hǽfde hē Eástdenum gilp gelǽsted, B. 829. Þā hleahtras and þā ārleásan gylpas, Bl. H. 195, 16. (4) *glory, applause, fame, name, renown :*—Hwæt rūmedlīces odde micellices hæfþ se eówer gilp *quid habet amplum magnificumque gloria ?*, Bt. 18, 1 ; F. 62, 22 : 19 ; F. 70, 17. Is þé geeówad þāra eásena gesælþa anlīcnes, þ is ǽhta and weordscipe and anweald and gelp (gielp, *v. l.* Cf. þæt mon seó foremǽre and hæbbe gōdne hlīsan, 24, 1 ; F. 82, 10) *habes ante oculos propositam formam felicitatis humanae, opes, honores, potentiam, gloriam*, 24, 3 ; F. 84, 20. Bid wēn lǽdlicre scome . . . geótende gielp *there will be chance of foul shame, good fame will be failing*, Fä. 41. Gītsung gilpes, Met. 7, 15. Gelpes, 10, 13. Gif c wiste hū wid þām āglǽcan elles meahte gylpe (*with glory*) widgrīpan, B. 2521. Sē de bid ūpāhafen mid dý gefeán and nid dý gielpe (gilpe, *v. l.*) disse worulde *quos consolatio gloriae temporalis extollit*, Past. 183, 4. Đonne se mon nō his āgenne gielp (*gloriam*) mid ne sécd, ac dæs ūplican Fæder . . . hē hæfd gewitnesse . . . dæt hē hit for Gode dyde, næs for gielpe, 451, 15–18. Mā manna hæfþ mīcelne gilp (gielp, *v. l.*) . . . for dysiges folces wēnan, þonne hē hæbbe for his gewyrhtum *plures magnum nomen falsis vulgi opinionibus abstulerunt*, Bt. 30, 1 ; F. 108, 3. Þū goda ūssa gilp gehnǽgdest, An. 1321. Hē nallas on gylp seled beágas *he gives not rings to gain glory*, B. 1749. v. dol-, īdel-, leás-, unriht-, weorold-gilp.

**gilpan.** *Add :* I. *to boast.* (1) *absolute :*—Gelpd *jactat*, Kent. Gl. 1051. Gylpad gramhýdige, þā þīn ǽhtan *gloriati sunt qui oderunt te*, Ps. Th. 73, 4. Ne mōt nān preóst beón tō mōdig ne tō gilpende, Ll. Th. i. 386, 10. (2) *to boast of* (*gen.*) :—Gif þū þæs gilpst, hū ne gilpst þū þeora gōdes, næs þīnes ?, Bt. 14, 1 ; F. 42, 26. Geþenc be dǽm gebyrdum, gif hwā þæs gilpþ (gelpd, *v. l.*), 30, 1 ; F. 108, 19. Hē mordres gylped, B. 2055. Þā gealp hē æt fægnode Godes fultumes, Ps. Th. 4, irg. Đā hē ongeat dæt hié gulpun hiera fæstenes *dum de abstinentiae virtute gloriantium praecepta perstringeret*, Past. 313, 1. (3) *to glory in* (*inst.*) :—Lífe ne gielped, hláfordes gifum, Rä. 59, 12. Þā hine wīg pegeat, nealles folccyning fyrdgestealum gylpan þorfte, B. 2874. Hē :wǽd þ hý gilpan ne þorftan dǽdum wid Dryhtnes meahtum, Gū. 210. (4) *with prep. :*—Đonne dæt mōd for his cræfta geearnunga gilpd and orsorglíce fægnad on him selfum *cum animus de virtutum meritis laeta apud se securitate gloriatur*, Past. 463, 27. Tō þǽm tīdun þe ūs Rōmāne oþwītad and tō dǽre genihtsumnisse þe hié ūs ealneg fore gielpad, þ ūre ne sién dǽm gelīcan, Ors. 4, 7 ; S. 182, 16. Þæt sindon þā gōdan tīda þe hié ealneg fore gielpad, 5, 1 ; S. 214, 4. Tō dǽm gōdan tīdan þe Rōmāne fore gulpon, S. 4, 18. Odde hie for his gōda mierringe gielpe (*glorietur*), Past. 149, 20. (5) *with clause giving the boast :*—Þā vēnde hē þæt hit Godes āgen wǽre ; and se deófles man gealp þæt hē eác wā wǽre, Wlfst. 99, 18. Hwæþer đū durre gilpan þ heora fægernes ǽn sié ? *num audes alicujus talium splendore gloriari ?*, Bt. 14, 1 ; F. :0, 22. Gylpan þ þū mǽge Crīstes þegnas oferswíþan, Bl. H. 175, 32.

(6) *uncertain construction :*—Ne gilp đū *ne innitaris* (v. ? Prov. 3, 5), Wrt. Voc. ii. 62, 2. (7) *with acc. ? :*—Swā [ne] gylpan þearf Grendles māga [ǽnig] ūhthlem þone [*the MS. is defective, but as Thorkelin's transcript gives* b *after* swā *perhaps* begylpan *may have been the original form :* it is not found elsewhere however], B. 2006. **II.** *to speak highly of* (*gen.*), *praise, applaud :*—Ic gilpe *subplaudo*, Wrt. Voc. i. 22, 29. Þā gylpaþ *applaudunt*, An. Ox. 4196. Gulpan, Wrt. Voc. ii. 85, 5 (this and the preceding are glosses to Ald. 59, 5) : 3 ; 38 : 5, 33. Đā welwillendan sint tō manianne dæt hié suā gielpan (gilpan, *v. l.*) hiera niéhstena dǽda sic *proximorum facta diligendo laudent*, Past. 229, 14. Gelpende *subplaudans*, Wrt. Voc. ii. 121, 46. v. for-gilpan.

**gilpen.** *Take here* gilpna *in Dict., and add :*—Odde se gielpna (gilpna, *v. l.*) and se āgīta for his gōda mierringe gielpe, and wēne dæt hē sié kystig and mildheort *aut cum effuse quid perditur, largum se quasi miserando glorietur*, Past. 149, 19. Đǽm gielpnan (gilpnan, *v. l.*) bid leófre dæt hē secge on hine selfne gif hē hwæt gōdes wāt *eligit arrogans bona de se jactari*, 217, 14. [The Latin original of Past. 216, 9 is : Bona, si qua sibi occulta sunt, ostentare conatur, atque sic per impatientiam usque ad arrogantiam ducitur.]

**gilp-georn.** *Add :* (1) *in a favourable sense.* v. Dict. (2) *in an unfavourable sense, vainglorious, arrogant, proud, boastful.* Cf. lof-georn :—Men beód ofergrǽdige woruldgestreóna and tō manege weordaþ tō wlance and ealles tō rance and tō gylpgeorne *erunt homines cupidi, elati, superbi ;* men sholl be covetous, boasters, proud (2 Tim. 3, 2), Wlfst. 81, 15. Ne beón gē tō rance ne tō gylpgeorne, 40, 19. *See next word.*

**gilpgeorn-ness,** e ; *f. Vainglory, arrogance, pride, boastfulness ;* jactantia, superbia :—Þā deófllican eahta leahtras . . . dæt is . . . gylpgeornys (cf. se seofoda leahter is *jactantia* gecweden, Hml. S. 16, 300), Wlfst. 68, 16. Hohfulnes and gylpgeornes (cf. se eahteoda leahter is *superbia* gehāten, Hml. S. 16, 306), 188, 37.

**gilping,** e ; *f. Boasting, arrogance, vainglory :*—For īdelre gylpincge *pro vana gloria*, Scint. 144, 11.

**gilp-lic.** *Add : arrogant :*—Pharao him filigde æt đām hōn mid his gilplicum riddum, Hml. Th. ii. 194, 23.

**gilp-líce.** *Add : arrogantly :*—Gilplíce *arroganter*, Wrt. Voc. ii. 1, 21. Gylplíce *jactanter*, Scint. 35, 4, 5 : An. Ox. 954.

**gilpna.** v. gilpen.

**gilp-ness,** e ; *f. Boastfulness, pride :*—Þurh gelpnesse heortan *per jactantiam cordis*, Ps. L. fol. 182 b.

**gilp-plega.** *Add : play that is glorious with pomp, pride and circumstance :* gilp-sceaþa. *After* Gen. 96 *add :* cf. Hæfdon gielp micel, Gen. 25 : gilp-sprǽc. *l.* -sprǽc.

**gilte.** *Add :*—Swínes blǽdran untýdrendes, þ is gylte, Lch. ii. 88, 24.

**gim.** *Add :* I. *a precious stone :*—Gim þe bid on coches micga *flestria*, Wrt. Voc. i. 38, 32. Gim *gemma*, Kent. Gl. 597. Se giem (gim, *v. l.*) *jacintus*, Past. 85, 5. Ne mǽg hit steorra ne stān ne se steápa gim beswīcan, Sal. 284. Is seó eággebyrd hīwe gelícast gladum gimme, þonne in goldfate smida orþoncum biseted weorded, Ph. 303. Đā giemmas, Past. 135, 3, 4, 16. Gimmas, 7. Gimmas hæfdon bewrigene weordlíce wealdes treúw, Kr. 16. Sum bid searocræftig goldes and gimma, þonne him gumena weard hāted tō mǽrdum māddum rēnian, Crä. 59. Hē hit gihrínade mid golde and mid gimmum, Jn. p. 188, 5. Wīntreówa blōstman beód gimman gelíce, Ælfc. Gr. Z. 295, 12. Is glisnad glæslūttur gimmum gelícast, Rūn. 11. Mon sceal sécan þe sǽwarode and be eá ōfrum þele gimmas, hwíte and reáde and hīwa gehwæs, Met. 19, 22 : Bt. 32, 3 ; F. 118, 17. Gymmas, Coll. M. 27, 7. **II.** *used of the heavenly bodies :*—Hālge gimmas, sunne and mōna, Cri. 692. Swegles leóht, gimma gladost, ǽdeltungla wyn *the sun*, Ph. 289. **II a.** *where a person is spoken of as a sun :*—Cyning þrymlíce of his heáhsetle scíned, wlitig wuldres gim, Ph. 516. v. god-, heáfod-, searo-, sinc-, tungol-, wæl-, wuldor-gim.

**gíman.** *Take here* gýman *in Dict., and add :* I. *to take care of* (*gen.*) (1) *to treat so as not to injure :*—Hit is fūllic þingc . . . þæt hī ne gýmad heora sylfra æt þām unþeáwe . . ., þæt hī ne gýmad heora sylfra, swā hī beþorfton, ac befýlad hī selfe, Wlfst. 305, 7–11. (2) *to treat so as to restore.* (a) *to cure.* v. gím-ness ; I :—Đone blindo gémed *caecum curat*, Mk. p. 3, 20 : Lk. p. 5, 10. From crypelnise gémed ī gehǽled, 1. Gémde unhǽlo, Mt. L. 9, 35. Gémde ī hǽlde hiá *curevit*, 19, 2. Lēcnade ī gémde, Mk. L. 1, 34. Gémes *curate*, Mt. L. 10, 8. Gémad, Lk. 10, 9. Gēme ī gelécnia *curare*, Mt. L. 12, 10. (b) *to correct :*—Wē gēmes ī boetas *corrigimus*, Mt. p. 2, 2. Gēmendum *correctis*, 17. (c) *to reprove.* v. gím-ness ; I. 2 :—Gife synngiga in đec brōđer, geong and gēm (*corripe*) hine ; gif đec gehéres boetend đū bist brōđeres đínes, Mt. L. 18, 15. (3) *to provide for the wants of* a person :—Sē đe ne gímd đāra đe his beód *qui suorum curam non habet* ; if any provide not for his own (1 Tim. 5, 8), Past. 139, 1. (4) *to see after the proper condition of things, attend to :*—Hē suíde wel gíemed đāra uterra đinga *provide exteriora subministrat*, Past. 141, 16. Gýme hē ǽgder ge đæs sēlran ge þæs sǽmran, þ nāđor ne misfare, Angl. ix. 260, 9. Đā hǽdengyldan đā đe þæt templ and þǽra goda gýmdon, ii. 482, 33. (4 a) *with gen. and acc. :*—Hē gýmd grǽdelíce his teolunge, his gafoles, his gebytlu, Hml. Th.

**i. 66, 10.** (5) *to take charge* of, *act as guardian* or *keeper*. (a) the object a person :—Him (*John*) befæste se Hǽlend his mōdor, þæt his clǽne líf ðæs clǽnan mǽdenes gýmde, Hml. Th. i. 58, 22. Ðæt hié tō slāwlíce ðǽra ne giémen ðe him befæste sién *a commissorum custodia minime torpescant*, Past. 191, 23. Se hierde bið ídel ðe scolde ðǽre heorde giéman *a gregis custodia vacat cura pastoris*, 129, 13. Nis tō wēnanne þætte wolde God hiora gāsta mid him gýman, Ps. Th. 77, 10. Biwœdded *desponsata* (in margin : Tō gēmanne nalles tō habbanne fore wíf), Mt. L. i, 18. (a *a*) *to have charge* as *ruler*, *to rule*. v. gímend; **I a,** gímen; **II** :—Hē gesette hig (*sun and moon*) þæt hig gímdon þæs dæges and þǽre nihte *posuit eas*, *ut praeessent diei ac nocti*, Gen. 1, 18. (b) the object a thing, *to take charge* or *possession* of :—Ðonne him fordsíð gebyrige, gýme his hláford ðæs hē lǽfe *si mortem obeat*, *rehabeat dominus suus omnia*, Ll. Th. i. 434, 27. (6) *to take care* that something is or is not done. (a) with positive clause :—Gýme swān þ hē æfter sticunge his slyhtswýn wel behweorfe, Ll. Th. i. 436, 15. Ðā ðe ofer ðǽre bióð giémen hié geornlíce ðætte ... *studeant qui praesunt, ut ...*, Past. 119, 13 : 403, 19. Him is tō giémenne ðæt hē ætiéwe his híeremonnum ðæt hē sié hiera fæder on lāre *curandum est, ut rectorem subditis patrem exhibeat disciplina*, 123, 24. Giémanne, 455, 10. Is ðǽm lǽce swíðe geornlíce tō giémanne ðæt hē ... *studet qui medetur, ut ...*, 28. (a *a*) with gen. pronoun and clause :—Hē ðæs giéme ðæt hē lustas ātemige *curet suggestiones edomare*, Past. 383, 6. (b) with negative clause :—Giémað ðæt gē eówre ryhtwísnesse ne dōn beforan monnum *attendite, ne justitiam vestram faciatis coram hominibus*, Past. 335, 21. Ðæt hié giémen ... ðætte of ðǽm gōde ne weorðe wyrse ysel ākenned *ut sollicite aspiciant, ne ...*, 313, 18. Ðæt hié geornlíce giémen ðæt hié eft ðā synne ne gefremmen *ut sollicite custodire studeant, ne ...*, 327, 13. Ufone sceal ðæt heáfod gíman ðæt ðā fēt ne āslíden *caput debet ex alto providere, ne pedes torpeant*, 131, 25. (b *a*) with gen. pronoun and clause :—Ealde witan þe þæt mynster geondgangen and þæs gýman, þæt þǽr nān bróðor ymbe ídelnesse beó, R. Ben. 74, 15. **II.** *to care for.* (1) *to have a liking* or *desire* for. (a) the object a person :—Wǽrleás mon and ... ungetreów, þæs ne gýmed God, Gn. Ex. 164. (b) the object a thing. (a) material :—Eádige beóð þā þe þissa eorþwelena ne gýmaþ, Bl. H. 159, 30. Seolcenra hrægla hí ne gímdon, Bt. 15; F. 48, 11. Gēmdon, Met. 8, 10. (β) non-material :—Hē ðisses middangeardes orsorgnesse ne gímð *prospera mundi postposuit*, Past. 61, 8. Waa ieów welegum ðe iówer lufu is on eówrum woruldwelum, and ne giémað ðæs ēcan gefeán, 181, 24. Hí gūðe ne gýmdon *they had no stomach for the fight*, By. 192. Ðæt sélre geceós, oferhýda ne gým, B. 1760. Heó mē sagað, þæt heó mǽglufan mínre ne gýme, Jul. 70. (2) *to take interest in, be concerned* about, *be affected* by a matter. (a) with gen. :—God sylfa þonne ne gýmeþ nænges mannes hreówe, Bl. H. 95, 29. Hē swelces lyt gýmð, Met. Einl. 8. (b) with clause, *to care* whether, what, &c. :—Sē ðe ne giémð hwæðer hē ðā sibbe healde *qui servare pacem non curat*, Past. 345, 12. Hié ne giémað tō hwon ōðerra monna wíse weorðe *non aliorum lucra cogitant*, 41, 24. Hē giémde hwæt hē hæfde monna gerímes, and ne nōm nāne wære hūlíce hié wǽron, Ors. 5, 4; S. 224, 21. Ne hē ne giéme hwelce hylde hē mid ðǽre ælmessan gewriexle, Past. 323, 17. Ne hí nā for þon ōþre men feormiað, þ hí mycclum gýman hwæþer heom þ gōd sý þ hí dóð, Gr. D. 76, 29. Hwý nelt þū gēman þ mín sweostor mē lǽt āne þegnian *non est tibi curae quod soror mea reliquit me solam ministrare?* (Lk. 10, 40), Bl. H. 67, 30. (c) with gen. pron. and clause :—Þonne þæs gíman nele Waldend, hū þā womsceaþan grēten, Cri. 1569. (3) *to be anxious, troubled* about :—Ðæt hié tō georne ne giémen ðissa eorðlicena ymbhogena *ut curare nimis terrena desuescant*, Past. 431, 12. Ne gēmende gié sié saúles iúrres *ne solliciti sitis animae vestrae*, Mt. L. 6, 25, 28, 31. Nǽlleð gē sié gēmende in merne. Morgen for ðon dæg gēmende (*sollicitus*) bið him seolfum, 34. (4) *to pay attention to, heed* advice, command, &c., *keep* a covenant, law, rule, *act in accordance with, in obedience to*. (a) with gen. :—Gif se brimhengest brídles ne gýmeð, Rūn. 21. Þā þe Godes willan wyrcað and wísdómes gýmað þā hwíle þe hý libbað, Wlfst. 5, 6 : Ll. Th. i. 334, 20. Hí þæs cynges worda ne gýmdon, for ðám his ríce ne wæs ofer hí, Bd. 2, 6; Sch. 134, 10. Hí wǽre ne gýmdon, Exod. 140. Muneca gehwylc þe ... regoles ne gýme, Ll. Th. i. 306, 2. Gýme hē his crístendomes georne, 310, 4. Godes laga gýman, 350, 10 : 318, 20. (b) with acc. :—Wē bebeódað þte Godes þeówas hiora rihtregol gýman and on riht healdan, Ll. Th. i. 102, 15. (c) absolute :—Bisceopas sceolan bodian ... gýme sē þe wylle, Ll. Th. i. 374, 21. **III.** *to observe, notice, consider.* (a) with gen. :—Ðā spone hē ðe his ðeáwa giémað *spectatores suos ad sublimia invitet*, Past. 83, 3. (b) with acc. :—Hig āspyriað þæs solecismus un þeáwas, ... and eác hig prūlíce gýmað þæs miotacismus gefleard, Angl. viii. 313, 25. (c) with clause :—Ne furðum ne giémað hwæt hié dōn, oððe hwonne hié hwæt dōn *nequaquam, quae quando agant, inspiciunt*, 287, 7. Dū slāwa, gā ðe tō ǽmetthylle, and giém hū hié dóð (*considera vias ejus*), Past. 193, 1. Ðæt hié geornlíce giémen (*ut sollicite considerent*) hwæðer him ðæt geðóht cume of fǽrlicum luste, ðe of gewilnunga, 417, 4, 32. Gíman hwæt se Waldend tō wrace gesette, Cri. 1600. (d) with gen. and clause :—Ðæt hié ontýnen hiera mōdes eágan and giémen

ðissa eorðlicena gesceafta (*mentis oculos ad consideranda ea, quae in infimis versantur, aperiant*) hū ðā fuglas ... gesibsumlíce farað, Past. 349, 20. v. ā-, be-, mis-gíman ; un-gímende.

**gim-bǽre.** *Substitute : Containing gems, set with gems* :—Gimbǽre belt *bullifer* (*gimmifer*) *baltheus*, An. Ox. 487. Gimbǽrum ringum *gemmiferis anulis*, 1191 : 4827.

**gim-cyn.** *Add :* (1) *a kind of gem* :—Smaragdus þ gimcyn, Nar. 5, 1. Hwelc fremu byþ þám gítsere þ hē ælces gimcynnes genóg begite, Bt. 26, 3; F. 94, 13. Eárhringas of mænigfealdan gimcynne geworhte, Nar. 26. 32. His brýdbūras wǽron eorcnanstānum, unionibus and carbunculis þǽm gimcynnum swíþast gefrætwode, Nar. 5, 4. (2) *a gem of a particular kind :*—Golde geglengde and gimcynnum (cf. mid ælces cynnes gimmum. Bt. 28 ; F. 100, 27), Met. 15, 4 : 25, 6. Þā rōde golde beweorcean and gimcynnum, mid eorcnanstānum besettan, El. 1064. Sēcan ǽgþer ge hwíte gimmas ge reáde, and ælces cynnes gimcyn, Bt. 32, 3 ; F. 118, 18.

**gíme.** *care. Take here* **gýme** *in Dict., and add :*—Gif wē habbað suā micle sorge and suā micle giéman ūrra niéhstena suā suā ūre selfra *si ut nostram, sic curam proximi gerimus*, Past. 45, 11.

**gíme-leás ; adj.** **I.** *that does not take care* or *trouble, careless, negligent :*—Wē wēnað þ mænige gímeleáse menn ne rēccean hū heora yrfe fare, Ll. Th. i. 238, 5. Útādrǽfdum gýmeleásra preósta fýlþum *ejectis neglegentium clericorum spurcitiis*, Angl. xiii. 366, 16. **I a.** *negligent in spiritual matters, in discharge of duty*, &c.—Gif hwylc bróðor beó gemēt swā gýmeleás (-lēs, v. l., gímeleás *neglegens*, R. Ben. I. 83, 16), þæt hē nelle hǽlige bēc smeágan, R. Ben. 75, 3. Críst sylfa cwæþ þ hē nelle gehýran þæs gímeleásan mannes gebedrǽdene, Bl. H. 57, 4. Ðǽm unbealdum is tō cýðanne hū giémeleáse hié bióð ðonne hié hié selfe to suíðe forsióð *inconstantibus intimandum est, quod valde se despicientes negligunt*, Past. 305, 16. Þá hálgan weras ... heora gemynd þurhwunað ... þā gímeleásan men þe heora líf ādrugon on ealre ídelnisse, heora gemynd is forgiten, Ælfc. T. Grn. 1, 12. Sume ic funde būtan Godes tācne gýmeleúse ungebletsade, Jul. 491. Seó gehýrnes ne bið nyt on þǽm ungelýfdum monnum and on þǽm gýmeleásum, Bl. H. 55, 32. Yfellibbendum and gímeleásum (*neglegentibus*), R. Ben. I. 118, 10. ¶ with gen. *careless* of :—Swā bið ðæt mōd slǽpende gewundad swā hit ne gefrēt, ðonne hit bið tō gímeleás his āgenra þearfa *mens a cura suae sollicitudinis verberatur et non dolet*, Past. 431, 19. **II.** *that is not cared for, that is not guarded.* (1) of a person, *without protection :*—Hí cwedað, wuton cunnian hwænne hine God lǽte swā swā gýmeleásne *dicentes, Deus dereliquit eum*, Ps. Th. 70, 10. (2) of cattle, *stray, untended, unwatched* :—Gif þē become ōðres gímeleás fioh on hand *si occurreris bovi inimici tui aut asino erranti* (Ex. 23, 4), Ll. Th. i. 54, 9. Wē nellen nān gýmeleás yrfe forgyldan *nolumus aliquod pecus incustoditum et per inobseruantiam perditum reddere*, 238, 10. **III.** *incurable.* Cf. gíman; **I.** 2 :—Gēme[me]leáse *incurabiles*, Mt. p. 18, 5.

**gímeleásian.** *Take here* **gýmeleásian** *in Dict.*

**gímeleáslic ; adj.** *That is done without care, careless, thoughtless :*—Unwǽrlicu and giémeleáslicu sprǽc menn dweled *incauta locutio in errorem pertrahit*, Past. 89, 8. In manegum gýmeleáslicum wordum þe steórleáslicu cildru gewuniað tō sprecanne, Gr. D. 289, 9.

**gímeleáslíce ; adv.** *Take here* **gēmeleáslíce** *in Dict., and add :* **I.** *carelessly, without taking pains, negligently :*—Gif heora hwylc fúllíce oðþe gýmeleáslíce mynstres þing behwyrfe *si quis sordide aut neglegenter res monasterii tractaverit*, R. Ben. 56, 11. Ðāra stōwa sum raþe rotaþ gif hire mon gímeleáslíce tilað, Lch. ii. 84, 25. Þā wēnde hē þ hē þā leóhtfatu gýmeleáslícor bette þonne hē sceolde *lampades negligenter exstinxisse se credidit*, Gr. D. 237, 1. **II.** *without care for good :*—Ús þe yfele and gýmeleáslíce mid unrihte libbað *nobis male viventibus atque neglegentibus*, R. Ben. 133, 12. **III.** *without notice* or *observation :*—Suā gímeleáslíce oft sceacað ūre geðóhtas from ūs, ðæt wē his furðum ne gefrēdað *cogitationes ex sensu negligenti quasi nobis non sentientibus procedunt*, Past. 139, 19. **IV.** *without care being taken.* Cf. gímeleás; **II.** :—þæt þā hālgan mynstru tōrorene ... gýmeleáslíce ættredon *quod sacra coenobia diruta ... neglegenter tabescerent*, Angl. xiii. 366, 13.

**gímeleás-ness, e ; f.** *Carelessness :*—Be speres gēmeleásnesse of *carelessness with a spear*, Ll. Th. i. 84, 11. Be ðám forþgewitenum gēmeleásnissum (*praeteritas neglegentias*), þā þe hē on cildháde gefremede, Bd. 27; Sch. 320, 1. Fore synnum and gemeleásnisum (*neglegentiis*) ūsum, Rtl. 178, 11. Heora gímeleásnesse *neglegentias suas*, R. Ben. I. 84, 12.

**gíme-líst.** *Take here* **gýme-leást** *in Dict., and add :* **I.** *the not taking proper care* of, *carelessness* with. Cf. gíman; **I.** 4 :—For ðǽre giémelēste his hǽlo *per negligentiam suae salutis*, Past. 463, 3. Be speres gýmeleáste of *carelessness with a spear*, Ll. Th. i. 84, 11. **II.** *the want of care to do or not to do something, negligence.* Cf. gíman; **I.** 6 :—Būtan hit gelimpe þæt man lator ārīse þonne hit gebyrige ... þæt ne geweorðe, þæt þyllic gýmelēst gelimpe ... gif hit gelimpe, dǽdbēte sē ... þe hit þurh his gýmelēste (gímeleástum *neglectum*, R. Ben. I. 42, 7) gelamp, R. Ben. 36, 2–7. Hē Gode nolde ðíówigan ... hē ðone demm his giémeliéste (*damna neglegentiae*) gebētan ne mæg, Past. 251, 17

Ðæt wē geðencen ðā gód ðe wē forgiémeleásodon, næs ðā wē dydon . . . wē genunað ūre giémelēste, 467, 10. Mid dædbōte his gýmeleáste, R. Ben. 68, 15. Hý mēde habbað, gif hý swā dōð, eác swylce wīte, gif hī . . . for gýmeleáste hit ne bētað (si neglegant), R. Ben. 119, 16. Gémeleáste, 68, 20. Þæt hý ǽr on ōþrum tīdum mid gémelēste forlēton omnes neglegentias suas aliorum temporum, 76, 7. Hī for gímelēste and for rēccelēste forlēton unwriten hiora dǣda, Bt. 18, 3; F. 64, 34. Giémeleste (-līste, v. l.), Past. 165, 6: 339, 21. Gif geneátmanna hwilc forgýmeleásað his hláfordes gafol . . . gif se hláford . . . þā gýmeleáste tō forgyfenesse lǽte, Ll. Th. i. 270, 18. Gif hwā cwydeleás . . . gewīte . . . þurh his gýmeleáste (-lýste, v. l.), 412, 28. Gímelīste, ii. 292, 7. Oðþæt hē þæs gyltes gýmeleáste gebēte until he make reparation for the negligence he was guilty of when he committed that fault, R. Ben. 69, 15. III. want of interest or concern, indifference. Cf. gíman; II. 2:—Oft ðā cræftas and ðā mægenu weordað te fǽrwyrde ðǣm ðe hī hæfð, ðonne hī for hira giémelēste hié fortrūwiað on þǣm cræftum ðe hī habbað, and hī nyllað iécan, Past. 463, 6. Folc ðe on clǽnum felda sige gefeohtað, and eft innan hira burgum belocene ðurh hiera giémeliéste (negligentiam) hié lǣtað gebindan, 229, 1. IV. want of anxiety, security. Cf. gíman; II. 3:—Hē forhtode þ hē forlure þā gýmelēste his þearfednesse metuebat paupertatis suae securitatem perdere, Gr. D. 201, 14. V. heedlessness, inattention, neglect. Cf. gíman; II. 4:—Hē lǣt his mód tōflōwan on ðæt ofdele giémeliéste and ungesceádwīsnesse æfter eallum his willum neglectam (animam) se inferius per desideria expandit, Past. 283, 15. Hē lǣt his hláfordes gebod tō giémeleáste, 121, 14. Gē forsáwon eall mīn geðeaht, and lēton eów tō giémelēste ðonne ic eów cīdde (increpationes meas neglexistis), 247, 23. Synu ðurhtogen hwīlum for giémeléste (negligentia), hwīlum for untrymnesse, 435, 15. Gē ðás getācnunga tō gýmeleáste dōð, Hml. Th. ii. 70, 15. Ðæt hē ðāra giémeliéste wolde gedíeglan ut horum negligentiam velaret, Past. 207, 22. V a. want of proper consideration, presumption:—Þæt bið swīðor tō gýmelēste and tō ídlum gylpe tō tellanne presumtioni deputabitur et vane glorie, R. Ben. 77, 5.

gímen. Take here gēmen, gýmen in Dict., and add:—Gýmen vel hoga studium, Wrt. Voc. ii. 137, 59. Gýmen exercitio, i. meditatio, 144, 66. I. care for a person or thing, seeing after the welfare, proper condition of. Cf. gíman; I. 3, 4. (1) with gen.:—Godes engel bebeád him þæt [hē] sceolde habban gýmene ǽgðer ge ðǽre mēder ge þæs cildes, Hml. Th. i. 196, 19. Hē ne forlǣte ðā giémenne hira ūterran ðearfe exterioris vitae providentiam non relinquat, Past. 137, 13. Ealle ðā ðe for beón sculon sculon habban giémenne ðissa ūterrena ðinga (habere sollicitudines exteriores debent), ond ðeáh ne sién hī tō fæste tō gebundene, 139, 23. Ðæt hē suā geornfullīce sié ymb ðā giémenne ðissa hwīlendlicra ðinga suā suā hit niédðearf sié ut curae temporalis sollicitudinis et quantum necesse est prodeant, 141, 4. Hē for niédðearfe hæfð giémenne his flǽsces curam carnis ex necessitate tolerat, 395, 19. (2) with prep.:—Ðonne hē gebint hine selfne tō ōðrum menn mid his wordum ðæt hē sceal niéde ðā giémenne and ðā geornfulnesse ymb ðone habban ðe he ǽr ne ðorfte, Past. 193, 9. I a. of medical care. Cf. gíman; I. 2 a:—Gif hē hwǣr ǽnigne freónd mētan meahte þe his gýmenne dyde and his wunde lācnian wolde sicubi amicos, qui sui curam agerent, posset inuenire, Bd. 4, 22; Sch. 455, 13. II. care of a pastor, ruler, cure of souls, charge, management, rule, administration. Cf. gíman; I. 5:—Sió manigfealde giémen ðæs underfangenan lāreówdōmes suscepta cura regiminis, Past. 37, 13. Ðā byrðenne ðǽre hirdelecan giémenne (gēmenne, v. l.) pastoralis curae pondera, 23, 11 : 27, 10. Ðæt dūst ðisse eorðlican giémenne (administration of secular matters), 131, 12. Gýmene regimine, i. regula, An. Ox. 3423: 5301. Ne forlǣte se reccere ðā inneran giémenne ðæs godcundan ðíowdōmes, Past. 127, 11. Gímenne, 13, 6. II a. with gen. of object of care:—Sió giémen (gíman, v. l.) ðǽre hálgan ciricean sié ðām beboden ðe hiere wel rǣdan cunne cura sanctae ecclesiae ei, qui hanc bene regere praevalet, imponatur, Past. 43, 24. Hine lǣs ōðerra monna giémen bisegað. Ðā ofergesettan sint tō monianne ðæt hié ōðerra monna giémenne gefyllen, 191, 20–22. II b. with prep. governing object of care:—Ne sié his (the bishop's) giémen nā ðý lǣsse ymb ðā gehīrsuman, Past. 75, 14. III. care that something is or is not done. Cf. gíman; I. 6:—Nū sceole wē hogian mid mycelre gýmene þ ūre līfe beó swā gelōgod, Hml. S. 16, 6. IV. care for a person (gen.), liking, affection. Cf. gíman; II. 1:—Sē ðe suā hígað tō andweardnesse his Scippendes, and ágiémeleásað ðǽre giémenne his nīhstena, oðða eft suā singallīce folgað ðǽre giémenne his niéhstena, ðæt hē ágiémeleásað ðā godcundan lufe, Past. 87, 10–13. V. care, pains, trouble in doing something:—Līchamlicere gepeódnesse lustum gýmene carnalis copulę uoluptatibus operam i. studium (dedissent), An. Ox. 1607. VI. with gen. or prep. (cf. II. a, b), care, anxiety, solicitude. Cf. gíman; II. 3:—Þeáh se wind þāra earfoþa and seó singale gémen þissa woruldsēlþa (se ymbhoga þyssa woruldsēlþa hine drecce, Met. 7, 53) him on blāwe, Bt. 12; F. 36, 28: Met. 7, 51. Hit is ðearf ðætte sió giémen, ðe hié hira hīremonnum ūtan dōn scylen, sié wel gemetgod sollicitudo, quae subditis exterius impenditur, sub certa necesse est mensura teneatur, Past. 139, 10. Se cræft ðǽre giémenne ymbe ðā fore-

sceáwunga ðæs heofonlican līfes vis sollicitudinis et erga coelestem vitam providae circumspectionis, 169, 6. Ðā giémenne (giémen, v. l.) ðisse ondweardan līfes ðæt getācnað curas vitae praesentis designant, 139, 18. VII. observation, consideration. Cf. gíman; III:—Þus gerǣddre besceáwunge gýmene hujuscemodi contemplationis intuitu, An. Ox. 245. v. ungemet-, weorold(?)-gímen.

gímend, es; m. I. a keeper. v. gíman; I. 5 a :—Gēmendum custodibus, Mt. p. 20, 4. I a. a ruler, governor. v. gíman; I. 5 a a:—Þǣr þǣr nys gýmend folc hrýst ubi non est gubernator populus corruit, Scint. 117, 7. II. an observer. v. gíman; III:—Ealra ðǣra tācna ðe ðǣr gelimpað ic eom sceáwere and gýmend, Hml. Th. i. 504, 3. v. be-gímend.

gíming (-ung). Take here gēmung in Dict., and add: I. a taking care of a person, entertaining, an entertainment, a wedding feast, nuptials. v. gíman; I. 3. [Cf. O. Sax. gōma; pl. a marriage feast; nuptiae:—Hē at ðēm gómum was ( = se Hǽlend geceiged wæs tō ðǣm fǽrmum ł hǽmdum (ad nubtias), Jn. L. 2, 2), Hēl. 2002]:—Gēmung nuptias (a gloss. on Mt. 22, 2. Cf. sē ðe dyde ðā fǽrmo ł brýdlōpa qui fecit nubtias, Mt. L. 22, 2), Wrt. Voc. ii. 73, 11. Gīming, 60, 52. Gēmung nuptiae, i. 288, 84. Tō gēmungum þæs heofoulican brýdguman ad nuptias sponsi caelestis, Bd. 3, 24 ; Sch. 311, 9. [Oð þæne dæg incre geámungæ, Hml. A. 132, 525. Tō hwan forhǽle þū ūs þīne gēmunga 135, 650.] II. care, management:—Þām gewunode hē bringan grēne wyrta, and eft hweorfan tō þǽre gýmingce (gíminge, v. l.) his wyrtgeardes (ad curam horti), Gr. D. 181, 4. III. care, keeping, guarding:—Wē þe ūs befæst is seó gýming Godes folces, Ll. Th. ii. 402, 10. In ðām dagum þe hē dyde his sceápa gýminge dum gregis sui curam gereret, Gr. D. 215, 9. [Hic am God ðe in min geming nam Jacob, Gen. and Ex. 2783.] IV. ruling, rule:—Hēr onfēng Pilatus gýminge ofer Jūdēas, Chr. P. 293, 23. V. caring, being anxious:—Behealdað eów ðæt gē ne gehefigien eówre heortan mid monigfaldre giéminge ðisse worolde attendite ut non graventur corda vestra in curis hujus vitae, Past. 129, 20. v. be-, un-gíming.

gímingian, gíming-lic. Take here gēmungian, gēmung-lic in Dict.

gimmian; p. ode To put forth gems (fig.), to put forth buds:—Sume sind gehǽtene tropi . . . swā swā is gecwedeu gemmare uites, þæt wintreówa gimmiað, for ðan ðe wintreówa blōstman beóð gimmum gelīce, Ælfc. Gr. Z. 295, 10.

gimmod. v. ge-gimmod.

gím-ness, e; f. I. care that repairs, restores. (1) medical care, curing. v. gíman; I. 2 a:—Ne is ðarf ðǣm hālum gēmnisse non est opus valentibus medico, Mt. L. 9, 12. Ðā ðe gēmnisse (cura) bihōfadon gehǽlde, Lk. R. L. 9, 11. Hē salde him mæhte gēmnisse (-nisses, L.) tō untrymnissum dedit illis potestatem curandi infirmitates, Mk. R. 3, 15. Of gēmnisse about healing (on the Sabbath); de cura (Sabbati murmurantes), Lk. p. 8, 4. Hē gēmnise his dyde (hine lācnude, W. S.) curam eius egit, Lk. L. 10, 34. (2) reproof. v. gíman; I. 2 c:—Mið gēmnisse brōðres correptione fratris, Mt. p. 18, 6: Rtl. 43, 27. II. care for the wants of a person. v. gíman; I. 3:—Dryhten gēmnisse hafað mīn Dominus curam habet mei, Ps. Srt. 39, 18: Lk. L. 10, 35. III. care for an object that affects with pleasure, fear, &c. v. gíman; II. 2:—Nis ðe gēmnis (gēmeniso, L.) be ǽngum non est tibi cura de aliquo, Mt. R. 22, 16. Ne is ðē gēmnise, þte . . ., Lk. L. R. 10, 40. IV. care, anxiety, trouble. v. gíman; II. 3:—Gēmnisse (sollicitudo) woruldes ðisses, Mt. L. 13, 22. Gēmnise mettes and woedes, Lk. p. 7, 15. Mið gēmnisum līfes sollicitudinibus uitae, Lk. L. 8, 14. Gēmnisum (-nisse, R.) ðisses līfes curis huius uitae, 21, 34. v. fore-, ofer-gímness.

gímran, gýrman; p. de to mourn:—Ic weóp ł ic gýrmde for geómrunge . . . wōp ł geómrung mīn fram ðē nis behýdd rugiebam a gemitu . . . gemitus meus a te non est absconditus, Ps. L. 37, 9–10. v. geómrian.

gim-rodor. Add:—Gimroder dracontia, An. Ox. 1075. Gimrodur, 7, 73: Angl. xiii. 30, 60. Ginrodor, Wrt. Voc. ii. 77, 28 : 25, 68. Gimro[dor], 106, 68. [The first four are glosses to Ald. 16, 1, probably also the last two.]

gim-stān. Add:—Tō þām geweorce (the tabernacle) brōhte þæt folc deórwirðe gimstānas . . . þā gimstānas getācnodon mislice fægernissa on Godes mannum (v. Ex. 35, 27), Ælfc. T. Grn. 23, 40–45. Gymstāna gemmarum, An. Ox. 1073. Of gimstānum gemmis, 3194.

gímung. v. gíming : gin, es ; n. v. ginn : gin ; adj. Vast. v. ginne.

gin (?) ; adj. Gaping (?), opening wide :—Capturam in amne Derentan constructam, quae usitato æt Ginanhecce nuncupatur uocabulo, C. D. iii. 199, 8. Tō ginun hōcum, 413, 10. [Cf. (?) O. H. Ger. ginun ore (vasto).]

ginan to yawn. Dele Cot. 23, and add : cf. gānian.

ginan; p. de To turn (trans.) back, drive back:—Hī man gýnde (gínde, gēnde [glossed drāf], v. ll.) ongeán eft tō Jūdan (cf. they, turning back upon them that pursued them, i Macc. 7, 46), Hml. S. 25, 636. [Cf. O. H. Ger. gaganen obviare: Icel. gegna to meet.] v. wiþ-gínan; on-geagn.

gin-fæst. Substitute: ample, liberal, noble (an epithet of God's gifts):—Þū glǽm hafast, ginfæste giefe, geoguðhādes blǣd, Jul. 168.

Hē gemunde mægenes strenge, ginfæste (gim-, MS.) gife, þe him God sealde, B. 1271. Hē ginfæstan gife, þe him God sealde, heóld, 2182. Abraham leófa! þū scealt þurh hand heofoncyninges sigorleánum onfón, ginfæstum gifum, Gen. 2919. Þū, ēce God, selest weorðlica ginfæsta gifa be geearnunga ānra gehwelcre, Met. 20, 227.

**gin-fæsten**, es ; *n. A noble, spacious closet (used of the Scriptures ?).* v. fæsten ; III :—Gif onlūcan wile bānhūses weard ginfæsten gōd gāstes cægum *if the mind with spiritual keys will open the noble, spacious chamber,* i.e. if a man will study the Scriptures (?), Exod. 524.

**gingra.** *Take here* geongra *in Dict., and add:* I. *of time-relations, a descendant.* Cf. ildra *an ancestor :*—Ðis is þ frið þ . . . ealle gecweden habbað . . . for hȳ sylfe and for heora gingran, ge for geborene ge for ungeborene (ge for hȳ sylfe ge for heora ofspryng, *v. l.*), Ll. Th. i. 152, 5. II. *denoting inferiority of position.* (1) in a general sense, *an inferior, a low* (as opposed to *a high*) *person :*—Eallum folce, ge yldrum ge gingrum, Ll. Th. i. 246, 18. (2) in special senses. (a) *a vassal, follower, servant of a prince* (human or superhuman) [cf. liberata ab pastu regis et principis, uel *iuniorum* eorum, C. D. ii. 25, 7] :—Hwane manaþ God mǣran gafoles þonne þone biscop ? for þon þe se biscop biþ Godes gingra, Bl. H. 45, 17. Him (*Lucifer*) tweó þūhte þæt hē Gode wolde geongra weorðan, Gen. 277. Hē mæg mē geofian, þeáh hē his gingran ne sende, 546. Erōdes forcōm æt campe cyning Iūðēa . . . Ic nū bebeóde þegnum mīnum þ hié þe hnǣgan gingran (*his follower*) æt gūðe, An. 1332. His gingran *Satan's followers* (*the fallen angels*), Sat. 191. Þā (*Adam and Eve*) him tō gingran self Metod mearcode, Gen. 458. Mōton wē hié ūs tō giongrum habban, 407. (b) *the official representative of a person in authority, a subordinate, deputy.* v. gingre, II :—Ne dorste se heáhgerēfa nāht ongeán þā hǣðengyldan, ac forlēt his gingran (cf. Aspasius se undergerēfa, 216) tōgeánes þǣre ceáste, Hml. S. 7, 212. Gif þises hwæt beforan cyninges ealdormonnes giungran gelimpe, Ll. Th. i. 86, 18. Ne derige se scírman his gingran, ne se hlāford his mannum, ii. 314, 2. Hēt se dēma his gingran þus dōn . . . þā hēt se undergerēfa hī ealle gebringan, Hml. S. 4, 329. Ne sceal him nān ealdorman settan dysige dēman ne unrihtwīse tō geongrum, Ll. Lbmn. 475, 9. Oft þā gōdan dēman habbað yfele gingran, 29. (c) *the follower of a teacher, a disciple :*—Gōd lāreów, ðonne hē his gingran suingð, Past. 267, 8. Ongan Gūðlāc geongran rētan, Gū. 1035. Se Wīsdōm sǣde þ his gingran hæfdon hine swā tōtorenne, Bt. 3, 1 ; F. 6, 2. Se Hǣlend wiste þ his gingran woldan unrōte beón, Bl. H. 135, 15. Hē hine his gingrum æteówde, 89, 36. Geongrum, 109, 7. Paulus cuæð tō his gingrum, Past. 181, 14. Giongrum, 451, 28. Hē hæfde twēgen gingran, 291, 14 : Sat. 526 : An. 427. [*O. Sax.* jungaro : *O. H. Ger.* jungiro *subditus, alumnus, discipulus.*]

**gingre**, an ; *f.* I. *a follower, servant* (cf. gingra ; II. 2 a). v. Dict. II. *a deputy.* Cf. gingra ; II. 2 b :—Heó arn tō þǣre fǣmnan þe þā ðæs mynstres abbodesse wæs, Hilde gingre (geongra, *v. l.*) *cucurrit ad uirginem, quae tunc monasterio abbatissae uice praefuit,* Bd. 4, 23 ; Sch. 478, 17.

**ginian.** *Take here* geonian *in Dict., and add :*—Geongendi oscitantes, Wrt. Voc. ii. 115, 75. Þā giniendan *hiulcas,* 42, 49. I. *of living creatures.* (1) *to open the mouth ;* of the mouth, *to be open :*—Geonath, ginath *battat, batat,* Txts. 43, 269. Geót on bollan and geona ymb, Lch. ii. 50, 12. Se wōda man stōd gynigende and þȳwde mid mūþe þ hē Martinum ābite, Hml. S. 31, 538. Geoniendum bile *hiulco rostro,* i. *aperto ore,* An. Ox. 2409. Draca mid giniendum (geniendum, *v. l.*) mūðe, Gr. D. 156, 11. Hī cleopodon giniendum (geniendum, *v. l.*) mūþum, 241, 8. Þā geoniendan þrotbollan *hiulcos* (i. *apertos*) *gurguliones,* An. Ox. 3574. (2) *to open the mouth and utter a sound :*—Gionat *garrit,* Wrt. Voc. ii. 109, 49. Geonaþ *garret,* 40, 55. Ginað *barrat* (cf. barrit elefans cum uocem emittit, Corp. Gl. H. 23, 34), 10, 69. II. *of material, to gape, yawn, be wide open :*—Beneoðan swīðe deóp niwolnys ginode (geonode, *v. l.*) *profundum subter praecipitium patet,* Gr. D. 52, 18. Þǣr geonode (gynude, *v. l.*) in þǣre hracan swylce þǣr hwylc seáð wǣre *quasi quoddam barathrum patebat in gutture,* 241, 12. Hū Marcus Curtius besceát on þā genigendan (gyniendan, *v. l.*) eorþan, Ors. 3, 3, tit. ; S. 2, 32.

**gin[n]**, es ; *n. A wide expanse :*—Wīddra and sīddra þonne befæðman mæge eorðan ymbhwyrft and ūprodor, gārsecges gin and þeós geómre lyft, Exod. 430. v. ginne.

**-gin[n].** v. on-gin[n].

**ginnan.** *Add : to begin :*—Þā gunnon (ongunnon, *v. l.*) hī þæt apostolice līf onhyrgan *coeperunt apostolicam uitam imitari,* Bd. 1, 26 ; Sch. 56, 21.

**ginne ;** *adj. Wide, spacious, ample, broad (lands).* I. *having a large area :*—Of þǣre ginnan byrig, Jud. 149. Seó æftre eá Ethiopia land and leódgeard beligeð ūton, ginne rīce (*a broad realm*), Gen. 230. Ic weóld folce Deniga and heóld ginne rīce (gim merice, MS.), B. 466. Ia. *as an epithet of the earth :*—Bið eal þess ginna grund (*this wide world*) glēda gefylled, Dōm. 12. In þȳs ginnan grunde, Jud. 2. Ic geondfērde fela fremdra londa geond ginne grund, Vīd. 51. Under gynne grund *under the broad earth,* B. 1551. II. *ample,*

*of great amount :*—Hē him grundwelan ginne sealde, hēt þām sinhīwum sǣs and eorðan tūddorteóndra teohha gehwilcre wæstmas fēdan, Gen. 457. [Cf. *Icel.* ginn- ; *and see* Grmm. D. M. 297.] v. un-ginne. **-ginnendlic, -ginness.** v. on-ginnendlic, on-ginness.

**gin-ness,** es ; *f. A gap in time, an interval, break :*—Ginnisse *intercapidine,* Wrt. Voc. ii. 111, 62. Cf. giniau.

**ginung.** *Substitute :* **ginung, geonung, genung, gynung,** e ; *f.* I. *an opening of the mouth and the uttering of sound.* Cf. ginian ; I. 2 :—Genung *barritus,* Wrt. Voc. ii. 101, 47. Giuung oððe rāringc, 10, 68. Geonung, geþota, rārung, 125, 18. Geonung *garrulitas,* 40, 24. II. *an opening of the mouth to bite :*—Gynung *morsus,* Germ. 399, 271.

**gin-wised.** *Add :* l. (?) **gin-wīse** (gynn-) *of noble manners* (wīse). Cf. gin-fæst *for the sense of* gin- *in this compound.*

**giofolnes.** v. gifolnes : **giolu.** v. geolo : **gió-man.** v. geó-man : **giów.** v. gīw : **-gīpe.** v. æ-gīpe.

**gipian ;** *p.* ode. *To gape, yawn :*—Gypigendum *hiulcis,* Germ. 398, 113.

**gipung,** e ; *f. A gape, yawn :*—Gypunga *oris patuli,* Germ. 402, 39.

**gird.** *Take here* gerd, gyrd *in Dict., and add:* I. *of material.* (1) *a long thin bough of a tree or stem of a plant* whether growing or cut off :—Tōh gerd, tōch gerd *lentum vimen,* Txts. 75, 1207. Tōh gerd, Wrt. Voc. ii. 50, 74. Gerd *virgultum,* 123, 66. On gerde *hysopo,* Jn. L. R. 19, 29. Mid gerd (gerdum, R.) ł mið hreáde *harundine,* Mk. L. 15, 19. Gerd bifiende *harundinem quassatam,* Mt. L. 12, 20 : Lk. L. 7, 24. Wudebǣre gyrda *vimina siluestria,* An. Ox. 1806. Þæt hē menige tō þām wuda . . . and gefēdrige hys wǣnas mid fegrum gerdum, þæt hē mage windan manigne smicerne wāh, Solil. H. 1, 11. (2) *a rod, staff :*—Girde snace āwendre *uiminis* (Aaron's rod) *ex colubro transfigurati,* An. Ox. 156. Hē him bebeád þ hī nāht on wege ne nāmon būton gyrde (gerde, R., gerd, L.) āne, Mk. 6, 8. (3) *a rod* for chastisement or punishment :—Mid gierde mon bið beswungen, and mid stæfe hē bið āwreðed. Gif ðǣr ðonne sié gierd mid tō ðreágeanne, sié ðǣr eác stæf mid tō wreðianne, Past. 127, 1 : 117, 8. Ōstig gyrd *scorpio,* Wrt. Voc. i. 21, 17. Cild ic eom under gyrde drohtniende, Coll. M. 34, 23. Lāreów mīn āwecþ mē stīþlīce mid gyrde, 35, 31. Hē hēt hī ealle beswingan mid gyrdum, and sidðan beheáfdian, Hml. S. 29, 283. Ia. *a straight line* drawn as a mark :—*Ymniscus* ys seó gyrd þe byð betwyx þām twām pricon ligende, Angl. viii. 333, 44. II. *as a measure* (1) of length, *a rod, pole.* v. *passage under* weall-stellung *and* met-gird :—Ðæs landes . . . xxiii. gerda on lange, and on brǣde ðǣr hit brādest is fīf geurda, and ðǣr hit unbrādost is ānne geurde . . . ðonne eástrichte. .xliii. geurde and .vi. fēt tō ðǣre eáststrǣte ; ðonne sūðrichte .xx. geurde and .vi. fēt, C. D. V. 163, 13-30. (2) of area, *a virgate, fourth part of a hide, thirty acres.* v. Seebohm's Vill. Comm., Andrews's Old English Manor, s. v. *yardland :*—Ic gesealde hym āne gyrde landes tō underwedde . . . Ðis sind þā landgemǣro þǣre gyrde, Cht. Crw. 9, 119-122. Be gyrde (girde, *v. l.*) londes. Gif mon geþingað gyrde landes oþþe māre, Ll. Th. i. 146, 1-2. Gebūre gebyreð þ him man tō landsetene sylle .ii. oxan, and .i. cū, and .vi. sceáp, and .vii. æceras gesāwene on his gyrde landes, 434, 24. Hȳ lētan him tō þā twā hīda landes æt Āweltūne and āne gyrde, and æt Weattan īgge þreó gyrda, C. D. B. i. 543, 38-544, 1. v. breóst-, cyne-, hefeld-, hreód-, met-, segl-, sige-, sund-gird.

**gird-weg.** *Take here* gyrd-weg *in Dict., and add: A road made with faggots* (?) :—Of fearnhege an gerdwege ; of gerdwege tō fīf ācan, C. D. iii. 54, 27. Cf. beám-weg.

**gird-wīte.** *Take here* gyrd-wīte *in Dict.*

**girela, gierela, am ;** *m.* : **girelu, e ;** *f. Take here* gerela *in Dict., and add:* I. in a collective sense, *attire, apparel, clothing, garments :*—Ðā gimmas . . . scoldon scīnan on ðæs hiéhstan sācerdes hrægle . . . ðonne ne beóð hira gimmas on ðǣm gerēnum ðæs biscepes gierelan, Past. 135, 12. On lǣwedum hāde and on lǣwedum girelan, 411, 35. Macheus his āgenne sunu gemētte mid purpuran gegieredne on biscephāde. Hē hiene for þǣm girelan gebealg, and hiene hēt āhōn, Ors. 4, 4 ; S. 164, 32. Gyrlan *cultu,* An. Ox. 1194. Gyrle *habitu,* 3364. Hēt hē mīne gefēran þ hié ealne heora gerelan him of ādydon *ponere amicos uestes imperauit,* Nar. 27, 13. II. *a garment, robe :*—Wudewan gierela *theristotedes* (sumpto viduitatis *theristro,* Ald. 76, 8), Wrt. Voc. ii. 87, 46. Gyrlan *stola,* Germ. 397, 10. God reáfian lǣteð eówere dohtra heora gyrla and tō oferrancra heáfodgewǣda, Wlfst. 45, 25. Ðā ðe Crīste folgiað on hwītum gyrlum, Hml. Th. i. 88, 34. Gierelum gielplicum, Gū. 390. Ðā ðe mid hnescum gerelum (gyrlum, W.S.) gescirped biðon *qui mollibus vestiuntur,* Mt. L. 11, 8. v. cyne-, cyning-, godweb-, hrōþ-, mæsse-, weorold-girela (-u).

**girel-gyden** *the goddess of dress,* Vesta (the name has been connected by the glosser with *vestis*) :—Gyrlgyden *Uesta,* Germ. 397, 511.

**girelian, girelic.** v. ge-girelian, ge-girelic.

**girian.** v. girwan.

**girnan.** *Take here* geornan, gernan, gyrnan *in Dict., and add :*—Ic gewilnie ł gyrne *glisco,* An. Ox. 18 b, 39. I. *to desire possession of something* (*gen. or indecl. pron.*) :—Gilpes þū girnst ? ac þū hine ne miht habban orsogne *gloriam petis ? sed securus esse desistis,* Bt. 32, 1 ;

F. 114, 18. Hé gierneð (girneð, *v. l.*) ðæs folgoðes *magisterium appetit*, Past. 55, 21. Hé mid wilnunga his gæstes giernð ðæs écan gefeán *aeterna. gaudia spiritus ex desiderio expectat*, 395, 20. Anweald þe gé swíþost girnaþ *vestra expetibilis potentia*, Bt. 16, 1 ; F. 50, 32. Ða recceras ðe hira ágnes gilpes giernað *rectores qui semetipsos diligunt*, Past. 143, 22. Ðú wást þ . . ic ealles for swíþe ne girnde þisse eorþlican ríces ; búton ic wilnode andweorces . . . *scis ipsa minimum nobis ambitionem mortalium rerum fuisse dominatam ; sed materiam . . . optavimus*, Bt. 17 ; F. 58, 25. Þæs leánes þe heó lange gyrnde, Jud. 347. Diórwyrþra hrægla hí ne girndan, Bt. 15 ; F. 48, 5. Gyrnan þæs écean geférscipes, Bl. H. 197, 16. Gif hí on écnesse næren, ðonne nære hiora swá swíðe tó girnanne, Bt. 34, 9 ; F. 146, 25. **I a.** where the object is not expressed :—Ðæt hié cunnen hiora ægen gehealdan, and siððan ðæt hié ððerra monna ne giernen *ut tenere sua sciant, et tunc ut aliena non ambiant*, Past. 341, 9. **I b.** *intrans. To have a desire* for something, *long* for :—Þá gierndon æfter þám onwalde, Ors. 6, 28 ; S. 278, 10. **II.** *to desire to do, or attain an object.* (1) construction uncertain :—Gyrneð *gestit* (*saturare*), Wrt. Voc. ii. 96, 44. Gernað *gestiunt* (*incumbere*), 76, 26. Girnað, 40, 19. Ic girnde *nitebar*, 59, 79. Gernde *satagit* (*praeferre*), 95, 11. Gyrndon *satagistis*, i. *desideratis* (*dictare*), An. Ox. 5426. Giornende *ambientes*, Rtl. 87, 10. (2) with dat. infin. :—Gif se man gyrneð (*desideret*) Crístes líchaman tó underfónne, Ll. Th. ii. 176, 18. Hí náht ne gyrndon tó hæbbene, Bl. H. 53, 25. (3) with clause :—Þá gierað (girnð, *v. l.*) ðæt hé his welan íece *augere opes, ambit*, Past. 331, 15. Gé girnað þ gé woldon eówerne naman tóbrædan geond eall eorþan, Bt. 18, 2 ; F. 64, 4. **III.** *intrans. To desire to go, endeavour to get* to an object or place :—Mid ðý ða menigo giorndon on him *cum turbae inruerent in eum*, Lk. L. 5, 1. Ús gedafenað mid micelre eáðmódnysse gyrnan tó þám écan gefeán, Ll. Th. ii. 400, 2. **IV.** *to ask for, demand, require.* (1) with gen. or indecl. pron :—Swá micel swá þæs wífes wer girnð (*expetierit*), Ex. 21, 22. Se abb. þes biscophádes gernde, and se arceb. him forwernde, Chr. 1048 ; P. 172, 10. Þá gyrnde hé griðes and gísla, P. 174, 27 : 1093 ; P. 227, 32. Hí georndon friðes, 1011 ; P. 141, 10. Begann se cyngc gyrnan his sweostor him tó wífe, ac hé and his menn lange wiðcwædon, 1067 ; P. 201, 13. (**I a**) giving person to whom the request is made :—Nis þám sácerde þám men tó forwyrnane scriftes þe him þæs tó gyrnð (*qui eam ab eo desiderat*), Ll. Th. ii. 176, 7. Gif hí tó him friðes tó ne girndon, Chr. 1009 ; P. 139, 11. (2) with clause (and person to whom request made) :—Þá eorlas gerndon tó him þ hí móston beón wurðe . . ., Chr. 1052 ; P. 180, 6. Girne hé tó Godes þeówum þæt hý him *absolutionem* macigan, Wlfst. 180, 11. (3) used absolutely, *to ask* from a person :—Gyrn fram mé and ic selle [þé] þeóda *postula a me et dabo tibi gentes*, Ps. Rdr. 2, 8. **IV a.** *to beg* :—Blind sum gesætt giornðe í bæd (giornde, R.) *caecus quidam sedebat mendicans*, Lk. L. 18, 35. Ne mæg ic tó giornanne *non ualeo mendicare*, 16, 3. **IV b.** *to pray for* evil, *imprecate* :—Swá swá hé bæd, gyrnde *ut imprecabatur* i. *optabat*, An. Ox. 2820. **IV c.** the subject not personal :—Gif þing gesceádlic swá gyrnþ (*exigerit*), Angl. xiii. 374, 130. v. ge-girnan.

**girnend-líc** ; *adj. Desirable* :—On gyrnendlicum wurðscypum *in appetendis honoribus*, Scint. 111, 13. v. ge-girnendlic.

**girning**, e ; *f.* **I.** *desire to possess.* v. girnan ; **I** :—Sé ná wiðsæcð middanearde, þám eorðlicre æhte gegladað gyrnincg *is non renuntiat mundo, cui terrenae possessionis delectat ambitio*, Scint. 59, 12. Gyrninge *cupiditatis*, An. Ox. 5289. Fram middaneardes gyrninge fæstað *a mundi ambitione ieiunant*, Scint. 53, 18. **II.** *desire for doing.* v. girnan ; **II** :—Hié beóð onælede mid ðære gierninge (girn-, *v. l.*) ðára smeáunga Godes wísdómes ánes *solius contemplationis studiis inardescunt*, Past. 45, 17. **III.** *desire expressed in words, petition, prayer* :—Gyrninge (*desiderium*) þearfana gehýrde [Dryhten], gyrnenga (*desideria*) heortan heora gehýrde eáre his, Ps. Rdr. 9, 38. Drihten sylð ðé gewilnunga í gyrningce í béna (*petitiones*) heortan þínre, Ps. L. 36, 4. v. ge-girnung.

**girn-ness**, e ; *f.* **I.** *desire for something.* v. girnan ; **I** :—Sió hæfð góde girnesse metes, Lch. ii. 220, 27. Gyrnesse *voto*, Wrt. Voc. ii. 95, 15. **II.** *desire for action, endeavour, purpose.* Cf. girnan ; **II** :—Gyrnessæ *industria*, Txts. 70, 527. Gif hwá of giernesse and gewealdes ofsleá his þone néhstan *si quis per industriam occiderit proximum suum* (Ex. 21, 14), Ll. Th. i. 46, 26. Girnesse *operam*, Wrt. Voc. ii. 62, 56. **III.** *desire expressed in words, petition, prayer* :—Heora módes gyrnesse gehýrað þíne eáran *desideria cordis eorum audivit auris tua*, Ps. Th. 9, 37. v. georn-ness.

**girran.** *Take here* **georran** *in Dict., and add* :—Ic (*a file*) gyrre *garrio* (*garrio*, voce carens, rauco cum murmure stridens, Ald. 252, 25), An. Ox. 26, 13. Gyrran *grunnire* (porcinus paganorum strepitus *grunnire* desisteret, Ald. 60, 36), 4337. [v. *D.D.* yirr, yerr *to snarl, growl, yell* : *N.E.D.* garre : *O. H. Ger.* cherran *stridere, strepere.*] *See next word.*

**girrettan, gyrrettan** *to roar* :—Leó gyrretynde í grymetende *leo rugiens*, Ps. L. 21, 12. v. *See preceding word.*

**girst** : v. gríst : gírstan. v. gistran.

**girwan.** *Take here* **gierwan, gerwan, gyrwan, gierian, gerian,**

---

**gyrian** *in Dict., and add* : **I.** *to prepare, make ready* for some action, *set in order* for a purpose :—Fela þæra wæs wera and wífa þe þæt wínreced geredon, B. 994. Healf þæt blód hé dyde on geryde (*or under* **IV.** Or could possibly geryde *be a corruption of* (ge)eárede ? Cf. eárede fæt *cratera*, 24, 25) orcas (*in crateras*), Ex. 24, 6. **II.** *to prepare* oneself *to do something* :—Hió hié tó deáþe gerede, Ors. 5, 13 ; S. 246, 30. Hié giredon hié tó wíge, 3, 5 ; S. 106, 17. Hié hié tó gefeohte geredon, 4, 10 ; S. 202, 13. Ongan hine fýsan and tó fíote gyrwan, An. 1700. **III.** *to dress* :—Hié wuldres weard wædum gyrede, Gen. 941. **III a.** *to arm* :—Hé gyrede hine mid gæstlicum wæpnum, Gú. 148. Ic hié hét þ hié hié mid heora wæpnum gereden, Angl. iv. 144, 139. **IV.** *to ornament* :—Hié gyredon mé golde and seolfre, Kr. 77. **V.** *to prepare* food, a meal, &c. :—Geruað (*parant*) ðá ðegnas eóstro, Lk. p. 11, 2. Ðonne ðú feorme gierwe, Past. 323, 22. **VI.** *to prepare, make ready* for a purpose by some process :—Se háta sumor hæleða bearnum giereð and drígeð sæd and bléda, Met. 29, 59. Ne hí siarocræftum godweb giredon *nec norant lucida vellera Serum Tyrio miscere veneno*, 8, 25. **VII.** *to make* for a purpose :—Hé girað (*parat*) eorðan rén, Ps. Spl. 146, 8. On þám stedewange girwan Godes tempel, El. 1022. **VII a.** *to make* fit for a purpose (*with complement*) :—Sæ cýðde hwá hine gesette . . . , forþon hé hine tredne him ongeán gyrede, þonne God wolde ofer síne ýðe gán, Cri. 1167. **VIII.** *to make the necessary preparations for* :—Þæt ic þé symbledæg sette and gyrwe, Ps. Th. 75, 7. **IX.** *to direct* :—Ðonan hine hlódan hálge and gecorene siððan hine gierdon ðá ðe Gode hérdon ðurh hálgan béc hider on eorðan, Past. 469, 1. v. ge-, on-, un-girwan.

**girwung.** v. ge-girwung.

**giscian** *to sob. Add* :—Ic nú wépende and gisciende misíó, Bt. 2 ; F. 4, 8. [ȝyxyn, yexen *singulcio*, Prompt. Parv. 539. To ȝyske *singultire*, Cath. Ang. 426. v. *D. D.* yox. *O. H. Ger.* geskón *oscitare*.] v. gesca, *and next word.*

**giscung, geocsung, geoxung,** e ; *f. Sobbing* :—Geocsung *singultus*, Wrt. Voc. i. 54, 64. In sicettunge and geoxunge *in singultum*, ii. 46, 9. [ȝyxynge *singultus*, Prompt. Parv. 539. ȝiskynge *singultus*, Cath. Ang. 426. Cf. *O. H. Ger.* gesgizunga *singultum*.]

**gise.** *Take here* **gyse** *in Dict., and add* :—Wéne gé ðæt ægðer sié mid mé ge gise ge nese ? (*ut sit apud me est et non*), Past. 308, 9. 'Ne sæde ic þ . . . ?' 'Gyse,' cwæþ ic, ' þú þ sædest,' Bt. 34, 6 ; F. 142, 5. Hwí wolde God swá lytles þinges him forwyrnan . . . ? Gyse hú mihte Adam tócnáwan hwæt hé wære, búton hé wære gehýrsum on sumum þince his Hláforde ? *why, would God refuse him so small a thing . . . ? Yes ; how could Adam know what he was, unless he were obedient in some thing to his Lord?*, Hml. Th. i. 14, 4.

**gísel.** *Add* :—Gísel *obses*, An. Ox. 45, 4. Philippus, þá hé cniht wæs, wæs Thebanum tó gísle geseald (*obses Thebanis datus*), Ors. 3, 7 ; S. 110, 20. Gísl *obsidem*, Wrt. Voc. ii. 84, 3. Gíslas *obsides*, 115, 10. Hé siex hund gísla on his geweald underféng *sexcentis equitibus in obsidatum receptis*, Ors. 3, 8 ; S. 122, 3. Man gíslas (gýslas, *v. l.*) sylle friðe tó wedde, Ll. Th. i. 156, 5. In tó West-Sexan þyder hý scylan gafol and gíslas syllan, 350, 20. v. fore-, friþ-gísel.

**gísel-hád**, es ; *m. The state of being a hostage* :—Gíslháda *obsedatus*, Wrt. Voc. ii. 115, 27.

**gíslþu** (?) ; *f. The giving of hostages* (? v. gíslian) :—Gísldu *obsedatu* (as if connected with *obses* and *dare* ?), Wrt. Voc. ii. 63, 25. [*For a verbal abstract in* þ *see* -brecþ.]

**gi-sprunt.** v. ge-sprintan.

**gist.** *Take here* **gæst, gest, giest, gyst** *in Dict., and add* :—Gast *hospes*, Wrt. Voc. ii. 43, 37. **I.** *a stranger* :—Gest ic wæs *hospes eram*, Mt. L. 25, 36, 43, 44. Ne aron gié gestas . . . ah gié aron burgwaro háligra *non estis hospites . . . sed estis cives sanctorum*, Rtl. 82, 30. **II.** *a guest, one who is entertained at another's house* :—Si tertia nocte hospitatus fuerit . . . habeat eum ad rectum tanquam de propria familia, quod Anglice dicitur : ' Twá niht gest, þridde niht ágen héwe,' Ll. Lbmn. 648, 21. Gystes *hospites*, R. Ben. I. 94, 5.

**gist-ærn, -ern.** *Take here* **gest-, gyst-ærn** (*-ern*) *in Dict., and add* : **I.** *a place of entertainment for strangers* :—Gestærn *diversorium*, Wrt. Voc. ii. 25, 62. Eódon hí in sumes túngeréfan healle (giæstern, *v. l.*) *intrauerunt hospitium cujusdam uilici*, Bd. 5, 10 ; Sch. 600, 7. **II.** *a place of shelter* :—Gewát sió lió út of þám scræfe . . . and hió unc forgeaf þ gestern, Hml. A. 207, 407.

**gister-dæg** *yesterday* :—Giosterdoeg (gestordæge, R.) ðió seofunda heri hora septima, Jn. L. 4, 52.

**gistern-líc** (gyst-, *q. v. in Dict.*) ; *adj. Of yesterday* :—Ðám dæge ne fyligð merigenlic dæg, for ðan ðe him ne forestóp se gysternlica, Hml. Th. i. 490, 20. Dæg se georstenlica *dies hesterna*, Hy. S. 47, 10.

**gist-hús** (gæst-, *q. v. in Dict.*), es ; *n. A place of entertainment for strangers, a guest-chamber, hostel, hospice, an inn* :—Gisthús ælðeódigra manna *zenodochium*, Wrt. Voc. i. 58, 51. Gysthúses méd *hospitii merces*, Nap. 57, 10. Mæg hé witan þ hé bið on sýðfæte and wel gysthúses beþearf, Ll. Th. ii. 430, 25. Ðone gewundedan ðe mon lædde helfcuicne tó ðæm giesðhúse (giest-, *v. l.*) (*ad stabulum*), Past.

125, 8. In gesthúse *in diversorio*, Lk. R. L. 2, 7 : Hml. Th. i. 116, 1. Befrán se hálga wer on hwæs gesthúse hí metes onbirigdon, ii. 168, 2. Onféng hé þá in his gesthúse (*hospitio*), Gr. D. 194, 13. Ic wæs cuma and gé mé underféngon on eówrum gesthúsum, Wlfst. 288, 16 : Hml. Th. ii. 286, 12. ¶ used of permanent lodging :—Eustachius gelædde hí intó his gesthúse (cf. hé ðær drohtnode fíftýne geár, l. 216) ... þá cwæð hé tó þám húshláforde ..., Hml. S. 30, 258. [*O. H. Ger.* gast-hús *diversorium, hospitium.*]

**gistian;** *p.* ode *To be a guest, be lodged in another's house :*—On wrigylse fiðra þínra ic gystige (*I will lodge?* The Latin is *exultabo*), Ps. Cam. 62, 8. Líf mánfull tó gystigenne of húse on hús *uita nequam hospitandi de domo in domum* (it is a miserable life to go from house to house, Ecclus. 29, 24), Scint. 153, 15. [*v. N. E. D.* guest; *vb. Icel.* gista *to. pass the night at another's house.*]

**gistig.** v. gestig *in Dict.*

**gisting, e;** *f. The being a stranger, exile :*—Gestinccum (*one* c *above the line*) exilia, Wrt. Voc. ii. 107, 66. Gestincum, 30, 2.

**gist-líc** *hospitable* [cf. *O. H. Ger.* un-gastlíchi]. v. gast-lic *in Dict.* : **gist-líþe.** *Add :* v. un-gistlíþe ; cf. cum-líþe.

**gist-líþian** *to be hospitable :*—Gæstlíþiende *hospitales,* Nar. 38, 18 note.

**gistlíþ-ness** (gæst-, gest-, *q. v. in Dict.*) *hospitality :*—Swilce hé gest-líþnysse gegearwode *quasi hospitalitatem exhiberet,* Gr. D. 76, 19. Gestlíþnesse begangan, Bd. 1, 27 ; Sch. 64, 3. ¶ on gistlíþnesse *as a guest :*—Gif bescoren man gange him an gestlíðnesse, gefe him man ænes if a tonsured man go from house to house seeking entertainment, let it be given him once, Ll. Th. i. 38, 12. Hé sumne Godes mann preósthádes on gestlíðnysse onféng *clericum quendam hospitio recepit,* Bd. 1, 7 ; Sch. 20, 1. For þám cuman þe hé on gestlíðnysse (gyst-, *v. l.*) gefeormode *pro hospite quem susceperat,* Sch. 21, 8. On gestlíðnysse onfón *in hospitalitatem suscipere,* Gr. D. 77, 3. Wæs hé on sumum húse inne þe hé hwílum on gæstlíþnesse wunode (*hospitari solebat*), Guth. Gr. 171, 16. Cf. cum-líþnes.

**gistran.** v. giestron *in Dict., and add :*—Dæg gestran *dies hesterna,* Ps. Vos. 89, 4.

**gistran-æfen, es;** *m. Yesterday evening :*—Gyrstanæfenne (gyrstandæg on æfenne, *v. l.*) *vespere hesterno,* Gr. D. 190, 12. Gierstanæfenne (gyrstanæfen, *v. l.*) *hesterno die sero,* 22, 21. Þá hláfas þe ús gyrstanæfen cómon, Hml. S. 23, 469, 517.

**gistran-dæg** (gyrstan-, *q. v. in Dict.*), *es ; m. Yesterday :*—Swá geostrandæg (deg geostran, Ps. Srt.) *dies hesterna,* Ps. Th. 89, 4. Gierstandæge *horno,* Wrt. Voc. ii. 43, 35. Be þám hú gyrstandæge cwæð, Guth. 74, 4. Gyrstandæg *heri,* Jn. 4, 52 : An. Th. 22, 1. Gyrstandæg (girston-, georsten, *v. ll.*), Ælfc. Gr. 224, 2. Gyrstandæg gemedemode úre Drihten hine sylfne ..., nú tó dæg Stephanus ... tó heofenum férde, Hml. Th. i. 56, 28 : ii. 286, 26 : Hml. S. 23, 468.

**gistran-niht, e;** *f. Yesternight :*—Gystranniht, B. 1334.

**gist-sele.** v. gest-, gyst-sele *in Dict.* : -**git.** v. and-, on-git.

**git** *ye two. Add :*—Cwæð hé tó him (cf. handþegnas twégen, 62, 5) : 'Ac tó hwon sweriað git mán?', Guth. 64, 6. v. inc.

**git** *yet.* l. gít. [*The word is often accented in the MSS., and only in such cases is the accent given in the following passages.*] I. when doing or being is continued up to, and exists at, a time stated or implied, *yet, still.* (1) alone :—Hé bútan ælcre synne wæs and giet is, Past. 261, 25. Rómáne þe giet rícsiende sindon, Ors. 2, 1 ; S. 58, 30 : 64, 2. Him mon áscóp þá noman þe hié giet habbað, 2, 4 ; S. 72, 14. Se sácerd sceolde and git (giet, *v. l.*) sceal gedéncean, Past. 77, 24. Giet (gitt, *v. l.*), 79, 5. Gett *adhuc,* Jn. L. R. 12, 35. (2) with defining words (*nú, þonne, þá, tó dæg(e),* &c.) :—Hé nú giet (git, *v. l.*) wilnað, Past. 361, 3. Hié nú giet rícsiende sindon, Ors. 2, 1 ; S. 62, 30 : 2, 4 ; S. 76, 1 : 2, 8 ; S. 92,16. Nú get, Met. 17, 5. Nú geot, Bt. 36, 2 ; F. 174, 22. Nú gyt *adhuc,* Bt. 41, 27 ; Sch. 73, 3 : Ps. Th. 91, 13. Gé sint ealle míne gewietan ðæt ic eom cléne nú giet (git, *v. l.*) tó dæg eówres ælces blódes *contestor vos hodierna die, quia mundus sum a sanguine omnium,* Past. 379, 14. Nú giet tó dæge (*usque ad nunc*) hit is on leóðum sungen, Ors. 2, 4 ; S. 72, 10. Nú giet tó dæge mon hætt ðæt lond ' Mánfeld' *campus nunc* 'Sceleratus' *vocatur,* 108, 19. Nú get æt þysne andweardan dæg, Bl. H. 125, 16. Hé þá giet lytel landríce hæfde, Ors. 2, 2 ; S. 66, 14. Hwæðer sincende sæflód þá gyt wære, Gen. 1437. Þá giet ðá, Gr. D. 36, 15 : Ll. Th. i. 56, 5. Þá giet þá Alexander hám cóm, þá giet wæs on him se mæsta þurst monnes blódes *Alexander apud Babyloniam adhuc sanguinem sitiens,* Ors. 3, 9 ; S. 136, 11. Þá gyt þe ic wæs gehefaldod *dum adhuc ordirer,* Cant. Ez. 12. Ðá ðe ðanne gít (git, *v. l.,* giet, 319, 13) willniað, Past. 17, 19. Gif hié ðonne giet (git, *v. l.*) tueónað, 103, 9 : 63, 14 : Gr. D. 322, 29. Seó stów gewearþ swiþe mære, and giet tó dæge is, Ors. 3, 8 ; S. 120, 21. Gé giet tó dæge wæron Somnitum þeówe *hodie Romani Samnio servierunt,* S. 122, 12. Giet tó dæge *usque in hodiernum dæg,* Ors. 2, 2 ; S. 216, 3. Giet oð þisne dæg, 3, 5 ; S. 104, 27. II. in negative sentences, where doing or being has not existed up to, and does not exist at, a time stated or implied, where the time of an action or condition has not been reached (*not*) *as yet.* (1) alone :—Þá þe gyt ne mihton breóstnet wera

werigean, Exod. 235. Ic ne beládige gýt mé for ylde, Hml. Th. ii. 516, 27. (2) with defining words. Cf. I. 2 :—Gé hit ne magon nú giet (git, *v. l., nunc*) áberan, Past. 237, 13. Ic cóm ... and nú git ic ná minne múþ ne ontýnde, and hé cóm and slóh cymbalan, Gr. D. 62, 21. Hé næfde gefylled ðá giet (git, *v. l.*) ðone rím his gecorenra, 43, 21 : 213, 24. Hé ðá giet nolde hí læran, 459, 21. Þá giet, Ors. 3, 11 ; S. 152, 14. Gif Críst geboren nære þá giet, 6, 9 ; S. 264, 13. Þá get, Bt. 18, 3 ; F. 64, 9. Þá gýt, Bl. H. 213, 14. Ná þá gyt næs *nondum,* An. Ox. 1296 : Jud. 107. Ne mæg ðonne git cuman tó ðæm betstan, Past. 399, 11. Ðonne git, 383, 35. Gít (giet, *v. l.*), 183, 6. Git (giet, *v. l.*) 233, 1. Giet (git, *v. l.*), 19, 10. Æppel þe þonne gyt (git, *v. l.*) ne reádige, Lch. i. 330, 21. Ne ænig nédþearf næs æfre giet, Met. 20, 20. II a. with the verb in the imperative (*do not*) *yet :*—Gemiltsa ús swiðor, and swá gýt ne forlæt, Hml. Th. ii. 516, 24. III. where doing or being exists at, and is continued from, a time stated or implied, *still, yet.* (1) alone :—Ic sceal sellan eów giet mioloc drincan, Past. 459, 18 : Gen. 2663. Wundor ðær weorþ and gýt beóð æteówed, Bl. H. 209, 15. Ne wiðcweðe ic tó deorfenne gýt, gif ic nýdbehéfe eom gýt ðínum folce, Hml. Th. ii. 516, 26. *Tempore futuro amabor* ic beó gelufod gyt, Ælfc. Gr. Z. 140, 16, 18 : B. 2512. (2) with other words :—Medmicel fæc nú gyt wuna mid ús, Bl. H. 247, 33. Hé wolde ðá giet yfel dón, Past. 457, 25. Gif þám folce þá giet misspeówe *si adversa belli perseverassent,* Ors. 2, 5 ; S. 82, 34 : 5, 9 ; S. 232, 15 : 1, 1 ; S. 17, 12 : Chr. 918 ; P. 98, 16. Þá gyt, Gen. 1189 : B. 1127. Philippuses yfel mehte þeh þá giet gemetlic þyncan ... þeh ic nú his dæda sume hwíle gesugian, Ors. 3, 7 ; S. 120, 15. Ic sóhte þíne ansýne, ic séce gyt symle (*requiram*), Ps. Th. 26, 9. III a. in negative sentences, (*not*) *any longer, henceforth :*—Ne þearft þú þe ondrædan nú giet, Gen. 1038. III b. in hypothetical clauses, *at any future time :*—On ealra gebedrædenne þe Crístene wæron oþþe gýt sýn, Bl. H. 47, 1. IV. with the idea of addition, extension, resumption, repetition, &c., *yet further, yet again.* (1) alone :—Þá word þe ic hér git (gyt, *v. l.*) secgan wille *ea quae subjungo,* Gr. D. 42, 19. Nú wille wé eác læran ... And git wé willað myngian, Ll. Th. i. 326, 1–6. Ic ðé wolde get (giet, *v. l.*) hwæthwega sweotolor gereccan, Bt. 36, 3 ; F. 176, 3. Nú wé sprǽcon be cynegum, wé willað be sumum cynincge eów cýðan git, Hml. S. 24, 82. (2) with other words :—Hé him wæs wániende his ágene heardsælða, and hé þá giet him selfum gedyde þæt þæt wyrrest wæs *he was lamenting his hard fortune, and then went on to do himself the worst evil of all,* Ors. 4, 5 ; S. 166, 21. Þá git hé him gesealde máðmas xii, B. 1866 : þá gyt, 47 : 1050. Wífa þá gyt, An. 1041. Wæs þára manna þe þær ofslegene wæron ... and þá hí gýt genáman þæs folces ..., Bl. H. 79, 20. Hé þá giet þriddan síþe wæs wilniende ..., Ors. 2, 5 ; S. 82, 7 : 3, 9 ; S. 126, 9. Þá git him wæges weard wið þingode, An. 632. Þá gyt, 1197 : Gen. 1476 : 1510. Him þá gyt gewát Abraham ..., 1793. V. where an event is certain but the time not fixed, *yet :*—Giet cymð se micla Godes dæg, Past. 245, 4. Þás gyldnan gatu giet sume síðe God wile gefælsian, Cri. 318. Hí habbaþ manega sáula on heora gewaldum þe him wile git God miltsian, Bl. H. 47, 7. God hine onwrýhþ gyt, þeáh þe wit hine ne geopenian, 187, 17. VI. with the idea of incompleteness, where an end is not reached, where something remains to be done, *still, yet.* (1) alone :—Twelf wítegan syndon tó eácan þisum git, Ælfc. T. Grn. 10, 8. Git mæg þeáh bót cuman, Ll. Th. i. 348, 23. Gyt (gett, L. R.) ic hæbbe eów fela tó secgenne, Jn. 16, 12. (2) with other words :—Nú gít þrý dagas tó láfe syndon, Bl. H. 231, 19. Ic wát manig nú gyt mære spell, An. 815. Him þæt þá git tó lytel yfel þúhte búton hié eác hié þæs naman benáme, Ors. 2, 8 ; S. 94, 3. Æfter þám þá giet þæs ilcan hærfestes *afterwards still in the same autumn,* Chr. 921 ; P. 102, 17. Ðær tó láfe ðá get wæs ..., 973 ; P. 119, n. 6. His módor þá get wolde sorhfulne síð, B. 1276. Þá gyt (get, L.) þá hé wæs feorr his fæder *cum adhuc longe esset,* Lk. 15, 20. Ðeáh hió him ðonne giet feorr sié, Past. 363, 19. VII. with degrees of comparison. (1) alone :—Giet swiðor hié syngiað, Past. 123, 1. Hé hæfde giet þe má unþeáwa þonne his eám hæfde *avunculi sui erga omnia vitia sectator, immo transgressor,* Ors. 6, 5 ; S. 260, 28. Gét wyrse, Bl. H. 41, 7. Git swiðor on scræfes onlicnesse, 207, 19. Gýt mære, 101, 6. Gyt lator, Chr. 1089 ; P. 225, 14. Gyt gelícra, Ps. Th. 88, 5. Swiðor giet, Met. 28, 71. Get, 21, 25. Wyrse get, 25, 67. Giet sceal ic monigfealdlecor sprecan, Ors. 2, 1 ; S. 62, 9. Git, An. 1489. Hé dyde git eallra wærst, Chr. 1087 ; P. 223, 22. (2) with other words :—Þá giet leng winnan, Ors. 2, 5 ; S. 78, 18 : 82, 32. Té þon þ hié þá git swiþor blóten þonne hié ær dyden, 4, 4 ; S. 162, 30. Þonne git læssan, Ll. Th. i. 342, 3. [*Goth.* ju bita.]

**gita.** l. gíta, *and add:* I. 1. Cf. gít ; I. 1 :—Ic þæt gýta geman, Kr. 28. I. 2. Cf. gít ; I. 2 :—Ðeáh ðú hí nú géta forgiten hæbbe, Met. 24, 46. On Angelcirican þú ána nú gýta (*accented in MS.*) ár biscop geméted *in Anglorum ecclesia adhuc solus tu episcopus inueniris,* Bd. 1, 27 ; Sch. 73, 3. II. in negative sentences. (1) cf. gít II. 1 :—Ne can þára idesa ówðer giéta beorna neáwest, Gen. 2466 (2) cf. gít ; II. 2 :—Ic cóm tó þyses gereordes mýsan, and ic nú gýt ne geopenode minne múð (*os adhuc ad laudem Dei non aperui*) tó Gode,

lofe, and hé cóm and slyhð cymbalan, Gr. D. 62, 19. Næs ðeós eorðe besmiten þá gēta beornes blóde, Met. 8, 33. **III.** in interrogative sentences :—Hwæðer sǽ þá gýta dǽl ǽnigue eorðan ofgifen hæfde, Gen. 1453. **IV.** 1. Cf. gít; **IV.** 1 :—þá þing þe ic hér tó gíta geþeóde *ea quae subjungo*, Gr. D. 42, 18. **IV.** 2. Cf. gít; **IV.** 2 :—Se Wísdóm gól gyd æfter spelie, song sóðcwida sumne þá gēta, Met. 7, 3. **V.** with idea of incompleteness. Cf. gít; **VI.** 2 :—Hé þá gíta feorron *adhuc longe positus*, Gr. D. 36, 15. **VI.** with comparatives. Cf. gít; **VII.** :—þás þeófas willað ríxian gýta (*accented in MS.*) swíðor þonne hig ǽr dydon, Ll. Th. i. 238, 23.

**gíta**, an; *m.* v. á-gíta.

**gitan.** Add :—Oð ðæt hé mid dǽdbóte forgifennesse gite (cf. R. Ben. 49, 9 *which has* begyte) *usque dum satisfactione veniam consequatur*, R. Ben. I. 56, 15.

**gítan, gētan**; *p.* te To *destroy* :—Mēces ecgum gētan, B. 2940. v. á-gítan.

**-gitel, -gitelness.** v. for-, ofer-gitel, -gitelness: -gíten. v. forgiten: -gitenness. v. on-gitenness.

**giþ-corn.** Add :—Giðcorn *herba munda*, Wrt. Voc. i. 30, 60. Giþcorn *citocacia*, 31, 45. [*Spurgia* spurge, guþcorn (? *printed* guweorn), 140, 32 (*middle of* 13th cent.). Cf. *O. H. Ger.* getto lolium. For giþ cf. *Lat.* git(i), gith(i) *name of a plant*. v. *N. E. D.* gith. *See also* Lch. ii. 248, 2 : Gitte hātte suþerne wyrt.]

**giþ-rife.** Add :—*Lassar vel æsdre* gyþrife, Wrt. Voc. ii. 54, 25.

**-giting.** v. for-giting: gitness. v. ofer-, on-gitness.

**gitsere.** Add : **gíetsere, gídsere** :—Gítsere *avarus vel cupidus*, Wrt. Voc. i. 47, 48. Gýtsere *avarus*, 76, 7. Ðæt se gítsere (gídsere, *v. l.*), him on geheápige ða byrðenne eorðlíca ǽhta, Past. 329, 20 : 331, 7. Gíetsere (gídsere, *v. l.*), 341, 6. Ne ða ðiófas, ne ða giétseras *neque fures, neque avari*, 401, 28. Þá gítseras (gýtseras, *v. l.*), Ll. Th. i. 420, 1. v. feoh-, weoruld-gítsere.

**gítsian.** Add : **giétsian, gídsian** :—Ðonne hié gítsiað ealdordómes, Past. 63, 16. Gítsiað (gídsiað, *v. l.*), 335, 8. Giétsiað (gídsiað, *v. l.*), 299, 10. Ðæt hié ðissa eorðlícena góda tó suiðe ne giétsien (gítsien, *v. l.*), 263, 10. Ðæt wé his ne gítseden (gídsoden, *v. l.*), 33, 18. Giétsian (gítsian, *v. l.*) and reáfian, 341, 4. Giétsiende (gídsiende, *v. l.*), 61, 11. (2) with dat. :—Reáflácum gýtsian *rapinas concupiscere*, Ps. Spl. 61, 10. v. ge-gítsian.

**gítsiend-ness**, e; *f. Avarice* :—Ða deóflican eahta leahtras . . . gítsiendnes (*avaritia*), Wlfst. 188, 36.

**gítsung.** Add : **giétsung, gídsung** :—Gídsung, gítsung *appetitus*, Txts. 41, 184. Gítsung, Wrt. Voc. i. 287, 68 : ii. 8, 61. Se þridda leahter is *auaritia*, þ is seó yfele gítsung (gýttsung, *v. l.*), Hml. S. 16, 280. *Radix omnium malorum est cupiditas* gítsung is wyrtruma ǽghwylces yfeles, Wlfst. 69, 9. For ðǽre gewilnunga woruldgielpes and giétsunga (gídsunge, *v. l.*), Past. 157, 2. Gítsunge *philargiria*, Wrt. Voc. ii. 96, 67 : An. Ox. 7, 226. Ðiófento, gítsunge (gítsungas, L.) *furta, auaritiae*, Mk. R. 7, 22. Deóflíce dǽda . . . on gítsungan and on gíernessan, Ll. Th. i. 310, 17. v. deófol-, feoh-, náwiht-, unriht-, weoruld-gítsung.

**giúluling** *July* :—Giúluling *quintus* (*mensis*), Wrt. Voc. ii. 118, 48. Cf. Quintilis, iulius, Corp. Gl. H. 100, 53. Quintilis in honorem Iuli Caesaris Iulius vocatur, Bede De Templ. Rat. c. xii.

**giw.** *l.* gíw, *and add*: gíu, gíg :—Gíu *gripem*, gíu *griphus*, Wrt. Voc. ii. 41, 3-4. Gíg *gripem*, 110, 1. Geówes hé hafað fiðeru and griffus fēt, Sal. 264.

**giwian.** Add :—Giowað (giuiað, giueð, giuað, L.) *petit, petierit*, Lk. R. 11, 10-12. Giuias, Mt. L. 7, 9. Giuiað *postulat*, Rtl. 92, 32. Giueð *petit*, Mt. L. 5, 42. Ue giugað *poscimus*, Rtl. 52, 10. Gié giuigas *petieritis*, 21, 22. Gé giowigas (giuað, L.), Jn. R. 16, 26 : Mk. R. (L.) 11, 24. Giowigas (giwiged, L.), 10, 28. Giwas, Mt. L. 20, 22. Giuað *petunt*, Lk. L. 12, 48. Giwude, Mt. L. 20, 20. Giuede, Mk. L. 15, 43. Giuede, Lk. L. 23, 52. Giowias (giuiað, L.) *petite*, R. 11, 9. Giowigas (giuað, L.), Jn. R. 16, 24. Ic giowade (giude, L.) ł giowigia (giuge, L.) walde *exigissem*, Lk. R. 19, 23. Giwigende *postulante*, Lk. p. 9, 13 : *poscenti*, Jn. p. 6, 17. Giwende *petendum*, Lk. p. 7, 4. Giowendum (giuendum, L.) *petentibus*, Lk. R. 11, 13. Giugiende *petenti*, Lk. L. 6, 30. v. ge-giwian.

**glade** (?); *adv. Joyousiy, gladly* :—Hié of þám grimman gryre glade treddedon, Dan. 439. Hí fore góddǽdum glade blissiað, Cri. 1287. [Glade *here might be n. pl. of* glæd.]

**gladian.** Add : **I.** intrans. (1) *to be bright, shine, gleam* (of polished metal) :—On him gladiað gomelra láfe, B. 2036. (2) *to be glad, rejoice* :—Hwílon heó besárgað hyre líchoman sárnissa, hwílon heó gladað on gódum gelimpum, Hml. S. 1, 221. (2 a) *to rejoice in something possessed* :—Februarius and Martius gladiað on fífum, Angl. viii. 302, 1. **II.** trans. (1) *to make glad.* (a) of physical effect, *to make of cheerful appearance* :—Ðæt hé gleadie onsíene in ele *ut exhiberet faciem in oleo*, Ps. Srt. 103, 15. (b) of mental effect, *to gladden, cheer* :—þ hí widuwan and steópcild georne gladian, Ll. Th. i. 326, 26. (2) *to please* :—Þá þe mid clǽnnysse him gecwēmað on life and on gódum weorcum hine gladiað nú, Hml. A. 15, 54. Utan gladian georne God, Wlfst. 112, 12. (3) *to make gentle, soften, appease* :—Mildode man-

*suescit*, gladode *mitigat*, Germ. 399, 436. Gladode *demulcet, pro demulcebat* (mentem . . . nec blandimentorum lenitas *demulcet*, Ald. 40, 36), An. Ox. 3004. v. ge-gladian.

**gladung**, e; *f.* **I.** *rejoicing, an expressing of gladness.* Cf. gladian; **I.** 2 :—Mid heora handum wyrcende sealmas singaþ, swylce hý heora geswinc mid godcundre gladunge (*divino celeunate.* Cf. *celeuma* sǽleóþ, Wrt. Voc. ii. 22, 24 : *celeuma*, i. *leta cantatio*, 130, 19 : *celeuma* cantus nautarum quem in prosperis praesertim concinnebant, Ducange) gefremmen, R. Ben. 137, 15. **II.** *a gladdening, cheering.* Cf. gladian; **II.** 1 b :—Ne bið ðǽr árfæstnys ne sibb ne hopa ne ǽnig gladung, ðýhð se frófur áweg *nec pax nec pietas immo spes nulla quietis flentibus arrideret, fugiunt solatia cuncta* (v. ge-gladian; **I.** 1 b), Wlfst. 139, 13. **III.** *an appeasing.* v. gladian; **II.** 3 :—Gladunge *placationem*, Ps. L. 48, 8. [v. *N. E. D.* gladding.] v. ge-gladung.

**glæd**; *n.* Add : [v. *N. E. D.* glad; *sb.*]

**glæd**; *adj.* Add : **I.** of living things, *cheerful, joyous, lively* :—Glæd *alacer*, Ælfc. Gr. Z. 44, 8 : *ludibundus*, Germ. 397, 409. (1) *of cheerful disposition* :—Swíðe glæd on móde, Ælfc. T. Grn. 16, 41. Þǽr ic (a *woodpecker*) glado sitte, Rä. 25, 7. Ðone gladan giefan *hilarem datorem*, Past. 323, 12. On óðre wísan sint tó manianne ða gladan (*laeti.* Cf. ða blíðan, 14), on óðre ða unrótan (*tristes*), 187, 12. Hé heóld þenden lifde glæde Scyldingas, B. 58. (2) *cheerful in appearance* :—Hé weard glæd on his ansýne *hilari facie*, Guth. Gr. 108, 27. (3) *well-disposed, kindly, gentle* ; *placatus, placabilis, placidus* :—Glæd bið se Godes sunu gif þú gnorn þrowast and þe sylfum dēmst *aeternus fuerit placidus te vindice judex*, Dóm. L. 86. Críst, eádiges mǽdenes glæd hálgum bēnum *Christe, beatae Virginis placatus sanctis precibus*, Hy. S. 119, 8. Gladum suna Fródan, B. 2025. Ic mínne can glædne Hróðulf, 1181 : 863. Ðæt wē ðone Hǽlend hæbben ús glædne, and hé ús gewissige and úrne eard gehealde and æfter geendunge ðæt ēce líf ús forgife *ut nos Deum placatum rectorem habere queamus*, C. D. iii. 60, 8. (3 a) *well-disposed* towards (*wiþ*) :—Mín Drihten hine gedó glædne wið eów *Deus meus faciat vobis eum placabilem*, Gen. 43, 14. (4) *glad* on account of a particular circumstance. (a) the circumstance given in the context :—Herodes gesēne ðone Hǽlend glæd wæs *Herodes uiso Iesu gauisus est*, Lk. L. R. 23, 8. Se middangeard bið glaedde (*gaudebit*), Jn. L. 16, 20. Glǽde uēron gauisi sunt, 20, 20. (b) with prep. :—Hé bið glæd (*gaudet*) fore stefne ðæs brýdgumes, Jn. L. 3, 29. Þ folc wæs glæd on allum ðǽm wundrum *populus gaudebat in universis quae fiebant*, Lk. L. R. 13, 17. Monigo in ácennisse his biðon glæde, Lk. L. R. 1, 14. (c) with clause :—Him mæg beón þe glædre his heorte þe hē sum þing hēr of undergyte, Angl. viii. 317, 39. **II.** of things. (1) of thoughts, looks, *expressing gladness* :—Hí gesáwon hine habban glædne andwlitan, Hml. Th. i. 72, 27. Him Godes engel þurh glædne geþonc þá wísan onwráh, Cri. 315. (2) of a place, *suggestive of gladness, delightful* :—In þám gladan hám *in that home of pure delight*, Ph. 593. (3) *mild, gentle* :—Beón dagas blíþe and glæde nihta sint dies laeti placideque noctes, Hy. S. 143, 12. v. ǽr-, mód-, un-glæd.

**glǽdan** *to cause to slip or totter. A compound form,* á-glǽdan, *seems to be concealed in the gloss* :—Labefacare agleddego, Txts. 111, 9. Cf. *O. Sax.* biglēdda. Labefactat, Gall. 23.

**glǽdene.** *Substitute:* **glǽdene**, an; *f. Gladdon* :—Glaedine, gladinae, gledinae *scilla*, Txts. 95, 1815. Glǽdene *gladiolum*, Wrt. Voc. i. 30, 49 : ii. 42, 30 : *scilla*, 68, 58 : 286, 38 : *scilla et gladiola*, 69, 5. *Lappatium* docce, ł. gledene, ł. *carix, gladiolum* secgg, Wülck. Gl. 297, 25-26. Þás wyrte þe man *bulbis scillitici* and óðrum naman glǽdene nemneð, Lch. i. 144, 22. *Gladiolum* and óþrum naman glǽdeue, 182, 14. Hand fulle secges and glǽdenan, ii. 356, 1. Wyl secg and glǽdenan neoðewearde, iii. 20, 4. [*From Latin?*]

**glǽdlic.** Add : **I.** *kindly, gentle.* v. glæd; **I.** 3 :—Tunge glætlic treów lifes *lingua placabilis lignum uitae*, Scint. 78, 10. **II.** of a thing, *delightful.* Cf. glæd; **II.** 2, 3 :—Glǽdlicne drenc *delectabilem potum*, Scint. 13, 12. v. un-glǽdlic.

**glǽdlíce.** Add : **I.** *with feelings of gladness, cheerfully, joyously* :—Manna gehwylc tó weorðunge his Drihtne dó tó góde þæs þe hē mæge wordes and dǽde glǽdlíce (*hilariter*) ǽfre, Ll. Th. i. 424, 22. Wē tódǽlað þá dagas þurh seofon, and swá glǽdlíce wē becumað tó þám andgite swá myceles gerēnes, Angl. viii. 302, 39. **II.** of ready, willing action, *cheerfully, with alacrity* :—þ Crístes lufu neádwíse wē gelǽstan glǽdlíce (*alacriter*), Hy. S. 120, 11 : Wlfst. 73, 22. v. un-glǽdlíce.

**glǽd-man**; *adj.* Add : *Take here from* glæd *in Dict.* :—Glǽdman *hilaris*, Wrt. Voc. i. 50, 67. Glǽdman Hróþgár, B. 367. [*Kluge suggests that man is cognate with Gothic* muns. v. E. S. xx. 335.]

**glǽd-mód.** **I.** *having glad thoughts, cheerful, joyous.* (1) of permanent disposition. v. glæd; **I.** 1 :—Sē þe wǽre hohmód, weorðe sē glædmód, Wlfst. 72, 8. (2) of an occasional frame of mind. Cf. glæd; **I.** 4. (a) of joy caused by temporal conditions :—Þǽr beorn monig glædmód, wlonc and wíngál wíghyrstum scán, Ruin. 34. Eáðhréðige glædmóde gégan hæfdon tó þám wealgeate, Jud. 140. (b) of mægð . . . *of spiritual joy, with gladsome mind* :—Se biscop glædmód eóde gumena þreáte God hergendra, El. 1096. Biseah tó heofona ríce glædmód, Gú.

1277: 1035. **II.** *of ready mind, having a mind that prompts to quick action.* Cf. glædlíce; II:—Hé fíyhđ yfia gehwylc ... glædmód gyrneđ (*is quick to desire*) þæt hé gódra mǽst dǽda gefremme, Ph. 462. **III.** *of gentle mind, having kindly thoughts:*—Eóde þá fromlíce fǽmnan tó sprǽce ... þær hé glædmód geonge wiste wíc weardian (cf. the later prose version : Affrican hire feader feng on earst feire on to lokin ʒef he mahte wiđ eani luue speden, Juliana, 11, 13), Jul. 91.

**glædnes.** *Add* : **I.** *the state or feeling of being glad.* v. glæd; **I. 1:**—Syndon eahta heálíce mægnu ... glædnes (*laetitia*, cf. Hml. S. 16, 345) and ánrædnys (*the opposites of* unrótnys *and* ásolcennys), Wlfst. 69, 1. Þte glædnise (*gaudium*) mín in iúch sié, Jn. L. 15, 11. Hí gesíđodon tó Críste ... fram eallum costnungum tó ealre glædnysse *from all temptations to joy,* Hml. A. 26, 42. Mid ege and mid micle glædnise, Mt. L. 28, 8. Fore gladnise *prae gaudio,* 13, 44. Unródtnis iuero gecerred bið in glædnise, Jn. L. 16, 20. **I a.** *gladness on account of something.* v. glæd; **I. 4:**—Wíf đín beres đé sunu ... And bið gefeá đé and glædnise (*gaudium tibi et exultatio*), Lk. R. L. 1, 14. Đis for đon glædnise mín gefylled is *hoc ergo gaudium meum impletum est,* Jn. L. 3, 29. **II.** *a pleasurable condition, state of happiness :*—Glædnys *ludus,* Germ. 398, 64. Geong iu glædnisse hláferdes đínes, Mt. L. 25, 23. On xxvii and on xxviii nihta þ tácnađ ealne gefeán, and ealle angnysse and uneáđnysse smyltnysse and glædnesse gehátađ, Lch. iii. 156, 14. **III.** *alacrity, cheerful readiness.* Cf. glædlíce; II:—Gode man sceal dón mid glædnysse ǽfre þá betstan behát, Hml. A. 35, 272. Þá Godes þegnas mid glædnysse efston, ástræhton heora swuran tó slæge for Críste, Hml. S. 28, 70. **IV.** *kindness, gentleness, favourable consideration, favour.* v. glæd; **I. 3:**—His glednes *hilaritas eius* (sicut ros super herbam, ita et *hilaritas eius* (sc. regis)), Kent. Gl. 688. Mycel glædnysse on him wæs *humilitatem in corde praeferebat.* Guth. Gr. 170, 175.

**glæd-scipe.** *Add:*—Þæt wé magon cuman tó þám eásterlican dæge þe aa byð mid fullum glædscipe and wynsumnysse and ēcere blisse, Angl. viii. 323, 40. [v. *N. E. D.* gladship.]

**glǽm.** *Add:* [v. *N. E. D.* gleam.]

**glæppe,** an; *f. Buck-bean* (?) :—Þás wyrta ... bisceopwyrt and glæppe and ribbe and gearwe, Lch. iii. 292, 5. Ælcre namcúþre wyrte dæl bútan glappan ánon, i. 398, 9. Cf. On glæppan felda, C. D. ii. 411, 20 : iii. 227, 34. An gleppan felda, ii. 74, 3. [Glapthorne occurs several times as a place-name in Latin charters.]

**glær,** es; *n. Substitute* : **glær,** es; *m. Amber* :—Smilting *vel* glær *electrum,* Wrt. Voc. i. 34, 66. Glær *succinum,* 286, 68. Glæres *sucini,* An. Ox. 1074: *sucine,* Wrt. Voc. ii. 77, 26. Glaeres *sucini,* 121, 63. Glæsas (glæras?) *sucina* (sucinum est electrum arboris, i. resina), Germ. 397, 21. [*O. H. Ger.* clases *electri.* Cf. Tacitus : 'Succinum quod ipsi *glesum* vocant,' and Pliny : 'A Germanis appellari *glessum* ... et a nostris unam insularum ob id *glessariam* appellatam.']

**glæs,** es; *n. Add:*—Án wurđlic weorc of glæse and of golde, Hml. S. 5, 252. Hwylce þinc gelǽdst þú ús? Mǽstlingc, ǽr and tin, swefel and glæs (*vitrum*), Coll. M. 27, 11. Hafa gebrocen glæs geara gegrunden ... sóna swá se wyrm þæs onbirigð, þonne swilt hé, Lch. ii. 114, 16. Cnúa glæs tó dúste, dó huniges teár on, lácua þ dolg mid, 128, 4.

**glæs,** es; *m. A glass vessel.* (1) *a glass for drinking:*—Hé sende him glæs fulne wínes *misit ei calicem uini,* Bd. 5, 5; Sch. 572, 7. (2) *a cupping-glass:*—Teóh mid glæse on þá sculdru, Lch. ii. 262, 5. Hwílum þú teóh mid glæse ođđe mid horne blód of þám sáran stówum, Lch. ii. 280, 23: 200, 13. Lǽt him blód þus; sete glæs on ođđe horn, and teó þ blód út, 232, 25: 206, 23.

**glæsen.** *Add:*—Beó ælc calic geworht of myldendum antimbre, gilden ođđe seolfren, glæsen ođđe tinen; ne beó hé ná hyrnen, ne húru treówen, Ll. Th. ii. 384, 7. Þ glæsene fæt *vas vitreum,* Gr. D. 104, 28 : 103, 13. Ele in ánum glæsenum fæte, 159, 9. Glæsene leóhtfatu, 49, 21. [v. *N. E. D.* glassen. *O. L. Ger.* glesín.]

**glæsen-eáge;** *adj. Grey-eyed:*—Glæseneáge *glaucus,* Wrt. Voc. ii. 42, 24. [Cf. glasen as an epithet of eyes; instances are given in *N. E. D.* under glassen. *O. L. Ger.* glesen-ógi *glaucus.* Cf. *O. H. Ger.* glas-augi *si visus tactus fuerit in oculo ita ut quasi vitrum remaneat.*]

**glǽs-fæt.** *Add:* (1) *a flask, bottle:*—Bebeád Benedictus þ hí út áwurpon þ ilce glæsfæt (*ampulla vitrea*) in þám wæs gesewen sum dæl eles ... þ hé útáworpene glæsfæt (*vas vitreum*) cóm in þá stánas, Gr. D. 159, 20–27. Gedó þreó pund on glæsfæt wel micel, gedó wínes tó v sestras, Lch. ii. 252, 8. (2) *a drinking-glass:*—Þ glæsfæt on þám wæs se wólberenda drync gehæfd, Gr. D. 104, 30. Gedó on glæsfæt, and þonne mid hláfe lapa on and nytta; ge þeáh þú mid cuclere þ súpe, þæt hylpþ, Lch. ii. 184, 23. (3) *a lamp:*—Hú Bonnosus þ tóbrokene glæsfæt geedstađelode ... Hé hóf upp glæsene leóhtfatu ... þá feóll án of his handum, þ hit weard tóbrocen, Gr. D. 49, 18.

**glæs-gegot,** es; *n. What is made of molten glass:*—Templ of ísernum geweorcum and of ǽrenum (of glæsgegotum, *v. l.*) geworht *templum aereo et ferreo opere constructum,* Nar. 37, 23 (v. note, p. 78).

**glæterian.** *Add:*—Of glæteriendum híwe beorhtmeð *flaua (auri) specie splendescit,* An. Ox. 532 : Wrt. Voc. ii. 149, 20.

**glæterung,** e; *f. Glittering, brilliance, bright light :*—On glæterunga *in matutino,* Ps. Rdr. 48, 15.

**glappe.** v. glæppe.

**glasin** ? :—*Baista,* ḡ. (=graece) glasin (*printed* glaisin, Wrt. Voc. ii. 125, 3), Wülck. Gl. 192, 3. See Angl. xxxiii. 137 for a Celtic origin of the word.

**gleáw.** *Add:*—Glēu *sagax,* Wrt. Voc. ii. 119, 47. Gleáwe *cati,* An. Ox. 56, 117. Wísra t gleáwra *augustior,* Germ. 399, 28. Swá swá þá gleáwestan *desertissimi,* Wrt. Voc. ii. 28, 54. **I.** *of physical sight, of the eye, sharp, gleg :*—Him ádimmiað þá eágan þe ǽr wǽron beorhte and gleáwe on gesihđe, Wlfst. 147, 31. **II.** *of mental vision.* (1) *quick to discern, of quick intelligence, clever :*—Hwá is nú đæra đe gesceádwís sié, and tó đǽm gleáw sié đæt hé swelces hwæt tócnáwan cunne, đætte nyte đætte ...?, Past. 411, 26. Ne eom ic dēma (dóma?) gleáw, wís for weorude, Hy. 4, 81. Gleáwum úþwitum *gymnosophistis,* An. Ox. 3095. Þurh gleáwe glígmen *per gymnosophistas,* 39. Him þá gleáwestan on wera þreáte wordum mǽldon, El. 536. (1 a) *where the seat of intelligence is given.* (α) in gen.:—Hié gemétton módes gleáwne, An. 143. (β) *with prep.* :—Melchisedech gleáw in gǽste, Cri. 139. (1 b) *where mode of expressing intelligence is given.* (α) in gen.:—Þonces gleáw, Ph. 144: An. 557. Hygeþances gleáw, 818. (β) *in dat.* (inst.) :—Searoþoncum gleáw, wordum wísfæst, Rä. 36, 13. ¶ *as epithet of the mind:*—Gleáwes *sagacis* (*animi*), An. Ox. 3109. Þú mē ongeáte gleáwe móde *cognovisti me,* Ps. Th. 138, 1. Gleáw *sagax* (*ingenium*), An. Ox. 3213. Gleáw, 7, 234. (2) *clever in a special department, skilled in an art, pursuit, having knowledge of a subject:*—Gleáw *gnarus* (*culter vineae*), An. Ox. 8, 143. Se gleáwa *argutus* (*poeta,* Ald. 137, 9), Wrt. Voc. ii. 89, 4. (2 a) *with gen., skilled in the use or practice of, having good knowledge of :*—Fród wita ... snottor ár ... wordhord onwreáh, beorn bóca gleaw, Mód. 4: El. 1212. Rece, gif þú cunne, wís, worda gleáw, Rä. 33, 14. Sum bið meáres gleáw, wiccrǽfta wís *one knows all about horses,* Crä. 69. Gleáw módes crǽfta, 32. Wísfæstne wer, wordes gleáwne (*skilled in speech*), An. 1650. Hí sumne gemétað gydda gleáwne (*a connoisseur of song*), Víd. 139. (2 b) *with prep., skilled in, clever at:*—Wæs hé wel gleáw on huntunge, Hml. S. 30, 16. Ic geseah swefen and ic ne mæg nánne man findan þe mé secge hwæt hit behealde; ic gehírde secgan þæt þú wǽre gleáw þǽron (*quae audivi te sapientissime conjicere*), Gen. 41, 15. (3) *quick to see the proper course of action or conduct, discreet, sagacious, prudent:*—Gleá wíf *uxor prudens,* Kent. Gl. 693. Ongitan sceal gleáw hæle hú gæstlic bið, Wand. 73: Jul. 131. Seó gleáwe, Jud. 171. Ofer feónd míne gleáwne (*prudentem*) mē dydes, Ps. Srt. 118, 98. Se cyning him ceóse sumne wísne man and glǽwne (*virum sapientem et industrium*), Gen. 41, 33. ¶ *as epithet of the mind :*—Ælc gleáw mód behealt hwelce ende hí habbaþ *rerum exitus prudentia metitur,* Bt. 7, 2; F. 18, 23. Dó mē wegas wíse þæt ic wite gearwe on hwylcne ic gange gleáwe móde, Ps. Th. 142, 9. (3 a) *prudent of or in mind, in thought.* Cf. (1 a), (1 b):—Him mæg wís sefa wyrda gehwylce gemetigan, gif hé bið módes gleáw, Sal. 439. Gleáw on móde, Gen. 2373. Judith, gleáw on geþonce, Jud. 13: El. 807. (4) *good.* Cf. gleáwe; III:—For þan þú eart se gooda, gleáw on gesyhđe þára háligra þe þínne held curan *quoniam bonum est nomen tuam ante conspectum sanctorum tuorum,* Ps. Th. 51, 8. God mín and gleáw hældend *Deus meus et salutaris meus,* 61, 6. Hé (*Abraham*) is gód and gleáw, Gen. 2657. Hé gleáw ne wæs, rēđe and rǽdleás, Dan. 176. Ic andette Drihtne ... đám gleáwan forđan ic hine gódne wát *confitemini Domino, quoniam bonus,* Ps. Th. 105, 1. Ic andette ... þám gódan Gode, ic hine gleáwne wát *confitemini Domino, quoniam bonus,* 117, 1: 53, 3. For his þæt gleáwe folc *coram populo suo,* 67, 8. **III.** *of things.* (1) *of that which is done with skill:*—Ic nīwne cantic Gode, gleáwne singe, Ps. Th. 143, 10. On þǽre gleáwan *sagacissima,* i. *argutissimo* (*serie*), An. Ox. 9, 9. (2) *of non-material objects, characterized by skill or prudence:*—Gleáw *sollers* (*sapientia*), Wrt. Voc. ii. 91, 42. Gleáwum *sollerti* (*praescientia*), An. Ox. 5200. Þone þe rǽdgeþeaht þurh gleáwe mihte georne cúđe, El. 1163. Swá bebeád Godes ǽrendgást gleáwan sprǽce, Gen. 2296. Þurh Júdithe gleáwe láre, Jud. 334. (3) *good:*—Þú wǽre mē on geoguđe hyht gleáw *Domine, spes mea a juventute mea,* Ps. Th. 70, 4. Þæt hí gleáwne hiht tó Gode hæfdan *ut ponant in Deo spem suam,* 77, 9. Him gangað ongeán gleáwe crǽftas, mildheortnesse mód and mihte sóđ, 84, 9. Byð sægd his lof gleáwast and mǣrust *annuntietur laus ejus,* 101, 19. [*O. H. Ger.* glau *perspectus, prudens, ingeniosus, diligens.*] v. crǽft-, ferhþ-, fore-, freá- (frǽ-), hreþer-, hyge-, mód-, steor-, un-, word-gleáw.

**Gleáw-ceaster.** *Add:*—Gleáwanceaster (Gleáw-, -cestre, *v. ll.*), Chr. 577; P. 18, 32. Of Gleáwecestre, 918; P. 98, 18: 941; P. 110, 8: C. D. v. 140, 9. Intó Glēweceaster, iii. 208, 25; Chr. 918; Th. 193, 18. Of Gleáwcestre, 1043; P. 163, 32: 1052; P. 175, 6. Tó Glēwcestre, 1053; P. 182, 38. ¶ *Latin forms:*—In uicecomitatu Gloucestre, C. D. iv. 172, 20. In Gloecestria, 254, 9. Tota ciuitas Gloucestriae, vi. 180, 17.

**Gleáwceaster-scír,** e; *f. Gloucestershire:*—Intó Gleáwecesterscýre,

C. D. ii. 132, 30. Tó Gleáweceastrescîre (Gleáwcestrescîre, *v. l.*), Chr. 1016; P. 152, 10. Tó Gleáwcestrescîre, 1038; P. 161, 18. ¶ *Latin form:*—In Glocestriae schira, C. D. iv. 273, 24.

**gleáwe**; *adv.* *Add:* I. *with skill:*—Hê is gleáwest ûre gelæred, and hê mæg þê ealle þá þinc gecýþan þe þú ûs âcsost *he is the best instructed of us, and he can tell you all the things you ask us,* H. R. 11, 9. II. *with prudence:*—Guman . . . gleáwe beþuncan hyra hǽlo, Rä. 49, 7. III. in the metrical psalter the word occurs with a vaguely favourable meaning. Cf. gleáw; II. 4:—Mê þín se gôda gâst gleáwe lǽdde, þæt ic on rihtne weg fêrde, Ps. Th. 142, 11. Gê þe on Godes hûse gleáwe standað and on cafertûnum Godes hûses gearwe syndan *qui statis in domo Domini, in atriis domus Dei nostri,* 134, 2. Ic wât and can þæt þú mín God gleáwe wǽre *agnovi quoniam Deus meus es tu,* 54, 8. Eart þú ednéowe, earne gelícast, on geogoðe nû gleáwe geworden, 102, 5. [Cf. Goth. glaggwaba (-uba) *diligently, accurately.*]

**gleáwlíc.** *Add:*—Þus gleáwlice (or *adv.?*) gâstgerýnum sægdon sigorôfum, swá fram Siluestre lǽrde wǽron *thus skilled in spiritual mysteries they told the victor (Constantine) as they were taught by Sylvester,* El. 189.

**gleáwlîce.** *Add:* I. *skilfully:*—Eart þú gleáwlîce swá limwǽdum leôhte gegyrwed *amictus lumine sicut vestimento,* Ps. Th. 103, 2. Hû glǽwlîce hê þæt swefen rehte *quod prudenter somnium dissolvisset,* Gen. 40, 16. II. *with discernment, appropriately:*—Hû þu gleáwlîce mid noman ryhte nemned wǽre Emmanuhel, Cri. 130. III. *with discretion, wisely:*—Ongan gleáwlîce gingran sîne wordum trymman . . . Swá hleóðrode hâlig cempa þeáwum geþancul, An. 427. Paulus eóde þá gleáwlîce and heora godas sceáwode ealle be endebyrdnesse, Hml. S. 29, 20. IV. *with verbs of inquiry, understanding, discriminating, with clear mental vision, clearly, accurately, diligently:*—Nû wê sceolon georne gleáwlîce þurhseón ûsse hreðercofan heortan eágum, Cri. 1328. Gif wê gleáwlîce æfter gâstlicum andgite tôcnáwað þæt se arc getácnode Godes gelaðunge, Hml. Th. ii. 60, 1. Hit gleáwlîce undergeat, i. 122, 18. Ic þæs wênde þæt ic mid wisdôme full gleáwlîce ongitan mihte *existimabam ut cognoscerem hoc,* Ps. Th. 72, 13. Ongitan gleáwlîce gâstgehygdum, An. 863: Jul. 181: Hy. 4, 77. Gleáwlîce *sollerter* (*animadverteret*), An. Ox. 3131. Geornfullîcor, gleáwlîcor *enixius,* i. *sagacius* (quicquid scrutando *enixius* rimaretur, Ald. 42, 36), 3104. [O. H. Ger. glaulîhho *intente, adtente, diligenter, prudenter, solerter.*] v. fore-, un-gleáwlîce.

**gleáw-môd.** *Add:*—Ryhtspell monig Gregorius gleáwmôd gendwôd ðurh sefan snyttro, Past. 9, 10.

**gleáwnes.** *Add:*—Gleáunes *industria,* Wrt. Voc. ii. 46, 2. Gleáwnes, 25, 43: *dissertitudo, astutia,* 141, 5. Gleáwnisse *astu,* 9, 27. Gleáwnesse *argumento,* 2, 10, 11: 3, 14: *dissertitudinem,* 26, 37: *peritiam,* 67, 13. Gleáunisse *argutiae,* 100, 70. I. *ability, cleverness, talent:*—Hê wæs gôdre gleáunesse (*bonae indolis*) cniht, Bd. 5, 19: Sch. 655, 2. II. *sagacity:*—Gleáw[nesse] *sagacitatis,* An. Ox. 853. Gleá[wnesse], 5, 9. Mid ealre gleáwnesse *omni sagacitate,* R. Ben. I. 58, 9. III. *skill, skill in speech, eloquence:*—Gleáw[nesse] *eloquentiae,* 2314. Gleáwnesse *dissertitudinis,* 5490. Glǽwnysse, 2, 493. IV. *diligence:*—Gleáwnysse *industria,* i. *curiositate,* An. Ox. 618: *industria, assiduitate,* 1324. Geornfulnysse, gleáwnesse *industriam,* 43. Glǽwnesse, R. Ben. I. 59, 14. V. *a sign, token, distinguishing mark:*—Se eásterlica dæg wæs on þǽre ealdan ǽ tribus argumentorum indiciis preceptum, þ ys mid þrým gleáwnyssum hê wæs beboden: þ ys, þ hê wǽre æfter þǽre eásterlican emnihte, and on þám forman mônðe, and on þǽre þriddan wucan, Angl. viii. 330, 6. v. gereord-, un-gleáwnes.

**gleáwscipe.** *Add:* I. *sagacity:*—Se abbod sceal gýman and mid eallan gleáwscîpe hogian (*omni sagacitate curare*), R. Ben. 51, 9. On gleáwscype swîþe bescáwede, Lch. iii. 436, 11. II. *diligence:*—Gif hê ongyt þæt eal his hogu and gleáwscipe nâht framað *si viderit nihil suam prevalere industriam,* R. Ben. 52, 14. III. *an argument, proof, calculation:*—On þrim geárum ne mæg þes gleáwscipe standan, Angl. viii. 327, 16. v. un-gleáwscipe.

**glêd.** *Add:* *a coal of fire:*—Gloed *carbo,* Wrt. Voc. ii. 103, 12. Gloede *prunas,* 118, 18. (1) *a live coal, coal of fire* (lit. or fig.):—Glêd *carbo* (*torridus altaris*), Wrt. Voc. ii. 89, 14. Swá rîcels býð þonne hit gîfre glêda bærnað, Ps. Th. 140, 2. Hî feallað on fýres glêde *cadent super eos carbones,* 139, 10. Strêie of glêdon (*carbonibus*) âhyrde, 119, 4. Licge þ îsen uppan þám glêdan, Ll. Th. i. 226, 27. Se hláf wæs mid þám glêdum (*prunis*) bewrigen . . . þá worhte hê Crîstes rôde tácen ongên þám glêdum (þá glêdu, *v. l.*, *contra prunas*), Gr. D. 87, 9-16. Hê þone bisceop on îsenum bedde âstrehte and byrnenda glêda dyde under his nacode lîc, Hml. S. 29, 242. Gisêgun gloeda (gloedi, L.) âsetede *uiderunt prunas positas,* Jn. R. 21, 9. Glêda *pruinas* (*prunas* congregabis super caput ejus, Prov. 25, 22), Kent. Gl. 970. (1 a) in pl. *a fire, æt þám glêdum at the fire:*—Sum man sæt æt þám (his, *v. l.*) glêdum (*sedebat ad prunas*) in his hûse mid his wîfe and mid his lytlan suna . . . þ hê sǽte mid him æt þám glêdan . . . se âwyrgda

gâst þone sunu âwearp in ðá glýda (on þá ylcan glêda, *v. l.*), Gr. D. 75, 13-25. Stôdon ðá esnæsæt gloedum (*ad prunas*), Jn. L. R. 18, 18. (2) *a flame, a spark:*—Hýðað wîde gîfre glêde, Cri. 1045. Gloetas and ðæccillas *scintillae et lampades,* Mt. p. 9, 20. Him wiht ne sceód grim glêda nîð, frêcnan fýres, Dan. 465. In þæs wylmes grund, . . . in glêda gripe, El. 1302: Jul. 391: Sal. 48. (3) *fire, flame:*—Fretan sceal frêcne líg fægne monnan, . . . reað rêðe glêd, Vy. 46. Nû sceal glêd fretan wigena strengel, B. 3114. v. glêde.

**gleddian.** *Add:* v. be-gleddian.

**glêde, an**; *f.* *A live coal:*—Mid his gyldenan tange þǽre glêdan spearcan tô mínre tungan gebringan (cf. Is. 6, 6), Angl. viii. 325, 31. Glêdan (*carbones*) onǽlde syut, Ps. L. 17, 9. v. glêd.

**-glêded.** v. ge-, þurh-glêded.

**glêd-fæt.** *Add:* *a censer, incense-pan:*—Glêdfæte *acerra* (Ald. 195, 27), Wrt. Voc. ii. 95, 56: 5, 66. Cf. Ps. Th. 140, 2 *under* glêd, (1).

**glêd-scofl, e**; *f.* *A fire-shovel:*—Gloedscofl *vatilla,* Wrt. Voc. ii. 123, 8. v. fýr-scofl.

**glemm.** *Add:*—Godes cyrice . . . wê sculan nǽfre hyre derian wordes ne weorces, ac griðian hý symle and healdan unwemme and â bûtan glemme (bûtan womme *vel* glemme, *v. l.*), Wlfst. 67, 18.

**glendran** to *devour.* l. glendrian, *and add:*—Fisc hyne gearwað þ hê glentrige (*gluttiat*) ǽs, Scint. 107, 8. v. for-glendrian.

**glendrian** to *throw down.* v. fore-glendra, ge-glendrian.

**gleng, e**; *f.* *Add:* gleng, es; *m.* I. *ornament, decoration, adornment, glory:*—Saga mê hwæt ðæs lifigendan mannes gleng sý. Ic ðê secge, ðæs deádan swât, Sal. K. p. 200, 9. Glenge *crustu,* i. *ornata* (cf. *crustu,* i. *ornatu* frætwunge, Wrt. Voc. ii. 25, 8), An. Ox. 7, 370: 8, 371. On mænigfealdre glencge ic glencyde mînne lîchaman, Angl. xi. 371. II. *pomp, splendour* in appearance, *display:*—Ðeáh þe 113, 51. wlance men him hâton gewyrcan heora byrgene of marmanstâne and ûtan emfrætewian mid reáðum golde, þeáhhwæðere se deáð hit eal tôðǽlt: þonne bið seó gleng âgoten, and se þrym tôbrocen, Wlfst. 148, 22. Se glencg, 263, 8. Ne cêpð nán man deórwyrðra reáfa bûton for ýdelum gylpe þæt hê sý tôforan ôðrum mannum þurh his glencge geteald, Hml. Th. i. 328, 30. Ic andette . . . îdel word . . . and ǽlcne glængc þe tô mînes lîchaman unrǽde ǽfre belimpe, Ll. Th. ii. 262, 28. Sigoriþe ende mid glengan æþclan *triumphans pompa nobili,* Hy. S. 85, 9. Tô woroldlican îdelan glengan, Ll. Th. i. 328, 9. Mid dislicum glencgum stolidis (*ornamentorum*) *pompis,* An. Ox. 1217. Glencgu *pompas,* 63. Ic ondette . . . unnyttes gylpes bîgong and îdle glengas, Angl. xi. 98, 27. III. *an ornament:*—Glencg *monile,* Germ. 396, 305. Æresð alra glengea scolde scînan gold on his hrægle . . . Tôeácan ðǽm golde ealra glenga fyrmesð . . . se giem iacintus, Past. 85, 1-5. Cume manna gehwilc tô circan bûton golde and glæncgum, Wlfst. 181, 2. Þæt folc âlêdon hira glenga *deposuerunt ornatum suum,* Ex. 33, 6. Brôhte se cniht tô ðám mǽdene deórwurða gimmas and woruldlice glencga, Hml. S. 7, 22. Menas, glencga *crepundia,* i. *monilia,* An. Ox. 538: Wrt. Voc. ii. 23, 29. (Cf. *crepundia, ornamenta,* 76, 9.) v. forlegis-, weorold-gleng.

**glengan.** *Add:* I. *to adorn* with material ornaments:—Glensþ (= glengst) *comas* (si tu te sumptuosius *comas,* Ald. 75, 5), An. Ox. 8, 332. Glencað *comunt* i. *ornant,* 11. Hî glencgað heora wîf mid þám þe hî weófoda sceoldan, Ll. Th. ii. 328, 7. On mænigfealdre glencge ic glencgde mînne lîchoman, Angl. xi. 113, 52. Manege mid oferrence glengdan hý sylfe, Wlfst. 46, 2. II. *to adorn, be an ornament to, be becoming to:*—Ne glenget *non decet* (non *decent* stultum verba *com-be becoming to:*—Ne glenget *non decet* (non *decent* stultum verba com-posita,* Prov. 17, 7), Kent. Gl. 594. III. *to arrange gracefully.* (1) of dressing the hair:—Geglencendlîce glencan *delicate componere,* An. Ox. 1203. (2) of arranging words:—Glengede *composita,* Kent. Gl. 595. (v. II.) v. ge-glengan; ofer-, un-glenged.

**glenge.** *Dele, and see* gleng: **glenge (?);** *adj.* v. glengista.

**glengendlîce**; *adv.* Elegantly:—Glencendlîce *delicate,* Hpt. Gl. 435, 12. v. ge-glengendlîce.

**gleng-full**; *adj.* Adorned:—Glengfulre burge *urbis ornatæ,* Germ. 395, 10.

**glengista.** The translator seems to have misunderstood the passage to mean: 'In order that thy diligence and genius may add somewhat to the knowledge of these things of mine.' In some way *ingenium* is represented by *glengista.* Could this word be the superlative of an adjective, *glenge* well-ordered, and the passage be completed [þín] *glengista* [orþanc ?]; cf. glengan; III.

**gleng-lic.** *Substitute:* Splendid, *full of pomp:*—Sió glenglice *pompulenta,* Wrt. Voc. ii. 67, 34.

**gleng-ness, e**; *f.* Ornamentation, adornment, Verc. Först. 123, 15.—ûre glengnesse and on ûre myclan gestreóne, Verc. Först. 123, 15.

**gleó.** v. glîw: gleomu. *Add:* cf. glǽm: **gleómung.** v. glômung: **glêsan.** *Add:*—Hê ðás bôc gloesde, Jn. p. 188, 15 [cf. Low Lat. glôsa.] v. ofer-glêsan.

**glid.** *Substitute:* glid[d] (?) *a slippery place:*—Sîen wegas hira ðeóstre and glidd (glid, Ps. Spl. C., glidd, Ps. Srt., slidornis, Bl. Gl. *lubricum*), Ps. Vos. 34, 6. v. glidder.

**glida.** *Add:* Glioda *miluus*, Wrt. Voc. ii. 114, 18. Sĕ đe reáflác lufađ, hē biđ glida, and nā culfre, Hml. Th. ii. 46, 16.

**glīdan.** *Add:* I. *to pass from one place to another by a smooth and continuous movement.* (1) of motion on or through a liquid:—Hornfisc glád geond gārsecg, An. 371. (2) of motion through the air:—Þonne glád þæt deófol ūt mid his leásunge swā swā smýc æt his eágdura, Shrn. 52, 32. (2 a) of the motion of the heavenly bodies:—Se steorra cymeð eástan ūp ǣrror sunnan, and eft æfter sunnan on setl glīdeð, Met. 29, 27. Se steorra glád him beforan (cf. se steorra him beforan fērde *stella antecedebat eos*, Mt. 2, 9), Hml. Th. i. 78, 23. On đām earde đe se tungel ofer glád, 106, 28. Hwonne ūp cyme eástan glīdan swegles leóma, Ph. 102. II. *to pass from one state to another, slip, fall*:—Oft đæt hefige mōd glīt niđor and niđor stæpmǣlum, oð hit mid ealle áfielð, Past. 279, 2. III. *of movement along a surface*:—Þonne hié mon slōg oþþe sceát, þonne glád hit on þǣm scillum, swelce hit wǣre smēđe īsen, Ors. 4, 6; S. 174, 7. His sceadu gehǣlde ealle þā untruman þe heó ofer glád, Hml. S. 10, 20. Beswepe þ hió áweg ne glīde, Lch. ii. 250, 19. IV. *to pass away*:—Þæt þā sáule wunde . . . glīdan mōte, Ps. C. 145. V. *of revolution*:—Is efneúđe ūp and ofdūne tō feallanne foldan þisse, þām anlícost þe on ǣge bið gioleca on middan, glīdeð hwæđre ǣg ymbūtan, Met. 20, 170. [*O. Frs.* glīda : *O. Sax.* glīdan : *O. H. Ger.* glītan.] v. æt-glīdan.

**glidder.** *Substitute:* glidder, glider; *adj.* I. *slippery*:—Beđearf seó sáwel on dōmes dæg . . . stađolfæstre brycge ofer þone glideran weg hellewītes brógan, Wlfst. 239, 14. II. *lascivious*:—Gehydge glidderre *sensu lubrico*, Ps. Srt. ii. p. 202, 17. Scild glidder *culpam lubricam*, 201, 10. v. glid[d].

**gliddrian.** *Add:*—Tealtriendum, gliddriendum *nutabundis*, An. Ox. 4104.

**glidering,** e; *f. An apparition, unreal appearance*:—Þǣre glyderinge *fantasmate* (v. (?) Ald. 57, 12), Wrt. Voc. ii. 34, 66.

**glig-.** v. glīw-: **glimith.** v. glýman.

**glind** *a fence of boards* (?), *a railing* (?):—Andlang rīđe on wican glinde, C. D. B. i. 296, 29. Cf. Æt Glindleá, C. D. iii. 426, 22. Glynde is a place-name in Sussex. [*O. L. Ger.* gi-lindi *railings*. v. Gall. 439.]

**glisian.** *Add:* [v. *N. E. D.* glise.]

**glitnian.** *Add:* I. *of light or of that which emits light*:—Glitenaþ hālig dæg and beorht þearle *rutilat sacrata dies et splendida valde*, Hy. S. 47, 6. Betwux þæs heortes hornum glitenode gelícnys þǣre hālgan rōde breohtre þonne sunnan leóma, Hml. S. 30, 42. Leóhtes dægrima glitnigende (*rutilans*) scīnþ, Hy. S. 8, 21. Gliteniend(r)e *corusco* (*immensi luminis splendore*), An. Ox. 4310. I a. *of the miraculous appearance of a person*:—Đā stōdon þā hālgan hāle of þām fýre glitiniende swā swā gold, Hml. S. 4, 338. II. *of objects that reflect light* (metal, liquid, gems, plumage, &c.):—Đū (*the phenix*) glitenest swā reád gold, E. S. viii. 476, 46. Glite[naþ] *fulgescit* (*pavonis pennae glauco coloris virore*), An. Ox. 539. Glitenaþ *coruscat*, i. *micat* (*limpida pupilla*), 1719. Glitenat *flavescit* (*vinum*), Kent. Gl. 908 : *flavescit, albescit*, Txts. 63, 894. Glitenaþ, Wrt. Voc. ii. 35, 72. *Flavescit*, glitenaþ *vel* geolwaþ *splendescit*, 149, 17. [*See for the preceding four instances*, Prov. 23, 31.] Mynum glitenian (*auratis*) *monilibus rutilare*, An. Ox. 1196. Gliteniendum *uernantibus* (*atque coruscantibus gemmis*), 4295. III. *to be splendid from excellent qualities*:—Agustus mid feówrum rihtingum glitnaþ gerisenlice swýđe, Angl. viii. 302, 2.

**glīw.** *Take here instances under* gleów, glig, *and add:* I. *jesting, pleasantry*:—Glió, gliú *facetiae*, Txts. 61, 825. Gleó, Wrt. Voc. ii. 34, 70. II. *jeering, mockery*:—Glió *cabillatio*, Txts. 47, 354. Gliú *gannatura*, 65, 948. Đe lǣs đe đū wegfērendum wurđe eft tō glīge (cf. *ne omnes qui vident incipiant inludere ei*, Lk. 14, 29), Hex. 38, 11. III. *any activity intended to amuse, a game, diversion, pastime, sport, play*:—Hē (*Herod*) đæs wītegan deáð þǣre lydran hoppystran hire glīges (*dancing*) tō mēde forgeáf, Hml. Th. i. 484, 3. In glīuuae (glíowe) *in mimo*, Txts. 70, 550. Gliú *mimum*, Wrt. Voc. ii. 56, 51 : 70, 35 : 46, 42. Stód þǣr sum man mid ānum apan and slōh cymbalan. Þā sōna se hālga wer wæs forhycgende þ glīg *cum simia vir adstitit, et cymbala percussit. Quem sanctus sonitum audiens dedignatus*, Gr. D. 62, 18. Pleglican glīa beclyppinga *iocosos ludorum amplexus*, Au. Ox. 3173. v. bismer-, chor-, gefiit-, sealm-glīw.

**glīw-bydenestre,** an; *f. A female player on the timbrel*:—Glýw-bydenestra *tympanistriarum*, Ps. L. 67, 26.

**glīw-cræft,** es; *m. The art of playing on an instrument, minstrelsy*:—Stód þǣr æ:toran þǣre dura sum man mid ānum apan and slōh cymbalan, and bæd him metes, swā swā sume men gewuniað þ hī mid glīgcræfte (*ludendi arte*) heom andlyfene sēceað, Gr. D. 62, 13. [Ne cuđe na mon swa muchel of song, of harpe . . . of lire . . . he wes god of alle gleocræften, Laym. 7012.]

**glīw-cynn** (?) *a kind of music* (?):—On glywcū *in tibiis* (tibiis *seems to have been taken in the sense of pipes, and to be explained as* glýwcyn, *a kind of music* (?)), Ps. L. 146, 10.

**glīw-dreám.** *Take here* gleó-dreám *in Dict., and add:* [Brutus and his duȝeđe makeden halinesse mid mete and mid drinchen and mid murie gleodreme, Laym. 1823.]

**glīwere.** *Substitute:* I. *a jester, buffoon*:—Glīwere *scurra*, Germ. 396, 320. II. *one who unworthily aims at pleasing, an obsequious follower, a parasite*:—Spilra, glīwera *parasitorum* (cf. *parasitus* leás ōlecere, Wrt. Voc. i. 74, 36), An. Ox. 679: 6, 13. Glīwra, forspillendra þēna, 4165. III. *a player on an instrument, minstrel.* v. cimbal-glīwere. [*Icel.* glýjari *a jester.*]

**glīw-gamen,** es; *n. Musical entertainment, music*:—Hearpe and pīpe and mistlic glīggamen drēmað eów on beórsele *cithara et lyra et tympanum et tibia et vinum in conviviis vestris* (Is. 5, 12), Wlfst. 46, 16.

**glīw-georn;** *adj. Eager for amusement, fond of jesting* or *minstrelsy*:—Bisceopum gebyreð þ hī ne beón tō glīggeorne, ne hunda ne hafeca hēdan tō swýđe, Ll. Th. ii. 316, 29.

**glīw-hleóþriend.** *Substitute:* glīw-hleóþriendlic; *adj. Musical*:—Þā glīwhleóđriendlican *musica*, Wrt. Voc. ii. 57, 35.

**glīwian.** *Take here* gleowian *in Dict., and add:* of the sound made by metal (?), *to play, sound*:—Mec (*a book*) siđđan wrāh hæled hleóbordum, hýde beþenede, gierede mec mid golde forð (*for a similar verse* cf. An. 1110); on mē glīwedon wrǣtlic weorc smiđa *me then a man enclosed between sheltering boards, stretched a covering of skin, went on to adorn me with gold; on me played the fair work of smiths* (referring to the sound made by the metal ornaments and clasps when the book was moved about or opened?), Rä. 27, 13. [*Icel.* glýja *to be gleeful.*]

**glīwian** *to adorn.* See preceding word.

**glīwing** (-ung), e; *f. Jeering, mockery*:—Tāle, i. glīwunge gecance gehispende *ganniturae*, i. *cachinnatione ludibrio insultantes*, An. Ox. 1472.

**glīwing-mann,** es; *m. A 'gay' woman* (?):—Glīwingmanna *ganearum* (ganea *meretrix*, Migne: but perhaps *ganeonum* should be read), *cauponum, tabernariorum*, An. Ox. 50, 9:

**glīwlic;** *adj. Jesting, mocking*:—Glīwlicre hyspinge *cauillo mimico* (*scurrili* ł *ioculari*), Germ. 396, 318.

**glīw-mægden, -mæden.** *Take here* gliéw-mēden *in Dict., and add*:—Glīwmǣdena *tympanistriarum*, Ps. Rdr. 67, 26.

**glīw-mann.** *Take here* gleó-mann *in Dict., and add*:—Glīgman *parasitus* (cf. glīwere), Hpt. Gl. 504, 20. Glīgmanna yppe *orcestra vel pulpitus*, Wrt. Voc. i. 39, 36. Suā micle mēde . . . suā wē habbað đæs hleahtres, đonne wē hliehað glīgmonna unnyttes cræftes. Wē herigað hira cræftas, and đeáh nyllað hī habban *sic eis virtutum sanctitas sicut stultis spectatoribus ludicrarum artium vanitas placet. Illi aurigarum et histrionum gesta favoribus efferunt, nec tamen tales esse desiderant*, Past. 231, 7. Þurh witige plegmen ł gléawe glīgmen *per gymnosophistas*, An. Ox. 39. Swā hweorfað gleómen geond grunda fela . . . simle sumne gemētað gydda gleáwne, Vīd. 136. [King Blæđgabreat . . . ne cuđe na mon swa muchel of song . . . gleomen him weoren deore, Laym. 7004. Þar was gleomenne song, þar was piping among, 5109.]

**glīw-stōl.** *Take here* gleów-stōl *in Dict., and add:* A seat of music and song (cf. þǣr (*at Hrothgar's court*) wæs gidd and gleó, B. 2105; cf. also seledreám), *a joyous home* (cf. hleów-stōl *for similar compound*). The subject of the riddle is a stag's horn, which is shed and its place taken by a new one. This process is represented as the expulsion of a man from his home and country by a younger brother who takes his place.

**glīwung.** v. glīwing.

**glīw-word,** es; *n. A word in a song*:—Se Wīsdōm glíowordum gōl (cf. ongan glíowian and geoddode, Bt. 12; F. 36, 6), Met. 7, 2.

**glof.** *Dele*, and see next word.

**glōf.** *Add*:—Gloob, glōb, glōf *manica*, Txts. 76, 631. Glōf, Wrt. Voc. ii. 55, 40: 71, 19. Hafuc sceal on glōfe wilde gewunian (cf. sum sceal wildne fugel ātemian, hafuc on honda, Vy. 86), Gn. C. 17. Đonne þū glōfan abban wille, Tech. ii. 127, 21.

**glōfed.** v. ge-glōfed: **glōma.** v. ǣfen-glōma.

**glōmung.** *Add*:—Glōmung *crepusculum*, Wrt. Voc. i. 21, 49. In sumre glōmunge ūres mōdes *in quodam mentis crepusculo*, Gr. D. 331, 14. v. ǣfen-glomming.

**gloria,** a, an; *pl.* glorian; *m. A Gloria*, a name for a liturgical formula:—Se gloria þæs forman sealmes, R. Ben. 69, 3: 68, 8. Under ānum gloria (glorian, R. Ben. I. 47, 6), 40, 22. Tōdǣled on twēgen glorian, 38, 3: 42, 13.

**glōwan.** *Add: p.* gleów:—Gleów, scān *fulminauit*, An. Ox. 4409. Þæt fýr weard þā ācwenced, þ þær ān col ne gleów, Hml. S. 7, 240. Gewyrme mid hāte glówende īsene, Lch. ii. 236, 31: 216, 1. Lecgað đā īsenan clútas hāte glówende tō his sīdan, Hml. Th. i. 424, 35. [Cf. the wk. verbs *O. Sax.* glōian: *O. H. Ger.* gluoen: *Icel.* glóa.]

**glydering.** v. glidering.

**glýman** (?) *to rage*:—Glimith ( = glýmith? for the vowel cf. rihum

= rȳhum, 114, 120) *sevtt*, Txts. 115, 125. [cf. *N. E. D.* gloom ; *vb.*, *where is quoted* M. H. Ger. (13th cent.) ein glümender hunt *a savage dog*. In Ld. Gl. G. 3, 59 *is given from another Leiden MS.* glimnit *sevit. Perhaps here for* glimnit *might be read* grimmit. v. grimman.]

**glyrendum** (?) *retortis*, Germ. 394, 288 : glywcum. v. glīw-cynn.

**gnæt.** *Add :*—Gnæt *scinifes* vel *tudo*, Wrt. Voc. i. 24, 3 : *scinifes* 77, 56. Gneat, Ps. Srt. 104, 31. Þā gnættas mid swīþe lytlum sticelum him (*man*) deriaþ, Bt. 16, 2 ; F. 52, 10. Heó (*fleabane*) gnættas and micgeas and fleán ācwelleþ, Lch. i. 266, 1.

**gnagan.** *Dele bracket at end, and add :*—Gnæhð, cīwþ *sulcat* (*corpora vermis*), An. Ox. 23, 49. Wyrmas heora bān gnagað byrnendum tóðum *vermes lacerant ignitis dentibus ossa*, Wlfst. 139, 10 : Dóm. L. 211. Wē hēdað þæra crumena ðæs hlāfes and ðā Iūdéiscan gnagað þā rinde, Hml. Th. ii. 114, 34. Sceal se hund bān gnagan, Lch. ii. 48, 12. Gnægen *conrosus*, Wrt. Voc. ii. 24, 35. Gnagene (gragene, MS.) *roderentur* (*leonum rictibus*), An. Ox. 2, 224. [O. H. Ger. gnagan : Icel. gnaga.]

**gneáþ.** *Add :*, gneád :—Hī cwædon þ him gneáðe wære heora wist and scrūd, Hml. S. 31, 1296. v. gnīþe, *and two following words*.

**gneáþlicness** (gneád-), e ; *f. Frugality, parsimony :*—Gneáðlinesse *frugalitatis*, gneádlicnys *frugalitas*, Hpt. Gl. 463, 74. Gneádlicnys, An. Ox. 2437.

**gneáþness** (gneád-), e ; *f.* I. *frugality, moderation in a person :*—Gneáðnys (gneád-, Hpt. Gl. 494, 41) swā spærlic *parsimonia tam frugalis*, An. Ox. 3748. Gneáþnysse *frugalitatis*, i. *temperantiae*, 2437. II. *scantiness of material, scarcity :*—Ne him wære hwætes gneádnes (genēðnys, *v. l.*) ne ōðerra worldwelena, Mart. H. 68, 9. v. gnīþness.

**gnēþe.** v. gnīþe : **gnēðen.** *Dele.*

**gnīdan.** *Add :*—Ic gnīde *frico*, Wrt. Voc. ii. 40, 11. *Frico* ic gnīde, *fricui* ic gnād, *frictum* geguiden, Ælfc. Gr. Z. 137, 15. I. *to rub an object :*—Hit biþ geornlic þæt mon heardlīce gnīde þone hnescestan mealmstān, Ors. 4, 13 ; S. 212, 27. I a. *to rub one object against another :*—Beóres tācen is þæt þū gnīde þīne hand on þā ōþre, Tech. ii. 125, 21. I b. *to rub a surface with material, cover a surface by rubbing :*—Reóde gnīdan *fucare*, Wrt. Voc. ii. 37, 49. Hē hēt hine mid sealte gnīdan, Hml. S. 14, 46. II. *to rub material on a surface :*—Hē gnād on ansȳne þæs mannes þ dūst . . . hē lange hwīle gnād, Gr. D. 216, 15. [v. *N. E. D.* guide.] v. ā-, be-gnīdan.

**gnidel** (-il), es ; *m. A pestle :*—Guidil *pistillus*, Wrt. Voc. ii. 117, 43.

**gnīding.** *Add :*—Sceal hē þā eágan weccan mid gnīdingum, Lch. ii. 30, 28.

**gnirran** *to snarl, gnash* or *chatter* (with the teeth) :—Hwỹlon þā tēð for mycclum cyle maūna þær gnyrrað (gryrrað, Dóm. L. 195) *nunc nimio stridentes frigore dentes*, Wlfst. 138, 29. Hlihhan oððe gnyrende gesihð unrōtnyssa getācnað *ridere aut stridentes uiderit tristitiam significat*, Lch. iii. 210, 12. [v. *N. E. D.* guar.]

**gnīþe** (gnēðe) ; *adj.* Of persons, *frugal, sparing* ; of things, *scanty, scarce :*—Gnēþre *mediocri*, Wrt. Voc. ii. 55, 10. Of gnæþum *parcis*, Germ. 391, 31. On ðām mægenum eáðmódnesse and hỹrsumnesse nôhte þon læssa ne gnēðra (gnēðra, *v. l. : these forms might be mutated comparatives of* gneáþ(-d)) wæs, Bd. 5, 19 ; Sch. 656, 11. [O. H. Ger. ge-nōti *parcus*. v. *N. E. D.* gnede.] v. un-gnīþe, gneáþ.

**gnīþelīce** ; *adv. Scantily, sparingly :*—Geótende swīþe gnēðelīce *exigue fundendo*, Gr. D. 51, 13. v. un-gnīþelīce.

**gnīþelicness**, e ; *f. Frugality :*—Spærnes, gnēþelicnes *frugalitas*, *temperantia*, *parcitas*, Wülck. Gl. 244, 6. Gnēðelicnesse *frugalitatis*, Angl. xiii. 32, 117 : Wrt. Voc. ii. 147, 34.

**gnīþness**, e ; *f.* I. *frugality :*—Gnēðnes *parsimonia*, Wrt. Voc. ii. 65, 73. Mid gnēþnesse *frugalitatis*, 33, 50. II. *scarcity :*—Hwætes genēðnys, Mart. H. 68, 9. v. gneáþness.

**gnohioc.** *l.* guohioc.

**gnorn** *sorrow. Add :*—Nū is hælwende þæt man hēr wēpe . . . Glæd bið se Godes sunu gif þū gnorn þrowast, Dóm. L. 86. v. grorn.

**gnorn** ; *adj.* v. grorn ; *adj.* : **gnornan.** v. gnornian.

**gnorne** ; *adv. Complainingly :*—León hwelpas grymetigað gnorne (or *adj.?*), georne sēcað *the lion's whelps roar their complaints, seek eagerly*, Ps. Th. 103, 20. Cf. grorne.

**gnorn-hof.** *Add :* cf. grorn-hof.

**gnornian.** *Take here* gnornan *in Dict., and add :* I. *to feel grief, regret*, &c. :—Ic gnornige *contristatus sum*, Ps. Th. 54, 2. Ā mæg gnornian sē þe nū fram þis wīgplegan wendan þenceð, By. 315. Gnorniendum *merentibus*, Kent. Gl. 1129. I a. *of things :*—Tȳdrað þis bánfæt, greóthord gnornað, Gū. 1240. Beám sceal on eorðan leáfum líðan, leomu gnornian (*the bare branches grieve*), Gn. Ex. 26. Hyge gnornende, Gū. 1182. II. *to feel* or *express discontent, murmur :*—Suā ðām ðe gnornað on ðære godcundan suingellan *qui in percussione positus erumpit ad sonitum murmurationis*, Past. 269, 1. Gnornadun *murmuraverunt*, Ps. Srt. 105, 25. Suelce hē cuæðe tō ðæm unryhtwīsan mōde ðe innan bið gnornigende (-iende, *v. l.*) *ac si*

*dicatur menti iniquae interius dolenti*, Past. 225, 10. Gnorniað *murmurabiunt*, Ps. Srt. 58, 16. v. be-gnornian ; grornian.

**gnornung.** I. *a feeling* or *expression of grief, sorrow*, &c. :—Oṇ gnornunga mōdes *in merore animi*, Kent. Gl. 517. Hit nāuht elles nāt būtan gnornunga *crescit in immensum noxia cura*, Bt. 3, 2 ; F. 6, 12 : Met. 3, 10. Þær is wōp wīde gehēred . . . and gnornunge mecga, Sat. 334. Him gnornunga gæste ne scōdun, Gū. 516. II. *a feeling* or *expression of discontent* or *complaint, a grudge :*—For eówerre āgene gnornunge ðe gē wið ðæm crīstendōme habbað, Ors. 3, 8 ; S. 122, 11. v. grornung.

**gnuddian** *to rub :*—Gnudda *frica*, An. Ox. 56, 33. [v. *N. E. D.* gnodde.]

**gnyran.** v. gnirran : **gōað.** v. gón.

**god** ; *m. and* god ; *n. Take these together, and add :* I. *of a heathen god :*—Heá gotho *manes*, Archiv 85, 310, 15 ; An. Ox. 53, 15. Þæra hæðenra godas synd gramlice deófla, Hml. S. 14, 18. In god *in divos*, Wrt. Voc. ii. 93, 57. Ic swerige ðurh ealle godas and gydena, Hml. Th. i. 426, 7. Gē habbað manega godas, Hml. S. 4, 134. I a. *with a defining addition :*—Wīnes god *Bachus*, Wrt. Voc. ii. 93, 42. Fỹres god U[u]lcanus, 95, 6. II. *an image which is worshipped, idol :*—god U[u]lcanus, 95, 6. Eówer godas synd āgotene oððe āgrafene, Hml. S. 4, 136. Þīne godas syndon gyldene and sylfrene . . . manna handgeweorc, 14, 20. 'Geoffra ðīne lāc ūrum gudum . . . .' 'Ðū cwyst þæt ic mē gebiddan sceole tō dumbum stānum, ðā ðe sind āgrafene ðurh manna handa,' Hml. Th. i. 422, 35. III. *of a person having godlike attributes :*—Ælc gesælig mon biþ god *omnis beatus deus*, Bt. 34, 5 ; F. 140, 2 : 35, 5 ; F. 164, 23. Ic gesette þē Pharaone tō gode, Ex. 7, 1. Ic sæde gē synt godas (goddo, L., godo, R.), Jn. 10, 34. IV. *in the Christian, monotheistic sense, God.* (1) *as a proper name :*—On anginne gesceóp God heofenan and eorðan, Gen. 1, 1. Goddes *Dei*, Rtl. 109, 11 : Mk. L. 9, 1 : Jn. p. 3, 4. (1 a) *with epithet :*—Se Ælmihtiga God hī āhredde, Chr. 1016 ; P. 150, 13. Þone ēcan mildan God, Cht. E. 231, 8. (2) *where the triune character of the Deity is marked.* (a) *of the first person of the Trinity :*—Drihten God, Fæder Crīstes, Hml. Th. i. 426, 24. God . . . Fæder Ælmihtig, Cri. 319. (b) *of the second person :*—Crīst þæs līfgendan Godes Sunu, Bl. H. 11, 30. (b) *of the second person :*—Hælend Crīst, God of Gode, Hml. Th. i. 426, 2. God tō ūs niþer āstāhg, Bl. H. 17, 29. Hié God sylfne āhēngon, El. 209. (c) *where the three persons are given :*—Se Ælmihtiga Fæder is God, and his Sunu is Ælmihtig God, and se Hālga Gāst is Ælmihtig God ; nā ðrỹ Godas, ac hī ealle ān Ælmihtig God untōdǽledlic, Hml. Th. i. 248, 6-9. (3) *where the genitive is used with a noun as an intensive :*—Þonne is þ Godes riht þ hē beó clǽne *it is the most perfect justice, that he be clear*, Ll. Th. i. 418, 12. V. *a Being such as is understood by the proper name God, God according to some particular conception or in regard to some special attribute or relation :*—Ic eom Abrahames God, and Isaaces God, and Iacóbes God. Nys God nā deádra, ac lybbendra, Mt. 22, 32. Se gōda God, Bt. 36, 1 ; F. 172, 5. Se āna sōða God . . . sē ān is sōð God þe ealle ðing gescōp, Wlfst. 105, 27-31. Þone God ic eów bodige þone ðe gē hātað uncūðne . . . hē sitt on his Fæder swīðran hand sōð God and sōð man, Hml. S. 29, 37-42. Tō Abrahames Gode, Ps. Th. 46, 9. Hig gesāwon Israhēla God, Ex. 24, 10. VI. *in special forms of speech.* (1) *where a strong wish is expressed :*—God him geunne þ . . ., Chr. 959 ; P. 115, 14. God eów gehealde, Ll. Lbmn. 486, 14. Āwende hine God Ælmihtig hrædlice of þisan lǽnan līfe intō helle wīte, C. D. iv. 87, 10. (2) *where dependence on, or gratitude to, the Deity is expressed :*—Mid Godes gæfe, C. D. i. 292, 21 : 299, 12. Gode Ælmihtigum sié ðonc ðætte . . ., Past. 3, 18. Swǽ gelǽrede biscepas swǽ nū, Gode ðonc, siendon, 9, 4. Nǽfde se here, Godes þonces, Angelcyn ealles for swīðe gebrocod, Chr. 897 ; P. 89, 30. (3) *where there is pious intention, conduct influenced by religion :*—Ǣghwæt þæs þe him ǣnig mon for Godes noman geselle, Ll. Th. i. 92, 11. Þæt hē his freónd nā for middangearde, ac for Gode lufige, Hml. Th. i. 584, 7. Seó is sōð lufu, þæt gehwā his freónd lufie on Gode, and his feónd for Gode, 528, 32. (4) *in earnest appeal, affirmation* or *exhortation :*—Ic bebióde on Godes naman ðæt . . ., Past. 9, 2. Ic eów bidde on Godes naman . . . þ . . ., Ll. Th. i. 194, 4. Wē biddað and on Godes naman beódað þ . . ., 364, 21. On Godes Ælmihtiges naman, Cht. E. 231, 11 : Ll. Th. i. 180, 22 : 182, 6. Nū hālsige ic ðē þurh God þ . . ., Hml. Th. i. 426, 31. Gif hwelc mon hine on Godes naman geandette, Ll. Th. i. 64, 21. VII. *in language concerned with church matters.* (1) *of spiritual things :*—Wē habbað āne gāstlice mōdor, seó is *Ecclesia* genamod, þ is Godes cirice, Ll. Th. i. 336, 8. Biscopas syndon Godes lage (*the doctrines of Christianity*) lāreówas, 332, 27. Hē Godes lage gebrǽdde, Chr. 963 ; P. 115, 4. Godes lof rǽran *to promote the Christian religion*, 5 : Cht. E. 229, 25. (2) *of ecclesiastical procedure, arrangement, constitution :*—Þā hālgan hādas þe Godes folc (*the Christian laity*) lǽran scylan, Ll. Th. i. 244, 9. Þridda dǽl þære teóðunge þe is Gode gebyrige gā . . . Godes þearfum (*the needy to whom church-alms are given*), 342, 9. . . . From ǽlcum Godes dǽle āworpene *cast out from church-communion*,

246, 15. Mid Godes bletsunge *with the blessing pronounced by the priest*, 256, 7. Muneca gehwylc ... geþence word and wedd þe hē Gode betǣhte, 306, 5. Gyf gehādod man gefeohte ... for Gode bēte swā canon tǣce, 168, 6. ¶ Godes þeów *a cleric :*—Ealle Godes þeówas ... and hūru þinga sácerdas, Ll. Th. i. 364, 10. Gif se Godes þeów nelle þǣre cyrican on riht þeówian, þ hē þonne mid lǣwedum monnum onfō þeówdōmes, Bl. H. 49, 3 : C. D. i. 293, 33 : Past. 5, 11. (3) of ecclesiastical property or dues :—Godes feós ðeóð *sacrilegium*. Wrt. Voc. i. 21, 31. Godes feoh and ciricean, Ll. Th. i. 2, 4. Godes gafel lǣstan, 350, 8. Þæs neádgafoles þe crīstene men Gode gelǣstan scoldon, 270, 14. (4) of churches :—Be ciricena gebētunge. þ ǣlc biscop bēte Godes hūs ... and eác þone cyning myngige þ ealle Godes cyrcan sȳn wel behworfene, Ll. Th. i. 246, 9–12. Hī Godes hūs griðedan, 334, 24. Hē eóde intō Godes (Goddes, L.) hūs *in domum Dei intrauit*, Lk. 6, 4. (5) where ecclesiastical and secular are contrasted :—For Gode and for worulde, Chr. 959 ; P. 115, 7 : Ll. Th. i. 168, 17. Wið God and wið men, Gode, 307 : 314, 26. v. heah-, hel-, wealdend-god ; cof-, deáþ-, gedwol-godas ; ūp-godu.

**gōd.** *Add:* I. *good, having in due measure the properties which an object of its kind ought to have.* (1) of material things :—Ǣlc treówu byrð gōde wæstmas, Mt. 7, 17. Ælfheres lāf (*a corslet*), gōd ..., golde geweorðod, ealles unscende, Vald. 2, 17. Hēt him ȳdlidan gōdne gegyrwan, B. 199. (1 a) of food or drink :—Ánan esne gebyreð tō metsunge xii. pund gōdes cornes, Ll. Th. i. 436, 26. xxx. ombra gōdes uuelesces alod, C. D. i. 293, 12. Ðō on gōd ealu, Lch. ii. 318, 13. Ǣlc man sylþ ǣrest gōd wīn ... Ðū geheólde þ gōde wīn oð þis, Jn. 2, 10. (1 b) of land, *fertile :*—Þæt land ys swīðe þearle gōd ... Drihten sild ūs þā moldan þe meolce and hunige flēwð, Num. 14, 7. Neorxna wang stōd gōd (cf. Gen. 2, 9), Gen. 209. Sum feóll on gōd land, Mk. 4, 8. (1 c) of a place :—Wē on þan gōdan rīce gesǣlige sǣton, Gen. 410. (2) of non-material things :—Mid gefyllednesse gōddere þēnunge wē weorðaþ heofena rīces yrfeweardas, R. Ben. 4, 24. Woruldgerihta ic wille þ standan swā gōde swā hȳ mon on betste ǣredian mæge ... And ... mid Denum be swā gōdum lagum swā hȳ betst geceósan mægen, Ll. Th. i. 272, 23–31. Swā gōde lage swā hȳ betste geceósen, 276, 17. (3) of animals :—Hors tō healfan pund gif hit swā gōd sȳ, and gif hit mǣtre sȳ ..., Ll. Th. i. 232, 25. .i. gōd metecū, 436, 27. Ne gōd hafoc geond sǣl swingeð, B. 2263. (4) of persons, as a term of indefinite commendation :—Higelāces þegn gōd mid Geátum, sē wæs moncynnes mægenes strengest, æðele and eácen, B. 199. Hēr lið ūre ealdor ... gōd on greóte, By. 315. Frōdne and gōdne fæder Unwēnes, Vid. 114. Geongne æðeling sceolan gōde gesīðas byldan tō beaduwe and tō beáhgife, Gn. C. 14. (4 a) as an epithet in courteous address :—Nū hæbbe ic his hēr on handa, herra se gōda, Gen. 678. Þū meaht nū þē self geseón, Eve seó gōde, 610. (4 b) as an epithet along with a title :—Forþfērde se gōda pāpa Marinus, Chr. 885 ; P. 80, 5. Seó gōde cwēn Margarita, 1093 ; P. 228, 11. (5) of qualities or attributes, *good* (*courage*) :—Ðā bæd ic þā fyrde þ hié hæfdon gōd ellen þāra þinga þe ūs on becwōmon *orabam Macedones ne aduersis casibus cederent neue deficerent*, Nar. 14, 22. Hē hæfde gōd geþanc, By. 13. (6) of a state of things, *commendable, right :*—Hū gōod is and hū wynsum þ mon eardige on ðāra gebrōðra ǣnnesse, Bl. H. 139, 29. Gōod is þæt ..., Ps. Th. 72, 23. II. of moral excellence. (1) in respect to general character or conduct, *virtuous.* (a) of persons :—Ǣlc man sceal his gōdan dǣda āhebban, gif hē sceal gōd and medeme weorþan, Bl. H. 129, 35. Noe wæs gōd ... dōmfæst and gedēfe (cf. Noe wæs rihtwīs, Gen. 6, 9), Gen. 1285. Ic þe gōdne wāt, fæsthȳdigne, 1346. Oft þā gōdan dēman (cf. þā unrihtwīsan dēman, 21) habbað yfele gingran, Ll. Lbm. 475, 28. Þā gōdan bióþ simle wealdende and þā yfelan nabbaþ nǣnne anweald, Bt. 36, 1 ; F. 172, 22. ¶ where a special virtue or excellence is implied. (a) bravery :—Sē þe worna fela gumcystum gōd gūða gedīgde, B. 2543. Hyne Geáta bearn gōdne ne tealdon ... wēndon þæt hē sleac wǣre, æðeling unfrom, 2184. Hē ūsic gārwīgend gōde tealde, hwæt helmberend, 2641. (B) wisdom or learning :—Is nū feala fordgewitenra frōdra and gōdra, gleáwra monna, El. 637. (b) of conduct, actions, words, feelings, &c. :—Titus wæs swā gōdes willan þæt ..., Ors. 6, 8 ; S. 264, 2. Būton hē hwæt mid gōdum willan for Gode gedyde, Bl. H. 97, 27. Gif hine hwā tō gōddre drohtunge tihte, Hml. Th. i. 524, 4. God him geunne þ his gōde dǣda swȳdran weardan þonne misdǣda, Chr. 959 ; P. 115, 14. Mid bysene gōdra weorca, Ll. Th. i. 272, 23. Gōddra, R. Ben. 16, 14. (b β) *brave* (*deed*), cf. II. 1 ¶ α :—Weorða ðē selfne gōdum dǣdum, Vald. 1, 23. (2) as an epithet of the Deity :—God simle biþ full gōd, Bt. 34, 7 ; F. 144, 20. Se gōda God, 36, 1 ; F. 172, 5. (3) *kind, gentle, gracious.* (a) of persons :—Þæt wē þeóden swā gōdne grētan mōton, B. 347. Cam freóndlīce on his fæder āre ne wolde gescéawian ... gōde wǣron Sem and Iafeð, Gen. 1587. Freónda gōdra, Rä. 27, 22. ¶ in a special sense, *liberal :*—Wes þū ūs lārena gōd, B. 269. Ic gumcystum gōdne funde beága bryttan, 1486 : 1969. (b) of actions, feelings, words, &c. :—On eorðan sȳ sybb mannum gōdes willan, Lk. 2, 14 : Bl. H. 93, 10 : Hy. 8, 6. Is gōd willa, þæt hē ōðres mannes ungelimp

besārgige, and on his gesundfulnysse fægnige, Hml. Th. i. 584, 5. Wolde ic freóndscipe þinne begitan gōdne, An. 480. Þā gāstas gōde word sprecað ... 'Wine leófesta ...,' Seel. 134. (4) *good* in a religious sense, *pious, devout :*—Gōd wæs Gūðlāc ; hē in gǣste bær heofoncundne hyht, Gū. 141. Symle Crīstes lof in Gūðlāces gōdum mōde weóx, 365. Cnihtas ǣfæste ... gōde in godsǣde, Dan. 90. Hē bið þām gōdum glædmōd on gesihðe ... Hē bið þām yfum egeslic tō geseónne, synnegum monnum, Cri. 911 : 1576. (4 a) *religious* by profession, *ecclesiastical, clerical.* (α) of persons :—Mid mīnra witena geþeahte, ge hādedra (gōdra, *v. l.*) ge lǣwedra, Ll. Th. i. 246, 20. Se cyng Willelm wæs milde þām gōdum mannum þe God lufedon (*humble to the servants of God*, Henry of Huntingdon), Chr. 1086 ; P. 219, 22. (β) of procedure :—Bēte man mid āne punde, and mid gōdre bōte (*with confession*) þingige georne (cf. twā (þreó, &c.) pund tō bōte mid godcundan scrifte *in the next six paragraphs*), Ll. Th. ii. 240, 13. (5) *proceeding from God.* Cf. godcund ; II. 1 :—Æfter þǣre gōdan sprǣce *iuxta oraculum*, Bd. 2, 12 ; Sch. 161, 15. III. *favourable, advantageous.* (1) *happy, prosperous.*—Wyrd ... þeáh hit ūs manigfealdlic ðince, sum gōd, sum yfel, hit is þeáh him ānfeald gōd, for þām þe hit eall tō gōdum ende bringþ, Bt. 39, 6 ; F. 220, 6–9. Nis se ende tō gōd, Seel. 38. On þām ēcean līfe syndon gōde dagas ... þeáh hwā wille hēr on līfe habban gōde dagas ... bið se ān gōda dæg mid Gode, Hml. S. 12, 80–89. Þæt hē geseó gōde dagas, Ps. Th. 33, 12. (1 a) of a season, *favourable to production*, (a) *good* (*year*) :—Cōm gōd geár and swā eác micel genihtsumnys wæstma on Breotone lond *tantis frugum copiis insula affluere coepit*, Bd. 1, 14 ; Sch. 38, 12. Cōm gōd gēr and wæstmberende *annus laetus et frugifer*, 4, 13 ; Sch. 419, 12. (2) *pleasant to the senses :*—Þæt treów wæs gōd tō etanne, Gen. 3, 6. Spica is gōdes stences, Bl. H. 73, 22. Mid ðǣm nosum wē tōsceádað gōde stencas and yfele, Past. 433, 22. (3) *conducive to well-being, beneficial, profitable, wholesome, salutary :*—þ bið gōd dolhsealf, Lch. ii. 92, 8. Wiþ nǣdran bite, fīfleáfe ... wiþ wīn gemenged gōd biþ tō drincanne, 110, 20. Þ tō nāhte nyt ne biþ þ man gōdne mete ete, gif hē hit eft spīwende ānforlǣteþ, Bl. H. 57, 5. (3 a) with dat. of object benefited :—Sió wiþerwearde wyrd is þǣm gōd þe winnaþ wiþ unþeáwas, Bt. 40, 2 ; F. 236, 17. Þ seó niównes þāra metta mæge him gōde beón, Lch. ii. 240, 16. (3 b) with dat. and dat. infin. :—Nis nā gōd þisum men āna tō wunienne, Gen. 2, 18. God is ūs hēr tō beónne, Mt. 17, 4. (4) of reputation, report :—Gōd *faustus* (*faustam famam*, Ald. 162, 12), An. Ox. 18 b, 35. IV. with reference to a purpose or effect. (1) *adapted to an end, useful, suitable :*—Sió biþ gōd tō dolhsealfe, Lch. ii. 92, 27. Blōd lǣtan mōna gōd ys, iii. 184, 11, *and often.* Stede hafað gōdne, Rä. 45, 3. (2) *having the characteristics required in a particular capacity, able, skilful :*—Swā sceal gōd scȳrman his hlāfordes healdan, Angl. ix. 260, 16. Sum bið gewittig æt wīnþege, beórhyrde gōd, Crä. 75. Hē ne bið him lǣce gōd, Sal. 102. (3) *reliable, trustworthy :*—Hæbbe hē in āðe ōðirne ǣwdan gōdne, Ll. Th. i. 42, 8. Mid gōdum ǣwdum, 28, 2, 8. Beforan gōdum weotum geceápod, 118, 14. Mid twām gōdum þegenum, 294, 12. V. *adequate, effectual, valid.* (1) of personal actions or activities, *thorough, effectual :*—Hē hit heóld on gōdre geþuǣrnesse, Chr. 860 ; P. 68, 1. Hī gōdne frið heóldon, 877 ; P. 74, 21. Nis nā tō forgytane þ gōde frið þe hē macode, 1086 ; P. 220, 12. (2) *valid, sound :*—Ā þīn dōm sȳ gōd and genge, Az. 109. (3) *sufficient or abundant in quantity :*—Eów byþ geseald gōd gemet and full, Lk. 6, 38. Swā mycel swā wolde beón gōd handebrād, Vis. Lfc. 72. Bið hē gōdes leánes weorðe, Ll. Th. i. 440, 18. Hē gegaderode gōdne dǣl feós, Hml. S. 25, 468. Hē gōde hwīle þone here gefiémde, Chr. 837 ; P. 62, 32. (4) qualifying a definite statement of quantity :—Drince gōdne bollan fulne, Lch. ii. 108, 6. Dō ǣlcre gōde hand fulle, 106, 15. v. ǣr-, cyne-, efen-, un-gōd.

**gōd**, es ; *n. Add:* I. *that which is good.* (1) *whatever is good in itself, or beneficial in its effect.* (a) *what is right, virtuous, &c. :*—Gōd bið genge and wið God lenge, Gn. Ex. 121. Gōd sceal wið yfele, Gn. C. 50. Þ him þ gōd mōte tō ēcum mēdum gegangan, þ him his freónd æfter gedēþ, Bl. H. 101, 17. Þ heofonlice rīce is gehāten eallum þe nū syndan gōdes wyrhtan, 111, 12. Þeáh hē gōdes hwæt onginne gǣstlice, Jul. 397 : Met. 9, 62. Seó sāwl bið forð lǣdende eall þā weorc þe heó ǣr fremede gōdes oððe yfeles. Gif þonne byð þæra misdǣda mā and þæs gōdes tō lyt, Wlfst. 254, 2–5 : Dōm. 43. Gōdes oððe gāles, Cri. 1035. Hī sién āsigen tō yfele ... þæt mōd ne mæg āredian tō gōde, Bt. 24, 4 ; F. 84, 28–34. Hē dyde māre yfel þonne gōd, Bl. H. 43, 34. Hē nolde nān gōd gehȳran, Hml. Th. i. 534, 7. (b) *what is beneficial, advantageous, pleasant, &c. :*—Gōdes and yfies ic cunnade, Vid. 51. Gōdes and yfeles, ... welan and wāwan, Gen. 465. Eów ǣfre ne bið þurh gife mīne gōdes onsién, Cri. 480. Ic geþolade gōdes ealles, wonn mōdearfoða mā, Hy. 4, 85. Onfōh þū þīnum esne fægere mid gōde *elige servum tuum in bonum*, Ps. Th. 118, 122. Ne mē ǣnig mid gōde ongitan wolde *non erat qui agnosceret me*, Ps. Th. 141, 4. Hē mē gōde dohte, mē beág forgeaf, Vīd. 89. Gōde gewircean, feohgiftum, B. 20. Mīne geornnesse mid gōde þū gefyldest, Bl. H. 89, 5. Þæt ic

gód æt him begitan môte, Ps. Th. 121, 9 : Gen. 2420. Gif wē gód underfēngon of Godes handa, hwî ne sceole wē éac yfel underfôn?, Hml. Th. ii. 452, 31. (2) *goodness, virtue, excellence* :—Gif hit gewurþ þæt se anweald becume tô gôdum men, hwæt biþ ðǽr lícwyrþe bûton his gôd, nas ðæs anwealdes? . . . hit biþ ðæs monnes gôd, nas ðæs anwealdes, Bt. 16, 2 ; F. 50, 14–19. God simle biþ full gôd, and þ his good and sió his gesǽlþ him nâhwonan ûtane ne côm, 34, 7 ; F. 144, 20. (3) *prosperous condition, well-being, good estate.* (a) as a condition actually existing :—Unryhtlicu iersung is ðæt mon iersige on ôðerne for his gôde (*on account of his prosperity*), Past. 189, 8. Gif ðu hwene gesihst gedeón on góde . . . gif him hwæt mistîmað, Hex. 44, 29. Forlǽt ðæt ðu næbbe tô ôðres mannes gôde andan, Prov. K. 33. (b) as a condition to be produced :—Hê dyde swâ mycel tô gôde intô þ mynstre of Burh on golde and on seolfre swâ nêfre nân ôðre ne dyde, Chr. 1066 ; P. 198, 16. Gemiltsa þîn môd mē tô gôde, Hy. 2, 2. Tô bealwe . . . tô gôde, Cri. 1107 : Verc. Först. 129, 28. For gôde, R. Ben. 116, 20. Weard of heofonum þæt môd in ðæs gǽstes gôd georne trymede, Gú. 78. (4) *good, benefit resulting* from something :—Heora nân him ne mehte bión nâne gôde (on nânum gôde, *v. l.*), Ors. 6, 30 ; S. 282, 19. Cweþaþ cræftige men þ him þ tô gôde cume, Lch. i. 88, 19. (5) tô gôde (gedôn *to act so as to bring about a good result, to do good*) :—Hê ne mihte nân ðing tô gôde gedôn-*bona facere non poterat*, Hml. Th. i. 534, 7. Ðeáh se mann ælmessan wyrce and fela tô gôde gedô, 528, 29. Nân man ne dēð bûtan Gode nân ðing tô gôde, 292, 36. Âsolcennys dēð þæt ðâm men ne lyst nân ðing tô gôde gedôn, ac gǽð him âsolcen fram ælcere dugeðe, ii. 220, 23 : Chr. 81 ; P. 8, 8. II. *a particular thing that is good.* (1) something, material or non-material, that it is an advantage to attain or to possess :—Of ðære sôþan gesǽlþe cumað ealle ðâ ôþre gôd . . . þâ fíf gôd . . . þ is anweald and weorþscipe and foremǽrnes and genyht and blis, Bt. 34, 6 ; F. 140, 16–23. Ealle þâ líchamlican gôd, 24, 3 ; F. 84, 5. Þû mē noldest þanc witan mînra gôda (*my good gifts*), Wlfst. 261, 10 : Ph. 624 : Cri. 1400 : Gen. 546 : Ps. Th. 102, 2. þæt folc ne cûðe ðæra gôda þæt hî cwǽdon þæt hê God wǽre, ac sǽdon þæt hê wítega wǽre *the people did not know of the advantages they had, to wit that they might call him God, but said he was a prophet*, Hml. Th. i. 190, 31. Nât hê þâra gôda, þæt hê mē ongeán sleá, rand geheáwe *he knows not of such advantages as striking at me, hewing my shield* (Grendel could not do these things as he had no sword), B. 681. Weán dreógan, gôda bedǽled, Sat. 186. Fremde from eallum ðǽm gôdum þe þu ûs gegearwodest, Bl. H. 233, 32. Hingriende hê mid gôdum gefylde, Lk. 1, 53 : B. 1861. Ðætte þ gé fore uueorolde sién geblitsade mid ðǽm weoroldcundum gôdum and hiora sáula mid ðǽm godcundum gôdum, C. D. i. 293, 35. (1 a) (*the highest*) *good* ; summum bonum :—Swâ hwæt swâ ǽghwelc man ofer ealle ôþre þing swîþost lufaþ, þ biþ his hēhste gôd . . . Ne onsace ic nâuht þ þâ gesǽlþa and seó eádignes sié þæt hēhste gôd þises andweardan lífes, Bt. 24, 3 ; F. 84, 11–15 : 34, 3 ; F. 138, 5. (2) *a good quality, virtue* :—Crîst ûs ælces gôdes bysene onstealde, Bl. H. 29, 7. Hî sceolon ælce gôdes bodian, Hml. A. 146, 60. (3) *a good deed* :—Þý lǽs hê ǽnig þâra gôda forylde þe hê þý dæge gedôn mihte, Bl. H. 213, 24. Þâ gôd dôn þe ûs Godes bêc lǽraþ, þæt is fæsten . . . and ælmessylena, 73, 26 : 101, 22. Hê ne mihte dôn þâ gôd þe hine man lǽrde, Gr. D. 324, 9 : Past. 87, 4. þæt wē bugon fram yfele and dôn gôda (*bona*), Coll. M. 33, 9. (3 a) of the services of the church :—Ðættæ mon unce tîde geuueorðiae on godcundum gôdum and æc on aelmessan, C. D. i. 292, 32 : 293, 3. Ic bidde hîgon ðette hié ðâs godcundan gôd gedôn fore hiora sáwlum, ðaet éghwilc messepriôst gesinge twâ messan . . . and aeghwilc diácon ârēde twâ passione . . . Aec ic biddo hîgon ðaet gē mē gemynen mid suilce godcunde gôde suilce iów cynlic ðynce, 293, 28–294, 1. (4) *property, wealth, goods* :—Sum tô lyt hafað gôdes grǽdig, Sal. 344. Þ gé of mínum âgenum gôde (mínes âgenes æhtes, *v. l.*) âgifan þâ teôðunga ǽgðer ge on cwicum ceápe ge on þæs geáres eorðwæstmum . . . and þâ biscopas þ ilce dôn on heora âgenum gôde, Ll. Th. i. 194, 5–9. Yrfes hyrde gôde mǽre, Gen. 2198 : B. 1952. Hî lǽddon Loth and leóda gôd, suðmonna sinc, Gen. 2016. Hê ðǽr mycel gôd tô gegaderode, Chr. 1065 ; P. 191, 24. (4 a) in pl., *goods* :—Ne gold ne seolfor ne þînra gôda nân . . . ne þîn boldwela ne nân þâra gôda þe þû iú âhtest, Seel. 58–60. Þ wē gefyllon þæs þearfan wambe mid ûrum gôdum, Bl. H. 39, 30. Of hîgna gemēnum gôdum aet hâm mon geselle .cxx. gesufíra hláfa, C. D. i. 293, 16. Þû hæfst mycele gôd (feolo gôdo, L., feolu gôdz, R., *multa bona*), Lk. 12, 19. v. feoh-, un-, unrîm-, weorold-gôd.

**gód-æpple.** *Substitute* : **gód-æppel** *a quince* :—Goodaeppel *citonium*, Wrt. Voc. ii. 104, 9. Gôdæppel (*the MS. has the accent*), 14, 36. Cf. cod-æppel.

**god-bearn.** *Add* :—Godfæder his godbearn lufie and lǽre, Wlfst. 74, 13. Beóð heó rihtlice ealswâ hý genamode beóð, godfæderas, gif hý heora godbearn Gode gestrýnað, 121, 5.

**god-borh.** *Substitute* : *A pledge confirmed by an appeal to God, one that is accompanied by the formulae of religion* :—Be godborgum (-borhgum, *v. l.*). Gif hwâ ôðerne godborges oncunne and tión wille þ hê hwelcne ne gelǽste þâra þe hê him gesealde *if any one bring against*

*another a charge in the matter of a pledge whose validity was confirmed by invoking the name of the Deity* (*where solemn formulae were used to give validity*). Cf. *the formulae* pp. 178–182 *beginning on* þone Drihten, on Ælmihtiges Godes naman, on lifiendes Godes naman), *and will accuse him that he do not carry out any of the pledges that he gave him*, Ll. Th. i. 82, 4–6.

**god-bót,** an. *l.* god-bót, e.

**god-cund.** *Add* : I. *of or pertaining to God* :—Godcund andgit and godcund foretiohhung, Bt. 39, 4 ; F. 216, 31. Se godcunda anweald, 16, 4 ; F. 58, 13. · Ðâ ðe sió godcundde stefn ðreáde, Past. 91, 7. Þæs godcundan mægenþrymmes, Bl. H. 103, 3. On þǽre godcundan dǽde (*the deed done by Christ*), 215, 28. Godcund gecynd *diuinam naturam*, Mk. p. 2, 3. Hî heora môd neár godcundum ðingum lǽtaþ, Bt. 40, 7 ; F. 242, 26. II. *given by or proceeding from God, having the sanction of or inspired by God.* (1) *of things.* (a) *a law, command, doctrine, &c.* :—Godcundre spæce *oraculorum*, i. *diuinorum eloquiorum*, An. Ox. 1531. Godcundre gesettnesse *diuine sanctionis*, 423 ; 1628. Mid þon worde þæs godcundan gewrites, Bl. H. 33, 20. Onbryrde tô godcundre lâre, 23. Þǽre godcundan ǽ gehýrsume, 163, 3. On þâm godcundan gebede *in the Lord's Prayer*, Ll. Th. i. 372, 28. Þâ godcundan lâre gehýran . . . þǽr mon þ godspel sægþ, Bl. H. 47, 28. Sum mæg godcunde reccan ryhte ǽ, Cri. 670. Godcundra beboda, Bl. H. 37, 8. On godcundum bôcum God beád þ . . . , Bt. 41, 3 ; F. 246, 32. (b) *a benefit, good, &c.* :—Biddan ðone godcundan fultum, Bt. 33, 3 ; F. 126, 34. Hié helpe findað, godcunde gife, El. 1033. Þâ sint tô tellanne tô godcundan gôdum, . . . God hî gesceóp tô gemâgum, Bt. 24, 3 ; F. 82, 30. Geweorþod mid godcundum geofum, Bl. H. 133, 3 : Gen. 2810. Mid godcundum wuldrum, Bl. H. 125, 17. (2) *of persons* :—Godcunde bydelas, Ll. Th. i. 424, 17. ¶ *having the sanction of the church, prescribed by the church* :—Eówr manaþ eówer lâreów þæt gē hýrsumian godcundum lârum (*divinis disciplinis*), Coll. M. 35, 35. Wǽron woroldwitan þe gesettan tô godcundan rihtlagan worldlaga, Ll. Th. i. 334, 22 : 348, 13 : ii. 242, 13. Ǽghwylc crîsten man unrihthǽmed forbûge and godcunde laga rihtlice healde, i. 306, 25 : 364, 18. III. *devoted to God*, of persons, worship, service, dues, &c., belonging to the church. (1) of persons :—Godcunde hâdas wǽron nû lange swîðe forsawene *those in holy orders have now for long been despised*, Wlfst. 158, 9. Micelne sinoð ǽgðer ge godcundra hâda ge woruldcundra *a great synod of churchmen and laymen*, Ll. Th. i. 244, 3. Þ hî godcundum lâreówan hýran, 326, 14 : 424. 7. (2) *of worship, services, &c.*, of the church :—Ic biddo hîgon ðaet gē mē gemynen mid suilce godcunde gôde suilce iów cynlic ðynce *I pray that you have such a memorial service for me as may seem to you fitting*, C. D. i. 294, 1. Mid godcundan scrifte, Ll. Th. ii. 240, 15. On godcundan scriftan and woruldcundan steóran, i. 328, 19 : 412, 11. Ðæt mon hiora tîd geuueorðiae mid godcundan gôd gedôn . . . ðaet ǽghwilc messepriost hîgon ðette hié ðâs godcundan gôd gedôn . . . ond ǽghwilc Godes ðiów gesinge twâ fíftig, C. D. i. 293, 1–33. Godes þeówum þe þâ cyrican mid godcundum dreámum weorþiað, Bl. H. 41, 27. Godcunde lâc bringan, 47, 4. Godcund gebed, Lch. ii. 140, 21. Godcunde gebedo *prayers addressed to God*, Wlfst. 240, 16. (3) *of dues, penalties, discipline, &c.* :—Gif hwâ forwyrne godcunde gerihta *de ecclesiae debita vi detinente*, Ll. Th. i. 404, 4–6 : 170, 7. Tô mid wîge godcundra gerihta forwyrne, Ll. Th. i. 404, 4–6 : 170. 7. Tô godcundre bôte gebûgan, 166, 15. Swâ mid godcundre bôte swâ mid woruldcundre steóre, 328, 3. Ǽr hē hæbbe godcunde bôte underfangen, 248, 24. Tô godcundan neódan *for the needs of the church*, 328, 9. Bisceope gebyreð ǽlc rihting ge on godcundan þingan ge on woruldcundan, ii. 312, 9. III a. *of a heathen deity* :—Þonne môton hié gongan in þone godcundan (cf. þone hâlgan bearo, 29, 23) bearo (*diuinum lucum*), Nar. 27, 10. On þâ godcundan stôwe, 31, 15. IV. *partaking of the nature of God, spiritual* :—Ðǽm godcundan heáhstan *anagogen*, Wrt. Voc. ii. 9, 7. Bisceopas þe godcunde heorda bewarian sceolan þ se wôdfreca werewulf tô fela ne âbîte of godcundre heorde, Ll. Th. i. 374, 29–31. Bodian godcunde þearfe *predicare spiritualem utilitatem*, 424, 18. Bodian and bysnian godcunde þearfe (*spirituale proficuum*), 374, 21 : 332, 30. Habban godcunde blisse and eác worldcunde, Bl. H. 83, 20. Sē ðe wille godcundne wîsdôm sécan, Bt. 12 ; F. 36, 9. Ðaette gē fore uueorolde sién geblitsade mid ðǽm weoroldcundum gôdum and hiora sáula mid ðǽm godcundum gôdum, C. D. i. 293, 36. In godcundum gǽstgerýnum, Gú. 219. IV a. *celestial, heavenly.* (1) *coming from heaven* :—Coludes burh forbarn mid godcundum fýre, Chr. 679 ; P. 39, 6. (2) *belonging to heaven* :—Hê nǽfre nǽnige godcunde englas nǽfde bûton hundlice englas, Bl. H. 181, 28. V. *that makes godlike* :—Þǽre godcundre besceáwunga *deifice contemplationis* (v. Ald. 11, 5), Wrt. Voc. ii. 139, 62.

**godcundlic.** *Add* : I. *of God* :—For his godcundlicum anwealde hê is ǽghwǽr andweard, Bt. 42 ; F. 258, 11. II. *proceeding from God, inspired by God* :—Godcundlicum wordum (*with words from the Scriptures*) heó hyre bearn lǽrde, Lch. iii. 428, 28. III. *devoted*

to God, religious:—Godcundlicere drohtnunge diuinę conuersationis, An. Ox. 2566. **IV.** partaking of the nature of God:—Gē hwæt-hwega godcundlices on eówerre sáule habbaþ, Bt. 14, 2; F. 44, 24. **IV a.** spiritual:—Godcundlic theoricam, i. contemplatiuam, An. Ox. 2516. **IV b.** celestial, heavenly:—Óþre hwīle hē smeáþ ymb þis eorþlice līf, óþre hwīle ymb þ godcundlice, Bt. 39, 7; F. 222, 5. Ealle godcundlice gesceafta standaþ on Drihtnes gewealdum, Hml. A. 154, 61. **V.** that makes godlike:—Godcundlicere deifice, An. Ox. 705.

**godcundlíce.** Add: **I.** of action by the Deity, by God, from heaven:—Þā cōm micel wæl and moncwild godcundlíce (dininitus) sended, Bd. 4, 3; Sch. 357, 22. Hē wæs godcundlíce (dininitus) gefultumod, 4, 24; Sch. 482, 2. **II.** in respect to religion or to the church, ecclesiastically:—Ne sīn ealle circan nā gelícre mæðe worldlíce wyrðe, þeáh hī godcundlíce habban hálgunge gelíce, Ll. Th. i. 340, 27: 360, 17.

**godcund-meaht** (?) divine majesty:—In seðel godcunndmæhtes his in sede majestatis snae, Mt. L. 19, 28. Ofer seðel godcundmæht his, 25, 31. Mið mægne menigo and godcundmæht cum virtute multa et majestate, 24, 30.

**godcundnys.** Add: **I.** the quality of being divine. (1) in a general sense:—Hū ne hæfdon wē ǽr gereaht þ ðā gesǽlþa and sió god-cundnes ān wǽre?... swā wē cwedaþ þ þ sié God þe þā godcundnesse hæfð and ðā gesǽlða, and ælc gesǽlig bið God beatitudo uero est ipsa divinitas ... divinitatem adeptos, Deos fieri necesse est. Omnis igitur beatus, Deus, Bt. 34, 5; S. 85, 27–86, 1. (2) of the persons of the Trinity:—His godcundnyss wæs on þǽre menniscnysse tō ānum sōðan Crīste ... æfre unbegunnen on ðǽre godcundnysse, Hml. A. 25, 23. Ðeós is seó hálige þrynnys ... on ānre godcundnysse æfre wunigende, on ānum mægenþrymme and on ānum gecynde, 2, 24: 26, 56: 59, 199. Arrius wolde wanian Crīstes godcundnysse, 198: 152, 17: 155, 84. **II.** a divine being:—Hit is gecynd ðǽre godcundnesse þ hió mæg beón ungemenged wið óþre gesceafta būton óþerra gesceafta fultume, swā swā nān óþer gesceaft ne mæg, ne mæg nān óþer gesceaft be him selfum bión ea est divinae forma substantiae, ut neque in externa dilabatur, nec in se externum aliquid ipsa suscipiat, Bt. 35, 5; F. 166, 4–7. Mē þincþ þ þū hwerfest ymbūton sume wunderlice sprǽce ymbe þā ānfealdnesse þǽre godcundnesse an mirabilem quendam divinae simpli-citatis orbem complicas?, F. 164, 18. Be þǽm dǽle þe sió mennisce gesceádwīsnes mæg ongitan ðā godcundnesse, 39, 10; F. 226, 28. **III.** divine service:—Ic wille ðet ðā hīwan ā hwīlæ ðæ crīstendōm sié fullícæ mid hira godcundnessæ for mē sién uolo ut familia ... quamdiu christianitas permanserit sint illi mei intercessores ad Dominum, C. D. v. 218, 32. Ne preóst ne forlǽte his godcundnesse, Ll. Th. ii. 354, 2. **III a.** a pious offering:—Gif hwā þ fæsten āberan ne mæg ðe his scrift him tǽcð, him ys ālýfed þ hē mót his fæsten ālýsan mid godcundnysse and mid his worldæhton (pietate et mundanis suis possessionibus); þ is þonne, gif hē byð welig, sylle for .xii. mōnða fæstene xxx scillinga, Ll. Th. ii. 220, 27. **IV.** a quality that is consonant with Deity, a godlike quality:—Ðeós wyrt hæfð sume wund-orlice godcundnesse, þ is þonne þ hyre blōsman hý æfter þǽre sunnan ryne wendað, Lch. i. 152, 24.

**gód-dǽd.** Add: **I.** a good deed, virtuous action:—Sume synd ealles tō īdele ælcere góddǽde, Ll. Th. ii. 322, 13. Þīn sāwl sceal wunian oðða on wīte for þīnum gyltum oðða on blisse for þīnum góddǽdum, Wlfst. 248, 6. For þām his góddǽdum (almsgiving), Gr. D. 320, 20. Þeáw is þ hī æfæstiað óþra manna góddǽda mos est invidere aliis virtutis bonum, 117, 5. **II.** a benefit; Ps. Th. 77, 13.

**god-dohtor.** Add:—'Ic þē wille biddan, Drihten, þ þ wæter ge-wurðe mē tō fulluhtes bæðe' ... 'Ic eom þīn godfæder and þū mīn goddohtor', Hml. A. 178, 298. Sum gerēfman wǽre þára þe onfēnge ānum mægdene æt fullwihte ... hē bæd þā ylcan his goddohter, þ heó mid him þā niht wunode, Gr. D. 308, 17.

**gód-dónd, -dénd.** Substitute: **gód-dónd, -dóend, es; m.** **I.** one who does good, one who acts righteously:—Næs þā góddóend, sē þe God wiste non est qui faciat bonum, Ps. Th. 52, 2. **II.** one who does good to another, a benefactor:—Þā neát ongitað hira góddénd, El. 359. Cf. yfel-dónd.

**góde-líc, gode-webb.** v. gód-líc, god-webb.

**god-fæder.** Add: **I.** a godfather:—Se godfæder wæs þæs cildes forspreca and borh wið God, Hml. Th. ii. 50, 17: 52, 4–15. God-fæder his godbearn lufie, Wlfst. 74, 13. Petrus wæs his (St. Mark's) godfæder and hine Gode gestrýnde, and hē lange folgode his fulluht-fædere Petre, Hml. S. 15, 143. Ic eom þīn godfæder and þū mīn god-dohtor, Hml. A. 178, 297. Ðā unsprecendan cild beóð gehealdene on ðām fulluhte ðurh geleáfan þæs fæder and þǽre mōder and þæs forespre-cendan godfæder, Hml. Th. ii. 116, 16: 52, 2. Beóð þā þe cildes onfōn rihtlíce ... godfæderas, gif hý heora godbearn Gode gestrýnað, Wlfst. 121, 4. **II.** God the Father:—Godfæder efenlæcend Dei Patris imitator, Scint. 13, 11. Sča Maria is Godfæder snoru, Shrn. 118, 6. Sča Maria onfēng on hire bōsm Godfæder sunu, Bl. H. 5, 33: 29, 27.

Se ilca Sunu wæs ācenned fram Godfæder, 31, 25. Hē fram Godfæder āsended wæs and eft tō Godfæder fēran wolde a Deo exivit et ad Deum vadit, Hml. A. 154, 77.

**god-frēcnes** (?). v. god-wrecnes.

**god-fyrht.** Add:—Ioachim wæs godfyrht man, Hml. A. 118, 42. Þā synna yrnað æfter þǽre earman sāwle and hire tō cwedað ... 'Wē wēndon þæt þū wǽre godfyrht, ac þu hæfdest deófles geþanc, Wlfst. 240, 27. v. N. E. D. god-fright. Cf. O. H. Ger. got-forht timoratus.]

**god-gesprǽce.** Substitute: **god-gesprǽce, es; n.** An oracle:—Wæs þis godgesprǽce (-sprec, -sprǽcen, -sprecen, v. ll.) þisses gemetes erat oraculum huiusmodi, Bd. 2, 12; Sch. 152, 12. Æfter þām godgesprǽce (-sprece, þǽm gódan sprǽce, þǽm gódgesprece [the MS. has the accent], v. ll.) iuxta oraculum, Sch. 161, 15. Cf. godcund; II. 1, god-sprǽce.

**god-gesprec** (gód- ?). See preceding word, and god-sprec.

**god-gesprecen, -sprǽcen** [cf. O. H. Ger. ge-sprochani]. v. god-gesprǽce.

**god-gild.** Add: a rite or practice of a heathen religion:—God-gildum ceremoniis, Wrt. Voc. ii. 23, 65: Lupercalibus, 50, 40. Se dēma stōd æt his godgyldum and deóflum onsægdnesse bær judex aris adsistebat, ac daemonibus hostias offerebat, Bd. 1, 7; Sch. 21, 1. Hē heora godgieldum eallum wiðsōc and hié æfter þǽm mid ealle tōwearp cunctam Aegypti religionem abominatus, ceremonias ejus et templa deposuit, Ors. 2, 5; Swt. 78, 4.

**godgild-líc; adj.** Of heathen worship:—Godgildlícere phanaticae, Wrt. Voc. ii. 66, 67.

**gódian.** Add: **I.** intrans. To be or to become good, be prosperous. Cf. gód; III. 1. (1) with a noun as subject:—Eówer kynedōm gódað þurh heora gódan geearnunga, Hml. S. 5, 444. Hié beóð suīðe un-gesǽlige, ðonne hié yfeliað for ðǽm ðe ōðre menn gódigað (gódiað, v. l.) quantae infelicitatis sint, qui melioratione proximi deteriores fiunt, Past. 231, 19. (2) with hit as subject:—Wolde man geswīcan þára māndǽda, þonne gódade hit sōna if people would cease to do evil, then would it soon be well with us, Wlfst. 243, 21. Hý āgunnon rǽdes gýman and hit āgann mid heom gódian, 14, 14. **II.** trans. (1) the object a person. (a) to make good, to give an appearance of being good:—Gē wǽron þā þe eów sylfe gódiaþ (rihtwīsiað, v.l.) beforan mannum vos estis qui justificatis vos coram hominibus, Gr. D. 40, 10. (b) to endow, furnish with (a) a material good:—Gódede indemtam (cirris crispan-tibus), Hpt. Gl. 513, 77. (β) non-material:—Mattheus ... þæt is Donatus, on Englisc 'Forgifen' oððe 'Gegódod.' God hine gódode swā þæt hē hine āwende of tollere tō apostol, Hml. Th. ii. 468, 15. (2) the object a thing, material or non-material. (a) to set right, put in good order:—Gódiað eówre āgene wegas and ealle eówre dǽda, Wlfst. 49, 29. Á hē mæig findan hwæt hē mæig on byrig bētan ... hūs gódian, ... hegas gódian, Angl. ix. 262, 15–20. (b) to endow:—Ðā bohte se abbot landes feola and gódede þ mynstre, Chr. 963; P. 117, 23. (c) to make abundant, accumulate. Cf. gód. V. 3:—Gódende cumulantem, i. multiplicantem, An. Ox. 1932. [v. N. E. D. good; vb.] v. ge-gódian.

**god-líc; adj.** God-like, divine:—Þǽre godlícan besceáwunga deifice contemplationis, Wrt. Voc. ii. 139, 61. Godlicum dealibus, i. deificis, 81. v. god-cund.

**gód-líc.** Add:—Gódelic pulchra, Germ. 394, 266.

**gód-líf, es; n.** A good, virtuous life:—Waltear swīðe gódlīfes man, Chr. 1095; P. 232, 5. [Cf. Icel. góð-lífi, -lifnaðr a good life.]

**god-mōdor.** Add:—Godmōdra matrenas, Wrt. Voc. ii. 57, 69.

**gódnes.** Add: **I.** the quality or condition of being good:—Óðer biþ se mon, þ biþ sāwl and līchoma, óðer biþ his gódnes, þ gegæderaþ God and eft ætgædre gehelt, Bt. 34, 3; F. 136, 33. Swā swā manna goodnes hī āhefþ ofer þā menniscan gecynd cum ultra homines quemque provehere sola probitas possit, 37, 4; F. 192, 8. **II.** goodness in one's relations to others. (1) as an attribute of the Deity:—Se Hǽlend þæt hungrige folc mildheortlíce fēdde, ægðer ge þurh his gódnysse ge þurh his mihte. Hwæt mihte seó gódnys āna, būton ðǽr wǽre miht mid þǽre gódnysse?, Hml. Th. i. 184, 19. Is swīþe sweotol þte God æghwæs wealt mid þǽre helman his gódnesse Deus omnia bonitatis clauo gubernare jure creditur, Bt. 35, 5; F. 160, 15. Hī þancodon Gode eallre his gódnysse, Hml. S. 25, 361. For þīnre gódnesse, Drihten, þū eart swēte universae viae Domini misericordia, Ps. Th. 24, 8. (2) of men, kindness, benevolence:—Hwæt is gód willa būton gódnys, þæt hē ōðres mannes ungelimp besārgie, and on his gesundfulnysse fægnige?, Hml. Th. i. 584, 5. **III.** advantage, benefit, profit; useful object:—Hwæt sind ðā gód þe men syllað heora cildum? Hwīlwendlíce gódnyssa, swylce swā þæt godspel hrepode, hlāf, and fisc, and ǽig, Hml. Th. i. 252, 24. **III a.** good fortune, prosperous circumstance:—Þū geseó gódnessa uideas bona (Hierusalem), Ps. L. 127, 5. **IV.** a good act or deed:—Hē þancode Gode eallra his gódnyssa, þ hē hine gescylde ... and him sige forgeaf, Hml. S. 14, 163. Habban ūs on handa ūre leóhtfatu þ sýn hálige weorc, on ælmesdǽdum and on eallum gódnessum, Ll. Th. ii. 368, 38. **IV a.** that which is good in any-

*thing, the good part of anything* :—Ðās þing wē habbað be him gewritene, ǣgðer ge gōde ge yfele, þ þā gōdan men niman æfter þeóra
gōdnesse (*may imitate the good part of his actions*), Chr. 1086; P.
221, 24.

**god-sǣd.** *Substitute : A divine progeny* (?), *children of God.* In Dan.
901 the same meaning seems to be intended as in 89 : *ginge and gōde* =
*ǣdele cnihtas* and *in godsǣde* (among the children of God ?) = ǣfæste.

**god-scipe.** *l.* gōd-scipe.

**god-sibb.** *Add : One who has become spiritually related to another*
(a baptized child or its parents) *by acting as sponsor at baptism* :—Hine
(*Malcolm*) slōh Moræl ; sē wæs Melcolmes cynges godsib, Chr. 1093 ;
P. 228, 9. Nān man on his godsibbe ne wīfige (cf. Si quis *commatrem*
*spiritalem* in conjugio duxerit, anathema sit, 20, 15. Si quis cum
*spiritali matre* peccaverit, sicut superius dictum est, anathematizetur, 21,
17), Ll. Th. ii. 300, 15. [Cf. *Icel.* guð-sefi *a godfather,* guð-sifja *a*
*godmother.*]

**godsibb-rǣden**[n], e ; *f. The condition of ' gossips '* (v. god-sibb) :—
Gif gē nellað healdan þā godsibbrǣdenne þe gē habbað for Gode and for
Sce Iōhannes dǣle begetene, Wlfst. 228, 3. [v. *N. E. D.* gossip-red.]

**god-spell.** *Add : I. the body of doctrine taught by Christ and his*
*apostles* :—Þis godspel byð bodod ofer ealle eorðan *praedicabitur hoc*
*evangelium regni in universo orbe,* Mt. 24, 14 : 26, 13. On ealle
þeóda ǣrest gebyrað beón þ godspel gebodud, Mk. 13, 10. Þā apostolas
wǣron gefylde þurh godspelles lāre, Bl. H. 133, 32. Cōm se Hǣlend
Godes rīces godspell bodigende and cweðende : . . . 'Gelýfaþ þām godspelle,' Mk. 1, 14-15. Þonne ge faran godspel tō lǣrenne, Bl. H. 233,
17. **I a.** *the Christian dispensation* (in contrast with the Mosaic) :—
Sē þe Godes beboda forsyhð nū on þæs godspelles tīman, Hml. S. 18,
477. þ is nū mānfullic . . . on þām crīstendōme þe Crīst āstealde, on
þæs godspelles tīman nū under Godes gyfe, Hml. A. 16, 75. **II.** *the*
*record of Christ's life and teaching.* (1) *contained in the books written*
*by the four evangelists* :—Drihten selfa swā on his godspelle be him
(*John the Baptist*) cwæþ, Bl. H. 165, 2 : 213, 21. On þæm godspelle
cwið þ . . ., 133, 36. (1 a) *one of the books written by the four*
*evangelists* :—Iōhannes ūs cýðde on þǣm godspelle and þus cwæþ :
'Hǣlend cwōm . . .,' Bl. H. 67, 23. Se godspellere (*St. Luke*) on
fruman his godspell wrāt and cwæð : 'On Hērodes dagum . . .,' 161, 25.
Ðā godspella ðerh Matheum . . . ðerh Marcun, Lk. p. 2, 5. Ān fore
feówer godspellum, Mt. p. 10, 14. Ðās fēwera godspelles, p. 9, 8.
(1 b) *a particular copy of the gospels* :—Ðerh syndriga stōwa godspella
tal gesegen bið tōgeseted, Mt. p. 11, 11. Foregesettum þām swīþe
hālgum godspellum, Bd. 4, 17 ; Sch. 431, 14. [ referred to in case
of solemn appeal :—Ic eów hālsie . . . þurh þā hālgan godspel and ðā
reliquia þe on ðisse cyrcan syndon, Ll. Lbmn. 415, 5. (1 c) *the* (*Latin*)
*text of a gospel* :—Ic cweðe nū þæt ic nǣfre heononforð ne āwende godspel of Lēdene on Englisc, Hml. Tb. ii. 594, 19. (2) *contained in*
*books written by others* :—Monige werun ðā ðe godspellas (*evangelia*)
āwritton, Mt. p. 7, 1. **III.** *the gospel, as used in the services of the*
*church* :—Wē gehýrdon þā þæt hālige godspel rǣdd wæs, Bl. H. 161, 9.
Þeh hē gehýre þā word þæs hālgan godspelles, 55, 7. Þonne wē gehýron
Godes bēc rǣdan and godspell secggean, 111, 17 : 47, 31. Acolitus
candele byrð þonne mann godspell rǣt . . . Diaconus godspell rǣt æt
Godes þēnungum, Ll. Th. ii. 348, 4-14 : Vis. Lfc. 13. **III a.** *where*
*the special portion of the gospel is specified, the gospel of the day* :—
Ðys godspel sceal on cylda-mæssedæg, Mt. 2, 18 rbc (*and often*) : Hml.
Th. i. 84, 26. Þis dægðerlice godspel, 220, 25. On þyssum godspelle,
Bl. H. 39, 14. Lucas sǣde . . . wē nū gehýrdon þis hālige godspel
beforan ūs rǣdan 15, 3-30. Gregorius trahtnode þis godspel (*the*
*parable of the talents*), Hml. Th. ii. 550, 1.

**godspell-bodung,** e ; *f. Gospel-preaching, the period during which*
*the gospel has been preached, the Christian dispensation.* Cf. godspell ; **I a** :—Seó ealde ǣ and wītegan wǣron oð Iōhannes tōcyme ;
siððan ongann godspelbodung (*lex et prophetae usque ad Iohannem ; ex eo*
*regnum Dei euangelizatur,* Lk. 16, 16), Hml. Th. i. 354, 16. Æt him
ongann seó godspellbodung, Ælfc. T. Grn. 12, 16. Iūdas Machabēus is
eall swā hālig on þām ealdan gecýðnysse swā swā Godes gecorenan on
ðǣre godspelbodunge, Hml. S. 25, 682. Wē sceolan mid earfoðnyssum
þ ēce līf geearnian, and seó earfoðnys ongan on ðǣre godspellbodunge,
16, 241. Seó ealde ǣ getācnode godspelbodunge under Godes gife.
Þreó tīda sind on ðysse worulde . . . ōðer is seó ðe wæs under ǣ ; seó
ðridde is nū æfter Crīstes tōcyme. Þeós tīd is gecweden 'under Godes
gife,' Hml. Th. i. 312, 28.

**godspellere.** *Add : I. an evangelist* :—Isaias wītegode be Crīste
swilce hē godspellere wǣre, Ælfc. T. Grn. 9, 8. **II.** *one of the*
*four evangelists* :—Matheus se godspellere, Hml. A. 49, 1. Swā swā ūs
sǣde se godspellere (v. Mt. 28, 12), 78, 151. Sce Marcus ðrowung þæs
godspelleres, Shrn. 74, 17. Ðe godspellere (*Lucas*) *Evangelista,* Mt.
p. 7, 1 : Bl. H. 15, 3. Fēwer godspelleras, ðāra endebrednis ðes is :
Matthaeus, Marcus, Lucas, Iōhannes, Mt. p. 2, 14. Feówer godspellara
naman, Lch. ii. 140, 17. Þā lāra þāra feówer godspellera, Bl. H.
35, 11.

**godspellian.** *Add : I. to proclaim good tidings to* :—Ðū ðe wilt
godspellian Sion *tu qui evangelizas Sion,* Past. 81, 9. Godspelliendum
mid micelre mihte *euangelizantibus uirtute multa,* Fs. L. 67, 12. Þām
godspelgendum mǣgenu manega *euangelizantium uirtutes multas,* Ps.
Rdr. 67, 12. **II.** *of the good tidings of the gospel.* (1) *intrans.*
*To preach the gospel* to a person :—Ongan hē þām foresprecenan brēþer
godspellian *praefato Fratri Verbum Dei evangelizare coepit,* Guth. Gr.
163, 45. (2) *trans. To preach* the gospel :—Hē bodade and godspellade
rīc Godes *praedicans et euangelizans regnum Dei,* Lk. L. 8, 1. Hī
Godes word Engla þeóda godspellodon, Chr. 596 ; P. 21, 17. [v.
*N. E. D.* gospel ; *vb.*]

**godspellic.** *Add : I. of the gospel, contained in the gospel* :—Swā
ūs seó godspellice racu cýð, Hml. Th. i. 76, 30. Godspellicere race
*euangelice relationis,* An. Ox. 1797. Godspellicere sprǣce *euangelico*
*oraculo,* 3067. **II.** *belonging to the times of the gospel, belonging*
*to the Christian dispensation* :—Endebrednise ðæs godspellica gesetnise
*ordo euangelicae dispositionis,* Lk. p. 2, 8. Cf. god-spell ; **I a** :—Iōhannes
wæs ǣgðer ge ǣlic ge godspellic *John belonged both to the Law and to*
*the Gospel,* Hml. S. 16, 101.

**godspell-traht,** es ; *m. An exposition of a portion of the gospels, a*
*homily* :—Ic gemune mē sylfne secgan þæs wīsan in þām godspelltrahtum
þe ic sylf wrāt *in Homiliis evangelii rem narrasse me recolo,* Gr. D.
283, 1. Ic cweðe nū þæt ic nǣfre heononforð ne āwende godspel-
trahtas of Lēdene on Englisc, Hml. Th. ii. 594, 19.

**god-sprec.** v. god-gesprec.

**god-sunu.** *Add* :—Hē (*St. Mark*) wæs Sce Petres godsunu on
fulwihte, Shrn. 74, 18 : Ælfc. T. Grn. 12, 35. Hine onfēng æt fullwihtes bæþe him tō godsuna Æþewald Eástengla cyning *suscepit eum*
*ascendentem de fonte sacro Aediluald rex Orientalium Anglorum,* Bd. 3,
22 ; Sch. 298, 10.

**god-þrymm.** *Add* :—Hwilc se godþrym sý þǣre ēcan Godes gesihþe
*quae sit majestas aeternae visionis Dei,* Gr. D. 245, 10. Hē geyfelsacode
þone naman þæs ælmihtigan godþrymmes *majestatis nomen blasphemavit,*
289, 22.

**god-webb.** *Add : I. fine woven material, material woven from*
*silk or cotton, fine linen* :—Twihīwe godweb *coccum bis tinctum,* Wrt.
Voc. ii. 135, 44. Godeweb *purpura,* An. Ox. 1378. Seolcen godwebbes *bombicinum purpurae* (*peplum*), 461. Genim þone æppel and
hine bewind on weolcreādum godwebbe, and seóð eft mid sceáte ōþres
godwebbes, Lch. i. 332, 5. Hæfð hē ānforlǣten ðæt twēgea bleó god-
webb ðæt hē habban sceolde on ðǣm hālgan hrægle . . . For ðon is
tōeácan ðǣm twiblíon godwebbe ðæt scyle beón twiðrǣwen twīn on-
ðǣm mæssegierelan *in superhumeralis ornamento habere coccum bis*
*tinctum nescit . . . Unde et bis tincto cocco torta byssus adjungitur,* Past.
87, 13-19. Sum welig man wæs mid purpuran and godewebbe geglenged
(*induebatur purpura et bysso,* Lk. 16, 19), Hml. Th. i. 328, 12. Hē
wæs gegyred mid baswum godwebbe and hwītum, Gr. D. 310, 1. Þeáh
wē ūs gescirpen mid þý reádestan godwebbe, Wlfst. 262, 21. Handstocu mid godwebbe gestefnede *manicae sericis clavatae,* Hpt. Gl. 526,
38. Hié of þæs treówes leáfum and of his flýse spunnon and swā eác tō
godwebbe wǣfon and worhtan *foliis arboris ex siluestri uellere uestes*
*detexunt,* Nar. 6, 18. Of þām cnihtum hī ālǣddon āweg tō wircenne
godweb, Ælfc. T. Grn. 21, 20. Iūdas funde gold and seolfor, godeweb
(god-, *v. l.*) and purpuran (*they got much gold and silver, and blue silk,*
*and purple of the sea,* 1 Macc. iv. 23), Hml. S. 25, 359. Bærn ymb
rēcels and godeweb, Lch. iii. 56, 12, 6. Mid godewebbum *sericis* (v.
Hpt. Gl. 526, 38 *supra*), An. Ox. 5322. **II.** *something made with*
*such material.* (1) *a* (*splendid*) *garment* :—Godweb *clamidis,* Wrt.
Voc. i. 291, 9 : *calamidis,* ii. 17, 30 : *calmidus,* 127, 56. Reád godweb *ostrum,* 64, 10. Fasces .i. *honores, dignitates* cynedōmas *vel*
aldor[dōmas] *vel gegerla vel* godweb, Wrt. Voc. ii. 146, 52 : 35, 2.
Goduueb, 108, 13. Goduuebbe *toga,* 122, 55. Þā wōhgeornan
woruldrīcan mid heora golde and seolfre and godwebbum (gode-, *v. l.,*
cf. godweb-girla), Wlfst. 183, 9. (2) *a curtain.* See also (3) :—Godweb *curtina,* Wrt. Voc. ii. 127, 56. (3) *a flag* :—Pater Noster hafað
gyldene fonan, and seó fone is mid .xii. godwebbum ūtan ymbhangen,
and ānra gehwylc godweb hangað on hundtwelftigum hringa gyldenra
. . . ðæt ðridde godweb wæs on ðæs godwebbes onlicnisse ðe geó ymb
mīnes fæder Dauides columban hangode on ðissum ilcan temple : ðæt
feórðe godweb wæs on ðæs godwebbes onlicnisse ðe geó Abimelech
brōhte Crīste tō lācum, Sal. K. p. 152, 16-28. *See next word.*

**god-webb ;** *adj.* **I.** *of purple or costly material* :—For þām god-
webum hræglum *ex purpureis vestibus,* Gr. D. 13 , 18. **II.** *made*
*of silk or cotton* :—Of ealseolcenum, sidenum *olosericis,* godewebbum,
sidenum *bombicinis* (the passage is : Olosericis et bombicinis indutum
vestibus. Perhaps *godewebbum* might be intended to represent *bombicinis*
*vestibus.* Cf. god-webb ; **II.** 1. In Hpt. Gl. 480, 61 bombicinis is
glossed by godwebbenum), An. Ox. 3162. [Mid godewebbum *sericis,*
5322. Here the word seems to be a noun : see last passage under god-
webb ; **I.**] v. eall-godwebb.

**god-webben.** *Add : I. of purple or costly material* :—For þām

godwebbenum hræglum *ex purpureis vestibus*, Gr. D. 131, 18. Ástreht mid godwebbenum (godewebnum, *v. l.*) pællum *strata palliis*, 176, 1. **II.** *of silk* or *cotton*:—Godwebbenum *olosericis*, Hpt. Gl. 480, 61. Godwebbenum, sidenum *bombicinis*, 66. v. eall-godwebben.

**godweb-cynn**, es; *n. A kind of cloak* or *pall*:—In ðām godwebcynne bið Sanctus Mihhael gescyrped on dômes dæg, Sal. K. p. 152, 22. v. god-webb; **II.** 1, 3.

**godweb-girela**, an; *m. A costly robe*:—Þá þe hê ne mæg tô him gebîgean mid golde ne mid seolfre ne mid godwebgyrlum, Wlfst. 197, 1.

**god-wræc, -wrec.** *For* -wrec *substitute* god-wrece (*short i-stem?*), *and add*: *Exiled from God* (cf. Meh leásne, mê ceigendæ þ ic siê Godes wracco *me falsarium, me clamans sacrilegum*, Mt. p. 1, 9), *impious:*—Goduureci *scevum* (cf. sceuo, i. iniquo ł falso, An. Ox. 4205: sceuitas, iniquitas, Corp. Gl. H. 106, 198), Wrt. Voc. ii. 120, 23. Sió godwrǣce *infandum*, 48, 19. Þæt godwrǣce *nefandum*, 59, 77. Of ðǣre godwrǣcan *a fanatica*, 3, 11. Þá forlegenan and þá godwracan, Nap. 50, 7. [Cf. *Icel.* guð-rækr *wicked.*] *See next word.*

**godwrǣc-lic**; *adj. Sacrilegious:*—Þ hê nâme æt his handa þ hûsl þǣre godwrǣclican (-wræt-, -wret-, *v. ll.*) gehálgunge *ut ex ejus manu sacrilegae consecrationis communionem perciperet*, Gr. D. 238, 12. Gehrînan þǣm godwrǣclican (-wræt-, *v. l.*) mete *contingere cibum sacrilegum*, 232, 13. [Cf. *Icel.* guðrǣki-ligr *wicked.*]

**godwrætlic.** *See preceding word.*

**godwrecnis.** *Add:*—Hefig mân is and godwrecnes (Godes wrecnys, godfrecnis, *v. ll.*), Bd. 1, 27; Sch. 69, 17. Godwrecnes *fanaticia*, Wrt. Voc. ii. 147, 36. Godwrecnissum *uaemonibus* (*l. facinoribus*. v. Bd. 1, 14; Sch. 39, line 1 of Latin text. See Hpt. 31, 29), Txts. 180, 36.

**gôian** *and* **gên** *to sigh, groan, lament:*—Hê swîþe gôað (gǣþ, gêþ, Bd. S. 497, 33, *v. ll.*) and geómrað *uehementer ingemiscat*, Bd. 1, 27; Sch. 97, 24. Se apostol gôiende (gênde, *v. l.*) and geómriende cwæð *gemebat dicens*, Sch. 98, 5. v. gôung.

**gold.** *Add:* **I.** *gold* in the ground:—Se forma gîtsere þe ǣrest þá eorþan ongan delfan æfter golde, Bt. 15; F. 48, 23. **II.** *gold* as a form of wealth:—Hwǣr côm þ unmǣte gestreón goldes and seolfres, Bl. H. 99, 28. Wênst þú þæt wê þínes hláfordes gold oþþe his seolfor stǣlon?, Gen. 44, 8. **III.** *gold* used as an ornament. (1) for personal ornament (dress, jewellery, &c.):—Cume manna gehwilc tô circan bûton golde and glæncgum, Wlfst. 181, 2. Godweb mid golde gefágod, Bl. H. 113, 20. Golde fǣted sweord, Ll. Th. i. 188, 8. Mid golde gesiwud bend *nimbus*, Wrt. Voc. i. 40, 47. Golde siowode *segmentata* (*veste*), ii. 95, 49. Nymað eall eówer gold (cf. gyldene eárhringas, 4), Ex. 32, 24. (2) used to ornament objects:—Seó cirice nalles on goldes wlite ne scîneþ, Bl. H. 197, 8. Fæt mid golde gefrætwod, 127, 7. Hê hit (*the binding of the book*) gehrînade mið golde and mið gimmum, Jn. p. 188, 5. (2 a) used in writing:—Bôca mid golde áwritenra, Bt. 5, 1; F. 10, 18. **IV.** *gold* as material:—Nam hê þæt gold and gêt án celf, Ex. 32, 4. **V.** *gold* used in payment:—Stent ðām bisceope eahta marca goldes; and gif hig hām cuman gylde ðām bisceope his gold, and gif heora nâðer ne cymð, ðô se bisceop for heora sâule swá mycel swá ðæt land is betere ðene ðæt gold sý, C. D. iv. 288, 8–12. Mid þridde healf hund mancusan goldes be gewihte, iii. 361, 24. Tô .viii. healfmarcum ásodenes goldes, Ll. Th. i. 154, 2. Twá and twêntig þúsend punda goldes and seolfres mon gesealde þām here wið friðe, 288, 12. Hî mid nânum þingum ne gebicge, ne mid golde ne mid seolfre, 380, 12.

**gold-bleoh**; *n. A golden colour.* Substitute: **gold-bleó[h]**; *adj. Gold-coloured.* v. gylden-hîwe.

**gold-blôma.** *Add: A gold-bloom* (v. *N. E. D.*), *marigold* (?). In favour of the meaning 'golden mass' it may be noted that *blôma* is not found in A. S. with the sense 'bloom', 'blossom'; and the occurrence of *hordfǣte* and *gewelegade* in the passage seems to suggest that with *goldblôma* is connected the idea of 'wealth', 'treasure'. In favour of 'marigold' it may be said that both O. Sax. and O. H. Ger., as well as Goth. and Icel., have forms meaning 'bloom' corresponding to A. S. *blôma*, and the actual compound, *golth-blômo* = amellus occurs in O. L. Ger. (Gall. 117). Cf. too *Du.* goud-bloem : *Ger.* gold-blume : *Swed.* guld-blomma *marigold*:—Críst se goldblôma, Bl. H. 105, 5 Se goldblôma on ðás weoruld becôm . . . þurh þone tôcyme wê wǣron geweorðade and gewelegade and geárode, Wlfst. 251, 11–17. (It is the same homily in Bl. H. and Wlfst.) *See next word.*

**golde**, an; *f. A marigold*:—Golde *solsequia* (cf. *solsequia* sigelhueorua, Lch. iii. 305, col. 1), Wrt. Voc. i. 68, 76. [v. *N. E. D.* gold *marigold.*] v. gold-wyrt.

**gold-fǣt.** *Add* Ph. 303 (*given under* gold-fǣt *a plate of gold*) *and* [Hwar beoþ þeo goldfæten þeo þe guldene comen to þine honden, Frag. Phlps. 6, 5.]

**gold-fǣt** *a plate of gold. Dele.*

**gold-fǣted**; *adj. Adorned with gold*:—Goldfæted (ofergyldene, *v. l.*) sweord *deauratum gladium*, Ll. Lbmn. 460, 28.

**gold-fell.** *Add:*—Goldfel *bratheas*, Wrt. Voc. ii. 11, 15. [*O. H. Ger.* golt-fel *auratas pelles*.] v. gold-fyll.

**gold-fellen**; *adj. Of gilded leather:*—Mid purpuran gescrýd and mid kynelicum gyrlum, mid gyldenum cynehelme and mid goldfellenum sceón, Hml. S. 31, 752. *See preceding word.*

**gold-finc.** *Add:*—Goldfinc *cintus* vel *frugellus*, Wrt. Voc. i. 29, 59: *florulus*, 281, 26: ii. 36, 55: *auricinctus*, 10, 33.

**gold-finger.** *Add:* [*O. H. Ger.* golt-finger *annularis*: *Ger.* goldfinger.] v. lǣce-finger.

**gold-frætwe.** *Add:*—Reste gewyrcan of marmanstáne and mid goldfrætwum and mid gimcynnum ástêned, Wlfst. 263, 3.

**gold-fyld**; *adj. Gilt, covered with gold-leaf:*—Goldfyld fel *petala* (*furva*, Ald. 142, 3), Wrt. Voc. ii. 89, 48. *See next word.*

**gold-fyll** (?) *gold-leaf, gold-foil*:—Him an rǣd hiów rudaþ on þām ricge goldfylle (-felle [*in a later MS.*], 476, 58) gelîc glitonaþ Fênix, E. S. viii. 478, 61. [Fyll *from* (?) *Lat.* folium. Cf. (?) *the forms in* Prompt. Parv., *fule of golde, quod dicitur* gold-fule *brateum vel bratea. For another explanation of* fyll *which connects it with* fedel *in O. H. Ger.* fedel-gold = filo dunne gold, gefedelgoldôte *bratteatas* (*comas*), *see* Beiblatt xiii. 13. *The Icel.* gull-fjallaðr *gilt, seems to point to yet another, and to make* gold-fyld, -fyll = gold-feld, -fell.] v. gold-fell.

**gold-gearwe**; *pl. Gold ornaments*:—Ðára goldgearwo wlænco þe hê his líchaman oterflôwnesse mid frætwað, Nap. 34. v. gold-wlencu.

**gold-gerêne** (?), **-regne** *a gold ornament. See next word.*

**gold-gewefen**; *adj. Woven with gold*:—Wimple goldgewefenum (Hpt. Gl. 506, 64 *has* goldgerenum, *and in margin* goldgereie) *cyclade auro texta*, An. Ox. 4297. Goldgeweuenum, 2, 316.

**gold-hilted.** *Add:* [Cf. *Icel.* gull-hjalt *a gold hilt.*]

**gold-hord.** [*In* Wrt. Voc. i. 58, 63 *the MS. has* gold-hold. v. Wülck. Gl. 187, 17.] *Add:*—On þām þe wæs behýdd se heofonlica goldhord, Ælfc. T. Grn. 13, 2. Se goldhord þe þú gemêttest, Hml. S. 23, 603. Swíðe ealdne goldhord, 570. Unárîmedlicu goldhord *innumeri thesauri*, Nar. 5, 10. Hêr Rômáne gesomnodon al þá goldhord þe on Bretene wǣron, and sume on eorþan áhýddon and sume mid him on Gallia lǣddon, Chr. 418; P. 10, 17: Shrn. 115, 32. Goldhordu goldes *thesauros auri*, Scint. 156, 6: 178, 13.

**goldhordian.** *Add:*—Goldhordað (*thesaurizat*) and nát hwǣm gesomnað þá, Ps. Srt., Rdr., L. 38, 7. Se ðe him sylfum goldhordað, and nis on Gode welig, Hml. Th. ii. 104, 23: Wlfst. 286, 25. Ná scylon bearn mágum goldhordian (*thesaurizare*, i. *lucrari*), ac mágas bearnum, Scint. 173, 12.

**gold-hwǣte.** *l.* -hwæt: **gold-lǣfra** . . . Lye. *Substitute:* goldlǣfer. v. reádgold-lǣfer.

**gold-leaf**, es; *n. A thin plate of gold*:—Reste gewyrcan of marmanstáne . . . mid goldleáfum gestrewed ymbûtan, Wlfst. 263, 6.

**gold-mǣstling.** *Add:* [Cf. *O. H. Ger.* golt-messinc *auricalcum.*]

**gold-ôra**, an; *m. A mass of gold*:—Wudebǣre gyrda bearewum on smǣtum rêdes goldôrun, [gold- ?] wecgum *vimina siluestria* (*e frondosis*) *nemoribus* (*allata mutauit*) *in obrizum flauentis auri metallum* (cf. ðá grênan gyrda wurdon tô reádum golde áwende, Hml. Th. i. 64, 1), An. Ox. 1810. v. gold-wecg.

**gold-siowod.** *Dele, and see* gold; **III.** 1.

**gold-smith.** *Add:*—Þæs wîsan goldsmiðes bán, Wêlondes, Bt. 19; F. 70, 1. 'Gád tô smiððan and fandiað þises goldes' . . . 'Ealle ðás goldsmiðas secgað þæt hí nǣfre ǣr swá clǣne gold, ne swá reád ne gesáwon,' Hml. Th. i. 64, 8. [*O. H. Ger.* gold-smid *aurifex*: *Icel.* gull-smiðr.]

**gold-smiþu.** *l.* -smîþ, *and add*: [*Icel.* gull-smíð *the goldsmith's art, working in gold.*]

**gold-þrǣd**, es; *m. A gold thread*:—Þá áþráwenan goldþrǣdas *bratea fila, torta aurea fila*, Wrt. Voc. ii. 127, 19. [*Icel.* gull-þráðr.]

**gold-wecg**, es; *m. A lump of gold*:—Goldwecg (-wecd, MS.) *auri metallum*, An. Ox. 451. v. gold-ôra.

**gold-wlencu.** *l.* -wlencu(-o); *indecl.*: -wlenc, e: gold-wrecen. v. wrecan; I c.

**gold-wyrt**, e; *f. Goldwort, marigold*:—Goldwyrt *solsequium*, An. Ox. 26, 36. v. golde.

**golfettung** (?) *mockery:*—Golfetung (gaffetung ?) *subsannatio*, Ps. L. 78, 4.

**gôma.** *Add:* (1) *the palate:*—In gôman, þǣr mon þone smæc tôdǣleþ *in palato*, Wrt. Voc. ii. 48, 3. (2) in pl. *the jaws:*—Gôman *fauces*, Wrt. Voc. ii. 38, 52. Ðá deôflu . . . hý sealdon suman fýrenan dracan; se ontýnde his þá fýrenan and þá scearpestan gôman and big swealh, Ll. Th. ii. 398, 39. (2 a) *fig.:*—Hê ûs álýsde of gômum þæs êcan deáþes, Wlfst. 145, 2. v. feorh-gôma.

**gop.** *Add:* The metre makes gôp probable, though perhaps not quite certain : at least a short vowel occurs in the similar verse : Is þæs gores sunu, Rä. 41, 72.

**gor.** *Add:* **I.** *dirt:*—Gor *letamen*, Wrt. Voc. ii. 50, 38 : *fimus*, An. Ox. 53, 39. Gores *fimi*, 4769 : Wrt. Voc. ii. 34, 51. Goor (*for* oo = o

v. boor = bor, 98, 7, hool = hol; 124. 13) *fimum*, 108, 65.  **II.**
*pulp* (?) :—Mængc wiþ þa sápan and þæs æpples gor, Lch. iii. 36, 31.

gōr = gár. *See* gár; **IV,** *where add* :—Tó ðes gáres súðende, C. D.
v. 86, 28. Cf. on ðone gáran ufwerdne, 356, 16 (the three passages
refer to the same place).

gorettan; *p. te.* **I.** *intrans. To stare about.* (1) of persons, *to let
the eyes rove* :—Ðæt hine lǽrð se deófol, þæt hē stande and gorette and
lócige underbæc út ; þæt bið gymeleás gebed, Wlfst. 234, 18. (2) of the
eyes or looking, *to rove* :—Þær (*in hell*) wēpað ðá eágan þe nú ðurh
unálýfedlíce gewilnunga goretende hwearftliað, Hml. Th. i. 530, 31.
Ne gán hí goretyndum eágum *non vagis oculis incedant*, Nap. 34.
Gorettende *passiuos* (*oculorum obtutus*), An. Ox. 5, 3. Wídlese
(= -lǽste ?) goretende *passiuis*, Archiv lxxix. 89. **II.** *trans. To
pour forth* :—Gorette *egerit* (spumasque frendens *egerit*), Germ. 398,
204. v. gorian.

gorettung, e ; *f. A roving look, wandering gaze* :—Wídgille em-
wlátung ł goretunge *passiuos oculorum obtutus*, Hpt. Gl. 405, 65.

gor-gráf, -grǽfe *a muddy copse* (?) :—Æt gorgráfes slǽde . . . eft in
on gorgráfes slæd, C. D. vi. 120, 8–26. Of gorgráfan, v. 579, 18. On
gorgráues, 380, 4.

gorian *to look, gaze* :—Swylce eác be ðám micelum muntum and
dúnum þá þe hýhst standaþ and goriaþ ofer ealne middangeard, An. Ox.
5, 3 note. Goriende *passiuos*, 7, 6. v. gorettan.

gorst. *Add* :, gors :—Gors *aegesta*, Wrt. Voc. ii. 99, 46. Gorst
*voluma*, 124, 16: *acidinetum*, 10, 39: *egella*, 142, 72 : *herba iras*, 43,
53 : i. 68, 13 : *tribulus*, 48.

gōs. *Add* :—Goos *anser*, Wrt. Voc. ii. 100, 37. Gós, 6, 69. Grǽg
gós *ganta*, Wrt. Voc. i. 62, 11 : *canta*, 280, 15. Grǽge gós *gans*, ii.
42, 15. Hwít gós *anser*, i. 62, 10. Wilde goos *cente*, ii. 103, 68 :
*gente*, 109, 63. Wilde gós *gante*, 40, 65. Genim góse rysele, Lch. ii.
40, 12, 15. Heorotes smera oþþe gáte oþþe góse, 68, 26. Sē þe on
þýs ylcum þrim dagum góse flǽsces onbyrigeð binnan feówortiges daga
fyrste hē his líf geændað, iii. 76, 27. Gése bróc scýt on mór, C. D. iii.
215, 33. .v. goes and .x. hennfuglas, i. 293, 9 : 297, 1 : 299, 23. Gósa
tungan gebrǽdde and geþicge, Lch. ii. 90, 8. v. hwíte-, wild-gós.

gōs-fugol. *Substitute for* Th. Chart. 471, 31 :—Sex gósfuglas, tén
hennfuglas, C. D. i. 312, 8.

gōs-hafoc. *Add* :—Góshafuc *accipiter*, Wrt. Voc. ii. 7, 69 : i. 280,
18. *Accipiter* góshafoc vel *aucarius*, Wülck. Gl. 285, 2.

-got. v. ge-got : gota. v. leád-gota.

Gota. *Add* :—Sum Gota þearfa on gáste *Gothus quidam pauper
spiritu*, Gr. D. 113, 15. Hú se Gota geneádod ágeaf Furtunate þá
cnapan, 79, 8. Wisle lond, and be-eástan þǽm sint Datia, þá þe iú
wǽron Gotan, Ors, 1, 1 ; S. 16, 18. Hú Bonefatius þám Gotan gefyllde
þá flaxan. Hit gelamp þ him cómon twēgen men tó of Gotena þeóde,
þá sǽdon þ hí tó Rauennan faran woldon, Gr. D. 66, 3–7. [Cf. *Goth.
Gut-þiuda the Gothic people.*]

Gotisc; *adj. Of the Goths* :—Þær æfter cóm Gotiscra manna here
*Gothis supervenientibus*, Gr. D. 194, 14.

Gotonisc; *adj. Of the Goths* :—Gotonisce cerme *Gothorum clangorem* An. Ox. 4606.

gōt-wope. *Add* : got- (?) :—Gótwoþe, eluhtre, betonice, Lch. ii.138,
9. Gótwoþan lǽst, 94, 6. Gótwoþan (*the accent is in the MS.*), 96, 7.
Nim gótwoþan and mageþan, 156, 19.

goung. *Substitute* : gōung *and* gēong, e ; *f. Sighing, groaning,
lamentation* :—In þæs túdres forðlǽdnesse bið gēong (gooung, góung,
*v. ll.*) and sár *in prolis prolatione gemitus*, Bd. 1, 27 ; Sch. 79, 3. Hér
is Brytta gēong *gemitus Brittanorum*, 1, 13 ; Sch. 36, 24. v. góian
(gén).

grad. l. grád, *and add* :—In grádum *in gradibus*, Ps. Srt. 47, 4.
[*Compare* Hml. Th. ii. 512, 11 *with* :—Martinus stáh tó ánre úpflóra ;
þá wǽron þǽre hlæddre stapas álefede . . . þ hē feól ádúne, Hml. S. 31,
601.] [*O. H. Ger.* grád.] v. rǽding-grád.

grǣd, es ; *pl.* grǽdas *and* (?) grǽde ; *m. Grass* ; pl. greeds (v
*N. E. D.*) :—Swē swá scúr ofer grēd *sicut imber super gramen*, Ps. Srt.
ii. p. 191, 28. Grǽdas *gramina*, Wrt. Voc. ii. 40, 21. Grǽde (i-stem
pl. ?, or ja-stem sing. ?, or wk. ? cf. *ulua* greden, Lch. iii. 329, col. 1),
*ulva*, ii. 31, 33. v. grǽde ; *adj.*

grǣd *a cry.* [*N. E. D.* grede.] v. han-grǽd : grǽdan *to cry out.
Add* : [v. *N. E. D.* grede ; *vb.*] : grǽde *grass.* v. grǽd.

grǣde ; *adj. Grassy* :—Gang nú of þǽre grǽdan (grēnan, *v. l.*) dúne,
Hml. S. 18, 245. v. grǽd *grass.*

grǣdig. *Add* : **I.** *having an excessive appetite for food.* (1) of
persons :—Consumptor, i. *devorator* gífre, grǽdig *gluto*, Wrt. Voc. ii.
134, 2. Grēdge *ambrones*, 100, 12. Grǽdige gúðrincas (*the cannibals*),
An. 155. (2) of animals :—Geogud myrwe grǽdig, Rä. 39, 2.
Grǽdigne scelfre *voracis mergulae*, Hpt. Gl. 418, 69. Earn, grǽdigne
gúðhafoc, Chr. 937 ; P. 109, 22. Moldwyrmas, gífre and grǽdige,
Seel. 74. (3) of some part of the consumer which is connected with
eating :—Tóþas grǽdige (to þas idge, MS.), Ph. 407. Mid grǽdigum
lippum *labris lurconibus*, i. *uorantibus*, An. Ox. 700 : Wrt. Voc. ii.

53, 51. Mid grǽdigum byrenre grimnysse ceáfium *rabidis ursinę
ferocitatis rictibus*, i. *faucibus*, An. Ox. 1475. (3 a) figuratively :—
Grǽdigum múþes ceáfium *ambronis* (taken to be dat. pl.) *orci*, i. *mortis
faucibus*, An. Ox. 836. **I a.** *with gen. of food* :—Se fisc bið
grǽdig þæs ǽses, Hml. Th. i. 216, 12. **II.** *of sexual appetite* :—
Grǽdig wemmend *lasciuus*, i. *feruidus in luxuria scortator*, An. Ox.
3338. **III.** *eager for gain, covetous, avaricious* :—Ná bútan ofer-
módignysse mæg grǽdig (*cupidus*) beón funden, Scint. 111, 7. Were
grǽdigum and fæsthafelum bútan geráde ys ǽht, 110, 15. God nele þ
wē beón grǽdige gýtseras, ne eác for woruldgylpe forwurpan úre ǽhta,
Hml. S. 16, 329. His gingran, gífre and grǽdige (cf. ágan ús þis
wuldres leóht eall tó ǽhte, 253), Sat. 192. Grēdige, 32. Grǽdige
*cupidas*, Wülck. Gl. 253, 28. Gítsung ontent ðæs mannes mód tó máran
ǽhte, and swá hē máre hæfð swá hē grǽdigra bið, Hml. Th. ii. 220,
9. ¶ here probably belongs :—On grǽdigum *cupidineo*, Wrt. Voc. ii.
137, 61. **III a.** *with gen.* :—Nis nán leódscipe swá grǽdig goldes
and seolfres swá ðá Iúdēiscean and ðá Rómāniscean, Hex. 54,
21. **IV.** *keen, eager* :—Grēdig *inians*, Wrt. Voc. ii. 110, 59.
Grǽdig *inhians*, 43, 75. Mín módsefa hweorfeð wíde . . . , cymeð eft tó
mē gífre and grǽdig, Seef. 62. **IV a.** *with gen.* :—Hē weard eft
suá ungemetlíce grǽdig ðæs gódan deáþes *in bonorum necem post didicit
anhelare*, Past. 37, 2. **V.** *that manifests eager desire* :—Hire on
hafelan hringmǽl ágól grǽdig gúðleóð, B. 1522. v. æle-, ofer-grǽdig.

grǣdlīce. *Add* : **I.** *with inordinate appetite* :—Éstmettas ná tó
grǽdiglíce mon ne sceal lufian, R. Ben. 17, 1. Gefrēdde se deófol þone
angel þe hē ǽr grǽdelíce forswealh, Hml. Th. i. 216, 32. **II.** *with
manifestation of strong desire, eagerly* :—Grǽdelíce *inhianter*, Wrt. Voc.
ii. 43, 74. Hí swíþe grǽdilíce (*inhianter*) eorþcundum lustum filigaþ,
R. Ben. 139, 27. v. un-grǽdiglíce.

grǣdignes. *Add* : **I.** *covetousness, cupidity* :—Wyrtruma ys ealra
yfela grǽdignyss *radix est omnium malorum cupiditas*, Scint. 110, 8 :
111, 5 : 112, 2. Ungefyllendlíc eáge grǽdignysse, 110, 16 : Prud. 57.
Be grǽdignesse *de cupiditate*, Scint. 110, 3. Grǽdignyssa *cupiditates*
(cf. honoribus aut prosperitatibus, 13–14), 111, 17. **II.** *eager
desire.* (1) in a good sense :—Þonne wē lífes word mid grǽdignysse
underfóð, Hml. Th. ii. 280, 16. (2) in an unfavourable sense :—Ealle
flǽsclíce grǽdignyssa mid forhæfednysse beóð forcorfene *omnes carnales
cupiditates abstinentia resecantur*, Scint. 55, 4.

grǣf. *Dele last passage, and add* : **I. a.** *pit, place dug out.* v. hyl-,
ísen-, stán-græf. **II.** *a grave* :—Græf sceal deádum men *a grave
is the place for a dead man*, Gn. Ex. 149. On brádnysse scræfes, grǽfes *in
superficie antri*, i. *monumenti*, An. Ox. 1889. Grafe, screafe eorþenum
(*cadavera*) *in cuniculo subterraneo* (*humata*), 33, 11. Míu Drihten, sié
þē þonc þæs þe þú léte þínne líchoman on græf álecgan, Angl. xii. 507,
8. Þeáh þe græf wille golde strēgan bróðor his geborenum, Seef. 97.

grǣf *a writing-style. Add* :—Gref *graffium*, Txts. 67, 997. Synd
gesealde from þám abbode ealle neáubehēfe þing, þæt is . . . seax, græf
(*gravium*) . . . weaxbreda, R. Ben. 92, 3 : 56, 20. Ðonne þú græf
habban wille, þonne sete þú þíne þrí fingras tósomne swilce þú græf hæbbe,
and styra þíne fingras swilce þú wríte, Tech. ii. 128, 6. [*From Latin
graphium.*]

grǣf (?), e ; *f. A bush, bramble* :—Dumas, spinas vel grǽfe, Wrt.
Voc. ii. 142, 12. v. grǽfe *to which perhaps the quotation belongs.*

grǣfa. v. grǽfe : grǽfa, grēfa. *Dele, and see* grafu.

grǣfe, an ; *f.* : grǽfa, an ; *m.* (? v. mearc-grǽfa.) **I.** *a thicket,
copse* :—Ðis syndon ðá gemǽru. Ǽrest grǽfan hrycg se wudu tó dúnhám
styde, C. D. iii. 388, 29. Úp on ðá blacan grǽfan ; of ðǽre grǽfan,
v. 339, 7 : ii. 172, 29. On hincstes grǽfan ; of hincstes grǽfan (but
grāfan, C. D. B. iii. 655, 13), iii. 134, 27. On grǽfan, Cht. Crw. 4, 2.
Þǽm gehilmdum grǽfum *frondosis dumis*, Wrt. Voc. ii. 93, 76 : 37,
37. Geþúfum grǽfum, 151, 22. Þurh grǽfan *per dumos*, 89, 44.
¶ in place-names :—Æt Brēmes grēfan, C. D. i. 222, 22. Brēmes
graefan, 227, 32. **II.** *brushwood* :—Sixtiga fóðra wuda, and twælf
fóður grǽfan, and sex fóður gearda, Chr. 852 ; P. 65, 25. [v. *N. E. D.*
greave.] v. gor-, þorn-, wír-grǽfe : græf, gráf, gráfa.

grǣfere. v. grafere.

grǣft. *Dele* græft, e ; *f.* (?), *and last passage, and add* :—Græft
*sculpture*, Wrt. Voc. i. 75, 24 : *celatura*, i. *sculptura*, ii. 130, 58.
Grǽftas *emblemata, uarietates, uasa uarię sculpta*, An. Ox. 50, 26.
Ísenum grǽftum *carpenta*, Wrt. Voc. ii. 15, 77. On heora grǽftum *in
sculptilibus suis*, Ps. L. 77, 58 : Ps. Vos. 105, 36. Ealle ðá grǽftas gē
ofergyldað, Hml. S. 8, 61. [*Icel.* gröftr ; *m. a digging ; engraving.*]
v. heáh-græft.

grǣg. *Add* :—Greig *feruginius*, Txts. 63, 850. Grei *gillus*
(= gilvus), 67, 967. Hęuui vel grei, hāuui vel grei, heáuui, grei
*glaucum*, 66, 473. Grǽg, hǽwe ísene oþþe sinderóme *ferrugine* (cf.
*ferrugine*, i. *ferreo colore* ísengrēg gesweorf, 31), Wrt. Voc. ii. 35, 34.
Grēge gós *gans*, 42, 15. Tó ðám grǣgan stáne, C. D. iii. 446, 8. Tó
grǽwan stáne, ii. 29, 3. On grēgan stán, v. 233, 2. Oþ þá grāgan
hārnesse *usque cigneam canitiem*, An. Ox. 1876. Nis ná Godes wunung
on ðám grǽgum stánum, Hml. S. 7, 135. v. æsc-. deorce- (*perhaps*

deorce *should be taken as an independent adverb*), dun-, flint-, fold-, īsen-, īsern-grǣg.

**grǣg-gos.** *Add:*—Grēgōs *anser silvatica*, Txts. 108, 1104. (*Perhaps* grǣg gōs *should be read.*)

**grǣg-hama.** *Add:* If the word denotes a living creature the verb *gylleð* would point to a bird rather than to the wolf. The verb *þeótan* (q. v.) and the noun *geþot* are the words used for the howl of the wolf, while *gellan* (q. v.) is used of the scream of a bird. As the epithet *grǣg* is applied to the mew, *grǣghama* might be a mew or gull. It may be noted that in the passage both birds and armour, two objects of which *gellan* may be predicated, are mentioned:—Fugelas singað, gylleð grǣghama, gūðwudu hlynneð, scyld scefte oncwyð.

**grǣg-hiwe, -hēwe.** *Dele, and see* grǣg *and* hēwe.

**grǣg-mǣl.** *Add:* with grey marks, having inlaid ornamentation. v. mǣl; II.

**grǣp.** *Dele:* grǣppian. v. ge-grǣppian.

**grǣf.** *Add:* [*The word seems feminine in the compound* wīþig-grǣf *in the following passage:*—On beorg; ðonne on wīðiggrǣfe; ðonne on ðone weg, C. D. v. 147, 32.]:—Ic ongyte þæt þā worlde lustas ne sint eallunga āwyrtwalode of ðīnum mōde, þeáh se grǣf gerýd sī (v. ge-rýd), Solil. H. 39, 5. Tō grǣfes owisce, C. D. iii. 388, 24. Be Tātan grǣfes wurtwale, 405, 29. On dynninces grǣfes wyrttruman (cf. dinninggrǣfes, 208, 5). 34, 14. Seó wudung on gemǣnan grǣfe tō Ðorndūne, 463, 10. On Cynæbeorhtæs grǣf sūðæwæardnæ; fram grǣfæ, v. 255, 31: iii. 302, 1: 427, 19: 81, 6. In Æðelstānes grǣf; of grāue, 80, 19. Of þǣre brādon strǣt be þām grǣfe innan ðā portstrǣt, Cht E. 239, 6. Ðām twām hīdan and ðā mǣde and ðone grǣf ðe þǣrtō mid rihte tō ligeð, 248, 12. Ofer mid ðone grǣf, C. D. iii. 52, 23. Ofer ðæt grǣf, 389, 1. In ðone lytlan grǣf, v. 126, 30. On Leómmannes grǣf westeweardan, iii. 406, 15. ¶ In a place-name:—Westgrǣf (*in a Latin charter*), C. D. iii. 374, 29. v. gor-, þir-, wīþig-, wyn-grǣf; grǣfa.

**grǣfa,** an; *m. A grove, copse:*—Be-westan ðā leáge eft tō grǣfan hrycge (cf. grǣfan hrycg, 388, 29), C. D. iii. 389, 2. Tō ðyrnan grǣfan; of ðyrnan grǣfan, v. 262, 9. ¶ in a compound:—Tō erscgrǣfan, C. D. iii. 434, 22. v. ellen-grǣfa; grǣfe.

**grǣfere,** es; *m. Take here* grǣfere *in Dict., and add:*—Grafere *sculptor*, Wrt. Voc. i. 75, 23.

**grafet.** *Substitute:* grafet[t], es; *n. An excavation, a trench:*—Of ðām crundele on ðæt lange grauet; of ðām lange grafette, C. D. v. 193, 34. Tō ðon lytlan grafette ūp an wuncges dūne; and ðér west hwōn tō ðon norðlangan grafette, 195, 5–7. On ðone miclan hæslwrīd wiðneoðan ðæt grafet, 194, 14. Cf. stān-hīwet.

**grafu;** *gen.* grǣfe; *f. A cave, den:*—Grǣfe (*the MS. has the accent*) ðeáfana (cf. illvirkja gröf *in the Icelandic version of* Mt. 21, 13) *speluncam latronum*, Mt. L. 21, 13. v. grǣf.

**gram.** *Add:*—Gram, wrāþ *furibundus*, An. Ox. 4484. Gram *mordicus*, Germ. 401, 29. Hē beforan þone graman cyning (*tyrannum*) gelǣd wæs, Bt. 16, 2; F. 52, 22. *See next word.*

**grama,** an; *m. A fiend:*—þ heó wǣre gramena mǣge, þeóstra gefǣra, Hml. S. 2, 173. Forligr macað of Godes temple gramena wununge, 16, 279. [*O. Sax.* gramo *a fiend, devil:*—Gramonō hēm *hell.*]

**grama.** *Add:* I. *anger, wrath* as an emotion in a person:—Wēn is þ þæs hlāfordes grama weaxe, Ll. Th. i. 270, 22. Mid mōdes graman, 272, 11. þā nam hē micelne graman and andan tō þām mannum, Hml. Th. i. 16, 30. Hē nam tō Malche fulne graman, Hml. S. 23, 694. II. *wrath, ill effect on another as a consequence of a person's anger:*—Becōm Godes grama ofer hī ealle, Hml. Th. i. 10, 29. Wolde hē tōbrecan Godes templ mid teónfullum graman, Hml. S. 25, 723. Godes graman habban, Ll. Th. i. 380, 5. Nā sē þe þolað ac sē þe dēþ graman (*contumeliam*) earm hē ys, Scint. 9, 6. Graman tǣlendra mid geþylde oferswýð *contumelias detrahentium patientia supera*, 12, 14. v. nīþ-grama.

**gramatic, -isc.** v. grammatic, -isc.

**gram-bǣre.** *Add:*—Ðā monðwǣran ... ðā grambǣran *mansueti ... iracundi*, 289, 5.

**grambǣrnes.** *Take here the passage in Dict. under* gramfǣrnys.

**gramian;** *p.* ode. I. *to be furious, rage:*—Gramigende *inæstuans*, Germ. 402, 58. II. *to be offensive to, vex* (with dat.):—þonne se feónd þis gesihð, ... þonne gramað (ofþingað, v. l.) him þæt swīðe hearde, Wlfst. 199, 2. [þanne ne þarf us noðer gramien ne shamien, O. E. Hml. ii. 69, 22. Ful swiðe us mæi gromien (gramie, 2nd MS.), Laym. 25216.]

**gramlic.** *Add:* I. *of persons:*—Ongeán Godes ege se gramlica deófol syled dyrstignysse, Wlfst. 59, 19. Bāal ... wæs gramlic ðeófol, Hml. S. 18, 48. Apollonius sum gramlic heretoga, 25, 289. Sum gramlic dēma hine gemartyrode mid micclum wītum, 27, 200. Se gramlica Antiochus, 25, 379. Þone gramlican feónd, 4, 58. Ealle þǣra hǣðenra godas synd gramlice deófla *omnes dii gentium demonia*, 14, 18. Ne cwæð þū nā goda, ac gramlicra deófla, 8, 59. II. *of things:*—Nǣron hī geneádode tō ðām gramlican geþeahte, Hml. S. 27, 166. Hē genam āne cuppan mid cwealmbǣrum drence ... and begōl

þone gramlican drenc, 14, 76. Gebīgan fram Godes geleáfan þurh ðā gramlican wītu, 19, 132. þurh gramlice steóra, Wlfst. 133, 18.

**gramlice.** *Add:*—Gramlīce God his hālgena þrowunga on him gewræc, Hml. Th. i. 526, 2. Geoffra ðām godum þ ic ðē gramlīce ne fordō, Hml. S. 8, 83.

**grammatic;** *adj. Grammatical, of grammar:*—Hē leornode grammatican cræft, Hml. S. 35, 14. [*O. H. Ger.* gramatich *grammaticus.*]

**grammatic-cræft,** es; *m. Grammar:*—On gramaticcræft (gramatisccræfte, v. l.), Bd. 4, 2; Sch. 344, 17.

**grammaticere,** es; *m. A grammarian:*—Grammaticeras and rīmcræftige þegnas, Angl. viii. 327, 34. [*O. H. Ger.* gramatichare *grammaticus.*]

**grammatisc;** *adj. Grammatical, of grammar:*—In gramatiscne cræft, Bd. 4, 2; Sch. 344, 19. v. grammatic.

**grammatisc-cræft.** v. grammatic-cræft.

**gram-mēde (?), -mēdu (?)** *anger:*—Gramme (grammēdes (?), -mēdu (?); An. Ox. 5032 *has only* gra) *irae*, Hpt. Gl. 521, 20. Cf. eáþ-, ofer-mēde, -mēdu.

**grana (?)** *one who has a moustache (?):*—*Polopis et crinitus*, i. grona, Hpt. 33, 251, 18. v. granu.

**granae.** v. granu.

**grānian.** *Add:*—þonne grāniað and wāniað þā þe hēr blissedon and fægnedon, Wlfst. 245, 2: Angl. viii. 336, 41. Grānode *rugiebam*, Bl. Gl. Seó grāniende gesceaft, Wlfst. 186, 5: 187, 1.

**Grantabrycg-scīr,** e; *f. Cambridgeshire; the people of that shire:*—þā sōna flugon Eást-Engla; þā stōd Grantabrycgscīr fæstlīce ongeán, Chr. 1010; P. 140, 9. Hī heafdon þā ofergān Eást-Engla ... Oxenafordscīre and Grantabrycgescīre, 1011; P. 141, 13.

**Granta-ceaster.** *Add:*—Ys sum fenn þæt onginneð fram Grante eá, nāht feor fram þǣre cestre, ðǣre ylcan nama ys nemned Granteceaster *est palus, quae a Grontae fluminis ripis incipiens haud procul a castello, quod dicunt nomine Gronte*, Guth. Gr. 113, 3.

**granu** (-ae, -e), an; *f. A moustache:*—Granae, granæ, gronae *mustacia*, Txts. 79, 1343. [*For the termination* ae *in wk. fem.* cf. clonae, 79, 1327, slahae, 87, 1576; *but the same form is found in the pl. of strong fem.*, cf. nabae, 79, 1322. If granae *could be taken as pl. its declension would correspond with that of the Icel.* grön, *pl.* granar. *O. H. Ger. has weak forms.* v. Grff. iv. 327, Grana gene, *loca super bucca*, granen grenones. *From a statement of Isidore it appears that the word was used by the Goths:*—Videmus cirros Germanorum, granos et cinnabar Gothorum. See Dief. ii. 427.] v. grana.

**grānung.** *Add:*—þér is wānung and grānung and ā singal sorh, Wlfst. 26, 8. Hēðenra grānung and reáfera wānung, 186, 13. Nis ðér ādles grānung, ac þér is geogoð būtan ylde, 142, 27. Grānung and murnung and sworetung, Verc. Först. 121, 18. Ic swince on mīnre grānunge (*gemitu*), Ps. Th. 6, 5.

**gran-wisc** *chaff (?):*—Gronuisc ̄acus (cf. acus sifeþa, i. 83, 19) Wrt. Voc. ii. 99, 16. Gronwisc, 4, 37. [Cf. *Ger.* granne *awn, beard of plant. For* wisc *see* weoxian.]

**grāp.** *Add:*—Heardecg cwacað ... grāpum gryrefæst (*dreadfully firm from the grasp that grips it*), El. 760. v. eorþ-, feónd-, hilde-, nearu-, nīd-grāp.

**grāpian.** *Add:*—Se lǣce grāpað suīðe fægre ymbūtan ðæt ðæt hē snīðan wile ... Suā se wītga dyde ... mid his wordum ... hit wæs betre ðæt hē grāpude mid ðǣm bīspelle ǣr ðon ðe hē cīdde, suā se lǣce grāpað and strācað ... ǣr ðon ðe hē stingan wille, Past. 187, 1–5. Ðeáh þū mē tǣhtest ǣr þā duru, ic hire ne mihte māre ǣredian būton þ ic hire grāpode ymbūton, Bt. 35, 3; F. 158, 31. Grāpade *adtreetat* (*poplitem debilitate curvatum*, Bd. 1, 21), Txts. 182, 82. Grāpode *adtrectaverit*, Wrt. Voc. ii. 6, 30. v. ā-, ge-grāpian; un-grāpigende.

**grāpung,** e; *f.* I. *the sense of touch:*—þā andgitu sint gehātene þus ... *tactus*, hrepung oððe grāpung on eallum limum, ac þeáh gewunelīcost on þām handum, Hml. S. 1, 199. II. *action of touching or handling:*—Hī ne mihton undergitan būton hit wǣre reáf ne mid heora grāpunge ne mid heora sceáwunge, Hml. S. 31, 819. Cunna mid grāpunge hwæðer hī stānas synd ... þū miht witan gewislīce mid grāpunge gif þū geseón ne miht þ hī synd stānas, 34, 334, 337. Ðurh his (*St. Thomas'*) grāpunge (cf. Lk. 24, 39 *under* grāpian) wē sind geleáffulle, Hml. Th. i. 234, 21.

**grā-scinnen;** *adj. Of grey fur:*—Grǣschynnene, Chr. 1075; P. 209, 32. [*Icel.* grā-skinn *grey fur;* grā-skinnaðr *lined with grey fur.*]

**grasian.** *Add:* The Latin is: Boues pascentes uiderit.

**grātan.** l. grotan; q. v.

**grapul** *a gradual, an antiphon sung between the Epistle and the Gospel at the Eucharist, so called because it was sung at the steps of the altar:*—[Alleluia] *for* graþulum byþ gesungen *Alleluia pro gradualibus canitur*, Angl. xiii. 436, 1020.

**gratian.** v. on-gratian.

**greáda.** *Add: a lap:*—Behýdað þá ælmessan on þæs þearfan greádan (*sinu*), Hml. A. 141, 91. Ðā hē beseah on his āgenne grǣdan (sceát, v. l.) betweoh his āstrehtan earmas, þā gemētte hē on his greádan (sceáte,

v. l., sinu), twelf mancosas ... hē āwearp þā mancosas on þæs mæsse-preóstes greádan (sceáte, v. l., sinum), Gr. D. 65, 13, 23. Suæ suæ cild irnð tō his mōder greádan (ad matris sinum), Past. 103, 23. Dryhten tōbræt ðone greádan (sinum) his mildheortnesse, 405, 9: 407, 11. Grǣdum gremiis, An. Ox. 2954. [v. N. E. D. greade.]

**greát.** Add:—Greátre grosse, greát and smæl grossas et graciles, Wrt. Voc. ii. 41, 67, 68. I. coarse of grain or texture:—Twēntig ambra ealoð, and tū hund greátes hlāfes (coarse bread) and þridde smales, Cht. Th. 158, 25. Āscrep þā greátan rinde of scrape the coarse rind off, Lch. ii. 270, 17. II. of persons, big, stout:—Hlǣne macer, greát grossus, smæl gracilis, Wrt. Voc. i. 83, 50. IIa. of parts of the body:—Se earm wæs swā swīðe greát and āswollen brachio in tantum grossescente, Bd. 5, 3; Sch. 565, 3. Se greáta līra beneoðan þām þūman, Vis. Lfc. 84. Gif mon þā greátan siuwe forsleá, Ll. Th. i. 100, 3. Mycele cneówu and hindan greáte genibus nodosis, Guth. Gr. 128, 126. III. of things. (1) material, massive, bulky, big:—'Ðū ne meaht gefrēdan micelne beám on ðīnum āgnan eágan' ... se yfela willa on ðǣre heortan is se greáta beám (trabes), Past. 224, 4. Lǣt niman ǣnne greátne cwurnstān, Lch. iii. 38, 15. Hē (Stephen) orsorh betwux ðām greátum hagolstānum þurhwunode, Hml. Th. i. 52, 18. Swingan mid greátum gyrdum, Hml. S. 35, 189. (1 a) of finely grown trees:—Of ðǣm greátan helebeáme ... on ðā greátan apeldre; of ðǣre greátan apeldre, C. D. iii. 135, 18–22. Onefen ðone greátan æsc, ii. 172, 23. On greátan þorn, v. 150, 8. Gif mon ððres wudu bærned ... forgielde ǣlc greát treów mid .v. sciłł., Ll. Th. i. 70, 5. (2) non-material things:—Of gealādle ... cymeþ greát yfel; sió biþ ealra ādla rīcust, Lch. ii. 106, 19.

**greáte wyrt.** Add:—Greáte wyrt beribabum, Wrt. Voc. i. 67, 67. Ādelfe þā greátan wyrt, Lch. ii. 270, 16. [Elna enula gret uurt, 139, 10.]

**greátian.** Add: [v. N. E. D. great; vb.] v. ge-greátian; grītan.

**greátnes.** Substitute: I. coarseness of material:—Ne cīden nō þā munecas ymb þā deáge oþþe greátnesse (grētnysse, R. Ben. I. 92, 2) hyra reáfa de colore aut grossitudine non causentur monachi, R. Ben. 89, 15. II. bigness, thickness:—Deós wyrt hafað elne lange stelan on fingres greátnesse, Lch. i. 270, 20: 278, 17. IIa. great bulk, swollen form:—Swilce man siwige āne bytte and blāwe hī fulle windes, and wyrce siððan ān þyrl, þonne heó tōþunden bið, on hire greátnysse, Hml. S. 34, 319.

**Grēcas.** Add: v. Crēcas, Crēce.

**Grēcisc.** Add:—Athēnas ... þǣre Grēgiscra heáfodburh, Hml. S. 29, 5. v. Crēcisc.

**gregg.** v. grīg: **grei-hund.** v. grīg-hund: **gremetunc.** For 'Prov. 19, Lye' substitute 'Kent. Gl. 686.'

**gremian.** Add:—Gremið, graemid, gremid lacessit, Txts. 73, 1170. Grema lacesse, An. Ox. 46, 52. Gremman lacessere, Wrt. Voc. ii. 112, 50. Gremmende lacessiens, 50, 56. I. to irritate, provoke. (1) the object a person:—Hý ðē gremiað exacerbaverunt te, Ps. Th. 5, 11: Hml. Th. i. 100, 22. Gremede exacerbauit (neminem sermonum seueritas), An. Ox. 7, 384: Wrt. Voc. ii. 88, 6. Ne grǣma þū ūre godas, Hml. S. 7, 109. Þ gē God ne gremian (grymman, v. l.), Ll. Th. i. 270, 28. Ne gremigen (gremige, v. l.) gē eówru bearn nolite] ad iracundiam provocare filios vestros, Past. 189, 23. Hū hī God gremion, Hml. Th. i. 588, 11. (2) the object an animal:—Wyrmgalere galdra sangum gremede Marsus (virulentos matrices) incantationum carminibus irritabat, prouocabat, An. Ox. 4942. Gremede irritat (torvam carmine gypsam), Wrt. Voc. ii. 96, 13. Gremedan irritabant i. prouocabant (venenatos aspidum rictus), An. Ox. 4478: Wrt. Voc. ii. 85, 57. II. to provoke to action. (1) with prep. (a) of a muscular movement:—Hine mon scel tyhtan and gremian tō spīwanne, Lch. ii. 184, 1. (b) of a course of action:—Ne sceole wē þā ðwyran tō ūre ēhtnysse gremian, Hml. Th. i. 554, 5. (2) with clause:—Tyht hié and gremeð ðæt irre ðæt hié wealwiað on ðā wēdenheortnesse impellente ira in mentis vesaniam devoluuntur, Past. 288, 6. III. to vex, behave ill to, be hostile to:—Grǣmaþ wiþerwinna þīnne naman irritat adversarius nomen tuum, Ps. L. 73, 10. Ðonne hié mon gremeð cum gravantur, Past. 218, 14. Gif gē nellað forgyfan þām þe eów gremiað (si non dimiseritis hominibus peccata eorum, Mt. 6, 15), Hml. Th. i. 266, 32. [v. N. E. D. greme.] v. ge-gremian.

**gremung, gremming, e;** f. Irritation, provocation:—On grǣmunge in irritatione, Ps. L. 94, 9. On gremminge in exacerbatione, Ps. Rdr. 94, 9.

**Grendel.** Add: The form Grendel occurs several times in place-names:—On Grendles mere (in Wilts.), C. D. B. ii. 364, 11. In Grendelsmere; of Grendelsmere (in Staffs.), iii. 223, 29. Tō Grendles gatan, 605, 14. On Grendles pyt; of Grendeles pytte, 667, 5. The forms Grindel, Gryndel also occur:—Of Grindeles pytt ... on Grindeles pytt, C. D. B. i. 176, 27–177, 1. Of Grindles bece, iii. 588, 22. Tō Gryndeles syllen; from Gryndeles sylle, 189, 25. Grimm connects Grendel with grindel (q. v.). See Grmm. D. M. (trans.) p. 243.

**grēne.** Add: I. green. (1) of grass, foliage, &c.:—Bebeád se

Hǣlend þ ðæt folc sǣte ofer þ grēne hīg (ofer groene gers, L., ofer groenum hegge i grese, R., super uiride faenum), Mk. 6, 39. Siððan Adam stōp on grēne græs, Gen. 1137. Þā geseah hē ānre stōwe fæc þām ōþrum felda grēnre (viridius), Bd. 3, 10; Sch. 233, 1. (2) of other things:—Groeni prassus, Hpt. 33, 251, 20. Groeni ār aurocalcum, Wrt. Voc. ii. 101, 36. Grēne ār auricalcos, i. 286, 66. Grēnum vernantibus (gemmis), ii. 85, 26. II. covered with herbage or foliage. (1) ot land:—Beorg sceal on eorðan grēne standan, Gn. C. 35. Grēnes gehæges uernantis prati, An. Ox. 550. Se munt is sum mid grēnum felda oferbrǣded, Bl. H. 207, 28. Tō grēnan hlince, C. D. v. 365, 29. Æfter ðām grēnan wege, iii. 389, 9. On grēnan dūne, v. 135, 36. On grēnan pytt, ii. 28, 31. Andlang ðæs wuduweges on ðone grēne pað, iv. 98, 23. Brāde synd on worulde grēne geardas, Gen. 511. Grēne wongas, 1657. Foldweg tredan, grēne grundas, An. 777. (1 a) fig. of a path, pleasant:—Gearwian ūs tōgēnes grēne strǣte ūp tō englum, Sat. 287. (2) of a tree, in leaf:—Hwæðer gē willen on wuda sēcan gold þæt reáde on grēnum triówum? non aurum in viridi quaeritis arbore, Met. 19, 6. III. where the colour is taken as a sign of a particular condition of a plant. (1) newness or tenderness:—Pīntreówes þā grēnan twigu, Lch. ii. 216, 5. Wunian wyrtruman þæs wudubeámes eorðan fæstne, oð þæt eft cyme grēne blēda, Dan. 518. (2) vigorous life. v. grēnnes; II:—Grǣs and wyrtan and treówu foraldiað and forsēriað, and cumað oððer, grēnu wexað and gearwað and rīpað, Solil. H. 10, 5. Brōhte seó culufre elebeámes twig ... grēne blǣde, Gen. 1474. (3) the presence of natural moisture:—Grēne beregrǣs (-cræs, MS.) farrago, Wrt. Voc. i. 38, 46. Ic sylfa slōh grēne tāne (cf. eleva virgam tuam, Ex. 14, 16) gārsecges deóp, Exod. 281. IV. unprepared for use. v. grēnnes; III. (1) of vegetable food:—Gif gē mē (the cook) ūt ādrīfaþ fram eówrum gefērscype gē etaþ wyrta eówre grēne (viridia), and flǣscmettas eówre hreáwe, Coll. M. 29, 11. (2) of a hide:—Grēnre hýde recentis i. noue corii, An. Ox. 3281. v. æle-, eal-, gærs-, hǣwen-, sām-, sin-, un-grēne.

**grēne-hǣwen (grēn-);** adj. Greenish:—Grēnehǣwen ceruleus, i. glaucus, Wrt. Voc. ii. 130, 34. Ðā hǣwengrēnan oððe þā grēnhǣwenan ceruleos, 22, 39.

**grēnian.** Add:—On lengtentīman springað oððe grēniað wæstmas, Angl. viii. 312, 22. [v. N. E. D. green; vb.]

**grēnnes.** Substitute: I. greenness of grass, foliage, &c. :—Þǣre stōwe grennes (uiriditas) and fægernes, Bd. 3, 10; Sch. 233, 5. Grēnnesse uiriditate (foliorum), An. Ox. 1581. (2) of other things:—Blǣhǣwenre hīwes grēnnysse glauco coloris uirore, i. uiriditate, An. Ox. 530. II. flourishing growth. v. grene; III. 2. (1) lit.:—Se wæstm on tō nymenne tō þām tīman þonne hē æfter his grēnnysse fealwað, Lch. i. 324, 7. (2) fig.:—Hē wile forlǣtan ðǣre lufan grēnnisse, and forseárian on ðǣre ungeðwǣrnesse qui separantur a uiriditate dilectionis arefiunt, Past. 359, 15. Ne næfð ǣnig bōh grēnnysse (printed spen-; uiriditatem) gōdes weorces, sē þe nā wunað on wyrtruman sōðre lufe, Scint. 3, 18. III. of wood, want of seasoning. Cf. grēne; IV:—Wē ceorfað heáh treówu on holte ðæt wē hī eft ūp ārǣren on ðǣm botle ðǣr ðǣr wē timbran willen, ðeáh wē hī for hrædlīce tō ðǣm weorce dōn me mægen for grēnnesse, ǣr ðǣm ðe hī ādrūgien (tamen non repente in fabrica (lignum) ponitur, ut prius vitiosa ejus viriditas exsiccetur), Past. 445, 2. IV. a green thing, plant:—On þām þriddan dæge hē gesceóp ealle trýwcynna and ealle grēnnyssa (cf. Germinet terra herbam virentem, Gen. 1, 11), Angl. viii. 310, 19.

**grennian.** In l. 5 for 'ringentibus,' '55, Lye' substitute 'dissolutis,' '172, 16,' and add: to grunt:—Grennigan grunnire, Wrt. Voc. ii. 42, 36. [Cf. O. H. Ger. granôn grunnire. v. N. E. D. grin.]

**grennung.** For 'Som.' substitute:—Grennung, graennung rictus, Txts. 93, 1738. [v. N. E. D. grinning.]

**greofa, greaua.** Substitute: greófa, an; m. A pot:—Greóva olla, Wrt. Voc. i. 288, 39: ii. 64, 15. [O. H. Ger. pfanna vel griupo frixorium.] v. ele-greófa.

**greóp** a ditch, drain:—Cuniculum, puteum vel greóp, Wrt. Voc. ii. 137, 33. v. grīpe; grēp(e).

**greósn, e;** f. Gravel:—Of griósne calculo, Kent. Gl. 745.

**greót.** Add:—Hē on greut giswom the whale was stranded, Txts. 127, 7.

**greótan.** Add:—Hwī ne bidst þū þe beþunga lífes lǣcedōmes nū þū scealt greótan, teáras geótan cur tua non purgas lacrymis peccata profusis, et tibi non oras placidae fomenta medelae?, Dōm. L. 82. [v. N. E. D. greet.] Cf. grǣtan.

**grēp** a furrow. Substitute: grēp, e; f. (v. feltūn-grēp); es; n. (? grēp, Wrt. Voc. ii. 82, 20 seems pl.) A ditch, drain:—[Ou] gengan grēp in latrinae cuniculum, Wrt. Voc. ii. 80, 66. Grēp (the MS. has the accent) cuniculum, 18, 24. Grēp cuniculi (cloacarum), 82, 20. Â hē mæcg findan hwæt hē mæcg on byrig bētan ... grēp hegian, dīcsceard bētan, Angl. ix. 262, 19. v. grōp, grēpe.

**grēpe, an;** f. A ditch, drain, privy:—Latrina genge, groepe atque ductus cloacas (aqueductus cloacae?), Txts. 73, 1172. Groepum scrobibus, 95, 1819. See preceding word.

**grétan** *to bewail.* *Add:*—Groeto (greóto (?), gréto (?)) *mereo,* Wrt. Voc. ii. 113, 83. [v. *N. E. D.* greet. *O. Sax.* grātan; *p.* griat.]

**grétan** *to greet.* *Add:* **I.** *to touch, handle:*—Ealle ða hearpan strengas se hearpere grēt mid ānre honda, ðeáh hē hié ungelīce styrige *chordae uno quidem plectro, sed non uno impulsu, feriuntur,* Past. 175, 9. Hē gomenwudu grētte *he played the harp,* B. 2108. Hē him con leóða worn oððe mid hondum con hearpan grētan, Gn. Ex. 171. Sum mæg fingrum wel hearpan stirgan, gleóbeám grētan, Cri. 670. **II.** *to touch, have to do with* a person. (1) *to treat medically:*—Gif se brīw and se drenc inne gewuniað, þū meaht þone man gelācnian; gif him of fleóged, him bið sēlre þ þū hine nā ne grēte, Lch. ii. 320, 20. (2) *of sexual intercourse:*—Hē fēng wīfe his and ne groette hire (*non cognoscebat eam*) oþ þæt hit gebær sunu his, Mt. R. 1, 25: Wrt. Voc. ii. 72, 15. Grētte, 60, 48. **III.** *of the effect produced on the mind:*—þonne māga gemynd mōd geondhweorfed, grēted glīwstafum *when the memory of friends brings joy to the mind,* Wand. 52. **IV.** *to set about* a task:—Lādsīð grētan, Exod. 44. **V.** *to touch, lay hands on, attack.* (1) *with personal subject and* (a) *personal object.* (a) *to treat ill, cause injury or trouble to:*—Ðeáh hié nān mann mid lāðe ne grēte, Past. 293, 19. Ealle þe mē unrihte grētan *qui injuste iniquitatem fecerunt in me,* Ps. Th. 118, 78. Hē ne gedyrstlǣhte tō þon þ hē āht grētte (hrepode, *v. l.*) þone Godes þeówan *ne servum Dei contingere auderet,* Gr. D. 38, 33. Ne sceolon gē mīne þā hālgan hrīnan ne grētan *nolite tangere christos meos,* Ps. Th. 104, 13. Of þære tīde þā werigan gāstas hine mid nǣnige ege ne mid geswencednesse grētan dorstan *neque aliquid ex eo tempore nocturni timoris aut uexationis ab antiquo hoste pertulit,* Bd. 3, 11; Sch. 242, 20: Gū. 348. Wyrd þone gomelan grētan sceolde, sēcean sāwle hord, B. 2421. (β) *to attack with weapons:*—Ic þē bæd þæt þū þone wælgæst ne grētte, B. 1995. Næs se folccyning ... þe mec gūðwinum grētan dorste, 2735. (b) *the object a thing.* (a) *material, to try to injure:*—Hī ne dorston ofer þ geþrýstlǣcan þ hī ōhte grēttan þā hālgan stówe rihtgeleáffulra manna *nequaquam ulterius praesumserunt catholica loca temerare,* Gr. D. 235, 6. Hī ne dorston grētan (hreppan, *v. l.*) þā hālgan stówe, 43, 11. (β) *non-material:*—Hē ðone aað gesæh and gesceáwade ... ond hē hine hweðre ne grētte *he examined the sworn statement, but did not attempt to refute it,* C. D. i. 279, 15. (2) *the subject an animal:*—Gif him þince þ hē hundas geseó and hī hine grētan, beorge him wið his fýnd, Lch. iii. 172, 21. (3) *the subject a thing that has a painful or destructive effect:*—Hwīlum cnysseþ þ sār on þā rib ... hwīlum becymð on þā weoþoban, and eft ymb lytel þā gesculdru þ sār grēt, Lch. ii. 258, 6. þā studu āne ... þæt fýr grētan ne mihte (seó studu ... ungehrinen fram þām fýre stód, *v. l.*) *sola illa destina ... ab ignibus absumi non potuit,* Bd. 3, 17; Sch. 269, 19. Hine (*Adam after death*) se(ó) eorðe grētan ne meahte þ hē fúlode and brosnode, Angl. xi. 1, 8. þone synscaðan gūðbilla nān grētan nolde, B. 803. **VI.** *to greet* with words. (1) *to address, accost:*—Ic groetu *convenio,* Txts. 53, 526. Ne sculon mæssepreóstas būton ōðrum mannum mæssan syngan, þ hē wite hwone hē grēte and hwā him oncwæðe, Ll. Th. ii. 406, 23. Wilt þū fremdne monnan ... wordum grētan, fricgan ymb forðgesceaft, biddan þē gesecge, Sch. 2. Ongan fūsne grētan, bæd hine þurh Scyppend þ ..., Gū. 1130. Grētende *conpellens* (rector Olympi *compellans* sobolem verbo currente, Ald. 148, 3), Wrt. Voc. ii. 90, 45. (1 a) *to address the Deity:*—Hē his sigedryhten grētte, and þus wordum cwæð, An. 61. Hī hwīlum tō gebede feóllon and sigedrihten grētton, Gen. 779. Grētende *interpellans* (*Deum curvo poplite*), Wrt. Voc. ii. 83, 13. (2) *to use courteous terms on meeting* a person, *salute:*—þonne hȳ æt frymðe gemētað ... grēted gǣst ōðerne, Cri. 1670. þā gāstas gōde word sprecað ... þone līchaman lustum grētað, Seel. 136. Cōm Dryhten ... and wine sīnne wordum grētte ... hēht his līchoman hāles brūcan, An. 1466: Hö. 58. Grētað (grōetas, L.) hit, cweðende, 'Sȳ syb þyssum hūse,' Mt. 10, 12. Nānne man be wege ne grētað (groetað, L., *salutaueritis*), Lk. 10, 4. Hē (*Lot*) grētan eóde cuman cūðlīce, Gen. 2430. (3) *to bid farewell:*—Hē hié grētte and hié forlēt, Bl. H. 247, 36. Hī ðā grētton and him cýððan hī nǣfre mā hī sēcan woldan *ualedicunt sociis tanquam ultra non reuersuri,* Bd. 1, 12; Sch. 34, 12. Apollonius hī bæd ealle grēton, and on scip āstāh, Ap. Th. 10, 23. (4) *to address respectfully, salute* a superior:—þ cild his Hlāford hālette and grētte, Bl. H. 165, 31. Hī sēcað ðæt hī mon grēte and weorðige on ceápstówum, Past. 27, 6. Eall folc þæne Hǣlend geseónde ... and hine grētende (groeton, L. R.) him tō urnon (*accurrentes salutabant eum*), Mk. 9, 15. (4 a) *to have audience of:*—Hróðgār grētan, B. 2010: 347: Gen. 2104. (5) *of formal speech:*—Ic Ælfric abbod on ðisum gewrite freóndlīce grēte Wulfget, Hml. A. 1, 1. þ gewrit þus cwæþ: 'Pilatus grēteþ Claudium his hlāford,' Bl. H. 177, 5. Ælfðrȳd grēt Ælfrīc arcebiscop and Æðelwerd ealdarman eádmódlīce. And ic cýðe inc, C. D. iii. 353, 3. Eádward king grēt Eádnóð bisceop ... And icc kȳðe, iv. 190, 9 (cf. Ego Eadwardus rex saluto Aylmerum ... Notifico uobis, 243, 15). Leófgiue grēt hire lēuedi Godes grētinge. And ic kīðe, 268, 12. Sende se cyng ... and hēt grētan ealne his leódscipe, Chr. 1014; P. 145, 5. v ā-, mis-grētan.

**greþe** (?):—Greðe *sodalem,* An. Ox. 29, 2. Gr[eðe?] *sodalis,* 56, 275.

**grēting.** *Add:* **I.** *of speech.* (1) *courteous terms of address on meeting:*—þā Elizabeth gehȳrde Marian grētinge (groeting[e], L., R.), Lk. 1, 41. (2) *respectful address, saluting of a superior:*—Ðā bōceras lufiað grētinga (groetingo(-e), L., R.) on strǣte, 20, 46. Groetengo (hǣlettunga, R.), Mt. L. 23, 7. (3) *of formal address in letters, &c.* v. grētan; **VI.** 5:—Ic Ælfric abbod on ðisum gewrite freóndlīce grēte mid Godes grētinge Wulfget, Hml. A. 1, 2. (4) *term applied to a person or thing, appellation:*—Heofenlicere grētinege synderlic gifu *celestis eulogię* (the name Benedict) *prerogatiua,* An. Ox. 2571. Brȳdleópes grētinge *epithalami elogium,* 3182. **II.** *of respectful action or worship:*—Hāt mē unmedemre for þære godcundan rōde grētinge (*for adoration of the divine cross*) þā duru beón untȳnede, Hml. S. 23 b, 448.

**grēting-hūs,** es; *n. An audience-chamber:*—Grētinghūs *salutatorium,* Wrt. Voc. i. 57, 49.

**grēting-word,** es; *n. A word of greeting, a salutation:*—Ðā stōp se encgel tō þām mǣdene and cwæð hire tō, 'Ave', þ is on ūrum gereorde grētingword, Archiv ci. 313. Ave and salue synd grētingword, Ælfc. Gr. Z. 209, 14.

-**grētlic.** v. ge-grētlic.

**grig** (?), **gregg** *a paltry fellow, a coward:*—Gryre sceal for greggum, græf deádum men, Gn. Ex. 149. [Cf. *Icel.* grey *a paltry fellow. For similar correspondence between Icelandic and English forms* cf. *Icel.* hey; *W. S.* hīg; hegg(e) *in* Rushworth Gloss. Mk. 6, 39.] *See next word.*

**grig-hund,** es; *m. A grey-hound:*—Grīghund *unfer,* Wrt. Voc. i. 288, 28. Canem quem Angli dicunt greihund, Ll. Lbmn. 367, note. [*Icel.* grey *a grey-hound.*] *See preceding word.*

**grillan.** *Add:* [v. *N. E. D.* grill.] v. gryllan.

**grim.** *Add:*—Grim *dira,* Wrt. Voc. ii. 27, 64. Seó grimme *atrox,* 1, 23. Grimme *acri,* 5, 25. Grymme *anxii,* Germ. 399, 262. **I.** *of persons:*—Mē feóndsceaða fæste hæfde grim on grāpe, B. 555. Babilone weard grim and gealhmód, Dan. 230. Of þæs grimman deófles gewealdum ālēsan, Bl. H. 63, 3. Cyrichatan hetole and leóðhatan grimme, Wlfst. 164, 11. Twēgen menn deófulseóka hæbbende grimme (*saeui*) swīðe, swā þætte nǣnig mæhte faran þurh wegge þæm, Mt. R. 8, 28. **II.** *of personal actions, character, feelings, or utterances:*—Weard seó feohte tō grim, Mód. 66. Wæs æt þām geongum grim andswaru, B. 2860. Him bið grim sefa, 2043. Onda tō ungemetlīce grim *zelus immoderate saeviens,* Past. 127, 3: Rä. 34, 5. Grimre gūðe, B. 527. Grimne gripe, 1148. Hē hit mid swīðe grimmum edleáne geðryscd *animum per asperam retributionem premit,* Past. 239, 17. Hē fǣhðo wið God grimme gefremede, An. 1389. Grim gárgewinn, 960. Grimra geþonca, Jul. 367. Ic mā fremede grimra gylta, Hy. 4, 27. Heó him handleán forgeald grimman grāpum, B. 1542. Hē fiȳhð grimme gieltas, Ph. 461. Hē habbað in gāstcofan grimme geþōhtas, Leás. 13. In þām grimmestan gǣstgewinne, Gū. 561. **III.** *of pain, disease, painful or destructive conditions:*—þonne bið grimm winter, Archiv cxx. 297, 61. Hell, grim græfhūs, Sat. 708. Grim glēda nīð, Dan. 465: B. 2650. Se grimma hungor, Rä. 44, 2: B. 102. Grim gǣstcwalu, Gū. 651. Grimre helle wīte *trucis tartari tormento,* An. Ox. 2217. On hū grimmum seáðe swinced þæt sweorcende mód, Met. 2, 1. Grimme sorge *acri angore,* Wrt. Voc. ii. 84, 38. Of þām grimman gryre, Dan. 439. Feallan on grimne grund, Cri. 1527. þone grimman þurst *diram sitim,* Nar. 9, 20. On þā grimman tīd, Cri. 1081. Poliað wē þreá, þæt syndon þȳstro and hǣto grimme, grundleáse, Gen. 390. þē sind wītu þæs grim weotud, An. 1367. Storm holm gebringed in grimmum sælum, Gn. Ex. 52. Grimre wræc *acrior ultio,* Bd. 1, 14; Sch. 39, 12. **IV.** *of a painful or destructive implement or agency:*—Heora geoguðe grimme līge fýr fǣdmade *juvenes eorum comedit ignis,* Ps. Th. 77, 63. Þū mē tōbrǣce bendas grimme *disrupisti vincula mea,* 115, 7. Hē ymbe þā herehūðe hlemmed tōgædre grimme gōman, Wal. 62: 76. Mid þȳ heardestan ... and mid þȳ grimmestan gumena gestreóna, Rä. 29, 3. **V.** *of crime, sin, &c., horrible, grievous:*—Wrace þæs grimman mānes *ultio diri sceleris,* Bd. 1, 14; Sch. 39, 13. Grimre synne (*this is a gloss to the preceding passage*), Txts. 181, 37. v. ferþ-, heaðu-, heoru-, hete-, hyge-, nīþ-, searo-, sin-, wæl-grim.

**grīma.** *Add:* **I.** *a visor, mask:*—Grīma *mascus,* Wrt. Voc. ii. 113, 54: 55, 46. **II.** *a spectre, goblin, nightmare:*—Grīma *masca* (masca *striga; nocturna imago quae animam dormientis perturbat; larva,* Migne), Wrt. Voc. ii. 113, 53: 55, 48: *larbula,* 70, 42. Grīma *scina* (l. scena), Txts. 94, 904: *scina, nitatio,* 98, 953. *See next word.*

**grimena.** *The passage is:*—Kymð gerstæpæ and grimenæ þus ne wes rīm *venit locusta et bruchus cuius non erat numerus.* Grīmenæ seems *a pl. gen. of the preceding word, governed by* rīm, *but the meaning is not clear.*

**grimetan.** v. grymettan.

**grim-full;** *adj. Fierce, terrible:*—Gif on Wōdnesdæg bið ācenned, sē bið scearp on gewinne and grimful, E. S. 39, 348. [v. *N. E. D.* grimful.]

grīming *witchcraft.* *Substitute:* grīming, es; *m. A spectre:*— Grīming *mascam,* Wrt. Voc. ii. 57, 25. v. grīma; II.

grimlic. *Add:* I. cf. grim; I :—Ongeán þām ānfealdan Godes ege se grimlíca deófol lǣrð dyrstignysse, Wlfst. 54, 2. II. cf. grim; II :—Grimlic gedrecednys *atrox uexatio (lictorum),* An. Ox. 3947. Mid grimlicum gebannum *feralibus edictis,* 3435. III. cf. grim; III :—Gehnexad þurh grimlice steóra and heardlíce ðreála, Wlfst. 133, 18. IV. cf. grim; IV :—Grimlice spyrringe *rapaci arpagine,* An. Ox. 5340. Grimlicum ceáflum *feroces rictus,* 4379. [v. *N. E. D.* grimly. *Icel.* grimmligr.]

grimlíce. *Add:*—Grimlícor *atrocius,* Wrt. Voc. ii. 5, 26. L of personal action:—Hergiendum grimlíce bereáfiendum *grassatoribus atrociter* (i. *crudeliter*) *uastantibus,* An. Ox. 2714. Grimlíce geþrǣste *acriter artabantur,* 4875. Be þām spæc se wītega and grymlíce þus cwæð, Wlfst. 177, 2. Ús mon nēnigre dǣda grimlícor ne mengaþ þanne þæs Seternes dæges weorces, 225, 25. Ðá hēt se cing þone hyra ealra grimlícost ácwellan, Shrn. 111, 22. II. of action by animals or things:—þá deór gewrǣðað grimlíce ongēn, Nar. 34, 7. þet fýr grǣfeð grimlíce, Cri. 1004. [*O. H. Ger.* grimlícho *cruenter; Icel.* grimmliga.] v. wæl-grimlíce.

grimman. To I. *add:*—Glimnit (grimmit (?)) *sevit.* v. glýman. For II. *substitute:* *to be fierce:*—Gūþmód grummon *martial minds were fierce,* B. 306. [For gūþ-mód *as a noun* cf. miht-mód, Exod. 149, *the only other case in which* mód *occurs compounded with a noun.*] *Add* (?): III. *to make angry:*—Beóde ic þ gē God ne grymman (gremian, *v. l.*), Ll. Th. i. 270, 28. [Perhaps the verb here is weak.]

grimme. *Add:* I. of personal action. (1) where pain, injury, &c., are caused by agent, or where anger, displeasure, &c., are felt or expressed:—Forgrípan gumcynne grimme and sáre, Gen. 1275. Grimme ic eom begangen, for ðon ic gnornige *contristatus sum in exercitatione mea,* Ps. Th. 54, 2. Hē eorlum onmǣlde grimme, Dan. 211. Hē hæfde styrne mód gegremed grymme, Gen. 61. (2) where the agent suffers:—Ðǣr is mǣðma hord grimme geceápod (*dearly purchased*), B. 3012. Grimme gegongen, 3085. Banan heardlíce grimme ongieldað, Sal. 132: Gú. 959. Grimme greótan *to bewail bitterly,* Sal. 376. I a. of personifications:—Wiga is on eorðan . . . leánað grimme þe hine wloncne weorðan lǣteð, Rä. 51, 9. Án wiht . . . grimme grymetað . . . Mōdor is . . . , 81, 3. II. of the effect or condition of things:—Bryne grimme gemencged, Wlfst. 26, 7: 94, 2. Smylte sǣ suðerne wind oft grimme gedrēfeð, Met. 5, 8. Him grimme on woruldsǣlða wind wrāðe blāweð, 7, 51. þæt sceal wrecan sweart líg sáre and grimme, Gen. 2415: Cri. 971. Secg wundað grimme, Rún. 15. Ofn wæs gegléded swá hē grimmost mihte, Dan. 227. [*O. H. Ger.* grimme *atrociter, saeve.*]

grimmettan. v. grymettan.

grimnes. *Add:*—Grimnes *atrocitas,* Wrt. Voc. ii. 2, 38. I. *fierceness, ferocity* of a living creature:—þǣra feónda grimnes, Wlfst. 186, 18. Byrenre grimnysse *ursinę ferocitatis,* An. Ox. 1477. II. *severity* of pain, disease, &c.:—Mid swiþre wealreówre grimnysse *satis crudescente* (*poenarum*) *atrocitate,* An. Ox. 4714. For þǣre grimnesse þára ōmena, Lch. ii. 278, 13. [*O. L. Ger.* grimnussi *seueritas.*] v. wæl-grimnes.

grimsian. *Add:*—Grimsaþ *deseviet,* Wrt. Voc. ii. 25, 71. [*O. H. Ger.* grimmisōn *saevire, desaevire.*]

grin, gryn, e; *f.:* es; *n. Substitute:* grin, giren, geren, e; *f.:* grin, es; *n., and add:* I. *a snare for taking game,* &c. (lit. and metaph.):—Hē cymð suá suá grin ofer ealle ðá ðe eardiað ofer eorðan, Past. 129, 22. Úre sáwl is áhred of grine (girene, Ps. Srt. 123, 7) swá swá spearwa, þ grin (giren, Ps. Srt.) is tóbrýt, Hml. S. 11, 252. Cyme him giren ðá hié neoton *inruat illis laqueus quem ignorant,* Ps. Srt. 34, 8. Fleógende fugel . . . gesihð ðæt ǣs on eorðan, and . . . forgiet ðæt grin ðæt hē mid áwierged wirð. Swá bið ðǣm gītsere. Hē . . . nē geliéfð ðæs grines ðe hē mid gebrogden wyrð, Past. 331, 17–20. For- wyrd girene heara *interitum laquei sui,* Ps. Srt. 34, 7. Hē hit gewearp mid synne grine, Past. 309, 18. Gefón myd heora grine, swá swá man deór oððe fugelas fēht, Solil. H. 46, 11. From girene ðá gesettun mē *a laqueo quem statuerunt mihi,* Ps. Srt. 140, 9 : 24, 15 : 90, 3. Of gerene ðisse *de laqueo isto,* 30, 5 : 9, 31. In grin ðissum gegripen *in laqueo isto compraehensus,* 9, 16. Án spearwa on gryn ne mæg befeallan, Chr. 1067; P. 201, 25. In gerene *in laqueum,* Ps. Srt. 65, 11. Gerene deáðes *laquei mortis,* 17, 6. Girenum *laqueis* (insidiator inimicus casualibus *laqueis præparatis* Germani pedem contrivit, Bd. 1, 19), Txts. 181, 69. Sē befealt on ðæs costneres grinu, Hex. 52, 25. Giren laqueos, Ps. Srt. 10, 7. Girene, 56, 7 : 63, 6 : 139, 6 : 141, 4. Gerene, 118, 110. II. *fig. a snare, means of enticing to wrong-doing :*—Nis preóstes cwene ǣnig óðer þing būtan deófles grin, Ll. Th. ii. 336, 25. Grin *reticulum (superbiae),* An. Ox. 961. III. *a noose :*—Hē ácwealde hine sylfne on heálicum grine, Hml. S. 19, 212. [v. *N. E. D.* grin, girn.] v. lust-, syn-grin.

grind. v. for-, ge-grind. [v. *N. E. D.* grind.]

grindan. *Add:* I. *to grind corn in a mill :*—Tuoege biðon grindas (grundas, R.) *duae erunt molentes,* Lk. L. 17, 35. Hí hēton hine (Samson) grindan æt hira handcwyrne, Jud. 16, 21. þá hē ne myhte úte wyrcan, þá wolde hē grindan mid his hálgum hondum . . . Ðá hē þǣre cweorna neálǣhte, and þ corn þǣr on lægde, þá orn seó cweorn, Shrn. 145, 21. Gif hió grindende þeówa sió, Ll. Th. i. 6, 6. I a. of the action of the teeth :—*Molides* . . . wē hǣteð grindigtēþ, fore hý grindeþ æl þ man byg leofaþ, Lch. iii. 104, 3. II. *to grind, crush, oppress :—Eliquat,* . . . *minuit, depremit vel* grint, Wrt. Voc. ii. 143, 5. III. *to scrape* or *rub against something :*—Wǣgas grundon, An. 373.

grindel. *Add:* [*See* Grn. D. M. (trans.) p. 243, *and N. E. D.* grind *a gate of horizontal bars.*]

grindere, es; *m. One who grinds corn :*—Se .iiii. nihta mōna byð gód þǣm ergendan hys sul út tō dōne and þēm grindere his cweorn, Lch. iii. 178, 1.

grind-tóðas. *Substitute:* grinde-tōþ (grindig-) *a molar tooth :*—þat þá tēþ þoligean ne mæge ne hǣte ne ceald, and swýþest þá grindigtēþ, Lch. iii. 104, 15 : 3 (v. grindan; I a). Grindetōþum, tuxum *molaribus,* Wrt. Voc. ii. 54, 46.

grindle. v. gryndle: grinian. *Add:* [v. *N. E. D.* grin *to snare.*]

grinu. *Substitute:* grinu, grionu; *adj. An adjective denoting some colour :*—Wann bruntus, grinu *avidius,* dun *natius,* geoluhwít *gilvus,* Wrt. Voc. i. 46, 42. (The word occurs in a list with the title 'Nomina colorum'.) Hwít *albus,* grionu *avidius,* giolu *aureus,* ii. 10, 29.

griósn. v. greósn: grip. v. ge-grip.

gripa. *Add:* gripu(?), e; *f. :*—Gripe (*acc. fem. from* gripu? *or acc. masc. from* gripe? *q. v.*) *pugillum (farinae)* (cf. *quantum pugillus capere potest farinae,* 1 Kings 17, 12), An. Ox. 2, 266. Gripan, 3877 (*both glosses refer to the same passage,* Ald. 53, 31). þe grípan [Ps. L. has gripa (*acc. pl. from* gripu? *or* gripā = gripan?) í handfulla] gæderað *qui manipulos collegit,* Ps. Rdr. 128, 7. v. frum-grípa.

grípan. *Add:* I. *intrans.* (1) with personal subject. (a) *to grasp at :*—Heó gráp þá tōgeánes, gūðrinc gefēng atolan clommum, B. 1501. (b) *to take hold of, lay hands on.* (a) *a material object :*—Heó on mec (an onion) grípeð, Rä. 26, 7. þú on beám gripe, blǣda nāme on treówes telgum, Gen. 891. (aa) *to take hold* of with an instrument :— Grāp on heofones tōðe, Rä. 84, 4. (β) *a non-material object, to seize on, take for use or as a possession :*—Him on fultum grāp heofonríces weard *God took speedy means to help him,* Gen. 2072. Ðæt hiera nān ne durre grípan suá orsorglíce on ðæt ríce and on ðone láreówdōm *ne quique culmen arripere regiminis audeant,* Past. 41, 5. Ðá ðe willað grípan on swelcne folgað *qui praeesse concupiscunt,* 53, 6. (2) the subject a thing. (a) material, *to seize on, make attack on, assail :*— Mere swíðe grāp on fǣge folc *ocean fiercely assailed the doomed folk,* Gen. 1381. Gripon (cf. gáres gripe, An. 187), unfǣge under sceát werum scearpe gáras *sharp spears fixed cruel fangs within the breasts of men,* 2062. (b) non-material :—Grāp heáh þreá on hǣðen cynn, Gen. 2545. II. *trans.* (1) *to seize.* v. grípend :—Grípeð *capessit, capit sumitque,* An. Ox. 50, 31. (a) with personal subject. (a) the object material :—Hí mē tōbeótodon þæt hí mec mit ðám tangum grípan (*comprehendere*) woldon, Bd. 5, 12; Sch. 621, 16. (β) the object non- material :—Sē ðe ðás ðing gecneordlíce begǣð, hē grípeð þæt behātene ríce, Hml. Th. i. 360, 25. Hié grípað ðone cwide ðæs apostoles Paules hiora gídsunge tō fultume *ad usum suae libidinis instrumentum apostolici sermonis arripiunt,* Past. 52, 4. (b) the subject a thing (snare), *to seize, take, catch :*—Ðet ðú ne sió gripen *ne capiaris* (*Dominus custodiet pedem tuum*), Kent. Gl. 50. Bióð gribene *capientur* (*iniqui in insidiis suis*), 350. (2) *to seize and carry off :*—Ic be hondum mæg grípan tō grunde Godes andsacan, Sat. 269. v. grippan.

gripe. *Add:* I. *grasp, clutch, embrace :*—Seó ǣrene gripu ofer gléda gripe wealleð, Sal. 48. II. *attack, assault.* (1) *by living creatures :*—Grimne gripe Gūðláf and Ōsláf mændon, B. 1148. þú þurh deóra gripe deáðe sweltest, Jul. 125. (2) *by things.* v. grípan; II. 2. (a) material :—þurh gáres gripe gást onsendan, An. 187. Hē hæfde him on handa hilde frófre (frore, MS.), gūðbilla gripe *he had in his hand aid for war, for the assault of battle-bills,* Vald. 2, 13. (b) non-material :— þǣr is wyrma slite and ealra wǣdla gripe, Wlfst. 209, 18. III. *grasp, power, control, mastery.* (1) by persons :—þín feorh beran in gramra gripe, An. 217 : 953. (2) by things :—in gléda gripe, Jul. 391. In þæs wylmes grund . . . in gléda gripe, El. 1302. v. níd-, on-gripe, *and passages at* gripa.

grípe, an; *f. A ditch, drain :*—Adelseáþa grýpan *cloacarum cuniculi,* An. Ox. 3320. Grýpan, adelseáþes *cloace,* 4290. Tō wiþersacunge adelseápe, grýpan *ad apostasię cloacam,* 4744. [v. *N. E. D.* grip.] v. greóp, grēp, grēpe.

grípend, es; *m. One who seizes* (v. grípan; II), *a robber :*—Strúdend oððe grípend *raptor,* Wrt. Voc. ii. 88, 69.

grípendlic. v. be-, un-grípendlic: gripennes. v. ge-gripennes.

gripol (-ul); *adj. Able to grasp much, capacious :*—Gripul, numul *capax, qui multum capit,* Wrt. Voc. ii. 128, 29.

grippan; *p. de* To seize :—Sōhton hine tō grioppanne (gigripanne,

R.) *querebant eum apprehendere*, Jn. L. 7, 30. [v. *N. E. D.* grip.] v. ge-grippan.

**gripu** (?) *a handful.* v. gripa: **gripu** *a cauldron. Add:* cf. gropa.

**grisla** *terror.* [Ant te grisle ant te grure þe bið et te dome, Marh. 15, 3. To grisle and to grure, O. E. Hml. i. 251, 14.] v. on-grisla.

**grislic.** *Add:* [Þær inn eode an grislic deofol, Hml. A. 175, 182.] v. on-grislic.

**grist.** *l.* grīst, *and add:*—Grīst *molitura* (molitura *granum molendum,* Migne), Wrt. Voc. ii. 58, 15.

**grist** (?) *gnashing of teeth, in the cpds.* grist-bātian, -bātung, -bite, -bitian, -bitung. [Cf. *O. Sax.* grist-grimmo *gnashing of teeth in rage:* O. H. Ger. gris-gramōn *stridere, fremere dentibus;* gris-grimmōn *stridere;* grist-grimmung *stridor.*] *See next word.*

**gristan** (?) *to gnash the teeth :*—Cyrmiende, gyrst t crim̄ (=? gyrstende t crimende) *stridule,* An. Ox. 4605. [v. *N. E. D.* grist *to gnash the teeth.*] *See preceding word.*

**gristbātian.** *Add: to rage :*—Fremit, i. *perstrepit, furit, indignabatur* gristbātaþ, Wrt. Voc. ii. 150, 58. v. gristbitian.

**gristbātung.** *Add :*—Tōþa gristbātung, Mt. R. 25, 30. Hē ongan beón swīðe geswænced mid gristbātingum (*stridoribus*) and gehlówum, Gr. D. 223, 8. v. gristbitung.

**grist-bite,** es ; *m. Gnashing of teeth :*—In tōða gristbitum, Wlfst. 188, 5. [Cf. þer wes muchel gristbat, Laym. 5189.]

**gristbitian.** *Add :*—Hē gristbitað (*fremet ; stridebit,* Ps. L. : grystbitað, Ps. Spl.) mid his tōþum ongeán hine, Ps. Th. 36, 12. Gristbites, Mk. R. 9, 18. Hȳ gristbitoton (*striderunt*) on mē tōþum heora, Ps. Rdr. 34, 16. [v. *N. E. D.* gristbite.]

**gristbitung.** *Add :*—Girstbitung *stridor* (v. Mt. 8, 12), Wrt. Voc. ii. 72, 28. Gristbitung (grisgbitung, MS.), Dōm. L. 226. Gristbiotung, Mt. L. 13, 50. Nallæs nā rihtstefnum ac mid gristbitingum (-bitunge, *v. l.*) clypigan *non vocibus, sed stridoribus clamare,* Gr. D. 28, 29 : 223, 8. [v. *N. E. D.* gristbiting.] v. gristbātung.

**gristel,** es ; *m. Substitute :* **gristle,** an ; *f. :*—Gristle *cartilago,* Wrt. Voc. i. 283, 39 : ii. 41, 23. Ic ondette mīne synna for ealne mīnne līchoman, for . . . tungan and gristlan and gōman, Angl. xi. 98, 49. For grislan and for tungan, Ll. Th. ii. 264, 5. [*O. Frs.* gristel, grestel.] v. næs-, nos-gristle ; grost.

**gristel-bān.** *Dele :* **gristian.** *Dele, and see* gristan (?).

**gristra.** *Substitute :* **grīstra,** an ; *m. A baker of bread :*—Mylenwyrd *molendinarius,* grīst *molitura,* grīstra *cerealis pistor* (or *cerealis, pistor.* v. Migne cerealis *pistor*), bæcere *pistor,* Wrt. Voc. i. 34, 37 : ii. 130, 17.

**grītan** ; *p.* te *To become great, flourish :*—Grȳtte *floruit,* Wrt. Voc. ii. 149, 52. Cf. greátian.

**grip.** *Add :*—Sē ðe Godes cyrican rȳpe oððe reáfige oððe hālignesse grið brece *si quis ecclesiam Dei denudauerit vel sanctimonia violauerit,* Wlfst. 68, 1. v. un-griþ.

**grip-bryce.** *Add :* **I.** *a breach of* '*griþ*' :—Griðbryce (*De militum rapinis*). Gif hwā on fyrde griðbryce fulwyrce, þolige līfes, Ll. Th. i. 408, 21. **II.** *the fine for such breach, the revenue derived from such fines :*—Ic cȳðe eów þ ic hæbbe geunnen him þ hē beó his saca and sōcne wyrðe and griðbryces, Cht. E. 233, 3. Ic habbe gegeofen . . . saca and sōcna, . . . griðbryce and scipbryce, C. D. iv. 208, 23. On Dena lage cyning āh griðbryce (*mulctas pacis violatae*), Ll. Th. i. 384, 6. [v. *N. E. D.* grith-breach.]

**gripian.** *Add :*—Deóres fnæstum griþode (*plebem*) *bestiæ flatibus eripuit* (i. *liberauit*), An. Ox. 2473. Godes cyrican wē sculan griðian and healdan unwemme, Wlfst. 67, 17. Griðian and friðian, 143, 9. v. ge-griþian.

**grito**(-u) *greatness. Take here* grȳto *in Dict., and add :* [O. H. Ger. grōzī *grossitudo.*] **gritta** *bran.* v. grytta : **grīwan.** v. be-, tor-grīwan : **grona.** v. granu : **gronung.** v. grornung : **gron-wisc.** v. gran-wisc.

**grōp** *a ditch, drain :*—Groop *scropis,* Txts. 115, 150. [v. *N. E. D.* groop.]

**gropa,** an ; *m. A pot :*—Mycel gropa *congius* (the gloss is : Congium *reddit* tala *vel* mycel gropa), Wrt. Voc. ii. 130, 78. [O. L. Ger. gropo *olla.*]

**grorn** ; *adj. Troubled, sad :*—Warð gāsrīc grorn þær hē on greút giswom *the whale got sad when he ran ashore,* Txts. 127, 6. Cf. gnorn.

**grornian.** *Add :*—Grornodon *murmurabant,* Ps. Vos. 105, 25. [Nēnig man hine geseah swīðe grorniende ac hē ā heofonlice blisse ber on his onseóne, Angl. x. 147, 256.] [O. Sax. grornōn.] Cf. gnornian.

**grornung.** *Add :*—Mid grornunge (gnornunge, sārinysse, *v. ll.*) *cum maerore,* Gr. D. 148, 30. Þurh nytlice gro[r]nunge *per utilem maerorem,* Scint. 20, 1. Cf. gnornung.

**grost** *gristle :*—Grost *cartillago,* Txts. 112, 56. [Cf. *O. H. Ger.* crostila *cartilago.*] v. gristle.

**grot.** *Add : meal :*—Grot *pollis,* Txts. 115, 149. [v. *N. E. D.* grot.] v. mere-, sand-grot, -grota ; grotan ; greót, gryt, grūt ; grotig.

**grotan** (?) *groats :*—Nim ātena gratan (grotan ?), Lch. iii. 292, 24. [v. *N. E. D.* groats.] *See preceding word.*

**grotig** ; *adj. Earthy :*—Grotig *terrulentum,* Germ. 396, 195.

**grōwan.** *Add :* **I.** *of a plant, to shew vigorous life, flourish, be green :*—Florescit blēwþ, crescit grēwþ, Wrt. Voc. ii. 149, 48. Þeós wyrt byð seldon funden, ne hȳ man gecnāwan ne mæg būton ðonne heó grēwð and blēwð, Lch. i. 98, 4. Swā nū lencten and hærfest, on lencten hit grēwþ, and on hærfest hit fealwaþ, Bt. 21 ; F. 74, 22. Greów *fronduerat,* Wrt. Voc. ii. 151, 23. Greóuue *viresceret,* 123, 70. Grōwende leáf *virens folium,* Kent. Gl. 387. Þonne gē geseóþ grōwende and blōwende ealle eorþan wæstmas, Bl. H. 59, 2. Grōwen *frondescere,* Wrt. Voc. ii. 151, 11. **I a.** figurative, of persons or things, *to flourish :*—Grōwað *germinabunt* (*tabernacula justorum*), Kent. Gl. 482. Ic greów swā þ treów þe mid wæstnium bið fægre gefrætwod, Hml. S. 30, 190. Þone rihtan geleáfan fæste staðelian on ūrum heortum, þ hē ðær mæge grōwan and blōwan, Bl. H. 111, 5. Hwæðer sī þīn ealde gȳtsung of ðīnum mōde āwyrtwalod, þæt heó gȳt grōwan ne myht, Solil. H. 37, 15. Seó cirice mid gefeán and mid blisse grōwende standeþ, Bl. H. 197, 24 : Gen. 88. **II.** *of land, to produce vegetation, be verdant :*—Ic grōwe *glesco* (ut *glisceret* foecundo germine tellus, Ald. 143, 23), An. Ox. 18 b, 42. Regn . . . þe þeós eorðe fram æfter grōweð, Ps. Th. 146, 8. Seó eorþe biþ geleht, þ hió grēwþ and blēwþ and westmas bringþ, Bt. 33, 4 ; F. 130, 6. Þā land greówan and blōstmedon *terra refloruit,* Bd. 4, 13 ; Sch. 419, 10. Greówan land heora āloden wæstmum, Ps. Th. 106, 36. Forst sceal freósan, . . . eorðe grōwan, Gn. Ex. 73. Geseah hē ānre stōwe fæc þām ōþrum felda grēnre (grōwenre, *v. l.*) *uidit unius loci spatium cetero campo uiridius,* Bd. 3, 10 ; Sch. 233, 1. **II a.** figurative :—Se sōðfæsta blōweð swā palma, and swā Libanes beorh grōweð, Ps. Th. 91, 11. **III.** *to have vegetative life, develop as a living plant :*—Se metod fēt eall þætte grōweð wæstmas on weorolde, Met. 29, 70. Swā longe swā heora gecynd biþ þ hī grōwan mōton, Bt. 34, 10 ; F. 148, 30. Ealle grōwende westmas, 39, 13 ; F. 234, 19. **IV.** *of seeds* (lit. or fig.), *to germinate :*—Ðonne grēwð ðæt sǣd ðāra worda *tunc verbi semen germinat,* Past. 137, 7. And þ sǣd grōwe and wexe *et semen germinet et increscat,* Mk. 4, 27. Þæs sǣdes corn bið āweaht mid āscunga . . . gif hit grōwan sceal, Met. 22, 42. God geunne ūs grōwende gife þ ūs corna gehwylc cume tō nytte, Lch. i. 404, 12. **V.** *of immaterial things, to arise, be developed :*—Him on ferhþe greów breósthord blōdreów, B. 1718. **VI.** *of a plant, to increase in size by natural development :*—Licgende beám lǣsest grōweð, Gn. Ex. 159. **VII.** *of things, to increase gradually :*—Ēce standeð Godes handgeweorc, grōweð swā þū hēte, Hy. 9, 35. Þā þā ðū ðōre men reáfodest, ðā greówon on þā ēcan wītu, Nap. 60, 2. **VIII.** *to increase in a specified respect :*—Grōwan in Godes sibbe, Sal. 484. **IX.** *to approach maturity :*—Grȳwe *pubesceret,* An. Ox. 17, 30. Grōwan, mitescian *mitescere* (perhaps this gloss belongs to Ald. 53, 19, *mitescere ac maturescere,* in which case *grōwan* may apply to, or be influenced by, *maturescere*), Wrt. Voc. ii. 55, 8. v. full-, ofer-grōwan.

**grōwnes.** *Add :* **I.** *flourishing condition, prosperity :*—Drihten ingc syleð swā myccle grōwnysse on ingcran beorðre swā hē nǣfre nǣnigan hālgan ǣr ne sealde (*vobis deus talem dabit fructum qualem nunquam habuerunt prophetae*), Hml. A. 124, 257. **II.** *offspring* (?) :—Flind *genitrix,* mīnes cynnes *gentis,* mid mīnre grōwnesse *germine,* Wrt. Voc. ii. 41, 71–73.

**gruncan.** *Substitute :* **gruncian** ; *p.* ode *To have an itch for, desire :*—Gruncaþ *prurit,* i. *desiderat,* Germ. 396, 254.

**grund.** *Add :* **I.** *the bottom, the lowest part of anything.* (1) *of the sea :*—On deópum, niwellicum grunde sǣwe *in fundo profundo maris,* An. Ox. 1942. (2) *the furthest point reached by the root :*—Gif ðū āwyrtwalast of ðīnum mōde ðā leásan gesǣlþa and þā of ātīhst oð ðone grund, Bt. 23 ; F. 80, 1. Hē hēt āceorfan on grund heom heora tungan of *eorum linguas abscidi radicitus fecit,* Gr. D. 240, 19. **II.** *the solid bottom or earth underlying the sea or other water :*—Þæt seó sǣ seofan dagas drīgne grund þām folce gegearcige, Hml. Th. i. 564, 24. Þā scipu tōscuton and hē ðone grund (*the bottom of the river*) gesōhte mid horse mid ealle, ii. 304, 28. **III.** *a deep place, abyss :*—Grund *profundum* (ne absorbeat me *profundum*), Bl. Gl. Āworpen tō sǣs grunde, Past. 31, 18. Grundas *abys*[s]*i,* Kent. Gl. 262. **IV.** *the solid base or foundation on which a structure is raised :*—Ðȳ mon sceal fæsðne weal wyrcean, ðȳ mon ǣr gehāwige ðæt se grund fæsð sié, ðǣr mon ðone grundweall on lecge, Past. 308, 3. Staþolas t grundweallas t grundas munta *fundamenta montium,* Ps. L. 17, 8. **V.** *the surface of the earth :*—Mon tōwearp þone weal niþer oþ þone grund *muros everti aequarique solo imperauit,* Ors. 5, 11 ; S. 238, 13. **VI.** *the earth as contrasted* (1) *with heaven :*—Wē men cwēdað hēr on grunde, Hy. 9, 39. (2) *with sea :*—Þone þe grund and sund, heofon and eorðan and hreó wǣgas āmearcode, An. 747. **VII.** *a land, country :*—Hweorfað gleómen geond grunda fela, Vīd. 136. **VII a.** *a portion of cultivated land :*—Se God sē þās grundas geworhte geunne ūs grōwende gife þ ūs corna gehwylc cume tō nytte, Lch. i. 404, 11. v. eár-, eormen-, hell-grund.

**grunde-hirde.** *l.* grund-hirde.

**grunde-swelge.** *Add:* **gunde-**, **grund-swelge**—Gundesuilge, gundaesuelgiae, -suelgae *senecen*, Txts. 97, 1850. Grundeswelge *sin(i)tea vel senecion*, Wrt. Voc. i. 31, 26. Grundeswelige *sinitia*, 79, 7. Grundeswylie *senicia*, An. Ox. 56, 379. Grundswylige *senecio*, Wrt. Voc. i. 68, 42.

**grundinga;** *adv. From the foundation, completely, totally:*—Biꝺ æghwilc syn grundinga (*funditus*) ādwæsced, Bd. 1, 27; Sch. 78, 3. *v.* grundlinga.

**grund-leás.** *Add:* **I.** *of an earthly pit, gulf, &c.* (1) *lit. bottomless, whose bottom has not been reached:*—Andlang hagan tó ꝺām grundeliésan pytte, C. D. v. 148, 10. On ꝺone grundlésan pyt, vi. 41, 23. (2) *fig.:*—Ne biþ se ꝺurst gefylled heora gītsunga, ac seó grundleáse swelgend hæfþ swīþe manegu wēste holu on tó gadrianne, Bt. 7, 4; F. 22, 32. On hú grundleásum seáꝺe þ mod þringþ *quam praecipiti mersa profundo mens hebet*, 4, 2; F. 6, 7. **II.** *of the pit of hell and of its characteristics:*—Grundleás seáꝺ *tartarus*, An. Ox. 23, 39. Hē helle séceꝺ . . . grundleásne wylm, Wal. 46. Þreá on helle, þæt syndon þýstro and hǽto grimme, grundleáse, Gen. 390. **III.** *of immaterial things, boundless, insatiable:*—Ne mæg se wela þá grundleásan gītsunga gefyllan *nec opes inexpletam restinguere avaritiam queunt*, Bt. 16, 3; F. 56, 2, 16.

**grundlinga.** *Add:* **I.** *where a building is razed to the ground, is destroyed to its foundations:*—Ðá sæde hē þæt his (*of the temple*) sceolde weorꝺan æghwylc stán grundlinga tóworpen *dico uobis, non relinquetur hic lapis super lapidem, qui non destruatur*, Wlfst. 88, 20. Seó burh wearꝺ tóworpen grundlunga, swá swá se Hǽlend sǽde, Ælfc. T. Grn. 21, 18: Hml. Th. i. 404, 12: Hml. A. 102, 11. Wearꝺ swá micel storm þ eall þ ormǽte weorc wearꝺ tówend grundlunga, Hml. S. 31, 1244. Þ tempel grundlunga tófeóll, 2, 387. Āhreás þæt tempel grundlunga, Hml. Th. i. 72, 5. **I a.** *fig.*—Þǽre ǽrran gerecednyssa dimhoua grundlunga (*funditus*) fordwinan, An. Ox. 1678. **II.** *of complete destruction or removal of other objects.* (1) *material:*—Ealle ꝺá godas gruudlunga suncon intó þǽre eorꝺan, Hml. S. 14, 143. (2) *non-material:*—Biꝺ æghwilc syn grundlinga (cf. *eallinga funditus*, Sch. 77, 13) ādwæsced *omnis culpa funditus exstinguitur*, Bd. 1, 27; Sch. 78, 3. Synna grundlunga (cf. *mid ealle*, R. Ben. 13, 18) of ādōn *peccata radicitus amputare*, R. Ben. l. 15, 6. *v.* grundinga.

**grundsópa.** *Substitute:* **grund-sopa**, an; *m.* The word translates *cartilago* in the following glosses:—Grundsopa (-suopa) *cartilago*, Txts. 49, 402: Wrt. Voc. ii. 13, 50. *Cartilago* grundsopa, *coriza, sternutatio* fnora, 128, 79, 80. In the glossary from which the last instance is taken the Latin words are arranged alphabetically, so that probably *coriza*, . . . fnora is not an independent entry but should be taken with *cartilago*. This supposition is made still more probable by a later gloss, where *coriza* occurs correctly among co- words—*coriza*, i. *sternutatio*, *cartilagines* nebgebræc *vel* fnora, Wrt. Voc. ii. 135, 77. According to these two glosses *cartilago* should have much the same meaning as *coriza* (v. nebgebræc), and so too should grundsopa. This meaning would not be far from that given for the word in Prompt. Parv.—growndesope (growndsope, grounsop) of any lycoure *fex*, *sedimen*, a meaning belonging also to Dutch grondsop. Apparently a different meaning is given to the word in another M. E. vocabulary. In a list 'Nomina arborum et earum fructuum' are these consecutive items—*Cortex* bark; *liber, interior pars corticis; suber, intima pars corticis; abdomen* grundsope, Wrt. Voc. i. 229, 24–27. Elsewhere (Wrt. Voc. i. 200, 46) *abdomen* is explained by *pinguedo porci:* could *abdomen* in the previous case refer to exudation on the bark of a tree? [Cf. *grurzapa cartilago*, Gall. 121.]

**grund-stán.** *Add:* A ground-stone (v. *N. E. D.*):—Grundstānas *cementa*, i. *petre*, Wrt. Voc. ii. 130, 64.

**grund-staþelian.** [Cf. grounstaþeling *fundamentum*, Ps. 136, 7.] *v.* ge-grundstaþelian: **grund-wæg.** *l.* grund-weg, -wæg, *dele* 'A foundation,' *and add:* Cf. eorþ-, fold-, mold-weg.

**grund-weall.** *Add:* **I.** *physical.* (1) *the foundation* of a building:—Hūs būtan grundwealle, Lk. 6, 49. Swylce eall seó cyrice wǽre tóworpen fram þām grundweallum (*a fundamentis*), Gr. D. 236, 14. (2) *the lowest part* of a mountain:—Grundwellas munta, Ps. L. 17, 8. **II.** *figurative.* (1) *of persons:*—God sceal beón grundweall þīnes lífes, Wlfst. 247, 6. Ne mæg nān man lecgan óþerne grundweall on ꝺǽre hālgan gelaꝺunge būton ꝺone ꝺe ꝺǽr geléd is, þ is Hǽlend Críst. Hē is se grundweall þǽre hālgan cyrcan, Hml. Th. ii. 588, 19–22. (2) *of things:*—Mid tealtriendum grundwealle *nutabundo* (*integritatis*) *fundamento*, An. Ox. 3880.

**-grundweallian.** *v.* ge-grundweallian: **grund-weg.** *v.* grundwæg.

**grunian.** *Add: and* **grunnian. I.** *to grunt:*—Grunian (grunnian, An. Ox. 4337) *grunnire*, Hpt. Gl. 507, 15. **II.** *to make a noise when chewing the cud:*—Grunaꝺ *ruminat*, Scint. 54, 15. [*Ayenb.* grunni: *M. H. Ger.* grunnen.] *v.* grunung *and next word.*

**grunnettan;** *p.* te *To grunt:*—Grunnettan *grunnire*, Wrt. Voc. ii. 110, 13. [*O. H. Ger., Ger.* grunzen.]

**grunnian, grunnung.** *v.* grunian, grunung.

**grunung.** *Add: and* **grunnung**—Grunung *barritus*, Hpt. Gl. 462, 55. Onhyrgan swȳna grununge (swīna grunnunge, *v. l.*), Gr. D. 185, 4. Grununga (grunnunge, An. Ox. 2387) *barritus*, i. *mugitus*, Hpt. Gl. 462, 54. Grununge (grunnunge, An. Ox. 4378) *rugitus*, 508, 40.

**grut.** *v.* grutt.

**grūt;** *indecl. and* grūt; *pl. n.* Take these under grūt; *gen.* grȳt (?), grūt (?); *dat.* grȳt, grūt; *f.*, *and add:*—Grūt *far*, Wrt. Voc. ii. 39, 76. Gruiit (= grȳt (?), grūt (?)) *pollinis*, 117, 64. Clam wiþ þon; þá reádan tigelan, gecnūwa tó dūste, gemeng wiꝺ grūt, Lch. ii. 114, 25. [*v. N. E. D.* grout. *O. L. Ger.* grūt *magaria; fermentata cerevisia quod uulgo* grūt *nuncupatur.*]

**grutt, es;** *m.* or *n.* **I.** *an abyss, a gulf, whirlpool.* (1) literal:—Déopnysse, grutte, sweliende *uoragine* (*inferni*), An. Ox. 4340. Grut edwindan *barathrum uoraginis* (*Charybdis*), 4, 9. Grut swelgendes, 7, 41. (2) figurative:—Swylce betwyx stānhricgum gruttes and stæfleahtres swelgend *quasi inter Scyllam solocismi et barbarismi baratrum*, An. Ox. 5466. Edwindan, grutte *in uoraginem* (*gastrimargiae*), 701. **II.** *a rock?:*—Stānrocca stāncyslas and sinewealte scylua, grutta (or ?? scylua grutta *of the rocks of the depths;* cf. (?) first passage under **I.** 2: if this explanation be correct the quotation belongs to **I.** 1) popelstānas of sandigum stranda stāncyslum *scopulorum glareas et rotundos scrupearum lapillulos de arenosis litorum sablonibus*, An. Ox. 1814. *v.* helle-grutt.

**gryllan;** *p.* de *To gnash the teeth, rage, be angry:*—Grylde *frendit*, Germ. 399, 393. Gryllendum *stridentibus*, 398, 173. [*Ger.* grollen.] *v.* grillan.

**grymetan.** *l.* grymettan, grymetian. *Take here* grimetan *in Dict., and add:*—Ic grimette (grymetige, [grimmete, 12 cent.] *v.ll.*) *fremo*, Ælfc. Gr. Z. 168, 1. Grymetteþ *frendit*, i. *stridet dentibus*, *rugiet*, Wrt. Voc. ii. 150, 55: *gemit, clamat*, 59. Grymettende *irascens, frendens*, 53. **I.** *of persons:*—Ic grymetige and stēne mid ealle móde *rugiebam a gemitu cordis mei*, Ps. Th. 37, 8. Þá grimetede se wælhreówa swá swá grǽdig leó, Hml. S. 11, 62. Grimetode (gegrimmetode, *v. l.*), 25, 540. Hī wēddon and egeslīce grymetodon, 6, 197. Hī hrȳmdon and grimetodon for ꝺám tintregum, Hml. Th. ii. 490, 12. Þá ongunnon ꝺá deóflu grimetian and cweꝺan, 494, 18. Þ folc tealde þ tó drȳcræfte grymetende mid gehlȳde, Hml. S. 7, 242. **II.** *of animals:*—Leó þonne hē grymetaꝺ (leó grymetende, Ps. L. 21, 14) *leo rugiens*, Ps. Th. 21, 11. Swá swá leó grimmeteꝺ (grymmetteꝺ, grimmetteþ, *v. ll.; perhaps this form should be taken as belonging to a verb* grimmettan, *frequentative to* grimman), Hml. S. 15, 189. Þá beran grymetedon (*rugiebant*), Gr. D. 229, 23. Þæt hors ongan blāwan and grymetigean (gremetian, *v.l.*) *coepit flatu et fremitu*, 183, 11. Leó grymetigende (*rugiens*), Scint. 207, 12. Grymetiende *rugientes*, Ps. Vos. 103, 21. Urnon þá beran grymetende, Hml. S. 24, 53. Grymetendra *rudentium*, i. *seuientium* (*leonum*), An. Ox. 3684. **III.** *of things:*—Þá neólnessa grymeteaþ, Bl. H. 93, 12. Gefeoht grimettaþ *bella fremunt*, Wülck. Gl. 255, 7. *v.* ā-, ge-grymettan (-etian).

**grymetung.** *l.* grymettung, *and add:*—Grymetting *vel* brēmung *fremitus*, i. *mugitus*, Wrt. Voc. ii. 150, 60. Cumaꝺ . . . mycele deór . . . heora grymetung biꝺ gelīc crætena cearcetunge, Wlfst. 200, 17. Gremetunc *fremitus* (*leonum*), Kent. Gl. 686. Grimetung *rugitus*, 726. Grymetunge *murmure*, Wrt. Voc. ii. 57, 36. Wē rǽdaþ þe þǽre león . . . þ ꝺá óꝺre deór þurh hyre grymetunge beóꝺ swá āfyrhte þ hí fleón ne durron, Hml. A. 63, 278. Lāþlice grymetunga *truculentos fremitus*, An. Ox. 2388. Grymetunge *rugitus* (*seueros*), 4378.

**gryn, es;** *m. n* (?). *Substitute:* **gryn[n]** (cf. hlyn[n]) *or* **gryne** (? cf. dyne, dyn[n]), es; *m.* Dele 'Or does gryn = grin?': **-grynd.** *v.* ge-grynd.

**gryndan. II.** *For* 'Cot. 68, Lye' *substitute* Wrt. Voc. ii. 28, 9, *and add:* [The sonne . . . and many sterren By easte aryseth . . . By weste hy grendeth, Shoreham.]

**gryndle, an;** *f.* A herring:—Grindle *alleh* (cf. *taricus vel allec* hærinc, Wrt. Voc. i. 77, 62), Wrt. Voc. ii. 10, 16. [*O. H. Ger.* grundela *turonilla, sanatilis: Ger.* gründel. *v. N. E. D.* grundel, grindle.]

**grynel, es;** *m. Add:* A swelling in the neck:—Grynlas *toles*, Wrt. Voc. i. 64, 60. Cf. cyrnel.

**gryntan.** *l.* on-gryntan: **grȳpe.** *v.* grīpe.

**gryre.** *Add:* **I.** *the state of being terrified:*—Ðurh hine gewyrꝺ swá micel gryre, swá nǽfre ǽr on worulde ne geweárꝺ, Wlfst. 19, 6. Gryre se mǽsta, 25, 19: 203, 4. Āsprang micel ōga and gryre ofer ealle ꝺá ungeleáffullan, Hml. Th. i. 470, 8. Gryre and ege, Hml. S. 23, 83. Gryre sceal for greggum, Gn. Ex. 149. Siꝺꝺan þæs gǽstes gryre āgiefen weorꝺeꝺ *after terror has become the portion of the spirit*, Dóm. 21. God sealde him wītes clom and egsan gryre (*inspired him with terror*), Sat. 454: Dan. 593. **II.** *terribleness, what causes terror or horror:*—Se lēgdraca, grimlic gryre, B. 3041. Ne mæg nǽnig gryre māre geweorꝺan *nor can any terrible time exceed this*, Dóm. 43. Hié of þām grimman gryre (*the fiery furnace*) glade treddedon, Dan. 439.

Gyllende gryre (*with the roaring waves of the Red Sea*), Exod. 489. Hine God ūs onsende wið Grendles gryre (*the terror caused by Grendel*), B. 384 : Exod. 20. Þā wudubeámas wagedon and swēgdon þurh winda gryre *flamine ventorum resonantibus undique ramis*, Dôm. L. 8. Þæt næfre Grendel swā fela gryra (*terrible deeds*) gefremeðe, hýndo on Heorote, B. 591. Gryrum horrendum, Wrt. Voc. ii. 43, 32. Ān deófol ārehte ānum ancran ealle helle gryras and yrmða and þāra synfulra sāwla tintregan and sūsla, Wlfst. 146, 18. v. heort-gryre.

**gryre-lic.** Add:—Ic eom gryrelic *horrida*, Wrt. Voc. ii. 43, 33. Gryrelicum *horrisonis*, 30. v. on-gryrelic (?).

**gryre-meaht, -miht,** e ; *f. A power that inspires terror, terrible power*:—His (*Antichrist's*) hlīsa and gryremiht bið from sǽ tō sǽ, Wlfst. 195, 20.

**gryrran** *to gnash, chatter* (of teeth) :—þā tēþ for miclum cyle gryrrað *nimis stridentes frigore dentes*, Dôm. L. 195. v. gnyrran.

**gryt.** v. grytt : **grȳtan.** v. grītan : **grȳto.** v. grīto.

**grytt,** es ; *n. Dust, meal* :—Grytt *pollis*, Txts. 89, 1620. Gryt *grues* (the word occurs in a list headed ' Incipit de frugibus.' The same gloss is given in Wrt. Voc. ii. 41, 30. In this case comparison may be made with Wrt. Voc. ii. 91, 22 where *grues* is written for the *caries* of Ald. 153, 28), Wrt. Voc. i. 287, 25. Gryttes *polline* (cf. mealewes *poline*, i. *farine*, An. Ox. 3872, both glosses of Ald. 53, 28), ii. 83, 66. v. grot, grotig.

**grytta.** *Dele last passage, for which see* hwǽte-gryttan, *and add*: *Hic furfur* þās grytta, Ælfc. Gr. Z. 48, 17. Berene gryta (gritta, *v.l.*), Lch. i. 354, 2.

**grytte** *a spider*:—Grytte *aranea*, Ps. Vos. 89, 9. Gongeweafre, grytte, Ps. Srt. 89, 9. [v. *N. E. D.* grit *a kind of crab.*]

**gullisc**?:—Mid ðȳ gulliscan seolfre oferworht, and mid ðām neorxnawonges compgimmum āstǽned, Sal. K. 150, 9.

**guma.** *Add*:—Þǽr læg secg mænig, guma norðerna, Chr. 937; P. 106, 26. Rinc mænig, gūðfrec guma, An. 1119. Guman ūt scufon, weras . . . , B. 215. Mōdige magoþegnas, māgas sine, godfyrhte guman, An. 1518. Wītgan, gāsthālige guman, El. 562. Guman rīce and heáne, Rä. 33, 12. Ðā foremǽran bisna þāra gódena gumena and þǽra weorþgeornena wera, Bt. 40, 4 ; F. 238, 29. Gumena mænigeo, hæleð in healle, Dan. 728. Folcstede gumena, hæleða eðel, An. 20. Gūðsearo gumena . . . sǽmanna searo, B. 328. Tō secganne gumena ǽngum, 474. Gumena sum, 1499. Gumena nāthwylc, 2233. Him God sealde gumena rīce, worlde tō gewealde in wera life, Dan. 607 : Vīd. 133. Hē weóld ealles þisses middangeardes, swā swā . . . gārsecg embegyrt gumena rīce, secga sitlu, Met. 9, 41. Metod weóld gumena cynnes, B. 1058 : An. 582. Hæleða leófost gumena cynnes, Gū. 1177. Þā heó sēleste mid Iūdéum gumena wiste hæleða cynnes, El. 1203. ¶ in epithets, (1) of the Deity :—Gumena Dryhten, Gen. 515 : An. 621 : Hy. 6, 14. Gumena weard, Crä. 59 : Hy. 6, 19. Gumena brego, An. 61. (2) of earthly princes :—Gumena baldor, Gen. 2693 : Jud. 9. Gumena aldor, Dan. 549. Gumena drihten, 613 ; B. 1824. Gumena weard, Dan. 636. Sigecyning . . . gūðweard gumena, Exod. 174. Hē wæs riht cyning, gūðweard gumena, El. 14. Sinces brytta . . . goldwine gumena, B. 1171: 1476 : El. 201 : Jud. 22. ¶ of other than mere men :—Feásceaft guma (*Grendel*), B. 973. Ic wæs mid blôde bestēmed begoten of þæs guman (*Christ's*) sīdan, Kr. 49. v. seld-guma.

**gum-cynn.** *Substitute*: I. *mankind* :—Gumcynnes gehwone (cf. moncynnes gehwone, Cri. 1027), B. 2765. Hē þæt wera cneórissum gewrecan þôhte, forgrīpan gumcynne, Gen. 1275. II. *a (noble) race, family, tribe, people* (cf. Idisi . . . gumkunnies wíf, Mariun munilīka, Hēl. 5785) :—Eom ic gumcynnes ānga ofer eorðan *I am the only one of the race* (cf. his sunu . . . , āngan ofer eorðan yrfelāfe *his only son and heir*, Isaac, Exod. 401), Rä. 85, 12. Wē synt gumcynnes Geáta leóde *we are of the noble race of the Geats*, B. 260. Swā hwylc mægða swā þone magan (*Beowulf*) cende æfter gumcynnum, 944.

**gum-cyst.** *Add:* cf. mann-cyst : **-gumian.** v. ofer-gumian : **gumrīce.** *Add:* cf. gumena rīce, Dan. 607 : Vīd. 133.

**gund.** *Add*:—Ātīhð hió þā yfelan wǽtan ūt and þone gund, Lch. ii. 44, 23. [v. *N. E. D.* gound. *Perhaps Goth.* gun[ds] *cancer.*]

**gunde-swilge.** v. grunde-swelge : **gungling.** v. geongling : **-gunnenness.** v. on-gunnenness.

**gupe,** an ; *f. A buttock* :—Gupan *clunis, renibus, coxe*, Wrt. Voc. ii. 131, 77. [*O. L. Ger.* gopon *terga* : *O. H. Ger.* goffa *clunis.*]

**gūþ-fana.** *Add:* and gūþ-fan, es ; *n.* (?) *a flag, pennon* :—Hē (*Constantine*) mearcode on his gūðfanan hālig rôde tācn, Hml. Th. ii. 304, 15. Gūðfanan geleá[fa]n wē beorað *vexillum fidei ferimus*, Ps. Srt. ii. p. 203, 23. Beran þā gūðfanan (*vexilla*) in on ðā ceastre, Prud. 74. ¶ *in the following instances the form* gūþ-fan ; *n. seems to be used*:—Gūþfan *labarum*, An. Ox. 2130. Sigefæst gūþfana *uictricia uexilla*, 1746. Segnes gūðfana *labara*, Wrt. Voc. ii. 49, 74. ii. mycele candelsticcan . . . viii. læflas and .ii. gūðfana, C. D. iv. 275, 25.

**gūþ-frec.** *Substitute* : *greedy for war* or *destruction.* The epithet is applied to the cannibals who, distressed by hunger, were eager for the

death of the victim they meant to eat :—þā wæs rinc manig, gūðfrec guma, ymb þæs geongan feorh breóstum onbryrded tō þām beadulāce, An. 1119.

**gūþ-gewǽd.** *l.* -gewǽde : gūþ-mód ; *adj. Substitute*: gūþ-mód, es ; *n. A martial mind.* v. grimman : **gūþ-prǽc.** *l.* -þracu.

**gutt,** es ; *m. A gut, an entrail* :—Guttas, innoðas *receptacula* (*viscerum*), Hpt. Gl. 408, 52.

**gyccae.** v. gicce : **gycel.** v. gicel: **gyce-nes.** v. gice-nes : **gycer.** v. gicer.

**gyden.** *Add*:—Hē wēnde þ heó Diana wǽre seó giden, Ap. Th. 24, 5. On Ueneris hīwe þǽre fūlan gyden, Hml. S. 31, 716. þ heó þǽre gydenan Diane godes wurðmynt gebude, 2, 385. Hē hyre anlīcnysse wurðode swā swā hālige gydenan, 115. Hæþene godas and þǽre gydena, Wlfst. 107, 19 : Hml. S. 4, 134 : Hml. Th. i. 426, 7. Clypiað tō eówrum godum and tō eallum gydenum, 150. ¶ as an explanatory gloss on the name of a divinity :—*Veste* gydene, Wrt. Voc. ii. 92, 81: *Ueneris,* An. Ox. 4449. *Proserpinam,* proprium nomen tō gidenan, 4187. Gydene, Wrt. Voc. ii. 67, 12. *Castalidas nympas* þā mānfullan gydena *vel* dūnelfa, 129, 33 : 61, 19. v. girel-gyden.

**gyden-lic.** *Substitute*: *Of a goddess, vestal* (virgin) :—Gedenlic *vestalis, Vestam colens* (*virgo*), Hpt. Gl. 481, 37 : An. Ox. 3193. Gyddenlic, 7, 233 : 8, 170. Gydenlice, Wrt. Voc. ii. 81, 73. Gydenlic, 92, 78.

**gydig ;** *adj. Possessed by an evil spirit, mad*:—þæne gidigan *limphaticum*, s. *Saul* (gy[digne], þæne gidigan *limphaticum*, i. *vecordem*, Hpt. Gl. 520, 63 : cf. *limphaticum* wōdan, Wrt. Voc. ii. 53, 56), An. Ox. 5009. Cf. god.

**gyldan.** *Add*: v. be-, ofer-gyldan ; ge-gyld.

**gylden.** *In* l. 8 *for* gyldenum *l.* gyldnum, *and add*:—Gelden trendel *circulus aureus*, Kent. Gl. 373. Gylden, 963. Hafað hē gyldene gāde, Sal. 91. Man hit cleopede þā Gildene burh, Chr. 1052 ; P. 183, 20. Gyldenu fatu and silfrenu, Bt. 36, 1 ; F. 172, 19. Twā hund gildenra pænega, Ap. Th. 27, 26. On gyldenan faton, Chr. 1075; P. 209, 33. Ne wyrc þū þē gyldne (gyldēne, *v. l.*) godas, Ll. Th. i. 44, 22. Gyldene, Ex. 20, 23. v. ge-, ofer-gylden.

**gylden-feaxa.** *Substitute* : **gylden-feax[e]** ; *adj. Golden-haired* :— Gyldenfeaxa *auricomus*, Wrt. Voc. ii. 6, 39. [Cf. *O. H. Ger.* goldfahs *auricomus.*]

**gylden-hilt[e]** ; *adj. Golden-hilted* :—Hē an ii. gyldenra rōda and ii. gyldenhiltra sweorda, C. D. B. iii. 74, 27.

**gylden-hīw[e]** ; *adj. Golden-hued* :—Gyldenhīwe *auricolor*, An. Ox. 43, 5.

**gylden-mūþ[e]** ; *adj. Golden-mouthed* (translating Chrysostomos) :— Gyldenmūða (-mūðe, *v. l.*) *crisostomus, os aureum habens*, Hpt. 31, 7, 113. Gregorius mid Grēcum Crysosthomas is gehāten . . . þysum wordum se ilca gyldenmūða Gregorius wæs sprecende, Gr. D 94, 20.

**gylding-wecg.** *Add*:—Gyldingwecg *aurifodina*, clympre *metallum*, smiþ *faber*, Wrt. Voc. i. 286, 72. Gyldingwegc, ii. 8, 55.

**gylece (-a?),** an ; *f.* (*m?*) *Some part of a monk's dress* :—Gylecan tācen his þæt þū strece forð þin wenstre handstoc and plyce innan mid þinre wynstran hande, Tech. ii. 127, 14.

**gylian.** *Add* (?) :—Gyli[ende] *garrula*, gylien[de] *garruli*, An. Ox. 56, 142, 138. v. gylung.

**gylt.** *Add*: I. *a failure of duty, a sin, crime, an offence* :—Getriówe bediólað gelt (*qui*) *fidelis* (*est animi*) *celat* (*amici*) *commissum* (Prov. 11, 13), Kent. Gl. 302. Gereónedes gyltes *concinnati sceleris* i. *culpe*, An. Ox. 2919. Gylte *reatu*, Ex. 32, 35. Gylt *noxam*, Wrt. Voc. ii. 61, 50. Mānfulne gylt *probrosum facinus*, i. *peccatum*, An. Ox. 2784. Eówerne gylt þe gē worhton, þæt wæs þæt cealf *peccatum vestrum, quod feceratis, id est vitulum*, Deut. 9, 21. Hē heánlīce hāmweard oðfleáh . . . þā bæd his fæder þæt þā senatum forgeáfen þǽm suna þone gylt (*pater . . . ignominiam filii deprecatus*), Ors. 3, 10 ; S. 140, 16. Gif ǽnig man ôðerne wrēge and him hwilcne gilt on secge (*accusans eum praevaricationis*), Deut. 19, 16. Gif hwilc preóst āgilte . . . hē þone gilt gebēte, Ll. Th. i. 290, 19. Gyltum gehrodene, Wal. 74. II. *a debt* :—Eallne þīnne gylt (*debitum*) ic þē forgeaf, Mt. 18, 32. Borhhande for geltum *vades pro debitis*, Kent. Gl. 849. II a. *a penalty, payment on account of crime*, Cht. Th. 423, 3 (v. Dict.). III. *responsibility for an offence, a (person's) fault*, Chr. 1048; P. 173, 11 (v. Dict.). IV. *desert of a penalty* ; buton gylte *without having done anything to deserve one's fate*, Chr. 1055 ; P. 184, 27 (v. Dict.). V. *state of being guilty, criminality, culpability* :—Hē gecnāwan mæg hwæt tælwierðe bið, and suāðeáh . . . forwandað ðæt hē bēte and ðreáge his hiéremenn be ðæs gyltes andefne *quae reprehendenda sunt cognoscit, sed tamen . . . dignis ea increpationibus non emendat*, Past. 195, 10. Gif hē þæs wiliuaþ þ him hiora yfel unwrecen sié be þæs gyltes andefne, Bt. 38, 7 ; F. 210, 8. Sceal ǽghwylc man bētan his wôhdǽda be his gyltes andefne, Bl. H. 45, 29. v. ǽ-, heáfod-gylt.

**gyltan.** *Add*:—Be ðām ðe on lytlum ðingum gyltað (*delinquuntur*), R. Ben. 71, 12. Þ ic nā gylte (*delinquam*) on mīnre tungan, R. Ben. 9. 25, 16. Ǽlcum gemete ne sceal ārung beón þǽre gyltendan geogoðe,

Nap. 17, 3. Dryhten aee gesette gyltendum (*delinquentibus*), Ps. Srt. 24, 8. Se abbod carige embe þā gyltendan gebrôðru (*circa delinquentes fratres*), R. Ben. 50, 18. v. ge-gyltan.

**gylte.** v. gilte.

**gyltend.** *Add:*—Þā þe nū nāne mildheortnesse nabbað wið hyra gyltyndum, Ll. Th. ii. 400, 25.

**gyltig.** *Add: culpable, delinquent:*—Gif hit gelimpð for oferflôwennysse metes oððe drinces, hē byð gyltig (*culpabilis*), Ll. Th. ii. 200, 31. Se brôðor, sē þe giltig āmeldod bið þām abbode þurh ôðerne man and nô þurh hine selfne, R. Ben. 71, 13. Gif heora hwilc mid deófles costnunge beswicen for Gode oþþe for worulde gyltig biþ, Lch. iii. 442, 35. Gif cinges geréfena hwylc gyltig biþ wiþ Gode oþþe wiþ men, 444, 6. v. un-gyltig.

**gylting.** *Add:*—Gyltinge *commissum*, Rtl. 114, 3. v. ā-gylting.

**gyltlíce; adv. Faultily:*—Gyltlíce (*culpabiliter*) handa tō Dryhtne upp ārærð sē þe dǣda his gebiddende gylplíce geypð, Scint. 35, 3.

**gylt-ness.** v. ā-gyltness.

**gylt-wíte, es; n. Fine for a crime:*—Poenam delicti quae Anglice dicitur giltwíte, C. D. ii. 406, 23. Gyltwíte, vi. 240, 35.

**gylung[?], e; f. Garrulity:*—Gy[lung] *garrulitas*, An. Ox. 56, 141. v. gylian.

**gýman.** v. gíman: **gýme-.** v. gíme-.

**gymmian.** *Substitute:* gymian, gymm[i]an *to cut, pierce* the flesh:—Gesyrewede [héapas] hī sylfe tō gymmienne *armatas catervus* (*jam jamque strictis mucronibus alternatim*) se jugulaturas (i. *perfossuras*), An. Ox. 3799. v. ge-gymian.

**gýnan.** v. gínan: **gynan** *to gain. Dele:* **gynung.** v. ginung.

**-gýpe.** v.-gípe: **gypian.** v. gipian: **gypung.** v. gipung.

**gyr** *a fir-tree.* For Lchdm. iii. 328, col. 1 *substitute:*—Gyr *abies*, Wrt. Voc. i. 285, 40.

**gyr** *mud.* v. gyru: **gyrd** *a rod.* v. gird: **gyrd** *a band, girth.* v. forþ-, þearm-gyrd: **gyrdan.** *Add:* v. for-, in-, un-gyrdan; ofer-gyrd.

**gyrdel.** *Add:*—Gyrdel *vel* āgimmed gerdel *clavus vel strophium*, Wrt. Voc. i. 40, 51. Swyrdes gyrdel *baltheus*, 58. Gyrdel oððe belt *balteum*, ii. 11, 51. Gyrdel oððe brêc *lumbare*, 51, 15. Synd gesealde from þām abbode ealle neádbehéfe þing, þæt is . . . gyrdel (*bracile*), R. Ben. 92, 3. Þā begyrde hē hine mid his gyrdele (*cingulo*) . . . Sôna swā hē wæs mid þām gyrdele begyrd, Guth. Gr. 148, 7. Hē stód on ðām wætere tō his gyrdle (*usque ad lumbos*, Bd 5, 12), Hml. Th. ii. 354, 18. Mid gildenum girdle his breóst wæs befangen, Ll. Th. ii. 370, 4. Ðonne þū gyrdel (-er, MS.) habban wylle, þonne sete þū þíne handa forewearde wiðneoþan þínne nafolan and stríc tō þínum twām hypum, Tech. ii. 119, 21. Hī cuwon heora girdlas, Ælfc. T. Grn. 21, 9. v. bí-gyrdel.

**gyrdel-bred.** *Substitute: A writing-tablet:*—Gyrdelbred *pugillaris*, Wrt. Voc. i. 288, 75.

**gyrdel-hring.** *Substitute:* gyrdel-hringe, an; f. A girdle-buckle, clasp for a girdle:*—Gyrdelhringe *lingula, legula*, Wrt. Voc. ii. 50, 66, 67. v. gyrdels-hringe.

**gyrdels.** *Add:*—Gyrdils *vel* broec; gyrdils, broec *lumbare*, Txts. 72, 573. Hyt byð tōsliten, swā wæs Abdias gyrdels þæs wítegan (cf.? computruerat *lumbare*, Jer. 13, 7), Lch. i. 328, 3. Tō gyrdylse *ad cingulum*, An. Ox. 3767. Hē hēt ādelfan seáþ oþ gyrdyls deópne, and bebeád þon þone Godes wer bebyrgde in þām seáðe oþ þone gyrdels, Shrn. 125, 32. Gerdels *cingulum*, Kent. Gl. 1149. In gyrdelsum *in zonis* (Mt. 10, 9), Wrt. Voc. ii. 72, 43.

**gyrdels-hringe,** an; f. A girdle-buckle, clasp for a girdle:*—Gyrdislrhingae, gyrdilshringe *legula*, Txts. 74, 582. Gyrdilshringe *lingula*, 75, 1226. v. gyrdel-hringe.

**gyrian.** v. girwan: **gýrla.** v. girela: **gyrman.** v. gíman: **gyrnan.** v. girnan: **gyrnes.** v. girn-ness: **gyrning.** v. girning: **gyrran.** v. girran: **gyrretynde.** v. girrettan: **gyrst** *stridor. Dele:* **gyrst** *stridulus.* v. gristan (?): **gyrstan.** v. gistran.

**gyru (?),** gen. **gyrwe; f. Mud, filth, dung:*—Gyr (gyru?, gor.?? cf. *letamen* gor, scear[n], Wrt. Voc. ii. 50, 38), dincge *letamen*, An. Ox. 4773. Gyrwe fen (the 12th cent. MS. has gurufen) *palus*, Ælfc. Gr. Z. 60, 10. ¶ giving rise to a local name:—Æt wíre mūðan and be Tínan þǣre eä, on ðǣre stôwe þe is gecýged on Gyrwum (*in loco, qui uocatur In Gyruum* (Yarrow)), Bd. 5, 21; Sch. 677, 12. [Cf. O. Frs. gere, iere *filthy water.*] v. gor, Gyrwas *and next word.*

**gyru (?);** adj. Muddy, marshy:*—On heán hangran middeweardne; ðanon on hwītau beorh . . . ðonon ūp on gyran torr, C. D. iii. 412, 9. See preceding word.

**gyrwan.** v. girwan.

**Gyrwas (-an).** *Add: The people of the fen district, which contained twelve hundred hides, six hundred in each of its two divisions.* v. Norþ-, Sūþ-Gyrwas:*—On Gyrwan (Gyrwa, v. l.) lande *in regione Gyruiorum*, Bd. 4, 6; Sch. 381, 19. On þǣre stôwe þe is genemned Crūland; þæt mynster is on middan Gyrwan (Girwan, v. l.) fænne (Crowland is called elsewhere 'Monasterium Gyruensis', Chr. P. ii. 37), Guth. Gr. 176, 2. v. gyru.

---

**gyse.** v. gise: **gýsel.** v. gísel.

**gyte.** *Add:* (1) *a flood of water, downpour of rain:*—Gyte inundatio, Wrt. Voc. ii. 111, 63: 45, 63. Swā mycel ýðgiung and regnes gyte (*inundatio*) forþ côm, Gr. D. 167, 25. (2) *a shedding of tears:*—Hwî ne feormast þū mid teára gyte torne synne? *cur tua non purgas lacrymis peccata profusis ?*, Dôm. L. 79. Bôte dôn mid teára gytum and mid gebedum, Wlfst. 264, 13. (3) *a flux of blood:*—Blôdes gytt *sanguinis profluvium*, Mk. p. 3, 7. Sum earm wíf wæs geswenct þurh blôdes gyte, Hml. Th. ii. 514, 27. (4) *effusion, shedding* of blood, *shed in blood-shed:*—Gyte blôdes on sace ofermôdigra *effusio sanguinis in rixa superborum*, Scint. 83, 7. Þæt hī heora handa fram ðām blôdes gyte ne wiðbrúdon, Hml. Th. i. 88, 5: Nap. 22, 25. Hit getácnað gefeoht and gete (*effusionem*) blôdes, Archiv. cxx. 53, 15. v. blôd-, in-, wæter-gyte.

**gyt-feorm** *an entertainment where there is pouring of drink, a feast.* Cf. ge-beórscipe, brýd-ealu (-oþ):*—On sumere ðeóde gebyreð winterfeorm, Eásterfeorm, bênf(e)orm for ripe, gytfeorm for yrðe, Ll. Th. i. 440, 26.

**gyþ-rife.** v. giþ-rife.

# H

**hā** *a thole:*—Þ wæs .viii. marc æt hā (hamelan, v. l. *see* hamele in Dict.), Chr. 1040; P. 160, 3. [Icel. hár *a thole.*] v. hā-sǣta, hān.

**haal-staan.** v. heall-stān.

**habban.** A. For I *and* IV *substitute:* I. *to have, hold* in or with the hand (*lit. or fig.*):*—Hē hafað in hondum heofon and eorðan, Gū. 619. Hine se mǣg Higeláces hǣfde be honda, B. 814. Wit hæfdon swurd nacod on handa, 539. Þā mǣdenu hæfden hī sylfe be handa heom betweónum, Gr. D. 119, 13. Þæt þíne englas þē on hondum habban, Bl. H. 27, 14. I a. *of the hand:*—Gif man frigne man æt hæbbendre hauda (*while the hand still holds the stolen goods*) gefô, Ll. Th. i. 42, 15: 198, 26. Habbendre, 220, 11. II. *to have, possess.* (1) *absolute:*—Ǣlcon þǣra þe hæfð man sylð . . . þām ðe næfð (nafeþ, R., ne hæfis, L.) *omni habenti dabitur . . qui non habet*, Mt. 25, 29. Sién ðā hæbbendan swelce hié nôwiht hæbben, Past. 387, 35. God ne hēt ūs gewelgian þā hæbbendan, Wlfst. 287, 24. (2) *with object.* (a) *to hold as property, possess* material or non-material objects:*—Mín lond þe ic hæbbe and mē God láh, C. D. i. 310, 5. Wealh, gif hē hæfæð (hæfð, v. l.) fíf hýda, Ll. Th. i. 118, 10. Hē hæfde mycele ǣhta, Mt. 19, 22. Þā cýððo þæs crístenan geleáfan þe hī hæfdon, Bd. 5, 22; Sch. 682, 19. Gif hē wite hwā þæs deádan ierfe hæbbe, Ll. Th. i. 136, 5. Ǣlc man þe hors habbe, 232, 20. Þā hālgan þe nǣht ne gyrndon tō hæbbenne, Bl. H. 53, 25. (b) *to hold as something at one's disposal or service, under one's control.* v. heofon-hæbbend:*—Þis leóht (this world) wē habbaþ wið nýtenu gemǣne, Bl. H. 21, 13. Hámtúnscíre hē hæfde oþ hē ofslôg þone aldorman, Chr. 755; P. 46, 21. Hié him hæfdon siþþan ealle þā anwealdas þe hié ealle ǣr hæfdon, Ors. 3, 11; S. 152, 24. Him his nefa gesealde Ircanian on onwald tō habbanne *eum Hyrcanorum genti praeposuit*, 1, 12; S. 54, 12. ¶ habban and healdan *to have and keep:*—Þā his mǣre word habbað and healdað, Ps. Th. 102, 19. Þā þe Godes ríces geleáfan habbað and healdaþ, Bl. H. 55, 17. Hafa and geheald húsa sēlest, . . . waca wið wráðum, B. 658. Þā word þæs godspelles his heortan habban and healdan, Bl. H. 55, 7. III. *denoting various kinds of connexion between subject and object, e. g. kindred, relative position:*—Ic hæbbe (hafo, L., R.) fíf gebrôþru, Lk. 16, 28. Ic lýt hafo heáfodmága, B. 2150. Sē ðe brýde hæfð (hæfes, L., hæfeð, R.), sē is brýdguma, Jn. 3, 29. Hæfde hē āgenne brôþor, Bd. 4, 22; Sch. 456, 19. Sume þā apostolas hæfdon him gemacan, Hml. A. 14, 34. Būton hē yruenoman hæbbe, Ll. Th. i. 290, 10. Būton hē hæbbe manigne man þe him hēre, Bt. 29, 1; F. 104, 9: Solil. H. 3, 12. Swā hē hæbbe freónda mā, Bl. H. 123, 1. Heó cwæð þ heó hine ne nänne habban (have as husband) wolde, Chr. 1067; P. 201, 16. Nis mē þearf hearran tō habbanne, Gen. 279. III a. *with complement or adverbial extension defining the connexion, cf.* VI. (1) the object a person:*—Wē habbað (habbas, L.) Abraham ūs tō fæder *patrem habemus Abraham*, Mt. 3, 9. Wē habbað ānne god tō fæder *unum patrem habemus deum*, Jn. 8, 41. Æþelwulf his dohtor hæfde him tō cuēne, Chr. 885; P. 78, 27. Þā hæfdon hī him tō wífum, Ors. 2, 2; S. 64, 30. Hine grame hæfdon tō hæfte, Ps. Th. 104, 15. Hæbbe hē him twēgen ceorlas tō gewitnesse, Ll. Th. i. 34, 4. Hæbbe hē him in āðe ǣwdan gôdne, 42, 8. Þ ǣlc man hæbbe æt þǣre syhl .ii. wel gehorsede men, 208, 12. Þ hī hī tō wífe habbon, Hml. S. 17, 158. (2) the object a thing. (a) a noun or pronoun:*—Nim þ ic þe tō sillenne habbe, Ap. Th. 12, 2. Hē hæfde þriddan dǣl his firde beæftan him, Ors. 1, 12; S. 52, 32. Theodosius hæfde þone wind mid him, 6, 36; S. 294, 26. Be þām sācerde . . , hwæt hē on him hæbbe, Ll. Th. ii. 128, 19. Hæbbe hē him gemǣne þ wið God, i. 332, 31. Þām þe heora dǣl getýnede hæbben, 128, ᴖ Būton se biscep hié mid him habbau wille, Past. 9, 6.

Habban mē ðæt tō gamene, 249, 1 : Bl. H. 113, 34. (β) a clause :—Hæfdon monige unwīse menn him tō worde þ siŏ hǣte nǣre for heora synnum, Ors. 1, 7 ; S. 40, 7. þ hē oft and gelóme hæbbe on gemynde þ mannum is mǣst þearf oftast tō gemunenne, þ is þ hī rihtne geleáfan habban, Ll. Th. i. 326, 10. **IV.** *to have* as a part or adjunct, *to contain* as parts of itself :—Habbaþ þā hwīla hwæthwugu onlīces, þ is þ heora ǣgþer hæfþ ende *utrumque spatium definitum est*, Bt. 18, 3 ; F. 66, 9. September hæfð .xxx. daga, Angl. viii. 300, 37, 39. Hæfde cista gehwilc tȳn hund geteled tīreádigra, Exod. 230. Hē hæfde blæc feax and blācne andwlitan *uir nigro capillo, facie macilenta*, Sch. 179, 6. Ân fictreów þe leáf hæfde, Mk. 11, 13. Gif se mōnð sceal habban .xxx. nihta ealdne mōnan, Angl. viii. 300, 33, 35. **V.** *to have* as an attribute, a quality, function, right, wrong, &c. (1) of persons :—Ic hæbbe geweald micel tō gyrwanne gōdlecran stōl, Gen. 280. Ylde hē hæfð (haefeð, L., hæfeð, R.), Jn. 9, 21. Eác wē habbað ðā synne, Ll. Th. i. 196, 7. Manege beóð ðe hæbbað ðā unðeáwas ealle . . . , Past. 455, 7. Seleucus hæfde seofon and seofontig wintra and Lisimachus hæfde þreó and seofontig wintra *Lysimachus annos septuaginta et quatuor natus, Seleucus autem septuaginta et septem*, Ors. 3, 11 ; S. 152, 17 : Gen. 1117. Ðæt cild hæfde lǣsse þonne þrȳ mōnðas þæs þriddan geáres, Shrn. 104, 18. Jūdas hæfde onlīcnesse (*was a type*) þæra manna þe willaþ Godes cyricean yfelian, Bl. H. 75, 23. Hē ne mehte habban þæs onwaldes noman, Ors. 6, 36 ; S. 294, 14. (2) of things :—Þā word þe geendiað on *or* habbaþ ðreó getācnunga, Ælfc. Gr. Z. 121, 18. Þā þing þe be mē synt habbað ende *the things about me are sure to come to pass*, Lk. 22, 37. **VI.** *to have, be affected with, experience, enjoy* or *suffer* :—Ne ic þæs deáðes hafu sorge on mōde, Gū. 1040. Þonne hafað hē mycelne lust, Lch. i. 358, 20. Heó hæfð unrōtnysse . . . Gē habbað (habað, L., habbas, R.) nū unrōtnysse, Jn. 16, 21, 22. Wē habbaþ nēdþearfe þ . . . , Bl. H. 23, 1. Swā fela swā untrumnessa and unclǣne gāstas hæfdon, Mk. 3, 11. On þām ðingum þe hī won (wana, *v. l.*) hæfdon, Bd. 5, 22 ; Sch. 682, 15. Hæbbe þæs gefeán folca ǣghwilc, and blessien þeóda *laetentur et exultent gentes*, Ps. Th. 66, 4. Gif hīwan hiora cirican māran þearfe hæbben, Ll. Th. i. 64, 14. Ðæs gefeán habban, B. 2740. **VII.** with object and dat. infin. expressing what is to be done by the subject, *to have* as a duty or thing to be done. Cf. II a :—Ic hæbbe (hafo, L.) þē tō secgenne sum ðing *habeo tibi aliquid dicere*, Lk. 7, 40. Ic hæbbe (hafo, L. R.) þone mete tō etanne þe gē nyton, Jn. 4, 32. Hæfst ðū æceras tō erigenne *habes agros ad arandum*, Ælfc. Gr. Z. 135, 7. Hæfst ðū cild tō lǣrenne *habes pueros ad docendum*, 151, 13. Uton wē geþencean hwylc handleán wē him forþ tō berenne habban, Bl. H. 91, 14. **VIII.** with dat. infin., *to have, be obliged* to do something :—Mage gyt drincan þone calic þe ic tō drincenne hæbbe *potestis bibere calicem quem ego bibiturus sum?*, Mt. 20, 22. Gif hē hæbbe ealle on fōðre tō āgifanne, Ll. Th. i. 140, 9. Hit hæfde (*would have*) ðonne tō wilnianne sumes gōdes, Bt. 24, 1 ; F. 80, 16. **IX.** *to hold, keep, retain*. (1) *to hold* in the same position :—Hafa lange hwīle þīne hand on, Lch. ii. 32, 22. (2) *to keep possession of* :—Ðone onwald mæg wel reccan sē ðe ǣgðer ge hine habban cann ge wiðwinnan *quam potentiam bene regit qui et tenere illam noverit et impugnare*, Past. 113, 21. (3) *to keep* in some relation to oneself, *have* in mind, in keeping, &c. :—Þ ic hæbbe feste on gemynde, Bt. 36, 3 ; F. 176, 24. Gēr ēce in mōde ic hefde *annos eternos in mente habui*, Ps. Srt. 76, 6. Regollícor libban þonne hī ǣr þisan on gewunan hæfdon, Ll. Th. i. 346, 28. Hæbbe ǣlc hlāford his hīredmen on his āgenon borge, 282, 9. Þā hwīle þe wē þ līf on ūrun gewealde habban, Bl. H. 101, 11. Æghwylc þára is wyrðe in gemyndum tō habbanne *sunt digna memorie singula*, Angl. iv. 140, 22 : 142, 75. (4) *to keep* a person in some particular place or condition, as guest, prisoner, &c. :—Þā þe þū ǣr on hæftnēde hæfdest, Bl. H. 85, 23. Hē hī feáwa dagas mid him hæfde *eos aliquot diebus secum retinuit*, Bd. 5, 10 ; Sch. 601, 9. Hē hæfde (*detinuit*) þone ǣrendracan hwylcnehugu fyrst in þām mynstre, Gr. D. 39, 23. Hē hæfde ǣnne līcðrowere belocen on ānum clyfan, Hml. S. 3, 480. Se gerēfa þe hine hæfde *comes qui eum tenebat*, Bd. 4, 22 ; Sch. 457, 17. Gif hwā Godes flȳman hæbbe on unriht, āgīfe hine tō rihte . . . Gif hwā āmānsodne oþþe ūtlahne hæbbe (*habeat*) and healde, Ll. Th. i. 410, 15–18. Harold þōhte þone kinge þǣr tō hæbbenne for huntnoðes þingon, Chr. 1065 ; P. 190, 28. Mid þȳ hē hwylcehugu tiid mid þone gesīþ hæfd (*hæfed, v. l.*) wæs (*teneretur*), Bd. 4, 22 ; Sch. 458, 13. Fram þām hī beóð hæfde and gehæftnede *a quo captivi tenentur*, Gr. D. 336, 5. Hī nǣron onlȳsde ah on bendum hié wǣron hæfde, Bl. H. 87, 26. **X.** *to hold* or *entertain* in the mind :—Hī hæfdon Godes elnunge, Bd. 5, 22 ; Sch. 681, 29. Sē þe nū forhogaþ þ ǣnig gemynd hæbbe Drihtnes eáþmódnesse, Bl. H. 83, 16. **X a.** *to entertain* a feeling towards (tō) an object :—For þǣre hatunge þe hē hæfð tō his Scyppende, and for þām andan þe hē hæfð tō þām men *propter odium in Creatorem et invidiam in hominem*, Angl. vii. 8, 65. Hig habbaþ andan tō hym, Nic. 4, 19. Þ man tō ōþrum lǣþþe hæbbe, Bl. H. 63, 36. Hē sceal habban andan tō hira yfele, Past. 75, 13. *See* cȳþþe habban *under* cȳþþu ; I. 2 a. **XI.** *to treat, use* :—Ic sende ofer eów geswinc and mettrumnesse . . . þā eów habbað oð deáðes tōcyme swīðe hearde, Wlfst. 230, 7.

þ folc hine hæfde swā yfele swilce hē sumes þinges scyldig wǣre, and ealle men hine fram stōwe tō stōwe brūdon and tō wundre tawedon, Hml. S. 23, 652. For hwig þ folc þone Hǣlend swā yfele hæfde. Nic. 4, 18. **XII.** *to hold* in some specified estimation, *to esteem* or *account as, consider as.* (1) with gen. :—Sum munuc, sē wæs hæfd and wēned fram mannum mycelre ārfæstnesse, and hē wæs gesewen gōdra þeáwa *quidam monachus magnae aestimationis habebatur, bonis quippe cernebatur moribus*, Gr. D. 326, 24. (2) with prep. (a) habban for *to consider* or *regard as* :—Eall þeódscipe hine heafde for fullne cyning, Chr. 1013 ; P. 144, 6. Heó hyt for Crȳstes andwlytan ǣfre hæfde, Hml. A. 187, 180. Hig hæfdon hyne for ǣnne wītegan *they counted him as a prophet*, Mt. 14, 5 : Ors. 1, 6 ; S. 36, 20 : Met. 26, 44. Þ him þā geþūhte swelc þæt mǣste wæl swelc hié oft ǣr for nōht hæfdon, Ors. 4, 7 ; S. 184, 15. Hié wilniað ðæt hié mon hæbbe for ðā betstan and for ðā hālgestan, Past. 135, 20. Ne magon wē . . . hātan oððe habban deádne mon for cwucene, Bt. 36, 6 ; F. 182, 19. Is þæs folces hlīsa ǣlcum men for nāuht tō habbenne, 30, 1 ; F. 108, 17. (b) habban on *to hold* in honour, esteem, &c. :—Þā hǣþenan selfe hæfdon his wundor on þǣre mǣstan āre, Shrn. 119, 33. Þone Eástordæg on weorðunge habban, Bd. 5, 22 ; Sch. 685, 6. Is seó stōw on micelre ārwurðnesse hæfd (hæfed, *v. l.*), Bd. 3, 2 ; Sch. 194, 3. **XIII.** *to carry on* some proceeding, *have dealings, engage in as principal, have* or *hold* a meeting, council, suit, &c. :—Þā tihtbysian men þe mid þām gerēfan sace habbað, Ll. Th. i. 294, 7. Hæfde se cyng his hīred æt Gleáweceastre, Chr. 1094 ; P. 228, 30. Hæfde se cyng mycel geþeaht, 1085 ; P. 216, 15. Hæfde Eádweard cing witenagemōt, 1050 ; P. 171, 36. Þe arceb and gehādode men hæfdon sinoð þreó dagas, 1085 ; P. 216, 12. Ælc gerēfa hæbbe gemōt, Ll. Th. i. 164, 20. Þ man habbe gemōt on ǣlcum wæpentace, 294, 2. Cwæð þ hē wolde mid his ealdormonnum and mid his wytum gesprec and geþeaht habban *cum principibus et consiliariis suis sese de hoc conlaturum esse dicebat*, Bd. 2, 13 ; Sch. 163, 23. Gif hwilc wið ūre bige habban wille, oþþe wē wið heora, Ll. Th. i. 156, 3. Hē wolde his hǣþengild habban *he would have his idolatrous worship*, Hml. S. 28, 26. Ðās wīsan hē ealle on him hæbbende wæs, 23 b, 32. **XIV.** *to declare, maintain, express the conditions of a case* :—Ðæs [s]prēce nǣnig mon on nǣnge ōðre halfe oncærrende sié nymne suǣ þis gewrit hafað (*except as this writing lays down the conditions*), Txts. 442, 17. **XIV a.** willan habban *to maintain as a fact* that a thing is so and so :—Þā lǣwedan willað habban þone mōnan be þām ðe hī hine geseóð (*the unlearned will have it that the moon is as they see it*), and þā gelǣredan hine healdað be þisum foresǣdan gesceáde, Lch. iii. 266, 10. **XV.** *to possess by taking or receiving, to have, get, take.* (1) of persons (a) without idea of compulsion :—Hwanon hæfst (hæfis, L.) þū līfes wæter?, Jn. 4, 11. Sē hæfð ðone weordscipe, sē ðe ǣr gedyldelíce ðā scande forbær, Past. 227, 4. Ymb .xxii. wint þæs þe hē rīce hæfde, Chr. 874 ; P. 72, 26. Hafa þē wunden gold, Gen. 2128. Hwæt gōdes dō ic þ ic ēce līf hæbbe?, Mt. 19, 16. Hæbbe hē him þ deáde (cf. þæt þǣr deád byð, byð his (*ipsius erit*), Ex. 21, 34), Ll. Th. i. 50, 8, 13 : 436, 13. Sǣdere gebyreð þ hē hæbbe ǣlces cynnes ǣnne leáp fulne, 438, 9, 18, 22. Ælc friðmanna frið hæbbe, 286, 5. Swælc monn se ðæt mīn lond hebbe *whoever gets my land*, C. D. i. 311, 1. Þ wē habban heora ealra fultum, Ll. Th. i. 284, 15. Bið hire rǣd þ frȳnd þā forword habban, 256, 2. Gif leornere gebuge þ hē hād hæfde (*got ordained*), 192, 12. Ðonne þū antifonariam habban wille, þonne wege þū þīne swīþran hand, Tech. ii. 119, 3 (and often). Earnion þæt wē Godes miltse habban mōton, Wlfst. 180, 21. Swā hwelce dæge swā hié hit habban wolden, Chr. 874 ; P. 72, 32. (a a) *to get in marriage* :—Lisimahhus his sweostor hæfde *cujus sororem Lysimachus in matrimonio habuerat*, Ors. 3, 11 ; S. 152, 17. Sē wæs lūþyttan fæder þe Æþelwulf cyning hæfde (hæfde tō cwēne, *v. l.*), Chr. 885 ; P. 80, 2. (a β) of parents, *to have* a child :—Hæfde heó cild, næbbe heó, Hml. Th. ii. 10, 7. Be ðon ðe ryhtgesamhīwan bearn hæbben. Gif ceorl and his wīf bearn hæbben gemǣne, Ll. Th. i. 126, 1–3 : 254, 15. Gif Maria unbeweddod wǣre and cild hæfde, Hml. Th. i. 196, 11. (a γ) *to have granted* what has been forfeit :—Gif hwā sié deáðes scyldig, and hē cirican geierne, hæbbe his feorh, Ll. Th. i. 104, 14. (a δ) ende habban *to come to an end, cease to exist* :—Hē standan ne mæg ac hæfð ende, Mk. 3, 26. (b) with idea of compulsion, *to get* as a result of conflict, pressure, &c. :—Emilianus ofslōg Gallus and hæfde him þone anweald, Ors. 6, 23 ; S. 274, 14. Þā Seaxan hæfdon sige, Chr. 885 ; P. 78, 29 : 909 ; P. 95, 30. Hī woldon hine besyrewian æt his līfe and habban syþðan his rīce, 1003 ; P. 135, 4. Þā hié angeáten þ hē ungemetlic gafol wið þǣm friþe habban wolde *cum intolerabiles conditiones pacis audissent*, Ors. 4, 6 ; S. 174, 25. (c) where the source from which the object comes is given :—Hwæt hæfð hē æt þām hlīsan, Bt. 18, 4 ; F. 68, 11. Gif cniht wǣpn brēde, gilde se hlāford ān pund, and hæbbe se hlāford æt þ hē mǣge, and him eal gldscipe gefylste þ hē his feorh of hæbbe, Cht. Th. 612, 23–28. Gē woldon habban mēde æt frǣmdra monna cwiddunge, Bt. 18, 4 ; F. 66, 24. Swilce getrȳwða swā se cyng æt him habban wolde, Chr. 1093 ; P. 228, 22. (2) of things. (a) *to get* some condition fixed :—þ gehwilc sprǣc hæbbe āndagan *let a term be appointed to each*

*suit*, Ll. Th. i. 158, 7. **XV a.** *to take* as guardian :—Gif se ceorl fēre forð, hæbbe sió mōdor hire bearn and fēde *if the husband die, let the mother take the child and bring it up*, Ll. Th. i. 126, 4. **XVI.** *to cause to move*. (1) *to cause to go, take* or *bring* with one :—Hī bundon hine, and reówan tō scipe, and dydon hine þæron, *v. l.*), Urnon þā west ... and hæfdon hine mid heom (wendon þā þanon mid him, *v. l.*), Chr. 1046 ; P. 169, 11. Cōmon ðā drȳmen, and hæfdon him mid twēgen ormǣte dracan, Hml. Th. ii. 474, 5. Gif gesīðcund man fare, þonne mōt hē habban his gerēfan mid him and his smið, Ll. Th. i. 144, 2. (2) *to get* to or from a place, *bring, take* :—Hāt twelf weras nyman twelf stānas ... and habban forð mid eów tō eówre wīcstōwe ... þā twelf weras ... nāmon twelf stānas ..., hæfdon forð mid him tō hira fyrdwīcum *praecipe eis ut tollant duodecim lapides ... portaverunt duodecim lapides usque ad locum in quo castrametati sunt*, Jos. 4, 3–8. Þ treówa hī hæbben ǣr .xxx. nihta of þām lande, Ll. Th. i. 70, 11. Hē wolde gefeccan þā lytlan and gebringan ūp tō his rīce. Hwæt synd ðā lytlan ðe hē wolde habban ūp tō his rīce?, Hml. Tb. i. 138, 6 : Bt. 41, 5 ; F. 254, 15 : Met. 31, 20. (2 a) *to get to take part in* action :—Seó swuster hī wolde habban tō hire bysegan, Hml. Th. ii. 440, 20. (3) *to put, place* :— Hē hefde his swīðran hand ofer Ephraimes heáfod *extendens manum dexteram posuit super caput Ephraim*, Gen. 48, 14. Ðā hēt ic eald hrægl tōslītan and habban wið þǣm fȳre *jussi scissas uestes opponere ignibus*, Nar. 23, 30. **XVII.** with object and complement. (1) adj. complement, *to get* something into a specified condition :—Þonne magon wē ūs God mildne habban *then can we get God gracious to us*, Bl. H. 107, 17. Eall þās þing þǣre þeóde Ongelcynnes gedafenað cūð habban *quae omnia Anglorum genti oportet haberi comperta*, Bd. i. 27 ; Sch. 76, 22. (2) with past ptcpl. complement, *to get* something done, *cause* to be done :—Þā hié tō ðǣm gemǣre cōmon mid heora firde, þā hæfdon hié hiera clūsan belocene *when they came to the boundary with their army they had the pass closed* ; Athenienses angustias occupavere, Ors. 3, 7 ; S. 112, 35. **XVIII.** *to allow to be* :—His gingran dohtor hē nolde būton hæftniéde habban *parvulas filias crudeli captivitate retinebat*, Ors. 3, 9 ; S. 128, 19. **B. habban** ; **II, IV, V.** *Add*: **I.** with gen. :—Gyf hē þǣre ylde and ðæs andgytes hæfd þæt hē hit under-standan mæg, Wlfst. 32, 8. Gif hē þǣra freónda hæfð þe þ dōn durron, Ll. Th. i. 290, 14. Gif hē mægnes habbe þ hē his gefān berīde, 90, 4. Gif hē þæs mægenes ne hæbbe þ hē hine inne besitte, 11. Gif mon hæbbe healfe (healfes, *v. l.*), 122, 10 : 144, 11. Hwǣr hié landes hæfden þæt hié mehten an gewīcian, Ors. 2, 5 ; S. 80, 9. Wē beóð hæbbende ðæs ðe wē ǣr hopedon, Hml. Th. i. 250, 34. **II.** as an auxiliary. (1) present forms making a perfect tense. (a) with inflected participle :— Ic hæbbe ðē nū tōdæg gesetne ofer ðióda *constitui te hodie super gentes*, Past. 441, 31. Hiá hebfað ðæs wīsan ðus fundene, C. D. i. 296, 5. Þām þe hiora dǣl getȳnedne hæbben, Ll. i. 128, 9. (b) with uninflected participle (or uncertain) :—Ðis ... ðet ic beboden hebbe, C. D. i. 300, 4. Heregȳð hafað ðas wīsan binemned, 312, 3. Þonne þū hig gefangen hæbbe *apprehensis*, Gen. 44. 4. Gif hæbben sume getȳned hiora dǣl, Ll. Th. i. 128, 6. Ær ælc man hæbbe āne rīde geriden, 232, 19. ¶ a curious use of the negative participle occurring in the following :—Ðā ðe ungefandod habbað flǣsclicra scylda *peccata carnis ignorantes*, Past. 407, 19 : 409, 22. Gehiéren ðā ðe ungefandod habbað ðara flǣsclicana scylda *audiant peccatorum carnis ignari*, 16. (2) past forms making a pluperfect tense :—Hig hæfdon sumne dǣl weges gefaren *processerant paululum*, Gen. 44, 4. (2 a) where the participle has to be supplied from the context :—Gelǣdde Theodosius eft fird wið him twǣm tō þǣre ilcan clūsan þe hē ǣr hæfde (*had* [*led an army*]) wið Maximus, Ors. 6, 36 ; S. 294, 17. hand-, land-, mis-, yfel-hæbbende ; for-hæfed.

**haca.** *For* Gl. Mett. 658 *substitute* :—Haca (hǎca, 87, 1559) *pessul*, Txts. 88, 803, *and add* : *Perhaps the word occurs in the following* :— On hacapenn foreweard ... on hacapenn foreweardne, C. D. iii. 412, 2, 14. An hacan penne, *v.* 238, 30. On hacan pundfold, of hacan pund-falde (haccan *is the form in the MS. printed* C. D. B. iii. 395, 18), vi. 41, 24. *Here there might be reference to the enclosures being bolted, or to their construction with hurdles, cf.* hæc, *and see* hake *in* N. E. D. [*O. L. Ger.* haco *uncus.*]

**hacce** (?). v. tyrf-hacce.

**haccian.** *Add*: v. ā-haccian ; hæccan.

**hacele.** *Add* : hacole (-ule), hæcile :—Haecilae, hecæle, haecile *palu-damentum, genus vestimenti bellici*, Txts. 88, 740. Haecilae, hecile, haecile *lacerna*, 72, 572. Hacele, Wrt. Voc. ii. 53, 65 : *capsula*, 16, 68 : *ependiten*, 32, 49 : *subucula*, 87, 54 : An. Ox. 5316. Hacole colomata, Wrt. Voc. ii. 134, 31 : *burrus* (*birrus* ? *v. birrus* unsmeðe hrægel, i. 40, 25) *panno*, 126, 78. Hacule *calamuca*, 127, 74. Albanus eóde ūt mid ðæs preóstes hakelan (cf. Scs Albanus gegyrede hine þæs preóstes munucgegyrelan (*caracalla*), Bd. 1, 7 ; Sch. 20, 24), Hml. S. 19, 36. Hē lēt þā hacelan (cf. wæstels *pallium*, 2) tō þǣm þe hine tunecan benǣmde, R. Ben. 28, 5. Gyf þū mæssan hacelan habban wille, Tech. ii. 119, 25. Hacelan *mantilia*, Wrt. Voc. ii. 57, 29. v. mæsse-, ofer-hacele. [*O. L. Ger.* hacul *casula* ; hekila *lucerna*.]

**hacine.** v. hæcine.

**hacod.** *Add*: hæced (-id), hecid. *The word translates both* lucius *and* mugil :—Haecid *lucius*, Txts. 74, 587. Haecid, hecid, haeced *mugil*, 78, 660. Hacod, Wrt. Voc. ii. 55, 81. *Lucius* hacud, *mugil idem* (cf. *mugilis vel mugil* mæcefisc, 77, 61 : cf. too names in other languages, *Icel.* gedda (cf. gaddr *a spike*), Fr. brochet (cf. broche *a spit*)), i. 65, 73. [*O. L. Ger.* hacud, hakith *lucius.*]

**hād.** *Add*: **I.** *person*; persona. (1) *a character in a drama or the like* :—Þonne se sceop in gebringð ōðre hādas þe wið hine wurdlion, swylce hig him andswarion, Angl. viii. 330, 43. (1 a) (*one's own*) *person* :—Swylce āgenum hāde ł naman *ceu propria persona*, An. Ox. 2329. (2) *an individual* :—Þ ænum untrumum hāde wæs forgyfen *quod uni personae infirmanti conceditur*, Bd. i. 27 ; Sch. 83, 10. Swȳðe yfelice mæn and þyses woroldlican līfes hādas *viles et saeculares vitae personae*, Gr. D. 232, 5 : Gū. 2. Ðā hādas ðǣre hālgan endebyrdnesse *personae sacrorum ordinum*, Past. 135, 13. (3) *the living body of a human being* :—Ic hæbbe mē on hrycg þæt ǣr hādas wreáh fold-būendra flǣsc and gǣstas, Rä. 2, 12. (4) *of a mode of divine being, person of the Trinity* :—Hē wæs on ānum hāde twēgra gecynda, Bl. H. 33, 33. Ān ælmihtig God is on þrȳm hādum ǣfre wunigende, Hml. S. 16, 1. (5) *as a grammatical term* :—*Uerbum* ys word, ān dǣl leden-sprǣce mid tīde and hāde būtan cāse ... him gelimpð ... *persona* hād, Ælfc. Gr. Z. 119, 8–16. Manega word synd þe ne magon habban þa twēgen forman hādas, ac habbað þone þriddan, 128, 15. (6) in the phrase 'to accept or respect the *person* of any one ' = to show partiality :— Ne onfōh ðū nænigne hād on dōme (*non accipies personam*, Deut. 16, 19), Ll. Lbmn. 476, 21. **II.** *sex* :—Hādes *sexus*, An. Ox. 3890. Hāde *sexu*, 2326. Swā hē nǣfre þone hād (wǣpnedhād, *v.l.*) on his līchaman nǣfde *ac si sexum non haberet in corpore*, Gr. D. 26, 30. **III.** *condition*. (1) in respect to mode of life, of profession, &c. :—Hine missenlices hādes (*of different condition*, i. e. laity and clergy) men sōhton, ægðer þāra ge ealdormen ge bisceopas, Guth. 66, 4. Ælces hādes men ... hūruþinga Godes þeówas, Ll. Th. i. 304, 24. Betre him wǣre ðæt hē on lǣssan hāde (*as a layman*) his līf geendode, Past. 31, 25. Swā bið on ðisse menniscan gecynde manige on beteran hāde wyrsan and on wyrsan hāde beteran ; swā ðætte oft on lǣwedum hāde ... man oferðihð ðone munuchād, 411, 32–36. (1 a) of the ecclesiastical pro-fession :—Hē wæs underfange of þām (þæs?) hādes mannum þe him ealra unēaðest was, þ was clerican, Chr. 995 ; P. 128, 19. Settan þas ylcan hādes menn (i. e. *they were to be regular, not secular, clergy*) ... þa hē sylf wes, and eác þ ælc oþer þ sceolde beón munuchādes mann, 40. Sume him þæs hādes hlīsan willað wegan on wordum and þa weorc ne dōð, Gū. 31. Sē þe þ nelle þ his hāde gebyrige, Ll. Th. i. 306, 22 : 346, 24 : 244, 11 : Chr. 1086 ; P. 219, 31. (1 b) phrases expressing the receiving, conferring, or holding of holy orders :—Ðone noman and ðā endebyrd-nesse ðæs hālgan hādes underfōn *nomen vel ordinem sanctitatis habere*, Past. 31, 11. Tō hālgum hāde becuman *ad sanctitatis speciem deduci*, 23. Æfter hālgum hāde *after taking holy orders* ; post sanctitatis habitum, Past. 133, 25. Þone ǣfæstan hād underfōn *habitum religionis accipere*, Bd. 4, 11 ; Sch. 404, 20. Hād underfōn, Hml. Th. ii. 48, 31. Hād onfōn, Mt. L. 10, 8 note. Gif leornere wǣre þ þurh lāre geþuge þ hē hād hæfde and þēnode Crīste, Ll. Th. i. 192, 13. Hē nolde þ ænig ōðer man sceolde hire hād on sættan *he would not have her take the veil from any one else*, Hml. S. 31, 584. (1 c) *the persons in holy orders* :— Hwæt getācniað ðā stānas ðæs hālgan hūses būton ðone hād ðǣre hālgan endebyrdnesse *quid sanctuarii lapidibus nisi sacrorum ordinum personae signantur*?, Past. 133, 13. (2) in respect to natural relations :—Heó (*Eve*) bæd meotod miltse þurh Marian hād (*as Mary was her daughter and Christ's mother*) : 'Þū fram mīnre dohtor, Drihten, onwōce,' Sat. 438. (2 a) defined by a genitive giving the class to which an object belongs :—Se manna wæs Crīste leófast on weres hāde, Ap. 27. Dīnes wuduwan hādes, Past. 207, 12. Heó wæs wunigende on wudewan hāde, Hml. Th. i. 146, 32. Þurh fǣmnan hād, Sat. 495. Þurh briddes hād, Ph. 372. In cildes hād cenned, El. 336 : 776. (2 b) by an adj. :— Þurh horscne hād, Crī. 49. Þurh clǣnne hād, 444. Þurh leóhtne hād, El. 1246. **IV.** *an order of beings* or *things, a kind, race* :—Swā þæt ænig ne wāt eordbūendra ... ne þæt ænig ne wāt engla hādes, Hy. 3, 34. Wuldres āras ... þāra on hāde sint syx genemned, El. 740. Þū fremest eorðwelan þurh monigne hād, Az. 98. Hlǣsfdige wuldorweorudes and worldcundra hāda and helwara, Crī. 286. Gerceafte under heofonum hādas cennað micle and mǣte, Gū. 23. **V.** *an order in a society, a rank, degree, an office* :—Men ælces hādes, heáne and rīce *men of every degree, high and low*, Guth. 66, 6. Swā man bið mihtigra oþþe mǣran hādes, Ll. Th. i. 398, 20. Ðǣm ðe lǣssan hādes bið, Past. 411, 23. Ðā ðe mon tō hiéran hāde dōn wille, 7, 15. Onwent sió geearnung ðone hād and ðā geðyncða, Past. 411, 25. Se engel hafað yldran hād, Crī. 1669 : Reim. 15. **V a.** in an ecclesiastical sense :—Seofon stapas sindon ... hālegra hāda ... Sē ðe Godes þeówum gederige ... gebēte hit be þām þe seó dǣd sȳ and be þām ðe se hād sȳ, Ll. Th. ii. 240, 1–8. Gif hwā gehādodne man bende ... bēte ... be hādes mǣðe, i. 400, 23 : 404, 16. Gif mæssepreóst manslaga wurð ... þonne þolige hē ægðres ge hādes ge eardes, 346, 5 : 400, 15. Þā Zacharias his sācerdes hādes (sācerdhādes,

*v. l.*) breác *cum sacerdotio fungeretur*, Lk. 1, 8. Gif þū þæt wāst þæt ic unrihtlíce bisceophāde onfénge, ic lustlíce fram þǽre þénunge gewíte, for þon ic mē sylfne nǽfre þæs hādes wurdne ne dyde (*libenter ab officio discedo, nunquam me hoc esse dignum arbitrabar*), Bd. 4, 2 ; Sch. 346. 24. Mǽde on hāde gecnāwan *to recognize distinctions in rank*, Ll. Th. i. 362, 4 : ii. 294, 5. Ne genéd þū (*a priest*) nǽfre þ þū gā tō þām hālgan hāde (cf. ne geneálǽc ðū Godes ðénungum, Hml. Th. ii. 170, 5), oððe māran underfó þonne þū nū hæfst ; sóðlíce on swā hwilcum dæge swā þū geþrístlǽcst þ þū underféhst þone hālgan sācerdhād, sóna þū bist eft mid deófles anweald gehæftned *ad sacrum ordinem nunquam accedere praesumas ; quacumque die sacrum ordinem temerare praesumseris, statim juri diaboli iterum mancipaberis*, Gr. D. 135, 9-16. Under Móyses ǽ móste se bisceop habban wíf . . . þ se sunu sceolde fón tō þām hāde æfter his fæder geendunge, Hml. S. 10, 220 : Past. 27, 22. Se preóst . . . hāligne hād underféng (cf. geeóde tō þām hālgan sācerdhāde *ad sacrum ordinem accessit*, Gr. D. 135, 31), Hml. Th. ii. 170, 10. Gif preóst ūt of scíre hād begite . . . and diácon . . . þolian his hādes būton scíre biscop heom hādes geunne, Ll. Th. ii. 292, 13-15. Mīn fulwiht and mīn[n]e hād . . . ic swíðe unmeodomlíce gehealdan hæbbe, Angl. xi. 99, 57. Ðone micclan hād (*the office of pope*), Hml. Th. ii. 122, 27.    V b. in a personal sense, *those belonging to an order* or *rank :*—Cwæð ǽlc hād ciricean þǽre mǽgðe ánmódlíce (cf. cum consilio omnium ecclesiasticorum graduum, C. D. i. 45, 12), Ll. Th. i. 36, 10. Ðā godcundan hādas giorne wǽron ymb lāre, Past. 3, 9. Wǽran heáfodstedas and heálíce hādas (i.e. cyning, arcebiscop, æðeling, leódbiscop, ealdorman, ll. 10, 11, 14) micelre mǽðe wyrðe, Ll. Th. i. 330, 6. þā hālgan hādas þe Godes folc lǽran scylan, 244, 9. *De reverentia sacerdotibus praestanda*. Eallum crístenum mannum gebyrað þ hig . . . hādas . . . ǽfre griðian and friðian, and þ hī hāda gehwylcne weorðian be mǽðe, 360, 25-28 : 336, 1 : 334, 33.    v. ciric-, heáh-hād, *and next word*.

-hād. *Add :* I. *with nouns.* (1) *marking condition of life*, weoroldhād. cf. hād, III. 1. (2) *with nouns of persons*, (a) *marking natural condition*, cild-, cniht-, fǽmn-, hægstealâ-, mægden-, mægþ-, man-, wer-, wíf-hād. cf. III. 2 a. (b) *marking office, rank*, apostol-, bisceop-, mæssepreóst-, martyr-, munuc-, pāpan-, preóst-, sācerd-hād. cf. hād ; V, V a. (3) *with abstract nouns* (a) *of condition*, fulwiht-, geoguþ-, mǽgþ-hād. (b) *of action*, camp-, níd-hād.    II. *with adjs.*, cyne-, untrum-, wǽpned-hād.

-hāda. v. efen-, ge-hāda.

hād-ārung, e ; *f. Respect of persons* (v. hād ; I b), *partiality* in judgement :—Dómas sceolon beón būtan ǽlcere hādārunge : þ ys þ hē ne murne nāðer ne rýcum ne heánum, ne leófum ne lāðum folcriht tō recceanne, Ll. Lbmn. 474, 18.

hād-bōt. *Add :*—Sē ðe Godes þeówum gederige seofonfealdre bōte gebéte hit be þām þe seó dǽd sý and be þām ðe se hād sý . . . Tō hādbóte, gif líflyre wurþe . . . þone forman stæpe béte man mid āne punde, and mid gódre bóte þingige georne, Ll. Th. ii. 240, 6-13 : 14. Tō hādbóte, gif fulbryce (*plena infractio*, 549, § 5) wyrðe, 20 : 23. Hādbót . . . ān dǽl þām biscope, óðer þām wíbedde, and þridde þām geférscipe, 242, 17.

hād-breca. *Substitute :* One who commits hād-bryce (q.v.), *who injures a person in holy orders :*—Hādbrecan (*the old Latin versions render this by* 'sacrorum ordinum contemptores', 'ordinum uiolatores', 'ordinis infractores'), Ll. Th. i. 380, 2. Hér syndan . . . hādbrecan. Wlfst. 165, 31.

hād-bryce. *Dele* 'a violation of holy orders'. *In* l. 4 *after* hād *add*, swā be were swā be wíte swā be lahslite swā be ealre āre (*secundum omnia quę habet malefactor*. This is the rendering in the 'Instituta Cnuti', which gives the first clause of the law thus : Quicunque uiolauerit ordinem, sicut est aut monachum aut presbyterum aut aliquem ordinatum uerberauerit aut aliquid huiusmodi fecerit). *For* Swt. A. S. Rdr. 109, 148 *substitute :*—Þurh hādbrycas, Wlfst. 164, 4 : 130, 4.    v. hād-bót.

hādelíce. *Substitute :* In respect to person :—God . . . ān myhtylíce and þrylic hādelíce *Deus . . . unus potentialiter, triuusque personaliter*, Hy. S. 29, 13.    v. hād ; I. 4.

haderung. v. hād-ārung ; hād-grip. *Add : See* hād ; V b.

hādian. *Substitute : To ordain.* v. hād ; III. 1 a, 1 b ; V a. (1) absolute :—Sende hē hine tō hādianne (*hādigenne, v. l.*) *misit eum ordinandum*, Bd. 3, 28 ; Sch. 323, 16. (2) with acc. of person :—Gif ðū cwest nū : 'Hwā lǽrde ðē ? ', þonne cweðe ic, 'Dūnstān'. 'Hwā hādode ðē ? ' 'Hē mē hādode', Ælfc. Gr. Z. 8, 15. Ne hādige man ǽfre tō hrædlíce, Ll. Th. i. 416, 15. (3) with acc. of person and order to which :—Hē gedyde þ hine man hādode tō mæssepreóste *eum presbyterum fecit ordinari*, Gr. D. 225, 23. Hē lét hig hādian tō bisceopum, Chr. 1053 ; P. 184, 11. Þæt hē hine hādian sceolde tō þ intō Lundene, 1048 ; P. 172, 17. Hét se pāpa hine hādigean (gehālgian, v. l.) tō bysceope *iussu pontificis in episcopatus consecratus est gradum*, Bd. 3, 7 ; Sch. 212, 10. ·(4) with acc. of person and complementary acc. of office, *to ordain* a person bishop, &c. :—Hér mon hādode Byrnstān bisceop tō Wintanceastre, Chr. 931 ; P. 106, 1. (5) with acc. of person :—Ðā apostolas hæfdon him mid fela leorningcnihta, of þām hī hādodon mæssepreóstas and diáconas, Hml. Th. ii. 490, 25. Hē aldorlicnesse onféng þ

hē bisceopas hādian (hādigan, *v. l.*) móste *data sibi ordinandi episcopos auctoritate*, Bd. 2, 8 ; Sch. 141, 18. Se bisceop bið gesett tō hādigenne preóstas, Ll. Th. ii. 348, 26 : 378, 22.    v. be-, ge-, on-, un-hādian.

hādod. *Add :*—Gif gehādod (hādod, *v. l.*) man hine forwyrce, Ll. Th. i. 400, 27.    v. ge-, un-hādod.

hād-swǽpa, hād-swāpe. *For these two substitute :* hād-swǽpe, -swāpe, an ; *f. A woman who attended to the necessary arrangements for a wedding on the part of the bride, a bridesmaid :*—Hādswǽpe (-a, MS. ; *but cf.* mínra *for* mínre, 20) *pronuba ; ipsa est et paranimpha*, Wrt. Voc. i. 52, 29. Brýdlofta *sponsalia*, wógere *procus*, brýdiguma *sponsus*, hādswǽpe *pronuba*, brýd *sponsa*, hādswǽpe *paranymphus*, 50, 35-40. Dryhtmon *paranimphus*, hādswǽpe *pronuba*, brýdguma *sponsus*, brýd *sponsa*, brýdbūr *thalamus*, iémung *nuptiae*, 288, 79-85. Cf. heorþ-swǽpe.

hādung. *Add :*—Be ðæs abbodes hādunge. On abbodes hādunge . . . *de ordinando abbati. In abbatis ordinatione* . . ., R. Ben. 117, 15. Heó weard þā gefullod and hādunga underféng (*took the veil*) . . . and manega óðre mǽdenu wurdon Críste gehālgode, Hml. S. 7, 284. Hine man hādode tō mæssepreóste. Þā sóna æfter his hādunga (*ordinatione*), Gr. D. 225, 23.    v. bisceop-, un-hādung.

hādung-dæg, es ; *m. The anniversary of a person's ordination :*—Þā gelamp hit embe geáres ryne þ hit wæs þæs abbodes hādingdæg. Þā sende ānne bróðor tō Pafnuntie and laþode hine tō þǽre symbelnesse, Hml. S. 33, 59. Hādungdæg, 91.

haeb. v. hæf.

hæbbed-ness (hæbbend- ? v. hæbbend-líc), e ; *f. Continence* (?), *restraint :*—þ wē ne gefremmon gylta ǽnigne, ac þ þonne se dæg gewít sýn wē clǽne þurh líchaman úres hæbbednysse, Angl. viii. 320, 3.    v. hæfedness.

hæbbend. v. for-, heofon-hæbbend.

hæbbend-líc. *Add : That may be held.* Cf. habban ; I.

hæbbenga. *Substitute :* hæbbung, e ; *f. Holding, constraint :*—Hæbbenga *conibentia* (simulata matrimonii *cohibentia*, invitus annulo subarratam sortitur virgunculam, Ald. 49, 34), Wrt. Voc. ii. 82, 67 : 18, 40.

hæbbere. v. sulh-hæbbere ; habban ; I.

hæc. *Substitute for all but the bracket :* hæc[c], e ; *f. and* hæc[c], hæcce, es ; *m. A hatch, heck.* [*hatch* a gate or wicket ; a flood-gate or sluice ; a contrivance for trapping salmon : *heck* a grating or frame of parallel bars . . . used to catch fish at a weir, N. E. D.] In the following instances it is not easy to determine which of the meanings just given should be assigned in each case. In stánweges hæc the word seems to mean a gate ; in the compound forms æt hacceburnan, C. D. iii. 292, 22 : v.136, 12 : on haccaburnen, 21 : of haccebroce, 13 : vi. 70, 13 : on hæccebróc, 21, one of the other meanings seems appropriate. Cf. too, hæcceleás díc, vi. 17, 20 ; *but see* (?) hæcce.    I. fem. or uncertain :—Ðis synd ðā landgemǽra intō Passefelde. Ðæt is, ǽrest of ðāre ealden hæcce æt freoðene felde . . . eft intō ðǽre ealdan hæcce . . . tō ðāre wudehæcche ; of ðǽre hæcce . . . wið æffan hecce . . . æt werdhæcce ; of werdhacce . . . intō stánweges hacce ; of stánweges hacce : In Angrices burne tō ealdermannes hæcce, tō ðær cynges hæcce . . . tō ðær cynges hæcce . . . tō Ælsyges hæcce . . . of cerlen hacce—tō cerlen hacce, C. D. iv. 157, 4-158, 14. Ford tō bindhæcce ; fram bindhæcce tō tudanhæcce ; fram tudanhæcce tō giddincgforda, iii. 275, 6. Innan þone reádan weg ; ollung þæs reádan weges ; þ innan þā hecce ; ollung þā hecce ; þ innan þā hecce firn geán þǽre cyrcan, Swt. Rdr. II. 203, 10.    II. masc. :—Swā west ðæt hit cymð tō ðan hæcce be sūðan Cranmere, C. D. iii. 399, 22. Capturam in amne Derentan constructam, quae usitato æt Ginan hecce nuncupatur uocabulo, 199, 8. Of ðám hæcce . . . eft innon ðane hæcc, vi. 171, 5-8. Ðæne hæcce, 76, 29. Andlang weges tō ðan hæcce, 234, 23. Of þǽre díc on þone burnan ; of þām burnan on þone hæc ; of þām hæcce on eobban slæd, C. D. B. iii. 63, 33.    v. hæc-geat, hæc-wer ; hæcce ; hec[c].

-hæc[c]. v. ge-hæc : -hæcca. v. ge-hæcca : hæccan *to hack.* v. of-hæccan ; haccian.

hæcce a crosier. l. hæcc, *and in line 2 for* dære l. þǽre.

hæcce, an ; *f. A fence of rails* (?) :—Andlang hæccan (heccan, *v. l.*), C. D. B. iii. 147, 25. [Cf. (?) On haccan bróc ; andlang haccan bróces, C. D. v. 298, 4. v. hæc.] [Cf. *Du.* hek *a fence, rail : Ger.* hecke *a hedge.*] v. haca.

hæccel. v. mearh-hæccel.

hæcce-leás ; *adj. Without a hatch* (hæc[c], *q. v.*) ?, *without a fence* (hæcce, *q. v.*) ?:—On hæcceleás díc ; ðonne andlang ðǽre díc, C. D. vi. 70, 20.

hæcewol. l. cæce-pol *a catch-pole, tax-gatherer :*—Kæcepol (*printed* hæcewol, *but see* Angl. viii. 449) *exactor*, Wrt. Voc. i. 18, 44. [Matheus wes cachepol, O. E. Hml. i. 97, 30.]

hæc-geat, es ; *n. A hatch-gate* (hatch-gate *a wicket* ; *a floodgate*, N. E. D. : *a gate at the junction of parishes or manors*, D. D.) :—On ðæt hæcget, C. D. v. 376, 14.

hæcine, an ; *f. A drink made of vinegar and water :*—Hæcine *pusca*

(*printed* hacine (*but see* Angl. viii. 451) *pusta*), Wrt. Voc. i. 28, 4 (in a list 'de generibus potionum').

**hæc-wer.** *Add :* See Seebohm Vill. Comm. pp. 150–3.

**hæf**, es ; *n. Sea. Take here* heaf *in Dict., and add :*—Haeb *salum* (cf. *salum* vel *mare*, 65), Wrt. Voc. ii. 119, 57.

**hæf** *what is lifted.* v. hand-hæf.

**hæfe** *leaven. l.* hæf, *and add :*—Hæf vel beorma *fermentum*, Wrt. Voc. ii. 147, 72. Hæf *fermentum*, i. *condimentum, blandimentum*, An. Ox. 57, 3. Wærniað fram hæfe (*fermento*) sundorhálgena, Scint. 75, 3.

**-hæfedness.** v. be-, for-hæfedness.

**hæfen** *having. Add :* , hafon. I. abstract, *the having* or *possessing* of something :—Mid gôdra weorca biggenge and mid hâligra mægena hæfene, R. Ben. 3, 7. Se brôðor þe mid swærra gylta hæfene bið gedered *frater qui gravioris culpe noxa teneatur*, 49, 13. II. concrete, *what is possessed* :—Sê ðe eallunge ðâ eorðlican gestreón forlætan ne mæg . . . fremige hê hafenleásum mid his hæfene, Hml. Th. ii. 400, 2. Hî biddað and wilniaþ þâ heafene þysse gestreónfullan wædle *petunt et exigunt sumptum lucrosae egestatis*, R. Ben. 136, 1. Hêr syndon .xxx. bôca on Leófstânes hafona, Nap. 46, 41. v. land-hæfen.

**hæfen-blæte.** v. hæfer-blæte.

**hæfen-leás.** *Take here* hafen-leás *in Dict., and add :* (1) used substantively :—Þearfa and se hæfenleása (*inops*) heriaþ þînne naman, Ps. L. 73, 21. For yrmþe hæfenleásra (*inopum*), 11, 6. Helpað earmum and hæfenleásum, Wlfst. 48, 23. (2) as adjective :—Þâ þe unrîce synd and hæfenleáse (hafen-, *v. l.*) þearfan *pauperiores*, R. Ben. 105, 8. Áspende hê his feoh on ælmyssum hafenleásum mannum, Hml. S. 14, 15 : 23, 200: Hml. Th. ii. 400, 1.

**hæfenleást.** *Take here* hafenleást *in Dict., and add :*—Genôh wære þâm wædlan his untrumnys, þeáh ðe hê wiste hæsfde ; and eft him wære genôh his hafenleást, ðeáh ðe hê gesundful wære, Hml. Th. i. 330, 17. Þis earme wîf mê gesôhte . . . Gif þu mihtest myltsian, and noldest, gebringe þê se Hælend tô hyre hafenleáste, Hml. S. 3, 187. Ðær wana þurh þære stôwe hæfenleáste sý *ubi necessitas loci exposcit*, R. Ben. 65, 6.

**hæfenness.** v. wan-hæfenness.

**hæfer.** *Add :* Heber *caper*, Wrt. Voc. ii. 103, 15. Hæfer, gât *caper*, 128, 35. Hæferes *capri*, 13, 51. Blôd heffera *sanguis hyrcorum*, Rtl. 21, 10.

**hæfer-bíte.** v. hæfern-bite.

**hæferblæte**, es ; *m. Substitute :* **hæfer-blæte** (-a), an ; *f. (m.) A snipe,* or *bittern* (?) (the word translates *bicoca* and *bugium*) :—Hraebreblêtae, hebreblêtae, hæbreblête *bicoca*, Txts. 44, 2. Hæferblæte *vel* pur, Wrt. Voc. i. 21, 42 : 280, 28 : ii. 11, 7. Hæferblæta, 126, 9. Hæuerblêta, Ælfc. Gr. Z. 307, 24. Hæferblæte *bugium* (cf. *scorellus* clodhamer and feldeware *uel bugium*, Wülck. Gl. 287, 18), Wrt. Voc. ii. 12. 63. Hæfenblæte (hæfer-?) *bugium*, mæw *alcedo*, i. 29, 23. [*From* hæfer *goat*, blæte (-a) *a bleater.* The snipe is associated in other languages with the goat. Cf. *Ger.* himmel-ziege : *Fr.* chèvre-volante. The second part of the compound is kept in hammer-*bleat*, v. D. D., heather-*bleat*, v. N. E. D., both names for the snipe.]

**hæfern.** *Substitute :* **hæfern** (hæf *sea*, ærn (ræn), ern *house*), hræfn (*q.v. in Dict.*), es ; *m. A crab, crab-shell* (?) :—Haebrn, hafaern *cancer*, Txts. 47, 379. Hefern (nefern, MS.), 108, 1106. Ostre *ostrea*, muxle *geniscula*, hæfern *cancer*, Wrt. Voc. i. 281, 63 : ii. 13, 30 : 16, 30. Hafern *concern* (? *concha*, cf. of muscellan *de conca*, ii. 75, 71), i. 291, 31. Haebern, habern, hafern *nepa*, Txts. 81, 1370. Hæfern, Wrt. Voc. ii. 60, 11 : Crabba oððe hæfern, 61, 48. Hebernum *choncis* (= *conchis*), Txts. 114, 106. v. wæter-hæfern.

**hæfern-bite** *a crab's claw :*—Cancer crabba, forceps hæfer[n]bite, Wrt. Voc. ii. 128, 7.

**hæft** *a captive. Add :* v. helle-hæft, ge-hæft ; *subst. and adj.*

**hæft.** I. *a bond. Add :*—Þâ hæftlingas þe hê hêt lædan of þâm hæftum, Hml. S. 5, 134. II. *captivity, prison. Add :*—Se cásere hêt hine gebindan and him tô gebringan bysmorlîce on hæfte *the emperor ordered him to be bound and brought to him ignominiously in custody*, Hml. S. 3, 191. On hæft settan, Chr. 1036 ; P. 158, 23.

**hæft** *a handle. Add :*—Sceaft *asta*, sceáð *vagina*, hæft *manubrium*, Wrt. Voc. i. 84, 26. ¶ *in* Jud. 263 *perhaps* hæste *should be read.*

**hæft**, e ; *f.* I. *taking, capture, holding :*—Hæft *captura, detentio, captio*, Wrt. Voc. ii. 128, 30. v. ge-hæft. II. *possession, having.* v. næft.

**hæfta.** v. helle-hæfta.

**hæftan.** *Add : to give in charge* to, *hand over* to :—Ne ænig man ôðerne tô nearwe ne hæfte, ne on unriht ne geþeówige *let not any man imprison other too straitly, nor wrongfully enslave*, Wlfst 70, 6. Fûlum wîtehûsa adelseáþe tô hæftenne *putido ergastulorum latibulo mancipande*, An. Ox. 4755.

**-hæftedness.** v. ge-hæftedness.

**hæft-encel.** *Substitute :* **hæftincel**, es ; *n. An enslaved captive, a captive bought and made a slave.* Cf. hæft ; II :—Hæftincel *emptitius* (cf. *emptitius* geboht þeówa, i. 50, 16), Wrt. Voc. ii. 30, 34.

**hæfte-neód.** *Add :* v. hæft-níd.

**hæft-líc;** *adj. Captious, sophistical :*—Of hæftlicon loces betýningum *captiosis sillogismi conclusionibus*, An. Ox. 3208.

**hæftling.** *Add :*—Þâ hæftlingas þe hê hêt lædan of þâm hæftum, Hml. S. 5, 133. Besæriga hæftlingas beón þîne þeówtlingas *dole captivos esse tuos servatos*, Hy. S. 125, 5. Þâ þe hæftlingas gelæddon ûs *qui captiuos nos duxerunt*, Ps. L. 136, 3. Hell forlêt hyre hæftlingas ût, Hml. Th. i. 228, 17. v. helle-hæftling.

**hæft-méce.** *Add :* [Cf. *Icel.* hefti-sax (*in* Grettis Saga). v. Vigfusson's Sturlunga Saga, Vol. i. xlix, note.]

**hæft-néd, hæftnédan, hæftnéd-nes, -hæft-nes.** v. hæft-níd, hæftnídan, hæftníd-ness, ge-hæftnys : **hæftnian.** *Add :* v. ge-hæftnian.

**hæft-níd**, e; *f.*; es; *n. Take here* hæft-néd *in Dict., and add :* *custody, durance, confinement :*—Hê âlædde mê of þâm drôsnum ælces ðeówdômes and ælcere hæftnýde, Ps. Th. 39, 1. His gingran dohtor hê nolde bûton hæftniéde habban *parvulas filias crudeli captivitate retinebat*, Ors. 3, 9 ; S. 128, 19. On þâm hæftnéde, Ælfc. T. Grn. 8, 21. Ic on hæftnýd hider geléd wæs *I was brought here into captivity*, Hml. S. 30, 345. Drihten ne dyde þæt hê ûs on hearde hæftnýd sealde *non dedit nos in captionem*, Ps. Th. 123, 5. Hæftnêd hefige, 125, 1. Þâ graman hæftnéd, 84, 1. Hê hî on hæftnýd heán gesealde, 77, 61. On heaftneád and on þeówdôm, Angl. xi. 2, 51. Ic hwîlum hæftnýd árære *I bring about captivity*, Rä. 80, 10. ¶ with gen. of person or thing by which one is held captive :—Hê mancynn of deófles hæftnýd âlýsde, Ll. Lbmn. 413, 6. Of deófles onwalde and of helle hæftnéde, Bl. H. 87, 13. Fram hæftnýde hellewítes, Hy. 6, 36. ¶ pl. with force of sing. :—Wæs sum wyln gehæft tô swinglum, and læg on hæftnêdum, Hml. S. 21, 167. Hê ûs âhredde fram deófles hæftnýdum, Hml. Th. i. 338, 4. v. hæfte-neód.

**-hæftnídan.** v. ge-hæftnídan.

**hæft-nídling**, es ; *m. A captive :*—Wæs þær sum hæftnédling (*captivus*), Gr. D. 293, 14. Hæftnýdlincg, Hml. S. 30, 194. XL. hæftnýdlinga, *xl captivos*, Gr. D. 232, 24. Of ðâm hæftnýdlingum, 233, 3. Hî læddon mid him micele herehûþe and manige hæftnýdlingas, Hml. S. 30, 391.

**hæftníd-ness**, e ; *f. Captivity :*—Hwylc mihte beón mâre wælgrimnes þonne ûre hæftnýdnes on helle þeóstrum, Nap. 35. Wê gehýrdon þ sum man wæs geseted in hæftnêdnesse (*in captiuitate positum*), Gr. D. 346, 22.

**hæft-noþ.** *Add :*—Ofer ðære reádan sæ eóde Israéla folc of Egipta hæftnoðe, Sal. K. 198, 18. Hæftnoð *captiuitatem*, Ps. L. 52, 7.

**hæftnung.** *Add :*—Hæftnunge *captiuitatem*, Ps. L. 125, 1. Hæfnunge, 84, 2. Ic sende ofer eów . . . hæftnunge : þæt is . . . man sceal þâ geoguðe lædan gehæft heánlîce mid heardum bendum, Wlfst. 295, 14.

**hæg** *a fence ; a hag, an enclosure :*—Terram nominatam Haeg, C. D. i. 49, 23. *The word is found forming the first part of local names,* Hægdûn, Hæghyll, Hægleá ; *also in other words,* hæg-steald, hæg-þorn. See, too, ge-hæg, *and cf.* haga ; hecg, hecge, hege.

**hæg-hâl.** *Add :* [Cf. (?) *Icel.* hagr *advantage, favour* ; there are several cpds. with *hag-*, which gives a favourable sense to the following form.]

**hæg-steald.** *Add : a tiro, novice :*—Warna ær cniht beón þænne hægesteald I geong cempa *caue ante miles esse quam tiro*, Scint. 205, 9. Sê ðe hehstald (*uirgo*) gecoren is . . . þte ðâ hehstald hehstald gehealde (*ut uirginem uirgo seruaret*), Jn. p. 1, 2–5. Ðær hehstalde *uirgini*, 2, 4. Of heghstald *ex uirgine*, Mt. p. 13, 2. Swylce geongum hægstealde, rince, hysse *ut effebo hircitallo*, An. Ox. 3476. Ðerh þ hehstald *per uirginem*, Jn. p. 1, 13. Alle hehstalde ðâ ilco, Mt. 25, 7. Hehstaldo, 11. ¶ *In a local name :*—Ad locum qui dicitur Hægstaldescumb, C. D. B. i. 97, 23. Hegsteldescumb, C. D. v. 104, 1. [*The word seems to mean at first the owner* (cf. *Goth.* staldan *to own*) *of a* hæg, *a small piece of land insufficient to maintain a household.* ] Cf. Hagustaldes-ea.]

**hæg-steald ;** *adj. Add :* v. hago-steald ; *adj.*

**hægsteald-hâd.** *Add :*—Hægstealdhâdes *celibatus*, An. Ox. 1395. **hægsteald-mann.** *Add :*—Hægstealdman *celeps*, Wrt. Voc. i. 291, 28 : ii. 17, 39. Hægstealdmen *coelibes*, 18, 59. Hægstealdmen *colibates*, 134, 67. Hegstealdman *celibes*, 85, 24. v. hagosteald-monn.

**hæg-sugga**, an ; *m. A hedge-sparrow :*—Hægsugga *ficitula*, Hpt. 33, 241, 48. [*See* N. E. D. hay-sugge.] v. hege-sugge, sucga.

**hægtesse.** *Add :* hægtiss (-ess), e : hætse, an ; hæts, e. I. *a fury of the classical mythology :*—Haehtess *furia*, Wrt. Voc. ii. 109, 47. Hægtesse, 36, 29. Hægtes *erenis*, hægtesse *eumenides*, 29, 41, 42. Haehtisse, hegitisse *eumenides, filiae noctis*, Txts. 59, 772. Hægtessa *furiarum*, Wrt. Voc. ii. 96, 82. Hegitesum *furiis*, An. Ox. 4, 85. II. *a hag, witch :*—Haegtis, hegtis *striga*, Txts. 99, 1913. Gâð tô þére hætse *vel* sceande (*Jezabel*) and bebyriað hire lîc *ite et videte maledictam illam, et sepelite eam* (2 Kings 9, 34), Hml. S. 18, 350. Sume wîf wyrcað heora . . . wôgerum drencas . . . Ac þyllice sceandas sceolan sîdian tô helle . . . Crîstene men sceolan forhigian þâ hætsan, M. 164. [*O. H. Ger.* hagazissa (-ussa) *furia* ; hâzus(-is) *strihia, erynnis* : *Ger.* hexe.] Cf. heah-rûn.

**hæg-þorn.** *Add :* (hægu-) *haythorn* (v. N. E. D. hawthorn):—Haeguthorn *alba spina*, Txts. 36, 19 ; haeguthorn, heguthorn *spina alba*,

98, 956. Wel hægþornes blóstman, Lch.ii. 54, 1. Ǽlces treówes dǽl þe man begitan mæg bútan hægþorne, 86, 9. [*Cinus* an haythorne, Wlck. Gl. 572, 45.] v. hagu-, hege-þorn.

**hæg-weard.** *Add*: [v. (*N. E. D.* hay-ward.]

**hǽl** *omen. Add*:—Hael omen, Wrt. Voc. ii. 115, 52. Nǽfre hé on aldordagum ǽr ne siððan heardran hǽle healþegnas fand *never in all the days of his life, before or since, less auspiciously* (cf. Icel. illu heilli *malo augurio* ; in evil hour) *did he come upon hall-thanes*, B. 719.

**hǽl** *health. Add*: I. *sound physical condition* (1) of a person :—Him sió hǽl losað *salus corporis amissa*, Past. 249, 6. Þeáh ðe him (*the old man*) ádl on ne sitte, þeáh oft his hǽl him bið ádl, Hml. i. 614, 16. Hyt tó hǽle gelǽdeð, Lch. i. 114, 21. Þǽre ǽrran hǽle *incolomitati pristine*, An. Ox. 4866. Twégen líchaman ou þá ǽran hǽle *gemina cadauera in pristinum uite statum* (*restituit*), 1875. Tóscádan welan and wǽdle, hǽle and unhǽle, Ll. Th. i. 328, 20. Suá hwá suá hæfð fulle hǽle his líchoman (*valetudinem corporis*), Past. 251, 3. Nis nánum crístenum menn álýfed þæt hé his hǽle gefecce æt nánum stáne, Hml. Th. i. 474, 30. (2) of a person's health :—Þǽre ǽran hǽle *incolomitati pristine* (*ualetudinem restituit*), An. Ox. 4354. II. *healing, cure* :—Hyt þ sár gelíþegað and þá hǽle gegearwað (*effects the cure*), Lch. i. 122, 9. II a. with gen. (1) of person :—' Gehǽle ðe Críst ' . . . Þá gelýfde seó burhwaru þurh þæs' bæddrydan hǽle, Hml. S. 10, 50. (2) of disease :—Þú scealt underfón ðínra wunda hǽle, 7, 276. III. *welfare, well-being, prosperity* :—On ðé ys eall úre hǽl, Ps. Th. 3, 7. Hé þæs hǽl gehleát, 105, 24. ¶ in form of salutation :—Hé þám cásere hǽle bodade, Lch. i. 326, 2. Hǽle Gode (hǽletode, Hpt. Gl. 467, 32) drē[mende] *osanna persultans*, An. Ox. 2607. III a. *a means to produce well-being* :—Þissere worulde hǽl is þ heó witan hæbbe, and swá má witena beóð swá hit bet færð, Hml. S. 13, 128. Nýd weorðeð oft . . . tó hǽle niða bearnum, Rún. 10. IV. *mental* or *spiritual health* or *healing, salvation* :—Tódæg is ðisum hírede hǽl gefremmed . . . Ic cóm tó gehǽlenne þæt þe ou mancynne losode, Hml. Th. i. 582, 5. Þú fulneáh mid ealle forwurde . . . Wé habbað nú þone mǽstan dǽl þǽre tyndran þínre hǽle (*habemus maximum tuae fomitem salutis*), Bt. 5, 3 ; F. 14, 10. Hǽle (hǽles, L., hǽlo, R.), Lk. i, 77. Sáwlum tó hǽle and ús sylfum tó þearfe, Ll. Th. i. 358, 14 : Hy. 6, 16. Tó hǽle and tó rǽde, Bl. H. 227, 4. Oncnáwan hwá him tó hǽle and tó helpe and tó feorhnere on þás world ástág, 105, 32. Hé wolde þrowian for ealra manna hǽle and ús gefreólsian from deófles þeówdóme, 65, 33 : 73, 7 : 129, 14. Þæt þú hire on hǽle gestóde *that you would be her salvation*, Ps. Ben. 34, 3. Þæt mín mód næbbe náne hǽle æt his Gode, Ps. Th. 3, 1. Þíne hǽle ic sǽde *salutare tuum dixi*, 39, 10. Þá wæs geworden werude Iúdéa þæt heó hǽl gehlutan háliges *facta est Iudaea sanctificatio ejus*, 113, 2. v. múþ-hǽl.

**hǽl.** *l.* hǽle q. v.

**hǽlan.** *Add*: I. *to heal* (1) a person sick in body or mind :—Sé hǽleð (*sanat*) gedrēste in heortan, Ps. Srt. 146, 3. Þ wíf of herning blódes hǽleð (*sanat*), Mt. p. 16, 3 : 15, 15. Monige lécneð † hǽles *multos curat*, 16, 15. Hǽled, 18, 1. Þ wíf of iorning blódes hǽled (*saluat*), Lk. p. 6, 1. Gémde † hǽlde hiá *curavit eos*, Mt. L. 19, 2. Haelde hiá *sanavit eos*, 21, 14. Ðý lǽs . . . hwærfa hiá and ic hǽle (*sanem*) hiá, 13, 15 : Jn. L. 12, 40. Ðte hǽlde ðrael his *ut saluaret seruum eius*, Lk. L. 7, 3. Críst hié hǽlan wolde, Bl. H. 105, 26. Hǽla ðá unstronga *sanare infirmos*, Lk. L. 9, 2. (2) *to cure* an infirmity of body or mind, a disease, &c. :—Bledsa sáwul mín Dryhten, sé hǽleð (*sanat*) alle áðle ðíne, Ps. Srt. 102, 3. Sé þe wunde lácnian wille geóte wín on . . . and eft ele ðæt sé hié líðe and hǽle, Past. 124, 12. Ðæt úre haele wunde *ut nostra cures vulnera*, Ps. Srt. ii. p. 204, 9. Þ hig hǽldun (*curarent*) ádle and ǽlce untrumnysse, Mt. 10, 1. Mihtig ǽlce untrumnesse tó hǽlenne, Bl. H. 223, 22. II. *to save* (1) from physical harm or destruction :—Dryhten, hǽl (*salva*) úsic, wé forweorðað, Mt. R. L. 8, 25. Hǽl þec seolfne . . . ástíg nú of róde, 27, 40. Of weorum blóda hǽl mec, Ps. Srt. 58, 3. (2) from destruction of the soul :—Hǽl ús on eorþan, wé þe synt on líchomum lifgende, and eác þá þe on helle synt biddaþ þínre onlésnesse and þínre hǽlo, Bl. H. 81, 21. Cwóm sunu monnes tó soecanne and tó hǽlenne þte losade, Lk. L. R. 19, 10. Ne tó doemenne ah tó haelanne middangeard, Jn. p. 6, 19. ¶ *hǽlan as epithet of Christ, Jesus.* Cf. hǽlend :—Ic eom Hǽlende Críst, Hml. S. 30, 60 : Ll. Th. i. 54, 28 note. Utan wé úre gyfe ðám syllan þe hyre onfón cann, þæt is úre Drihten Hǽlende Críst (úrum Drihtne Hǽlendum Críste, *v. l.*) *nostra donaria offeramus ei, qui nouit accipere, Domino Deo nostro*, Bd. 3, 24 ; Sch. 307, 20 : Rtl. 114, 15. Ðú Hǽlende Críst *Iesu Criste*, Angl. ii. 365, 10, 17. Æt úrum Hǽlendum Críste *per Christum*, Ors. 4, 10 ; S. 194, 28. On Hǽlendum Críste, Bl. H. 187, 8. Tó Drihtne Hǽlendum Críste, 155, 15. Wið úrne Drihten Hǽlendne Críst, 159, 33. v. for-, ge-, þurh-, un-hǽlan.

**hǽlan** *to castrate* :—Móna se syofoða, blóð lǽtan . . . temian, hǽlan (*castrare*) gód ys, Lch. iii. 186, 22. [For corresponding forms in other languages see Dief. ii. 498, Angl. xxx. 131.] v. tó-hǽlan.

**hǽl-bǽre.** v. hál-bǽre.

---

**hǽle.** *Add*:—Hǽle sceal wísfæst and gemetlic, Fä. 86. Sum bið heardsǽlig hǽle, bið hwæðre gleáw, Crä. 32. Láð bið wineleás hǽle, Vy. 32. Þá cóm in gán ealdor þegna (*Beowulf*), dǽdcéne mon, hǽle hildedeór, B. 1646 : (*Wiglâf*), 3111. Se æðeling (*St. Andrew*) . . . Crístes cempa . . . þær in eóde elnes gemyndig hǽle hildedeór, An. 1004. Hié gemǽtton háligne hǽle under heolstorlocan bídan beadurófne, 144. v. hǽleþ.

**hǽle.** *adj.* *Hale, sound, whole, safe* :—Sýne hǽle *pupillam incolumem*, Hpt. Gl. 487, 69. Þá woldan hié on écnesse hǽle and trume wið deófla níþum and helle wítum, and deáþ geþrowodan for Godes naman, Bl. H. 171, 30. v. ge-, wan-hǽle ; hál.

**hǽle.** *an*; *f.* *l.* hǽle, es; *n.*, and *add*: [Cf. *Goth.* un-haili *ill-health*.]: -hǽled. v. on-hǽled: -hǽleddlic, hǽledness. v. un-gehǽledlic, un-gehǽledness.

**hǽlend.** *Add*: I. used of the Deity in reference to pre-Christian times (1) as a noun denoting an agent, *a saviour* :—Freá mihtig, hǽlend manna, Ps. C. 137. Drihten is mín hǽlend *Dominus salus mea*, Ps. Th. 26, 1. Þú eart mín hǽlend *salutare vultus mei*, 42, 6. Úre hǽlend God helpe ússes *salutaris noster, Deus noster, Deus salvos faciendi*, 67, 20. Hǽlynd Drihten, 107, 6. Mín gást wynsumaþ on God mínum hǽlende, Bl. H. 7, 3. (2) with weakening of force and tending to become a mere title (cf. Christ). (a) where it is not definitely applied to the second person of the Trinity :—Him wæs Hǽlend God wráð geworden, Sat. 281. Bearn Hǽlendes, Sat. 153. Hǽlendes, 86. Þú (*Satan*) ús (*the fallen angels*) gelǽrdest þæt wé Hǽlende hýran ne sceoldan, 54. · Herigean Hǽlynd Drihten *Laudate Dominum*, Ps. Th. 112, 1 : 98, 10. (b) applied to the second person :—Frumbearn Godes sǽde : ' Ic eów geworhte . . . Ic on neorxna wonge ǽsette treów . . .' git oferhýrdon Hǽlendes word . . . Næs þá monna gemet . . . þæt eów míhte helpan, nimðe Hǽlend God, sé þæt wíte ǽr tó wrece gesette, férde tó foldan ', Sat. 470-95. II. of the Deity in Christian times. (1) denoting a saviour, used of Christ :—Þú hǽlend eart middangeardes, El. 809. Þæt hé mundbora mín geweorðe, helpend and hǽlend wið hellsceaðum, Jul. 157. Ic wille hýran mínum hǽlende, Gú. 576. Heó cende ealles middaneardes hǽlend, Bl. 105, 18. Hǽlend tillfremmendra, Rä. 60, 6. (2) passing into a title. Cf. I. 2. (a) used of God the Father :—Dryhten Hǽlend (cf. þín sunu, 778), El. 726. (b) used of Christ. (a) *the Saviour* :—Ðá se Hǽlend ðæt ongeat, Past. 33, 15 : Bl. H. 17, 25. Se Hǽlend ús helpe gefremede þurh his líces gedál, Ph. 650 : El. 862. Se gehálgoda Hǽlend, Cri. 435. Maria smerede þæs Hǽlendes fét, Bl. H. 69, 2 : Cri. 505. Martha gearwode þám Hǽlende ǽfengereordu, Bl. H. 67, 26. ¶ with other titles of the Deity :—Þú eart Hǽlend God, Hy. 3, 9. Hí lǽrdon ǽnne willan beón on Dryhtne Hǽlende Críste (Dryhtne Hǽlende, *v. l.*) (*in Domino Saluatore*), Bd. 5, 19 ; Sch. 666, 8. (β) rendering *Jesus* :—His nama wæs Hiesus, þæt is Hǽlend, for ðan ðe hé gehǽlð ealle ðá þe on hine gelýfað, Hml. Th. i. 198, 12. Hǽlend genam his twelf þegnas sunder, Bl. H. 15, 6, 15, 23. Hit is Hǽlend se Nazarenisca *it is Jesus of Nazareth*, 18. Hire sweostor gesæt big Hǽlendes fótum, 67, 27 : Sat. 382 : An. 574 : Kr. 25. Lazarus sæt mid Hǽlende, Bl. H. 67, 36. Didimus mid hondum Hǽlend genóm, Sat. 544. ¶ with other titles of the Deity :—Úre Drihten Hǽlend . . . wæs Hǽlend Críst, Bl. H. 67, 4-5 : Sat. 219 : An. 1409. Úre Drihten Hǽlend Críst, Bl. H. 11, 21. v. hǽlan ; II. 2 ¶.

**hǽlend-líc.** *Substitute: That heals* or *saves, salutary* :—Hálwende, hǽlendlíc þæs heofenlícan [heretogan] cynnincg *saluatrix superne ducis natiuitas*, An. Ox. 1538. v. ge-hǽlendlic.

**hǽleþ.** *Add*: [*The declension of this word is like that of ealu; both are t-stems, and the regular nominative should be* hæle *q. v. See* Kl. Nom. Stam. § 29, Sievers Grammar § 281]. I. used with complimentary force of both temporal and spiritual persons : (1) implying excellence in worldly matters :—David wæs háten diórmód hǽleð, Israéla brega æðele and ríce, cyninga cýnost, Ps. C. 1. Weorð eác ádrǽfed deórmód hǽleð Óslác of earde, Chr. 975 ; P. 120, 20. Ing wæs ǽrest mid Eást-Denum . . . þus Heardingas þone hǽleð nemdun, Rún. 22. Byð for eorlum æðelinga wyn hors hófum wlanc, þǽr him hæleþe ymb welege on wicgum wrixlað sprǽce, 19. (1 a) transferred to Christ :—Ongyrede hine geong hǽleð, þæt wæs God ælmihtig, strang and stíðmód, gestáh hé on galgan, módig on manigra gesyhðe, Kr. 39. (2) in spiritual matters :—Iôhannis hǽleð helwarum sprǽc, Hö. 24. Wís hǽleð (*St. Andrew*), An. 921. Tírfæst hǽleð . . . bisceop se góda . . . ðám wæs Cyneweard nama, Chr. 975 ; P. 120, 9. (3) expressing courtesy in address :—Nú þú miht gehýran, hǽleð mín se leófa, Kr. 78 : 95 : El. 511. II. *a man* :—Nǽnig manna wát, hǽleða under heofenum, Sal. 50. Fira gehwylc hǽleða cynnes, Wal. 40. Nǽnig manna under heofonhwealfe hǽleða cynnes, An. 545. Drihten ealra hǽleða cynnes, El. 188. Heofonengla here and hǽleða bearn, ealle eorðbúend and atol deófol, Cri. 1278. Þonne heofon aud hel hǽleða bearnum, fíra feórum fylde weorðeð, 1592. Mith heliðum, Txts. 151, 12. ¶ in phrases applied (1) to an earthly ruler :—Eádward cing . . . hæleða wealdend, Chr. 1065 ; P. 193, 31. Hæleða waldend (*the king of Sodom*), Gen. 2139. (2) to the Deity :—Sóð Sunu Metodes, sáwla Bergend, hæleða Helpend, Dan. 403. Hæleða

Scyppend, An. 396. Bearn Wealdendes, hæleða hyhtgifa, El. 852. Hæleþa Wealdend, Ps. Th. 1416. [Cf. *Icel.* hölðr.]

**hæleþ-helm.** *Take this at* heoloþ-helm: hæletoþ. *Dele, and see* hæl; III ¶.

**hælettan(-ung).** v. hâlettan(-ung).

**hælftre,** e; *f. Substitute:* hælfter, e; *f., and* (?) es; *m.:* hælftre, es; *m. or n.; or,* an; *f., and add:*—Hælfter *capistrum,* Wrt. Voc. ii. 128, 45. Hê breác on þâm (horse) hælftre (hælftres, *v. l.*) for brîdelse *in quo (jumento) capistro pro freno utebatur,* Gr. D. 34, 12. On hælftre ł on wealdleðre *in chamo,* Ps. L. 31, 9. Haelftreo, Ps. Srt. 31, 9. [*O. L. Ger.* heliftron *(in) chamo.*]

**hælhiht.** v. healhiht: **hælig.** v. hâlig: **hælnes;** I. *Add after* 'salvation,' l. 2 : nuuc dies salutis, *and at end:* cf. hâlignes.

**hælsend.** *For* 'Cot. 73, Lye' *substitute:*—Haelseut *extipices,* Wrt. Voc. ii. 107, 76. Hælsendas *extipices, aruspices,* 30, 4.

**hælsere,** *For* Cot. . . . Lye' *substitute:*—Hælsere *augur,* Wrt. Voc. ii. 101, 34. Hælsera *aruspicum,* 84, 51 : 3, 30. v. wyrm-hælsere.

**hælsian** *to take omens* (v. hæl). *For* 'Cot. . . . Lye' *substitute:*—Haelsadon *auspicantur,* Wrt. Voc. ii. 101, 32. Hælsadon, 7, 47.

**hælsung.** *For* 'Cot. 11, Lye' *substitute:*—Hælsunga *auguria,* Wrt. Voc. ii. 6, 28. v. hâlsung.

**hælþ.** *Add:* I. *(good) health* (1) *of body:*—Hê cwæð þæt hire cild gesund beón sceolde, and eal hire hîwisc hælðe brûcan, Hml. Th. ii. 150, 19. Gif þû gesihst þê on wætere cealdan þw[e]án, hælðe lîchaman *(sanitatem corporis)* getâcnaþ, Lch. iii. 214, 14. (2) *of soul, salvation:*—Eallon þâm tô êcere hælðe þe his lîchaman sêceað, Chr. 1023; P. 156, 25. II. *healing.* (1) *physical:*—Heó ârâs andsund of þâm bedde . . . þâ wundrode se þegn his wîfes hælðe, Hml. S. 22, 55. Hê sumne blindne man gehælde . . . and manega gelŷfdon þurh ðæs mannes hælðe, 34. (2) *spiritual :*—On hâlwendlican þînum ł hælðe *in salutare tuum,* Ps. L. 118, 81. v. un-, wan-hælþ.

**hælu.** *Add:* I. *sound physical condition:*—Sió hælo ðæs lîchoman *(salus corporis)* . . . ðonne hê ðære hælo benumen wierð, Past. 251, 9–10. Ðæt gôde môd ðe sió hælo (hælu, *v. l.*) ful oft âweg âdrîefð, 255, 16. Sint tô manianne ðâ hâlan ðæt hié ne forhycgen ðæt hié hêr on ðære hwîlendlican hælo him gearuigen ðâ êcan hælo, 247, 12. Hond geednîuad wæs tô hælo *(sanitate),* Mt. L. R. 12, 13. Swæ hwâ swæ hæfð fulle hælo his lîchoman *(valetudinem corporis),* Past. 250, 3. Waldend him mæg syllan hælo on heáfodgimme, Gu. Ex. 44. II. *a making whole, healing, a cure:*—Hê gehæledum gewitte ârâs . . . þâ ealle men on þæt gefêgon hwilc wundor ðære hælo þu:h Drihtnes gyfe geworden wæs *(quid ibi sanitatis Domino largiente consequeretur),* Bd. 4, 3; Sch. 366, 5. Alle mið hælo untrumige *omnes sanando languores,* Mt. p. 14, 9. Hê monge gehælde . . . hî symle æt Godes cempan gearwe fundon helpe and hælo, Gû. 862 : El. 1216. Gewuniaþ . . . gelômlice wundor hælo geworden beón *solent crebra sanitatum miracula operari,* Bd. 4, 3; Sch. 365, 16. Wundra manega hælo (monig wundur hælo, *v. l.*) gefremede wæron *multa sanitatum sint patrata miracula,* 5, 15; Sch. 649, 11. Haelo (cf. *potestatem curandi,* Mk. 3, 15) *sanitatum,* Mk. p. 3, 10. Ic hæla (hælo, L. R.) gefremme *sanitates perficio,* Lk. 13, 32. III. *well-being, welfare, prosperity:*—Hê hî on hælo hŷþe gelædde, swâ bê hira willan wyste fyrmest *eduxit eos in portum voluntatis eorum,* Ps. Th. 106, 29. Sige bêc onsendað . . . hælo hŷðe þâm þe hŷ lufað, Sal. 245. ¶ *in forms of greeting or address* (1) *on coming to or meeting a person:*—Sié þê êce hælo and in eorð:n lof, Cri. 411. Him hælu and lof secgean *laudent eum,* Ps. Th. 106, 31. Hê hælo âbeád Maria mycle, Men. 50. Mê Gabrihel hælo bodade, Cri. 202. Beádas hælo ł groetas *salutate,* Mt. L. 10, 12 : Mk. p. 4, 6. (2) *on parting:*—Hælo âbeád heordgeneátum goldwine Geáta *the lord of the Geats* (Beowulf at the point of death), *liberal and kind, bade farewell to his hearth-sharers,* B. 2418. (3) *in written communications:*—Eusebius ðæm brôðer in Drihten haelo *Eusebius fratri in Domino salutem,* Mt. p. 10, 12. Hê þâm câsere hælo bodade þyssum wordum, Lch. i. 326, 2. III a. *safety against attack, deliverance* from unfavourable conditions :—Horn hælo ûs . . . Hælo (hê âlŷsde ûs, W. S., R.) from fîondum ûsum *cornum salutis nobis . . . salutem ex inimicis nostris,* Lk. L. 1. 69–71. (1) *with gen. of the saver :*—Syle ûs on earfoðum fultum, for ðon hælu byð manna gehwylces îdel *(vana salus hominis),* Ps. Th. 59, 10. (2) *with gen. of the saved :*—þæt hî for sibbe and hælo heora êðles campedon *ut hi pro patriae pace et salute militarent,* Bd. i, 15; Sch. 41, 10. Gemicligende hælo kyningces his *magnificans salutes regis eius,* Ps. L. 17, 51. IV. *mental or spiritual health or well-being :*—Ðâ truman sint tô manianne ðæt hié gewilnigen mid ðæs lîcuman trumnesse ðæt him ne losige sió hælo ðæs môdes *admonendi sunt incolumes ut salutem corporis exerceant ad salutem mentis,* Past. 247, 7. Genôh ryhte þû hit ongitst, and þ is tâcn ðînre hælo *indicium est erectae naturae,* Bt. 36, 4; F. 178, 25. Sió sâul, ðonne hió gebædd wierð ðæt yfel tô forlætanne . . . sêcð ðonne ðâ forlorenan hælo *(salutem amissam),* Past. 251, 14. IV a. *safety, deliverance, salvation.* Cf. III a :—Hine God freoðade on foldan, swâ hê feora gehwylc healdeð in hælo (cf. nô God wolde þæt seó sâwl sâr þrowode, 379), þæt se gæst þîhð in þeáwum, Gû. 368. 'Gehæle mê *(salvum*

me fac)* ðîn sió swîðre ' . . . Hê gecŷðde ðæt hê ðæs êcean lîfes hælo *(aeternam salutem)* sôhte, Past. 389, 22. Ic his sâcerdas mid hælu gegyrwe *sacerdotes ejus induam salutare,* Ps. Th. 131, 17. (1) *with gen. of saver :*—Sæle mê, Dryhten, þîure hælo heht *redde mihi laetitiam salutaris tui,* Ps. C. 100. þ mîn gâst wynsumige on þîure hælo, Bl. H. 159, 3. Gesêgon êgo mîn hælo ðîn *(salutare tuum),* Lk. L. R. 2, 30. Sæcgeað Drihtnes hælu, Ps. Th. 95, 2. (2) *with gen. of saved.* See next paragraph. ¶ *the salvation effected by Christ's death :*—Hæl ûs, wê þe synt on lîchomum lifgende, and eác þâ þe on helle synt biddaþ þînre onlêsnesse and þînre hælo, Bl. H. 81, 23. þæt þû ûs âhredde and ûs hælo giefe sylle, Cri. 374: 613: 1575. Him selfum tô êcere hælo, Chr. 855; P. 66, 8 : Ll. Th. i. 102, 7. Eal þis hê þrowode for ûre lufon and hælo, Bl. H. 23, 35. For manna hælo, 79, 3. Fore uncerra sâula hêla and uncerra bearna, C. D. i. 292, 26. (Cf. pro remedio animae meae et filii nostri, 287, 31.) Sancta Maria brôhte eallum geleáffullum êce hælo, 5, 31. IV b. *that which produces spiritual health or well-being :*—Is wel gecueden ðætte ðæt flæsclice lîf sié ðære heortan hælo *vita carnium sanitas cordis,* Past. 235, 22. Ðæt hié geðencen hû micel hælo ðæt bið ðære heortan ðæt se lîchoma sié medtrum *ut considerent, quanta salus cordis sit molestia corporalis,* 255, 14. [v. *N. E. D.* heal; *sb.*] v. un-hælu.

**hælu-tîd,** e; *f. A time of well-being, a happy time:*—Eádward cing . . . hælotîd weóld Walum and Scottum and Bryttum, Chr. 1065 ; P. 193, 31. [Cf. William of Malmesbury, who notes that in Edward's reign ' all was calm and peaceable both at home and abroad', and says that 'the happiness of his times had been revealed in a dream . . . in the time of Canute', Bk. ii. c. 13.]

**hæl-wyrt,** e ; *f. Penny-royal:*—Hælwyrt *pollegia,* Wrt. Voc. i. 68, 61. v. hyll-wyrt.

**hæman.** *Add:* I. *in a not criminal sense.* (1) *to have sexual intercourse:*—Gif wer and wîf hŷ gesomnien, and heó secge þ hê ne mæge hæman *(coire)* mid hire . . . nime hire ôðerne, Ll. Th. ii. 146, 37. (2) *to marry:*—Ne beþærfeþ þ mon hæme *non expedit nubere,* Mt. R. 19, 10. (2 a) *of concubinage, to cohabit:*—Gif hê . . . þe hié bohte . . . âlêfe his suna mid tô hæmanne, Ll. Th. i. 46, 16. II. *in a criminal sense, to have illicit intercourse, commit adultery, fornicate:*—Ðŷ læs hî on unryht hæmen . . . Hê egesode ðâ ðe on unryht hæmdon *propter fornicationem . . . Fornicationis metum praemisit,* Past. 397, 20. Næs ic nâ genihtsumigende on þâm geongum ðe on þære sæ nid mê hæmdon, Hml. S. 23 b, 396. þone þe hæme wið nŷten *qui coierit cum jumento,* Ex. 22, 19 : Ll. Th. i. 52, 11. Sê þe mid nunnon hæme, 246, 6. II a. *figurative:*—Þû fordydest ælcne man sê þe hæmþ *(fornicatur)* fram þê, Ps. L. 72, 27. v. ge-, unriht-hæman ; diru-, wôh-hæmende ; un-, unriht-hæmed.

**hæmdere.** v. unriht-hæmdere: **-hæme;** *adj.* v. ge-hæme.

**-hæme;** *pl. m. This form is found in many words denoting the inhabitants of places whose names end in* -hâm, e. g. Æschæma gemæru, C. D. iv. 70, 26. *For a list of such words see* Cht. Craw. 116. *Also the form* -hæminga *occurs with the same meaning :*—Wanhæminga gemære, C. D. v. 264, 1. Wealthæminga gemearc, iii. 405, 7.

**hæmed.** *Add:* I. *of legitimate connexion:*—Gif ðâ gesinhîwan tô ungemetlîce hié gemengað on ðæm hæmede *conjuges immoderatae admixtioni servientes,* Past. 397, 11. Gif hire liófre sié ôðer hêmed tô niomanne *if she prefer to make a second marriage,* C. D. i. 310, 20. Æulic hæmæd *legitimum conubium,* An. Ox. 416. Hæmeda *matrimonii,* 3617. Hæmedu (hæmedru, Hpt. Gl. 525, 13) *lenocinia* (spreto spousali peplo blanda procorum *lenocinia* contemnens, Ald. 76, 9), 5245. ¶ *a marriage feast;* nuptiae :—Of hæmdum ł of brŷdlópum *de nuptiis,* Jn. p. 1, 3. Tô ðæm færmum ł hæmdum *ad nubtias,* 2, 2. I a. *of the intercourse of animals:*—Sindon sume gesceafta þe tŷmað bûton hæmede, Hml. Th. ii. 10, 15. II. *of illegitimate connexion:*—Hæmed *incestum,* Wrt. Voc. ii. 44, 44. Nys mê þŷnes weales hæmed næfre þe leófre þe mê nædre tôslyte, Shrn. 154, 22. Hæmedes, forligeres *prostibule,* An. Ox. 4219. Hæmede *stupro,* 2942: 5043. Sê nunnan hæmede and forligete. Sê þe mid nunnan hæme, Ll. Th. i. 246, 5 : 66, 14. Ælþeódige mæn gif hió hiora hæmed rihtan nyllað, 38, 1. Ceorlisc man . . . þ hæmed mid hreówe forlæte, 7. þâ forbodenan gyfta ł hæmeda *uetitos hymeneos,* An. Ox. 1781. Hæmedo, Txts. 69, 1036. Hæmeda, Wrt. Voc. ii. 78, 29. Wîfþing, gifta, hæmed, 43, 13. v. mæg-, nîd-, riht-, unriht-, wôh-hæmed.

**hæmed-dreám** (?), **-drîm, -drîme**(?), es; *m. The pleasure of a vicious life* (?), *a life of pleasure:*—Hæmedrîmes (hæmeddrîmes, [hæmed-] scipes *lenocinii* (antequam Samson illecebrosis *lenocinii* nexibus nodaretur, Ald. 72, 15), An. Ox. 5046. (Cf. 5245, *under* hæmed; I.)

**hæmed-gemâna.** *For* 'Cot. 129, Lye' *substitute:*—Hæmedgemânan *matrimonia,* Wrt. Voc. ii. 55, 4.

**hæmed-gifta.** *Dele, and see last instance under* hæmed: **hæmed-rim.** v. hæmed-dreám.

**hæmed-scipe.** *Substitute :* (1) *in a good sense, the state of matrimony :*—Hæmedscipes gemânan *hymenei* ł *connubii commercio,* Hpt. Gl. 482, 7. (2) *in a bad sense, cohabitation without marriage :*—Hæmed-

rimes ‡ [hæmed]scipes *lenocinii, seductionis*, Hpt. Gl. 521, 40. v. hæmed-dreám.

**hǽmed-þing.** *Add:* (1) with no sense of criminality :—Þes bisceop sǽde ... Þ hé nǽfre on his lífe ne cóme neáh wífe þurh hǽmedþing, ac heóld his clǽnnysse, Hml. S. 3, 204. Mycel wundor hit wæs þæt þæt mǽden gebær cild þe nǽfre náhte þurh hǽmedþing weres gemánan, Wlfst. 15, 16. Mǽssepreóstas witan þæt hig nágon mid rihte þurh hǽmedþing wífes gemánan, 269, 21 : Ll. Th. i. 306, 18. (2) of criminal intercourse :—Gif hwá nunnan mid hǽmedþinge (*fornicationis causa*) on hire hrægl ... gefó, Ll. Th. i. 72, 8. Gif hwylc geong man hǽmedþing gewyrce bútan rihtum gesinscipe *si juvenis quis absque legitimo conjugio fornicatus fuerit*, ii. 164, 23. Be hǽmedþingam. Gif mon hǽme (*fornicetur*), i. 68, 8.

**hǽmed-wíf.** For ‘Cot. 136 Lye’ *substitute :*—Hǽmedwíf *matrona*, Wrt. Voc. ii. 59, 19.

**hǽmend**, es; *m. An adulterer, a fornicator :*—Hǽmend *incestatur* (*-or ?*), Wrt. Voc. ii. 44, 47. v. unriht-, wóh-hǽmend.

**hǽmere.** *Add:*—God fordémð þá dyrnan forligeras and þá unrihtan hǽmeras, Hml. A. 19, 145. v. unriht-, wóh-hǽmere.

**hǽmestre.** v. níd-hǽmestre: **-hǽmingas.** v. -hǽme; *pl. m.*: **hǽn.** v. hen: **hǽnan.** *Add:* v. ge-hǽnan.

**hǽnep.** *Add:*—Hǽnep *canafel sylvatica*, Wrt. Voc. i. 69, 16 : *cannabum*, ii. 128, 4 : *cannabin*, 6. Hǽnep (henep, *v. l.*). Deós wyrt þe man *cannaue silfatica* and óþrum naman hǽnep (henep, *v. l.*) nemneþ, Lch. i. 228, 15–17.

**-hǽp, -hǽplic, -hǽplicnes.** v. ge-hǽp, ge-hǽplic, ge-hǽplicnes.

**hǽppan** (?); *p.* te *To move accidentally* (?), *to slip :*—Þá slóh sum hǽþen man tó þám hálgan were, ac mid þám swenge hǽpte þ swurd him of handum (*the sword slipped out of his hand*), and ne mihte man hit nǽfre syððan findan (cf. þæt wǽpen wand áweg mid þám slege of þæs réðan handum, Hml. Th. ii. 510, 22 : nyste hé fǽringa hwǽr þ seax cóm þe hé ǽr on handa hæfde, Bl. H. 223, 17 : *all three passages refer to the same event in the life of St. Martin*), Hml. S. 31, 477. [Cf. *N. E. D.* hap *to go by chance.*]

**hǽpse.** *Add:*—Ne sceolde hé nán ðing forgýman ðe ǽfre tó note mehte ; ne forða músfellan, ne, þ gít lǽsse is, tó hæpsan pinn, Angl. ix. 265, 9. Hæpsan, *loca clustella* (*arcarum reserantur*), An. Ox. 4003.

**hǽpsian.** *Add:*—Sero, seras, ic hæpsige, is ðǽre forman geðeódnysse, Ælfc. Gr. Z. 166, 1. v. be-hæpsian.

**hǽr.** *Add:* I. *a hair :*—Hǽr *pilus*, Wrt. Voc. ii. 117, 40. (1) *a human hair, hair of a person's head :*—Hǽr (*capillus*) of heófde iówrum ne bið forloren, Lk. R. L. 21, 18. Þ fýr heora ne æthrán, ne furþum án hǽr heora heáfdes, Hml. S. 30, 454. Ne mæhtú énne hér (*unum capillum*) húit geuirce, Mt. L. 5, 36. Him þá hǽr (his hǽr, *v. l.*) áfeóllon *þilis cadentibus*, Gr. D. 157, 8. Hǽras (*capilli*) heáfdes, Mt. L. 10, 30. Héro (hér, R.), Lk. L. 12, 7. Heora wæs má þonne hǽr on mínum heáfde, Ps. Th. 39, 14. Ne efesiad eów ne eówre hǽr ne sciron (*non facietis calvitium*), Deut. 14, 1. (2) *a hair of an animal :*—Of hǽrum (of hérum ðæra camella, Mt. L. 3, 4) *de pilis*, Wrt. Voc. ii. 71. 61. Wullan fliásum, hérum, Txts. 151, 4. Hǽran, Rä. 36, 4. II. *a number of hairs together* (1) *a lock.* v. hǽr-locc :—Hǽra *cincinnorum.* An. Ox. 1199. (2) *a fringe :*—Ðá hér *fimbrias*, Mt. L. 23, 5. III. with collective force, *hair* (1) *of persons :*—Hǽr *cesaries, pilos*, Wülck Gl. 290, 11. Unbegánum locca fexe and fúliendum hǽre *inculta criniculorum cesarie et squalente capillatura*, An. Ox. 1214. (2) *of animals :*—Sume bróhton gáte hǽr ... þæt gáte hǽr getácnode þá stíþan dǽdbóte, Ælfc. Gen. Thw. 3, 31–6, v. heáfod-hǽr.

**hǽre.** *Add:* I. *sackcloth* used as a garment, *a hair-shirt :*—Hé scrýdde hine mid hǽran and mid axan bestreowode, Hml. S. 31, 445. Mid héran *cilicio*, Ps. Srt. 34, 13. Heó (*St. Cecilia*) wæs gegyred myd hǽran æt hyre líchaman, and onufan þǽre hǽran heó wæs gegyred myd golde áwefenum hrægelum, Shrn. 149, 20. Hí mid hǽran hí gescrýddon tó líce *they wore sackcloth next their skin*, Hml. S. 12, 36 : Hml. A. 108, 207. Heó áwearp hire hǽran and hire wudewan reáf, 109, 228. II. *sackcloth* used to lie on :—Hé oftost læg uppon ánre hǽran on þǽre baran flóra, Hml. S. 31, 853. On stíþre hǽran licgende, 1351 : Hml. Th. ii. 516, 31. [v. *N. E. D.* haire.]

**hǽrean-fagol.** Have the glossers misunderstood the word *herinaciis*, and supposed it to be the name of a bird ? Can the *hǽrean* represent *herin* and *fagol* be a mistake for *fugol?* and in the other gloss, *hattefagol*, is *hatte* = *hátte*, and *fagol* for *fugol*, so that the gloss would mean *herinacius is the name of a bird?*

**hǽren.** *Add:*—Heó gegyrede hý mid hǽrenre tunecan and mid byrnan, þ is mid lytelre hacelan, Shrn. 140, 30.

**hǽrfest.** *Add:* I. *autumn, the third of the four seasons.* [It began on August 7 and November 6 was its last day :—þæs (*after Lammas day*) hærfest cymð ymb seofon niht bútan ánre wonan ... Syþþan (*after All Saints’ day*) wintres dæg on syx nihtum genimð hærfest mid herige *six days after Lammas autumn comes ... six days after All Saints’ day winter time captures autumn*, Men. 140–204]:—Tó hǽrfestes emnihte, Chr. 1048 ; P. 174, 21. On hærfeste gefór se here on Miercna lond,

877 ; P. 74, 21. Ætforan hærfeste forbarn þ hálige mynster sĉe Paule, 1086 ; P. 218, 22. Wé weorðiað heáhengles tiid on hærfeste, Michaheles, Men. 177. Ðis wæs on hærfest, Chr. 918 ; P. 100, 2. Hé sæt on þám biscoprice ealne þone sumor and þone hærfest, 1048 ; P. 172, 14. Herfest, 1006 ; P. 136, 16. I a. *as the season for the ripening and gathering of fruits :*—Hærfest byð hreðeádegost, hæleðum bringeð géres westmas, Gn. C. 8. Swá nú lencten and hærfest, on lencten hit gréwð, and on hærfest hit fealwað, Bt. 21 ; F. 74, 22. Se wæstmbǽra hærfest bryngþ rípa bléda, 39, 13 ; F. 234, 15. Hærfest cymð, wlitig wæstmum hladen, Men. 140. Me mæcg on hærfeste rípan, in Agusto and Septembri and Octobri ... fela tilða hám gæderian ... ǽr tó túne tó stíð winter cume, Angl. ix. 261, 14–20. II. *the part of Autumn in which the fruits of the earth are gathered in, harvest.* v. hærfestlic ; II., hærfest-mónaþ, hærfest-tíd ; II :—Agustus síhð tó mannum nid genihtsumum hærfeste and *autumnus* cymð tó mancynne binnan seofon nihta fyrste, Angl. viii. 311, 18. On hærfeste wícode se cyng on neáweste þǽre byrig, þá hwíle þe hié hira corn gerypon, Chr. 896 ; P. 89, 8. Mon eorðan wæstmas on hærfeste hám gelæded ... on rypes tíman, Ph. 244. II a. rendered in late Latin versions by *Augustus* (cf. Augustus *messis, messis tempus*, Migne) :—On hærfeste (*in Augusto*), ðá fullan wican ǽr Scá Marian mæssan (*Sept.* 8), Ll. Th. i. 92, 6. Berebryttan gebyreð corngebrot on hærfeste (*in Augusto*), 440, 2. iii dagas ǽlcre wucan on hærfest (*in Augusto*), 432, 22 : 434, 7. ¶ in a late MS. it is used as the name of the month, *August :*—On Iuli mónðe ... On hærfest ... On Setembre, Angl. x. 185, 10.

**hǽrfest-líc.** *Add:* I. *autumnal.* v. hærfest ; I. :—Hærfestlicere *autumnali* (*tempore*), An. Ox. 3838. On hærfæstlíce (árfæstlíce, MS.) tíde (*in autumnali tempore*, i. e. *August* 20), fíf dagum ǽr Scé Bartholomeus mæssan (*August* 25), Guth. Gr. 157, 59. II. *of harvest.* v. hærfest ; II :—Hé weard ofslagen þurh þǽre sunnan hǽtan on hærfestlicre tíde *mortuus est in diebus messis hordeaceae*, Hml. A. 108, 198.

**hǽrfest-mónaþ.** *Add:* cf. hærfest ; II a.

**hǽrfest-tíd,** e ; *f.* I. *autumn.* v. hærfest ; I :—Þú þá treówa on hærfesttíd heora leáfa bereáfast, and eft on lencten ðpru leáf sellest, Bt. 4 ; F. 8, 6. II. *harvest-time.* v. hærfest ; II :—On sumera and on hærfesttíde, þonne mon wæstmas in somnode *tempore aestatis, quo fruges erant colligendae*, Bd. 4, 4 ; Sch. 369, 7.

**hǽrfest-tíma,** an ; *m. Autumn :*—Autumnus, þ ys hærfesttíma, cymð tó mancynne binnan seofon nihta fyrste *autumn comes on the seventh of August*, Angl. viii. 311, 18.

**hériht.** *l.* hériht(e), *and for* ‘ crinitus. ... Lye’ *substitute :*—Þá hérihtan *setosa* (*vervecum vellera*), Wrt. Voc. ii. 87, 27.

**hǽring.** *Add:*—Hǽring *sardina*, Wrt. Voc. i. 281, 64. Heringas *sardinas*, Txts. 94, 910.

**hǽr-loccas,** Hpt. Gl. 526, 45. *Perhaps this should be read* hǽr, loccas. Cf. fexa ł hǽra *cincinnorum*, 435, 5.

**hǽrn.** *Substitute for passage :*—Hraen, raen *flustra, undae*, Txts. 60, 400. Flód oððe hærn *flustra*, Wrt. Voc. ii. 33, 32. Hærn eft onwand árýda geblond, An. 531.

**hǽr-nǽdl.** For ‘ Lye’ *substitute :*—Mid þráwincspinle, hǽrnǽdla *calamistro*, An. Ox. 1200.

**hǽr-sife,** es ; *n. A hair-sieve :*—Man sceal habban ... hérsyfe, Angl. ix. 264. 14. [O. L. Ger. hâr-sif *setatium* : O. H. Ger. hâ[r]-sib(-sip) *cribellum, sedatium*.]

**hǽs.** *Add:* I. *a bidding, an order :*—Streclicere hǽse (*quod*) *violenti precepti* (*imperio complendum jubetur*), An. Ox. 1294. Petrus and Andreas be Crístes hǽse forléton heora nett ... hí æfter stemne ánre hǽse þæt þæt hí hæfdon forgeáton, Hml. Th. i. 578, 24. Deóflu be eówere hǽse þá deófolseócan forléton, 64, 26. Seó menigo háligra sáula mid Drihtnes hǽse wǽron of þǽm cwicsúslum áhafena, Bl. H. 87, 18. Be hyre ágenum cyre, ná geneádod mid nánre hǽse, Hml. A. 32, 204. Þurh his hálige hǽs, An. 1522 : 1588 : El. 86 : Wlfst. 255, 1. Féran sceal þurh freán hǽse sundor ánra gehwæs sáwl of líce, Az. 92. Hé hét him tó clypian ealne þone here þ hí his hǽse gefyldon, Hml. S. 28, 27 : Angl. vii. 52, 406. Hé gehýrde þá word þæs hátendan, ac hé yldode þ hé þás gefyllan nolde *audivit jubentis verba, sed implere distulit*, Gr. D. 159, 16. Hé beád þæs apostoles hǽsa (-e, *v. l.*) Dyonisie, Hml. S. 29, 63. II. *an invitation* from a superior :—Scé Paulinus þǽre cyricean scíre onféng mid þæs arcebisceopes hǽse and Eádboldes þæs cyninges (*inuitatione Honorii aniistitis et Eadbaldi regis*), Bd. 2, 20 ; Sch. 188, 12. III. *an office, service one is bidden to perform* (?) :—Þénunge. hǽse *munia*, Wrt. Voc. ii. 57, 8. v. níd-hǽs ; hátan.

**hǽsel** *galerus. Dele.*

**hǽsel** *hazel. Add:*—[H]aesil, haesl *auellanus*, Txts. 38, 50. Hæsl *abellanus*, Wrt. Voc. ii. 7, 42 : *abellanus vel colurnus*, i. 285, 24. Haesil, haesl *corylus*, Txts. 50, 236. Of ðǽre apoldre on ðæne hwítau hæsl, ðonnæ of ðám hwítan hæsle on hnuttwíc eástewearde, C. D. v. 221, 18. [The word occurs in a great many local names. [v. C. D. vi. 293, col. 2.]

**hǽsel-hnutu.** *Add:*—Hæselhnutu *abelena*, Wrt. Voc. ii. 98, 14. Haslhnutu *abellana*, 4, 52. Hæslhnute cyrnel *nucleus sive nucleus*, 62, 37.

**hæsel-ræw**, e; _f. A row of hazels_:—On ðã hæselræwe, C. D. iii. 77, 4.

**hæsel-wrid**, es; _n. m_ (?). _l._ hæsel-wríd, -wríþ, es; _m., and add_:—On ðone miclan hæslwríd wiðneoðon ðæt gráfet; of ðãm hæslwríðe, C. D. v. 194, 14. v. wríd.

**hæsel-wyrt**. _Dele_: hæssec. v. hassuc.

**hae-swealwe**, an; _f. A kind of hawk_:—Haesualwe (_Sweet suggests_ sæ-) _astur_, Txts. 43, 234. Cf. heoru-swealwe.

**hæt**. _Add_:—Haet mitra, Wrt. Voc. ii. 114, 13. Hæt _tiara_, 85, 42 : _capitium_, An. Ox. 5320. Hættes _mitre_, 5242 : Wrt. Voc. ii. 87, 45. Camb on hætte oððe on helme _crista_, 19, 10. Eówre hættas _mitre_, 55, 21 : 70. Haetas _mitras_, Txts. 113, 75.

**hǽt** _heat_. _For forms that might be taken as oblique cases of such a nominative see_ hǽtu : **hǽta**. v. scyld-hǽta.

**hǽtan**. _Add_: I. _trans._ (1) _to communicate heat to_:—Gedô on calic, menge æfter þon wið wæter, and hǽte, Lch. ii. 24, 25. (2) _to cause the sensation of warmth in_:—Lǽcedôm . . . tô hǽtenne untrumne magan, Lch. ii. 158, 21. II. _intrans. To be warm_:—Haetendae _calentes_, Txts. 48, 206. v. for-, ge-, in-, on-hǽtan.

**hǽte**. _Dele last passage, and add_:—Hǽte _calor_, . . . hǽte _micel fervor_, Wrt. Voc. i. 53, 40, 42 : 76, 73, 75. I. _the quality of being hot_:—Belimpð seó hǽðung tô ðære hǽtan, Hml. Th. i. 286, 3. Þ seó sunne mid hyre hǽtan middaneardes wæstmas ne forbærne, Lch. iii. 250, 16. Þurh ðære sunnan hǽtan, 276, 16. Þæt hellice fýr hæfð unásecgendlíce hǽtan and nán leóht, Hml. Th. i. 532, 2. I a. _the sensation caused by contact with fire_:—Ne undergyte gê þæt eówre glêda náne hǽtan mínum líchaman ne gedôð, ac swiðor cêlinge?, Hml. Th. i. 430, 12. II. _heat_ as an element present in all bodies, _fire_ as one of the four elements:—Ðunor cymð of hǽtan and of wǽtan. Seó lyft týhð ðone wǽtan tô hyre neoðan and ðã hǽtan ufon, and þonne hí gegaderode beóð, seó hǽte and se wǽta binnon ðære lyfte, þonne winnað hí him betweónan mid egeslicum swêge, and þ fýr ábyrst út ðurh ligett gyf hê mǽre biþ þonne se wǽta; gyf se wǽta byð mǽre ðonne þ fýr þonne fremað hit, Lch. iii. 280, 2-9. Nis nán lichamlic þing ðe næbbe ðã feówer gesceafta him mid, þ is lyft and fýr and eorðe and wæter . . . Úre líchaman habbað ægðer ge hǽtan ge wǽtan, eorðan and lyft, 272, 27-274, 8. III. _a hot condition of the atmosphere, hot weather_:—Sió hǽte hæfð genumen þæs súðdǽles mǽre þonne se cyle þæs norððǽles hæbbe, Ors. 1, 1 ; S. 24, 28. Côm swá micel hǽte (_ita jugis et torrida siccitas_) giend Rômáne þæt ealle heora eorðwæstmas forwurdon, 2, 6 ; S. 88, 15. Cýtan árǽran þ hí wið cyle and wið hǽton hí sylfe geburgon, Hml. S. 23, 419. For þæs sumores hǽtan, Bl. H. 59, 4. Se hara þonne hê on sumura for swiðlicre hǽtan geteórud byþ, Lch. i. 226, 23. III a. _a region of hot atmosphere, a torrid zone_:—Án þæra dǽla is on ælemiddan weallende . . . þonne beóð on twá healfa þære hǽtan twêgen dǽlas gemetegode, Lch. iii. 260, 24. IV. _of bodily condition, a state of feeling hot_:—Tô eácan þǽm hié derede ægþer ge þurst ge hǽte _besides this their being so thirsty and hot injured them_, Ors. 5, 7 ; S. 230, 17. Him côm on swá nicel hǽte and swá micel þurst þ hié him heora feores ne wêndan _they got into such a state of heat and thirst that they gave up hope of life_, 6, 13 ; S. 268, 12. IV a. _a feverish or inflamed condition of body_:—Wið ðæs magan hǽtan, Lch. i. 268, 1. Deós wyrt gehǽled mænigfealde untrumnyssa . . . eágena sárnysse and hǽtan, 272, 2. V. _of intense feeling or passion_:—Hǽtan _incentiua_ (_Melantiae carnis incentiua illecebrosis stimulis agitabant_, Ald. 59, 18), An. Ox. 4226. v. lencten-, sumer-hǽte; hát.

**hǽtera**. _In bracket dele_ '_O. H. Ger._ hadarun . . . _clout_', _and add_: v. _N. E. D._ hater.

**hǽþ** _a heath_, **hǽþ** _a plant. Take these together, for_ ' e ; _f._' _substitute_ es ; _n. m., and add_: I. _a heath, a tract of uncultivated, waste land._ (1) masc. :—Andlang ðære díc tô ðǽm hǽðe foreweardan . . . ; ðonne westweard ofer ðone hǽð, C. D. iii. 264, 2-4. Úp on ðene hǽð ; ofer ðene hǽð, 384, 26. (2) neut. :—Ofer ðæt hǽð, C. D. iii. 392, 3, 5. On ðæt hǽð westeweard, 427, 33. On ðæt hǽð westeweard, v. 212, 18. v. môr-hǽþ. II. _a plant-name_:—Haeth, haet (cf. haet-colas, 53, 570), hêt _calomacus_ (-_chus_), _calomancus_, Txts. 52, 269. Hǽþ _colomacus, genesta_, Wrt. Voc. ii. 134, 35. Hǽð _calomacus_, 13, 33. Haeth, haedth, haet _thymus_, Txts. 102, 1007. Hǽþ _timus_, Wrt. Voc. i. 285, 68. Hǽð _alucurus vel thimus_, ii. 10, 38. Hǽþ _brogus_, 127, 25 : _mirica_, i. 33, 54. Smeóce mid hǽþe and þ ylce on wíne drince, Lch. i. 354, 24. ¶ _the word is found in many compounds._ (1) _as the first part of words ǽnoting localities_, hǽþ-beorh, -burh, dún, -feld, -gára, -hricg, -leáh, -slæd, v. C. D. vi. 293, 294. (2) _as part of proper names._ v. Txts. 595.

**hǽþ**, e; _f Dryness from heat, parched condition_:—Mycel hǽte _ferfor_, swaloð _cauma_, drúgað oððe hǽð _siccitas_, Wrt. Voc. i. 76, 77. [Cf. _O. H. Ger._ hei _uredo_, ge-hei _cauma_; ar-, far-heien.] _See next word, and_ hǽþung, for-hǽþan.

**hǽþa**, an; _m. Parching by heat_:—Hê gebæd þ God forgeáfe þǽre eorðan rênas, for þan ðe se hǽða þã hýnde ðã eorðan . . . þá ásende Drihten rênscúras and þã eorðan gewæterode þe ǽr wæs forburnen, Hml.

S. 14, 168. v. æfter-hǽþa (_where dele queries as to form and gender_), _and preceding word._

**hǽþan**. v. for-hǽþan; hǽþung, _and two preceding words._

**hǽþ-cole**. _Substitute_: hǽþ-cole _a plant-name_:—Haetcolae _colomata_, Wrt. Voc. ii. 105, 16. Hǽðcole _colomate_, 15, 20. Hǽþcole _stena_, i. 68, 68 (in a list of plant-names).

**hǽþen**. _Add_:—Hǽþene _geneliatici_, Wrt. Voc. ii. 40, 53. A. _as adj._ (but sometimes where used predicatively might belong to B.) I. _referring to times covered by Old and New Testaments._ (1) _of persons._ (a) _not believing in Jehovah, not of the Jewish religion_:—Giethro, ðeáh hê hǽðen and eldiódig wǽre, Past. 130, 12. Hǽðen heriges wîsa (_Nebuchadnezzar_), Dan. 203. Þ wíf wæs hǽðen Sirofênisces cynnes _erat mulier gentilis Syrophoenissa genere_, Mk. (W. S., L., R.) 7, 26. Hǽðenes heáðorinces (_Holofernes_) heáfod, Jud. 179. Hǽðnum _folce (the people of Sodom)_, Gen. 2416. Þone hǽðenan _hund (Holofernes)_, Jud. 110. Oðre þeóda, hǽðene herigeas, Ps. Th. 78, 10. (a a) _gentile_ (as used in the A.V.) v. B. I. aa :—Gerihtnes hǽþenra þeóda, Bl. H. 163, 23. Hê bið geseald hǽþnum mannum _he shall be delivered unto the Gentiles_ (Lk. 18, 32), 15, 9. Betwuxn hǽðenum monnum _among the Gentiles_ (i. Cor. 5, 1), Past. 211, 8. ¶ _the part put for the whole_:—Áhangen hǽðenum folmum, El. 1076. (b) _used of a Samaritan as opposed to a Jew_:—Samaritanus, þ is hǽðin monn, Lk. L. 10, 33. Ðes wæs hǽðin _hic erat Samaritanus_, 17, 16. (2) _of things._ Cf. II 3 :—Hǽþenu godu _dii gentium_, Ps. Th. 95, 5. Gê sǽdon þ þá hǽðnan tída wǽron beteran þonne þá crístnan, Ors. 6, 37 ; S. 296, 18. Ne swerigen gê nǽfre under hǽðene godas (_per nomen externorum deorum non jurabitis_, Ex. 23, 13), Ll. Th. i. 54, 23. II. _referring to Christian times._ (1) _of persons._ (a) _not of the Christian religion_:—Swá hwylc hǽþen (_gentilis_) man swá forlǽt hǽþen wíf . . . Gyf hyra óðer biþ hǽþen, oþer gefullod, Ll. Th. ii. 144, 12-14. Heó wæs ǽryst hǽðen and wǽlgrim . . . þá gelýfde heó on God and onfêng fulwihte, Shrn. 139, 4-7 : Hml. S. 7, 264. Astrias, hǽðen and hygeblind, Ap. 46. Hǽðen _hildfruma_, Jul. 7. Se hǽþena man, Bl. H. 223, 10. Þǽm hǽþnan _cásere (Nero)_, 171, 29. Þæt hǽðene weorod, 221, 30. Eác weard on Ispanie þ þá hǽðenan _men (the Moors)_ fôran and hergodan uppon þám Xpênan mannan . . . hí áweg ádrifan eall þet hǽðena _folc_, Chr. 1086 ; P. 221, 33-222, 3. Þeh hié (_the Goths_) hǽþene wǽre, Ors. 2, 8 ; S. 94, 9. Heora fæder and môdor [wǽron] hǽþena þá gýt, Hml. S. 5, 36. Hǽðne, Bl. H. 211, 20. Þær hǽþene men deófum onguldon, 221, 3. Manige hǽþne men ungeleáfsume, 129, 24. Be þára hǽþenra manna fleáme, 203, 4. Of hǽþenum mágum _ethnicis_ (i. _gentilibus_) _parentibus_, An. Ox. 2416: Hml. S. 31, 13. Þ man crístene menn of earde ne sylle hûru on hǽðene leóde, Ll. Th. i. 304, 16. ¶ _the part put for the whole_:—Þurh hǽðene hand, Ap. 60. (a a) _used specially of the Scandinavian invaders of England._ v. (c), B. II. 1 a :—Wit begêtan ðás bêc æt hǽðnum herge mid uncre claene feó, Txts. 175, 4. Hié wǽl geslôgon on hǽþnum herige (hǽþene here, _v. l._), Chr. 851 ; P. 64, 22 : 853 ; P. 64, 32. Hér hǽþne (hǽðene, _v.l._) men oferhergeadon Sceápige, 832 ; P. 62, 9. Ofslægen from hǽþnum monnum, 838 ; P. 62, 35. Ceorl gefeaht wiþ hǽðene men, 851 ; P. 64, 11. (b) _not baptized_:—Æghwilc cild sí gefullod binnon nigon nihton . . . and gif hǽðen cild binnon .ix. nihton þurh gímeliéste forfaren sí, Ll. Th. ii. 292, 6. Cild gyf hit hǽðen swelte. . . . Sê þe ofsleá his beam hǽðen . . . Hǽðen cild gif hit bið preóst beboden . . . and hit hǽðen swelte, 144, 32-35. Gif ungefullod cild fǽrlíce bið gebrôhte tô þám mæssepreóst, þ hê môt fullian sôna, þ hit ne swelte hǽðen, 352, 17. Cf. Gif hit bútan fulluhte gewît, 412, 24. (c) _barbarous._ Cf. (a a) :—Hǽðen _hreáfere_ [oþþe] _flotman_ ł _wícing barbarus praedo_ [_vel crudelis_] _archipirata_, Hpt. Gl. 501, 32. (2) _of monstrous beings._ Cf. B. II. 2 :—Hǽðenes _hilderinces (Grendel's)_, B. 986. Hê (_Grendel_) feorh álegde hǽðene sáwle, 852. (3) _of things, pertaining to non-Christian people, or to their religion and customs_:—Hearhlicre, þæs hǽþenan _vel templicre fanatice_, i. _profani_, Wrt. Voc. ii. 147, 38. Of hǽþenum gewunan _apostatico ritu_, An. Ox. 4920. Ic hine áwende fram hǽðenum gylde tô ðám sôðan Gode, Hml. Th. i. 468, 14. Tô þám hǽðenan temple getogen, Hml. S. 2, 384. In þære hǽþenan byrig, An. 1493. Hǽðnum horde, B. 2216. Heora hǽþenan gild wǽron ealle ídelu, Bl. H. 223, 1. Wê lǽrað þ man geswíce freólsdagum hǽðenra leóða and deófles gamena, Ll. Th. ii. 248, 11. [H]ǽðenra [bôca] _indegitamentorum_, An. Ox. 4442. Ou hǽðnum þeáwum dweligende, Bl. H. 201, 20. Hê offrode his lác þám hǽðenum godum, Hml. Th. ii. 482, 7. Hǽðeniscipe bið þ man ídola weorðige, þ is þ man weorðige hǽðene godas, Ll. Th. i. 378, 19. (3 a) _profane as opposed to sacred or Christian literature_:—Hê leornoðe grammatican cræft and þá hǽðenan bêc (cf. Shrn. 152, 11-18) oþ þá hálgan godspel him becômon tô hande, Hml. S. 35, 15. B. _as subst._ I. _of pre-Christian times._ v. A. I. (1) _of persons._ (a) _one who is not a believer in Jehovah_:—Hwurfon hæleð geonge tô þám hǽðenan (_Nebuchadnezzar_) foran, Dan. 434. Ðone ufemyston hêton þá hǽþenan Saturnus, Angl. vii. 14, 122. Wê nú hǽðenra þeówned þoliað, Dan. 307. Hǽþenra _allophilorum (the Philistines)_, An. Ox. 881 : 5018. Hê hí on handgeweald hǽðenum

sealde, Ps. Th. 105, 30. Hǽþnum, Bl. H. 171, 22. (aa) *a gentile*, in pl. *the Gentiles*. v. A. I. aa:—Alle hǽðno (hǽðno, R.) i̇ cynno middangeardes, Lk. L. 12, 30. Hǽdna i̇ cynna, Mt. L. 12, 21. Þec gelegdon on lǽðne bend hǽðene mid hondum, Sat. 540 (cf. Lk. L. R. 18, 32). Cyningas hǽðna, Lk. L. R. 22, 25 : Mt. L. 20, 25. Gesald bið hǽðnum, Lk. L. R. 18, 32. Hǽðnum, Mk. L. 10, 33, 42 : Lk. L. 21, 24. Haedno *gentiles*, Mk. p. 4, 15. (b) *a believer who is not of Jewish nationality*:—Sume wǽron hǽðene (hǽðno summo, L., hǽðno sume, R. *gentiles quidam*) þe fôron þ hig woldon hî gebiddan on ðam freólsdæge, Jn. 12, 20. Sæccendum hǽðnum (*gentilibus*) hine geseá uilnandum, Jn. p. 6, 14. (b β) *any one not of Jewish nationality*, in pl. *nations* other than the Jewish :—Ofersuíðnesse hǽðno i̇ hǽðnra (hǽðnana, R., þeóda, W. S.) *pressura gentium*, Lk. L. 21, 25. On allum hǽðnum, Mk. L. 13, 10. Gelǽeded biðon in alle hǽðno (þeóda, W. S., cynn, R. *gentes*), Lk. L. 21, 24. **II.** referring to Christian times. (1) of persons :—Nû se hǽþena ne con ûre gyfe onfôn *si paganus* (Penda) *neseit accipere nostra donaria*, Bd. 3, 24 ; Sch. 307, 16. Þ hî gehǽlan þises hǽðenan eáge, Hml. S. 4, 151. Hûsl sceal hâlgum men, hǽðnum synne, Gn. Ex. 132. Hǽðene swǽfon dreóre druncne, An. 1004. Þá hǽðnan heora þá leásan godas him lapodan on fultum, Bl. H. 201, 30. Sê þe Godes bebod oferhogaþ, hê biþ on hǽþenra onliċnesse, 49, 13. Hê wæs crîsten lǽce and hê eardode in hǽþenra midlene, Shrn. 125, 7. On hǽðenra gildum libban *paganis erroribus implicari*, Bd. 2, 1 ; Sch. 109, 21. (1 a) of the Scandinavian invaders of England. v. A. II. 1 a :—Feallan sceolon hǽðene at hilde, By. 55. Þá hǽþenan for his geleáfan wurdon wôdlîce yrre, Hml. S. 32, 113. Þá wunda þe þá wælhreówan hǽþenan on his lîce macedon, 181. Under Norðmannum gebêgde on hǽþenra hæfteclommum, Chr. 942 ; P. 110, 21. (2) of the devil. Cf. A. II. 2 :—Heó þæt deófol teáh bendum fæstne, hâlig hǽðenne, Jul. 536.

**hǽþen-dóm.** *Add :* **I.** *the belief and practice of a heathen people* :—Hǽþendômes *gentilitatis* (Gregorius nostris parentibus errorem tetrae *gentilitatis* abstulit, Ald. 74, 13), An. Ox. 5156. Hû hê of hǽþendôme mæge tô crîstendôme ðurh rihtne geleáfan and ðurh fulluht cuman, Wlfst. 32, 10. Ænne crîstendôm ânrǽdlîce healdan and ǽlcne hǽðendôm georne forbûgan, Ll. Th. i. 314, 9. Ælcne hǽðendôm oferhogian, 350, 12. Ænne God lufian and ǽlcne hǽðendôm georne âscunian, 316, 19. **II.** *people among whom (or district in which) paganism prevails*. v. Crîsten-dóm ; II :—Þ man crîstene men . . . on hǽðendôme (cf. on hǽðene leóde, 304, 16) hûru ne gebringe, Ll. Th. i. 378, 1. v. hǽþen-nes.

**hǽþen-gild.** *Dele passages from* Num. 25, 2 : 31, 16, *in* l. 10 *for* 454 *read* 456, *and add :* **I.** *idolatry* :—Swutele synd þæs flǽsces weorc . . . hǽðengild *manifesta sunt opera carnis . . . idolorum servitus* (Gal. 5, 20), Hml. S. 17, 25. Hý fulwihte onfêngon and wǽron blîðran tô ðam deáðe þonne hý hêr on hǽðengilde lifden, Shrn. 142, 13. Nis nânum crîstenum menn âlýfed þæt hê his hǽle gefecce æt nânum stâne . . . sê ðe elles dêð, hê begæð untwýlîce hǽðengild, Hml. Th. i. 474. 33. On þǽre ôþerre ylde man ârǽrde hǽðengild wîde geond þâs woruld, Ælfc. T. Grn. 4, 15 : Jul. 15. **I a.** *a particular form of idolatry* :—Tô manega of þâm folce . . . tô þâm hǽðengilde bugon *filiae Moab vocaverunt eos ad sacrificia sua. At illi comederunt et adoraverunt deos earum*, Num. 25, 2 : 31, 16. **I b.** *idolatrous worship, an idolatrous rite or practice* :—Se mânfulla wolde his hǽðengild habban (*celebrate his idolatrous worship*), Hml. S. 28, 26. Hî lêton him betweónum tân wîsian . . . hluton hellcræftum hǽðengildum (*with idolatrous rites*) teledon berymnan, An. 1104. **II.** *an idol*. Cf. deófol-gild ; II :—Þá þe hǽðengildum þeówiað *idolis servientes*, Hml. S. 17, 39. Bartholamêus þá hǽðengild hýran ne wolde, wîg weorðian (cf. Hwî tôwurpe ðû (*St. Bartholomew*) ûre godas?, Hml. Th. i. 468, 16), Ap. 47. Oft hê hǽðengield ofer word Godes weóh gesôhte, Jul. 22.

**hǽþen-gilda.** *Add : gen. pl.* -gilda :—Se fæder âna hǽðengilda wunode *the father alone remained a heathen*, Hml. Th. ii. 504, 7. Fêrde sum æðelboren man fram Alexandrian byrig tô Rôme byrig Polemius gehâten ; sê wæs hǽþengilda, Hml. S. 35, 4. Eóden þá hǽðengyldan intô heora temple clypigende tô ðam leásan gode, 4, 153. Se ealdorman wolde ðá hǽðengildan forbǽrnan . . . 'Geðafiað hûru þæt man heora ǽhta æyle sylle' . . . þá wurdon getealde ân hund þǽra hǽðengylda þe ðæs temples gýmdon, and nân man ne mihte heora ǽhta geriman, Hml. Th. ii. 484, 22. Hê ofslôh ðá hǽðengildan (cf. deofolgildan, 112) *he slew the priests of Baal*, Hml. S. 18, 155.

**hǽþenisc.** *Add :*—Þá wæs Hannibale æfter hiera hǽðeniscum gewunan þ andwyrde swiþe lâð *abominatus dictum Annibal*, Ors. 4, 10 ; S. 202, 6. Gê sǽdon þ eów selfum wǽre betere þ gê eówerne crîstendôm forlêten and tô þǽm hǽðeniscan þeáwum fênge þe eówre ieldran ǽr beeódon, 6, 37 ; S. 296, 21. [*Icel.* heiðneskr.]

**hǽþen-mann.** *l.* hǽþen mann. v. hǽþen ; A. I. 1 b.

**hǽþen-nes.** *Add :* **I.** *paganism* :—Hǽðennesse *gentilitatis*, Wrt. Voc. ii. 40, 30. Hê frægn hwæþer þá ylcan landleóde crîstene wǽron þe hî þá gýt on hǽþennesse gedwolum lifdan (*an paganis adhuc erroribus essent implicati*), Bd. 2, 1 ; Sch. 109, 19. Hê monige wæs gecîgende

fram hǽþenesse (hǽðennesse, *v. l.*) and fram gedwolan heora lîfes *multos ab errore reuocans*, 5, 11 ; Sch. 611, 5. **II.** *people among whom (or district in which) heathenism prevails* :—Wit begêtan ðás bêc æt haeðnum herge mid uncre claene feó. And ðæt wit deodan . . . for ðon ðe wit noldan ðæt ðás hâlgan beoc lencg in ðǽre haeðenesse wunoden, Txts. 175, 4-7. [v. *N. E. D.* heathenesse.] v. hǽþen-dóm.

**hǽþen-scipe.** *Add :* **I.** *the belief and practice of the heathen* :—Mânfulles hǽþenscipes bîgengcas *fanatice gentilitatis ceremonias*, An. Ox. 2623. Albanus gelýfde on ðone sôðan God, and wiðsôc þám hǽðenscype, and weard sôþlîce crîsten, Hml. S. 19, 28. His fæder wæs . . . on hǽðenscipe wunigende and his gemæcca samod, Hml. Th. ii. 498, 26. Hê âwende his môder of mânfullum hǽðenscipe . . . and his fæder forweard on fûlum hǽðenscipe, 504, 5-11. Se gerêfa þreátode hine tô hǽþenscipe, Shrn. 33, 10. Îdele leóð þe ymbe hǽðenscipe geworhte syndon, Hml. A. 142, 120. **II.** *a particular form of heathen belief* :—Þá þrý cnihtas wiðcwǽdon his (*Nebuchadnezzar's*) hǽþenscipe, Hml. A. 70, 131. **III.** *the condition of being heathen* :—Heó nolde his sanda brûcan for his hǽðenscype (*on account of his being a heathen*), Hml. A. 110, 271. Heó nolde þurh his hǽþenscype habban ǽnige synne, 115, 428. **IV.** *a heathen practice* :—Þonne heó nele âbûgan tô nânum hǽðenscipe, Hml. A. 28, 97. Hǽðwylcne hǽðenscype wordes and weorces forhogie man ǽfre, *id est idolatria et ueneficia*, . . . , Wlfst. 73, 17. **V.** *a time when (or place where) heathendom prevails* :—Þá þe secgaþ þæt þeós world sý nú wyrse on ðysan crîstendôme þonne hió ǽr on þǽm hǽþenscype wǽre, Ors. 1, 8 ; S. 40, 25.

**hǽþ-feld,** es ; *m. Open uncultivated land, a heath* :—Tô mǽde, and se hǽðfeld eal gemǽne, C. D. v, 78, 32. On ðone hǽðfeld, 177, 27. Up on þone lytlan (*printed* hone lytland) hǽþfeld, C. D. B. i. 296, 25. Forheregian swâ swâ fýres lêg ðeð drígne hǽþfeld, Bt. 16, 1 ; F. 50, 4. ¶ For the word as local name see C. D. vi. 294.

**hǽþfeld-land,** es ; *n. Moorland* :—Lindesfarona landes is syfan þû·end hýda mid hǽþfeldlande, C. D. B. i. 414, 18.

**hǽðiht.** *l.* hǽþiht(e).

**hǽðung.** *Substitute :* hǽþung, e ; *f. Parching* or *drying by heat* :—On ðǽre sunnan is hǽtu and beorhtnys ; ac seó hǽtu drýgð, and seó beorhtnys onlýht. Oðer ðing ded seó hǽtu, and ôðer seó beorhtnys, belimpð seó hǽðung tô ðǽre hǽtan, and seó onlîhting belimpð tô ðǽre beorhtnysse, Hml. Th. i. 284, 34-286, 4. v. hǽþan.

**hǽting.** *Add : Heating, warming :* hǽts, hǽtse. v. hægtesse.

**hǽtsan.** *Add :* , hǽtsan (?). *Perhaps the word may be connected with* hǽts(e) (v. hægtesse). cf.(?) *later English* hag *to incite, urge.* v. *N. E. D.*

**hǽtt.** v. hǽt : **hǽttende.** v. hatian : **hǽttian.** *Add :* v. be-hǽttian.

**hǽtu.** *Add : gen.* e :—Hǽto *calor*, Wrt. Voc. i. 291, 11. **I.** *the quality or property of being hot* :—On ðǽre sunnan is hǽtu and beorhtnys ; seó hǽtu drýgð, Hml. Th. i. 284, 35. Þǽre sunnan hǽtu wyrcð fîf dǽlas on middanearde, Lch. iii. 260, 18 : Ph. 17. Hǽto, Bl. H. 51, 21. Fýres hǽto, Dan. 262. Swîðe sweartes lîchaman heó wæs for þǽre sunnan hǽto, Hml. S. 23 b, 176. From haeto (*calore*) his, Ps. Srt. 18, 7. Þæs folces wæs fela forworden ægðer ge for þurste ge for hǽte (*ardore solis*), Ors. 6, 31 ; S. 286, 21. **II.** *heat* as an element in all bodies :—Gedweorod sint . . . cele wið hǽto, wǽt wið drýgum, Met. 20, 73. Se cyle ðið ðá hǽto and þ wǽt wið ðǽm drýgum, Bt. 33, 4; F. 128, 33 : Met. 20, 113 : 29, 50. **III.** *a hot condition of the atmosphere, hot weather* :—Deostru and lêht, cele and haetu (*caumas*), Ps. Srt. ii. p. 197, 32. Hý hit ne magon eall gebûgian, sum for hǽto, sum for cyle, Bt. 18, 1; F. 62, 10. Ælc wiht mæg bet wyð cyle þonne wið hǽte (*omnia animantia patientius ad summum frigoris quam ad summum caloris accedant*), Ors. 1, 1 ; S. 24, 30. Feáwe men mehten beón eardfæste . . . for þǽre hǽte and for þǽm stence . . . ge ealle þá fiscas âcwǽlan for þǽre hǽte, 5, 4 ; S. 226, 2-7. Ic drîfe sceáp mîne tô heora lǽse, and stande ofer hig on hǽte (*aestu*) and on cyle, Coll. M. 20, 13. **IV.** of sexual passion :—Seó gecyndelice hǽtu þurh þ mægen þæs Hâlgan Gâstes gestilleþ on þe (*the Virgin Mary*), Bl. H. 7, 27. **V.** *great warmth of feeling, fervour* :—Se rehtgeleáfa mid haetu (*calore*) walle, Ps. Srt. ii. p. 201, 17. v. lencten-, sumer-hǽtu hǽte.

**hǽtung.** *Dele.*

**hǽwe ;** *adj. Blue, grey* :—Haeuui, hâui, heáwi *cerula*, Txts. 50, 221. Hêuui *vel* grêi, hâuui *vel* grêi, heáuui, grêi *glaucum*, 66, 473. Grǽg, hǽwe *ferrugine* (cf. îsengrǽg *ferrugine*, i. *ferreo colore*, 31 : *ferrugo vel ferrugineus*, i. *color purpurae subnigrae*, Wülck. Gl. 236, 32), Wrt. Voc. ii. 35, 34. v. wann-hǽwe, *and next word*.

**hǽwen.** *Add : green* :—Hǽwen oððe grǽg gla[u]cum, Wrt. Voc. ii. 40, 72. Basu, hǽwen *indicum*, 49, 55. Grêne, hǽwen, fâh, deorc *ceruleus*, i. *glaucus. Color est inter album et nigrum, subniger*, 130, 24. Hǽwen stân *cyanea lapis*, 137, 74. Hacele hǽwen *subucula iacinthina*, An. Ox. 5318 : Wrt. Voc. ii. 87, 56. Hêwen (*ex*) *iacintho*, 77, 19. Hǽwen, *hiacineto, viridis*, An. Ox. 35, 2. Hǽwenre deáge, 1058. Þá hêwnan sǽs *marmora glauca*, Wrt. Voc. ii. 90, 43. v. blǽ-, grên-, lîn-, sweart-, wel-hǽwen, *and preceding word*.

**hǽwen-gréne;** *adj. Bluish green :*—Đā hǽwengrēnan *ceruleus,* Wrt. Voc. ii. 22, 38.

**hafa.** v. wan-hafa : **hafe,** Hpt. Gl. 504, 72. v. hafetian : **hafecere.** v. hafocere.

**hafe-geat,** es ; *n. A gate that has to be raised* (?) :—In tō hafegeæte ; of hafegeæte, C. D. iv. 157, 11. Cf. tyrn-geat.

**hafela.** *Add :*—Ne hēdde hē þæs heafolan, B. 2697. Hē him of dyde helm of hafelan, 672 : 1521. Heáfde, heafolan (heofulan, lxx. 3) eágum *capiti, fronti, oculis,* Lch. i. lxxiv. 4. Men hafelan bǽron . . . Grendles heáfod, B. 1635 : 1614. Hī Æscheres heafelan mētton, 1421. Hē hafelan onhylde, Gū. 1244. Hī woldon on þām hysebeorðre heafolan gescēnan, An. 1144. Hēt Hildeburh hire suna sweoloðe befæstan . . . hafelan multon, B. 1120. Se beorhta beág . . . eádigra gehwǽm hlífað ofer heáfde. Heafelan lixað þrymme biþeahte, Ph. 604. v. wīg-heafola.

**hafenian.** *Add: The meaning 'grasp, hold' seems supported by* O. H. Ger. hebinōn *tractare,* inthepinōt pin *sustentor, but in later English* heven *means to raise, a sense which would suit the passages.* v. N. E. D. heven (*where is quoted* Noe hiuened up an auter, Allit. Pms. 53, 506).

**-hafen-ness.** v. ā-, ūp-hafenness.

**hafetian.** *Add:* , hafettan, haftian :—Ic hafetige (afetige, hafecige, *v. ll.*) oððe fægnige *plaudo,* Ælfc. Gr. Z. 171, 7. Hafet *plaudet,* Kent. Gl. 611. Flōdas feágað t hafetiað *flumina plaudent,* Ps. L. 97, 8. Gilpað t gulpan, hafe¸tiað, -ttað?] *applaudunt,* Hpt. Gl. 504, 72. Hafetiað mid handum *plaudite manibus,* Ps. L. 46, 2. Haftud *plauditur,* Germ. 394. 220. v. beaftan.

**-hafness.** v. wan-hafness.

**hafoere.** *Take here* hafecere *in Dict., and add :*—Hafocere *falconus,* Wrt. Voc. ii. 147, 3.

**hafocung,** e ; *f. Hawking :*—On hafocunga leáhge, C. D. B. i. 280, 26.

**-hafol.** v. fæst-, wan-hafol : **-hafolness.** v. wan-hafolness : **hafud-æcer, -land.** v. heáfod-æcer, -land.

**haga.** *Add:* I. *a fence* or *a fenced enclosure :*—Haga *sepis* (*spinarum*), Kent. Gl. 527. Fram earnes beáme Cregsētna haga an eást-halfe scēd hit tō Liówsandene . . . fram swelgende Cregsētna haga tō sioxslihtre, C. D. ii. 73, 25–28 : iii. 227, 20–23. Þær se haga ūt ligeþ, Cht. E. 294, 23. Swā se haga scȳt *secundum quod sepes declinat,* C. D. B. ii. 386, 20. Andlang hagan oð cyninges healh . . . oð þone hagan, C. D. i. 257, 33–258, 1 (*and often*). On ðone hagan tō pitan wyrðe . . . ofer þone feld on hagan . . . anlang herepaðes tō ðas hagan ænde, v. 13, 23–28. Úp on Afene oð ðæt ðe se alda suīnhæga ūt sciōted tō Afene ; ðonne be ðǽm hagan, ii. 29, 11. Inn on brōc ; of ðām brōke inn on ðone hagan : æfter ðām hagan, iii. 382, 14. On ðone healdan hagan, v. 273, 6. II. *an enclosed dwelling in a town :*—In ciuitate Dorouernia duas possessiunculas et tertiam dimediam, id est in nostra loquella ðridda half haga, C. D. i. 243, 13. Duas mansiones et dimidiam quod Angli dicunt þridda hialf haga, v. 68, 24. Unam uillam quod nos Saxonico ān haga dicimus, ii. 57, 19. Se haga an Hāmtūne, iii. 443, 16. Ðis is ðes hagan embegang *circuitus eiusdem hospicii,* vi. 135, 14. Ðis is ðæs hagan bōc on Winceastre, 136, 10. Cum nouem praefatae ciuitatis habitaculis, quae patria lingua Hagan appellari soleunt, iii. 297, 11. Twēgen hagan binnan þorte, Cht. E. 239, 16. v. bōc-, deór-, gemǽr- (v. gemǽre ; II. ¶), heáfod-, imb-, mǽr-, wulf-haga ; hǽg.

**haga** *a berry.* *Add:* I. *a haw :*—Hagan *cinum,* Wrt. Voc. ii. 131, 11. [*Cinus* an haythorne and an hawe, Wlck. Gl. 572, 45.] II. *used as a type of a thing of no value :*—Hagan *gignalia,* Wrt. Voc. ii. 42, 16.

**-haga.** v. ān-haga.

**hagal** (-ol, -ul). *Add:* [*m.* and] *n.* (v. Ps. L. 147, 17). I. *hawl* (v. N. E. D. hail) :—'Ic sende micelne hagol . . . sweltað ealle þā þing þe ūte beoð and se hagoi him onufan feald.' . . . Drihten sende hagul, Ex. 9, 18–23. Eall þæt se hagol lǽfde, 10, 15. Ic āsende ælcne untīman, þæt bið egeslīce greát hagol, s¸ fordēð eówre wæstmas . . . , Wlfst. 297, 7. On hagule in *pruina,* Bl. Gl. Ia. *A hailstone :*—Hē āsendeþ gycelstān his swā swā hagalu (*buccellas*), Ps. L. 147, 17. II. *a hail-storm :*—Smelt hagol *imber serotinus,* Kent. Gl. 560. Hagelum t scūrum *imbribus,* An. Ox. 360.

**hagalian.** *Add:*—Hit hagolade seofon niht ofer ealle Rōmāne *per septem dies grando lapidum terram verberavit.* Ors. 5, 10 ; Swt. 234, 6.

**hagal-scúr.** *Add :*—Ne bið þǽr hagulscūras hearde mid snāwe *non veniet . . . nix, grando, procella,* Dōm. L. 264.

**hagal-stán.** v. haga-þorn : **hagian** *to please.* *Add:* v. ge-, of-hagian : **hagian** *to fence.* v. ymb-hagian.

**hagol-stán.** *Add :*—Ic seude ofer eów hagelstānas, and ælc ān hagel-stān weged fīf pund, Wlfst. 228, 6. Cymð rēn and hagolstānas ofer eów, 212, 24.

**hago-spind ;** *m. n.* ?l. *n., and add :*—Feger i¸ leúr t higospind ðīn *pulchra est gena tua,* Rtl. 4, 1. Heagospind *genae,* Wrt. Voc. ii. 41, 21. Heagospinnum *genis,* Lch. i. lxx, 5 : lxxiv, 6. Heagaspen *genas,*

Wrt. Voc. ii. 109, 62. Haguspind oððe þunwange *malas,* 57, 30. Hē his eagospind mid teárum leohte *lacrymarum rivulis genas rigavit,* Guth. Gr. 162, 34. v. spind.

**hago-steald ;** *adj. Young and brave, warrior :*—Æðelum kinge hȳrdon holdlīce hagestealde men, Chr. 1065 ; P. 192, 39. v. hæg-steald ; *adj.*

**hago-stealdmonn.** *Add:* v. hægsteald-mann.

**Hagustaldes-eá, -hám** *Hexham. Substitute :*—Hagustaldes-eá, Chr. 681 : 766 : 685. Hagstaldes-ee, Hagustaldee, 780. Hagustaldes-ee, Hagustaldee, 789. Eanberht Hagestaldes biscop, Hagusteald bð, t of Hagestaldes-ee, 806. Mon gehālgode on Agustald tō biscope, 685. Sum Godes þeów of þām brōþrum þǽre cyrican æt Heagostealdes-eá (Hægestealdes-, Agostaldes-, *v. ll.*) *quidam de fratribus Hagustaldensis ecclesiae,* Bd. 3, 2 ; Sch. 196, 19. Tō cyrican [tō] Heagostealdes- (Hægestealdes-, *v. l.*) eá, 4, 12 ; Sch. 414, 18 : 5, 23 ; Sch. 691, 18. Hē Cūðberht gehālgode tō biscope tō Hagustaldes-hām, Chr. 685. v. hæg-steald.

**hagu-þorn** (**hago-**), es ; *m. A hawthorn.* *Take here* haga-þorn *in Dict., and add :*—Hagudorn, heagoðorn *alba spina,* Txts. 36, 19.

**hal** *a corner.* v. healh.

**hál.** *Add:* I. *whole.* (1) *not divided :*—Gif hit tōdǽled biþ, þonne ne biþ hit nō hál, Bt. 34, 12 ; F. 152, 28. (2) *with no part wanting :*—Befeste þē hālne Gode *Deo te totum committe,* Solil. H. 53, 12. II. *of physical well-being.* (1) *whole, hale, sound, in good health.* (a) *of a living thing :*—Hē is gīt hāl and gesund *viget incolumis,* Bt. 10 : F. 28, 14. Þū eart swīþe geselig nū þū gīt liofost and eart hāl, 35. Ælc wuht wolde bión hāl and libban ðāra þe mē cwica ðincþ, 34, 10 ; F. 148, 15. Cild full hāl and full æltǽwe geboren, 38, 3 ; F. 200, 22. For hwī se gōda lǽce selle ðām hālum men sēftne drenc and ōþrum hālum strangne, 39, 9 ; F. 226, 11. Ne mæg se unhāla þām hālan gelīce byrðene āhebban, Ll. Th. i. 412, 8. Hig gemētton hālne (*sanum*) þone þe ǽr untrum wæs, Lk. 7, 10. Ne beþurfon nā ðā hālan (*sani*) lǽces, Mk. 2, 17. Ðā hālan (ðā truman, 5) *incolumes,* Past. 247, 3. Nys hālum *valentibus*) lǽces nān þearf, ac seócum, Mt. 9, 12. Sume mid þǽre rāde earniaþ þ hié sién ðy hālran, Bt. 34, 7 ; F. 144, 8. (b) *of a part of a living thing :*—Næfð nān man tō þæs hāl eágan þæt . . . , Solil. H. 34, 21. Swā swā þæs līchoman æágan hālren beóð, 44, 27. Þām hālestan hālestum æágum, 47, 9. (b a) *figurative :*—þ hē beleác on hālre tungon (*in plain, unequivocal language.* The later Latin version renders the passage : Qui statim conclusit et omnino confirmavit totum quod pater suus in vita sua fecerat), Cht. E. 212, 9. Forgif ūs hāle eágan ūres-mōdes, Bt. 33, 4 ; F. 132, 31. (c) *of a person's condition :*—Be his hālan lȳfe *while in a sound state of health,* Chr. 614 ; P. 22, 22 : 616 ; P. 22, 34 : 1052 ; P. 183, 17. (2) *uninjured :*—Nō þȳ ǽr inn gescōd hālan līce, B. 1503. Hāl and uuscendede hond gilǽde *salvam et inlesam manum educat,* Rtl. 102, 37. Hyssas hāle hwurfon iu þām hātan ofne, Dan. 271. (3) *where health is gained, freed from sickness, cured, whole after injury :*—Ic beó hāl (*salva*) gyf ic hys reáfes æthrīne, Mt. 9, 21. þ heó hāl (*salva*) sȳ and lybbe, Mk. 5, 23. Hāl bið (byð gehǽled, W.S. *sanabitur*) cnæht mīn, Lk. 7, 7. Gif hē slǽpð, hē byþ hāl (*saluus*), Jn. 11, 12. Dryhten wine sunne grētte, . . . hēht his līchoman hāles brūcan . . . Ārās þā mægene rōf . . . hāl, næs him gewemmed while, . . . bān gebrocen, An. 1472. Hālne *valentem sospitem* (Ald, 40, 1), Wrt. Voc. ii. 81, 4. Hié hine on rōde āhēngan . . . hē hine hālne and gesundne ðy ðriddan dæge æteówde, Bl. H. 177, 27. Þīn (*the blind man's*) geleáfa þē hāle (*saluum*) gedyde, Mk. 10, 52. Hī wurdon hāle *salui fiebant,* Mk. 6, 56. Hālum monnum *sanatis hominibus,* Mt. p. 15, 19. (3 a) *of a part of a living body :*—þæt mǽden (*a girl born dumb*) hæfde hire sprǽce mid hālre tungan, Hml. S. 31, 1118. Hālne *incolumem* (*pupillam evulsam*), An. Ox. 3471. (3 b) *where the sickness from which a person is freed is given.* (a) *with gen. :*—Hē byþ þæs sāres hāl, Lch. i. 352, 2. (β) *with inst. :*—Hē bið ece hāl, Lch. ii. 308, 2. (γ) *with prep. :*—Hāl from februm (ridesohte, R.), Mk. 1, 31. Hāl uēre (wearþ gehǽled, W.S.) from ādle *sanus fiebat a languore,* Jn. L. R. 5, 4. Hē wæs hāl geworden of ðām eórede *sanus factus est a legione,* Lk. 8, 36. III. *of mental health, sane, sound* (mind) :—Wōd *rabidus vel insanus,* hāl *sanus,* Wrt. Voc. i. 75, 57. Hāl angyt, Solil. H. 28, 3. Hāles mōdes *sane mentis,* Mk. 5, 15. Hālum mōde *sana mente,* Lk. 8, 35. Þū ǽr witan scalt hweðer wit hāle sién *videamus utrum sani simus,* Solil. H. 32, 13. Andgit swā swā þæt hālre byð swā hyt māre geseón mæg þǽre ǽcean sunnan, 45, 2. IV. *of moral or spiritual health :*—Dōð eówre heortan hige hāle and clǽne, Ps. Th. 61, 8. V. *safe.* (1) *secure against impending danger :*—Gefultuma mē, ðonne beó ic hāl (*salvus ero*), Ps. Th. 118, 117. Dryhten, dō mē hālne *Domine, salvum me fac,* 117, 23. (β) *uninjured by danger incurred, saved from peril :*—Būton þā dagas gescyrte wǽrun, nære nān mann hāl geworden (*non fieret salua omnis caro*), Mt. 24, 22. þ hit mǽge hāl and orsorg fleógan tō his earde *ut perturbatione depulsa sospes in patriam revertaris,* Bt. 36, 1 ; F. 172, 33. Hē þone hilderǽs hāl gedīgeð, B. 3co : Gn. Ex 106. Gedō mē hālne, ālȳs mē fram lāðu⁽ᵘⁱ⁾, Ps. Th. 53, 1. þā hē wearð

gedofen hē cwæð, 'Drihten, gedó mē hālne,' Mt. 14, 30. Óðero hālo dyde, hine seolfne ne mæge hālne dōa, Mt. L. 27, 42. Hē hyne hālne gefēng, Lk. 15, 27. (ββ) with gen. of peril from which one is saved. Cf. II. 3 b :—Hē lifigende cwōm heaðolāces hāl tó hofe gongan, B. 1974. (2) saved from spiritual danger :—Sē ðe þurhwunað oð ende, sē býð hāl (salvus), Mt. 24, 13 : 10, 22. Hwā mæg hāl beon ?, Mt. R. L. 19, 25. Sē þe gelýfð and gefullod biþ, sē biþ hāl, Mk. 16, 16. Hē hys folc hāl gedeð fram hyra synnum, Mt. 1, 21. God wile þ ealle menn hāle beón, Hml. S. 30, 92 : Lk. 8, 12. VI. in forms of greeting. (1) with verb :—Hāl westū, Maria ave, Maria, Bl. H. 143, 17 : Lch. iii. 54, 18. Wes þū, Hróðgār, hāl, B. 407. (2) alone :—Hāl (hāl beó þū, W.S.), lāruwa have, Rabbi, Mt. L. R. 26, 49. Hāl (hāl wæs þū, W.S.), cynig Jūdēana, 27, 29 : Mk. L. R. 15, 18 : Lk. L. R. 1, 28. v. hæg-, sām-, wan-hāl.

-hala. v. ge-hala.

halan. Substitute for 'halan . . . afterbirth': hala, an; m. The after-birth; secundae, secundina (cf. cild-hama secundae, Wlck. Gl. 159, 31 : secundina pellis in qua concipitur infans, 677, 42), and add: [cf. O. H. Ger. halu tegmine.]

hāl-bǽre. For 'Scint. . . Lye' substitute: (1) of things :—Gesceád hālbǽre ratio salutaris, Scint. 206, 14. Sīþfætes hǽlbǽres itineris salutaris, 206, 17. Him hí syllan andetnesse hālbǽrne lǣcedóm sibi dent confessionis salubre remedium, Angl. xiii. 394, 408. Hālbǽre salutiferam, Germ. 389, 6. (2) of persons, that promotes the wellbeing of others :—Freónd hālbǽrne ic nā gescynde amicum salutarem non confundor, Scint. 195, 11.

hāletttan. Add: , hǽlettan :—Gif gē hālettaþ (salutaveritis) eówre bróþer, Mt. R. 5, 47. Hǽleteþ þæt hús salutate domum, 10, 12. Þā se biscop tó mē cwōm, ðā grētte hē mē sóna and [h]ālette his leóðþeáwe cum me more rituque salutaret, Nar. 27, 17. Ic, Bēda, Crístes ðeów and mæssepreóst, sende grētan þone leófostan cyning and hālettan Ceólwulf gloriosissimo regi Ceoluulfo Baeda famulus Christi et Presbyter, Bd. praef. : Sch. 1, 3. [O. H. Ger. heilazen salutare.] v. ge-hālettan.

hālettend. Add: cf. scyte-finger.

hāl-fæst. For 'Lye' substitute :—His sáule gyltas . . . onwreoða . . . suman swā gāstlicum brēðer þe hālfæst sý and his sáule wundela gehǽlan cunne (spiritali seniori qui sciat curare sua vulnera), R. Ben. 72, 6.

hālga. Add :—Þū eart Godes hālga, Mk. 1, 24. Wē sungon be eallum hālgum cantavimus de omnibus sanctis, Coll. M. 33, 27. v. sundor-hālga.

hālgian. Add: I. to make holy, sanctify :—Hālgig t hālga ðū (gehālga, W.S., R.) hiá . . . Fore him ic hālgiga (hālgige, W.S., gihālgo, R.) mec seolfne sanctifica eos . . . þro eis ego sanctifico me ipsum, Jn. L. 17, 17-19. II. to consecrate, set apart as sacred to God, dedicate to a religious office or use :—On þissum geáre man hālgode þet mynster æt Westmynster . . . hine man bebyrgede innan þǽre nīwan hālgodre circean on Westmynstre, Chr. 1066 ; P. 195, 3-197, 2. Ciricean hālgian, Bl. H. 205, 24. II a. to consecrate a person to an office :—Þeodorus biscop hine hālgode, Chr. 670 ; P. 35, 17. Þīs ilcan geáre man gehālgode Tatwine tó arcebiscop . . . hine hālgodan Daniel and Ingwold . . . and Aldwine . . . and Aldulf, 731 ; P. 45, 8. Hine man hālgode tó cinge, Ll. Lbmn. 214, 25. II b. to bless a thing so that it possesses special virtue :—Þū sunnandæg sylf hālgodest and gemǽrsodest hine manegum tó helpe, Hy. 9, 25. Gif hwā ordāles weddige þonne cume hē . . . tó þǽm mæssepreóste þe hit hālgian scyle, Ll. Th. i. 210, 27. Hālgiende exorcizans (vir Deo deditus liquidas fontium limphas exorcizans et sacrae benedictionis ubertate foecundans, Ald. 37, 30), Wrt. Voc. ii. 80, 42. Hālgiende, 31, 11. II b β. to consecrate the Eucharistic elements :—Swā oft swā man hūsel hālgað, Ll. Th. i. 360, 33. III. to honour as holy :—Hy. 5, 2 (in Dict.). IV. to keep a day holy, Bl. H. 37, 32 (in Dict.). v. ge-hālgian, un-hālgod.

hālgung. Add: I. consecration. v. hālgian ; II :—Ne sind ealle cyricean nā gelícre mǣde weoruldlíce wurðscipes wyrðe, þeáh hig godcundlíce hālgunge habban gelíce, Ll. Th. i. 360, 17. I a. consecration of a person to an office. v. hālgian ; II a :—Hér forðférde biscop Aðelwold, and seó hālgung þæs æfterfilgendon bisceopes . . . wæs xiii. Kt. Noū, Chr. 984 ; P. 124, 3. Þǽr wǽron æt his hālgunge twēgen ercebisceopas, 979 ; P. 122, 23. I b. blessing that imparts special virtue. v. hālgian ; II b :—Hālgunge gecrīstnad exorcismi catacizatus (ecclesiastico exorcismo catechizatus, Ald. 57, 24), Wrt. Voc. ii. 84, 55 : 31, 12. Nā bēte nān man þ fýr (the fire at the ordeal) nā læuge þonne man þā hālgunge onginne, Ll. Th. i. 226, 26. I b β. consecration of the Eucharistic elements. v. hālgian ; II b β :—Micel is seó hālsung and mǣre is seó hālgung þe deófla āfyrsað . . . swā oft swā man fullað oþþe hūsel hālgað, Ll. Th. i. 360, 32. II. hallowing, holding in honour as holy. v. hālgian ; III :—Seó hālgung þæs mǣran naman Godes ongann ūs mannum þā þā Críst weard geflǣschamed ; ac seó ylce hālgung wunað on ēcnysse, for ðan ðe wē on ðām ēcan lífe bletsiað and herigað ǽfre Godes naman, Hml. Th. i. 270, 20-23. v. ciric-, crism-,

fant-, ge-, getimber-, healh-(?), hūsel-, sealt-, templ-, wæter-hālgung.

hālgung-bóc a benedictional :—Ic eom hālgungbóc, healde hine Dryhten þe mē fægere þus frætewum belegde, Nap. 35.

hālian. Add : , hālig(e)an. I. of physical health, to heal (intrans.). (1) the subject a person, to recover from wounds or illness :—Hē ongan trumian and hāligean sanescere coepit, Bd. 4, 22 ; Sch. 456, 11. (2) the subject a body or part of it :—Ðonne cōlað se līchoma and hālað, Lch. i. 82, 10. Smyre þ neb mid ; þonne smeþað hyt and hālað, 86, 9. Smyre þā sāran gōman mid oþ þ hý hāligen, 348, 17. (3) the subject a wound, sore, &c. :—Lege on þā wunde ; þonne hālað heó sóna, Lch. i. 88, 23. Sió wunde wolde hāligean (hālian, v. l.), æfter ðæm ðe hió wyrmsde, Past. 258, 1. (4) the subject an indefinite hit :—Gif men his leoðu acen . . . ðonne hālað hyt sóna (cf. gif hund man tóslíte . . . ðonne bið hit sóna hāl, 15), Lch. i. 86, 23, 4. Wyrc him sealfe ðæt hit hālige, iii. 40, 16. II. to be saved. v. hāl ; V. 2 :—Geþencean wē eác, gif óþer nýten wǽre tó hāligienne and geteód tó þon ēcan lífe, þonne onfénge hē (Christ) heora híwe, Bl. H. 29, 5. [O. H. Ger. heilēn sanescere.] v. ge-, wan-hālian.

hālig. Add: A. adjectival. I. set apart for religious use, consecrated, sacred :—Hālig leger cimiterium, Wrt. Voc. i. 34, 9. Seó stōw þe þū on stynst ys hālig eorðe (sancta terra), Ex. 3, 5. Æfter gewuna dæges hālges (diei festi), Lk. L. R. 2, 42. On ðāge hāligum (hāligum, R.), Mk. L. 14, 2. On hālgum beorge in monte sancto, Ps. Th. 98, 10. On hāligre stōwe, Mt. 24, 15. On þā hālgan ceastre, 4, 5. On þ hālige templ, Bl. H. 71, 17. Hālig tiber, Exod. 415. Hālige dagas kalendae, Wrt. Voc. i. 53, 35. Hūslfatu hālegu, Dan. 705. Is þeós tíd ealra tíd hēhst and hālgost, Bl. H. 83, 19. Alh heáhst and hāligost, Exod. 394. Betwux ðām hālegestan (hālgestan, v. l.) hālignessum, Past. 135, 9. I a. where the person to whom a thing is dedicated, in respect to whom a thing is holy, is given :—Ælc wǽpned býð Drihtne hālig (sanctum) genemned, Lk. 2, 23 : El. 1195. Hē wæs sācerd in þǽre hālgan cirican, seó wæs hālig þǽre eádigan fǽmnan, Gr. D. 88, 4. On þone Drihten þe þes hāligdōm is fore hālig, Ll. Th. i. 178, 3, 12. Intó Níwan mynstre ǽnne sylfrene hwer on þǽre hālgan þrynnesse naman þe seó stōw is fore hālig (cf. wið Godd geborgen znd Sēs Iōhannes and ealra ðǽra hālgena þe seó hālige stōww is fore gehālgod, 391, 26), Cht. Th. 559, 1. II. used of Deity ;—Hālig, hālig, hālig, Drihten God allmæhtig, Mt. p. 10, 7 : Gen. 97 : 642 : Ps. Th. 98, 9. Hālig is heofonríces Weard, 10. Hāliga Fæder Pater Sancte, Ju. 17, 11. Hālig Godes Sunu, Bl. H. 7, 24. Þū eart þæt hālige lamb, Hy. 8, 22. Se Hālega (Hālga, v.l.) Gǽsð, Past. 93, 1. On þǽre hālgan þrynnesse naman, Cht. Th. 558, 36. Úres þæs hālgan Godes Dei nostri, Ps. Th. 133, 2. II a. of a heathen deity :—God, hēhst and hālgost (Jupiter), Met. 26, 38. III. of persons considered to be specially devoted to, or directed by, God, e. g. angels, prophets, apostles, saints ; the epithet tends to become a mere title, cf. saint, reverend :—Sió hālge gecynd angels, Cri. 1018. Se hāliga (hālga, v. l.) wer (Moses), Past. 51, 17 : (Nathan), 185, 22 : (St. Paul), 99, 17 : (St. Andrew), An. 168 : (St. Guthlac), Gū. 79. Se hālga Bēda, Hml. S. 26, 272. Heáhfæderas hālige, An. 877. Hālige wītigan, Sat. 460. Þā gesetton hālige fæderas and Godes folces lāreówas þā tíd þæs fæstenes, Bl. H. 27, 25. Þā hāligan martyras, Bt. 11, 2 ; F. 36, 5. Mid hālgum englum, Mk. 8, 38. III a. used of any part of such persons :—Se hālga innoð þǽre ā clǽnan, Bl. H. 11, 20. Hālgan stefne, Exod. 257 : An. 56. Martiras herigað Hēhfæder hālgum steinum, Sat. 656 : An. 723. Hē (St. Guthlac) his eágan ontýnde hālge heáfdes gimmas, Gū. 1276. IV. of things. (1) that pertain to God :—Is þín nama hālig, An. 542. Seó ród . . . hālig, El. 625. Ðǽre hǽlga rōdes sancte crucis, Rtl. 94, 9 : 120, 9. Of his þǽm heán hālgan setle de excelso sancto suo, Ps. Th. 101, 17 : Gen. 260. Hē þē gebohte blōde þý hālgan, Seel. 30. Flōd wæs āðæled hālgum mihtum, Gen. 151. (2) that have their origin or sanction from God :—Hālig gewrit sancta scriptura, Wrt. Voc. ii. 6, 2. Hāliges gewrites scripturae, An. Ox. 40, 7. Hē (Peter) onféng þone ealdordōm ðǽre hālgan cíericean, Past. 115, 8. On cyrclicere t hāligere hālsunge ecclesiastico i. sancto exorcismo, An. Ox. 4082. Hē hí heofonhlāfe hālige (pane caeli) gefylde, Ps. Th. 104, 35. Þis hālige godspel, Bl. H. 15, 30. Þurh þ hālige fulwiht, 77, 3. Gif gē gehealdað hālige lāre, Exod. 560. Þurh þín hālig word, An. 1420. Gāstgifu vel hāligu carismata, dona, Wrt. Voc. ii. 129, 5. Hālige gewreotu, Bl. H. 17, 21. (3) of divine operations (ordinary or extraordinary) in the physical world :—Wæs hālig leóht ofer wēstenne, swā se wyrhta bebeád, Gen. 124. Cōm morgen . . . hālig of heolstre, An. 243. Cōm wuldres tācen hālig of heofenum swylce hāðre sægl, 89 : 1020. Hālig God oferbrǽdde hālgan nette (the pillar of cloud) hāt-weudne lyft, Exod. 74. Hālge gimmas, sunne and mōna, Cri. 692. Hihte ic tó þínra handa hālgum dǣdum in operibus manuum tuarum exultabo, Ps. Th. 91, 3. V. conformed to the will of God, free from sinful affection. (1) of persons, of godly character and life :—Ælc gefullod man sý æfter his fulluhte hālig, Wlfst. 154, 19. Þ nǽre nǽfre nǽnig tó þæs hālig mon, Bl. H. 117, 26. Hē wiste þ hē wæs

rihtwís and hálig, Mk. 6, 20. Hié (*Abraham and Sarah*) sǽton bútú hálig on hige, Gen. 2780. Hié wilniađ đæt hié mon hæbbe for đá betstan and đá hálgestan, Past. 135, 20. (1 a) used of any part of such persons :—Herian God hálgum reorde, Hy. 3, 58. Eorþe wældreóre swealh hálge, Gen. 1017. Manige hálige líchaman *multa corpora sanctorum*, Mt. 27, 52. (2) of actions, feelings, &c. :—Biþ þ clǽre fæsten and hálig, Bl. H. 37, 31. Hálegu treów, Gen. 2118. Hælges hygtes *sanctae spei*, Rtl. 3, 26. Hálgan hyhtes, Cri. 58. Hálgum *sanctae* (*uirginitati*), An. Ox. 960. Hálgum sige *sancta uictoria*, 2936. Be hálgum lífe *de conuersatione*, 4533. Fæsten and hálige wæccan, Bl. H. 73, 27. þæt wē tó þám hýhstan hrófe gestígan hálgum weorcum, Cri. 750. þǽr þǽr mon mete and drync for sóđre Godes lufan seleđ, hyt biđ swíđe gód weorc, and hit biđ gemong óđrum hálgum weorcum geteald, Ll. Th. ii. 432, 15. **VI.** of animals, *not destructive* or *dangerous, tame* cattle as opposed to *wild* beasts :—Inc is hálig feoh and wilde deór on geweald geseald, Gen. 201. **B.** substantival. **I.** *that which is holy, a holy thing.* Cf. **A.** **I.** :—Húse þínum hálig gedafenađ *domum tuam decent sancta*, Ps. Th. 92, 7. þæt weófod biđ hálegra hálig *altare erit sanctum sanctorum*, Ex. 29, 37. þ hálige đe of þē ácenned býđ *that holy thing that shall be born of thee*, Lk. 1, 35. Ne sellađ gē hálig (þ hálige, W.S. *sanctum*) hundum, Mt. R. L. 7, 6. **II.** *a holy place* :—Ic đē on hálgum ætýwe *in sancto apparui tibi*, Ps. Th. 62, 2. **III.** *a holy person.* (1) of a divine person. Cf. **A.** **II.** :—Háliges (*Christ's*) hyhtplega, Cri. 737. Gréne stondađ gehroden háliges meahtum beorhtast bearwa, Ph. 79 : Met. 29, 55 : Ps. Th. 113, 2. Hálges, Th. 399 : Gú. 814. Gif wē ús tó þám hálgan (*Christ*) helpe geléfađ, Sat. 291. Hálgostes blǽd on blá[wende] *Sacrosancti flatus* (i. *spiritus*) *inspirans*, An. Ox. 1526. (2) *a saint, prophet,* &c. Cf. **A.** **III.** :—Hē (*St. Matthew*) geseh swǽsne geféran (*St. Andrew*), hálig hálgne, An. 1012, Heó (*St. Juliana*) þæt deófol teáh, ... hálig hǽdenne, Jul. 536. Seó hálge ongon frignan, 345 : 589. Háliges (*Moses'*) láre, Exod. 307 : (*St. Andrew's*), An. 895 : 1391. Hálges (*St. Guthlac's*) lára, Gú. 979. Háligre (*St. Juliana's*) fæder, Jul. 61. Weard þǽre hálgan hyht geníwad, 607. þæt þám hálgan (*Noah*) wæs sár on móde, Gen. 1592 : An. 48. þǽre hálgan, Jul. 246. Englas and heáhfæderas and wítgan and ealle hálige, Bl. H. 103, 33. Hálge and gecorene, Past. 467, 32. Hí hálge cwelmdon, bærndon gecorene, Jul. 15. (3) *a godly person.* Cf. **A.** **V.** I :—þurh Crístes sige ealle hálige wǽron gefreólsode, þá þe him þeówiaþ on hálignesse, Bl. H. 31, 33. Eardungstów Godes his hálgan (*sancti eius*) synt, An. Ox. 40, 38. On gesyhđe þára háligra *ante conspectum sanctorum*, Ps. Th. 51, 8. Háligra helm, Cri. 529. Scyldigra scolu áscyred weorđed from hálgum, 1609. þínum þám hálgum, Ps. Th. 73, 4. Ne forlǽt God nǽfre his hálge, 36, 27. Mánfulle ... hálige under heora sótum þryccaþ, Bt. 4 ; F. 8, 14. Hí þíne hálgan yfeladan, Ps. Th. 82, 3. **IV.** *a sacred rite* (?), *consecration* :—Níuæs timbredes húses hálgum (hálgung?) *encenia*, Jn. p. 6, 6. v. eall-, efen-, fant-, gást-, heofon-, þurh-, un hálig.

**hálig-dæg.** Add :—Giward háligdæg (-doeg, L.) *facto sabbato*, Mk. R. 6, 2.

**hálig-dóm.** Add : **I.** *holiness, sanctity.* (1) of human beings. Cf. hálig ; **A.** **III.** **V.** :—Háligdóm is fullneáh ásprungen and sóđfæstnes swýđe gelytlod *defecit sanctum, diminutae sunt veritates*, Ps. Th. 11, 1. Háligdómes *sanctimonie* (Christus, zelotypus *sanctimoniae* informator, Ald. 6, 35), Wrt. Voc. ii. 75, 58. Hē for his háligdómes (*sanctitatis*) mycelnesse weard manigra mynstra fæder, Gr. D. 26, 13 : 246, 22. (2) of the Deity. Cf. **A.** **II.** :—Bespreng mē mid þínum háligdóme, swá swá mid ýsopon, þæt ic beó geclǽnsod, Ps. Th. 50, 8. **II.** *a holy thing, something held sacred.* (1) *from its connexion with the Deity* :—Beforan đǽre earce đe se háligdóm (*the two tables of stone*) on wæs đæs temples *coram testamenti arca*, Past. 103, 5. (2) *from its connexion with Christ or a saint, a relic or collection of relics.* (a) *a single relic* :—Hēr swutelađ be þám hálgum reliquium þe Æþelstán geaf in tó sancta Marian mynstre on Exancestre ... Nú wille wē eów secgan ... hwæt ánra gehwilc þǽra háligdóma bié. Ǽrost of þám sylfan deórwyrđan treówe þǽre hálgan róde ..., C. D. B. ii. 389, 3-38. (b) *a collection of relics* :—Se ilca kyning Æþelstán sende ofer sǽ getríwe men and gesceádwíse and hig férdon swá wíde landes swá hig faran mihton and begeáton þá deórwurđestan mádmas þe ǽfre ofer eorđan begiten mihton beón, þ wæs háligdóm se mǽsta of gehwilcum stówum wýdan and sýdan gegaderod ... Hē ... þone þryddan dǽl þæs foresǽdan háligdómes þyder inn (*into St. Peter's Minster at Exeter*) lēt dón .. eallum þám tó hylpe þe þá hálgan stówwe þe se háligdóm on is mid geleáfan gesēcađ. Nú wille wē eów secgan ... hwæt se háligdóm is ... Ǽrost ..., C. D. B. ii. 389, 19-39. Hæbbe hē Godes unmiltse and æalles đæs háligdómes (cf. ic eów hálsige fer ealle đá hálgan reliquias đe gind ealne middangeard sindon, Rtl. 114, 18) đe ic (*Æthelstan*) on Angelcyn begeat, 315, 22. Hire scrín mid hiræ háligdóme, C. D. iii. 360, 8. Sende Benedictus twǽgen his muneca tó Maure mid lácum, þ is mid háligdóme of þæs Hǽlendes róde and of Marian reáfe and of Stephanes líchaman and of Martines reliquium, Hml. S. 6, 72. Sum

wudewe wolde efsian ǽlce geáre þone sanct (*St. Edmund*) and his næglas ceorfan and on scrýne healdan tó báligdóme on weófode, 32, 194. Gá man mid háligdóme út and mid háligwætere, Wlfst. 173, 13. Út ealle mid hálidóme, 181, 3. Gif hwá mǽne áđ on háligdóme (*super sancta*) swerige, Ll. Th. i. 398, 4. **III.** *a holy place, place specially appointed for worship* :—þá burh Hierusalem, þǽr biđ heora háligdóm, Hml. A. 106, 136. **IV.** *holy doctrines* :—Đonne hē wilnađ đæt hē háligdóm lǽre *cum sancta studet dicere*, Past. 383, 7.

**háligdóm-hús,** es ; *n. A place where holy things are kept, a sacrarium* :—Beón út ágáne diácon and pistelrǽdere of (on, MS.) háligdómhúse mid líchaman Drihtnes *egrediantur diaconus ac subdiaconus de sacrario cum corpore Domini*, Angl. xiii. 422, 818.

**hálig-ern.** Add :—Háligern *archanum*, Germ. 395, 42. Đæt háliern weard geopenod and þá !ác wǽron in gebróhte, Ap. Th. 24, 6. On hálierne *sacello*, An. Ox. 3237. Ođ ic ingá on háligern *donec intrem in sanctuarium Dei*, Ps. Rdr. 72, 17. Of háligetnum *de sacrariis*, Germ. 392, 43.

**háliglíce ;** *adv. Holily* :—Sē byđ Gode geþeódd, sē đe hyt háliglíce dēđ, Nap. 35.

**hálig-mónaþ.** Add :—Se mónaþ (*September*) þe wē nemnađ háligmónođ, Mart. H. 182, 26.

**hálig-nes.** Add : **I.** *holiness.* v. hálig ; **A.** **V.** :—Hēr wæs Ósuuald ofslagen ... þæs hálines and wundor wǽron manig'ealde gecýdde geond đis ēgland (cf. cujus quanta fides in Deum, quae deuotio mentis fuerit, etiam post mortem uirtutum miraculis claruit, Bd. 3, 9), Chr. 641 ; P. 27, 24. þǽre hálignesse hús *domus sanctitatis*, Bl. H. 163, 11. **II.** *holiness of* God. v. hálig ; **A.** **II.** :—Heriađ Drihten, and andetađ þæt gemynd his hálignesse (*sanctitatis ejus*), Ps. Th. 29, 3. On munt hálignesse hís (*sanctificationis suae*), Ps. Vos. 77, 54. **III.** *sanctity, saintliness.* v. hálig ; **A.** **III.** :—Đonne biđ đæt gold ásueartod, đonne sió hálignes monnes lífes (cf. hwelc æfter hálgum háde, 25) biđ mid eorđlicum weorcum gewemmed *aurum obscuratur, cum terrenis actibus sanctitatis vita polluitur*, Past. 133, 21. **IV.** *holiness, sanctity of a rite.* v. hálig ; **A.** **IV.** 2 :—Đurh þæs hálgan fulluhtes hálignesse, Wlfst. 154, 19. **V.** *an object held sacred* :—Ic hálsige þe þurh ealle háliguyssa (*sanctitates*) þe synt on heofonan and on eorđan, and þurh þæne fulluht ařd Crístendóm þe þú underfangen hæfst, Ll. Lbmn. 413, 20. **VI.** *a holy place.* Cf. hálig ; **B.** **II.** :—Đu on đínre hálignesse hēr ásprǽce *Deus locutus est in sancto suo*, Ps. Th. 59, 5. **VII.** *religious worship, rites* or *practices* :—Fram þám bisceope hiora hálignesse þe hí ǽr beeódon *a pontifice sacrorum suorum*, Bd. 2, 13 ; Sch. 167, 16. [Cf. Ich wulle halinesse to mine goden halden and swiđe heom wurđen, Lanm. 8049.]

**hálig-portic,** es ; *n. A sanctuary* :—Ic ingá on Godes háligportic (*sanctuarium*), Ps. Vos. 72, 17 : 73, 7 : 82, 13. (*Perhaps* hálig portic *should be taken* ; portic *seems neuter*, Hml. Th. i. 508, 10).

**hálig-rift,** e ; *f. Substitute :* es ; *n., and add* :—Mynecena tácen is þæt þú sette þíne twégen scytefingras on þín heófod foran and stríce siþþan áđúne andlang þínra hleóra on þæs háligryftes tácnunge, Tech. ii. 129, 6. Háligrefte *theristro* (*viduitatis*), An. Ox. 2, 441. Hálirefte 5243.

**hálig-wæter.** Add :—Gá man mid háligdóme út and mid háligwætere, Wlfst. 173, 13. Sprænge se mæssepreúst háligwæter ofer hig ealle, Ll. Th. i. 226, 23.

**hál-ness.** v. wan-hálness.

**háls.** In l. 1 *after* 'forgeaf' *add* : , gefreóde and gefreođade folc under wolcnum, *and at end* : v. mund-heáls : **háls-bóc.** v. heáls-bóc : **halscod.** v. healsed.

**hálsere.** Add : *a soothsayer* (?), *diviner, an augur* :—Hálsere *commentarius* (cf. commenta, i. ficta, fraudes, 39), Wrt. Voc. ii. 132, 42. Hálseras *extipices*, i. *auruspices*, 145, 18. v. hælsere.

**hálsian, héalsian.** *Substitute* : **hálsian, halsian** (?), **healsian.** **I.** *to beseech, entreat, make solemn appeal to* :—Ic hálsie *obtestor, deprecor*, Germ. 402, 88. (1) *where entreaty is made in the interests of the speaker.* (a) *with acc. of person addressed* :—Beó þú Gode underþýd, and hálsa hine (*obsecra eum*), Ps. Th. Srt. Vos. 36, 7. (b) *with acc. of person and clause of entreaty* :—Ic đē halsige (healsige, *v. l.*) þ đú mē secge *quaeso te*, Bt. 38, 4 ; F. 202, 21. Ic þe halsige þ þú mē nó leng ne lette, 36, 3 ; F. 174, 32. Ic þē hálsie þæt þú ús miltsie, Hö. 107. Ic hálsige and gebidde mē tó đē þæt ..., Hy. 3, 47. Hē halsaþ (healsaþ, *v. l.*) ǽlcne ... þ hē for hine gebidde, Bt. prooem. ; F. viii. 11. Đec wē hálsiađ đæt úre haele wunde, Ps. Srt. ii. p. 204, 9. (b a) *where the entreaty is emphasized by connecting it with something sacred or highly esteemed* :—Ic hálsige (hálsigo, L. R. *adinro*) þē đurh God þ đú mē ne þreáge, Mk. 5, 7 : Gú. 1176. Ic þe hálsige fore þínum cildháde, Hö. 118. Wē biddađ and hálsiađ on Godes noman, Txts. 175, 15. Heó hyne hálsode þurh God þ hé đám rinclige ... Dryhten cwæđ : 'Hē wæs þurh mē gehálsod', Shrn. 135, 18-25. Hē mec þíne lífe healsode þ ..., B. 2132. (2) *where the entreaty is made in the interests of the person addressed.* (a) *with acc. of person* :—

Lǽre hié and healsa (*obsecra*), Past. 291, 16. (b) with acc. and clause :—
Ic þē healsige þ ðū gesceádwíslíce þ ongite *quaeso te, vide quam id
sancte probes*, Bt. 34, 3; F. 136, 18. Ic eów hálsige þ gē gongan tō
byrgenne weligra manna, Bl. H. 99, 12. Hē hý hálsode (*the accent is in
the MS.*) þæt hý nānuht þǽra ǽrenda ne underfēngon, Qrs. 4, 6; Bos
86, 25. (bα) emphasized. v. (1 bα):—Ic eów healsige for dǽm tōcyme Dryhtnes ðæt gē nō tō hrǽdlíce ne sién ástyrede *rogamus vos per
adventum Domini, ut non cito moveamini*, Past. 213, 14. Ic eów
hálsige on ðoᴉne Drihten . . . þæt gē forlǽtan . . ., Wlfst. 232, 12.
(3) of solemn appeal made in legal proceedings, *to adjure* :—Ic eów
hálsige on Fæder noman . . . and fer ðaere hālgen faemnan naman, þ gē
tō ðǽm ordāᴉe ne gangen, gif gē scyld on eów witen, Rtl. 114, 14–22.
Ic hálsige þē þurh þǽne ælmihtigan God *adiuro te per omnipotentem
Deum*, Ll. Lbmn. 413, 1. Ic hálsige *obsecro*, 12 : *obtestor*, 19. Hálsie
man ðone man hēr. Ic eów hálsie, 415, 1. (4) *to exorcize* :—Exor-
cismus aquae. Ic hálsige ðec *exorcizo te, creatura aque*, Rtl. 100, 27.
Salthālgcincg. Ic l álsigo ðec, giscæft saltes, 117, 34. (5) *to imprecate* :—Háls[ode] *inprecabatur*, An. Ox. 4, 45. II. *to augur,
divine*. v. hálsung; II. On wīgbedde tō hálsienne *ariolandi*, Wrt.
Voc. ii. 9, 15. v. ā-hálsian; eofulsian.

**hálsigend.** *Add* :—Hē beád him þ hē wǽre gehádod tō exorcista, þ
wē hātað hálsigend þe ðe bebȳt deóflum þ hí of gedrehtum mannum
faran, Hml. S. 31, 141.

**hálsigendlic.** *Add: that earnestly entreats* (of a prayer) :—Sum
wíf bær hire deádan sunu ongeán Libertinum . . . Heó mid āðsware him
tō cwæð : 'Ne fǽrst þū heonon būton þū mínne sunu mē cukenne ágife'.
Hē áforhtode for hire hálsiendlican (*geornfullan, v. l.*) bēne (*expavit
petitionis illius juramentum*), Gr. D. 17, 23.

**hálsigendlíce.** *Dele : hal-stān.* v. heall-stān.

**hálsung.** *Add :, halsung (?), healsung.* I. *en'reaty, solemn
appeal.* (1) on one's own behalf. Cf. hálsian; I. 1 :—Geneálǽcige
gebed † hálsung mín (*deprecatio mea*) on gesíhþe þínre, Ps. L. 118, 169
Bēne † hálsunge míne *deprecationem meam*, 16, 1. God gehírde míne
healsunge (*deprecationem*), and Drihten onfēng mín gebed (*orationem*),
Ps. Th. 6, 7. Healsunga, 38, 14. Healsunge (*obsecrationem*), Ps. Vos.
142, 1. Mid hálsungum *cum obsecrationibus*, Kent. Gl. 659. ¶ of
a form of prayer used in the church service :—Hálsung, þæt is Kyrieleison
*letania*, R. Ben. 37, 1 : 38, 12. Hálsunge bēn, þæt is Kyrieleison
*supplicatio letanie, id est Kyrieleison*, 34, 2. (1 a) where the appeal is
emphasized by an oath. Cf. hálsian; I 1 bα :—Heó þus cwæð and mid
āðe geswór . . . Hē áforhtode for ðære bēne hálsunge (*expavit petitionis
illius juramentum*), Gr. D. 17, 30. (2) *adjuration.* Cf. hálsian; I 3 :—
Hálsung. Ic hálsige þē . . ., Ll. Lbmn. 413, 1 : 415, 10. Hálsuncge,
Rtl. 114, 13. (3) *exorcism.* Cf. hálsian; I. 4 :—Hálsunge *exorcismo*,
i. *adjurationem*, An. Ox. 4083. Mid þæs sácerdes hálsunge se deófol wyrð
āfȳmed fram þáre menniscan gesceafte, Wlfst. 33, 21. (4) *imprecation.*
Cf. hálsian; I 5, Bl. H. 99, 21 *in Dict.* II. *divination.* Cf.
hálsian; II :—Hálsung *divinatio*, Wrt. Voc. ii. 141, 56. v. hǽlsung.

**hálsung-gebed.** *Substitute : A prayer in the service of the church :—*
Hálsunggebedu *supplicatio letanie*, R. Ben. I. 39, 6. Cf. Gebedu
*letania*, 42, 18.

**hálsung-tíma,** an; *m. A time of supplication* :—Swylce fram þæs
dæges úpspringe tō hálsungtíman þreó tíða sȳn forð āðenede, Nap. 35.

**hálwenda.** v. hálwende; B.

**hálwende.** *Add : , hálwynde.* A. *adjective.* I. *conducive to
physical health* :—Hálwende cleoþan *medicinale*, i. *salutiferum cataplasma*, An. Ox. 1972. Þone hálwendan cleoþan *malagma*,
3051. I a. figurative :—Ðætte hié ðone hálwendan (*-wyndan, v. l.*)
drenc ðæs æðelan wínes ne gehwyrfen him selfum tō áttre, Past. 365, 8.
Hálwe[n]dne lǽcedóm *saluberrimum malagma*, An. Ox. 374. II.
*conducive to well-being* :—Scildend þára hálwendra (*þǽre hǽlo, Ps. Th.*)
Crīstes his *prctector salutarium xpi sui*, Ps. Vos. Srt. 27, 8. Hálwende
*prosperos* (*successus*), An. Ox. 4550. III. *conducive to moral or
spiritual health* or *well-being* :—Hálwende cynnincg *salutatrix natiuitas*,
An. Ox. 1538. Hē wolde ðǽm fortrúwodum monnum andrysno hál-
wendes eges (*saluberrimi timoris*) on gebrengean, Past. 385, 16. Mid
dȳ hálwyndan wætre *aqua salutis*, 261, 8. On hálwyndre hreówsunga
(*salubris tristitia*), 425, 17. On hálwende láre *in doctrina sana*, 91, 15.
Ðá hálwendan forhæfdnesse *difficultatem salutis*, 401, 31. Þǽne hálwendne *saluberrimum*, i. *salutare* † *congruum* (*Christi adventum*), An.
Ox. 1773. Hē ús sealde hálwendne geþóht, Bl. H. 11, 35. Manig
þing þe him sylfum swíðe hálweude (*salubria*) wǽron tō witanne, Bd. 3,
19; Sch. 280, 10. B. *in weak declension used as substantive.*
(1) personal. *Take here* **hálwenda** *in Dict., and add* :—God,
se hálwynda mín *Deus, salutaris meus*, Ps. Srt. 26, 9 : 61, 3. Ūre
hálwenda, Ps. L. 84, 5. Hálwynde ūr, Ps. Srt. 78, 9. Se hálwynde
ūr, 67, 20. In Gode ðǽm hálwyndan mínum, 61, 8 : 94, 1 : ii. p. 193,
13. (2) of a thing :—Þíne sóðfæstnesse and hálwendan þínre (þínne ?,
þíne ?) *veritatem tuam et salutare tuum*, R. Ben. I. 12, 13. v. hálwend-lic.

**hálwend-lic.** *Add : used in weak declension as substantive.* v.

hálwende ; B. (1) personal :—Hē is hálwendlica mín *salutaris meus*,
Ps. L. 61, 3. Ūre hálwendlica, 64, 6 : 78, 9. (2) of a thing :—On
hálwendlican þínum † hǽlde *in salutare tuum*, Ps. L. 118, 81. v. un-
hálwendlic.

**hálwendlíce.** *Add : so as to promote or produce bodily or spiritual
health; salubriter* :—Ðis fæstin þ ðóhtum líchomum ǽc gemendum
hálwoendlíce gesetted is *hoc jejunium quod animis corporibusque curandis
salubriter institutum est*, Rtl. 9, 29. I. of bodily health :—Heó is
gehǽled hálwendlíce ðurh Críst *she is restored to perfect health by Christ*,
Hml. S. 9, 29. I a. figurative :—Synne áttor hálwendlíce byð
geopenud on andetnysse, þ cwyldbǽrlíce lutude on geþance *peccati uirus
salubriter aperitur in confessione quod pestifere latebat in mente*, Scint.
39, 6. II. of spiritual health :—Oft weorðað men swíðe hálwendlíce (*salubriter*) áfǽrde mid ðǽm ilcan ðingum ðe hí ǽr unnytlíce lufedon,
Past. 441, 24. Is ús micel ðearf ðæt wē hálwendlíce (*to our spiritual
profit ; salubriter*) geðencen ðá gód ðe wē forgiémeleásodon, 467, 7.
Hálwendlíce (*salubriter*) gebreád, Gr. D. 160, 20. Críst wolde ðá
ealdan ǽ ǽr gefyllan, and siððan ðá níwan gecȳðnysse hálwendlíce (*with
salutary effect*) onginnan, Hml. Th. ii. 244, 29.

**hálwendnes.** *Add : safety, salvation; salutare* :—Ic sette on hǽlo
(hálwendnesse, MS. T.) *ponam in salutari*, Ps. Spl. 11, 6. Sóðfæstnesse
þíne and hálwendnesse (*salutare*) ic gesǽde (Ps. 40, 10), R. Ben. 11, 8.
God hálwendnyssa ūra *Deus salutarium nostrum*, Ps. L. 67, 20.

**ham** *a garment. Add* :—*Colobium, dictum quia longum est et sine
manicis* lopa, hom *vel* smoc, mentel, Wrt. Voc. ii. 134, 37. Hom
*colobium*, i. 288, 34. Ham, hom, Txts. 46, 167. Haam *camisa*, 50,
244. Ham, cemes, Wrt. Voc. ii. 13, 23. Ham, hacele *subucula*,
An. Ox. 5316.

**ham** *a ham. Add* :—Hom *copla, poples*, Wrt. Voc. ii. 132, 80.
Hamme *publite*, Txts. 111, 25. [H]omme *poplite*, 182, 81. Hamme
*suffragine*, An. Ox. 38, 3. Gebígedum hamme *curvo poplite*, Hpt. Gl.
493, 75. Homme *puplites*, Txts. 114, 102. Homme *cambas*
(= *gambas*), Lch. i. lxxi. 10.

**ham** *a piece of enclosed land, a ham* (v. *N. E. D.*). *Add* :—Hæfde
hió hire gebógod on ánan wyrtigan hamme, Hml. S. 30, 312. On
brádan leá on ênne ham; þurh út ðone leá súð út on óðerne ham; of
ðan hamme . . . on brádan ham westeweardne; of brádan hamme . . . of
mǽde on flexhammas; of flexhamman on minthammas . . . of ðan
wæterwege on waterhammes; of ðan hamman, C. D. v. 374, 14–32.
v. fleax-, flód-, mint-, mylen-, sceáp-, stigel-, wæter-hamm. See Midd.
Flur, s. v.

**hám.** *Add :* I. *a farm, estate* :—Tō hyre ágenum háme *ad prǽ-
diolum suum*, An. Ox. 4741. Háme *prǽdia* (*ut ab urbe ad propria
praedia ducerentur*, Ald. 69, 4), 4840. Hē forgeaf summe hám tō
þǽre hálgan stówe, Hml. S. 6, 232. Hē cwæð þ hē ne mihte embe
munuclíf þá smeágan . . . ac wolde beón embe his þincg . . . and gedreóhlǽcan his hámas, 121. I a. as a technical English term, a *vill,
manor* (v. Se.bohm Vill. Comm. s. v.) :—Fela sceal tō holdan hámes
gerēfan and tō gemetfæstan manna hyrde, Angl. ix. 265, 10. Þone hám
æt Beccanleá . . . and æt Felhhamme and þá land þe þǽrtó hȳran, Cht.
Th. 489, 12–18 : 2 : 9 : 19. Weard ádrǽfed Óslác of earde . . . háma
bereáfod, Chr. 975; P. 120, 24. Tō geeácnode intó Élegmynstre byð
þrý hámas ðe ðus sind gehátene, Meldeburna, Earmingaford, Norðwold,
C. D. iii. 60, 33. II. *a dwelling, an abode.* (1) on earth. (a) a
habitable building, a house :—Þurhwuniendum eallum þám getimbre
þæs hámes *perdurante tota domus fabrica*, Gr. D. 119, 27. Sum bið
bylda til hám tō habbanne, Crǽ. 76. (b) the fixed residence of a
person or family, an inhabited house, a residence :—Gelaðode se gesíð
hine tō his hám, and hē hine gesóhte and on his hús eóde and his swǽs-
enda breác *rogatus a comite intrauit epulaturus domum eius*, Bd. 3, 22;
Sch. 297, 1. Æt Finnes hám, B. 1156. Hē bewiste swá hwæt swá
man dyde on his háme (hám, *v. l.*) *quaeque in ejusdem domo agebantur
noverat*, Gr. D. 299, 30. Ic wunode in mínum háme (hám, *v. l.*)
þe mē gelamp in þissere byrig of mínes fæder yrfe, 313, 27. Decius
áwédde . . . and ásprang sárlic wóp on ðám háme, Hml. Th. i. 434, 15.
Sē ðe forlétes hús † hám, Lk. L. 18, 29. Geþenca hweðer áwiht mani
mann cynges hám séce þǽr ðǽr hē on túne byð, Solil. H. 44, 2.
Hē Hróðgáres hám bringe, B. 717. Hē þǽr háligne hám ǽrærde, Gú.
120 : 242. Hȳ hleóleáse háma þoliað, 193. [On] ǽlces cynges háma
[hȳrede] beóð sume on búre, sume on healle, sume on óðene, sume on
carcerne, Solil. H. 44, 18. Sume wuniað on wéstennum, gesittað hámas
on heolstrum, 54. Gewiton him þá wígend wíca neósian . . . Frysland
gesēon, hámas and heá burg, B. 1127; Chr. 937; P. 106, 18 : Exod.
453. Ic hire beád gymmas . . . and mǽre gebytlu, hámas and hȳred,
Hml. S. 8, 37. (α) a place that used to be a person's home :—Gif
man mægð gebiged . . . gif hit fácne is, eft æt hám gebrenge, Ll. Th. i.
22, 2 : 10, 8. (β) in connexion with marriage. v. VII. 2 :—
Abraham idese bróhte tō háme, þǽr hē wíc áhte, Gen. 1721. Þǽm tō
hám forgeaf Hréðel ángan dohtor, B. 374. (2) not on earth :—Hē on
norðdǽle hám and heáhsetl heofena ríces ágan wolde, Gen. 33 : Sat. 276.
Þǽra ēcena háma, Solil. H. 2, 15. Sēcan þá hámas and þá árleásan

eardungstôwe, Seel. 70. (3) figurative, (long) home:—Hé foresǽde þone dæg þe hé sceolde cuman tô Cofantreó tô his langan hâme, Vis. Lfc. 90. Ic sceal lange hâm, eardwíc uncúð, âna gesêcan, Ap. 92. III. an inhabited place, district, region, neighbourhood. (1) on earth:—Ne mêtte hé ǽr nán gebún land, siþþan hé from his âgnum hâm fôr, Ors. 1, 1 ; S. 17, 24. Trôia burg ... lengest burne hâma under hefonum, Met. 9, 18. (2) not on earth:—Is hâm sceapen ungelíce englum and deóflum, Cri. 898. Nis þæt betlic bold, ne nôht ryhtlic hâm, ac þǽr is helle grund, Dôm. 24. Eádig eorl heofona hâmes earnað, Ph. 483 : Gú. 768. In þǽm deóran hâm (heaven), Sat. 219. Tô þǽm hâlgan hâm heofona ríces, An. 1685. On þâm ecan hâme, Solil. H. 1. 18. Trumlicre hâm. beorhte burhweallas, Sat. 294 : 362. Hé wolde him tô helpe hâm gesêcan (visit their dwelling (hell) ), 436. In álefan, êðel tô ǽhte, 278. IV. a place where rest, refuge, or satisfaction is found:—Þǽr he hungrium hâm staðelude collocavit illic esurientes, Ps. Th. 106, 35. Úton wé hycgan hwǽr wé hâm âgen, Seef. 117. V. native country:—Lyt eft becwôm hâmes niósan, B. 2366. Þá hé tô hâm becôm, 2992 : Víd. 94. Tô hâme, Exod. 456. Þára þe hâm eahtoðe, B. 1407. VI. in prepositional phrases. (1) æt hâm. (a) at or in one's own house:—Of hígna gemǽnum gôdum ðaer aet hâm, Txts. 444, 24. Þá hí æt hâm (húse, L., R. domi) wǽron, Mk. 9, 33. Hit cýþan þâm ðe æt hâm (húse, R.) synt, Lk. 9, 61. Maria sæt æt hâm (hâme, L., R.), Jn. 11, 20. Se gesíð him nolde ǽr yfles gestiéran æt hâm, Ll. Th. i. 134. 6. On ælcum treówo ic geseah hwæthwuga þæs þe ic æt hâm beþorfte, Solil. H. 1, 8. (b) in one's own neighbourhood, town, etc. :—Ne gesêce nân man þone cyng for nánre sprǽce, búton hé æt hâm rihtes wyrðe beón ne môte, Ll. Th. i. 266, 10. Hæfde se cyning his fierd on tú tônumen, swá þ hié wǽron simle healfe æt hâm, healfe úte, Chr. 894; P. 84, 32. Þá cinges þegnas þe þá æt hâm æt þǽm geweorcum wǽron, P. 87, 15. (c) in one's own country. not abroad:—Hié heora here on tú tôdǽldon, ôþer æt hâm beón heora lond tô healdanne, ôðer út faran tô winnanne, Ors. 1, 10; Swt. 46, 16, Higelác æt hâm wunade, B. 1923. (2) fram hâm from native sources: þæt fram hâm gefrægn Higeláces þegn gôd mid Geátum, B. 194. (3) tô hâm hweorfan, faran, etc., to return to one's house or neighbourhood:— þá hwurfan hí eft tô hâme (hâm, v. l.) redierunt, Bd. 4, 25 ; Sch. 497, 21. Hé eft gewát tô hâm faran, B. 124. Gecerdon ðá ðe gesended wæron tô hâm reuersi qui missi fuerant domum, Lk. L. 7, 10. Cuôm tô hús í tô hâm ueniens domum, 15, 6. Hié swá sigebeorhte tô hâm fôran, Bl. H. 203, 31. On burh rídan hâle tô hâme, By. 292. VII. hâm as adverb; home:—Hâm wegað advehunt, Wrt. Voc. ii. 1, 5. Hié hâm fêrdan abscedunt, 3, 20. Hâm feredan advectabant, 5, 5. (1) to one's home, house, or abode:—þonne hé hâm cymð ueniens domum, Lk. 15, 6 : 7, 10 : Ll. Th. i. 274, 21 : 232, 21 : Solil. H. 1, 5. Dæt sceáp ðæt forloren wæs gé hâm né brôhtan (non reduxistis), Past. 123, 10 : Solil. H. 1, 6. Hé nolde hâm tô his gemæccan gehweorfan, Hml. A. 125, 269. Gif hwilc man forstolen þingc hâm tô his cotan bringe, Ll. Th. i. 418, 17. Begyte þá bâde hâm sé þe heó fore genumen sý, 354. 7. Fela tilða hâm gæderian, Angl. ix. 261, 17. ¶ with verb of motion implied:—Búton heó fram þâm ceorle wille eft hâm ongeán, Ll. Th. i. 416, 14. (1a) In connexion with marriage. v. II. 1 b β. [Cf. O. H. Ger. heim-bringa domi duca ( domi duca dea quae praeesse existimabatur cum sponsa duceretur domum, Migne)]:—Ne hí ne beóþ hâm gebrôhte neque nubentur, An. Ox. 1265. (2) to one's own district or neighbourhood (a) on earth:—Ðá ôþre hâm cômon, Chr. 917; P. 98, 4. (b) not on earth :—Côm þegen Hǽlendes hâm tô helle, Sat. 427. (3) to one's native country :—Ic hâm síþie repatrio, Wrt. Voc. i. 22, 30. Æfter wræcsíðe hâm cumenum, Chr. 792 ; P. 55, 29. Se cyning (Ulysses) hâm cerde, Bt. 38, 1 ; F. 194. 8. Hit Scipia oftrǽdlíce hâm onbeád (sent home orders) þæt hié hit ne angunnen, and eác self sǽde, þá hé hâm of Ispanium côm, Ors. 4, 12 ; S. 208, 34. Lida ... hâm cymeð, nefre him holm gestýreð, Gn. Ex. 106. v. bisceop-, cyne-, heofon-, mynster-hâm.

hama. Add: a natural covering, integument, membrane, skin, slough of a serpent:—Inluvies secundarum hama in quo fit parvulus, Wrt. Voc. ii. 110, 61. Mædenlicum haman virginali puerperio, Hpt. Gl. 414, 50. Matrice cildhaman puerperio, utero haman, 436, 6. Seó nǽddre âwurpð ǽ'ce geáre hire ealdan haman, and bið ðonne befangen mid eallnîwum felle, Nap. 35. Hér côm in gangan in spíðer (inspíðer?) wiht hæfde him his haman on handa, Lch. iii. 42, 12. [v. N. E. D. hame. Cf. Icel. hamr a skin, especially of birds.] v. feorh-, fiþer-hama.

hâma. Add:—Hâma grillus, Wrt. Voc. ii. 110, 2 : 41, 6: cicada, 16, 27. Hâman cicade, Txts. 52, 256. v. hyll(e)-hâma.

hamacgað. The word glosses convalescet, so probably the true form is part of a verb corresponding to O. H. Ger. ge-magên convalescere; cf. magian.

hâm-brigan. Dele, and see hâm; VII. 1 a.

hâm-cyme. Add:—þá þá hé hâm ne côm in ðá tíd þe him beboden wæs, Florentius þá wênde his hâmcymes cum hora qua jussus fuerat non rediret, Florentius suspectus est redditus, Gr. D. 207, 2. Hí mycelne gefeán hæfdon be his hâmcyme, Hml. A. 125, 278. Gebiddende for his hâmcyme of þâm wræce and of þâm earfoðan þá hé þá on wæs, Ps. Th. 30, arg. [v. N. E. D. homecome.]

hamel (?) ; adj. Broken, rugged:—Æt hamelan dene, C. D. iii. 362, 36. On þonne þriddan hlinc ðe tô hamelan dúnæ hýrð ... on ðá mearce ðe tô hamelan dúne hýrð, v. 361, 30–362, 1. Cf. Andlang streámes tô brocenan beorge, C. D. B. ii. 245, 34. [Cf. O. H. Ger. hamal-scorrun praeruptum (montis): M. H. Ger. hamel a rugged height, crag.] v. hamelian.

hamela (-ola). A person with cropped hair. [Cf. O. Frs. berdes hemilinge (homelenga) barbae truncatio.] Take here the article under homela, and add: The Latin version of the law is : Si eum radat in contumeliam ad collificum ( = ? colobicum).

hamele porticulo. v. hamer ; I.

hamelian. Add: [v. N. E. D. hamble: D. D. hammil. O. Frs. homelia ên hûs to demolish a house; homelenga, hemilinge truncatio (barbae).] v. be-hamelian ; hamel.

hamer. Add: I. a hammer used for beating, breaking, &c., a workman's hammer:—Hamer malleus, Wrt. Voc. i. 287, 1. Slecg, hamur, ii. 57, 78. Beátendes hameres stíþnes tundentis mallei durities, An. Ox. 481. Mín (a key's) heáfod is homere geþuren, sworfen feóle, Rä. 87, 1. Þeáh ðæra manna æghwylc hæfde ǽnne hamor on handa, and þeáh man ... mid þâm hameron beóte on þæt ísene þell ... ne âwacode hé nǽfre for eallum þissum, tô ðám wêrig hé wǽre, Wlfst. 147, 3–8. Hameras sleánde mallei percutientes, Scint. 171, 14. Wæ þæt deór uneáþe mid ísernum hamerum and slecgum (malleis) ofbeóton, Nar. 21, 5. II. a hammer used by the master of the rowers to give signals for the stroke; porticulus, porticulus:—Hamere porticulo (crepante naucleri porticulo, Ald. 3, 3), Wrt. Voc. ii. 75, 12. Hamure porticulo, An. Ox. 7, 13 : 8, 7. Hamele, 1, 33 : 3, 22. (All these are glosses to the same passage.) v. clod-, dúþ-(dýþ-), hand-hamer.

hamer-secg. Add: [Hammer-sedge carex hirta, E. D. S. Plant Names.]

hamer-wyrt. Add: 'Hammerwort is Pellitorie ot the wall', Gerarde's Herbal:—Homorwyrt perdicalis, Wrt. Voc. i. 68, 60. (Cf. þás wyrte þe wé perdicalis (glossed in a later MS. by halmer wet) nemdan, Lch. i. 186, 17). Hamorwyrte blôstman, Lch. i. 374, 5 : iii. 4, 8. Nim hamorwyrte hand fulle, 6, 27. With heáfodwrǽce ; genim hamorwyrt, 2, 1. Cnûwa niðewearde hamorwyrt and secg, ii. 74, 30.

hâm-fæst. Add:—Sum deácon wæs feor þanon hâmfæst (living far from the place; longe positus), sé gewilnode fêran tô him, Gr. D. 208, 13. 'Gefyrn ic hine cúðe, leóf, ac hé fêrde heonon, and ic nât tô gewissan hwǽr hé wunað nú.' Þá cwæð se hâlga wer, 'Witodlíce hé wunað nú on Wincelcumbe hâmfæst (he is settled at Winchelcombe), Hml. S. 21, 33. Ic and míne gefêran on Ephesa byrig hâmfæste wǽron I and my companions had our home in Ephesus, 23, 739-

-hâmian. v. ge-hâmian.

ham-land, es ; n. Enclosed pasture land:—Is þæs londes þridde half híd þe Oswold seld Cynelme tô bóclonde swá hé hit him ǽr hæfde tô forlǽten tô lǽnlonde ǽgðær ge on earðlonde ge on homlonde, Cht. E. 208, 11.

hâm-leás. Add: of a place, without a habitation:—Andlong paðes tô hâmleásceagan, C. D. v. 194, 8.

hamm. v. ham : -hammen. v. be-, ge-, seolfor-, ymb-hammen : hâm-scír. For ' Cot. 71, Lye' substitute:—Hâmscíre edilitatem, Wrt. Voc. ii. 106, 79. Hâmscír, 29, 4: hâm-scyld. v. riht-hamscyld.

hâm-síþ, es ; m. A journey home:—Drihtnes encgel hyre gecígde þone hâmsíþ hyre gemæccan, Hml. A. 125, 273.

hâm-sôcn. Add:—Ic cýðe eów þ ic hæbbe geunnen him þ hé beó his saca and sôcne wyrðe, and griðbryces and hâmsôcne, Cht. E. 233, 3. [v. N. E. D. hamesucken. See Steenstrup's Normannerne, iv. 348 sqq.] v. riht-hâmsôcn.

hâm-steall. Add:—On hâmstealle in praedium (in praedium (tô ânum tûne, W.S.) cui nomen Gesemani, Mk. 14, 32. Cf. on þone tûn (in tûn, L., R.) in villam, Mt. 26, 36), An. Ox. 61, 55. On Coftûne aet þâm hâmstealle .v. cassatorum, C. D. ii. 167, 28. Of ealdan hâmstealle ðe Ædelere ǽhte, iii. 424, 15. In deópan hâmsteale (-stealle?), 381, 4. [v. N. E. D. home-stall.]

hâm-stede. Add: ¶ The word occurs as a place-name in the charters, but in some of the following instances (e. g. vi. 35, 34) it is or may be a common noun, and in some perhaps to ham rather than to hâm should the first part of the compound be referred:—On hâmstedes wyllas norðewearde, C. D. iii. 131, 18. Tô hemstedes geate ; from hæmstedes geate, 172, 37–173, 1. xx hídas in Heomstede, iv. 177, 21. Tô niulæs hâmstæde, v. 136, 9. Onbútan ðone ealdan hânistede, vi. 35, 34. Ðis sind ðára .III. hída landgemæra tô Hâmstede (cf. loco qui celebri Hamstede nuncupatur uocabulo, 12), 37, 29. Ðis syndon ðá landgemæra tô Hâmstede (cf. in loco qui celebri æt Hámstede nuncupatur uocabulo, 17), 105, 35.

Hâm-tún. Add: v. Norþ-, Súþ-hâmtún.

Hâmtúnisc ; adj. Of Northampton:—Harold sǽde þ hé Cnutes sunu wǽre and Ælfgyfe þǽre Hâmtúnisca[n], Chr. 1035 ; P. 159, 29.

**Hámtún-scir.** *l.* scír, *and add:* **I.** *Northamptonshire:*—Hí (*the Danes*) heafdon þá ofergán East-Engla i, and Eást-Seaxe ii, . . . and healfe Huntedúnscíre ix, and micel on Hámtúnscíre x, Chr. 1011; P. 141, note 3. In tó Bedanfordscíre, and þanon tó Huntadúnscíre and swá in tó Hámtúnscíre, 1016; P. 149, 12. **II.** *Hampshire:*—Him (Alfred) tó cóm Sumorsæte alle and Wilsætan and Hámtúnscír, Chr. 878; P. 76, 8. Be-súðan Temese . . . Bearrucscíre and Hámtúnscíre and Wiltúnscíre, 1011; P. 141, 17.

**hám-weard.** *Add:* **I.** *towards one's place of abode* (temporary or permanent). Cf. hám; **VII.** 1:—Sé ðe þyder (*to church*) mid clænum móde færð . . . and tó Gode georne þencð . . ., hé þe blíðra mæg syððan hámwerd eft gewendan, Wlfst. 281, 24. **I a.** (*arrived*) *at one's place of abode:*—þá wé hámweard wæron *cum venissemus ad diversorium*, Gen. 43, 21. **II.** *of a body of people, e.g.* troops, *towards the place or district dwelt in by them, on the way home,* cf. hám; **VII.** 2. (1) with substantive verb:—þá hié þá hámweard wæron, þá métton hié micelne sciphere, Chr. 885; P. 78, 18: 911; P. 96, 13: Ors. 2, 4; S. 70, 19: 3, 11; S. 152, 20. þá hié from ðære byrg hámweard wæron, S. 144, 28. (2) with verb of motion:—þonne hie hámweard fóran, þonne sceoldan hiera senatus rídan wiðæftan þæm consulum, Ors. 2, 4; S. 70, 27. Israhéla folc mid sige wendon him hámweard, Hml. A. 113, 379. Se cyng þá hámweard gewende, Chr. 1095; P. 231, 24. **III.** *towards one's native country, on the way home.* Cf. hám; **VII.** 3. (1) with substantive verb:—Hé mid heora here wæs in Asiam; þá burgware bædon þ hié tídlíce hámweard wære *Agesilaus, arcessitus ex Asia*, Ors. 3, 1; S. 98, 14. Mid þære herehýþe Rómáne oferhlæstan heora scipa ða hí hámweard wæron *cum Romana classis ad Italiam praedis onusta remearet*, 4, 6; S. 176, 18. (2) with verb of motion:—þá hié hámweard wendon, ealle Asiam hié geniéddon þ hié him gafol gulden, Ors. 1, 10; S. 44, 17. Hí fóron tó Róme and gebidan mycele earfoðnysse þá hí hámward fóran, Chr. 1061; P. 191, 2.

**hám-weardes.** *Add:* **I.** cf. hám-weard; **II.**:—Fór Swegen eorl in tó Wealan, and him man gíslode. þá hé hámwerdes wæs, Chr. 1046; P. 164, 28. **I.** cf. hám-weard; **III.**:—Hú hý sceoldon beón áléd of Bábilonia þeówdóme, and Gode þancian þæra ára þe hí be wege hæfdon hámweardes, Ps. Th. 22, arg.

**hán** (?) *a thole:*—Ænne scegð .lxiii. áre, hé is eallgearo bútan þám hánon; hé hine wolde fulgearwian his hláforde tó gerisnum, Crw. Cht. 23, 8. [*Icel.* hár. *v.* há; *and for a double declension like* há, hán *see* fíá, fíán; íá, íán *a toe;* tá, tán *a twig.*]

**hán,** e; *f.* *A projecting stone that forms part of a boundary:*—þis synt þá gemæro . . . tó þære háne; þonan norð on gerihte andlang hrycges, C.D. ii. 215, 31. Ǽrest on þane hwítan weg; ðonon on ðá reádan háne; of ðære háne on ðone herpað, iii. 415, 30: v. 297, 32: 376, 9. Of ðám byrigelse tó ðære reádan hánæ; of ðære reádan hánæ andlang stræt, 217, 4. On þá grægan háne; of þære grægan háne, Cht. E. 294, 25. [*Icel.* hein *a hone.*]

**hana.** *Add:*—Hana *gallus*, Wrt. Voc. ii. 41, 16. Sumes wífes gást wunode mid hire oð hana sang, Shrn. 30, 29. Hana (*gallus*) þá licgenda[n] áwecð and þá slápolon hé þreáð, cocc (*gallus*) þá wiþsacendan cít; hanan (*gallo*) cráwendon hopa gehwer[f]þ, Hy. S. 6, 36–7, 5. On hanan welle, C.D. iii. 403, 11. Seó leó þone lytlan hanan hyre ondrǽt, gif heó him on besyhð, and ealra swíðost gif se hana hwít bið, Hml. A. 63, 282. ¶ The word is given by runes contained in the text of Rä. 43, which has a cock for part of its subject. *v.* holt-, mór-, wór-, wudu-hana.

**han-créd.** *Add:* **I.** *cock-crowing:*—Scyllendre cocca fiþerslehte and . . . hancréde *concrepante pullorum plausu et sonante gallicinio,* An. Ox. 4893. **II.** *a division of the night:*—Betwux hancréde læg se hálga wer geedcucod, Hml. Th. ii. 334, 30. Cf. han-grǽd.

**hancréd-tíd,** e; *f.* *Cock-crow, a division of the night:*—Honcrédtíd *gallicinium,* Wrt. Voc. ii. 41, 17.

**hand.** *For B.* 2137 *see* hand-gemǽre, *dele the passage from* Ll. Th. i. 18, 1, *and add:* **I.** *a hand:*—Gif hé heáhre handa dyntes onféhð *if he receives a blow from an uplifted hand,* i. e. *a violent blow.* (*For the force of* heáh cf. (?) *its metaphorical use in:* Úre hand ys heáh Deut. 32, 27; *and for the idea of force suggested by the position of the hand* cf.: Hé his handa ál.óf and hí wolde wíde tódrífan, Ps. Th. 105, 21), Ll. Th. i. 18, 1. Gif men sié se earm mid honda mid ealle of ácorfen beforan elmbogan, 96, 28. On sumre stówe se hróf wæs þ man mid his handa neálíce geræcean mihte, Bl. H. 207, 22. Mid handa, Hml. Th. i. 508, 20. Forlét hé daroð of handa fleógan of folman, By. 149. Ne wolde hé óðer wæpen habban bútan áne girde him on handa (on hand nyman, *v. l.*), Bd. 3, 18; Sch. 275, 9: Gen. 678: B. 495: 540. Ánra gehwylc wið earm gesæt, hleonade wið handa, Sat. 433. Hé hond álegde, earm and eaxle . . . Grendles grápe, B. 834. On þám háligdóme swerian þe him man on hand sylð, Ll. Th. i. 292, 15. Fét sint gebundene, handa gehæfte, Gen. 380. Mínra handa geweald, Handa þuman *palmarum pollices,* An. Ox. 3547. Onfón mid geglófedum handum, Solil. H. 42, 12. Betwuh hondum *intra tenentis manus,* Past. 241, 12. Hí hyra handa on hine wurpon and námon hine, Mk. 14, 46.

Handa sendan, El. 457. **I a.** brád hand *the palm of the hand:*—Bráde hand *palmam,* Wrt. Voc. ii. 74, 22. þu mid þíne brádre hand (*alapa*) þá nunnan þaccodest, Gr. D. 190, 13. Ongan heó þerscan heó sylfe mid hire sýste ge eác mid hire brádum handum (*alapis pugnisque*), 68, 29. Sume hyne slógun on his ansýne mid hyra brádum handum *palmas in faciem ei dederunt,* Mt. 26, 67. ¶ The loss of the hand was the penalty for certain crimes:—Gif hwá on cirican hwæt geþeófige . . . sleá mon þá hond of þe hé hit mid gedyde, Ll. Th. i. 66, 4. Be cirliscum þeófe gefongenum . . . sleá mon hond of oþþe fót 114, 7. Gif se mynetere fúl wurðe, sleá mon of þá hand þe hé þ fúl mid worhte, 206, 20. ¶ The hand was used in various ways in formal proceedings. (1) legal. *v.* Grmm. R. A. 137 sqq.:—Clíroc feówra sum hine clænsie (and áne his hand on wiófode...), Ll. Th. i. 40, 17. Ic hebbe tó heofena míne hand and ic swerie, Deut. 32, 40. þ hý ealle gemǽnum handum of ǽgðere mægðe on ánum wæpne þám sémende syllan þ cyninges mund stande, Ll. Th. i. 174, 21. (2) in religious ceremonial:—Hé heóld hine tó ð handa *eum ad confirmandum tenuit,* Chr. 855; P. 67, 27. Hine nam se cing tó bisceopes handa, 993; P. 126, 8. **II.** in figurative expressions arising from the use of the hand (1) *to grasp, hold, retain;* where possession, custody, control, authority, &c., are denoted:—Sé þe at habbendre handa (*with stolen goods upon him;* cf. hand-hæbbende) gefangen sý, Ll. Th. i. 220, 11. Ámanige þære scíre bisceop þá bóte tó þæs cynges handa, 266, 20. Twégen cempan . . . þá ǽr wæron under Eustachius handa *two soldiers . . . they had served under Eustace,* Hml. S. 30, 231. Under cynges hand, Ll. Th. i. 284, 14. Áhrede of þæs hundes handa mín líf, Ps. Th. 21, 18. Ælc þing þe tó Godes handa belimpan sceolde, Wlfst. 211, 3. Gást mínne ágifan on þínes sylfes hand, An. 1419: Hy. 7, 83. Sé hafað in hondum heofon and eorðan, Gú. 619. (I a) *referring to a thing* (not a person):—Deáð and líf on þære tungan handa, R. Ben. 21, 21. (2) *to give:*—Griþ þ hé mid his ágenre hand sylð, Ll. Th. i. 292, 5. Unnendre handa lǽtan *bona voluntate dimittere,* Cht. Th. 202, 37. Eorðe wældreóre swealh of handum þínum, Gen. 1017. **III.** in expressions arising from considering actions as performed by the hand. (1) where the hand is spoken of as the agent:—Sum mæg wrætlíce weorc áhycgan . . . hond bið gelǽred, wís and gewealden, Crä. 45. Nú seó hond ligeð, seó þe eów welhwylcra wilna dohte, B. 1343. Hond gemunde fǽhðo genóge, feorhsweng ne ofteáh, 2488. Sceal hond and heard sweord ymb hord wígan, 2509. Him sió swíðre swaðe weardade hand on Hiorte, 2099. (2) where the word denotes agency, instrumentality in general:—Oft him bonena hond on herefelda gesceóde, An. 17. Úre hand ys heáh and ne worhte Drihten þás þing, Deut. 32, 27. Mín hand býð ofer þíne æceras and ofslihð þíne hors, Ex. 9, 3: Gú. 230. Monnes hond, 429. Under þære mihte Godes handa, Bl. H. 99, 3: Ps. Th. 88, 12. Hé mid árleásre hond (handa, *v. l.*) hí ácwealde, Bd. 3, 1; Sch. 192, 6. God þás fyrd wereð mid þære miclan hand, Exod. 275. Se ælmihtiga lét his hond cuman . . . hyht wæs geníwod, Gú. 924. Gif se mon áhefþ his handa tó ælmesdǽdum, Bl. H. 37, 24. Waldend his honda árǽrde wið þám herge, Gen. 50: Ps. Th. 105, 21. **IV.** in reference to the position of the hands one on each side of the body. (1) (right or left) *hand:*—þær stent cwén þe on þá swýðran hand (*a dextris tuis*), Ps. Th. 44, 11. Sited nú on þá swíðran hond sunu his fæderes, Sat. 580. Tó þám yflum þe him bið on þá wynstran hond, Cri. 1364. (2) of relative position generally (every or any) *side:*—Beón hí ðǽr on ǽlce hand beclýsede, Hml. S. 23, 326. (3) of relative position of opponents, *side:*—þær wearþ monig mon ofslægen on gehwæþere hond (ǽgðre hand, *v. l.*), Chr. 853; P. 66, 2. On swá hwæðere hond Dryhten mǽrðo déme, B. 686. **V.** used of a person considered (1) as a protector, custodian, &c., cf. **II.**:—Ic wylle ðæt man ágyfe ðám híwum hyra freóls swylce hand (*lord*) tó ceósenne swylce him leófast sý, C. D. ii. 116, 35. (2) as an agent. Cf. **III.**:—Gestǽle on ryhtran hand gif hé mæge, Ll. Th. i. 76, 7. (3) as a recipient of property, *an heir:*—Nú hit eall ágán is on ðǽron oð ðíne hand (*until you inherited*); ðonne ðú hit becweðe and sylle swá gesibre handa swá fremdre swaðer ðe leófre sý, C. D. ii. 114, 7. Sylle heó hit on ðá hand ðe hire ǽfre betst gehýre, vi. 138, 27. **VI.** *skill in using the hand, skill:*—Ælfwine hæfde moncynnes míne gefrǽge leóhteste hond lofes tó wyrcenne, Víd. 72. **VII.** as a measure, *v.* hand-brǽd:—Wæs swá mycel þæs treówes gesýne swá wolde beón gód hande brád (handbred ?), Vis. Lfc. 73. **VIII.** in prepositional phrases. (1) æt. (a) *at hand, within reach:*—ðá sæt hé æt beóde, næfde þá æt handa hwær hé þ gebróhte lác healdan sceolde, Bd. 3. 2; Sch. 197, 20. (b) expressing immediate source, *at* (a person's) *hand:*—nǽh nán rihte óþres mannes tó onfónne æt fullunte ne æt biscopes handa, Wlfst. 307, 28. (2) be, *by hand(s), with the hands:*—Hine Beówulf hæfde be honda (*Beowulf's hand clutched Grendel*), B. 814. Ic be hondum mæg hǽðenra sceal grípan tó grunde, Sat. 268. (3) for, *on behalf of, in the interest of, on account of:*—Ælfríc nam þ toll for þæs kynges hand, Cht. Th. 635, 24: 631, 39: 639, 16: 636, 2. (4) of, *from subjection* to:—God hé álýsde láðum of handa, Ps. Th. 106, 2. (5)

on. (a) with dat. (a) *in one's possession, charge* or *keeping* :—Mann sette Ælfgār Leófríces sunu ðane eorldóm on handa, Chr. 1048; P. 177, 4. ¶ on handa habban *to have on hand, be engaged in some business* :—Swā hwilce bysiga swā hȳ on handa hæfdan hȳ unfulworhte lǽtað *ex occupatis manibus quod agebant imperfectum relinquentes*, R. Ben. 20, 3. Forlǽte ǽghwylc swā hwæt swā hē on handa (handum, R. Ben. 9, 75, 16) hæfde *relictis omnibus quelibet fuerint in manibus*, 67, 21. (β) said of evil affecting a person :—For ðǽre neóde þe ús nú on handa stent (*is now pressing on us*), Wlfst. 181, 25. Þā hwíle þe eów unfrið on handa stód, Cht. E. 229, 28. [Cf. wind heom stod on honde þe scaf heom to Irlonde, Laym. 22313.] (b) with acc. (a) *into one's possession, charge* or *keeping* :—Beówulfe ríce on hand gehwearf, B. 2208. (aa) of a pledge :—Ealle him on hand sealdon (*fidem dantes spondent*) þ hī woldon efenwyrhton beón, Chr. 972; P. 119, note 13. (β) *into one's presence, in one's way* :—Gif þē becume ōðres monnes giémeleás feoh on hand *si occurreris bovi inimici tui erranti*, Ll. Th. i. 54, 10. (γ) wel on hond *favourably, prosperously* :—Him for ðissere worulde wel on hand eóde *things went well with him as regards this world*, Hml. S. 23, 14. [Here tuder swiðe wexeð, and wel dieð, and goþ wel on hond, O.E. Hml. ii. 177, 18.] (δ) on hand gān *to submit*. (For examples see Dict.). (6) tō. (a) *within reach, so that a thing may be held* or *touched* :—Seó culufre brōhte elebeámes twig ān tō handa (*columba venit portans ramum olivae*), Gen. 1473. Sīgan tō handa hālgum rince (cf. *extendit manum et apprehensam (columbam) intulit in arcam*, Gen. 8, 9), 1463. Heó lið wǽge bær hǽlum tō handa, B. 1983. Hnāg ic (*the cross*) þām secgum tō handa, Kr. 59. Him tō honda fleág fugla cyn (cf. hē him (*birds and beasts*) andlyfene sealde of his āgenre handa, Guth. Gr. 142, 30), Gū. 888. (b) *into the possession, custody, &c., of a person* :—Wæs se hālga stede gehwyrfed ðām cyninge tō handa, C.D. iii. 60, 28. Gif hē bócland hæbbe gā þ þām cyninge tō handa, Ll. Th. i. 420, 12. Hē him tō honda hūðe gelǽded, Gū. 102. Hærfest tō honda hērbüendum rípa blēda receð (cf. se wæstmbǽra hærfest bryngþ rípa blēda, Bt. 39, 13; F. 234, 15) *remeat pomis gravis autumnus*, Met. 29, 62. Gyrnde se cyng ealra þāra þegna þe þā eorlas hæfdon, and hī lētan hī ealle him tō handa, Chr. 1048; P. 174, 30. Belandod of þām þe se eorl him tō handa gelǽten hæfde, 1091; P. 226, 21. Tō handan, 4. (b a) tō handa weorpan. (1) *to throw on a person's hands* (with the idea of rejection) :—Gif mon hwelcne ceáp gebygeð and hē onfinde him hwelce unhǽlo on, þonne weorpe þone ceáp tō handa, Ll. Th. i. 138, 12. (2) *to hand over* (under compulsion) :—Gif neát mon gewundige weorpe þ neát tō honda, Ll. Th. i. 78, 10. (b β) tō hand :—Būton man āgeáfe Eustatius and his men heom tō hand sceofe, Chr. 1052; P. 175, 13. (c) *into subjection, under control* :—Se heafoc weorðeð tō hagostealdes honda gelǽred, Vy. 92. (d) *on behalf of, for the benefit of, in trust for* :—Þæne āð nam Wulfrige se scīrigman tō þæs cinges handa (*ad opus regis*), Cht. Th. 273, 29. Hætde heó gehealdan þ cynerīce þrittig wintra hyre suna tō handa, Lch. iii. 432, 3. Man gerædde þ Ælfgifu Hardacnutes mōdor sǽte on Winceastre mid þæs cynges hūscarlum hyra suna, and heóldan ealle West-Seaxan him tō handa, Chr. 1036; P. 161, 4. Hū seó heord fare þe se bisceop tō Godes handa gehealdan sceall, Ll. Th. ii. 312, 26. (7) under. *in subjection, under control* or *rule* :—Under hand hǽðenum dēman, Dan. 71. (8) ymb. (a) local, *at hand, near, close by* :—Hȳ (*birds*) him ymb hond flugon (cf. 888), Gū. 709. (b) temporal, *at once, straightway* :—Jam jam embe hand, hrædlíce, somninga, sōna, þǽrrigte, Germ. 388, 73. v. borh-, here-, irfe-, riht-, spere-hand.

hand *also*. *Add*: adv. *Just, exactly* :—Dōn hand swā gelíce (*similiter*; swā gelíce, R. Ben. I. 86, 4) þā ðe on fare synd, R. Ben. 78, 9: 105, 7. Sȳn eác hand swā gelíce geþreáde þā ðe on þām sylfum cildum mid ungesceáde gehātheortað, 130, 6. [*The W.S. version of* Mt. 20, 5 (*the passage rendered in* Anal. Th. 74, 4) *translates* similiter *by* þām swā gelíce.]

hand-æx, e; f. *An axe that could be used with one hand, a hatchet* :—Handæx *dextralis* (dextralis *securis genus, idem quod manuaria*, Migne. Cf. *Spanish* destral *a small axe or little hatchet*), Wrt. Voc. ii, 140, 1. [v. *N.E.D.* hand-ax. *Icel.* hand-öx.]

hand-belle, an; f. *A hand-bell* :—Þǽr synd . . . iiij handbellan and vj hangende bollan (bellan?), C.D.B. iii. 660, 34. [*Icel.* hand-bjalla.]

hand-bóc. *Add*: I. *a book containing the order of service for extreme unction, baptism and catechisms*; manuale :—Mæssepreóst sceal hūru habban . . . handbōc, penitentialem, . . . Ll. Th. ii. 384, 1. II. *a hand-book, manual* :—Wē gesetton on þissum enchiridion, þ ys manualis on lyden and handbóc on englisc, manega þing ymbe gerím-cræft, Angl. viii. 321, 34. [*Icel.* hand-bók.]

hand-brǽd, -brēd. *Perhaps* hand-bred *should be read and the quotation be taken to the next word. But in support of* hand-brǽd *may be noted the form* breð (= brǽð) *odor*, Wrt. Voc. i. 42, 58, *and the phrase* gód hande brād. v. hand; VII. *Wiclif has* handibreede v. *N.E.D.* handbede.

hand-bred. *Add* :—Handbred *vola*, Wrt. Voc. i. 283, 15. Of werlicum folman, handbrede *uirili uola*, An. Ox. 1549. Handbrede *palmula*, Germ. 399, 462. Āstrehtum handbredum tō heofenlicum rodore, Hml. Th. ii. 138, 10. Ūpāwendum handbredum wiþ þæs heofones weard, Hml. S. 26, 118. Fýste, hondbryda (folme, lxxiv, 16), fingras mid þām næglum *pugnas, palmas, digitos cum unguibus*, Lch. i. lxxi, 6. Hē his handbredu (folmas (-e, v.l.) *palmas*, Gr. D. 166, 7) āstrehte wið heofenas weard, Hml. Th. ii. 182, 16. [He his handbreden up to heofene astrehte, Shrn. 15, 24.]

hand-clāþ. *Add*: [Hire handcloðes and hire bordcloðes ben makede wite, O.E. Hml. ii. 163, 34. A handcloðe *hoc manutergium, hic towalus*, Wülck. Gl. 756, 15.] Cf. hand-hrægl.

hand-cops. *Add* :—Sweórcopsas *vel* handcopsas *boias, catenas*, Wrt. Voc. ii. 126, 43.

hand-cræft. *Add* :—Gif hwylc neód sȳ tō becȳpenne ǽnig þing heora (*artifices monasterii*) handcræftes, R. Ben. 95, 16. [v. *N.E.D.* handcraft.

hand-cræftig. *Dele.*

hand-cweorn. *Add* :—Nime þonne clǽnne lengtenbere and grinde, on handcwyrna; nime siþþan mǽderan and drīge on handcwyrna, Archiv. lxxxiv. 326 (d).

hand-dǽd. *Dele*: hand-dǽda. *Add*: v. riht-handdǽda: -handede, v. wōh-handede: hand-fæstan. *Dele.*

hand-fæstung, -fæstnung, l. hand-fæstnung, *and add* :—Handfæstnung *mandatum*, Wrt. Voc. ii. 58, 58. [v. *N.E.D.* hand-fastening.]

handfangen(e)-þeóf. *The word seems to have the same force as* infangeneþeóf (q.v.), *which is the usual form in lists similar to those in which it occurs* :—Hámsócn and forsteall, griðbrice and handfangenðeóf, C.D. iv. 233, 9. Handfangeneðeóf, 17: 23: 30.

hand-full. *Add* :—Hondful beówes *manticum*, Wrt. Voc. ii. 113, 52. Handful, 55, 45: 71, 13. 'Horse mete is bere þ hē ús forgeaf, underfó hē gærs.' Þā underféng se hālga þā handfulle, Hml. S. 3, 218. Sē ðe gripa † handfulla gæderaþ *qui manipulos colliget*, Ps. L. 128, 7. Genim þreó handfulla mucwyrte, þreó sealtes, Lch. ii. 38, 10. v. hærfest-handful.

hand-gang. *Substitute*: *Submission, surrender*. Cf. on hand gān. v. hand; VIII. 5 b δ :—Houdgong *deditio*, Txts. 56, 337. Handgong, Wrt. Voc. ii. 25, 23. Handgang *deditio, l. traditio*, 139, 66. Freódōm *emancipatio*, handgang *manus impositio* (cf. (?) manus impositio reconciliatoria *ea est per quam poenitentes haeretici sive excommunicati sanctae ecclesiae reconciliantur*, Migne), i. 60, 3. [In the Ormulum hand-gang is used of the laying on of hands by the Apostles (All þiss gæfeun forþ þe posstless þurrh hanndganng upponn alle þa þatt fulluhht unnderrfengenn, 15992), or in confirmation (þurrh fulluht ga þurrh hanndgang att hadedd mannes hande, 13254).] [Cf. *Icel.* hand-ganga *submission to a lord, surrender*.]

hand-gemaca, an; *m. A close companion* :—Þā hyrdecnapan mid heora handgemacan ymbe þ wǽron, Hml. S. 23, 421. Cf. hand-gesella, -gestealla.

hand-gemǽne *in the phrase* handgemǽne beón (cf. *Germ.* handgemein werden *to fight hand to hand*) :—Ðǽr unc hwíle wæs handgemǽne *there for a time it was for the two of us hand-to-hand fighting*, B. 2137.

hand-gesella, -gestealla. *Add*: cf. hand-gemaca, hand-preóst.

hand-geweorc. *Add*: I. *what is made with the hands* :—Þine godas syndon gyldene and sylfrene . . . getreówleásera manna handgeweorc Hml. S. 14, 21. Handgeweorce *manufacta*, An. Ox. 3710. I a. *of what is made by the Deity* :—Ic beó þīn hondgeweorc, Bl. H. 147. 35. Swiðor wile God ārian mannum his handgeweorce, Hml. Th. i. 68, 25. His handgeweorc, Adames ofspring, ii. 260, 25: Ll. Th. i. 304, 21. II. *work done by the hands, work in general* :—Fram nænigum eordlicum handgeweorce næs seó bóc āwriten, Wlfst. 214, 10. His handgeweorc þū bletsadest *operibus manuum ejus benedixisti*, Hml. Th. ii. 448, 30. II a. *of the operations of the Deity* :—Hē (*Adam*) wæs gehiwad þurh Godes handgeweorc, Angl. xi. 1, 10. v. hand-weorc.

hand-gewrit. [*The reference for the last passage is* Hml. Th. i. 448, 14.] I. *handwriting, autograph, signature* (cf. *N.E.D.* hand-writ) :—Sóðne geleáfan hē wæs andettende and mid his handgewrite (*cum subscriptione sua*) getrymede, Bd. 5, 19; Sch. 667, 9. II. *a document in a person's own handwriting* :—'Þā deóflu habbað thín on hande mín ágen handgewryt' . . . Cóm se deófol . . . þā cwæð se hālga wer, 'Wē clypiað tō ðām Hǽlende . . . oð þ þū þ handgewryt āgife' . . . Æfter fyrste feól þ ylce gewryt of þǽre lyfte . . . Se biscop āxode one cnapan gif hē oncneówe þ gewryt. Hē cwæð, 'Ic oncnáwe þæs cartan, þis ic sylf āwrāt', Hml. S. 3, 423–457. Drihten sende his āgen hand-gewrit on Scs Petrus heáhaltare.— Ðā wæs þæt gewrit āwriten mid gyldenum stafum, Wlfst. 212, 3.

hand-gift. *Add* :—Næs þæt gefremed firen æt giftum, ac þǽr Hālig Gāst handgift sealde. [The passage seems based on Mt. i. 20: Noli timere accipere Mariam conjugem tuam; quod enim in ea natum est, de Spiritu Sancto est. The Holy Ghost, as it were in the place of husband, makes the *gift* (q.v.) which is required before marriage can take place.] Cf. hand-leán.

**hand-gripe.** *Add:* [v. *N. E. D.* hand-grip.]

**hand-grip.** *Add: security granted by a person in authority*, cf. hand; II. 2 :—Cyricgrið binnan wāgum and cyninges handgrið, Ll. Th. i. 166, 21. Godes cyricgrið and crístenes cynincges handgrið, 358, 261. Gehālgodes cyninges handgrið, Wlfst. 266, 11.

**hand-hæbbende.** *Add:* v. hand; **II.** I. [v. *N. E. D.* hand-habend. Cf. *Icel.* hand-hafandi *seizing, laying hands* on :—þit muuit handhafandi at orðit, Sturlunga Saga (ed. Vigfusson) i. 42, note 5.]

**hand-hamer.** *Add: a hammer that can be used with one hand, a small hammer* :—Handhamur *malleolus*, Wrt. Voc. ii. 58, 1.

**hand-hefe,** es; *m. l.* hand-hæf. es; *n., and add* :—Hondhafum, Lk. R. 11, 46. [cf. on haudum hebban *to bear on the hands* (v. hebban): Goth. hafans *portatus*.]

**hand-hrægl** *Add:* cf. hand-cláþ.

**hand-hwíl.** *Add:* cf. *span* used of time :—On ánre handhwíle *uno momento*, R. Ben. I. 24, 3. Tídum and handhwílum *horis et momentis*, Hy. S. 145, 5. [v. *N. E. D.* hand-while.]

**-handla.** v. sulh-handla.

**handle,** es; *n. l.* handle, an; *f. A handle* :—Haudle *stiba*, Wrt. Voc. ii. 121, 10: i. 287, 31. v. sulh-handla.

**hand-leán.** *Add:* —þonne hē þā handleán hafað and sceáwað, Hy. 2, 7, 12. Cf. hand-gift.

**hand-leng(u)** *hand's length* :—Gyf þū peran wille . . . geþeód þīne fingras tōsomne forð handlenge *if you want a pear . . . join your fingers together projecting out their full length*, Tech. ii. 124, 19.

**handlian.** *Add:* **I.** *to touch with the hands* :—Sē ðe handlað wífhādes mannes líc, Hex. 50, 11. Handla *contrecta*, i. *palfa*, Wrt. Voc. ii. 135, 35. Handlian *contrectare* (*mea membra*), An. Ox. 17, 44. **II.** *to treat* a subject :—Nū wylle ic bysne ætýwan ymbe þā þiug þe wē nū handledon, Angl. viii. 304, 24. v. ge-handlian.

**hand-lín.** *Substitute:* **I.** *a napkin* :—Handlín *maniterium*, W t. Voc. ii. 56, 47. Handlín (-lind, MS.) *maniteorium*, i. 290, 71. **II.** *a maniple*, one of the Eucharistic vestments :—Albe *alba*, stole *stola*, sculdorhrægl *superhumerale*, cæppe *planeta*, handlín *manualis*, Wrt. Voc. i. 81, 41–46. Scrýde hine mid superhumerale and mid alban and stolan and handlíne and planētan, MS. Laud. 482, fol. 48 a. [Take here the two instances given in the Dictionary.] Ðonne þū handlín habban wille, ðonne stríc þū mid þínre swýðran handa eclinga ofer þíne wynstran, Tech. ii. 120, 1.

**handlinga.** *In the passage l.* handlinga, *and add* : , handlunga *in the hands* :—Hine man healfcwicne handlunga þanon āhōf *in manibus jam semivivus levatus est*, Gr. D. 63, 1. Ðā men handlunga (mid heora handum, *v. l. in manibus*) genāmon þ wíf of þām gebedhūse, 73, 7. Þā ongunnon ðā hæðenan hí handlinga āteón, Hml. S. 11, 247. [Cf. *N. E. D.* handlings.] v. handlung.

**handlung.** *Add:* Cf. *the corresponding passage in* Gr. D. 164, 29 :—Þone þe se Godes wer (*Benedict*) nā gehrínende ac on lóciende (*non tangendo, sed respiciendo*) álýsde.

**hand-mitta.** *Substitute:* —Handmitta *exagia*, Wrt. Voc. ii. 70, 13. v. an-mitta.

**hand-preóst** *a priest at a person's hand* (using the phrase as in 'they were first at the kyngis hond', 1 Chron. xviii. 17 (Wicklif), where the A. V. has 'chief man of the king') :—Þrengde hē his handpreóstas and eác sume of his tūnpreóstan þ hí scoldan helpan þan feáwan munecan *precepit capellanis clericis suis, ut essent cum monachis*, Chr. 870; P. 284, 1. Cf. hand-þegn, -gesella.

**hand-sceaft.** *Dele:* **hand-sceát.** *Dele.*

**hand-scío** *a glove.* Dele. The word is dative of a proper name, which may be seen in the place-name of the following passage: In loco qui dicitur Andscōheshām, C. D. i. 102, 9. Graff vi. 418 gives Hant-scōhasheim as a German place-name.

**hand-scōlu, -scālu.** *l.* scolu, -scalu.

**hand-seax.** *Add:* —Lytel swurd oððe handsex *sica*, Wrt. Voc. i. 84, 23. Handseax *coarim* (*cultrum*?), ii. 16, 10.

**hand-selen.** *For* 'Cot. 136, Lys.' *substitute:* —Handselen *mancipatio*, Wrt. Voc. ii. 8; 59.

**hand-seten.** *Add:* —Ðis synt ðāra witena handsetena and ðære hína ðe on ðære geþafunge wēron, C. D. v. 162, 30.

**hand-sliht.** v. and-sliht.

**hand-spitel** *a kind of spade* :—Mattoc *vel* handspitel *fovessoria*, Wrt. Voc. ii. 150, 25.

**hand-spor.** *Substitute:* —hand-sporu, an; *f. A dagger of the hand, a long, sharp nail* :—Hæþenes handsporu (hūnsporu ?), egl unheóru, B. 986. [Cf. hūnsporan *dolones* (v. stæf-sweord), Wrt. Voc. ii. 106, 65.]

**hand-stoc.** *Substitute: A sleeve* :—Gylecan tācen his þæt þū strece forð þín wenstre handstoc and plyce innan mid þínre wynstran hande, Tech. ii. 127, 14. Ymbe þæt ūtan þe þæs scapularæs handstoca āteóriað, 20. Handstocu mid godewebbum gestefnede *manicæ sericis clauatæ*, An. Ox. 5321: 2, 452: 3, 373: 8, 375. Handstocan(-e, Hpt. Gl. 525, 6) *manicas*, 5240.

**hand-swyle,** es; *m. A swelling in the hand* :—Haudswyle *cidaricus*, Wrt. Voc. ii. 131, 46.

**hand-tam;** *adj. So tame that it may be handled;* mansuetus :—Gif ðū mid wilddeórum mē nū bētan wylt hí beóð sōna handtame, Hml. Skt. 8, 86. [v. *N. E. D.* hand-tame. *O. H. Ger.* hant-zam *subjugatus, edomitus.*]

**hand-þweál.** *Add:* —Handþweál *manulauium*, Wülck. Gl. 146, 9. (*Omitted after* Wrt. Voc. i. 37, 16.)

**hand-weorc.** *Add:* [v. *N. E. D.* hand-work.] v. hand-geweorc.

**hand-wyrm.** *Add:* —Hondwyrm, handyrp, honduyrp *briensis*, Txts. 45, 320. Houdwyrm *ladascapiae, briensis*, 73, 1193. Handwyrme *uerme* (minor exiguo sulcat qui corpora *uerme*, Ald. 272, 31), An. Ox. 23, 50. Hondweorm *uerme*, i. *briensis*, 25, 1. (The same passage is glossed in both cases.) [v. *N. E. D.* hand-worm.]

**hand-wyrst.** *Add:* —Handwyrst *articulus*, Wrt. Voc. ii. 10, 24. Elnboga *vel* hondwyrst *cuba*, 137, 40. Se earm betweónan elnbogan and handwyrste *cubitus*, 22, 62. [v. *N. E. D.* hand-wrist.]

**hanga(?),** an; *m. A slope* (?), *declivity* :—On líchangan; oł líchangan, C. D. v. 321, 32.

**hangelle,** an; *f. An implement that hangs*, Rä. 45, 6. [cf. (?) *D. D.* hangle. *O. L. Ger.* hangilla *alligatura; a bunch* of grapes. v. 2 Sam. 16, 1.]

**hangian.** *Add:* **I.** of the position taken by a body under the action of gravity when supported only from above :—Ic (*a horn*) hongige wlitig on wāge, Rä. 15, 11. Him ne hangað nacod sweord ofer þām heáfde be smalan þræde, Bt. 29, 1; F. 102, 27. Hangaþ þær leóhtfæt, Bl. H. 227, 28. Wearþ hē gefæstnod be þære swíþran handa tō þære bære þ hē hangode tō eorþan (*he hung by his right hand without being able to reach the ground with his feet*), 151, 19. Wæron wit twēgen on ānum olfende, and wit unc simble ondrēdeu hwonne wit sceoldon feallan of þām olfende, and miccle mā wit hangodan be þām olfende þonne wit þæron sæton, Shrn. 38, 17. On ðæm clife hangodon on ðæm ísgean bearwum manige sáula be heora handum gebundne . . . and ðonne ðā twigo forburston þonne gewitan þā sáula niþer þā þe on ðæm twigum hangodan, Bl. H. 209, 34–211, 4. On ðæs sācerdes hrægle scolde hangian bellan, Past. 95, 3. On þære-sculon hangian ðā feówer hringas, 171, 3. Ic on wāge geseah wlitig hangian eald sweord, B. 1662. **I a.** of persons, *to be suspended on a gallows* or *cross* :—His sunu hangað hrefne tō hróðre, B. 2447. For hwon āhēnge þū mē hefgor on þínra honda róde þonne iú hongade?, Cri. 1489: 1457. Wearh sceal hangian, fægere ongildan þ hē ær fācen dyde manna cynne, Gn. C. 55. Hongende *crucifixum*, Lk. p. 11, 8. **II.** *to be attached, hold fast* :—þā spācan sticaþ, oþer ende on þære selge . . . Ðā felga hangiaþ on ðām spācan, ðeáh hí eallunga wealowigen on þære eorðan . . . þā felga ne magon bión on þām færelde, gif hí ne bióþ fæste on þām spācum, Bt. 39, 7; F. 222, 7–20. **III.** *to remain suspended without visible support, float* in the air :—Gif him fore wolcen hangað, Met. 5, 4. Tōdrīf þone mist ðe nū hangaþ beforan úres mōdes eágum, Bt. 33, 4; F, 132, 32. Hangode, Met. 20, 266. **IV.** *to have the top bending beyond the lower part, to lean over* :—Ofer þæm mere hongiað bearwas, wudu wæter oferhelmað, B. 1363. **V.** *to hang on, cling to, be unwilling to abandon* :—Hangaþ úre mōd ealne weg on þæm þe wē æfter spyriaþ, Bt. 35, 5; F. 166, 14. Ne þurfon gē nō hongian on ðām anwealde, ne him æfter þrīngan; gif gē wíse bíþ hē wile folgian eów þeáh gē his nō ne wilnian, 16, 1; F. 50, 29. **VI.** *to rest for authority* on, *depend* on :—In ðissum twæm bebodum ealle ae hongað (stondes í honges, L.) and witga in his *duobus mandatis universa lex pendet et prophetae*. Mt. R. 22, 40. v. ā-, ge-hangian.

**hangra.** *Substitute: A wood on a hill-side*, and add :—Tō foxhangran; of ðām hangran, C. D. vi. 106, 1. Of ðām ellenstubbe on ðone yfemestan hangran, iii. 384, 5. [For a discussion of the word and for a number of compound forms in which it occurs see Cht. Crw. p. 134. Other forms which occur, and which connect the word with trees, are :—Tō byrichangran, C. D. iii. 412, 8. Tō perhangran, C. D. B. iii. 97, 3. Tō ðan þriddan þorne æt wírhangran, C. D. v. 297, 18. On sealhangran (cf. tō sahlbeorge (sealh-?), iii. 451, 17; tō sealhyrstæ, v. 256, 1), vi. 234-18. See also *N. E. D.* and *D. D. s. v.* hanger, and *Midd. Flur. s. v.* hangra.] v. wrōht-hangra.

**han-grēd,** es; *m. Cock-crow* :—Gif on [h]angrēde hit þunrað *si gallicantu tonitruaverit*, Archiv. cxx. 50, 15. [v. E. S. 39, 348.] v. grēdan; han-crēd.

**hár.** *Add:* **I.** *grey-haired with age, old* :—Wæs frōd cyning, hár hilderinc, on hreón mōde, B. 1307: By. 169: Chr. 937; P. 108, 20. Ic (*a plough*) geonge swā mē wísað hár holtes feónd (*the grey-haired ploughman?, the enemy of the holt, because the wood has to be cleared away from the land which is to be brought under cultivation*), Rä. 22, 3. Gamele ne mōston hāre heaðorincas hilde onþeón, Exod. 241. ¶ used substantively, *a grey-haired person* :—Hí hāres hyrste Higelāce bæron, B. 2988. Tunge þínre hārra *lingua canum* (as if *canorum*?) *tuorum*, Ps. L. 67, 24. **II.** *grey.* (1) of an animal's coat :—Wulf, hár hæðstapa, Vy. 13. (2) of bright metal :—Hāre byrnan (cf. On him (*Beowulf*) byrne (ísernbyrne, 671) scān, B. 405.), Vald. 2, 17: B. 2153. (3) of a bright star :—Hárwengnes *canities*, se hāra steorra *canis* (as if

connected with *canus?*) vel *canicula, stella quae Sirius vocatur*, Wrt. Voc. ii. 128 25. (4) of frost, *hoar* :—Hwílum hára scóc forst of feax[e], Rä. 88, 7. (5) of stone (cf. ræg-hár :—Ofer hárne stán, B. 1415: An. 843. **II** a. the word occurs often as epithet of stones and trees used as boundary-marks :—Tó ðám háran stáne ; of ðam stáne, C. D. iii. 389, 10. Of ðære brádan ác ðæt hit cymð tó ðære wóhgan apeldran, ðanon norðrihte ðæt hít cymed tó ðære háran apeldran, 33. An háran stán, ii. 29, 6. Of ðan háran stáne on ðone háran wíðig ; of ðan háran wíþie, iii. 313, 27. **III**. fig. of things, *hoary, of great age* :—Hárne middengeard *canescentem mundum*, Mt. p. 1, 5. [*O. Sax., O. H. Ger.* hér : *Ger.* hehr.] v. feax-, healf-, ræg-, un-hár.

**hara.** *Add* :—Hara, hæra *lepus*, Txts. 74, 608. Hara and swýn synd forbodene tó æthrínenne, Lev. 11, 6. Haran *lepusculi*, Kent. Gl. 1104.

**haran spreeel.** *Add* :— Haran spreccil *eccios*, Wrt. Voc. i. 68, 16.

**hár-hune.** *l.* -húne, and *add* :—Háre húne *marrubium*, Wrt. Voc. i. 67, 66. v. húne.

**harian, horian.** *Dele: for* horige *in note to* Ps. 27, 1 *read* hopige.

**hár-ness, e** ; *f. Greyness of hair, grey hair* :—[Eld]ra hárnes *senum canities*, Kent. Gl. 762. Oþ þá grǽgan háruesse *usque cigneam (vetulae senectutis) canitiem*, An. Ox. 1877. Hárnessa *canos (suos cum dolore ducentes ad inferos)*. 3367.

**hárung.** *Add* : **I.** *greyness* :—Hárung *canicies*, Ælfc. Gr. Z. 82, 14. **II.** *a growing grey-haired, old age* :—Oð ylde and hárunga *usque in senectam et senium*, Ps. L. 70, 18.

**hár-wenge.** *Add* : *grey-bearded* [cf. wang (wenge)] :—Cóm sum hárwencge manu (*St. Peter* )intó þám cwearterne . . . þá cwæð se hárwencga, Hml. S. 8, 131–138. Sum geleáfful bócere hárwencge and eald, sé hátte Eleazarus (*Eleazar, one of the principal scribes, an aged man, and of a well-favoured countenance*, 2 Macc. vi. 18), 25, 33 : 28, 91.

**hárweng-ness, e** ; *f. Greybeardedness, old age* :—Hárwengnes *canities, gravitas, senectus*, Wrt. Voc. ii. 128, 22.

**hás.** *Add* :—Ic swanc hrýmende (clypiende, Ps. Rdr., Spl., Srt.), háse gewordene synt míne góman, Ps. L., Rdr., Spl., Srt. 68, 4. [Mid haswre ( = hásre) hwoðrunge *rauco cum murmure*, An. Ox. 26, 14.]

**hás-hrímian**(?) *to cry hoarsely* :—Hié háshrýmedon on heora stefnum (hásrúnigendun stefnun, *v. l.*) *erant clamoribus raucisonis*, Guth. Gr. 128, 127.

**hás-rúnigende.** *See preceding word.*

**hassuc.** *Add* : , hæssuc (-ec) :—Út on Prilleces hæssecas ufewearde, C. D. v. 198, 29. ¶ *as part of a compound* :—Innon hæssucmór ; of hæssuc-mór, C. D. iii. 384, 18. Cf. Ab illo loco usque ad hássukes more, 387, 3. [v. *N. E. D.* hassock.]

**hás-swēge** ; *adj. Hoarse-sounding* :—Hásswége *raucisonos, rugientes*, Germ. 391, 38.

**hasu.** *Add* :—Wegas syndon drýge, haswe herestrǽta (*perhaps herestrǽta here is used as in An. 200 of watery ways, and haswe might be equivalent to* glaucus (cf. *the passage under* haswe), *an epithet of waves, glaucae undae*), holm gerýmed, Exod. 284. Haswe bléde, Rä. 14, 9.

**haswe** ; *adv. Greyly* :—Ic eom wráþre þonne wermód sý [þe] hér on hyrstum heasewe (cf. wermód se hára, Lch. iii. 30, 14) stondeþ *durior quam glauca absinthia campi*, Rä. 41. 61.

**hát** *heat.* *Add* :—Hát ácólað *ardor frigescit*, Angl. i. 285, § 2 : ii. 374, 3. Nánwiht þæs hátes ne þæs cealdes, Wlfst. 184, 19. Wið wunda hátum, Lch. i. 84, 20. v. sumer-hát.

**hát** ; *adj. Add* : **I.** *having or communicating heat.* (1) of the sun, atmospheric conditions, &c. :—Seó háte sunne scíneþ, E. S. viii. 478, 82. Scíned sunne swegle hát, Met. 28, 61. Sceal eft cuman sumor swegle hát, Gn. Ex. 78. Se háta sumor drýgþ and gearwaþ sǽd and bléda, Bl. 39, 13 ; F. 234, 14. Helle þǽre hátan, Gen. 362. Hátum bærnete *torrido solis chaumate*, An. Ox. 3243. Twégen dǽlas (*the temperate zones*) náðor ne tó háte ne tó cealde, Lch. iii. 260, 25. Seó sunne mid hyre hátum leómum, 252, 5. Forbærned hátan heofoncolum, Exod. 71. Sumurlange dagas swíðe háte, Met. 4, 19. Swegl byð hátost, Gn. C. 7. (2) of fire, or anything burning or glowing :—Líg . . . hát ofer helle, Gen. 377. Bryne . . . hát, Cri. 1060. Þone deópan grund þæs hátan léges, Bl. 103, 15. Betwux þére cealdan eorþan and þám hátan fýre, Bt. 334 ; F. 128, 38. Hátum mearcísene *torrido* (i. *ignito*) *cauterio*, Hpt. Gl. 453. 21. Gá hé tó þám hátum írene, Ll. Th. i. 206, 22 : 226, 7. Wið þone hátan bryne þe wealled on helle, 424, 16. Stæppe on hát col . . . stæppe on swá hát swá hé hátost mæge, Lch. ii. 124, 6. Licgad mé ymbútan heardes írenes háte geslægene (*forged while the iron glowed*) grindlas greáte, Gn. 383. Ær hé bǽl cure, háte heaðowylmas, B. 2819. Lége hátra, Rä. 41, 57. Bǽl, háttost heaðowelma, El. 579. (3) of material affected by sun, fire, &c. :—Hé geworhte ánes fearres anlícnesse of áre, tó ðon þonne hit hát wǽre . . ., Ors. 1, 12 ; S. 54, 24. Gif hit wæter sý, hǽte; man hit oð hit hleówe tó wylme . . . hit swá hát sý swá wé ǽr cwǽdon, Ll. i. 226, 13–20. Wæs þǽre burnan wælm heaðofýrum hát, B. 2547. Hé of þám hátum bæðe (*a vat of boiling oil*) eóde, Hml. Th. i. 58, 29. Wel on swá hátum, hafa on múþe swá hát swá þú hátost mæge, Lch. ii.

50, 15. Styre mid sticcan gif þú hǽttre wille, 76, 26. Innon ðone hwær þá ðá hé háttost wæs, Hml. S. ix, 107. (4) of the heat of the body :—Wæs þæt blód tó þæs hát, B. 1616. Hát heáfodwylm *hot tears*, El. 1133. Háte hleórdropan, Gú. 1315. Þæt blód gesprang, hátost heaðoswáta. B. 1668. **II.** of a person, *having the sensation of heat* :—Ic sceal þysne wítes clom beoran beornende . . . hát on helle, hyhtwillan leás, Sat. 159. **II** a. where the sensation is caused by disease :—Þis sint tácn þæs hátan magan ómihtan, Lch. ii. 192, 24. **II** b. of bodily conditions producing the sensation of heat :—Se ece of mínum earme, ðǽr hé hǽttra wæs and byrnendra, eall áweg álǽded wæs *dolor omnis de brachio, ubi ardentior inerat, funditus ablatus est*, Bd. 5, 3 ; Sch. 566, 10. **III.** denoting one of the fundamental qualities of elements and bodies in general :—Hwæt is heora (*the four elements*) ǽlces gecynd? Ðæs fýres gecynd is hát and dríe *ignis calidae et aridae est naturae*, Angl. vii. 12, 105. Be wambe missenlicre gecyndo . . . þonne heó beð hátre gebyrdo and gecyndo . . . Be hátre gecyndo wambe. Sió womb seó þe bið hátre gecyndo, sió melt mete wel, Lch. ii. 220, 14–23. **IV.** of persons or their affections, actions, &c. (1) *having or showing intensity of feeling, ardent, fervent* :—Eálá, wǽre hé áðer, oððe hát, oððe ceald, Past. 445. 36. Þǽr manegum wæs hát æt heortan hyge weallende, An. 1711. Wæs seó treówlufu hát æt heortan, Cri. 539. Him wæs geómor sefa, hát æt heortan hyge murnende, 500 : El. 628 : Gú. 1182. On hátum *torrido* (*castitatis ardore*), An. Ox. 1779. Hé gnornsorge wæg háte æt heortan, Gú. 1310. (2) *excited with anger, wrathful, fierce*, v. hát-heort :—Hordweard hát and hreóhmód hlǽw oft ymbehwearf, B. 2296. Hát and heaðogrim, 2691. Æt helle durn dracan eardigað háte on hreðre, Sat. 99 : 281. Is onbærned þin yrre fýre hátre, Ps. Th. 78, 5. **V.** *that excites strong feeling.* (1) in a favourable sense *exciting warm feelings of affection*, dear to a person :—Mé hátran sind Dryhtnes dreámas þonne þis deáde líf lǽne on londe *dearer to me are the joys of the Lord than this mortal life and frail on earth*, Seef. 64. (2) unfavourable, *causing pain, suffering, &c., severe, violent, intense* :—Him in gesonc hát . . . flacor flánþracu, Gú. 1116. Se grimma hungor ne se háta þurst, Rä. 44, 3. Sume hí cuwon heora gescý . . . for ðære micclan angsumnysse ðæs hátan hungres, Hml. Th. i. 404, 6. Hátum bryne *torrido* (*coenobialis vitae*) *rigore*, An. Ox. 2705. Þæt mé sorgna is hátost on hreðre, Gú. 993. v. brand-, bryne-, fýr-, ofer-, ongemet-, sunn-, þurh-, weall-, wilm-hát.

**hát** *a promise.* *Add* :—þ hát fadores *promissum patris*, Lk. p. 11, 14.

**hata.** v. ciric-, dǽd-, ge-, leód-, mynster-, scyld- hata.

**hátan.** *Add* : **I** a. with acc. and infin. :—Háat meh gecuma tó ðé, Mt. L. 14, 28. **I** b. where there is no subject to the verb in the infinitive :—Ðæt ðú dóa hátes i héhtes *quod tu fieri jubes*, Mt. p. 1, 11. For þǽm gylte hiene eft hétt his fæder ofslean, Ors. 3, 6 ; S. 108. 12. Hé hiene hétt bebyrgean, 128, 16. Hát wyrcean stengas, Past. 169, 22. **I** c. with clause :—þ nǽngum cuoede gehéht i hæt *ut nemini diceret imperat*, Mk. p. 3, 20. **I** d. absolute :—Lǽr ðæt folc, and ðreáta, and tǽl, and hát, Past. 291, 18. Hé þ cwæð hátende (*jubendo*) má þonne biddende, Gr. D. 250, 20. ¶ (in glosses) with dat. of person :—Gástum unclǽnum hátas *spiritibus immundis imperat*, Mk. i. 27. Windum hátted, Lk. L. 8. 25. **I** e. verb of motion implied by a preposition :—Hét (héht, *v. l.*) hé his lǽce tó him *vocavit medicum*, Bd. 5, 6 ; Sch. 581, 6. **II.** *to promise* :—Ðá ðing ðe hé tó Gode hétt (Gode gehét, *v. l.*), Past, 84, 17. Éce héht *aeterna promittit*, Lk. p. 9, 17. **III.** *to call* so and so. (1) where the complement is the proper name used in speaking of a person, people, or place :—Neáh þére byrig ðe mon nú hǽt Babilonia, Bt. 35, 4 ; F. 162. 20. On þá sǽ þe mon hett Euxinus, Ors. 1. 1 ; S. 8. 21. Hé wæs hátan (-en, *v. l.*) Agesilaus, 3, 1 ; S. 99, 29. Craccus wæs hǽten (háten, *v. l.*) án þára consula, 5, 3 ; S. 222, 24. (2) where the complement is an official title :—Rómane him gesetton ládteów þone ðe hié tictatores héton, Ors. 2, 4 ; S. 70, 2. (3) where the complement is a general term used technically :—Deófas wé hátaþ oð .vii. men ; from .vii. hlóð oð .xxxv. ; siþþan bið here, Ll. Th. 1. 110. 13. (4) where the complement is the title of a book :—On þǽre béc þe wé hátað *De Videndo Deo*, Solil. H. 64, 25. (5) where the complement is a class or common noun (a) in the nominative :—Deós wyrt þe . . . sume men hennebelle hátað, Lch. i. 94, 6. Þæt þú sóðfestnes hǽtst, þæt ys God, Solil. H. 52, 12. Tó þám deórcynne þe mon hát tigris, Bt. 38, 1 ; F. 196. 1. Þonne háte wé hine morgensteorra, 39, 13 ; F. 234. 3. (b) in the accusative :—þone dæg and ðá niht þe wé hátað bissextum (*for nominative see* 262, 7, þ bissentus cume), Lch. iii. 246, 14. (6) where the complement is the name bestowed on an object hitherto unnamed :—God gecígde þá drígnesse eorþan and þǽra wætera gegaderunga hé hét sǽs *vocavit Deus aridam terram congregationesque aquarum appellavit maria*, Gen. 1. 10. (7) Where the complement is an abusive epithet :—Gif man mannan an óðres flette mánswara háteð, oþþe hine mid bismærwordum scandlíce gréte, Ll. Th. i. 32, 4. Hine mon scyle on bismer hátan se ánscóda, Past. 45, 8. v. á-, be-, for-, ge-, on- hátan.

**hátan**, _p._ hátte. _Add._: _To be called_ so and so. (1) the complement a proper name:—Meroe hátte án ígland, Lch. iii. 258, 18. þý wege þe háte Appia, Bl. H. 193, 12. In tún þone þe hátte (háta, L.) Gezemani _in uillam quae dicitur Gesemani_, Mt. R. 26, 36. On þære ðióde þe Deira hátte, swiþe neáh þære byrig ðe mon nú hæt Babilonia, Bt. 35, 4; F. 162, 20. Mid Latinus wífe Lucrettie hátte, Ors. 2, 2; S. 66, 31. Themestocles hátte Atheniensa ládteów, 2, 5; S. 82, 13. Marcus þe óþre noman hátte Curtius, 3, 3; S. 102, 30: 3, 6; S. 108, 24. Hé þæm munte gesette þone ilcan naman swá swá hé hátte, Bl. H. 197, 29. Under þæm twæm consulum Tita and Publia hátton, Ors. 2, 4; S. 70, 8. (2) the complement the title of a book:—On ðære béc ðe _Morales_ hátte, Past. 107, 18. On bócum ðæm ðe _Ecclesiastis_ hátton, 275, 16. (3) the complement a class noun:—Frige hwæt sc (_an anchor_) hátte, Rä. 17, 10. Se hearda stán, sé ðe aðamans hátte, Past. 271, 3. Saga mé ðæt andweorc ðe Adam wæs of geworht. Ic ðé secge, of viii punda gewihte. Saga mé: hwæt hátton ðáge? Ic ðé secge ðæt æroste wæs foldan pund . . ., Sal. K. 180, 3–7.

**háte**. _Substitute_: I. of the sun, _hotly, hot._ (1) cf. hát; I. 1:—Of heofnum háte scíned þeós beorhte sunne, Gen. 810. Þonne sunne hátost scíned, Ph. 209. Ðonne þære sunnan scíma hátast scínþ, Bt. 5, 2; F. 10, 29. (2) of glowing iron. Cf. hát; I. 2:—Lecgad ðá ísenan clútas háte glówende tó his sídan, Hml. Th. 1. 424, 35. Gewyrme mid háte glówende ísene, Lch. ii. 236, 31. (3) of the effect produced by fire, sun, &c; cf. hát; I. 3:—Geond helle háte onæled, Sat. 341. II. of intense feeling, _fervently, passionately._ Cf. hát; IV. 1:—Hí geheóldan hálge láre háte æt heortan hige weallende, Ph. 477. Gewrec nú, Dryhten, þæt mé ys þus torne on móde háte on hreðre mínum, Jud. 94. III. _with violent exertion, furiously_:—Stánhofu stódan, streám háte wearp wídan wylme _there stood the stone courts, the stream furiously flung its broad boiling waters_, Ruin. 39. [O. Sax. héto: O. H. Ger. heizo.]

**háte** _a bidding, an invitation._ v. wín-háte.

**háten** (?). _Perhaps for._ hátene _in the passage should be read_ háte (cf. _for case_ mid glówende ísene, Lch. ii. 216, 1), _or_ hátum; _in either the termination of_ ísene _may have influenced the scribe?_

**hát-heort**. _Add_:—Hátheort _furibundus, iratus_, Hpt. Gl. 477, 29. þære hátheortan _furibundae_, Wrt. Voc. ii. 34, 45. þæm hátheortan _funesto_, 14. Háthort were _viro furioso_, Kent. Gl. 845. [Cf. O. H. Ger. heaz-herzi _furor_.]

**hátheort-nes**. _Add_:—Reþscipas _vel_ hátheortnessa _furias, iras_, Wrt. Voc. ii. 151, 77.

**hát-hirtan**. _Add_:—Háthert _stomachatur_, An. Ox. 18. 4. Hé hiene ne háthierte, Past. 297, 6. _v._ ge-háthirtan.

**hatian**. _Add_: I. the subject a person. (1) the object a person. (a) _to hate_ as deserving reprobation:—þá þe ic hatige, ðá ic hatige for þí þe hí þæt gód þære gesceádwísnesse wendad on yfel, Solil. H. 16, 14. þú hatast ealle þá þe unriht wyrcead, Ps. Th. 5, 5. Ðá cwædon þá hálgan þ hí hine hatedon for his geleáfleáste, Hml. S. 11, 60. (β) _to feel the strongest dislike towards_:—Ne mæg nán man twám hláfordum þeówian; hé sóþlíce ænne hatad and óðerne lufad, Mt. 6, 24. Ne scyle nán wís mon nænne mannan hatian; ne hataþ nán mon þone gódan, búton se ealra dysegosta; ne þ nis nán riht þ mon þone yfelan hatige, ac hit is rihtre þ him mon mildsige, Bt. 38, 7; F. 210, 15–18. (γ) _to bear malice to_:—Ælc ðæra þe his bróðor hatad is manslaga, Hml. Th. i. 54, 7. Ne scealt þú nænne mann unscyldig hatian _thou canst not hate any man and be innocent_, Angl. xii. 517, 21. ¶ where malicious action is expressed or implied, _to show hate_ by deeds. Cf. II. 2, hatung; II:—þe þæt wíf feod, hatad under heofnum and þín heáfod treded, Gen. 912. Eádige beó gé þonne eów men hatad and ehtad and onhiscaþ, Lk. 6, 22. Wæs þæs wyrmes wíg wíde gesýne . . . hú se gúdsceaþa leóde hatode and hýnde, B. 2319. Lufa þínne néxtan and hata þínne feónd, Mt. 5, 43. þreóra cynna syndon morþras, þ is þ árest þ man tó óþrum læþþe hæbbe and hine hatige and tæle behindan himsylfum, Bl. H. 65, 1. Ne meahte hé on þám feorhbonan fæhðe gebétan, nó hé þone heaðorinc hatian ne meahte láðum dædum, B. 2466. (2) the object a thing. (a) material:—On þæm dæge hié hatigaþ þisse worlde welan and þá þing þe hié nú lufiaþ, Bl. H. 93, 21. (b) non-material. Cf. (I a):—Ne hatad hé nán yfel, Ps. Th. 35, 4. Hatiaþ yfel and fleóþ, Bt. 42; F. 258, 24. Lufie mon þone man and hatige his unþeáwas, 39, 1; F. 212, 8. Hatian, Met. 27, 32. Mé is álýfad þæt yfel tó hatianne, Solil. H. 16, 17. II. of an animal. (1) cf. I. 1 β:—Ðá styriendan nétenu . . . hyrigaþ monnum, lufiaþ þ hí lufiaþ and hatiaþ þ hí hatiaþ, and flióð þ hí hatiaþ and sécaþ þ hí lufiaþ, Bt. 41, 5; F. 252, 24–28. (2) cf. I. 1 γ ¶:—Mýs hættende _sorices insectanda_, An. Ox. 8, 388. v. ge-hatian.

**hátian**. _Add_:—Hátende, háttendae, haetendae _calentes_, Txts. 47, 357. I. _to be made hot_ by the sun, _get dried up by heat_, cf. hát; I. 3:—Sunne upp cuóm hátedun _sole orto aestuaverunt_, Mt. R. 13, 6. II. of a person, _to get hot_. Cf. hát; II:—Úre líchama oft of ðám fýre hátad ðe him on wunad, Hex. 22, 24. III. of the effects

of strong feeling, _to be excited, troubled_, &c., cf. hát; IV. 1:—Mín gást mé hátad _spiritus meus aestuat_, Först. Verc. 137, 10. þá ongan hé hátian on his geþance _aestuare coepit in cogitatione_, Gr. D. 64, 2. Hé wæs byrnende and hátiende for þám heáfe þære ásteópnesse _orbitatis luctu aestuans_, 165, 12. Hátigendre synne _aestuante culpa_, Germ. 391, 23. IV. of that which causes pain, _to be fierce, intense, raging._ Cf. hát; V. 2:—Hátode, barn _incanduisset_ (cum fervor torridae persecutionis et ardor crudelitatis acrius _incanduisset_, Ald. 67, 22), An. Ox. 4731. v. á-, ge-, on-hátian.

**hátigend-líc**; _adj._ _Hateful, detestable_:—Ys hatigendlic (_odibilis_) sé þe gemáh ys tó specenne (_another by much babbling becometh hateful_, Ecclus. 20, 5), Scint. 79, 15. Hatigendlic (_odibilis_) beforan Gode and mannum ofermódignyss (_pride is hateful before God and man_, Ecclus. 10, 7), 83, 1. Ic wiðsace þám hatigendlicum bígengum þe ðá Iúdéiscan healdad, Hml. S. 3, 605.

**hátlíce**; _adv._ _Ardently, fervently_:—þ hí tó heofonlicre gewilnunge hátlíce beóð áweahte _ut ad caeleste desiderium ardentius excitentur_, Scint. 62, 6. Gebede hátlícor onstandan wé scylon, 31, 19. þ wé God hátlícur lufian, 163, 4. Cf. hát; IV. 1.

**hát-ness**, e; _f._ _Hotness, heat_:—Se(ó) háte sunne scíneþ and þurh þára sunnan hátnesse se heáp wyrdeþ onæled, E. S. viii. 478, 82.

**hatol**. _Add: Odious, hated, hateful_:—Letig wer hatol _vir versutus odiosus (est)_, Kent. Gl. 488. Hatol _odiosam (mulierem)_, 1098.

**hatte-fagol**. v. hærean-fagol.

**hatung**. _Add_: I. Cf. hatian; I. 1 a, β:—Hatung áwecþ saca _odium suscitat rixas_, Scint. 1, 12. Gif ænig þing ungeþwærlices on his geþance ríxade . . . hé hine sylfne geclænsige fram ælcre hatunge leahtre, R. Ben. 38, 19. Hwí is se deófol swá onweard þám men? For þære hatunge þe hé hæfþ tó his scyppende (_propter odium in creatorem_), Angl. vii. 8, 65. Heora gelícan næron on þæs cáseres lande, ne him swá leóíe, gif hí noldon áwendan þá lufe tó hatunge, Hml. S. 11, 59. Bið rihtwísnys on dóme forhwyrfed for ege and for gýtsunge and for hatunga and for lufe, Hml. A. 148, 108: 113. Ælce yrsunge and andan and hatunge áworpan fram úrum heortum, 142, 112. II. _hatred that finds expression in acts._ Cf. hatian; I. 1 a, γ ¶:—Hé him fremede mid þære rédan éhtnysse hatunge, Hml. Th. i. 84, 12. Hine se kyning hider and þider áfiýmde, and hé his éhtnysse and his hatunge fleáh, Guth. 76, 15.

**háw**. Kemble says, 'In all probability, _a look out_, or _prospect_'; Middendorff compares the word with _-hau_ in German place-names, and takes it to mean a clearing, a place where trees are cut down (cf. heáwan). But perhaps in the one passage where the word occurs _hláwe_ should be read:—Haec sunt supradictarum uocabula terrarum, aet Uuineshauue (cf. scuccanhlau, 196, 1), C. D. i. 195, 30.

**-háwe**. v. earfoþ-háwe.

**háwian**. _Add_: I. absolute, _to look._ (1) with the eyes:—Hé eóde út, and háwode and hercnode _egressus est, et erectis auribus adstans_, Guth. Gr. 136, 8. Hé wæs eft cyrrende tó þære spyrtan, and wærlíce and forðonclíce háwode, and geseah þ seó nædre þær in wæs qui reversus ad sportam caute ac sollicite attendit, sed eam serpens tenebat, Gr. D. 203, 17. (2) with the mind's eye:—þære sáule háwung is gesceádwísnes and smeáung. Ac manige sáwle háwiad mid ðám, and þeáh ne geseóð þ þ hí wilniad (_non sequitur ut omnis qui aspicit videat_), Solil. H. 28, 7. II. _to look at, observe_ an object (_gen._) (1) with the eyes:—Ælc man ðára þe æágan heft ærest háwad þæs þe hé geseón wolde, Solil. H. 27, 6. Hý mín háwodon and mé beheóldon _ipsi consideraverunt et conspexerant me_, Ps. Th. 21, 16. (2) figurative:—Creft ealra crefta is þæt man spurige æfter Gode, and hys háwie and hine geseó, Solil. H. 30, 24. Ðreó þing sint neódbehéfe ðám eágan ælcere sáwle; án is þæt hál sién, óðder þæt heó háwien ðes þe heó geseón wolden, þridde þæt hí magen geseón þæt þæt hí geháwian _tria ad animam pertinent, ut sana sit, ut aspiciat, ut videat_, 4. III. where the direction or end of a look is marked by a preposition, _to look after, on, to._ (1) physical:—Hé beseah on æghwilce healfe; and hé háwode on þá róde _he looked about on every side, and his gaze rested on the cross_, Hml. S. 23, 504. Críst sende swægende fýr of heofonum, þ menn on háwoden (_that men might look on_), 2, 261. Hé hét his cnapan háwian tó ðære sæ gif ænig mist árise, 18, 145. (2) figurative, where the mind is directed to a subject:—Hwónlíce fremad ðæs mannes líf ðe bið nýtene gelíc, ðe háwad symle tó ðære eorðan, þ is, tó eorðlicum ðingum, Hml. Th. ii. 442, 8. þæt man geseó þæt ðæt hé æfter háwode _ut aspiciat, ut videat_, Solil. H. 27, 4. Is ðearf þæt þú rihte háwie mid módes æágum tó Gode swá rihte swá swá scipes ancerstreng býd áþenæd on gerihte fram þám scype tó þám ancre, 22, 3. IV. _to look after, guard, watch_ (with _acc._):—Hire fóstermóder hí hét gán mid óþrum fæmnon on feld sceáp tó háwienne, Hml. A. 171, 50. V. _to look on, regard with_ (_kindly_) feeling:—Háwa nú mildelíce þás earman eorðan _jam miseras respice terras_, Bt. 4; F. 8, 20. VI. _to secure that a thing is_ (_or is not_) _done, to see to it_ that:—Háwa þæt se inra wind þe ne tówende, Hml. Th. ii. 392, 32. þý mon sceal fæsðne weal wyrcean, ðý mon ær geháwige ðæt se grund fæsst sié, ðær mon ðone grundweall on lecgge tunc fabrica

*robusta construitur, cum prius locus solidus, in quo fundamentum poni debeat, providetur*, Past. 308, 3. **VII.** where a condition, stated in a clause, is to be ascertained by looking :—Drihten lócað of heofenum ofer manna bearn and háwað hwæðer hé geseó ænigne þæra þe hine séce *Dominus de coelo prospexit super filios hominum, ut videat si est requirens Deum*, Ps. Th. 13, 3. Háwa hwæðer hys ceáflas sín tóswollene, Lch. iii. 140, 8.

**háwung.** *Add* :—Þære sáule háwung is gesceádwísnes and smeáung *aspectus animae ratio est*, Solil. H. 28, 6.

**hé.** [*In* p. 513, col. 1, l. 60 Enachis (Num. 13, 29) *should be read for* Enac his : cf. *the accusative* Enachim *in* Jos. 11, 21. For -*is* as gen. in foreign names cf. Num. 13, 11, 12.] *Add* : nom. sing. m. hé, hee, hí, hié; f. heó, hió, hé : [also *North*. hiá, hiú, hiuu : *Kent*. hí, hiá]; n. hit, hyt : *gen. m. n.* his, hys, is; f. hire, hyre, hiere, heore, hiore : n. hit, hyt : *gen. m. n.* his, hys, is; f. hire, hyre, hiere, heore, hiore : *dat. m. n.* him, hym, heom, him; f. (as gen.) : *acc.* hine, hyne, hiene, higne, hin; f. hié, heó, hió, hé, hí, hý : [*North*. hiá, heá; *Kent*. hiá]: *nom. acc. pl.* hí, hig, hié, hii, hió, heó, hé, hý : [*North*. heá, hiá, hié, hiá; *Kent*. hiae]; *gen.* hiera, hira, hiora, heora, hieora, hera, hyra : [*North*. hiara, heara]; *dat.* him, hym, heom :—*Ille* hé, *ipse* hé sylf . . . *sui* his, Ælf. Gr. Z. 93, 13–14. *Ille* hé, *illius* his, 96, 15 (*and often pp*. 96–119). **A.** masculine and feminine forms. [The want of clearness that results from the pronoun material being so limited in Old English may be illustrated by the following passages :—Romulus . . . his ágenne sweór tó ðeáðe beswác, þá hé hiene tó him áspón and him gehét ðæt hé his ríce wið hiene dǽlan wolde and hiene under ðǽm ofslóg, Ors. 2. 2 ; S. 66, 7–22. þonne lǽte hé (*God*) his (*the reward*) hine (*Lucifer*) lange wealdan, Gen. 258.] **I.** where the pronoun refers to persons or personifications. (1) the persons definite individuals. (*a*) *masculine singular* :—Se apostol his stírde ðá hé cuæð, Past. 33, 10. Him ætwát Petrus . . . Ðá andwyrdon him ðá Iúdéas, 443, 14. Geonduearde him Philippus . . . cuoeð tó him án of ðegnum his, Jn. L. 6, 8. Gefrugnun him ðá æláruas, 9, 15 : Lk. L. 10, 30. Hé him tó gehét monigne lǽce, and heora nán him ne mehte beón náne góde, Ors. 6, 30 ; S. 282, 18. Mid heora ealra fultume, 3, 10 ; S. 140, 18. (*a a*) where the person is a male, but the noun is of the neuter gender, cf. B. I. 1 a :—Þ cild . . . ǽr hé on innoðe geeácnod wǽre, Lk. 2, 21. Hig cómon þ cild ymsníþan, and nemdon hyne, 1, 59. (*a β*) where the pronoun represents either a male or female, cf. III. 1 a :—Uncer (*Malchus and his wife*) lǽþette ǽgþer óþer þeáh þe hé hit óþrum ne sǽde, Shrn. 39, 22. (*a γ*) pronoun omitted :—þá wandode se bisceop, ac hine bǽdon þá óþre, and fylston þám fæder, þ gefremode his béne, Hml. S. 31, 1109. (*a δ*) pleonastically with noun (proper or common) :—Hé þá Malchus nyste, Hml. S. 23, 688. Hé ðá Drihten Críst cwæð, Wlfst. 261, 2. Nú hælþ þ þes man, Nic. 1, 27. ¶ anomalous construction :—Ic nolde þ ðú wéndest þ se God þe fæder is eallra gesceafta, þ him útane cóme his gódnes, Bt. 34, 3 ; F. 136, 23. (*b*) *fem. sing.* :—Mín dohter is deád ; ac cum . . . and heó (hiú, L., heó, R.) lyfað, Mt. 9, 18. Hí (*sapientia*) clepað, Kent. Gl. 6. Mín dohtor . . . sete þíne hand ofer hí (hiá, L., hiá, R.) þ heó (hiá, L.) hál sý and lybbe (hiá hlifige L., hió lifge, R.), Mk. 5, 23. (*b a*) where the person is a female, but the noun is (i) masculine :—Hé geworhte þæt ribb tó wífmen and gelædde hig tó Adame, Gen. 2, 22. (ii) neuter :—Hí seldon þ cild . . . Heó úp eóde . . . Hml. A. 125, 295. Mín wíf ðá hwíle hiá hit gehaldan wile, C. D. i. 310, 12. Án wíf . . . heó (hió, L., heó, R.) cwæð, Mt. 9, 21 : Gen. 3, 15. Nys þis mæden (þæt mægden, R.) deád ac heó (hió, R.) slǽpð, Mt. 9, 24. (*b β*) pleonastically, cf. A. S. 66, 32. (*c*) *plural* : definite individuals, either males or females, or where both sexes are represented :—Zacharias . . . and his wíf . . . Sóðlíce hig wǽron búta rihtwíse, Lk. 1, 16. Latinus . . . Brutus . . . þá heó on fríe wǽron . . . hié brémuste wǽron tó ðǽm cyninge, Ors. 2, 2 ; S. 66, 30–32 : 2, 8 ; S. 92, 29–31. Hí (*the Romans*) hié (*the daughters of the Sabines*) begeáton, 2, 2 ; S. 64, 28. (*c a*) pleonastically :—Hí ðá þá bydelas . . . férdon, Hml. S. 23, 52. Hí ðá hálgan . . . ealle hí forhtedon, 236. Hí þonne ðá seofon geómredon, 125. Móyses and Helias hí fæston, and se Hǽlend . . . hé fæste, Guth. Gr. 124, 26. (*c β*) placed immediately before the name of the person associated with the person spoken of :—Wæs Sarran sár on móde þæt him Abrahame (*her and Abraham*, cf. the similar construction with the duals of the first and second persons) ǽnig ne weard bearn gemǽne, Gen. 2215. (2) the persons indefinite. (*a*) any one of a class or with certain characteristics :—Hí (*one suited to be a bishop*) sceal tilian swǽ tó libbenne swǽ hé mǽge . . ., Past. 60, 18. Sé bið siweníge sé ðe his andgit bið ðǽr tó ðon beorhte scínende ðæt hé (hié, *v. l.*) mǽge ongietan . . ., 67, 25. Hé (*mulier fortis*) bohte emit, Kent. Gl. 1140. Mæg þone wísan . . . scamian, þonne hine . . . lysted, Met. 10, 14. Ðeáh hé (hí, *v. l.*) fela wundra wyrcen, eft þonne hit tó him cumað, Past. 26, 22. Eówre wítgan . . . ðæt hé (hié, *v. l.*) eów gebróhton on hreówsunge, 90, 3. Heó, 87, 4. Hié (hió, *v. l.*), 271, 20. Sume ðá ðá wénað ðæt hié eáðmóde síen, hii dóð, 301, 26. Ðonne hé (hié, *v. l.*) dóð . . ., ðonne hié . . . gehwierfað, 368, 19. Ic bebeóde mínum aefterfylgendum . . . ðaet hiae . . ., C. D. i. 293, 23. Se

færlica deáð hé (hié, *v. l.*) bereáfode ðæs ðe hí (hié, *v. l.*) stríndon, Past 333, 16. ¶ anomalous constructions. (*a*) the pronoun repeated :—Hié sint tó manianne ðætte hié ðá Godes ǽ þe ús forbiét deófium tó offrianne, ðæt hié þá ilcan ǽ ne gehwierfen tó diófulgilde, Past. 368, 1–4. (*β*) a singular pronoun referring to a plural antecedent :—Sume beóð . . . gesewen swelce hé (hié, *v. l.*) fæsðlicu weorc wyrce, and ðeáh, ðeáh hé (hié, *v. l.*) swá dó . . ., hé (hié, *v. l.*) bið áswunden oninnan him selfum, Past. 235, 18–21. (*γ*) where the noun which the pronoun should represent is not given, but is to be inferred :—Wé cwædon he hláfordsearwe, þ hé (i. e. *any one that commits the crime in question*) beó his feóres scyldig, Ll. Th. i. 202, 2. (*δ*) where the pronoun is omitted :—Nánan þeófe . . . þonne þe wé geáxian þ fúl sý, Ll. Th. i. 229, 13. Ælc mynetere þe man tíhð þ fals feoh slóge, 296, 12. Gódfremmendra swylcum gisefde bið þæt þone hilderǽs hál gedígeð, B. 300. Swá fela manna swá man wite þ ungelygne sýn, Ll. Th. i. 222, 10. (*b*) any one at all, v. man :—Gif hig ǽnig man út ábréde, hæbbe hé Godes curs, Cht. E. 253, 13. Hwelc fremu bið menn ðæt hé (hié, *v. l.*) gestríene eal ðæt him ymbútan sié, Past. 333, 11. Ðý lǽs ǽnig durre . . . forcweðan, swelce hé licette eáðmétto . . . gif hine (hiene, *v. l.*) gecíst sió úplice gifu, 51, 2–4. Ælc mon hæfþ ðone friódóm þ hé wát hwæt hé wile, Bt. 40, 7 ; F. 242, 19. Mon mæg geþencean þ hé on riht gedémed, Ll. Th. i. 56, 29. Gif hwá wrace dó ǽr þon hé him ryhtes bidde, 108, 4. ¶ (*a*) the pronoun omitted :—Nó þæs fród leofað gumena bearna þæt þone grund wite, B. 1368. (*β*) where there is no antecedent noun, *they* used like older *man* :—Gif se oxa hnitol wǽre for dæge oððe for twám and hig hit his hláforde cýðdon, Ex. 21, 29. Eádige synt gé þonne hí (hiá, L., mennisc, R.) wyriað eów . . . swá hí (hiá, R.) éhton þá wítegan þe beforan eów wǽron, Mt. 5, 11–12. (*c*) where the pronoun represents a person of a class described in a preceding relative clause :—Sé ðe hwæt yfeles ongiet on his níhstan and hit forswugaþ, hé déð . . ., Past. 275, 7 : 343, 19. Sé þe segð . . ., hé byð scyldig, Mt. 5, 22 : Vald. 2, 28 : Sal. 86. (*c a*) where the pronoun is antecedent :—Hæbbe hé Godes curs þe þis ǽfre undó, Cht. E. 253, 24, 32. Críst him wurðe wráð þe hí hæfre geþýwie, 253, 17. (3) where the oblique cases of the pronoun, having any of the values given in (1) and (2), refer to the subject of the sentence. (*a*) reflexive :—Hé his on ðá ilcan wísan tielað ðe hié dóð, Past. 133, 8. Se yfela ðeów . . . itt him and drincð, 121, 13. Hé þóhte his sunu tó beswícanne, and him siþþan fón tó þǽm onwalde, Ors. 6, 30 ; S. 282, 9. Hé him tó gehét monigne lǽce, 17 Ne mót sé óðrum onfón, sé ðe him (*qui ipse*) bið unfullod, Ll. Th. ii. 140, 19. Gegadorode micel here hine, Chr. 921 ; P. 101, 23. Gif mín wiif hiá nylle swǽ gehaldon, C. D. i. 310, 19. Hié wǽron hiera tilgende, Chr. 876 ; P. 74, 13. Alchere and Aeðelwold fón him tó ðǽm londe, C. D. i. 310, 24. (*a a*) strengthened with *self*, q.v. :—Fét hé þonne higne seolfne, Ll. Th. ii. 430, 1. Ús manode sió sóðfæstnes ðurh hé (hié, *v. l.*) selfe, Past. 280, 8. Gif hié hiera níhstan lufien suá suá hié selfe, 275, 2. (*b*) reciprocal :—Antigones and Perthica gefeohtedan þæt hié wolden him betweónum gefeohtan, Ors. 3, 11 ; S. 144, 34. Ealle gesceafta þú gesceópe him gelíce and eác on sumum þingum ungelíce, Bt. 33, 4 ; F. 128, 26. Hí ne beóð fram him sylfum tótwǽmede, Hml. Th. i. 500, 5. (4) as relative. (*a*) alone, cf. sé ; III. :—Wé feohtan ne dorston ongeán ðone ormǽtan here, hé (þe?) hæfde þá burh beseten, Hml. S. 7, 348. (*b*) combined (*a*) with þe to express the relative. v. þe ; I. 3 :—Sé bið siweníge sé ðe his andgit bið tó ðon beorhte scínende, Past. 67, 24. Sende Galerius him ongeán Severus þe him se onweald ǽr geseald wæs, Ors. 6, 30 ; S. 282, 5. Wá þǽm menn þe swicdóm þurh hyne cymð *vae homini per quem scandalum venit*, Mt. 18, 7. (*β*) with *sé*. v. sé ; IV. 2 a. (5) the genitive as possessive. (*a*) the pronoun as in (1). (*a*) with noun. (*a a*) alone :—Þú nemst hys naman (noma is, L.) Hǽlend, Mt. 1. 21. Weard hyre (hire, L., R.) blódes ryne ádrúwod, Mk. 5, 29. Fanius hieora consul, Ors. 3, 10 ; S. 140, 12 : Bl. H. 249, 2. (*a β*) with other words :—His seó heáhe gódnes, Bt. 34, 3 ; F. 136, 23. Þ his gód and sió his gesǽlþ, 34, 7 ; F. 144, 20. (*β*) without noun, *his*, *hers*, *theirs* :—Wé his syndon, Ps. Th. 99, 2. Hé gean Ælfriðæ ðæs cyninges wífæ . . . and ðám æðelingæ, ðæs cyngæs suna and his feóran, C. D. iii. 127, 26. Ðá weard Eustatius uppon his horse, and his gefeóran uppon heora, Chr. 1048 ; P. 173, 1. (*b*) the pronoun as in (2). (*a*) with noun. (*a a*) alone :—þæt on hys heortan (hearta is, L.) ásáwen is, Mt. 13, 19. (*β*) without noun, *his*, *hers*, *theirs* :—Búton heó fram þám ceorle wifte eft hám ongeán, and nǽfre eft heó his ne weorðe, Ll. Th. i. 416, 15. (*c*) the pronoun as in (3). (*a*) with noun. (*a a*) alone :—Swá man spricð wið his freónd *sicut solet loqui homo ad amicum suum*, Ex. 33, 11. Gif hwá fare fram his hláforde, Ll. Th. i. 126, 9. Heó onwríhð hire ǽwelm þonne þ hé beó his feóres scyldig, 202, 2. Heó geopenaþ hiore ðeáwas, Bt. .20; F. 70, 25. Ðæt hié hera mód gestrongien, Past. 307, 20. ¶ where the subject is not expressed :—On þám dagum wæs álýfed tó álecgenne his fýnd, Hml. S. 25, 684. Be unálésedum fære fram his hláforde, Ll. Th. i. 126, 8. (*a β*) with other words :—Þeáh se rihtwísa áfealle, ne wyrð his nán bán tóbrocen, Ps. Th. 36, 23. God on his þǽre heán ceastre, Bt. 40, 7 ; F. 242, 31. Hé

bioð anlíc þára his þegna sumum, 37, 1 ; F. 186, 12. Sendon hý ymb heora þæt mæste bismer, Ors. 3, 11 ; S. 146, 28. (β) without noun :— Ǽr þá Crístnan mehten hira út áscúfan, Chr. 897 ; P. 91, 13. (β β, as substantive :—Hé bið gelícost ðǽm men ðe his tówirpð, Past. 445, 18. Ðá ðe hiera (hiora, v. l.) sellað qui sua largiuntur, 327, 12. II. where the pronoun refers to an animal. (1) masculine :—Feóll se assa ... and Balaam beót hine. Þá geopenode Drihten þæs assan múð, and hé cwæð : 'Hwí bæátst þú mé?' Num. 22, 27-28. Þǽr wæs begyten se mǽsta bera .., sé wæs gewunod þ hé manna líchaman slát ... þá wæs hé mid réðnesse onǽled, and ðone biscop gesóhte ; ac hé forgeat ealle þá his réðnesse and his heáfod ofdúne ásænde, Gr. D. 194, 24-195, 3. Fleógende fugel, ðonne hé gífre bið, hé gesihð ðæt ǽs, Past. 331, 17. Gif se hund má misdǽda gewyrce, and hé (the owner) hine (the dog) hæbbe, Ll. Th. i. 78, 6. (2) feminine :—Hé ásende áne culfran, þ heó sceáwode. ... Heó fleáh, and ne mihte findan hwǽr heó hire fót ásette, Gen. 8, 8-9. Seó leó, ðeáh hió wel tam sé, and hire mágister lufige, Bt. 25 ; F. 88, 9. Seó leó mid hire clifrum scræf geworhte, Hml. S. 23 b, 787. Beseó hé tó þǽre nǽddran, and hé leofað sóna swá hé besihð on hig. Num. 21, 8. (3) for genitive as possessive see instances under (1) and (2). III. where the pronoun refers to an inanimate thing. (1) masculine :—Ðæs mónan ryne is nearo, for þan þe hé yrnð ealra tungla niðemest, Lch. iii. 248, 9. Of ðám wǽtan þe byð gefroren ǽr þan hé tó dropum geurnen sý, 278, 25. Þá lǽwedan willað habban þone mónan be þám ðe hí hine geseóð, 266, 10. Hé nam þá hláfas and hig gedǽlde, Jn. 6, 11. (1 a) where the pronoun refers to either a masc. or fem. noun, cf. I. 1 a β :—Gyf þín hand oððe þín fót þe swicað áceorf hyne of, Mt. 18, 8. (2) feminine :—Sió sprǽc ..., hié (hió, v. l.) ... gelǽrð, Past. 275, 4. Sió gesceádwíslice gecynd ... ðonne hé ... forlíesð, 351, 1. Nilus seó eá hire ǽwielme is néh þǽm clife ... and þǽr hió ǽrest úp wield ... Ond þonne of þǽm sé þǽr hé úp of þǽm sonde scýt hé is eást irnende ... and þǽr mon hæt þá eá Ion, Ors. 1, 1 ; S. 12, 19-27. Man wísdóm and láre hieder on lond sóhte, and wé hié (hí, v. l.) nú sceoldon úte begietan, gif wé hié habban sceoldon. Swá clǽne hió wæs oðfeallenu ..., Past. 3, 13. Ǽlc sǽ, þeáh heó deóp sý, hæfð grund on ðǽre eorðan, Lch. iii. 254, 20. 'Teóh ðíne hand' ... þá teóh hé hig ongeán and bróhte hí eft út, and heó wæs gelíc þám óðrum flǽsce, Ex. 4, 7. Seó Ægyptus ... be norþan hire ..., and be eástan hiere, Ors. 1. 1 ; S. 12, 16-17. Genim þás wyrte ... cnuca hý, Lch. i. 122, 2. Hié hiora (books) nánwuht ongiotan ne meahton for ðǽm ðe hié nǽron on hiora ágen geðióde áwritene, Past. 5. 12. (2 a) pleonastic :—Seó eorþe þe Lazarus deádan líchaman heóld, heó hyne cwycne ágeaf, Nic. 14, 37. v. Ors. 1, 1 ; S. 12, 16 supra. (2 b) possessive :—Heó (the sun) mid heore beorhtan scíman, Bt. 4 ; F. 6, 33. Hiore, 41, 1 ; F. 244, 7. Hyre, Lch. iii. 260, 10. IV. where the pronouns are used to mark sex :—Sum cyn is gecweden epicena, þæt is on Englisc gemenged : hic coruus ðes hremn, swá hwæðer swá hit byð, swá hé, swá heó ; hic miluus ðes glida, ǽgðer ge hé ge heó ; haec aquila ðes earn ; ǽgðer ge hé ge heó, Ælfc. Gr. Z. 19, 10-14. Ursus bera, ursa heó, Wrt. Voc. i. 78, 12, 13. B. neuter forms. I. where the pronoun refers to a neuter noun. (1) the noun denoting a person. (a) a male. cf. A. I. 1 a a :—Underfóh þis cild (puerum istum) and féd hit, Ex. 2, 9. Áxiað þe þám cilde, and þonne gé hyt gemétað, Mt. 2, 8. (b) a female, v. (4). (c) sex not determined :—Manig wíf swelt for hire bearne ǽr heó hit forðbringan mæge, Bt. 31, 1 ; F. 112, 11. (2) the noun denoting an animal :—Ongan his hors wérigean ... oð ðæt hit on eorðan hreás, Bd. 3, 9 ; Sch. 230, 3 ; Ps. Th. 32, 15. Þ nán man ne sylle nán hors ofer sǽ bútan hé hit gifan wille, Ll. Th. i. 208, 19. Hé genam án cealf ... and se cnapa hit ofslóh, Gen. 18, 7. (3) the noun denoting an inanimate object :—Ðæt hefige mód glít ..., oð hit áfield ...; for ðǽm hit ǽr hit nolde behealdan ..., hit sceal áfeallan, Past. 279, 2-5. Hé ðæs áliéfdan nánwuht nolde forlǽtan, ac his swíðe ungemetlíce breác, 339, 5. Wé cwǽdon be hláfordsearwe, þ hé beó his feóres scyldig, gif hé his ǽtsacan ne mihte, Ll. Th. i. 202, 3. Hé ástígende on án scyp ... bæd hyne þ hé hit fram lande tuge, Lk. 5, 3. Wæs micel licggende feoh funden ; sum hit Scipia tó Róme sende, sum hé hit hét þǽm folce dǽlan, Ors. 4, 10 ; S. 196, 30. (3 a) pleonastic :—Hit is welig þis eálond on wæstmum, Bd. 1, 1 ; Sch. 8, 6. Hit hafað þis land sealtseáðas, and hit hafað hát wæter, 24. Brittania þæt ígland hit is norðeástlang ; and hit is eahta míla lang, Ors. 1, 1 ; S. 24, 1. Mýn rýce nys ná on þysum myddanearde ; gif hyt on þysum myddaneard(e) mýn ríce wǽre, þonne ..., Nic. 4, 37. Uton oðwendan hit monna bearnum, þæt heofonríce, nú wé hit habban ne móton, Gen. 403 : B. 1705. (3 b) pronoun omitted :—On þám gemótan, þeáh wurðan on namcúðan stówan, Ll. Th. i. 348, 17. (4) possessive, its (his, her) :— þ hús feóll ; and his hryre wæs mycel, Mt. 7, 27. Þ mægden cuoeð móder his puella dicit matri suae, Mk. L. 6, 38. Þ geheáld hond his (hyre hand, W. S.) cuoeðende, 'Lá, mægden, árís,' Lk. 8, 54. II. where the pronoun represents a masculine or feminine noun. (1) masc. (a) a living creature :—Gif se oxa spyrnð ongeán ðá gáde, hit dereð him sylfum, Hml. Th. i. 390, 10. (b) an inanimate object :—Se wǽta ..., gyf hit sealt sý ..., hit byð ... tó ferscum wæterum áwend, Lch. iii.

278, 10. Hié wurdon geuuræt mid moncwealme, and sé wæs swá ungemetlic, ðæt hié ... sóhton hú hí hit gestillan mehte, Ors. 3, 10 ; S. 140, 8. Þisne middangeard ... hit, S. 142, 23 : Past. 5, 5. (2) fem. (a) a living creature :—Geseah hé león (cf. seó leó, 777) ... and hit his fótlástes liccode, Hml. S. 23 b, 773. (b) an inanimate object :— Ðára byrðenna hefignesse, eall ðæt ic his geman, ic áwríte, Past. 23, 12. Ne gæð ná máre tó métinge búton þæt þú hit geseó and herige, Hml. Th. i. 186, 7. Þá þe landáre hæfdon, hí hit beceápodon, 316, 10. ¶ possessive :—Þonne seó leó bringð his hungregum hwelpum hwæt tó etanne, Ors. 3, 11 ; S. 142, 24 : Hml. S. 23 b, 778. III. the pronoun representing a personal pronoun or noun :—Cwyst þú eom ic hyt (ah ic hit eam, R.) numquid ego sum?, Mt. 26, 22. Ah hit sié ic numquid ego?, Mk. R. 14, 19. Gif þú hyt eart (þ sié, R.) si tu es, Mt. 14, 28. Hí wiston þ hit wæs Drihten scientes quia Dominus est, Jn. 21, 12. III a. the pronoun omitted :—Se Hǽlend cwæð : 'Hé ys (he it is, A. V.) sé ðe ic rǽce hláf,' Jn. 13, 26. Him weard gesǽd þ wǽre Martinus, Hml. S. 31, 994. IV. where the pronoun represents an object which is described in, or may be inferred from, the context :—þá þá þú tó þám gefeohte férdest þú offrodest deóflum, and nú ðú sigefæst cóme þú gebǽde þe tó Críste ; cýð mé hú hit sý, Hml. S. 7, 342. Genim þá ylcan wyrte, and wyl on ealdan wíne tó þriddan dǽle, hit hælp wunderlíce, Lch. i. 72, 24 : 122, 9. Genim þǽre ylcan wyrte þreóra trymessa wǽge, seóð on ealdum wíne, and gníd þǽrtó xxvii piporcorn ; gedrinc his þreó full fulle, 74, 1. Sete ðín wín, and lege ðínne hláf ofer ryhtwísra monna byrgenne, and ne et his nánwuht, Past. 327, 2. Æfter ðǽm þe him swá oftrǽdlíce mislamp, hié angunnan hit wítan heora látteówum and heora cempum heora earfeþa, Ors. 4, 4 ; S. 164, 25. IV a. where hit stands in apposition to a following clause or infinitive phrase :—Hycgað his ealle, hú gé hí beswícen, Gen. 432. Unc hit Waldend hêht for wera synnum Sodoma and Gomorra sweartan líge fýre gesyllan and þás folc sleán, 2504. V. hit as indefinite subject :—On lencten hit grêwð, and on hærfest hit fealwaþ, Bt. 21 ; F. 74, 22. Swylce hit ealle niht dagie, Lch. iii. 260, 1. Hit segð on hálgum bócum, þæt ..., Wlfst. 146, 16. Þæs ylcan scyldige þe hit hér beforan cwæð, Ll. Th. i. 248, 18. Winnende þǽr hit þonne þearf wæs, Ors. 6, 23 ; S. 274, 29. Harold þǽr his líðes ábád, for þám þe hit wæs lang ǽr hit man gegaderian mihte, Chr. 1066 ; P. 196, 14. ¶ with plural verb :—Fór Hannibal, þêh þe hit (the earlier MS. omits hit) ymbe þone tíman wǽron swá micel snáwgebland, Ors. 4. 8 ; Bos. 90, 5.

heador. v. heaþor : heá-dor. v. heáh-deór : heaf. l. hæf, q. v.

heáf. Add :—Weard micel morcnung and ormǽte wóp, swá þ se heáf swégde geond ealle þá ceastre ... þá cwæð hé : 'Sege mé for hwilcum intingum þeós ceaster wunige on swá micclum heáfe and wópe,' Ap. Th. 6, 8-20 : Exod. 35. Nales þæt heáfe bewinded, ne hûru wæl wêped wulf se grǽga not heard were his howls about that, nor cared the grey wolf for the carnage, Gn. Ex. 150. Byrnende for þám heáfe þǽre ásteópnesse orbitatis luctu aestuans, Gr. D. 164, 12. Þú scealt þurh wóp and heáf cennan, þurh sár micel in dolore paries, Gen. 923. Heáf in helle habban, Gú. 588 : Sal. 467. Helle heáfas, Gen. 38.

heáfan. Take the passages to heófan : -heáfda. v. efen-heáfda [cf. O. Sax. oðar-hobd(i)o]: heáfdede. v. micel-, þri-, twi-heáfdede.

heáfdian ; p. ode To behead :—Sóna swá hig man heáfdode, þá cóm þǽr fæger culfre of þám líchaman, Shrn. 154, 11. Heó lócode his goldes þe hí belífian (vel heáfdian) wolde, Hml. S. 12, 221. [v. N.E.D. head ; vb. and O. Frs. hâvdia : O. H. Ger. houbeten decollare.] v. be-heáfdian.

heáfod. Add : A head :—Heáfod caput, heáfud cephal, Wrt. Voc. ii. 16, 40, 41. I. the head of a living creature. (1) of a human being :—Bróht wæs heáfud (-od, L.) his on disce, Mt. R. 14, 11. Þeáh him mon sleá mid sweorde wiþ þæs heáfdes though one strike at his head with a sword, Bl. H. 47, 14. Wið ðæs heáfodes sáre, Lch. i. 286, 22. Him ne hangað nacod sweord ofer þám heáfde (pendentis supra verticem gladii terror), Bt. 29, 1 ; F. 102, 27. Hé slóg mid his heáfde on þone wág caput pariete collidens, Ors. 5, 2 ; S. 250, 12. Þ sigbég gesetton hæfde (on heófod, R.) his coronam inposuerunt capiti eius, Jn. L. 19, 2. Hé Iôhannes bibeád heáfde biheáwan, Jul. 295 : Met. 1, 43. Heáfde beneótan, Ap. 46 : Jul. 604. Ic heáfde forceart Grendeles módor, B. 2138. On ðæt heáfud (-od, v. l.), Past. 261, 14. Tó sácerdan heáfod áhyldan, Ll. Th. i. 334, 33. Þweh mín heáfod (heáfut, L., heófod, R.), Jn. 13, 9. Hnigon mid heáfdum him tógeánes, Gen. 237 : 742. Heora heáfda of áceorfan, Ors. 2, 3 ; S. 68, 12. Hí wecgað heora heáfdu, Ps. Th. 21, 6. Heáfda, Mt. L. 27, 39. (1 a) where the head is used in measurement :—Dura þ mannes heáfod ge þá sculdro magan in, Bl. H. 127, 9. Se hróf on sumre stówe wæs þ man mid his handa neálíce gerǽcan mihte, in sumre eáþelíce mid heáfde gehrínan, 207, 23 : Hml. Th. i. 508, 19. (2) of an animal :—Ðæs íles heafud (-od, v. l.), Past. 241, 16. Scêpes heáfod, Bl. H. 183, 22. Slóg hê hors mid his sweorde þ him wand þæt heáfod of, Ors. 5, 2 ; S. 216, 24. Ðá heáfudu (heáfdu, v. l.), Past. 105, 5. Hí hine oftorfodon mid hrýðera heáfdum, Chr. 1012 ; P. 142, 23. Ceruerus sceolde habban

þrió heáfdu, Bt. 35, 6; F. 168, 17. **II.** *the head* (1) as the seat of thought :—Ðæt heáfod sceal wísian ðæm fótum, Past. 131, 24. Hond sceal heófod in wyrcan, Gn. Ex. 68. (2) as part essential to life, cf. heáfod-æ.—Ne sý nán óðer bót bútan þ heáfod (cf. forgá þýfðe be his feóre, 210, 3), Ll. Th. i. 282, 2, 23. Sý hē þeóf, and þolige heáfdes, 276, 13. For þon ðín éþel (wyrd?) hit swá be þínum heáfde and fóre hafað áræded *fata ita de tuo capite statuerunt*, Nar. 29, 13. **III.** *the head* in reference to hair :—Eówres heáfudes loccas, Mt. 10, 30. Heáfdes (heófdes, R.), Lk. 12, 7. Loc of heáfde, An. 1425. Of heófde iówrum, Lk. R. 21, 18. þ hié eal hiera heáfod besceáren, Ors. 4, 11; S. 204, 8. Ðá sácerdas ne scoldon nó hiera heáfdu scieran mid scierseaxum, Past. 139, 12. **IV.** (1) in enumeration, as in *per head* :—Æt heáfde peninc, Wlfst. 170, 20. (2) in numbering cattle :—Mid xii heáfdon sceápa, Cht. Th. 641, 1. **V.** *the extremity of a thing* :—Stæfes heáfda *apex*, Mt. L. 5, 18. Heáfod (*of a key*), Rä. 62, 5. Þurh his (*a battering-ram*) heáfdes mægen, 54, 9. **V a.** *the rounded part of a plant* :—xii hund heáfda (cf. *capitum* (*heads of garlic*) milia multa, Prehn, p. 255), Rä. 83, 4. Genim gárleáces þreó heáfdu, Lch. ii. 234, 20. **VI.** *the top* of a building :—Þæt þu heáfod sié healle mærre and gesomnige síde weallas fæste gefóge, Cri. 4. Se stán ys geworden tó þære hyrnan heáfde (in heafut, L., heáfod, R.), Mt. 21, 42. **VII.** of places. (1) *a summit, eminence* :—Of hēfdes welle on nunnene linc; of nunnene linche on litiges hēuede; of litiges hēuede anlang díche, C. Ð. iii. 420, 10–12. Of ðére dúne on beran heáfde; of beran heáfde, 376, 7. Of ðám stáne tó ðám heáfde; big ðám heúfde, 384, 16. On ðám beorge ðat hit sticað on cheotoles heáfde, 434, 14. Tó dúnan heáfde; ðæt tó Hunes cnolle, v. 313, 13. Æt Biédan heáfde, Chr. 675; P. 34, 28. (2) *the upper end of that which is, or is thought of as, sloping.* (a) of land. Cf. æt ðas akeres úpende, C. D. iii. 434, 2. *In pl. the word seems often equivalent to* and-heáfdu, *q. v.* :—Andlang cumbes tó ðæs cumbes heáfde, 434, 35 : ii. 29, 3. Æt ðæs croftes heáfod, iii. 37, 23. On þæs hlinces heáfod, v. 217, 21 : iii. 420, 27. On móres heáfod, C. D. B. iii. 336, 19. On hanslædes heáfdan . . . on catedenes heáfdan, C. D. iii. 380, 26–29. Tó ceólan heáfdan, 462, 21. Be ðæra æcera heáfdan, vi. 79, 12 : iii. 420, 16. Be heáfdan, 444, 14. Andlang fyrh tó ðon heáfdon, 437, 22. Of ðære fyrh á be þæm heáfdan, Cht. E. 208, 33, 34. Of þám heáfodon andlang fúra . . . Ondlong weges oþ þá heáfdo, C. D. iii. 436, 16–27. (b) of water :—Of horspóles heáuede . . . on horspóles heáued, C. D. iii. 445, 25–35. In ðes pulles heáfod, 382, 10. On þæs fennes heáfod, C. D. B. iii. 517, 30. On seohteres heáfod, 624, 20. (3) *head*, as in *bed's head*, the part of a couch where a person's head would rest :—Scē Adrianes hand heó ásette æt hire heáfdum on hire ræste, Shrn. 59, 35. Setton him tó heáfdum hilderandas, B. 1242. **VIII.** *head* as in fountain-*head*, *source.* (1) literal :—Andlang weges tó mearcbróces heáfde, C. D. iii. 445, 4. On beueres bróces heáfod, v. 48, 8. On ðæs wælles heáfod, ii. 28, 34 : 29, 4. On secgwælles heáfod, 7. On wulfwælles heáfod, 13. (2) figurative :—Wyrd . . ., weána wyrtwela, wópes heáfod, Sal. 444. Of edwittes ýða heáfdum, 29. **IX.** *the beginning* of a period of time :—Heáfdes fæstenes *capitis ieiunii*, Angl. xiii. 404, 566. Fram heáfde fæstenes, 563. Fram heáfde lenctenes oþ tó gereorde Drihtnes *a capite quadragesime usque ad cenam Domini*, 407, 596. **X.** *the figure-head* of a ship :—Harold his scipes heáfod þám kynge bróhte, Chr. 1063; P. 191, 16. **XI.** used of persons. (1) *one to whom others are subordinate, a chief, leader* :—Israhéla folc geceás Ionatham, biddende þ hē wære heora heáfod and heretoga wið þá hæþenan þeóda; and hē fēng ðá tó ealdordóme swá swá hí bædon, Hml. S. 25, 717. Þone arcð . . . sē þe ær wæs Angelcynnes heáfod and Xpendōmes, Chr. 1011; P. 142, 5. Þú mē gesettest ðeódum tó heáfde *constitues me in caput gentium*, Ps. Th. 17, 41. Hwæt áwriten is be hira heáfde and be hiera láreówe, ðæt is deóful *quod de eorum capite scriptum est*, Past. 301, 6. Ðæt hálige heáfoð (-od, *v. l.*) ðære hálgan gesomnunge, ðæt is Dryhten, 101, 22. (2) *one who is more intelligent than others, who can instruct others* :—Is ðearf ðæt ðæt dúst disse eorðlican giémenne ne áðisðrige ðæt eáge ðæs recceres, for ðæm ealle ðá ðe ofer óðæ bióð, bióð heáfda (-u, *v. l.*) ðæra ðe ðærunder bióð, and ðæt heáfod sceal wísian ðæm fótum, Past. 131, 23. **XII.** used of places, *a capital, chief town* :—Constantinopolim is nú þ hēhste cynesetl and heáfod ealles eástríces, Ors. 3, 7 ; S. 116, 13. Babilonia þe wæs Persa ríces heáfod, Wlfst. 194, 11. **XIII.** phrases. (1) with prep. *ofer.* (a) local, *over* (*one's*) *head, aloft* :—Hí him ásetton segen heáh ofer hieora heáfod, Bl. H. 249, 2. (b) with the idea of protection, influence, &c. :—Þú hand þíne mē ofer heáfod holde gesettest *posuisti super me manum tuam*, Ps. Th. 138, 3. Þá þe him Godes egsa hleonað ofer heáfdum, Gū. 44. (2) with another noun :—Hē tóbærst mid wundum from ðám heáfde oð ðá fēt, Shrn. 132, 9. (3) with a verb. (a) heáfod brecan *to destroy, crush* an enemy :—Heáfod hē gebreceð hæleða meniges, Ps. Th. 109, 7. (b) heáfod (á)hebban. (a) *to take courage, regain cheerfulness* or *confidence* :—Eówre heáfdu (heófodo, R.) úp áhebbaþ; for þám þe eówer álýsednes geneáléceð, Lk. 21, 28. (β) *to feel proud* or *elated* :—Hí

beóð þý dædfromran, and for ðon hiora heáfod hebbað, Ps. Th. 109, 8. (γ) *to be defiant* :—Hí heora heáfod wið þe hófan, Ps. Th. 82, 2. (c) heáfod niman *to accept as a slave.* Cf. *Icel.* fœra einum hófuð sitt *to surrender oneself to an enemy*, and see Grmm. R. A. pp. 146–7, 327–8 :—Ealle þá men þe heó nam heora heáfod for hyra mete on þám ýsium dagum, Cht. Th. 621, 9. [*Goth.* haubiþ : *O. Frs.* hâved : *O. Sax.* hôbid : *O. H. Ger.* houbit : *Icel.* haufuð, (*later*) hofuð.] v. foran-, fore- (for-), healf-, ofer-, oferhealf-, súþ-, úp-heáfod; and-heáfdu; wulf-heáfod-treów.

**heáfod-æ** (?) *a law that affects life.* v. heáfod; **II.** 2 :—Heáfod[æ?] *capital*[*is*] *lex* (Wright prints : Capital lex-heáfod), Wrt. Voc. ii. 128, 43.

**heáfod-æcer**, es; *m.* *A strip of land, an acre in extent, lying at the head* (cf. heáfod ; **VII.** 2 a) *of a field* [*and so forming its upper boundary* (? cf. heáfodland)] :—Fines gemære, limites h(e)áfudland, decumanus tióðe h(e)áfudæcer, Wrt. Voc. i. 38, 2–4. Bæ ðæs heáfdæcres westfurh, C. D. v. 253, 14. Be fenne on þonne heáfodæcer, C. D. B. iii. 517, 24, 27. On þone heáfodæcre, C. D. iii. 442, 6.

**heáfod-bæþ**, es; *n.* *A head-bath, wash for the head* :—Heáfodbæþ wið þon (*falling off of hair*). Weliges leáf wylle on wætere, þweah mid þý, Lch. ii. 156, 1.

**heáfod-beáh.** *Add* :—Mon hehþ þone heáfodbeáh æt þæs ærneweges ende *currenti in stadio jacet praemium corona*, Bt. 37, tit. ; F. xviii. 9.

**heáfod-beald** ; *adj.* *Bold-faced, shameless* :—Mid heáfodbaldre *frontosa* (cf. sió balde *frontosa* [*moecharum impudentia*, Ald. 60, 16], 85, 27), Wrt. Voc. ii. 34, 44.

**heáfod-bend** ; *m.* *A head-band* (v. *N. E. D.*). (1) *a crown* :—Þ bið cyninga þeáw and cásera þ hí oft habbað gyldenne heáfodbænd ymb heora heáfod, Nap. 15, 20. (2) *a band put round the head as punishment* :—Sum mann wæs gebunden onbútan þ heáfod for his hefigum gylte; sē cōm tó þám hálgan and his swára heáfodbend sóna tóbærst swá hē hine gebæd, Hml. S. 21, 423. [*O. H. Ger.* houbit-bant *corona, diadema, strophium, sertum.*]

**heáfod-beorg**, es; *m.* *A chief hill* (?) :—On cissan beorg middanweardne . . . ; swá tó heáfodbeorge westeweardon, C. D. v. 179, 26–30. Ðis synt ðá landes meære tó Bryningtúne. Ærest on heáfdbeorh; ðonne on wyrtwalan . . . swá tó herpaðe; andlang herpaðes tó Imman beorge; of Imman beorge eft on heáfodbeorge, 300, 7–22.

**heáfod-bolla.** *Add* :—Hē hí bær tó þére stówe seó is gecweden cwealmstów and heáfodbollan stów, Nap. 36.

**heáfod-bolster.** *Add* :—Heáfodbolster *cervical*, Wrt. Voc. i. 284, 59. Heáfedbolster, ii. 16, 67. Heáfodbolstor *capitula*, 128, 41. Tó bedreáfe genihtsumige tó hæbbene meatte and hwítel and bedfelt and heáfodbolster (*capitulae*), R. Ben. 91, 16. [*O. H. Ger.* houpit-polstra *cervicalia.*] Cf. heáfod-hrægel.

**heáfod-botl.** *Add* : *chief messuage.*

**heáfod-burh.** *Add* :—Heáfodburg (*Decapolis*), An. Ox. 61, 3. Þá gesætton þá wytan þá cnihtas on twám heáfodburgum, Hml. S. 2, 320. Cf. ealdor-burh.

**heáfod-cláþ.** *Add* :—Heáfodcláþ *capitale*, Wrt. Voc. ii. 128, 44. ¶ *the cloth used for wrapping the head of a dead person* :—Ic his líc behwearf mid gewunelicre þénunge, and þá þá gē mē wrehton, þá næs his heáfodcláþ eallunga fuldón, Hml. S. 31, 1425.

**heáfod-cyrice.** *l.* -cirice, *and add* : v. heáfod-mynster.

**heáfod-ece.** *Add* :—Heáfodwærc *vel* [heáfod]ece *cephalia*, i. *dolor capitis*, vel *cephalargia*, Wrt. Voc. ii. 130, 84. Wið heáfodece, Lch. i. 188, 15 : 190, 20 : 196, 22, and often. Laurentius ðá wudewan fram hefigtýmum heáfodece gehælde, Hml. Th. i. 418, 22. Hē mid ele gesmyrode án licgende mædum on langsumum sáre ðurh hefigtýmum heáfodece, and hire sóna wæs bet, ii. 150, 6.

**heáfod-fæder.** *Add* : [?; but cf. *Icel.* hófuð-faðir *a patriarch, a father of the church.*]

**heáfod-frætewness.** *For* 'Cot. 65, Lye' *substitute* :—Heáfodfretennesse *decriminalia* (*discriminalia* capitum, Ald. 68, 31, *glossed by* eárpreónas, An. Ox. 4821), Wrt. Voc. ii. 86, 48. Heáfodfrætennesse, 26, 77.

**heáfod-gemaca.** *Add* :—Heó geheóld hyre fóstormódor sceáp mid óþrum fæmnum hire hefdgemacum *ipsa pascebat oves nutricis suae cum ceteris puellis coaetaneis suis* (Hml. A. 209, 40), Nar. 40, 18.

**heáfod-gewæde.** [The Latin of Gen. 20, 16 is : Hoc erit tibi in velamen oculorum.] *Add* :—God bereáfað eówere dohtra heora gyrla and tó oferrancra heáfodgewæda (v. Isaiah iii. 18, sqq.), Wlfst. 46, 1.

**heáfod-gold.** *Add* :—Ne beóð þær forþ borene sigele ne beágas ne heora heáfodgold, Wlfst. 254, 1.

**heáfod-gylt.** *In l.* 2 *after* wyrðe *insert* ne, *and add* :—Þá men þe mid openan heáfodgyltan hý sylfe forgyltað, Wlfst. 153, 9. Cf. heáfodsynn.

**heáfod-hær.** *Add* :—Heáfodhær *capilli*, Wrt. Voc. ii. 128, 37.

**heáfod-haga**, an; *m.* *A fence running at the head* (v. heáfod; **VII.** 2 a) *of a piece of land* (?) :—On ðone ealdan heáfodhagan, C. D. vi. 64, 7.

**heáfod-hebba**, an; m. I. of a person, *an author, originator.* Cf. heáfod; VIII:—Ðá bisceopas swíðost ælces gedweldes tiledon, and ælc gedwyld hí upp árærdon. Twégen ðær wæron bisceophádes men þe ælces yfeles heáfodhebban wæron, Hml. S. 23, 365. II. of a thing, *a beginning*:—Ærest wé wyllað fón on Ianuarium, for þon hé is heáfodhebba and eác þæs geáres geendung, Angl. viii. 305, 29. [Cf. *O. H. Ger.* ur-hap *causa, fermentum:* Ger. ur-heber *originator.*]

**heáfod-hrægel**, es; n. I. of clothing. The word glosses *oraria* in the verses which tell the medicinal virtues of St. Cuthbert's clothing, 'tegmina corporis almi', 'veneranda vestis'. One whose eyes were affected 'sancti accipiens oraria vatis' was cured. v. Nap. 36. It also glosses *poderis*:—Gif þú fyligst rihtwísnysse þú gegrípst hí, and þú on dést swylce heáfudhrægl wyrðscype (*indues quasi poderem honorem*), Scint. 74, 2. II. of bedding, *a bolster, pillow*:—Bedreáf bedda genihtsumiað ... hwítel ... and heáfudrægel *stramenta lectorum sufficiant* ... *sagum ... et capitulae,* R. Ben. I. 93, 3. Cf. heáfod-bolster.

**heáfod-land**. *Take here* hafud-land *in* Dict., *and add*: [v. land; IV.]—Of ðære stréte on ðá díc ðe scýt tó ðam heáfodlande; ðonne on westhealfe ðæs heáfodlandes, C. D. v. 275, 17-19. Tó þám heáfodlonde, iii. 384, 32. Of þæm wege á be þæm heáfodlande; þ eft in þ óþer heáfodlond áne hwíle; þænne in þá furh; þ andlong fyrh anbútan þ heáfodlond ... of þæm heáfodlonde eft on þone weg, Cht. E. 208, 25-29: 35. On þæt heáfodlond; of þám heáfodon andlang fúra, C. D. iii. 436, 16: 21. See Seebohm Vill. Comm. p. 4, and *N. E. D.,* D. D. headland.

**heáfod-leahter**. *Add*: , *a deadly sin*:—Sceolon crístene men ðá eahta heáfodleahtras oferwinnan ... Se forma heáfodleahter is gýfernyss ... eahteoða módignyss. Þás eahta heáfodleahtras geniðeriað þá unwæran intó hellewíte, Hml. Th. ii. 218, 16-24: Hml. S. 16, 267: Hml. A. 76, 101. Cf. heáfod-synn; heáfod-mægen.

**heáfod-leás**. *Add*:—Se cwellere slóh þone cniht þ hé læg heáfodleás, Hml. S. 12, 208: Hml. A. 113, 369. Þæs bisceopes líc ... árás and nam his ágen heáfod þe of áheáwen wæs, and eóde forð ... his Drihten herigende ... þ wæs syllic wundor þ se martyr heáfodleás mihte gán God herigende, Hml. S. 29, 307. Þonne hí heáfodleásne heora ealdorman findað, Hml. A. 113, 353: 364. Þá heáfodleásan man héngc on ðá portweallas, Hml. S. 23, 74.

**heáfod-lencten-fæsten**. *Dele, and see* heáfod; IX.

**heáfod-líc**. *Add*: I. marking position, *placed at the top*:—Heáfodlíc, ufeweard swer *epistilia*, Wrt. Voc. ii. 30, 29. Heáfudlicum *capitellis,* 21, 19. II. marking degree, rank, *chief, principal.* (1) of places, offices, &c.:—Ðæs heáfodlícan hearges *capitolii,* Wrt. Voc. ii. 20, 38. Dóme [heáfod]lícum *auctoritate principali,* An. Ox. 5150. Þás feówer heáfodrícu (heáfodlíc rícu, *v.l.*) *quatuor regnorum principatus,* Ors. 2, 1; Bos. 38, 20. (2) of sins, *deadly, mortal*:—Heáfod[lícra] *principalium* (*vitiorum*), An. Ox. 773. Ne wé heáfodlíce leahtras ne lufian, Wlfst. 253, 9. [v. *N. E. D.* hedly.]

**heáfod-lín**. [*Icel.* höfuð-lín *a linen hood,* belonging to a priest's dress.] v. biscop-heáfodlín.

**heáfod-ling**. v. efen-heáfodling.

**heáfod-loca**, an; m. *A skull*:—Heáfodlocan (cf. heáfudponnan, lxx, 9) *capitali,* Lch. i. lxxiv, 10.

**heáfod-mægen**, es; n. *A cardinal virtue*:—Nú syndon eahta heáfodmægnu, ðá magan oferswíðan þás deóflu, Hml. S. 16, 312. Cf. heáfodleahter.

**heáfod-mann**. *Add*: I. *a head-man, a person of high position or rank*:—Híredmanna gehwilc sille pænig tó ælmessan ... and héafodmen teódian, Wlfst. 181, 17. Hé sende tó Scotlande, and bæd ðá heófodmenn (ealdormenn *maiores natu,* Bd. 3, 3; Sch. 199, 6), Hml. S. 26, 49. II. *a person high in office*:—Se heáfodman þæs gehergodan folces hine (*Ezechiel*) ácwealde, Ælfc. T. Grn. 9, 41. Æt nýxtan næs nán heáfodman þ fyrde gaderian wolde, Chr. 1010; P. 140, 30. Ozias heora heáfodmann (*princeps,* governor of the city), Hml. A. 107, 156. Hí hine læddon tó heora heáfodmannum (*duxerunt ad Caiapham principem sacerdotum, ubi scribae et seniores convenerant,* Mt. 26, 57), 75, 47, 70. II a. where the office is military:—On þám flotan wæron þá fyrmestan heáfodmen Hinguar and Hubba, Hml. S. 32, 29. Þára heáuodmanna naman wæran Ingware and Ubba, Chr. 870; P. 71, n. 6. Mann sceolde forðian út scipu, and setton Raulf eorl and Oddan eorl tó heáfodmannum, 1052; P. 177, 10. Hé gesette þá heáfodmenn tó gehealdenne þ folc (*captains of the people,* i. Macc. 5, 18), Hml. S. 25, 403. ¶ heáfdes-mann. Cf. *Icel.* höfuðs-maðr:—Cóman twá hund scypa, þæron wæron heáfdesmenn Cnut and Hácon, Chr. 1076; P. 211, 37. II a a. *the head, captain* of a band:—'Alædað mé tó ... eówerne ealdor.' Hig (*the robbers*) clipodon þone cniht him tó þe hira heáfodman wæs, Ælfc. T. Grn. 18, 19.

**heáfod-panne**. *Add*:—Heáfodpanne *cephalus,* Wrt. Voc. ii. 130, 82: *capitale,* 22, 51. Heánnes þáre heáfodpannan *cacumen capitalis,* seám þáre heáfodpannan *cerebrum,* 52-54. Heófodponna (hefid- [*altered from* heáfud-]) stów, Jn. R. 19, 17. Heáfudponnan *capitali,* Lch. i. lxx. 9. [v. *N. E. D.* head-pan.]

**heáfod-pyle** (?) *a pillow*:—Wangere, heáfod-(= þ-pyle?) *cervical.* Wrt. Voc. ii. 73, 29.

**heáfod-ríce**. *Add*:—Hú hit gelomp ymb ðás tú heáfodrícu, Asiria and Rómána, Ors. 2, 1; S. 62, 12.

**heáfod-sár**. *Add*:—Wið heáfudsáre, Lch. i. 300, 6. Wið heáfodsár (-ece, *v.l.*), 212, 25.

**heáfod-sealf**, e; f. *A salve for the head*:—Tó heáfodsealfe, aluwan gegníd in eced, smyre þæt heáfod nid, Lch. iii. 2, 14.

**heáfod-segn**, es; m. *An ensign having a head (not a flag*?):—Hét þá in beran eafor heáfodsegn, ... helm, herebyrnan, gúðsweord, B. 2152-4. These are the 'feówer madmas' (l. 1027), given to Beowulf by Hrothgar, of which the first is elsewhere (1021-2) described as 'segen gyldenne, hroden hiltecumbor'. It would seem, then, to have been an ensign, which had at the head of its shaft (*hilte*) the figure of a boar. Perhaps the poet of the Exodus had the same kind of ensign in mind where he says that the tribe of Judah, 'Hæfden him tó segne ... gyldenne león,' Exod. 319-21.

**heáfod-slæge**. *Add*: , -slege *a cross-beam resting on columns, an architrave* (?); *and for* 'Cot. 50, Lye' *substitute* Wrt. Voc. ii, 20, 58.

**heáfod-smæl**. *Substitute: The opening in a tunic for the head to pass through, the collar of a tunic*:—Heáfodsmæl *capitium* (*tunica coccinea, capitium et manicae sericis clavatae,* Ald. 77, 15. Glosses to the same passage elsewhere are: *Capitium* hæt, An. Ox. 5320: Hpt. Gl. 526, 35: healsed, Wrt. Voc. ii. 87, 57), Angl. xiii. 37, 286: Wrt. Voc. i. 288, 43: ii. 17. 9. Þá ræsde án næddre æt þám heáfodsmæle and him on þone bósm *evenit ei, ut coluber per caput eius inter tunicam et ventrem irreperet,* Mart. H. 200, 2. [Cf. *O. H. Ger.* houpit-loh *capitium* (*tunicae*). See Ld. Gl. H. s.v. *capitio.*]

**heáfod-stede**. *Add*: [*Icel.* höfuð-staðr.]

**heáfod-stíg**, e; f. *A path along the head of a field* (?):—Tó ðære heáfodstíge, þæt swá in ðá heáhstræt, C. D. iii. 167, 23.

**heáfod-stocc**, es; m. This word, which occurs several times in charters that describe the boundaries of land, seems from the following passage to mean *A stock or post on which the head of a criminal was fixed after beheading*:—Heora lima man ealle tóbræd ælc fram óðrum ... and ðá heáfodleásan man héngc on ðá portweallas, and man sette heora heáfda swilce óþra ðeófa búton ðám portweallon on ðám heáfodstoccum, Hml. S. 23, 71-76. Instances of occurrence in charters are:—Æfter Foss tó ðám heáfodstocce, C. D. iii. 384, 29. Of ðære hylle andlang ðære díc úp tó heáfodstoccan; of heáfodstoccan andlang stræt, v. 110, 34: 217, 14. Tó weáwan hócan; ðanon on ðá heáfodstoccas, 207, 26. Be gemære: ðæt on ðá heáfodstoccas; of ðan stoccan on ðone inærstán, iii. 439, 6. On gerihte on ðá heáfudstoccas; of ðan heáfodstoccum, vi. 62, 7. On gréne wei on neðe héuedstokes; of ðanne héuedstocken, iii. 201, 32.

**heáfod-stól**. *Add*:—Heáfedstól *capitella,* Wrt. Voc. ii. 15, 84.

**heáfod-wærc**. *Add*:—Heáfodwærc *cephalia,* i. *dolor capitis* vel *cephalargia,* Wrt. Voc. ii. 130, 84. Gif hwá sý on heáfodwræce æfter bæþe, Lch. i. 328, 18. Wið heáfodwræce (-wærce, l. 8), iii. 2, 4.

**heáfod-weard**; m. *Add: One who performs* heáfod-weard (*see next word*), *one who is on guard*:—Heáfodweardas *excubitores,* Wrt. Voc. ii. 146, 16.

**heáfod-weard**; f. *Guarding the (lord's) head. Add*: See Kemble's Saxons in England, ii. 63.

**heáfod-weard** *a title of a section of a book, heading of a chapter. Add*:—Gesaegd aron heáfudwearda ðára réda *expliciunt cabitula lectionum,* Mt. p. 20, 9. Onginneð heáfudweardo *incipiunt capitulae,* Mk. p. 1, 1.

**heáfod-weg**, es; m. *A road along the head* (v. heáfod, VII. 2 a) *of a field, valley,* &c. (?):—Of ðæn cumbe on Tetanhylle; of Tytanhylle tó ðæn heáfodwege; ondlong cumbes, C. D. V. 401, 35. Of þæm heáfodlonde eft on þone weg; of ðæm wege on hlydan, ondlong hlydan on þon heáfodweg; of þæm wege on þone hyll, Cht. E. 208, 29.

**heáfod-wræc**. v. heáfod-wærc.

**heáfod-wund**. *Add*:—Þá hét hé his læce tó him, and bebeád him þ hé þá tolýsdan geþeódnesse mínre heáfudwunde gesette *uocauit medicum, et dissolutam mihi emicranii iuncturam conponere iussit,* Bd. 5, 6; Sch. 581, 8.

**heáf-sang**. *Substitute: A dirge, lament*:—Heúfsang *lamentabile* (*canticum*: cf. canticum *lamentabile,* quod epithrenion uocatur, Ald. 13, 23), Wrt. Voc. ii. 49, 69.

**heago-rún**. *Add*: cf. heah-rún: Heago-stald-. v. Hagu-stald-.

**heáh**. *Add*:—Héum *minacibus* [cf. oferhlífiende *minaci* (turrem *minaci* proceritate in edito porrectam, Ald. 62, 12), 85, 47], Wrt. Voc. ii. 57, 65. Heáran *editiorem,* 32, 43. A. *as adj.* I. in a physical sense. (1) *extending to a (relatively) great distance from the lowest point.* (a) of persons, plants, &c. (α) a person:—Geseah hé weorud ... and wæs án þæra swyþe heáh and swýðe mycel ofer eal þæt óþer folc, Vis. Lfc. 14. Silhearwan swá heáge swá entes, Hml. S. 4, 286. (β) a tree, plant, &c.:—Of heán beáme feallan, Vy. 21. Macian ænne heágan gealgan, Hml. A. 98, 204. Þæt treów on holte

hỹhst geweaxe, Met. 13, 52. (b) of buildings, hills, &c. (a) of buildings, lofty structures:—Tempel heáh and horngeáp, An. 668. In sele þǽm heán, B. 713. Máran cyricean and hỹhran timbrian, Bd. 2, 14; Sch. 170, 16. Tó gyrwanne gódlecran stól heárran on heófne, Gen. 282. Þá scipu wǽron hiéran (heárran, v. l.) þonne þá óðra, Chr. 897; P. 90, 17. (β) of hills, high :—Of þám heóhan (heáhan, F. 14, 28) munte, Bt. 6; S. 14, 16. On ánre heáre dúne, Ors. 3, 11; S. 142, 14. Ofer heánne (heáne, v. l.) munt, Past. 81, 13. Heáne, Met. 7, 4. Heáhne (hēhne, R.), Mk. 9, 2. Muntas heáche (heáe, Srt.), Ps. L. 103, 18. Be ðǽm heán muntum and dúnum, þá þe heáh standað ofer ealne middangeard, Wlfst. 262, 13. (c) of water. (a) rising water, high :— Seó eorðe weóll ongeán þám heofonlican flóde oð ðæt þæt wæter wæs heáhre þonne ǽnig munt ǽfre wǽre, Wlfst. 206, 22. Loc hwenne þ flód byþ ealra hēhst, Chr. 1031; P. 158, 4. (β) deep, high (seas):— Se pytt hēh (deóp, W. S.) is, Jn. L. 4, 11. Heánne holm, Sat. 17; Wand. 82: El. 983. Heá holmas, Az. 123. Ic heán streámas cunnige, Seef. 34. (d) raised above a surface :—Gif þæs dolges ófras synd tó heá, Lch. ii. 96, 5. (2) having a specified upward extent :—Se arc wæs þrittig fǽdma heáh in altitudine triginta cubiti, Angl. vii. 34, 324. Fæt úp oþ mannes breóst heáh, Bl. H. 127, 6. Hú hēh hell seó, Sat. 707. Hí woldon witon hú heáh hit wǽre tó þǽm hefone, Bt. 35, 4; F. 162, 22. Þæt fær gewyrc . . . þrittiges heáh elngemeta, Gen. 1308. Þæt hié nǽren x fóta heá bufan wætere, Ors. 5, 13; S. 246, 11. Mon dyde ǽlces consules setl áne pyle hiérre þonne hit ǽr wæs, 5, 11; S. 236, 7. (3) having a lofty position :—Híge þám þe on húses þece heáh (or under (1 a β)?) áweaxeð foenum aedificiorum, Ps. Th. 128, 4. Fæder . . . in heofonsetle heáh Deus altithronus, Dom. L. 276: Ph. 449. On dúnum gesæt heáh . . . earc Nóes, Gen. 1422. Þeós heá lyft ' the lift sae hie,' Rä. 8, 4. Þá tungla þæs heán heofnes, Bt. 39, 13; F. 232, 25. Heáhre handa dynt a blow from an uplifted hand, Ll. Th. i. 18, 1. Þ mynster wæs geseted in heánum cnolle þæs muntes (in summo montis cacumine), Gr. D. 49, 3. On þǽm heán cnolle sumes muntes, Bl. H. 197, 18. Of heán rodore, Dan. 236: Gen. 545. On þone heán heofon, 476. Ofer ðone heán hróf þæs heofones, Bt. 36, 2; F. 174, 5. Ofer ealle heá hwammas, Past. 245, 6. Þæt hiéhste editissima (arx), Wrt. Voc. ii. 88, 57. (3 a) metaphorical :—Úre hand is heáh, Deut. 32, 27. In earme heám (þǽm hǽhstan, Ps. L.), Ps. Srt. 135, 12. II. non-physical. (1) of persons or their attributes, of exalted rank, dignity or estimation. (a) human beings :—Him onwóc heáh Healfdene, B. 57. Hēh sácerd summus sacerdos (Pope Damasus), Mt. p. 1, 10. (v. heáh-sácerd.) Ic sette hine heáne fore cyningum eorðan, Ps. Srt. 88, 28. Heáge lǽcas archiatros, i. summos medicos, An. Ox. 3027. Se hiéra folgoð, Past. 189, 17. Hē wæs hiérra þonne consul, Ors. 5, 12; S. 242, 29. Hiérra ofer þá consulas, 4, 9; S. 190, 28. Þurh geþingða heárra on háde, Ll. Th. i. 328, 14. Maara ł hēra maior, Mk. L. R. 10, 43. Huelc hēra (yldra, W. S.) is quis maior est?, Lk. L. 22, 27. Arð ðú mára ł hēra (mǽrra, W. S.) from feder ūrum, Jn. L. 4, 12. Gē eów on hiéran (hiérran, v. l.) folgoðe áhebbað, Past. 52, 14. Rómane him gesetton híran lǽdteów þonne hiera consul wǽre Romani dictatorem creant, cujus auctoritas et potentia consulem praeiret, Ors. 4. S. 70, 1. Beforan ðǽm hírrum hádum, Past. 411, 22. Sē wæs on láre and on dǽde se hỹhsta uir doctrina et actione praecipuus, Bd. i. 23; Sch. 47, 25. Þeáh þú heágust (summus) sí, eáðmódnysse heald, Scint. 22, 3. Sē ðe hēist (ylıst, W. S. maior) is iúer, Mt. L. 23, 11. Hēest, 20, 26. Heeist ł maast, p. 18, 3. Ofer eorðcyningas ealra heáhstne excelsum prae regibus terrae, Ps. Th. 88, 24. God þē gedeð heáhst and mǽrost ealra þeóda faciet te Deus excelsiorem cunctis gentibus, Deut. 28, 1. (b) divine or angelic beings :—Heáh and hálig þrynes, Cri. 379. Dryhten in Sion micel and hēh ofer ealle folc, Ps. Srt. 98, 2. Lá hēh fæder abba pater, Mk. L. R. 14, 36. Se heá and se hálga heáhengel, Bl. H. 199, 35. Seó heá miht on þysne wang ástág, 105, 13. Þæs heán fæder summi Patris, Gr. D. 240, 25. Swá heágum Gode wiþcweþan, Bt. 35, 4; F. 160, 29. Þone heán cyning gásta hyrde, Dan. 198. Þára heán handa Drihtnes, Ps. Th. 76, 9. Þæt hē (Jupiter) god wǽre hēhst and hálgost, Met. 26, 38. Se hēhsta god, Bt. 38, 1; F. 194, 17. Hyldo þæs hēhstan dēman, Jud. 4. Sunu Godes ðæs hēista (hēsta, R.), Mk. L. 5, 7. Ðæs hēsta, Lk. L. 8, 28. Þone heáhestan hǽleða cynnes, Ps. Th. 91, 1. (2) of exalted quality, of superior kind :—His seó heáhe (sió heá, v. l.) gódnes, Bt. 34, 3; F. 136, 24. Þá forhæfdnesse ðæs heán gesinciges, Past. 399, 12. Þǽre heán gecynde gesǽlþa, Bt. 14, 3; F. 44, 29. Mid ðǽm heigra mǽht uirtutem ex alto, Lk. p. 11, 17. Hí gereafiað swá heáne láriówdóm, Past. 27, 19. Wið swá heáne anwald, Bt. 2: Met. 29, 2. Cýðan higecræft heáne, Dan. 98. Wrát hē heáh [ = heáh-lice ?] bóc and weorðlice scripsit librum eximium, Bd. 5, 15; Sch. 651, 5. Heánum meahtum, Rä. 2, 10. On þá heán þrymmas heofona ríces, Bl. H. 67, 22. Se mægðhád is hírra ðonne se gesincipe, Past. 409, 23. Hwæt mæg hiérre bión ðonne sió sóðe eáðmódnes?, 301, 21. Hyhta hỹhst, Gú. 34. Sió hēhste gesǽlþ, Bt. 34, 4; F. 138, 24. Ðára hēhstena góda, 24, 4; F. 86, 15. Tó ðǽm hēistum bodum ad altiora, Mt. p. 9, 17. (2 a) of great importance, grave, serious :—Hē hēht

þæt segn (circumcision) wegan heáh gehwilcne, Gen. 2371. (2 b) difficult, arduous :—Ðæs heán hádes ardui (propositi), Wrt. Voc. ii. 75, 68; 4, 66. (3) chief, principal :—Drihten þá cynelican burh forhogodlíce naman nemde . . . seó ceaster þonne wæs hēh and aldorlic, Bl. H. 77, 25. Þeós tíd ealra tída hēhst and hálgost, 83, 19. Seldon bútan þám hỹhstan symbelnessum (heáhtídum, v. l.), Bd. 4, 19; Sch. 443, 6. v. heáh-tíd. (4) of great amount, degree or force :—Heáh bliss exultatio, Ps. Th. 118, 114. Ðá gestód hine heáh weder, Bt. 38, 1; F. 194, 10. Heáh wæs þæt handleán, Exod. 19. Hí him heánne blǽd gestrýnað, Ph. 391. Heá mihte handa þínre, Ps. Th. 88, 12. Þær is brógna hỹhst, Dóm. 23. (5) of time, fully come, complete :— From ǽrmorgenne oð heáne (heáhne, v. l.) undern a mane usque ad tertiam plenam, R. Ben. 74, 11. B. as subst. I. a high place. v. N. E. D. high; B. 1 :—Quinta terra appellatur Badoríces heáh, C. D. i. 44, 13. II. the superlative denoting the Deity :—Se hēhsta (heáxta, Ps. L., hēhsta, hỹhsta, Bd. 4, 3; Sch. 361, 21) salde stefne his, Ps. Srt. 17, 14. Ðú hēhsta (heáxta, Ps. L.), 9, 3. Þæs hēhstan (hēiste, L., hēsta, R., hēxtan, Hml. Th. i. 198, 14) sunu, Lk. 1, 32: 76. Þæs heáhstan, Ps. Th., Ps. L. 106, 10. Hēstan (heáxstan, Ps. L.), Ps. Srt. 20, 8. v. efen-, heofon-, ofer-, úp-heáh.

heáh; adv. Add: I. physical. (1) so as to extend to a great height :—Be ðǽm heán muntum and dúnum þá ðe heáh standað ofer ealne middaneard, Wlfst. 262, 13. Hlǽw sceal heáh hlífian, B. 2805: Ph. 23: Dan. 603. (2) at or to a position of great height :—Hí him ásetton segen gyldenne heáh ofer heáfod, B. 48: 2768. His meahta spéd heáh ofer heofonum wunade, Ph. 641. Wæs nán tó gedále nymðe heá wæs áhafen on þá heán lyft, Gen. 1401. Hí woldon þone stán heár and gerysenlícor ásettan ut lapis amoueretur et altius reponeretur, Bd. 3, 8; Sch. 224, 9. II. fig. (1) in an exalted position :—Swá micelum swá hē deóppur byð ásliden swá micelum swá hē hēgur (excelsius) byþ upp áhafen, Scint. 84, 17. (2) of mental operations :—Þú hyt sēest hwílum swá heá, hwílum swá deópe, Solil. H. 48, 9. (3) proudly, arrogantly :—Ne áhebbað gē tó heá eówre hygeþancas nolite extollere in altum cornu vestrum, Ps. Th. 74, 5. His mód ástáh heáh fram heortan, Dan. 528. [O. Sax., O. H. Ger. hôho.]

heáh-altar, es; m. A high altar :—Þæs heáhalteres ofergeweorc cibborium, Wrt. Voc. ii. 23, 15. On Scs Petrus heáhaltare in his circan, Wlfst. 212, 3. Hēhaltare, 214, 11. [Icel. há-altari.] Cf. heáh-wígbed (-weófod).

heáh-beorg. Add: cf. heáh-clif, -torr.

heáh-biscop. Add: (1) of a Christian priest :—Sæt se arcebisceop Augustinus . . . Cwæð hē se heáhbisceop tó him, Bd. 2, 2; ch. 118, 7. Þæs heáhbyscpes (þæs heán biscopes, v. l.) leomu pontificis summi (Gregory) membra, 2, 1; Sch. 107, 23. (2) of one not Christian :— Se heáhbiscop (the high priest) Isachar, Hml. A. 129. 430. Þú eart sácerd æfter endebyrdnesse þæs heáhbiscopes (Melchisedech), Ps. Vos. 109, 4.

heáh-bliss. v. heáh; II. 4: heáh-bytlere. Dele.

heáh-cásere, es; m. The supreme emperor :—Þú gewurðod eart on heofonríce heáhcásere, Hy. 7, 60. Cf. heáh-cyning.

heáh-cléofa. l. -cleofa.

heáh-clif. Add:—Swá bið eác gelíce þǽm heáclifum þonne hí hlífiað feor úp ofer þá óðre eorðan, Wlfst. 262, 10. Cf. heáh-torr.

heáh-cræft. Add :—Ðerh hēhcræft, Txts. 151, 4.

heáh-cræftiga, an; m. I. a master-builder, an architect :—Bæd se cyning hine þ hē him onsende sumne heáhcræftigan stángeweorces . . . se abbud sende him cræftige wyrhtan architectos sibi mitti petiit . . . abba misit architectos, Bd. 5, 21; Sch. 678, 1-17. Heáhcræftegan (-igan, v. l.) architectos, Sch. 676, 7. II. a highly skilled artist, a physician (?) :—Heáhlǽcas oððe (heáh)cræfgan archiatros (or has architectos been read?), Wrt. Voc. ii. 2, 60.

heáh-cyning. Add :—I. of Deity. (1) God the Father :—Heáhcyning, freá ælmihtig, Gen. 172. Siððan heáhcyning, wuldres wyrhta, woruld staðelode, Ph. 129. (2) God the Son :—Þú sylfa cum, heofones heáhcyning, . . . Críst nergende, Cri. 150: Ps. Th. 118, 146. Heofena heáhcyning, Cri. 1340. II. of an earthly king, B. 1039.

heáhdeór-hund. Add: The Latin version of the charter has: Omnes canes suos venaticos, Cht. Th. 504, 1.

heáh-ealdorman. Add :—Valerianus se heáhealdorman (patricius), Gr. D. 340, 34.

heáh-engel. Add :—Gabrihel, heofones heáhengel, Cri. 202. Heáhengles tíd, Men. 177. Fæder onsende heáhengel his, 50. Heáhengla brego, Cri. 403. Þurh eall engla wered and heáhengla, Ll. Lbmn. 413, 9.

heáh-fæder. Add: I. the first person of the Trinity, God the Father :—Be þám áncennedan suna þæs heáhfæder (heán fæder, v. l.) de Unigenito summi Patris, Gr. D. 240, 5: Wlfst. 230, 29. Martiras herigað hēhfæder, Sat. 656. II. (1) a patriarch of the Old Testament :— Iacób se heáhfæder, Ll. Th. i. 196, 2. Arones þæs heáhfæder, Bl. H. 161, 28. Rachel hátte Iacóbes wíf ðæs heáhfæderes, Hml. Th. i. 84, 28. Ealra óþerra heáhfædera mægen hē (John the Baptist) oferstígeþ, Bl. H. 167, 23. Heáhfædra fela, Hö. 47. Apostolas wið þám heáh-

fǽdrum and wið wîtgum, Ps. Th. 44, 17. Þurh þâ mǽran wîtegan and heáhfæderas, Ll. Lbmn. 413, 10. (1 a) in a special sense, *one of the twelve sons of Jacob* :—Twelf tîda beóð on ðâm dæge, and twelf mônðas on geáre; twelf heáhfæderas sind, twelf wîtegan, twelf apostoli, Hml. Th. i. 396, 9. (2) in Christian times. (a) *a father of the church* :—Rǽde him mon lîf þǽra heáhfædera (*vitas patrum*), R. Ben. 66, 17. (b) *the chief of a religious community, an archimandrita* :—Hêhfæder, lâreów archimandrita, i. *princeps ouium*, An. Ox. 3720. (3) *a patriarch* in a heathen community :—Hire (*St. Margaret's*) fæder wæs hǽþenra monna heáhfæder (of þ heðene folc patriarke ant prince, Marh. 2, 14; patriarch he was wel hei, Marg. 4; *erat gentilium patriarcha et idola adorabat*, Hml. A. 209, 25), Shrn. 101, 11.

heáh-fore, e. *Substitute* : heáh-fore (-u), an, e; heáh-fru, e, *and add* :—Ænlic hêhfore *aurea quadrupes*, i. *uacca*, An. Ox. 1462. Heáhfru *antile*, Wrt. Voc. ii. 8, 57. Hiord *arimentum*, oxa *bova*, heáhfru *antile*, cû *vacca*, i. 287, 53–56. Farra mîno and hêhfaro (*altilia*) gislægno, Rtl. 107, 21. Ðerh blôd heffera and calfra *per sanguinem hyrcorum et vitulorum*, 21, 10.

heáh-freá, an; m. *A high and mighty lord* :—Heofona heáhfreá (*Christ*), Cri. 253 : 424. Cf. heáh-cyning ; I. 2.

heáh-fȳr, es; n. *High-leaping flame* :—Heáhfȳr ǽlað, Wal. 22.

heáh-galdor, es; n. *A powerful charm, a charm of great virtue* :—Seó nǽdre dytteð hyre eáran, þæt heó nele gehȳran heáhgaldor sum, þæt snotre men singað wið attrum, Ps. Th. 57, 4.

heáh-gást, es; m. *The Holy Ghost* :—Inc (*the Father and the Son*) is gemǽne heáhgǽst hleófæst, Cri. 358. Cf. heáh-cyning.

heáh-geréfa. *Add* : I. as an English title :—Ósulf ad bebb. hêhgr̄ [= ad Bebbanburh hêhgeréfa], C. D. ii. 292, 34. II. rendering foreign titles :—Olibrius se heáhgeréfa (*praefectus*, 209, 41), Hml. A. 171, 51. Æghwilc heáhgeréfa on Iûdêum, Bl. H. 177, 14. Ðæs câseres heáhgeréfa, Hml. Th. ii. 122, 29. Getengde se Aristodemus tô ðâm heáhgeréfan and genam on his cwearterne twêgen ðeófas, i. 72, 18 : 426, 33. Heáhgeréfan *preside* (*Marciano*, Ald. 47, 29), Wrt. Voc. ii. 66, 52. Hê (*Domitian*) sende sumne heáhgeréfan Sisinnius gehâten, Hml. S. 29, 203. Þonne gê beforan kyningum gestondan and heáhgeréfan (*ante praesides* (dêmum W. S.) *et reges stabitis*, Mk. 13, 9), Bl. H. 171, 17.

heáh-gestreón, es; n. *Treasure of great value, costly treasure* :—Þá þe firena lange lǽstað, hýdað heáhgestreón, Sal. 317. Hǽfde gumena sum goldes gefandod, heáhgestreóna, B. 2302. Ceól gehladenne heáhgestreónum, An. 362.

heáh-geþring, es; n. *Mounting waves* :—Bîdað stânhleoðu streámgewinnes, þonne heáhgeþring on cleofu crȳðeð, Rä. 4, 27. Cf. heáh; A. I. 1 c a.

heáh-getimbrad. *Add* : cf. Gú. 556.

heáh-geþungen. *Add* : v. heáh-þungen.

heáh-geweorc, es; n. *Sublime work* :—Úpheofon is heáhgeweorc handa þînra *opera manuum tuarum sunt coeli*, Ps. Th. 101, 22. Nis þæt monnes gemet þæt hê mǽge in hreðre his heáhgeweorc furðor áspyrgan, Sch. 28. Cf. heáh-weorc.

heáh-græft; adj. *Substitute* : heáh-græft *a carving in relief* :—Heáhgræfte *anaglifa*, Wrt. Voc. ii. 6, 13.

heáh-heall (?), e; f. *A palace* :—Bold wæs betlic brego rôf cyning heáhealle *the building was splendid, a brave king was the prince of the palace* (?), B. 1926. Cf. heáh-sele.

heáh-helm; adj. *Having foliage high up*; of a light, *having far-reaching rays* :—þone heáhhelman leóman *iubar alticomum* (the passage is : Modio lateat ne tecta lucerna, sed iubar alticomum Domini diffundat in aedem, Vita S. Cudbercti c. 21, 50), Hpt. 33, 238, 1.

heáh-heolope, an; f. *Elecampane* :—Heáhhiolope, Lch. ii. 104, 1 : 138, 16. Genim heáhheolopan, 18, 22. Heáhhiolopan, 102, 23 : 274, 2. v. eh-heolope.

heáh-hirde, es; m. *A chief pastor, an archimandrite* :—Hêhhyrde archimandrita, i. *excelsus magister*, An. Ox. 910. cf. heáh-fæder; II. 2 b.

heáh-hlip. *Add* :—Hê ofer heáhhleoðu (heáh hleoðu?) stylde, Cri. 745.

heáh-hlútor; adj. *Of great purity* :—Heáhhlútrum môde and bilewitum *simplici ac pura mente*, Bd. 4, 24 : Sch. 491, 10.

heáh-hweólad ; adj. *High-wheeled* :—Hêhhwiólad wǽn *carrucutium*, Wrt. Voc. i. 34, 26.

heáh-hylte; n. *A high-placed shrubbery* :—Eall swâ ðæt heáhhylte scæt tô scagan, C. D. v. 234, 24. Â be þâm hêhhylte in on þone langan þorn, Cht. E. 206, 27. Cf. scôm-hylte.

heáh-ildest; adj. *Most excellent* :—Ðyses heáhyldestan cyncges *huius precellentissimi regis*, Angl. xiii. 368, 36.

heáh-lǽce. *Add* :—Heálecas *archiatros*, Wrt. Voc. ii. 101, 1. Heáhlǽcas, 81, 36. Hêhlǽcas (hehhlæces, MS.) *archiatros* .i. *summos medicos*, Hpt. Gl. 477, 43 (all three glosses refer to the same persons as does Shrn. 135, 13). Heáhlæces, Wrt. Voc. ii. 2, 69.

heáh-land, es; n. *High ground* :—Heáhlond stigon sibgemágas (*Abraham and Isaac*) on Seone beorg, Exod. 385.

heáh-landrîca. v. land-rîca.

heáh-lâreów. For 'Lye' *substitute* :—Heáhleáreów archimandrita, Wrt. Voc. ii. 3, 23. Heáhlâreówum *gymnosophistis*, 40, 40 : didascalis, magistris doctorum, Hpt. Gl. 485, 21.

heáh-leornere, es; m. *A great scholar, a master* :—Heáhleornere archimandrita i. excelsus magister, An. Ox. 910.

heáh-mægen, es; n. I. *an exalted virtue, one of the three theological virtues* :—Nú synd ðreó heáhmægnu ðe menn sceolan habban, Fides, Spes, Caritas, Hml. S. 16, 246. II. *sublime power, divine might* :—Is þæs wuldres ful heofun and eorðe and eall heáhmægen tîre getâcnod, El. 753. Ongit Godes heáhmægen, 464. Þæt hine werþeóde and eal engla cynn úp on roderum hergen heáhmægen, þǽr is help gelong, Jul. 645. Cf. heáh-miht.

heáhmæsse-dæg, es; m. *A day on which high mass is celebrated* :—An heáhmæssedagum, þ is Sancte Stephanes and Sancte Iôhannes . . ., Nap. 36.

heáh-môd. *Add* : *high-spirited* :—Hû þâ wihte (*a cock and a hen*) mid ûs heáhmôde (heán-, MS.; but cf. wrǽtlice twâ, 1) twâ hâtne sindon, Rä. 43, 17.

heáh-môr, es; m. *A lofty mountain* :—In heáhmôrum (heáum (heágum) môrum, v. ll.), *in arduis montibus*, Bd. 4, 27 ; Sch. 515, 13.

heáh-nes. *Add* : I. in a physical sense. (1) *height* :—Ǽr þon þe seó heáhnes (*altitudo*) þæs wealles gefylled wǽre, Bd. 2, 14; Sch. 170, 19. Egeslicere heáhnysse (heánnesse, Wrt. Voc. ii. 85, 48) (*turrem*) *minaci proceritate*, An. Ox. 4436. Þá triówa heánnisse ic wundrade, Nar. 28, 1. (2) *depth* :—Ne hæfdon heánisse eorðes, Mt. L. R. 13, 5. Heónisse, Mk. R. 4. 5. (3) *a height, high place, high part, top* :—Ord, cnol, heánes *apicem* (v. Lk. 16, 17, and cf. apex, cacumen litere, 72, 6), Wrt. Voc. ii. 73, 74. Heánnes þǽre heáfodpannan *cacumen capitalis*, 22, 52. Under haehnisse (heánes, 77, 73) *sub cono* (*sublimi verticis* [*arboris*]), 121, 65. Heánnesse *caucumine* (*collis*, v. Ald. 21, 36), 22, 1. On heáhnysse *in edito*, An. Ox. 2458. Fleógan on ðâ heáhnesse (*in altum*), Bt. 36, 1 ; F. 172, 33. On heáhnise *in conum*, Wrt. Voc. ii. 82, 45. Oð ðæs heáfdes heáhnesse (heánesse, lxxii, 13) *usque ad uerticem*, Lch. i. lxxiv, 36. On hêgnessum *in altum*, An. Ox. 1559. Hergað Dryhten in heánissum, Ps. Srt. 148, 1. (4) *a deep place* or *part* :—Lǽd on heánise *duc in altum*, Lk. L. 5, 4. II. non-physical. (1) *of persons* or *their attributes, loftiness of rank* or *character, high rank* or *quality, majesty, dignity* :—On heálicere hêhnysse ł geþinþe geuferede *edito* (*uirginitatis*) *fastigio sublimati*, An. Ox. 930. On heálicere dêmendre hêhnysse ł geþinþe *in alto tribunalis culmine*, 3456. Þá wón wyrd on unrihtwîsra anwealda heánesse, Bt. 5, 1 ; F. 10, 21. Æfter heáhnysse ł heánnysse þînre *secundum altitudinem tuam*, Ps. L. 11, 9. Ne wællað gié in heánnise (heónisse, R.) genime *nolite in sublime tolli*, Lk. L. 12, 29. (2) *a position of dignity* or *supremacy* :—Ðæt mynster on eallum Norðscottum ealldorðóm and heánnesse onfêng (ealdordôm onfêng mid heánessum, v. l.) *monasterium in cunctis septentrionalium Scottorum monasteriis arcem tenebat, regendisque eorum populis praeerat*, Bd. 3, 3 ; Sch. 201, 20. (3) *exaltation* of mind, *elevation beyond ordinary conditions* :—In môdes heáhnnesse *in extasi* (*figuram vidit*, Ald. 152, 23), Wrt. Voc. ii. 91, 16.

heáh-reced, es; n. *A splendid house, temple, palace* :—Eorðan ic bidde and úpheofon, and ðâ sôþan Sancta Marian, and heofones meaht and heáhreced, Lch. i. 400, 4. Geond heáhræced (*the temple*), An. 709.

heah-rún, e; f. '*A damsel having a spirit of divination*' :—Heahrún *pithonissa* (pithonissam necromantie spiritu vaticinantem, Ald. 26, 11. The reference is to Acts 16, 16 : Puellam quandam habentem spiritum pythonem), Wrt. Voc. ii. 78, 47. Cf. hel-rún, -rȳnegu, helle-rúne; heago-rún, hægtesse.

heáh-sácerd. *Add* :—Hî lǽddon þæne Hǽlend tô þâm heáhsacerde (hêhsácerd, L. *ad summum sacerdotem*) . . . Petrus him fyligde oþ ðæs heáhsácerdes (*summi sacerdotis*) cafertûn. . : . Ðâ árás sum heáhsácerd (ðæ hêhsácerd, L.) . . . eft hine áxode se heáhsácerd . . . þá cwæð se heáhsácerd (se hêh ðâ sácerd, L. R., *summus autem sacerdos*), Mk. 14, 53–63. Þá biscopas and ðâ heáhsácerdas, Hml. A. 135, 661. Cyninga bearn and wîtegena and heáhsácerda, 129, 437 : 131, 489. Hî lǽddon hine (*Joseph*) tô ðâm biscope and tô þâm heáhsácerdum, 135, 648.

heáhsácerd-hâd (?), es; m. *Highpriesthood* :—Ðes êce hæfeð h sácerhâd *hic sempiternum habet sacerdotium*, Rtl. 90. 30.

heáh-sǽl. *Add* :—Nú is hire helpe heáhsǽl cumen *venit tempus miserendi ejus*, Ps. Th. 101, 11.

heáh-sǽþeóf. For '*Cot. 9, 191*' *substitute* :—Heáhsêðeáf *archiparratta* (archipirata, Ald. 56, 31, the gloss to which in An. Ox. 4039 is : Archipirata, i. *summus latro* flotman), Wrt. Voc. ii. 84, 44. Heáhsǽðeóf, 5, 28. See next word.

heáh-sceaþa, an; m. *An arch-robber, arch-pirate* :—Heáhsceaþa *archipirata*, An. Ox. 8, 228.

heáh-seld. *Add* : [seld = setl, Sievers, Gram. 196, 2] I. *a throne* :—Satanus wolde on heofonum hêhseld wyrcan (cf. hú hê him stôl

geworhte on heofonum, Gen. 273), Sat. 372. Stondað hæleð ymb hêhseld, 47. **II.** *an elevated platform :*—For heáhseldum *pro rostris,* An. Ox. 2322. Hêhseldum, Wrt. Voc. ii. 68, 47. v. heáh-setl.

**heáh-setl.** *Add:* **I.** *a seat of honour :*—'Ðê is leófre on ðisum wâcum scræfum þonne ðû on healle heálic biscop sitte.' Ðâ cwæð hê þæt hê wurðe nǽre ðæs heáhsetles, Hml. Th. ii. 146, 30. **II.** *an official seat.* (1) of a king, *a throne :*—On hêghseðel Godes *in throno Dei,* Mt. L. 23, 22. Bifore hêhseðle Godes, Rtl. 48, 3. Hêhseðlo *thronos,* 113, 12. (2) *a judgement-seat :*—Fore hêhseðle (dômsetle, W. S.) *pro tribunali,* Mt. L. 27, 19. Biforan hêhseðle Crîstes *ante tribunal Christi,* Rtl. 13, 7. Gié sittað ofer hêhseðlo (-e, R.) dôemende *sedeatis super thronos iudicantes,* Lk. L. 22, 30. (3) *of a teacher, speaker,* &c.:—In hêhseotle aeldrena hergen hine *in cathedra seniorum laudent eum,* Ps. Srt. 106, 32. Haehseðlum *prorostris* (for *pro rostris,* v. heáh-seld; II.), Wrt. Voc. ii. 118, 26.

**heáh-sittende ;** *adj. High-sitting, seated on a lofty throne :*—Heáh-sittendum *celsithrono,* Angl. xiii. 368, 39.

**heáh-steáp ;** *adj. Lofty :*—Se hâlga heáhsteáp reced timbrede, Gen. 2839.

**heáh-strǽt.** *Add :*—Of þælbricge tô ðǽre hêhstrǽte ; of ðǽre hêhstrǽte, C. D. vi. 60, 21. [v. *N. E. D.* highstreet.] Cf. heáh-weg.

**heáh-strengþu(o) ;** *f. Great strength :*—Heáhstrengðu heáfdes mînes *fortitudo capitis mei,* Ps. Th. 107, 7.

**heáh-sunne (?),** an ; *f. The arch-sun, the Deity :*—Wǽre þu forinwordlîce dysig ðâ þû wilnodest þæt þû scoldest myd swilcum ǽagum þâ heáhsunnan (heán sunnan ?) and ǽce geseón (*velle illum solem videre*), Solil. H. 34, 17.

**heáh-þegen.** *Add :*—Wæs sum heáhþegen gehâten Tetradius, Hml. S. 31, 506. Mid ânum heáhþegene Lisias gehâten (*Lysias a nobleman and one of the blood royal,* 1 Macc. 3, 32), 25, 330. Datianus hâmweard wæs mid his heáhþegenum, 14, 181. Feormode Holofernes his heáhþegnas (cf. ealle þâ yldestan þegnas, Jud. 10), Hml. A. 111, 283.

**heáh-þeód.** *Substitute: An illustrious race :*—Sum æþela man on þǽre hêhþeóde Myrcna rîce *vir de egregia Merciorum stirpe,* Guth. Gr. 104. 2 : 152, 19.

**heáh-þreá,** an ; *m. Extreme punishment :*—Grâp heáhþreá on hæðencynn, Gen. 2545.

**heáh-þrymm,** es ; *m. Exalted glory :*—Heáhþrym Godes, Gû. 1298.

**heáh-þrymme (?) ;** *adj. Of exalted glory :*—Hû andrysne heáhþrymme (*or a case of preceding word ?*) cyningc hêr wile dêman *quam celsithronus metuendus adveniet Judex,* Dôm. L. 95.

**heáhþu.** v. hîhþu.

**heáh-þungen.** *Add :*—Heáhþungen *perspicuus,* Wrt. Voc. ii. 68, 5. Cnæht mîn hêhðungen bið suîðe *puer meus sublimis erit valde,* Rtl. 1, 27. Bûtan þæt þâ bysena heáhþungenra lǽrað *nisi majorum cohortantur exempla,* R. Ben. 29, 19.

**heáh-tíd.** *Add :*—Heó seldan on hâtum baþe baþede bûton þâm heáhtídum tô Eástron and æt Pentæcosten and þy twelftan dæge ofer Geohhel (*praeter sollemniis maioribus, uerbi gratia paschae, pentecostes, epifaniae*), Bd. 4, 19; Sch. 443, 6 : Hml. S. 20, 45.

**heáh-torras.** *Substitute:* heáh-torr, es ; *m. A high rock, high mountain :*—Þâ giceligan heáhtorra bearewæs *glaciales alpium* (i. *montium*) *saltus,* An. Ox. 2035. Cf. heáh-beorg, -clif.

**heáh-weg ;** *m. A highway, main road :*—Hiis terminibus circumcincta. Ab oriente cyninges hêiweg ; a meritie strêt tô scufelingforde ... an cyninges strǽte, C. D. ii. 66, 31–67, 2. Cf. heáh-strǽt.

**heáh-weofod.** l. -wîgbed, -weófod, *and add :* cf. heáh-altar: **heáh-weorc.** *Add :* v. heáh-geweorc.

**heal** *a corner.* v. healh : healc. v. healoc.

**heald** *a hold.* *Add :*—Hald *firmum,* Wrt. Voc. ii. 147, 71. v. môr-, ûp-heald ; fæst-heald ; *adj.*

**heald** *inclined.* *Add :*—Hald *cernua,* Txts. 49, 455. Haldi, haldi *penduloso,* 84, 754. Suae haldae (halde) *reclines,* 92, 865. **I.** literal: —Of greátan hlinces ende on healdan weg ; andlang heldan weges, C. D. iii. 420, 5. Tô healdan hlince, 431, 11. Tô healdan grǽfe, v. 212, 4. On ðone heáldan weg, ii. 29, 5. On ðâ healdan stîge, iii. 462, 11. **II.** figurative. (1) *inclined* to :—þ ǽlc gesceaft bið heald onlocen (-loten ?) wiþ hyre gecynde, Bt. 25; F. 88, 7. (2) *that tends to mean things :*—Þâ healdan *divexa* (ardua sectari necnon *devexa* cavere, Ald. 157, 2), Wrt. Voc. ii. 91, 54 : 27, 12. v. forþ-, freónd-, in-, môr- (?), niþer-, norþ-, ô-, scyte-, sûþ-, tô- heald ; neowol ; hilde.

**healdan.** *Add:* **A.** *trans.* **I.** *to keep watch over, keep in charge.* (1) *to keep* a flock (*lit.* or *fig.*), sheep, swine, &c.:—Beóceorle ... gif hê gafolheorde healt, Ll. Th. i. 434, 36. Healde gê ðâ heorde mid suelcum eorneste suelce hirdas scoldon, Past. 89, 13. Abel ǽhte heóld fæder on fultum (*fuit Abel pastor ovium,* Gen. 4, 2), Gen. 973. Nyste hê hwâ hî (*four sheep*) heólde, Gr. D. 206, 11. Se hyrde ... þe nele þâ heorde þe hê healdan sceal bewerian, Ll. Th. i. 374, 23. (2) *of persons in positions of authority or trust, to watch over, keep, govern, rule,* the people, places or things under their authority or care. (a) the head of a family or

clan :—Him on lâste heóld land and yrfe Malalehel, Gen. 1167. Heóld mâga yrfe, 1218. Heóld leódgeard, 1224 (cf. Enoch ... hyrde wæs heáfodmâga, 1200). (b) a king :—Crîstes gespelian crîstendôm and cynedôm healdað and wealdað, Ll. Th. i. 350, 4. Ic (*Beowulf*) heóld þâs leóde fîftig wintra, B. 2732. Offa wîsdôme heóld êðel sînne, 1959. Nabochodonossor weardode wîde rîce, heóld hæleða gestreón and þâ heán burh, Dan. 666. ¶ *used absolutely :*—Eall folc geceás Eádward tô cynge, healde þâ hwîle þe him God unne, Chr. 1041 ; P. 163, 10. (b a) of superhuman rulers :—Tô þâm þe wera gâstum wealdeð and healdeð, Ps. Th. 75, 9 : Rä. 41, 5. Satan helle forð healdan sceolde, gŷman þæs grundes, Gen. 348. (c) a high official :—Sum rîce gerêfa eard weardode, in þǽre ceastre heóld hordgestreón, Jul. 22. Þâ mâþmhyrdas ðe þ feoh heóldon, Bt. 27, 4 ; F. 100, 14. Ic beóde eallum mînum gerêfum ... þ hŷ mîn folc rihtlîce healdan, Cht. E. 230, 29. Ðâ munecas beádon þone abbod þ hê sceolde healdan hî rihtlîce, Chr. 1083 ; P. 214, 19. Hê befæste þâ burg Æþerêde aldormen tô haldonne, 886 ; P. 80, 13. (d) of a lord's relation to his man :—Ic wille beón N. hold ... wið þâm þe hê mê healde swâ ic earnian wille, Ll. Th. i. 178, 7. (e) a legal guardian or keeper of property, one legally responsible for the safety of a thing :—Healden þâ mǽgas þone frumstôl oþ þæt þæt bearn gewintrod sié, Ll. Th. i. 126, 6. Hig .xi. healdan þǽre hyndene feoh, 232, 3. Hié hit (*a sword*) gesund âgifon .. bûton hiora hwæðer ǽr þingode þ hê hit ângylde healdan (*be responsible for it while in his keeping*) ne þorfte, Ll. Th. i. 74, 12. Man sumne berigean geselle his feoh tô healdenne oþ þæt hê x. wintra sié, 30, 5. Tô healdenne *vel* ædfæst, tæht *vel* becwyddod *depositum,* Wrt. Voc. i. 21, 4. (3) in a more general sense, *to keep, guard, be a guardian of.* (a) the object a person :—Sê ðe healdeð þê *qui custodit te,* Ps. Th. 120, 3. Englas healdað hâligra feorh, Gû. 61. Healdað hine nihta gehwylce twâ hund wearda, Sal. 259. Hê þâ geogoðe wile ârum healdan, B. 1182. ¶ of a bird and its eggs: Mec (*a cuckoo*) ... heóld and freoðode, Rä. 10, 5. (a a) the subject a thing :—Dæg and niht þâs werþeóda weardum healdað, An. 101. (b) the object a place or thing :—Se weard þæt mǽre lîf healdeð, Gen. 951. Weard goldmâðmas heóld, B. 2414. Sume heaðoreáf heóldon, 401. Weard Scyldinga sê þe holmclifu healdan scolde, 230. Sceótend þâ þæt hornreced healdan scoldon, 704. Neorxna wang and lîfes treó lêgene sweorde healdan, El. 758. Gif ðu ǽnigne gôdne heorde hæbbe þe wel cunne healdan þæt þæt ðû gestreóne and him befǽste, Solil. H. 3, 13 : 17. Tô healdenne, 4, 2. (4) in a hostile sense, *to watch, keep under observation :*—Sittende heóldun hine *sedentes servabant eum,* Mt. R. L. 27, 36. Haldende ðe Hǽlend *custodientes Iesum,* 27, 54. ¶ *used absolutely :*—Gê habbað heordrǽdenne : farað and healdað, Mt. 27, 65. (5) *to defend* against attack, *preserve from injury.* (a) the object a person :—Ic þe friðe healde þæt þê ne môton mângenîðlan gâste gescéððan, An. 917 : 1434. Hê (*God*) mê friðe healdeð ... ne gê mê lâðes wiht gedôn môtun, Gû. 281. Wit þê friðe healdað and mundbyrde, Gen. 2528. Þâ englas sceldað and healdað ealle hâlige sâwla, Bl. H. 11, 27. Heald mê herewǽpnum wið unholdum, Ps. Ben. 34, 3. Þæt hê þâ weálâfe heólde þæt ǽnig mon wordum ne weorcum wǽre ne brǽce, B. 1099. (b) the object a place or thing :—Mîne þincg ic heóld nû nigon geár wið ealle hŷnða, Hml. S. 9, 42. Æt niéhstan wæs nân tô gedâle, ... þâ se egorhere eorðan tûddor eall âcwealde, bûton þæt earcebord heóld heofona freá, Gen. 1404. His templ healdan wið þâ hæðenan, Hml. S. 25, 338. Wið ælfycum êðelstôlas healdan, B. 2372. Wið feónda gehwone flotan eówerne healdan, 296. **II.** *to hold.* (1) *to lay hold on, take :*—Ah ne haldas (genimeð, R., hû ne nymð hê, W. S.) and gehebbes ðâ ilco *nonne tenebit et levabit eam ?,* Mt. L. 12, 11. (1 a) in a hostile sense, *to take prisoner, arrest :*—Haldað (genimeð, R., nimað, W. S.) hine *tenete eum,* 26, 48. Haldas, Mk. L. 14, 44. Hê hêht folcgesîþas healdon þone hererinc ... hê hine inne hêht on carcerne [bringan], Met. 1, 71. Eódon tô haldanne hine (þ hî hine nâmon, W. S.), Mk. L. R. 3, 21. Sôhton hine tô haldanne (þ hine genôman, R.), Mt. L. 21, 46. (2) *to have hold of, prevent from escaping.* (a) the subject a person :—Hê heóld hine tô fæste, B. 788. (b) the subject a thing :—Ðæt sint þâ þreó anceras þe þæt scyp healdað ongemang ðâm brôgan þâra ŷða, Solil. H. 29, 17. Ðone streng þæt ðæt scyp healdan sceal, 22, 17. **III.** *to hold, keep from falling.* (1) the subject a person. (a) *to hold* in or with the hand, arm, &c. :—Haldas hearpas and fato *tenentes citharas et phialas,* Mt. p. 10, 2. Healdende palmtwigu on heora handum, Hml. Th. i. 538, 17. (b) *to hold up* by supports :—Se scyppend þâs eorðan wreðstuðum and þâs world healdeð, Rä. 41, 2. (2) the subject a thing :—þ þæt hnesce wæter hæbbe fiôr on þǽre fæstan eorðan, for þâm þe hit ne mæg on him selfum gestandan. Ac seó eorþe hit helt (hilt, Met. 20, 95), Bt. 33, 4 ; F. 130, 5. Seó eorþe on nânum þinge ne stent, ne nânwuht eorþlices hî ne healt þ hió ne sîge, 37. Healdeð, Met. 20, 166. Hê seah hû þâ stânbogan eorðreced innon healde, B. 2719. **IV.** *to maintain, support, uphold.* (1) the subject a person. (a) the object a person :—þâ hwîle þe gê mê rihtlîce healdað, Cht. E. 230, 6. Heóld mec and hæfde Hrêðel cyning, geaf mê sinc and symbel, B. 2430. Nô hî findan meahton æt þâm æþelinge þæt hê Heardrêde hlâford wǽre, ...

hwæþre hē hine on folce freóndlárum heóld, 2377. Hine Metod heóld wilna wæstmum, Gen. 1947. Gif hwā þǽre friðleásan man healde oþþe feormige, Ll. Th. i. 384, 7 : 410, 18. (a a) *to support life* :—þū of foldan fódder neátum lǽtest ālǽdan, on þǽm hī līf healdað, Ps. Th. 103, 13. (b) the object a thing :—þæt hē healde his mǽga rǽd *that he uphold what is to the advantage of his kinsmen*, Sal. 491. Sǽte haldan (*to keep in repair*), Ll. Th. i. 432, 15. (2) the subject a thing :—Mē mǽra dǽl in gǽstgerýnum wunað, sē mē wraðe healdeð, Gū. 220. **V. *to hold and control, manage* :**—Dryhten . . . scyreð and scrīfeð and gesceapo healdeð, Vy. 66 : Gen. 2827. Eal þū hit geþyldum healdest, mǽgen mid mōdes snyttrum, B. 1705. þā þe unwīse heora heortan hige healdað mid dysige *insipientes corde*, Ps. Th. 75, 4. **V a.** reflex. *to hold, bear* or *conduct* oneself, *to behave* :—Wǽre þū tōdæg beswungcen? Ic næs, for þām wærlice ic mē heóld (*tenui*), Coll. M. 34, 9. Loth þǽre monwīsan fleáh, and hine fægre heold, Gen. 1941. Eów manaþ eówer lāreów þæt gē healdan eów selfe ǽnlīce, Coll. M. 35, 37. Gif hē hine heólde swā swā hē sceolde, Ll. Th. i. 192, 15. Dryhten hine ðreáde for his ǽrgedōnan weorcum, ǽr ðǽm ðe he him sǽde hū hē hine forð healden sceolde *Dominus facta ejus corripuit, nec tamen illico, quae essent facienda, monstravit*, Past. 443, 28. **VI. *to handle, treat, deal with*.** (1) a person :—Is rihtlic þ ūre ǽlc ōðerne healde mid rihte, Ll. Th. i. 336, 10. (2) a subject :—Gode þanc þæs dǽles þe ic wót. Ic wille þis nū smeigan and haldan swā ic geornost mæg *ista diligenter cauteque tractabo*, Solil. H. 53, 10. **VII. *to hold, contain within itself*** :—Hit eorðe oninnan hire heóld, Met. 29, 55. **VII a. *to be capable of containing*** a certain quantity :—Wæterfatu healdende ǽnlīpige twyfealde gemetu oððe þrysfealde (*hydriae capientes singuli metretas binas uel ternas*, Jn. 2, 6), Hml. Th. ii. 56, 20. **VIII. *to hold as owner* or *as tenant, to have possession* or *enjoyment of*.** (1) the subject a person :—Þīn āgen bearn frætwa healdeð, þonne þīn flǽsc liged, Gen. 2188. Wē wunian mōton grimme grundas ; God seolfa him rīce healdeð, Sat. 260. Ofer þan heofonfugelas healdað eardas *super ea volucres coeli habitabunt*, Ps. Th. 103, 11. Þǽr sylfǽtan eard weardigað, ēðel healdað, An. 176. Grendel mōras heóld, B. 103. þā þe heóldon hyge-þancum hæleða rǽdas, El. 156. Þ Ælfgifu sǽte on Winceastre mid þæs cynges hūscarlum, and heóldan eall West-Seaxan him tō handa, Chr. 1036 ; P. 161, 4. Hī cuǽdon þæt hié þæt tō his honda healdan sceoldon, Chr. 887 ; P. 80, 21. Hū mæg hē gāstlicne wæstm habban and healdan?, Bl. H. 55, 10. Þeáh mē genōh cume, ne fagnige ic hys swīðe, . . . ne mǽran getilige tō haldænne, Solil. H. 35, 17. Heó Myrcna anweald mid rihthlāforddōme haldende wæs, Chr. 918 ; P. 105, 28. (2) the subject a thing :—Hald þū nū, hrūse, nū hæleð ne mōston, eorla ǽhte, B. 2247. Hī forleton eorla gestreón eorðan healdan, 3167. **VIII a. *to hold, occupy* an office, a position** :—Sē ðe scīre healt (*the reeve*), Angl. ix. 265, 6. Hē heóld þridde healf geár bīsdōm, Chr. 931 ; P. 106, 2. Tō tācne þæt mon endebyrdlīce ðone biscepdōm halde (*healde, v.l.*), Past. 52, 22. Sē þe scīre healde, Ll. Th. i. 434, 33. Rōmāne lādteówas gesetton, þe hié consulas hēton, þ heora rīce heólde ān geár ān monn, Ors. 2, 2 ; S. 68, 3. Lāreówdōm healdan, Hml. Th. ii. 320, 12. Ealdorscype, ealdordōm healdan *primatum tenere*, Coll. M. 30, 17, 23. **VIII b. *to hold, keep forcibly* against an adversary** :—Hig fuhton fīf dagas, . . . ac hig þā duru heóldon, Fin. 42. Hē frægn . . . hwā þā duru heólde, 23. Wǽron innan þǽm castele manige þe hine healdon woldan ongeán þone cyng, Chr. 1087 ; P. 224, 5. Hē his ealdormen hæfde beboden þā clūsan tō healdanne, Ors. 6, 36 ; S. 292, 27. **VIII c. *to remain in*, retain possession of** :—Gif þū fǽrst tō þǽre winstran hælfe, ic healde (*habebo*) þā swīðran healfe, Gen. 13, 9. Hié hiera heres þone mǽstan dǽl hām sendon mid hiora herehýþe, and þone oþerne dǽl þǽr lēton þæt lond tō healdanne, Ors. 1, 10 ; S. 46, 22. **IX. *to retain, detain, not to let go, not to lose*.** (I) the object a person. (a) *to keep, not to abandon* :—Gif hwā his rihtǽwe forlǽte . . . Ac healde gehwā mid riht his ǽwe, Ll. Th. ii. 300, 26. (b) *to detain as prisoner, keep* in prison :—Gif cirican fāh mon geierne . . . Gif hīwan hiora cirican þearfe hæbben, healde hine mon on ōðrum ærne, l.l. Th. i. 64, 14. Ne dýde man nǽfre on Sunnandæges freólse ǽnigne forwyrhtne, ac wylde and healde þ se freólsdæg āgan sié, 172, 14 : 402, 12. 'Hāt hī healdan þý lǽs ðe hī fleámes cēpon.' Ðā andwyrde se heretoga : 'Ic hāte healdan hī and eów, oð þæt heora sagu āfandod sý,' Hml. Th. ii. 484, 1–3. (2) the object a thing, material or non-material :—Hē woruldwelan lufað and hielt (hilt, *v.l.*) *eas diligendo retinet*, Past. 331, 10. þā welan beóþ leóftælran þonne þonne hié mon selþ þonne hié beón þonne hī mon gadraþ and healt (hilt, *v.l.*), Bt. 13; F. 38, 15. þā ðe þ word healdað *qui uerbum retinent*, Lk. 8, 15. Hē gife, þe him God sealde, heóld, B. 2183. Hald (heald, *v.l.*) ðīne ælmessan, ðý lǽs ðū hié forweorpe, Past. 324, 3. þæt hē healde Godes miltse, Sal. 491. Ge-healdsum on ðǽm ðe hē healdan scyle oððe dǽlan, Past. 149, 19. Nis nān gesceaft ðe hē tiohhige þ hió scyle winnan wiþ hire Scippendes willan, gif hió hire gecynd healdan wile *nihil est, quod naturam servans, Deo contraire conetur*, Bt. 35, 4; F. 160, 23 : 34, 12; F. 152, 20 : 36, 6; F. 182, 22. **X. *to keep* for use when needed, *keep in store*** :—Hē him ēce leán healdeð on heofonum, Cri. 1681. **X a.** with

extension or complement, *to keep* in a place, condition, relation, &c. :—þū hī gaderast and heltst on þīnum horde, Bt. 14, 2 ; F. 44, 4. Hē feora gehwilc healdeð in hǽlo, Gū. 368. Hē healdeð mē on heaðore, Rä. 21, 13. þā þe þē on heora lufan healdað *diligentes te*, Ps. Th. 121, 6. Hī hýdað heáhgestreón, healdað on fæstenne, Sol. 317. Gif hit unwitan ǽnige hwīle healdað būtan hæftum, hit þurh hrōf wadeð, 411. Heald mē on þīnre sōðfæstnesse, Ps. Th. 142, 1. þā word on his heortan habban and healdan, Bl. H. 55, 8. **X b.** reflex. *to keep oneself, remain* :—Heóld hyne syððan fyr and fæstor sē þǽm feónde ætwand, B. 142. Wīf ic lǽrde þ hié heora weras lufedan . . . ; and ic lǽrde weras þ hié be him ānum getreówlīce hié heóldan, Bl. H. 185, 24. **X c.** *to continue to occupy, not to leave* :—Æsc byð stīð on staðule, stede rihte hylt, Rūn. 26. Hī heora ryne healdað, stōwe gestefnde, Gen. 159. **XI. *to hold, keep together, without interruption*.** (I) *to hold together* a number of people, *hold* a meeting, court, &c. :—Hū mon ðæt hundred haldan sceal. Ǽrest þ hī heó gegaderian ā ymb feówer wucan, Ll. Th. i. 258, 3. (2) *to keep in force* or *operation*, continue a practice, habit, arrangement, &c. :—Ic healde mīne wīsan, Rä. 9, 4. Sió gesomnung ðǽre hālgan ciricean ðurh ondetnesse hielt (hilt, *v.l.*) ðā gewitnesse ðǽre sōðfæsðnesse, Past. 367, 6. Ǽt þām unþeáwe þe dysige men on ungewunan healdað, Wlfst. 305, 9. Hē þæt gerýne þǽre hālgan fulwihte mid gōdum dǽdum heóld and fullade, Bl. H. 213, 16. Hié þæt heóldun mid micelre unsibbe, Chr. 887 ; P. 80, 26. Ic āwrītan hēt monege þāra þe ūre foregengan heóldon (*many laws that were in force with our predecessors*) . . . and manege . . . ic āwearp . . . and on ōðre wīsan bebeád tō healdenne (*I ordered that other laws should be in force*), Ll. Th. i. 58, 17–20. Ðeáw healdan, 440, 22. Hwylce steóre hý be þan healdan willað, 276, 28. Ǽlc þāra þe healdan wile hālige þeáwas, Gen. 1531 : Ll. Th. ii. 300, 29. (3) *to maintain* a condition, relation, &c., *keep* company, silence, &c. :—Hié healdað mā gefērrǽdenne and efnlīcnesse ðonne ealdordōm wið ðā yfelan, Past. 123, 2. Ðyllicne gebrōðorscipe hié heóldon him betweónum, Ors. 3, 11 ; S. 152, 28. Hié on symbel wið Rōmānum sibbe heóldon, 4, 8 ; S. 186, 3. Hié hié selfe nīðað tō healdonne swīgean, Past. 271, 16. (4) *to perform* a function, office, &c., *keep* watch :—Eorl ofer ōðrum healdeð heáfod-wearde, B. 2909. Ic ǽgwearde heóld, 241. Sceaft nytte heóld, 3118. þæt gē wæccende wið hettendra hildewōman wearde healden, Jul. 664. Wið þām fǽrscyte wearde healdan, Cri. 767. Wið wrāð werod wearde healdan, B. 319. (5) *to keep* a day, festival, ceremonial observance, &c. :—Ðes man restedæg ne healt, Jn. 9, 16. On þǽre stōwe þe wē nū bissextun healdað, Angl. viii. 306, 41. Tōdāl þǽra metta wē nā ne healdaþ . . . þā bīgengu þe nāwan mōnan wē nā ne healdaþ, An. Ox. 40, 26, 34. Healde man ǽlces Sunnandæges freólsunga fram nōntīde þæs Sæternesdæges oþ þæs Mōnandæges līhtinge . . . and man ǽlc beboden fæsten healde, Ll. Th. i. 264, 18–22 : 320, 10. Hāligra tīd þā man healdan sceal, Men. 229. **XII. *to keep* unbroken, inviolate.** (1) *not to pass* a limit :—Healdeð georne mere gemǽre, Sch. 52. Mearce healdan, Met. 11, 73. (2) *to keep* a command, law, pledge, promīse, &c. :—Word his ic haldo, Jn. L. R. 8, 55. Treów þū wið rodora weard healdest, Gen. 2119. Gif gē lufað mē, healdað mīne beboda : þe þe lufað mē healt mīne sprǽce, Ælfc. T. Grn. 14, 31. Hylt, Ps. Th. 18, 10. Hī swincað wið synnum, healdað sōð and riht, Gū. 782. Hē wǽre wið þec heóld, El. 824. Hī hyra þeódnes wordum and weorcum willan heóldon, Cri. 1237. Hī gōdne friþ heóldon, Chr. 877 ; P. 74, 21. Heald forð tela nīwe sibbe, B. 948. Hē hī stearclīce healde *eos artissime constringat*, Chrd. 54, 26. Þte Godes þeówas hiora ryhtregol on ryht healdan, Ll. Th. i. 102, 15. Þæt ic ǽ þīne heólde and lǽste, Ps. Th. 118, 61. Hwæt hié wyrcean and healdan scoldon, Past. 103, 3. Uton healdan þ wedd and þ frið, Ll. Th. i. 238, 24. Clǽnnysse healdan *to keep the vow of chastity*, 306, 20. **XIII. *to constrain, compel*** :—Gif gehādod man hine forwyrce mid deáðscylde, gewilde hine man and healde tō biscopes dōme, Ll. Th. i. 168, 23 : 402, 1. **XIV. *to keep back from action, restrain, stop*** :—Hī heóldon heora eáran (*continuerunt aures suas*, Acts 7, 57), Hml. Th. i. 46, 33. Heald þīne handa, Hml. S. 13, 256. Nǽnig monn mǽhte hine temma i halda (*domare*), Mk. L. 5, 4. **XIV a. *to restrain oneself, refrain*** :—Healde hine ðæt hē ne cnytte ðæt underfongne feoh on ðǽm swātlīne, 59, 13. Þ wē ūs healdan wiþ þā heáfodlican leahtras, Bl. H. 37, 2. Gif hié hié nyllað healdan wið ðǽm ǽfste, Past. 233, 17. **XV. *to hold in the mind*.** (I) *to entertain, have* a feeling :—Hió hióld heáhlufan wið hæleða brego, B. 1954. Hī gefeán healdað, Ph. 391. þæt hē gāstlice lufe healde, Leás. 38 : Sal. 491. (2) *to keep in mind, remember* :—Hī his wīsdōmes hlīsan healdað, Gū. 128. þā þe Dryhtnes bibod heóldon on hreðre, Cri. 1160. (3) *to hold* a belief, an opinion, &c. :—þā men þe Godes rīces geleáfan habbað and healdaþ, Bl. H. 55, 17. (4) *to hold* in esteem, *regard* :—Se bisceop þone iungan cniht deórwurðlīce heóld, Ælfc. T. Grn. 17, 8. Heó wæs sumne dǽl hæbbende of þām reáfe þæs Hǽlendes and hyt swýðe deórwyrðlīce heóld, Hml. A. 187, 180. Þī hé elcað þæt wē sceolon deórwyrðlīce healdan Godes gife, Hml. Th. i. 248, 28. (5) with object and complement or extension, *to hold as, regard*

as:—Buton hiora hwæðer ǽr þingode þ hē hit āngylde healdan (or under I?) ne þorfte, Ll. Th. i. 74, 12. Hié him þæt gold tō gode noldon healdan, Dan. 198. **B.** *intrans.* **I.** of things, *to hold, remain unbroken, not to give way:*—Weallas him (waves) wiðre healdað, Gn. Ex. 54. **II.** of persons, *to hold one's ground, not to give way before an adversary:*—Gūðweard gumena hēht his hereciste healdan georne, fæst fyrdgetrum, Exod. 177. **III.** *to proceed, move on:*—Cōm þ lið intō Temese, and lāgon þǽr twā niht, and heóldon syððan tō Denmarcon, Chr. 1071; P. 206, 21. **IV.** with dat. of person to whom a thing is offered, and dat. of thing, *to perform for a person the action suggested by the noun:*—Hē him (the birds) ǽte heóld, þonne hý him hungrige ymb hond flugon, Gū. 708. Hý hine bǽron and him bryce heóldon (they served him), 701. þæt se wudubeám wildeór scilde, ǽte eallum heólde (should feed them all), swylce fuglas eác heora feorhnere on þæs beámes blēdum nāme, Dan. 506. Dracan þū gehéoðwadest, hēte him bysmere healdan *draco quem formasti ad illudendum ei*, Ps. Th. 103, 25. **C.** with adverbs. **I.** forð, *to continue, go on with:*—Heóldon forð ryne eástreámas heora, Gen. 215. **II.** on, *to go on:*—Heóld on heáh gesceap *high destiny held on its course*, B. 3084. v. ā-, æt-, mis-, of-, ofer-, on-, oþ-healdan; dreám-healdende; be-, full-, ge-healden.

**-healden**; *adj.* v. scyte-healden: **-healden[n]**, e; *f.* v. ge-healden[n].

**healdend.** *Add:*—Adam neorscna wonges nīwre gesceafte hyrde and haldend, Gen. 172. v. be-, duru-, ge-, rīce-healdend.

**-healdendlic.** v. ge-healdendlic: **-healdennes.** v. be-healdennes: **-healdfæst.** v. ge-healdfæst.

**healding**, e; *f.* *Holding, keeping* of a command:—In haldinge *in custodiendo (sermones tuos)*, Ps. Srt. 118, 9. v. healdan; **A. XII.** 2.

**-healdlic.** v. freóndheald-lic.

**heald-ness.** *Add: the office of a bishop.* v. healdan; **A. I.** 1:—Healdnessa *flaminia* (v. Ald. 25, 35), Wrt. Voc. ii. 33, 71. v. be-, for-, ge-healdness.

**healdsum(?)**; *adj. Taking care of, protective:*—Sē bið halsum in his líf, Archiv. cxxix. 25, 6. v. ge-healdsum.

**-healdsumlíce, -healdsumness.** v. ge-healdsumlíce, ge-, mis-healdsumness: **healede** *calcanosus.* v. hélede.

**healf**, e; *f.* Substitute: *Side, part:*—Hac on ðäs healfe, *illac* on ðā healfe, Ælfc. Gr. Z. 225, 4. **I.** as a specification of position or direction. (1) *one of two sides of an object* (v. (3)):—þ tōswollene lim (the foot) fram þǽre uferran healfe beþe, Lch. ii. 68, 14. Lǽt blōd of earme, næs on þā healfe þe þ sár biþ, 262, 16. On ðā healfe þe heó scínð, þǽr byð dæg, and on þā healfe þe heó ne scínð, ðǽr byð niht. Ǽfre byð on sumre sīdan þǽre eorðan dæg, and ǽfre on sumre sīdan niht, Lch. iii. 234, 25–28. An bā halbae (halbe, halfe, *v. ll.*) *altrinsecus*, Txts. 38, 51. On twā healfa, Wrt. Voc. ii. 1, 8. þ wē sendan on twā healfa tō þām gerēfum, Ll. Th. i. 236, 14. **¶** (the right or left) side, hand:—Gif þū fǽrst tō þǽre winstran hælfe, ic healde þā swiðran healfe; gif þū þā swiðran healfe gecíst, ic fare tō þǽre winstran healfe, Gen. 13, 9. *Dextrorsum* on ðā swyðran healfe, *sinistrorsum* on ðā wynstran healfe, Ælfc. Gr. Z. 225, 7–9. (a) of a person:—þū sittest on sínre swiðran healf, Hy. 7, 42. Hē sette Mannaseh on his winstran hand, þæt wæs on Israhéles swiðran healfe. Gen. 48, 13. (β) of a thing:—Fram swiþre healfe *dextro cornu*, Wrt. Voc. ii. 140, 2. Hit (the cross) ongan swǽtan on þā swiþran healfe, Kr. 20. (2) *one of more than two sides* (v. (3)) (a) a definite number:—On āne healfe, Chr. 892; P. 82, 33. Him mon on þreó healfe onwinnende wæs, Ors. 4, 7; S. 184, 3. On seofon healfa swōgað windas, Cri. 950. Bið seó tunge tōtogen on týn healfa, Seel. 115. (b) indefinite:—On healfe gehwäre, Ph. 206. Heó ne helt on nāne healfe, Bt. 33, 4; F. 130, 36: Met. 20, 164. On ǽlee healfe, Chr. 892; P. 82, 34. On hwilce healfe, Gen. 1918. Him mon sceolde an mā healfa on feohtan þonne on āne, Ors. 2, 5; S. 80, 27. Hí on healfa gehwone þringað, Ph. 336. Hié on healfa gehwone heáwan þōhton, B. 800. (c) where *feówer* is used indefinitely:—þā burgware self þæt fæsten onbærndon an feówer healfa *succensis domibus suis*, Ors. 3, 11; S. 144, 32. For þǽm gewinnum þe hié þā hæfdon on feówer healfa, 4, 10; S. 196, 19. (3) with force as in either (1) or (2) and (a) gen. of object:—Hí (sun and moon) be healfe heofones þisses on āne ne lǽt God *God does not let them be on the same side of heaven*, Met. 29, 43. Beón on þā swiþran healfe Drihtnes, Bl. H. 95, 21. On þā swiþran healfe mínes dǽles, 147, 30. Wǽles healfe *aluei marginem*, An. Ox. 3679. On oþre healfe Donua þǽre ié, Ors. 1, 1; S. 16, 12. On þā healfe muntes *ultramontana*, Chr. 887; P. 80, 26: Bt. 18, 2; F. 64, 11. Hí ne lǽt God on āne healfe þæs heofones biön, 39, 13; F. 234, 8. þā twā ǽdran on twā healfa þāra eágena, Ors. 4, 6; S. 178, 23. Hē gesette twā folc on twā healfa his, S. 174, 32. Hié selfe wǽron on þǽm midmestan, and þā oþre on twā healfa hiera, 5, 12; S. 242, 4. Behealde hē on feówer healfe his, Bt. 19; F. 68, 22: Ll. Th. i. 224, 8. (b) with dat. of object:—Hē gesæt Godfæder on þā swiþran healfe, Bl. H. 91, 5. Mé bið gongende grēne on healfe, and mín swæð sweart on ōðre, Rä. 22, 9. Him on healfa gehwäm hettend seomedon, Exod.

209. Him on healfa gehwone, Cri. 928. Beóð twēgen dǽlas on twā healfa þām gemetegodum dǽle, Lch. iii. 262, 1. (4) *with prep.* be healfe *beside* (with dat.):—Hæleðum be healfe fēran, B. 2262. Him be healfe sittan (standan, eardian), An. 1065: By. 152: Rä. 85, 20. (5) of the position occupied by two opponents:—Twēgen gewin drugon ... hý hine trymedon on twā healfa, Gū. 104: El. 955. Fyrdhwate on twā healfe tohtan sēcað, 1180. (6) *one of the opposite sides in a conflict:*—Hwæðer healf hæfð sige, Ors. 3, 1; S. 100, 9. Wæs swiðe feala manna forfaren on Cnutes healfe, Chr. 1025; P. 157, 18. Weard swiðe stranglic gefeoht on bā halfe, 1066; P. 199, 13. (7) *one of the parties to a transaction, dispute, &c.:*—Gān twēgen menn of ǽgðre healfe, Ll. Th. i. 226, 19, 20. Gerǽdden þā witan on ǽgðer halfe þ man yfeles geswác, and geaf se cyng his freóndscipe on ǽgðre healfe, Chr. 1048; P. 174, 17–19. Man freóndscipe gefæstnode mid wædde on ǽgðere healfe, 1014; P. 145, 11. Hergodon hí on heora healfe and Cnut on his, 1016; P. 147, 16. Beó on nāðre healfe nā mā manna þonne .xii., Ll. Th. i. 212, 7. Hié getrúwedon on twā healfe frioðuwǽre, B. 1095: 1305: 2063. (8) *behalf, account:*—Swā oft swā þā ôþre hergas ūt fōron, þonne fōron hié oþþe mid oþþe on heora healfe on, Chr. 894; P. 84, 22. **II.** *side, quarter, direction:*—ðæt hē ne ðyrfe an nāne healfe anbūgan tō nānum synlicum luste, Past. 83, 15. Ne lēten hié nō hié on ǽlce healfe gebígean *nequaquam eos per tot varietates latera mutabilitatis aura versaret*, 306, 4. ðā sprǽce nǽnig mon on nǽnge ōðre halfe oncaerrende sié nymne suǽ þis gewrit hafað, C. D. B. i. 446, 13. þū ondrǽdan ne þearft on þā healfe (in that quarter, i. e. from Grendel) aldorbealu eorlum, B. 1675. þeóðbealu on þreó healfa. Ān is þāra þæt hý him yrmða tō fela andweard seóð ..., Cri. 1268. Weras þeahtedon on healfa gehwǽr, sume hyder sume þyder *they considered the matter on all sides*, El. 548. [*Goth.* halba: *O. Sax.* halba: *O.Frs.* halve: *O. H. Ger.* halba: *Icel.* hálfa.] v. eást-, fæderen-, mōdor-, norþ-, sǽ-, spere-, spinel-, sūþ-, ūt-, wǽpned-, west-, wíf-healf.

**healf** *a half.* See next word.

**healf**; *adj.* *Add:* **A.** **as adj.** **I.** (1) immediately preceding a substantive, *denoting the thing which is halved:*—Ān healf tūn ... healfne tūn, C. D. ii. 66, 29–30. Healf wer ætfeald, Ll. Th. i. 354, 21. þolige hē healfes weres, 398, 5: 254, 15. Be healfan were gyldan, Ll. Th. i. 354, 19: 408, 20. Tō healfre hīde, 188, 1. Forgielde þone wífman fullan gielde and þ beam healfan gelde, 68, 2. Be healfum wurðe, 208, 24. Gebycgan mid halfe weorðe, C. D. ii. 120, 28. Healfne bannuc *buccellam semiplenam*, An. Ox. 2402. Healfne leód, Ll. Th. i. 8, 7: 22, 4, 6. Twelf tīda and lytle māre þonne āne healfe tíde, Lch. iii. 258, 20: Angl. viii. 298, 17. Healfre hīde landes, C. D. iv. 136, 32. Healf geár, Chr. 901; P. 93, 1. Healf pund, Ll. Th. i. 258, 18. On ðone healfan æcer, C. D. iii. 437, 21: iv. 300, 10. Twēgen healfa hlāfas ic brōhte, Hml. S. 23 b, 518. þreó healfe elne, Ll. Th. i. 212, 2. (a a) with pronoun:—Gif hit biscepsunu sié, sié be healfum þām, Ll. Th. i. 150, 20. Sē þe hine gefó and gegange healfne hine āge, 42, 18. (b) denoting one of the parts into which the division is made, healf dǽl *a half:*—Hió hire folc on tū tōdǽlde ... Hió mid þǽm healfan dǽle beforan þǽm cyninge farende wæs ... and se healfa dǽl wæs Ciruse æfter fylgende, Ors. 2, 4; S. 76, 25–30. Geteald tō healfan dǽle middaneardes, Hml. Th. i. 68, 35. Hē sealde healfne dǽl þām þearfan, and þone healfan dǽl hē dyde on his hricg, Hml. S. 31, 70: Ll. Th. i. 228, 20. (2) following a substantive:—Hec sunt prata ... stocmēd healf, C. D. ii. 65, 26. Donne seó eahteoðe tíd bið healf āgān *mediante octava hora*, R. Ben. 73, 15. þyringas and Begware healfe, Ors. 1, 1; S. 16, 11. (2 a) following a pronoun:—Gif hió (the hand) healf onweg fleóge, Ll. Th. i. 98, 9. Sié hit healf forgifen, 64, 22. þām āgende hine man healfne āgielde, 42, 22. Gesette hē .cxx. sciłł. Dǽle hē þ healf (half of it) in þā scíre þe hē ǽr folgode, healf in þā þe hē on cymð, 86, 6. Āsmeáge hwæt his biglifen sý, and dǽle þ healf on ælmyssan (*dimidium in eleemosynas distribuat*), ii. 134, 31. Mid þǽm miclan wōlbryne monncwealmes ... hié healfe belifene wurdon, Ors. 2, 9; S. 86, 25. Man ne mihte macian hí healfe ūp, Hml. S. 21, 434. (3) where the adj. (a) precedes a substantive with demonstrative or defining words:—Nū ys healfe (healf? *or can* healfe *be taken as adverb qualifying* fornumen?) hire līchama mid hreófnisse fornumen *ecce jam medium carnis ejus devoratum est lepra*, Num. 12, 12. Ic gean healfes ðæs landes, C. D. iv. 300, 6, 28. Be healfre þǽre bōte, Ll. Th. i. 70, 1. Genim healf þā sealfe, Lch. ii. 78, 16. Hē nam healf ðæt blōd (*dimidiam partem sanguinis*), Ex. 24, 6. Hē behēt þām apostole healf his ríce, Hml. Th. ii. 476, 21. Hē āge healf þ wíte, Ll. Th. i. 40, 2. (b) follows the substantive:—þā þ weorc þǽre cyrícean hūhugu healf (*or adv.?*) wæs geworht *cum opus ad medium ferme esset perductum*, Bd. 3, 8; Sch. 225, 10. Is þ land æt Snōcescumbe healf þæs cinges, healf uncer Brentinges, C. D. ii. 250, 23. On þām fíftan dǽle healfum, Bt. 18, 1; F. 62, 23. Ealne þysne middangeard ... healfne, Ors. 1, 1; S. 8, 9. ðet land healf and healfne tūn, C. D. ii. 66, 30. (4) preceding a relative clause:—Agustus ādrāf of Rōmebyrig healfe þe þǽrbinnan wǽron, Ors. 6, 1; S. 254, 16. **II.** used with ordinal numerals where a half unit is to be expressed. (1) where the cardinal number for the units is

given:—Ðá hé on þǽre mǽgþe twá gér and þridde healf (twa geár and ðrydde healf geár, v.l.) þá cyricean rehte cum in illa provincia duobus annis ac dimidio ecclesiam rexisset, Bd. 4, 3; Sch. 351, 13. (2) generally the cardinal is not given:—Duas possessiunculas et tertiam dimediam, id est in nostra loquella ðridda half haga, C. D. i. 243, 13. Underwed þ sý þæs orfes óðer healf weorð, Ll. Th. i. 352, 9. Ðæt wǽre óðer healf hund M ofslagen þára féðena peditum centum quadraginta millia trecenti et triginta, Ors. 3, 10; S. 138. 16. þæs gehorsedan heres fífte healf M equitum quatuor millia ducenti, 3, 9; S. 124, 12. Cuóm feórðe healf hund scipa, Chr. 851; P. 64, 17. Sé þe hæbbe þreó hída tǽcne óðres healfes [hýdes gesettes], Ll. Th. i. 144, 11. On óðerre healfre míle sǽce unius ferme miliarii et dimidii spatio, Bd. 5, 2; Sch. 556, 5. Tó ðriddan healfan geáre, Hml. S. 6, 300. Óþerne healfne pening gewege, Lch. ii. 288, 8. Óðre healfe elne, Ll. Th. i. 212, 2. Hé heóld þridde healf geár bísdóm, Chr. 931; P. 106, 2 : 946; P. 112, 2. Hiera mon áhéng fífte healf hund quadringenti et quinquaginta servi in crucem acti, Ors. 5, 3; S. 222, 30.      III. as a measure of degree:—Se áð sceal bión healf be húslgengum, Ll. Th. i. 112, 4.      IV. where no substantive precedes or follows the adj. (1) where a substantive may be supplied from the context:—Gif Wylisc mon hæbbe híde londes . . . gif hé hæbbe healfes (cf. 144, 11. v. II. 2 supra) (healfe, v.l.), Ll. Th. i. 122, 10. þæt hié him óðer fiet gerýmdon, healle and heáhsetl, þæt hié healfre geweald ágan móston, B. 1087. Hé wolde hýdan eal heofona ríce and him ðær on healfum [ríxian], Sal. 454. (2) where a substantive may be inferred from the 'context. Cf. I. 1 b:—Saluie, rude be healfan (dǽle) þǽre saluian, Lch. ii. 292, 17. Tódǽle man þá eahta dǽlas on twá, and fó se landhláford tó healfum, tó healfum se bisceop, Ll. Th. i. 264, 4 : 342, 19 : 228, 18. Tó healfan, 268, 20 : 274, 31. Gielde hé hine þriddan dǽle. Gif mon spere selle, healfne. Gif hé horses onlǽne, ealne hé hine gylde, 120, 14. Gielden þæs mǽgas þæs weres þriddan dǽl . . . Gif hé mǽgas nǽge, gieldan þá gegildan healfne (dǽl weres? or wer?), for healfne hé fleó, 78, 24. Gielde mon healfne cyninge, healfne þám gegildan, 80, 3. Swylce ic tódǽle ǽnne penig on twá, þonne hæbbe ic healfne, and mín cleric healfne, and mín dǽl byð semis, and his semis, Angl. viii. 335, 28.      V. adverbial use of instrumental. Cf. micle :—Þynceð þegua gehwelcum huniges bíbreád healfe þý swétre, Met. 12, 9.      B. substantive. a half :—Healf medium (hanc vestem findi placuit . . . servatur medium signi index), An. Ox. 32, 12. Gif mon hæbbe híde londes . . . Gif hé hæbbe healfes (healfe, v.l.; but see IV. 1), Ll. Th. i. 122, 10. þá ásweóll him se líchama ofer healf fram þám lendenum oþ þá fét tumore dimidia pars corporis ipsius a lumbis tenus planta turgescens, Guth. Gr. 153, 12. þæt híg bringan melwes þone teóðan dǽl þæs gemetes þe man nemð ephi, healf ǽr undern, healfe ofer undern (medium ejus mane, et medium ejus vespere), Lev. 6, 20. Gif hé hæbbe ealle on fóðre tó ágifanne, ágífe ealle : gif hé nǽbbe, ágífe healf on fóðre, healfe (healf, v.l.) on óðrum ceápe (dimidium in annona, dimidium in alio captali), Ll. Lbmn. 116, 14. Ðáh sé á half ríces mínes licet demedium regni mei, Mk. L. 6, 23. Half (hlaf, R.) gódra mínra ic sello ðorfendum demedium bonorum meorum do pauperibus, Lk. L. 19, 8. Gif mon elþeódigne ofsleá se cyning áh twǽdne dǽl weres, þriddan dǽl sunu oþþe mǽgas. Gif hé mǽgleás sié, healf kyninge, healf se gesíð, Ll. Th. i. 116, 16. Geselle .cxx. sciłł, healf (dimidium) cyninge, healf biscepe, 66, 17 : 296, 8 : 294, 8, 9. Half, 258, 12, 17. Gelde healf, 20, 3.

**healf**; adv. Half :—Healf man and healf hors centaurus vel ippocentaurus, healf mann and healf assa onocentaurus, Wrt. Voc. i. 17, 39, 40. Þæt (the Minotaur) wæs healf mon, healf leó Minotauro, utrum fero homini, an humanae bestiae aptius dicam nescio, Ors. 1, 8; S. 42, 29. Centauri, þæt sindon healf hors, healf menn equites veluti unum corpus equorum et hominum viderentur, S. 44, 1. See the following compounds.

**healf-brocen**; adj. Half-broken :—þám sticcum healfbrocenra ísa semifractarum crustis glacierum, Bd. 5, 12; Sch. 633, 9.

**healf-clungen**; adj. Half-frozen :—Halbclungni (half-) semigelato, Txts. 96, 931.

**healf-cwic.** Add :—For þám slege hé feóll ádúne, and hine man healfcwicne (-cwicc-, v.l.) upp áhóf (semivivus levatus est), Gr. D. 63, 1. Healfcwice seminecem, An. Ox. 17, 46.

**healfe** adv. (?) v. healf; adj. A. I. 3 a.

**healf-fers** glosses emistichium, Hpt. 31, 10, 203.

**healf-féþe**; adj. Half-lame :—Healfféþe semipes, Germ. 396, 150.

**healf-freó**; adj. Half-free :—Hwílum be freótmen, hwílum be healffreón, Wlfst. 171, 4 note.

**healf-gemet** glosses diametra, Hpt. 31, 10, 199.

**healf-hár**; adj. Half-grey :—Healfhár semicanus, fulhár canus (omitted after) Wrt. Voc. i. 45, 34. v. Angl. viii. 451.

**healf-híd**, e; f. A half-hide :—Gif hé ne bið bútan tó healfhýda (healfre híde, v.l.) gerysen, Ll. Th. i. 188, 16.

**healf-mearc**, e; n. A half-mark :—Hé hæfð geboht healfe híde landes mid healfmarce goldes and mid áne punde seolfres and twégan óran, C. D. iv. 136, 34. Fylste ǽlc gegylda he[alf]mearc tó fylste. Cht. Th. 611, 32. Ic an míne láuedy healfmarc goldes, C. D. iv. 308,

2 : Cht. Th. 573, 13. Tó .viii. healfmarcum ásodenes goldes, Ll. Th. i. 154, 1. Gylde .xxx. sciłł. mid Englum and mid Denum þreó healfmarc (cf. ii. 292, 12), 168, 10. Gilde heora ǽlc .vi. healfmarc, 298, 5, 8 : ii. 298, 4, 12. .x. healfmarc. 2. ¶ the following seem anomalous in form or construction :—Béte man þ æt deáðum menn mid .vi. healfmarce, and æt cwicon mid .xii. óran, Ll. Th. i. 292, 10. Heora ǽlc sylle .vi. healfmarc wedd, 294, 7. Æt cynges spǽce lecge man .vi. healfmarc wedd, and æt eorles .xii. óran wedd, and æt ǽlcum þegene .vi. óran wedd, 296, 25.

**healf-nacod**; adj. Half-naked :—Gesáwon wé mennisce men feá healfnacode (seminudos), Nar. 10, 16.

**healfpenig-wurþ.** Add :—Healfpeningwurð wexes tó candelmæssan, Wlfst. 117, 1.

**healf-rúh**; adj. Half-rough :—Án healfrúh tæppet sipla, Wrt. Voc. i. 40, 35.

**healf-scyldig**; adj. Half-guilty :—Healfscyldig temeson, medius sons, Hpt. 31, 12, 251.

**healf-sester**, es; m. A half-sester :—Healfsester mine, Wrt. Voc. ii. 56, 1.

**healf-sinewealt**; adj. Half-round :—Healfsinewealt semirotundum, Wrt. Voc. i. 55, 20.

**healf-slǽpende.** Add :—Him þúhte on healfslǽpendon líchoman, ná eallinga swylce on swefne, Vis. Lfc. 3.

**healfunga.** Add : I. from the side, indirectly :—Hit is nytte ðæt ðæt him mon on tǽlan wille, ðæt hit mon healfunga sprece, swelce hit mon hwón gebríne major profectus adducitur, si hoc, quod in eis reprehenditur, quasi ex latere tangatur, Past. 207, 7. Ðæt wé him sume opene scylde healfunga onwíeten, ðæt hié for ðǽm scamige si culpae manifestioris ex latere requisitae improperio confunduntur, 209, 22. II. slightly, to some extent, half :—Geseah hé hwǽr þá weorcstánas lágon ofer eall þǽr onbútan, and hé healfunga þæs wundrode, þeáh ná swíðe embe þ ne smeáde, Hml. S. 23, 491. [v. N. E. D. halfing.] Cf. eallunga.

**healf-weard.** Dele, and see hláf-weard.

**healf-weg**, es; m. Half-way, a point equidistant from two extremes :—Ægelríc æt healfwege, C. D. iv. 234, 3.

**healf-wudu.** Add : [Widebalme i. halue wude, Wrt. Voc. i. 140, 66.]

**healh.** Add : I. a corner, an angle. v. healhiht :—Ǽlc wág bið gebíeged twiefeald on ðǽm heale duplex semper est in angulis paries. Past. 245, 13. Gemétte hé hine hleonian on þám hale his cyrcan wið þám weófode invenit eum recumbentem in angulo oratorii sui contra altare, Guth. Gr. 163, 50. Hé gefeall him in ánan heale and . . . slǽp, Vis. Lfc. 37. II. a retired or secret place, cave, closet, recess :—Oð ðá ýtemestan helle heala[s?] to the most remote of hell's recesses; ad inferni nouissima, Ps. L. fol. 193 a, 5. Swá hwelp leóna eardiende on halum (in abditis), Ps. Spl. 16, 13. On þýstrum healum (scræfum, Dóm. L. 139) þissere worulde tenebrosis in antris, Wlfst. 138, 1. Healum cubilibus, Germ. 402, 54. III. a bay :—Strénæs hale (alch, halch, v. ll.) quod interpretatur sinus fari, Txts. 140, 210. Streánes halh, 200. In streánæs halæ (hęle, hale, v. ll.), 147, 378. IV. the word occurs not infrequently in the charters, and in the single instance where it appears to be explained it seems to mean a stony slope: In quoddam petrosum clivum et ex eo Baldwines healh appellatur, Txts. 427, 8. (1) qualified by an adj. :—On þone sídan healh ; of þám sídan heale á be þám héhhylte, C. D. B. iii. 517, 36. (2) with gen., or as second part of a compound. (a) gen. of person :—Æt Iddes hale, C. D. i. 315, 22. On Oddan heal ; of Oddan heale, v. 270, 8. On Beocces heal, vi. 94, 15. In Puttan ealh, C. D. iii. 383, 20. (b) compounded with names of animals :—On nédderheal ; of nédderheale, C. D. v. 270, 11 : 281, 33. On calfheals, iii. 385, 31. On horshealgæt, vi. 94. 14. (c) gen. or cpd. of plant-growth :—On bærheal, of bærheale, C. D. B. ii. 247, 7. Tó hǽcfeldheale, C. D. iii. 131, 8. On braccon heal ; of brachan heale, C. D. v. 277, 17. Tó rischeale ; of hrischeale, iii. 79, 9. On hrischalh ; of hrischalh, 460, 15. Tó ceaggon heale, v. 262, 8. On brómhalas ; of brómhalan, iii. 81, 27. v. wír-heálh. (d) gen. of thing, or uncertain :—Tó cuntan heale, C. D. B. ii. 246, 33. Innan crypeles heale, 374, 12. On farsthalh ; of forsthalh, C. D. iii. 460, 18. On bioton halh ; of bioton hale, 24. Tó curdan heale, v. 207, 33. On stenges healh, of stenges heale, C. D. B. iii. 49, 28. On scæccan halh, C. D. iii. 463, 14. Innan cucan healas, 450, 3. Andlang bróces on swyllan healas ; of ðan healan, vi. 2, 12. ¶ the word occurs also as the first part of compounds :—On halhford, C. D. iii. 439, 4 : 442, 31. Ond long healhtúnes gemǽres, 436, 27. Æt healhtúne, 294, 21. Æt healtúne, iv. 184, 14 : 198, 1. Andlang eú tó healwhwere, v. 392, 33. Of ðǽre syrfan tó healwícum, 262, 14. [v. N. E. D. hale a corner.]

**healhiht**; adj. Having many angles :—Healhihtum (hælhihtum, Hpt. Gl. 409, 8) angulosis (cellulis), An. Ox. 121. v. healh; I.

**heá-lic.** Add : I. local. (1) reaching to a great height, lofty, tall :—Heofon is wundorlíce heálíc and wíd on ymbhwyrfte ; sé gǽð under ðás eorðan ealswá deóp swá bufan, Hex. 10, 1. Man áhéng hí on

healicum gealgan, Hml. A. 95, 119. Heálicum sǽnesse *edito* (*alto*) *promontorio*, An. Ox. 576. Heálicne pīntreówes bōh *procerum pini stipitem* (cf. ǽnne heáhne pīnbeám, Hml. Th. ii. 508, 24), 2221. Heálicum boga bīgelsum *celsis arcuum fornicibus*, 510. Mid heálicum cederbeámum, Hex. 12, 4. (2) *situated at a great height, high up :*—Heálic sittende mǽden *sublimis residens virgo*, Hy. S. 108, 7. On heálicere hēhnysse *in alto* (*tribunalis*) *culmine*, An. Ox. 3454. Hē gewát tō đan Hǽlende þe hē on heofenan heálicne standende geseah (cf. Video filium hominis stantem a dextris Dei, Acts 7, 56), Hml. Th. i. 48, 7. Heálice heofona heáhnyssa ástīgan *summa polorum culmina scandere*, Hy. S. 88, 7. II. *of persons*. (1) *of high rank, position or dignity :*—Gedæf on gehwǽdum forbūge heálic beón gehæfd *contentus modicis uitet sublimis haberi*, Wülck. Gl. 257, 33. Heálic *atrox* (quasi *atrox* regina imperium usurpans, Ald. 10, 29), Hpt. Gl. 422, 21. Đē is leófre on đisum wācum scræfum đonne đū on healle heálic biscop sitte, Hml. Th. ii. 146, 28. Uton wē þus heálices and đus foremǽres mundboran lāre folgian, Bl. H. 169, 17. Stefn heálices fæderes *vox excelsi Patris*, Hy. S. 49, 7. Hī đone Hǽlend wurđodon and nǽnne ōđerne swā heálicne ne tealdon, Hml. S. 11, 97. Đā yfelan (*Venus*) wurđiađ þā hǽđenan for heálice fǽmnan, Wlfst. 107, 17. (2) *of noble qualities :*—Geearnungum heálic *meritis celsus*, Hy. S. 104, 15. III. *of material things*. (1) *of superior kind, of high class or degree :*—Gif hē gesōhte heálicne heáfodstede, Ll. Th. i. 330, 15. (2) *of excellent quality, precious* (stone) :—For heálicum gymstānum, Hml. S. 20, 60. Se heofon is betera and heálicra and fǽgerra đonne eall his innung, Bt. 32, 2 ; F. 116, 10. IV. *of non-material things*. (1) *reaching a high degree*. (a) *of the voice, elevated, raised, loud* (v. heálíce ; III a.) :—þā hǽþenan clypodon mid heálicre stemne, Hml. S. 31, 1031. (b) *high in respect to worth, dignity, &c.* :—Heálic hēþ *edita* (*pudicitiae*) *proceritas*, An. Ox. 1698. Heálic wyrþment, synderlic gifu *prerogatiua*, i. *excellentia*, 2572. On heálicere hēhnysse ꝼ geþinþe *edito* (i. *alto*) *fastigio*, 929 ; *precelso*, 4407. Sum heálic gōd *quandam claritudinem*, Bt. 24, 3 ; F. 82, 23. Þū forsihst đone heálican wurđmynt (*gloriam mundi*), Hml. Th. ii. 146, 27. Abel hæfde þreó heálice mihta (*tria maxima justitiae praeconia*), Angl. vii. 8, 78. (c) *of feeling, condition, profound, intense, extreme :*—Sȳ heálic swige æt þǽm gereorde *summum fiat silentium ad mensam*, R. Ben. 62, 13. Heálicra mildheortnysse *summe clementiae*, Hy. S. 29, 7. Mid heálican geþylde, Hml. A. 21, 176. Mid heálicere gecneordnisse, Ælfc. T. Grn. 16, 46. Hié hæfdon miccle lufan and eác heálico ondrysnu, Bl. H. 205, 8. (d) *as an epithet of what is evil, deep guilt, grievous sin, profound error :*—Nis nán leahter swā heálic þ man ne mæg gebētan, Hml. S. 12, 157. On þām heálicon gedwylde þæt hī swā fūle [men] him tō godum gecuran, Wlfst. 107, 24. On đæt heálice gedwyld, Sal. K. p. 123, 106. Hī þǽr heálicne on hryre gefremedan *multiplicata est in eis ruina*, Ps. Th. 105, 23. Wiđ eallum þǽm heálicum synnum, Bl. N. 7. Þurh heálice misdǽda, Ll. Th. i. 404, 1. (2) *of a high degree of excellence, noble, excellent :*—Heálic lār *praecipuum documentum*, Hpt. Gl. 455, 27 : Wrt. Voc. ii. 66, 19. Þæt is heálic dæg, bēntíd brēmu, Men. 74 : 37. Þæt is heálic rǽd mouna gehwylcum, Cri. 430. Mid heálicum ealdordōme *authentica auctoritate*, An. Ox. 2597. Mid heálicere *superna* (*potestate*), 3531. Heálicre gife *charismate*, Wrt. Voc. ii. 23, 25. Heálice synde[r]gife *felix priuilegium*, An. Ox. 2588. Heálicum *eximia, nobilia, insignia*, Wrt. Voc. ii. 145, 5. þā heálican gewyrhto Sce Iōhannes, Bl. H. 167, 5. [v. *N. E. D.* highly. *O. H. Ger.* hōhlīh *sublimis* : *Icel.* hā-ligr.]

**heá-líce.** *Add :* I. *in a local sense, on high :*—Pilatus ásette đis gewrit tō đǽre rōde bufon Crīstes heáfde heálíce, Hml. Th. ii. 254, 27. Stōd se earming ætforan þām deófle þær hē heálíce sæt, Hml. S. 3, 372. Se wītga cwæđ þæt āhæfen wǽren heálíce upp sunne and mōna, Cri. 693. II. *in or to a high position or rank :*—Se fæder þōhte hwām hē hí (*his daughter*) mihte heálícost forgifan, Ap. Th. 1, 13. II a. *specially :*—Heálícust on tíde gebedes *precipue in tempore orationis*, Scint. 36, 16. III. *in or to a high degree or extent, greatly, extremely :*—Ealle mægene hergan heálíce, Cri. 383. Swā swā heálicor ic geswu[telige] *ut altius pandam*, An. Ox. 5058. Hit nis gīt se tīma þ ic þē heálícor mæge onbryrdan *firmioribus remediis nondum tempus est*, Bt. 5, 3 ; F. 14, 14. III a. *with elevated voice :*—Seraphines cynn unāþreótendum þrymmum singađ ful heálíce (*or under* IV ? *but see* heálic ; IV. I a) hlūdan stefne fægre, Cri. 389. IV. *with high quality, nobly :*—Hē biđ genied mid đǽm folgođe đæt hē sceal heálíce sprecan *loci sui necessitate exigitur summa dicere*, Past. 81, 6. IV a. *of workmanship, with perfect workmanship, elaborately :*—Heofon ongeat hwā hine heálíce torhtne getremede tungolgimmum, Cri. 1150. [v. *N. E. D.* highly ; *adv.*]

**heálicness.** *Add :* I. *in a local sense :*—Heálicnysse *conum* (ut pyrae cacumina sphaerae apicem triginta cubitis in *conum* praecellerent, Ald. 48, 26), An. Ox. 3529. II. *of rank, dignity, &c. :*—Eálá þ swā mycel heálicnys swilces weres ūs þeówode, Hml. S. 30, 281.

**heall.** *Add :* I. *a large room forming part of the residence of a great man, in which the social, public life of the household is carried*

on :—Hūs *domus*, heall *aulea*, cavertūn *vestibulum*, Wrt. Voc. i. 289, 82 : ii. 8, 66. Hwearf þā tō healle . . . þæt hē ofer his ealdre gestōd, ābeád for þǽre dugeđe deóp ǽrende, Az. 166. Swā swā ǽlces cynges hāma ; beođ sume on būre, sume on healle, sume on ōdene, Solil. H. 44, 19. Cyning sceal on healle beágas dǽlan (cf. B. 1020 sqq.), Gn. C. 28 : Rā. 56, 13. 'Miht þū mē ārǽran on Rōmānisce wīsan cynelice gebytlu ? . . . Hē cwæđ þ hē wolde wyrcan þā healle . . . and þā ōþre gebytlu bæftan þǽre healle . . . twelf hūs tōgædere, Hml. S. 36, 91–99. I a. *as the place for meals :*—Swylc þū æt swǽsendum sitte mid đīnum ealdormannum and þegnum on wintertīde, and sié fȳr onǽled and þīn heall gewyrmed (*calido effecto cenaculo*), Bd. 2, 13 ; Sch. 165, 18. Wæs þeós medoheal dreórfāh, eal bencþelu blōde bestȳmed, heall heorudreóre, B. 487. Healle *cenaculi*, An. Ox. 5251. Tō healle gang Healfdenes sunu, wolde self cyning symbel þicgan, B. 1009. Wē on bence . . . hǽleđ on healle, By. 214 : Dan. 729. I b. *as a sleeping-place for the retinue, the lord having his separate apartment* (cf. Hrōđgār gewát ūt of healle . . . wolde sēcan cwēn tō gebeddan, B. 663. Hrōđgār gewát tō hofe sīnum rīce tō rǽste, 1236. Wæs tō būre Beówulf fetod, 1310) :—Sigon tō slǽpe . . . þā wæs on healle heardecg togen sweord, B. 1288. II. *a residence, habitation of a great man, palace :*—Þisse healle hornas ne byrnađ, Fin. 4 : 20. Hē sæt ætforan þǽre healle dura (beforan þǽre healle, *v. l.*) *residens ante palatium*, Bd. 2, 12 ; Sch. 155, 11. Manege scīran wurdon gedrehte þurh þæs cynges healle geweorc (*through work at the king's hall*) þe man on Westmynstre worhte (cf. se cyng . . . his hīred innan his nīwan gebyttlan æt Westmynstre heóld, 1099 ; P. 234, 34), Chr. 1097; P. 234, 8. Wæs hē tō þǽre fæderlican healle gelǽdd and þǽr gefēdd *aulis in paternis imbuebatur*, Guth. Gr. 107, 20. Đē is leófre on đissum wācum scræfum đonne đū on healle heálic biscop sitte (*Bede's Latin is :* Tui claustra deserti huic gradui (*the episcopal*) praefers), Hml. Th. ii. 146, 28. Ūre Scyppend . . . his gecorenan on þisum middanearde geágnađ swā swā hlāford his hīred on his healle, 72, 29. Þā eóde heó (*queen Alexandria*) on hire palatium, þ is on hire healle, Shrn. 75, 25 : An. Ox. 4368. Āsettan healle hrōffæste (cf. fæst hūs timbrian, Bt. 12 ; F. 36, 10) *perennem ponere sedem*, Met. 7, 6 : 11. Gif mon on nīwne weall unāđrūgodne micelne hrōf and hefigne onsett, đonne ne timbređ hē nō healle ac hryre (*non habitaculum, sed ruina fabricatur*), Past. 383, 33. Se Hǽlend cōm intō þæs ealdres healle (*in domum principis*), Mt. 9, 23: Sal. 380. II a. *figuratively :*—Wel þē gerīseđ þæt þū heáfod sié healle mǽrre, Cri. 4. III. *an official building*. (1) *a building for worship, a temple :*—Weardiađ Dryhten in halle đǽre hālgan his *adorare Dominum in aula sancta ejus*, Ps. Srt. 28, 2. (2) *a building for legal business, a court of law :*—In đæs giroefa halle ꝼ mōtern (on þ dōmern, W.S.) *in praetorium*, Jn. L. R. 18, 28. v. gegild-, heáh-, heofon-heall.

**heall,** es ; *m.* A *stone, rock :*—þām strengestan(-e, MS.) stāne, healle *robustissimæ petre* (cf. Mt. 7, 24), An. Ox. 4111. ¶ *in place names, as the name of a person*. Cf. *Icel.* Hallr :—In halles burge, C. D. iii. 377, 24. Heallingwara mearc wiđ Halles meres, 400, 27. In locum qui dicitur halles meri, 386, 24. Cf. In loco ubi nominatur Hallingas, i. 194, 15 (*the last two passages are parts of the same charter*). De Heallingan, 264, 11. Hallinga homme, weallan, iii. 389, 7, 19 (*the last three occur in the same charter, which refers to* Halhagan). [*Goth.* hallus *petra* : *Icel.* hallr *a rock, boulder.*] The word is used also as a proper name. v. heal-stán.

**heall-ærn, -gamen.** v. heal-ærn, -gamen *in Dict.*

**heall-hālgung** (?), e ; *f.* *Celebration of rites in a hall* (?), *Bacchanalian rites :*—Geld, haealhālgung *ceremoniae* (cf. *ceremoniae*, i. *ritus sacrificandi* geld, Wülck. Gl. 202, 27), g. *orgia*, Wrt. Voc. i. 28, 54.

**heal-lic.** *For* 'Cot. 194, Lye' *substitute :*—Tō heallicum geseton *ad palatinas zetas*, An. Ox. 2996. Đā heallican seld, Wrt. Voc. ii. 81, 23. þā heallican *palatinas* (*infulas*), An. Ox. 4622.

**heall-reced, -sittende.** v. heal-reced, -sittende *in Dict.* : **heallstán.** v. heal-stán : **heall-þegen, -wudu.** v. heal-þegen, -wudu *in Dict.*

**healm.** *For* II *substitute* I a *below, and add :* I. *in a collective sense, stubble, straw :*—Hēg *foenum*, healm *stipula*, Wrt. Voc. i. 289, 46. Healm *stramen spicarum*, ii. 137, 48. Swā hwylc man swā ofer þisne staþol seteđ . . . hīg ođđe healm (*stipulam*) . . . þeáh þe þ hīg and þ healm forbyrne, Gr. D. 328, 23–27. Wiđ liđseáwe, genim beren healm, Lch. ii. 134, 2. Sete hié swē swā halm (*stipulam*) biforan onsiéne windes, Ps. Srt. 82, 14 : ii. p. 187, 26. Đæt halm *paleas*, Lk. R. 3, 17. I a. *stubble as representing the arable land from which a crop has been gathered :*—Ciricsceat mon sceal āgifan tō đǽm healme and tō đǽm heorđe (*according to the amount of cultivated arable land and to the kind of house*. But the old Latin version has : A culmine et mansione de se mon on biþ tō middum wintra, Ll. Th. i. 140, 13. II. *a straw, stalk :*—Eár *spica*, egla *arista*, healm *culmus*, codd *folliculus*, Wrt. Voc. i. 38, 49 : 67, 36. Healm *vel stela culnus*, ii. 137, 48. Đā halm geberneđ *paleas comburet*, Lk. L. 3, 17. Đa halmas, Mt. L. 3, 12. v. bere-, hwǽte-healm.

**healm-streáw.** *Add:* [*Icel.* hálm-strā.]

**healoc.** *Substitute:* **healoc, healc,** es; *m.* [*diminutive* of healh. Cf. holoc] *A little corner* or *recess, concavity* :—Hēr sint tācn áheardodre lifre ge on þām læppum and healocum and filmenum, Lch. ii. 204, 5. On ðām liferbylum and læppum þe on þām liferholum and healcum (τὰ σιμὰ), 20. On þǽre lifre healcum and holocum, 206, 7. [v. *N. E. D.* halke.] Cf. hilc.

**healre ?** :—On healre dūne; of healre dūne, Cht. Crw. 4, 25. Tô healre mere; of healre mere, C. D. iii. 79, 1. Cf. In loco siluatici ruris usitato nomine hellere lēge, i. 63, 9.

**heals.** *Add:* I. as part of a person :—Dyde him of healse hring gyldenne þeóden, B. 2809 : 3017. Cyning þegn be healse genam, 1872. Hire wið halse grápode, 1565. Wiþ healswærce . . . þonne þone heals wærc[e], smire ðā þeóh; gif þā þeóh wærce, smire þone heals, Lch. ii. 312, 5–7 : 8. II. as part of an animal :—Hals is mín (*a badger's*) hwít and heáfod fealo, Rä. 16, 1. Ic (*an ox*) beáh hæfde on healse, 71, 11. III. as part of a thing. Cf. fāmig-, wunden-heals *as epithets of a ship* :—Heó (*bagpipes*) hafað hyre on healse bróðor síne, Rä. 32, 21. [v. *N. E. D.* halse.] v. freóls.

**heals-beág.** *Add:* a collar :—Healsbeága mǽst . . . þone hring hǽfde Higelác . . , B. 1195.

**heals-beorg.** *For* 'Hpt. . . . 423' *substitute* :—Halsbearh *thoraca,* i. *lorica,* An. Ox. 5021. Healsberga *lorica* (*spoliatos*), 725. Halsbearga *loricam,* 759.

**heals-bóc.** *l.* (?) heals-bóc. v. hálsian, healsian.

**heals-brynige,** an; *f. A gorget, hauberk* :—Healsbrynige *thoraca,* An. Ox. 2, 418. [*For the form* brynige *cf. Icel.* brynja.]

**healsed.** *For* 'caputium, Cot. 170, Lye' *substitute :* capitium, Wrt. Voc. ii. 87, 57, *and add :* See next word.

**healseta.** *Add: The opening in a tunic for the head to pass through, the neck of a tunic.* The Latin of the original narrative is : Evenit ei, ut coluber per caput eius inter tunicam et ventrem irreperet et latus suis morsibus laniaret, Mart. H. 238.

**heals-fæst.** *Substitute: With unbending neck, defiant, unsubmissive, proud, contemptuous* :—Hire (*Hagar*) mód āstāh þā heó wæs magotimbre eácen worden, ongan æfþancum āgendfreán halsfæst herian (cf. *Agar concepisse se videns despexit dominam suam,* Gen. 16, 4), Gen. 2238.

**heals-fang.** *Substitute: A legal payment of varying amount according to the status of a person, to be paid by him as a due or fine, or to be received by him or on his account for injury done to him.* (1) to be paid as a due :—Medemra þegna heregeata : hors and his gerǽda and his wǽpn oððe (*in L. H.,* et suum hal[s]fang, 559, 7) his healsfang (halsfangc, *v. l.*) on Wessexan, Ll. Lbmn. 358, 14. (2) to be paid as a penalty :—Gif for godbótan feohbót áríseð, swā swā wíse woroldwitan tô steóre gesettan, þ gebyreð . . . for woroldsteóran tô godcundan neódan, hwílum be wíte, hwílum be wergylde, hwílum be halsfange, Ll. Lbmn. 258, § 51. (a) where it is the *heals-fang* of the payer :—Gif fríman an ðane forbodenan tíman [wyrce], sió hē healsfange scyldig . . . Gif ceorl búton wífes wísdóme deóflum gelde, hē sié ealra his ǽhtan scyldig and healsfange. Gif būtwū deóflum geldaþ, sión hió healsfange scyldigo and ealra ǽhtan . . . Gif mon his heówum in fæsten flǽsc geſe, frigne ge þeówne halsfange ālýse, Ll. Lbmn. 13, 11–21. Gyf freoman freólsdæge wyrce, þonne gebēte þ mid his halsfange (decem solidos persoluat, Inst. Cnut.), 342, 26. Gyf hláford his þeówan freólsdæge nýde tô weorce . . . gylde lahslit se hláford mid Denum, wíte mid Englum (dominus det halsfang, Inst. Cnut.), 345, 1. Gyf hwā on leásre gewitnesse openlíce stande . . . gylde hē þām cingce oððe landrícan be healsfange (persoluat regi aut domino terre x solidos, quod Dani uocant halsfang, Inst. Cnut.), 338, 24. Reddat regi . . . helsfang, 557, 10. (b) where it is the *healsfang* of the injured person :—Gif man æt unlagum man bewǽpnige, forgilde hine be halsfange (x sol. ei emendet, Inst. Cnut.; halsfangium eius emendet, 606, 12); gif hine man gebinde, forgilde be healfan were, 350, 15. ¶ It formed the first part of the compensation (*wer*) paid to the friends of a slain person, and it is in this connection that most detail is given, the amount, time of payment, and recipients of the *healsfang* being stated :—Twelfhyndes mannes wer is twelf hund scyllinga . . . Gif man ofslægen weorðe, gylde hine man swā hē geboren sý. And riht is ðæt se slaga . . . finde wærborh . . . þonne þæt gedón sý, ðonne rǽre man cyninges munde . . . Of ðǽm dæge on .xxi. nihtan gylde man Lxx. sciłł. tô healsfange æt twelfhyndum were. Healsfang gebyreð bearnum, bróðrum and fæderan; ne gebyreð nánum mǽge ðæt feoh būte ðām ðe sý binnan cneówe. Of ðām dæge ðe ðæt healsfang ágolden sý on .xxi. nihtan gylde man ðā manbóte . . . 392, 3–23: 190, 10. Further details concerning the *healsfang* in the case of the ceorl may be gained from the laws of Henry I, which show that the *healsfang* was part of the wer :—In omni weregildo debet halsfang primo reddi, sicut were modus erit . . . Qui natus sit ad iiii. libras [= twihindus homo] . . . halsfang eius sunt v marc, que faciunt xii. sol. et vi. den. Si quis ad IIII. libras persoluendus occidatur, et ad id res ueniat, ut precio natalis eius componendus sit, primo debent reddi xii. sol. et vi. den. et in wera numerari. Reddantur uero patri uel filio uel fratri . . . et

ipsi diuidant inter se. A die qua wera uadiata est in xxi diem debet halsfang reddi, et hoc indiuisum habeant a ceteris . . . reddatur vii sol. et vi den. ad expletionem xx sol. (i. e. *the* healsfang (=12s. 6d.) + 7s. 6d. *made the first pound*) [Then three successive pounds were to be paid, making four pounds in all, the amount of the slain man's *wer*], 581, 8–582, 17. According to the laws of William I the widow of a slain man shared (or received) the *healsfang,* 498, 499, § 9. [*Heals-fang* means literally the seizing by the neck or throat (*collicipium* is the rendering of the word in the old Latin version of Cnut's Laws, Ll. Lbmn. 339, 24 : 343, 25). Cf. the passage in Beowulf, where in the description of such an action *heals* and *fón* are used: Fýrdraca . . . rǽsde on þone rófan, . . . heals ealne ymbefēng biteran bānum, 2691. Its formation may be compared with that of *feax-fang* (an action to which the law attached a penalty), a word which with the similar *berd-fang* is found in the Frisian laws. In these laws, too, is mentioned the offence of seizing by the *hals* (Huaso orem grypt oen syn hals, dat di adema hor ut ner in mey), to which the term *heals-fang* might very well have been applied in Old English. As in the Old English legal phraseology the word which denotes an offence denotes also the fine which is to be paid for that offence, *healsfang* in the first instance might have denoted the action, then the fine paid for the assault, and then, like *wergild,* have come to be regarded as a standard for fines in the case of other offences (cf. first passage under (2) above :—Hwílum be wergylde, hwílum be halsfange). And it may be noted that in two of the instances where a fine is determined by *healsfang* the offences involve violence, unlawful disarming, and manslaughter. *Halsfang* occurs in Frisian law, but its meaning is not defined. Richthofen explains it as a ' Menschen- oder Mädchen-raub '. The word occurs in Icelandic, as well as a verb *háls-fengja,* meaning respectively *an embrace* and *to embrace.*]

**heals-gang,** es; *m. A tumour in the neck* :—Halsgang *struma,* Wrt. Voc. i. 61, 15. *See next word.*

**heals-gund.** *Add* :—Lǽcedómas wið healsgunde, and þæs tācn hwæðer hē hit sié . . . wið healsgunde, þonne ǽrest onginne se healsgund wēsan . . . Wiþ þone ilcan . . . dô on þone gund, Lch. ii. 44, 7–26. Gif se gund biþ ouginnende, 46, 3.

**heals-mǽgeþ,** e; *f.* Dele ' e '; *mægeþ is not inflected in the singular.*

**heals-mene.** *Add: an ornament for the neck* :—Brýcð wíf healsmene *utitur mulier anabola* (*ornamentum muliebre*), Hpt. 31, 7, 91. Healsmyna frætewunge *crepundiorum lunulas,* An. Ox. 2203. Halsmenum, sweórbeágum *lunulis,* 1188. Menas gimbǽrum heal[s]mynum *crepundia* (*collo*) *gemmiferis lunulis* (*pendentia*), 4828.

**heals-ome.** *l.* heals-óme (or -ôman; *pl., only plural forms of the simple word seem to occur.* v. -óman), *and add* :—Se man sē ðe biþ on healsóman nime healswyrt.

**heal-stán, healstan**(?), **helsta**(?) [v. heall *a stone.* Cf. *Icel.* hellu-steinn *a flat stone;* Hall-steinn (*a proper name*). Perhaps the word, which seems little used, occurring only in glosses, may have ceased to be recognized as a compound, and the vowel of the second element may have been shortened. In this case it is possible that *healstan* may have been taken for the oblique case of a weak noun *healsta* (cf. (?) fián, fiá), and this might account for the form *helsta,* and the adjective *hilsten, q.v.*]. *A flat cake with a hard crust,* so called because of the hardness of its crust [cf. for similar terms *pflasterstein* in German, *pavé* in French, for a hard kind of cake], *a crust* :—Crustula similis haalstaan (*crustalla* halstān), Txts. 55, 604. Helsta *vel* rinde *crustula,* Wrt. Voc. ii. 137, 22. Healstānes *crustule* (buccellam *crustulae* semiplenam peniger praepes hiulco advexerat rostro, Ald. 33, 19), 79, 33. Healstán *colliridam* (v. (?) *collyridam* conspersam oleo, Lev. 8, 26), 11, 14, 56. Halstánum *crustulis* (sportulas *crustulis* (rindum, An. Ox. 3858) et tortellis refertas, Ald. 53, 22), 83, 62. Healstānum, 18, 50.

**heals-wærc,** es; *m. Pain in the neck* :—Wiþ healswærce . . . þonne þone heals wærc[e], smire ðā þeóh; gif þā þeóh wærce, smire þone heals, Lch. ii. 312, 5.

**heals-wiþa.** *l.* -wriþa.

**heals-wyrt.** *Add* :—Halswyrt *auris leporis,* Wrt. Voc. i. 30, 57 : *auris leporis* ł *auris folia,* Lch. iii. 300, col. 1 : *epicosium,* 302, col. 1 : *epicurium,* Wrt. Voc. i. 79, 22. Helswyrt, An. Ox. 56, 44. Heleswyrt *epigurium,* 393. Halswyrt *narcissus,* Lch. iii. 304, col. 1. Þysse wyrte ðe man *narcissum* and óðrum naman halswyrt nenneð, i. 158, 14. *Bulbum* þā wyrte ðā man óþrum naman halswyrt hāteþ, 222, 10. *Sinfitum album* and óþrum naman halswyrt, 240, 3. Se man sē ðe biþ on healsóman nime healswyrt, iii. 4, 26. [v. *N. E. D.* halswort.]

**healt.** *Add* :—Healt (healt, MS.) *catax,* Wrt. Voc. i. 45, 52. Sió healte *catax* (Vulcanus, Ald. 172, 32), ii. 93, 51 : 19, 51. Gif mon þā greátan sinwe forsleá . . . Gif se mon healt sié, . . . geselle .xxx. sciłł. tô bóte, Ll. Th. i. 100, 5. Hē wæs healt *claudicabat pede,* Gen. 32, 31. Gif ðín fót swicað þē, ceorf hine of ; betere þē is þ þū healt (halt, L., R.) gā on ēce líf . . , Mk. 9, 45. Þ hē þām healtan cnapan (cf. se cnapa wæs creópere, 20) his hǽle ābǽde, Hml. S. 6, 28. Blinde geseoð, healte (*claudi*) gāð, Mt. 11, 5. Underföð þā blindan gesihðe . . . and

þā healtan fǽreld, Hml. S. 29, 337. Ðā eodan tō him þā healtan, 21, 14. Mycel menigeo blindra and healtra, Jn. 5, 3. v. lemp-healt.

**healtian.** _Add:_—Hū lange wille gē healtian on twā healfe ðus? (_usquequo claudicatis in duas partes?_, I Kings 18, 21), Hml. S. 18, 98. Gangas rihte dōð mid fōtum eówrum þæt nā healtigende (_claudicans_) worige (Heb. 12, 13), Scint. 186, 3. [_O. L. Ger._ haltōn.] v. ā-healtian.

**heámol, hamal**(?); _adj._ Substitute: **heámol**; _adj._ Parsimonious, miserly, niggardly:—Uncystig _vel_ heámol (heámul) frugus, Txts. 62, 413. Uncystig oððe heámol, fercūþ _frugus_, Wrt. Voc. ii. 36, 5. Tō hwan wurd ðū swā heámul (fæsthafol, Wlfst. 258, 12) mīnra gōda þe ic ðē sealde?, Nap. 36.

**heámol-scipe, es;** _m._ Parsimony, miserliness, niggardliness:—Forlǣtan wē . . . nīðas and nearoþancas and heámolscipas, Nap. 36.

**heán.** _Add:_ **I.** of persons. (1) _of low degree, of humble condition, low, poor, as opposed to_ rīce, welig, wlanc:—Se hālga (_Noah_) cwæð þæt hē (_Ham_) wesan sceolde heán . . hleómāga þeów (_servus servorum erit fratribus suis_, Gen. 9, 25), Gen. 1595. Ic mē ceóse þæt ic heán gange on hūs Godes _elegi abjectus esse in domo Dei mei_, Ps. Th. 83, 11. Heán sceal gehnīgan, Gn. Ex. 118. Doem ðǽm freóndleásan and ðǽm heánan (_humili_), Ps. Srt. 9, 39. Heánne and ðearfan, 81, 3. Ic eom se ilca God þe þone weligan and þone heánan geworhte, Wlfst. 259, 3. Deáð þone rīcan gelīce and þone heánan ofswelgþ and swā geemnet þā rīcan and þā heánan _mors involvit humile pariter et celsum caput, aequatque summis infima_, Bt. 19; F. 68, 33. Ealle gelīce on woruld cumað, wlance and heáne, Met. 17, 6. Ne mæg ǽnig . . . rīcra ne heánra, Gū. 968. Wloncum and heánum, Wal. 43. (I a) _human as opposed to celestial beings_:—Þū (_Christ_) dugeðum cwóme heánum tō hrōðre, Cri. 414: 632. (I b) _of inferior rank_:—Heánra cempa _miles ordinarius_, Wrt. Voc. ii. 59, 14. (2) _of little worth, mean, ignoble, base_:—Heán wæs lange, swā hyne Geáta bearn gódne ne tealdon, ne hyne micles wyrðne Drihten gedón wolde, swýðe wēndon þæt hē sleac wǽre, æðeling unfrom, B. 2183. Þū scealt andettan yfeldǽda mā, heán helle gǽst, Jul. 457: 615. Helm sceal cēnum and ā fah þæs heánan hyge hord unginnost, Gn. Ex. 206. Āhrede mē hearmcwidum heánra manna, Ps. Th. 118, 134. (2 a) _applied to a thing personified_:—Hió (_day_) sceal wreccan lāste hāmleás hweorfan, nō þý heánre bið, Rä. 40, 9. (3) _reduced to a low position or condition, brought low, rendered abject, humbled_:—Ic sceal heán and earm wadan wrǽclāstas wuldre benēmed, duguðum bedēled, Sat. 120: Cri. 265. Ǣr þon ic gehēned heán gewurðe _priusquam humiliarer_, Ps. Th. 118, 67. Gē magon geþencan hū heán hē wearþ his geblōta and his diófolgilda (_how low he was brought through his sacrifices and idolatries?_), þā þā gē hiene gebundenne hæfdon and hiene ātugon swā swā gē woldon, Ors. 6, 37; S. 296, 22. Þē (_Satan_) se Ǽlmihtiga heánne gehnǽgde, An. 1193. Wrǽcstówe wērige gāstas . . . heáne gefōran, Gen. 91: Ps. Th. 87, 5. Sē þe hine sylfne āhefeð heáhmōdne, sē sceal heán wesan, Mōd. 54. (4) _depressed, dejected, cast down, miserable_:—For hwon wāst þū weán, gesyhst sorge, sagast līfceare heán, hygegeómor, Gen. 879: 866. Feásceaft hæleð . . . heán, hygegeómor, heófende sprǣc, An. 1559: 1089. Hē sceal heán þonan, geómor hweorfan, þām bið gomenes wana, Gū. 1327 (cf. 1353): An. 893: Ph. 554: B. 2099: 2408. Hē heán gewāt, dreáme bedǣled, 1274. Beornas wēpað wānende, heáne, hygegeómre, hreówum gedreahte, Cri. 994: El. 1216. (5) _low in fortune, wretched, in evil plight_:—Wend þē from wynne, þū scealt mid weres egsan hearde genearwod heán þrowian þīnra dǣda gedwild, Gen. 921. Ic fleáh weán, wana wilna gehwilces, heán of wícum, 2273. Þū hreósan sceoldes heán in helle helpendra leás, Cri. 1414. Þū scealt wērigmōd, heán, hrōðra leás hearm þrowigan, An. 1369. Ic eów hālsie þæt gē mē of þyssum earfeðum ūp forlǣten heánne, El. 701. Heáne, hrōðra bidǣled, hyhta leáse helle sōhton, Jul. 681. **II.** of things. (1) _of little importance_:—Dryhten ðā heánan gelōcað _Dominus humilia respicit_, Ps. Srt. 112, 6. (2) _of actions, mean, base, low_:—Ne þǽr ōwiht inne ne belīfe on heortscrǽfe heánra gylta _nec lateat quidquam culparum cordis in antro_, Dōm. L. 39.

**heán** _to elevate._ _Add:_ , **hȳn**:—Ðū ūp hēst mec of geatum deáðes _exaltas me de portis mortis_, Ps. Srt. 9, 15. Þā staðolas þǽre cyrican . . . hē ongann hȳn (heán, v. l.) and mīclian, Bd. 2, 4; Sch. 127, 10. [v. _N. E. D._ high; _vb. O. Frs._ ge-heid; _pp._] v. ge-heán; hīgan.

**heáne.** _Add:_—Þū miht oferhýdige . . . heáne gehnǽgean _tu humiliasti superbum_, Ps. Th. 88, 9.

**heán-lic.** _Add:_ **I.** _of little worth_ or _importance, paltry, common; vilis_:—Man wōt oft māre þe þām heálicran ðonne be þām heánlicran, Solil. H. 17, 14. **II.** _vile, contemptible, base_:—Heánlic slǣp, Dōm. L. 257. Eów mæg gescomian þ gē swā heánlic geþōht on eów geniman for ānes monnes ege, Ors. 6, 37; S. 296, 17. Swā heánlice ofermētto, 2, 5; S. 84, 11. Þā hlāfordas hæfdon heánlicne sige (_indignam victoriam_), 2, 6; S. 88, 1. Þā āscedan hiene his þegnas hwý hē swā heánlicne word be him selfum gecwǣde, þ hē oferwunnen wǣre, 4, 1; S. 156, 29.

**heán-līce.** _Add:_—Man sceal þā geoguðe geómorlīce lǣdan gehæft

heánlīce mid heardum bendum and swā bysmorlīce bringan of heora ēðle, Wlfst. 295, 17. Sume hī man heánlīce hǽttode, Chr. 1036; Th. i. 294, 7, col. 2. [_O. H. Ger._ hōn-līhho _infandum, deformius_ (cpv.).] v. un-heánlīce.

**heán-mōd,** Rä. 43, 17. v. heáh-mōd.

**heáp.** _Add:_ **I.** of persons. (1) _in a general sense, a band, company_:—Se eádmōda heáp (_the apostles_), Hml. Th. i. 318, 13. Þǣr wæs preósta heáp, micel muneca ðreát, 'Chr. 973; P. 118, 12. Hī mid þý heápe helle sēcað, fleógað mid þām feóndum, Dōm. 17. Hē (_Peter_) āna sprǣc for ealne ðone heáp, Hml. Th. i. 394, 1. His þone gecorenan heáp _electos suos_, Ps. Th. 104, 38. Hellwarena heáp, Cri. 731. Leófra heáp, El. 1206. Hālige heápas _the multitudes of saints_, Wlfst. 190, 3. Ān engla þreát . . , heápa wyn, Hö. 18. Iunge heápas _inuestes_ (_puerorum_) _cateruas_ i. _multitudines_, An. Ox. 2877: Wrt. Voc. ii. 44, 40, 41. (2) _of a regulated company, one under discipline._ (a) _ecclesiastical._ (a) _the clergy._ Cf. preóst-heáp:—Betwux middeweardum heópe _inter medios cleros_, Ps. L. 67, 14. (β) _a choir_:—Heápum _classibus_ (v. Ald. 35, 28), Wrt. Voc. ii. 79, 58. (b) _secular._ (a) _an army, a host_:—Heáp (_the host of the Huns_) wæs gescyrted, lāðra lindwered: lythwōn becwōm Hūna herges hām eft þanon, El. 141. Of þām heápe fleág giellende gār, Vid. 127: Exod. 192. (β) _a division of an army, a troop, company_:—Heáp _cuneus_ (cf. _cuneus_ getrimmed fēða, i. 18, 31), Wrt. Voc. ii. 16, 241 Heápum _maniplis_ (v. Ald. 191, 6), 95, 12: 54, 51. Fēþena heápum _peditum turmis_, i. _agminibus_, An. Ox. 827. Heora ǽgðer hæfde his folc on þrīm heápum _cohortes triplici ordine disposuit_, Ors. 5, 12; S. 242, 3. Hǽfde wuldres beám werud gelǣded, hālige heápas, Exod. 568. (γ) _an_ (armed) _retinue_:—Ic and gelǣded, hālige heápas, Exod. 568. (γ) _an_ (armed) _retinue_:—Ic and gelǣded mīnra eorla gedryht, þes hearda heáp, B. 432. Elene heápe gecoste mīnra eorla gedryht lindwīgendra land gesōhte, El. 269. (δ) _a crew_:—Heápum _agminibus_ (_remigantum_), An. Ox. 5, 5. **II.** of other living things:—Fiþerbǣre heápas _pennigeras_ (_volucrum_) _turmas_, An. Ox. 1566. **III.** of heápas _per turmas_ (Prov. 30, 27), Kent. Gl. 1109. **III.** of inanimate objects or of material:—Heáp _strues_, Wrt. Voc. ii. 121, 18. (1) _a collection_ of objects:—Heáp _congeries_ (_canonum_, v. Mt. p. 4, 3), Wrt. Voc. ii. 71, 48: 17, 42. Weartene heáp _satiriasis_, i. 20, 9. Þǣr wæs wlitig weoroda heáp, An. 872. Āwrīteþ hē on his wǣpne wællnota heáp, Sal. 161. Ǽtýwdon monige heápas sweartra līgea (swearte heápas þāra līga, v. l.) _apparent crebri flammarum tetrarum globi_, Bd. 5, 12; Sch. 618, 16. Þā ylcan heápas þāra fýra _idem globi ignium_, 619, 5. (2) _a raised mass_ of material:—In heáp bið gesamnod _comprehenditur_, Wrt. Voc. ii. 58, 56. On heáp _in cumulum_ (_turgescens pontus in cumulum creuit_, Ald. 34, 26), An. Ox. 7, 163. **IV.** _in the phrase_ on heápe. (1) _of persons, in company, in a body, together_:—Þæt feórðe cyn fyrmest eóde, wigan on heápe, Exod. 311. Nealles him on heápe handgesteallan ymbe gestōdon, B. 2596. [Þa þe uerde wes isomne of ælche moncunne, þa heo weoren þer on hepe an hunddred þusende, Laym. 28292. v. _N. E. D._ on heap.] (2) _of things_:—Gewīteð mid þý wuldre on westrodor tungol faran on heápe _the sun and its glory together depart journeying to the western heaven_, Sch. 69. v. efen-, eóred-, mægden-, mægen-, munuc-, preóst-, wuldor-heáp.

**heápa.** v. heópa.

**heápian;** _p._ ode _To heap up, accumulate, bring together_:—On heápedon _ingesserunt_ (ubi cloacarum cuniculi putores stercorum _ingesserunt_, Ald. 45, 27), Wrt. Voc. ii. 82, 21. Heápedan _concinnant_ (qui sacramentis _concinnant_ (cf. _concinnatas, cumulatas_, 80, 50) frivola falsis, Ald. 162, 2), 92, 17: 19, 41. Heápian _accumulare_, 2, 5. v. ge-, ymb-heápian; hīpan.

**heáp-mǽlum.** _Add:_ **I.** _in troops, in crowds_:—Heápmǽlum _gregatim_, Wrt. Voc. ii. 40, 17: _cateruatim, gregatim, multipliciter_, 19, 51: _manipulatim_ (legiones, quae heápmǽlum ongunuon tō hyra hūsum ladian _currere viri et feminae, nobiles atque ignobiles coeperunt, certatim que eum in suis rapere domibus conabantur_, Gr. D. 200, 28.

**heard.** _Add:_—Heard _dira_, heardre _dirae_, Wrt. Voc. ii. 27, 64, 72. **I.** of material:—Wæs hió (_an iceberg_) hetegrim . . . bordwealla (_the sides of a ship_) grōf heard (_or under_ VI?) and hīþende, Rä. 34, 7. Gūðbyrne . . . heard, handlocen, B. 322. Heardes īsenes grindlas, Gen. 383. Mid hefegum helme oððe heardre byrnan, Hml. Th. ii. 502, 13. Ic læg on heardum stāne, Cri. 1425. Hearde mēde (cf. on Heardanlēge, ðǣre is ōðer noma Drȳganlēg, C. D. v. 141, 27), Txts. 436, 5. Hī fuhton heardum heoruwǣpnum, Jud. 263. Iornan on hearde wegas, Shrn. 72, 2. Eorðan līm symle bið þý heardra þe hit sǽstreámas swīðor beātað, gen. 1325. Flinte heardra, Rä. 41, 78. **I a.** _used of a tree; cf._ hard-beam:—Hē āstāg in treé heard (treó heord, R.) _ascendit in arborem sicomorum_, Lk. L. 19, 4. Ǽlces treówcynnes dǣl . . . būtan heardan beáman, Lch. i. 398, 8. **I b.** _used substantively_:—Ealle þā sār and þ hearde hyt gelīðigaþ and gehnesceaþ, Lch. i. 368, 1. **I c.** _used figuratively_:—Þū heardeste strǣl tō ǽghwilcre unrihtnesse,

Bl. H. 241, 3. **II.** of persons. (1) *capable of great physical endurance or exertion, hardy, bold in fight* (lit. or fig.) :—Is his eafora nū heard hēr cumen, B. 376. Rōf ōretta heard under helme, 2539. Þǣr on-innan bær eorlgestreóna hringa hyrde, hard wyrðne dǣl fǣttan goldes *there in bore of treasures, of plated gold, the rings' keeper bold a noble portion,* 2245. [For hard wyrðne *several emendations have been suggested :* hard-fyrdne, hard-fyndes, hord-wyrðne, hord-wynne.] Ārās þā se ríca (*Beowulf*) . . sume þǣr bidon . . . swā him se hearda bebeád, 401. Wracu sceal heardum men (cf. sēlre bið æghwǣm þæt hē his freónd wrece, B. 1385), Gn. Ex. 153. Ecg sceal on sweorde and ord spere, hyge heardum men, 205. Frægn Scipia hiene an hwíg hit gelang wǣre þ Numentie swā raðe āhnescaden, swā hearde swā hié longe wǣron. Ðā sǣde hē þ hié wǣren hearde þā hwíle þe hié hira ānrǣdnesse geheóldon him betweónum *Scipio Tiresum consuluit, qua ope res Numantina aut prius invicta durasset, aut post fuisset eversa. Tiresus respondit: ' Concordia invicta . . .',* Ors. 5, 3 ; Swt. 222, 13-18. Hearde hild-frecan, B. 2205. Gūðfrecan gāras sendon on heardra gemang, Jud. 225. (1 a) with gen. of noun defining form of activity :—Beadwe heard, B. 1539. Wíges heard Crēca drihten (*Ulysses*), Met. 26, 13. Níðweorca heard (*Edgar*), Chr. 973; P. 118, 23. ¶ figuratively of a saint :—Beorn (*St. Andrew*) beaduwe heard, An. 984. (2) *firm, steadfast, resolute :*—Þeáh þe se líchoma wǣre mid þǣre untrumnesse swā swíðe geswenced, hweþre his mōd wæs ā heard and gefeónde on Drihten, Bl. H. 227, 9 : Gū. 950. Ārās eorla wynn heard, hygesnottor . . mēðe for þām miclum bisgum, 1082. Heard and higestraug, Men. 42 : An. 1401. Se hearda hyge, Gū. 517. Þā þrý cōmon tō þeódne foran hearde and higeþancle, Dan. 94. **II a.** of word or thought, *bold, resolute :*—Ā scyle geong mon wesan geómormód, heard heortan geþōht swylce habban sceal, blíðe gebǣro, Kl. 43. Him þā brōðor þrý æt sprǣce þǣre hǣldon hygesorge heardum wordum, Gen. 2035. **III.** of things. (1) *capable of resisting wear or injury :*—Þā treówa þe beóð āheáwene on fullum mōnan beóð heardran wið wyrmǣtan and lengsǣrran þonne þā ðe beóð on níwum mōnan āheáwene, Lch. iii. 268, 10. **IV.** of *a character not easily impressed or moved.* (1) of persons, *obdurate :*—Manige men beóð heardre heortan, Bl. H. 57, 18. Mōdblinde men flintum heardran, Cri. 1189. Heó wǣron stearce, stāne heardran, El. 565. Ic wæs þæs heardestan geþōhtes mann (*a man of a mind impervious to good influences* (?) : the Latin is : *homo obscurae opinionis*), þæt ic mē míne dagas tō nytte ne gedyde, Först. Verc. 137, 18. (2) of non-material things, *rigid, unyielding :*—Heardum rigido (*imperio*), An. Ox. 1293. **V.** *difficult to bear, oppressive, rigorous, strict.* (1) of things not necessarily painful :—Him heard (*durum*) wæs þ hí on ealdum mōde wǣron geneádode níwe þing tō smeágenne, Gr. D. 104, 20. Heard wæs hinsíð, Hö. 7. Ðū seó wyrd scyðed heard and hetegrim, An. 1564. Heardan ceápe, B. 2482. Þurh heard gelāc, An. 1094. Feala ðū ætýwdest folce ðínum heardra wīsan *ostendisti populo tuo dura,* Ps. Th. 59, 3. Hearde laga *rigidas* (i. *duras*) *leges,* Wülck. Gl. 256, 33. Heardran hǣle, B. 719. Sēr ic geférde heardran drohtnoð, An. 1404. Nýd bið wyrda heardost, Sal. 310. (2) of painful things :—Næs nā mid Rōmānum ǣr ne siþþan swā heard gefeoht swā þǣr wæs *numquam ulla Romano militi tumultuosior pugna et terribilior fuit,* Ors. 5, 7 ; S. 230, 12. Nīð heard and hetegrim, An. 1397. Heardes heolewītes, Gen. 303. Ðone kyning ðe hine on swā heardum wrǣce gebrōhte, Past. 37, 4. Sume hē lēt þreágan mid heardum broce *alios duris agitari sinit,* Bt. 39, 11 ; F. 228, 24. Longe ic wæs nū on ðǣm heardan campe, Bl. H. 225, 31. Hōn on hearde hengene, Hml. Th. ii. 308, 30 : Hml. S. 37, 101, 157. Morðorleán heard and heorogrim, Cri. 1613. Þincð sió sōðe gesǣld þý wynsumre þe hē mā heardra hēnða ādreóged, Met. 12, 21 : B. 166. Heardra hearma, An. 1447. Þeáh ðe þæt wīte hwēne heardre and strengre gedōn sý *cum paulo districtius agitur,* Bd. 1, 27; Sch. 66, 16. Wīta heardost, Kr. 87. Þ hē onfó þæs heardestan þeówdōmes, Bl. H. 49, 5. (3) of a time in which there is suffering :—Se hearda dæg (*the day of doom*), Cri. 1065. Nǣnig bihelan mæg on þām heardan dæge wom unbēted, 1311. **VI.** of persons, *harsh, severe in dealing with any one :*—Symble hē þā steóre dyde būtan mildheortnesse, and hit mā dyde on wælgrimnesse wyllan þonne mid ǣnigre mildheortlicre forgifnesse . . . hē wæs swā heard and unforgyfende þām forwyrhtum mannum, Gr. D. 320, 1. Weard Tiberius Rōmānum swā wrāð and swā heard swā hē him ǣr wæs milde and līþe *inmutata est Tiberii modestia, atque ex mansuetissimo principe saevissima bestia exarsit,* Ors. 6, 2 ; S. 254, 30. Hēt mec hláford mín hēr heard (? her-heard, MS.; *see* heard-eard). Grein *suggested* eard, *but the alliteration seems to require* heard. Cf. oððe þis waroð þe hēr āworpen liged, Rä. 41, 49) niman, Kl. 15. Gē him æghwæs oftugon þurh heardne hyge hrægles nacedum, mōses meteleásum, Cri. 1506. **VI a.** of a person's actions, qualities, &c. :—Þāra cyninga wælhreównes wæs tō þām heard, Bt. 29, 2 ; F. 104, 33. Heard spēc *sermo durus* (*suscitat furorem,* Prov. 15, 1), Kent. Gl. 503. Hē þōhte forgrīpan gumcynne grimme and sāre heardum nihtum, Gen. 1276. **VI b.** of a thing with which injury may be inflicted by a person :—Heardum mēce *dira framea,* An. Ox. 890. **VII.** *intense in force or degree :*—Gif seó sealf sié

tō hear[d], geswēt mid hunige, Lch. ii. 36, 16. Þonne heard gebrec, hlūd, unmǣte, swār and swiðlic, swēgdynna mǣst, ældum egeslic, eáwed weorðeð, Cri. 954. Se líchoma on þone heardestan stenc and on þone fūlostan bið gecyrred, Bl. H. 59, 12. **VIII.** of energetic, vehement action :—Heard handplega, Exod. 327. Heard gripe hrūsan, Ruin. 8. Heorosweng heardne, B. 1590. Is þē gūð weotod heardum heoruswengum, An. 954. v. ecg-, ellen-, feól-, for-, fȳr-, gūþ-, hrímig-, íren-, mægen-, níþ-, regn-, scūr-, slíþ-, stearc-, stede-, þrǣc-, þroht-, wíg-heard. The word is found in many person-names : for a list of such see Txts. pp. 485-6.

**heard**, es ; *n. What is hard :*—Nān wiht þæs heardes ne þæs hnesces, Wlfst. 184, 20. Him on hand gǣð heardes and hnæsces, Sal. 286. v. hnesce ; *n.*

**hearde.** *Add :* **I.** of falling or striking (*lit.* or *fig.*):—Hē sume āc āstāh, . . . and hē hearde feóll (cf. in arborem ascendens deciderat deorsum, et contrito corpore spiritum exhalavit, Vit. Cuth. c. 34), Hml. Th. ii. 150, 32. Ic wæs hearde cnyssed *impulsus,* Ps. Th. 117, 13. **II.** of seizing, pressing (*lit.* or *fig.*) :—Hē (*a sea-beast*) weard mid eoforspreotum hearde genearwod, B. 1438. Mid weres egsan hearde genearwod, Gen. 921. Hearde genyrwad, gebunden bealorāpum, Cri. 364. Þē tō heortan hearde grīped ādl unlīðe, Gen. 936. **III.** of binding, fastening, *firmly, tightly :*—Helm on heáfod āsette, and þone full hearde geband, Gen. 444. Unrōtnesse gerǣped, hearde gehæfted (cf. gerǣpte mid þǣre unrōtnesse, and swā gehæfte, Bt. 37, 1 ; F. 186, 22), Met. 25, 49. Wītum gebunden, hearde gehæfted, Jud. 116. Þurh þā ic hongade hearde gefæstnad, Cri. 1457. [The last three passages might be taken under IV.] **IV.** *in a way that involves pain :*—Hrinon hearmtānas hearde and sāre drihta bearnum, Gen. 992. Þæs wrāðe ongeald, hearde mid hīwum, hægstealda wynn, 1862 : Dan. 598. Him þæt hearde weard forgolden, Jud. 216. Wē þæs hearde sceoldon bīdan in bendum, Hö. 87. Him bonena hand hearde gesceóde, An. 18. Wyrd bið wended hearde . . . and hwæðre him mæg wíssefa wyrda gehwylce gemetigian, Sal. 435. Þeáh þe þ wīte hwæne heardor and strangor dōn sý *cum paulo districtius agitur,* Bd. 1, 27 ; Sch. 66, 13. **V.** with intensive force. (1) with verbs implying pain, injury, &c. :—Ūs hearde sceód fǣmne þurh forman gylt, Gen. 997. Gē sceolon hearde ādreógan wīte, Cri. 1514. Mē is heorte and flǣsc hearde geteórad, Ps. Th. 72, 21. Hwílum mē bryne stīged, hyge heortan neáh hearde (hǣdre, *v. l.*) wealleð, Sal. 62. (2) of painful physical sensation, e. g. thirst, Hml. Th. ii. 256, 31 (in Dict.). (3) of painful, violent, intense emotion :—Hē (*St. Martin*) cōm tō hūse hearde gedrēfed (cf. Martinus cōm micclum dreórig, Hml. S. 31, 213), Hml. Th. ii. 504, 25. Ne wē cunnun þurh hwæt þū þus hearde ūs eorre wurde, El. 400. Lengað hine hearde, þynceð þæt sý þria xxx þūsend wintra ǣr hē dōmdæges dyn gehȳre, Sal. 270: Seel. 155. Hearde ondrǣdan, Cri. 1018. Hē hiene geeáðmēdde tō þǣm folce þe hē him þǣr heardost ondrēd, Ors. 3, 7 ; S. 112, 33. Þonne hine þæs hlīsan heardost lysteð, Met. 10, 14.

**heard-fyrde.** *Dele, and see* heard ; II. 1.

**heard-hara, heardra,** an; *m. The name of a fish. Take here* heardra *in Dict., and add :*—Heardhara *cefalus,* Txts. 52, 270. Haerdhera *caefalus,* 115, 167. Heardra *cephalus,* Wrt. Voc. i. 66, 4 : *ceffalus,* 281, 70 : *cefalus,* ii. 14, 20. Heardhara *mugil,* 114, 40. Hacod oððe heardra, 55, 81. Heardran *mullos,* An. Ox. 56, 339. [*Ger. harder.*]

**heard-heáwa.** *Substitute :* **heard-heáw, -heáwa, -heáwe, hēwe, -hīwe, -hēui** *a cutting implement, chisel :*—Heardheáu *cisculus,* Txts. 51, 467. Heardhēui *ciscillus,* 52, 262. Haerdhaeu, 116, 199. Heardheáw, Wrt. Voc. ii. 14, 34. *Circillus, navicula vel* heardheáwa, 131, 23. Heardheáwe *vel* nafogār *foratorium,* 149, 74. [Cf. *N. E. D.* hard-hewer *a stonemason.*]

**heard-heort.** *Add :* [*The Latin of* Ex. 33, 3, 5 *and of* Deut. 9, 6 *is* populus durae cervicis *and* durissimae cervicis populus.] **I.** *not affected by pity* (see first two passages in Dict.). **II.** *impervious to good influences :*—Gif hiora hwilc swā heardheort wǣre þ hē nāne hreówsunge ne dyde, Bt. 41, 3 ; F. 248, 15. Jōseph weard āhred swā þ þā heardheortan (*the Jews*) his næfdon nān þing, Hml. A. 79, 173. Þā unstillan and þā heardheortan abbud sceal þreágean *indisciplinatos et inquietos debet arguere,* R. Ben. 13, 12. [v. *N. E. D.* hardheart.]

**heardheortness.** *Add :* [*The Latin of* Deut. 31, 27 *is* cervicem tuam durissimam :]—Losiað tō fela for heora heardheortnysse wið þone Hǣlend, Hml. S. 25, 529.

**heard-hēwe, -hīwe.** v. heard-heáw.

**heardian.** *Add :*—Heardadun (*gelaverunt*) swē swē wall weter heardadon ȳðe in midre sae, Ps. Srt. ii. p. 187, 30. [v. *N. E. D.* hard. *O. Sax.* hardōn : *O. H. Ger.* hartēn, hartōn.] v. ā-, wiþ-heardian ; hirdan.

**heard-lic.** *Substitute :* **I.** *bold, warlike.* Cf. heard ; II. 1 :—Wīglice, heardlice *bellicosas* (*cohortes*), Hpt. Gl. 425, 8. **II.** *resolute, stern.* Cf. heard ; II. 2 :—Heardlic eornost and wíslic wærscipe and stydefæst mōdstaþol . . . bið witena gehwilcum weorðlicre micle, þonne

hē his wîsan fāgige tô swîðe, Ll. Th. ii. 318, 37. **III.** *hard to bear, dire, grievous.* Cf. heard; **V**:—Egeslic ǽled eágsýne wearð, heardlic hereteám, An. 1556. Heom þūhte heardlic (*durum*) þ hî wǽron genýdede on ealdum môde þ hî scoldon nîwe wîsan hycgan, Gr. D. 104, 21. Silla wið Marius heardlice gefeoht þurhteáh and hiene gefliémde *Sulla gravissimo praelio vicit*, Ors. 5, 11 ; S. 236, 21. þē sind heardlicu, wundrum wǽlgrim wîtu geteohhad, Jul. 263. **IV.** *harsh, severe, pitiless.* Cf. heard; **VI**:—þæt bið þearlic gemôt, heardlic heremægen, Dôm. 37. [*Icel.* harð-ligr *hard, severe.*]

**heardlíce.** *Add*:—Heardlíce *dure*, i. *pertinaciter, pessime*, Wrt. Voc. ii. 142, 16. **I.** *boldly, hardily.* Cf. heard; **II.** 1:—Hē þæt folc bewerode wið þā hǽðenan leóda heardlíce mid wǽmnum, Ælfc. T. Grn. 7, 3. **II.** *hardly, without ease.* Cf. heard; **V.** 1:—Se man, sē ðe wile on ǽlce tîd heardlíce and forwernedlíce lyfigean, sē bið fulfremed, Wlfst. 284, 8. **III.** *severely, inflexibly:*—Tô ēcre forwyrde heardlíce (*districtius*) gedēman, Bd. 4, 25 ; Sch. 504, 1. **IV.** *in a way that causes pain.* Cf. hearde; **IV** :—Banan heardlíce, grimme ongieldað, Sal. 131. **V.** *with intensive force with verbs implying pain, injury, &c.* Cf. hearde; **V.** 1:—Þēh se mennisca deófol synfullum môte heardlíce derian, Wlfst. 273, 22. Se bealofulla hýneð heardlíce, Cri. 260. **VI.** *of energetic action, physical or mental.* Cf. heard; **VIII** :—Þæt mon heardlíce gnîde (*collidendo vehementius*) mealmstān, Ors. 4, 13 ; S. 212, 27. Ongunnon hî heardlíce feohtan, By. 261. Ic nimo ꝥ heartlíce (geteá (?), cf. 21, 6 geteá *trahere*) traham, Jn. L. 12, 32. Hē genam þā heardlíce þurh heora lāre on his orþance þā egeslican dǽda, Ælfc. T. Grn. 17, 20. **VII.** *not easily, only by degrees:*—Ðone blindo heartlíce gemeð *caecum paulatim curat* (v. Mk. 8, 22–25), Mk. p. 3, 20. Heartlíce onginnes *paulatim incipiens*, Mt. p. 11, 11.

**heardlicness.** *Add* :—The Latin of the passage is : Alii asperitatem vitae ipsius disputabant.

**heard-môd.** *Add*:—Heardmôd bið se mon þe ne mæge þysum gelýfan, Hml. S. 36, 326. v. heard; **IV.** 1.

**heardness.** *Add*:—Heardnissae *rigore*, Txts. 92, 871. **I.** *hardness, callosity, hard material*:—Wið ǽlce heardnysse, fearres smeru mylt . . . ealle þā sār and þ hearde hyt gelíðigað and gehnesceaþ, Lch. i. 366, 26. Ealle yfele heardnyssa and gegaderunga heó tôfereþ, 270, 16. **II.** *obduracy.* Cf. heard; **IV**:—Tô heardnisse (*duritiam*) heortan eówre, Mt. R. 19, 8 : Mk. L. R. 10, 5. **III.** *strictness, severity, austerity.* Cf. heard; **V**:—Hē in heardnesse munuclîfes lifde *in monachica districtione uitam duxit*, Bd. 4, 26 ; Sch. 508, 5.

**heardra.** v. heard-hara : **heard-sélig.** *Add* :—Hwîlum gebyrede ðām heardsǽlgan (-sǽlegum, *v. l.*) þ him wǽre betere þ he bearn næfde ðonne he hæfde *carentem liberis infortunio dixit esse felicem*, Bt. 81, 1 ; F. 112, 20 : heard-sǽlnes. *After* heardsǽlnes in l. 2 *add*: (heartsǽlnes, *v. l.* see Mod. Lang. Rev. viii. 60, 25).

**heard-sélþ.** *Add* :—Se cyning . . . him wæs wāniende ægþer ge his āgene heardsǽlða ge ealles þæs folces *rex . . . nunc suam, nunc publicam infelicitatem deflet*, Ors. 4, 5 : S. 166, 20.

**heardung**, e; *f. A hardening, a being or becoming hard:*—Heardung þǽre lifre būtan gefélnesse and būtan sāre, Lch. ii. 198, 13. Be þǽre lifre heardunge, 160, 21. [*Cf. O. H. Ger.* hartunga *exercitatio.*] v. ā-heardung.

**hearh.** *Add*:, her(i)g, here : **hearga**, an ; *m.* [*For pl.* hearga ; *f.* substitute : The form hearga, Past. 153, 22, is perhaps a mistake, as at 157, 5, 7 the form is heargas, which is also the reading of the Cotton MS. at 152, 22. Another explanation might be that hearga is a remnant of the u-declension, and this may aptly to the form in Ex. 34, 15 : Lev. 26, 1, 30. Herge in Az 110 seems a verbal form parallel with bletsien.] **I.** *a place sacred to a god, with an idol and an altar.* (1) *a grove:*—Hearga *lucum* (the word occurs among glosses to Aldhelm between one on Ald. 50, 25 and another on 50, 27 : in the text between these *lucum* does not occur), Wrt. Voc. ii. 82, 81 : 51, 26. (2) *of a building.* (a) *a temple, fane:*—Se ylca hearg (hearh, here, *v. ll.*) *fanum*, Bd. 2, 15 ; Sch. 175, 5. Haerg *lupercal* (lupercal *templum panos*, Ld. Gl. H. 22, § 27, 11), Wrt. Voc. ii. 113, 28 : 51, 25. Hearges *sacelli*, 90, 20. Ðæs heáfodlican hearges *capitolii*, 20, 38 : 128, 46. Hearge *Herculis* (the gloss belongs to *sacello*, v. Herculis *sacello*, Ald. 44, 28. In Hpt. Gl. 482, 37 the gloss is placed rightly :—On hālierne ꝥ hergan, temple *sacello*), 81, 78 : *Herculus*, 43, 24. Herige, herge *delubro*, *templo*, Hpt. Gl. 493, 37. Þæt hē becrupe on þæs Amones anlícnesse þe inne on þǽm hearge (*templo*) wæs, Ors. 3, 9 ; S. 126, 28. Haerga *sacellorum*, Wrt. Voc. ii. 119, 51. Hergana *sacellorum* (sacellum *templum idolorum*), Hpt. Gl. 451, 23. Templicere hærgana *fanatica delubrorum superstitione*, 482, 27. Hergas *fana*, Bd. 3, 30 ; Sch. 331, 20 : 333, 1. (b) *the part of a temple in which the altar and idol stood:*—Hearh *delubrum* (Roma fregit *delubra sacelli*, Ald. 151, 22), An. Ox. 18 b, 21. ¶ the word occurs in place-names:—In loco cuius uocabulum est Besingahearh, C. D. v. 35, 17. Bituih Gumeningahergae and Liddinge, i. 142, 7. In quattuor locis, id est, æt hearge . . . and æt geddincggum, 282, 17.

Wæs gesewen ātîfred ealle ðā heargas (*idola*) . . . sió gîtsung ðe Scs Paulus cuæð ðæt wǽre hearga (*idolorum*) gefēra, Past. 157, 4–6. Hergas ðeóda *simulacra gentium*, Ps. Srt. 113, 4. Heargas hǽþenra ðeóda, Ps. Spl. 134, 15. Herga *simulacrorum, idolorum*, Hpt. Gl. 440, 63. In hergum heara *in simulacris suis*, Ps. Srt. ii. p. 183, 29. Þ hē þeówige unclǽnum deófum, and þām unwittigum heargum, Hml. S. 30, 52. Se hālga herigeas þreáde, deófulgild tôdrǽf, An. 1689. **III.** the word is also applied to a Christian temple :—Heargas *fana* (but Giles gives *templa :* Nescitis quod *templa* Dei sint ilia vestra, Ald. 140, 19), Wrt. Voc. ii. 89, 21.

**hearh-eard** (?) *a grove-dwelling* (?), *a dwelling in a grove, a grove as a dwelling.* v. hearh ; **I.** 1 :—Hēt mec hlāford mîn herheard niman (cf. hēht mec mon wunian on wuda bearwe, 27. Cf. *too, the phrase* ūpeard niman, Gû. 1051. *But for another rendering of the passage see* heard ; **VI.**

**hearh-lic** ; *adj. Pertaining to a fane.* v. hearh ; **I.** 2 a ; *fanaticus :*—Hearhlicre *vel* templicre *fanatice*, Wrt. Voc. ii. 147, 37.

**hearm.** *Add :* **I.** *evil, physical or otherwise, as done to or suffered by a person or thing :*—Gif him ǽnig hearm of þām drence becymð, Ælfc. T. Grn. 21, 32. þā cýdde man mē þ ūs mǽra hearm tô fundode þonne ūs wel lícode, and þā fôr ic . . . intô Denmearcon þe eów mǽst hearm of côm . . . wē ne þurfon þanon nēnes hearmes ūs āsittan, Cht. E. 230, 1–10. Him eallum tô hearme, Hml. S. 13, 127. Næbbe hē his nā māran hearm, Ll. Th. i. 276, 11. Wē þis wîte þolien, hearm on þisse helle, Gen. 368. Hearm þrowigan, sāre swyltcwale, An. 1369 : 1073. Swurdbcran hine gewordene gesihð, hearm fūllic getācnað *gladiatorem se factum uiderat: dampnum fedum significat*, Lch. iii. 204, 26 (v. Archiv. cxxv. 56, 300). **I a.** *an evil, injury, a calamity :*—Hearme *discrimine*, i. *damno* (*imminentis famis*), An. Ox. 3869 : *discrimine*, i. *periculo*, 46, 13. Seó dǽd wearð Rômānum tô ðǽm mǽstan hearme þæt him nān folc ne getrūwode *the deed was the cause of this very great injury to the Romans, that no people trusted them*, Ors. 4, 12 ; S. 210, 11. Gif hwilc man þ wǽpn gelæcce and hwylcne hearm gewyrce, þonne is þ riht þ sē þe þone hearm geworhte, þ sē þone hearm gebēte, Ll. Th. i. 418, 7–10. Hē unc þisne hearm gerǽd, Gen. 797. Hearma *calamitatum*, Wrt. Voc. ii. 24, 61. Wîte, hearma mǽstne, Gen. 802. Feala mē se Hǽlend hearma gefremede, nîða nearolicra, El. 912 : An. 1200. Æt ealre þǽre hergunge and æt eallum þām hearmum þe ǽr þām gedôn wǽre, Ll. Th. i. 288, 2. Ic þā myclan hearmas þe ūs tô fundedon gelôgod hæbbe, Cht. E. 230, 8. Wit hearmas, þreáweorc þoliaþ, Gen. 736. **II.** *grief, affliction :*—Gehýrde heó hearm galan (cf. hearmleóð āgôl, 615) helle deófol, Jul. 629. **III.** *injurious speech, calumny.* Cf. hearm-cwide :—Ic worn for þē worda hæbbe . . . hearmes gehýred and mē hosp sprecað, Cri. 171. Hearma *calumniarum*, An. Ox. 8, 233. **III a.** *a calumny :*—Ālēs mec from hearmum (*calumniis*) monna, Ps. Srt. 118, 134.

**hearma.** *Substitute : A field-mouse or a dormouse :*—Hearma *megale* (= μνγαλῆ), Wrt. Voc. ii. 114, 2 : 55, 60. [Cf. *migale ignota nisi similis est* cameloni, Shrn. 29, 12. This is in a list of glosses to Leviticus c. xi : in v. 30 mygale occurs in the Vulgate and the A.V. has *ferret.*] Hearma *netila*, ii. 114, 61 : 60, 10 : i. 22, 50. Herma, Txts. 116, 225. [*O. H. Ger.* harmo *mygale, cameleon.*] *See next word.*

**hearma-scinnen** ; *adj. Of ermine :*—On merðene pyleceon and hearmascynnene, Chr. 1075 ; P. 209, 32.

**hearm-beorg**, es ; *m. A hill of calamity* or *of affliction :*—Sitæþ on hærmbergæ, E. M. Furn. 373.

**hearm-cwalu.** *Add :* [Cf. *Icel.* harm-kvæli *torments.*]

**hearm-cwedelian.** *Add :* , -cwidelian, -cweodelian :—Þætte ne hearmcwidelìgen (-cweodelien, Ps. V.), Ps. Vos. 118, 122.

**hearm-cwéþan.** *Add :*—Harmcwēdun, Mk. R. 15, 32. Hearmcwēðendne *calumniatorem*, Ps. Vos. 71, 4. Gebiddað fore ðǽm harmcuoed[end]um iuih *orate pro calumniantibus uos*, Lk. L. 6, 28.

**hearm-cwiddian.** *Add :*—Ne hearmcwyddigan (*calumpnientur*) mē þā môdigan, Ps. L. 118, 122. Þæt mē oferhýdige ne môtan hearmcwyddian, Ps. Th. 118, 122. [*O. H. Ger.* harm-quetôn *maledicere.*]

**hearm-cwide.** *Add :* Cf. hearm-sprǽc.

**hearm-full** ; *adj. Evil, injurious :*—Tô hearmfullum *in peruersos*, An. Ox. 46, 13.

**hearm-fullic.** *Dele*, and see last passage under hearm ; **I.**

**hearm-georn.** v. un-hearmgeorn.

**hearm-heort** ; *adj. Of evil, malicious heart.* v. hearm ; *adj., and next word.*

**hearm-heortnen.** *Substitute :* **hearmheort-ness**, e ; *f. Ill-will, malice :*—Būtan hearmheortnesse *sine murmure*, Wrt. Voc. ii. 86, 45.

**hearmian.** *Add : to do harm to* (dat.) :—Se synfulla man hearmað him sylfum egeslice swýðe, Wlfst. 34, 13. Hearmað þē þîn gewinn tôgeánes mē, Hml. Th. i. 390, 11. Ælc man þe yfel dēþ . . . þeáh þe hit sumum fremige, and ælc man þe gôd dēð . . . þeáh þe hit hearmige sumum, Hml. S. 27, 173. Hē him hearmian nolde, 23, 311. An manncynn wunað under þînum anwealde . . . and þū wel wāst þ hit

wile hearmian þīnum cynerīce heora rēceleásnysse gyf him man ne gestȳrð heora stuntnysse *est populus . . . et optime nosti, quod non expediat regno tuo, ut insolescat per licentiam,* Hml. A. 96, 152. v. of-hearmian.

**hearm-leóþ.** *Add:* [Cf. *Icel.* harm-söngr *a dirge.*]

**hearm-lic.** *Add: calamitous :—*Ðȳ hearmlican *calamitosa,* Wrt. Voc. ii. 18, 49.

**hearm-plega.** *Add:—*Oft wǽron teónan wǽrfæstra wera weredum gemǽne, heardum hearmplega (cf. *Facta est rixa inter pastores gregum Abram et Lot,* Gen. 13, 7).

**hearm-sprǽc** *calumny. For* 'Som.' *substitute :—*Hosp, hearmsprǽc *calumpnia, accusatio falsa,* Wrt. Voc. ii. 127, 76. Cf. hearm-cwide.

**hearm-sprǽcol, -sprǽcolnes.** *Dele.*

**hearn(?)** *In the line:* Salpicis et clangor, necnon et classica sistri, Ald. 207, 36, sistri *is glossed by* hearnes, Wrt. Voc. ii. 96, 77.

**hearpe.** *Add:—*Hearpe *cythara,* Ps. L. 56, 9. Hearpa, 107, 3. Hearpe *psalterium,* Ps. Srt. 107, 3. Scyl wæs hearpe, hlūde dynede, Reim. 27. Hearpan stapas *cerimingius,* hearpan stala *ceminigi,* Wrt. Voc. ii. 130, 40, 66. Hwelce sīn ðā ingeðoncas monna būton suelce sumere hearpan strengas áðenede, ðā se hearpere suīðe ungelīce tiéhð and styreð, and mid ðȳ geðēð ðæt hí nāwuht ungelīce ðǽm sōne ne singað ðe hé wilnað ?, Past. 175, 6. Hé hearpan wynne, gomenwudu grētte, B. 2017. Hū ic þē mid 'hearpan hlyste cwēman, Ps. Th. 91, 3. Mid his hearpan (Bt. F. 168, 14 *has* hearepan), Bt. 35, 6 ; S. 102, 11. Heriað hine mid hearpum, and on þǽre tȳnstrengean hearpan *confitemini Domino in cithara; in psalterio decem chordarum psallite illi,* Ps. Th. 32, 2. Hearpan *liram,* Wrt. Voc. ii. 53, 11. Sum mæg fingrum wel hlūde fore hæleðum hearpan stirgan, gleóbeám grētan, Cri. 669. Þonne ic (*the devil*) mīne hearpan genam and mīne strengas styrian ongan, heó þæt lustlīce gehȳrdon and fram þē (*God*) ácerdan and tō mē urnan, Wlfst. 255, 8. Hearpan *cymbala* (*but the word in* Prov. 23, 21 *is* symbola), Kent. Gl. 891. Hearpas *citharas,* Mt. p. 10, 2. v. wīf-hearpe.

**hearpene.** *Dele.* The (unintelligible?) gloss upon which the word has been based is : *Aidoneae* hearpen, Wrt. Voc. ii. 9, 70.

**hearpere.** *Add :—*Dauid . . . wæs under hiofenum hearpera mǽrost, Ps. C. 4.

**hearp-slege.** *Add: An instrument for striking the strings of a harp :—*Hearpslege *plectro,* An. Ox. 52, 1. v. slege ; VIII.

**hearp-swēg.** *Add:* Ps. Rdr. 56, 9.

**hearpung.** *Add:* Ceruerus ongan plegian wiþ hine for his hearpunga, 18 : 33.

**hearr.** v. heorr : **hearste-panne.** v. hirste-panne : **-hearwa.** v. Sigel-hearwa : **hearwian.** *Dele.*

**heaþor** *restraint, confinement :—*Cyning . . . healdeð mē (*a sword*) on heaðore, Rä. 21, 13. Ǽghwā mec (*an onion*) reáfað, hafað mec on headre, 66, 3.

**heaðu.** *l.* heaþu, *and add :* v. heaþu-līþende, -sigel.

**heaþu-līþende.** *In support of* heaþu = *sea note the other compounds of* līþende, *five denoting water, and the sixth* (scip-līþende) *motion on water.*

**heaþu-sigel.** *Add :* For a passage connecting the sun with the sea v. Ph. 120 :—Sōna swā seó sunne sealte streámas heá oferhlīfað (the original Latin has no reference to the sea : Ubi sol pepulit fulgentis limina portae).

**-heáw.** v. ge-, heard-, on-heáw : **-heáwa.** v. heard-heáwa.

**heáwan.** *Add :—*Heáwed *secate,* An. Ox. 56, 32. I. *intrans. To strike with a cutting weapon, deal blows :—*Hī on healfa gehwone heáwan þōhton, B. 800. II. *trans. To strike forcibly with a cutting weapon, to hack, gash :—*Mē (*Christ*) on beáme beornas sticedon gārum on galgum, heów se giunga þǣr (cf. *unus militum lancea latus eius aperuit,* Jn. 19, 34), Sat. 511. Hine heówon heðene scealcas and bēgen þā beornas þe him big stōdon, By. 181. Hī heówan heaþolinde hamora lāfan, Chr. 937 ; P. 106, 14. Ðeáh þe lāðra fela ðīnne byrnhomon billum heówan, Vald. 1, 17. III. *to shape with a cutting implement,* Bd. 4, 11 ; Sch. 407, 21 (*in Dict.*). IV. *to hew, fell wood :—*Hī slōgon þā crīstenan . . . swā swā mann wudu hȳwð, Hml. S. 28, 69. V. *to cut off, sever a part from the whole by a blow :—*Sume heówun (*caedebant*) þǣra treówa bōgas, Txts. 21, 8. VI. *to form by hewing :—*Deórhege heáwan, Ll. Th. i. 432, 15 : Angl. ix. 262, 8. v. ā-, be-, for-, ge-, tō-heáwan.

**-heáwe.** [Cf. *O. H. Ger.* hauwa : *Ger.* haue.] v. heard-heáw : **heáwere.** v. flǽsc-, wudu-heáwere : **hebba.** v. heáfod-hebba ; **hebbe.**

**hebban.** *Add : A weak past* hefde *occurs with* Add. Hml. S. 8, 212. I. *trans.* (1) *to raise material to a higher level or towards a vertical position :—*Se esne his āgen hrægl ofer cneó hefað, Rä. 45, 5. Hine gelæhte ān hors mid tōðum and hefde him upp, Hml. S. 8, 212. Hyse hōf his āgen hrægl hondum ūp, Rä. 55, 3. Þecene hebban, 46, 2. Geworhton mē (*the cross*) feóndas him tō wæfersȳne, hēton mē heora wergas hebban, Kr. 31. (1 a) *to lift up* what is to be borne out :—Ðonne hī hebbað (hæbbað, *v. l.* eleuent) ðā earce ūp, Past. 173, 4.

---

Hié hōfan þā bǽre and hié bǽron mid heora handum, Bl. H. 149, 20. (1 b) *to lift* what is to be used, *lift* a weapon, *raise* a standard :—Hē bord ongeán hefeð, hāligne scyld, Jul. 386. Hōfon herecyste hwīte linde, segnas on sande, Exod. 301. Hwate weras hōfon herecombol, El. 25. Ic gefrægn mōdes rōfan hebban herebȳman, Exod. 99. Sceal gār wesan monig . . . hæfen on handa, B. 3023. Hafen, 1290. Wæs þūf hafen, segen for sweótum, El. 123. (c) where part of the body is moved, *to lift* the hand, head, eye, &c :—Ðonne hē hōf his hond upp tō hiofonum, ðonne hōfon ðā deór fōtas (fēt, *v. l.*) upp, Shrn. 72, 6. Mið hebbendum upp ēgum *eleuatis sursum oculis,* Jn. L. 11, 41. ¶ in figurative expressions where feeling is symbolized by such action :—Hī heora heáfod wið þē hōfan swīðe, Ps. Th. 82, 2. Cf. horn hebban, Ps. Th. 148, 14 : Past. 425, 22. (2) In various figurative expressions. (a) *to raise, lift* up the voice, *give utterance to* words, *make* a sound :—Wē hōfan lofsonga word, Sat. 154. Cleopa, hefe ūp ðīne stefne suā bīme *quasi tuba exalta vocem tuam,* Past. 91, 19 : Wlfst. 283, 1. [Þæt hē] hōfe hāligu word, Dan. 543. Wæs lof hafen . . . hī Fæder weorðodon, and þone Sunu wordum heredon, El. 890 : Jul. 693. Wæs wōp hæfen, hlūd heriges cyrm, Au. 1157 : Gū. 233. (b) *to raise* in position, or in well-being, *to exalt, elevate :—*Ābīd Dryhten and [hē] hefeð ūp (*exaltabit*) ðē þæt ðū ineardie eorðan, Ps. V. 36, 34. Hī hōfun Pendan suna tō cyninge *leuato in regem filio Pendan,* Bd. 3, 24 ; Sch. 314, 21. Tō ðǽm ðæt hī hī hæbben (āhebben, *v. l.*) ofer ðā ðe hié heora sellað *ne super eos se, quibus terrena largiuntur, extollant,* Past. 319, 17. Hād tō hebban swā heofonsteorran, Az. 37. Tō hebbanne, Dan. 321. (c) *to extol, exalt :—*Hī heáð and hebbað þone hālgan blǽd, Sch. 42. Hebbað ūrne God *exaltate Dominum,* Ps. Th. 98, 10. (d) *to set up, institute.* Cf. rǽran :—Hī feóndscype rǽrdon, hōfon hǽðengield, Jul. 15. (e) *to raise* a question, *bring up* a case :—Wolde se cing ðā spǽce beforan eallon his witan ūp hebban, C. D. iii. 315, 11. (f) *to direct* the mind to a lofty object :—Dō þīnes scealces sāwle blīðe, for ðon ic hī tō ðē hebbe *ad te animam meam levavi,* Ps. Th. 85, 3. Tō ðē ic hōf sāwle mīne, Ps. Srt. 85, 4. Hebbað eówer mōd tō him, Bt. 42 ; F. 258, 22. (3) *to lift and carry, bear* to or from :—Þā apostolas hōfon Marian līchoman ūp and hine āsetton on neorxna wanges gefeán, Bl. H. 157, 33. Hōfon hine wītigan ūp tō ēðle, Sat. 460. Hȳ hine hōfun on þā heán lyft, Gū. 383. Him wæs hafen beód tō, Bd. 3, 6 ; Sch. 209, 13. II. *intrans. To rise, mount :—*Hē stāh ūp tō ðām stēpele and of ðām stēpele hōf upp on lyfte, swylce hē wolde wið þæs heofones weard, Wlfst. 100, 3. Hefe ūp ofer heofenas *exaltare super caelos,* Ps. Srt. 56, 6, 12. v. ā-, æt-, ge-, in-, ofer-, oferā-, on-, oþ-, under-hebban.

**hebbe.** v. ūp-hebbe ; **hebba :** **hebbendlic.** *Add.* v. ofer-hebbendlic : **hebbing.** v. ūp-hebbing : **hec.** v. fōdder-hec ; **hæc,** *and see N. E. D.* heck.

**hēcen,** es ; *n. A kid :—*Nime ǽghwylc hīwrǽden of ǽlcum hūse ān lamb . . . æfter þām ylcan gewunan nymað þ hēcyn, Angl. viii. 322, 10. Assan oððe hēcenu (*printed* netenu, Lch. iii. 198, 9) gesihð gylt ceápes hit getācnað *asinos uel edos uiderit, crimen negotii significat,* Archiv cxxv. 48, 13. ¶ in place-names :—On hēcenes hangran, C. D. iv. 49, 11. [*' Mndl.* hoekijn *Böckchen von Schafen und Ziegen : mnd.* hoken.' *See* Jord. p. 140.]

**hecg, hegg,** e ; *f. A hedge, fence :—*In ðā hegce wið westan ðā cotu ; ondlonges hegce, C. D. iii. 52, 25. Æt ðǽre lange hegge ænde, 385, 7. Bebbanburh wæs ǽrost mid hegge betȳned, and þǣr æfter mid wealle, Chr. 547; P. 16, 20. [*O. H. Ger.* hecka, hegga : *Ger.* hecke.] Cf. hæg, hege, *and next word.*

**hecge,** an ; *f. A place provided with a hedge* (?), *an enclosure ; a fence* (?), *hedge :—*On Beówanhammes hecgan . . . tō ðǽre rūwan hecgan, C. D. ii. 172, 28, 32. Tō rūgan hegcan ; swā andlang hegerǽwe, 137, 14. Ǽrest of þām gāran innan þā blacan hegcean ; of þǽre hegcean innan þone fūlan brōc, C. D. B. ii. 259, 7. Cf. haga *and preceding word.*

**hēdan.** *Add:* I. *to take charge or possession of* (*with gen.*). (1) the object a person :—Gif hē næbbe mǽgburg, hēden his þā gefān, Ll. Th. i. 148, 19. (2) the object a thing. [Hml. Th. ii. 114, 33 : Exod. 583 : Ll. Th. i. 436, 9 : Hml. Th. i. 330, 31 *in Dict.*] II. *to have a care for, take notice of* (*with gen.*) [B. 2697 : Ll. Th. ii. 316, 30 : Hml. Th. iv. 534, 16 *in Dict.*] III. *to care for, take notice of* (*with acc.*) [Hml. Th. i. 116, 4 *in Dict.*] IV. *to take care* that (*with clause*) :—Hēde se ðe scīre healde þ hē friðige and forðige ælce be ðām ðe hit sēlest sȳ, Angl. ix. 259, 13. V. *to observe, take note of* (*gen.*) :—Næs him nā þe sēl þæs þe hē georne hēdde, ne mihte hē þǣr nænne geseón þe hē gecnāwan cūþe, Hml. S. 23, 638. Gelamp hit þ sume hlosniende menn ðǣr betweónan eódon and þisra seofona georne hēddon, 137.

**hēdd-ern.** *Add :* , hēd-ern *a store-room :—*Būton hit under þæs wīfes cǽglocan gebrōht wǽre . . . ac þǣra cǽgan heó sceal weardian ; þæt is hire hēddernes cǽge and hyre cyste cǽge and hire sticel(?), Ll. Th. i. 418, 21 note. On kycenan oþþe on hēderne (*cellario*) oþþe on mynstres bǽcerne, R. Ben. 71, 17 : R. Ben. I. 82, 2. Hwā gefylþ cleafan

(*cellaria*) his oþþe hědderna (-e, Coll. M. 28, 17 : *promptuaria*) būton cræfte mīnon (*the salter's*)?, Wrt. Voc. i. 9, 23. v. melu-hēdern.

heden *an overcoat, a mantle, cloak* :—Heden *casla*, Wrt. Voc. ii. 103, 25 : 13, 56 : *gunna*, 110, 19. Crūsne (*q. v.*) *vel* heden *cocula*, 135, 39 : 136, 49. þurh lārēwlicum basincge, hedene, scicelse *magistri mēlote*, An. Ox. 1471. ¶ *in the gloss* : *mastruga* hæðen, Wrt. Voc. ii. 59, 30, *perhaps* hæðen, *not* hæðen (= heden) *should be taken. In* Isid. Orig. mastruca *is explained as* 'vestis Sardonica ex pelliculis ferarum', *and* hæðen *might refer* (?) *to* Sardonica.

hědend-líc ; *adj. Captious, sophistical* :—Of hæftlicon and hēdendlicum (hyndenlicum, An. Ox. 3028) betynungum *captiosis conclusionibus*, Hpt. Gl. 481, 63.

hēdendlíce ; *adv. Captiously* ; captiose, Wrt. Voc. ii. 128, 32.

hēf. v. hyf : hefalsian. v. eofulsian (yfelsian).

hefe. *Add* : I. *the property of being heavy* :—Ænne swer ormætes hefes, Hml. S. 31, 1248. Se hālga gāst hī heóld and mid hefe gefæstnode, þ þā mānfullan ne mihton þ mǽden ástyrian, 9, 98. God is būtan hefe and hē ealle gesceafta gelōgode on gemete, and on getele, and on hefe, Hml. Th. i. 286, 12–15. **I a.** *weight in a high degree* :—Hefe wæstma brycð bōh *pondus fructuum frangit ramum*, Scint. 85, 4. **II.** *figuratively.* (I) *oppressive effect* or *influence* :—þonne gehwylce synfulle menn ōðre geólǽcað, and mid gegaderodun hefe þǽre wyrstan lyffetunge ofðriccað, Hml. Th. 494, 4. (2) *importance* :—Hefe *mole* (*virtutes amplas, quae modulum et numerum excedunt pro mole gestorum*, Ald. 159, 21. **III.** *a heavy mass of material, a burden* :—Hefe *gleba* (*spurci glebula ruris*, Ald. 140, 34), An. Ox. 18 b, 41. Hefe *fasce*, i. *onere*, Wülck. Gl. 234, 21. Hefe gehefdum *mole grauatis*, 251, 16. Hefe mole (*ingentis scopuli mole connexas*, Ald. 68, 12). Ne ðā gēt . . . ahefegum (an hefegum?) hefe ásette wǽron *necdum montes gravi mole constiterant*, Kent. Gl. 265. **IV.** *a weight* as measure :—Hefe *pondus* (*abominatio est apud Deum pondus et pondus*, Prov. 20, 23), Kent. Gl. 752. Getelum, hefum *numeris, ponderibus*, Wülck. Gl. 250, 25. Hefum *minis*, i. *talentis*, Germ. 396, 122.

-hefed. v. ge-hefed : -hefedness. v. on-hefedness.

hefe-full ; *adj. Grievous* :—Sy hē āna wuniende mid dǽdbōte and hefefulre hreówesunge *solus sit persistens in poenitentie luctu*, R. Ben. 49, 18.

hefeld. For '*m.* (?)' *substitute n., and add* :—Hebeld *licium*, Wrt. Voc. ii. 113, 5. Hefeld, 51, 13. Hefelda *liciorum* (*filis flamma combustis*), An. Ox. 3550. Hefeldum *liciis*, 7, 256. Heueldun, 4, 65. ¶ Hebild *seems a mistake for* hebild-gerd *in the gloss* hebild *liciatorium*, Txts. 74, 602. Cf. hebelgerd, 75, 1219. [*v. N.E.D.* heald, heddle. *O. L. Ger.* hebild *licium* : cf. *Icel.* hafald ; *n. the perpendicular thrums that hold the weft.*]

hefeld-gyrd. *Substitute* : hefeld-gird, e ; *f. A weaver's beam* :—Hebelgerd *liciatorium* (*the word is glossed by* hebild, 74, 602), Txts. 75, 1219. Hefeldgyrd, Wrt. Voc. ii. 51, 3. (For *liciatorium* v. i. Sam. 17, 7.)

hefeldian. *Add* :—Wæs heueldad, ongunnen *ordiretur*, Hpt. Gl. 494, 11. v. ge-hefeldian.

hefeld-prǽd. *Add* :—Hebeldðrēd *licia*, Wrt. Voc. ii. 113, 6. Hefeldprǽde, 51, 12. Hefeldprǽdum *liciis*, 82, 47 : An. Ox. 3545.

hefe-lic. *Add* : **I.** *of fighting, heavy* (cf. hefig ; III), *with great bodies of troops*, Chr. 868 ; P. 70, 1 (*in Dict.*). **II.** *grave, serious* :—Hefolices gyltes *gravioris culpe*, R. Ben. I. 56, 17. **III.** *hard to bear, grievous, oppressive* :—Geweard swīðe hefelic and swīðe wōlberendlic geár, Chr. 1086 ; P. 217, 27. þ hit him hefelic ne beó, Lch. iii. 282, 10. þæt heom hefelice ne þince þǽs þing, Angl. viii. 321, 43, 1083 ; P. 215, 25 (*in Dict.*). **IV.** *hard to do, laborious* :—Gif hwylcum brēþer hwæt hefelices and unácumenlices (*aliqua gravia aut impossibilia*) beboden sy, R. Ben. 128, 10. **V.** *causing sorrow* or *distress, grievous* :—Swīðe hefelic (or *at* III ?) geár and swīðe swincfull and sorhfull geár, Chr. 1085 ; P. 217, 17. **VI.** *overpowering to the senses* :—Ne cymð þǽr sorh ne sār ne ǽnig geswinc ne hungor ne ðurst ne hefelic slǽp, Wlfst. 139, 27.

hefelíce. *Add* : **I.** *grievously, seriously* :—Sió stillness oft swīðe hefelíce (*gravius*) dered hira ingeðonce, Past. 351, 6. Oðre syngodon hefelícor þonne þū, Wlfst. 299, 3 : Past. 313, 3 (*in Dict.*). **II.** *with slow action of mind or body, dully*, Mt. 13, 15 (*in Dict.*). **III.** *severely, in a way that is hard to bear* :—Hefelícor steóre (†) styðlícor stīre hē sī underþeód *districtiori discipline subdatur*, R. Ben. I. 65, 3. **IV.** *sadly, mournfully* :—Hefelíce *lugubriter*, Wrt. Voc. ii. 53, 50. v. hefiglíce.

heffere. v. heáhfore.

hefig. *Add* : **I.** *of great weight, ponderous* :—Mid rōde tācne gewǽpnod, nā mid reádum scylde, oððe mid hefegum helme, oþþe heardre byrnan, Hml. Th. ii. 502, 12. Wiht hafað hefigne steort, Rä. 59, 7. **I a.** fig. :—Hiá gebindas byrðenna hefiga (hæfige, R.) in scyldrum monna, Mt. L. 23, 4. **II.** *of great specific gravity, dense* :—þ leóhte fyr ūp gewīt, and sió hefige eorþe sit þǽr niþere *ut*

*pendulus ignis surgat in altum terraeque graves pondere sidant*, Bt. 39, 13 ; F. 234, 12 : Met. 29, 53. Wā dǽm ðe gaderað an hine selfne ðæt hefige fenn . . . Ðæt is ðæt mon gadrige ðæt ðicke fenn . . . *vae ei qui aggravat contra se densum lutum. Contra se densum lutum aggravare est* . . ., Past. 329, 18. Sió eorþe is hefigre and þiccre þonne ōþra gesceafta, Bt. 33, 4 ; F. 130, 19 : Met. 20, 133. Hefigere ic eom þonne se hāra stān, Rä. 41, 74. **III.** *of fighting where many troops are engaged.* Cf. hefelic ; I :—Būtan hefigum gefeohte and blōdgyte *sine ullo proelio ac sanguine*, Bd. 1, 3 ; Sch. 15, 2. **IV.** *weighty, important* :—Ðā ðe hefigo (hæfigra, R.) aron ðæs ǽs *quae graviora sunt legis*, Mt. L. 23, 23. **V.** *grave, severe, serious, deep, profound.* (I) in a good sense :—Sié in ðǽr hefig giwoednise *sit in ea gravis lenitas*, Rtl. 105, 1. Sceomfullnis hefig *verecundia gravis*, 110, 3. (2) in an unfavourable sense :—Hū hefig þ dysig is ðe ðā earman men gedwelaþ, Bt. 32, 3 ; F. 118, 6 : Met. 19, 1. Āhrede mē hefiges nīðes feónda mīnra *eripe me de inimicis meis*, Ps. Th. 58, 1. Gyf hwā hwylce hefige yfelnysse on his hofe geseó, Lch. i. 248, 11. Sace hefige *litem gravem* (Archiv cxxv. 49, 47), Lch. iii. 198, 24 (*in Dict.*). Sint folces firena hefige, Gen. 2410. Ðā ðe ǽfellað on hefegum scyldum (cf. on micla scylda, 7) *qui gravibus noxis immerguntur*, Past. 437, 3. Wið hefigum synnum, Angl. viii. 320, 1. Hī habbaþ sum yfel hefigre and frēcendlicre þonne ǽnig wīte sié, Bt. 38, 3 ; F. 200, 27. þā hefegastan *gravissimam* (*valetudinem*), An. Ox. 4348. **VI.** *having the aspect of heaviness, thick* mist, fog, cloud, &c. :—Tōdrīf þone þiccan mist þe hangode hefig and þystre, Met. 20, 266. **VII.** *slow, dull* :—Hefig is hearta folces ðisses *incrassatum est cor populi hujus*, Mt. L. 13, 15. Ðæt hefige mōd glīt niðor and niðor *desidiosa mens in lapsum casus impellitur*, Past. 279, 2. **VIII.** *of persons.* (I) *troublesome, oppressive* :—Wæs hē nāwiht hefig his yldrum *nullius molestiae parentibus fuit*, Guth. Gr. 107, 22. Nælle ðū mē hefig (*molestus*) wosa, Lk. L. R. 11, 7. Hefig is mē ðiós widwe, 18, 5. Huæd hir hefigo (hefge, R. *molesti*) gié sint?, Mk. L. 14, 6. (2) *expressing strong disapproval.* Cf. colloquial *to be down on* a person or thing :—Tō hwon syndon gē þyses weorces swā hefige?, Bl. H. 69, 15. **IX.** *hard to bear, onerous, burdensome, oppressive, grievous* :—Wæs hit on ǽlce wīsan hefig tyma, for ðām þe hī nǽfre heora yfeles geswicon, Chr. 1001 ; P. 133, 30. Carfull, hefi *scrupulosa* (*ecclesiastici regiminis sollicitudo*) An. Ox. 5429. Hwelc wīte sceal ūs tō hefig ðyncan *quae poena gravis est* ?, Past. 255, 3. þeáh hit nū hefig seó . . þeáh hit biþ gesǽlþ gif hit mon geðyldilíce ārǽfnþ, Bt. 11, 1 ; F. 32, 30. Hū hefig sorg men beoþ seó gēmen his bearna, 31, 1 ; F. 112, 17. Gif þ riht tō hefig sy, sēce hē þā līhtinge tō þām cynge, Ll. Th. i. 266, 11. **I.** 'Mē þincað þā bebodu swīðe hefige.' **G.** 'Mē ne þincð nānwiht hefig ðes þe man lufað.' **I.** 'Ne þincð mē nān geswinc hefig, gif ic habbe þ ðæt ic æfter swince', Solil. H. 25, 26–26, 2. Hefig sār, 40, 9. Hē sceolde cuman tō hefegum martyrdōme *ad martyrii tormenta ducebatur*, Past. 53, 21. Be þǽre hæfegan gēmenne bearna, Bt. 31, 1 ; F. 112, 19. Hefig geoc hē beslēpte on ealle, 16, 4 ; F. 58, 16 : Met. 9, 55. Swǽre hæftnēd hefige, Ps. Th. 125, 1. Mōdsorge hefige, Gū. 1025. þā myclan byrþenne and þā hefian āberan þǽre myclan langunga, Bl. H. 135, 8. Gebūrgerihta syn mislice, gehwǽr hy syn hefige (*onerose*), gehwǽr medeme (*leviores aut medie*), Ll. Th. i. 434, 4. Hefigra wīta, Gū. 857. Ðeós landlagu stǽnt on suman lande, gehwǽr hit is hefigre (*gravior*), gehwǽr leóhtre (*levior*), Ll. Th. i. 434, 30. Helle wīte þæt him hefegore ys, Ælfc. T. Grn. 21, 23. Māran and hefigran frēcennesse wyrðe, Bt. 22 1 ; F. 76, 16. Beóð þy hefigran heortan þenne, Wand. 49. **X.** *hard to perform, difficult, requiring exertion, laborious, toilsome* :—Hefig ł uneáðe *difficile*, Lk. L. 18, 24 : Mt. L. 19, 23. Hū hefig and hū earfoþe þis is eall tō gereccanne *quanti oneris est*, Bt. 39, 4 ; F. 216, 32. Mec sorg bicwōm, hefig hondgewinn, Jul. 526. Ðynceað him sumu weorc suīðe hefug (hefgu, *v. l.*) *quaedam sibi difficilia opponit*, Past. 285, 1. Hefigast gewinna, þæt hī mid welerum geworht habbað *labor labiorum ipsorum*, Ps. Th. 139, 9. **XI.** *causing sorrow* :—Hē fond his mondryhten ādlwērigne : him þæt in gefeól hefig æt heortan, hygesorge wæg, micle mōdceare, Gū. 982. **XII.** *oppressive to the bodily senses, overpowering* :—Hefies *ferrei* (the passage is : Ferreus lethi somnus, Ald. 80, 19), An. Ox. 2, 487 : 5481. Ðeós wyrt hafað hefigne smæc, Lch. i. 264, 20. **XIII.** *weighed down.* (I) with care, trouble, &c. (a) *feeling trouble* :—Alle gē ðā ðe winnes and hefege gē aron *omnes qui laboratis et onerati estis*, Mt. L. 11, 28. (b) *expressing sorrow* :—Mē is swǽre stefn, hefig, gnorniende *a voce gemitus mei*, Ps. Th. 101, 4. Hē sealde hine sylfne in hefige cwīðnesse *sese in gravibus lamentationibus dedit*, Gr. D. 120, 7. (2) with sleep, weariness, &c. :—Woeron ēgo hiora hefigo *erant oculi illorum ingrauati*, Mk. L. R. 14, 40. v. þurh-hefig.

hefig *action as of a heavy body, force, violence* :—All in þ hefig wyrcas *omnis in illud uim facit*, Lk. L. 16, 16.

hefige. *Add* : **I.** *with difficulty* :—Swīðe uneáðe ł hefige ðā ðe gestrióne habbas in rīce Godes ingāð *quam difficile qui pecunias habent in regnum Dei introibunt*, Mk. R. 10, 23. Hefge, Lk. R. 18, 24. **II.** *with slow or reluctant action, under pressure* :—Gāst

nēd ꝉ hefia (nēde, R.) fearras *spiritus uix discedit*, Lk. L. 9, 39. **III.** *grievously, painfully*, Ps. Th. 57, 2 (*in Dict.*). [*O. H. Ger.* hebigo *grave, sublime.*]

**hefigian.** *Add:* **I.** *intrans.* *To become heavy.* (1) *to increase in weight :*—Se wǣta āsīgð tó ꝥǣm lime, ꝺonne āswilð hit and hefegað, Past. 72, 10. (2) *of disease, to grow worse :*—Hefiendre (hefigende, *v. l.*) þǣre ādle *ingravescente molestia*, Gr. D. 297, 14. **II.** *trans.* *To make heavy* or *dull, to weary :*—Þý lǣs ic lengc þone þanc hefige þára leornendra mid gesegenum þára fremdra tǣlnysse *ne sensus legentium prolixae sententiae molesta defensio obnubilet*, Guth. Gr. 102, 31. [*O. H. Ger.* ge-hebigón.] v. a-, ge-hefigian.

**hefig-líc.** *Add:* **I.** *of fighting, heavy :*—Nán hefilic gefeoht ne weard, Chr. 868; P. 71, 2. **II.** *grave, deep, profound :*—Hefiglices gedwolan *erroris*, Past. 367, 19. v. hefe-líc.

**hefig-líce.** *Add:* **I.** *sluggishly, dully :*—Mið eárum hefiglíce (*graviter*) gehērdon, Mt. L. R. 13, 15. **II.** *with grief, displeasure,* or *anger :*—Þá hǣðenan weras his word hefiglíce (*moleste*) onfēngcon, Gr. D. 250, 20. Hefiglíce *dure*, Gen. 21, 11 (*in Dict.*). Fela sprǣc se Hǣlend and hefiglíce be rícum; ac hē hí eft gefrēfrode, Hml. Th. ii. 328, 2. **III.** *vehemently, deeply, intensely :*—On langre lengtenādle hefiglíce swenced (*graviter vexatus*), Bd. 3, 12; Sch. 243, 8. Ongunnun ꝺá ǣgieáwan hefiglíce (hefi-, *v. l.*) him āgēn stondan (*grauiter insistere*) *the scribes began to urge him vehemently*, Lk. (W. S., L., R.) 11, 53. Þ þte swiþe hefiglíce beswicþ þára monna mód, Bt. 18, 1; F. 60, 21. Sió stilnes swiðe hefiglíce (*gravius*) dereð hiora ingeðonce, Past. 350, 6. Hē ofermódegað innan micle ꝺy hefiglícor *graviter interius superbitur*, 312, 3. v. hefe-líce.

**hefig-mód.** *Substitute:* **I.** *having an oppressive disposition, troublesome, vexatious.* v. hefig; **VIII.** 1 :—Hefigmóde hí wǣron mē *molesti erant mihi*, Ps. Spl. T. 54, 3. **II.** *sad-hearted, having a heavy heart.* v. hefig; **XIII.** 1 a :—Þǣr (*in heaven*) him nǣfre ne hingrað, ne hē hefigmód ne bið, Nap. 36.

**hefig-ness.** *Add:* **I.** *oppressiveness, burdensomeness :*—Synna ūsra hefignesse uē bioðn āðryhto *peccatorum nostrorum pondere premimur*, Rtl. 51, 23. Hū ꝺu gehǣled beón miht fram þysse ādle hefignesse (hefi-, *v. l.*) *quomodo cureris ab huius molestia langoris*, Bd. 3, 12; Sch. 243, 16. Ne þincð mē nán geswinc hefig, gyf ic geseó and habbe þæt ꝺæt ic æfter swince. Ac se tweónung wyrcað þá hefinesse, Solil. H. 26, 3. Wē bēron hefignise (*pondus*) ꝺæs dæges and hǣto, Mt. L. 20, 12. **I a.** *a trouble; a difficult matter :*—Hū ne witon wē þ nán nearewnes ne nán earfoþu ne nán unrótnes ne nán sár ne nán hefignes nis nán gesǣlð? *nam non esse anxiam, tristemque beatitudinem, nec doloribus, molestiisque subjectam quid attinet dicere?*, Bt. 24, 4; F. 86, 21. Gif hwilcum brēðer ǣnig hefines ... beóð geþeódde *si cui fratri aliqua gravia ... injunguntur*, R. Ben. I. 114, 5. **II.** *oppressed condition of body* or *senses, want of animation, dullness :*—Þu cwǣde þ ic hæfde forgiten þ gód þ ic oninnan mē hæfde for ꝺæs líchoman hefignesse *quod memoriam corporea contagione pressus amisi*, Bt. 35, 2; F. 156, 16. Seó sául þá hwíle þe heó on þám lícuman byð ne mæg God geseón swá swá heó wilnað for þæs lícuman hefenesse and gedrēfednesse, Solil. H. 29, 14. **II a.** *disease :*—Ðe ilca ūsra untrymnise ꝉ hefignise gebær *ipse nostras aegrotationes portavit*, Mt. L. 8, 17. **III.** *oppression :*—Ðreátuncg ꝉ hefignise ꝺǣra byrðenra *invitatio* (cf. geþreátod and genīded *invitus*, genīddan *invitant*, Wrt. Voc. ii. 44, 59–60) *oneratorum*, Mt. p. 16, 12.

**hefig-tíme.** *Add:* **I.** *heavy, weighed down :*—Hefitýme *grauidum*, Germ. 402, 53. **II.** *weighty, of great importance, serious :*—Ðence se abbod hū mycele byrðene and hū hefigtýme hē underfēncg mid ꝺǣm háde *abba cogitet quale onus suscepit*, R. Ben. 118, 19. **III.** *grave* (*offence, &c.*), *severe, serious in its effects :*—Hū micel wíte is and hú hefigtýme þæt man on āmánsumunge sié *quanta pena sit excommunicationis*, R. Ben. 54, 1 : 48, 10. Hit byþ swiðe hefigtýme gylt *grave delictum est*, 138, 26. For swǣrum and hefigtýmum (heálicum, R. Ben. I. 78, 8) gylte *pro gravi culpa*, 70, 3. Þurh swiðe hefigtýme hunger þe þisne eard swíðe gedrehte, Chr. 1096; P. 233, 4. Oft hit getímað þæt swýþe hefigtýme sacu and ungeþwǣrnessa (*scandala gravia*) on mynstre āspringað, R. Ben. 124, 3. Be hefigtýmum gyltum *de gravioribus culpis*, 49, 12, 14. **IV.** *of persons, oppressive, annoying, troublesome :*—Hefigtýme hig wǣron mē *molesti erant mihi*, Ps. L. 54, 4. **V.** *of things, hard to bear, grievous; in a weaker sense, tedious.* (1) *used attributively :*—Hē geðafað þæt ꝺá árleásan his hálgan ꝺearle geswencað mid hefigtýmre ehtnysse, Hml. Th. i. 574, 23. Án licgende mǣden on langsumre sáre ꝺurh hefigtýmum heáfodece (cf. *per integrum annum intolerabili capitis dolore vexata*, Vit. Cuth. c. 30), ii. 150, 5. (2) *used predicatively, where the source of trouble is given,* (a) *by a noun* (or *pronoun*) :—Weard his líf swíðe hefigtýme ꝺám gebróðrum, ac hí hit forbǣron for his bróðer gódnysse, Hml. Th. i. 534, 5. Þæt hit (þis godspel, 21) tó hefigtýme ne ðince þám heorcnigendum, ii. 72, 23. (b) *by a clause* or *pronoun representing one :*—Þincð ūs hefigtýme þ wē him gehýrsumian, Hml. A. 6, 134. Him hefigtýme wæs þ hí hine gesāwon, 75, 74. God gelácnað his

gecorenra gyltas mid mislicum brocum; and þeáh ꝺe hit hefigtýme sý ꝺám ꝺrowigendum, Hml. Th. i. 472, 19. (c) *by a dat. infin. :*—Þúhte nē hefigtíme þē tó tiþienne þæs, Ælfc. Gen. Thw. 1, 6. Hit is láð and hefitýme lǣwedum folce tó gehíranne ... hwæt on ꞌhálgum bócum áwriten is, Wlfst. 304, 15. ¶ *of a period in which weather or other conditions are unfavourable :*—On þám tíman wæs swiðe hefigtíme wynter, and se mere wæs mid forste oferþeaht, Hml. S. 11, 142. Ðis wæs swiðe hefigtíme geár ǣgðer ge þurh mænigfealde gylda and eác þurh hefigtýme hunger, Chr. 1096; P. 233, 3. Eall þ geár wæs swíðe hefigtíme on manegum þingum and mislicum, ge on unwæderum, ge on eorðwæstmum, and mycel orfes wæs þæs geáres forfaren, 1041 ; P. 163, 11. **VI.** *oppressive to the senses* or *faculties :*—Nis crístenum monnum nán ðing swá hefigtýme swá swá oferfyl. Be ðám se Hǣlend clypað, ꞌWarniað þæt eówere heortan ne sýn ofersýmedeꞌ (*grauentur*) mid oferfylle,ꞌ R. Ben. 63, 21. v. hefe-tíme.

**hefigtím-ness.** *Add :*—Náne ūs lífes cwylmige hefigtēmnessa *nulla nos vitæ crucient molesta*, Hy. S. 143, 10. Út ānýddum wæteres hefigtēmnyssum *pulsis aquæ molestiis*, 19, 31.

**hefli** (*for* be-héflic) *useful;* commodum, An. Ox. 56, 190.

**-hefness.** v. úp-hefness : **hefung.** *Dele:* heg (*l.* hēg). v. híg : **hēgan** *to exalt.* v. hígan : **-hēgan** *to hold a meeting.* v. ge-hēgan, mæþel-hēgende.

**hege.** *Dele second example, for which see* **hecg**, *and add :*—Tó ꝺǣm mǣrhege; ondlong ꝺæs mǣres heges, C. D. iii. 32, 30. Tó bysceopes swýnhege; ondlong heges, 77, 11 : 78, 6. Oð ꝺone cwichege; súð andlang heges, 380, 13. Longan mēd iacit be norðan hege, ii. 26, 27. Tó ꝺám ráhhege; æfter ꝺam hege á be ꝺám ófre, iii. 77, 29. Æfter ꝺám ealdan hege tó ꝺáre grēnne æc, 274, 34. On Wiferꝺes mǣduan hege; of ꝺám hege, 78, 21. Tó ꝺám mǣrhege; of ꝺám hege on Sæfern, 79, 13. Stǣnenum hæge útaþýdum *maceriae depulsae*, Ps. L. 61, 4. Gehega þíne eáran mid þornigum hege *sepi aures tuas spinis*, Wlfst. 246, 9. Of línaceran innan þone hege; æfter þám hege, Cht. E. 239, 11. On hína hege; of hína hege, C. D. iii. 461, 32. Gewunode án þeóf þ hē stáh ofer þone hege *fur consueverat per sepem ascendere*, Gr. D. 23, 24. Hē stáh upp on þone hege *ascendit sepem*, 24, 21. Hyrdel, hege *cratem*, i. *flecta*, Wrt. Voc. ii. 136, 51. Hegas *crates*, 105, 49 : 15, 47. Hegum *sepibus*, Germ. 401, 15. Ne læg ǣldeoðig man wiðútan mínum hegum, ac mín dura geopenode symle wegfērendum *foris non mansit peregrinus, ostium meum viatori patuit* (Job. 31, 32), Hml. Th. ii. 448, 22. ꞌFar geond wegas and hegasꞌ ... Hē hēt faran tó wegum and hegum getācnigende þæt wilde folc þe hē gegaderode of eallum middanearde, 376, 13–19. Deós wyrt byþ cenned wið hegas, Lch. i. 226, 2. Á hē mæig findan hwæt hē mæig on byrig bētan ... hegas gódian, Angl. ix. 262, 20. [Ælfred fērde lutigende geond heges and weges, geond wudes and feldes, swá þ hē becóm tó Æðelingége, Shrn. 16, 11. v. *N. E. D.* hay.] v. ꞌ æcer-, burg-, cwic- (C. D. iii. 180, 12), deór-, fearn- (C. D. iii. 54, 26), gemǣr(e)- (v. ge-mǣre ; **II.** ¶ *where add* gemǣr-hege, C. D. vi. 234, 1), mǣr-, ráh-, snǣd-, stán-, swín-, tyrig-, wyrttún-hege ; hæg, hecg, haga.

**hege-clife.** *Add :*—Reád clæfre ... hegeclife, Lch. ii. 312, 20 : iii. 12, 30. Hegeclifan leáf, 58, 27. Genim hegeclifan, ii. 54, 8.

**hegegian.** v. hegian.

**hege-hymele,** an ; *f. Hedge* (or *wild*) *hop plant :*—Cicena mete *muronis*, hegehymele *humblonis*, Wrt. Voc. i. 69, 27–28. Þis is seó grēne sealf ... brócminte and óþre mintan, cicena mete, hegehymele, Lch. iii. 6, 8–15.

**hege-rǣwe.** *l.* -rǣw, *and add :*—Andlang hegerǣwe, C. D. iii. 388, 24. Andlang ꝺǣre hegerǣwe, 461, 23. Ollung þǣre hegreáwe, Swt. Rdr. ii. 203, 4, 5. Innan þá hegreáwe, 9. In ꝺá hegreáwe ; æfter þǣre heghreáwe, Cht. E. 239, 2. On Dæneheardes hegerǣwe, C. D. ii. 54, 11. Hegerǣwe, v. 71, 7.

**hege-rife.** *Add: hairif* (*N. E. D.*) :—Wiþ cneówwærc, wuduweaxe and hegerife, Lch. ii. 66, 11 : 140, 3. Wyl æscrinde, ... hegerife, marubian ... and þ líc gníd mid þǣre hegerifan. Wyrc sealfe of marubian, ... hegerifan, 78, 11–16. Hegerifan corn, 344, 11. Genim hegerifan, 76, 11 : iii. 16, 16. Wyl hegerifan, ii. 342, 2. Wyl hegerifan ufewearde, iii. 38, 25.

**hege-ságol,** es ; *m. A hedge-stake :*—Weard his óðer fót be his scó fæst on ánum hegesáhle (on ánum ságle þæs geardes, *v. l. in sude sepis*), Gr. D. 24, 28.

**heges-sugge.** v. hege-sugge.

**hege-stæf** (heg-), es ; *m. A bar used to stop an opening in a fence* (?) :—Hegstæf *clatrum* (= ? κλεῖθρον *a bar, bolt; Latin* clathri, clatri *a trellis, grate*), Wrt. Voc. ii. 131, 67. Cf. Dorebar *clatrus*, i. 203, 35. Barre *clatrus*, 237, 34.

**hege-steall,** es ; *m. The site of a hedge* (?), *a place with a hedge* (?) (cf. *Haystall* a small portion of wood on the outskirts of a large wood (in Herefordshire), Halliw. Dict.) :—Æfter ꝺám hegestealle, C. D. iii. 391, 10. v. geard-steall.

**hege-stów,** e ; *f. A place with a hedge :*—On ꝺá hegestówe ufewardre; ondlong hegstówe, C. D. iii. 213, 9. In ꝺá hegestówe ; andlong

ǽre hegestówe, 263, 28. On ðá aldan hegestówe; and syððan á ondlang ðǽre ealdan hegestówe on ðone folchearpað, 393, 13. On ðá hegstówe; of ðǽre hegstówe, 77, 27. Ofer ðǽre strǽte in ðá hegestówe, 263, 25.

**hege-sugge**, an; f. *A hedge sparrow :*—Hegesugge *cicada, ŭicetula,* Wülck. Gl. 131, 34. [*N. E. D.* hay-sugge.] v. hæg-sugga.

**hege-þorn** (?) *hawthorn, haythorn* (v. *N. E. D.* hawthorn). *The word seems to occur in the compound* hegeðonhyrs (*l.* (?) hegeðornhyrst), C. D. i. 261, 8. v. hæg-þorn.

**hege-weg**, es; m. *A road that runs between hedges :*—Andlang heges on ðane brádan hegewai, C. D. iii. 380, 13. Cf. weall-weg.

**hég-hús.** v. híg-hús.

**hegian, hegegian** *to hedge, fence :*—Hega éaran þíne mid þornum *sepi aures tuas spinis,* Scint. 80, 3. Á hé mæig findan hwæt hé mæig on byrig bétan . . . grép hegiau, dícsceard bétan, Angl. ix. 262, 19. Geneát sceal . . . burh hegegian (v. burg-hege), Ll. Th. i. 432, 16. v. ge-, ymb-hegian; hagian.

**hég-síþe.** v. híg-síþe: **heg-stæf.** v. hege-stæf: **heg-stów.** hege-stów: **héh-faro.** v. heáh-fore: **héhþu.** v. híhþu.

**hel, hæl** (?, for form cf. tæl, tel), es; m. *A hidden spot* (?), *a shelter* (?) :—Tó Dudemǽres hele; of Dudemǽres hele, C. D. vi. 171, 5 : 76, 26. On Ecgerdes hel ufeweardne, iii. 48, 16. [Cf. From her frendes hy stelen And gon to wode and maken hem helen, And crepen thereinne, Alis. 4959. Heal *a hidden spot; a shelter,* D. D.]

**hel** (?) *a pretext. Substitute :* hél, es; m. *Calumny, a false charge :*—Ne teó ic N. ne for hete ne for hóle (héle, *v. l.*) . . . and ic sylf tó sóðe talige þ hé mínes orfes þeóf wǽre, Ll. Th. i. 180, 11. þá geréfan rýpað þá earman bútan ǽlcere scylde . . . and mid yfelan hélan earnne men beswicað (*they defraud the wretched folk with wicked false charges*), ii. 320, 18. v. hól.

**hel, hell, helle,** e; f. *Substitute:* **hel, hell, hyll,** e; f.: **helle,** es; m. *In* l. 22 *for* ǽfengife *l.* ǽfengifi, *and add:* I. *the lower world, the abode of the dead.* (1) in Jewish and Christian use:—' Leófe dohtor gif ǽnig andgyt sý on helle lǽt þú þæt cwicsúslene hús '. Dæt mǽden ðá forð eóde . . . and cwæð : ' Dionisia, hál wes þú, ic grǽte þé nú of helle gecíged ', Ap. Th. 26, 11–16. Dryhten from helle ástág, Gú. 1077. Hí sculon gán libbende on helle (*in infernum*), Past. 429, 24 : Ps. Spl. 54, 16. Hafað se hálga helle bereáfod, Cri. 558. (2) in classical mythology :—þǽre helle hund . . . þæs nama wæs Ceruerus, Bt. 35, 6 ; F. 168, 15. Of helle *ex herebo,* Wrt. Voc. ii. 97, 37 : 31, 67. II. *the abode of the fallen angels, the place of punishment of the wicked after death :*—Ic wénde þ þ hell (hel, *v. l.*) wǽre be ðám tintregum unárǽfnendlicum ic oft secgan hýrde . . . ' Nis þis seó hell þe þú wénest,' Bd. 5, 12 ; Sch. 617, 11–18. Hwæþer helle sý þe ofer þyssere eorðan þe under þissere eorðan . . . Manige men wénað þ seó hell sý on sumum dǽle þyssere eorðan . . . þ wé hátað helle in gewritum . . . mé is geþúht þ seó ufere hell sý on þissere eorðan, and seó neoþere hell sý under ðissere eorðan, Gr. D. 332, 10–20. Se gífra helle bið á open deófium and þǽm maunum þe nú be his lárum lifiaþ, Bl. H. 61, 12. Heom (*the fallen angels*) wearð hyll gegearwod, Wlfst. 8, 8. Geatt helles *portae inferi,* Mt. L. 16, 18. Tó botme helle þǽre hátan, Gen. 362. þǽre stýlenan helle, Sal. 490. Tó þám (þǽre, *v. l.*) deópan helle, Hml. S. 27, 159. þæs þú in helle scealt werhðo dreógan, B. 588. On þǽre fýrenan helle, Bl. H. 45, 5. Wið þone weallendan bryne þe weallað on helle, Ll. Th. i. 364, 13. In helle (*in inferno*) áhóf ðá ǽgo his mið ðý wǽre in tintergum, Lk. L. 16, 23. Ne sceal nán man wénan þ æalla þá þe on helle beóð habban gelíc wíte, Solil. H. 65, 21. Tó þǽre sweartan helle, Hml. S. 4, 290. Hylle, Sat. 338 : 717. Satan . . . helle forð healdan sceolde, Gen. 348. þá sweartan helle, grǽdige and gífre, 792. Helle, morðorhúsa mǽst, fýres fulle, Cri. 1624. III. *used personally :*—Hell ongeat þ se Scyppeud cwóm, þá heó þ weorud ágeaf, Cri. 1160. Nales hel (*infernus*) ondetteð ðé, Ps. Srt. ii. p. 185, 23. v. níþ-hell.

**héla.** *Add :*—Héla *calcaneus, exterior pars pedis,* Wrt. Voc. ii. 127, 40. Hélan *calce,* 21, 20. þám hélum (cf. ilum, lxxii, 13) ðæt ðæs heáfdes heánnesse *a plantis usque ad uerticem,* Lch. i. lxxiv, 36. Hélan *talos,* lxxi, 11. Heálan, lxxiv, 22. Hí habbað feax oð hélan *habentes comas usque ad talos,* Nar. 35, 3 : 38, 8.

**helabr.** v. heolfor.

**hélade ;** *adj. Having large heels :*—Hélade *calcanosus,* Wrt. Voc. ii. 22, 73. Heálade, 127, 41.

**helan.** *Add :* I. *to prevent something becoming known :*—Hí lǽrdon hira synna, and hí hí nánwuht ne hǽlon (*absconderunt*), Past. 427, 29. Strengre is þ ic morðor hele, scyle mánswara lifian, Cri 193. I a. *with dat. of person to whom something is not made known :*—Míne scylde ic dyde þé cúðe, and míne unrihtwísnysse ic þe ne hæl, Ll. Th. ii. 426, 21. Gif ðú hyt ongitten hæbbe, ne hel hyt mé, Solil. H. 53, 7. Ne mæg ic ðé náuht helan þæs þe ic wát, Bt. 42 ; F. 256, 13 : Gen. 1582 : El. 703. Sió heá lár is betere manegum monnum tó helanne, and feáwum tó secganne, Past. 459, 9. I b. *with preps. to conceal from* (wiþ, fram) :—Ðonne hí he[o]lað (*the o is written*

*above the line*) from monnum (*hominibus occultando*) ðæt hí secggan scoldon, and secgað ðæt hí he[o]lan scoldon, Past. 449, 5. Ne hel ic (*celavi*) mildheortnisse ðíne from gesomnunge micelre, Ps. Srt. 39, 11. þéh þe hé hit fæste wið þá senatus hǽle, Ors. 4, 10 ; S. 196, 16. II. *to keep silence* about :—Ic ne mæg leng helan be þám lífes treó, El. 706. v. ge-helan ; helian.

**hélan** *to calumniate.* v. hoelan *in Dict., and* hólian.

**Helcol** *Hercules :*—Helcol *Alcidis,* Wrt. Voc. ii. 93, 46 : 5, 58. [*The* o *is accented in both instances.*]

**heldan** *to incline.* v. hildan : **helde** *a slope.* v. hilde : **helde** *allegiance. Dele, and see* hyldu.

**helde** *tansy. Add :*—Helde *tanicetum,* An. Ox. 56, 395 : *tenedisse,* Wrt. Voc. i. 68, 24. Genim heldan leáf, Lch. iii. 58, 26.

**hele** *a covering* (?) [Cf. *O. H. Ger.* halu *tegmine* ; helí ; f. *velamentum.*] v. eorþ-hele.

**helerung.** v. heolorung : **helfe.** v. hilfe : **helfling.** *l.* hilfling : **helian.** *Add :* v. á-, be-, for-, ge-, ofer-, un-helian : **heling.** v. ofer-heling.

**hell-cniht,** es ; m. *An infernal servant, a devil as servant :*—Stód se earming ætforan þám árleásan deofle þær hé heálíce sæt mid his hel-cnihtum, Hml. S. 3, 372.

**hell-cund ;** *adj. Infernal, devilish :*—þæt helcunde wered *the host of devils,* Wlfst. 254, 15.

**hell-deófol.** *Add : the god of the infernal regions :*—Heldióbul *Orcus,* Wrt. Voc. ii. 115, 64. Heldeófol, 63, 49. Cf. helle-deófol.

**helle-bryne.** *Add :*—Wið hellebryne beorgan his sáwle, Wlfst. 271, 16 : Ll. Th. i. 318, 20.

**helle-cǽge,** an ; f. [*Under* cǽg *the weak fem.* cǽge *has been incorrectly deleted ; it should be restored*] :—Hé bereð hellecǽgan (cf. seó cǽge, 20) on handa, Verc. Först. 128, 5.

**helle-duru.** *Add :*—Tó þám sweartum tintrehstówum helleduru (tintreges gómum helledures ( = -dores ?), *v. l.*) hí hine gebróhton *ad nefandas tartari fauces perducunt,* Guth. Gr. 131, 185. þonne wendeð Sćs. Petrus fram þære helleduru, and hé belúceð þá helleduru, Verc. Först. 128, 12. On helleduru gelǽded, Bd. 5, 14 ; Sch. 644, 21.

**helle-fýr.** *Add :*—On hwylc gerád is hit tó gelýfanne þ þ líchamlice hellefýr mage geniman þá unlíchamlican wísan þære sáwle ?, Gr. D. 303, 18. Hweþer hit sý tó gelýfanne þ sý án hellefýr (*unus gehennae ignis*) . . . witodlíce án hellefýr is, 333, 13–16. Cwælmed in þǽm mǽstan hellefýre, Wlfst. 218, 15. Hé ne fédde hellefýrum náht lytel synfullne *qui non parvulum peccatorem gehennae ignibus nutrisset,* Gr. D. 290, 4.

**helle-gást.** *Add : a spirit of hell, an infernal spirit :*—þ hé sigor hæfde betwyh þám óþrum hellegástum, Gr. D. 189, 26.

**helle-geat.** *Substitute :*—Úre Hǽlend tóbræc hellegatu . . . And is nú hellegeat belocen rihtwísum mannum, Hml. Th. i. 228, 1–5. *But see* geat, (4).

**helle-god.** *Add :* v. hell-god : **helle-grund.** *Add :* v. hell-grund.

**helle-grut.** *Substitute :* **helle-grutt,** es ; m. or n. *The abyss of hell :*—Hellegrut *baratrum,* i. *infernum,* An. Ox. 689.

**helle-hinca.** *Add :* v. hancettan.

**helle-hús.** *Add :*—Hellehús hafað forclas micle, Verc. Först. 109, 6. þ hellehús is mid swíðe láðlicum gástum áfylled, 112, 2.

**helle-loc** *an enclosure in hell ; in pl. hell as a prison :*—þ hí scoldan hine gelǽdan tó hellelocum (*ad inferni claustra*), Gr. D. 325, 30. *See also* loc ; I.

**helle-mægen** *the force or host of hell :*—þæt eall hellemægen for þæs fýres hǽto forweorðeð, Verc. Först. 166.

**helle-smiþ.** v. smiþ.

**helle-stów** *an infernal region :*—Be þám wítelicum hellestówum *de locis poenalibus inferni,* Gr. D. 332, 9.

**helle-súsl.** v. súsl, (2).

**helle-tintreg** *hell-torment :*—In helletintrego, Verc. Först. 128, 19. *See also* tintreg, *and cf. next word.*

**helle-wíte.** *Add :*—Wé gebyrian sceolon oððe heofonwarena cyninge oððe hellewítes deóflum, Wlfst. 151, 20. Hellewíte *tartari tormento,* An. Ox. 2218. Hellewite *tartara,* 1249. Hé underféng hellewíte *eum ultrix gehenna suscepit,* Past 339, 3. Drífad ðá deófla þá synfullan sáwla in hellewítu, Verc. Först. 128, 10. *See next word.*

**hellewíte-bróga** *terror of hell :*—þæt man ús foresegð embe hellewíte-brógan (*or?* helle wíte-brógan. v. wíte-bróga. *But cf. be fyrhto þæs tintreglican wítes be leóþ geworhte de horrore poenae gehennalis carmina faciebat,* Bd. 4, 24 ; Sch. 487, 15), Wlfst. 151, 24.

**hell-god** *the god of hell, Dis :*—Helgodes *Ditis,* Wrt. Voc. ii. 95, 3 : 27, 24.

**hell-grund** *the depth of hell :*—þú in hellgrundes (helle-, *v. l.*) ástige, Angl. xii. 507, 8. v. helle-grund.

**hell-heort ;** *adj. Faint-hearted* (?) :—For ðám egsan þæs engles ansýne þá weardas wǽron áfǽrede and hellheorte, and efne swá forhte gewordene swá heó deáde wǽron, Nap. 37. [Cf. (?) *M. H. Ger.* hell weak.]

**hell-heoþo.** *Add :*—Wite þú hú wíd and síd helheoðo dreórig (*l.* heoro-dreórig), Sat. 700.

**hel-lic.** *Add :* **I.** *referring to classical mythology.* Cf. hell ; **I.** 2 :—þǽm hellicum gorgoneo (*maculata cruore*, Ald. 208, 21), Wrt. Voc. ii. 96, 83 : *gorgoneis* (*molitur damna venenis*, Ald. 166, 11), 92, 66 : 41, 44. **II.** *of hell.* Cf. hell ; **II** :—On þám blindan cwearterne þǽre hellican súsle, Hml. A. 8, 205. On ðám hellican líge, Hml. S. 17, 34. Ætwindan þám hellicum wítum, Hml A. 34, 251. **III.** *worthy of hell, infernal, diabolic, exceedingly wicked :*—Ǽlcne crístenne man warnian wið þás egeslican and þás deófollican coðe, þ ys wyð þás hellican unþeáwas, Angl. viii. 337, 7.

**hell·rún, e ; . f.** *A sorceress, one who has a spirit of divination :*—Helrún *pithonis* (cf. pithonissa, spiritus inferni, Corp. Gl. H. 6, 252), Wrt. Voc. ii. 68, 64 : 69, 20. Fram helrúnum *a pithonibus*, 3, 37. Cf. heáh-rún ; hell-rúne.

**hell-rúna.** (*l ?*) **hell-rúne,** *and add :*—Helhrúnan, wiccan *pitonissam, diuinatricem,* An. Ox. 1926. Helrúnan, 2, 60 : 7, 106 : 8, 106. *v.* helle-rúne, hell-rún, -rýnigu.

**hell-rýnigu** *a sorceress :*—Helrýnegu *pithonissa,* Wrt. Voc. ii. 69, 21. *See preceding words.*

**hell-sceaþa.** *Add :* **I.** *a fiend :*—þ hié ús sýn on fultume wið helsceaðum, Bl. H 209, 28. **II.** *hell personified, the grave.* Cf. hell ; **I.** 1 :—For ðon ná helsceaða andet ðé and ne deáþ herede *quia non infernus confitebitur te neque mors laudabit te,* Ps. Rdr. 277, 18.

**hell-waran.** *Add :* **I.** Cf. hell ; **I.** 1 :—þú átuge fram helwarum (*ab inferno*) sáwle míne, Ps. Spl. 29, 3. **II.** Cf. hell ; **I.** 2 :—Se hellwarana cyning, Bt. 35, 6 ; F. 170, 6. **III.** Cf. hell ; **II** :—Him þá getealdan stówe mid helwarum *deputatum sibi apud inferos locum,* Bd. 5, 14 ; Sch. 643, 7.

**hell-ware.** *Add :* **I.** Cf. hell ; **I.** 2 :—Eall helwara wítu gestildon, Bt. 35, 6 ; F. 170, 4. **II.** Cf. hell ; **II :**—þá unrótsodon helware. Hml. S. 4, 292. Helwara hreám, Wlfst. 186, 7. On helwara ríce is seó miccle byrnuys þǽs écan wítes, Nar. 50, 22.

**hellwendlic ;** *adj. Infernal, of the lower regions.* *v.* hell ; **I.** 2 :—þǽm helwen₍d₎llican *lethea,* Wrt. Voc. ii. 53, 20.

**hell-weorod, es ;** *n. The host of hell :*—Bið ástyred ge heofonwered ge eordwered ge hellwered, Wlfst. 25, 21.

**hell-wiht, e ; f.** *A creature of hell :*—Engla þrym and helwihta hryre and eorðan forwyrd, Wlfst. 186, 2.

**helm.** *Add :* **I.** *a covering for the head.* (1) *a helmet :*—Helm *galea,* Wrt. Voc. i. 84, 10 : *cassium,* ii. 103, 38 : 14, 5 : 129, 24. þǽr wæs helm monig, eald and ónig, B. 2762. Helm sceal cénum, Gn. Ex. 205. Wæs of þǽm hróran helm and byrne álýsed, B. 1629. Weox his helm þyrl, Fin. 45. Helmes *cassidis,* Wrt. Voc. ii 103, 34 : 13, 61 : 129, 25 : An. Ox. 2, 417. Ymb þæs helmes hróf heáfodbeorge wírum bewunden wál an útan heóld, B 1032. Ecg sceal wið helme hilde gebídan, Gn. C. 16. Sweord swín o:er helme ecgum dyhtig andweard scired, B. 1286. Seó ecg helm oft gescær, 1526 : 2973. þonne rond and hand on herefelda helm ealgodon, An. 10. Módcræftig snid gewyrced tó wera hilde helm oððe hupseax, Crä. 64. Helmas *cassida,* Wrt. Voc. ii. 14, 1. Fóron tó gefeohte hæleð under helmum, Jud. 203. Hæleð . . . helmum þeahte, Gen. 1089. Ád helmum behongen, hilde-bordum beorhtum byrnum, B. 3139. ¶ *epithets of the helmet are* brún, Jud. 318 : brún-fáh, B. 2615 : entisc, B. 2979 : gold-fáh, B. 2811 : heard, B. 2255 : heaþo-steáp, B. 1245 : 2153 : hefig, Hml. Th. ii. 502. 12 : hwít, B. 1448 : scír, Jud. 193. (1 a) *where the helm has a technical significance :*—Eorles heregeata syndon . . . feówer helmas and feówer byrnan . . . Cyninges þegenes . . . helm mid byrnan, Ll. Th. i. 414, 4–11. Of viii hídum helm and byrnan, Chr. 1008 ; P. 138, 6. þeáh ceorlisc geþeó þ hé hæbbe helm and byrnan . . . gif hé þ land nafað hé bið ceorl swá þeáh, Ll. Th. i. 188, 8. (2) *a crown, diadem :*—Sitt þonne swegles brytta on heáhsetle helme beweorðod (gewurþod, Wlfst. 137, 17), Dóm. L. 118. Cóm se deófol mid purpuran gescrýd and mid helme (mid gyldenum cynehelme, Hml. S. 31, 752) geglengd, Hml. Th. ii. 512, 24. Mid helme (cynehelme, Hml. S. 31, 764), 30. Aman gelædde Mardocheum, mid helme (cf. cynehelm *diadema* 232) gescrýdne, Hml. A. 99, 242. Durh ðone ðyrnenan helm on ðone Hælend beslagen, Hml. Th. ii. 254, 10. **II.** *the top, crown* of a thing, mostly of *the foliage of a tree* or *plant.* *v.* helm-bǽre, helmiht :—Gebúf sícbeám *vel* helm *frondea ficus,* Wrt. Voc ii. 151, 16. Coppe helmes (*sub*) *cono* (*sublimi*) *verticis,* i. *capitis* (*arboris*), An. Ox. 1564 Mid wexendum helme *florenti fronde,* 1132. Ic sæt innan bearwe mid helme beþeht, Dóm. L. 2. Helm *conum,* Wrt. Voc. ii. 129, 24. Gebúfe beámas *vel* helmas *frondea robora,* Wrt. Voc. ii. 151, 13. Huníbǽrum clǽfran helmum *melligeris caltarum frondibus,* An. Ox. 95: 924. **III.** *cover, concealment :*—Nó heó on helm losað, ne on foldan fæðm, ne on fyrgenholt, ne on gyfenes grund, gá þǽr heó wille *she will not escape into concealment, neither into earth's bosom, nor into the mountain wood, nor into ocean's depths, go where she will,* B. 1392. **III a.** *a covering :*—Helme *porticulo* (cf. *porticulus* minor porticus seu aedicula quae sepulcris mortuorum superstruebatur, Migne.

But *porticulus* in the passage glossed, Ald. 3, 3, is the hammer used in giving signals to rowers), An Ox. 33. Helme *tiro* (the line to which the gloss belongs is : Sed tyro infracta tectus testudine Christi, Ald. 210, 12 ; *helme* seems to belong to *testudine*), Wrt. Voc. ii. 97, 7. *v.* cyne-, íseru-, leþer-, wuldor-helm.

**helma.** *Add :* **I.** *a helm :*—Helma *clavis,* Wrt. Voc. ii. 98, 4. **II.** *a person who directs affairs :*—God is wealdend and steóra and steórróþer and helma, for þǽm hé riht and rǽt eallum gesceaftum swá swá gód steóra ánum scipe *Deus est veluti quidam clavus atque gubernaculum, quo mundana machina stabilis atque incorrupta servatur,* Bt. 35, 3 ; F. 158, 25.

**he·m-bǽre ;** *adj. Bearing foliage, leafy :*—Helmbǽres bearuwæs *frondiferi nemoris,* Wrt. Voc. ii. 151, 17.

**helm-berende ;** *adj. Having foliage, leafy :*—Helmberendum wuldor-beágum *frondigeris coronis,* Wrt. Voc. ii. 151, 19.

**helmian.** *Add :* *v.* be-, ge-, ofer-helmian ; cynehelmian : **helmig.** *v.* leáf-helmig.

**helmiht.** *l.* helmiht(e), *and for* ' Cot . . . Lye ' *substitute :*—Of ðǽm helmihtum bearwum *e frondosis nemoribus,* Wrt. Voc. ii. 78, 37 : 31, 7.

**help.** *Add :* ; hylp (*an i-stem noun?* Cf. u-grade forms, hulpa, hulfa *in O. L. Ger. and O. H. Ger. But cf. also* hylpan = helpan) : **I.** *help, assistance, succour :*—Nú is hire helpe heáhsǽl cumen *venit tempus miserendi ejus,* Ps. Th. 101, 11. Is micel þearf ealre þisse þeóde helpes and rǽdes, Wlfst. 243, 4. Sende se túnræd his helpes biddende, Hml. S. 31, 1220. Hé hyne bæd hylpes, Shrn. 147, 9. Ælcum swyncendum on helpe beón, Ll. Th. ii. 414, 36 : Ps Th. 98, 3. Hý on náure helpe néron ne heom sylfum ne heora freóndum, Solil. H. 68, 24. Hé út blǽde lǽded, hió tó helpe hæleða bearnum *qui producit foenum, et herbam servituti hominum,* Ps. Th. 146, 9 : 77, 18. Hé geþolade láðlicne deáð leódum tó helpe, Cri. 1174. þu onwóce mannum tó helpe, Sat. 440 : B. 1961 : Kr. 102 : El. 679. Hé geseah þá gesihþe þám mannum tó nytnesse þe hit gehýrad, ná him sylfum tó ǽnigre helpe Gr. D. 327, 17. Heó þæt cild gebær eallum middangearde tó sóðan helpe, Wlfst. 22, 10. Ic helpe tó þé holde gelýfe *ad te confugi,* Ps. Th. 142, 10 : Sat. 291 : Vald. 2, 27. Ne mæg se hreó hyge helpe gefremman, Wand. 16 : Cri. 263 : 424 : Ph. 650 : B. 1552 : An. 91 : 426 : 1616 : Jul. 696 : 722. Hé him helpe (helpan, MS., *the verb having been written in error under the influence of mæg which follows?*) ne mæg eald and infród ǽnige gefremman, B. 2448. Hí æt him helpe geniétton, Gú. 894 : El. 1032 : Ps. Th. 105, 24 : 117, 13. Ic helpe æt þé hæfde symble *factus es refugium meum,* 58, 17. **II.** *any thing or person that affords help, a means of assistance or support, an aid.* (1) *a* person :—þú eart ealra cyninga help, hálig lǽce, Hy. 7, 62. Ic gewéne on milde mód mínes Drihtnes, and mé þæt wát tó helpe, Ps. Th. 51, 7. Ne him áhwǽr were ǽnig fultum, ne his steópcildum stande tó helpe *non sit illi adjutor, nec sit qui misereatur pupillis ejus,* 108, 12. þú scealt leódum þínum tó helpe weorðan, B. 1709. (2) *a thing :*—Heó cwæð þ þæs geáres help (bigleofa, *v. l. subsidium*) hire forspilled wǽre, Gr. D. 68, 23. Nýd weorðeð oft niða bearnum tó helpe, Rún. 10. Hé gewende tó his gewunelican helpe, scrýdde hine mid hæran . . . and fæstende þurhwunode on singallum gebedum, Hml. S. 31, 661. Hé geaf six and twéntig cottlífa eallum tó hylpe, C D. B. ii. 389, 33. Nim þe þis ofæt on hand . . . þe sende God þás helpe of heofonríce, Gen. 521. Helpas *solacia,* R. Ben. I. 65, 10 : *praesidia,* Wülck. Gl. 252. 5. þá eorþlican helpas dón *terrena subsidia prebere,* Chrd. 66, 22. (2 a) *a place, a refuge :*—Stán help ílum *petra refugium herenacis,* Ps. Rdr. 103, 18. **III.** *a cure, remedy* of disease :—Gif þás fultumas ne sýn helpe *if these remedial measures are not effectual remedies,* Lch. ii. 262, 15. *v.* mid-, níd-help.

**helpan.** *Add :* **I.** *to add one's own action or effort to that of another so as to make it more effectual, to further the action or purpose* of :—Hé his mǽges healp, B. 2698. Uton clypian tó heofonum þ God úre helpe and tóbrýte þisne here, Hml. S. 25, 349. Ic wolde helpan þæs þe ðǽr unscyldig wǽre and hénan þone þe hine yfelode, Bt. 38, 6 ; F. 208, 17. Is se dæg cumen þ úre mandryhten mægenes behófað gódra manna ; wutun gangan tó helpan hildfruman, B 2649 : 2879. Of suoester ne hiá helpende *de sorore non eam adiuuante,* Lk. p. 7, 1. **II.** *to relieve the wants* or *necessities* of a person, *to succour :*—þonne hý him tó eów árna bǽdun, þonne gé hyra hulpon, Cri. 1354. Help (cf. ára, Met. 4, 31) þínum earmum moncynne, Bt. 4 ; F. 8, 11. Milsa ús þ help úsig *miserere nostri,* Mt. L. 20, 30. Gif se hierde ágiémeleásað ðæt hé hiera útan ne helpe *si cura exterioris subsidii a pastore negligatur,* Past. 137, 15. Hí wolde tóweorpan wuldres aldor, þær heora Móyses mægene ne hulpe, Ps. Th. 105, 19 : 118, 92. Bibeád ic eów þ gé of þám ǽhtum þe ic eów geaf earmra hulpen, Cri. 1503. **II a.** *used absolutely :*—Gif limlǽweo lama þe forworht wǽre weorðe forlǽten, and hé æfter þám þreó niht álibbe, siþþan man mót hylpan, sé þe wyllen beorgan sáre and sáule, Ll. Th. i. 172, 18. **III.** *to be serviceable, to profit, avail.* (1) *the subject a* person :—Ne helpað hí mid óðrum hira niéhstum, mid óðrum hí him deriað *in uno proximorum vitam minus adjuvant, in altero multum*

*gravant*, Past. 449, 28. (2) the subject a thing. (a) given by a noun :—Oft sió ilce lár ðe óðrum hielpeð (óðre hilpeð, *v. l.*), hió dereð ðǽm óðrum *saepe aliis officiunt, quae aliis prosunt*, Past. 173, 19. Ðǽm synfullan náuht ne helpað his gódan gedóhtas, . . . ne ðǽm ryhtwīsan ne deriað his yflan gedóhtas, 423. 25. Wisse hé þ him holtwudu helpan ne meahte, B. 2340 : 2684. (b) given in a clause :—Ic wát þ þe nā ne helpeð (fremað, *v. l.* expedit) þ þū gā fram mē þus unrótum, Gr. D. 81, 13. Hwæðer þū on ǽngum geþrahte swā twioræde sié þ ðe helpe hwæþer hit gewyrþe þe hit nó ne gewyrþe, Bt. 41, 3 ; F. 250, 9. **IV.** reflex. *to put forth needed effort on one's own behalf* :— þ heora hǽþenan gild nāwðer ne him sylfum helpan ne mihton, ne nānum ðāra ðe tó him āre wilnodan. Bl. H. 223. 3. **V.** *to relieve* a *malady, remedy* a *weakness* :—Ic geléofo, help (tóhelpe, R. *adjuva*) ungeleáffulnisse mīnne, Mk. L. 9, 24. v. tó-helpan.

**helpe.** *Dele, and see help* ; III, I.

**helpend.** *Add* :—Hé symble untrumum and þearfum ārede and hiora helpend wæs on hiora sāre *infirmis et pauperibus consulere, opem ferre non cessabat*, Bd. 3, 9 ; Sch. 229, 11. Helpend am þīnes *auxiliatus sum tui*, Rtl. 19. 9.

**helpend-bǽre.** *Dele, and see* helpend-rāp.

**helpend-líc.** *For 'auxiliary' substitute : To be released.* Cf. helpan ; II :—Helpendlicum *soluendis, i. liberandis hominibus*, Germ. 402, 68.

**helpend-rāp,** es ; *m. A rope used to help or support* :—Helpendrāp *opiffera*, Wrt. Voc. ii. 65, 47. [Cf. Icel. hjálp-reip.]

**hel-rún.** v. hell-rún : **hél-spure.** *Add* : -sporu. Ps. Vos. *has* hélspuran *in the two passages quoted* : **helto.** *l.* hilto : helur, helerung. v. heolor, heolorung : **helwenlic.** v. hellwendlic.

**hem.** *Add* :—Hem ora *lorīcę*, An. Ox. 50, 51. Feald þū mid þīnre swíðran hande þane bem þínes wynstran earmstoces ofer þīnne wynstran scytefinger, Tech. ii. 128, 2.

**hemeþe,** es ; *n. An undergarment with short sleeves, a shirt* :—Loþa, serc. smocc, hemeþe *colobium*, An. Ox. 3725. Gescrýdd mid hemeþe (*interula*), Angl. xiii. 443, 1114. Gif þū hemeþe habban wille, þonne nim þū siýfan þē on hand and wege hī, Tech. ii. 127, 6. [O. L. Ger. hemithi *camisa* : O. H. Ger. hemidi *supparus, camisa, tunica.*]

**hemlíc.** v. hymlíc.

**hemming, himming,** es ; *m. A boot made of raw hide* :—Hemming, i. rūh scó *pero*, Wrt. Voc. ii. 68, 6. Himming, 117, 5. [Cf. Icel. heming *the skin of the shanks of a hide*. Hemingr *as a proper name in Icelandic*, and Hemming *in O. H. Ger.* v. N. E. D. hemming.]

**hen.** *Take here* hæn *in Dict., and add* :—Hen *gallina*, Wrt. Voc. i. 77, 35. Henn, 281, 29 : 41, 18. Ǽn henne ǽg *unum ovum gallinaceum*, Bd. 3, 23 ; Sch. 301, 18. Dó henne ǽges þ hwíte tó, Lch. ii. 110, 2. Hænne flǽsc næs swíþe gesoden, 194, 7. Oþ henne stigele, Cht. Crw. 7, 53. Hū Bonefatius ādýdde þone fox þe bāt his módor henna. His módor gewunode tó fédenne henna on hire hūses cafortūne, ac hig gelómlíce āweg bær ān fox . . . Cóm se fox, swā hys gewuna wæs, and gelæhte āne henne (hæn, *v. l.*), Gr D. 69, 22-70, 2. Mettas þe gód blód wyrceað, swā swā sint wilda henna, Lch. ii. 244, 25. Beóð henna (*galline*) gelíce þām þe mid ūs beóð reádes híwes ; and gyf hī hwylc man niman wile oððe hyra æthríneð, þonne forbærnað hī sóna eall his líc, Nar. 33, 26. Henna hróst, Angl. ix. 262, 4. Æt .x. hīdum tó fóstre . . . .x. gees, .xx. henna, Ll. Th. i. 146, 18. v. edisc-, ersc-, hām-, wōr-hen.

**hénan.** v. hīnan : **-hendan.** v. ge-hendan : **-hende.** *Add* : v. æf-, īdel-, strang-hende : **henep.** v. hænep.

**Hendrícas** (?) *the name of the inhabitants of a district in England* :—Hendríca landes is þrýu þúsend hýda, C. D. B. iv. 444, 25.

**hen-fugol.** *Take here* hæn-fugul *in Dict., and add* :—Sex gósfuglas, tén hennfuglas. C. D. i. 312, 9.

**henge-clif.** *Add* :—Haengiclif *preruptum*, Hpt. 33, 251, 19. [Cf. Icel. hengi-flug *a precipice* ; hengi- *occurs in several compounds.*]

**hengen.** Under **I.** add after 'hanging,' racking ; and in the second passage substitute *racking for hanging*. Under **II.** substitute : an *apparatus for punishment or torture to which the sufferer is attached.* (1) *a cross* :—Críst hī mid hospe on hengene fæstnodon, Hml. Th. ii. 256, 22. Se déma hēt wyrcan āne hengcene, and hēt hōn þone bisceop þǽron, and hē swā hangigende þone Hǽlend bodode, swā swā Andreas dyde (cf. Sc̄s Andreas wæs āhangen on róde, Shrn. 153, 12). þā hēt se déma dōn hine of þǽre hengcene, Hml. S. 29, 252-256. (2) *a rack, framework on which a person is stretched, and to which the limbs are fastened* :—Se heáhgeréfa hēt on hengene āstreccan Crisantum, and mid candelum bærnan būta his sídan, þā tóbærst seó hengen (in nodosi cippi claustrum viri Dei tibias et suras astringunt. statim cippi duritia ad nihilum redigitur, Ald. 44, 33). Hml. S. 35, 311-313. Hé hēt hī on hencgene āstreccan and ðrāwan swā swā widdan . . . Agathes andwyrde on ðǽre hencgene . . . 'Ne mæg nān sāwl beón gebroht tó heofonum būtan mīn līchama beó on þínre bendum genyrwod and fram ðínum cwellerum on þínum copsum āgrápod.' þā hēt hē hī gewríðan on ðām breóste mid þǽre hencgene, Hml. S. 8, 112-122. Hēt se wælhreówa

hine hōn on heardre hengene, and his sídan bærnan mid hātum līgum, and mid hengene ðrāwan tó langere hwíle, Hml. Th. ii. 308, 30. 'Āhóð hine on þǽre hengene and hetelíce āstreccað ealle his lima þ þā liþa him tógaan.' þā gefæstnodon þā cwelleras hine on þǽre heardre hengene, and hine hetelíce tihton, swā swā man web tiht . . . Hé hēt hī swíðor witnian þone hālgan wer on þǽre hengene . . . Dacianus hēt hine gedón of þǽre hengene and hine eft āhón on heardum gealgan, Hml. S. 37, 98-157. Hé hēt ðone hālgan wer on hencgene āhæbban, and mid ísenum cláwum clifrian his lima, and ontendan blysan æt bām his sídum, 14, 42. 'Āstreccað hine, and swingende geangsumiað.' Laurentias ðā āstreht on ðǽre hengene (cf. hē hine (St. Laurence) hēt āþenian on īrenum bedde, Shrn. 116, 2) ðancode his Drihtne . . . Hé hēt ālýsan hine of ðǽre hengene, Hml. Th. i. 426, 21-35. **III.** *here add* :—Hengen *ergastulum*, Wrt. Voc. ii. 30, 60 : 70, 15. In the passage from Alfred's Laws *hengen* might refer to the actual constraint of the limbs as in the stocks. See the first two passages under II. 2, where such constraint is noted. And the whole section, which is entitled ' Be cierlisces monnes byndellan,' seems to apply to such constraint. In the two glosses and in the passage from Cnut's Laws the word seems used in a more general sense of confinement. v. róde-hengen ; hengen-wítnung, heng-wíte.

**hengest.** *Add* :—Hengest *canterius*, Lch. i. lxi, 4 : *caballus*, Wrt. Voc. ii. 16, 77 : *cabullus*, i. 287, 43. The word occurs in several local names. v. C. D. vi. 297, col. 2.

**heng-wíte.** *Add* : Cf. hengen ; **III.** hé-nis. v. hín-nes.

**henne-belle,** an ; *f. Henbane* :—Hennebelle *simphoniaca*, Wrt. Voc. i. 30, 42 : 79, 4 : An. Ox. 56, 374. Hennebelle. Ðeós wyrt þe man *symphoniacam* nemned, and óðrum naman belone, and eác sume men hennebelle (hænne-, *v. l.*) hātað, Lch. i. 94, 3-6. Beolonan sǽd, þ is hænnebelle, iii. 72, 10. Genim hænnebellan sǽd, 60, 7. [v. N. E. D. hen-bell.]

**hen-streát** (?). v. streát.

**hentan.** *Substitute* : **I.** *with gen.* (1) *to seize, take.* (a) *to arrest* a person :—Gif hé man tó deáðe gefylle . . . his hente mid hreáme (hearme, MS. The old Latin version has 'persequatur eum cum clamore.' Cf. too : Gif hwā þeóf gemēte, and hine āweg lǽte būton hreáme, 392, 15) ǽlc þāra þe riht wille, Ll. Th. i. 170, 10 : 404, 11 (here the Latin version has 'capiat eum cum clamore '). Se cāsere beád þ man swíðe georne sceolde cépan crístena manna, and gehwā þǽr hē mihte heora be feore hente, Hml. S. 23, 49. (b) *to capture* an animal :—þā woldon þā hǽþenan he[n]tan þǽre leó, ac heó gelæhte ǽfre ǽnne and ǽnne, Hml. S. 35, 280. (2) *to take and carry off* :—Āgeóte man heora blód on ðā eorðan, and swā hwā swā þæs blódes hent and him tó mete macað, hé losað of his folce, E. S. viii. 62, 39. (3) *to get at with a blow, strike* with a weapon :—Dioclitianus hēt hine (St. Sebastian) lǽdan tó ānum felda and hine þǽr gefæstnian and hentan mid flānum (cf. mid strǽlum ofstician, Shrn. 55, 8), Hml. S. 5, 424. [Cf. Moyses hente ðe cherl wið hise wond, And he fel dun in dedes bond, Gen. and Ex. 2715.] **II.** *with prep.* hentan *æfter to try to get* :—Nime hé leáfe þ hē móte hentan æfter his āgenan (licentiam accipiat ut suum audeat perquirere, Lat. vers.), Ll. Th. i. 386, 17. [v. N. E. D. hent.]

**heóf.** *Add* :—Heóf *luxus* ( = *luctus*), weópan *luxerunt*, Wrt. Voc. ii. 51, 33. þǽr (in hell) is wānung and grānung and aa singal heóf, Wlfst. 94. 3. Se hlúda heóf, 186, 19. Nān þincg gehýred næs būton seó geómerung þæs heófes, Hml. S. 23 b, 203. In þām heófse þæs feóndes deáðes *in luctu mortis inimici*, Gr. D. 120, 17. Ic fór mē tó Egipta lande feówertēne geár on heófe, Ap. Th. 24, 27. Mid blisse and heófe ealre þǽre mǽgðe heó fór mid hire were, 25, 19. Heófum *questibus*, An. Ox. 2829. v. heáf.

**heófan.** *Add* : *also strong forms occur.* p. heóf, hóf (*an Old Saxon form A. S.* heáf?) ; *pl.* heófon. **I.** *absolute* :—Heófde *luxerat*, Wrt. Voc. ii. 53. 35. þæt wíf gnornode, heóf hreówigmód, Gen. 771. Ongan ic of inneweardre heortan heófsonde forðbringan þā geómorlicau siccetunga, Hml. S. 23 b, 428. **II.** *with acc., To lament* :—Godes andsacan . . . heófon deóp gehygd . . . þæt heó woldon benǽman Críst rodera ríces, Sat. 344. **III.** *with gen., To be sorry for, grieve* at :—þæt hié swā gefeón ðissa andweardena góda ðæt hí him ondrǽden ðā ēcan yfl., and swā ðāra yfela ðisse worulde hiófen ðæt hī hiora tóhopan gefæstnigen tó ðǽm ēcum gódum *sic de bonis praesentibus gaudeant, ut mala aeterna pertimescant ; sic de malis temporalibus lugeant, ut spem in bonis perennibus figant*, Past. 393, 28-31.

**heófe-líce.** *Dele, and see* heófend-líc.

**heófend-líc** ; *adj. Lamentable, expressing grief, funereal* :—Heófendlíce *funebre* (*carmen*), Wrt. Voc. ii. 76, 76 : 37, 4 ; *funebre, luc uosum*, 151, 59 : *lamentabile* (*carmen*), An. Ox. 900.

**heófian.** *Add* : **I.** *absolute* :—In þām dæge heofene and eorðe cwāciað and heófiað and ealle þā ðing þe on him syndon *in quo omnis creatura congemescit.* Wlfst. 182, 9. Eádige beóð ðā þe heófiað *beati qui lugent*, Hml. Th. i. 550, 27. Hī biterlíce on wópe heófodon, Hml. S. 23, 66. For þām earmlican swǽsnyssum þissera heófiendra (-igendra,

*v. l.*), 5, 56. **I a.** where the occasion for mourning is given:—Þá þe for hýndum heófiað, Hml. Th. i. 550, 29. Þ hé heólige for middangeardes hryrum . . . þá sceolon heófian for middangeardes tóworpennysse, 612, 20–28. **II.** *trans.:*—Þænne wé heófiað þ wé yfele dydon *dum plangimus quod male gessimus*, Scint. 47, 17. Árleás sáwl byð heófud *inþia anima plangitur*, 42, 11.

**heófing.** v. heófung: **heofinga** orbes, Wrt. Voc. ii. 64, 57. [Cf. Hringa hóhwerfinge (hóhhwyrfinge, 64, 21), Wrt. Voc. ii. 75, 6: hófringas hófum, An. Ox. 18–19, glosses to *orbes orbibus*, Ald. 2, 36. Perhaps heofinga *orbes* is a corruption of one or other of these glosses]: **heófað.** v. heáfod.

**heofon.** *Add:* In later specimens the word is often feminine, e. g. :— *Hoc caelum* þeós heofen, Ælfc. Gr. Z. 86, 11. **I.** *the overarching vault of sky, the sky, firmament.* v. heofon-hróf, -hwealf :—Hé cwæð, ' Geweorðe heofen ', and þærrihte wæs heofen geworht (cf. Gen. 1, 6, 8), Hml. Th. i. 6, 1–2. Heofon biþ open on þæ.n eástdæle, and mycel mægen forþ cymeþ, and þone heofon oforþecþ . . . and seó heofon biþ gefeallen æt þæm feówer endum middangeardes, Bl. H. 93, 1–5. Swelce eal se hefon birnende wære, Ors. 2, 6; S. 86. 23. Se heofen, 4, 7; S. 184, 22. Hié gesáwon swelce se hefon wære tóhliden *Falescis coelum scindi velut magno hiatu visum*, 4, 8; S. 188, 26. Hí woldon witon hú heáh hit wære tó þæm hefone, and hú ðicke se hefon wære and hú fæst, oððe hwæt þær ofer wære, Bt. 35, 4; F. 162, 21–23. Behealde hé on feówer healfe his hú wídgille ðæs heofones hwealfa biþ, 19; F. 68, 22. Þá gigantas woldon tóbrecan ðone heofon under him (*Jove*), 35, 4; F. 162, 12. Byrnendne heofon, Exod. 73. **I a.** as the expanse in which the sun, moon, and stars are fixed :—*Firmamentum* is þeós roderlice heofen mid manegum steorrum æmett, Lch. iii. 254, 8 : 232, 21. Tunglena heofon, Angl. vii. 12, 109. Þá þá Críst ácenned wæs, þá sende seó heofen níwne steorran, Hml. Th. i. 298, 26. Heofon ongeat hwá hine getremede tungolgimmum, Cri. 1150. Beheald þá tunglu þæs heán heofnes, Bt. 39, 13; F. 232, 26. Heofones tungul. Ors. 3, 5; S. 104, 18. Mon geseah swelce hit wære án gylden hring on heofonum brædre þonne sunne; and wæs from þæm heofone brádiende niþer oþ þá eorþan, and wæs eft farende wið þæs heofones, 5, 10; S. 234, 8–11. Ðonne seó sunne on hádrum heofone beorhtost scíneþ, Bt. 9; F. 26, 15. Þá steorran synd fæste on þære heofene; þæt (*what*) menn geseoð feallan of þære heofone, swylce hyt sýn steorran, hyt beoð spearcan, Angl. viii. 320, 31 : Cri. 940. Sceáwa heofon, hyrste gerím, rodores tungel, Gen. 2180. **I b.** considered as a revolving sphere :—Seó heofon belýcð on hyre bósme ealne middaneard. And heó æfre tyrnð onbútan ús swiftre þonne ænig mylenhweól eal swá deóp under þyssere eorðan swá heó is bufan. Ealle heó is sinewealt and ansund, Lch. iii. 232, 17–21. *Firmamentum* is þeós roderlice heofen . . . seó *firmamentum* tyrnð symle onbútan ús . . . ac þær is ungerím fæc betweón hyre and þære eorðon, 254, 8–13. *Firmamentum*, þ ys þeós heofon, heó ys gesewenlic and líchamlic . . . and heó æfre tyrnð onbútan ús, Angl. viii. 309, 44. Hwylces gecyndes is seó heofon? Fýres gecyndes and sinewealt and symle turniende, vii. 12, 107 : 14, 137. Se heofen mót brengon leóhte dagas and eft þ leóht mid þeóstrum behelian, Bt. 7, 3; F. 20, 20. Wé wendað úre neb tó eástdæle þær seó heofen árist, Hml. Th. i. 262, 11, 6. Behealdaþ ðá hrædiérnesse þisses heofenes, Bt. 32, 2; F. 116, 6. ¶ used figuratively :—Míne þeówas sindon wísdómas and cræftas; mid þám þeówum ic eom ealne þone heofon ymbhweorfende, and þá niþemestan ic gebrenge æt þám héhstan, and þá héhstan æt þám niþemestan *rotam volubili orbe versamus, infima summis, summa infimis mutare gaudemus*, Bt. 7, 3; F. 20, 35. **I c.** the plural used with the same sense as the singular :—Þæt weorc þínra fingra, þæt synd heofonas and móna and steorran, Ps. Th. 8, 4. Hé geseah áne hlædre standan æt him on eorðan. Óðer ende wæs uppe on hefenum (-onum, *v. l.*), Past. 101, 19 : Chr. 773; P. 50, 20. On heofonum *coelo*, Ors. 5, 10; S. 234, 9 : 2, 6; S. 86, 22. God hét hyne lócian tó heofonum *suspice coelum*, Gen. 15, 5 : Bt. 39, 7; F. 222, 6: Hml. Th. ii. 150, 23. Holm under heofonum, Gen. 161 : 1387 : Ph. 58. Hæled under heofonum, B. 52. Ic gesié heofenas (*caelos*), werc fingra ðínra, Ps. Srt. 8, 4. **I d.** as the object towards which eyes or hands are directed under the influence of reverence or strong emotion :—Hé his handa wæs uppweardes brædende wið þæs heofones (*manus ad coelum tendens*), and mid oferheortnesse him wæs wæniende, Ors. 4, 5; S. 166, 19. Ic hebbe tó heofena míne hand and ic swerie, Deut. 32, 40. Hé nolde furðun his eágan áhebban úp tó þám heofone (-heofena, L., R.), Lk. 18, 13. Hé beseah on þone heofon (heofun, R.), Mt. 14, 19. On þone heofon behealdende geómrode, Mk. 7, 34. Mid ábrædedum handum and in þá heofon lócigende, and mid teárum geómrigende, Hml. S. 23 b. 701. **I e.** where great height is expressed by saying a thing reaches heaven. (1) physical :—Micle burga and oð heofun fæste *urbes magnae et ad coelum usque munitae*, Deut. 1, 28. Þá tó heofenum úp heáh ástigað *ascendunt usque ad coelos*, Ps. Th. 106, 25 : Exod. 460 : 492. Bryne stígeð heáh tó heofonum, Ph. 521. Dúst stonc tó heofonum, Rä. 30, 12. (2) of exalted position :—Þú, Cappernaum, cwyst þú byst þú úpáhafen oð heofon, Mt. 11, 23. **II.** *the region of the atmosphere*

*in which birds fly, clouds float, moisture is stored.* v. heofon-fleógende, -flód, -fugol, -fýr, -wolcen :—Seó heofon (hefon, L., heofunn, R.) wæs belocen þreó gér and syx mónþas, Lk. 4, 25. Heofon réce swealg, B. 3156. Of heofenes deáwe *de rore coeli*, Gen. 27, 28. Heofenes (heofnes, L., R.) fugelas, Lk. 13, 19. Se swéta mete ðe him cuóm of hefonum (cf. hét hé þá wídan duru wolcen ontýnan heá of heofenum, and hider rignan mannum tó mōse, Ps. Th. 77, 25), Past. 125, 20. Mon geseah weallan blóð of eorþan, and rínan meolc of heofonum, Ors. 4, 3 ; S. 162, 7. **III.** *the region beyond the visible sky* :—Ær þám þe gewíte heofon and eorþe, Mt. 5, 18. Þeós wlitige gesceaft, heofon and eorðe, An. 1440. **III a.** plural with force of singular :—Bið gehýred mycel stefn on heofenum *fyrdweorodes getrymnesse*, and heofon biþ open on þæm eástdæle, and mycel mægen forþ cymeþ þurh þone openan dæl, Bl. H. 91, 35. Ealle gesceafta, heofenas and englas, sunnan and mónan and eorðan, sæ and ealle fixas God gesceóp on syx dagum, Hml. Th. i. 14, 27. **IV.** *one of the spheres into which the realms of space round the earth were divided by the early astronomers* :—Siofon heofonas sindon in gewritum leornode; þ is se lyftlica heofon, and se oferlyftlica and se fýrena heofon and se stronga heofon þe wé rodor hafað. and se egeslica heofon and engla heoton and heofon þære há'gan ðrinnisse, Nap. 50. Ðonne bist þú bufan ðám swiftan rodore and lætst behindan þe þone héhstan heofon, Bt. 36, 2 ; F. 174, 16. **V.** *the celestial abode of immortal beings.* (1) of God and his angels :—Heofon is his þrymsetl, Hml. Th. i. 262, 4. Heofan, El. 753. Heofones waldend, Gen. 300. Ic hæbbe geweald tó gyrwanne stól on heofne, 282. (1 a) plural with same meaning as singular :—Heofona freá, Gen. 1404. On heofona ríce, 254. Heofna ealdor, Sat. 567. On heáhsetle heafena ríces, Hy. 8, 29. Hé ær worolde rícsode on hefenum (-onum, *v. l.*), Past. 33, 13. Hé tó heofonum ástág, on his ealdcýððe, Cri. 737. Ic gefylle mid mé sylfum heofenas and eorðan, Hml. Th. i. 262, 3 : Men. 65. (2) of beatified spirits :—Sié þára manna gehwám heofones duru ontýned, El. 1230. (2 a) pl. as sing. :—Seó sáwl færð tó heofonum, Bt. 18. 4 ; F. 68, 14. Þú forgeáfe þám sáwlum eard on heofonum, 33, 4 ; F. 132, 19. (3) *one of the seven heavens recognized by the Jews* :—Paulus árímde ðá diógolnissa ðæs ðriddan hefones, Past. 99, 8. Þæt ðære heofenan þe bufan hyre (*the firmament*) synd and beneoðan synd ungesegenlice and mannum unásmeágendlice. Synd swá þeáh má heofenan (heofena. Angl. viii. 310, 3), swá swá se wítega cwæð, ' Coeli coelorum,' þ is heofena heofenan. [Þæs heofona tácniað þá apostolas and þá wítegan; be heom ys gecweden, ' Celi enarrant gloriam Dei,' Angl. viii. 310, 5.] Eác se apostol Paulus áwrát þ hé wæs gelædd oð ðá þriddan heofenan, Lch. iii. 232, 21–26. Þeáh hé (*Christ*) on eorðan cenned wære, hwæðre hís meahta spéd heáh ofer heofonum (*or under I c?*) wunade, Ph. 641. Hefonas hé (*St. Paul*) ðurhfór mid his módes sceáwunga, Past. 99, 23. (4) *the abode of heathen deities* :—Þte Job sceolde beón se héhsta god . . . and sceolde rícsian on heofenum, Bt. 35, 4 ; F. 162, 7. (5) applied figuratively to a righteous person :—Se rihtwísa is heofen geháten, for ðam þe on rihtwísum mannum is Godes wunung, Hml. Th. i 262, 15. **VI.** *the power* or *majesty of heaven; the ruler of heaven* :—Se wísdóm nis ufan cumen of hefenum . . . ac sé sé ðe of Gode cymð, hé bið gesibsum *non est ista sapientia desursum descendens . . . Quae desursum est sapientia, pacifica est*, Past. 347, 25. Ic syngude on heofon, Lk. 15, 21. **VI a.** referring to heathen mythology :—Job sceolde bión ðæs heofenes sunu, Bt. 35, 4 ; F. 162, 7. **VI b.** in asseveration or oaths :—Ðæt gé ne swerian þurh heofon, Mt. 5, 34. Ic hæbbe tó gewitnisse heofen and eorðan *testes invoco coelum et terram*, Deut. 4, 26. **VII.** *a condition of peace or happiness* :—Gif þú ðe ofsceamian -wilt ðínes gedwolan, þonne onginne ic þé sóna beran and þé bringe mid mé tó heofonum, Bt. 3, 4 ; F. 6, 16. Ic gebrenge eáþmódnesse on heofonum, 7, 3 ; F. 22, 2. Ic wát þ manegum men ðúhte þ hé wære tó heofonum áhafen gif hé ænigne dæl hæfde þára þinra gesælða þe ðú nú gét hæfst, 11, 1 ; F. 32, 25. **VIII.** *a ceiling* :—Húshefen oððe heofen, hróf (heofenhróf? *but cf. lacunar* hróf, 55, *and for two alternatives after* oððe v. 5, 70 : 36, 5 : 47, 13) *lacunar*, Wrt Voc. ii. 50, 58. Heben, hús[heben] (? hebenhús, MS.) *lacunar*, 112, 34. v. hús-, úp-heofon; heofone.

**heofon-beácen.** In Mod. Lang. Rev. vi. 164 Prof. Napier makes the very probable suggestion that ll. 86–107 and ll. 108–124 in the Exodus should be transposed. If this be accepted *heofon-beácen* would *be the sun.*

**heofon-bígenged, -biggenged;** *adj. Practising the heavenly virtue of chastity.* Cf. heofonlíc; V. [See also : *superni celibes* (altered from *cælitis*) heofenlíce bígenge clæne (*superni coelites* (*virginitatis*) heofenlíce bígendce ł clæne, Hpt. Gl. 436, 26), An. Ox. 1256.] :—Wé beón éce heofonbígende *simus perennes celibes*, Hy. S. 36, 32. Heofanbiggende *celibes*, 5, 27. v. bí-geng.

**heofon-cenned;** *adj. Heaven-born* :—Ofer heofancennede roderes ealle *supra celigenas aetheris omnes*, Hy. S. 108, 9.

**heofon-cund.** *Add:* Ðá cóm ðær gán in tó mé heofoncundu wísdóm, Bt. 3, 1 ; F. 4. 17. From ðæs hefencundan Fæder éðle ádrifene, Past. 249, 15. Mid ðæm: heofoncundan fíre wæron ðá lác forbærndu on ðæm

altere, 222, 23. Gē ne ongitað þone heofoncundan anweald, Bt. 16, 1; F. 48, 31. Þu gemengest þā heofoncundan hider wið eorðan sáula wið líce, Met. 20, 235. Þā heofoncundan þing þē sint gecynde, Bt. 14, 1; F. 40, 34.

**heofoncund-líc**; *adj. Heavenly, celestial :*—Becuman tó ðām ēcan lífe þæs heofoncundlican ríces, Wlfst. 215, 10. Mid heofoncundlicre bletsunge gebletsod, 293, 29.

**heofon-cyning.** *In* l. 6 *for* -cyning l. -cyninga, *and add :* I. of the first person of the Trinity :—Heofoncyninges lof singað Ceraphin, El. 748 : An. 723. Hefoncyninges, Gen. 659. Hí hnigon mid heáfdum heofoncyninge, 237. Abraham hýrde heofoncyninge, Exod. 410. II. of the second person :—Ród bestēmed heofoncyninges hlútran dreóre, Cri. 1087. Eall gē þæt mē dydon tó hýndum heofoncyninge, 1514.

**heofone.** *Add :* I. *the overarching vault of sky :*—Ic gedó þæt eów bið ægðer heard ge heofone ge eorðe *dabo vobis coelum desuper sicut ferrum et terram aeneam,* Lev. 26, 19. Sí þé heofone swilce ór and eorðe swilce ísen, Deut. 28, 23. Under þære heofenan fæstnisse, Gen. 1, 20. Geseah hē standan āne hlædre fram eorðan tó heofenan, 28, 12. God hēt þā fæstnisse heofenan, 1, 8. On ðām ōðrum dæge gesceóp God heofenan, seó ðe is gehāten *firmamentum,* Lch. iii. 232, 13. Hē getimbrode ðā heálican heofenan, Hml. Th. ii. 586, 29. I a. *as the* expanse in which the stars are fixed :—Seó heofene and ealla tungla heore rina behealdað, Solil. H. 9, 14. Hí (*the planets*) ne synd nā fæste on þære rodorlican heofonan swā swā ōðre tunglan, Angl. vii. 14, 121. II. *the region of the atmosphere in which clouds float, moisture is stored, birds fly,* &c. :—Eal woruld winneð ongeán þā ofer-hogan ... Seó heofone ús wind wið þonne heó ús sendeð styrnlice stormas, Wlfst. 92, 16. Þære heofenan wæterþeótan wæron geopenode, Gen. 7, 11 : 8, 2. Hwí is þ tācn (*the rainbow*) on þære lyftenan (-ran, MS.) heofonan (cf. arcum meum ponam in nubibus et erit signum, Gen. 9, 13) gesewen?, Angl. vii. 38, 357. III. *the region beyond the visible sky* (the combination *heaven and earth* denotes the universe) :—In þām dæge heofene and eorðe cwaciað, Wlfst. 182, 9. Nān man Godes mihte ne forflíhð on nānum heolstrum heofenan oðða eorðan oþþe sǽ ðriddan (*nec judicium superni Gubernatoris ustpiam effugere queo,* Vit. Cuth. c. 24), Hml. Th. ii. 146, 31. On anginne gesceóp God heofenan and eorðan, Gen. 1, 1. IV. *the celestial abode of immortal beings :*—Swā micel is betwux gódum mannum and yfelum, swā micel swā bið betwux heofenan and eorðan, Hml. Th. i. 262, 20. Ic geseah englas ferigan gesǽlige sáwle tó heálicre heofenan, ii. 150, 27. Godes ríce on rodorlicere heofonan, 330, 27. IV a. *one of the seven heavens recognized by the Jews :*—Hē becóm tó ðære ðriddan heofonan, Hml. Th. ii. 332, 10. Þā ōðre heofenan synd ungesewenlice and mannum unāsmeágendlice. Synd swā þeáh mā heofenan swā swā se wītega cwæð, ' Coeli coelorum ', þ is heofena heofenan. Eác se apostol Paulus āwrāt þ hē wæs gelædd oð ðā þriddan heofenan, Lch. iii. 232, 21–26 : Angl. viii. 310, 2 : Ps. L. 148, 4. V. *used in forms of asseveration or in oaths :*—Sē ðe swereð on heofonan, hē swereð on Godes þrymsetle, Mt. 23, 22. *See* heofon.

**heofon-fleógende**; *adj. Flying in the air.* v. heofon; II :—Heofonfleógende fuglas *volucres cœli,* Ps. Vos. 103, 12.

**heofon-flód,** es; *m. Flood produced by heavy rain :*—Wæs seó eá for regna micelnesse swíðe rēðe, and heofonflód micel on sæt (on gesett, *v. l.*) *fluuius prae inundantia pluuiarum late alueum suum immo omnes ripas suas transierat,* Bd. 3, 24; Sch. 309, 18.

**heofon-fýr,** es; *n. Lightning.* v. heofon; II :—Be ðām muntum ... þā ðe heáh standað ... heó beóð genehhe mid heofenfýre gebreáde, Wlfst. 262, 15.

**heofon-hæbbende.** *Substitute :* **heofon-hæbbend,** es; *m.* An epithet of the Deity, *he that holds the citadel* (arx) *of heaven.* v. habban; I 2 b :—Heofenhæbbend *arcitenens,* Wrt. Voc. ii. 9, 59. v. heofon-wealdend.

**heofon-hróf;** II. v. heofon; VIII.

**heofon-hús** (?) *a house with a ceiling* (?). v. heofon; VIII.

**heofonisc.** *Add :*—Hié ne mehton from Galliscum fýre forbærnede weorþan, ac hí hefenisc fýr (*e coelo ignis*) forbærnde, Ors. 2, 8; S. 94, 15.

**heofon-leóht.** *Add :*—Ðæt ofer his reliquias þ heofonleóht (*lux caelestis*) ealle niht wæs ofer gestondonde, Bd. 3, 11; Sch. 235, 9.

**heofon-líc.** *Add :* I. *Of, in, or belonging to heaven, as the abode of God.* v. heofon; V :—Heofonlíc hleóðor and se hālga song gehýred wæs, Gū. 1297. Seó sáwl mót brúcan þæs heofonlican, siþþan heó biþ ābrogden from þām eorþlican, Bt. 18, 4; F. 68, 17. On þ ēce wuldor þæs heofonlican ríces, Bl. H. 61, 6. Mid heofonlicum þreáte hāligra gāsta, 95, 6. Ðone weg þe ðē gelǽt tó þære heofenlican byrig, Bt. 36, 1; F. 172, 29. Nū míne fēt gongað on heofonlicne weg (*I am dying*), Bl. H. 191, 21. Hié þā ongehýd heora heortan fæstlíce on þām heofon-lican hyht gestaþelodon, 135, 29. Hér Dūnstān forlēt þis líf and geferde þ heofonlíce, Chr. 988; P. 125, 15. Hē ús forgeaf heofonlicne hám, Kr. 148. Geearnian ðone hefonlican ēðel, Past. 255, 4. Heofon-licra ceastriwarena *supernorum* (i. *angelorum*) *ciuium,* An. Ox. 328.

Geimpod tó ðǽm hefenlicum (hefon-, *v. l.*) diógolnessum, Past. 99, 18. Þū gegæderast ðā hiofonlicon sáwla and ðā eorþlican líchoman, Bt. 33, 4; F. 132, 23. II. *proceeding from* or *belonging to the Deity, divine.* Cf. heofon; VI :—þæt heofenlíce gehāt, Bl. H. 135, 27. Wæs Drihten cweþende tó Marian líchoman, ' Aris þū, ... þū eart þ heofenlíce templ ', 157, 13. Seó onblāwnes þære heofonlican onfæðm-nesse, 7, 26. Mid þām heofonlicon wísdóme þe him se Hǽlend forgeaf, Angl. vii. 2, 10. Gesión ðā birhtu þæs heofenlican leóhtes ,cf. þā ēcan birhtu Godes, 5) mid módes eágum, Bt. 34, 8; F. 146, 2. Ōþer dæl sceal beón geclǽnsod on þām heofonlicon fýre, 38. 4; F. 204, 1. Ic eów freoþige tó Fæder þ hē eów gehealde þurh þ heofenlíce anwald, Bl. H. 135, 26. Wealdend þe gife heofonlicne hláf, An. 389. Ic gebrenge þā heofonlican gód æt þām eaþmēdum, Bt. 7, 3; F. 22, 2. II a. *applied to miraculous manifestations :*—Ofer his reliquias heofenlíc leóht (*lux caelestis*) ealle niht wæs oferstandende, Bd. 3, 11; Sch. 235, 9 : Gū. 1264. Seó ætýwnes heofonlices wundres *miraculi caelestis ostensio,* Bd. 3, 11; Sch. 237, 3. Hē getrymede heora geleáfan mid þon heofonlicon weorce (*with working of miracles*), Bl. H. 17, 8. III. *of or from heaven.* v. heofon; II :—þā hine man on þ fýr wearp, þā ālýsde ic hine mid heofonlicon rēne *Croesum rogi flammis traditum, misso coelitus imbre defensum,* Bt. 7, 3; F. 22, 13. Hit wearð fram heofonlicum fýre (*igne caelesti*) forbærned, Ors. 1, 3; S. 32, 3. Úre fæderas ǽton heofonlicne mete (heofunlica, R., heofunlíc, L.) *manducauerunt patres nostri manna,* Jn. 6, 58. IV. *having relation to heaven and divine things :*—þætte eal ... sié ymb ðā heofon-lícan lufan ... ðý lǽs him losige ðæt hefenlíce ondgit *ut per omne ... ad amorem coelestium surgat, ne ... ipso veritatis intellectu vacuetur,* Past. 84, 6–8. Heofenlicere lác[nunge] celestis medicinae, An. Ox. 381. Heofenlicun angite *anagogen,* i. *superno sensu,* 184. þ gāstlice, heofenlíce contemplatiuam (*uitam*), 2432. Ic lufige þæt heofenlíce and þæt gāstlíce ofer þis eorðlíce, Solil. H. 12, 14. Heofonlíce blisse mon mihte ā on his móde ongytan, Bl. H. 223, 34. Sē ðe wile brúcan ðāra godcundra ðinga and ðāra hefonlicra lāra, Past. 81, 14. Ðū bescylst mid óþre eágan on þā heofenlican þing, mid óþre þū lócast on þas eorþlican, Bt. 38, 5; F. 206, 18. V. *having the purity that belongs to heaven, chaste.* Cf. heofon-bigenged :—Hic et haec et hoc caelebs clǽne oððe heofonlíc, Ælfc. Gl. Z. 66, 3. Clǽngeorne *celibes,* i. *casti, celestem vitam ducentes,* heofonlicre *celibea,* Wrt. Voc. ii. 130, 54.

**heofonlíce.** *Add :*—Heofonlíce *coeliter,* Wrt. Voc. ii. 20, 23.

**heofon-ligende.** *Dele, and see* heofon-bigenged.

**heofon-ríce.** *Add :* I. *heaven as the abode of God and angels :*—Heóldon englas forð heofonríce hēhðe þe Godes hyldo gelǽston, Gen. 321. Þām stede þe wē cúðon on heofonríce, 358. Wit noldon on heofonríce hnígan mid heáfdum hālgum Drihtne, 741. Hē (*Satan*) hefonríce forworhte *coelum perdidit,* Past. 233, 20. ¶ in phrases describing the Deity as the ruler of heaven. (1) of God the Father :—Hæfð geheaðerod hefonríces weard (cf. se ælmihtiga God, Bt. 21; F. 74, 9) mid his anwealde ealle gesceafta, Met. 11, 31. Spræc heofonríces weard tó Abrahame, éce Drihten, Gen. 1744 : Exod. 485 : Dan. 12 : An. 52 : Jul. 212 : Gū. 583 : El. 197. Fæder mancynnes, ... God lifigende ... hiofonríces weard, Ps. C. 113 : Hy. 8, 2. Wuldres cyning, heofonríces helm, Cri. 566. Wuldorcyning, heofonríces God, Jul. 239 : El. 1125. (2) of Christ :—Ic (*Eve*) ðe hálsige, heofonríces weard ... þū fram mínre dóhtor, Drihten, onwóce, Sat. 422. Críst wæs ācenned ... Hǽlend gehāten, heofonríces weard, Men. 4. On þā dúne þe Dryhten ǽr āhangen wæs, heofonríces weard, El. 718. II. *heaven as the abode of beatified spirits :*—þū ús lǽrdest þ wē ongeáton þæt ðæt ys úre ágen ... þæt ys þæt heofonríce, Solil. H. 8, 1. On fullum geleáfan heofonríces *de vitae aeternitate securus,* Ors. 6, 34; S. 290, 13. Bið open eádgum heofonríces duru, Ph. 12. Heofonríces hyht, helle wītu, An. 1054. Hefonríces þolian, Gen. 633. þæt wē sculon cuman of þisse worulde tó úres Fæder oeðle, þ is tó heofonríce, Ors. 5, 14; S. 248, 28 : Sat. 216. On heofonríce eádge mid englum, Cri. 1246 : 1639. In heofonríce habban eard mid englum, El. 621. III. *a place or condition of the greatest pleasure of which a person is capable :*—Hē hæfde his heofonríce hēr on eorðan, þā him nānes willan næs forwyrned hēr, ne nānes lustes on þysse weorulde *anima ejus in vita ipsius bene-dicetur,* Ps. Th. 48, 18.

**heofon-setl,** es; *n. The heavenly dwelling :*—In heofonsetle heán *in sede polorum,* Dóm. L. 276. v. ge-rinnan.

**heofon-steorra.** *Add :*—Heofonsteorran (cf. steorran, Bt. 33, 4; F. 132, 22) ealle efenbeorhte ne scínað, Met. 20, 222.

**heofon-waran;** *pl. m. The inhabitants of heaven :*—Gebyrian oððe heofonwarena cyninge oððe hellewītes deófium, Wlfst. 151, 20.

**heofon-ware.** *Take here the plural forms given under* **heofon-waru** *in Dict., and add :*—Ealle heofonware him tógeánes fērdon, Hml. S. 31, 1432. Críst þe sibb is heofonwara and eorðwara, Ors. 3, 5; S. 106, 29.

**heofon-waru.** *Add :* I. *the inhabitants of heaven :*—Gesamnod wyrð eall heofonwaru, Wlfst. 25, 11 : Ll. Th. ii. 132, 21. Gehýrað heofonwaru *audite, celi,* Wlfst. 44, 28. II. *heaven, the region*

*occupied by beatified spirits :*—Hē hefenware cǽga him (*St. Peter*) befǽste, 176, 15.

**heofon-wealdend,** es; *m. The ruler of heaven :*—Hefonwealdend *arcitenens* (Nullus me superat . . . ni Deus aethrali summus qui regnat in arce . . . Dum pater *arcitenens* concessit, jure guberno, Ald. 271, 13–21), An. Ox. 23, 10. v. heofon-hǽbbend.

**heofon-weorod,** es; *n. The heavenly host :*—Þurh Godes mihte bið eal āstyred heofonwered (heofon-, *v. l.*), Wlfst. 25, 21 : 203. 5.

**heofon-wlitig,** adj. *Of heavenly beauty :*—Wē magon gedōn þæt eorðcundlíce men magon gewiorðan hiofonwlitige, Först. Verc. 115, 11.

**heóf-sang.** *Dele, and see* heáf-sang : heofula. v. hafela, hnifol.

**heóf-sīþ** (?), es; *m. A lamentable condition :*—Nū mín hreþer is hreóh, heówsīþum (heóf-? Cf. heowaþ = heófaþ, Ps. Th. 46, 1) sceóh, Reim. 43.

**heófung.** *Add :*—Cōm seó mōdor mid mycelre sárnysse tō þǽre heófunga, Hml. S. 4, 315. Þās bemǽndon mid swýðlícre heófunge þ̄ hī swylce yrmðe gesāwon, 25, 213. þ̄ folc feóllon tō eorðan mid flōwendum teárum, cweðende mid heófunge (*communi lamentatione et fletu dicentes*), Hml. A. 107, 162. Hlehter eówer on heófincge (*luctum*) sī gehwyrfe∴; Scint. 26, 9. Heófun[ge] *querimoniam,* i. *singultum,* An. Ox. 3366. Þū gecerdest wōh mínne ł míne heófunge (*planctum meum*), Ps. L. 29, 12. Heófunga sicetungum *lamentorum singultibus,* Hpt. Gl. 472, 57. Mid mycclum heófungum hī heora geleáfan woldon āwendan, Hml. S. 5, 38. Hefige synna hefige heófinga (*lamenta*) gewilniaþ, Scint. 29, 12. ¶ In the gloss *jubilationis* heófunge, An. Ox. 1345, the passage referred to, 2 Tim. 4, 7, seems to have been misunderstood.

**heolfor.** *Add :*—Helabr *tabo,* An. Ox. 53, 19. Heolfre *tabo* (Jezebel discerpunt denſe molossi, membraque purpureo *tabo* perfusa ruebant, Ald. 207. 29), Wrt. Voc. ii. 96, 76.

**heolor** (-er), **helur** '(-or), e; *f. A scale of a balance, a balance :*—Heolor, helor *lanx,* Txts. 73, 1177; *trutina* vel *statera,* 103, 2041. Laxhe. holor (Ep. Gl. laxhe. olor) *l. lanx* heolor, Corp. Gl. H. i. 16. Helur *momentana* (cf. lytle wǽga *momentana* vel *statam,* i. 38, 42), Wrt. Voc. ii. 59, 6. Heolere (heolora, Hpt. Gl. 447, 73) *lance,* An. Ox. 1757. Heolore, 2, 46. Gelícere heolre *equa bilance,* 4602. Heolore, 2, 354. Hiolore, Hpt. Gl. 512, 77. Twyfealdre heolra, Wrt. Voc. ii. 86, 3 : 12, 1 (*the last five are glosses to* Ald. 65, 13). v. twiheolor.

**heoloran.** v. heolorian.

**heolor-bledu,** e; *f. The scale of a balance :*—Mid þā efnan helurblede *justa lance,* Wrt. Voc. ii. 48, 40.

**heolorian, heolrian, holrian** *to weigh in a balance :*—Hē heolrede *pensauit,* An. Ox. 1597. Holrede, Hpt. Gl. 443, 75. Heolrode *trutinabat,* Wrt. Voc. ii. 86, 4. Heolorende *librantis,* 78, 23 : 52, 29. v. ā-heolorian.

**heolorung,** e; *f. Weighing in a balance :*—Helerunge *momentum,* Wrt. Voc. ii. 59, 7.

**heoloþe.** v. eh- (eoh-), heáh-, hind-heolope : heolra. *Dele, and see* heolor.

**heolstor.** [*In the first passage perhaps* hrúse *might be read for* hrúsan *and* heolstre *be dat.* (*inst.*), *as in* El. 1082 :—þā þe in foldan deópe bedolfen sindon, heolstre behýded. *Or possibly* (?) *a form* heolstre *exists alongside* heolstor. v. Germ. 399, 447 *infra, and cf.* eówestre (?).] *Add :* m. :—Heolstr, heolstr *secessus,* Txts. 94, 901. Heolstre *latebra,* Wrt. Voc. ii. 50, 18. Heolstre, dígelnesse *latibulo,* i. *tenebrositate* (*taciturnitatis*), An. Ox. 3354. Heolster *latebram,* 3289. Hē sette ðeóstru heolstur (*latibulum*) his, Ps. Srt. 17, 12. Þē (*Satan*) se ælmihtiga gehnǽgde, and (on?, and on?) heolstor besceáf, An. 1193. Helustras, heolstras *recessus,* Txts. 92, 867. Hiolstra latebrarum, An. Ox. 2052. Holstrum (heolstrum, Hpt. Gl. 476, 9) *latebra, loca occulta,* 2968. Of díglum dimhofum ł heolstrum *obstrusis latibulis,* Hpt. Gl. 405, 61. Of heolstrum *de recessibus,* Wrt. Voc. ii. 81, 10 : 26, 51. Of heolhstrum, of díglum *de recessibus,* i. *de occultis* vel *de secretis,* 139, 5. Nán mon Godes mihte forflíhð on nánum heolstrum heofenan oððe eorðan oþþe sǽ ðriddan, Hml. Th. ii. 146, 31. Hleostrum *bibulis buccis,* Wrt. Voc. ii. 126, 6. Blāce stōdon scíre leóman (*the brilliant light from the pillar of fire*) . . . neowle nil.tscuwan ne mihton heolstor āhýdan *the shades of night could not hide the secret places of the earth because of the light from the pillar of fire,* Exod. 115. Betwyx clūdige heollstru *inter recessus scrupeos,* Germ. 399. 447. *See next word.*

**heolstor;** adj. *Add :*—Of heolestrum *de latebrosis* (*animae recessibus*), An. Ox. 11, 93. *See preceding and following words.*

**heolstrig;** adj. *Full of hiding places, dark, secret :*—On heolstrigere dígelnesse *in latebrosum* (*lautumiae*) *latibulum,* An. Ox. 3317. Of heolstriccum *de latebrosis,* Wrt. Voc. ii. 28, 38. ¶ *used substantively, a secret place :*—Of dígelnessum, heolstrigum (of dígelnessum, of heolstrigum, Hpt. Gl. 475, 53) *de recessibus,* An. Ox. 2952. *See two preceding words.*

**heon, hion.** v. heonan.

**heonan.** *Add :*—Heonon *hinc,* Ǽlfc. Gr. Z. 225. 3 : *dehinc,* 237, 10. Heonan *istinc,* Wrt. Voc. ii. 44, 55. I. local. (1) where

there is motion. (a) *from this place* or *spot :*—Mē lǽrdon Rōmāne þ̄ ic gewāt heonon (*from Rome*) onweg, Bl. H. 191, 14. Ic heonon nelle fleóu fōtes trym, By. 246 : Gen. 2149 : B. 252 : Jul. 253 : Gen. 415. Dōð þās þing heonon (hiona, L., R. *hinc*), Jn. 2, 16. (b) *from this* (*the speaker's*) *country :*—Heonon of lande wǽron twēgen abbudas gesende, Chr. 1050; P. 170, 27. Mín hlāford gewāt heonan of leódum ofer ýða gelāc, Kl. 6. (2) where distance is measured or direction determined :—Nis þæt feor heonon mílgemearces þæt se mere standeð, B. 1361 : Gen. 2279 : 2513. Sūð heonon, Bo. 26. (2 a) where relative position is marked :—Hiona and ðona (on twā healfa, W. S.) *hinc et inde,* Jn. L., R. 19, 18. (3) with verbs of looking. showi.g, calling, &c. :—Þone (*quem*) nǽnig heonon ne sceáwaþ, Bl. H. 31, 9. Heonan of þisse weurlde geseón þā sunnan sylfe, Solil. H. 47, 10. Hriucg þæs landes þe ic þē heonon getǽce, Gen. 2854. Heonan ic cleopige tō Heáhgode, Ps. Th. 56, 2. (4) *from this world, from this life.* v. heonansīþ :—Heonon *istinc,* i. *ex hac uita,* An. Ox. 3503. Hí tō ðē hionan (hion, Met. 20, 239) fundiaþ, Bt. 33, 4; F 132, 25 : Met. 18, 11. Heouon, Gen. 476. Hié forð heonon gewiton of worulde dreámum, Kr. 132. Āstigon heó on helle heonan lifigende, Ps. Th. 54, 14 : Cri. 754 : Mōd. 73. (5) *from this source* or *origin :*—Ðis is mín rihteþel, hionon ic wæs ácenned, Bt. 36, 2 ; F. 174, 23 : Met. 24, 51. Mín ríc nis heona (of ðyson middanearde, W. S.) *meum regnum non est hinc,* Jn. L. 18, 36. II. temporal. (1) *from this time onward :*—Ne driuco ic heone (*amodo;* heonun forð, W. S.) . . . oð ðone doege, Mt. L. 26, 29. Ne mec geseáð gié nū hena (heonon forð, W. S.), 23, 39. (1 a) *along with* forþ :—Heonon forþ *amodo,* An. Ox. 56, 67. Heonon forð on ēcnesse (*iam non amplius in aeternum*) ne ete ǽnig mann wæstm of þē, Mk. 11, 14. Gif hwā heonan forð ǽnigne man ofsleá, Ll. Th. i. 248, 2 : Hml. S. 7, 371. Forð heonon, Exod. 287. Sib sceal gemǽne englum and ǽldum ā forð heonan wesan, Cri. 582. (2) *at some time from now, at some time in the future, afterwards :*—Heona ł ǽfter ðisse (*amodo*) gié geseáð sunu monnes cymmende in wolcnum heofnes, Mt. L. 26, 64. (2 a) (at some definite time in the future) *from now :*—Heonan on þisse eahteþan niht *eight days hence,* Gū. 1009. v. be-heonan.

**heonane.** *Add :* I. *from this world.* v. heonan; I. 3 :—Ne mōt hē hionane lǽdan of þisse worulde wuhte þon mǽre hordgestreóna þonne hē hider bröhte, Met. 14, 9. II. *from existence :*—Gedwināð heonone þysse worulde gefeán (*hujus cessabunt gaudia saecli*) . . . wrǽnnes eác gewīteð heonone, Dom. L. 231–235.

**heonu.** *Add :* , eonu, enu, onu:—Heonu (henu, R.) *ecce,* Mk. L. 1, 2. Heonu (heono, R.), 2, 24 : 3, 32. Heono (henu, R.), M.. L. 11, 10 : 17, 5. Heona, 24, 6. Henu, 2, 1. Heunu, 12, 47. Heno, 2, 9. [H]eono, Lk. L. 23, 15. [H]eono (heono, R.), Jn. L. 3, 26 : 4. 35. [H]eno (henu, R.), Mt. L. 1, 20. (*In the last three instances the* h *is written above the line.*) Eonu porro (gewisslíce, W. S. sōðlíce ł uutedlíce, L. Mt. 8, 27), Wrt. Voc. ii. 72, 32. Eno nū hwæt wæs seó Salomones rǽste elles ?, Bl. H. 11, 19. Eno ic þē gecýþe, Andreas, 237, 4. Onu þonne gif, Gr. D. 303, 5. For many instances in the translation of Bede's History see Bd. M. p. xxix.

**heópa.** *Add :*—Heópan *sicomoros,* Wrt. Voc. ii. 120, 51. [If by *sicomorus* is meant a tree or shrub. this entry perhaps might belong here. But if a fruit is meant, the gloss belongs to heópe. *Sicomorus* seems used with the former meaning in the gloss *sicomorus* vel *celsa æps,* Wrt. Voc. i. 33, 27 : in the latter in the gloss *celsa agreste, sicomorus* heortberge (cf. *mora* heorotberge, 114, 27 ; *mora, celsa agreste,* Corp. Gl. H. 79, 271), ii. 131. 55.]

**heóp-brémel.** *l.* -brēmel, *and add:* [cf. hiaf-brāmi *tribulus,* Gallée.]

**heópe.** *Add :*—Heópe *buturnus,* Wrt. Voc. ii. 126, 84. ¶ in a local name (?) :—Tō Heópeoricge, C. D. iii. 71, 30. v. heópa.

**heorcnian.** *Add :* I. *absolute :*—Þā hēt se bisceop þ̄ hē heorcnode geornlícor; hē stōd þā and hlyste . . . and ne mihte nān þing þǽre myrþe gehýran, Hml. S. 31, 1391. Suwian and heorcnian (*audire*) leorniccnihtum gedafenað, R. Ben I. 26, 10. Þone weig tō ðǽra heorcnigendra heortan, Hml. Th. i. 362, 11. Heorc[niendum] *auscultan ibus,* Hpt. Gl. 472, 52. II. *with gen.* :—Ðā fēringa oðsuīgde hē, suǽ hē hwæshwegu hercnade . . . Cuæð hē, 'Hū meahte ic bū somod ge in heofon gehēran ge hēr sprecan,' Shrn. 72, 24. Hié hyrcnodon hāliges lāre, An. 654. Hē wolde hyrcnigan hālges lāra, mildes meðelcwida, Gū. 979. III. *with dat.* :—Hē heora wordum heorcnode, Hml. Th. i. 422 (*not* 442 *as in Dict.*), 2. IV. *with acc.* :—Maria sæt heorcnigende his lāre (cf. his word heorcnigende, 440, 16), Hml. Th. ii. 438, 33. v. ge-heorcnian.

**heorcnung.** *Add :* I. *the action of hearkening :*—Ǽlc ðǽra manna ðe hine forhæfð fram unālýfedlícere heorcnunge, Hml. Th. ii. 564, 4. II. *the faculty of hearkening, power of hearing :*—Stemn is geslagen lyft gefrēdendlíc on hlyste, swā micel swā on ðǽre heorcnunge is *voice is stricken air perceptible by the sense of hearing so much as is within the capacity of a person to hear,* Ǽlfc. Gr. Z. 4. 6. Underfōð þā deáfan heorcnunge, Hml. S. 29, 337.

**heord.** *Add :* I. *a company of domestic animals of one kind kept*

*together under the charge of one or more persons.* v. hirde :—Heorda *armentorum*, Wrt. Voc. ii. 6, 7. (1) *a herd* of oxen :—Sum fearr þǣre heorde drǣfe oferhogode, Hml. Th. i. 502, 12. Oxanhyrde mōt lǣswian .ii. oxan mid hlāfordes heorde, Ll. Th. i. 438, 14. (2) *a herd* of swine :—Wæs mycel swȳna heord (worn, L., R. *grex*) lǣsgende, Mk. 5, 11. Heord swȳna (sunor bergana, L.) *grex porcorum*, Lk. 8, 32 : suner berga, L. (swīna, R.). Mt. 8, 32. Ðonne se inswān his heorde tō mæstene drīfe, Ll. Th. i. 434, 21. (3) *a flock* of sheep :—Sceáphyrdes riht is þ hē hæbbe . . . his heorde meolc .vii. niht æfter emnihtes dæge. Ll. Th. i. 438, 24. His gebrōðru wǣron mid heora fæder heordum on lǣsum . . . ' Þīne gebrōðru healdað scēp on Sichima,' Gen. 37, 12 : 47, 4. Geseah hē þreó heorda sceápa sittende wið þone pitt . . . þǣra hyrda gewuna wæs, þonne hig heora heorda gegaderodon, 29, 2-3. (4) *in pl. flocks and herds* :—Hi fōrun . . . būton lītlingum and heordum (*absque parvulis et gregibus atque armentis*), Gen. 50, 8. (5) *a swarm* of bees. v. gafol-heord. II. *a spiritual flock* :—Ðonne se hirde gǣð on frēcne wegas sió hiord ðe unwærre bið gehrīst, Past. 29, 23. Sió hiord (heord, *v. l.*) sē ðe folgað ðǣm ðeáwum ðæs hierdes, 81. 3. Micel bið betwux ðæs hirdes līfe and ðǣre heorde, 75, 4. Þǣre heorde þe hī Gode healdan sceoldan nǣnige gōde beón, Bl. H. 45, 15. Ðæt gē fēden Godes heorde ðe under eów is, Past. 137, 17. Se hyrde þe þonne þā heorde intō Godes rīce mōt lǣdan, Ll. Th. i. 424, 10. III. *a family under the care of its head* :—Siððan mē se hálga (*God*) of hyrde freán mīnes fæder [hæfde] fyrn ālǣded (cf. Postquam eduxit me Deus de domo patris mei, Gen. 20, 13. *For* freá *used by a son of his father,* cf. Gen. 2889. *where Isaac addresses Abraham as* freá mīn. Freán and mīnes fæder *are in apposition, and the insertion of* hæfde *after* fæder *completes the else too short half verse* mīnes fæder, *and at the same time fits in with* ālǣded, *so making the alteration to* ālǣdde *unnecessary. Of* hyrde mīnes fæder *seems to be a translation of* de domo patris mei, *but perhaps* hyrd *might mean* keeping, care. v. IV.), Gen. 2695. Ic eom mundbora mīnre heorde, Rä. 18, 1. Herde bearn *filii*, Ps. Th. 126, 4. IV. *keeping, custody, care, guard. Take here the last two passages under* heorde *in Dict., and add* :—Hē ūt wæs gongende tō neáta scypene þāra heord (heorde, *v. l.* custodia) him wæs þǣre nihte beboden, Bd. 4, 24 ; Sch. 483, 2. Þæt hȳ feoh gestrȳnen and on hyrde lecgen *ut acquirant pecunia*, quas recondant, R. Ben. 136, 17. Gif hǣden cild binnon .ix. nihton þurh gīmelīste forfaren sī . . . gilde .xii. ōr for þǣre heorde þe hē wæs hǣden swā lange (i. e. *the priest was to pay a fine, because his care of his flock had been such that an infant member of it had been allowed to perish*), Ll. Th. ii. 292, 9. Of hyrde mīnes fæder, Gen. 2695. (See above under III.) v. gafol-, in-, sceáp-heord.

**heordan.** *Substitute*: heorde, an ; *f. The coarse part of flax, tow, oakum* ; *in pl.* hards *of flax* :—Of heordan wearpe *de stuppe* [i. *lini*] stamine, An. Ox. 3726 : Wrt. Voc. ii. 24, 30. (*For both see* Ald. 51, 23.) Heordan *stuppa*, Wrt. Voc. ii. 121, 14. Heordena (*altered from* heorþena) tendre *naptarum fomite* (heordan fomitum), Wrt. Voc. ii. 78, 7 : heordena *naptarum*, 59, 5ˢ. For all three see Ald. 23, 5), An. Ox. 1649. Heorþena *stupparum*, 3292. [*v. N. E. D.* hards.]

**heorde** *custody.* v. heord ; IV. **heord-ness.** v. hird-ness.

**heord-rǣden[n].** *Add* : I. *watching* as a sentinel on guard :— Swylce hyrdrǣdenu on nihte þā þe for nāhte beóþ gehæfde *tamquam custodia in nocte quae pro nihilo habentur.* Ps. L. 89, 4. II. *watching over* as a protector or guide, *watchful care* to prevent another suffering or doing wrong :—Se abbod mid ealre emhȳdignesse carige embe þā gyltendan gebrōðru . . . on eallum gemete hȳ scylun lǣca þeáwe on heora heordrǣddenne notian, R. Ben. 51, 2. Sȳn þā cild ā beheáldene mid steóre and mid mycelre heordrǣdenne ǣghwǣr (*cum omni custodiam habeant*), 117, 11. Heordrǣdene, R. Ben. I. 106, 12. Mid ealre heordrǣdenne (*custodia*) geheald heortan þīne (*keep thy heart with all diligence*, Prov. 4, 23), Scint. 100, 10. Ofer dohter gālfulle fæstna heordrǣdene (*keep a sure watch over a shameless daughter*, Ecclus. 42, 11), 177, 3. III. *watching over animals, care* of a herdsman :—Hire hyrdeman ðurh holdrǣdene sume āc āstāh and his orf lǣswode . . . and hē hearde feóll gewāt of worulde tō Gode for ðǣre hylde his hirdrǣdene (*for the fidelity of his care of the cattle*), Hml. Th. ii. 150, 33. IV. *a guard, watch, persons or things that guard* :— Neorxnawanges get is gehealden þurh engla þēnunge and fȳrene hyrdrǣdene, Angl. vii. 30, 288. Sete, Drihten, heordrǣdene mīnum mūðe, Hml. S. 30, 209. Heordrǣdena sē þe gesihð swīcunge hit getācnað *custodias qui uiderit deceptionem significat*, Lch. iii. 202, 13. V *a place for keeping* :—Hig gesetton þā burh æppla tō hyrdrǣdenne *posuerunt Hierusalem in pomorum custodiam*, Ps. L. 78, 1.

**heóre.** *l.* hīre. v. un-hīre.

**heorot.** *Add* :—Heort *cervus*, hind *cerva*. Wrt. Voc. i. 22, 63. Heorot, ii. 23, 9 : Ps. Vos. 41, 2. Geseah hē micelne floc heorta . . . æteówde him sylfum ān ormǣte heort. Hml. S. 30, 29. Heorutes (heorotes, Ps. Vos., heortes, Ps. Srt. 17, 34. Heoretes (heorotes, Ps. Vos.), 103, 18. Heortes heáfod *brunda* (cf. a harte horne *hec brunda*, 222, 3), Wrt. Voc. i. 17, 42. Heortes hȳd *nebris*, 26, 26. On heán muntum heortas wuniað, Ps. Th. 103, 17 :

28, 7. Hearta *cervorum*, Mt. p. 8, 5. Heorotum *cervis*, Ps. Th. 17, 32. Hē forbeád þā heortas, swylce eác þā bāras, swā swiðe hē lufode þā heádeór swilce hē wǣre heora fæder, Chr. 1086 ; P. 221, 9. ¶ the word occurs in many place-names as the first part of a compound :—On heortbrōc, C. D. iii. 430, 12. On hiortburnan, 459, 5. Tō heortdūne, 430, 11. Tō heorotfelda geate, ii. 215, 34. Tō Heortforda, iii. 462, 6. Tō heorthamme, vi. 120, 22. Fram heortleáge. iii. 406, 22. Heortmere, i. 195, 34. In ðā heortsole, iii. 380, 6. On ðæt heorotsol, ii. 249, 37. On heortwyllan, iii. 438, 33. On þ mynster þe is nemned Heo:oteá (*quod nuncupatur Herutea, id est insula cervi*), Bd 3, 24 ; Sch. 310, 18. Heorteá, 4, 23 ; Sch. 466, 3. v. buc-heorot.

**heorot-beg** *some kind of berry* :—*Murus eorum* i. *pro omni feraci arbore posuit* .i. *aliquando fructus eius albus, aliquando rufus, aliquando niger* .i. herutbeg (*note on* Ps. 78, 45), An. Ox. 54, 2. *See next word.*

**heorot-berge.** *Add* :—Heorotberge *mora*, Wrt. Voc. ii. 114, 27. Heoru.berge, 55. 77. Heortberige, Lch. iii. 304. 7. Heortberge *celsa agreste, sicomorus*, Wrt. Voc. ii. 130, 55. Heorotberge *fragus*; 38, 63. [v. D. D. hart-berry.]

**heorot-brembel.** *l.* -brēmel, -brēmbel, *and add:* See next word.

**heorot-bremel-leáf**, *es* ; *n. A leaf of the buckthorn* :—Cnūa heorotbrēmbelleáf, Lch. ii. 332, 6.

**heorot-brēr.** *Add* :—Heartbreer, Lk. L. 17, 6. Cf. heorot-beg, -berige.

**heorot-clǣfre.** *l.* -clǣfre, *and add* :—Heortclǣfre *cynocephaleon*, Wrt. Voc. i. 31, 4 : Lch. iii. 301, 27 : *camedus*, Wrt. Voc. i. 67, 6. Heortclǣfre. Ðeós wyrt þe man *chamedris* and ōþrum naman heortclǣfre nemneð, heó bið cenned on dūnum, Lch. i. 120, 18. [v. N. E. D. hart-clover.]

**heorot-crop.** *Add* :—Genim heorotcrop neoþeweardne, Lch. ii. 50, 11.

**heorot-smeoru** *hart's grease* :—Hiorotsmera, Lch. ii. 118, 13.

**heorr.** *Add* : I. *glossing* cardo :—Heor *cardo*, Wrt. Voc. ii. 103, 39. II. *a hinge; the bar which forms part of a hinge* :—Heorras *serras* (seras portarum tuarum, Ps. 147, 13), Bl. Gl. III. *a cardinal point* (local) :—Heorras eorðan *cardines terrae*, Ps. Srt. ii. 186, 29. Heorra, Ps L. Lnd. 238, 12. Æfter þām feówor heorren heofenes and eorðan, Lch. iii. 84, 11. IV. *an essential point* :—Heort *cardo.* i. *finis*, Germ. 388, 3. For þām wē cweþaþ þ þ hēhste gōa sié se hēhsta hrōf eallra gōda, and seó hior ðe eall gōd on hwearfaþ, and eác þ þing ðe mon eall gōd fore dēþ quo fit uti summa, cardo, atque caussa expetendorum omnium, bonitas esse jure credatur, Bt. 34, 7 ; F. 142, 35. [v. N. E. D. harre.] *See next word.*

**heorra.** *Substitute*: heorre, hearre, hyrre, an ; *f.* I. *glossing* cardo :—Hic cardo þeós heorre (heorr, *v. l.*), Ælfc. Gr. Z. 37, 9. Heorre (hearre, *v l.*) cardo, 317, 2. II. *a hinge; the bar which forms part of a hinge* :—Swē forhwerfed bið on hiore hyrran *sicut* (*ostium*) *vertitur in cardine suo*, Kent. Gl. 991. Hē gestrangode heorran þ scytielsas gata þīnra confortauit seras portarum tuarum, Ps. L. 147, 13. III. *a cardinal point* :—Hearran *cardines orbis terrae*, Kent. Gl. 268. *See preceding word.*

**-heort.** *Add* : -heort, es ; *n.* v. wēden-heort ; -heort ; *adj.* v. clǣn-, eaþmōd- (? Az. 152), efen- (?), ge-, hearm-, hell-, unge-, wēden-heort ; wōdheortness.

**heort-angness** (?). v. cnyss.

**heort-cōðu**, es ; *f.* *Substitute*:—heort-coþu, e ; *f.* : -coþa, an ; *m.* *Heart-disease* :—Cardiacus dicitur qui patitur laborem cordis, vel morbus cordis heortcoþa vel ece, mōdseócnes vel unmiht, Wrt. Voc. ii. 128, 65. Hwīlum wyrmas heortcoþe wyrceað, Lch. ii. 176. 13.

**heorte.** *Add* : I. *the heart as organ of an animal's body* :—Gif þīn heorte ace *ad cardiacos*, Lch. iii. 42, 1. Þǣre heortan þā līflican *cordis uitalia*, i. lxxiv, 26. Bān bið funden on heortes heortan, Lch. i. 338, 6. Gyf hwā onbūtan his heortan oþþe on his breóstum sār þolie, 206. 18 : Gū. 1116 Nim his (a badger's) lifre . . . and þā heortan æt þīnum burhgeatum behele, Lch. i. 328, 24. II. *the heart as seat of life* :—Mē is heorte and flǣsc hearde geteórad, Ps. Th. 72, 21. Deáðes wylm hrān æt heortan, B. 2270 : Gen. 724. Þē tō heortan grīped ādl unlīðe, 936. Bīdan hwonne of heortan hunger oððe wulf sāwle and sorge sonede ābregde, 2276. Ic (the baker) heortan mannes gestrangie, Coll. M. 28, 36 : Ps. Th. 103, 15. Heáfodswīma heortan clypte, Gen. 1369. Heora heortan onfōð mægene (leofað heorte heara, Ps. Srt.) and libbað ā worlda world *vivet cor eorum in seculum seculi*, 21, 2ᶜ. III. *the region of the heart, breast, bosom* :—Sum heó hire on handum bær, sum hire æt heortan læg, Gen. 636. IV. *the heart as seat of feeling, will, intellect, mind* :—Hwæt getācniað ðā heán hwammas būton unclǣnu and twiefeald mōd ? For ðǣm ǣlc wāg bið gebīeged twiefeald on ðǣm heale. Suā bið ðæs monnes heorte, Past. 245, 14 ; Ps. Th. 77, 36 : 56, 9. Hwæt is se ealdordoom bū an ðæs mōdes storm, sē simle bið cnyssende ðæt scip ðǣre heortan mid ðāra geðōhta ȳstum, Past. 59, 5. Gē tælde hyra heortan (heartes, L.) heardnesse, for ðām ðe hī ne gelȳfdon, Mk. 16, 14. Heortan cræftas, Dan.

394. þæt hié weorðeden móde and mægene þone mǽran dæg heortan gehigdum, El. 1224: Cri. 747. Mínre heortan hyge, Ps. Th. 72, 17: 85, 13: 118, 69. His módor geheóld ealle þás word on hyre heortan (hearta, L., heorte, R.) smeágende, Lk. 2, 51. Hálig in heortan, Gú. 554. Se deófol sǽwð mánfullice geþóhtas intó þæs mannes heortan, Angl. vii. 28, 263. þám þe mid heortan hycgeað rihte *his qui recto sunt corde*, Ps. Th. 72, 1: Dan. 491: 598. Fór se deófol on Iúdas heortan þ hé hine belǽwde, Jn. 13, 2: Hy. 7, 79: Dan. 570. Hí berað on breóstum heortan clǽne, Gú. 771. Eall geþanc manna heortena wæs gewend on yfel, Gen. 6, 5. Ic hí lifian hēt lustum heortena (*secundum desideria cordis eorum*), Ps. Th. 80, 12. IV a. *where eyes or ears are attributed to the heart* :—Hé gehwyrfde his heortan eáge, Past. 99, 22. Wē sceolon gleáwlíce þurhseón ūsse hreðercosan heortan eágum, Cri. 1329. Anhyld þīnre heortan eáre, R. Ben. 1, 3. V. *the seat of one's inmost thoughts, one's inmost being, soul* :—Of þǽre heortan willan se mūð spicð, Mt. 12, 34. Opene weorðað monna dǽde, ne magon weras heortan geþóhtas fore waldende bemīðan, Cri. 1048: 1056: 1039. Bedeáglian hwæt hé dearninga on hyge hogde heortan geþoncum, Gú. 1227. His heortan diégennesse hit geopenað, and þæs óðres heortan belocene hit þurhfærþ, Bt. 13; F. 38, 26. Nā swilce God nyte ǽlces mannes heortan, Angl. vii. 50, 490. VI. *intent, will, desire, inclination* :—Adame his hyge hwyrfde and his heorte ongann wendan tó hire willan, Gen. 716. Selle ðē Dryhten efter heortan ðínre (cf. ðínum willan, Ps. Th.), Ps. Srt. 19, 5. Utan ealle ánmódre heortan georne ūrum Drihtne cwēman, Ll. Th. i. 424, 14. Eallum þám þe his líchoman mid ēstfulre heortan sēceað, Chr. 1023; P. 156, 25. VII. *disposition, temperament, character* :—Ðwerre heortan (*qui peruersi cordis (est)*, Kent. Gl. 612. For eówer heortan heardnesse hē eów wrát þis bebod, Mk 10, 5. Ic eom bilwite and eádmód on heortan, Mt. 11, 29. Oferhýdegum eágum, unsǽdre heortan, nolde ic mid þǽm men mínne mete ðicgean *superbo oculo et insatiabili corde, cum hoc simul non edebam*, Ps. Th. 100, 5. Hē hæfde heortan unhneáweste hringa gedáles, Vid. 73. Sumum hē syleð monna milde heortan, Crä. 108: Alm. 2. VIII. *the seat of the emotions generally* :—Him mæg beón þe glædre his heorte, Angl. viii. 317, 39. Heorte mín āhlyhheð, Ps. Th. 85, 11. Ys mē on hreðre heorte gedréfed, 54, 4: 68, 21: 101, 4. Heorte ys onhǽted, Jud. 87. þá þíostro þínre heortan (þínre gedréfednesse, Bt. 6; F. 14, 30) willað mínre leóhtan lāre wiðstondan, Met. 5, 21. Hē heortan sorge wæg, B. 2463. God mæg gehǽlan hygesorge heortan mínre, Cri. 174: Gú. 1178. Hē geblissað on his heortan, Ex. 4, 14. Būte him ǣr cume hreów tó heortan, Met. 18, 11 Wǽron heaðowylmas heortan getenge, Exod. 148: Dan. 609: Ps. Th. 101, 4. Him wæs leóht sefa heortan néh, An. 1254. Hit wyrs ne mæg on þínum hyge hreówan þonne hit mē æt heortan dēð, Gen. 826. þæt wæs torn were hefig æt heortan, 980: Cri. 500: 1494. Is mín mód gehǽled, hyge ymb heortan gerūme, Gen. 759: 354. Hē hafað wērige heortan, seán sorhfulne, Sal. 377. IX. *the seat of love or affection* :—Þǽr þín goldhord is, þǽr is þín heorte (hearta, L., eorta, R.), Mt. 6, 21. Utan God lufian innewerdre heortan, Ll. Th. i. 350, 9. Heó cwæð þ heó hine ne nānne habban wolde mid líchoman (líchomlicre, *v. l.* licre *is written above* an) heortan (*with carnal affection?*), Chr. 1067; P. 201, 19. X. *the seat of courage* :—Hige sceal þe heardra, heorte þe cēnre, mód sceal þe māre þe ūre mægen lytlað, By. 312: B. 2561. Getrymed is heorte his, Ps. Srt. 111, 8. Heard heortan geþóht habban, Kl. 43. Hē sent on eów forhte heortan, Deut. 28, 65. Herd hige þínne, heortan staðola, An. 1215. Heardrǽdne hyge, heortan strange, Gen. 2348. Hí beóð heortum þý hwætran, Rä. 27, 20. XI. *the seat of the intellectual faculties* :—Eálá dysegan and on heortan lǽte, Lk. 24, 25. Hē āblende hyra eágan and āhyrde hyra heortan, þ hí ne geseón mid hyra eágon and mid hyra heortan ne ongyton, Jn. 12, 40. Drihten eów ne sealde undergitende heortan, Deut. 29, 4. XII. *the central part of anything* :—Byð mannes sunu on eorðan heortan þrý dagas and þreó niht, Mt. 12, 40. XIII. *in phrases with prepositions.* (1) æt heortan *in (one's) inmost thoughts* :—Heó wuldorcyning herede æt heortan, Jul. 239. (2) *in (on)* heortan *in (one's) inmost thoughts* :—Gyf se yfela þeówa þencð on his heortan and cwyð, 'Mīn hlafurd uferað his cyme,' Mt. 24, 48: Leás. 6. Abraham hlōh cweðende on his heortan, 'Wenst þū . . .', Gen. 17, 17: Ps. Th. 52, 1 (cf. on his móde, 13, 1). Hē in breóstum þā gīt herede in heortan heofonríces weard, An. 52. Ic herge in heortum (-an?) heofonríces weard, Gú. 583. (2 a) on ealre heortan *with all (one's) heart* :—Ic andete Drihtne on ealre mínre heortan (*in toto corde meo*), Ps. Th. 9, 1. (3) mid . . . heortan *with (all) one's heart, with great sincerity or devotion* :—þæt wē mid heortan hǽlo sēcen, Cri. 752. Fæder and mōder freó þū mid heortan, Fä. 9. Hē gebǽrd suā geðyldelíce suelce hē hit hæbbe mid ealre heortan forlǽten, Past. 225, 18. Gelýfst ðū mid ealre heortan?, Hml. Th. i. 420, 35. Ne herede heó hine nō mid wordum ānum, ac mid ealre heortan, Bl. H. 13, 6. Biddað mid inweardre heortan ðysne apostol, Hml. Th. i. 68, 8. Ic þe mid ealre innancundre heortan (*in toto corde meo*) sēce, Ps. Th. 118, 10. ¶ Cf. *the use of the instrumental case* :—Inwerdre heortan

biddan, Ll. Th. i. 312, 23. XIV. *in the phrase* in heortan and heortan *with duplicity* :—In heortan and heortan spreocende syndun ðā yflan *in corde et corde locuti sunt mala*, Ps. Srt. 11, 3. v. hát-heorte.

**heort-ece.** *Add* :—*Cardiacus dicitur qui patitur laborem cordis vel morbus cordis* heortcoþa *vel* [heort]ece, Wrt. Voc. ii. 128, 66. Wiþ heortece, gif him oninnan heard heortwærc sié, Lch. ii. 60, 6. Wiþ heorotece, 11. Wiþ hiorotece, 14.

**heort-gesíða.** *Substitute*: heort-gesidu(-a); *pl. The vitals, entrails* :—þone rysle þe þá heortgesida mid beóð oferwrigen *adipem qui operit vitalia* (v. heorte, I, *and* cf. *uitalia, uiscera*, Corp. Gl. H. 120, 209: *uitalia, uiscera, renuncule* i. lundlagan, Wülck. Gl. 29, 37), Lev. 3, 3. v. heort-hama.

**heort-gryre**, es; *m. Terror of heart, mortal terror* :—Fela cynna egesan geweorþað on eorðan folce tó heortgryre, Wlfst. 86, 15.

**heorþ.** *Add*: I. *a hearth, fire-place* :—Fyrpannae *vel* herth *arula*, Txts. 36, 5. Hearth, 123, 17. Heort *foculare*, Wrt. Voc. ii. 39, 38. Íren hiorð *arula*, 10, 21. Heorðe *fornacula*, 109, 7: 35, 77. Wermōd gesodenne on wætere on nīwum cytele, dō of heorðe, Lch. ii. 44, 2. Brǽdingce on heorþum tó mōse *assaturam (alimentorum) in focularibus (praeparatam) ad edulium*, An. Ox. 376: Wrt. Voc. ii. 82, 30. II. *as typical of the household or home* :—Ān mylen . . . and .vii. heorðas būtan ðon, and þreó cyrcan, C. D. v 316, 2. v. wigbed-heorþ.

**heorþa.** *Add* :—Herþa (*is the reading of the MS. given in*) Ælfc. Gr. Z. 321, 5. Ǽlce geáre tó preósta gescý finde man biccene heorðan (*pelles buccinas*), Chrd. 48, 26.

**heort-hama.** *Add* :—Heorthama *bucleamen*, Wrt. Voc. ii. 126, 67. Smælþearmas, geallan mid þý heorthoman (*bucliamine*), Lch. i. lxxii, 7. [The Latin of Ex. 29, 22 is: Tolles arvinam quae operit vitalia. v. heort-gesidu.

**heorþ-bacen.** *Add* :—His gebrōðra worhton heom heorðbæcenne (axbakenne, *v. l.*) hláf (*panem subcinericium*), Gr. D. 86, 32.

**heorþ-hogu.** *Add*: ; Wlfst. 177, 7.

**heorþ-pening.** *Add*: Cf. Nū dōð hig æt ǽlcum heorðe tó gecnáwnisse þām canonicon ānne penig . . . and ealswā æt ǽlcum forðfarenum gildan æt ǽlcum heorðe ǽnne penig tó sáwulsceote, Cht. Th. 609, 6–12.

**heorþ-swǽpe.** *For 'Som.' substitute* :—Heorðsuaepé (herdusuēpe, Leiden Gl.) *pronuba*, Txts. 89, 1660. v. hád-swǽpe.

**heortian** (?) *to encourage* :—Heortendum *cohortante*, Hpt. Gl. 425, 23. v. hirtan.

**heort-leás**; *adj. Without courage or spirit, cowed* :—Ic bidde, man, þ þū gemune hū micel bið se brōga beforan dómsetle Drihtnes þænne, stent hē (ealra hergea mǽst, Wlfst. 137, 22) heortleás and earh, āmasod and āmarod, mihtleás, āfǽred *sis memor illius qui tum pavor ante tribunal percutiet stupidis cunctorum corda querelis*, Dóm. L. 124.

**-heortness.** v. ofer-heortness.

**heort-scræf**; *n. The heart-cavern, the heart with its dark recesses* :—Ne þǽr ōwiht inne ne belífe on heortscræfe heánna gylta *nec lateat quidquam culparum cordis in antro*, Dóm. L. 39.

**heort-seóc, -seócness.** *Dele.*

**heort-wærc.** *Add* :—Gif him oninnan heard heortwærc sié, þonne him wyxþ wind on þǽre heortan, Lch. ii. 60, 6: iii. 74, 21. Wið heortwærce, 18.

**heoru-drync.** *Substitute: Drinking by the sword, a wound.* [For the personifying of the sword and its drinking of blood when making a wound cf. such passages as : Gladius Domini repletus est sanguine, Is. 34. 6. Qui prohibet gladium suum a sanguine, Jer. 48, 10] :—Hreðles eafora hiorodryncum swealt (cf. wundum sweltan, By. 293) bille gebeáten, B. 2358.

**heoru-flā** *an arrow for war* :—Wǣpna and heoruflān *arma et sagitte*, Ps. L. 56, 5.

**heoru-hóciht.** l. -hóciht(e): heow. l. heów. v. híw: heów-síþ. v. heóf-síþ: heówung. v. híwung.

**hér.** *Add* :—Sume (*adverbs*) synd *localia*, þæt synd stōwlice, for ðan ðe hí getácniað stōwa . . . hér, Ælfc. Gr. Z. 224, 15. Sume cumað of naman speliendan, *hic* hér, 233, 9. I. *in this place* :—Wē nabbað hér (*hic*) būtun fíf hlā ās, Mt. 14, 17. Gōd ys ūs hér tó beónne, 17, 4. Ic hér on sōðre gewitnesse stande, Ll. Th. i. 180, 27. Hē ārās, nis hé hér (hír, L.), Mk. 16, 6. ¶ marking place to which a person has come to get something :—þ ic ne durfe hér feccan *ut non ueniam huc haurire*, Jn. 4, 15. I a. *in this country, region, place of residence* :—Ūre ieldran, ðā ðe ðás stōwa ǽr hióldon, hié lufodon wisdóm . . . Hér mon mæg giét gesión hiora swæð, . . . Hér woldon ðæt hér ðý māra wísdóm on londe wǽre, Past. 5. 13–25. Hē onfehð friccan scíre and foryrneles ðā hér iernað beforan kyningum, 91, 21. Hér mid ūs, Ph. 23: 31. Hér is ǽghwylc eorl ōðrum getrýwe, B. 1228. Hér used with a noun qualified by *this* :—Rufinus wolde habban him self þon anwold þǽr eást, and Stileca wolde sellan his suna þisne hér west, Ors. 6, 37; S. 296, 7. Hér sǽged on þissum bócum, Bl. H. 45, 3. Ic in answer to a call :—'Hwǽr eart þū?' Him andwyrde þ heáfod, 'Hér, hér, hér,' Hml. S. 32, 151. II. *in a weakened sense, more or less*

directly indicating something present to the sight or mind, where attention is called to what the speaker has, brings, or offers, or discovers :—Hér is seó stów *ecce locus*, Mk. 16, 6. Hláford, hér ys þín pund *domine, ecce mna tua*, Lk. 19, 20 : 22, 38 : Gen. 2226. Hér þú hæfst þ þín ys *ecce habes quod tuum est*, Mt. 25, 25 : Gen. 2889. Hér ys geswutelod úre forwyrd, Jud. 177. 289 : Gen. 75. 1. Nú hæbbe ic his hér on handa, 678 : Vald. 2, 18. **III.** *on earth, in this world or life :*— Ne wæs hér þá giét nymðe heolstersceado wiht geworden, Gen. 103. Æghwilc man sceolde mid sáre on þás world cuman, and hér on sorhgum beón, Bl. H. 5, 28. Þ gé hér on mínum naman syllaþ, 41, 17. Ne mæg ic hér leng wesan, B. 2801. Ge hér nytwyrðe tó beónne, ge þider tó cumane, Solil. H. 2, 16. Hér for worulde, Bt. 37, 3 : F. 190, 10 : Bl. H. 49, 19 : Ll. Th. i. 328, 13. ¶ with defining phrase :—Hér ofer eorðan, Crä. 30. Sê þe hér on eorðan eáðmód leofað, Mód. 68. On eorðan hér, Ph. 638. Wê men cweðað on grunde hér, Hy. 9, 39. Hér on life, Ll. Th. i. 372, 35 : Seel. 150. In life hér, Gú. 1222. Hér on þyssum lænum lífe, Kr. 108. Libban hér on worulde, Bt. 19 ; F. 70, 15 ; Bl. H. 35, 35. Þ ðá yfelan hér on worulde habban sceoldan, Bt. 38, 2 ; F. 198, 15 : Gen. 474. In worulde hér, Gú. 864. **IV.** in reference to speech or action. (1) *at this point* of a book :—Hér endaþ seó ǽreste bóc, Bd. 1, 34 ; Sch. 105, 14. Hér endaþ nú seó æftre fróferbóc and onginþ seó þridde, Bt. 21 ; F. 76. 2 : Solil. H. 54, 6 : 55, 1. (2) *at this juncture :*—Uton gebyddan unc hér dæglanges, and spurian tó morgen furður *hodie satis scripsimus*, Solil. H. 45, 22. (3) referring to what has just been said :—Nú ic þyses Alexandres hér gemyngade *Alexandri istius mentione commonitus*, Ors. 3, 7 ; S. 110, 9. Hér (*in the lesson just read*) sagaþ Matheus, Bl. H. 27, 3 : 49, 3 : 23, 12. (4) referring to what immediately follows :—Hér is Eádgáres cyninges gerædnes, Ll. Th. i. 262, 1. Hér seó clænnes þá fúlnesse þreáð, Prud. 14 (*and often*). **V.** with verbs of coming or bringing :—Þæt hý hí wið þæt warnien þæt hý hér (*in locum hunc tormentorum*) ne cumen, Solil. H. 68, 6. Þá ic hér ǽrest cómen, Gen. 2711: Bo. 7 : B. 244 : 376. Hér syndon gesferede Geáta leóde, 361 : An. 1175. **VI.** hér . . . þær *here . . . there* (with indefinite force) :— Gyf eów hwá segð, ' Nú Críst ys hér, oððe þær,' Mt. 24, 23. **VII.** along with other adverbs, from which juxtaposition arise later compound forms. (1) æfter, bæftan :—Swá swá wê eft hér æfter secgað *ut in sequentibus dicemus*, Bd. 3, 30 ; Sch 332, 3 : Angl. viii. 317, 37. Hýr efter, Ll. Th. i. 26, 6 : 36, 13. Is hér bæftan gecweden on endebyrdnesse þæs godspelles, Hml. Th. ii. 80, 24. (2) be-eástan cf. I a. :— Wê witan ófer égland hér be-eáston (*to the east of this country*), Chr. P. 3, 11. (3) beforan :—Ðeára sáula ðe haer beforan hiora namon áuuritene siondon. C. D. i. 294, 3 : Hml. Th. ii. 368, 5. Swá hit hér beforan gecweden is, Ll. Th. i. 204, 2 : 390, 9. (4) be-ufan :—Ðás gewriotu ðe hér beufan stondað, C. D. ii. 121, 23. (v. hér-bufan *in Dict.*) (5) inne. Cf. I. :—Bróðor gang hider in tó ús ; se ylca is hér inne ðe áhredde ðá cnihtas, Hml. Th. ii. 312. 4 : Gen. 436. Hér syndon inne dôhtor mine, 2464. (6) neáh :—Ic wât heáhburg hér áne neáh, Gen. 2517. (7) of :—Hê sum þing hér of undergyte, Angl. viii. 317, 39. (8) on-gemang. v. hér-ongemong *in Dict.* (9) tó :—Hér tó bið understanden se Hálga Gást, Hml. Th ii. 362, 25. (10) tó-eácan :— Ðás ðing . . . and fela hér tóeácan, Wlfst. 48, 11 : 67, 4. (11) wiþ-neoþan :—Be þyssa witena gewitnysse þe hér wiðnyðan áwritene standað, Cht. E. 236. 15.

**hér** ; adj. *Dele, and see* here-spel : **héra**. v. **híra** : **hér-æfter**. v. **hér** ; **VII** : **herbid**. v. **hilfan**.

**here** glosses fornaculum, Wrt. Voc. ii. 109, 12 : 36, 2. Cf. (?) dur-here.

**here** an army. *Add :* **I.** *a body of armed men.* (1) not referring to England. (a) *an army, a host* :—Cempa *miles*, here *exercitus*, Wrt. Voc. i. 72, 69 : faccus, *exercitus*, ii. 146, 70. Fird, here *expeditio*, 29, 69. Bið se here eal ídel, ðonne hê on óðer folc winnan sceal, gif se heretoga dwolað *in exploratione hostium ; rustra exercitus velociter sequitur, si ab ipso duce itineris erratur*, Past. 129. 8. Here wícode égstreáme neáh, El. 65. Handrófra here, Exod. 247. Dauid miclum his ágenes herges ; leah *cum damno exercitus*, Past. 37, 7 : Bl. H. 193, 2. Ic ríde herges on ende, Rä. 78, 8. Heriges wísa, Dan. 203. Herges wísa, freom folctoga, Exod. 13. Mennen þe þú áhreddest herges cræstum, Gen. 2127. Títus cóm mid Rómána herige . . . þá leóde flugon þá hié þone here tóweardne wiston, El. H. 79, 11–13. Se eorl of Normandíge sende tó Francena cynge, and hé cóm mid mycelan here, and se cyng and se eorl mid ormætre fyrde besǽton þone castel, Chr. 1090 ; P. 225, 28. Út of þám herige, Jud. 135. Se cyning sende his here tó *missis exercitibus suis*, Mt. 22, 7. ¶ in an epithet of the Deity, the Lord of *hosts* :—God sylfne, herga fruman, El. 210 : Cri. 845. (b) *a division of an army, army corps, legion, cohort, troop* :—Wæs eft here hider onsended *rursus mittitur legio*, Bd. 1, 12 ; Sch. 33, 6. Ðá onsendon hí him micelne here tó fultume *quibus legio destinatur armata*, Sch. 32, 7. Hergas wurdon feówer on fleáme, Gen. 2073. Wéron gesendeno hergas his *missis exercitibus suis*, Mt. L. 22, 7. Heria *manipulorum*, An. Ox. 2, 443. Herium *cohortibus*, 23. Hóf for

hergum hlúde stefne lifgendra leód, Exod. 276. Faraon bróhte sweordwígendra síde hergas. 260. Twelf hergas engla *duodecim legiones angelorum*, Mt. 26, 53. Him Perse mid heora twégen ealdormannum ongeán cóman . . . Sóna swá hê wiste þ hê wið þá twégen heras sceolde, Ors. 3, 1 ; S. 96, 15. (c) *a particular kind of armed force*, e. g. infantry, cavalry :—Pharon hæfde syx hund wígwægna, and fela þæs óðres heres wæs *exercitum curribus equitibus instructum egit*, Ors. 1, 7 ; S. 38, 24. On his fêðehere wæron xxxii M, and þæs gehorsedan (*equitum*) fífte healf M, 3, 9 ; S. 124, 12. Of rædum here *aequitatu*, fótgangendum here *peditatu*, An. Ox. 5253–4. (2) *referring to* English military affairs. [In that part of the A. S. Chronicle which deals with the struggle between the English and Danes, *here* is always used of the latter, *fyrd* being the term denoting the native force. But in the annals of the eleventh century *here* is used in speaking of the English.] (a) *an army* :—Harold feaht eár þan þe his here cóme eall, Chr. 1066 : P. 198, 5. Cóm Harold úre cyng . . . mid micclan here Englisces folces (cf. mid ealre his fyrde, 33), P. 197, 27. Se cyng mid his here férde tó Hrofeceastre, 1087 ; P. 224, 8, 10, 12. On here cringan, By. 292. Penda teáh here and fyrde wið Eástengle, Bd. 3, 18 ; Sch. 274, 9. Ne onhagode him (*Godwine*) tó cumenne . . . ongeán þone cyng and ágeán þone here (fyrd *is used of Godwine's force* ll. 11, 23, *and of the force gathered to help the king*, l. 19) þe him mid wæs, Chr. 1052 ; P. 175, 36. Hét se cyning bannan út here, 1048 ; P. 174, 22. Þis weard Harolde cyng gecýdd, and hê gaderade þá mycelne here (cf. Harold gegæderade sciphere (-fyrde, *v. l.*) and landhere (-fyrde, *v. l.*), P. 195, 38), 1066 ; P. 199, 27. Willelm cyng lædde Englisene here (fyrde, *v. l.*) and Frencisce ofer sǽ, 1073 ; P. 209, 6. (b) *used of a raiding v. l.*) *and ravages a country* :—Leófgár fór tó fyrde ongeán Griffin force, one that ravages a country :—Earfoðlic is tó ætellanne seó gedrecednes . . . þe þone Wyliscan cing . . . Earfoðlic is tó ætellanne seó gedrecednes . . . þe eall Engla here dreáh, Chr. 1056 ; P. 186, 33. Penda cóm mid Myrcna here (*hostili exercitu*), and ealle þá þe hê mihte mid ísene and fýres lýge hê fornam, Bd. 3, 17 ; Sch. 269, 9 ; Chr. 1052 ; P. 178, 39 : 1054 ; P. 184, 14. Ecgferð sende here on Scottas . . . and earmlíce hí Godes cyrican hýndan and bærndon, 684 ; P. 39, 13. (c) *an army that comes from abroad to England* :—Willelm férde intó Englalande mid myccian here ridendra manna and gangendra of Francríce and of Brytlande, Chr. 1085 ; P. 215, 35. ¶ *especially of the Scandinavian invaders.* (1) *as raiders of the country* :—Ðis man gerǽdde ðá se micela here cóm tó lande, Wlfst. 180, 18 : Ll. Th. i. 286, 7. Unrím heriges here cóm tó lande, Ll. Th. i. 286, 7. Ðis synd þá friðmál þe Æðelred cyng and ealle his witan wið ðone here gedón habbað ðe Anláf and Iustin and Gúðmund mid wǽron. Æt ǽrost, þ woroldfrið stande between Æðelréde cynge and eallum his leódscipe and eallum þám here þe se cyng þ feoh sealde, Ll. Th. i. 284, 6–11. Twá and twéntig þúsend punda mon gesealde þám here wið friðe, 288, 12. (1 a) *the reference is probably to the Scandinavians in the following :*—Gif hit cucu feoh wære and hé secgge þ hit here nǽme (cf. jumentum . . . captum ab hostibus, Ex. 22, 10), Ll. Th. i. 52, 2. Ðá earman men beóð wyrs bereáfode from þám unrihtwísan déman þonne fram þám wælgrímmestan here : ne bið nán heretoga swá gífre on frændrea monna yrfe swá se unrihtwísa déma byþ on his hýremonna. Hê beóð wyrsan þonne herigende here, here man mæg oft befleón, Ll. Lbmn. 475, 14–23. (2) *as settlers* :—Oslác eorl and eal here þe on þis ealdordôme wunað, Ll. Th. i. 278, 5. Þ he þeówe ne freó ne mótun in þone here faran bútan leáfe, ne heora nán þe mã tó ús, 156, 1. Gefæstnode Eádweard cyng frið wið Eást-Engla here (wið Eást-Engle, *v. l.*), Chr. 906 ; P. 95, 2. (3) *the word is applied to both the English and Danish forces in the following :*— þá heras him sylfe tóeódan (cf. Eádmund gegaderode fyrde and þone here áflymde, 1.), Chr. 1016 ; P. 150, 2. **II.** *used of things that can injure* :—Mid herige hrímes and snáwes, Men. 204. **III.** *a large number of people, multitude, host.* (1) *of persons engaged in acts of violence.* v. Ll. Th. i. 110, 14 *in Dict.* :—þ here (wered, W. S.) turba, Lk. L., R. 22. 47. Weard eal here burhwarena blind, Gen. 2490. Cirm hæðnes heriges (*the crowd that attacked St. Andrew*), An. 1240 : 1204 : Ap. 21. Hí here samnodan, An. 1126 : 1189. ¶ in pl. to express great numbers :—Síde herigeas, An. 1069. (2) *of a regular company* :—Heofenengla here, Cri. 1278. Heres *classis regular company* :—Heofenengla here, Cri. 1278. Heres *classis (monasticae)*, An. Ox. 5502. Gê cunnon hwæt se hláford is, sê þisne here lædeð, Cri. 574. Ælbeorhtra scolu, hergas háligra, 930 þæt heregas þreó, se heofonlica þreát . . . þæt helcunde heregas þreó, se heofonlica þreát . . . þæt helcunde wered, Wlfst. 254, 11–15. (3) *of a fortuitous collection of people, a crowd, multitude* :—Wæs forléten here (*turba*), Mt. L. 14, 23. Þ here, Mk. L. 12. 41 : Lk. L. 23, 48. Synfulra here, Cri. 1533. Mid monigfald here *plurima multitudine*, Mk. L. 10, 46. On alle ðiosne here (*turbam*), Lk. L. 9, 13. Þ here, 18, 36. ¶ in pl. to express great numbers :— Ðegnas saldon ðæm hergum (*turbis*), Mt. L. 14, 19 : Lk. L. 7, 24. Weard Godes ágen bearn áhangen for herigum, El. 180 : Met. 26, 57. Ðá gesæh ðe Hælend hergas menigo *videns Jesus turbas multas*, Mt. L. 8, 18. **IV.** *harrying, devastation, plundering, ravaging :*—Ic eów áwerige wið hearma gehwilcne, þæt eów bíte ne slíte here ne hunger, Wlfst. 132, 18. Gyf hit geweorðe þæt on þeódscype becume heálic

ungelimp, here ođđon hunger, bryne ođđon blodgyte, unwæstm ođđon unweder . . . 169, 16. Hé þá mægđe mid grimme wæle and herige on gebræc *prouinciam illam saeua caede ac depopulatione attriuit*, Bd. 4, 15; Sch. 423, 10. v. bil-, féþe-, gang-, hors-, land-, norþ-, rád-, ræde-, ríde-, stæl-, unfriþ-here. The word occurs in many proper names.

hére dignity. *In the passage* Hwæt is hiora here, *perhaps* hér *might be read, which would correspond with the phrase in the prose* nú tó láfe.

here-beácen. *Substitute:* I *a war-signal* (lit. or fig.):—Herebaecon, -bécon, -béuc *simbulum*, Txts. 96, 919. Herebæcun, 101, 1971. Hé sealde háligra fædera herebeácen him, id est, credo *sanctorum patrum tradidit symbolum*, Bd. 4, 17; Sch. 432, 4. I *a. a beacon:*—Úpstandende herebeácn *pira*, Wrt. Voc. i. 41, 43. Hí átendon heora beácna (herebeácen, herebeácna, *v. ll.*) swá swá hí férdon, Chr. 1006; P. 137, 2. II. *an ensign:*—Mín weorod . . . herebeácen and segnas beforan mé læddon *totum agmen me sequebatur cum signis et uexillis*, Nar. 7, 16. III. *a signal for a fleet, a lighthouse* (lit. or fig). Cf. fýr-tor:—Herebeác[n] *farus*, Wrt. Voc. i. 37, 2: 41, 45. Herebécun héal cum sænesse *farus in edito promontorio*, An. Ox. 575. Herebeácn, 1701.

here-beorg, e; f. *Harbour, shelter, lodgings, quarters:*—þá genam hé þær hereborge, Nap. 82. [v. *N. E. D.* harbour. *O. H. Ger.* hereberga; f. *hospitium, diversorium, tabernaculum:* Icel. her-bergi; n. *an inn.*] *See next word.*

herebeorgian; p. ode *To take up one's quarters, lodge:*—Wolde his án mon herebeorgian æt ánes mannes (wícian æt ánes búndan húse, *v. l.*) his untances, Chr. 1048; P. 173, note 1. [v. *N. E. D.* harbour. *O. H. Ger.* heribergôn *hospitari:* Icel. herbergja *to harbour*.]

here-býme. *l.* -bíme, *and add:*—Herebýme *classica, tubas*, An. Ox. 50, 21. Herebýmum *classibus*, 2602.

here-fêþa. *Add:* , herig-fêþa *a troop of infantry, a phalanx:*—þreát, herigfêþa *falanx*, i. *exercitus, multitudo militum, cohors*, Wrt. Voc. ii. 147, 6.

Herefinnas; *pl. The name of some people occupying a district in Mercia:*—Herefinna landes is twelf hund hýda, C. D. B. i. 414, 21.

here-fong. *Add:*—Herefong *ossifragus*, Wrt. Voc. ii. 63, 69. Herlsong *ossigragus*, Hpt. 33, 241, 66.

here-gang. *Add:*—*capture and devastation made by an army:*—Hé ofslóh þone cing and þá mægđe mid grimmum wale and heregange ábræc *interfecit regem, ac prouinciam illam saeua caede ac depopulatione attriuit*, Bd. 4, 15; Sch. 423, 8. Seó feórđe yld is geteald of Dauide tó đám myclan heregange (*the Babylonish captivity*), fífte of đám heregange tó Crístes gebyrdtíman, Wlfst. 312, 1.

here-geatu. *Add:* [*The word occurs very rarely in the singular; indeed* be hergeate, Ll. Th. i. 412, 26, *seems the only instance of that number. Plural forms are* n. ac. -geatwe(-a), -geata(-u, -e); *dat* -geatwum, -geatum.] I :—Eahta hund éoredmanna ealle mid heregeatwum gegerede, Nar. 4, 13. Twégen englas gesceldode and gesperode and mid heregeatwum (heora geatwum, *v. l.*; *but see* Bl. N. 24), Bl. H. 221, 28. II :—Beón þá heregea a (-e. *v. l.*) swá hit mædlic sý, Ll. Th. i. 414, 4: 15. Beón þá heregeata forgyfene, 420, 16. Hé becwæđ đæt man . . . tilode to his herg-atwæn đæs đe man habban sceolde, C. D. iii. 352, 16 Man selle mínum hláforde đæt gold tó mínum heregeatum, iv. 300, 20. Đám cinge mínne hæregeatwa. v. 333, 10. His láf his hergeatu đám cincge bróhte, iii. 315, 8. Heregete, iv. 292, 5. Ne teó se hláford ná máre bútan his rihtan heregeate (-a, *v. l.*), Ll. Th. i. 412, 30. Geláste ælc wuduwe þá heregeata (-u, *v. l.*) binnan twelf móndum, 416, 16. ¶ For instances of heriots see C. D. ii. 380, 27: iii. 127 22: 304, 30: 360, 19: iv. 299, 19 (*of a woman*): vi. 147, 5: Cht. Th. 573, 3: 592, 5 (*of a bishop*): Cht. Crw. 23, 5. see Ll. Lbmn. ii. 500.

here-gild. *Add: tax levied to provide money to buy off the Danes* (v. here) I. 2 c ¶ 1):—On þan ylcan geáre áléde Eádweard cyng þ heregyld þ Æþelréd cyng ær ástealde, Chr. 1052; P. 173, 18. Ic Eádweard king kýđe . . . đat só fele síđe só men gilded hire gilde tó heregilde, C. D. vi. 205, 23. Ab illa magna heregoldi exactione quae per totam Angliam fit, 180, 11. ¶ The following passages give instances of the amounts paid to secure peace:—On þám geáre man gerædde þ man geald ærest gafol Deniscan mannum . . . þ wæs ærest .x. þúsend punda; þæne ræd gerædde Síríc arceb., Chr. 991; P. 127, 2-6. þá gerædde se cyng and his witan þ him man gafol behéte . . . wiđ þon þe hí þære hergunge geswicon . . . him man geald .xvi. þúsend punda, 994; P. 129, 10-15. Twá and twentig þúsend punda goldes and seolfres mon gese lde þám here wiđ friđe. Ll Th. i. 288, 11. To Wulfstan such taxes were 'scandlice nýdgyld,' and he reproaches his countrymen, 'Wé him (*the Danes*) gyldad singallíce and hý ús hýnađ dæghwámlíce,' Wlfst. 163, 10. That payment of the Danes was not always prompt will be seen from the following passage: Gens pagana . . . promittebant se ad ecclesiam sancti salvatoris . . . ituros, et eam suis incendiis funditus delere, nisi pecunia, quae eis ab archiepiscopo Sirico promissa fuerat, ad plenum daretur, C. D. iii. 285, 5-11. See Ll. Lbmn. ii. 344: Chr. P. ii. 173-175.

here-hlóþ. *Add:*—Ne ic mé herehlóđe helleþegna swíđe onsitte *nor do I fear much a crew of hell's ministers*.

here-hýþ, -húþe. *l.* -húþ, *and add:*—Hí læddon mid him micele herehúþe and manige hæftnýdlingas, Hml. S. 30, 390. Sé þe fint herehúđa manige *qui inuenit spolia multa*, Ps. L. 118, 162.

here-láf. *Add:*—Se cyninge féng tó friđe wiđ hí . . . Hé cyrde đá hámwerd mid his herelâfe, Hml. S. 25, 592. Cf. fird-láf.

here-lic. *Substitute: Relating to an army:*—þá herelican *classica*, Wrt. Voc. ii. 19, 57. v. sciphere-lic, *and cf.* flot-lic.

here-lof. *Substitute:* I. *warlike glory, fame:*—Herelof, hlísa *rumusculus*, An. Ox. 4564. Hlísfulles mæg[đhádes] herelofe (herelofa *rumore, fama*, Hpt. Gl. 511, 25) *famosae uirginitatis rumore* (*comperto*), 4521. II. *a sign of victory, trophy:*—Herelof *tropeum*, i. *signum uictorie*, An. Ox. 1908. Siges herelof *triumphi tropeum*, 1761.

here-nes. *Add:*—Herenis *favor*, Txts. 61, 824. Đæs lof ł herenis in godspell *cujus laus in evangelio*, Mt. p. 8, 13. þær is Godes lof and þæs héhstan cyninges herenes, Wlfst. 265, 14. Hernises *laudis*, Lk. p. 6, 17. Behealden in Godes hyrnessum (here-, *v. l.*) *Dei laudibus intentus*, Gr. D. 224, 14.

hére-nes. v. hír-nes: here-nitig. *Dele*, *and see* nytig.

here-numa, an; *m. A captive, prisoner of war:*—On hernumena bygenum; Ll. Th. ii. 328, 11. [*Icel.* her-numi *a captive*.]

here-pæþ. *Add:* , e; *f.* (?) [Herepæþ *seems distinct from* stræt *and from* weg:—On đá stræt; andlang stræt . . . on đone herepađ; of đám herepađe . . . on đá stræt; of đære stréte, C. D. iv. 49, 6-13. *For* weg *see* C. D. iii. 414, 23 *infra*:—þanon súþ tó þane herepađe (to the lawepathe, later version; ad illam legalem semitam, Latin version) . . . and swá weast andlange herepađes (alonge the lawepathys; per longum legales semitas), C. D. B. ii. 386, 25-27. On þone herepađ; andlang herepaþes, C. D. iii. 406, 18. Andlang herpaþes, 413, 26. Herpaþes, 406, 32 : 407, 3. On herpađ; andlanges herpađes, Cht. Crw. 1, 11. Tó herepađe; swá west on herepađe anlang hrygges; đæt of herepađe on rúgan díc . . .; đonne ford ofer herepađ, C. D. iii. 403, 15-17: 416, 1. Andlang weges of đæt hit cumđ tó đám herpađe; đonne ofer đone herepađ, 414, 23. Eást tó hearpađe; â be hearpađe, 404. 29. On đone herepađ, ii. 29, 14: iii. 416, 19. On đone herpađ. 415, 30. ¶ perhaps the word may be taken as also feminine (v. pæþ), e. g. :—On đére herepađe . . . of đane ordcearde on đáre ordere erepađ, C. D. iii. 415, 20-23. [The word remains in the local name Harepath. See Cht. Crw. p. 46.] v. ceaster-, folc-, friþ-, port-, sealt-, wíc-, wuduherepæþ.

herepæþ-ford *a ford where a herepæþ crosses a stream:*—Andlong bróces on herpaþford, C. D. iii. 436, 30. ¶ *as a local name:*—Hae sunt uillulae eorum . . . Herpođford, C. D. iv. 164, 27

here-rǽs, es; *m. An inroad by an army, a raid by the Danes:*—Gif hwæt færlíces on þéode becynuđ, beón hit hererǽsas, beón hit færcwealmas, beón hit niswyderu, Wlfst. 271, 2.

here-reáf. *Add:*—Seó sýfernes and óđre mægnu forhæfdon heó fram herereáfe (*a spoliis*), Prud. 54. Herereáf *manubias, quae manu capiantur*, An. Ox. 1925. Herereáfu *spolia*, Scint. 19, 8: 82, 15.

here-spel. v. hér. *Substitute:* here-spell, es; *n. A story of praise, panegyric, eulogy:*—Gehýr nú þis herespel (*the story of creation*), Sch. 37. Cf. here-word.

here-strǽt. *Add:*—Innan þone wege; þonne of þám wege út æt norđgæte on þone smalan pæþ, of þám smalan pæþ innan þá herestrét; þonne andlang þære herestrét, C. D. B. iii. 468, 14-16. Tó đære wíde herestrǽt; ætter đære herestrǽt, C. D. iii. 73, 19. Cf. fird-strǽt.

here-teám. *Add:*—*Excidium, casus, ruina vel* hereteám, Wrt. Voc. ii. 145, 8.

here-téma. *l.* -tíma, *and in l. 6 for* 'prince' *read* 'captain' *or* 'general': hereþ. v. hergaþ: here-þreát. *For* 'cohortes, Lye' *substitute:*—Heređreátas *choortes*, Wrt. Voc. ii. 21, 53.

here-þrym. *Substitute:* here-þrymm, es; *m. A martial force:*—Hereþrym *falanges*, Wrt. Voc. ii. 40, 10. Cf. mann-þrymm.

here-toga. *Add:*—I. *the acting leader of an army:*—Scotta sumdæl gewát on Brittene, and þes landes sumdǽl geeódon, and wes heora heratoga Reóda geháten, Chr. pref.; P. 5, 1. Đonne se heretoga wácađ, þonne biđ eall se here gehindred, 1003; P. 135, 15: Ll. Lbmn. 475, 18 (see *2nd passage under* here; I. 2 c ¶ 1 a). Swá hwylcne heora swá him se táu ætýwde, þonne gecuron hí þone him tó heretogan and tó ládþeówe (*hunc tempore belli ducem omnes sequuntur*), Bd. 5, 10; Sch. 600, 19. Þá onstealdon þá heretogan ærest þone fleám, Chr. 993; P. 127, 29. II. *as an official term:*—Ealdorman *princeps*, heretoga *odđe* láteów *dux* ealdorman *odđe* geréfa *comes*, Wrt. Voc. i. 72, 60. Gércyning *odđe* heretoga *consul*, ii. 20, 4. II *a. used of an English official:*—Ic Óswald mid geđafunge and leáfe Eádgáres Angulcyningces and Ælfheres Mercna heretogan (cf. Ælfhere ducis Merciorum, 33), C. D. iii. 5, 5: 49, 29: 159, 20. Cf. Ælfhere ealdorman, Chr. 975; P. 121, 24. III. *applied to a civilian:*—Hú þ wæs weallende spelboda and ungeþyldig heretoga (*John the Baptist*), Bl. H. 165, 34.

here-wíc. *Add:*—Herewíc *castra*, Wrt. Voc. ii. 96, 19. Herewíc, fyrdwíc, 20, 6. *Castra, oppida, loca altissima sita, dicia quasi casa alta* herewíc *vel* gefylco, 129, 36.

here-word. *Add:*—Hlísan. herewurd (-ward, An. Ox. 717) *rumusculos, famas,* Hpt. Gl. 423, 31. Cf. here-spell.

herᵹaþ. *Add:*, hereþ *booty:*—Cóm se þeóf, and genam ǽnne weðer ... þá ongan hé þǽr standan. earm mid his hereðe (*cum praeda sua*), Gr. D. 224, 26.

hergere. *Add:*—Þte úsig ðú hæbbe hergeras (*laudatores*).

hergian. *Add:*—Hergaþ *praedat,* Wrt. Voc. ii. 146, 1. **I.** *to harry, plunder:*—Hié aᵹgunnan hergean and hiénan þá þe hié friþian sceoldon *octava legio omnes. quibus subsidio praeerat, interfecit, praedam sibi omnem vindicavit,* Ors. 4, 1; S. 160, 9: 4. 6; S. 172, 26. Sum his folc hé sende þæt lond tó bærnanne and tó hergenne, 4, 8; S. 188, 11. þá unrihtwísan déman beóð wyrsan þonne herigende here, Ll. Lbmn. 475, 22. **I a.** *used ot the action that rescued the inhabitants of hell:*—On þone dæg Críst reste deád on byrgenne, and his sáwl somod and his godcundnes somod hergode geond helle grund, Shrn 68. 3. **II.** *of things, to harrass:*—Hit is wén ðæt se ne mǽge óðerra monna scylda of ádueán, sé se ðe hine ðonne giét his ágena on herigeað *ne profecto diluere aliena delicta non valeat is, quem adhuc propria devastant,* Past. 73, 19. v. for-hergian.

hergiend, hergend, es; *m. A plunderer, robber, spoiler:*—Hergiend and áhíðend *grassator,* Wrt. Voc. ii. 40, 38. Hergiendum, rýperum *grassatoribus,* i. *inpugnatoribus,* An. Ox. 2712. v. for-hergend.

hergung. *Add:*, herigung, herung:—Hergiung *expeditio,* Wrt. Voc. ii. 108, 8. Hergung, ferd *expeditio,* i. *praeparatio, exercitus.* 145, 41. Næs his (*Alexander's*) hergiung oþ þá fremdan áne, ac hé gelíce slóg and hiénde þá þe him on siml wǽron mid farende *nec minor in suos crudelitas, quam in hostem rabies fuit,* Ors. 3, 9; S. 130, 19. Æt eallum slyht and æt ealre hergunge and æt eallum þám hearmum þe ǽr þám gedón wǽre ǽr þ frið geset wǽre, man eall onweig lǽte, Ll. Th. i. 288, 1. Seó fífte yld wæs fram Babiloniscre heregunge oð Crístes ácennednysse, Hml. Th. ii. 58, 7. Hé hý gefríðode fram þǽre herunge þára twéga kyningca, Ps. Th. 45, arg. Sum his folc hé sende tó hergenne ... se consul wæs þencende þæt hé hié on þǽre hergunge beswíce, Ors. 4, 8; S. 188, 13. Búton miclan hergiungum *extra has clades,* 3, 9; S. 128, 23. [*O. H. Ger.* heriunga *devoratio, direptio.*] v. for-, neáh-hérgung.

herian. *Add:* **I.** *to extol the merits of, express approbation of:*—Wé heriað (-igað, *v. l.*), Past. 230, 7. Herigeað (-igað, *v. l.*), **I.** Heriegeað, 39, 8. Hé hit herede, 53, 8. Lǽrað hí hit ælcne ðára ðe hit gehíerð herian, 427, 17. Herigean, 55, 7. Tó herianne (-igeanne, *v. l.*), 52, 19. Tó herigenne, 353, 25. Hered, 451, 19. **II.** *to extol the attributes of Deity:*—Heraþ *concelebrat,* An. Ox. 2612. On dægred man sceal God herian, Bt.wk. 194, 20. v. á-, efen-, ge-, wið-herian; mæþel-hergende un-hered.

herian *to despise.* v. hirwan.

herigend, es; *m. One who praises:*—Ne gelýf þú herigendrum þínum *nec creda- laudatoribus tuis,* Scint. 205, 15.

herigend-líc. *Add:* **I.** *praiseworthy, deserving praise* or *approbation:*—Hergendlic *probabilis,* Wrt. Voc. ii. 67, 31. Ic wolde beón gehered þeáh ðe ic herigendlic nǽre, Angl. xi. 113, 49. Se man nǽre herigendlic, gif hé for þí ne syngode þe hé ne mihte; ac hé wǽre herigendlic, gif hé ne syngode þá þá hé mihte ... drecð deófol mancyn mid costnungum, þ þá beón hergendlice and hálige þe him wiðstandað *magnae laudi non esset, si ideo homo non peccasset, quia male facere non potuisset ... genus humanum ex insidiis diaboli tentantur, ut ex eo virtus tentati probetur, et palma non consentientis gloriosior appareat,* Angl. vii. 24, 225–229. Hé gewilnode þ hé hæfde herenesse þæs clǽnan lífes, ac hé nolde in him habban þ hergendlic (heriend-, *v. l.*) líf (*laudabilem vitam*), Gr. D. 117, 34. **I a.** *that deserves to be celebrated or eulgiz-d:*—Hí wuldrodon þá hergendlican þrynesse and sungon Godes lofsang, Hml. S. 30, 452. Hergendlíce mé wǽron ðíne ryhtwísnessa *cantab les mihi erant iustificationes tuę,* Ps. Vos. 118, 54. Ðás herigendlicestan gehwyrfednysse ... þǽre árwurðan Marian, Hml. S. 23 b, 1. **I b.** *having qualities that deserve praise, excellent:*—Ðeós wyrt is tó þám herigendlic þ hý man wið gewune drenceas gemencgeað, Lch. i. 172, 6. **II.** *that expresses praise, that praises:*—Heriendlic *fauorabile,* i. *laudabile (praeonium),* An. Ox. 2774. Hergendlíce, Wrt. Voc. ii. 34, 6. Swá swá sume men gewuniaþ þ hí singað mid hergendlicum cræfte ǽr hí etan (the translator has misunderstood the Latin, which is: Sicut quidam ludendi (laudandi *seems to have been read*) arte victum solent quaerere), Gr. D. 62, 13. v. ge-, un-herigendlic.

herigendlíce. *For last passage substitute:*—Ðæt ilce ðæt hé untælwyrðlíce ondréd tó onsónne, ðæt ilce se óðer swíðe hergeondlíce (herᵹendlíce, *v. l.*) gewilnode *quod laudabiliter alter appetiit, hoc laudabiliter alter expavit,* Past. 49, 19. Herigendlíce (hergendlíce, *v. l.*), 295. 5: Bd. 1, 27; Sch. 82, 7. Án ðæra is þes hálga wer þe wé nú tódæg wurðiað, for ðan ðe hé áspende swíðe herigendlíce þæt feoh þe him God befæste, Hml. Th. ii. 560, 9.

herigend-sang, es; *m. A song of praise:*—Fausta adclamantes, i. *alto canendo vel* herigendsang *vel* lofsang, Wrt. Voc. ii. 147, 11.

herig-feþa. v. here-feþa: herig-weard. v. hearg-weard: hering *emulation.* v. hyring: hering *praise.* v. herung: hér-inne. v. hér; **VII.** 5.

hér-, hǽr-líc. *Substitute:* her-líc, hær-líc; *adj. Laudable, noble:*—Hé hét Jóhannes, gódne pápan, heáfde beheáwon; næs ðæt hærlíc dǽd, Met. 1, 43. Næs þæt herlíc dǽd þ hine swelces gamenes gilpan lyste, 9, 18.

her-numa, -næp. v. here-numa, -næp.

hér-rihte; *adv. Just here, at this point:*—Uton ændian þás bóc nú hǽrrihte, Solil. H. 49, 10. Cf. þǽr-rihte.

herste. v. hirste: herpa. v. heorpa.

herþan. *Add:* [Cf. *Goth.* hairþram (*d. pl.*) *visceribus.*]: herþ-land, C. D iii. 18, 29; 399, 30. *l.* (?) irþ-land.

hér-tó; *adv. Up to this point:*—Hértó *actenus,* An. Ox. 56, 80. v. hér; **VII.**

herung. *Add:* **I.** *praise, approbation:*—Mon sceal ðone ingong ðǽre tælinge wið heringe gemengan, ðætte hié for ðǽre licunga ðǽre heringe ... eác geðafigen ðá tælinge *ipsa invectionis exordia permixta sunt laude temperanda, ut dum admittunt favores etiam correptiones recipiant,* Past. 303, 17–20. Ongin nú stranglíce, and þín gemynd stent on neorunge, Hml. S. 29, 272. Herunge *favorem* (nisi Deorum *favorem* repropitiarent, Ald. 67, 13), An. Ox. 4723. Herunga *opinionum* (cujus vitam tantis *opinionum* rumusculis extollit, Ald. 33, 29), 2424: *precoriorum,* 4950. Benedictus gewilnode má þ hé þrowode þysses middaneardes yfel þonne þá herunga (*laudes*), and þ hé wǽre for Gode swýðe mid gewinnum geswænced þonne hé wǽre úp áhafen on þám herungum (*favoribus*) þisses andweardan lífes, Gr. D. 98, 9–12. Lofu, herunga *preconia, fauores,* An. Ox. 3982. Heruncga *preconia,* i. *laudes,* 64. **II.** *praise, extolling of the Deity:*—Sé þe ... his Drihten, þe is ealra gereorda gifend mid herincge ne ðancað, R. Ben. 69, 11. Dionisius þancode his Drihtne mid herunge, Hml. S. 29, 286 Heofon mid herungum (*laudibus*) swégþ, Hy. S. 84, 30. **II a.** *praise in song:*—Mid swíþ wégum dreámes (†) herunge sangum *dulcisonis melodie concentibus,* An. Ox. 402. **II b.** *a service of praise, lauds:*—Begém herunga lofsangas þe wé hlyniende syngað *attende laudum cantica quę excubantes psallimus,* Hy. S. 26, 6. v. lof-, samod-herung.

herut-beg. v. heort-beg: herwan. v. hirwan.

hése, hoese, haese, hýse *woodland country, land with bushes and bushwood.* [The character of the land to which this name is applied seems marked by the fact that a *denbǽre* is called *hése*:]—Adiectis quatuor denberis ... heáhden, hése, helmanhyrst, C. D. i. 317, 20. Adiectis denberis in commune saltu ... Meredaen ... and Teppan hýse, 194, 36. De patrimonio meo. ... nomine Hýse, 29ᶺ, 36. In loco qui dicitur on Linga hoese, 192, 13. Terra ... pertinens tó haese, 294, 25. Cf. Ðonon on hésleá, C. D. V. 121, 34. On hésleábróc, iii. 97, 29: vi. 102, 31. [*O. L. Ger.* (Gall.) hési-penning *a forest-tax.* See Jellinghaus. *s. v.* hees. Low Lat. heisia *silva sepibus septa,* Migne.]

hese *a youth.* v. hyse.

hete. *Dele passage* (Rä. 34, 5) *in l. 4, and add:* **I.** *as a human passion:*—Wæs here and hete on gehwilcum ende oft and gelóme, Wlfst. 162, 14. Hit ná næs búton hete and gewinnum, Ors. 3, 11; S. 142, 17. Ic mé wið heora hete hýde, Ps. Th. 54, 12. Ne teó ic N. for hete ne for hóle, Ll. Th. i. 180, 10. Hé nam tó Malche fulne graman, and him mid eallum hete cídde, Hml. S. 23, 695. Hine þurh hete héngon fæderas ússe, El. 424. Hannibal gecýþde þone níþ and þone hete (*odium*) þe hé beforan his fæder geswór, Ors. 4, 8; S. 186, 9. **I a.** *an act or thought prompted by hate:*—Hé heom beheþ ælcne hete, Hml. S. 23, 230. Ðá ðóhton heatas in heortan *qui cogitaverunt malitias in corde,* Ps. Srt. 139, 3. **II.** *used in reference to the Deity:*—Him nið Godes ... hete gesceóde, Dan. 620. Þú mé forlǽred hæfst on mínes herran hete, Gen. 819. **II a.** *punishment that is due to God's anger:*—Þone mǽstan hete (*magnas plagas*) hé sent on eów, Deut. 28, 59. v. ellen-, sǽ-hete.

-hete (?) *a foe.* v. níþ-, scyld-hete.

hete-grim. *Add:*—Wæs hió hetegrim, Rä. 34, 5.

hete-líc. *Add:* **I.** *of persons, malignant:*—Dydon þá heáfodmenn swá swá þ hetelíc wíf (*Jezebel*) him bebeád, Hml. S. 18, 194. **II.** *of things, hard, severe:*—Hé mæg him wénan hetelíces leánes, Wlfst. 191, 23. Hé férde on hetelícum wintra, on swá swiðlícum cyle þ sume nien swulton þurh þone, Hml. S. 31, 59.

hetelíce. *Add:* **I.** *of action or motion, violently, furiously, fiercely:*—Hét hé him his seax árǽcan ... and hine sylfne hetelíce ðýde, þæt him on ácwehte, Hml. Th. 88. 10: Hml. S. 15, 24. Þá þæt Engliscan hí hindan hetelíce slógon, Chr. 1066; P. 199, 15. Þá gestódon hine hundas hetelíce swýðe *dogs attacked him furiously.* Hml. S. 12, 52. Hé sǽde þ sum hund burce hetelíce on ánne man, 31, 1132. Manega hús hetelíce feóllon *many houses fell with great violence,* 15, 94. Þá fýnd hine úp geond þá lyft sume hwíle feredon, þæt hé on his fylle þý þá fýnd hetelícor hreósan sceolde, Hml. Th. i. 380, 28. **II.** *of disposition,*

*malignantly, with ill-will* :—Þyses cyninges cwēn wæs forcūþost wīfa, Gezabel gehāten, hetelīce gemōdod, Hml. S. 18, 50. Ðā Malchus þās word gehýrde þe se portgerēfa him swā hetelīce wæs tō spræcende, 23, 718. [v. *N. E. D.* hately.]

**hēþir.** v. æd[d]er; III.

**hetol.** *Add :* I. applied to persons. (1) of disposition, *malignant :*—Sē (*Jove*) wearð hetol seónd (hetol and þrymlic, Sal. K. p. 121, 24). Hē āflýmde his āgene fæder, ... and wolde hine forfaran georne, Wlfst. 106. 9. Þ hetole wīf (*Jezebel*), Hml. S. 18, 194. Leódwatan hetele, Wlfst. 310, 4. Ðā hæðenan þe him hetole wæron, Hml. S. 25, 685. Cwædon þā weardmenn tō þām hetelum Jūdēiscum, Hml. A. 79, 176. þā hæðengildon þe þær heteloste wæron, Hml. S. 29, 166. (2) of appearance, *having a malicious expression, that shows ill-will :*—Se nīðfulla wer wyrð geswutelod ðurh his hātheortnysse on hetolum and wlitan, Hex. 46, 31. II. of an animal, *ferocious.* v. hetol-ness; II :—Hetelum *rabidis,* i. *ferocibus* (*molossi rictibus*). An. Ox. 3640. III. of punishment, *severe.* Cf. hetollīce; II :—Sý hē gewītnod mid hetolre steóre, R. Ben 67, 16. v. un-hetol.

**hetollīce;** *adv.* I. of action, *violently, fiercely :*—Se wælreówa deófol wolde geniman þone cnapan of Basilius handum hetolīce teónde, Hml. S. 3, 443. II. *severely.* Cf. hetol; III :—Hē āgelt hetollīce wercendum mōdignysse *retribuet abundanter facientibus superbiam,* Ps. L. 30, 24.

**hetol-ness, e; f.** I. as an attribute of a person, *violence, severity :*—Weámōde lāreówas þurh hetolnysse (*rabiem*) heora rēðscipes gehwyrfað þære lāre gemet tō ungefōge þære wælhreównysse, Chrd. 70, 15. II as an attribute of an animal, *ferocity, rapacity.* v. hetol; II :—Hetelnessa *rapacitatis* (feroces ursinae *rapacitatis* rictus, Ald. 61, 19), An. Ox. 11, 152.

**hettan.** *Add :* [O. H. Ger. hezzen *incitare :* Ger. hetzen.] v. on-hetting.

**hetting.** v. on-hetting.

**hī, hig** *an interjection :*—Hig lā mē *heu me,* Ps. Rdr. 119, 5. Hyg lā, Ps. L. 119, 5. Hī lā hī, Ælfc. Gr. Z. 280, 13.

**Hiccas.** v. Hwiccas.

**hice** *the name of a bird* (?) :—Hicae *paruca* (*parula*?), Wrt. Voc. ii. 116, 50. Yce *parruca,* 67, 69. Cf. (?) Hykemeres strēme, C. D. iii. 467, 25. v. hice-māse.

**hicel** *a woodpecker* (?) :—On hicleshām, C. D. iii. 202, 4. Æt hiceles wyrðe, 427, 21. [v. *N. E. D., D. D.* hickwall.]

**hice-māse.** *Add :*—Hicemāse *sagittula,* Hpt. 33, 241, 44. v. hice.

**hīd, hīgid.** *Add :* [A neuter form, hīde, seems to occur once certainly :*—Ic sello Berhtsige ān hīde bōclondes, C. D. ii. 121, 4, *and to such a form might belong the following genitives :*—Ānes hīdes, 120, 33. Ānes hīdes lond, C. D. B. ii. 268, 9. *The nominatives* hīde, gyrde *in,* 'Þ næs ān ælpig hīde ne ān gyrde landes,' Chr. 1085 ; P. 216, 27, *are perhaps really incorrect late forms*] I. *a portion of land :*—Hīd *cassatum,* Wrt. Voc. ii. 129, 21. Ðis syndon ðære halīre hīde landgemæru, C. D. iii. 52, 7. Ðāra fīf and twēntig hīgda, C. D. B. ii. 142, 1. Myrcna landes is þrittig þūsend hýda, i. 414, 15 (*and often*). Hū fela hundred hýda wæron innon þære scīre, Chr. 1085 ; P. 216, 18. Ic sello ii hīda on Hwætedūne, C. D. ii. 120, 33. ¶ the construction is twofold. (1) a (so many) hide(s) of land :—Næs ān hīd landes innon Englælande þ hē nyste hwā heó hæfde, Chr. 1086 ; P. 220, 20. Tēn hīda ðaes londes, C. D. i. 315, 30. iii. hīda bōclondes, ii. 120, 32. (2) land of so many hides :—Ic sylle Wulfsige ānes hīdes lond on Eásttūne, C. D. B. ii. 268, 9. Mid ðý tēn hīda londe aet felda ... end ðaet tēn hīda lond æt crogleáge, C. D. i. 315, 22–25 : 33 : ii. 100, 9–24. Ic sile Forðrēde nigen hīgida lond ... tū hīgida lond, 5, 24–30. I a. *where assessment is made according to the number of hides :*—Sē þe hæbbe þreó hīda tæcne ōðres healfes hýdes gesettes, Ll. Th. i. 144, 11. Leóhtgesceot ... æt ælcere hīde, 366, 32 : Chr. 1083; P. 215, 25 Sceóte man æt æghwilcre hīde þænig, Wlfst. 181, 5. Geswicne sē hine be cxx hīda, Ll. Th. i. 110, 17. Be sixtegum hīda, 68, 19 : 114, 11 : 130, 13 : 138, 5. Be twelf hīdum, 4 : 146, 16. Of þrým hund hīdum and of x hīdum ænne scegð, and of viii hīdum helm and byrnan, Chr. 1008; P. 138, 6. Sē þe hæfð xx hīda, sē sceal tæcnan xii hīda gesettes landes, Ll. Th. i. 144, 5, 8. I b. *where status is fixed by the number of hides :*—Gif hē ne geþeó būton tō healīre hīde, þonne sī his wer lxxx scītt., Ll. Th. i. 188, 1. Gif Wylisc mon hæbbe hīde londes, his wer bið .cxx. scītt.; gif hē hæbbe healfe .lxxx. scītt., 122, 9. Wealh gif hē hafað fīf hýda, hē bið syxhynde, 118, 10. Gif ceorl geþeáh þ hē hæfde fullīce fīf hīda āgenes landes, 190, 15 : 188, 5. II. in Bede translating *familia :*—Mycel eáland, þ is syx hund hīda micel æfter Angelcynnes æhte *insula non modica, id est magnitudinis juxta consuetudinem aestimationis Anglorum familiarum sexcentarum,* Bd. 1, 25; Sch. 52, 1. Twelf hund hīda ... þreó hund hīda *mille ducentarum familiarum ... trecentarum familiarum,* 4, 16; Sch. 425, 20, 23. v. healf-hīd.

**hiden.** v. hider; I 2 b.

**hider.** *Add :*—Hider *istuc,* Wrt. Voc. ii. 112, 11. I. local.

(1) *to the place where the speaker is.* (a) with a verb expressing movement :—Gā hider neár *accede huc,* Gen. 27, 21. Hū eódest þu hider (hidir, L.) inn? *quomodo huc intrasti?,* Mt. R. 22, 12. Þæt ic ne cymo hider (hidder, L.), Jn. R. 4, 15. Ic mægenbyrðenne hider ūt ætbær, B. 3092. Mec mīn fæder hider onsende, Jul. 322. Bringað hyne tō mē hider (hidir, L.) *afferte huc illum ad me,* Mt. 17, 17. Gā hē hider tō mē *jungatur mihi,* Past. 383, 1. (b) where a verb of motion is implied :—Hē hine sōna hider læt, Mk. 11, 3. Hē āstyrað þis folc lærende þurh ealle Jūdēam āgynnende of Galiléa oð hyder (*usque huc*), Lk. 23, 5. Ne þec mon hider mōse fēded *they won't come hither to feed you,* Gū. 245. (2) *to the country or region to which the speaker belongs.* (a) with a verb expressing movement :—þ wæs ymb twā gēr þæs þe hié hider ofer sæ cōmon, Chr. 895; P. 89, 1 : 937; P. 110, 3 : B. 240. For þām hīrede þe þū hider (*Hell*) læddest, Sat. 423. Cōm seó hlæfdige hider tō lande, Chr. 1002; P. 134, 10 : 1057; P. 188, 1. Nū gē þus feor hider on ūrne eard in becōmon, By. 57. Wē synd āworpene hider on þas deópan dalo, Gen. 420. (b) where motion is implied :—Gē him syndon ofer sæwylmas hider wilcuman, B. 394. Man ūtanbordes wisdom and lāre hieder (hider, *v. l.*) on lond sōhte, Past. 3, 11. Gyf Wealh Engliscne man ofsleá, ne þearf hē hine hider (-en, MS. ; cf. spon *for* spor *in* § 1. v. Ll. Lbmn. 374) ofer būton be healfan were gyldan, ne Ænglisc Wyliscne geon ofer, Ll. Th. i. 354. 19. Se aldor þæm heaðorincum hider wīsade, B. 370. Hē ūtlændisce hider in tihte, Chr. 959; P. 115, 12. (c) where relation is expressed :—Man hālgode Trumwine Pihtum, for þan hý hýrdon þā hider, Chr. 681 ; P. 39, 11. (3) *to this world, to this life :*—Ne læt hē his nānwuht of þis middangearde mid him māre þonne hē brōhte hider, Bt. 26, 3 ; F. 94, 17 : 33, 4 ; F. 132, 24 : Crī. 760 : 295 : Crä. 21 : Ps. Th. 56, 3 : Hy. 10, 10. Hider on eorðan, Past. 469, 1. Hē his spræce hider on þas eorðan sended *emittit eloquium suum terrae,* Ps. Th. 147, 4. Antecrīst nū gēt hider on middangeard ne cōm, Bl. H. 117, 33. Hider hē fundað on þysne middangeard, Kr. 103. Nænig eft cymeð hider under hrófas, Gn. C. 64. (3 a) motion implied :—Hafað him geþinged hider þeóden ūser on þām mæstan dæge, Dōm. 5. (4) *in this world.* Cf. (3 a) :—þū gemengest þā heofoncundan hider (cf. on ðisse worulde, Bt. 33, 5 ; S. 82, 3) wið eorðan, sāula wið līce, Met. 20, 235. II. marking the end to which an action or an operation of the senses or mind is directed :—Fōh hider tō mē *stretch hither thy hand and take from me,* Sat 686. Hlyst hider *listen to me,* Past. 381, 14. Þonne bearn Godes þurh heofona gehleodu hider oðýweð (*shews himself to us*), Crī. 905. III. *to this point :*—Forlētað wið hider (lætað þus, W. S. *sinite usque huc*), Lk. R. L. 22, 51. IV. with other adverbs. (1) þider(es) *hither and thither, in various directions :*—Hider and þider *ultro citro,* Wrt. Voc. i. 289, 68. Hider ond hider (hidir an didir, III, 10) *ultroque citroque,* Txts. 107, 2148. (a) local :—Hider and þyderes *ultro citroque* (*inter densa filorum stamina decurrant*), An. Ox. 1040. Sandigum wara cyslum hider and tyder (þider, Hpt. Gl. 503, 1) tealtriendum *harenosis sablonum glareis ultro citroque nutabundis,* 4103. (b) describing confused thought or action :—Ðæt scip ðære heortan bið drifen hider and ðider *navis cordis huc illucque impellitur,* Past. 59, 5. Þā wes hē on þām unrōtan mōde hider and þyder þencende *moestam mentem huc illucque jactabat,* Guth. Gr. 171, 17. Mē þincþ þ þū mē dwelige and dyderie ... lætst mē hider and ðider, Bt. 35, 5 ; F. 164, 13. Hī irnaþ hider and ðider dwoligende, 36, 5 ; F. 180, 12. (2) geond *to and fro :*—Brǣd þ heáfod hider and geond ofer þ fýr, Lch. ii. 38, 3. v. hidere, hideres.

**hider-cyme.** *Add :* I. Cf. hider; I. 2 :—Angelcynnes hidercymes on Breotone *adventus Anglorum in Brittaniam,* Bd. 1, 23; Sch. 48, 7. II. Cf. hider; I. 3 :—Eall þæt man ūs foresægð ymbe Cristes hidercyme (hidertōcyme, *v. l.*), Wlfst. 241, 22. [v. *N. E. D.* hithercome.]

**hidere;** *adv. Hither :*—Hidere *istuc,* Wrt. Voc. ii. 91, 43. Cf. hwidere.

**hideres.** *Take here* hidres *in Dict., and add :* I. local :—Hē þær lange hyderes and þyderes sēcende fōr, Hml. S. 236, 730. II. figurative :—Sió ābisgung hine scofett hidres ðædres, Past. 169, 13. Mē þincþ þ þū mē dwelige and dyderie and lædst mē hidres and þidres, Bt. 35, 5 ; F. 164, 13. Hidres þidres, 36, 5 ; F. 150, 12.

**hider-ryne;** *adj. Of this* (the speaker's) *country :*—Hidirrine *nostratis,* Txts. 115, 131. Cf. hwider-ryne.

**hider-tōcyme** *advent.* v. hider-cyme; II : **hidres.** v. hideres : **hiéwet.** v. hīwet: hifcund. v. hīw-cund.

**hīg** *hay, mown grass. Take here* heg (*l.* hēg) *in Dict., and add :*—Hēg *foenum,* Wrt. Voc. i. 289, 45. Græs oððe hīg *fenum,* ii. 35, 30. Swǣ swǣ hēg (*faenum*) hreðlice ādrūgiað, Ps. Srt. Ps. Spl. 36, 2. Hīg, Ps. L. 36, 2. Hýg, 101, 5. Ic sceal fyllan binnan oxan mid hīg (*foeno*), Coll. M. 20, 1. 'Hē māweþ heig (gærs, *v. l.* fenum) on þissere dene' ... þā geseah hē þ hī ealle meówon þ heig ... 'Ber þis grēne hīg (gærs, *v. l.*) þām horsum tō mete.' Gr. D. 36, 2–29.

**hīgan, hēgan** *to exalt, worship :*—Hié þis [hæðengild? cf. hē þā hæðengild hýran ne wolde, wīg weorðian, Ap. 47] hēgan (hēran?) ne willad ne þisne wīg wurðigean, Dan. 207. v. heán; hīran (?).

higdi. v. hýdig: hi-geára. v. geó-geára.

higera. [In Rä. 25, 8 *the rune is that for œ not for a.* v. Beiblatt. xxiv. 41] *Add :*—Fína *vel* higrae, higre *picus,* Txts. 88, 808. Higrae, *traigis,* 103, 2064: *cicuanus,* 51, 476. Higere, Wrt. Voc. ii. 14, 30. Higre *berna,* 11, 5. Higrae (-ę), Txts. 44, 156. ¶ *in a local name :*— On higran hongran, C. D. v. 135, 37.

hig-hús. *Take here* heg-hús (*l.* hēg-) *in Dict., and add :*—Hēghús *fenile,* Wrt. Voc. ii. 148, 22.

higian. *l.* hígian, *and add :*—Hē hígode oðde tilode *nititur,* Wrt. Voc. ii. 59, 69. Hígien wē *contendamus,* 24, 36. Hígiendre *intento,* 48, 63. (1) *with preps., to strive after, to, towards.* (a) æfter :—Hú mæg þ yfel beón þte ælces monnes ingeþanc . . . æfter hígaþ and wilnaþ tô begitanne *neque enim vile quiddam . . . quod adipisci omnium fere mortalium laborat intentio,* Bt. 24, 4; F. 86, 13. Ðæt ierfe ðæt gē ǣrest æfter hiēgiað (hígiað, *v. l.*) *hereditas ad quam festinatur in principio,* Past. 331, 24. Nota þæs wísdómes þe þū habbæ . . . and híga georne æfter māran, Solil. H. 47, 17. Is ælcum þearf þ hē hígie eallan mægne æfter þǣre mēde, Bt. 37, 2; F. 188, 16. (b) on :—Ne hígion hí on feohgafole usuris nequaquam incumbant, Chrd. 76, 32. (c) tô. (a) *of movement :*—Hē hígode tô þǣre stôwe *ad locum tetendit,* Gr. D. 99, 20. (β) *of effort, endeavour, &c. :*—Hē hiēgað (hígað, *v. l.*) tô andweardnesse his Scippendes *ad auctoris speciem anhelat,* Past. 86, 10. Hē hígode tô þǣre lufan þæs heofonlican ēþles *ad amorem coelestis patriae exarsit,* Gr. D. 11, 5. Ðæt ðā weras hígien (hígigen, *v. l.*) tô māran byrðene *ut viros magna exerceant,* Past. 178, 17. (d) wiþ (*gen.*) :—Hē hígað wið ðæs ðæt hē wolde hū hē eallum monnum wunderlicost ðúhte *satagit ut mirabilis cunctis innotescat,* Past. 463, 36. Wiþ þæs ic wât þū wilt hígian Bt. 11, 2; F. 34, 8. (2) *with dat. infin. to strive to do,* Past. 105, 14 (*in Dict.*). (3) *with clause :*—Hié hígiað ealle mægene ðæt hié ðæt gedwellen ðæt ôðre menn ryhtlíce ongieten habbað *student summopere ab aliis recte intellecta destruere,* Past. 365, 23. Tô þām þ þū hígie þ þū mæge becuman tô þām gesǣlþum þe ēce þurhwuniaþ, Bt. 22, 2; F. 78, 18. v. ofer-, on-hígian.

hígid. v. híd: hig-lá. v. hí: higo-spind. v. hago-spind.

higre *berna.* v. higera.

hig-síþe, es; *m.* A *hay-scythe :*—Se Godes wer . . . bær on his eaxle his hēgsíþe *falcem fenariam in collo deferens,* Gr. D. 37, 14.

hígþ, e; *f. Exertion, effort :*—Mid sceorpum hígðum *acutis nisibus,* Hpt. 31, 14, 360. [*v. N. E. D.* hight *exertion.*] v. hígian, hígung.

hígung, e; *f. Striving, endeavour, effort :*—Se flǣscbana hæfde þ getogene sweord on his handa and mid stranglice hígunge (*nisu forti*) āhôf þone earm upp in heānesse and mynte sleán þone Godes wer, Gr. D. 254, 34. v. tô-hígung; hígþ.

híhþ, híhþu(-o). *Take here* heáhþu *in Dict., and add :* I. *distance from the base upwards, altitude, elevation above the ground :*—þæs stānes hēhþe *obolisci proceritatem,* i. *altitudinem,* An. Ox. 3525. I a. *figurative :*—Heálic hēþ *edita* (*pudicitiæ*) *proceritas,* An. Ox. 1699. Swā mycelum swā hē on hýþe upp āhefð *quanto in alto se erigit,* Sci.it. 84, 16. II. *high degree of a quality :*—Heálicere hēhþe (*in tam*) *præcelso* (*puritatis*) *fastigio,* An. Ox. 4408. III. *a high point or position :*—On hēhþe ārǣredne *in edito,* i. *in fastigio porrectam,* An. Ox. 4437. IV. *the highest part of anything, a summit, top :*—Hēhþ[þe] *apicem,* i. *summitatem,* An. Ox. 3528. Hēh[þe] *verticem,* i. *cacumen,* 384. Heáhðo *culmina,* Wrt. Voc. ii. 25, 2. Heáhþo, 6. V. *the highest point, extreme degree :*—Mæg[en] sôðes gebedes ys hýhð (*celsitudo*) sôðre lufe, Scint. 4, 20. VI. *the regions above, the heavens :*—þænne hýhð heofonlic (*celsitudo caelestis*) byð openud, Scint. 180, 15. Ástág in middangeard freóbearn Godes of heáhðu, Cri. 789. Hē his þone hālgan líchaman āhôf úp in heofene hýhðo, Först. Verc. 129, 5. On heáhðum, Cri. 867: Gú. 768: 1061. Englas twēgen cleopedon of heáhðum, Cri. 508. VII. *in the phrase* on híhþu (-um). (1) *in an exalted condition or estimation :*—Geþanc heortan úre swā micelum mid Gode on neowlum ys swā hit mannum on hýhþe (*in alto*); and eádmôdnys heortan úre swā micelum mid Gode on hýhþe ys swā micelum swā mannum on neowlum, Scint. 21, 11-14. (2) *in the highest degree :*—þæt hí lof Godes hergan on heáhðu, Dôm. 48. On hēhðo, An. 1000. On heáhðum, Jul. 560.

hild *grace. Substitute :* hild, es; *m.* I. *watchful care, safe keeping exercised by a person with respect to* (1) *persons :*—þū eart se gooda gleáw on gesyhðe þāra hāligra þe þínne held curan, Ps. Th. 51, 8. Hālgum gāstum þe his hyld curon, Dan. 481. Hié on friðe Drihtnes of þām grimman gryre glade treddedon, gleáwmôde guman on gāstes hyld 440. Folc wæs on lande; hæfde wuldres bearn werud gelǣded on hild Godes, Exod. 568. (2) *things :*—Onbyhtscealcas þe on Godes húse gearwe standað, and on cafertúnum Crístes húses, úres þæs hālgan Godes, held begangað (-eð, MS.) *who are caretakers in the house of God; servi qui statis in domo Domini, in atriis domus Dei nostri,* Ps. Th. 133. 2. II. *preservation, safety experienced by a person :*—þæt hí fore his hyldon (gehylde, *v. l.*) heora bēne geóten *pro eius custodia preces fundant,* Bd. 1, 27; Sch. 73, 14. v. ge-hild.

hildan *to bend, incline. Take here* hyldan *in Dict., and add :* I.

*trans. :*—Ne drinc ðū of þǣre fiascan, ac hyld (*inclina*) þū hí wǣrlíce, Gr. D. 142, 5. þā þā hē helde ł bígede *cum* (*membra sopori*) *dedisset* i. *inclinasset,* An. Ox. 2105. II. *intrans. :*—Men gesáwon āne hand . . . of heofonum cumende; and seó hæfde āne gyldene rôde, and wæs æteówod manegum mannum, and helde tôweard tôforan þæs húses duru *ecce humana manus ab olympi nubibus ante ostium domus . . . porrecta videbatur,* Guth. Gr. 105, 18. [v. *N. E. D.* hield.] v. ge-hildan.

hilde, an; *f.* A *slope, declivity :*—Helde, burhsteall *clivium* (*cliuium,* ascensus singularis uiae, Ld. Gl. H. *s. v.* glebum) i. *discensum,* Wrt. Voc. ii. 131, 72. On Owunes hyldan ufewyrde, C. D. v. 293, 25. Of ðæs clifes nordhyldan . . . on æccan dene nordhyldan, iii. 418, 25, 33. [v. *N. E. D.* hield. *O. H. Ger.* halda; *f. clivus.* Cf. *Icel.* hallr; *m. a slope.*] v. heald.

-hilde (cf. healdan). v. earfoþ- (earfoþ-hilde = discontented, not *hard to incline,* the meaning given above), iþ-, ôþ-hilde : -hilde (cf. hildan). v. iþ-hilde.

-hildedness. v. on-hildedness.

hilde-frôfor. v. gripe; II. 2 a : -hildelic. v. ge-hildelic.

hilde-rinc. *Add :*—þū scealt gyltas þíne swíðe bemurnan, hār hilderinc, hefie þe ðincaþ synna þíne, Dôm. L. 30, 56.

hilding, e; *f. Bending, curving :*—Crymbing, hylding *curvatura,* Wrt. Voc. ii. 23, 66. [*Prompt. Parv.* heldynge *or* bowynge *inclinacio.*] -hildness. v. ge-hildness.

hilfan (?), helfan *to halve, divide into two parts :*—Herbid (helbid?) *bipertitum* (cf. bipertitum, in duobus pertitum, 128), Corp. Gl. H. 25, 138; Wrt. Voc. ii. 102, 2. [Cf. Scipen gunnen helden, bosmes þer rendden, seiles þer helfden (*split in half*), Laym. 7851.]

hilfe, es; *n. Take here* helfe; *m. n.* (?) (*l. n.*) *in Dict., and add :*—Ðā þā se Gota mid eallum his mægene heów . . . , þā fǣringa rǣsde forð þ ísen of þām hylfe (*manubrio*) . . . Benedictus genam þ hylfe (*manubrium*) of þæs Gotan handa and scēt hit on þone seað; and þǣrrihte gehwearf þ ísen of þām grunde and weard on þām hylfe (in þ hylfe, *v. l.*), Gr. D. 113, 23-114, 15. Heora ān his exe úp ābrǣd, wolde hine sleán, ac him forwyrnde sum ôþer swā þ hē þ hylfe gelæhte and wiðhæfde þ slege, Hml. S. 31, 154. [v. *N. E. D.* helve.]

hilfing. *Take here* helfling *in Dict., and add :* [*O. L. Ger.* helfling. Cf. *N. E. D.* halfling.]

-hilmed. v. ge-hilmed.

hilsten (?); *adj. Having crust.* v. heal-stán :—And hylstene hláfas *et tortam* (*torta?*) *panis* (cf. (?) : et daretur ei torta panis, Jer. 37, 20), Wrt. Voc. ii. 30, 21.

hilt. *Dele all derivates but* fetel-, *and add :*, helt :—Helt *capulus,* Wrt. Voc. ii. 102, 15 : *capulum,* 103, 30. Oð hielt *capulotenus,* 86, 68. Wolde hē þurhþýn hí mid þām swurde, ac se ord bígde upp tô þām hiltum, Hml. S. 12, 226. Oð ðā hylta hē behýdde þæt swurd *capulotenus abdidit ensem,* Ælfc. Gr. Z. 272, 17. [*O. L. Ger.* hilt : *O. H. Ger.* hilz *capulum* : hilzi *capulus.* v. Gall, *s. v.* hilt.] v. ge-hilte; holt.

-hilt, -hilte. v. fealo-, gylden-, seolfor-, wreoþen-hilt (-hilte) : -hiltan. v. ā-hiltan.

hilte. *Add :*—Oþ þā hiltan *capulotenus,* An. Ox. 4945. v. mid-hilte.

-hilted. v. gold-, seolfor-hilted.

hilting a *sword :*—Mēce, hiltinge *macheram,* i. *gladium,* An. Ox. 758.

hilt-sweord a *hilted sword, sword with a hilt :*—Hiora þegnas bióþ mid fetlum and mid gyldenum hyltsweordum gehyrste, Bt. 37, 1; F. 186, 5. Cf. gold-hilted.

hiltu(-o) *lameness. Take here* helto *in Dict., and add :* [*O. H. Ger.* halzî : *Icel.* helti.]

himming. v. hemming.

hínan. *Take here* hýnan *in Dict., and add :* I. *to humble, humiliate :*—Ðý læs hē his eádmôdnesse forleóse, geðence hē ðæt hē bið self swíðe gelíc ðǣm ilcan monnum þe hē ǣr ðreátað and hiénd, Past. 116, 16. II. *to treat with dishonour, degrade, insult :*—Hē hié for þǣre gewilnunga swíþe bismrade, and bebeád þ hié mon on ælce healfe hiénde . . . , and bebeád þ mon āfylde deófolgielda þā cirican spreta legatione sacras aedes repleri statuis imperavit, Ors. 6, 3; S. 258, 6. III. *with the idea of violence.* (1) *to conquer, subject :*—Læssan sige hæfð sē sē ðe burhware ofercymð, for ðon him bióð fremde ðā ðe hē ðǣr hínd and ðreátað *minor enim est victoria urbium, quia extra sunt quae subiguntur,* Past. 218, 19. þā hié mon slôg and hiénde and on ôþru land sealde *populis bello victis, pretio vinditis,* Ors. 5, 1; S. 214, 13. (2) *to oppress, afflict :*—Hē côm tô ānre byrig Bosor gehäten, on ðǣre wǣron ðā hǣðenan þe hýndon his mágas (cf. many of their brethren were shut up in Bosor, i. Macc. 5, 26), Hml. S. 25, 414. (3) *to lay low, destroy.* (a) *the object a person.* (a) *of the action of an individual :*—Næs his hergiung on þā fremdan āne, ac hē gelíce slôg and hiénde hé þe him on siml wǣron mid farende. Hē ofslôg Amintas and his brôðor and Parmenion and Filiotes . . . and monege ôþre . . . and Clitus *nec minor ejus in suos crudelitas, quam in hostem rabies fuit.*

*Docent hoc Amyntas occisus, fratres ejus necati, Parmenio et Philotas trucidati . . . multique exstincti, Clitus . . . interfectus,* Ors. 3, 9; S. 130, 19–24. Sum ōðer hine wolde slēán on his heáfde mid heardum ísene, ac þ wǽpen wand āweg mid þām slege of þæs reðan handum þe hine hȳnan wolde, Hml. Th. ii. 510, 23: By. 324. (β) of the operations of troops :—Se eahteþa dǽl þāra legion . . . angunnan hergean and hiénan þā þe hié friþian sceoldon *octava legio . . . omnes, quibus subsidio praeerat, interfecit,* Ors. 4, 1; S. 160, 10. (b) the object a thing, *to lay waste, destroy.* (a) the subject personal :—Hí hēndon and hergedon Godes cyrican and yfeledon and slógan crístene men *uastari ecclesias, affligi interficique Christianos praeceperunt,* Bd. 1, 6; Sch. 18, 16. Noldon ða hǽðenan þām hālgan geðafian þæt hē swā hālig treów ǽfre hȳnan sceolde (hí ne mihton on heora mōðe findan þ hē þ treów forcurfe, Hml. S. 31, 395), Hml. Th. ii. 508, 26. (β) of the operations of nature :—Hí gebǽd . . . þ God forgeáfe þǽre eorðan rēnas, for þan ðe se hǽða þā hȳnde ða eorðan, Hml. S. 14, 168. IV. *to accuse* :— From hēnendum *ab accusatoribus,* Jn. p. 5, 9.

**hinca.** *Add: See next word.*

**hincian** (?); p. ode *To limp, hobble, halt* :—Hincodon (? printed luncodon) *claudicauerunt,* Ps. L. 17, 46. [*In support of a verb* luncian Lindelöf cites Swed. lunka *to jog on*; Norw. lunke, *and the dialect* (*Shetland*) lunk *to limp. In support of* hincian cf. Icel. hinka; p. aði: O. H. Ger. hinchan; p. hanch *claudicare. See also* hinca.]

**hind.** v. hynd. *Substitute:* hind :—Seó þridde hind (*this seems a mistake for* híd. Cf. seó þridde híd æt Dydincotan, 400, 8) æt Dydincotan . . . Ðonne is ealles ðæs landes þreó hída, .II. æt Penedoc and .I. æt Dydinecotan, C. D. iii. 19, 7–9. See, however, Kemble's Saxons in England i. 113, where hind is taken as *hynd,* and so connected with numeral hund.

**hind.** *Add* :—Hind *cerva,* Kent. Gl. 110: *dammula,* 128. Cwæð se cyning tó hire hwylcne dǽl þæs landes hió onfón wolde hyre bróðrum tó wergilde. Hió cwæð þ hió his nā māran ne gyrnde þonne hire hind ūtan ymbe yrnan wolde þe hire ealne weg beforan arn ðonne hió on rāde wæs . . . Hió ða hind swā dyde þ hió him beforan hleápende wæs, and hí hyre æfter fílígende wǽron, Lch. iii. 426. 23–32. Hinde meolc, 4, 1.

**hindan** *Add:* I. where there is movement towards the back of an object. (1) of the direction of an action :—Hē hēt Matheum hindan mid sweorde þurstingan, Shrn. 131, 33. þā Engliscan hí hindan hetelíce slógon, Chr. 1066; P. 199. 15. (2) with verbs of pursuit :—Hē ofi nþ þā sunnan hindan and cymþ wiþforan þā sunnan ūp *it comes up with the sun from behind and rises be ore the sun,* Bt. 39, 13; F. 234, 2. II. marking position, *at the back, behind,* Ph. 293 (*in Dict.*). v. on-, wiþ-hindan.

**hind-berigʒ.** *Add* ·—Hindberiae *acinum,* Wrt. Voc. ii. 99, 9. Hindberige, 8, 42. Hindberge, i. 285, 65: *erimio,* ii. 107, 34. Hindberige *erimio,* 29, 40. ¶ the word seems to be used of the strawberry also :—Hindberian *flaga,* 38, 62. [v. N. E. D. hindberry. O. H. Ger. hint-beri *frambores, frambrones.*]

**hind-brēr,** e; f. *Add* :—Hindbrēr *erimius,* Wrt. Voc. ii. 144. 2. Hindbrēre *erimia,* Txts. 58. 352.

**hind-cealf.** *Add:*—Hindcaelf *inulus,* Wrt. Voc. ii. 111, 84. Hindcealf *hinnulus,* 43, 41. Eálá ðu liófestæ hind (*cerva*) and gecwēmest hindcealf (*hinnulus*), Kent. Gl. 110. [v. N. E. D. hindcalf. O. H. Ger. hint-kalp *hinnulus.*]

**hinder.** (1) where there is movement backwards :—Slincan on hinder, Dōm. L. 240. (2) where there is reversal of movement :—Sȳn mīne fýnd on hinder gecyrde *convertantur inimici mei retrorsum,* Guth. Gr. 126, 75: Ps. Spl. T 9, 2. (3) where there is inversion of proper order :—Bið þæs mannes líf on hinder gefadad, gif þ flǽsc sceal gewyldan þone gāst, Hml. S. 17, 12.

**hinder-ʒeap, -gep.** *l.* -geáp, -gép, *and in the bracket of* l. 6 *for* hiþer *l.* luþer.

**hinder-genga,** an; m. I. one that goes backward (epithet of a crab) :—Hindergenga *retrograda* (Nepa m hi nomen . . . passibus Oceanum *retrograda* transeo versis, Ald. 254, 30), An. Ox. 26, 23. II. one that goes back from the faith he has professed, an *apostate* (cf. Manega his leorningcnihtas cyrdon onbæc and ne eódun mid him, Jn. 6, 66. Homo apostata, i. retrogradiens, Kent. Gl. 141) :—Hindergengena *apostatarum,* An. Ox. 5, 16.

**hinderling.** *Add:* [v. N. E. D. hinderling]: -hinderling. v. on-hinderling.

**hinder-scipe.** *Substitute: Evil craft. fraud, knavery, guile, treachery* :—Feóndlices hinderscypes *spiritalis nequitiae,* An. Ox. 378. Ongeán feóndes hinderscype scyld geleáfan *contra hostis nequitiam scutum fidei,* Hy. S. 135, 25.

**hind-fald.** *Dele the bracket:* hine. *The word seems constructed as a nominative to the genitive* hína (*from* hígna): -hine. v. ge-híne: **hinend** *an accuser.* v. hínan; IV.

**hin-gang.** *Add:*—Aer his hiniongae, Txts. 149. 18.

**hin-ness,** e; f. I. *a trampling upon, subjecting* :—Ic salde iów mæhte hennisse (hénisæs, L.) ł niðrunge ofer nēðre *dedi uobis potestatem calcandi supra serpentes,* Lk. R. 10, 19. II. *a laying waste, destruction* :—Godes cyricena hȳnnysse (bærnesse, *v. l.*) and slege martyra unblinnendlíce dōn wæs *incendiis ecclesiarum, caedibus martyrum incessabiliter acta est,* Bd. 1, 6; Sch. 19, 1.

**hin-síþ.** *Add:*—Heard wæs hinsíð . . . þe hȳ æt þām beorge blíðne fu]ndon *hard had been* (*Christ's*) *death* (*on the cross*) . . . *which at the grave* (cf. *for the meaning of* beorg : Wēndon þæt hē on þām beorge bídan sceolde āna in þǽre eásterniht, 14) *they found to be joyous* (cf. exierunt de monumento magno gaudio, Mt. 28, 8), Hö. 7. ¶ *as a gloss to* exitus ? :—In síðas *exitus* (the passage is : Sicut euidentias rerum exitus probauit, Bd. 1, 14. Perhaps the glosses took the word to be plural and used in the sense 'end of life', and intended to express the idea by hinsíðas. Cf. insíðgryre for hinsíðgryre, Sat. 456), Txts. 181, 39.

**hinþ(u, -o).** *Take here* hȳnþ *in Dict., and add:* I. *misery, poverty* :—Sume beóþ wīdcūþe on heora gebyrdum, ac hí beóþ mid wǽdle and mid hēnþe (hǽnþe, *v. l.*) ofþrycte, þ him wǽre leófre þ hí wǽran unæþele þonne swā earme *hunc nobilitas notum facit, sed angustia rei familiaris inclusus esse mallet ignotus,* Bt. 11, 1; F. 30, 33. Ðíos of hēnðu ł unspo.d (hēnðum ł unspoednum, R.) hire sende *haec de penuria sua misit,* Mk. L. 12, 44. II. *hurt, injury, destruction* :—Hié fæstor tōsomne beóð gefēgde tó gōdra monna hiénðe in bonorum *gravius nece glomerantur,* Past. 361, 21. Hýnðe (*vitae*) *detrimento,* i. *dispendio,* An. Ox. 3156. Is geswenced of hēnðe (*innocens*) *afflictus est damno,* Kent. Gl. 811. Hēuðo *damnum* (*sustinebi',* qui impatiens est), 704. Hȳnða *damna* (*rerum formidans*), An. Ox. 2993. Ic heóld nū nigon geár wið ealle hȳnða þínes fæder gestreón, Hml. S. 9, 42.

**hioful** *the face. Dele, and see* hnifol.

**hion.** *l.* hión, *and add:* cf. Heáfodwunde tó bōte . . . Gif þ ūterre bān bið þyrel, Ll. Th. i. 92, 15. [*Liebermann proposes to read* hionne *with the meaning* '*membrane*'. Cf. Dan. hjerne-binde *membrane of the brain,* and see note on the word in Ll. Th.]

**hion** *hence.* v. heonan; I. 3: -hípan. v. be-, ge-, ymb-hípan.

**hípe** *a heap. Take here* hȳpe *in Dict., and add* :—Hȳpe *congeries,* An. Ox. 4780. Hȳpum *cumulis,* Germ. 401, 22. On reáde hȳpan *in rubicundas congeries,* An. Ox. 1822. v. stán-hípe.

**hípel.** *Take here* hȳpel *in Dict., and add:*—On hȳpel *in aceruum,* Scint. 95, 17. Hȳplas *montes,* Germ. 395, 56.

**-hípian.** v. be-hípian.

**híra** *one who obeys. Take here* hēra, hȳra *in Dict., and add* :— Æþelbyrhtes hēra *sub potestate positus Aedilbercti,* Bd. 2, 3; Sch. 123, 5. Mid glædum geþance þā underþeóddan leorneras heora ealdrum hȳran sceolan, for ðī þæne glǽdan hȳran God lufað, R. Ben. 20, 24. Mid þām gecorenum Crístes hērum (hȳrede, *v. l.*), Wlfst. 256, 19.

**híran.** *Take here* hȳran *in Dict., and add:* I. *to perceive sound* :— Ðý lǽs mið eárum hērað, Mt. L. 13, 15. Earo tó hērraunne, 13, 9. Tó hēraune, Lk. p. 8, 15. II. *trans. to hear* a sound or that which causes sound :—Ne hēres ðū hū micla wið ðec coeðas?, Mt. L. 27, 13. Hērde from ðæm menigum lā hǽl ūsic *audit a turbis osanna,* Mk. p. 4, 17. Gié hērdon efolsungas *audistis blasphemiam,* Mt. L. 27, 65. Ðā ðing gié hērdon, Lk. L. 7, 22. III. with object and infin. *to hear* a person say :—Ne hȳrde ic snotorlícor guman þingian, B 1842. þā ic Freáware fietsittende nemnan hȳrde, 2023. Nǽfre wē hȳrdon hæled ǽnigne þyslic cȳðan, El. 538. IIIa. with infin. only, *to hear* say :—Ic hiérde secgan þæt . . ., Ors. 3, 10; S. 138, 18. Hȳrde, B. 582: Reb. 1. Þone ic Andreas nemnan hērde, An. 1178. Swā wē hit secgan hiérdon, Ors. 6, 31; S. 286, 7: Chr. 851: P. 64, 23. Wē þæt hȳrdon ł æiēdum cȳðan, El. 670. Ne hērdon . . . fira nān ymb gefeoht sprecan (cf. gehērde nān mon . . . ymbe nān gefeoht sprecan, Bt. 15; F. 48, 14), Met. 8, 31. IV. *to give ear, hearken, listen* :—Hērað, Mk. L. 4, 3. Gemoeton hine hērende (hlystende, W. S.), Lk. L. R. 2, 46. IVa. *trans. To listen to* a person or thing attentively :— Suæ hua ne hēres worda iúera (nyle hēran wordum eówrum, R.), Mt. L. 10, 14. Oðero bíspell hēres gē, 21, 33. Hēres gié mec alle, Mk. L. 7, 14. Cuēn sūððēnes cuōm tó hēranne snytro Salomones, Mt. L. 12, 42. V. *to listen with compliance or assent to* a person or thing :— þū mīnum lārum hȳre and þæt land gesēc, Gen. 1750. Hȳre brȳde þīnre, 2797. Gif ða cirica ne hēre, Mt. L. 18, 17. Is nū þearf mycel þæt wē wísfæstra wordum hȳran, An. 1169. Þær þū þām ne hiérde þe unc þisne hearm gerǽd, Gen. 797. Gif him mon hȳran nelle, þonne mōt se mæssepreóst hit wrecan, Bl. H. 49, 2. Gif þū wilt his wordum hȳran and his beboda lǽstan, 183, 36. Wē þe beóð holde, gif þū ūs hȳran wilt, Gū. 251: Gen. 542. Hērende *obsecundans* (*precibus et monitis*), Wrt. Voc. ii. 82, 68. VI. *to obey* :—Hírde *paruit,* Wrt. Voc. ii. 67, 27. VIa. *to obey* a person :—Wind and sǽ hērað ł hērsumiað him *uentus et mare oboediunt ei,* Mk. L. R. 4, 41. Þū mīn bibod bræce þe þīnes bonan worde, feónde hȳrdest þonne þīnum Scyppende, Cri. 1395. Nōe fremede swā hine Nergend hēht, hȳrde heofoncyninge, Gen. 1315: 1493. 'Hāt būtū āweg fēra.' . . . þā se wer hȳrde his waldende, 2803: Exod. 410. Suna ic lǽrde þ hié hȳrdon heora yldrum (cf. Filii, obedite parentibus vestris, Eph. 6, 1), Bl. H.

185, 20. Ús is mycel þearf þ̄ wē godcundan lāreówan geornlíce hýran (*pareamus, obediamus*, Lat. vers.), Ll. Th. i. 424, 7 : 326, 15 : 332, 34. Wíf sceal hire ealdore (hláforde, *v. l.*) hiéran, 138, 18. Ic wille þ bisceop and þá gerēfan hit beódan eallum þām þe him híran (*parere*, Lat. vers.) sculon, 194, 11. Hýran. 240, 15. 'Nū þū lungre geong hord sceáwian' . . . þá ic gefrægn hine dryhtne hýran, B. 2754. **VI** b *to obey an order :*—Hēred *pareat (praecepto)*, Wrt. Voc. ii. 75, 48. Ealla gesceafta hýraθ (heórsumiaþ, Bt. 4 ; F. 8, 8) þīnre hǣse, Met. 4, 26. Hēt se cyning tō him cnihtas gangan ; hyssas hýrdon lāre, Dan. 432. Noldan Crēcas þǣm bebode hiéran, Ors. 3, 11 ; S. 144, 16. **VII** *to be subject to.* (1) *of the relation between subject and ruler (human or divine) :*—Ic Críste hēro *Christ is my king*, Ps. C. 74. Þone cyning þām þū hýrdest ǣr *the king whose subject you were*, El. 934. Harold hýrde holdelíce herran sīnum, Edw. 32. Eádwearde cinge hýrdon holdlíce hǣgstealde menn, 14 : B. 66. God rícsaþ ofer hí . . . gif hī hiora unwillum hīm hērden, Bt. 35, 4 ; F. 160, 19. þ wē ānum cynehlāforde holdlíce hýran, Ll. Th. i. 314, 11. þ hē wǣre on gehealtsumnysse þæs bebodes his Scippende underþeód and þurh þ wiste þ hē him hýran sceolde *ut in observatione mandati sciret subjectum creatori suo*, Angl. vii. 6, 46 ; Sat. 54. Hēran, 183 : 234 : Met. 9, 45. (1 a) *the relation between a subject and a dominant race :*—Hié wiθsōcon þ hié leng Lǣcedemonium hiéran nolde *a regno Macedonum defecerunt*, Ors. 3, 11 ; S. 144, 19. (2) *of the relation between man and lord :*—Sē byθ earming þe . . . deófle campaθ . . . Sē byθ eádig þe . . . Dryhtne hýreθ, Hy. 2, 10 : Dóm. 96. Đā θe deóflum hýrdon, Bl. H. 201, 20. Manegum men þincþ þ hē nǣnne anweald næbbe būton hē hæbbe manigne man þe him hēre, Bt. 29, 1 ; F. 104, 9. Đence ǣlc mon hū nytwyrðe hē sié and hū gehiérsum ðǣm ðe hē mid ryhte hiéran scyle on ðām ðe hē dēþ *penset quisque quid subjectus egerit*, Past. 57, 14. Ne gebyraθ him (*a priest*) nān þingc tō worldwíge, gif hē Gode wile rihtlíce hýran *fighting is no concern of a priest, if he means to have God for his lord and master*, Ll. Th. i. 346, 23. Ic wille hýran holdlíce mínum hǣlende, Gū. 576. (3) *of the relation between servant and master, to serve :*—Þonne esne his hláforde hēreθ and cwēmeθ, Ps. Th. 122, 2. Hērde Drihtne *serviens Domino*, Lk. p. 2, 3 : 2, 37. Hēre wē him *seruiamus illi*, I, 74. Ǣnig mon ne mæg tuǣm hláferdum hēra *servire*, Mt. L. 6, 24. Nelle ic unbunden ǣnigum hýran, Rä. 24, 15. Sunu monnes ne cuóm him tō hēranne (*ministrari*), Mt. L. 20, 28. (4) *to be under the dominion* of evil, error, &c. :—þæt hē ūs ne lǣte leng in disse deáθdene gedwolan hýran, Cri. 344. Synne hýrendra *Hismahelitum*, Ps. Rdr. 82, 7. **VIII.** híran tō *to belong to.* (1) *to be subject to the dominion, authority, jurisdiction, &c., of :*—Man āgife ǣlce teóðunge tō þām ealdan mynstre þe seó hýrnes tō hýrd, Ll. Th. i. 262, 7. Hwílon Wentsǣte hýrdon intó Dūnsǣtan, ac hit gebyreθ rihtor intó West-Sexan ; þyder hý scylan gafol and gíslas syllan, 356, 18. Man hālgode Trumwine Pihtum, for þan hý hýrdon þā hider *addidit . . . Trumwini ad prouinciam Pictorum, quae tunc temporis Anglorum erat imperio subiecta* (Bd. 4, 12), Chr. 681 ; P. 39, 11. Eádweard fēng tō Lundenbyrc and tō Oxnaforda, and tō ðǣm landum eallum þe þǣr tó hiérdon, 912 ; P. 96, 18. Ealle þā land þe intó Rōme hýrdon, Hml. S. 30, 232. On þ geráð þæt þā īgland Sicilia and Sarþinia hiérden tō Rōmānum, Ors. 4, 10 ; S. 202, 21. (2) *of a due, privilege, &c.* :—Gelǣste man sáulsceat intó þām mynstre þe hit tó hýrde, Ll. Th. i. 308, 7. Þrýfealdne áθ swā wíde swā hit tó þære byrig hýre, 388, 13. (3) *of persons, to be attached to a place* by residence, occupation, office, &c. :—þā biscopas and þā gerēfan þe tō Lundenbyrig hýraθ, Ll. Th. i. 228, 7. Þā burh æt Ligraceastre, and se mǣsta dǣl þæs herges þe ðǣr tó hýrde wearθ underþeóded, Chr. 918 ; P. 105, 23. Æt þām tūne þe hē tō hýre, Ll. Th. i. 30, 1. Þā yldestan men þe tō þǣre byrig híron, 208, 30 : 210, 5. **IX.** *to get to know by hearing, hear of, be told.* (1) *with acc.* :—Huætd ðis ic hēro from ðē?, Lk. L. 16, 2. þā hē þæt hiérde, Chr. 835 ; P. 62, 17. Unryhthǣmed suā unryht suā wē betwuxn hǣθnum monnum ne hiérdon, Past. 211, 9. Menigo hērdon (hērende wērun, R.) ðā ðe hē wyrcende wæs, Mk. L. 3, 8. Cwǣdon þæt heó ōwiht swylces ne ǣr ne sīθ ǣfre hýrdon, El. 572. (2) *with clause* :—Hýrde ic þæt þām frætwum feówer meáras lást weardode, B. 2163. Hērdes þū ǣfre þætte ǣnig mon on sondbeorgas settan meahte fæste healle?, Met. 7, 9. Wē hírdon (hiérdon, *v. l.*) ðætte . . . Past. 381, 8. Hýrdon, Gū. 79. Hýrde wē þæt . . . , Ap. 70. Hērde gē for ðon ācueden is, Mt. L. 5, 33. (3) *with acc. and infin.* :—Ne hýrde ic gumena ǣnigne ǣfre bringan ofer sealtne mere sēlran lāre, Men. 101. (3 a) *with infin.* :—Ne hýrde ic cymlícor ceól gegyrwan, B. 38. (4) *intrans.* :—Hí ne gesáwon sundbúende ne ymbūtan hí ne hērdon, Met. 8, 14. Ymbe sciphergas hí ne hērdon (cf. ne gehērde nān mon nānne sciphere, Bt. 15 ; F. 48, 14), 31.

híran (?) *to exalt, worship* [v. híra, *cpve.* of heáh, heáh ; II. 1.] :— Hē þā hǣðengild hýran ne wolde, wíg weorþian, Ap. 47. v. hígan.

hirdan. *Take here* hyrdan *in Dict.*, and *add :* v. geond-hirdan.

hirde. *Add :* I. *one who has charge of cattle :*—Gātbuccan hyrde *capra aegida*, Wrt. Voc. i. 22, 78. Ān hirde (hierde, S. 5, 12), Ueriatus hāten *Viriathus, homo pastoralis*, Ors. 5, 2 ; S. 216, 6.

Ceápes heorde *gregarius*, Nar. 18, 26. Swā hiorde (*pastor*) āscādeþ scēp from ticnum, Mt. R. L. 25, 32. Hyrdas (ðā hiordas, R., ðā hiorde, L. *pastores*) wǣron nihtwæccan healdende ofer heora heorde, Lk. 2, 8. Hyrdas (hiordas, R., hiorda), 15. Bodan hyrdum cýðdon, Cri. 450. Oxena hierdas *hobulcos*, Wrt. Voc. ii. 80, 17. **II.** *a keeper, guardian, protector, director* of people :—Būton ic hyrde (*custos*) ǣtwere eów, Coll. M. 28, 21. Mec sǣwelcund hyrde bihealdeθ, Gū. 289. Under hāligra hyrda gewealdum, 386. (1) *used of a person in authority, one who bears rule :*—Is ōþer (*St. Peter*) cyricean hyrde tō Crístes handa, Bl. H. 171, 7. Se cyning and se biscop sceoldan beón Crístenra folca hyrdas, and hī from eallum unrithwīsum āhweorfan, 45, 26. ¶ in phrases denoting a king, ruler, head of a house, leader, &c. (a) :—Ríces hyrde, werodes wīsa (*Moses*), Exod. 256. Wine Scyldinga, ríces hyrde (*Hrothgar*). Leóf þeóden, ríces hyrde (*Beowulf*), 3080. Ríces hyrde (cf. ríce gerēfa rondburgum weóld, 19), Jul. 66. Bregowearda fela, ríces hyrdas, Gen. 2334. Se wīsa and se fæstrǣda folces hyrde (cf. se wīsa and fæstrǣda Cato, sē wæs eác Rōmāna heretoga, Bt. 19 ; F. 70, 8), Met. 10, 49. Brego Beorhtdena, folces hyrde (*Hrothgar*), B 610 : (*Hygelac*), 1849 : (*Beowulf*), 2644. Enoch siððan ealdordōm āhóf, folces wīsa . . . hē hyrde wæs heáfodmāga, Gen. 1200. (1 a) applied to the Deity :—Wæs hiin hyrde gōd heofouríces weard, Dan. 11. ¶ in phrases :—Wuldorcyning . . . ríces hyrde, An. 808. Lífes weard, dugoθa hyrde, Gen. 164. Þone heán cyning, gāsta hyrde, Dan. 199. Þeóda hyrde, Az. 150. (2) *used of a teacher, guide, pastor :*—Đā hierdas næfdon andgit, Past. 27, 25. Đām gāstlicum hyrdum, þæt sind lāreówas, Hml. Th. i. 36, 10. **III.** *the keeper* of a thing. (1) with the idea of possession or control. (a) material :—Malalehel wæs æfter larede yrfes hyrde . . . Siððan Mathusal māgum dǣlde gestreón, Gen. 1067 : 1545 : 219. Sinces hyrde, 2101. Hringa hyrde, B. 2245. (a a) used of a dragon :—Wyrm, hordes hyrde, B. 887. Frætwa hyrde, 3 33. (b) non-material :—Fyrena hyrde, B. 750. Synna hyrdas, Gū. 522. (2) with the idea of protection, caretaking of a place :—Adam neorxnawonges nīwre gesceafte hyrde and healdend, Gen. 172. Beorges hyrde (*the fire-drake*), B. 2304. Ic ofslōg húses hyrdas, 1666. (2 a) the subject a thing :—Ne biθ sond wið micelne rēn manna ǣngum húses hyrde, Met. 7, 22. (2 b) non-material :—Þonne se weard (*conscience*) swefeθ, sāwele hyrde, B. 1742. (3) in phrases denoting the Deity :—Leóhtes hyrde, Az. 121 : Hy. 4, 7. Þrymmes hyrde, Jud. 60 : Jul. 280 : El. 348 : 859. Wuldres hyrde, B. 931. Tungla hyrde, Hy. 4, 9. Lífes waldend, heofona hyrde, Dóm. 8 **IV.** *a keeper* of a prison, one on the watch to prevent, *a guard, watchman :*—Hié gemēton þæs carcernes duru opene and þā seoton hyrdas deáde licgan, Bl. H. 239, 25 : An. 1079. **IV a.** fig. :—Wer þū giedda wīs, wær wið willan, worda hyrde, Fä. 42. v. cǣg-, cwēn-, heáh-, hríþ-, mǣþum-, mūl-, oxan-hirde.

hirde-cnapa, an ; *m. A (young) herdsman :*—Hē lēt ðǣr ārǣran his hyrdecnapan cýtan, þ hí ðǣr gehende mid heora hláfordes yrfe lāgon. . . . And þā hyrdecnapan . . . ymbe þ wǣron, Hml S. 23, 417-421.

hirde-leás. *Add :* I. *without a shepherd :*—Swā swā hyrdeleáse sceáp *sicut oves quibus non est pastor*, Hml. A. 110, 260. **II.** *without a pastor, without an ecclesiastical ruler :*—Seó cyrice æt Hrofesceastre wæs hyrdeleás *Hrofensis ecclesia pastorem minime habebat*, Bd. 2, 20 ; Sch. 188, 5. Wæs mynster unfeorr fram heora húse þ wæs forlǣten and hyrdeleás for heora hláfordes deáðe and forþfore of þām mynstre *non longe erat monasterium, quod rectoris sui morte erat destitutum*, Gr. D. 205, 23.

hirde-líc. *Add :*—Hū mæg se biscep brūcan ðǣre hierdelican āre, Past. 132, 3. Hyrdelicere gýmene *pastoralis curg*, An. Ox. 5423. Hyrdelicere care *sollertia pastorali*, 2986. Þā scylon gýmene hyrdelice underfōn, Scint. 121, 17.

hirde-mann, es ; *m. A herdsman, shepherd :*—Hire hyrdeman sume āc āstāh and his orf lǣswode mid treówenum helme, Hml. Th. ii. 150, 10. Se engel cýdde Crístes ācennednysse hyrdemannum, i. 36, 9. Sacu betwux Abrames hyrdemannum (*inter pastores gregum*) and Lothes, Gen. 13, 7. [v. *N. E. D.* herd-man.]

hirdnan, e ; *f. A hardening :*—xii ðūsendum sīða sceaprpra ðonne seó ān flān ðā sý fram hundtwelftigum hyrdenna geondhyrded, Sal. K. p. 150, 28.

hirde-wyrt. *Add :*—Hirdewyrt, þ is eorðgealla, Lch. ii. 202, 22. Hyrdewyrt, 30, 21. Centaurian, þ is hyrdewyrt, ōþre naman eorþgealla, 248, 13. Hirdewyrt seó lǣsse, 250, 11. Nim centaurian, þ is fel terrae, sume hātaþ hyrdewyrt, sume eorðgeallan, 186, 27.

hirdmann. v. in-hirdmann.

hird-ness. *Add :* I. *watchful care, taking charge, taking care* that a thing be not damaged :—þām mynstre fore wæs mid geornlicre heordnysse *monasterio solerti custodia praefuit*, Gr. D. 52, 15. On hū mycelre Godes heordnysse (*custodia*) beóð þā þe cunnon hī sylfe forseón on þysum life, 39, 30. þā þā hē nam þā hyrdnysse (hiordnisse, *v. l.*) þæs regollican lífes in þām mynstre *cum in monasterio regulari vitae custodiam teneret*, 104, 2. **II.** *a watch, guard* to prevent evil :— Ic gesette mínum mūþe heordnesse *posui ori meo custodiam*. R. Ben. 21, 11. **III.** *a watch, period during which watch is kept :*—þūsend

geára . . . swā swā heordnes (*custodia*) on nihte, Ps. Rdr. 89, 4. Fram heordnesse dægredlicre oð on niht *a custodia matutina usque ad noctem*. 129, 6. **IV.** *a place for keeping things in :*—Hig gesetton þā burh on æpplena hyrdnesse *posuerunt Hierusalem in pomorum custodiam*, Ps. L. 78, 1. Cf. heord-ræden.

**hírd-preost.** v. híred-preóst : **hird-ræden.** v. heord-ræden : **hird-ung.** *Take here* hyrdung *in Dict.*: **híre** *pleasant. Take here* heóre *in Dict.* : -híre. v. ofer-híre : -híre ; *adv.* v. un-híre.

**híred.** *l.* híred, *and add :* **I.** *a family, wife and children :*—Gif hwā stalie swā his wíf nyte and his bearn . . . Gif hē stalie on gewitnesse ealles his híredes, Ll. Th. i. 106, 15–17. Gif hig (*priests*) hwylc árwyrðe hýredes fæder tō his hūse geladige, sē þe wyle mid his wífe and mid bearnum on gāstlicum gefeán blissian. ii. 410, 21. Hē sette swā swā scēp heóredas *posuit sicut oves familias*, Ps. Vos. Srt. Rdr. 106, 41. Heórdas, Ps. L. 106, 41. **II.** *a family, body of relatives, house :*—Nān monn hiera cynnes ne hiera híeredes (hióredes, *v.l.*) ne offrode *homo de semine tuo per familias non offeret*, Past. 65, 1. Gif ðū (Cyrus) hine forstenst wē fordýlegiad þē and þīne hýred, Hml. Th. i. 570, 26. **III.** *a (great) man's household :*—Gif sum ríce mann mē cūð ne bið, ne nān monn his híredes (híeredes, *v.l.*), Past. 63, 4. Faeder hiórodes (fæder hīna. R.) *pater familias*, Mt. L. 21, 33. Fader hiórodæs (heóredes, R.) ł hígna, 13, 27. Hiórades, 10, 25. Feder iórodes (hína, R.), 13, 52. Hírodes, Lk. L. 12, 39. Gerēfan mid his hírede hē tō geleáfan gecyrde *praefectum cum domo sua conuertit*, Bd. 2, 16 ; Sch. 177, 21. Hírede *familia*, An. Ox. 3307. Hýrede, Rä. 60, 6. Ðone ðegn gesette hlāferd his oïer hiórod (heórod, R. *familiam*) his, Mt. L 24, 45. Híred, Past. 459, 12. On .xiiii. nihte mōnan is gód on nīwne híred tō fǽrenne. Lch. iii. 178, 32. Ða eorðlican blāfordas sint tō ðǽm gesette ðæt hié ðā endebyrdnesse and ðā ðegnunga hiora híeredum gebrytnige *terrenae domus dominus famulorum ordines ministeriaque dispertiens*, Past. 319, 20. ¶ *the place of residence of a man and his household :*—Orceard hírede, synt orceardas gedafenlice æpplum *pomerium curti, sunt pomaria congrua malis*, Lch. i. lxii, 8. **III a.** *where the Deity is regarded as the father of a family.* (1) the family being the good :—Ðū þe ūs gedydest þínes hýredes *Deus qui nos munis*, Solil. H. 8, 9. [Æt] woes hiórodes ðínes beodum *adesto familiae tuae precibus*, Rtl. 86, 3. Hiórad ðín giheald *familiam tuam custodi*, 17, 5. (2) the family, those in heaven :—Híred *familiam* i. *congregationem* (*coeli beatam*), An. Ox. 817. **III b.** *where the devil is the father :*—Forgit þæt hūs and þone híred þínes leásan fæder, þæt ys deófol *obliuiscere domum patris tui*, Ps. Th. 44, 12. **IV.** *the household (and house) of a king, court :*—Se cyning ne his híred (*domestici eius*), Bd. 3, 14 ; Sch. 260, 1. Híredes begímen *aulica cura*, Lch. i. lx, 3. Hié an ānum híerede wǽron āfedde and getýde (cf. Alexandri commi'litones, Alexandri duces, 153, 16, 17), Ors. 3. 11 ; S. 152, 29. Gif þegen geþeáh þ hé þénode cynge and his rādstefne rād on his hírede, Ll. Th. i. 190, 20. Wille wē be him (*William I*) āwrītan swā swā wē hine āgeáton, and ōðre hwīle on his hírede wunedon, Chr. 1086 ; P. 219, 19. Hýrede, 1074 ; P. 210, 3. Hié tō his healle ne tō his (*Nero's*) hírede eft wendan noldan, Bl. H. 173, 18. Be ðām ðe on cyninges hírde feohteð (cf. on cynges healle feohte, 66, 7) *de dimicatione in regia*, Ll. Th. i. 408, 12. Hēr se cyng heóld his híred on Winceastre tō þām Eástran, Chr. 1085 ; P. 216, 32. On .xii. nihte mōnan byð gód on hírd tō fǽrenne, Lch. iii. 178, 27. **IV a.** *where the Deity is king :*—Wē moton sittan mid Drihtne . . . þǽr his híred nū hālig eardað, Sat. 592. Āworden wæs mid engle menigo hiórodes heonionlic *facta est cum angelo multitudo militiae caelestis*, Lk. 2, 13. Ic þe hālsige, heofonrīces weard, for þām hírede þe þū hider lǽdest, engla þreátas, Sat. 423. Hē geheóld híred heofona, and þæt hālige seld, 348. **IV b.** *of the followers of Satan :*—Hē tō helle hnīgan sceolde and his híred mid, Sat. 376. **IV c.** *where a thing is personified :*—Swā hit bið be þām wísdōme. Ælc . . . hym mæg cuman tō and on hys hýrede wunian (cf. cynges hām sēcan, 2), Solil. H. 44, 16. **V.** *the inferior clerks attendant upon the mass-priest :*—Se biscop sceal þrafian þā mæssepreóstas þ hié þone híred þe hié ofer beóþ, and þā lǽwedan men þe hié aldormen ofer beón sceoldan, þ hié þǽm ne geþafian þ hié heora líf on wōh lifgean, Bl. H. 45, 9. **VI.** *the members of a religious house.* v. híred-preóst ; II :—Ðæt bió geselle ðæt land ðām hírode . . . būtan hit hit unt unnan híredes ofgān tō rihtan gafole . . . and his ðonne se híred hit geearnian . . . and staude simle seó bōc on ðæs híredes handa, C. D. ii. 58, 21–29. Æt ǽlcan tīdsange eal híred aþeneJum limum singe þone sealm, Wlfst. 181, 26. Nime gē ðā ðe on ðæm hírede (hiórode, *v.l.*) unweorðuste síen, Past. 131, 7. On hírede *in clero*, An. Ox. 8, 369. Mathēus dǽl Sēe Cūðberti, Marcus dǽl biscope. Lucas dǽl ðæm hiórode, Jn. p. 188, 8. Wiste hē sumne híred on his bisceopscíre þe þā ungeþwǽre him betweónum wǽron (cf. wǽron on ðām tīman ungeþwǽre preóstas on sinum his mynstra, Hml. Th. ii. 516, 4), Bl. H. 225, 5. Mid geþeahte bēgra þǽra híreda þe æt þām cyrcean syndon *cum consilio amborum sodalitatum quae in ecclesiis istis sint*, Ll. Th. ii. 236, 18. [v. *N.E.D.* hird.] v. bisceop-, nunn-, preóst-, wíf-híred.

**híred-cniht.** *Add :* **I.** *a domestic.* v. híred ; **III** :—Oncneów Philippus, swā swā fæder, Eugenian, and Auitus and Særgius hyra āgene swyster, and hyra hýredcnihtas hī eádmódlīce cyston, Hml. S. 2, 249. His híredcnihton eallon .v. pund tō gedāle, ǽlcon þe þām þe his mǽd wǽre, Cht. Crw. 23, 25. [**II.** *an official of a court.* v. híred ; **IV** :—Hírtcynihttes *satrapae* (cf. gesīþmen, þeignes *as glosses to the same passage*, 874 : dēman *satrape*, 4,760), An. Ox. 11, 116.]

**híred-cūþ** ; *adj. Familiar, domestic :*—Betere ys þincg híredcūþ beón gewanud þænne sāwle hǽle forwyrþan *melius est rem familiarem minui quam animę salutem perire*, Scint. 203, 13.

**híred-gerefa**, an ; *m. An officer of a king's court* (? cf. híred ; **IV**) :—Gerēfa *consul*, undergerēfa *proconsul*, híredgerēfa *exconsul*, ānwalda *monarces*, burhgerēfa *praetor*, Wülck. Gl. 110, 4–9.

**híred-leóf** (?) ; *adj. Dear to a family, friendly, familiar :*—Gif of ōþrum mynstre cūþum and híredlofum (-leófum ?) brōþor ǽnig gecýdd byþ forþfaren *si ex alio monasterio noto ac familiari frater quis nuntiatus fuerit defunctus*, Angl. xiii. 445, 1146. Cf. hiw-cūþ.

**híred-lic.** *Substitute :* **I.** *of a family.* v. híred ; **III** :—Híredlicere þenrǽdene híwcūþ carfulnys *familiaris clientele domestica sollicitudo*, An. Ox. 4181. **II.** *of a court.* v. híred ; **IV** :—Þæs híredlican *palestinę* (*palatine* has been misread), An. Ox. 2414. Tō hýredlicum (hýrdelicum, 2996. Híredlicum, Angl. xiii. 33, 156. Hýrdlicum, Hpt. Gl. 476, 57) gesetum *ad palatinas zetas*, 7, 215. Hýrdlice *palatinas*, 8, 266.

**-híredlic.** v. ge-híredlic : **híred-lof.** v. híred-leóf.

**híred-mann.** *Add :* **I.** v. híred ; **III** :—Ælcon híredmen (*bp. Alfwold's*) his onrid þe hē ālǽned hæfde, Cht. Crw. 23, 24. Híredmanna gehwilc sille pænig tō ælmessan, oððe his hlāford sille for hine, Wlfst. 181, 16. Be híredmonnum *de hero proprio familiae fidejussore*, Ll. Th. i. 394, 25. Norðhymbra ūtlagodon heora eorl Tostig, and ofslōgon his híredmenn, Chr. 1064 ; P. 190, 15. **II.** v. híred ; **IV** :—Se cyningc ābræc intō þām būre þær heó inne læg, and hēt his hýredmen ealle āweg gān, Ap. Th. 2, 1. [v. *N.E.D.* hird-man.] Cf. híred-wífman.

**híred-preóst. I.** *a domestic chaplain.* v. **hírd-preóst** *in Dict.* **II.** *a member of a religious house.* v. híred ; **VI** :—Þys sint þāra manna naman ðe man freóde . . . on Wynstānes gewytnysse mæssepreóstas and on eallra þāra híredpreósta, Cht. E. 255, 14 : 23 : 25 : 256, 2 : 6. Cf. Ðæs wæs on gewitnesse Ælfheáh mæssepreóst and se híred, Cht. Th. 622, 5. Is tō gewitnesse eall se híred on Baðan, 642, 6. Hē hié hēt lǽdan hider tō mynstere and hēr gefreógian on þæs hírydes gewitnesse, 627, 5. On ealles þæs híredes gewitnesse on Baðon, 641, 27 : 642, 2 (*and often*). Coram istis testibus : clerici Sancti Petroci, 623, 21.

**híred-wist.** *Substitute : A being, as it were, of a family, familiarity :*—Geornfullnyss híredwiste gearwað *assiduitas familiaritatem parat*, Scint. 203, 12. v. uu-híredwist.

**híre-mann.** *Take here* hýre-mann *and* hýrig-mann *in Dict., and add :*—Oft for ðæs lāreówes unwísdōme misfarað þā híremen, Past. 28, 5. On ðām breóstum ðæs gódan recceres sceal bión gierd. Ðæt is ðæt hē ðreáge his híremenn, 125, 22.

**hírend**, es ; *m.* **I.** *a hearer :*—Ðā hērend (gihērend, R.) gehērað *audientes audiant*, Mk. L. 4, 12. Hērdon ł hērend wēron *audientes*, 3, 8. **II.** *one who is subject.* v. híran ; **VII.** 4 :—Synne hýrendra (*or pres. part.* ?) *Hismahelitum*, Ps. Rdr. 82, 7. v. gehírend.

**-hírendlic.** v. ge-hírendlic : **hír-lic.** v. hír-líc : **hírlíce.** · v. un-hírlíce.

**hír-ness.** *Take here* hýr-ness *in Dict., and add :* **I.** *hearing :*—Eára hērnisse (-nisses, L.) *aures audiendi*, Mk. R. 4, 23. Hērnisses, Mt. L. 11, 15. Hērnises, Lk L. 8, 8. From hērnise *auditu*, Mt. L. 13, 14. Te hērnise *auditui*, Jn. L. 12, 38. **II.** *subjection :*—Hī him gehēton eádmóde hýrnese and singale underþeódnesse *subiectionem continuam promittebant*, Bd. 1, 12 ; Sch. 32, 3. **III.** *service :*—Hē þā twelf bócland gefreóde eorðlices camphādes and eorðlicre hērenesse (hēr-, *v.l.*) *ablato studio militiae terrestris*, Bd. 3, 24 ; Sch. 310, 6. Hērnisse *officio*, Rtl. 50, 37 : 106, 22. Hērnese *servitio*, 9, 31 : *servitutem*, 29, 30 : 106, 13. Hērnise engla *ministerium angelorum*, Mk. L. 1, 17. Hērnise ríces Godes *ministerium regni Dei*, Mk. L. 4, 11. Embehtsum[n]ise ł hērnisse hē gefe Gode *obsequium praestare Deo*, Jn. L. 16, 2. Hē gefealh singallíce his þegnungum and hýrnessum *ejus obsequiis sedule atque incessanter adhaerebat*, Gr. D. 299, 29. **IV.** *a parish :*—Man āgife ǽlce teóðunge tō þām ealdan mynstre þe seó hýrness (hēr-, *v.l.*) tō hýrð (*ad matrem ecclesiam, cui parochia adjacet*), Ll. Tb. i. 262, 7. v. ge-, in-, níd-, ofer-hírness.

**hirstan** *to fry. Take here* hyrstan *in Dict., and add :*—Bān mín swā swā on herstan herste (*confrixa*) sint, Ps. Vos. Srt. 101, 4. v. gehirstan.

**hirste**, an ; *f.* **I.** *a frying-pan :*—Bān mīne swā swā on herstan (*frixorio*) herste sint, Ps. Vos. Srt. 101, 4. **II.** *a gridiron :*—Hyrste *craticula*, Wrt. Voc. ii. 136, 53. Herst[um ?] *graticulis, ferreis factis* (*flectis*?), Ld. Gl. H. 36, 175. Herst[an ?] *latriuncula, craticulas prunis impositas*, 9, 75 (v. 138, col. 1).

hirste-panne, an; *f. A frying-pan:*—Hyrstepanne *frixorium*, i. *sartago, cremium*, Wrt. Voc. ii. 150, 1 : *cremium*, i. *frixorium*, 136, 67. Hē him tǣhte ðæt hē him genāme āne īrene hierstepannan (hearste-, *v. l.*) *sume tibi sartaginem ferream*, Past. 160, 7 : 163, 22 : 165, 9.

hirsting, e; *f. Frying, burning:*—Wylm *vel* hyrsting *frixura*, Wrt. Voc. ii. 150, 84. Mid ðisse pannan hierstinge wæs Paulus onbærned *Paulus hujus sartaginis urebatur frixura*, Past. 165, 3. [Cf. *O. H. Ger.* harsta *frixura*.]

hirsting (*a diminutive of* hirste?) *a frying-pan:*—Hyrstyngc *frixorium*, Wrt. Voc. i. 82, 69. *Frigo* ic hyrste, of ðām is *frixorium* hyrstung, Ælfc. Gr. Z. 175, 3. Hyrstincg *cremium*, Ps. L. 101, 4.

hirsting-hlāf. v. hyrsting-hlāf *in Dict.*

hirsting-panne, an; *f. A frying-pan:*—Hyrstingpanne (*printed* dyrsting-, Wrt. Voc. i. 25, 1) *sartago vel frixorium*, Wülck. Gl. 123, 14.

hīrsum. *Take here* hȳrsum *in Dict., and add:*—Hērsum oð tō deāðe *obediens usque ad mortem*, Rtl. 21, 26. v. un-hīrsum.

hīrsumian. *Take here* hȳrsumian *in Dict., and add:*—Hȳrsumian *obtemperare*, Wrt. Voc. ii. 63, 8. Hīrsumiendum *parentibus*, 67, 28. I. *to obey a person:*—Hērsumað *obedit* (*malus linguae iniquae*), Kent. Gl. 589. Hērsumað *optemperat* (*fallax labiis mendacibus*), 590. Be ðām ðæt ǣlc ōðrum hȳrsumige *ut obedientes sibi sint invicem fratres*, R. Ben. 130, 10, 14. Gif gē hæfdon geleáfan . . . hit hȳrsumode (*obediret*) eōw, Lk. 17, 6. I a. *to obey a person in authority, civil or ecclesiastical:*—Hū ðā kyningas Godes ǣrendwrecum hērsumedon (hīr-, *v. l.*), Past. 3, 6. Þæt ealle Rōmāne him (*the senate*) hīrsumeden, Ors. 2, 4 ; S. 72, 4. Þ edleán þe ðū gehēte ðām monnum þe ðē heórsumian woldan, Bt. 3, 4 ; F. 6, 20. ¶ *where the Deity is the object of obedience:*—Þē ealle gesceafta heórsumiaþ and þā gesetnessa þīnra beboda healdaþ, Bt. 4 ; F. 8, 8. Drihten cwyð, 'Of eáres hlyste hē hȳrsumode (*obedivit*) mē,' R. Ben. 19, 21. Ðā kyningas Gode hērsumedon (hīr-, *v. l.*), Past. 3, 6. I b. *of a people, to be subject to another:*—Þæt Crēcisce and þæt Affricanisce wǣron swā swā hié him hiérsumedon and him underþiéded wǣre, Ors. 2, 1 ; S. 60, 8. II. *to obey a thing.* (1) *an order, injunction:*—Gebudon him Perse þæt hié hæfden iii winter sibbe wiþ hié (*rex Persarum quiescere in pace Graeciam praecepit*) . . . Hié þā lustlīce þǣre sibbe hīrsumedan (*they submitted to the peace imposed upon them*), Ors. 3, 1 ; S. 94, 26. (2) *a feeling, desire, an impulse, &c.:*—Hī āgenum lustum and heora gītsunge fyliað and hȳrsumiað *propriis voluptatibus et gule illecebris servientes*, R. Ben. 9, 24. Þæt hē āgenum lustum ne hȳrsumige *non voluptatibus suis obediens*, 20, 12. III. *to serve:*—Gif hē tōbrǣc ǣnig þing on þǣre hȳrsumnesse þe hē on hȳrsumode, āþer on kycenan . . ., oðþe on ǣnigum ōðerum cræfte þe hē mid līchomlicum geswince on hȳrsumode, R. Ben. 71, 16–72, 1. III a. *to serve God, follow a religious life:*—Twēgen hālige menn þe hȳrsumedon Gode on ancersetle wuniende, Chr. 1086 ; P. 218, 33.

hȳrsum-līc; *adj. Ready* (of service), *willing:*—Hē gegearwode heom his hȳrsumlice gegnunge *eis obsequium praebebat*, Gr. D. 152, 1.

hīrsumlīce. v. un-hīrsumlīce.

hīrsum-ness. *Take here* hȳrsumness *in Dict., and add:* I. *obedience:*—Hē (*Peter*) eádmōdnysse wiðsōc, and hwæðere for hȳrsumnysse geðafode *he refused to allow Jesus to humble himself by the washing of feet, and yet in order that he might be obedient he consented*, Hml. A. 157, 135. I a. *obedience to one in authority:*—Be hȳrsumnesse. Ðǣre forman eádmōdnesse stepe is hȳrsumnes būtan elcunge . . . sōna swā heom ǣnig þing fram heora ealdre geboden bið, hī þæt būtan elcunge mid weorce gefremmiað, R. Ben. 19, 14–19 : 12, 12. Se arð āxode hȳrsumnesse mid āþswerunge at him, and hē hit forsōc, Chr. 1070 ; P. 206, 21. I b. *subjection of one people to another:*—Hē hié (*the Welsh*) tō eáþmōdre hērsumnesse gedyde, Chr. 828 ; P. 62, 3. Þā elreordegan kyningas ðe ic mid nēde tō hȳrsumnesse gedyde, Nar. 32, 19. II. *readiness to obey or serve, humility:*—Hērsumnisse mid bisene ædeáwed (cf. sié hē īwer hēra ł embehtmonna (*minister*), Mk. L. 10, 43) *humilitatis exemplo monstrato*, Mk. p. 4, 15. III. *service, appointed work:*—Sȳ heom swylc hȳrsumnes betǣht swylc him sȳ, R. Ben. 67, 6. Þurh þā gemǣnan þēnunge þysse hȳrsumnesse (*the work of the kitchen which all took in turn*), 58, 16. On þǣre hȳrsumnesse þe hē on hȳrsumode, āþer oðþe on kycenan, oþþe on hēderne, oðþe on mynstres bæcerne . . . oðþe on ǣnigum ōðerum cræfte þe hē mid līchomlicum geswince on hȳrsumode, 71, 16. Faran tō swylcan weorce and hȳrsumnesse swylce him beboden sȳ, 85, 15. Hē gesealh his þegnungum and hȳrsumnessum (*obsequiis*), Gr. D. 299, 29. v. un-hȳrsumness.

hirtan. *Take here* hyrtan *in Dict., and add:* to refresh, revive, comfort:*—Hē ongan mid his gehāte hī hyrtan (*sublevare*). Gr. D. 145, 19. Earme men ðū scealt hyrtan, Angl. xii. 516, 21. Hyrttende *refocilando*, Wrt. Voc. ii. 81, 43. Suā se micla cræftiga hiertende tō scȳfð *magnus regendi artifex favoribus impellit*, Past. 53, 16. Hyrtendum *cohortante*, An. Ox. 791. Hyrtende *refocilantes*, i. *confirmantes*, 3866. v. ge-edhirtan.

hirting, e; *f. Refreshing treatment:*—Hyrtinge *fotu* (*medicus* . . .

*putrida fibrarum procurans ulcera fotu*, Ald. 150, 16), An. Ox. 17, 10. [v. *N. E. D.* hearting.]

hīru. v. hūru : -hīrung. [*O. H. Ger.* hōrunga *auditio*.] v. ge-hīrung.

hirwan. *Take here* hyrwan, herewian, herian, *in Dict., and add :* I. *to feel (and express) contempt for, to despise, scorn :*—Ealle hié hié swā wundige hyrwað *omnes ut ulcerosum contemnunt*, Verc. Först. 139, 10. Hȳ nū hyrwað hāligra mōd, þā þe him tō heofonum hyge staðeliað, Gū. 36. Sume weorþað egeslīce godcundnessa hyrwende, Wlfst. 82, 1. II. *to speak evilly of.* (1) *of mockery, derision, scorn :*—Man mid hōcere gōde dǣda hyrweð, Wlfst. 164, 18. Alle ðā gesēgun mē herwdun (*aspernabantur*) mē, spreocende wērun mid weolerum, Ps. Srt. 21, 8. ¶ *in contrast with* herian :—Man eal hyrweð þæt man sceolde herian, Wlfst. 165, 3. Man oft herede þæt man scolde hyrwan, and tō forð hyrwde þæt man scolde herigean, 168, 12 : Ll. Th. i. 334, 1. (2) *of calumny, backbiting :*—Ne ǣnig man ōþerne bæftan ne tǣle ne hyrwe tō swȳðe, Wlfst. 70, 15. (3) *to blaspheme, blame :*—Nā þās gereccende þīne [Dryhten in mē] ic hyrwe gesceafte *non haec narrans tuam Domine in me blasphemo creaturam*, Angl. xi. 118, 58. Golias Godes naman hyrwde, Hml. S. 18, 19. III. *to show contempt of* by action :—Ðā brǣc Leófsunu, þurh ðæt wīf ðe hē nam, ðæne cwide, and herewade ðæs arcebiscopes gewitnesse, C. D. vi. 127, 28. v. un-hirwan ; hirwend.

hirwend. v. hyrwend *in Dict.*

hirwend-līc; *adj. Contemptible :*—Hyrwendlic *contemtibilis*, An. Ox. 5503. Ðā hirwendlican *contemtibiliora*, Wrt. Voc. ii. 15, 62. ¶ Heruuendlicae, haeruendlicae, heuuendlice *contemtum* (-*im*?), Txts. 46, 186. The word might be the acc. fem. of an adjective, or it might be an adverb, in which case *contemtim* must be read.

hirwing, e; *f. Evil-speaking, blasphemy :*—Of heortan manna . . . forðstæppað . . . hyrwincga (*blasphemia*), Scint. 137, 12.

hirw-ness. *Take here* hyrw-ness *in Dict., and add :*—Ne ǣnig man ne gewunie þæt hē huxlīce onhisce, ne ðurh hyrwnesse (hyruw-, *v. l.* *blasphemiam*) God ne gegremie, Wlfst. 70, 12.

his-līc; *adj. Fit, suitable :*—Þonne him man ōþer hislic hors findan mihte *cum aptus equus inveniri potuisset*, Gr. D. 183, 5. Cf. þeslic.

hīw *fortune. l.* hīw.

hīw *shape. l.* hīw, *and add :* I. *of material things.* (1) *form, shape, figure :*—Manig wyht is mistlīce fērende geond eorþan, and sint swīþe ungelīces hīwes *quam variis terras animalia permeant figuris*, Bt. 41, 6 ; F. 254, 24. Þā feówer gesceafta hē . . . on ōþrum hīwe gebrengð *elementa . . . alterna commutatione transformat*, 39, 8 ; F. 224, 9. Hē sceolde hī āwendan of þām wyrmhīwe . . . and tō manna gelīcnysse of þām lāðum hīwe, Hml. S. 10, 106. Fæger hīwe *formosa* (*frontis*) *effigie*, An. Ox. 3411. Gāst se hālig mid līchomlic huiu (*specie*) suelce culfra, Lk. L. 3, 22. (1 a) *a figure :*—Hē geseah ealra wihta . . . hīw in cuman *variorum monstrorum diversas figuras introire prospicit*, Guth. Gr. 139, 4 : 140, 4. (1 b) *a form, shape, something formed* by carving, writing, &c.:—Hēr āmearcod is hāligra hīw þurh handmægen āwriten on wealle, An. 725. Hīwe *simulacro*, i. *statua*, An. Ox. 2285. Hīw (hīf, An. Ox. 3784) *effigiem* (*frivolam simulacri*), Hpt. Gl. 495, 28. Mid manifealdum hīwum *diversis* (*imaginum*) *thoraciclis*, i. *imaginibus*, An. Ox. 1044. Tȳn hīw habbað þā bōceras mid þām hig āmearkiað heora accentas, Angl. viii. 333, 21. (2) *appearance, aspect :*—Of scilfrium hīwe beorhtmeð flaua (*auri*) *specie splendescit*, An. Ox. 533. Se fugel is on hīwe onlīcost peán, Ph. 311. Hīw sceolan ārīsan . . . on swylcum heówe swā hié ǣr hié sylfe gefrætwodan, Bl. H. 95, 24. (2 a) *beautiful appearance, beauty :*—Grēne stondað gehroden . . . beorhtast bearwa. Nō gebrocen weorðeð holt on hīwe, Ph. 81. (3) *colour :*—Apricitas, color hió, Wrt. Voc. ii. 100, 51. Hīw *apricitas*, 7, 10. Ðæt ædeleste hiéw (hīw, l. 23) *color optimus*, Past. 133, 11. Hwītes hīwes (hiéwes, *v. l.*), 87, 20. Hiówes, Nar. 15, 32. Ungelīces hīues *discolor*, Mt. p. 3, 19. Blaccum hīwe *nigro colore*, ib. Iacintus is lyfte onlīcuð on hīwe, Past. 85, 5. (4) *form, kind, nature, character :*—Ðā ældeódegan weras ðe on cuman hīwe him mid wunedon (*peregrinos viros in hospitalitatem receptos*, Gr. D. iv. 14), Hml. Th. ii. 96, 35. Sē þe wæs on Godes hīwe onfēng þ hīw ūre tȳddran gecynde, Bl. H. 29, 3. Undernim ðū leorningcnihtes hīw, þ þū ðæs gerýnu leornian mæge, Hml. Th. i. 590, 21. In monnes hīw, Cri. 657. In cildes hīw, 725. Eom ic þāra twelfa sum þe hē getreóweste under monnes hīw mōde gelufode, Gū. 682. II. *form of* non-material things. (1) *of speech.* (a) *technical grammatical terms :*—De specie. Species is hīw, *primitiua* and *diriuatiua*. Ealle ðā eahta *partes* forneán habbað þās twā hīw . . . Ōðer hīw is gehāten *inchoatiua*, Ælfc. Gr. Z. 211, 1–14. De figura. Figura is gefēgednys oððe hīw. Twā hīw synd, *simplex* and *composita*, 217, 10. Sume sind gehātene *scemata*, þæt sind mislīce hīw on lēdensprǣce, hū heó betst gelōgod beó, 295, 4 : Angl. viii. 331, 2. (b) *in a more general sense, formula, form of words :*—Hīwum (*praedictis exemplorum*) *formulis*, An. Ox. 79. Nā beseah on spǣce heów leáse *non respexit in insanias falsas*, Ps. Rdr. 39, 5. (2) *of abstractions, form, type, model, appearance that shews evidence* of a quality :—Mæþhādes hīwe

*uirginitatis typum*, i. *speciem*, An. Ox. 299. On ymbsnidenesse hîwe (*tipo*), 40, 17. Of hîfe (hîwe, Hpt. Gl. 465, 74), gelícnysse *liniamento .i. similitudini* (*puritatis*), 2530. Fǽmnhâ[d]licum hîwe *uirginali formulae*, i. *specie*, 536. Þæt hê hîwige swylce hê ârfæstes môdes sý, and under þâm leáslican hîwe gederige, Wlfst. 53, 27. Ðý lǽs ǽnig durre on eáðmôdnesse hîwe (*sub humilitatis specie*) hit forcweðan, Past. 51, 3. Sume men onderfóð eáðmôdnesse hîw, sume ofermôdnesse, 301, 25. (3) *a pretext* :—Hîwe *praetextu*, An. Ox. 2684: 3930. (4) *an imaginary form, a fancy* :—Scinlâc *vel* hîw *fantasia*, i. *imaginatio, delusio mentis*, Wrt. Voc. ii. 147, 42. **III.** *a kind, species* :—On seofen hîwum *septem speciebus* (*dirimuntur*), An. Ox. 3113. v. ǽ-, wyrm-hîw; dim-hîw; *adj.*

**hîwan.** *Add* : **I.** *the domestics of a household* :—Þâ hîwan *familiares domus illius*, Bd. 3, 9; Sch. 231, 15. Ðâ côm sum þâra hîna, cleopode mec, 5, 3; Sch. 565, 12. Twêgen æceras on gemang hîna lande (*land let to the members of a household*?), C. D. iii. 400, 7. Hîna herdlandes, 399, 30. Hîna gemǽre *boundary of land held by the hîwan* (?), 24. Gif mon his heówum in fæsten flǽsc gefe, Ll. Th. i. 46, 9. Hî âxodon æt þâm hîwum hwæðer Petrus ðǽr wuuunge hæfde, Hml. S. 10, 111. ¶ Hî(g)na ealdor *the head of a household* :—Gemêtte hê þǽr fǽmnan wæs nift þæs hîna ealdres (*patris familias*), Bd. 3, 9; Sch. 231, 11. Wæs sum hîwscypes fæder and hîna ealdor *erat pater familias*, 5, 12; Sch. 612, 18. **II.** *a king's household* :—Se cyning ne his hîwan (hîred, *v. l. domestici eius*), Bd. 3, 14; Sch. 260, 1. Him (*the king*) and his hîwum *sibi suisque*, 3, 28; Sch. 323, 16. **III.** *the members of a religious house* :—Ceólfreð abbud and ðâ hîgan on Medeshâmstede, C. D. ii. 46, 15. Ðis syndan ðæs londes gemǽru ðe hîgen biscope gesald habbað. Ǽrest of Sæuerne be hîgna gemǽre, iii. 463, 13. Mid ærcebiscopes geðeahte and ðâra hióna et Crîstes cirican, i. 299, 14. Ic Werferð biscop mid mîra hîgna leáfe, ii. 132, 9. Ðem biium tô Crîstes cirican, i. 299, 35. v. riht-hîwa.

**hîw-cund;** *adj.* *Domestic* :—Hîwcundum (hîf-, MS. *for* hîf = hîw *see* An. Ox. 2530: 3784 *given under* hîw) *domesticis*, Hpt. Gl. 413, 16.

**hîw-cûþ.** *Add* : **I.** *of a house or family, domestic.* (1) :—Hîwcûþum *domesticis* (*sodalibus*), An. Ox. 5132. Se cyngc betwux his hîwcûðum mannum blissode, Ap. Th. 3, 4. (1 a) *figuratively* :—Hwæt is þ þǽm men sý mâre þearf tô þencenne þonne embe his sâuwle þearfe, ... and hwylce lǽtteówas hê hæbbe, and hwyder hê gelǽded sý ... Sweotollîce wê magon ongeotan þ þâ syndon heówcûðe (*there are those belonging to the household*, i. e. good or evil spirits?) þe wê geseón ne magon, Bl. H. 97, 23. (2) *of things* :—Hîwcûþ carfulnys *domestica sollicitudo*, An. Ox. 4183. Hîwcûþre *domestice* (*sodalitatis*), 2808. **II.** *familiar* :—Þone hîwcûþestan *familiarissimum*, Wrt. Voc. ii. 147, 32. (1) *of persons* :—Ic ne eom him swǽ hiéwcûð, Past. 62, 6. Ðyses weres hîwcûðesta wæs Julianus *hujus viri familiarissimus fuit Julianus*, Gr. D. 71, 11. (2) *of things* :—Ðeós wyrt ys culfran swîðe hîwcûð (*doves are very fond of this plant*), þanon hý sum þeódscipe *columbinam* hâteð, Lch. i. 170, 13. Þone deófol þe sit on þînum hneccan ic þê of âbleów, and se deófol his hîwcûðe setl sóna forlêt, Hml. S. 31, 1191. *See next word.*

**hîwcûþa,** an; *m.* *A member of a household* :—Incnîhtas, hîwcûþan *clientes*, An. Ox. 870. Hîwcûðum geleáfan *domesticis fidei*, R. Ben. I. 87, 16.

**hîwcûþ-lic;** *adj.* **I.** *domestic* :—Hîwcûðlic geter *domestica scissura*, Wrt. Voc. ii. 141, 70. Of hîwcûþlicere geférrǽddene *domestica sodalitate*, An. Ox. 2531. ¶ *used substantively* :—On hîwcûðlicum ðînum *in domesticis tuis*, Scint. 194, 9. **II.** *familiar* :—Mid hîwcûþlicre byldo *familiaritatis ausu*, Gr. D. 32, 9.

**hîwcûþlîce.** *Add* :—Þû scealt þînon Drihtne hîwcûðlîce æt his weófode þênian *ad altare cum Domino famularis*, Chrd. 67, 37. Hê wæs gebunden tô mê hîwcûþlîce (heów-, *v. l.*) mid freóndlîcre lufan *amicitiis familiariter obstrictus*, Gr. D. 3. 28. Hê hîwcûðlîce mid him wæs *ei familiarissimus fuit*, 14, 10. Þâ þe Gode hîwcûþlicor (hiówcûðlucor, *v. l.*) and freóndlîcor þeówiað *qui Deo familiarius serviunt*, 164, 31.

**-hîwcûþlician.** v. ge-hîwcûþlician.

**hîwcûþ-ness,** e; *f.* *Familiarity.* (1) *with a person* :—Seó swǽslice hîwcûþnes þǽre sôðan lufe *caritatis familiaritas*, Gr. D. 250, 8. Mid bylde þǽre hîwcûðnysse *ausu familiaritatis*, 71, 24; 140, 7. (2) *with an action* :—Bûtan tô rǽdenne hîwcûðnysse *nisi legendi familiaritate*, Scint. 220, 2.

**hîwe.** *Add* : v. ǽ-, ân-, fiþer-, gylden-, manig-, þûsend-, un-hîwe; hîw-ness.

**-hîwe.** v. heard-hîwe: -hîwede. v. twi-, þri-hîwede: -hîwen (?). v. sin-hîwen: -hîwendlic. v. ge-hîwendlic: hîwene. *Dele.*

**hîwere.** *Add* : **I.** *one who forms*; *of mental operation, one who fabricates falsehood.* v. hîwian; **I b** :—Fâcenfulle hîweras, wyrh[tan] *strofosi* (*fallaciarum*) *fabricatores*, An. Ox. 2781 : *fabricatores* (*falsitatum*), 4244. **II.** *a pretender.* v. hîwian; **III** :—Hê cwæð þ hê Crîst sylf wǽre ... and sum bisceop ... gelýfde þâm hîwere, Hml. S. 31, 838. **III.** *a decoy* (?) :—Hîweres (hireres, MS.) *aucupis*, Kent. Gl. 129.

**hîwe-stân.** *Take here* **hiéwe-stân** *in Dict.*

**hîwet[t],** es; *n.* *Hewing, cutting* :—Tô ðǽm ðæt wê sién gefêged tô ðǽm gefôgstânum on ðǽre Godes ceastre bûtan ðǽm hiéwete ǽlcre suingean *ut in templum Dei sine disciplinae percussione disponamur*, Past. 253. Hýwyt *dolatum*, Wrt. Voc. ii. 141, 63. v. stân-, wudu-hîwet.

**hîw-fæger;** *adj.* *Fair of form*, Verc. Först. 166.

**hîw-fæst;** *adj.* *Beautiful* :—Hîwfæst *formosa*, i. *speciosa*, An. Ox. 1054. Hîwfæstre *formosior*, i. *speciosior*, 453.

**hîw-gedâl.** *Add* :—Hîwgedâl *divortium*, i. *divisio conjugiorum*, Wrt. Voc. ii. 141, 54 : 28, 27. Hîwgedâle *divortio*, 14.

**hîwian.** *Add* : *to form, give shape to* :—Hîwað *confingat*, Wrt. Voc. ii. 23, 56. Hîwade *finxit*, i. *figurabat*, 148, 64. **I.** *to shape an object.* (1) *material* :—Ðû heówodest mê *tu formasti me*, Ps. Rdr. 138, 5. Sê þe hîwude (hiówede, Ps. Srt.) eáge, 93, 9. (2) *non-material* :—Þû þe hîwast (hiówas, Ps. Srt. *fingis*) sâr on bebode, Ps. Rdr. 92, 20. **I a.** *to give form to what is unreal, cause an illusion* :—Galdra hîwung ... hîwedan *prestigiarum scena* (*quam callido phantasmate falsi nebulones*) *schematizarunt*, An. Ox. 4061. **I b.** *to shape in the mind* (*falsely*), *fabricate.* v. hîwere; **I** :—Îdele and leáse spel hî hýwiaþ and mannum reccaþ *quae non viderunt confingunt*, R. Ben. 135, 24. Hîwiende *musitantes*, i. *fingentes* (presbyteros contra Susannam *mussitantes*, Ald. 38, 17. Cf. *fabricatores falsitatum potius quam presbyteri*, 59, 23), An. Ox. 2804. **II.** *to change the form of an object to that of another in order to deceive* :—Hê hine tô ôþrum men hîwað, and his gebyrda mid þâm bediglað, þ hê heonan mæg ætberstan, Hml. S. 23, 692. Mænig cimeþ ... and leáslîce leóged and egeslîce gylped, namað hine sylfne and hîwaþ tô gode (*calls himself god and pretends to be so*), swylce hit Crîst sý *multi uenient in nomine meo dicentes : ego sum Cristus; et multos seducent*, Wlfst. 89, 3. Sê þe litelîcost cûðe leáslîce hîwian unsóð tô sóðe (*to make untruth appear truth*), 128, 9. Hîwian yfel tô gôde, 81, 36. **III.** *to make an object appear other than it really is.* (1) *with complement* :—Se man hýwað hine sylfne mihtine and unforhtne þe nâh on his heortan ǽnigne câfscype, Wlfst. 53, 14. Þ hê hîwige hine sylfne mihtigne, Angl. xi. 109, 54. (2) hîwian, swilce ... *to make appear, as if* ... :—Se man hîwað hine sylfne, swylce hê deóp inngehýd hæbbe, þe nât nâ mycel gescâd ǽniges gerâdes, Wlfst. 53, 19. **IV.** *to assume an appearance or character that does not belong to the subject, to feign* :—Bilewite cild ue hîwað mid wordum, þæt hit óðer ðence and óðer sprece, Hml. Th. i. 512, 15. Ic eom eald tô hîwigenne, Hml. S. 25, 94. Anatolius hâtte sum hîwigende munuc, and hê behýdde his yfelnysse, 31, 792. **IV a.** *to make as if* :—Ne hîwa ðû, mîn bearn, swilce ðu mid bilewitnysse mæge gân orsorh tô mǽdena hûsum, Hex. 48, 9. Þæt hê swicollîce hîwige, swylce hê ârfæstes môdes sý, Wlfst. 53, 26. Ongeán þâm andgyte se deófol forgifð stuntnysse, and eác þ se man hîwige swylce hê andgytful sý, Angl. xi. 109, 49 : 51 : 59. Ne sceal hê hîwian, swilce hit him uncûð sý *non dissimulet*, R. Ben. 13, 16. **IV b.** *with clause* :—Þ hî hîwion þ hî ingehýd habban, Angl. xi. 109, 56. **V.** *to dissemble* :—Ne hîwige synna *neque dissimulet peccata*, R. Ben. S. 15, 5. **VI.** *to show figuratively* :—Gâstlîce hîwedon *typice obumbrabant* (*septenos vitiorum cuneos*), Au. Ox. 11, 104. v. be-, geed-, ofer-, twi-hîwian; un-hîwed.

**hîwian** *to marry* : *Add* : [*O. H. Ger.* hîwen *nubere*.] v. ge-hîwian; sin-hîwan (?).

**hîwiend** (?), es; *m.* *One who forms* :—Gestaþeliend, nîwiend (hîwiend? Cf. *plasmatio* hîwunga, Wrt. Voc. ii. 148, 77) *informator*, i. *plasmator*, An. Ox. 365.

**hîwisc.** *l.* hîwisce, hîwisc. For suffix cf. *îdisc*(e). *After the bracket in the last line but one insert* Hml. Th. i. 310, 28. Æt hîwisce, *and add :* **I.** *a family, house* :—Fæder hîwisc *pater familias*, Rtl. 190, 21. Se fæder hîuuisc ł hiórodes fæder ł hîgna fæder, Lk. L. 13, 25. Se fæder hîuuisc (ðe fæder ðæs hiórodes, R.), 14, 21. Cuoedas gié ðǽm fæder hîuuisc ł hiórodes, 22, 11. [*In the Northern specimens the word shews no inflection, and might almost be taken for an adjective qualifying fæder, if it were not for the last passage, where fæder is dative.*] Laurentius him ðæs getîðode, and nigontýne wera and wîfa his hîwisces gefullode, Hml. Th. i. 422, 23. **II.** *a hide of land with a household settled on it, a family-holding of land* [cf. the two forms given to the same regulation :—Gif wilisc man geþeó þ hê hæbbe hîwisc landes, *and* Gif hê beó tô þâm gewelegod þ hê hýred and êht âge, Ll. Th. i. 186, 13 *and* 23. See Andrews' *Old English Manor*, p. 167, n. 2 : Seebohm, *Vill. Com. s.v.* : Sax. Eng. i. 92]. v. hîw-scipe; **II** :—Æt Bitelanwyrthe ân hîwisce, and æt Brômleáge ân hîwisce, C. D. B. iii. 133, 18. In loco qui dicitur heregeardingchîwisce, C. D. ii. 51, 19. Æt Cemele tién hýda, æt Domeccesîge þridde half hîwisce, 53, 16. Þæt half hêwisse, iii. 410, 12. Ðis his ðâra .v. hîda bôc æt Dydylingetûne and ðas ânes hîwisces æt Uddinge (cf. Ðis sint ðâre .v. hîda landgemǽre tô Dydylingtûne and ðas syxtan æt Udding, 444, 27. In the Latin charter the grant is described as ' aliquam terrae partem duobus in locis, id est v mansas ubi uulgariter dicitur aet Dydylingtûne, et *unam mansam*

ubi uocitatur aet Uddinge', ii. 330, 1), iii. 445, 22. On ôðre healfe ânes hîwisces, 435, 13. Ðis synt ðâ landgemæro ðæs hîwisces æt Winterburnan . . . Ðis his ðæs hîwisces landgemæro on Wiht (cf. duas mansas, unam mansam in Uecta Insula, aliam . . . æt Uuinterburnan, ii. 299, 6-10), 431, 7-16. Æt hilcan hîwisce, v. 147, 13. Oð îdel hîwisce (land where no family was living? see first passage under îdel in Dict.) eásteweard, 319, 21. Geaf hê him týn hîwisca (hîda, v. l.) landes . . . and æfter medmiclum fæce sealde him mynster þrîtiges hîwisca (hîda, v. l.) donauit terram x familiarum . . . et non multo post monasterium xxx familiarum, Bd. 5, 19; Sch. 662, 3-7. [O. Sax. hîwiski : O. H. Ger. hîwiski domus, familia.]

**hîwisclîce** ; adv. As forming part of a family or household :—In ealdum tîdum biscop mid his geférum ge eác abbud wunade mid munucum ; hwæþere hié tô þæs biscopes scîre heówesclîce (hiów-, v. l.) belumpen a temporibus antiquis et episcopus cum clero et abbas solebat manere cum monachis ; qui tamen et ipsi ad curam episcopi familiariter pertinerent, Bd. 4, 27 ; Sch. 517, 10. [Cf. O. H. Ger. hîwisc-lih domesticus.]

**-hîwlæcan.** v. ge-hîwlæcan.

**hîwleás-ness.** For ' deformitas, Som.' substitute :—Hîwleás (hîwleásnes ?, hîwleást ? Cf. hîwlǽs-lǽs, Hpt. Gl. 510, 7) deformatio, An. Ox. 4462.

**hîw-lic.** Add : I. beautiful. In Lch. iii. 204, 8 : 212, 6 the original Latin is formosam. II. of language, figurative :—Hîwlice l þeáwlice spæce tropologiae, i. similitudinis l figurati sermonis, Hpt. Gl. 432, 12.

**hîw-lic.** For ' matronalis . . . Lye' substitute : adj. Of a married woman :—þære hîwlican matronalis (cf. (?) matronalis pudicitiae obliviscens, Ald. 59, 16), Wrt. Voc. ii. 55, 19. [O. H. Ger. hîw-lîh conjugalis.]

**hîw-ness** (?), e ; f. Beauty, fairness :—Sindon ôðre wîf . . . heora lîc bið on marmorstânes hwîtnysse (hîwnesse, v. l.) aliae sunt mulieres . . . specioso corpore quasi marmore candido, Nar. 38, 10. v. hîwe.

**-hîwodlíce.** v. ge-hîwodlíce.

**hîw-rǽden.** Add : In Ps. L. the word is neuter :—Hîwrǽden oððe hîred familia, Wrt. Voc. i. 72, 28 : ii. 147, 30. Hîwhrǽdenne domui, 141, 75. I. a family, household of a private person :— ' Ic hâlsige ðê þæt eal mîn hîwrǽden gefullod wurðe.' Hê nigontýne wera and wîfa his hîwisces gefullode, Hml. Th. i. 422, 21. Nime æghwylc hîwrǽden of ælcum hûse ân lamb (cf. nyme ælc mann ân lamb tô his hîwrǽdene tollat unusquisque agnum per familias et domus suas, Ex. 12, 3), Angl. viii. 322, 6. Ænne man ic ofslôh of þînre hîwrǽdene (cf. hýrman, 783), Hml. S. 31, 778. Hîwrǽdenu familias, Ps. L. 106, 41. II. the household of a great man :—þegnrǽdenne oððe hîwrǽdenne clientele, Wrt. Voc. ii. 24, 44. Hîwrǽdene, Hpt. 31, 18, 504. II. a house, body of people living together with common interests and occupations, a religious house :—þæt heó sién þæm biscope holde and þære heórædene æt Weogornaceastre, Cht. Th. 168, 24. ¶ in the gloss untrum hîwrǽden abbaso, Hpt. 31, 12, 275, abbaso = infirma domus, not infirmatorium as given by Migne. III. a house, family, tribe, nation :—Ne eom ic nâ âsend bûton tô ðâm sceápum Israhêla hîwrǽdene ðâ þe losedon (ad oves quae perierunt domus Israhel, Mt. 15, 24), Hml. A. 69, 110. On ûtgange hîwrǽdenes Jacobe in exitu domus Jacob, Ps. L. 113, 1. Ân esne of Leuies hîwrǽdene vir de domo Levi, Ex. 2, 1. Ealle hýwrǽdena þeóda universae familiae gentium, Ps. L. 21, 28.

**hîw-scipe.** Add : I. a house, family :—On eardungstôwe hûses l hîwscipes mînes in tabernaculo domus meae, Ps. L. 131, 3. Wæs sum hîwscipes man erat quidam vir paterfamilias, Guth. Gr. 172, 1. II. a hide of land. v. hîwisc ; II :—Hê geann þæs landes æt Sandforda in tô þâm mynstre . . . and ânes hîwscypes hê geann Godríce þærof, Cht. Crw. 23, 4.

**hîwung.** Add :—Figmenta, i. plasmatio, mendacia hîwunga, Wrt. Voc. ii. 148, 78. I. shaping, forming of material :—Adam lifde æfter þære menniscan hîwunge .dcccc. wintra and þrittig wintra ; and þê sexteoþegan geáre fram his hîwunge hê gegylte, Angl. xi. 1, 13-16. II. shape of a material object, frame, make, constitution :—Hê sylf oncneów hîwunga l gescapennysse (figmentum) ûre, Ps. L. 102, 14. II a. shape, form, species, kind of non-material object :—Nis nân âsecgendlic oððe unâsecgendlic fracodlicnysse hîwung þæs ic ne sih tihtende and lærende, Hml. S. 23 b, 383. III. transformation, taking of another shape :—Hî woldon mid heora hîwunge (the taking by evil spirits of the figures of various animals) þæs hâlgan weres môd âwendan, Guth. Gr. 139, 10. IV. an illusory shape, deceptive appearance :—Galdra hîwung litigum hîwunge hîwedan fordwan præstrigiarum scena (i. umbra) (quam) callido fantasmate (falsi nebuloso) schematizarunt . . . disparuit, An. Ox. 4057. Smeágende hwæðre hit gâst wære þæt þær mid hwylcere hîwunga gebæde hî putans ne spiritus esset, qui se fingeret orare, Hml. S. 23 b, 281. V. pretending to do what is not really done :—Ðâ bædon hî . . . þ . . . hê dyde swilce hê æte . . . and swâ mid ðære hîwunge him sylfum geburge. Ðâ cwæð hê : ' Ic eom eald tô hîwigenne . . . bið mîn hîwung þâm geongum tô forwyrde, Hml. S. 25,

90-97. V a. a pretence, trick :—Heówunga praestigias, An. Ox. 2238. VI. pretending to be what one is not, simulation :—Ælc hîwung is antsæte Gode, Hml. S. 12, 246. Hê wiste þ hê mid feóndlicum cræfte ne mihte bedydrian Martines gesihðe . . . wæs ðâ geswutelod his hîwung, 31, 827. Wæron ôþre gedwolan Antecrîstes lima, mid ârleásra hîwunge, 832. Hû hê ârâsode þâ hîwunge Totillan de simulatione Totilae deprehensa, Gr. D. 130, 13. Se deófol gedeð þ se man þurh lîcetende hîwunge deð, swylce hê andgytful sý, þe lytel can tô geráde, Wlfst. 53, 4. þurh leáse hîwunge, 8. VI a. pretence of piety or goodness, hypocrisy :—Hî sceolon habban eáðmôdnysse on heora ædelum þeáwum mid nânre hîwunge, Hml. A. 39, 385. Manega geleáfan Crîstes nâ lufiað, ac þæne þurh leáse hîwunge gehealdan hî gehîwiað multi fidem Christi non amant, sed eandem per hypochrisin tenere se simulant, Scint. 129, 12. VII. of speech. (1) false speech, fiction :—Hîwung oððe leásspel figmentum, Wrt. Voc. ii. 34, 43. Hîwungum commentis (haereticorum lenocinantibus illectus), An. Ox. 2911. Hîwunga frivola (falsitatis vaticinantem), 1929. (2) speech in which the apparent meaning is not the real, irony :—Hironiam þurh smicernesse and hîwunge, Wrt. Voc. ii. 42, 54. v. frum-, ge-hîwung.

**hîwung** marriage. Add : [O. H. Ger. hîwunga matrimonium, connubium, contubernium.]

**hlacerian** ; þ. ode To scoff at, mock :—Ne ne tælun l hlakerian l gebysmerian [mê] mîne fýnd neque irrideant me inimici mei, Ps. L. 24, 3. [Cf. (?) O. Frs. hlacka to laugh.] See next word.

**hlacerung**, e ; f. Scoffing, mockery, scorn :—þu gesettest ûs tâle l bysmur l on hlacerungum and hleahter þæm þâ þe synt onbûtan ûs posuisti nos subsannationem et derisum his qui sunt in circuitu nostro, Ps. L. 43, 14. Hit is swîðe unþæslic þ wê on Godes hûse îdele spellunga and hlacerunga begân, Nap. 38. See preceding word.

**hladan.** Add : I. to load a vessel with a freight :—Wæs naca hladen herewædum, mearum and mâðmum, B. 1897. II. to load, furnish abundantly with something. (1) the object a person. (a) the thing material :—Goldhladen þegn, Fins. 13. (b) the thing non-material :—Guma gilphlæden, B. 868. (2) the object a thing :—Hærfest wæstmum hladen, Men. 142. Windhladen (q. v.) ventuosus. III. to put as a burden, freight, or cargo, to load something on a porter or vehicle :—Ic mê [on] hrycg hlade, þæt ic habban sceal, Rä. 4, 65. Hý ne môston on bæl hladan leófne mannan, B. 2126. Ic gefrægen hond reáfian . . . ânne mannan, him on bearm hladan bûnan and discas sylfes dôme, 2775. Ongunnon stîgan on wægn weras, and hyra wicg somod hlôdan under hrunge, Rä. 23, 10. IV. to draw ; haurire :—Nômun, hlôdun auserunt, Wrt. Voc. ii. 101, 28. (1) to draw water (lit. or fig.) :—Gê hladaþ wæteru of wyllum haurietis aquas de fontibus, Ps. L. fol. 184 a. Ðonan hine hlôdan hâlge, Past. 467, 32. Hladað iów nû drincan, 469, 7. Ne in huon ðu hlada hæfis ðu neque in quo haurias habes, Jn. L. 4, 11. Úp hladen exantlamus, hauriamus, Hpt. Gl. 418, 33. Tô hladanne ðæt wæter, Past. 373, 9. Tô ladanne (hladanne, R.), Jn. L. 4, 7. (2) to draw breath :—Swâ þæs halgan wæs ondlongne dæg oroð ûp hlæden, Gû. 1252. (3) to draw, obtain favour, inspiration, &c. :—Hê hlet hauriet (salutem), Kent. Gl. 282. (4) to scoop out grain from a vessel :—Hig worhton him âne anlícnesse þe on ðâre stræte stôd, and mid ðâre swîðran hand þone hwæte hlôd, and mid þâm winstran fêt þâ mittan træd, Ap. Th. 10, 13.

**hladung.** Substitute : A drawing, draught :—Gelustfulligende hladungum genihtsumum oblectans haustibus affluis, Hy. S. 58, 12.

**hlæd-disc.** Dele ' (?)', and add : a dish containing various kinds of fruit.

**hlædel.** Add :—Wæterseáþes wæg, þænne wê mid hlædele, [þ is mid] hlædtrendle ûp hladan cisterne limpham, quam anthlia, hoc est rota hauritoria exanthlamus, i. haurimus, An. Ox. 501. Man sceal habban . . . cytel, hlædel, pannan, crocca, Angl. ix. 264, 9.

**hlæder**, e ; f. : hlæddre, an (?). l. hlæder ; e : hlædre, an ; f. I. a ladder, set of moveable steps (lit. or fig.). Seó hlædder (hlæddra, R. Ben. I. 28, 7) (scala) tâcnað ûre lîf . . þære hlædre sîdan tâcniað lîchoman and sâule ; on ðæm twâm sîdum missenlice stæpas eáðmôdnesse sió geladung gefæstnode, R. Ben. 23, 9-14. Bið hê þâm men gelîc þe ârærþ sume heáge hlæddre, and stîhð þe þære hlæddre stapum oð þ hê tô ðæm ænde becume, and wylle þonne git stîgan ufor, Hml. S. 1, 22. Sum heora mid hlæddre (hlædre, v. l.) wolde unlûcan þ ægðyrl, 32, 205, 212. Hê stôd on treówenre hlædre (treówene hlædran, v. l. in ligneis gradibus) and gefyllde þâ leóhtfatu, Gr. D. 45, 27. Hê (Jacob) geseah âne hlædre standan æt him on eorðan, Past. 101, 18. Hê sceal habban . . . hlædre, Angl. ix. 263, 8. Lytlum and lytlum stîgan stæpmælum swilce hê on sume hlædre stîge, and wylle weorðan uppe on sumu sæclife, Solil. H. 45, 17. II. a set of fixed steps in a building, flight of steps, stairs :—Martinus stâh tô ânre ûpflôra. þâ wæron þære hlædre stapas âlefede on ær and tôburston færinga, Hml. S. 31, 602. Sês Petrus cyrice . . . on þæra hlæddre twâ and feówertig stæpena, Angl. xi. 4, 8 : 5, 10. þær wæs gewuna þæm folce . . . þ hié æfter hlæddrum ûp tô ðæm glæsenum fæte âstigon (cf. þæs folces gewuna is . . . þæt hî . . . stæpmælum tô ðâm fæte âstîgað, Hml. Th. i. 510, 3),

Bl. H. 209, 7. Suǽ suǽ on sume hlǽdre (hlǽdere, *v. l.*) stæpmǽlum, oð ðæt hió gestonde on ðǽm solore, Past. 23, 17. v. scip-hlǽder.

**hlæd-hweól.** *Substitute*: **hlæd-hweogol, -hweogl,** es; *n.* *A wheel used in drawing water* :—Hlædhwiogl (*rota*) *hauritoria* (v. Ald. 8, 29), Wrt. Voc. ii. 76, 1 : 43, 1. Hlædhweogl, 5, 47. v. hlæd-trendel.

**hlædred[e]**; *adj.* *Laddered, provided with steps* :—On þone hlæd-dredan (hlædreadan, C. D. vi. 94, 13) beám, C. D. B. iii. 492, 27.

**hlæd-trendel.** *Add* :—Hlædtrendle *rota hauritoria*, An. Ox. 502. v. hlædel, hlæd-hweogol.

**hlǽfdige.** *Add*: I. *the mistress of a household* (lit. and fig.) :—Hýredes hláford *paterfamilias*, hýredes móder oððe hlǽfdige *materfamilias*, Wrt. Voc. i. 73, 21. Seó sáwl is ðæs flǽsces hlǽfdige, and hire gedafnað þ heó simle gewylde ða wylne, þ is þ flǽsc tó hyre hǽsum. Þwyrlíce færð æt ðám húse þær seó wyln bið þære hlǽfdigan wissigend, and seó hlǽfdige bið þære wylne underðeódd, Hml. S. 17, 8-12. Þære hláfdian *matrone*, Wrt. Voc. ii. 54, 65. Swé swé égan menenes hondum hláfdian hire (*dominae suae*), Ps. Srt. 122, 2. I a. *the lady superior of a convent* :—Eálá þú hlǽfdige, ealles middaneardes cwén, Hml. S. 23 b, 487 : 472. Bide þá eádigan Sanctan Marian þíne leófan hlǽfdian, Angl. xii. 515, 2. II b. *as title of an English king's wife.* (1) *in the king's lifetime* :—Hugon þe seó hlǽfdige (*Ethelred's queen*) heafde hire gesett tó geréfan, Chr. 1003 ; P. 135, 6. Se cyng (*Edward*) geaf þære hlǽfdian (cf. seó cwén, 182, 7) eall þ heó ǽr áhte, 1052 ; P. 183, 12. Ǽrest his kynehláforde ǽnne beáh on hundeahtotigan mancysan goldes . . . And þære hlǽfdian (hlǽdigan, C. D. ii. 380, 29) (*dominae suae reginae*, 504, 1) ǽnne beáh on þrittigan mancyssan goldes, Cht. Th. 501, 10. Ic ann mínæn cinæhláforðæ . . . and þám æþelingæ . . . and þære hlǽfdigan . . ., 553, 37. (2) *after the king's death* :—Hér forðférde Cnut cing . . . and Ælfgyfu Imme seó hlǽfdie sæt ðǽr (*Winchester*) binnan, Chr. 1035 ; P. 158, 11. On þýs ylcan geáre forðférde seó ealde hlǽfdige (*the queen dowager*), Eádwerdes cinges móder, Imme hátte, 1051 ; P. 172, 32. Eadweard cingc and Ælfgyfu seó hlǽfdige (cf. Ego, Eadward rex . . . Ego, Ælfgyfa praedicti regis mater . . ., 75, 8), C. D. iv. 76, 13. Eádgyð seó hlǽfdie forðférde, seó wæs Eádwardes cynges geresta, Chr. 1076 ; P. 212, 19. III. *as a form of courteous address, lady* (?) :—Cueð hir tó se Hǽlend, 'Maria' (*in the margin* þ is on Englis, hláfdia), Jn. L. 20, 16.

**hlǽfþe** *preparation of material for making bread* (?) :—Hláf *panis*, bráð hláf *paximatium*, daag *sparsum*, dáges hlǽfþe *sparsio*, Wrt. Voc. i. 288, 65-68.

**-hlæg.** v. ge-hlæg : **hlénan.** *Add*: v. be-hlénan, *and see* ymb-hlennan.

**hlǽne.** *Add* :—Hlǽne *macer* vel *macilentus* Wrt. Voc. i. 83, 48. v. þyn-hlǽne.

**hlǽnian.** *Add* :—Lǽnede *marcebat*, Wrt. Voc. ii. 57, 64. [v. *N. E. D.* lean ; *vb.*] v. ge-hlǽnian.

**hlǽn-nes.** *Add* :—Hungor *esuries*, hlænnys *macies*, Ælfc. Gr. Z. 82, 15 : Wrt. Voc. ii. 56, 2 : *exhilitas*, 145, 6. Mid hlænnesse *macie* (me dira fames *macie* torquebit, Ald. 272, 16), An. Ox. 23, 33. Hlænnesse *atrophiam, tenuitatem corporis*, Hpt. 31, 14, 338.

**hlénsian.** *Add* :—Ic hlǽnsige *macero*, An. Ox. 1156. v. á-, ge-hlǽnsian.

**hlæst**; *m.* (not *n.*). *Add*: [*O. H. Ger.* hlast *onus*.] v. scip-hlæst : **hlæstan.** *Add*: [Þay wyth lyf wern laste and lade, Allit. Pms. 35, 1145.] v. ofer-hlæstan.

**hlæsting** *toll claimed by the king in harbours, and on transport by road or stream* :—Nomina consuetudinum Anglice praecepi ponere, scilicet . . . hlæstinge, Cht. Th. 411, 30. Hleastynge, 359, 4. See Sax. Engl. ii. 75 : *N. E. D.* lastage.

**hlæst-scip,** es ; *n.* *A merchant-vessel* :—Hlaestscip *honeraria*, Wrt. Voc. ii. 110, 46.

**hléw.** *Add* :—Wæs þær in þám sprecenan íglande sum mycel hléw of eorþan geworht . . . Ða wæs þér on óðre sídan ðæs hléwes (hláwas, *v. l.*) . . . seað *erat in praefata insula tumulus agrestibus glebis coacervatus . . . in cujus latere . . . cisterna*, Guth. Gr. 117, 7. Of ðære díc on ðone hláw ; of ðǽm hláwe, C. D. iii. 217, 12. ðét hleówede hláwe, 385, 18. Hláwum *aggeres*, Wrt. Voc. ii. 9, 42. Inn on Kett ; of Kette in ða hláwas ; of ðám hláwan . . . of ðám sló ine on ða hláwas ; and of ðám hláwan *ad tumulum uocitatum Kett ; ex Kette usque ad monticulos . . . ad sloh; deinde ad alios monticulos*, C. D. iii. 382, 14-19. Be ðǽm heáfdum on þreó hláwas ; of þreóm hláwan, 220, 5. v. brér-hléw.

**hláf.** *In l. 27 after 'bran' add* Cht. Th., *and add* : I. *bread made from meal or flour* :—Þú him of eorþan út ǽlǽddest hláf (*panem*) tó helpe . . . hláf trymeð heortan mannes, Ps. Th. 103, 14, 15. Sý ánes pundes gewihte hláf tó eallum dæge. Sý gehealden þæs pundmǽtan hláfes se þridda dǽl *panis libera una propensa sufficiat in die . . . de eadem libra tertia pars reservetur*, R. Ben. 63, 14-16. Hú mæg þǽm geweorðan þe . . . him hláf and stán on gesihðe geweorðað . . . þæt he þone stán nime, . . . hláfes ne gíme, El. 611-616. Hé his líchoman him sealde on hláfe, Bl. H. 73, 5. Gé etað hláf be gewihte and gé ne beóð fulle, Lev. 26, 26. Hí hláf ne éton (cf. næs þér (*Mermedonia*) hláfes wist werum, An. 21) . . . ac æton manna líchaman, Bl. H. 229, 8. ¶ *bread as a food for penitents, &c.* :—Gif hwá ordáles weddige . . . féde he hine sylfne mid hláfe and nid wætere and sealte and wyrtum, Ll. Th. i. 210, 28. Fæsten tó berenan hláfe, Wlfst. 173, 10. I a. *in phrases implying the eating of bread.* (a) *hláf brecan to break bread for distribution to others* :—Brec ðǽm hyngriendum ðínne hláf *frange esurienti panem tuam* (Is. 58, 7), Past. 315, 14 : Bl. H. 37, 20. Áféng se Hǽlend hláf and hine brǽc, Mk. 14, 22. Cf. Hú hig-hine oncneówan on hláfes brice, Lk. 24, 35. (β) *tó hláfe gan to go to eat bread.* Cf. hláf-gang :—Ðǽre wucan rǽdere gange tó hláfe (hláue, *v. l.*) and drince ǽr ðám þe hé beginne tó rǽdenne *frater ebdomedarius accipiat mixtum priusquam incipiat legere*, R. Ben. 63, 1. Ðá wicþénas ǽnre tíde ǽr gemǽnum gereorde gán tó hláfe (*accipiant panem*), 59, 14. I b. *with qualifying words* :—Cruman berenes hláfes, Lch. ii. 134, 9. Hé þære ytemestan yldo his lífes mid medmiclum hláfe and cealde wætere (*pane cibario et frigida aqua*) áwreþede, Bd. 5, 12 ; Sch. 630, 19. Fæsten tó berenan hláfe, Wlfst. 173, 10. Eton hig þeorfne hláf, Angl. viii. 322, 14. His synna beóð ádýlegode þurh þone drihtenlican hláf (= þ húsel, 5), Ll. Th. ii. 392, 6. II. *a loaf, cake* :—Smal hláf *artocobus* (cf. *artocopus* a symynel, Wülck. Gl. 564, 43), Wrt. Voc. ii. 10, 47. Þu nymst ánne holne hláf and ánne gebígedne hláf of þǽm þeorfra hláfa windle *tolles tortam panis unius crustulam, laganum de canistro azymorum*, Ex. 29, 23. Cuoeð þ stánas ðás hláfa i tó hláfum sié gewordeno *dic ut lapides isti panes fiant*, Mt. L. 4, 3. Gé ne gedencas fíf hláfana (hláfa, R.) *non recordamini quinque panum*, 16, 9. Æt .x. hídum tó fóstre .x. fata hunies, .ccc. hláfa, Ll. Th. i. 146, 16. Fíf hláfum onfangenum . . . hé . . . þá hláfas brǽc, Mk. 6, 41 : An. 590. Hé nam þæt flǽsc mid þám heorðbacenum hláfum (cf. focan *subcinericios panes*, 6), Gen. 18, 8. Æt ánre feorme þone mon þá hláfas wrát tó þicgeanne *cum panes per convivia frangerentur*, Ors. 5, 10 ; S. 234, 5. Mé wǽran míne teáras for hláfas, Ps. Th. 41, 3. Ælc gebúr sylle .vi. hlátas ðám inswáne, Ll. Th. i. 434, 21. Hylstene hláfas *tortam panis* (v. Ex. 29, 23), Wrt. Voc. ii. 30, 21. Hláfas *turtas*, 94, 24. Hláfas of bere, Jn. R. 6, 9. II a. *a bit of bread* :—Hláfes *cruste*, Wrt. Voc. ii. 21, 1. Hláue *crusta*, 94, 3. Þá-þe wilniað fretan mín folc swá ánne hláf (*sicut escam panis*), Ps. Th. 13, 9. III. *bread as representing food in general* :—On swáte þínes andwlitan þú brícst þínes hláfes *in sudore vultus tui vesceris pane*, Gen. 3, 19. Wurdon wíde menn wǽdlan hláfes, Ps. Th. 104, 14. Hé eóde on sumes Fariséa ealdres hús þ he hláf ǽte (tó brúcanne hláf, L. R. *manducare panem*), Lk. 14, 1 : 15. Þonne hiæ hláf etað (mete þicgeað, W. S.), Mt. R. L. 15, 2 : Ps. Th. 101, 4 : Gen. 935. Þú senst úsne hláf dæghwámlíce, Hy. 7, 68. Hingrendum hláf and hrægl nacedum, Cri. 1355. III a. *where bread is taken to represent the food of a meal* :—'Gerestað eów . . . oð þæt ic eów lecge hláf ætforan, þæt gé eów gereordian' . . . Abraham þa nam buteran and meoloc and þæt flǽsc mid þám hláfum and léde him ætforan, Gen. 18, 4-8. III b. *in special phrases*, e. g. *bread of affliction* :—Ðú ús fédest teára hláfe, Ps. Th. 79, 5. Þá þe sáres hláf ǽton, 126, 3. III c. *of spiritual sustenance, bread* of life :—Ic eom lífes hláf, Jn. 6, 35. Críst, se sóða hláf be him sylfum cwæð, 'Ic eom se líflíca hláf,' Hml. Th. i. 34, 16. Ðú ús sillest þone hláf éces lýfes, Solil. H. 8, 13. Þé sóðfæst Meotud wist gife, heofonlícne hláf, An. 389. IV. *material like bread, manna* :—Hé sealde him heofenes hláf *panem coeli dedit eis*, Ps. Th. 77, 25. V. *a loaf-shaped mass, cake* of material :—Hláf wexenne (cf. weax-hláf) niman freó[n]d-scipas níwe gefégd *panem cerarium accipere, amicitias nouas iungit* (Archiv, cxxv. 63), Lch. iii. 210, 2. v. ælmes-, bréad-, hirsting-, hwíte-, oflæt-, oster-, þeorf-, weax-hláf.

**hláf-brytta,** an ; *m.* *One who distributes food to a household, a steward,* cf. hláf-ǽta [cf. gleáw þeów þone geset hys hláfurd ofer his híred, ðæt hé him on tíde mete sylle, Mt. 24, 45] :—Eádgifu gefreóde Ælfgiðe Birhsies dohtor hláfbryttan, C. D. B. iii. 537, 10 ; Cht. E. 255, 18.

**hláf-gang.** *Substitute: The going to eat bread.* Cf. tó hláfe gán *under* hláf; I a β. (1) *of ordinary bread* :—Ða wicþénas ánre tíde ǽr gemǽnum gereorde gán tó hláfe . . . ðehhweþere freólstídum beón bútan þám hláfgange . . . oð þæt hí mæssan hæbben *septimanarii ante unam horam refectionis accipiant panem . . . in diebus tamen solemnibus usque ad missas sustineant*, R. Ben. 59, 13-18. (2) *of the Eucharistic bread* :—Hwilcan geþance mæg ǽnig man geþencan on his móde þ hé tó sácerdan heáfod áhylde, and heora mæssan on circan gestande, and æt

hláfgange (*when he goes to receive the consecrated bread*) heora hand cysse, Ll. Th. i. 334, 34.

hláf-gebrece, es; *n. Substitute*: hláf-gebrecu, e; *f. A fragment of bread*:—Hé his cristallum cynnum sendeð swylc swá hláfgebrece *mittit crystallum suum sicut frusta panis*, Ps. Th. 147, 6.

hláf-hús *a house of bread* (translation of Beth-lehem):—Bethlehem is gereht 'Hláf-hús', Hml. Th. i. 34, 15.

hláf-mæsse. *Add*:—Blódlǽs is tó forgänne fíftýne nihtum ǽr hláf-mæsse, Lch. ii. 146, 9. *See next word*.

hláfmæsse-tíd, e; *f. Lammas-tide*:—Hú sié ǽttres ful sió lyft on hláfmæssetíd, Lch. ii. 14, 30.

hláf-ofen, -ofn, es; *m. An oven for baking bread*:—*Fornum* hláfofn, *a farre dictum*, Wrt. Voc. ii. 39, 65.

hláford. *Add*: I. applied to non-English persons, or in a general sense. (1) *a master of servants, a male head of a household*:—Gléaw þeów hone geset hys hláfurd (hláferd, L., dryhten, R.) ofer his híred, ðæt hé him on tíde mete sylle, Mt. 24, 45. Se ðeówa nát hwæt se hláford (hláfard, L. R.) déð, Jn. 15, 15. Gif þeów næbbe wíf and his hláford him wíf sylle . . . þæt wíf and hire winclo beóð þæs hláfordes . . . Gif se wiel cwið: 'Mé is mín hláford leóf,' Ex. 21, 4–5. Se apostol beád ðeówum mannum þæt hí wǽron heora hláforde getreówe and holde, wǽre se hláford good, wǽre hé yfel, Hml. Th. ii. 68, 9. Wénst þú þæt seó mengio þínra monna þé mæge dón gesǽligne? . . . yfele þegnas beóþ heora hláforde fiénd *an te longus ordo famulorum facit esse felicem? qui si vitiosi moribus sint . . . ipsi domino inimici*, Bt. 14, 1; F. 42, 23. Swǽ swǽ ǽgan ðiówa in hondum hláfarda heara, Ps. Srt. 122, 2. Ne mæg nán man twám hláfordum þeówian, Mt. 6, 24. (1 a) where the servant is a thing personified:—Hláford mín (*a plough's*), Rä. 22, 3. (2) *a ruler, one who has subjects, one to whom obedience is due*. (a) *sovereign* of a country, *governor* of a city or province, *an ecclesiastical chief*:—Se hláford (*Nero*), Met. 9, 55. Se hláford (cf. v. 2) ðe ðǽm here waldeð, 25, 15. Hyra hláford (Caldéa cyning, 668) læg, Dan. 675. Þæt hé Heardréde hláford wǽre oððe þone cynedóm ciósan wolde, B. 2375. Gif hwelc swíþe ríce mon on his hláfordes ǽrende færþ, Bt. 27, 2; F. 98, 21. Gyf þínes hláfordes ǽrendgewrit and hys insegel tó ðé cymð, Solil. H. 23, 14. Geðenc nú hweðer mani mann cynges hám séce . . . hí cumað ealle tó ánum hláforde, 41, 1–10. Heretoga hláforde leóf, Met. 1, 47. Þegnas síne mynton forlǽtan leófne hláford (cf. Ðracia cining, 22), 26, 72. Þeóda ǽghwilc hæfdon heora hláford for þone héhstan god (cf. hiora cyningas hí weorþodon for godas, Bt. 38, 1; F. 194, 15), 44. Pílatus gréteþ Claudium his hláford, Bl. H. 177, 5. Rómwarena hláford, El. 983. Úrne hláford (cf. Heliseus hæfde ealdordóm micelne, 25), Jul. 129: 681. Dryhten hláforda *Dominus dominorum*, Ps. Srt. 135, 3. Hwæt tácnað ús Saul búton yfle hláfurdas (*mali rectores*)? oððe hwæt Dauid búton góde ðeówas (*boni subditi*)?, Past. 197, 22. ¶ applied to Deity:—Gif ðá gesceafta heora unwillum hláforde hérden, Bt. 35, 4; F. 160, 21. Þ hí þeówian swilcum hláforde and fægniaþ þæs þ hé heora wealt, 39, 13; F. 234, 29. Áhóf ic riicnæ kyningc, heafunæs hláford, Txts. 126, 5. Heofeones hláford and ealles middangeardes, Bl. H. 69, 13. Þane ǽcan hláford, Solil. H. 25, 2. Hláford eallra, engla and elda, El. 475. (3) used in addressing a ruler:—Se biscop wrát ǽnne pistol Theodosio cásere þus cweðende: 'Hyt gedafenað, lá wynsuma hláford . . .,' Angl. viii. 322, 48. (b) *a military officer, captain*:—Hundraðes monna hláford *centurio*, Mt. p. 15, 13. (c) *a master of disciples*:—Hláford mín (cf. þone leófestan lǽreów, 977), Gú. 1331. Hé his hláford geseah ellorfúsne . . . ongan þá duguda hleó geongran rétan, 1026–1035. Hý þæs lǽreówes word ne gehyrwdon; sóna wǽron gearwe hǽleð mid hláford, Cri. 461. (d) *a major-domo*. v. hláf-weard:—Gesette hine hláford húses his, Ps. Srt. 104, 21. (e) figurative (a) where the ruler or master is a thing:—Se wela and se anweald and þá woruldgesǽlþa sint eówre hláfordas and eówre wealdan-das, Bt. 16, 2; F. 50, 36. Ðá unrihtwísan cynges hí underþiódaþ unþeáwum; sceal ðonne néde tó þára hláforda dóme þe hine ǽr underþeódde, 37, 1; F. 186, 29: Met. 25, 65. (β) where the ruled is a thing:—Is þ forweorþfullic wela þe náuþer ne mæg hine selfne ge-healdan ne his hláford, Bt. 29, 1; F. 102, 15. Hwí wæs Adame án treów forboden, þá þá hé wæs ealles óðres hláford?, Angl. vii. 6, 42. Þás woruldgesǽlþa and þes anweald willaþ clifian on þǽm wyrstan monnum, and him geþafiaþ þæt hí bióð heora hláfordas, Bt. 16, 3; F. 54, 20. (f) used of animals:—Gif gé gesáwen hwelce mús þæt wǽre hláford ofer óþre mýs and sette him dómas and nídde hié æfter gafole *si inter mures videres unum aliquem jus sibi ac potestatem prae caeteris vendicantem*, Bt. 16, 2; F. 52, 2. (3) *an owner, a proprietor*:—Gif oxa hníte wer oððe wíf . . . his hláford (*dominus bovis*) bið unscildig. Gif se oxa hnitol wǽre . . . and hig hit his hláforde cýðden . . . ofsleah þone hláford, Ex. 21, 28–29. Sum fearr weard ángencga . . . Se hláford ðá gegaderode micele menigu his incnihta, Hml. Th. i. 502, 12; Bl. H. 199, 9. (4) *a husband*:—Nerónes wíf, Libia, and Agrippan wíf, Agrippina, noldan leng heora hláforda ne heora wera restgemánan sécan, Bl. H. 173, 15. II. used of Englishmen in technical senses. (1) *a master of free or servile labourers*:—Gif þeów mon wyrce on Sunnandæge be

his hláfordes hǽse . . . se hláford geselle .xxx. sciłł. tó wíte . . . Gif se frígea þý dæge wyrce bútan his hláfordes hǽse, Ll. Th. i. 104, 2–6. Gif hláford his þeówan freólsdæge nýde tó weorce . . . gylde lahslit se hláford, 402, 17–19. Gif wíteþeów hine forstalie, hó hine mon, and ne gylde his hláforde, 118, 7. (2) *the male head of a household*. (a) *the master of domestics*:—Hæbbe ǽlc hláford his híredmen on his ágenum borge, Ll. Th. i. 394, 27. Híredmanna gehwilc sille pæníg tó ælmessan, oððe his hláford sille for hine, Wlfst. 181, 17. (b) *the master of a wife, a wife's lord and master, the husband*:—Ðis is geðinge Eádwaldes and Cyneðrýðe, Eðelmódes láfe ymbe ðet lond ðe hire Eðelmód hire hlábard salde, C. D. i. 295, 34. Æfter Byrhtwara (cf. Byrhtwaru Ælfríces láf, 380, 23) dæge . . . for Ælfríc hire hláford; and Brómleáh . . . swá Ælfríc hire hláford hit becwæð, ii. 381, 20–23. Eádgyð seó hlǽfdie fordférde, seó wæs Eádwardes cynges geresta . . . and se cyngc . . . leide heó wið Eádwearde cynge hire hláforde, Chr. 1076; P. 212, 22. Þæt wíf sceal hire ealdore (hláforde, v. l.) hiéran, Ll. Th. i. 138, 18. (3) *a lord spiritual, the chief of an ecclesiastical establishment*. v. hláford-dóm:—Gif preóst mon ofsleá . . . hine mon of þám mynstre ágife, búton se hláford þone wer foreþingian wille, Ll. Th. i. 76, 3. Fóe se hláford tó and ðá hígon æt Krístes cirican . . . an ðás rédenne ic hit ðider selle ðe se monn, sé ðe Krístes cirican hláford sié, sé mín and mínra erfewearda forespreoca, and an his hláforddóme wé bión móten, C. D. i. 311, 17–22: 310, 31. Bútan þæs munuces hláfordes léfnesse, Ll. Th. i. 74, 16. Healf cyninge, healf biscepe and þǽre cirican hláforde þe þá nunnan áge, 66, 17. Wiib and cild ðǽm hláforde and hígum and ðǽre stówe befestan, C. D. i. 316, 10. Geunnan healfes Gode and sancte Petre and ðǽre cyrcean hláforde, v. 143, 2. Ðá menn ðá ðaer (*Canterbury*) hláfordas wǽron, 292, 29. Aet hláforda tídum, 293, 17. (4) *a lord of vassals or retainers, a feudal lord*:—Godríc þone gódan forlét þe him mænigne oft meár gesealde; hé gehleóp þone eoh þe áhte his hláford, By. 189. Wé cweðað þ mon móte mid his hláforde feohtan orwíge, gif mon on þone hláford fiohte; swá mót se hláford mid þý men feohtan. Æfter þǽre ilcan wísan mon mót feohtan mid his mǽge . . . búton wið his hláforde; þ wé ne liéfað, Ll. Th. i. 90, 19–25: 120, 3: 220, 22: 228, 27. Ne teó se hláford ná máre on his ǽhte búton his rihtan heregeate, 412, 29. Sé þe ymb his hláfordes feorh sierwe, 64, 4. Sé ðe ðone ándagan brece, búton hit sý þurh hláfordes geban, 260, 13. Gif hwá fare unáliéfed fram his hláforde, 126, 9: 150, 15. Þá þe hine ǽr hláforde befæston, 162, 17. On cinges sele hé his hláforde þénode, 192, 1. Se man þe ætfleó fram his hláforde . . . on scypfyrde oþþe on landfyrde, 420, 7. Se man þe on fyrdunge ætforan his hláforde fealle, 15. Gif mon wille of boldgetale in óðer boldgetæl hláford sécan, dó þ mid þæs ealdormonnes gewitnesse þe hé ǽr in his scíre folgode, 86, 3: 134, 3. Gif hwá embe cyningc oþþe hláford syrwie, 408, 3. (4 a) with special reference to the grant of land:—Fó se hláford tó his lande þe hé him ǽr sealde, Ll. Th. i. 420, 10. Hláfordes gifu, 292, 16: 422, 2. Ælcne man lyst, siððan hé ǽnig cotlýf on his hláfordes lǽne getimbred hæfð, þæt hé hine móte þár on gerestan . . . oð ðone fyrst þe hé bócland and ǽce yrfe þurh his hláfordes miltse geearnige, Solil. H. 2, 7–13. Ymb mín lond þe ic (Abba geroefa) hæbbe and mé God láh and ic æt mínum hláfordum begæt, C. D. i. 310, 6. (5) *the lord of a manor*:—Gif se hláford him wile þ land árǽran tó weorce and tó gafole, Ll. Th. i. 146, 3: 436, 9. Gif geneátmanna hwilc forgýmeleásað his hláfordes gafol . . . gif se hláford mildheort bið . . ., 270, 16–18. Æt hláfordes falde, berne, 434, 13, 16. Gescádwís geréfa sceal witan ge hláfordes landriht ge folces gerihtu, Angl. ix. 259, 4. (5 a) *the lord of a manor* in legal relations:—Fó se hláford (landhláford, v. l.) tó healfan, tó healfan þ hundred, Ll. Th. i. 268, 20: 258, 12–13. Gif se hláford sæcge þ him naðor ne burste ne áð ne ordál . . . niman se hláford him twégen getreówe þegenas innan þám hundrede and swerian . . ., 280, 10–13. Gif se hláford hine ládian wylle, 294, 12. Gif þeós lád teórie, gylde twygylde, and hláforde his wíte, 354, 31: 282, 3. (6) *a ruler*. (a) of a country, (*our*) *lord* (*the king*):—Gif úre hláford ús ǽnigne eácan geþæncean mæge tó úrum friðgildum . . . uton healdan þ frið swá hit úrum hláforde lícige, Ll. Th. i. 238, 15–25. Þone man þe úres hláfordes grið tóbrocen hæbbe, 296, 29. Úres hláfordes gerǽdnes and his witena, 304, 9, 14, 18. Ælc mæssepreóst mæssige for úrne hláford and for ealle his þeóde, Wlfst. 181, 22. (b) of a province:—Ær Æðelred wæs Myrcna hláford, C. D. ii. 131, 28. Æþelrédes dohtor Myrcna hláforde, Chr. 399; P. 105, 31. Æþred aldorman and Æthelflæd Myrcna hláfordas, C. D. ii. 151, 1. Hé hit geearnode hit æt Mercna hláfordum, 111, 29. See Chr. P. ii. 118. v. land-, riht-, scip-hláford.

hláford-dóm. *Add*: , *jurisdiction*:—Hláforddómes *consulatus*, i. *principatus*, An. Ox. 271. Constantinus him æfterfyligde in þæs mynstres rihtinge and hláfordóme (ealdordóme, v. l.) *Constantinus ei in monasterii regimine successit*, Gr. D. 96, 8. An ðás rédenne ðe se monn, sé ðe Krístes cirican hláford sié, sé mín and mínra erfewearda mundbora, and an his hláforddóme wé bián móten, C. D. i. 311, 21. Wiib and cild ðǽm hláforde and hígum and ðǽre stówe befestan tó mundbyrde and tó hláforddóme on ðǽm ðingum ðe him ðearf sié, 316, 11. On

ælcum ðǽra gerihta ðe tô heora hlāforddôme gebyrað, v. 142, 33. Hē hæfde þone rǣcenddôm and hlāforddôm þæs mynstres *monasterii regimen tenebat*, Gr. D. 20, 21. v. riht-hlāforddôm.

**hlāford-gift.** *Substitute*: hlāford-gift, es; *m.* or *n.* *Grant by a lord* (? cf. hlāford; II. 4 a), *appointment by a lord to a command* (?) :—Rǣdgiftes ł hlāforddômes, hlāfordgiftes *consulatus*, i. *principatus* (the passage is: Si cogente peregrinandi necessitate illa, cui *consulatus* vice regimen caeterarum commissum est, externa quaerere regna maluerit, Ald. 5, 26), Hpt. Gl. 412, 65.

**hlāford-hold;** *adj. Loyal to a lord* :—Yfele þegnas beóþ heora hlāfordes fiénd. Gif hī gôde beóþ and hlāfordholde, Bt. 14, 1 ; F. 42, 24. *See next word.*

**hlāford-hyldo.** *Add*: v. rihthlāford-hyldu.

**hlāfording,** es ; *m.* I. *a prince, sovereign* :—Nis nā mā hlāfordinga on worulde þonne twēgen, God Ælmihtig and deófol, Wlfst. 298, 7. II. *a prince, noble, lord spiritual or temporal* :—Hit wes gesitolad þām hlāfordingan þā þēron wēron, þæt wes Adelwold bisceof and Ælfstān bisceop and Æþelgār abbod and Ælfríc cild . . . and swīðæ manega ôðra ðegenas, C. D. B. iii. 547, 9. [v. *N. E. D.* lording.]

**hlāford-lic;** *adj. Lordly, heroic, noble* :—Hlāfordlic *heroicus*, id est nobile, An. Ox. 18 b, 46.

**hlāford-scipe.** *Add*:—Gange ðæt land tô ðām ðe sē wylle ðe ðonne bisceoprīces wealde on Wigeraceastre; and hig sȳn ǽfre underþeódde and ðām hlāfordscipe folhgien ðe ðonne bisceop beó, C. D. iv. 137, 22. Ðā forlēt se deófoll ðone ælmihtigan . . . and nolde habban his hlāfordscipe, Hex. 16, 29 : Hml. A. 2, 42. Þā munecas ǽfre hefdan þone hlāfordscipe ofer ðā preóstas, Chr. 870 ; P. 284, 11.

**hlāford-swica.** *Add*:—Hlāfordswican losiað on ende mid þām getreówleásan deófle þe hī tihte tô ðām swicdôme, Hml. S. 19, 231 : 194. Tô helle scylon hlāfordswican, Wlfst. 203, 25.

**hlāford-swīcung,** e ; *f. Treachery to a lord* :—Ús mon þonne nēnigre dēda grimlīcor ne mengaþ, þonne þæs saternesdeges weorces . . . būton manslihte and ciricbryca and hlāfordswīcunga, Wlfst. 225, 28. Uton forlǣtan . . . hlāfordswīcunga, Verc. Först. 167.

**hlāford-þrymm,** es ; *m. Lordly greatness, majesty* :—For heora woroldwuldre and for hlāfordþrymme, Chrd. 66, 20.

**hlāf-ræce (-u),** an ; *f. An instrument for stirring a fire for cooking* :—Hlābrecæ *rotabulum* (rotabulum *furca vel illud lignum quo ignis movetur in fornace causa coquendi*, Migne), An. Ox. 53, 43. Cf. ofen-raca.

**hlāf-weard,** es ; *m. A steward, major-domo.* v. hlāford ; I 2 d :—Hē sette hine on his hûse tô hlāfwearde (*printed* hālf-) *constituit eum dominum domus suae*, Ps. Th. 104, 17.

**hlagol.** For 'Lye' *substitute* :—Ne ǽnig man tô hlagol sȳ ne fǣringa tô fǣgen ne eft ne beó tô ormôd, Wlfst. 70, 13. Ne beón gē tô felawyrde ne ealles tô hlagole ne eft tô āsolcene ne tô unrôte, 40, 13.

**hlanc.** *Add*: *loose from emptiness, not filled out.*

**hland.** *Substitute*: Lant (v. *N. E. D.*, s. v.), *urine* :—Hlond *lotium*, Wrt. Voc. ii. 113, 9. Hlom (hlond?) *vel* micga, i. 21, 63. Hland, ii. 71, 9. Mid þām fūlestum hlondes (micgan) stengcum *putentissimis lotii nidoribus*, An. Ox. 3264: 3274. Hlande *lotio*, Wrt. Voc. ii. 82, 5. Nim wulle and wǣt mid biccean hlonde, Lch. i. 362, 18. Genim hlond, gehǣt mid stānum, þweah mid þȳ hlonde, ii. 156, 14. Hrȳþeres geallan wiþ gǣten hland gemenged, 40, 20. Hlond *lotia*, Wrt. Voc. ii. 93, 9.

**hleahtor.** *Add*: I. *the action of laughing.* (1) *as an expression of joy, merriment* :—Plega and hleahtor . . . þær wigan sittað on beórsele blīðe ætsomne, Rūn. 14. Hlehter (*risus*) eówer on heófunge byþ gehworfen and bliss on gnornunge, Scint. 171, 6. Hlehter sáre byð gemineged, 11. Be hlehtre and be wôpe, 1. Hwelce cehhettunge gē woldon þæs habban and mid hwelcre hleahtre gē woldon beón āstyred *quanto moveris cachinno*, Bt. 16, 2 ; F. 52, 5. Dyde ic mē tô gomene ganetes hleóðor and huilpan swēg for hleahtor wera, Seef. 21. Leahter *risum*, Scint. 171, 12. (1 a) *attributed to other than human beings* :—Wæs engla þreāt hleahtre blīðe, Cri. 739. Ic (*the devil*) þā rôde ne þearf hleahtre herigean, El. 920 : An. 1705. (2) *as an expression of contempt, scorn* :—Gif þū mid þan þeáwe tǣlendra mē hleahtrige, warna þē sylfne þǽr þū þē hleahtres (leóhtes?) wēne þæt þū þǽr ne wurðe mid dymnysse þȳstro āblend *if you after the manner of critics laugh at me, look to yourself lest where you expect laughter* (light?) *you can see nothing for the darkness* (the Latin is: si more obtrectatoris succensueris, cave, ut ubi *lucem* putaveris, ne a tenebris obcaeceris), Guth. Gr. 101, 23. Bysmredon of hleahtre *deriserunt derisu*, Ps. Rdr. 34, 16. Bysmrodon mē mid hleahtre (*printed* mildhleahtre) *subsannaverunt me subsannatione*, Ps. Spl. 34, 19. Þæt wīf āhlôh wereda drihtnes nalles glædlīce, ac heó þone hleóðorcwide husce belegde on sefan swīðe . . . on būre āhôf hihtleásne hleahtor, Gen. 2387. II. *a laugh, a burst or peal of laughter* :—Þā higeleáslican ceahhetunga, hlehtras *ineffrenatos cachinnos*, An. Ox. 3171 : Wlfst. 233, 18. v. tǣl-, ungemet-hleahtor.

**hleahtor** vice. v. leahtor.

**hleahtor-bǽre.** *Substitute*: *Productive of laughter* :—Ne sceal

hē fela sprecan, ne īdele word ne hleahtorbǽre (leahtor-, *v. l.*) *multum loqui non amare, verba vana aut risui apta non loqui*, R. Ben. 18, 8.

**hleahtor-lic.** *Dele the passage given, for which see* leahtor-lic, *and add* :—Hlehterlic hit ys wanhālnysse tôbrocene ealles līchaman wunda feáwa geswutelian *ridiculum est debilitate fracta totius corporis uulnera pauca monstrare*, Scint. 38, 7.

**hleahtrian;** *p.* ode *To laugh to scorn, deride* :—Ealle geseónde mē hlehtredon ł tǣldun [mē] *omnes uidentes me deriserunt me*, Ps. L. 21, 8. Gif þū mid þan þeáwe tǣlendra mē hleahtrige, Guth. Gr. 101, 23. (v. hleahtor ; I. 2.)

**hleáp** *a leap, run.* [*O. H. Ger.* hlouf *cursus*: *Icel.* hlaup *leap.*] v. ût-hleáp.

**hleápan.** *In the last passage for* 452 *read* 482, *and add*: I. *to run, go hastily or with violence, rush* :—Hī gebundon þone bysceop be þam fôtum on sumne fearr, and þone gegremedon þ hē hleóp on unsmēðe eorðan, Shrn. 152, 1. Hēr Rôðbert þæs cynges sunu hleóp fram his fæder, Chr. 1079 ; P. 213, 32. Hleópon (*so in the* [*facsimile of the*] MS., *not* hleówon) hornboran, hreópan friccan, El. 54. Gif hē ût hleápe . . . And gif mon þone hlāford teó þ hē be his rǣde ût hleópe, Ll. Th. i. 282, 2-5. II. *to jump, spring* :—Hē āwearp his hrægl him of and hleóp on ðone mere (cf. hē unscrȳdde hine sylfne and scǣt intô ðām mere, Hml. S. 11, 211), Shrn. 62, 9. II a. *to leap on to a horse* ; hleápan ûp *to mount* :—v. hleápere ; II :—Hleóp *ascendit* (equum), An. Ox. 2142. Þā hēt ic þā hors gerwan and eóredmen hleápan ûp *imperaui equitibus ut ascenderent equos*, Nar. 21, 22. III. *to spring up and down, jump about.* v. hleápettan :—Hē gefēng his swīðran, ārǣrde hine upp, and hē hleóp sôna cunnigende his fēðes hweðer hē cūðe gān (*apprehensa manu ejus dextera, allevavit eum . . . Et exsiliens stetit, et ambulabat*, Acts 3, 8), Hml. S. 10, 32. IV. *of non-material things, where there is rapid extension, to mount up at a bound* :—Mīn unriht mē hlȳpð nû ofer heáfod *iniquitates meae superposuerunt caput meum*, Ps. Th. 37, 4. v. oþ-hleápan.

**hleápend.** v. ofer-hleápend.

**hleápere.** *Add*: I. *one who runs about the country, a landleaper* (v. *N. E. D.*), *vagrant* :—Fīfte cyn is wīdscrīþelra hleápera (*circumcellionum*), R. Ben. 135, 20. II. *one who mounts a horse, a horseman.* v. hleápan ; II a :—Hleáperas (-es, MS.), rǣdehere, *cerethi*, An. Ox. 775. Ineóde rǣdehere mid fyrhweohlodum crætum and hleáprum on sǣ *introïuit equitatus Pharaonis cum quadrigis et ascensoribus in mare*, Ps. Rdr. 282, 19.

**hleápettan;** *p.* te *To jump about, skip* :—Cwið seó bôc þæt hē ūp āstôde and ongunne hleápettan (hleáppettan, *v. l.*) . . . and ā wæs gangende and hleápende (hleáppetende, *v. l.*) and Dryhten herigende, Bd. 5, 2 ; Sch. 560, 5-10. v. hleápan ; III.

**hleápe-wince.** *Add*:—Hleápewince *cucu*, Wrt. Voc. ii. 16, 17 : cucurata, Hpt. 33, 240, 26. [*With* wince, *describing the peculiar flight of the bird, compare* wancol.] v. lǣpe-wince.

**hleáppettan.** v. hleápettan.

**hlec.** *Add*: *leaky* :—Hlec (hlecen, MS., *but* hlec, 2, 480: Hpt. Gl. 529, 11), tôcinen bāt *rimosa, scissurosa barca*, An. Ox. 5456. Lecum *rimose*, Germ. 400, 69. [v. *N. E. D.* leak ; *adj. Icel.* lekr, *leaky.*]

**hlecan** *to join.* *Add*: v. tô-hlecan.

**hlēcan** ? :—Grunnian, hlēcan (hlētan, Hpt. Gl. 507, 54) *grunnire*, An. Ox. 4337.

**hlēda.** *Substitute*: hlēda, an : hlēde, es ; *m.* *A seat, bench* :—Þes hlēda (hlȳda, hlēde, *v. ll.*) hoc *sedile*, Ælfc. Gr. Z. 34, 3. Man sceal habban . . . hlȳdan, sceamelas, Angl. ix. 264, 20.

**hlēfan.** v. á-hlēfan.

**hleglende.** *Substitute*: hlegelende, hlaegulendi ; *adj.* (*ptcpl.*) *Deep-sounding* :—Hlaegulendi *bombosa*, Wrt. Voc. ii. 102, 13. Hleglende, 11, 29. (Cf. ? *vocibus humanis fantem testantur asellam, garrula quae pridem bombosa fauce rudebat*, Ald. 137, 37.)

**hlehhan.** v. hlihhan : **hlemman.** *Add*: v. be-hlemman : **hlennan.** v. ymb-hlennan : **hlenor-teár.** For 508, *l.* 50, 9 : **hleó-hrǽscness.** v. hleów-hrǽscness.

**hleomoc.** *Substitute*: hleomoc, es ; *m.*: hleomoce, an ; *f.* *Brook-lime* :—Hleomoc *fafida*, Wrt. Voc. ii. 40, 3. Hleomoce hātte wyrt, seó weáxeð on brôce . . . gecnūwa þā hleomocan, Lch. ii. 92, 13-16. Nim lilian and hleomoc, 324, 13 : 320, 14 : 330, 5, 14 : 3. Genim wād and hleomocan . . . wyl hleomoc and gearwan, 36, 23-25. Niman leomucan, iii. 38, 17. Genim lemocan, 46, 13. [Leomoc *fafida*, Lch. iii. 302, col. 2. Leomche *favida*, Wrt. Voc. i. 139, 37. v. *N. E. D.* lemeke and brook-lime.]

**hleonaþ.** *Substitute*: hleónaþ, es ; *m.* *A shelter* :—Ic mē ānum hēr eáðe getimbre hûs and hleónaþ, Gū. 222. v. hleów, *and* cf. fôdnoþ *for form.*

**hleónian;** *p.* ode *To shelter, protect, take care* (hleów) *of* :—Ic hǣle and hleónie curam, Wrt. Voc. ii. 21, 41.

**hleór.** *Add*: I. *a cheek* :—Lege þīne hand brālinga tô þīnum hleóre, Tech. ii. 121, 3. Leóre 120, 27. Lege þū þīne swȳðran hand under

þín hleór, 121, 5. Stryc þú mid þínum twám scytefingran andlang þínra hleóra, 119, 18: 129, 6. On hleórum *on the cheeks (of a badger)*, Rä. 16, 4. Ic bidde þ gé wylspringas ontýnan on hleórum . . . dreórige hleór (*moestam faciem*) drecaþ mid wópe, Dóm. L. 26–35. Hleór *genas*, Wrt. Voc. ii. 42, 20. **II.** *a face* :—Hleór *frons*, Txts. 64, 438: *facies*, Wrt. Voc. ii. 36, 44. Hleór *vel* wlita *frons*, 151, 4. Mín þrowade heáfod hearmslege, hleór geþolade árleásra spátl, Cri. 1435. Hé hēt hī mid handum sleán on þ hleór þ heó hlýdan ne sceolde, Hml. S. 8, 70. Hé legde hleór on eorðan *cecidit in faciem suam*, Gen. 2337. S. gegrípeð feónd be þám fótum, lǽted foreweard hleór on strangne stán and stregdað tódas, Sal. 113. [v. *N. E. D.* leer.]

**hleór-beran.** *Another suggestion, which accepts a compound form, is to read* hleór-bergan *face-protectors* : **hleostrum.** v. heolstor.

**hleótan.** *Add* : **I.** *to cast lots* :—Ic eów forbeóde þ eówer nán ne áxie þurh ǽnigne wiccecræft be ǽnigum ðinge . . . for ðan sē ðe þys dēð . . . bið þám hǽðenum gelíc, þe hleótað be him sylfum mid ðæs deófles cræfte . . . Hleótan man mót mid geleáfan swá þeáh on woruld-ðingum bútan wiccecræfte, þ him dēme seó tā gif hí hwæt dǽlan willað, Hml. S. 17, 73–86. Hleáte (hleátte, L.) wē *sortiamur*, Jn. R. 19, 24. **II.** *to receive by appointment, be appointed to* an office :—Hé wæs hleótende þá ændebyrdnysse biscophádes *ad episcopatus ordinem accessitus est*, Gr. D. 192, 1. v. tó-hleótan.

**hleótend,** es; *m.* *One who obtains* :—Swá þēh his sylfes wyllan hé wæs lytel (hleótend, *v. l.*) in ðám midle Crístes þegna *tamen sponte fit parvulus in medio discipulorum*, Gr. D. 218, 1.

**hleóþian.** v. hlóþian.

**hleóþor.** *In bracket at end read* O. H. Ger. hliodar, *and add* : **I.** *a sound, noise* :—Ongan þær beón gehýred swýþe mycel swég and hleóðor swylce þær wǽre sum mycel mænigo in gangende *coepit quasi cujusdam magnae multitudinis ingredientis sonitus audiri*, Gr. D. 284, 24. Hleóðor gryrelic, An. 1553. **II.** *the sound of a bell or musical instrument, voice of the trumpet* :—Hyre is on fóte fæger hleóðor, wynlíc wóðgiefu, Rä. 32, 17. For þære bellan hleóðre (*ad sonum tintinnabuli*) hē ongǽte hwænne Rómánus him þone hláf bróhte, Gr. D. 99, 5. Gehýrde heó cúðne swēg and hleóðor heora bellan *audiuit notum campanae sonum*, Bd. 4, 23 ; Sch. 477, 16. Ðeáh ðe . . . ánra gehwylc . . . hæbbe gyldene býman on múðe, and ealra býmena gehwylc hæbbe .xii. hleóðor, and hleóðra gehwylc sý heofone heárre and helle deópre, ðonne géna ðæs hálgan cantices se gyldena organ hē hý ealle ofer-hleóðrað, Sal. K. p. 152, 7–12. **III.** *the sound produced by the mouth of an animate creature, voice* :—þá wróhtsmiðas hleóðrum brugdon, hwílum swá wilde deór cirmdon, hwílum cyrdon eft on mennisc híw breahtma mǽste, Gú. 878. (1) *voice of a rational being* (a) *in speech* :—Him stýran cwóm stefn of heofonum, wuldres hleóðor, word æfter spræc, Exod. 417 : An. 740. Wæs stefn geworden, seó forðgelǽd-dum hleóðre swá gecleopode and þus cwæð *vox facta est, quae producto sonitu clamaret, dicens*, Gr. D. 52, 23. Hé ne meahte ellensprǽce hleóðor áhebban, Gú. 1129. Hé þurh hleóðor ábeád ege earmum gǽstum, 657. Hié tóhlŏdon hleóðrum gedǽlde . . . siððan metod tóbrǽd monna sprǽce, Gen. 1693. ¶ *where a thing is personified* :— Ic (*a horn*) wæs wǽpenwiga . . . hwílum ic tó hilde hleóðre bonne wilgehlēdan, Rä. 15, 4. (b) *in song* :—þæs sealmsanges hleóðor and dream *psalmodiae sonitus*, Gr. D. 286, 2. Ðonne wit song áhófan, hlúde bi hearpan hleóðor swinsade, Vid. 105. Engla hleóðres (cf. Engla þreátas sigeleóð sungon, 1289), Gú. 1293. (2) *voice, note of a bird* :— Ic þurh múð sprece . . . hleóðres ne míne, Rä. 9, 4. Dyde ic mē tó gomene ganetes hleóðor, Seef. 20. þonne hē gehēráð hleóðrum brægdan óðre fugelas, hí heora ágene stefne styriað, Met. 13, 47. v. efen-swēg-, word-hleóþor ; ge-, ofer-, unge-hleóþor ; *adj.*

**hleóþrere** (? v. hleóþrian), es ; *m.* *A rhetorician* :—Se hleóðere (hleóðrere ?, leóþere ? *The passage glossed is* : Versibus heroicis Prosper *Rhetor* insinuat, Bd. 1, 10 ; S. 48, 28) *rethor*, Txts. 180, 4.

**hleóþrian.** *Add* :—Hleóðrien *crepitaret*, Wrt. Voc. ii. 21, 29. Hleóðrian *crepitare*, 38. Hleóðriende and bēcniað *ciebant*, 50. Hleóþrende *increpitans*, 48, 66. Hleóðrendi, hlaeóðrinde, hleóðendri, Txts. 69, 1065. **I.** *intrans.* (1) *To make a sound.* (a) *the subject a person.* (a) *of speech* :—Hleóðriað *proclamant*, Ps. L. p. 247, note 2. Him sylfa oncwæð, heán hleóðrade, Gen. 866. Hleóðrade hálgan stefne cempa . . . and þus wordum cwæð, An. 537 : Gú. 484. David býmende stefne hleóðriende cwæð, Angl. viii. 331, 12. (β) *of song* :—Hleóðriað Drihtne *praecinite Domino*, Ps. L. 146, 7. Hleóðriað *concinant*, Ps. Srt. ii. p. 202, 5. þ hleóðrigende folc *turba psallentium*, Prud. 75. (b) *the subject a thing* :—þá hleóðriendan ligettas, Wlfst. 182, 10. þá hleóðriendan lígeas, Verc. Först. 87, 3. þǽm swógendum, hleóðregendum *argutis* (*fibrarum fidibus*, Ald. 71, 28), Wrt. Voc. ii. 5, 36. (2) *the subject a sound, to sound, resound* :—Hú manige dreámas and lofsangas nū hleóþriaþ in heofonum *quantae resonent laudes in coelo*, Gr. D. 282, 15. Him stefn oncwæð, word hleóðrode, An. 1432. In þæs eárum hleóþredon (swēgdon, *v. l.*) þá word þæs muneces geþóhtes *in cujus auribus tacita cogitationis verba sonuissent*, Gr. D. 144, 34. Þunode oððe hleóþrede *increpuerit* (*salpicum clangor*, Ald. 23, 3),

Wrt. Voc. ii. 44, 14. Hleóþriende *concrepans*, i. *resonans* (*clangor buccinae*), An. Ox. 1916. Mid hleóþriendum dreáme *consona armonia*, 2593. Dreámas hleóþriende *concentus concrepantes*, 4914. **II.** *trans. To speak words* :—þæra worda gemyndig þe hē hleóðrade tó Abrahame, Ps. Th. 104, 37. v. á-, efen-, ofer-hleóþrian.

**hleóþriend-líc.** v. glíw-hleóþriendlíc.

**hleóþrung.** *Add* :—*Sound, noise of a trumpet* :—þæt is bēmena dæg and hire leóþringa, Verc. Först. 130, 20. v. efen-hleóþrung.

**hleów.** *Add* : **I.** *cover, shelter* furnished by an object :—Under hrófes hleó, Rä. 28, 5. Hé holtes hleó gemēteð, Ph. 429. **II.** *protection* afforded by a person :—Hē ácenned weard tó hleó and tó hróðre hæleða cynne, An. 567 : 111. Hē (*Alfred*) becóm tó Æðelingēge, and on sumes swānes húse his hleów gernde (*desired the protection of the swineherd*) and eác swylce him and his yfele wífe hērde, Shrn. 16, 13. **II a.** *in a personal sense,* a *protector* :—Wígendra hleó cwóm heaðolāces hāl tó hofe gongan, B. 1972. þá cwæð wígendra hleó, An. 1452. [v. *N. E. D.* lee.]

-**hleów**; *adj.* v. ge-, un-hleów ; hleów-ness : **hleówan.** v. hlīwan.

**hleówe**; *adj. Warm. Substitute* : hleówe; *adv. Warmly, snugly.*

**hleów-fæst.** *Add* : *warm* :—On cealdum eardum is neód þ ðæs reáfes māre sig, on hleówfæstum (*calidis*) læs, R. Ben. 88, 7.

**hleów-hræscnes.** *For* forcæncednysse *l.* forsc[r]æncednysse, *and add : destruction of protection or shelter* (?). v. á-hræscian.

**hleów-ness,** e ; *f. Warmth, sunniness* :—Hleównys *apricitas* (omitted after Wrt. Voc. i. 47, 33), Angl. viii. 451.

**hleówsian, hlīwsian** ; *p. ode. To shelter, protect* :—þú hlīwsast *favis*, Wrt. Voc. ii. 147, 21.

**hleów-stede.** *Add* : Angl. viii. 451, 34 : hleówþ. v. hlīwþ: hleówung. v. hlīwung. hlēp-. v. hlíp-: hlēt. v. hlít: -hlēta. v. -hlíta : hlētan. v. hlēcan: -hlēþa. v. ge-hlēþa.

**hlid.** *Add* : **I.** *that which covers the opening at the top of a vessel or closes the mouth of an aperture* :—Bytte hlid *cordias*, Wrt. Voc. ii. 135, 80. 'Gange hē him tó mínre byrgene and áteó āne hringan úp of ðære þrýh' . . . 'Getīða mē þ ic áteó þās hringan úp of ðysum hlide (hlyde, *v. l.*)' . . . Hē teáh ðā þ īsen úp of ðām stáne, Hml. S. 21, 67. Hī gemētton āne mǽre þrūh . . . and þ hlid (hlyd, *v. l.*) ðǽr tó gelimpĭce gefēged, 20, 82. Þrýh hlid *sarcophagi tumbam*, i. *tumulum*, An. Ox. 3970. Ðonne þú cuppan wylle . . . Ðonne þú hlid habban wylle, Tech. ii. 125, 6. **I a.** *figurative* :—Gerýna hlidum beclýsinega (*mysticis*) *sacramentorum operculis clausa* (*coelitus reserantur*), An. Ox. 1521. **II.** *that which closes an aperture in a wall, fence, &c., a gate, door* :—On Lullan hlyd on ðā hegestōwe, C. D. iii. 213, 8. v. eág-, ceaster-hlid.

**hlīdan.** *Add* : ; *p.* hlád, *pl.* hlidon ; *pp.* hliden *To cover with a lid* :—Ðonne þú hlid habban wylle, þonne hafa þ þíne wynstran hand sámlocene and eác swá þā swýþran and hwylf hý syþþan ofer þā wynstran eal swylce þú cuppan hlīde, Tech. ii. 125, 8. [He heled hit and wrihð (lides, *v. l.*), A. R. 84.]

-**hlidede.** v. twi-, þri-hlidede.

**hlid-geat.** *Add* :—Ǽrest on dīc ; ðonne upp wið hlidgeatas ; ðonne on brādan hærpað, C. D. v. 109, 8. Andlang weges tó hlidgeate, Cht. E. 290, 24. Beforan hlidgeate *ante postes*, Wrt. Voc. ii. 6, 5. [v. *N. E. D.* lidgate.]

-**hlidian.** [*O. Frs.* hlidia.] v. ge-, un-hlidian ; -hlidede.

**hlīfan** ; *p.* hláf, *pl.* hlifon ; *pp.* hlifen *To stand out prominently, tower up* :—Hlībendri *minaci*, Wrt. Voc. ii. 114, 12. Hlīfendre *miniaci*, 55, 71. v. ofer-hlīfan ; hlīfian.

**hlīfendre** *minium.* Dele and see preceding word.

**hlīfian.** *Add* : **I.** *of position* :—þæt treów þe wexeð on þám wudu-bearwe þæt hit hlīfað úp ofer eall þá óðre treówu . . . bið hit swiðlicor geweged þonne se óðer wudu. Swá þe þam heáclífum þonne hí hlīfiað feor úp ofer þā óðre eorðan, Wlfst. 262, 5–11. þǽre byrig hlīfað ān munt *urbi mons praeeminet*, Gr. D. 225, 14. Of ðám munte þe ofer his mynstre hlīfade *ex eo monte qui ejus monasterio in excelso prominet*, 12, 8. Hlifode ofer mycel stānclif and swá hlifiende . . . þ stānclif þe him ofer hlifode *magna desuper rupes eminebat . . . prominens . . . saxum quod desuper incubuerat*, 213, 10–24. **II.** *of degree* :—Fore golde and fore gimmum forð hlīfað seó reádnes and bryne ðæs swyles *pro auro et margaritis rubor tumoris ardorque promineat*, Bd. 4, 19 ; Sch. 450, 10.

**hlifung.** v. ofer-hlifung : **hlīgan.** *Dele* 'or hligan?', *for the Latin in the second passage substitute* 'scientiae sibi nomen extendunt', *and add* : [*O. Frs.* hlīa ; *subj.* hlīge.] v. be-hlīgan.

**hlihhan.** *Take here* hlehhan *in Dict., and add* : **I.** *to laugh* :—Ic hlīhe *ridebo*, Kent. Gl. 11. Hlihcaþ *rident*, Germ. 391, 17. Weard micel gehlýd hlihhendra deófla, Hml. S. 31, 810. **I a.** *to have an emotion which may be expressed by laughing, to rejoice* :—Hió hlíhð *ridebit* (*mulier fortis in die novissimo*), Kent. Gl. 1150. ¶ *used of the mind* :—Wæs him frófra mǽst geworden . . . hlihende hyge, El. 995. **II.** *to laugh at* (with gen.) :—Seó eáðmódnes hlôh þǽre ofer-módignesse fylles *humilitas deridet superbiam iacentem*, Prud. 34 a. þá hlôgon his geféran þæs forcorfenan basinges, Hml. S. 31, 72. **II a.**

with phrase expressing scorn, *to laugh* to scorn :—Hē getǽlde his fæder . . . and his tō bismere hlôh, Angl. xi. 2, 53. Hlôgen men his worda on bysmer (cf. hlôgan men Nôes worda . . . and bismerodan hine, 216, 28), Wlfst. 206, 11. **III.** with prep. :—Ofer hine hig hlihchađ (hlichađ, Ps. Rdr., blehhađ, Ps. Vos., hlæhađ, Ps. Srt.) *super eum ridebunt*, Ps. L. 51, 8. Þeáh þe monn hwelces yfeles on hlihge (cf. *M. E.* to laugh on a person) and þū þe unscyldigne wite *though scorn is poured on you for some evil and you know yourself to be innocent* (see Prov. Kmbl. 12 in Dict.), Prov. M. 12. **IV.** *trans. To laugh at, deride, scorn* :—Hlôgun and tēldun hine *deridebant eum*, Lk. R. 8, 53. v. ge-hlihhan.

**hlinaþ.** *Dele, and see* **hleónaþ.**

**hlinc.** *Add :* **I.** *a bank separating strips of arable land on a slope* (v. Seebohm, Vill. Comm. p. 5), *a bank forming a boundary :*—Andlang đæs hlinces on đâra þreóre acra ende, C. D. v. 71, 6. Tô þæs niþærlangau hlincæs eástendæ; andlang hlincæs ūt on eá, 243, 3. Úp od landscare hlinc; fram đâm hlinche, iii. 434, 3. Andlang mǽrfyrh on đane wôn hlinc; of đæm wôn hlince tô wege; andlang weges tô mǽrhlince; andlang mǽrhlinces . . . on đone mǽrhlinc; đonne andlang mǽrhlinces od đâra þreóra æcera heáfod; đonne eft be đâra þreóra æcera heáfdum on ôđerne mǽrhlinc, 414, 9–21. Of twelf ækeran ūt forđ bufon scortan hlince æt đæs fūrlanges ende, v. 111, 6. Tô đam hlince . . . tô mearchlince, vi. 33, 20. On bibban hlincg norđæweardnæ; đonan be đâra æcere handheáfdum, v. 256, 14. On wyrđhlinc; of wyrđhlinc, iii. 76, 36. Andlang đêre ealdan landsceare od þornhlince; of þornhlinh on dinnes hlinch; of dinnes hlince, vi. 36, 11–13. On þone hlinc bufan Friþelinga dîc *to the lynk above Frythelyng dyche*; ad marginem superius Frythelyng dyche (*late versions*), C. D. B. ii. 260, 34. **I a.** *land separated by banks* (?) :—Tô burchlinken, C. D. iii. 409, 29. On burhhlincas; of burhhlincun, 396, 14. **II.** *a rising ground, ridge :*— Tô hǽđhylle; đonon on stânhlinces ende, C. D. iii. 82, 6. Andlang hlinces on þæt sūþheáfod; þonne âdūne on þæt slæd, 414, 2. Of hlinces heáfod, 420, 27 : v. 217, 21. On đæs hlincæs norđændæ; đæt andlang hlincæs sūđ on đæs cumbæs heáfod; đonon on đæs hlincæs wæstændæ, 242, 30–33. Be wirtrune on hlinches brôc, iii. 410, 5. On earnes hlingc; of earnes hlince, 412, 31. Úp ofer deórhlinc; of đâm hlince tô đâm beorge, 420, 24. Swâ seó Læfer scæt tô bealdan hlince (cf. scæt on Byrhtferđes hlæw, 15), 431, 11. On steápan hlince; of steápan hlince, 82, 4. Andlang weges tô fearnhlince, v. 147, 29. On đonæ miclan hlinc; of đâm hlincæ on đonæ ford, 256, 17. On clofenan hlinc (cf. od đone tôbrocenan beorg đe đæt is tôclofen, ii. 251, 6 : æt đâm litlan tôclofenan beorge, iii. 421, 9), v. 179, 27. Ofer dûne on meóshlinc westeweardne; đonne âdûne on đâ ŷfre, ii. 172, 26. On cealdan hlinc westewearde; þonne on wyrtrum oþ cealdan hlinc eásteweardne; on wyrtrum þonne gît norđ, C. D. B. iii. 682, 13. Of đære æc tô stânhlincan, C. D. iii. 78, 36. [v. *N. E. D.* linch, link.] v. mǽr-, stân-hlinc.

**hlinc-gelâd,** es; *n. A watercourse on a slope* (?). The word occurs as a place-name :—Đis sind đâ landgemǽru tô Hlincgelâde (cf. quoddam ruris praediolum . . . cui solicolae antiquum indiderunt uocabulum æt Lhincgelade, 78, 21), C. D. vi. 79, 4.

**hlinc-rǽw,** e; *f. The boundary line formed by a link* or *bank :*— Andlang hlingrǽwe tô đæs niđærlangan hlincæs eástendæ; andlang hlincæs æît ūt on eá, C. D. v. 243, 2. Andlang hlincrǽwæ . . . đonne andlang hegærêwæ, 255, 35. Andlang đêre ealdan hlinchrêwe, vi. 36, 7. Of đâm andheáfdum on đâ hlincrǽwe (-rêwe, iv. 66, 7) úp tô đêre dîc, iii. 408, 29. Of đâm stâne on âne hlincrǽwe od hit cymđ tô grâfum, 455, 1.

**hlinian.** *Add :*—On hlingo (-u, *written over* o) *innitor*, Wrt. Voc. ii. 111, 73. **I.** *to recline, lie on a couch* for rest (or to eat; in translation of Latin *-cumbere* forms) :—Se wulderfulla on godewebbenum beddum hlinađ, E. S. viii. 473, 18. Wîf ongeat þte hlionade (sæt, W. S., *accubuit*) in hūs, Lk. L. 7, 37. Hê æt gereordum hlenode on þæs Hǽlendes bearme, Shrn. 32, 18. Se ele gewǽtte þone fiôr þǽre stôwe þe hî on hlinedon (*incubuerant*), Gr. D. 160, 14. Hlioniga (hlinig, L., site, W. S., *recumbe*) on đâ lætemestu stôwwe . . . biđ đê wuldor bifora đæm hlingendum (sittendum, W. S., *discumbentibus*), Lk. R. 14, 10. Hlengendes æt gereordum *recumbentis*, Mt. R. 26, 7. Đâ đe hliongende woeron, Lk. L. 7, 49. **II.** *to lean* for support :—Þâ studu þe se bysceop on hleonigende forđfêrde *illa destina cui incumbens obiit*, Bd. 3, 17; Sch. 269, 18. **III.** *to incline in thought, be favourably disposed to :*—Eallra willa hlinede (hleonade, hleonodon, *v. ll.*) tô gehŷranne þâ gefeán þæs heofonlican rîces *omnium uota ad nuper audita caelestis regni gaudia penderent*, Bd. 4, 2; Sch. 345, 8. v. wiþer-hlinian.

**hliniend,** es; *m. One who reclines :*—Đrihtenlices breóstes hliniend *dominici pectoris accubitor*, Hpt. Gl. 414, 57.

**hlinung.** *Add :*—Hlynung (hnylung, MS.) *accubitus*, Wrt. Voc. i. 41, 9. Þâ forman hlinunga *primos recubitus* (Mt. 23, 6), An. Ox. 61, 37. v. ge-hlinung.

**hlíp,** es; *m. Take here* **hlŷp,** es; *m., and add :*—Se forma hlŷp, Cri. 720. Ymbe đæne *saltus lunae*, þæt ys ymbe þæs mônan hlŷp, wurdlian, Angl. viii. 308, 16. v. ǽ-, æt-, clif-, ofer-hlíp.

**hlíp,** e; *f.* **I.** *a leaping-place, a place to be jumped over* (v. *N. E. D.* deer-*leap* a lower place in a hedge or fence where deer may leap) :—On hinde-hlŷp; of hinde-hlŷpe, C. D. iv. 19, 24. ¶ Hindehlíp occurs as a local name :—Landes sumne dǽl, đæt synd .iii. hîda đe fram cūđum mannum Hindehlêp is gehāten, C. D. iii. 5, 7. **II.** *a precipitous fall in a river* (cf. stæþ-hlípe), *leap* as in salmon *leap* :—Of đêre ealdan hæcce into prêsta hlŷpe, intô đâm bece . . . tô Freóbearnes hlŷpe . . . Of đâm æssce tô đêre ældan hlŷpe; of đâre hlŷpe tô đâre ealden wudehæcciæ . . . of đâm brôce tô đan æssce : . . of Werdhæcce tô eácrofte . . . intô Æđerîces hlŷpe, of đâre hlŷpe intô wulfhlŷpe, C. D. iv. 157, 4–35. v. hlípe.

**hlíp-cumb** *a valley with steep sides* (? cf. stæþ-hlípe) :—Upp tô hlŷpcumbe; of hlŷpcumbe, C. D. iii. 204, 19.

**hlípe,** an; *f.* **I.** *a place to leap from, a place to mount a horse from.* v. hleápan; **II a.** *Take here passage under* **hlŷpa** *in Dict.* **II.** *a place to jump over :*—On hlŷpan; of hlŷpan, Cht. Crw. 3, 14. Tô hindehlŷpan, C. D. iii. 385, 29. On đone holan weg æt hindehlŷpan; þonne of hindehlŷpan, ii. 249, 35. Hyndehlŷpan, 421, 19. **III.** *a precipitous fall in a river* (?) :—Andlang slades tô Wullâfes hlŷpan, C. D. iii. 431, 17. Tô preóstan lŷpan, C. D. B. ii. 310, 25. On swealewan hlŷpan . . . tô swacan hlŷpan, C. D. iv. 27, 13–21. v. hlíp; *f.* -hlípe. v. stæþ-hlípe.

**hlípe-burna,** an; *m. A brook with a fall in it* (? v. hlíp; **II:** **hlípe; III**) :—Of þâm cumbe on hlŷpeburnan, C. D. iii. 457, 4.

**hlíp-geat** (hlípe-), es; *n. A leap-gate, a low gate in a fence, which can be leaped by deer, while keeping sheep from straying* (*N. E. D.*) :— Ondlong geardes on đæt hlŷpgeat; of đêm hlŷpgeate, C. D. iii. 180, 28. Tô đâm hlŷpgete; of đêm hlŷpgete â be wealle, 456, 8. Tô đâm wealle; of đâm wealle intô hlŷpgete; of đâm hlŷpgete intô đâm hachan, 424, 20. Tô đâm hlŷpgeate, 77, 16. On þ hlŷpiget; of þâm hlŷpgete, C. D. B. iii. 44, 20. On đæt ealde hlŷpgeat, C. D. iii. 406, 31.

**-hlíplíce.** v. stæþ-hlíplíce : **hlírian.** *Take here* **hlŷrian** *in Dict.* : **hlís[e].** v. uu-hlís[e].

**hlísa.** *Add :* **I.** in reference to persons. (1) where knowledge of a person's greatness is widespread, *fame :*—His hlísa âsprang tô Syrian lande, Hml. S. 16, 137. Âsprang his hlísa geond þâ land wíde, 26, 239. Gif hæleđa hwone hlísan lyste, Met. 10, 1. Sê þe wile wíslíce æfter þâm hlísan spyrian, þonne ongit he swiþe hraþe hū lytel hê biđ, Bt. 18, 1; F. 60, 28. Heora gemynd onweg gewât mid þâm myclan hlísan *the memory of them passed away along with the great fame* (? the Latin is: Periit memoria eorum *cum sonitu*), Ps. Th. 9, 7. Gê þone hlísan habban tiliađ ofer đióda mâ þonne eów þearf sié, Met. 10. 22. (2) where a certain character is attributed to a person, *reputation, repute :*— Sint tô manienne đâ đe yfel đegellíce dôđ and gôd openlíce, đæt hî geđencen hū hrædlíce se eorđlíca hlísa ofergêđ (*humana judicia quanta velocitate evolant*), Past. 447, 30. Gôd word and gôd hlísa ǽlces monnes biþ betera þonne ǽnig wêla, Bt. 13; F. 38, 23. Iôhannes wæs wanigende on his hlísan, for đan đe hê weard oncnâwen wítega, sê đe wæs lytle ǽr Crîst geteald, Hml. Th. i. 356, 35. Beó â getreówra đonne đe mon tô wêne, đŷ læs men wênan đæt đū nâne næbbe búton wiđ hlísan (*unless you get credit for it*), Prov. K. 76. Wilnigaþ monige men anwealdes đe hié woldon habban gôdne hlísan, þeáh hî his unwyrþe sién, Bt. 18, 1; F. 60. 26. ¶ used of the Deity, *glory :*—Næfre hlísan âh Meotud þan mâran þonne hê wiđ monna bearn wyrceđ welđædum *no more glorious attribute has the Maker than his mercy to man*, Az. 85. (2 a) where special characteristics are attributed, *reputation* (a) for something, the thing expressed (or implied) by a noun :— Hlísa *rumusculus* (*speciali castimonia*), An. Ox. 717. Hlíse singalre *opinio crebra* (*lectionis assiduitate*), 11, 162. Wilnung ungemetlices hlísan gôdra weorca. Bt. 18, 1; F. 60, 24. Hî willađ habban đone hlísan hâligdômes *odorem de se extendere sanctae opinionis quaerunt*, Past. 439, 34: Gû. 31. (β) of being or doing something, with clause :—His hlísa weóx . . . þæt hê sôđ God wæs, Hml. Th. i. 356, 33. Ne hê ne scrîfe đæs hlísan búton hū hê ryhtosđ wyrce, Past. 323, 17. For đâm gôdan hlísan (đæt hié gifule đyncen), 339, 25. Monige men noldan đone hlísan habban đæt hié unwíese sién, *nonnulli aestimari hebetes nolunt*, 67, 2. Monig mon dêđ micel fæsten, and hæfđ đone hlísan đæt hê hit dô for forhæfdnesse . . . monig biđ âgiéta his gôda, and wilnađ mid đŷ geearnigan đone hlísan đæt he sié rûmgiful *saepe sub parsimoniae nomine se tenacia palliat, contraque se effusio sub appellatione largitatis occultat*, 149, 4–8. Hê wæs . . . beorn bôca gleáw. Boitius se hæle hâtte, sê þone hlísan geþah, Met. 1, 53. Þone eádegan hlísan *faustam famam* (Ald. 161, 12), Wrt. Voc. ii. 92, 16: 37, 31. (3) *report* of those who no longer exist :—Hwæt is hiora here búton se hlísa ân?, Met. 10, 54. (4) *what is told* about a person :—Nis ús se hlísa tô forswigianne þe be đâm eádegan Gregorie đurh ealdra manna sage tô ús becôm *nec silentio praetereunda opinio, quae de beato Gregorio traditione maiorum ad nos usque perlata est*, Bd. 2, 1; Sch. 108, 20. **II.** in reference to a thing. (1) *fame* of something admirable or remarkable :—Se gesǽliga hlísa hire geornfulnesse *felix industriae eius rumor*, Bd. 4, 23; Sch. 472, 16. Hî þancunge dydon

for heora gemētinge. Þā āsprang se hlīsa (*the fame of this event*) geond ealne þone hīred, Hml. S. 30, 384. Þ tācnode þone hlýsan þǣre fǣmnan hālignysse, Shrn. 149, 3. Hī his wīsdōmes hlīsan healdaþ, Gū. 128. (2) *approbation, applause* :—Herelof, hlīsa *rumusculus* (*virtutum*), An. Ox. 456, 4. Hlīsena *rumorum*, i. *opinionum* (*integritatem immensis rumorum laudibus prosequitur*, Ald. 26, 7), 1918. Hlīsum *rumusculis* (*cujus vitam tantis opinionum rumusculis extollit*, Ald. 33, 29), 7, 150. v. mǣr-, un-, weorold-hlīsa.

**hlīs-bǣre.** For 'Som.' substitute :—Hlīsbǣre *rumigerula* (*meritorum gloria*), An. Ox. 2836 : *rumigerula*, i. *opiniosam*, 2, 112. v. un-hlīsbǣre.

**hlīs-eádig.** Add :—Se hlīseádgesta *opinatissimus*, Wrt. Voc. ii. 62, 64. v. un-hlīseádig.

**hlīs-ful.** Add : I. *famous* :—Sum wer wæs swýðe namcūð and hlīsful (*nominatissimus*) þurh his drohtnunga, Hml. A. 195, 15. Se seofoða heáfodleahter is gehāten īdel wuldor, þæt is gylp, þonne se man gewilnaþ þ hē hlīsful sȳ, Hml. Th. ii. 220, 28. Hlīsfulles *rumigerulę* (*Virginitatis gloriam*), An. Ox. 4397 : *famosae*, Hpt. Gl. 511, 23. Hlīsfulne sigor *famosum tropheum*, Wrt. Voc. ii. 147, 29. Þone hlīsfullestan *devulgatissimum*, i. *opinatissimum*, 139, 60. II. *of* (*good*) *repute, honourable* :—Hlīsful *favorabilis, laudabilis, famosus*, Wrt. Voc. ii. 147, 15. Wæs on þǣre byrig ān ǣnlic wimman (*Judith*) ... hlīsfull on þeáwum, rihtlīce lybbende, Hml. A. 108, 195. v. un-hlīsful.

**hlīsful-líce.** Add :—Iōhannes wæs ... ðæs folces heretoga and hī hlȳsfullíce geheóld wið þā hǣðenan ðeóda (cf. John ... and his wars and worthy deeds which he did, i. Macc. 16, 22), Hml. S. 25, 743.

**hlīsig** ; *adj. Famous* :—Hlīsies *famosae*, An. Ox. 8, 250. v. un-hlīsig.

**hlīt**, es ; *m.* (but in Ps. L. 30, 16 *the word seems feminine*). Take here hlēt, hlyt (*l.* hlȳt) *in Dict., and add* : I. *a lot* (*the object which is used*) :—*Cleros* an Crēcisc getācnaþ hlȳt an Englisc *cleros sors interpretatur*, Chrd. 75, 28. Ofer hrægl mīn sendon hlēt (hlȳt, Ps. L.) *super vestem meam miserunt sortem*, Ps. Vos. Srt. 21, 19. Hlētt, Mk. R. 15, 24. I a. *the urn in which the lots were placed* :—Hlēte *urna* (*matronam, quam suprema sors gemina mortis mulctaverat urna*, Ald. 25, 9), Hpt. Gl. 449, 58. II. *the casting of lots* :—Wiðercwidas ofðrect hlēt, and tōscēd *contradictiones comprimit sors, et* (*inter potentes*) *diiudicat*, Kent. Gl. 655. Be hlēte *sorte* (*territorii dirempta*), Hpt. Gl. 426, 42. Hlēte tōdǣlde him eorðan *sorte divisit eis terram*, Ps. Vos. Srt. 77, 54. III. *the share assigned to a person* :—Seó sāwel ðe bedǣled is þām gōdnyssum, heó gewilnige þæt se cystiga wealdend hī geðeóde þām hlȳte his gecorena, Hml. Th. i. 346, 29. Ne forlǣt Dryhten gird synfulra ofer hlēt (*sortem*) ryhtwīsra, Ps. Vos. Srt. 124, 3. IV. *lot, fate, fortune* :—Hē Mercna rīce twā and twēntig wintra missenlice hlēte (hlȳte, *v. l. varia sorte*) fore wæs, Bd. 2, 20 ; 184, 1. Þone hē gelīce hlēte (hlȳte, *v. l.*) genīðrade and ofslōh *Eanfridum simili sorte damnavit*, 3, 1 ; Sch. 192, 22. Nū syndon gesette þā apostolas in hlēt ǣ hié bodian *now are the apostles appointed to the task* (?) *of ever proclaiming her*, Bl. H. 157, 35. On handum þīnum hlȳta mīne *in manibus tuis sortes meae*, Ps. L. 30, 16. IV a. *of death* :—Þǣre ȳtemeste hlȳtes *sortis suppremę*, An. Ox. 2294. Þǣm ētemestan hlēte *suprema sorte*, Hpt. Gl. 453, 34. v. mid-hlīt ; hlyte.

**-hlīta.** [*O. H. Ger.* hlōzo *clerus*.] v. efen-, ge-hlīta : **-hlīte.** v. efen-hlīte.

**hlītere** (?), **hlytere** (?), es ; *m.* I. *one who casts lots.* v. tān-hlītere. II. *one who has a share of an inheritance* :—Hī preóstas an Crēcisc *clericos* [cf. Clericus, sors Dei (cf. Dominus est hereditas eorum (*the Levites*), Deut. 18, 2), Corp. Gl. H. 4, 61. Clericus, hereditas, sors, 32, 440] hātað, þ is an Englisc hlȳteras, Chrd. 75, 30. [Cf. *O. L. Ger.* eðan-hlōtere *consors*.]

**hlīþ.** Add :—Siððan þū gehȳrde on hlīðes ōran galan geác on bearwe, Bo. 21. Geworhton hī hlǣw on hlīðe, sē wæs ... wǣglīðendum wīde tō sȳne, B. 3158. Beorga hlīða (hlida, MS.) būgað and myltað (cf. ðā beorgas būgað and myltað, Wlfst. 137, 6) *colles liquescent*, Dōm. L. 101. Hliuða *scuporum*, Wrt. Voc. ii. 120, 37. Streámas weorpað on stealc hleoða stāne and sonde, Rä. 3, 7. Stealc hliðo stīgan, 88, 3. ¶ as the first part of compounds :—On þone hlíðwege, C. D. iii. 436, 25. Þis sint þā denstōwa ... hliþwīc, ii. 318, 30.

**hlīwan.** Take here hleówan *in Dict., and add* :—Hlȳwan *fouere*, An. Ox. 252. Uton hlȳwan ofcalene and wǣfan nacode and syllan mete þām gehingredum, Wlfst. 119, 6.

**hlīwe**, an ; *f. A shelter* (?) :—Tō ðǣre strǣt ; on ðā streátan hlȳwan ; of ðǣre hlȳwan, C. D. iii. 229, 28. Tō poshlīwan ; ðonne of poshlīwan, 82, 2. v. hleów.

**hlīwsian.** v. hleówsian.

**hlīwþ.** Take here hleówþ *in Dict., and add* :—God forgifð ūs mannum menigfealde wæstmas ... þ se līchama hæbbe hlȳwðe and fōdan, Hml. S. 11, 358. Hlȳwþa *caumene*, Wrt. Voc. ii. 130, 7.

**hlīwung**, e ; *f. Shelter, protection* :—Hlīwing *favor*, Wrt. Voc. ii. 147, 14. Sconde hlēwung *sive fraceþu ignominium*, 49, 30. Stōw gecwēme ... þæs fȳrhȳses hlȳwing winterlices cyles ... wiþerrǣdnes

sī gelȳht *locus aptus* ... *cuius caumene refugio hybernalis algoris* ... *aduersitas levigetur*, Angl. xiii. 397, 461. v. ge-hlīwung.

**hloccettan** (?) *to utter a sound, groan, sigh* :—Ic loccete (roketto, R.) deiglo *eructabo abscondita*, Mt. L. 13, 35. Loceteð *eructavit*, p. 9, 7. See next word, unless l is substituted for r ; see roc[c]ettan.

**hloccettung**, e ; *f. Sighing, groaning* :—Hloccetunge *gemitu*, Hpt. Gl. 421, 7. See preceding word.

**hlocian.** v. ā-hlocian : **hlom.** v. hland : **-hlóp.** v. brȳd-hlóp.

**hlóse**, an ; *f. A pigstye, lewze, looze* (v. D. D.) :—Swīna hlóse *ceni, luti* (the gloss seems to refer to the dirt of a pigstye ?), Wrt. Voc. ii. 130, 77. Fald weoxian, scipena behweorfan and hlōsan eác swā, Angl. ix. 261, 19. ¶ hlōs- occurs in a number of local names :—Oth hlōscumbes heáfud, C. D. B. ii. 392, 32. Ðis synt ðā denbǣra ... hlōsdionu, swānadionu ..., C. D. ii. 195, 16. On hlōshām sūewerdne, C. D. B. iii. 474, 34. (Cf. hlossanhām, C. D. iii. 377, 18.) Tō hlōshrycge, C. D. iii. 434, 15. Oþ hlōsleáge, Cht. Crw. 7, 48. On hlōsmoc, C. D. iii. 412, 25. On hlōsstedes crundles sūðecge, 465, 15. On hlōswuda middeweardne, v. 177, 28. Cf. centum viginti porcis ... in Hliossole et Ægelbertinherst, 88, 21.

**hlosnere.** Add : *a disciple* :—Gerysenlīce þās þing byð þām lāreów þ hē nā forhele his hlosnere þ riht þe on þām cræfte can, Angl. viii. 304, 22. Āblicgedum hlystendum and nitendum hlosnerum bemīþende *attonitis auditoribus et ignavis auscultatoribus* (*arcana mentis ipsorum*) *recludentes*, An. Ox. 2333. [Cf. *O. H. Ger.* hlosari *auditor, discipulus*.]

**hlosnian.** Add : I. *to listen with astonishment, listen spellbound* :—Hlosnendum *attonis* (l. *attonitis*, Ald. 32, 11, see An. Ox. 2333 under hlosnere), Wrt. Voc. ii. 79, 21. Tō hircniendum oððe hlosnendum *attonitis*, 2, 47. II. *to listen as an eavesdropper or spy* :—Gelamp hit þ sume hlosniende menn ðǣr betweónan eódon and þisra seofona georne hēddon, Hml. S. 23, 136. v. hlysnan.

**hlōs-stede**, es ; *m. A place where there is a pigstye* :—Tō litegan hlōsstede ; of litegan hlōsstede, C. D. vi. 153, 8. v. hlōs.

**hlot.** Add : I. *a lot that is cast* :—Hig wurpun hlotu (hlott, R.) *miserunt sortes*, Lk. 23, 34. Hȳ āsendan hlota ofer þā xii cyn Israhēla, Hml. A. 130, 456. I a. *the urn in which the lots are placed* (fig.) :—Hlote *urna*, An. Ox. 1838 (v. hlīt ; I a). I b. *the result determined by lot, the lot falls on a person* :—Ðā gefeóll þæt hlot ofer Jūdan cyn, Hml. A. 130, 457. II. *a casting of lots* :—Of hlotti (hlote, R.) eóde þte roecels gesette *sorte exiit ut incensum poneret*, Lk. L. 1, 9. Mið hlod *sorte*, p. 3, 4. Hǣdenscipe bið þ man mordweorc gefremme on ǣnige wīsan, oþþe on blōte (hlotæ, *v. l., which the old Latin version renders* in sorte ; *but the better reading seems to be* blōt. Cf. ǣnige hǣðenscipe oþþe on blōt oþþe on firhte, ii. 296, 25) oþþe on fyrhte, Ll. Th. i. 378, 22. III. *an allotted portion, a share, lot.* v. mans-lot :—On Fearnes felda gebyrað twēga manna hlot landes ... and þreóra manna hlot on Normantone ... and feówer manna hlot, C. D. B. iii. 230, 31-231, 2. Ne forlǣt Dryhten gyrde synfulra ofer hlot rihtwīsra (*super sortem iustorum*), Ps. L. 124, 3. III a. (*part or*) *lot* with another :—Gif þu nylt mē ofsleán, nafa þū nān hlot mid mē on heofena rīce, Hml. A. 180, 350. IV. *an allotted amount to be paid, lot* (*and scot*) :—Omnis Francigena qui tempore Eadwardi fuit in Anglia particeps consuetudinum Anglorum quod ipsi dicunt *an hlote et an scote*, Ll. Th. i. 491, 9. V. *lot, fate, fortune* :—Þām ytemestan hlote supprema sorte, An. Ox. 1990. v. ge-hlot, hwōn-hlotum.

**hlóþ.** Add : I. *prey* :—Tō hlóþe (hlōwe, MS.) ī reáfiáce *ad praedam*, Ps. Spl. T. 16, 13. [*O. L. Ger.* hlōtha *praeda*.] II. *a gang* :—Þeáh him feónda hlōð feorhcwealm bude, Gū. 887. Swylt ealle fornōm secga hlōðe and hine sylfne mid ... xxx and feówere ... mid hlāford, Jul. 676.

**hloþa.** v. loþa : **hlopere** *rhetor.* v. hleóþrere.

**hlóþere** *a robber.* For 'praedator' ... Lye' substitute :—Hlōþere praedo, Wrt. Voc. ii. 84, 43.

**hlōþian.** Add :—Hleóðedon, Bd. 1, 14 ; Sch. 38, 9 : **-hlōw**, es ; *n.* v. ge-hlōw : **-hlōw** ; *adj.* v. stefn-hlōw.

**hlōwan.** Dele passage from El. 54, for which see hleápan, and add : I. *of animals or uncertain* :—Gehlōw hlōwan *mugitum reboasse*, An. Ox. 1466. Hlōwende *mugitans* (*taurus*), 36, 12. Hlōwende, þutende *bombosa*, Wrt. Voc. ii. 126, 51. II. *of other things* :—Hlōwed *remugiet* (*totus mundus*, Ald. 65, 21), Wrt. Voc. ii. 86, 6. Ongeán hlēwþ, An. Ox. 4609. v. ā-hlōwan.

**hlōwung.** For 'Hlōweng ... Lye' substitute :—Hlōwung *balatus*, Wrt. Voc. ii. 125, 6. *Bombus* hlōwung *vel sorbellus, clamor tubis cyrm*, 126, 48. Hlōwengum *bombis* (aurea hunc *bombis* nascentem vacula (bacula, Giles ; but cf. aurea quadrupes, Ald. 20, 34) vatem signavit, Ald. 144, 6), 90, 6. Hlōwengum *vel* swoegum, 12, 8.

**hlúd.** Add : I. *of sound, voice, &c.* :—Hlúd herges cyrm, Exod. 107 : An. 1158. Þeódegsa bið hlúd gehȳred, cwāniendra cirm, Cri. 835. Swēg ... hlúd, 492. Se dyne becōm hlúd of heofonum, Sat. 467 : 607. Stefn æfter cwōm hlúd, An. 740. Hlúd bȳman stefn, Cri. 949. Hlúd wōp, 999. Hlúdan reorde, Ps. Th. 92, 4. Hē dreám gehȳrde hlúdne, B. 89. II. *of a person, noisy, talkative, clamorous* :—Hlúd

*garrula (mulier)*, Kent. Gl. 188 : *clamosa (mulier)*, 300. Wærwyrde sceal wísfæst hæle breóstum hycgan, nales breahtme hlúd, Fä. 58. Ne eom ic sylfa hlúd, Rä. 82, 1. **III.** of things. (1) of wind or water :— Winde gelícost þonne hē hlúd ástíged, El. 1273. Wæter hlúd and undióp, Past. 469, 6. Sió hlúde ýd on dǽre hreón sǽ, 437, 16. Ýþa hlúde, Ps. Th. 64, 7. (2) of material or instrument with which sound is made :—Þǽr bið hlúd wudu, Rä. 4, 24. Hlúdum *argutis (fidibus)*, An. Ox. 8, 309. Nǽfre mon þæs hlúde býman ábláwed dæt ne sý seó beorhte stefn hlúdre, Dóm. 1. (3) of action that makes a sound, e. g. *a blow, a crash :*—Heard gebrec hlúd unmǽte, Cri. 954. Se micla anweald dára yfelena gehríst swíþe fǽrlíce, swá swá great beám on wyda wyrcd hlúdne dynt donne men lǽst wénaþ, Bt. 38, 2 ; F. 198, 9. Sē bið swēga mǽst and gebreca hlúdast, Rä. 4, 40. v. ofer-, un-hlúd.

**hlúd-clipol.** *Add :*—Hē ná beó hlútclipol on stefne *non sit clamosus in voce*, R. Ben. I. 35, 11.

**hlúde.** *Add :*—Hlúdur *concisius*, Wrt. Voc. ii. 22, 29. **I.** with reference to the voice, with verbs of calling, speaking, laughing, &c. :— Ne hí on hracan áwiht hlúde ne cleopiad *non clamabunt in gutture suo*, Ps. Th. 134, 19. Hlúde cígan, cirman, styrman, Gen. 2908 : Jud. 270 : 223 : Ps. Th. 129, 6. Hlúde hlihhan, Hml. Th. ii. 350, 30 : Gen. 73. Hlúde reordian, El. 406. On lofsongum waldend hlúde hergan, Crä. 93. Clypiad gít hlúddor (hlúdor, *v. l.*), Hml. S. 18, 119. Hlúdor, Bl. H. 15, 22. **II.** cf. hlúd ; **III.** 1 :—Hwælmere hlúde grimmed, Rä. 3, 5. **III.** cf. hlúd ; **III.** 2 :—Dynedan scildas hlúde hlummon, Jud. 205. Frætwe míne swógead hlúde, Rä. 8, 7. Býman sungon hlúde, El. 110 : Dóm. 109. Hlúde hearpan stirgan, Cri. 669. **IV.** cf. hlúd ; **III.** 3 :—Biersted hlúde heáh hlódgecrod, Rä. 4, 62. v. ofer-hlúde.

**hlúd-ness**, e ; *f. Loudness, clamour :*—Clamor on Englisc ys hlúdnys, Angl. viii. 332, 3. [*O. H. Ger.* hlút-nussi *clangor.*]

**hlúd-stefn.** *Substitute :* hlúd-stefne (-stefn ?) ; *adj. Loud-voiced :*— (Seó ?) hlúdstefne býme *grandisona tuba*, Wrt. Voc. ii. 42, 41.

**hlúd-swēge.** *Add :*—Hē hlúdswēge (hlúdon swēge, *v. l.*) clypode swá swá leó grimmeted, Hml. S. 15, 188.

**hlutor.** *l.* hlútor, *and add :*—Hlútrae (-e) *liquentes*, Txts. 74, 578. Þá hlútresdan *limpidissimos*, Wrt. Voc. ii. 51, 38. **I.** of a liquid, *free from mixture or impurity* (lit. or fig.) :—Gif swá hlútor wæter tódñówed æfter feldum, Past. 469, 6. Éstfulle hlúttres wínes wista *delicatas defruti delicias*, An. Ox. 3167. Fram hlúttrum (þám hlútrum, Wrt. Voc. ii. 88, 41) wíne *a merulento temeto*, 5493. Rôd bestēmed heofoncyninges hlútran dreóre, Cri. 1087. Dá lāreówas drincad suíde hlúter (-or, *v. l.*) wæter *aquam limpidissimam pastores bibunt*, Past. 31, 4. Hlútru wín *merulenta defruta*, i. *pura uina*, An. Ox. 2649. Hlúterra wella wæter hí druncon, Bt. 15 ; F. 48, 12. Swín þe . . . nyllaþ hí áspyligan on hlúttrum wæterum, 37, 1 ; F. 192, 27. **II.** of air, weather, *clear, not cloudy :*—Þurh þá hlútran *per sudum*, Wrt. Voc. ii. 88, 64. **III.** of bright objects, *bright, shining, splendid, not dimmed* (lit. and fig.) :—Hlúttor (hlýttor, *clarus* hlútter, Hpt. Gl. 418, 18) *luculentus*, i. *splendidus (limpidissimi solis splendor)*, An. Ox. 494. Hlúttor heofones gim scíned, beód wolcen tówegen, Ph. 183. Hē scíned of his heáhsetle hlútran lēge, Cri. 1336. Geseón done hlúttran æwellm ðæs hēhstan gódes (*boni fontem visere lucidum*), and of hām selfum áweorpan dá diostro his módes, Bt. 35, 6 ; F. 166, 25. Hiofones leóhtes hlútre beorhto, Met. 21, 39. Mônan leóhte leóman . . . . hædre and hlútre, Az. 79. **III** a. *bright, untroubled, pure* joy, peace, &c. :—Kyning sceal on Drihtne clǽne blisse, hlúttre habban *rex laetabitur in Domino*, Ps. Th. 62, 9. On heofonríce hlútre dreámas ágan, Cri. 1246. **IV.** of (mental) vision, intellect. (1) *clear, having unobstructed sight :*—Mid hlútrum móde ongitan *pura mente cernere*, Bt. 39, 13 ; F. 232, 24. Gesíon mid hlúttrum eágum his módes, 34, 8 ; F. 146, 2. Þú scealt habban dínes módes eágan clǽne and hlúttre, 42 ; F. 256, 13. (2) *that is clearly seen or understood, freed from obscurity :* —Elucubratum, i. *meditatum, accensum, purum* hlútor, Wrt. Voc. ii. 143, 14. (2) *Of persons, splendid, glorious, illustrious, brilliant :*— Wæs hē on wordum hlúttor and scínende *sermone nitidus*, Bd. 5, 15 ; Sch. 651, 13. Freá, hlúttor heofones weard, Sch. 52. **V** a. *of personal attributes :*—Þín willa mid ús weorde gelǽsted on eardunge eordan ríces, swá hlúttor is in heofonwuldre gewlitegod, Hy. 6. 12. **VI.** *clear* from evil, guilt, deceit, &c., *pure, sincere :*—Þæt gebed sceal beón scort and hlúttur (*pura*), R. Ben. 45, 22. Ne him hlúttur gást on hracan eardad *neque est spiritus in ore ipsorum*, Ps. Th. 113, 16. Is mínre heortan hige hlúttor and clǽne, 72, 17. Hē hæfde hlúttre lufan, An. 1065. Hē þæt hlúttre mód in þæs gǽstes gód trymede, Gú. 77. Háligra hlúttre sáule, Az. 151. Mid clǽnre heortan and mid hlútrum gebedum, Bl. H. 81, 17. v. heáh-hlútor.

**hlútor-líce.** *Add :* **I.** *clearly, plainly, simply.* Cf. hlútor ; **IV :** Dis spell ic for þǽra hǽlo þe hit leornade odde gehýrde hlúttorlíce áwrát and sǽde *hanc historiam simpliciter ob salutem legentium siue audientium narrandam esse putaui*, Bd. 5, 13 ; Sch. 643, 5. Allum lútorlíce æteáwas *cunctis perspicue ostenditur*, Mt. p. 10, 8. **II.** *with sincerity.* Cf. hlútor ; **VI :**—Þǽr man cyrcean rǽre, þǽr mon Gode árwurdlíce and

hlúttorlíce (*with reverence and sincerity*) offrigean mæge, Ll. Th. ii. 408, 17.

**hlútorlíc-ness**, e ; *f. Sincerity, purity :*—Syþþan hí þá hlúttorlicnysse his módes and þá clǽnnysse his lífes ongeáton *probantes vitae illius sinceritatem et serenae mentis modestiam*, Guth. Gr. 111, 84.

**hlútor-ness.** *Add :* sincerity, simplicity :—Micle swýdor is tó hálsienne ealra gesceafta Drihten mid ealre eádmódnesse and mid ealre underþeódnesse and módes hlútternesse (*cum omni humilitate et puritatis devotione*) . . . Mid úre heortan hlútternesse (*puritate*) . . . úre gebeda beód andfenge, R. Ben. 45, 17–22. Seó eahtode miht is seó sóde eádmódnyss . . . mid módes hlúttornysse ; for dan sē de wís byd, ne wurd hē nǽfre módig, Hml. S. 16, 369.

**hlútre.** *Add : without trouble* (of rejoicing. Cf. hlútor ; **IV** a) :— Heorte hygeclǽne hlútre blissad (-iad, Th.) þám þe sódlíce sēcad Dryhten *laetetur cor quaerentium Dominum*, Ps. Th. 104, 3.

**hluttran.** *Dele :* hlúttran. *Add :* v. ge-hlúttrad ; hlýttrian.

**hlýd**, es ; *n.* l. *m., and add : noise, tumult :*—Druncennys is hlídes full *tumultuosa res est ebrietas*, Chrd. 73, 36.

**hlýd**, e ; *f. Rumour, noise made in discussing an event :*—Mardocheus weard þurh þá micclan hlýde cúd þám cyninge *the matter made such a great noise that Mordecai became known to the king*, Hml. A. 95, 120. [In Ps. Spl. T. 9, 7 *perhaps* hlydne *arises from confusion between* hlynne (v. hlyn) *and* hlýde.] [*O. H. Ger.* hlúti *sonus, sonitus, clangor*.]

**hlýda** *March. Add :* [v. *N. E. D.* lede.] v. hréþ-mónaþ : hlýda *a seat.* v. hlēda.

**hlýdan.** *Add :*—Hlýdad *strepunt*, Germ. 388, 14. **I.** of persons. (1) *to speak loud, cry aloud, chatter :*—Ic hlýde *garrio*, Wrt. Voc. ii. 41, 62. Hē ongan clypian and hlýdan *clamare coepit*, Bd. 3, 11 ; Sch. 240, 1. Þá ongan hē mid micelre stefne hlýdan (*perstrepere*), Gr. D. 64, 23. Sió hlýdende *garrula (pagina)*, Wrt. Voc. ii. 89, 5 : 40, 56. Hlýdendra *garrulorum (loquacitas)*, An. Ox. 5437. Hlýdendum *garrientibus*, 4195. (1 a) *with object :*—Stefn smoeda hlýded *vox canora concrepet*, Ps. Srt. ii. p. 202, 5. Hlýde *garriat* .i. *uociferet (eundem adisse)*, An. Ox. 1955. (2) *where there is disorderly conduct :*—Sē de wile drincan and dwǽslíce hlýdaþ, drince him æt hám, ná on Drihtnes húse, Hml. S. 13, 84. Hē onfēng þæs hlýdendan folces andgyte *tumultuantis turbae suscepit sensum*, Gr. D. 265, 6. Hlýdende menio *turbam tumultuantem*, An. Ox. 61, 7 : Wrt. Voc. ii. 72, 39. **II.** of animals :—Hlýdan *reboasse* (*aurea quadrupes mugitum reboasse* describitur, Ald. 20, 35), An. Ox. 11, 126. **III.** of things :—Píplic swegelhorna hlýdende blende *musica sambucorum (harmonia) persultans insonuerit*, An. Ox. 1646.

**hlýde**, an ; *f. A noisy brook* (? v. hlúd, *and* cf. hlyn, hlynn), *torrent :*—Andlang díc ; þ on hlýdan ; andlang hlýdan on brádan mór, C. D. B. ii. 374, 14. Andlang cumbes innan hlýdan ǽwylmas ; swá andlang hlýdan, C. D. v. 107, 13. In dá hlýdan ; of dǽre hlydan, iii. 80, 10 : 37. On þá hlýdan ; of dǽr hlýdan on þá stánbricge, 436, 26. Cf. (?) Andlang bróces on lýdeburnan, 396, 24. Andlang hlúdeburnan ; of hlúdeburnan. v. 358, 16. Cf. (?) Hí cómon tó Hlýdanford, Chr. 997 ; P. 131, n. 3. [*Loudwater* is a place-name in Buckinghamshire.]

**hlýde** *a seat.* v. hlēda : -hlýde. v. ofer-hlýde : hlýdend. *Dele, and see* hlýdan.

**hlýdig.** *Add :*—Wordig gehlýd odde hlýdig gewyrd *uerbosa garrulitas aut garrula uerbositas*, An. Ox. 1418.

**hlýding**, e ; *f. Clamour, cry, noise :*—Middum næht lýdeng (cirm ł cleopung, R.) geworden wæs *media nocte clamor factus est*, Mt. L. 25, 6. [*O. H. Ger.* hlútinga *harmonia*.] v. hlýdan.

**hlýd-mónaþ.** *Dele :* hlyn *a maple.* *Add* (Could this be the word which in M.E. becomes lyn in lyntre *tilia*, and later linn. v. *N. E. D.* linn, a linden or lime ?) :—Þǽr wæs hlin and ác. [*The metre might seem to require* hlin *or* hlinn, *but* hlin *perhaps is possible.* Cf. *such verss as :* Wæs hió hetegrim, Rä. 34, 5 : is þæs gores sunu, 41, 72.]

**hlyn[n].** *Add :*—Ðunorráda hlynn, Wlfst. 186. Mid hlynne *cum sonitu*, Ps. Rdr. 9, 7. Hlynnum *clangoribus* (cum tuba raucisonis reboat *clangoribus*, Ald. 146, 19), An. Ox. 17, 7.

**hlynian.** *The passage here may be taken under* hlynnan : **hlynn** *a torrent. Add :* [v. *N. E. D.* linn.]

**hlynnan.** *Add :*—Hlynþ *reboat*, Hy. S. 8, 13. Hlynde of heofone (Dryhten) *intonuit de celo Dominus*, Ps. Rdr. 17, 14. Hlende *insonuerit*, An. Ox. 1647. Scyl wæs hearpe, hlúde hlynede, Reim. 28. Gif þunorráde bid hlynende of eástdǽle, Archiv cxx. 47, 18.

**hlynsian.** *Add :*—Hlynsedan *tonant* (printed hlynredan *tomant*), Wrt. Voc. ii. 90, 44.

**hlýp.** v. hlíp : hlýpa. v. hlípe.

**hlysnan** *to listen, to listen with astonishment :*—Geheras ł lysnas *audite*, Mt. L. 13, 18. Hlysnende *adtonitus*, Wrt. Voc. ii. 99, 34· Hlysnende, áfyrhte *attoniti*, 101, 19. Hlysnendum, tó hircniendum *adtonitis*, 4, 45. Hlysnendi *arectas*, 101, 4. v. hlosnian.

**hlyst.** *Add :* **I.** *hearing* as one of the five senses, *faculty of hearing :*—Stemn is geslagen lyft gefrēdendlic on hlyste, Ælfc. Gr. Z.

4, 6. Ic syngode on gesihðe and on hlyste, eác on swæcce, on stence, and on hrepunge, Angl. xi. 112, 16. Hē his hlyst næfde, Hml. S. 21, 271. **II.** *the action of hearing, hearing* of something :—Hū ic þē mid hearpan hlyste cwēman mihte, Ps. Th. 91, 3. **III.** *the action of intent hearing, listening* :—Hē ābeád for þǽre duguðe deóp ǽrende ... hlyst wæs þǽr inne (*there was attentive hearing given*), Az. 169. Hlyst ȳst forgeaf, An. 1588. Þonne swīað hē and hlyst gefeð, Ph. 143.

**hlystan.** *Add:* **I.** *to pay attention with the ear to an utterance or a speaker* :—Cwæð Crīst tō him : ' Hlyst nū, Placida ; ic eom Crīst,' Hml. S. 30, 59. Ic sceal sprecan . . . hliste sē þe wille, Met. Einl. 10. **I a.** *of the regular attention of a learner* :—Ðē gedafenað tō lērenne and mē tō hlistenne, Solil. H. 32, 16. **II.** *to listen* to speech or speaker. (1) with gen. :—Wē byddað ðē þ þū hāte hyne cuman tōforan þȳnum dōmsetle, and hlyst hys worda, Nic. 2, 5. Ðā fundon hié hiene tōmiddes ðāra wietena . . . hlystende hiora worda *invenerunt illum in medio doctorum audientem illos*, Past. 385, 23. Seó mōdor sæt geornlíce hlystende hira tale, Hml. S. 30, 321. (1 a) *to listen as a learner, be a regular auditor* :—Hē hine þǽr āfēdde feówer geár . . . and hine sōhton þā crīstenan and his lāre hlyston, Hml. S. 22, 190. (1 b) *to give heed* to a person or to advice, *be persuaded to follow* :—Nȳd weorðeð 'niða bearnum tō helpe, gif hí his blystað ǽror, Rūn. 10. Hlest *ausculta* (*sermones meos*), Kent. Gl. 74. (2) with dat. or prep. (a) *of regular auditors* :—Sē ðe fundige wíslíce tō sprecanne, ondrǽde hé him ðȳ lǽs his sprǽc gescynde ðā ānmōdnesse ðǽra ðe ðærtō hlystað (*ne ejus eloquio audientium unitas confundatur*), Past. 93, 25 : 95, 20. Ne ic stæfcyste ne leornode, ne þǽfa nānum ne hlyste þe þā smeádon and ræddon, Hml. S. 23 b, 594. Bodian lāreówas godcunde þearfe, and ælc þ gescād wite hlyste him georne, Ll. Th. i. 424, 19. Hú hē lǽran mæge ðā ðe ðærtō hlystan willað, Past. 95, 22. (b) *to listen and be persuaded* :—Hlyst mínum rǽde gif ðū lufast megðhād, þ ðū gebūge mid biggengum tō þǽre gydenan Vesta, Hml. S. 7, 99. Sē ðe oferhogie þæt hē heom hlyste, Wlfst. 176, 27. v. ge-, under-hlystan.

**-hlyste.** v. ge-hlyste.

**hlystend.** *Add* :—Ǽr beó þū hlystend, syþþan lāreow *antea esto auditor, postea doctor*, Scint. 126, 1. Hlystendum *auditoribus*, i. *auscultoribus*, An. Ox. 2331. v. geleáf-, lār-, leáf-, tō-hlystend.

**-hlystfull.** v. ge-hlystfull : **hlystung.** v. under-hlystung : **hlyt.** v. hlīt.

**hlyta, hlytta.** *Add* :—Hlutan (*but* y *is written over* u) *sortilegos*, Txts. 97, 1886. [*The form here is peculiar,* hlotan *or* hlyttan *would seem the form to be expected. In* tān-hlyta *perhaps* tān-hlīta (cf. -hlīta) *might be read.*] v. ge-hlytta.

**hlyte,** es ; m. *A portion, lot, share* :—Hlyte *portio*, Wrt. Voc. ii. 117, 53. [*Icel.* hlutr.]

**-hlyte ;** *adj.* v. or-, wan-hlyte : **hlytere.** v. hlītere : **hlytm.** *Add* : v. un-hlytm.

**hlytman.** *to allot* (?) :—Wē sculon tilian þæt wē tō þām ēcan gefeán becuman mōton, þæt bið ælc man tō his yldrum hlytmeð(-ed?), Verc. Först. 167.

**-hlytto.** v. ge-hlytto : **hlȳttor.** v. hlūtor : **hlȳttrian.** *Add* : [O. H. Ger. hlūt[t]aren *clarere, clarificare*.] v. ā-, ge-, ofer-hlȳttr[i]an : **hlȳwan.** v. hlīwan : **-hnād.** v. ge-hnād.

**hnǽcan.** *Substitute* : **hnǽcan ;** *p.* te *To destroy, crush* :—Ic hnǽce (nǽce, v. l.) oððe ācwelle *neco,* Ælfc. Gr. Z. 138, 15. [Cf. (?) O. H. Ger. neihhan *immolare*.] v. ā-hnǽcan.

**hnǽgan** *to neigh. Add* :—Hnǽgende *frendens,* Wrt. Voc. ii. 150, 52.

**hnǽgan** *to bow. Add* : [O. L. Ger. hneigan *inclinare*.]

**hnǽgung.** *Add* :—Hnaeggiung *hinnitus*, Wrt. Voc. ii. 110, 40.

**hnæpf, hnæpp.** *l.* hnæpp, hnæpf (??), *and add* :—Steápes, hnæppes *poculi,* i. *calicis,* An. Ox. 1847. Se cyning genam þone hnæp (steáp, v. l. calicem) . . . þā se Godes wer onfēng þām hnæppe (steápe, v. l.), Gr. D. 186, 7–11. [Drinc ælce dæg fæstende nœpp fulne caldes, Lch. i. 374, 23. v. N. E. D. nap. O. L. Ger. napp *scyphus*.]

**-hnǽst, -hnǽstan.** v. ge-hnǽst, ge-hnǽstan.

**hnappian.** *Add* : *to sleep lightly or for a short time, get drowsy* :—Ic neapiu and gerestu *obdormiam et requiescam,* Ps. Srt. 4, 9. For hwí hnappas þū ł hwí slǽpst þū *quare obdormis*?, Ps. L. 43, 23. Gehwēde hneppast *paululum dormitabis,* Kent. Gl. 135. Þonne wē gebærað for ūre rēcelíesðe swelce wē hit nyten, ðonne hnappige wē. Ac ðonne wē slāpað fæste, ðonne . . ., Past. 195, 5. Ic hneappode and slēpan ongon *ego dormivi et somnum coepi,* Ps. Srt. 3, 6. Zosimus nænige þinga hnappode and geornlíce þ wēsten beheóld *Zosimus did not close an eye, and gazed earnestly on the desert,* Hml. S. 23 b, 666. Hí heom betweónan ān and hnappodon *one after another they got drowsy,* 23, 247. Ne hneppien *nec dormitent,* Kent. Gl. 126.

**hnappung.** *Add* :—Hnappung *dormitatio,* Wrt. Voc. ii. 141, 76. Hneappunge *dormitationem,* Ps. Srt. 131, 4.

**hnātan.** *Dele* : hneápan ; *p.* hneóp. v. ā-hneápan.

**hnecca.** *Add* :—Hnecca *occipitium,* Wrt. Voc. i. 282, 41 : *occiput,* ii. 63, 22 : *cervix, posteriora colli,* Txts. 110, 1165. Hnecca (snecca,

MS.) *occipitium,* 82, 720. 'Beſleh ǽrest ǽune þwang þām biscope fram þām hneccan oþ þone hōh (*a vertice usque ad calcaneum*) and him þ heáfod syþþan of āceorf' . . . Sume men gesetton þ ācorfene heáfod eft tō ðām sweóran (*cervici*), Gr. D. 198, 4–12. Sege him þ mē sȳ þ heáfod fram þām hneccan ācorfen, Ap. Th. 8, 17. Þæs hneccan āhylt eádmōdnyss *cuius ceruicem inclinat humilitas,* Scint. 20, 2. v. hracca.

**hnescan ;** *p.* te *To make soft* :—Hnesce *mulceat,* Wrt. Voc. ii. 57, 19. Þā mettas ðe gōd seáw wyrcen and wambe hnescen, Lch. ii. 226, 12. v. ge-, tō-hnescan ; hnescian.

**hnesce.** *Add* : **I.** *of material or its quality.* (1) *soft to the touch, yielding easily to pressure* :—Wē habbað hrepunge þæt wē magon gefrēdan hwæt bið heard, hwæt hnesce, Hml. Th. ii. 372, 32. Wæter wolde wīde tōscrīðan wāc and hnesce, Met. 20, 93. Þæt hnesce and flōwende wæter, Bt. 33, 4 ; F. 130, 3. Wring on hnesce wulle, Lch. i. 86, 3. Wyrce him hnesce bedd, iii. 112, 1. Næscum hrǽglum gegearwæd, Mt. R. 11, 8. Þ wæter and sió lyft bióþ hwēne hnescran gecynde ; hí bióþ swíþe eáþe tō tōdǽlenne, 34, 11 ; F. 150, 27. Eóde heó onuppan þā hnescan ȳþa, Hml. S. 23 b, 684. ¶ figuratively used :—Ðæt hí āfeóllen on ðæt hnesce bedd ðæs gesinscipes, næs on ðā heardan eorðan ðæs unryhthǽmdes, Past. 397, 22. (2) *soft, tender* (of young growth) :—Telge his hnesc bið, Mt. L. 24, 32. Telge his nesc bið (telgu his hnisca bióðon, R.), Mk. L. 13, 28. (3) *yielding easily to force* :—Þæt mon heardlíce gníde þone hnescestan mealmstān, Ors. 4, 13 ; S. 212, 28. **II.** *of movement, action, soft, gentle* :—Hnescum fealle *guttatim,* Hpt. Gl. 408, 33. **III.** *of condition, soft, free from hardship* :—Tō hnesscere wununge *ad mollem sinum,* Germ. 400, 500. **IV.** *lacking in energy* :—Ðone hnescan ðafettere, Past. 453, 25. **V.** *tender, gentle* :—Lufu, næs tō hnesce, Past. 127, 2. Hnesce andswore *responsio mollis,* Kent. Gl. 502. **VI.** *yielding to temptation, inclined to wantonness, effeminate* :—Se ōðer heáfodleahter is gecweden forliger oððe gālnyss, þæt is þæt se man sȳ hnesce on mōde tō flǽsclicum lustum, Hml. Th. ii. 220, 4. **VII.** *unable to endure hardship, &c.* :—Hwilc sió gecynd siě þæs líchoman, hwæþer hió sié strang þe heard and eáþelíce mæge þā strangan lǽcedōmas āberan, þe hió sié hnesce and mearwe and þynne and ne mæge āberan þā lǽcedōmas, Lch. ii. 84, 13.

**hnesce ;** *n. What is soft* :—For gehwæt heardes oððe hnesces, wætes oððe dríges, Angl. xi. 98, 53 : Wlfst. 184, 20. Næscum gegearwode *mollibus vestiti,* Mt. R. 11, 8. v. heard ; *n.*

**hnesce ;** *adv. Softly* :—Ic eom hnesce understreówod, Hml. S. 37, 201.

**hnescian.** *Add* : **I.** *intrans. To become soft* :—Wylle ealle ðas rinda on hāligwætere oð ðæt hȳ wel hnexian, Lch. iii. 14, 6. **II.** *trans. To make soft* :—Sió hnescað *que mollit* (*sermones suos*), Kent. Gl. 25. [v. N. E. D. nesh, vb.] v. ge-hnescian ; hnescan.

**hnesc-ness.** *Add* :—Mið hnescnissum gewēded *mollibus vestitum,* Mt. L. 11, 8.

**hnifol.** *Add* : , hneofola (-e?) :—Hnifol oððe foreweard heáfod *frons,* Wrt. Voc. ii. 36, 45. Onsíðn hiora ondwlita ł hnioful (h *over* n) monnes *vultus eorum facies hominis,* Mt. p. 9, 11. Hneofulan (heofulan, v. l. heafolan, lxxiv, 4) *fronti,* Lch. i. lxx, 3.

**hnifol-crumb.** *Substitute : with the face bent downwards* :—Hnifolcrump, gebíged *cernua curvaque* (cf. *cernua curvaque vetustas,* Ald. 18, 17), Wrt. Voc. ii. 23, 46, 47. Nióle oððe hnifolcrumbe *cernuas,* 18, 42.

**hnigan.** *Add* : **I.** *to bend* from an upright position :—Hnāg ic (*the cross*) þām secgum tō handa, Kr. 59. Āsitte hē þonne ūplang, hnīge þonne forð, Lch. iii. 2, 12. **I a.** *to bend* in reverence, *make obeisance* :—Heó hnāh ādūne tō Sebastianes fōtum, Hml. S. 5, 92. Tō ðām æðelan hnigan him sanctas, Sat. 240. Hí feóllan on foldan, and tō fōtum hnigon, 533. **II.** *to sink to a lower position,* Rä. 4, 63: Sat. 375 (*in Dict.*). *See next word.*

**hnigian.** *In* l. 2 *after* hnigie *add* forð.

**hnīpan** (?) *to bow, bend the head* :—Āsige ł hnípte (hnimpte, An. Ox. 1579) *procumberet, caderet,* Hpt. Gl. 443, 50. Hnípendre (hnipendre = hnipiendre?) *curua,* An. Ox. 1279. Hnipenre *cernua,* Hpt. Gl. 436, 61. [*In support of this form might be cited the Icel.* hnípa ; *p.* hnípti ; *pp.* hnipinn, *where trace of the strong conjugation remains only in past participle, and such a pair of strong and weak verbs as* hnīgan, hnigian. *But more probably the past tense* hnípte *may be assigned to a weak* hnippan, *and the two participles to* hnipian.]

**hnipend.** *Dele, and see* hnīpan, hnipian.

**hnipian.** *Add* :—Hē nyste hwæt hē cweðan sceolde, ac stōd þǽr and hnipode (*hung his head*), Hml. S. 23, 689. Hí hnappodon and swā lange hí hnipedon (*they drooped their heads so long*) þ hí ealle on slǽpe wurdon, 23, 248. Sete þū þíne hand on þín heáfod foran, and hwōn hnipa (*printed* hniwa) swilce þū þē forgyfenesse bidde, Tech. ii. 122, 5. Hnipendre, gebígedre *curua,* An. Ox. 1279. Hnipen[d]re *cernua,* Hpt. Gl. 436, 61. Bitere teáras hí symle ālēton and hnipiende eódon, Hml. S. 23, 46. v. hnīpan.

**hnippan.** v. hnīpan.

**hnītan.** *Add:* I. *of an animal, to gore:*—Ān þearle wōd cū hnāt yfele ǣlcne þe heó gemǣtte, Hml. S. 31, 1042. II. *of things:*—þonne cumbol hneotan, An. 4.

**hnitu.** *Add:*—Hnitu *lendina,* Txts. 74, 590 : Wrt. Voc. ii. 50, 70 : *ascarida,* 8, 56. v. sweór-hnitu.

**hnoc.** v. gadinca. [Cf. (?) *D. D.* nocky *a simpleton.*]

**hnol.** *Add:*—Hnoll *cervix,* Wrt. Voc. i. 64, 66. Men gesāwon scīnan æt his hnolle (cf. bufan his heáfde, Hml. S. 31, 937) swilce fýren clýwen, Hml. Th. ii. 514, 2. Hnoll *gygram,* Lch. i. lxix, 9. Hē forcyrfð hnollas (*ceruices*) synfulra, Ps. L. 128, 4.

**hnoppa.** *Add:* v. wull-hnoppa, *and next word.*

**hnoppian** *to pluck:*—Hnoppian *vellere* (Mt. 12, 1), Wrt. Voc. ii. 72, 57. [*N. E. D.* nap; *vb.*]

**hnossian.** *Add:* cf. ge-hnyssan.

**hnot.** *Add:* I. *of animals, without horns, that has lost a horn:*—Hnot *mutilum,* hnottum *mutilatis,* Wrt. Voc. ii. 56, 16, 17. [*Perhaps* hnoc (*q. v.*) *should be read* hnot, *and taken here.*] II. *of trees, cropped, pollarded :*—Tō ðām hnottan stocce (cf. Usque la notte stokke, iii. 374, 6), C. D. v. 303, 3. On þone hnottan þorn, 289, 1. III. *cleared of bushes* (?) :—On hnottan ford, C. D. iii. 25, 23. On hnottan mǣræ norðæweardna, v. 112, 27. [v. *N. E. D.* not. *D. D.* not (*of a field*) *smooth, well-tilled.*]

**hnut-beám.** *Add:*—Hnutbeám *nux,* Wrt. Voc. ii. 115, 4. Hnut-beám oððe walhhnutu, 60, 23.

**hnut-scill**(?), e; *f. A nut-shell. Perhaps the word may be inferred from the form* hnutscyllingas *in* hnutscyllinga mearc, C. D. iv. 105, 5.

**hnutu.** *Add: gen. dat.* hnyte. v. pīn-hnutu :—Hnutu *avilina,* Wrt. Voc. i. 285, 25 : *abilina,* ii. 4, 9. Nyte *ficos,* Mt. R. 7, 16. ¶ *the form* hnut- *is found in many local names :*—On hnutclyf, C. D. iii. 48, 6. In hnutfen, v. 126, 32. Aet Hnuthyrste, i. 63, 5. On hnutleáge, v. 207, 20. Tō hnutstede, iii. 275, 8. On hnutwīc, 176, 17. v. eorþ-, wealh-hnutu.

**-hnycned.** v. ge-hnycned : **hnydele.** v. hydele.

**hnygela.** *Add:*—Hniglan *putamine* (*stuppae,* Ald. 51, 23), Wrt. Voc. ii. 83, 17 : An. Ox. 7, 267. Of hnīlan, Angl. xiii. 35, 206. Æcemban hniglan *stuparum putamina* (Ald. 45, 11), Wrt. Voc. ii. 82, 16. Hnyglan, 118, 36. Þā hnyglan, 66, 60. Hnīlan, Hpt. 33, 239, 17.

**hnȳlung.** v. hlinung : **-hnyscan** *to crush.* v. ge-hnyscan : **-hnyscan** (= -hyscan). v. ā-, on-hnyscan, -hyscan : **-hnyssan, -hnyst.** v. ge-hnyssan.

**hoc.** *Add:*—Hocc, cottuc *vel* gearwan leáf *malva,* Wrt. Voc. ii. 113, 62. Hoc, 56, 36.

**hōc.** *Add:* I. *a hook* at the end of a pole, chain, &c. for catching hold, dragging, &c. (lit. or fig.):—Manna heortan þe beóð ðurh un-rihtwīsnysse hōcas āwegde, Hml. Th. i. 362, 27. v. tyge-, web-, wīngeard-hōc. II. *a fish-hook* :—Hōc *hamus,* Wrt. Voc. ii. 43, 36. Sende ongul ł hōc (hōc ðīn, R.) *mitte chamum,* Mt. L. 17, 27. III. *a curved implement* :—Hōce *cauterio* (torrido dogmatum cauterio, Ald. 26, 34), Wrt. Voc. ii. 78, 54 : 18, 13. v. weód-hōc; hōc-īsern. IV. *bent timber used in shipbuilding* (?) [v. *N. E. D.* hook; 8] :—Hōcas *uncini,* spreotas *trudes,* Wrt. Voc. i. 57, 15. Þoll *scalmus,* bord *tabule,* hōcas *uncinos* (v. Wülck. Gl. 289, 11), 63, 81 (both glosses occur in lists of words connected with ships). V. *a sharp bend or angle in the length of anything.* v. hōced :—Tō ginum hōcum, C. D. iii. 413, 10. Swā tō weáwan hōcan, v. 207, 26.

**hōced.** *Add:*—On ðā hōcedan dīc; of þǣre hōcedan dīc, C. D. B. ii. 260, 36 : C. D. vi. 30, 5. v. hōc; V.

**hocg.** v. hogg.

**hociht** *full of mallows. l.* hōciht(e) *having many bends, and add :*—On ðā olde lake tō hōctan ýðe, C. D. vi. 227, 9. v. hōced. [*For* ii *in* l. 3 *read* iii.]

**hōc-īsern,** es; *n. A reaping-hook, sickle:*—Hōcīsern *falcicula,* Wrt. Voc. ii. 146, 78. v. hōc; III.

**hoc-leáf.** *Add:*—Hocleáf *malva,* Wrt. Voc. ii. 56, 35. Hocleáfa *maluarum,* An. Ox. 97.

**hōcor.** *l.* (?) hocor. [v. *N. E. D.* hoker.]

**hōd.** *For* 'Cot. 31, Lye' *substitute* :—Hood *capitium,* Wrt. Voc. ii. 102, 65. Hōd, 128, 49 : 13, 22. Ðonne þū cuglan habban wylle, þonne wege þū þīnne earmellan and fōh tō þīnum hōde, Tech. ii. 127, 17. Nim þū þē be þīnum hōde, 129, 4. Gif hē godspel rǣde lecge him þæne hōd ofer þā sculdra *si evangelium legit, cucullum vel cappam super humeros dejiciat,* Ll. Th. ii. 140, 25.

**hof.** *Add: a temple:*—Hof *sacellum, templum,* Germ. 391, 21. On hāligum hofe þīnum *in sanctuario tuo,* Ang.. xi. 118, 50. Hofa *edes,* i. *templum,* Wrt. Voc. ii. 142, 32. v. cyne-, dim-hof.

**hōf.** *Add:*—Befealdende hōfringas (= hōf-hringas) hōfum *inplicans orbes orbibus* (Ald. 2, 36), An. Ox. 19.

**-hōf.** v. be-hōf.

**hofer.** *Dele* '[?]', *and add :*—Hofr *gibbus,* Txts. 64, 459. Horer, ofer *tuber,* 103, 2074. Wæs sum earm ceorl egeslīce gehoferod and ðearle gebīged þurh ðone brādan hofor . . . Hē wearð gehǣled . . . swā þ næs gesýne on his hricge hwǣr se hofor stōde, Hml. S. 21, 95-106.

**hoferede.** *Add:*—Hoferede *gibbus,* Wrt. Voc. ii. 41, 12. *See next word.*

**hoferian** *to be humpbacked :*—Houeriendne (hoferiiendne, An. Ox. 3662) *gibbum,* Hpt. Gl. 492, 40. Hoferedne *cyppum* (= *gibbum,* Ald. 50, 21, the passage to which this and the preceding gloss belong), Wrt. Voc. ii. 82, 78. v. ge-hoferod, hoferede.

**hoffingas.** *Substitute:* **hōf-hring,** es; *m. The circle described by the horse's feet.* v. hōf, hōh-hwirfing.

**hōfian** (?) *to need :*—Sē ðe lǣs hōfad (behōfað?) *qui minus indiget,* R. Ben. I. 64, 14. v. be-hōfian.

**hof-lic;** *adj. Pertaining to a court or palace :*—Tō hoflican geseton *ad palatinas zetas,* An. Ox. 2996.

**-hōflic.** v. be-hōflic : **-hōfod.** v. ge-hōfod : **hofoton?** :—Tō cwenn hofoton ; of cwenn hofoton, Cht. E. 248, 17 : **hōf-ring.** v. hoffingas : **hof-pela.** *Dele, and see* þyle : **hoga.** *Add:* v. ofer-, un-, wan-hoga.

**hoga** *care. Substitute: effort:*—Hogan *conamine,* An. Ox. 8, 283. v. ymb-hoga.

**hogcende.** v. hogian : **-hogd, -hogdlīce, -hogdnes.** v. for-hogd, for-hogdlīce, for-hogdness.

**hogg, hocg,** es; *m. A hog:*—.xx. sugena . . . swýn, and .xl. hogga . . . xliiij hogga, Cam. Phil. Soc. 1902, p. 15. Cf. Ðæs landes æt Hocgestūne, C. D. iii. 294, 22. Ðǣs dæn wæs Hocgetwisla, Lindhyrst, vi. 243, 16.

**hogian.** *Add:* I. *to think, have such and such thoughts :*—Gif ne eaðmōdlīce ic hogade *si non humiliter sentiebam,* Ps. Srt. 130, 2. I a. *with an object, to have as an object of thought :*—Gē on heortan hogedon inwit, Ps. Th. 57, 2. II. *to be wise, prudent,* &c. :—Ne hogedon ongeatan *non sapuerunt intellegere,* Ps. Srt. ii. p. 195, 1. Dysge hwīlum hogiað *stulti aliquando sapite,* 93, 8. III. *to think about, employ thought* about a matter :—Þū tō lyt hogedest ymbe þone ende þīnes līfes, Wlfst. 260, 20. Hē lithwōn hogode embe his sāwle þearfe, Hml. S. 26, 243. Seó burhwaru orsorhlīce wæs underðeódd flǣsclicum lustum, and hwōnlīce hogode ymbe ðā tōweardan yrmða, Hml. Th. i. 404, 32. Hwilce mēde hæfde hē for þām þ hē swā holdlīce hogode embe mē? *quid pro hac fide praemii consecutus est?*, Hml. A. 98, 218. IV. *to take thought* in order to do something, *busy oneself:*—Reáðre deáge ceácan on heore wīsan deágian hogaþ *rubro stibio mandibulos suatim fucare satagit,* An. Ox. 1209. Hogiaþ *satagunt* (*ornamentis vestium decorari*), 5121. Mid ðām þe ic hogede helpan þīnum wīfe *while I was busy trying to help your wife,* Hml. S. 36, 363. Hogede *satageret,* An. Ox. 4218. V. *to take heed, take care* to secure a result :—Hogode *curauit* (*pastor et foeminas prohibere*), An. Ox. 5160. Nū sceole wē hogian mid mycelre gýmene þ ūre līf beó swā gelōgod þ ūre ende endige on God, Hml. S. 16, 5. Wē sceolon carfullīce hogian þæt wē tō ðǣre ēcan freólstīde becumon, Hml. Th. i. 548, 4. VI. *to have anxious thought, be anxious, troubled :*—Hē swīðe hogað and geómerað hine swā gebundenne *ligatum se uehementer ingemiscat,* Bd. 1, 27 ; Sch. 97, 21. Hī ne hogodon nā þeáh hī eallunga hyre sāwle ādwǣscton, Gr. D. 73, 18. Se apostol hogiende and geómriende cwæð *gemebat dicens,* Bd. I. 27 ; Sch. 98, 4. VII. *where thought implies intention, purpose, endeavour.* v. hogung :—Hogiende (? *printed* hogcende) *imminens,* Germ. 392, 41. (1) *with acc. :*—Gif þæt mōd mid ðwyrlicum geðōhtum hogað ōðrum dara, Hml. Th. i. 412, 28. Hogiende, serwiende *molientes* (*aliud argumenti genus*), An. Ox. 2939. (2) *with infin. :*—þ þ ofer byð ic hohgie gedēlan, Solil. H. 35, 19. Snytrian hog[iað], menegiaþ *philosophari decreuimus,* An. Ox. 5393. Hogode *moliretur* (*euertere*), 3446. Wæccum hoga gehēodan fæstenu *uigiliis stude copulare ieiunia,* Scint. 55, 10. Hogige ælmyssan syllan *studeat eleemosynam dare,* 110, 1. Hogede leoþewǣcan *mitigare niteretur,* An. Ox. 3803 : *moliretur,* 4230. (3) *with clause :*—Gefirn ic hyt hohgode þ ic hine sceolde forseón, Solil. H. 35, 12. Ic hohggode þ ic scolde nān habban, 36, 10. Ic on mōde mīnum hogade þæt ic wolde tōworpan bearn Hēlendes, Sat. 84. Hogien[dum] *nitentibus* (*ut . . .*), An. Ox. 4374. (4) *with preposition :*—Hī on heortan hogedon tō nīðe, Ps. Th. 77, 20. Hī tō swice hogedon, 82, 3. [v. *N. E. D.* how, howe.]

**-hogiend.** v. for-, ofer-hogiend : **-hogiendlic :** -hogendlic. v. for-hogiendlic : **-hogness.** v. for-hogness : **-hogod.** v. ā-, for-hogod : **-hogodlīc.** v. for-hogodlīc : **-hogodness.** v. for-, ofer-hogodness.

**hogu.** *Add:*—Studium *vel medecina, curatio vel* lācnung *vel* gýmen *vel* hogu, Wrt. Voc. ii. 137, 59. Gif hē ongyt þæt eal his hogu and gleáwscipe nāht framað *si viderit nihil suam prevalere industriam,* R. Ben. 52, 14. Sý seó mǣste hogu þǣm abbode þæt hý forgýmeleásede ne sýn *cura maxima sit abbati ne aliquam negligentiam patiantur,* 60, 18. Beó ðām abbode seó mǣste hogu (*cura*) þæs andfencges þearfena, 84, 1. Þæt hý būtan hoge and care sýn ealra þinga þe tō heora līchoman belimpeð *ut neminem illorum cura sui corporis tangat,* 137, 18.

[Dryhten] hoge hæfð *Dominus curam habet mei*, Ps. Rdr. 39, 18. Hýrað mid ege, and gladiað mid hogum (*exultate cum tremore*), Chrd. 33, 16. [v. *N. E. D.* how, howe.]

**hogung.** *Substitute: effort, endeavour.* v. hogian; **VII** :—Mid hogungum eallum uton biddan ealle þæne Ælmihtigan *nisibus totis rogitemus omnes cunctipotentem*, Hy. S. 8, 23. v. for-hogung.

**hóh** *a heel. Add* :—Befieh ænne þwang þám biscope fram þám hneccan oþ þone hóh (*calcaneum*), Gr. D. 198, 5, 9. Fyrsnum, hóum *calcibus*, Wrt. Voc. ii. 127, 48. [v. *N. E. D.* hough.] *See next word.*

**hóh** (*applied to land*). *Add: a promontory* :—Hooh *promontorium*, Hpt. 33, 251, 21. Hóg, III, 4. Tó ðám hó; of ðám hó á be wuda tó ðám æsc, C. D. iii. 79, 9–10. Tó micle hóh; fram micle hóhe tó middelhille, 71, 33. On Healdenes hó; of ðám hó, vi. 100, 10. On þone hó foreweardne, v. 381, 27. ¶ the word occurs mostly in local names, from one of which (Clofes-hóh) the declension may be shewn :—Seó stów is nemned Clofeshooh (-hóh, *v. l.*) *locus appellatur Clofeshoch*, Bd. 4, 5; Sch. 378, 12. Clofeshóh, C. D. i. 227, 8. Cloueshó, v. 58, 9. Apud Cloueshó, 59, 22 : i. 105, 5. Æt Clofeshoo (-hó, *v. l.*), Chr. 822; P. 60, 9. On ðære mæran stówe ðe mon háteð Clofeshóas, C. D. i. 278, 29 : 201, 5 : 204, 16 : v. 66, 25. Clofeshós, i. 222, 6. Txts. 432, 14. Æt Clofeshóum, C. D. i. 223, 9 : 280, 5. *Other instances of the occurrence of the form are* :—In regione qui uocatur Hóhg, C. D. i. 102, 8. Hóhtún, v. 33, 8. Æt Cægeshó, i. 197, 23. Þ is fingringahó, iii. 274, 8 : 272, 11. Hwítingahó, 275, 8. On lindhóh ; of lindhó, 76, 34. De Poddenhó, 376, 32. In Strengeshó, 375, 24. Þurh Wippan hóh, vi. 234, 3. [v. *N. E. D.* hoe.]

**hoh-fæst.** *Add* : cf. hyge-fæst.

**hoh-full.** *Add* : **I.** *careful, that takes care or pains* :—Emhýdi, hohful *zelotypus*, An. Ox. 2277. Hé sí gewordan hohful *reddatur de suis ratiociniis sollicitus*, R. Ben. I. 17, 7. Hohfullum (carefullan, R. Ben. 72, 12) bréðer betæce þás gímene *solicito fratri injungat hanc curam*, 80, 15. **II.** *thoughtful, prudent* :—Sum sácerd . . . hohful on móde (cf. *edoctus monitis*, Vit. Cuth. poet. c. 30), Hml. Th. ii. 152, 6. **III.** *anxious, troubled* :—Hé bið oððe untrum oððe hohful, Hml. S. 12, 84 : Wlfst. 142, 6. Ne beó ðú hohful, lá wíf, þín sunu leofað, 152, 19. Hé ða swíðe hohful weard and feól tó his fótum fíówendum teárum (cf. *provolutus ejus pedibus fusis cum gemitu lacrimis*, Vit. Cuth. c. 28), Hml. Th. ii. 152, 10. Nelle þú leng beón hohful be þínre dehter, Hml. S. 33, 290. **IV.** *denoting anxiety* :—Æmtig wamb and gyrla hohfull Drihten bitt *inanis uenter et habitus luctuosus Dominum deprecatur*, Scint. 43, 5. **V.** *persistent, persevering.* Cf. hogian; **VII** :—Þá þá se munuc lange þurhwunode on þære ánwilnysse, þá cwæð se hálga tó þám hohfullum munece, Hml. S. 31, 1084.

**hohful-ness.** *Add* : **I.** *solicitude, care* :—Hohfulnesse be þingum gewítendlicum *sollicitudinem de rebus transitoriis*, R. Ben. I. 16, 10. Þurh médderne hohful[nesse] *per maternam sollicitudinem*, Hpt. Gl. 404, 72. **II.** *trouble, sadness, anxiety* :—Þá eahta leahtras . . . hohfulnes (cf. se fífta leahtor is *tristitia*, þ is þissere worulde unrótnyss, Hml. S. 16, 289), Wlfst. 188, 37.

**hóh-hwyrfing.** *l.* -hwirfing, *and add* :—Hringa hóhhwerfinge *orbes orbibus*, Wrt. Voc. ii. 75, 6. Hóhhwyrfinge, 64, 21. v. hóf.

**hohinge-ród.** *Substitute* : **hóhing,** e; *f. Hanging* :—Ðú for hæle cynnes mennisces róde hóhinge þe þoludest *pro salute generis humani crucis patibulum pertulisti*, W. Cat. 294, 12.

**hoh-mód.** *Add* :—Sé ðe wære hohmód, weorðe sé glædmód, Wlfst. 72, 8.

**-hohsnian.** v. on-hohsnian : **hó-hylde.** v. ó-heald, -hilde.

**hol** *a hole. Add: and* holl. [*It is not always possible to distinguish between forms that belong to* hol *and those that belong to* holh; *some of those here given to the former may belong to the latter.*] **I.** *a cave, pit, deep place in water* :—Hool *vorago*, Wrt. Voc. ii. 124, 13. Hol *cava* (*or adj.?*), 129, 63. Hola *speleo, spelunca*, An. Ox. 2047. Holum *caverniculis*, Wrt. Voc. ii. 103, 32 : 13, 59 : *cavernis*, 22, 11. On holum *in antris*, 46, 4. Þá iermingas út of þæm holan crupon þe heó on lutedan, Ors. 2, 8; S. 92, 30. Holu *cavernas*, Wrt. Voc. ii. 103, 52 : 129, 66. Seó grundleáse swelgend hæþ manegu wéste holu on tó gadrianne, Bt. 7, 4; F. 22, 33. ¶ the word occurs in local names :—Bulan hol, C. D. v. 43, 8. Of ðære stánhlæwe innan ðan hwítan hole; of ðám hwítan hole intó ðám reádan hole; of ðám reádan hole intó ðám dunnan hole; of ðám dunnan hole, 253, 1–4. On ðá æaldan hola; of ðám holum, 112, 34. Haec sunt nomina pastuum porcorum . . . Húnbealding hola, i. 258, 10. **I a.** *a hole made to live in by an animal, burrow* :—Of oteres hole, C. D. iii. 418, 17. Foxas holas (holo, R.) habbað *uulpes foueas habent*, Lk. L. 9, 58. Holo, p. 6, 12. **II.** *a den used to keep animals in* :—Hola *cabearum* (patefactis *cavearum clustellis*, Ald. 49, 3), An. Ox. 3560. **III.** *an aperture passing through anything; a pore* :—Hol *spiramentum*, Wrt. Voc. ii. 121, 6. v. brocc-, fox-, lifer-, stán-, wulf-hol; holh.

**hol** *a covering. Add* :—Mt. L. 5, 18 *has* stæfes heáfod.

**hol** *hollow. Add* :—Hol *cava* (*or under* hol *a hole?*), Wrt. Voc. ii.

---

129, 63. Holum *cavo*, 21, 60. **I.** *having a void space within* :—Ræsde án næddre of holum treówe, Shrn. 144, 27. Þú nymst ánne holne hláf (*a loaf with the crumb taken out?*) *tolles tortam panis unius crustulam*, Ex. 29, 23. Séc án hol treów (*cavam arborem*) and bring mé þá hrægl þe þú þær inne finde, Gr. D. 202, 23. Befieáh hé in sum hol treów and hine sylfne áhýdde, 293, 14. On þone holan æsc, C. D. B. ii. 247, 4. Leápas hole (*c?*)*orbes cauatos*, Germ. 396, 146. **II.** *having a cavity or depression in the surface* :—Holan beorges burna, C. D. i. 317, 19. Mín þegn funde wæter in ánum holan stáne (*in lapide concauo*), Nar. 8, 3. Fram kincges stáne úp tó holan stáne, C. D. v. 111, 2. **III.** *concave, arched* :—Holum stánum *fornicibus*, Wrt. Voc. ii. 40, 5. **IV.** *deeply excavated or depressed*, of a valley, road, &c. :—Tó ðám holan móre; andlang ðæs holan móres, C. D. B. ii. 247, 1. Æt holan cumbe, C. D. iii. 327, 15. Tó holan díc, v. 365, 31. On holan dene, iv. 108, 27. On holan weg, v. 302, 37. **IV a.** *lying in a hollow or depression*, of a stream, pool, &c. :—On holan bróc, C. D. iv. 95, 36 : 287, 27. On holan ford, iii. 436, 12. In fontem holan wielle, 379, 10. And lang eá tó holan wylle, v. 302, 36. **V.** of the shape of a vessel or plant :—Holo pannae *patena*, holo ponne *paneta*, Txts. 86, 784. (Cf. *M. E.* hol basin *in contrast with* flat basin. v. *N. E. D.* hol basin, *s.v.* holl.) Hole cersan, Lch. ii. 78, 26. Þá holan cersan, 34, 9. [v. *N. E. D.* holl.]

**hol** *having a cover. Dele and see* hol; **I.**

**hól.** *Add* :—Sacu and clacu, hól and hete, Wlfst. 86, 10. Stalu and cwalu, hól and hete, 129, 3 : 268, 23. Sennacheríb mid hóle (v. 2 Kings xviii. 19 sqq.) him (*Hezekiah*) on wan, Hml. S. 18, 396. Se feónd cwæð : 'Maledicte, non Benedicte', and þ swá gecwæð se deófol for hóle and for æfste, Gr. D. 122, 19. v. hél.

**-hola.** v. ge-hola.

**holc.** *Add* :—On ðære lifre *holocum*, Lch. ii. 206, 7.

**hold** (*a title*). *Add* :—Symbel worhte ðæm aldormannum and holdum and forwostum Galileæs *cenam fecit principibus et tribunis et primis Galileae*, Mk. L. R. 6, 21.

**hold** *a carcase. Add* :—Líc oððe hold *cadaver*, Wrt. Voc. i. 85, 54. Hold *ferinum*, ii. 108, 39 : 70, 23 : 35, 20.

**hold; adj.** *Add* : **I.** of a superior to an inferior :—Ic (*Edgar*) beó eów swýðe hold hláford þá hwíle þe mé líf gelæst, Ll. Th. i. 278, 11. Ic (*Cnut*) cýðe eów þ ic wylle beón hold hláford and únswícende tó Godes gerihtum and tó rihtre woroldlage, Cht. E. 229, 21 : Chr. 1066; P. 200, 17. **II.** of inferior to superior :—God is mín gewita ic wæs ðínum fæder swá gehýrsum swá ic fyrmest mihte and fullíce hold on móde and on mægene and ðé æfre on fullum hyldum hold and on fulre lufe, ðæs mé is God gewita, C. D. iv. 300, 35–301, 2. Urias slæge his ágenes holdes ðegnes, Past. 35, 23. Fela sceal tó holdan hámes geréfan, Angl. ix. 265, 10. Lilla ðæs cyninges þegn him se holdesta (heoldesta, *v. l.* amicissimus), Bd. 2, 9; Sch. 147, 6. His gesíþ þe hé him ær þone holdestan gelýfde, 3, 14; Sch. 255, 7. **III.** in a religious sense, *devout* :—Ðære holdan mægsibbe *deuotae germanitatis*, An. Ox. 9, 1. Eálá hwilc heófung holdra geleáffulra (holdra and geleáffulra, Hml. Th. ii. 518, 14), Hml. S. 31, 1382. **IV.** in a general sense, *friendly, well-disposed* :—Boetius . . . wæs on Greácas hold *was friendly towards the Greeks*, Met. 1, 56. Micel heáp holdra freónda úre andbidað þær (*in heaven*), Hml. Th. ii. 526, 31. Þá þeóde symble Angelcynne þá holdestan *gentem nationi Anglorum semper amicissimam*, Bd. 4, 26; Sch. 504, 15. **V.** of things, *pleasant* :—Heriað hine on hleóðre holdre béman, Ps. Th. 150, 3. Mid þý sélestan hwætecynnes holde lynde *adipe frumenti*, 147, 3. Hí holdne begeáton, fælne fultum, 113, 18. v. drýhten-, hláford-, in-, þeóden-hold.

**-holda.** v. un-holda : **hold-áþ.** *Add* : v. hyld-áþ.

**holde.** *Add* : **I.** *graciously.* v. hold; **I** :—Ic him míne hælu holde ætýwe, Ps. Th. 90, 16 : 118, 73. **II.** *loyally, devotedly.* v. holde; **II, III** :—Þíne hælu holde lufigean, Ps. Th. 69, 5.

**holdigean.** *Substitute* : **holdian;** *p.* ode. *To flay; to embowel* (?) :—Man þá hálgan swang and bærnde and swilce ofsticode swín holdode (v. ge-wyrce), Hml. S. 23, 106 : 73. Tó holdigenne, tó befleánne *euiscerandum*, Germ. 393, 109. v. holding-stów, hyldan; æt-hýdan.

**holding-stów,** e; *f.* *A place where slaughtered animals are dressed, a slaughter-house* :—Súð ðonan oð hit cymð tó ðære holdingstówe, C. D. v. 184, 23. v. holdian.

**hold-líc;** *adj. Friendly, kindly* :—[H]wæt hý holdlíces *quid amicum, fidum*, An. Ox. 50, 29.

**holdlíce.** *Add* : **I.** *graciously.* Cf. hold; **I** :—Hú holdlíce God spræc be his clænum þegenum, Hml. A. 22, 190. **II.** *loyally.* Cf. hold; **II** :—Befrán se cyning . . . 'Hwilce méde hæfde Mardochéus for þám þ hé swá holdlíce hogode embe mé?' Ait rex : 'Quid pro hac fide þraemii Mardochaeus consecutus est?', Hml. A. 98, 218. Utan ænne cynehláford holdlíce healdan, Ll. Th. i. 312, 21. Holdlíce hýran, 314, 11 : Wlfst. 266, 8. Holdlíce (holdelíce, *v. l.*), Chr. 1065; P. 194, 20. **III.** *devoutly.* Cf. hold; **III** :—Holdlíce *devote* (*but the text in* Ald. 81, 29 *is* : Iuxta quod vestra vota *devota* sposponderunt), Wrt.

Voc. ii. 88, 50 : 27, 2. **IV.** *in a friendly way.* Cf. hold ; **IV :**—Holdlíce *affectuose,* Wrt. Voc. ii. 4, 5. [v. *N. E. D.* holdely.]

**hold-ræden.** *Add :* v. hyld-ræden.

**holen.** *Add :* , holig[n] :—Holegn *acrifolus,* Wrt. Voc. ii. 99, 4. Holen *ruscus,* Hpt. Gl. 530, 6. Tó ðǽm beorge ðe mon háteð æt ðǽm holne, C. D. ii. 29, 6. In ymman holig ; of ymman holigne, C. D. B. iii. 223, 25. Tó ðám gemǽre æt ðám holignan ; of ðám holigena gemǽra, C. D. iv. 287, 27.

**holen-hyrst** *a holly-copse :*—Holenhyrst (*a place-name*), C. D. ii. 228, 1.

**holen-leáf,** es ; *n.* *A holly-leaf :*—Genim holenleáfa micle twá handfulla, Lch. ii. 356, 11. Genim eald holenleáf, 50, 10.

**holen-rind,** e ; *f.* *Holly-rind, bark of the holly :*—Holenrinde niþewearde, Lch. ii. 96, 2 : 98, 8. Amber fulne holenrinda and æscrinda, 332, 15.

**holen-stybb,** es ; *m.* *A holly-stump :*—Æt ðǽm holenstypbum, C. D. iii. 383, 27.

**holh.** *Add :*—Of ðám ylcan stáne, in þám wæs þæt holg þæs nearwan scræfes *ex petra eadem, quae in semetipsa concava angustum specus fecerat,* Gr. D. 211, 7. Gif þonne seó nǽdre befleáh hine in hwylc holh, gif hé þonne gebletsode þæs hóles múð mid þǽre halgan róde tácne, sóna ofer þ wæs seó nǽdre getogen deád of þám hóle *quem si quando serpens in foramine fugerit, signo crucis os foraminis benedicit, statimque ex foramine serpens jam mortuus trahitur,* 247, 5–7. [v. *N. E. D.* hollow.] v. hol.

**holian.** *Add : trans.* *To make a hole in, dig* ground :—Gáþ gé and þ stánclif hwæðhugu holiað *ite et rupem in modico cavate,* Gr. D. 113, 5. Hé hét ðá heardnysse swíðe holian on middan ðǽre fióre his botles (cf. *fodiamus in medio tuguriunculi mei,* Vit. Cuth. c. xviii), Hml. Th. ii. 144, 3. [v. *N. E. D.* hole.] v. ge-, þurh-holian ; holing.

**-holian** *to get.* v. ge-holian : **hólian.** *In* l. 3 *read* hólón. *Add :* [v. Goth. af-holón *in* Lk. 19, 8] cf. hélan.

**holing,** e ; *f.* *Digging, excavation :*—Þá ongunnon hí on þám stánclife hwylcehugu holinga dón, Gr. D. 113, 11. v. under-holung.

**hol-leác** *a kind of onion :*—Holleác *duricorium,* Wrt. Voc. i. 286, 11 : ii. 26, 21 : Lch. iii. 20, 16 : 46, 23. [v. *N. E. D.* holleke.]

**holm.** *Add :* [*For the use of* holm *in the sense of* hill v. (?) holm-wudu ; *and for the later use of the word in this sense* cf. þe vox ulih to þam holme (cleoue, 2nd MS.), Laym. 20861.] **I.** *sea :*—Brym *vel* holm *cataclismus, diluvium,* Wrt. Voc. ii. 129, 42. Sǽýþa *vel* holmas *equo[r], maria,* 143, 74. **II.** *low-lying land by a stream,* occurring in local names :—Man beónn ealle Cantware tó wigge tó Holme, C. D. ii. 387, 19. Þ land æt Húnstánestúne be ǽstan bróke mid þan lande et Holme, iv. 58, 27. Into Holme minstre, 113, 29. Of elkanleighe tó hilisbrók on þane holm ; þane endelanges þrókes in on wryng ; þanen endlang wryng, C. D. B. ii. 264, 18. [v. *N. E. D.* holm.]

**holm-wudu** *wood growing on a hill :*—Mé (*the Cross*) geweorþode wuldres ealdor ofer holmwudu (holtwudu ?), Kr. 91. [cf. He wes iflozen into þan haze wude, in tó þan haze holme, Laym. 20712.] cf. firgen-beám.

**hol-ness,** e ; *f.* *A hollow, depression in the earth's surface :*—Hé sóhte þone Godes wer geond þá holnessa (holenesse, *v. l.*) þára dena *virum Dei per concava vallium quaesivit,* Gr. D. 99, 22.

**holt.** *Add :* **I.** *a wood, copse :*—Hár holtes feónd, Rä. 22, 3. For ðǽm wé ceorfað heáh treówu on holte ðæt wé hí eft úp árǽren on ðǽm botle, Past. 443, 36. Hwá áspyreð ðæt deófol of geofones holte, Sal. K. p. 146, 28. Hé rád þurh ǽnne heáhne holt, Hml. S. 19, 219. On pápan holt súðweardne, C. D. B. ii. 246, 2. Seó eorðe sóna swá swá hyre God bebeád stód mid holtum ágrówen, Hex. 12, 3. ¶ *compounds of* holt *with tree-names are not infrequent in charters.* v. ác-, alor-, birc-, bóc-, hæsel-holt. Cf. *too* beorh-holt, C. D. B. ii. 246, 34 : gehæg-holt. **II.** *wood, a piece of wood, handle* or *shaft of a weapon* (?). v. gár-holt :—Holt *capulus* (armet dextram *capulus,* ceu parma sinistram, Ald. 214, 17), Wrt. Voc. ii. 97, 33 : 20, 17.

**holt-hana.** *Substitute for* 'acegia . . . 138' :—Holthana, holtana, holthona *acega,* Txts. 38, 41. Holthana, Wrt. Voc. ii. 4, 28. Cf. wudu-hana.

**hól-tihte.** *Add :*—Calumpnia *hosp,* hearmspreác, *accusatio falsa* hóltihte, Wrt. Voc. ii. 127, 77.

**holt-wudu.** *In* Kr. 91 *the MS. has* holmwudu : **holung.** v. underholung.

**hólunga.** *Add :*—Hólunga *nequaquam, nequicquam, nequiquam,* Txts. 80, 683. Hólenga *nequiquam,* Wrt. Voc. ii. 59, 61. Hólenga (on ídel, *v. l.*) ic wénde *incassum aestimabam,* Gr. D. 25, 25. Hólinga (on idel, *v. l.*) hé cleopað, E. S. 43, 164. Hólinga (*in vano*) winnað þá þe timbriað, Ps. Vos. 126, 1.

**hóme.** v. óme. *l.* hóman. v. óman : **homela.** v. hamela : **hómig.** v. ómig.

**hón** (?). *Dele.* *The words* 'his hon' *in* l. 3 *seem to be a repetition of* 'his hon[godon]' *in* l. 2.

**hón.** *Add :* **I.** *to place* a thing *so that it is supported from above :*—Mon héhþ ǽnne heáfodbeáh æt ærneweges ende, Bt. 37, 2 ; F. 188, 8.

Hí gedydon ánne scyld and áne anlícnysse, and áhengon (hēngon, *v. l.*) hí úp on heora Capitolium, Ors. 6, 25 ; Bos. 125, 2. Gá án mǽdenman tó and hó hit on his sweóran, Lch. iii. 42, 10. **II.** *to suspend on a cross or gibbet as a punishment :*—Gif wíteþeów hine forstalie, hó hine mon, Ll. Th. i. 118, 6. Sleá man hine, oþþe hó, swá man þá yldran ǽr dyde, 242, 6. **III.** *to let droop* or *bend downward :*—Þæt heáfod hó ofdúne, Lch. ii. 18, 14. **IV.** *to put* clothing on :—Gif þú . . . cláþa þe má on hæfst (hēhst, *v. l.*) þonne þú þurfe, Bt. 14, 1 ; F. 42, 15. v. ofer-, ymb-hón.

**hónede** ; *adj.* *Having (large ?) heels :*—Hónede *calcaneus,* Wrt. Voc. i. 45, 41.

**honsteorc.** v. hop-steort.

**hóp.** *Substitute :* hop, es ; *n.* *A piece of raised* or *enclosed land in the midst of fen, marsh,* or *waste land, a hope* (v. *N. E. D.* s. v.) :—Mǽdwǽgan hop, C. D. vi. 243, 14. *Perhaps in the gloss* fennegan hopu *stagnosa* ligustra (An. Ox. 36, 14–15), hopu *should be taken* here. *The passage glossed is :* Avis cernitur, cursumque suum inter stagnosa paludis ligustra deflectens, sese subito ab eorum obtutibus velut evanescens abdidit. *Could the gloss belong to* stagnosa paludis, *the Latin words being understood as describing parts of the marsh ?* *In another gloss,* Wrt. Voc. ii. 51, 57, *which may belong to the same passage,* lygistra *is glossed by* hopu ; *but other glosses give* ligustra blóstman, Wrt. Voc. ii. 53, 5 : hunisuge, 89, 43 : *and* ligustrum *is always glossed by* hunisuge. *The epithet* fennig *seems more appropriate to a* hope *than to a tree.* ¶ *in local names :*—In marasco terram unius aratri inter haec quatuor confinia . . . ab austro Bedlinghope in palude, C. D. v. 68, 14. In Eásthope, ii. 137, 1. In wiðingmere ; ðæt út wið hopwudes wíca, iii. 391, 23. In hopwuda, ii. 33, 18 : 167, 30. v. fen-, mersc-, mór-hop ; how (?).

**hopa.** *Add :* **I.** *expectation of what is desired, desire combined with expectation :*—On hopan (*spe*) hǽle wé beóð gewordene : hope sóðlíce sē þe gesewen ys nys hopa (Rom. 8, 24), Scint. 130, 3. Geanbidung rihtwísra bliss ; hopa sóðlíce árleásra forwyrð, 8. Hopa þe byð gelencged geswenceð sáwle (Prov. 13, 12), 9. Fandung wyrcð hopan ; hopa ná gescynt, 7, 19. Ne þǽr árfæstnes, ne sib, ne hopa, ne swige geglaðað *nec pax, nec pietas, spes nulla quietis flentibus arrident,* Dóm. L. 220 : Wlfst. 139, 12. Þá þe yfele dón ná geswícað mid ídelum hopan (*uana spe*) forgyfenysse be Godes miltsunge sēceað, Scint. 130, 13. Hé ealle his geþóhtas and hopan on God beset, R. Ben. 3, 24. **I a.** *where the object of hope is given :*—Se miccla hopa tó þínum Hǽlende þ hé þíne synna ádwǽscan wylle, Dóm. L. 28, 9. **I b.** *personified :*—Se hopa árǽhte sweord þǽre eáðmódnesse, Prud. 35 a. Seó ofermódnes stellan wile ofer þone hopan, 32 a. **II.** *a feeling of trust* or *confidence :*—On ege Drihtnes trúwa strencðe, and bearnum his byð hopa *in timore Domini fiducia fortitudinis, et filiis eius erit spes* (Prov. 14, 26), Scint. 65, 1. **III.** *a person* or *thing that gives hope for the future,* or *in which hopes are centred :*—Þú eart hopa þínra se mǽsta *tu spes tuorum maxima,* Hy. S. 98, 15. Ys dǽdbót lǽcedóm wunde, hopa hǽle (*spes salutis*), Scint. 47, 2.

**hopian.** *Add :* **I.** *to look (mentally) with expectation* to (*tó*), *hope* for :—Án is þæt ðú hefst and brícst and lufast þæt ðæt þú ǽr tó hopedest. Eálá hweðer ic ǽfre cume tó ðám ðe ic tó hopie, Solil. H. 27, 15. Hé forsihþ þás eorþlican gód and hopaþ tó þám tóweardum, Bt. 12 ; F. 36, 26. Gehíeren ðá unblíðan ðá leán ðæs gefeán ðe hié tó hopiað *tristibus inferenda sunt laeta, quae promittuntur,* Past. 187, 18. Hú sóðlíc sió heánes is ðe hié tó hopiað and eác habbað *quam sit vera excellentia, quam sperando tenent,* 299, 5. Þonne man wát þæt hé ǽr tó hopede, Solil. H. 29, 6. Se sige þe eall Angelcynn tó hopode, Chr. 1009 ; P. 139, 8. Hí tó ðám sceatte hopedon *they hoped to get the offered reward,* Hml. S. 23, 53. Ðý lǽs hé eallunga áfealle ðonon ðe hé fæstlícost tó hopian scolde *ne ab eo, quod robuste sperare debuit, funditus cadat,* Past. 395, 11. **II.** *to be hopeful about* (*with gen.*) :—Hé ðá wæs geortrúwod þæs cildes, and gehwearf geðyldelíce hopiende þæs óðres *he was in despair about the one child, and returned patient, being hopeful about the other,* Hml. S. 30, 179. **III.** *to trust, have confidence :*—Tó þé ic hopige, Drihten *ad te, Domine, clamabo,* Ps. Th. 27, 1. Hopa, mín móð, tó Drihtne and gebíd his willan *expecta Dominum,* 26, 16. Þ is se hiht, þ hé hopige tó Gode ǽgðer ge on gelimpe ge on ungelimpe and nǽfre ne ortrúwige be Godes árfæstnysse, Hml. S. 16, 250. Ús is tó hopigenne on þæs Hǽlendes gescyldnesse, sē ðe ús tihte þus : 'Confidite, ego uici mundum,' Angl. vii. 28, 270. **III a.** *to trust that (with clause or* (?) *acc. and infin.) :*—Hopiað *confidimus* (laetabundos fore fiducialiter *confidimus*), An. Ox. 3034. Hopiað *confidunt* (caeterorum praeconia se transcendere *confidunt*), 940. **III b.** *combining* III *and* III a :—Ic hopige on Drihten þ hé mé wylle áhreddan, Hml. S. 14, 111. **IV.** *to hope for :*—Witodlíce þæt gesiht ǽghwylc hwæt hé hopige ? Gif sóðlíce þæt wé ná geseoð wé hopiað, þurh geþyld wé geandbidigað, Scint. 130, 5. Forgyfenysse wé hopian *ueniam speremus,* 19. **IV a.** *with clause, to hope* that :—Ic hopige þ cherubin se mǽra sí wesan wylle, Angl. viii. 325, 30. **IV b.** *to hope of* (*tó*) *a person that :*—Hopode and gewil-

node þ hē hine þām abbode befæste *petiit ab eo ut eum abbati committeret*, Gr. D. 27, 23. v. ā-, ge-hopian.

**-hopp.** v. ge-hopp.

**hóp-páda.** *Substitute*: hop-pāda, an; *m. An upper garment* :— *Ependeton* cōp *vel* hoppāda *vel* ufre scrūd, Wrt. Voc. i. 59, 52. Cf. hopsteort.

**hoppe.** *Add*:—The 12th century Latin version of the first passage is : Nola bouis, collarium canis (Anglice dicitur *hundes hoppe*, quasi canis circularium, quia *hóp* circulus) . . . unumquodque ualet unum sol., et uniuscuiusque modus computatus *melda*. [**v.** *N. E. D.* hoppe *seed-vessel of flax.*] v. ge-hopp.

**-hoppe.** v. gærs-hoppe: **hoppere.** *Dele.*

**hoppetan.** *Add*: , hoppettan:—Se hrefn mid openum mūðe and mid āþenedum fiðerum ongann yrnan hoppetende ymbūtan þone hlāf *coruus aperto ore, expansis alis circa panem coepit discurrere*, Gr. D. 118, 25.

**hoppian.** *Add*:—Sum man gesette his ðeówan man on fetera. Hē sæt lange on ðām bendum oð þ hē bestæl ūt mid his stafe hoppende (hoppegende, *v. l.*), Hml. S. 21, 417.

**hopp-scýte** *a coverlet* (?). *Substitute*: hop-scīte (hopp-) *a bed-curtain*, and add :—Heó (*Judith*) nam þ heáfod and his hopscýtan *abstulit conopeum eius* (cf. An. Ox. 7, 365 where *conopeum*, occurring in the story of Judith, is glossed by *wáhreft*. In the poem of Judith the word is rendered by *fleóhnett*, Jud. 47), Hml. Aʂ. 118, 307.

**hop-steort** *the train of a dress* :—Hopsteort (*printed* honsteorc, *but v.* Du Cange '*limpus in veteri glossario Saxonico* hopsteort ') *limpus*, Wrt. Voc. ii. 53, 41. Cf. hop-páda.

**hopu.** v. hop: **-hopung.** v. tō-hopung.

**hór-cwene.** *Add*:—Hóringas oððe hórcwenan, Wlfst. 309, 22.

**hord.** *Add*: I. *an accumulation of valuable things hidden away or laid by for preservation or future use* (*see also* IV.). (1) *of precious metals, jewels, &c.* :—Sege ūs nū hwær se ealda hord (*of coins*) sý þe þū digellīce fundest, Hml. S. 23, 661. Hord sceal in streónum bīdan, Gn. Ex. 68. Wyrm, hordes hyrde, B. 887. Māðma hord mīnne, 2799. Scealt þū þīnes unþances þone hord āmeldian, þe þū sylfwilles ǽr noldest cýðan, Hml. S. 23, 716. Ne hýdeþ eów hord in eorþe *nolite thesaurizare vobis thesauros in terra*, Mt. R. 6, 19. Draca hord beweotode, B. 2212. Se gūðsceaða hord gesceát, dryhtsele dyrnne, 2319. Gong hord sceáwian under hārne stān, 2744. Hord warian, Rä. 32, 21 : 88, 22. (2) *of material valuable for its properties* :—Sege eallum mannum þ sóna swā hī geopeniað mīne byrgene, þ hī magon ðǽr findan swā deórwurðne hord (*the miracle-working remains of St. Swithin*) þ heora dýre gold ne bið nāhte wurð wið þā foresǽdan māðmas, Hml. S. 21, 54. II. *a valuable article* :—Bið seó móddor hordum gehroden, Rä. 81, 17. III. *of non-material things*, (1) *that are valued* :—Hýdeþ eów hord in heofonum, Mt. R. 6, 20. Ðurh sefan snyttro, searoðonca hord, Past. 9, 11. Sceal þæs heánan hyge hord unginnost, Gn. Ex. 206. Hē (*Christ*) æteówde mē eác his ǽnlican hordas, ðā hē mē gehēt, Hml. S. 7, 38. (2) *that are concealed* :—Synna hord, Ps. C. 155. Dyrne hordas *abdita* (*secretorum*) *archana*, An. Ox. 4216. IV. *a place where treasure is deposited; the condition of being deposited* (in the phrases *of horde*, *on hord*, but perhaps the passages might be taken under I. See *N. E. D.* hoard; 2) :—þū hī gaderast and helst on þīnum horde *tuis ea divitiis annumerare maluisti*, Bt. 14, 2 ; F. 44, 5. Wæs gold āhæfen of horde, B. 1108. Bēg and siglu, eall swylce hyrsta swylce on horde ǽr nīðhýdige genumen hæfdon, 3165.

**hord-cleófa, -clýfa.** *l.* hord-cleofa, -clyfa, *and add*: See next word.

**hord-cófa.** *l.* hord-cofa, *and add* :—Ic (*the devil*) wolde . . . þæt hý (*the wicked*) wunedon on mīnum hordcouan (hwæt woldon hý on mīnum hordcleofan, *v. l.*) and þīne circean forgeáton, Wlfst. 255, 14.

**hordere.** *Add*:—Be mynstres hordere (*cellarario*). Se mynstres hordere sī gecoren of þǽre gesamnunge, sýfre and nā oferettol. . .; sý hē ealre geśerrǽdenne swā swā fæder. Hē hogige embe ealle ðing ; ne dō hē nān ðing būtan þæs abbodes hǽse; healde þæt him beboden sý, R. Ben. 54, 6–12. þæs horderes tǽcen is þæt mon wrænce mid is hande swilce hē wille loc hunlūcan, Tech. ii. 118, 10.

**hord-ern.** *Add*:—Hordren *proma cella prumptuaria*, Hpt. 33, 245, 41. Se munuc þe þ hordern heóld *monachus qui cellarium tenebat* (cf. Hml. Th. ii. 178, 22 *under* hordere), Gr. D. 159, 15.

**horder-wíce.** *l.* -wíce.

**hord-fæt.** *Add*:—Būrþēn *cancellarius vel scriniarius* [hordfæt *scrinium vel cancellaria*, Angl. viii. 452, omitted after], Wrt.Voc. i. 61, 3.

**hord-weorþung.** *Substitute*: *Treasure given to honour a person* (cf. Hē þām bātwearde bunden golde swurd gesealde, þæt hē syððan wæs māðme ðý weorðra, B. 1902), *costly reward* :—Ful oft ic for lǽssan leán teohhade, hordweorðunge, hnāhran rince, sǽmran æt sæcce, B. 952. Cf. hring-, sinc-weorþung; weorþung; III.

**hóre.** *Add*:—Leás fyrnhicge, hóre *prostituta pellax*, i. *meretrix quae prostat*, i. *mendax*, An. Ox. 2940. Hórena *meretricum*, 3329.

**horh.** [*The* hor(g)-, hor(e)w- *forms seem to belong to the same*

*original nominative, but they are so far differentiated in meaning that they are taken separately.*] *Add* :—Horh *flegma*, i. *saliua*, Wrt. Voc. ii. 149, 38 : *flegma*, 35, 65. Nytta þāra lǽcedōma þe þone horh of þām heáfde teó, Lch. ii. 282, 25. Þū forlēte on þīnne ondwlitan þā earman heora horh (spātl) spīwan, Angl. xii. 505, 13. Horh *flegmata*, Wrt. Voc. ii. 108, 71 : 35, 64. Swiling wið hōrum (hrum, MS.) and gillistrum tō heáfdes hǽlo, Lch. ii. 2, 3. [Hᴊóras, i. 358, 13. Dracontjan wiþ fūle hóras on men, ii. 174, 5. [**v.** *N. E. D.* hore. *Icel.* horr *mucus from the nose.*]

**horheht.** *l.* horheht(e): **horh-leahtras.** v. or-leahter: **horian**, Ps. Th. 27, 1 note. *Dele, and see* hopian; III : **horian** *to defile.* v. horwian.

**horig.** *Add*: , hórig (? cf. *Wick.* hoory) :—Horig *spurcus*, An. Ox. 18 b, 82. Ne līchoma wunige horig ł fūl *nec corpus adsit sordidum*, Hy. S. 26, 26. Hē bið āðwogen fram his synnum ðurh ðā untrumnysse, swā swā horig hrægl þurh sāpan, Hml. Th. i. 472, 6. Tō horgan wege ; ðonne of horgan wege, C. D. B. ii. 245, 25. On horegan ford ; of horegan forda, C. D. vi. 153, 5. Scīnende hýd horig (*sordidum*) ge-swutelað mōd, Scint. 87, 6. Horie *purulenta*, Germ. 396, 259. Gif þū bere horige reáf (*ceruleas* (*nigras*) *uestes*), Hpt. 31, 13, 325. [**v.** *N. E. D.* hory.]

**hóring.** *Add*:—Gif hóringas oððe hórcwenan innan þysan earde weorðan āgytene, Wlfst. 309, 21.

**horn.** *Add*: I. *the horn* of an animal :—Swýþor þonne æþele cealf, þeáh þe him upp āgā horn on heáfde *super vitulum nouellum cornua producentem*, Ps. Th. 68, 32. Hē geseah ánne ramm betwux þām brēmelum be þām hornum gehæft, Gen. 22, 13. Ūr feohteð mid hornum, Rūn. 2. Atol deór monig īrenum hornum, Sal. 470. I a. *where horn is used medically* :—Heortes horn hafað mægen ǽlcne wǽtan tō ādrīgenne, Lch. i. 334, 3, and often. Wið hōmum, nim gāte horn, 350, 17 : 21. Fearres horn gebrǽdedne tō acsan, 366, 9. v. cū-, wesend-horn. II. *horn as emblem of power and might* (Biblical use) :—Hē ūs hǽle horn ārǽrde, Lk. i. 69. Ealle hornas synfulra ic tōbrece and beóð ūp āhefen hornas ryhtwīses, Ps. Rdr. 74, 11. Ic cwæð tō ðǽm ðe syngodon : 'Ne hebbe gē tō ūp eówre hornas.' Ðonne āhebbað ðā synfullan swīðe ūp hira hornas, ðonne hī hī nǽfre nyllað geeáðmēdan . . ., Past. 425, 21–24. III. *a vessel formed from a horn.* (1) *a drinking-horn.* v. drync(e)-, wīn-horn; *and cf.* Contulit magno regi duo *cornua* (*or under* IV ?) auro argentoque decorata (cf. mec (*a drinking-horn*) mon þeced golde and sylfore, Rä. 15, 2) ut eo liberius hoc praerogatiuum roboretur, C. D. ii. 293, 17. Offero refectorario dicti monasterii . . . cornu meae mensae, ut senes monasterii bibant inde in festis sanctorum, et in suis benedictionibus meminerint aliquando animae donatoris, i. 305, 3–13. (2) *a receptacle for other liquids or powder.* v. blæc-, ele-, pipor-horn. (3) *a horn for cupping* :—Him cōm ongēn se ealda feónd sittende on ānum mūle on lǽces ansýne and bær horn and his blōdsex (*cornu et tripedicam ferens*), Gr. 161, 2. v. tyge-horn. (4) *a horn tube for inhaling* :—Genim . . . swefl and recels . . lege on hātne stān, drinc þurh horn þone rēc, Lch. ii. 316, 11 : 56, 11. IV. *a horn for blowing, a trumpet.* v. blǽs-, swegel-, trūþ-horn :—Hornblāwere *cornicen*, horn *cornu*, Wrt. Voc. i. 73, 64. Horn *salpix*, An. Ox. 18 b, 86. Nǽfre mon þæs hlūde horn āþýteð ne býman āblāweð, Dōm. 109. V. *a projection like a horn at each corner of the altar in the Jewish temple* :—Tō horne weófedes, Ps. Rdr. Spl. 117, 27. Oð horn wībed, Ps. Vos. 117, 27. Oð horn *ad cornua*, Ps. Srt. 117, 27. VI. *each of the pointed extremities of the moon in her first and last quarters*, Rä. 30, 2 (*in Dict.*). VI a. *each end of a bow.* Cf. horn-boga :—Hē forbricþ hornas bogana *confringit cornua arcum*, Ps. Rdr. Vos. Srt. 75, 4. See Rä. 15 for various uses of the horn, and Tupper's notes on the riddle.

**horn-blǽwere.** *Add*:—Hornblāuuere *cereacus* (cf. cereacas, tubicines, Corp. Gl. H. 30, 298), Wrt. Voc. ii. 103, 71. Hornblāwere *ceriacus*.

**horn-boga.** *Add*: [**v.** *N. E. D.* horn-bow.]

**horn-bora.** *Add*:—Hornbora *cornicen*, Wrt. Voc. i. 291, 21 : ii. 17, 35. *In* El. 54 *the MS. has* hleópon *not* hleówon.

**hornede**; *adj. Provided with horns* :—Hornede nǽdran, carastis þ nǽdercyn, Nar. 13, 15.

**horn-fótede**; *adj. Horn-footed, hoofed* (of a horse) :—Hornfōtedne *cornipedem* (-*um*, MS. Cf. horsa *cornipedum*, 21, 69), Wrt. Voc. ii. 135, 71.

**horn-leás**; *adj. Without horns* :—Gif hē hornleásne oxan geseó, þonne ofercymeð hē his fīnd, Archiv cxx. 304, 28 ; E. S. 39, 349.

**hornnaap** ? :—Hornnaap *decurat*, Wrt. Voc. ii. 98, 8. [Decurare = *nimium curare* (Migne). Could naap (= nāp) be *p. t.* of nīpan, used here figuratively of mental gloom ? Further could horn = orn (ran) ? ; and could two quite different glosses have been suggested for the same Latin word, because the glosser was uncertain whether to connect the word with currere or curare ?]

**horn-píc**; *n.* (?). *l. m.*: **hornung.** *See next word.*

**hornung-sunu.** For Cot. 142 *substitute* :—Hornungsunu *nothus*, Wrt. Voc. ii. 61, 67, *and add*: [*The form* hornung(-ing) *seems to occur*

*in several local names in the charters :*—Horninggeseie *Horningsea* (in Cambridgeshire), C. D. iv. 245, 20. Horninggeshǣð *Horningsheath* (in Suffolk), 293, 4. Horningadene, vi. 66, 33. Horninganǣre, iv. 92, 32. Đat land at Horninggen (cf. uillam noto nomine cognominato Horningga, 28, 24: uillam de Horninghe, 111, 7), 29, 27. Hornning-dūn et ōðer Horningdūn, 164, 12.]

**horrat** ? :—Horrat *sub*[*si*]*stit*, Germ. 402, 79.

**hors.** *Add:* I. *a horse, as a general term* :—Hors *sonipes,* wildecynnes hors *equifer,* Wrt. Voc. i. 23, 3–4. Hors hnǣgð *equus hinnit,* Ælfc. Gr. Z. 129, 2. Gif hors on hricge oððe on þām bógum āwyrd sȳ, Lch. i. 290, 10. Weard his hors ofslagen þe hē on sæt *the horse he was riding was killed,* Chr. 1079 ; P. 214, 6. Gif hē aferað ne ðearf hē wyrcan ðā hwíle ðe his hors úte bið, Ll. Th. i. 434, 9. Gif mon horses onlǣne ōðres esne, and hē losie, ealne hē hine gylde, 120, 14. Ic gean mínon feder . . . þæs horses þe Đúrbrand mē geaf, and þæs hwítan horses þe Leófwine mē geaf, Cht. Th. 559, 6–19. Ic geann mínon mæsse-preóste . . . þæs mālswurdes . . . and mínes horses mid mínon gerǣdon, 560, 34. Þā hē on ðām horse sæt *when he was riding,* Bd. 3, 14 ; Sch. 257, 10. Đa weard Eustatius uppon his horse and his gesceóran uppon heora *Eustace got on his horse and his men on theirs,* Chr. 1048 ; P. 172, 24. Wē forbeódað ǣlce lāde ǣgðer ge on wǣne ge on horse, Ll. Th. ii. 298, 23. Forfang æt men fíftene peningas, and æt horse healswā, i. 224, 26. Sum bið hafeces cræftig. Sum bið tō horse hwæt, Crä. 81. Nān man ne sylle nān hors ofer sǣ, būtan hē hit gifan wille, Ll. Th. i. 208, 18. Geaf Oswine þæt betste hors Aidane . . . þæt hē mihte fordas oferrídan, þonne hē tō hwylcre eá cōme, Bd. 3, 14 ; Sch. 256, 24. Wē becōmon on smēðne feld and rúmne, and wæs gescroepe ærneweg. Þā ongunnan þā iungan biddan þone bysceop þ hē him ālȳfde þ hī ærnan mōsten and gecunnian hwylc heora swiftost hors hæfde, 5, 6 ; Sch. 575, 7 : Ors. I, I ; S. 20, 34. Iōhannes heów þæt hors mid þām spuran, Ælfc. T. Grn. 18, 22. Hwæt sylþ hē (*the king*) þē (*the huntsman*) ? Hwílon hē sylþ mē hors, Coll. M. 22, 35. Horsa *cornipedum,* Wrt. Voc. ii. 21, 69. Horsa scip *ypogavus,* i. 56, 14. Þæt hors þȳ gewunelican þeáwe horsa æfter wērinesse ongan wealwian and on gehwæþere sídan gelōmlíce hit oferweorpan, Bd. 3. 9 ; Sch. 230, 17. Mā þurh his fōta gang þonne on horsa rāde *magis ambulando quam equitando,* 4, 3 ; Sch. 349, 16. Hió becwið Cynelufe hyre dǣl þæra wildera horsa, Cht. Th. 538, 33. Þā Deniscan hæfdon miclne dǣl þāra horsa freten, Chr. 894 ; P. 87, 25. Þā landleóde āhreddon eall þæt hié (*the Danes*) genumen hæfdon, and eác hira horsa and hira wǣpna micelue dǣl, 917 ; P. 98, 8. Hié āsettan him on ānne síþ ofer mid horsum mid ealle, 893 ; P. 84, 4. Fleáh ðæt Englisce folc, for ðan þe hig wǣran on horsan, 1055 ; P. 186, 6. Ælc man wite his getȳman be mannum and be horsum and be oxum, Ll. Th. i. 154, 14. Hēt hē hyssa hwǣne hors forlǣtan, By. 2. Hí (*the Danes*) nāman heom hors and ridon swā wíde swā hí woldon, Chr. 994 ; H. 129, 9. Ōðer healf hund æcera and þærtō þrittig oxna and twēntig cūna and tȳn hors, Cht. Th. 312, 20. Hæbbe Eádwold hyre taman hors, 539, 6. Hors anstyllan, Angl. ix. 262, 23. Swā wildu hors (*equos indomitos*), ðonne wē hié ǣresð gefangnu habbað, wē hié ðacciað ; tō ðon ðæt wē eft . . . ðā temian, Past. 303, 9. Hēht se cāsere gesponnan fíower wildo hors tō scríde and hine in ðæt scríd āsetton ðæt ðā wildan hors scealden iornan . . . and him ðā limo all tōbrecan, Shrn. 71, 34. ¶ *as horses, in varying numbers, form part of the heriot, they are frequently mentioned in wills.* v. here-geatu. II. *a male of the horse kind.* (1) *as distinguished from* mare :—Hors *equus,* myre *equa,* Wrt. Voc. i. 78, 5 : 287, 42. Hors mon sceal gyldan mid .xxx. scill. . . . myran mid .xx. scill, Ll. Th. i. 356, 2. (2) *as distinguished from* hengest :—Hors *equus,* hengest *cabullus,* Wrt. Voc. i. 287, 42. Ān hundred wildra horsa and .xvi. tame hencgestas, Cht. Th. 548, 11. [Horses were used by those who had to journey or whose business required them to move about ; for the drawing of vehicles in which either people (especially invalids (?) v. under wægn, Bd. 3, 9 : Lch. ii. 30, 29 : *and see* hors-bǣr) or goods (v. lād ; III) were carried ; and as beasts of burden (v. Ll. Th. ii. 298, 23 *supra:* seám-hors). They were used, too, in hunting. When the Danes came Byrhtnoth seems to have been hawking : He lēt him of handon fleógan hafoc, By. 7 ; the huntsman of Ælfric's Colloquy receives a horse from the king (Coll. M. 22, 35 *supra*) ; and from the story in Bd. 5, 6 [*supra*] it seems that racing was not altogether unknown at a very early time. But if a passage in Alfred's translation of Boethius describes English feeling, riding as an amusement was little known (v. rídan). In war, too, and in farming horses were less used than in later times. In the Chronicle under the year 1055 (v. *supra*) a defeat of the English is attributed to their being on horses, a mode of fighting which according to Florence of Worcester was 'contra morem' ; and Byrhtnoth, who bids his men drive away their horses (By. 2 *supra*), himself alights (By. 23). According to the colloquy ploughing was done with oxen, and the difference between the English and Scandinavian practice may explain the reason for Alfred's noting Ohthere's account of the use of horses in ploughing (Ors. I, I *in Dict.*).] v. ge-stēd-, rād-, seám-, stōd-hors. Cf. *too* eoh, hengest, mearh, mere, stēda, wicg.

**hors-ærn.** v. hors-ern.

**hors-ærnnes** (?) *horse-running* (a gloss to hippo-*dromus*) :—Horsernysse *ypodromi,* An. Ox. 2, 133. v. ærnan ; hors-hūs, hors-ryne.

**hors-bǣr.** *Add:*—His horsbǣr þe hine mon untrumne on bær wæs gehealden, Bd. Sch. 382, 13. Sum þegn læg on paralisyn . . . þā cwæð hē þ hē wolde tō Wynceastre sȳðian hūru on his horsbǣre, Hml. S. 21, 181.

**horsc** *quick.* *Dele passage from* C. D. iii. 456, 15, *and see* horsc foul.

**horsc ;** *adj.* *Foul, dirty* :—On horscum wyllan (cf. in fūle wyllan, 367, 18 : *contrast,* tō þām fægran wille, C. D. B. iii. 352, 14), C. D. iii. 456, 16. v. horh, horu, horsc-lic, foul.

**hors-camb.** *Add:*—Hē sceal habban horscamb and sceára, Angl. ix. 263, 8.

**horsc-lic, horx-lic ;** *adj.* *Foul* :—Horxlic *fædus,* An. Ox. 2, 499. Horxlices *squalentis,* i. *sordentis* (*eremi*), 2430. Heora heortan horxlice wyrmas (cf. Dante's 'fastidiosi vermi') ceorfað, Dōm. L. 167. Hors-lice wītehūsa *squalentium ergastulorum,* An. Ox. 4752. Horslice fȳlþu *putidos squalores,* 1789. v. horsc *foul.*

**horslíce.** *Add:*—Horslícae (-e) *naviter,* Txts. 78, 668. Horslíce, hwætlíce, Wrt. Voc. ii. 59, 47.

**hors-cniht ;** *m.* *A groom* :—Aman gelǣdde Mardochēum geond þā burh swylce hē his horscniht wǣre, Hml. A. 99, 242.

**hors-cræt.** *For* 'Lye' *substitute* :—Horscræt *biga, ubi ii° equi currui junguntur,* Wrt. Voc. ii. 126, 18.

**hors-elene.** *Add:*—Horselene *helena,* An. Ox. 56, 413. [v. *N. E. D.* horse-heal.]

**hors-ern.** *Add:*—Horsern *equiale,* Wrt. Voc. ii. 30, 53.

**hors-here.** *For* Lye *substitute* :—Horshere *Phæræones,* Cant. Moys. Thw. 23.

**hors-hirde.** *Add: an ostler* :—Ne ne sȳ þín horshyrde wǣpenleás *neque sit tuus agason* (= *prouisor equorum*) *inermis,* Hpt. 31, 12, 269. Horshierde *mulio,* Wrt. Voc. ii. 71, 29. Horshiordas *pabulatores,* 116, 59. Horshyrdas, 67, 70.

**hors-hūs** (?) *a hippodrome* :—Mōðhúses, horshyses (-húses ? The passage glossed is : Ad imperialis ypodromi vestibulum, Ald. 40, 33, to which refer also *yppodromi* þæs húses, Wrt. Voc. ii. 81, 24 : *imperialis hypodromi* þæs cāserlican húses, 48, 45), An. Ox. 2998. v. hors-ærnnes.

**hors-minte.** *For* Lye *substitute* :—Nim twā mintan, þ is tūnminte and horsmiute, Lch. iii. 72, 6. [v. *N. E. D.* horsemint.]

**hors-pæþ,** es ; *m.* *A horse-track* :—Ādúne on streáme tō horspæðes forda, C. D. v. 157, 25. Cf. hors-weg.

**hors-ryne** (?) *horse-running* (a gloss to hippo-*dromus*) :—Mōðhúses, horsyrnes *prodromi* (*see the passage glossed under* hors-hūs), Hpt. Gl. 476, 61.

**hors-syðða.** *Dele.*

**hors-þegn.** *Add:*—Horsðegn *mulio,* Wrt. Voc. ii. 114, 39 : *agaso,* 10, 15. 'Æfter mē fēhð tō mín horsþegn' . . . Him ðā forðfērdum Andreas onfēng þære heordelican scíre gȳmnysse, sē wæs gefyrn þæs biscopes horsþegn '*post me, mulionem*' . . . *Quo defuncto ecclesiae pastoralem suscepit curam Andreas, qui in stabulis itinerum cursum servaverat equorum,* Gr. D. 191, 22–27. Horsþēnes wācnys *mulionis uilitas,* An. Ox. 1383. Horsþegnes, Wrt. Voc. ii. 54, 52.

**hors-weard.** *Add: Perhaps as* horsweard *is coupled with* heáfod-weard (*q.v.*), *the duty of the geneát, which has this name, was the care of the lord's horses when out on an expedition.*

**hors-weg.** *Add:*—On horsweg ; of horswege innan gātānstíge, C. D. B. i. 417, 12.

**hors-yrnes.** v. hors-ryne.

**horte,** an ; *f.* *A whortleberry* :—Hortan *facinia,* Wrt. Voc. ii. 146, 69. Wīnberigena (i. hortena) deáge deághian *bacciniorum fuco inficere,* Hpt. Gl. 524, 22. Hortena, An. Ox. 2, 433 : 8, 340. (The last three are glosses to Ald. 75, 17.) Cf. (?) On hortan ford, C. D. vi. 48, 15.

**horu.** *Add: n.* [A weak form occurs, Hml. S. 7, 129.] I. *of physical impurity* (or *uncertain*) :—Fūles horewes *squalentis ceni,* An. Ox. 3598. Mixe, horwe *ceno,* i. *luto,* Wrt. Voc. ii. 130, 71. Fūle horewas *putidos* (*ergastuli*) *squalores,* An. Ox. 11, 134. II. *of moral impurity* :—Mōd mid horuwe (*sorde*) gewæht, Hy. S. 37, 12. Hwæt ligst þū on horwe leahtrum āfylled, Dōm. L. 77. Mid þām fūlestan horwe (*incest*), Ap. Th. 24, 14. Micel tōdǣld betwuh clǣnnysse fǣmnenlicre sāwle and horwu (*sordes*) hyre, seó þe manegra gǣlsum underlæg, Scint. 69, 14. Þā āfeormadan fram horwum *expiatos sordibus,* Hy. S. 4, 22 : Dōm. L. 156 : Cant. M. ad fil. 5. Fram eallum horwum heálicra leahtra, Hml. Th. ii. 242, 31. Þurh ælfremede horwan gefȳled, Hml. S. 7, 129. [v. *N. E. D.* hore.]

**horu-weg.** *Dele the second passage, and add* (?) :—On horweges norðende ; of horweges norðeude andlang weges eástweard, C. D. B. ii. 246, 11. Cf. tō horgan wege, 245, 25.

**horweht.** *l.* horweht(e): **-horwian.** v. ge-horwian : **horx-.** v. horsc-.

**hós** *a bramble. Substitute :* **hos,** *pl.* hossas *and* (?) hosa *a shoot, tendril :—*Hos *butrus* (cf. cyprus, arbor est habens . . . butros sicut erba pratorum, Ld. Gl. H. 90, col. 2), Wrt. Voc. i. 285, 27 : ii. 11, 56. Mænifealde hosses *spissos* (palmitum) *pampinos,* An. Ox. 564. Hisses, hosses, Hpt. Gl. 419, 69. Twigu ł hosa *ramnos* (ramos seems to have been read. Cf. *ramus* twig, Wrt. Voc. i. 285, 80 : but *hosa* from its form seems to belong to *hosu*), Ps. Cam. 57, 10. v. hyse.

**hosa.** v. hosu.

**hose-bend.** For 'Lye . . . 517' *substitute :—*Hosebendas *periscelides* (crurum), An. Ox. 4822.

**hosp.** *Add :—*Hosp, lehter *probrum,* Wrt. Voc. ii. 67, 35. Hosp, hearmspréc *calumpnia,* 127, 77. *Factio,* i. *conjuratio, conventus, narratio vel* hosp, 146, 67. Ðá cempan . . . bígende heora cneówu and cweðende mid hospe (milites . . . *genu flexu ante eum inludebant dicentes,* Mt. 27, 29) . . . Ðæra cempena hosp hæfde getácnunge on gástlicum dingum, Hml. Th. ii. 254, 3. Of unrihtum unhlísfulles hospes edwíte *de sceuo infamis calumnie inproperio,* An. Ox. 4207. [For] teóna hospe *pro calumniarum contumelia,* 4268. Ceachetunge, hospe *cauillatione,* i. *uituperatione,* 4500. Hospe *inproperio,* Wrt. Voc. ii. 44, 71. Hosp *calumniam,* i. *opprobrium,* An. Ox. 471 : 1261. Hux, hosp (husp, Hpt. Gl. 524, 30) *hironiam,* 5201 : Wrt. Voc. ii. 116, 80. Hé smeáde hú hé mihte his hosp on þám hálgum gewrecan *he considered how he might avenge on the saints the insult he had received,* Hml. S. 11, 114. Ælcne hosp hí forbæron, 28, 131. Hospas hyspendra *obprobria exprobrantium,* Ps. Rdr. 68, 10. Gemyndig beó ðú hospa (inproperiorum) þínra, 73, 22. Álýs mé fram hospum (calumniis) manna, 118, 134. Hospas *strofas,* i. *uersutias,* Germ. 396, 318. Sé bið eádig þe for Críste ðolað wyriunge and hospas, Hml. Th. i. 554, 21.

**hospettan ;** *p.* te *To mock :—*Hospetet *subsannat,* Txts. 101, 1963.

**hosp-líc ;** *adj. Insulting, contumelious, opprobrious, blasphemous :—*Hí (the Jews) tó Críste hosplíce word wédende spræcon, Hml. Th. ii. 232, 31.

**hospul ;** *adj. Contemptible :—*Hospula *inrita* (cf. *irritum* forhogd, Wrt. Voc. ii. 112, 7), Ps. Rdr. 88, 35.

**hosp-word.** *Add :—*Sæde se deófol him hospword and mid manegum tálum hine týnde, ac hé næs gestirod for his leásum tálum, Hml. S. 31, 723. Se Hælend ðæra Iúðéiscra hospword gehýrde. . . . 'Wé oncnáwað þæt þú eart wód,' Hml. Th. ii. 232, 16.

**hoss.** v. hos.

**hosu,** e (an ?) ; *f.* (and ? hosa, an ; *m.* ; but *perhaps* hosa, Wrt. Voc. i. 81, 48, might be *pl.,* or a mistake for hose (cf. eága for eáge, 70, 42, or for hosu) :—Hosa *caliga vel ocrea,* Wrt. Voc. i. 81, 48. Synd gesealde from þám abbode ealle neádbehéfe þing, þæt is . . . hosa (hosan. R. Ben. l. 93, 9, *calige*), R. Ben. 92, 3. Habbon hig tó fótgewædum hosa (hosan, R. Ben. I. 92, 1), 88, 14. Hý habbaþ pohhede hosa (caligas follicantes), 136, 23. Gyf þú hosa habban wille, þonne stríc þú uppweard on þínum sceancum mid þínum twám handum, Tech. ii. 127, 12. II. *a husk, pod :—*Hose *glumulâ,* An. Ox. 8, 94. Pisan hosa *siliqua,* Wrt. Voc. ii. 120, 58. See hosa *in Dict.* v. leþer-, scin-hosu ; læs-hosum.

**how** (hop ?), es ; *n. A hill* (?), *mound* (?) :—Oð ðæt wæstmæste how, C. D. v. 84, 1 : 243, 4. [v. (?) N. E. D. *how a hill, mound.*]

**hraca.** v. hrace.

**hráca.** *Add :—*Hráca of breóste *flegma ex pectore,* Chrd. 23, 7. Flegmata, þ byð hráca oððe geposu, deriað þám ealdan, Angl. viii. 299, 36. Hráca ł snofol *flegmata,* An. Ox. 31, 3. v. hræcan.

**hracca.** *For Som. substitute :—*Hracca *occiput,* Wrt. Voc. ii. 65, 33. Hreacca, hreca, hrecca, Txts. 82, 715.

**hrace.** *Add :* [A dat. fem. hraca *occurs in* Kent. Gl. : *this might =* hrace *from a strong* hracu, *or might =* hracâ = hracan. *In the same glossary the nom. is* hraca] :—I. *of living creatures :—*Hrace *gula,* Wrt. Voc. ii. 40, 46. Hrace ł þrotu *guttur,* Ps. L. Spl. Rdr. Vos. 5, 11 : Ps. Rdr. Vos. 13, 3. Hraece, Ps. Srt. 5, 11. Hraecae, 13, 3. Hraca, Ps. Cam. 5, 11 : 13, 3. Raca ł þrotu, Ps. L. 13, 3. Mín hraca *guttur meum,* Kent. Gl. 234. Ðínre hraca *gutturi tuo,* 29 : 157. In hreacan his, Ps. Srt. 113, 7. Hracan, 134, 17. Hracan (hræcean, lxx, 8) *guttori,* Lch. i. lxxiv, 9. Fram eallum þám þigenum þe hracan oþþe innoþ tó miclum luste getýhþ *ab omnibus quae ventris et gutturis prouocant appetitum,* R. Ben. 138, 14. Hracan *fauces,* Wrt. Voc. ii. 39, 56. II. *of places, a gorge, narrow outlet at the upper end of a valley* (?) :—Anlang cumbes hracan (cf. andlang cumbes tó ðæs cumbes heáfde, 434, 35), C. D. iii. 440, 22. [v. N. E. D. *rake.*]

**hræcing.** *Dele, and see* hræcing : **hracod.** *Dele :* **hracu.** v. hrace.

**hradian.** *Add :—*Geefst ł hrada þæt þú álýse *accelera ut eruas me* Ps. L. 30, 3. Is tó hradienne and tó efstenne *currendum et agendum est,* R. Ben. 5, 8.

---

**hradung.** *For Lye substitute :—*Ofst and hradung gódra weorca is tó þǽm ríce weges færeld, R. Ben. 3, 11.

**hraebre-bletae.** v. hæfer-blǽte : **hræca** *occiput.* v. hracca.

**hrécan.** *Add : to reach* (v. N. E. D. s. v.). I. *intrans. :—*Hréceo *excreo,* An. Ox. 53, 40. Wiþ þæs magan springe, þonne þurh múð bitere hræcð oþþe bealcet, oððe him on þám magan súged, Lch. ii. 192, 13. Þám men þe . . . on magan untrum sié oþþe bitere hréce, 62, 16. Gif heora ænegum for unhǽle hráca of breóste derige, hréce bæftan him (*post dorsum flegma proiciat*), and þæt fortrede, Chrd. 23, 8. I a. with dat. of what is expectorated :—Wið þ man blóde hréce, Lch. i. 278, 48. II. *trans. To spit* blood, &c., Lch. i. 142, 1 (in Dict.). Swá hwæt swá man him fram hréce *quod spuitur,* Chrd. 23, 12. v. á-hrécan.

**hræce** *the throat.* v. hrace : **hrécettan.** *Take here passage under* **hréctan** *in Dict., and* cf. hrǽcetung.

**hrǽcetung.** *Add :—*Sé þe bitere hrǽcetunge þrowað, Lch. ii. 158, 19. Lécedóm þe bitere hrǽcetunge áweg déþ, 188, 19 : 256, 11.

**hrǽc-gebrǽc,** es ; *n. l.* hrǽc-gebrǽc, e ; *f.,* and add :—Hrǽcgebrǽc *brancos,* Wrt. Voc. ii. 13, 1.

**hrǽcing.** Rtl. 65, 27. v. rǽcing : **hréctan.** v. hrécettan.

**hrǽc-tunge.** *Add : the tongue of the throat, the uvula :—*Tóðum, tungan, múðe, hrǽctungan (uvae), hracan, protbollan, Lch. i. lxxiv, 9 ; lxx, 8.

**hrǽcung.** *Add : phlegm :—*Hóras *vel* hrǽcunga (-da, MS.) *vel* spátlung *pituita,* i. *minuta saliva,* Wrt. Voc. i. 46, 15. v. blóð-, wyrms-hrǽcung.

**hræd.** *Add :—*Hraed, hrad *percitus,* Txts. 85, 1539 : *perpes,* 87, 1574. Hraede *propero,* 89, 1675. I. *of rapid movement.* v. hrædlíc ; I :—Swá hrædlíce swá hradu ýst windes scip tóbrycð, Ps. Th. 47, 6. Eal swá earn þonne hé mid hrædum flyhte wyle forð áfleón, Nic. 14, 36. Heora hors mid swá hræde ryne (tanto cursu) þá eá oferférdon, efne swá seó eá in hire nænigne wætres streám hæfde, Gr. D. 15, 31. Hrædne gang *rapidum* (i. *uelocem*) *gressum,* An. Ox. 50, 43. Ðá hradan *perpeti* (praepeti *volatu,* Ald. 22, 6), Wt. Voc. ii. 77, 74. Hradum *prepedibus* (praefectibus *catervis,* Ald. 136, 27), 88, 78. I a. *fig. to denote prompt action :—*Hred *festinus* (qui, *festinus* est pedibus offendet, Prov. 19, 2), Kent. Gl. 663. Hrede (veloces) foet heara tó ágeótenne blóð, Ps. Srt. 13, 3. II. *quick in respect to time.* (1) *not lasting long.* Cf. hræd-líc :—Þeáh ðe gýt wǽre óðer þúsend geára tó ðam dæge, nǽre hit langsum ; for ðan swá hwæt swá geendað, þæt bið sceort and hræd, Hml. Th. i. 618, 28. On manegum landun tild bið redre ðonne on óðrum, ge yrðe tíma hrædra ge mǽda rædran, Angl. ix. 259, 8–11. (2) *that comes without delay, speedy.* v. hræd-líc ; III :—Hym byþ hræd bót (cf. sóna bið sél, 18), Lch. i. 354, 11. III. *of prompt action.* (1) *by persons :—*Gemedema hræd beón ongebróht úrum breóste *dignare promptus ingeri nostro pectori,* Hy. S. 10, 6. Ðá ðe bióð tó late . . . ðá ðe bióð tó hrade *pigri . . . praecipites,* Past. 281, 17. Hræde, 176, 1. (I a) *where the kind of action is given, prompt* to do (tó), *prompt in* (on), *ready with* (mid) *a matter :—*Suiðe hræd (velox) tó gehiéranne and suiðe læt tó sprecenne, Past. 281, 5. Hræd tó singienne *ad peccandum ualde procliua,* Chrd. 54, 22. Ne tó hræd ne tó stíð tó ðære wrace, Past. 79, 11. Eáðe and hræd on hlehtre *facilis ac promptus in risu,* R. Ben. 30, 9. Þú wǽre hrædra tó his fultume þonne hé wénde, Ps. Th. 20, 3. Hræd tó yfle *prona in malum,* Chrd. 54, 31. Ic lǽre þ þú beó hrædra mid hreówlicum teárum, Dóm. L. 75. (2) *applied to things :—*Ræddre anwealhnysse *strenue integritatis,* An. Ox. 2343. IV. *of mental quickness* (cf. hræd-sprǽce), Crä. 73 (in Dict.). [v. N. E. D. rad.] v. flán-, frǽ-hræd.

**hræd-bíta.** *l.* -bita, *and add :—*Hrædbita *blata,* Wrt. Voc. ii. 11, 53. Hræþbita, i. 281, 44. v. bitela.

**hræding.** *Add :—*For hrædince *compendio,* An. Ox. 3347. ¶ *the word occurs mostly in the phrase* on hrædinge *hurriedly, without allowing enough time :—*Hit is on hrædinge earfoðrecce *it is difficult to relate unless plenty of time is allowed,* Wlfst. 22, 14. Man ne mihte on hrædinge ásmeágean hú earmlice gefaren is, 166, 11. Hí hæfdon árǽred on hrædincge áne cyrcan, Hml. S. 15, 43. Hí bebyrigdon hine swá swá hí sélost mihton on swylcere hrædinge, 32, 168.

**hræd-líc.** *Add :* I. *quick, swift.* v. hræd ; I :—Hyra hors mid swá hrædlicum ryne (tanto cursu) oferférdon þá eá swylce . . ., Gr. D. 15, 28. II. *of time, coming soon to an end.* Cf. hræd ; II. 1, Ors. 1, 10 ; S. 44, 28 (in Dict.). III. *happening within a short time.* v. hræd ; II. 2 :—Se hrædlíca ende mínes lífes (cf. ymb ánes geáres fyrst and eahta mónað þú swylst, 31, 25), Nar. 32, 26. Þte hrædlíc ús ðínræ milsa ginyhtsamnisse ágesaiga *ut celerem nobis tuae propitiationis habundantiam largiatur,* Rtl. 124, 34. IV. *happening before the natural* or *fitting time, early, premature :—*Hrædlicre *mature* (mutare, MS.), Wrt. Voc. ii. 56, 11. V. *that comes unexpectedly, sudden :—*Him cóm swá hrædlíc sár swá þám cennendan wífe cymð færlic sár, Ps. Th. 47, 6. Ðá ðe mid hrædlíce luste (repentina concupiscentia) bióð oferswíðde, Past. 431, 11 : Chr. 977 ; P. 122, 9 (in Dict.).

**hrædlíce.** *Add :* I. *of quick movement.* (1) *literal :—*'Farað hrædlíce (cito)' . . . Ðá férdon hig hrædlíce, Mt. 28, 7, 8. Cume ðonne án spearwa and hrædlíce (citissime) þ hús þurhfleó, Bd. 2, 13 ; Sch. 165, 23. Mid hræs geeáde all sunes ðerh hrædlíce ł oefestlíce in sǽ *impetu*

abiit totus grex per praeceps in mare, Mt. L. 8, 32. Áris hrædlíce surge velociter, Rtl. 58, 9. Hreód wrít[eres] hredlíce wrítendes, Ps. Srt. 44, 2. (2) figurative:—Hrædlíce cursum (l. cursim, v. Ald. 202, 15, cursim festinat credere Christo), Wrt. Voc. ii. 96, 15.    II. promptly, actively:—Hrædlíce naviter (qui laboriosi certaminis coronam viribus naviter nanciscuntur, Ald. 2, 17), Wrt. Voc. ii. 74, 58.    III. in respect to time at which action takes place:—Hræd[líce] quantotius, An. Ox. 56, 321: B. 963.    (1) immediately after a point of time fixed by the occurrence of an action or defined by an adverb, directly, straightway, at once:—Ðá ætsóc hé ... And hrædlíce (continuo) þá créow se cocc (immediately the cock crew), Mt. 26, 74. Hrædlíce confestim, 21, 3. Up ásprung[n]um leóman hrædlíce geondgeótað exorto iubare extimplo diffundunt, An. Ox. 89. Rædlíce, 3676. Hé him word onsende, þurh þæt hí hrædlíce hælde wæron, Ps. Th. 106, 19. Hwearf hé þá hrædlíce, B. 356. Arís nú hrædlíce, An. 938: 1507: El. 1087. (2) soon, within a short or reasonable time, without delay:—Nis hit him nó swá longe áléfed swá þé dyncþ, ac ðú miht ongitan þ him biþ swíþe hrædlíce gestýred hiora orsorgnesse, Bt. 38, 2; F. 196, 23: C. D. iv. 87, 11: Ll. Th. i. 334, 35: Bl. H. 107, 14. Gehýr mé hrædlíce and mé help freme velociter exaudi me, Ps. Th. 68, 17: 142, 6: Cri. 263. Hredlíce, Ps. Srt. 36, 2. Tídlícor, hrædlícor maturius (ut disputatio maturius terminetur, Ald. 77, 29), Wrt. Voc. ii. 55, 24. Uton habban úre mód úp swá swá wé yfemest mægen wið ðæs heán hrófes þæs héhstan andgites þ þú mæge hrædlícost cumon tó þínre ágenre cýððe, Bt. 41, 5; F. 254, 17. (3) (too) soon, without (sufficient) delay:—Ðæt gé nó tó hrædlíce ne síen ástyrede from gewitte ut non cito moveamini a vestro sensu, Past. 213, 16: 220, 12. Míne sælþa ... náne sælþa ne sint, for ðám hí swá hrædlíce gewítaþ, Bt. 10; F. 26, 28: Bl. H. 21, 11. Manige men lustlíce gehýraþ, and þeáh hrædlíce forgytaþ, 55, 26. Ne hádige man æfre wudewan tó hrædlíce, Ll. Th. i. 416, 16.    IV. in respect to time during which action continues, quickly, shortly, briefly:—Hý wæron gebrytte swá hrædlíce swá swá hradu ýst windes scip tóbrycð, Ps. Th. 47, 6. Be þám æfteran is hrædlíce tó witanne de secundo breuiter intimandum est, Bd. 4, 23; Sch. 469, 13. And þæt ic hrædlíce cwede ut enim breuiter dicam, 5, 8; Sch. 587, 13: 5, 12; Sch. 612, 15.    V. suddenly, unexpectedly:—Færinga, hrædlíce inprovisu, Wrt. Voc. ii. 45, 41. Hú hrædlíce se færlica deáð hié bereáfode ... Ðeáh hí hit hrædlíce ætsomne ne gestriéndon quibus festina mors repente et simul abstulit, quidquid eorum nequitia nec simul nec repente congregavit, Past. 332, 16–18. Hrædlíce perniciter (catechumeni cadaver, quem fortunae ferocitas perniciter oppresserat (cf. hé swá færlíce swealt, Hml. Th. ii. 504, 25), Ald. 30, 26), 78, 79. [v. N. E. D. rathely.] v. for-hrædlíce.

**hrædlicness.** Add:—Cóm sum wíf mid miccle rædlicnysse yrnan of þám húse and cleopode ex aula mulier immensa velocitate currens clamabat, Guth. Gr. 105, 27.

**hræd-mód;** adj. Hasty, quick-tempered:—Se heofonlica wísdóm cwæð þ þ yrre hæfð wununge on ðæs dysegan bósme, þ is þonne hé bið tó hrædmód (cf. ne sis velox ad irascendum: quia ira in sinu stulti requiescit, Eccl. 7, 10), Hml. S. 16, 342.

**hræd-mónaþ.** v. hréþ-mónaþ.

**hræd-ness.** Add: I. where there is rapid movement:—Rædnis pernicitas (pedum), Txts. 182, 75. Wit geségon sittan twégen men on twám olfendum and þá efstan mid þære mæstan hrædnesse, Hml. A. 206, 361. Þone ðóðor mid swiftre rædnesse geslegene, Ap. Th. 13, 4. Rædnisse concursionibus, Wrt. Voc. ii. 105, 24. Rædnessum, 15, 26.    II. where little time is taken:—Se stán weard upp áhafen mid swá mycelre hrædnysse (celeritate) swylce hé ær náne hefinysse hæfde it took as little time to lift the stone as if it had no weight to start with, Gr. D. 123, 13. Hé mid ealre hrædnysse onféng his ærran hæle salutem pristinam citius recepit, 157, 14. Wundorlícre hrædnysse hé ongyt þæs innoðes líðunge in a wonderfully short time he will perceive relief in the stomach, Lch. i. 112, 1.    III. promptness, readiness:—Ic eom ondetta þæt ic onféng on mínne múð wealworda and yfelre rædnesse (cf. reþnesse, 101, 43) unnyttra blissa, Angl. xi. 98, 37. On rædnesse in maturitate, Bl. Gl.

**hræd-rípe.** See instances given under ræd-rípe. (l. ræd-rípe.)

**hræfn** a raven. Add:—Hraebn, hraefn [nycti]corax, Txts. 52, 285. Ðá cóm þær sum hrefen (corvus) inn; sóna swá hé þá cartan geseah, þá genam hé hig sóna and gewát mid on þæne fenn, Guth. Gr. 140, 5. Hí sædon þæt seó glóf of ánes hrefnes múþe feólle, 145, 27. Þá geségon hí þone hræfn mid þan swearton nebbe þá glóse teran uppe on ánes húses þæce, 144, 16. Flugon tó hrócas and hremmas and þára martyra eágan út áhaccedon, Hml. S. 23, 77.

**hræfnes fót.** Add:—Hraebnes (hræfnæs, hraefnes) foot quinquefolium, Txts. 90, 848. Hraefnaes fót, 106, 1084. Hræfnes fót quinquefila, Wrt. Voc. i. 68, 27: Lch. iii. 30, 4. Hrefnes fót, ii. 38, 16: 326, 1. Hræmnes fót, iii. 12, 14. Hremnes fót, i. 382, 16. Hremmes fót polipedium, Wrt. Voc. i. 79, 13: An. Ox. 56, 384.

**hræfnes leác.** Add:—Hreafnes leác ... Ðeós wyrt ðe man satyrion and óðrum naman hræfnes leác nemneð, Lch. i. 108, 16.

**hrægl.** Add: I. a garment, vestment:—Þynwefen hrægl levidensis

(vestis), Wrt. Voc. ii. 54, 17.    Hrægl peplum, An. Ox. 18 b, 74.    Ðæt hrægl superhumerale, Past. 83, 22. Sceolde beón áwriten sió racu ðæs dómes on ðæm hrægle ðe mon hæt rationale ... On ðæm selfan hrægle ðe hé on his breóstum wæg ... Swíðe ryhte ðæt hrægl is geháten ðæt se sácerd beran sceolde ðæs dómes racu, 77, 8–23. Hrecgli, hraecli amiculo, Txts. 41, 155. Preóst hine clænsie in his hálgum hrægle (or under II a? v. mæsse-hrægel) ætforan wiðfode, Ll. Th. i. 40, 15. Gearwende hine mið hrægle (clamyde), Mt. L. 27, 27. Mið fellereóde hrægle purpura, Mk. L. 15, 17. Cyrtel ł hrægl ðin and hrægl ł hæcla tunicam tuam et pallium, Mt. L. 5, 40. þ purbþle hrægl purpureum uestimentum, Jn. L. 19, 5. Gif mon næbbe búton ánfeald hrægl hine mid tó wreónne oþþe tó werianne, Ll. Th. i. 52, 24. Hí scínaþ on manegra cynna hræglum (cf. wædum, Met. 25, 4) purpura claros nitente, Bt. 37, 1; F. 186, 3. 'Bring mé þá hrægl (uestimenta)' ... þá hí þás hrægl gesáwon ... hí onféngon heora ágenu hrægl, Gr. D. 202, 23–203, 2. Hrægla, Mt. L. 26, 67: 27, 35. Woedo ł hræglo ł cláþas, Mk. L. 14, 63.    II. with collective force, dress, garments, clothes, clothing, raiment:—Sió mennisce wædl wilnað ... ægðer ge hrægles ge metes ge dryncges, Bt. 26, 2; S. 60, 18. Hí hine hrægles bædon (vestimenta petebant) ... Se þegn þ hrægl (uestimenta) bróhte tó þám láreówe ... hé cwæð: 'Cumað, nimað þis hrægl and scrýdað eów mid,' Gr. D. 202, 20–28. Horses hýde hí habbað him tó hrægle gedón pelliculas equorum ad uestimentum habentes, Nar. 38, 2. Mid swelce hrægle (veste) hé in eóde, mid swelce gange hé út, Ll. Th. i. 46, 3.    II a. clothes that a person is wearing, (a person's) dress:—Gif hwá nunnan ... on hire hrægl gefó, Ll. Th. 72, 9.    III. cloth, material of which clothing for persons or coverings for things are made:—In huítum hrægle (or under I?) and on asca in cilicio et cinere, Lk. L. R. 10, 13. Sý on wintra seó cuhle of þiccum hrægle, R. Ben. 8, 11.    III a. a cloth (e. g. an altar-cloth, v. wígbed-hrægel), a sheet, a covering (e. g. of a wall. v. wág-hrægl):—Is ofer his byrgenne stówe treówgeweorc on gelícnesse medmycles húses geworht mid hrægle (hrægele, v. l.) gegearwod (coopertus), Bd. 4, 3; Sch. 366, 10. Líchoma innbewand mid línene hrægle corpus inuoluit sindone, Lk. L. 23, 53. In hrægle (scétan, R., scýtan, W. S.) clænum in sindone mundo, Mt. L. 27. 59. Hiá biuundun hine mið linninum hræglum (mid línenum cláðe, W. S.) ligauerunt eum linteis, Jn. L. 19, 40. Wæfelsum, hræglum sabanis (in sabanis et sindonibus bajulabantur aegroti, Ald. 49, 18), An. Ox. 3588. Rægelum, 2, 229. v. bearm-, deád-, hand-, heáfod-, líc-, mæsse-, més-, on-, sculdor-, stríc-, wág-, wíf-, wígbed-hræg(e)l.

**hrægel-gewæde.** For Cot. 118, Lye substitute:—Hloðan, gegirelan liniamento, hræglgewædum liniamentis, Wrt. Voc. ii. 50, 4–5.

**hrægel-hús.** Substitute: A place where clothes are kept:—Hræglhús vestiarium, Wrt. Voc. i. 58, 46. Be mynstermonna hræglelhúse, R. Ben. 89, 2. Ágifen á þá ealdan þonne him man níwe reáf sylle and tó hræglelhúse (rægel-, R. Ben. I. 92, 8, vestiario) betæcen þearfum tó dælenne ... Ðá þe on ýtinge farað nimon him bréc of hrægelhúse ... Sýn eác on hrægelhúse gehealden ægðer ge cugelan ge syr. cas beteran þonne þá þe hý gewunelíce weriað, 91, 1–12.

**hrægel-sceára;** pl. f. Cloth-shears, scissors for cutting out clothes:—Ræglsceára forfices, fexsceára forpices, Wrt. Voc. ii. 150, 21.

**hrægel-talu.** Substitute: The clothes to which the brethren of a monastery had a claim, which had to be furnished by the abbot, as no brother had a right to separate property. Cf. Synd gesealde from þám abbode calle neádbehéfe þing, þæt is cugele, syric, &c., þæt hý þurh neóde náne tale tó syndrigre æhte næbben, R. Ben. 92, 2–5:—Be mynstermonna hrægelhúse and be hyra hrægeltale (this is the heading of a chapter containing an account of the clothing to be furnished to the members of a monastery by the abbot. It was for the purchase of such clothing (ad uestimenta) that the land mentioned in the charter quoted in Dict. was given), R. Ben. 89, 3.

**hrægel-þegn.** Add: I. as officer of royal household:—Ælcan gesettan hrægleðene hundeahtatig mancusa goldis, C. D. B. iii. 75, 30 (from K. Eadred's will).    II. as officer of a monastery:—Beón eác on hrægelhúse (hrægl-, v. l.) gehealden ægðer ge cugelan ge syricas ... and notian þára þe ... on ýtinge farað, and þá eft þám hrægelþéne (vestiario) betæcen swá hý hám cumen, R. Ben. 91, 13. Be hrægelþénum gebróðra de vestiariis fratrum, R. Ben. I. 91, 9.

**hræglung.** Add:—Zosimus hire tó cwæð: 'Ne beþorftest þú nánre andlyfene oððe hræglunge?' Heó him andswarode: '... se gegyrla þe ic hæfde sóna swá ic Iordanen oferfór mid swiðlicre ealdunge tótorene forwurdon,' Hml. S. 23 b, 567.

**hraen.** v. hærn: -hræscian. v. á-hræscian.

**hrætele, hrætel-wyrt.** Substitute: hrætel-wyrt, e; f. Rattle-wort:—Hrætelwyrt hierobotanum, Wrt. Voc. i. 68, 73. v. hratele.

**hræþe-mús.** v. hreaþe-mús.

**hræw.** Add: I. A living body:—Sceal þín hrá dælan ... Hié þín feorh ne magon deáðe gedælan, An. 954: 1033.    II. a dead body, corpse:—Eálá þú earma líchama, nú þú scealt gewurðan tó fúlan hræwe and wyrmum tó mete, Wlfst. 141, 1. Ræwe (reáwe, Hpt. Gl. 441, 14) cadaueri, An. Ox. 1480. [Geed]cuced ræw (reáw, Hpt. Gl. 458, 45)

rediuiuum cadauer, 2213. Ræw (ræáw, Hpt. Gl. 518, 23) funera, 4871. Fore þám wyrmum þe of þám hreáwum (hreáwe, v. l.) creópað, Gr. D. 302, 19. Se feónd gespearn fleótende hreáw, Gen. 1447. Eów in beorge bæl fornimeð, and eówer hrá bryttad lácende líg, El. 579.

hrá-gífre. Substitute for citation :—Þá wælhreówan oððe þone hrágífran funestam (cf. þæs réþan and þæs deádberendan funesti, 34, 12 : þá deádlicostan funestissima, 36, 25), Wrt. Voc. ii. 38, 21.

hrágra. Add :—Hrágra ardea et dieperdulum (cf. deperdulus, auis i. negra, id est reig, Steinm. iv. 185, 42), Txts. 38, 42. Ardea hrágra diomedea, Wrt. Voc. i. 29, 9. Hrágra ardea, ii. 7, 69 : 10, 34. Hráhra (hrágra, v. l.), Ælfc. Gr. Z. 307, 3. Rághgre, Hpt. 33, 240, 30. ¶ in compounds :—On hrágraþorn, of hrágraþorn, C. D. iii. 31, 19. Siluam quae dicitur Rágreholt, v. 5, 23.

hrá-líc. Substitute : hrá-líc, hráw-líc ; adj. Funereal :—Heófendlíce, hráwlíc funebre (cf. ii. 76, 76 where carmen funebre, Ald. 13, 22, is glossed), Wrt. Voc. ii. 37, 4.

hram-gealla. v. ram-gealla.

hramma. Add :—Of þæs magan ádle cumað monige ádla, ... hramma, Lch. ii. 174, 25.

hramsan. Substitute : hramsa, hramse, an ; m. f. Wild garlic :—Hramsa, hromsa acitula, Txts. 40, 59. Hramse, Wrt. Voc. i. 286, 19. Ramese, 67, 2. Hramsa caepinica, Txts. 108, 1108. Hromsan (hramsa, 40, 60) crop acitelum, 37, 57. Hramsan crop, Wrt. Voc. i. 286, 20. Hrameson ramuscium, Lch. iii. 304, col. 2. Ramesan ramusium, Wrt. Voc. i. 30, 44. ¶ in compounds ? :—On hramæshangran ; of ðám hangran, C. D. iii. 229, 27. Beneoðan hramesleá, v. 297, 14. [v. N. E. D. rams, ramson.]

hran. Add : a small kind of whale :—Hran, hron, horn ballena, Txts. 44, 146. Hran oðð e hwæl, Wrt. Voc. ii. 10. Manducat unumquodque animal in mari alterum. Et dicunt quod vii minoribus saturantur maiores, ut vii fiscas sēlaes fyllu, sifu sēlas hronaes fyllu, sifu hronas hualaes fyllu, Lch. iii. 304, col. 2 ... (seven seals are plenty for a smaller whale, and seven smaller whales are plenty for one of the larger kind), Au. Ox. 54, § 1. Sǽfisce ꝥ hrane ballenā (grandior), 23, 48. Hran ballenam, coetum, 7, 47 : ballenam, 4, 16. Ran balenam .i. diabolum (crudelissimam superbiae balenam virtutum devoratricem, Ald. 10, 26. Cf. the poem on the whale), 668.

hran-fisc. Add : The word seems used of some other fish than the whale in the following :—Hié of ðæm neáhēum and merum þá hronfiscas ūp tugon, and þá æton, and be þæm lifdon, and þ wæter æfter druncon (this very imperfectly translates the Latin, which is : Hii assueti fluminibus necnon et stagno quum terris erant crudo pisce tantummodo et aquarum haustu viventes), Nar. 22, 9.

hratele. Add : n ; f. The name of some plant :—Hratele bobonica, Wrt. Voc. i. 67, 1. Hrate[le?] bobonaca, Lch. iii. 300, col. 2. [v. N. E. D. rattle ; I. 3.] v. hrætel-wyrt.

hraþe. Add : I. of quick movement. (1) with verbs of motion :—Hræðe gangaþ cito euntes, Mt. R. L. 28, 7. Hié eódun hraþe of byrgenne, Mt. R. 28, 8. Þú hræðe (cf. on hrædum færelde, Bt. 4 ; F. 6. 31) hefon ymbhwearfest, Met. 4, 3. Giurnun twoege somen and ðe óðer ðegn hraðor (hraður, L. citius) arn ðon Petre, Jn. R. 20, 4. Hwearf þá tó healle swá hé hraðost meahte, þæt hé ofer his ealdre gestód, Az. 166. (2) of quick movement of the body :—Hió ðæt gihérde árás hræðe (raþe, W. S. cito), Jn. 11, 29. Hraðe (with a quick movement) heó æðelinga ánne hæfde fæste befangen, B. 1294. II. in respect to time, where the relation of the time of a circumstance to a fixed point of time is given. (1) immediately, straightway, at once :—Ðá ongann hé sueriga ... And hraeðe (hræðe, R. continuo) hona gesang, Mt. L. 26, 74. Hræðe (hraðe, R.), 13, 20 : 27, 48. Heá hraðe (statim) forleorton netta, 4, 22 : Mt. p. 1, 8. Mid ðý wæs gefulwad hraðe (hræþe, R. confestim), Mt. L. 3, 16. Hraðe, 21, 3. Mid þí hé þus cwæð, hraþe sió onlícnes sendde mycel wæter þurh hiore múþ, Bl. H. 245, 24 : 19, 30. Þá ongeat hé hraðe ꝥ ..., Gen. 1474 : Dan. 242 : Jud. 37. Ne þæt hé yldan þóhte, ac hé geféng hraðe rinc, B. 740 : El. 669. Wæs him swíðe hraðe geandwyrd respondetur protinus, Past. 443, 23. (2) within a short time, soon, without delay :—Beó þú onbúgende þínum wiþerwinnan hraðe (cito), þá hwíle þe þú eart on wege mid him, Mt. 5, 25. Hreðe, Ps. Srt. 36, 2. Þ ðú wyrces dó bræðe (citius), Jn. L. 13, 27. Hræðe (statim) úp iornende wæs, Mk. R. L. 4, 5. Hraðe (hræðe, v. l.) sóna þæs æfterfylgendan wóles mox subsequentis pestilentiae, Bd. 4, 1 ; Sch. 334, 12. Ic ne mæg hit nú swá hraþe ásingan hanc oportet paullisper differas voluptatem, Bt. 39, 4 ; F. 218, 8. Þænne wangas hraðe blóstmum blówað, Men. 90 : B. 224 : Met. 13, 31. Ðǽm mæg beón suíðe hraðe (hræðe, v. l.) geholpen quibus citius succuritur, Past. 225, 22. Ðá gecýðde hé swíðe hræðe æfter ðǽm paulo post adjunxit, 465, 18. Sume hé bereáfaþ hiora welan swíðe hraþe þæs ðe hí ǽrest gesǽlige weorþaþ some he strips of their wealth very soon after they have begun to be fortunate, Bt. 39, 11 ; F. 228, 22. Ful hræðe ðæs paulo post, 22, 1 ; S. 50, 11. Ðæt wé magon ongitan hræðor bi úrum ágnum gewunan quod citius ex ipso usu colligimus, Past. 411, 15. Árás þá eorla wynn swá hé hraðost meahte (as soon as his weariness would permit), Gú. 1082. III. where action or process goes on rapidly :—Hrægle gelíc þe hraðe ealdað, Ps. Th. 108, 19. Weaxaþ swíþe hraþe feldes blósman, Bt. 9 ; F. 26, 18. Hraður þonne ic mæge án word gecweþan dicto citius, Wrt. Voc. ii. 28, 2. Þær þær hit gefrēt þ hit hraþost weaxan mæg and latost wealowigan, Bt. 34, 10 ; F. 148, 22. IV. suddenly :—Swíðe hræðe for sumum ungesǽldum tó ungemetlíce unblíðe eum repente tristitia oborta immaniter deprimit, Past. 455, 9. V. readily :—Hraþe ultro (Christus contritis corde ultro miserescit, Ald. 58, 8), Wrt. Voc. ii. 84, 65. ¶ þý hraþor the rather, the sooner. (1) in respect to time :—Mon mæg ðý hraðor ðára reáfera gítsunga gestillan, gif ... citius raptorum avaritia corrigitur, si ..., Past. 333, 13. (2) (all, none) the more for this reason, on this account :—þeáh hí eówre sín, ne þincþ eów nó þý hraþor (raþor, v. l.) heora genóh, Bt. 13 ; F. 38, 31 : 30, 1 ; F. 108, 9, 11 : 32, 2 ; F. 116, 25 : 33, 2 ; F. 124, 24. Hræþor (hraþor, v. l.), 41, 4 ; F. 252, 3. þeáh man deádne mannan mid reáfe bewinde, ne árist þæt reáf ná ðe hraðor eft mid þám men, Hml. Th. i. 224, 6. þ hé sumne rǽd funde þ þe hraðor nære heora gemynd ádýlegod, Hml. S. 29, 196. [v. N. E. D. rathe ; adv., rather ; adv.] v. for-hraþe, raþe.

hráw-líc. v. hrá-líc : hreá indigestion. v. hreán in Dict.

hreác. For last citation substitute :—Múwan, hreácas acervos, Wrt. Voc. ii. 9, 55. Dele ' v. hrycce,' and add : v. scíd-hreác.

hreacan. v. hráce : hreád. v. earm-hreád : hreáfetian. v. wín-reáfetian : hreáfigende. v. hwearfian.

hreám. Add : I. cry, clamour :—Hwæt gemǽnð þ word : ' Þára Sodomotiscra hreám (clamor) ástáh úp tó heofenum.' Seó syn bið mid stemne (voce) þonne se gylt bið on dǽde ; and seó syn bið mid hreáme (clamore) þonne se man syngað freólíce bútan ælcere sceame swylce hé his yfel óþrum mannum bodige, Angl. vii. 46, 446-452 : Gen. 18, 20-21. Þá weard hreám áhafen ... wæs on eorðan cirm, By. 106. I a. where the voice is raised under the influence of strong emotion (pain, terror, anger, &c.), a cry of pain, &c. :—Mid Dryhten dreám, mid deóflum hreám, Cri. 594. Þæt folc fleáh áfirht for heora hreáme omnis Israel fugit ad clamorem pereuntium, Num. 16, 34 : Hml. S. 13, 229. Se sceocca sóna fordwán mid swíðlicum reáme, swá þ ðá munecas micclum áfyrhte wurdon áwrehte, 6, 316. Ic geseah mínes folces geswinc, and heora hreám (clamorem) ic gehýrde, Hml. Th. ii. 192, 5. Heó ongan swá fela stefnum and hreámum (tot vocibus clamoribusque) hlýdan, swá fela swá heó mid áwyrgedum gástum wæs geþreád, Gr. D. 74. 4. II. where the cry (proclaiming, appealing, &c.) consists of articulate words :—On middre nihte wæs mycel hreám geworden (man hrýmde and cwæð clamor factus est, Mt. 25, 6) : ' Nú cymð se brýdguma,' Angl. viii. 307, 13. Ic offrode onsægdnesse hreámes ꝥ stefne lofes immolaui hostiam uociferationis, Ps. L. 26, 6. Gif wé þurhwuniað on úrum gebedum, þonne mage wé gedón mid úrum hreáme þæt se Hælend stent, Hml. Th. i. 156, 26. Þeáh ðe hé mid hreáme ðæs bǽde, ii. 500, 21. Hé mid hreáme clypode : ' Mære is se god ...,' Hml. S. 22, 116. [v. N. E. D. ream.]

hreáþe-mús. Add :—Hreáthamús, hraeðemuus stilio vel vespertilio, Txts. 99, 1924. Hreádaemús, hreádamús, hraeðemuus vespertilio, 106, 1098. Hreáþemús vespertilio, Wrt. Voc. i. 281, 34.

hreáw hreów. Add : [for the double form cf. hreáw and hreów (p. tense of hreówan), streáw and streów, eáwan and eówan.] I. of food, not cooked :—Þær syndon menn ðá be hreáwan flǽsce and be hunige lifigeað ubi sunt homines cruda carne et melle uescentes, Nar. 38, 16. Næs þæt folc gewunod tó hreáwum flǽsce, þeáh ðe God him bebude þ hí hit hreáw ne æton ... Sé wile ðicgan Godes líchaman hreáwne ..., Hml. Th. ii. 278, 29-32. Be hreáwum fixum hý libbað and þá etaþ pisces crudas manducant, Nar. 35, 4. II. of hides, undressed. v. hreáwness :—Wǽtum [and] hreáwum sina [bendum] udis et crudis neruorum nexibus, An. Ox. 3241. Hreáwum crudis (neruorum flagris, Ald. 58, 3), 4113 : Wrt. Voc. ii. 24, 20. [v. N. E. D. row for the hreów form.]

hreáwan ; p. de To get raw :—Reáwde vel blódgade crudescit, Wrt. Voc. ii. 137. [Rawe as fiesche crudere, crudescere, Cath. Ang. 301.]

hreáw-ness, e ; f. Rawness of a hide. v. hreáw ; II :—Grēnre hýde hreáwnesse recentis corii cruditate, An. Ox. 3283.

hrecca. v. hracca : hreddan. Add : [v. N. E. D. redd.]

hreddere, es ; m. A defender :—For þig is þǽre hálgan cyrcan neód þ heó hæbbe hredderas (defensores), Chrd. 94, 4.

hredding. Add :—Ælc rihtwís man hæfde fultum and hreddinge, sé ðe mid fullum geleáfum on his earfoðnyssum tó ðám Ælmihtigan clypode, Hml. S. 13, 48. Hræddinge, 2, 219. v. á-, land-hredding.

hréfan. Add : v. ofer-hréfan.

hregrése the groin :—Hregrési inguen, Txts. 110, 1181 : Hpt. 33, 244, 1. [Cf. (?) O. H. Ger. hega-drósc inguen.] Cf. (?) ræge-reóse.

hréman. Substitute : hréman ; p. de To vaunt, boast :—Nó ꝥ ðú þín aldor ǽfre wolde Godes goldfatu in gylp beran, ne þý hraðor hrémde þeáh þe here brohte Israéla gestreón in his ǽhte geweald, Dan. 756.

Hār hilderinc hrēman ne þorfte mecga gemānan, Æðelst. 39. [*O. Sax.* hrōmian : *O. H. Ger.* hrōmen, hruomen *gloriari, jactare.*]

**hrēman** *to cry out.* v. hrīman : **hrēmig.** *Add* : [v. *O. Sax.* hrōmag : *O. H. Ger.* hruomag *gloriosus.*] v. wil-hrēmig.

**hremman.** *Add* :—Hē mid smeágungum smeálíce ūs hremð (*v. l.* dereð), Hml. S. 13, 59. Þā gecorenan hē hræmde ł gelette (*impediuit*), Ps. L. 77, 31. v. ge-hremman.

**hremming.** *Add* :—Lettingge, remmincge *offendiculo*, An. Ox. 971 : *obstaculo*, 5135 : 5450. Wearne, remmincge *obstaculo*, i. *impedimento*, 2080. Remmincga *obstacula, impedimenta*, 1426. Remmingcum *obstaculis*, i. *contrariis*, 3563. v. weorold-hremming.

**hrenian.** *For* 'redolere . . . Lye' *substitute* : *to smell of something* :—Æfæst næfre wīn hrenige, þ he nā gehȳre þæt þeodwitan : 'Þ nys coss ræccean ac scencan' *religiosus nunquam uinum redoleat, ne audiat illud philosophi* : '*Hoc non est osculum porrigere, sed propinare,*' Scint. 106, 5.

**hreócan.** v. reócan : **hreoce.** *Dele.*

**hreód.** *Add* : I. as a collective or generic term, *reed, the reed, reeds; a reedy place* (?) :—Hreód (reód, 112, 46) *carectum* (v. Numquid crescere potest *carectum* sine aqua ?, Job 8, 11), Txts. 47, 387 : Wrt. Voc. ii. 13, 37 : 129, 15. Þær synd . . . manige eáland and hreód and beorhgas and treówgewrido *crebris insularum nemoribus*, Guth. Gr. 113, 5. On þære eá ōfre stōd hreód *fluminis ripas harundo vestiebat*, Nar. 8. 20: Wæs seó burh mid þȳ hreóde . . . þe wē ǽr sægdon geworht *oppidum ex his arundinibus quas ante descripsimus erat edificatum*, 10, 13. In heáhmórum and hreódum (hreódeum, hrēþum, rēþum, *v. ll.*) *in high mountains and in rough places covered with reeds* (? cf. Guth. Gr. 113, 5 *supra*; but the Latin is 'in arduis asperisque montibus'), Bd. 4, 27 ; Sch. 515, 13. II. *a reed* :—Hreód *harundo, canna*, Wrt. Voc. ii. 110, 22 : *ferula*, 98, 9 : *calamus vel canna vel arundo*, i. 79, 27. Hiá genōmon hreád (*harundinem*) and slōgun heáfud his, Mt. L. 27, 30. II a. *a reed for writing* :—Hreód bōceras (*scribe*, Ps. Cam. has writ *scribe*, Ps. Srt. Vos. have writ *scribę*. Is it possible that scribe has been taken as imperative and glossed by wrīt ? Or should wrīteres be read for writ ? The best version is given in Ps. Rdr. where *calamus scribę is rendered* wrītingfeþer bōceres) hrædlíce wrītendes *calamus scribae uelociter scribentis*, Ps. L. 44, 2. Hangode seó carte on þām hreóde *conspicit unam arundinem . . . in cujus fastigio . . . schedulam . . . pendentem*, Guth. Gr. 141, 18. ¶ the word forms part of many compounds in local names, e. g. hreód-brōc, C. D. iii. 79, 26 : hreód-burne, 25, 18 : hreód-īg, v. 121, 30 : hreód-leáh, iii. 246, 19 : hreód-mǣd, vi. 153, 9 : hreód-mōr, C. D. B. ii. 433, 29 : hreód-pōl, C. D. ii. 29, 10 : hreód-slǣd, vi. 137, 17.

**hreódan.** v. ge-, on-hreódan ; hroden.

**hreód-aler** *some kind of alder* (?) :—On Hreódalras ; of Hreódalron, C. D. B. ii. 270, 26.

**hreód-cynn,** es ; *n. A kind of reed* :—Þā genāmon hié sume spingan and gefyldon mid ecede . . . and dydon on sum hreódcynn, and ræhton ūp tō his mūþe, Nap. 39.

**hreódeum.** *Add* : v. hreód ; I.

**hreód-gird,** e ; *f. A reed, cane* :—[H]reó[d]gyrde *calamum*, Germ. 390, 48.

**hreódig.** v. hreódeum *in Dict.* : **hreódiht.** *l.* hreódiht(e).

**hreódihtig ;** *adj. Reedy, full of reeds or sedge* :—*Carecta, loca caricis plena, spinacurium*, secgihtig *vel* hreódihtig, Wrt. Voc. ii. 129, 14.

**hreód-pípere,** es ; *m. A reed-piper, player on a flute* :—Reódpípere *auledus*, Wrt. Voc. i. 60, 46.

**hreód-writ.** *Dele, and see* hreód ; II a.

**hreóf.** *Add* : I. of persons :—Hreóf *scabiem habens*, Bd. 5, 2 ; Sch. 557, 7 : *colosus*, i. *infirmus*, Wrt. Voc. ii. 134, 34. Seó fāgung wæs tōbrǣded geond eallne his líchaman, þ hē wæs geþúht swylce hē hreóf wǣre *ita ut diffusa in corpore ejus varietas leprae morem imitari videretur*, Gr. D. 159, 2. Scs Martinus gecyste þone man þe wæs egeslíce hreóf, and hē wæs sóna hāl, Shrn 147, 6. Hreófe oððe wearrihtum *callosi* (but the passage is : Corpore *calloso venere leprosi*, Ald. 175, 18), Wrt. Voc. ii. 93, 72 : 19, 53. Ðā wunda on ðǣm hreófan líce *vulnera quae erumpunt membris per scabiem*, Past. 437, 17. Ðes Scs Marcus hǣlde untrume men and hreófe, Shrn. 74, 27. Hreófe *larbatos* (the glosser seems to have misunderstood the passage : *Larvatos* et comitiales ac caeteros valetudinarios sanitati restituit, Ald. 70, 16), Wrt. Voc. ii. 86, 64 : 52, 47. *a disease* :—Cniht geþreád mid þǣre hreófan ādle *puer morbo elephantino correptus*, Gr. D. 157, 6. II. *of a thing*, Wal. 8 (*in Dict.*).

**hreófian.** v. ā-hreófian.

**hreófl,** e ; *f. Add* :—Gif sió hreófl (*scabies*) ðæt líc ofergǣð, Past. 437. 18. Hē swā mycel hreófle and sceorfe (micle hreófle and scurf) on his heáfde hæfde *scabiem tantam ac furfures habebat in capite*, Bd. 5, 2 ; Sch. 557, 12. v. hreófla *leprosy.*

**hreófl ;** *adj. Add* :—Hē wæs ge dumb and hreófl (hreóf, *v. l.*) *scabiem habebat*, Bd. 5, 2 ; Sch. 557, 8.

**hreófla.** *Add : one covered with sores* :—Hreófla *ulcerosus*, Wrt. Voc. i. 45, 63. Tiberius wæs swā unhāl myd myslȳcum wundum þ hē wearð hreófla, Hml. A. 181, 17.

**hreófla** *leprosy. Dele passage from Bede, and add* :—Ðā geslōh hine sóna se snāwhwíta hreófla (*statim orta est lepra in fronte ejus*, 2 Chr. 26, 19), Hml. A. 58, 186. Se hreófla wearð nyðer āfeallen, þ hys lȳchama wæs clǣne, 192, 319. Heliseus gehǣlde Naaman fram ðām atelicum hreóflan, Hml. S. 18, 310. Ðū mínue hreóflan (cf. heó on eallum limum egeslice wunda hǣfde, 266) gehǣldest, 7, 322. Heó (Miriam) wearð mid hreóflum (-an, *v. l.*) geslagen, Hml. A. 58, 177. v. hreófl ; *f.*

**hreóf-lic.** *Substitute* : *Leprous*, as epithet of a disease :—Sió hreóflíce *elephantina*, Wrt. Voc. ii. 33, 6. Hreóflic *regalis* (*morbus*), An. Ox. 18 b, 79. Hreóflicum *elephantino* (*tabo*), 7, 262. Cniht geþreád mid þǣre hreóflican ādle (*morbo elephantino*), Gr. D. 157, 7.

**hreóf-lig** (*l.* hreóflig). *Add* : I. used (often as substantive) of persons :—Seó ealde ǣ bebeád þæt gehwilc hreófli man gecōme tō þām sácerde . . . Gif se sácerd hine hreófligne tealde . . . Swā sceal sē ðe mid heáfodleahtrum wiðinnan hreóflig bið cuman tō Godes sācerde, Hml. Th. i. 124, 5, 12. Hē hreóflig wunode oð ðæt hē weard deád (*fuit rex leprosus usque ad diem mortis suae*, 2 Chr. 26, 21), Hml. A. 59, 187. His líchama wæs geþúht swylce hē hreófli wǣre *in corpore ejus varietas leprae morem imitari videretur*, Gr. D. 159, 2. Hē forgeaf . . . hreóflium smēðnysse heora líchaman, Hml. Th. i. 26, 11. Hī reóflige geclǣnsodon, ii. 490, 23. Hreóflige, Hml. S. 15, 6. II. used of a disease :—Wǣrrehte, hreóflic *elefantinosa*, i. *regia* (*corporis incommoditas*), An. Ox. 2072. Hreófligum wyrmse *elephantino tabo*, 3584. Hreóflige þicnysse *elefantina* (*cutis*) *callositate*, 4927. v. un-hreóflig.

**hreógan** *to get rough* (of weather) :—Mid þȳ hit ǣfenne neálǣhte, ðā ongunnon þā windas eft weaxan and þ weder hreógan (*printed* breogun, *but see* Angl. 1. 511), Nar. 23, 11.

**hreóh** *storm. Add* : hreów *a stormy, troublous time* :—Manige yfelice mæn becōmon tō þām wuldorbeágum þæs sōðan martyrdōmes, þonne hwylc hreów oððe ehtnes upp ārās (*oborta occasione*), Gr. D. 232, 7. v. hreóh-nes.

**hreóh.** *Add* : hreów, reów. (*For forms with* w *see* hreóh *storm*, hreóh-nes ; I.) I. *rough* of weather, sea, &c., *tempestuous* :—Sió hlúde ȳð on ðǣre hreón sǣ *procella saeviens*, Past. 437, 16. Good scipstióra ongit micelne wind on hreóre sǣ ǣr ǣr hit geweorþe, Bt. 41, 3 ; F. 250, 14. II. *fierce, cruel* of pain, &c. *Take here* reów *in Dict., and add* :—Swā se þeódsceaða reów rícsode, An. 1118. Nis þǣr unrótnes, ne hryre, ne caru, ne hreóh tintrega *non tristitiae, curae, tormenta, ruinae*, Dōm. L. 261. Nis ðǣr hryre, ne caru, ne hreóge tintregu, Wlfst. 139, 30.

**hreohehe.** *l.* hreohche.

**hreóh-full.** *For citation substitute* :—Kł. Januarius gif hē byþ on Mōnandæg, þonne biþ . . . windig sumor, and hreóhfull geár (cf. estas uentuosa et tempestuosa, 12) biþ, Archiv cxx. 297, 46. *See next word.*

**hreóh-lic ;** *adj. Stormy, full of trouble* :—Hū feallendlic and hū lǣnendlic and hū hreóhlic þeós woruld ys, Wlfst. 136, 27. *See preceding word.*

**hreóh-nes.** *Add* : , hreów-nes. I. *storm, tempest* (lit. or fig.) :—Wearð ðāre sǣ smiltnesse āwænd fǣringa and wearð micel reównes āweht, swā þ seó sǣ cnyste þā heofonlican tungla, Ap. Th. 10, 26. Ystendre (wealcendre) sǣ (reóhnesse) fiódas *feruentis* (i. *furentis*) *oceani flustra*, An. Ox. 2475. On reþre þreóhnesse *in seuo turbine*, Wülck. Gl. 252, 32. Ne lǣt ūs besencan on ðissere cealdan hreóhnysse, Hml. S. 11, 187. Ystendre reóhnesse *tumentem* (*aequoris*) *insaniam*, An. Ox. 2500. Gedrēfednesse ðreóhnessum *tribulationum turbines*, Wülck. Gl. 251, 41. Scúra hreóhnessa *procellarum turbines*, An. Ox. 4415. Gif þunor cymð æt þǣre xii tíde dæges, hreóhnessa and stormas sē bēcnað, Archiv cxx. 48, 33. II. *a stormy, troublous time* :—þonne hwylc hrīnnes oððe ehtnes upp ārās *oborta occasione*, Gr. D. 232, 7. On þǣre hreóhnesse, gedrēfnesse *ea tempestate* (*florens*), An. Ox. 2420. III. *a rough place, desert* (?) :—Hine hig tihton on unwæterigre stōwe ł on reóhnesse (*in inaquoso*), Ps. L. 77, 40. v. breóh *a storm.*

**hreól.** *Add* :—Reól *alibrum*, Wrt. Voc. ii. 7, 71 : i. 282, 16. Riul, 66, 32. Spinte, reól, gearnwindan, Angl. ix. 263, 10.

**hreónian.** v. reónian : **hreopian.** v. hrepian.

**hreósan.** *Add* : I. *to fall* from an upright position, *fall to the ground* :—Hrýst *cespitat*, Hpt. 31, 17, 478. Hreás *occubuit* (machera percussus *occubuit*, Ald. 49, 14), An. Ox. 3582. Reósende *nutabunda* (*arbor*), 1575 : 2234. II. *to fall from a state of material or spiritual well-being* :—Hreósþ *corruit* (*impius in impietate sua*, Prov. 11, 5), Kent. Gl. 349. Úp āhefð [Dryhten] ealle þā þe hreósað *alleuat Dominus omnes qui corruunt*, Ps. L., Srt., Rdr. 144, 14. On hrorenum folke *in populo graui*, Ps. L. 34. 18. III. *to fall from a higher to a lower level* :—Hié under grund hruron, An. 1602. On þæt ēce fȳr gē breósan sceal, Cri. 1524. Hreósende *cassabundus* (cf. (?) in tetrum

tartarum *cassabundus*, Ald. 10, 35), Wrt. Voc. ii. 129, 19.    **IV.** *to*
*fall* into a state or condition, *fall* into a person's hands :—Hrure *incidisti*
(*in manum proximi tui*, Prov. 6, 3), Kent. Gl. 124.    **V.** *to move or*
*act with violence, fall* upon, *attack* :—Þá áwyrgedan gástas betwux þá
grimlican léga in hruron and feóllon *maligni inter favillantium vora-*
*ginum atras cavernas discurrentes*, Guth. Gr. 132, 3.   [Reoseđ (falleþ,
2nd MS.), Laym. 15887. Reosen (falle, 2nd MS.), 24016: 26719.
Ras (2nd MS. rees) ; *p.* 15518.]

**hreósend-lic**. *Add : ready to fall.*    **I.** v. hreósan ; **I** :—Hreósend-
lice *cassabundum*, i. *corruendum* (*stipitem*), An. Ox. 2237.    **II.** v.
hreósan ; **III** :—Hreósendlic *cassabundus*, i. *corruendus* (*in tartarum*),
An. Ox. 686.    **III.** v. hreósan ; **V** :—Hreósendlicum scúrum *ruituris*
*imbribus*, An. Ox. 3973.

**hreóđan**. *l.* hreódan.

**hreów** *storm.* v. hreóh : **hreów** ; *adj.* v. hreóh ; *adj.*

**hreów** *sorrow.* *Add :*—Hé in hreówe teárum (*lacrimis paenitentiae*)
Drihtne þeówode, Bd. 4, 25 ; Sch. 496, 13.  Hæbben wé góde hreówe
úra synna, Verc. Först. 95, 15.  v. ge-hreów, *and next word.*

**hreów** ; *adj. Penitent :*—Hé on hreówum teárum . . . Dryhtne
þeówode *totum se lacrimis paenitentiae . . . mancipauit*, Bd. 4, 25 ;
Sch. 496, 13.  v. **hreówe** in Dict.

**hreówan**. *Add : p.* hreów. With dat. or acc. of person, or used
absolutely.    **I.** *to affect with sorrow, to distress, grieve, vex.*  (1)
with pronoun (in apposition to clause) as subject :—Þæt mé on mínum
hyge hreóweđ, þæt hié heofonríce ágan, Gen. 426.  (2) with clause as
subject :—Mec ongon hreówan þæt mín hondgeweorc on seónđa geweald
séran sceolde, Cri. 1415.    **II.** *to affect with pity or compassion.*  (1)
the subject a noun (pronoun).  (a) a person :—Hé þám folce mid his
eáđmódnysse cwéman wolde þ hé þurh his fullan eáđmódnysse hreówan
sceolde (*should excite compassion*), Hml. S. 23, 623.  (b) a thing :—Hé
đæs cáseres mycclan hreówsunga geseah, him þ hreów, Hml. S. 23, 401.
Earfođsýnde wæs se man þe swilc ne mihte hreówan, 82.  (2) no subject
expressed :—Hreáw hine *penituit eum*, Ps. Rdr. 105, 45.    **III.** *to*
*affect with regret, to make* a person *wish that he had not done something,*
or *that something had not happened.*  (1) the subject a noun (pronoun) :—
Ne doo đú nánwuht búton geđeahte, đonne ne hríwđ hit đé đonne
hit gedón biđ *sine consilio nihil facias, et post factum non poenitebis,*
Past. 287, 11.  Him þæt ne hreóweđ, Gú. 783.  Hit þé wyrs ne mæg on
þínum hyge hreówan þonne hit mé æt heortan déđ, Gen. 826.  (2) with
clause or subject :—Hreáw hine swíđe þæt hé áweahte adelinga ord,
Gen. 1276.  Nú mé mæg hreówan þæt ic bæd God, 816 : 819.  (3)
where no subject is expressed and the cause for regret is in the genitive :
—Ne þé hreówan þearf ealles swá micles swá þú mé sealdest *you need not*
*regret all you gave me, much as it was*, Seel. 150.    **IV.** *to affect*
*with sorrow* for sin, *make penitent.*  (1) the subject a noun (pronoun) :—
Gif him his yfel ne hreówþ, Bt. 36, 6 ; F. 182, 21.  Đý læs him tó
hwón hreówen đá geđóhtan synna *si cogitata mala minus cruciant*, Past.
417, 35.  Hié (*sins*) ne magon ealla on áne tíd emnsáre hreówan, 413,
29.  (2) where no subject is expressed and the cause of sorrow is in
the accusative :—Þonne hreóweđ hyre swíđe þá yfelan dǽda, Verc. Först.
105, 9.  [v. *N. E. D.* rue.]

**hreów.** *l.* hreów, q. v.

**hreówian**. *Add :*—Đǽm hrǽwende bróđer *paenitenti fratri*, Lk.
p. 9, 4.

**hreów-lic**. *Add :* **I.** *exciting pity, lamentable :*—Him tó hreówlic
þúhte þ man swá geongne man cwealde . . . swá hé geáxod hæfde
þe man gehwǽr dyde, Ll. Th. i. 240, 25.    **II.** *suffering distress,*
*hapless, miserable :*—Hreówlíce *calamitosum* (*uulgus*), An. Ox. 4868.
[v. *N. E. D.* ruly.]

**hreówlíce**. *Add : in a way to excite pity :*—Ic wille geswigian . . .
hú hreówlíce hé wearđ ádrǽfed of his ágenre þeóde *praetermitto Pandio-*
*nis flebilem fugam*, Ors. 1, 8 ; S. 42, 18.  Swíþe hreówlíce swá gebend
hé wæs wuniende *lacrymabile spectaculum praebuit*, 5, 2 ; S. 220, 1 :
Hml. S. 23, 575 : 639.  þá wearđ hé hreówlíce deád *he died*
*miserably*, Hml. Th. i. 478, 14.  v. wæl-hreówlíce.

**hreów-ness**. *Add :*—Hrewonise wyrcas gié *paenitentiam agite*, Mt.
p. 14, 4.  Hrewunisse, p. 16, 10.  v. swíþ-hreówness.

**hreówsian**. *Add :* **I.** *to grieve, lament* for :—Ongan se wísdóm
hreówsian for þæs módes týdernesse, and ongan giddian *his versibus de*
*nostrae mentis perturbatione conquesta est*, Bt. 3, 2 ; F. 6, 6.    **II.** *to*
*grieve* for sin, *repent* of evil.  (1) absolute :—'Hreówsiađ' . . . Ærest
hé lǽrde đæt hí hreówsodon '*paenitentiam agite*' . . . Praemisit paeni-
*tentiae lamenta*, Past. 425, 35.  Is micel đearf . . . đæt hé sóna hreówsige
*necesse est, ut apud se semper ad poenitentiam recurrat*, 165, 21.  Đæt
hí mǽgen be đǽm ilcan gemete hreówsian *ut mensura lamentationis*
*erigantur*, 417, 34.  Hwílum him đyncđ đæt hé hæbbe fierst genógne
tó hreówsianne *modo adhuc tempus subsequens ad poenitentiam pollicetur*,
415, 35.  Mára gefeá wyrđ on hefonum for ánum hreówsiendum, 411,
13.  (2) with acc. or uncertain :—Sé đe his synna forlǽt and hí ne
hreówsađ, Past. 425, 29, 27.  Đá đe đá geđóhtan synna hreówsiađ,
417, 32 : 419, 19.  Đá đe đá gedónan scylda hreówsiađ, . . .

đæt mon hreówsige his synna, 421, 24-29 : 437, 21.  Đæt hié hira
unryhtwísnesse hreówsian, 425, 24.  Hé sceal his ágnu yfelu hreówsian,
461, 22 : 421, 13.  (3) with gen. :—Đæt mód innan hreówsađ đæs
unnyttes þe se líchoma ǽr dyde *magis intus quod fecimus, dolemus*,
Past. 259, 23.  Đæt mód đæs hreówsađ, 415, 27.  Sceal hé đára
lǽstena worda hreówsian, 199, 16.  (4) with clause :—Hé hreówsade
đæt hé him ǽfre suá ungeriesenlíce geđénigan sceolde, Past. 199, 18.
(5) with prep. :—Đonne hié for ánre hwelcre hreówsiađ, đonne hreówsiađ hié for ealle *dum per unumquodque erroris sui inquinationem deflent*
*simul se ac totos lacrymis mundent,* Past. 413, 24.    **II a.** of penitence in an ecclesiastical sense, *to do penance :*—Hí sceolon seofon geár
mid micelre angsumnysse hreówsian, Hml. A. 149, 125.  v. ge-hreówsian.

**hreówsung**. *Add :*—Hreówsunge *penitudinis*, Wrt. Voc. ii. 66, 15.
Swelce hí hí mid đǽre hreówsunga tó đǽm áđweán đæt hí hí mægen
eft áfýlan *cum idcirco se lacrymis lavant, ut mundi ad sordes redeant*,
Past. 419, 25.  Hé forhogde đá forgifnesse đe hé mid đǽre hreówsunga
begiten hæfde . . . đæt đæt hé ǽr mid đǽre hreówsunga geclǽnsode . . . mon
æfter his hreówsunga gewyrce đæt hé eft scyle hreówsian . . . sé đe
æfter đáre hreówsunga hine ryhtlíce nyle gehealdan . . . sé đe áđwihđ
mid hreówsunga his unclǽnnesse *ipsam, quam flendo potuit impetrare,*
*veniam contemnit . . . dum fletibus suis vitae munditiam subtrahit . . .*
*post fletum committeret, quod rursum necesse sit flere . . . quisquis post*
*lacrymis vitae innocentiam non custodit . . . qui mundatur fletibus a*
*peccato*, Past. 421, 6-22.

**hrépan** ; *p.* te *To call, cry out :*—Hrépađ (*printed* hrewađ) *cient,*
Wrt. Voc. ii. 96, 63.  Hrépađ, 20, 11.  v. hróp, hrópan.

**hrepian** and **hreppan**. [The two forms may be taken together.]
*Add :* **I.** *to touch* with the hand, *come in contact with :*—þ wíf wearđ
gehǽled þá đá heó hrepode (æthrán, Mt. 9, 20) þæs Hǽlendes reáf,
Hml. S. 9, 13.  Wearđ án líc gebróht tó đæs hálgan byrgene . . . þá
árás se deáda mid đám þe hé hrepode þá byrgene, 18, 307.  ' Ic sette
míne hand ofer đé untrumne ' . . . se cyning wearđ gehǽled sóna swá hé
hine hrepode, 24, 157.  Heora handa ástífedon, swá hwá swá hreopode
þá róde mid handum, Hml. Th. i. 598, 12.    **II.** *to touch, make use*
*of, have to do with* :—Ic þé swá gehoóld, þæt þú hig ne hrepodest, Gen.
20, 6.  Ne hrepa þú þæs treówes wæstm, for þan đe þú bist deádlic,
gif đú đæs treówes wæstm geetst *de ligno . . . ne comedas . . . in*
*quocumque enim die comederis ex eo, morte morieris*, Hml. Th. i.
14, 1.    **III.** with the idea of hostility.  (1) where injury is caused,
*to lay hands on, attack, seize.* (a) the subject a person :—Ástrece þíne
hand and hrepa his bán and his flǽsc, Hml. Th. ii. 452, 19.  Hý ne
dorston þá hálgan stówe hreppan (grétan, *v. l. temerare*), Gr. Đ. 43, 12.
(b) the subject a thing :—þá wolde hé þurhþýn hí mid þám swurde, ac
se ord ne dorste hí hreppan, Hml. S. 12, 227.  (2) where blame is expressed [cf. *N. E. D.* touch, 19 = *to take to task, censure*] :—Gif hé
gesceádwíslíce and mid eáđmódnesse sóđre lufe hwylce þinc repađ ođđe
geswutalađ *si qua rationabiliter et cum humilitate karitatis reprehendit*
*aut ostendit*, R. Ben. I. 102, 2.    **IV.** *to touch* the mind or heart :—
Nán lustfullung ne hrepede his mód, Hml. Th. i. 176, 6.    **V.** *to touch*
*on, treat* of a matter.  (1) the subject a person :—Đás þing wé swá
hwónlíce hér hrepiađ on foreweardum worce, for đan wé hig þenceađ
oftor tó hrepian and tó gemunanne, Angl. viii. 300, 21.  (2) the subject
the writing in which the matter is treated :—Đyses godspelles anginn
hrepode úres Hǽlendes þrowunge, Hml. Th. i. 152, 27.  Hwílwendlíce
gódnyssa, swylce swá þæt godspel hrepode, hláf, and fisc, and ǽig, 252,
25.  [v. *N. E. D.* repe.]  v. á-, for-, ge-hrepian (-hreppan).

**hrepsung**. v. ræpsung.

**hrepung**. *Add :* **I.** *the action of touching* with the hand or other part
of the body, *exercise of the faculty of feeling :*—Godes æugel þ cweartern
geopenode mid his handa hrepunge, Hml. S. 4, 234.  Ic gesyngode on
gesihđe . . . and on hrepunge, Angl. xi. 112, 16.  Repunge, 102, 87.
Wé sceolon áwendan úre handa and ealne líchaman fram fúllicum and
leahterlícum hrepungum, Hml. Th. ii. 374, 7.    **I a.** *sexual contact :*
—Clǽne hrepunga flǽsclicre *mundus contactu carneo*, Hy. S. 42.
37.    **I b.** (*medical*) *examination by feeling :*—Án æþele lǽce . . .
cúđe tócnáwan, gif hé cunnode þæs mannes, be his ædrena hrepunge
hweđer hé hrađe swulte, Hml. S. 3, 569.    **II.** *the sense of touch :*—
þá fíf andgitu sint gehátene þus, *Uisus*, þ is gesihđ . . . *tactus* hrepung
ođđe grápung, on eallum limum, ac þeáh gewunelícost on þám handum,
Hml. S. 1, 199.

**hrér**. *Add :*—Sule hym súpan gebrǽddan hrére ǽgeran, Lch. iii. 106,
17.  [v. *N. E. D.* rear.]  v. hrére.

**hreran**. *The form* hréron *seems to point to a verb of the class to*
*which* beran *belongs. To this* hryre (= hrere) *might be assigned : but it*
*might, perhaps, be looked upon as a. mutated form of* hrure, *though*
*there are few traces outside of the preterite-present verbs of such muta-*
*tion.*  Cf. þætte ic hrure l̃ þ ic feól, Ps. L., þ ic hrure, Ps. Rdr. 117, 13.

**hréran**. *Add :*—Ic wæs syxtýne síđum on đá mere hrérendum . . .
eágorstreámas *I have been sixteen times on a sea-going boat that ploughed*
*through the waves*, An. 491.  v. á-, ge-, ofer-, tó-hréran ; cwic-, fold-,
mold-hrérende ; for-hréred.

**hrére**; _adv. Lightly (cooked)_:—Nim ân hrére bréd ǽg, Lch. iii. 136, 24. Sing on ân hréren bréden (hrére bréd?) ǽg, 294, 8. v. hrér.

**hrére-mûs.** _Add_:—Hrýremûs _stelio (read as_ vespertilio?), Kent. Gl. 1110. [v. _N. E. D._ rear-mouse.]

**hréred-ness.** v. hrér-ness: **hréren-bréden.** v. hrére: **hrére-ness.** v. hrér-ness.

**hrér-ness.** _Add_:—On his ymbehwyrfte bið swíþe mycel hréreues, Verc. Först. 133, 16. Þysne dæg wé ús on mycelre rémesse tóweardne ongytan magon, 130, 20. On hrérnisse _in commotione(m)_, Bl. Gl. (_under_ onhrérnisse; _but see_ Angl. xxi. 237).

**-hresp.** v. ge-hresp: **hrespan.** v. ge-hrespan: **hrétan.** _Dele, and see_ hrútan.

**hréða.** _Add: a mantle_:—Hréðan _melote_ (the mantle of Elijah), Wrt. Voc. ii. 77, 61. Hréðan _melote_ (Amos, dum spoliare se _melote_ et amiculis erubesceret, Ald. 50, 25), 82, 79: 56, 63.

**hréð-mónaþ.** _Add_:—Hrédmónað _Marche_, Chr. P. 274.

**hréð-ness.** v. réþ-ness.

**hrícian**; _p._ ode _To cut open_:—Hí man holdode and hí ealle hrícode (_the MS. has the accent_); swilce óðer wæterflód swá fléow heora blód, Hml. S. 23, 73. Hrýcigende _resulcans_ (cf. manus _resulcans_, iterum aperiens, _the passage is the same in both cases_, An. Ox. 46, 49), Germ. 398, 144. v. tó-hrícian.

**hricsc.** v. hrýsc.

**hriddel.** _Substitute_: [hrídel,] **hriddel,** es; _n. A riddel, coarse sieve_:—Man sceal habban . . . syfa, sǽdleáp, hriddel, hérsyfe, Angl. ix. 264, 13. [v. _N. E. D._ riddle.]

**hridder.** _Add_: , **hríder, hriddern**:—Hríder _glebulum_, Wrt. Voc. ii. 98, 12. Hridder _capisterium_, 92, 3: 19, 38. Hú hé geedstaðelode, þ tóbrokene hridder (_capisterium_) . . . hé genam þá sticcu þæs tóbrocenan hriddres (hridderes, _v. l._) . . . and hire ágæf þ hriddern (hridder, _v. l._) . . . þá landleóde áhéngon þ ilce hriddern (hridder) in þære cyrcan ingange, Gr. D. 96, 30–97, 34. [The second passage in Dict., and all but the first here refer to the same incident.] [v. _N. E. D._ ridder. _O. H. Ger._ rît(e)ra _cribrum_.]

**hridir.** v. mid-hriþere: **hridrian.** _l._ hrídrian, _and add_: [v. _N. E. D._ ridder. _O. H. Ger._ rîtarôn.] v. ge-hrídrian.

**hrif.** _Add_: I. _of human beings_:—Gif hrif wund weorðeð, Ll. Th. i. 18, 6. Healt geboren of his môdor hrife (innoðe, _v. l._), Bd. 5, 2; Sch. 560, 1. Of méddernum rife _de uulua_, An. Ox. 1496. Gif mon bið on hrife (hrif, _v. l._) wund _si quis in ilio (ilibus, v. l.) vulneretur_, Ll. Th. i. 96, 10. Mín Drihten, sié þé þonc þæs þe þú mid þínum þám clǽnan hrife hungor and þurst and cyle þrowodest, Angl. xii. 507, 20. II. _applied to things_:—Þæt mé (_a bow_) of hrife fleógeð, Rä. 24, 12: 18, 6.

**hrífe** (?); _adj. Rapacious, fierce_. (1) _of animals_:—Wé ús warnigan scoldon wið þá missenlican cynd nǽdrena and hrífra wildeóra (_serpentes et rapida ferarum genera_), Nar. 5, 28. Þurh þá lond þe þá unárefnedlican cyn nǽdrena and hrífra wildeóra (_execrabilia serpentum et rapida ferarum beluarumque genera_) in wǽron, 6, 18. Þurh þá stówe þe missenlicra cynna eardung in wæs nǽdrena and rífra wildeóra _per bestiosa serpentiosaque loca_, 10, 5. Alle ðá ǽttrena and gett ðá rífista feerrǽsenda ǽc nétna sceðende _omnia venenata et aduc ferociora repentia et animalia noxia_, Rtl. 125, 31. [(2) _of things, destructive_:—Ðére vii. niht gyf win[d] byoð, fír byð swýðe rýfe þý geáre _si in septima nocte fuerit ventus, ignis multa destruet in illo anno_, Archiv cxxviii. 57, 2.] [v. _N. E. D._ rife. _Some of the early instances there given might be taken in the sense which is here given to_ hrífe.] v. hrífnian.

**-hrifian.** v. ge-hrifian: **hrífing.** _Take here_ hrýfing _in Dict._

**hrífnian** (?) _to become rapacious or ferocious_ (hrífe). [_See_ ge-hrífnian, _where the verb has been connected with_ hrif; _the better sense may be obtained if the word is connected with_ hrífe; _and in this case should be written_ ge-hrífnian.]

**hrif-téung,** e; _f. Stomach-ache_:—Hrifteung (_printed_ hrig-, Wrt. Voc. i. 19, 24) _yleos_, Wülck. Gl. 112, 23.

**hrífþo.** _Add_:—Sió hwíte riéfþo þe mon on súþerne _lepra_ hæt, Lch. ii. 228, 12. v. heáfod-hrífþo.

**hrif-wund.** _For passage substitute_:—Gyf mon rifwund (on hrife wund, gewundod _v. ll._) . . . gif hé ðurhwund bið _si quis in ilibus uulneretur . . . si transforatus sit_, Ll. Lbmn. 82, 23.

**hrilæcung.** _Dele, and see_ riht-lǽcung.

**hrím.** _Add_:—Hrím _pruina_, Wrt. Voc. ii. 118, 14. Hríme _pruina_ (frigidior candente _pruina_, Ald. 271, 31), An. Ox. 23, 14.

**hríman** _to shout. Take here_ hrýman _in Dict._ (_with the exception of_ Dan. 756: Æðelst. 39, _for which see_ hréman) _and add_:—Is gewriten ðætte swíðe wǽre gemanigfaldod Sodomwara hreám and Gomorwara. Sé cliopað, sé ðe dearninga syngað; ac sé hrémð, sé ðe openlíce and orsorglíce syngað _peccatum cum voce est culpa in actione, peccatum vero etiam cum clamore est culpa cum libertate_, Past. 429, 1. Wæterfrocgan brímað blúdum stefnum ranᵹ . . . _procaces efferunt uoces_, Chrd. 96, 29. [v. _N. E. D._ reme.] v. ge-hríman.

**hríman** (?); _pp._ ed _To cover with hoar frost_:—Nis þæt feor heonon þæt se mere standeð, ofer ðǽm hongiað hrímde (hrinde, MS.) bearwas

(cf. wǽron . . . swíðe _hrímige_ bearwas . . . and on ðǽm clife hangodan on ðǽm _isgean_ bearwum manige swearte sáula, Bl. H. 209, 32–35), B. 1363. [v. _N. E. D._ rime.] _See_ **hrind** _for other suggested emendations._

**hrím-forst,** es; _m. Hoar-frost_:—Deáwas and rímforst (_pruina_), Ps. L. p. 249, 6. Hé ofslóh heora morbeámas on rímforste (_in pruina_), Ps. L. 77, 47. [v. _N. E. D._ rime-frost.]

**hrímian** (?). v. hás-hrímian.

**hrímig.** _In_ Bl. H. 207, 27 _the passage is_:—Se munt is styccemǽlum mid hsomige wuda oferwexen, sum mid grénum felda oferbrǽded. _Perhaps_ brómige _should be read, rather than_ hrímige. [_On the strength of_ Bl. H. 209, 32 hrímge _has been suggested as an emendation for_ hrinde, B. 1363. v. hrind.]

**hrimpan.** v. ge-hrimpan.

**hrínan.** _Add_: [_a pp._ hríned _occurs._] I. _to touch with the hands_:—Hé hrán þ ceiste, Lk. L. 7, 14. Duru sóna onarn siððan þé hire folmum hrán, B. 722. Ðá hrínendo him _tangentes eum_, Lk. p. 5, 5. I a. _to touch, be sensitive to_:—Scíneð þe leóht fore . . . nú þú his hrínan meahte, Gen. 616. I b. _to touch_ the hand, finger, &c , to something, _bring into contact with_:—Send Lazarum þte indépe þ hrínæ útaweard fingeres his in wætre _mitte Lazarum ut intinguat extremum digiti sui in aquam_, Lk. L. 16, 24. II. _to come into contact with_:—Nó hafað hió fót ne folm, ne ǽfre foldan hrán, Rä. 40, 10. III. _to touch, strike_ with a (pointed) weapon:—Siððan ic hríno hildepílum láðgewinnum, Rä. 16, 28. Gif hine hríneð þæt mé (_a bow_) of hrife fleógeð, 24, 12. IV. _to affect by contact, make an impression upon_:—Him heardra nán hrínan wolde íren ǽrgód, B. 988. V. _to have to do with, meddle with_:—Þám hringsele hrínan ne môste gumena ǽnig, B. 3053. V a. _to lay hands on, or meddle with so as to hurt, to injure, hurt._ (1) the agent a person:—Ic hríno ðone hiorde _percutiam pastorem_, Mk. L. R. 14, 27. Ne wæs ǽnig þára þæt mé þus þríste swá þú nú þá mid hondum hrínan dorste, Jul. 512. (2) the agent non-personal:—Hé on þá tíd ðe hé inne bið ne bið hrinen (hríned, _v. l._) mid þí storme ðæs wintres (_hiemis tempestate non tangitur_), Bd. 2, 13; Sch. 165, 25. Fǽre ne môston wætres brógan hrínan, Gen. 1396. VI. _to reach, attain to_:—Nǽfre hió heofonum hrán, Rä. 40, 20. [v. _N. E. D._ rine.] v. oþ-hrínan.

**hrind.** _For_ B. 1363 _see_ **hríman.** A hrind- _form occurs in_ C. D. iii. 394, 6: On hrindan bróc, _but there is nothing to show its meaning._

**hríne.** _Add_: I. _an act of touching, the action of touching_:—Þone þe ná ne gedyde swylcne se hríne ǽniges mannes, Gr. D. 87, 24. II. _the touch_ of an inanimate object:—Hí þære eá wæteres hrine him ondrédon, Gr. D. 15, 8. III. _the sense of touch_:—Þú þe wé ne magon líchamlíce ongytan . . . ne mid smecce, ne mid hrine _quem sensus ignorat_, Solil. H. 6, 15. v. hand-, on-hrine.

**hrine-ness.** _Add_:—hrinen-ness:—Heó tó hrinennesse (hrinenesse, _v. l._) þære drihtenlican handa árás _ad tactum manus dominicae surrexit_, Bd. 5, 4; Sch. 569, 21.

**hring.** _Dele_ 'hrincg ansa . . . Lye' _in ll._ 4, 5, _and add_: I. _a ring as ornament encircling a finger, an arm, a neck_:—Bewrít ðá wyrte mid ánum gyldenan hringe, Lch. i. 112, 22. Dyde him of healse hring gyldenne, B. 2809. Ne gé ne sceolon beón rance mid hrínggum geglengede, Ll. Th. ii. 358, 5. Gimbǽrum ringum _gemmiferis (digitorum) anulis (comi)_, An. Ox. 1192. Hringas an[nul]os, Wrt. Voc. ii. 6, 61. I a. _a betrothal ring_ (lit. or fig.):—Ic hæbbe óðerne lufiend (_Christ_) . . . hé his geleáfan hring mé ʒet tó wedde (cf. hé haueð iweddet him to mi meiðhad mit te ring of rihte bileaue, Kath. 1508), Hml. S. 7, 30. II. _a ring_ of a coat of mail. v. Hring-Dene:—Hringum _hamis, circulis loricæ_, An. Ox. 50, 50. III. _a ring_ employed as a means of attachment, suspension, compression, &c. Cf. hringe:—Mé habbað hringa gespong, slíðhearda sál, síðes ámyrred . . . fét synt gebundene, handa gehæfte, Gen. 377. Ic sceal þegne mínum hringum hæfted hýran georne, Rä. 5, 2: 87, 4. Wyrc feówer hringas (_circulos_), and áhôh hié on ðá feówer hyrnan ðære earce; and hát wyrcean twégen stengas . . . and sting út ðurh ðá hringas, Past. 169, 20–24. IV. _the border of a circular object,_ of land as bounded by the horizon:—Siððan þú gestígest steápe dúne, hrincg ðæs heán landes, Gen. 2854. IV a. fig. _the limit of a jurisdiction_:—Þonne þæt gecnáwed feónd, þætte gehwylc hæleða cynnes on his hringe bið fæste geféged, Wal. 40. V. _an object having a circular form._ Cf. hring-mere, -pytt, stede, -will:—Hri[ng] _circulus (teres lunaris globi)_, An. Ox. 8, 47. Se hring (_a chalice or paten_), Rä. 49, 8: 60, 1. V a. _a circular fold, coil._ Cf. hring-boga, -burne:—In hringe _in spira (chelydri)_, Wrt. Voc. ii. 96, 14: 47, 40. Hringum _spiris (anguis)_, 86, 25: An. Ox. 4944. V b. _a wreath_:—Hringas _serta (purpureis floribus contexta)_, Wrt. Voc. ii. 84, 19. VI. _a circular mark_:—Þæs sinewealtan hringes _teretes cycli (cycli_ has been taken as gen. sing., it is nom. pl. and describes the marks on a peacock's feathers, v. Ald. 142, 23), Wrt. Voc. ii. 89, 60. Hí ymb hine gemearcodon ânne hring (_circulum_) on þære eorðan and héton þ hé mid his fét þone hring ne oferstôpe, Gr. D. 196, 27–197, 1: Lch. ii. 112, 1. VI a. _a circular band of light or colour_:—Is ymb þone sweóran swylce sunnan hring beága beorhtast (cf. his (the

*Phenix's*) sweóra is swylce *smǽte gold*, E. S. viii. 478, 57; *and* Ors. 5, 14; S. 248, 9 (*in Dict.*). In this latter passage, however, the original seems to intend a halo with prismatic colouring), Ph. 305. **VII.** *a group of persons standing in a circle* :—Wuldorful apostolan hring *gloriosus apostolorum chorus*, Angl. ii. 357, 10. Fugla cynn þone hálgan hringe beteldað, Ph. 339. **VIII.** *an enclosed circular space, sea* or *land enclosed by the horizon* :—Wíde rád wolcnum under ofer holmes hrincg hof sēleste, Gen. 1393. **IX.** *a circular course* or *orbit* :—Hringa hōhwerfinge *orbes orbibus*, Wrt. Voc. ii. 75, 6 : 64, 21. Hringum *orbibus*, 63, 10. **X.** in reference to the revolution of time and its computation :—Ǽr sunne twelf mōnða hringc ūtan ymbgán hæbbe *priusquam sol bis senis voluminibus annilem circumvolverit orbem*, Guth. Gr. 172, 28. [Bd. 4, 18 ; Sch. 437, 11 : 5, 21 ; Sch. 680, 6 *in Dict.*] v. gedwol- (v. Bd. 5, 21; Sch. 680, 8), hōf-, mídl-, wíngeard-hring.

**hring.** *in* wōpes hring. *Add : Though a noun,* hring, *denoting sound may be inferred from the compounds* bel-, nōn-hring, *it is hardly with this meaning that the word occurs in the phrase* wōpes hring ; *for the epithet* blát (An. 1281) *is not applicable to sound, and the parallel phrase,* hát heáfodwylm (El. 1133), *denotes tears. Perhaps, though, there is the same extension of meaning as in the cases of* hlimme, hlynn, hlýde (?), *where words denoting a stream or torrent are connected with words denoting sound (see next word).*

**hringan.** *Add* : I. *intrans. To give out a sound* :—[Sal. 266 : B. 327 *in Dict.*] II. *trans.* (1) *to ring* a bell :—Dô þú mid þínum twám handum swylce þú bellan ringe, Tech. ii. 118, 20. (2) *with cognate object* :—Tácnu þænne hí hringað *signa dum sonant*, Angl. xiii. 392, 382. Cyrcwerd hringe tā[c]n *edituus sonet signum*, 384, 272. (3) *to announce* a time *by ringing* :—Sý þæs abbodes gýmen þæt mon ealle tída þæs godcundan þeówdómes on rihte tíman hrincge, oþþe hé sylf ǽlce tíd getácnige, oðþe swylcum brēðer þá gýmene betǽce þe ǽlce tíd . . . mid beácne geswytelige *nuntianda hora operis Dei sit cura abbatis, aut ipse nuntiare, aut tali fratri injungat hanc curam ut omnia compleantur*, R. Ben. 72, 10–14. Wē lǽrað þ man on rihtne tíman tída ringe, Ll. Th. ii. 254, 5 : 296, 3. v. ge-hringan.

**hringan** *to surround.* [*Icel.* hringja *to surround* : O. H. Ger. gehringen *congyrare.*] v. ymb-hringan.

**hring-burne** (?), an ; *f. A brook with many windings* (? cf. hring ; **V** a) :—On hringheburne, C. D. iii. 416, 31.

**Hring-Dene,** *pl. The Danes, the mailcoated* (?) *Danes* (v. hring ; II, and cf. Gár-Dene) :—Hū hit Hring-Dene gebūn hæfdon, B. 116 : 1279. Ic Hring-Dena weóld, 1769.

**hringe,** an ; *f. A ring employed as a means of attachment, suspension, compression, &c., a buckle, clasp.* v. hring ; III :—Hringiae, hringae, hringe, sigl *fibula*, Txts. 62, 410. Sigel oððe hringe, Wrt. Voc. ii. 35, 42. Hringe *ansa*, 8, 5 : i. 284, 7 : 66, 34 (*not* hringc). Geheáfdod hringce *samothracius*, 40, 60. Smēðe ringce *tinius*, 56. 'Gange him tô mínre byrgene and āteó āne hringan úp of ðǽre þrýh ; and gif seó hringe him folgað æt þám forman tige . . . Gif seó hringe nele úp . . .' Se smið . . . genam āne hringan . . . Hé teáh þ íren úp eáðelíce of ðám stāne, Hml. S. 21, 43–69. Hringan *legulam*, Wrt. Voc. ii. 87, 18. [*Icel.* hringja *a buckle.*] v. gyrdel-, gyrdels-hringe.

**hringed.** *Substitute for citations* :—Hringedu byrne *lorica hamata* (*anata*, MS.), Wrt. Voc. ii. 51, 37. Hringed byrne, B. 1245. Hringde byrnan, 2615.

**-hringend.** v. ymb-hringend.

**hring-fáh.** *For* -fēgh *in* l. 2 *l.* fágh, *and add* :—*Having circular bands of different colours* (?. v. hring ; **VI** a) :—Tonica polimita hringfaag, *a rotunditate circulorum*, Txts. 100, 984. Hringfaag *polimita*, 88, 798. Hringfāg, Wrt. Voc. ii. 68, 26.

**hring-gewindla,** an ; *m. Something rolled into a circular form* (v. ge-windan ; I. 1 a), *a sphere* :—On hringgewindlan *in spera*, Wrt. Voc. ii. 47, 61.

**hringian.** *Dele, and see* hringan.

**hring-mǽl,** es ; *n. A sword with ring-shaped markings* :—Hire on hafelan hringmǽl āgōl, B. 1521. Hé . . . hringmǽl gebrægd, 1564. *See next word.*

**hring-mǽl ;** *adj. For* 'Beo . . . 1564' *substitute* :—On him gladiað gomelra láfe heard and hringmǽl Heaðobeardna gestreón, B. 2037. *See preceding word and cf.* wunden-mǽl.

**hring-pytt,** es ; *m. A circular pit* :—On hringpyt, C. D. v. 325, 14 : 340, 19. Hryngpyt, 291, 23. Hrungputt, 112, 32.

**hring-seta, hring-sete.** *Substitute* : **hring-set,** es ; *n. A circus* :—Hringsete *circio* (*accipit in* circo *victor serta*, Ald. 141, 29), Wrt. Voc. ii. 89, 45. Hringseta *circentium* (*gymnicorum exempla . . . praeconia circensium* (cf. *circenses circus*, Migne) *adipiscuntur*, Ald. 3, 22), 75, 18 : 17, 64. *See next two words.*

**hring-setl,** es ; *n. A circus* :—On hrincgsetles openre wafunge *in circi spectaculo*, An. Ox. 3510. Rincsettles, 3535.

**hring-sittend,** es ; *m. A spectator in a circus* :—Hrincsittendra *circensium* [v. hring-set (*second example*)], An. Ox. 65. Ringsittendra *circentium*, Wrt. Voc. ii. 131, 31.

**hring-stede.** *Substitute : An enclosed place circular in form.* Cf. hring ; **V** :—Æt Ringstyde, C. D. iv. 208, 25.

**hring-weorþung.** *Substitute : A ring given to do honour to the receiver, a costly ring.* v. weorþung ; III, *and* sinc-weorþung.

**hring-will,** es ; *m. A circular well* or *spring.* Cf. hring ; **V** :—On hringwylle ; *of* hringwylle, C. D. iii. 449, 10 : 450, 9.

**hring-windel.** *Dele, and see* hring-gewindla.

**hrínung.** *Add : the sense of touch* :—Mē þincð þæt þú ne trúwie þám uttram gewitte, nāðer ne þám eágum . . . ne ðám hyrínunge *respuis omne testimonium sensuum*, Solil. H. 18, 13.

**hríran.** v. ā-, ge-, tō-hríran.

**hrís.** *Substitute : Twigs, small branches, brushwood* :—Frondes, s. dicuntur *quod ferant virgultas vel umbras*, geleáf rís *vel* bōgas, Wrt. Voc. ii. 151, 7. Geleáf hrís *frondes*, 39, 69. Oð birnan hrís, C. D. v. 157, 16. ¶ Perhaps in a local name :—Hē cóm tō Hrísbeorgan, vi. 184, 14 : 197, 31. (Cf. *Icel.* Hrís-hóll as a local name). [v. *N.E.D.* rice.] *See next word.*

**hrís** (?) ; *adj. Covered with brushwood* (?) :—Tō hrýsan beorge ; of ðám beorge, C. D. v. 348, 26. ¶ *in a local name* :—Heó ann ðæs landæs æt Hrísan beorgan, C. D. iii. 360, 4. Cf. Ultra flumen Tamense, Hrísebeorgam, 347, 11. *See preceding word.*

**hríseht.** *l.* hríseht(e), *and for* 'Cot. 186, Lye' *substitute* :—Ðý hrísehtan, þá hǽrihtan *setosa* (*vervecum vellera*), Wrt. Voc. ii. 87, 27 (cf. *bushy* as an epithet of the hair or beard). [Cf. *Icel.* hrís-ottr *bushy, grown with shrub.*] v. hrísig.

**hrísel.** *Add* : hrísel (?v. Rä. 36, 7) :—Hrisl, hrisil *radius* (-*m*), Txts. 93, 1704. Hrisle *ebredio* (*ab radio* ?), Wrt. Voc. ii. 106, 73 : 28, 74. Hríslum hrístlendum *radiis stridentibus*, Wrt. Voc. ii. 83, 23 : An. Ox. 2, 246. Rislum, 3739.

**hrísian.** *Add* : , hrissan :—Risaendi, risende *fibrans*, Txts. 62, 434. Hrissende, Wrt. Voc. ii. 35, 54. Hrysiende, 148, 56. I. *trans.* :—Hig hrysedon † hig cwehton heáfda heora, Ps. L. 108, 25. Ðonne þú sealt habban wylle, þonne geþeóddum þínum þrím fingrum hryse þíne hand swylce þú hwæt seltan wylle, Tech. ii. 124, 4. II. *intrans.* :—Syrcan hrysedon, B. 226. Gūðsearo gullon, gáras hrysedon, An. 127. [v. *N.E.D.* rese *to shake.*] v. ge-hrisian.

**hrísig ;** *adj. Bushy* :—Rýsige *setosa*, An. Ox. 8, 337. v. hríseht.

**hristenda.** *Substitute* : **hristende.** v. hrýscan : **hristlan.** v. hrystlan.

**hristlung.** *Dele* : hristung. v. hrýscung.

**hrís-weg,** es ; *m. A road made by laying down brushwood, and covering it with earth* (?) :—On hrísweg, C. D. iii. 384, 6.

**hrið** *fever. Add* : v. hridian : **-hriþer.** v. mid-hriþer.

**hriþer.** *Add* :—Hrýðeres belle . . . bið ānes sciłł weorð, and is melda geteald, Ll. Th. i. 260, 16. Begete hē þára syxa ǽnne æt ānum hrýðere, oþþe æt þám orfe þe þæs weorð sý, 160, 1. Be .xxx. pæñ. oþþe be ānum hrýðere, 232, 7. Nán man hrýðer ne sleá būton hē habbe twēgra trýwra manna gewitnesse, 296, 17. Án hríðr, C. D. i. 311, 3. Án eald hríðr, 312, 7. .i. eald hríðer, 297, 1. Tú hriéðeru, ōðer sealt, ōðer fersc, v. 164, 29. Hríðero *armenta*, Wrt. Voc. ii. 80. 16. Hríþeru, An. Ox. 2448. Hruþeru, 2, 86. Tú eald hríðeru (.ii. ealde hrýðeru, *v.l.*), Ll. Th. i. 146, 18. Gíf hrýðera (hríð-, *v. l.*) hwelc sié þe hegas brece, 128, 12. Hrýðeran styllan, swýn stician, Angl. ix. 262, 1. Man slôh þǽr hrýðera and gehwilces cynnes nýtenu, Hml. S. 23, 34. [Hríþer (*and* hríþ) *occurs in local names, as an independent form or in compounds* :—Hec duo aratra a quibusdam campus armentorum, id est *hríðra leáh*, appellantur, C. D. i. 232, 21. Wiðeástan hríðres heáfod, v. 71, 1. On rýðæres heáfod, 358, 11. Be westan hríðerleá, 109, 12. Hríðden, i. 261, 8.] [v. *N.E.D.* rother.] v. fald-, fearr-, feld-, sleg-hríþer ; hríþ *in* hríþ-fald, -hirde.

**hríþeren.** *Add* : [v. *N.E.D.* rotheren]: **hríþer-flǽsc.** v. eald-hryter-flǽsc.

**hríðer-freóls.** *Substitute* : **hríþer-freóls,** es ; *m. A sacrifice at which a bull was offered* :—Hrýþerfreólsas *taurilia* (*suove taurilia turificando*, Ald. 67, 12), An. Ox. 4719.

**hríþer-heord.** *Add* : Hrýþerheord *armentum*, An. Ox. 18 b, 2.

**hríþer-hirde.** *Add* :—Hreóðarhyrde *armentarius*, Hpt. 33, 238, 3. Wæs sum cniht hrýðerhyrde, Gr. D. 300, 4. v. hríþ-hirde.

**hríþ-fald,** es ; *m. A cattle-fold* :—Ríþfald *buccetum* (cf. hrýðra fald *bucetum*, i. 15, 22), Wrt. Voc. ii. 126, 68.

**hríþ-hirde,** es ; *m. A herdsman* :—Hríðhiorde *bobulcus*, Wrt. Voc. ii. 102, 9. Hríðhierde, 11, 25. Hríðheorda *armentarius*, Gr. D. 300, 4. v. hríþer-hirde.

**hríþian.** *Dele first citation, and add* :—Hwíle hé líþaþ swylce hē on dueorge sý, Lch. iii. 118, 1. [*Icel.* riða *to tremble* as in fever or ague.]

**hríung.** v. hreóung.

**hróc.** *Add* :—Hrooc *grallus*, Wrt. Voc. ii. 110, 6. Hróc *grauculus* (*garrulus . . . graculus* ater, Ald. 142, 19), 89, 56. Flugon tō hrócas and hremmas . . . and þára martyra eágan ūt āhaccedon, Hml. S. 23. 77. v. niht-hróc.

**hroden.** For **hreóðan** *l.* hreódan, *in bracket for* hroðian *l.* hroðinn, *and add :* v. fǽtan, fǽted.

**hróf.** *Add :* I. *the outside upper covering of a building, ceiling of a room, upper surface of a cave,* &c. :—Hróf *lacuna*[r], Txts. 76, 109 : *lacunar*, Wrt. Voc. ii. 50, 55 : *camara*, 17, 16 : *tholus (tholus* tectum de petris sine ligno, Ld. Gl. H. 40, 19), 122, 30. Wæs þæt bold tóbrocen swíðe ... hróf ána genæs ealles ansund, B. 999. Of þám stáne þǽre ciricean hrófes, Bl. H. 209, 1. Gebrosnad is hús under hrófe, Cri. 14. On heáhsetlum hrófe getenge *celsos solii culmine,* Met. 25, 5. Gif mon on níwne weall unádrúgodne micelne hróf and hefigne on sett, Past. 383, 32. Hí openodon þone hróf (*tectum*), Mk. 2, 4. Hé geseah steápne hróf golde fáhne, B. 926. Hrófas *tecta,* An. Ox. 2257. Hrófum oððe bígelsum *arcibus,* Wrt. Voc. ii. 96, 79. I a. used of the covering of a pit where some one is hiding :—Hrófes *tecta et tigilli* (cisternae latebram ... quae lymphis vacua praestabat *tecta tigilli,* Ald. 1648), Wrt. Voc. ii. 92, 40. I b. in phrases that denote entering, or being in, a house, chamber :—þæt hié bewisten eal þ licgende feoh under ánum hrófe, Ors. 2, 4 ; S. 72, 5. Hrófe *tigillo* (in proprii domatis *tigillo* conflagrasse memoratur, Ald. 38, 22), An. Ox. 2, 110. Biðon tuoege in hrófe ánum, Lk. L. R. 17, 34. Under þám fýrenan hrófe *in the fiery furnace,* Dan. 239. Snyredon ætsomne under Heorotes hróf, B. 403. Under geápne hróf, 836. Eall under hróf gefór *all entered the ark,* Gen. 1360. Ne wyrðe am þte under hróf mínum inngáe, Lk. L. 7, 6. Róf, Mt. L. 8, 8. I c. *house-top* as the most public place to proclaim anything :—Ðætte in eárum giherdest and sprecende gé wérun in cotum ábodad bið on hrófum, Lk. R. L. 12, 3. Ofer hrófa, Mt. L. 10, 27. I d. *where a part represents the whole* (?) *a house* v. hróf-leás ; II. II. *something which in form or function may be compared to the covering of a house* :—Helmes hróf *the covering which the helmet forms,* B. 1030. Georges hróf *the roof which the hill makes for the cave in its side,* 2755. Wætera hrófas *the waves that curled their heads over those walking over the bottom of the Red Sea,* Exod. 571. ¶ *used of the sky, clouds,* &c., *considered as the roof of the world* :—Under rodores hrófe, Hy. 5, 5. Ofer ðone heán hróf þæs heofones, Bt. 36, 2 ; F. 174, 5. Oþ wolcna hróf, Exod. 298. Hyrstedne hróf hálgum tunglum, Gen. 656. Ofer worulde hróf, Dan. 407. III. *the roof of the mouth* :—Hrófes and gómena *palati et faucium,* Germ. 392, 6. IV. *the top* of anything, *the highest point* :—Ic eów mæg gereccan hwæt se hróf is eallra geselþa *ostendam tibi summae cardinem felicitatis,* Bt. 11, 2 ; F. 34, 7. Hrófe *apice,* Wrt. Voc. ii. 3, 56. þeáh man gesette án brád ísen þell ofer þæs fýres hróf, Wlfst. 147, 3. Cwóm wiht ofer wealles hróf, Rä. 30, 7. v. first-, múþ-hróf.

**hróf-leás.** I. *of a building, without a roof* :—Rófleáse and monleáse ealde weallas *parietinae,* Wrt. Voc. i. 59, 8. II. *of land, having no houses upon it* (?) :—Ealdréd hæfð geunnen Ædestán sumne dǽl landes, ðæt synd twá hída mid ðám ðe hé ǽr hæfde and mid ðám hrófleásan lande, C. D. iv. 262, 14.

**hróf-stán.** *Add after* hrófstáne : yrnð dropmǽlum swíðe hluttor wæter (cf. wæs of þǽm ilcan stáne þǽre ciricean hrófes swíðe hluttor wǽta út flówende (cf. þ ilce hús (*the church*) on scræfes onlícnesse wæs æteówed, 207, 19), Bl. H. 209, 1.)

**hróf-tigel.** *Add :*—Hróftiglum *imbricibus,* Wrt. Voc. ii. 88, 37. Hróftigelum, 45, 29. Hróftig[el]um, 79, 7. [v. *N. E. D.* roof-tile.]

**hróf-timber.** *Add :*—Hróftimbrum (róf-, Hpt. Gl. 459, 43) *imbricibus,* An. Ox. 2256.

**hróf-wyrhta.** *Add :*—Hrófuuyrhta (-uuyrcta, -huyrihta) *tignarius,* Txts. 101, 2020.

**hromige.** v. brómig.

**hróp.** *Add :* v. ge-, on-hróp.

**hrópan.** *Add :* [v. *N. E. D.* rope.] v. hrépan : **hrops.** v. ofer-hrops : **-hror.** v. ge-hror : **hroren-lic.** v. hroren-ness. v. ge-hroren-ness : **hróst.** For 'Lye' *substitute :* Angl. ix. 262, 5 : **hrot.** *See* rot *for two more instances.*

**hróp-girela,** an ; *m. Splendid dress, a crown* :—Ðú settest on heáfde his hróðgirelan (*coronam*) of stáne deórwyrðum, Ps. Rdr. 20, 4.

**hrúm.** *Add :*—Hrúm *cacobatus,* Wrt. Voc. ii. 17, 37. Hrúme *fuligine,* 34, 42. Nim ceteles hrúm, Lch. ii. 148, 10.

**hrum** = hórum, Lch. ii. 2, 3. v. horh : **hrúmig.** *For* 'Cot. 31, Lye' *substitute* :—Hrúmig *caccabatus,* Wrt. Voc. ii. 13, 17. v. rómig : **-hrúmod.** v. be-hrúmod : **hrung.** *Dele* v. scil-hrung.

**hrúrol ;** *adj. Deciduous* :—Hrurulne *deciduum,* Nap. 39. v. hreósan.

**hruse.** *l.* hrúse, *and add* : I. *the ground.* (1) *as a surface* :—Crungon hergas tó hrúsan, Ruin. 30. Ðonne se forst tó hrúsan cymeð, Rä. 41, 55. Hwǽr seó ród wunige under hrúsan, El. 625. Se wínsele on hrúsan ne feól, B. 772. þonne ic hrúsan trede, Rä. 8, 1. Hé hrycge sceal hrúsan sécan, 28, 11. (1 a) *the floor* of a subterranean place :—Hwá wát on hwelcum hlǽwa Wélandes bán hrúsan þeccen?, Met. 10, 43. (2) *as a solid stratum* :—Treów hrúsan fæst, Rún. 13. (2 a) *as a place of burial or concealment* :—Hald þú, hrúse, eorla ǽhte, B. 2247. Heard gripe hrúsan, Ruin. 8. Se þeódsceaða heóld on hrúsan hordærna sum, B. 2279. þonne flǽsc onginneð hrúsan ceósan tó gebeddan, Rún. 29.

(3) *as suitable for cultivation, soil, land* :—Rén, hagal and snáw hrúsan leccað (cf. leccaþ þá eorþan, Bt. 39, 13 ; F. 234, 16) on wintres tíd ; for þǽm eorðe onféhð eallum sǽdum, gedéð þ hí grówað, Met. 29, 64. (3 a) *as productive* :—Ic (*a spear*) on wonge áweóx, wunode þǽr mec féddon hrúse and heofonwolcn, Rä. 72, 2. þonne God lǽteð hrúsan syllan bléda beornum, Rún. 12. II. *the world we live in.* (1) *dry land* as opposed to sea :—Ic holmmægne biþeaht hrúsan styrge, Rä. 3, 9. (2) *earth* as opposed to the material heaven :—Sé ðe heofon worhte, hrúsan swylce, Ps. Th. 120, 2 : 133, 4. III. *the material of which the surface of the ground is composed, earth* :—Hrúsan bið heardra, Rä. 81, 30. IV. *earth* as one of the four elements :—Ligeð him behindan heiig hrúsan dǽl (cf. sió hefige eorþe sit þǽr niþere, Bt. 39, 13 ; F. 234, 12), þeáh hit (*fire*) hwílan ǽr eorðe sió cealde oninnan hire heóld, Met. 29, 53.

**hrut.** *Substitute :* **hrút** *dark-coloured* (?). *In form* hrút *agrees with* Icel. hrútr *a ram, but the word it glosses is treated as an adjective in the other two instances of its occurrence* :—Wonn *bruntus,* hrút (*the MS. has the accent*) *balidus* (cf. *balidus* dunn, Wrt. Voc. i. 289, 28 : dun, ii. 125, 4), Wrt. Voc. ii. 12, 59. v. hrýte.

**hrútan.** *Add :* I. *to make a noise, rumble, rattle* :—Went hié sió wamb and hrýt and gefelð sár þonne se mon mete þiged, Lch. ii. 216, 20. Ne mé hrútende (v. Angl. xxxii. 386) hrísil scelfaeð, ni mec ðuuana aam sceal cnyssa (cf. nec radiis carpor, duro nec pectine pulsor, Ald. 257, 23), Txts. 151, 7. II. *to snore* (perhaps this is a different word. v. *N. E. D.* rout) :—Sé ðe hrét *qui stertit,* Kent. Gl. 322. Reát *dester*(t)*uit, somniavit,* Wrt. Voc. ii. 139, 17. Ðá hé þæne cyrcward gehýrde ofer eall hrútan, Vis. Lfc. 31. Hrútende *stertens,* Wrt. Voc. ii. 121, 30.

**hruxl** (*l.* hrúxl). v. ge-hrúxl.

**hrúxlian** *to make a noise* :—þá hé geseah menigu rúxlende (*turbam tumultuantem*), Mt. R. 9, 23. [Hence later (?) *rustle* ; but see *N. E. D.* s. v.]

**hrycce.** *Dele, and see* hwicce.

**hrycg.** *Add :* I. *the spine of man or animal* :—Hryg *dorsum,* bæc *terga,* Wrt. Voc. i. 283, 43. Hricges *spinæ* (*draconis*), An. Ox. 2467. Geseah hé þ þǽr sæt án deóíol on þǽre cú hrycge, Hml. S. 31, 1047. II. *a ridge.* v. gráf-, læg-, middel-, sand-, stán-, timber-hrycg, *and* Midd. Flur. s. v.

**hrycg-bán.** *Add :* [v. *N. E. D.* ridge-bone.]: **hrycg-brǽdan** *l.* (?) hrycg-brǽd. v. brǽd.

**hrycg-hrægel.** *Add :*—Eádgyfe his swyster .i. hrigchrægl and .i. setlhrægl, Cht. Crw. 23, 22.

**hrycg-mearh.** *Add :*—Hricgmearh (*printed* -meard) *spina,* Wülck. Gl. 292, 7.

**hrycg-téung.** *Dele, and see* hrif-téung : **hrycigan.** v. hrícian : **-hrydran.** v. á-ryddan : **-hrýman.** v. hríman : **hrýme.** *Dele.*

**hrympelle.** *Substitute :* **hrympel** (?) *a wrinkle* :—Hrypellum (hrympellum? v. ge-hrimpan, *and N. E. D.* rimple), Wrt. Voc. ii. 95, 73.

**hrypel.** *See preceding word.*

**hryre.** *Add :* I. *a fall from a height.* (1) *a dropping from a high position under the force of gravity* :—Hý hófon hine hondum and him hryre burgun, Gú. 702. (2) *a descent of rain, hail,* &c. :—Ne hægles hryre ne hrímes dryre, Ph. 16. (2 a) *of a shower of stones,* Hml. Th. i. 50, 23 (*in Dict.*). (3) *fig. a descent from high estate, flourishing condition* :—Ær ðæs monnes hryre bið ðæt mód úp áhæfen, Past. 299, 18. Hié náþer næfdon siþþan ne heora namon ne heora anweald. Ac heora hryre wearð Ahténum tó árærnesse, Ors. 3, 1 ; S. 98, 8. II. *a sinking to a lower level, precipitate descent* (lit. or fig.), *hasty action* :—Ealle word hryres *omnia uerba praecipitationis,* Ps. Rdr. 51, 6. On myclum hryre seó beord wearð on sǽ besceofen *magno impetu grex praecipitatus est in mare,* Mk. 5, 13. Se druncena wénð þ hé sum þing gódes dó, þonne hé bið an hryre besceofen *ebriosus putat se aliquid obtimum agere, cum fuerit precipitio deuolutus,* Chrd. 74, 24. III. *a falling from an upright position* (lit. or fig.). (1) *a falling to the ground* of a building :—Wearð swá micel eorþbeofung þæt on þǽm íglondum wurdon micle hryras ond Colosus gehreás *magno terraemotu insulae adeo concussae sunt, ut labentibus vulgo tectis ingens quoque ille Colossus rueret,* Ors. 4, 7 ; S. 184, 25. (2) *a fall from an independent status, fall* of a town, country, &c. :—Gif on tíde (.x.) þunrað fram eástdǽle ryras buruga (*rui*[n]*as urbium*) getácnað, Archiv cxx. 51, 45. (3) *a yielding to temptation, moral fall* :—Besende se áwyrgeda gást mænigfealde geþóhtas on heora mód, and wurdon þearle gecostnode þurh his fægernysse ... 'Mín bearn, þín ansýn is wlitig, and þissum bróþrum cymð micel hryre for heora tyddernyssum', Hml. S. 33, 166. Wín swýþe gedruncen graman and yrre and hryras fela hit deð *uinum multum potatum irritationem et iram et ruinas multas facit,* Scint. 106, 1. (4) *destruction.* (a) of persons. (a) of natural death :—þér (*in heaven*) sóðfæstra sáwla móton æfter líces hryre lífes brúcan, An. 229. Oð þæt him cwelm gesceód ... oð þæt him God wolde þurh hryre

hreddan heá ríce, Dan. 671. (β) of violent death in battle, &c. :—Hryre excidium, Wrt. Voc. ii. 32, 40. Æfter deófla hryre *after the fall of Grendel and his mother*, B. 1680. Æfter hæleða hryre, 2052. Winemǣga hryre, Wand. 7. (b) *destruction* of a place :—þy ilcan geáre þe Cartaina tôworpen wæs, æfter hiere hryre hî tôwurpon Corinthum *eodem anno quo Carthago deleta est, ruinam Carthaginis eversio Corinthi subsecutus est*, Ors. 5, 2; S. 214, 27.

**hrysc.** Substitute : **hrȳsc** *a bang* (?), *knock. Take here the passage given under* hricsc, *and add* :—Wiþ geswelle þām þe wyrð of fylle oððe of slege oþþe of hrȳsca hwilcum, Lch. ii. 6, 28. *See next word.*

**hryscan.** Substitute : **hrȳscan** *to make a creaking, grating, whirring noise;* stridere :—Ðǣre hristendan (hrîscendan ? v. hrȳscung) tô swēge (*this is almost certainly a gloss to* Ald. 65, 15 : Ad stridulae buccinae sonum) *ad stridulae*, Wrt. Voc. ii. 3, 46. Strengce rîscendum *nervo stridente*, Hpt. Gl. 405, 75. Rîslum hrîscendum *radiis stridentibus*, An. Ox. 3740. Mid hrȳscendum þearma strengum *argutis (i. stridolis) fibrarum fidibus*, 5006. [*For connexion of this word with* Mod. E. rush *and* Ger. rauschen *see for one view* N. E. D. rush, *for another* E. S. xxxix. 345.] v. ge-hrūxl, hrȳsclan.

**hrȳsclan** (?), **hrȳxlan**, **hrȳstlan.** *To make a noise* :—Hrîslum hrîstlendum *radiis stridentibus*, Wrt. Voc. ii. 83, 24. v. hrȳscan, hrūxlian.

**hrȳscung** (?) *a wheezing, whistling, hissing sound. See the passage given in Dict. under* hristung, *where read* (?) hrîscung. Cf. *first passage under* hrȳscan.

**hrȳtan** *to scatter. Dele, and see* **hrūtan**; II.

**hryte** *or* **hrȳte.** *l.* hrȳte. *v.* hrūt : **hrȳxlan** (?). *v.* hrȳsclan.

**hū.** Add : I. in direct questions. (1) qualifying a verb. (a) *in what way ?* :—Hū mæg þis þus geweorþan ?, Bl. H. 7, 21. Hū mæg ic andsware ǣnige findan ?, Cri. 183. (a a) with ellipsis of the rest of the sentence, *how* (would it be) if . . . :—Hū þonne gyf þū ne meaht ?, Solil. H. 40, 1 : 6 : 39, 20. (b) *with what reason ?* :—Hū (*quo modo*) miht þū secgan þînum brēþer, 'Læt . . . ?,' Lk. 6, 42. Hū (*hûmeta*, W. S.) cwepestū . . . ?, Mt. R. L. 7, 4. Hū þearf mannes sunu mâran treówe ?, Exod. 425. (c) *with what meaning ?, to what effect ?* :—Hwæt is gewriten on þǣre ǣ ? hū rǣtst þū ?, Lk. 10, 26. (d) with intensive addition :—Sē ðe eáran worhte, hū sē oferhleóður ǣfre wurde ? *qui plantavit aurem, non audiet ?*, Ps. Th. 93, 9. (2) used interjectionally to introduce a question, *what ?, why ?* :—Dū, Capharnaum, hū wið in heofonum ðū ðec āhefes ? *tu, Capharnaum, numquid usque in caelum exaltaberis ?*, Mt. L. 11, 23. Hū ! onsuæræstū suæ ðǣm biscobi ? *sic respondis pontifici ?*, Jn. L. 18, 22. (2 a) mostly with negative questions :—Hū nys seó sâwl selre þonne mete ? *nonne anima plus est quam esca ?*, Mt. 6, 26 : Lk. 17, 17. Hū lā ! ne wurpe wē þrȳ cnihtas intô þām fȳre ?, Hml. Th. ii. 20, 12. Lā hū ne gewîdmǣrsude ? *nonne percrebruit ?*, An. Ox. 2374. Hū ne nū [God] sēcð þās ? *nonne Deus requiret ista ?*, Ps. Rdr. 43, 22 : 38, 8. (3) qualifying adj. or adv. :—Hū fela blâfa (monigo (feola, R.) hlâfas, L.) hæbbe gē ? *quot panes habetis ?*, Mt. 15, 34. Hū lange beó ic mid eów ? hū lange forbere ic eów ? *quousque ero vobiscum? usque quo patior vos ?*, Mt. 17, 17. Wilt þū hū lange edwît þolian feóndum ? *usque quo improperabit inimicus ?*, Ps. Th. 73, 10. (3 a) with the case of a noun used adverbially :—Hū gerâdes (*qua mente*) mæg se biscep brūcan ðǣre hirdelican âre ?, Past. 133, 3. II. in direct exclamations :—Hū beorht O! *preclara*, An. Ox. 1266. Hū (hū swîðe, R., L.) beó ic geþreád, Lk. 12, 50. Efne hū glædlic bið and gôd swylce *ecce quam bonum et quam jucundum*, Ps. Th. 132, 1 : Bt. 16, 2 ; F. 52, 3. Hū þǣr wæs unefen racu om gemǣne, Cri. 1460. III. in dependent questions and exclamations. (1) qualifying a verb (a) in dependence on verbs of ordering, telling, asking, hearing, remembering, thinking, knowing, caring, trying :—Ic cýðe and wrîtan hâte hū mîn willa is, C. D. i. 310, 3 : 316, 3. Hî rehton him hū (*qualiter*) hit gedôn wæs, Mk. 5, 16. Hwanon hē cymð and hū hē bȳð and tô hwan hē gewyrð wē âmearkodon, Angl. viii. 312, 47. Se godspellere sǣde hū Drihten cwæþ tô Petre, Bl. H. 23, 12 : 15, 3. Seó cwén ongan fricggan . . . hū on worulde ǣr wîtgan sungon be Godes bearne, El. 561. Wurdon hî blîðe syððan hî gehȳrdon hū seó hâlige sprǣc, Jud. 160. Geþencað hū hē sprǣc wið eów *recordamini qualiter locutus est uobis*, Lk. 24, 6. Ūton geþencan hū (hwæt, *v. l.*) Iacôb cwæð, Ll. Th. i. 196, 1 : An. 639 : 962. Geðohte huu wæs þ wēre ðiós groeteng *cogitabat qualis esset ista salutatio*, Lk. L. R. 1, 29. Tô gewitane hū gedôn mann hē wæs, Chr. 1086 ; P. 219, 16. God âna wât hū his gecynde bið, Ph. 356. Men ne cūðon hū âfæstnod wæs feldhūsa mǣst, Exod. 85. Nū is undyrne hū þā wihte hâtne sindon, Rä. 43, 16. Þ gē ne sorgige . . . hū gē eówic gearwige (*quid induamini*), Mt. R. 6, 25. Hē cunnode hū hié cweðan woldon, Dan. 531 : Jud. 259. On sefan sêcan hū . . ., El. 474. Sirwan hū . . ., Sat. 499. (a a) where the verb on which the clause depends is not expressed :—Hū man sceal gyldan twelfhyndes mann, Ll. Th. i. 174, 12 : 178, 1 (*a form like* Hēr cȳð *might be supplied*). (a β) where the verb on which the clause depends has an object, to which the clause is in apposition :—Árece ūs þæt gerȳne, hū þū eácnunge onfēnge, Cri. 75. Þisses fugles gecynd fela gelîces bi Crîstes þegnum beácnað, hū hî beorhtne gefeán heal-

dað, Ph. 389. Wyrd ne cūðe freóndrǣdenne, hū heó from hogde, Jul. 34. Hū magon wē swā dȳgle āhicgan on sefan þinne, hū þe swefnede, Dan. 131. Bið wundra mā þonne hit ǣnig mǣge āþencan, hū þæt gestun and se storm brecað brâde gesceaft, Cri. 991. Feorh ne bemurndan . . . hū þæs gâstes sîð æfter swyltcwale geseted wurde, An. 155. ¶ the object a pronoun :—Hycgað his ealle hū gē hî beswîcen, Gen. 433. Ne mæg ic þæt gehicgan, hū ic in þǣm becwôm, Sat. 179. Þæs gîman nele waldend, hū . . ., Cri. 1570. (a γ) where the verb on which the clause depends has an object to which the clause is not in apposition :—Englas beweardiað þananforð manna gehwylcne, hū hē gelǣste . . ., Wlfst. 144, 19. Gewât neósian hūses, hū hit Hring Déne gebūn hæfdon, B. 115. Wæs þæs wyrmes wîg wîde gesýne . . . hū se gūðsceaða Geáta leóde hýnde, 2318 : 2948. (b) in dependence on nouns of meaning akin to the verbs mentioned in (a) :—Dis is seó gerǣdnyss hū mon ðæt hundred haldan sceal, Ll. Th. i. 258, 2. Tô bēhðe, hū hyre æt beaduwe gespeów, Jud. 175. Þā ealdan race, hū þū yfle gehogdes, Cri. 1398. Þæt is fyrn sægen, hū hē weorna feala wîtu geþolode, An. 1492. (b a) in dependence on adjectives :—Weard þ mǣden mycclum hohful hū heó ǣfre wæras wissian sceolde, Hml. S. 2, 122. (2) with weakened meaning, nearly with the force of *that*, introducing indirect statements. (a) after verbs as in (1 a) :—Hig rehton . . . hū hig hine oncneówan on hlâfes brice, Lk. 24, 35. Gehêrað . . . hū Drihten wolde cuman tô þære stôwe þe hē on þrowian wolde, Bl. H. 15, 5. Hî tô rǣde gerǣddon . . . hū hî God weorðodon, Ll. Th. i. 350, 7. Geþencan wē hū Drihten cwæð, 'Eádige beóþ þā þe nū wēpað ', Bl. H. 25, 19. Hē þôhte hū hē him strenglicran stôl geworhte, Gen. 273. Fyrd eall geseah hū þǣr hlifedon hālige seglas, Exod. 89. (a a). (1 a a) :—Hū þā deófla on Brytisc sprǣcon, Guth. Gr. 135, 1, and often (cf. similar use of þæt v. þæt ; V. 2). (a β). Cf. (1 a β) :—Gē on lôciað . . . fǣrwundra sum, hū ic sylfa slôh . . . gârsecges deóp, Exod. 280. Cýðan godspelles gife, hū se gâsta helm . . . âcenned weard, El. 176. Gē wîtgena lâre onfēngon, hū se liffruma in cildes hâd cenned wurde, 335. Ussa yrmða geþenc, hū wē hwearfiað heánlîce, Cri. 371. (b) Cf. (1 b) :—Þā angan Thomas his sprǣce, hū hē côm tô Cantwarebyri, and hū se arb āxode hȳrsumnesse, and hē hit forsôc, Chr. 1070 ; P. 206, 10. (b a). Cf. (1 b a) :—Þǣr hē gemyndig, hū hē in yrmðum wunade, An. 163. (3) introducing a noun clause :—Bið þridde tâcen, hū (cf. ân is . . . þæt, 1239, ôðer is . . . þæt, 1244) . . . þæt gesǣlige weorud gesihð þæt fordône þrowian, Cri. 1248. Nis ǣnig wundor, hū seó unclǣne gecynd ondrǣde, 1016. Þæt is wundres dǣl, hū mec seaxes ord and seó swîðre hond . . . geþýdan, Rä. 61, 12. Hē hæfde him tô gamene . . . hū hē eordcyningas yrmde, Met. 9, 47 : Sat. 196 : Exod. 244. (4) qualifying an adj. or adv. :—Gē ne geþenceað . . . hū fela (hū monige, R. *quot*) wylegena gē nâmon, Mt. 16, 9. Gemyne hū mycel yfel þe gelamp, Bl. H. 31, 13 : 33, 25 : Wand. 30. Hū þū æþele eart, Hy. 3, 14 : 18. IV. introducing a relative clause. (1) *in what way* :—Gefada embe lôca hū þū wylle, Hml. S. 3, 285. (v. lôc(a) *in Dict.*) Âbîdan miclan dômes, hū him metod scrîfan wille, B. 979. (2) qualifying an adj. or adv., *to what extent* (in a correlative phrase) :—Â hū lenge swîðe, Ps. Srt. 37, 9. (3) with antecedent noun (or pronoun) :—Hē geworhte ânes fearres anlîcnesse of âre tô ðon, þonne mon þā earman men oninnan dôn wolde, hū se hlynn mǣst wǣre *he made a bull's image of brass in the way, in which the sound would be greatest, when the wretched men were put inside*, Ors. 1, 12 ; S. 54, 25. V. with indef. adj. or adv. :—Ac elcra, elles hū *sed secus*, i. *aliter*, An. Ox. 3202. Þū hit nâ hū elles begitan ne miht, Bt. 32, 1 ; F. 114, 8. VI. in phrases :—Gelîc ðâm scipe ðe ðā ȳða drîfað ūt on sǣ swā hū swā se wind blǣwð, Hen. 46, 21. Begite hē, swā hū swā hē mæge, septies cxx manna, Ll., Th. ii. 286, 22. v. hū-meta.

**hūdenian.** Dele the suggested connexion with *hȳd*, and add ' *Húdenian* . . . gehört offenbar mid ndd. *húdern* vor Kalte zittern ' . . . und bildet die s-lose nebenform von me. ndd. *schudderen* ', Beiblatt xv. 350.

**hūf.** v. ūf.

**hūfe.** Add : **hūf**, e :—Hūfe *cuphia vel mitra*, (omitted after Wrt. Voc. i. 16, 65, see) Angl. viii. 450. Hættes, hūfan *mitre*, An. Ox. 5242. Hūfan *mitre* i. *tigera*, 2, 440. Mitrae hættes, hūfan *tigera*, snôda, Hpt. Gl. 525, 9. [v. N. E. D. houve.]

**hūfian.** Add : v. ge-, un-hūfod(-ed) : **-hugende.** v. stîþ-hugende.

**hū-hwega.** Add : I. used where measurement is only approximately given :—Hūhugu *circiter*, Wrt. Voc. ii. 24, 35. (1) of space measurement :—Is þ eáland fram þǣre cyrican feor ūt on gârsecge seted hūhugu (-hwega, hūru, v. ll.) on nygan mîlum (*nouem ferme milibus passuum*), Bd. 4, 27 ; Sch. 511, 7. Hūhugu (neáh, hugu, v. ll.) on twēgra mîla fæce *duum ferme milium spatio*, 4, 4 ; Sch. 567, 10. Nôht feor . . . þ is hūhwega (swilce, v. l.) on ôþere healfre mîle fæc, 5, 2 ; Sch. 556, 4. (1 a) of extent :—Þā þā þ weorc hūhugu (hwæthwugu, v. l.) healf wæs geworht *cum opus ad medium ferme esset perductum*, Bd. 3, 8 ; Sch. 225, 10. (2) of time measurement :—Hūhugu (hwæthwega, v. l.) ymb þā teóþan tîd dæges, 3, 27 ; Sch. 316, 13. Hūhugu (hūru, v. l. *ferme*) feówertig daga, Bd. 5, 4 ; Sch. 567, 12. Nū for ânum .xii. nihtum

hūhugu (hwæthwega, v. l.) swā (neálíce for twelf dagum, v. l.) ante dies fere duodecim, Gr. D. 79, 12. Nū for seofon wintrum hūhugu swā ante septem ferme annos, 305, 21. (3) numeral:—Hūhugu (hwæthwega, v. l.) syx hund hída, Bd. 4, 19; Sch. 451, 23. Þeós circe mid þýs portice mihte hūhwego fíf hund manna befón, Bl. H. 207, 14. II. marking degree:—Gloriosas saltim hūhugu, Wrt. Voc. ii. 41, 52.

hū-ilpa. v. hwilpa : hūlas. v. sceald-hūlas.

hulc a ship. Add:—Hulc liburna, Wrt. Voc. i. 63, 33. [v. N. E. D. hulk.]

hulc a hut. Add:—Hulce tugurio, An. Ox. 2515. [v. N. E. D. hulk.]

hulfestre. Add:—Hulfestran (printed hulfstan, Wrt. Voc. i. 63, 24) ciapella, Wülck. Gl. 287, 14.

hulfstan. See preceding word.

hū-lic. Add: I. in direct questions. (1) qualifying a noun, what sort of:—Hūlic heáfod hæfst se Pater Noster?, Sal. K. 148, 14. (2) predicative, of what sort?—Hūlig is ðes? qualis est hic?, Mt. L. 8, 27. II. in indirect questions. (1) qualifying a noun, what sort of:—Gecunnia and ásca huulic monn sē, Mt. L. 10, 14 marg. Gif hē wiste hūlic wíf (qualis mulier) wēre, Lk. L. 7, 39. Sceáwa hūlice (hūlco, L.) stānas and hūlic (huulig, L.) timber aspice quales lapides et quales structurae, Mk. R. 13, 1. (2) predicative, of what sort:—Þ hī him bróhtan þ heáfod tó, þ hē gesēge hūlic þ wēre, Shrn. 76, 27. Hē giémde hwæt hē hæfde monna gerímes, and ne nóm nāne ware hūlice hié wēron, Ors. 5, 4; S. 224, 22. (3) used substantively:—Ðā ðe gesēgon hūlic (hwelce, R.) geworden wēre, Mk. L. 5, 16. Hē ædeáude hūlco (qualia) wēro ðrouendo hreáferas, Lk. p. 9, 3. Hūluco, Jn. p. 7, 12. v. hū.

hulu. For 'Gl. Prud... 439' substitute:—Hulu siliqua, Germ. 390, 63. Cornbērum eára scale, hule, egle granigera spicarum glumula, An. Ox. 1412. Hulæ, 2, 41. [v. N. E. D. hull.] v. beren-hulu.

huma. v. uma.

humele, an; f. The hop-plant. [Cf. (?) Æt humelcyrre, C. D. iii. 274, 32.] v. eówo-humele, hymele.

hū-meta. Add: I. in direct questions. (1) in what way?, by what means?:—Hūmeta wāt God? quomodo scit Deus?, Ps. Spl. 72, 11. (2) with what reason or right:—Hūmeta cwyst þū tó þínum brēðer?, Mt. 7, 4. (3) how is it that?, why?:—Gif heó turniende is, hūmeta ne fealð heó? si volubile est, cur non cadat?, Angl. vii. 12, 109. Hūmeta wēnde Adam þ hē mihte hine behýdan fram Godes gesihðe? unde a Domini praesentia abscondi posse putabat?, 26, 239. II. in indirect questions. (1) qualifying a verb. (a) cf. I. 1:—Hē āxodon þā weardmenn hūmeta se ān wēre tó þām hālgum geþeód?, Hml. S. 11, 236. (b) Cf. I. 2:—Hē āxode þā weardmen hūmeta hī dorston hī swā wel fēdan, Hml. S. 37, 61. (2) with ellipsis of the rest of the clause ntroduced by how:—Wē hērdon þ sum sunu ofslóge his fæder, ic nāt hūmeta, būton wē witon þ hit unmennisclic dǣd wæs, Bt. 31, 1; F. 112, 16. v. hū.

hun. Substitute: hun (?), hunu (?), hūn (?) diseased matter, disease; tabum:—Hune vel ādle tabo (elephantino deturpans, Ald. 49, 16. The passage is glossed: Hreófligum wyrmse āwlǣtende, An. Ox. 3585), Wrt. Voc. ii. 82, 55.

hūn a bear-cub, in proper names, e. g. Hūn-bald, Ælf-hūn. v. Txts. 635 for many examples. [Icel. húnn a young bear. The word occurs in local names.]

huncettan; p. te To limp, halt:—Hý healtodon ł huncetton claudicauerunt, Ps. Rdr. 17, 46. [Cf. O. H. Ger. rendering of same passage: Sié hunchen, halzeten.] v. helle-hinca, hincian.

hund. Add: I. a dog:—Hund canis, bicce canicula, Wrt. Voc. ii. 23, 7. Hwīlum ic beorce swā hund, Rä. 25, 2. Ne ðu murnþ nāuþer ne friénd ne fiénd þe mā þe wēdende hund, Bt. 37, 1 ; F. 186, 8. Hrýðeres belle and hundes hoppe ... ælc bið ānes sciłł. weorð, and ælc is melda geteald, Ll. Th. i. 260, 16. Be hundes slite. Gif hund mon tóslíte oþþe ābíte ... Gif se hund mā misdǣda gewyrce, 78, 1–6. Wiþ hundes slite, Lch. i. 148, 7. Cōmon hundas forþ on wundorlícre mycelnesse and rǣsdon on þone apostol, Bl. H. 181, 20. Hunda hūs canile, domus canis, Wrt. Voc. ii. 128, 20 : 23, 13. Of þēre þeóde þēr men habbað hunda heáfod, Shrn. 76, 17. Gif hwā þās wyrte mid him hafað ne mæg hē fram hundum beón borcen (brocen, v.l.), Lch. i. 170, 16. I a. a dog used for hunting, a hound:—'Syle mē (the huntsman) ænne hafoc.' 'Ic (the fowler) sylle lustlíce, gif þū sylst mē ænne swyftne hund,' Coll. M. 25, 31. Nān hara ne onscunode nænne hund, Bt. 35, 6 ; F. 168, 10. Wildu diór wolde stondan swilce hī tamu wēron ðeáh hī men oðde hundas wið eódon, 3. Hū wēre þū dyrstig ofstikian bār? Hundas bedrifon hyne tó mē, Coll. M. 22, 15. Hwæþer gē willen wēþan mid hundum on sealtne sǣ þonne eów sēcan lyst heorotas, Met. 19, 15 ; B. 1368. 'Ic (the huntsman) brēde mē max, and sette híg, and getihte hundas mīne, þ wildeór híg ēhton ... Būton nettum huntian ic mæg.' 'Hū?' 'Mid swiftum hundum ic betǣce wildeór, Coll. M. 21, 27. Hwæþer gē eówer hundas and eówer net ūt on ðā sǣ lǣdon þonne gē huntian willaþ?, Bt. 32, 3 ; F. 118, 13. I b, in the passages in

which the dog is mentioned in the Bible more or less of contempt is implied:—Hundes tungan habbað feóndas, Ps. Th. 67, 23. Hundas cōmon and his wunda liccodon, Lk. 16, 21. Þæt flǣsc þæt wildro ābiton ne ete gē, ac worpað hit hundum (cf. the rendering of this passage in Ll. Th. i. 54, 2 : Sellað hit hundum, where perhaps the difference of verbs marks a difference of feeling towards the animal, but see (3 a)), Ex. 22, 31. Sealdon flǣsc heora fuglum tó mōse, hāligra líc hundum and deórum (carnes eorum bestiis terrae), Ps. Th. 78, 2. Perhaps the influence of the feeling noted in I b may be traced in theological writings (but see II):—Se mann þe nyle geswícan unnytre sprǣce ... bið wyrsa þonne hund oððe ǣniges cynnes nýten, þonne hē intó cyrcan cymð ... ælc mon hatað þone hund and drífð hine ūt of þēre cyrican, Wlfst. 234, 27–235, 5. I c for the use of the dog in medicine see Lch. i. 370. II. applied as a contemptuous epithet to a man. Cf. I. b:—Þone rēþan þe biþ þweórtēme þū scealt hātan hund, nallas mann ferox atque inquies linguam litigiis exercet? cani comparabis, Bt. 37, 4; F. 192, 16. Se cāsere nýdde þone biscop and ðone diácon tó hæþenscipe: þā swygode se biscop. Ðā cwæþ se diácon tó þām biscope: 'Clypa ongēn þissum deófles hunde þe þē on beorceð,' Shrn. 56, 22. Æt hundum, þ is unwyrðum and unclǣnum monnum, Mt. L. 7, 6 marg. III. some sea-beast, a seal (?), a dog-fish (?):—De Scilla ... hī gewiton on sǣ and wurdon tó hundum. Scilla, ðet is sǣhund gecweden, An. Ox. 26, 61. IV. the word occurs in local names:—On þone hundes þýfel; of hundes þýfel, C. D. iii. 425, 29. See, too, Hunda-hām, -leáh, Hundes-geat, -hlǣw, vi. 304. v. gríg-, regn-, roþ-, sǣ-hund.

hundes beó. l. peó, and see píe : hundes cwelcan. Add:—Hundes cwelcan colocinthidae, Wrt. Voc. ii. 14, 51. [Cf. Dan. kvalke gelder-rose] : hundes fleóge. Add:—Hundes fleóge ricinus, Wrt. Voc. i. 23, 38 : cinomya, 73 : hundes tunge. Add:—Hundes tunge canis lingua, Wrt. Voc. i. 67, 28. Ribbe, hundes tunge, ii. 13, 13. [v. N. E. D. hound's tongue.]

hund. Add: The word is used both as substantive (governing a noun in the genitive) or as adjective (agreeing with noun). The dative plural, though sometimes like the nominative, also has both e and um as inflection. I. as abstract numeral:—Twēntig síðon seofon beóð ān hund and feówertig, Angl. viii. 303, 6. II. as substantive. (1) without lesser numerals:—Þæt þanon wēre tó helle duru hund þūsenda míla gemearcodes, Sat. 723. Hund scillinga gelde se āgend, Ll. Th. i. 28, 5. Hē hæfde ān hund þūsenda gehorsedra, Ors. 3, 9 ; S. 124. 34 : B. 2994. Þæt wæs nigon x hund þūsenda decies novies centena millia virorum, Ors. 2, 5 ; S. 84, 29. Þreóm hundum sciłł. gylde se āgend, Ll. Th. i. 26, 9. Mid twām hunde scipa, Ors. 4, 6; S. 178, 27 : 176, 10 : 180, 5. Fór hē mid siex hund monna, 3, 9 ; S. 128, 13. Genōm Calatinus iii hund monna mid him, Ors. 4, 6 ; S. 172, 20. (2) with lesser numerals, and (a) followed by the lesser numeral:—Æfter þǣm þe Rōmeburg getimbred wæs ii hunde wintra and hundeahtatigum post urbem conditam anno ccxc, Ors. 2, 6 ; S. 86, 19. Mid feówer hunde scipa and þritigum cum trecentis triginta navibus, 4, 6 ; S. 172, 31. Mid iii hund scipa and lxgum cum ducentis sexaginta navibus, 176, 25. Æfter þǣm þe Rōmeburg getimbred wæs iii hunde wintra and ān, 2, 7 ; S. 90, 5. Ymb feówer hund wintra and seofone (vii winter, v. l.) anno cccc° vii°, Bd. 1, 11 ; Sch. 30, 12. Feówer hund wintra and þæs fíftan hundseofontig post annos ferme ccclxx, 26. (a a) where a preposition is used with both numbers:—Mid þrim hunde scipa and mid xxx, Ors. S. 4, 5. Ymb feówer hunde wintra and ymb feówertig, 2, 2 ; S. 64, 20. An feówer hund eá and on lx, 2, 4 ; S. 74, 1. (b) preceded by the smaller number:—Hiora scipa xxx gefangen, and iiii and ān hund ādruncen centum et quatuor naves demersae, triginta captae, Ors. 4, 6; S. 176, 13. Þēr wēron xxx and c gearora (centum triginta), 172, 5; C. D. vi. 243, 12. Æfter i wintra and feówer hundum post annos quadringenti et quadraginta, Ors. 4, 7; S. 182, 19. Wintra hæfde fíf and hundnigontig ... and eahta hund, Gen. 1179. (3) with ordinals:—Cuōm feórðe healf hund scipa, Chr. 851 ; P. 64, 17. Heora mon āhēng fífte healf hund quadringenti et quinquaginta servi in crucem acti, Ors. 5, 3; S. 222, 30. III. as adjective. (1) without lesser numerals:—Þæt wǣron fíeftiéne hund þūsend monna quinquies decies centena millia peditum equitumque, Ors. 3, 9; S. 128, 22. iiii hund wintrum æfter þǣm þe Rōmeburg getimbred wæs anno ab Urbe condita cccc, Ors. 3, 7 ; S. 110, 14. Hund síðon centies, twā (þreó, &c.) síðon du- (tri-, &c.) centies, Ælfc. Gr. Z. 286, 6, 12. (2) with lesser numerals, and (a) followed by them:—iii hund and siex men of ǣgðerre healfe, Ors. 2, 6; S. 86, 21. iiii hunde wintrum and hundeahtatigum, 1, 10; S. 44, 3 : 4, 9; S. 188, 29. v hunde wintrum and vii, 4, 7 ; S. 180, 15. Feówer hunde wintrum and feówer and siextigum, 4, 1 ; S. 154, 1. On þrím hund dagum and fíf and sixtigum, Angl. vii. 14, 128. On þrím hund dagum and eahta and sixtigum dagum, 130. Eahta hund and feówertigum feórum, Gen. 1161. (b) where the lesser numeral precedes:—Seofon winter ond eahta hund, Gen. 1140. v. hundred, hund-teóntig.

hund-eahtatig. Add: I. as (singular) substantive :—Þæs folces

him eóde on hundeahtatig burga, Ors. 4, 10 ; S. 198, 15. Hē hundeahtatig scipa gegaderade, 4, 6 ; S. 170, 34. **II.** as adj. :—Hundeahtatigon síðon *octuagies*, Ælfc. Gr. Z. 286, 5.

**hundeahtatigoþa** *eightieth* :—Se hundeahtatigoða *octogesimus*, Ælfc. Gr. Z. 283, 13.

**hunden.** *Add :*—Hē sende on hý fleógan hundene (*muscam caninam*), Ps. Rdr. 77, 45.

**hund-feald.** [*In the first passage perhaps* hundfealdgetel *should be read.* v. þúsendfeald-getel.] *Add :*—Heó næfð þone wurðmynt þæs hundfealdan wæstmes, Hml. A. 34, 250. Hē underfēhð þā mēde be hundfealdum edleáne, 15, 51. Hundfealde mēde, 21, 186 : Hml. Th. i. 148, 18. Tēn ðúsend síðan hundfealde ðúsenda him mid wunodon *decies millies centena millia assistebant ei* (Dan. 7, 10), 348, 3. Hundfealde *centeni*, Ælf. Gr. Z. 13, 16. ¶ be hundfealdum *a hundredfold* :—Be hundfealdum hē onfēhð leán *centuplum accipiet*, Mt. 19, 29. Þ hí be hundfealdum habbað þā mēde Þ Þ hí be ánfealdan for his lufon dydon, Hml. A. 15, 55.

**hundfeald-getel.** v. hund-feald.

**hundfeald-lic** ; *adj. Hundred-fold* :—Hundfealdlic hē onfēhð *centuplum accipiet*, Scint. 58, 2.

**hund-freá (?)** *a centurion* :—Hundfre[-á?] *centurio*, Mt. L. 22, 19 marg.

**hunding.** v. healf-hunding.

**hund-lic.** *Add :*—Hundlice oððe tuxas *canini*, Wrt. Voc. ii. 16, 50 : Bl. H. 181, 28.

**hund-nigontig.** *Add :* **I.** as substantive with gen. :—Hē wæs nigon and hundnigontic geára *nonaginta et novem erat annorum*, Gen. 17, 24. Ofer nigon and hundnigontigum (hundneántig, L., hundniontig, R.) rihtwísra *super nonaginta nouem iustis*, Lk. 15, 7. Ofer nigon and hundnigontig ryhtwísra, Past. 411, 13. **II.** as adj. :—Hundnigontig síðon *nonagies*, Ælfc. Gr. Z. 286, 5. Hē lēt him behindan ciólas nigon and hundnigontig, Met. 26, 24. **III.** where the governed or qualified noun is not expressed :—Māre bliss bið . . . be ánum synfullan men . . . þonne be nigon and hundnigantigan þe dædbóte ne behófiað, Angl. xi. 114, 68. Hū ne forlǣt hē þā nigon and hundnigontig (-neántih, L. ; hundnigontig and nigon, R.) on þām muntum ?, Mt. 18, 12, 13. Ðā nigona and hundneóntig (ðā hundnióntig and nióne, R.), Lk. L. 15, 4.

**hundnigontig-geáre** ; *adj. Ninety years old* :—Enos leofode hundnygontyggeáre *vixit Enos nonaginta annis*, Gen. 5, 9.

**hund-nigontigoþa** *ninetieth* :—Se hundnigontigoða *nonagesimus*, Ælfc. Gr. Z. 283, 14. On þæm seówer-and-hundnigontigoðon psalme, Past. 415, 5. Oð ðæt hundnigonteóþe geár, Hml. A. 37, 330.

**hundnigontig-wintre.** *Add :*—þā hē wæs nigon-and-hundnigontigwintre, Gen. 17, 1.

**hundred.** *Add :* **I.** as an abstract numeral :—Þrittig síðon seofon beóð twā hundred and týn ; feówertig síðon seofon beóð twā hundred and hundeahtatig ; fíftig síðon seofon beóð þreó hundred and fíftig, Angl. viii. 303, 7-9. **II.** as substantive. (1) governing a gen. :—Half hundred fóðra cornes, C. D. iv. 263, 20. Cýswyrhtan gebyreð hundred cýse (-a?) *caseum facienti reddere convenit centum caseos*, Ll. Th. i. 438, 31. Hundraðes monna hlāfard *centurio*, Mt. p. 15, 13 : Mt. L. 8, 5. Heora man āhēng fífte healf hundred (hund, *v.l.*), Ors. 5, 3 ; Th. 442, 24. Hundrað (hundteóntig, R., hund, W. S.) scípa *centum oves*, Mt. L. 18, 12. Hundrað (hundred, R., hund, W. S.) scillinga *centum denarios*, 18, 28. Hundreð, Lk. R. 15, 4. Þǣr wæs þreó þúsend gerēfena and þreó hundrǣd, Angl. xi. 4, 13. Þ hit .xii. hund (hundred, *v.l.*) sciłł., Ll. Th. i. 190, 3. Ðrím hundredum peninga *trecentis denariis*, Mk. R. 14, 5. Twā hundred and twēntig sciłł., Ll. Th. i. 366, 21. Hæfde hē sume hundred scipa, Bt. 38, 1 ; F. 194, 7. (2) *a group of a hundred persons or objects* :—Hí wurpon fela hundreda forð ofer þone weall, Hml. A. 68, 80. *Ducentesimus* sē ðe byð on ðām twǣm hundredum æftemyst, Ælfc. Gr. Z. 284, 1. Ofer ðrím hundradum *tribunus* bið forwost, Mk. L. 6, 21 marg. Hundredum *centuriis* (*exercitus in centuriis* et *millibus conglobatos*), An. Ox. 882. Ðerh hundrað (-eð, R.) *per centenos*, Mk. L. 6, 40. (2 a) used of things denoting value, where the thing is to be inferred. Cf. modern use of *hundred* = hundred pounds. *Icel.* hundrað = 120 *yards of wadmal* :—Bēte man þ mid .xii. hund. : Bēte man vi. hund. .vi. hundꝼ . . vi. hundꝼ . . bēte man þ mid hundꝼ, Ll. Th. i. 292, 6-9. Lecge hē án .C. (*unum hundretum*) tō wedde . . . gilde ān .C., 296, 7-11. Ðā ðe wæstmiað, ān drittig, . . . ān hundrað (-eð, R.) *qui fructificant unum trigenta . . . unum centum*, Mk. L. 4, 20 : 8. Wæstm gebrenges, óðer hundrað (hundteóntig, R., hundfealdne, W. S.), Mt. L. 13, 23. Hundrað *centesimum*, 8. Þreó [hundr]ed æt cwicum men, Ll. Lbm. 473, [4]. In Danelage per xviii hundreda, qui numerus complet septies xx. libras et iiii. ; forisfacturam enim hundredi Dani vocabant viii. libras, Ll. Th. i. 454. 10-12. [As 15 óran are said to make a pound, the hundred seems to be the great hundred (= 120), and the óra to be the unit.] **III.** as adjective :—Sē ðe hæfeð hundrað scíp (*centum oues*), Lk. L. 15, 4. Mid ān hundred and twēntigum scillingum, Ll. Th.

i. 360, 21. Mid penigum twǣm hundreðum *denariis ducentis*, Mk. R. 6, 37. Ðriim hundraðum scillingum, Mk. L. 14, 5. **III a.** as ordinal :—Hundraðes ðæs nióða salmes *centesimi noni psalmi*, Mt. p. 19, 9. Twā hundredum and seofen and sixtigum fíftýne geáres getel *olimpiade ducentesima sexagesima septima*, An. Ox. 3036. **IV.** character uncertain :—In feng ðǣra fiscana hundrað fíftih ðríu *in captura piscium centum quinquaginta trium*, Jn. p. 8, 9. v. hund, hund-teóntig.

**hundred** *a territorial division.* *Add :*—Nis ǣni man on lífe þe ǣfre gehýrde þ man crafode hine on hundrǣde oþþon āhwār on gemóte, Ll. Th. i. 184, 11.

**hundredes ealdor.** *Add :*—Hundredes ealdor *centurio*, Wrt. Voc. i. 18, 12. Hē (*Cornelius* 'centurio cohortis quae dicitur Italica', Acts 10, 1) is hundredes ealdor, Hml. S. 10, 119. Andswarode se hundredes ealdor, Mt. 8, 8. Þæs hundredes ealdor, 27, 54. v. hundred-mann.

**hundred-mann.** *Add :*—Þā se hundredman geseah *uidens centurio*, Lk. 23, 47. Wæs sumes hundredmannes þeówa untrum, 7, 2.

**hundred-seten**, e ; *f. The ordinance of the hundred ; the fine for not attending the hundred-court* (?) :—In multis locis debent habere constitutionem hundredi, quod Angli dicunt hundrǣdsetene, Ll. Lbmn. 615, 15. Omnes forisfacturas . . . id est hundredsetena, āthas et ordēlas, C. D. ii. 252, 12. Cf. next word.

**hundred-sócn**, e ; *f. Attendance at the hundred-gemot ; fine for non-attendance* :—Omnes forisfacturas terrarum suarum, id est, burgbrice, hundredsócna, āthas, ordēlas, . . . hāmsócna et frithbrice et foresteall, Cht. Th. 187, 23. Cf. Of Hylle . . . hāmsócne and forsteall, griðbrice . . . áþ and ordēl, and iii gemót on geáre, 433, 26-32.

**hund-seofontig.** *Add :* **I.** as abstract numeral :—Týn síðon seofon beóð hundseofontig, Angl. viii. 303, 5. **II.** as substantive (sing. or pl.). (1) with gen :—Þǣr on ríme forborn fíf and hundseofontig hǣðnes herges, Jul. 588. Þæt synd eall tōgedere twā and hundseofontig geára (MS. geáre), Hml. S. 6, 361. His ymbgong is hundseofontig míla, Ors. 2, 4 ; S. 74, 16. Sió wæs getimbred lxxiitigum wintra ǣr Rōmeburg, 4, 4 ; S. 164, 10. Hundsiofontig wintra, Past. 317, 1. Wintra hundseofontig, Gen. 1158. Hē hiora sprǣce tōdǣlde on twā and hundseofontig geþeóda, Bt. 35, 4 ; F. 162, 26. Cynno hundseofontig seofon, Lk. p. 4, 9. (2) as pl. *(the) seventy* :—Ðā gecyrdon þā twā and hundseofontig (-sifuntig, R.), Lk. 10, 17. Æfter þǣra hundseofontigra gefadunge *according to the Septuagint*, Angl. viii. 336, 9 (cf. **III.**). Twǣm and unseofontigum eftcerrendum, Lk. p. 6, 15. Se Hǣlend gemearcude ōðre twā and hundseofontig (-sifontig, R.), Lk. 10, 1. **III.** as adj. :—Æfter þǣra hundseofontigra wealhstoda geset-nyssa, Angl. viii. 336, 4. Hundseofontigon síþon *septuagies*, Ælfc. Gr. Z. 286, 4. Hundseofontigum síþon seofon síþon, An. Ox. 61, 22. Or. þām hundseofontigum geárum (geára, Ps. Vos. Srt.) *in ipsis septuaginta annis*, Ps. Rdr. L. 89, 10. Oðrum twǣm and unseofontigum ðeáðum, Lk. p. 6, 14. Æfter unseofuntigum trahteras, Mt. p. 2, 11. Fram unsefuntig aldrum, 3. Hundseofuntig seofo síða, 18, 7. **IV.** where a governed or qualified noun is not expressed :—Heora sprǣc is tōdǣled on twā and hundseofontig, Bt. 18, 2 ; F. 62, 33.

**hundseofontig-geáre** ; *adj. Seventy years old* :—Cainan lyfode hundseofontiggeáre *vixit Cainan septuaginta annis*, Gen. 5, 12.

**hundseofontigoþa** *seventieth* :—Se hundseofontigoða *septuagesimus*, Ælfc. Gr. Z. 283, 12.

**hundseofontigseofon-feald** ; *adj. Seventy-and-sevenfold* :—Seofonfeald wracu bið gesealde for Cain and hundseofontigseofonfeald (*septuagies septies*) for Lamech, Gen. 4, 24.

**hund-teóntig.** *Add :* [*The word as substantive may be treated as singular*, v. Nar. 36, 12 ; *or as plural*, v. Lev.. 26, 8. *Cf. the singular construction with much larger numbers in* Bl. H. 79, 25, *and* Past. 409, 9 : *the plural in* Ll. Lbmn. 415, 21.] **I.** used as substantive. (1) governing a genitive. (a) alone :—Hundteóntig ǣla, Ll. Th. i. 146, 20. Ealles þæs folces wæs . . . þrittigum sýþum hundteóntig þúsenda, Bl. H. 79, 25. Fíf eówer filiað hira hundteóntig, and hundteóntig eówer fleóð hira týn þúsendu, Lev. 26, 8. Mid hundteóntegum sciłł. gebēte, Ll. Th. i. 70, 21. Hundteóntig sciłł. geselle hē, 72, 14. Hí genāman þæs folces . . . hundteóntig þúsenda . . . and ehtatýne sýþum hundteóntig þúsenda hī tōsendon, Bl. H. 79, 20-23. Gif hæbbe hwā hundteóntig *libras centum*, Jn. L. R. 19, 39. Hunteántig punda síða monigfald *centuplum*, Lk. L. 8, 8. (b) in combination (by addition) with lesser numbers :—Þā beóð on lenge hundteóntiges fótmǣla and fíftiges lange, Nar. 36, 12. Mid .L. sciłł. and hundteóntegum gebēte hē, Ll. Th. i. 70, 19. Wintra hē hæfde twā and hundteóntig, Gen. 1227 : 1131. Hundteóntig daga on ān and hundeahtatig daga, Hml. A. 92, 11. Þurh ðā hunteóntig and feówer and feówertig þúsenda þrowera, Hml. Lbmn. 415, 21. (c) with a number as multiplier :—Wintra hæfde twā hundteóntig geteled ríme and fífe eác (cf. Thare leofode twā hund geára and fíf geár, Gen. 11, 32), Gen. 1741. (2) without a genitive. Cf. hundred ; **II.** 2 a :—Mid hundteóntigum ic hit him forgylde, Wlfst. 258, 18. Sume saldun wæstem, sume hundteóntig (*centesimum*), sume sextig, Mt. R. 13, 8 : (*centum*), 23. **III.** as adjective. (1) alone :—

**Hundteántih** ombras *centum cados*, Lk. L. 16, 6. (2) with other numerals :—Nán mon elles singan ne mæg búton ðæt hundteóntig and feówertig and feówer þúsendo, Past. 409, 9. Þurh heondteóntig and feówer and feówertig þúsendu martira, Ll. Lbmn. 414, 26. **III a.** as ordinal :—In psalme hunteánteige nióða *in psalmo centesimo nono*, Lk. p. 10, 11. **IV.** construction uncertain :—Þ nett full mið miclum fiscum hunteántig (hund-, R.) and fíftig ðriim i ðreó, Jn. L. 21, 11. v. hund, hundred.

**hundteóntig-feald.** *Add:*—Hunteóntifealdes *centenę* (*frugis*), An. Ox. 950.

**hundteóntigfealde**; *adv. A hundredfold* :—Hundteántigfalde (hundrað síða monigfallíce, L.) onfooð *centuplum accipiet*, Mt. R. 19, 29.

**hundteóntigfealdlíce**; *adv. A hundredfold*:—Þa englas sǽdon þæt him wǽre hundteóntigfealdlíce máre myrhð tóweard, Wlfst. 237, 9.

**hundteóntigoþa** *hundredth* :—Se hundteóntigoða *centesimus*, Ælfc. Gr. Z. 283, 14. Se hundteóntigeþa-and-twá-and-feówertigeþa, R. Ben. 37, 23. Fram ðám hundteóntigeðan-and-þám-nigeðan oð þene hundteóntigeþan-and-þane-seofan-and-feówertigeþan . . . fram ðám hundteóntigeþan-and-seofonteóðan oð þone hundteóntigeðan-and-seofon-and-twéntigeðan . . . bútan þám hundteóntigeþan-and-þreó-and-prítigeðan and þám hundteóntigeþan-and-twá-and-feówertigeþan . . . se hundteóntigeþa-and-se syxteóða, 43, 8–25.

**hundteóntig-wintre**; *adj. A hundred years old*:—Hundteóntigwintre cild byð ǽwyrged *puer centum annorum maledictus erit*, Nap. 39.

**hund-twelftig.** *Add:* **I.** as substantive [in which case the word may be treated as singular, v. Ors. S. 174, 17 ; or as plural, v. Hml. S. 21, 318]. (1) governing a genitive. (a) alone :—Cyninges burgbryce bið .c.xx. (hundtwelftig, *v. l.*) sciñ., Ll. Th. i. 88, 7. Heó wæs hundtwelftiges fóta lang, Ors. 4, 6 ; S. 174, 17. Ánra gehwylc godweb hangað on hundtwelftigum hringa gyldenna. And ðæt æreste godweb is háten *Aurum caeleste*, ðǽm ðióstre ne magon cxxtigum míla neáh gehleonian, Sal. K. 152, 17–20. Mid hundtwelftigan sciñ. . . . mid sixtigan scillinga, Ll. Th. i. 342, 2 : 410, 9. Be .cxx. (hundtwelftigum, *v. l.*) hída, 110, 17 : 198, 23. Gylde hé þám cynge hundtwelftig scillinga (sciñ., *v. l.*), 264, 12 : 62, 5 : 66, 16 : 86, 17. Cômon tó ðám hálgan hundtwelftig manna, mislíce geuntrumode, Hml. S. 21, 318. (b) with units :—Hundtwelftig scíra hé hætde and seofon scíra, Hml. A. 92, 6. **II.** as adjective. (1) alone :—Hé bodode húru hundtwelftigum wintrum, Wlfst. 206, 8. Mid .c.xx. (hundtwelftig, *v. l.*) sciñ. (scillingum, *v. l.*), Ll. Th. i. 110, 12. (2) with units :—Mid óþrum fíf and hundtwelftigum his efenbisceopum *cum aliis cxxv episcopis*, Bd. 5, 19 ; Sch. 666, 24. **III.** where the governed or qualified noun is not expressed :—Wæs ungemetlic wæl geslagen Persa, and Alexandres næs ná má þonne hundtwelftig on þǽm rǽdehere, Ors. 3, 9 ; S. 124, 21.

**hund-twéntig.** *Add:*—Mid hundtwéntigum sciñ., Ll. Th. i. 410, 9. Mid hundtwéntigum sciñ. (hundtwéntig scillinga, *v. l.*), 402, 6. Geselle hé·hundtwéntig sciñ, 66, 16. Hundtwéntig scillinge, 390, 25.

**hund-wille, -welle** *hundredfold* :—Hundwelle *centesimum*, Mt. L. 13, 8.

**hund-wintre.** *Add:*—Seth wæs hundwintre and fíf *Seth vixit centum quinque annis*, Gen. 5, 6.

**hune.** *l.* húne, *and add:*—Húnae *vel* bióuuyrt *marrubium*, Txts. 78, 657. Húne *marubium*, Wrt. Voc. i. 286, 32 : *prassion*, 68, 32.

**Hungerie** *the Hungarians*; later, *Hungary* :—Seó þeód þe mon þá hét Basterne, and nú hié mon hæt Hungerre (Hungerie, *v. l.*), Ors. 4, 11 ; S. 206, 36. Þes folces þe be Hungrie fór fela þúsenda þǽr earmlíce forfóran, Chr. 1096 ; P. 232, 36.

**Hunger-land** *Hungary* :—Þisne æþeling Cnut cyng hæfde forsend on Ungerland, Chr. 1057 ; P. 188, 10.

**hungor.** *Add:*—Hungor *fames* vel *popina*, Wrt. Voc. i. 51, 3. **I.** *the feeling caused by want of food* :—Ne biþ þǽr hungor ne þurst, Bl. H. 65, 19. **I a.** *exhaustion caused by want of food :*—Gif hé for hungre libban mǽge, Ll. Th. i. 64, 13. **I b.** *lack of food* (lit. or fig.) :—Hungres *fame*, i. *inedia* (non te hordeo alam, sed paleis et *fame* conficiam, Ald. 34, 1), An. Ox. 2440. **I b a.** with gen. of food :—Ne ádl ne hláfes hungor, Shrn. 104, 27. Hié lǽtað ða sáwla ácwellan for hungre hira worda *fame verbi animae pereant*, Past. 377, 11. **I c.** personified, An. 1089 : 1116 (in *Dict.*). **II.** *lack of food in a country, a famine* :—Wæs geworden mycel hunger (-or, R.) *facta est magna fames*, Lk. 4, 25. Hunger suíðe strong *fames ualida*, Lk. L. 15, 14. Côm micel hǽte . . . þæt ealle eorðwæstmas . . . forwurdon . . . Æfter þǽm weard se mǽsta hunger *siccitas fuit, ut praesentis tunc futurique anni spem gignendis terrae fructibus abnegarit*, Ors. 2, 6 ; S. 88, 17. Hié þæs hungres ne mehte hié gerestan *fames Urbem corripuit*, 2, 4 ; S. 70, 9. Hié for þǽm hungre þa burh werian ne mihton, Bl. H. 79, 16. Bið̃on monncwalmo and hungro *erunt pestilentiae et fames*, Mt. L. 24, 7 : Lk. L. 21, 11. Wé geáxiað hungras wexende, Bl. H. 109, 1. **III.** *a strong desire, craving* :—Hit wirð gewundod mid ðǽm huugre ðæs nyðemestan and ðæs fúlestan geðóhtes *cupiditatis infimae fame sauciatur*, Past. 283, 17. Þonne wé beóþ mid mycclum hungre yfelra geþóhta ábisgode, Bl. H. 19, 15. **III a.** *a craving for something* (*gen.*) :—Hit hæfð ðæs suíde micelne hunger, Past. 283,20.

**hungor-geár.** *Add:* (*n*) and *m.* :—Ær þá hungorgeáras cômon *antequam veniret fames*, Gen. 41, 50. [*O. H. Ger.* hungor-jár.]

**hungor-lǽwe.** *Add:* cf. lim-lǽweo.

**hungor-lic**; *adj. Hungry:* of things, *meagre, scanty* :—Hungerlicre gnéðelicnesse *familicae frugalitatis*, Wrt. Voc. ii. 147, 33. Þá ungerlican *familice*, 80, 8. Þá hungerlican, 34, 28. *See* hungrig ; **II.**, *where the same passage is glossed.*

**hungrian.** v. hyngrian.

**hungrig.** *Add:* **I.** of living creatures, *hungry:*—Swá þ se hund hungrig sý, Lch. i. 246, 2. Þæt hé líchamlicne bigleofan þám hungrian Danihele bróhte, Hml. Th. ii. 174, 3. Þæne hungrian *familicum*, i. *ieiunum* (*prophetam*), An. Ox. 3685. Hungrigum *familicis* i. *abstinentibus* (*turmis*), 3860. Þonne seó leó bringð his hungregum hwelpum (*avidis catulis*) hwæt tó etanne, Ors. 3, 11 ; S. 142, 24. **II.** of things, *meagre, scanty.* v. hungor-lic :—Hungrigre gneáþnysse *familicę frugalitatis* (Ald. 33. 36), An. Ox. 2436 : 4634.

**hunig.** *Add:*—Þis hunig *hoc mel*, Ælfc. Gr. Z. 38, 10. Hunig oððe mildeáw *nectar*, Wrt. Voc. ii. 61, 38. Seóð oþ huniges þicnesse, Lch. ii. 30, 8. Æt .x. hídum tó fóstre .x. fata hunies, Ll. Th. i. 146, 16. Mon ðás ðing selle . . . mittan fulne huniges oðða twégen uuínes, suǽ hwaeder suae ðonne begeotan mæge, C. D. i. 293, 14 : 299, 23. Sester fulne huniges, 312, 10. Mid ús is geræd þ beóceorl sylle .v. sustras huniges tó gafole, Ll. Th. i. 436, 2. Swétra þonne þú beóbreád blénde mid hunige, Rä. 41, 59. Ne nánne wǽtan hí ne cúþon wiþ hunige mengan, Bt. 15 ; F. 48, 10. Wiþ dorena hunig gemenged, Lch. ii. 28, 19. Se feld ús gearcode swéte hunig, Angl. viii. 299, 45. Beón ætterne tægel habbað on hindon, hunig on múðe, Leás. 21. v. dún-hunig.

**hunig-æppel.** *For '* Pastillus . . . Lye *' substitute:* A lozenge or pastille containing honey :—Hunaegæpl, hunigæppel *pastellus*, Txts. 90, 830. Hunigæppel, Wrt. Voc. ii. 67, 65 : *passtellus*, i. 289, 75.

**hunig-bǽre.** *Substitute:* **I.** of flowers, *containing honey* :—Huni bǽrum clǽfran helmum *melligeris caltarum frondibus*, An. Ox. 93. **II.** fig. *honied, mellifluous* :—Hunibǽre *mellifluam* (*dogmatum dulcedinem*), An. Ox. 2153.

**hunig-binn,** e; *f. A receptacle for honey* :—Man sceal habban . . . hýfa, hunigbinna, Angl. ix. 264, 15.

**hunig-camb.** *For '* Lchdm. . . . col. 1' *substitute:* Angl. xiii. 368, 46, *and add:*—Sáwl gefylled trytt beóbreád i hunigcamb *anima saturata calcabit fauum*, Scint. 50, 9.

**hunig-flówende.** *Add:* **I.** lit. of flowers, Gú. 1250 (in *Dict.*). **II.** fig. :—Huniflówende gecnordnessa *melliflua studia*, Hpt. Gl. 404, 17.

**hunig-súce.** *Add:*—Hunaegsúgae (huneg-), hunigsúge *ligustrum*, Txts. 76, 615. Hunigsúge, Wrt. Voc. ii. 51, 5 : *ligustra* (fronde *ligustra* fatiscunt, Ald. 141, 25), 89, 43. [v. *N. E. D.* honey-suck.]

**hunig-swǽs.** *Dele.*

**hunig-swéte.** *For '* Th. An. 45, 4 ' *substitute:* Hml. Th. ii. 118, 22, *and add:* **I.** lit. :—*Gutta*, þ ys hunigswéte dropa, Angl. viii. 299, 48. Huniswéttre *mellitę* (*dulcedinis gustum*), An. Ox. 336. **II.** fig. :—Huniswé[te] lippan *mellea labia*, An. Ox. 3183. Orþiende wyrtbrǽþa swétnyssa lıffiicra hunigswéte *spirans odorum balsama vitalium melliflua*, Hy. S. 98, 21. [v. *N. E. D.* honey-sweet.]

**hunig-teár.** *For first two passages substitute:*—Áhlúttredes hunigteáres *defecati nectaris*, Hpt. Gl. 468, 37. Hunigteáres *carene*, Wrt. Voc. ii. 17, 65.

**hunig-teáren.** *For '* Gl. . . . 140' *substitute* Germ. 389, 24.

**hunigteár-lic.** *For '* Cot. . . . Lye *' substitute:*—Þone hunigteárlican *nectareum*, Wrt. Voc. ii. 59, 49.

**hún-spuran.** *Substitute:* hún-sporu, -spuru, an; *f. A sword-stick* :—Húnsporan *dolones* (cf. dolones, tela absconsa, Corp. Gl. H. 44, 351), Wrt. Voc. ii. 106, 65. Húnspuran, 25, 66. v. hand-sporu, stæf-sweord.

**hunt.** *Add:* [v. *N. E. D.* hunt.]

**hunta.** *Add:*—Wæs Esau gléw hunta (*vir gnarus venandi*), Gen. 27, 27. Deáð æfter moncynne, egeslic hunta, á bið on waðe, Met. 27, 13. Of huntan gríne losian, Ps. Th. 123, 6. Tó huntan wícan, C. D. iii. 219, 9. Ðis is ðára .iii. hída landbóc . . . ðe Æðelréd cing gebócode Leófwine his huntan, 230, 5. On huntena weg, 48, 10. Tó huntena forda, v. 267, 24. Hé mé álýsde of láðum gríne huntum unholdum *liberavit me de laqueo venantium*, Ps. Th. 90, 3. Ic ásende míne huntan (*venatores*), and hí huntiað hí of ǽlcere dúne, Hml. Th. i. 576, 27. Hét se cásere his huntan hine ðær gefeccean and hine mid sueorde ofsleán, Shrn. 72, 8. ¶ in place names :—Duas mansas iuxta Huntandúne, C. D. iii. 101, 17. Huntedúne, 94, 3. **III.** cassatos aet Huntenatún, i. 207, 1. Hae sunt uillulae, Huntanawoð, Herþordford, iv. 164, 27. [v. *N. E. D.* hunt *a huntsman*.] v. heáhdeórhunta.

**hunta** *a spider.* Dr. Bradley suggests that in l. 2 *spiþra* should be read for *spiþra* which is the MS. reading.

**huntaþ.** Add: I. *hunting, the chase :*—Bið gód huntoð on þám mónþe, Lch. iii. 182, 1. Se cyng, for þan hé of huntaþe (-oþe, *v. l.*) cóm (*uenerat enim de uenatu*), gestód æt þám fýre and hine wyrmde, Bd. 3, 14; Sch. 258, 17 : Gen. 27, 30. Hé férde út on huntað mid eallum his werode ... þa geseah hé micelne floc heorta, and hé ða gestihte his werod ... hú hí on þone huntað fón sceoldon. þa hí ealle ymb þone huntað ábysgode wæron ..., Hml. S. 30, 25-28. II. *what is taken by hunting, venison* (cf. *N. E. D.* hunt, sb.[2] 2 b) :—Hwæt wæs sé þe mé ǽr bróhte of huntoðe and ic æt þǽrof? *quis ille est qui dudum captam venationem attulit mihi et comedi ex omnibus?*, Gen. 27, 33, 31, 19, 25. v. huntnaþ.

**huntian.** Add : I. *intrans.* :—þa gelamp þ hig huntedon on mærgen. þa gearn sum hynd betweox þám gebróðrum and hig sceoton hyra strǽlas, Shrn. 148, 3. Ælcne man lyst, siððan hé ǽnig cotlýf ... getimbred hæfð, þæt hé móte ... huntigan and fuglian and fiscian, Solil. H. 2, 10. Hwæþer gé nú eówer hundas and eówer net út on ða sǽ lǽdon ðonne gé huntian willaþ?, Bt. 32, 3; F. 118, 14. Huntgendra (huntiendra, Ps. L., Vos., Srt.) *venantium*, Bl. Gl., Ps. Rdr. 90, 3 Huntendra, Ps. Srt. 123, 6. II. *trans.* :—Hml. Th. i. 576, 28 (*in Dict.*). v. ge-huntian.

**hunticge,** an; *f.* *A huntress :*—Huntigystran (hundicgean, *v. l.*) *uenatrices*, Nar. 38, 3.

**huntnaþ.** *Dele second passage, and add :*—Harold þóhte þone kincge Eádward þár tó habbenne for huntnoðes (huntoðes, *v. l.*) þingon, Chr. 1065 ; P. 190, 28. Weard se cyng Willelm on huntnoðe fram his ánan men mid ánre fíá ofsceoten, 1100 ; P. 235, 16.

**huntnold** *hunting* :—'Hunta ic eom' ... 'Wǽre þú tó-dæg on huntnolde (*venatione*)?, Coll. M. 21, 34. Cf. (?) fǽreld *for suffix*.

**huntung.** Add :—Wæs hé wel gléáw on huntunge, and þ ælce dæge beeóde, Hml. S. 30, 16.

**-hupian.** v. on-hupian: **hurnitu.** v. hyrnetu.

**húru.** Add : , híru, hýru. I. *qualifying measurements, at least, about :*—Wé wið þám wyrmum wunnan húru twá tída þǽre nihte (*prope duas horas*), Nar. 13, 27. Húru *ferme* (*centies exorans ferme*), An. Ox. 17, 38. Húru embe seofon niht, Bl. H. 45, 31. Hé ðone miclan flód bodade húru hundtwelftigum wintrum, Wlfst. 206, 7 : Gen. 2343. Gearwige hé hine tó húselgange húru þriwa on geáre, Ll. Th. i. 322, 8. Ðæt hyra ǽgðer hýru hæbbe .lx. penega wyrð, C. D. vi. 133, 23. *See other instances under* hú-hwega. I a. *where a limiting date is fixed, at latest, at last :*—Utan gelǽstan ælce geáre úre sulhælmessan fíftǽne niht onufan Eástran ... and úre eorðwæstma be emnihte oððe húru (cf. *latest*, 208, 5) be ealra hálgena mæssan, Wlfst. 116, 3. Sulhælmessan húru .xv. niht ofer Eástran, Ll. Th. i. 318, 30. þæt hí húru beón gecyrrede *ut uel sero conuertantur*, Scint. 63, 6. II. *introducing a limiting or determining condition, at least, at any rate :*—Ða sint tó manienne ðe hiera líchoman synna onfunden habbað, ðæt hié húru æfter ðæm scipgebroce him ða sǽ ondrǽden (*ut mare saltem post naufragium metuant*), Past. 403, 12. Ondrǽden hí him húru ðonne hí hí hrímað, 437, 11 : 313, 8. þa bǽdon hine his discipulos þ hié móstan húru sume uncýme streównesse him under gedón, Bl. H. 227, 12 : Ll. Th. i. 356, 21. Bútan gé hit on Léden geleornian magan, geleorniað hit húru on Englisc, Wlfst. 125, 7. Wé beóðað þ man crístene men for ealles tó lytlum húru tó deáðe ne forrǽde, Ll. Th. i. 376, 21. III. *where an extreme point is considered, even :*—Gif hé his unrihtwísnysse húru on his forðsíðe behreówsað, Hml. Th. ii. 344, 34. Húru gif hé cwǽde þæt hé nǽre sumum óðrum mannum gelíc, ac hé cwæð, 'Ic ne eom swilce swá óðre men,' 428, 21. Hé on his ágenum fæder áre ne wolde gesceáwian, ne þa sceonde húru hleómsgum helan, Gen. 1581. IV. *introducing the most essential or considerable circumstance, above all, especially :*—Bæþ .. hálum and húru (*maxime*) þám geongum sý seldor getíðod, R. Ben. 60, 23 : Past. 25, 21 : 361, 7. For ðý ðe hé ongeat ðæt sió ungeðld oft dereð ðám mannum ðe micle forhæfdnesse habbað, ða lǽrde hé ðæt hié húru sceoldan geðylde habban tóeácan ðǽre forhæfdnesse, 311, 22, 19 : Bl. H. 47, 19. Ic wylle cýðan eów eallum and þám húru þe hit ǽr nystan, Wlfst. 153, 7 : B. 3120. Wolde his mæg húru álynnan of láðscipe, Gen. 2047 : Bl. H. 225, 8. Húru secgan hét Simon Petre (cf. Go, tell his disciples and Peter, Mk. 16, 7), Sat. 523. Wé ealles sculon secgan þonc ... and húru þǽre hǽlo, Cri. 613. Gebéte þ ... swá be were swá be wíte ... and for Gode húru béte swá canon tǽce, Ll. Th. i. 168, 6 : 402, 14 : 340, 19 : ii. 292, 2 : 302, 7 : Solil. H. 2, 17 : 30, 11. Ǽfre hé mæig findan on ðám hé mæig nyt beón ... húru is mǽst neód ..., Angl. ix. 261, 3. Hit is earfoð tó witane þára biscopa (naman?) þe cómon, and húru abbuda, Chr. 1050; P. 170, 26. þ gé nǽðer ne geearnian, ne þone deáð þises andweardan lifes ne húru þone tóweardan écere helle, Ll. Th. i. 270, 29. V. *giving emphasis* (I) *to a statement, certainly, indeed.* (a) *introducing a clause :*—Húru cúð dyde Nergend ... þæt hé þæt gyld on þanc ágísen hæfde, Gen. 1503 : Jud. 346 : Cri. 22 : 82 : 789 : Hö. 15 : Seel. 1 : B. 369 : Ap. 42 : An. 549. Ic lufige ælc ðing ... and húru þæt þing swíðost þe mé tó wísdóme fultumað, Solil. H. 43, 1 : 35, 1. (b) *in the body of the clause :*—Hwæt þú húru lyt geþóhtest, Seel. 22. Hwæt

þonne húru seó mennisce gecynd þæs mæg lof secgean, Bl. H. 123, 2. þæt dysige sceáp þætte forweorðan wolde húru, Ps. Th. 118, 176. Nú dú húru scaelt *usquequo*, An. Ox. 54, 3. ¶ *in negative clauses :*—Hit tó ælcum men ne cymþ be his gewyrhtum, ne húru nánum ealne weg ne wunað, Bt. 30, 1; F. 108, 18 : 33, 2 ; F. 124, 28 : Met. 20, 38 : Met. 8, 10 : 22, 4 : Seel. 38 : B. 862 : 1071. Ne húru wundur wyrceað deáde *numquid mortuis facies mirabilia?*, Ps. Th. 87, 10 : Wrt. Voc. ii. 115, 8. Efne sé on hygde húru ne slǽpeð, 120, 4. Ne wæs þæt húru fracoðes gealga, Kr. 10 : Gú. 741. (2) *to a wish or prayer, on* (*no*) *account* :—Ne ofgif þú mé húru *ne elonges a me*, Ps. Th. 70, 11. Ne forgit húru gódra manna stefna, 73, 22. þæt þú húru mé ǽnne ne forlǽte *non me derelinquas usquequaque*, 118, 8. Ne mé húru forswelge sǽgrundes deóp *ne me demergat tempestas aquae*, Ps. Th. 68, 15. (3) *to a question :*—On hwám mæg húru ǽfre ǽnig man on worolde swíðor God wurðian þonne on circan?, Ll. Th. i. 334, 25. *See next word.*

**húru-þinga.** Add : *an emphatic modification of* húru. I. v. húru ; II :—Tó þám þ hí þone mete, þone hí þágýta fullfremedlíce geblissiende þicgean ne mihton, húruþinga (húru, *v. l.* saltem) geómriende onbyrigdon, Gr. D. 170, 7. Sé þe ... dæghwámlice his circan gesécan ne mæge, hé húruðinga on ðám Sunnandagum þider cume, Hml. A. 144, 9. II. v. húru ; III :—Mt. 14, 36 (*in Dict.*). III. v. húru ; IV :—Wé willað þ ælces hádes menn georne gebúgan tó rihte ... and húruþinga (*praecipue, praesertim*) Godes þeówas, ... and ealle Godes þeówas ... and húruþinga (*maxime*) sácerdas, Ll. Th. i. 364, 5-11. On eallum tídum gedafenað crístenum mannum þæt hí góde weorc begán, ... and swíðost on þisum fæstene. Sé ðe on óðrum dagum sleac wǽre tó gódnysse, hé sceal húruðinga on ðisum dagum ácucian on gódum bígengum, Hml. Th. ii. 100, 23 : Hml. A. 141, 87. IV. v. húru ; V. 3 :—Hwilcan geþance mæg ǽnig man ǽfre húruðinga þ dón?, Ll. Th. i. 334, 28.

**hús.** Add : I. *a building for human habitation :*—Hús *domus* vel *lar*, Wrt. Voc. i. 25, 37. Insæte hús *vel* lytel hús *casa* vel *casula*, 58, 28. Húses *domatis* (in proprii *domatis* tigillo conflagrasse memoratur), ii. 80, 54 : Kent. Gl. 971. Se scyppend gesceóp þone middaneard swylce hé þám men hús getimbrode, and hine syððan intó þám gelǽdde swá swá þæs húses hláford, Angl. vii. 6, 51. Ælces húses wáh biþ fæst ægþer ge on ðǽre flóre ge on þǽm hrófe, Bt. 36, 7 ; F. 184, 12. þeáh hwá his spere sette tó óðres mannes húses dura, Ll. Th. i. 418, 5. Fyrst on húse *tignum* vel *tigillum*, An. Ox. 18 b, 92. Swá swá oferdruncen man wát þ hé sceolde tó his húse and tó his ræste, Bt. 24, 4 ; F. 84, 30. Gif hwá gefeohte on cyninges húse, Ll. Th. i. 106, 2 : 330, 22. Gif ceorl ceáp forsteld and bireð intó his ærne (huse, *v. l.*), 138, 16 : 286, 11. Sylle him man tól tó his weorce and andlaman tó his húse, 434, 27. Beón hí áwergode on húse and on ǽcere, Ll. Lbmn. 438, 23. Gif þeóf brece mannes hús nihtes, Ll. Th. i. 50, 18 : Ex. 22, 4. Hús settan and tún timbrian, Solil. H. 1, 13. Ic mé hér getimbre hús, Gú. 222. Húsa sélest, B. 146. Hié eft hwyrfende wǽron tó heora húsum, Bl. H. 207, 31. Se Treówyrhta segþ :—Hwilc eówer ne notað cræfte mínon, þonne hús (*domos*) ... eów eallum ic wyrce (*fabrico*)?, Coll. M. 31, 11. Hús *gurgustia* (virginibus condunt *gurgustia* cellae, Ald. 171, 21), Wrt. Voc. ii. 41, 45. Húso (hús, *v. l.*) *domos*, Mk. L. 10, 30. Ofer hrófa ł húsa *super tecta*, Mt. L. 10, 27. I a. *the portion of a building occupied by one tenant or family :*—Candel ǽfre on ðám ylcan húse (*cella*) byrne, R. Ben. I. 54, 17. Hús *cellam* (*cellulam* in qua praefatae Virgines psalmodiae concentum celebrabant), An. Ox. 4659. I b. *a temporary erection, tabernacle :*—Ic gedó ðreá húso *faciam tria tabernacula*, Mt. L. 17, 4. Wyrce wé ðriá hús (húsa, L.), Mk. R. 9, 5. I c. *house, as in* wash-*house*, *of a separate building forming part of a residence :*—Hé wolde wyrcan þá healle ... and þá óþre gebytlu bæftan þǽre healle, bæðhús and kycenan and winterhús and sumerhús and wynsume búras, twelf hús tógædere, Hml. S. 36, 99. II. *a building for human occupation, for some purpose other than that of an ordinary dwelling :*—þæt hús þǽr man ðweað heora handa *consistorium*, Wrt. Voc. i. 57, 50. Seóccra manna hús *abaso, infirmatorium*, 58, 36 : *nosocomium*, 52. Sútera hús *sutrina domus*, 59, 3. Leornigmannes hús *gymnasii*, An. Ox. 2, 175. þæs cáserlican húses *imperialis hypodromi*, Wrt. Voc. ii. 48, 46 : 81, 24. Forligeres húses *prostibuli*. i. *locus fornicationis*, An. Ox. 2940. Tó meltestrum húse *ad lupanar*, 4018. Álǽd mé of þyses carcernes húse, Bl. H. 87, 34 : Ll. Th. i. 64, 15. Ymbe þæt háte hús (*the place of the fiery furnace*), Az. 162. II a. *the house of a deity, a place of worship, church, temple, tabernacle :*—Hús Godes *tabernaculum Dei*, Rtl. 71, 3. Mín hús sceal beón gebedhús gecéged, Bl. H. 71, 19. þæt hús (seó myccle cirice, 25), 125, 30 : 207, 17. Húses *sacelli*, Wrt. Voc. ii. 91, 5 : *sanctuarii*, An. On. 56, 164. þæs temples segl geworht tó wlite þæs húses, Cri. 1140. þám hálgan húse, 1136. þæt hús (*the temple of Janus*), Ors. 3, 5 ; S. 106, 11. Húss *edem* (v. Lk. 11, 51), Wrt. Voc. ii. 73, 47 : 30, 67. Ælc biscop béte Godes hús on his ágenum, and eác þone cyning myngige þ ealle Godes cyrcan sýn wel behworfene, Ll. Th. i. 246, 10. Gehálgode Godes hús, 336, 1. II b. *a building for*

*the entertainment of travellers, a public house, an inn :*—Fald oððe hús be wege *stabulum*, Wrt. Voc. i. 85, 72. **III.** *a building for the keeping of animals :*—Sceápa hús *ovile*, gáta hús *caprile*, Wrt. Voc. i. 58, 26, 27. Gáta hús *caprile*, hunda hús *canile*, ii. 23, 12, 13. Hunda hús *canile, domus canis*, 128, 20. Sió leó ábít hire ágenes húses hirde, Met. 13, 31. **IV.** *a building for storage, for the keeping of material :*—Wæterscipes hús *colimbus*, Wrt. Voc. i. 57, 56. v. æppel-, corn-, híg-hús. **V.** *the place of abode of a religious fraternity ? :*— Eádige weorðað þá þe eardiað on þínum húsum (or *under* **II** a ?), hálig Drihten *beati qui habitant in domo tua, Domine*, Ps. Th. 83, 5. **VI.** *a building* (without specifying its purpose) :—Gif preóst on unhálgodon húse mæssige, Ll. Th. ii. 292, 16. **VII.** *a household :*—Gilêfde hê and hús (híwræden, W. S.) his all, Jn. R. L. 4, 53. Nán hús næs binnan þære byrig þ hit næfde þære wrace angolden, Ors. 6, 23; S. 274, 12. **VIII.** *a family, race :*—Jacobes, Israhéla, Aarones hús, Ps. Th. 113, 1, 18, 19. **IX.** used figuratively :—Nú gebrosnad is hús under hrófe, Cri. 14. Þære hálignesse hús (*Elizabeth's womb*), Bl. H. 163, 11. Drihten, þú eart . . . mín hús, and mín êðel *domus mea, patria mea*, Solil. H. 11, 7 : Cri. 1482 : Gú. 774 : El. 1237. Sê ðe gisceóp mec (*the Virgin Mary*) eftgireste in úse mínum (*in tabernaculo meo*, Rtl. 65, 17. Timbrian þ hús his módes on þám fæstan stáne eáðmetta, Bt. 12 ; F. 36, 21. Drihten ásette on sunnan his hús (*tabernaculum*), Bl. H. 9, 31. In ða êco húso *in aeterna tabernacula*, Lk. L. 16, 9. ¶ used of heaven and hell :—Oþ þ ic þe in gelæde on mínes Fæder hús, Bl. H. 191, 20. Ingong in þæt atule hús, Gú. 534 : 649 : Sat. 710. v. æppel-, bæþ-, bel-, bóc-, capitol-, cípe- (cæpe-), corn-, deófolgild-, dim-, drenc-, eala(-u)-, eardung-, fisc-, flæsc-, fore- (Vis. Lsc. 33), forliger-, fýr-, gebed-, gemót-, gereord-, gereording-, goldhord-, grêting-, háligdóm-, helle-, heofon-(?), híg-, hláf-, hors-(?), hrægel-, læce-, lár-, leorning-, mangung-, máþum-, mealt-, melu-, mere-, miltestre-, mót-, neód-, offrung-, pleg-, reord-, rest-, sceand-, sealt-, snæding-, snytro-, spic-, spræc-, sumer-, symbel-, þegnung-, þyrl-, tócir-, tów-, úp-, wæsc-, wæfer-, wæpen-, weorc-, wín-, winter-, wundor-hús.

**hús-ærn,** es ; *n. A dwelling-house, private house :*—Ðá ðe næfre gystas on húsærne onfóð (*nunquam hospes in domum recipitur*), búton sellendlices gysthúses mêd ær ápinsod sý, Chrd. 102, 1.

**hús-bonda.** *Add :*—Þonne gê tó gereorde geládode beóð, ne sitte gê on þám fyrmestam setlum, þe læs ðe árwurðra (*honoratior te*, Lk. 14, 8) wer æfter ðê cume, and se húsbonda (-bunda, *v. l.*) háte þê árísan and rýman þám óðrum, Mt. 20, 28. [In the old Latin version of Ine's laws *húslgenga* is misunderstood, and (written *hulsgenga*) is explained as 'duodecimhindus uel husbonda', Ll. Lbmn. 97, § 19. In a previous section (15) it is explained as 'duodecimhyndus'.]

**hús-bonde.** *l.* (?) -bonda. v. ge-bedda, ge-maca *for* a- forms.

**hús-bót,** e ; *f. House-repair ; wood for the repair of a house: the right to cut such wood :*—Ðis is seó wudung ðe ðærtó gebyreð, ælce geáre fíftig fóðra and án hund of ðæs cinges ácholte and húsbót, C. D. vi. 243, 13. [*v. N. E. D.* house-bote.]

**hús-brycel ;** *adj. Burglarious :*—Húsbrycel *clasmatorius efractor*, Wrt. Voc. ii. 131, 64.

**husc.** *For* 'Cot. 186, Lye' *substitute :* Wrt. Voc. ii. 87, 30, *and add :*—Hux, hosp *hironiám*, An. Ox. 5201. (*Both glosses belong to* Ald. 75, 20.) v. hyscan.

**hús-carl.** *Add :*—Hêr lêt Harðacnut hergian eall Wihracestrescire for his twêgra húscarla þingon, Chr. 1041 ; P. 162, 6. [**v.** *N. E. D.* housecarl.]

**husc-líc.** *Take here* hux-líc *in Dict., and add :* **I.** of material things, *unseemly :*—Gif bwá wyle wyrcan weófodsceátas Gode . . . of his ealdum cláðum, gesylle þá ealdan and geceápige níwe, þ hí tó huxlice tó his lácum ne beón, Hml. A. 35, 287. **II.** of conduct, action, treatment, &c. :—Þæt nán cyning . . . ne sceolde þincan tó huxlic þæt hê gebúge tó Crístes fulluhte, Hml. Th. ii. 40, 24. Ne ðúhte him tó huxlic þæt hê mid gesceáde hine betealde unsynnine, 226, 11. Næs on þære þeóde nán deáþ swá huxlic swá swa on ródehengenne, Hml. A. 76, 81.

**husc-líce.** *Take here* huxlíce *in Dict., and add :*—Sleánde mid handbredum huxlíce and gelóme, Hml. Th. ii. 248, 13. Huxlíce gebundene, Hml. A. 107, 157. Þá hors hí oftrædan huxlíce under fótum, Hml. S. 18, 347. Ne ænig man ne gewunie þæt hê huxlíce onhisce, Wlfst. 70, 11. Tælende þone Hælend huxlíce mid wordum, Hml. A. 60, 208 : Hml. S. 15, 83.

**-húsed.** v. ge-húsed.

**húsel.** *Add :* **I.** *a sacrifice* ; sacrificium :—Miltheortnisse ic willo, and nis húsul *misericordiam volo, et non sacrificium*, Mt. L. 12, 7. Húsul eóstorlic *sacrificium paschale* (*fecisti*), Rtl. 34, 36. **II.** *the consecrated elements at the Communion ; the service at which these are administered, the Eucharist, the Lord's Supper :*—Húsl *eucharistia*, Wrt. Voc. ii. 30, 59 : 70, 12. Hwî is þæt hálige húsel gecweden Crístes líchama oððe his blód, gif hit nis sóðlíce þ þ hit geháten is ?, Hml. Th. ii. 268, 21. Þis húsel is gemynd Crístes líchaman and his blódes, 276, 6. Þæt hálige húsel is ægðer ge Crístes líchama ge ealles geleáffulles

folces æfter gástlicere gerýnu, 15. Seó snæd þæs húsles ðe heó ðicgan sceolde, 272, 26. Hálige bêc beódað þæt man gemencge wæter tó ðám wíne ðe tó húsle sceal, 278, 6. Twêgen munecas bædon æt Gode sume swutelunge be ðám hálgan húsle, and æfter ðære bêne gestódon him mæssan. Ðá gesáwon hí licgan án cild on ðám weófode þe se mæssepreóst æt mæssode, and Godes engel stód mid handsexe . . . þá tóliðode se engel þæt cild on ðám disce, and his blód intó ðam calice ágeát. Eft ðá ðá hí tó ðám húsle eódon, ðá wearð hit tó hláfe and tó wíne, and hí hit ðygedon, 272, 14-21. Gif man mæssepreóst tihtlige . . . mæssige gif hê durre, and ládige hine on þám húsle, Ll. Th. i. 344, 13, 14. Gif preóst húsl forgíme, ii. 292, 23. Gif wê sceáwiað þæt hálige húsel æfter líchamlicum andgite, þonne geseó wê þæt hit is gesceaft brosniendlic . . . Hit is on gecynde brosniendlic hláf and brosniendlic wín . . . his gástlica líchama ðe wê húsel hátað is . . . búton blóde and báne . . . þæt húsel is hwílwendlic, ná êce ; brosuiendlic, and bið sticmælum tódæled ; betwux tóðum tócowen, and intó ðám búce ásend, Hml. Th. ii. 270, 6-34. **II a.** in phrases having reference to the administration and receiving of the Eucharist. (1) húsl (ge)hálgian *to consecrate the elements :*—Þis húsel ðe nú bið gehálgod æt Godes weófode, Hml. Th. ii. 276, 6. Gif preóst on treówenan calice húsl gehálgige, ii. 292, 20 : i. 360, 33. Hê gehálgode húsel of hláfe and of wíne, Angl. vii. 44, 415. (2) tó húsle (ge)hálgian *to consecrate (bread and wine) for the Eucharist :*—Hí hálgodon hláf and wín tó húsle, Hml. Th. ii. 268, 3, 5 : 270, 17 : 274, 14. (3) húsl tóbrecan *to break the bread :*—Oð þæt se preóst þæt húsel tóbræc, Hml. Th. ii. 272, 18. (4) húsles wirþe *entitled to go to communion* (see first passage under (5)) :—Hér on lífe húsles beón wyrþe, Ll. Th. i. 372, 35. (5) tó húsle gán, gangan *to go to communion, receive the sacrament, communicate* (cf. húsel-gang, -genga) :—Swá hwilc man swá tó húsle ne gá (sê ðe húselganges unwurðe sý, Hml. Th. ii. 174, 17) *si quis non communicat*, Gr. D. 152, 26 : 153, 11. Sê ðe ete ær þám þe tó húsle gá *qui edit antequam eucharistiam acceperit*, Ll. Th. ii. 140, 12. Wíf mót tó húsle gán (*eucharistiam accipere*) ær þám heó cenne, 156, 12. Gange ælc tó húsle *ad communionem accedat*, R. Ben. 115, 4. Gá hê tó húsle þý dæge þe hê tó ordále gán scyle, Ll. Th. i. 210, 30. Þ gê tó þýs húsle ne gangen, ne tó ðæm ordále, gif gê scyld on eów witen, Rtl. 114, 21. Tó þisum húsle tó gánne, Ll. Lbmn. 414, 2. Þæt folc æfter godcundum ðeáwe tó húsle gange, Hml. Th. i. 508, 4 : ii. 272, 24 : 278, 1. (6) húsles onbyrgan, húsl þicgan (cf. húsles þigen, Hml. Th. i. 266, 8 : Angl. xii. 514, 5) *to partake of the Lord's Supper, to take the Sacrament :*—Sê ðe ete . . . æfter þám þe hê húsl þicge *qui edit . . . postquam eucharistiam sumserit*, Ll. Th. ii. 140, 13. Þ þu ná geþrístláce þ þú þises húsles onbyrige *ut non audeas hanc eucharistiam percipere*, Ll. Lbm. 413, 31 : Hml. Th. ii. 278, 4. Þ gê ne genéðon þ gê þis húsl ðicgon and tó ðisson weófode ne gán, Ll. Lbmn. 415, 7 : Hml. Th. ii. 266, 18-278, 20.

**húsel-disc.** *Add : See the passage* Hml. Th. ii. 272, 19 (*given under* húsel; II.).

**húsel-fæt.** *Add :*—Nelle wê þ in cyrcean mon ænig þing inne healde, bútan þá þe tó þære cyrcean frætwum belympað, þ is hálige bêc, and húselfata, and mæssereáf . . . , Ll. Th. ii. 406, 33.

**húsel-gang.** *Add : the receiving of the Eucharist, Communion.* v. húsl ; II a. 5 :—Wê beóð geclænsode þurh ðæs hálgan húselganges, Hml. Th. ii. 266, 24. Þá wæs þeáw ær þám húslgange þ se diácon cleopode, ' Swá hwilc man swá tó húsle ne gá, þonne búge sê of þissere stówe' *cum missarum solemnia celebrarentur, atque ex more Diaconus clamaret, 'Si quis non communicat, det locum'*, Gr. D. 152, 25 : 30 : Hml. Th. ii. 174, 17 : 24. Be æte ær húslgange *de cibo ante eucharistiae acceptionem*, Ll. Th. ii. 128, 20 : 130, 18. Æfter mæssan and húsl-gonge *post missas et communionem*, R. Ben. 62, 7. Gancge ælc æfter óðrum tó húselgancge (húsle, *v. l.*) (*ad pacem, ad communionem*), 114, 4 : Hml. S. 236, 754.

**húsel-hálgung.** *For* 'Se . . . gehálgaþ' *in* l. 4 *substitute :*—Þæt fulluht ús áþwehð fram eallum synnum, se húselgang ús gehálgað, seó dædbót gehæld úre misdæda. (*From this passage it would seem that* húsel-hálgung *and* húsel-gang *have the same meaning.*) *Add : holy communion, the sacrament of the Lord's Supper :*—Húselhálgung næs ær þám se Hælend gehálgode hláf and wín tó húsle, Hml. A. 71, 155. Twá ðing syndon þurh Godes mihte swá myccle and swá mære þæt æfre ænig man ne mæg ðæron ænig ðing áwyrdan ne gewanian, fulluht and húsl-hálgung. Nis se mæssepreóst on worulde swá synfull, gyf hê ðæra þênunga áþere dêð, swá swá ðærtó gebyreð, . . . ne byð seó þênung þæs ná þe wyrse. Ne eft nis ænig swá mære þæt áðor ðæra þênunga gegódian mæge, Wlfst. 34, 3-11.

**húsel-þegn.** *Add :*—Accolitus, þ is húsolþegn, Chrd. 97, 21.

**hús-heofon.** *For* 'Cot. 119, Lye' *substitute :* Wrt. Voc. ii. 50, 58.

**hús-hláford.** *Add :*—Eustachius gelædde hí intó his gesthúse, and . . . cwæð tó þám húshláforde : 'Þás men synd mê cúðe . . . gif mê nú mettas and wín, and ic hit þé gilde eft of míre hýre,' Hml. S. 30, 259.

**hús-hleów.** *Add :*—Dæle man . . . mete þám ofhingredum, drenc þám ofðyrstum, húshleów gefarenum, wæfels þám nacedum, Wlfst. 74, 4.

húslian. _Add:_—Man sceal húslian þone seócan þa hwýle hē hit forswelgan mæg, and man ne sceal hit nā dōn nānum sámcwyce men, for
þan þe hē hit sceal etan, Ll. Th. ii. 390, 23. Gē sculon húslian þá cild
þonne hí gefullode beóð, and hý man bere tō mæssan þ hyg beón
gehúslode ealle þá .VII. dagas þā hwíle þe hig ungeþwogene beóð, 392, 12.
v. ge-húslian.

húslung. _Add: houseling, communion:_—Háligra húslung is and
on crístendóme háligra gemana, Wlfst. 24, 13 note. [v. _N. E. D._
houseling.]

hús-ræden. _Add:_—Húsræden Aarones _domus Aaron,_ Ps. L. 117, 3 :
134, 20.

hús-scipe, es ; _m._ _A house, family:_—Hē gebletsode húses (_domui_)
Israéles, hē gebletsode hússcipes (_domui_) Aarones, Ps. L. 113 second, 12.
v. ge-hússcipe.

hús-wist. _Add:_ [Cf. _O. H. Ger._ heim-wist : _Ger._ haus-wesen.]

húðe. _l._ húþ, _dele_ [v. herehúðe], _and add:_—Húþa _praeda_ (_ineffa-
bili_), An. Ox. 219. Húðe _praedam,_ Kent. Gl. 1137. þá ýþwōrigendan
húþa _fluctivagam praedam,_ Wrt. Voc. ii. 149, 72. Ungerīme húþe
_numerosas preþas,_ An. Ox. 5084.

húung. v. ymb-húung : hux-líc, huxlíce. v. husc-líc, husclíce.

hwá. _Add: pl. n._ hwá; _dat._ hwám, hwǽm.        I. in direct
questions. (1) hwá _who:_—Hwǽm (hwám, _v. l._) beóð ðás ðyllecan
gelícran? _quibus isti sunt similes?,_ Past. 226, 23. Æt hwám (_from
hwǽm,_ R. _a quibus_) nimað cyningas gafol?, Mt. 17, 25 ; Hml. Th. i.
510, 32. (2) hwæt _what,_ where the subject of the question may be of
any gender or of either number. (a) _alone,_ questions asking for the
nature, character, extent, &c., of person or thing:—Hwæt is se dumba,
sē þe on sumre dene rested?, Sal. 229. Hwæt is þeós wundrung?, Cri.
89. Hwæt is wuldor þín þe þú upp árærdest, þá þú goda ússa gilp
gehnægdest?, An. 1319. Hwæt sindon þá gimmas búton God sylfa?,
Cri. 694. (b) _strengthened_ by æfre:—Hwæt þis æfre beón scyle?,
Hml. S. 23, 532 : 516. (c) _with partitive_ gen. :—Hwæt wæs seó
Salamones ræste elles búton se hálga innoð?, Bl. H. 11, 19. (d) _with
gen., what manner_ of :—Ac hwæt wile ðæt nū beón weorca ðæt ús on
óðerre stōwe forbiét ðæt wē hit beforan mannum dōn, on óðerre lǽrð
búton ðæt wē hit helen? _quid est ergo, quod opus nostrum et ita faciendum
est, ne videatur, et tamen, ut debeat videri praecipitur?,_ Past. 451, 2.
Hwæt þis æfre beón sceole fǽrlices _whatever manner of marvellous thing
must this be?,_ Hml. S. 23, 516. Hwæt gifest þú mē freómanna tō
frófre?, Gen. 2174.      II. introducing an exclamatory clause. Cf.
III. I β iii a ; hwilc ; II:—Eálá ! hwæt se forma gítsere wǽre, þe ǽrest
þá eorþan ongan delfan æfter golde, Bt. 15 ; F. 48, 22 : Met. 8,
55.        III. in dependent clauses. (1) after verbs (or verbal nouns
or adjectives) of asking, learning, knowing, seeing, saying. (a) hwá :—
Hē frægn . . . hwá þá duru heólde, Fin. 23. Heofon ongeat hwá hine
getremede, Cri. 1150. Þonne bið gecýðed hwá unclǽnnisse líf álīfde,
Dóm. 62. Hwæt wille gē cueðan hwæs oððe hwæs gē sién? _quid vos
hujus vel illius dicitis?,_ Past. 211, 13. (b) hwæt (_for meaning see_ I. 2
_above._) (a) _alone._ (i) of persons :—Ðá áxode Paulus þone engel hwæt
seó góde sáwel wǽre. Ðá sǽde hē him þæt heó wǽre mildheortnesse
fyligende and staðolfæst . . ., Wlfst. 237, 11. Hū mihte Adam
tōcnáwan hwæt hē wǽre . . .?, Hml. Th. i. 14, 4. Ic wát ge hwæt þú
eart ge for hwon þú gnornast _scio qui es, et quare maeres,_ Bd. 2, 12 ;
Sch. 156, 14. þám deófle wæs micel twínung hwæt Críst wǽre, Hml.
Th. i. 168, 10. Hē hine hēt secgan hwæt his geféran wǽron, Bt. 16,
2 ; F. 52, 23. (ii) of things :—Sum blind þearfa gehýrde myccle menigo
fēran ; þá áhsode hē hwæt þæt wǽre, Bl. H. 15, 17. Hē áscode hwæt
hyt sóðes wǽre for hwig hym man swá fǽrlíce æfter sende, Hml. A.
184, 94. Hū ne wást þú hwæt (þ, _v. l._) wē cweþaþ, Bt. 34, 5 ; F. 138,
34. Uton spyrian hwæt þá geföran, þá þe God lufedon, and hwæt þá
geföran, þá þe God græmedon, Wlfst. 130, 11-13. Oð ðæt ic wite
hwæt God wylle hwæt be mē gewurðe _donec sciam quid de me fieri
uelit Deus,_ Bd. 5, 19 ; Sch. 670, 12. þá frægn Scipia hiene an hwý hit
gelang wǽre þ . . ., Ors. 5, 3 ; S. 222, 15. Ic nát mid hwí ic delfe,
Hml. S. 23 b, 764. Uton gehýran hwæt hē dyde and mid hwý hē ús
freó gedyde, Bl. H. 83, 31. Hē him sægde þurh hwæt seó sául eádegust
gewurde, 159, 28. (β) _with_ gen. (i) where the noun in the genitive
denotes a class or kind, _how many_ or _how much_ of which is in question :—
Hē befrán hwæt hí him feós geúðon _he asked what (how much) money
they would give him,_ Hml. Th. ii. 242, 16. Mē lysteþ þ ic wite hwæt
sóþes sý be þǽre wísan _quid hac de re veritas habeat,_ ignoro, Gr. D.
303, 6. Be þǽm hringum mon mehte witan hwæt Rómána dugude
gefeallen wæs, Ors. 4, 9 ; S. 190, 13. Árīman hwæt þǽr mancynnes
forweard, 1, 11 ; S. 50, 13. Tō secganne hwæt hiera folces forwurde,
5, 2 ; S. 220, 9. (ii) where the genitive denotes a single object, _what
part_ of :—Sege mē hwæt his (_wealth_) þē deórast þince, Bt. 13 ; F. 38,
10. (iii) where the noun in genitive denotes that, the manner or kind
of which is in question, _what kind of_ :—Befrínende hwæt þ fǽrlices
wǽre, Hml. S. 31, 243. (iii a) _what wonderful kind of._ Cf. II :—Hit
is on hrædinge earfoðrecce hwæt hē gesáwenlicra wundra worhte, Wlfst.
22, 14. (iv) where the genitive denotes objects the number of which is

in question :—Saga mē hú fela sí fugela cynna. Ic ðē secge twá and fíftig.
Saga mē hwæt fisccynna si. Ic ðē secge six and þrittig, Sal. K. 204, 5-
10. (2) after other verbs. (a) hwá :—Hié ofergeáton . . . hwá him
dugeða forgeaf blǽd, Gen. 2581. (b) hwæt. (a) _alone:_—Ne in huon ðú
hlada hæfis ðú _neque in quo haurias habes,_ Jn. L. 4, 11. þú wille cweþan
þ þá welgan habban mid hwám hí mægen þæt eall gebētan, Bt. 26, 2 ;
F. 92, 35. Eall hwæt (þæt, _v. l._) hí willniaþ hí begitaþ, 40, 7 ; F. 242,
22. Hwæt seó rǽding cwyð . . ., hyt ys tō gýmanne, Angl. viii. 323, 32.
(β) _with_ gen. Cf. I β i :—Hē giémde hwæt hē hæfde monna gerímes,
and ne nōm náne ware húlice hié wǽron, Ors. 5, 4 ; S. 224, 21. (3)
where the hwæt-clause is subject to the verb of the main clause :—
Bið æt Gode ánum gelang eal hwæt wē gefaran scylon, Wlfst. 122,
9.        ¶ with elliptical construction, the main clause not expressed :—
Ælc man hwæt ((_it did not matter?_) _what_) . . . his háde tō belumpe
folgade, sē þe wolde, Chr. 1086 ; P. 219, 31.        IV. as an indefinite
pronoun. (1) hwá (a _alone, with much the same sense as_ man, _any
one:_—Ne selle mon tō fela ðǽm ðe lytles ðyrfe, ðý lǽs hwá him self
weorðe tō wǽdlan, and him ðonne gehreówe sió ælmesse _ne, cum pauca
oportet, plurima praebeant, et ipsi postmodum minime inopiam tolerantes
ad impatientiam erumpant,_ Past. 325, 7. ðæt is ðæt mann (mon, _v. l._)
forwierne his sweorde blódes, ðæt hwá forwirne his láre ðæt hē mid ðǽre
ne ofsleá ðæs flǽsces lustas _gladium a sanguine prohibere est praedicationis verbum a carnalis vitae interfectione retinere,_ 379, 2. Hwá þe
heom þises bereáfie, God sié heom wráð, Cht. Th. 621, 22. Gif ðú
hwene gesihst geðeón on góde, blissa on his dǽdum, Hex. 44, 28.
(b) _with_ gen. :—Gif hwá þonne þegena sý þe on bóclande cyricean
hæbbe, Ll. Th. i. 262, 11. (2) hwæt. (a) _alone_ :—Gif him hwæt
mistímað, Hex. 44, 30. Weald hwæt heom tíde, Ll. Th. ii. 316, 25.
Gif hí on hwon (ówiht, _v. l._) ágylton _siqua delinquissent,_ Bd. 3, 5 ; Sch.
204, 22. Gif þú tōdǽlst hwæt on feówer, Angl. viii. 335, 24 ; Bl. H.
97, 27. (b) _with_ gen. :—Gif hié hwæt suá heálicra yfela on him
ongieten sý qua _valde sunt eorum prava,_ Past. 197, 5. Gif him gebyrige
ðæt hē on ðæs hwæt befoo ðe wið his willan sié, 198, 23. Hwæt
swylces, Gr. D. 138, 2. Gif hí hwæt litles understandaþ of þám Lýdenbócum, Ælfc. Gen. Thw. 2, 10.        ¶ anomalous construction where
V. i is used as well :—Mē bet lícað þ swá hwæt swá þú in Rómána
cyrican . . . oððe on hwilcre óþre hwæt þæs gemēte, þ Gode má lícode
_mihi placet, ut siue in Romana . . . seu in qualibet ecclesia aliquid
invenisti quod plus Deo possit placere,_ Bd. 1, 27 ; Sch. 65, 5.      V. in
combination with swá. (1) swá hwá (hwæt) swá. See also (7 a) :—
Swá hwá swá hild his gódan weorc, . . . ne lǽt hē nánne óðerne æfter
him, Past. 449, 29. Swá hwá þonne swá þæs wyrþe biþ þ hē . . ., Bt.
5, 1 ; F. 10, 13. Gif twēgen eówer geþafigaþ be ǽngum þinge swá
hwæs swá hé gebiddan (be ǽlcum þinge þe hig biddað, W. S.) _si duo ex
vobis consenserint de omni re quamcumque petierint,_ Mt. R. 18, 19. Hē
gelýfd swá hwæt swá hē cwyð, gewurðe þis, Mk. 11, 23 : Lk. 10, 35.
Swá hwæt swá (_quicquid_) . . . gelumpe, þæt eall þ (_totum hoc_) se ofen
. . . of ásude, Bd. 4, 9 ; Sch. 393, 11. (1 a) with gen. :—Hē forgifeþ
eall swá hwæt swá þes middangeard . . . æbyligða geworhte, Bl. H. 9,
11. (2) swá hwá (hwæt) :—Suá huá dringe selles _quicumque potum
dederit,_ Mt. L. 10, 42 : Mk. R. 11, 23. Swá hwæs hé gewilnode him
ne forwyrnde God, Hml. S. 34, 193. Swá hwæt hē gewyrce, Ll. Th. i.
78, 7. Swá hwæt (huæd, L.) gecweoðas, dōað þ, Jn. R. 2, 5.
(3) hwá (hwæt) swá :—Hwæt swá þín hand mæge wyrcan, Gr. D. 327,
26. (4) swá hwá (hwæt) swá :—And suá chuæt ðá _quamcumque,_ Mt.
L. 18, 19. (4 a) Swá hwá (hwæt) sē þe :—Suá huá sē ðe wælle _qui-
cumque uoluerit,_ Mk. L. 10, 43. Suá huá sē ðe ne hæfeð . . . genumen
bið from him I ðǽm, Lk. L. 8, 18. Hú, Mk. L. 10, 44. Hú, 11,
23. (5) Sē swá hwá (hwæt). Cf. (7 b) :—Sē ðe suá huá _quicumque,_
from mē ðe gewæxe, Mk. L. 7, 11. þ suá huæd, Lk. L. 10, 35.
(5 a) Sē þe swá hwá (hwæt). Cf. (7 b) :—Sē ðe suá huá _quicumque,_
Lk. L. 9, 5 : 48. þte swá hwæt (_quodcumque_) is of mē, Mk. R. 7, 11.
Ðá ðegnas sægdun him ðá ðe swá hwæt (huæd, L.) hiæ dydun _narrauerunt
illi quaecumque fecerunt,_ Lk. R. 9, 10. (6) Sē I swá hwá (hwæt) :—
Ðá I suæ huæt (chuæt) _quaecumque,_ Mt. L. 18, 18. (6 a) Sē þe I hwá
(hwæt). Cf. (7 c) :—Sē ðe I suá chuá ðec genédes . . . geong mið him,
Mt. L. 5, 41. (7) where eal _qualifies the indefinite form._ [Though
probably eal in every case is adjective in the following passages, they may
suggest that the construction might easily come to be considered as one
in which eal was substantive, and the hw- forms were relatives.]
(a) Cf. (1), (1 a) :—Þǽr mē æteówde hit self eall swá hwæt swá mē
mislícode _ubi omne quod displicebat se patenter ostenderet,_ Gr. D. 3, 18.
þá gemētton hí . . . eall swá hwæt swá mihton beón gesewene . . .
_invenerunt . . . quaeque poterant . . . videri,_ 129, 5. Hweþer hí magen
ábiddan eall swá hwæt swá heó biddað, and begytan eall þ hi gewilniað
_si omnia quae volunt possunt, et cuncta impetrant quae desiderant obtinere,_
166, 21. Eall swá hwæt swá hē findan mihte, hē dǽlde _quidquid habere
potuit, expendit,_ 293, 7. Eal hē mót ástundian swá hwæt swá fram his
gingrum forgýmeleásod bið _ad ipsum respicit quicquid a discipulis
delinquitur,_ R. Ben. 61, 7. Eal swá hwæt swá ic þe gehēt, eal ic hit
gesette, Bl. H. 147, 8 : 21, 23. Eall swá hwæt swá hē geseah, ealles hē

his gyrnde, Ll. Th. ii. 398, 20. (b) Cf. (5), (5 a):—Hē gitríówed
iówih alle ðā ðe swā hwæt (alle ðā suæ huæd, L. *omnia quaecumque*) ic
cwedo iów, Jn. R. 14, 26 : 16, 15 : Jn. R. 4, 29. (c) Cf. (6 a):—Sē
ðe cued mē tó alle ðā ðe ł suæ huæd ic dyde, Jn. L. 4, 29. **VI.** as
relative:—Nān man ne dorfte hine beládian ꝥ hē fæt næfde on hwý hē
hit wyrman mihte, Hml. A. 141, 84. ¶ Instances of *hw-* forms used
as true relatives are found only in late O. E., but there are many earlier
instances in which such forms are used in a way to suggest that the
transition to the relative force would be easy. See above Angl. viii. 323,
32 : Bt. 40, 7 ; F. 242, 22 (III. 2 b a) : Wlfst. 122, 9 (III. 3) : Cht.
Th. 621, 22 (IV. I a) : In. R. 2, 5 (V. 2) : Lk. L. 8, 18 (V. 4 a), and
all the passages under V. I, V. 7. To these may be added:—Ne rǣdde
gē ꝥ hwæt (the later version has, Ne rēdde gē hwæt . . .) Dauid dyde
*nec hoc legistis quod fecit Dauid*, Lk. 6, 3. [Here *hwæt* is not a
relative to antecedent *ꝥæt*, but the *hwæt*-clause is in apposition to *ꝥæt*.
Cf. the A. V. rendering 'Have ye not read so much as this, what David
did '.] v. ā-, æt-, wel-hwā, nāt-hwæt.

**hwæcce**, an ; *f. A chest*[:—Weard gemēt ꝥæt feoh uppon ānre
cornhwyccan (*printed* -hryccan; -hwæccan, *v. l.* Cf. Ofer ꝥæs mynstres
earce, seó wæs hwǣtes full *super arcam monasterii, quae erat frumento
plena*, Gr. D. 158, 13. *The same incident is described in the two
passages*, Hml. Th. ii. 178, 8.] [Nether wheche ne leede to be leyde
in, bote a grete Clothe to hely my foule Caryin, E. W. 27, 4].
v. hwicce.

**hwǣde** ; *adj. Small, petty*:—His lytlan hwǣdan geþóhtas *parvulos
cogitatus ejus*, R. Ben. I. 4, 8. v. ge-hwǣde.

**hwæder.** *Add:*—Elles hwæder *aliorsum*, Ælfc. Gr. Z. 225, 10.
Ic fylige þē swā hwæder swā þū færst, Mt. 8, 19.

**hwæg.** *l.* hwǣg, *and add*:—Huaeg, huuaeg, hwǣg *serum, liquor casei*,
Txts. 98, 982, 979. Gáthyrde gebyred his heorde meolc . . . and his
dǣl hwǣges, Ll. Th. i. 438, 28.

**-hwæga.** v. -hwega : **hwæl** *impudent.* v. hweall.

**hwæl.** *Add: A large kind of whale* (*as compared with* hran,
q. v.):—Hran odde hwæl *ballena*, Wrt. Voc. ii. 10, 67. Hwæl *ballenam*
.i. *diabolum*, An. Ox. 6, 12. God gesceóp þā micelan hwalas (*cete
grandia*), Gen. 1, 21. Hwælas, Angl. viii. 310, 18.

**hwæla.** *Dele, and see next word.*

**hwælen** ; *adj. Of the nature of a whale*:—Hē is onmiddan hwælen,
Sal. 263. *See* Angl. i. 153.

**hwæl-weg,** es ; *m. The path of the whale, the ocean*:—Hweted on
[h]wælweg hreder unwearnum, Seef. 63.

**hwǣnan.** v. ā-hwǣnan.

**hwǣr.** *Add:* , hwāra. **I.** in direct questions. (1) with verbs
denoting rest, *where, in what place*:—Adam, hwār eart þū?, Gen. 3, 9.
Hwǣr is þæt tiber?, Gen. 2890. (1 a) where it is implied that the
question cannot be satisfactorily answered:—Hwǣr sint nū þæs Wēlondes
bān?, Bt. 19 ; F. 70, 4. Hwǣr bid lā þonne se ídla lust? . . . Hwǣr beóþ
þonne þā symbelnessa?, Bl. H. 59, 15–17. Hwǣr is þín gilp and þín
hiht?, 243, 9. Hwār (buoer, L.) is eówer geleáfa?, Lk. 8, 25. Hwǣr
syndon þíne word, Drihten?, Bl. H. 243, 31. ¶ *strengthened by*
āhwǣr, ǣfre:—Hwǣr is heora God āhwǣr nū ðā?, Ps. Th. 113, 10.
Hwǣr āgylte hē ǣfre on his gegerelan, sē þe mid þon ānum hrægle wæs
gegyrwed?, Bl. H. 167, 36. (1 b) elliptical:—Ðā cwēdon big tó him,
' Hwār (huēr, L., hwēr, R.), Drihten? ' Lk. 17, 37. (2) with verbs
denoting motion (or change), *to or from what place.* Cf. (1 a):—Hwǣr
cōm eówer God?, Ps. Th. 78, 10. Hwǣr cōm seó frætwodnes heora
húsa? . . . oþþe hwǣr cōm heora snyttro?, Bl. H. 99, 27–31 : Sat. 36.
Se pytt hēh is ; huona ł huǣr (hwēr, R. *unde*) hæfis ðū uætter?, Jn. L.
4, 11. **II.** in dependent clauses. (1) with verbs denoting rest. (a)
after verbs of asking, enquiring, seeking, saying:—Ic āxige hwǣr seó
offrung sig, Gen. 22, 7 : Angl. vii. 26, 236 : Mt. 2, 4. Ic sóhte . . .
hwǣr ic feor odde neáh findan meahte . . . , Wand. 26 : El. 217. Ge-
secgad mē hwonne þæt gewurde and hwāra, Ors. 4, 10 ; S. 194, 25.
Gesecge hē hwǣr ǣnig gewin swā gehwurfe, 6, 4 ; S. 260, 6. Hwǣr
(huer, L., hwēr, R.), Jn. 20, 15. (a) with force similar to that in
I. I a:—Frīned hē hwǣr se man sié, sē þe for Dryhtnes naman deádes
wolde onbyrigan, Kr. 112. (b) after verbs of knowing, making known,
seeing, learning:—Gif hwā wiste hwār (huēr, L., hwēr, R.) hine hǣfde,
Jn. 11, 57. Ic nāt hwār hī hine lēdon, 20, 13. Ic ne wāt hwǣr þū
eart, Bl. H. 241, 7. ꝥ Adam understóde hwār (hwǣr, *v. l.*) hē þā wæs,
Angl. vii. 26, 238. Þām folce gecýdan hwǣr se wealdend wǣre, An.
800. Þū gesyhst hwǣr þā synfullan forweordad *cum pereant peccatores
videbis*, Ps. Th. 36, 33. Þā ofseah hē hwǣr sum ūdwita lǣdde twēgen
gebródru, Hml. Th. i. 60, 22. Wē nū gehýrad hwǣr ūs hearmstafas
onwócan, Gen. 939. (b a) with emphatic genitive:—Ic ne wāt hwǣr mín
bródor eordan scéata eardian sceal, Rǣ. 85, 18. (c) after verbs of considering, observing, caring:—Uton wē hycgan hwǣr wē hām āgen, Seef.
117. Dryhten sceáwad hwǣr þā eardien þe his ǣ healden, Gū. 26. Se
cyng gehāwade hwǣr mon mehte þā eá forwyrcan, Chr. 896 ; P. 89, 11.
Hī beheóldon hwār hē gelēd wǣre, Mk. 15, 47. (c a) with emphatic
genitive:—Hæfde ic ūhtceare hwǣr mín leódfruma londes wǣre, Kl. 8.

(c β) where the clause is in apposition to a pronoun:—Hié ymb þæt siredon
hwǣr hié hié gemētan wolden, Ors. 3, 11 ; S. 144, 35. (c γ) elliptical:—
Hī woldon on elþiódignesse beón, hī ne róhton hwǣr, Chr. 891 ; P. 82,
22. (d) where the clause is the equivalent of a noun governed by a
verb or preposition:—Stearra gestód ofer ðǣr ł hwēr (þǣr, W. S., R.)
wæs ðe cnæht, Mt. L. 2, 9. Foxas habbad holu . . . mannes sunu næfd
hwǣr hē hys heáfod āhylde, Mt. 8, 20. Hwóer, p. 15, 16. þæt wē
oncnāwan magun hwǣr wē sǣlan sceolon sundhengestas *that we may
recognize the port*, Cri. 863. (e) where the clause is equivalent to an
adverbial phrase of place:—Mid ðý cuōme ðǣr ł huoer (þǣr, W. S., ðǣr,
R.) uæs se Hǣlend, Jn. L. 11, 32. (2) with verb of motion:—Nān
mon nyste hwǣr hē cōm, ac fóran hwærfigiende geond þ wēsten, Ors. 6,
31 ; S. 286, 19. **III.** with indefinite force:—Wē niton þeáh sǣ
wunion for on neáwiste hwǣr, Jos. 9, 7. Wundur hwār þonne eorl
ellenróf ende gefēre lífgesceafta, þonne leng ne mæg mon mid his māgum
meduseld búan. Swā wæs Bíówulfe . . . seolfa ne cúðe þurh hwæt his
worulde gedāl weordan sceolde *it comes as a surprise anywhere whenever
a stout warrior may come to his end, when no longer can a man with
his kindred inhabit the meadhall. So it was with Beowulf . . . he himself knew not through what his parting with the world should come to
pass*, B. 3062 : 2029 (?). **IV.** in combination with swā. (1) *with
verbs denoting the being in a place.* (a) swā hwǣr swā:—Swā hwǣr swā
(suǣ huēr, L.) hold byd, þæder beód earnas gegaderude, Mt. 24, 28 : 26,
13. Swā hwār swā (suā huēr, L., swā hwēr, R.), Mk. 14, 9 : Lk. 17,
37. (b) swā hwǣr [*see also* (a)]:—Swā hwǣr (þǣr, W. S., suā huēr, L.)
gistrión goldes iówer is, ðǣr heorte bid *ubi thesaurus uester est, ibi cor
uestrum erit*, Lk. R. 12, 34. Suā huēr (hwǣr, W. S.) ic am, ðǣr ǣc
ðegn mín bid, Jn. L. 12, 26. Hī ꝥ mǣste yfel worhton swā hwār hī
fērdon, Chr. 1094 ; P. 128, 4. (2) where there is movement to or from
a place:—Heó heofdon sige swā hwǣr swā heó cōmon, Chr. 449 ; P. 13,
12. **V.** as a relative:—Ðǣr ł huēr (þǣr, W. S., R.) is strión ðín,
ðǣr is hearta ðín, Mt. L. 6, 21. Hwēr am ic, ðǣr ðegn mín bid, Jn. R.
12, 26. See also Mt. 24, 28 (IV. I a) : Lk. R. 12, 34 (IV. I b) : Jn.
L. 12, 26 (IV. I b). v. nāt-hwǣr.

**-hwǣrn.** v. nā-hwǣrn.

**hwǣr-hwega** ; *adv. Somewhere*:—Syle mē ðinne wíngeard . . . and
ic þē óderne finde on fyrlene forhwega (hwærhwega, *v. l.*), Hml. S. 18,
174. Nis nān tweó þæt ǣlc þing þæt ys hwǣrhwugu is *quidquid est,
alicubi esse cogitur*, Solil. H. 51, 10. Þā bæd hē æt þæs mynstres
hláforde, þ hē him ālýfde hwǣrhwugu (-hugu, *v. l.*) þ hē him móste
byrgenne gegearwian, Gr. D. 225, 25.

**hwǣrlǣcan.** v. þwǣrlǣcan.

**hwæs.** *Add:* v. ecg-hwæs [ecg wæs (ecghwæs?) íren, B. 1459:
2778.]

**hwæst,** es ; *m. Breathing, blowing*:—Ordas ł hwǣstes (hfæstes, MS.)
*spiritus*, Hpt. Gl. 464, 25. Huǣsttum *flatibus*, 55. Cf. fnǣst, *and next
two words.*

**hwǣstrian.** *Take here* hwāstrian *in Dict., and add*: [cf. *Wick.*..
whistren *to whisper, murmur.*] v. þwāstrian.

**hwǣstrung.** *Take here* hwāstrung, *and add*:—Hwāstrung (hurast-
rung, MS.) *mussitatio*, Hpt. Gl. 476, 19.

**hwæt** ; *adv. or interjection. Add:* **I.** in direct questions. (1) *why*:—
Hwæt ofermódgad ðiós eorde and ðis dúst? *quid superbit terra et cinis?*,
Past. 299, 22 : 211, 12 : Mt. 19, 17 : Nic. 14, 14. Ac hwæt ofermódige gē
þonne, oþþe hwý āhebbe gē eów?, Bt. 42 ; F. 258, 15 : Hml. Th. ii. 164,
28. Hwæt seofast þū wid mē? *quid igitur ingemiscis?* (cf. hwī (*quid*)
murcnast þū wid mín?, 3), Bt. 7, 3 ; F. 20, 14. Hwæt (cf. tó hwī,
W. S., for hwon, L., R. *quid*, Mt. 27, 46 : hwī, W. S., tó hwon, L., R.
*quid*, Mk. 15, 34) forlǣtest þū mē?, An. 1415. Hwæt standaþ gē hēr
and ūp on þysne heofon lóccaþ? *quid statis aspicientes in coelum?* (Acts
I, 11), Bl. H. 123, 21 : Cri. 510 : An. 1318 : Jul. 505. (1 a) strengthened by ǣfre:—Hwæt þū ǣfre wilt aldre lǣtan þæne þe hēr leofad rihtum
þeáwum, Gen. 2642. (2) as a particle of interrogation:—Hwæt lā nis
hē fæder þín? *numquid non ipse est pater tuus?*, Cant. M. ad fil. 6. Lā
hwæt is ǣnig óðer on eallum þām gelimpum būtan Godes yrre swytol?,
Wlfst. 163, 13. **II.** in indirect questions:—Ic ðē mæg eówian ðæs
bisna þā ðe magon getrymian tó þām þ þū nāst hwæt þū læng siofige, Bt.
36, 1 ; F. 172, 28. **III.** in clauses expressing astonishment, *how,
what*:—Eálā hwæt Drihten deófles costunga geþyldelíce ābær *O how
patiently our Lord bore the devil's tempting*, Bl. H. 33, 28 : Sat. 316.
Juliana, hwæt þū glǣm hafast, Jul. 167. Hwæt hē frēcnu gestreón funde,
Met. 8, 58. **III a.** preceding a question:—Hwæt lā hwæt ! sint
þis nū þā gód?, Bt. 3, 4 ; F. 6, 18. **IV.** as an introductory particle
of vague meaning, *why, well, so, indeed, certainly*:—Gif þonne hwā ne
rēcþ hwæþer hē hæbbe . . . þe nabbe . . . , hwæt þ beóþ forlytla sǣlþa
þæt mon swā eáþe forlǣtan mæg an *vel si amiserit, negligendum putat* ?
*sic quæque perexile bonum est, quod aequo animo feratur amissum*, Bt. 11,
2 ; F. 34, 30. Sē þe gedyrstigad onwreón þā scandlicnesse his steópmēder
. . . hwæt (*profecto*) sē sódlíce onwrihd his fæder scondlicnesse, Bd. 1,
27 ; Sch. 70, 4. Hwæt seó gítsung gedēþ heore gítseras lāþe *siquidem
avaritia semper odiosos facit*, Bt. 13 ; F. 38, 15. Hwæt hē is God mín

*etenim ipse est Deus meus*, Ps. Th. 61, 2, 6. Hwæt wē witan *nouimus namque*, Bd. 1, 27; Sch. 81, 21. And hwæt þā se ylca God manna cynn ādwǣscan ne wolde *quia itaque isdem Deus humanum genus exstinguere noluit*, 77, 12. Hwæt hī dydon swā swā hē cwæð *fecerunt, ut dixerat*, 2, 2; Sch. 117, 20: 1, 27; Sch. 78, 9: Hml. S. 22, 141:24, 12: Angl. viii. 330, 23. Hwæt ic þīnra bysna ne mæg wuht oncnāwan, Gen. 533. **V.** *somewhat, any, at all.* Cf. ā-wiht :—Gif hit hwæt elles geselde *if it happened at all differently*, Cht. Th. 166, 20. Gif hit hwæt ælcor (elles, *v.l.*) bið *sin alias*, Bd. 4, 28; Sch. 519, 7.

**hwæt;** *adj. Add* :—Huæt, huet, huæt *licidus, lucidus*, Txts. 75, 1223. Hwet *licidus, liquidus*, Wrt. Voc. ii. 51, 7, 8. *Efficax*, hwæt, i. *citus, expeditus, astutus, acutus, sollers, peritus* arud, 142, 54. **I.** *swift* :—Gif hē hwæt biþ, ne tweóþ nænne mon þ hē hwæt ne sié *cuicumque velocitas adest, manifestum est esse velocem*, Bt. 16, 3; F. 54, 30. Hī mid hwatum hȳrsumnesse fēt gefolgiað, R. Ben. 20, 3. **II.** *active, nimble* :—þā handa āwindað þā ðe ǣr hæfdon ful hwæte fingras, Wlfst. 148, 4. **III.** *keen, bold, active* :—Hē ūsic gārwīgend gōde tealde, hwate helmberend, B. 2642 : 2517. Ōsfriþ his sunu . . . se hwatesta fyrdesne *filius eius Osfrid, iuuenis bellicosus*, Bd. 2, 20; Sch. 184, 11. v. eofor-, secg-hwæt.

**hwǣte.** *Add : corn, grain* :—Of hwǣte *cœreri*, Wrt. Voc. ii. 22, 5. (1) **as a plant** (a) *growing* :—Ātíò hē ǣrest of þām lande þā þornas, . . . þ se hwǣte mæge ðȳ bet weaxan *liberat arva prius fruticibus, . . . ut nova fruge gravis Ceres eat*, Bt. 23; F. 78, 23. Ūre hwǣte and ealle ūre eorþan wæstmas beóþ gebletsode, Bl. 51, 12. Hē ofersevów hit mid coccele onmiddan þām hwǣte (in midle þæs hwǣtes, R. *in medio tritici*), Mt. 13, 25. Þe lǣs gē þone hwǣte (*triticum*) āwurtwalion, 29. (b) *gathered* :—Gadriaþ þone hwǣte (hwēte, R., hwætte, L.), 33. (2) *as part of the plant*. (a) *the grain with the husk* :—Heó ābæd ān hrīdder tō feormianne sumne dǣl hwǣtes (*triticum*), Gr. D. 97, 3. Þ hē eów hrīdrude swā swā hwǣte, Lk. 22, 31. (b) *the grain separated from the chaff* :—Corn huǣtes *granum frumenti*, Jn. L. 12, 24. Wæs hwǣtes wana *triticum deerat*, Gr. D. 145, 9. Seó earc wæs hwǣtes full (*frumento plena*), 158, 14. Þ hē him hwǣtes (*tritici*) gemet sylle, Lk. 12, 42. Hund mittena hwǣtes, 16, 7 : Ap. Th. 10, 2. Hī þone hwǣte ūp bǣron, 5. Huīt corn sonuuald for huǣtte cuóm of heofenum, Jn. L. 6, 31 note on *manna*. Hē āfeormað his þyrscelflóre, and hē gegaderað his hwǣte on his bern; þā ceafu hē forbærnð, Mt. 3, 12. Hwǣtas sume [h]andlian untrumnysse getācnað *frumenta aliqua tractare infirmitatem significat*, Lch. iii. 204, 12. [The word occurs in local names, see C. D. vi. 304, col. 2.]

**hwǣte-corn.** *Add* :—Nim hwǣtecorn, meng wið hunig, lege on þone finger, Lch. ii. 80, 20.

**hwǣte-croft.** v. croft : **hwǣte-god.** *Dele* : **hwǣte-smedeme,** an; *f. l.*-smedema, an; *m.*

**hwǣte-wæstm, es;** *m.*(?) *Substitute* : **hwǣte-wæstm** *wheat-produce, wheat-crop, wheat* :—Eorþan mōder, geunne þē Drihten æcera wexendra . . . þǣre brādan berewæstma and þǣre hwītan hwǣtewæstma and ealra eorþan wæstma, Lch. i. 402, 6. Hwǣtewæstm (hwętewestem, Surt.) sende him on genyhtsumnesse *frumentationem misit eis in habundantiam*, Ps. Vos. 77, 25.

**hwæþer.** *Add* : **I.** *in direct questions.* (a) *alone* :—Hwæðer (cf. hwæt, Mt. 9 5) is ēðre tō secgenne? *quid est facilius dicere*?, Mk. 2, 9 : Lk. 5, 23. Hwæþerne woldest þū dēman wītes wyrþran, ðe [þone þe] þone unscyldgan wītnode, þe ðone þe þ wīte þolode?, Bt. 38, 6; F. 208, 15. Hueðerne (*quem*) wallas gié hic forlēto iówh, Barabban í ðone Hǣlend?, Mt. L. 27, 17. Hwæþer wēnst þū nū? *what* (*there being two alternatives*) *do you think*?, Bt. 36, 4; F. 178, 9. (b) *with gen.* :—Hwæþer ðāra twēgra þincþ þē mihtigra?, Bt. 36, 4; F. 178, 14. (2) *with the force of* hwæt (v. hwā; I. 2 a), *where the answer is confined to two alternatives* :—Hwæþer ðincþ þē þ þā ðing sién, þe þāra sōþena gesǣlþa limu, ðe sió gesǣlþ self?, Bt. 34, 6; F. 142, 9. **II.** *in dependent clauses.* (1) *as substantive.* (a) *alone. which of the two.* (a) *where the alternatives are not expressed* :—Nāst ðū hwæðer bið þæs rīcan wīfes cild, hwæðer þæs earman, Hml. Th. i. 256, 14. Geþence þonne þāra tīda and nū þissa, hwæþre him bet līcien, Ors. 1, 11; S. 50, 22. (β) *where the alternatives are given* :—þā angunnon hī reahtigean hwæðer mā mǣrlecra dǣda hæfde þe Philippus þe Alexander, Ors. 3, 9; S. 130, 26. (ββ) *where the alternatives are expressed in a dependent clause introduced by the conjunction* hwæþer :—Gesege mē hwæþer þē betere ðince . . . , hwæþer . . . þe . . . , Bt. 8; F. 26, 10. (b) *with genitive, which of the two.* (a) *the alternatives not expressed* :—On ðǣm gefilte hwæðer hiera mehte māran fultum him tō geteón, Ors. 3, 11; S. 144, 36. Hit is on hiora āgenum anwealde hwæþre (hwaþre, *v.l.*) ðāra hī gecēosan, Bt. 40, 3; F. 238, 23. (β) *the alternatives expressed* :—Hē āscade hwæþer heora sceolde on ōþrum sige, habban, þe hē on Rōmanum, þe Rōmane on him, Ors. 4, 1; S. 156, 1. (2) *as adjective, which* object of two :—Mid ðǣm worde bið gecȳþed hwæðer healf hæfð sige, Ors. 3, 1; S. 100, 9. Gehwā mōste cȳðan tō hwæþeran hlāfordscipe hē wolde gebūgan, Hml. S. 23, 116. Saga mē on hwæðere Adames sīdan nam ūre Dryhten ðæt rib, Sal. K. 198, 8. **III.** *one*

*or other* of two, *either* :—Twā ðing sindon . . . gif hwǣm þāra twēga hwæþeres (hwæðres, *v.l.*) wana biþ *duo sunt, quorum si alterutrum desit*, Bt. 36, 3; F. 176, 7. Ðonne him mon ðissa twēga hwæðer ondrǣtt suiður ðonne ōðer, Past. 189, 9. **IV.** *each* of two :—Weard mycel wælsliht on hwæðre (gehwæþere, *v.l.*) hand, Chr. 871; P. 73, 3. **V.** *in combination with* swā. (1) swā hwæþer swā :—An feó oþþe an āðe, swā hwæðer swā him leófre sió, Ll. Th. i. 32, 1. (2) swā . . . swā . . . swā hwæðer swā :—Swā werðādes swā wīfhades, swā hwæðer (swæðer, *v.l.*) swā hit sȳ, Ll. Th. i. 244, 11. (3) swā . . . swā . . . swā hwæþer :—Swā wæterordāl swā ȳsenordāl, swā hwæðer him leófresȳ, Ll. Th. i. 224, 16. (4) swā hwæþer swā . . . swā . . . swā . . . :—Cēóse se man . . . swā hweðer swā hē wylle, swā ānfeald ordāl, swā pundes wurðne āð, Ll. Th. i. 280, 16 : 394, 1. (5) swā hwæþer . . . swā . . . swā :—Ǣlc tiónd āge geweald swā hwæðer hē wille, swā wæter swā īsen, Ll. Th. i. 296, 3. **V a.** *as adverb, however* :—Gebēte hit swā hwæðor swā hit gebyrige, swā mid godcundre bōte, swā mid woroldcundre steóre, Ll. Th. i. 328, 2. Werian his man swā hwæðer him þincð þ hē hine eáð āwerian mæge, swā for frigne, swā for þeówne, 388, 2. Gewylde man hine swā hwæðer swā man mæge, swā cucne, swā deádne, 390, 21. Swā hwæðer swā (swaðor, *v.l.*), 268, 17. v. ge-hwæþer, swæþer.

**hwæþer;** *conj. Add* : *generally with subjunctive. For instances of indicative see* Mt. 20, 15 : Solil. H. 3, 9. Cri. 1307. **I.** *in direct questions, whether . . .* [*or* (*whether*)] :—Hwæðer wæs Jóannes fulluht þe of heofonum þe of mannum? *baptismus Johannis unde erat? e cælo an ex hominibus*?, Mt. 21, 25 : Hml. Th. i. 222, 20 (*in Dict.*). Ic þe bidde, cwyst þū hwæþer hit tō gelȳfenne sȳ . . . hwæþer þe . . .? *dic, quaero te, numquid non credendendum est . . . an . . .*?, Gr. D. 146, 1–6. **I a.** *where the question is introduced by a pronominal* hwæþer, cf. **II.** 1 b a :—Hwæðer (*quid*, cf. hwæt, Mt. 9, 5) is ēðre tō secgenne, 'þē synd ðīne synna forgyfene', hwæðer þe (*an*) cweþan, 'arīs, nim ðīn bed and gā'?, Mk. 2, 9 : Lk. 5, 23. **I b.** *where* hwæþer *occurs only in the second alternative* :—Wæs Jōhannes fulluht of heofone, hwæðer þe of mannum? *baptismus Johannis de coelo erat, an ex hominibus*?, Lk. 20, 4. **I c.** *where the question asks for yes or no as an answer, the second alternative not being expressed*. In later English the introductory *whether* is omitted : in O.E. the question is often introduced by *cwist þū, cweþe gē*, &c. :—Cuiðestū í hueðer (cwyst þū, W.S.) somnigas of ðornum wīnbēger? *numquid colligunt de spinis uvas*?, Mt. L. 7, 16. Cweðe wē hwæþer þā ealdras ongyton? *numquid cognouerunt principes*?, Jn. 7, 26 (cf. cweþe gē *numquid*, 31). Hwæðer (*numquid*) ǣnig man him mete brōhte?, 4, 33. Hueðer (cweðe gē, W.S.), Mt. L. 9, 15. Hueoðer (cweþe wē, W.S.), 12, 23. Hwæþer Rōmāne hit witen tō secganne hwæt hiera folces forwurde?, Ors. 5, 2; S. 220, 9. Eálā! hwæðer heó hider cumende syó, and mē ne gȳme?, Hml. S. 23 b, 667. Hwæþer (*si*) seó næddre þurh hyre āgen andgit sprǣce?, Angl. vii. 24, 238. **II.** *with dependent clauses.* (1) *where both the alternatives implied in* hwæþer *are given, whether . . . or.* (a) hwæþer . . . þe :—Hī ne scrifon hwæðer hit wǣre ðe dæg ðe niht, Past. 427, 31. (b) hwæþer þe . . . þe :—Andswarode mē sum ðing, ic nāt hwæt, hweðer þe ic sylf þe ōðer þing (*sive ego ipse, sive alius quis*), Solil. H. 3, 8. (b a) *where a pronominal* hwæþer *precedes the dependent clause*, cf. **I a** :—Gesege mē hwæþer þū hȳ forseó . . . þe þū gebīde hwonne hī þe forlētan, Bt. 8; F. 26, 12. (c) hwæþer . . . hwæþer þe :—Hē gecnǣwþ be þǣre lāre, hwæþer (*utrum*) heó sī of Gode, hwæþer þe (*an*) ic be mē sylfum spece, Jn. 7, 17. (d) hwæþer . . . þe :—Sié on cyninges dōme hwæþer hē līf āge þe nāge, Ll. Th. i. 106, 3 : 224, 18 : 330, 24. Sē þe ne giémeð hwæðer his gǣst sié earm þe eádig, Cri. 1553. Geseón hwæðer him mon sóð þe lyge sagað, 1307. Hwæðer him yfel þe gōd under wunige, 1333 : Bl. H. 119, 5. Ic nāt hwæðer hit wæs innan mē ðe ūtan (*extrinsecus sive intrinsecus*), Solil. H. 3, 9. (e) hwæþer . . . oþþe :—Deófol mōt ælces mannes āfondian, hwæðer hē āht sȳ oððe nāht; hwæðer hē God mid inweardlicre heortan lufige oððe hē mid hīwunge fare, Hml. Th. i. 268, 11–14. Hueðer . . . oþþe (í MS.) *utrum . . . an*, Jn. L., R. 7, 17. (e a) *where the alternatives are not mutually exclusive* :—Beseah Drihten hwæðer his mihta andgyt ǣnig ealra hæfde, oððe God wolde sēcan (*si est intelligens, aut requirens Deum*), Ps. Th. 52, 3. (f) *in combination with* swā :—Inseglige mon þā hand, and sēce man ofer þæne þriddan dæg swā hwæðer swā heó beó fūl swā clǣne binnan þām insegle *insigilletur manus, et inquiratur die tertia si inmunda sit uel munda intra sigillationem*, Ll. Th. i. 226, 31. (2) *where one alternative only is given*. **v. I c.** *whether, if* :—Ðæt ðū nyte hwæðer (hwiðer, *v.l.*) ðū māran wilnige, Past. 331, 4. Ne wæs mē cūð hwæðer . . . egesa wære, Gen. 2710. Geseón hwæðer (*an*) Helias cume, Mt. 27, 49. Hī gȳmdon hwæþer (gif í hueðer, L. *si*) hē gehǣlde, Mk. 3, 2. Hié wǣron orwēne hwæðer ǣfre Rōmāne tō heora anwealde becōmen, Ors. 4, 9; S. 192, 4. Hē āxode hwæþer (gif í huoeðer, L. *si*) hē āht gesāwe, Mk. 8, 23: Lk. 23. 6. Āfandað God . . . hwæðer hē ānrǣde sȳ, Hml. Th. i. 268, 16: Gen. 1437. Sorgian hwæðer . . . Met. 9, 34: Sat. 277. Hyne fyrwet bræc hwæðer hē cwicne gemētte þeóden, B. 2785. (2 a) *where the clause is in apposition to* hit :—Ys hit

on þýnum anwealda hwæðer hî leng þâr binnan beón môtan, Chr. 995;
P. 130, 11. His scrift hit gecýðe þâm biscope, hweðer hê tô þâre bôte
cirran wolde, Ll. Th. i. 212, 24. v. ā-, nā-hwæþer.

**hwæþere.** _Add_: **I.** _in a principal clause with which is connected a
dependent clause introduced_ (1) _by_ þeáh. (a) þeáh... hwæþere:—
Þeáh hê hié mannum missenlíce dâle, hwæþere hê bebeád þ wê...
gedâlan... þone teóþan dâl, Bl. H. 39, 18. Þeáh hê latode...,
hwæþre hê... þegnunga gefylde, 167, 8 : Ph. 640. Þâh... hueoðre
_etsi_... _tamen_, Lk. L. 18, 5. (aa) þeáh þe... hwæþere:—Þeáh þe þ
hûs ufan open sý,...hweþre hit biþ... wið âghwylc ungewidro gescylded, Bl. H. 125, 31 : Dan. 234. (b) hwæþere... þeáh:—Hwæþre
hê getrymede heora geleáfan mid þon heofonlicon weorce, þeáh hié word
þæs heofonlican gerýnes ne ongeáton, Bl. H. 7, 7. (ba) hwæþere...
þeáh þe:—Hwæðre þæt gegongeð, þeáh þe hit sý greóte beþeaht, Dôm.
98. Nô hwæþre... þeáh þe..., Gen. 952. (2) _by gif_:—Gif (_etsi_)
ne selles for ðon friónd his bið, fore giornise huoeðre (_tamen_) his seleð
him, Lk. L. 11, 8. Gif se hund losige, gâ þeós bôt hwæðre forð, Ll.
Th. i. 78, 6. (3) _by a particle expressing time_:—Syþþan hié ðæt feoh
onfengon, ne mihtan hié hweðre forswîgian, Bl. H. 177, 31. Ðâ hê þâ
gesihþe geseah, þâ ne wæs hê hweðre nôht feor on oferhygd âhafen,
215, 32. **II.** _in a co-ordinate clause._ (1) _introducing the clause_:—
Wandode se wîsa ; hwæðre hê cwæð, Dan. 550 : An. 504 : Kr. 38 : 101 :
Ps. 68, 3. ¶ _with another particle_:—God swâ forlâteþ sweltan his
corenan, þâ þonne hwæþre (_tamen_) hê ne lâteþ nâ beón forholene æfter
deáþe, Gr. D. 294, 5. (2) _within a clause._ (a) _however, yet_:—Manigfeald
wundor ðâr beóð æteówed, ealles oftost hweðre on ðâm dæge, Bl. H. 209,
16. Ðegnas his geuundradon... nânig monn hueðre (_tamen_) cueð...,
Jn. L. R. 4, 27. Gesæh gegesettedo ðâ hræglo, nô hueoðre 'inn eóde, 20,
5 : Crâ. 32 : Met. 28, 170. (b) _however, but_:—Alle swæ huelce
cuoeðas, ðôas ; æfter werc hueðre (_uero_) hiora nallas gê gedôa, Mt. L.
23, 3. Nû hueðre (_uero_) cuoeð, Jn. L. 9, 41. Ðis gedd cuæð se
Hâlend, ðâ ilco huoeðre (_autem_) ne ongetton, 10, 6 : 13, 7 : 15, 24 :
17, 25. Hê wæs on Pannania on woruld cumen ; wæs hê hweðre in
Italia âfêded, Bl. H. 211, 17 : 19. **III.** _in a clause referring to
a previous sentence or group of clauses._ (1) _introducing the clause, yet_:—
Geþencean wê þ Drihten his englas gesceóp...; ealle stôwa hê gefylleþ
... and âghwâr hê biþ andweard ; hwæþere hê hine geeáþmêdde, Bl. H.
23, 21 : B. 574 : 970 : 2298 : An. 51. ¶ _with another particle_:—
Þonne hwæþre (_tamen_) ûs is genôh cûð, Gr. D. 320, 26. (2) _within
a clause._ (a) _however_:—Se bisceop þâ þær gesette gôde sangeras...: næs
hweðre nânig man þe nihtes tîdum dorste on þâre ciricean cuman, Bl. H.
207, 34 : Dan. 168 : (_tamen_) Jn. L. R. 7, 13. Ongeat hwæþre...,
Gen. 1863 : Men. 68 : Ph. 443 : Met. 20. 74. (b) _however, but_:—
Inhlôgan hine. Hê hueðre (_uero_)... genôm ðone fæder..., Mk. L.
R. 5, 40. Ne ðus is huoeðre (_autem_) in iúih, 10, 43 : Jn. L. 20, 17.
Huæðre, 6, 6. Dâle hê hwæðre..., Ll. Th. i. 86, 6. **IV.** _in a
clause connected with a preceding one by another conjunction._ (1) _and_:—
Hê ûs lârde hû wê ûs gebiddan sceoldan, and hwæþere cwæþ, 'Eówer
Fæder wât hwæs eów þearf biþ, âr gê hine biddan,' Bl. H. 19, 36 : 23,
28 : 75, 24, 28 : 103, 19. Ll. Th. i. 100, 6 : Sal. 438 : Cri. 1378 :
El. 719. Þæt wundra sum monnum þûhte..., and þæt hwæþre gelomp, Gû. 491. (1 a) _and þâ_ (_þonne_) hwæþere:—Ne dorstan hî nô
him geneálâcan, and þâ hwæþre fêrde hê mid him, Shrn. 76, 29. Cwyst
þû þ þe nâre cûð þ ic ne cûðe Grêcisc geþeóde? and þonne hwæþre (_et
tamen_) sprec nû on Grêcisc, Gr. D. 300, 16. (2) _eác_:—Eorðe ælgrêno,
eác hwæþre ceald, Met. 20, 78. (3) _ac_:—Genôh wel wât God hû hit
getîmað on þâre fandunge ; ac hwæðere se man næfð nâ mycele geðincðe
bûton hê âfandað sý, Hml. Th. i. 268, 17. Þâ hâþenan men tô lôcodan,
ah hié hweþre wâron tô ðæs swîðe gefyrhte þæt heora nânig him wiþstandan ne dorste, Bl. H. 221, 34. Ah miltsa þû hweþre ûs, 225, 20.
Ac hê him tô frôfre lêt hwæðere forð wesan..., Gen. 955. v. ge-, sôþ-
hwæþere.

**hwæt-hwâra**; _adv._ A _little, somewhat, slightly_:—Þâ þeáhhwæðre gebyrede him þæt hié hwæthwâra gebugan tô fleónne _cum Persarum acies
paulatim cederet_, Ors. 1, 12 ; S. 54, 11. Þæt þâ munecas hwæthwâra
furþor restan þonne healfe niht _ut modice amplius de media nocte pausentur_,
R. Ben. 32, 13. Gelencged hwæthwâra, 37, 8. Syricas hwæthwâra
(-hwega, _v. l. modice_) beteran, Lch. 1, 374, 22. Þeáh hwet teartlíces hwæthwâra
stîdlíce (hwæthwega stîdlíces, _v. l._) geset sý, 5, 11. Cf. æt-hwâra.

**hwæt-hwega.** _Add_: **I.** _as substantive._ (1) _alone_:—Þeáh hit wêne
þ hit sylf hwæthwega (-hwuga, _v. l._) sî _si se esse aliquid existimat_, Gr. D. 8,
22. Hwæthwugu bið betweoh ðâm irsiendan and ðâm ungeðyldgan, þæt is
ðæt... _in hoc ab impatientibus iracundi differunt, quod..._, Past. 293,
15. Ðonne him hwæthwugu wiðstint, 455, 16. Huoeðer huoðhuoegu
(_aliquid_) woere wona?, Lk. L. 22, 35. Him biþ hwæshweg (-hwugu,
_v. l._) wana, Bt. 34, 1 ; F. 134, 12. Suæ hê hwæshwegu hercnade, Shrn.
72, 24. Nân gesceaft swâ clâne ne forwyrð, þæt hê tô hwanhwugu ne
weorðe, Solil. H. 63, 1. Hió wirpð on ðæt geðôht hwæthwugu tô
begietenne _adipiscenda quaeque cogitationi objicit_, Past. 70, 22. Hwæthugu _aliquid_, Bd. 1, 27 ; Sch. 66, 1. Hwæthweg (-hwugu, _v. l._), 5, 2 ;
Sch. 559, 16. Huothuoegu, Jn. L. 13, 29. Hwothwoego (hwæthwugu,

R, ænig þing, W. S.), Mt. L. 5, 23 : (ôwiht, R., ænig þing, W. S.), 24,
17. Huothuoego t sum ðing, 21, 3 : Lk. L. 7, 40. Huothuogu (hwæt-
hwoegu) _quid_, Jn. L. 4, 33. Hwæthwogu _aliquid_, Jn. R. 13, 29.
Huodhuoge _quid_, Mk. L. 15, 24. (2) _with genitive_ (a) _following_:—
Âbiersð hwæthwugu (_aliquid_) ût ðæs ðe hê sugian sceolde, Past. 165,
15. Hê wilnað hwæshweg (-hwugu, _v. l._) þæs þe hê þonne næft, Bt. 11,
1 ; F. 34, 1. Hwæshwugu (hwæthweg, _v. l._) þisses woruldwelan
wilnian _aliquid poscere_, 26, 2 ; F. 94, 3. Þû scealt habban hwæthweg
(-hwugu, _v. l._) wiþerweardes _per aspera quaeque distractus_, 32, 1 ; F. 114.
19. Hwæthwugu swilces _tale aliquid_, Bd. 4, 3 ; Sch. 354. 11. Hwæthwugu
stiórwierðes, Past. 194, 3 : 147, 1 : 171, 25. Hwæthwugu þæs þe ic
beþorfte, Solil. H. 1, 7. (b) _preceding_:—Þte ne yfles ðê huodhuoegu
blimpe _ne deterius te aliquid contingat_, Jn. L. 5, 14. Gif mon medmycles hwæthwega (_exigui quid_) deóðum onsægð, Ll. Th. ii. 156, 15.
Swâ þ hê hire hwæthwegu nabbe on his Môde, Bt. 35, 1 ; F. 154, 31.
(c) _both preceding and following_:—Lytles hwæthwegu underfôn þæs þe ic
hider brôhte, Hml. S. 23 b, 712. (3) _with an adjective._ (a) _following,
something_ (_good_):—Tô þon þ hê him forgeáfe hwæthwega (-hugu, _v. l._)
getâse (sume getâse hýðde, _v. l._) his gewinnes _ei laboris sui commodum
dedit_, Gr. D. 39, 27. Manige men beforan ôþrum mannum hwæthwugu
gôd begangaþ, Bl. H. 57, 2. (aa) _with an adjective clause_:—Habbað
gié hêr huoethuoego þte ðtlic sê? _habetis hic aliquid quod manducetur?_,
Lk. L. 24, 41. (b) _preceding_:—Þte ne wyrse ðê huodhuoegu blimpe
_ne deterius tibi aliquid contigat_, Jn. L. 5, 14. Lyttel hothuoego
_modicum quid_, Jn. L. 6, 7. **II.** _as adjective_:—Seó cyrice hwæthwugu fæc (sum fæc, _v. l._) sibbe hæfde _ecclesia aliquantulam... pacem
habuerit_, Bd. 1, 8 ; Sch. 28, 3. On hwæthwuga fata (_g. pl._? or _acc. pl._?)
(hwylchwugu fatu, _v. l. in uasa quaelibet_) gehîwod, 3, 22 ; Sch. 291, 6.
_In the two following passages_ hwæthwegu _seems adjective, but perhaps
should be considered as adverb and the passages put under_ III. v. Gr.
D. 88, 23 _under_ III. 1:—Hit nis êce gifu..., ac is hwæthwegu
(hwilc-, _v. l._) eldung, Bt. 38, 3 ; F. 202, 17. Hæfde ic þâget hwæthwega
(hwilc-, _v. l._) gemynd on mînum môde þâre uurôtnesse _ego nondum
penitus moeroris oblitus_, 36, 1 ; F. 170, 26. **III.** _as adverb._ (1) _some-
what_:—Wæs seó suðduru hwæthwega hâde mâre, Bl. H. 201, 15. Se
Wisdôm... mîn geþôht hwæthwegu (-hwugu, _v. l._) ûp ârârde, Bt. 3, 1 ;
F. 4, 26. Mîn lâr hwæthwugu ingâð on þîn ondgit, 13 ; F. 36, 33.
Him hwæthwugu sió sôðfæsðnes on geeácnod bið _jam aliquid de veritatis
intellectu conceperant_, Past. 367, 17. Hê gedyde hwylcehugu (hwæthwega) yldinge _paululum moram fecit_, Gr. D. 88, 23. (2) _almost._
v. hû-hwega:—Fornéah t hwæthwega hî fordydon mê _paulo minus
consummauerunt me_, Ps. L. 118, 87.

**hwæt-hweganinga** (-unga); _adv. Somewhat, a little_:—Gif þû hî
hwæthweganinga wiþ fýr ne gemengdest, Bt. 33, 4 ; F. 130, 10. _See
next word._

**hwæt-hweganunges.** _Add_:—Mê ðincþ þ þû sadige hwæthweg-
nunges (-hwugununges, _v. l._), Bt. 39, 4 ; F. 218, 5. _See preceding
word._

**hwæt-hwoegno.** _l._ -hwegno(-u) _and add_: **I.** _alone._ v. hwæthwega, I.:—Hwæthwoegnu wêre wona iów? _numquid aliquid defuit
uobis?_, Lk. 22, 35. **II.** _with an adjective._ v. hwæt-hwega; **II.**
3:—Mæge hwæthwoegnu gôd (_aliquid boni_) wosa?, Jn. R. 1, 46. Ðætte
ne wyrsa ðê hwæthwoegnu bilimpe, 5, 14. Þ ân gihwelc lytel hwæt-
hwoegno onfôe, 6, 7. **II a.** _with an adjective clause._ v. hwæt-hwega;
**II.** 3 a a:—Habbað gê hêr hwæthwoegno þte ettlic sié?, Lk. R. 24, 41.

**hwætlíce.** _Add_: **I.** _of quick movement_:—Þâ ârn se cniht and
eóde hwætlíce on þâ mædwe (_pratum velociter ingressit_), Gr. D.
36. 11. **II.** _of prompt action._ (1) _of persons, with activity of
body or mind_:—Hors[c]líce, hwætlíce _naviter_ (cf.? triumphum...
viribus _naviter_ (v. Wrt. Voc. ii. 74, 58) nanciscuntur, Ald. 2, 17), Wrt.
Voc. ii. 59, 47. Swâ hwylc swâ hwætlíce tô þeógincge efstað, bûtan
tweón hrædlíce hî beóð geendude _quicumque ad profectum tendunt, sine
dubio celeriter finiantur_, Scint. 101, 16. Nû wê hwætlíce þis habbað
gegaderod, þæt is on Lýden _actiuum opus_, Angl. viii. 330, 35. (2) _of the
operation of things, e.g. diseases_:—Hwæt[líce] _perniciter_ (quos lethale
virus _perniciter_ prostraverat), An. Ox. 1874. **III.** _quickly, in a
short time_:—Swâ swâ wyrta felda hwætlíce (_cito_) hî feallaþ, Ps. L. 36,
2. Þæt tô þâm hwætlícor hê mæge becuman _quatinus ad eam quantocius
valeat peruenire_, Scint 29, 3.

**hwæt-ness.** _Add_:—Hê ys gecweden for þâra tungla hwætnysse
_momentum_, þ ys styrung, and on Lýden, _a motu siderum_, Angl. viii, 318,
6. v. ge-hwætness.

**hwæt-scipe.** _Add_:—Gê eówerra gewinna and eówres hwætscipes
hwetstân forluran _cotem splendoris et acuminis sui perdiderunt_, Ors. 4,
13 ; S. 212, 23.

**hwall.** v. hweall: **hwalwa.** _Dele_: -hwâm. v. dæg-hwâm:
-hwâmlic. v. dæg-hwâmlic, ge-hwâmlic: -hwâmlíce. v. dæg-,
geár-hwâmlíce; ge-hwâmlíce.

**hwamm.** _Add_:—Ic mê âna gestôd on sumum hwomme þæs cæfertûnes,
Hml. S. 23 b, 422. Hwommas _angulos_, Germ. 403, 14 : _porticus_, 396,
175.

**hwanan.** *Add:* **I.** in direct questions. (1) local:—' Hwanon cômon gē?' þā cwǣdon hig: 'Of Chanaon lande,' Gen. 42, 7: An. 256. Hwanon ferigeað gē fǣtte scyldas?, B. 333. (2) asking for source, cause, &c. (a) local source from which material things are obtained:—Hwanon (huona, L., hwona, R.) mæg ǣnig man þǣs mid hlāfum on þisum wēstene gefyllan?, Mk. 8, 4. Huona (hwǣr, W.S.) bycge uē hlāfo?, Jn. L. R. 6, 5. Hwanon hæfst þū lifes wæter?, Jn. 4, 11. (b) source from which things are derived:—Hwanon ys þysum þes wīsdôm and þis mægen?, Mt. 13, 54: 56. (c) origin of a person or thing:—Hwanon eart þū?, Jn. 19, 9. Fullwiht Jôhannes hwonan wæs; of heofonum ðe of monnum?, Mt. R. 21, 25. Hwonan côm se nama ǣrest? *what was the origin of the name?*, Bt. 40, 6; F. 242, 1. (d) the conditions from which a conclusion may be drawn:—Cwæð Zacharias: 'Hwanun wât ic þis?, Lk. 1, 18. Hwanon cûðest ðū mē *unde me nosti?*, Jn. 1, 48. Hwanan sceal mē cūþ beón þ ic mid līchomlicum eágum geseón ne mæg?, Bl. H. 21, 19. Dauid sylf nemde hine drihten and hwanon is hē his sunu?, Mk. 12, 37. (e) the cause or reason for a result:—Hwanun is mē ðis þ nīnes drihtnes môder tô mē cume?, Lk. 1, 43. Hwanon is þes þus strang?, Bl. H. 85, 10. Hwonon wurde þū mid þissum woruld-sorgum þus swīþe geswenced?, Bt. 3, 1; F. 4, 20. **II.** with dependent clauses. (1) cf. **I. 1**:—þū nāst hwanon hē cymþ, ne hwider hē gǣþ, Jn. 3, 8. Frægn heó . . . hwonan his cyme wǣre . . . ' Ic eom . . . tô þē sended of heáhdu,' Jul. 259. Hwanan, B. 257. (1 a) *from what position or state:*—þ Adam understôde . . . hwanon hē āfeólle, Angl. vii. 26, 238. (2 a) cf. **I. 1 a**:—Hig næfdon hwanon hī hyt āguldon, Lk. 7, 42. Gif hwā befô þ him losod wæs, cenne sē þe hē hit æt befô hwanon hit him côme, Ll. Th. i. 288, 16: 22: 388, 21. (2 b) cf. **I. 1 b**:—Wundrigende . . . hwonon him þā gereordo côman, Bl. H. 153, 8. Hwanon, Solil. H. 51, 7. þ hī ongiten hwonan him se wela côme, Bt. 39, 11; F. 230, 18. (2 c) cf. **I. 1 c**:—Wē witon hwanon þes is. Ðonne Crīst cymþ, þonne nât nān mann hwanon hē biþ, Jn. 7, 27: 28: 8, 14: 9, 29, 30. Wæs Jôhannes fulluht of heofone, hwæðer þe of mannum? . . . Ðā swaredon hig þ hig nyston hwanun hē wæs, Lk. 20, 4-7. Ongitan hwæt hié send and hwonan hī send, Bt. 14, 3; F. 46, 5. 'Wâst ðū hwonan ǣlc wuht côme?' 'Ic wât ǣlc wuht fram Gode côm, 5, 3; F. 12, 21. þæt is cûð hwanon þǣm ordfruman ǣdelu onwôcen, An. 683. Hē nyste hwanon hyt (*the wine made from water*) côm, Jn. 2, 9. (2 d) *from what quarter* action should proceed:—þæt ic ongiton mæge hwonan ic þīn tilian scyle (*from what side I am to set about thy care*) and hū *ut, qui modo sit tuae curationis, intelligam*, Bt. 5, 3; F. 10, 34. (2 e) cf. **I. 2 e**:—Nān mon nyste hwonon sió wrôht côm, Ors. 6, 4; S. 260, 19. Gif ðū witan wilt hwonan hȳ cumaþ, þonne miht þū ongitan þ hī cumaþ of woruldgītsunga, Bt. 7, 1; F. 16, 14. Ne mæg ic geþencan hwonon him ǣnig unrôtnes cuman sceolde, 33, 1; F. 122, 8. **III.** as a relative:—Maria gegroeted wæs from Elizabeth . . . huona eftgecierred wæs in hūs hire, Lk. p. 3, 15.

**hwanon-hwega;** *adv.* *Whencesoever:*—Huuananhuuoega (huuonan-), huonanhuegu *undecunque*, Txts. 106, 1095.

**hwænne.** *Add:* **I.** in direct questions:—Hwænne (huoenne, L., hwonne, R.) gesāwe wē þē hingrigendne?, Mt. 25, 37. Huonne L., hwanne, R., 38. Hwǣnne (huoenne, L., hwenne, R.) beóð þās þing?, Lk. 21, 7: Jn. 6, 25. Hwenne gewyrð þæt?, Solil. H. 46, 20. **II.** in dependent clauses. (1) where the time at which the action of the main clause takes place is fixed by the dependent clause:—Hwænne (huonne, L., hwenne, R.) ic bræc fīf hlāfas . . ., and hū fela wyligena gē nāmon fulle?, Mk. 8, 19: 20. Hē sceal winnan and sorgian hwonne se dæg cume . . . būton hē ǣr hwæt for Gode gedyde, Bl. H. 97, 26. (2) after verbs expressing attempt to know, knowing, or causing to know:—þā āhsodon hī hine hwænne (huoenne, L., hwenne, R.) Godes rīce côme, Lk. 17, 20. Wuton cunnian hwænne hine God lǣte, Ps. Th. 70, 10: Sal. 414. Bewitigan hwonne ûp cyme ǣdelast tungla, Ph. 93: 102: 114. Gē nyton hwænne seó tīd ys, Mk. 13, 33. Hwonne, Bl. H. 117, 27: Gen. 2601. Sege ûs hwænne (hoenne, L., hwænne, R.) þās þing gewurðan, Mt. 24, 3: Ors. 4, 10; S. 194, 24: An. 136. Him se reogolweord gebeóde foran tô hwonne sió tīd sié, Cht. E. 81, 13: Ll. Th. i. 160, 12. (3) after verbs expressing desire, expectation with hope or fear, waiting, (to desire, &c.) *the time when:*—Hæleð langode . . . hwonne hié of nearwe stæppan môsten, Gen. 1433. Ic wēne mē . . . hwænne mē Dryhtnes rôd . . . gefetige, Kr. 136. Wit unc simble ondrēdon hwonne wit sceoldon feallan of þām olfende, Shrn. 38, 15. Hié wǣron on þǣre ondrǣdinge hwonne hié on þā eorþan besuncene wurden, Ors. 2, 6; S. 88, 14. Beóð beofigende hwonne . . ., Sat. 622. Menn ne magon gebīdon hwonne hē him tô cume, Bt. 39, 1; F. 212, 2: 8; F. 26, 1: Exod. 250. (3 a) where the verb in the main clause has an object to which the dependent clause is in apposition:—Hine ðæs heardost langode hwanne hē of ðisse worulde môste, Bl. H. 227, 1. Ic þæs fǣres on wēnum sæt, hwonne mē wrāðra sum aldre beheówe, Gen. 2700: 1028. Hē bād sôðra gehāta, hwonne him līfes weard . . . reste āgeáfe, 1426: 2276. Hē wyrde bīdeþ, hwonne God wille þisse worlde ende gewyrīcean, Bl. H. 109, 32. (4) *until:*—Hire þynced lang seó ylding and seó uferung hwænne heó cume tô Gode *the time when she*

*may come to God seems long delayed;* differtur a regno, Gr. D. 245, 7. Him þūhte ǣfre tô lang hwonne hē môste beón ymbe þæs līchaman oferfylle, Wlfst. 236, 11: By. 67. **III.** with indefinite force. (1) *of time, at some time or other, some day:*—Hē nū hwonne bið ārīsende *quandoque resurrecturus*, Bd. 2, 1; Sch. 107, 10: Bl. H. 123, 32. þeáh hī seldum hwonne (*on rare occasions*) beswemde weorþon, Bt. 37, 4; F. 192, 28. (2) in other connections:—Ic wēne nū hwonne þ dysige men willon wundrian *quod quidem cuipiam mirum forte videatur*, Bt. 36, 6; F. 182, 15. Ic wât ðeáh ðū cweþe nū hwonne tô mē: 'Hwylc unryht mæg bión māre . . .?,' 'quae' vero *inquies* 'potest iniquior esse confusio . . .?,' 39, 9; F. 224, 27. **IV.** as co-ordinating relative:—Se forma dæge ðaere dær-stana, ðonne I huoenne eóstro āsægcas *primo die azymorum, quando pascha immolant*, Mk. L. R. 14, 12. Siððan hundtwelftig wintra wræce bisgodon fǣge þeóda; hwonne (*and then*) freá wolde on wǣrlogan wīte settan, Gen. 1265. v. seld-hwnne.

**hwāra (-e).** v. hwǣr: -hwāra. v. æt-, hwæt-hwāra.

**hwarne, hwergene (?);** *adv.* [*Not*] *at all:*—Wæs ne huarne long from him sunes berga *erat non longe ab illis grex porcorum*, Mt. L. 8, 30. v. hwergen, nā-hwern, nā-hwǣr; **III.**

**hwarum,** Hpt. Gl. 434, 12. v. þweorh: **hwast.** *In l. 2 for* 'Som.' *substitute* Wrt. Voc. ii. 55, 72: **hwǣstrian.** v. hwǣstrian: **hwǣstrung.** v. hwǣstrung: **hwat, es;** *n.* *Dele, and see* hwatu: **hwata.** *Dele the passage from* Deut. 18, 10: **hwatend.** *For* 'Lchdm. . . . col. i.' *substitute:*—Hwatend *iris Illyrica*, Wrt. Voc. i. 67, 41: ii. 49, 58.

**hwaþerian, hwoþerian;** *p.* ode To roar:—þ gewealc þāra ȳða hwaðerode mid windum *the tumult of the waves roared, lashed by the winds*, Ap. Th. 11, 2. Drihten côm gangende on ðære sǣ; þā ȳða ārison, ac hē hī oftræd; se brym hwoðerode under his fôtswaðum (*the sea roared beneath his footsteps*) ac swā ðeáh hē hine bær, wolde hē nolde hē, Hml. Th. ii. 388, 19. See next word.

**hwaþerung, hwoþrung, e;** *f.* A (*hoarse*) *sound:*—Ic (*a file*) gyrre mid hāsre hwoðrunge *garrio rauco cum murmure* (*stridens*), An. Ox. 26, 14. See preceding word.

**hwatu, e;** *f.* An *augury, omen:*—Hwata omina, Wrt. Voc. ii. 65, 12. Ne gȳman gē galdra ne īdelra hwata, Wlfst. 40, 14. Warna þē þæt þū ne gīme drȳcræfta ne swefena ne hwatena *nec inveniatur in te qui ariolos sciscitetur et observet somnia atque auguria*, Deut. 18, 10. [þ is liðer custume þ man leueð get, and þ is . . . hwate, and fele swilche deueles craftes, O. E. Hml. ii. 11, 13; Werpeð þ gilt . . . uppen hwate, and seið: 'Nahte ich no betere wate, 105, 24-28. Alas! þe luþur wate (desteny, *v. l.*), R. Glouc. 34, 16.]

**hwealf, e;** *f.* Dele last passage, and add:—H[w]alf clima (climas partes celi ad superna conuexas uocamus, Ld. Gl. H. s.v. clima), Wrt. Voc. ii. 104, 20. Hwealfe *climatis*, hwealfum *climatibus*, 23, 52, 53. *See next word.*

**hwealf;** *adj.* *Add:*—Hualb, halb, hualf *convexum*, Txts. 46, 179. þæs hwalfan *divexi*, Wrt. Voc. ii. 27, 45. Ðā hwalfan *convexa*, 20, 59.

**hwealfian.** *Dele, and see* hwilfan.

**hweall, hwall;** *adj.* *Wanton:*—Huuæl procax, Wrt. Voc. ii. 117, 70. Hwal ymbclypte (*quem nefandis ulnarum gremiis*) procax obun-cabat, 81, 11. Hwalie *procaci* (*voce*; the laughter of Ham), 96, 55. [O. H. Ger. hwell *procax*; hwellī procacia.]

**hwearf** *a troop.* *Add:*—Beorg ymbstôdan hwearfum wrǣcmæcgas (cf. thin menigī stôd aftar themu hôe hwarbôn, Hēl. 5180), Gū. 234. [Hē þer wærf makede he made an assembly there (cf. obarmôdie man (*the chief priests and Pharisees.* v. Jn. 11, 57) an irô hwarþe gisprākun (cf. colligerunt concilium, Jn. 11, 47), Hēl. 4172), Laym. 17485. (Wace has 'feste tint')]. v. fêþe-hwearf.

**hwearf.** [*The word is neuter in the two instances given in the (late) charter*]. *Add:*—Nô man ne worðe suuā dirsty ðat ðis ilk whari (*commutationem*) and ðis ilk forward breke, C. D. iv. 242, 29. [þus is þis eitlond igon from honde to hond þet alle þa burhȝes þe Brutus iwrohte . . . beoð swiðe afelled þurh warf of þon folke, Laym. 2070.] v. be-hwearf.

**hwearf** *a wharf.* *Add:*—Ic wille ðat sainte Petre and ðā gebrôðera in Westminstre habben ðat land and ðone wearf ðe Ulf and his wīf . . . gāfon, . . . and ic ann alswā ðat hī habben fulne frīdôm on allen þingen ðā ðær ûp āspringeð be lande and be strande, C. D. iv. 221.

**hwearf;** *adj.* Dele. *For* and hwearf *l.* andhwearf, *pp. of* andhweorfan *to oppose.*

**hwearfian.** *Add:* **I.** *to turn* on a hinge, pivot, axle, &c. (lit. or fig.):—Seó hior ðe ealle gôd on hwearfaþ, Bt. 34, 7; F. 142, 35. Eall ðiós hwearfiende gesceaft hwearfaþ on ðām stillan Gode, 39, 6; F. 220, 24. Sió sāul sceolde hwearfian on hire selfre, swā swā eall þes rodor hwerfþ, oðóe swā swā hweól onhwerfþ, 33. 4; F. 132, 11. **II.** *to revolve* round a centre, *move round* in an orbit. (1) of a material body:—Ðā tunglu lengestne ymbhwyrft habbaþ þe ymb þā eaxe middewearde hwearfaþ swā nū Boeties deþ, 32, 3; F. 214, 24. Eall tungla hwerfiað on þām ylcan wīsan, Solil. H. 9, 23. (2) of the revolution of the seasons:—Ðū recst þæt geár þurh þæt gewrixle þāra

feówer týda ... þára wrixlað ælc wyð óððer and hwerfiað swá þæt heora ǽgðer byð eft emne þat þæt hyt ǽr wæs, Solil. H. 9, 20. (3) of processes that may be said to move in a circle:—Hwerfiað on þám ylcan wîsan sê and eá (cf. of ðáre sǽ cymþ þ wæter innon þá eorþan ... wyrþ tó eá ... wyrþ eft tó sǽ, Bt. 34, 6; F. 140, 17-20), Solil. H. 9, 23. (4) of change, where similar objects succeed one another:—On ðám ylcan wîsan hweorfiað ealle gescæafta, Solil. H. 9, 24. III. *to change* :—Hû meahtes þú bión on midre þisse hwearfunga þ þú eác mid ne hwearfode?, Bt. 7, 3; S. 18, 28. IV. *to wander about, be tossed about* on sea :—Hwerfigo *versor* (in delictorum fluctibus *versor*, Ald. 81, 15), Wrt. Voc. ii. 88, 47. Swá oft swá hé wæs hwearfiende mid þám ilcan scipe *quoties cum eodem fuisset carabo versatus*, Gr. D. 347, 20. Geond þis wéste hreafigende (hwearfigende?), Hml. S. 23 b, 544. [Gief hie wunienge hwareíed, hie turned fram iuele to werse, O. E. Hml. ii. 173, 20. Winess drinnch þe wharrfeþþ all þin herrte, Orm. 14121. Crist hise name shollde wharrfenn, 13289. Win þatt wass off water wharrfedd, 15323. All þiss middellærdess þing turrneþþ her and wharrfeþþ ... swa summ þe wheol, 3641. v. un-hwearfiende.

-hwearfness. v. ge-hwearfness: hwearft. *Add* : v. be-hwearft.

hwearftlian. *Add: to wander about, be tossed about* on the sea :—Hwearftlige *versor* (v. hwearfian; IV.), An. Ox. 2, 500. Ic hwearwlie (= hwearftlie) *er*[*r*]*o*, 23, 57. Hwearft (= hwearftlað) *errat*, 26, 37.

-hweg. v. æt-, hwæt- (*under* hwæt-hwega) -hweg.

hwega. *Add* : I. as substantive with gen., *somewhat*, v. hwæthwega; I. 2 b, hwilc-hwéga; II. 2 :—Lytles hwega for þæs lîchaman nédbehǽfednyssum mid him hæbbende, Hml. S. 23 b, 150. II. as adverb, *about*. v. hwæt-hwega; III. :—Neáh (hugu, hûhugu, *v. ll.*) on twégra mîla fæce *duum ferme milium spatio separata*, Bd. 5, 4; Sch. 567, 11. v. ælc-, æt-, for-, hwǽr-, hwanon-, hwidor-, swilc-, tó-hwega.

-hweganinga (-unga), -hweganunges, -hwegno. v. hwæthweganinga, hwæt-hweganunges, hwæt-, hwilc-hwoegno: hwegl. v. hweogol: hwelan: hwylan. *Dele* hwylan.

hwelca, hwylca, an; *m.* *An inflamed swelling, a pustule* :—Cwydele *vel* hwylca *varix*, Wrt. Voc. i. 45, 32. [*Prompt. Parv.* whelke, soore *pustula* : *Wck.* whelk *pustula* : *Chauc.* whelkes white (on a ' fyr-reed face'), *D.D.* whelk, whilk *sty, pimple*.] v. hwelian; cwidele; swelca.

hwele. *Dele.*

hwelian. *For* ' Lchdm. ... col. 1' *substitute* Sciut. 76, 19 *and add* : *to waste away, pine* :—Mænige andan mid wunde hweliað *multi inuidiæ liuore tabescunt*, Scint. 77. 2. Be oþres fremum þu ná hwela *de alterius profectibus non tabescas*, 8.

hwelp. *Add* : , hwelpa, an; *m.* :—On hwelpes dell, C. D. B. ii. 246, 7. Gyf þú on foreweardon sumera þigest hwylcne hwelpan þonne gýt ungeseóndne, Lch. i. 368, 26. Gif þú wille þ wíf cild hæbbe, oþþe tife hwelp, ii. 172, 21 : Rä. 1, 16. Huoelpas (welpas, R.), Mt. L. 15, 27. Beran ongeányrnan gegripenum hwealpum *urso occurrere raptis foetibus*, Scint. 95, 5. Hwelpum, Kent. Gl. 607.

hwelung. *For* ' Hwelung ... Lye ' *substitute* :—On hwelunge in *clangore*, Wrt. Voc. ii. 46, 16.

hwem. *Add* : I. *a corner* of a building :—Godes engel fleáh geond ðá feówer hwemmas þæs temples and ágróf mid his fingre róde tácn on þám fyderscýtum stánum, Hml. Th. i. 466, 13. II. *a corner* of the earth (north, &c.) :—Drihten wæs gefæstnod mid feówer nægelum tó westdǽle áwend, and his wynstra heóld ðone scýnendan súðdǽl, and his swiðra norððǽl, eástdǽl his hnol ; and hé ealle álýsde middaneardes hwemmas swá hangiende, Hml. Th. ii. 256, 3.

hwemman. *Add* : v. ge-hwemman.

hwéne. *Add* : I. Almost always with comparatives. (1) with adj. :—Syxtig mîla brád, oþþe hwéne brádre, Ors. 1, 1 ; S. 18, 31. Sió lyft bioþ hwéne hnescran gecynde, Bt. 34, 11 ; F. 150, 27. (2) with adv. :—Þæt is tó herianne hwéne rihtlícor, Bt. 14, 3 ; F. 46, 13. Hwéne æfter hé cuið, Past. 99, 14. Hwéne æfter þon hé cwæð, Bd. 1, 27 ; Sch. 86, 2. II. with verb (ptcpl.) :—Hwéne *pusillum* (progressus inde *pusillum* (hwón, W.S., lytel hwón, R., L.), Mk. 1, 19), An. Ox. 61, 48.

hweogol. *Add* : , hweogola (?), an ; *m.* I. *a wheel* (1)of any kind :—Ǽlc gesceaft hwearfað on hire selfre swá swá wheól, Bt. 25 ; F. 88, 33. Hweowlu *rotas*, Germ. 392, 54. (2) of a vehicle :—On wænes eaxe hwearfiað þá hweól and sió eax stent stille ... þ hweól hwerft ymbúton, Bt. 39, 7 ; F. 220, 27-29. Sum cild ... bearn under ánum yrnendum hweóle, and weard tó deáðe tócwýsed, Hml. Th. ii. 26, 25. (3) a fixed wheel as (part of) a machine :—Wǽg þænne wé mid hlædele, hlædtrendle (hweowla, hweowl; hweowlan, Hpt. Gl. 418, 32) úp hladan *limpham, quam anthlia, hoc est, rota hauritoria exanthlamus*, An. Ox. 502. Hét se cásere gebindan Georium on ánum brádum hweowle ... Hé weard gebroht on þám hweowle, þá tyrndon þá hǽðenan hetelíce þ hweowl, and hit sóna tóbærst, Hml. S. 14, 85-94. (4) *the wheel* of Fortune :—Gif þú þé selfne tó anwealde þám woruldsælþum gesealdest ... Wénst þú þ ðú þ hwerfende hweól þonne hit on ryne wyrþ mæge oncyrran ? *fortunae e regendum dedisti ... Tu vero volventis rotae impetum retinere con-*

*aris ?*, Bt. 7, 2 ; F. 18, 35. II. *a circular band* :—Hé sǽde þ þá Drihtnes fótlástas wǽron beworht mid ærne hweóle and þæs heánes wǽre oð monnes swýran, and þ þér wǽre ðyrel on middum þám hweóle (cf. Is þér geworht emb þá lástas útan hwéne wiððre þonne bydenfæt úp oþ mannes breóst heáh ; wæs þ ǽreste of grénum áre geworht ; ... is on westan medmycel duru, Bl. H. 127, 5-8), Shrn. 81, 11-14. III. *a circle* or *cycle used in computation* :—Gým þisses hweóles, hyt þé ætýwþ genóh openlíce þæs mónan ryne, Angl. viii. 328, 33. v. hlæd-, mylen-, sceard-(?) hweogol.

-hweóle. v. twi-hweóle: hweóled. v. feówer-hweohlode, heáh-hweólad.

hweól-fág. *For second line substitute* :—Hwiólfáge *cyclade*, Wrt. Voc. ii. 20, 33.

hweól-godwebb, es ; *n.* *A robe of fine material circular in form* :—Hweglgodwebbum *cycladibus*, Wrt. Voc. ii. 24, 15.

hweól-lást, es ; *m.* *The track left by a wheel*, fig. *an orbit, a circuit* :—Geáres hweóllást *anni orbita*, Hy. S. 93, 33.

hweól-rád, e ; *f.* *A wheel-road, rut* ; fig. *an orbit* :—Huueólrád, hueólrád, -raat *orbita*, Txts. 82, 710. Hweoglrád, Wrt. Voc. ii. 63, 52.

hweól-rîþig, es ; *n.* *A brook that turns a wheel ?* :—Of ðám forda andlang hweowelrîðiges, ... eft on hweowelrîðig, C. D. iii. 289, 4-7. On hweólrîðig, 381, 8.

hweól-weg, es ; *m.* *A cart-road* :—On hweogelweg, C. D. iii. 386, 4. hweop. *Dele.*

hweorf *the whorl of a spindle* :—Huerb *vertil* (*þrinted* ventil), Wrt. Voc. ii. 123, 39. v. hweorfa ; II.

-hweorf. v. ge-hweorf.

hweorfa. *Add* : I. *a joint, vertebra*. v. hweorf-bán :—Þá hweorfan and ðá cneó *popliies et genua*, Lch. i. lxxiv, 20. II. *the whorl of a spindle*. v. hweorf :—Hwyorfa *vertigo* (among words connected with spinning), Wrt. Voc. i. 59, 23. ¶ Here probably belong the two glosses :—Hweorfan *molam*, Wrt. Voc. ii. 94, 1 : 57, 13. *The passage glossed is* : Si parcae ... mortale vitae fusaque rotante minantur, quod vehet in collo tereti vertigine molem, Ald. 175, 35. To vertigine, *not to* molem (*wrongly written* molam) *must belong the gloss*, hweorfan.

-hweorfa (-e). v. sigel-hweorfa (-e).

hweorfan. *Add* : *p.* hwearf, *pl.* hwurfon, hweorfon ; *pp.* hworfen. I. where there is motion from one place to another. (1) *to move about, wander* :—Þá gástas þe for Gode hweorfað, Gn. C. 59. Londrihtes mót monna æghwylc îdel hweorfan, B. 2888. Holt hweorfende, Rä. 57, 3. Hweorfende *spatiantes*, Wrt. Voc. ii. 83, 74. (1 a) fig. of non-material objects :—Mîn hyge hweorfeð ofer hreðerlocan, mîn módsefa ... hweorfeð wîde, Seef. 58-60. (2) where the point to or from which motion is directed is marked. (a) of living creatures :—Hwiðer hweorfað wé (*whither shall we turn*) ... gif wé swîcað þé ?, An. 405. Hwearf hé tó healle swá hé hraðost meahte, Az. 166 : Sat. 190. Hwurfon hæleð geonge tó þám hǽðenan foran, Dan. 434. Hé wæs miclum geswenced ǽr hé þanon hwurfe, Chr. 982 ; P. 124, 29. Þú scealt hweorfan of earde þînum, Gen. 1018 : Wal. 81. Hweorfan tó þis enge lond, Cri. 31. Þider hweorfan, Dan. 203. ¶ with reflexive dative :—Hé him siþþan hwearf tó Róme *postea quam Romam venit*, Ors. 5, 12 ; S. 242, 27. (b) of an inanimate object :—Þæt fýr scýde tó þám þe þá scylde worhton, hwearf (hweorf, MS.) on þá hǽðenan hæftas fram þam hálgum cnihton, Dan. 267. (2 a) where the point to which is that from which motion originally took place, *to return, go back* :—Gǽstas hweorfað in bánfatu, Ph. 519. Hé siþþan hwearf hámweard tó Babylonia *post Babyloniam rediit*, Ors. 3, 9 ; S. 136, 3. Paulinus huerf eft tó Cantwarum (hwearf eft tó Cent *rediit Cantiam*, Bd. 2, 20 ; Sch. 186, 24), Chr. 633 ; P. 24, 20. Þá hwearf sé ána in tó him *rediit ipse solus*, Bd. 4, 3 ; Sch. 357, 21 : 5, 19 ; Sch. 660, 22. His geféran hwurfan tó cyricean *sociis ad ecclesiam reuersis*, 4, 3 ; Sch. 352, 14. Hwurfon wîf on willan þ *the women returned with delight*, An. 2086. Gé nú eft hweorfað (hwurfað, *v. l.*) and biddað *reuertentes dicite*, Bd. 4, 3 ; Sch. 357, 8. Þonne hé eft tó his éðle hweorfan (hwurfan, *v. l.*) wolde *cum patriam reuerteretur*, 5, 19; Sch. 659, 23. Wæs Maria eft hweorfende tó hire húse, Bl. H. 139, 3. (3) where the space through which or into which, or the line along which, motion is directed is given :—Mægen monna cynnes hweorfað on wîdne lég, Cri. 958 : Gú. 784. Hwearf heó bî bence, B. 1188. Hæleða bearn sculon on þæt líg tó þé hweorfan, Gen. 754 : Sat. 419. ¶ with reflex. dat. :—Wand hé him úp þanon, hwearf him þurh þá helldora, Gen. 447. (4) of the passage to the next world :—Gástas hweorfon, sóhton swegles dreámas, An. 640. II. of the course of events, *to proceed* :—Gif seó wyrd swá hweorfan mót on yfelra manna gewill, Bt. 4 ; F. 8, 18. III. *to turn*. (1) of persons, *to direct the mind* to or from a person or subject :—Búton se mon hweorfe tó góde, Bt. 31, 2 ; F. 112, 28. Létaþ hine eft hweorfan tó mínum lárum, 3, 1 ; F. 4, 24. (2) of things, *to pass* to or from the possession of a person :—Þonne þá þing hwám from hweorfende beóð, hé hí sceal mid þám mǽstan sáre his módes forlǽtan ... And hý þé willaþ on murcnunga gebringan þonne hié þé fram hweorfaþ, Bt. 7, 2 ; F. 18, 16-20. IV. *to change* (intrans. and trans.) :—Swá

hit oft gesǽleð on þǽm sélran þingum þæt seó wyrd and sió hiów hié oft oncyrreð and on óþer hworfeð *ut aliquid plerumque in secundis rebus fortuna obstrepit*, Nar. 7, 28. Hiǽ weorfaþ heóra andwliotu, Mt. R. 6. 16. Se móna is ǽfre se ylca þeáh ðe his leóht gelómlíce hweorfe, Lch. iii. 242, 16. Hweorfende *versicolor* (*versiculos*, MS. but the passage is : *Versicolor* penna pavonis, Ald. 142, 22), Wrt. Voc. ii. 89, 59. v. and- (B. 548), est-, for-, ymb-hweorfan ; sin-hweorfende ; mis-, níw-hworfen.

**hweorf-bán.** *Add:*—Hwiorfbán *poplites*, Lch. i. lxxi, 11. v. hweorfa [?].

**hweorfness.** v. ymb-hweorfness : **hweoðerian.** *Dele, and see* hwaþerian : **hweoðerung.** *Dele, and see* hwaþerung.

**hwer.** *Add:*—Huuer, huer *lebes*, Txts. 72, 563. Hwer (hwyr, *v l.*), Ælfc. Gr. Z. 316, 5. Hweres ł cyteles *sartaginis*, Hpt. Gl. 503, 34. Hwer, þollan *sartaginem*, An. Ox. 4115. Man sceal habban . . . hwer, leád, cytel, hlǽdel, pannan, crocca, dixas, Angl. ix. 264, 9. Hét hé feccan ǽnne ǽrene hwer, and hine ealne áfyllan mid weallendum leáde and lecgan Georium innon ðone hwer, Hml. S. 14, 104–107 : 25, 117. Hwerum *caccabis*, Wrt. Voc. ii. 95, 62 : 19, 71. Hweras *lebetes*, An. Ox. 4670 : Wrt. Voc. ii. 50, 60. v. crocc-hwer.

**hwerfan.** v. hwirfan : **hwerfel.** v. hwurful : **hwerfere.** *l.* hwirfere : **hwerf-lic.** *l.* hwirf-lic : **hwerflung.** v. hwirflung : **hwerfung.** v. hwirflung : **hwergen.** *Add:* v. á-hwergen ; ná-hwǽrn.

**hwer-hwette.** *Add:*—Hwæerhwætte *cucumeris*, Wrt. Voc. i. 67, 11.

**hwésan.** *Dele, and see* hwósan : **hwet.** v. hwæt.

**hwet-stán.** *Add:*, **hwete-stán:**—Huetistán (huete-) *cox*, Txts. 54, 294. Hwetstán *cox*, hwetestán *cotem*, Wrt. Voc. ii. 15, 4, 5. Lytel hwetstán *coticulus* vel *coticula*, 135, 37. Hwettstán *cotem*, An. Ox. 56, 21. Mon heardlíce gníde þone hnescestan mealmstán æfter þǽm þ hé þence þone soelestan hwetstán on tó geræceanne, Ors. 4, 13 ; S. 212, 29.

**hwettan.** *Substitute:* To whet, sharpen:—Ic hwette (hwætte, *v. l.*) *acuo*, Ælfc. Gr. Z. 167, 1. **I.** *to sharpen the edge of* an implement (*lit. or fig.*):—Se lǽce hýt his seax and hwett (hwæt, *v. l.*), Past. 166, 6. Þá undeádlican wyrmas hwettað hyra téð tó þon þ hig . . . fírne líchoman slítan, Ll. Th. ii. 396, 6. Hí hwetton tungan heora *acuerunt linguam suam*, Ps. Spl. 139, 3. ¶ hwett stán *a stone used for whetting* (?):—Tó hwettan stánes wylle ; of hwættan stánes wylle, C. D. iii. 430, 11. **II.** *to make a person keen* (hwæt), *incite, excite, egg on.* (1) absolute:—Swá þin sefa hwette, B. 490. (2) with acc. :—Þonne wín hweteð beornes breóstsefan, Mód. 18. Oðer gást hine tyhteð . . . ýweð him earmra manna misgemynda and þurh þæt his mód hweteð, Sal. 495. Þone síðfæt him snotere ceorlas lythwón lógon, hwetton higerófne, B. 204. (2 a) where the course or action to which a person is incited is given:—Ic dysge dwelle and dole hwette [on] unrǽdsíðas, óðrum stýre nyttre fóre *I silly ones lead astray and stupid ones egg on to ill-advised ways, others keep back from profitable proceeding*, Rä. 12, 3. Úsic lust hweteð on þá leódmearce, micel módes hiht tó þǽre mǽran byrig, An. 286. Hweteð on [h]wælweg, Seef. 63. Ic hig hwette tó fleánne, Shrn. 41, 25. [He whæite his særes, Laym. 14215. He wette his tossches, S. S. 911. O. H. Ger. wezzen *acuere, exacuere, provocare : Icel.* hvetja *to whet, incite.*] v. á-, ge-hwettan.

**Hwiccas.** *Add:*—In ðǽre stówe ðe man gýt nemneð Agustinus aac, in Myrcna (Hwicna, *v. l.*) gemǽre and Westseaxna (*in confinio Huicciorum et occidentalium Saxonum*), Bd. 2, 2 ; Sch. 113, 4. In Hwiccia mǽgþe. 4, 23 ; Sch. 470, 14. Wilfrid is Hwiccia biscop, 5, 23 ; Sch. 690, 16. ¶ Perhaps the word is used in a limited and in a wider sense. In a list of territorial names in one group occurs the following :—Hicca (Wicca, 416, 7, a Latin form of the list) landes is þrý hund hýda. The next group begins :—Hwinca (= Hwicna ?) landes is syfan þusend hýda, Cilternsǽtna feówer þusend hýda, C. D. B. i. 414, 22–25. The suggestion may receive some support from the forms, Hec-, Hwicc-, used by Florence when speaking of the Magesǽte. v. Chr. P. ii. p. 197.

**hwicce, hwice** (?), an ; *f. a box, chest:*—Huice *tria* (tria *columbarium species*, Migne), Wrt. Voc. ii. 122, 76. Hwicce *clustella* (ut doctor verbi *claustella* resolvat, Ald. 138, 23), An. Ox. 18 b, 11. ¶ as part of a local name :—In loco ubi ruricoli nominantur Huiccewudu, C. D. ii. 10, 5. [Til . . . Perneles porfyl be put in heore whucche, Piers P. A. 4, 102. Alle woned in þe whichche (*the ark*), Allit. Pms. 49, 362. Whyche *cista, archa*, Prompt. 242. Make a luytel whucche forte do in þ blod, Jos. 39.] v. corn-hwicce ; hwæcce.

**hwice.** *See preceding word.*

**hwicung, e ;** *f. Squeaking :*—Se ealda feónd ongan onhyrgian . . . swína grunnunge and músa hwicunge (*stridores soricum*), Gr. D. 185, 4. [*v. D. D.* weak *to squeak.*]

**hwida,** Hpt. Gl. 430, 67. v. hwítel.

**hwider.** *Add:* **I.** in direct questions. (1) *to what place ?:*—Hwider fundast þú síðas dreógan ?, Gen. 2269 : An. 405 : Cri. 1691. Hwyder (hwidder, L.) wylt þú þ wé faron, Mk. 14, 11. Huidir, þn. L. 16, 5. (1 a) with emphatic genitive :—Hwider mæg ic þinne andwlitan befleón eorðan dǽles ? *a facie tua quo fugiam ?*, Ps. Th. 138, 5. (2) *to*

---

*what state ?:*—Hwyder gewiton þá welan and þá ídlan blissa ? hwyder gewiton þá mycclan weorod þe him ymb stódan ?, Bl. H. 99, 23–25. **II.** in dependent clauses. (1) *after verbs of asking, finding out, knowing, considering.* (a) with local force :—Eówer nán ne áhsað mé hwyder ic fare, Jn. 16, 5. Hié sendon hlot him betweónum hwider hyra gehwylc faran sceolde, Bl. H. 229, 5. Ic wát hwyder (huidder, L., hwider, R.) ic gá, Jn. 8, 14 : 14, 5 : Gn. C. 58 : B. 163. (a a) where the place is marked by condition existing in it :—Tó þencenne . . . hwyder hé gelǽded sý, þe tó wíte, þe tó wuldre, Bl. H. 97, 22. (b) of the operations of the mind :—' Hwæðer ðú nú ongite hwider þiós sprǽce wille?' Ða cwæþ ic : 'Sege mé hwider hió wille', Bt. 40, 1 ; F. 234, 32–33. Oð þæt hé cunne hwider hreðre gehygd hweorfan wille, Wand. 72. (2) as relative adverb :—Ðú waldes geonga huidir (hwider, R., þǽr, W. S. *ubi*) ðú waldes . . . óðer ðec lǽdes hiddir ðiddir (dider, R., W. S. *quo*) ðú nuilt, Jn. L. 21, 18. **III.** indefinite, *to some place or other* :—Sé ðe hwider faran wille singe his paternoster, Hml. S. 17, 96. Elles hwider *aliorsum*, Ælfc. Gr. Z. 225, 10. Elles hwyder ofer þ (ne) *aliorsum ulterius (progredi valentes)*, An. Ox. 3781 : Wrt. Voc. ii. 83, 35. **IV.** combined with swá, whithersoever. (1) swá hwider swá :—Ærendian swá hwyder swá him mon tó tǽcð *in nuncium ire quocunque dicetur ei*, Ll. Th. i. 432, 18 : Lk. 9, 57. Hé þurhférde eall Breotone eálond swá hwyder ymb swá (swá hwyder swá ymb, *v. l.*) Angelðeóde on drohtedon *peragrata insula tota quaquauersum Anglorum gentes morabantur*, Bd. 4, 2 ; Sch. 343, 22. Hé swá hwider ymb swá hé beden wæs férde *ubicumque rogabatur diuertens*, 4, 12 ; Sch. 412, 1. (2) swá hwider :—Ic fylgo ðec suá huider ðú færes *sequor te quocunque ieris*, Mt. L. 8, 19. Suæ huiddir, Lk. L. 9, 57. (3) hwider swá :—Ic wille folgian þé hwider swá þú ganges, Mt. R. 8, 19. v. ǽg-, ge-, ná-hwider ; hwidere.

**hwidere, hwidre ;** *adv. Whither :*—Ac ðǽr ðú ongeáte hwidre ic þe nú teohhie tó lǽdanne, Bt. 22, 2 ; F. 78, 1. Cf. hidere.

**hwider-hwega ;** *adv. Somewhither :*—Gange hé him út hwiderhwega sume hwíle, Lch. ii. 182, 11.

**hwider-ryne ;** *adj. Of what country :*—Huidirryne *cujatis*, Txts. 115, 130.

**hwidre.** v. hwidere : **hwien.** v. hwítel.

**hwifer** (?) ; *adj. Quaking, quivering, shaking.* Perhaps this adjective may be inferred from the following words in Suffolk names :—Tó hwifermirsce, C. D. iii. 275, 1. Wifærmyrsc, 273, 26. Tó hwifrǽme-[ra, *v.* C. D. B. iii. 603, 40], 275, 12. Ic gǽan þæs landes æt hwifersce, 272, 16. [*v. D. D.* wiver, whiver, *to shake, quiver ; wivery : hivering, quaking.*]

**hwíl.** *Add :* **I.** *an indefinite space of time :*—Næs þá nán hwíl tó þám þæt . . . *nec mora* . . ., Guth. Gr. 139, 3. Næs þá nǽnig hwíl tó þan sóna swá hí út eódon, þá geségon hí þone hræm *nec mora, egredientes conspiciunt corvum*, 144, 15 : 145, 23. Næs þá nǽnig hwíl tó þan sóna swá hé wæs mid þám gyrdele begyrd *confestim ut se cingulo illius succinxit*, 148, 7 : 154, 22. On ðǽre gǽlinge ðe hé ðá hwíle ámierreð, Past. 39, 1. Uncúð bið ǽghwylcum ánum men . . . hwilce hwíle hine wille Drihten hér on worlde lǽtan, Bl. H. 125, 9. ¶ in oblique cases, alone or with other words, with adverbial force. (1) acc. (a) alone :—Ne racentégum hwíle (*jam*) ǽnig mon hine mǽhte gibinda, Mk. R. L. 5, 3. Ic hwíle wæs Heodeninga scop, Deór. 36. (b) with an adverb :—Þá þe hwíle ǽr edwít þoledon, Jud. 214. Þá wítu ðe ic nú hwíle (*now for a time, already*) þolode, Solil. H. 12, 4. (c) with a qualifying word (a) pronominal (demonst. or indef.) :—Þá hwíle *donec*, i. *dum*, Wülck. Gl. 251, 9 : *dum*, 21. Heora nǽnig þá bǽre þá hwíle (*the while, meanwhile*) áhóf, Bl. H. 153, 3. Ic nát hú nyt ic þá hwíle beó þe ic þás word sprece, Ors. 4, 13 ; S. 212, 26. His ríce hé heardlíce werode þá hwíle (hwíla, *v. l.*) þe his tíma wæs, Chr. 1016 ; P. 149, 2. Sume hwíle *paulisper*, An. Ox. 4740. Næs ic nǽfre gít náne hwíle swá emnes módes, Bt. 26, 1 ; F. 90, 25. Monige hwíle bið þám men full wá, Gen. 634. Oðer hwíle *aliquando*, Lk. L. R. 22, 32. Óþre hwíle bið tó tǽlenne, óþre hwíle hit bið tó heriganne *nunc splendorem accipit, nunc amittit*, Bt. 27, 4 ; F. 100, 18. (β) adjective :—Hé lange hwíle on þám gebede wæs, Bl. H. 217, 28. Lytle huíle (*modicum tempus*) mið iúh am, Jn. L. 7, 33 : Past. 333, 15. (2) in prepositional phrases :—Hú hrædlíce se fǽrlica deáð hié on lytelre hwíle bereáfode ðæs þe hié on longre hwíle mid unryhte striéndon *quibus festina mors repente et simul abstulit quidquid eorum nequitia nec simul nec repente congregavit*, Past. 332, 16. Hé heom on ealre hwíle metes tilian sceolde, Hml. S. 23, 219. Tó hwíl (*ad tempus*) geléfað, Lk. L. 8, 13. Þá wæs ymb hwíle ðá gefelde hé . . ., Bl. H. 217, 30. **II.** (with constructions as in I) *an hour* ; hora. (1) as a definite space of time :—Ðás hlætmesto án tíd ł huíl (*una hora*) worohton, Mt. L. 20, 12. Ne mæhtest áne hwíle (huíle, L.) áwæccan ?, Mt. R. 26, 40. (2) as a subdivision of the day :—From þǽre syxta hwíle . . . oþ þe nigoþan hwíle. Æt þǽre nigoþan tíd (huíl, L.), Mt. R. 27, 45–46. (3) *the time of day* :—Tíd ł hwíl (*tíma*, W. S.) forð gewát *hora praeteriit*, Mt. R. L. 14, 15. (4) *the time* of an event :—Tó neálíceþ hwíl (ðíu huíl ł tíd, L.) *appropinquavit hora*, Mt. R. 26, 45. On þǽre hwíle cwæð se Hælend,

55. Be ðǽm dæge and þára hwíle nǽnig wát, 24, 36. Tíd ɫ huíl (hwȳl, R.), Mk. L. 13, 32. v. beorht-, brac-, niht-, preówt-hwíl.

**hwilc.** *Add*: I. in direct questions (1) as adjective (a) qualifying a noun, *what* :—Hwylc man is þ mǽge áríman ealle þá sár?, Bl. H. 59, 33. Hwelc gesceádwís mon mihte cweþan þæt . . .? *quis putet* . . .?, Bt. 28; F. 100, 30. On hwylcre mihte wyrcsð þú þás þing? *in qua potestate haec facis?*, Mt. 21, 23. Hwelce twá synd wiþerweardran betwuh him þonne gód and yfel?, Bt. 16, 3; F. 56, 6. For hwilcum (hwylcum, *v. l.*) óþrum ðingum woldest ðú þ sprecan? 38, 3; F. 200, 10. (b) where the noun is not expressed :—'Heald þá beboda.' (Ðá cwæð hé: 'Hwylce (huelca, L., hwælc. R.'?) '*serva mandata.*' *Dicit*: '*Quae*'?, Mt. 19, 18. (c) as predicate :—Hwylc bið hé þonne búton swylce stán?, Bl. H. 21, 26. Hwilc beóð þá lytlan godas on tó gelýfenne nú þá fyrmestan godas swá fúllíce leofodon?, Hml. S. 35, 117. Huelcne (huat, R.) cueðas menu sié sunu homnes? *quem dicunt homines esse Filium hominis*, Mt. L. 16, 13. (2) as substantive, (a) *who* :—Hwylc (cf. hwá, Mt. W. S., L., R. 3, 7) æteówde eów tó fleónne?, Bl. H. 169, 9. Hwelc (hwá, W.S., R. *quis*) wénes ðú maast is?, Mt. L. 18, 1. (b) *which* of many :—Hwylc (hwilc, R., hualc, L.) eówer mæg geþencan . . .? *quis vestrum cogitans* . . .?, Mt. 6, 27. Hwelc úre mæg áreccan . . .?, Bt. 34, 10; F. 150, 11. Hwylc is of ús þ hæbbe swá hwíte sáule . . .?, Bl. H. 147, 18. II. in an interjectional clause, *what* (*excessive*), cf. hwá; II :—Gif gé gesáwen hwelce mús þæt wǽre hláford ofer óþre mýs, and sette him dómas . . . hú wunderlíc wolde eów þæt þincan, hwelce cehhettunge gé woldon þæs habban, and mid hwelcum hleahtre gé beón ástyred (*quanto moveris cachinno!*), Bt. 16, 2; F. 52, 4. III. in dependent clauses. (1) as adjective (a) qualifying a noun, *what, what sort of* :—Þǽr ðú gemunan woldest hwylcra gebyrda þú wǽre and hwylcra burgwara for worulde, oþþe eft gástlíce hwilces gefērscipes ðú wǽre on dínum móde, Bt. 5, 1; F. 10, 3-5. Þonne secge ic eów on hwylcum (wilce, R.) anwealde (*in qua potestate*) ic þás þing wyrce, Mt. 21, 24. Gé nyton on hwylcre tíde eówer hláford cuman wyle, 24, 42. Ongitan hwylce men bióþ underþíed þǽre wyrde, hwylce ne bióþ, Bt. 39, 6; F. 220, 22. Hí witon on hwelcum wæterum hí sculun sēcan fiscas *norunt* . . . *necnon quae tenero pisce praesentent litora*, 33, 3; 118, 18. Nú þú wást hwelce þeáwas þá woruldsǽlþa habbaþ, 7, 2; F. 18, 5. (a a) where a high degree in the quality of the noun is implied. Cf. (b a) :—Mé þynceþ wundor mid hwylcne byldo þú sceole beforan cininge gylpan, Bl. H. 175, 31. (b) as predicate, *of what sort* :—Hé wiste hwæt and hwylc (húlic, L.) þis wíf wǽre *sciret quae et qualis mulier esset*, Lk. 7, 39. Ic þé wille secgan hwelc se lǽcecræft is . . . Hé is swíðe biter on múþe and hé tir þ on ðá protan . . . Ac hé werodaþ, siþþan hé innaþ, Bt. 22, 1; F. 76, 28. Wé nyllað geþencan hwelc hit þá wæs, Ors. 3, 11; S. 152, 33. Ús gedyde tó witanne Alexander hwelce þá hǽðnan godas sindon tó weorþianne, 3, 9; S. 126, 31. Ne nóm náne ware húlice (hwilce, *v. l.*) hié wǽron, 5, 4; S. 224, 22. Hwý gé nellan ácsian æfter ðám wísum monnum . . . hwilce hí wǽron . . . and siþþan gé hiora þeáwas geácsod habben, him onhyrian, Bt. 40, 4; F. 240, 2. Smeáþ hwelc þǽs flǽsclican gód sién, 32, 2; F. 116, 28. (b a) where a high degree is implied. Cf. (a a) :—Gefrēd hé hwelc sió hǽl tó habbanne wæs *salus, quanti sit muneris, sentitur*, Past. 249, 7. (2) as substantive, *which* :—Hí smeádon hwylc (huá ɫ huelc, L. *quis*) hyra yldost wǽre, Mk. 9. 34. IV. with indefinite force. (1) as adjective, *some, any* (a) with noun :—Gif hwelc bróðer (huælc ɫ ǽnig bróðer, L.) deód sié, Mk. R. 12, 19. Wēn is þæt hwilc wundor ineóde, Bl. H. 239, 30. Gif þú wēnst þte wundorlíce gerela hwelc weorþmynd sié, Bt. 14, 1; F. 42, 18. Gif hwelc swíþe ríce mon wyrþ ádrifen of his earde, 27, 3; F. 98, 20: 41, 2; F. 244. 24. Ðæt mon wilnode hwelcre gítsunge, Past. 73, 3. Þonne hwylcum men gelimpeþ þ . . ., Bl. H. 131, 24: Bt. 37, 4; F. 192, 14. Hwelcum earmum men, Bl. H. 215, 26. Þeáh ðú teó hwelcne bóh, Bt. 25; F. 88, 22. Gif gé gesáwen hwelce mús, 16, 2; F. 52, 1. Gif hé hwlyc lim forlýst, 34, 9; F. 148, 7. Gif mon hwelcne ceáp gebygeð, and hé onfinde him hwelce unhǽlo on, Ll. Th. i. 138, 10-11. Gif þú hine gesáwe on hwilcum earfoþum, Bt. 10; F. 28, 16: Bl. H. 51, 28. (b) *with* án, óþer :—Būtan þǽr hwylc óðer mettrum man sý, Wlfst. 285, 8. Ic wolde witon hwæþer þú wēndest þ hwilc án ðǽra fíf góda worhte ðá sóþan gesǽlþe, 34, 6; F. 140, 26. Hí ǽlce synne geþencen . . . for ðǽm ðonne hié for ánre hwelcre hreówsiað, ðonne hreówsiað hié for ealle, Past. 413, 24. Be him sylfum þe he óþrum men hwylcum *de se an de alio aliquo*, Bd. 4, 3; Sch. 365, 2. (2) as substantive. (a) alone, *any one, any thing, some one, some thing* :—Hwona ðǽs mæg hwelc ɫ hwa (ǽnig man, W.S.) gefylle? *unde istos poterit quis saturare?*, Mk. R. L. 8, 4. Gif hwylc gelýfe on God, Bl. H. 153, 19. Þ man wite gehwæt hwylces, Gr. D. 138, 3. (b) with gen., *any one of, some one of* :—Búton hine þǽra þreóra þinga hwylc (cf. ǽnig, 4) forwyrne, Wlfst. 285, 14. Búton heora hwelc gecirre, Bt. 3, 1; F. 6, 5. Þeáh hwá wéne þ hé on heora ánra hwylcum mæge habban fulle gesǽlþa, ne byþ hit nó swá.' . . . Þú cwist þ wé ne magon on ðǽra ánra hwilcum þ hēhste gód habban . . . ne wé wēnaþ þ úre ánra hwelc ðá fíf ealle ætgædere begite,' 33, 2; F.

124, 23-29. Þonne úre Drihten úre hwylces neósian wille, Bl. H. 125, 12. Mid þǽm þe hié þára dura hwelce opene gesáwon, Ors. 3, 5; S. 106, 16. Ðeáh hé ðára góda hwylc forleóse, Bt. 34, 6; F. 140, 34. Gif mon ánra hwilc ofslóh, 39, 4; F. 216, 21. V. *combined with* swá. (1) adjectival :—Swá hwylc man swá mildheortnesse nafað, Bl. H. 13, 22: 49, 22. Swá hwylc lác swá *munus quodcumque*, Mt. 15, 5. (2) substantival :—Swá hwylc swá ne gelýfeþ, Bl. H. 153, 17. Swá hwilcne swá hí tó hospe habban wolde, Hml. Th. ii. 228, 31: Bl. H. 49, 15. Swá hwylce swá (*quaecumque*) gé gebindað ofer eorðan . . . swá hwylce (hwælc, R.) swá gé ofer eorðan unbindað, Mt. 18, 18. Swá hwylc swá (and suá chuelc, L.) segð *quicumque dixerit*, Mt. 15, 5: 20, 26: Mk. 10, 43. Sé ðe swá hwelc (chuælc, L.) onfóeð ðone cnæht, mec onfóeð; and swá hwelc swá (sé ðe suá huá, L.) mec onfóeð . . ., Lk. R. 9, 48. (2 a) with genitive :—Swá hwylcne heora swá (*quemcumque*) him se tán ætýwde, Bd. 5, 10; Sch. 600, 17. v. á-, gewel-, nát-, sam-hwilc; húlic.

**hwilc-æthwega.** *See second passage under* **hwilc-hwega** *in Dict.*

**hwilc-hwega.** *Add*: I. adjectival. (1) of extent, degree, *little, some, not much* or *great* :—Hé spræc gelícost ðǽm ðe hit hwelchwugu syn wǽre *culpa quippe esse innuitur*, Past. 397, 28. Hit nis éce gifu . . . ac is hwilchwugu eldcung, Bt. 38, 3; F. 202, 17. Þæt forneáh náht tó láfe ne wunode búton hwylchugu lytel ele *ut pene nihil nisi parum quid olei remaneret*, Gr. D. 159, 9. Of hwylcumhugu dǽle, Bl. H. 103, 17. Hé gedyde hwylcehugu (sume lytle, *v. l.*) yldinge *paululum moram fecit*, Gr. D. 88, 23. Hǽfde ic þá gíet hwylchwugu gemynd þǽre unrótnesse *ego nondum penitus moeroris oblitus*, Bt. 36, 1; F. 170, 26. Þæs flǽsces hwylcnehwugu dǽl, Hml. A. 205, 345. (2) of number, *some, a few* :—Wé magan hwylcumhwega wordum seccgan be ðǽre gebyrdo . . . Sancte Martines, Bl. H. 211, 12. Hwylcumhwego, 115, 28. Hé hí hwylcehwugu (-hugu; feáwa, *v. ll.*) dagas mid him gehǽfde *eos aliquot diebus secum retinuit*, Bd. 5, 10; Sch. 601, 8. (3) with indefinite force, *some, any* :—Sum hálig man hwylchugu (-hwugu, *v. l.*) *sanctus uir aliquis*, Bd. 3, 10; Sch. 233, 6. In hwylcumhugu ánum þinge *in una qualibet re*, Gr. D. 41, 17. Cweð hwylchugu (sum, *v. l.*) word *dicito aliquod uerbum*, 5, 2; Sch. 558, 16. Þ hé Angelþeóde onsende hwylcehugu (sume, *v. l. aliquos*) lǽreówas, 2, 1; Sch. 111, 15. On hwilchugu (hwylchwugu, *v. l.*) fatu gehíwad *in uasa quaelibet formatus*, 3, 22; Sch. 291, 6. Hwelchugu word (sume þing, *v. l. aliqua*) ic wille gereccean, Gr. D. 23, 14. II. substantival. (1) alone, *anything, something* :—Giwude huelchuoegu (hwæthwugu, R., sum þingc, W. S., *aliquid*) from him, Mt. L. 20, 20. Huoelchuoego (áht, W. S.), Mk. L. 8, 23: Lk. L. 11, 54. Hwelchwoego, Mt. p. 1, 9. (2) with gen. :—Of Nazareth mæge huelchuoegu gódes (ǽnig þing gódes, W. S.) wosa *a Nazareth potest aliquid boni esse, jn. L. 1, 46. See next word.

**hwilc-hwegno** (-u), **-hweogne, -hwoene, -hwóne.** I. adjectival, *some, any* :—Hé hyhtade bécon hwelchweogne from him gesegen wēre (bécon huoelchuoene tó geseánne *signum aliquod uidere*, L.), Lk. R. 23, 8. Gif huæt gié habbað wið hwelchuóne óðer (hwelchwoegu óðer ðing, R. *si quid habetis aduersus aliquem*, Mk. L. 11, 25. II. substantival, *anything, something* :—Hé gefrægn hine gif hwelchwoegnu (*aliquid*) gisēge, Mk. R. 8, 23. Welchwoegnu, Lk. R. 11, 54.

**hwilc-hwēne.** *Dele, and see* **hwilc-hwegno.**

**hwilc-ness.** *Add* :—Æfter ǽghwylces hwylcnysse *secundum uniuscujusque qualitatem*, R. Ben. I. 16, 4: Chrd. 96, 22. For þeáwa hwylcnysse *pro qualitate morum*, 95, 22.

**-hwíle.** v. óþer-hwíle.

**hwílen.** *Add*: *temporal* :—Him Paulines se hwílena hláford andswarude *cui Paulini temporalis dominus respondit*, Gr. D. 181, 12. v. (?) óþer-hwílen.

**hwílende.** v. hwíl-wende.

**hwíl-fæc, es**; *n.* For 'Lye' *substitute* :—Hwílfæc *interuallum*, An. Ox. 1178. Cf. hwíl-stycce, -þrág, -tídum.

**hwilfan**; *p.* te *To arch, vault, make* hwealf (*q.v.*) :—Ðonne þú hlid habban wylle, þonne hafa þú þíne wynstran hand sámlocene, and eác swá þá swýþran, and hwylf hý ofer þá wynstran eal swylce þú cuppan hlíde, Tech. ii. 125, 7. [Icel. hvelfa *to arch, vault*: O. Sax. be-hwelbian.] v. á-, be-, ofer-hwilfan.

**hwilpa** (-e?), an; *m. f.* (?). *Some kind of bird* :—Dyde ic mé tó gomene ganetes hleóþor and huilpan swēg fore hleahtor wera, Seef. 21. [Cf. (?) Scotch quhaip, whaup *a curlew*. *See also* yar-whelp *a godwit* in D.D.]

**hwíl-stycce.** *Add*: —Leáf þ hé moste him sum hwílstycce gebiddan *licentia paululum orandi*, Gr. D. 254, 24. Þéh þe þes middangeard sum hwílstycce cwēme, 258, 26. Hwílsticcu *intervalla*, Wrt. Voc. ii. 44, 61.

**hwíl-þrág, e**; *f.* A space of time :—Ic þrowode þurh hwílþráge (*per horarum momenta*) swilce ic neálǽðte mínum ende, Gr. D. 243, 19.

**hwíl-tídum.** *Substitute*: **hwíl-tíd, e**; *f.* A time :—Ic bidde eów þæt gé þises gewrites gíman and on hwíltídum hit on gemynde habban, Wlfst. 108, 17. ¶ the word occurs almost only in the dat. pl. used as an adverb. Add to the examples in Dict.: (1) *sometimes*, as opposed to never, *from time to time, now and again* :—Gehwilce untrumnyssa hwíltídum þǽr wurdon gehǽlede, Hml. S. 36, 420. (2) *at times, at intervals*, as opposed to always or continuously :—Cwyst þú hwæþer hit

tô gelýfenne sý þ þysum Godes þeówan mihte symble æt beón se wíte-dômes gâst, hwæþer þe hwíltídum (*per intervalla temporum*) his môd gefylde þæs wítedômes gâst ?, Gr. D. 146, 5. (3) *correlative, sometimes . . . at others* :—Hwílt[ídum] . . . hwíltídum *modo*, An. Ox. 92-107. Sculan þâ gebrôðra hwíltídum (*certis temporibus*) beón âbyse-gode mid heora handa geswince, hwíltídum (*certis iterum*) mid rædinge, R. Ben. 73, 4-6. Se môna is hwíltídum weaxende, hwíltídum wani-ende, Hml. Th. ii. 214, 32.

**hwílum.** In l. 3 for *quandam* l. *quondam*, and add :—Hwílum *nunc*, Wrt. Voc. ii. 61, 43. (1) *of more or less repeated action, sometimes, at times* :—Ðâ ðe hwílum (cf. hwíltídum, 3) gedúfað on ðæm miclum scyldum *qui aliquando in gravibus noxis demerguntur*, Past. 437, 33 : Bt. 24, 4 ; F. 84, 33 : 39, 9 ; F. 226, 12 : Bl. H. 227, 7. (1 a) *of alternate or con-trasted action.* (α) hwílum . . . hwílum *sometimes . . . at others* :—Hwílum þurh wífes geweald, hwílum þurh weres, Bl. H. 195, 4-5 : 203, 14-15. (β) hwílum *in the second clause only* :—þær hê hæfþ weallendne lêg and hwílum cyle þone grimmestan, Bl. H. 61, 35. (2) *of a single past event, once, some time ago* :—Sêtnung hwílum í for longe âworden *seditio quondam facta*, Lk. R. L. 23, 19. Hwílon wacodon menn swâ swâ gewunelic is ofer ân deáð líc, Hml. S. 21, 289. (3) *of a future event, at some future time* :—Hwílum (æt sumum cyrre, W. S.) gicerred *aliquando conuersus*, Lk. R. L. 22, 32. v. ǽr-, geó-, nû-hwílum.

**hwíl-wende.** *Add* : , hwílende. I. *of duration, temporary, not lasting long, not permanent* :—Medemmicel hwíl is þ gê mê ne geseóð, and eft is lytel fæc þ gê mê eft geseóð . . . Þeós hwílwende gesihð . . ., Hml. A. 74, 40. Hí nâ tô þære hwílendre (*ad illam momentaneam*) mihtan dædbôte becuman. Wê forsceamiað nû on lytlum timan dædbôte dôn, Scint. 49, 9. II. *of a person, concerned with the things of time* ; *of things, temporal, not spiritual or eternal* :—Sê þe hwílende (*tempo-rarius*) ys on blisse, êce hê byð on wíte, Scint. 172, 7. Him sihð on þyssa hwílwendra þinga lufu *inter hos amor temporalium rerum grassatur*, R. Ben. 139, 26. Þû wêre nû oð þis úpâhafen on þisse worulde æhtum and hwílwendum weorcum ; nú gedafnað þê þ þú beó úpâhafen on gâst-licum welum, Hml. S. 30, 118. [Þeos world is whilende, O.E. Hml. i. 7, 20. Þis world fareþ hwilynde, hwenne on cumeþ an oþer goþ, Misc. 94. 31.]

**hwílwend-líc.** *Take here the passages under* hwílend-líc, *and add* : I. *of duration, temporary, not of long duration, not eternal* :—Ðreó þing synd on middanearde, ân is hwílwendlic, þe hæfð ǽgðer ge ordfruman ge ende . . . Oðer þing is êce, swâ þ hit hæfð ordfruman and næfð nênne ende . . . Ðridde þing is êce, swâ þ hit næfð nâðor ne ordfruman ne ende, Hml. S. 1, 25-31. Ân líf is hwílwendlic, ôðer êce, Hml. Th. ii. 440, 4. Hí wæron gehælede tô hwílwendlicum lífe, 240, 15. Þæra hæðenra wíta synd hwílwendlice, Hml. S. 11, 127. For þissum hwíl-wendlicum yfrum brúcað ðæra êcera gôda on worulda woruld, 30, 449. II. *temporal, not spiritual* :—Ðâm rícan wæs forgolden mid ðâm hwílwendlicum spêdum, Hml. Th. i. 332, 5. Hú hê geheólde þâ hwílwendlican geþincþu, Hml. S. 26, 113. II a. *physical, not spiritual and eternal* :—Hit gedafenode Godes weorcum þ se ælmihtiga, sê þe is êce leóht, ǽrest þ hwílwendlice leóht geworhte *congruit operibus Dei, ut a luce aeterna lux temporalis primo fieret*, Angl. vii. 18, 159.

**Hwinca.** v. Hwiccas.

**hwirfan.** *Take here* hwerfan *in Dict., and add* : I. *of motion.* (1) *to move about* :—Ic hider and þider mê (*reflex. dat.*) hwyrfde (hwerfde, *v. l.*), Bd. 5, 6 ; Sch. 576, 5. Hwerfende *errabilis, vertibilis*, Wrt. Voc. ii. 144, 17. Hwerbende *errabiles*, 107, 33. Hwyrfende, 29, 47. (2) *to go to or from, to return* :—Hié eft hwyrfende wæron tô heora húsum, Bl. H. 207, 30. (3) *to revolve* :—þære eaxe ðe eall þes rodor on hwerfþ, Bt. 39, 3 ; F. 214, 21. Þ hweól hwertþ ymbúton, 39, 7 ; F. 220, 29. (3 a) *reflex.* :—Be þínre hêse heó hwyrfð seó heofene, and ealla tungla heora rína gehealdað *tuis legibus rotantur poli, cursus suos sidera peragunt*, Solil. H. 9, 13. II. *of action, conduct, to proceed, go on* :—Hwý þú ǽfre woldest þ seó wyrd swâ hwyrfan sceolde ? (*cur tantas lubrica versat fortuna vices ?*). Heó þreáþ þâ unscildigan, and náuht ne þreáþ ðâm scildegum, Bt. 4 ; F. 8, 12. III. *of the operations of the mind* :—Mê þincþ þ þú hwerfest ymbúton sume wunderlice sprǽce, Bt. 35, 5 ; F. 164, 17. Nú wê sculon eft hwierfan neár Rôma þær wê hit ǽr forlêton *Romae ut ad id tempus redeam unde digressus sum*, Ors. 2, 5 ; S. 86, 13. IV. *trans. To turn, give direction to* :—Arewan ongeán hwyrfde *catapultas retorsit*, An. Ox. 4241. Hié heora wǽpen hwyrfdon wiþ Bryttas, Bd. 1, 15 ; Sch. 40, 8. v. tô-hwirfan ; ongeán-hwirfende ; mis-, níw-hwirfed.

**-hwirfedlíc.** v. for-hwirfedlíc : **-hwirfedness.** v. for-, ge-, on-hwirfedness.

**hwirfel.** *Add* : In local names :—Tô hwerfeldíc, C. D. iii. 316, 29. Ouer worfuldoune, vi. 233, 16. On wirfelmere, C. D. B. iii. 606, 16. [D. D. whirl *an eddy* ; *a whirlpool.*]

**hwirfe-pól**, es ; *m. A whirl-pool* :—Hwyrfepôlum *charybdibus*, Wrt. Voc. ii. 24, 56.

**hwirfere** *a changer, an exchanger. Take here* hwerfere *in Dict.* : **hwirfing.** v. hôh-hwirfing.

**hwirflede** ; *adj. Rounded, round* :—Sinewealt (and) hwyrflede *teres*

---

*atque rotunda* (*ut globus astrorum*, Ald. 272, 22), An. Ox. 23, 42. Cf. hwirfling.

**hwirf-líc.** *Take here* hwerf-líc *in Dict.*

**hwirfling**, es ; *m. Something round, an orb* :—Hwyrfliences (hwurf-linces, Hpt. Gl. 453, 37) begýmendum rícetere *orbis gubernante monarchiam*, An. Ox. 1992.

**hwirflung.** *Take here* hwerflung *in Dict., and add* : *change, vicissitude* :—Huoerflunges *vicissitudinis*, Rtl. 28, 11. Ðæt gêr byð âwend mid twi six hwyrfolunga, and hyt hæfð twâ and fíftig wucan, Angl. viii. 301, 36.

**hwirf-ness.** v hwyrf-ness ; ge-hwirfness : **hwirf-pól.** *Dele, and see* hwirfe-pól : **hwirlic.** v. þweorh-líc.

**hwiscettung**, e ; *f. Squeaking* :—Mid músa hwiscetunge *stridores soricum*, Gr. D. 185, 4. [Cf. (?) *Dan.* hviske *to whisper.*]

**hwisprian.** *Add* :—Hwisprendo *murmurantes*, Jn. p. 4, 20.

**hwistle.** *Add* : v. wistle : **hwistlere.** *l.* (?) wistlere.

**hwistlian.** *Add* :—Hwyslaþ *exsibilat*, Germ. 398, 176. Wistlaþ ot þâm dæle þe þ sâr biþ, Lch. ii. 258, 19. Hwistliende *sibilans* (*coluber linguis trisulcis*), An. Ox. 4703. Swisliende, 2, 370. v. â-hwistlian.

**hwistlung.** *Add* : I. *hissing, whistling* :—Leóhtlic hwyslung (*sibilus*) mæg hors tamcyan, Chrd. 96, 18. Þ lond hleódrade for þâra wyrma [hw]istlunge *sibilabat tota regio*, Nar. 13, 22. Mislice fugela hwistlunge, Guth. 48, 5. Næddrena hwistlunge *sibilos serpentium*, Gr. D. 185, 3. II. *piping, playing on a pipe* [*l.* (?) wistlung. v. wistle], Lk. L. 15, 25 (*in Dict.*).

**hwít.** *Add* : I. *simply of colour, white* :—Hwít *byssina, candida*, Wrt. Voc. ii. 126, 32 : *bysina*, 87, 55 : *candens* (*lilium*), An. Ox. 5249. Ic geán mínon feder . . . ðes hwítan horses ðe Leófwine mê geaf, C. D. iii. 362, 18. Þâ leáf beóþ hwítran, Lch. i. 278, 15. Hægl bið hwítust (*crocorna*, Rún. 9. I a. *without substantive, white dress* :—Hwíte (*cr corna*, Rún. 9. I a. *without substantive, white dress* :—Hwíte (*cr adv. ?*) oðde beorhte hine gescrýdan *alba aut splendida se uestire*, Lch. iii. 198, 26. ¶ *The weak form used substantively, the white* (part) *of an egg* :—On ânum æge . . . þæt hwíte ne bið gemenged tô ðam geolcan, Hml. Th. i 40, 27. Smyre mid henne æges þe hwítan, Lch. iii. 50, 4. Gemeng wiþ æges þ hwíte, ii. 74, 24. Nim þ hwíta of æge, iii. 96, 19. II. *denoting refinement or purity in material* :—Þonne ytst ðú azima, þ ys hwít hláf þære sífernesse, Angl. viii. 323, 18. Hwítes hláfes cruman, Lch. ii. 24, 3. Hwítes seolfres (cf. reád *as an epithet of gold*), Jos. 7, 21. Dô on hwít sealt, Lch. ii. 94, 8 : 124, 10. II a. *denoting spiritual purity* :—Hwylc is of ús þ hæbbe swâ hwíte saúle swâ þeós hálige María ?, Bl. H. 147, 18. III. *as an epithet of the Sunday on which white garments were worn* :—On Hwítan Sunnandæg, Chr. 1067 ; P. 202, 30. IV. *in personal names* :—Hwíta, Hwítze (-e), Txts. 632. Brâda hátte wæs gebúr tô Hædfelda, and Hwíte hátte ðæs Brâdan wíf . . ., seó Hwíte wæs Wynburge þridde môdor, C. D. vi. 212, 15-18. Cf. Hwíting, ii. 3, 30. The word also occurs in many local names. v. C. D. vi. 305. v. meolc-, mêre-, þurh-hwít.

**hwít**, es ; *n.* I. *whiteness* :—Hwít âsolað *nitor squalescit*, Angl. i. 285, § 2 : ii. 374. 3. II. *something white, the white* of an egg. Cf. hwít ; I. :—Mid æges þý hwíte, Lch. ii. 82, 9. Dô æges hwít tô, 342, 18. Nim ægra hwít, iii. 134, 10. III. *certain kinds of food, cheese, eggs, butter, fish, allowed at times when flesh was for-bidden* :—Fæste ælce dæge on his lengtene tô nônes and forgang hwít (*abstine te ab albo*), Ll. Th. ii. 132, 5. Fæst ælc dæge tô nônes and tô ânes mêtes búton sunnandæg, and forgâ hwít, Wlfst. 289, 25. Cf. Ðâ ðe on þâs hálgan tíde magon cýse and ægra and fisc forgân, swíþe heálic fæsten þ bið, Ll. Th. ii. 438, 11. Gif hit festendæg sié selle mon uuêge cêsa and fisces and butran and aegera ðaet mon begeotan mæge, C. D. i. 293, 10. v. searu-hwít.

**hwíte** ; *adv. Whitely, with white colour* :—þ ðridde cyn mintan þ blôwed hwíte, Lch. iii. 16, 11. Hwíte (or *adj. ?* v. hwít ; I a.) hine gescrýdan *to dress in white*, 198, 26.

**hwíte-.** *The compound character of the following words with* hwíte *as first component seems supported by the instances given under* hwíte-clǽfre (Lch. ii. 326, 21) *and under* hwíte-hláf.

**hwíte-clǽfre** *white clover* :—Hwíteclǽfre *calcesta*, Wrt. Voc. ii. 13, 29 : i. 67, 42. Hwíteclǽfr *ca*[*l*]*cista*, 291, 4. Nim hwíteclǽfran wísan, Lch. ii. 326, 21. Nim hwíteclǽfran, 64, 2.

**hwíte-cylle** *some kind of bag or vessel* :—Hwítecylle *folle bubulum, i. vas piceum* (cf. culleum, folle bubulum, Corpl. Gl. H. 39, 956 : culleum uas pice oblitum, 926 : in culleum, in follem bobulum, et aliter machina contenta et bitumine lita, 67, 224), Wrt. Voc. ii. 150, 14.

**hwíte-gôs** *a white goose* :—Hwítegôs *anser*, Wrt. Voc. i. 280, 14 : ii. 7, 60.

**hwíte-hláf** *white bread, a white loaf* :—Willa ic gesellan . . . CL. hláfa, L. hwítehláfa, cxx. elmeshláfes, Cht. Th. 474, 26.

**hwíte-leác** *white leek* :—alba cipa, Wrt. Voc. ii. 8, 47.

**hwítel.** *Add* :—Tô beddreáfe genihtsumige tô hæbbenne meatte and hwítel (*sagum*), R. Ben. 90, 15. Hí ne mihton hine beran búton on ânum hwítle (*sago*), Gr. D. 125, 18. Rúhne hwítel (*printed* hwien,

Lch. i. lxi, 3) *amphiballum*, Hpt. 31, 8, 140. Hwitla *stragularum*, An. Ox. 1035. v. under-hwítel (*printed* hwida, Hpt. Gl. 430, 67.)

**hwiða.** *Add:*—Whiðe *aura* (abl.), An. Ox. 2, 420.

**hwítian.** *Add:*—Hwítað heofon *albescit polus*, Hy. S. 21, 23. Hwæs blód reádaþ on rosan gelicnysse, and hwæs líchama hwítað on lilian fægernysse, Hml. S. 34, 113. v. ge-hwítian.

**hwíting,** e; *f. Substitute:* **hwíting-melu,** wes; *n.:* **hwít-loc.** *For* Rä. 48, 3 *l.* 43, 3: **hwít-locced.** *l.* -loccede, *and add:*—Cwēn hwítloccedu.

**hwol?,** An. Ox. 37, 6. The word is given as a gloss to *infingens* in the passage: Inruit in quamdam spinulam . . . medelanium plantae ipsius *infigens*, Guth. Gr. 153.

**hwón.** *Add:* [*For construction* cf. feáwa.] **I.** substantival (1) of number. (a) alone, *a few persons* or *things:*—Ofer lytla þ huón ðú wēre leáffull, ofer monigo ðec ic setto *super pauca fuisti fidelis, super multa te constituam*, Mt. L. 25, 21. (b) with gen.:—Hrippes feolo, wyrcendra huón *messis multa, operari pauci*, Lk. L. 10, 2. Hiæ hæfdum lytelra fisca hwón (huón, L.) *habebant pisciculos paucos*, Mk. R. 8, 7. (2) of quantity, *a little*. (a) alone:—Ádó þ pic of, súpe hwón wearm, Lch. ii. 318, 5. Dō on breówende wyrt, hwón, 332, 22. (b) with gen.:—Dó hwón sealtes tō, Lch. ii. 78, 2. Hwón berenes melwes, 322, 27. Hwón wínes, 344, 6. **II.** adjectival (1) of number. (a) qualifying a noun:—Of seofa hláfum and hwón lytle fiscas (*paucis pisciculis*), Mk. p. 3, 18. Huón fiscðrútas *pisciculos*, Mt. 15, 34. (b) predicative:—Hrípes monigo, wercmenn huón *messis multa, operarii pauci*, Mt. L. 9, 37. Rípes feolu, wyrcende hwón, Lk. R.10, 2. Gif huón sint ðá ðe gihæled biðon *si pauci sunt qui saluantur*, 13, 23. (2) of quantity. (a) *little:*—Gié huóno þ lytlo geleáfas (hwón þ lytle þ læssa gileófa, R.) *uos pussilae fidei*, Lk. L. 12, 28. Lch. ii. 32, 3: 124, 22 (*in Dict.*). **III.** adverbial. (1) local, *a little way:*—Hine from eorða eft-lǽda huón *eum a terra reducere pusillum*, Lk. L. 5, 3. (1 a) in a phrase:—Foerde þonan lytel hwón *progressus inde pusillum*, Mk. R. L. 1, 19. (2) temporal, *a little while:*—Lǽt þonne hwón gestandan, Lch. ii. 264, 27. (3) of degree, *a little, slightly:*—Sete on glēda, gewyrm hwón, Lch. ii. 310, 4. Swēt hwón, 318, 13: 324, 6. Man tó hwón stýrde þám þe syngodon, Wlfst. 168, 2. Fērde hē hwón feorr (*paulo longius*) fram þám mynstre, Gr. D. 28, 17. (3 a) in a negative phrase *not at all, not in the least, in no wise:*—Ná tó þæs hwón (*nullatenus*) ne færst þú heonon, búton þú mínne sunu áwecce, Gr. D. 17, 20: 38, 15: 80, 27: Hml. S. 30, 412. Ne magon hí tó þæs hwón (*nequaquam*) begitan þá þing þe him geteohhode næron, Gr. D. 54, 13. Ná tó þes hwón *minime*, An. Ox. 40, 5. Ná-te-þes-hwón, 4, 47. v. ātes-, nátes-hwón.

**hwón-lic.** *In last line* l. Skt. *for* Swt., *and add:*—Wurdon æteówode fela ðúsend engla, þý lǽs ðe wǽre geþúht ánes engles ealdordóm tó hwónlic tó swá micelre bodunge, Hml. Th. i. 38, 6. Hit wǽre hwónlic geþúht þ . . ., bútan mennisce eágan mihte geseón þ . . ,, Hml. S. 31, 1252.

**hwónlíce.** *Add:* **I.** *for a little while:*—Mín sylfes gást wæs hwónlíce ormód worden *defecit paulisper spiritus meus*, Ps. Th. 76, 4. **II.** *slightly, little*. (1) with adjectives:—Hwónlíce gelýfede menn *men slightly endowed with belief*, Hml. Th. i. 566, 28. Hwónlícor *minus* (*compta*), An. Ox. 1015. (2) with verbs, where action is slight in operation or result:—Hwónlíce (wónlíce, 2, 55) hwapelaþ *sensim scaturiat*, An. Ox. 1890. Scortlíce and hwónlíce (wónlíce, 2, 235) *strictim et summatim* (*commemorandum*), 3656. Hwónlíce summatim (*expletis exemplis*), 3878. Ic and míne dohtra . . . hí ǽfre tihton tó þínre geþafunga, þeáh ðe ús hwónlíce speówe (*though our success has been slight*), Hml. S. 8, 34. Þá þe hwónlíce understandan magan hú micel wíte is þæt man on ámánsumunge sié *qui minus intelligere possunt quanta pena excommunicationis*, R. Ben. 54, 1. Tó-dæg wē habbað hwónlíce be hláf, ac tó-merigen wē sceolon habban genihtsumlíce (cf. *quare de panis inopia vester animus contristatur? Hodie quidem minus est, sed die crastina abundantes habebitis*, Gr. D. c. 21), Hml. Th. ii. 172, 2.

**hwón-lotum.** *Substitute:* **hwón-hlotum,** *adv. In small portions, moderately* (?):—Huónhlotum *parumper* (cf. parumper, satis modice, Corp. Gl. H. 88, 96), Txts. 85, 1515.

**-hworfen-ness.** v. ongeán-hworfenness.

**hwósan;** *p.* hweós *To cough*:—Wite þú gif hē mid earfodnysse hwēst and hyt út hrǽcþ; þanne ys þ clǽnsunga þára breósta, Lch. iii. 122, 3. Hē hwēst swýþe hefelíce . . . and þat hē út hrǽcþ byþ swýþe þicce and hæfet hwýt híw, 126, 9. Þá men hwósað gelóme, hwílum blóde hrǽcaþ, ii. 258, 7. Hē egeslíce hweós and angsumlíce siccetunga teáh, swá þæt hē earfoðlíce orðian mihte, Hml. Th. i. 86, 7.

**hwósta.** *Add:*—Wiþ angbreóste, gif men sié dríge hwósta, Lch. ii. 58, 15.

**hwoþerian, hwoþrung,** v. hwaþerian, hwaþerung: **hwurf.** v. **hwyrf: hwurfling.** v. hwirfling: **hwurful.** *Add:* v. sin-hwurfol.

**hwurful-ness.** *Add:*—Hine ne meahte nán scúr hwurfulnesse (*mutabilitatis aura*) ástyrigean, Past. 308, 10.

**hwŷ.** *Add:* **I.** in direct questions:—Hwŷ (hwí, *v. l.*) forcwið hē . . .

---

ðæt hē ne fēde his heorde?, Past. 42, 6. Hwŷ (hwié, *v. l.*) wolde hē hié lǽran?, 250, 24. Hwig eart þú swá gedréfedes mōdes?, Ap. Th. 2, 9. **I a.** *strengthened with* ǽfre, á:—Hwŷ gē þonne ǽfre ofer-mōdigen?, Met. 17, 15. Hwí eów á lyste?, 10, 18. **II.** used interjectionally to introduce a question, cf. hú; **I. 2,** hwá, **II:**—Hŷ cweðað: 'Hwí! ne synt wē mūðfreó? hú ne mōton wē sprecan þæt wē willað? hwæt! ondrǽde wē hwylc hláford mæg ús forbeóden úrne willan?, Ps. Th. 11, 4. **III.** in dependent clauses. (1) after verbs of asking, telling, thinking, &c. cf. hwá, **III.:**—Wundrian hwí þ ís weorþe, Bt. 39, 3; F. 214. 35. Uncúð hwí sió wyrd swá wō wendan sceolde, Met. 4, 40. Gehycgan hwŷ . . . , 15, 9. (2) where the matter referred to in the indirect question is the cause of the action stated in the main clause, so that almost the same meaning as that intended would be got if the dependent clause were introduced by *because* and expressed affirmatively:—Scipia mǽnde his earfoða tó Rōmana witum . . . hwý hié hiene swá unweorðne on his ylde dyden, Ors. 5, 4; S. 224, 26. Hē gehēt him Godes yrre, hwý hē nolde gelýfan þ hē hálig wǽre, Hml. S. 31, 804: Hml. Th. i. 48, 16 (*in Dict.*).

**hwylca.** v. hwelca: **hwyrf.** v. geán-hwyrf: **hwyrfe-pól.** v. hwirfe-pól: **hwyrfling.** v. hwirfling.

**hwyrft.** *Add:*—Þú leornodest ymbe þises rodores hwyrft, Solil. H. 21, 8. v. ge-, geán-, twi-hwyrft.

**hwyrftness.** v. ge-hwyrftness.

**-hycga.** v. firen-hycga.

**hycgan.** *Add: p.* hygde, hygede (v. for-hycgan). **I.** *to think, have such and such thoughts:*—Þá þe mid heortan hycgeað rihte *qui recto sunt corde*, Ps. Th. 72, 1. On fyrenfulra geðancas, þá wiðerwearde mē wráðe hycgeað *cogitaverunt adversum me*, 139, 8. **I a.** where the subject matter of thought is given as object:—Þá inwit and fácen hycgeað on heortan *qui cogitaverunt malitias in corde*, Ps. Th. 139, 2. **I b.** where a pronoun representing the thought is object:—Ne meahte monna ǽnig bedeáglian hwæt hē dearninga on hyge hogde heortan geþoncum, Gú. 1227. **I c.** *to conceive, understand:*—Hicgan, understandan *collegi*, i. *intelligi* (*colligi datur quod virginitas sit*); An. Ox. 1391. **II.** *to think* of, about (1) with gen.:—Hycgad his ealle, hú gē hí beswícen, Gen. 432. (2) with prep.:—Míne þearfan symle hycgað ymb heora Drihten, Wlfst. 260, 13. **III.** expressing purpose, endeavour. (1) with acc.:—Hycgan *moliri* (quicquid *moliri* deliberaret), An. Ox. 4710. (2) with infin.:—Sē þe framian higþ *qui proficere studet*, Scint. 100, 14. Hí higdon *nitebantur*, i. *moliebantur* (*flectere*), An. Ox. 2, 198. Higde, 3375. Fylian fótswaþu . . . mid mycelre hygdan geblissunge *sequi uertigia . . . cum magna studuerint hilaritate*, Angl. xiii. 367, 20. (3) with clause:—Uton hycgan þæt wē Hǽlende hēran georne, Sat. 594. (4) with prep.:—Ne hycge hē tó slǽpe *let him not think of sleep* (i.e. *don't let him have any intention of going to sleep*), Ps. Th. 120, 3. **IV.** *to call to mind, remember:*—Uton wē hycgan hwǽr wē hám ágen, and þonne geþencan hú wē þider cumen, Seef. 117. v. twi-hycgan.

**-hycge.** v. firen-hycge: **-hycgend.** v. firen-, fram-hycgend.

**hŷd.** *Add:* **I.** *the skin of an animal, raw* or *dressed:*—Hiera sceldas wǽron betogen mid elpenda hýdum (*scuta elephanti corio extento habilia*) . . elpendes hýd wile drincan wǽtan gelíce and spŷnge dēð, Ors. 5, 7; S. 230, 26. Hŷde *bysse*, i. *corii*, An. Ox. 3285: 3283: Wrt. Voc. ii. 82, 14: 11, 75: 93, 13. Mec (*a book*) wráh hæleð hleóbordum, hŷde (hŷþe, MS.) beþenede (cf. the following citation), Rä. 27, 12. Hŷda *tergora* (De pugillaribus . . . Calceamenta mihi tradebant *tergora dura*, Ald. 263, 10), An. Ox. 26, 19. **I a.** *the skin of a serpent*, Ors. 4, 6; S. 174, 15 (*in Dict.*). **I b.** *the shell of an oyster:*—Sǽ mec fēdde . . nú wile monna sum mín flǽsc etan . . . siððan hē mē of sídan seaxes orde hŷd árýpeð, Rä. 76, 7. **II.** *the skin of a human being:*—Úteweardre hŷde *cute summa*, An. Ox. 50, 23. Bið se líchoma hreóf ðonne se bryne ðe on ðǽm innoðe bið út áslihð tó ðǽre hýde (*ad cutem*), Past. 71, 6. Sindon ðá loccas tó sparienne ðǽm sácerde ðæt hí ðá hŷd behelien (*ut cutem cooperiant*), 141, 9. **II a.** in technical phrases relating to penal flogging:—Gif þeówetlingas þæt fæsten rihtlíce ne fæsten, þolian þǽre hŷde [oþþon hŷdgyldas], Wlfst. 172, 1 [and note]. Gebēte hē þæt swá swá hit gelagod is, . . . þrǽl mid his hŷde, þegn mid xxx scillingan, Wlfst. 181, 9. v. ǽl-hŷd.

**-hŷd.** v. ge-hŷd.

**hŷdan.** *Add:*—Ongunnun sume efnegespita on hine and hŷdde onsióne his (*uelare faciem eius*), Mk. R. 14, 65. Ðá wǽron hié þý swŷðor áfyrhte and hié fæstor hŷddan *tanto magis cunctis propter timorem abditis*, Nar. 10, 26. v. oþ-hŷdan.

**-hŷdan** *to bind with a rope.* v. ge-hŷdan.

**hydele, hnydele,** an; *f. The name of a plant:*—Hǽwen hydele. Genim þás wyrte þe Grēcas brittanice and Engle hǽwen hydele nemnað, Lch. i. 126, 4-6: 16, 21. Hǽwen[h]y[l]dele (h *has been blotted out and* l *struck out*, Wülck. Gl. 296, 23) *brittanice*, Wrt. Voc. i. 67, 22. Hǽwene hnydele, Lch. iii. 24, 8. Neoðewearde lilian and hǽwene h[n]ydelan (hydelan *altered by a caret mark to* hnydelan), 4, 10.

**hŷdels.** *Add:* [v. N.E.D. hidels.]

**hýdig** *of hide*. *Add*:—Hídig fatu (higdi, MS.) *calidilia* [perhaps the reading is *casidilia*. v. Wülck. Gl. 97, 20. Cf. punᵹ *cassidele* (*-ile*)], Coll. M. 27, 35.

**hýf**. *Add*:—Tó hýfen *ad aluearium*, An. Ox. 3822. Hýfa *cerea castra*, i. *aluearia*, 113. Þes náhte náht óþres tó his áᵹnum bryce búton feáwa hýfa beona (*pauca apum vascula*), Gr. D. 229, 12 : Angl. ix. 264, 15. ¶ the following glosses belong to passages referring to bees:— Hýfe *gurgustio*, i. *cellula*, An. Ox. 307. Hýfa *tuguria*, i. *cellulas*, 253.

**hygd**. *Add*: v. el-, ymb-hygd: **-hygd**; *adj.* v. ofer-, stíþ-hygd : **-hygde-**. v. -hygdig- : **-hygdig**; *sbst.* v. ofer-hygdig : **-hygdig**; *adj.* v. ymb-hygdig : **-hygdigian**. v. ofer-hygdigian : **-hygdiglic**. v. for-, ymb-hygdiglic : **hygdiglíce**. *Add*: v. ofer-, ymb-hygdiglíce : **hygdig-ness**. *Add*: v. hræd-, ymb-hygdiᵹness : **-hygdlic**. v. ge-, ofer-hygdlic : **hyge**. *Add*: v. ofer-hyge.

**hyge-leás**. *Add*: I. of persons. (1) *senseless*, Gen. 51 (*in Dict.*). (2) *spiritless* (?), *without courage*:—Be milte wærce . . . tácn ðære ádle hú higeleáse hí beóð (cf. *the section to which this heading refers*: Tácn þære ádle hú híwleáse hié beóð . . . þa men beóð mægre and unróte, bláce on onsýne, 242, 2–4. Higeleáse *might be taken to correspond with* unróte, *or it might be an error for* híwleáse), Lch. ii. 166, 12. I a. of a person's actions, conduct, &c.:—Higelæs *effrenatus* (*cachinnus*), Hpt. Gl. 481, 2. II. of things, *unsuitable*, *extravagant*:—Wé lǽrad þ man geswíce higeleásra gewǽda and dislicra gerǽda and bismorlicra efesunga, Ll. Th. ii. 248, 15.

**hygeleás-lic**; *adj.* *Foolish*, *senseless*, *extravagant*:—Þá higeleáslican ceahhetunga *effrenatos cachinnos*, An. Ox. 3170.

**hygeleáslíce**; *adv.* *Thoughtlessly*, *with levity*, *carelessly*:—Efston ealle preóstas tó cyrcan, and ná higeleáslíce (*non inhoneste uel inconposite*) gangon in, Chrd. 34, 5.

**hyge-leást**. *Add*: , -líst. (1) *folly*, *buffoonery*, *extravagance*:— Þ ne higeleást gemǽte (ge higeleás méte, MS.) tende *ut non scurilitas inveniat fomitem*, R. Ben. I. 75, 17. Hé ætbréde his líchaman . . . of sprǽce and of higeleáste (*de loquacitate*, *de scurilitate*), 86, 6. Þ se man . . . on deáwum hæbbe módes clǽnnysse and forhæfednysse bútan higeleáste (líig-, *v. l.*), Hml. S. 17, 59. (2) *a foolish act or word*:— Higlísta (*scurilitates*) oðþe ídel word wé fordémað, R. Ben. I. 26, 13.

**hyge-méþe**. *Substitute*: *weary or sad in mind*:—Bróðor ofscét óðerne . . . þæt wæs feohleás gefeoht fyrenum gesyngad hreðre hygeméðe *one brother shot the other . . . that was a fight where no bót could be claimed* (cf. Wedra helm ne meahte on þám feorhbanan fǽhðe gebétan, 2465), *evilly done*, *with a breast filled with sad thoughts* (i. e. the slayer was bitterly grieved for the dreadful act he had perpetrated?), B. 2442.

**hyge-sceaft**. *For gender* cf. frum-sceaft.

**hyht**. *Add*: I. *hope*, *expectation of something desired*:—Ðæt sió manung hine tó hyhte gehwierfe *ut admonitio eum ad spem reducat*, Past. 265, 21. I a. *where the object of hope is given*. (1) in gen.:—Ne bið him wynne hyht, Ph. 480. Þú mé gelǽddest mid lufan hyhte *deduxisti me quia factus es spes mea*, Ps. Th. 60, 2. Þone onwriᵹenan hyht reste þǽre écean wé habbaþ *revelatam spem quietis aeternę tenemus*, An. Ox. 40, 19 : An. 1054. Sǽle blidse mé, Dryhten, þínre hǽlo heht *redde mihi laetitiam salutaris tui*, Ps. C. 100. (2) marked by a preposition:—Gúðlác upp gemunde hám in heofonum. Him wæs hyht tó þám, Gú. 69. Utan ús tó þǽre hýðe hyht staðelian, Cri. 865. (3) expressed in a clause:—Hyht is onfangen, þæt bletsung mót bǽm gemǽne symle wunian, Cri. 99. II. *feeling of trust or confidence in a person or thing*:—Þá gehýrde hé hú þá menn . . . Crístes helda swóron . . . Ðá cwæð hé on his móde . . . 'Gyrstanǽfen nán man ne mihte Crístes naman nemnian mid hihte,' Hml. S. 23, 534. Hé (*Abraham*) forð gebád langsumne hiht (cf. *fide obtulit Abraham Isaac*, Heb. 11, 17), Exod. 405. II a. *where object of trust is given*:— Byð his heorte gearo hyhte tó Drihtne *paratum cor ejus sperare in Domino*, Ps. Th. 111, 7. Good is þæt ic on God mínne hiht sette *bonum est ponere in Deo spem meam*, 72, 23 : Gú. 406 : Hy. 4, 36. Ðæt hí heora hiht ne besetton on ðám swicelum welum, Hml. Th. ii. 326, 35. Ic in mínne fæder hyht staðelie, Jul. 437 : El. 798. Ðá ðe hiht on hine habbað fæste, Ps. Th. 129, 7 : 143, 3. Ic God gemyndgade þæt ic hæfde mæstne hiht, 76, 3. III. *hope of doing*, *intent*, *desire*:— Þǽr mín hyht myned tó gesécenne, Gú. 1061. Hí gehátað holdlíce, swá hyre hyht ne gǽd, Leás. 14. Úsic lust hweteð on þá leódmearce, micel módes hiht tó ðǽre mǽran byrig, An. 287. Mé bið forwyrned þurh widersteall willan mínes hyhtes, Jul. 442. IV. *joyous expectation*, *joy*, *exultation*:—Hyht wæs á in heofonum, Dóm. 64 : Seef. 122. Lufu, lífes hyht, and ealles leóhtes gefeá, Cri. 585 : Gú. 631. Hierusalem, þú bist full hálgan hyhtes, swá þú geháten eart (cf. Gerusalem is gereht ' sibbe gesyhþ ', Bl. H. 81, 1), Cri. 58. Manna gehwám mód bið on hyhte, fyrhð áfréfred, An. 637. Dréam wæs on hyhte, 876. Þæs þú gife hleótest, háliᵹne hyht on heofonþrymme, 481. Ic þe háte þæt þú hellwarum hyht ne ábeóde, ah þú him secgan miht sorga mǽste, Sat. 695. Hyht geceósed, woruld wynsume sé þe wís ne bið sáwle rǽdes, Leás. 40. V. *a person or thing that gives hope or promise*:— Middaneardes Álýsend . . . heofonwara hyht and eorþwara, and eác úre

hyht, Bl. H. 87, 10. Þú mé eart se héhsta hyht, Drihten *tu es*, *Domine*, *spes mea*, Ps. Th. 90, 9 : El. 197 : Hy. 7, 9 : Ph. 423 : Pa. 73. Gér byð gumena hyht, þonne God lǽteð hrúsan syllan beorhte blǽda beornum, Rún. 12. Weoruda Scyppend hafa þé tó hyhte, Fä. 63. Gemunað wigena wyn, háligra hyht, heofonengla God, Jul. 642. VI. *an object of hope*, *what is hoped for*:—Híðendra hyht, Rä. 89, 5 : 65, 3. Is mín hyht mid God, Gú. 289 : 61. VI a. *what is expected*:—Nabbað hié tó hyhte nyniðe cyle and fýr, Sat. 335 : 176. VII. *ground of hope*, *promise*. v. hyht-full ; II, hyht-lic ; III. v. ge-hyht.

**hyhtan**. *Add*: [*forms as from* hyhtian *occur*.] I. *to look* (*mentally*) *with expectation and desire*, *look forward with hope to*:—Wé tó þínum hidercyme hopodan and hyhtan, Bl. H. 87, 12. Uton tó þám beteran hycgan and hyhtan *let us turn our thoughts and hopes to the better*, Leás. 44. II. *to trust*, (1) *have confidence in*:—Eádig wer sé ðe hihtaþ (*sperat*) on him, Ps. L. 33, 9. Móises in ðǽm gié hyhtas, Jn. L. 5, 45. In noman his þeóde hyhtað, Mt. L. R. 12, 21. On Drihtne hihtiende, Ps. L. 25, 1. (2) *to look with confidence to*:—For ðon hé hyhte tó mé, ic hine lýse *quoniam in me speravit*, *liberabo eum*, Ps. Th. 90, 14. III. *to hope for* something:—Hé hyhtade bécon hwelc-hweogne from him gesegen wére (tó geseánne, L.) *sperabat signum aliquod uidere ab eo fieri*, Lk. R. 23, 8. IV. *to expect* (*without idea of desire*):—Cymeð ðe hláferd in dæg of ðǽm ne hyhtas ꞇ ne woenas (*sperat*), Mt. L. 24, 50. Hyhtað ꞇ woenað, Lk. L. R. 12, 46. Gif gié sellas ðǽm from ðǽm gié hyhtað tó onfóane, Lk. L. 6, 34. Nóht on ðec hyhtendo *nihil in te sperantes*, 35. V. *to entertain feelings of joy*, *to exult* (?):—Þ cild onsprang and ongeán his Hláford hyhte (cf. *exultauit in gaudio infans*, Lk. 1, 44), Bl H. 165, 29. Hyhton nú and blissian eall geleáffull folc, 91, 6. Swá se hyhtenda gigant (cf. *exultauit ut gigas*, Ps. 18, 6), 9, 34. v. be-hyhtau.

**-hyhtendlic**. v. ge-hyhtendlic.

**hyht-ful**. *Add*: [I. *full of hope*, *joy*, &c. v. Dict.]. II. *giving abundant grounds for hope*, *promising*:—Hyhtful *vel* ðiéndi *indolis*, Wrt. Voc. ii. 111, 54. Hyhtful, þiónde, þone gleáwan, 45, 58. v. hyht-lic.

**hyht-lic**. *Add*: I. *feeling joyous*, *exultant*:—Hergas wurdon on fleáme . . . him on láste stód hihtlic heorðweorod, Gen. 2076. II. *causing joy* or *pleasure*, *pleasant*:—Þæt is sió án rest ealira geswinca, hyhtlicu hýð heáum ceólum módes usses, Met. 21, 11. Nis þæt betlic bold . . . ne nóht hyhtlic hám, ac þǽr is helle grund Dóm. 24. Wile mon mec hátan hyhtlic gewǽde, Rä. 36, 12. III. *giving ground for hope*, *hopeful*, *promising*. v. hyht-ful ; II :—Þá weard lafede geogoð áféded, hyhtlic heorðwerod heáfodmága, Gen. 1605.

**hyhtlíce**; *adv.* *Pleasantly*:—On þám græswonge gréne stondað ge-broden hyhtlíce beorhtast bearwa, Ph. 79.

**hyhton**? :—Betwux middele hyhton (hlyttan? v. ge-hlytta) *inter medios cleros*, Ps. Spl. 67, 14.

**hylc**. *Substitute*: I. *a bend*, *winding*, *tortuous way* ; anfractus (cf. anfractum, iter tortuosum *vel* difficile, Corp. Gl. H. 18, 657):—Stíge mistlicum hylcum dweliende (*a recto*) *tramite errabundis anfractibus exorbitans*, An. Ox. 3696 : Wrt. Voc. ii. 9, 54. Fram stíge geond wóge hylcas on þá swýþran hand búgende *a tramite per obliquos anfractus dextra* (*levaque*) *declinantia*, 3427. II. *an inequality of surface*, *a hump*, *roughness of land*:—Ábrocen land *vel* hilcas (-es, MS.) *anfractus*, Wrt. Voc. i. 55, 12. Wóge smeþiende hylcas *salebrosos* (i. *asperos*) *conplanans anfractus*, An. Ox. 1772. Hyllceas, 4, 28. [v. N.E.D. hulch *a hump*.] v. ge-hylced.

**-hylced**. v. ge-hylced : **hyld**, held, es ; *m.* *Dele*, *and see* hild, es ; *m.*, *and* hyldu ; *f.*: **hyldan** *to bend*. v. hildan : **hyldan** *to flay*. *Add*: [v. N.E.D. hild.] v. holdian: **hyld-áþ**. *Add*: [Ðá Wylisceen kingas cóman tó him and becóman his menu and him heldáðas swóron, Chr. 1114 ; P. 245, 25.] : **hylde** *a slope*. v. hilde : **-hylde**. v. -hilde.

**hyldere**. *Add*: *one who flays by scourging*:—Hyldere *lictor* vel *virgifer*, Wrt. Voc. i. 66, 26. Cf. hýd ; II a. *and* tintreg-þegn.

**hylding**. v. hilding.

**hyldu**. *Add*: held[u]. I. *kindness*, *affection*, *good will*:—For hylde and lufe *affectu*, Wrt. Voc. ii. 3, 65. I a. *good will towards a benefactor*, *gratitude*:—Ðonne hé his ælmessan dǽld . . . ne gíeme hé hwelce hylde hé mid ðǽre ælmessan gewriexle *ne impensae gratiae vicissitudinem requirant*, Past. 323, 18. II. *of the relation between lord and man*. (1) *the favour*, *grace of a lord* (human or divine) *shown to the man*:—Æfter þám eall þeós worold geceás Agustuses frið and his sibbe ; and eallum monnum nánuht swá gód ne þúhte swá hié tó his hyldo becóme, and þ hié his underþeówas wurden *Agustus cunctis gentibus una pace compositis*, Ors. 5, 15 ; S. 250, 18. Oft ágyltað ðá hláfordas and ðá menn wuniað on Godes hyldo *plerumque offendunt qui regunt*, *et in patrisfamilias gratia permanent qui reguntur*, Past. 321, 3. Hé ús eft laðude tó his hyldo *ad recuperationem nos gratiae vocavit*, 407, 1. Hete hæfde hé æt his hearran gewunnen, hyldo hæfde his ferlorene, Gen. 301. (2) *the loyalty*, *devotion of the man to the lord*:— Sægde Clitus for ealdre hyldo (*from devotion to his old lord* (*Philip*)) þæt Philippus mǽre hæfde gedón þonne Alexander, Ors. 3, 9 ; S. 130, 28. Þám þe egsan his healdað mid hyldo, Ps. Th. 84, 8. Hí lybbað

on ēcnysse mid þām heáhfæderum for heora hylde wið God, Hml. S. 25, 740. Ic þē mīn gehāt, . . . hyldo gylde *vota tua quae reddam*, Ps. Th. 55, 10. For eówrum hyldum þē gē mē symble cȳddon, Ll. Th. i. 276, 19. Ic wæs ðīnum fæder fullīce hold on mōde and on mægene, and ðē ǣne on fullum hyldum hold and on fulre lufe, C. D. iv. 301, 1. (2 a) on hyldum (*with gen.*) *as the vassal* or *officer* of a person :— Hē fōr on þæs cynges heldan (in loco regis, Florence of Worcester, Chr. P. ii. 282) uppon heora brōðer, Chr. 1095; P. 230, 18. His mæg Eádgār hē ʒær on þæs cynges Willelmes heldan tō cynge gesette, 1097; P. 234, 15. (2 b) *devotion* to the service of a lord :—Hire hyrdeman ðurh holdrǣdene sume āc āstāh, and his orf lǣswode . . . and hē hearde feóll, gewāt of worulde tō Gode for ðǣre hylde his hirdrǣdene, Hml. Th. ii. 150, 33. III. in adjuration, or affirmation, swearing, where the possession of the lord's favour is connected with a course of action :— Swā ic āge Pharaones helde, ne farað gē heonon *per salutem Pharaonis non egrediemini hinc*, Gen. 42, 15. ‘Ic hālsige eów for þæs Cāseres helda þ gē mē secgon hwæðer hē of forligere sig ācenned.’ Hig cwǣdon : ‘ Hyt nys nā on ūre ǣ ālȳfed tō swerigenne, and swā ðēh swā wē þæs Cāseres helda habban mōton and swā wē deáþes scyldige ne wurþon, þ nys hē nā of forligere ācenned,’ Nic. 4, 6–11. Gecȳþe seó gewitnysse þ on Godes helde and on hlāfordes (*the Latin versions have* in fide (fidelitate) Dei et domini sui; per sacramentum, þ heó him on sōðre gewitnysse sȳ (*for the forms of oaths see* pp. 178 sqq.), Ll. Th. i. 388, 23. Gehȳrde hē hū þā menn him betwȳnan sprǣcon and oft and gelōme Crīstes helda swōron (*swore by Christ* ?), Hml. S. 23, 529. [v. *N. E. D.* held.] v. rihthlāford-hyldu.

**hylfe.** v. hilfe: -hylian. [*Goth.* huljan: *O. Sax.* be-hullean: *O. H. Ger.* hullen: *Icel.* hylja.] v. be-hylian.

**hyll.** *Add*:—Hyl odðe beorh *collis*, Wrt. Voc. i. 80, 43. On ðā rūgan hylle, C. D. iii. 454, 1. Dena ł hylla *colles*, Ps. L. 113, 4. [The word occurs as the second element of many local names. v. Midd. Flur.] v. ǣmett-, ciric-, eág-hyll.

**hyl-lic** (?); *adj. Hilly :*—Þis syndon þā tūnas . . . ōþer is hillic lēg . . . feorþe healf burhlēg, fīfte gislic lēh, C. D. B. iii. 577, 17.

**-hylman.** v. for-hylman: **-hylmend.** v. ofer-hylmend: **hylp.** v. help: **hylte**, es; *m. Substitute*: -hylte, es; *n.* v. heáh-, scōm-hylte.

**hylu**, e; *f. A hollow :*—Of ðǣre wylle on þā hyle; ðonne be ðǣre hyle, C. D. iii. 407, 12.

**hymblīcae.** v. hymlīce: **Hymbre.** *Add*: v. Sūþan-hymbre.

**hymele.** *Add*: The word translates several foreign plant-names:— Hymele *volvula* (cf. wudu-winde), Wrt. Voc. i. 289, 63. Hymele. Ðeós wyrt ðe man *politricum* and ōðrum naman hymele nemneð byþ cenned on ealdum hūsstedum, and eác on fuhtum stōwun, Lch. i. 154, 23–26. Hymele. Genim þās wyrte ðe man *bryonia* and ōþrum naman hymele nemneð, Lch. i. 172, 1–3. Hegeclife and hymelan, gearwan and geáces sūran, iii. 12, 30. ¶ *in local names* :—Hymelbrōc, C. D. iii. 443, 22: Hymel-mōr, 206, 32 (Ymel-, 26.): Hymel-tūn, 259, 29. v. hege-hymele; humele, eówo-humele.

**hymen.** v. ymen: **hymener.** v. ymener.

**hymlīce** (-lice ?), an; *f.: hymlīc* (-lic ?), es; *m. Hemlock. Take here* hemlīc *in Dict.*, and *add* :—Hymblīcae, huymblīcae, hymlīce *cicuta*, Txts. 46, 185. Hymlīc, Wrt. Voc. ii. 14, 32. Hymelīc, i. 67, 30 : *septiphilos*, 66, 64. Hymlīc *leptefilos*, ii. 54, 20. Slǣpdrænc; rædic, hymlīc . . . , Lch. iii. 22, 27. Wyrc sealfe of netlan and of hemlīce, ii. 128, 7. Well hemlīc, 78, 6. ¶ *in a local name* :—On hemlēclēge, C. D. iii. 437, 3.

**hȳn.** v. heán: **hȳnan.** v. hīnan.

**hynden.** *Add*:—On þāra hyndenna gehwelcere, Ll. Th. i. 136, 14. **hynden-lic.** v. hēdend-lic.

**hyngrian.** *Add*: I. *with nom. of person* :—Gif ic hyngre (hyngriu, Ps. Srt.) *si esuriero*, Ps. Vos. 49, 12. Ðā ðe hyncgrað *qui esuriunt*, Mt. L. 5, 6. Hyugcerde *esuriit*, 21, 18. Hiá hyncerdon *esurientes*, 12, 1. Hyngran (hingran, *v. l.*), hātian, calan, Bd. 1, 27; Sch. 82, 24. Hyngrende (hyncgerende, L.) *esurientem*, Mt. R. 25, 44. Sāwle ðā hyngrendan, Ps. Vos. 106, 9. Bidon gié hyngrendo, Lk. L. 6, 35. ‘ Brec ðǣm hyngriendum ðīnne hlāf, Past. 315, 13. Ðā hyngerendo (hy[n]crende, R.) gefylde, Lk. L. 1, 53. Hē gesamnode hungrigendan, Ps. L. 106, 36. II. *with dat. or acc. of person.* (1) *acc. or uncertain* :— Ðæt ungeornfulle mōd hyngreð (cf. 329, 2 for case), Past. 283, 12. Þonne ūsic hyngreð (-að, *v. l.*) . . . ūsic hingrian (hyngran, *v. l.*) mihte, Bd. 1, 27; Sch. 84, 5–8. Gif mē hingreð *si esuriero*, Ps. Th. 49, 13 : Bl. H. 39, 30. Sē ðe cymes tō mē ne hyncgreð (hyucre, R., hingrað, W. S.) hine *qui uenit ad me non esuriet*, Jn. L. 6, 35. Þā þe hié hyngrið (*qui esuriunt*, Mt. R. 5, 6. Leornernas his hyngrede (hingrede, W. S.), 12, 1. Mē hyngrede, Past. 329, 2. Þā welegan eódon biddende, and hī hingrode (*esurierunt*), Ps. Th. 33, 10. Hwæþer þā welgan nǣfre ne hingre (hingrige, *v. l.*), Bt. 26, 2; F. 92, 34. Þā þe hié on eorþan lēton hingrian for his naman, Bl. H. 159, 17. (2) *with dat.* :—Gif ðīnum fȳnd hingrige, fēd hine, Hml. S. 21, 375. v. of-hyngrod.

---

**hȳn-ness.** v. hīn-ness: **hynni-laec.** v. ynne-leác: **hȳnþ.** v. hīnþ (u, -o).

**hype.** *Add*:—Þeóh *vel* hype *femur*, Wrt. Voc. ii. 148, 18. ‘ Hæbbe eówer ǣlc his sweord be his ðió (*super femur suum*)’ . . . Is ðearf ðæt hē hæbbe his sweord be his hype (*super femur suum*), Past. 433, 15. Ðæt mon his sweord doo ofer his hype, 383, 4. Þurh þ swyrd þe him on hype hangode ðā hē ādranc, Cht. Th. 208, 22. Þonne þū gyrder habban wylle, þonne sete þū þīne handa forewearde wiðneoþan þinne nafolan and strīc tō þīnum twām hypum, Tech. ii. 119, 22.

**hȳpe** *heap.* v. hīpe.

**hype-bān.** *Add*:—Lendenu *vel* hypebān *renes vel lumbi*, hypebān *catacrina*, Wrt. Voc. i. 44, 36, 37. Hypbān *catacrinas*, ii. 129, 39.

**hypebān-ece**, es; *m. Sciatica* :—Wiþ hypebānece, Lch. i. 170, 8. Cf. hype-wærc, þeóh-ece.

**hȳpel.** v. hīpel: **hype-werc.** *l.* -wærc, *and add* : cf. þeóh-wærc : **hyppede** (?) *figit*, An. Ox. 46, 11 : hypsan. v. hyspan.

**hȳr.** *Add*: I. *payment contracted to be made for the temporary use of anything* :—Sume men syllað eác cyrcan tō hȳre swā swā wāclice mylna . . . ac hit ne gedafenað þ man dō Godes hūs ānre mylne gelīc for lydrum tolle, Hml. S. 19, 248. I a. *where the thing is money, interest, usury* :—Hȳre *fęnoris, usurę*, Germ. 389, 45. II. *payment contracted to be made for personal services, wages* :—Gif mē nū mettas and wīn, and ic hit þē gilde eft of mīre hȳre *I will pay it you back out of my wages* (cf. hē bæd þ hē mōste healdan heora æceras and him mēde earnian, 216), Hml. S. 30, 261. Hī ealle wǣron on ðǣre hȳre gelīce, Hml. A. 44, 509.

**hȳra.** *In* l. 5 *for* 38 l. 88, *and add* : I. *one who hires, a tenant* :— Hȳra *conductor*, Wülck. Gl. 213, 10. II. *one who takes wages* :— Hȳrena þeáwe gē fleóð. Suā se hȳrra ðonne hē ðone wulf gesiehð *mercenariorum vice deseruiunt, quia veniente lupo fugiunt*, Past. 89, 15. Hȳra *mercennarius*, Wülck. Gl. 213, 10.

**hȳra** *a subject*, **hȳran** *to hear.* v. hīra, hīran, hȳran *to exolt.* v. hīran.

**hyrd**, *parchment* (?), *a parchment covered with writing* (?) (cf. (?) herdo *vellus*. Stalder führt die Herde, Härde als ein in berner Oberlande gebräuchliches Wort für Schaaf- oder Ziegenfell, Grff. iv. 1030) :— Ic þæt gewrit þisse andweardan hyrde gesette *textum praesentis cartulae digessi*, Guth. Gr. 103, 53.

**hyrdan.** v. hirdan.

**hyrdel.** *Add*:—Hyrdel *cleata*, Wrt. Voc. i. 82, 16. Hyrthir (-il ?) *cratis*, An. Ox. 53, 37. Hyrdle *plecta*, 3888. Hyrdla, fȳrþollena *catastarum*, 4485. ¶ *of the bone-frame of an animal* :—Ostige ribba hyrdlas *squamigeras costarum crates*, An. Ox. 2466. v. loc-hyrdel.

**hyrd-lic.** v. hīred-lic: **hyrdung.** v. hirdung: -**hȳre.** v. ofer-hīre : **hȳred-ness.** *Dele.*

**hȳre-gilda.** *Substitute*: *One who pays hire* or *wages* :—Hȳre-gildan *mercedarii* (mercedarius *qui mercedem dat pro labore sibi inpenso*, Corp. Cd. H. 78, 181), Wrt. Voc. i. 18, 46.

**hyrel.** *Add*:—Hit cymð tō hyrel, tō ðām clife; and swā andlang clifes tō asdene; ðonne gǣð hit norð ofer hyrel, C. D. iii. 435, 14–15. The word seems the name of a stream?

**hȳre-mann.** v. hīre-mann: -**hȳreness.** v. on-hyreness: **hȳr-geoht.** *See* gecht *in Dict.*

**hyrian** *to imitate.* *Add* :—Ðā cild . . . hyriað ealdum monnum, Bt. 36, 5; F. 180, 10 note. v. of-hyrian.

**hȳrian.** *Add*: v. be-hȳran : -**hyriend.** v. on-hyriend : **hȳrig-mann.** v. hȳr-mann.

**hyring**, e; *f. Imitation, emulation* :—Ðurh þis beóð āwecte . . . herincga *hinc suscitantur . . . emulationes*, R. Ben. 128, 14. v. on-hyring.

**hȳring** *hiring.* v. be-hȳring.

**hȳr-mann.** *Add* :—*A hireling, mercenary* :—Iób cwæð : ‘ Mannes līf is campdōm ofer eorðan, and swā swā mēdgidlan dagas swā sind his dagas (*sicut dies mercenarii, dies ejus*, Job 7, 1)’ . . . Se hȳrman his edleánes anbidað, Hml. Th. ii. 454, 31. ‘ Ænne man ic ofslōh of þīnre hīwrǣdene’ . . . Wæs ān hȳrman tō wuda āfaren; sē læg gewundod, Hml. S. 31, 783. Symle sceal gōd scȳrman his hȳrmen scvrpan mid manunge, and him eác leánian be ðām ðe hȳ earnian, Angl. ix. 260, 22. [v. *N. E. D.* hireman.]

**hyrne.** *In* l. 6 *for* norð hyrnan *l.* norðhyrnan, *and add* :—Andlang ðǣre dīc; of ðǣre dīce hyrnan, C. D. B. ii. 434, 37. Anlang weges on ðǣre dīce hyrnan, C. D. iii. 411, 13. Hirnan, ii. 205, 16. Tō herpaðe; ðonan tō ðǣre dīcan hyrnan; ðonan andlang dīc, v. 78, 30 : vi. 170, 34. Of ðām wealle swā norð ðæt ðū cyme tō ðæs wealles hyrnan; of ðǣre hyrnan ā be wealle, iii. 424, 27. Tō garstūnæs hyrnan, v. 74, 6. Be eástwardan mōre oð ðā hyrnan, C. D. B. i. 296, 29. ¶ *in a local name* :—Oð Doddinghyrnan, C. D. i. 1, 16. [In the following perhaps þyrnan should be read for hyrnan :—On ðā brēmbelhyrnan; of ðǣre hyrnan, C. D. v. 112, 30.] [v. *N. E. D.* hern.] v. beáh-, norþ-, norþeást-hyrne.

**hyrned.** (v. ofer-hyrned.) *Add* :, hyrnede (v. eahta-, six-, þrī-hyrnede).

hyrnen; *adj.* *Full of corners* :—Hyrnynum *angulosis*, An. Ox. 7, 20. Cf. hyrn-full.

-hyrnende. v. ān-hyrnende : **hȳr-ness.** v. hīr-ness.

hyrnetu. *Add* : I. *a hornet* :—Hirnitu *crabro*, Txts. 52, 275. Hyrnetu, Wrt. Voc. i. 281, 41 : ii. 136, 60. Hyrnette (hyrnete, *v. l.*) *scabro*, Ælfc. Gr. Z. 307, 13. II. *a gad-fly* :—Beáw *vel* hyrnette *vestrum*, Wrt. Voc. i. 23, 64.

hyrn-full. *Add* :—Hyrnfullum, hyrnigum *angulosis* (*cellulis*), An. Ox. 121.

hyrnig. *See preceding word.*

hyrn-stān. *Add* :—Of hyrnstáne gecȳþnessa *angulari* (*duorum*) *testamentorum lapide*, An. Ox. 1546.

hyrst. *Add* : I. *a wood, copse* :—Hec sunt pascua porcorum . . . illa silua sandhyrst nominatur, C. D. ii. 65, 8. II. *an eminence, knoll* :—Wermód on hyrstum heasewe standed (cf. wermód byd cenned on dúnum and on stǽnilicum stówum, Lch. i. 216, 19) *glauca absinthia campi*, Rä. 41, 61. ¶ The word occurs in a great many place-names. Where the first part of the compound is the name of a tree hyrst probably belongs to I, e.g. æsc-, hæsel-, hnut-, holen-, mapolder-, seal-, þorn-hyrst. So, too, perhaps in earnes, úlan hyrst. But in some others it might belong to II, e.g. cysel-hyrst. [v. *N. E. D.* hurst.]

hyrstan *to murmur.* v. ge-hyrstan : **hyrstan** *to fry.* v. hirstan : **hyrste, hyrsting.** v. hirste, hirsting.

hyrsudon. *Substitute* : **hyrsian** (v. hors?); *p.* ode. *To go on horseback*(?) :—Ǽghwanon hyrsudon of eallum þissum bīfylcum tó his folgode and tó his þénunge dā æþelestan menn *ut undique ad eius ministerium de cunctis prope prouinciis uiri nobilissimi concurrerent*, Bd. 3, 14 ; Sch. 256, 13.

hyrsum. v. hīrsum : **hyrtan.** v. hirtan : **hyrthir.** v. nyrdel : **hyrwan.** v. hirwan.

hyscan. *Add* :—Hyscd *inridebit*, Ps. L. Rdr. 2, 4. Hisctun (*exprobrauerunt*) mē fȳnd mīne, Ps. L. 41, 11. Fram stefne hiscendre *a uoce exprobrantis*, 43, 17. Hihsendes bysmeres *subsannantis gannitures*, An. Ox. 5229. v. ā-, on- (*not* in-) hyscan.

hyscend, es ; *m. One who taunts, reviles, mocks* :—Hiscend *convitiator*, Germ. 398, 102.

hyse. *Add* : I. *a man* :—Swylce geongum hægstealde, rince, hysse *sicut effebo hircitallo*, An. Ox. 3476. Swā ungebyrdum hysse, 7, 247. Ungebarde hysse, Wrt. Voc. ii. 82, 33. (All three are glosses to Ald. 48, 2.) II. *a shoot, scion* :—Hisses, hosses *pampinos*, Hpt. Gl. 419, 69. v. hos.

hyse-beorþor. *Add* :—Hyseberþres *puerperii* (Maria post caelestis *puerperii* praeconium virgo remansit), An. Ox. 3908. Hysebyrþre *puerperio* (postquam Virgo Virginem sancto *puerperio* peperit), 4947.

hyse-byrding, e ; *f. Child-bearing* :—Mid heofenlicre heseberdincge *celesti puerperio*, An. Ox. 946.

hyse-byrþre, an ; *One who bears a* (*male*) *child* :—Ácende hyseberþre þæue þe (Gabriel) foresǽde *enixa est puerpera quem Gabriel praedixit*, Hy. S. 50, 34.

hyse-cild. *Add* :—Hé ofslóh ealle dā hysecild *occidit omnes pueros*, Hml. Th. i. 80, 15.

hyse-rinc, es ; *m. A young man* :—Adam wæs swíde weordlic hiserinc þā hine God ǽrest gehíwad hæfde tó mænniscum gesceape on þrýtiges wintres ylde, Angl. xi. 2, 25. Wæs sum hysering (*adolescens*) in þām mynstre . . . þysum cnihte seócendum, Gr. D. 338, 22.

hyspan. *Add* :—Sē de hespd . . . hespd his wer[h]tan *qui calumniatur* (*egentem*), *exprob*[r]*at factori eius*, Kent. Gl. 497-499. Hespd *exprobrat*, 591. Hyspd *subsannat*, 1089. Hȳ hypston *exprobrauerunt*, Ps. Rdr. 41, 11. Hyspendes bysmeres *subsannantis ganniture*, An. Ox. 4756. v. ā-hyspan.

hyspend. *Add* : A *mocker, reviler* :—Hé geeádmēd hyspend *humiliabit calumniatorem*, Ps. Rdr. 71, 4.

-hyspendlic. v. ge-hyspendlic.

hysp-full ; *adj. Scornful* :—Hipsfulre gebism[r]u[n]gce *ridiculoso ludebrii*, An. Ox. 11, 180.

hysping. *Add* : *Scoffing* :—Hyspyncge *cauillatione*, Hpt. Gl. 8, 247. Glíwlicre hypsingce *cauillo mimico*, Germ. 396, 318.

hȳþ *a port.* (*In* l. 4 *for* 131 *read* 133.) *Add* :—Hȳþ *recessus*, Germ. 400, 506. Hȳdae *de confugione. statione*, Wrt. Voc. ii. 106, 6. Hȳde *portum*, 67, 50. þā þā hé cóm tó Rómāna hȳþe (*ad Romanum portum*), Gr. D. 347, 16. Of dǽre hȳde andlang streámes, C. D. vi. 100, 6. Æ[t] hȳdum (æt[h]ȳdum wǽran gesette, Wrt. Voc. ii. 86, 30) *portunalia* (v. hȳþ-gild), An. Ox. 11, 186.

hȳþ. *l.* hȳþ, hȳþþ(u) :—Lyre *jactura*, hȳd *commodum*, Wrt. Voc. i. 74, 52. Swā hwæt on hȳdþe and on temprunge byd hālwende hit ys *quicquid cum modo* (but *commodo* has been read) *et temperamento fit, salutare est*, Scint. 54, 19. Tó þām þ hé him gedyde sume getǽse hȳdde his geswinces *ei laboris sui commodum dedit*, Gr. D. 39, 27. v. ge-hȳþþa.

hȳþan. *Add* :—Seó réde þeód Langbeardna . . . wæs hȳþende (hīþ-, *v. l.*) and éhtende úres sweóran *effera Langobardorum gens . . . in*

*nostram cervicem grassata est*, Gr. D. 258, 12. Hīdendum *grassantibus* (ad diram prostrata necem *grassantibus* armis, Ald. 204, 10), Wrt. Voc. ii. 96, 37. v. ge-hȳþan.

-hȳþe. v. ge-hȳþe : -hȳþegian : **hȳþegung.** *Add* :—þencende hȳþegunge *excogitando commoda*, Scint. 12, 6 : -hȳþelice. v. ge-hȳþelice : -hȳþend. -ā-hȳþend.

hȳþ-gild. *Substitute* : *A festival held at a harbour in honour of the god of harbours* :—Hȳdgylda *portunalia* (spurcas caeremonias exhibentes, aut lupercalia celebrando, vel *portumnalia* perpetrando, Ald. 67, 11), An. Ox. 4717. v. hȳþ.

-hȳþig. v. ge-, un-hȳþig : **hȳþ-lic.** *Add* : v. hȳþ-gild : -**hȳþness.** v. ge-hȳþness : **hȳwyt.** v. hīwet.

# I

ī, es ; *m. A letter* i :—Ān getitelad I getacnad ān þūsend, and twēgen īas getitelode, II, getācuad twā þūsend, and swā ford tó ǽlcum getele, Ælfc. Gr. Z. 282, 10-12.

iacinct. *Substitute* : iacinctus ; *gen.* iacin(c)tes ; *m. Jacinth* :—Se giem iacinctus *hyacinthus*, Past. 85, 5. On gimma gecynde carbunculus bid diórra donne iacinctus, and swadeáh dæt bleoh dæs iacintes bid betera donne dæs carbuncules ; for dǽm dæs de dæt gecynd forwiernd dǽm iacinte se wlite his beorhtnesse hit eft geiécd, 411, 27-30. Mid dǽm stāne iacincta (iecinta, *v. l.*), 83, 24. Iacincde (iacincte, *v. l.*), 87, 3.

ic. *Add* :—Of lāme ic þē leodo gesette, geaf ic þē lifgendne gǽst, ārode þē ofer ealle gesceafte, Cri. 1382. Ic þurh Iūdas ǽr hyhtful geweard and nū gehȳned eom þurh Jūdas eft, El. 922.

ican. *Add* : I. *to add.* (1) with the idea of supplementing or completing :—Huelchwoego in aldum bócum tó éccanne *aliquid in veteribus libris addere*, Mt. p. 1, 9. (1 a) *to add to.* (a) with dat. :—Dā eádigan fundon þās dómas and Cantwara rihtum þeáwum ǽcton, Ll. Th. i. 36, 13. (β) with prep. :—Hé þām bisceope gesealde on ǽht þreó hund hída and þær eác ȳhte tó, Bd. 4, 16 ; Sch. 425, 23. Gif wē þonne gyld ārǽrdon þ him man ȳhte ufon on þ be his wlites weorde, Ll. Th. i. 234, 6. (2) with the idea of increase, augmentation :—Meotud umbor ȳced, Gu. Ex. 31. Hé ūs monna mǽst mordra gefremede and swȳdor gȳt ȳcan wolde, Jud. 183. (2 a) *to add* after, to :—Man ȳhte yfel æfter ódrum, Wlfst. 156, 12. Ican āne elne tó his anlícnesse, Lk. 12, 25. II. *to add to.* (1) by way of supplement or completion :—þās lāreówas ne sceolan Godes dómas nāwþer ne nā wanian ne ne ēcan, Bl. H. 81, 4. (1 a) the material of addition given (a) in dat. Cf. I. 1 a a :—Hlódhære and Eádríc écton þā ǽ, þā þe heora aldoras ǽr geworhton, þyssum dómum, Ll. Th. i. 26, 5. (β) with *mid*. Cf. I. 1 a β :—Yc þ mid wīne, Lch. ii. 208, 2. Yc þonne mid ecede, 184, 20 : 190, 12. Críst cwæd þ hé ne cóme nó þās bebodu tó brecanne ac mid eallum gódum tó ícanne (*non veni solvere, sed adimplere*, Mt. 5, 17), Ll. Th. i. 56, 2. (2) *to increase, augment, enlarge* :—Under hū micelre frécenesse hié liecgad, and hū hié ícead (iécead, *v. l.*) hira forwyrd *quantis lapsibus succrescentis ruinae subjaceant*, Past. 233, 24. Hié hiera undeáwas iécead (iécad, *v. l.*) *culpa cumulatur*, 289, 14. Dæt hē wunda tó suíde ne íce (iéce, *v. l.*), 125, 15. Dā cræftas hí nyllad iécan, 463, 7. Éced *mactus*, Wrt. Voc. ii. 54, 71. (2 a) *to increase* with (a) with dat. :—Hé iécte mægdum and mæcgum mǽgburge síne, Gen. 1122. (β) with *mid* :—Hé ícte (iécte, *v. l. cumulavit*) his āgne scylde mid dǽm æfste, Past. 233, 21. Nimen hié him bisene on hira gódan weorcum, and ícen (iécen, *v. l.*) hié simle mid hira āgenum *proximorum facta imitando multiplicent*, 229, 16. v. æt-, ge-, oþ-(ot-), tó-, under-ícan.

ice. v. yce. *l.* íce. v. ȳce.

Icenhilde strǽt or weg *the old road running from the coast of Norfolk through Bedfordshire, Buckinghamshire, and Berkshire, thus connecting the east with south-west Britain.* Cf. Green's *Making of England*, p. 121 :—Dis synd dā landgemǽre intó Uffentūne (*Upton in Berkshire*) . . . intó Ikenilde strǽte ; of Ikenilde strǽt, C. D. v. 252, 30. Úp on Icenhilde weg, 107, 21 : 153, 33 : 332, 10, 17. Tó Iccenhilde wege, v. 153, 16. On Icenilde weg, vi. 102, 28. Ycenylde, iii. 97, 27. Ichenilde, v. 297, 17. On Icenhylte ; andlang Icenhylte, C. D. B. ii. 259, 11. .IIII. chimini ; scilicet Watlingestrete, Fosse, Hikenildestrete, Ermingestrete, Ll. Th. i. 447, 16. Hykenild, 478, 12. See Ll. Lbmn. ii. 522.

icge. *In* B. 1107 *the MS. has* ꝺicge=andiége (?). Cf. *Goth.* andaugjo *openly.*

-icge *a suffix of nouns denoting a female agent.* v. ācennicge, bar[r]icge, drȳicge, galdricge, hunticge, sericge (scern- ?), sealticge, synnicge. See Kl. Nom. Stam. § 44.

Iclingas. *Add* : The original Latin describing Guthlac's family is : Hujus viri progenies per nobilissima illustrium regum nomina antiqua ab origine ICLES digesto ordine cucurrit. Icel is mentioned in Mercian royal genealogies :—Cnebba wæs Iceling, Icel Eámæring, Chr. 626 ; P. 24, 11 : 755 ; P. 50, 6. Cnebba Icling. [Ic]il Eámæring, Txts. 170, 93.

See Chadwick's Origin of the English Nation s.**v.** [The name occurs in a charter :—On Icæles æwilmas tó Æðelbrihtes mearce, C. D. iii. 130, 33.]

**-ícness.** v. æt-, tó-ícness: **-ídan.** v. á-ídan.

**ídel.** *Dele* Past. 457, 20 *under* III, *and add*: I. *empty.* (1) of places, *unoccupied, without inhabitants :*—Stód seó dýgle stów ... ídel and æmen, Gú. 187. Oð ídel híwisce, C. D. v. 319, 21. Gif hé ðæt hús ídel (æmtig *vacantem*, Mt. 12, 44) gemétt, hé hit gefylleð mid monigum, Past. 283, 24. Duguð eal gecrong ... ýðde þisne eardgeard ælda Scyppend, oð þæt burgwara breahtma léase eald enta geweorc ídlu stódon, Wand. 79-87. (2) of persons, *not having anything, empty-handed.* (a) in respect to material things :—Nán man náh tó Godes cyrican ídel tó cumene, Wlfst. 238, 2. Samson nolde gán ýdel of ðære byrig, ac hé ábær ðá gatu úp tó ðære dúne, Hml. Th. i. 226, 31. Ðene forleorton geonga ídelne *eum dimiserunt uacuum*, Mk. L. R. 12, 3. (β) in respect to non-material things :—Ne fremda þú þære gesihðe þe þú mé ærest æteówdest, þ ic húru ídel heonone ne hwyrfe, Hml. S. 23 b, 671. (γ) *without food* (fig.) :—Gereorde sáwle ídle and sáwle hyngrende gereorde, Ps. Srt. 106, 9. Hingriende hé mid gódum gefylde and ofermóde ídele (ðá ídlo, L., R. *inanes*) forlét, Lk. i. 53. I a. *devoid of* something, *destitute of.* (a) with gen. :—Hwonne se dæg cume þ hé sceole þæs ealles ídel hweorfan, Bl. H. 97, 26. (β) with inst., *unprovided* with :—Hælu byð manna gehwylces mægene ídel *vana salus hominis*, Ps. Th. 59, 10 : 107, 11. Man byð merwe gesceaft, mihtum ídel *homo vanitati similis factus est*, 143, 5. II. of actions, feelings, thoughts, words, &c., *void of worth* or *usefulness, vain, ineffective, frivolous :*—His æfæstnes bið suíðe ídlu *hujus vana est religio*, Past. 281, 4. Riht spræc sý and behéfe, næs ídel *recta locutio sit et utilis, non anilis*, Coll. M. 18, 16. Éghwelc word ídil (*otiosum*), Mt. L. 12, 36. Ídel wuldor, þæt is gylp, Hml. Th. ii. 220, 27. Mid ídelum wuldre *coenodoxia*, i. *uana laude*, An. Ox. 1109. Mid ídelre dæde, Wlfst. 279, 8. Mid ídelre gewilnunge *effeta* (i. *exinanita*) *uoluntate*, An. Ox. 4677. Mid iédelre (ídelre, *v. l.*) ólicunge orsorgnesse hié gehátað ðæm scyldegan *incassum delinquentibus promissa securitate blandiuntur*, Past. 91, 10. Onæled mid ídele geseán, Bt. 14, 1 ; F. 40, 29. For þínum ídlan gilpe (v. ídel-gilp), Bl. H. 31, 14. Ymb ídelne gilp, Past. 85, 7. Mid ídelum gescotum *iactibus uacuis*, An. Ox. 49, 2. Be ídelstum wordum *de otiosis uerbis*, Scint. 217, 2. II a. of persons. (a) in respect to their actions, *useless, ineffective, unprofitable :*—Læreð þ ðá ídlo hiá gefyldon ðá ðe beboden woeron geondetað sint *docet ut inutiles* (cf. ðorleáso, Lk. L. R. 17, 10) *se implentes quae praecepta sunt fateantur*, Lk. p. 9, 7. Heora hæþenan gild wæron ealle ídelu and unnyt, and þ hié náwðer ne him sylfum helpan ne mihton, ne nánum ðára ðe tó him áre wilnodan, Bl. H. 223, 2. Ídle, orfeorme, unbiþyrfe, Jul. 217. Wutun hí ídle gedón (*exinanite*) oð þæt hí heora eard gecéosan, Ps. Th. 136, 7. (β) with regard to thought, words, &c., *foolish, without intelligence :*—Sé ðe cueðas bróðre his ðú unwís † ídle (ídla, R. *racha*) ... sé ðe cueðas ðú ídle † unwís (dysig † dole, R., þú stunta, W. S. *fatue*), Mt. L. 5, 22. Fífo wéron ídlo (dysige, W. S., R *fatuae*), 25, 2 : 3 : 8. Gif hwelc of ðæm ídlum (*curiosis*) wellæ wutta, Mt. p. 3, 2. III. of things, *useless, having no useful effect, serving no useful purpose, superfluous :*—Þæs restedæges æmethwíle ídle (*superuacuum*) wé tellað, An. Ox. 40, 18. Uton teolian þ ús þás tíida ídle ne gewítan, Bl. H. 129, 36. Hwær beóþ þonne his ídlan gescyrplan ?, 111, 35. IV. *idle, doing nothing :*—Hwý sceal ænig monn bión ídel þ hé ne weorce ?, Bt. 41, 3 : F. 248, 24.

**ídel, es ; n.** *Add*: I. *that which is useless, vain, or frivolous :*—Swá hwylc ídel swá him tó geþance yrnð and him gecoren bið, þæt hié taliað hálig, R. Ben. 9, 18. Ðá ðe willað tó fela ídles and unnyttes gespræcan *verbosi*, Past. 271, 7. Ídle *casso*, Wrt. Voc. ii. 103, 37 : 14. 4. Wá þám þe cyrican mid ídele sécað : þæt syndan þá ungesáligan þe ðær fleardiað mid ídelre spæce and hwílum mid ídelre dæde, Wlfst. 279, 5-8. Ðoune ongitt ðín sáwl ðæt ðú sylf lufodest ídel, Hex. 50. 22. ¶ on ídel. *Take here the passages in Dict. under* ídel ; III, *and add*: (1) *in vain, to no purpose :*—Hí on ídel sóhton sáwle míne, *ipsi in vanum quaesierunt animam meam*, Ps. Th. 62, 8. (2) *without cause :*—Ne flít ðú on ídel *ne contendas* (*contra hominem*) *frustra*, Kent. Gl. 57. Ne nemn þú Drihtnes naman on ýdel (*in vanum*) ; ne byð unscyldig sé þe his naman on ýdel (*frustra*), nemð, Ex. 20, 7. Ne dwela ðú on ídel *be not deceived without cause* (2 Macc. vii. 18), Hml. S. 25, 157. II. *idleness*, Prov. Kmbl. 1 : 61 (*in Dict.*) [The Latin translated in Lch. iii. 214, 11 is : Si uideris multas capras, uanitatem significat ; the Latin original of Guth. 70, 2 is : Non est praetereundum silentio ...] *See next word.*

**ídel-georn.** *Add*: I. *frivolous, useless, unprofitable.* v. ídel ; **n.** I :—Sé ðe wære ídelgeorn, weorðe s† notgeorn, Wlfst. 72, 9. II. *lazy.* v. ídel ; **n.** II. See examples in Dict.

**ídel-gilp, es ; n. m?** *Vain glory, arrogance :*—Hí befeallað on ídelgelp ... Is betere ðæt mon læte sume hwíle weaxan ðæt ídelgielp *inanis gloriae tentatione fatigantur* ... *Tolerandum est, ut . . . interim arrogantia crescat*, Past. 457, 19-23. [*For* ídel *as adjective qualifying* gilp *see* ídel ; II.]

**ídel-hende.** *Add :*—Nán man náh tó Godes cyrican ídelhende tó cumene, Wlfst. 238, 2. Hí eft of þám mynstre ídelhænde (-hende, -hynde, *v. ll.*) hwurfon *a monasterio vacui sunt regressi*, Gr. D. 16, 31.

**ídeling (-ung), e ; f.** *A worthless* or *trifling thing :*—Ídalinga (idalalinga, MS.) *friuola* (cf. *frivola* leásunga, Wrt. Voc. ii. 34, 55 : *fribula* híwunga, An. Ox. 1929), Germ. 389, 89.

**ídel-líc ; adj.** *Idle, vain, useless :*—Hwæt is swá ídellic oððe swá untrumlic swá swá þ man fordéme þone sóþan déman ?, Nap. 40.

**ídellíce ; adv.** I. *in vain, to no purpose :*—Haldende ídelnisse ídellíce (*supervacue*), Ps. Srt. 30, 7. Mon hwæðre ídellíce (*vane*) bið gedroefed, 38, 7 : 88, 48. II. *without cause :*—Ídellíce (*vane*) edwíttun sáwle míne, 34, 7. v. on ídel *under* ídel ; **n.**

**ídel-ness.** *For passage in l. 18 see* IV, *and add*: I. *emptiness.* Cf. ídel ; I. 2 :—Þá welegan hé forlæteþ on ídelnesse (*diuites dimisit inanes*, Lk. 1, 53), Bl. H. 5, 10 : 159, 19. II. *worthlessness ; a worthless, useless thing, a vanity.* Cf. ídel ; II :—Idelnessa *uana*, Wülck. Gl. 253, 29. Hwær beóþ þá symbelnessa, and þá ídelnessa, and þá ungemetlican hleahtras ?, Bl. H. 59, 18. II a. *a vain, false religion :*—Ýdelnysse *superstitionis*, An. Ox. 4429. Ýdelnysse *superstitione*, i. *uanitate*, 4021. Nú is se tíma þ ðú forláte þíne ýdelnysse, and lác ðám godum geoffrige, Hml. S. 22, 213. III. *lack of result, ineffectiveness.* Cf. II, II a a :—Hí ealne dæg mid ídelnesse (*frustra*) wunnon, Gr. D. 250, 21. On ídelnesse mon ongit Godes ðæt hefonlice wuldor, gif . . . *incassum gloria patriae coelestis agnoscitur, nisi . . .*, Past. 160, 17. In ídelnesse mec wordiað *in uanum me colunt*, Mk. L. R. 7, 7. IV. *idleness, lack of energy :*—Nys eác mid ídelnysse tó forelætanne þæt wundor *non me quoddam spiritale praesagium narrare piget*, Guth. Gr. 159, 1.

**ides.** *The word occurs as a gloss to* virgo, Kent. Gl. 1196, *and a weak form*, idesan, *glosses* juvenculam (Ald. 29, 14), An. Ox. 2136. *It is also found as a gloss to* virgo *in Aldhelm's poems* (Ald. 191, 7), An. Ox. 15, 4 ; 17, 52 : (Ald. 194, 14), An. Ox. 15, 5 ; 17, 59 ; 18, 29.

**idig.** *Perhaps for* to þas idge *should be read* tóþas grædige. *If* idge *be an independent word the vowel should be long.*

**ídisc . . . m. n** [?]. *Substitute :* ídisce, ídisc (ýdd-), es ; **n.**, *and add :*—Árís and ágif þyses ceorles ýddisce (æhta, *v. l.*) þe þú underfénge *surge et res istius rustici redde quas accepisti*, Gr. D. 164, 3. [*The suffix* -isc(e) *has a collective force.* Cf. híwisc(e).]

**ídlian.** *Add*: I. *to be* or *become empty, be unoccupied.* v. ídel ; I. 1 :—Fram ælce bígonge þis land ligeð tólýsed and ídlað in wéstenne *ab omni cultura destituta in solitudine vacat terra*, Gr. D. 258, 19. II. *to make vain, render nugatory.* v. ídel ; II :—Ídlod *cassaretur* (*cum quicquid molire deliberaret cassaretur*, Ald. 67, 7), An. Ox. 4711. III. *to render worthless, profane* sacred things :—Monige þone geleáfan þe hí hæfdon mid unrihtum weorcum ídledon *multi fidem quam habebant iniquis profanabant operibus*, Bd. 4, 27 ; Sch. 513, 7.

**ieó** (= geó), Ll. Th. ii. 366, 7 : **iescæ.** v. gesca : **iesen.** v. gesen.

**ífe** (?), an (?) ; **f.** *Some kind of plant :*—Rúde *ruta*, íue *iva*, brócminte *sisymbrium*, Wrt. Voc. i. 69, 1-3. [Cf. Span. *iva tenerium iva* ; and see *N. E. D.* herb ive.]

**ífig.** *l.* ífig, *and add* : [íf-ig ⟨ íf-hég. Cf. O. H. Ger. eba-hewi] :—Ífeg *edera*, Txts. 60, 392. Ibaei *hederam*, 112, 44. Ífig *eder*, Wrt. Voc. ii. 29, 3. Þæs blacan ífiges croppan, Lch. ii. 248, 21 : 268, 3. Hífia crop *hederarum corimbos*, An. Ox. 115. Íuia, 7, 17.

**ífig-beara (-o)** *a grove of ivy-covered trees* (? cf. ífiht) :—On ífigbeare, of ífigbeara, Cht. Crw. 1, 15.

**ífig-cropp.** *Add :*—Dó ðær tó ífigcroppas, Lch. iii. 12, 32.

**ífig-croppa.** *Add :*—Genim ífigcroppan, Lch. ii. 86, 20.

**ífig-rind, e ; f.** *Bark of ivy :*—Genim ífigrinde, Lch. ii. 338, 12.

**ífig-tearo.** *Add* : , -teoru, -teru :—Wensealf ; hiorotes mearh, ífigtearo, and gebeáten pipor, and sciptearo, Lch. ii. 128, 19. Íbigteru *cummi*, An. Ox. 53, 12. Ýuiterum (*printed* yuk- ; *for* k=i v. 392, 59, 94) *ederas*, Germ. 389, 26.

**ífig-twig, es ; n.** *An ivy-twig :*—Wiþ sunbryne ; merwe ífigtwigu, wyl on butran, smire mid, Lch. ii. 324, 16.

**ífiht.** *l.* ífiht(e).

**íg.** *Add* : [*Besides* íg *there seems to be a form* íge ; *m.* e. g. on Meldaníge éastewerdne, C. D. v. 303, 2. Of eallum Lindesíge (v. Lindes), Bd. 3, 11 ; Sch. 237. 10. In insula quae dicitur Seolesíge, C. D. v. 41, 27 : 52, 10. *Moreover there are instances of* íg *in the accusative*, e. g. Wið-westan hunddes-íg (cf. tó hu[u]ddes-íge, 5), C. D. v. 298, 7. On swannes-íg, vi. 108, 1 : *such forms seem to belong neither to* íg ; *f. nor to* íge ; *m.*, jó-, ja- *stems respectively.*] The word occurs in place-names :—Locum qui apud Anglos nuncupatur Ceroteég, id est Cirotis insula, C. D. ii. 122, 27. Hengestes-íg, v. 401, 26. On Beseríge ; ðonne on Fyrsíge, 300, 17. On meldaníge . . . tó Ceólesíge. 303, 2-3. Ðis sind ðá landgemæra tó Gósíge, vi. 8, 19. Æt Weattaníge, C. D. B. i. 544, 1.

**igeoþ.** *Add* : , ígeþ, ígþ :—Tó ðon crundele ðe se ígð on stent, C. D. v. 193, 33. Út ongeán stréam tó snítan-íge, on norðhealfe þæs ígeðes,

C. D. B. ii. 374, 15. Ofer ðonæ īgað, C. D. v. 173, 23. Andlang eaxan oþ focgan īgeþas, of focgan īgeþum, Cht. Crw. 3, 3; C. D. B. iii. 667, 2-3. v. īw-īgaþ.

**igil.** *Add:* , iil:—Iil *ericius*, Txts. 59, 765: *histrix*, 69, 1023. Stān gebeorg īles (igles, Txts. 336) *petra refugium erinacis*, Ps. Vos. 103, 18. Ilum *herenacis*, Ps. Rdr. 103, 18. ¶ in a local name:— Tō īlmere, C. D. vi. 4.

**īg-land.** *Add:* , iég-, ī-land:—Ān īglond ligð ūt on gārsecg ... þeáh nū ānra hwā wealde þæs īglandes, Met. 16, 12-17. On þām iéglande þe Sicilia hātte, Bt. 15; F. 48, 20. On ān īglond ūt on Wendelsǣ, Bt. 38, 1; F. 194, 11. Oþ þæt īland þe wē hātað Thyle, 29, 3; F. 106, 23. Ic īglanda eallra hæbbe bōca onbyrged, Sal. 1.

**-iht.** *Add:* , -eht; -ihte, -ehte (-i), -ecti. *As most adjectives with one or other of these forms occur in the oblique cases only, it is impossible to say which form should be given in the nominative; but the* -iht *is found in* þorniht, *and the* -ihte (-ehte, -ecti) *in* ĕcilmehti, bogehte, clibecti (clifihte), ōmihte, stānihte, þōchte; *uncertain instances are* cambiht(e), clufeht(e), flāniht(e), hǣriht(e), hǣþiht(e), helmiht(e), hōciht(e), horheht(e), horweht(e), hreódiht(e), hrīsiht(e), īfiht(e), īsiht(e), rysciht(e), siniht(e), sandiht(e), þyrniht(e), wāriht(e), wudiht(e), wundiht(e). [Cf. *O. H. Ger.* -ohti.]

**iht** *yoked.* v. ge-iht.

**-ihtig, -ehtig.** v. clifihtig, hreódihtig, secgihtig, wurmsihtig. [Cf. *Du.* steenachtig.]

**ilca.** *In bracket for 'only' substitute:* '*as a rule, but for strong forms see* An. Ox. 5050, Bd. Sch. 450, 15', *and add:* I. in weak declension. (1) as adjective:—Se ilca wiþerwearda þe him ǣr þā synna lǣrde, Bl. H. 61, 17. Be þǣm ilican (ilcan, ylcan, *v. ll.*) andgyte, R. Ben. 4, 9: 64, 3. Þāra ilcena engla geféran, Gr. D. 260, 20. (2) as substantive:—Se ilca sē ðe wénde ðæt hē wǣre ofer ealle, Past. 39, 24. Þis is se ilca þe þū for his deáþe plegodest, Bl. H. 85, 18. Ne sý him nānre ōðere þigene getīðod būton þæs ilican (ilecan, ilcan, *v. ll.*) þe hē ǣr forsóc, R. Ben. 69, 22. Dauid sang þysne sealm ymb swýðe lang þæs þe hine God ālýsed hæfde ... for þǣm ylcan hine sang Crīst þonne hē ālýsed wæs ..., Ps. Th. 17, arg. Hē spone ðā ðe his ðeáwa giémað tō ðǣm illcan (ilcan, *v. l.*), Past. 83, 3. His freónda forespræc forstent him eal þæt ylce þe hit sylf sprǣce, Wlfst. 110, 4. II. in strong declension:—Þǣre ylcre geþinþe *eiusdem propositi*, An. Ox. 5050. Mid þǣre gehrinennesse þāra ylcra (ilcena, *v. l.*) gegyrela (gegyrelena, *v.l.*) *tactu indumentorum eorundem*, Bd. 4, 19; Sch. 450, 15. v. ge-ilca.

**ilce.** *Add:*—Sume unðeáwas cumað of ōðrum suā ilce suā hié cōmon ǣr of ōðrum *quaedam vitia sicut ex semetipsis gignunt alia, ita ex aliis oriuntur*, Past. 306, 19. Þā yfelan hyne geseóð swā ylce swā þā gōdan, Solil. H. 67, 16. Weaxe sió bōt ... swā ilce swā sió manbōt dēð, Ll. Th. i. 150, 15. Swā ilce (same, *v. l.*) swā, 17: 19. And swā ylce be þǣre ōðerre sunnan, 45, 13.

**ild.** *Add:* II.—Seó mearewǣste cildes yld *tenerrima infantis etatula*, An. Ox. 2867. Hē his ealdan ylde ofergetiligende ... arn, Hml. S. 23 b, 185. Hē hit eác gefremode, gif hē þā ylde hæfde *he would have done it too, if he had had the requisite age*, 31, 27. III. of a particular time of life. (1) *old age*:—Ābogenre, hnīþendre ylde *cernua, curua uetustate*, An. Ox. 1280. Ic mid ylde (for yldum, *v. l.*) gewǣht eom, Hml. S. 23 b, 782. (1 a) of things:—Ǣlc hūsl þe bið on ylde *omne sacrificium quod est vetustate corruptum*, Ll. Th. ii. 218, 9. (2) *youth*:—Mīne ylde *iuuentutem meam*, Ps. L. 42, 4. v. cild-, for-, ofer-ild.

**-ild(e).** v. frymþ-ild(e).

**ildan.** *Add:* I. *to delay.* (1) with acc.:—Ne yllde (ylde, *v. l.*) hē hit þā leng, Bd. 2, 12; Sch. 152, 4. (2) with clause:—Tō won yldest þū þ þū tō Gode gecyrre?, Archiv cxxii. 257, 9. Ne yld þū nā þ þū gecyrre ... Sē þe yldeð þ hē ne gecyrre. Ne yldon wē nā fram dæge tō dæge þæt wē tō Gode ne gecyrron, Wlfst. 151, 15. (3) with dat. infin., Bl. H. 7, 33 (*in Dict.*). (4) absolute or uncertain:—Ic ylde *elongo, prolongo*, Wrt. Voc. ii. 143, 23. Ylde, elcode *distulit, i. moram fecit, abduxit*, 141, 46. Hē þā lange wiðsakende yllde *diu negando distulit*, Gr. D. 103, 31. Aelden *tricent*, Wrt. Voc. ii. 122, 81. Bið ilded *differtur*, 26, 7. II. *to dissimulate*:—Ne sceal hē hit nō yldan and hīwian, swilce hit him uncūð sý *neque dissimulet peccata deliquentium*, R. Ben. 13, 16. III. *to decay with age.* Cf. ildu; III a.:—Ielde *cararit* (for *curarit*, Ald. 157, 8), Wrt. Voc. ii. 91, 55: 19, 37. v. ā-, ge-ildan.

**ildcung**, e; *f. Delay:* [Ild-, eld-, yld-]cung[e] *dilatione*, An. Ox. 56, 129. v. eldcung.

**ildend.** *The proper reading in the passage given is* ylding:—Næs þā nǣnig ylding tō ðǣm *nec mora*, Guth. Gr. 129, 135.

**ildenn**, e; *f. Delay, deferring, putting off:*—Ildenne *dilatione*, Wrt. Voc. ii. 25, 75. Būtan ǣnigre yldenne (yldinge, *v. l.*) *sine ulla dilatione*, Bd. 1, 27; Sch. 80, 2.

**ildest.** *Add:* I. *eldest:*—Seó mǣgð āsprang of Nōes eltstan suna, Hml. Th. i. 24, 7. II. *chief.* (1) as adjective:—Yldest burhwara *proceres* vel *primores* vel *primarii*, Wrt. Voc. i. 18, 40. Ðæt ieldesðe

---

setl on gemētengum hī sēcað, Past. 27, 8. Þā yldestan cāseras *Aggusti*, Wrt. Voc. ii. 8, 18. (2) as substantive, a *chief person*:—Sē ðe eówer yltst sý, Mt. 23, 11. Clypa tō þē þā yltstan of Israhēla folce, Ex. 17, 5. v. heáh-ildest.

**ild-full**;- *adj. Causing much delay, dilatory:*—Þeús yldfulle (ylfulle, Hpt. Gl. 529, 6) letting *hec morosa tricatio*, An. Ox. 5454. I[l]defulle, 2, 478.

**ildian.** *Add:* I. with oblique case. (1) acc.:—Hē wæs lange wiðsacende and hit eldode *diu negando distulit*, Gr. D. 103, 32. (2) with dat. (?), Hml. Th. i. 350, 14 (*in Dict.*). II. with (negative) clause:—Se munuc gehýrde þā word þæs hātendan, ac hwæþre hē yldode þ hē þā hǣsa gefyllan nolde *monachus audivit jubentis verba, sed implere distulit*, Gr. D. 159, 16. III. absolute:—Gehýrde Dryhten and yldode (*distulit*), Ps. L. 77, 21.

**ilding.** *Add:*—Aelding *dilatio*, Wrt. Voc. ii. 106, 38. Elding *dilatio*, i. *mora*, 140, 33. Næs þā nǣnig ylding tō þām *nec mora*, Guth. Gr. 129, 135. Gif fǣrunga cymð se ýtemesta dæg, þonne bið losod seó yldi[u]g *if the last day comes suddenly to the man who has deferred his conversion, the time during which he has delayed will be lost* (?), Archiv cxxii. 257, 17. Ylding *dilationis*, Wrt. Voc. ii. 28, 67. Yldinge *fascis* (*mentis cervicem gravi fascis sarcina deprementibus*, Ald. 80, 1), An. Ox. 8 b, 1. Yldincga *tricarum*, i. *morarum*, 2079.

**ildra;** *adj. Add:* I. *of greater age:*—Hē is wintrun yldra þonne ic *me aetate praeibat*, Gr. D. 218, 26. I a. of parents in contrast with children:—Bearn, beó gē underðiódde eówrum ieldrun māgum *filii, obedite parentibus vestris*, Past. 189, 22. I b. where persons of the same name are distinguished by age, *elder, senior:*—Rōmāne besǣton þone ieldran Hannibalan *inclusus ea obsidione senior Annibal*, Ors. 4, 6; S. 170, 29. II. where difference of date is marked, *earlier, former* in contrast with present:—His mæsse bið geseted on ðǣm eldran mæssebōcum, Shrn. 90, 34. II a. qualifying terms of relationship in direct ascent, *grand-, great-[great ...] grand-:*—Mīn yldra fæder *my grandfather*, C. D. ii. 116, 16. Felix mīn eldra (yldra, *v. l.*) fæder *Felix atavus meus* (cf. Felix wæs his (*Gregory's*) fīfta fæder, Hml. Th. ii. 118, 9), Gr. D. 286, 12. Sió gifu hiora fæder and heora eldran (eolldran, *v.l.*) fæder *vel paterni vel aviti specimen ingenii*, Bt. 10; F. 28, 32. Yldran fæder *avitum*, Wrt. Voc. ii. 96, 61. Þurh ildran fæderas *per atavos*, 65, 72. III. *belonging to an earlier time:*—Ne dyde hē swā eldran cynne, Ps. Th. 147, 9. IV. denoting position, rank, *greater, superior, elder:*—Ðā Apostolas and þā eldran (ældran, yldran, *v. ll.*) brōður *Apostoli et seniores fratres*, Ll. Th. i. 56, 13.

**ildra;** *m. Add:* I. *of relationship.* (1) *a parent:*—Sume habbað bearn genóge, ac ðā beóþ hwīlum unhāle oþþe yfele ... þ ðā eldran for þām gnorniaþ, Bt. 11, 1; F. 32, 9. Mið ðý in lǣddun ældru his (*parentes eius*) ðone cnæht, Lk. R. 2, 27. Ældro, 43. Manige bearn beóþ gestrýned tō heora eldrena forwyrde, Bt. 31, 1; F. 112, 9. (2) in pl. *more or less distant kinsfolk of a person in direct ascent:*—Se mon sē þe bócland hæbbe and him his yldran (mǣgas, *v. l.*) lǣfdon, Ll. Th. i. 88, 16. Manigne mon sceamaþ þ hē weorþe wyrsa ðonne his eldran wǣron *imposita nobilibus necessitudo ne a majorum virtute degenerent*, Bt. 30, 1; F. 110, 4. Hē hiene hētt bebyrgean an his ieldrena byrg *hunc referri in sepulchra majorum sepelirique praecepit*, Ors. 3, 9; S. 128, 16. (2 a) of an animal:—Seó leó gemönd þæs wildan gewunan hire eldrana, Bt. 25; F. 88, 13. (3) *ancestors, fathers of a people:*—Ūre ieldran þisne ymbhwyrft þises middangeardes on þreó tōdǣldon *majores nostri orbem totius terrae triquadrum statuere*, Ors. 1, 1; S. 8, 1. Eówre ieldran, 4, 13; S. 212, 24. Eoldran, Bt. 16, 1; F. 50, 7. Gif hié gemunan willað hiora ieldrena (*majorum suorum*) unclænnessa, Ors. 2, 1; S. 64, 14. Þ burg seó wæs on ǣrdagum heora ieldrena ēðel *urbem auctorem originis suae*, 4, 5; S. 168, 11. II. of position, rank, &c., *a superior, a noble:*—Bituīn aeldrum *inter primores*, Wrt. Voc. ii. 111, 42. Betweón ieldrum, 45, 55. Betweoh yldrum, 49, 1.

**ildu.** *Add:* I. *an age, one of the six ages of the world:*—Yldo *evo* (*primo*), Wrt. Voc. ii. 94, 80. Þes middangeard néde on ðās eldo endian sceal þe nū andweard is; for þon fīfe þāra syndon āgangen on þisse eldo, Bl. H. 17, 35. II a. *age, time of life:*—Hāt baðo ǣlcere yldo and hāde gescrǣpe (*omni aetati et senui accommodos*), Bd. 1, 1; Sch. 9, 1. II a. of a thing:—On þæra sex fīfa ǣlcon on þæs mōnan eldo, Lch. ii. 16, 3. III. *old age:*—Hī (*Adam and Eve*) ne mihton forealdian, ne deáde beón ... ðā underðeóddon hī selfe ... tō eldo and tō deáðe, Shrn. 66, 20. III a. *decay from old age.* Cf. ildan; III:—Yeldo *grues* (l. *caries*; the line glossed is: Quae quassat *caries*, et frangit fessa vetustas, Ald. 153, 28), Wrt. Voc. ii. 91, 22. Eldo *cnues* (l. *caries*, and cf. *caries*, *putredo lignorum vel ferri sindor vel vetustas*, 129, 10), 19, 35. v. cild-, for-, or-ildu.

**ile;** *m. Add:* ill, es; *n.* I. *sole of the foot:*—Illa *plantarum*, Lch. i. lxxi. 12. Ila, lxxiv. 23. II. *hard skin:*—Ile *callus*, Wrt. Voc. ii. 127, 51. Wearras, ilas *callos*, 13, 48.

**ilf.** [*The gender of* ælf, ilf *seems nowhere decisively fixed, but the*

*forms* dūn-ylfa, -ælfa *seem to show that at any rate sometimes it is feminine.*] *Add*:—Sȳ þ ylfa þe him sié, þis him mæg tō bōte, Lch. ii. 290, 29.

**ilfig.** *Add*:—Ylfige, An. Ox. 4937. Cf. gydig.

**ilfette.** *Add*:—Æluetu *cicnus*, Hpt. 33, 240, 10. Iluetu (*printed* ilnetu) *ciciris* (*cicnus*? cf. i. 280, 10 where *ciciris* is given in a list of birds, but without an English equivalent. A similar list is given on p. 62, and there *cignus* occurs just before *mergulus*, as at p. 250 does *ciciris*), Wrt. Voc. ii. 16, 15. Cf. Æt ylfethamme, C. D. iii. 130, 34.

**ilnetu.** *Dele, and see preceding word.*

**ilpen.** v. ylpen.

**imbe** *a swarm of bees. Take here* ymbe *in Dict., and add*: Cf. Of ðām mōre on imbaleá, C. D. v. 277, 13. v. imb-stocc.

**imb-haga.** *Take here* ymb-haga *in Dict.*

**imb-stocc,** es; *m. A stump with a swarm of bees in it*:—On ðæne ymbstocc; of ðām ymbstocce, C. D. v. 234, 26.

**impian** *to imp, graft*:—On længtene eregian and impian, Angl. ix. 262, 7. [*O. H. Ger.* impfōn: *Ger.* impfen. v. *N. E. D.* imp.] v. ge-impian.

**in;** *prep. Add*: **A.** with dat. inst. **I.** of position or location. (1) *within* any place or thing:—Gif in cyninges tūne man mannan ofsleá, Ll. Th. i. 4, 4. In (on, *v. l.*) cyninges healle, 66, 8: 82, 8. Sié þe in heáhnessum ēce hǽlo and in eorðan lof, Cri. 411. Gekȳþe hē þ hē þ feoh in wīc gebohte, Ll. Th. i. 34, 10. Gif in feaxe (*in the part of the head covered by hair*) bið wund, 92, 18. Seó sceal in eágan, Gn. Ex. 123. Hiora in ānum weóll sefa, B. 2599. (1 a) where a place is defined by a characteristic:—Mēde on heofonum, sigorleán in swegles wuldre, Jud. 345: Dan. 404. (1 b) with proper names of countries, towns, &c.:—In (on, *v. l.*) Breotone, Bd. 2, 12: Sch. 157, 12: Men. 40. Gif hit man in Cænt ætfō, Ll. Th. i. 34, 6. Hē wæs ǽr in Mercum preóst in Breódūne, Chr. 731; P. 45, 8. Þā þe in Norþhymbrum būgeað and on Eást-Englum, 894; P. 86, 7. (2) of position. (a) *on*:—Of ðǽm mere ðe Trūsō standeð in staðe, Ors. 1, 1; S. 20, 9. Hē wrāt in wāge worda gerȳnu, Dan. 723. Ðǽr bād in cynestōle cáseres mǽg, El. 330: B. 1952. Þes wudu āworpen ligeð in eorðan, Rä. 41, 50. Gekȳþe hē in wiófode (cf. Cliroc hine clǽnsie . . . āne his hand on wiófode, 40, 18) mid his gewytena ānum, Ll. Th. i. 34, 8. (b) *at*:—In midle *in centro*, Wrt. Voc. ii. 92, 13. Cwæþ hē þus in fruman þæs epistoles, Nar. 1, 8. (3) with collectives. (a) as singular, *in*:—Mǽrsiað mīnne restendæg in eówrum cynne, Wlfst. 210, 21. In mǽgða gehwǽre, B. 25. Þā wæs gefrēge in þǽre folcsceare, El. 968. In þām gārheápe, Exod. 321. (b) as plural, or with plurals, *among*:—Gif man in Lencten hālig ryht in folce ālecge, Ll. Th. i. 88, 13: Gen. 2834: Hy. 4, 87. Swǽse men in leódum, Ll. Th. i. 38, 3. In þǽm gāstlicum þrymmum, Bl. H. 21, 15. (4) defining the particular part of anything in which it is affected:—Gif mon bið in (on, *v. l.*) exle wund, Ll. Th. i. 98, 5. Godes ōrettan in sefan swencan, Gū. 542. (5) expressing relation to that which covers, clothes, &c.:—Freóst hine clǽnsie in his hālgum hrægle, Ll. Th. i. 40, 14. Þā hié in hyra gryregeatwum gangan cwōmon, B. 324. Gefrætwed in eádwelum, Ph. 586. (6) marking a whole where the parts forming it are stated:—Þrȳ sind in naman ryhte rūnstafas, Rä. 59, 14. (7) *in a book, in* a company, where the subject matter of a book, or a member of a company, is referred to:—Þæne heriað in gewritum rincas regolfæste, Men. 43. Sint in bōcum his wundor cȳðed, El. 826. Þrītiga sum þāra monna þe in þām here weorþuste wǽron, Chr. 878; P. 76, 17. (8) with non-physical objects considered as having extension or content:—Healded Meotudes ǽ in breóstum, Ph. 458: An. 51. Hē herede in heortan heofonrīces weard, 52. Him wæs Godes egsa in gemyndum, Gū. 139. In mōde, Mōd. 83: B. 180: Dan. 218. In wera līfe, Cri. 416. **II.** of situation, condition, occupation, form, &c. (1) of situation, kind of position:—In līge sār wānian, Gū. 1085. (1 a) situation expressed by material instruments, *in* bonds, set *in* silver, &c.:—Ic sceal bīdan in bendum, Sat. 49: Gū. 545: Rä. 54, 6. Stān in goldfate smiða orþoncum biseted, Ph. 304. (1 b) situation as to light, darkness, &c., and atmospherical environment:—Þā þe in þeóstrum sǽton, Cri. 116. Þæt wē ūs behȳdan magon in þissum neowlan genipe, Sat. 102. Þeóf sceal gangan in þȳstrum wederum, Gn. C. 42. (1 c) situation within the range of sensuous observation or the sphere of action of another, *in* the sight, hearing, power, care, &c.:—In gemōtes gewitnesse, Ll. Th. i. 82, 16. In gesihðe, Gū. 731. In gewealdum wuldorcyninges, Gū. 568: 666. In his meahtum sind ealle gesceafta, Jul. 182. In Godes dōme, Gū. 82. In dracan fæðme, El. 766. Sāwla ne mōton in mīnum ǽhtum wunigan, 907. In Godes wǽre, Gū. 718. In freoðu Dryhtnes, Ph. 597. (2) of condition or state:—Hē in oferhygde lifde, Dan. 107. Ic in wīte sceal bīdan, Sat. 48. In sibbe, Ph. 601. In hǽlo, Gū. 368. Lifgan in lisse, Ph. 672. In yrmðum, An. 163. In cearum, Gū. 193. In wrǽcsīðe, 595. In sorgum, El. 694. In dȳgle, Gū. 437. In līfe, Ph. 607. In līfe *when alive*, An. 597. Wunian in gewinne, Cri. 622. (2 a) with concrete substantive:—Ne mæg þǽr manna gecynd gefēran in līchoman, El. 737: Gū. 732. In flǽschaman, Ps. C. 143. (3) of occupation:—Hē leofað in leahtrum,

Mōd. 76: Sal. 316. Hē in gylpe wæs, Dan. 636. In lofe, Wal. 88. Gē in gestalun stondað, Gū. 481. (3 a) *in the act* or *process of*:—Hine synnigne man gefō in ceápe oþþe elles æt openre scylde, Ll. Th. i. 124, 22. Gē weorðmyndu in dolum dreáme Dryhtne gieldað, Gū. 435. (4) of form, order, &c.:—Se þreát þāra Godes þeówa in wīfhāde *ancillarum Dei caterva*, Bd. 4, 7; Sch. 385, 15. (5) of manner in speech or writing:—Tō þǽre ceastre þe in Englisc is hāten Kalcacester, Bd. 4, 23; Sch. 466, 15. (6) of means or instrumentality, *with*:—Mynstres aldor hine cænne in preóstes canne, Ll. Th. i. 40, 13. Ic beóm onsended þæt ic in mānweorcum oncyrre hyge from hālor, Jul. 439. Monige þeówiað in þeáwum, Gū. 473. Þām þe his in weorcum willan ræfnað, 594. Ic in līchoman and in mīnum gǽste Gode campode, 615. (7) of measure, *within*:—Ne geweorðe þ crīsten man gewīfige in .vi. manna sibfæce, Ll. Th. i. 318, 13. (8) expressing object, aim, purpose, &c.:—Ne wē swylc ne gefrugnan gelimpan þæt þū in sundorgiefe swylce befēnge, Cri. 80. In egesan engel Drihtnes lēt his hand cuman in þæt heá seld, Dan. 721. (9) expressing reference or relation to something, *in reference* or *regard to, in the case* or *matter of*:—Ðū in (on, *v. l.*) mihte and on rīce hī oferstīgest, Bd. 2, 12; Sch. 157, 12. Se gǽst þīhð in þeáwum, Gū. 369. **III.** with special forces. (1) *belonging to* as an attribute:—Ne ic culpan in þē, incan ǽnigne, ǽfre onfunde, Cri. 177. (2) *partaking in, associated in*:—Hæbbe hē ǽnne mid in āðe, Ll. Th. i. 28, 12. Hæbbe hē him in āðe ōðirne ǽwdan, 42, 8. (3) of representative character, *in* the name of:—In Crīstes noman . . . and in þǽre hālgan rōde naman, Wlfst. 224, 9–11. **IV.** expressing relation. (1) of the action of a verb to an indirect object, to rejoice *in*, &c.:—Gē gefeóð in firenum, Gū. 479. (2) of an adjective (or participle) to some department to which its qualification is limited:—Æþele in (on, *v. l.*) weoruldgebyrdum, Bd. 4, 23; Sch. 464, 3. Snottor in sefan, Exod. 438. In dǽdum deór, Seef. 41. Gleáw in gǽste, Cri. 139. Trum in breóstum, Men. 134. Gleáw in geþance, El. 807. (3) of substantive to a certain sphere:—Geofu in godcundum mægne, Gū. 501. Dǽl in godcundum gǽstgerȳnum, 219. **V.** temporal. (1) within the limits of a period or space of time:—In foreweardum Danieles dagum, Chr. 709; P. 40, 25. In ǽrdagum, Cri. 79. In ealddagum, 303. In geárdagum, 251: 822. In fyrndagum, Exod. 559: Dan. 317: Ph. 570: Gū. 601. (1 a) with sbs. implying time:—Ic ǽfre in ealdre ǽngum ne wolde þæs melda weorðan, Gū. 1202. In woruldlīfe, Dan. 103: Crä. 15: Gū. 1142. In geoguðe, Seef. 40. (2) of a limit of time, *within the space of*:—Ne wē þǽre wyrde wēnan þurfon tōweard in tīde, Cri. 82. (3) where other preps. or none are now more usual. (a) *on*:—Þone dæg in þām seó hālige rōd gemēted wæs, El. 1224. (b) *during*:—Ic þone dēman in dagum mīnum wille weorðian, Gū. 590. Þīn geleáfa in līfdæge on ūrum mōde þurhwunige, Hy. 6, 8. In hyra līfdagum, Wal. 75. (b a) with words implying time:—Gehalde hine heofones cyning in ðissum līfe ondwardum and eác swā in ðǽm tōwardan līfe, C. D. ii. 121, 32. In þone dēman wille lufian in līfe (*during life*), Gū. 592. (c) where no prep. would be used:—Siendon þīne dōmas in daga gehwārm sōðe, Dan. 287. **B.** with acc. **I.** of motion. (1) after verbs of coming, going, bringing, putting, sending, &c. (a) where a material object moves to a position:—Gif man in mannes tūn geirneð, Ll. Th. i. 6, 16. Þ ne þeówe ne freó ne mōton in (on, *v. l.*) þone here faran būtan leáfe, ne heora nān þe mā tō ūs, 156, 1. In þæt seld gangan, Dan. 151. Scūr sceal in þās woruld cuman, Gn. C. 41. Lǽtað gāres ord in gedūfan in fǽges ferð, An. 1334. ¶ with proper names:—Ðā fērdon Peohtas in (on, *v. l.*) Breotone, Bd. 1, 1; Sch. 11, 20. (1 a) *with* innan:—Engel in þone ofn innan becwōm, Dan. 638. Hē biered in þæt treów innan torhte frætwe, Ph. 200. (b) where the subject of the verb is non-material:—Oð ðæt wintra rīm gegǽð in þā geoguðe þæt se gǽst lufað onsȳn yldran hādes *until years come upon youth* (*until a man gets older*), *so that the spirit loves the appearance of an older state*, Gū. 470. Oðer cōm geár in geardas, B. 1134. Lēt his bēn cuman in þā beorhtan gesceaft, Gū. 749: El. 1089. (2) after verbs in which the idea of motion is not explicitly expressed:—Hī feor þonan in þās deáðdene drohtað sōhton, Ph. 416: Gū. 1343. His sefan trymman tō wuldre in þā wlitegan gesceaft, 1090. Heó þā rōde hēht in seolfren fæt locum belūcan, El. 1026. ¶ in a figurative expression. v. sceát; **IV.**—Gif hió ōðrum mæn in sceát bewyddod sī, Ll. Th. i. 24, 5. (2 a) with verbs expressing birth or creation:—Þū fram mīnre dohtor onwōce in middangeard, Sat. 440: B. 60. Bearn in woruld cennan, Vy. 2: Cri. 452: 640: El. 336. God sāwle in wuldor āwecað, Ph. 567. Ne ǽnig þāra dreáma þe Dryhten gescōp gumum tō glīwe in þās geómran woruld, Ph. 139. (2 b) with collectives, expressing entrance or admission to membership:—Þæt wæs wīglic werod, wāce ne grētton in þæt rincgetæl ræswan herges, Exod. 234. (3) in reference to non-physical regions. Cf. A. I. 8:—Geác sorge bodeð in breóstheord, Seef. 55. Ic onsende in breóstsefan bitre geþoncas, Jul. 405. Nalæs hȳ him gelīce lāre bǽron in his mōdes gemynd, Gū. 89. **II.** of situation or position, condition or state. (a) *into* the embrace, clutch, &c. (*lit.* or *fig.*):—Þū scealt þīn feorh beran in gramra gripe, An. 217: 953. Sāwle bescūfan in fȳres

fǽdm, B. 185. (b) *into* the power, possession, care of, *into* the sight. Cf. **A. II.** 1 c:—In feónda geweald, An. 1621. Him wundra fela Alwalda in ǽht forgeaf, Exod. 11. Him engla God hálige heápas in gehyld bebeád, 382. In gehyld Godes, An. 117. In Godes wǽre, Men. 39: Gú. 662. In eágna gesihð, Rä. 60, 9. (2) in reference to state or condition. Cf. **A. II.** 2:—Woldun hý geteón in orwénnysse Meotudes cempan, Gú. 547. In ècne gefeán, Men. 173. Ne lǽd þú ús in costunge, Hy. 6, 28. In wíta forwyrd, An. 1620: El. 765: Leás. 10. In þeóde þrym gestígan, Crä. 19. In líf onwæcnan, Ph. 640. Hé ácenned wearð in cildes hád, El. 776. Hé in binne wæs in cildes híw cláðum biwunden, Cri. 725. (3) introducing that into which anything turns or is made:—Hí hogedon þæt heán mægen ne hwyrfe in hǽðendóm, Dan. 221. Hí setton mè in edwít þæt ic eáðe forbær rúme regulas, Gú. 459. (3 a) introducing the condition or result brought about by some action:—Hé þæt hluttre mód in þæs gǽstes gód georne trymede, Gú. 78. (3 b) of exchange. Cf. to turn *into* money = sell *for* money. Cf. on ; **B. III.** 8:—His freónd in gold (on gold, wiþ goldes, *v. ll.*) bebycgan *amicum suum auro uendere*, Bd. 2, 12; M. 130, 33. (4) introducing parts produced by division:—Wæs tódǽled in tuā bisèscíra West-Seaxna lond, Chr. 709; P. 40, 26. **III.** of direction without motion of the agent. Cf. on ; **B. III.** 3:—Gúðlác his in Godes willan mód gerehte, Gú. 66. Onstèp mínne hige in gearone rǽd, Hý. 4, 39. **IV.** expressing the relation (1) of a verb to some indirect object, to believe *in*, trust *in*:—Ic þæt gelýfe in liffruman, ècne onwealdan ealra gesceafta, Gú. 609: An. 562. Hé in his meahte gelýfeð, Seef. 108. þú in ècne God getreówdes, Jul. 434: Gú. 617. (1 a) corresponding verbal nouns have a similar construction:—Hæfde hé geleáfan in liffruman, Dan. 643. (1 b) where a verbal noun with another verb is equivalent to a simple verb in (1):—Gúðlác sette hyht in heofonas, Gú. 406. Ic in mínne fæder hyht staðelie, Jul. 436. (2) of adjective to some department to which its qualification is limited. Cf. **A. IV.** 2:—Sum bið á wið firenum in gefeoht gearo, Crä. 90. **V.** temporal. (1) *within* the limits of a space of time:—Gif mon in Lencten hálig ryht álecge, Ll. Th. i. 88, 13. (1 a) with other sbs. implying time:—Hé in þá ǽrestan ældu gelufade frécnessa fela, Gú. 80. (1 b) with processes occupying time:—Gif þisses hwæt gelimpe in Lenctenfæsten, 88, 12. þám bið Dryhten scyld in síða gehwane, Ph. 464. (2) of a limit of time, *before* or *at the expiration of, within the space of*:—þæt þus his unrím in wintra worn wurðan sceolde, Dan. 325. Durupegnum wearð in áne tíd hildbedd styred, An. 1093. (3) where other preps. or none are now more usual. (a) *at*:—On þǽre þeóde wæs in þá tíd Sæbyrht cyning *in qua gente tunc temporis Saberct regnabat*, Bd. 2, 3; Sch. 123, 3. In ǽlce tíd, Cri. 406. In þá þpelan tíd (*at Christ's birth*), 455; Ph. 509: 517: An. 912. In swá hwylce tíd swá gé tó mè hweorfað, Reb. 5. (b) *on*:—Eánfléd wæs gefulwad in þone hálgan ǽfen Pentecosten, Chr. 626; P. 24, 8. (c) *during*:—In þá slíðnan tíd, Mod. 52: Gú. 1058. Lǽran þæt hié sylfra betweónum freóndrǽdenne gelǽston in hira lífes tíd, El. 1209. (d) *without prep.*:—In ealle tíd *all the time*, Ph. 77: Edw. 32. v. on-, þǽr-in.

**in-ádl.** *Add*: Cf. in-copu.

**in-ǽlan.** *Add*:—Holen sceal inǽled, yrfe gedǽled deádes monnes, Gn. Ex. 80. Gesáwon hí ǽnne ofen inǽledne (*succensum clibanum*), Gr. D. 219, 12.

**in-bærniss, -bærnniss.** *Add*:—Mid inbernisse *cum incensu*, Ps. Srt. 65, 15.

**in-betýnedness, e; f.** *Inclusion, shutting in, confinement*:—Hé wæs manig gǽr ána belocen in þám nearwestan scrǽfe . . . on þǽre frumtíde his inbetýnednesse, Gr. D. 210, 27: 212, 5.

**in-bláwan.** *Add*: *To inflate*:—Mid oferhigde gáste inbláwen *superbiae spiritu inflatus*, Gr. D. 200, 10. Gif ǽnig sý inbláwen on þá oferhýda þǽre geǽttredan deófles láre, Cht. E. 242, 20.

**in-boren; adj.; in-borena, an; m. [Ā]** *native*:—Inborena *indigena*, Germ. 390, 32.

**in-bryrdan.** *Add*: v. ge-inbryrdan.

**in-bryrdness.** *Add*:—Hú manega cynn sýn þǽre inbyrdnesse (on-, *v. l.*) *quot sunt genera compunctionis*, Gr. D. 244, 23 : 242, 1.

**in-búan.** *Add*: v. ge-inbúan.

**in-burh.** *Add*:—Inbirig *uestibule*, i. *atrii*, An. Ox. 3828. In[byrig?] *atria*, 8, 274.

**in-byrdling.** *Add*: **I.** *a native*:—Sicelic inbyrdlinc t bur[h]leód *siculus indigena*, i. *ciuis*, An. Ox. 3957. Inbyrdling, 2, 275. **II.** *a slave*:—Inbyrdlincg *uerna*, i. *seruus*, An. Ox. 7, 185.

**inc.** *Add*: **I.** alone:—Ne fornime incer nóðer óðer ofer will, . . . ac geǽmtigeað inc tó gebedum, Past. 399, 34–36. ' Fæder, wé ábidon þ þú cóme ' . . . 'Cwepað git þ ic ne ætýwde inc (inc bám, *v. l.*) slǽpendum ?', Gr. D. 149, 11. Lǽt inc gesèman, Past. 349, 12. **II.** *with* bègen:—þé and . . . þín ágen bearn . . . inc bám ic geháte, Hml. S. 23 b, 449 : Sat. 488 : Wlfst. 259, 15, 16 : Gr. D. 149, 9. ¶ plural and dual forms are used of the same persons:—Se ealdor and his prófost cómon, þus cweðende: 'Wé andbidodon ðín, . . . and þú ne cóme ' . . .

' Hwí secge gé þæt ic ne cóme ? Hwæt lá ! ne æteówode ic inc bám slápendum ? Farað and árǽrað þæt mynster swá swá ic eów on swefne dihte ' (cf. swá swá git gehýrdon slǽpende þurh gesihðe, Gr. D. 149, 15), Hml. Th. ii. 172, 18–28. ' Úre hláford hèt eów (*John and Paul*) gebiddan tó þyssere anlícnysse, oððe ic inc bègen ofsleá.' þá cwǽdon þá hálgan : ' Ne cunne wè . . .' Hé hèt þá twǽgen gebróðra beheáfdian, Hml. S. 7, 411–418.

**inca.** *Add*: **I.** *an occasion, opportunity*:—Beháten þá mágas þæt hý nǽfre nǽnne incan ne sécan, hú him tó syndrigum ǽhtum gerýmed sý *promittent quia numquam ei tribuant occasionem habendi*, R. Ben. 103, 18. Ne gedyrstlǽce heora nán . . . þæt hé Godes áre gewanige oþþe ǽnigne incan sèce, hú heó gewanod weorþe, Lch. iii. 442, 17. **II.** *a cause of complaint*:—Hyra nán ne gedyrstlǽce þæt hé . . . ǽnig ðing áhsige . . . þe lǽs þe ǽnig inca (incca, *v. l.*) gesæld sý (*ne detur occasio*), R. Ben. 62, 19. **III.** *a scruple, doubt*:—Ynca *scrupulum*, Wrt. Voc. i. 16, 46. Incan, tweónunge *scrupulum*, i. *dubitationem*, An. Ox. 4198. Nú tóbræc and tólýsde swíðe cúð gesceádwísnes þone incan and tweón mínes geþóhtes *scrupulum cogitationis meae aperta ratio dis-olvit*, Gr. D. 228, 2.

**-incel.** *Add*: v. bóg-, cof-, dóc-, hæft-, liþ-, stán-, súl-, tún-, þeów-, wíl-incel. [v. Kl. Nom. Stam. § 63 : Beiblatt. 15, 238 sqq.]

**incer.** *Add*:—þurh hincre *per uestram* (of you two) (*doctrinam*), An. Ox. 2, 204. Tó hwon sweriað git mán ? ac wǽron æt þisse wydewan háme and þǽr þus incer líf leofodon, Guth. 64, 7. ¶ plural and dual forms used of the same persons:—Ic geseó þæt eówer mód is áwend, for ðan ðe gé eówre spéda þearfum dǽldon : gáð nú tó wuda, and heáwað incre byrðene gyrda . . . Bicgað eów landáre . . . Bicgað eów pællene cyrtlas þæt gé tó lytelre hwíle scínon, Hml. Th. i. 62, 31–64, 14. Hundas licciað eówre blód and fugelas fretað incer flǽsc Shrn. 148, 3.

**in-cerran** (= on-cirran, *q. v.*) *to pervert, divert*:—Gif aenig monn ðás úre gewitnisse incerre on ówihte, C. D. ii. 6, 11.

**incfullian.** v. ge-incfullian.

**incge.** *Add*: l. (?) Incge[s] láfe. Incg- *occurs several times in local names*. v. C. D. vi. 306.

**in-cígan.** *Add*: v. ge-incígan ; on-cígan.

**in-cleofð[u, e; f.?]** *an inner chamber, a lair*:—Swá swá leó on incleofe, Ps. Rdr. 9, 30. Unryhtwísnesse hé smeáde on incleofe his, 35, 5. v. in-cleofa.

**in-cniht.** *Add*:—Incniht *parasitus*, Hpt. Gl. 504, 21. Incnihtas, híwcúþan *clientes*, i. *socii*, An. Ox. 870. Incnihtum (-cnihttum, Hpt. Gl. 514, 54) *clientibus*, 4684 : *parasitis*, Hpt. Gl. 483, 74.

**in-cofa.** *Add*:—Eóde Martinus tó ánes mannes húse. þá ætstód hé fǽrlíce ætforan þám þrexwolde, cwæð þ hé egeslicne feónd on þám incofan gesáwe, Hml. S. 31, 530. [Tó] incofu[m] [*ad cordis*] *penetralia*, An. Ox. 5407.

**in-copu.** *Add*:—Incoþa *colera*, An. Ox. 31, 2 : *incommoditates*, i. *infirmitates*, 1981. Colera rubea, þ synt reáde incoða, beóð on sumera . . . On hærfeste beóð colera nigra, þ synt swearte incoðan, Angl. viii. 299, 30–34. Incoþan *melancolias*, i. *nigrum fel*, An. Ox. 3049. ¶ In the gloss *fibras* þearmas incoþe, An. Ox. 1978, perhaps innoþas or innoþa should be read : the passage is : Viscerum fibras, Ald. 26, 33.

**in-cund.** *Add*: **I.** physical, *of the inner part of the body*:—Búton þæt incunde blód ðe anbútan þǽre heortan is út yrne, E. S. viii. 62, 40. Tó incundum *ad intima* (*ventris*), Kent. Gl. 999. Incundum *imis* (*ilibus*), An. Ox. 5, 23. **II.** non-physical, in reference to mind, feeling, spirit. (1) denoting earnestness, sincerity:—Hé geoffrode his lác mid incundre heortan, Hml. S. 25, 795. His Drihten heriende mid incundre heortan, 37, 193. Gif gé þá hálgan láre underniman wyllað on incundre heortan, Hml. A. 26, 53. (2) of deep feeling, *coming from the heart*. v. incundlíce:—Incundre ábryrdnesse *infimi* (*intimi*?) *amoris*, An. Ox. 1184. Gif hé mid eallre heortan and incundre geómerunge clypað tó Gode, Hml. S. 19, 183. Mid sóðre behreówsunge and mid incundan wópe, 192. þ hí hine lufion mid incundre lufe and mid eallre heortan, Hml. A. 42, 445. (3) *of the inward parts, of spiritual nature*:—Ðæt hí mǽgen ðǽm inncundan (in-, *v. l.*) Déman on hira ágnum inngeðonce lícian *ut interno judici in semetipsis placere studeant*, Past. 195, 22. Ne hé him ne ondrǽde nánne eorðlicne ege ðyses andweardan lífes, ac geðence hé ðone inncundan (in-, *v. l.*) ege Godes (*respecto intimo terrore*), 83, 5.

**incundlíce; adv.** *From the heart, with deep feeling.* Cf. in-cund ; **II.** 2:—Uictor incundlíce geómerode and hlúde clypode, Hml. S. 28, 99.

**incund-ness, e; f. I.** *feeling that comes from the heart, heartiness, earnestness.* v. in-cund ; **II.**:—Wé hine lufiað and wurðiaþ mid gewissum geleáfan cweþende mid múðe and mid módes incundnesse þæt sè án is sóð God, Wlfst. 105, 30. **II.** *an inner part.* Cf. incund ; **I.**:—Beón clǽne heortan incundnes *sint pura cordis intima*, Hy. S. 9, 18.

**in-cyme, es; m.** *In-coming, entrance*:—Ðá hé þæne cyrceward gehýrde hrútan, þá ne wénde hé him nánes incymes (*there was no hope for him of any getting in*), Vis. Lfc. 32.

**Indea.** *Dele, and see next word and* India.

**Indéas.** *Add:* , Indie *Indians;* or using the name of the people for that of their country, *India:*—þ deór Indéos hátað *dentes tyrannum,* Nar. 15, 15 : 22, 8. Indos, 26, 19. On Indéa londe is XLIIII þeóda *India habet gentes xliiii,* Ors. 1, 1 ; S. 10, 17. India, 15. Æfter þǽm hé fór on Indie . . . hé geeóde Nisan, India heáfodburg . . . Æfter þǽm þe hé hæfde ealle Indie him tó gewildon gedón . . . Hé cóm on India eástgemǽra *post haec Indiam petit . . . Nyssam urbem adiit . . . Perdomita India . . . Ad Chofides ventum est,* 3, 9 ; S. 132, 4–29. Þá þá hé wæs on Indéum, 136, 6. Deáh hé rícsige ofer eallne middangeard . . . from Indéum þ is súðeástende þisses middaneardes *licet Indica tellus tua jura tremiscat,* Bt. 29, 3 ; F. 106, 22.

**India, Indéa;** *f. India:*—Wyrdwríteras secgað þæt ðrý leódscipas sind gehátene India. Seó forme India . . . , seó óðer . . . , seó þridde ; þeós þridde India . . . , Hml. Th. i. 452, 11–14. Þurh þá uncúðan land Indie *per ignota Indie loca,* Nar. 6, 12. Ðá wynstran dǽlas Indie *sinistram partem Indie,* 20, 19 : 21, 7. Wé cwómon in Indie lond *in India peruenimus,* 4, 2. On óþer þeódlond India (*or under* Indéas ?) *in alias Indie regiones,* 22, 2. Þá wilnode ic Indeum innanwearde tó geseónne *interiorem Indiam perspicere cupiens,* 5, 17. On Indea, Chr. 883 ; P. 79, 7.

**in-digolness,** e ; *f. A secret place:*—Hé ásette ðýstro his indígelnesse *posuit tenebras latibulum suum,* Ps. Rdr. 17, 12.

**Indisc.** *Add:* I. as adjective:—Astriges, se Indisca cyning, Hml. Th. i. 524, 33. II. as subst. (1) Indisca *an Indian:*—Ðá hǽðengyld þe ðás Indiscan wurðiað, Hml. Th. i. 456, 14. Þá Indiscan willað beón eówere gafolgylderas, ii. 482, 31. Þæra Indiscra kyning ásende tó sécenne sumne wyrhtan . . . 'Sende mé þyder þe þú wille búton tó þám Indiscum' . . . ' Þú mé gestrýnst þá Indiscan, Hml. S. 36, 18–25. Þá bodan cómon fram ðám Indiscum, Hml. Th. ii. 484, 6 (2) on Indisc *in Indian language:*—Þá wǽron wunderlicum nomum on Indisc gecéged *Indica lingua erant uocitate,* Nar. 26, 11.

**in-drencan.** *Add:*—Indrencu straelas míne *inebriabo sagittas meas,* Ps. Srt. ii. p. 196, 27. Ðú indrenctest hié *inebriasti eam,* Ps. Srt. 64, 10. v. ge-indrencan ; on-drencan.

**in-drincan.** *Add:*—Rinnellan his indrincende, Ps. Srt. 64, 11. v. on-drincan.

**in-eardian.** I. *to dwell:*—Ic ineardiu (*inhabitabo*) in getelde ðínum, Ps. Srt. 60, 5. Ðú ineardas in him, 5, 12. Ðá rehtwísan ineardiað ofer hié, 36, 29. Ðæt ic ineardie in húse Dryhtnes, 22, 6. From hete ineardiendra in hire, 106, 34. II. *to inhabit:*—Dryhten cwildeflód ineardað *Dominus diluvium inhabitat,* Ps. Srt. 28, 10. Inearda eorðan, 36, 3. Þæt ðú ineardie eorðan, 34. v. on-eardian.

**in-eardiend,** es ; *m. An inhabitant:*—Hwylc wæs þǽr áweht tó þám eorre bútan þám ylcan temples ineardiend ? *quis alius ad irascendum nisi ejusdem templi inhabitator excitatur ?,* Gr. D. 63, 12.

**in-fær.** *Add:* m. I. *an entrance, a way by which a place is entered:*—His folce ðú scealt heofenan ríces infær geopenian, Hml. Th. ii. 134, 15. Þæt se ungesewena wulf infær ne geméte hwanon hé in tó Godes eówde cume *ne lupus inuisibilis aditum inueniat, quo ouile Domini ingredi ualeat,* Chrd. 21, 13. II. *a going into a place:*—Hig geseágon þine infæras (*ingressus*), infæras mínes Godes, Ps. L. 67, 25. III. *right or permission to enter:*—Wíte hé þæt him ælces infæres forwyrned bið *sciat omnem sibi aditum denegari,* R. Ben. 53, 16. Ne sig him ná eáðelíce þæs infæres getíðod (*non ei facilis tribuatur ingressus*) . . . Gif hé bit þæt him mon infæres tíþige, 95, 4–8. Hí noldon geðafian þám bisceope þ hé infær hæfde his ǽrende tó ábeódenne, Hml. S. 31, 655. Þæt hé preósta gatu . . . lúce and unlúce, þ man næbbe infær bútan leáfe (*ut nulli nisi per licentiam aditus pateat intrandi*), Chrd. 20, 10.

**in-færeld.** *Add:* I. *an entry, a place or way by which one enters, a vestibule:*—Hé hý lǽdde intó þám infærlde þære cytan, and hé sylf into þǽre inran eóde and ðá duru him tó beclýsde, Hml. A. 196, 30. Deáð wið infereld gelustfullunc[ge] is *mors secus introitum delectationis est,* R. Ben. I. 30, 13. Godcundre lage infæreldu eádmódum geopeniað *diuine legis penetralia humilibus patent,* Scint. 221, 5. Foredura, infærelda *uestibula,* i. *introitum* (*alvearii*), An. Ox. 135. Infærelda *uestibula* (*coelestis regni*), 3894. II. *right or permission to enter:*—Ne sí him eðelic forgifen infæreld *non ei facilis tribuatur ingressus,* R. Ben. I. 95, 12. Sí forgifen infæreld *annuatur ingressus,* 17.

**infangene-þeóf.** *Add:*—Ic an heom þ hý habben . . . infangeneðeóf (In the Latin version of the charter this is rendered : Concedo ut habeant . . . potestatem fures in terra sua cum re furtiua deprehensos in ius uocandi et puniendi), C. D. iv. 202, 8. Mid tolle and teáme and infangeneðéf, 217, 29. Ic an toll and teám and infangeneðéf, 216, 5, and often. [v. *N. E. D.* infangthief.] v. handfangen[e]-, útfangene-þeóf.

**inflǽscness.** *For* 'Lye' *substitute:*—Hælendes inflǽscnisse ðý gére . . . DCCCC wintra and IIII winter, C. D. B. ii. 268, 5 ; Cht. E. 161, 23. v. onflǽscness.

**in-fóster.** *Add: breeding on one's own farm, rearing from one's own stock.*

**in-fyrde,** es ; *n. Entrance to a ford (?):*—Andlang díces tó infyrde á be mǽre on Temese ; andlang Temese, C. D. vi. 84, 19. On ðá rǽwe ; of ðære reáwe on Temese, on ðæt infyrde ; andlang Temese, v. 275, 21.

**ing.** v. inn ; *adv.*

**-ing.** *Add:*—Ealderas Neptalinga *principes Neptalim,* Ps. L. 67, 28. v. god-, wædl- (?), Wóden-ing.

**in-gán.** *Add:*—Hé hine swá swýþe deóplíce mid his láre ineóde þæt hé nǽfre ǽr ne syþþan swylc ne gehýrde *numquam ante neque post tam magnam profunditatem scientiae se ab ullius ore audisse testatur,* Guth. Gr. 163, 46. Wé ðá cynelican burh Porres mid úrum wǽpnum ineódon (*printed* metdon) *urbem regiam Pori armis inuasimus,* Nar. 4, 19.

**in-gang.** *Add:* I. *an entrance, a place or way by which one enters, a doorway, vestibule:*—Seó byrgen is on Hierusalem . . . Se ingang is eástan in, and on ðá swíðran healfe þǽm ingange is stǽnen bedd, Shrn. 69, 2–4. Æðelíc ingong . . . duru ormǽte, Cri. 308. Bið se torr þyrel, ingong geopenad, Jul. 403. Æt ánes scræfes inngange (cf. an sumes scræfes dura, Bl. H. 199, 16), Hml. Th. i. 502, 16. Fram þǽre heortan inngange (*ostio*), Gr. D. 35, 18. In þám ingange (cafortúne, *v. l.*) hire húses *in hospitii sui vestibulo,* 69, 26. On þǽre cyricean inngange *in ecclesiae ingressu,* 97, 33. Tó ingangum *ad fauces, ad introitum,* An. Ox. 50, 47. II. *an entering, a going into:*—Inngong Godes mínes *ingressus Dei mei,* Ps. Srt. 67, 25. Hí ne dorston þæt hálige hús mid ingange (*by entering*) geneósian, Hml. Th. i. 504, 10. III. *an entering upon action, a beginning, first step:*—Suá mon sceal on ðæm úpáhæfenum monnum ðone fruman and ðone ingong ðære ðreátunga gemetgian *ipsa in elatis invectionis exordia sunt temperanda,* Past. 303, 18. [þis was his ingang, of his útgang ne cunne wé iett nóht seggon, Chr. 1127 ; P. 258, 27.] IV. *right or permission to enter.* (1) *the right of a person to enter and remain* in a place:—Æt heldore þǽr sǽge gǽstas æfter swyltcwale sécan onginnað ingong in þæt atule húse, Gú. 534. (2) *admission* to a religious house as one of its members:—Wið ðan ðe mín wiif benuge innganges . . . Gif hláford nylle hire mynsterlífes geunnan, C. D. i. 310, 29. Hé læg fíf dagas beforan ðæs mynstres geate, swá hé ne æt ne dranc, ac hé bæd ingonges. Þá underféng se abbod hine on þ mynster, ðá geleornede hé his saltere on feówer mónðum, Shrn. 109, 5. Cf. on-gang.

**in-geat.** *Dele.*

**in-gehygd.** *Add:* I. *mind, thoughts:*—Hié þá eorþlican sorga forléton and þá ingehyd heora heortan on þone heofonlican hyht gestaþelodon, Bl. H. 135, 29. On þám is godcundnesse wén þe manna ingehygd wát and can, 179, 26. Mé þingð þ on þæs hálgan weres inngehigdum wǽre Heliseus gást *ego sancti viri praecordiis Elisaei spiritum video inesse,* Gr. D. 130, 9. II. *conscience:*—Þá déglan ingehygde úre gesiónde swete *secreta conscientiae nostrae videns vestigia,* Ps. Srt. ii. p. 203, 39. III. *knowledge:*—*Scientia* gód ingehýd on Englisc, Wlfst. 51, 8 ; Angl. xi. 107, 8. Gewít fram ús, nelle wé þane weg þínre ingehýde (*recede a nobis, et scientiam viarum tuarum nolumus,* Job 21, 14), Ll. Lbmn. 438, 16. Hé tǽcþ men ingehýd *docet hominem scientiam,* Ps. L. 93, 10. Godes Gást hæfð ingehýd ælces gereordes, Hml. Th. i. 280, 12. IV. *meaning, import:*—Onfangenum rǽdelse hé smeáde ymbe þ ingehýd, and hit gewan mid wísdóme, Ap. Th. 4, 19. V. *a course of life; propositum:*—On gemǽnum naman muneca ingehýd byð gehyrwed *sub generali nomine monachorum propositum blasphematur,* R. Ben. 136, 4. Stípes híwe ingehýdes *ardui formam propositi,* An. Ox. 411 : Wrt. Voc. ii. 65, 60. Ingehéde *proposito, initio,* i gradu, Hpt. Gl. 420, 70. Geþínge, ingehýde *proposito* (*summo virginitatis*), An. Ox. 968 : 1609. Ingehúde (-hýde, Hpt. Gl. 491, 55) *proposito* (*sanctae conversationis rigido*), 3628. Tó þes hálgan þeówdómes ingehýde cumaþ ná þá áne þe freó synt *ad cuius :anctae militiae propositum veniunt non solum liberi,* R. Ben. 138, 19. For fǽm[n]há[d]licum ingehýde (-héde, Hpt. Gl. 459, 78) *propter uirginale* (*pudoris*) *propositum,* i. *gradum,* An. Ox. 2281. Ingehýd (-héd, Hpt. Gl. 498, 3), 3893. v. in-geþóht.

**in-gelǽdan.** *Add:*—Is ingelǽded *inditur,* Wrt. Voc. ii. 48, 61.

**in-gemang** ( = on-gemang), Hml. A. 205, 351.

**in-geótan.** *Add:*—Lióma hálges gǽstes ingeót úrum gehygdum *jubar Sancti Spiritus infunde nostris sensibus,* Ps. Srt. ii. p. 201, 3.

**in-geóting.** *Add:*—Ingeóting *lustramentum,* An. Ox. 2, 184. þweál, yn-geotincg, 3275.

**in-geseted** *inserted;* insertum, Wrt. Voc. ii. 48, 22.

**in-geþanc.** *Add:* I. *the seat of thought, intellect, mind, heart, spirit, breast:*—Ðæt hé selle Gode his ágne breóst, ðæt is his inngeðonc (ingeðanc, *v. l.*), Past. 83, 1. Hú mæg þ yfel beón þte ælces monnes ingeþanc wénþ þte gód sié, Bt. 24, 4 ; F. 86, 12. Hé ongann smeálíce þencan on his módes ingeþance *velut in angustum suae mentis sedem recepta,* 24, 1 ; F. 80, 6. Hweðer geleornodest þú þe myd þám eágum þe mid þám ingeþance (*intellectu*) ?, Solil. H. 21, 13 : 19, 1, 3. Mid eádméde ingeþance, Ps. C. 152. Ic wolde þ ðú wendest þín ingeþanc from þám leásum gesǽlþum *deflecte in adversum mentis intuitum,* 33, 3 ; F. 126, 5. Hit bið getǽsed on ðæt ingeðonc *in intimis tangitur,* Past. 297, 18. Ingeþanc *precordia,* i. *intima,* An. Ox. 3566. Hwelce sín ðá

inngeðoncas monna búton suelce sumere hearpan strengas áþenede? *quid sunt intentae mentes nisi quaedam in cithara tensiones stratae chordarum*?, Past. 175, 6. II. *conscience:*—Gē forseóþ þá cræftas eówres ingeþonces and eówres andgites *relicta conscientiae virtutisque praestantia*, Bt. 18, 4; F. 66, 23. III. *a thought, cogitation:*—Ðá ingeðoncas ðe wealcað in ðæs monnes móde *cogitationes quae volvuntur in mente*, Past. 155, 21. IV. *intention, purpose;* intentio:—Ðæt inngeðonc (in-, *v. l.*) ðære heortan *cordis intentio*, Past. 141, 7. Ne gehwyrfde hine næfre ðæt unryhtwíse ingeðonc (*intentio perversa*) tó ðæm wón andgiete, 365, 18. On swelcum ... ælces mennisces módes ingeþanc bið geswenced *in talibus humanorum actuum votorumque versatur intentio*, Bt. 24, 3; F. 82, 21: 36, 3; F. 176, 6, 20. Mid ealles módes geornfullan ingeþance hígian, 22, 2; F. 78, 18. Sió synn ðe longe gesíred bið, sió cymð symle of yfium ingeðonce *in studiis malitiosa semper intentione peccatur*, Past. 435, 17. v. in-gehygd.

**in-geþeóde.** The MS. reading in l. 2 belongs to the second passage.

**in-geþóht** *conscience:*—Þá gewordenum þám ærmergene heó weard on hire ingeþóhte (geþóhte, *v. l.*) áfyrhted for þon þe heó þá þurhtogenan lustas on hire líchaman gefremede *cum mane facto conscientiam deterreret perpetrata carnis delectatio*, Gr. D. 72, 12. v. in-gehygd; II: in-geþanc; II.

**in-geweaxen** *ingrown:*—Ingeweaxenra *inolitorum*, Wrt. Voc. ii. 48, 23.

**in-gyte,** es; *m. Infusion:*—Þurh ingyte háliges gástes *per infusionem sancti spiritus*, Angl. xiii. 395, 424.

**in-gewitness.** *Add:*—Of his ingewitnesse *de scientia ejus*, Gr. D. 95, 22.

**in-hǽtan;** *p.* te *To inflame:*—Þ seó nunne wǽre inhǽted mid un-mǽtum feferádlum *quod sanctimonialis illa immensis febribus aestuaret*, Gr. D. 29, 10. v. on-hǽtan.

**in-heald.** *Substitute: Sloping inwards, worked in low relief:*—Inheald *interrasilem*, Wrt. Voc. ii. 46, 24.

**in-hebban.** *Add:*—Hé wénde swíðe þæt ǽnig ælda ǽfre [ne] meahte swá fæstlice forescyttelsas on écnesse ð inhebban (o in hebba, MS.), oððe þæs ceasterhlídes clústor onlúcan, Cri. 313. v. on-hebban; IV.

**in-híred.** *Add:*—Híwcúþum inhíredes *domesticis clientelę* (*sodalibus*), An. Ox. 5133. Geférrǽdene, inhírede *clientela*, i. *obseruatio domestica*, 2809. Hírede þeówtlicum inhírede þénum (*cum omni*) *familia* (*et*) *vernacula clientela* (*una cum*) *parasitis*, 3309.

**in-híwan.** *Add:*—Mon ágefe ðæt lond iunhígum tó heora beóde, C. D. i. 316, 17.

**inhoh.** Dele, and see An. Ox. 5161.

**in-hold.** *Add:*—Hí nystun hwá rihtlucur þá land áhte þonne þǽre scíre bisceop, þá hé innhold wæs, and Godes geleáfan on riht bodude, and his hláford lufude, Cht. Crw. 19, 24.

**in-lǽdan** *Add:* [*O. H. Ger.* in-leiten *inducere.*]

**in-land.** *Add:*—Ic selle mínum geréfan ánes hídes lond on eásttúne, swá swá Herred hit hæfde, on ðreóra monna dæg, and all ðæt innlond beliged án díc útane, Cht. E. 169, 29. Wulfēge ðæt inland, and Ælfēge ðæt útland, C. D. ii. 381, 16. [v. *N. E. D.* inland.]

**in-laþian.** *Add:* [*O. H. Ger.* in-ladón *invocare.*]

**in-laþigend,** es; *m. One who invites:*—þ inlaþigendum þínum þú gearwige mettas *ut inuitatori tuo prebeas cibos*, Scint. 170, 12.

**in-lenda.** *Add:*—Inlenda *habitator*, i. *incola*, An. Ox. 2434: *accola*, i. *habitator*, 3591. Ælc ðæra manna ðe blód ytt sceal losian of his folce, beó hé inlenda beó hé ælðeódig (*homo quilibet de domo Israel et de advenis qui peregrinantur inter eos*, i. *comederit sanguinem, disperdam animam illius de populo suo*, Lev. 17, 10), E. S. viii. 62, 36.

**in-lende.** *Add:*—Þá hig wǽron his inlǽnde *cum essent incolae eius*, Ps. L. 104, 12. [Cf. *O. H. Ger.* in-lente *incole*.]

**in-lendisc.** *Add:* The definite form used substantively, *a native, an inhabitant:*—Inlendisca *accola*, i. *habitator*, An. Ox. 2415.

**in-líc.** *Add:*—Inlíces módes ecge *internę mentis acie*, Scint. 62, 15. Þá inlecan *interna*, Wrt. Voc. ii. 48, 60. On inlicum inelfum *in imis*, i. *intimis ilibus*, An. Ox. 986.

**inlíce.** *Add:*—Bitere scel hit him wyrþan forgolden, búton hé hit mid ælmessan inlíce forgilde, Wlfst. 277, 7. þæt is heálic rǽd monna gehwylcum ... þæt hé symle inlocast and geornlícost God weorðige, Cri 432.

**in-lígian;** *p.* ode *To inflame:*—Gesprec Dryhtnes inlígagede (= in-lēgade) hine *eloquium Domini inflammavit eum*, Ps. Srt. 104, 19.

**in-líhtan.** *Add:*—Ne inlíhteð (on-, *v. l.* *irradiat*) se wítedómes gást þá mód þára wítegena, Gr. D. 146, 7. v. ge-inlíhtan.

**in-líhtness;** *f. Illumination:*—Dryhten, inlíhtnis (*illuminatio*) mín, Ps. Srt. 26, 1. In inlíhtnisse fýres, 77, 14.

**in-liþewác.** v. un-leoþuwác.

**in-mḗde;** *adj. Of profound concern, of great solicitude:*—Þonne ne sceal ús nán woruldgestreón swá inméde swá úres Drihtnes lufu, Nap. 40. Gode náne ǽhta ne synd swá inméde swá him syud tó ágenne úre sáwle clǽne, ib. Hí nán þing him inmédre ne lǽten, ne besorhre, þonne hira Drihten *Christo omnino nihil praeponant*, R. Ben. 132, 8.

**inmest;** *adv.* v. inn; *adv.*

**inn** *a lodging,* &c. *Add:*—Hí gelógodon his bǽd on þæs mynstres sprǽchúse ... þ inn wæs swýþe nearo, Hml. S. 31, 856. His healle oððe innes *ipsius tabernaculi*, R. Ben. I. 4, 2. Týnum and twéntigum on ánum inne ætgædere hí restan ... Leóht on ðǽm selfum inne (*cella*) byrne, R. Ben. 47, 7. Se Gota gewennde tó his inne (húse, *v. l.*) *Gothus ad hospitium reversus*, Gr. D. 81, 15. Án lang gealga stǽnt æt Amanes inne *lignum stat in domo Aman*, Hml. A. 100, 280. Hí heom in gecuron mid hyra mēder, Hml. S. 30, 317.

**inn;** *adv.* *Add:* , ing [cf. (?) ingang *where other MSS. have* innan, Chr. 1016; P. 147, 19]. *Of motion or direction, inwards:*—Inn *introrsum*, Wrt. Voc. ii. 44, 18. Móyses oft eóde inn (in, *v. l.*) and út on ðæt templ, Past. 101, 24. Nán mann ne mihte ne inn (ing, *v. l.*) ne út, Chr. 1016; P. 149, 6. Se ingang is eástan in, Shrn. 69, 3. Be cumbe ing on holan bróc; þ andlang streámes ing on hlósmoc, C. D. iii. 412, 24. Ing tó ealdan mynstre, Cht. E. 185, 7. Hē tíhð his fét suá hé inmest mæg, Past. 241, 12. *See also verbs where* in *has been taken as a prefix.*

**innan.** *Add:* A. as adverb. I. local, *within, inside.* (1) in reference to a place or thing:—Gif hē þone oxan innan betýnan nolde, Ll. Th. i. 48, 31. Sió sunne ne mæg ealle gesceafta innan geondscínan, Bt. 41, 1; F. 244, 9. Ufan hit is enge and hit is innan hát, Dóm. 22: B. 2412. Heó is innan mid éce mægene geweorþod, Bl. H. 197, 11: Gen. 1366. (2) in reference to a person, *within the body:*—þá smalan wyrmas ðone man ge innan ge útan werdaþ, Bt. 16, 2; F. 52, 12. Gif men innan wyrmas eglen, Lch. i. 82, 22. (2a) where the non-physical part of man is in question, mind, heart, soul:—Heora heortan beóð innan gemanode, Bl. H. 129, 8. Hreðer innan weóll, Cri. 539. Ússe hreðercofan innan uncyste, 1330. Hungor innan slát merewērges mód, Seef. 11. II. *inwardly, in the mind, heart,* &c., *in respect to the spiritual part of man:*—Ðý lǽs hié sién innan gehæfte mid ofermētum *ne intus a superbia captivi teneantur*, Past. 307, 7. Ðæt hí innan ne áfeallen ðonon ðe hí wēnað ðæt hí útan stonden *ne, ubi se stare extrinsecus aestimant, ibi intrinsecus cadant*, 439, 9. Ne þúhte hē him nó innon swá fæger swá hē útan þúhte, Bt. 32, 2; F. 116, 24. Mid hwylcum ceasterwarum hý beóð in áre getealde innan (*intus*), Gr. D. 39, 33. Hié mid þǽre lufan Drihtnes innan onbryrde wǽron, Bl. H. 119, 18: 217, 6. þæt hē his selfes on sefan áge anwald innan, Met. 16, 3. B. as preposition. I. with gen.:—Gif þ gebyrige þ ǽnig mǽgð tó þan strang sý innon landes oþþe úton landes, Ll. Th. i. 236, 10. II. with dat. (1) local, (a) of rest, *within:*—Him þæs tácen weard for eorlum innan healle, Dan. 719. Hē is bebyrged innan þám mynstre innon Scs Nicolaus portice, Chr. 1072; P. 209, 5. Innan híra burgum *intra urbis claustra*, Past. 227, 25: An. 1237. Sittað eów innan ceastre *sedete in civitate*, Past. 385, 4. Gē eówer net setton úp on dúnum and innon wudum, Bt. 32, 3; F. 118, 15. Innan þám hundrede, Ll. Th. i. 280, 12. Innan þisan earde, 304, 13. Sý hit innan lande, sý hit út of lande, 420, 15: Gn. C. 43. (b) of motion or direction, *within, into:*—Nán mann ne cume innon þǽre ciricean, Ll. Th. i. 226, 9. Hē eóde innon þám mynstre, Hml. S. 23 b, 64. Gif heó þ heáfod innan þám men bestincð, Angl. vii. 28, 259. Hē hēðene þeáwas innan þysan lande geciered, Chr. 959; P. 115, 10. (2) of time, *within the limits of* a period, in:—Hí wendon tó Wǽringscíre innon (ingang, *v. l.*) þǽre middewintres tíde, and hergodon, Chr. 1016; P. 146, 21. (3) *within* a person. Cf. A. II:—Answarode mē sum ðing, ic nát hwæðer hit wæs innan mē ðe útan *sive alius quis extrinsecus sive intrinsecus*, Solil. H. 3, 9. Ýþende mód innan hreðre, Ps. Th. 54, 22. Adame innan breóstum his hyge hwyrfde, Gen. 715. III. with acc., *into:*—Hér rád se here ofer Mierce innan Eást-Engle, Chr. 870; P. 70, 5. Of ðǽre sǽ cymþ þ wæter innon þá eorþan, Bt. 34, 6; F. 140, 18. Gif heó þ heáfod innan þone man bestincð, Angl. vii. 28, 259. v. on-, wiþ-innan.

**innan-burhware.** *Add:*—Ðá þreó geférscipas innanburhwara and útanburhwara, C. D. B. iii. 491, 11.

**innane.** *Add:* I. of position:—Hié wǽron innane (*intus*) eágna full, Past. 194, 20. II. *inwardly, in reference to the mind, heart,* &c.:—Hié beóð innane áhafene on ofermēttum *mens in superbiam extollitur*, Past. 271, 21. Innane (*intus*) hē hit geþafode, 417, 17. Hí þindað innane on ídlum gilpe, 439, 5.

**innan-earm,** es; *m. The side of the arm towards the body:*—Lǽt him blód of innanearme, Lch. ii. 234, 6.

**innan-fortog.** v. for-tog, *where read* Wiþ innanfortoge.

**innan-onfeall** *an internal swelling:*—Wiþ innanonfealle, Lch. ii. 10, 11. v. on-feall.

**innan-tíderness,** e; *f. Internal weakness:*—Se petra oleum is gód andfeald tó drincanne wið innantíédernesse and útan tó smerwanne, Lch. ii. 288, 15. Innantýderness, 174, 8. v. innoþ-tíderness.

**innan-weard.** In l. 4 *after* B. 1976 *add* cf. innor; II.

**innan-wund,** e; *f. An internal wound:*—Wiþ innanwunde sealf, Lch. ii. 8, 30.

**inne.** *Add:* A. as adverb. I. of rest. (1) local. (a) *inside* a

room, house, &c.:—Leóht inne stód, B. 1570. Gæst inne swæf, 1800: 1866. Cyning inne gebond feónda foresprecan . . . , þær hē liged in carcerne, Cri. 732. Þæt hē inne oþþe ūte cirican berȳpe, Ll. Th. i. 334, 30. (a a) with prepositional phrases:—Īsene gelíc inne on dǣm ofne (in fornace), Past. 269, 6, 8. Wæs hē on sumum hūse inne, Guth. Gr. 171, 15, 16. Inne on healle, B. 642. Inne in ræcede, Mód. 17. Þām þe inne gehȳdde wrǣte under wealle, B. 3059. (a β) with þǣr (i) demonstrative:—Hē fand þǣr inne æðelinga gedriht swefan, B. 118: Dan. 275. Þ þū þǣr tō morgue mæssan inne gesinge, Bl. H. 207, 5: 205, 6: Ll. Th. i. 226, 29. (ii) relative:—Hē eóde intó ðām būre þār his dohtor inne wæs, Ap. Th. 22, 18: Jud. 45: Bl. H. 217, 25. (a γ) with hēr:—Hēr syndon inne dohtor mīne, Gen. 2464. (b) indoors:—Witan ge lǣsse ge mǣre ðæs ðe tó tūne belimpð, ge on tūne ge on dūne . . . ge inne ge ūte, Angl. ix. 260, 1. (c) where there is idea of confinement:—Gif hē hine (an ox) inne betȳnan nolde (cf. si non recluserit eum, Ex. 21, 29), Ll. Th. i. 48, 31. Be fæhðum. Gif se mon mægnes hæbbe þ hē his gefán berīde and inne besitte, 90, 4. Gif hē torngemōt þurhteón mihte þæt hē eotena bearn inne genunde (that he might remember how his foe had been besieged (see the preceding passage)), B. 1141. (d) inne on, mid, within a region, with a people:—Gylde lahslitte inne on Deonelage, wīte mid Englum, Ll. Th. i. 172, 3. Hēr inne on þyssum fȳre, Gen. 436. Þus hit stód inne mid Englum, Ll. Th. i. 330, 9. Inne mid Denum, 414, 15. (e) where there is detention:—Stande þriddan dǣl þǣre bōte inne a third part of the fine shall not be paid out, Ll. Th. i. 94, 7. (2) of the inner man:—Hreðer inne weóll, B. 2113. Tō ūpáhæfen inne on mōde, Met. 25, 19. II. of motion:—Hȳ hine þǣr inne gebringan, Ll. Th. i. 198, 26. On æghwylcue þe þǣr inne cōm, Jud. 50. Þǣr inne fealh secg, B. 2276. B. as preposition (following case):—Án þunor tōslóg þ hūs þe hiora godas inne wǣron, Ors. 6, 14; S. 268, 30. On þ hūs þe heó hié inne reste, Bl. H. 147, 2. v. þǣr-inne.

**inne-cund.** Add: [v. Goth. inna-kunds domesticus.]

**innefare.** Add:—Rop and smælþearme, wambe and inneforan and magan þá geondblāwað, Lch. ii. 246, 22.

**inn-geþanc, -elfe.** v. in-geþanc, -ylfe.

**innemest; adj.** Add:—Innemyste his fulle synd fācne interiora eius plena sunt dolo, Scint. 19, 14.

**innera.** Add: , **innerra.**    I. local:—Rif vel seó inre wamb alvus, Wrt. Voc. i. 44, 38. Hē fērde forð ofer þ wæter in þā inran land þǣra hǣðenra, Hml. S. 30, 309.    II. concerned with the inner man:—Se earma innera man, þ is seó wērige sāwl, Verc. Först. 93, 4. Se inra dēma internus iudex, Scint. 44, 15. Inran gewitnesse eágan, 185, 7. Ymb ðā geornfulnesse ðǣre inneran (innerran, v. l.) ðearfe his hiéremonna, Past. 137, 12. Forlǣtan ðā inneran (innerran, v. l.) giémenne ðæs godcundan ðiówdōmes for ðǣre ābisgunge ðāra ūterra weorca, 127, 8. Forlǣtað ðā ūterran sibbe and habbað ðā innerrau fæste, 357, 9.

**inne-weard.**   I. as adj. (1) physical:—Inneweard eáre auris, Wrt. Voc. ii. 10, 22. Inneweard þeóh femina, 36, 48. (2) nonphysical:—Swā hwā swā wille dióplíce spirigan mid inneweardan mōde æfter ryhte quisquis profunda mente vestigat verum, Bt. 35, 1; F. 154, 19: 38, 3; F. 200, 23    II as subst. :—Āwergode beón heora þeóh and eall heora inneweard, Ll. Lbmn. 438, 32. Fugelas on heora blōdigon bilon ðǣra martyra flǣsc bǣron, ðearmas and inneweard, Hml. S. 23, 81.

**innian.** Add: v. innung : **innihte.** l. in rihte, and see riht; II : **in-nīwian.** Add: v. ge-innīwian.

**innor.** Add : I. with reference to a place or thing:—Innor bið se hierde, se hielt ðā leoma ūtan interior est custodia, quae servat exterius membra, Past. 359, 4. Fērde hē forð . . . in þā inran land . . . ; þā gīt hē wilnode þ hē innor fērde, Hml. S. 30, 310. Hine seó ȳð gegrāp and hine fram lande innor āteáh quem unda rapuit et eum a terra introrsus traxit, Gr. D. 114, 32.    II. with reference to position in a room, a place further from the door being a more honourable one. Cf. B. 1976:—Hē mōt him innor tǣcan stede and setl liceat eum in superiorem constitueret locum, R. Ben. 111, 4.

**innoþ.** Dele 'f[?]' (in Ps. Th. 108, 18 siô does not refer to innaþ, but to wyrgðu), and add: I. the inner part of the body:—Inneþas ilia (nescitis quod templa Dei sint ilia vestra, spiritus in vobis habitat, Ald. 140, 19. Cf. 1 Cor. 3, 16), Wrt. Voc. ii. 89, 22. II. the stomach, womb, belly:—Se hālga innoð þǣre ā clǣnan. Þone innoþ geceás Crīst, Bl. H. 11, 20. Of innoþe uulua, An. Ox. 4086. Innoþas receptacula (viscerum), 105. II a. the intestines, bowels:—Him eóde se innoð (cf. eall his innewearde, Hml. Th. i. 290, 19) ūt æt his forðgange, Hml. S. 16, 207. Wiþ innoþes forhæfdnese, Lch. ii. 174, 3. Se bryne on ðǣm innoðe fervor viscerum, Past. 71, 6. III. used with reference to feeling, emotion, &c.:—Þá wæs eall hire heorte āstired and hire innoð, Hml S. 30, 340. Hē wolde ðæt of ðǣm innoðum ā libbendu wætru fleówen ðe on hine gelífden, Past. 467, 30. IV. as seat of appetite:—Frǣcum innoþes gȳfernesse gulosa uentris ingluvie, An. Ox. 2446. V. a gut, an entrail:—Se wǣta ðāra innoða

---

humor viscerum, Past. 73, 9. Hē þǣre mōdor innoþas āweahte ipse viscera matris exsuscitat, Bl. H. 167, 6.

**innoþ-tyderness.** l. -tīderness, and add: v. innan-tīderness.

**innung.** Add: I. what is contained in something, contents:—Mīn is eall eorðan ymbhwyrft, and eall hyre innuncg meus est orbis terrae, et plenitudo ejus, Ps. Th. 49, 13.    II. lodging. v. innian:—On geþances his wununge innunge hē gearwað Crīste in mentis suae hospitio mansionem preparat Christo, Scint. 11, 18.

**in-orf.** Add:—Inorf suppellex (culinae), An. Ox. 4664.

**in-sceppende** innocent:—Āgutun blōd inscedðende effuderunt sanguinem innocentem, Ps. Srt. 105, 38. v. un-sceþþende.

**in-segel.** Add: I. a seal attached to a document as evidence of authenticity, Shrn. 176, 10 (in Dict.). Seó sprǣc weard ðām cynge cūð. Ðā ðā him seó talu cūð wæs, ðā sende hē gewrit and his insegl tō ðām arcebisceope, C. D. iv. 266, 19.    II. a seal placed on a lock, receptacle, &c., so that an opening cannot be effected without breaking it :—Hē beleác þæt wīnern and āsette his āgen insegl on þ loc and forlét hit swā belocen apothecam clausit, atque impresso sigillo proprio munitam reliquit, Gr. D. 59, 5. Þā insǣgla wǣron tō swutelunge . . . þā fēng se portgerēfa tō þǣre tēge, and hē hī uninsǣglode, Hml. S. B. 758–765. Hī ðæt gewrit mid twām sylfrenan inseglum (insæglan, 756) on ānre teáge geinsegledon, 343. Cōm tācn of heofenum, and þæt bearn swytelíce mid inseglum beclȳsde Omnitenens sigillum manifestandi militis sui in aeternae memorationis iudicium praemisit, Guth. Gr. 104, 13. Unȳðe þe wæs þæt þū hit eall ne mihtest mid inseglum beclȳsan, Wlfst. 259, 20. Bōc mid seofon inseglum (sigillis) geinseglode . . . þā bōc uutȳnan and hire inseglu tōbrecan, Gr. D. 332, 22–24.    III. a seal, an engraved stamp of hard material to make an impression upon wax, &c.:—Þonne wē sceáwiað þā inseglu and onlícnessa þe þonne gȳt fullfremedlíce ne beóð āgrafene sicut necdum perfecte sculpta sigilla conspicimus, Gr. D. 283, 23. [v. N. E. D. inseil.]

**in-seglian.** Add: [v. N. E. D. inseil; vb.] v. be- (Ps. Rdr. 290, 34), un-inseglian.

**in-seten[n], e; f. An institution:**—Þte folc ðīn ēcelicum gefeága insetenum ut populus tuus sempiternis gaudiat institutis, Rtl. 8, 11.

**in-settan.** Add: v. ge-insettan.

**in-siht.** Add:—Ic wille mid tintregum æt ðē ofgán ðises ðinges insiht, Hml. Th. i. 590, 23.

**in-smoh; gen. -smōs [?]; m.** Substitute: **in-smoh, -smog; gen. -smoges; n.,** and add v. æ-smogu.

**in-snæd, es; m.** A piece of woodland kept in the lord's hand (?):—Tō Ōswaldingtūne hiérð holenhyrst . . . and triphyrst and insnādis (-as ?) intó Ōswaldingtūne, C. D. ii. 228, 4. Cf. in-wudu.

**in-stæppan** should follow instæpes.

**in-stæpe; adv.** Add:—Hȳ farað, and instepe æft cumað, Solil. H. 62, 31.

**in-sting.** Add:—Him mon betǣhte þá þreó land tō innstinge inn tō Defenum (to be under the authority of Devonshire), Cht. Crw. 19, 16.

**in-styrian** to move, excite:—Þ ðā hālgan triów swíðe wēpen and mid micle sāre instyred wǣron (commoueri), Nar. 28, 12. v. on-styrian.

**in-sweógness.** v. in-swōgenness.

**in-swōgan.** v. geond-swōgan; in-swōgenness.

**in-swōgenness.** Add: Insweógnesse is a v.l., Bd. Sch. 133, 23.

**in-timbrian.** Add:—Trymede hē hī mid his lāre and mid his manunge heora heortan intimbrede, Guth. 64, 19.

**in-tinga.** Add: I. a cause from which a result follows. (1) a thing:—Wæs seó lǣsse synn intinga þǣre māran, Hml. Th. i. 484, 14. Wāst þū þone intingan þīnre ádle? scisne tuae infirmitatis cau-am?, Guth. Gr. 162, 24. (2) a person:—Hī wǣran intinga þāre wrǣðe ðe wæs betwyx him and ðan cinge, Chr. 1051; P. 183, 31.    II. reason, account, ground of action:—Ne wiston wē for hwylcan intingan þ gedōn weard, Chr. 1057; P. 188, 16.    III. occasion, fitting opportunity:—Under intingan sub obtentu (deuorant domos uiduarum sub obtentu prolixae orationis, Mk. 12, 40), Wrt. Voc. ii. 73, 43. Sēcende intingan heora gedāles quaerentes occasionem diuortii, Bd. 1, 15; Sch. 42, 26. For æghwæþerum ðyssum mānum hē intingau sealde for ðām, þæt hī hwurfon tō ǣrran ðǣre unclǣnnesse quo utroque scelere occasionem dedit ad priorem uomitum reuertendi his, 2, 5; Sch. 133, 12. Se hlīsa him hǣlo intingan ðēnade ad quos rumor occasionem salutis ministrauit, 4, 23; Sch. 472, 18.    IV. sake; gratia:—Uuordes intinga uerbi gratia, Wrt. Voc. ii. 123, 46. For intingan forhebbendran lífes continentioris uitae gratia, Bd. 3, 27; Sch. 317, 18. Se storm for ūrum intingan (nostri gratia) gestillde, 5, 1; Sch. 553, 20. For intingan ūre hǣlo nostrae euasionis gratia, 554, 8. For huntoðes intingan, Hml. S. 30, 104.

**in-tó.** Add: I. expressing motion to a position within a space or thing. (1) with verbs of going, bearing, sending. (a) with dat. :—Maria eóde intó Zacharias hūse Maria intrauit in domum Zachariae, Lk. 1, 40: Hml. S. 23, 754. Gāð eów intó ðǣre cyrcan, Hml. Th. i.

508, 1. Orn hē eft inntō (in-, *v. l.*) ꝺǣm temple *ad tabernaculum recurrit*, Past. 103, 4. Mid þām mannum þe mē mid fōron intō Denmearcon, Cht. E. 230, 3. Hēr cuōm se here intō Escanceastre from Werhām, Chr. 877; P. 74, 14. Hiene bestæl se here intō Werhām, 876; P. 74, 7. Þēh þā menn ūp ætberstan intō þǣre byrig, Ll. Th. i. 286, 2. Hē āscōc hī (*a viper*) intō byrnendum fȳre, Hml. Th. i. 574, 16. Gif ceorl ceáp forsteld and bired intō his ærne, Ll. Th. i. 138, 15 : 286, 11. Intō þām hūse gelǣdan, Angl. vii. 6, 51. (b) with acc. :— Hié hié bestǣlon intō Escanceaster, Chr. 876; P. 74, 11. (2) where motion is not explicitly expressed :—þæt hī onfōn eów intō ēcum eardungstōwum (cf. on ēce eardungstōwe *in aeterna tabernacula*, Lk. 16, 9), Hml. Th. i. 334, 28. Hē bepǣhte hī intō his būre, Chr. 1015; P. 146, 1. Hī unrǣd reddon intō ꝺissum earde, 1052; P. 182, 2. II. with special force. (1) *into the possession of* :—Æfter hiera dæge eft intō ꝺǣre hālgan stōwe, C. D. iii. 50, 5. Gā intō Glǣstingabyrig, 128, 7. Hē gesealde twā gegrynd intō Niwan mynstre, 29. Gesylle hē þone þriddan dǣl his teóðunge intō his cyricean . . . Gā ǣlc cyricsceat intō þām ealdan mynstre, Ll. Th. i. 262, 12-16 : 308, 6 : 340, 17 : 360, 4. (1 a) of political supremacy :—Hwīlon Wentsǣte hȳrdon intō Dūnsǣtan, ac hit gebyreð rihtor intō West-Sexan; þyder hȳ scylan gafol and gīslas syllan, Ll. Th. i. 356, 18-20. (2) implying residence as an inmate :—þ muneca gehwylc þe ūte sȳ of mynstre . . . gebūge intō mynstre, Ll. Th. i. 306, 3. III. in reference to non-physical regions :—Bescȳt se deófol yfel geþōht intō þām men . . . Hē sǣwð mānfullice geþōhtas intō þæs mannes heortan, Angl. vii. 28, 260-263. IV. in reference to a state or condition :—Gā intō (cf. on, 23) þīnes hlāfordes gefeán *intra in gaudium Domini tui*, Mt. 25, 21. Ascofene of heofonlicere myrhðe inntō hellicere sūsle, Hml. Th. i. 540, 4. Intō Godes rīce lǣdan, Ll. Th. i. 424, 11. V. *to a person or thing within a place* (perhaps in the following instances *in tō*, rather than *intō*, should be read) :—Hī sōna intō þām ciningce eódon, Hml. S. 23, 142. Þā eóde Simon intō Nerōne, Bl. H. 175, 10. Þā heó intō hire mōddrian eóde, 165, 28. Þā ōþre brōþra þe þǣr ūte wǣron eódan intō him, 217, 35. Malchus on foreweardan intō his þām hālgan geféran, and se bisceop æfter him inn eóde, Hml. S. 23, 752. VI. marking direction :—Hē hæfde þā geatu forworht intō him, Chr. 901; P. 92, 8. VII. marking position, *in* :—þā yldestan þægenas intō seofon burgum, Chr. 1015; P. 146, 1. Þet hē hine hādian sceolde tō ꝺ intō Lundene, 1048; P. 172, 7.

**in-trepettan** *to trip, dance, hop* :—Intrepetan *subsaltare*, Ld. Gl. H. 37, 197. [*O. H. Ger.* trepizente *quadrupedante*.] Cf. treppan.

**in-trifelung.** *Dele, and see* trifelung.

**in-wǣre,** es; *m. Internal pain* :—Ic þrowode mycelne ece mīnre heortan and līflicra leoma . . . þā mettrumnesse lǣcas hātað mid Grēciscre sprǣce *sincopia*, inwræc (cf. *sincopia, defectio stomachi*, Ld. Gl. H. 41, 47), Gr. D. 243, 21. Wið innwrǣce (inwerce, *v. l.*), Ll. Th. ii. 162, 37.

**in-waru,** e; *f. Performance of services due in the case of* in-land. v. werian; III c :—.iii. hīda tō inware, and ōðer healf tō ūtware, Cht. E. 235, 28.

**in-weard;** *adj. Add* : , -wyrd :—Swā hwilc man swā hine lufað mid clǣnre and mid inweardre heortan, Hml. A. 168, 123 : 178, 279. Oþ inwyrde swētnesse *ad medullam* i. *ad intima*, An. Ox. 175.

**in-weard;** *adv. Add* :—Suā huelc suā inweard hīgige tō gangenne on ꝺā dura ꝺæs ēcean līfes *quisquis intrare aeternitatis januam nititur*, Past. 105, 14.

**inweardlíce.** *Add* :—Hū mæg ǣnig man hine inweardlíce tō Gode gebiddan, būton hē inwerdlíce (-weard-, *v. l.*) on God hæbbe rihtne geleáfan, Wlfst. 21, 2-4. Inweardlíce *medullitus* (*dilexerit*), An. Ox. 7, 114. Inwurdlíce, 2007. Inwerdlí[ce] *uoluntatiue*, 56, 147. Gebide þē fǣawum wurdum swā þū inweardlicost mage *ora brevissime ac perfectissime quantum potes*, Solil. H. 55, 14. ¶ for-inweardlíce. *In* Bt. F. 236, 9 *and in the following passage* for *is a prefix rather than an independent adverb* :—Wǣre þū forinwordlíce dysig ꝺā þū wilnodest þæt þū scoldest mid swylcum ꝺāgum þā heáhsunnan geséon *quaenam talium oculorum impudentia est velle illum solem videre*, Solil. H. 34, 15.

**in-weorc,** es; *n. Indoor work* :—On wintra . . . mænige inweorc wyrcean, ꝺerhsian, wudu cleófan, Angl. ix. 261, 24.

**in-wise.** *l.* -wīse.

**in-wrītere,** es; *m. A resident scribe* (?), *a private secretary* (?) :— Inwrītere *antigraphus, cancellarius* (cancellarius in ecclesiis cathedralibus dignitas cujus officium erat . . . litteras capituli facere et consignare, Migne), *scriptor* (cf. būrþēn *cancellarius vel scriniarius*, cyrcweard *sacri scriniarius*, wrītere *antigrafus*, Wrt. Voc. i. 61, 3-5), Hpt. 31, 8, 123; Lch. i. lx, 10.

**in-wudu,** a; *m. Woodland reserved to the lord* :—Se wuda gemǣne þe intō lōceres leáge hȳrð oð ꝺæs cinges inwuda, C. D. B. iii. 189, 2. Cf. in-snǣd.

**in-wunung,** e; *f. In-dwelling, residence* :—Forlǣtað hí þone godcundan þeówdōm and þæs mynstres inwununge, Chrd. 10, 29. v. onwunung.

---

**in-wyrm,** es; *m. An internal worm, worm in the intestines* :—Wiþ inwyrmas (cf. Gif men innan wyrmas eglen, 82, 22), Lch. i. 4, 25.

**in-ylfe.** *Add* : , -elfe, -ifle, -efle :—Innifli (in-) *interamen*, Txts. 69, 1059. Inilfe, Wrt. Voc. ii. 70, 33. Innelfe *extis*, 31, 67. On inlicum inelfum (-elmum) *in imis ilibus* i. *visceribus*, Hpt. Gl. 429, 64. Him mon selle gōse innefle, Lch. ii. 176, 24. Wiccgan innelbe; 134, 4.

**ipping-íren.** v. ypping-íren.

**Ira-land.** For argument in favour of taking Iceland to be the country intended where this word is used in Ohthere's narrative see Dr. Craigie's note in Mod. Lang. Rev. vol. xii, p. 200.

**īr[e, es; *n.?] The projecting back of an axe* :—Somnige mon ealle þā bān . . . and cnocie man þā bān mid æxse ȳre, Lch. iii. 14, 12. Hī hine þǣr oftorfodon mid bānum and mid hrȳðera heáfdum, and slōh hine þā ān heora mid ānre æxe ȳre (ēre, *v. l.*), Chr. 1012; P. 142, 24. [v. N. E. D. ear. Cf. Ger. öhr handle.]

**īre,** es; *m. A monetary unit.* [*This form seems to be a singular corresponding to Icel. eyrir, while ōran is plural corresponding to aurar. For this entry I have to thank Professor Max Förster*] :— Ægylsige bohte Wynrīc æt Ælfsige abbude mid ānon ȳre goldes, C. D. vi. 210, 24. Bohte man .lx. æcera mid þrīm pundum and mid ānum ȳre, C. D. B. iii. 371, 2. [Cf. Icel. eyrir.] v. ōra.

**īren,** es; *n. Add* : I. iron :—Ylda oferstīged stȳle, heó ābīted īren mid ōme, Sal. 300. II. *an instrument, tool, appliance, &c., made of iron* :—Swā æscǣre beó hē þ īren ne cume on hǣre ne on nægle, Ll. Th. ii. 280, 21. II a. *a sword* :—Gūðbill geswāc, swā hyt nō sceolde īren ǣrgōd, B. 2586. Wæs þǣm hæftmēce Hrunting nama . . . ecghwæs (ecg wæs, MS.) īren, B. 1459 : 2778. Īren ecgheard, An. 1183. Mēce, . . . dȳre īren, B. 2050. Him īrenna ecge ne mihton helpan æt hilde, 2683. Īrenum *chalibis*, Wrt. Voc. ii. 19, 40. II b. *a fetter* :—Gehēndun in fōtcospum foet his, īren ꝺorhleórde sāwle his, Ps. Srt. 104, 18. Gebundne in īrene, 106, 10. II c. *the iron used in the ordeal, the ordeal by hot iron* :—Hē lādige hine mid īrene *adlegiet se per Dei judicium*, Ll. Th. i. 489, 19, 21. v. brand-, cimb-, gād-, lǣce-, writ-, ypping-íren.

**īren;** *adj. Add* :—Īren hiorꝺ *asula*, Wrt. Voc. ii. 10, 21. Āne īrene hierstepannan, Past. 160, 7 : 162, 23. Mid īrenum þīslum sleán, Bl. H. 189, 30.

**īren-byrne.** *Add* : v. īsern-byrne.

**īren-gelōma.** *Add* :—Sealde hē him īrengelōman þ is hāten wudubill (*ferramentum quod falcastrum vocatur*), Gr. D. 113, 18. Hē hēt weorpan īrengelōman (*ferramenta*) in þæs mynstres wyrtgeard, þā īrengelōman wē hātaþ spadan and spitelas, 201, 19. Īrengelōman *ferramenta ruralia*, Bd. 4, 28 ; Sch. 520, 22.

**īren-helm.** *Add* : v. īsern-helm.

**Īren-sīd** *epithet of Edmund* :—Eádmund cing Īrensīd wæs geclypod for his snellscipe, Chr. 1057; P. 187, 36. [Cf. Icel. Iárn-sīða *name of a mythical king.*]

**īren-smiþ,** es; *m. A blacksmith* :—' Hēt ic hider lǣdan Stephanum þone īrensmið (*ferrarium*)' . . . Stephanus se īrensmið wæs forðfēred . . . seó gefremednes Stephanes deáðes þæs īrensmiðes, Gr. D. 318, 10-15. [*Icel.* jārn-smiðr.] v. īsen-smiþ.

**irfa,** an; *m. An heir* :—Ꝺet hē ꝺis wel healde his dei and siꝺꝺan forð bebeóde his erbum tō healdenne, C. D. i. 297, 5. [*Goth.* arbja : *O. H. Ger.* arbio, erbo *haeres.*]

**irfe.** *Add* : I. *inherited property, property that passes to an heir* :— Ierfe *hereditas*, Wrt. Voc. ii. 43, 47. Ꝺæt ierfe ꝺæt gē æfter hiégiað *hereditas ad quam festinatur*, Past. 331, 24. Ūre worldcunde fædras wilniað ꝺæt wē hira irfes (ierfes, *v. l.*) wierꝺe sién, 255, 2. Yrfes lyre *patrimonii iacturam*, An. Ox. 3151. Gif . . . gesibbra ærfeweard forþ cymeð . . . ꝺanne ann ic ꝺǣm ofer mīnne dæg alles mīnes erfes tō brūcanne swā him liófust sió, Cht. Th. 483, 20. Ūrum cildum wē tiochiað ūrne eard and fūrne ēꝺel and ūre ierfe eall ætsomne tō forlǣtanne *pueris tota simul patrimonia hereditas reservamus*, Past. 391, 28. II. *property* :—Willa ic gesellan of ꝺǣm ærfe ꝺe mē God forget . . . lx ambra maltes . . . , C. D. i. 299, 15. Ꝺā ꝺe æfter ōðerra monna ierfe flītað and hié reáfigeað *qui aliena rapere contendunt*, Past. 177, 6. Sculon hié niédenga gadrian ōðer ierfe on ꝺæs wriexle ꝺe hié ǣr for mildheortnesse sealdon *violenter exquirunt, quae misericorditer largiuntur*, 341, 18. Hē wolde his irfe (ierfe, *v. l.*) geteóðian (cf. cunctorum quae dederis mihi decimas offeram tibi, Gen. 28, 22), 101, 17. II a. on ēce irfe *in perpetuity* :—Mon āgefe ꝺæt lond innhīgun on ēce ærfe, C. D. i. 316, 17, 26. III. *cattle,* (*live-*)*stock.* v. ge-irfian. [*The passages given in Dict. under* yrfe *may be taken here*] :—Be yrfes ætfenge. Sié þe yrfe befō *de illis qui pecus intertiant. Si quis pecus aliquod interciet*, Ll. Th. i. 204, 9. Wæs þæt lond ierfælæás . . . And ic ꝺā sælf þæt ierfæ tō gestrīndæ þæt ꝺǣr mon siꝺꝺan bī wæs . . . Ꝺonnæ is þær nū irfæs nigon eald hrīꝺru . . . and fiftig wæþera *terra omni pecunia caruit. Tunc ego ipse peccuniam meam in ea reparare studui, unde interim pauperes vixerunt . . . Modo habetur ibi pecunia ix veteres boves . . . et l arietes*, Cht. Th. 162, 27-

163, 5. Ic sello ... þás lond mid cwice erfe ... Feó sió nēste hond tổ þēm londe and tổ þēm erfe, 480, 29–481, 23. [v. *N. E. D.* erf.] v. in-i fe.

**irfe-béc.** *Add:—Olographum testamentum est* eallwritene yrfebēc, Wrt. Voc. ii. 65, 40.

**irfe-cwealm** (?). v. yrf-cwealm.

**irfe-gewrit.** *Add:—*Þā spræc ic on þā māgas mid þē erfegewrite, Cht. Th. 167, 19.

**irfe-leás;** *adj. Without live stock.* v. irfe; III.

**irfe-numa.** *Add:—*Swē hit mīne ærfenuman ǽr onstellen, C. D. i. 316, 22. Eihwelc mon mīnra ærbenumena, 299, 22. v. mid-irfenuma.

**irfe-weard.** *Add:—*Gewriten yrfeweard *legaturius*, Wrt. Voc. ii. 54, 2. Ēghwylc ðāra erfewearda ðe æfter him tổ ðǽm londe fōe ... Ðǽs gewriotu sión getrymed mē and mīnum ærfeweardum. Gif ... gesibbra ærfeweard forð cymeð wēpnedhādes, C. D. ii. 121, 12–27. Monega land wǽron būtan ǽlcum ierfwearde *largissimae hereditates et nulli penitus heredes*, Ors. 5, 2; S. 218, 2. Mīne ærfeweardas, C. D. i. 316, 24. Gestrÿnendlicra yrfwearda (erf[w]erda, Hpt. Gl. 439, 30) *liberorum procreandorum*, An. Ox. 1402. Ic beóde mīnum erfeweardum, C.D. ii. 132, 15. Wē ūre cildru tiochiað ūs tổ ierfeweardum tổ habbanne, Past. 391, 29. v. efen-irfeweard.

**irfeweardnes.** *Add:—*'Ðonne God sylð his leófum slǽp, þæt is Drihtnes yrfwyrdnys (*hereditas*).' þonne Goðes gecorenan becumað tổ deáðe, ðonne gemētað hī yrfwyrdnysse, Hml. Th. ii. 526, 29. Tổhopa ðǽre ēcan ierfeweardnesse (*hereditatis*), Past. 391, 30. Mid yrfweardnysse, Ps. L. 36, 34. On yrfwerdnysse *in hereditate*, Scint. 148, 4.

**irfeweardian.** *Add:—*Þū yrfwyrdast, Ps. L. 81, S. v. ge-irfeweard an.

**-irfian.** v. ge-irfian.

**ir-furlang** (?):—On irfurlanges dīc; and of irfurlanges dīc ðæt on mǽrdīc, C. D. iii. 405, 32. Cf. (?) furlang; II.

**-irgan.** v. ge-irgan.

**irgþ.** *Add:—*On yrhþe ɫ on fyrhto *formidinem*, Ps. L. 88, 41. Hwī wolde geðafian hē þæt his ðegen (*St. Peter*) hine for yrcðe swā oft wiðsóce?, Hml. Th. ii. 250, 3.

**Iringes weg.** *Substitute:* Īringes weg *the milky way* [Mirari tamen non possumus in tantum famam praevaluisse ut Iringi nomine, quem ita vocitant, lacteus coeli circulus usque in praesens sit notatus, Grm. D. M. (trans.) 358 q. v.]:—Īringes (Iuuaringes, Erf. Cf. (?) Iúring, 159, 199) uueg (uuec) *via secta* (v. Virgil, Georgics i. 238, where, however, the zodiac is intended), Txts. 105, 2118.

**ir-lic.** *Add:—*Of yrlicere (hyrlicre, Hpt. Gl. 449, 78) rēþnesse *furibunda ferocitate*, An. Ox. 1844. Crīst sylf wrāt gewrit swýðe eorlicum wordum for Sunnandæges weorcum, Wlfst. 207, 3. *See next word.*

**irlíce;** *adv. Angrily:—*Heó gebealh heó swīðe eorlíce wið hire suna *with fierce anger was she incensed against her son*, C. D. iv. 54, 30.

**irming.** *Add:—*Ealle mīne synna þe ic ermingc gefremede, Angl. xi. 102, 80. Hié fægniað irmingas hiera āgnes hearmes *de damnis suis miseri exultant*, Past. 245, 2. Tổ bodianne ermingum (*captiuis*) forgefnise, Lk. L. R. 4, 18.

**irmþ.** *Add:* I. *misery, wretchedness, calamity:—*Se cyning ... hæfþ māran ermþe *majorem regibus inest miseriae portionem*, Bt. 29, 1; F. 102, 25. Þā monigfealdan iermþo þā wērigan burg swīþe brociende wǽran *maxima omnium malorum abominenta fessam urbem corripuere*, Ors. 2, 4; S. 70, 10. Yrmþa (eormða, Hpt. Gl. 519, 68) *calamitatum*, An. Ox. 2973. Hié on ðām iermþum heora līf geendodon, Ors. 2, 2; S. 66, 19. II. *in a moral sense, badness:—*Gif hine mon leahtorfulne ongit ... him mon secge þæt hē þanon gewīte, þe lǽs hē mid his yrmðe (*miseria*) ōþre geleahtrige, R. Ben. 109, 20. III. *poverty, destitution:—*Hū ne hæfdest þū ðā earmþe (yrmþe, *v. l.*) þā þā þū welegost wǽre? *tu hanc insufficientiam plenus opibus sustinebas?*, Bt. 26, 1; F. 92, 6. Ermðe (wǽdle, *v. l.*) *indigentiam*, 26, 2; F. 94, 9. Ðonne hē ongiet ðæt ðone earman ne magon his iermða (*paupertas*) geeaðmēdan, Past. 183, 15. Ðone ðe on ðǽm ofne āsoden bið his iermða *quos caminus paupertatis excoquit*, 3. On ðīnum iermðum (*paupertate*), 181, 13.

**irnan.** *Add:—*Iornð *cursat*, Wrt. Voc. ii. 21, 51. A. *intrans.* I. *of persons or animals.* (1) *to move quickly:—*Swā swā gigant yrnð on his weg, Ps. Th. 18, 6. Tógægnes iorned *occurrit*, Lk. R. L. 22, 10. Forerynelas iernað beforan kyningum, Past. 91, 21. Ān plegende cild arn under wǽnes hweowol, Shrn. 32, 12. Cūðberhtus arn plegende mid his efenealdum ... Cūðberhtus þā gýt mid his plegan forð arn, Hml. Th. ii. 134, 2–16. Stǽnene manlīcan hié styredan and urnon him sylfe, Bl. H. 173, 24. Þæs cyninges þegnas þider urnon, Chr. 755; P. 48, 7: Sat. 532. Him urnon ealle hellwaran ongeán, Bt. 35, 6; F. 168, 29: Jud. 164. Þā men onwōcan and ūt urnon, Ors. 4, 2; S. 160, 22. Þā wīfmen urnon wið ðara wealla, 4, 10; S. 194, 11. Iern *discurre*, Past. 193, 18. Irnn, Kent. Gl. 125. Yrn *curre*, Gr. D. 115, 5. Eom, 325, 29. 'Gāð from geate tổ geate ...' Ðæt is ðæt mon

ierne from geate tổ ōðrum, Past. 383, 8. Hē hiene hēt iernan fela mīla beforan his rǽdwǽne, Ors. 6, 30; S. 280, 12. Wildu diór þǽr woldon tổ irnan, Bt. 35, 6; F. 168, 1. Ðā wildan hors scealden iornan on hearde wegas and him ðā limo tōbrecan, Shrn. 72, 1. Se hrefn mid āþenedun fiðerum ongann yrnan hoppetende ymbūtan þone hlāf *coruus expansis alis circa panem coepit discurrere*, Gr. D. 118, 24. Iornende *currens*, Mt. L. 27, 48. Eornende *currentes*, Mt. R. 28, 8. (1 a) figurative:—Sió eáðmōdnes iernð beforan ðǽm gielpe, Past. 299, 16. (2) *to go about freely, without check or restraint:—*Ðā dysegan irnaþ hider and ðider dwoligende, Bt. 36, 5; F. 180, 12. Gif þū gesēge ðeóf, somud ðū urne mid hine, Ps. Srt. 49, 18. (2 a) figurative:—Yrnende *uagans, circumiens* (vestrum mentes ingenium per scripturarum arua late *uagans*, Ald. 4, 15), An. Ox. 141. (3) *with an idea of violence, attack:—*Gif man in mannes tūn ǽrest geirneð, .vi. scillingum gebēte; sē þe æfter irneð .iii. scillingas, Ll. Th. i. 6, 17. (4) *to run* to shelter, fig. *to have recourse to, resort to:—*Irnð *currit* (turris fortissima nomen Domini; ad ipsum *currit* justus, Prov. 18, 10), Kent. Gl. 641. Tổ ðǽm gebanne ðæs tōhopan nān man ne mæg cuman, būtan hē ðider irne (ierne, *v. l.*) mid ānmōdnesse, Past. 344, 20. (5) *of a course of action:—*Ðæt mōd iernð on ðā unāliéfedan unðeáwas, and hit swā ðeáh ne onwæcneð tổ ðon ðæt hit eft on ierne mid hreówsunga, Past. 431, 22. Þā he on eallum ðingum wadaþ on hiora āgenne willan, and æfter hiora līchoman luste irnaþ, Bt. 41, 2; F. 246, 24. Būton hē tổ ǽlcum men mæge gebeácnian þ hē irne on his willan, 11, 1; F. 32, 21. Ðæt hē ierne ðreátigende from ðāra unðeáwa ǽlcum tổ ōðrum, Past. 383, 8. (6) *to run* for a prize:—Mon hēhþ ǽnne heáfodbeáh gyldenne æt sumes ærneweges ende. Fǽrþ þonne micel folc tổ and irnaþ ealle endemes ... and swā hwilc swā ǽrest tổ ðām beáge cymþ, þonne mōt sē hine habban him ... swā dēþ eall moncynn on þ̄s andweardan līfe, irnaþ and onettaþ and willniaþ ealle þæs hēhstan gōdes, Bt. 37, 2; F. 188, 8–14. II. *of things.* (1) *of the heavenly bodies, clouds, &c., to move rapidly through space:—*Sió sunne ne onhrīnþ nō ðæs dǽles þæs heofenes ðe se mōna on irnþ, ne se mōua nō ne onhrīnþ þæs dǽles ðe sió sunne on irnþ, Bt. 39, 13; F. 232, 28. Yrnþ, Ps. Th. 18, 6. Steorran yrnaþ wiþersýnes, Bl. H. 93, 19. Him arn on lāst þýstre genip, Gen. 138. Gif se mōna urne swā ūp swā seó sunne dēþ, Lch. iii. 248, 6. Ǽfre seó sunne byð yrnende ymbe ðās eorðan, 234, 22. (2) *of a vessel or those on it:—*Hī tugon ūp heora segel and urnon west tổ Axamūðan, Chr. 1046; P. 169, 11. In sīdum ceóle hē under segle yrne, Gn. Ex. 186. Þā gesāwon hié Rōmāna scipa on ðæm sǽ irnan, Ors. 4, 1; S. 154, 5. Þæt scip wæs ealne weg yrnende under segle, 1, 1; S. 19, 34. (3) *to spread quickly:—*His word yrneð (eorneð, Ps. Srt.) wundrum sniōme, Ps. Th. 147, 4. (4) *of thoughts:—*Mē arn tổ gemynde oft and gelōme *it often occurred to me*, Ll. Lbmn. 269, 16. (5) *of a plant, to grow rapidly:—*þ þæs wæstmes yrð þǽr mā upp yrnende wǽre ... þā georn (arn, *v. l.*) sōna ūp genihtsumlic yrð *ut illius frugis ibi potius seges oriretur ... mox copiosa seges exorta*, Bd. 4, 28; Sch. 521, 14–22. Ūp yrnendre *luxuriante*, i. *crescente*, An. Ox. 1580. (6) *of machinery* (a mill or millstone):—Þā orn seó cweorn ðurh godcunde miht, Shrn. 145, 23. Ne mylnum nis ālÿfed tổ eornenne, Wlfst. 227, 11. III. *of a liquid or a moist substance, sand, &c.* (1) *to flow.* v. irning; I.:—Oft of denum yrnað deópe wyllan *emittis fontes in convallibus*, Ps. Th. 103, 10. Orn blōd ūt, Ors. 5, 10; S. 234, 5. Þ hālige blōd orn æfter eorðan swā swā flōd, Shrn. 132, 21. Hwider arn þ wæter on þām widgillan flōde? *quo reversae sunt aquae* (the waters of the Deluge)?, Angl. vii. 36, 339. Tōfleówan, ūt urnon *defluxerunt* (ilia Arii), An. Ox. 2857. Swā sum ǽwelm and irnon manige brōcas of, Bt. 34, 1; F. 134, 10. Lǽt ðīne willas iernan (irnan, *v. l.*) wīde, Past. 373, 5. Wæter yrnende, Ps. Th. 64, 11: Gen. 211. Eornende, Ps. Srt. 57, 8. (1 a) *of the action of a purgative or emetic draught:—*Drinc swīðne drenc sē þe wille ūp yrnan and ofdūne, Lch. ii. 116, 24. (2) *where* liquid *is discharged from a receptacle, to flow with a liquid:—*Hié þrowiað ormǽtne þurst, and oft ūt yrnað gemengde ūtgange, Lch. ii. 230, 20. Gif mon blōde āne ūt yrne ... oþþe gif mon for roppes untrumnysse ūt yrne, 170, 20–22. (3) *to discharge a liquid:—*On ðone yrnendan mōr, C. D. v. 393, 3. IV. *of time, to pass, elapse:—*God gesceóp ealle ðā seofon dagas þe yrnað on þǽre wucan oð þysre worulde geendunge, Hml. S. 17, 95. Ernendum emrenum *labentibus*, i. *currentibus lustris*, An. Ox. 395. B. *trans. To follow* a course, way:—Weg beboda þīnra ic arn *uiam mandatorum tuorum cucurri*, Ps. L. 118, 32. Hié biōð gehwerfde eft tổ þām ilcan ryne þe hié ǽr urnon, Bt. 21; F. 74, 12. Hē blissode swā swā ent tổ yrnenne weg, Ps. Spl. 18, 6. v. fore-, of-irnan; tổ-, ūt-irnende.

**irnend.** v. fore-irnend.

**irnere.** *Add:—*Yrneres *Pelethi*, Hpt. Gl. 424, 73.

**irning, e;** *f.* I. *a running, flux.* v. irnan; A. III. 1 :—Iorning (Herning, Mt. p. 16, 3) blōdes *profluvium sanguinis*, Lk. p. 5, 20. Blōdes flōuing ɫ iorning *sanguinis fluxus*, Mt. L. 9, 20. II. *a course:—*Erningc ɫ ymbgeong *decursus*, Mt. p. 12, 14. v. on-, ūt-irning; ærning.

**ir-ness, e;** *f. Anger:—*Se sārlica cwide þe ūre Drihten þurh eornesse

tổ þæm ǽrestan men cwǽþ, Bl. H. 123, 8, 11. Wē sceolon ūrum þām nēxtan forlǽtan ealle þā eornesse (yr-, v. l.) and þā æfþancan þe hī wið ūs gewyrcað, Hml. A. 160, 196, 201.

**irre** *anger. Add:*—Hierre, Past. 289, 12. Bið onǽled yrra (*ira*) his, Ps. L. 2, 13. God ūs forgyfeð his erre gif wē ūre monnum forgeofað, Shrn. 80, 11. On mē þurhfōron eorru (*irae*) þīne, Ps. Rdr. Vos. Srt. 87, 17.

**yrre**; *adj.* II. *Add:* (1) of persons (or things personified) or personal attributes :—þā weard Símon erre, Bl. H. 181, 17. Se yrra C., Sal. 123. Erre mōde git mē gedydon, Bl. H. 189, 25. Wǽron hié swíþe erre on heora mōde, 149, 28 : 223, 6. (1 a) *angry* with. (a) with dative (i) preceding :—Him weard ierre (irre, v. l.) se gōda wyrhta, Past. 337, 7 : 381, 23 : Gen. 342 : 742. Ealle godas him irre wǽren, Ors. 3, 7 ; S. 114, 4. (ii) following :—Sum man weard yrre his ðeówan men, Hml. S. 21, 414. þā wæs yrre God Abimelehe, Gen. 2741. þū yrre ūs wurde and eft milde *iratus es, et misertus es nobis*, Ps. Th. 59, 1. (1 β) with preposition :—Hē wæs yrre wið Aaron *adversum Aaron iratus*, Deut. 9, 20. Se cyning wæs yrre wið mē *iratus rex servis suis*, Gen. 41, 10. (2) of an animal :—Siþþan hē (*an elephant*) irre wæs and gewundod, Ors. 4, 1 ; S. 156, 11.

**irsian.** *Add:* (1) absolute :—Iersað *stomachatur*, Wrt. Voc. ii. 90, 48. Ðý iræs eorsie Dryhten, Ps. Srt. 2, 12. Tō iorsienne *ad irascendum* (*facilem*), Kent. Gl. 645. Ne beó hē tō slāw, ne beó hē tō eorsigende (*printed* eornigende), Ll. Th. ii. 416, 16. (2) with dat. :—Ǽlc þ yrsaþ (eorsaþ, R.) hys brēðer *omnis qui irascetur fratri suo*, Mt. 5, 22. (3) with prep. :—Hwī irsast þū wiþ ūs?, Bt. 7, 5 ; F. 22, 36. Ðonne hē wið hine iersað, Past. 63, 3. Fram þām þeódum þe wið mē yrsiað *de gentibus iracundis*, Ps. Th. 17, 46. Unryhtlicu iersung is ðæt mon iersige (irsige, v. l.) on ōðerne for his gōde, Past. 189, 8.

**irþ.** *Add:* I. *ploughing* :—On manegum landum tild bið redre ðonne on ōðrum ; ge yrðe tíma hrædra, Angl. ix. 259, 10. Yrðe georne fordian, 261, 21. Yrðe, 5. II. *a crop* ; *seges* :—Eard, Bd. 4, 28 ; Sch. 521, 15. [v. *N. E. D.* earth.] v. bēn-, for-irþ.

**irþ-land.** *Add:*—Ierðland *arvo* (-*a*?), Wrt. Voc. ii. 8, 2. Ægðer ge etelond ge eyrðlond ge eác wudoland, C. D. ii. 95, 14. Sextig æcera eardlondes . . . and twelf æceras mædwelandes, 150, 16 : vi. 219, 1. Ter duodenas segetes . . . quod Anglice dicitur xxxvi æceras yrðlandes, Midd. Flur. 47, 31. Ægðer ge on eardlonde ge on homlonde, Cht. E. 208, 11. Bī ðæm eordlande foreweardum, C. D. iii. 391, 14. Be ðæs hlinces niðerecge oð ðæt hit cymð tō ðǽm yrðlande, 418, 20, 26. Of ðǽre díc widnorðan ðæt yrðland, ðonne bī ðam yrðlande, v. 298, 1. Ic tōwurpe ðás burh and hí gesmēðige, and tō yrðlande æwende, swā þæt heó bið cornbǽre swíðor þonne mannbǽre, Hml. Th. i. 450, 11. His deácon sǽde þ seó eá wǽre of hire rihtryne on þǽre cyrican yrðland (*agros*) ūp yrnende, Gr. D. 193, 15.

**irþling.** *Add:* I. *a husbandman* :—Far tō wēstene þǽr nān fugel ne flýhð, ne yrðling ne erað, ne mannes stemn ne swēgð, Hml. Th. i. 464, 25. Gif se yrðlincg behylt underbæc gelōme, ne bið hē gelimplic tilia . . . Se yrðlincg āmyrð his furuh gif hē lōcað tō lange underbæc, Hml. S. 16, 178-180. Nū swincð se yrðlincg embe ūrne bigleofan, and se woruldcempa sceall winnan wið ūre fýnd, 25, 819. Críst geceás hyrdas and yrðlingas and fisceras, and hí tō lāreówum gesette, Hml. S. 5, 225. II. *a bird* (some of the same Latin words are used for the wren. v. wrenna) :—Irðling *cucuzata*, Wrt. Voc. ii. 16, 21. Eorþlinc *birbiacaliolus*, Hpt. 33, 241, 56.

**irþ-mearc,** e ; *f A boundary of arable land* :—Be ðǽre yrðmearce, C. D. iii. 419, 2. Andlang westcumbes betweah ðā twā yrhmearca (yrþ-?), 420, 4.

**irþ-tilia,** an ; *m. A husbandman* :—Yrðtilian (*but* y *altered to* e) *agricolas*, Hpt. Gl. 464, 20. v. eorþ-tilia.

**is.** *Add:*—On ðǽm mere wæs micel īs and yfel . . . þā on forewearde niht snāð þ īs ðāra hāligra líchoman, Shrn. 61, 35-62, 2. þā wæs Donua seó eá swā swíþe oferfroren þæt hié getrūwedon þæt hié ofer þǽm īse faran mehten ; ac hié mǽst ealle þǽr forwurdon, Ors. 4, 11 ; S. 208, 2.

**-isc.** *Add:* v. militisc.

**-isc(e).** v. hīwisc(e), īdisc(e).

**ís-earn,** es ; *m. A kingfisher* :—Ísern (-ęrn, -aern) *alcion, alchior,* Txts. 39, 115. Ísen *alcion,* Wrt. Voc. ii. 6, 44 : *alchior,* 7, 11. [Cf. Ger. eis-vogel *a kingfisher.*]

**ísen** ; *n. Add:* I. *iron* :—Glād hit on þǽm scyllum swelce hit wǽre smēðe, Ors. 4, 6 ; S. 174, 8. Grǽghǽwe ísene *ferrugine,* Wrt. Voc. ii. 35, 34. Gewyrme mid hāte glōwende ísene, Lch. ii. 236, 32 : 218, 24. Hié him wǽpeno worhton þā þe īsen hæfdon, Ors. 4, 13 ; S. 210, 25. II. *an implement, a tool, &c., made of iron* :—þ rǽsde forð þæt īsen (īren, *v. l.* ferrum · head of a hatchet) of þǽm hylfe, Gr. D. 113, 26. Aðamans mon mid nāne īsene ceorfan ne mæg, Past. 271, 3. Ðæt téah þæt hié men mid lācnian sculdon, 364, 10. Hē teáh þ ísena under his nacodum fōtum, ac arn wæter ūp and cēlde þā ísena, 36, 392. v. bærn-, brǽd-, ceorfing-, mearc-, mynet-, screádung-, snid-ísen.

**ísen** ; *adj. Add :*—Ísen randbeág *ferreus umbo,* Wrt. Voc. ii. 147, 79. þ ísene tōl, Gr. D. 114, 1. Hié nāmon treówu and slōgon on ðerne ende monige scearpe ísene næglas, Ors. 4, 1 ; S. 158, 5. Hwæt ylst þū ūs on smiþþan þīnre būton ísene fýrspearcan (*ferreas scintillas*), Coll. M. 31, 5.

**ísen-feter** (-or) *an iron fetter* :—Ísenfetor *balus,* Wrt. Voc. ii. 10, 58. Ísenfeter, i. 288, 6. v. ísern-feter.

**ísen-grǽf,** es ; *m. An ironstone quarry* :—On ísengrafas ; ot ísengrafan, C. D. v. 234, 30. Cf. ísern-ōre.

**ísen-grég.** *Add:*—Ísengrǽg *ferrugine,* i. *ferreo colore,* Wrt. Voc. ii. 35, 31. v. ísern-grǽg.

**ísenian.** *Add:*—Hísnedum bārsperum *ferratis uenabulis,* An. Ox. 736. v. ge-ísned.

**ísen-smiþ.** *Add:* v. íren-smiþ.

**ísen-tanga,** an ; *m. Substitute* : **ísen-tange,** an ; *f. A pair of snuffers* :—Ísentange *munctorium,* Ælfc. Gr. Z. 314, 9.

**ísern** ; *n. Add:* I. *iron* :—Hē bið ðǽm íserne (ísene, *v. l.*) gelíc, Past. 268, 5 : 267, 18, 21. II. *an iron tool or implement* :—Ísern *chalibem* (*chalybem* prolapsum gurgite Gothi, Ald. 159, 32. v. Gr. D. 113, 26 *under* ísen ; II.), Wrt. Voc. ii. 92, 7 : 19, 39. v. mynet-, ríp-ísern.

**ísern** ; *adj. Add:*—'Sete íserne weall . . .' ðā isernan hierstepannan hē tǽhte for íserne weall . . . tō ísernum wealle, Past. 165, 8-12. Ðæt hē him genāme āne íserne (írene, *v. l.*) hierstepannan, 161, 7 : 163, 22. Íserne gelōman, Gr. D. 201, 19. *See following compounds.*

**ísern-feter** *an iron fetter* :—Ísernfeotor (ísern-, ísaern-fetor) *balus,* Txts. 45, 272 : Wrt. Voc. ii. 125, 5. Ísernfeter, i. 21, 34. Ísernfsetor *forfix,* ii. 35, 76. [Cf. *Goth.* eisarna-bandi.] v. ísen-feter.

**ísern-gelōman.** *Substitute:* **ísern-gelōma,** an ; *m. An iron tool* :—þā íserngelōman wē hātaþ spadan and spitelas, Gr. D. 201, 19. þ him mon íserngelōman (issern-, *v. l.*) brōhte, Bd. 4, 28 ; S. 520, 20. Ðæt wǽron IIII stāncræftigan . . . hý gesénedon ælce morgen heora íserngelōman, Shrn. 146, 15. v. íren-gelōma.

**ísern-grég** ; *adj. Iron-grey* :—Íserngréi *ferrugine,* Wrt. Voc. ii. 108, 49. v. ísen-grǽg.

**ísern-helm** *an iron helmet* :—Írsenhelm (*Wright prints* íren) *cassis,* Wülck. Gl. 142, 2.

**ísern-ōre** *an ironstone quarry* :—Ísernōre *ferri fodina, in quo loco ferrum foditur,* Wrt. Voc. ii. 148, 11. Cf. ísen-grǽf.

**ísern-scúr** *a shower of iron missiles* :—þone þe oft gebād ísernscúre, B. 3116.

**ísig.** *Add:*—On ðǽm clife hangodan on ðǽm īsgean bearwum manige swearte sāula be heora handum gebundne, Bl. H. 209, 35.

**ísiht(e)** ; *adj. Icy* :—Ic earfeðu dreāh, hwílum þǽre ísihtan cealdnysse þæs wintres, hwílum þæs unmǽtan wylmes þǽre sunnan hǽto, Hml. S. 23 b, 572.

**Ispánia.** *Add:*—Seó ūs neárre Ispánia, Ors. 1, 1 ; S. 22, 31. Seó ūs fyrre Ispánia, S. 24, 7. Weard on Ispánie þ þā hǽðenan men hergodan, Chr. 1086 ; P. 221, 33. On þǽre firran Ispánia, Ors. 4, 11 ; S. 206, 6. Wið þā firran Ispánie, 33. On þā neárran Ispánie, 5, 2 ; S. 220, 6.

**Ispánie** ; *pl.* Spaniards, Spain :—From Sceltiuerin, Ispánia folce, Ors. 4, 12 ; S. 208, 24. Hē monega gefeoht on Ispánium þurhteáh, 29 : 4, 8 ; S. 188, 19. Scipia gefiēmde Hasterbal on Ispániun (*in Hispania*), 4, 10 ; S. 198, 14. Hē fōr of Ispánium (*ab Hispaniis*), 22. Wæs ān hirde on Ispánium, 5, 2 ; S. 216, 6. Áscien Ispánie þe þæt ilce wǽron dreógende, 5, 1 ; S. 214, 14.

**Ispánisc** ; *adj. Spanish* :—Leandro þām Ispániscan biscope, Gr. D. 237, 21.

**Italia,** e, an (*Latin forms also occur*) ; *f. Italy* :—On Ticinis hē wæs āfēd Italian landes (cf. hē wæs āfēd on Italia, Hml. Th. ii. 498, 24), Hml. S. 31, 12. Hē gefōr on Italie (cf. in Italiam, 1, 11 ; S. 50, 24), Ors. 3, 2. Hié sendon on Italie æfter Hannibale . . . hē sceolde Italiam forlǽtan, 4, 10 ; S. 200, 30-33. Hē fōr of Ispánium on Italie (*ab Hispaniis ad Italiam*), S. 198, 23. v. Eotol.

**Italie.** *Add:*—Wǽron ealle Italie Rōmānum on fultume, rs. 4, 11 ; S. 208, 7. Áscian Italie hiera āgne londleóde, 5, 1 ; S. 214, 11. v. Eotol-ware.

**Isra(h)élisc** ; *adj. Of Israel* :—Israéliscan folces *Israhelis,* Ps. L. 146, 2. Sum Egiptisc man gestrínde sunu be Israhéliscum wífe . . . þa fiāt hē wið ānne Israhéliscan man, Num. 24, 10. þā Israéliscan bearn *Israel,* Ps. L. 123, 1.

**íþ.** *Add:*—þæt hié iéð mehton þā burg āwēstan, Ors. 2, 7 ; S. 90, 13 : 5, 7 ; S. 228, 20. þæt hé iéð mehte winnan, 2, 3 ; S. 68, 14 : 3, 1 ; S. 96, 16 : Past. 211, 15 : 459, 2. Suā micle hē mæg iéð his hiéremenn geteón, 81, 16. Micle ðý iéð, 397, 6. þe íð, Ors. 4, 3 ; S. 162, 8. v. un-eáþe.

**íþan** *to lay waste. Take here* éþan *in Dict., and add:*—Hē hine gegyrede mid wyrgðu . . . and sió his innað ýþde (? ydwe, MS.) wylce wan wætere gelíc *he clothed himself with cursing . . . it laid waste his inward parts, fought like a flood;* induit se maledictione . . . et

intravit sicut aqua in interiora ejus, Ps. Th. 108, 18. Íðende *depopulans*, Wrt. Voc. ii. 95, 84.

**-íþan** *to be gentle.* v. ge-íþan.

**íþast.** *Add:*—Wē magon hié suā íðesð gebētan, Past. 306, 20.

**íþ-begēte.** v. ēþ-begēte : **íþ-belig.** *l.* íþ-belge, *and add :* v. eáþ-bylgness.

**íþe.** *Take here* ēþe *in Dict., and add :*—Ǣdre *levius*, Wrt. Voc. ii. 53, 58. **I.** *easy, not difficult to do :*—Swā ēþe swā hit is tō ongitanne, Bt. 41, 4 ; F. 250, 21. Þā þing þe ne sint ēðe tō forlǣtanne, 7, 2 ; F. 18, 16. Hī bióð swīðe ēðe tō tedǣlenne, 34, 11 ; S. 92, 27. Him wǣre iéðre ðæt hē hira gearra wēnde, Past. 433, 29. Nāwuht nis iéðre tō gesecganne, 239, 10 : Ors. 2, 5 ; S. 80, 11. Micle iéðre, Past. 203, 17. Micle ðe iéðre, 277, 25. Éþre is *facilius est*, Mt. R. 19, 24. Nis hire ēþre tō feallanne of dūne ðonne ūp, 33, 4 ; F. 130, 38. Éðre *facilis*, Kent. Gl. 479. Nāwðer ne on ēðnum (ēðrum ?, ēðum ?) þingum ne on rēnum, Shrn. 204, 3. **II.** *easy, not troublesome, pleasant :*—Hē sǣde þæt him nǣre nǣfre ǣr swā ēðe ne swā myrige, swā him þā wæs, Wlfst. 237, 7. **III.** *of persons, not exacting, not harsh :*—Weard Tiberius Rōmānum swā wrāð and swā heard swā hē him ǣr wæs milde and iéþe, Ors. 6, 2 ; S. 254, 30. [*O. Sax.* ōði : *O. H. Ger.* ōdi *facilis.*] v efen-, sin-íþe, un-eáþe.

**íþe** *desert, waste. Take here* ēþe *in Dict., and add :* [*Goth.* auþs : *O. H. Ger.* ōdi : *Ger.* öde : *Icel.* auðr.]

**íþe-lic** ; *adj.* **I.** *easy to do :*—Hū iéðelic bið tō forgiefenne sió gedóhte synn, Past. 419, 10. Gif ðū ne wilt ūs geðafian in swā ýðelicum (ǣðelicum, *v. l.*) þinge (*in tam facili causa*), Bd. 2, 5 ; Sch. 135, 3. **II.** *of a material object, inconsiderable, slight, of moderate size :*—Man swā mearcað mid ēþelicum (medmicelum, *v. l.*) treówe þeorfe hlāfas þ hī beóþ swylce gesewene swylce hī sýn on feówer feórðan dǣlas tōdǣlde, Gr. D. 87, 2. v. eáþe-lic, un-eáþelic.

**íþelíce.** *Add:*—Hē hié iéðelíce ofercōm *facile agrestium hominum inperitam manum compescuit*, Ors. 6, 30 ; S. 278, 23 : 6, 36 ; S. 294, 5 : Past. 399, 18 : 441, 14. Íðelíce (iéðlíce, *v. l.*), 141, 5 : 335, 16. Swā micle swā hió ēstelícor ofdūne āstígeð, swā hió iéðelícor ūp āstígeð, 103, 19. Micle iéðelícor, 107, 2. Ðý iéðelícor, 304, 5. Micle ðý iéðelícor, 80, 8.

**íþ-georn** ; *adj. Pleasant, gracious, amiable :*—Éþgeorn *deliciosa*, i. *amabilior, leta*, Wrt. Voc. ii. 138, 42. Cf. ēst-georn.

**íþ-gesýne.** *Add:* [Cf. *Icel.* auð-sēnn.]

**íþ-hilde** ; *adj. Easily held, content* (cf. ge-healdan : **XI a.**). *Take here examples given under* ēþ-hylde *in Dict., and add :*—Éþhelde *vel* fulhealden *contentus*, Wrt. Voc. ii. 135, 1. Nā his ēðhylde weldǣde *non suo contentus officio*, Scint. 133, 2. Hæbbende fódan and mid hwǣm wē beón oferhelede þām ēðhylde (*contenti*) sýn wē, 143, 12. Éðhelde *contentiae*, An. Ox. 11, 26. *See* earfoþ-hilde *under* -hilde.

**íþ-hilde** ; *adj. Easily inclined* (v. hildan *to incline*) ; *of a person, easily moved to anything, compliant :*—Gif nā bið ēðhylde (cf. eáðe, R. Ben. 30, 9) *si non sit facilis*, R. Ben. I. 35, 6.

**-íþian.** v. un-íþian.

**íþ-ness.** *Add:*—Swā him ðiós stillnes and ðiós iéðnes mā lícað, swā him lǣs lícað ðæt ðæt hié tō gelaðode sindon *quo non sunt molesta quae tenent, eo minus amabilia fiant quae vocant*, Past. 351, 7. Ūs wæs ānes þinges ēþnes (*una res fuit saluti*), þ se snāw leng ne wunede þonne āne tīde, Nar. 23, 21. Hié for hira āgenre iéðnesse ðæt fleóð *quietem propriam spectando refugiunt*, Past. 41, 10. Þāra þe ǣrest on earfoðum byð and eft on ēðnesse, Ps. Th. 40 arg. : Solil. H. 44, 13. Hī maciað eall be luste and be ēþnesse, Ll. Th. ii. 322, 25. Þāra góda and þāra ýðnessa þe God hafað gegearwod þām þe hine lufiað, Verc. Först. 101, 17. v. un-eáþnes.

**íþ-rǣde** ; *adj. Easy to guess* (v. rǣdan : **VI a.**) :—Cunna mage þū ārǣdan hwæt þis mage beón. Ic wēne þæt hit nis ēðrǣde, E. S. xxxvi. 326.

**-íþrian.** v. ge-íþrian.

**íþrung** (?), e ; *f. Amelioration, a making easier :*—Ne mæg ēðrunge (? edringe, MS.) ǣnge gehātan geómrum gāste, geóce oðθe frófre, Seel. 107. *See preceding word.*

**íþ-togen** *easily deferred* (?) :—God wolde þ hī ðǣr stille reston and on ðām scræfe slēpon oþ þás ýðtogenan tīde þe hē hī eft mancynne geswutelian wolde, Hml. S. 23, 317.

**íþ-wilte** ; *adj. That may be easily turned* (v. wiltan) :—Éþwiltum mēce *romphea uersatili*, i. *mobili* † *uolubili*, An. Ox. 1151.

**Iudēas.** *l.* Iúdēas, *and add :* Iúdan, Iúdēan ; *gen.* ena, ana :—Iúdēas cōmon, Past. 33, 14 : Jn. 11, 8. Alle Iúdēas (eal Iúdēa þeód, W. S.) *omnis Iudaea*, Mt. L. 3, 5. Wǣron Iúdan on miclum gedrefe Ors. 6, 10 ; S. 266, 1. Ðis ys se Hǣlynd Iúdēa (Iúdēana, L., R.) cyning, Mt. 27, 37 : Jn. 2, 13. Manega þāra Iúdēa, 11, 19. Þēra Iúdēa (Iúdēana, L.) gearcung, 19, 42. On Iúdana lond, Ors. 3, 5 ; S. 104, 24. Iúdea, 6, 7 ; S. 262, 23. Mid Iúdēum *apud Iudaeos*, Mt. 28, 15. Iúdēum, Jn. p. 5, 3. Iúdēum, Jn. L. 19, 40. Dryhten tǣlde ðā scamlēasan Iúdēas, Past. 207, 8. Hē hēt ūt ādrīfan ealle þā Iúdan, Ors. 6, 4 ; S. 260, 21. Cōm Godes wracu ofer Iúþan, 6, 3 ; S. 256, 34.

iue. v. ífe : iuht. v. geoht.

**íw.** *Take here* eow (*l.* eów) *in Dict., and add :*—Íuu *taxus*, Wrt. Voc. ii. 121, 76. Eów *ornus*, 65, 8. Tō íwes heáfdan . . . on íwdene, C. D. iii. 444, 4-6. On Íwwcumb, of Íwwa cumbe, 218, 34. Cf. Tō íwígað, v. 240, 25.

**íwan.** *Add:* v. on-(an-)íwan : **íw-berige.** *Take here* eówberige *in Dict.*

**íwed-, eáwed-ness,** e ; *f. Showing :*—Eáudnise *ostensionem*, Rtl. 113, 40. v. æt-íwedness.

**-íwness.** v. æt-íwness.

# K

In one instance *k* seems used for *g* :—Ðæt mód ðe ǣr wæs kelēd (ālēd, *v. l.*) of his gewunan *cum cogitatio extra usum ducitur*, Past. 57, 9.

# L

**lā. I.** *Add:*—Lā *aue*, An. Ox. 56, 133. Wā lā wā *eheu*, Wrt. Voc. ii. 32, 44. **II.** *Add: giving emphasis* (1) *to interrogation or exclamation :*—Lā whǣr nū þā . . . lā whǣr sind *ubi nunc . . . ubi sunt*, Wülck. Gl. 253, 34, 37. Lā hū, ne mōt ic dōn þæt ic wille?, *aut non licet mihi quod volo facere?*, Hml. Th. ii. 80, 25. Hwæt dō ic lā?, 104, 16. Suwiað : hwæt lā, ne gehýre gē hū myrige lofsangas swēgað on heofonum ?, 98, 4 : Hml. S. 8, 48. Ne eart þū lā Sebastianus ?, 5, 449. (2) *to entreaty or command :*—Swuga, lā, swuga *tace, obsecro, tace*, Solil. H. 48, 7. Gecier lā, ne folga mē, ðæt ic ðē ne dyrre ofstingan, Past. 295, 15. (3) *to statement or affirmation :*—Geá, lā, geá ; gyf hyt nū fǣrenga gewurde . . . *vere aliquantum ; imo si haec repente provenerint . . .*, Solil. H. 34, 11. Lā ah ðeáhhwæðre se foreðancula wer bæd his fultumes *sed videlicet vir providus solatium petivit*, Past. 305, 1. Hit is lā ful gōōd þæt ǣfre ūre eágan mōston geséon þæt wē wilnodon, Ps. Th. 34, 21. (4) *to negation :*—Uton ǣndian þás bōc nū hǣrrihte . . . Nǣse, lā, nǣse ; uton ne forlǣtan gyét ðás bōc *concludamus hoc volumen . . . Non sinam omnino concludi hunc libellum*, Solil. H. 49, 12.

**laber.** v. lawer.

**lāc.** [*If* ðinne *in* Hml. S. 7, 119 *is correct,* lāc *is there masculine, but perhaps* ðīne *should be read.*] **II.** *Add:* v. lāc-lic :—Se mægðhād sceal God beón geoffrod be his āgenum cyre, þ seó lāc beó leófre þām Hǣlende, Hml. A. 33, 234. Nolde Drihten āsendan þone ðe hē sylf gehǣlde tō þām sācerde mid ǣnigre lāce, Hml. Th. i. 124, 19. Gān mid lāce tō Godes hūse, and beran þæt cild forð mid þǣre lāce, 134, 22. Þ synd þā mǣstan lāc, Hml. A. 35, 289. Ðā lāc beóð God ealra andfengeost, Past. 222, 21. Freó lāca *oblationes*, Ps. L. 50, 21. Ic hatige þā lāc þe bióð on wōh gereáfodu . . . Sē þe mē brengð lāc of earmes monnes āhtum on wōh gereáfodum, ðonne bið ðæt swelce hwā wille blōtan ðǣm fæder tō ðance and tō lācum his āgen bearn *ego odio habens rapinam in holocausto. . . . Qui offert sacrificium de substantia pauperis, quasi qui victimat filium in conspectu patris*, Past. 342, 2-10. Ðā offrunga and ðā lāc (*holocausta*) ðe mon brōhte tō ðǣm weóbude, 217, 20. **III.** *Add:*—Laac *elogia*, Wrt. Voc. ii. 107, 13 : *exenium*, 69. Lāc, 83, 48 : *munuscula*, 55, 16. Ne sí munece ālýfed þæt hē ǣnig gewrit oððe sende oððe lāc fram hyra māgum underfón *nullatenus liceat monacho a parentibus suis litteras, eulogias vel quelibet munuscula accipere*, R. Ben. 87, 11. **IV.** *Dele ; in the instances given here* lāc = lācnung. *Add to compounds* ælmes- (Nap. 5), bríw-, drý-, sib-, word-, wrōht-, wund-lāc.

**lācan.** *Add:* **IV.** *to delude, trick :*—Óðer gāst lǣdeð hine and lǣced (lǣced ? v. lǣccan) and geond land spaneð, Sal. 496. Swilce þā woruldsǣlþa wǣron rihte þā hī ðē mǣst geólecsan swilce hī nū sindon, þeáh þe hý þe liólcen (ōleccan, *v. l.*) on þā leásan sǣlþa *fortuna talis erat, cum blandiebatur, cum tibi falsae illecebris felicitatis alluderet*, Bt. 7, 2 ; F. 18. 2. Cf. for-, ge-lācan, *and Icel.* leika *to delude.*

**lāc-dǣd.** *Add:*—Lācdǣde, *cystinesse munificentie*, An. Ox. 3833.

**lāc-fæsten** *a fast considered as an offering :*—Ne gelýfe þæs nǣnig mon þ him ne genīhtsumige þ fæsten tō ēcere hǣlo, būton hē mid ōþrum gódum hit geēce, and sē þe wille Drihtne bringan gecwēme lācfæsten, þonne sceal hē þ mid ælmessan and mid mildheortum weorcum fullian, Bl. Hml. 37, 18.

**-lācian.** v. ge-lācian.

**lacing.** The word seems to occur only as a local name :—In loco qui dicitur Lacinge, C. D. ii. 93, 22. On Dýðmere ; ðonon on Lacing ; andlang Lacing on cealcford, v. 397, 15 : vi. 28, 12. Cf. Lacingbrōc, vi. 8, 13 : 72, 31. In uilla quae cognominatur Lakingheðe, iv. 16, 28. Quandam telluris particulam qui appellatur æt Lacingahið, v. 301, 11.

lácnian. *Add*:—Lácnie *medor*, Wrt. Voc. ii. 58, 45. 'We lácno-don Babylôn, and hió ðeáh ne wearð gehǽled'. Ðonne bið Babylôn gelácnad, nales ðeáh fullíce gehǽled. . . . '*curavimus Babylonem, et non est sanata.*' *Babylon quippe curatur, nec tamen ad sanitatem reducitur*, Past. 267, 9 Hǽlwende cleoþan lácniende *medicinale cataplasma pro-curans*, An. Ox. 1974. Mid lácniendum tôlum *medicinalibus instru-mentis*, 3047. v. un-lácnod, *and next word*.

lácnigend-líc. *Add*:—Mid lácniendlicum tôlum *instrumentis medi-cinalibus*, Hpt. Gl. 478, 2. v. un-lácnigendlic.

lácnung. *Add*: I. *healing, medical care*:—*Studium vel medecina, curatio vel* lácnung *vel gȳmen vel hogu*, Wrt. Voc. ii. 137, 59. Ne cann ic nâht on lácnunge, Hml. S. 22, 41. Wite hê þæt hê þá gȳmenne þára umtrumra sáula tô rihtre lácnunge underféng *noverit se infirmarum curam suscepisse animarum*, R. Ben. 51, 12. Gif hê his seócum dǽdum ealle lácnunge gegearewade *si morbidis earum actibus universa fuerit cura exhibita*, 11, 5. II. *a medicine, medicament, means of heal-ing*:—þá hálan lǽces ne lácnunge ne behôfiað, R. Ben. 50, 19. Lác[nunge] *medecinae*, An. Ox. 382 : *medicamine*, 4352. Lácnunge, cliþan *cataplasma*, 3050. Godcundra myngunga sealfunga, háligra gewrita lácnunga *unguenta adhortationum, medicamina scripturarum divinarum*, R. Ben. 52, 12.

lác-sang. *Add*: cf. offrung-sang.

lactuca. *Add*:—Gif se ríca ágylte, þreá hine ; þonne ytst þú þíne eástru mid grénum lactucum, mid biternesse. Þ wát eall ceorlisc folc þ gréne lactucas beóð bitere ; swá synt þá rícan men tô þreágenne, Angl. viii. 323, 22.

lacu. For '*A pool . . . lake*' *substitute*: *A stream, water-course*, and add :—In australi atque in occidente habens torrentem cuius uocabulum Fiscesburne . . . in oriente aquam quae Anglorum lingua Lake nominatur habens, quae est duarum, quae ibi sunt, ulterior . . . Insuper memoratam aquam, id est Fiscesburnam . . ., C. D. i. 122, 31. On scegbrôc oð seó lacu scȳt west þanon út on hǽdfeld, C. D. B. iii. 624, 19. Oþ wogg-gawilllacu út scȳt ; on þá lace oð wocggawilles heáfod, Cht. E. 266, 24. Be healfan stréme intô Sandfordes lǽce ; swá andlang ðære lace intô Sandforda ; of Sandforda eást andlang ðære lace, C. D. iv. 134, 21–24. Oð ðá lace ; andlang lace út on Temese, v. 302, 34 : 330, 28 : vi. 2, 12 : vi. 8, 26. On þá fúlan lace, v. 13, 22. On stréam oþ þá laca tôlicgaþ, Cht. Crw. 3, 12. ¶ *as second part of a compound* :—Út on æsclace ðær æsclace fylð út on Wuorf . . . of ðære ealdan díc on Grindewylles lace . . . on Ættanpennes lace, C. D. vi. 48, 8–14. On brômlace ; ðonne andlang streámes, iii. 452, 13. On ðá gemǽrlace ; andlang lace, vi. 8, 26. On þá mǽrlace, 9, 2. On sandlace ; andlang sandlice tô ceóles íge, v. 303, 3. [v. *N. E. D.* lake, *and see* Cht. E. 465 : Cht. Crw. 54.] v. fisc-, mǽd-lacu.

lád. II. *Add*:—In monasterio quod iuxta ostium aquilonale flúminis Génládae positum Raculfe nuncupatur, Bd. 5, 8. Haec sunt termina huius agri . . . æt aquilone génlád, C. D. i. 238, 6. [v. *D. D.* yenlade ; *Halliwell Dict.* yenlet.] IV. *Add*: ¶ *In the phrase* cyrcan lád, *which seems sometimes* (?) *to have the same meaning as* ciric-sceat. *All the following passages occur in charters of Oswald, bishop of Worcester* :—Si hit ǽlces þinges freoh bútan ferdfare and walgeworc and brycggeworc and circanláde, C. D. iii. 5, 14 : 159, 31. *The corresponding forms in Latin are seen in the following passages* :—Sit praedictum rus liberum ab omni mundiali seruitio . . . excepta sanctae Dei basilicae suppeditatione ac ministratione, 173, 30 : 241, 35. Exeptis snctDei aecclesiae necessitatibusus atque utilitatibus, 177, 32, Libera omnis rei nisi aecclesiastici census, 212, 29 : 259, 23 261, 15. Aeclesiastici census, id est duos modios de mundo grano, ii. 386, 30. Aecclesiae manus et sepultura praesulis in Wigurna ceastre dinisci deueniat ; alias plena glorietur libertate, excepta expeditione rata, pontis arcisue constructione, 385, 15. V. *leading, guiding* :—Blind gif blinde lát forelǽdas *caecus si caeco ducatum praestet*, Mt. L. 15, 14. v. corn-, from, ofer-, wudu-lád.

lád. I. *Add*:—Lád *excussatio*, Wrt. Voc. ii. 146, 25. Heora ǽlc ôþerne myngige þæt þá slápulan náne láde næbben (*propter somnolento-rum excusationes*), R. Ben. 47, 17. II. *Add*:—Gif hwá þeóf fridige, sȳ hê emscyldig wið mē þa þe þeóf scolde, búton hê hine mid fulre láde wið mē geclánsian mæge, Cht. E. 231, 11. III. (mistaken for) *accusation* :—Fram þrím ondréd heorte mín . . . . láde (*delaturam*) ceastre, Scint. 224, 17.

ládian. I. *In* l. 3 *read* 241 *for* 244, *and add* : (1) *to clear, excuse, defend a person* :—Manigra manna gewuna is ðæt hié hié mid ðissum wordum ládiað and cueðað : 'We brucað úres ægnes, ne gítsige wē nánes ôðres monnes,' Past. 337, 19 : 439, 21. Sume þá biscopas wiðstôdan strang-líce and scyldon and ládedon þá sôðfæstnesse *quidam in defensione veritatis episcopi persistentes*, Gr. D. 240, 10. (1 a) *to clear* of a charge, Past. 308, 7 (*in Dict.*). (2) *to excuse* a fault, Ors. 5, 2 ; S. 216, 31 (*in Dict.*).

ládigend-líc. *Add* : v. be-ládigendlic.

lád-mann. *Add*:—þá cwæð Esau : 'Ic bidde þē þæt þú nyme þē ládmenn of mínum geférum, þæt þē wegas wissigeon, Gen. 33, 15. [v. *N. E. D.* lodeman.]

lád-rinc. For '*The word, . . . vehicularius*' *substitute* : In attempt-ing to determine the meaning of this word it should be noticed that *lád* in all its other compounds, *lád-mann, -scipe, -teáh, -teów*, has the force of leading, guidance. The *lád-rinc* seems to be a guide, and his special character in the passage given above may be inferred from the following passage :—Si aduenae de aliis regionibus aduenirent, debebant ducatum habere ad aliam regalem uillam quae proxima fuisset in illorum uia, C. D. v. 159, 8–11. Cf. *too* : *ductor*, qui ad conducendum aliquem in via per alterius regionem datus est a quovis principe, Migne.

lád-scipe. *Add*:—Ládscipe *ducatum*. (*See passage under* lád ; V.)

lád-teów. *Add*: [*from* lád-þeów]. I. *a leader, guide* :—Ne forlǽt ûs, ac beó úre ládteów (*ductor*), ðú cans eal ðis wésten, and wásð hwǽr wē wícian magon, Past. 304, 15. II. *a military leader, general* :—Marcellinus, Iuliuses ládteów, Ors. 5, 12 ; S. 240, 24. Alexandres æfterfolgeras wǽron gehátene ládteówas, 3, 11 ; S. 150, 8. Pompeiuses legian mid his þrím ládteówum *Pompeiani duces cum legionibus*, 5, 12 ; S. 240, 21. v. ǽ- (Ps. Vos. 9, 21), fore-ládteów ; lættēwestre.

ládteów-dôm. *Add*:—Under lætteówdôm *sub* (*discipline*) *pedagogio*, An. Ox. 3014.

ládung. I. *Add*:—þ se man gecyrre fram his synnum, gif hê wile, oððe hê bútan ládunge losie mid ealle, Hml. A. 62, 265.

-lǽca. For *l.* ág-, *and add* : v. ge-lǽca : lǽcan. *Add* : v. cneord-, cúþ-, cȳþ-, fá- (tǽ-), fremed-, ge-, gecneord-, gecúþ-, gecȳþ-, geed-, gelôm-, geong-, gesamod-, ge-swǽs-, geþwǽr-, gewundor-, swǽs-, þwǽr-, wiþer-lǽcan : lǽccan. *Add* : v. á-lǽccan ; lácan ; IV.

lǽccan (?) *to blame, find fault with* [v. *N. E. D.* lack ; 5]. v. on-leccan.

lǽccung (?), e ; *f. Blaming* :—Ðá forðgáð of welerum mínum ne onsién (*faciem* seems to have been read) on leccungæ (tô bysmre, Ps. Spl. C.) *quae procedunt de labiis meis non faciam irrita*, Ps. Cant. 88, 35. [v. *N. E. D.* lacking, *and see bracket at end of* lǽcing *in Dict.*]

lǽce. I. *Add*:—Leáces sex *camilema*, Wrt. Voc. i. 22, 28. v. riht-, un-, weorold-lǽce. II. *Add*:—On lǽces mere, C. D. v. 325, 19. On lǽcemere, vi. 72, 25. Tô lǽces forda, 9, 11. On lǽces ford, 120, 9.

-lǽce, an ; *f.* v. scín-lǽce : -lǽce ; *adj.* v. eáþ-lǽce *and* efen-lǽce.

lǽce-cist, e ; *f. A medicine chest* :—Fundon hí þá áhȳdde mancas in his lǽcecyste *aureos invenerunt absconsos in medicamine*, Gr. D. 344, 17.

lǽce-cræft. *Add*: I. *the art of medicine* :—Lǽcecræft *medicina*, An. Ox. 3124. Wæs sum munuc, þám wæs nama Iustus, and wæs gelǽred on lǽcecræfte (*medicinali arte imbutus*), Gr. D. 344, 6 : 11. Hê áxode gif hê cúðe áht on lǽcecræfte, Hml. S. 22, 40. II. *medical treatment* :—þ word wind on ûs swá swá wís lǽce dêð þe mid stíðum lǽcecræfte gelácnað þone untruman, Hml. A. 6, 129. III. *a recipe, remedy, medicine* :—Lǽcecræftas (cf. lǽcedômas, 44, 7) wiþ healsgunde, Lch. ii. 2, 16. [v. *N. E. D.* leechcraft.]

lǽce-dôm. *Add*: I. *healing* :—Medecina, þ ys lǽcedômes cræft, Shrn. 152, 17. Se getȳda lǽce ðæs heofonlican lǽcedômes ǽgðer ge ðá hálan lǽrde ge ðám unhálum lǽcedôm eówde *peritus medicinae coelestis apostolus non tam sanos instituit, quam infirmis medicamenta mon-stravit*, Past. 397, 15–17. Hê forgeaf wanhálum mannum mid his worde lǽcedôm, Hml. S. 22, 24. II. *a medicine, remedy* :—Lǽcedôm *malagma*, i. *medecinam*, An. Ox. 375. Cleoþan, lǽcedôm *cataplasma*, i. *medicamentum*, 1973.

lǽcedôm-ness. *Add*:—Lǽcedômnessa *cataplasma*, Wrt. Voc. ii. 81, 55.

lǽce-finger. *Add*:—Middelfinger *medius*, lǽcefinger *medicus*, Wrt. Voc. ii. 58, 6. [v. *N. E. D.* leech-finger.]

lǽce-getawu ; *pl. n. Medical apparatus* :—Hí wǽron geondsmeágende eall his lǽcegeteá. þá fundon hí þá mancas in his lǽcecyste *illius omnia medicamenta perscrutantes aureos invenerunt in medicamine*, Gr. D. 344, 16.

lǽce-íren, es ; *n. A lancet* :—Hê ásette his lǽceíren (*medicinale ferra-mentum, id est phlebotomum*) on míne tungan, Gr. D. 32, 25.

lǽcend, -lǽcend, -lǽcestre. v. efen-lǽcend, -lǽcere, -lǽcestre.

lǽce-wyrht, e ; *f. Leech-work, medical treatment* :—Mín ádlige cneów is yfele gehæfd, þæt ne mihte nán lǽcewyrht áwiht gelíðian, þeáh ðe heó gelôme tô geléd wǽre (*diu est quod molestia genu tumentis oppressus nulla cuiuslibet medicorum industria possum sanari*, Vit. Cuth. c. 2), Hml. Th. ii. 134, 33.

lǽce-wyrt. I. *Add*:—Abgarus wundrode þ hê wearð gehǽled bútan lǽcewyrtum þurh ðæs Hǽlendes word, Hml. S. 24, 160.

lǽcing. *Dele, and see* lǽccung : -lǽcne. v. eáþ-lǽcne : -lǽcness. v. gelôm-, þríst-lǽcness : lǽcung. *Add* : [v. *N. E. D.* leeching.] : -lǽcung. v. ed-, efen-, gedyrst-, gelôm-, geþríst-, neá[h]-, riht-lǽcung.

lǽdan. *Add* : I. *to cause to move* (*liþan*) *with oneself*. (1) *to bring* or *take* a person to a place or person. (a) *with the person's consent* :—Ezechias lǽdde ðá ælldeódgan ǽrenddracan on his máðmhús, Past. 39, 3. Orfeus lǽdde his wíf mid him oþ þe hê côm on þ gemǽre

leóhtes and þeóstro; þá eóde þ wíf æfter him, Bt. 35, 6; F. 170, 12. Gif heó léng libbe þonne sé þe hié út lædde, Ll. Th. i. 66, 18. Læd under earce bord eaforan þíne, Gen. 1332. Se sióca áh þearfe þ hine mon læde tó þám læce, Bt. 38, 7; F. 210, 1. Þá men þe hié úp mid him læden, Ll. Th. i. 82, 11. Gif hý man út of lande lædan wille on óðres þegnes land, 256, 1 : Gen. 1774. Hát síðian Agar and Ismael lædan mid hié, 2785. (b) of enforced movement :—Héton hiene Rómäne gebindan and gebringean beforan fæstennes geate. Þá náwþer ne hine þá hám lædan ne dorston þe hiene þider læddon, ne his þá onfón þe hiene mon tó brohte, Ors. 5, 2; S. 218, 34 : Chr. 796; P. 56, 9 : Gen. 2016. Læddon þá leóde lääne gewinnan tó carcerne, An. 1251. Læde hine tó Róme, Ll. Th. i. 264, 8. Hét hé niman þone eorl and tó Bæbbaburh lædan, Chr. 1095; P. 231, 27. In þone lääan lég lädan, Gú. 567. On gemót læded, Cri. 795: Ph. 491. ¶ figurative :—Óðer willa feohtende wið ðæm willan his módes hine gehæftne lædde on synne gewunan, Past. 423, 19. (b a) to bring or take (to the place of) an action, lead to execution, bring to justice, &c. :—þ hine man tó rihte læde, Ll. Th. i. 396, 15. Gif hé hine forstalede, þ hine man lædde tó þære torfunge, 234, 8. (2) to take, carry, convey. (a) the object material :—Ne læt hé his nánwuht of þýs middanearde mid him máre þonne hé bröhte hider, Bt. 26, 3; F. 94, 15. Þone gewundedan ðe mon lædde helfcuicne tó ðæm giesðhúse, Past. 125, 8. Hé hét smiðian of smätum golde áne lytle róde, ðá hé lædde on his swýðran, Hml. ii. 304, 16. Æþelhelm lædde Wesseaxna ælmessan tó Rome, Chr. 887; P. 80, 30. Rómäne gesomnodon al þa goldhord þe on Bretene wæron . . . and sume mid him on Gallia læddon, 418; P. 10, 20 : Past. 333, 19. Hý læddun hyne of lyfte tó earde, Gú. 398. Hwæþer gé eówer hundas and eówer net út on sæ lædon ðonne gé huntian willaþ?, Bt. 32, 3; F. 118, 14. Tíd is þ þú fére and þa ærendu læde, Gú. 1271. Ne miht ðú náht lædan of þysum lífe mid þé, Hml. S. 9, 47. Héton þá lædan ofer landsceare, teón torngeníðlan, An. 1231. Wæs líc læded tó moldgrafe, Jul. 689. ¶ lädе lädan, v. läd; III. (b) the object non-material :—Se þeóden bebeád þrýðweorc . . . Godes ærendu lædan tó Channanéum, An. 778. Frið lädan, 174. (3) to bring evidence, a case, an action, &c., into court :—þá lædde ic Aðulfes cinges yrfegewrit on úre gemót æt Langandene, Cht. Th. 486, 13. Sceal ic his word and his weorc in gewitnesse Dryhtne lædan, Gú. 693. Godwine hæfð geläd fulle läde æt ðan unrihtwíse ðe Leófgár hyne tihte, and þ wæs läd æt Licitfelda, Cht. Th. 373, 34. (4) to produce, bring forth :—Wæstme lädað (-eð, MS.) cederbeámas, Ps. Th. 103, 16. Cynna gehwylc cucra wuhta þára þe lyft and flód lædað and fédað, Gen. 1298. Læde seó eorðe forð cuce nítenu and creópende cinn and deór, Gen. 1, 24. (4 a) to be productive :—Wudu mót him weaxan, tänum lædan (cf. týdran), Hy. 4, 105. II. to accompany and show the way to, conduct, convoy, guide (lit. or fig.) :—Þú lätst mé hider and ðider on swä þicne wudu, Bt. 35, 5; F. 164, 13. ‘Ic oudreðe þ ic ðe läde hidres þidres of þínum wege.’ . . . ‘Ic beó swíþe fægn gif ðú mé lädest þider ic þe bidde, 40, 5; F. 240, 21-25. Hí lädað mid wynnum æðelne tó earde, Ph. 345. God self hine lädde ðurh ðæt wësten, Past. 304, 7. Him urnon ealle hellwaran ongeán, and läddon hine tó hiora cyninge, Bt. 35, 6; F. 168, 29. Gif hwelc forworht monn cymð, and bitt úrne hwelcne ðæt wé hine läden tó sumum rícum menn, Past. 63, 2. þ ælc man hæbbe þá men gearowe on his lande þe läden þá men þe heora ägen sécan willen, Ll. Th. i. 162, 24. Nú þú móst féran . . . ic þec lädan sceal, Cri. 1672. Lädan weorode lāreów tó lides stefnan, An. 1708. Ðá ðe óðerra monna säula underfoð tó lädanne, Past. 77, 4. III. of a commander, to march at the head of :—Mægenwísa is trum, sé þás fare lädeð, Exod. 554. Fyrd wæs gefýsed, fram sé þe lädde, 54. Mægen lädan, El. 241. Godcunde lāreówas sceolan ús lädan forð æt þam dóme . . . Gesǣlig bið se hyrde þe þá heorde intó Godes ríce mót lädan, Ll. Th. i. 424, 8-11. Se cyng betǣhte þá fyrde tó lädene Ealfríce, Chr. 992; P. 127, 11. IV. to guide by holding :—Blind gif blindne lädeþ, Mt. R. 15, 14. Óþerne ealdne man lädden feówer äwyrgde englas mid mycelre rēðnesse, and hine besencton on þá fýrenan eá, Bl. H. 43, 28. Hí genämon þone ð., leáddon hine tó heora hūstinga, and hine þær oftorfodon, Chr. 1012; P. 142, 21. ¶ wíf lädan to marry, Lch. iii. 190, 7 : 212, 8. V. to guide with reference to action or opinion, to lead to a conclusion, induce to do :—Óðer gást lädeð hine and lǣceð, oð þæt his eáge bið æsþancum ful, Sal. 496. Tó hwon lǣddest þú hider þeosne? why did you cause this man to come hither? Bl. H. 85, 25. Hé lädde hié mid ligenum and mid listum speón, Gen. 588. ‘Ðær ðú ongeáte hwidre ic þe nú teohhie tó lädenne.’ . . . ‘Hwider wilt þú mé lädan?’ ‘Tó þǣm sóþum gesǣlþum ic tiohhie þ ic þe läde,’ Bt. 22, 2; F. 78, 1-7. Hé teohchode hine tó lädanne on lífes weg, Past. 305, 5. VI. of a road, to serve as a passage to :—Weg þe lädeþ (lädas, L.) tó forwyrde . . . se weg þe lädeþ (lädes, L.) tó lífe, Mt. R. 7, 13-14. Gän on ðone weg þe ús lētt tó heofonan ríce, Chr. 1086; P. 221, 25. VII. the object inanimate, to guide, give direction to something flexible :—Sé þe foran lädað brídels on blancan, El. 1184. VII a. to trace a line, boundary, track, &c. :—Gif ðá landgemǣre ealswä wǣron swä man heó on fruman lädde, C. D. iv. 234,

34 : 235, 4. Þá þe lífes weg lädan cunnon, Wlfst. 75, 2. Gif mon secge þ man þ trod äwóh drífe, þonne mót sé þe þ yrfe áh trod oð tó stæde lädan, Ll. Th. i. 352, 11. VIII. to guide a ship, steer :—Gé þe þus brontne ceól ofer lagustræte lädan cwómon, B. 239. IX. to deal with, treat :—Ic naman Drihtnes herige, and hine mid lofsange läde swylce laudabo nomen Dei mei cum cantico, et magnificabo eum in laude, Ps. Th. 68, 31. X. to engage or take part in, perform :—þá wurdiað þín weorc wordum and dædum . . . and Críst heriað and him lof lädað, Hy. 7, 25. Hé wæs eft swä ær lof lädende, An. 1479. XI. to pass, go through life :—Líf lädan on gefeán, Bt. 12; F. 36, 24. Ancorlíf, munuclíf lädan, Bd. 4, 27; Sch. 511, 2 : 3, 27; Sch. 316, 4 (see all three in Dict.). XII. intrans. to take a certain direction :—Hé äna is ealra beáma on eorðwege úp lädendra beorhtast geblówen, Ph. 178. v. be-, mis-, ofer-, ymb-lädan; under-läded.

-läde. v. un-läd, -läde : Läden. Add : [v. N. E. D. leden.] v. bócleden.

Läden ; adj. Add :—On Lýdenre sprǣce, Angl. viii. 313, 19.

Läden-bóc. Add :—Ðá ungelǣredan preóstas gif hí hwæt litles understandaþ of þám Lýdenbócum, Ælfc. Gen. Thw. 2, 11.

lädend a bringer :—Æs lädend legislatorem, Ps. Rdr. 9, 21.

-lädendlic. v. ge-lädendlic.

Läden-gereord. Add :—Leornian sprecan on Lädengereorde discere sermocinari Latina lingua, Coll. M. 18, 34.

Läden-lár, e ; f. Latin lore, knowledge of Latin :—Sé þe þurh Lädenláre rihtne geleáfan understandan ne cunne geleornige húru on Englisc, Wlfst. 124, 29 : 126, 23.

Läden-lic ; adj. Latin :—Nú hæfst þú mé ofte gebedon þ ic þe út ärehte mid Lädenlicre sprǣce þæs eadigestan Nicholaes gebyrdtída, Nap. 40.

Läden-sprǣc. Add :—Sé þe þurh Lädensprǣce rihtne geleáfan understandan ne cunne geleornige húru on Englisc, Wlfst. 126, 1.

läd-lic, -líce. v. un-lädlic, -líce : lädness. Add : v. onwegä-, wiþ-lädness.

lǣfan. Add : to cause to remain (lifan). I. of a deceased person, to have as remainder after one :—Se gesibsuma lǣfð symle yrfeweard æfter him sunt reliquiae homini pacifico, Ps. Th. 36, 36. Hé lǣfde æfter him þreó sunan, Chr. 1086; P. 221, 11. Nam se óðer hí and weard deád, ne se sǣd ne lǣfde . . . And ealle seofon hí hæfdon and sǣd ne lǣfdon, Mk. 12, 21, 22. Gif hwä gefare and nän bearn ne gestríene, gif hé bróðor lǣfe, fó sé tó his wífe, Past. 43, 13. II. to transmit at death to heirs or successors, bequeath :—Manige for bearnlēste eallne þone welan ðe hí gegaderigaþ hí lǣfað frǣmdum tó brúcanne orbus liberis alienum censum nutrit heredi, Bt. 11, 1; F. 32, 7. Hí lǣfað fremdum heora ǣhte relinquent alienis divitias suas, Ps. Th. 48, 9. Hé þám yldestan eaforan lǣfde folc, Gen. 1214: 1179. Hé eaferum lǣfde, swä dēð eádig mon, lond and leódbyrig, þá he of lífe gewät, B. 2470. Hí of lífe gewyton and lǣfdon heora ǣhta þám æðelum mannum. Iulianus ðá dǣlde . . . heora landäre, þe him lǣfed was, Hml. S. 4, 79-82. Þonne þú heonan cyrre . . . lǣf ús ēcne gefeán, Cri. 159. Ic wilnode . . . æfter mínum lífe þám monnum tó lǣfanne þe æfter mé wǣren mín gemynd on gódum weorcum, Bt. 17; F. 60, 16. III. to allow to remain, not to take, consume, remove, &c. :—Hí nymað ælc wiht, and uneáðe hí þám þearfiendum lytles hwæt lǣfað, Ll. Lbmn. 476, 11. Hí näman æt heora mägon sceattas genóge . . . and þä spendon and dēldon hafenleásum mannum . . . Þæt feoh þ hí ǣr lǣfdon (had not spent before) hí mid heom tó þám scræfe hæfdon, Hml. S. 23, 198-213. Eal monncynnes þæt þǣr lǣfed wæs, Ors. 2, 6; S. 88, 6; Bt. 11, 1; F. 30, 19. ¶ where the object is food, not to eat :—Wulfas on ǣfne ne lǣfað näwiht oð morgen, Ll. Lbmn. 476, 3. Þæt þæt hí lǣfon healdan heora bearnum reliquerunt quae superfuerunt parvulis suis, Ps. Th. 16, 14. Eal þ flǣsc þ wildeór lǣfen carnem quae a bestiis fuerit praegustata, Ll. Th. i. 54, 1. III a. to leave after subtraction :—Dó of ðám feórþan deále eall þæt seó sió his ofseten hæfþ . . . ðonne miht ðú ongitan þætte þær ealles nis monnum märe lǣfed tó búgianne búton swelce än lytel cafertún, Bt. 18, 1; F. 62, 16. IV. to leave, to leave, not to take with one :—Þá men þe hé bæftan him lǣfde, Chr. 755; P. 48, 14.

lǣfel. Add :—Læfel manile, Wrt. Voc. ii. 56, 46. Hé hét geótan wæter on læfel misit aquam in pelvem, Hml. A. 155, 102. Man sceal habban . . . læflas, Angl. ix. 264, 21.

lǣfend. Substitute : v. lǣrend.

lǣfer. I. Add : In local names :—Ad uadum qui uocatum Leuerford, C. D. i. 64, 12. Leuuremer Livermere (in Suffolk), iv. 245, 30. Cf. Liversedge, Liverpool; cf. eá-lifer. II. Add :—Lǣfer lamina (auri), An. Ox. 2, 26. Læfrum petalis (deauratis), 5497. Leafrum, 2, 497. In Hml. Th. ii. 498, 3 lǣfrum translates laminis. v. reádgold-lǣfer.

-lǣg. Add : ge- (at ge-lagu), ofer-læg.

lǣge (?) ; adj. Fallow, unploughed ; in cpds. lǣg-æcer, C. D. iii. 442, 9: lǣg-hrycg, 437, 18. v. N. E. D. lea.

lǣl. I. Add :—Lǣla uibices, An. Ox. 7, 246. Lǣlo, 8, 184. II.

*Add:*—Læl *liuor*, An. Ox. 32, 24. ¶ *The word glosses liuor =*
*envy:*—Lēla liuoris (rancida *liuoris* inuidia, Ald. 40, 14), An. Ox. 4,
52. Cf. lǽlian.

lǽlian. *Substitute:* I. *to hurl* a dart (?):—Þte nales ðā sweartan
deóblu in mīnre sīdan lēligen, swā swā gewuniað, scytas *ut non tetri dae-*
*mones in latera mea librent, ut solent, iacula,* Lch. i. lxxiii, 33. II.
*to get black and blue:*—Æfestian, lǽlian *libescunt* (cf. lǽl; II. ¶),
Wrt. Voc. ii. 50, 41.

lǽmen. *In* l. 8 *read* lǽmena *for* lǽmina (v. Wülck. Gl. 404, 39),
*and add:*—Se līchoma lǽmen is, for ðǽm þe hē of ðām geworht wæs,
Verc. Först. 148, 21. Ðā ðæs æfter sextēne geárum forlēt hē þone
lǽmnan ofn ðæs menniscan līchoman, Shrn. 50, 33.

lǽn. *Add:*—Gif ðæt God geteód hæbbe, and mē ðæt on lǽne gelīð
(*it is to be granted me*) ðæt gesibbra ærfeweard forðcymeð wēpnedhādes,
C. D. ii. 121, 26. Þæt þæt þe heó tō lǽne onfēng, Gr. D. 97, 12.

lǽnan. *Add:* I. *to lend, grant temporary possession of a thing on*
the condition of the return of the same or its equivalent:—Be ðām
monnum ðe heora wǽpna tō monslyhte lǽnað. Gif hwā his wǽpnes
ōðrum onlǽne (lǽne, *v. l.*), Ll. Th. i. 74, 1-3. I a. *to lend for a*
consideration, *lend* (money) at interest:—Gif bisceop . . . oððe hwylc
Godes þeów lǽnð his feoh tō unrihtun gafole (*pecuniam suam injusto*
*foenore mutuam dederit*), Ll. Th. ii. 198, 14. Be þām gehādodum
mannum þe hyra feoh lǽnað tō hȳre, 194, 31. Ys forboden þ hē his
feoh, ne his ǽhta (*pecuniam suam vel possessiones*) tō nānum unrihtum
gafole ne lǽne; þ is þ hē hine mǽran ne bidde tō āgyfanne þonne hē
him ǽr lǽnde; ac for lufe lǽne gehwā ōðrum his feoh and his ǽhta,
194, 15-19. II. *to grant:*—Se gōda līchama þancode Gode ealre þǽre
āre . . . þe hē him lǽnde, Wlfst. 237, 6. Wīsdōm lǽnende i tȳdiende
*sapientiam praestans*, Ps. L. 18, 8.

lǽne. *Add:*—Ðæt wæs tō suīðe scortre hwīle, for ðǽm ðiós woruld
is suīðe lǽnu *in tempore paucorum dierum*, Past. 255, 11. Sē ðe ǽgðer
wilt ge þissa lǽnena stōclīfa ge þāra ēcena hāma, Solil. H. 2, 14.

lǽn-lic. *Add:*—Wē sculon geþencean þ þis līf is lǽnlic þe wē nū on
libbað, Ll. Th. ii. 400, 15.

lǽnend-lic. *Add:*—Ealle þās lǽnendlican earfeðnessa ende habbað;
ac þā tōweardan ende nabbaþ, Verc. Först. 141, 7: 142, 11.

lǽn-land. *Add:*—þonne is þæs londes þridde half hīd þe Oswold
seld Cynelme his þegne tō bōclonde, swā hē hit him ǽr hæfde tō forlǽten
tō lǽnlonde, Cht. E. 208, 11.

lǽpe-wince, an: *f. A lapwing:*—Laepaeuincae, lepeuince, laepi-
uince *cucuzata*, Txts. 52, 264. v. hleápe-wince (*of which* læpewince
*seems the earliest form*).

-lǽpped. *Add:* v. twi-lǽpped; *and take after* læppa.

læppa. *Add:*—Lappa *lanna*, *angulus auris*, Hpt. 33, 244, 8.

-lǽr, *empty.* v. ge-lǽr; lǽre, lǽr-ness. [*v. N. E. D.* leer.]

lǽran. *Add:* I. *to show the way* (*lit. or fig.*) *to* a person:—Gāþ
ealle on þone weg þe eów lǽraþ ðā foremǽran bisna þāra gōdena
gumena, Bt. 40, 4; F. 238, 29. Simle ic þīne weogas wanhogan lǽrde
*doceam iniquos vias tuas*, Ps. C. 105. II. *to show* a person the way
*to or from, guide, direct:*—Hē mec lǽred from þē on stearcne weg,
Jul. 282. Hē lǽrde þā leóde on geleáfan weg, An. 1682. III. *to*
*guide the action of* a person:—Sió godcunde foretiohhung lǽrde ðone
þe hē wolde þ he gold hȳdde, and eft þone þe hē wolde þ hit funde,
Bt. 40, 6; S. 140, 16. IV. *to show* what should be observed or
done. (1) where there is advising, exhorting, admonishing, persuading,
instigating, &c. (a) absolute:—Lǽrdan *hortantur*, lǽrað *hortamini*,
Wrt. Voc. ii. 42, 47, 48. Dióule lǽrende *diabolo instigante*, Rtl. 114, 5.
(b) with personal object. (a) alone:—Salomon cuæð: 'Dō, mīn sunu,
suā ic ðē lǽre' *exhortatio subditur: Fac quod dico*, Past. 193, 17.
Wīgend lǽrde helle deóful . . . and þæt word gecwæð: 'Sleað synnigne
ofer seolfes mūð,' An. 1299. On ōðre wīsan sint tō lǽranne (cf.
manianne, 19) ðā scamleásan, on ōðre ðā scamfæstan. Ðǽm scamleásan
ne wyrð nō gestiéred būtan micelre tǽlinge, Past. 205, 21: 179, 21.
(β) *to exhort.* &c. *to* something:—þū þrīstlīce þeóde lǽrest tō beadowe,
An. 1187. Oðer hine tyhteð and on tǽso lǽred, Sal. 493. (γ) with
clause:—Ic þē lǽre . . . þæt þū hospcwide . . . ǽfre ne fremme, El. 522.
Oðer hine lǽreð þæt hē lufan healde, Sal. 491. Ðās leásan spell lǽraþ
gehwilcne man . . . þ hē hine ne besió tō his ealdum yfelum, Bt. 35, 6;
F. 170, 15. Þū synfulle simle lǽrdes þ hió cerrende Crīste hērdon, Ps.
C. 55. Se deófol þone Iūdas lǽrde þ hē Drihten belǽwde, Hml. A.
154, 66. Ic leófra gehwone lǽran wille þ hē ne āgǽle gǽstes þearfe,
Cri. 816: Dōm. 47: El. 1206. Sint tō lǽranne ðā ofersprǽcan ðæt
hié wacorlīce ongieten *admonendi sunt multiloquio vacantes, ut vigi-*
*lanter aspiciant*, Past. 277, 3. (2) of authoritative utterance, *to*
*prescribe, order, enjoin, direct.* (a) absolute:—Dō swā ic lǽre, Ll. Th. i.
184, 14. (b) with clause:—Ic lǽre þ hit dō swā ic ǽr cwæð, Angl. ix.
260, 8. Ǽt ǽrestan wē lǽrað þ ǽghwelc mon his ǽð and bēote and
wǽrlīce healde, Ll. Th. i. 60, 2. Wē lǽrað and biddað and on Godes
naman beódað þ . . ., 364, 21. Ǽghwilc cild sī, wē lǽrað, gefullod
binnon nigon nihton, ii. 292, 5. (c) with personal object. (a) alone:—
Hē self dō swā swā hē ōðre lǽrð, Past. 453, 15. (β) with a noun

object, of that which is enjoined or commended:—Ōðerne hē lǽrde
gedyld *alteri patientiam proponit*, Past. 291, 21. Ðæt hē lǽre ðā ōðre
eáðmětta, . . . ond lǽre ðā slāwan geornfulnesse gōdes weorces . . . and
ðā ōðerne cysta lǽre . . . lǽren hī ðā wīsgālan gesinscipe . . . and
ðā forhæbbendan lǽren forhæfdnesse *superbis praedicetur humilitas* . . .
*torpentibus praedicetur sollicitudo boni operis* . . . *tenacibus infundatur*
*tribuendi largitas* . . . *incontinentibus laudetur conjugium* . . . *continen-*
*tibus laudetur virginitas corporis*, 453, 19-32. (γ) with dat. infin.:—
þe nān neóðdearf ne lǽrde tō wyrcanne *quem non externae pepulerunt*
*fingere caussae*, Bt. 33, 4; F. 128, 11. (δ) with clause:—Hwæt wile
ðæt beón weorca ðæt ūs on ōðerne stōwe forbiét ðæt wē hit beforan
mannum dōn, on ōðerre lǽrð (cf. hēt, l. 8) ðæt wē hit beforan mannum
dōn *quid est quod opus nostrum et ita faciendum est, ne videatur, et*
*tamen ut debeat videri praecipitur*, Past. 451, 3. Hē ðone ōðerne lǽrde
ðæt hē him anwald on tuge *alteri imperium proponit*, 291, 20. Wē
willað biddan freónda gehwylcne and eal folc lǽran georne þ hī
inwerdre heortan God lufian, Ll. Th. i. 316, 18: 326, 1. V. *to*
*impart knowledge.* (1) *to declare, proclaim:*—Hī lǽrden hira synna, and
hī hī nānwuht ne hǽlon *peccatum suum praedicaverunt, nec absconderunt*,
Past. 427, 28. (2) *to teach, give instruction in* a subject, *preach:*—Hē
gewritu lǽred, Sal. 50. Monige wīse lǽreówas winnað mid hira ðeáwum
wið ðā bebodu ðe hī mid wordum lǽrað *quod verbis praedicant, moribus*
*impugnant*, Past. 29, 22. Nān cræft nis tō lǽranne ðǽm ðe hine ǽr
geornlīce ne leornode *nulla ars doceri praesumitur, nisi intenta prius*
*meditatione discatur*, 25, 15. (3) *to teach* a person something. (a)
with acc.:—þū hine þeódscipe þīnne lǽrest *de lege tua docueris eum*,
Ps. Th. 93, 12. Hē ūs lǽrð nytwyrðlicu ðing, Past. 255, 12. (b)
with clause:—Sint hié tō lǽranne hū hié scilen dǽlan, Past. 341, 16.
(c) *to instruct* a person in a subject:—Lǽre mon furður on Lǽden-
gedióde ðā ðe mon furður lǽran wille, Past. 7, 13. (4) *to teach*
something to a person:—Hē þām folce Godes gerihta lǽrde, Hml. Th.
i. 74, 22. (5) *to teach* a person, *give instruction to, educate, train:*—
Se Wīsdōm þe hit lange ǽr tȳde and lǽrde, Bt. 3, 1; F. 4, 30. Hē in
Effessia ealle þrāge leóde lǽrde, Ap. 31. Ūre flǽsclican fædras lǽrdon ūs
*patres carnis nostrae habuimus eruditores*, Past. 255, 7, 10. Hié lǽrdon
hira tungan, and wenedon tō leásunge *docuerunt linguam suam loqui*
*mendacium*, 239, 18. Hū mislice mon sceal menn lǽran, 173, 13.
Hit bið swīðe geswincful ðæt mon ǽlcne mon scyle on sundrum lǽran,
hit is ðeáh earfoðre ealle ætsomne tō lǽranne, 453, 10-12. Ongan hine
brȳd wīshȳdig wer wordum lǽran, Gen. 1823. Hī sǽgdon swā fram
Siluestre lǽrde wǽron, El. 191. (6) absolute, *to teach, act as teacher:*—
Ǽlc wyrd is nyt þāra ðe áuþer dēþ, oððe lǽrþ oþþe wrícþ *quae aut*
*exercet, aut corrigit, prodest*, Bt. 40, 2; F. 236, 16. Sió stōðfæstnes
self lǽrde *docente veritate*, Past. 125, 7. Wē rehton hwelc se hierde
bión sceal; nū wē him willað cȳðan hū hē lǽran sceal *qualis esse debeat*
*Pastor ostendimus, nunc qualiter doceat demonstremus*, 173, 15. Wæs
hē gemēt tōmiddes ðāra lǽreówa frignende, nalles lǽrende (*docens*);
for ðæm hē ūs wolde ðæt tō bīsene dōn ðætte ðā unlǽredan ne dorsten
lǽran (*docere*), 385, 27. Ǽr þām þe his Apostolas tōfarene wǽron
geond ealle eorðan tō lǽranne, Ll. Th. i. 56, 4. (7) intransitive, *to*
*give instruction* about something:—Se hālga heáp . . . hī āsendon tō
lǽrenne eallum leódscipum be Crīstes tōcyme for middangeardes ālȳsed-
nysse, Hml. Th. i. 388, 16. v. mis-, þurh-lǽran; fore-, yfel-
lǽrende.

lǽre *should be taken here:* -lǽre. v. earfoþ-, eáþ-lǽre: -lǽred.
*Add:* v. gestæf-lǽred.

lǽrend, es; *m. One who teaches, instigates*, &c. v. lǽran:—
Bepǽcend *deceptor*, lǽrend (*printed* læfend) *seductor*, lǽwend *proditor*,
Wrt. Voc. i. 49, 16-18. Drihten þ ongeat, þ se deófol þone Iūdas
lǽrend (*printed* læfend) . . . Wiste hē þ hē on his godcundre mihte
hæfde ǽghwæðer ge ðone lǽwend ge ðone lǽrend, Hml. A. 154, 71.

lǽrest. *l.* lǽrest. The *r* for *s* may be explained by Verner's
Law.

lǽrestre. *In* l. 3 *for* 543 *read* 548, *and add:*—Lār hyrde hopan . . .
lǽrestre mægenes *disciplina custos spei* . . . *magistra virtutis*, Scint.
206, 18.

lǽrig *the border of a shield.* v. ymb-lǽr(i)gian.

lǽring-mann. *Add:*—þæs lāreówes hǽs and þæs lǽrincmannes
(leornincgmannes, *v. l.*) weorc *magistri jussio et discipuli opera*, R. Ben.
20, 6.

lǽs. *Add:*—Seó lǽs is tōforan eallum mannum gemǽne on ðām
hǽðfelda *the pasture on the heathfield lies open to admit all men*, C. D.
iii. 419, 21. Ān lǽs on waruðe, 429, 16. Sceáp lǽsuwe (lēswe, Ps.
Srt.) his *oues pascuae eius*, Ps. L. 99, 3. On stōwe lǽswen (lēswe?,
lǽswena?; lēswe, Ps. Srt.) *in loco pascuae*, 22, 2. Hȳ lǽtan him tō
lǽswena?; lēswe, Ps. Srt.) *in loco pascuae*, 22, 2. Hȳ lǽtan him tō
. . . þā hlǽfordes and his sceápa lǽse æfter þæs hlāfordes, C. D. B. i. 544, 3.
þone þe ðis land gelytlede on lǽsu[m?] oððe on gemǽru[m?] *qui istam*
*terram diminuerit in pascuis siue metis*, C. D. v. 253, 36. Cf. Beó-leáh,
lǽs *pasture where there were many flowers for bees:*—þurh beóléase,
C. D. iii. 75, 37:—On beólése . . . ūt þurh beóléase, C. D. B. iii. 249,

31, [v. *N. E. D.* lease, leasow.] v. fearn-, feld- (C. D. iv. 96, 2 : vi. 39, 9), mór-, út-, wudu-lǽs.

**lǽs** *allowance.* v. beód-lǽs.

**˙lǽs.** *l.* lǽs, *and in last citation* þinga *for* þing, *and add :* **I.** *adv. or conj.* :—Nǽfð nán man tó þæs hál eágan þæt hé ǽni hwíle mage lócigan ongeán þás sunnan þe wé hǽr geseóð, and húru þæs þe lǽs (*all the less*) gyf heó hefð unhále, Solil. H. 35, 1. Hys mé lyst swá læng swá lǽs, 36, 17. Ðú hǽtst mé forlǽtan þá unrótnesse, ðý lǽst ic . . . þý mettrumra sí, 49, 1. Þe lǽste ( = lǽs þe) gehremde *ne offenderet,* An. Ox. 3675. Þe lǽste (*ne forte*) beó gemétt bróþor ásolcen, Angl. xiii. 434, 982. **II.** *as subst.* :—Ic oft wíscte þ hyra lǽs wǽre swá gewinfulra, Nar. 2, 29.

**lǽs-hosum.** *Perhaps for* fótleáste lǽshosum *should be read* fótleáse lǽsthosan *footless hose, hose that did not cover the sole of the foot.* v. lǽst ; *f.*

**lǽssa.** *l.* lǽssa, *and add :* **A.** *as adj.* agreeing with a substantive expressed or understood. **I.** of size, extent in space :—Ic eom mǽre þonne þes middangeard, lǽsse þonne hondwyrm, Rä. 67, 2. Lǽssan ymbgang hæfð se mann þe gǽð ábútan án hús þonne sé ðe ealle ðá burh begǽð. Swá eác ðe móna hæfð his ryne hraðor áurnen on þám lǽssan ymbhwyrfte þonne seó sunne hæbbe on þám máran, Lch. iii. 248, 10-15: Met. 28, 12. Lýssan *minima,* Kent. Gl. 1100. Hé þára lǽssena ríca reccend is, Ors. 2, 1 ; S. 58, 25. Senepes sǽd . . . is ealra sǽda lǽst (lǽsest, L.), Mk. 4, 31. Se móna eala tungla hæfð lǽstne embegang, Angl. vii. 14, 134. **II.** of number, in the case of collective unities :—þǽr mǽre folc sig . . . þǽr lǽsse folc síg, Ll. Th. i. 232, 14. Hié werod lǽsse hæfdon þonne Húna cyning, El. 48. **III.** of time :—Scyld wel gebearg líf lǽssan hwíle, B. 2571. **IV.** of qualities, emotions, conditions, actions, or occurrences, expressing extent or degree :—Wæs se gryre lǽssa efne swá micle swá bið wíggryre wífes be wǽpnedmen, B. 1282. Ne þincð mé þæt wundur wuhte þe lǽsse, Met. 20, 117. On ǽnigum þingum cræftig, on máran wísdóme oþþe on lǽssan, Bl. H. 49, 28. Ǽnigne creft gelíorman, oððe leásan oððe máran, Solil. H. 30, 22. Lǽssan sige hæfð sé sé ðá burhware ofercymð, Past. 218, 18. Hé forlǽt ðá máran gód and went hine tó ðǽm lǽssum *relictis amplioribus bonis ad minima retorquetur,* 403, 5. Nó þæt lǽsest wæs hondgemóta, B. 2354. **IV a.** having a quality mentioned to a slighter extent, *less* in respect to (*on*) :—Ic eom on mægne mínum lǽsse þonne se hondwyrm, Rä. 41, 95. **V.** of things. (1) with respect to value :—þ man nǽnne ne slóge for lǽssan yrfe þonne .xii. pæniga weorð, búton hé fleón wille . . . þ man ne wandode þonne þeáh hit lǽsse wǽre, Ll. Th. i. 242, 8-11. Nalæs hí hine lǽssan lácum teódan, þeódgestreónum, þonne þá dydon þe hine æt frumsceafte forð onsendon, B. 43. (2) with respect to importance or interest :—Ne sceolde hé nán ðing forgýman ðe ǽfre tó note mehte ; ne forða ( = furþum) músfellan ; ne þ gít lǽsse is, tó hæpsan þinn, Angl. ix. 265, 9. Ðæt hié be ðǽm lǽssan ðingum ongieten hú suíðe hié gesyngiað on ðǽm máran *ut ex minori consideratione colligant, quantum in majoribus rebus delinquant,* Past. 375, 23. Lǽstra þinga (unge)drýstlǽcende áht secgan þæs ðe hé geseah, Hml. S. 23 b, 644. **VI.** of persons or places, in reference to rank, dignity, &c. :—Ic eom lǽssa þonne ealle þíne miltsunga, Gen. 32, 10. Man þe bið lǽssan maga þon[n]e se cyninges þegn, Ll. Th. i. 154, 7. Heáfodmynstres griðbryce . . . medemran mynstres . . . gít lǽssan, 342, 3. Hé mǽðe cann on óðrum mannum, on his gelícum ge on lǽssan mannum, Wlfst. 51, 31. Seó ilce burg Babylonia, seó ðe mǽst wæs and ǽrest ealra burga, seó is nú lǽst and wéstast, Ors. 2, 4 ; S. 74, 23. Úre Áliésend ðe mára is and mǽrra eallum gesceaftum, hé hine gemedomode tó bíonne betwiux ðǽm lǽsðum (lǽstum, *v.l.*) and ðǽm gingestum monnum, Past. 301, 13. **VI a.** applied to the inferior or smaller of two persons or places of the same name :—Ðæs Jacóbes leásse (lǽssa, R.) móder *Jacobi minoris mater,* Mk. L. 15, 40. Se lǽssa middangeard *michrocosmos,* Wrt. Voc. i. 282, 22 : 64, 13. **VII.** referring to (mean) conduct :—þætte ealra lǽst wæs, his gingran dohter hé nolde búton hæftníede habban, and þ wæs lytel cild *etiam parvulas filias crudeli captivitate retinebat,* Ors. 3, 9 ; S. 128, 18. **VIII.** of quantity :—Him gebyriað .v. æceras tó habbanne, mǽre gyf hit on lande ðeáw sý, and tó lytel hit bið beó hit á lǽsse, Ll. Th. i. 432, 25. Sume beóð on máran áre, sume on lǽssan, sume fulneah búton, Solil. H. 44, 13. On lǽsse plihte, Ll. Th. i. 226, 6. Ánra gehwylc þe hafað lǽsse mægen, Sal. 356. **B.** as substantive. (1) *the less* :—For hwan ne déþ hé þ lǽsse nú hé þæt mǽre dyde?, Bl. H. 181, 6. (2) *less, a smaller amount* :—Ne wǽron þás ealle gelíce lange, ac on þyssum wæs þreó þúsend wintra, on sumre lǽsse, on sumere eft mǽre, Bl. H. 119, 4. Ic for lǽssan leán teohhade, B. 951. Sé þe lǽsse hæbbe, Ll. Th. i. 414, 19 note : Bl. H. 53, 16. Hweðer ðú mǽre wisse þonne ðú nú wást, þe lǽsse, Solil. H. 59, 8. (2 a) with gen. :—þæt hire þý lǽsse on þearf lytlan ne bið ánum fingre þe hire on eallum bið þǽm líchoman, Met. 20, 179. Hí lǽsse ongietað ðæs ðe him hreówan ðyrfe, Past. 411, 4. Hé hit gehíwað swá þæt lǽst manna wát hú hé him wið þone ðeódfeónd gescyldan sceal, Wlfst. 54, 19. Ða ðe Lǽdensprǽce lǽste (lǽsde, *v. l.*) cúðon, 9, 16. (3) *what is of less importance* :—He mót ǽgðer witan

---

ge lǽsse ge máre, ge betere ge mǽtre, Angl. ix. 259, 23. **C.** as adverb :—Sé þe lǽsse maga sý, Ll. Th. i. 414, 19. Swunce máre sé þe unriht gestreón on his handa stóde, and lǽsse sé þe þǽr áriht onsprǽce, 290, 5. Ic lufige ǽlcne mínra freónda, sume lǽsse, sume máre. Solil. H. 16, 18. Ic ðóhte þæt hit wǽre lǽsse ðrýt (*less wearisome* ; or? *a less weariness*) tó gehýrenne, Hml. Th. ii. 2, 11. Ǽlc fagnað þæs þe lǽste (*to a very slight extent*) hé ongytan mæg, Solil. H. 31, 23. v. lǽs.

**lǽst,** e ; *f. A fault, sin* :—Wé sceolon biddan georne God þæt hé úre neóda gecnáwe and úre lǽsta gebéte, Nap. 41. [*Icel.* lǫstr. v. *N. E. D.* last *a fault.*]

**lǽstan.** *Add :* v. ge-lǽstan : **lǽste.** *Add :*—Laesti *vordalium,* Wrt. Voc. ii. 124, 17 : -lǽstfullian. v. ge-lǽstfullian : **lǽst-wyrhta.** *Add :*—Lǽstwyrhta *caligarius,* Wülck. Gl. 112, 9, om tted at Wrt.Voc. i. 19, 17.

**lǽswian.** *Add :* **I.** *trans.* (1) with acc. :—Hé lǽsode (fédde, *v. l.*) his swýn *porcos pavit,* Gr. D. 106, 28. (2) with dat. :—Hé gewunode þ hé lǽswode þám eówde his sceápa *ovium suarum gregem pascere solebat,* Gr. D. 215, 5. **II.** *intrans.* of animals, *to take food, graze, feed* :—þá leásiendan *pascentes* (*agnos*), An. Ox. 5210. [v. *N. E. D.* leasow.] v. ed-, ge-lǽswian.

**lǽt.** *Add :* **I.** *slow, sluggish* :—Be lattre meltunge sumra metta, Lch. ii. 160, 9. Late *lento,* Wrt. Voc. ii. 49, 62. On óðre wísan sint tó manianne ðá ðe bióð tó late (*pigri* : cf. ðá sláwan 19), on óðre ðá ðe bióð tó hrade, Past. 281, 18. **I a.** where the matter in which slowness is shown is noted. (1) with gen., B. 1529 : Dóm. 89 (*in Dict.*). (2) with prep., An. 46 : Ll. Th. ii. 404, 20 (*in Dict.*). (3) with dat. infin., Past. 281, 6 : Lk. 24, 25 (*in Dict.*). (4) with clause, Bl. H. 43, 20 (*in Dict.*). **II.** *delayed or deferred in time, late* :—Gif se biscop þá gýt lættra wǽre þ hé inne eóde *si adhuc episcopus tardius intrasset,* Gr. D. 59, 18. **III.** *advanced in point of time in the course of the day or night, late* :—Ðá seó lǽtre (lættre, *v. l.*) tíd weóx *cum hora tardior excrevisset,* Gr. D. 128, 12. Hí wǽron genýdde þ hí for þǽre lǽttran tíde (*tardiori hora*) wunedon læng þonne hí sceoldon, 126, 26. Oð ðá lǽtran tíde, 24.

**-lǽt.** [*Goth.* -léte : *O. H. Ger.* -laz.] v. for-, ge-lǽt.

**lǽtan.** *Add :* **I.** *trans.* (1) *to leave, allow to remain, abstain from taking away.* (a) with noun object :—Hé on fæstre stówe lét sum his folc, Ors. 4, 9 ; S. 190, 1. Hié þone óþerne dǽl þǽr léton þæt lond tó healdonne, 1, 10 ; S. 46, 21. Hwilce hwíle hine wille Drihten hér on worlde lǽtan, Bl. H. 125, 9. Þú ne scealt nǽnne cláð betweón lǽtan þínum eágum and hym, Solil. H. 43, 16. (b) with clause :—Lǽt þe on gemyndum (*keep in mind*) hú þæt manegum weard gefrége, An. 962. (1 a) *to loose one's hold of, let go* :—Hé hǽt fealdan þ segl, and eác hwílum lecgan þone mæst and lǽtan þá bætinge, Bt. 41, 3 ; F. 250, 15. (2) *to leave undone, unaffected, &c.* :—Gif preóst óðerne unwarnode lǽte, Ll. Th. ii. 294, 25 : 296, 15. Hit is wóh þ hí mon lǽte unwítnode . . . ðú ǽr cwǽde þ hé unriht dyde, þ hé lǽte unwítnod þá ýfelan, Bt. 38, 3 ; F. 202, 6-13. Lǽtan wrǽce stille, Gú. 170. (2 a) *intrans. To desist from* :—On þane .vii. dæg lét Drehten fram ǽghwilcum weorce, Wlfst. 218, 26. His sunu féng tó his eorldóme and lét of ðan þe hé ǽr hæfde, Chr. 1053 ; P. 182, 26. Lǽtan *desistamus,* An. Ox. 56, 320. (3) *to leave the control or management of something to some one else* :—þú þonne lǽtst eal eówer færeld tó þæs windes dóme, Bt. 7, 2 ; F. 18, 32. Ne lǽt ðú tó aldiódgium ðinne weorðscipe *ne des alienis honorem tuum,* Past. 249, 10. Þonne sceal ic beó þæs geðafa and lǽtan hyt tó þínum dóme, Solil. H. 32, 19. Ic hæbbe ealle þá spǽce tó Ælfhége lǽten, Cht. Th. 208, 32. (4) *to leave* to an heir, *bequeath* :—Míne sibbe ic lǽte eów, Past. 351, 12. Eallne þone welan hí lǽtað (lǽfað, *v. l.*) frǽmdum tó brúcanne *alienum censum nutrit heredi,* Bt. 11, 1 ; F. 32, 7. (5) *to quit, abandon* :—Wuton cunnian hwænne hine God lǽte *Deus dereliquit eum,* Ps.Th. 70, 10. Hé sceal lǽtan his wyrignesse and lufian his gebedu,Wlfst. 239, 19. Beódan Abrahame of eorðscræfe ǽrist fremman, lǽtan landreste, An. 782. (6) *to allow or cause the escape of* a confined fluid, *to discharge* a missile :—þú þurh lyft lǽtest milde morgenrén, Az. 82 : 135. Hé hygegár lǽteð, Mód. 34. Hé lǽteð foreweard hleór on strangne stán, Sal. 113. ' Tódælnessa ðára wætera út léton mín eágan.' Tódǽldu wæteru wé lǽtað út of úruin eágum ' *Divisiones aquarum deduxit oculus meus.' Divisas ex oculis aquas deducimus,* Past. 413, 27. Hé of stáne lét strange burnan, Ps. Th. 77, 17. Hí þára bearna blód léton swá man gute wæter *effuderunt sanguinem eorum sicut aquam,* 78, 3. ' Lǽt forð ðíne willas.' . . . Ðæt is ðæt mon his wætru út lǽte ' *Deriventur fontes tui foras.' . . . Fontes foras derivare est,* Past. 373, 12-16. (7) *to allow to have* :—þá bæd Eustachius þ hí him fyrst léton þ hí him tó Gode gebǽdon, Hml. S. 30, 424. (8) *to grant temporary possession of something to* (*to*) a person :—Úre Drihten is swíþe gemyndig ealra þára gifena þe hé ús tó lǽteþ, Bl. H. 51, 24. Eádmund oferhergode Cumbraland and hit lét tó eal (eall tó, *v. l.*) Malculme, on þ geráð þ hé wǽre his midwyrhta, Chr. 945 ; P. 110, 34. Hé geann Leófsige þæs mannes þe hé him ǽr tó lét, Cht. Crw. 23, 18. Dúnsǽte beþyrfan, gif heom se cyning an, þ man húru friðgíslas tó heom lǽte *Dunsetis expedit, si*

rex concedat, ut saltem pacis obsides habeant, Ll. Th. i. 356, 21.
(9) to allow or cause to pass or go, lǽtan of to let off:—Ic lǽte hǽþen
folc ofer iów I will send heathen folk upon you, Wlfst. 223, 12. Hé
hine sóna hider lǽt continuo illum dimittet huc, Mk. 11, 3. Hé ne lǽt
nã of gebedum his gãst he did not let his spirit off prayers, Hml. S. 31,
1357. Dêm þú hí tó deáðe, swã tó lífe lǽt, swã þé leófre sý, Jul. 88.
Gif se hláford mildheort bið, þ hé þã gýmeleáste tó forgyfenesse lǽte,
Ll. Thi. 270, 19. Hét se cásere lǽtan león and beran tó þám cynegum,
Hml. S. 24, 29. Hé hét lǽtan him tó twégen león, 51. Hé hét áne
strange leó lǽtan intó him, 30, 416. Heó hire mód ongan lǽtan æfter
þám lárum Gen. 592. Swã mycele furðor swã hé on háde is lǽten,
R. Ben. 112, 2. **II.** followed by an infinitive. (1) to permit,
allow, suffer. (a) where the infinitive has a subject, and is (a)
intrans.:—Hí ne lǽt God on áne healfe þæs heofones bión, Bt. 39, 13;
F. 234, 8. Ic wundrige for hwý God lǽte ǽnig yfel beón, oððe gif hé
hit geþafian wile . . . , 36, 1; F. 172, 5. Ðæt hé his feax lǽte weaxan,
Past. 139, 25. (β) trans.:—Ne lǽte gé eów ǽlcre láre wind áweccgan,
Past. 306, 8. Him wǽre micel ðearf ðæt hié lǽten Godes ege hié
geeáðmédan, 321, 12. (b) where the infinitive is without subject and
where now a passive construction may replace the earlier active:—Lǽt
þé fullian let yourself be baptized, Hml. S. 5, 204. Ne lǽten hié nõ
hié on ǽlce healfe gebígean they would not let themselves be inclined to
every side, Past. 306, 4. (2) to cause, let (in to let a person know).
(a) where the following infinitive has a subject:—Hé lǽt hig ætwindan
tó wuda dimitto eos avolar ad sylvam, Coll. M. 26, 3: Gen. 438. Ic
sígan lǽte wælregn, 1349. Hé leórt tácen forð úp éðigean, El. 1105.
(b) where the infinitive is without subject (cf. 1 b):—þú of foldan
fódder neátum lǽtest álǽdan producens foenum jumentis, Ps. Th. 103,
13. Se cyng lǽt tóscyfton þone here geond eall þis land, Chr. 1085;
P. 216, 1. Lǽt inc geséman, Past. 349, 12. (3) in the,imperative as
an auxiliary:—Lǽt gán ðín eágean beforan ðínum fótum palpebrae tuae
praecedant gressus tuos, Past. 287, 12. Lǽt ðíne willas iernan wíde,
and tódǽl hié deriventur fontes tui foras, et divide, 373, 4. Hláford,
gif þín willa sý, lǽt sendan (sǽnde man, v. l.) ǽrendracan mittaris, si
placet, qui huc eum exhibeat, Gr. D. 35, 9. **III.** to behave, appear,
think. (1) intrans. to behave so and so, have the appearance of being,
make as though:—Hé lǽt him eáðelíce ymbe þæt he takes that very
easily, Wlfst. 298, 30. þæt mancyn . . . þæs him náht ne ondrǽdað,
ac him orsorh lǽtað (profess to be unconcerned), 182, 15. Se kyngc
lǽt lihtlíce of þ hé cóm tó Englalande, and hine lét syððan tacan the
king made light of it till he came to England, and afterwards had him
taken, Chr. 1076; P. 211, 34. Ealle hí léton swilce hí on ǽfen slépon,
and sóna ðæs on morgen of ðám slǽpe áwacedon they all comported
themselves as if they had gone to sleep in the evening and soon after in
the morning had waked from their sleep, Hml. S. 23, 440. (1 a)
reflex., to show oneself so and so:—Heó efenwyrðe hí lét on eallum
þingum þám bisceope condignam se in omnibus episcopo praebuit, Bd. 4,
6; Sch. 384, 4. (2) trans. (a) with object and complement. (a) the
object a noun, or pronoun, to regard as:—Ic for náht lǽte floci fero,
Germ. 393, 140. Ic hine gelícne lǽte wísum were similabo eum uiro
sapienti, R. Ben. 4, 12. Hé bið tó eáðmód ðám yflan mannan, and
lǽt hine him tó gelícne (regards him too much as an equal), Past. 121,
21. Wé ðisses middangeardes welan foresettað and ús leófran lǽtað
ðonne ðã lufan þára heofonlicra eádignessa cum mundi diuitias amori
caelestium praeponimus, Bd. 3, 19; Sch. 279, 2. Ǽlc wôh gé lǽtað
tó rihte, Wlfst. 297, 27. þám þe nán þing him leófre ne lǽtað þonne
Críst his qui nihil sibi Christus carius aliquid existimant, R. Ben. 19,
15. þára hrægla þe nú drihtguman diórost lǽtað, Met. 8, 11. Drihten
lét hine him swã leófne þ hé ne gegeólde þ hé wǽre medmycelne fyrst
geunrótsod hunc quam dilectum Dominus attendet, quem contristari nec
ad modicum pertulit, Gr. D. 90, 15. Apollinis þe hí mǽrne god léton,
Wlfst. 197, 19. Lǽt ðé ǽlcne mannan . . . swã leófne swã bróðor,
Hex. 44, 24: Fä. 12: Angl. xii. 516, 24. Ðæt hé ðã ðe him underðiédde sién lǽte him tó genyhte ðæt hié hié sellen, 320, 1. Ðǽr hié
ne wénden ðæt hié selfe beteran wǽren ðonne ôðre menn, ðæt hié ne
lǽten hiera geðeaht and hiera wénan suã feor beforan ealra ôðerra
monna wénan nisi meliores se ceteris aestimarent, nequaquam cunctorum
consilia suae deliberationi postponerent, 306, 1. Him þǽs woruld úttor
lǽtan þonne þæt éce lif, Gú. 97. Gif þú ðé wilt dón manegra beteran,
ðonne scealt þú ðé lǽtan ánes wyrsan, Bt. 32, 1; F. 114, 14. Tó
hwǽm wé gelíc létan welle ríce Godes? cui adsimilabimus regnum Dei?,
Mk. R. L. 4, 30. (b) with object alone. (a) the object a noun, to
suppose something:—Nán þridde be him sylfum ne lét hé búton swilce
hé of his gemynde wǽre he had no third supposition about himself
except it was as if he were out of his mind, Hml. S. 23, 634. (aa) to
esteem (?):—Him ne bið lǽten gold ne seolfor neither gold nor silver is
held precious by them, Verc. Först. 106, 15. (β) the object a clause,
to consider that:—Swã ic lǽte on mínum geþance þ mé tó nánre
byrig swã rihte ne gebyrige swã tó þissere byrig, Hml. S. 23, 675.
Hé lǽt þæt hé ána sý strengra þonne hí ealle, Wlfst. 197, 21. Ic

lǽte riht (justum censeo) . . . þ sé þe þone hearm geworhte, þ sé
þone hearm gebéte, Ll. Th. i. 418, 4. Hé lét him tó rǽde þ (what)
hé þá gerǽdde, Hml. S. 23, 319. þæt hé lǽte him tó bysne hú þá
feónd forwurdon that he regard the fall of the angels as an example
for himself, Sat. 196. **IV.** in phrases (1) with adj., án lǽtan, to
let alone, not to meddle with:—Gif hié þone wæstm án lǽtan wolden,
Gen. 644. (2) with verb in infin., beón lǽtan to let be, cease from:—
Uton lǽtan bión þás sprǽce, Bt. 34, 7; F. 144, 18. (3) with adverb.
(a) behindan, (a) to leave behind (one), go away without:—þe behindan
ne lǽt, þonne þú heonan cyrre, mænigo þus micle, Cri. 155. (β) to
pass beyond, outstrip:—Ðonne bist þú bufan ðám rodore, and lǽtst
behindan þe þone hêhstan heofon, Bt. 36, 2; F. 174, 16: Met. 24, 29.
(b) fram, to start from a port:—Wé nõ geseóð þá stilnesse þǽre hýþe
þe wé ǽr fram léton, Gr. D. 6, 19. (c) ofdúne, to let down, to cause
or allow to descend:—Hié léton hiera hrægl ofdúne tó fótum, Ors. 3, 5;
S. 106, 19. (d) úp, to put ashore:—Hé cóm tó Sandwíc and lét þǽr
úp (lét dón úp, v. l.) þá gíslas, Chr. 1014; P. 145, 23. (e) út, to put
to sea:—Godwine eorl . . . lét út áne dæge ǽr midsumeres mæsseǽfene,
Chr. 1052; P. 177, 11. Sóna þæs ðe hí on scip eódon and út léton, Bd.
3, 15; Sch. 263, 6.

**-lǽte.** Substitute: -lǽte; sbst. v. ǽ-, blód- (Lch. ii. 16, 8), ge-lǽte:
-lǽte; adj. v. ǽ-, earfoþ-lǽte: -lǽtedness. v. for-lǽtedness.

**lǽtemest;** adj. Add:—On latemystum in nouissimo, Scint. 105, 8.
**-lǽtende.** v. for-lǽtende: -lǽtennesse. v. for-, tó-lǽtenness: lǽtere.
Add: v. for-lǽtere.

**lǽp:**—Presumat, i. audeat læþ ( = geþrístlǽ[h]þ?), An. Ox. 955.
v. ge-þrístlǽcan.

**lǽp land, lǽp** a lathe. Take these together, and add:—On westan
Cænt ðær ðæt land and ðæt lǽd tó lið, C. D. vi. 81, 19. Of Æglesforda
and of ellan þám lǽþe þe þǽr tó líþ de Æilesforda et de toto illo lesto
quod ad illum manerium pertinet, C. D. B. iii. 659, 25. [v. N. E. D.
lathe.]

**lǽþan** to cause to be hateful, cause a person (dat.) to shun:—Eal þæt
hé forbeóde and his gingrum lǽþe omnia que discipulis docuerit esse
contraria, R. Ben. 11, 18. v. for-lǽþan (Wlfst. 165, 13).

**lǽþettan;** p. te To make hateful:—Se oferlyfa on ǽte and on wǽte
dêð þone man unhálne, and his sáwle Gode lǽðetteð, O. E. Hml. i. 296, 6.
v. láþettan.

**lǽþ-leás.** v. láþ-leás.

**lǽþþ[u].** Add:—Hí mé sǽdon þ sum wer wunne on þǽre hefigestan
hatunge his gesacan, þæs lǽþþu (lǽðð, v. l.) and feóndscipe forð weóx
tó þon swíðe þ . . . quidam vir gravissima adversarii sui aemulatione
laborabat, cujus ad hoc usque odium prorupit, ut . . . , Gr. D. 158, 27.
Mid wordum laeððu (odii), Ps. Srt. 108, 3. Laeððu unrehtwísre odio
iniquo, 24, 19. Lǽðu odium, 35, 3. Hé beseah eáðmódlíce þá lǽþþe
(lǽððo, v. l.) and feóndscipe þæs æfstigau mæssepreóstes ejus odia
humiliter declinavit, Gr. D. 119, 23. þ wé hí lufian and lǽððe tó
nabban, Hml. S. 16, 265.

**-lǽðu.** v. mót-lǽðu.

**-lǽting.** v. for-lǽting: lǽtlíce. Add: , latlíce:—þane latlíce
(morose) wé wyllað beón gesǽd, R. Ben. I. 76, 4. Lǽtlícor tardius,
68, 3.

**lǽt-ness, e; f.** **I.** slowness in movement:—þǽre sunnan lǽtnys
binnan feówer geára fæce gewyrcð ǽnne dæg, Angl. viii. 308, 30. Hé
þá lǽtnysse ðæs geáres rynes geanbidode, Hml. S. 23 b, 647. **II.**
slowness of intellect:—þín gerecenes weóx fram mínre lǽtnysse and
dysegan swongernesse ex tarditate mea crevit expositio tua, Gr. D.
174, 23.

**-lǽtness.** v. á-, æt-, for-lǽtness.

**lǽttewestre, an; f.** A female guide:—Ongan ic biddan míne lǽttew-
estran, Sancta Maria, Hml. S. 23 b, 508. v. lád-teów.

**-lǽttu.** v. un-lǽttu.

**lǽw, léw, e; f.** Injury, weakening:—Gelíce þám dwǽsan þe for
heora prýtan léwe (through the disastrous effect of their pride?) nellað
beorgan, Wlfst. 165, 9. v. lim-, syn-lǽw, -léw.

**lǽwa.** Add:—Hé is mín lǽwa hic me tradet, Hml. Th. ii. 244, 5.
Hwílon cwepað preóstas þ Crístes lǽwa . . . mage wið Críst hine betellan,
swilce hé neádunge gefremode þá fácn wið hine, Hml. S. 27, 157. v. be-
lǽwa; lǽwe.

**lǽwan.** Add:—Be Iúdan Scarioth þe hine lǽwde, Ps. Th. 3, arg.

**lǽwe (?), e; m.** A betrayer:—Him wǽre betere þ hé geboren nǽre
þonne hé his lǽwe (lǽwa, v. l.) wǽre. Nǽron þa Iúdéiscan ne se dyrna
lǽwe (lǽwa, v. l.) þurh God geneádode, Hml. S. 27, 163–166. Cf. (?)
ge-fére, ge-síþe for declension.

**lǽwe** mutilated, weakened. [v. N. E. D. lew weak.] v. hungor-,
lim-lǽwe.

**lǽwed** a layman. Dele, and see leód: -lǽwed, -léwed injured.
v. á-, ge-léwed given under á-léfian, ge-léfed, but better separate as á-,
ge-lǽwed. v. lǽwe, lǽwa.

**lǽwend.** Add:—Wiste Drihten hwá his lǽwend and myrðra wæs,
Hml. A. 162, 235: 154, 70. v. be-lǽwend.

**læw-finger.** *Take here* **leáw-finger** *in Dict.:* **læwing.** v. be-læwing: **læx.** v. leax.

**léwsa, léwsa.** *Take here* **léwsa** *in Dict.*

**láf.** I. *Add:* (1) *what is left, a remainder:*—Éce láf (v. éce ; I), Exod. 370. Láfa, beliuendras *superstites, i. uiui,* An. Ox. 3313. ¶ *in the phrase* tó láfe *as remainder, remaining, left:*—Þrý dagas nú tó láfe syndan, Bl. H. 231, 14. Hwæt is heora nú tó láfe bútan se lytla hlísa and se nama mid feáum stafum áwriten? *signat superstes fama tenuis pauculis inane nomen litteris,* Bt. 19 ; F. 70, 10. Þá gebródru út fóron, and hé sylf on þám mynstre tó láfe weard, Hml. S. 23 b, 651. Wæs se mæsta mancwealm . . . swá þæt heora feáwa tó láfe wurdon *pestes pene usque ad desolationem exaestuauerunt,* Ors. 1, 6 ; S. 36, 16. Án of him tó láfe ne wunode *unus ex eis non remansit,* Ps. Vos. 105, 11. Ic ænlípigu on þám cafertúne tó láfe opstód, Hml. S. 23 b, 410. (1 a) *what is left* of something:—Hí námon þára hláfa and fixa láfe (ðá hláfo (láfe, R.) ðára screádunga, L. *reliquias fragmentorum*), Mk. 6, 43. (1 b) *what is left* by something (*gen.*):—Þú miht hér geseón moldan dæl and wyrmes láfe, Bl. H. 113, 20. Weard se mæsta dæl mid hungre ádýd, and þá láfe ðæs hungres ofslóh se here, Hml. Th. i. 404, 11. II. *Add:*—Him féla láf (*used with collective force and taking verb in plural?*) ne meahton sceddan, B. 1032. IV. *Add:*—Þét Alexandres láf wæs and his sunu, Ors. 3, 11 ; S. 148, 31. Of wífe í hláfe seofa bródra *de uxore septem fratrum,* Mt. p. 19, 6. Þte læda bróder his láf tó wíf þæs *ut ducat frater ejus uxorem illius,* Mt. L. 22, 24. v. beód-, fird-, mete-láf.

**laga.** *Add:*—Laga *statutum,* Wrt. Voc. ii. 137, 80. v. lagu.

**-laga.** v. lund-laga.

**lagian.** *Add:*—Ic smeáde hú ic mihte eallum mínum leódscype rihtlícast lagian þá þing tó þearfe þe wé scylan healdan, Ll. Lbmn. 269, 14. v. ge-lagian.

**-lagol.** v. æ-lagol.

**lagu.** I. *the body of rules binding on the members of a state or community:*—Hé hit béte swá swá lagu tæce (*as the law directs*), Ll. Th. i. 418, 14. Swá man swýdor spæc embe rihte lage swá mann dyde máre unlaga, Chr. 1086 ; P. 218, 19. Hí eallum folce góde lage (fulle lagu, *v. l.*) behéton, 1052 ; P. 180, 33. (*In the passages from the Chronicle the word might be plural,* v. II.) I a. where the state is named :—On Cantwara lage, Ll. Th. i. 330, 17. On Engla lage, Wlfst. 311, 4. I b. *where the name of the ruler with whom a code of laws is connected is given :*—Dene and Engle wurdon sammæle tó Eádgáres lage, Chr. 1018 ; P. 154, 16. Ic (Cnut) wylle þ eal þeódscype Eádgáres lage healde, Cht. E. 231, 3. I c. *the regulations that concern a particular class :*—Be leódgedingdum and lage. Wæs hwílum on Engla lagum þ leód and lagu fór be gepincdum, and þá wæron þeódwitan weordscipes wyrde ælc be his mæde, Ll. Th. i. 190, 11. Ðegenes lagu is þ hé sý his bócrihtes wyrde, and þ hé dreó ðinc of his lande dó, 432, 4. Nordhymbra preósta lagu, ii. 290, 1. Ðeów swán and ðeów beócere æfter fordside beón ánre lage wyrde, i. 436, 20. I d. *what is fixed by law in a particular case :*—Gif hwá þæne fridleásan man healde, béte þ swá hit ær lagu wæs, Ll. Th. i. 384, 8. Gif hine man æniges þinges teó, andswarie . . . swá hit lagu (riht lagu, *v. l.*) sý, 396, 1. II. *one of the individual rules which constitute the law* (v. I):—Ælfrédes laga cyninges, Ll. Th. i. 152, 13. Ðis syndon þá laga þe Ædelréd cyng and his witan gerædd habbad, 292, 1. Cyninges lage lytledon, 348, 19. Tuá lagena í æa *bis legum,* Germ. 388, 16. On Engla lagum, Ll. Th. i. 190, 11. Man rihte laga úp árære, 316, 25 : 328, 1. Lage, 228, 1. III. *a particular branch of law :*—Mid cynelicere lage *fiscali jure,* An. Ox. 4844. IV. *the action of the courts of law, law* (in *to go to law*):—Þár þegen áge twégen costas, lufe oþþe lage, Ll. Th. i. 298, 6. Sé þe rihte lage and rihte dóm forsace, 384, 16. V. *of divine law.* (1) (*God's*) *law or laws :*—Gif hwá Godes lage oþþe folclage wirde, Ll. Th. ii. 296, 22. Crístene lage healdan, i. 318, 11. Crístes lage wanodan, 348, 18. Godes laga healdan, 346, 24. Godcunde laga, 306, 25. (2) *the law of Moses :*—Þis is lagu and wítigan, Scint. 4, 8. God gesette þá fíf béc on þám þe is Godes lagu, and Móyses hí áwrát . . . and seó lagu forbeád mancynne sinna tó gefremmenne, Ll. Th. ii. 366, 17–23. Móyses cwæd on Godes lage, i. 196, 3. (3) *the Mosaic dispensation :*—Under Móyses lage men móston lybban on máran sóftnysse þonne nú æfter Crístes ácennednysse, Hml. A. 15, 58. VI. *customary rule or usage :*—Landlaga sýn mistlice :—laga sceal on leóde luslíce leornian sé þe on lande sylf nele leósan *leges et consuetudines terrarum sunt varie . . . leges debet in populis libenter addiscere, qui non vult in patria solus amittere,* Ll. Th. i. 440, 23. VII. *what is considered right and proper :*—þæt wé beón wære þ wé náhwár ne gán of lage, Angl. viii. 308, 18. VIII. *a rule of action or procedure :*—Hé lærde þæt manna gehwilc ódrum beóde þæt, þæt hé wille þæt man him beóde. Þis is rihtlic lagu, Wlfst. 67, 3. Þis is seó lagu þe wé healdan sculan, 274, 13. Mid stípum lagum *strictis* (*pudicitiae*) *legibus,* i. *ordinibus,* An. Ox. 2178. VIII a. *a rule laid down by one in authority for the treatment of a subject :*—Laga áwritenum gesettnessum gedémdan (*orthodoxorum patrum*) *scita* (i. *de-*

*creta*) *scriptis decretalibus sancxerunt,* An. Ox. 1964. Rædborena laga *iuris peritorum scita,* 5226. v. burg-, folc-, grið-, mæg-, preóst-, regol-lagu.

**-lagu** (?). v. út-lagu. Cf. -lah ; *adj.*

**lagu-flód.** *Add:*—Lagoflód *diluuium,* Scint. 200, 6 : *pelagus,* Germ. 401, 8.

**-lah** ; *adj.* v. út-lah.

**lah-breca.** *For* 'Scint. 2, Lye' *substitute :*—Widstandan þám lah-brecan *resistere sacrilego,* Scint. 9, 10.

**lah-brecende** ; *adj. Sacrilegious :*—Wid God múde mid lah-brecendum woffigende *erga Deum ore sacrilego blasphemantem,* Scint. 9. 9.

**lah-lic.** *For* 'Scint. 9, Lye' *substitute :*—Sé þe gylt his bóte lah-licre (*legitima*) beheófad, Scint. 46, 2. Gif hé nelle þ ornest oþþe ne mage, begyte him lahlicne spalan, Ll. Th. i. 489, 16.

**lahlíce.** *Add:*—Þæt hý læran þæt gehádode regollíce and læwede lahlíce heora líf fadian, Wlfst. 307, 15. Laglíce *legitime,* Angl. xiii. 394, 413.

**lám.** *Add:*—Lám *hoc argillum,* An. Ox. 28, 32. Ic eom láme widmeten *comparatus sum luto* (Job 30, 19), Hml. Th. ii. 456, 13. v. mistel-lám.

**lama.** *Add:*—Lama *debilis,* Wrt. Voc. i. 75, 40. Sum mæden weard lama *quaedam puella paralytica,* Gr. D. 228, 9. Seó wæs ær fíf geár loma, Shrn. 128, 20. Þes lama wædla bútun handcræfte (cf. sé læg bedryda fram cildháde od his geendunge, 96, 21), Hml. Th. ii. 98, 16.

**lamb.** *Add:* , lemb :—þ lemb *agnum,* Rtl. 47, 36, 14. Swá swá lamb þonne hit man scyrd, Hml. Th. ii. 16, 21. Sceáphyrdes riht is þ hé hæbbe . . . .i. lamb of geáres geogede, Ll. Th. i. 438, 23. Lombur scépa *agni ovium,* Ps. Srt. 113, 4. Lomberu, 6. Lo[m]bra *agnorum,* ii. 193, 1. .xx. lamba, C. D. ii. 64, 31. Lamba pæd, iii. 413, 29. [¶ *the word does not occur frequently in local names, but* Lambehíde, C. D. iv. 156, 11, Lambahám, i. 298, 3, *are instances.*] v. cilfer-, púr-lamb.

**lambes cerse.** *Add:*—Lambes cerse *thiospis,* Wrt. Voc. i. 68, 52.

**lám-pytt.** *Add:*—Tó ðám lámpytte, C. D. iii. 407, 1.

**lám-seáde** [?], an ; *f. Substitute :* **lám-seáp,** es ; *m.* Cf. lám-pytt *for use of the plural.*

**land.** I. *Add:*—Hé sende ofer sæ getríwe men, and hig férdon swá wíde landes swá hig faran mihton, C. D. B. ii. 389, 20. II. *Add:*—Lond *territorium,* Wrt. Voc. ii. 122, 14. Landes manna scipa .xlii., Chr. 1046 ; P. 168, 11. Ealle þá þe þær on lande (ealle þá landleóde, *v. l.*) *all those in the country,* Gr. D. 145, 7. Ánum ðára burgawará londes (ríces, W. S. *regionis*) ðæs, Lk. L. 15, 15. Wæs se fruma egeslic leódum on lande, B. 2310. Wé þé willad ferigen tó þám lande þær þe lust myned tó gesécanne, An. 294. Seó æftre Ethiopia land and leódgeard beliged úton, Gen. 229. Créca land, El. 250. Þec landa gehwilc herige, Dan. 376. Wé biód láðe on landa gehwám, folcum fracode, An. 408. Hit wæs eald þeáw on þissum landum, Ll. Th. ii. 408, 2. II c. *fig. realm, domain :*—In lifgendra londes wynne, Cri. 437 : Gú. 790. On lande *in terra* (*viventium*), An. Ox. 4273. III. *Add:* (1) *ground, cultivated land, soil, field :*—Brocen land *vel* geworht land *novalis ager,* Wrt. Voc. i. 37, 53. Hé hám cyrde fram þám weorce þæs landes, Gr. D. 165, 19. Hé mót neótan londes frætwa, Ph. 150. Londes ceorl *the husbandman,* Met. 12, 27. Swá hwá swá wille sáwan wæstmbære land, Bt. 23 ; F. 78, 21. Wé sceolon bletsian úre land, and Drihten biddan þ þá wæstmas þe on eordan syndon geþeón mótan, Verc. Först. 129, 26. Blósmige land *florea rura,* Wülck. Gl. 256, 3. Lond beód gefrætwad *the fields are made fair,* Ph. 116. Land wæron freórig, An. 1261. Seówun lond *seminauerunt agros,* Ps. Srt. 106, 37. Land wæterad *arua rigat,* Scint. 118, 14. Storm landu (*arua*) forhwyrfd, 51, 17. (1 a) *land* attached to a dwelling and in contrast with it :—Benedictus wunode uppon lande *Benedict was out in the fields of the monastery,* Gr. D. 165, 14. Sé þe on londe sý *he that is in the field,* Mt. R. 24, 18. Wæs sunu his ældra on lond (*in agro*), Lk. L. 15, 25. Hé eóde út on þæt land þencende *egressus fuerat ad meditandum in agro,* Gen. 24, 63. (1 b) *ground in a general sense :*—Hé nolde fleógan fótmæl landes, By. 275. Licgad æfter lande loccas tódrifene, fex on tindan, An. 1428. Þý læs þe hwæte cída leás licge on þám lande, Met. 12, 6. (2) *ground as property, landed property :*—Landes læn *precarium,* Wrt. Voc. i. 21, 2. Ic gean him and his wífe þæs landes æt Stoctúne wid án hund mancosa, Cht. Th. 597, 33. Hé sealde hiora gehwærdum hund þúsenda landes and locenra beága, B. 2995. Ic þe hneáw ne wæs landes, Gen. 2824. Næbbe ic . . . welan . . landes ne locenra beága, An. 303. Þegenes lagu is þ hé . . . dreó ðinc of his lande dó, Ll. Th. i. 432, 5. Hé him brád syled lond tó leáne, Vy. 76. (2 a) *an estate in land :*—On Dyddanhamme synd .xxx. hída . . . Ofer eall ðæt land gebyrad æt gyrde .xii. pænegas . . . and náh man nænne fisc wid feó tó syllanne ðonne hláford on land byd ær man hine him gecýde. Of Dyddanhamme gebyred micel weorcræden. Se geneát sceal wyrcan swá on lande, swá of lande. C. D. iii. 450, 11–32.

Monega land binnan þǽre byrig wǽron būtan ǽlcum ierfwearde *largissimae introrsum hereditates et nulli penitus heredes*, Ors. 5, 2 ; S. 218, 1. Taurus brōhte þone bisceop tō sumum his landa, Hml. S. 22, 187. Ic gean Alfmǽre and Ælfstāne þára twēgra landa æt Hættanleá, Cht. Th. 597, 24 : 520, 18 : 523, 27 : 524, 19. Of manegum landum mǽre landriht árīst tō cyniges gebanne, Ll. Th. i. 432, 6. (2 b) *where the extent of the land is defined* :—Ic selle Cyneswīðe ðreóra hīda lond. . . . Nū gewrīte ic hire ðæt ðreóra hīda lond . . . and ic hire lēte tō . . . ðæt twēga hīda lond . . . and ic bidda ðæt ðis ðreóra hīda lond and ēc ðæt twēga . . ., C. D. ii. 100, 9-24 (*and see* hīd ; I. 2). (3) *country in contrast with town* :—Be ciépemonna fōre uppe on londe, Ll. Th. i. 118, 11. (3 a) *an estate in the country* :—Hē genēbuade ānum ðára burgawarā and sende hine on lond his (*uillam suam*) ðte gelēsuade ðā bergas, Lk. L. 15, 15.          IV. *a land, ridge in a ploughed field.* v. heáfod-land, land-gewyrpe :—Eást on ðā furh ; ðæt tō ðām sceortan lond, C. D. iii. 437, 24. Tō ðon eásteran lande, v. 194, 27. On ðæt scorte land sūðeweard, 379, 32. On ðæt reáde land ; fram ðām reáden lande, iii. 419, 19. [v. Philol. Trans. 1898, p. 532.] v. át- (Cht. E. 208, 34), beán-, behát-, beód-, ber[c]-, bōc-, būr-, ceáp- (C. D. iv. 294, 18), ciric-, dene-, dūn-, eald-, earnung-, eriung-, ete-, fen-, feoh-, fōster-, Franc-, friþ-, gafol-, gebūr-, gedál-, gehát-, geneát-, geréf-, hǽþfeld-, hām-, hwǽte-, lǽn-, mǽd-, mǽdwe-, mǽst-, mersc-, munt-, mynster-, neáh-, norþ-, Peác-, sácerd-, scrūd-, sūþ-, teóþung-, timber-, unfriþ-, uppe-, wīn-, wudu-land ; ūtan-landes.

**land-ár.** *Add* :—Þæt hē ná cīde be lǽssan landáre *ne causetur de minori substantia*, R. Ben. L 16, 13. Gehealdenum him sylfan landáre *reservato sibi usufructorio*, 100, 1. Hī lǽfdon heora ǽhta . . . Iulianus þā dǽlde heora landáre þe him lǽfed wæs, Hml. S. 4, 82. Heó beceápode þā gymmas and eác hire landáre wið licgendum feó, 9, 54.

**land-bōc.** *Add* :—Ðis is ðára feówer hýda landbōc æt Wīdigleá ðe Eádgár cing hæfð gebōcod Cēnulfe on ēce yrfe, C. D. iii. 457, 23.

**land-bygen.** This form in the following passage seems an error, as the law, in the title of which it occurs, deals with the sale of a fellow-countryman :—Be landbygene (= landleóda[n] bebygene ?), Ll. Th. i. 110, note 1. v. land-leóda.

**land-efne,** es ; *n.* *Amount of landed property* :—Se cyng lēt tōscyfton þone here geond eall þis land tō his mannon, and hī fǽddon þone here ǽlc be his landefne, Chr. 1085 ; P. 216, 3.

**land-feoh** *land-tax.* Cf. wudu-feoh.

**land-firding,** e ; *f.* *Military operations on land* :—Æt ðām ende ne beheóld hit nán þing seó scipfyrding ne seó landfyrding būton folces geswinc and feós spylling, Chr. 999 ; Erl. 134, 36.

**land-folc.** *Add* :—Cōm þ landfolc tō þe þǽr tō láfe wæs þǽr heora hláfordes līc læg, Hml. S. 32, 134. Hē wunode on þǽre byrig and bodode þām landfolce, 29, 83.

**land-gehwearf.** *Add :* The Latin note is : Abbas Athelwoldus commutationem terrę egit aput Brihtelmium. In cujus vicissitudine, &c.

**land-gemǽre.** *Add* :—Landgemǽres *territorii*, An. Ox. 844. Nū hæbbe wē scortlīce gesǽd ymbe Asia londgemǽro ; nū wille wē ymbe Europe londgemǽre (e *altered to* o) āreccean swá micel swá wē hit fyrmest witon, Ors. i, 1 ; S. 14, 26-28. Hē on Rōmāna londgemǽro hergeade *cum oram Italiae maritimam vastaret*, 4, 6 ; S. 172, 1. Ǽrest ymbe ūre landgemǽra. Úp on Temese . . ., Ll. Th. i. 152, 8. v. riht-landgemǽre.

**land-gewyrpe.** *Add: the ridge formed by a land* (?). v. land ; IV.

**land-hláford.** I. *Add* :—Æt ǽlcum were ðe binnan ðám .xxx. hīdan is, gebyreð ǽfre se ōðer fisc ðām landhláforde, C. D. iii. 450, 26.

**land-hredding,** e ; *f.* *Redemption of mortgaged land* :—Ic onborgede .xxx. mancsa goldes tō mīnre landhreddinge æt Beorhnōðe, Cht. Crw. 9, 118.

**-landian.** v. be-landian ; ge-landod : **-landing** *one of a country.* v. Lindisfarnea-landing.

**land-leód.** *Add: a native of a country* :—Landleód i[n]digena, Wrt. Voc. ii. 44, 69. Londleód *incola*, Ps. Srt. 38, 13 : 118, 19. Londleóde *incolae*, 104, 12. Þá landleóde hī hátað Parcoadras, Ors. 1, 1 ; S. 14, 9. Þá landleóde on þǽre stōwe *incolae*, Gr. D. 97, 31. Ealle þá landleóde (ealle þá þe þǽr on lande wǽron, v. l.), 145, 7. Men þe þǽr landleóde wǽron *ejusdem loci accolae*, 230, 8. Næs ná án þ seó stōw wæs ungewunelic, ac eác swilce uncūð þám landleódum him selfum, Hml. S. 23 b, 107. Landleóde *indigenas*, An. Ox. 17, 18. v. land-leóda.

**land-leód** *a people.* *Add* :—Wunode á syððan se sōða geleáfa on þǽre landleóde, Hml. S. 24, 190. Hē æt Somnite gemǽre and Rōmāne gesæt, and þá nīhstan landleóde on ǽgþere healfe him on fultum geteáh *circa finitimas Romae urbes auxilia sibi adquirere studens*, Ors. 3, 7 ; S. 110, 7. Þ cynebōt tō þám landleód (leódum, v. l.). [The passage seems very corrupt and should read (?) : Seó cynebōt tō þám landleódum], Ll. Th. i. 186, 18.

**land-leóda** (?), an ; *m.* *A native of a country* :—þǽre stōwe landleódan *incolae*, Gr. D. 97, 31. Heom cōm tōgēnes Eádgár cild . . . and

ealle þá landleóden, Chr. 1068 ; P. 204, 16. Godwine betealde hine wið Eádward cyng his hláford and wið ealle landleódan, 1052 ; P. 183, 8. [Be land(leódan *written above the line*) bygene, Ll. Th. i. 110, note 1.] v. leóda.

**land-mearc.** *Add* :—Mín is Galaaþes landmearc *meus est Galaad*, Ps. L. 107, 9. Þis sind þá landmearca tō Byligesdýne, C. D. iii. 274, 31. Þegnas and ceorlas habbað landmearke, hū mycele má gerīst hyt þ seó tíd hæbbe mearke, Angl. viii. 326, 12.

**land-mearc ;** *adj.* *Substitute* : **land-mearca,** an ; *m.* *A territory.* [v. mearc ; III. (*in Dict.*)] :—Se landmearca Galaad, Ps. L. 59, 9. (*Similar glosses in Ps. L. are :* Arabiae þæs landes, 71, 15. Sylo þǽre mearke, 57, 61. Libanum þone holt, 71, 16. Iuda þǽre mǽgþe, 67, 28. Hermon þǽre dūne, 132, 3. Cf. *Horeb* Choreb þǽre dūne, 105, 19.) *See preceding word.*

**land-rīce.** *Add* :—Wē Darium oferswýðdon and ūs in onweald geslōgon eal his londríce *Dario superato acceptaque in conditiones omni eius regione*, Nar. 3, 23.

**land-riht.** *Add :* I. *rights due to the owner of land from those living on it.* Cf. land ; III. 2 :—Gescádwīs geréfa sceal ǽgðer witan ge hláfordes landriht ge folces gerihtu, Angl. ix. 259, 4.          II. *rights of country districts.* Cf. land ; III. 3 :—Hit gebyreð þ be bisceopes rǽde fare ǽghwylc lahriht, ge burhriht ge landriht, Ll. Th. ii. 312, 20.

**land-sceap.** *Dele, and see next word.*

**land-scearu.** I. *Add* :—Swá hē on lansceare (*printed* -sceape, *but see* Nap. 41) stille stande ðǽr hine storm ne mæg áwecgan, An. 501.          II. *Add* :—Ðis ys seó landscaru tō trefwurabo, Cht. E. 296, 1 : 8 : 12. (Cf. landgemǽro, 17.) On landscare hrycg, Cht. Crw. 3, 3. *See note* p. 48.

**land-sidu.** *Add* :—Uton lufian ūre ágenne landside, eallswá ūre yldran dydon þe tōforan ūs wǽron, Wlfst. 130, 17.

**land-spēdig.** *Add* :—Landspēdig ǽhta *locuples* (i. *diues*) *gadzarum* (*opulentia*), An. Ox. 3154.

**land-stycce.** *Add* :—Hē hine sylfne beeóde swá him þearf wæs būtan racenteáge in swá mycclum landsticce ungebunden swá hē ǽr gebunden on wunode *in tanto se spatio sine catena coercuit, in quanto antea ligatus mansit*, Gr. D. 214, 16.

**lane.** *Add* : **, lanu** :—Andlang lanan tō Beorhtnaðes stáne ; of ðám stáne andlang lanan tō ðæs mōres heátde, C. D. iii. 431, 18. v. strǽtlanu.

**lang.** *Add* : I. *of space relations.* (1) *great in measurement from end to end.* (a) *of a line, way, journey, &c.* :—Lang and stearc weg *itiner*, Wrt. Voc. i. 37, 36. Rūmre racenteáge, langre līnan, Sal. 294. Sume habbað swīðe langne weg, Solil. H. 44, 7 : Gen. 554. Werod Waldend sende on langue sīð, 68. (b) *of a material object* :—Hafað tungan lange, Rä. 59, 8. Gyrde lange, Sal. 90. Habbað leóht speru, lange sceaftas, 120. (b a) *of a particular build of ship* :—Gelamp hit þ Pyhtas cōman sūþan of Scithian mid langum scipum ná manegum (*longis nauibus non multis*, Bd. 1, 1), Chr. P. 3, 6. Hēt Ælfrēd cyng timbran langscipu (lang scipu ?, *the other MSS. have* lange scipu) ongēn ðá æscas, 897 ; P. 90, 14. (c) *of vertical measurement, tall, high* :—Lá, leóf cynehláford, án lang gealga stænt æt Amanes inne, Hml. A. 100, 279. Andlang stánweges tō ðám langan cýrstelmǽle . . . ðonne . . . tō ðan langan þorne, C. D. v. 297, 15. Þá geongan cnihtas wǽron lange on wæstmum, Hml. S. 30, 303. Þæt hē hangie on þám lengestan treówe ufeweardum, Verc. Först. 110, 5. (2) *having (more or less, or a specified) extension from end to end* :—Wund inces lang, Ll. Th. i. 92, 18. Fíftiges fōtgemearces lang, B. 3043. Þú þæt fǽr gewyrc þreó hund lang elngemeta, Gen. 1308. Þá wǽron tū swá lange swá þá ōðru, Chr. 897 ; P. 90, 15. Sume tunglu habbaþ lengran ymbhwyrft þonne sume habban, and ðá lengestne þe ymb þá eaxe middewearde hweorfaþ, Bt. 39, 3 ; F. 214, 22-24. (2 a) *of vertical measurement ; v.* lengþ :—Men fíftýne fōta lange . . . twēntiges fōta lange *homines habentes staturam pedum .xv. . . . pedibus .xx.*, Nar. 35, 23-30. On þám lengestan treówe þe standeð on þám hýhstan sǽclife, Verc. Först. 110, 5.          II. *with reference to serial extent or duration.* (1) *of a series of words, e. g. a long tale* :—Mē ðincþ þ þe þincen tō ǽlenge þás langan spell . . . Hit is swīþe long spell, Bt. 39, 4 ; F. 218, 5-9. Ic sǽde ðe swīþe lang spell and wundorlic, 35, 5 ; F. 166, 1. (2) *having a great extent in duration.* (a) *of a period of time* :—Tēn ðūsend geára þeáh hit lang þince, Bt. 18, 3 ; F. 66, 12. Wæs seó hwíl þæs lang, Gen. 584. ¶ *in adverbial phrases* :—Tō langre hwíle, Gen. 489. Hī swá langne fyrst hafað leáf yfel tō dōnne, Bt. 38, 4 ; F. 204, 13. Hē lange hwíle on þǽm gebede wæs, Bl. H. 217, 28. Se hálga bád . . . lange þráge, Gen. 1426. (b) *of a process, state, or action viewed as extending over a period of time* :—Seó lange mettrumnes, Bl. H. 59, 28. Se hlísa, ðeáh hē hwīlum lang sié and fela geára þurhwunige, Bt. 18, 3 ; F. 66, 17. Gif hī hiora yfel earme gedēð, hū ne biþ þ lange yfel wyrse ðonne þ scorte, 38, 2 ; F. 198, 11. Se longa gefeá, Ph. 607. Næs þ onbid long, Gū. 876. For longum geselþum . . . on ðam langum geswince, Bt. 39, 11 ; F. 228, 23-26. Þæt longe líf, Cri. 1464. Ic sceal langne hám gesēcan, Ap. 92. (3) *having more or less, or a specified extension*

serially or temporarily. (a) of a period of time :—Swā swā se fyrst lengra biþ, swā hī bióþ ungesǣligran, Bt. 38, 4; F. 204, 14: Lch. iii. 266, 18: B. 134. Þonne byđ seó nyht .xvi. tȳda lang and se dæg .viii. tȳda, Shrn. 153, 21. On swā langum fyrste swā hit bufon hēr āwriten is, Chr. 1052; P. 173, 21. Ne wæron þās (ages of the world) ealle gelīce lang², Bl. H. 119, 3. (b) of state or action, cf. (2 b) :—Ne biđ þæs lengra swice sāwelgedāles þonne seofon niht, Gū. 1007. Lengran līfes, Gen. 1841. (4) where excessive duration is implied, tedious, prolix :—Nū ys lang æall tō ārīmanne, Solil. H. 10, 7. Tō lang is tō recenne hū . . ., B. 2093. For langsumre, for langre prolixa, i. longa, An. Ox. 3997. Þoue sōfte langan morosam, Wrt. Voc. ii. 32, 6. (4 a) with þyncan :—Tō lang hit him þūhte hwænne hī tōgædre gāras bēron, By. 66. Þeáh hit lang þince, Met. 10, 66. (5) with a substantive denoting a period of time to indicate an extent greater than that expressed by the substantive :—Þæt biđ daga lengast, Sat. 606. Ealle lange dagas līfes þīnes, Ps. Th. 127, 6. (6) that continues in action or operation for a long period, lasting, permanent :—Hē him þās eorđan ealle sægde lǣne under lyfte, and þā longan gōd herede on heofonum, Gū. 91. (6 a) in the comparative, cf. (2 b), (3 b) :—Ođ þæt lengre ne biđ westem wudu-beámes, Vy. 23. (7) as a grammatical term :—Seó ōđer declinatio geendađ hire genitiuum on langne i . . . seó feórđe declinatic macađ hire genitiuum on langne us, Ælfc. Gr. Z. 21, 8–12. Hēr æfter ys makros, Þ ys ou Lȳden longa virgula, and on Englisc lang gyrd, Angl. viii. 333, 29. III. as substantive. (1) with preposition :—Gif hē hit dierneđ and weorđeđ ymb long yppe, Ll. Th. i. 116, 7. David sang þryne sealm ymb swȳđe lang þæs þe hine God ālȳsed hæfde, Ps. Th. 17, arg. (2) without prep. :—Þā dysegan menn þe þysum drȳcræftum long lȳfdon, Met. 26, 99. Ne biþ him hyht þ hȳ þis lǣne līf long gewunien, Ph. 481. (2 a) as predicate of an impersonal clause :—Næs þā long tō þon þæt . . ., B. 2591 : 2845. Lang biđ syđđan þæt se gāst nimeđ æt Gođe . . ., Seel. 5. Ne biđ lang ofer þæt þæt Israhēla æđelu mōten rīcsian, El. 432. v. efen-, furh-, niþer-, ūp-lang.

-lang. v. ge-, gerēf-lang : -lang. v. and- (on-) lang.

Langbeardas. Add : , -bearde :—Hū þā rēđan Langbearde āwēddon, Gr. D. 42, 16 : 141, 1. Langbearde (-an, v. l.), 43, 6 : 293, 10, 15. Langbearde (-as, v. l.), 43, 9. Langbearde (-a, v. l.), 235, 4. In Langbearda (-beardana, v. l.) landes sumum dǣle, 16, 7. Þāra un-geleáffulra Langbeardna (-ena, v. l.), 234, 10 : 293, 1. Leódbrond, Longbearda kyning, Shrn. 122, 26. Þā wyrcendan Langbearde hē grētte, 250, 17. v. Sūþ-Langbeardas.

Langbeardisc ; adj. Lombard, of the Lombards :—Sum Langbeardisc man, Gr. D. 229, 13. Cōmon Langbeardisca leóda, 229, 13. Hit gelamp in sume tīd þā þā Langbeardisce mæn wrungon elebergan, 250, 12.

lange. Add : , lenge? I. of time. (1) for or during a long time. (a) of continued action :—Gif se lāreów hié gemyndgađ đāra weligera đe lange striéndon and lytle hwīle brucon si eorum ad medium memoria deducatur, qui et ditari in hoc mundo diu conati sunt, et tamen in adeptis divitiis diu manere nequiverunt, Past. 333, 15. Þurh sum fæc līf ādreógan, ac nā lancge (diu), Coll. M. 28, 32. (a a) where the period within which the time is measured is given :—Hié longe on dæg sige āhton, Chr. 871; P. 72, 1. Hié fuhton lange on dæg on, 921 ; P. 101, 25. Paulus þær lange dæges geleáfan bodode, Hml. S. 29, 46. (a β) where too long a time is implied :—Lange prolixe, longe, An. Ox. 2726. (b) of action that takes place at some time or other within a long time :—Þæt wæs Hrōđgāre hreówa tornost þāra þe leódfruman lange begeáte, B. 2130. (2) where relative duration is expressed. (a) by the comparative or superlative :—Þ land stent oferslēde hwīlon mōnađ, hwīlum leng, Lch. iii. 254, 1. Leng þonne þū þurfe, Dan. 430 : Gū. 1031. Leng swā sēl (wel, MS.), B. 1854. Hē lufade hine lenge (lengc?) hū geornor, Gū. 109. Lenge swiđor āwa usquequaque, Wrt. Voc. ii. 79, 18. Ā hū lenge swiđur, Ps. Srt. 118, 8, 43, 51, 10. Swā leng swā mā magis magisque, An. Ox. 3594. Iōhannes leofode heora lengst, Ælfc. T. Grn. 15, 43. Þā hwīle þe hié þær lengest mete hæfdon, Chr. 894; P. 85, 23 : 1036; P. 161, 1. Sigehere lengest Sǣdenum weóld, Vid. 28 : B. 2008 : Exod. 423 : Gen. 1219. Lencten byđ lengest ceald, Gen. C. 6. Hū ic lengest mæge þīne sōđfæstnesse, sēlest gehealdan, Ps. Th. 118, 26. (b) by preceding adverbs of comparison :—Swā lange swā mē līf gelǣst, Ll. Th. i. 276, 19. Swā lange quamdiu, An. Ox. 250. ¶ Swā lange þæt, oþ until :—Þ man tȳmde þær hit ǣrest befangen wǣre swā longe þ man wiste hwǣr hit ætstandan wolde ut aduocaretur ubi deprehendebatur, donec innotesceret in quo stare uellet, Ll. Th. i. 290, 2. Lengde hit man swā lange þ seó scipfyrd eall belāf, Chr. 1052; P. 177, 23. Hē leofode swā lange þ man his cynn nyste, Angl. vii. 44, 417. Hē forweornde swā lange ođ his sciperes gefēngon hine, Chr. 1046; P. 169, 8. Tō lange, B. 905. (3) with reference to a point of time far distant from one indicated, long before, long after :—Hē langa (lang, v. l.) ǣr wunode wreclāstum, Chr. 1065 ; P. 195. 6. Hē wæs longe ǣr swiđe earfæcierre tō Godes geleáfan, Shrn. 100, 17 : Exod. 138 : Cri. 115. Hwæđer hē lenge ǣr āfeólle, Lch. ii. 258, 24. Be þǣre rōde þe ǣr in legere wæs lange bedyrned, El. 602. Gelǣstan þæt hē lange gehēt . . . in fyrndagum, Exod. 557. Lange siđđan woruld

bryttade, Gen. 1215. Nōht longe ofer þis, Gū. 1144. (4) the comparative in the sense, after the point of time indicated by the context, (no, any) longer :—Siđđan ofer þ ne rīxodan leng Rōmāna cinigas on Brytene, Chr. 409; P. 11, 19. Beáhhordum leng wyrm wealdan ne mōste, B. 2828 : An. 1044. Nō þy leng leofađ lāđgeteóna, B. 974. Ne dorston þā gelettan leng ōwihte, An. 801 : 1662. Ne oncnāwđ ofer þ i ā lengc (amplius) stōwe, Ps. L. 102, 16. Ne scealt þū ā leng sār þrowian, An. 1469. Gif þū leng ofer þis gedwolan fylgest, Jul. 201 : El. 576. For hwām lifađ se wyrsa leng?, Sal. 357. II. of extension in space, to a great distance, far ; in the comparative, of relative distance, further :—Lange procul, An. Ox. 2250. Lange and feor longiuscule, 3743. Sume scrīđađ leng, Met. 28, 8. v. ungemet-lange.

-langes. v. dæg-, geár-, niht-langes.

lang-fēre. Add :—Langfēre, langsum diuturna ,i. longeua, An. Ox. 2072. Treówa . . . langfērran, Angl. viii. 327, 24.

langfǣrness, e ; f. Long duration :—On þyses līfes langfērnysse in huius uitae longinquitate, Scint. 29, 1.

lang-gestreón, es ; n. Treasure that had existed long, ancient treasure :—Wēnde hē þæt hē lytel fæc longgestreóna brūcan mōste, B. 2240.

langian to grow long, langian to cause longing, may be taken together. Add : I. to lengthen (intrans.) :—Syđđan langađ seó niht and wanađ se dæg, Angl. viii. 311, 28. Ēfern longeđ aduesperascit, Lk. R. 24, 29. II. impers. to cause longing, &c. :—Mē ā langađ (it ever distresses me) þæs þe ic þē on þyssum hȳndum wāt, Seel. 154. Longađ þonne þȳ lǣs þe him con leóđa worn he that knows many songs sorrows the less, Gu. Ex. 170. Ongan mē langian for mīnre hæftnȳde (my captivity began to be irksome to me), and ic ongan gyrnan þ ic sōhte mīn mynster, Shrn. 41, 17. v. of-langod.

langlīce. Add :—Langlīce þrowian, Hml. Th. i. 594, 31. Langlīce tǣcan, Hml. S. 36, 244.

lang-līfe. Add :—þ þū sī langlīfe (longeuus) ofer eorđan, Scint. 173, 9. þ þū langlīf wunie, Hml. Th. ii. 36, 1.

lang-mōd. Add :—[Langmōde, Ps. Cant. 7, 12.] [Cf. Goth. lagga-mōdei.] See two following words.

langmōdlíce ; adv. Patiently, with long-suffering :—Brōþerlice yfelu sōđ lufu langmōdlíce (longanimiter) byrđ, Scint. 5, 2.

langmōd-ness, e ; f. Patience, long-suffering :—Geþyldig þurh lang-mōdnysse patiens per longanimitatem, Scint. 10, 17.

lang-ness. Add :—Eorþena langnyss nā syndrađ þā þe sōđ lufu geþeód terrarum longitudo non separat quos caritas jungat, Scint. 5, 13.

langsum. Add : I. in reference to time. (1) of a space of time, long :—Seó eorþe byđ mid þām winterlican cyle þurhgān, and byđ langsum ǣr đam đe heó eft gebeđod sȳ, Lch. iii. 252, 7. Langsumum fæce prolixa (i. longo) (temporum) intercapedine (i. spatio), An. Ox. 3625. (2) of action that goes on long, or state or thing that lasts long :—Langsum diuturnum (trophaeum), An. Ox. 800. Langfēre, langsum diuturna i. longeua (valetudo), 2072. Mid langsumere gestra[n]gunge diuturna uegetatione, 1444. Hē gebād langsumne hiht, Exod. 405 : Gen. 1757 : B. 1722. Đæt hió hiom līf mid đē langsum begēton, Ps. C. 57. (2 a) where the time seems too long. (a) prolix, tedious, wearisome :—Lagu byđ leódum langsum geþūht, gif hī sǣyđa swiđe brēgađ, Rūn. 21. Nān mann on līfe on đyssere langsuman worulde, Hex. 2, 11. For langsumere prolixa (valetudine fatigatam), An. Ox. 3997. (β) dilatory, tardy :—Hwæt sceall hit swā langsum, efne nū is se tīma, Hml. S. 22, 212. II. of space relations, lengthy, extended :—Langsum[um] wrǣda bīum prolixis fasciarum ambagibus, An. Ox. 3498. III. of a person, patient, long-suffering ; longanimis, Ps. Spl. 102, 8 : Wrt. Voc. ii. 53, 52 (in Dict.).

langsum-líc ; adj. Too long, tedious :—Langsumlic biđ ūs tō gereccenne and eów tō gehȳrenne ealle đā deópnyssa đæs Fulluhteres bodunge, Hml. Th. i. 362, 32.

langsumlíce ; adv. I. long, during or for a long time :—Hit God siþþan longsumlíce wrecende wæs, Ors. 2, 1 ; S. 58, 17. Hē tō þære dura cōm and þǣr langsumlíce swȳđe cnucede (he knocked long and loudly), Vis. Lfc. 29. II. patiently, with long-suffering :—Hē nele þæs synfullan deáđ, ac langsumlíce his gehwyrfednesse biđ (anbīt, v. l.), Hml. S. 23 b, 391.

langsum-ness. Add : I. length :—Langsumnys longitudo, An. Ox. 1699. Langsumnyssa, Angl. viii. 336, 39. II. patience, long-suffering :—Geþyld and līđnes and sybb and hyrsumnes and langsumnes, Nap. 4?.

lang-toh(-g) (?), -togen (?) ; adj. Long-drawn, extensive :—Þæt lengtogran leahtras seócnyss lengre bærnđ ut prolixiora uitia egrotatio prolixior exurat, Scint. 161, 18. For double comparative cf. lang-fǣre.

lang-wyrpe ; adj. Oblong :—Gyf þū hwilce langwyrpe bōc habban wille, þonne strece þū þīne wynstran hand and wege hī, and sete þīne swȳþran ofer þīnne wynstran earm be þǣre bōce læncge, Tech. ii. 119, 13. [v. N. E. D. long-warped oblong.]

lanu. v. lane.

**lapian.** _Add:_—Swā swā hundas lapodon Naboðes blōd, swā hī sceolon lapian and liccian þīn blōd _in loco hoc, in quo linxerunt canes sanguinem Naboth, lambent sanguinem tuum,_ Hml. S. 18, 209. Lapa _bibe, lambe,_ Germ. 398, 152.

**lár.** _Add:_ I. _the act of teaching_ or _instructing:_—Monige fleóð ða nyttwyrðan hiérsumnesse ðǣre lāre (_praedicationis_), Past. 45, 18 : Gr. D. 35, 4. Lāre _pedagogio,_ An. Ox. 1099. On rīme wæs þreó þúsend þǣra leóda ālesen tō lāre (_to instruct Elene about the cross_), El. 286. Wē beódað þǣm mǣssepreóstum . . . þ hig swīðe geornlice ymb þæs folces lāre sȳn . . . Ne mæg eówer nān hyne lāre belādian; ǣlc eówer hafað tungan; sē þe gōd sprecan wile, symble hē mæg sumné mon gebētan, Ll. Th. ii. 424, 14–25. I a. _a piece of teaching_ or _instruction, a lesson:_—Hē gebād leódum tō lāre longsumne hiht, Exod. 405. II. _the condition of being taught, learning, study:_—Lāre _disciplinae,_ An. Ox. 1098. His frȳnd hine befǣstan tō lāre, Hml. S. 3, 4. Marcus wæs mid Petre on lāre, Ælfc. T. Grn. 12, 33. Hē wæs lange on lāre on Mediolana byrig, Hml. S. 5, 2 : 3, 10. Befæst tō woruldlicre lāre, 4, 185. Smeágunge, lāre _studium,_ An. Ox. 2010. III. _that which is taught, a ( person's) doctrine_ or _teaching:_—Mīn lār (laar, L.) nis nā mīn _mea doctrina non est mea,_ Jn. 7, 16. Eów is lār Godes ābroðen of breóstum, Exod. 268. Hié hyrcnodon hāliges lāre, An. 654. Tō bodianne þā hālgan lāre, Gr. D. 35, 5. III a. _in pl. doctrines, precepts, ordinances:_—Þȳ lǣs tōworpen sién frōd fyrngewritu and þā fæderlican lāre forlǣten, El. 432. Lāra _dogmatum,_ An. Ox. 2088. On wordsnoterlicum lārum _in philosophicis dogmatibus,_ 2270 : 2305. Lārum _traditiones (Pharisaeorum),_ 5100. Lārum and trymnessum, cȳðnessum _adstipulationibus_ (scripturae _adstipulationibus_ ornatus foeminarum rapina virorum vocatur, Ald. 76, 23), Wrt. Voc. ii. 3, 63. Rihtwrītera lāra _orthographorum disciplinas,_ An. Ox. 196. IV. _advice, counsel, suggestion, instruction, order:_—Exantipus him Rōmāne andrēd for þon hié for his lāre æt hiora gemēttinge beswicene wurdon, Ors .4, 6 ; S. 176, 7. Hió Offan fiet be fæder lāre gesōhte, B. 1950. Lāre _sugestiones,_ Kent. Gl. 1175. IV a. _an instance of malicious counsel, a plot:_—Ðā hǣþnan bisceopas ðæt wrēgdon . . . Ealle ðā hǣþenan bisceopas swulton, þā ðe in þǣre lāre wǣron, Shrn. 121, 5. V. _speech intended to instruct_ or _inform:_—Lār _paradigma_ (_evangelicum_ the parable of the good seed), An. Ox. 1406. Hāliges lāre _the story of St. Andrew,_ An. 1480. Lāra, bodunga, _cathegorias,_ i. _nuntiationes ł praedicationes,_ An. Ox. 3128. VI. _that which is learned, learning, erudition:_—Hié ne wēndon ðætte sió lār sceolde swǽ oðfeallan, Past. 5, 23. Sió lār Lǣdengeðíódes, 7, 15. Of his lāre bit ancnāwen, Kent. Gl. 399. Hē wæs on bōclicum lārum getȳd, and hē on ðǣre lāre ðeáh. . . . Hē gefæstnode his lāre on fæsthafelum gemynde, Hml. Th. ii. 118, 16–20. VI a. _a particular branch of learning, a study:_—On bōclicum lārum getȳd _trained in literary studies,_ Hml. Th. ii. 118, 16. VI b. _cunning, craft:_—Ic mē gūðbordes sweng lāre gebearh, Gen. 2693. v. fore-, Lǣden-, word-lār.

**lár-bōc.** _Add:_—Hē āwearp his lārbōc _he flung away the book he was learning from,_ Hml. S. 4, 189. Paulus cwæð on his lārbōcum (_in his epistles_), Hml. A. 77, 108.

**lár-bodung,** e ; f. _Preaching:_—Dō man þā lārbodunge (_predicationem_) be þām þe þ folc understandan mage, Chrd. 50, 10.

**lár-cræft.** In l. 1 _after_ hæbbe _add_ bōca onbyrged, _in_ l. 2 _after_ onlocen _add_ Libia and Grēca, _and add: knowledge acquired by study, erudition:_—Tō rǣdingum . . . geǣmtigion hī silfe . . . and eác tō drihtlicum lārum and tō mænigfealdum lārcræftum _lectioni . . . uacent aut etiam doctrinis sacris et diuersarum artium erudiantur disciplinis,_ Chrd. 66, 36.

**láreów.** _Add:_ [_from_ lār-þeów _a form which is represented in later English, e. g._ Se æðele þeóde lārðeáw, Angl. xi. 374, 59. _See N. E. D._ lorthew, _and_ Verc. Först. 167]:—Hēhfæder, lāreów _archimandrita,_ An. Ox. 3720. Æs lārwu (lāruw, R.) _doctor,_ Mt. L. 22, 35. Ðū lāruu (lāreu, R.) _magister,_ 36. Lā lāruua (lārwa, R.), Mk. L. 9, 17. Hāl lāruwa (lareu, R.) _have Rabbi,_ Mt. L. 26, 49. Þæs æþelgan lāreówes _egregii dogmatistę (doctrina),_ An. Ox. 4363. Lēdene lāreówas maciað on sumum namum _accussatiuum_ on im, Ælfc. Gr. Z. 75, 4. On middum ðǣra lāruua (lārwara, R.), Lk. L. 2, 46. Lāruum (lārwum, R.) _magistratibus,_ 22, 4 : 23, 13. [v. _N. E. D._ larew.] v. ǣ-lāreów.

**láreów-dōm.** _Add:_ I. _the authority_ or _office of a teacher:_—Lāreówdōm _discipulatus_ (cf. discipulare _edocere,_ Migne), Wrt. Voc. ii. 141, 10. Hwylc sprǣc þæs godcundan lāreówdōmes _quis sermo divine auctoritatis,_ R. Ben. 133, 2. Ongunnon hī him tō befæstenne heora cild tō Godes lāreówdōmes (_coepere suos ei filios omnipotenti Deo nutriendos dare,_ Gr. D. l. 2, c. 3), Hml. Th. ii. 160, 2. Sume þā apostolas þe sīþodon mid Crīste on his lāreówdōme (_as his disciples_), Hml. A. 14, 33. Sume men wyllað betǣcan heora lāðostan cild tō Godes lāreówdōme, 35, 265. Lāreówdō[mum] _magistratibus,_ An. Ox. 4547. II. _the action of a teacher, instruction, guidance;_ applied to a thing:—Hit (_a mechanical contrivance_) gewissað ūs þurh wīsne lāreówdōm, Hml. S. 5, 269. III. _what is taught by a teacher, a study:_—Bōclicum lāreówdōmum _liberalibus studiis,_ An. Ox. 3100.

**láreów-lic.** _Add: of a teacher_ or _master, having the character of a master:_—þurh lārewlicum basincge _magistri melote,_ An. Ox. 1471. On eallum þingum lāreówlicum hī fylian regole _in omnibus magistram sequantur regulam,_ R. Ben. 9. 18, 9.

**láreów-setl.** _Add:_—Lārewsetle _pulpito,_ An. Ox. 7, 206.

**lár-fæsten,** es ; _n. A fast imposed as discipline:_—Æfæstenu . . . and mīnra dǣda gewitena lārfæstenu ic oft āgælde, Angl. xi. 99, 63.

**lár-hlystend.** _Add:_—Gecrīstnode lārhlystendras _caticuminos,_ An. Ox. 2881.

**lár-leást.** _Add:_—Hī nā cunnan nāþor þurh lārleáste ne lǣdan ne lǣran, Wlfst. 276, 6.

**lár-lic.** _Add:_ I. _that is under instruction:_—Hē campdōme fyligde betwux lārlicum gefylcum (_among the troops in training_), Hml. S. 31, 17. II. _doctrinal._ Cf. lár ; III :—þā sind blinde þe þæt leóht ðæs lārlican andgites nabbað, Hml. Th. ii. 374, 30. III. _persuasive._ Cf. lár ; IV, lǣran ; IV. 1 :—Hē hine getrymede mid his lārlicum wordum (_verbis persuasoriis_), Gr. D. 299, 2. IV. _concerned with learning, of learning, learned._ Cf. lár ; VI :—Hē underfǣng þone cnapan tō lārlicre scōle, Hml. S. 3, 14. Lārlicere bīgenge _gymnicum (philosophiae) studium,_ An. Ox. 2282. Lārlice cræftas _scolares disciplinas,_ 41.

**lár-spell.** _Add:_—Lārspell (_as heading to a homily_), Wlfst. 232, 11 : 242, 22 : 250, 14 : 266, 1. Mid lārspelle bodian _predicare,_ Chrd. 50, 7. Marcus, þe wæs mid Petre on lāre, wrāt þā ōðre bōc (_the second gospel_) be Petres bodunge be þām þe hē geleornode on his lārspellum (_the discourses in which he (Peter) instructed Mark_), Ælfc. T. Grn. 12, 35. Se mǣssepreóst sceal mannum mid rihte bodian þone sōðan geleáfan and him lārspel secgan, Ll. Th. ii. 384, 25.

**lár-sum ;** _adj. Ready to learn, docile:_—Sién wē snotre . . . and lārsume, Verc. Först. 95, 23.

**lár-swic,** es ; _m. n._ (?). _Substitute :_ lár-swic, es ; _n._ or -swice, es ; _m._ (Cf. ǣ-, be-swic.)

**laser.** _Add:_—Laser _zizania,_ Wrt. Voc. ii. 124, 28. þurh þæs sǣd þe ægðer sǣwð ge laser ge coccul, Angl. viii. 300, 24. Lasera, coccela _loliorum, zizaniorum,_ Hpt. Gl. 462, 23.

**lást.** _Add:_—Lēst _orbita,_ Germ. 400, 102. Lāst _orbitae,_ Wrt. Voc. ii. 115, 73. ¶ on lāst _afterwards, at last:_—Heó on lāst tiliað tō cwēmanne Gode and mannum mid wordum _postea in ore suo benedicent,_ Ps. Th. 48, 12. Paulus fērde wīde geond þás woruld oð þæt hē on lāst becōm intō Rōmebyrig, Ælfc. T. Grn. 15, 18. v. sweart-lāst ; _adj._ -lāstfull. v. ge-lāstfull.

**lást-weard.** _Add: a follower:_—Lāstðwerdas _sequipedas,_ Angl. xiii. 31, 97.

**lát** _leading._ v. lád ; V.

**lata.** _For the passage substitute:_—þeáh þe heó þæs bearnes lata wǣre, heó þonne Gode (þæs bearnes MS., _but see Latin_) nōht lata ne wæs _erat tarda soboli, sed non tarda Deo,_ Archiv cxxii. 248, 20–22 ; Bl. H. 163, 8. v. dǣd-lata.

**late.** _Add:_ I. _slowly:_—þā mettas þe late melten, Lch. ii. 176, 23. Listnie and late gange _let him listen and go slowly_ (?) ; _gradu lento [but_ late _might be instrumental of_ læt], Wrt. Voc. ii. 41, 76. Nis hē swār swā sume fuglas, þā þe late þurh lyft lācað, Ph. 316. Hē āgeaf andsware æfter longre hwīle, swā hē late meahte oreðe gewealdan, Gū. 1198. II. _after the proper_ or _usual time, after delay, after a long time, at an advanced period_ or _stage:_—Hē wile āfeallan, ðeáh hit late sié _non quidem repente, sed cadit,_ Past. 437, 22. Heó wile late āþreótan þæt heó fǣhðo ne tȳdre, Sal. 447. II a. _late in the day, at a late hour:_—Ðā þā hī eft late (lator þonne hī sceoldon, _v. l._) gecyrdon tō mynstre, Gr. D. 126, 28. II b. _in the comparative_ or _superlative, or with adverb of comparison:_—Hī beóð ðæs ðe lator ðe hī oftor ymbðeahtiað, Past. 435. 2. þȳ lator, Ors. 3, 1 ; S. 100, 16. Būtan hit gelimpe þæt man lator ārīse þonne hit gebyrige, R. Ben. 36, 3. Se mōna dæghwāmlíce feówer prican lator ārīst þonne hē dyde on þām ōþrum dæge. Swā eác seó sǣ symle feówer prican oððe fíf lator flōwð, Angl. viii. 327, 26–28. II c. _where_ late _is contrasted with_ early _or_ soon:—Hasterbal swā late fleáh for þon þe hē elpendas mid hæfde, Ors. 4, 10 ; S. 198, 27. Hē hēt sendon æfter, þēh hē þ tō late dyde, 6, 34 ; S. 290, 31 : Past. 249, 8. Sume lator fēlað þāra lǣcedōma, sume raþor, Lch. ii. 84, 25. Lengten ne mæg beón ǣr .v. id. Febr., ne lator þonne .ii. id. Martii, Angl. viii. 324, 42. III. _the comparative used in the sense after the point of time indicated by the context:_—Gif se bisceop þā ā lator inn eóde _si adhuc episcopus tardius intrasset,_ Gr. D. 59, 19. IV. _recently, lately:_—þeáh hē latost tō mynstre cōme and ȳtemest sȳ on endebyrdnesse, R. Ben. 119, 4.

**láþ,** es ; _n. Add:_—Nis him nān lāð, hē rest hine eáðe, Ps. Th. 40, 9. þæt nān wiht ne sȳ . . . þæs leófes ne þæs lāðes þæt hig þonne mihte fram ūres Drihtnes lufan āsceádan, Wlfst. 185, 2. Ne cweðe gē nān lāð ðǣm deáfan _non maledices surdo,_ Past. 453, 1. Gif hit þ wǣre, swā hit feor þām sȳ, þ þīn dohtor on ǣnig lāð āsliden wǣre, Hml. S. 33, 223. Ðā fugelas ūs nǣnige lāðe ne yfle ne wǣron _aues non nobis perniciem ferebant,_ Nar. 16, 18.

**láþ;** adj. Dele passage in l. 19, and add:—Láþe exosas, Wrt. Voc. ii. 30, 25. **I.** hateful, repulsive:—Láþ unclǽnnys detestanda obscenitas, An. Ox. 4301. Láþera inuisorum (uitiorum), 885. **I a.** hateful to a person:—Hú láð eów selfum wæs tó gelǽstanne eówre áþas, Ors. 3, 8; S. 122, 16. Ingeþanc Gode láþe precordia Deo inuisa, An. Ox. 3567. Ic wát þæt nán swá gód man ne leofað swá he is, þéh þe he mé sié se láþesta, Ors. 5, 12; S. 244, 1. **I b.** antithetical to leóf:—Leóf carus, láð odiosus, Wrt. Voc. i. 85, 63, 64. Sume men wyllað betǽcan heora láðostan (least loved) cild tó Godes láreówdóme. Ac hí ne geefenlǽcað ná Abrahame þe his leófran sunu tó láce geoffrode, Hml. A. 35, 265. **II.** unwilling, loath(?):—Láþ inuitam (but perhaps the glosser has read inuisam), An Ox. 5406.

**láþettan.** [In the last two passages láþettan translates infestare, which however is for infestari. The original Latin of the two translations is: Canes latrantes uiderit uel eis infestare, and: Camelos uidere et ab eis se uiderit infestare.] For 'To be odious . . . hate' substitute: **I.** to abhor, execrate, hate, hold in detestation:—Þíne goda ic láðette and him teónan dó ego diis tuis abominationem feci, Angl. xvii. 116, 4. Man tó forð láþet þæt man scolde lufian, Wlfst. 165, 3 [: 168, 13: Wrt. Voc. ii. 26, 8: Shrn. 39, 22, in Dict.]. Ongunnon hí hine onscunigean and láðettan mid máran orwyrðum fracoðlicra worda majoribus hunc uerborum contumeliis detestari coeperunt, Gr. D. 250, 28. **II.** to make hateful, render odious. v. lǽþettan:—Ðás gyltas ne magon úre sáwla ofsleán, ac hí magon hí áwlǽtan and Gode láðettan, Hml. Th. ii. 590, 29.

**laþian.** Add:—Hé mé lathath inuitat me, Wrt. Voc. ii. 49, 38. Laðode accessiuit, 4, 21. Ðætte hé cígende óðre ðider tió and laðige ut illuc clamando alios trahat, Past. 379, 20. Ongan óðer ríce man hí laðian tó his gesynscipe, Shrn. 60, 2. v. ge-, in-laþian.

**laþian.** Add:—Heom láðode eallum þ hí swá oft árisan, hwílon þrywa on niht, hwílon feówer sýðum, tó singenne þone lofsang þonne hí slápan sceoldon, Hml. S. 21, 231. v. á-laþian.

**laþigend.** v. in-laþigend.

**láþ-leás.** Add:—Ǽr he sý láðleás (lǽðleás, Ll. Th. i. 164, 17) wið ælce hand, Ll. Lbmn. 144, 13. [v. N. E. D. loathless.]

**láþ-lic.** Add:—Þám líchaman bið láðlic legerbed gegyrwed, Wlfst. 187, 12. Láðlic lurida, An. Ox. 23, 59. Hé hrýmde mid grimlicre stefne and láðlicre, Shrn. 120, 30. Láþlice grymetunga truculentos fremitus, An. Ox. 2388. [v. N. E. D. loathly.]

**láþlíce.** Add:—Mid ealswylcan láran Antecríst láðlíce forlǽred ealles tó manege, Wlfst. 56, 3. Þǽr losað þ cild láðlíce hæðen, Hml. S. 17, 155.

**laþung.** Add: a church; ecclesia:—On háligre laþunge gelǽred bodigend in sancta ecclesia doctus predicator, Scint. 124, 9.

**láþwend-ness,** e; f. Malignity, hostility:—Þte ðú áscúfe from mec ðá ungesewenlican næglas þá fæstniað láðwendnesse ut retrudas a me inuisibiles clauos quos figunt odibiles, Lch. i. lxxiv. 13.

**latian.** Add:—For hwí latodest þú? quare tardasti?, Gr. D. 88, 33. Ne lata þú tó mínum fultume, Ps. Th. 39, 15. Uilesceret, i. tardaret uel latode, Angl. xv. 208. 100 b. v. á-, ge-latian.

**latlíce.** v. lætlíce.

**latu,** e; f. Add: delay:—Þá gesettan bíleouene his gebróðrum gebeóde hé on rihtne tíman búton late fratribus constitutam annonam sine mora offerat, R. Ben. 55, 12. 'Álǽdað mé nú tó bútan late eówerne ealdor.' Hig clipodon þá þone cniht him raðe tó þe hira heáfodman wæs, Ælfc. T. Grn. 18, 17. v. ge-latu.

**latung,** e; f. Delay:—Latunga tricarum, i. morarum, An. Ox. 7, 129.

**laur-beám.** Add:—Laurbeámes lauri, Wrt. Voc. ii. 53, 12. **-laured.** v. ge-laured.

**laur-treów.** Add:—Þá geseah heó spearwan nest on ánum lawertreówe, Hml. A. 120, 117.

**láwerce.** Add:—Láuwerce tilaris, Wrt. Voc. i. 281, 13. Láuuercae, láuricae, Txts. 102, 1012.

**Lazarus;** gen. Lazares; pl. Lazaras Lazarus:—Ic bidde eów þæt gé beón gemyndige ðæs Lazarus reste . . . manega Lazaras gé habbað nú licgende æt eówrum gatum, Hml. Th. i. 334, 25–29.

**leá.** v. leó.

**leác.** Add:—Laec ambila, Wrt. Voc. ii. 100, 20. Leác alium, 6, 53: allium, i. 78, 72. Hé leác sette he planted vegetables, Shrn. 61, 20. v. cípe-, rysc-leác, fugeles leác.

**leác-blæd,** es; n. A leek leaf:—Þis man sceal wið þ gedrif wrítan on þreóm leácbladan, Nap. 41.

**leác-cærse.** Add:—Leáccersan, túnc[ersan] nasturcium, Wrt. Voc. i. 286, 14.

**leác-tric.** See leáh-tric.

**leác-trog.** Substitute: A cluster of berries carved for the ornamenting of a ship:—Leáhtrog corimbus, cacumen navis, Wrt. Voc. ii. 135, 76. Leáctrogas corimbos, 14, 78. Leáctrogas, -trocas, Txts. 53, 540. Cf. corimbis nauibus uel cacumen, Corp. Gl. H. 35, 661. Corimbus nauibus, Ld. Gl. H. 47, 5. v. trog.

**leád.** Add: **I.** lead:—Hét se cásere his cwelleras feccan ænne ærenne hwer and hine áfyllan mid weallendum leáde . . . Hé (St. George) bletsode þ leád and læg him onuppan, and þ leád wearð ácolod, Hml. S. 14, 104–115. Leádes clynun mastigiis, Wrt. Voc. ii. 54, 75. Lēde plumbo, Germ. 393, 117. **II.** a cauldron:—Man sceal habban . . . hwer, leád, cytel, hlædel, pannon, Angl. ix. 264, 9. [vi. bidenfate and .ii. cuflas and .þrý. trogas and leád and trefet, C. D. B. iii. 367, 39. v. N. E. D. lead; 5.]

**leáden.** Add:—Hí þás race on ánum leádenum tabulan ágrófen, Hml. S. 23, 342. Hé ðá líc léde on áne leádene (lǽdene, v. l.) ðrúh, 24, 71. Se cásere hét hý cwice belúcan in leádenum cistum, Shrn. 146, 24. Lédene plumbeos, Germ. 393, 122.

**leád-gewiht,** es; n. Some scale of weight (cf. (?) lead-pound:—Sex waxpunde makiet .j. leed pound, N. E. D. s. v.):—Ic onborgede .xxx. mancsa goldes be leádgewihte, Cht. Crw. 9, 118. See note, p. 77.

**leád-gota,** an; m. A lead-founder:—Gif hé smeáwyrhtan hæfð . . . Mylewerde, sútere, leádgotan (leód-, MS.) and óðran wyrhtan ælc weorc sylf wísað hwæt him tó gebyreð, Angl. ix. 263, 18.

**leáf.** Add: **I.** a leaf of a tree, plant, &c. :—Leáf folium, rind cortix, Wrt. Voc. i. 285, 77. Næfre brosniað leáf under lyfte, Ph. 39. Lytle hwíle leáf beóð grēne, Sal. 312. Hleófa (leáf, R.) folia, Mt. L. 24, 32. Þú þá treówa on hærfesttíd heora leáfa bereáfast and eft on lencten óþru leáf sellest, Bt. 4; F. 8, 4–7. Hié heora líchoman leáfum beþeahton, Gen. 845. Beám sceal on eorðan leáfum liðan, Gn. Ex. 26. **I a.** an artificial leaf:—Gylden is se Godes cwide gimmum ástæned, hafað silfren leáf, Sal. 64. **II.** a leaf of a book:—Hér on þysan óþran leáfe ongind seó æftere bóc, Gr. D. 92, 2. Se æresta heofon gefealden swá swá bóca leáf beóð, Verc. Först. 122, 14. Feówer leáfum oþþe fífum of þære bóce geræddum, R. Ben. 67, 7. v. cawel-, fíc-, hoc-, holen-, íþig-, wín-leáf.

**leáf.** Add: **I.** leave:—Búton se abbod him geþafunge mid leáfe sylle; sý þeáh seó leáf on ðá wísan þ þær seó foresǽde bót fylige nisi forte abbas licentiam dederit per permissionem suam; ita tamen ut satisfaciat reus ex hoc, R. Ben. 69, 7. Þrowode Meotud on galgan þe Fæder leáfe, Men. 87. Bútan Freán leáfe, Met. 11, 67. Þonne hé hæfð Drihtnes leáfe, 10, 67. **II.** what is right as being permitted:—[Mennisc]lice lēfe fas humanum (contra jus divinum et fas humanum, Ald. 72, 32), An. Ox. 5070. v. ge-leáf.

**-leáf;** adj. leafy. v. ge-, reád-leáf: **-leáf;** adj. believing. v. geleáf.

**leáfa** (?). l. leáfa, and add:—Hié gesetton . . . þ þá woruldhláfordas móston mid hiora leáfan . . . fiohbóte onfón, Ll. Th. i. 58, 7. Bútan bisceopes leáfan sine uenia episcopi, ii. 170, 21. Be his scriftes leáfan cum confessarii sui uenia, 224, 33. v. ge-leáfa.

**-leáfe.** v. fíf-, seofon-, þri-leáfe.

**leáf-full.** Add:—Leáfulre fideli, An. Ox. 1329. v. ge-leáffull.

**leáf-helmig.** For 'frondicoma, Germ. 390' substitute:—On lēþhelmigum frondicomis, Germ. 390, 102.

**leáf-leóht;** adj. Easy to believe (?):—Se gewuna þisse hálgan drohtnunge þe gedēþ leáfleóht and eáþe þæt ðe ær earfoðe and ancsumlic þúhte (the English version here does not follow the Latin closely, the only part of which that seems the foundation of the English is: Processu conversationis et fidei. In some way fidei seems to have occasioned leáf-leóht), R. Ben. 5, 19.

**leáfnes-word,** es; n. A pass-word:—Ne gē leáfnesword gúðfremmendra gearwe ne wisson, B. 245.

**leágung.** Dele, and see Angl. i. 508.

**leáh;** m. In l. 12 after Kmbl. insert ii, and add:—Þurh ðone leá on ðám leáge; þurh ðone lytlan leá westeweardne . . . þurh ðone leá norðeweardne, C. D. v. 207, 12–23. v. brēmel-, ort-geard-, sealt-, wíþig-leáh.

**leáh;** f. Add:—Fram ceddan leáge tó langan leáge . . . fram langan leáge, C. D. ii. 73, 21. In illud septum tó brádan leáge, transitque illo septo brádan leáge, iii. 383, 18. On ceaforleáhe; of ðære leáhe, 77, 26: 79, 2. v. fyrs-, gemōt-, lín-, styfic-, tigel-leáh, and see Midd. Flur. for numerous compounds.

**leáh** lye. Add:—Leág, læg lexiva, Txts. 74, 591. Lǽcedómas wiþ miclum heáfodece . . . and sealf tó þon ilcan, and leáh and eágsealfa, Lch. ii. 172, 28 : 302, 23.

**leahter.** Add: [The word is made feminine in Hml. S. 16, 306:—Seó eahteóðe leahter, but in other MSS. it is masculine, and so in the other seven instances]:—Scyld, lehter, mándæd crimen, i. peccatum, Wrt. Voc. ii. 137, 2. Hwæt ne cann sē ðe ealle ðing cann? Hē ne cann nænne leahter, and hí wæron mid leahtrum áfyllede, Hml. Th. ii. 572, 35. Ne mæg synne on mē fácnes frumbearn fyrene gestǽlan, líces leahtor, Gú. 1045. Þæs líchoman leahtras and þá unþeáwas, Met. 22, 25. Leahtra conuitiorum, An. Ox. 5363. Leahtra firene geseón on þám sáwlum, Cri. 1281. Gelácnigan leahtras gehwylcne, yfel unclǽne, 1309. Líchoman leahtra clǽne, Ph. 518. Fácnes clǽne, leahtra leáse, Jul. 566. Leahtrum flagitiis, An. Ox. 2678. Lahgtrum l gyltum facinoribus, 4, 50. Lehtrum scyldige, An. 1218. Lǽnan lífes leahtras, Ph. 456. Forgif ús gyltas and synna, and úre leahtras álǽt, líces wunda, and mándǽd, Hy. 6, 20, 23. v. heáfod-, or-, stæf-leahter.

**leahter** *laughter.* v. hleahtor.

**leahter-full.** *Add:*—Ne beó se carsulla leahterful, ne sē ne lufige īdelnysse, sē đe on stilnysse is, Hml. Th. ii. 442, 34. Hē is Gode deàd, for þan þe hē leahterfull and geleáfleás ætbærst, and hē ys geworden tô wealdgengan, Ælfc. T. Grn. 18, 5. Gif se prāfast hlehterful (hleahter-, *v. ll.*) *si propositus repertus fuerit vitiosus,* R. Ben. 126, 1. Gif hine mon leahtorfulne ongit (ǽnigne unđeáw on him āgitt, *v. l.*) *si vitiosus inventus fuerit,* 109, 16.

**leahter-lic;** *adj. Vicious, faulty, defective:*—Ic bidde þone gelǽredan and þone geleáfullan, gif hē hēr hwylc hleahterlic word onfinde *obsecrans, si illic vitiosus sermo aures eruditi lectoris perculserit,* Guth. Gr. 101, 11.

**leahtre.** v. or-leahtre.

**leahtrian.** I. *add:*—Leahtrian *insimulare,* An. Ox. 4255. Leahtrode, tǽlede *criminemur, derogemur,* 8, 392. II. *add:*—Leahtrað mægen yfelnyss; and coccelas oferstīgað hwǽte *uitiat uirtutem malitia; et zizania transcendunt frumentum,* Scint. 101, 1. v. ge-midleahtrian.

**leáh-tric.** *l.* leahtric, *take here* leác-tric *in Dict., and add:*—Be þǽre nunfǽmnan þe bāt þone leahtric, Gr. D. 30, 33. [*Lat.* lactuca.]

**leahtrung.** *Add: opprobrium, abuse, reproach:*—Ic eom worden mannum tô leahtrunge *ego sum opprobrium hominum,* Ps. Th. 21, 5. þū hī gescyldst wið ǽlcere tungan leahtrunge *proteges eos a contradictione linguarum,* 30, 23. On heora ofermēttum and on heora leahtrunga (leahtungra, MS.) *in superbia et contemptu,* 20.

**leán.** *Add:*—Fultum odđe leán *emolomentum,* Wrt. Voc. ii. 29, 29. Mǽnifealde leán gelumpon *copiosa (animarum) emolumenta (Christo) prouenerunt,* An. Ox. 2633. þēh þe hié him leána tô þǽre dǽde wēnden, Ors. 5, 2; S. 218, 18. Ic bidde đæt se monn . . . đā ilcan wīsan leste . . . and đā godcundan leán mīnre sáule mid gerēce, C. D. i. 316, 21. v. weorold-leán.

**leán.** *Add: pp.* lagen. I. *to blame* a person or thing. See examples in Dict. II. *with dat.* of person, *to speak with disapproval of* something to a person, with the idea of dissuading or prohibiting:—Ne leá ic đē nā đæt đū ǽgđer lufige *I do not tell you that loving both is a bad thing,* Solil. H. 61, 17. Hē him lōh đæt hē hæfde his brōđor wíf (cf. dicebat illi, 'Non licet tibi habere eam,' Mt. 14, 4), Shrn. 123, 1. Se consul forseah þā sægene þe þā hlyttan him sǽdon, and him lōgan þ hē æt þǽm gefeohte ne cōme wið Gallie *contemtis auspiciis quibus pugnare prohibebatur adversum Gallos,* Ors. 4, 7; S. 184, 27 : Nar. 6, 27 (*in Dict.*). þone sīđfæt him snotere ceorlas lythwôn lōgon, þeáh hē him leóf wǽre, hwetton higerōfne *they said nothing to dissuade him from the journey, dear though he were to them, urged him on,* B. 203. Gif hē self drohtað on đām eordlicum tielongum đe hē đōrum monnum leán sceolde, Past. 133, 5. Tô gehiéranne suā hwæt suā wē him áuđer odđe leán odđe lǽra[n] wiellen *to hear whatever we may dissuade them from or persuade them to,* 303, 7. v. for-leán.

**leánian.** *Add:*—Drihten leánigende ys *Dominus retribuens est,* Scint. 108, 13. Leániendum *remuneratore,* An. Ox. 767: *largitore,* Hpt. Gl. 492, 1. Leániende wrace *ultricem uindictam,* An. Ox. 3816. v. ed-, geed-leánian; un-leánod.

**-leániend.** v. ed-, eft-, geed-leániend.

**leás.** II. *add:*—Sōđfæst *verax,* sōđsagol *veridicus,* leás *fallax* vel *mendax,* unsōđsagol *falsidicus,* Wrt. Voc. i. 76, 17-20. (1) of persons (or personifications). (a) *not truthful:*—Ic cwæđ þæt wǽron ealle menn ungemete leáse *ego dixi,* '*Omnis homo mendax,*' Ps. Th. 115, 2. (b) *not real, false, pseudo-*:—Leáse crístas and leáse wītegan, Mk. 13, 22. þā leásan godu, Ap. 49. (c) *not to be trusted, perfidious, deceitful:*—Leás fyrnhicge *prostituta pellax,* An. Ox. 2940. Leás wiht (leáswiht?) (*Satan*), Sat. 727. Sió ōđru wyrd is leás and beswīcþ ealle hire gefēran *illa fortuna fallit,* Bt. 20; F. 70, 33. Fram leásum aþume geypt *a pellaci genero proditus,* An. Ox. 2377. Leásum *perfido (fratre),* 5068. Hī weorþaþ bereáfode ǽlcre āre fram heora leásan cyninge, Bt. 29, 2; F. 104, 17. Leáse sceáweras *spies,* B. 253. þā leásan men, þā þe mid tungan treówa gehātað, fácenlīce þencað þonne hié æt nēhstan beswīcað, Leás. 24. (d) *of conduct, loose, licentious,* cf. leásung; IV.:—Ualerianus wæs swīđe leás man and wrǽne aa *Valerianus levis ac lubricus extitit,* Gr. D. 341, 2. (2) *of things.* (a) *in reference to speech, untruthful, lying, false:*—Leásre wrōhte *strofose accussationis,* An. Ox. 4236. Swilce hē gebringe đā sōđan lāre tô leásum gedwylde, Hml. Th. ii. 2, 24. For hwī đē hātan dysige men mid leásre stemne wuldor?, Bt. 30, 1; F. 108, 2. Leásum (leás, Met. 26, 1. (b) *sham, not genuine:*—Hēt Maxentius mid micclum swicdōme oferbricgian đā eá mid scipum, and syđđan đylian swā swā ōđre bricge . . . hē ne gemunde đǽre leásan bricge þe hē ālecgan hēt, Hml. Th. ii. 304, 27. Leása gesǽlþa *falsa bona,* Met. 12, 27. þās feówer (*the four evangelists*) syndon tô underfónne, . . . and forlǽtan þā ōđre þe leáse gesetnysse (*pseudo-gospels, apocryphal writings*) gesetton, Hml. S. 16, 224. (c) *false, not to be trusted, deceptive, vain, worthless:*—Ic nolde þ unc beswice ǽnegu leás anlīcnes (*cassa imago*) for sōþa gesǽlþa, Bt. 34, 1; F. 134, 8. Se leása wēna þāra dysigena monna *hominum fallax opinio,*

27, 3; F. 98, 32. þ leáse lot bewrigen mid wrencum *fraus mendaci compta colore,* Met. 4, 46. Eálá hū leás is þysses middaneardes wela, Chr. 1086; P. 219, 6. (d) *faulty, incorrect, false* (as in *false quantity*):—Solocismus bið sum leás word on đām ferse, Ælfc. Gr. Z. 294, 10. v. un-leás.

**leás;** *n. Add:* I. *what is untrue, untruth:*—Sege ūs nū þ sōđe būton ǽlcon leáse, Hml. S. 23, 590. II. *what is incorrect:*—Micel yfel dēđ sē đe leás writ, būton hē hit gerihte, Hml. Th. ii. 2, 23.

**leás-bregd.** *Add:* , -bregda:—Ne beó þū nā leásbrēda oþþe swicol, ac beó sōđfæst and symle getrýwe, Hml. S. 12, 129.

**leás-bregden.** *See next word.*

**leás-bregdness.** *For* 'Leo 220, 22' *substitute:*—Se sceocca eów lǽrd þyllice scíncræftas þ hē eówre sáwla hæbbe đonne gē gelýfađ his leásbrǽdnysse (-brēdene, *v. l.*), Hml. S. 17, 107. Mercurius wæs swīđe fácenful and swicol on dǽdum, and lufode stala and leásbrēdnysse, Sal. K., p. 122, 74.

**leáse;** *adv. Falsely:*—Hē leáse fieswede (leáslīce ongann), Bd. 2, 9; Sch. 147, 1.

**leásere;** II. *add:*—Heó ongan lǽran þone leásere, Shrn. 47, 5.

**leásettan.** *Add:*—þonne hý sume mid geficum wið þone ānne þeódað and leásettað, sume wið þone ōþerne *dum adulantur partibus,* R. Ben. 125, 2.

**leás-ferhþ, -fyrhþ;** *adj. False, fickle* (?) :—Næs hē ofermōd ne nīđig ne leásferhþ (-fyrhþ, *v. l.*), Nap. 41.

**leás-fyrhte.** *Add:*—Be đām árleásum . . . and be đām leásfyrhtum, Nap. 42.

**leás-gewita,** an; *m. A false witness:*—þā leásgewitan lēdon heora hacelan ætforan fótum sumes geonges cnihtes, sē wæs gecīged Saulus, Hml. Th. i. 46, 35.

**leás-gewitness.** *Add:*—Sume æfter fácne and æfter leásgewitnysse tô sōđre dǽdbóte gecyrrað, Hml. Th. ii. 398, 3.

**leáslíce.** *Add:*—Hié ná leng ne beheóldon þá līgeas þæ se ealda feónd leaslíce gehīwode þurh his scíncræft *ut flammas quas antiquus hostis finxerat non viderent,* Gr. D. 124, 16. v. un-leáslíce.

**leás-ōleccan** *to flatter:*—Wæs hit þ seó tunge þára leásōlecendra (*adulantium*) cweleþ þæs sáwle þe hī gehiéran lysteþ, Gr. D. 34, 27.

**leás-ōleccend.** *See preceding word:* leás-ōleccere. v. ōleccere.

**leás-sagol.** *Add:*—þus hī dweledon mid heora leássagelan sprǽce, Hml. S. 23, 378.

**leás-spellung.** *Add:*—Swá heora scopas on heora leóđum giddiende sindon and on heora leá(s)spellungum, Ors. 3, 1; S. 94, 29.

**leás-tyhtend.** v. leás-tyhtan *in Dict.*

**leásung.** *Add:* I. *lying; a lie:*—þý læs on mē mæge ídel spellung oþþe scondlic leásung beón gestæled *ne aut fabulae aut turpi mendacio dignus efficiar,* Nar. 2, 21. Hī tieligeað đæt hié ne sculen leásunga secgan (*falsa dicere*), Past. 237, 8. II. *vain or foolish speech:*—Leásung *famfaluca,* Wrt. Voc. ii. 34, 75. III. *deceitful action:*—Gereónung, leásung *factio, mendacium,* An. Ox. 2243. þā gereónedan leásunga *concinnatas factiones, i. falsitates,* 2803. IV. *light (immoral) action.* Cf. leás; II. 1 d:—Hē wæs swīđe wrǽne man and ābysgod in manigum leásingum *vir valde lubricus et cunctis levitatibus occupatus,* Gr. D. 341, 21. v. folc-leásung.

**leásung,** e; *f. Release on giving an equivalent* (?), *compensation:*—Leásung *hostimen* (cf. hostimentum *requital*), Wrt. Voc. ii. 70, 26: 43, 20. Cf. līsing.

**leás-wiht** (?). *A false creature, seducer, pander:*—Lôcade leáswiht (leás wiht? *Satan*) geond þæt lāþe scræf, Sal. 727. Leásuhta bepǽcunge *lenonum lenocinio,* An. Ox. 4014.

**leás-wyrcend,** es; *m. A deceiver, a doer of what is false:*—Deófol is yfeltihtend and leáswyrcend, synna ordfruma and sáwla bepǽcend, Hml. Th. i. 102, 1.

**leáw-finger.** v. lǽw-finger.

**leax.** *Add:*—Hē wearp ūt his net, and þēr weard oninnan ān ormǽte leax, Hml. S. 31, 1275. Him mon þá mettas selle þá þe late melten, leax and þā fixas þá þe late meltan, Lch. ii. 176, 23.

**leax-heáfod.** *Dele, and see* heáfod-ǽ (?) : lec (?). *Dele, and see* leóf.

**lēc.** *Add:*—Hwæt secge ic be eágum mīnum . . . þā mē mid lēce forhwyrfdon unrihtum? *quid dicam de oculis meis . . . qui me intuitu perverterunt iniquo?,* Angl. xi. 118, 50. Hē wæs gestæđđig on his lēce, Hml. S. 31, 296.

**leccan** *to moisten.* *Add:*—Leccan *humectare,* Hpt. Gl. 421, 71.

**leccan** *to blame.* v. læccan : **leccing.** *Add:* v. geond-leccing.

**leccung** *reproach.* v. læccung : -lēce. v. fram-lēce : -lecg. v. gelecg.

**lecgan.** *Under* II. *dele* 'L. Eth.', *and add:* I. *to cause to take a horizontal position:*—Swá swá gôd scipstýra hǽt fealdan þ segl and eác hwīlum lecgan þone mæst, Bt. 41, 3; F. 250, 15. I a. *to fell a person, slay:*—Gif hine hwā lecge binnan þǽm fyrste, Ll. Th. i. 222, 29. Wē rīdan ealle tô . . . and þone þeóf lecgean, 236, 18. Būton hē hine werian wolde . . . þ hine man þonne lēde, 240, 30. II. *to deposit.* (1) *to place in a position of rest on the ground or other sup-*

porting surface, *place* in a receptacle:—Đā lāc ðe mon on ðæt weóbud legde, Past. 219, 6. Wē bōca tōbrǣddon and on bearm lægden, Sal. 431. Ðió mengu giwēdo hiora legdun on woeg, Mk. R. L. 11, 8. Nim sume tigelan and lege beforon ðē, Past. 161, 3. Sete ðīn wīn and lege ðīnne hlāf ofer ryhtwīsra monna byrgenne *panem tuum et vinum super sepulturam justi constitue*, 327, 1. Lecge man þ īsen uppan þām stapelan, Ll. Th. i. 226, 28. Gif man ōðer wǣpn gedreóhlīce lecge þǣr hig stille mihton beón, 418, 6. Hēt se cāsere lecgan Georium innon ðone hwǣr, Hml. S. 14, 106. (2) *to deposit in the grave, bury:*—Gif man ǣnig līc of rihtscriftscīre elles hwǣr lecge, Ll. Th. i. 308, 6. Sleá hine man and on fūlan lecge, 396, 17. (3) *to lay* an egg, Lch. iii. 204, 30 (*in Dict.*). (4) *to deposit* a pledge. (a) a material pledge:—Ǣt cynges spǣce lecge man .vi. healfmearc wedd, Ll. Th. i. 296, 25. Sette mon inborh oþþe underwed lecge, 356, 10 : 352, 8. (b) a verbal pledge :—Hē forbeád him ǣlc wedd tō syllanne, būtan þysan wedde þe hē ūp on Crīstes weófod lēde . . . 'Ic þreó þing behāte . . .', Ll. Lbmn. 214, 26. (4 a) *to deposit* something as pledge:—Gif hwā þeóf clǣnsian wylle, lecge ān .c. tō wedde, Ll. Th. i. 296, 7. (5) lecgan in *to ȝut into the possession of, assign to*:—Đā land ðe hig ðider in lecgeað, Cht. Th. 370, 25 (*in Dict.*). **III.** *to place, set, apply.* (1) *to place close to, place on* :—Wið tōþwǣrce, gebærn hwīt sealt, . . . gegnīd eal tōsomne, lege on, Lch. ii. 50, 23 : 64, 1, *and often* :—[Gen. 2336: Rä. 4, 14; Chr. 1083; P. 205, 22 : Gen. 21, 7 *in Dict.*]. (1 a) *to annex, attach* : —Lagiað gōde woroldlagan, and lecgað þǣr tōeácan, þæt ūre crīstendōm fæste stande, Wlfst. 274, 7. (2) *to lay before, bring* to the notice of, Gen. 31, 37 (*in Dict.*). (3) with object denoting a member of the body, Rä. 78, 4 (*in Dict.*). **IV.** *to bring forward as a charge:*—þ hē mōste hine betellan æt ǣlc þǣra þinga þe him man on lēde, Chr. 1048; P. 175, 3. **V.** *to impose* a burden, Past. 293, 17 : Gū. 685 : Chr. 1052; P. 178, 2 : 1064; P. 190, 24 (*in Dict.*). **VI.** *to dispose* or *arrange over a surface.* (1) *to place* in a *proper or designed condition:*—Ic lecge grundweall *fundo*, Ǣltc. Gr. Z. 220, 1. Ðǣr mon ðone grundweall on lecgge, Past. 308, 4. Þā hēt hē hī bindan and on balcan lecgan, Bt. 16, 2 ; F. 54, 3. (2) *to fix as a covering :*—þ nān scyldwyrhta ne lecge nān scēpes fell on scyld, Ll. Th. i. 208, 10. (3) with non-material object, *to establish* a law, *lay down* a principle :—Hē sætte mycel deórfrið, and hē lægde laga þǣr wið, Chr. 1086; P. 221, 6. (4) *to direct* one's steps, Seef. 57 : Gen. 2536 : 2400 (*in Dict.*). (4 a) *intrans.* (v. *N. E. D.* lay; 43) on lāst lecgan *to follow* :—Wesseaxe forð ondlongne dæg on lāst legdun lāþum þeódum, Chr. 937; P. 108, 3. v. for-lecgan; on-lecgende.

**lecgung.** v. niþer-lecgung.

**lēf;** *adj. Add:*—Lēf *debile*, Germ. 389, 79. Mē is gelīcost þām þe on lēfan scipe byþ, Gr. D. 5, 14. v. ge-lēf.

**lēf;** *n. Dele.* The Latin which the citation translates is: Si in quarta ventus fuerit parui *panes* sunt in illo anno, so that *léf* seems = *hláf.* v. Archiv cxxviii. 56, 12.

**-lēfed, -lēfedness, -lēfian.** v. ge-lēfed, ā-lēfedness, ā-lēfian : **lēft.** *Dele.*

**Lega-ceaster,** e ; *f. Chester :*—Hié gedydon on ānre wēstre ceastre on Wirhealum, seó is Legaceaster (Leg-, Liege-, Lige-, *v. ll.*) gehāten, Chr. 894; P. 88, 6. Hē micele fyrd gelædde tō Legaceastre (Leige-, *v.l. ad Legionum, quae a gente Anglorum* Legacaester, *a Brettonibus autem rectius Carlegion appellatur*), Bd. 2, 2; Sch. 120, 5. Hē lædde his ferde tō Legaceastre, Chr. 605; P. 23, 5. Tō Legeceastre, 1016; P. 147, 16 : 1055; P. 186, 18. Lægeceastre, 972; P. 119, 10. Ābūton Legceastre, 1000; P. 133, 14.

**Legaceaster-scīr,** e ; *f. Cheshire :*—þȳ ilcan geáre wæs Legeceasterscīr gehergod, Chr. 980; P. 124, 9.

**-lege.** v. feorh-, or-lege : **-legen,** e ; *f.* v. ge-, on-, ūp-legen : **-legen;** *adj.* v. for-legen : **-legennes.** v. for-legennes.

**leger,** II. [*the last passage under* II. *should be transferred to* III.]. *add :*—Hē ābād on ðām legere āne feáwa dagas (cf. hē læg þā swā forþ āne feáwa daga, Hml. S. 31, 1349) mid fefore gewæht, Hml. Th. ii. 516, 29. Basilius weard gebrōht on legere tō his fordsīde, Hml. S. 3, 564. Heó wæs gestelled mid līchamlicre mettrumnesse and seomode (seon- MS.) laman legre *ea quam medici paralysin vocant molestia corporale percussa est*, Gr. D. 284, 2. **III.** *add :*—Sē þe þæt ne can, ǣr he hit geleornige, ne hē rihtlīce ne bið hūsles wyrðe . . . ne furðon clǣnes legeres æfter his fordsīde, Wlfst. 302, 8. Đā beád se biscop his wer þām cynge. Đā cwæð se cyng þ mihte beón geboden him wið clǣnum legere (*to obtain burial in consecrated ground* [cf. C. D. i. 310, 33, *given at* leger-stōw]), Cht. Th. 208, 31. v. dirne-, sib-leger.

**-leger;** *m.* v. sib-leger : **-leger;** *adj.* v. dirne-leger.

**leger-bedd.** *Add :*—Marcellus sǣde þ heó læge on paralisin. þā āxode Tītus þone apostol hwī hē geþafode þ heó swā lāge on þām legerbedde, þonne hē ōðre ālēfede ealle gehǣlde, and heó āna læg swā, Hml. S. 10, 237.

**-legere.** *For* 'v. for-legere' *substitute:* adj. v. ān-legere : **-legere;** *adv.* v. dirne-legere : **lēgere.** v. leógere.

**leger-fæst.** For ' R. Ben . . . Lye' *substitute :*—Ealle fram flǣscǣte hī forhæbben būtan þām wanhālum and þām legerfæstum (*preter debiles et aegrotos*), R. Ben. 64, 7.

**-leger-scipe.** v. dirne-legerscipe.

**leger-stōw.** *Add :*—Āgefe mon tēn hund peñd. inn mid līce mē wið legerstōwe *let ten hundred pence be given for me with my body in consideration of my being allowed burial there*, C. D. i. 310, 33.

**lēgian.** v. līgian.

**legie,** an; *f. A legion :*—þā hēt Pompeius þæt mon þ fæsten brǣce and on fuhte dæges and nihtes, simle ān leg(ie) æfter ōþerre unwērig *cum alias aliis legiones dies noctesque succedere sine requie cogeret*, Ors. 5, 11 ; S. 238, 9. Ealle þā legean, 5, 12 ; S. 240, 6. Eahta legian, 5, 13 ; S. 246, 7 : S. Augustus sende Quintilius on Germanie mid þrim legian, 5, 15 ; S. 250, 10. Rōmāne hæfdon gegaderad feówer legian heora folces, 4, 9 ; S. 192, 7 : 5, 12 ; S. 240, 12. Seofon legan (legion, *v. l.*), S. 238, 16.

**-legis.** v. for-legis : **-legu.** v. ealdor-legu : **-lēgu** (?). v. ge-lēgu (?): **lemb.** v. lamb : **lēmian.** *Add:* v. ge-lemian.

**lemp-healt.** *Substitute:* Limp-halt (v. *N. E. D. s. v.*), *halting :*—Laempihalt, lemphihalt, lemp-halt, lemphald *lurdus* (cf. *lordicare* dorso incurvato incedere, Migne), Txts. 74, 589. Lemphealt, Wrt. Voc. ii. 71, 3 : 51, 20.

**lempit,** e ; *f. A dish, basin :*—Lempite *patellas*, Txts. 108, 1123. [*M. L. Ger.* lampet, lempet : *Du.* lampet *basin.*]

**lencten.** *Add:* , lenten. **I.** *spring.* The season according to the poetical calendar began on Feb. 7 and ended on May 8 :—Æfter seofentȳnum þrowade nihtgerīmes Mathias (*his day was* Feb. 24) þæs þe lencten on tūn geliden hæfde, Menol. 28. Hēr wæs mycel gefeoht on Norðhymbra lande on lengtene (*in spring* or *in Lent* ?) on .iiii. Nō. Apr̄, Chr. 798; P. 57, 35. On længtene eregian and impian, beána sāwan . . , Angl. ix. 262, 6. þū þā treówa on hærfesttīd heora leáfa bereáfast, and eft on lencten ōþru leáf sellest, Bt. 4 ; F. 8, 7. Lengten, 39, 13 ; F. 234, 18. **II.** *Lent* (with this sense the word seems neuter, taking the gender of *fæsten* ?) :—Fram idus Septembris oð lenctenes (*quadragesime*) anginne hȳ on ān mǣl tō nōnes gereorden. Ofer eal lencten (*in quadragesima*) oþ eástran hȳ oð æfen fæsten, R. Ben. 66, 4–6. Be lenctenes gȳmene *de Quadragesime observatione*, 76, 2. On lænctenes fæstenes dagum *in quadragesime diebus*, R. Ben. I. 82, 15. Sume menn dyslīce fæstað ofer heora mihte on gemǣnelicum lenctene, Hml. S. 13, 94. Ic þe lǣre þ þū þīn lengten rihtlīce gehealde, and tō ānes mǣles þæt fæsten gefæste, Wlfst. 247, 33. Fæste hē ān lengten (*unam quadrigesimam*), Ll. Th. ii. 210, 25. On þām þrim lengctenum, 134, 31. Fæste hē .ii. lengtenu, 210, 27. iii. lengctenu, 194, 12. Lengteno, 192, 5. [v. *N. E. D.* lenten.] v. foran- (Lch. ii. 256, 1), mid-lencten.

**lencten-ādl.** *Add:* , dysentery :—Hara bið gōd wið lengtenādle (*contra dysenteriam*), Ll. Th. ii. 162, 23. Wið lenctenādle, þ is fefer, Lch. ii. 12, 28.

**lencten-bere** *spring-sown barley* (? cf. lenten corne as . . . otys, pecys, barley. v. *N. E. D.* lenten-corn) :—Nime þonne clǣnne lengtenbere and grinde on handcwyrna, Nap 42. Cf. lencten-eorþe.

**lencten-dæg.** *Add :*—On Lengtendagum *quadrigessimali tempore*, Chrd. 51, 23 ; 42, 29.

**lencten-fæsten.** *Add :*—þ Lengtenfæsten *Quadragessima*, Chrd. 113, 19. þeós clǣne tīd læntenfæstenes, Angl. xii. 513, 31. Ealra swīðost healdan hȳ forhæfednesse clǣnsunge on lenctenfæstenne, R. Ben. 76, 5. Fram kalendas Octobris oð lenctenfæsten *a kalendis octobribus usque ad caput quadrigesime*, 74, 3.

**lencten-hǣte,** an; -hǣt(u), e ; *f. Spring-heat,* heat *in spring :*—Of rēðre lenctenhǣtan (-hǣte, *v.l.*) *repentinus calor veris*, Ors. 3, 3 ; Bos. 55, 22.

**lencten-lifen,** e ; *f. Lenten* fare :—Ymbe heora lenctenlifene (*de quadragessimali alimento*) smeágian þā ealderas georne, Chrd. 15, 13.

**lencten-tīd.** *Add :*—Lenctentīd *vernum tempus*, Wrt. Voc. i. 76, 62.

**lencten-tīma,** an ; *m.* **I.** *spring-time, spring :*—Lengtentīma and cildiugoð geþwǣrlæcað . . . Lengtentīma ys wæt and wearm, Angl. viii. 299, 25–28. Lententīma *vernale tempus*, An. Ox. 3837. **II.** *the season of Lent :*—Læsse pleoh bið þām Crīstenan men þæt hē flǣsces brūce on Lenctentīman, þonne hē wīfes brūce, Hml. Th. ii. 608, 18.

**lencten-time.** *Dele, and see preceding word.*

**lencten-wicu.** *Add:* Jn. 5, 1, 17 rbc. : 8, 21 rbc.

**-lend.** v. ge-lend : **-lenda.** v. ge-lenda; in-, ūt-lenda : **-lendan** *to endow with land.* v. ge-lendan : **-lende;** *adj.* v. el(e)-, in-, ūt-lende : **-lende;** *n.* v. ele-lende.

**lenden-ādl,** e ; *f. Disease of the loins :*—Wēnaþ unwīse lǣcas þ þ sié lendenādl, Lch. ii. 232, 8.

**lenden-brǣda.** l. -brǣde, *and add :*—Gif sió lendenbrǣde bið forslegen *si lumbi truncentur*, Ll. Th. i. 98, 1. [*O. L. Ger.* landi-brēda *reniculus.*]

**lenden-ece,** es ; *m. Pain in the loins :*—Wiþ lendenece, Lch. ii. 64, 16, 21 : 234, 29.

lenden-reáf. *Dele, and see* lenden-sîd.

lenden-seóc; *adj. Diseased in the loins:*—Þis ilce deáh wiþ lendenseócum men, Lch. ii. 248, 27. Lendenseóce men mîgað blóde and sande, 232, 9.

lenden-sîd; *adj. Of a garment, reaching to the loins:*—Lendensîd reáf *lumbare* vel *renale*, Wrt. Voc. i. 40, 22. Cf. fót-sîd.

lendenu. *Add:* , lendnu (-a):—Lendena *lumbia*, Wrt. Voc. i. 283, 52 : ii. 51, 73. Lendnum, laendum *clunis*, Txts. 48, 216. Lâreówas ûs secgað þ on þâm lendenum is þæs lîchaman gâlnyss, Hml. A. 17, 95. Begyrd sweord ðîn ymb lendna [lendynu, Ps. Cam.: lendan (= lendna), Ps. Srt.] *accingere gladium tuum circa femor*, Ps. Vos. 44, 4. [v. *N. E. D.* lend.]

lendis lieg. *Add:*—Laembis lieg, Wrt. Voc. ii. 126, 41.

-lendisc. *Add:* v. ele-lendisc: -lendiscness. v. inlendisc-ness: leng *length*. v. lengu.

lengan *to be long. Add:*—Þonne wê eác for ðî on ðâm sancge lencgað *propter hoc protrahendo et morose volumus dici psalmum*, R. Ben. 68, 9. Lenged *protractum*, An. Ox. 28, 17. [In l. 5 for *prophet's* l. *prophets'*.]

lenge *length.* v. lengu: lenge ; *adv. long.* v. lange ; I. 3 ; *longer.* v. lange ; I. 2.

lengþ. *Add: height.* v. lang ; I. 2 a :—Ðone munt ðe sŷ in ðære lengoðe seó lîne ðe wile .xxxiii. sîþa ealne eorðan ymbehwyrft ûtan ymblicgan, Sal. K. p. 152, 5.

leng-togran. v. lang-toh.

lengu. *Take here* leng *in Dict., and add:* , lenge. I. of space relations. (1) cf. lang ; I. 2 :—Tô ðon þ him nære nâ âlŷfed furður tô gânne þonne swâ swâ þære racenteáge længe (leng, *v. l.*) âþened wæs *ne ei ultra liceret progredi, quam catenae ejusdem quantitas tendebatur*, Gr. D. 214, 8. Wæs seó wîcstôw on lengo .xx.es furlonga long, Nar. 12, 16. Gyf þû hwilce langwyrpe bôc habban wille . . . sete þîne swŷþran ofer þîne wynstran earm be þære bôce læncge, Tech. ii. 119, 15. (1 a) cf. lang ; I. 2 a :—Lencge, hîh[þe] *proceritate, summitate*, An. Ox. 1640. II. of time relations. Cf. lang ; II. 3 a :—Ær þon ðe seó sunne cyrre hig tô þæs dæges lenge *ere the sun turn herself (before the winter solstice) and as' an effect the length of the day increases*, Shrn. 153, 28. Þâ lengce his lîfes hê him eall gerehte *longitudinem dierum suorum et finem vitae suae sibi in ordine manifestavit*, Guth. Gr. 172, 31. Mihst þû swâ manegra tîda lencgu oferfaran, Hml. S. 23 b, 522.

lent *a lentil. Substitute: lentils, pulse:*—*Legumine* .i. lent ł fað, Germ. 390, 64. [Take thou to thee . . . bene and lent *tu sume tibi . . . fabam et lentem*, Wick. Ezech. 4, 9.]

leó. *Add: gen. f.* leó:—Þâs Grêcisce naman . . . *hic leon* þeós leó ; ac wê forlætað þone *n* on Lêdensprǽce and cweðað *leo*, Ælfc. Gr. Z. 42, 1. Swê swê leá *sicut leo*, Ps. Srt. 16, 12: ii. 184, 40. Hê hêt âne strange leó lǽtan in tô him . . . þâ arn seó leó . . . se leó heora ne oðhrân, Hml. S. 30, 415-420. Woldon þâ hǽþenan hentan þære leó (cf. þurh ðâ león, 306), 35, 280. Hwelp þæs león *catulus leonis*, Ps. L. 16, 12. Onsíon leás *facies leonis*, Mt. p. 7, 11 : 14. Þâ cwôman hwîte león in fearra gelícnisse, Nar. 14, 26. God geworhte . . . ðâ rêðan león ðe hêr on lande ne beóð, Hex. 14, 32.

leód, es ; *m. Add : pl.* leóda. *A man of a particular country :*—Itthamar wæs Cantwara leód *Ithamar oriundus de gente Cantuariorum*, Bd. 3, 14 ; Sch. 253, 13. Gif man leúd ofsleá an þeófðe, Ll. Th. i. 42, 13. Beeástan him sindon Osti þâ leóde, Ors. 1, 1 ; S. 16, 29 : 22, 7. Gê Rômâniscan leóda *ye men of Rome*, Hml. S. 35, 291 : Hml. A. 65, 7 : Lch. iii. 246, 15. Se wer gebirað mâgum, and seó cynebót þâm leódum, Ll. Th. i. 186, 5. Forweard se consul mid eallum his folce from Etusci þǽm leódum *L. Baebius a Liguribus circumventus cum universo exercitu occisus est*, Ors. 4, 11 ; S. 206, 9. v. ceaster- (Nap. 12), norþ-leóde ; leóda.

leód, e ; *f. Add:*—Gelamp on þǽre leóde gewinn, Hml. Th. ii. 502, 3. Hê þâm cyninge and his leóde bodade, 128, 21. Hê gecyrde tô his âgenre leóde, i. 400, 15. Þâs land syndon Crêca leóde, Ors. 1, 1 ; S. 22, 12. v. burg-, ceaster- (Nap. 12) leód.

leóda. *Add:*—L(e)ódan *ciues*, An. Ox. 56, 272. Rômânisce leódan (leóde (-a), *v. ll.*) ongynnað heora geár æfter hǽðenum gewunan, Lch. iii. 246, 15. Þær mihton geséon Winceastre leódan (leóde, *v. l.*) rancne here, Chr. 1006 ; P. 137, 10. Eádweard bewarede land and leódan (leóde, *v. l.*), 1065 ; P. 195, 15.

leódan. *Add:*—Him brega engla of lîce âteáh liódende bân (*the rib from which Eve was made*), Gen. 182.

leód-bisceop. *Add:*—Cnut cyning grêt his arceb and his leód-biscopas, Cht. E. 229, 18. [*Dan.* lyd-biskop *suffragan bishop*.]

leód-geþyncþ, es. *l.* , e ; leód-hata. *Add:*—Gr. D. 163, 32.

leód-hwæt. *In the passage* l. leódhwata, *and add:* cf. brego-rôf, cyning-beald.

leódisc. v. þider-leódisc.

leód-rǽden[n], e ; *f. A population ; people, the country of a people :*—Hwylc wundor is, þeáh þe wê þis be mannum secgan, nû seó

---

ûplice leódrǽden þǽre ængellican gecynde of sumum dǽle æfwerdlan ârǽfnede of hyra efenceasterwarum *quid mirum quod hoc de homine dicitur, quando illa superna regio in civibus suis ex parte damna pertulit*, Gr. D. 204, 28. Cf. leód-scipe.

leód-sceaþa. *Add:* cf. þeód-sceaþa.

leód-scipe. *Add:*—þæt folc of gehwilcum leódscipe þâ stôwe geneósiað, Hml. Th. i. 510, 12. For ðone cincg and ealne his leódscipe, C. D. iii. 315, 16. Cf. leód-rǽden.

leód-stefn. *Add:* cf. þeód-stefn: leód-wita. *Add:* cf. þeód-wita.

leóf, *as a form of address. Add:* I. to one person :—' Hæfst þû ǽnig gedeorf?' 'Geá, leóf, ic hæbbe,' Coll. M. 20, 11, 7. Ealra manna hlâford . . . wê biddað þînne cynescipe . . . hî under ðê, leóf, on yfele þurhwunedon, Hml. S. 23, 284. Leóf, ic ðê cŷðe hû hit wæs ymb ðæt lond, C. D. ii. 133, 3. Leóf, Æðelwold Ealdarman cŷð his leófan cynehlâforde hû ic wille ymbe ðâ landâre, v. 333, 3. II. to more than one person :—Wulfstân arceb grêt Cnut cyning his hlâford and Ælfgife þâ hlǽfdian ; and ic cŷþe inc, leóf . . ., Cht. E. 232, 15. Ðâ cwæð hê tô heom eallum ; 'Lâ leóf, ic bidde eów', Hml. S. 23, 580, 720. v. leóf; I. 1 a.

leóf. *Add:* I. as *adj.* :—Leóf *carus*, þurhlâð *odiosus*, Wrt. Voc. i. 28, 65. (1) of persons :—Leófre *optatæ (generationis)*, An. Ox. 3369. Leó(fe) *dulcia (natorum pignora)*, 220. (1 a) as an epithet in address ; *see preceding word* :—Leófan men, Wlfst. 6, 2 (*and often*). Men þâ leófestan 232, 12. (2) of things :—Mid leófre fèrrǽdene *contuberniali sodalitate*, An. Ox. 2353. Ðê is leófre on ðisum wâcum scræfum ðonne ðû on healle heálic biscop sitte, Hml. Th. ii. 146, 27. Biþ hit swâ him leófost bið, Lch. ii. 144, 23 : By. 23. Mê is eal leófast þæt þê lâþost is, Ors. 5, 12 ; S. 242, 9. II. as *subst.* (1) of persons, *a dear one, friend, leman* (v. *N. E. D.* lief, 3 b) :—Ne biþ hê Godes leóf, Bl. H. 21, 35. Leóf *succubam*, Germ. 394, 192. (2) of things :—Leóf âlâþað *amor abolescit*, Angl. ii. 374, 3. Nân wiht ne þæs leófes ne þæs lâðes, Wlfst. 185, 1. v. efen-, ge-, hîred-(?)leóf.

-leofa. v. big-leofa.

leófan. *Dele. The passage given here is in full :*—Israéla éðelweardas lufan lîfwelan þenden hié lêt metod. *It may be noted that* Israéla *occurs 12 times in this poem, but only in this instance does it seem to form a half line. A word seems missing, and it might be suggested by l. 43 þær Israéla æhta wæron, and the line might read:* Âhton Israéla, &c. *Cf. too eorlas* Israéla *for a similar half line.*

leóf-lîc. *Add:*—Leóflicere *laudabili* .i. *honorabili (fervore)*, An. Ox. 3919.

leógan. *Add:*—Ic leóge *fallo*, Ælfc. Gr. Z. 180, 3. I. of speech. (1) *to say what is not true in order to deceive:*—Gif ic Dâuide lêgu si *Dauid mentiar*, Ps. Vos., Srt. 88, 36. Ne leóh þû (*non loqueris falsum testimonium*), Wlfst. 66, 18. Ðeáh hê nyte hwæt hê sôðes secge, him is ðeáh leófre ðæt hê leóge ðonne him mon ǽnigra ungerisna tô wêne *eligit bona de se vel falsa jactari, ne mala possit vel minima perpeti*, Past. 217, 16. Heó wolde hire lîf forlǽtan ǽr þan þe heó luge, Hml. S. 12, 179. Lêgende (leógendu, Ps. Vos.) wes unrehtwîsnis *mentita est iniquitas*, Ps. Srt. 26, 12. Þâ þâ hê gehŷrde þæs leógendan (*mentientis*) cnihtes word, Gr. D. 40, 30. Lîgende wêrun *mentiti sunt*, Ps. Srt. 17, 46. Lêgende, 77, 36. (1 a) leógan *on to make a false charge against* :—Se cniht leáh on hine sylfne *the lad accused himself falsely*, Hml. S. 12, 247. Gif ðê mon on leóge, fægena þæs, Prov. K. 70. (2) *to state what is not correct, make a mistake* :—Se âwergda gâst ongan Godes bêc trahtian, and þâ sôna leáh (*and at once made a mistake*) ; forþon þis næs gecweden be Crîste . . ., ah be hâlgum monnum, Bl. H. 29, 30 : Môd. 81. II. *to give (or have) a wrong idea, deceive* another (or one's self) (with dat.) :—Hû ðæt môd ðætte wilnað for óðre beón lîhð him selfum, ðonne hit ðencð fela gôdra weorca tô wyrcanne, Past. 55, 14. Oft eác ðâ grambæra[n] leógað him selfum, ðonne hié wênað ðæt hié ryhtne andan hæbben *saepe iracundi rectitudinis falluntur zelo*, 289, 17. Þâ stuntan môd leógað, ðonne hî wênað þ þæs mannes ærnung beó of his lîchaman missenlicnysse, Gr. D. 46, 7. Nis þæt seldguma . . . næfne him his wlite leóge, B. 250. III. *trans.* (1) *To state incorrectly, make a mistake in* what is said :—Gif ǽnig þonne hê âgind sealm leógð rǽdinge *si quis dum pronuntiat psalmum fallitur lectionem*, R. Ben. I. 79, 12. Hê ne leág fela wyrda ne worda, B. 3029. (2) *to deceive a person (as a translation of Latin* fallere) Hymn. Surt. 33, 15 (*in Dict.*). v. be-leógan.

leógere. *Add:* I. *one who knowingly makes a false statement:*—Þâ fêrde sum leógere (-ore, *v. l.*) (cf. *that wicked Simon had misinformed*, 2 Macc. 3, 11) and belǽwde þ feoh, Hml. S. 25, 756. Hê sceal leógeras and lîceteras hatian, Wlfst. 266, 28. II. *one who makes a false pretence, a hypocrite* :—Lâ lêgere *hypocrita*, Lk. L. 6, 42. Ðû lêgere ł gíé lêgeras, Mt. L. 15, 7. Mið lêgerum, 24, 51 : Mk. L. R. 7, 6.

leóht *a light. Add:* I. *light.* (1) *the medium of visual perception generally ; the condition of space in which light is present :*—Leóht hafað hîw and hâd Hâliges Gâstes, Sal. 408. Æt sunnan setlgange . . .

nǽnig leóht ne æteóweþ, Bl. H. 93, 17. Þǽr is þ éce leóht búton þeóstrum, 65, 17. Hí sôhton ôðer land (*hell*): þæt wæs leóhtes leás and wæs líges full (cf. Milton's 'from those fiames no light'), Gen. 333: Bl. H. 63, 2. Leóhtes hyrde God, Az. 121: Dôm. 53. Þone þe leóht gescôp, Jul. 117: Gen. 122. (I a) *light* as a mark of a habitable region, *a region or condition in which there is light*, used of this world and the next:—Hê sáwla lǽded on úprodor, þǽr [is] leóht and líf, Exod. 545. Ús is wuldres leóht ontýned *heaven is opened to us*, Sat. 556: Cri. 1673: An. 1613. Hê ús hafað þæs leóhtes bescyrede *he has deprived us of heaven*, Gen. 392: 401. Heó on wyrse leóht under eorðan neoðan God sette sigeleáse, on þá sweartan helle, 310. Gif hit forget his ágen leóht, þ is éce geseá, Bt. 3, 2; F. 6, 9. (2) *light* as itself an object of perception, *an individual shining or appearance of light*:—Mycel leóht and freábeorht onlýhte þ carcern, Bl. H. 229, 28. Ðá him ðæt leóht côm of heofonum and hine gebrêgde, Past. 443, 19. Nú scíneð þe leóht fore glædlic ongeán, þe ic from Gode brôhte, hwít of heofonum, Gen. 614: B. 727. Mid beorhtum leóhte *luce serena*, An. Ox. 3324. Mid his þǽm scínendan leóhte, Bl. H. 85, 9. (3) *light* residing in or emanating from a luminary:—Þæs blácernes leóht næs gesýne, Vis. Lfc. 55. Se môna mid his blácan leóhte, Bt. 4; F. 6, 35. Se môna hys leóht (lêht, L.) ne sylð, Mt. 24, 29. Siððan hié sunnan leóht geseón meahton, B. 648. (4) fig. of a beloved object:—Þú eart dohtor mín seó dýreste . . . mínra eágna leóht, Jul. 95. II. *the illumination which proceeds from the sun in daytime, daylight, daytime, the light of day*:—Þancwyrhe biþ þæs dæges leóht for þǽre egeslican þióstro þǽre nihte, Bt. 23; F. 78, 28. Þá côm ôðer dæg, leóht æfter þeóstrum, Gen. 144. Leóht eástan côm, B. 569: An. 124. On leóhtes deorcunge *in lucis crepusculo*, Angl. xiii. 398, 475. Æfter leóhtes cyme, Jul. 161. Ær leóhte *ante lucem*, Ps. Vos., Rdr. 77, 34. Onginnendum leóhte *incipiente luce*, R. Ben. I. 37, 15. ¶ cf. the phrase by God's light:—Dæg byð Dryhtnes sond, mǽre metodes leóht, Rún. 24. III. *the state of being visible or exposed to view*, as in to come to *light*:—Sceal on leóht cuman sínra weorca wlite, Cri. 1037: Ph. 508. IV. *power of vision, eyesight*:—Cwæþ se godspellere þ leóht cyrde tô þon blindan, Bl. H. 17, 36. Sæge Adame hwilce þú gesihðe hæfst . . . gife ic him þæs leóhtes genóg, þæs ic þe swá gôdes gegired hæbbe, Gen. 619. Se blinda leóht onfêng, Bl. H. 19, 11. ¶ where sight is taken as a mark of life:—Sê þe wile eorlscipe æfnan, oð þæt eal scæceð leóht and líf somod, Vîd. 142. V. *a body which emits illuminating rays*. (1) a heavenly body:—Þonne swegles leóht, gimma gladost, ofer gársecg úp ædeltungla wyn eástan líxeð, Ph. 288. Cwôm leóhta mǽst *the sun rose*, Gú. 1256. God cwæð: 'Beó nú leóht (*luminaria*) on þǽre heofenan fæstnysse . . . and beón tô tácnum . . . God geworhte twá micele leóht (*luminaria magna*) þæt mǽre leóht tô þæs dæges lihtinge and þæt lǽsse leóht tô þǽre nihte lihtinge, Gen. i. 14–16. (2) *a lighted candle, lamp*, &c.:—Wê sceolon beran úre leóht tô cyrcan and lǽtan hí ðǽr bletsian, Hml. Th. i. 150, 20. (3) with collective force:—þ hí Godes circan mid leóhte and lácum gelôme gegrêtan, Ll. Th. i. 326, 17. Wê sculan gán mid þám leóhte betwux Godes húsum and singan ðone lofsang . . . þeáh ðe sume men singan ne cunnon, hí beron þeáhhwæðere þæt leóht on heora handum, Hml. Th. i. 150, 28–31. (4) used figuratively:—Se Godes cwide is leóht wincendra, Sal. 77. Ðý lǽs sió gídsung ðæs lǽnan lofes ádwæsce ðæt leóht ðǽre geofolnesse, Past. 321, 22. VI. *illumination as a possession of the mind*:—Hí onfêngon ðæt leóht ðæs ondgietes, Past. 429, 12. VII. *in a spiritual sense*:—Brôðor Pawlus, árís þú and gebide þê ǽr, for ðon þú eart leóhtes swer, Bl. H. 141, 1. Men forlêton þá beorhtnesse þæs heofonlican leóhtes, 17, 16. Gehwilcne man þǽra þe wilnaþ tô ðǽre sôþan gôdes liohte tô cumenne, Bt. 35, 6; F. 170, 17. Hê wæs onǽled mid ðý úpcundan leóhte, Past. 379, 24. Neálǽcan þǽm leóhte ðǽre sôðfæstnesse, 461, 7. Hê hafaþ leóht éces lífes, Bl. H. 103, 31. VII a. applied to Deity as the source of divine light or to those who manifest it:—Ic eom middaneardes leóht, Jn. 8. 12. Wealdend God . . . sôðfæstra leóht, El. 7. Þú eart heofonlic lióht and þæt hálige lamb, Hy. 8, 22. Þý þriddan dæge ealles leóhtes leóht lífgende árás, El. 486. Gê synt middaneardes leóht, Mt. 5, 14. v. ælmes-, candel-, frum-leóht.

leóht *bright*. *Dele last passage but two, and add*: I. *bright, shining, luminous*:—Wolcen lêht (líht, R., beorht, W.S.) *nubes lucida*, Mt. L. 17, 5. Lyftwundor leóht (*the pillar of fire*), Grod. 90. Se leóhta beám leódum byrhted, Cri. 1090. Ic him þá máðmas geald æt gúðe leóhtan sweorde, B. 2492. Mid þá leóhtan gedryht *with the band in shining robes*, El. 737. Dryhtnes onsién sunnan leóhtre, Cri. 1652. Sceán leóht inn . . . þá wæs hit swá leng swá leóhtre, Vis. Lfc. 54. I a. figurative. (1) *illustrious, splendid*:—On his dagum sceolde weorþan geboren sê se þe leóhtra and scínendra (*clarior*) þonne sió sunne þá wǽre, Ors. 5, 14; S. 248, 11. (2) *giving mental illumination*:—Swá dôð nú þá þeóstro þínre gedréfednesse wiðstandn mínum leóhtum lárum, Bt. 6; F. 14, 31. II. *of a place, time of day*, &c., *having a considerable amount of light*:—Eálá dæg leóhta, Sat. 166. In þám leóhtan hám, Gú. 806. Sió sunne bringþ leóhte dagas, Bt. 21; F. 74, 24. II a. fig. (1) in respect to the mind:—Crisantus leornode mid

leóhtum andgite and mid gleáwun môde grammatican cræft, Hml. S. 35, 13. (2) in respect to spiritual purity:—Gif êgo þín bið bilwit all líchoma ðín lêht (*lucidum*) bið, Lk. L., R. 11, 34. Hê onfêng leóhtne geleáfan, El. 491. (3) *cheerful, untroubled*:—Beó leófwende, leóht on gehygdum, Fä. 92. III. *of appearance, fair*:—Wáláwá! þ is sárlic þ swá fæger feorh and swá leóhtes andwlitan men (cf. swá fægeres híwes menn, Hml. Th. ii. 120, 26) sceolan ágan þýstra ealdor *heu, pro dolor! quod tam lucidi uultus homines tenebrarun auctor possidet*, Bd. 2, 1; Sch. 110, 5.

leóht *not heavy*. *Add*: I. *of little weight*:—Hwílum þ leóhte fýr úp gewít and sió hefige eorþe sit þǽr niþere, Bt. 39, 13; F. 234, 12. Hêt ic .cc. mínra þegna leóhtum wǽpnum (*levibus armis*) hié gegyrwan, Nar. 10, 27. II. *of a vessel or receptacle, adapted for light loads*:—Leóht leáp *imbilium*. Wrt. Voc. i. 287, 27: ii. 46, 40. Leóhte scypa, Ors. 1, 1; Swt. 19, 8 (*in Dict.*). III. *of meat or drink, that does not lie heavy on the stomach*; *of intoxicating drink, without much alcohol*:—Leóht beór *melle dulci*, Wrt. Voc. i. 290, 77: ii. 56, 49. Hwílum him deáh þ him mon selle leóhte wyrtdrencas, swilce swá bið wel geteád alwe, Lch. ii. 226, 13. Leóhte mettas þicge hê, 264, 4. IV. *of little moment, trivial*; *of sin, venial*:—For lǽhton suman gylte *pro leui qualibet culpa*, Angl. xiii. 434, 984. Be sumum leóhtum (*levibus*) scyldum, Gr. D. 328, 5. Leóht *paucula* i. *parua* ł *exigua* (*exempla*), An. Ox. 1692. V. *light, wanton, frivolous*. Cf. leóht-brǽdnes. VI. *moving quickly*:—Brimwudu scynde leóht, láde fús, Gú. 1306. Hê hæfde monncynnes leóhteste hond lofes tô wyrcenne, Vîd. 72. VII. *of what is imposed, easy to bear, not onerous, not oppressive*:—Ðyncet him suíðe leóht sió byrðen ðæs láreówdômes, Past. 25, 9. Ðára byrðenna hefignesse, eall ðæt ic his geman, ic awríte, þý lǽs hí hwǽm leóhte (*levia*) ðyncen tô underfônne, 23, 13. Benedictus ús bôc áwrát leóhtre be dǽle (*the Benedictine rule was in some respects less severe than that of Basil*. Cf. Basilius áwrát munucregol . . . þeáh þe hê hefegra sý þonne sê ðe Benedictus ús gebysnode, Hml. S. 3, 147) ðonne Basilius, Hex. 32, 9. Ðyncað him ðý leóhtran ðá geswinc ðe ofergán sculon *leve fit, quod transeundo laboratur*, Past. 407, 31: Bt. 10; F. 30, 13. Þá gesetness þe þǽr tô stronge wǽron and tô hearde hê hié ealle gedyde leóhtran and líþran, Ors. 5, 12; S. 244, 15. VIII. *easy, not offering difficulty* to what is to be done to one:—Swá mycclum swá þæs mannes gecynd unmihtigre wæs, swá hit wæs leóhtre tô miltsunge *homo quanto fragilior in natura, tanto facilior ad veniam*, Angl. viii. 4, 36. IX. *easy to do*:—Þá fêt habbaþ þæs þe leóhtran gang, Lch. i. 342, 12. X. *of sleep, not producing heaviness, easily shaken off*:—Mê leóht slǽp ofernam, Bd. 5, 9; Sch. 592, 7. XI. *free from bodily or mental oppression*:—Þonne is se ǽresta lǽcedôm dægfæsten, þ mon mid þý þá wambe clǽnsige, þ hió þý þe leóhtre sié, Lch. ii. 218, 1. Wið innoþes (l. (?) môdes) hefignesse, syle etan leóhtre . . . sôna bið þ môd leóhtre, iii. 50, 23. v. leáf-leóht.

-leóht. v. el-, em-leóht: leóhtan. v. líhtan.

leóht-berende. *Add*:—Steorra leóhtberende *lucifer*, Ps. Lamb. 109, 3.

leóht-bora, an; m. A *light-bearer*:—Ðá wærð his leóhtbora áfyrht swýðe, Vis. Lfc. 36.

leóht-brǽdness. *Substitute: Wantonness, levity, frivolity*:—Þonne ys se ôðer heáfodleahter gecweden gífernes . . . of þǽre bið acenned ungesceád bliss and scеandlícnes and leóhtbrǽdnes and ídelsprǽc (*inepta laetitia, scurrilitas, levitas, vaniloquium*), Verc. Först. 168. Gálre leóhtbrǽdnesse *petulantis lasciviae*, An. Ox. 4706. Hý hý georne bewerian wið leóhtbrǽdnesse ídelra worda and unnyttra gebǽra *subtrahat corpori suo de loquacitate, de scurrilitate*, R. Ben. 76, 19. Uton forlǽtan . . . gálnysse and sceandlicnessa and leóhtbrǽdnessa and ídele sprǽca and ealle unclǽnnessa, Verc. Först. 167, 6.

leóhte *brightly*. *Add*: [O. H. Ger. liohte *lucide*.]: -leóhtend. v. geond-leóhtend.

leóht-fæt. *Add*:—Lêhtfaet *lanterna*, Wrt. Voc. ii. 112, 49. Leóhtfæt *lampas*, i. 284, 33: *lampas vel lucerna vel lanterna*, 81, 30. Leóhtfætes *lanterne*, ii. 52, 2. Man sceal habban . . . leóhtfæt, blácern, Angl. ix. 264, 21.

leóht-fǽtels, es; m. A *lamp, lantern*:—Leóhtfætels ł leóhtfæt *lucernam*, Ps. L. 17, 29.

leóhtian. *Add*: I. *to give light, shine*:—Þá sceán þǽr fǽringa leóht inn æt þám eástende . . . þá wæs hit swá leng swá leóhtre, swá lange hit leóhtode, Vis. Lfc. 54. II. *to grow light* (cf. leóht; II), *to dawn*:—In þá dagunge, þá þá hit ǽrest leóhtode *in ipso subsequentis lucis crepusculo*, Gr. D. 234, 21. Oð ðæt hit leóhtige *usquoque lucescat*, Angl. xiii. 398, 474.

leóht-leás. *Add*:—Hê hêt hí lǽdan tô leóhtleásum cwearterne, Hml. S. 29, 240: 35, 36.

leóht-lic *of little weight*. *Add*: , *of sin, venial*:—Durh ðám streáwa and ðám ceafe sind getácnode leóhtlice synna, Hml. Th. ii. 590, 14. Hû deóp seó bôc ys on gástlicum andgite, þeáh þe heó mid leóhtlicum wordum áwriten sig, Ælfc. Gen. Thw. 3, 22. [v. N. E. D. lightly; *adj.*]

leóhtlíce. *Add*: I. *without much pressure or force*:—Þweah leóht-

líce mid wylle wætre, Lch. ii. 308, 11. II. *to no great amount :—*
Wyl on ealað swíþe, geswét mid hunige leóhtlíce, Lch. ii. 62, 20. II a.
*to no great degree, slightly, not elaborately :—*Þeáh wé þás þing leóhtlíce
unwreón, hig magon fremian bet þonne þá þe beóð on leóðwísan fægre
geglenged *though our exposition of these matters be slight, they may do
more good than those that are prettily ornamented with versification,*
Angl. viii. 304. 2. III. *without being oppressive* or *harsh :—*Fæste
hé .VII. winter heardum fæstene oððe .xv. leóhtlícor.*VII. annos jejunet duro
jejunio, vel .XV. levius,* Ll. Th. ii. 146, 12. IV. *easily, with little
inconvenience :—*Sume nunnan tellað tó lytlum gylte þ hí hí forlicgon
and þ hí leóhtlíce magon swá lytel gebétan, Hml. A. 115, 431. V.
*of sleeping :—*Hé þá dyde swylce hé leóhtlíce slépe *ille ac si leviter
dormiens,* Gr. D. 85, 7.

**-leóhtness.** v. on-leóhtness: **leóht-sáwend.** v. sáwend: **leóht-
sceáwigend.** *Substitute : One who sees light.*

**leóma.** *Add :* I. *radiance, splendour :—*Leóma *iuvar,* Txts. 72, 554.
Seó sunne hæfð ðreó ágennyssa on hire ; óðer is se leóma oððe beorhtnys
æfre of ðære sunnan, seó ðe onlíht ealne middangeard, Hml. Th. i. 282,
9. Þonne se móna beó full, and his leóma ealne middaneard oferscíne,
Angl. viii. 323, 6. Glitenode gelícnys þære Crístes róde breohtre þonne
sunnan leóma, Hml. S. 30, 43. Úp ásprungum leóman *exorto (solis)
jubare,* i. *splendore,* An. Ox. 88. II. *a ray, portion of brilliant light.*
(1) *of the light of a heavenly body :—*Swá under ánum leóman þære
sunnan (ánum sunnan leóman, *v. l.*) *sub uno solis radio,* Gr. D. 171, 12.
Under ánum leóman (sunnan leóman, *v. l.*), 172, 22 : An. Ox. 2970.
Reáde leóman *roseos radios,* 18, 24. (2) *of other light, e.g. a tongue of*
flame :—Leóma, leúma *globus,* Txts. 66, 478. Leóman *radio* (angelus
limpidissimo lucis *radio* resplendens, Ald. 52, 2), An. Ox. 3772. Leómum
(*flammarum*) globis, 2813. Leóman (*clibani*) globos, 1658. [v. N. E. D.
leám.] v. dægred-, sunnan-leóma.

**-leómod.** v. ge-leómod: **león.** *Add :* p. leáh; pp. ligen. v. á-león.

**leóran.** *Add :* , leórian. I. *to pass from one place to another, pass
over or through (transivimus)* þurh fýr and wæter, Ps.
Vos. 65, 12. Þé gedafenaþ þ þú leóre on þíne bære *tu debes procidere
lectum,* Bl. H. 149, 17. On swá hwelcre stówe swá mín gemynd sý
mærsad . . . se unclæna ne leóre on ðá stówe, Shrn. 104, 28. II. *to
pass away at death, pass from this world to the next :—*Tódæg þú leórest
tó þære upplican eþelnesse, Shrn. 119, 29. Gehwylc man swylc hé
heonan leóreþ (leóraþ *v. l.*), swylc hé byð andweard in ðám dóme *qualis
hinc quisque egreditur, talis in judicio praesentatur,* Gr. D. 328, 4. Hé
tó Drihtne leórde (hleórde, *v. l.*), Hml. S. 23 b, 804. Heó of þám líchoman leórdon, Shrn. 64, 4. Leóran on ðá écean reste, 75, 1. Hé cýðde
hwylce sceoldou beón sweltende and leórian (lióran, *v. l.*) *of þám mynstre
innotuit qui et qui essent in brevi ex eadem cella morituri,* Gr. D. 298, 16.
Him wæs cúð þ hé sylfa and þá óþre mid eallre hwætnesse sceoldon beón
leóriende (leórende, *v. l.*) *of þisum lífe certum tenuit se et illos de hac
vita esse sub celeritate migraturos,* 299, 15. Hwylce men sceoldon beón
sweltende and leóriende (leórende, *v. l.*) *qui morituri sunt,* 300,
11. II a. *of things, to pass away, come to nothing :—*Word mín
næfre ne leóraþ *verba mea non praeteribunt,* Mt. R. 24, 35. v. á-, forþ-,
of-leóran.

**-leórendlic.** v. be-leórendlic.

**leórend-ness,** e ; *f. Passing away, departure* from this world :—
Manige men hí gesomnodon tó swá háligre sáwle leórendnesse of þysum
middanearde, Gr. D. 291, 14.

**leornend.** v. leornian.

**leornere.** *Add :* I. *a learner, scholar, pupil, disciple :—*Eálá gé wynsume leorneras (*discipuli*), eów manaþ eówer láreów, Coll. M. 35, 33.
Wæs se Hálga Gást áhafen ofer þá Godes leorneras, Bl. H. 135, 3. II.
*a reader, student :—*Lá, þú leornere o *Lector,* Guth. Gr. 101, 22 ; 102,
29. Ic wilnige ðætte ðeós spræc stigge on ðæt ingeðonc ðæs leorneres
(*lectoris*), Past. 23, 17. III. *a man of learning, a scholar :—*Scs
Augustinus tíd ðæs bisceopes and þæs æþelan leorneres, Shrn. 122, 23.
Hieronimos tíd þæs mæssepreóstes and þæs æðelan leorneres, 136, 23.
v. heáh-, stær-leornere.

**leór-ness.** *Add :* v. for-leórness.

**leornesse (?).** *Substitute :* leorn-ness (?), e ; *f. Learning :—*Hé monige
him tó discipulum genam, and þá æfter fæce tó sácerdháde þurh his
leornesse getýde and gelǽrde *multos suos discipulos fecit, atque ad sacerdotalem usque gradum erudiendo atque instituendo prouexit,* Bd. 3, 5 ;
Sch. 205, 13.

**leornian.** *Add :* I. *to acquire knowledge* of a subject, *skill* in an art,
&c., as a result of study, enquiry, experience or teaching. (1) with object :—Sélre mé wæs þæt þú mé gehnægdest, and ic syþþan þín sóðfæst
weorc leornade *bonum mihi quod humiliasti me, ut discam justificationes
tuas,* Ps. Th. 118, 71. Hú ne wást þæt þú leornodest on Ptolomeus
bócum ? *sicut Ptolomaeo probante didicisti,* Bt. 18, 1 ; F. 62, 6. Him
þæs Wedera þeóden wræce leornode (cf. Milton's 'study of revenge '),
B. 2336. Wé ǽ leornedon, El. 397. Hí leornedan láð weorc Gode
*didicerunt opera eorum,* Ps. Th. 105, 26. Hé wolde þæt þá cnihtas cræft
eornedon, Dan. 83. Leorna þás láre, Sch. 23 : Fä. 61. Leorniaþ wís-

dóm, and þonne gé hine geleornod hæbben, ne forhogiaþ hine þonne, Bt.
16, 1 ; F. 50, 25. Þæt hí leornigen ðone cræft geþylde on þám langan
geswince, 39, 11 ; F. 228, 25. Þisne cræft (bóccræft) leornian, Angl.
viii. 308, 26. Syndon þrý deáðas leornode on bócum, Verc. Först. 102,
15. Siofon heofonas sindon in gewritum leornode, Nap. 50. 2. (2) with
a clause :—Ic wolde þ þú leornodest hú þú mihtest becuman tó þám
sóþum gesǽlþum *superest, ut unde veram hanc beatitudinem petere possis
agnoscas,* Bt. 33, 3 ; F. 126, 29. Leorna þé seolfa and geþancmeta þíne
móde on hwilce healfe þú wille hwyrft dón, Gen. 1916. Leornigeað
(*discite*) hwæt is, ' Ic wylle mildheortnesse næs onsægdnesse,' Mt. 9, 13.
Ðá ongan hé smeágan and leornigan on him selfum hú hé þ ríce þám
cyninge áferran·mihte, Bt. 1 ; F. 2, 18. Þonne is leornod on bócum þæt
on þysse worulde sýn fíf onlícnessa þe helle gryre, Verc. Först. 106, 11 :
109, 4. (3) with infin. :—Sé þe nǽfre ne leornde specan *qui numquam didicit loqui,* Scint. 80, 17. I a. *to learn* a book, *read
with the intention of gaining knowledge :—*Hú ne sæde ic þé ǽr þæt þú
hyt scealt sécan on þære béc þe wit þá ymbspræcon ? Leorna þá bóc,
þonne findst þú hyt þær, Solil. H. 65, 8. Hé forbeád openlíce þæt mon
náne fæste bóc ne leornode *aperto praecepit edicto, ne quis Christianus docendorum liberalium studiorum professor esset,* Ors. 6, 31 ; S. 286, 4. II.
*intrans.* (1) *to acquire knowledge of a subject, to receive instruction,
study :—*Tó Lædensprǽce on þære ðe wé leorniað, Hml. S. 15, 110.
Forlét hé fæder and módor and on óðrum earde leornode, Hml. Th. ii.
334, 3. Hé hiene beménde . . . þære scóle þe hé on leornode, Ors. 6,
31 ; S. 284, 24. Húmeta cann þes stafas þonne hé ne leornode ?, Jn. 7,
15. Ðá þe firwetgeorne weorþaþ and onginnaþ leornian, Bt. 39, 3 ; F.
216, 5. (2) with prep. :—Wé leornodon be þám wælhreówan Bisi-
ridem . . . þæs leódhatan gewuna wæs þ . . . , Bt. 16, 2 ; F. 52,
29. II a. *to read :—*þý læs ic lenge þone þanc hefige þára leornendra (*legentium*), Guth. Gr. 102, 32. III. *to acquire knowledge*
of a fact, *hear* of something :—Wé leornodon þ hwílum gebyrede swíþe
ungecyndelic yfel, Bt. 31, 1 ; F. 112, 12. v. þurh-leornian.

**leornung.** *Add :* I. *the action of learning :—*Ðá ðe beóð gesette tó
ðære ðénunga ðæs láreówdómes ðæt hí nǽfre ne gewíten from ðære geornfulnesse ðære rǽdinge and leornunge háligra gewrita *ut qui ad officium
praedicationis excubant, a sacrae lectionis studio non recedant,* Past. 171,
21. Him bið ðearf ðæt hé hine genime simle be ðære leornunge háligra
gewrita, and be ðám áríse, *studere incessabiliter debet, ut per eruditionis
studium resurgat,* 169, 15. II. *the condition of a learner, pupilage :—*
Láreówdóm *vel* leornung *discipulatus,* Wrt. Voc. ii. 141, 10. III.
*what is learnt* or *taught :—*Sió fóstermódur ælcre leornunga and ælces
cræftes *mater omnium virtutum,* Past. 217, 1. v. for-leorning.

**leornung-hús.** *Add :—*Leorninghúses *gymnasii,* An. Ox. 3223. On
leorninghúse in *gymnasio,* Wrt. Voc. ii. 74, 55.

**leornung-mann.** *Add :—*Leornigmannes hús *gymnasium,* An. Ox.
2, 175. ¶ with reference to the teacher :—' Wénað wé hwæþer hé
ænigne láreów hæfde ?' ' Ne gehýrde ic nǽfre þ hé æniges mannes leor-
ningmann (*discipulus*) wǽre,' Gr. D. 12, 24. Ne mæg hé beón mín
leorningmau, Hml. S. 33, 114. Þæs láreówes hǽs and þæs leornincgmannes weorc, R. Ben. 20, 6. Þæra fíf bóca andgit geopenode se
Ælmihtiga Láreów his leorningmannum, Hml. Th. ii. 396, 12.

**leornung-scól,** e ; *f. A school for* (book-) *learning :—*Hé wæs þæs
mynstres láreów þe is genemned Flundis. In þæs leornungscóle drohtnigende and gelǽred wæs (*in discipulatu illius conversatus atque eruditus
est*) sum man, Gr. D. 14, 6.

**leóþ.** *Add :—*On tælsumum leóðe (smicere leóðe, Wrt. Voc. ii. 23, 24)
*carmine rythmico* i. *numerali,* Hpt. Gl. 415, 55. Sigarlic (þæt sigorlíce,
Wrt. Voc. ii. 23, 49) leóþ hé sinþ *carmen triumphale decantet,* An. Ox.
1347. Eác mé sceal áðreótan ymbe ealra þára Tróiána gewin tó ásecgenne, for ðon on spellum and on leóðum hiora gewin cúðe sindon (*certamina, quae in fabulis celebrari solita sunt*), Ors. 1, 8 ; S. 42, 14. [v.
N. E. D. leoth.] v. byrgels-, scop-, sealm-leóþ.

**leóþ-cræft.** *Add :—*An þára wæs Sibylla þe áwrát on leóðcræftes wíson
be Crístes ácennednesse, Hml. Th. ii. 18, 16.

**leóþere (?)** *a poet.* [*Goth.* liuþareis *a singer : O. H. Ger.* liudari
*bardus.*] v. hleóþrere (?).

**leóþ-gidding.** *Add :—*Hér mæg findan foreþances gleáw, sé ðe hine
lysteð leóðgiddunga, hwá þás fitte fégde, Hpt. 33, 72, 2.

**leóþian** *to sing.* Dele, *and see* liþian.

**leóþ-líc.** *Add :—*Hé mid leóðlicum metre be þám móndum þus giddode, Angl. viii. 301, 34.

**leóþ-sang.** *Add :—*Byriensang, leóþsang *epitaphion,* An. Ox. 902
(*where see note*).

**leóþubig-ness,** e ; *f. Supple bending of a joint :—*Hí þone líchaman
ealne ansundne, swá hé þágýt lifigende wǽre, and on liþobígnyssum
invenerunt corpus totum integrum, quasi adhuc viveret, et lentis artuum
flexibus,* Guth. Gr. 169, 147. v. bíg-ness.

**leóþu-cǽge ;** *f.* l. -cǽga ; *m.*

**leóþu-cræft.** For bracket *substitute (by nimble fingers),* B. 2769,
*and add :—*Mægencyning báncofan onband, breóstlocan onwand, leóðu-
cræft onleác, El. 1251.

**leóþu-cræft.** *Dele, and see preceding word.*

**leóþu-rún.** *Substitute* : leoþu-rún, e; *f.* ? :—Ic þé lǽre þurh leoðorúne þ ðú hospcwide ǽfre ne fremme wið Godes bearne, El. 522.

**leoþu-wác.** *For* leoþuwác *in middle of* l. 2 *l.* lioþuwác, *dele last passage, and add* :—Of liþewácum helmum *lentis frondibus*, An. Ox. 923. Liþewácum, tógum (tagum, Hpt. Gl. 514, 69) *lentis (viminibus caedentes*, Ald. 66, 29), 4693. Liþewácum *lentis (artuum flexibus*, Guth. Gr. 168, last line), 37, 8. v. in-liþewác.

**leoþuwácian.** v. ge-liþewácian.

**leoþu-wǽcan.** *Dele first passage (for which see* :—Sǽs geliþewǽcað brymmas *ponti mitescunt freta*, Hy. S. 6, 28), *and for last passage substitute* :—Leoþewǽcan *mitigare, pacificare*, An. Ox. 3802.

**leóþ-wís** (?); *adj. Poetical, rhythmical* :—*Celeuma, idem et toma,* i. *leta cantatio* lewis (leóþwís ?) plega *(for celeuma see* gladung), Wrt. Voc. ii. 130, 20.

**leóþ-wíse.** *Add* :—Þás þing magon freman bet þonne þá þe beóð on leóðwísan fǽgre geglenged, Angl. viii. 304, 3.

**leóþ-wrenc, es;** *m. A trick in a poem, a doubtful or spurious passage* (?) :—Dyple obolismene . . . byð oft on Uirgilius bócum and on his leóðwrencum gesette, Angl. viii. 334, 19.

**leów; pl.** (?). *Dele* ' (?)', *and bracket* : leów. v. mund-leów : leówe. *Add* : [On ríme þæs læssan mílgetæles þe *stadia* hátte fíf hund and þæs miclan mílgetæles þe *leuua* hátte þreó hund and eahta and syxtig, Nar. 33, 9-11 : 19 : 23.]

**lesan.** *Add* :—Ic lese *lego*, Wrt. Voc. ii. 49, 66. Lisit *legit, collegit,* Txts. 73, 1200. Uton helpan þám raðost þe helpes betst behófað, þonne lese (nime, *v. l.*) wé þæs leán *(metemus inde mercedem nostram, accipiemus inde premium*, old Latin versions) þær ûs leófast bið, Ll. Th. i. 412, 3.

**lesca** *the groin* :—Lesca *inguen*, Txts. 110, 1181 : Hpt. 33, 244, 1. [v. *N. E. D.* lisk.]

**lesu; f.** *Dele* : lesung. v. stán-lesung : letanîa. *Add* :—Wé sungon seofon seolmas mid letanîan *(letaniis*), Coll. M. 33, 29 : leþer. *Add* : spor-leþer : leþeren. *Add* :—Liþrine trymsas *asses scorteas*, Txts. 43, 226.

**leþer-hose** (-hosu ?). *l.* leþer-hosu, *and add* :—Leþerhosa *ocreae uel tibiales*, Wülck. Gl. 125, 31. v. hosu.

**lettan.** *Add* : (1) *to hinder* a person, thing, action, &c. :—Ne leteð *non tricaverit* (si lethi somnus palpebrarum convolatus *non tricaverit*, Ald. 80, 20), Wrt. Voc. ii. 88, 36. Let, An. Ox. 8 b, 6. (2) the action from which one is hindered given in genitive :—Wé þe þæs nû nellað lettan þæs þû ǽr geþóht hæfdest *propositi tui orthonomias dirumpere nolumus*, Guth. Gr. 123, 20.

**letting.** *Add* : [*In the passages from* Lch. iii. letting *glosses* impeditio] : (1) *hindering, hinderance, impediment* :—Hí ealle þyder inn onfangene wǽron bútan ǽlcere lettinge, þæt wæs ic âna ût âsceofen, Hml. S. 23 b, 414. Lǽttinge, 407. Hé lettincge (*impedimentum*) gegearwað ôðrum, Scint. 180, 17 : R. Ben. I. 87, 10. (2) *delay* :—Se arð þá bútan ǽlcre lettinge férde anân tó ðám cinge, Chr. 995 ; P. 130, 14. Lettincga *morarum*, An. Ox. 1671.

**léw, léwsa.** v. lǽw, lǽwsa : lewis. v. leóþ-wís.

**libban.** *Take here* lifian *in Dict., and add* : I. *to be alive, have life* :—Þú eart swíþe geséelig nû þú gít liofost and eart hál. Hwæt, þæt is sió mǽste âr deáðlicra manna þæt hié libban and sién hále, Bt. 10 ; F. 28, 24–27. Ic wât þæt nán swâ gód man ne leofað swâ hé is, Ors. 5, 12 ; S. 242, 33. Wé þe lybbað (lifgeað, Ps. Vos., lifgað, Ps. Srt.) *nos qui vivimus*, Ps. Rdr. 113, 18. Seó orþung . . . is seó lyft þe wé on libbað . . . swâ swâ fixas cwelað gyf hí of wætere beóð, swâ eác cwelð ǽlc eorðlic líchama gif hé byð ðǽre lyfte bedǽled, Lch. iii. 22–27. Heora nâ mâ ne lifde, Ors. 3, 11 ; S. 152, 15. Ælces libbendes monnes môd, Bt. 31, 2 ; F. 112, 25. I a. *to remain alive* after risk of death, *be saved from death* :—Hé sceal fleón . . . and libbe, Past. 167, 3. Ðæt hé fleó tó ðára burga ânre, ðæt hé on sumre ðára weorðe genered, ðæt hé móte libban, 166, 18. Hió is ân lytel and ðeáh ic mæg ðǽron libban *modica est, et vivet anima mea in ea*, 399, 24. Tó tácne þæt hié ôþer woldon, oþþe ealle libban oþþe ealle licgan, Ors. 3, 10; S. 138, 32. I b. fig. of things :—Gif wé ne gebétað ðæt on ûs deádbǽres is þurh synna, ðonne ácwild ðæt ðætte on ûs ǽr lifde ðurh gód weorc, Past. 445, 25. II. *to supply oneself with food, feed, subsist* (lit. or fig.) :—Þá gástlican láre . . . þe ûre sául big leofað and féded bið, Bl. H. 57, 9. Þ yrfe þe wé big leofiaþ, 51, 18. Sume hí leofodon be ofete and wyrtum, Hml. Th. i. 546, 4. III. *to procure oneself the means of subsistence* :—Hí be heora âgenum handgewinne lifigeað (lifiað, *v. l.*) *proprio labore manuum vivunt*, Bd. 4, 4; Sch. 371, 7. Þás eorþan þe ealle cwice wyhta bí libbað *terra haec in qua vivimus*, Ors. 2, 1 ; S. 58, 20. Sume leofodon be âgenum geswince, Hml. Th. i. 546, 4. Ðá beóð bútan ierre ðe be hiera giefum libban sculon *sine offensione perdurant qui ex aliena dispensatione subsistunt*, Past. 321, 5. IV. *to pass life* in a specified fashion, indicated by an adv., adverbial phrase, or adj. or complementary subst. (1) with regard to conduct :—Sé þe ungereclíce liofaþ, Bt. 36, 6 ; F. 182, 21 : Past. 61, 7. Ðá gelǽredan ðe swâ nyllað libban swâ hié on bócum leornedon . . . hié on ôðre wísan libbað, on ôðre hí lǽrað, 29, 18–25. Hié on wôh libbað, 109, 21. Hé wel libbe, 193,

22. Wille ic þ þá Godes þeówas . . . libban clǽnan lífe, Ll. Th. ii. 272, 16. Ic wilnode weorþfullíce tó libbanne, Bt. 17 ; F. 60, 15. Tó libbenne (-anne, *v. l.*), Past. 61, 19. (2) with regard to personal conditions. (a) with adv. or adv. phrase :—Þá þe sôftor libbaþ, Bt. 39, 10 ; F. 288, 17. An hwelcum brocum þá lifdon þe ǽr him wǽron, Ors. 3, 9 ; S. 136, 20. (b) with adj. or compl. sbst. :—Þ tácen þ hé cwaciende and geómeriende and woriende and útlaga leofode symle ofer eorþan *ipsum signum quod tremens et gemens vagus et profugus semper viveret*, Angl. vii. 32, 308. (3) with regard to the rule or principle, or to the object and purpose of one's life :—Ælc ídel mon liofað æfter his âgnum dôme, Past. 283, 21. Hí libbað ôðrum monnum, and cwelað him selfum, 449, 19. Wé ûres fíæsces lustum ne libben, 43, 11. Ðæt hié scylen be hira rǽdum libban, 319, 22. V. with cognate object :—Lifde hé his líf on micelre eáðmôdnesse *duxit uitam in magna humilitatis perfectione*, Bd. 3, 27 ; Sch. 322, 3. Diácon þe regollíf libbe, Ll. Th. i. 344, 21. VI. *to continue in life, be alive for a longer or shorter time, have one's life prolonged* :—Ðá hwíle þe hí libbaþ, Bt. 37, 3 ; F. 192, 7. Hé leofode swâ lange þ man his cynn nyste, Angl. vii. 44, 417. Hié twégen þe þǽr lengest lifdon, Ors. 3, 11 ; S. 152, 23. Gif Eádwald leng lifige ðonne Cynedrýd, C. D. i. 296, 6. Embe twelf mônaþ sé þe lifge, hé betre sý þonne hé nú is, Bl. H. 131, 5. Gif hé môste þá gýt twá geár libban *if he could have lived two years more*, Chr. 1086 ; P. 220, 27. VI a. said of Deity and spirits :—Ðǽr Drihten leofaþ â bûton ende on écnesse, Bl. H. 83, 3. Sé þe leofað on écnesse gesceóp ealle ðing, Angl. vii. 10, 96. Beón gehiérsume ðǽm ðe ûre gǽsta Fæder bið wið ðǽm ðæt wé môten libban on écnesse, Past. 255, 9. Hú ne witon wé þ ealle men líchomlíce sweltaþ, and þeáh seó sáwl bið libbende, Bt. 18, 4 ; F. 68, 13. ¶ of man before the fall :—Tó þon þ wǽre geswutelad þ ealle men mihton ǽfre bútan deáþe lybban, gif nán man ne syngade, Angl. vii. 10, 86. VII. *to continue in the memory of men* :—þæt lifigende *vivacem* (Ceciliae *vivacem* condere laudem, Ald. 182, 24), Wrt. Voc. ii. 94, 45. VIII. *to make one's abode, reside* :—Þám cynnum Scotta and Pehta, on þám hé on ellþeódignesse lifde (*in quibus exulabat*), Bd. 3, 27 ; Sch. 322, 11. v. mis-, ofer-libban ; un-, wel-, yfel-libbende.

**líc.** *Add* : I. *the living body of a man or animal* :—Hí wǽron mid olfendes hǽrum tó líce gescrýdde, Hml. Th. ii. 506, 23 : Hml. S. 31, 333. Hí mid hǽran hí gescrýddon tó líce, 12, 36. Ðý læs hié mid ðý tôle ðæt hále líc gewierden, Past. 365, 11. Hine lyst bet þaccian and cyssan ðone ôðerne on bær líc, Solil. H. 42, 4. Þá men forbrédan and weorpan hí an wildedeóra líc, Bt. 38, 1 ; F. 194, 31. I a. *the body* in contrast with the soul or vital principle of which it is the seat :—Sáwel mid líce, Ph. 525. Seó eádge sáwl hió wið þám líce gedǽled, Cri. 1668. Gedǽlan líf wið líce, B. 2423 : Ap. 83. Of líce aldor onsendan, Gen. 2789. Ânra gehwylc hafað ætgædre bû líc and sáwle, Cri. 1037. I b. *the corporeal or material nature or state of man, the material body and its properties, the flesh.* (1) of kinship :—Þú sægdest þæt Sarra þín sweostor wǽre, líces mǽge (*kinswoman according to the flesh*), Gen. 2789. (2) of sins of the sense :—Fyrene gestǽlan, líces leahtor, Gú. 1045. II. *a dead body* :—Gewát seó sáwul of ðám líchamon tó Gode . . . His líc wearð gesewen sôna on wuldre, beorhtre ðonne glæs, Hml. Th. ii. 518, 10. Open wæs þæt eorðærn, æðelinges líc onféng feóres gǽst, Hö. 19. Mín líc scyle on moldærn molsnad weorðan, Ph. 563. Wacodon menn swâ swâ hit gewunelic is ofer ân deád líc, Hml. S. 21, 290. Gif man ǽnig líc of rihtcryftscíre elles hwǽr lecge, Ll. Th. i. 368, 7. III. *the trunk* in contrast with the limbs :—Siððan líc and leomu and þes lífes gǽst âsundrien somwist hyra þurh feorhgedál, Gú. 1149. Leomu líc somod and lífes gǽst, Ph. 513. [v. *N. E. D.* lich.]

**líc; adj.** *Like* :—Ân þæra feówer nýtena wæs gesewen swilce mannes ansýn, þ ôðer wæs líc (gelíc, *v. l.*) ânre león híwe, Hml. S. 15, 182. [þ líce getæl, Angl. viii. 318, 24 *here* lice *seems an error for* ilce.] v. ge-, on- (an-), swâ-(?)líc.

**-líc.** *In the suffix the vowel seems early to have been shortened, though the long i was at any rate occasionally preserved*, e. g. Swâ swâ him þincæ þæt mǽ for Godæ þearflíicustþ sí, Cht. Th. 554, 36.

**líc-burg, e; f.** *A city of the dead, a cemetery* :—Lícburg *cimiterium*, Txts. 51, 472.

**licceras.** v. ôleccere.

**liccian.** *Add* : I. *to pass the tongue over* a surface :—Seó leó his fôtlástas liccode, Hml. S. 23 b, 773. Ðá men þá írengelôman liccodan *milites ferramenta lambendo*, Nar. 9, 19. Þá hundas liccedan (*lingebant*) his wunda, Gr. D. 310, 6. Se bera ongan liccian (*lambere*) þær biscopes fét, 195, 4. I a. *to lick the dust, suffer defeat* :—Feónd his eorðan liciað *inimici ejus terram lingent*, Ps. Srt. 71, 9. II. *to lick up* a fluid, *lap* :—Hundas liccað eówre blôd and fugelas fretað incer flǽsc, Shrn. 148, 2. His blôd ðá fleów binnon ðám cræte, þæt liccodon (*linxerunt*) hundas, Hml. S. 18, 226. Swâ swâ hundas lapodon Naboðes blôd, swâ hí sceolon lapian and liccian þín blôd *in loco hoc, in quo linxerunt canes sanguinem Naboth, lambent sanguinem tuam*, 210. Liccigan *linxere* (v. Ald. 207, 23), Wrt. Voc. ii. 96, 75. II a. of an inanimate agent, Lch. iii. 276, 12 (*in Dict.*).

-lîce, es; *n.* v. self-lîce: -lîce; *adj.* v. self-lîce: -lîce; *adv. Add:* v. on-, swā-lîce.

**licettan.** *Add:* I. absolute. (1) *to dissemble, pretend, be hypocritical:*—Swā bioð ðā ðe hira gōd eówiað beforum monnum and hira yfel helað oninnan him selfum: hi līcettað, and woldon līcian for manna eágum ūtane būton gōdum weorcum innane *vitiorum mala intus contegunt, humanis vero oculis quorumdam demonstratione operum de solo foris justitiae colore blandiuntur,* Past. 449, 10. Cōm Nathan tō cīdanne Dāuide, and līcette, suelce hē ymb sumes ðearfan ryht sprǣce, 185, 18. (1 a) of speech:—Mid þȳ hē geswiperum mūðe līcetende ǣrende wrehte *cum simulatam legationem ore astuto uolueret,* Bd. 2, 9; Sch. 146, 25. (2) *to carry favour* with (?):—Hē him sǣde þ hē ofslōge Saul, and wolde mid þǣre leásunge līcettan wið Dāuid, Hml. S. 12, 250. II. *to feign* something. (1) with acc., *to present a false appearance* of a quality, property, &c., *feign* humility, &c. :—Hē līcet mildheortnesse ðǣr ðǣr nān ne bið, Past. 220. 23. Tō ðǣm mōde ðe innan bið gnornigende and ūtan līcet geðyld *menti interius dolenti, et sanctam se exterius per patientiam demonstranti,* 225, 11. Se gōda cræft ðe hē ðǣr līcette *virtus ostensa,* 222, 3. Swelce hē līcette eáðmētto, and doo ðeáh for gilpe, 51, 3. (2) with acc. and complementary adj. :—Hī līcettað hié unscyldge *they present an appearance of innocence;* se hominibus, quod iniqui sunt, tegunt, Past. 439, 20. (3) with a clause, *to give to understand* what is not the case, *to pretend* that :—Mid þǣre hīwunga ðe hió līcet þ hió sié gōd, Bt. 20; F. 72, 1. Hié līcettað ðæt hié ðæt dōn ðurh eáðmōdnesse, Past. 302, 8 ; 9: 427, 17. Hē līcette þ hē ūþwita wǣre, Bt. 18, 4; F. 68, 1: Met. 26, 36: Past. 121, 17. (3 a) *not to refrain from showing* what is the case, *to profess* that :—Hit is micel sceand gif wē nyllað līcittan (-ettan, *v. l.*) ðæt wē sién ðæt wē sindon *nimis turpe est non imitari, quod sumus,* Past. 233, 11. (4) with dat. :—Hē līcett (līcet, *v. l.*) wið hié mā gefērrǣdenne ðonne ealdordōme, Past. 121, 22. III. *to produce an unreal appearance :*—Hīwunge hīwedan, līcettan *scenam scematizarunt,* An. Ox. 4061. IV. *to pretend, bring a false charge :*—Līccitan *insimulare,* An. Ox. 2944. IV a. *to make a false claim :*—Hī līcettaþ þ hī gelǣstan magon *they pretend to be able do what they cannot,* Bt. 26, 1; F. 90, 16.

**līcettere.** *Add:*—Lēcetere *simulator,* Kent. Gl. 353.

**līcettung.** *Add:*—Līcetunga *commenta* (cf. commenta, i. machinationes, ficta, Wrt. Voc. ii. 132, 39), Germ. 399, 268.

**līc-fæt.** *Add:*—L[ic]f[æt] beofað, seomað sorgcearig, Jul. 708. [*The* l *and* f *are given by the runic characters.*]

**licgan.** *Add:* I. of persons or animals. (1) *to be in a prostrate or recumbent position :*—Godes þeówa lið æt þīnum gatum, Hml. S. 31, 1153. Dā læg se king and āsweartode eall, C. D. iv. 57, 13. Se wītega læg and slēp, Hml. Th. i. 246, 2. Læg sum wædla æt his geate, 328, 13. Þā se Hǣlend geseah þysne licgean (licgende, L., licende, R.) *hunc cum uidisset Iesus iacentem,* Jn. 5, 6. Anlīcost swīnum þe simle willað licgan on fūlum solum, Bt. 37, 4; F. 192, 26. Hī gesāwon on nǣshleoðum nicras licgean, B. 1427. Ænne laman on bedde licgende (liccende, L., licende, R.), Mt. 9, 2: Mk. 7, 30. (1 a) with predicative complement expressing condition, *to lie sick, dead, &c. :*—Mīn ealdor ligeð forheáwen, By. 222. Manige licgaþ deáde, Bt. 19; F. 70, 13. Wæs se king binnan Oxanaforde swȳþe geseócled, swā þ hē læg orwēnæ his līfes, C. D. iv. 57, 4. Hē læg linnacod, Gen. 1566. Hē læg wīne druncen, 2634. Hī lǣgon āswefede, B. 566. Lāgan, An. 1085. Lāgon, Jud. 30. Þā þe on sāre seóce lāgun, Cri. 1356. Suelce hié ǣr lǣgen on longre medtrymnesse, Past. 229, 2. Hē on ræste geseah Grendel licgan aldorleásne, B. 1586. Hē smyrode ān licgende mǣden on langsumum sāre, Hml. Th. ii. 150, 5. (2) *to lie sick or injured, keep one's bed :*—Ðēr wæs ðæt mǣgden licgende (licende, L.), Mk. R. 5, 40. Bide þone Hǣlend þ hē līf forgife þysum licgendum cnihte (cf. hī wēndon þ se cniht þǣrrihte sceolde sweltan, 326), Hml. S. 21, 333. Geseah hē his swegre licgende and hriðgende, Mt. 8, 14. (3) expressing the posture of a dead body :—Se līchoma inne læg þæs deádan mannes, Bl. H. 219, 15. Hē nolde fleógan ... þā his betera læg, By. 275–279. (3 a) *to lie in the grave :*—Æt Æðeldrȳðe byrgene ... de ðǣr gehāl lið oð ðis on eallhwītre ðrȳh of marmstāne geworht *Æðeldrydae ... quae incorruptibili corpore hactenus condita mausoleo marmoreo albo perdurat,* C. D. iii. 60, 20. Gif hē fūl beó, licge þǣr hē læg, Ll. Th. i. 296, 10. Eorðe āgeaf, þā hyre on lāgun, eft lifgende, Cri. 1156. (3 b) without direct reference to posture or place, *to be dead :*—His æferan eád bryttedon ... þā hyra hláford læg, Dan. 675. Hit wæs Godes gifu þæt ealle þā lāgon þe hit dōn sceoldon, Ors. 5, 2 ; S. 218, 7. (4) *to be in one's bed or sleeping place for the purpose of sleeping or resting :*—Se engel him gramlīce tō cwæð, 'Līst ðū and rest þē, and Godes þeówa liþ æt þīnum gatum,' Hml. S. 31, 1152. Tō his bedde þe hē an lið, Ps. Th. 40, 3. Ic læg on heardum stāne licgende in crybbe, Cri. 1425. Þ cild þe læg on cradele, Ll. Th. i. 418, 25. Wæs his ræst ... on nacodre eorðan ... cwæð hē: 'Ne gedafenað Crīstenan men þ hē elles dō būtan swā hē efne on axan and on dūste licge,' Bl. H. 227, 15. Heó cwæð þ Eugenia eóde tō hyre licgendre and hī wolde forlycgan, Hml. S. 2, 185. Hana þā licgenda[n] āwecð, Hy. S.

6, 36. (5) of sexual intercourse, *to lie* with a person :—Ne lige þū dearnenga *non moechaberis,* Ll. Th. i. 44, 18. Ne lig dernunga *non adulterabis,* Mt. L. 19, 18. Gif hē mid gehǣme ... Gif ōðer mon mid hire lǣge ǣr, Ll. Th. i. 68, 17. II. *to assume a recumbent or prostrate position,* of a wounded or slain person, *to fall :*—Hē tō þām ylpe cōm, and stang hine æt ðām nauelan þ hī lāgon ðǣr bēgen, Hml. S. 25, 586. III. *to be or remain in a specified position of subjection, misery, captivity, sin,* &c. :—þū his sorge ne þearft beran, þǣr þū gebunden ligst, Gen. 734. Þǣr hē ligeð in carcerne clommum gefæstnad, Cri. 734: Sal. 265. Hē liþ on his līchaman lustum *foedis libidinibus immergitur,* Bt. 37, 4; F. 192, 25. Đā ðe on ðǣre synne ealnuweg licgað (-ead, *v. l.*), Past. 179, 3. Hē hiene hēt on carcern bescūfan, and hē þǣr læg oþ hē his līf forlēt, Ors. 5, 4; S. 224, 16. Lāgon þā ōðre fȳnd on þām fȳre, Gen. 322. Đeáh hē ðonne giét on ðæs flǣsces lustfulnesse licge, Past. 395, 6. Hié sculon for ðȳ ofdrǣdde licgean āstreahte ōðrum monnum underðiódde, 109, 23. Sceal þeós menego licgan on leahtrum, Sat. 263. III a. *to lie under, be subject to* disadvantage or obligation :—Ðonne hē suā suīðe ōðre oferhlifað ðætte ealle licggeað under his willan, Past. 111, 2. Đætte hié ongieten under hū micelre frēcenesse hié liecgað (licggeað, *v. l.*), 233, 24. IV. *to remain in a state of inactivity or concealment :*—Seldum ǣfre his leomu licgað *his limbs are hardly ever still,* Sal. 270. Ne meahton wē gelǣran leófne þeóden rǣd ǣnigne, þæt hē ne grētte goldweard þone, lēte hyne licgean, B. 3082. Licgende heó gespæc deór *latitantem alloquitur bestiam,* An. Ox. 4898. V. *to dwell, sojourn, lodge temporarily :*—Hē liþ him on londe, Gn. Ex. 100. Hē sceal licgan of Martinus mæssan oð Eástran æt hlāfordes falde swā oft swā him tō begǣð, Ll. Th. i. 434, 12. VI. of material things. (1) *to be at rest on the ground or other surface :*—On eorðlicere cyrcan lið stān ofer stāne, Hml. Th. ii. 582, 17. On meoxes gelīcnysse þe lið under fōtum, Hml. S. 8, 38. Licgað æfter lande loccas tōdrifene, An. 1428. Hit on eorðan læg on twām styccum, Cri. 1138: B. 1532. Discas lāgon and dȳre swyrd ... swā hié wið eorðan fæðm þūsend wintra þǣr eardodon, 3048. Hē geseah þā līnwǣda licgan *uidet posita linteamenta,* Ju. 20, 5. Licgende beám lǣsest grōweð, Gn. Ex. 159. (1 a) of things that rest on the body :—Licgað mē ymbe īrenbendas, Gen. 371 : 382. Him on eaxle læg breóstnet, B. 1547. (2) *to be deposited, remain in a specified place :*—Ligeð him behindan hefig hrūsan dǣl, Met. 29, 52. Sum heó hire on handum bær, sum hire æt heortan læg, Gen. 636. Genim þās wyrte ... lege tō þǣre wunde ... ac ne geþafa þ heó lengc þǣr æt licge þonne hyt þearf sȳ, Lch. i. 100, 5. (3) *not to move;* licgende feoh *other property than cattle, treasure :*—þā (the senators) wǣron binnan Rōmebyrg wuniende tō þon þæt hié bewisten eal þ licgende feoh under ānum hrōfe þæt hié begeáton oþþe on gafole oþþe on hergiunga, Ors. 2, 4; S. 72, 4. þēh þe hié swīðe gebrocode wǣren on heora licgendan feó *cum pudenda penuria esset aerarii,* 4, 10; S. 196, 18. (4) *to remain* unused, unproductive, &c. :—Eall þ his (the earth) fennas and mōras genumen habbað, and eall þ on ealdum ðeódum wēstes ligeþ, Bt. 18, 1; F. 62, 15. þȳ lǣs se hwǣte cīpa leás licge on þām lande, Met. 12, 6. (5) of the wind, the tongue, *to be still, be at rest :*—Đonne wind ligeð *tum ventos claudit Aeolus antris,* Ph. 182. Đeáh sió tunge eáðmōdlīce licge, ðæt mōd bið suīðe ūpāhafen *linguam premit, mentem elevat,* Past. 271, 24. (6) *to be situated, have a position :*—Ān īgland ligð ūt on gārsecg, Met. 16, 12. On ðām endum ðe tō etenlǣse licgan, Ll. Th. i. 440, 13. Gif ōðres mynstres ār on ōðres mynstres rȳmette lēge, C. D. iii. 128, 24. (6 a) of a road, way, stream, &c., *to have a specified direction :*—þone weg þe lið tō līfes treówe *viam ligni vitae,* Angl. vii. 30, 287. Ligð, Met. 20, 279. On þæt crundel þǣr se haga ūt ligeþ, Cht. E. 294, 23. Swā swā æddran licgeað on ðæs mannes līchaman, swā licgaþ þās wæterǣddran geond ðās eorðan, Lch. iii. 254, 23. VII. fig. of immaterial things, *to exist, reside* in some specified place or quarter, *be placed in certain conditions :*—Se wīsdōm and eác ōþre cræftas licgaþ forsewene, Bt. 36, 1; F. 172, 11. Wīsna fela þe ǣr under hoðman biholen lǣgon, Cri. 45. Licge se ealdordōm on unfriðe, Ll. Th. i. 286, 34. VII a. of thoughts, inclinations, &c., *to have a specified direction or object :*—Đā ingeðoncas ðe ǣfre willað licgean on ðǣm eorðlicum gewilnungum *cogitationes quae a terrenis desideriis numquam levantur,* Past. 155, 22. VIII. *to appertain* to. v. III. *in Dict.* v. of-, under-, wiþ-, ymb-licgan.

**-licgend.** v. for-licgend.

**līc-hama.** *Add:*—Līchama *soma,* Wrt. Voc. i. 49, 23. I. *the material frame of man.* (1) living :—On healfslāpendum līchaman, nā eallinga swylce on swefne, Vis. Lfc. 3. Þȳ lǣs heó þone hālan līchoman fornime, Lch. i. 100, 6. Hié heora līchoman leáfum beþeahton, Gen. 845. (2) dead :—His līchama (corpus) ne mihte on þām ylcan dæge beón bebyrged, for þām þe hē wæs feorr tō berenne, Gr. D. 83, 31. þæt his līchoma legerbedde þæst swefeþ, B. 1007. Mē is leófre þæt mīnne līchaman mid mīnne goldgyfan glēd fæðmie, 2651. Þǣr þā līchoman lange þrāge, heáhfædera hrā, beheled wǣron, An. 791. Nelle wē þ mon þā līchoman þe ǣr on cyrcean bebyrgde wǣron ūt weorpe, Ll. Th. ii. 408, 9. Twēgen līchaman, twā līc *gemina (defunctorum) cadauera,* An. Ox. 1870: Ph. 489. I a. *the trunk* as opposed to the limbs :—Hē leomum onfēng and līchoman,

Cri. 628. **I b.** *the body in contrast with the soul* :—Ic forlēt of mīnum līchoman lifgendne gǣst, Cri. 1454. God ūs gesceóp on sāwle and on līchaman, Hml. A. 11, 289. **I c.** *the material body with its properties, corporeal nature* :—Swyltendes līchaman gewǣht tīdder[nes] *moribundæ carnis fessa fragilitas*, An. Ox. 1275. For līcuman (līchoman, *v. l.*) tiédernesse, Past. 61, 10. Hē on līchaman lengest worulddreáma breác, Gen. 1219. Enoch heonon on līchoman lisse sōhte . . . , nales deáðe swealt, 1204. Hyra waldend fōr of līchoman, Cri. 1187 : B. 3178. **II.** *used in reference to the eucharistic elements* :—Ic ofþyrsted wæs līchoman, gāstes drynces, Seel. 41. **III.** *used of a plant* :—Wið gewitleáste, genim of þām līchoman þysse wyrte mandragore þreóra penega gewihte, Lch. i. 248, 4.

**līcham-leás.** *Add* :—Ðā englas hē geworhte . . . ealle līchamleáse lybbende on gāste, Hex. 6, 27.

**līcham-lic.** *Add* : **I.** *bodily, corporeal, physical* or *material as opposed to spiritual or immaterial* :—Nān līchamlic gesceaft nǣfð nāne sāwle būton se man āna, Hml. A. 12, 294. Ic eom þurh mīne gecynd līchamlic man and þū eart ēce God, 156, 123. Līchamlicere geþeódnesse *carnalis copulæ*, An. Ox. 1604. Līcamlices cweartenes *carnalis ergastuli*, 2552. Hē līchamlicne deáð geðrowade, Hml. A. 152, 31. Hē þurh his līchamlice þrowunge ūs generede, 154, 58. **II.** *of appetites, desires*, &c., *carnal as opposed to spiritual* :—Līchamlicere unālēfednesse *corporalis inlecebre*, Wrt. Voc. ii. 135, 83. Līcamlicere gǣlse *carnalis luxus*, An. Ox. 610. Līchamlicere, 1723.

**līchamlīce.** *Add* : **I.** *physically* :—Þe lǣs hig þone deáð on heora sāwle þolian, ðe hig līchamlīce (līcumlīce, *v. l. in corpore*) ðoledon, R. Ben. 94, 14. Ealle men līchomlīce sweltaþ, and þeáh seó sāwl bið libbende, Bt. 18, 4 ; F. 68, 13. Maria ācende Críst līchamlīce, Hml. A. 30, 163. Maria is his mōdor līchamlīce and gāstlīce his swustor, 33, 219. His micelnesse ne mæg nān monn āmetan ; nis þ nō līchomlīce (līcum-, *v. l.*) tō wēnanne, ac gāstlīce, Bt. 42 ; F. 258, 13. **II.** *carnally, having no regard to spiritual interests* :—Þā lufedon hī hyre māgas līchamlīce (*carnaliter*) . . . and ne hogodon nā þeáh hī eallunga hyre sāwle ādwǣscton, Gr. D. 73, 12–19.

**līcian.** *Add* : **I.** *to please.* (1) *with person or thing as subject.* (a) *absolute* :—On ǣlcum lande ne līcað þ on ōþrum līcaþ, Bt. 18, 2 ; F. 64, 26. Hē wilnað ungemetlīce līcigean (līcian, *v. l.*), Past. 143, 6. Hī woldon līcian for manna eágum, 449, 10. (b) *with dat. of person pleased* :—Ic Gode līcie swýðor þonne æðele cealf *placebit Deo super vitulum novellum*, Ps. Th. 68, 32. Hū eów līcaþ (*placet*) þeós spǣc?, Coll. M. 32, 7. Þæt ic gearewe Gode līcode *ut placeam coram Deo*, Ps. Th. 55, 11. Hwî ne sceolde mē līcian fæger land?, Bt. 14, 1 ; F. 40, 17. Sió wilnung ðæt hē scyle monnum līcigean (līcian, *v. l.*) *cupido placendi hominibus*, Past. 141, 14. Hē wilnað Gode tō līciganne (līcianne, *v. l.*), 371, 21. (b a) *with wel*, (i) *to be* (*well*) *pleasing* :—Wel heó līcað ūs, Coll. M. 32, 9. Hē þīn mōdsefa līcað leng swā wel, B. 1854. Ðām wîfe þā word wel līcodon, 639. Gif hē wilnað ðæt hē hire līcige bet ðonne sē ðe hine sende, Past. 143, 4. (ii) *to be sufficient* :—Wel līcas ðǣm dæg werignise his *sufficit diei malitia sua*, Mt. L. 6, 34. (2) *impersonal, with dat. of person* :—Ne þē on þīnum selegescotum swīðe līcað *neque in tabernaculis viri beneplacitum erit ei*, Ps. Th. 146, 11. On ðee līcað mē *in te complacui mihi*, Lk. L. R. 3, 22. ʻGif eów swā līcige . . .ʼ Hit him līcode, Bl. H. 241, 20–24. Hié cwēdon þ hit þ līcode eallum tō healdenne *dixerunt omnes* : ʻ*Placet ea custodire*,ʼ Ll. Th. i. 58, 29. Līcige þē . . . þæt þū mē ārige *complaceat tibi, ut erip[i]as me*, Ps. Th. 39, 15. Uton healdan þ frið swā hit ūrum hlāforde līcige, Ll. Th. i. 238, 25. Hū wolde þē nū līcian gif hwylc swīþe rīce cyning wǣre . . . , Bt. 41, 2 ; F. 244, 24. (2 a) *with wel.* (i) *to be* (*well*) *pleasing* :—In ðǣm wel līcade sāwle mīne *in quo bene complacuit animae meae*, Mt. L. 12, 18. Ūs māra hearm tō fundode þonne ūs wel līcode, Cht. E. 230, 2. (ii) *to be sufficient* :—Wel līcas *sufficit*, Mk. L. 14, 41. **II.** *to take pleasure in* :—On þē ic wel līcade *in te complacui*, Mk. R. L. 1, 11. v. of-līcian.

**līc-leóþ.** *Add* :—Līcleóð *epicedion*, Wrt. Voc. ii. 76, 77 : *carmen funebre*, Hpt. Gl. 427, 62 : *epitaphion, carmen super tumulum* ł *mortuorum*, 70.

**līc-lic** ; *adj. Belonging to a funeral* :—Līclicum wordum *uerbis exequialibus*, Germ. 401, 51.

**līc-lic** ; *adj. Likely, apparently suitable* for a purpose :—Īdele word oðde hlehtre oðde gamene lī(c)lic *verba vana aut risui apta*, R. Ben. I. 21, 11. v. ge-līclic.

**līc-mann.** *Add* :—Gewāt se Gād of worulde tō helle. Man heóld þā þ līc on þā hēðenan wīsan . . . þā on þone feórðan dæg fǣrlīce on mergen ārās se ylce Gād ārǣred þurh God, and þā līcmen wurdon wundorlīce āfyrhte, Hml. S. 36, 130.

**-līcness.** *Add* : an-(on-)līcness.

**līc-rest.** *Add* : **I.** *a vehicle or bier in which a corpse is borne* :—Man slōh án geteld ofer þā hālgan bān binnan þǣre līcreste (cf. tentorio maiore supra *carrum* in quo reliquiae (*þā bán*) inerant extenso, Bd. 3, 11), Hml. S. 26, 181. **II.** *a grave, tomb, sepulchre* :—Hē wilnode þ his līcræst sceolde beón æt Cridiantūne, Chr. 977 ; P. 122, 10. **III.** *a*

*place of burial, a cemetery* :—On līcreste, līctūne *in cimiterio*, An. Ox. 4347. [v. *N. E. D.* lich-rest.]

**līc-sang.** *Add* :—Līcsang *epichedieon*, An. Ox. 901 : 2, 19. Hī sungon þā ealle sealmas and līcsang þā hwīle þe man ðā byrgene bufan geopenode, Hml. S. 20, 88. [v. *N. E. D.* lich-song.]

**līc-þegnung.** *Add* :—Ðǣr wæs sumre tīde ylding tō gefyllanne þā līcþenunge his bebyrginge (þā līcþegnunge and þā gedæfenu þǣre byrgene gefyllan, *v. l.*) *cum mora esset temporis ad explendum debitum sepulturae*, Gr. D. 84, 5. Hē sǣde þ hē æt þæs hālgan weres līcþenungum wǣre, Hml. S. 31, 1429.

**līc-þrowere.** *Add* :—Týn līcþroweras wurdon gehǣlede fram heora langsumum broce, Hml. S. 27, 129.

**līc-stōw, e ; f.** *A place of burial* :—Hē mē sǣde þ se biscop him forgǣfe līcstōwe in his cyrcan *episcopus locum in ecclesia praebuit, in quo sepeliri debuisset*, Gr. D. 340, 35.

**līc-þrúh** *a tomb, sepulchre* :—Þā eóde hē and his līcþrúh (*sepulcrum*) gegearwode . . . ʻSeó þīn līcþrúh eáðe unc bēgen ymbfēhðʼ . . . þā ontýndon hī þā þrúh (*sepulcrum*) . . . þæs abbodes līchama hæfde āfylled ealle þā līcþrúh (*sepulcrum*) . . . þā fǣringa se līchama þæs abbudes . . . hine sylfne cyrde and ǣmtige stōwe þǣre līcþrúh gegearwode þām mæssepreóste, Gr. D. 225, 28–226, 23.

**līc-tún.** *Add* :—Hit wæs eald þeáw on þissum landum þ mon oft forðgefarene men innan cyrcean byrigde, and þā stōwa þe wǣron tō Godes þeówdōme gehālgode . . . mon worhte tō līctūnum . . . Gif þonne on hwylcere stōwe swā fela þǣra byrgena sý þ hit tō earfoðlic sý tō dōnne, þonne lǣte man þā stōwe tō līctūne, Ll. Th. ii. 408, 2–15.

**līcung.** *Add* : v. ge-onlīcung.

**līc-wyrþe.** *Add* : , -weorþ :—Wið his līcwyrðan scætte, C. D. B. iii. 491, 12. Hī gegearwodon ealle þā þing þe mihton beón gesewene þ wǣron nýdbehēfe and līcwyrðe þām þe mid swā mycelum fæder þyder cuman mihton, Gr. D. 148, 8. Þā geseah ic týn geonge men . . . ful līcwyrðe mē þúhte tō mīnes līchaman luste, Hml. S. 23 b, 371. v. ge-, un-līcwyrþe.

**līcwyrþlīce** ; *adv. In an estimable, praiseworthy manner* :—Swīðe līcwyrðlīce þū gefyldest, Hml. S. 23 b, 57.

**lida.** *Add* : v. frum-lida : -liden. v. for-liden : -lidenness. v. for-lidenness.

**līf.** *Add* : **I.** *the condition or attribute of being alive, animate existence* ; *opposed to* **death.** (1) *the condition, quality, or fact of being a living person or animal* :—Hē of līfe gewāt, B. 2471 : Edg. 29. Hē (*the Phenix*) cymeð tō līfe, Ph. 367. ¶ *in phrases describing the Deity* :—Metod, līfes brytta, Gen. 122. Līfes weard, 1889. Līfes leóhtfruman, Cri. 227. (1 a) *continuance* or *prolongation of animate existence* ; *opposed to* **death** :—Līfes beám (cf. deáðes beám, 478), Gen. 468. Līfes ēðel (*Eden*), 1576. Hē āhte geweald līfes and deáðes, Gū. 495. Þū līfes word lǣstan noldes, Cri. 1393. (1 b) *animate existence viewed as dependent on sustenance* :—Līfes tō leofne, An. 1125 : 1113. Hwæþer būtan þē (*the baker*) wē magon līf ādreógan?, Coll. M. 28, 27. (2) *fig. a condition of power, activity, or happiness, in contrast to a condition conceived hyperbolically or metaphorically as* **death** ; *the state of existence of the souls of the blessed, in contrast with that of the lost* :—Hē sōðfæstra sāwla lǣded on ūprodor, þæt is leóht and līf, Exod. 545. Þonne līf and deáð sāwlum swelgað, Cri. 1603. Naman āwritene on līfes bēc, Hml. Th. i. 34, 8. Līfes treó (*the cross*), El. 706. Hē on þone hālgan beám āhongen wæs . . . , þǣr hē līfes ceápode moncynne, Cri. 1096 : 1367. Līfes weg sēcan *to die and go to heaven*, Ap. 31. Līfes brūcan, An. 229. Hē leóde lǣrde on līfes weg *he showed them the way to heaven*, 170. Līfes wīsdom *saving knowledge*, Cri. 1052. Līfes leóht, Bt. 5, 3 ; F. 14, 13. (3) *animate existence viewed as a possession of which one is deprived by death* :—Þ is gīt deórwyrþre þonne monnes līf, Bt. 10 ; F. 28, 38. Sié þ on cyninges dōme, swā deáð swā līf, swā hē him forgifan wille, Ll. Th. i. 60, 10. Bið his līf scæcen, Vy. 39 : Vid. 142. Þ hē him ne unne nāðer ne ǣhta ne līfes, Ll. Th. i. 270, 23. Þolige hē landes and līfes, 358, 21. Līfes lyre, Ph. 53. Þā sāwla þe Críst mid his āgenum līfe gebohte, Ll. Th. i. 304, 17. Līfe gebeorgan, Hml. S. 5, 332. Nelle ic him þ līf on geniman, Wrt. Voc. ii. 32, 33. Līf ofǣtan, Gen. 1073. His līf be his were man ālíese, Ll. Th. i. 110, 8. (3 a) *be* līfe *on pain of losing life* :—Ic beóde eallum mīnum gerēfum . . . be heora āgenum life, Cht. E. 230, 29. (3 b) *in adjuration, asseveration*, &c. :—Se þeóden mec þīne līfe heálsode, B. 2131. (4) *the cause* or *source of living* ; *the vivifying* or *animating principle* :—Þæs līchoman līf is seó sāwl, and þǣre sāwle līf is God, Hml. Th. i. 160, 7. Sāwelleásne, līfe belidenes līc, El. 878. Sundur gedǣlan līf wið līce *to separate body and soul*, B. 2423. Of þæs weres handa ic ofgange þæs mannes līf *de manu viri requiram animam hominis*, Gen. 9, 5. Līf *spiraculum* i. animam (*exhalavit*), An. Ox. 2822. (5) *a living person* (?) :—Wite þū, lā arwurða līf (= leóf?), Angl. viii. 334, 34. **II.** *with reference to duration, the animate terrestrial existence of an individual with regard to its duration, the period from birth to death* :—Swā lange swā mē līf gelæst, Ll. Th. i. 276, 29. Lytle hwīle sceolde hē his līfes niótan, Gen. 486. Gif mē Drihten an lengran līfes, 1841 : Cri. 1323.

Lífes æt ende, B. 2823. Þára þe hyra lífes þurh lust brúcan, Gú. 388. On hira lífes tíd, 766 : El. 1209. Oft getímað yfelum teala for lífe *often it goes well with the wicked while he lives*, Hml. Th. i. 332, 15. On lífe ... æfter his dæge *during his lifetime ... after his death*, Ll. Th. i. 298, 9. Ge on lífe ge on legere, 306, 22 : 184, 13. Seó on lífe wæs wintrum yldre *she was at a more advanced time of life*, Gen. 2610. Hé lífa gehwæs lengu wealdeð, Gú. 483. ¶ Ná on lífe *never* :—Ne ge-wurðe hit ná on lífe þ wé álecgan úre wulder mid earhlicum fleáme, Hml. S. 25, 660. **III.** *course, condition, or manner of living*. (1) *the series of actions and occurrences constituting the history of an individual from birth to death*. In a generalized sense, *the course of human existence from birth to death* :—Þá hálgan hádas þe Godes folc læran scylan lífes bysne, Ll. Th. i. 244, 10. Hé ongan ácsian be þæs scóhwyrhtan lífe, Gr. D. 322, 5. Þ abbodas and abbodessan heora ágen líf rihtlíce fadian, 314, 14. Se wísa mon eall his líf læt on gefeán, Bt. 12 ; F. 36, 24. Þá hwíle þe ic on þisum lýcuman and þisse weorulde sié fultuma mé þæt ic simle þone ræd áræðige ðe mé for þám lýfum best sí, Solil. H. 13, 25. (1 a) where the life is recorded in a book :—Be hálgum lífe hi[re] béc *de conversatione illius opuscula*, An. Ox. 4533. Scē Ceaddan líf Béda wrát on Angelcynnes bócum, Shrn. 59, 11. Þeáh hí eall hiora líf and hiora dæda áwriten hæfden, Bt. 18, 3 ; F. 64, 36. (2) with reference to either of the two states of human existence separated by death :—God þá gehealde for bæm lífum, C. D. ii. 132, 19. (a) (*this*) *life* :—Þis deáde líf, læne on londe, Seef. 65. Adam hæfde xxx and c lífes wintra on worulde, Gen. 1120 : D. 197. Ende lænau lífes, 2845. Ende worolde lífes, 1387 : 2343 : Gú. 904. Eorþan lífes ende, Leás. 47. Hér on lífe (*in hac vita*) húsles beón wyrðe, Ll. Th. i. 372, 35 : Seel. 150. Is seó bót æt þé gelong æfter [lí]fe, Hy. 4, 110. (See Mod. Lang. Rev. 12, 71.) Þis deorce líf, Wand. 89. (b) (*the next*) *life* :—Hwonne him betre líf ágyfen wurde, Gú. 751. Hálig gæst gehæted him lífes ræste, 334. Hú monna gehwylc ær earnode éces lífes, Cri. 1052. Tó þám úplican lífe, An. Ox. 2214. Se rinc sóhte óðer líf, Gen. 1627. (2 a) with reference to states separated by conversion :—Þæs ealdan lífes yfelnesse *ueteris uitae malitia*, An. Ox. 40, 24. (3) *a particular manner or course of living* :—Þæs nyþeran lífes, An. Ox. 594. Hád hálgan lífes, Dan. 300. Tó rihtum lífe, Ll. Th. i. 36, 18. Libban clǽnan lífe, 272, 16. Mid þweorum lífe, Bd. 5, 13 ; Sch. 642, 7. Orsorg líf lǽdan, Met. 7, 40. Hwá unclǽnnisse líf álífde, Dóm. 63 : Mód. 48. (3 a) *a life spent in a particular kind of work* :—II. weras in lífe and in háde háliges drohtoðes *duo viri in vita atque habitu sanctae conversationis*, Gr. D. 205, 16. On ancersetle and lífe geseted *in anchoretica uita*, Bd. 5, 1 ; Sch. 549. 3. (3 a) *the place in which such a life is passed* :—Hé áræ̃rde him munuclíf (cf. hé gestaðelode him mynster, Hml. S. 31, 312) ... þæt mynster hé gelógode mid wellybbendum mannum ... Næs heora nánum álýfed on ðám lífe ǽnig cræft búton hálgum gebedum and heora gewritum, Hml. Th. ii. 506, 14–20 : C. D. iii. 117, 25 (*in Dict.*) (4) *the active pleasures or pursuits of the world* :—Æghwylc ælda bearna forlǽte ídle lustas, læne lífes wynne, Sch. 100. **IV.** phrases with prepositions. (1) on lífe *alive* :—Nis ǽni man on lífe þe ǽfre gehýrde þ ..., Ll. Th. i. 184, 10. (2) tó lífe *alive* :—Hé áxode hwí hý heóldon þá wífnem tó lífe *cur feminas reservastis ?*, Num. 31, 15. Dém þú hí tó deáde, swá tó lífe lǽt, swá þé leófre sý *condemn her to death or leave her alive, as you would liever*, Jul. 88. Þá þe him tó lífe (*when living*) lǽdost wǽron cwicera cynna, Jud. 323. **V.** *adv. gen.* lífes *alive* :—Hé bið lang lífes *vitalis erit*, Lch. iii. 156, 18, 23. Unlǽde bið on eorðan, unnyt lífes ... sé þurh þone cantic ne can Críst geherian, Sal. 21. (For other instances see Dict.) v. á- (Verc. Först. 108, 15), cot-, cyre-, gód-, nunn-, preóst-, riht-, stoc-, un-líf; un-lífes.

-líf. v. -life : -lifa. v. ofer-lifa.

**lífan** *to permit. Add* :—Úre Hǽlend lýfde þ mann his lífe gebeorge, Hml. S. 5, 322. Hý lýfdon ðe þær ofer wǽron lytlingum heora *reliquerunt que superfuerunt paruulis suis*, Ps. Rdr. 16, 14. v. á-, ge-, un-lífed ; á-, ge-lífedlic ; ge-lífedlíce ; ge-lífedness ; ge-lífen ; ge-lífenscipe.

**lífan** *to believe. Add* : v. be-lífan ; be-, ge-lífed ; ge-lífedlic ; ge-lífedlíce ; ge-lífen ; ge-lífend, -lífende ; ge-lífendlic ; ge-líf(en)ness.

**líf-brycgung.** v. ge-brýcgan *in Supplement* : **líf-dæg.** *Add* : [v. N. E. D. life-day] : -lífe. v. lang-líf : **lífen.** v. lencten-lífen.

**lifer.** *Add* :—Lifre *jecor*, Wrt. Voc. i. 45, 10. Wiþ þǽre lifre swile. Lch. ii. 200, 1 (and often). His lifere *iecor eius*, Kent. Gl. 218. Swát ýðum weóll þurh báncofan, blód lifrum swealg (*the blood streaming out brought with it parts of the inside of the body? Cf. his líchama wæs ge-menged mid þǽre eorðan, swá þæt blód fleów ofer eorðan swá wæter*, Bl. H. 241, 26), An. 1278.

lifer = (?) læfer, q. v. v. eá-lifer.

**lifer-ádl.** *Add* :—Liferádl *ypaticus*, Wrt. Voc. i. 19, 40. Hwæt him sié tó forgânne on liferádle, Lch. ii. 210, 13. Wyrtdrencas wið eallum liferádlum, 212, 23.

**lifer-seóc.** *adj. Having the liver diseased* :—Gif se lifersióca mon blódes tó fela hæbbe, Lch. ii. 210, 7. Wyrce mon tó drencum liferseócum mannum, 212, 24. Heó liferseócum wel fremað, i. 236, 13.

**lifer-seócness,** e ; *f. Disease of the liver* :—Wið liferseócnysse, Lch. i. 286, 24 : 304, 9.

**lifer-wǽrc.** *Add* :—Gelíc liferwǽrces tácnum, Lch. ii. 258, 1. Be sex þingum þe þone liferwǽrc wyrceað, 198, 9.

**líf-fæst.** *Add* : **I.** *having life, quickened*, Vy. 6 (*in Dict.*) **II.** *life-giving* :—Þá lýffæstan gerýnu (*the eucharistic elements*), Hml. S. 23 b, 625. **III.** *settled in respect to domicile* :—Ic wille ǽrist mé siolfne Gode forgeofan tó ðere stówe æt Crístes círican, and mín bearn ðér líffest gedóan, C. D. i. 316, 9.

**líf-fæstan.** *Add* : [cf. O. H. Ger. líb-fastigón *vivificare*] : -líffæst-nian. v. ge-líffæstnian.

**líf-gedál.** *Add* :—Tó þon þ hí heom ne ondréden on þám deáðe æt heora lífgedále *ut in morte minime pertimescant*, Gr. D. 337, 27.

**lífian.** v. libban : lífian. v. be-lífian : -lifiend. v. mid-lifiend : -lifigende. v. un-lifigende.

**líf-lád.** *Add* : **I.** *course of life, lifetime* :—Þæt feórðe muneca cyn ... ealle heora lífláde (*tota vita sua*) geond missenlice þeóda farað, R. Ben. 9, 21. **II.** *conduct, conversation, mode of life* :—Þéh þe seó tunge þǽre helle tintregu forswígode, seó his líflád hí spræc and cýðde *etiamsi taceret lingua, conversatio loqueretur*, Gr. D. 317, 21. Þá ge-bróðra ongǽn hine sylfne wǽron spelliende and his ágenre lífláde (droht-nunge, *v. l.*) swíðe ungelíce (*suae conversationi longe dissimiles*), 106, 2. Hé gebeáh intó þám mynstre ... and hine beeóde [on] gódre lífláde, Hml. S. 33, 328. Hé ongan tælan his lífláde (drohtnunge, *v. l.*) *coepit conversationi ejus derogare*, Gr. D. 117, 15. [v. N. E. D. livelihood.] v. riht-líflád.

**líf-leás.** *Add* : **I.** *that has ceased to live* :—Sum man ... his feorh forlét. ... Se hálga wer geneálǽhte þám lífleásan men (cf. þone sáwlleás-an líchaman, Hml. S. 31, 249), Hml. Th. ii. 504, 35. **II.** *not endowed with life* :—Geoffrian heora lác þám lífleásum godum, Hml. S. 29, 278. **II a.** *not having animal life* :—Þá treówa þe on æppel-túne wexað, þá þe sind lífleáse, sáwulleáse, and andgitleáse, Hml. Th. ii. 406, 11.

**líf-leást.** *Add* :—Gif þás lác ne beóð bebrocene þurh Bél, beó hit úre lífleást (*let us die*), Shrn. 4, 5. Wé synd ealle beléwde tó úre líf-leáste *traditi sumus ego et populus meus, ut conteramur*, Hml. A. 99, 254. Wé gemétað lífleáste on eorðan gif we his láre folgiað, Hml. S. 34, 136.

**líf-lic.** *Add* : **I.** *having life, living, animate* :—God gesceóp .III. líflíce gástas *tres vitales spiritus creavit Deus*, Gr. D. 263, 11. Ic eom se líflíca hláf, Hml. Th. i. 34, 16. **II.** *long-lived* :—Sé þe acenned bið, líflíc (*vitalis*) hé bið, Archiv cxxix. 18, 11. On ánre nihte ealdne mónan þ cild þ swá bið ácenned, þ bið líflíc (lang lífes, *v. l.*), 21, 7. **III.** *vital, necessary to life.* (1) physical :—Swilce hí ðone líflícan blǽd forðrǽstne ácwellon, Hml. Th. ii. 92, 12. (2) spiritual :—Þurh líflíce láre, .Hml. Th. i. 408, 1. **IV.** *lively* :—Líflíces orþa[nces] *uiuacis ingenii*, An. Ox. 72. Wel manega on scearpnysse andgytes líflíce wuniað *plerique in acumine intelligentiae uiuaces existunt*, Scint. 220, 20.

-lífne. v. ǽ-lífne.

**lifrig.** For 'Connected with the liver' substitute, *Clotted, coagulated* (cf. N. E. D. livered, *clotted*, *coagulated* ; livery (of soil) *heavy, tenacious*).

**lift.** v. lyft-wynn : **líf-welle.** *Add* : life-giving. Cf. deáð-wille.

**líg.** *Add* : **I.** physical :—Lǽgas (*fulgura*) on regn hé dyde, Ps. Rdr. 134, 7. **II.** figurative :—Ðá lác þe se líeg ðére lufe forbǽrnð on ðǽm altere gódra weorca, Past. 222, 22. Ðætte se spearca ðára gódra weorca birne héalíce ligge on ðǽre incundan lufan, 86, 7. v. ád-, deáþ-, teón-líg (-lég).

**líg-berend.** *Substitute* : **líg-berend,** es ; *m. A flame-bearer* ; flam-miger, Wrt. Voc. ii. 149, 9. Líg-berende ; *adj. Flame-bearing* ; flam-miger, Wrt. Voc. ii. 36, 52.

**líge-leóht** (?) ; *adj. Bright with flame* ; the neuter used substantively, as abstract noun :—Þis fýr is án lég, and hwæðre se án lég þreó þing on him hafað ... He is hwít ... þonne is þæt þridde þæt líhteð eall geond eorðærn ... and þonne is hit hwæðre án lég, and ne mæg þæt háte fram ðám hwíte áscádan, ne ðæt hwíte fram þám légeleóhte (þæt háte, þæt hwíte, þæt légeleóhte *seem all substantive forms of the same kind, and an adjective* lége-leóht *seems to be implied as much as the adjectives* hát *and* hwít), Verc. Först. 168.

**lígen.** *Add* :—Lígen *flammeum*, Wülck. Gl. 239, 21.

-ligenness. v. for-ligenes.

**Liger** *the Loire* :—Wið þá mycclan eá þe menn hátað Liger, Hml. S. 6, 159.

-liger. v. for-ligr : ligere. v. ge-ligere : -ligerian. v. firen-ligerian : ligerness. v. ge-ligerness.

**líget.** *Add* : **I.** n. or m. :—Léget *fulgor*, Wrt. Voc. i. 76, 35. Micel líget fleáh swilce flán, Hml. Th. i. 504, 29. Þæs lígettes, ii. 202, 27. Légedes (légeð, L.) *fulgoris*, Lk. R. 11, 36. Sendan ðunras and lýgetu, Bt. 35, 4 ; F. 162, 3. Sceotiende fýrene lígettas, Hml. S. 25, 495. **II.** *f.* :—Hwanon cymð lígetu ? Hit cymð fram winde and fram wætere, Sal. K. 186, 14. Lýgtu *flamma*, Ps. L. 105, 18. Légitu *fulgur*, Ps. Srt. ii. 196, 19. Légite *fulgoris*, 190, 15. On þá gelicnesse tungles oððe ligite, Nar. 7, 14. For ðæs þunres ege and þǽre

ligette, Wlfst. 207, 26.　Līgita *fulmina*, Wrt. Voc. ii. 34, 69.　Lēgite *fulgura*, Ps. Srt. ii. 197, 34.　Līgeta, Bt. 35, 4; F. 162, 13 note.

liget-sliht, e; *f. l.* es; *m., and add:*—Swā lēgedslæht scīnende *sicut fulgor coruscans*, Lk. R. L. 17, 24.　Mycel mægn ligetslehta (liégietslyhta, *v. l.) tanta coruscationis virtus*, Gr. D. 167, 24.　For hreónessum and līgetslehtum (-slihtum, *v. l.) tempestatibus coruscis*, 133, 31.　Leigeðslæhtas *fulgura*, Mt. p. 10, 3.

-līgian. *v.* in-, on-līgian: līg-loccod *l.* -loccode: -līgne. *v.* unlīgne: lignian. *l.* lignan, *and in bracket for* laugnen *l.* láugnen.

Ligora-ceaster *Leicester:*—Rād se here ūt of Ligeraceastre, and bræcon þone friþ, Chr. 917; P. 98, 2: 921; P. 101, 6.　Æt Ligraceastre (Legra-, Ligran-, *v. ll.*), 918; P. 105, 22.　On Legraceastre, 943; P. 111, 16.　Eádmund Myrce geeóde . . . Ligoraceaster and Lindcylene, 942; P. 110, 17.

līg-ræscet[t]ung. *Add:*—Lȳghræscetunge *choruscationem*, Ps. L. 143, 6.

līg-spiwol. *Add:*—Of līgspiwelum flōde *de Flegetonte*, Germ. 391, 199. *The Latin translated by* Dōm. L. 209 *is:* Os flammivomum implebitur igne.

līhtan *to shine. Take here* leóhtan *in Dict., and add: to be light:*—Þā sceán leóht inn, swylce nīwe mōna ārise, swā þ hit līhte under þære rōde swȳdran earme . . . hit līhte geond ealle þā cyrcan, Vis. Lfc. 51–56. On þære ylcan nihte þe se behātena dæg æfter līhte *nocte eadem, qua promissus illucescebat dies*, Gr. D. 148, 12. *v.* frum-, ge-, ofer-līhtan.

līhtan *to lighten. Add:*—Þā lȳhte (hlīhte, līhte, *v. ll.*) hē sōna desiliens, Bd. 3, 14; Sch. 257, 12.　Hī þā sōna līhton *descendentes*, Gr. D. 15, 27. *v.* ofer-, under-līhtan.

-līhtend. *v.* in-, on-līhtend: -līhtian. *v.* in-līhtian.

līhting *shining. Add:*—Swā micel swā þæs dæges līhting geþafige *quantum hora permittit*, R. Ben. 67, 8.　Ealle þās þing þurh lifes līhtincge gefyllan *haec omnia per hanc lucis viam* (*has* vitam *been read?*), 5, 8. *v.* rodor-līhting.

līhting *alleviation. Add:* v. dædbōt-līhting: līhtingness. *As the word translates* levitas *perhaps* līhtnes *should be read:* līhtness. *Add:* v. in-, on-līhtness.

lilie. *Add:*—Lilige *lilium*, Wrt. Voc. i. 79, 59.　Hwylc wyrt is betst and sēlust? Lilige hātte seó wyrt, for ðām ðe heó getācnað Crīst, Sal. K. 186, 9.

lim. *Add:* I. *any organ or part of the body:*—Behōfað þæt heáfod þæra ōðera lima, swā swā ðā lima behōfiað þæs heáfdes. Gif ān lim bið untrum, ealle ðā ōðre þrowiað mid þām ānum, Hml. Th. i. 274, 7–9. Leoma līfgedāl, Gū. 1019.　Hē (*the Phenix*) of æscan onwæcneð leomum geþungen, Ph. 649.　Is āwriten ðæt hē bīcne mid ðām eágum, and sprece mid ðæm fingrum, and trit mid ðæm fēt; for ðæm ðe innor bið se hierde þe hielt ðā leomu (limu, *v. l.*) ūtan (*interior est custodia, quae ordinata servat exterius membra*), Past. 359, 5.　II. *a part or member of an animal body distinct from the head or trunk:*—Ne mæg se mūð clypian . . . , ne eáge geseón . . ne nān limn (lim? *or* lima?) ne dēð nān ðing, Hml. Th. i. 160, 10.　Þā geongan leomu, liffæstan leoþu geloden weorðað, Vy. 5.　Seldum æfre þæs fugeles leomu licgað, Sal. 270.　Bið se līchama leorde on strangum breóste, on fullum limum and hālum, Hml. Th. i. 614, 12.　Hē leomum onfeng and līchoman, Cri. 628.　II a. = gecynd-lim:—Se wǣta ðāra innoða āstīgeð tō ðǣm lime *humor viscerum ad virilia labitur*, Past. 73, 10.　II b. *the leg:*—Hē gebǣd hine tō Gode gebīgedum limum, Hml. S. 25. 623.　III. fig. *of persons.* (1) *a member of the chnrch, Christ's body, a subordinate where Christ is the head:*—Mec, þīn lim, Hy. 4, 52.　Wē ðe his (*Christ's*) liomu (limo, *v. l.*) sindon *membra ejus*, Past. 33, 21.　Wē (*the angels*) ymb hine (*Christ*) hōfan, leomu ymb leófne, lofsonga word, Sat. 155.　Ðā gōdan lāreówas nō ðæt ān wilniað sēcean ðæt hālige heáfoð ðǣre gesomnunge, ðæt is Dryhten, ac wiln[i]að ðæt hié ofdūne āstīgen tō his limum, Past. 101, 24.　Crīst is crīstenra heáfod, and ealle Crīstene men syndon tō Crīstes limum getealde, Wlfst. 37, 7.　(2) *a limb of Satan:*—Þeáh hine deófol mid his lymum wylle gedreccan, Angl. viii. 324, 19.　IV. *not referring to animals.* (1) *part of a tree, a branch*, Gn. Ex. 26: B. 97 (*in Dict.*).　(2) *a member of a sentence:*—Tōdāl *comma*, lim *cola*, An. Ox. 18 b, 10.　Lim *cola*, lines ðǣl *commata*, 26, 1, 2.　Mid lime (lima, MS.) ł tōdala *colopho*, 131.　Lime colo, 7, 196.　Þur[h] lim, 2850.　Þurh lim and tōdāl *per cola*, i. *membra et commata*, 201.

līm. *Dele last passage, and* '*cola*, 20, 24:' *in l.* 6, *and add:*—Liim *cementum lapidum*, Txts. 49, 449.　Līm tō wealle *cementum*, Wrt. Voc. i. 75, 22.　Hrīm on lime, Ruin. 4. *v.* weall-līm.

līman; *p.* de *To emit rays, beam, shine:*—þ þ leóht þe þær lȳmde betweoh þām þȳstrum wæs beorhtre þonne dæges leóht *ut diem vinceret lux illa inter tenebras radiasset*, Gr. D. 171, 5. [*v. N. E. D.* leam *to shine, cf.* Icel. ljóma.] *v.* ā-līman; leóma.

līman *to join.* [*v. N. E. D.* lime *to cement.*] *v.* ge-līman(-ian); līming.

limb-stefning. The gloss at Wrt. Voc. i. 61, 46 is: *Peripetasma* limb-stefning. Comparison with 26, 6, *limbus* stemning *vel* hem, suggests (?) that the gloss should read, *peripetasma, limbus* stefning.

lim-fīn, e; *f. A lime-heap:*—Ðanon on gerihte on cyneges līmfīne, of ðære fīne niðer, C. D. B. i. 518, 41.　Cf. wudu-fīn.

lim-gelecg. *Add:*—Limgelecg *liniamentum* (cf. Hpt. Gl. 465, 73, where the same passage is glossed: *Liniamento, specie ł similitudine* of hīwe ł gelícnysse, *imagine*), Wrt. Voc. ii. 79, 47. *v.* lim-rǣden.

lim-gesihþ *physical vision, sight by means of the bodily eye* (? cf. A man has na lym þat he is warere wiþ þan wiþ his eghe, Hamp. Ps. 16, 9. þe lyme of syȝte *organum visus, N. E. D.* under limb; I):—Ealle menn ārīsað mid limgesihðum (*corporibus*), Ps. Rdr. 301, 4.

līmian. *v.* līman.

līming. *Add:*—Līming *liture*, Wrt. Voc. ii. 85, 51. The passage to which all three glosses belong is: Turrem . . . forti *liturae* compage constructam erexit, Ald. 62, 13. *In* Hpt. Gl. 509, 54 *and* An. Ox. 4439 *the reading is* linunge.

lim-leás. *Add:* , *not having all one's limbs:*—Gif hwā ālēfed wǣre, oððe limleás . . . Hwæt sceole wē smeágan embe ðā þe gewītað tō ðām ēcum forwyrde, hwæðer hī ālēfede beón oððe limleáse?, Hml. Th. i. 236, 28–33.

limpan. *Add:* I. *to befall, happen:*—Hē hiene ofslōg, swā him eác selfum siþþan æfter lamp, Ors. 4, 5; S. 170, 10.　II. *to belong, pertain:*—Būtan ðǣm wioda ðe tō ðǣm sealtern limpð, Txts. 438, 25. Limpeð, 444. 16.　Mēdu mid riahte tō ðǣm lande limpað, 439, 7: 438, 15.　III. *to pertain to, be concerned with, have relation to:*—Rǣdincga tō þæs hālgan ārwyrþnesse limpende *lectiones ad ipsius sancti uenerationem pertinentes*, Angl. xiii. 430, 936.　IV. *expressing a relation of equivalence where the same amount is expressed in different units:*—.xxx. ombra gōdes uuelesces aloð, ðet limpeð tō .xv. mittum, Txts. 444, 21.　V. *to be suitable, be applicable:*—Gif [lī]þe wyrtdrenc ne limpe, sele strangne, Lch. ii. 264, 3.　[*v. N. E. D.* limp.] *v.* mis-limpan.

-limpfull, -limplǣcan, -limplic, -limplicness. *v.* ge-limpfull, &c.: limplīce. *Add:* v. ge-limplīce.

lim-rǣden. The passage where this word is given as a gloss to *chlamide* is: Pro chlamide, quam angelicae puritati liniamento . . . adsciscebat, Ald. 35, 10. In Wrt. Voc. ii. 79, 47, which refers to the same passage, *liniamento* is glossed by *lim-gelecg*: it is probable, then, that *lim-rǣden* is a gloss to *liniamento* rather than to *chlamide*, and has the same meaning as *lim-gelecg* (*q. v.*).

lim-wērig. *Add:*—Limwǣrigne, Txts. 126, 16.

līn. *Add:*—Liin *manitergium*, Txts. 76, 634.　Līn, Wrt. Voc. ii. 55, 42.　Hī befealdan hī mid līne *uoluant crucem sindone*, Angl. xiii. 421, 808.　Hē onfēng līne (*linteum*) and hine mid begyrde, Hml. A. 155, 92, 103.　[*v. N. E. D.* line.] *v.* bisceop-heáfod- (*not* bisceop-, heáfod-) līn.

līn-æcer (?), es; *m. A field where flax is grown:*—In līnæceran (be?) wege þām innmæstan; of līnaceran innan ðone hege, Cht. .239, 10.　Cf. līn-leáh, fleax-æcer.

lind. *Add:* I.:—Lindan *tilig*, An. Ox. 2, 8.　In ðā geápan linde, C. D. iii. 375, 5.　II:—Stōd under linde, under leóhtum scylde, Lch. iii. 52, 19.　[The word occurs in many local names. v. C. D. vi. 309–310.]

Lindcylene *Lincoln:*—Burga fīfe, Ligoraceaster and Lin[d]cylene (the d *is erased;* Lindcylne, -kylne, Lincolne, *v. ll.*), Chr. 942; P. 110, 17. Lindcylene (-cylne, -colene, *v. ll.*) ceastre gerēfan *praefectum Lindocolinae ciuitatis*, Bd. 2, 16; Sch. 177, 20.　On Lindcylene, 2, 18; Sch. 181, 19.　Tō Lindcylne (-cylene, -colne, *v. ll.*) *Lindocolino*, Sch. 182, 6. Honorius wes gehālgod on Lincollan, Chr. 627; P. 25, 27.　On Lincolna, 1067; P. 202, 34.　¶ Lincolna-scīr, Chr. 1064; P. 190, 21.

Lindisfaran. *l.* Lindisfaran. *Dele the bracket after* '*Northumbria*', *and add:*—Lindesfarona landes is syfan þūsend hȳda mid hæðfeldlande, C. D. B. i. 414, 17.　Myrcna þeóde and Lindesfearena (-pharona, *v. l.*), Bd. 4, 3; Sch. 350, 8.　Myrcna mægþ and Middelengla and Lindesfarena (-farona, *v. l.*), Sch. 367, 7.　Hē hine āsænde Myrceon tō biscope and Middelenglum and Lindesfarum, Shrn. 59, 14.　[The form in the last passage in Dict. seems taken from Bede's Latin Life of Cuthbert : Insula *Lindisfarnea*, c. xvi.　The same chapter has the form Lindisfarnensium insula.]

Lindesfarnea-landing, es; *m. A native of Lindisfarne:*—Ediluald Lindisfearneolandinga biscop, Jn. Skt. p. 188, 3.

Lindesse, . . . Lindesīge. *l.* Lindes[s], e; *f.:* Lindes-īg, e; *f.:* Lindes-īge, es; *m.:* Lindes-īgland, es; *n.:*—On Lindesse lande (in Lindesīglande, *v. l.*), 3, 27; Sch. 318, 18.　On Lindesigge mægðe, Bd. 2, 16; Sch. 177, 10.　Mon mihte of ealre Lindesse stōwum sweotole geseón (of eallum Lindesīge geseón swutule of eallum þām stōwum, *v. l.*) *omnibus Lindissae prouinciae locis conspicua stabat*, 3, 11; Sch. 237, 10. On Lindese (Lindesīge, -ēge) *in prouincia Lindissi*, præf.; Sch. 4. 20.

lind-gestealla. *Add:*—Ongan . . . helle hæftling galan: 'Hwæt weard eów wrāð rōfum, rincas mīne, lindgesteallan?, An. 1346.

lind-hwæt. *v.* leóð-hwæt.

līne. *Add:* I. *a cord:*—Ne magon hȳ ðā lifes līnan on middan ymbfæðmian, Sal. K. 150, 31.　II. *a line, stroke made on a surface:*—

'þú leornedest be ánre línan wæs áwriten anlang middes þæs þóþeres' ... 'Ic wót hwæt seó líne tácnað,' Solil. H. 20, 16-20. þá línan þe on þám þóþere átéfred wæs, 21, 6. **III.** *a continuous extent of length without breadth or thickness:*—On ðone munt þe sý in ðære lengoðe seó líne ðe wile .xxxiii. síða ealne eorðan ymbehwyrft útan ymblicgan, Sal. K. 152, 5. **IV.** *a series of objects arranged on a line:*—þá rímcræftige men wyrcað heom circul of þám fíf stafum, and betæcað þrý dagas ánum stæfe. þonne getímað hyt þ hig wrixliað twía on ánum mónðe, and on þám circule fiftýne niht hig onfóð on þære néxtan línan, and on þrittig hig geendiað, Angl. viii. 327, 40. v. fleax-líne.

**línen** *linen.* *Add:*—Línin rýe *villa,* Wrt. Voc. ii. 123, 60. Línen heáfodes wrigels *anaboladium* vel *sindo,* i. 40, 28.

**línete.** *In* Wülck. Gl. 286, 21 *the word is given as* línece.

**líne-twige.** *Add:*—Línaethuigae *carduelis,* Txts. 54, 309. [v. *N. E. D.* lintwhite.]

**-ling,** es; *m.* *Add:* v. byrd-, cýþ-, efen-, heáfod-, mæst-, ráp-, reád-, sib-, þeów-, þeówet-, under-, wædl- (?), wiþer-ling.

**-ling, -linga,** *adv.* *Add:* v. bråd-, ecg-, neód-, níd-, níw-, un-myndlinga, -lunga.

**lín-leáh;** *f.* *A flax-field:*—On línleáge geat, and ðonne on línleáge middewearde, C. D. ii. 172, 14. On línleáge éastewearde, v. 207, 21.

**linnan.** *Dele:* v. á-linnan, *and add:* v. of-linnan.

**lín-sæd.** *Add:*—Genim línsæd, gegrind, bríwe wið þám elmes drænce; þ bið gód sealf foredum lime, Lch. ii. 66, 25. On længctene ... línséd sáwan, Angl. ix. 262, 10.

**linung.** v. líming: **lín-wæd.** *Add:*—þá línwæda *linteamina,* Angl. xiii. 428, 894: **-lípe.** v. án-, sundor-, synder-lípe: **-lípes.** v. sundor-, synder-lípes: **-lípig.** v. án-lípig:—**lípum.** v. án-lípum.

**lippa.** *Add:* [Weler *is generally used where modern English would have* lip, e. g. *in* Ps. 51, 15 *(quoted at* R. Ben. I. 69, 9) labia *is rendered by* weleras *in* R. Ben. 62, 10, *and in all the versions of the Psalter.*] **I.** *either of the two fleshy structures which form the edges of the mouth:*—Hunigswéte reádum andþraciaþ lippan smérum *mellea (tunc) roseis herescunt labia labris,* An. Ox. 3186. **II.** *with special reference* (1) *to feeding:*—Smérum gifrum and mid grædigum lippum *buccis ambronibus et labris lurconibus,* An. Ox. 699. (2) *to speech:*—Míne lippan þú geopena *labia mea aperies,* R. Ben. I. 69, 9.

**líra.** *l.* líra, *and add:*—ðonne þú sealt flæsc wille, þonne twenge þú mid þínre swíðran neoþewearde þíne wynstran þær se lýra þiccost sí, Tech. ii. 125, 2. Fægere fingras, smale and lange, and þéra nægla tósceád, and se greáta líra beneoðan þám þúman, Vis. Lfc. 84. [v. *N. E. D.* lire.] v. sceanc-, scot-líra.

**-lipprica.** v. eár-lip[p]rica: **-lírede.** v. spear-lírede: **líreht.** *l.* líreht: **-lis.** v. -les.

**lísan.** *Add:*—Lýs þíne synna mid ælmessum on þearfena gemiltsunge *(peccata tua eleemosynis redime, et iniquitates tuas misericordiis pauperum,* Dan. 4, 24), Ll. Th. ii. 434, 25. [v. *N. E. D.* leese.] v. un-lísan.

**-lísedness.** v. á-, to-lísedness: **-lísend.** v. á-, on-, tó-lísend: **-lísendlíc.** v. á-, on-, tó-lísendlíc: **-lisfullíce.** v. ge-lisfullíce: **-lísian** *to slide.* v. ge-lísian: **lísing.** *Add:* v. eft-, tó-lísing: **lísness.** *Add:* v. ge-, on-lísness.

**liss.** *Add: mitigation, cessation:*—Swégde út ormæte wyllspring ... Hí micclum blissodon, and Gode þancodon heora geswinces lisse *(they thanked God for the alleviation of their hardship),* Hml. Th. i. 562, 17. [v. *N. E. D.* liss.]

**lissan.** *Add:* [v. *N. E. D.* lisse.]

**list.** *Add:*—Sníð lythwón and listum, Lch. ii. 208, 17. [v. *N. E. D.* list.]

**list-wrenc.** *For* 'Lye' *substitute:*—Mid listwrence híwian unsóð tó sóðe, Wrfst. 128, 5. þ þæ yfel cunnon híwian tó góde and unsóð tó sóðe þurh lytigne listwrencg, 81, 37.

**-lísu** (?). v. weg-lísu.

**lið.** *Add: a joint,* especially *a finger-joint:*—Swilce ðær læge on ðám disce ánes fingres lið, Hml. Th. ii. 272, 27. Nim. VIII. and sete hine on þám forman lyðe þæs þúman, Angl. viii. 326, 32: 29. Liþo *artus,* Wrt. Voc. ii. 81, 18. Liþa *articculus (palmae coelestis),* An. Ox. 1587: *articulos (digitorum),* 3546 [v. *N. E. D.* lith.] v. finger-lið.

**lið** *a fleet. Add:*—þá lét Eádward cyng scypian .xl. snacca, þá lágon æt Sandwíc ... þá geáxedon þ lið þ on Sandwíc læg embe Godwines fare, setton þá æfter, and hé heom ætbærst, and þ lið wende ongeán tó Sandwíc, and swá hámweard tó Lundenbyrig, Chr. 1052; P. 179, 13-22. [v. *N. E. D.* lith *a body of men.*] v. scip-lið.

**Lída.** *Add:*—Líða-mónað, Chr. P. 277, margin. v. þri-líþe: -liþa. v. haþo-liþa.

**líþan.** *Add:*—þonne wé líðað *(navigamus)* feor, æt néhstan wé nó geseóð þá stilnesse þære hýþe þe wé ær fram léton, Gr. D. 6, 7. þá eódon hí of þám scipe, þá þe líþon and fóron mid Maximiane *(qui cum Maximiano navigabant),* 249, 14. þá wæs heofones smyltnes tósliten, þære þe wé ær úton leoþon (liþon, *v. l.) interrupta est serenitas, qua uehebamur,* Bd. 5, 1; Sch. 551, 12.

líðan *to suffer loss* (?). *Add:* v. be-líðan: líðan *to assuage.* *Add:*—Líþende *hospita,* Germ. 392, 59.

**líþe.** *Add:*—ðæt hé him sié líeðe (líðe, *v. l.*), Past. 125, 23. Líþe *blandus, lenis,* líþe, swæs *blanda, jocunda,* líþum *vel* swétwyrdum *blandis sermonibus, lenis verbis,* Wrt. Voc. ii. 127, 1-4. Sprecende mid líðum wordum (líðre spræce, *v. l.) blando sermone alloquens,* Gr. D. 80, 15. Ealle þá gesetnessa þe þær tó stronge wæron and tó hearde hé hié ealle gedyde leohtran and líþran, Ors. 5, 12; S. 244, 16. v. freónd-, meolc-líþe.

**-líþe.** v. þri-líþe.

**líþe-líc.** *Add:*—Mid líðelicre ðlicunga *blandimento,* Past. 183, 19. Hit bið mid ðære líðelican manunga áredod ... hine mon sleá mid líðelicre andsuare, 297, 17-22.

**líþelíce.** *Add:*—þænne se munuc sprece, líþelíce *(leniter)* clypige, R. Ben. 30, 13. Swá myccle ufur swá gestigon þá þreátas þæra singendra, swá myccle líþelícor *(lenius)* wæs gehýred se sealmsang, Gr. D. 286, 1.

**líþend.** *Add:* v. scip-líþend.

**líþere.** *In l.* 2 *for* leðera *l.* líðera, *and add:*—Turniendre líþeran *rotantis fundibali,* An. Ox. 695. [v. *N. E. D.* lither.]

**líþian.** *Add:* , leoþian; *p.* ode *To unloose, release:*—þá wæs eft swá ær ealdfeónda níð onwylled: wóð óðerne lythwón leodode, þonne in lyft ástág ceargesta cirm *then again as before the hate of old foes was hot, cries for a time gave vent to a second outburst of hate, when to the heavens rose the clamour of the fiends,* Gú. 363. Foldan ic freoþode folcum ic leoþode (as leoþode *rimes with* freoþode *its root vowel should be short),* Reim. 40. [Cf. (?) *O. H. Germ.* lidôn *secare.*] v. á-, ge-, on-, tó-líþian.

**líþian.** *Dele* ', *or make,' and add:*—Líþian *mitescere,* An. Ox. 3852.

**líþig.** *Add:*—Genim þás wyrte on mortere wel gepunude oð þ heó wel líþi (líþe, *v. l.*) sý, Lch. i. 312, 11.

**líþigian.** *Add:*—Hé his folc gegladode and líþegode him on mislicum geswincum for ðære mærðe *dedit requiem universis provinciis juxta magnificentiam principalem,* Hml. A. 95, 107.

**líþ-ness.** *Add:*—Heó heóld on hyre þeáwum hálige drohtnunge þurh módes líþnesse, Hml. S. 2, 96. Líðnysse *lenocinio (the English word seems to be a gloss to the phrase* blandimentorum lenocinio, *rather than to the single word. The passage is:* Blandimentorum lenocinio *(by gentleness)* natum flectere nititur, Ald. 43, 25), Angl. xiii. 34, 172. *(See next passage).* Hé sceal mencgan þá réðnesse wið þá líðnesse *miscens terroribus blandimenta,* R. Ben. 13, 10. Líédnesse, Past. 125, 13. Eáwlá, wíf, tó hwan wenest ðú þínes líchoman hæle mid smyringe and oftþweále and óðrum líðnessum *(lenitivis)* ?, Verc. Först. 166.

**líþrian.** *l.* líþran, *and add:* v. á-, ge-líþran.

**líþ-seáw.** *Add:*—Wiþ liþseáwe and gif liþseáw sió, Lch. ii. 12, 14.

**líþule.** *Add:*—Gif lioþole út yrne, Lch. ii. 12, 24.

**líþung.** *Add:*—Líþunge *ueniam (indulgentiae),* An. Ox. 8, 398.

**líþ-wærc.** *Add:*—Wiþ liðwærce sing viiii síþum þis gealdor, Lch. ii. 322, 6.

**líþ-wyrde;** *adj. Of gentle speech:*—Hé wæs líðwyrde on þære tíde þe hé wolde þæt ic næfre in écnesse nære mid wordum getyrged, Nap. 84.

**líxan.** *Add:*—Líxte *fulminavit* (v. Ald. 61, 35), Wrt. Voc. ii. 85, 43. Gemétte hé .XII. mancessas, and þá wæron swá líxende (scínende, *v. l., fulgentes)* swá swá hí wæron on þá ylcan tíd of fýre út átogene, Gr. D. 65, 17.

**ló;** *pl. n.* lóan, lón; *dat.* lóum *a strap.* v. mæst-, sceaft-ló; lóh-sceaft.

**lobbe.** *Add:* [þou madest his soule to stumblen as a lob *(sicut araneam),* Prose Psalter 38, 15. Our ʒeres shal þenchen as þe lob, 89, 10.]

**loc.** *Add:* **I.** *a bolt, lock:*—Hé beleác þ wínern and ásette his ágen insegl on þ loc, Gr. D. 59, 6. Hæpsan, loca *clustella (arcarum reserantur),* An. Ox. 4003. Wurdon Ianes dura fæste betýned, and his loca rustega, Ors. 5, 15; S. 250, 21. Locum *clustellis (cavernarum patefactos),* An. Ox. 7, 258. Benedictus wunode binnan þám locum his mynstres *(intra cellae suae claustra),* Gr. D. 124, 24. **I a.** *fig.:*—Hit oferstáh þá sylfan locu þæs líchaman *ipsa carnis claustra transibat,* Gr. D. 4, 21. **II.** *an enclosure:*—On ðære ylcan circan wæron onfæste þá locu þæra bróðra sceápa *(caulae ovium),* Gr. D. 224, 16. Locu *caulas,* i. *munimenta ovium* vel *sepimenta ovilium,* Wrt. Voc. ii. 129, 81. **III.** *a clause.* v. clýsing:—Locu *periodos,* An. Ox. 7, 195. **IV.** *a conclusion, settlement:*—Getrýwe gewitnes, and riht dóm, and ful loc, Ll. Th. ii. 302, 6. v. helle-, meaht-loc.

**lóc.** *Add:* , lóce. *The word is used with* nú *and with indirect interrogatives, pronouns or adverbs. Its force in the latter combination, ever, is seen in the following gloss:*—Lóc hwæt tó láfe beó *quodcumque restat,* Germ. 388, 78. **I.** *with* nú, *bespeaking attention:*—Lóce nú age, Germ. 393, 168. Lóca nú be þære sunnan ... , Bt. 6; F. 14, 21. Ac lóca nú hwæþer ðú wille ... *sed visne* ..., 35, 5; F. 162, 30. **II.** *forming indefinite relatives:*—Lóca hwylce concurrentes beón, Angl. viii. 302, 23. Lóca hwylce hig beóð, 304, 46. Lóca hwæt þær ofer sý, 300, 34, 36. Lóca hú God wylle, Hml. A. 62, 253, 257. Lóc hú lange se sóða læce hit foresceáwige, Hml. Th. i. 474, 25. Lóce

hwænne mîn tîma beó, Angl. xii. 499, 7. Lôca hwær beó se môna nîwe, viii. 322, 31 : 333, 21. Lôca hwær se ealdor him tǽce, R. Ben. 82, 15. [v. *N. E. D.* look; 4.]

**loca.** *Dele : ' That which closes, . . . lock,' and first passage (for which see* loc ; I) ; *for : '* 72 b . . . Sal. 185' *substitute :* Bôca cǽga, [le]ornenga locan *the keys of books, the locked place of learning,* Sal. 135. Ic sume in bryne sende, in liges locan (*into the cloister of flame, hell*), Jul. 474; *and add :* v. cǽg-, cealf-, heáfod-loca.

**loca** *a lock of wool. Add :*—Loca *floccus,* Txts. 64, 448.

**locc.** *Add :*—Loc *crinis,* Wrt. Voc. ii. 137, 4. Loccas *antiae,* 87, 60. Winde loccas *circinni,* 104, 6. Gewanedum locca fexe *dempta cincinnorum cesarię* (the reference is to Samson), An. Ox. 5048. Fexa loccum (*rasis*) *cincinnorum criniculis,* 4173. Þá Ismahéli hæfdon geþwinglode loccas and scearp sex on hiora hiáfde, Hml. A. 202, 218. Þá tær hê his loccas heófende and wolde hine sylfne ádrencan, Hml. S. 30, 180. v. fore-locc.

**-locced.** v. loccod[e] : **loccettan.** v. hloccettan.

**loccian.** *Add : to allure, entice, win over by gentle means :*—Mon sceal ðone welegan ofermôdan tô him loccian mid liðelicre ôlicunga *superbus dives exhortationis blandimento placandus est,* Past. 183, 19. [*O. L. Ger.* loccôn *allicere, attrahere, mulcere : O. H. Ger.* locchôn : *Icel.* lokka.] v. á-loccian.

**loccod[e]** ; *adj. Having locks, provided with hair :*—Loccad *crinitus,* An. Ox. 56, 13. v. hwît-, líg-loccod[e].

**locer.** *Add :* , es; *m.* [*Icel.* lokar ; *m. a plane.*]

**loc-hyrdel,** es; *m. A hurdle used in making a sheepfold :*—Lochyrdla tilian, Angl. ix. 261, 9.

**lócian.** *Add :* I. *intrans.* (1) *to give a certain direction to one's sight, direct one's eyes upon some object or towards some portion of space,* (a) *with phrase or adv. expressing the direction or the intended object of vision :*—Lôcað geneahhe fram þám unlǽdan ǽngan hláford *from the wretched solitary often are his lord's looks turned,* Sal. 382. Gê nú eágum tô on lôciað . . . fǽrwundra sum, Exod. 278. Eall engla cynn lôciaþ þurh þá ontýnnesse on manna cynn, Bl. 93, 23. Ðá welan ðe hié on lôciað, Past. 183, 7. Hê úp lôcade þurh wolcna gang, Dan. 623. Hê lôcade geond þæt láðe scræf, Sat. 727. Lôca ofer londbúende, 684. Lôcian ongeán þá sunnan *oculos ad lucem soiis attollere,* Bt. 38, 5 ; F. 204, 27. Þeáh heó ǽr gladu wǽre on tô lôcienne, 6 ; F. 14, 27. (b) *with the object or direction left indeterminate, to possess the power of vision, to see :*—Eágan hî habbað and hig ne lôciað (*uidebunt*), Ps. L. 134, 16. Sume swîðe scearpe lôciað; sume uneáðe áwiht geseóð, Solil. H. 44, 22. Sê ðe ealra scearpost lôcian mæg, ne mæg þeáh þá sunnan selfe geseón swiice swiðe heó ys, 43, 21. Him biþ swá þǽm fuglum þe magon bet lôcian on niht ðonne on dæg *similes avibus sunt, quarum intuitum nox illuminat, dies caecat,* Bt. 38, 5 ; F. 206, 4. Simle hê bið lôciende, ne slǽpþ hê nǽfre, 42 ; F. 258, 8. Sum wíf wæs six geár blind, and weard gehǽled . . . and côm beorhte lôcigende, Hml. S. 36, 266. (2) *with indirect questions, to apply one's sight to ascertain :*—Hê lôcað hwonne úp cyme glîdan swegles leóma, Ph. 101. Seó byren lôcade tô þǽre fǽmnan hwæþer heó sceolde hine cucene þe deádne, Shrn. 47, 2. Hêt hê ǽnne mon stîgan on þone mæst and lôcian hwæþer hê þæt land gecneówe, Ors. 4, 10 ; S. 202, 1. (3) *fig. to direct the intellectual eye,* (a) *to turn or fix one's attention or regard :*—Ic ðê bidde ðæt ðú nô ne lôcige on mîne synna, for ðæm ðe ic self him ealneg on lôcige *peccatum meum ne respicias postulo, quia hoc respicere ipse non cesso,* Past. 413, 20. Hê ne lôcað mid ðǽm eágum gesceádwîsra geðeahtes, 287, 18. Lôciað, Bt. 38, 5 ; F. 206, 15. (b) *to take care that, see that :*—Lôca nú þæt þú ofer gemet ne wilnige *vide ne impudenter velis,* Solil. H. 17, 9. Lôcige hê þ hió hæbbe hrægl *providebit puellae vestimenta,* Ll. Th. i. 46, 17. (4) *specialized uses with prepositions.* (a) *lôcian on to regard :*—Ðeáh hê forsió ðæt hê him on lôcige *ex aequo respicere ceteras dedignatur,* Past. 111, 20. (b) *lôcian tô.* (a) *to direct one's attention to, select for consideration :*—Tô hwǽm lôcige ic búton tô ðǽm eáðmódum *ad quem respiciam nisi ad humilem ?* . . . On psalmum gecueden is ðætte Drihten lôcige (*respicit*) tô ðǽm eáðmódan, Past. 299, 19–25. (ß) *to take care of, attend to :*—Lôca tô mînre generennesse *ad defensionem meam aspice,* Ps. Th. 21, 17. (γ) *to direct one's expectations to, rely on, be dependent on :*—Úre eágan tô ðê lôciað, Ps. Th. 122, 3. Þú and þá þe þê tô lôciað *tu et omnia quae tua sunt,* Gen. 20, 7. ' Lǽdað út þæt wíf and þá þe hire tô lôciað.' . . . Hê lǽddon hí of þǽre birig mid eallum hire mágum, Jos. 6, 22. (γ a) *of things, to belong to :*—Ðás þreó béc lôciað intô Strætforda, C. D. iii. 6, 23 : 19, 22. II. *with gen.* (1) *to look into, make examination of :*—Þá wæs þ gesáwen fram þám mannum þe his lôcodon (*those that looked into the matter ;* a respicientibus), þ þ wæs sóð þ hí sǽdon, Gr. D. 241, 11. (2) *to have regard to :*—Gôdra bysena lôcendra wera, Gr. D. 8, 20. (3) *to take care of, watch over :*—þú eáðmôdra ealra lôcast *humilia respicit,* Ps. Th. 137, 6. Þám cwellere ætfeóll fǽrlíce his gold. Þ wíf him cwæð ð, ' Cniht, nim þín gold þe læs þ hit losige.' Swá orsorh wæs þ wíf . . . þ heó lôcode his goldes þe hí belîfian wolde, Hml. S. 12, 221. [*O. Sax.* lôcôn. Cf. *O. H. Ger.* luogên.] v. be- (Ps. Rdr. 44, 5), ge-, ymb-lôcian.

**-lôciend.** v. on-lôciend.

**locod[e]** (?) *having flocks of wool* (v. loca) ; *shaggy :*—Hrúhge wulla raggie, loc[ode ?] flýs *hirsutas (bidentum) lanas (et) setosa (vervecum) vellera,* An. Ox. 5191.

**loc-stán,** es; *m. A stone that closes the entrance to a cave :*—Ðæs scræfes locstán hî wel fæste beclýsdon, Hml. S. 23, 345. Ðæs scræfes locstán hî út álynedon, 426.

**lôcung.** v. eft-, þurh-lôcung : **-loda.** v. ge-loda.

**loddere.** *Add :* The word occurs in local names :—Lodderþorn, Loddere-lacu, Loddæræs-sæccing, Lodres-wei, Loddera-beorh, -strǽt. v. C. D. vi. (Index).

**-lodr.** v. ge-lodr.

**lof.** *Add :* I. *praise, the expression of a favourable opinion.* (1) *from the point of view of the giver,* (a person's) *praise, praise* (expressed by that person) :—Gedyde se lǽreów ðæt hié ǽresð gehiérdon ðá heringe . . . ðætte ðæt lof hié getrymede, Past. 213, 21. Heó nis nánes lofes wyrþe *she does not deserve the praise of men,* Bt. 20 ; F. 70, 23 : Vid. 72. Wið þám lofe ðæs folces, 18, 4 ; F. 66, 21. Hæfde sigora weard wǽre betolden leódfruman mid lofe sínum *God had protected St. Andrew at the same time praising him,* An. 991. Lofum *laudibus,* i. *preconiis (uirginitatis*), An. Ox. 1903. (2) *from the point of view of the receiver,* (a person's) *praise, praise* (received by that person) :—Wyrþ oft gôdes monnes lof álegen, Bt. 18, 3 ; Fox. 64, 31. Ne biþ his lof ná ðý læsse, Bt. 40, 3 ; F. 238, 11. Þám wîsan men côm tô lofe and tô wyrðscipe þ se cyning him teohhode tô wîte, Bt. 16, 2 ; F. 52, 26. Ôþre cræftas næbbaþ nán lof ne nænne weorþscipe, 36, 1 ; F. 172, 10 : 18, 2 ; F. 64, 25. Lof sê gewyrced, hafað heáhfæstne dôm, Vid. 142. II. *the ascription of glory to the Deity :*—Lofe leánian leóhtes hyrde, Az. 121. Of lofe hweorfan þinre eádgife, Jul. 275. Lof Godes hergan, Dôm. 48. ¶ as object of verbs, forming with the verb a phrase meaning (1) *to praise :*—Þǽr wæs lof hafen fæger mid þý folce ; Fæder weorðodon, and þone sôðan Sunu wordum heredon, El. 890. Þám þe his lof bǽron, Dan. 476 : An. 1297. Hî Críst heriað and him lof lǽdað, Hy. 7, 25 : An. 1479. Crístes lof rǽran, Cri. 1689: Jul. 48. Hé Dryhtnes lof reahte and rǽrde, Gú. 130. Lof Drihtnes wyrcean, Gen. 256. (2) *to be praised :*—Á þær dôm áge, leóhtbǽre lof, sê ús þis líf giefeð, Crä. 112. III. *a hymn :*—Loob *ymnus,* Wrt. Voc. ii. 124, 27. Lof *ymnum,* i. 289, 72. III a. *certain psalms (cxlviii-cl) used in the church service :*—Lofu *laudes,* R. Ben. I. 42, 15 : 44, 4. [v. *N. E. D.* lof.] v. ǽfen-, neód-, ôret-, sealm-, word-lof.

**lôf,** es; *m.* ? *Substitute :* lôf, es; *m. A fillet, band :*—Wrǽdas, cynewiþþan, lôfas (*the MS. has the accent*) *redimicula,* An. Ox. 5241. [Cf. *O. L. Ger.* (Gail.) hâr-lôf *snood for the hair ;* licium.]

**lof-georn.** *Add :* I. in a good sense, *eager to deserve praise,* B. 3183 (*in Dict.*). II. in a bad sense, *ostentatious, boastful :*—Se seofoða leahter is *iactantia* gecweden, þ is ýdel gylp ; þ is ðonne se man bið lofgeorn and mid lícetunge fǽrð, and dêð for gylpe gif hê hwæt dælan wile, Hml. S. 16, 302. Ne sý nán man lofgeorn, ne wilnigende þæt his dǽda hálige gesǽde sién, ǽr hié hálige weorðan, R. Ben. 18, 18. Ná hê lofgeorn (*but the Latin has* prodigus) ne sý, 55, 3.

**lofian.** *Add :*—Woeron in tempel lofando (hergende, W. S., herende, R. *laudantes*) God, Lk. L. 24, 53. v. sealm-, ymb-lofian ; un-lofod : **lof-lic.** *In l.* 2 *for* 45 *l.* 55.

**lof-sang.** *Add :* I. *a song in praise of a person :*—Fausta adclamantes, i. *alto canendo vel* herigendsang *vel* lofsang, Wrt. Voc. ii. 147, 11. II. *as part of a religious service, a canticle.* v. lof ; II :—Ôþrum dagum on ðǽre wucan sý cantic gesungen, þæt is lofsang, þe tô þám dæge belimpð, R. Ben. 38, 4. Lofsang of þám godspelle, þæt is : ' Benedictus Dominus Deus Israhel,' 36, 21. [v. *N. E. D.* lof-song.]

**lof-sealm,** es; *m. Lauds, psalms* (cxlviii-cl taken together) *used in the church service :*—Þone lofsealm (*laudes*), þæt is, 'Laudate Dominum de celis,' R. Ben. 36, 18 : 38, 9.

**lofung.** *Add :*—Wynsum sié him lofung (*laudatio*) mîn, Ps. Rdr. 103, 34.

**log** (?) *water :*—Mid lande and mid loge *cum terra et cum aqua,* C. D. iv. 202, 1. [The grant in which this phrase occurs is of land that had been held by a 'húskarll' of king Edward. The alliterative phrase 'land and lögr' is common in Icelandic, so perhaps *loge* shows Scandinavian influence and is the same as English *lage* (<*lagu,* q. v.), or it may be from a nominative *log.* v. *N. E. D.* lough.]

**-lôg.** v. feá-lôg : **loga.** *Add :* v. þeód-loga : **-logen.** v. for-logen : **-lôgendlic.** v. ge-lôgendlic.

**lôgian.** *Add :*—Wê lapiað and lôgiað crístene men intô Godes hûse, Wlfst. 154, 17. Hit biþ tô langsum eall hêr tô lôgigenne be ðám clǽnum nýtenum oððe be þám unclǽnum on ðǽre ealdan ǽ *it is too tedious to give here an ordered account of everything in the old law concerning the clean and unclean animals,* Hml. S. 25, 82.

**-lôgung.** v. ge-lôgung.

**loh-sceaft.** *l.* lôh-sceaft, *and add : a stick with a strap to it* (?). v. lô.

**-lôm, -lôme, -lômlǽcing, -lômlǽcness.** v. ge-lôm, &c.

**lōm-lic,** *adj. Frequent* :—Lōmlicum siccetungum (*per*) *crebra suspiria,* An. Ox. 984. v. ge-lōmlic.

**-lōmlīce, -lōmlician, -lōmrǣd[e].** v. ge-lomlīce, &c.: lopystre. *Add* : [*Adapted from Latin* locusta.]

**loppe.** *Dele* '*flea* (?),' *and the query after* '*spider,*' *and add* : [v. N. E. D. lop.] Cf. lobbe.

**lor.** *Add* :—Þȳ lǣs hiora ǣnig tō lore wurde, Nar. 12, 25. Tō lore (lose, *v. l.*), Bd. 5, 9 ; Sch. 595, 13 (v. los). Hē þæs scipes geþrowode æfwyrdlan and lore (lyre, *v. l.*) ealra þāra þinga þe in him wǣron *navis rerum omnium jacturam pertulit,* Gr. D. 141, 14. [v. N. E. D. lore.]

**-lora.** v. hleów-lora : **-lorenness.** v. for-lorenness.

**lorh.** *Add* :—Hē sceal fela towtōla habban : flexlīnan, spinle, reól, stodlan, lorgas, Angl. ix. 263, 11. In this passage the word seems to belong to the *a*-stem masculine declension, but in the Epinal-Erfurt glossaries to the *i*-stem feminine, with *i*-umlaut of o. [*For the meaning* pole, cf. fugol-treów.]

**lorian.** *Add* : v. for-lorian.

**losian.** *Add* : A. *intrans.* I. *to be lost, perish.* (1) *of living creatures.* (a) *in a physical sense.* (a) *to die, be destroyed* :—Mid hungre ic losige *fame pereo,* Lk. L. 15, 17. Se līchoma losaþ þurh ðā oferfille, Hml. A. 6, 153. Lā, haesere, wē losaiaþ *praeceptor, perimus,* Lk. L. 8, 24. Sē ðe losade bitwih wigbed and þ wāghrǣle, Lk. L. R. 11, 51. Þā ōðre losodon, Hml. S. 4, 367. Gif se hund losige (*perierit*), Ll. Th. i. 78, 5. (β) *to lose strength, fail, faint* :—Ne losiga hiá in woeg *ne deficiant in via,* Mt. L. 15, 32. (b) in reference to temporal prosperity, *to fail, be ruined* :—Mið ðȳ gē losigað *cum defeceritis,* Lk. L. 16, 9. Ūs fremað þ ān man swelte for folce and nāteshwōn ne losige (losaige, L., (loesige, R.) *pereat,* Jn. L. 11, 50) seó mǣgð tōsomne, Hml. A. 66, 13. (c) *to perish spiritually* :—Gif se synfulla gecyrran selle . . . hē swelt (losaþ, *v. l.*), Hml. A. 139, 29. Þæt losað þ cild lādlīce hǣðen, Hml. S. 17, 155. God hī swā gebīgde tō his sōðan geleáfan þ heó ne losode, 4, 359. Ðā ārleásan ǣfre for heora yfelnysse losodon . . . Ðā ārleásan magon nǣfre ætwindan ðām ēcum wītum āhwǣr, 16, 89. (2) *of inanimate things, to decay, be destroyed, come to nothing* :—Hēr of heáfde iúero ne losað (*non peribit*), Lk. L. 21, 18. Mett sē ðe losað (*perit*), Jn. L. 6, 27. Ðā bytto losas, Mt. L. 9, 17. Se wela and se anweald losiaþ swā swā sceadu oþþe smēc, Bt. 27, 3 ; F. 98, 31. Hū ne forealldodon ðā gewritu and losodon ?, 18, 3 ; F. 64, 38. II. *to be lost to a person* (*dat.*). (1) where the subject is a material or immaterial possession lost by negligence or misadventure :—Him losað beforan Gode his ryhtwīsnes *coram Deo innocentia amittitur,* Past. 265, 11. Butergeþweor ǣlc and cȳsgerunn losaþ eów, Coll. M. 28, 19. Hē beorna reáf manige mēteð, þǣr hit mannum losað *invenit spolia multa,* Ps. Th. 118, 162. Eall heora ǣhta losodon, Hml. S. 30, 151. Seó gesceádwīsnes þurh nān ðing ne mæg þām men losian, Bt. 11, 2 ; F. 34, 18 : Met. 10, 37. (2) the subject life or limb :—þonne him feorg losað, Seef. 94 : Rä. 13, 3. (3) the subject something undesirable, which is got rid of :—Gif hié geornlīce wilnigen ðæt him yfel ðing losie *si malis veraciter carere desiderant,* Past. 263, 15. (4) the subject the loss suffered :—hē geðencan ne con hwæt him losað on ðǣre gælinge *ne ipsa quidem, quae patitur damna consideret,* Past. 39, 1. II a. *to be lost to a place, taken from a place* :—Hig . . . þæt bið forwisnad, ǣr hit āfohten foldan losige *foenum . . . quod priusquam evellatur arescit,* Ps. Th. 128, 4. III. *to be lost, be out of one's own possession or custody.* (1) of that which has strayed or been mislaid :—Gaað tō ðer ilca, ðió losade (losigað, R.), oð ðæt gemoete ðā ilca, Lk. L. 15, 4. (1 a) figurative :—Ne eom ic nā āsend būton tō ðām sceápum, ðā ðe losedon, Hml. A. 69, 110. (2) of a living creature, *to escape, abscond* :—Gif mon sweordes onlǣne ōðres esne, and hē losie, Ll. Th. i. 120, 12. Him swā geborgen sȳ heora unwilles þ heora tō fela ne losien, 274, 5. (2 a) *to escape from a person or place.* (a) with dat. :—Him se ōðer þonan losað, B. 2062. Gif þīn geneát stalie and losie þē, Ll. Th. i. 116, 10. Gif þeóf losige þȳ dæge þām monnum þe hine gefōð, 148, 6. Þǣr ǣnig ne mæg losian caldan clommum, Cri. 1629 : 1002 : Rä. 3, 11. (β) with prep. :—Swā swā spearuwa of huntan grīne losige *sicut passer erepta est de laqueo venantium,* Ps. Th. 123, 6. IV. *to be lost, not to be obtained,* the subject something one might have had :—Gíf him þæt rīce losað *if they fail to get heaven,* Gen. 434. Ðȳ lǣs him losige ðæt heofenlice ondgit *ne ipso veritatis intellectu vacuetur,* Past. 85, 7. þæt him hālig gǣst losige þurh leahtras on þās lǣnan tīd, Cri. 1559. V. *to be wasted, not to be used to advantage* :—Somnigas ðā screádunga ðætte ne loesige (losia, L.), Jn. R. 6, 12. Gif fǣruuga cymð se ȳtemesta dæg, þonne bið losod seó eldi[n]g, Archiv cxxii. 257, 17. B. *trans.* (in the Lindisfarne Gospels for the most part). I. *to destroy.* (1) in respect to temporal matters :—Ðā wyflo yfle losas *malos male perdet,* Mt. L. 21, 41. Ðeóf ne cymeð būta þte . . . spilleð ᛏ losað (-as, L.), Jn. R. 10, 10. Ðe cynig fordyde ᛏ losade morðorslago ðā ilco, Mt. L. 22, 7. Hine se diówl losade (*dissipauit*), Lk. L. 9, 42. Cuōm þ flōd and losade ᛏ spilde (*perdidit*) alle, 17, 27. Hine in fýr sende þte hine losade ᛏ fordyde, Mk. L. R. 9, 22. Cwōme ðū losige ᛏ tō losane ūsig, 1, 24. Losiga, Lk. L. 6, 9. Sōhtun hine tō losanne, Jn. R. 10, 39. (2) of spiritual

destruction :—Hē sāuel his losað, Lk. L. R. 9, 24, 25. Ðā sāuel losige ᛏ fordōa in tintergo, Mt. L. 10, 28. II. *to lose, be deprived of* :—Ne losade (losa, R.) ic of ðǣm ǣniht, Jn. L. 18, 9. Þte all þ salde mē ne ic losige (loesge, R.) of ðǣm, 6, 39. III. *to lose, cease to know the whereabouts of* an object :—Gif losað ēnne of ðǣm, . . . mið ðȳ gemoetað hiá, Lk. L. 15, 4. Gif wīf losað cāsering ēnne, Lk. L. R. 15, 8. IV. *to fail to obtain* :—Ne loseð mearda his, Mt. L. 10, 42. Losað, Mt. L. R. 9, 41. v. for-losian.

**los-wist.** This word is taken out of its order between los and lose.

**lot.** *Add* :—Met. 4, 46. Ðonne hié ōðre menn mid hira lote bismriað, ðonne gielpað hié suelce hī sién micle wǣrran ðonne hié *dum perversa et duplici actione ceteros fallunt, quasi praestantius ceteris prudentes se esse gloriantur,* Past. 243, 24. þū wylt þysre byrig ealde witan mid þīnan lote bepǣcan, Hml. S. 23, 711. Of lote *astu, astutia doli,* An. Ox. 50, 48. Lotu (locu, MS.) *uersutias,* i. *callidates* (Zabulus . . . novas *versutias* adversus Guthlacum . . . versare coepit, Guth. Gr. 137), 37, 2. v. wǣr-lot.

**loten.** v. forþ-loten : **lotendra**? *madendum.* *Substitute* :—Bītendra mandentium. [Wrt. Voc. ii. 57, 44–47 reads :—*Mandit* eteð, *mando* ic ete, *madendum* lotendra, *mandeo* ic bīte.]

**loþa.** *Add* :—Loþa heordan of wearpe, of ācumban wæs gehefeldad *colobium* (*cum*) *de stuppae stamine* (*vel potius*) *putamine ordiretur,* An. Ox. 3725.

**lot-wrenc.** *Add* :—Ðā beóð gesǣlige þe deófles swicdōmas tōcnāwað and his lotwrencas mid geleáfan oferswȳðað, Hml. S. 16, 224.

**lūcan.** [*The transitive and intransitive uses should be separated.*] *Add* :—Luce *conderet,* i. *clauderet,* An. Ox. 28, 18. [v. N. E. D. louk *to close.*] v. sām-locen.

**lūcan** *to pull up.* *Add* : [v. N. E. D. louk *to pull up or out.*] v. tō-lūcan : lūcung (?). v. an-lūtung.

**lufen.** *Add* :—Nabochodonossor him on uýd dyde Israēla bearn ofer ealle lufen tō weorcþeówum (*forced them into hopeless slavery*), Dan. 73.

**lufestre.** *Substitute* : A (*female*) *lover* :—Nȳðhǣmedra lufiestran (*Veneris*) *stuprorum amatricis,* An. Ox. 2, 334. Nēdhǣmestran, lufestran, 4451.

**lufian.** *Add* : I. with object a person or personal adjunct. (1) *to have a great affection or regard for, hold dear.* (a) the subject a person :—Ic lufiu (*diligam*) ðē, Ps. Srt. 17, 1. Sē þe his feónd lufað, Mód. 70. Hī his naman lufiað *diligunt nomen ejus,* Ps. Th. 68, 37. þæt þū sōð godu lufian wolde, Jul. 195. (b) the subject an animal :—Ðeáh seó leó hire mǣgister swīðe lufige, Bt. 25 ; F. 88, 10 : Met. 13, 20. (c) the subject love :—Sió lufu ðonne hió lufað ætsomne ǣgðer ge God ge his niéhstan, Past. 87, 8. (2) with reference to love between the sexes :—Isaac underfēng Rebeccan tō wīfe and lufode hig swīðe, Gen. 24, 67. Gif ðū hwilc ǣnlic wīf lofodest swīðe ungemetlīce (*amore flagrares*), and heó nolde þē lufian, Solil. H. 42, 15 : Bt. 38, 1 ; F. 194, 25. His mōd ongon fǣmnan lufian, Jul. 27. (3) *to express affection in words* :—Hē gearnode þ hē eác ðā hālegan hǣrenesse gehȳrde, hū hī God lufodon (lofodon, *v. l.*) and heredon *laudes beatas meruit audire,* Bd. 3, 19 ; Sch. 277, 20. Þegnas heredon, lufedun leófwendum lifes āgend, Cri. 471. Wuton wuldrian hālgan hliððorcwidum hiofenríces weard, lufian liófwendum lifes āgend, Hȳ. 8, 3. (4) *to express affection by action or conduct, to caress, cherish* :—Ic lufige *foveo,* Wrt. Voc. ii. 38, 11. Swilc God wyrceð gǣsta lifes tō trumnaðe . . . Swā se almihtiga ealle gesceafte lufað in līchoman, Gū. 733. Ic geteáh his mōd tō þon þ hē lufode mid his brādre hand þā nunnan and ofer þā sculdru geþaccode *cujus mentem traxerit, ut in terga ejusdem sanctimonialis feminae blandiens alapam daret,* Gr. D. 189, 22. Heó lufode þā leóde, liðwǣge bær hælum tō handa, B. 1982. Frofre gǣst in Gūðlāces geóce gewunade, lufade hine and lǣrde, Gū. 109. Cōmon earnas . . . lissum lufodon, An. 870. Nemne hē God lufige mid lācum, Jul. 111. Hī beádon hīne þ hē sceolde healdan hī rihtlīce and lufian hī, Chr. 1083 ; P. 214, 19. II. with object a thing. (1) *to be strongly attached to, be unwilling to part with* :—Sē ðe lufað sāuel his spildeð ᛏ losað hiá, Jn. L. R. 12, 25. (2) *to have a strong liking for, be very fond of* :—Hē līcett ðæt hē lufige ðæt hē ne lufað, ðisses middangeardes gilp hē lufað, and hē līcett swelce hē ðone onscunige *fingit se de bono opere amare, quod non amat, de mundi autem gloria non amare, quod amat,* Past. 57, 1. Ðonne heó lufaþ þās eorþlican þing. Bt. 33, 4 ; F. 132, 17 : Met. 20, 223. Hig lufigeað þā fyrmystan setl on gebeórscypum, Mt. 23, 6. Lufiað, Lk. 11, 43. Snottre men lufiað midwist nīine, Rä. 89, 7. Wē lufedon ūra wamba fylnesse, Verc. Först. 123, 14. Þām þe þrowera þeáwas lufedon, Gū. 132. Nǣfre þū geþreátast . . . þ ic þeódscipe þīnne lufie, Jul. 178. Gyf wē sēlre geleorniað þ we willað georne lufian (*gaudenter amplectimur*), Ll. Th. i. 440, 22. (3) *to regard with favour, approve of* :—Gif wē ōðerra monna welgedōna dǣda ne lufigað and ne herigað *si aliena bene gesta non diligimus,* Past. 231, 1. Eal swilc is tō leánne and nǣfre tō lufianne, Ll. Th. i. 322, 22. (4) *to be devoted to a practice* :—Hǣðenscipe biþ þ man . . . wiccecræft lufige oþþe morðweorc gefremme, Ll. Th. i. 378, 21. (5) *to take pleasure in the existence of* a virtue, practice, state of things (*acc. or clause*) :—God lufað þæt man sī mildheort (*miseri-*

*cordiam diligit Dominus*, Ps. Th. 83, 12. Đū đæt ne lufedest þæt ic þē bernelāc brengan mōste, Ps. C. 122. ¶ in the legal formula :—Ic wille beón N. hold and getrīwe, and eal lufian þ hē lufađ, and eal āscunian þ hē āscunađ, Ll. Th. i. 178, 4. (6) *to take pleasure in*. (a) doing something, *love* to do (*clause*) :—Þā lufiađ þ hig gebiddon hī standende on gesomnungum *qui amant in synagogis stantes orare*, Mt. 6, 5. (b) something being done :—Hig lufigeađ þ hig man grēte on strǣtum, Mt. 23, 7. III. with prep. (?) *to bestow affection* on :—Wē lufedon ūra wamba fylnesse and on ūre gold and on ūre glengnesse and on ūre myclan gestreóne and on reáflācum. Swīđor wē þæt lufedon, þonne wē dydon Godes beboda, Verc. Först. 123, 14-17. v. sceand-lufiende, *and next word.*

**lufiend.** *Add* : I. *a lover* of a person. (1) cf. lufian ; I. 1 a :—Swā swā lufu byđ betweóna þām lufiende and þām þe hē lufađ, Solil. H. 28, 16. (2) of love between the sexes. Cf. lufian ; I. 2 :—Ic hæbbe ođerne lufiend . . . sē đe his geleáfan hring mē lēt tō wedde, Hml. S. 7, 27. (3) *a protector, cherisher.* Cf. lufian ; I. 4 :—Hē wæs þearfena lufiend *cultor pauperum*, Gr. D. 329, 13. II. *a lover* of a thing. (1) cf. lufian ; II. 4 :—Þū cwēn, lāre lufigend, Ap. Th. 18, 12. Đæs wŷsdōmes lufiendas *amatores sapientiae*, Solil. H. 42, 2. (2) cf. lufian ; II. 5 :—Geornful lufiend *cupidus* (*castitatis*) *amator*, An. Ox. 363. Brōđerrǣd-enne lufigendras, Scint. 14, 3.

**lufiend-lic.** *Add* :—Heó wæs swīþe lufigendlic eallum onlōciendum *omnium oculis gratiosa et anabilis videbatur*, Hml. A. 95, 98. Lufiendlices (*omne quicquid*) *delectabile*, An. Ox. 334.

**luf-lic.** *Add* :—Crīst hlinode on his (*John's*) luflicum breóste, Ælfc. T. Grn. 13, 2. Hē frēfrode hī mid luflicum wordum *eos verbis consolabatur*, Gr. D. 251, 20 : Hml. A. 73, 9.

**luflíce.** *Add* : I. of conduct, treatment, *courteously, pleasantly* :—Luflíce *affabiliter* (*instruendo*), Wrt. Voc. ii. 80, 64. Hié ūs luflíce (*benigne*) onfēngon, Nar. 17, 18. Hē þære fǣmnan grētinge luflíce (*gratanter*) onfēng, Guth. Gr. 158, 9. II. of speech :—Mid þām þe luflíce sprecađ tō heora nýhstum *cum his qui loquuntur pacem cum proximo suo*, Ps. Th. 27, 4. Đā munecas hit mǣndon lufelíce (*complained in courteous terms*) tō him, Chr. 1083 ; P. 214, 18.

**luf-rǣden.** *Add* :—L[u]fr[ǣdenne] *caritatem*, An. Ox. 56, 224. [v. *N.E.D.* love-red.]

**luf-sum.** *Add* : [v. *N.E.D.* lovesome.]

**lufsum-lic** ; *adj. Pleasing, desirable* :—Đā sende se pāpa Ōswió lufsumlic (*desiderabilem*) ǣrendgewrit, Bd. 3 ; 29 ; Sch. 329, 2.

**lufsumlíce.** *Add* : [v. *N.E.D.* lovesomely] : **lufsum-ness.** *Add* : [v. *N.E.D.* lovesomeness.]

**luf-tíme.** *Add* : *agreeable* :—Luftŷme *affabilis*, An. Ox. 56, 217. Đeós sylfe hŷrsumnes biđ Gode antfenge and mannum luftēme (*dulcis*), R. Ben. 20, 17. Gif đæm mǣdenum likiađ hyra luftŷman sprǣce, Hex. 48, 16. Luftēmpre *dulcius*, R. Ben. I. 3, 8.

**luftim-lic** ; *adj. Agreeable, pleasant* :—Luftŷmlica *amplectende*, An. Ox. 56, 254.

**lufu.** *Add* : I. *warm affection, attachment* :—Unc gemǣne ne sceal elles āwiht nymđe lufu langsumu, Gen. 1906. His þegnas for hiora eardes lufan tilodon hine tō forlǣtanne, Bt. 38, 1 ; F. 194, 28. Ic hæfde brōdor and eđel on Egyptum and þǣr mid mīnum māgum wunode . . . þā ongan ic heora lufu (lufa, *v.l.*) forhycgan, Hml. S. 23 b, 326. ¶ plural with force of singular :—Đeáh hē hit for lufum (*spiritu dilectionis*) dō, Past. 167, 12. Hit is nū đearf đæt wē for lufum (*caritatis studio*) eft cierren, 461, 10. I a. *an act of kindness, action prompted by love* :—Ān lufu is þe þū miht mē gegearwian *unum est quod mihi impendere beneficium potes*, Gr. D. 182, 5. Bescirede duguđa gehwylcre, lufena and lissa, Gū. 1049. I b. *amicable settlement as opposed to litigation* (v. *N.E.D.* love ; I d), Ll. Th. i. 298, 5 (*in Dict.*). II. in a religious sense, *love*; caritas. (1) of God towards man :—Seó godcunde lufu, Bt. 10 ; F. 30, 8. Swā se ælmihtiga ealle gesceafte lufađ . . . Nis þæt lǣsast þæt seó lufu cýđeđ, Gū. 741. Fore monna lufan mīn (*Christ's*) þrowade heáfod hearmslege, Cri. 1434. Ic lufan symle lǣstan wiđ eówic *I will ever show my love to you*, 477. Lufan Dryhtnes wyrcan *to gain the love of God by deeds*, Dōm. 49. Lufe wyrcean, Gen. 624. (2) of man towards God :—Him Dryhtnes lof born in breóstum, brondhāt lufu, Gū. 937. Seó lufu . . . byđ geēced þonne þæt andgyt byđ gefæstnod on Gode ; ne þǣre lufu ne byđ nān ende, Solil. H. 29, 6-8. Hī feorh āgēfan for Meotudes lufan, Men. 82. Ealle gesceafta habbaþ gemǣnelíce đā āne lufe, þ hī þeówian swilcum hlāforde, Bt. 39, 13 ; F. 234, 28 : Solil. H. 28, 11. On breóstum wegan byrnende lufan Meotodes, Edg. 40. His lufan ādreógan, Gū. 63. For Godes lufum and for Godes ege *supernae formidinis et dilectioni spiritu afflatus*, Past. 169, 3. (3) of God's creatures to one another :—Sybb sŷ mid eówic, symle sōđ lufu, Jul. 669. Sybbe healdan, gǣstlice lufu, Leás. 39. III. *strong feeling, passion, affection* :—Sē þe nū gehæft sié mid đǣre unnyttan lufe þisse middangeardes *quos fallax ligat terrenis habitans libido mentis*, Bt. 34, 8 ; F. 144, 25. Flǣsclicra gewilnunga lufa *carnalium desideriorum affectus* (acc. pl.), Scint. 28, 13. III a. *strong liking* for, or *devotion* to something (*gen.*) :—Sybbe lufu, Ps. Th. 84, 9. Hwæđer đē ǣnig lufe

ođđe lust sī ǣnigre wemnesse, Solil. H. 36, 13. Eall sió lufu đæs hǣmeđđinges biþ for gecynde *haec caritas ex naturali intentione procedit*, Bt. 34, 11 ; F. 152, 14. For đāra leásena spella lufan, 35, 5 ; F. 166, 16. IV. *love* between man and woman :—Gif đū hwilc ǣnlic wīf lofodest, and heó nolde þē lufian on nān ođer gerād būtan þū woldest ǣlce ōđer lufe ālētan for hyre ānre lufe, Solil. H. 42, 16. Lufan, Bt. 38, 1 ; F. 194, 26. Hit þūhte him feáwa daga for þǣre lufe þe hē tō hire hæfde, Gen. 29, 20. Heó þæs beornes lufan wiđhogde, Jul. 41. Hē sinhīgscipas gesamnaþ mid clǣnlicre lufe *hic conjugii sacrum castis nectit amoribus*, Bt. 21 ; F. 74, 38. Đā lufe mon mæg swīþe uneáþe, ođđe nā, forbeódan, 35, 6 ; F. 170, 11. Druncen beorg þē . . . and idese lufan, Fä. 26. IV a. personified :—Đec lufađ clene lufe *te diligat castus amor*, Ps. Srt. ii. p. 202, 7. V. *an object of desire* :—Hē sægde hire his lust and willan, þ his lufu wǣre þ hē þā stōwe neósode þāra eádigra apostola *indicauit ei desiderium sibi inesse beatorum apostolorum limina uisitandi*, Bd. 5, 19 ; Sch. 657, 14. VI. in phrases with a preposition. (1) *with* for, for the *love* or *sake* of :—Ic ācsige þē hweđer þū ađer ođđe for heora lufum ođđe for ǣniges þinges lufum hym eft tō geēnan wille . . . hweđer þū for heora lufum woldest đās þing underfōn, Solil. H. 38, 4-9. (2) *with* on :—Gif him sŷ Meotud on lufan, Fä. 10. Ic hī on lufan mīnre hæfde *quae dilexi*, Ps. Th. 118, 47 : 121, 6. v. brōþor-, mōder-, weorold-lufu.

**lufung**, e ; *f. Loving, action of loving* :—Þā lufedon hī hyre māgas līchamlíce and on þǣre lufunge wǣron hyre ēhtende (*amando persequentes*), Gr. D. 73, 14.

**luf-wende.** *Add* : *loving, affectionate* :—Amans *homo byđ* lufwende man, Angl. viii. 331, 41. Lufwyndre sage *amico fatu*, An. Ox. 18, 26. [Ich luuie þe tō leofmon, luuewende lauerd, Jul. 65, 5.]

**lufwendlic** *friendly.* For 'amabilis, Lye' *substitute* :—Lufwendlic wer *vir amicabilis*, Kent. Gl. 661.

**lufwendlíce** ; *adv. In friendly fashion* :—Lufwendlíce *blande* (*ingreditur*), Kent. Gl. 912.

**luh.** *Add* : [v. *N.E.D.* lough (1)] : **luncian.** v. hincian.

**Lunden.** *Add* : , e ; *f.* :—Nam man đæt wīf and ādrencte hī æt Lundene brigce, C. D. iii. 125, 14. Innan Lundene fenn ; andlang sūđ on Temese, 73, 20. Lundene ware biscop, iv. 291, 33. Lundene waru grīđede wiđ þone here, Chr. 1016 ; P. 153, 8. Tō Lundene weard, P. 148, 14 : 1052 ; P. 179, 7. On Paules byrig binnan Lundene, C. D. iv. 290, 15. On Sūđrian wiđ Lundenne, iii. 349, 36. Hēr wæs micel wælsliht on Lundenne, Chr. 839 ; P. 64, 3. Gemōt on Lunden, 1050 ; P. 171, 37. Abb tō Lunden, 38. Hī on þā burh Lundene (*or gen.* ?) gefuhton, 1009 ; P. 139, 25.

**Lunden-burh.** *Add* :—On Lundenbyrig, C. D. vi. 80, 12.

**Lundenisc.** *Add* : [Stephne cōm tō Lundene and te Lundenisce folc him underfēng, Chr. 1135 ; P. 263, 14. Te Lundenissce folc, 1140 ; P. 266, 30.]

**Lunden-tūn** *London* :—From þǣm nēdbāderum in Luundentūnes hŷđe, C. D. i. 114, 21.

**Lunden-waru**, e ; *f. The Londoners, people of London* :—Lundenwaru grīđode wiđ þone here, Chr. 1016 ; Erl. 159, 22.

**Lunden-weg**, es ; *m. The London-road* :—Andlang đæs mylanweges on đone Lundenweg ; andlang đes Lundænes weges, C. D. vi. 31, 29.

**lund-laga.** *Add* :—Lundlagan (-leogan, lxxii, 5) *veniculos*, Lch. i. lxxiv, 28.

**-lunga.** v. -linga.

**lungen.** *Add* :—Wiđ miltan sāre foxes lungen . . . gesoden, Ll. i. 340, 4, 11. Smyre mid þām wǣtan þe drýpe of healfsodenre rammes lungenne (-ene, *v.l.*), 356, 19. Hē āsceat āne flān and ātǣsde đone cyning betwux þǣre lungene (*inter pulmonem et stomachum*, 2 Kings 22, 34), Hml. S. 18, 221.

**lungen-ādl.** *Add* :—Dolhsealf wiđ lungenādle, Lch. ii. 92, 13.

**lungen-ǣder**, e ; *f. A lung-vein* :—Lǣt him of lungenǣdre blōd, Lch. ii. 106, 24.

**lungen-sealf.** *Add* :—Wyrc lungensealfe, nim cost . . . , Lch. iii. 70, 1.

**lunger** ; *adj. Quick to act* [:—Ceáslunger *contentiosus*, Chrd. 19, 12]. [*O. Sax., O. H. Ger.* lungar *strenuus, expeditus.*] *See next word.*

**lungre.** *Add* : I. of prompt action :—Eódon lungre under linde, nalæs late wǣron eorre æscberend, An. 46. Lungre leórdan, nalas leng bidon, 1044. II. of violent action :—Ic lungre eam deópe gedrēfed, Cri. 167. Flōdwylm ne mæg manna ǣnigne ofer Meotudes ēst lungre gelettan, An. 518 : 1423 : 1474. III. of unchecked action :—Ne magan wē him lungre lāđ ætfæstan (cf. hine God forstōd, 1337), An. 1349. *See preceding word.*

**lūs.** *Add* :—Wiđ lūsan sealf . . . sōna đā lýs swyltađ, Lch. iii. 54, 21-25 : 28. Wyrc sealfe wiđ lūsum . . . seó sealf gedēđ þ þær biđ þāra lūsa lǣs, 50, 16-18.

**lust.** *Add* : I. *pleasure, delight* :—Þū hæfst ongyten þā wonclan trūwa þæs blindan lustes *deprehendisti caeci numinis ambiguos vultus*, Bt. 7, 2 ; F. 18, 3. Hē hæfde his heofonricre hēr on eorđan, þā hine nānes willan næs forwyrnd hēr, ne nānes lustes on þysse weorulde, Ps. Th. 48,

18. Luste *oblectamento* (*verborum fraudulento*), An. Ox. 5285. Hwæðer him ðæt geðóht cume of færlicum luste (*delectatione*), Past. 417, 5. Hé lust wigeð, B. 599. Hú manige þu forléten hæbbe þisse worlde lusta for Gode, Solil. H. 23, 4, 7. Ic ongite þætte ... seó héhste blis nis on þám flǽsclicum lustum *video* ... *nec laetitiam voluptatibus posse contingere*, Bt. 33, 1; F. 120, 6. ¶ with prep. or oblique case used adverbially. (v. II. ¶) *with pleasure, gladly.* (1) *with prep.* on luste, on lust :— Wíf bæd hine blíðne æt þære beórþege ... Hé on lust geþeah seleful, B. 618: Vy. 76: Rä. 71, 7. Sceal lof Drihtnes on lust sprecan mín múð, Ps. Th. 144, 21. (2) dat. (inst.)—Seó sáwl mid gefeán séceð lustum þæt lámfæt, Seel. 133: 136. Wé þás sǽlác lustum bróhton tíres tó tácne, B. 1653. Hé (*Christ*) lustum dreág ehtendra níð, Gú. 495. God weorðiað mid lofsangum lustum myclum, Ps. Th. 99, 3. Hé (*Noah*) stáh ofer streámweall lustum miclum, Gen. 1495. II. *desire, appetite* for something :—Monað módes lust ferð tó féran, Seef. 36. Úsic lust hweteð on þá leódmearce, An. 286. þæt ic þé mæge lust áhwettan *that I may whet your appetite*, i. e. *make you more ready* (*to take us as passengers*), 303. Ne lyst mé nú þæs; ac gyf hyt mé æfre on lust becymð *I do not desire it, but if ever it becomes a desire to me*, Solil. H. 36, 16. ¶ in a bad sense, *greed* :—Ús þurh þíne lust and gítsunga onscunian sceal Scippend, Bt. 7, 5; F. 24, 5. II a. with gen. of thing desired :—Ic wolde witan hwæðer ðé ænig lufe oððe lust sí ænigre wemnesse, Solil. H. 36, 14. On ðǽm luste yfles weorces, Past. 71, 14. Lust leófes síðes, Exod. 53. þurh firena lust, Cri. 369. II b. with clause giving that which is desired :—Him wæs lust micel þæt hé þiossum leódum leóf spellode, Met. Ein. 3. Se Sceoppend eallra gesceafta hæþ forgifen ǽnne lust eallum his gesceaftum, þ is þ hí woldon á bión, Bt. 34, 12; F. 152, 17. Hé sægde hire his lust and willan, þ his lufu wǽre þ hé þá stówe neósode, Bd. 5, 19; Sch. 657, 13. II c. (*one's*) *desire* or *wish*—Hé wénþ gif hé ðonne lust begite *if he get his desire*, Bt. 34, 7; F. 144, 4. þæt bið eádig wer, sé ðe á þenceð þ hé his lust on þon gefylle *beatus vir qui implevit desiderium suum ex ipsis*, Ps. Th. 126, 6. Hí hiora lusta lifdon hwíle *desiderium eorum attulit eis*, 77, 29. Hé hí lífian hét lustum heortena (*secundum desideria cordis eorum*), 80, 12. þ mon fulgá eallum his lustum, Bt. 24, 2; F. 82, 13. II. ¶ with prep. or oblique case used adverbially (v. I. ¶), *with alacrity, willingly, eagerly*. (1) *with prep.* on luste, on lust :—Wǽron æscwigan ... síðes gefýsde ..., fóron on luste cáseres bodan, El. 262. (2) *with case* :—Heó (*Hagar*) lustum ne wolde þeówdóm þolian, Gen. 2239. þá clǽnan folc ... ǽr sinne cwide georne, lustum lǽstun, Cri. 1225. Ic þé gearuwe tó, æt leóhte gehwám, lustum wacie, Ps. Th. 62, 1. Mé lustum álýs, and mé lungre weorð, ... georne þeccend, 70, 2. Hú ic ǽ þíne lustum lufode, 118, 97. Lustume (lustum ?) *voluntarie*, Rtl. 28, 13. III. *sensuous appetite* or *desire, considered as sinful* or *leading to sin* :—Se lust ðe hine geunrótsað, Past. 417, 8. Sió scyld ðe hiene ðurh sciénesse costað for his luste, 79, 22. Ðá ðe mid færlice luste (cf. *unryhtgewilnunge*, 30) bióð oferswíðde *qui repentina concupiscentia superantur*, 429, 33. þá þe æfter hiora líchoman luste irnaþ, Bt. 41, 3; F. 246, 24. Lusta *libidinum*, An. Ox. 1907. Líchamlicere geþeódnesse lustum *carnalis copulæ voluptatibus*, 1606. Se þe líþ on his líchaman lustum, he bið anlícost féttum swínum, Bt. 37, 4; F. 192, 25. Hé ofðrysce ðá lustas his unðeáwa, Past. 85, 12. Wé á sculon idle lustas, synwunde forseón, Cri. 756. IV. *sexual appetite* or *desire* :—Ðá ðe ofðryscað ðá styringe ðæs flǽsclican lustes, Past. 409, 2. Wrǽne on lust áslád (*praeses*) *petulcus in luxum labescit*, An. Ox. 4650. V. *lust, passionate desire* for something :—Wæs se leódhete þrohtheard ... þrymman sceócon módige maguþegnas morðres on luste, woldon on þám hysebeorþre heafolan gescénan, 1142. VI. *of a thing, vigour, lustiness* (?) :—Úp gewát líg and þurh lust (*by its violence* ?) geslóh micle máre þonne gemet wǽre, Dan. 249. v. geoguþ-, unriht-, wamm-, weorold-, wyn-lust.

lust-bǽre. *Add*: I. *pleasant, desirable* :—Hié beóð tó myndgianne ðára góda ðe hié ǽr dydon, ðæt hié sién ðe lustbǽrran tó gehiéranne ðæt him mon beódan wielle, Past. 303, 8.

lustbǽre; *adv.* *With pleasure, gladly, willingly*—Ic wolde lustbǽre mid tácne þære hálgan róde mé bletsian, ac ic næbbe ðá mihte *volo me signare, sed non possum*, Hml. Th. i. 534, 23. Sum eáwfæst ðegen bæd ðone hálgan wer ..., and hé lustbǽre ðæs getíðode, ii. 172, 9. Hé efne móde and gladum þá ðénunga lustbǽre gefylle *ipso aequo animo impleat officium*, R. Ben. 55, 17.

lustbǽr-líc. *Add* :—Seó andweardnes þære lustbǽrlican onsýne *praesentia concupitae formae*, Gr. D. 188, 12.

lust-full. v. ge-lustfull.

lustfullian. *Add*: I. *to take delight.* (1) absolute, Bd. 1, 27; Sch. 96, 20: 97, 11: 96, 7 (*in Dict.*). (2) *to delight* in (*on*), Hml. S. 8, 116 (*in Dict.*). (3) with dat. *to be delighted* with :—Ic lustfullode ðære stówe swétnesse and wlite *delectata suauitate ac decore loci illius*, Bd. 5, 12; Sch. 629, 12. Ongan hé lustfullian þæs bisceopes wordum *uerbis delectatus*, 2, 9; Sch. 148, 8. Ongan se bysceop lustfullian þæs iungan snytro and his wíslicra worda *deleciabatur antistes prudentia uer-

borum iuuenis*, 5, 19; Sch. 658, 23. Lustfulliende (-igende, *v.l.*) þám écum médum *delectatus praemiis*, 4, 25; Sch. 497, 10. Wæs heó lustfulliende (-igende, *v.l.*) þære gódan foresetenesse *delectata bono proposito*, 5, 19; Sch. 657, 17. (3 a) with acc. (and dat. ?) :—Se cyning ongan lustfullian þ clǽneste líf háligra and (mid, *v.l.*) hiora gehátum *rex delectatus uita mundissima sanctorum et promissis eorum*, Bd. 1, 26; Sch. 58, 14. (4) with infin. :—Ic lustfulliende wæs (lustfullode, *v.l.*) þára gemánan brúcan þe ic on þære stówe sceáwade *delectatus consortio eorum, quos in illo loco uidebam*, Bd. 5, 12; Sch. 629, 10. II. *to give delight* :—Ðeáh ðæt ðǽm móde lícige and lustfullige (*delectat*), Past. 71, 23.

lustfull-nes. *Add* :—þá þá hé geseah þá lustfullnesse þæs líchaman (*delectationem carnis*) ... hé sprǽc þysne cwyde : 'Eall seó lustfulnes and swétnes þæs líchaman weorðeþ tó wyrma geride (*dulcedo illius vermes*), Gr. D. 323, 1–3 : 8. His lustfullnysse him ne belífð nán ðing, Hex. 50, 25. Sió gítsung ðæt mód ðæt hió gebindeð mid ðære lustfulnesse, hió hit gewundað *avaritia capti. animum, dum quasi delectat, exulcerat*, Past. 71, 21. Gehíren hí ðæt ðás andweardan gód bióð from ǽlcre lustfulnesse (*a delectatione*) gewítende, 441, 20: Gr. D. 322, 27. Lustfulnes[sa] *inlecebras, uoluptates*, An. Ox. 50, 6.

lustfullung. *Add*: I. in a not unfavourable sense :—Gehwilce untrume and forsewenlíce on ðissum middanearde swá miccle hraðor Godes stemne gehýrað, swá micclum swá hí lytle lustfullunge on ðisum lífe habbað, Hml. Th. ii. 376, 6. I a. *pleasure in something* (*gen.*) :—þæt þú on míne heortan getryme þínra beboda lustfullunga, Angl. xi. 101, 28. II. in an unfavourable sense :—On þreó wísan bið deófles costnung ; þæt is on tihtinge, on lustfullunge, on gefawunge. Deófol tiht ús tó yfele, ac wé sceolon ... geniman náne lustfullunge tó ðære tihtinge ... Se Hǽlend mihte beón gecostnod þurh tihtinge, ac nán lustfullung ne hrepede his mód, Hml. Th. i. 174, 30–176, 7. Ic gesyngode on yfelre geðafunge, and on unclǽnre lustfullunge, Angl. xi. 112, 14. Nihtsumere wynne þá ásmeádan lustfullunga *opulenti luxus exquisita oblectamenta*, An. Ox. 325. v. ge-lustfullung.

lust-grin. l. -grín : -lustian. v. ge-lustian.

lustlíce. *Add* :—Yfel biþ gesælþ gif hit mon lustlíce dẽð and geðyldlíce áræfnþ *beata sors omnis est aequinamitate tolerantis*, Bt. 11, 1 ; F. 32, 31 : 38, 7 ; F. 210, 14. Ic lióða fela lustlíce (v. lustbǽrlíce) sanc, Met. 2, 1. Sẽ ðe Godes beboda lustlíce gehýrð, and lustlícor mid weorcum gefylð, Hml. Th. i. 552, 2. Hé sylþ mẽ hors oþþe beáh þæt þe lustlícor cræft mínne ic (*the hunter*) begange, Coll. M. 22, 38.

lustsum-líc. *Add*:—Ðá syndon swýþe fægere and lustsumlíce on tó seónne, Ors. 1, 3 ; S. 32, 14.

lustume. v. lust ; II. ¶ 2.

lútan. *Add* :—Heó leát tó slege, and hé slóh þá tó mid eallum mægene *she bent to receive the blow, and he struck at her with all his might*, Hml. S. 12, 211.

lutian. *Add*:—Ic lutie *delituo*, An. Ox. 18 b, 20. Synne áttor lutude (*latebat*) on geþance, Scint. 39, 7. Lutode *torpebat*, Germ. 401, 23. þisne lutigendne (*latitantem*) in þám scræfe þá hyrdas gemétton, Gr. D. 100, 8. Lutiende *delitescente*, i. *latitante*, An. Ox. 3745. Wunda lutigendra *vulnerum latentium*, Hy. S. 33, 25. [Cf. *Goth.* lutôn.] v. æt-, be-, ge-lutian.

lybean. *Add*:—Lybisne *dilaturas* (*ligaturas* ?), Hpt. 33, 250, 8.

lyb-lác. *Add* :—Úton forbúgan þá synleahtras þe ús forbodene synd, þ is ... lyblác and ealle þá unþeáwas þe deóflu on mancynn gebringað, Wlfst. 135, 3.

lyb-lǽca. *Add*:—þá lyblǽcan and þá ðe manige galdor cunnon and þá ðe gelóme galaþ ... þá þe hér bióð þá mǽstan drýicgan and gealdorcræftigan ne cumað nǽfre of þæra wyrma seáðe, Nap. 43. Lyblaecan *caragios*, Wrt. Voc. ii. 103, 24.

lyffetere. *Add*:—Lyftere (lystere, MS. ; *but cf.* liffetere *favisor*, Wrt. Voc. i. 49, 14. Ólececeþ *favet* ii. 147, 19) *fautoris* (*strophosi fautoris instinctu*, Ald. 66, 19. Cf. *instinctu strophosi hostis*, 37, 3, *in both passages the devil is meant*), An. Ox. 4674. Lyffeterum *parasitis*, An. Ox. 11, 183.

lyffettan. *Add* :—þænne hí lyfetað *dum adulantur*, R. Ben. I. 110, 11. Mardocheus sæt þǽr úte and nolde álútan ne lyffettan þám Amane *cum Aman vidisset Mardochaeum sedentem ante fores palatii, et non solum non assurrexisse sibi, sed nec motum quidem de loco sessionis suae*, Hml. A. 97, 194. Hé nolde nǽfre lyffettan ne mid ólecunge sprǽcan, Hml. S. 31, 626. Swá gewuna is þ þǽra liffettendra (*adulantium*) tunge cwylmeð þæs sáwle þe hí gehýran wile ... preóstas liffetende syrwdon, Gr. D. 34, 26–35, 1.

lyffetung. *Add*:—Ðæt mód undercrýpð seó léase liffetung (*adulatio*), Gr. D. 35, 16. Manna lyffetunge ic lufode tó swíðe, Angl. xi. 113, 51. þás magon þyllíce óðre mid lyffetungum tó leahtrum gehnexian, Hml. S. 16, 174.

lyft. *Add*: I. *air as one of the four elements* :—Sié eorþe is drýge and ceald, and þ wæter wǽt and ceald ; sié lyft ... is ǽgðer ge ceald ge wǽt, Bt. 33, 4; F. 128, 35. þ lyft ys wǽt and wearm ... fýr býð wearm and drigge ... eorðe ys ceald and drigge ... wæter is ceald and

wǽt, Angl. viii. 299, 28–35. **II.** *the body of air surrounding the earth, the atmosphere:*—Swā swā lyft and lagu land ymbclyppað, Met. 9, 40. Stille þynced lyft ofer londe and lagu swīge, Rä. 4, 11. Cómon twēgen deófiu tō him of þǣre lyfte *velut ex aere lapsi*, Guth. Gr. 123, 7. Fliógan ofer þām fȳre þe is betwux þām rodore and þǣre lyfte, Bt. 36, 2; F. 174, 10. Hē ongan fleógan on þā lyfte, Bl. H. 187, 28. Deófiu fleód geond þās lyft ungesewenlīce, swā swā fugelas dōd gesewenlīce, Hml. Th. ii. 90, 21. On lyft scacan, fleógan ofer foldan, Sat. 263. In lyft āstāg cirm, Gū. 363. **III.** *the upper region of the air, sky, heaven :*—Tō morgen hyt byð smylte weder ; þes heofon (*caelum*) ys reád ... Tō dæg hyt byð hreóh weder ; þeós lyft (*caelum*) scīnd unwederlīce, Mt. 16, 3. Lyft ūp geswearc *heaven above grew dark*, Exod. 461. Lyft bið onbærned, hreósad heofonsteorran, Cri. 1043. Oðeówdon fȳrena tácnu on norð-dǽle þǣre lyfte, Chr. 926; P. 107, 19. Nis ǽnig nū eorl under lyfte, Cri. 219 : Ph. 39 : Gū. 91. Hȳ hine hōfun on þā heán lyft, 383. **IV.** *a cloud :*—Lyft *nubes*, An. Ox. 3711 [: Mk. 9, 7 : Lk. 21, 27 : 12, 54, *in Dict.*]. **V.** *contaminated air :*—Wólberende lyft hwītes heówes, Nar. 15, 32. Ealle sūðfolc worhton eorþhūs for þǣre lyfte wylme and ǽternesse, Lch. ii. 146, 16. **VI.** *air in motion, a breeze :*—Mec lyft ūphāhōf, wind of wǽge, Rä. 11, 9. Hē sǽde þ ān gehwǽde wolcn efne þā upp āstīge mid þǣre unstæddigan lyfte. Efne ðā āræs se wind, Hml. S. 18, 150. Ne windig wolcen, ne þǣr wæter fealled lyfte gebysgad, Ph. 62. Hē gesette ȳsta his on lyftu (*auram*), Ps. L. 106, 29. v. ǽr–, un–, ūp-lyft.

**lyft-lic** ; adj. *Of the atmosphere.* v. lyft ; **II.**—Se lyftlica heofon, Nap. 50, 2. [*O. H. Ger.* luft-līh *aerinus.*] v. ofer-lyftlic ; lyften.

**lyft-wynn.** *Add:*—*Joy in the realms above* (?) :—Ūs bōceras beteran secgad lengran lyftwynna ; þis is lǽne dreám, wommum āwyrged, Exod. 531.

**lyge.** *Add:*—Lyges *mendacii*, Bd. 1, 14; Sch. 38, 20 : 3, 19 ; Sch. 278, 19.

**lygen** ; adj. *Lying, false.* [*O. H. Ger.* lugīn *falsarius* : *Icel.* lyginn.] v. un-lygen, un-gelygen.

**lyg-ness.** *Add:*—Figmenta, i. plasmatio, mendacia hīwunga, lignes, Wülck. Gl. 239, 9.

**-lynian (-lynnan).** v. ā-, tō-linian (-linnan) : **lyni-bōr.** *l.* lyni-bor, *and for* Wrt. Voc. ii. *l.* Wrt. Voc. i.

**lynis.** *Add:*—Lynis *axredo*, Txts. 43, 258. Lynisas *axredones*, 257 : *axedones*, 36, 8.

**lyre.** *Add :* **I.** *perdition, destruction :*—Lyre, forwyrd *perditio*, An. Ox. 56, 35. God heóld hine wið his sāwle lyre, Hml. Th. ii. 454, 4. Þæt hē ne sȳ on lyre forswolgen, R. Ben. 51, 6. **II.** *the fact of losing* something. (1) *the being deprived* of*, failure to keep* a possession, faculty, &c. :—Þonne se man geunrōtsad for his ǽhta lyre, Hml. S. 16, 291. Lyre gehealtsumnesse *dispendio castitatis*, An. Ox. 353. Lyre wæs lustlīce þone lyre þæs horses þoliende *jumenti perditi damnum libenter ferens*, Gr. D. 14, 19. Hē þolode lyre (*jacturam*) eallra þāra þinga þe on þām scipe wǽron, 141, 13. (2) *loss of a living creature by death :*—Hē nolde ābūgan fram Godes lufe for bærna lyre, Hml. S. 16, 48. Him tō cȳdenne his ǽhta lyre (cf. se deófol ācwealde ealle his ǽhta), 4), Hml. Th. ii. 450, 30. (2 a) *loss by death in battle :*—Būtan þǣra manna lyre þe him mid cōmon, Hml. S. 27, 53. **III.** *detriment, disadvantage, damage :*—Forðelgiad leras *sustinuere dispendia*, Kent. Gl. 1019.

**lyre-wrenc, es ; m.** *A trick that causes damage* or *loss :*—Lā, hwī ne mōt ic habban þæt ic mē sylf beget mid mīnum lyrewrencum ?, Verc. Först. 168.

**-lyrtan.** v. be-lyrtan : **lysnan.** v. hlysnan.

**lystan.** *Add :* **I.** *to cause pleasure in* a person. (1) absolute :—Lysted *juvabat*, Wrt. Voc. ii. 48, 2. (2) with acc. of person. (a) alone :—Gif þē lyste *si placet*, Bt. 7, 3; F. 22, 7. Ūre frid is wyrs gehealden donne mē lyste (*placeat*), Ll. Th. i. 220, 2. (b) with gen. of that in which pleasure is taken :—Suā hiene swīdur lysd (lyst, *v. l.*) disses and-weardan *quo delectant praesentia*, Past. 351, 8. (c) with clause :—Mē lyste bet þ þū sǽdest ymbe þ donne dū mē ācsodest, Bt. 34, 6 ; F. 142, 12. (d) with dat. infin. :—Ic hys hæbbe goodne dǽl gehȳred, and ic hys eác gelīfe ; ac mē lyste hyt nū bet tō wītanne þonne tō gelȳfanne *it would be pleasanter to me for it to be known than to be believed*, Solil. H. 59, 33. (3) with dat. of person, Bd. 3, 16; Sch. 266, 8 (*in Dict.*). **II.** *to cause desire.* (1) with acc. of person and (a) gen. of thing desired :—Ne lyst mē nū þæs *nihil hujusmodi quaero, nihil desidero*, Solil. H. 36, 15. Ðæt hié eác selfe ðæs ilcan lyste *ut habere propria concupiscant*, Past. 229, 14. Ðē ongan lystan ūre, nas ūs þīn, Bt. 7, 5; F. 24, 1. (b) acc. of thing desired ?:—Hē on ðǽm ōdrum hæfde ðæt hine lyste, Past. 459, 3. Hū done cealdan magan ungelīclice mettas lyste, Lch. ii. 160, 8. (c) with clause :—Ǽlcne man lyst ... þæt hē hine mōte hwīlum þāron gerestan, Solil. H. 2, 8. (d) with infin. *to make* a person *willing and ready* to do something :—Þū meaht ongitan gif his þē gēman lyst, Met. 31, 1. Hī eall witon þæt hȳ witan lyst, Solil. H. 67, 22. Ðæt hine ne lyste sum nytwyrde weorc wyrcean *agere quae debet bona dissimulat*, Past. 285, 9. Swā hwelcne mon swā lyste

þæt witan, Ors. 1, 11 ; S. 50, 17. (e) with gen. and dat. infin. cf. (2 d) :—Fela mē lyste witan ðes þe ic nāt. Ne lyst mē þeáh nānes þinges swīdor tō witanne þonne þises *there is nothing I desire more to be known than this*, Solil. H. 14, 22. (2) with dat. of person :—[Hml. Th. ii. 220, 22, *in Dict.*]. Lyste þām þe lyste þisne cræft leornian, Angl. viii. 308, 25. v. of-lysted (*not* -lystōn).

**lystan** ; *p.* te *To desire.* **I.** with gen. :—Þonne seó sāwl þyrsted and lysted Godes rīces *Deum sitiens anima*, Gr. D. 244, 27. **II.** with infin. :—Manige men hine geornlīce lystan geseón *multi hunc anxie videre sitiebant*, Gr. D. 45, 22. [v. *N. E. D.* lust ; 2. Cf. *Goth.* lustōn *to desire* : *O. H. Ger.* lustōn.]

**lystere** ( =? hlystere). *Substitute :* lystere. v. lyffetere.

**lyt.** *Add :* [v. *N. E. D.* lite.] v. un-lyt.

**lytel** ; adj., *and neut. of* adj. *Add :* , lȳtel (?). **A.** adj. **I.** as the opposite of *great.* (1) *of material objects, portions of space, &c., small in size, not large :*—Ne bið nǽnig tō þæs lytel lid on lime āweaxen, Seel. 96. Swilce ān lytel (lytlu, *v. l.*) pricu, Bt. 18, 1 ; F. 62, 4. Lyttel scipp *naviculam*, Mt. L. 13, 2. Sē de lytelo bȳ (*domicilium*) hæfde in byrgennum, Mk. L. 5, 3. .ii. lytle bollan fulle, Lch. ii. 214, 11. ¶ of a person's stature :—Hē wæs lytel (lyttel *pusillus*, L.) on wæstmum, Lk. 19, 3. (1 a) used to designate species or varieties which are distinguished by their smallness from others belonging to the same genus or bearing the same name :—Brūne wyrt, hāre wyrt lytelu, Lch. ii. 132, 8. (1 b) with superlative force in *little* finger, toe :—Gif se lytla bið of āslegen, Ll. Th. i. 96, 7. Sió lytle tā, 23. On dǽm lytlan ... ānum fingre (cf. on dām lǽstan fingre, Bt. 33, 4 ; F. 132, 1), Met. 20, 179. (2) used of young children :—Lytel cnæht des *parvolus iste*, Mt. L. 18, 4. Syle þicgean on wīne geongum men fīf cuceleras fulle, and gingrum and un-trumum and wīfum þrȳ cuceleras, litlum cildum ānne, Lch. i. 122, 24. Lytlo cild *parvolos*, Mk. 10, 13. (3) *of collective unities, having few members, inhabitants, &c. ; small in number :*—Hér is ān lytele (*parva*) burg swīde neáh ... Hió is ān lytel (*modica*), Past. 399, 23. Is hiora here ... tō lytel swelcra lāriówa, Met. 10, 55. Lytlo ēdo *pusillo gregi*, Lk. p. 7, 15. Lytle werede, Gen. 2093. Ic wāt hēr āne neáh lytle ceastre, 2578. Lytle worado *pauci*, Lk. L. 13, 23. (4) *of immaterial things, considered in respect of their quantity, length in series, &c. :*—Gē eów ondrǽdaþ þ gē onfōn tō lytlum leánum, Bl. H. 41, 21. Lytlum sticcum leódworda dǽl reccan, An. 1490. (5) *of distance or period of time.* Cf. B. **II.** 3 :—Ðā geswigode se wīsdōm āne lytle hwīle, Bt. 7, 1 ; F. 16, 5. Lytle hwīle, B. 2030. Þone lytlan fyrst, Cri. 1323. (6) *of qualities, conditions, &c., small in extent* or *degree :*—Mē þūhte þæt sār swīde lytel odde ealles nāwiht, Solil. H. 41, 4. Mē ne þincþ nāuht lytel gōd þisses andweardan līfes gesǽlþa, ne eác nāuht lytel yfel his ungesǽlþa *in hac ipsa fortuna populari nonnihil boni malive inesse perpendo*, Bt. 39, 2 ; F. 212, 14. Nales fore lytlum ... ac fore þām mǽstan mægeneardedum, Cri. 963. (7) *not of importance.* (a) *of things, trifling, trivial :*—Þonne ongit hē hū lytel se hlīsa bið and hū lǽne and hū tēdre and hū bedǽled ælces gōdes *fama quam sit exilis et totius vacua ponderis*, Bt. 18, 1 ; F. 60, 29. Hē bið for swīþe lytlum þingum gedrēfed, 11, 1 ; F. 32, 18. Ǽnne of bebodum ðissum lytlum (*minimus*), Mt. L. 5, 19. For dǽm de þū wǽre getrȳwe ofer lytle þing, ic gesette þē ofer mycle, Mt. 25, 21. (b) *of persons, inferior in rank* or *condition, not distinguished :*—Lytel hē bið genemned in rīc heafna ... des micil bið geceigd, Mt. L. 5, 19. Lytel þūhte ic leóda bearnum, læg on heardum stāne, Cri. 1425. Swā hwylc swā syld ānne drinc ānum þyssa lytylra manna, Mt. 10, 42. Ānum of ðisum brōdrum mīnum lytlum, Mt. L. 25, 40. (b a) *of a town :*—Dū, Bethlem, undærfe ðing lyttel arð (*nequa-quam minima es*), Mt. L. 2, 6. (8) *mean, vile.* (a) *of things :*—Tō þām þæt dū hwylce þēnunga mīnon lytlan līchaman tō gehȳdnysse gegearwige, Hml. S. 23 b, 252. (b) *of persons :*—Ic eom se lytla for þē and se lȳdra man, se hēr syngige swīde genehhe ... þearle scyldig, Hy. 3, 41. **II.** as opposite of *much.* (1) *not much, only a slight amount* or *degree of, barely any :*—Sceáwige mon georne hwilc se ūtgang sié, þe micel, þe lytel, þe þǣr nān ne sié, Lch. ii. 218, 11. Hwæt is heora nū tō lāfe būtan se lytla hlīsa and se nama mid feáum stafum āwriten *signat superstes fama tenuis pauculis inane nomen litteris*, Bt. 19 ; F. 70, 10. Gȳt lǽssan mynstres þǣr lytel þeówdōm sȳ, Ll. Th. i. 360, 22. Byþ lytel frēcne fram fȳre, Lch. i. 330, 2. Tō lytel hit biþ, beó hit ā lǽsse, Ll. Th. i. 432, 24 : B. 1748. Lytles geleáfes, Mt. L. 6, 30 : 14, 31. Wē habbaþ litelne gearowitan būton tweón, Bt. 41, 5 ; F. 254, 10. Ic him līfwrade lytle meahte ætgifan, B. 2877. (1 a) forming with its sb. a kind of privative combination, with the sense *absence* or *scarcity* of what the sb. denotes :—Gemune hwæt sī mīn lytle spēd *memorare quae mea substantia*, Ps. Th. 83, 40. (2) *a small quantity of, some, though not much :*—Nū gȳt ys lytel (lyttil, L., lyttel, R.) leóht on eów *athuc modicum lumen in uobis est*, Jn. 12, 35. .ii. lytle bollan fulle mid lytle hunige gemengde, Lch. ii. 214, 11. Þǣr dydon Rōmane lytla triéwþa þæt him þā wǽron unweorþe þe hiera hlāford beswican *in hoc solo Romanis circa eum fortiter agentibus quod percussores ejus indignos judicarent*, Ors. 5, 2 ; S. 218, 17. (3) with pl., *few :*—Wræccum lytlum (feáwum, W.S.) *plagis paucis*, Lk. R. L. 12, 48. Hȳ sculan nyttian lytlum and

forhtlicum metum, Lch. ii. 30, 30. Þā nolde hē him geceósan welige yldran, ac þā þe hæfdon lytle worldspēda (*few worldly goods*), Bl. H. 23, 25. **B. absolute and substantive. I. absolute.** (1) *those that are little.* (a) cf. **A. I.** 2 :—Ðāra lyttelra *parvulorum*, Mt. p. 1, 6. (b) cf. **A. I.** 8 b :—Drihten gehealdeð þā lytlan, Ps. Th. 114, 6. (2) *few.* Cf. **A. II.** 3 :—Woèg lytelra *uia paucorum*, Lk. p. 8, 7. Ofer lytla *super pauca*, Mt. L. 25, 21 : 23. (3) *not much, only a small amount* or *quantity* :—Betere ys þām rihtwīsan lytel (*modicum*) þonne þām synfullan mycel wela, Ps. Th. 36, 14. Ðǣm lyttel bið forgefen, Lk. L. 7, 47. On lytlum (lytelum, L.) getrȳwe . . . on lytlum unriht-wīs, I.k. 16, 10 : 19, 17. Hē sceal of swīðe lytlum hyt onginnan, Solil. H. 45, 16. Þonne wāt ic swīðe lytel ōðer nānwiht, 66, 17. Ðȳ lǣs hié fela sellen ðǣm ðe hié lytel sceoldon, oðče lytel ðǣm ðe hié micel sceoldon, Past. 321, 17. Lytel āgan, Bl. H. 49, 20. Gē sāwað micel sǣd and rīpað litel (*modicum*), Deut. 28, 38. ¶ with adverb :—Wund-rum lytel mæg gedōn . . . , Bt. 11, 1 ; F. 32, 21. Þā þurfon swīþe lytles, 14, 2 ; F. 44, 13. Þ man crístene menn for eall es tō lytlum tō deáðe ne fordēme, Ll. Th. i. 304, 19. (3 a) with gen. :—Ic hys mæg swīðe litel ongytan oðče nāwiht, Solil. H. 25, 15. Hyre þā gýt tō lytel þūhte þæs anwaldes ðe se cyningc ǣr gewunnen hæfde *non contenta ter-minis mulier quos a viro suo acquisitos*, Ors. 1, 2 ; S. 30, 17. Wē witon swīþe lytel þæs þe ǣr ūs wæs būton þe gemynde, Bt. 42 ; F. 256, 25. (3 b) in the genitive depending upon an indefinite pronoun :—Gif þā ǣnies willan wana biþ, ðeáh hit lytles hwæt sié *si absit aliquid tuae beati-tudini*, Bt. 11, 1 ; F. 30, 22 : 32, 20. Nānwuht ne lytles ne miceles, 30, 25 : Met. 22, 47. (3 c) qualified by a demonstrative :—Þíne seofunga for þām lytlan þe þū forlure, Bt. 11, 1 ; F. 30, 21. (4) *unimportant condi-tion, inferior position* :—Oft hē of lytlan ārǣrde tō miclan þā þe him hȳrdan, Ll. Th. i. 334, 6 : 14. **II. as substantive.** (1) *a small quantity, piece, portion, a small thing, a trifle*, Lch. ii. 336, 4 [*in Dict.*] (1 a) with gen. :—Ān lytel febbres, Past. 229, 3. Wudugāte geallan and lytel wīnes, Lch. i. 348, 18. Lytel eles, ii. 76, 13. Diles sǣd lytelne, 228, 21. Glǣdenan rinde lytelra gedō þreó pund on glæsfæt, 252, 7. (2) of per-sons. (a) cf. **A. I.** 2 :—Suā huā ne onfóas rīc Godes swelc lyttel (*parvulus*), Mk. L. 10, 15. Būta gié geworðe suǣ lytlo (cnehtas, R., lytlingas, W.S. *parvoli*), Mt. L. 18, 3. Of mūðe ðāra lytla (cildra, R., cilda, W.S. *infantium*), 21, 16. Būta wīfum and lytlum ł cildum (cneh-tum, R.) *exceptis mulieribus et parvulis*, 14, 21 : 15, 38. Forlētas ðā lytlo (þā cild, R.), 19, 14. Brōhton tō him lytle (lytlo cild, L.), Mk. R. 10, 13. (b) cf. **A. I.** 8 b :—Ēnne of lytlum ðisum *unum de pusillis istis*, Mt. L. 18, 6. Of lytlum ðassum *ex minimis istis*, 10, 42 : 25, 45. (3) *a short time* :—Æfter lytle huíle ł ymb lytle (ymbe lytel, W.S.) *post pusillum*, Mk. L. 14, 70. Embe lytel (æfter lytlum ł ymb lytle huíle, L., æfter lytlum hwíle, R.), Lk. 22, 58. **C. adverbial use of various cases. I.** *to only a small extent, but slightly, not much.* (1) acc. :—Lytel fremað þeáh crísten man būtan crístenum dǣdum, Wlfst. 65, 21. Lyttel lufað *minus diligit*, Lk. L. 7, 47. (2) with inst. :—Sam hē hine miclum lufige, sam hē hine lytlum lufige, Solil. H. 58, 14. Þū hine gedēst lytle lǣssan (*paulo minus*) þonne englas, Ps. Th. 8, 6 : 118, 87. Ful lytle ðe gearor, Solil. H. 26, 15. **II.** *lytlum a little at a time* :—Geót þriwa lytlum on hāte þā ahsan, Lch. ii. 32, 13 : 176, 22 : 230, 21. **II a.** lyt-lum and lytlum *little by little, gradually* :—Hē sceal lytlum and lytlum stīgan neár and neár stæpmǣlum swilce hē on sume hlǣdre stīge, Solil. H. 45, 16. **III.** *a little.* (1) of distance :—Gefoerde lytel ðona *progressus pusillum*, Mt. L. 26, 39. (2) of time. (a) with acc., *for a little time* :—Ðā-gēt lyttel (lytel, R. *modicum*) mið iúh ic am, Jn. L. 13, 33. (b) with inst., *a little* (*before*) :—Swā swā þū mē nū lytle ǣr gehēte, Bt. 22, 1 ; F. 76, 22 : Met. 12, 13. v. for-, un-, ungemet-lytel ; lytle, an ; *f.* : lǣs, lǣssa.

**lytel-fóta.** *l.* (?) fitel-fóta (*q. v.*).

**lýþer-lic.** *Add* :—Ðā ālēde ic mínne kynegyrylan, and mē mid uncūþe hrægle and mid lýþerlice gerelan gegerede, Nar. 18, 3. [*v. N. E. D.* litherly, *adj.*]

**lýþerlíce.** *Add* : [*v. N. E. D.* litherly ; *adv.*]

**lýþre.** *l.* lýþre, *and add* : **I.** of persons :—Se lýðra man āna (*the vile man alone*), þonne hē forsihþ Godes beboda . . . þonne bið hē deófles ðeówa, Hml. Th. i. 172, 17. Mín lýðra lātteów (*my rascally guide*) forlēt mē þus ǣnne, Hml. S. 21, 211. Wē sceolon forseón þone lýðran deófol (*the foul fiend*), Hml. Th. i. 270, 13. Hwæt synt þā wyrmas būton lýðre men ?, Angl. viii. 323, 31. Hwǣr syndon þā wiðersacan eówre lýðran māgas (*your vile kinsmen*)?, Hml. S. 23, 296. Lýþrum monnum *to vile cravens*, Ors. 6, 36 ; S. 292, 27. **II.** of things :—Hū lǣne and hū lýðre þis líf is on ðō getrūwianne, Wlfst. 189, 3. Hit ne gedafenað þ man dō Godes hūs ānre mylne gelíc for lýðrum tolle (*for sordid gain*), Hml. S. 19, 253. Lýðre gesetnyssa *vitiosa compositio*, Angl. viii. 313, 26. Ne sceall nān Godes þegn for sceattum riht dēman, ac healdan þone dōm būton lýðrum sceattum (*without infamous bribes*), Hml. S. 19, 246. Þurh lýðra sǣd *by seed that does harm*, Angl. viii. 300, 24. [*v. N. E. D.* lither.]

**lyt-hwón.** *Add* : **I. as substantive** :—Monigo sint geceigdo, lythwón gecoren *multi sunt vocati, pauci electi*, Mt. L. 20, 16. Lythuón gecor-

eno, 22, 14. **I a. with gen.** :—Lythwón becwōm Hūna herges hām eft þanon, El. 142. Lythwón monna gefīit *paucorum hominum contentio*, Mt. p. 2, 10. **II. as adv.** (1) of distance :—Þā hē wæs lythwón þanon āgān *progressus pusillum*, Mt. 26, 39. Onwende hē his neb āweg lythwón, Lch. ii. 284, 16. (2) of time :—Lytle huíle (*modi-cum*) gesēne wēre hine cuæð and eftsōna lythuón (*modicum*) ne uēre gesēne, Jn. p. 7, 14 : Gū. 363. (3) of extent, degree :—Hē lithwón hogode embe his sāwle þearfe, Hml. S. 26, 243 : 28, 139. Se scamfæsta hǣfð genōh on ðǣm tō his bettrunge ðæt his lāreów hine suíðe lythwón gemyndgige his unðeáwa *verecundis ad conversionem sufficit, quod eis doctor mala sua saltem leniter ad memoriam reducit*, Past. 207, 4. (3 a) where the word is equivalent to an emphatic negative :—Þone siðfæt him snotere ceorlas lythwón lōgon . . . hwetton higerōfne (*far from blaming them, they urged him on*), B. 203. (4) *gradually, little by little* :—Lythuón onginnes from fruma, æfter ðon ðȳ æfterra . . . *paulatim inci-piens a primo, deinde secundo* . . . , Mt. p. 11, 11.

**lytig.** *Add* : **I.** in a good sense, *prudent* :—Letig *astutus* (Prov. 13, 16), Kent. Gl. 450 : 485 : *callidus* (Prov. 22, 3), 809. Leti, 412 : *versutus* (Prov. 12, 23), 424. **II.** in a bad sense :—Litig and pǣtig *versuta et callida*, Germ. 389, 21. Letig wer hatol *vir versutus odiosus*, Kent. Gl. 487. Wēnst þū þæt seó mengio þīnra monna þe mæge dōn gesǣligne ? Nese, nese. Ac gif hié yfele sint and lytige, ðonne sint hié þe pleólicran gehæfd þonne genæfd, Bt. 14, 1 ; Fox 42, note 10.

**lytle, an ;** *f.* A *servant-maid, female slave* :—Heó (*Judith*) hire lytlan (*Abram.* Cf. mid ānre þīnene *Abra*, 109, 231), Hml. A. 114, 401.

**lytlian.** *Add* : , lytlan :—Ǣlc riht lytleð for Gode and for worulde, Wlfst. 243, 10. [*v. N. E. D.* little.] v. ge-lytlian.

**lytling.** *Add* : **I.** *a child* :—Lǣtað þā lytlingas *sinite parvulos*, Mt. 19, 14. Lytlungas, Ps. L. 1369. **II.** *a person of little account, of inferior position.* Cf. lytel. **A. I.** 7 b :—Gif ǣgðer ge biscopas ge preóst-as æfter heora rihtan gesettednesse lifdon, þonne wǣre hit oferflōwennis ūs litlingum (*nobis exiguis*) āwiht nīwes tō trahtnienne, Chrd. 2, 4.

**lytlung, e ;** *f.* *Diminution* :—Seó godcundnyss underfōhð nāne lyt-lunge, Angl. vii. 56, 537. v. ge-lytlung.

# M

**mā.** *Subst.* or *adj.* *Add* : **I. as subst.** (1) with partitive genitive sing., *something in addition, an additional quantity* or *amount* :—Ne wilnige ic heora nānes nāwyt mycle mā ðonne ic nēde sceol habban tō mȳnes līichaman hēle, Solil. H. 37, 11. Ne wē wítegan habbað þæt ūs andgytes mā ǣfre secgan, Ps. Th. 73, 9. (2) *a greater number, more individuals of the kind specified.* (a) with partitive genitive plural (or of noun of multitude) :—Næs his folces nā mā ofslagen þonne nigon, Ors. 4, 1 ; S. 156, 24. Þǣr bið wundra mā þonne hit ǣnig mæg āþenc-ean, Cri. 989. Februarius hæfð þý geáre (*leap-year*) ānum dæge mā daga þonne þý ōðrum geáre, Angl. viii. 305, 43. Hē āferede mancynnes mā þonne gemet wǣre, An. 1180. (b) without partitive genitive :—Gif mā tō scyle, Ll. Th. i. 160, 3. .xii. būton gē mā willan, 274, 11. Sý hit ofer āne scíre, sý hit ofer mā, 224, 27. Þū hæfst mē manega bysna gereihte, and ic hæbbe sælf gesegen on bōcum mā þonne ic āreccan mage, Solil. H. 66, 13. (c) to express an indefinite excess over a number stated approximately :—Sume habbað twā oþþe mā, Ll. Th. i. 316, 9 : 438, 13. Twā hund oðče mā, El. 634 : Ælfc. Gr. Z. 32, 16. (3) *other individuals of the kind specified, other persons or things in addition to those mentioned* :—Þ unriht ālegde ūre hlaford ; þ hē mā mōte, Ll. Lbmn. 244, 36. Þæt hē ienige tō þām ilcan wuda þǣr ic ðās sceaftas cearf, fetige hym þǣr mā, Solil. H. 1, 11. Hwæt wille ic mā cwæðan ?, 37, 6. (3 a) with gen. :—For þǣm hē ne uþe þæt ǣnig mā folca for his þingum forwurde þonne þe self mid his āgenre þeúðe, Ors. 2, 5 ; S. 80, 33. Ge on londum ge on mā ðāra þinga ðe heó on forhaldne wēran, C. D. v. 140, 15. Ic wæs on ceóle and mínes cnōsles mā, Rä. 19, 4. **II. as adj.** v. Dict.

**mā ; adv.** *Add* : **I.** *in* or *to a greater degree, extent*, or *quantity* :—Hī forseoð hī selfe lǣs on þysum middanearde þā þe þæncað þ hī sýn sylfe mā gōde þonne ōðre men *ut minus se in hoc mundo despiciant qui plus se ceteris aliquid fuisse meminerunt*, Gr. D. 151, 27. Swā leng swā mā *magis magisque*, An. Ox. 2542. Þā menn magon geseón heora freónd, and ne magon heom þeáh nā nāne gōde ne beón, ne hī hym þe mā, Solil. H. 68, 30. **II.** *longer, further, again, besides* :—Woldest þū āwiht mā witan ? *nihilne plus scire cutis ?*, Solil. H. 14, 21. Hwí ācsast þū mā æfter ðǣm ?, 36, 15. Ne secge ic nǣfre mā þæt ic hāla ǣágan habbe, 48, 16. Be ūre sāwle lífe ic nū ðon mā nāwuht ne twæóge, 59, 25. **III.** qualifying a predicate as being applicable in a greater measure or degree than another, *more, rather* :—Eówra sāwla mā (*potius*) forhwerfdon þonne hié gerihton, Ll. Th. i. 56, 18.

**macian. I.** *to bring into existence by construction* or *elaboration.* (1) *to construct, frame, fashion* :—Wurdon tōbrocene þǣra hæþenra goda

hūs and anlícnyssa þurh þǽra manna handa þe hī macodon and guton, Hml. S. 29, 181. Me mæig in Maio and Iunio ... fiscwer and mylne macian, Angl. ix. 261, 13. Hēr weard getimbrod ð mynster on Winceastre þ Cynwalh lēt macian, Chr. 648; P. 28,17. Mæssereáf of ealdum cláðum macian, Hml. A. 35, 279. (2) *with a substance as object* :—Cȳs-wyrhtan gebyreð þ heó of wringhwǽge buteran macige tō hláfordes beóde, Ll. Th. i. 438, 31. (2 a) *to produce* an article of food or drink by culinary or other operations :—Bring mē twā þā betstan tyccenu þæt ic macige mete þīnum fæder þǽr of (*ut faciam ex eis escas patri tuo*), Gen. 27, 9. (3) *to produce by action, bring about* a condition of things, a state of feeling :—þā Frencisce menn macodon mǽst þet unseht betweónan Godwine eorle and þām cynge, Chr. 1052; P. 183, 14. (3 a) *to cause* something *to happen* to a person (*dat.*), cause a person *to experience* something :—þā bǽdon hig sume þæt Samson mōste him macian sum gamen, Jud. 16, 25. (3 b) *to make peace*. (*a*) *to bring about a condition of* :—Nis nā tō forgytane þ gōde frið þe hē macode on þisan lande, Chr. 1086; P. 220, 13. (*β*) *to make peace between enemies* :—Leófríc eorl cōm wið, and Harold eorl and macedan seht þǽr betweónan, Chr. 1056; P. 186, 34. (4) *to give rise to, have as a result, be the cause of* :—Gýfernyss macað þām menn mycele untrumnysse, Hml. S. 16, 272. Gītsung is wyrtruma ǽlcere wōhnysse. Heó macað reáflác and unrihte dōmas, stala and leásunga, 282 : 288. (5) in grammar, *to form* a case, tense, &c., in a specified manner :—Ðeós *declinatio* ne macað nā hire *vocatiuum* on eallum namum on āne wīsan, Ælfc. Gr. Z. 31, 15. *Elicio* macað *elicui*, 175, 10. Sume ðás maciað *femininum* on *a*, 40, S. þā maciað *praeteritum* on *aui*, 138, 11. (6) *to prepare* or *provide* a meal, feast for guests :—Gelíc þām cyninge þe macode hys suna gyfta *simile regi qui fecit nubtias filio suo*, Mt. 22, 2. (7) used with *of* to designate the action of causing what is denoted by the regimen of the prep. to become what is denoted by the object of the verb :—*Fornicatio* macað of Crīstes limum myltestrena limu, Hml. S. 16, 278. (8) said of constituent parts, *to amount to* :—þǽrtōeácan syx tīda ; þā māciað ǽfre ymbe þ feórþe geár þone dæg and ðā niht þe wē hātað *bissextum*, Lch. iii. 246, 13. **II.** *to subject to operation, manage, use* :—Iubal wæs fæder herpera and þǽra þe organan macodun *Iubal fuit pater canentium cithara et organo*, Gen. 4, 21. **III.** *to cause to be or become* something specified. (1) with sb. as complement :—*Superbia* geworhte englas tō deóflum and ðone man macað eác, gif hē mōdigaþ tō swȳðe, þæs deófles gefēran, Hml. S. 16, 310. (2) with sb. preceded by *tō*, or simple dative :—Ic macige þē mycelre mǽgðe *faciam te in gentem magnam*, Gen. 12, 2. Hē wolde hine macian tō gode, Ælfc. T. Grn. 2, 43. **IV.** *causative uses*. (1) with dependent clause, *to cause* something *to happen, bring it about* that :—Hī macedon hit þā þ ǽr wæs ful rīce, þa (þ?) hit weard tō nānþing, Chr. 870; P. 71, 11. (2) *to cause to move, put* :—Seó ealde cyrce wæs eall behangen mid criccum ... and man ne mihte swā ðeáh macian hī healfe ūp (*not half of them could be put up on the walls*), Hml. S. 21, 434. **V.** *to do, perform*. (1) with a noun of action as object :—Hī ealle sǽdon þ sē is sōð God þe swilce wundra macað, Hml. S. 22, 56. Sweriað þæt gē dōn wið mē swilce mildheortnisse swā ic macode wið eów *jurate ut quomodo ego misericordiam feci vobiscum, ita et vos faciatis cum domo patris mei*, Jos. 2, 12. (2) *to conclude* a bargain, contract :—Mid þām mannan þe ǽr þ loc makeden, Chr. 1094; P. 229, 9. (3) with sbs. expressing the action of vbs., and forming with them phrases approximately equivalent in sense to those verbs :—Manega drȳmen maciað menigfealde dydrunga þurh deófles cræft, Hml. S. 21, 465. Ǽnig man ciricmangunge nid unriht ne macie, Ll. Th. i. 306, 28. þæt hȳ him *absolutionem* macigan, Wlfst. 180, 12. **VI.** *to behave, act*. (1) with *hit* and adv. denoting manner :—Ic nāt nā forgeare hū ic hit þus macige *I do not quite know how it is I behave so*, Hml. S. 23, 556 : 672. þā hālgan martyras on þām scræfe sǽton, and þām biscope he endebyrdnysse rehton hū hī hit macedon on Decius cāseres timan (*how they had acted in the time of the emperor Decius*), 786. (2) without *hit* :—Riht is þ mynecena mynster-líce macian, efne swā wē cwǽdon ǽror be munecan (cf. riht is þ munecas ... regollíce libban, 2-4), Ll. Th. ii. 322, 32.

**mād.** *Substitute* : mád-mōd ; *adj. Senseless* (v. ge-mád) :—Sum on oferhygdo þrymme þringeð, þrinted him oninnan ungemēde mádmōd (*senseless arrogance*), Mōd. 25.

**mæc.** *In* l. 2 *for* mecca *read* mecea.

**mæcca** ; an ; m. *A consort* :—Ic hæbbe crístenne fæder ... and his mæcca mīn mōdor is of þyssum lífe gewiten, Hml. S. 33, 103. v. ge-mæcca.

**mæcga.** *Add* : v. ōret-mæcga : -mæclic. v. ge-mæclic.

**mǽd.** *Dele the passage from* C. D. iii. 52, 15, *and add* : *meadow-land* :—Ðāra oxena wīc and seó mǽd ðe ðǽr mid rihte tō gebyreð ... and seó meád benorðan eá, C. D. v. 383, 14-18. Feówer æceras mǽde bewestan eá, i. 175, 2. On hreódmǽde lace, vi. 153, 9. Mōrmǽde, iii. 449, 20.] .xII. æcras an westhealfe ðǽre strǽte, and ān (æcer) mǽdwa beneoðan ðǽm hlíde, iii. 52, 15. Hec sunt prata ... stocmǽd healf be-norðan hegforde, be stūre mēda suē ðǽr tō limpað, ii. 65, 27. On sūð-mǽdwan ; of ðǽre mǽde, iii. 77, 18. Æt ðǽra hína mǽde, vi. 4, 26.

On cuttes mǽd ; of þǽre mǽde, iii. 456, 30. Onbūtan ðā mǽdewe, iii. 386, 5. On miclan mǽdua (*or pl. ?*), iii. 81, 7. Hē eóde on þā mǽdwe (mǽde, *v. l.*) *pratum ingressus*, Gr. D. 36, 11. On bulan mǽdæ, C. D. v. 112, 29. On clǽnan mǽde, 325, 17. On smēðe mētue, iii. 460, 19. [On hreódmǽde, vi. 102, 31 : iii. 97, 30.] On ðā mǽd norðeweardæ, v. 340, 24 : vi. 234, 7. Mǽda *prata*, An. Ox. 138. On manegum landum tild bið redre ðonne on ōðrum, ge yrðe tīma hrædra, ge mǽda rǽdran, Angl. ix. 259, 10. Feldlǽs, mǽda, and yrðland, C. D. vi. 39, 9. Tō mǽdwuum, iii. 386, 1. *Una prata* on burgwara mǽdum and an norðeweardum burgwara mǽdum healf mǽd, ii. 66, 34. [Æt westmǽdu-wan ; of westmǽdwan, iii. 82, 14.] v. dāl-, sundor-, mǽr-, wīþig-mǽd.

**mǽd-æcer,** es ; m. *A meadow* :—þæne hagan þe Eádwerd āhte, and þæne mǽdæcer þe þǽr tō hȳrð, Swt. A. S. Rdr. ii. 203, 13. .viii. mǽdæc-eras ... gebyriað tō Cenelmestūne, C. D. vi. 33, 28.

**mǽd-díc** ; f. *A meadow-dike* :—Of þām mere on þa ealdan mǽddíc ; þonne andlang díc, C. D. B. iii. 396, 32.

**mæder** (?). *Another version of this prescription has* : Ofgeót mid hlūttrum ealaþ, Lch. ii. 354, 19.

**mǽdere.** *Add* :—Mǽdre *sandix*, An. Ox. 8, 345. Mǽdere, wād *sandix, i. iacinto*, 2, 436. Wealhbasu † mǽdre *uermiculo*, 35, 4. On længtene ... mederan settan, línsēd sāwan, Augl. ix. 262, 10.

-**mǽdla.** v. ge-mǽdla.

**mǽd-lacu,** e ; f. *A meadow-stream* :—On þā mǽdlace ; of þǽre lace, C. D. iii. 457, 6.

**mǽd-land.** *Add* :—.xII. æceras gōdes mǽdlandes (mǽdwe-, *v. l.*), C. D. B. ii. 266, 26.

**Mǽd-mónaþ** *July* :—Mǽdmónaþ (Mēd-, *v. l.*), Menol. Fox (*at end*) ; Hickes i. 215.

**mæg** (?) *power, might, virtue* :—Mæg (mægen ?) sōðes gebedes ys hȳhð sōðre lufe *uirtus vere orationis est celsitudo caritatis*, Scint. 4, 19. Micel ys mæg (*uirtus*) gif þū nā dera fram þām þe þū gederod ert, 12, 17. Hē Godes ríce ... eallum mæge (mægene ?) fyrþrode, Lch. iii. 438, 2. Cf. maga, and (?) v. mægen-þrymnes.

**mǽg.** *Add* : **I.** *a kinsman* :—Gif āðer oþþe mǽg oþþe fremde þā rāde forsace, Ll. Th. i. 268, 21. Lǽte heó hit tō sweolcum hire mēga swelce hit hire tō geearnigan wille, C. D. ii. 100, 22. Ðis wæs gedōn on gewitnesse hís āgenra mága Æðelstānes and Æðelhúnnes and eác Alhmundes his āgenes sunu, v. 141, 22. Ic hātu cȳðan ... mínum mēgum and gefeórum, ii. 120, 5. On mínum geongum mágum, 176, 3. **I a.** *a parent, kinsman of an earlier generation* :—On Ines dæge mínes (*Alfred's*) mǽges, Ll. Th. i. 58, 24. Be wurþscipe māga (*parentum*) ... ne scylon bearn (*filii*) māgum (*parentibus*) goldhordian ac māgas bearnum, Scint. 173, 7-13. Bearn, beó gē underðiódde eówrum ieldrum māgum *filii, obedite parentibus vestris*, Past. 189, 22. Of hǽþenum māgum *ethnicis parentibus (oriundus)*, An. Ox. 2417. **II.** *kindred* involved legal responsibility of its members to one another. (1) where one member was criminal, or subject to criminal prosecution :—Að syllan þ hȳ on heora mǽge nāne þȳfðe nyston, Ll. Th. i. 206, 2. Gif hē clǽne beó nime hē upp his mǽg, 296, 10. Beó hē feówertig nihta on carcerne ... and his mǽgas (mágas, *v. l.*) hine fēden gif he self mete næbbe, 60, 10 : 120, 6 : 124, 7 : 148, 18 : 164, 11 : 202, 15 : 206, 5 : 228, 26 : 238, 31 : 286, 32. Gif hwylc his mága hine seormige, þonne beó hē scyldig ealles þæs he āhte, 248, 8. Gif cyninges þegn ætsace ... nime hē his mága .xII. ..., ii. 298, 8. Gehealden hī hine .xxx. nihta, and hié hine his mǽgum (mágum, *v. l.*) gebodien, i. 64, 19. His mǽgum and his fríondum, 90, 8. (2) of conditions when a kinsman was injured :—Ne gebyreð nānum mǽge þ feoh būte þām þe sý binnan cneówe, Ll. Th. i. 174, 25. Hæbbe hē his mǽg forworht *he shall have forfeited all claim to compensation in respect to his injured kinsman*, 90, 20. Gif mon elþeódigne ofsleá, se cyning āh twǽdne dǽl weres, þriddan dǽl suuu oþþe mǽgas (mágas, *v. l.*), 116, 15. Agífe mon þām māgum (mágum, *v. l.*) þ treów, 70, 10 : 118, 8 : 148, 15 : 164, 13 : 202, 16 : 250, 15 : 406, 26. Se wer gebirað māgum (mǽgde, *v. l.*), 186, 4. (3) where protection, assistance, support, is given :—Mon nōt feohtan mid his geborene mǽge, Ll. Th. i. 90, 24. Gif man gehādodne oþþe ældeódigne forrǽde ... , þonne sceal him cyng beón, oþþon eorl þǽr on lande and bisceop þǽre leóde, for mǽg and for mundboran, būton hē elles ōðerne hæbbe, 174, 8 : 348, 6. Healden þā mǽgas (mágas, *v. l.*) þone frumstōl oþ þæt hit (*a minor whose father is dead*) gewintred sié, 126, 6. Fōn māgas tō and weddian heora māgan tō wīfe, 254, 20. Ládige hē mid his māgan þe fǽhðe mōton mid beran, 344, 26 : 362, 23. Gif hwylc landleás man ... eft his mǽgas gesēce, 204, 6. (4) as cognisant of matters affecting the kindred :—þ on cyninges and on biscopes gewitnesse gerecce beforan his mǽgum, Ll. Th. i. 88, 22. **III.** by the law of the church marriage was forbidden within certain limits of kinship :—Wē lǽrað ... þ ǽnig crísten mann binnan .vi. manna sibfæce on his āgenan cynne ǽfre ne gewífie, ne on his mǽges láfe þe swā neahsib wǽre, Ll. Th. i. 364, 23. **III a.** of illicit intercourse :—Gif twēgen gebrōðra oþþon twēgen genyhe māgas wið ān wíf forlicgan, Ll. Th. i. 168, 19. [v. N. E. D. may a kinsman.] v. fædering-, níd-, un-mǽg ; ge-nídmágas.

**mæg**; _f._ _Add:_—Seó frĭðe mæg (_the bird that hatches the cuckoo's egg_), Rä. 10, 9. [v. _N. E. D._ may a _maiden_.]

**mæg-cnafa**, an; _m._ _A young kinsman_:—Ic gean mīnum mǣgcnafan (_cognato_) þæs landes æt Anne his dæg . . . and þæs landes æt Worþigum . . . mīnum mǣgcnafan, C. D. B. ii. 329, 21-25.

**mǣg-cŭð.** _Add:_—Mǣgcŭþre cognatę, An. Ox. 2700.

**mǣg-cynren.** _Dele, and cf._ mid cynrene, An. Ox. 1297.

**mægden.** _Add:_ v. glīw-mægden.

**mægden-cild.** _Add:_—Beó hit hyseciId, beó hit mǣdencild _sit masculus infans, sit femina_, Ll. Th. ii. 190, 22.

**mægden-hād.** _Add:_ _girlhood_:—On hyre mægdenhāde hió (_the Virgin Mary_) dyde fela wundra on webgeweorce, Shrn. 127, 15.

**mægden-lic.** _Add:_—Onfēng heó þis bebod þ heó nǣht ofer þ ne dyde leóhtlices ne mægdenlicere wīsan oððe merwelicre _mandatum accepit, ut nihil ultra leve et puellare ageret_, Gr. D. 287, 20. Gesáwon hī cuman mycel mǣdenlic werod, Hml. S. 7, 251.

**mægden-mann.** _Add:_—Hester, wlitig mǣdenmann, Hml. A. 94, 82. Crīst mǣdenmann him tō mēder geceás, 14, 15 : Hml. Th. i. 308, 28.

**mǣge.** _Add:_—Ic selle Cyneswīðe mīnre mēgan lond, C. D. ii. 100, 10.

**-mǣge.** v. un-mǣge.

**mǣgen.** I. _add:_—Swā hwæt swā tōforan þām neádbehēfum belifen byþ on heora mǣgenes tilunge _quidquid necessario victui superest ex operibus manuum_, R. Ben. 138, 17. Ic sylle Wulfsige mīnum gerēfan wið his holdum mǣgene (_for his loyal and able service_) ānes hīdes lond, Cht. E. 161, 27. Be sāre þæs magan. Gif se man þ magan hæbbe læt him blōd, Lch. ii. 180, 31. Hē (_Aidan_) munuclīce leofode . . . mid sōþum mægnum, Hml. S. 26, 82. II. _add: a virtuous action_:—þæt wē beón gōdum mannum gelīce in ðām mægenum þe wē dōn magon, Verc. Först. 169, 3. III. _add:_—þæt eorðlice mægn þe þū hēr samnast . . . eall þis mægn wāt, þe hēr tō gemōte cōm, þæt þīn heáhsetl is þrymmes āfylled, Wlfst. 254, 13-18. v. full-, god-, heáfod-, helle-, nīd-, stīþ-mægen.

**mægen-fæst.** _Add:_—þes eard nis eác ealles swā mǣgenfæst hēr on ūteweardan þǣre eorðan brǣdnesse swā swā heó is tōmiddes on mǣgenfæstum eardum, þǣr man mæg fæstan freólīcor þonne hēr, Hml. S. 13, 106-109.

**mǣgenig (?), mēnig**, _adj._ _Strong:_—þurh mēnige hand (_per manum fortem_) hē hig ūt forlǣt of þīs lande, Ex. 6, 1.

**mægen-leást.** _Add:_—Sum līcðrowere nāhte his fēðes geweald . . . hē wolde geneálǣcan his huice, gif hē mihte. þā ofhreów ðám munece þæs hreófsian mægenleást, Hml. Th. i. 336, 11. Sume hī bebyrigan woldon, ac hī hrædlīce for mægenleáste swulton, 404, 2 : Hml. A. 68, 79. Gif hē ongyt þæt þæs gebodes micelnes his mihta oferstīhð, hē . . . his mægenleáste his ealdre gecȳþe, R. Ben. 128, 15.

**mægen-stán.** _Add:_—Tō mǣgenstānes dæne, C. D. v. 45, 23. Anlang wæges tō ðǣm megenstāne, iii. 411, 21.

**mægen-strengo.** _Add:_ [_O. Sax._ megin-strengi.]

**mægen-þrymm.** _Add:_ I. _glory, majesty_:—Ðonne hē sit ofer setle his mǣgenþrymmes _tunc sedebit super sedem maiestatis suae_, Ælfc. Gr. Z. 237, 9 : Mt. 25, 31. On hys mǣgenþrymme _in sede maiestatis suae_, 19, 28. Swilce ic stande æt his wuldorfullan mægenþrymme foran, Hml. S. 23, 830. Seó hālige þrynnys on ānre godcundnysse ǣfre wunigende, on ānum mǣgenþrymme (v. mægen-þrymnes) and on ānum gecynde, Hml. A. 2, 25. II. _in a personal sense, a mighty host_:—þurh þā twelf apostolas, and þurh ealle andetteras and hālige fǣmnan, and þurh ealle þā heofonlican mægenþrymmas, Ll. Lbmn. 415, 19. III. _mighty power_:—Ðonne hē cymð mid his mǣgenþrymme tō dēmanne and his wuldor tō ætiéwanne _cum virtutis suae gloriam venit ostendere_, Past. 307, 17.

**mægenþrym-nes.** _Add:_—Ān is godcundnys, gelīce wuldor, emnēce mǣgenðrymnes (_maiestas_), Ath. Crd. 6 : Hml. Th. i. 276, 20. Mægnþrymnysse _maiestatis_, Ps. L. p. 247, 8. Mæg[en]ðrymnysse, Ps. L. 28, 3 : An. Ox. 3398. Mæg[en]þrymnesse _maiestati_, 428.

**mǣger.** _Add:_—Hig hæfdon mycele heáfda, and mǣgere (manigre, MS.) ansȳne _erant . . . capitibus magnis, macilenta facie_, Guth. Gr. 128, 114.

**mǣg-lic.** _Add:_—Ðes ðegen bæd for his þeówan hǣlðe mid sōðre lufe, for ðan ðe heó ne tōscæt nǣnne be mǣglicere sibbe (_true love does not make distinction of person in accordance with relationship_), Hml. Th. i. 128, 2. Sume for mǣiglicre sibbe hī bebyrigan woldon _some would have buried them because they were kinsmen_, 404, 1.

**mǣg-myrþra.** _Add:_—Se treówleása fæder and mǣgmyrþra (_parricida_), Gr. D. 239, 4.

**mǣg-ness.** v. un-mægness.

**mǣg-rǣdenn.** _Add:_—Gesibbre mǣgrǣdene _propinquę necessitudinis_, An. Ox. 2810. Hē cwæð tō his hlāforde þe him wæs þurh his dohtor on mǣgrǣdenne _accersito ejus domino sibi per filiam propinquo_, Gr. D. 181, 19. Be his freóndum þe him gesibbeste synt and þurh mǣgrǣdenne nēhste, Hml. A. 139, 36.

**mǣg-sibb.** _Add:_—Mǣgsibbe _parentelę_, An. Ox. 5131 : germanitatis, 9, 2. v. mǣgþ-sibb.

**mǣgþ.** I. _add:_—Mǣgþ _prosapia_, An. Ox. 11, 112. Cōm Crīst ou ðām tīman þe seó cynelice mǣigð āteórode, Hml. Th. i. 82, 4. Mid cynrene, mǣgþe _prosapia_, i. _genus_ ł _progenies_, An. Ox. 1297 : _stemmati_, Germ. 393, 131. Hē fērde embe Agathen ǣhta, and eác wolde gehæftan ealle hire mǣgðe, Hml. S. 8, 210. IV a. _add:_—þær is mid Estum ān mǣgð þæt hī magon cyle gewyrcan, Ors. 1, 1 ; S. 21, 14. IV c. _add:_—þaet mynster is geseted in Huicca maegðe, C. D. i. 114, 14. Ealle Breotone mǣgþe Crīstes geleáfan onfēngon _omnes Brittaniarum prouinciae fidem Christi susceperant_, Bd. 4, 16 ; Sch. 428, 14. v. neáhmǣgþ.

**mǣgþ-hād.** _Add:_ _virginity_ as regards man or woman:—Mǣgðhād is sē þe wunað on clǣnnysse ǣfre fram cildhāde ge wǣpmenn ge wīfmenn, Hml. A. 20, 162. Ðás hālgan nǣron nǣfre mid wīfum besmitene. Hī sindon mǣgðhāde gehealdenre clǣnnysse (_virgines sunt_), 19, 125. Heó cwæð þ heó hine ne nānne habban wolde, gyf hire seó ūplice ārfæstnys geunnan wolde þ heó on mǣgðhāde Drihtne on clǣnre forhafednysse cwēman mihte, Chr. 1067 ; P. 201, 16.

**mǣgþ-rǣdenn**, e; _f._ _Relationship_:—Mǣþrǣdene _necessitudinis_, i. _amicitię_, An. Ox. 2, 109. Mǣgðrǣdena _necessitudinum_ (_Osburga mihi contribulibus necessitudinum nexibus conglutinata_, Ald. 1, 12), 7, 2. Mǣgðrǣdena, Angl. xiii. 27, 2. v. mǣg-rǣdenn.

**mǣg-þrymm.** v. mægen-þrymm : **mǣg-tudor.** _Dele, and see_ mǣgcŭþ.

**mǣg-wine.** _Add:_ The word occurs as a proper name:—Mēguini, Txts. 159, 186, 202 : 161, 293. Iuxta terminos id est bereueg et Mēguines paeð, C. D. i. 50, 14. Mēguuines paeð, 54, 30.

**mǣg-wlite.** _Add:_—Hié oncneówon Crīstes rōde mǣre tācen on his mægwlite (cf. hié gesāwon Cristes rōde tācen on his onsiéne, Bl. H. 243, 13), An. 1340.

**mǣl** a measure, &c. II. _add:_ v. crīstel-mǣl. III. _add:_ v. undern-mǣl. IV. _add:_—Nȳtenu etað swā ǣr swā hī hit habbað, ac se gesceádwīsa man sceal cēpan his mǣles, Hml. S. 16, 318. Ðonne hī etað tō ānes mǣles on dæg _quando in die una refectio fuerit_, Chrd. 15, 7. Be hyre (_St. Æthelthrȳð_) is āwrytan þ heó wel drohtnode tō ānum mǣle fæstende, būtan hit freólsdæg wǣre (cf. seldon būtan māran symbelnesse mā þonne ǣne sīðe on dæg _semel per diem_) þ heó wolde mete þicgan, Bd. 4, 19 ; Sch. 443, 17), 20, 42. Gif hwām geboden sȳ tō ðigene, and hē hit mid gebelge forsace, ne sȳ him tō gewilnedum mǣle (_hora qua desideraverit_) nānre ōðere þigene getīðad, R. Ben. 69, 21. Hȳ on ān mǣl tō nōnes gereorden _ad nonam semper reficiant_, 66, 5. Eten gebrōþru on twā mǣl, þæt is ǣrest on ðǣre syxtan tīde and eft on ǣfen _ad sextam reficiant fratres et ad seram cenent_, 65, 14 : 63, 15. (See also lencten ; II.)

**-mǣl**; n. v. for-mǣl : **-mǣl**; adj. v. ge-, grǣg-, hring-, sceáden-, wunden-mǣl.

**mǣlan.** _Add:_—Hyt ys gerǣdd þ Mōyses lǣrde þ folc, and þus wordum mǣlde, Angl. viii. 322, 4. Hē mǣlde and him beforan sǣde _praedixit_, Gr. D. 103, 32. [v. _N. E. D._ mele.]

**mǣl-dropa.** _Add:_ [Cf. _Icel._ mēl-dropi _foam from a horse's mouth._ v. _N. E. D._ meldrop.]

**mǣle**, adj. _Marked, spotted_:—On mǣlan beorh middeweardne, C. D. v. 166, 3. v. un-mǣle.

**-mǣle**; n. v. ed-mǣle : **-mǣle**; adj. v. þūsend-mǣle : **-mǣle**; adj. sam-mǣle.

**mǣl-sceafa.** _Add:_—Mǣlscaua a caterpillar (described thus : Centenis pedibus gradior per gramina ruris, Ald. 272, 33), An. Ox. 23, 53.

**mǣl-tīd**, e ; f. _Meal-time_:—Hē sceal hyne gebiddan on āsettum tīdum, and ǣr mǣltīdum (-tīman, v. l., Nap. 84) metes ne ābītan, O. E. Hml. i. 303, 7.

**mǣl-tima.** _See preceding word._

**-mǣlum.** _Add:_ v. byrþen-, pric-, scȳr-, snǣd-, stefn-, sundor-mǣlum.

**mēnan** to mean. I a. _add:_—Hē cȳðde hwæðer hē mǣnde, ðe ðæs mōdes fōster ðe ðæs līchoman _qui pastionem corporis an corporis suaderet aperuit_, Past. 137, 18. I b. _add:_—'Ne sele eldiódigum.' Hē mǣnde ðā āwiergedan gǣstas '_nec sint alieni participes tui._' Alienos malignos spiritus vocat, Past. 373, 25. Hwæt mǣnde Sanctus Paulus, ðā hē his lāre suā cræftelīce tōsceád . . . būton ðæt hē ongeat Titum hwēne monðwǣrran . . . and Timotheus hē ongeat hātheortran . . . , 291, 19.

**mēnan** to relate. _Add:_—Scipia mǣnde (or _under_ mǣnan _to lament_; III ?) his earfoða tō Rōmana witum, þǣr hié æt hiera gemōte wǣron, hwȳ hié hiene swā unweorðne on his ylde dyden ; and ācsade hié for hwȳ hié nolden geþencan ealle þā brocu and þā geswinc þe hē for hira willan fela wintra dreógende wæs ; and hū hē hié ādyde of Hannibales þeówdōme ; and hū hē him tō þeówdōme gewylde . . . ealle Africe Scipionem pro concione de periculo salutis suae contestatum, quod sibi pro patria laborante ab ingratis denunciari cognovisset, Ors. 5, 4 ; S. 224, 24.

**mēnan** to lament. I. _add:_—Mǣnes (_plangent_) alle cynno eorðes, Mt. L. 24, 30. Mǣnæ lugere, 9, 15. Mǣnende tumultuantem (turbam), 23. Mǣnende (_dolentes_) wē sōhton ðec, Lk. L. 2, 48. Woependen and mǣnende (-iende, L.) _flentes et heiulantes_, Mk. R. 5, 38. Mǣnende

and woepende *lugentes et flentes*, 16, 10. **III.** *add :*—Hē wēpende mǣnde þā unāre þe mon him būton gewyrhton dyde *deplorans injurias suas*, Ors. 5, 12; S. 240, 9. Giweópun alle and mǣndun ðā ilca *flebant omnes et plangebant illam*, Lk. R. L. 8, 52. Hē wæs mǣnende þā dǣd mid micle wōpe *flevit*, Ors. 5, 12; S. 242, 19. v. ge-mǣnan.

**mǣne**; **II.** *add :*—Þā synleahtras þe ūs forbodene synd, þæt is ... leásunga and mǣne āþas, Wlfst. 135, 3. Ic eom anddetta mǣnra āða, Angl. xi. 101, 35.

-**mǣne-líc**, -**líce**, -**licness**, -**mǣn-ness**, -**scipe**. v. ge-mǣnelic, &c.: -**mǣnsumian**, -**ung**. v. ge-mǣnsumian, -ung: -**mǣnung**. v. ge-mǣnung.

**mǣra** ?:—Tō werbolde .XL. mǣra oðđe ān fōðer gyrda, C. D. iii. 451, 1.

**mǣran**, **māran**. *Dele* māran, *and in* Nar. 32, 22 *l.* mǣran (v. Angl. i. 512). *Add:* v. ā-, wíd-mǣran.

**mǣrian**, **mǣrian** *to bound, form the boundary of* land :—Ondlang riðies đæt hit cymð tō Cearwyllan; đonne mǣred hit Cerwylle seoðđan, C. D. iii. 404, 16. Ǣrest westan-norðan hyt mǣrað Wōdnes dīc, 456, 15. [v. *N. E. D.* mere, mear : *D.D.* mear.] v. ge-mǣrian.
-**mǣran**, -**mǣrian** *terminare.* v. ā-mǣran, -mǣrian.

**mǣr-brōc.** *Add :*—Of Afene in mǣrbrōc . . . on đone nearuan byge on Afene; upp andlang strēmes, đæt eft upp on mǣrbrōc, C. D. iii. 436, 33-437, 8.

**mǣr-cnoll** *a boundary* cnoll :—Of wealhgeate tō mǣrcnolle; of mǣr-cnolle, Cht. E. 445, 11.

**mǣr-cumb** *a boundary* cumb :—In mǣrcumb; of đām cumbe, C. D. iii. 399, 7.

**mǣr-díc.** *Add :*—Tō mǣrdíc; đonne andlang mǣrdíc, C. D. iii. 415, 1.

**mǣre** *a boundary.* *Add :*—Se ilca forwyrnd þǣre sǣ þ heó ne mōt þone þeorscwold oferstæppan þǣre eorþan (mǣru *follows* eorđan *above the line*), Bt. 21; S. 49, n. 3. In mǣru Magedan *in fines Magedan*, Mt. R. 15, 39. [v. *N. E. D.* mere, mear *a boundary : D.D.* mear.]
·**mǣre** *illustrious.* **I.** *add :*—Mǣran *illustris* (*Agnae gloriosum exemplar*), An. Ox. 4276. **II.** *add :*—Mǣre *sublimis* (*celsitudo*), An. Ox. 1007. Hū beorht, mǣre, ǣnlic o *preclara* (*virginitatis gratia*), 1266. Mǣre *celeberrimus*, i. *excellentissimus* (*Agathae rumor*), 3937. On þǣm mǣran fæstene *in celeberrimo* (*Alexandriae*) *municipio*, 3418. On mǣrum *in summo* (*virginitatis proposito*), 5, 21. Mǣran *potiorem* (*virginitatis gloriam*), 4153. Swearm þā mǣran mǣdo bereáfað *examen amoena prata populatur*, 137. [v. *N. E. D.* mere.]

**mǣre-mǣd** (?) *a boundary meadow* :—Đis syndon þā landgemǣro ... norðrihte on mǣremǣde westewearde, C. D. iii. 416, 18.

**mǣr-flōde** *a boundary channel* :—Forð on đā díc tō mǣrflōdan, C. D. iii. 408, 31.

**mǣr-ford** *a boundary ford* :—In mǣrford; of đan forda, C. D. iii. 126, 32.

**mǣr-furh** *a boundary furrow* :—Andlang mǣrfyrh, C. D. iii. 414, 9. Æt mǣrfurh, 28. [v. *N. E. D.* mere-furrow.]

**mǣr-geard.** v. geard.

**mǣr-haga** *a boundary fence* :—Andlang mǣrhagan . . . on þone mǣr-hægan, C. D. iii. 437, 1-6. v. gemǣr-haga *under* ge-mǣre; **II. ¶**.

**mǣr-heg.** *l.* -hege, *and add* :—Tō đām mǣrhege, C. D. iii. 79, 13. Ollonc þæs gemǣreheges (cf. gemǣrheges, 1) onbūtan Hreódlēge; đæt swā on þone mǣrhege đe sceót tō đǣre hālgan ǣc, vi. 234, 12 : v. 126, 26.

**mǣr-hlinc** *a boundary* hlinc :—Andlang weges tō mǣrhlinc; andlang mǣrhlinces, C. D. iii. 414, 10 : 18 : 19 : 21.
-**mǣrian.** v. -mǣran.

**mǣr-lacu** *a boundary stream.* v. lacu, *where also see* gemǣr-lacu.

**mǣr-líc.** *Add* :—Đā frægn ic hié and āhsode hwæþer hū ōwiht mǣrli[ces] in þǣm londum wisten *quos cum interrogarem si quid nossent in illa regione dignum aliquid ad spectaculum*, Nar. 24, 31.

**mǣrlíce.** *Add* :—Mǣrlíce *insigniter* (*edidit opusculum*), An. Ox. 4585. Hēt se cāsere hine Críst wiðsacan, and hē mōste beón mǣrlíce mid him, Hml. Th. ii. 310, 19. Wæs hyre willa mǣrlícor þ heó wolde hyre sylf hyre mægðhād behātan Gode, Hml. A. 32, 200. Se cyng þæt hūs (*the temple*) mǣrlícost tō Gode betǣhte þe ǣfre ǣr ǣnig gewurde, Wlfst. 278, 4. Hū hē be Gode mihte mǣrlícost wrītan, Hml. S. 15, 202.

**mǣr-pol** *a boundary pool* :—Andlang streámes đæt on mǣrpól; đonne of đǣm pōle on beánbrōc, C. D. v. 198, 31.

**mǣr-pull** *a boundary pull* :—On mǣrpul; ondlong pulles on Afene, Cht. E. 445, 13.

**mǣrsian.** **A.** *trans.* **III.** *add* :—Hī mid ege and micelan geleúfan mǣrsodon þǣre eádigan forðfōre dæg, Hml. S. 23 b, 800. His gemynd sceal beón mǣrsad mid mæssesongum, Shrn. 84, 3. **IV.** *add* :—Eástrun wē nā ne mǣrsiaþ *pascha non celebramus*, An. Ox. 40, 30. Hē mērsode micele symbelnesse for þām sige, Hml. S. 30, 396. Dreám mǣrsodan *concentum celebrabant* (*praefatae virgines*), An. Ox. 4661. **V.** *add* :—Hē worhte fela wundra . . . se Hǣlend hine mērsode (mǣrsode, *v. l.*) swā, Hml. S. 27, 205. Mǣrsi[an] *extollamus*, An. Ox.

56, 332. **B.** *intrans.* *To become famous*; clarescere :—Manige hālige martyras . . . daga gehwylce mǣrsiað and scīnaþ (*clarescunt*) for þām wundrum þe æt heora þām deádum bānum geweorðað, Gr. D. 292, 4. Manige wundra scīnaþ and mǣrsiað (*clarescunt*) þe lange ǣr wǣron mannum bemiþene, 330, 21.

**mǣr-sīc** *a boundary sike* :—On mǣrsīc; of mǣrsīce on mǣrdīc, C. D. vi. 60, 17.

**mǣr-stān.** *Add:* [v. *N. E. D.* mere-stone.] v. gemǣr-stān *under* ge-mǣre; **II. ¶**.

**mǣrsung.** **II.** *add:*—Wæs gemǣrsad mērsong (*fama*) of him, Lk. L. 4, 37. **III.** *add:*—On þæs regoles mǣrsunge, Hml. S. 23 b, 151. Ealle þās dǣda and mǣrsunga [*caelebrationes* (Sabbati observatio, circumcisio, &c.)] wē oncnāwaþ wesan gefyllede, An. Ox. 40, 10. **IV.** *add:*—Heora fixnoðe gelamp micel earfoðnys, þæt Crístes tācne gelumpe micel mǣrsung, Hml. Th. ii. 290, 6. Wē on lofsangum hyre mǣrða cýðað, þ heó ús þingige tō hyre suna, þ hē ús miltsige for đǣre mǣrsunge þe wē hyre gedōð, Hml. A. 25, 34. v. sealmsang-, wíd-mǣrsung.

**mǣr-þorn.** *Add :*—Of đǣre þyrnan on mǣrþorn; of mǣrþorne, D. D. vi. 221, 16.

**mǣrþu.** *Add :*—Þyses dæges þēnung and đyssere tíde mǣrð sprecað embe Godes tōcyme, Hml. Th. i. 600, 2. Æt þǣre mæssan weard his mǣrð geswutelod swā þ se hālga gāst hine ealne befēng on fýres gelýcnysse, Hml. S. 3, 475. Þū hine gewuldrast and geweorðast and him sylst heáfodgold tō mǣrðe *gloria et honore coronasti eum*, Ps. Th. 8, 6. Sceolde him man bringan ongeán crætwǣn . . . hiora consulum tō mǣrþe, þæt wæs triumpheum, Ors. 2, 4; S. 70, 35. **II.** *add:*—Mǣrþa *insignia* (*ornamentorum et vestium*), An. Ox. 5172. Eal swā feala mǣrþa ic gerime [swā] stīþnessa [þū] on belǣt[st] *tot ego glorias numerabo quot uiolentias inrogaueris*, 4762. Hī ealle Godes mǣrða wurðodon, Hml. S. 23 b, 799. Tō þām geweorce brōhte þ folc gold and seolfor and deórwirþe gimstānas and menigfælde mǣrþa, Ælfc. Gen. Thw. 3. 31.

**mǣr-pyrne** *a boundary thornbush* :—On đā blacan þyrnan . . . of đǣre þyrnan . . . andlang fūrena on mǣrðyrnan; đanan on mǣrdíc, C. D. vi. 220, 22.

-**mǣr-treów.** v. gemǣr-treów *under* ge-mǣre; **II. ¶**, *and see N. E. D.* mere-tree: -**mǣrung.** v. ge-mǣrung.

**mǣslere**, es; *m.* *A sacristan, keeper of a church* :—Gā tō Abundium þām mǣslere (cf. cyricweard, 4) *vade ad Abundium mansionarium*, Gr. D. 228, 15. [Cf. *O. H. Ger.* mesinari *mansionarius, ianitor, aedituus: Ger.* messner.]

**mæsse:** **I.** *add:*—Se Hǣlend gehālgode hlāf and wín tō húsle . . . and þā wæs seó mæsse āsteald þurh Críst, Hml. A. 71, 158. Gyf þū mæssan hacelan habban wille, þonne stríc þū mid tōsprǣddum handum niþer ofer þine breóst, Tech. ii. 119, 25. Gif þū (cf. se mæssepreóst, 18) wille mē hwylce þearfe gegearwian, geoffra þysne hlāf þām ælmihtigan Gode for mē æt þīnre mæssan, tō þon þ þū geþingie mīnum synnum, Gr. D. 348, 28. **I a.** *a particular instance of the service, a mass* :—Đæt ǣghwilc mæssepríost gesinge fore Ōsuulfes sāwle twā messan, C. D. i. 293, 31. Wæs his gewuna þæt hē wolde ǣlce dæge habban twā mæssan, būtan hit mā wǣre . . . Đā cwæð hē tō his geféran þ hit betere wǣre þ hig þā mæssan hæfdon, Vis. Lfc. 63-67. **I b.** *the service held on a saint's or martyr's day, a* (*person's*) *mass* :—Sci Rufi mæsse biþ gemēted on þām yldran mæssebōcum, Shrn. 121, 30. Sca Sabine mæsse bið gemēted on þām nīwran bōcum, 123, 17 : 124, 33. v. heáh-mæsse.

**mæsse-æfen.** *Add:*—Leóhtgesceotu þriwa on geáre, ǣrest on Eásteræfen, ōðre síðe on Candelmæsseæfen, þriddan síðe on Ealra Hālgena mæsseæfen, Ll. Th. ii. 256, 28.

**mæsse-bōc.** *Add:*—Þreú þēningbēc, mæssebōc and bletsungbōc and pistelbōc, Cht. Crw. 23, 27. Sci Rufi mæsse biþ gemēted on đām yldran mæssebōcum, Shrn. 121, 30 : 124, 33. On þām nīwran sacramentorum, þ ys on đām mæssebōcum, 119, 5.

**mæsse-dæg.** *Add:*—Eádmund cyning forðférde on Scs Agustínus mæssedæg, Chr. 946; P. 112, 2. On Scē Gregories mæssedæg, 951; P. 112, 7. Se cyng hēt ofsleán ealle đā Deniscan men þe on Angelcynne wǣron on Bricius messedæg, 1002; P. 135, 2.

**mæsse-hacele.** *Add:*—Hē stōd āþenedum earmum mid mæsse[reáfe] gescrýdd, and hæfde grēne mæssehacelan on him, Vis. Lfc. 39.

**mæsse-hrægel.** *Add: a vestment used in celebrating mass.* The Latin original for Shrn. 112, 19 is : Hic constituit sacerdotes et levitas vestes sacratas in usu cotidiano non uti nisi in ecclesia. Cf. mæsse-reáf.

**mæssian.** *This should be placed after* mæsse-wín.

**mæsse-niht.** *Add:*—Mōna āþīstrode on middes wintres mæsseniht, Chr. 827; P. 60, 23. On ealra hālgena mæsseniht, 971; P. 119, 23. On Scē Ambrosius mæsseniht, 1095; P. 230, 27.

**mæsse-preóst.** *Add:*—Leófgār wæs Haroldes eorles mæssepreóst, Chr. 1056; P. 186, 25. Se biscop sceal þrafian þā mæssepreóstas þ hié healdan Godes ǣwe on riht, and þone híred þe hié ofer beóþ, and þā lǣwedan men þe hié aldormen ofer beón sceolan; for þon se gōda lāreów sægde, þonne se mæssepreóst wǣre gelǣded on ēce forwyrd, þonne ne mihte hē þǣre heorde þe hē Gode healdan sceolde nǣnige gōde beón,

Bl. H. 45, 6–16. Mæssepreóstas sceolon symble æt heora húsum leorningmonna sceole habban, Ll. Th. ii. 414, 7.

**mæssepreóst-hád.** Add :—Se ylca mæssepreóst Constantínus on mæssepreóstháde (on preóstháde, v. l.) his líf geendode idem (presbyter) Constantius in presbyteratus officio vitam finivit, Gr. D. 66, 1. Ær his mæssepreóstháde, Shrn. 13, 23. Mæssepreóstháde onfónde sacerdotium accipientes (filii Leui), Scint. 108, 3.

**mæsse-reáf.** For 'Vestment' l. 'Vestments', and add :—Eall swá be mæssereáfe þe sume menn maciað of heora ealdum cláðum, Hml. A. 35, 279. Se hálga Swiðun on scínendum mæssereáfe stód swylce hé wolde mæssian, Hml. S. 21, 354. Mæssepreóst sceal habban clǽne mæssereáf, Ll. Th. ii. 384, 3. Þreó þéningbéc . . . and án mæssereáf, Cht. Crw. 23, 27. Habbað eów mid swylc mæssereáf and swylce húselfata swylce gé mid risnum þá þénunga þénian magon, Ll. Th. ii. 404, 26. Twá mæssereáf, C. D. B. iii. 660, 33.

**mæsse-sang.** Add : I. celebration of mass :—Nán mæssesang beón ne mæg bútan þǽm þrím þingum, þ is oflǽtan and wín and wæter (cf. panis et vinum et aqua sine quibus nequaquam missae celebrantur, 111, 30). Ll. Th. ii. 406, 2. Hé him swiðlíce ondréd in þám mæssesange (in illa missarum celebritate), Gr. D. 309, 4. His gemynd sceal beón mǽrsad mid mæssesongum on eallum ciricum, Shrn. 84, 3. II. the service held on a saint's day, a (person's) mass. v. mæsse; I b :—Scí Agapites mæssesang mæg gemétan sé þe sécð on þám níwran sacramentorum, Shrn. 119, 4. [Messe-song, Gen. and Ex. 2466.]

**mæsse-steall,** es ; m. The place where the priest stood when saying mass (?), the altar (cf. gif preóst búton gehálgodon weófode mæssige, Ll. Th. ii. 292, 18. Se pápa hét hine mæssian at S. Petres weófode, Ch. 995; P. 130, 28. Hé stód æt ðám weófode swylce hé wolde mæssian, Hml. S. 21, 355) :—Geearnian wé mid gódum dǽdum, þæt is mid clǽne ælmessan and mid leóhte tó úrum ciricean and tó úrum mæssesteallum, Nap. 43. [Prof. Max Förster suggests another meaning, and compares steall with stallum = a stall, seat in the choir of a church, Nap. 84.]

**mæsse-þegnung,** e ; f. The service of mass :—On óþran dagan on þǽre fíftan tíde and sixtan and seofoþan nis ná mæsseþénuug álýfed, ac man mót swíðe wel mæssan singan on ærnemorgen, Angl. xi. 8, 15.

**mæsse-úhta** the hour of matins on a feast day, the matins themselves :—Habbon þonne interuallum . . . bútan sunnanúhtan and mæsseúhtan (festiuitatibus sanctorum), þonne ne þearf nán interuallum beón, Chrd. 24. 7. Gé sculon singan sunnanúhtan and mæsseúhton, ǽfre nigon rǽpsas mid nigon rǽdingum, Ll. Th. ii. 384, 4. Cf. Crístesmæsse-úhta, Chr. 1021; P. 154, 31.

**mæssian.** Take here mæssian, placed wrongly in Dict. after mæssehrægel, and add :—Se pápa mid his ágenum handum him his pallium on sette . . . and hé syððan mid þám pallium þǽr mæssode (mæssan sang, v. l.), swá se pápa him gewissode, Chr. 1022; P. 157, 1. Messode, Hml. S. 3, 350. Se bisceop him eallum mæssode, 29, 261 : 22, 69. Hí (those under Moses' law) ne mæssoden nǽfre . . . húsel næs gehálgod ǽr þám ðe se Hǽlend cóm, 10, 222 : Hml. A. 17, 81. Hé hét mæssian for þæs forðfarenan sáwle, and árǽrde þone deádan, Hml. S. 6, 209. Hé stód æt ðám weófode swylce hé wolde mæssian, 21, 355. Smeáging . . . hwilcan tíman on sunnandagan oþþe on óðran dagan man mæssian móte, Angl. xi. 7, 3, 6. Se Hǽlend ne gecýst nú be nánum cynrene, ac of ælcere mǽgðe tó his þénungum him tó mæssigenne, Hml. A. 17, 87. Se þe geþrístlǽcð tó mæssianne oððon húsl tó ðicganne, and wát hine sylfne on synnum fúlne, Wlfst. 34, 14. [v. N. E. D. mass; vb.] v. ge-mæssian.

**mǽst,** adv. I. add : very much :—Þæt orþancum ealde reccað þá þe mǽgburge mǽst gefrúnon, Exod. 360. Alexandreas ealra rícost monna cynnes and hé mǽst geþáh þára þe ic ofer foldan gefrægen hæbbe, Víd. 16. Þeáh leahtras bysigen monna módsefan mǽst and swíðost, Met. 22, 31 : 62. Mǽst and fyrmest, Ps. Th. 121, 7. II. add :—Hé þár mycel gód gegaderode . . . þá hyt eall mǽst gegaderod wæs, Chr. 1065; P. 190, 28. Mǽst ealle Africe gecirdon tó Geoweorþan universam pene Africam regno suo junxit, Ors. 5, 7 ; S. 228, 26.

**mǽstan.** Add :—Þú mǽstest on ele heáfod mín inpinguasti in oleo caput meum, Ps. Rdr. 22, 5. v. ofer-mæstan.

**mæsten;** n. (not m.). In l. 5 for L. M. read L. In. and add :—Seó lǽs and ðæt mæsten is gemǽne tó ðám án and twéntigum hídum, C. D. v. 319, 28. Æceren oððe bóc oððe óðer mæsten, Chrd. 15, 10.

**mæstlíce;** adv. Very much :—Mǽstlícust magnopere, Angl. xiii. 447, 1169.

**mæst-ling,** es ; m. A fatling :—Mæstling altilia (Mt. 22, 4), An. Ox. 61, 29. v. mǽst, mǽstan, mǽstel-bearh.

**mæstling.** Add :—Mǽstlinges electri (stannique metalla), An. Ox. 2, 27. [v. N. E. D. maslin.]

**mæstling-smiþ.** l. -smiþ : mæst-lón. v. lóh.

**mǽtan.** Add : with acc. of person and of dream :—Tó þǽm sóðum geséldum ic tíohige ðæt ic þé lǽde, þǽr þín mód oft ymb rǽswed and eác mǽt te ducere aggredimur ad veram felicitatem, quam tuus quoque somniat animus, Bt. 22, 2 ; S. 51, 13. Þá gemunde Iósep þá swefen þe hine æt sumon cyrre ǽr mǽtte recordatus somniorum, quae aliquando viderat, Gen. 42, 9. Hé nán þincg þǽre byrig ne cúþe gecnáwan . . . and

hé wundrigende þóhte swilce hine on niht mǽtte . . . Hé cwæð : ' God gebletsige mé, hwæþer hit furþon sóð sý oððe hwæðer mé on swefne mǽte eall þ ic hér geseó fǽrlices wundres,' Hml. S. 23, 512–523. Nó hé gemunde þæt him mǽted (? metod, MS. ; for construction cf. 157) wæs, Dan. 119.

**mǽte.** Add :—Hé mót ǽgðer witan ge lǽsse ge mǽre, ge betere ge mǽtre ðæs ðe tó túne belimpð, Angl. ix. 259, 23. Hý getrymedon him word mǽte firmauerunt sibi uerbum malum, Ps. Rdr. 63, 6. Micle ge méttan, C. D. B. iii. 491, 12. Ðá druncengeornan synt micele mǽttran ðonne nýtenu, Hml. A. 145, 27. Swá bióð þá midmestan (mǽstan, v. l.) men onmiddan þám spácan, and þá betran neár þére nafe, and þá mǽtran neár ðǽm felgum . . . þá felga longiað on þǽm spácan . . . swá dóð þá mǽtestan (mǽstan, v. l.) men þám midmestum, and þá midmestan on þǽm betstan . . . þá mǽtestan (mǽstan, v. l.) ealle hiora lufe wenden tó ðisse weorulde, Bt. 39, 7 ; S. 130, 1–9. [v. N. E. D. meet.] v. byrþen-, pund-, úþ-mǽte.

**mǽte;** adv. Poorly, badly :—Him þúhte þ heora frið mǽttor (mǽctor, MS.) gelǽst wǽre þonne hit scolde, Ll. Th. i. 162, 3. v. or-, úþ-mǽte.

**mǽþ.** I. add :—Swá þæs gyltes mǽð beó secundum modum culpe, Chrd. 62, 1. II. add :—Nis nánes mannes mǽð þ cunne ásæcgan eal þ gód þe God hǽfð gegearwod þám þe hine lufiað, Angl. xii. 514, 29. Se man hæfð gold, þæt is gód be his mǽðe, Hml. Th. i. 254, 19. III. add :—Intingan beseoh ná mǽþe causam respice non personam, Scint. 185, 12. Riht dóm ys þár ná mǽþa (persone) ac weorcu beóþ besceáwude, 3. IV. add : v. mǽþ-leás, -lic. V. add : v. mǽþ-full :— On ðǽre sylfan grétinge ǽlc sí gegearcod him mǽð in ipsa salutatione omnis exibiatur humanitas, R. Ben. I. 88, 6. [v. N. E. D. methe.] v. hyge-, un-mǽþ.

**mǽþ,** mowing. Add :—Se Godes þeówa cwæð : ' Árís and ber þis gréne híg þám horsum . . . nú is lytel tó láfe þysses mǽþes (cf. hé máweþ heig on þissere dene, 2), and swá þis gedón byþ, ic gá æfter þé ' leua fenum viride, porta pabulum jumentis; ecce ego, quia parum superest, opere expleto te subsequor, Gr. D. 36, 31. v. mǽþ-méd ; máwan.

**mǽþel.** Add : v. ge-maþel.

**mǽþel-frið,** es ; n. Peace secured by law at a public assembly, the violation of which had to be compensated twofold :—Ciricfriþ II. gylde ; mæþlfriþ II. gylde, Ll. Lbmn. 3, 6.

**mǽþ-full.** Add : v. un-mǽþfull.

**Mǽð-hild.** If this be a woman's name, it could not be that which later becomes Matilda, cf. Mathild, Chr. 1067; P. 202, 28 : Mahtild, 1083; P. 215, 22. O. H. Ger. Maht-hilt.

**mǽþlan.** Add : [v. N. E. D. mell.]

**mǽþ-leás.** Add :—Bebeád Martínus þám mǽðleásum scealfrum þ hí geswicon þæs fixnoðes, Hml. S. 31, 1322. v. mǽþ ; IV.

**mǽþ-lic.** Add : v. mǽþ ; IV : **mǽþlíce.** Add : v. un-mǽþlíce.

**mǽþ-méd,** e ; f. Reward for mowing :—Gyteorm for yrðe, mǽdméd gutfirma ad arandum et firma pratorum fenandorum, Ll. Th. i. 440, 27.

**mǽþung,** e ; f. Measuring, determination of amount, assessment :— Seó mǽdung (modus correptionis) is on þám bisceope and on þám ealdre þe under him bið, Chrd. 35, 18.

**Mǽþ-ware** the Medes :—Médware, Shrn. 155, 33.

**mǽt-lic.** v. or-, un-mǽtlic : **mǽtlíce.** v. or-mǽtlíce : -mǽtu. v. ofer-mǽtu : **mǽwect.** v. mǽd-mǽwect.

**maffian;** p. ode To fall away from right conduct, be or become shameless :—Wín and druncene wíf gedóð hwílon þ witon maffiað uinum et mulieres ebriose apostatare faciunt sapientes; wine and women will make men of understanding to fall away (Ecclus. 19, 2), Chrd. 74, 2. Mid maffigendre and prútlicre stæppincge petulanti tumidoque gestu incedere, 77, 2.

**maga** the stomach. Add :—Hé cwæð ðæt gé móston drincan gewealden wínes for eówres magan mettrymnesse modico vino utere propter stomachum et frequentes tuas infirmitates, Past. 319, 7.

**maga** able. Add : having means :—Gif man þone man betýhð þe bið lǽssa maga (a person of less ability; qui minus possit) þone se cyninges þegn, Ll. Th. i. 154, 7. Sé þe lǽsse maga (mǽge, mage, v. ll.) sý (qui minus potest, qui impotencior est [old Latin versions), 414, 19. Þá preóstas þe áðer oððe ágen wylla oððe mage ælmeshand (a parent who had means but exhausted them by almsgiving; cf. Past. 325, 6–8) hæfenleáse gedyde clerici quos voluntas aut natiuitas pauperes fecit, Chrd. 12, 19. Cf. maþelian.

**magan.** For ' does not occur in W. S., but' substitute : magan = posse occurs in Angl. xiii. 389, 337 : Scint. 46, 6 : 159, 6 ; in l. 8 for mágon l. magon. I. add :—Ne magon hý ús þonne ǽnige góde, Wlfst. 122, 7. Ne ástyra ðú yrsunga unmihtigum men, ðeáh ðe ðú mæge bet, Hex. 46, 2. ¶ magan tó :—Þás ús magon tó geuðgon nobis ista sufficiunt, Chrd. 90, 8. Hé wæs smeágende hwæt tó bóte mihte æt þǽm fǽrcwealme, Ll. Th. i. 270, 9. ¶ magan wiþ. (1) dat. or uncertain :—Ǽlc wiht mæg bet wyð cyle þonne wið hǽte omnia pene animantia patientius et tolerabilius ad summum frigoris quam ad summum caloris accedant, Ors. 1, 1 ; S. 24, 29. Þá getweóde hié hwæðer hié wið him mæhten cum desistendum certamine propter metum periculi arbitrarentur, 1, 14 ; S. 56, 31. Mehte, 4, 6 ; S. 170, 21. (2) with acc. :—

Philippuse geþūhte þæt hē leng mid folcgeseohtum wið hié ne mehte, Ors. 3, 7; S. 118, 18. **III** i. expressing possibility where there are no prohibitive conditions :—Hæbbe hē ungeligenra manna gewitnesse þe man gelýfan mæge, Ll. Th. i. 158, 13. Hý smeádon hū heora frið betere beón mæhte, 162, 2. Begytan hine magan forgyfenysse gelýfe *consequi se posse ueniam credat*, Scint. 46, 6. Hē sǽde nāne gyltas magan beón ālýsede . . . *dixit nulla scelera posse redemi* . . , 159, 6. (2) expressing the admissibility or certainty of a supposition :—For ðām hē mæig wēnan, gyf hē þ ǽr forgýmð, þ . . . *qua scire debet, si minus hoc servabit* . . , Ll. Th. i. 440, 13. Wite þū for sōð, gif þ þīne āgne welan wǽron þe þū mǽndest þ þū forlure, ne mihtest þū hī forleósan, Bt. 7, 3; F. 20, 18. Hē geseþ swā eáþelīce crīstenne magan þolian *ipse testatur tam facile Xpianum posse carere*, Angl. xiii. 389, 337. **III** c. i. *add* :—Mid scipun þe mon dulmunus hǽtt, þe mon sægð þæt on än scip mæge ān þūsend manna *it is said that a thousand men can be put into one ship*, Ors. 1, 10; S. 46, 33. **IV**. expressing permission or sanction. *add* :—Āgyf þīne scīre, ne miht (mæht, L.) þū lencg tūnscīre bewitaı (*iam non poteris uilicare*), Lk. 16, 2. Gyf hē wel āginnan wile, ne mæig hē sleac beón, Angl. ix. 259, 21. Būtan hē þone gerēfan hæbbe þe þæs wyrðe sý þe þ dōn mæge, Ll. Th. i. 280, 15. **IV** a. in a legal statute *may = shall* or *must* :—x. wintre cniht mæg bión þiéfðe gewita *a boy of ten shall be liable for complicity in a case of theft*; *puer decem annorum debet scire ne furtum faciat*, Ll. Th. i. 106, 18. Gyf hit ðonne elles funden sý, ðonne mæg þ forfangfeoh leóhtre beón, 226, 5. Ic hæbbe gecoren and mīne witan hwæt seó ðeáre mæg witan, 276, 31. **IV** 3 c. ii. *add* :—On ǽghwelc þāra fata mihte twēgen mittan oþþe þreó (cf. *hyrdriae capientes singuli metretas binas vel ternas*, Jn. 2, 6), Shrn. 48, 29. v. ofer-mæg.

**maga-þiht;** *adj. Strong of stomach.* v. þiht.

**māge.** *Add :—*þ nān biscop ne nān mæssepreóst næbbe on his hūse wunigende ǽnigne wīfman, būton hit sý his mōdor oððe his swustor, faðu oððe mōddrige, oððe māge of þām þe ne mage nān unhlīsa āspringan, Ll. Th. ii. 376, 23. Fōn māgas tō and weddian heora māgan tō wīfe þām þe hire girnde, i. 254, 20. Gunnilde, Cnutes cynges māgan (*sister's daughter*), Chr. 1045; P. 165, 23. [v. *N. E. D.* mowe.] v. nīd-māge.

**Mage-sǽte.** *Add :—*In pago Magesǽtna, C. D. B. iii. 242, 23. See note, and Chr. P. ii. 197 : 219.

**magian;** *p.* ode *To be strong, prevail :—*Ic magude ongeán hine *preualui aduersus eum*, Ps. Rdr. 12, 5. Ic magude ł swīþige, Ps. Spl. T. 12, 5. [*O. H. Ger.* magēn *valere, vigere.*] Cf. maga.

**magister.** *l.* māgister, and *add :* **I.** *a director, chief, ruler :—*Ðonne hē gemētte ðā scylde ðe hē stiéran scolde, hrædlīce hē gecýðde ðæt hē wæs māgister and ealdormonn (*magistrum se esse resoluit*), Past. 117, 6: Gen. 40, 21 (*in Dict.*). Hē sette him weorca mægestras (*magistros operum*), Ex. 1, 11. **II.** *master* as correlative of *servant* or *man :—*Hit is niédðearf ðæt mon his hlāford ondrǽde, and se cneoht his māgister, Past. 109, 14. **III.** *the owner* or *tamer of an animal :—*Seó leó, ðeáh hió wel tam sē . . . and hire māgister (*magistrum*) swīðe lufige . . . heó ābīt hire lādteów, Bt. 25; F. 88, 10. **IV.** *a teacher :—*Se māgister (cf. lāreow, 3), Past. 455, 20. Mid þām lāreówdōme þæs heán māgistres Godes hē wæs on godcundlican þeódscipe getýd and gelǽred *summis providentibus magistris monasticis disciplinis erudiebatur*, Guth. Gr. 112, 96. Nerōn wolde hātan his āgenne māgister and his fōsterfæder (*familiarem praeceptoremque suum*) ācwellan þæs nama wæs Seneca, Bt. 29, 2; S. 66, 24. Hī hæfdon māgistras gearwe, ðā ðe hig lǽrdon and týdon (*magistros, qui docerent*), Bd. 4, 2; Sch. 345, 14. **V.** (*one's*) *master, he whose disciple one is :—*Be þǽre hæfegan gēmene bearna cwæþ mīn mægister Euripides *in quo Euripidis mei sententiam probo*, Bt. 31, 1 : F. 112, 20.

**māgister-dōm,** es; *m. The office of a master* or *teacher :—*Hefe mægsterdōmes *pondus magisterii*, Scint. 120, 9. On mægsterdōme *in magisterio*, 122, 13. [v. *N. E. D.* master-dom.]

**magu.** *Dele last passage, and add :* v. wuldor-magu: **magu-tudor.** *l.* -tūdor.

**māl.** **II.** *add :—*þ sciplið gewende tō Legeceastre, and ðǽr ābiden heora māles (*their pay*) þe Ælfgār heom behēt, Chr. 1055; P. 186, 19. v. frið-, wiþer-māl.

**māletung.** *Dele, and see* maþelung.

**malscrung.** *Add :—*Malscrung *pressicium* (*for prestigium?*), Hpt. 33. 246, 83. [*N. E. D.* masker.]

**māl-sweord.** *Add :—*Ic geann mīnon swurdhwītan þæs sceardes mālswurdes, Cht. Th. 561, 23.

**mamera,** an; *m. Deep sleep :—*Momra (*printed* momna) *sopor*, Wrt. Voc. ii. 120, 82. Mameran *sopore*, An. Ox. 3404. Mamran, 2, 203. v. mamor.

**mamor.** *Dele second passage, and see preceding word.*

**man.** *Add :* **I.** with correlative *he :—*Ðonne mon mā fæst ðonne hē ðyrfe, Past. 313, 1. On ðǽre gesundfulnesse mon forgiett his selfes, 35, 6. Hit is āwrieten ðæt mon ne scyle cweðan tō his friénd . . . , 325, 1. Seó hrōf wæs þ man mid his handa getǽcean mihte, El. H. 207, 22. Wudewanhād is þ man wunige on clǽnnysse æfter his gemacan, ægðer ge weras ge wīf, Hml. A. 20, 153. Þæt man drince swā swā him ne derede, Ælfc. T. Grn. 21, 36 : Past. 189, 9. Swā swā scyp brincð man ofer sǽ; syððan hē tō lande cymð, þonne forlǽt hē þ scyp, Solil. H. 21, 20. **II.** with correlative *they :—*Gif ǽnig . . . fluge . . . , þ hine mon slōge swā raðe swā mon hiora fiénd wolde, Ors. 1, 12; S. 52, 35. Þæt hūs þǽr man ðweað heora handa, Wrt. Voc. i. 57, 50. Nān mæssepreóst . . lǽre þ mon hys cyrcan gesēce, and him heora teoðinge syllan, and þā geryhtu þe hig þām ōþrum syllan sceoldan, Ll. Th. ii. 410, 32. **III.** with verb in plural :—Mīn āgen . . . man ofgān willað (wile, *v. l.*) æt mē, Hml. S. 23, 599.

**mān.** *Add :—*Mid deófium drohtnoð habban in morðre and on māne, Wlfst. 187, 18. Uton forbūgan mān and morðor, 188, 14. Mān *pro nefas*, An. Ox. 53, 7. Synt mān (*nequitiae*) on heora wunungum, Ps. L. 54, 16. Mānu *flagitia*, Scint. 88, 15. Hwǽr syndon ūre godas þe swylcra māna gyrnen swilce hiora wǽron, Ors. 1, 8; S. 40, 29.

**mān;** *adj. Add :—*þā oðswōran hié mid þǽm bismerlicestan āðe þæt hié him nǽfre on fultume nǽre, þēh þā āðas wǽron neár māne (*or sbst.?*) þonne sōðe *turpissimam rupti foederis labem adcumulavere perjurio*, Ors. 4, 3; S. 162, 12. Ic eom mānra āþa gewita, Angl. xii. 501, 19.

**mān-āþ.** *Add :—*Ælcum geleáffullum men is tō warnigenne wið mānāðas (-āða, māne āðas, *v. ll.*) . . . Manega men tellað tō lytlum gylte, þ hī ōðre men mid mānāðum beswican, Hml. A. 147, 89-93.

**mānāþ-swaru,** e; *f. Perjury :—*Be mānāðsware *de perjurio*, Ll. Th. ii. 130, 24.

**-mancian.** v. be-mancian.

**mancus.** *Add :—*Ǽgehwilcre sprǽce þe māre sý þonne .iiii. mancussas, Ll. Th. i. 154, 10. Ān æstel on fīftegum mancessa (mon-, *v. l.*), Past. 9, 1. Hē hæfde þrý mancas (*tres aureos*) āhýdde . . . þa fundon hī þā ylcan þrý āhýdde mancas . . . secge him se brōþer þ hē sý onscunod fram eallum þām gebrōðrum for þām mancessum (*pro solidis*) . . . tōweorpað þā .iii. mancossas (*aureos*) ofer hine, Gr. D. 344, 14-37. [The word is of Arabic origin. v. *E. H. D.* p. 78.]

**mān-cynn** (?) *an evil race.* v. mann-cynn; **II.** 2 (last passage).

**mān-dǽd.** *Add :—*Māndǽde *piaculo*, An. Ox. 2006. Māndǽda *facinorum*, i. *criminum*, 921 : *passionum*, i. *uitiorum*, 1137.

**mān-dǽda,** an; *m. An evil-doer, one that works iniquity :—*Morðslagan and māndǽdan . . . and wiccan and unlybbwyrhtan, Nap. 65, 36.

**mān-deorf.** *Add : bold in evil* (?). v. dearf: **-mane.** v. ge-mane.

**mān-full.** *Add :—*Mānful *nefarius*, Angl. xi. 117, 37. Mānfulne *probrosum*, An. Ox. 2783. Sittaþ mānfulle (*perversi*) on heáhsetlum, and hālige unden heora fōtum þryccaþ, Bt. 4; F. 8, 14. Mānfullan men þe wē ymbe specað wǽron getealde for godas, Wlfst. 106, 15. Þāra mānfulra forþforlǽtenesse on þās woruldspēda, Bt. 5, 1; F. 10, 22.

**mānful-lic.** *Add :—*Iacōb hæfde twā geswustru him tō wīfe . . . Ac þ is nū mānfullic ǽnigum menn tō dōnne on þām crīstendōme, Hml. A. 16, 73.

**mānfullīce.** *Add :—*Is sē þe mānfullīce (*nequiter*) geeádmētt hine (*se*), Scint. 19, 14. Þām gelīc . . . þe mangodon mānfullīce in þām temple, Ll. Th. ii. 352, 22: Wlfst. 295, 25. Hī ðone heofenlican Æðeling mānfullīce ācwellan woldon, Hml. Th. i. 402, 9. Gezabel mānfullīce leofode on fūlum forligere and on ǽlcere fracodnysse, Hml. S. 18, 270.

**-mang** *mixing.* v. æg-, ge-mang : **-mang** *mongering.* v. ge-mang: **-mang** *-mong.* v. ā-, ge-, on-mang : **-mangenness.** v. ge-mangenness.

**mangere.** *Add :—*Apollonius forlēt his þone wurðfullan cynedōm and mangeres naman genam mā þonne gifendes, Ap. Th. 10, 9. v. pening-mangere.

**mangestre.** v. smeoru-mangestre.

**mangian** (?) *to mix :—*Suā is tō mon[g]ianne (mengenne, *v.l.*) ðā liéðnesse wið ðā rēðnesse *miscenda est lenitas cum severitate*, Past. 125, 13.

**mangung.** *Add :—*Of mīnra yldrena gestreóne mē becōm þis feoh on handa, and of þyssere ylcan byrig mangunge ic mē þ feoh gerǽhte, Hml. S. 23, 670. Āworpan hī woruldþēnunga and mancgunga *secularia officia negotique abjiciant*, Chrd. 76, 35. v. cyric-mangung.

**manian.** **I.** *add :—*þ hē hié suā micle mā lufað suā hē hié suiður manað and suingð *ut eo se filios Dei sentiant, quo illos disciplinae flagella castigant*, Past. 251, 22. Him fylgð God, ðonne hē hine monað . . . and hine spænð ðæt hē tō him geciérre *Deus subsequens monet, qui ad se redire persuadet*, 407, 9. Wē maniað þ man Sunnandæges freóls mid eallum mægene healde, Cht. E. 231, 18. **II.** *add :—*Gif wē mid rīcan mannan hwæt embe ūre neóde manian willað *si cum hominibus potentibus volumus aliqua suggerere*, R. Ben. 45. 20. **III.** *add :—*On ōðre wīsan sint tō monianne (cf. lǽranne, 21) ðā iungan, Past. 179, 19. **IV.** *add :—*Mīnes sweóres fæder manode rihtes gafoles *pater soceri mei exactionem canonis egerat*, Gr. D. 305, 26. Ūre Drihten þreað þā þe on fæstendagum hiora borga manian, Ll. Th. ii. 438, 34. v. of-manian.

**maniend.** *Add : a creditor :—*Hē sǽde þ hē wǽre hefelīce geswenced fram his maniende (moniendan, *v. l.*) for twelf scillingum *quia a creditore suo pro duodecim solidis graviter affligeretur*, intimavit, Gr. D. 157, 32. Hē hēt þ hē āgeáfe his maniende (-um, *v. l.*), 158, 21.

**manig.** I. *add:*—Nôes and Abrahames and mæniges ôðres word beóð ofergytene, Wlfst. 3, 38. Monegum men gescrincað his fêt tô his homme, Lch. ii. 68, 2. Bûtan hergiungum þe gewurdon an monigre þeóde, Ors. 3, 9; S. 128, 26. Hê heora monig ðûsend ofslôg, 3, 7; S. 110, 33. Þâ Rômâniscan mædenu manega ðurhwunodon on mægðhâde, Hml. S. 7, 293. Nis þæt gôd þ þâ monegan godas sién, Shrn. 101, 1. Mid monegum þûsendum, Ors. 5, 4; S. 224, 19. Manega ðûsenda engla, Hml. Th. ii. 334, 16. Monege ôþre þeóda; and eác þâ monegan cyningas, Ors. 5, 1; S. 214, 15: 4, 8; S. 186, 15. Þâ monegan ǽrran, 3, 11; S. 142, 6. II. *add:*—Dâuid monigne forsende, Past. 36, 8. ¶ the forms in the following are peculiar:—Swâ monig (*indeclinable* = quot. ?) beóð men ofer eorðan, swâ beóð môdgeþoncas *quot homines, tot sententiae*, Gn. Ex. 168. Dâuid monig (monigne, *v. l.*) forsende, Past. 37, 8. Þâ heáfodmen . . . mænig man (mænig-man *as a cpd.*?) nnid þâm swîðe gedrehtan, Chr. 1096; P. 233, 7. III. *add:*—Monigum monna (monigum monnum, manegum menn, *v. ll.*) tô hæle *nonnullis saluti*, Bd. 4, 19; Sch. 450, 20. v. for-, fore-manig.

**manig-feald.** I. *add:*—Eów tîhþ swîþe manigfeald gedwola (*multiplex error*), Bt. 26, 1; F. 90, 8. Eárhringas of mænigfealdan gimcynne geworhte, Nar. 26, 32. Þæne mænifealdan cræft *multiformem machinam*, An. Ox. 119. Mislicu wîtu and manigfeald earfoþu *carcer, lex, ceteraque legalium tormenta poenarum*, Bt. 39, 2; F. 212, 27. Ælc deáþlic man swencþ hine selfne mid mistlicum and manigfealdum ymbhogum, and þeáh willniaþ ealle þurh mistlice paþas cuman tô ânum ende *omnis mortalium cura, quam multiplicium studiorum labor exercet*, *ad unum finem nititur pervenire*, 24, 1; F. 80, 17. Mid mænifealdum (*diuersis*) hîwum, An. Ox. 1043. Geswincfull geár þurh manigfealde ungyld and þurh mycele rênas, Chr. 1098; P. 234, 29. II. *add:*—Eówer mêd is menigfeald on heofonum (*mercis uestra multa in caelo*, Lk. 6, 23), Hml. Th. i. 556, 11. Mid mænifealdre *opulenta* (*ubertate*), An. Ox. 1028. Swâ manigfeald yfel and swâ micle unêþnesse *tot pericula*, Bt. 27, 2; F. 96, 12: 38, 3; F. 200, 3. Unârîmedum, mænifealdum *numerosis, i. multis*, An. Ox. 111. Þâ mænifealdam *collecta*, 324. Mænifealde *spissos*, 563.

**manigfealde;** *adv.* *In many ways, abundantly:*—His hâlines and wundor wæron syððan manigfealde gecýdde geond ðis êgland, Chr. 641; P. 27, 25. [v. *N. E. D.* Manifold; *adv. O. H. Ger.* managfalto.]

**manigfealdian;** *p.* ode *To multiply, become numerous, abundant,* &c. v. manig-feald; II.:—Weahsað gê and monigfealdiað *crescite et multiplicamini*, Past. 109, 6. Þte gié monigfaldiga *ut abundetis*, Rtl. 13, 17. Mænifeal[dian] *amplificare*, An. Ox. 5215. [v. *N. E. D.* manifold. *O. H. Ger.* managfaltôn.]

**manigfeald-lic.** *Add:*—Unârîmedlicu goldhord þǽr wæron inne and ûte, and monigfealdlicu hié wæron and missenlicra cynna, Nar. 5, 11. [Þurh mistlice and mænigfealdlîce unriht and gyld, Chr. 1104; P. 239, 22.]

**manigfealdlîce.** *Add:* I. cf. manig-feald; I:—Ðeáh ðe hié mon manigfealdlîce and mislîce styrede *eos per tot varietatis latera mutabilitatis aura versaret*, Past. 306, 5. Ætforan ôðrum gyldum þe man myslîce geald, and men mid menigfealdlîce drehte, Chr. 1052; P. 173, 23. Þý lǽs þæt eów seó sægen monifealdlîcor biþ onþûhte *ne sim scribendi multiplex*, Nar. 3, 29. Wê mihton ðâs rǽdinge menigfealdlîcor trahtnian *the passage admits of more complex treatment*, Hml. Th. i. 556, 13. II. cf. manig-feald; II.:—Hê ne cwæþ nâ menifealdlîce (*in the plural*), 'Tô ûrum anlîcnissum,' ac ânfealdlîce (*in the singular*), 'Tô ûre anlîcnisse,' Ælfc. Thw. Gen. 3, 16. Mænifealdlîce *affatim*, i. *abunde, ubertim*, An. Ox. 1689: Chr. 1086; P. 219, 5. Ealle þâ niht swîðe mænifealdlîce (*in very large numbers*) steorran of heofenan feóllan, nâht be ânan oððe twâm, ac swâ þiclîce þ hit nân man âteallan ne mihte, 1095; P. 230, 28. Scæl ic monigfeald!ecor sprecan wiþ þâ *I must speak more at large against them*, Ors. 2, 1; S. 62, 9.

**manigfeald-ness.** *Add:*—Hû micel monigfealdnes (*multitudo*) swêtnesse þîne, Ps. L. 30, 20. Þeáh hê mid þǽre mænigfealdnysse þǽre synne bysgunge âbysgod sig *licet multiplicitate negotii peccati suspensus sit*, Ll. Th. ii. 176, 8. Wê nô þurh ðâ mænigfealdnesse ûra gebeda sind gehýrede *non in multiloquio nos exaudiri scimus*, R. Ben. 45, 20.

**manig-hîwe** (?); *adj.* *Multiform:*—Þæne mænifealdan † [mæni]-hîwan *multiformem*, Hpt. Gl. 409, 5.

**manig-teáw;** *adj.* —Julius se mænigtýwa câsere, Angl. viii. 306, 40. Hê wæs smið and mænigteáwa wyrhta, Hml. A. 134, 591.

**manigteáw-ness.** *Add:*—Ðæt sunnan gêr byð gesett on þrîm hund dagum and fîf and syxtigum dagum and syx tîdum þæs þe âsmeáde séo mænigtýwnes gebungenra wera, Angl. viii. 298, 5.

**mân-lic;** *adj.* *Wicked, evil:*—Yrre and anda ûs synd forbodene, manslyht and morðdǽda and ealle mânlice þing, Hml. A. 8, 190. Hê (*Christ*) âmeldode heora (*the Jews*) mânlice geþôhtas, and heora unrihtwîsnysse hê him openlîce sǽde, 76, 75.

**mânlîce;** *adv.* *Wickedly* (of swearing) *falsely, criminally:*—Sê ðe fæder oððe môdor mânlîce wyrigð, hê sceal deáðe sweltan, Hml. Th. ii. 324, 29. Se gîtsere wyle mânlîce swerian his sâwle. tô forwyrde *the*

covetous man will swear falsely to the destruction of his soul, Hex. 52, 29. Ðâ forlæg se fæder (*Jove*) fûllîce, and manega his mâgan mânlîce forwemde, Sal. K. 121, 38.

**mann.** I. *add:* (1) *a human being irrespective of age or sex:*—Mîn sunu, ic ðe tô men gebær, Hml. S. 25, 175. (a) used explicitly as a designation applicable to either sex :—Nis nân wîfhâdes mann hire gelîca, Hml. Th. ii. 10, 12. Se man sê þe [ne] mæge bearn âfêdan, nime þonne . . . meoluc on hyre handæ, Lch. iii. 68, 12. Gif mon ungewintrædne wîfmon tô niédhǽmde geþreátige, sié þ swâ þæs gewintredan monnes bôt, Ll. Th. i. 78, 18. Þ hê tô þâm untruman men geeóde. þâ hê þâ in eóde tô þǽre fǽmnan, Bd. 5, 3; Sch. 564, 21. (b) in general or indefinite applications, *body, person*; in pl. *people :*—For ðære orsorgnesse monn oft âðint on ofermêttum, Past. 35, 2. Gif man ofslagen weorðe, ealle wê lætað efendýrne, Ll. Th. i. 152, 12. Gif hwâ gewerde ôðres monnes wîngeard, 50, 24. Gif man ôðrum steóp âsette þǽr mæn drincen, 32, 8. Leófan men, Wlfst. 6, 2, *and often*. Men ðâ leófestan, 232, 12, *and often*. Ic cwæð þæt wæron ealle men ungemete leáse (*omnis homo mendax*), Ps. Th. 115, 2. (*See also* æghwilc, ælc, ǽnig, gehwilc, hwilc, nǽnig, nân, sum.) (b a) where there is contrast of human and divine :—Se munuc trýwsie hine sylfne wið God and wið men, Ll. Th. i. 306, 7. Uneáðelic þ ys mid mannum; ac ealle þing synt mid Gode eáðelice, Mt. 19, 26. (b β) tô mannum cuman (cf. tô tûne cuman) *to happen, take place*, of a season, *begin :*—Gyf þû wylt witan ǽniges mônðes gesceád, hwylce dæge hê cume tô mannum, Angl. viii. 304, 8. (c) of a child :—Uuc næs gemæne man (cf. habban bearn gemæne. v. gemæne; I. ¶ 1 a a), Hml. S. 2, 157. (d) used predicatively, (*to be*) *man, to have human nature :*—Hê geswutelode þæt hê wæs sôð man, and for ði metes behôfode, Hml. Th. i. 178, 9. (2) in abstract or generic sense :—Drihten, hwæt is se mann . . . oþþe hwæt is se mannes sunu? *quid est homo . . . aut filius hominis?*, Ps. Th. 8, 5. Restedæg wæs geworht for þâm men, næs se man (*homo*) for ðâm restedæge, Mk. 2, 27. Nis mê ege mannes, Ps. Th. 117, 6. Þeáh ic God ne ondrǽde, ne ic man ne onþracige, Lk. 18, 4. (3) *man* as in inner *man :*—Se innra man, þ is séo sâwl, Ll. Th. ii. 224, 6: Verc. Först. 93, 4. (4) *an adult male person :*—Lîfes man *uir uitþ* (*uenerabilis*), An. Ox. 3699. Hê sǽde . . . heó man ne wæs, Hml. S. 2, 78. Gif bescoren man steorleás gange, Ll. Th. i. 38, 12. Habban þâ .xii. men heora metscype tôgædere, 236, 6: 230, 22. II. *add:* (1) of free men :—Gif mon wille . . . hlâford sêcan . . . sê þe hine tô men feormie . . . sê þe hine tô men onfô, Ll. Th. i. 86, 2–9. Oft âgyltað ðâ hlâfordas and ðâ menn wuniað on Godes hyldo *plerumque offendunt qui regunt, et in patrisfamilias gratia permanent qui reguntur*, Past. 321, 3. Gif hwâ ymb cyninges feorh sierwie þurh hine oþþe þurh wreccena feormunge oþþe his manna, Ll. Th. i. 62, 16. Se hlâford ne derige his mannum, ne forðan his nýdþeówan, ii. 314, 2. Âh hlâforda gehwylc formycle þearfe þ hê his men rihtlîce healde, i. 372, 13. (2) of unfree men (in a temporal or spiritual sense) :—Nis nâ mâ hlâfordinga on worulde þonne twêgen, God Ælmihtig and deófol. Sê þe Godes beboda hylt, hê is Godes man . . . ; and sê ðe deófles worc begǽð, hê is deófles man, Wlfst. 298, 7–11. Beó hys mann, næs þîn âgen, and beó geðafa þ þû æart hys þeówa *noli esse velle quasi proprius et in tua potestate, sed . . . Domini te servum esse profitere*, Solil. H. 53, 14. Gif man his mæn an wiófode freóls gefe, Ll. Th. i. 38, 15. Æt men fiftene peningas, æt horse healf swâ, 224, 25. Be manna metsunge. Ânan esne gebyreð tô metsunge . . . , 436, 25. Wê cwǽdon ûrum þeówum mannum, 234, 3. Gê hlâfordas, dôð gê eówrum monnum (*servis*) ðæt ilcce, Past. 201, 24. (2 a) of a female slave :—Se fruma wæs þ mon forstæl ǽnne wimman Ælfsige . . . Ðâ besêng Ælfsige þone mann æt Wulfstâne . . . Æfter þâm bæd Ælfsige ǽgiftes his mannes, Cht. Th. 206, 19–30. (3) where both free and unfree are included :—Manig strec man wyle werian his man swâ hwæðer him þincð þ hê hine ýð âwerian mæge swâ for frigne swâ for þeówne, Ll. Th. i. 388, 2. (4) applied to members of a fighting force :—Hê hié . . . on ðæm ýtemestan ende his monna âsette *in exercitu Antigoni dispersi sunt*, Ors. 3, 11; S. 146, 35. III. used of a lord :—Ic beóde þ hý nân man ne brocie . . . þ hý ne môtan ceósan swylcne mann swylce hý wyllan, Cht. Th. 492, 13. v. ǽhte-, æsc-, ǽwda-, ambiht-, brim-, burh-, carl-, ceáp-, celmert-, ciépe-, ealdor-, eórod-, esne-, fæsting-, fâh-, fêster-, fêþe-, fiot-, freó-, fyrn-, geneát-, geó- (iú-), gesîþ-, gleó-, gum-, hægsteald-, hæþen-, hagosteald-, heásod-, healf-, here-, hîre-, hîred-, hundred-, hundredes, hynden-, inhird-, lah-, land-, leorning-, lid-, mægden-, mynster-, neáh-, norþ-, rîpe-, rýne-, sǽ-, scegþ-, scip-, scîr-, scîrig-, steór-, steóres, sûþ-, teóþung-, tûn-, tûnes-, twi-, þeów-, un-, unfriþ-, wæpen-, wæpned-, weorc-, weorold-, wîg-, wræcmann.

**manna** *man.* *Add:*—Sió ungeðyld geniêt ðone monnan ðæt hê geopenað all his ingeðonc, Past. 220, 9. 'Ne hera ðû nænne man on his lîfe' . . . Sê ðe herian wille hâligne mannan, herige hine . . . æfter his geendunge, Hml. Th. ii. 560, 18. 'þû âcenst sunu.' Oncnâwað þurh þâs word sôðne mannan âcennedue of mædenlicum lîchaman, i. 198, 10.

**manna** *manna.* *Add:* , an; *m.* :—On ðære earce ðâ stênenan bredu . . . and se swêta mete ðe hié hêton monna . . . sceal bión on ðæm

breóstum ðæs monnan swētnes, Past. 125, 23. Hēt hē hider rignan mannum tō mōse manna cynne, Ps. Th. 77, 25.

**mann-cwild.** *Add:*—Ic ðæc biddo ðæt... him fiónd ne sceðde, ne hungor, ne monncwild, Shrn. 73, 5.

**mann-cynn.** II. *add:* (1) *men, a number of people:*—Hwæt þær moncynnes forweard on ǣgðere hand *quantas nationes, quantosque populos idem turbo involverit*, Ors. 1, 11 ; S. 50, 14. Hié gegæderedon eal moucynnes þ þær læfed wæs. 2, 6 ; S. 88, 6. Mann slóh eall þet mancynn þ man ārǣcan mihte, Chr. 1014; P. 145, 20. (2) *a race of men, a people:*—Ðis mannkynn lifað fela geára *hoc genus hominum multos vivit annos*, Nar. 38, 22. Mannkynn...þa man hāteð Silhearwan, 29. Seó burh (*Alexandria*) is mǣrost mid Egyptiscum mancynne, Hml. S. 15, 14. Manega of þām mancinne (*the Jews*), Ælfc. T. Grn. 20, 41. Ðreála ic on þæt mancyn (*the Israelites*) sǣnde, Wlfst. 133, 19. þæt is Gog and Magog, þæt beóð þā mancyn (māncyn?) þe Alexander beclýsde binnan muntclýsan (cf. *Exsurgent ab Aquilone spurcissimae gentes, quas Alexander rex inclusit, Gog et Magog.* See for this legend Bousset, 'The Antechrist Legend,' translated by Keane. v. mun-clýse). Ðā getācniað alle deófles lima, þæt beóð alle þā þe deófles weorc wyrcð, Wlfst. 84, 30. Manncynna ealdor *Christ*, Hml. Th. i. 588, 18.

**mann-cyst.** e ; *f. Manly virtue:*—Healdan wē þæt mid gódum dǣdum and mid æðelum mancystum, þæt wē beón gódum mannum gelíce in ðǣm mǣgenum þe wē dōn magon, and in ðǣm dǣdum þe wē þurhteón magon, Verc. Först. 169. Cf. gum-cyst.

**mann-fultum.** *Add:*—Ueriatus him geteáh tō micelne monfultum, ond monega tūnas oferhergeade, Ors. 5, 2 ; S. 216, 8.

**mann-myrþra,** an ; *m. A homicide, murderer:*—Þá wíf þe dóð āwegāworpnesse heora bearna ... sȳn hȳ geteald tō manmyrðrum *habeantur pro homicidis*, Ll. Th. ii. 154, 36.

**mann-rǣdenn.** I. *add:*—Him nicclum sceamode þæs deófles manrǣdenne þe hē on wæs oþ þ, Hml. S. 31, 1197. Hí lēton tō rǣde þ hí woldon ābūgan þām heretogan tō his mannrǣdene *omnes una voce:* '*Sponte tradamus nos omnes populo Holofernis*,' Hml. A. 108, 182. Geoffra þine lāc ApollIne, sē ðe mæg þinre nytenuysse gemiltsian and tō his manrǣdene gebígan, Hml. S. 14, 36. Seó burhwaru..budon him manrǣdene tō eallum his bebodum (*servi tui sumus, quaecumque jusseris faciemus*, 2 Kings 10, 5), 18, 364.

**mann-slaga.** *Add:*—Þá þe óðre men mid mānaðum beswícað beóð eal swā miceles wītes scyldige swā ðā manslagan, Hml. A. 147, 94. Betwuh þām manslagum *cum viris sanguinum*, Ps. Th. 25, 9. Þá manslagan, 5, 6.

**mann-sleán** (?) *to kill:*—Ne sceal mon mansleán (man sleán ?) *non occidere*, R. Ben. 16, 18.

**mann-swǣs;** *adj. Gentle, meek:*—Hē lǣrð ðā manswǣsan (*man-suetos*) wegas his, Ps. Rdr. 24, 9. Cf. mann-þwǣre.

**mann-(mān-?)swica.** [*In favour of* mān- *it may be noted that* mann- *does not occur as the first part of this compound, but does occur with* -slaga ; *in* Wlfst. 55, 6 *the* a *has the accent in two MSS.* (*though in one of these* mān- *is written in* mánslagan, Wlfst. 26, 14), *and at* 114, 13 manswican *is a v.l. for* mānsworan.] *In* l. 2 *read* mannslagan, *and add:* *a deceiver, cheat:*—Ān unlagu æt ðām ætfengan þe swicigende manswican lufedan be-westan, Ll. Lbmn. 244, 28. Swā gerāde manswican (mān-, *v.ll.*) þe on ðā wīsan swǣslíce on unriht, þæt syndan forbodan Antecrīstes, Wlfst. 55, 6. Mānsworan (manswican, *v.l.* and þá heora hlāford beswícaþ and hine forlǣtaþ his feónda(n) tō handa), 114, 13. Þyder scylan manslagan and þyder scylan manswican, 203, 21. Seó ēhtnes þe crīstene þoledon oft and gelōme þurh wælhreówe manswican, 83, 18.

**mann-þrymm,** es ; *m. Array of men, retinue, troop:*—Se cāsere fērde mid ealle his manþrymme (cf. mid ealle his werede, 15), Verc. Först. 97, 11. Cf. here-þrymm.

**mann-þwǣre.** *Add:*—Leorniað æt mē þ ic manþwǣre (*mitis*) eom, Hml. S. 16, 24. [*O. H. Ger.* man-duuāri *mitis*.] Cf. mann-swǣs.

**-mannþwǣrian.** v. ge-mannþwǣrian.

**mann-þwǣrness.** *Add:*—Dāuid for his manþwǣrnysse (-þwyrnysse, *v.l.*) and mildheortnysse weard Gode gecwēme, Hml. S. 16, 55.

**mann-weorþ.** *Add:* The amount seems to have been a hundred shillings. v. gildan ; III. 3 cc.

**mans-lot** *a man's lot* (v. hlot ; III.) *or share, the amount of land allotted to the head of a family when the hundred was divided up:*—On Elsingtūnhundred āh Sancte Eádmund xxvii manslot, Nap. 43 *q. v.*

**-mānsod.** [v. *N. E. D.* manse.] v. ā-mānsod.

**mān-swara.** *Add:*—Dider sculan mānsworan, Wlfst. 114, 13: 203, 23.

**mān-swaru.** *Add:*—Be mānsware *de perjurio*, Ll. Th. ii. 180, 37.

**mān-swerian.** *Add:*—Gif hē on ungehālgedum Crīstes mǣle mānswerað *si in cruce non consecrata perjuraverit*, Ll. Th. ii. 158, 37. Hē swāþeáh mid þām óðrum mānswerige *nihilominus cum aliis perjurium facit*, 19. Nū gȳt eástdæles men swergeað ðurh his noman, and ne geþristlæcað hí ō þ hí mānswergen on his noman, Shrn. 109, 17. [*Eác*

mānswered man māre þone hē scolde, Shrn. 17, 24. v. *N. E. D.* manswear.]

**mān-swica.** v. mann-swica.

**manu,** an ; *f. A mane:*—Manu, brystæ *juba, setes porci et leonis cabalique*, Txts. 110, 1182. Manu, biriste, Hpt. 33, 244, 5. Hȳ habbað horses manan *habent jubas equorum*, Nar. 34, 32. [*O. H. Ger.* mana *juba* : *Icel.* mön.]

**manung.** I. *add:*—Suā sceal ǣghwelc lāreów mid ānre lāre and mid mislicum manungum his hiéremonna mōd styrigean *ex una doctrina, non una eademque exhortatione tangere corda audientium debet*, Past. 175, 11. II. *add:*—Cóm eft þider sē þe geswænced wæs mid þæs gafoles manunge *cum is qui necessitate debiti affligebatur rediret*, Gr. D. 158, 13. v. gafol-manung.

**mān-wrǣc ;** *adj. Wicked:*—Þæt mānwrǣce, mānful *infandum*, Wrt. Voc. ii. 47, 55. Cf. sceþ-wrǣc.

**mapul-treów.** *Add:*—In ðæt rūge mapeltreów, C. D. iii. 379, 22.

**marc.** *Add:* [Twā hund marcas goldes ... fifti marcas rēdes goldes, Cht. Th. 512, 17, 27. Fíf markes goldes, 514, 20. Tō marc goldes, 570, 7.] v. healf-marc.

**-mārian.** v. ge-mārian. [*O. H. Ger.* mērōn *augere, exaggerare*.]

**marman-stān.** *Add:*—Deáh hit wǣre marmanstānas, ðā wǣron āswengde on ðāra onsýn þe þǣron sǣton, Shrn. 81, 2.

**marmel-stān,** es ; *m. Marble:*—Fægere geheówed swylce marmelstān mǣres cinnes, E. S. viii. 476, 56. [v. *N. E. D.* marble-stone.]

**marmor-stān,** es ; *m. Marble:*—Gehīwod swylce marmorstān, E. S. viii. 478, 59. Heora líc biþ on marmorstāns hwītnysse, Nar. 38, 9.

**marm-stān.** *Add:*—Se marmstān sceolde beón onwænded, sē wæs āseted ofer his byrgene. Þá þá se marmstān āweg genumen wæs, Gr. D. 302, 15–16. Hí gemētton āne mǣre þrūh geworht of marmstāne, Hml. S. 20, 80. Godes encgel sette ēnne marmstān æt þæs mǣdenes heáfde, 8, 201.

**Martes dæg** *dies Martis*, Archiv cxx. 297, 15.

**martyr.** *Add:*—Þeós wyduwe is māre þonne martyre, Shrn. 151, 8. For Agnes ðingunga þínes mǣran martyres, Hml. S. 7, 322. Wē witon unrím ðāra monna þe ðā ēcan gesǣlda sōhtun nallas ðurh þ ān þæt hí wilnodon ðæs líchomlican deáðes, ac eác manegra sārlicra wíta hié gewilnodon wið ðan ēcan lífe : þ wǣron ealle þā hāligan martyras, Bt. 11, 2 ; F. 36, 5.

**martyr-cynn,** es ; *m. A race or family of martyrs :*—Ðǣr flugen sóna tō feala cynna fugelas, and þāra hāligra martyra eágan ūt āhaccedon ... wundorlic wæs þ martyrcynn, Hml. S. 23, 85.

**martyr-dōm.** *Add:*—On ðā tiid ... suā huelc sua biscephād underfēng, hē underfēng martyrdōme ... nān twió næs ðæt hē sceolde cuman tō hefegum martyrdōme *illo in tempore quo quisquis plebibus praeerat, primus ad martyrii tormenta ducebatur... quemque dubium non erat ad supplicia graviora pervenire*, Past. 53, 18–21.

**martyr-hād.** *Add:*—Martyrhād underfōn *martirium subire*, Gr. D. 231, 5.

**martyr-racu,** e ; *f. An account of martyrs :*—Hí nǣron furðan wyrðe þ man heora naman on ðisre hāligra martyrrace sceolde āwrítan, Hml. S. 23, 367. Hí woldon ðisra hāligra martyra martyrrace āwrítan, 334 : 342 : 773.

**massere.** *Add:* [v. *D. D.* masser *a merchant.* Cf. *Low Lat.* massarius, *and see* Anglia xxxiii. 402.]

**maþa.** *Add:*—Him weóllon maðan geond ealne ðone líchaman, Hml. Th. i. 472, 30. Þǣr manna líc lāgon ... þa weóllon eall maðon and egeslíce stuncon, Hml. S. 4, 212. [v. *N. E. D.* mathe.] v. eorþmata (-maþa?).

**maþelere.** *Add:* [*A. R.* maðelere *a chatterer*.]

**maþelian.** *Add:*—Rǣdaþ, maþeliaþ *contionantur*, i. *sermocinantur* (*loquuntur*, Hpt. Gl. 461, 2), An. Ox. 2323. Wíglāf maðelode, word-rihta fela sægde gesīðum, B. 2631. Fela wē mihton ymbe þissum þingum maðelian, Angl. viii. 332, 34. Þás þing þe wē ymbe sȳn maðeligende, 307, 31. [Hore muð maðeled euer, A. R. 74. Ane maðelild þ maðeled hire al þe talen of þe londe, 88.]

**maþelig.** *Substitute: Talkative, talking much and loudly* as a drunken man :—Maðeli (*luxuriosa res, vinum, et*) *tumultuosa* (*ebrietas*), Kent. Gl. 725.

**maþelung.** *Add:*—Gewyrd, maþelung *uerbositas*, An. Ox. 1419. [Heó opened hire muð mid muche maðelunge, A. R. 80.]

**māþum.** *Add:*—Weard seó cwēn niclum gegladod þæt heó mōste ðone māðm (*the cross*) on moldan findan, Hml. Th. ii. 306, 11. 'Geswutela mē ðǣre cyrcan mādmas'... 'Gif ðū gelýfst, ic ðē geswutelige ðā mādmas'... 'Āgif ðā mādmas'... 'On Godes ðearfum ic hí āspende, and hí sind ðā ēcan mādmas ðe nǣfre ne beóð gewanode,' i. 422, 11–34. Hē hí hēt gān into his māðmum *iussit eam introire ubi repositi erant thesauri eius*, Hml. A. 110, 266.

**māþum-cleofa,** an ; *m. A treasure-chamber, place where treasures are placed :*—Gān ūt of þām māðmcleofan (cf. l. 266 ; *see preceding word*), Hml. A. 110, 277.

**māþum-fæt.** *Add:*—Hē bereáfode Godes templ and fela goldhordas

forð mid him gelæhte, and ðá hálgan máðmfatu and þ mǽre weófod, Hml. S. 25, 12.

**máþum-gestreón.** *Add :*—Þér se bróþer þám óþrum ne mæg gehelpan, ne se fæder þám suna, ne þá neáhmágas, ne þá máðmgestreón, Verc. Först. 134, 24.

**matt.** *Add :*—Tó bedreáfe genihtsumige tó hæbbenne meatte and hwítel and bedfelt and heáfodbolster *stramenta lectorum sufficiant matta et sagum, lena et capitula,* R. Ben. 90, 15. Þ hine man álegde on þá meattan þe hé him on gebæd *praecepit eum in psiathio, quo vulgo matta vocatur, in quo orare consueverat, projici,* Gr. D. 125, 26. [*From Latin* matta.]

**mattuc.** *Add :*—Ic nát mid hwí ic delfe nú mé swá wana is ægþer ge spadu ge mattuc, Hml. S. 23 b, 765. Of matucce and adesan hý út áwurpon hý *bipenne et ascia deiecerunt eam,* Ps. Rdr. 73, 6. Hé sceal habban æcse, adsan . . . mattuc, Angl. ix. 263, 3.

**máwan.** *Add :*—Hé mǽwð (máweþ, *v. l.*) gærs (heig, *v. l.*) *fenum secat,* Gr. D. 36, 2. Máwaþ *tondent,* An. Ox. 43, 15. Hé stóp on þá mǽde, and þá geseah hé þ hý ealle meówan (meówan þ heig, *v. l.*) *pratum ingressus, et omnes intuens fenum secantes,* Gr. D. 36, 12. On hærfeste rípan, in Agusto and Septembri and Octobri máwan, Angl. ix. 261, 16. v. á-máwan.

**mé.** *Add : dat.* mec:—Secgað mec *dicite mihi,* Nar. 25, 11. Hwæþer hié mec sóð sægdon, 30.

**meagol-mód.** *Add :* Angl. xi. 97, 3.

**meagol-ness.** *Add :*—Nú gerýst hyt tó swutelianne mid ealre heortan meagolnysse hwanon hé cóm, Angl. viii. 325, 37. Wé sceolon þére micclan lufan úrum Drihtne singallíce þancian æghwæþer ge mid wordum ge mid dǽdum ge eác mid ealre heortan meagolnysse, Hml. A. 153, 39.

**meaht.** *Add :* I. *the quality of being able to do what is desired, operative power* :—Wítiendlicere mihte geswuteled *prophetica uirtute propalatam,* An. Ox. 3652. Se feónd nǽnige mehte wið ús uasaþ, Bl. H. 31, 33. Sunu monnes hæfeþ mæhte (mæht, L. *potestatem*) tó forlǽtenne synne, Mt. R. 9, 6. I a. *as an attribute of impersonal agents* :—Genim þás wyrte, heó of sumre wundurlicre mihte helpeð, Lch. i.126,16. I b. *in pl. powers* :—Mihta (-um, MS.) *uirtutum* (Johannes . . . *miris uirtutum signis per totum orbem claruit),* An. Ox. 1805. Þér nú God swutelað þæs hálgan martires mihta, Chr. 1012; P. 143, 4. II. *bodily strength* :—Gif þé þince þ þú máran lǽcedóm dón ne durre for unmihte þæs mannes . . . gebíd oþ þ þú dyrre. Gif meht ne wyrne, lǽt him blód, Lch. ii. 254, 4. Sáh hé niðer sprǽce benumen and ealre his mihte, Chr. 1053; P. 182, 22. III. *great power or strength, mightiness.* (1) *as an attribute of God* :—His miht bið á éce, Bl. H. 31, 26. Mihte *potestatis (divinae),* An. Ox. 12, 11. Heofenlicere mihte reósende *cælesti numine nutabunda,* 1574. (2) *of persons, nations, &c.* :—Geweóx miht eorðlices ríces, Bd. 2, 9; Sch. 142, 16. (3) *an act of power, mighty work, miracle* :—Ne synd áwritene ealle Iúdan gefeoht for his feónda ware, and ealle ðá mihte þe hé mǽrlíce gefremede, Hml. S. 25, 678. Þus gerádra mihta *talium miraculorum,* An. Ox. 3062. Áwrítan þá wundra and mihta þe Martínus mihtiglíce gefremode, Hml. S. 31, 2. Hergan metudæs maecti, Txts. 149, 2. IV. *superiority of strength or power as used to enforce one's will* :—Neádunge, mihte uim, An. Ox. 1237. V. *associated with* mægen :—Hé on mihte (mahte, L.) and on mægene unclǽnum gástum bebýt *in potestate et uirtute imperat spiritibus immundis,* Lk. 4, 36. VI. *power over others, dominion, authority,* used of persons or things :—Wælhreówre mihte *tyrannici potentatus,* An. Ox. 1592. Mid wælhróŵre mihte *tyrannica potestate,* i. *imperio,* 1158: 2345. Hé salde him mæht (mæhtæ, R.) gaasta unclǽura, Mt. L. 10, 1. VI a. *an exercise of authority* :—Mid mihtum *nutibus,* i. *imperiis* (uernacula matronae nutibus mancipatur), An. Ox. 2351. VII. *a virtue;* virtus :—Seó óðer miht is *castitas* . . . Seó drydde miht is *largitas,* Hml. S. 16, 321, 326 : 334 : 345 : 356. Mihta *virtutum,* An. Ox. 959. VIII. *as a person or thing,* (1) *one who, or that which, exercises power or government* :—Stíþnes ungesáwenlicere tóbrocen mihte *duritia inuisibili contrita potestate,* i. *dominio,* An. Ox. 3259. Ðá heán mihta hér on worulde hreósað and tó lore weorðað, Wlfst. 262, 16. (2) *the fifth of the nine orders of angels* :—*Uirtutes* mihta, Hml. Th. i. 342, 27. (3) *a deity, divinity* :—Mihte *numina,* i. *deos,* An. Ox. 4722. Mihta, 2, 372. v. duguþ-, freá-, godcund- (?), gryre-meaht (-miht).

**meaht;** *adj. Add :* v. un-meaht, un-gemeaht.

**meahte-líce.** *Add :*—Heó ðone migðan mihtelíce gebet, Lch. i. 222, 4. [v. *N. E. D.* mightly.]

**meaht-full;** *adj. Powerful* :—Mín God is strang and mihtful, Hml. A. 174, 137. [v. *N. E. D.* mightful.]

**meahtig.** *Add :*—Se láreów sceolde beón miehtig (mihtig, *v. l.*) tó tyhtanne on hálwende láre, Past. 91, 14. Deáh þe ðá mihtegestan and þá rícestan hátan him reste gewyrcan of marmanstáne, Wlfst. 263, 2.

**meahtig-líc.** *Add :* [O. Sax. mahtig-líc : O. H. Ger. mahtig-líh.] v. fore-, un-meahtiglic.

**meahtiglíce.** *Add :*—Sulpicius wolde áwrítan þá wundra and mihta þe Martínus se mǽra mihtiglíce gefremede, Hml. S. 31, 3. Cúðberhtus

gefremode mihtiglíce wundra on ðám mynstre wunigende, Hml. Th. ii. 142, 23.

**meahtiglic-ness.** v. un-meahtiglicness.

**meahtig-ness.** v. un-meahtigness.

**meaht-leás.** *Add : weak, impotent, powerless.* (1) physically :—Þá fǽringa sáh hé niðer sprǽce benumen and ealre his mihte . . . hé þurhwunode swá unspecende and mihteleás forð oð þone Ðunresdæg and þá his líf álét, Chr. 1053; P. 182, 24. Hí wǽron mid þǽre meteleáste mihtleáse gedóne, Hml. S. 37, 54. (2) non-physical :—Hé bið him swá mihtleás on his módes strece þ hé his underþeóddan egesian ne dear, O. E. Hml. i. 301, 6. [v. *N. E. D.* might-less.]

**meaht-loc,** es ; *n. A bolt of might* :—Ne wáciað þás geweorc, ac hí wel healdað, stondað stíðlíce bestryþed fǽste miclum meahtlocum, Sch. 88.

**malm.** *Add :* [v. *N. E. D.* malm.]

**mealmiht.** *Add :*—On þone mealmihtan ford, C. D. B. iii. 63, 27. [Cf. *N. E. D.* malmy.]

**mealm-stán.** *Add :*—Wrít þysne circul mid þínes cnífes orde on ánum mealmstáne (*printed* mealan stáne ; *but see* Archiv cxxix. 48, n. 1), Lch. i. 395, 4. [v. *N. E. D.* malm-stone.]

**mealt.** *Add : Sour* (? cf. *Icel.* maltr *bitter* to taste).

**mealt-ealu;** *n. Malt-ale* :—Hwerhwettan moran and áne handfulle sperewyrte . . . wylle on mealtealoð, Nap. 44.

**mearc** *a mark,* **mearc** *a limit.* [These may be taken under one head, see *N. E. D.* mark.] *Add : a weak form* mearce *occurs* Angl. viii. 326, 11, *and a neuter* mearc Gr. D. 197, 4. I. *a boundary* (1) of land :—Istis terminibus terra circumgyrata esse videtur . . . Ǽrest Ælfgýðe mearc . . . oþ Eádgife mearce, þonne þonan tó þæs biscopes mearce, Cht. E. 176, 16-21. Eást tó mearchlince ; and swá eást be ðæs bisceopes mearce, ðonon be Byrhtswýðe mearce, C. D. vi. 33, 22-25. (2) of immaterial things :—Findan hwylce dæge seó mearke, þ ys se termen, gá on tún . . . gerýst hyt þ seó tíd hæbbe mearke hwænne heó tó síge crístenum folce tó blisse, Angl. viii. 326, 11-14. II. *a stone or other monument set up or standing as a memorial or as a guide* :—Hé ásette for tácne and tó mearce on þǽre stówe þrý stánas (cf. hé mearcode þá stówe, Hml. Th. ii. 160, 35) *tres petras in loco eodem pro signo posuit,* Gr. D. 112, 29. III. *a standard, an ensign* :—Nymað þá sigefæstan mearca *uictricia tollite signa,* Ælfc. Gr. Z. 71, 10. IV. *an object placed to indicate a point to be reached* :—Beó þér gemeten nygon fét of þám stacan tó þǽre mearce, Ll. Th. i. 226, 13. V. *a sign, token, indication, symptom* :—Him næs nán deáðes mearc on gesewen, Hml. S. 23, 436. VI. *a sign affixed or impressed for distinction,* (1) *a device, stamp, &c.,* placed on an article as an indication of ownership, *as a means of identification, &c.* :—Man mid mearce gecýþe þ man riht drífe, Ll. Th. i. 352, 6. (2) *a visible sign or badge assumed by or imposed on a person* :—Antecríst forbýt ælcum men aðor tó bycganne oððe tó syllanne, bútan hé on his foranheáfde habbe his mearce, Wlfst. 200, 4. Hé Pætres mearce onféng *accepta tonsura,* Bd. 3, 18; Sch. 274, 4. (3) *a character made with a pen by an illiterate person in place of a signature* :—Þ gewrit mid his ágenre hand he áuríte, oððe gif hé ná can stafas óðer fram him gebeden write ; and se nícumena mearce dó (cf. hé sylf on þám gewrite róde tácn mearcige *signum faciat,* R. Ben. 101,6), R. Ben. I. 98, 1. (4) *a written symbol* :—Ic hæbbe gesett áne mearke beforan þám rǽdingum, and þá ic wylle hér ámearkian, Angl. viii. 333, 14. VII. *a visible trace or impression diversifying a surface, as a line, written character, or the like* :—Hí ymb hine gemearcodon ánne hring on þǽre eorðan and hé wæs belocen binnan þǽm mearce (mearcan, *v. l.*) þæs hringes *ei in terra circulum designaverunt, et designatione circuli inclusus est,* Gr. D. 197, 4. Mearcum *caracteribus* (literarum), An. Ox. 8, 259. Notera mearca *notariorum caracteres,* 2847. v. Dene-, irþ-, wiht-mearc.

**mearca,** an ; *m.* I. *a mark, line.* v. mearc ; VII. II. *a territory.* v. land-mearca (*perhaps also* Dene-mearca, *the nominative of the weak form does not occur*).

**mearce,** an ; *f.* I. *a limit.* v. mearc ; I. 2. II. *a territory.* v. (?) Dene-mearce.

**mearcere.** *Add :*—Wrí[terum], mearcerum *notariis,* An. Ox. 5447.

**mearc-ford** *a boundary ford* :—Tó mearcforda ; andlang bróces, C. D. v. 330, 18.

**mearc-grǽfa,** an ; *m. A boundary grǽfa* (q. v.) :—Of ðes westlangan hlinces ende on ðonne mearcgréfan, C. D. iii. 135, 26.

**mearc-hlinc,** es ; *m. A boundary* hlinc (q. v.) :—Eást tó mearchlince ; and swá eást be ðæs bisceopes mearce . . . be Byrhtswýðe mearce, C. D. vi. 33, 32.

**mearcian** *to mark,* **mearcian** *to fix bounds.* [These may be taken together ; cf. mearc.] *Add :* I. *to trace out boundaries for, plan out* :—Hé mearcode þá stówa þe gé eówre geteld on sleán sceoldon *metatus est locum, in quo tentoria figere deberetis,* Deut. 1, 33. I a. fig. *to plan, design, draw up* a table :—Þæra geára getæl hæfð seó tabule þe wé mearkian willað, Angl. viii. 327, 41. II. *to march to, border upon, have as a boundary to one's land* :—Ðis sindon ðá landgemæro . . .

andlang brōces tō ðǣre dīc ðǣre se æðeling mearcode, C. D. v. 298, 3.     **III.** *to make a mark on* an object :—Man swā mearca𝔡 (*signat*) mid medmicelum treówe þeorfe hlāfas, þ hī beóð gesewene swylce hī beón on feówer feórðandǣlas tōdǣlede, . . . 'For hwī ne mearcodon gē (*signastis*) þysne hlāf swā swā hit þeáw is?,' Gr. D. 87, 1–13.    **III a.** *to mark* with a symbol :—Mid þām hāligan ele gē scylan þā hǣþenan cild mearcian on þām breóste . . . mid rōde tācne, Ll. Th. ii. 390, 10.    **IV.** *to mark* a symbol on something, *portray, design* :—Týn hīw habbað þā bōceras . . . mid þām hig tōdǣlað and āmearkiað heora accentas ; þ forme hīw . . . hērbæftan ic mearkye, Angl. viii. 333, 23. Hī mearcodon mid ðæs lambes blōde on heora gedyrum Tau, Hml. Th. ii. 266, 7. Hē sylf on þām gewrite rōde tācen mearcige *signum faciat*, R. Ben. 101, 6. Tācna on sǣlicum þā þā mearcode strandum *signa in glarigeris cum sulcaret litoribus*, An. Ox. 2492.    **V.** *to make with the hand* the sign of the cross on an object :—Hē mearcode him on heáfde hālig rōde-tācen and on his gūðfanan, Hml. Th. ii. 304, 14. Mearciað rōde tācen on eówrum foreheáfdum, i. 466, 20.    **V a.** *to mark* an object with the sign of the cross :—Hē mearcode hine sylfne mid rōde tācne *he crossed himself*, Hml. S. 31, 719. Wē sceolon mearcian ūre forewearde heáfod and ūrne līchoman mid Crīstes rōde tācne, Hml. Th. ii. 266, 11. Mearcian sē þe hine gesihð anxsumnesse getācnað *to see oneself cross oneself* (?) *betokens trouble;* the Latin is: Tricare qui se uiderit, anxietatem significat, Lch. iii. 210, 31.    **VI.** *where an object* is placed at a spot that the spot may be identified afterwards, *to mark* a place with something :—Hē mearcode ðā stōwe (v. mearc ; II.), Hml. Th. ii. 160, 35.    **VII.** *to indicate in writing, note* :—Ðā sciplīðende þ gehȳrende behȳdelīce hī mearcedon ðone dæg, Shrn. 86, 2.    **VIII.** *to make perceptible by some sign or indication* :—Ēdmōdnise under hiora (*paruulorum*) noma mercað (*significat*) tō haldenne, Lk. p. 9, 15. v. ā-mearcian.

**mearc-īsen.** *Dele last passage, and add* :—Mercīsene *cauterio*, An. Ox. 2, 61.

**mearc-īsern.** *Add* :—Gemearcod mid deófles mearcīserne, Hml. A. 201, 192, 206.

**mearc-mōt.** *Dele:* -mearcodness. v. tō-mearcodness: **mearc-pæþ.** *Take here* El. 233, *given under* mearc-wæd (*the facsimile reprint of the Codex Vercellensis has* mearcpaðu), mēarc-preát. *l.* mearc-.

**mearcung.** *Add:* **I.** as verbal noun. (1) v. mearcian; **III** :—Mearccinge, bærneytte *cauterio*, An. Ox. 1983. Wæs þæt Godes folc āhredd fram ðām fǣrlican deáðe þurh ðæs lambes offrunge and his blōdes mearcunge, Hml. Th. ii. 264, 14. (2) cf. mearcian; **VII** :—Gif ic āsceáde mid mearcunge (*praenotatione*) þāra namena, Gr. D. 7, 3.    **II.** *a mark* :—Wrītera mearcunga *notariorum caracteres*, An. Ox. 2847.    **III.** *a description* :—Steorwigele, mearcunge (stiorwigle ł mearcunge, Hpt. Gl. 468, 1) *constellationem* (cf. constellatio, notatio siderum, Corp. Gl. H. 33, 517), An. Ox. 2631.

**mearc-wæd.** *Dele, and see* mearc-pæþ.

**mearc-weg.** *Add* :—Andlang mearcweges *per longum limitosas vias,* C. D. B. ii. 260, 31.

**mearc-will,** es ; *m. A boundary spring* :—Ðonon on mearcwill ; of mearcwille, Cht. E. 293, 26.

**mearg.** v. mearh: **meargian.** v. ge-meargian.

**mearh** *marrow. Add* :—Wæl tōsomne in heortes mærige, Lch. i. 374, 8. v. hrycg-mearh.

**mearh** *a horse. Add* :—Wicgce, meare *equo*, An. Ox. 2, 32. Mera mengeo on onsióne māran . . . þonne ðā elpendas *maiores elephantorum corporibus hypopotami*, Nar. 11, 1.

**mearh-lic.** *Add* :—Mearglice *medullata*, Ps. Vos. 65, 15.

-**mearr.** v. ge-mearr: **mearþ.** *Add:* v. merþern.

**mearu.** *Add:* **I.** of material :—Genim ðone crop ūfeweardne swā mearune (mearuwne, *v. l.*), Lch. i. 224, 17. Mearewa smæras *tenera labella*, An. Ox. 2162. Merwe ǐfigtwigu, Lch. ii. 324, 16. Merwost sié, 194, 24.    **II.** of persons. (1) *not grown-up, not fully developed, inexperienced* :—Hē him wæs ondrǣdende þone slide þǣre synne in þām merwum (mearwum, *v. l.*) leorningmannum (*tenerioribus discipulis*), Gr. D. 119, 17. (1 a) of age, *tender* age or years :—Seó mearewæste cildes yld *tenerrima infantis etatula*, An. Ox. 2865. On mearuwes[tan] *in tenerrima* (*pubertate*), 1633. Mǣrewestan *gracillima* (*cunabulorum aetatula*), 5038. (2) *delicate, not robust* :—Ðām untrumum gebrōðrum oðþe þǣm mearewum (mearwum, *v. l.* delicatis) and þām unweorcheardum, R. Ben. 75, 7. [v. *N. E. D.* meruw.] v. meru.

**mearu-lic;** *adj. Soft, easy, luxurious* :—Þā onfeng heó þis bebod æt Sancta Marian, þ heó nāht ofer þ ne dyde leóhtlices ne mægdenlicre wīsan oððe merwelicre, ac þ heó forhæfde hī sylfe fram unnyttum hleahtre and plegan *mandatum accepit, ut nihil ultra leve et puellare ageret, et a risu et jocis abstineret*, Gr. D. 287, 20.

**mearulīce;** *adv.* **I.** *without hardship, tenderly, delicately, indulgently* :—Hē hæfde ǣnne sunu, and sē wæs .v.-wintre, þone hē lufode swiþe līchamlīce and fēdde mǣrwlīce (merwlīce, *v. l.*) and selfwillendlīce *filium habuit annorum quinque, quem nimis carnaliter diligens remisse nutriebat,* Gr. D. 289, 5.    **II.** *without vigour, weakly* :—Hī svlfe

---

mid gewilnungum hnescum mearulīce (*printed* nearulīce) nā underhnīgan *ipsi desideriis mollibus eneruiter non succumbant*, Scint. 122, 2.

**mearuw-ness.** *Add* :—Mearunesse *teneritudine*, i. *tenerum, fragile, molle, flexum, flexibile*, An. Ox. 1492.

**mēce.** *Add:* v. sige-mēce.

**mēce-fisc.** *Add* :—Þes mēcefisc *hic mugil*, Ælfc. Gr. Z. 39, 1.

**mēd.** *Add* :—Funde se his arcedeácon æt þām cnihte þe wæs þæs biscopes byrele mid mēdum (*praemiis*), þ hē þone geættredan drync him tō bǣr, Gr. D. 186, 22.    ¶ tō mēdes *as reward:*—Gyfe him Crīst heofona rīce tō mēdes, C. D. iv. 171, 21 : Hml. S. 12, 139. Swā hwæt swā hē begit his swinces tō mēdes, 36, 43. v. mǣþ-, weorold-mēd.

**mēdan.** *Substitute: to put courage* into a person (?) :—Ondsware ȳwe sē hine on mēde wordum secgan hū se wudu hātte *let him make answer that can encourage himself to say in words how the wood is called,* Rä. 56, 15. [*As on* is *the alliterating word it can hardly be a prefix, and the verse may be compared with:* Eard wæs þȳ weorðra þe wit on stōdan, Rä. 85, 6.]

**med-drosna.** *l.* -drōsna : -**mēde.** *Dele* 'subst. and', *and* (-mēdu) *at end, and add:* v. in-mēde.

-**mēde**, es ; *n.* v. ān-, eáþ-, gram- (?), ofer-mēde ; -**mēdu: medere.** v. mædere.

**mēd-gilda.** *Add* :—Beó þū gemyndig þīnes mēdgildan (mǣd-, *v. l.* : Lch. i. lxiii. 3) *esto memor tui gallonis* (i. *mercennarii*), Hpt. 31, 12, 262.

**mēdian;** *p.* ode *To reward* :—Þone Erminigeldum his fæder ongan lǣran and mid mēdum mēdian and mid beótum brēgan *quem pater et praemiis suadere et minis terrere conatus est,* Gr. D. 237, 23.

-**medla.** *l.* -mēdla.

**med-micel.** **I.** *add:* [The Latin to Guthl. 5 is : Adsumta hordeacei panis particula ; the diminutive *particula* seems to show that *medmicel* refers to quantity, not to quality, which *beren hlāf* suggests, cf. Bd. 5, 12, *infra.*]    **III.** *add:* with reference to quality, degree, &c. (1) of persons or personal attributes :—Ðā metmiclo *pussillanimes,* Rtl. 11, 39. Þonne þ mōd wile ymb his āgene þæncan, būton tweón hit gehweorfeþ þȳ medmāre tō his sylfes þearfe *cum animus interiora appetit, ad haec proculdubio minor redit,* Gr. D. 5, 7. Þonne þ mōd byð tōdǣled tō manegum wīsum, hit byð þȳ medmāre (lǣsse, *v. l.*) tō hwylcum synderlicum þingum *cum animus dividitur ad multa, fit minor ad singula,* 41, 14. Suā long gié ne dēdon ānum ðassa metdmaasta (*de minoribus his*), Mt. L. 25, 45, margin. (2) of things :—Hē þǣre ȳtemestan yldo his lifes on ancorsetle mid medmiclum hlāfe (*coarse bread*; pane cibario) and cealde wætere āwreþede, Bd. 5, 12 ; Sch. 630, 18.

**mēdren-cynn.** *In l.* 2 *for* reht meódrencynn *l.* rehtmeódrencynn, *and take the passage to* riht-mēdrencynn.

**mēd-sceatt.** **II.** *add:*—Seó aufengnes mēdsceata on dōmum ys sōðfæstnesse forlætnes, Ll. Lbm. 476, 30. Sē þe þām scyldegan scyldeþ for mētsceattum (*pro pecunia*), 475, 3. Nys nānwiht unrihtlycre ðonne ys þ man mēdsceattas onfō for dōmum *nichil iniustius est quam susceptio munerum pro iudicio subuertendo,* 474, 23. Ðā ðwyran dēman ne geendiað nā þā spǣce ǣr heora seód bið āfylled ; and þan þonne hȳ dēmað, ne scēwiað hȳ nā þā spǣce, ac þā mēdsceatas (*munera*), 475, 46.

**medtrum-ness.** *Add* :—Sió medtrymnes (mettrumnes, *v. l.*) ðæt mōd gehwierfð gehwelces monnes hine selfne tō ongietanne *molestia corporalis ad cognitionem sui mentem revocat,* Past. 255, 15.

-**mēdu.** v. eáþ-, gram-, ofer-mēdu ; -**mēde,** es ; *n.*

**meduma.** *For* 'A weaver's beam' *substitute* 'A treadle of a loom,' *in* l. 2 *for* 'insubulæ,' *l.* 'insubula,' *and add* :—Meðema *tramarium,* Wrt. Voc. i. 59, 27. (Wright prints: Tramarium-meðema wersa, *but the MS. has* persa, *which is Latin, and belongs to the next word.*)

**medume.** *Add:* , me(o)dum.    **I.** *add: small, little.* (1) of amount :—Hī cōmon ǣrest mid medemum fultume, ac sióððan hȳ wiston hū hit þǣr besūðan wæs, þā . . . lēton hī bēodan mycele fyrde, Chr. 1052 ; P. 175, 17. (2) of quality, status, &c. :—Þeáh þe Paulus wǣre se medmesta (*minimus*) þāra apostola, Gr. D. 91, 6.    **II a.** *add:*—Heom ðūhte ōðre hwīle þæt hē wǣre swylce hit cild wǣre, ōðre hwīle eft swylce hē medemre ylde man wǣre, and ōðre hwīle swylce hē eald geðungen man wǣre, Wlfst. 99, 14.    **II b.** *add:*—On meodumum (medemum) stōwum (*mediocribus locis*), R. Ben. 89, 9 : 107, 14. Se ðeóda lāreów lǣrde ðā rīcan . . . Se ylca apostol manode eác ðā medeman . . . þearfan hē lǣrde, Hml. Th. ii. 328, 14.    **III.** *add:*—Hē ðūhte him sylfum suīðe unlytel and suīðe medeme *se parvulum non videbat,* Past. 113, 12. Sceal hē þurh clǣne andetnysse and þurh medeme bōte (*through meet penance*) and þurh his teáras þā synna eft āðweán, Hml. A. 158, 158. Hē gecēð him tō geþingum ðīnne ðone medoman naman (*thy worthy name*), Shrn. 77, 8. Drihtne tō geearnienne medome folc (*plebem perfectum,* Lk. 1, 17), Bl. H. 165, 15. Rihtwīsra manna gāstas and full medemra *spiritus justorum et perfectorum,* Gr. D. 260, 21. Be full medemum (fulremedum, *v. l.*) werum *de perfectis viris,* 7, 22. Se God hæfð ealle creftas on hym gesunde and ful medeme, Solil. H. 52, 14. v. efen-medeme.

**medumian.** **I.** *add: to assign as one's proper place* :—Gif munuc eáðhylde bið and geþæf, þeáh hine man wācne and unweorðne talige and

an ūteweardum forlǣte and tō ūteweardum medemige *si omni vilitate vel extremitate contentus sit*, R. Ben. 24, 9.

**medum-lic.** I. *add : simple :*—Sume medemlice gesettednysse *paruum decretulum*, Chrd. 2, 11. Ne beó gē tō creásum reáfum gefrætwode, ac medemlicum (*simplici modo*), 90, 13. I a. *of middle rank.* Cf. medume ; II a :—On medomlicere stōwe *loco mediocri*, R. Ben. I. 101, 8.

**medumlīce.** I. *add : slightly :*—Gyf þū halban habban wille, þonne wege þū medemlīce þīn reáf mid þīnre handa, Tech. ii. 119, 19. Wē byddað þā bōceras þe þās þing fulfremedlīce cunnon þ heom hefelīce ne þince þās þing þe wē medomlīce iungum cnihtum settað, Angl. viii. 321, 43. Wē habbað medomlīce þās þing gehrepod, hyt þingð ūs gefædlic þ wē rūmlīcor þās gerēnu ātrahtnion, 324, 6. Wurdon eorðwæstmas eall tō medemlīce gewende, Chr. 1095; P. 232, 13. II. *add :*—Ðā ðe medomlīce lǣran magon *qui praedicare digne valent*, Past. 375, 18. Manige wē sceáwiað nū, and swā þeáh nū gȳt wē hī nā full medomlīce (*perfecte*) oncnāwaþ, Gr. D. 331, 13. Hwelc ūre mæg āreccan medemlīce ūres Sceppendes willan?, Bt. 34, 10; F. 150, 11. Būtan hē hit medomlīce gebæte ǣr his ænde, C. D. vi. 35, 2. v. ge-, un-medumlīce.

**medumlic-ness.** *Substitute : Mediocrity, insignificance, littleness :*—Gehwǣdnys, medemlicnys ealdordōme underwreoþod (*nostra*) *mediocritas* i. *paruitas auctoritate subnixa*, An. Ox. 5064.

**medum-micel ;** *adj. Little, short* (of time) :—Medemmicel hwīl is þ gē mē ne geseóð *modicum et non uidebitis me*, Hml. A. 73, 16. v. ge-medummicel.

**medum-ness.** I. *add :*—Seó gyfu ne bið oncnāwen of þǣre medemnysse, ac gewuna hī is tō getācnigenne of þǣre sāwle dǣdum, Hml. S. 23 b, 240. Ðā medomnesse ðǣre strengio se salmscop ongeat *hanc dignitatem fortitudinis Psalmista considerat*, Past. 85, 21.

**medu-scerwen.** v. scerwen : **Medu-wǣge.** *Add :* -wæg(u?), e.

**medu-wyrt.** *Add : meadwort :*—Mēdewyrt (*the accent is in the MS.*) *rubia*, An. Ox. 56, 40. Genime neoþewearde medowyrt, Lch. ii. 70, 17. Genim medowyrte nioþowearde, 134, 5. [v. *N. E. D.* meadwort.]

**Mēd-ware.** v. Mǣþ-ware.

**mēd-wyrhta, an ;** *m. A hireling, worker for pay, mercenary :*—Mēdwyrhta (*mercennarius*) ys sē þe stōwe hyrdes healt, ac gestreón sāwla nā sēcð, Scint. 123, 13. Mēdwyrhtena *lixarum*, An. Ox. 4, 24.

**melcan.** *Add :*—Gif þē meolce lyste, þonne strocca þū þīnne wynstran finger mid þīnre swyþra[n] handa þām gelīce swylce þū melce, Tech. ii. 123, 25. v. ā-, ge-melcan.

**meld.** *Add :* v. regn-meld : **melda.** *Add :* v. ster-melda.

**meldian.** *Add :*—þæt hors ongan . . . mid unāblinnendlicre brogdettunge ealles līchaman meldian and yppan (*prodere*), þ hit ne mihte witman beran, Gr. D. 183, 12. [v. *N. E. D.* meld.] v. ā-, be-meldian.

**mēle.** *Add :* Mēlas *charchesia, uasa pastoralia*, Hpt. 31, 5, 55. Man sceal habban bleda, mēlas, cuppan, Angl. ix. 264, 17. [v. *N. E. D.* meal.] v. stel-mēle.

**-melle.** v. ǣ-melle.

**meltan.** I. *perhaps some of the forms given here should be taken under* miltan, q. v. II. *add :*—Gerīst þ him mon lytlum þā mettas selle þā þe late melten, leax, and þā fixas þā þe late meltan, Lch. ii. 176, 22–24. v. ā-meltan.

**meltung.** *Add :*—Be lattre meltunge sumra metta, Lch. ii. 160, 9.

**melu.** *Add :* I. *meal, ground grain :*—þe ne āteórað melu on þīnum mittan (*hydria farinae non deficiet*, 1 Kings 17, 14), Hml. S. 18, 63. Orn seó cweorn ðurh godcunde miht . . . and wæs genihtsumnes meluwes, Shrn. 145, 26. Ðeós wyrt mid meoluwe gecnucud, Lch. i. 270, 23. Mid berenum meluwe, 15. Genim þās wyrte and meluw, 12. II. *a powdery substance resembling flour :*—Genim heorotes sceafoþan of þām horne, oþþe þæs hornes melo, Lch. ii. 72, 14. v. āc-, beán-, hwǣte-, hwīting-, wyrm-melu.

**melu-hēdern** *a meal-storehouse :*—Man sceal habban . . . meluhūdern, Angl. ix. 265, 2.

**men.** *Dele, and see* þrimen.

**mene.** *Add :*—Hē geg'ængde mē mid orle of golde āwefen and mid ormettum mynum mē gefretewode, Hml. S. 7, 37.

**-mened (?).** v. ofer-mǣned.

**menen.** *In line 8 for* mennen *is l.* mennenu, *and in last line dele* , þeów-, *and add : In* Ps. L. 85, 16 *the word is feminine :*—Galla, þ Godes mennen (mennen, *v. l.*), Gr. D. 280, 12. Þeów mennen, Agar, Gen. 2246. Sunu þīnre þīnenne i mennenne *filium ancillae tuae*, Ps. L. 85, 16. Be þām Godes mænnene (menn, þeówenne, *v. ll.*) *de ancilla Dei*, Gr. D. 29, 20. Gif hē þeów oþþe þeów mennen (þeówne, þeowene, *v. ll.*) ofstinge, Ll. Th. i. 50, 3 : Gen. 2233.

**menen-lic.** v. myniend-lic.

**mengan.** I. *add :* (1) *to mix one thing with another, interpose among :*—Mē ys neód þ ic menge ð Lýcen amaug þissum Englisce, Angl. viii. 317, 16. (2) *to mix two or more things together :*—Heora underngereordu and ǣfengereordu hié mengdon tōgædere, Bl. H. 99, 23. (3) *of immaterial things or fig. :*—Hē þæs preóstes heortan and geþanc mid his searwes āttre geondsprengde and mengde *ejus praecordia malignus spiritus ingressus pestiferis vanae gloriae fastibus illum inflare coepit*,

Guth. Gr. 137, 7. Ðǣm lāreówe is tō mengenne ðā liðnesse wið ðā rēðnesse *miscenda est lenitas cum severitate*, Past. 124, 13. III. *add : to confound, not to distinguish :*—Nā mengende hādas and nā spēde syndriende *neque confundantes personas neque substantiam separantes*, Angl. ii. 360, 4. IV. *of persons, to join to others so as to form one of a company :*—Ic ǣnlīpigu on þām cafertūne oþstōd . . . ic mē þā eft ongan mængan tō ōþrum, þ ic wolde on sume wīsan inn geþringan, Hml. S. 23 b, 411. [v. *N. E. D.* meng.] v. ofer(?)-, un-menged.

**-menged-lic, -līce, -ness, -mengness.** v. ge-menged-lic, &c.

**mengung.** *Add : a crowd of people :*—Wē þe wǣron gemǣngde tō þysum folclicum mængungum *nos turbis popularibus admixti*, Gr. D. 209, 13.

**mengdu.** *Perhaps* menigu *should be read :* **menige**, Ex. 6, 1. v. mægenig.

**menigu.** *Add :*—Hū micel menigu ðǣra getreówfulra byð, Past. 403, 21. Mengeo (menigu, *v. i.*), 5, 11. Seó ungemetlice mengeo þæs folces, Ors. 2, 5; S. 80, 11. For ðǣre menige (menge, *v. l.*) ðæs folces, Past. 113, 19. Ðæt mon ðā godcundan sprǣce ðǣre menigo (mengio, *v. l.*) tōdǣle, 373, 19. Binnon ðām weallum wǣron ungerīme meniu manna (cf. innumera hominum conuenticula, Bd. Sch. 623), Hml. Th. ii. 352, 10. Ðā gesomnode hē miclo mænigiu brōþra and sweostra, Shrn. 129, 6. v. eóred-menigu.

**men[n].** v. mere-men[n] : -menne. v. ǣ-menne.

**mennisc ;** *adj. Add :*—Ic andette Gode and ðǣm (ðe, MS.) menniscum men mīnum gāstlicum scrifte, Angl. xi. 99, 56. Hē āsende mennisce sprǣce on þone heort, Hml. S. 30, 44. Englas geþafodon ǣr Drihtnes tōcyme þæt mennisce men him tō feóllon, Hml. Th. i. 38, 27. Mennisce eágan hine ne mihton geseón, 598, 18. Gesāwon wē mennisce men feá healfnacode *paucos Indorum seminudos notavimus homines*, Nar. 10, 16. ¶ *used substantively :*—Ðū tīhst ðis mennisce tō ðǣre ȳdelan lāre, Hml. Th. i. 588, 5.

**mennisc ;** *n. Add :* I. *mankind, men in general :*—Bið unstrenge mennisc ðurh māran tӯddernysse, Hml. Th. ii. 370, 17. Eal mennisc wæs synfull, 472, 2. Nelle ic þis mennisc gehealdan tō þām ēcum wītum, for þām þe hī synd tӯddre *fragilis est in hominibus conditio, non ad aeternos servabo cruciatus*, Angl. vii. 48, 467. II. *a race, people :*—Hē āxode hwæt þ mennisc wǣre on þām muntum wunigende *quis sit populus iste qui montana obsidet*, Hml. A. 104, 80. Of Japhet cōm þæt norðerne mennisc, Ælfc. T. Grn. 4, 37. Hē lǣrde manega þæs Engliscan mennisces, Angl. viii. 2, 4. Þā fūlan forligeras þæs fracodostan mennisces Sodomitisce ðeóda, Hml. S. 13, 191 : Ælfc. T. Gm. 4, 16. III. *a number of people, men, people :*—Micel mennisc Iūðēiscre mǣgðe on Crīst gelȳfde, Hml. Th. ii. 420, 31. IV. *the human, human nature, humanity :*—Mon mæg gesión þ hī gió men wǣron, ac hī habbaþ þæs mennisces þone bestan dǣl forloren *fuisse homines adhuc ipsa humani corporis reliqua species ostentat ; quare versi in malitiam humanam quoque amisere naturam*, Bt. 37, 3 ; F. 192, 3.

**mennisc-lic.** *Add :* I. *human :*—Ne geseah hē . . . nāne mennisclice gesihðe, Hml. S. 23 b, 181. II. *that should characterize man, humane :*—Beó him gegearewod eal mennisclic fremfulnes *omnis ei exhibeatur humanitas*, R. Ben. 83, 18. Hī forlǣtaþ þ gecyndelice gōd, þ sint mennisclice þeáwas, Bt. 37, 3 ; F. 192, 5. v. un-mennisclic.

**mentel.** *Add :*—Hē cearf læppan of Saules mentle (mentelle, *v. l.*), Past. 199, 11.

**meó.** *Add :*—Synd gesealde from þām abbode ealle neádbehēfe þing, þæt is . . . meón (*pedules*), hosa . . . , R. Ben. 92, 3. Hæbben hȳ tō fōtgewǣdum hosa and meón, 89, 14 : 91, 6.

**meolc.** *Add :* I. *milk* as food. (1) *of an animal :*—Gehǣt scenc fulne cūwearmre meolce, Lch. ii. 354, 2. Wyl on eówe meolce, 144, 22. Gebyred þ hē hæbbe ealdre cū meolc, Ll. Th. i. 438, 18. Sceal mon lācnian mid cū meolcum oððe gāte . . . Eác hylpð gif mon mid eástānum onbærnedum þā meoluc gewyrð, Lch. ii. 218, 21–24. Hē lifde be þāra wildeóra meolcum, Shrn. 118, 17. (2) *of a woman :*—Genim wīfes meoluc þæs þe cild habbe, Lch. ii. 28, 8 : 42, 5. (3) figurative :—Ic sceal sellan eów gīet mioloc drincan, nalles flǣsc etan, Past. 459, 18. II. *a milk-like juice or sap :*—Genim þisse ylcan wyrte meolc (meoluc, *v. l.*), Lch. i. 224, 6. v. eówo-meolc.

**meolcen.** v. milcen.

**meolcian.** *Add :*—Hī on þǣm mōnðe þriwa on dæge mylcedon heora neát, Shrn. 78, 1. v. þri-milce.

**meolc-līþe ;** *adj. Soft as milk, gentle :*—Fram þām þe weg cynelicne beboda Drihtnes būton gylpes leahtre mealclīþe eádmódlīce stæppeð *ab his qui uiam regiam mandatorum Domini absque iactantis uitio lactei humiliter incedunt*, Angl. xiii. 369, 49.

**meolc-teónd.** *l.* -deónd. v. deón.

**meóning, es ;** *m. A garter, binding for a sock :*—Meóningas (*printed* weoningas) *fascellas*, Wrt. Voc. ii. 146, 53. v. meó.

**meord.** *Add :*—For intingan heofonlicre mēde (meorðe, *v. l.*), Bd. 4, 31; Sch. 540, 7. Tō mēde (meorde, *v. l.*) heora edleánes[1] *pro mercede retributionis*, Gr. D. 227, 16. For gelícnesse gōdra mēda (mēde, *v. l.*) and edleána *pro aequalitate praemiorum*, 312, 14. Cf. mēd.

**meornan.** *Take here examples given to* murnan.

**meós.** *Add :*—Man him sette of ꝺǣre foresǣdan róde sumne dǣl þæs meóses þe heó mid beweaxen wæs, Hml. S. 26, 37. ¶ as the first component in local names, e. g. :—On meósbróces heáfod, C. D. v. 339, 3. On meósdene, 303, 1. In meósdûne, iii. 373, 23. On meóshlinc, ii. 172, 26. Tó meósleáge, v. 215, 9 (cf. ge-lêgu). On meósmôr, iii. 81, 29. [v. *N. E. D.* mese. Icel. mýrr *a moor, bog.*]

**meox.** [*In* l. 6 *after* 'meox?' *insert :* and swá ꝺeáh, gif þu his wel notast, hwæt biꝺ wæstmbǣrre?]. *Add : manure :*—Ne forhtige gê for ꝺæs fyrnfullan þreátum, for ꝺan þe his wuldor is wyrms and meox, Hml. S. 25, 261. Hit ys bysmorlic dǣd þ ǣnig man ... þone mûꝺ ufan mettum áfylle and on ôꝺerne ende him gange þ meox ût fram, E. S. viii. 62, 16. Ic hine bewurpe mid meoxe *mittam stercora*, Lk. 13, 8. God áhefꝺ of meohse (*de stercore*) þone mann þe hê wile, O. E. Hml. i. 301, 26. Meoxa *stercorum*, An. Ox. 3331. [v. *N. E. D.* mix.]

**meox-beorh** (?) *a dunghill* (?) :—Tó meox beorhym (= meoxbeorgum?), Cht. E. 449, 35. Cf. *N. E. D.* mix-hill *a dunghill.*

**meox-scofl,** e ; *f.* A *dung-shovel :*—Man sceal habban ... ofnrace, mexscofle, Angl. ix. 265, 3.

**-merca.** v. in-, on-, sól-merca : **mercung.** v. ge-, ofer-mercung.

**mere.** I. *add :*—Hê hám cymeꝺ ... nefne him holm gestýreꝺ, mere hafaꝺ mundum, Gn. Ex. 107. II. *add : a natural pool :*—Æt Finchámstede áu mere blôd weóll, Chr. 1098 ; P. 234, 22. Hí þá hálgan gelêddon tó ánum brádum mere ... se mere wæs mid forste oferþeaht, Hml. S. 11, 141. Hí cwǣdon þ wê fundon sumne swîþe micelne mere in þǣm wǣre fersc wæter and swête genóg *ingens nos stagnum dulcissime aquae inuenturos*, Nar. 11, 26. On merum *in stagna*, Ps. L. 106, 35 ; 113, 8. [*The word occurs in many compounds.* v. Midd. Flur. s. v.] III. *add :*—Beforan ꝺǣm temple stôd ǣren ceác ... ꝺǣtte ꝺá menn ꝺe intô ꝺǣm temple gán woldon meahten hira honda ꝺweán on ꝺǣm mere *ante fores templi ad abluendas ingredientium manus mare aeneum, id est, luterem boves portant*, Past. 105, 4. v. sealt-, ûter-, wîþig-mere.

**mere.** *Add :* I. *the female of the horse :*—þ mǣden wæs swá forbroden swylce heó án myre wǣre, Hml. S. 21, 475. Gif man of myran folan áꝺrîfꝺ, Ll. Th. i. 70, 22. .x. mǣran mid .x. coltan . . . .vi. mǣran mid .vi. coltan, Shrn. 159, 17, 29. II. *the female of other quadrupeds :*—Olfenda myran and hyra folan and stêdan *camelos masculos et feminas illas quae habent foetas*, Nar. 35, 11. v. olfend-mere.

**mere-grot.** *Add :* I. material :—Heó hafaꝺ stánas hwîte and sinewealte swylce meregrotu (-grotan, *v. l.*), Lch. i. 314, 21. þá betstan meregrotu, Bd. 1, 1 ; Sch. 8, 18. II. figurative :—þás meregrota þám beforan lecgan þe þisra þinga gýman wyllaꝺ, Angl. viii. 308, 43.

**mere-grota.** *Add : See preceding word.*

**mere-men**[n]. *Add :*—Ic geháte gewîtan fram mê þá mǣremen þe synt smere (*sirene* ?) gecîged, and eác þá *castalidas nymphas*, þ synt dûnylfa, Angl. viii. 325, 25.

**mere-nǣdre.** *Add :*—Merenǣddre *murex*, An. Ox. 18 b, 56.

**mere-steall,** es ; *m.* A *pool of stagnant water, pond :*—Of þǣre oferfylle cumaꝺ þá unrihtan lustas, gelîce and on meresteallum wyrmas týddraꝺ, Verc. Först. 169.

**mere-swîn.** *Add :*—Mereswîn *luligines*, An. Ox. 41, 1.

**mergelle.** v. mear-gealla : **merg-lic.** v. mearh-lic : **merian.** *Add :* v. ge-merian.

**merigen.** I. *add :*—Wæs þá geteald ǣfen and merigen tó ánum dæge, Lch. iii. 232, 12. Drince on morgenne scenc fulne þises drences, tó middes mergenes stande eástweard, ii. 116, 7. Ofer ealle niht oꝺ leóhtne mergen, R. Ben. 47, 9. II. *add :*—Swá swá þ godspel sægꝺ : 'Ne þenc þû be mergene,' Hml. S. 31, 57. Heó swôr þ Helias sceolde ꝺæs on mergen (merigen, *v. l.*) sweltan, 18, 158. v. Sunnan-merigen.

**merigen-dæg.** *Add :*—Gif hê him þæs mergendæges geunnan wolde *si in crastino vitam servasset*, Guth. Gr. 110, 60.

**merigen-lic.** I. *add :*—Hê on merigenlicere tîde mynster gesôhte *he returned to the monastery in time for matins*, Hml. Th. ii. 138, 16. Ealle þás niht ic áne wunode biddende ... and þis mergendlican dæge gelîcode mê þ ic eówerne sum mê tó begeáte, Hml. S. 33, 108. Meriendlice lofsangas *matutini*, R. Ben. I. 45, 16. Merrigenlice, 37, 14. On mergenlicum lofsangum, 42, 9. Merigenlicum, 66, 13.

**mersc.** *Add :*—Hîredes seota tó prêsta tûne, and se mersc se tó ꝺam ilcan lande belimpꝺ ... isti sunt termini ... marisci ; in oriente hîredes mersc tó prêsta tûne, C. D. ii. 102, 29-33. Hî wendon ofer Temese ... and swá wiꝺ Caningan mærsces (mersces, *v. l.*), Chr. 1010 ; P. 141, 6. Segor stôd on midwege betweox ꝺǣm muntum and ꝺǣm merscum ꝺe Sodoma on wæs.

**mersc-hófe.** v. hófe.

**mersc-hop,** es ; *n.* A *hope* (v. hop) *in a fen :*—þá merschopa þe þǣr bûtan syndon, C. D. B. ii. 526, 10.

**mersc-mylen,** e ; *f.* A *mill in a fen :*—On hore paꝺe intô merscmylne ; of merscmylne, C. D. vi. 100, 12.

**mertze** (?) *substitute :* **mertze, myrtse,** *and add : trading dues.*

[For instances of such dues see Ll. Th. i. 300] :—Scipmanna (-e, MS.) myrtse, cêping *teloneum* (cf. teloneum *tributum pro mercibus*, Migne), Wrt. Voc. i. 37, 10. Cf. cîping ; I a.

**merþern ;** *adj. Of martin skins :*—Merꝺerne pyleceon, Chr. 1075 ; P. 209, 32. v. mearþ.

**mése.** *Add : a table at which a meal is taken :*—ꝺæs abbodes mýse sceal á beón gemǣne þearuum and elþeódegum mannum, R. Ben. 93, 3. Sý hê áscyred fram gemǣnre mýsan þigene *suspendatur a mensa*, 49, 15. Fram meósan and fram geꝼǣrǣdene *a mense consortio*, R. Ben. I. 56, 9 : 77, 9 ; 106, 12. Hê tó Furtunates mýsan (beóde, *v. l.*) becôm, Gr. D. 62, 8. Gebrôꝺra gereorde æt hyra mýsum (meósan *mensis*, R. Ben. l. 69, 2) ne sceal beón bûtan háligre rǣdinge, R. Ben. 62, 3.

**més-hrægel,** es ; *n.* A *napkin :*—Mýshrægel *mappula*, R. Ben. 1. 93, 10.

**met.** *Add : measure :*—Ealdes mannes eágan beóþ unscearpsýno ; þonne sceal hê þá eágan weccan mid gnîdingum, mid gongum, mid rádum, oþþe mid þý þe hine mon bere oþþe on wǣne ferige ; and hý sculan nyttian lytlum and forhtlicum metum (*these means are to be employed in small doses and with great caution* (?), Lch. ii. 30, 30. [*O. H. Ger.* mez *mensura : Icel.* met ; *n. pl. weights of a balance.*] v. or-, wer-met : -mét. v. métto.

**metan.** I. *add :*—Thômas eóde metende mid ánre metegyrde þone stede, Hml. S. 36, 94. IV. *add :*—Mê þincꝺ unêꝺe þæt hû hî tôgædere metst, Solil. H. 61, 8. Mest, 17, 10. v. efen-, tô-metan.

**métan** *to paint. Add :*—Wercaꝺ hió of weaxe ... mêtaꝺ Fenix, E. S. viii. 478, 50. v. on-mêtan.

**métan** *to meet. Add :*—Mon on þám feldum þára háligra gewryta swîꝺe eáꝺe þá wǣpnu mêtan mæg mid þǣm mon þá uncysta ofercuman mæg, Ll. Th. ii. 414, 20. Mid þǣm ꝺû geearnode Godes irre, ꝺǣr (*if*) ꝺá gódan weorc ǣr nǣren (*had not been*) on ꝺê mêtte (*inventa*), Past. 355, 5.

**met-cund.** The Latin word glossed is *catalectico.*

**mete.** *Add :* I. *food :*—Gif mete sý áwyrd, Lch. ii. 142, 14. Nys rîce Godes meta (*esca*) and drînc, Scint. 153, 7. Ægþer ge hrægles ge metes ge drinces, Bt. 26, 2 ; F. 94, 4. Wiꝺ genumenum mete, Lch. ii. 142, 7. Wermôd drincan ǣr þon þe hié mete þicgan, 32, 1. Ne reccaþ hî þára metta, Bt. F. 88, 19. Hû sió womb weorꝺe mid swôtlecustum mettum gefylled, Past. 311, 9. II. *a meal, meat* as in *at meat :*—þonne hî hira hláf brǣcon æt mete, Shrn. 30, 8. Ælce dæge ǣr mete þrié cucler fulle geþicge, Lch. ii. 152, 7. v. bleó-, fôr-, ofer-, searu-, smeá-, sufel-, swêt-, swôt-, wist-mete.

**-mete ;** *adj.* v. -met[t] : **mete-áflíung.** *l.* -flîung.

**mete-ærn.** *Add :*—a refectory :—þonne tǣce ic eów hwǣr þára brôꝺra metern (*refectorium*) wǣre, Gr. D. 147, 34.

**mete-awul** (?) *a meat-hook* (?) :—Mán sceal habban ... meteawel and tó odene fligel, Angl. ix. 264, 7.

**mete-cleofa,** an ; *m.* A *pantry :*—Met[e]clyf[a] *cellarium*, An. Ox. 56, 270.

**mete-cû.** *Add :*—Be oxanhyrde ... his metecû môt gán mid hláfordes oxan. Be cûhyrde ... gá his metecû mid hlafordes cû, Ll. Th. i. 438, 12-20.

**mete-cweorra,** an ; *m. Surfeit of food* (?) :—Wiꝺ metecweorran, Lch. iii. 60, 4. v. á-cweorran.

**-métedness.** v. wiþ-mêtedness : **mete-fætels.** *l.* -fætels.

**mete-láf.** *Add :*—For hwî ne môt se ꝺearfa onfón þînes metes, þe mid ꝺê is tó onfónne heofona rîce ? ... Hwî nis sê wyrþe þ hê onfó þînra metelâfe, þe mid þê is tó cumenne tó engla gebeórscipe ?, Hml. A. 142, 102-107.

**mete-leás.** *Add :*—Ne mihte Iûdas meteleás þǣr ábîdan, Hml. S. 25, 447. Hié (*the Danes*) sǣton on þám îglande ... oþ þone first þe hié wurdon swîþe meteleáse, Chr. 918 ; P. 98, 32. þá león leofodon be hungre seofon niht meteleáse, Hml. S. 16, 32.

**mete-leást.** *Add :*—þǣr onsæt mycel hungor, and seó mycele wǣdl þǣre meteleáste genyrwde ealle þá landleóde *fames incubuerat, magnaque omnes alimentorum indigentia coangustabat*, Gr. D. 145, 6. Hû mage wê þus feáwa feohtan ongeán þás meniu, nû wê synd gewǣhte mid gewinne and meteleáste, Hml. S. 25, 306.

**-métend.** v. ge-mêtend : **-metendlic.** v. á-, wiþ-metendlic : **-metendlîce.** v. wiþ-metendlîce : **meten-lic,** -lîce. v. wiþ-metenlic, -lîce.

**meter.** *Add : versification :*—Meteres crǣft *metrica ars*, Bd. 4, 2 ; Sch. 344, 18. Bêda mid leóꝺlicum metre be þǣm mônꝺum þus giddode, Angl. viii. 301, 34. Swîþswêgum metrum (-e ?) *heroico exametro*, An. Ox. 1437.

**mete-rǣdere,** es ; *m. The brother appointed for the week to read aloud to the others at meals.* Cf. Be ꝺǣre wucan rǣdere. Gebrôꝺra gereorde æt hyra mýsum ne sceal beón bûtan háligre rǣdinge, R. Ben. 62, 2-4, *and see the whole chapter :*—Gyf þû meterǣdere fyldstól habban wille, Tech. ii. 122, 20.

**meter-fers.** *Add :*—Furtunatus sette þás naman ealle tó meterferse, Angl. xi. 2, 35. Eall swylce sum getýd wer sitte and sum meterfers mid his feꝺere áwrîte, viii. 317, 22. Oft þá þeódwitan þus heora meteruers

gewurðiað, 332, 15. Hig gewurðiað heora spǽce and heora meterversa gesetnyssa, 313, 29. v. riht-meterfers.

**meter-lic.** _Add:_—Meterlicere getincnesse _metrica facundia_, An. Ox. 124.

**mete-sacca.** _Substitute:_ **mete-sticca,** an; _m. A spoon:_—Metesticca (_printed_ -sacca, _but see_ Angl. viii. 451, 1) _legula vel coclea vel cocle,_ Wrt. Voc. i. 26, 62 (_the word occurs in a list of objects connected with the table_). v. sticca; II.

**mete-þiht;** _adj. Strong from taking food_ (?). v. þiht.

**mete-þing,** es; _n. An operation connected with cooking:_—Hí man geornlíce tȳ þ hí góde bæcystran beón and tó ǽlcum meteþingum clǽngeorne, Chrd. 19, 19.

**mete-tíd,** e; _f. Mealtime:_—Þá þá seó mætetíd (mete-, _v. l., tempus refectionis_) cóm, Gr. D. 277, 24. Gif wē fæstað and þ underngereord tó þám æfengifle healdað, þonne ne bið þ nán fæsten, ac bið seó metetíd geuferad, and bið þ æfengyfel getwifealdad, Ll. Th. ii. 436, 30.

**metfæst-ness,** e; _f. Modesty:_—Mid metfæstnesse _cum modestia,_ R. Ben. I. 55, 6. v. gemetfæst-ness.

-**metgiend.** v. ge-metgiend.

**met-gird.** _Add:_ mete-:—Thómas eóde metende mid ánre metegyrde þone stede, Hml. S. 36, 94.

**metgung.** _Add:_ v. þanc-metegung: **mēþe.** _Add:_ v. hyge-, sǽmēþe: **medema.** v. meduma _a treadle._

**mēþ-ness,** e; _f. Weariness, lassitude:_—Méðnisse _lassitudine,_ Txts. 181, 55.

**mēting,** e; _f. Meeting, assembly:_—An mētincge þæs geféres sȳ þæt gebed gescyrt _in conventu brevietur oratio,_ R. Ben. 46, 2. v. gemēting.

-**meting.** v. wiþ-meting: -met-lécan. v. gemet-lécan: met-lic. _Add:_ v. gemet-lic: metlíce. v. un-metlíce, gemetlíce: -**metlicung.** v. gemetlicung: -**metness.** v. ge-metness: -**mētness.** v. ge-mētness: **metod,** Dan. 119. v. mǽtan.

**metod.** [_In the phrase se_ metoda drihten, metoda _is not a gen. pl., as suggested in Dict., but either a wk. noun or adjective, as will be seen from the following examples:_—Micel mildheortnys þæs metodan Dryhtnes, Hml. Th. ii. 316, 21. Menigfealde beóð þæs metodan Drihtnes egsan and swingla ofer scyldigum mannum, 328, 32 (_both passages are alliterative._)] _Add:_—Se metod eallra gesceafta (cf. se milda metod, Met. 29, 68) fēt on eorþan ealle grówende westmas, Bt. 39, 13; F. 234, 18.

**metod-sceaft.** _The word might be masculine._ Cf. fram-sceaft.

**metsian.** II. _add:_—Ǽghwilc hine sylfne metsode swá swá hē mihte oþþe wolde; sum him mid bær þæs líchaman genihtsumnysse, sum þæra palmtreówa æppla, sum beána mid wætere ofgotene _each provisioned himself as he could or would; one carried with him a sufficiency for the body, one dates, one beans soaked with water,_ Hml. S. 23 b, 126.

**met[t],** es; _n._ v. un-met[t]: -met[t]; _adj._ v. or-, un-met[t]: -mēt[t]. v. -mētto.

-**metta.** [Pacience and ich weren yput to be mettes, And seten by our selue at a syd-table, Piers P. C. xvi. 41.] v. ge-metta: -**mēttan.** v. ge-an-mēttan (v. ge-anmētan _where read_ -mēttan _not_ -mēdan), ge-eáþmēttan (v. Hml. A. 159, 183, _given under_ ge-eáþmēdan; IV. 2).

**mettian.** v. metian: -mētto. _Add:_ v. weá-mētto, -mēt[t]: -**metung.** v. ge-, þanc-metung.

**micel.** I. and III. _Add:_ I. _great_ (1) with reference to size, bulk, stature:—Geseah hē swȳþe mycele weorud ... and wæs án þæra ... swȳþe heáh and swȳðe mycel ofer eal þæt oþer folc, Vis. Lfc. 14. Hié him gesealdon án .c. þára miclena þrierēðrena, Ors. 3, 1; S. 96, 27: 5, 13; S. 246, 6. (1 a) as an epithet to distinguish objects of the same kind but of different size:—Nim þá miclan sinfullan, Lch. ii. 240. 8. (1 b) _great_ in extent:—Gif mon on miclum gangum (_long walks_) weorðe geteórad, Lch. i. 76, 4. (2) with reference to coarseness of material. v. greát:—Hē fēng tó þǽre teala myclan andleofone, þæt wæs tó þám berenan hláfe, Guth. Gr. 126, 85. (3) with reference to amount or degree:—Him wǽre micel ðearf ðæt hié léten Godes ege hié geeáðmēdan, Past. 321, 12. Micul, 405, 21. Is hit swȳðe micel cyn þ gehwylc crīsten man þone dæg weorðige, Ll. Th. ii. 420, 31. Oft se micla anweald ðára yflena gehrīst swíþe fǽrlíce, Bt. 38, 2; F. 198, 8. Lacedēmonie hæfdon máran unstillnessa þonne hié mægenes hæfden _Lacedaemonii, inquieti magis quam strenui,_ Ors. 3, 1; S. 98, 34. (4) with reference to power or importance:—Sēe Cristofores ðrowung þæs miclan martyres, Shrn. 76, 15. Úre Áliésend mára is and mǽrra eallum gesceaftum _Redemtor noster magnus manens super omnia,_ Past. 301, 12. Suā huelc suā wille betweoxn eów mǽst beón (_major fieri_), 121, 6. (5) of things material or immaterial, _of great excellence_ or _work, of importance_ or _significance:_—Hē (John) heóld þá clǽnnysse on móde and on líchaman on micelre drohtnunge, Hml. A. 14, 23: 16, 14. Hwǽr beóþ þá glengeas and þá mycclan gegyrelan þe hē þone líchoman ǽr mid frætwode?, Bl. H. 111, 36. For hwan ne dēþ hē þ lǽsse nū hē þ mǽre dyde?, 181, 7. (6) where a quality is possessed in a high degree:—Þú stunta and se mǽsta dwǽs þe ǽfre on þissere byrig mǽst wæs, Hml. S.

23, 695.

II. _add:_—Gif mon on mycelre ráde weorþe geteórad, Lch. i. 76, 4. Ðonne hē ús seleð micel siolfor, ðonne hē ús seld micle getyngnesse, Past. 369, 13. Æt mǽstra hwelcre misdǽde, Ll. Th. i. 58, 6. **IV.** _add:_ (a):—Hē micel þæs moncynnes sum ácwealde, sum on Mæcedonie lǽdde, Ors. 4, 11; S. 208, 15. Ic mycel folces tó helle geteáh, H. R. 15, 6. Genim þás wyrte ... ealra gelíce mycel, Lch. i. 218, 3. Máre ic þyses gemyndgade þonne ic his mid ealle ásǽde _haec commemorata sunt magis quam explicata,_ Ors. 3, 2; S. 100, 25. (b):—Hwílum hié oft on dæge út gáð and þonne lytlum, hwílum ǽne and þonne micel, Lch. ii. 230, 22. Sellan fela ðám ðe hié lytel sceoldon, oððe lytel ðǽm ðe hié micel sceoldon, Past. 321, 17. Þet hió him nēren máran ondeta þonne hit árǽded wæs on Ædelbaldes dæge, Cht. Th. 70, 25. **V.** _add:_—Ne Godwine eorl, ne oþre men þe mycel mihton wealdan, Chr. 1036; P. 158, 20. **V a.** in a prepositional phrase:—On ánum dæge, oððe on twám, oþþe be ðám mǽstan on þrim, Hml. Th. i. 594, 25. v. for-, med-, medum-, níd (?), un-, un-gesceád-micel.

**micel-ǽte.** _Add:_—Sífre, ná mycelǽte _sobrius, non multum aedax,_ R. Ben. I. 61, 5: 20, 14. Ne beó hē druncengeorn, ne beó hē tó slápol, ne beó hē tó micelǽte, Ll. Th. ii. 416, 15.

**micel-heáfded.** _l._ -heáfdede.

**micelian.** II. _add:_—Hiǽ brǽdaþ þwænge heora and micclaþ (miclas, L.) fasu heora _dilatant philacteria sua, et magnificant fimbrias,_ Mt. R. 23, 5. Mic[liaþ], An. Ox. 61, 36. **III.** _add:_—Miclade God _magnificens Deum,_ Lk. L. R. 18, 43.

**micel-ness.** I. _add:_ I a. _a mass:_—Weard upp áscoten swȳðlicu mycelnes þæs ungemētan stánclifes _ingentis saxi moles erupta est,_ Gr. D. 12, 9. Eall tōweaxen mid mycelnessum þára clífstána _saxorum molibus asperum,_ 159, 26. II. _add:_—Hū manigfeald is seó mycelnes þínre swētnesse _quam magna multitudo dulcedinis tuae,_ Ps. Th. 30, 21. Þá þe þǽre mycelnesse hiora spēda gylpað _qui multitudine abundantiarum suarum gloriabuntur,_ 48, 6. II a. _quantity, amount:_—Seó ylece mycelnes (_quantitas_) sealmsanges, R. Ben. 34, 9. **III.** _add:_ III a. _a great thing, great deed:_—God worhte mycelnessa (_magnalia_) on Egipta lande, Ps. L. 105. 21. v. ofer-micelness.

**micelu.** _Add:_—Heó hafað sǽd on grēnum coddum on ðǽre mycele þe pysan, Lch. i. 316, 10. [_O. L. Ger._ mikili.]

**micelung.** _Add:_ glory:—Áhefen ys þín myclung ofer heofonas _elevata est magnificentia tua super caelos,_ Ps. Th. 8, 2.

**micga.** _Add:_—Hí beguton hine ealne mid ealdum miggan ... se migga þurh Godes mihte weard tó swētum stence áwend, Hml. S. 35, 153-157.

**micge.** _Add:_—His micgge bið blódreád, Lch. ii. 198, 19. Beðe mid hættre cū micgan (cūmicgan?), iii. 10, 20. [v. _N. E. D._ mig. _O. L. Ger._ migge.]

**micgern.** _Take here_ mycgern, _where for bracket substitute:_ [v. _N. E. D._ midgern. _O. L. Ger._ (Gallée) mid-garni _aruina:_ _O. H. Ger._ mitti-garni.], _and add:_—Of micgerne _aruina .i. adeps_ l _pinguedo,_ An. Ox. 2, 105. Mycgernne _seuo,_ 2763. Micgernu _exugiam,_ Lch. i. lxxiv. 3. Midirnan, lxx. 2.

**mid.** II. _add:_—His here geseah þæt hē mid þȳ horse áfeóll, Ors. 3, 7; S. 118, 4. Se wer þe mid his ágene (-on, _v. l._) wíf bið slǽpende, Bd. 1, 27; Sch. 86, 1. Ána mid him sylfum _alone by himself,_ Gr. D. 105, 29: 32: 106. 24. **II a.** where there is combination to complete or form a whole:—Sumne dǽl landes, ðæt synd twá hída mid ðám ðe hē ǽr hæfde, and mid ðám hrófleásan lande _a portion of land, that is two hides with what he had before and with the roofless land,_ i. e. what he had before and the roofless land taken together make up the two hides, the portion granted, C. D. iv. 262, 13-14. **IV.** _add:_—Albanus eóde út mid ðæs preóstes hacelan (_wearing the priest's dress;_ cf. Sēs Albanus gegyrede hine mid þæs cuman munucgegyrelan _hospitis habitu indutus,_ Bd. 1, 7; Sch. 20, 25), Hml. S. 19, 36. Þá sprǽc ic on þá mǽgas mid þē erfegewrite (_having the deed with me_), Cht. Th. 167, 18. **VI.** _add:_—Henna gelíce þám þe mid ús (_apud nos_) beóð reádes híwes, Nar. 34, 1. Þone Hǽlend þe becōm tó manuum mid Iūdēiscum folce, Hml. S. 24, 89. Mid weálandum, Gen. 2706. **VII.** _add:_—Gestód Rōmeburg xii winter mid miclum welum, Ors. 6, 1; S. 254, 6. Hē geseah ǽnne wer standan mid átogenum sweorde _vidit virum stantem, evaginatum tenentem gladium,_ Jos. 5, 13: Hml. S. 25, 583. Is se lǽssa man betere ... mid gesundfulnysse þonne se unhála beó ..., Hml. A. 40, 410. His mánfulla gebedda mid Arrianiscum gedwylde dweligende lyfode, Hml. S. 31, 653. **VIII.** _add:_—Ðȳ lǽs hié mid ðȳ tóle ðæt hále líc gewierden, Past. 365, 11. Hí ne dorston þæt hálige hús mid ingange geneósian, Hml. Th. I. 504, 10. **IX.** _add:_—Hē mid ðám dæge eóde him út of ðám scræfe, Hml. S. 23, 489. Hē wæs mid eallum his lífe ymb Godes þeówdōm ábisgod, Bl. H. 211, 31. **X.** _add:_—Gehlade áne cuppan fulle forð mid ðám streáme, Lch. iii. 74. 14. **XI.** _add:_—Mitte þe hit þá þǽre eádegan tíde neálǣhte, Verc. Först. 96, 20: 97, 12. **XII.** _add:_ (1) cf. II.:—Hē þæt heáfod hēt Iuliuse onsendan and his hring mid, Ors. 5, 12; S. 242, 18: 6, 17; S. 270, 23. Cwōman mysce manige, mid wǽrun gnættas, Ps. Th. 104, 27. Hit eall mid fȳre forbærned, and hē sylf mid forwyrðeð, Verc. Först. 120, 19.

Hié sylfe gáð mid, 128, 10: Hml. Th. i. 598, 2. Him faraÞ mid Godes englas, 456, 23. Ælcum welwyrcendum God mid beó mydwyrhta, Solil. H. 30, 14. Nāman hí him wealhstodas mid, Bd. 1, 25; Sch. 52, 13. (2) cf. **IV.**:—NimaÞ þis hrægl and scrýdaÞ eów mid, Gr. D. 202, 28. Sóna swā se hræfu þā cartan geseah, þā genam hē hig sóna and gewāt mid on þæue senu *corvus, ut chartulam prospexit, rapido forcipe arripuit*, Guth. Gr. 141, 6. Þā gewǣda þe heó bewunden wæs mid, Hml. S. 20, 94. Mid ðӯ tóle ðe hié sceoldon mid ðæt unhāle āweg āceorfan, Past. 365, 12. v. þǣr-mid.

**midd.** **I.** *add:*—Be ānre līnan wæs āwriten anlang middes þæs þōþeres, Solil. H. 20, 17. Betwux þām eórode middan, Hml. S. 25, 583. On middum dǣm ofne, Past. 269, 1. On midre sǣ, 431, 30. On midde þā sǣ *in cor maris*, Ps. Th. 45, 2. On midde þā sceade deáðes *in medio umbrae mortis*, 22, 4. Betwih midde þreátas *inter medios cleros*, Ps. Vos. 67, 14. Heora ǣgþer hæfde his folc on þrim heápum, and hié selfe wǣron on þǣm midmestan, Ors. 5, 12; S. 242, 3. **II.** *add:* (cf. *the last passage with* midde-niht):—Hī tó ðām middan wintran eódou heom tó heora garwan feorme, Chr. 1006; P. 136, 24. v. efen-mid.

**midd,** es; *n. The middle:*—On midde manegra *in medio multorum*, Ps. L. 108, 30. [*O. H. Ger.* in mitte: *Icel.* mið; *n.*]

**mid-dæg.** *Add:*—Se middæg wæs fram Abraham oð Móysen, Hml. Th. ii. 74, 19. Seó tíd middæges, Hml. S. 23 b, 160. Hwæt dēstū gif ic tó mergen middeges gebíde? *what wilt thou do if to-morrow I live to see midday?*, Hml. S. 3, 590. Fram middæge oð nōn *a sexta hora usque ad horam nonam*, 27, 188.

**middæg-lic.** *Add:* Middæglecum, Ps. Vos. 90, 6.

**middæg-þegnung,** e; *f. Midday-meal, dinner.* v. þegnung; **V.**:—Sylle man tó middægþenunge (*ad sextam*) twām and twām ān tyl cӯssticce ... and on æfen ān cӯssticce, Chrd. 15, 2.

**middan-eard.** *Add:*—Þā tōweardan frēcednyssa þises losigendlican middaneardes, Hml. Th. i. 538, 7.

**middanearden;** *adj. Mundane, worldly:*—Lufu Godes streclíce āsyndraÞ manu fram middaneardenre (*mundano*) and flǣsclicre lufe, Scint. 16, 16.

**middaneardlic.** **I.** *add:*—Ealle middaneardlice ðing beóð geendode, Hml. Th. i. 538, 35. **II.** *add:*—His mód āwrecce hē of middaneardlicum gedwyldum, Hml. A. 53, 74. v. middangeard-lic.

**middan-geard.** **I.** *add:*—Lengra ðonne eal middangeard oð ðe eorðe, Sal. K. 150. 14. Beorhtran ðonne ealles middangeardes eorðe, 148, 21: 150, 6. His handa sint brādran ðonne xɪɪ middangeardas, 11. Ðeáh ðe seofon middangeardas sӯn ealle on efn ābrǣdde on þisses ānes onlícnysse, 29. **II.** *add:*—Ðeáh ðe eal middangeard sӯ fram Adames frymðe edniówe geworden, and ānra gehwylc ... mōte lifigan ðreó hund wintra, Sal. K. 148, 33.

**middangeard-lic.** *Add:*—Middengeatlicre werednesse *mundane suauitatis*, An. Ox. 11. 42.

**middangeard-tōdǣlend** *glosses* cosmographus, *mundi descriptor*, Hpt. 31, 8, 125.

**middan-sumor, -winter.** *Add:*—Ingang þære middanwintres (*this seems certainly a compound*) tīdæ, Chr. 1016; P. 147, 19.

**midde.** *Add:*—On middan þǣre flóre his botles *in medio tuguriunculi*, Hml. Th. ii. 144, 3. v. æle-midde.

**middel.** *Add:* **I.** *the middle point* or *part* of a line, area, volume, number, &c.:—Þ hīw byð gecīged omoeuteleuton swā oft swā se middel and se ӯtemesta dǣl geendað on gelícum stæfgefēge, Angl. viii. 332, 13. **II.** *the position of being among* or *surrounded by a number* of people or *within* a town, &c., *midst* of:—Hē hleóp on ðone mere and stód on ðāra midle *he jumped into the mere and stood in the midst of them* (the thirty-nine soldiers), Shrn. 62, 10. Hē wæs lytel in ðām midle Crīstes þegna (*in medio discipulorum*), Gr. D. 218, 1. Ne wyrð seó nǣfre onwend þā hwíle þe God byð on hire midle, Ps. Th. 45, 4. **III.** *the middle* of the body:—Oð middil þube (*puue*, MS.) *tenus*, Hpt. 33. 251, 25.

**middel;** *adj.* *Add:*—Foreweard fót *planta*, middel fót (middel-fót?) *subtel*, Wrt. Voc. i. 45, 3. Andlang eá on middel gewæd (middel-gewæd?) ... andlang fleótes tóemnes middelbyrum, C. D. B. ii. 519, 14. Gif gē slāpað betwih midle (middele, Ps. Spl.) þreátas *si dormiatis inter medios cleros*, Ps. Cam. 67, 14. Ondlong ðæs æceres tó ðǣm midlestan wícwege, C. D. iii. 260, 11. In þone midlestan holan weg, Swt. A. S. Rdr. ii. 203, 8.

**middel-ǣdr,** e; *f. A middle vein, median vein:*—Lǣt him blód of innanearme of þære miclan ǣdre þære middelǣdre, Lch. ii. 234, 6. Sceal mon on þǣre middelǣdre blód lǣtan, 210, 11.

**middel-bӯre** *a middle shed* (?). v. middel; *adj.*

**middel-fót.** v. middel; *adj.*

**middel-hrycg,** es; *m. A ridge of land lying between two streams:*—Of lyllan bróce on middelhrycg; of middelhrycge on herepaðford, Cht. Crw. 1, 19. v. p. 52.

**middel-ríce,** es; *n. A middle kingdom, a kingdom lying between two others:*—Earnulf wunode on þǣm londe be-eástan Rín, and Róþulf fēng tó þǣm middelríce, and Oda tó þǣm westdǣle, Chr. 887; P. 80, 24.

**midde-niht** (?) *midnight:*—Gif þunor cumeð on forautniht ... Gif hē cymð on middeniht (midde niht?) ... Gif hē on dæg cumð, Archiv cxx. 47, 12–16. [*In favour of* midde-niht *as well as* mid-niht *may be noted* midde-sumor, midde-winter *as well as* mid-sumor, mid-winter: *further the form* midne-dæg (q. v.) *seems to show that an oblique case might get compounded with a noun, and the compound be used as a nominative. The same may have happened with* midder-niht.] v. midd; **II.** *last passage.*

**midder-niht** (?) *midnight:*—On ēfentīd ł on middernæht (midder [= midre?] næht; middum næht, L.) *sero an media nocte*, Mk. R. 13, 35. Æd middernæht, Lk. p. 7, 3: Lk. L. R. 11, 5. [Cf. *Ger.* mitternacht *from O. H. Ger.* zi mittern naht.]

**middeweard.** *Add:*—Middeweard se spaca bið ǣgðrum (ende) emnneáh, Bt. 39, 7; F. 222, 8. On middeweardum hire ríce bió getimbrede Babylonia, Ors. 2, 1; S. 62, 14: 2, 4; S. 74, 11. On þā lytlan dūne middeweardre, C. D. ii. 249, 31. Tó gemēnan hylle middeweardne, v. 100, 21. ¶ *as a noun* :—On middaweardan hire (heora) *in medio eius* (*eorum*), Ps. L. 54, 11, 16. Middeweardum, 136, 2. On middeweardum þines freólsas, 73, 4.

**midde-winter.** *Add:*—Maria onfēng God on hyre innoð, and hine bær oð middewintres mæssedæg and hine þā ācende, Hml. Th. i. 200, 28. On myddewintres mæssenyht, Lk. 2, 1, rbc. In þære middewintres tíde, Chr. 1006; P. 137, 14: 1016; P. 146, 22. Tó þām midewintre wæs se cyng on Gleáweceastre, 1085; P. 216, 10. Hē wæs on Westmynstre þone midewinter, 1075; P. 212, 6. Ou ðon .xl. dæg ofer midewinter, 762; P. 51, 13. Tó þām ymbrene ǣr myddawintrau (-wintra?), Lk. 1, 26, rbc.

**mid-ferhtness.** The Latin original of the passage is: Si pueritia, si adolescentia, si iuuentus eorum exstitit sine querela ... qualis esse potuit eorum senectus?, Archiv cxxii. 247, 10–13.

**mid-gesíþ** (?):—Midgesíðum emhlenned *sodalibus vallatus*, Hpt. Gl. 422, 38. *Napier* (An. Ox. 680, *note*) *from this passage deduces a* midgesíþ (cf. *Goth.* miþ-gasinþa) *on the ground that* mid *as preposition here would be unsuitable. But if the construction with verbs similar to* emhlenned *is noted* (e.g. ymb-gyrdan, -habban, -hegian, -hīpan) *it will be seen that* mid *is a usual construction, so that* mid gesíðum *seems to be quite unobjectionable.*

**mid-hilte,** an; *f. The middle part of the hilt:*—Midhilte *capulus, manubrium gladii* vel *uniuscuiusque rei*, Wülck. Gl. 199, 21. [Cf. *Icel.* meðal-kafli *the middle piece of the haft.*]

**mid-hlít** *fellowship:*—Gyf hwylc ... tó andetnesse cuman nele fram cirycean hē is tó ānyðanne and fram gemǣnsumunge and midhlӯte geleáffulra (*a communione et consortio fidelium*), Nap. 45.

**-midian.** v. ā-midian, Ps. Rdr. 286, 6.

**mid-irfenuma,** an; *m. A co-heir:*—Þ on yrfwerdnysse his midyrfenuma (*coheres*) þū sӯ, Scint. 148, 4.

**midl.** *l.* mídl, mīþl, *and add:*—Swā horsum mídlu (*frena*) synd on tó āsettenne, Scint. 55, 11. [*O. H. Ger.* mindil *lupatum*.]

**-midleahtrian.** v. ge-midleahtrian.

**midlen.** *Add:*—Wē aufēngum þine mildheortnesse on þām midlene þínes temples (*in medio templi tui*), R. Ben. 83, 24.

**midlen;** *adj. That is in the middle, midmost:*—Sume syndon *localia, propinquus* gehende, *longinquus* fyrlen, *medioximus* midlen, Ælfc. Gr. Z. 14, 21.

**mid-lencten.** *Add:*—On mydlengtenes wucan on Tӯwesdæg, Jn. 7, 14 rbc. Hæfde Eádwerd cing witena gemōt on Lunden tó midlencten, Chr. 1050; P. 171, 37. Tó midlengtene, 1094; P. 229, 4. .vii. nihton ǣr midlenctene, 1055; P. 185, 5.

**midl-hring, midlian** *to bridle.* *l.* mídl-hring, mídlian.

**midlung.** *Add:*—Tó midlunge fyrdwícana heora *in medio castrorum eorum*, Ps. L. 77, 28. On midlunge mínra daga *in dimidio dierum meorum*, 101, 25.

**midnæddran:**—Ofer næddran and midnæddran (mid næddran (?) *basiliscum*: *the glosser seems to have taken* -cum *as a preposition suffixed, and to have thought* basiliscum = *cum basilis*) þū gæst, Ps. Spl. 90, 13.

**midne-dæg.** *Add:*—Se dæg wæs on þeóstre niht gecierred fram midnedæg (middum dæge, v. l.) oþ nōn, Shrn. 67, 18. On ærnemerigen, on undern, on midnedæg, and on ðǣre endlyftan tíde, Hml. Th. ii. 74, 9.

**mid-ness.** *Add:*—In hiora midnesse, Shrn. 36, 14.

**midne-sumor** (?) *midsummer:*—Ofer þone midnesumor (midne sumor (?), *but cf.* midne-dæg), Chr. 1006; P. 136, 12. v. midd; **II.**

**mid-síþegian** *to accompany:*—Midsӯðegodon *comitantur*, Hpt. 31, 16, 426: 13, 310. Midsӯðegod *comitata*, 12, 273. Cf. mid-síþian.

**mid-síþium** = (?) mid gesíþum, An. Ox. 680. v. mid-gesíþ (?).

**mid-spreca.** *Add:*—Sege ūs þ sóðe būton ælcon leáse, and wē beóð þíne geholan and ealne weg þíne midsprecan, Hml. S. 23, 590. Leahtra auspecan and manna midspecan (*liberatores*), Chrd. 62, 26.

**mid-sprecende** *speaking on behalf of:*—Ðū þe wǣre mydsprecende (-sprecend *later* MS. v. E. S. 49, 350) þām Hǣlende, Nic. 6, 24. v. mid-spreca.

**mid-streám**, es; _m. Midstream_:—Andlang midstreámes, C. D. v. 380, 12.

**mid-sumor.** _Add_:—On .xii. kl. Iulius byð sunstede, þ ys on Lýden _solstitium_, and on Englisc midsumor, Angl. viii. 311, 9.

**Midsumor-mónaþ** _June_, Menol. Fox (at end); Hickes i. 215.

**mid-þeahtian** _to consent_:—Ná midþeahtien wiþerwenglum _ne consentiant adversariis_, Ps. Rdr. 290, 1.

**mid-þeówan.** v. þeówan; I.

**mid-þolian** _to compassionate_:—Midþolian _conpati_, Scint. 149, 9. Mildheortnyss fram midþoligende fremedre yrmðe nama gehlét _misericordia a conpatiendo aliene miserie uocabulum sortita est_, 147, 3: 148, 16.

**mid-þrowung**, e; _f. Compassion_:—Midþrowung _conpassio_, Scint. 149, 5. Midþrowunge and frófre _conpassionis et consolationis_, 159, 9. þurh midþrowunge néhstes _per conpassionem proximi_, 148, 19.

**mid-weg.** _Add_:—Þá þá hé wæs on midwege _cum in medium iter venisset_, Gr. D. 314, 11. Ær þám þe hé tó midwege cóme _before he had gone half way_, Hml. S. 31, 946.

**mid-winter.** _Add_:—Fallum æhtemannum gebyreð midwintres feorm, Ll. Th. I. 436, 33. Se kyng wæs þone midwintres dæig on Eoferwíc, Chr. 1069; P. 204, 27. Se kyng wæs þone midwinter on Westmynstre, 1076; P. 212, 23.

**Midwinter-mónaþ** _December_, Menol. Fox (at end); Hickes i. 215.

**mid-wunung.** _Add_: _society, fellowship, communion_:—Neód ys þ hine tógeférlæce gódra midwununge _necesse est ut se associet bonorum consortio_, Scint. 6, 3. Be midwununge (_consortio_) gódra and yfelra, 191, 1. Leóhtes éces midwuninge _lucis æternæ consortium_, Angl. xiii. 380, 209. Yfelra þeáwas and midwununga (_consortia_), Scint. 192, 4.

**mígan.** _Add_: with dat. of matter discharged:—Se man míhð wormse, Lch. ii. 208, 5. Lendenseóce men mígað blóde and sande, 232, 10. Gif hé gemígan ne mæge, and gif hé blóde míge, 8, 24.

**migoþa.** _Add_:—Migeðan _lotia_, An. Ox. 17, 28.

**míl.** _Add_:—Þ lond is on lenge and on bræde þæs miclan mílgetæles .cxxxiii. and án half míl (_.cxxxiii. et dimidium miliarium_), Nar. 33, 24. Wæs se mere mid wudu beweaxen míle brædo _erat circumdatum silua mille passus tum patens_, 12, 8. For unfriðe man mót freólsæfenan nýde fulfaran betweónan Eferwíc and six míla gemeta, Ll. Th. ii. 298, 27.

**-milce.** v. þri-milce.

**milcen.** _Add_:—Gif eala sié áwerd oþþe meolcen mete, Lch. ii. 14, 18.

**milde.** I. _add_: Lufu bið mildu _caritas benigna est_, Past. 222, 5. II. _add_:—Þá wearð Tiberius Rómánum swá wráð and swá heard swá hé him ær wæs milde and iépe _inmutata est Tiberii modestia, atque ex mansuetissimo principe saevissima bestia exarsit_, Ors. 6, 2; S. 254, 30.

**mildelíce.** _Add_:—Mildelíce _misericorditer_, Chrd. 49, 11. Uton wendan ús tó úrum Drihtne, hé ús wyle mildelíce underfón, Wlfst. 142, 10. Se cyning andwyrde þære cwéne swíðe mildelíce, Hml. A. 101, 304. Hé hit swíðe mildlíce ágeaf ðám biscop, C. D. v. 140, 29.

**mild-heort.** II. _add_:—Ábiddaþ God eádmódlíce, for þám hé is swíþe rúmmód and swíðe mildheort, Bt. 42; F. 258, 22: An. 1287. Þú eart mín Drihten God dædum mildheort _tu, Domine, Deus meus, miserator et multum misericors_, Ps. Th. 85, 14. v. un-mildheort.

**mildheort-líc**; _adj. Merciful, compassionate_:—Hé hit má dyde on wælgrimnesse wyllan þonne mid ænigre mildheortlicre forgifnesse, Gr. D. 319, 29. Wer ábysgod on mildheortlicum weorcum _vir misericordiae actibus deditus_, 301, 18.

**mildheortlíce.** _Add_:—Críst ús mildheortlíce fram deófles ðeóstrum álýsde, Hml. Th. i. 604, 3: Hml. A. 163, 269. Wé sceolon déman for úres Drihtnes lufon æfre mildheortlíce . . . bútan wælhreównysse, 9, 221. Scel bión on ðæm reccere ðæt hé sié ryhtlíce and mildheortlíce rædende his hiéremonnum and mildheortlíce witniende _erga subditos suos inesse rectoribus debet et juste consulens misericordia, et pie saeviens disciplina_, Past. 125, 5. Hé suá micle iéðelícor bið gefriðod from his ágnum costungum suá hé mildheortlícor (_misericordius_) bið geswenced mid ððerra monna costungum, 107, 3.

**mild-hleahter.** _Dele, and read_ mid hleahtre _in_ Ps. Spl. 34, 19. v. Ps. Cam. 34, 16.

**mild-ness**, e; _f. Mildness, gentleness_:—Ne sceal swá liðe mildnes (_lenitas_) beón þ ne forhæbbe þá syngunge, Chrd. 62, 21. [_O. H. Ger._ miltnissa _misericordia_.]

**míl-gemearc.** _Add_: v. ge-mearcian; I a.

**míl-gemet.** _Add_:—Út on þone feld; ðæt út tó mílgemete, C. D. v. 382, 2.

**míl-getæl.** _Add_:—Þæs læssan mílgetæles .ccc. and þæs máran .cc., Nar. 33, 18: 22.

**milisc.** _Add_: v. súr-milisc: **miliscian.** _Add_: v. ge-milscod.

**milite**; _pl. Soldiers_:—Þá genámon hié þá milite . . . Wæron þá milite þæs geréfan men, Nap. 45. Þá milite geworhton þyrnene coronan and setton on his heáfod (_milites praesidis (þæs geroefe kempe, R.) . . . plectentes coronam de spinis posuerunt super caput ejus_, Mt. 27, 27–29), 13, 22. _See next word_.

---

**militisc**; _adj. Military_:—Sumes militisces mannes (sumes þegenes, _v. l._) hors _equus cujusdam militis_, Gr. D. 77, 32. Þæs militiscan mannes (þæs þegenes, _v. l._) béue, 78, 27. Wæron militisce men (_milites_) farende, 194, 13.

**miltan.** I b. _add_:—Wið þære wambe þe late mylt, Lch. ii. 194, 23. II. _these examples may be taken to_ meltan. v. á-, for-miltan; sám-milt.

**milte.** _Add_: milt, es; _m._:—Þindeþ him se milt, Lch. ii. 232, 11.

**-milte.** v. eáþ-, twi-, un-eáþ-milte.

**milte-seóc.** _Add_: milt-seóc:—Wið miltan sáre, genim þás wyrte . . . heó þone milteseócan gehæleþ, Lch. i. 276, 16.

**miltestre.** _Add_:—Sum myltestre þurh deófles tyhtince þóhte þ heó his hlísan ámyrran wolde, Hml. A. 195, 19. Sum wíf hátte Uenus, swá fracod on gálnysse ðæt hire fæder hí hæfde, and eác hire bróðor, on myltestrena wísan, Sal. K. 123. 91. [_Lat._ meretrix.]

**miltestre-ærn**, -ern (?) _a brothel_:—[Tó] myltest[re]erne (cf. meltestrum húse, 4018) [_ad_] lupanar, An. Ox. 8, 225. Cf. miltestre-hús.

**milts.** _Add_:—Ðá ongann hé (_Orpheus_) biddan hiora (_the Fates_) miltse; þá ongunnon hí wépan mid him, Bt. 35, 6; F. 168, 28. Milse _ueniam_, An. Ox. 5, 43. [v. _N. E. D._ milce.] v. un-milts.

**miltsian.** _Add_:—Ic mildsiende eom mínum þám getreówum, Wlfst. 229, 13. [v. _N. E. D._ milce.]

**miltsiend.** _Add_:—Mildheort and miltsigend (mildsend, Ps. Srt.) Drihten _misericors et miserator Dominus_, Ps. L. 110, 4. Bewépað eówere fyrnleahtras . . . þæt se árfæsta miltsigend eówere behreówsunge underfó, Hml. Th. ii. 420, 17. þ hé sý úre mildsigend and úre frefrigend, Verc. Först. 137, 3.

**miltsigend-líc.** _Add_: v. un-miltsigendlic.

**miltsung.** _Add_:—Mildsunga (_miserationes_) his ofer ealle weorc his, Ps. L. 144, 9. v. ge-miltsung.

**-mimorlíce.** v. ge-mimorlíce.

**min.** [_For another explanation of this word see N. E. D._ min, _where_ minne _is taken as the nominative form: but the word may be taken as belonging to the same declension as_ mid[d]; _pl._ midde, _so_ min[n]; _pl._ minne. _Holthausen rejects the word altogether._ v. Beiblatt, xvi. 228.] I. _add_ (?) :—On minnan linche, C. D. B. iii. 494, 31. II. _add_:—Wið feóndes hond and . . wið malscrunge minra wihta, Lch. iii. 36, 14.

**mín.** I. _add_:—Míre andetnysse leóhtfæt, Hml. S. 23, 810. III. _add_:—Ne þearf ic yrfestól eaforan bytlian ænegum mínra, Gen. 2177.

**min-dóm.** _The passage from_ Ps. Th. 54, 7 _is_:—Ic bíde þæs beornes þe mé bóte eft mindóm and mægenes hreóh. _The last line is too short, perhaps it might be completed by writing_ minne _after_ mindóm? _But see_ min.

**mín-líce.** _Add_: [cf. Icel. mín-ligr.]

**minsung.** _Add_:—Forhæfednys, minsung, gneáðnys _parsimonia, i. abstinentia_, An. Ox. 3748.

**minte.** _Add_:—Brócminte and óþre mintan, Lch. iii. 6, 14. ¶ the word occurs in several local names. v. C. D. vi. 315. [_From Latin_ menta, mentha.]

**mirce**, es; _n. For another rendering of_ An. 1315 _see_ ge-scirdan.

**-mirce**; _n._ v. ge-mirce: -mirce; _adj._ v. æ-mirce: mircels; IV. _add_: Hml. S. 26, 163: -mircian, -mircung. v. ge-mircian, -mircung.

**míre or mýre**, an; _f. An ant, mire in_ pis-mire. The word occurs in the nickname Mýran heáfod, Chr. 1010; P. 140, 13, applied to þurcytel, who is called in Fl. Wig. _Danicus_ minister. The nickname is in that chronicle glossed by 'equae caput,' but in H. Hunt. by 'caput formicae.' [Cf. _Dan._ myre : _Swed._ myra : _Icel._ maurr : _and Du._ mier. _See too_:—_Natura formicae._ Ðe mire is magti, Misc. 8, 234. Ðe mire muneð us mete to tilen, 9, 273. v. _N. E. D._ mire.]

**mirgan**, &c. v. myrgan, &c.

**mirran.** I. _add_:—Hú ðonne gyf ðé myrrað and lettað þæs líchoman mettrimnysse _dolor corporis te fortasse vi sua commovet_, Solil. H. 40, 6. Ælfere ealdorman and óþre manega munucregol myrdon, Chr. 975; P. 121, 26. II. _add_: v. mirrend. v. on-mirran.

**mirrend**, es; _m. A waster, squanderer._ v. mirran; II. :—Se hordere ne sceal beón myrrend (_prodigus_), Chrd. 19, 13. Ná se hordere ná sí cystig oðde myrrent æhte _neque cellarius prodigus sit aut stirpator substantiæ monasterii_, R. Ben. 1. 62, 3.

**mirt, myrt.** _Dele, and see_ mertze: miru. v. geoguþ-miru: **mis-beódan.** _Add_: [v. _N. E. D._ mis-bede.]: **mis-bregdan**; _pp._ -bróden (_not_ broden). _Add_: [cf. _H. S._ misbreyde _an offence, misdeed._]: **mis-can.** _For_ Ps. Th. 44, _l._ 41, _and add_: v. ge-miscan.

**mis-cenning**, e; _f. A wrong declaration_ (v. cennan; II.), _a shifting of the ground of an action after it has come into court; the fine for such variation, the right to accept such fines_ (often the subject of grant by the king):—Icc kíðe ðat icc habbe geunnen . . . miskenninge, C. D. iv. 213, 11: 215, 7, _and often._ [v. _N. E. D._ mis-kenning.]

**mis-crocettan** (-crócettan?). _Add_: v. crácettan.

**mis-cwéman** _to displease_:—Á hí ymbe þ wæron, hú hí ðé miscwémdon, Hml. S. 23, 287. [v. _N. E. D._ misqueme.]

**mis-cweþan.** I. *add:*—Miscwedenes wordes *barbarismi*, An. Ox. 2, 485.

**mis-dǽd.** *Add:*—Unrihthǽmed, árleásta fela, mān and morðor, mis-dǽda worn, Met. 9. 7. Úrum misdǽdum *impietatibus nostris*, Ps. Th. 64, 3. Âhwerf nū fram synnum and fram misdēdum mīnra gylta þīne ansíone *averte faciem tuam a peccatis meis*, Ps. C. 84.

**mis-fadian.** *Add:*—Se abbod nān þing ne misfadige (miss-, *v. l.*) ne unrihtlíce ne geendebyrde, swylce hē fréolíce dōn mōte þæt, þæt him lícige *nec abbas quasi libera utens potestate injuste disponat aliquid*, R. Ben. 113, 25.

**mis-faran;** I. *add:*—Nū secgað sume menn þ him sceole gelimpan swā swā him gesceapen wæs and geset æt fruman, and ne magon forbúgan þ hī misfaran ne sceolan. Nū secge wē gif hit swā beón sceal, þ hit is unnyt bebod . . . 'Declina a malo et fac bonum,' Hml. S. 17, 224. [v. *N. E. D.* misfare.]

**mis-feng,** es; *m. A mistake, fault, misdeed:*—Hē ūs gegearwað þa heofonlican for ðām eorðlicum . . . gif wē ælmyssan dōn willað on ūrum lífe, and gif wē dǽdbóte dōn willaþ ūrra misfenga, Nap. 45.

**mis-féran.** *Add:* [v. *N. E. D.* misfere.]

**mis-gewider.** *l.* -gewidere. Cf. un-gewidere.

**mis-healdan;** *p.* -heóld *To neglect, slight a person:*—Nū for mane-gum geárum, þā þā hī mishéoldon þone heofonlican God, hī wurdon gehergode *ante hos annos, cum recessissent a via quam dederat illis Deus, exterminati sunt proeliis*, Hml. A. 106, 130.

**mis-híran.** *Add:* [v. *N. E. D.* mishear.]

**mis-hworfen.** *Add:*—Mishworfenre tíde, An. Ox. 3836.

**mis-lǽdan.** *Add:*—Dysig bið se wegférenda man sē ðe nimð þone smēðan weg þe hine mislǽt, and forlǽt ðone sticolan þe hine gebrincð tō ðǽre byrig, Hml. Th. i. 164, 8.

**mis-lǽran.** *Add:* [v. *N. E. D.* mislear.]

**mis-lár.** *Substitute: Incitement to evil, suggestion:*—Sē þe gelustful-lunge gemīdlað gálfulre mislāre (*suggestionis*), Scint. 88, 7. Gif forman mislāre (*suggestioni*) nā byþ wiðstanden, 210, 10. Onþæslice gewilnunga flǽsclicra mislāra *inportunas desideriorum carnalium suggestiones*, 33, 20. Misl[āra?] *inlecebras*, An. Ox. 56, 323. [Þe defies tuihting and mislore, O. E. Hml. ii. 29, 2.]

**mis-libban.** *Add:* [v. *N. E. D.* mislive.]

**mis-lic.** I. *add:* (1) with a singular noun, where different instances of that which is denoted by the noun occur, *not uniform, different forms of:*—Hū mislic bið mægen þāra cynna, Rä. 81, 8. Þā ic þurh mislic cwealm slōg, Jul. 493. Ic sōðfæstum þurh mislic bleó mōd oncyrre, 363. (2) *different, various:*—Nǽron mislice mettas and drencas, Met. 8, 9. Þæt synt mistlice geearnunga fulfremedra manna, Ps. Th. 44, 15. Gode tō þancunga his mislicra and manigfealdra gesceafta, 18, arg. Þā wyrtge-mang tácniað mistlicu mægen Crístes, 44, 10. [Þe inre is euere iliche; the uttre is mislíche, A. R. 4.]

**mislíce.** I. *add:*—Ðeáh ðe hié mon manigfealdlíce and mislíce styrede, Past. 306, 5. Men mōston ǽr Móyses lage mistlíce libban *men might live according to various systems of law before the law of Moses*, Ll. Th. ii. 368, 13. Manega cynegas wǽron myslíce geworhte (*of various dispositions*), Hml. S. 18, 386. Ne geseah hine nān man náteshwōn yrre . . . ne mislíce geworhtne (*of varying disposition, irresolute*), ac on ánre ánrǽdnysse ǽfre wunigende, 31, 307.

**mis-lícian.** *Add:*—Gif hwæn þises sealmsanges fadung mislícað (*displicuerit*), R. Ben. 44, 14. Swā hwæt swā mē mislícode (miss-, *v. l.*), Gr. D. 3, 18. Ðý lǽs hē mislícige ðām þe hē ǽr hine selfne sealde *ut ei placeat, cui se probavit*, Past. 131, 3. Hira swā tilige ǽgðer ōðrum tō lícianne, ðæt hié ne mislícien hiera Scippende *sic eorum quisque placere studeat conjugi, ut non displiceat conditori*, 393, 26.

**mis-lícness.** *Add:*—For mislícnysse syngigendra sume tō berenne synd, sume tō þreágenne *pro diuersitate peccantium alii portandi sunt, alii castigandi*, Scint. 114, 19.

**mis-limpan.** *Add:*—Ic swīðor ceorude þonne mīn sáwul behōfode þā ðā ic ǽhte forleás . . . oððe mē hwæt mislamp (*any misfortune befell me*) on þises lífes ryne, Angl. xi. 113, 41.

**mis-rǽdan.** *Add: To misread a riddle, give a wrong answer to, misinterpret:*—Swā hwilc man swā mīnne rǽdels riht árǽde, onfó sē mýnre dohtor tō wīfe, and sē ðe hine misrǽde, sý hē beheáfdod, Ap. Th. 3, 11.

**miss** *loss:*—Mycel is mē unbliss mīnra dýrlinga miss, Hml. S. 23, 271. [cf. *Icel.* missir; *m. a loss*; missa; *f.*]

**mis-scrýdan.** *Add:*—Se misscrýdda wæs âworpen on ðā ýttran þeóstru, Hml. Th. i. 530, 21.

**missen-líc.** *Add:*—Is þes middangeard missenlicum wīsum gewliteged, Rä. 32, 1. Hī þā eádignesse begytaþ þurh missenlicu weorc (*per opera diuersa*), Gr. D. 315, 25. Him se steóra bibeád missenlíce gemetu, Sch. 46.

**missenlíce.** *Add:*—Swā nū missenlíce (*or adj.?*) geond þisne middan-geard winde biwáwne weallas stondað, Wand. 75. Hē gumena cynnes manige missenlíce (*under various conditions?*) men of deáðe worde âwehte, An. 583.

**missenlíc-ness.** *Add:*—þ is ân eádignes þe hī þǽr onfóþ, and ungelíc missenlicnes þæs edleánes (*dispar retributionis qualitas*), Gr. D. 315, 24. Seó missenlicnes (*diversitas*) manna líchamena . . . seó missen-licnes manna synna, 333, 23.

**mis-sprecan.** *Add:* [v. *N. E. D.* mis-speak.]

**mist.** *Add:* I. *a cloud of minute particles of water, vapour of water, cloud:*—Hē hēt his cnapan hāwian tō ðǽre sǽ gif ǽnig mist ārise of ðām mycclum brymme, Hml. S. 18,ˊ146. Ðā brǽdas ðæs flǽsces stigon upp on ǽlce healfe geond þā sǽwl swā hit wist wǽre, 23, 38. I a. *a fog, steam, haze:*—Of þǽre eá wǽre reócende se mist unâræfnedlicre fȳl-nesse and unswētes stences *foetoris intolerabilis nebulam exhalans fluvius*, Gr. D. 318, 28. Mid þȳ miste (*nebula*) þæs fūlan stences . . . seó fȳlnes þæs reócendan mistes, 319, 10–11. II. *dimness of eyesight:*—Wiþ eágna miste . . . þ bið lyb wiþ eágena dimnesse, Lch. ii. 30, 11–15. Wurdon his eágan yfele gehefegode mid tóswollenum breáwum and swiðlicum myste, swā þ his seón swȳðe þeóstrodon, Hml. S. 31, 587. III. *what obscures mental vision:*—Hē bið âblend mid ðǽm miste ðāra leásunga *aspersae falsitatis nebulis seductus*, Past. 240, 3. Gif þū ðone wīsdōm selfne geseón wilt, þū ne scealt nēnne myst betweón lǽtan þīnum eágum and hym, Solil. H. 43, 17.

**mis-þeón.** *Add:*—Hwæs cēpð hē, būtan hū hē mage þeónde mis-þeón? *quid agit nisi ut crescendo decrescat?* Chrd. 79, 18.

**mis-þyncan** *to give a wrong idea*, impers. with dat. of person, *to have mistaken ideas:*—Ðā cwæð hē tō ðām cynge: 'Þes man is swīðe æfestful.' Ðā cwæð se cyncg: 'Ðē misþingð (*you are mistaken*); þes iunga man ne æfestigað on nánum ðingum,' Ap. Th. 14, 25.

**mis-tǽcan.** *Add:* [v. *N. E. D.* misteach.]

**mistian.** For mistrian *at end l.* mistran, *and add:* [*Prompt. Parv.* mystyn or grow ropy as wedur and mysty *obnubilo*.]

**mis-tídan.** *Add:* [v. *N. E. D.* mistide]: **mis-timian.** *Add:* [v. *N. E. D.* mistime.]

**mis-tríwan.** *Add:* [cf. *N. E. D.* mistrow.]

**mis-tucian.** *l.* -túcian, *and add:*—Hē beót Libertinum on þ heáfod and on þā ansȳne, oð þ eall his andwlita weard tóswollen and âwannod. Ðā þā hē swā swīðe mid geþersce mistúcod wæs (*vehementer caesus*), Gr. D. 20, 33. Þā hors mid þām spurum mistúcode (geblōdgode, *v. l.*) *equi calcaribus cruentati*, 15, 5.

**mis-wendan.** *Add:* [v. *N. E. D.* mis-wend.]

**mis-wenian** *to misuse, abuse:*—Miswenige (*printed* -penige) *abutatur*, Scint. 224, 10: 225, 8.

**mis-wider** v. mis-gewider. *l.* mis-widere. v. mis-gewidere.

**míte.** For 'tamus' *substitute* 'ta[r]mus (tarmus *blatta, tinea,* Migne),' *and add* (?):—Bibiones vel mustiones muscfleotan *vel* wurma smite (sinite, Wrt., *but see* Wülck. Gl. 121, 23) *l.* (?) mustfleógan *vel* [must] wurmas, míte, Wrt. Voc. i. 23, 75. v. must-fleóge.

**míþan.** *Add:* [v. *N. E. D.* mithe.]

**míþian;** *p.* ode *To conceal, keep from appearing openly:*—Se ealda feónd ne mihte âdreógan þæs wīsan swígiende ne deógollíce þurh swefn míðgian (*the old enemy could not suffer these things in silence nor keep them from being generally known by entrusting them to the secrecy of a dream*), swā swā ǽfre his gewunan, ac mid openlicre gesihþe hē gebróhte hine sylfne beforan eágum þæs ârwyrðan fæder [the original Latin, which seems to have been misunderstood, is : Haec antiquus hostis tacite non ferens, non occulte vel per somnium, sed aperta visione ejusdem Patris oculis sese ingerebat], Gr. D. 122, 3. v. míþan.

**mitta.** *Add:*—Ne scyle nān man blǽcern ǽlan under mittan (*sub modio*), Past. 43, 3. Ðē ele ne âteóraþ ne melu on þīnum mittan (*hydria farinae non deficit, nec lecythus olei minuetur*, 1 Kings xvii. 14), Hml. S. 18, 63. On ǽghwelc þāra fata mihte twēgen mittan oþþe þreó (cf. *hydriae capientes singuli metretas binas vel ternas*, Jn. 2, 6), Shrn. 48, 29. 'Ic sille eów hundteóntig þūsenda mittan hwǽtes' . . . Hig worhton him âne anlícnesse þe . . . mid ðǽre swiðran hand þone hwǽte hlód and mid þām winstran fēt þā mittan træd, Ap. Th. 10, 1–13. [v. *N. E. D.* mit.]

**mittan.** *Add:*—þā heó eft cōm, þā mitte heó hire cild lifiende and gesund, Shrn. 32, 15.

**mixen.** *Add:*—Him (*Job*) wæs his myxen forlǽten þ hē þǽruppan sittan mihte, Hml. S. 30, 200.

**mixen-duncge,** an; *f. Dung from a mixen:*—Myxendincgan ūt drag-an, Angl. ix. 261, 9.

**moc** *muck?* in hlós-moc. v. hlós. [Cf. *Icel.* myki *dung*; moka *to clear away dung*. *M. E.* muk, mok.]

**mód.** I a. *add:*—On hālgum gewrite bið gelōmlíce heáfod gesett for þæs mannes mōde, for ðan ðe þæt heáfod gewissað þām ōðrum limum, swā swā þæt mōd gediht ðā geðōhtas, Hml. Th. i. 612, 11–14. Se wīsdōm is hālig and hine sylfne ætbrēt fram mōdes hīwunge and mynd-leásum geðōhtum, ii. 326, 3. þā onget heó on hyre mōdes gesyhðe hyre ætȳwed beón þæt heó geseah *intellexit in uisione mentis ostensum sibi esse quod uiderat*, Bd. 4, 23; Sch. 478, 12. Ús cōm tō mōde hū Dionisius ymbe bissextum wæs sprecende, Angl. viii. 306, 38. I b. *add:*—Neádian ōðerne tō mâran drænce þonne his mōd wolde *nolentem cogere*

ad bibendum, Hml. A. 93, 25. Eálá gē đeówan ... swā hwæt swā gē wyrcađ, wyrcađ mid mōde, swā swā Gode sylfum servi ... quodcumque facitis ex animo (heartily, A. V.) operamini, sicut Domino (Col. 2, 23), Hml. Th. ii. 326, 23. Ic eów sumes fyrstes geann þ gē eów sylfe beþencean and on beteran mōde gebringan, Hml. S. 23, 188. v. ge-, meaht-, þole-, un-mōd.

-mōd. Add: v. æ-, fæst-, ge-, geþyld-, hefig-, hoh-, hræd-, leás- [v. leásmōd-ness], lytel-, mād-, seóc-, stearc-, strang-, swǽr-, þole-, unrōt-, wāc-, weá-, wiþer-mōd.

mōdegian. v. mōdigian.

mōd-geþanc. Add: I. mind, thoughts:—þ mæg se mon begytan, sē þe his mōdgeđanc æltowe byþ, Gr. D. 2, 5. Ic ondette mīne synna ... for mūđ and mearh and mōdgeþonc, sionwe and sīdan and swýran, Angl. xi. 98, 50. II. a thought:—Swilce beóđ þæs mannes mōdgeþancas ita sunt casus mentis, Gr. D. 6, 6. Hwylc man wāt þæs mannes mōdgeþancas būtan þæs mannes gāst, þe on him sylfum byđ? quis scit hominum quae hominis sunt, nisi spiritus hominis qui est in ipso?, 137, 1.

-mōdian. v. ofer-mōdian.

mōdig. III. add:—Betere biđ þ wīf .. eádmōd on heortan ... þonne þ mǽden beó þe mōdig biđ on heortan, Hml. A. 40, 401. Se mōdiga deófol, Wlfst. 249, 2. Heó (Judith) ofercōm þone mōdigan (Holofernes), 114, 410. Mōdig[e] arrogantes, An. Ox. 56, 233. Drihten hēt ūs beón eádmōde þ wē tō heofonum becōmon, for đan þe þā mōdigan ne magon tō heofonum, Hml. S. 16, 129. III a. applied to a personal attribute:—Æfter þām mōdigan unþeáwe after the vice of pride, Wlfst. 249, 7. V. applied to an animal:—Sum mōdig fearr weorđ āngencga and þære heorde drāfe oferhogode, Hml. Th. i. 502, 11. Se micela ylp þe đā mōdigan fearras mid ealle ofbeát, Hml. A. 63, 285.

mōdigian. Add:—His wuldor is wyrms and meox; nū tō dæg hē mōdegađ, and tō-mergen hē ne biđ (his glory shall be dung and worms; to-day he shall be lifted up, and to-morrow he shall not be found, 1 Macc. 2, 63), Hml. S. 25, 262. Hī āfligdon đā hǽđenan þe mōdegodon ongeán God (cf. they pursued after the proud men, and the work prospered in their hand, 1 Macc. 2, 47), 242. God gewræc his forsewennysse on đǽm ænglum þe unrǣdlīce mōdegodon, 13, 183. þæt nā nān ænlīpig ne mōdige (mōdgige, mōdegige, v. ll.: mōdie, R. Ben. I 111, 2), ne hine nā ne anhebbe, þonne mynstres notu manegum biđ betǣht ut dum utilitas monasterii pluribus committitur, unus non superbiat, R. Ben. 125, 10. þe lǽs þe mōdegodan fýnd heora ne forte superbirent hostes eorum, Cant. M. ad fil. 27 : Hml. Th. i. 578, 13. Se đā wīs byđ, ne wurđ hē nǽfre mōdig. On hwan mæg se mann mōdigan þeáh hē wille?, Hml. S. 16, 373. Seó māre ne sceal mōdigan (mōdigian, v. l.) tō swīđe ofer đā lǽssan, Hml. A. 41, 415. Ontimber [him is] geseald tō mōtgenne materia ei datur superbiendi, R. Ben. I. 110, 4. Gif man āgyte þ hī wyllon mōdiggan odđe prūtian si reperti fuerint superbi aut elati, Chrd. 18, 30. v. eáþ-mōdigian.

mōdig-līce. Add: v. ofer-mōdiglīce.

mōdig-ness. I. add:—þæt byđ mōdignys, þæt ænig man forseó Godes beboda. Seó mōdignyss ys ealra unþeáwa angin and ealra mægna hryre, Wlfst. 249, 4-7. Ælc yfel cymđ of mōdignysse, Hml. A. 40, 405. Geseoh heora mōdignysse and ūre ǣdmōdnysse, 107, 163. Hē on assan hricge rād eádmōdlīce mannum tō bysne þ hī mōdignysse onscunion, Hml. S. 27, 99. v. ofer-, un-mōdignyss.

-mōdigung. v. ofer-mōdigung.

mōd-leás. Add: senseless; cf. mōd; I. a: þū druncena ... þe mōdleás (sine mente) rest, Chrd. 74. 13.

mōd-leást. Add: despondency:—Se syxta unþeáw is þ sē þe tō hlāforde biđ geset, þ hē for mōdleáste ne mæge his mannum dōn steóre, ac biđ hin swā mihtleás on his mōdes strece, þ hē his underþeóddan egesian ne dearr, O. E. Hml. i. 301, 5. Lǣcas cýđdan þām fæder þæs cnihtes mōdleáste (his despondency after being rejected by Agnes), Hml. S. 7, 68.

-mōdlic. v. ofer-mōdlic: mōdlīce. v. ān-, eád- (eáþ-), efen-, ofer-, rūm-mōdlīce.

mōd-lufu. Add:—Hē hine mid bām handum beclypte and mid eallre mōdlufan sette tō his breóstum, Nap. 45.

-mōdness. v. ān-, eád- (eáþ-), glæd-, heáh-, heard-, leás-, leóht-, meagol-, ofer-, or-, rūm-, swiþ-, þole-, wāc-, weá-, wiþer-mōdness.

mōdor. Add: I. a female parent. (1) a woman who has given birth to a child:—Suǣ suǣ cild irnđ tō his mōđer (-ur, v. l.) greádan, Past. 103, 23: Wlfst. 193, 9. Hē wæs Bryttisc on his mōđer healfe, Chr. 1075; P. 202, 7. Hī freónda ne rōhton, ne þæt odđe mēđer (mōđer, v. l.), Hml. S. 5, 45. For đām mycclum geleáfan þǽre mēđer, Hml. Th. ii. 116, 13. Habban gýmene ǣgđer ge đǽre mēđer ge þæs cildes, 196, 19. Wiđ suna moeder (matris) đīnre, Ps. Srt. 49, 20: 68, 9. Of mōdres (mōđer, R., mōđor, W. S.) hrif, Mt. L. 19, 12. Mōđeres, Jn. L. 3, 4. Moederes, Lk. p. 4, 5. Beæftaň his mēđer and his mǣgum, Past. 385, 20. Swā hwylc swā segđ his fæder and mēđer (moeder, L., mōđer matri), Mt. 15, 4. Nū ne sceolon þā mǣdenu heora mōđdru forseón of đām đe hī cōmon, þeáh đe hī beón on mægđhāde lybbende and heora mōđdru beón wīf, Hml. A. 37, 324: 32, 208. Đā mōđdru on heora cildra martyrdōme þrowodon; þæt swurd ... becōm tō đǽra mōđdra heortan, Hml. Th. i. 84, 17-19. Mōđero matres, Mk. L. 10, 30. (2) used of an animal:—Ylp is ormǣte nýten ... Feówer and twēntig mōnđa gǣđ seó mōđor mid folan, Hml. S. 25, 569. Fugelas ne týmađ swā swā ōđre nýtenu, ac ǣrest hit biđ ǣig, and seó mōđor brēt þæt ǣig tō bridde, Hml. Th. i. 250, 23. (3) in extended sense, an ancestress:—Heó (Eve) is ealra libbendra mōđor, Gen. 3, 20. I a. used figuratively of spiritual relationship:—Mǣdenu magon beón Crīstes mōđdru, gif hī wyrcađ on līfe his fæder willan. Eall Crīstes geladung is Crīstes mōđor, for đan đe heó ācenđ Crīstes sylfes limu þurh đā hālgan gife on đām hālgan fulluhte, Hml. A. 33, 216. v. fēster-, god-mōđor. II. applied to things more or less personified:—Geđyld is mōdur and hierde ealra mægena, Past. 215, 19. Se yfela willa ... is mōdur ælces yfeles, 222, 14. Wyrd seó swīđe ealra firena fruma, fǣhđo mōdor, Sal. 443. Ælc đyssera heáfodleahtra hæfđ micelne teám, ac gif wē đā mōdru ācwellađ, þonne beóđ heora bearn ealle āđýdde, Hml. Th. ii. 218, 28. III. applied to a person who acts like a mother. (1) one who shows motherly affection:—Hē ætiéwe his hiéremonnum đæt hē sié hiera fæder on lāre and hiera mōdur on mildheortnesse, Past. 123, 25. (2) one who exercises control, the superior of a female religious community:—Ealle þā sweostor ... for heora mōdor sāwle georne þingedon, Bd. 4, 23; Sch. 479, 10.

mōdor-cynn, es; n. Maternal kin:—Hire mōdorcynn gǣd tō Heinrīce cāsere on the mother's side she was descended from the emperor Henry, Chr. 1067; P. 202, 22.

mōdor-healf (?). v. mōdor; I. i.

mōdor-lic. Add:—Mid mōđerlīce[re] cennincge materna matrice, An. Ox. 1763.

mōdorlīce; adv. Like a mother:—Heó weard gehādod tō abudessan on Elīgmynstre ofer manega mynecena, and heó hī mōdorlīce heóld mid gōdum gebysnungum tō þām gāstlican līfe, Hml. S. 20, 39.

mōdor-lufu, an; f. Love for a mother, filial affection:—'Þis is þīn mōdor, and þū hēld þe for mōdor hafa.' And hē þā, Jōhannes, swā dyde, and hē hié þā in mōdorlufan hæfde, Nap. 45.

mōdrige. Add: A mother's sister:—Buhe hātte wæs Dryhtlāfes mōddrige, Cht. Th. 651, 4. Scē Seaxburh and Scā Æþeldrýđ ... wǣron Annan dohtra ... Đonne wæs Scē Eormenhild Ercenbrihtes dohtor and Seaxburge ... rested Scē Eormenhild on Elīgbyrig mid hyre mēder and mid hyre mōdrian Scē Æđeldrýđa, Lch. iii. 430, 11-25.

mōd-þrýđu. l. þrýþ, and add: cf. hyge-þrýþ.

mōd-þwǣrness. Add:—Se fæder weard tō mycelre mōdþwǣrnysse (monþwǣrnysse, v. l.) gelǣded (ad magnam mansuetudinem perductus), Gr. D. 22, 8 : 48, 29.

mōd-wēn. Substitute: mōd-wynn, e; f. Heart's delight, treasure:—þonne ic forđ āscūfan sceal þæt freán mīnes mōdwyn freodađ middelnihtum when I (a key) push forth what protects my lord's treasure at midnight, i. e. the bolt of the lock, Rä. 87, 7. v. wyn.

mogian. v. for-mogian.

molcen. Add:—Fela henne ǣgru gesleá on ān fæt swā hreáw, geþwere þonne and þicge, and gemenge ǣr wiþ flētan, and nān ōþer molcen þicge, Lch. ii. 264, 26.

molda. Add: [v. N. E. D. mould.] v. mold-gewind.

molde. I. add:—Moldum sablonibus, An. Ox. 7, 99. II. add:—Men ne mihton þā moldan būgian for đeówracan sweartra deófla, Hml. Th. ii. 142, 32.

mold-corn. This should be put before molde.

mold-gewind the top of the head:—þonne se untruma biđ gesmyred on þām moldgewinde (in vertice) and on foranheáfde and on þan þunwengon and on his nebbe, Nap. 46. v. molda.

molsn decay, corruption:—Hī gemētton þone līchaman þæs cildes mid molsne (tabe) gebrosnode and wyrma fulne, Gr. D. 198, 24.

molsniend-lic. v. un-molsniendlic: molsnung. v. for-molsnung.

mōna. I. add:—Setl his swā swā sunna ... and swā swā mōne, Ps. Vos. 88, 38. Đæs mōnan geár hæfđ seofon and twēntig daga and eahta tīda. On đām fyrste hē underyrnđ ealle đā twelf tācna þe seó sunne undergǣd twelf mōnađ ... Đæs mōnan ryne is swīđe nearo for þan þe hē yrnđ ealra tungla niđemest and þǣre eorđan gehendost ... þis is þæs mōnan geár; ac his mōnađ is māre, þ is þonne hē gecyrd nīwe fram þǣre sunnan ođ þ hē eft cume hyre forne āgeán ... and eft þurh hī beó ontend. On đām mōnđe synd getealde nigon and twēntig daga and twelf tīda: þis is se mōnelica mōnađ, and hys geár is þ hē underirne ealle đā twelf tunglan, Lch. iii. 246, 24-248, 21. II. add:—Swā hwær swā þe mōna byđ feówertýne nihta eald, Lch. iii. 244, 11.

mōnaþ. Add:—þæs eásterlican mōnđes angin, Angl. viii. 330, 2. Synt feówur mōnđas (mōneđo, L., mōnođas, R.) ǣr man rīpan mæge, Jn. 4, 35. Wīf his gedēgelde hiā mōneđam (monođas, R.) fīfo (mensibus quinque), Lk. L. 1, 24 : 4, 25. Ymb ānes geáres fyrst and eahta mōnađ, Nar. 31, 26. Đeós tīd cymđ ymbe twelf mōnađ (post annum), Ll. Th. ii. 224, 32. v. Midsumor-, Midwinter-mōnaþ. ¶ for the name of the months see Chr. P., Appendix A, and the Martyrology given in the Shrine.

**mónaþ-ádl.** *Add:*—Be mónaðádles hǽmede *de coitu in menstruali tempore*, Ll. Th. ii. 128, 26. Swā hwilc ceorl swā mid his wīfe hǽme on mónaðádlie (*in consuetudine ejus menstrua*), 144, 3.

**mónaþ-fyllen.** *Add:*—Mónoðfylene, An. Ox. 7, 366. Mónaþfylyne, 8, 360. Mónaþfulne, Angl. xiii. 37, 274. (These and Hpt. 525, 63 *all refer to the same passage.*)

**mónaþ-lic.** I. *add:* used substantively :—Wiþ ealle yfele gegaderunga þæs innoþes and wið wífa mónoðlican, Lch. i. 56, 24 : 276, 2 : 278, 4.

**mónaþ-seóc.** I. *add:*—Wiþ þon þe mon sié mónaþseóc; nim mereswínes fel, wyrc tō swipan, swing mid þone man; sóna bið sēl, Lch. ii. 334, 1. Mónoþseóc *inerguminum* (cf. deófelseócne, 4934), An. Ox. 2, 404. Man ferode ... myslīce geuntrumode, and mónaðseóce and wóde, Hml. S. 16, 139.

**mór;** I. *add:*—Hī eardiað an þæs gedwildes móre and meoxe (*in luto heresis*), Chrd. 96, 31. Móras *salebras*, i. *loca lutosa*, An. Ox. 17, 63. The word occurs often in charters. v. Midd. Flur. v. heáh-, wīþigmór.

**móraþ.** *Add:*—Drinc móraþ (-eð, *v. l.*) *pota diamoron*, Hpt. 31, 11, 240; Lch. i. lxii. 10.

**mór-beám.** *Add:*—Cyme tō þám treówe þe man hāteþ mórbeám, Lch. i. 330, 19. Heora mórbeámas, Ps. L. 77, 47. [*Lat.* morus.] See *next word, and* mūr-beám.

**mór-berige,** an; f. A mulberry:—Hī mid mórberium gebyldon þā ylpas (*to the end they might provoke the elephants to fight, they showed them the blood of grapes and mulberries*, 1 Macc. 6, 34), for ðam ðe mórberian him is metta leófost, Hml. S. 25, 576.

**more (-u).** *Add:*—Hē leofode on wǣstene be wyrta morum lange, Hml. S. 31, 195. [v. *N. E. D.* more.]

**morgen.** I. *add:*—Gehwilce morgene, Lch. ii. 108, 2. Ōþre morgne, 116, 21.

**morgen-colla.** *Add:* For colla cf. (?) cwelan. v. Angl. xxxi. 258.

**morgen-dæg.** I. *add:*—Ðā hit þā on morgendæg wæs *primo deinde aurore diluculo*, Nar. 22, 1.

**morgen-gebedtíd,** e; f. *Morning prayer-time;* in pl. *matins:*—Ðā hē þā his morgengebedtída wolde Gode gefyllan *cum matutinas laudes Domino impenderet*, Guth. Gr. 135, 272.

**morgen-gifu.** *Add:*—Ic gean intō Ælíg .. þāra þreó landa þe wit būta geheótan Gode, þ is æt rettendūne þe wes mīn morgangifu ..., C. D. iii. 274, 16. Gewāt Eádríc ǽr Ælfēh cwideleás, and Ælfēh fēng tō his lǣne. Ðā hæfde Eádríc lāfe and nán bearn. Þā geúþe Ælfēh hire morgengife (*concessit Ælfegus illi viduæ donum dotis suæ tantum quod ei dederat Eadricus, quando eam primum accepit uxorem*), Cht. E. 212, 19. (The Latin version is of much later date than the English.) Nabbe gē (*the suitors for the speaker's daughter*) nā gódne tíman āredodne ... āc — āwrítað eówre naman on gewrite and hire morgengife, þonne āsænde ic þā gewrita mínre dohtor þ heó sylf geceóse hwilcne eówer heó wille, Ap. Th. 20, 7. [v. *N. E. D.* moryeve.]

**morgen-mete.** *In* l. 3 *for* 129 l. 192.

**morgen-steorra.** *Add:*—Hē cóm beforan Críste on myddangeard swā se morgensteorra cymð beforan þǽre sunnan, Shrn. 95, 13. Ǽr morgynsteorran *ante luciferum*, Ps. Cam. 109, 3.

**morgen-tíd.** *Add:* a morning hour :—On morgentídum ic smeáde on þe *in matutinis meditabor in te*, Ps. L. 62, 7: Lch. ii. 182, 25.

**morgen-wlǽtung,** e; f. *Nausea in the morning:*—Wið morgenwlǣtunga, Lch. iii. 44, 19.

**mór-hǽþ,** e; f. l. es; m. n.: **mór-hana** (?). v. wór-hana: **-móringas.** v. West-móringas.

**mór-lǽs** *marshy pasturage:*—xxiii. acrae prati iacent in feormóre ... Item uilla habere debet in eodem prato communem pasturam, quae ymēne mórlǽse appellatur, C. D. iii. 408, 23.

**mór-seohtre** *a marshy ditch:*—Wæterfrocgan hwílon hí man gesihð of wætere, and swā þeáh sēcað tō fūllicum mórseohtrum (*in putridine paludis commorantur*), Chrd. 96, 28.

**mór-slǽd,** es; n. A marshy valley :—Norð on ān mórsleóc; norð tō ié, C. D. v. 124, 26. On ðæt mórslæde (-slæd?) ēstwærde, vi. 9, 1.

**mortere.** *Add:*—Murra hātte wyrt, gegnīd on mortere, Lch. ii. 18, 3. Genim ealdne rysle, getrifula on treówenum mortere, 180, 4. Cnuca on ānum trýwenum mortere, i. 220, 11. [*Lat.* mortarium.]

**morþ.** I. *add:*—Heora yfel is egeslic and endeleáslic morð, Hml. S. 17, 154. II. *add: a very evil deed, mortal wrong :*—Heora nán ne mihte þ morð gefremman, Hml. S. 32, 209. III. *add:*—Wīte ræfnian for þám gylte swā myceles morðes *poenas pro illa tanti homicidii culpa tolerare*, Gr. D. 186, 27. [v. *N. E. D.* murth.]

**morþ-cræft** (?) *deadly art:*—Hwæt is seó micele miht þínre morðcræfte, þ þū þyllic gefremast þurh feóndlicne drýcræft, Hml. S. 35, 173. [*As* cræft *is regularly masculine perhaps* morþdǽde (*see next word*) *should be read here,* cræfte *having been taken owing to the neighbouring* drýcræft.] v. morþor-cræft.

**morþ-dǽd.** *Add:* I. *evil-doing:*—Ofsceamod for þǽre morðdǽde þe hē gedón hæfde, and for þám manslihte þe hē slóh mid þǽre handa, Ælfc. T. Grn. 18, 34. II. *an evil deed:*—Irre and anda ūs synd

forbodene, manslyht and morðdǽda, Hml. A. 8, 190. Hē (*Jove*) manega manslihtas and morðdǽda gefremode, Hml. S. 35, 108.

**morþor.** *Add:* v. mæg-morþor.

**morþor-cwalu** *murder :*—Sumu (*one of the devil's arrows is made*) of reáflāce ... and of morðorcwale, sumu of þeófunga and of feóunga, Nap. 46.

**morþor-sliht.** *Add:*—Ic eom ealles anddetta, morðorslihta, mǽnra āða, .. and unsibbe, Angl. xi. 101, 35.

**morþ-wyrhta.** *Add:*—Ðider (*to hell*) sculan mánsworan and morðwyrhtan, Wlfst. 26, 16.

**mot.** *Add:*—Mote *atomo* (minor ... modico Phoebi radiis qui vibrat *atomo*, Ald. 272, 32), An. Ox. 23, 52: 26, 74.

**mótan.** I. *add:* expressing permission or possibility that comes from permission. I a. *add:* (1) the subject a person :—Eálā hū yfele mē dōþ manege woruldmenn mid ðām þ ic ne mót wealdan mīnra āgenra þeówa *an ego sola meum jus exercere prohibebor*?, Bt. 7, 3; F. 20, 20. Bið þē God hold ... and þū móst (*poteris*) mid him rícsian, Ll. Th. ii. 132, 16. Wóst þū genóh gif ic gedó þæt þū þæt wóst, þæt þū móst simle lybban? *quid, cum te immortalem esse didiceris, satisne erit*?, Solil. H. 56, 10. Gif þē ǽfre gewyrð þ ðū wilt oððe móst eft fandian þára þióstra þisse worulde *si terrarum placeat tibi noctem relictam visere*, Bt. 36, 3; S. 105, 25. Hū mǽg sē beón gesǽlig, sē ðe on ðām gesǽlþum ðurhwunian ne mót, 2; F. 4, 15. þǽr ic nū móste (*was permitted*) þīn mód gesiþerigan ... þ þū mihtest (*wast able*) mid mē fliógan, 36, 2; F. 174, 6. Þā bǽdon hí for heora ealdcyððe þ hí móston him beran flǽsc, Hml. S. 25, 91: Bt. 1; F. 2, 8: 35, 4; F. 162, 25. God sealde frīdóm manna sáulum, þæt hý móston dōn swā good swā yfel, swæðer hý woldon, Solil. H. 10, 18. Gedó mē þæs wyrðne, þæt ic þē mōte geseón *fac me idoneum ad videndum te*, 13, 15. Þæt þū ne mōte began þæt þæt þū wilnast, 46, 12. (2) the subject a thing : where the natural processes in connection with an object are given :—Se heofon mót brengan leóhte dagas, ... þ geár mót brengan blósman, ... seó sǽ mót brūcan smyltra ýþa, and ealle gesceafta mōtan heora gewunan and heora willan bewitigan, Bt. 7, 3; F. 20, 20–24. Me mæig, gif hit mót gewiderian (*granted good weather*), mederan settan, Angl. ix. 262, 9. þ se stemn and se helm mōte þý fæstor and þý leng standon, Bt. 34, 10; F. 148, 33. I b 2. *add:*—Hē gesealde Persum ... healfe Mesopotamiam wiþ þǣm þe hié of þǣm londe mósten būton lāþe *ut tutum et incolumem exercitum a locorum periculo liberaret, partem Mesopotamiae Persis concessit*, Ors. 6, 32; S. 286, 27. II. *add:*—Gif man eard wille rihtlíce clǣnsian, þonne mót man spyrian hwǣr þá mánfullan wununge habban, Ll. Th. i. 348, 25: 380, 8. Wē mōton þencan (ūs is tō geþencanne, *v. l.*), 196, 23. Drihten, hǽle ūs : wē mōton forweorðan *Domine, salva nos, perimus*, Mt. 8, 25. Mōton þá hyrdas beón swíðe wacore, Ll. Th. i. 374, 27 : 344, 27. Unðeáwas ðe hē ǽr ne cūðe wunnon him ðá on and on his cynne syððan, swā þæt hí móston mid micclum geswince ðá gódan ðeáwas healdan, gif hý hí habban woldon, Hex. 26, 5. II a. where the infinitive is to be inferred :—Hē fridige ælce be ðám ðe hit sēlest sý, and be ðám hē eác mót ðe hine weder wísað, Angl. ix. 259, 16. III. as an auxiliary :—Gif woe geslás t huoeðer mōto wē geslaa (sleá wē, W. S.) *si percutimus*, Lk. L. 22, 49. þ wīð wēdes his gehrīne móston (móstun æthrínan, R., æthrinon, W. S.) *ut fimbriam vestimenti ejus tangerent*, Mt. 14, 36.

**mótere.** *Add:* [v. *N. E. D.* mooter.] Cf. gemót-mann.

**moþ-freten;** *adj. Moth-eaten :*—Heora reáf nǣron nān þingc moðfretene, Hml. S. 23, 437.

**moþþe.** *Add:*—Swā swā on reáf moþþe (*tinea*), and wyrm forswylhð treów, eall swā unrótnyss deráð heortan, Scint. 168, 7. Ne behýde gē eówerne goldhord ... þǽr ðǽr moððan hit āwēstað, Hml. Th. ii. 104, 30. Moþþ[um] *tineis*, An. Ox. 50, 37.

**mót-hús.** *Add:* [v. *N. E. D.* moot-house.] Cf. gemót-hús.

**mótian;** I. *add:*—Hí lange mótodon, Hml. S. 34, 214: 310: 36, 365. Þā gehýrdon hí mótian wið Martine lange (*they heard a long conversation being carried on with Martin*), and hē wæs āna ǽr innan þám húse belocen, 31, 694. [v. *N. E. D.* moot.] v. ge-mótian.

**mót-lǽðu.** *Add:* For the prevalence of the three-meetings-a-year practice see Grmm. R. A. 823, where is quoted '*tria plebiscita, quae dicuntur ungeboten.*'

**mót-stów.** v. gemót-stów (1): **mót-weorþ.** *Add:* v. weorþ; VIII.

**múga.** *Add:*—Mūgan *aceruos* (*farris*), An. Ox. 26, 45.

**múl.** *Add:*—Absalon rād on his mūle ... þā gefēng hine ān treów be ðám fexe ... and se mūl arn forð fram þám ārleásan hláforde, Hml. S. 19, 222. Him cóm ongén se ealda feónd sittende on ānum mūle on lǣces ansýne, Gr. D. 161, 1. Martinus rād him wið gescrýd mid sweartum cláþum; þā scyddon þá mūlas þe þ cræt tugon, Hml. S. 31, 971. Ðá cempan þá woldon mid þám cræte forð, ac þá mūlas ealle endemes āstífodon tō þǽre eorðan āfæstnode, 985. Wæs þridde healf þūsend mūla ðe þá seámas wǣgon ... wæs unrīm getæl eác þon on horsum and on mūlum, Nar. 9, 9–14. ¶ *for* mūl *in local names see* C. D. vi. 316.

múl-hirde. Add :—Þín múlhyrde *tuus mulio* (*custos mulorum*), Hpt. 31, 12, 267.

-mun. v. ge-mun.

mund. Add : III. as representing control, grasp, &c. :—Lida bið longe on síðe . . . hâm cymeð, gif hē hâl leofað, nefne him holm gestýred, mere hafað mundum (*unless the sea has him in its clutches*), Gn. Ex. 107. III a. *add* :—Se crīstena man sceal clypian tô his Drihtne mid mōde and mid mūðe and his munde âbiddan, Hml. S. 17, 137. Mund *patrocinium*, An. Ox. 7, 61. v. sceaft-mund.

mund-bora. Add :—Mundbora *patronus* (*civitatis*), An. Ox. 4877. An ðâs rēdenne ic hit ðider selle ðe se monn sē ðe Kristes cirican hlâford sié, sē mín and mínra erfewearda forespreoca and mundbora and an his hlâforddôme wē bián môten, C. D. i. 311, 21. Iulianus úre ciricean mundbora (*defensor*), Gr. D. 71, 12.

mund-byrd. Add :—Mundbyrde *patrocinii*, i. *auxilii*, An. Ox. 3883.

mundbyrdan. Add : *to defend, protect* :—Hit gelamp þ se hâlga wer mundbyrde his âgene þegnas (bewerede his gingran, *v. l. discipulos defendit*), Gr. D. 43, 13.

mundbyrd-ness; II. *add* :—Ic mē sylfe myngode mínes forehâtes and þære mundbyrdnysse þe ic ær fore geceás, Hml. S. 23 b, 543.

mundian. Add :—God mundað þâ stôwe, and þâ slihð and gescynt þe þær sceaðian willað, Hml. S. 25, 804. Godes mynstra cyning sceal mundian æfre, O. E. Hml. i. 303, 2.

mund-leów. Add :—Munlēuu *vescada*, Txts. 104, 1055. Hē hēt geótan wæter on mundleów *misit aquam in pelvem*, Hml. A. 155, 102.

mund-wist, e; f. *Protection, guardianship* :—Đâ ænglas him and-sweredon, 'Ac sýó hige (*the soul*) ânumen of úre mundwiste, for ðan ðe mid fúlnesse hyó wæs in gangende,' Nap. 46.

-muning. v. ge-muning.

munt. Add : I. general :—Munt l̄ heofen *Olimpus*, An. Ox. 18 b, 62. þâ Wylisce â tôforan intô muntan and môran fērdan, Chr. 1095 ; P. 231, 23. II. special, *the Alps* :—Tô Longbeardna londe and tô þæm londum on þâ healfe muntes *regnum Longobardorum et alias terras quae sunt ultramontana*, Chr. 887 ; P. 80, 26. v. neáh-munt.

munt-clýse (-a?), an; f. (m.?). *A place shut in by hills, a moun-tain-prison* :—Gog and Magog, þæt beóð þâ mancyn þe Alexander beclýsde binnan muntclýsan, Wlfst. 84, 31. [Cf. Efter this Alexander went and closed in a maner of folkes þat are called Gog and Magog wiþin þe hilles of Caspy. . . . He garte close all þe entreeȝ wit stane and lyme and sand. Prose Life of Alexander, p. 104, E. E. T. S., no. 143. v. mann-cyn; II. 2.]

munt-geóf. Add : , -giú :—On Mauricius mynstre, þæt is on Muntgiú swâ men farað tô Rôme, Wlfst. 152, 9.

munuc. Add :—Ic (*Edgar*) wille nū ðâ forlǣtenan mynstru on mínum anwealde gehwǣr mid munecum gesettan . . . and ðâ munecas libban heora líf æfter regole ðæs hâlgan Benedictes, C. D. iii. 60, 1–7. Hēr drǣfde Eádgar cyng þâ preóstas (þa canonicas *canonici, v. ll.*) of Ealdan mynstre . . . and sette hý mid munecan, Chr. 964 ; P. 116, 3. Nū wille wē úre sprǣce âwendan tô þâm iungum munecum þe heora cildhâd habbað âbisgod on cræftigum bôcum, Angl. viii. 321, 26. v. riht-munuc.

munuc-behât, es ; n. *A monastic vow* :—'Ân munuc côm and gyrnde mîre dehter, sylle ic hī him oððe nâ ?' 'Asecge mē hwæðer hē his Gode wiðsace and his fulluhte and his munucbehâte,' Hml. A. 197, 81 : 198, 95.

munuc-cnapa, an; m. *A young monk* :—Se âwyrgeda gâst . . . tôcwýsde ǣnne munuccnapan (ǣnne þâra muneca, *v. l.*) sumes gerēfan sunu *malignus spiritus unum puerulum monachum cujusdam curialis filium contrivit*, Gr. D. 125, 7 : 93, 18. Sum Benedictes munuccnapana (cniht, sē wæs munuc, *v. l.*) *quidam Benedicti puerulus monachus*, 154, 9.

munuc-hâd. Add : I. general or of a man :—In munuchâde in *monachico habitu*, Gr. D. 27, 18. Ne môt man iungum men wíf for-gyfan, gif hē hine ǣr tô munuchâde (*monachismo*) gemynte, Ll. Th. ii. 142, 9. Oft on lǣwedum hâde and on lǣwedum girelan mid gôdum weorcum and mid ryhte lífe man oferðihð ðone munuchâd and ðâ ôðre ðe ðone hiérran hâd habbað *quidam in deteriori ordine sortem extremi habitus bene vivendo transcendunt*, Past. 411. 36. II. of a woman :—Heó wæs gelǣded tô ðâm munuchâde þe heó wilnode and gyrnde *ad eum quem desiderabat habitum perducta est*, Gr. D. 199, 19. Sum eald wíf in hâlgum munuchâde in þissere byrig wunode *anus quaedam in sancti-moniali habitu constituta in hac urbe manebat*, 283, 5.

munuc-líf. I. *add* :—Đâ mynstra on Wintancestræ Eádgâr cining tô munuclífe gedyde (cf. Chr. 964 ; P. 116, 3 *under* munuc), C. D. iii. 128, 20. II. *add* :—On ðâm munuclífe þe is Lindisfarneá gehâten, Hml. Th. ii. 142, 6. Hū wel hit fērde mid ūs þâ ðâ munuclíf wǣron mid wurðscipe gehealdene, Hml. S. 13, 149.

munuc-reáf, es ; n. *Monk's or nun's dress, monastic habit* :—Basilius on munucreáfe (*in monachico habitu*) fleónde gesôhte Ualeriam þâ mǣgðe, Gr. D. 27, 17. Eála swustor . . . âlege þíne woruldlican gegyrlan, and gegyre þē mid munucreáfe, Hml. S. 33. 82. þâm preóste

is ungedafenlic þ hē munucreáf (*uestem monachicam*) werige, Chrd. 63, 32. v. munuc-scrúd.

munuc-regol. Add : III. *monastic rule or mode of life* :—Hī munucregol myrdon, and mynstra tôstǣncton, and munecas tôdrǣfdon, Chr. 975 ; P. 121, 26.

munuc-scrúd, es ; n. *Monk's dress* :—Werige gehwâ swâ his hâde tô gebyrige, þ se preóst hæbbe þ þ hē tô gehâdod is, and hē ne werige munucscrúd ne lǣwedra manna, Ll. Th. ii. 358, 8. v. munuc-reáf.

múr-beám, es ; m. *A mulberry tree* :—Hē ofslôg múrbeámas hira on forste *occidit moros eorum in pruina*, Ps. Vos. 77, 47. [*From Latin murus*. Cf. *Murus* môr-beám, Wrt. Voc. i. 80, 36 : brēmel, ii. 55, 82 : braer, 114, 48. *Celsi murer*, murberien, i. 140, 54.] v. môr-beám.

murcian. Add : v. be-murcian.

murcnung. Add :—Weard ðâ micel morcnung and ormǣte wôp, Ap. Th. 6, 9. Murcnunge yfel nâ ætīwe *ne murmurationis malum appareat*, R. Ben. I. 64, 17. Se fæder forweard on môde and seó môdor mid murcnunge wæs fornumen, Hml. S. 2, 105. Þíne eáran âwend fram fúlre sprǣce and murcnunge, Wlfst. 246, 7. Forlǣt þíne murcnunge, . . . ic gedô þē welinge, Ap. Th. 16, 9. Ceórigum murcnungum *quaeru-losis questibus*, An. Ox. 624. Mid swâ biterum (âfrum) heófum, murc-nungum *tam rancidis l̄ amaris questibus*, i. *querimoniis*, 2829.

murn. v. un-murn.

murnan ; p. de. *Substitute* : murnan ; p. mearn ; *also wk*. murnde. *Take here the examples given under* meornan *in Dict., and add* : II :—Oferfyll bið þære sâwle feond . . . hit ne murneð for nânum men, ne for fæder ne for mēder ne for brôðer ne for swustor, Wlfst. 242, 6. II a. with dat. infin. :—Heó ne murnð leófðic leóð tô drýmanne, Angl. viii. 324, 16. III b. Cf. Bt. S. 111, 18, *where* myrnð *is the reading*.

murnlíce. v. un-murnlíce.

murnung. Add :—Of þæs magan âdle cumað monige and missenlica âdla . . . micla murnunga and unrôtnessa bútan þearfe, Lch. ii. 174, 26.

mús ; I. *add* :—Se micela ylp . . . ondrǣt him for þearle, gif hē gesihð âne mús, ðeáh ðe seó mús ne mage his micelnysse deran, Hml. A. 64, 258. Wiþ weartum, genim hundes micgean and múse blôd, meng tôsomne, smire mid, Lch. ii. 322, 12. Cwôman Indisce mýs in þâ fyrd in foxa gelícnisse *mures Indici in castra pergebant uulpibus similes*, Nar. 16, 5.

mús-fealle. Add :—Ne sceolde hē nân ðing forgýman ðe ǣre tô note mehte, ne forða músfellan, ne þ gīt lǣsse is, tô hǣpsan pinn, Angl. ix. 265, 8.

mús-hafoc. Add :—Múshafoce (mush, MS.) *accipitre*, An. Ox. 23, 18.

mús-þeóf? :—Músþeófum *furibus*, Wrt. Voc. ii. 38, 15.

must-wyrm (?), es ; m. *An insect found in wine* :—Mustfleógan *vel* [must]wurmas *bibiones vel mustiones*, Wrt. Voc. i. 23, 75. v. must-fleóge, míte.

múþ. Add : I. *the external orifice in an animal body which serves for the ingestion of food, together with the cavity to which this leads* :—Heó brôhte ân twig on hire mūðe (*in ore suo*), Gen. 8, 11. Mid nebbe, mūþe cýwat, pluc(ciaþ) *rostro*, i. *ore decerpunt*, i. *rodunt*, An. Ox. 100. Ne geunclǣnsað ðæt nô ðone mon ðæt on his mūð gǣð, Past. 317, 14. II. *the mouth considered as the receptacle of food or with reference to swallowing, devouring, tasting, &c.* :—Gefrīða mē of þæs león mūðe, Ps. Th. 21, 19. Hē is swíðe biter on mūþe and hē þe tirþ on þâ þrotan, Bt. 22, 1 ; F. 76, 29. Ne forbinde gē nô ðǣm ðerscend-um oxum ðone mūð, Past. 104, 8. Mūða gehwylc mete þearf, Gn. Ex. 125. II a. applied to things personified :—Grǣdigum mūþes ceáflum *ambronis orci faucibus*, An. Ox. 837. III. considered as the instru-ment of speech or voice :—Se crīstena man sceal clypian tô his Drihtne mid môde and mid mūðe, Hml. S. 17, 137. Đâ sylfan his lâreówas æt (æfter, *v. l.*) his mūðe writon and leornodan *doctores suos auditores sui faciebat*, Bd. 4, 24 ; Sch. 486, 20. His word þe hié æt his sylfes mūþe gehýrdon, Bl. H. 119, 32. Hē ne ontýnde mūþ his, An. Ox. 40, 33. Hī habbað dumne mūð, Hml. Th. i. 366, 26. III a. used as the subject of a verb of speaking :—Mín mūð wile sprecan wísdôm, Ps. Th. 48, 3. Se mūð þæs rihtwísan smeáð wísdôm, 36, 30. Of þære heortan willan se mūð spicð, Mt. 12, 34. Þâra mūðas sprecað mânidel word, Ps. Th. 143, 9 : 62, 9. III b. in various prepositional phrases. (1) with þurh :—Đâ Godes word ðe þurh his mūð beóð gesprecen, Past. 373, 22. Swâ hē spræc þurh his hâlegra witegena mūð, Lk. 1, 70. (2) with of, in, on :—Of ðæra cilda mūðe þū byst hered, Ps. Th. 8. 2. Of þínum mūðe ie ðē dême, Lk. 19, 22. Þ in mūðe twêgen oþþe þreó gewitnesse stonde gehwilc word, Mt. R. 18, 16. (2 a) Of ânum mūðe with one voice :—Hī sungon þysne sang swylce of ânum mūðe, Hml. S. 11, 164. III c. in other phrases : (1) *to shut the mouth, keep silence* :—Đeáh hié ðæs líchoman mūð belúcen, Past. 271, 23. (2) *to put words in another's mouth, tell him what to say* :—Sete mín word on his mūð, and ic beó on þínum mūðe and on his mūðe, Ex. 4, 15. (3) *to seek in a person's mouth, seek to be told by a person* :—Sió ǣ sceal beón sôht on ðæs sâcerdes mūðe, Past. 91, 17. IV. *the exterior opening of the mouth considered as part of the face* :—Gif mūð wôh weorðeð, Ll. Th. i. 14. 9. His (*the dead man's*) eágan beóþ betýnde, and his mūþ

and his næsþyrlo beóþ belocene, Bl. H. 59. 14. Hí setton áne spyngan
tó his múðe, Jn. 19, 29. Swingað hine on his múð, 243, 2. **V.** *the
opening of anything having a containing capacity, by which it is filled
or emptied* :—Hé þæt feoh geseah on þæs sacces múðe (*in ore sacculi*),
Gen. 42, 28. **VI.** *the outfall of a river* :—His líc ligð æt Tínan
múþe, Chr. 792; P. 55, 30.

**-múþ**; *adj.* v. gylden-múþ; reód-múþa.

**múþa.** *Add* :—On múþan *in portum*, Bl. Gl. *Aestuaria, ostia* ł
múþan, An. Ox. 41, 3. v. Wísle-múþa.

**múþettan**; *p.* te *To chatter, let out a secret* :—Hí (*the guards at
Christ's sepulchre*) námon þone sceatt and swá þeáh múþetton and on
synderlicum rúnungum þ riht eall ræddon, Hml. A. 79, 160.

**múþ-hǽl**, es; *n. l.* e; *f.*

**múþ-sár**, es; *n. A pain of the mouth* :—Haran geallan mæg wið
pipor gemenged wið múðsáre (*contra dolorem oris*), Ll. Th. ii.
162, 25.

**múþ-sealf**, e; *f. A mouth-salve* :—Gif mannes múð sár sié ... Tó
múðsealfe, Lch. ii. 48, 28.

**mycgern.** v. micgern: **mydd.** *Add* : [v. *N. E. D.* mud *a
measure*.]

**mýderce.** *Add* :—Man sceal habban ... cyste, mýdercan, bearmteáge,
Angl. ix. 264, 20. Lǽt hí ealle fordón and ic gedó þ þú hæfst týn
þúsend punda tó þínum mýdercum (*arcariis gazae tuae*), Hml. A. 96,
156. [Cf. (?) *Icel.* mjöł-drekka *a chest* ?] v. tow-mýderce; earce.

**myl.** *Add* : [v. *N. E. D.* mull.]

**mylen.** *Add* : *f. n. A water mill* :—Ligð bænorðan ðám porte .xxxvi.
æceras yrdlandes, and .x. æceras mǽde, and án mylen, C. D. v. 316, 1.
Gif hit beón mæg swá sceal mynster beón gestaþelod þæt ealle neádbehéfe þing þærbinnan wunien, þæt is wæterscype, mylen (myll *molen-
dinum*, R. Ben. I. 112, 15), wyrtún, R. Ben. 127, 6. Of lace andlang
watæres on Cortices mylne; of Cortices mylne ... tó ðære fúlan flóde,
C. D. vi. 31, 20. Sume menn syllað eác cyrcan tó hýre swá swá wáclice
mylna ... ac hit ne gedafnað þ man dó Godes hús ánre mylne gelíc for
lyðrum tolle, Hml. S. 19, 248-253. Fiscwer and mylne macian, Angl.
ix. 261, 13. Ic gean Ædwine muneke þá mylne þe Ringware áhte ...
and ic gean þ myln þe Wulnóð áhte into Scē Eádmunde, C. D. iv. 59,
11-15. Andlang streámæs on ðá mylne, v. 340, 21. [*Lat.* molina.]
v. mersc-mylen *and the* mylen-*compounds, almost all of which are connected with water.*

**mylen-burna** (-e) *a mill-stream* :—Ad riuulum qui Mǽlænburna
dicitur, C. D. v. 103, 2. Of dúne on Mylenburnan, 124, 34, 36 : 125, 2.
¶ *as a place-name* :—Ðæt land æt Mylenburnan, C. D. ii. 114, 33 : vi.
131, 12.

**mylen-díc**; *f. A mill-dyke* :—Andlang ðǽre mylendíc eft on ðá eá,
C. D. v. 383. 12. Andlong cærent on þá mylendíc, Cht. E. 208, 31.

**mylen-feld**; *m. A field where there is a mill* :—Tó mylenfelda,
C. D. v. 381, 34.

**mylen-fleót.** v. fleót.

**mylen-gafol** *revenue derived from a mill* :—Hér stent gewriten hwæt
Baldwine abbod hæfð geunnen his gebróþra tó caritatem, þ is ii mylne-
gafel æt Lacforde, hælf pund at þ án and xii óran æt þ óþer, Nap. 46.

**mylen-gear**, es; *m. A mill-yair* (yair *an enclosure for catching fish.*
v. *D. D.* yair) :—þæs hagan gemǽre æt Wintanceastre lið úp of þǽm
forda on þone westmestan mylengear westeweardne; þæt eást on þone
ealden welig, and þonan úp andlanges þæs eástran mylengeares ... on
þone ealdan mylengear; þæt þǽr andlanges þæs ealdan myle[n]geares oð
hit fácað on þǽm ísihtan æsce; þæt súð ofer þá twisealdan fordas ...
forð þæt hit sticaþ eft on þǽm westemestan mylengeare, C. D. B. ii. 305,
22-30. Andlang eá on ðone mulenger; ðonan andlang ðære mylendíc,
C. D. v. 383, 11. On ðone ealdan myliar ðǽr ðá welegas standað; ðæt
west andlang burnan, iii. 421, 32.

**mylen-hweogul.** *Add* :—Seó heofon ǽfre tyrnð onbútan ús; heó ys
swyftre þonne ǽnig mylenhwiól, Angl. viii. 309, 47.

**mylen-púl.** *l.* -pull.

**mylen-steall.** *Add* :—On ðone mylensteall; ðæt of ðǽm mylenstealle
andlang Ycenan, C. D. v. 121, 10.

**mylen-stede.** *Add* :—Se mylenstede and ðæt land benorðan eá ðe
ðǽrtó hýrð, C. D. v. 383, 13.

**mylen-streám**, es; *m. A mill-stream* :—Intó ðám milestreáme, of
ðám nylestreáme, C. D. v. 253, 18.

**mylen-troh.** *Add* : [v. *N. E. D.* mill-trough.] Cf. wæter-þeóte.

**mylen-tún** *a 'tún' with a mill, as a local name* :—*Aliquam partem
terre in prouincio Cantiþe ubi nominantur* Mylentún, C. D. i. 272, 14.

**mylen-weard.** *Add* :—Gif hé smeáwyrhtan hæfð, ðám hé sceal tó
tólan fylstan : mylewerde, sútere ..., Angl. ix. 263, 18. [v. *N. E. D.*
mill-ward.]

**mylen-weg** *a road to a mill* :—Andlang ðæs mylanweges on þone
Lundenweg, C. D. vi. 131, 29.

**mylen-wer.** *Add* : [v. *N. E. D.* mill-weir.]: **myliær.** v. mylen-
gear : **mylma.** *Add* : [cf. (?) Goth. milhma *cloud*] : -**mynde.** v. ǽ-
mynde.

**myndgian.** **II.** *add* : (1) *to bring to the notice of* a person :—
For ðám ic ðé mindgige, þ þú ongite ðætte nán gesǽlþ nis on þisse andweardan lífe *ut agnoscas in his fortuitis rebus beatitudinem constare non
posse, sic collige*, Bt. 11, 2 ; F. 34, 14. (2) *to remind* a person of something (*gen.*) :—Wé magon beón suá nyttran æt him, gif wé hié mynd-
giað hira gódna weorca *utilius apud illos proficimus, si et eorum bene
gesta memoramus*, Past. 211, 21. [Bt. 35, 3 ; F. 160, 7 ; 35, 2 ; F.
156, 14. v. mynegian.] Hié beóð tó myndgianne þǽra góda ðe hié
ǽr dydon, Past. 303, 8.

**myndgung.** *Add* :—Ðes sylfa þeáw for ðý lange þurh myndgunge
þæs hálgan weres on Angelcynnes mynsterum forþweard wæs, Lch. iii.
434, 19 : 440, 5. v. ge-myndgung.

**myndig.** *Add* : v. eft-myndig : **myndlinga.** v. un-myndlinga.

**myne.** **II.** *add* :—Wæs eall heora myne fæst on tóhopunge þæs écean
Drihtnes, Hml. S. 23, 155. **IV.** *a memorial, memory* :—Þá ðá hǽðenan
menn crístendómes leóman mid ealle ádwǽscan woldon, and ǽlcne myne
ofer eorðan ádýlgian, Hml. S. 23, 11. [v. *N. E. D.* min.]

**mynecenu.** *Add* : Mynecyna *sanctimonialium*, Angl. iii. 366, 21.
[v. *N. E. D.* minchen.]

**mynegian.** **I.** *add* : with reflex pron. :—Ic mé sylfe myngode
mínes foregehátes, Hml. S. 23 b, 542. **II a.** *add* :—Wel þú mé myne-
gast (*your reminder is opportune*); ic ðé gelǽste þæt ic þe gehét, Solil. H.
31, 4. **II b.** *add* :—Ic mynegige *moneo*, Ælfc. Gr. Z., 254, 13. Hé
hí tó þám myngode þ heó hine geefenlǽcende ..., hogode, Lch. iii.
440, 18. Myniendum *hortante*, i. *monente*, An. Ox. 29. Minigende
(*ammonentes*) búton ceorunge þ hí beón, R. Ben. I. 73, 1. ¶ *to urge* an
animal :—Nimað þás swipan þæt gé magan þis hors mid mynegian and
drífan (*minare*), Gr. D. 14, 21. v. un-mynegod.

**mynegiend-líc**; *adj. Hortatory* :—Myniendlícere tyhtincge *hortandę
suasionis*, An. Ox. 3381. Word mynegyendlíce *uerba exhortatoria*, Angl.
xiii. 367, 30.

**mynegung.** **I.** *add* :—Tóforan eallum þingum wé ðæs mynegunge
dóð þ hý bútan ceorunge sýn *hoc ante omnia ammonentes, ut absque
murmuratione sint*, R. Ben. 65, 10. Minegungum *oraculis*, i. *sermonibus*, An. Ox. 3384. **II.** *add* :—Þý lǽs seó mynegung forlǽge, Ll. Th.
i. 234, 29. **III.** *a memorandum* :—Ðis is myngung manna bíwiste,
Ll. Th. i. 440, 29. v. ge-mynegung.

**mynetere.** **I.** *add* :—Mynetere *trapezeta*, An. Ox. 18 b, 93.
**mynetian.** v. ge-mynetian.

**mynet-ísen**, -ísern, es; *n. A die for stamping coin* :—Feówer síðon
man áwende mynetísena (minetíserna, *v. l.*) on his dagum, Hml. S. 23,
477. Cf. stemping-ísern.

**mynet-slege**, es; *m. Striking of coin, minting, coining* :—Wæs þæs
feós ofergewrit ðæs ylcan mynetsleges þe man þ feoh on slóh sóna þæs
forman geáres þá Decius fếng tó ríce, Hml. S. 23, 475. v. frum-
mynetslege.

**mynster.** *Add* :—Wæs se abbud geháeod tó þæm mynstre þe Eádgár
cyning mid munecum gesette, Lch. iii. 438, 26. Þes þeáw lange on
Angelcynnes mynsterum forþweard wæs, 434, 20. Hé began georne
mynstera wíde geond his cyneríce tó rihtlǽcynne, 440, 1. Ðá mynstra
on Wintanceastræ hé þurh Godes gyfe tó munuclífe gedyde, C. D. iii.
128, 19. His mód wæs ǽfre embe mynstru smeágende oþþe embe cyrcan,
Hml. S. 31, 28. v. Élíg-, neáh-, West-mynster.

**mynster-bóc** *a book belonging to a monastery* :—Hér syndon xxx
bóca ealre on Leófstánes abbodes háfona bútan mynsterbéc, Nap. 46.

**mynster-clúse**, an; *f. A cloister, monastery, convent* :—His gemæccean mynecyna mynsterclúsan swá unearges mid gewunan hyrdes heó
bewerude swýþe wærlíce hé (*Edgar*) bebeád *coniugi suę sanctimonialium mandras* [mandra *monasterium*, Migne] *ut impauidi more custodis
defenderet cautissime precepit*, Angl. xiii. 366, 22.

**mynster-fǽder** *the head of a monastery* :—Sum mynsterfæder *quidam monasterii pater*, Gr. D. 293, 1.

**mynster-gang.** *Add* :—Heálíce gegaderunga ne mót mon gesceádan
bútan bégea geðafunga. Heora ǽgðer mót óðrum lýfan mynstergang
(*licentiam dare in monasterium ire*), Ll. Th. ii. 152, 4.

**mynster-geat** *monastery-gate* :—Æt þám mynstergeate (cf. beforan
þæs mynstres geate, 25), Gr. D. 145, 2 : 163, 25.

**mynster-hám.** *Add* :—Wé hine cúðon in þám mynsterháme þe hé
on wæs *nos eum in hac ecclesiastica domo novimus*, Gr. D. 319, 24.

**mynster-land.** *Add* : *n. Land belonging to a monastery* :—Ædelwold
sealde mé tó gehwerfe ðone hám Heartingas on sixtigum hídum wið ðám
mynsterlande ðe lið intó Élíg, C. D. iii. 60, 32.

**mynster-líc.** *Add* :—Mynsterlícere *monasticae* (*conuersationis*), An.
Ox. 9, 3. Ðá Godes þeówas, þonne heó intó cyrican cuman, habban
gástlíce þeáwas ... and mynsterlíce wísan, Wlfst. 234, 10.

**mynster-líf.** **I.** *add* :—Heó forhogode þæs fæder láre and onfếng
þám háde þæs hálgan mynsterlífes *contemto patre, conversationis sanctae
habitum suscepit*, Gr. D. 222, 24.

**mynster-mann.** *Add* :—Lá, mynsterman, wylt þú witan hwæt þis
tácnaþ ?, Angl. viii. 323, 16 : Wlfst. 224, 17. Wé þencað iunge mynstermen tó gegrétanne, Angl. viii. 321, 38.

**mynster-prafost.** *l.* -prāfost: **mynster-preóst.** *For 'monastery (?)' substitute 'minster.'*

**mynster-stede,** es; *m. A monastic edifice, monastery* (as a building):—Eall his mynsterstede full fæste gestód, būton þām gebedhūse ānum in þām hē læg seóc; eall hit ābifode *dum ejus omnis domus in sua soliditate persisteret, cubiculum in quo jacebat aeger contremuit,* Gr. D. 182.

**mynster-timbrung,** e; *f. Building of a monastery:*—Hū hē þurh gesihðe gedihte þā mynstertimbrunge neáh Terracinense *de fabrica monasterii Terracinensis per visionem ab eo disposita,* Gr. D. 147, 11.

**myntan. I a.** *add:* (a) of the action of an inanimate object:—þ āborstene clif hreás ofdūneweard, and wæs farende oþ þ hit cōm þær hit mynte feallan ofer þ mynster, Gr. D. 12, 11. **I d.** *add: to mean something for a person:*—Ic hit āgnian wille tō āgenre æhte þ þ ic hæbbe, and næfre þē myntan plot ne plōh, ne turf ne toft, Ll. Th. i. 184, 6. **I d a.** the subject an immaterial thing personified:—Nytende hwæt ofertōwerd mynte dæg *ignorans quod superuentura pariat dies,* Scint. 215, 1. [*v. N. E. D.* mint.]

**myrgan.** *Take here* mirgan, *and add:* [*v. N. E. D.* merry; *vb.*]: **myrgen.** *Take here* mirgen.

**myrige;** *adj. Take here* mirige *in Dict., and add:*—Wæs ðær gehende ān myrige dūn mid wyrtum āmēt mid eallre fægernysse and eác ful smēðe, Hml. S. 19, 108. Þeáh þe þes middaneard myrge wære, 28, 158. Hē sæde þæt him nære næfre ær swā eðe ne swā myrige, swā him þā wæs, Wlfst. 237, 7. Dōmesdæg ys se myrga dæg, Angl. viii. 336, 30. v. un-myrige.

**myrige;** *adv. Take here* mirige *in Dict., and add:*—Fegerne tūn timbrian, and þær murge and sōfte on eardian, Solil. H. 1, 13.

**myriglīce;** *adv. Pleasantly, melodiously:*—Myccle liþelīcor and myriglīcor (myrgelīcor, *v.l.*) wæs gehýred se sealmsang *coepit psalmodia lenius audiri,* Gr. D. 286, 1.

**myrigþ, myrhþ.** *Take here* mirigþ *in Dict., and add:*—Wel mæg gehwā witan þ gif āhwær is myrcð (myrhð, *v. l.*) and wuldor, þ þær (*in heaven*) is unāsecgendlic wuldor, Hml. S. 12, 92.

**myrre.** *Add:*—Tō eallum uncystum þe on gōmum beóð ācenned . . . myrre and pipor, Lch. i. 318, 14. Tō gehealdanne līchoman hælo mid Drihtnes gebede, þis is æþele læcedōm: Genim myrran and gegnīd on wīn . . . þonne is eft se æþelesta læcedōm tō þon ilcan. Genim myrran and hwīt recels . . . and þæs rēceles and myrran sý mæst, ii. 294, 17–25. [From Latin.]

**-myrþe, -myrþere.** v. self-myrþe (?), -myrþere (?).

**myrþra.** *Add:*—Hē sæde þ hē heora deáðes myrðra wære *se in eorum morte clamabat homicidam,* Gr. D. 207, 21. v. mann-myrþra.

**myrþrian.** *Add:* v. ā-myrþrian.

**myscan.** v. miscan.

# N

**nā. I.** *add:*—Ne gefúlle hē nō (næfre, *v.l.*) on swæ opene scylde, Past. 235, 2. Ne gewurðe hit nā on līfe, Hml. S. 25, 660. **II b.** *add:*—Hē hiene geniédde þ hē sealde Rōmānum þreó hund gīsla; and hē þeh siþþan nā þý læs ne hergeade on Rōmāne *ad deditionem coactus, trecentos obsides dedit. Enim cum inprobos non cohiberet excursus,* Ors. 5, 7; S. 228, 31.

**nabban.** *Add:*—Nafað ðæs monnes mōd nānne gāstes freódōm, Past. 265, 2. Hē næfde þæs cræftes þ hē hine tōcwȳsan mihte, Hml. S. 31, 1247. Hī næbbað ēce gewitnesse, Past. 449, 3. Hié hit tō nānum lāðe næfdon, Ors. 1, 10; S. 48, 13. Hý tō Gode næfdon nāþer ne lufe ne ege, Wlfst. 10, 5. Nabbe (næbbe, *v.l.*) gē nānne gemānan wið hine, Past. 357, 5.

**nacian.** [*In* Mart. H. 18, 20 *the passage is:* Hē wæs nacod on carcern onsænded, *so that* nacod *is an adjective, and not a participle from* nacian. v. *N. E. D.* nake.] v. ge-nacian.

**nacod. I a.** *add:*—Swā þām men þe wurde færinga nacod beforan eallon folce, and hē nyste þonne mid hwām hē þone sceamiendan līchaman bewruge, Wlfst. 238, 14: Mart. H. 18, 20. Þā hēt hē hī nacode (*propriis exutam vestibus* Ald. 60, 17) lædan tō sumum scandhūse, Shrn. 56, 8. **I a a.** *destitute of clothing* (implying poverty and wretchedness):—Hym cōm ongeán ān þearfende man nacod on cealdum wyntra, Shrn. 146, 35. Ðā næfde Martinus nān ðing tō syllenne þām nacodan ðearfan, Hml. Th. ii. 500, 22. Þone nacodan gefrēfrian, 25. Gemētte hē ænne þearfan nacodne, Hml. S. 31, 61. **I b.** *add:*—Se nacoda assa bið mid reáfum gesædelod, Hml. Th. i. 210, 29. **I c.** *add:*—Hī sceoldon underhnīgan nacodum swurde (nacedum swyrdum, *v.l.*), Hml. S. 5, 28. **I d.** of a surface, *bare, without a covering:*—Wæs his seó æþeleste ræst on his hæran (earan, MS., *but cf.* on flōre licgende, on stīðre hæran, Hml. Th. ii. 516,

31: *both passages refer to St. Martin*) oþþe elles on nacodre eorðan, Bi. H. 227, 11. **II b.** *add:*—Nū miht þū wel witan þæt weorc sprecan swīðor þonne þā nacodon word þe nabbað nāne fremminge, Ælfc. T. Grn. 21, 24. **II c.** of a narrative, *bare, without amplification or comment:*—Seó bōc is swīþe deóp gāstlīce tō understandenne, and wē ne wrītaþ nā māre būton þā nacedan gerecednisse; þonne þincþ þām ungelæredum þ eall þ andgit beó belocen on þære ānfealdan gerecednisse, Ælfc. Gen. Thw. 2, 30. v. healf-nacod.

**nacod-ness.** v. næced-ness: næ. v. ne: nēcan. v. hnēcan.

**næced.** *Add:*, næcedu:—Þær is hunger and næcedu, and þær is yrmðo and nearones, and þær is unmæte cyle and unāhefendlic hæto gemēted, Verc. Först. 169.

**-næced.** v. be-næced.

**næced-ness.** *Add:*, nacod-ness:—Scamfæst næcednys *pudibunda nuditas,* Hpt. Gl. 492, 56. Hī būtan næcednysse him bet mihton tīðian (*cf.* hī eðelīcor hine mihton scrýdan, Hml. Th. ii. 500, 30) *without stripping themselves they might better have given him clothes,* Hml. S. 31, 74. Be Crīstes līchoman nacodnisse, Angl. xi. 172, 34.

**næder-bīta.** *l.* næder-bita.

**næder-cynn,** es; *n. A kind of snake:*—Cwōman hornede nædran, carastis þ nædercyn, Nar. 13, 16. Saga mē hwæt næddercynna sī on eorðan. Ic ðē secge, feówer and þrittig, Sal. K. 204, 7. Wið scorpiones stingc and wið ealra næddercynna slitas, Lch. i. 304, 18.

**næder-fāh;** *adj. Spotted like a snake:*—Inn eóde ān grislic deófol. Hē wæs on dracan heówe and eall hē wæs nædderfāh, Hml. A. 175, 183.

**nædre.** *l.* nædre, *and add:*—Cōm of ðæm wætre ān nædre, seó wæs ungemetlīce micel (*serpens mirae magnitudinis,* and þā men ealle ofslōg þe nēh ðæm wætre cōman, Ors. 4, 6; S. 174, 4. Sió nēdre . . . lærde Euan on wōh. Ðā wæs Adam . . . ðurh gespan ðære næddran . . . oferswīðed, Past. 417, 26–29. 'Beó gē swā ware suā suā nædran . . .' For ðæm . . . sceal ðære nædran lytignes . . . ðære culfran biliwitnesse gescirpan, 277, 20–23. Nēdra (nēdre, R.) *serpentem,* Lk. L. 11, 11.

**næfe-bor.** v. nafu-bor.

**næfre.** *Add:*—Sē ðe nēbre (næfre, *v.l.*) ne āblind ungestæððignesse, Past. 71, 3: 425, 4: 445, 4. Næfra (næfræ, R.) *numquam,* Mt. L. 7, 23. Forebeádas næfræ gesueriga *prohibens omnino jurare,* Mt. p. 14, 16.

**næft,** e; *f. Poverty, indigence:*—Næfte *inopie,* Scint. 159, 13. Tō genim þearfan, and for næfte his ne forlæt hyne īdelne *adsume pauperem et propter inopiam eius ne dimittas illum uacuum,* 157, 3: 7. Of næfte, 198, 8.

**næftig;** *adj. Poor, indigent:*—Nā berýp ðū þeów wīsne, ne þū næftigne (*inopem*) forlæt hyne, Scint. 190, 1. N[æ]fti[ge] *inopes,* An. Ox. 56, 227. N[æ]f[tige] *egenos,* 231.

**nægel. II.** *add:*—Of þām scipe wæron þā næglas forlorene (*clavi perditi*) and þā þylinge tōslægene, Gr. D. 248, 23. v. hand-, wer-nægel.

**nægel-seax.** *Add: a razor* (*nouacula*) scearp þū dydest fācn, Ps. L. 51, 4. Nægelsexes tācn is þ þū mid þīnum scitefingre dō ofer þīnne ōþerne swilce þū ceorfan wille, and strāca syþþan on þīn leór mid þīnum fingre swilce þū scearan wille, Tech. ii. 127, 1.

**nægel-spere,** es; *n. A spear with a sharp point* (?):—Naeglsperu *unguana,* Corp. Gl. H. 121, 260. [*Cf.* Nægle oððe spere *cuspide,* Wrt. Voc. ii. 21, 24. Sceal ecg on sweorde and ord spere, Gn. Ex. 204. Ēn therō fīondo . . . druog negilid sper . . . mid heruthrummeon stak, Hēl. 5706.]

**nægen.** *l.* nægen = mægen.

**nægled-cnearr.** *Add: Cf.* Scip sceal genægled, Gn. Ex. 94. [*Cf.* Sie forlētun . . . nettiu and neglitskipu, Hēl. 1186.]

**næglian.** *Add:* v. ā-nægled.

**nǣm,** e; *f. A taking, acceptance:*—Be ælmessena nǣme *de elemosinis accipiendis,* Chrd. 49, 3. On þære nǣme cyrcan æhte *in accipiendis ecclesiasticis sumptibus,* 12, 7. Cf. nām.

**nǣman.** *Add:* v. for-, ge-nǣman: nǣmere. v. duguþ-nǣmere.

**nǣnig. I b.** *add:*—Þā fuglas ūs nænige lāðe ne yfle ne wæron *aues non nobis perniciem ferebant,* Nar. 16, 18.

**nǣnig-dǣl** *not a particle:*—Þ heó æt nýhstan nænigdæl (nænigne dæl, *v.l.*) leóhtes scīman geseón mihte *ut ne minimam quidem lucis alicuius posset particulam uidere,* Bd. 4, 10; Sch. 401, 10. Cf. sumdæl; nænig-, nān-wiht.

**nǣp.** *Add:*—Nǣp *rapa,* An. Ox. 56, 41. [From Latin. v. *N. E. D.* neep.]

**nǣrende** ?, Sal. 337.

**nǣs** *was not. Add:*—Hit nas (næs, *v.l.*) nā gecweden, Past. 108, 10.

**nǣs;** *adv.* **I.** *add:*—Ðæt ūs wære gearo his miltsung, næs ðæt ryht, Past. 405, 17. **II.** *add:*—Rīcsian næs nā suā ofer menn, ac suā suā ofer niétenu, Past. 109, 21. Næs nō . ., ac . ., 387, 32.

**nǣsc.** *Add:* [*In the last passage perhaps* ræscum (v. ræsc) *should be read for* næscum.] v. reód-næsc.

**næs-gristle.** *Add:* , an; *f.* :—Næsgristlan *internasso*, Lch. i. lxx, 6.

**næss.** I. *add* :—Næssas *cautes* (rupibus in celsis qua tundunt caerula *cautes*, Ald. 267, 24), An. Ox. 26, 56.     II. *add*: Cf. Hí nyþer ge-feallað under neowulne grund *descendunt usque ad abyssos*, Ps. Th. 106, 25.

**næster.** For *cancale l. caucale.*

**næs-þyrel.** *Add:*—Ðæt ádl þe wē hátað Cancer hym wæs on þām nebbe fram þām swýðran næsþyrle oð hyt cóm tó þām eáge, Hml. A. 181, 8. Næsþeorlu (*nares*) hí habbað and hig ne gestincað, Ps. L. 113, 6.

**nǽtan.** *Add: to afflict* :—Mínes módes nearunesse mē nǽtt *angustia animi affligit me*, Verc. Först. 137, 11. Hwí eom ic nǽted? *cur affligor?*, 142, 2. Swā mycle swíðor swā wē nū beóð nǽtte on þyssum lífe, swā mycle mā wē feógað on ðām tóweardan lífe, 141, 18.

**nafela.** *Add:*—Ylp is eall mid bánum befangen binnan þām felle bútan æt ðām nafelan, Hml. S. 25, 568. Ðonne þū gyrder habban wylle, þonne sete þū þíne handa forewearde wiðneoþan þínne nafolan and stríc tó þínum twám hypum, Tech. ii. 119, 22. Þǽr beóð kende *homodubii*, þ beóð twilice; hí beóð oð ðene nafolan (*usque ad umbilicum*) on menniscum gesceape, and syþþan on eoseles gelícnesse, Nar. 36, 19. v. eorþ-nafela.

**nafu-bor** *an auger* :—Hē sceal fela tóla tó túne tilian . . . æcse, adsan . . . sage, . . . næfebor, Angl. ix. 263, 3. Cf. nafu-gár.

**nafu-gár.** *Add:* [O. L. Ger. naðu-gēr.]

**nāgan.** I. *add* :—Hē nāh æfter forðsíðe crístenra manna gemáman, Ll. Th. i. 372, 34.     II. *add* :—Nāh man on ǽnigne tíman dæges ne nihtes æt Godes húse unnyt tó dónne, Wlfst. 278, 18 : 39, 16. Be þām magon Godes þeówas gecnāwan þ hí nāgon mid worldcampe tó farene, ac mid gāstlican wǽpnan campian, Ll. Th. ii. 388, 4.     III. *not to be obliged* or *bound to do* :—Ðā ðā Landfranc cræfede fæstnunge his gehērnesse mid áðswerunge, þā forsóc hē and sǽde þ hē hit náhte tó dónne (*he was not bound to do it*), Chr. 1070; P. 206, 2.

**nā-hwǽr.** I. *add* :—Hē áxode, 'Hwǽr ǽton gē?' Hí cwǽdon, 'Nāhwǽr (nō-, *v.l. nusquam*),' Gr. D. 127, 5. Hié ne dorston þæt land náwǽr (nāwǽrn, -wǽrn, *v.ll.*) gesēcan on þā healfe, Chr. 918; P. 98, 26. Hē of mynstere nolde náwǽr beón gemēt, Hml. Th. ii. 506, 4.    I a. fig. :—Gyf hyt nū sǽrenga gewurde, nyste ic náhwǽr eorðan hú ic ongynnan wolde (*I should not know how on earth to set about it*), Solil. H. 34, 12.

**nā-hwǽrn.** *Add: See preceding word.*

**nā-hwæþer.** *Add:* I. as adjective :—Nāðrum werode ne becymð nǽfre nān ende, Hml. Th. ii. 608, 9. God hine ne neádode on nāðre healfe, Hex. 22, 30.    I a. as a grammatical term, *neuter* :—*Neutrum* is nāðor cynn . . . ðis cyn gebyrað oftost tó nāðrum cynne, Ælf. Gr. Z. 18, 14–18.    as substantive :—Nāðer ne meihte on óþrum sige gerǽcan *velut invicti ab alterutro recesserunt*, Ors. 3, 1; S. 96, 33. Hí nóhwæþerum (-e, Bd. S. 647, 2) heora willunge habban ne magon *in neutro cupitum possunt obtinere propositum*, Bd. 5, 23; Sch. 693, 2. Hē ys swā gelógod þ hē nāðron ne derað, ne Februario ne Martio, Angl. viii. 307, 26. Hē wæs mid þām sáre geswenced þæt hē nāðer þāra ne gesittan ne standan mihte (*ut sedere aut stare nequivisset*), Guth. Gr. 153, 14.

**nā-hwider.** *Add:*—Hē nóhwider ofer þ cumon ne mæg, Bt. 36, 5; F. 180, 24. Martinus nolde út of þām mynstre nāhwider, Hml. S. 31, 257. Þā hig þā woldon hig lǽdan, þā ne myhton hig nāhwyder hig onstyrian, Shrn. 154, 25. Heora fiðera ne mihton nāhwider hí áberan, gif hí ne ābǽre seó lyft, Hex. 8, 23.

**nām.** *Add:* cf. nǽm.

**nama.** *Add:* I. as the individual designation of a single person, animal, place, or thing :—Mín nama ys Adonai, Ex. 6, 3. Mann wæs fram Gode āsend, þæs nama wæs Iōhannes (*cui nomen erat Iohannes*), Jn. 1, 6. Ðæs biscepes tíd and his módor, þǽre noma wæs Scē Anthiæ, Shrn. 71, 29. Brocceshám ðes dennes nama, ðes óðres dennes nama Sængethryg, Billanora is ðes ðriddan nama, C. D. ii. 74, 1–2. Brettisc cyning, þām wæs nama Natanleod, Chr. 508; P. 14, 26: 975; P. 120, 8. Eádbryht, . . . þām wæs óþer noma nemned Prǽn, 794; P. 56, 6. Him þ tó lytel yfel þúhte búton hié eác hié þæs naman benǽme *ipsum quoque Romae nomen persequentes*, Ors. 2, 8; S. 94, 4. Gregorius, se wæs óðrum naman genemned Nanzanzenus, Past. 173, 16. Laucius þe óþre noman wæs hāten Genutius, Ors. 3, 3; S. 102, 2. Þæt tācen nūgiét cúþ is on þǽre eá noman þæs consules sleges Fauiuses *testatur hanc Fabii cladem fluvius Allia, sicut Cremera Fabiorum*, 2, 8; S. 92, 17. Bizantium . . . be his noman wæs gehǽtenu Constantinopolim *a Constantino . . . Constantinopolis dicta*, 3, 7; S. 116, 12. Þǽr wǽron on āwritene ealra þāra rícestena monna noman, 6, 3; S. 258, 15. Naman, Past. 77, 16. Þām geatum mon āscóp þā noman þe hié giét habbað, Ors. 2, 4; S. 72, 14. Damascus getimbrode āne burh, and hire naman gesceóp be him sylfum Damascum *Damascus Damascum condidit et nomen civitati dedit*, Angl. vii. 44, 429.    II. *the particular word used to denote any object of thought not considered in a purely individual character* :—Ǽlc libbende

nýten, swā swā Adam hit gecígde, swā ys hys nama, Gen. 2, 19. Ðǽre wambe nama getācnað ðæt mód . . . Of Salomonnes cuidum wē nāmon ðætte ðǽre wambe nama scolde tācnian ðæt mód, Past. 259, 5–8. Ic him selle beteran noman ðonne óðrum mínum sunum oððe dohtrum *dabo eis nomen melius a filiis et filiabus*, 407, 36.    II b. *a title* of rank or dignity :—Ðā ðe ðone noman underfóð and ðā endebyrdnesse ðæs hálgan hādes, Past. 31, 11. Hē ne mehte self habban þæs onwaldes noman (*titulum imperatoris*), Ors. 6, 36; S. 294, 14.    III. *the name* of God or Christ, with implication of divine nature and power inherent in it :—Drihten úre God, hú wundorlic þín nama ys geond ealle eorðan, Ps. Th. 8, 2. Ðonne bistú daelniomende alra ðeára góda ðe ǽnig monn for his noman gedóeð, Txts. 174, 12. Men þā wilniað heora sáwla sellan for Dryhtenes naman *homines qui tradiderunt animas suas pro nomine Domini nostri*, Ll. Th. i. 56, 21: 92, 11. Ne nemn þū Drihtnes naman on ýdel, Ex. 20, 7. His noman wē sceolan weorþian mid wordum and dǽdum, Bl. H. 103, 27. Naman, Chr. 959; P. 115, 3.    IV. *the reputation* of some character or attribute, with gen. or clause :—Hí mē habbaþ benumen mínes naman þe ic mid rihte habban sceolde; þone naman ic sceolde mid rihte habban þ ic wǽre wela and weorþscipe, Bt. 7, 3; F. 20, 27. Hié wilniað ðæt hié gegítsien æt ðǽm ungetýdum folce wísdómes naman *ut apud imperitum vulgus scientiae sibi nomen extorqueunt, student*, Past. 365, 22.    IV a. *a distinguished name, reputation* :—Ic wille wyrcan mē naman and ofer-winnan Iūdam, Hml. S. 25, 300.    V. (*one's*) *repute* or *reputation* :—Ðæt is ðæt mon his mearce brǽde, ðæt mon his hlísan and his naman (noman, *v.l.*) mǽrsige, Past. 367, 13    Wurdon Læcedemonie swā swíðe forslagen þæt hié nāþer næfdon siþþan ne heora namon ne heora anweald, Ors. 3, 1; S. 98, 8.    VI. *the mere appellation in contrast or opposition to the actual person or thing* :—Hē gesette Eugenius tó þǽm ríces noman, þ hē cásere wǽre, and sēng him self tó þǽm onwealde, Ors. 6, 36; S. 294, 12. Ðonne naman ānne wē lufodon ðætte wē Crístne wǽren, and swíðe feáwe ðā ðeáwas, Past. 5, 7.    VII. in prepositional phrases, (1) be naman. (a) with verbs of naming :—Monega eá sindon be noman nemnede for þǽm gefeohte, Ors. 2, 4; S. 72, 12. Hē bebeád þ Hierusalem mon siþþan hēte be noman Helium *Hierosolymam Aeliam vocari praecepit*, 6, 11; S. 266, 18: El. 756: Chr. 975; P. 120, 28. (b) with verbs of calling upon, mentioning, &c. :—Heó ongan swegles weard be naman nemnan, Jud. 81. (c) with verb of knowing, *individually* :—Ic can þē be naman *novi te ex nomine*, Ex. 33, 12. (2) on (in) naman (a) in phrases expressing invocation of, reliance on, devotion to, (a) the persons of the Godhead :—Ðǽr twēgen oþþe þrý synt on mínum naman (in mínum noman, R.) gegaderode, Mt. 18, 20. Fulligeað hig on naman (in noman, R.) Fæder and Suna and þæs Hālgan Gāstes, 28, 19. Þ gē dóð on mínum naman ānum of þysum lǽstum, Hml. S. 31, 84. Hié on þínum naman wunnon, Bl. H. 141, 12. Hē hine þǽr on Godes naman geandette, Ll. Th. i. 64, 21. On Drihtenes naman (in noman, R.), Mt. 21, 9. In Dryhtnes noman, Cri. 413. (β) power of evil :—Hē clypode tó ðām fyrmestum deóflum, and on heora naman begól þone gramlican drenc, Hml. S. 14, 76. (b) in adjuration (a) by reference to the Deity or to saints :—Ic bebiáde Eádwealde an Godes naman and an ealra his hāligra ðet hē ðis wel healde, C. D. i. 297, 3. Ic bebióde on Godes naman (noman, *v. l.*) ðæt . . ., Past. 9, 2. Ic eów hālsige on Fæder naman, and on Suna naman . . ., and on ðaes Hālgan Gāstes, Rtl. 114, 14. (β) by reference to heathen gods or evil spirits :—Hē him geswór on his goda noman, Ors. 4, 6; S. 178, 9. (c) in case of dedication :—His mynster is æt Hwíterne, on Martines naman gehālgod, Chr. 565; P. 19, 14. (d) *under the character* or *designation of* :—Sē ðe underfēhð wítegan on wítegan naman (in noman wítgu, R.), Mt. 10, 41: 42. v. bí-, cúþ-, fore-, fulluht-, Lǽden-, tó-nama.

**nam-cíging,** e; *f.* A *calling by name, naming* :—An þǽre nam-cýginge ne sý nānon ālýfed þ heora ǽnig óðerne sindrium naman nemne *in ipsorum appellatione nominum nulli liceat alium puro nomine appellare*, Chrd. 9, 25.

**nam-cúþ.** *Add:* I. of persons :—Wæs sum ríce cyning, namcúð on worulde, Asuerus gehāten, Hml. A. 92, 2. Sum wer wæs namcúð and hlísful þurh his drohtnunga, 195, 15. His þ mǽre cynn wæs swiþe namcúð eallum folce, Hml. S. 23, 630.    II. of things :—*Asteriscus* ys namcúð tācen, Angl. viii. 333, 39. [v. N. E. D. namecouth.]

**namcúþlíce.** *Add: individually* :—Ǽnne God gē bodiað, and hūmeta namast þū namcúðlíce þrý godas, Hml. S. 34, 162.

**namian.** I. *add* :—Swā swā Abraham dyde . . . and þ wíf Anna . . . and fela óðre men ðe wē ne magan namian, Hml. A. 34, 261.    III. *substitute: to call by some title or epithet* :—Hwí namode Críst on his godspelle Abel rihtwísne tóforan óðrum? *cur Abel in evangelio singulariter justus nominatur?*, Angl. vii. 8, 76.    IV. *to name* (with the name as complement) :—Mercuries sunu þe hí Óðon namiað, Wlfst. 107, 11.    V. with cognate object :—Ne þū þínes Drihtnes naman ne namie on ídel, Wlfst. 66, 15. Hē ne gecneów þāra namena nān ðing þe hē þǽr namode, Hml. S. 23, 685. v tó-namian.

**namn.** v. ge-namn.

**nán.** I b. *add:*—Gif ic náne weorc ne worhte on him þe nán óðer ne worhte *si opera non fecissem in eis quae nemo alius fecit*, Jn. 15, 24. Næs nán rihtwís man ne nán hálig ǽr Abel, Hml. A. 129, 411. Flýhð se frófur áweg, ne byð þǽr fultum nán, Wlfst. 139, 14 : Dóm. L. 222. Nis on þám londe . . . ne wóp ne wracu, weátácen nán, Ph. 51. Ná on náre strencðe horses, Ps. L. 146, 10. Wé náne wiuht ne þurfon forlǽtan þæs wísdómes, Solil. H. 66, 4. Atýwde þ wilde fýr ðe nán mann ǽror nán swylc ne gemunde, Chr. 1032 ; P. 159, 5. Hí ne magon heom þeáh ná náne góde beón *they cannot be of any good to them*, Solil. H. 68, 29. Þú þe nelt þé geeówian openlíce nánum óðrum búton þám þe geclǽnsode beóð on heora móde, 5, 20. Þes iunga man ne æfestigað on nánum ðingum ðe hé hér gesihð, Ap. Th. 14, 26. Næbbe wé náne hláfas *panes non habemus*, Mk. 8, 16. Þú þe náne gesceaftas ne forlǽtst tó náhte weorðan, Solil. H. 5, 5. III. *add:*— Ne forlǽt þé nán þe gewityg byt, ne þé nán ne sécð bútan wýs, ne þé nán ne gemét búton geclǽnsod, Solil. H. 7, 1–3. Nǽfre welan ne beóð bútan synne begytene, ne nán þá eorþlican þing ne mæg bútan synne gebrytsnian, E. S. viii. 473, 32. ¶ a case used adverbially :—Hé þá stówe gódode tó þan swíþe þæt heó næs náne (*in no respect*) óþor ne wæccere þonne formænig þára þe his yldran ǽr gefyrþredon, Lch. iii. 438, 11.

**nán-wiht.** I. *add:*—Þæt hé þé nánwiht (náwiht, nóht, *v. l.*) láðes ne dó *ut nec tibi aliquid mali faciat*, Bd. 2, 12 ; Sch. 156, 23. Nát ic nánwiht betere þonne þú ðé gebidde, Solil. H. 4, 14. Nǽniht *nullam*, Lk. L. 23, 14.

**nasu.** *Add:* [*a wk. dat. occurs*] :—Dó brálinga þíne hand tó þínre nasan, swilce þú hwæt gestince, Tech. ii. 123, 12.

**nátes-hwón.** *Add:*—Hé suwode swilce hé ne gefrédde heora swingla náteshwón, Hml. S. 31, 977. Sume nellað wítnian mid náenre wrace þá máran synna on him sylfum náteshwón, Hml. A. 8, 185 : 16, 79 : 26, 43. Náteshwón (*nullatenus*) hé ne gedyrstlǽce, R. Ben. I. 100, 17.

**ná-teþeshwón** *by no means:*—Náteþeshwón *nequaquam*, Chrd. 116, 30. Nátyþeshwón *nullatenus*, 113, 20 : 114, 15. v. hwón ; III. 3 a.

**-naþ.** v. -noþ.

**ná-þing** *nothing:*—Náþing *nihil*, Germ. 395, 31. Ne gefrédde hé náþinc þæs brynes, Hml. A. 196, 48.

**ná-wiht.** I a. *add:*—Deófol mót ǽlces mannes áfandigan, hwæðer hé áht sý oððe náht, Hml. Th. i. 268, 12. Ne frign ðú unc nóhtes má ne ne áxa *caue ne nos ulterius scisciteris*, Nar. 32, 6. Ne byþ þ tó náhte *that will be good for nothing*, Lch. i. 344, 25. Oð hit mid ealle áfield, and tó náuhte wirð, Past. 279, 4. Tó náwuihte, Solil. H. 62, 28. Hé ne mihte on his móde áfindan þæt hé þone nacodan mid náhte ne gefréfrode, Hml. Th. ii. 500, 25. Him þá geþuhte swelc þæt mǽste wæl swelc hié oft ǽr for nóht hæfdon, Ors. 4, 7 ; S. 184, 15. I b. *add:*—Wé ús nówihtes. (náhtes, nóhtes, *v. ll.*) elles ne wéndon búton deáðes sylfes *neque aliud quam mortem sperare ualeremus*, Bd. 5, 1 ; Sch. 551, 17. Þ hé þé náwiht (nánwiht, nóht, *v. ll.*) láþes ne dó, 2, 12 ; Sch. 156, 22. Ne sceal hé náht (nóht, *v.l.*) unáliéfedes dón, Past. 61, 14. 'Ic nát nánwiht Godes gelíces.' 'Ic wundrie þín, hwí þú secge þæt þú Godes náwiht gelíces nyte,' (*nihil te nosse Deo simile*), Solil. H. 15, 16. Hí náht ðyllices ne gebudon, Hml. Th. i. 500, 29. II. *add:*—Næs ic on náuht (náuht on ?) ídlum anbide, þeáh hit mé lang anbid þúhte, Ps. Th. 39, 1. Æfter náht manegum dagum, Hml. S. 23 b, 350. Æfter nówiht manigum wintrum, Hml. A. 200, 183. Ne getweóge ic náwuht be Godes ǽcnesse, Solil. H. 59, 12. v. á-wiht.

**náwiht-líc.** *Add:*—Ongeán þám ingehýde se deófol syleð nytennysse náhtlicum mannum (*worthless men*), and eác þæt hý híwigon þæt hý ingehýd habban, Wlfst. 59, 15. Swá se gesibsuma wer swýðor blissað on góde, swá áswindeð se níðfulla swýðor tó náhtlicum ðingum, Hex. 46, 28. [The Latin original for R. Ben. 138, 30 is : Stulta mundi elegit et ignobilia mundi.]

**náwihtlíce.** *Add: ignobly:*—Ongeán þæs módes strengðe se mánfulla deófol forigð ábrodennysse, þæt se man ábreóðe on ǽlcere neóde náhtlíce ǽfre, and eác þæt hé híwige hine sylfne mihtigne, Wlfst. 59, 13 : Angl. xi. 109, 54.

**náwiht-ness.** *Add:*—Ignauia, þæt is ábrodennyss oððe náhtnyss, Wlfst. 58, 18 ; Angl. xi. 109, 39.

**Nazarenisc.** *Add:*—Se Nadzarenisca wítga, Bl. H. 71, 15.

**ne.** I. *add:*—Hé his ðǽr nó ne wénde, Past. 197, 14. Ne scírð hé nó hwæðer hié reáfoden oððe hwelc óðer yfel fremeden, 329, 7. Wé gesyngiað, gif wé óðerra monna welgedóna dǽda ne lufiað and ne herigað, 231, 1. Ðeáh ic nú ðis recce, nǽ (ne, *v.l.*) tǽle ic ná micel weorc, 41, 2. II. *add:*—Ðonne ne léten hié nó hié eallinga on ǽlce healfe gebígean, ne furðum nó áwecgean, Past. 306, 4.

**neádian.** *Add:* I. *absolute:*—Neádode *inuitos*, i. *coactos*, An. Ox. 1621. II. *to force to do something:*—Neádiende *compellens* (*scandere*), An. Ox. 2463. Neádod *conpellitur*, i. *angariatur* (*redire*), 2660. Neádude *cogerentur*, i. *compellerentur* (*redire*), 2484. III. *to force to or from something :*—Hé ofslóh þone óþerne

þe hine ðǽrtó neádode, Hml. S. 25, 227. Ne sceolon þá woruldcempan tó þám woruldlicum gefeohte þá Godes þeówan neádian fram þám gástlican gewinne, 828 : 834. Nán man ne móste neádian óðerne tó máran drænce þonne his mód wolde *nec erat qui nolentes cogeret ad bibendum*, Hml. A. 93, 24.

**neádian, neódian.** *Add:* v. ge-neódian.

**neádlunga.** *Add:*—Hí hine neádlunga (mid nýde, *v. l.*) áhófon úp on þ hors þe hí hine ǽr of áwurpon *invitum eum in caballum de quo deposuerunt, levauerunt*, Gr. D. 15, 24.

**neádung.** *Add:* of pressure due to persons or circumstances :—Hé him ásǽde hwylc neádung þæs gafoles hine áþreátode *quae eum urgeret debiti necessitas, indicauit*, Gr. D. 157, 28. Heó wolde lybban hyre líf on mægðháde sylfwilles for Gode, ná for neádunge, Hml. A. 32, 191. Þæne deófollican unðeáw, þ hé wile on his gebeórscipe þurh his hálsunge and ðurh his neádunge gedón, þ óðre men nimað máre ðonne hit gemet sý, 145, 23.

**neádunga (-e).** *Add:*—Is óðer ðeówt neádunge búton lufe, óðer is sylfwilles mid lufe, Hml. Th. ii. 524, 5 : i. 580, 1. Genam se sciphláford mé neádinga æt him, Hml. S. 30, 358. Þá þe hé bepǽcan ne mæg, þá hé wile neádunga nýdan, Wlfst. 84, 21.

**neáh ; adj.** *Add:*—Neáhne *proximum*, Germ. 400, 524. Neágum *proximis*, 399, 409. I. *add:* (1) local :—Sume synd stówlice, þá geswutelíað gehendnysse oððe ungehendnysse . . . *proximus* neáxð (neáhst néxt, nýxt, nýhst, *v. ll.*), Ælfc. Gr. Z. 14, 21. Þá gegaderode micel folc hit of þám niehstum burgum, Chr. 921 ; P. 102, 4. (2) marking relation, position, or order :—Cyninges þegenes (heregeata) þe him nýhste syndon, Ll. Th. i. 414, 9. II. *add:*—Se Sunnandæg wæs ealra daga se ǽresta, and hé bið eft se néxta t ǽitemesta, Wlfst. 210, 1. Ǽr his néxtan dæge, Hml. Th. ii. 152, 8. Þá þá hé sceolde álǽtan þæt níhste orað and ágyfan his gást *cum extremum spiritum ageret*. Gr. D. 324, 15. v. un-neáh, ende-néhst, and the neáh- compounds.

**neáh ; adv. prep.** I. (1) *add:*—' Hér is án lytele burg swíðe neáh ' . . . Hé cwæð ðæt hió wǽre swíðe neáh '*est ciuitas hic juxta . . . parua*' . . . *Iuxta dicitur*, Past. 399, 25 Sió sunne þǽr gǽð neár on setl þonne on óðrum lande, Ors. 1, 1 ; S. 24, 18. Scipia geáscade þ þá foreweardas wǽron feor ðǽm fæstenne gesette, and eác þ þǽr náne óðre neár wǽron, 4, 10 ; S. 200, 13. Þ se slaga móte mid griðe nýr, Ll. Th. i. 250, 17. Þá menn þe þǽr nýcst syndon, 236, 21. (1 a) figurative :—Sé ðe hyne myd hys módes ǽagum geseón wele, hé sceal . . . stígan neár and neár stæpmǽlum, Solil. H. 45, 17. I. (2) *add:* in superlative, of order in time, *last:*—Hét se cing þá módor ealra neáhst ácwellan, Shrn. 111, 22. Æðelstán and Eádmund, and Eádgár þe nýhst wæs, Ll. Th. i. 350, 7. Be ðám þe ic nú níehst ácsode, Solil. H. 65, 3. I. (3) *add:*—Hié selfe neáh forwurdon, Ors. 2, 6 ; S. 88, 16. Þá gemétte heó hire hwæte ealne beón neáh (*pene*) gedǽledne fram hire ágenum suna, Gr. D. 68, 23. II. (1) *add:*—Ealle ðá clifu þe neáh þǽm sǽ wǽron, Ors. 5, 4 ; S. 226, 4. Ðǽm ǽrestan godwebbe ðíostro nɛ magon cxxtigum míla neáh gehleonian, Sal. K. 152, 20. (1 a) figurative :—Nú wé sculon eft hwierfan neár Róma *we must now return in our story to Rome*, Ors. 2, 5 ; S. 86, 13. Þá áþas wǽron neár máne þonne sóðe, 4, 3 ; S. 162, 12. Þ frýnd móton bóte nýhst *that the friends may be most nearly concerned with the* '*bót*', Ll. Th. i. 256, 4. Godes grið is ealra griða sǽlast, . . . and þǽr néhst þæs cynges (*and next to that the king's*), 330, 3. II. (2) *add:*—Nú is þǽre tíde swíþe neáh *tempus nunc appropinquat*, Guth. Gr. 164, 3 : Jud. 287. Néh þǽre æftre Scā Marian mæssan, Chr. 1048 ; P. 173, 15. Hit wæs swíðe neáh his lifes ænde *ad extrema uitae ueniens*, Gr. D. 314. 3. Hwæðer is ðe leófre þe ðú nú onfó þá costnunga, þe neár þínum ende ?, Hml. S. 30, 132. II. (3 a) cf. I. (3) :—Neáh ðæm eall þá þing þe ðanan cumað wiþ ǽlcum ǽttre magan *omnia pene, quae de eadem insula sunt, contra uenenum ualent*, Bd. 1, 1 ; Sch. 13, 3. Neáh ðon eallum út ágangendum *cunctis pene egressis*, 1, 7 ; Sch. 23, 33. v. for-, ful-neáh ; neáh-compounds.

**neáh-ceaster** *a neighbouring city:*—Néhceastra gehwilce and land forhergiende *proximas quasque ciuitates agrosque depopulans*, Bd. 1, 15 ; Sch. 43, 11.

**neáh-cirice** *a neighbouring church:*—Sumre neáhcyrican mæssepreóst *uicinae ecclesiae presbyter*, Gr. D. 117, 3. Férdon hí tó þǽre neáhcyrican (*ad uicinam ecclesiam*), 216, 3.

**neáh-dǽl** *a neighbouring part:*—In þám neáhdǽlum Tuscie mǽgðe *in uicinis partibus Tusciae*, Gr. D. 71, 30.

**neáh-fæder** *a neighbouring father of the church, one not belonging to distant parts:*—Nú ic þus swíðe behealde þá neáhfæderas þe mid ús wǽron *dum uicinis ualde patribus intendo*, Gr. D. 179, 7.

**neáh-feald ; adj.** *Intimate:*—Tó his neáhfealdum freóndum, Nap. 47.

**neáhfeald-líc ; adj. Intimate:*—H gereordon hí sylfe mid neáhfealdlicre gesǽgne (the Latin is : *uicaria relatione*) þurh þá hálgan sprǽcu þæs gástlican lífes, Gr. D. 168. 17.

**neáh-gangol ; adj.** *In attendance on the person of the sovereign :*—þ eall hí dydon for ðæs cáseres ðingon, for þon hí him ǽr on hírede

swíðe neáhgangole wǽron (cf. *Icel.* þeir vóru svá nákvæmir konungi), Hml. S. 23, 130.

**neáh-gebúr.** *Add :*—Hēt hē makian ǽnne castel . . . and hine on his spǽce Malueisin hēt, þ is on Englisc Yfel nēhhebúr, Chr. 1095; P. 231, 9.

**neáh-gebȳren.** [*Put this before* **neáh-gebȳrild.**] *Add :*—His fōstormōdor ābæd ān hrìddern hire tō lǽne æt ōðrum wífe hire neáh-gebȳrene (-gebúrene, *v. l.*) *nutrix illius a vicinis mulieribus praestari sibi capisterium petiit,* Gr. D. 97, 1. þā wíf his nēhgebȳrne (neáh-gebúrena, *v. l.*) *vicinae mulieres,* 251, 25. Nēhgebȳrene (neáhgebúrena, *v. l.*), 252, 5.

**-neahhelíce.** v. ge-neahhelíce.

**neáh-hergung** *harrying in one's neighbourhood :*—Ne mihte ic gangan tō eástdǽlum for Rōmwarena cempena neáhhergunge *I could not go East because the Roman soldiers were harrying in the neighbourhood,* Hml. A. 200, 174.

**neahhige.** *Add :*—Ús neahge wearð gecȳðed hū Gūðlāc his in Godes willan mōd gerehte, Gū. 64.

**neáh-lǽcan.** *Add: with dat. or tō.* I. of movement in space :—Hē āna belāf and neálǽhte tō þǽre stōwe, Hml. S. 30, 105. þā apostolas ealle neálǽhton tō Drihtne, Bl. H. 155, 14. Hē weard āweht tō his neálǽcendan stefne, Gr. D. 85, 8. II. of movement in time. (1) with a noun or pronoun as subject :—Se dōm neálǽceþ, Bl. H. 91, 19. Nū neálǽceþ ǽgþer ge þin onwrigennes ge uncer gecȳþnes, 187, 22. Ic neálǽhte mínum ende, Gr. D. 243, 20. Þonne seó tíd neálǽce, Bl. H. 205, 28. Swā neálǽcende is þeós andwearde woruld tō ende *quantum praesens seculum propinquat ad finem,* Gr. D. 330, 25. (1 a) with clause :—Nū neálǽceþ þ wē sceolan ūre ǽhta gesamnian, Bl. H. 39, 11. (2) with impersonal construction, *to approach a season or event :*—Hit tō ðām dōme nū georne neálǽcð, Wlfst. 18, 14. Neólicað onlēsnisse eówrum *appropinquat redemtio uestra,* Lk. R. 21, 28. Þǽre tíde neálǽhte ūre ālēsnesse, Bl. H. 77, 14. Mid þȳ hit ǽfenne neálǽhte *uespertino tempore,* Nar. 23, 9. Þā þā hit neálǽhte þǽre tíde his deáþes *appropinquante mortis ejus tempore,* Gr. D. 301, 23. Hit neálǽhte his ænde *ad extrema pervenit pater,* 226, 1 : 307, 2.

**neáhlǽcung.** *Add :*—Seó tōwearde woruld mid hire neálǽcunge byð gecȳþed, Gr. D. 330, 26. Sē þe ne blissað on neálǽcunge middan-geardes geendunge, Hml. Th. i. 612, 23.

**neáh-land** *neighbouring country :*—þā henna āweg bær ān fox cumende of þám neáhlande (nǣht feorran, *v. l.*) *vulpis gallinas ex vicino rure veniens auferebat,* Gr. D. 69, 28.

**neáh-lic.** *Add :*—Hē dyde gelíce þon swylce hē swȳþe leóhtlíce slēpe and wæs āweht tō þǽre neálecan stefne (*ad vicinam vocem*), Gr. D. 85, 9.

**neáhlíce.** *Add:* I. *nearly, almost :*—Weard ān cnapa þurh nǣddran geslit neálíce ādȳd, Hml. S. 31, 951. II. *nearly, closely :*—Hī þeódað hī neálícor and fæstlícor tō þǽre rihtwísnesse *justitiae vicinius atque arctius inhaerebunt,* Gr. D. 336, 23. III. *hardly :*—Se hróf wæs on mislicre heánesse ; on sumre stōwe hē wæs þ man mid his handa neálíce (cf. earfoðlíce, Hml. Th. i. 508, 20 : both passages refer to the same place) gerǽcean mihte, in sumre eáþelíce mid heáfde gehrínan, Bl. H. 207, 22.

**-neahlíce.** v. ge-neahlíce.

**neáh-mǽg.** *Add :*—Se brōþer þám ōþrum ne mæg gehelpan, ne se fæder þám suna, ne þā neáhmágas, ne þá mādmgestreón, Verc. Först. 134, 24.

**neáh-munt.** *Add :*—Wæs se Godes man gelǽded in þone neáhmunt *in vicino monte ductus est,* Gr. D. 293, 13.

**neáh-mynster** *a neighbouring monastery* or *convent :*—In þám neáh-mynstre (neáhnunnmynstre, nēhnunmynstre, *v. ll.*) *uicino uirginum monasterio,* Bd. 4, 1; Sch. 337, 16.

**neáh-nunnan-mynster.** *Add:* neáh-nun[n]mynster. See *preceding word.*

**neáh-sibb** *near relationship. Add :*—Neáhsibbe *propinquę necessitudinis,* An. Ox. 2810.

**neáh-sibb; adj.** *Add: nearly related,* Wulfst. 271, 11. [Iosæþ wæss nehsibb wiþþ Sannte Marȝe, Orm. 13537. Cf. *O. H. Ger.* nāhsippa *proxima.*] Cf. feor-sibb.

**neáh-stōw.** *Add :*—Be þissere neáhstōwe *de vicino loco,* Gr. D. 48, 18. Hē þā lǽcas ǽghwanon of þám neáhstōwum (*ex vicinis locis*) gesomnode, 277, 22. His nama wæs cūð geond ealle þá neáhstōwa, 100, 13. Þ fȳr geondfērde ealle þá neáhstōwa *cum propinquiora sibi quaeque loca ignis invaderet,* 47, 28.

**neáh-tíd, neáh-þeód.** *Transpose these.*

**neáh-west.** I. *add :*—Anastasius wæs geþeóded tō Nonnoso, sē wæs prāfost on ðám mynstre þe geseted is in þám munte Soracte, and hē him þeódde tō fore þǽre stōwe neáwiste (*propinquitate loci*), Gr. D. 48, 26. Binnan ānes geáres fyrste næs gemēt hǽðengild geond hundteóntig mīla-neáwiste (*for a hundred miles round*), Hml. Th. i. 562, 27. II. *add :*—Ic wolde þæt hȳ mínre neáwiste wilnedon and þíne forhogedon, Wlfst. 255, 17. Būton hit sy elles hwylc þe mǽran Godes ege habbe,

þæt hit for his neáweste þe betere beó for Gode and for worolde, 269, 13.

**neáh-wudu** *a neighbouring wood :*—Ān hrefn wæs gewunod þ hē cōm of þám neáhwuda (*ex vicina sylva*), Gr. D. 118, 11 : 229, 20.

**nealles.** *Add:* , nals :—Hié ðæt folc bisenað on hira unðeáwum, nals (nalles, *v. l.*) on hira lāre, Past. 31, 6. Nals (nealles, *v. l.*) nā suā suā healt monn, 67, 10. Ðonces, nals nā (nalles nō, *v. l.*) for gestreónum, 137, 20. Þæt āttor nales þæt ān (nalæs þ ōn, *v. l.*) eallum middan-geardes ciricum þæt hē strǽgd, ac hit eác swylce in ðis eáland becōm *uirus non solum orbis totius, sed et insularum ecclesiis aspersit,* Bd. 1, 8; Sch. 29, 14. [*O. H. Ger.* nalles, nales, nals.]

**neán.** I. *add:* I a. *of time, from a time near at hand.* v. feorran :—Fela wítegan mid heora wítegunge bodedon Drihten tōweardne, sume feorran, sume neán (*some prophesied long before the event, some when it was near*), Hml. Th. i. 358, 7. III. *add :*—Mine neán āstyred fēt, neán āgoten stæpas míne *mei pene moti sunt pedes, pene effusi sunt gressus mei,* Ps. Rdr. 72, 2.

**-neán.** v. ge-neán.

**nearu.** I. *add :*—Leoniða angeán Xersis fōr on ānum nearwan londfæstenne and him þǽr mid gefeohte wiðstōd *Leonida in angustiis Thermopylarum obstitit,* Ors. 2, 5 ; S. 80, 14. Sume habbað swíðe scortne weg, and þeáh nearone, Solil. H. 44, 9. Ðæt scip bið drifen on swíðe nearwe bygeas, Past. 59, 6. I a. *fig. :*—Ǽghwylc Crísten mann smeáge hū nearo se síðfæt bið þǽre synfullan sāwle, Verc. Först. 138, 14. II. *add :*—þā synfullan berað nearowne wæstm and sceandfulne on ansȳne þes heáhstan Scyppendes, Verc. Först. 135, 10. III. *add: of material or non-material bonds :*—Neara arta, i. stricta (*conjugii continentia*), An. Ox. 578. Nearewum emsǽt-nunge arta obsidione, 5264. Se nearewecte stíþnes *artissima uiolentia,* 1239. IV. *add :*—Wiþ nearwum breóstum, Lch. ii. 174, 6. V. *evil, mean.* v. nearulíce ; V ; nearu-þanc.

**nearulíce.** II. *add :*—Heó nearolíce (angsumlíce, *v. l.*) geþreád wæs mid feferádle *anxietate febrium urgetur,* Gr. D. 29, 21. þā eóde hē hider and þider nearolíce geswænced in his geþōhte *cum huc illucque anxius pergeret,* 251, 24. IV. *closely, tightly :*—Nearolíce *strictim* (moecham manus *strictim* tollentis obuncat, Ald. 164, 3), An. Ox. 18 b, 90. V. *illiberally (?), evilly.* v. nearu-þanc :—Ne anhyre ðū þ nearolíce (*nequiter*) þū dō. Þe nearolíce (*nequiter*) dōþ beóð ge-teórode, Ps. Rdr. 36, 8–9.

**nearu-ness.** I. *add:* I a. *a narrow space, a place of small extent :*—Nearenesse *ergastulo* (e corporis *ergastulo* emigrare), An. Ox. 979. II. *add:*—þám men bið þurst getenge and nearones, Lch. ii. 194, 2. For manegum nearonessum ic neálǽhte mínum ende *crebris angustiis ad exitum propinquans,* Gr. D. 243, 19. II a. *physical inconvenience, difficulty, troublesome action :*—Hī gesāwon þā nearo-nessa and þā uneáðnesse þe him sylfum gedōn wæs *factam sibi difficultatem videbant,* Gr. D. 226, 17. III. *add :*—Geseah hē frēfrende gesyhðe, seó him ealle þā nearonesse (neara-, *v. l.*) þǽre gemyngedan sorge (*omnem anxietatem memoratae sollicitudinis*) āfyrde, Bd. 4, 11; Sch. 406, 9. Gif ealle wítegan wítegodon þæt Crist sceolde ðurh nearunysse his ðrowunge intō his heofonlican wuldre faran, hūmeta mæg sē beón crīsten, sē ðe nele . . . ðurh nānre earfoðnysse þæt beon wuldor mid Crīste geearnian?, Hml. Th. ii. 284, 27. Gefriða mē of eallum mínum nearonessum *redime ex omnibus angustiis meis,* Ps. Th. 24, 20. IV. *scantiness.* (1) *of space :*—Fore nearonesse (nearwnesse, *v. l.*) þǽre stōwe þe þæt mynster on getimbred is *propter angustiam loci, in quo monasterium constructum est,* Bd. 4, 10; Sch. 400, 6. (2) *of means :*—Ðeáh wē þisse worulde wlenca tilian swíðe . . . ; þeáh wē ūs mid þám deórwyrþestan gimmum ūton ymbehōn, hwæðere wē sceolon on nearonysse ende gebídan, Wlfst. 263, 1.

**nearu-searu.** *Add:* An *evil, mean trick (?).* Cf. nearu-þanc, -wrenc.

**nearu-þanc.** *Add :*—Feóndlices nearaþances ł hinderscypes *spiritalis nequitiae,* An. Ox. 378. Feóndlicra nearaþanca, bīswíca *spiritalium nequitiarum,* i. *fraudium,* 763. Forlǽten wē . . . tǽlnesse and twy-sprǽcnessa, nīðas and nearoþancas, Verc. Först. 94, 3. v. nearulíce ; V ; nearu-searu-, wrenc.

**nearu-wrenc.** *Add:* an *evil, mean trick (?) :*—Ǽfestum onǽled oferhygda ful, nīðum, nearowrencum, Mōd. 44. v. nearu-þanc, -searu.

**nearwe.** I. *add :*—Ān clīwen suíðe nearwe and suíðe smeálíce gefealden, Past. 241, 24. Ne ǽnig man ōðerne tō nearwe ne hæfte, Wlfst. 70, 5.

**nearwian.** *Add: to restrain :*—þám ūtyrnendan men (*the man with dysentery*) mon sceal sellan þā mettas þā ðe wambe nearwian, Lch. ii. 278, 17.

**neát.** *Add :*—Him mon scolde sellan ðā breósð ðæs neátes (cf. pectusculum de ariete . . . in partem Aaron, Ex. 29, 26–28), Past. 81, 25. Gyf man forstele feoðerfōt neát, hors oððe hrȳðer (*animal quadrupes, equum vel bovem*), Ll. Th. ii. 140, 33. Hē þás foldan gefylde swíðe mislicum neáta cynnum (cf. mid mistlicum cynrenum nētena, Bt.

33, 4; F. 132, 26), Met. 249. Men and neát (nýtenu, Ps. Th. Rdr.) *homines et iumenta*, Ps. Vos. Srt. Cam. 35, 7.

**nebb.** *add:*—Hér *pilus*, neb *piceca*, Wrt. Voc. ii. 117, 41-42. **I.** *Add:*—Mid nebbe pluc[ciað] *rostro* (*apes*) *decerpunt*, An. Ox. 100. **III.** *add:*—Nebb *uultus*, An. Ox. 2931. Dragað hine niwelne his neb tó eorðan, Hml. S. 14, 155. Ðá hé fleáh, ðá tórýpte hine án bré(m)ber ofer ðæt nebb. Ðá hé ætsacan wolde, ðá sǽde him mon ðæt tó tácne, C. D. ii. 134, 28. Þú gesceáwast ðæs mannes neb, and God sceáwað his heortan, Hml. Th. i. 288, 6. Eówer nebb sint suá scamleás suá ðára wífa ðe beóð forelegnissa *frons mulieris meretricis facta est tibi*, Past. 207, 9.

**-neb[b], -nebba, -nebbe.** v. geáp-, salo-neb[b], hyrned-nebba, twi-nebbe : **neb-gebræc.** *l.* -gebræc.

**neb-sealf,** e; *f.* *A face-salve:*—Nebsealfe *stibio*, An. Ox. 4, 25. Of nebsealue, 8, 269.

**neb-wlátung.** For 'frontositas . . . word' *substitute:*—Nebwlátung, ǽwyscnes *inpudentia*, An. Ox. 4306 : **neb-wlatung.** *Dele.*

**neb-wlitu.** *Add:* neb-wlite; es; *m.*:—Heora nebwlite þurh ðá mycclan sorhge mid ealle áhlǽnsode, Hml. S. 23, 126. Eall heora nebwlite ongann tó scínenne swilce seó þurhbeorhte sunne, 820. Him gelícode hire fægra nebwlite, Hml. A. 94, 89. Hé beseah on hire scínendan nebbwlite, 109, 245 : Hml. S. 29, 169. Heora nebwlite wǽron swilce rose and lilie, 23, 780.

**nefa.** **I.** *for other examples see* ge-nefa. **II.** *add:* in a general sense, *a descendant*, pl. *children's children :*—Nefena nefen[a] *pronepotum* (qui nepotum et pronepotum piacula abolere potuisset), An. Ox. 5029. Æftergengcum, nefenum *nepotibus* (haeredibus et futuris nepotum *nepotibus*), 3370.

**nefe** (?), an; *f.* *A grand-daughter :*—Se cyng blissode on his ylde þ hé geseah his nefan (nefenan?) mid hire were, Ap. Th. 27, 9.

**nefene.** *Dele second passage, for which see* nefa.

**nefne.** **II.** *add:* **II a.** *without negative, only, nothing but :*—Dó tó drence nǽdran geworhte swá lǽcas cunnon, and þonne hié ǽlcra drincan willen, drincan hié nemne wæter, Lch. ii. 202, 18.

**-nēhþ.** v. efen-ēhþ, -nēhþ : **-nēhwian.** v. ge-nēhwian.

**nemnan.** **I.** *add:* Monega eá sindon be noman nemnede for ðǽm gefeohte, Ors. 2, 4; S. 72, 12. **I a.** with cognate accusative :—þú nemst hys naman Hǽlend, Mt. 1, 21. **II.** *add:*—þ hěhste gód þe wé nemnaþ God, Bt. 39, 7; F. 220, 31. Þone swylcne seócne lǽcas nemniað gewitleásne, Gr. D. 247, 14. Hér wé magon gehiéran, ðá hé be ðǽm wróhtgeornan secgean wolde, ðæt hé hine nemde se áworpna, Past. 357, 23. Gif þú swá gewlǽtne mon mētst . . ., ne miht ðú hine ná mid rihte nemnan man, ac neát (*hominem aestimare non possis*), Bt. 37, 4; F. 192, 13. **IV.** *add:* (1) *to mention* a subject (person or thing) :—þonne ðú gehýrst nemnan þone Fæder, þonne understenst ðú þæt hé hæfð Sunu. Eft þonne þú cwyst Sunu, þú wást þæt hé hæfð Fæder, Hml. Th. i. 284, 10. Ðú sǽdest þ ðú nystest ǽlcre gesceafte ende; ac wite nú þ þ is ǽlcre gesceafte ende þ þú self ǽr nemdest, þ is God, Bt. 34, 12; F. 154, 14. **IV a.** *to mention the name of* a person, *mention by name:*—Se Hǽlend spræc be ðám rícan, 'Sum ríce man wæs.' Eft be ðám wǽdlan, 'Sum ðearfa wæs geháten Lazarus' . . . Ne nemde se Hǽlend þone welegan, ac ðone wǽdlan, 330, 6. **IV b.** *with cognate accusative, to give the name of:*—Hé his yldrena naman nemde *he gave the names of his parents*, Hml. S. 23, 683. v. tó-nemnan.

**nemning,** e; *f.* *Name, appellation :*—Hé his yldrena naman nemde, hwæt þæs ánes nama wæs and hwæt þæs óþres næmnincg wæs, Hml. S. 23, 684.

**-neód;** *adj.* v. ofer-neód.

**neód-.** v. níd-.

**neód-full.** *Add:*—Nú bidde ic míne arceð and ealle míne leóðb þ hý ealle neódfulle beón ymbe Godes gerihta, Cht. E. 230, 14.

**neódlíce.** *Add:*—þý neódlícor gehelpan þám ylcan tédriendum mannum *eisdem infirmantibus prodesse propinquius*, Gr. D. 267, 20.

**neom.** *Add:*—Þára þú neart gemyndig læng *quorum non es memor amplius*, Ps. Th. 87, 4.

**-neórþ.** v. ge-neórþ.

**neorxna wang.** *Add:*—Brúcað gě Godes neorxnewonges, Hml. S. 30, 101. Ðá ðá hí ǽrest gesceapene wæron on neorxna wonge, Past. 405, 27.

**neorxnawang-lic;** *adj.* *Of paradise:*—Hér onginneð se þridda flód of ðám neorxnawanglican wylle, Gr. D. 179, 1.

**neósian.** *Add:*—Untrum ic wæs and gé neósadun mín *infirmus eram, et visitasti me*, Mt. R. 25, 36.

**neósung.** *Add:*—Hú miccle swiðor is Godes andweardnys and his neósung ǽghwǽr . . . Godes gást áfandað ealra manna heortan, and ðá ðe on hine gelýfað, þá hé gegladað mid his neósunge, Hml. Th. i. 288, 2-9. Nis nánra georngra manna neósung tó þǽm *ad quas* (nuns) *juvenum nullus accessus est*, R. Ben. 139, 7. Ðǽle man . . . frófer þám dreórigan, neósunge þám seócan, Wlfst. 74, 5.

**neoþan.** *Add:*—Ðunor cymð of hǽtan and of wǽtan. Seó lyft týhð ðone wǽtan tó hyre neoðan, and ðá hǽtan ufon (-an, *v. l.*), Lch. iii. 280, 3. v. under-neoþan.

**neoþemest.** *Add:* v. under-neoþemest.

**neoþera.** *Add:* of degree, rank, &c., *inferior :*—þæs niðeran (nyþeran, An. Ox. 593) lífes *inferioris uitae*, Hpt. Gl. 420, 34. Ne onscunige ic nó þæs neoþeran and þæs unclǽnan stówe, Bt. 5, 1; F. 10, 15. Hú nearwe and hú ænge wǽron ealle ðá neoðerran gesceafta, Gr. D. 174, 16. Hit wirð gewundod mid ðǽm hungre ðæs nyðemestan and ðæs fúlestan geðóhtes *cupiditatis infimae fame sauciatur*, Past. 283, 17.

**neoþor.** *Add:*—Niðerer *inferius*, Hpt. Gl. 420, 10. Seó eorðe stent on ælemiddan swá gefæstned þ heó nǽfre ne býhð náþor ne ufor ne nyðor (neoðor, nyþror, *v. ll.*), Lch. iii. 254, 18.

**neówlinga.** v. níwlinga.

**neowol.** **I.** *add:*—Nimað þisne scyldigan . . . and dragað hine niwelne (neowelne, *v. l.*) his neb tó eorðan, Hml. S. 14, 155. **II.** *add:*—Drohtnoð habban . . . in neowulm ǽtre (*in the poison of the bottomless pit*), Wlfst. 188, 8. On neowulm *in imo*, Scint. 21, 12. Tó neowlum *ad ima*, 4, 17 : 20, 8. Neolum *imis*, Lch. i, lxxv, 3. þeáh se man gewíte in ðá neowelestan scrafa, Verc. Först. 103, 10.

**neowol-lic.** *Add:*—On deópum, niwelicum grunde *in fundo, profundo, i. imo maris*, An. Ox. 1942.

**neowol-ness.** *Add:* **I.** of a deep place on earth :—Ofer þá stówe ufon wæs hangiende unmǽte stánclif, and eác beneoðan swiþe deóp neowelnys (niwolnys, niolnes, *v. ll.*) ginode *in loco ingens desuper rupes eminet, et profundum subter praecipitium patet*, Gr. D. 52, 18. Under þám ylcan eáhþyrle geonode mycclu neolnes (niwelnes, *v.l.*), 199, 25. **II.** of the lower regions :—Seó gräniende neowelnys and seó forglendrede hell, Wlfst. 187, 1. þú átuge míne sáwle of neolnessum (*ab inferis*), Ps. Th. 29, 2.

**nepte.** *Add:* [From Latin] : **-nereness.** v. ge-nereness.

**nergend.** *Add:*—þis is þæs ælmihtigan Dryhtnes sylfes mūðes cwide . . . 'Ic eom se ælmihtiga Dryhten and eallra gásta nerigend,' Verc. Först. 121, 8.

**nergend-lic;** *adj.* *That should be preserved* (?) :—Q. For þám micel gód (*the MS. has the accent*) and nergendlic swýðe, and þú fintst blisse, Hpt. 21, 189.

**nerian.** *Add:* v. á-nerian : **nering.** *Add:*—Nerun[ge], An. Ox. 5395 : **-neru.** v. ealdor-, feorh-neru.

**nesan.** *Add:*—Hwílum ús earfoðlíce gesǽled on sǽwe, þeh wé síð nesan, An. 515. Gif hié brim nēsan and gesundne síð settan mósten, El. 1004.

**nese.** *Add:* (1) saying *no* to a question :—'Hwæþer ðín woruld eall wǽre æfter ðínum willan.' Ðá andsworode Boetius : 'Nese, lá, nese; næs ic nǽfre gít náne hwíle swá emnes módes . . .', Bt. 26, 1; F. 90, 24, Nese, lá, nese; ne mín ne nánes mannes nis ðá þám creftig . . ., Solil. H. 4, 3. (2) where a request, command, &c., is refused :—Críst sǽde þæt se yfela welega bǽde Abraham þæt hé sende Lazarus. . . . Ðá cwæð Abraham : 'Nese, . . .', Solil. H. 67, 30. 'Nese, næse,' 68, 7. 'Uton . . . spurian tó morgen furður.' Nese, lá, nese,' 46, 1. 'Næse, lá, nese,' 49, 12. (3) where a prohibition is assented to :—'þ án ic þé bebeóde, þ þú . . . ne forgite þ þ ic ǽr tǽhte.' Ðá cwæþ ic : 'Nese, ne forgite ic hit nó,' Bt. 34, 9; F. 146, 15. (4) where dissent is expressed :—'Hí ondrédon þ wé heom for ðon grame beón woldon, for ðon þe hí ǽr ús hýran noldon.' Ðá cwæð se cásere : 'Nese' (*there was no reason for them to think so*), Hml. S. 23, 275. Hé cwæð be him sylfum tó þám cýpemannum : 'Syllíce is mé ánum gelumpen . . . man mid wítum ofgán willað æt mé þ ic mid rihtan þingon begyten hæfde.' Ðá andwyrdon þá cýpemen : 'Nese, nese, leófa man, ne miht þú ús ná swá bepǽcean mid þínan smēðan wordan,' 601. (5) as representing a negative statement :—Oððe wēne gě ðæt ǽgðer sié mid mě ge gise ge nese *ut sit apud me, est et non*, Past. 308, 9.

**-ness.** *The suffix is attached to nouns,* v. hæftníd-, mægenþrym-, wyndreám-ness ; *to adjectives, e. g.* gód-, swēt-, gífer-, nearu-ness ; *to numerals or pronouns.* v. án-, hwilc-ness ; *to past participles.* v. álífed-, gedrēfed-ness ; for-sewen-, ágoten-, gecoren-ness ; *to verbal roots,* (1) *weak :* v. íc-, líf-, nere-, styre-ness. (2) *strong :* v. foreseó-, grōw-, weax-ness. (3) *pret. pres.* wit-ness.

**nestig.** v. nihstig.

**netele.** *Add:* netel, e :—þá geseah hé þǽr neáh him weaxan þicce scaldþýfelas netelena (netlenu, nytelena, *v. ll.*) and brēmela (*urticarum et veprium*) . . . hé hine sylfne nacodne wylede on þǽra netela (netlena, nytelena, *v. ll.*) tendingum, Gr. D. 101, 11-17.

**nēþan.** *Add:* (1) absolute :—Him wæs mycel ege tó þon þ hé hūru tó swýðe ne nýdde (gedyrstlǽhte, *v. l.*), gif hé þæs ungewunelican þinges tó Gode wilnode *he was very much afraid of venturing too far, if he desired that unusual thing of God*, Gr. D. 18, 10. (2) with preposition :—Ic swíðe unmeodum geneahhe nēðde tó Dryhtnes líchoman and tó his ðám deórwyrþan blóde *I ventured far too frequently to go to the Lord's Supper*, Angl. xi. 99, 70. (3) with clause :—Hwæt is þes

ceorlisca wer þe nēþeþ (gedyrstlǣceđ, *v. l.*) þus ungelǣred þ hē āgnađ him sylfum þā þēnunga ūres apostolican hlāfordes? *quis est iste vir rusticus, qui officium apostolici nostri domini sibimet indoctus usurpare praesumit?*, Gr. D. 35, 4.

**net-gearn.** *Put this before* nēþan.

**nett.** I. *add:*—Gif hwylc deór byđ on nette āwyrged *si fera aliqua in rete strangulata sit*, Ll. Th. ii. 214, 1. Fleótas (-es, MS.) tó nette *aestuaria*, Wrt. Voc. i. 57, 9. Hwæþer gē nū settan eówer nett on đā hēhstan dūne đonne gē fiscian willađ? ic wāt đeáh þ gē hit þǣr ne settađ. Hwæþer gē nū eówer hundas and eówer nett ūt on đā sǣ lǣdon đonne gē huntian willaþ? ic wēne þeáh þ gē hī đonne settan ūp on dūnum and innon wudum, Bt. 33, 3; F. 118, 11–15. v. feax-, fugol-, sǣ-, wíd(?)-nett.

**nettian.** v. ge-nettian.

**newe-seóþa.** *Add:*—Neuanseáda, naensīda *ilium*, Txts. 68, 505. Naensood, 110, 1180.

**nic.** *Add: no:*—Andswaredun þā snottre cwæþende, 'Ne sē ł nic,' Mt. R. 25, 9. v. niccan.

**niccan** *to say no* (v. nic), *refuse a person something:*—Ic bidde đē þurch đene Drictene gif ic ongēn ne cōme đat đū it nēfre ne lēt welden mīne unwynan æfter mē đe mid unrichte sitteđ đēron, and niccađ it mē ēuere tō undanke, C. D. vi. 201, 6. [v. *N. E. D.* nick *to deny.*]

**Nicēnisc** *Nicene:*—Se bisceopsinođ þæs Nicēniscan geþeahtes, Angl. xi. 8, 1.

**nicor.** *In* l. 2 *read* niccres, *and add:*—In þǣre eá āweóllon swā ǣmettan þā nicras (*printed* þam cras) *hypopotami ueluti formice efferbuere*, Nar. 11, 13. [*The form* crās *should be deleted.*] [v. *N. E. D.* nicker.]

**nicstig.** v. nihstig.

**nīd.** *Add: I. violence, force, compulsion,* exercised by or upon persons:—Hē cwæđ þ wǣre mid gafoles neáde (neóde, *v. l.*) geþrafod *sum geleáffull wer fidelis vir quidam necessitate debiti compulsus*, Gr. D. 157, 22. Hē wæs beótiende þ hē wolde mid nýde (*violenter*) gān in þā cyrican, 234, 15. Hī hine mid nýde (nēde, neádlunga, *v. ll.*) upp āhōfon and on his āgen hors āsetton *invitum eum in caballum levaverunt*, 15, 27. Arrianus þe þider cōm þ nýd tó wyrcanne *Arrianus, qui vim facturus aduenerat*, 23572. II. *for, of* nīde *of necessity, unavoidably:*—Gif đū for neóde āxsast æfter mīnum naman *if you must ask for my name*, Ap. Th. 15, 21. Seó þearlwísnes þæs heardan līfes him ǣrest of nýde (nēde, *v. l.*) becōm (*ex necessitate obuenerat*) for bōte his synna, Bd. 4, 25; Sch. 493, 19. III. *necessity from the* facts or circumstances of the case:—Nales ođ bewerenesse þā symbelnesse tó mǣrsienne mæssesanges, gif þæt nýd (nēd, *v. l.*) ābǣdeđ ođđe symbeldæg gelimpeđ ođđe ōđer sācerd in þǣre stōwe ne biđ *non usque ad prohibitionem missarum sollemnia celebrandi, cum fortasse aut festus dies exigit, aut exhiberi mysterium (pro eo quod sacerdos alius in loco deest) ipsa necessitas compellit*, Bd. 1, 27; Sch. 94, 23. IV. nýd is *it is necessary or needful* (with dat. infin. or clause):—Is mǣst neód þ hē āsēce, Angl. ix. 261, 4. IV a. with dat. of person:—Eal swā ūs neód is gelōme tó dōnne, Ll. Th. i. 326, 7. Mē ys neód þ ic menge þ Lýden amang þissum Englisce, Angl. viii. 317, 16. V. nīd habban *to be under a necessity to do something:*—Nabbađ hī neóde tó farenne, Mt. 14, 16. VI. *imperative demand* for the presence, possession, &c. of something:—Nis mē þæs horses nān neód *ego caballo opus non habeo*, Gr. D. 15, 23. Gif wē þām þearfan, þe þæs neód biđ (*who is in need of the water*), gerǣcađ cuppan cōles wæteres, Hml. A. 141, 82. VI a. (*to have*) need of:—Secgađ þ Drihten hæfđ his neóde, Mk. 11, 3. VII. (*to have*) need, *be in want:*—Đā nēd hæfde *quando necessitatem habuit*, Mk. L. 2, 25. VIII. *a condition of affairs placing one in difficulty or distress; a time of difficulty; exigency, emergency:*—Mōyses sǣde Drihtne þæs folces neóde, Ex. 15, 25. Þæt Crīstene menn tó cyrican faran magan and þǣr heora neóda tó Gode mǣnan, Wlfst. 278, 20. IX. *a condition marked by the lack or want of some necessary thing, or requiring some extraneous aid or addition:*—Hml. Th. ii. 340, 21 (*in Dict.*). X. *a matter requiring action to be taken, a piece of necessary business:*—Martinus fērde tó þām cāsere, wolde for sumere neóde wiđ hine sprecan, Hml. S. 31, 651. Eóde hē ymbe sume neóde, Vis. Lfc. 18. XI. *a particular point or respect in which some necessity or want is present or is felt:*—Heó sende þā gebrōđra tó sēcenne summe stān tó swilcere neóde, for đan þe on þām fenlande synd feáwa weorcstāna, Hml. S. 20, 76. XI a. *a necessary article, necessary of life:*—Āmang þām feó þe wē on þysum dagum ūre neóde mide bicgađ, Hml. S. 23, 706. v. ciric-, folc-, ofer-, sǣr- (?), weorold-nīd; nīde, nīdes.

**nīdan.** *Add: I. to exercise constraint or compulsion upon one:*—Hié in hātheortnisse nēddun (*conpulerent*) mec, Ps. Srt. ii. 193, 38. Hē nō æt ne cume, đeáh hiene mon niéde, Past. 59, 10. I a. *to force* in a particular direction, for a particular object:—Nā þ ān gōdu geheált, ac heó āweg nýt (*repellit*) wyþerwerde, Scint. 13, 10. His ealdormen niéddon hī æfter (v. æfter, I. 6) gafole, and micel gefiit hæfdon *propter auaritiam Maximi ducis in arma surgentes*, Ors. 6. 34; S. 290, 24. II. *to force* to something. (1) *with* tó *and noun:*—Hē

nænigne nýdde tō Crīstenum þeáwe *nullum cogebat ad Christianismum*, Bd. 1, 26; Sch. 59, 5. Hī hiene niéddon tō leornunga, þēh hē gewintred wǣre, Ors. 6, 31; S. 284, 21. (2) *with dat. infin.:*—Hié hié selfe nīdađ (niédađ, *v. l.*) tō healdonne swīgean, Past. 271, 16. Stinge him mon feþere on mūđ, nēde hine tō spīwanne, Lch. ii. 286, 17. (3) *with clause:*—þone hié nǣddun þ hē bǣre his rōde *hunc angariauerunt ut tolleret crucem ejus*, Mt. R. 27, 32. [v. *N. E. D.* need *to constrain.*] v. for-nīdan.

**nīd-bād.** *Add:* figurative:—Hwæt, wē nū wǣron fægne þæt wē ne mōston bedīglan on ūssum scræfum, þæt hē ūs ne swencte mid his mægnis nīdbāde, Mod. Philol. 1, 33.

**nīd-behēfe.** *Add: I. necessary:*—Nēdbehēfe ys þā gyltas forceorfan *necessarium est ipsas culpas succidere*, Scint. 8, 4. þ is nýdbehēfe, Chrd. 111, 6. II. *with dat. of person:*—Ūs ys þīn līf nýdbehēfe gīt, Hml. S. 22, 226: 28, 142: Scint. 8, 4. II a. *with dat. of person and dat. infin.:*—Is lenctentīd eallum Crīstenum mannum nēdbehēfe tō gehealdenne, Wlfst. 102, 13.

**nīd-behēfedness,** e; *f. A need, necessity:*—Lytles hwega for þæs līchaman nēdbehēfednyssum mid him hæbbende, Hml. S. 23 b, 150.

**nīd-behēfness,** e; *f. What is needful:*—Ealle nýdbehēfnysse hē wæs dǣlende þām þe þæs behōfodon, Hml. S. 30, 8.

**nīd-brýce.** *l.* -bryce.

**nīde;** II. *add:*—Hē gebint hine selfne tō him mid his wordum đæt hē sceal niéde đā giémenne ymb đone habban đe hē ǣr ne đorfte . . . đæt hē hine sceal nīde tela lǣran *apud curam, quae ante deerat, mens ligatur . . . commissis sibi cogitur bona dicere*, Past. 193, 8–12. III. *add:*—Đæt hē đonne tō sōo, gif hē niéde sciele *coactus ad regimen veniat*, Past. 59, 9.

**nīded-līc.** v. ge-nīdedlic: **nīdelīce.** v. un-nīdelīce.

**nīdes.** *Add:* [Gif þū hire nýdes (nēdinga, *earlier version*) on ne sōhtest, þone wǣre heó clǣne, Hml. A. 135, 656 (12th cent.). Se eorl . . . and þā muneces fiēmden se ōđer abbot ūt of þā mynstre, hī scolden nēdes; on fīf and twēnti wintre ne biden hī nǣfre ān gōd dæi, Chr. 1131; P. 262, 3.]

**nīd-faru.** *At end of first line l.* there *for* the, *see* Txts. p. 149.

**nīd-full;** *adj. Necessary, needful:*—Mid eádmōdre and neódfulre þēnunge *humili ac necessario officio*, Angl. xiii. 377, 174.

**nīd-grāp,** e; *f. A violent grasp, forcible clutch:*—Nýdgrāpum nimeđ, Reim. 73.

**nīd-hǣmdere,** -hǣmedre, es; *m. A violator of chastity, an adulterer:*—Nýdhǣmedra *stuprorum* (Venus *stuprorum* amatrix, Ald. 62, 19), An. Ox. 7, 304: 8, 240. Nýdhǣmedran, 2, 333. Cf. unriht-hǣmdere.

**nīd-hǣmestre.** *Add* (?): *an adulteress* (?). *Perhaps* nīd-hǣmestre *glosses* stuprorum amatrix *rather than* amatrix. *See preceding word, where the passage glossed is given.*

**nīd-hūs,** es; *n. A necessary room:*—Sýn eác binnan claustre slǣpern, beódern, hǣdern, and ealle þā neódhūs þe brōđra beþurfon (*cetere habitationes usibus fratrum necessariae*), Chrd. 21, 18.

**nīdige.** [Cf. *O. H. G.* nōtig *violentus.*] v. un-nīdige.

**nīdinga.** *Add:*—Đonne sculon hié eft niédenga gadrian ōđer ierfe on đæs wriexle đe hié ǣr for mildheortnesse sealdon *violenter exquirunt, quae misericorditer largiuntur*, Past. 341, 18. Nū đæt đæt hié lyst hī sculon nēde[n]ga forlǣtan, and đeáh đæt hī nū nēdenga forlǣtađ him biđ eft tō wīte gehealden *nunc; quod libet, invitis subtrahitur, et tunc, quod dolet, invitis in supplicium reseruatur*, 441, 22–24. Gyf đu nēdinga hyre on ne sōhtest, þonne wǣre heó clǣne, Hml. A. 135, 656. v. un-nīdinga.

**nīd-līc;** *adj. Necessary:*—Swīgendum nā þþelīce mæg lācnung gedafenlicre and neódlicre sprǣce beón gegearwnd, Scint. 41, 2. v. þreánīd-lic.

**nīd-ling.** *Add: a captive:*—Hit gelamp þ Langbeardisce men gehergedon .xl. neádlinga *dum fere quadringentos captiuos Longobardi tenuissent*, Gr. D. 232, 24. v. hæft-nīdling.

**nīd-mǣg.** *Add:* v. ge-nīdmāgas.

**nīd-māge.** *Add:*—Oft týne ođđe twelfe ælc æfter ōđrum scendađ þæs þegnes cwenan and hwīlum his dohtor ođđe nýdmāgan, Wlfst. 162, 21.

**nīd-micel.** *The full passage in* Bl. H. *is:* Medmycel ǣrende wē þyder habbađ, and ūs is þearf þ wē hit þēh gefyllon *we have an important errand thither, and we must however carry it out*, 233, 11. *The poem seems to support the idea contained in* nēdmicel, *that of urgency:* Ūsic lust hweteđ on þā leódmearce micel mōdes hiht, An. 286. *In support, too, of* nēdmicel *is the accent in the* MS. *Moreover St. Andrew would hardly have spoken of his mission as unimportant.*

**nīd-nǣman.** *Add:*—Ne neádnǣmde, ne ođbrǣd *non arripit, non eripit*, Angl. xxxii. 505.

**nīd-nīd,** e; *f. Absolute, unavoidable necessity:*—Gif ænig geþrīstlǣse būtan slǣperne tō slǣpenne būtan he neádneóde hæbbe (*absque causa ineuitabili*), Chrd. 61, 9.

**nīd-niman.** *Add:*—Se biscop eóde tō þǣre cyste and ārfullīce

nýdnimende (neódnymende, v. l.) hē tōslōh þā locu þǣre cyste, and þǣr genam þā .xii. mancossas accessit ad arcam, et pie violentus claustra arcae comminuit, duodecim aureos tulit, Gr. D. 64, 13.

níd-nimend, e; f. Rapine :—Fulle sindun nēdnimende and unclēnnisse pleni sunt rapina et immunditia, Mt. R. 23, 25. Cf. þeófend for suffix.

níd-sibb. Add :—Niédsybba necessitudinum (Osburgae mihi contribulibus necessitudinum nexibus conglutinatae, Ald. 1. 12), An. Ox. 9, 5.

níd-þearf. IV. add : need, a condition marked by the lack or want of something necessary, or requiring some extraneous aid or addition :— Ðonne hie eallenga ágiémeleásiað ðone ymbhogan woruldcundra ðinga, ðonne gefultumað hē nāwuht tō his hiéremonna niéddearfe subditorum necessitatibus minime concurrunt, Past. 137, 3.

níd-þearf; adj. Add :—Oft sē slāwa ágǣlð ðæt weorc ðe him niéddearf wǣre tō wyrceanne plerumque piger necessaria agere negligit, Past. 283, 25. [Cf. Goth. naudi-þaurfs necessary.]

nídþearf-líce. Add : usefully :—Mē sylfum þynceð þ ic nā ne ongyte fornytlíce and nýdþearflíce þā word þe þū sǣdest videor mihi utiliter non intellexisse quae dixeras, Gr. D. 174, 20.

nídþearf-ness. I. add :—Neádendre neádþea[r]fnesse tō wrǣcsíðiende cogente necessitate peregrinandi, An. Ox. 269. I a. what is unavoidable :—Neádþear[f]nysse débitum (naturae), An. Ox. 1987. II. add : where there is lack of want :—Hí wǣron gefédde mid þæs gecyndes neádþearfnysse (with what is needed by nature) . . . þ is mid þām wyrtum þe on þām wēstene weóxon, Hml. S. 23 b, 130 : 153. Hē cwæð þæt hē ðā sceolde swíðlíce befrínan his nýdþearfnysse (memento ut modo quicquid opus habes me interroges, Vit. Cuth. c. 28), Hml. Th. ii. 152, 8. III. add :—Gif hwilc man on micelre neádþearfnesse biþ þín gemyndig . . . ic gefremme þæs mannes nēdþearfnesse, Shrn. 77, 6–9.

níd-þeów. Add :—Hlāforda gehwylc āh swýþe micele þearfe þæt hē his men rihtlíce healde; and hit bið his āgen þearf þæt hē his neádþeówum beorge swā hē betst mæge, Wlfst. 300, 4.

níd-þrafung, e; f. Harsh reproof :—Sē ðe suá forbýgð ðone wielm and ðone onrǣs his hátheortnesse for ðǣm ðe hine mon sleá mid líðelicre andsuare, ðonne bið his undeáw ofslægen būtan ǣlcre niéddrafunga, suá suá Isael wæs deád būtan orde qui ergo a fervoris sui impetu sub lenitatis percussione resiliunt, quasi sine ferro moriuntur Past. 297, 22.

nídwrǣclíce; adv. As if acting under compulsion, as if forcibly driven :—Þā ongan ic nýdwrǣclíce gemang þām folce wið þæs folces þringan, Hml. S. 23 b, 404.

nieþer. v. niþer : nígan. Perhaps swígende should be read for nígende.

nigon. I. add: (1) inflected :—Mid nigonum þāra níwena scipa, Chr. 897; P. 90, 23. (1 a) with a pronoun :—Ðæt wē tellan á .x. men tógædere, and se yldesta bewiste þā nigene, Ll. Th. i. 230, 23. (2) uninflected :—Næs nā mā þonne hundtwelftig on þǣm rǣdehere, and nigan on þām fēðan, Ors. 3, 9 ; S. 124, 21. Þus feor sceal beón þæs cinges grið . . . .iii. míla, .iiii. furlang . . . .ix. fóta . . , .ix. berecorna, Ll. Th. i. 224, 9. Þára wæs án twelf geára, óþer nigan geára, and se þridda seofan geára, Shrn. 58. 11. (2 a) with a multiple of ten :—Ofer nigon and hundnigontig ryhtwísra, Past. 411, 13. Nigon and .xx. wintra, Chr. 973; P. 118, 23. (2 a a) with pronoun :—Hē forlēt þā nigon and hundnigontig, Mt. 18, 12. II. add: (1) alone :—Niogen hund wintra, Angl. xi. 4, 21. On nigon (nygan, v. l.) mílum nouem ferme milibus passuum, Bd. 4, 27; Sch. 511, 7 : Chr. 897; P. 91, 24. Beó þǣr gemeten nygon fēt of þām stacan tō þǣre mearce, Ll. Th. i. 226, 12. (2) with pronoun :—Þā nigon engla werod, Hml. Th. i. 12, 8. Þā nygon nǣdran, Lch. iii. 36, 25 : Ll. Th. i. 196, 25. Hē ús benimeð þāra nigon dǣla, 6. Of þǣm nigon dǣlum, 262, 15. Þā nigan dǣlas, Bl. H. 51, 2. Nigen, 209, 27. (3) as part of an ordinal :—On ðǣm nigon and hundsiofantigoðan sealme, Past. 413, 10 : R. Ben. 37, 19 : Ps. Th. 29, arg. On þām nigon and þrittigoðan geáre, Chr. 1052; P. 173, 19.

nigon-gilde; adj. Entitled to ninefold compensation :—On þām lagum is cynges feoh nigongilde, Ll. Th. i. 330, 20. Preóstes feoh .ix. gylde, 2, 5.

nigon-gilde; adv. With ninefold compensation :—Gif frig man cyninge stele, .ix. gylde forgylde, Ll. Th. i. 4, 3. Cf. án-, twi-gilde.

nigon-nihte; adj. Nine days old :—On nigannihtne ealdne mōnan, Lch. iii. 160, 27.

nigonteóþa. Add :—Neár þām neogonteóðan geáre, Lch. iii. 264, 25. On ðone nygentegðan dæg, Shrn. 92, 21 : 105, 29.

nigontíne. Add :—Ǣfre ymbe neogontýne geár, Lch. iii. 264, 22.

níhsta. Add :—Swā swā þām neáxtan quasi proximum, Ps. L. 34, 14. v. ge-nēsta in Dict.

nihstig. Add : , nicstig, and substitute :—Sūp wearme nyhstig, Lch. iii. 48, 2. v. niht-nihstig.

nihstnig. Add :—Syle drincan nyxtnig, Lch. iii. 58, 24. The Latin original for R. Ben. 138, 2–8 is : Dum adhuc jejuni sunt.

niht. I. add :—Leóht niht þǣr on sumera bið, Bd. 1, 1; Sch. 9, 16. Ðū settes ðeóstru and geworden wæs naeht (nyht, Ps. Rdr.), Ps. Srt. 103, 20. Nípende niht, B. 649. Niht helmade, brūnwann oferbrǣd beorgas steápe, An. 1307. Niht bið wedera þeóstrost, Sal. 310. Tō (on) middre nihte medio tempore noctis, Bd. 1, 1; Sch. 9, 17. On wanre niht, B. 702. On nieht, Past. 365, 16. Wintercealdan niht, An. 1267. I a. a time dark as night :—Hit wæs niht oð midne dæg nox usque ad plurimam diei partem tendi visa est, Ors. 3, 5; S. 104, 19; 4, 7; S. 184, 23. III. add :—Gyf ǣnig mann wǣre āne niht on helle, Wlfst. 146, 26. IV. (1) used to mark an occasion or a point of time :—Þǣre nihte þe hié þ fæsten gefæst hæfdon, Bl. H. 205, 34. On þǣre æfterfylgendan niht, 215, 15. Þrié wulfas on ānre niht brōhton ānes deádes monnes líchoman binnan þā burg, Ors. 4, 2; S. 160, 20 : 4, 5; S. 170, 2. Þǣre ilcan niht þe mon on dæg hæfde þā burg mid stacum gemearcod, 5, 5; S. 226, 17. Ǣghwylcre (-hwylce, v. l.) niht, Bd. 1, 33 ; Sch. 102, 19. On þǣre nýhstan wucan ǣr hālgan nyht (ante quadragesimam), Ll. Th. ii. 432, 36. Þás niht sceolon ealle Israhéla bearn begíman, Ex. 12, 42. Wæs hē sume niht on ānum níceal(c)tan hūse, Ors. 6, 32 ; S. 230, 18. Hí ǣghwylce niht byrnaþ, and beorhte scínaþ ǣlce niht, Bl. H. 127, 35. (2) as a division or period of time :—Ǣr þan ðe þæs dæges lenge oferstíge þā niht, Lch. iii. 256, 13. Ðis eálond leóhte nihte (lucidas noctes) on sumera hafað . . . hit hafað mycele lengran dagas on sumera and swā eác nihta on wintra þonne þā sūðdǣlas middangeardes, Bd. 1, 1; Sch. 9, 15–25. V. the time at which darkness comes on :—Hié þǣr gewunedon oþ niht, Ors. 2, 5; S. 80, 30. Hié ealne ðone dæg wǣron þ þafiende oþ niht, 5, 7; S. 230, 18 : Chr. 871 ; P. 70, 28. v. brýd-, foran-, freóls-, gistran-, midde-, midder-, þreó-niht ; sin-nihte.

-nihte. For compounds of this form with numerals see Lch. iii. 160 : see also feówer-, eahta-nihte.

nihtes. Add : I. alone :—Hē nihtes on ungearwe hí on bestæl, Ors. 1, 10; S. 46, 34. Hié . . . hié nihtes on frumslǣpe on bestǣlan, 2, 8; S. 92, 1 : Chr. 876; P. 74, 11. II. with dæges, continuously :— Dæges and niehtes hié fundiað, Past. 127, 20. Þā hēt Pompeius þæt mon þæt fæsten on fuhte dæges and nihtes, simle ān legie æfter óþerre unwêrig, Ors. 5, 11; S. 238. 9. Hit hagolade seofon niht dæges and nihtes, 5, 10; S. 234, 16. Ǣgþer ge dæges and nihtes, Bt. 35, 6 ; F. 168, 8.

niht-feorm the amount of provisions necessary for one night, entertainment due to the king. v. feorm ; I b. ¶

-nihþ. v. efen-nēþþ.

niht-hwíl, e ; f. The space of a day, four and twenty hours :— Gif ǣnig man wǣre āne niht on helle, and hē eft wǣre æfter þām of ālǣdd . . . ne áwacode hē nǣfre for eallum þisum, tō ðām wêrig hē wǣre for þǣre ānre nihthwíle, Wlfst. 147, 9. v. niht ; III.

nihtian to become night. [v. N. E. D. night : O. H. Ger. nahtēn : Icel. nátta.] v. ge-nihtian.

niht-nihstig. Add :—Hine mon scel neahtnestigne tyhtan tō spíwanne, Lch. ii. 184, 1. Gód wín þicgen hié and neahtnestige lapien on hunig, 12. ¶ on nihtnihstig after fasting a night :—Syle dríncan on mergene on nihtnihstig gódne bollan fulne, Lch. iii. 48, 15 : 50, 20 : i. 82, 13 : 84, 16. On nihtnistig (-nihstig, v. l.), 76, 7. On nihtnistig, 74, 1 : 6 : 76, 13. On nihtnestig, ii. 62, 18 : 88, 2. On nihtnicstig, iii. 22, 9 : 17. On neahtnestig, ii. 184, 12.

niht-slǣp; m. Sleep during the night :—þ ilce geþanc þe heom āmang þām nihtslæpe wæs on heora heortan, eall, þā hí áwacodon, hí þ sylfe geþōhton, Hml. S. 23, 442.

niht-waru. After nihtware in l. 2 add : (propter noctes).

niman. Add :—Nōmun, naamun, noumun (h)auserunt, Txts. 43, 247. I. to seize, grasp, capture, catch. (1) to get into one's hands by force or artifice. (a) by war, robbery, legal process, &c. :— Yfelra gerêfena þeáw ys þ hí nymað ǣlc wiht, Ll. Lbmn. 476, 9. Dæghwámlíce ic sæt mid eów on þām temple, and gē mē ne nāmon (nōmo, L., nōman, R.), Mt. 26, 55. Hí nāmon þone ð and þes cynges men and dydon hí on hæftnunge, Chr. 1087; P. 224, 27. Ðā cōm se here tō Hāmtūne . . . and þǣr nāmon ábuton swā mycel swā hí woldon sylfe, 1010; P. 141, 4. Gif hrýðera hwelc sié þe begas brece . . . nime sé hit þe on his ǣcere mête and ofsleá, Ll. Th. i. 128, 14. þ wē hine ofsleán and niman eall þ hē áge, 228, 15 : 208, 30 : 264, 1. þ hig niman þā tihtbysian men, 294, 6. Gif hē secgge þ hit here nāme, 52, 2. Hē hēt hiene niman and ðǣron bescúfan, Ors. 1, 12; S. 54, 31. Nimon, Chr. 1015; P. 146, 3. Mē tō nymenne comprehendere me, Mt. 26, 55. Fato stronges tō niomanne (niommanne, L.) uasa fortis diripere, Mk. R. 3, 27. Niomonde ðone Hǣlend tenentes Iesum, Mt. L. 26, 57. ¶ with cognate accusative :—Ne nime nān man nāne nāme, Ll. Th. i. 386, 11. (b) to catch fish, an animal, a bird, &c. :—Niman fisc, Gr. D. 11, 15. Menn bist ðu niomende homines eris capiens, Lk. L. 5, 10. (b a) of an animal, to seize prey :—Se wulf nimað (nimeð, L., R.) ðā sceáp lupus rapit oues, Jn. 10, 12. (2) to lay hold of with the hand, to seize and hold :—Ðū nōme (tenuisti) hond ðā swíðran míne, Ps. Srt. 72, 24.

Lǽdes mannes tācen is þæt þū ðē mid ealre hande be þīnum cynne nime, swilce þū þē be bearde niman wille, Tech. ii. 129, 17. (2 a) fig. :—Ðāra synna gē nimað *quorum peccata retinueritis*, Jn. L. 20, 23. (3) *intrans.* of a plant, *to take* to that on which it grows, *take hold, get rooted* :—Wiþ feallendum feaxe . . . smyre þ feax and þ heáfod; þonne nimeþ þ feax tō, and seó sealf genýdeð þ hyt weaxeð, Lch. i. 344, 20. (4) *with non-material agent* :—Namm hý ofermōdnis *tenuit eos superbia*, Ps. Rdr. 72, 6. Mē nearonessa nāmon [*tribulatio et*] *angustia invenerunt me*, Ps. Th. 118, 143. Þā þe wǽron āþer oþþe on līchaman untrumnysse oðða fram þām āwyrgdan gāste geswencte and numene *quos aut corporum aegritudo, aut immundorum spirituum infestatio . . . cogebat*, Guth. Gr. 152, 23. **II.** *without the idea of force or art.* (1) *with a material object.* (a) *to take* into one's hand or hold. (α) *with the instrumentality of the hand or hands explicitly or implicitly indicated* :—Nēdro hió niomas, Mk. L. R. 16, 18. In hondum niomað ðec, Lk. L. R. 4, 11. Þū blǽda nāme on treówes telgum, Gen. 891. Wit nāmon mid handum on þām treó blǽda, Sat. 417: Bl. H. 71, 8. Nim þā girde on þīne hand, Ex. 17, 5. Nim ǽnne sticcan and gnīd tō sumum þinge, Lch. iii. 274, 3. Ehera niomendra *spicas vellentium*, Mt. p. 16, 13. (β) *with the instrumentality not expressed or considered* :—Hū fela wyligena brytsyna gē nāmon (nōmon, L.)?, Mk. 8, 20. Nim ðīn bed and gā, 2, 9. Ne cyrre hē ongeán þ hē his reáf nime, 13, 16. Se wæstm ys tō nymenne . . . þonne hē . . . fealwað, Lch. i. 324, 6. Hē bebeád þ munecas wǽpena nāmen, and mid þǽm fuhte, Ors. 6, 34; S. 290, 2. (b) *to receive into one's body by one's own act, take* food :—Hē tō micel nimð on ǽte oððe on wǽte, Hml. S. 16, 270. Þ tō nāhte nyt ne biþ þ man gōdne mete ete oþþe þ betste wīn drince, gif þ gelimpeþ þ hē hit eft spīwende ānforlǽteþ, þ hē ǽr tō blisse nam and tō līchoman nyttnesse, Bl. H. 57, 7. (c) *to bring, receive,* or *adopt* a person into some relation to oneself :—Þā onfēng hē (Oswald) his and nam æt fullwihtes bæþe and æt þæs bysceopes handa him tō godsuna (*sibi accepit in filium*), Bd. 3, 7; Sch. 213, 6. Oswold hine tō fulluhte nam, Hml. S. 26, 132. Æt þām mannum þe . . . hý niton hwā hý tō born nime, Ll. Th. i, 204, 1. Neoman wē ūs tō wynne weroda Drihten, Sat. 198. Þ hī hine niman be his fullan were on borh, Ll. Th. i. 242, 2: 162, 16. (c c) in reference to marriage or cohabitation :—Þēh hē (*a priest*) folǽtte þā (*the woman*) hē ǽr hæfde, hē be lifiendre þǽre eft ōðere nimð, Ll. Th. i. 316, 11: Ex. 21, 10. Gif Iacób nymð wīf of þises landes mannum, Gen. 27, 46. Þonne man nīwan wīf nymð, ne fare hē ūt tō gefeohte, Deut. 24, 5. Þū scealt sweltan for þām wīfe þe þū nāme; heó hefð ōðerne wer, Gen. 20, 3. Hēr nōm (nam, *v. l.*) Beorhtrīc Offan dohtor Eádburge, Chr. 787; P. 54, 3. Gif preóst cwenan forlǽte and ōðre nime, Ll. Th. ii. 296, 1. (d) *to transfer by one's own direct act* something *into one's possession or keeping, to appropriate* :—Fyrenfulle foldan ǽhta and þysse worulde welan nāmon *peccatores obtinuerunt divitias*, Ps. Th. 72, 10. Ágyfe hē þā ǽhta, oþþon . . . oðsace . . . þ hē hit āriht nāme, swā hit ǽr geforword wæs, Ll. Th. i. 286, 18. Hī wilnodon þ þā hlāfordas nāman swā hwæt swā hī hæfdon and lēton hī libban, Bt. 29, 2; F. 104, 31. Ic hæbbe anweald mīne sāwle tō ālǽtanne, and ic hæbbe anweald hig eft tō nimanne, Jn. 10, 18. (2) *with non-material object.* (a) *to adopt* a custom, law, &c. :—Gif þū wilnast þ heó for ðīnum þingum ōþre þeáwas nimen, Bt. 7, 2; F. 18, 28. (b) *to assume, charge oneself with* a function, responsibility, &c. :—Gif hire liófre sié ōðer hēmed tō niomanne, C. D. i. 310, 20. (c) *to undertake and perform, to take* a part :—Þǽne nymendan dǽl *the participle*, Angl. viii. 313, 10. (d) *to assume as if one's own, to assume as if granted* :—Gif sē þonne berste, nime þonne leáfe þ hē mōte hentan æfter his āgenan, Ll. Th. i. 386, 16. (e) in grammar, *to have by right or usage, to take* a particular case, ending, &c. :—Sume nimað *datiuum casum*, Ælfc. Gr. Z. 249, 10: 19: 251, 1. **III.** with idea of choice, purpose, use, treatment, or occupation. (1) *with idea of choice, to pick out from a number*, at random or with intention :—Nim sume tigelan *take any tile* (*out of a number*), Past. 161, 3. Nim þisne and forgyf ūs Barrabban, Lk. 23, 18. Hū mæg geweorðan . . . þæt hē þone stān nime . . ., hlāfes ne gīme, El. 615. Swelce wē nimen ðone clǽnan hwǽte, and weorpen ðæt ceaf onweg, Past. 369, 9. Gif gē ymb worldcunde dōmas beón scylen, ðonne nime gē ðā ðe on ðǽm hīrede unweorðuste sién, 131, 6. (2) with idea of purpose, use, employment, *to choose or adopt* in order to use :—Uton niman ūs tō bysnan þ ǽrran worldwitan tō rǽde gerǽddon, Ll. Th. i. 350, 5. (3) *to adopt and enter upon a way* :—Dysig bið se wegfērenda man, sē ðe nimð þone smēðan weg . . ., and forlǽt ðone sticolan, Hml. Th. i. 164, 8. (4) with idea of treatment :—Ðā lytlan synna mon ne gelēfeð tō nānre synne, ac nimeð hī tō gewunan *minor culpa dum quasi creditur . . . in usu retinetur*, Past. 437, 26. (5) with idea of occupation :—Cuðm micel here . . . and wintersetl nāmon on Eást-Englum, Chr. 866; P. 68, 14. Þū mid sceame nyme þ ýtemeste setl, Lk. 14, 9. Siþþan hē binnan gemǽre wǽre, and wīcstōwa nāme, Ors. 2, 4; S. 76, 10. (5 a) *intrans. and fig.* (a) *to have a place* in :—Word mīn ne nimeð (niomað, R., wunaþ, W. S.) in iúh *sermo meus non capit in*

uobis, Jn. L. 8, 37. (β) *to take place, occur* :—Ne nimeð wītge losia būta Hierusalem *non capit prophetam perire extra Hierusalem*, Lk. L. R. 13, 33. (6) *to occupy, take up the time or attention of*, hold in suspense :—Huu long sáuel ūsra ðū nimes (gǽlst þū ūre līf, W. S.)? Gif ðū arð Crīst, cuæð ūs ēuunge, Jn. L. R. 10, 24. **IV.** *to obtain from a source, model, &c., derive.* (1) *to obtain by one's own act* from some source, material or non-material :—Swilce ǽ swylce wē habbað, and swylce þæáwas swylce habbað, ealle þā þe gōd sint wē nāmon of þīnum [*rīce*], and of þīnum rīce wē bysniað eall þæt wē gōdes dōð *Deus de cujus regno lex in ista regna describitur*, Solil. H. 6, 17. Nim þǽr gōde eáhsealfe *get a good eyesalve from the materials so used*, Lch. iii. 292, 15: 18. Fuglas heora feorhnere on þæs beámes blēdum nāme, Dan. 508. (2) *to infer, deduce* :—Þæs cýþnesse Drihten nam of þisse wīsan, Bl. H. 31, 16. (3) *to get information, evidence*, &c., by inquiry, questioning, &c. :—Heá sōhton tō niomanne huoelchuoego of mūðe his þte heá gehēndon hine, Lk. L. R. 11, 54. **V.** *to take* something given or offered. (1) *to receive* something given, bestowed, allotted, &c., *get* a share, a reward, &c. :—Uton dōn swā þearf is . . . þonne nime wē þæs leán, Ll. Th. i. 412, 3. Þis bebod ic nam (*accepi*) æt mīnum fæder, Jn. 10, 18. Nime se ágenfrīgea his fel and flǽsc, and þolie þæs ōðres, Ll. Th. i. 128, 14: 138, 19. (1 a) *to receive* a person delivered over to one's keeping :—Ðone Hǽlend hē salde him . . . Ðā cempo niomende ðone Hǽlend, Mt. L. 27, 27. (1 b) *to receive* something inflicted, *undergo, have done to one* :—Se gāst nimeð æt Gode swā wīte swā wuldor, Seel. 6. (2) *to receive or get* in payment, as wages, fine, tribute, &c. :—Gif mon nime æfesne on swīnum, Ll. Th. i. 132, 18. Gilde se landrīca þone pænig and nime ǽnne oxan æt þām men, ii. 300, 6. Hwæt hig forð syllan þonne man gildan sceole, and hwæt hig eft niman gif ūs feoh ārīse, i. 232, 4. (3) *to receive, accept, exact* a promise, engagement, oath, &c. :—Þæne að nam Wulsige se scīrigman *ipsum juramentum archiepiscopi accepit Uulfsi scirman*, Cht. Th. 273, 27. Niman þā þe hit tō gebyreð on his ǽhtan inborh, Ll. Th. i. 162, 19. Gif eówer hwylc . . . þ wedd æt his hýremannum niman nelle, 240, 16. (4) *to receive something offered, not to refuse, receive willingly, accept* :—Ne nim þū lāc *nec accipies munera*, Ex. 23, 8. Nim þ þīn ys, Mt. 20, 14. Gif hwā æt þeófe mēdsceatt nime, Ll. Th. i. 208, 15: 222, 5. (5) *to accept as true or correct* :—Ne ealle nimað (niomað, L.) word þās, Mt. R. 19, 11. (6) *to accept with the mind* or will in some specified way :—Þā ylcan sprǽce wē nimað lustlīce, Gr. D. 209, 21. (7) *to include, contain* :—Þte ne mæhte fōan þ nioman (nioma, L.) *ut non caperet*, Mk. R. 2, 2. Ðene niomende þ quem continens, Mt. p. 12, 4. **VI.** of intellectual action. (1) *to receive and hold with the intellect,* (a) *to apprehend, understand* :—Of Salamonnes cuidum wē nāmon ðætte ðǽre wambe nama scolde tācnian ðæt mōd *quia venter mens dicitur, ea sententia docetur*, Past. 259, 8. (b) *to keep in mind* :—Nim þe nū fæste (*fixum tene*) þ ic sprece, Gr. D. 172, 32. Gemynd neomendum (*retinentibus*) bebodu his, Ps. Vos. 102, 18. (2) *to begin to have or be affected by* a feeling or state of mind :—Se deófol nam micelne graman ongeán þone Godes man, Hml. S. 29, 184. (3) *to conceive and exercise* courage, pity, &c. :—Ellen niman tō ǽnigum gōdan weorce, Angl. xi. 113, 45. **VII.** with nearly the force of *make* or *do* :—Hū micel scyld ðæt sié ðæt monn nime sume sibbe wið ðā wierrestan, Past. 353, 11. Friþ niman. v. friþ. **VIII.** with idea of movement or removal. (1) *to carry, convey, cause* a person *to go with one, conduct, lead* :—Þonne hī þe from gewītaþ, ðonne nimað hī heora men mid him, Bt. 20; F. 72, 16. Ðā nam hē hig and fērde onsundron, Lk. 9, 10. 'Arīs and nim þ cild and his mōdor, and fleóh' . . . Hē árās þā, and nam þ cild and his mōdor, and fērde, Mt. 2, 12-13. Nim ǽnne oððe twēgen tō þe, Mt. 18, 16. Nime se hlāford him twēgen getreówe þegenas and swerian, Ll. Th. i. 280, 11: 344, 16: 394, 5. Hié nimen þā men mid him, 82, 13. (1 a) *to move* to a state or condition, *to promote* to a rank :—Þ hig beón wyrðe tō þām miclan hādum tō nimene *ad gradus ecclesiasticos digne possint promoueri*, Chrd. 54, 30. (2) *to carry* a thing *with one, bring* to a person or place, *draw* to oneself :—Alle ic nimo (*traham*) tō mē seolfum, Jn. L. R. 12, 32. Ne nyme gē nān þing on wege, Lk. 9, 3. Sē þe hæfð seúð gelīce nime codd, Lk. 22, 36. Hig forgēton þ hig hlāfas nāmon, Mt. 16, 5: Mk. 6, 8. (3) *to take away, remove* :—(a) *without employing violence* :—Nǽfre man þǽre moldan tō þæs feale ne nimeþ, þ . . ., Bl. H. 127, 17. Sē ðe nimeð (ðeð āweg, W.S. *tollit*) synne middangeardes, Jn. L. R. 1, 29. All þ palmung hē nimeð (ðeð āweg, W.S.), 15, 2. Niomað (dōð āweg, W.S.) ðone stān, 11, 39. Tō niomanne (nummane, L., āfyrran, W.S. *auferre*) telnisse mīne, Lk. R. 1, 25. (a a) where the point from which a thing is moved is marked by a preposition :—Hē nōm (*tulit*) mec of scēpum feadur mīnes, Ps. Srt. ii. p. 183, 19. Nim wuda of þǽre stōwe þe his eard biþ on tō weaxanne, Bt. 35, 10; F. 148, 25. (b) with idea of violence, deprivation :—Sē ðe nimþ (nimmeð, L. *auferet*) þā ðing þe ðīne synt, Lk. 6, 20. Gié nōmon (ætbrūdun, W.S. *tulistis*) cǽgo wīsdōmes, Lk. L. R. 11, 52. Þām þe wylle niman (tó niomanne, L.)

þîne tunecan, Mt. 5, 40. (b a) with prepositions:—Ne nimð hig nân man æt mê, Jn. 10, 18. Nân man ne nimþ eówerne gefeán fram eów, 16, 22. Ne nimð hig nân man of mînre handa, 10, 28. Þá strengran nimaþ þá welan of þám unstrengrum, Bt. 26, 2; F. 92, 14. Hê lêt nyman of hire ealle þá betstan gærsaman, Chr. 1035; P. 159, 30. (c) of removal by death or decay :—Se metod eallra gesceafta fêt on eorþan ealle grôwende westmas . . . and eówaþ ðonne hê wile, and nimþ þonne hê wile, Bt. 39, 13; F. 234, 20. Gif mec hild nime, B. 452. (4) to deliver, hand over:—Ne nime (nŷde, v. l.) man nâðer ne wîf ne mæden tô þám þe hyre sylfre mislîcige, Ll. Th. i. 416, 20. Wurdon hié âfærde and on fleám numen, An. 1342. (5) to bring to mind:—Ic nam mê tô gemynde þá gewritu and þá word þe mê se arceb mê fram þám pâpan brôhte, Cht. E. 229, 23. (6) intrans. To move oneself, go, proceed : cf. IX :—Gê ne gemunon . . . þonan gê nôman (cômon, v. l.), Bt. 16, 1; F. 48, 32. Nim (hef ðæc, R.), âhefe þê upp, W.S.) and worpas in sæ, Mt. L. 21, 21. (6 a) to get on, develop, flourish:—Bearwas blôstmum nimað, . . . wongas wlitigað, Seef. 48. IX. intransitive use in idiomatic combination with preposition. Cf. VIII. 6:—Þ þá gôdan men niman æfter þeóra gôdnesse, Chr. 1086; P. 221, 24. X. in combination with adverbs, forming the equivalents of compound verbs:—Gif hê clæne beó æt þám ordâle nime upp his mæg (he shall take his kinsmen's body from the grave, disinter, exhume), Ll. Th. i. 296, 10. Bûton þá mágas hine ût niman (release, redeem) willan be his wære, 228, 27. [v. N. E. D. nim.] v. nîd-, tô-niman.

-nimend, es; m. v. dǽl-nimend: -nimend, e; f. v. nîd-nimend: nimeness. v. dǽl-nimeness: -nimu. v. nîd-nimu: nim-ung. Add : v. be-, dǽl-nimung.

nip (?). v. râp.

nirwan. Add : I. to confine :—On dîglum dimnessum tô nirewiende latibulis carceralibus artandum, An. Ox. 3145. II. to rebuke:— Nâ neirwð (nirwed ?) hê non arguet, Ps. Rdr. 93, 10. Þû nyrwdest mann corripuisti hominem, 38, 12. v. for-nirwan.

nirwett; n. (not m.) II. add:—Rômâne on ungewis on ân nirewett befôran, Ors. 3, 8; S. 120, 29. II a. a place of confinement :—Godes Sunu wæs gelêd on nearuwre binne, tô ði þæt hê ûs fram hellicum nyrwette (the prison (or (?) confinement) of hell) âlŷsde, Hml. Th. i. 34, 32. v. breóst-nirwett.

nistan. Add :—Nistað nidificabunt, Ps. Vos. 103, 17.

nîten. Add :—Swâ swâ clǽne nêten (nŷten, v. l.) eodorcende quasi mundum animal ruminando, Bd. 4, 24; Sch. 486, 15. Be ælces nŷtenes weorðe gif hî losiað. Hors mon sceal gyldan mid .xxx. sciłł. . . . myran mid .xx. sciłł. . . . oxan mid .xxx. þ., cû mid .xxiiii. þ., swŷn mid .viii. þ., man mid punde, sceáp mid sciłł., gât mid .ii. þ., Ll. Th. i. 356, 1-6. Âþwer buteran þe sié gemolcen of ânes bleós nŷtne oþþe hinde, Lch. ii. 112, 26. Sê þe hǽme mid nêtene (niétene, nŷtene, v. ll.) qui coierit cum jumento, 52, 11. Wið nŷten, Ex. 22, 19. Bletsien þec deór and nŷten (wild beasts and cattle), Az. 145. Be niétena misdǽdum. Gif neát mon gewundige, 78, 8. Gif sió âdl nêtnum sié; and gif sió âdl wyrde mannan, Lch. ii. 14, 11. v. weorc-nîten.

nîten-cynn, es; n. A kind of cattle :—Hê gesceóp æf ðǽre eorðan eall nŷtencynn and deórcynn (jumenta et bestias), Hml. Th. i. 16, 5. Eall nŷtencynn and ðá wildan deór, Hex. 14, 29.

nîtenlîce; adv. Like an animal :—Þæt man môte æfter luste nŷtenlîce (nîten-, v. l.) libban, Wlfst. 55, 18.

nîþ. I. add:—Hê mid swâ lytle nîþe âbræc Rômebyrg, þ hê bebeád þ mon nǽnne mon ne slâge, Ors. 6, 38; S. 296, 30. Ne trûwige nân man be ælmesdǽdum bûtan lufe; for ðan ðe swâ lange swâ hê hylt ðone sweartan nîð on his heortan, ne mæg hê God gegladian, Hml. Th. i. 54, 13. IV. add: an instance of wickedness or malice :—Hê weard âcweald mid þŷ âttre his âgnes nîþes (malitiae), Gr. D. 187, 6. Hû mycelne nîþ hî hæfdon menniscum cynne æteówed unusquisque quantum nequitiae egisset, 189, 11. Æfestum onǽled, oferhygda ful, nîþum, nearowrencum, Môd. 44. Forlǽtan wê morðor and oferhŷdyg and æfeste, . . . nîðas and nearopancas, Verc. Först. 94, 3. Ne morðor tô begangenne, ne nîðas tô fremmanne, Wlfst. 253, 7.

nîþ; adj (?). Dele and see preceding word.

nîþan; p. de To envy :—Þweora manna þeáw is þ hî æfestiað ôþra manna gôddǽde and hefelîce nîþað þâ hî selfe nô ðŷ ǽr habban willað mos pravorum est invidere aliis virtutis bonum quod ipsi habere non appetunt, Gr. D. 117, 5. [Nîðede ðat folk him (Isaac) fel wel, and deden him flitten hire ostel (cf. me (Isaac) quem odistis et expulistis a vobis, Gen. 26, 27), Gen. and Ex. 1521. Þat þou be liþered nil þou niþe ne aemuleris ut nequiter facias, Ps. 36. 8. O. H. Ger. nîden, nîðôn to hate, envy: Icel. nîða to lampoon.]

nîþer. Add :—Ðonne sió lufu for mildheortnesse nieðer âstîged, Past. 103, 16. Þ wæter ic niðer (not neðer, v. Angl. i. 509) âgeat aquam effudi, Nar. 8, 10. Betwix deádum mannum bið þin eardingstôw niðer on eorðan, 50, 28. Wearþ hine niðer on þæt nióbedd, Gen. 343. Niðer under næssas, Sat. 31. Sê sceal heán wesan niðer gebîged,

Môd. 55. Funde þreó rôda under neólum niðer næsse gehŷdde, El. 832. v. niþere.

niþer-âstîgend, es; m.: -âstîgende; ptcpl. One who descends: descending :—Fram niðerâstîgendum on seáðe a descendentibus in lacum, Ps. L. 29, 4: 87, 5. v. niþer-stîgend.

niþere. Add :—Niðre deorsum in terra, Hpt. 33, 247, 114. Þ leóhte fŷr ûp gewît and sió hefige eorþe sit þǽr niþere, Bt. 41, 13; F. 234, 13.

niþer-ecg, e; f. The lower edge or brink :—Be ðæs hlinces niðerecge, C. D. iii. 418, 19.

niþer-flôr; f. A lower floor, a room downstairs :—Gelôgode Benedictus hine sylfne on sumes stŷpeles ûpflôra, and Seruandus gereste hine on þǽre nyðerflôre þæs ylcan stŷpeles (in turris inferioribus), Gr. D. 170, 17. Nyðerflôra, 20.

niþer-hryre, es; m. A falling down :—Mid fylle oððe mid niþer-hryre casu vel praecipitatione, Scint. 229, 12.

niþerigend-lic. Add : v. ge-niþerigendlic.

niþer-lang; adj. With the length stretching downwards :—Tô ðæs niðærlangan hlinces eástænde, C. D. v. 243, 3.

niþer-lecgung, e; f. A laying down, deposition :—Nyþerlecgunge lîchaman Hǽlendes ûres wê wyrþiaþ depositionem corporis Saluatoris nostri celebramus, Angl. xiii. 421, 801.

niþer-lic. I. add :—Se deáð is nyðerlic (death has its place deep down) : hê is for þan nyðerlic : þeáh se man gewîte in ðâ neowelestan scrafa þe on middangearde sŷ, þonne sceal hê þeáhhwæðere sweltan, Verc. Först. 103, 9-12. II. add :—Hû swŷþe ic sylf licge in þysum nyþerlicum þingum quantum ipse in infimis jaceam, Gr. D. 6, 28.

niþer-onwend; adj. Down-turned :—Hê hangode nyþeronwendum heáfde he hung head downwards, Gr. D. 24, 29.

niþer-sceótende down-rushing :—Nyþersceótende precipites, An. Ox. 2669.

niþer-sige. Add :—Ǽr nyðersige ante solis occasum, R. Ben. I. 22, 9.

niþer-stige. Add :—Se nyðerstige and se ûpstige descensus et ascensus, R. Ben. I. 28, 3.

niþer-stîgend, es; m.: -stîgende; ptcpl. One who descends: descending :—Ic beó geanlîcod niðerstîgendum on seáðe assimilabor descendentibus in lacum, Ps. L. 27, 1 : 142, 7. Wæs swîðe hefig frécednys þám niþerstîgendum, Gr. D. 112, 20. v. niþer-âstîgend.

niþerung. Add : v. ge-niþerung.

niþer-weard; adv. :—Nyþerwyrd in praeceps, An. Ox. 3668 (= Hpt. Gl. 499, 56 [not 66]).

nîp-full. Add : jealous :—Sâr heortan and heóf wîf nîþfull (zelotypica), Scint. 225, 1. Se nîðfulla (æfæstiga, v. l.) mæssepreóst (cf. hê ongann andian, 8), Gr. D. 117, 17 : 118, 17. Þá nîþfullum (i. æfestigum) æfestes qui rancida livoris (inuidia torquebantur), An. Ox. 2963. Nîðfulle (printed hîd-) hî synd, grame hî synd odiosi sunt, molesti sunt, Scint. 3, 4. Nîþfulra swicful feónda gereónung liuidorum (i. inuidorum) fraudulenta emulorum factio, An. Ox. 2240. [v. N. E. D. nithful.]

nîþfullîce. Add :—Ðá Iûdêiscan smeádon nîðfullîce ymbe Crîstes cwale (cf. Pilatus sciebat quod per invidiam tradidissent Iesum, Mt. 27, 18), Hml. Th. ii. 226, 26.

nîþ-grama; m. Malicious anger, anger and malice :—Geclǽnsige his heortan gehwâ fram ǽghwilcum nîðgraman and hetelîcan yrre, Wlfst. 180, 9.

nîþ-hell hell where malice and wickedness reign (?) :—Þû scealt faran intô þǽre nigenda nîþhelle (hnîgende intô þǽre nîþhelle (niþerhelle lower hell? The MS. is a late one)? Cf. hê tô helle hnîgan sceolde, Sat. 375), Hml. A. 174, 150.

nîþig; adj. Envious :—[Nî]þig inuidus, An. Ox. 56, 99. Næs hê ofermôd ne nîþig . . . þá nîðigan and þá æfstigan (given in note to preceding).

nîþing. Add : [v. N. E. D. nithing] : -nîþla. v. ge-nîþla.

nîþlîce. The passage in which muliebriter occurs is : Timidorum more militum horrorem belli muliebriter metuentium, Ald. 11, 22. Cf. nîþing.

nîþ-scipe, es; m. Wickedness :—Sî fornumen mân i nîðscipe synfulra consumetur nequitia peccatorum, Ps. L. 7, 10.

nîwan. Add :—Hê nû nîwan weard prǽfost þæs ylcan mynstres ejusdem monasterii nuper praepositus fuit, Gr. D. 23, 9 : 229, 6. Nîwan cumende noviter veniens, R. Ben. I. 95, 11. Ic þe andette þæt ic þæt wilnode oð mê nû âðreáð swîðe nîwan fateor eos modo, ac pene his diebus, cupere destiti, Solil. H. 35, 23.

nîw-cumen. I. newly come, just arrived :—Swilce hî nîcumene sŷn and swilce hî ealles dæges ǽr nâhtes ne onbirigdon, Hml. A. 146, 68. II. one newly come to a religious house, a novice :—S nîcumena mearce dô ille novitius signum faciat, R. Ben. I. 97, 17. Hê sî gelǽd on þám hûse nîcumenra (novitiorum), 96, 15. [Cf. O. H. Ger. nîw(i)-quemo novitius.]

nîwe. Add : I. not existing before, now made, or brought into existence, for the first time :—Ealdere timbrunga bôte instructio, nîwe timbrung constructio, Wrt. Voc. i. 39, 59. Sele nîwe, Gû. 714. Þá

(at the creation of Adam) wæs fruma níwe ælda túdres . . . : fæder wæs
ácenned Adam ǽrest, 795. Adam . . . neorxna wonges níwre gesceafte
hyrde, Gen. 171. God geswác þá þǽre níwan gesceapennysse *requievit*
*Deus a novarum conditione creaturarum*, Angl. vii. 4, 22. Gif mon on
níwne weall unástíðodne micelne hróf onsett, Past. 383, 32. Hé
getimbred eardwíc níwe, Ph. 431. Níwe flódas Nóe oferlád, Exod. 362.
Hié níwa ceastra timbredon, Ors. 1, 10; S. 48, 9. **I a.** *of a kind
now first invented or introduced:*—Níwe nihtweard (*the pillar of fire*)
sceolde wícian ofer weredum, Exod. 116. **II.** *not previously known.*
(1) of things spoken or heard:—Swég úp ástág níwe, B. 783. Þás
níwan spel ic þé ealle in cartan áwríte, Nar. 3, 17. (2) of feelings,
experiences, events, &c.:—Wæs him níwe gefeá befolen in fyrhðe, El.
195. Longe neótan níwra gefeána, Gú. 805. (3) of things or persons:—
Ne byð god on þe níwe geméted, ne þú fremedne God gebiddest, Ps. Th.
80, 9. Hí offrodon . . . þám godum þe hí ne cúðon; níwe cómun þe
hira fæderas ne wurðodon, Deut. 32, 17. **III.** *coming as a resumption or repetition of some previous act or thing:*—On þǽm æfterran
gére gelǽrdan Rómána biscepas swelce níwe rǽdas swelce hié fol oft ǽr
ealde gedydan, Ors. 4, 7; S. 184, 2. **III a.** *restored after demo-
lition, decay, disappearance, &c.:*—Feorh bið níwe, þonne hé his líc,
þæt ǽr líg fornóm, somnað, Ph. 266. Þá ealdan forþ gewitun, and
efne hí wǽrun gewordene níwe, An. Ox. 40, 36. ¶ *applied to the
moon:*—Gyf se móna byð ǽr æfenne fram ðǽre sunnan geedníwod, hé
byð þonne sóna æfter sunnan setlgange níwe geteald, Lch. iii. 266, 4.
Wé cwedað níwne mónan æfter menniscum gewunan, ac hé is æfre se
ylca þeáh ðe his leóht gelómlíce hwyrfe, 242, 15. Þ geár hæfð twelf
níwe monan, 248, 25. **IV.** *other than the former or old, different
from that previously existing, known, or used:*—Bið ús geset níwe
nama; swá swá se wítega cwæð, 'God gecígd his ðeówan óðrum
naman.' Eft se ylca wítega cwæð, 'Þú bist gecíged níwum naman,'
Hml. Th. i. 96, 27–29. Áfeormudre þæs ealdan lífes yfelnesse on
níwre geleáfan gyfe wé gangað, An. Ox. 40, 25. Bibod níówe (níua,
L.) ic sello iów, Jn. R. 13, 34. **IV a.** *of persons occupying a certain
position or relationship:*—Árás níwe cing, Ex. 1, 8. **V.** *with
demonstrative* se *to distinguish the thing spoken of from something old,
or already existing, of the same kind.* (1) of institutions, practices,
&c.:—Ðǽre níua (neówe, R.) gewitnesse *noui testamenti*, Mt. L. 26,
28. Nalæs þ án þ hé gýmenne dyde þǽre níwan cyricean þe of Angelcynne gesomnad wæs, ac swylce eác þára yldra bígengena Brytta and
Scotta, Bd. 2, 4; Sch. 127, 12. Se godspellere wæs fæstnung ægþer ge
þǽre ealdan ǽ ge þǽre níwan, Bl. H. 163, 25. Hé hié mid þǽm ilcan
wrence beswác þe hé æt heora ǽrran gemétingge dyde, and eác mid þǽm
níwan þe hié ǽr ne cúðon, Ors. 4, 9; S. 188, 33. (2) with things,
places, or persons:—Cóm Hasterbal se níwa cyning, Ors. 4, 6; S. 176,
33. Þá Scipia hæfde gefaren tó ðǽre níwan byrig Cartaina, 4, 10; S.
196, 23. **VI.** *of recent origin or growth, that has not yet existed
long:*—Níwes *recentis* (*paradisi*), An. Ox. 688. Ic tiohhie þæt hió þæs
níwan taman náuht ne gehicgge, Met. 13, 26. Heó forgit sóna hire
níwan taman, Bt. 25; F. 88, 12. Níwe sibbe, B. 949. Caelf níówe
*vitulum novellum*, Ps. Srt. 68, 32. **VI a.** *of articles of food or
drink, freshly made, produced, or grown, belonging to the fresh crop or
growth:*—Mid neówum ele gemencged, Lch. i. 350, 2. Gé etað ealde
mettas oð eów níwe cumon, Lev. 26, 10. **VI b.** *recently made,
not yet used or worn, still unimpaired by use:*—Heó wæsceð his wárig
hrægl, and him syleð wǽde níwe, Gn. Ex. 99. Hé forð bringð of his
goldhorde níwe þing and ealde, Mt. 13, 52. **VII.** *having but
recently come into a certain state, position, or relationship:*—Níwe
heofonlic *neotericus uranii, celestis nouus*, Hpt. 31, 13, 303. Ne aron
gié gestas and níwe cumo (*advenȩ*), Rtl. 82, 30. **VII a.** *new to
a thing, inexperienced:*—Níwe on geleáfan *neophitus*, Hpt. 31, 13,
304. Eall þás þing þǽre níwan þeóde Ongelcynne on Godes geleáfan
gedafenað cúð habban *quae omnia rudi Anglorum genti oportet haberi
comperta*, Bd. 1, 27; Sch. 76, 21. **VII b.** *inexperienced, unskilled,
rude:*—Níwum gebúrum *rudibus colonis*, An. Ox. 11, 88. **VIII.**
used substantively:—Wénst þú þ hit hwæt níwes sié, Bt. 7, 2; F. 16,
27. Hwæthwegu níwes and seldcúþes, 34, 4; F. 138, 29. Gelamp þé
áht (ǽnig þing *v. l.*) níwes?, Gr. D. 4, 2. Hwæt ic yrmða gebád . . .
níwes oðde ealdes, Kl. 4.

**níwerne** *is wrongly placed after* níwunga: **níw-fara.** *Add:* v.
níw-gefara.

**níw-gefara,** an; m. *A new-comer, a stranger:*—Nígefaran tó túne
feccan, Ll. Th. i. 432, 16. v. níw-fara.

**níw-gehálgod, -hálgod;** adj. *Newly consecrated:*—Se wítega
begeát his (*Jehu's*) heáfod mid ele . . . Ðá Hieu se nígehálgode (níghál-
goda, *v. l.*) cyningc férde, Hml. S. 18, 326.

**níwian.** *Add: to repeat:*—Wið foredum lime, lege þás sealfe on
þ forode lim, and forlege mid elmrinde, dó spilc tó; eft simle níwa oþ þ
gehálod sié, Lch. ii. 66, 23.

**níwi(g)end.** v. ed-níwigend *and* híwiend.

**níwlinga;** adv. *Anew:*—Þá nýtenu æfter deáþe ne lifiað, and se
man onginneþ þonne eft neówlinga (neówunga, *v. l.*) lifigean æfter þæs

líchaman deáþe, þonne hé geendeþ þis gesewenlice líf *jumenta post
mortem non vivunt, homo vero tunc vivere inchoat, cum per mortem
carnis hanc visibilem vitam consummat*, Gr. D. 226, 28.

**níw-slícod;** adj. *Newly-glossed, with the gloss fresh on it* (a garment):—Swá scýnende sunne oðde nigslýcod hrægel, Shrn. 149, 8.

**níw-soden;** adj. *Newly-boiled:*—Nísodenes wínes *defruti*, An.
Ox. 326.

**níwung.** *Add:* v. ed-, eft-níwung: **níwunga.** v. níwlinga.

**noctern,** es; m. *A nocturn, one of the divisions of the office of
matins:*—Syx nocternes þæs æftran sealmas *sex nocturnȩ posterioris
psalmi*, Angl. xiii. 404, 561. Tó nocterne *ad nocturnam*, 426, 870.
Æfter nocternum *post nocturnas*, 437, 1027. Tó nocternum *ad
nocturnos*, 434, 990. Tó nocternan *ad nocturnas*, 396, 448. Gedónum
nocternum *peractis nocturnis*, 380, 220. [From Latin.]

**nomementa?** v. nówend.

**nón;** m. (not n.) **I.** *add:*—Se ǽrmerigen . . . se undern . . . , se
middæg . . . se nón wæs fram Móyse oð Drihtnes tócyme, Hml. Th. ii.
74, 20. Se bere . . . nó tó middes dæges hám cóm, þonne him wæs
beboden þ hé tó nónes sceolde, ne hé hit nó ne ylde æt nón, þonne hé tó
middes dæges sceolde hám cuman, Gr. D. 206, 20–23. Fram Sæternesdæges nóne oð Mónandæges líhtincge, Wlfst. 117, 4. Se dæg wæs on
þeóstre niht gecierred fram midnedæg oð nón; hé æt þǽm nóne his gást
onsænde, Shrn. 67, 18. **II.** *add:*—Sí gedón tácn nónes þ fylige
se tídsang þæne nón ná fylige scenc, Angl. xiii. 399, 483.

**nón-belle,** an; f. *The bell rung at the hour for the service of
nones:*—Monegra monna gewuna is þonne hé fæstan sceolan, þ sóna swá
hig þá nónbellan gehýrað hig tó mete fóð, Ll. Th. ii. 436, 34.
v. nón-hring, -tíd.

**nón-hring,** es; m. *The ringing of a bell to announce the hour for
the service of nones:*—Sóna swá hý nónhringc gehýrað *mox ut signum
audierint ad horam nonam*, Chrd. 114, 14.

**nón-mete.** *Add:*—Nónmete *anteceniam, merendam*, Hpt. 31, 14,
353.

**nón-sang.** *Add:*—Sóna swá hig þá nónbellan gehýrað hig tó mete
fóð; ac nis hit náht gelýfedlic þ þ sý medeme fæsten. Ac þ is riht þte
æfter nónsange mon mæssan gehýre, Ll. Th. ii. 436, 36.

**nón-tíd.** *Add:*—Synd þá ðe wénað þ hý fæstende synd rihtlíce, gif
hý etað sóna swá hý þ belltácen (v. nón-belle) gehýrað þǽre nigoðan
tíde, þ is seó nóntíd, Hml. A. 140, 65. Ǽr nóntíde ábyrigan ne ǽtes
ne wǽtes, Wlfst. 102, 25. Fram nóntíde þæs Sæternesdæges oþ þæs
Mónandæges líhtinge, Ll. Th. i. 264, 19. Tó þǽre nóntíde hám
hweorfan, Gr. D. 206, 18. Hé is deád gyrstandæge on þá nóntíde, 306,
10. [Cf. *Icel.* nón-tíðir *the services at nones.*]

**norþ;** adj. *Add:*—Columba cóm tó Pihtum, and hí gecyrde tó
Crístes geleáfan. Þ synd þonne wærteras þe norðum mórum (cf. wæs
se Columba se ǽresta láreów þæs Crístenan geleáfan on þám mórlandum,
þá þe syndon tó norððǽle Pehta ríces *erat Columba primus doctor fides
Christianae transmontanis Pictis ad aquilonem*, Bd. 5, 9; Sch. 593,
1–4), Chr. 565; P. 19, 14. [This passage is added in a late hand.]
Hét Eádward cyning átimbrian þá norðan (norðran *other MSS.*) burh,
913; P. 97, 29. On ðám norðran dǽle wunað eall manncynn, Lch. iii.
260, 25. On ðone norðere steð, C. D. v. 148, 21.

**norþ;** adv. *Add:* **I.** with reference to movement, direction, or
extent:—Sum feówertig scipa fóron norþ ymbútan, Chr. 894; P. 86, 9.
Fela hund manna hí námon, and lǽddon norð mid heom, 1064; P. 192,
9. Hit is án hund and syfan and fiftig mila lang súð and norð, Ors. 1,
1; S. 28, 8. Ealle Asiam . . . súð fram þǽm Reádan Sǽ and swá norð
oþ þone sǽ þe man hǽt Euxinus, 1, 2; S. 30, 1. Him is ðæt heáfod
súð gewend and þá fét norð, Shrn. 66, 24. ¶ the word is of constant occurrence in the lists of boundaries given in charters. **II.** with
reference to place or location:—Swá hit súð licgeð ymbe Gealboe and
ymb Geador norð, Sal. 191: 188. Þá wæs hé swá feor norþ swá þá
hwælhuntan firrest faraþ, Ors. 1, 1; S. 17, 11. Ne bið nán niht . . . for
ðám þe seó sunne byð þonne swá feorr norð ágán, Lch. iii. 260, 6.
Wǽron norð of ðǽm stáne áwexene bearwas, Bl. H. 209, 32. Mid
fleáme cóm on his cýþþe norð Costontinus, Chr. 937; P. 108, 19.
Þonne þunor cumeð west oðde norð, Archiv cxx. 48, 20. Þæt hé west
and norð trymede getimbro, Gen. 275. Þætte súð ne norð óðer nænig
sélra nǽre, B. 858. Súð oðde norð, Vid. 138: Met. 10, 24. Norð
and eást, 13, 59. Se winterlica móna gǽð norþor þonne seó sunne gá
on sumera, Lch. iii. 252, 12. v. eást-, west-norþ.

**norþan.** *Add:*—Þá hwíle cóm Willelm . . . and Harold cóm norðan
and him wið feaht, Chr. 1066; P. 198, 4. Se here bræc þone friþ of
Hámtúne and of Ligeraceastre and þonan norþan (*from north of
Leicester*), 921; P. 101, 7. Þonne won cymeð nihtscúa, norðan
onsended hreó hæglfare, Wand. 104: Seef. 31: B. 547. Se feórða
heáfodwind hátte *septemtrio*; sé blǽwþ norðan, Lch. iii. 274, 23.
Wind norþan and eástan *Boreas*, Bt. 4; F. 8, 6: Met. 4, 23: *Auster*,
6, 12. Gefaren tósomne súðan and norðan, Gen. 1988: Dan. 52: Sal.
259. Súðan and norðan, eástan and westan, Cri. 885: Ph. 324. [*Icel.*
norðan. Cf. *O. H. Ger.* nordana.] v. be-, eástan-, on-, westan-norþan.

**norþ-and-eást-rodor.** v. norþeást-rodor : **norþan-wind.** *Add :* v. riht-norþanwind.

**norþ-dǽl. I.** *add :*—Hér oðeówdon fȳrena leóman on norðdǽle þǽre lyfte, Chr. 926 ; P. 107, 19. Hū wæs þes middaneard tódǽled æfter þām flóde ? Sem ... þone eástdǽl middaneardes þe is gehāten Asia ... Cham þone sūðdǽl ... Affrica, ... Iafeth ... norðdǽl ... Europa, Angl. vii. 40, 375. **II.** *add :*—Ic wille wyrcean mīn setl on norðdǽle *ponam sedem meam ad Aquilonem*, Past. 111, 24. Arcton hātte ān tungol on norðdǽle, Lch. iii. 270, 9.

**norþ-eást ;** *adv. Add : in the north-east, to the north-east :*—Gif þunor bið mycel eást oððe norðeást, Archiv cxx. 48, 23. Norð tō ðére lytlan dīc ... swā norðeást tō ðǽre lytlan rīðe, C. D. v. 195, 8. [Se leóma þe him from stód ... wæs swilce ormǽte beám geþūht norðeást scínende, Chr. 1106 ; P. 240, 22. Cf. Scipmen saeden þ hī sǽgon on-norðeást fīr micel, 1122 ; P. 250, 30.]

**norþeást-hyrne** *a north-east corner :*—Stód þǽr ān rōd on ðǽre eorðan on ðām norðeásthyrnan, Vis. Lfc. 71.

**norþeást-rodor** *the north-east sky, the north-east :*—Eóde wit ongeán norðeástrodor (norð-and-eástrodor, *v. l.*), swā sunnan uppgang bið æt middum sumera *incedebamus contra ortum solis solstitialem*, Bd. 5, 12 ; Sch. 615, 17.

**norþ-efes** *a northern margin :*—Be ðām wege oð ða norðefes, C. D. v. 221, 2.

**norþ-ende.** *Add :*—On ðæs hlincæs norðændæ, C. D. v. 242, 31. Man beád þā folce þider ūt ofer ealne þisne norðende, Chr. 1052 ; P. 175, 29.

**norþerne.** *Add :*—Griffin se norþerna cyng (*king of North Wales*), Chr. 1046 ; P. 164, 28. v. eást-norþerne.

**norþ-heald ;** *adj. Sloping to the north, bent northwards :*—Of þām hwītan tréowe on ðæt norðhealde tréow ; of ðām norðhealdan tréowe, C. D. B. ii. 246, 32.

**norþ-healf.** *Add :*—On norðhealfe þæs hīredes mearc, C. D. B. iii, 15, 12. Hē is bebyrged on ða norðhealfe on Sēe Paulus postice, Chr. 976 ; P. 122, 14. Hī gelōgodon Sēe Ælfeáges līchaman on norðhealfe Xpes weófodes, 1023 ; P. 156, 23.

**norþ-hilde** *a north-slope :*—Oð ðæs clifes norðhyldan, C. D. iii. 418, 25 : 33.

**norþ-hyrne** *a north-corner :*—Tō mōrmǽde norðhyrnan, C. D. iii. 449, 20.

**norþ-land.** *Add : land lying to the north :*—Hī hwemdon mid þām scypon wið þæs norðlandes, Chr. 1052 ; P. 180, 19.

**norþ-lang ;** *adj. Having its length extending northwards, running north and south :*—Tō ðon norðlangan gráfette, C. D. v. 195, 6. On ðone norðlangan hlinc, iii. 135, 24.

**Norþmandisc ;** *adj. Norman :*—Æfter Norðmandiscere lage, Ll. Th. i. 489, 11.

**Norþ-mann. I.** *add :*—þām wǽpenleásum menn onbugon þā Francan and þā fyrlenan Norðmenn, Hml. S. 29, 177.

**norþ-rihtes ;** *adv. Due north :*—Ðonne norðrihtes andlang cumbes, C. D. iii. 450, 5.

**norþ-sǽ.** *Add :*—Ðis synt ðára xxx. hīda landgemǽro tō Cawelburnan on Wiht. Ǽrest of sǽ ... ðanon on sūðsǽ ... andlang Cawelburnan ūtt on norðsǽ, C. D. v. 82, 24.

**norþ-sciphere** *a northern fleet :*—Wæs Legeceasterscīr gehergod fram Norðsciphere, Chr. 980 ; P. 124, 10.

**norþ-þunor** *thunder in the north :*—Se norðþunor bēcnað scēpa deáð, Archiv cxx. 48, 21.

**norþ-weard ;** *adv. Add :*—þonne se dæg langað, þonne gǽð seó sunne norðweard ... Ðonne heó norðweard byð, þonne macað heó lenctenlice emnihte on middeweardum hyre ryne, Lch. iii. 250, 20–25.

**nos-gristle.** *Add : an ; f.*

**nos-þyrel.** *Add :*—God gesceóp ūs twā eágan and twā eáran, twā nosþirlu and twēgen weleras, Ælfc. Gen. Thw. 4, 16.

**nostle.** *Add :*—Nostlæ *uitla* (*uicta*, MS.), An. Ox. 53, 28.

**nosu. I.** *Dele* ' *also an* ', *and add : a nostril ; pl. the nostrils, nose :*— ' Ðīn nosu is swelce se torr on Libano.' Ðæt is ðæt wē oft gestincað mid ūrum nosum ðæt wē mid ūrum eágum gesión ne magon. Mid ðǽm nosum (*per nasum*) wē tōsceádað gōde stincas and yfele. Hwæt is getácnod ðurh ðā nosu (*per nasum*) ...?, Past. 433, 19–22. Is sió lytle nosu ðæt mon ne sié gescádwīs ; for ðǽm mid ðǽre nose wē tōsceádað ðā stencas, 65, 19–21. Nosa habbað *nares habent*, Ps. Vos. 113, 6 second : 134, 17. **II.** *substitute :* nōse, an ; f. *taking it as a separate word.*

**not-georn ;** *adj. Busy in useful employment, profitably employed, diligent in business :*—Sē ðe wǽre idelgeorn, weorðe sē notgeorn, Wlfst. 72, 9.

**-noþ.** v. droht-, fisc-, fōd-, fōddor-, fōstor-, fugel-, hæft-, hleó-, hunt-, sǽd-, wig-noþ (-naþ).

**notian. I a.** *add :*—Ic notode þǽra hláfa, Hml. S. 23 b, 568. **I d. :**—Āmang þām feó þe wē on þysum dagum notiað Hml. S. 23, 706. Feoh þe man on fyrndagum slóh, and on ðǽra

yldrena cāsera tīman notode, 615. Ðis synd þǽra bōca tācn þe mon on cyrican tō godcundum þeówdōme notigan sceal ... Ðonne þū antiphonariam habban wille ... for þon hē is genotod, Tech. ii. 119, 1–4. Notian, 120, 24. Tyrn ... swilce þū notian wille, 119, 12. Underfēngon hī hyra horsa tō-brūcenne and tō notienne, Gr. D. 16, 4. Þǽra (hláfa) ic breác notigende, Hml. S. 23 b, 521. [v. *N. E. D.* note.]

**notu. I.** *add :*—Tō singenne sōðlīce notu unrōtnysse heortan gefrēfrað *psallendi enim utilitas tristitiam cordis consolatur*, Scint. 33, 7. Note *utilitati*, An. Ox. 7, 353. **II.** *add : occupation*, or *work*, as properly pertaining or assigned to a person :—Notu *ministerium*, Chrd. 52, 24 : 13, 21. Hit mīnra þegna .lii. tō loman gerēnode þæt hié mec ǽnigre note nytte beón ne meahton (*inutiles fecit*), Nar. 15, 27. Ne sceolde hē nān ðing forgȳman ðe ǽfre tō note mehte, Angl. ix. 265, 7 : 260, 14. [v. *N. E. D.* note.] v. hád-, sundor-notu.

**not-wirþe ;** *adj. Useful :*—Notwurðe hē bið *utilis erit*, Archiv cxxix. 18, 13. v. nyt-weorþ.

**nōwend,** es ; *m. A skipper, mariner, sailor :*—Þis is se heáhengel sanctus Michael and se æðela nōwend and se gleáwa frumlida ... sē ðe rhid heofonlicum wǽlum his scip gefylled, An. Ox. 32, note. His nōwent (*nauta*), þām wæs nama Uaracc ... se nōwent rihte þ lytle scip þe wiþhindan þām mǽran scipe gefæstnod wæs. Þā weard se rāp tōbrocen, and hē onweg gewāt ... Þȳ þryddan dæge þā þā se biscop ne geseah ǽtȳwan ... þone nōwent (*nautam*) ... hē hine deádne gelȳfde ... þā onwegānumenum þām nōwende ... se biscop fērde ... and þā þā hē cōm tō Rōmāna hȳþe hē gemētte þone ylcan nōwent (*nautam*), Gr. D. 346, 35—347. 16. Nōwendes, steórmannes *naucleri*, An. Ox. 32. Nōwendes *naucleri, nauclerus est dominus nauis*, 5, 8 : 7, 12 : 8, 6. Þā hwīle þe þā rōwendas (nōwentas, *v. l.*) þæs scipes gegearwodon ōþre gerēþru *dum nautae navis armamenta repararent*, Gr. D. 306, 3. Ðára nomementa (nōwenta ?) *nautarum*, Txts. 181, 53.

**nū. I.** *add :* (1) *at the present time :*—þū āna nū gēna (gȳta, *v. l.*) eart bysceop gemēted, Bd. 1, 27 ; Sch. 73, 3. (2) *in the time immediately following on the present moment, immediately :*—Hāt mē nū sillan þā hearpan, þonne wāst þū nū þ þū gīt nāst, Ap. Th. 16, 25. Nū ic sceall geendian earmlicum deáþe, Hml. S. 26, 249. (3) *in the time directly preceding the present moment :*—Ān wundor þæt ic ongæt nū for þrym nihtum (*adhuc ante triduum*), Gr. D. 234, 7 : 235, 19 : 232, 9. Ymbe þ ilce þū gyddodest nū hwēne ǽr, Bt. 5, 3 ; F. 12, 7. Þæt is gesewen þæt hē wæs gewiss his silfes fordfōre of þām þe wē nū secgon gehȳrdon (*ex his quae narrauimus*), Bd. 4, 24 ; Sch. 492, 2 : Ll. Th. ii. 348, 31. Ymbe þā þing þe wē nū handledon, Angl. viii. 304, 24 : 298, 19. Hē wæs ā mid Langbeardum of nū .iv. geár (*until four years from now*), Gr. D. 234, 9. (4) with weakened temporal sense in sentences expressing a command or request :—And nū, cyningas, ongeotað, Ps. Srt. 2, 10. Cleopian wē nū in eglum mōde, Bl. H. 19, 2. Gehȳran wē nū for hwon se blindo leóht onfēng, 11. (5) used to introduce an important point in an argument, or series of statements :—Nū ūs is gesæd þ ... nū gif þū ǽnig þincg hæfst ..., Hml. S. 26, 256–258. Nū cwæð se hālga Bēda ... þ ..., 272. (5 b) inserted parenthetically with similar force :—þeáh hē nū māran wilnige, hē ne mæg furðum ðæt fordbringan, Bt. 18, 3 ; F. 64. 23. Hwī nis nū anweald tō tellanne tō sumum ðára hēhstena gōda ? ... Hwæþer þ nū sié tō talianne wāclic ...?, Bt. 24, 4 ; F. 86, 14–16. (6) with preposition :—Oð nū *usque nunc*, Ps. Srt. 70, 17. **III.** *add :*—Nū, ic secge eów *ecce prædixi vobis*, Mt. 28, 7.

**nū-hwīlum ;** *adv. Nowadays, at present :*—þā þingeras þingiaþ nūhwīlum þǽm ðe lǽssan þearfe āhton *nunc contra faciunt oratores*, Bt. 38, 7 ; F. 208, 26. Cf. ǽr-, geó-hwīlum.

**-numa.** *Add :* here-numa.

**nume-stān.** *Add :* Cf. Calc *calculus*, Wrt. Voc. ii. 102, 39 : *calculus, ratio, vel sententia, vel numerus* teblstān, 43. *The gloss at 13, 6 seems to combine these two, and in this case* nume-stān *corresponds to the second. Could* nume-stān *be a mistake for* nume[rus tæfl]stān ?

**numol.** *Add :* **I.** of the mind, *able to grasp, capable :*—Andgytful, numel *capax* (*memoriae*), An. Ox. 3101. **II.** *biting :*—Swā swā deáðes gefēran, swā forfleóh þū þ numele wīn *ut mortis socium, sic mordax effuge vinum*, Chrd. 74, 10.

**-numolness.** v. dǽl-numolness.

**nunne.** *Add :* **I.** of a Christian woman :—þā berād mon þæt wīf þæt hē hæfde ǽr genumen ... ofer þára biscopa gebod, for ðon ðe heó wæs ǽr tō nunnan gehālgod, Chr. 901 ; P. 92, 14. Nunnena *sanctimonialium*, An. Ox. 8, 368. **II.** non-Christian :—Minutia hātte ān wīfmon þe on heora wīsan sceolde nunne beón *Minucia, virgo vestalis*, Ors. 3, 6 ; S. 108, 16.

**nunn-fǽmne** *a nun :*—Seó hālige nunfǽmne *sanctimonialis femina*, Gr. D. 223, 14. Hē nȳde genam āne nunfǽmnan and tō him gegaderode mid unālȳfedum synscipe, 230, 13.

**nunn-līf** *the life of a nun :*—þā þā ... hāliges nunlīfes drohtoþ (*sanctimonialis vitae conversationem*) heó sōhte, Gr. D. 199, 16.

**nunn-mynster.** *Add :*—þæt hē hine tō ðām befæste þ hē mōste beón lǽce þæs nunmynstres (on þām nunmynstre, *v. l.*) *ut eum sanandum monasterio commendaret*, Gr. D. 27, 27.

**nunn-scrúd.** *For* án *read* an: nu-seóþa. v. newe-seóþa.

**nyht-sum;** *adj. Abundant*:—Nihtsumere wynne *opulenti luxus*, An. Ox. 322. Nihtsume *abundantes*, Ps. L. 71, 12. þá nihtsumestan spryttinga *uberrima plantaria*, An. Ox. 1129. v. ge-nyhtsum.

**nyhtsumian** *to be sufficient*:—Ðý lés ne nyhtsumige ús and eów *ne forte non sufficiat nobis et vobis*, Mt. R. 25, 9. v. ge-nyhtsumian.

**-nyhtsuming.** v. ge-nyhtsuming.

**nyhtsum-ness,** e; *f. Abundance*:—Of nihtsumnesse (*abundantia*) blisse gesibsum mann byð oncnáwen, Scint. 11, 13. v. ge-nyhtsumness.

**nyllan.** *Add*:—Hí getácniað þá ðe tela nellað, ne nellað leornian hwæt Gode leóf sý, Hml. S. 25, 51-52. Oft monn bið ðære earfoðnesse láreówdóme underðiéded, ðeáh hé ǽr nolde his láreówes lárum bión, Past. 35, 11. Hwæt be him nellendum gewurðan sceoldon (hwæt hí sceolan nyllan, *v. l.*) *quid de eis nolentibus fiat*, Gr. D. 61, 18.

**nyme.** v. fore-nyme.

**nypel** *the trunk of an elephant*:—Se micela ylp ðá módigan fearras mid ealle ofbeát mid his egeslican nypele, Hml. A. 63, 286.

**nytan.** *Add*: (1) *Cf.* witan ; I. 2 :—þá nyston his leorningcnihtas nán andgit þyssera worda, Hml. Th. i. 152, 10. (2) *Cf.* witan; I. 4 :—Hé hí þærúte nyste *he did not know they were outside*, Hml. S. 31, 693. (3) *Cf.* witan; I. 7 :—Wé be him náþor nyton swá hí ðǽr libban, swá hí ðǽr deáde licgon, Hml. S. 23, 306. (4) with gen. ; I. 8 :—Nát hé þára góda þæt hé mé ongeán sleá, B. 681. Hí ðæs godcundan gesceádes nyston ðurh stemne, Hml. Th. i. 106, 4. Eom ic cnæpling and nytende mínes færes, ii. 576, 15. (5) with dat. infin. :—Wé nytan nánum óðrum þingum tó getrúwianne bútan hit þis sý, Ll. Th. i. 220, 16.

**nyten.** *Add*: v. nyten-lic.

**nyten-lic;** *adj. Ignorant*:—Cúðberhtus, ðá ðá hé wæs eahtawintre cild, arn swá swá him his nytenlíce yld tíhte plegende mid his efenealdum: ac God wolde stýran þǽre nytennesse Cúðberhtes þurh mynegunge gelimplices láreówes, Hml. Th. ii. 134, 3.

**nyten-ness.** I. *add*:—*Ignorantia*, þ is nytennys, Angl. xi. 109, 40. Þ hé on his ylde of ðám yfelan slǽpe his ǽrran nytennysse áríse, Hml. A. 53, 81: Hml. S. 14, 36: 25, 788. Þý lǽs þe ǽnig ungecyrred woroldman mid his nytnesse and ungewitte regules geboda ábrǽce, Lch. iii. 442, 2. Hé þurh his cildhádes nytenesse his ríce tóstencte, 434, 26. Ongeán þám ingehýde and gearawitolnesse þe of Godes ágenre gife cymð, se deófol sǽwð and sendeð nytennesse, Wlfst. 53, 18. I a. *want of knowledge on a particular point*:—Nytennessa míne (*ignorantias meas*) ne gemun ðú, Ps. L. 24, 7. I b. *a condition of not being known by others, a state of incognito*:—þá gesylde Smaragdus on þǽre netennysse eahta and þryttig wintra *Smaragdus* (*who was Euphrosyne in man's clothes*) *maintained her incognito for thirty-eight years*, Hml. S. 33, 260.

**nytig** (?) *usefulness* (?), *profit* (?):—Fird, here, nitig (hereiung ? Cf. faerd *expeditio*, 107, 62 ; hergiung *expeditio*, 108, 8. *Or could* nitig (= nytig) *be connected with the verb* expedire. Cf. expedit ei, proderit ei, 72, 78?) *expeditio*, Wrt. Voc. ii. 29, 69.

**nytlíce;** *adv. Usefully*:—Mé þinceð þ ic full nyttlíce (fornytlíce and nýðþearflíce, *v. l.*) ne undergite ná þá þing þe þú sǽdest *videor mihi utiliter non intellexisse quae dixeras*, Gr. D. 174, 18. v. un-nytlíce.

**nytlicness.** *Add*: *profit, advantage*:—Swá þ hit sí for micelre nyttlicnesse (*magnae utilitatis*) þ hyra weorc forholen beón ne magon, Gr. D. 61, 10. v. un-nytlicness.

**nytness.** *Add*:—Nyttnis *utilitas*, Ps. Srt. Cam. 29, 10. Hí heora hors tó bryce and tó nytnesse onféngon, Gr. D. 16, 3. v. un-nytness.

**nytt.** *Add*: **nytto**; *indecl.* I. *add*:—Hwelc nytto on blóde mínum? *quae utilitas in sangui[ne] meo?*, Ps. Vos. 29, 10. Wé woldon þ hit wurde tó nytte ðám gehérendum, Bt. 35, 5; F. 166, 17. Sum ðing ðe tó nyte mæge, Angl. ix. 262, 24. II. *add*: *useful work, charge, service*:—Paulinus onféng þá nytte þæs wyrtgeardes *Paulinus excolendi horti suscepit curam*, Gr. D. 180, 28. Ǽfre hé mæig findan on ðám hé mæig nyt beón aud ðá nytte dón ðe him fylstan scylan, Angl. ix. 261, 2. v. un-, weorold-nytt.

**nytt;** *adj. Add*:—Ǽfre hé mæig findan on ðám hé mæig nyt beón, Angl. ix. 261, 2. Hié mec ǽnigre note nytte beón ne meahton *inutiles facti sunt*, Nar. 15, 27. Hí (*friends*) beóð mé on sumum ðingum nytte, and ic eác heom, Solil. H. 40, 5. Ic ælcne mínra freónda lufige swá mycele má þonne ðone óðerne swá ic ongyte þæt hé betran willað þonne se óðer and his gesceádwisnesse nyttran willan tó dónne *tanto magis amo amicos meos, quanto magis bene utuntur anima rationali, vel certe quantum desiderant ea bene uti*, 16, 21. v. on-nytt, *and see next word*.

**nytt,** es; *n. What is useful, advantageous, profitable*:—Ic nát hwes ic bydde, hweðer ic bydde nyttes þe unnittes mé sylfum, Solil. H. 13, 18. v. un-nytt.

**nyttian.** *Add*:—Sume beóð stæreblind and nyttiað þeáh þǽre sunnan, Solil. H. 44, 23. Nǽfð nán man tó þæs unhále ǽagan þæt hé ne mage lybban þe þǽre sunnan, and hire (*printed* hine) nyttian gyf hé ænygwiht geseón mæg, 43, 25. Eald man sceal þá eágan weccan mid gnídingum, mid gongum ... and hý sculan nyttian lytlum metum (*they* 

---

*must use these remedies very moderately*), Lch. ii. 30, 30. v. ge-nyttian.

**nyttung.** *Add*: v. wuldor-nyttung.

**nyt-weorþ.** *Add*:—Forgife mé se wilega gifola þæt mé tó ǽgðrum onhagige, ge hér nytwyrðe tó beónne (cf. Alfred's words in the translation of Boethius: Ic wilnode weorþfullíce tó libbanne þá hwíle þe ic lifede, Bt. 17 ; F. 60, 14), ge húru þider tó cumane, Solil. H. 2, 16. Ic lufige ælc ðing be ðám dǽle þe ic hyt nytwyrðe ongyte, 43, 1. Hwæþer þæt (*anweald*) nú sié tó talianne wáclic and unnyt þte nytwyrþost is eallra ðissa woruldþinga ? *num imbecillum ac sine viribus aestimandum est, quod* (potentia) *omnibus rebus constat esse praestantius?*, Bt. 25, 4 ; F. 86, 16. v. un-nytwirþe.

**nytweorþlíce.** *Add*:—Ðæt hí ðæs ðe nytweorþlícor gehiérden ðá hálgan láre, ðe hí ǽr wilnodon ðæt hí gehíran mósten *ut quanto anxie quaererent, tanto utiliter audirent*, Past. 443, 12. v. un-nytwirþlíce.

**nytweorþ-ness.** *Add*:—Hwilc nytwyrðnes (*utilitas*) on mínum blóde?, Ps. L. 29, 10. Netwearnes *commoditas*, An. Ox. 8, 68. Gif se hýredes ealdor tó lytele note and nytwyrðnesse (-weorþ-, *v. l.*) on his heorde angyt *quicquid paterfamilias utilitatis minus potuerit invenire*, R. Ben. 11, 2.

# O

**oden.** *For first and third passages substitute*:—Se wítega segð, 'Frymþa odene þínre and wínwringan þínre (*primitias areae tuç et torcularis tui*) þu ná latast tó bringan mé, Scint. 109, 3. On odene cylne macian, Angl. ix. 262, 2. *Add*:—Ðá ðing tó bewitanne ðe tó scipene oððe tó odene belimpað, Angl. ix. 260, 5. Man sceal habban ... tó odene fligel, 264, 8.

**of.** I a. *add*:—Ic fleáh of wícum, Gen. 2273. Him gewát Hróðgár út of healle, B. 663. I β. *add*:—Wit unc simble ondrédon hwonne wit sceoldon feallan of þám olfende, Shrn. 38, 16. II. *add*:—þá Lapithe gesáwon Thesali of hiora horsum beón feohtende wið hié, Ors. 1, 9 ; S. 42, 33. Hé wyrðode wordum wuldres aldor ... of carcerne, An. 57. Sió stefn geweard gehérned of heofonum, 168. III. *add*:—Hwæðer him ðæt geðóht cume of fǽrlicum luste ðe of wilnunga, Past. 417, 5. Þú tída gehwane of sylfum þé symle inlíhtest, Cri. 108. III a. *denoting cause, reason*:—Hé in yrmðum wunode þe of his lufan (*from love of him*) ádrég, An. 164. V. *add*:—Ic ðweá beð mín of teárum mínum *lavabo lectum meum lachrymis meis*, Ps. Spl. 6, 6. Bebeád ic eów þæt gé bróðor míne áretten of þám ǽhtum þe ic eów geaf, Cri. 1502. Hé áfedde of fixum twám and of fíf hláfum fíra cynnes fíf þúsendo, An. 589. VI. *add*:—Of ðam (*báne*) worhte God fǽmnan, Gen. 183. VII. *add*:—*where removal, &c.*, is from a material object*:—Wæterfrocgan hwílon man gesihð of wætere, Chrd. 96, 28. Gif monnes tunge bið of heáfde, Ll. Th. i. 94, 20. (2) the object non-material:—Sume men of hiora scome (*pudore amisso*) þá wǽtan þigdon, Nar. 9, 21. Of þǽm seóndscipe þe ús ǽr betweónum wæs, þ hé seoþþan wæs mé freónd, 19, 19. Sé bið áðwægen of unclǽnnesse, Past. 421, 21. Hé Godes lage and láre forlǽt, and ðurh deófles láre of ðám deð ðe his cristendóme tó gebyreð, Wlfst. 78, 15. Of wlite wendað wæstma gecyndu, Gú. 15. Eów is lár Godes ábróden of breóstum, Exod. 269. ¶ *with instrumental*:—Ðý lǽs hié wyrðen áwyrtwalode of ðýs andwerdan lífe, Past. 339, 18. IX. *add*:—Ǽfter þysum ongunnon of ðám gegaderwyrhtum tǽlan ðone hálgan, Hml. S. 6, 186. Sum ridda geband on ánum claþe of þám hálgan dúste, 26, 223. Achan behýdde oð ðám herereáfe, Hex. 54, 4. Swilce hé ǽte of þám spice, Hml. S. 25, 92. Hé Pehta þeóde of þám mǽstan dǽle (*maxima ex parte*) Ongelcynnes ríce underþeódde, Bd. 3, 24; Sch. 313, 19. X. *add*:—Godes gást him wæs on wunigende ǽfre of ðám dæge, Hml. Th. ii. 64, 14. XI. (a) *add*:—Swelce hé plantige treówu, and ceorfe of ðá wyrtruman, Past. 449, 33. Þonne seó sául of þám bið, Bl. H. 57, 35 : 111, 32. Fleót þ fám of, Lch. ii. 104, 20. XI. (d) *add*:—Gif preóst miswurðige circan þe eal his wurðscipe of sceal árísan, Ll. Th. ii. 294, 10. v. þær-of.

**of-ǽte** (?), an ; *f. What one eats of* (?), *food*:—God hét spryttan menigfealde treówcynn mid heora wæstmum mannum tó ofǽte (cf. universa ligua ... ut sint vobis in escam, Gen. 1, 29), Hex. 12, 2.

**of-ǽte** (?); *adj. Fat, given to eat too much*:—Fór ofǽte (oferǽte ?) *porcaster obesus*, i. *pinguis*, An. Ox. 21, 4. (Of *seems to correspond to* ob, ǽte *to esus* ?) v. of-eten.

**of-áxian.** *Add*: *to find out by enquiry*. (1) *the source from which not given*. (a) *the object a person*:—Se Cásere is sneágende hwǽr hé ús mǽge ofáxian, Hml. S. 23, 453. Hé hét ácwellan ealle þá crístenan þe hé ofáxian mihte, 29, 201. (b) *the object a thing*:—Dó ús gewisse þæs þe þú ofáxie, Hml. S. 23, 467. (c) *with a clause*:—Þǽr hé ofáxode þ se cyning wæs, Chr. 1016; P. 152, 22. Ðeós lúdith ofáxode hú Ozias gespræc *haec cum audisset quoniam Osias promisisset*, Hml. A. 108, 209. þá Iúdéiscan ofáxodon hú úre Drihten árǽrde Lazarum of

deáðe, 66, 26. Ofáxa hwæt se cásere be ús geboden hæbbe, Hml. S. 23, 465. Ic bidde þe þ þú læte ofáxian gif þis folc hæbbe ǽnige unriht-wísnysse ongeán heora God *perquire si est aliqua iniquitas eorum in conspectu Dei eorum*, Hml. A. 106, 137. (2) where the source from which is given. (a) cf. (1 b) :—Sulpicius wrát be Martine þá ðing þe hē ofáxode oððe æt him sylfum oððe æt óðrum mannum, Hml. S. 31, 5. (b) cf. (1 c) :—Ic sceal mē gebiddan tó him, and æt him ofáxian hwænne þú eáþelícost mihte tó þám folce becuman *orabo Deum et dicet mihi quando eis reddat peccatum suum*, Hml. A. 110, 257. Hē hæfde ofáxod æt óðrum mannum ǽr þ hē wæs Iúdéisca *dixerat eis se esse Iudaeum*, 96, 139.

**of-beátan.** *Add* :—Se micela ylp þe þá módigan fearras mid ealle ofbeát mid his egeslican nypele, Hml. A. 63, 286.

**of-brǽded**, Sal. K. p. 148, 22. v. ofer-brǽdan : **of-brytsig.** *Dele, and see* **byrstig.**

**of-calen.** *Add* :—Utan hlýwan ofcalene and wǽfan nacode and syllan mete þám gehingredum, Wlfst. 119, 6.

**of-cyrf**; I. *add* :—Se abbod brúce ísene ofkyrfes *abba utatur ferro abscisionis*, R. Ben. I. 60, 2. Seó ród is wíde tódǽled mid gelómlicum ofcyrfum tó lande gehwilcum, Hml. S. 27, 144.

**of-dǽl**; *adj. l.* (?) of-dǽle (*as an i-stem*).

**of-dǽle**, an (?). *l.* of-dǽle, es, *and add* : v. gēn-dele, æf-dǽll (*which should be taken here*), *and* cf. æf-, geán-dýne.

**of-drǽd[d].** *Add* :—Se þridda cnapa wacode swíðor for ege þonne for his gebedum . . . se ofdrǽdda cnapa þ eall geseah, Vis. Lfc. 59. Daria cwæð tó þám ofdrǽddan men, Hml. S. 35, 269.

**of-drincan** *to intoxicate* :—Ælces cynnes drinc þe man mæg ofdruncen beón *omnis generis potus quo quis inebriari possit*, Ll. Th. ii. 134, 21 note. v. for-, ofer-drincan.

**of-dúne.** *Add* : I. of direction of movement :—Úp yrnan and ofdúne, Lch. ii. 116, 24. II. of attitude or posture, to lie, bow *down* :—Eadmódlíce ofdúne anlútan, Past. 467, 7. Ic ofdúne on ðá eorðan læg, Hml. S. 23 b, 575. III. of position in space :—Þá stód hē on hlǽddre . . . þá stód ðǽr ofdúne on þǽre fióre Sancte Peter, Gr. D. 227, 6.

**ofdúne-onwend**; *adj. Turned downwards* :—Hē hangode ofdúne-onwendum heáfde *he hung head downwards*, Gr. D. 24, 28.

**ofdúne-, ofdún-rihte**; *adv. Straight down* :—Sýn þá fēt gebundene tó ðám hēhstan telgan, and þ heáfod hangige ofdúnrihte and þá fēt úprihte, Verc. Först. 110, 10.

**ofdúne-, ofdún-weard**; *adv. Downward, down* :—þ áborstene clif hreás ofdúneweard (ofdún-, *v. l.*), Gr. D. 12, 10. Hē áfeóll ofdúne-weard (ofdún-, *v. l.*) (nyðerweard hreás, *v. l.*), 24, 25.

**ofdúne-weardes**; *adv. Downwards* :—Underfēng hine seó ýþ and teáh ofdúneweardes, Gr. D. 114, 33.

**of-earmung.** *Add* :—On ofearmunga and mildheortnesse *in miseratione et misericordia*, Ps. Rdr. 102, 5. Gemyne ofearmunga (*miserationum*) þínra and mildheortnesse þínre, 24, 6.

**ofen.** *Add* :—Hē sceolde beón forbærned on hátum ofne, Hml. Th. ii. 18, 26. þá forlēt hē þone lǽmnan ofn ðæs mænniscan líchoman, Shrn. 50, 33.

**ofen-raca.** *Add* : -racu, e; *f.* For '*an instrument for clearing out an oven or furnace*' substitute : '*A fork for stirring the fire in a furnace for cooking.*' [Cf. rotabulum *furca vel illud lignum cum quo ignis movetur in fornace causa coquendi*, Migne] :—Man sceal habban . . . ofnrace, Angl. ix. 265, 3.

**ofer.** I. (4) *add* :—Þú woldest mē laðian þæt ic swíðor drunce swilce for blisse ofer mínum gewunan ; ac wite þú þæt sē þe óðerne neádað ofer his mihte tó drincenne, þæt sē mót áberan heora bēgra gilt, gif him ǽnig hearm of þám drence becymð, Ælfc. T. Grn. 21, 29–32. (5) *add* :—þæt earme mancynn ofer him sylfum heófiað and wēpað, Wlfst. 183, 1. (8) *add* :—Dæg byð ofer dæg, Ps. Th. 60, 5. (8 a) marking sequence in time of events :—Ofer mínre gecígnesse þú gesettest ealle þíne apostolas tó mínre byrgenne (cf. 137, 25–27) *after I am called from this world thou hast appointed all thine apostles to attend my burial*, Bl. H. 143, 29. (9) denoting the object on which an action or feeling takes effect :—þá þe him Godes egsa hleonað ofer heáfdum, Gú. 44. (10) denoting the cause of an action :—God manna cynn eallinga ádwǽscan ne wolde ofer (for *v. l.*) hyra synnum (*pro culpa sua*), Bd. 1, 27 ; Sch. 77, 17. II. (2) *add* :—Ðá hē fleáh, ðá tórýpte hine án bré[m]ber ofer ðæt nebb, Gr. D. ii. 134, 28. Hē slóh hine ofer his wange, Gr. D. 200, 15. Ælc man ofer eall fērdon, Hml. S. 23, 266. (3) *add* :—Þá ásweóll him se líchama ofer healf *his body swelled through a half of it* ; dimidia pars corporis ipsius turgescens, Guth. Gr. 153, 12. Oð þæt hié máran lēfnesse onfēngon ofer eall (*per omnia*) tó lǽranne, Bd. 1, 26 ; Sch. 58, 8. Ofer eall hlýdende ǽlc man cwæð . . . *there was clamouring throughout the crowd and it was said by every one* , Hml. S. 23, 617. þá spræc man ofer eall and wíd-mǽrsude *auditum est et celebri sermone divulgatum in aula regis*, Gen. 45, 16. Gelæhton þá weardmen his wealdleðer fæste, þæt hē mid fieáme ne burste, ac hē nolde him ætfleón, ac hē clypode ofer eall (*he called out*

so *as to be heard by all round him*), Ælfc. T. Grn. 18, 16 : By. 256. (4) *add* :—Sē ealdorman hēt gelǽdan Erculanum ofer ðǽre burge weall and hine þǽr heáfde beceorfan *comes Herculanum super urbis murum deductum capite truncavit*, Gr. D. 198, 8. (5) *add* :—þá eóde hē·ofer sumne þorn *inruit in quamdam spinulam*, Guth. Gr. 153, 6. (6) *add* :—Wæs þeós sprǽc gefylled ofer Nabochodonosor, Hml. Th. ii. 434, 6. (8 a) *add* : of quantity :—Ofer fíftig míla, Hml. S. 9, 3. Ofer ynce, Ll. Th. i. 18, 17. Ofer .xii. winter and ofer eahta peningas, 198, 17 : 228, 12. Ne God gyltas ofer ǽnne sýþ wrecan wile ǽnigum men *nec Deus bis crimina vindicat ulli*, Dóm. L. 89. Hæbbe sylf þ hē ofer þ árǽre *ipse habeat super augmentum*, Ll. Th. i. 436, 14 (*see also* twelf-wintre). Gif þǽr beón má þonne seofon . . . gif þǽr byð án ofer þá seofon, Angl. viii. 304, 11 : 303, 44. (8 β) *add* :—Sē ðe ofer his ǽwe hǽmð, hē is forlír ðurh his ǽwbrice, Hml. Th. ii. 208, 17. Ofer þ mē lysteð þ þú mē secge sum þing be his módes eádmódnysse, Gr. D. 45, 13. *Non habeas Deos alienos* ; ðæt is, ne lufa ðú óðerne God ofer mē, Sal. K. 188, 22. (9) *add* :—Hí fuhton unwǽrlíce ofer Iúdan leáfe (cf. they were not obedient unto Judas, 1 Macc. 5, 61), Hml. S. 25, 456. (10) *add* :—Hē wæs on scipe ofer bolster slápende, Mk. 4, 38. (14) *add* : in reference to time, ⟨a⟩ *after* :—Þone lyttlan fyrst tó libbanne ofer þá óþre . . . wæs sum bróðor þe æfter (ofer, *v. l.*) hine libban nolde . . . libban æfter (ofer, *v. l.*) þē, Gr. D. 53, 15–28. He neaht ofer þ, Ll. Th. i. 32, 3. (β) *through* :—Hē wunode on sǽgrunde middan ofer dæg and ofer niht *die et nocte in profundo maris fuit* (2 Cor. 11, 25), Hml. S. 31, 900. Man bær þone ele hire. þá wæs se ele wexende ofer ealne þone weg (*all the while they were carrying it*), Hml. S. 31, 1123. Eall þ heó ofer gǽr habban scolde tó bygleofan (ealne þe heó hæfde hire begiten tó ealles geáres andlyfene, *v. l.*) *omne quod in stipendio totius anni paraverat*, Gr. D. 68, 26. Nán ðing belífan ne móste ofer niht (cf. nec remanebit quidquam usque mane, Ex. 12, 10), Hml. Th. ii. 280, 8. III. *add* :—Hider ofer . . . geon ofer, Ll. Th. i. 354, 29, 30. þæt þæt þǽr ofer byð, Solil. H. 35, 19 : Lk. R. 11, 41. Súþ ofer on hlýpan, Cht. Crw. 3, 14. Redempta stód hire ofer, Hml. Th. ii. 548, 1. þá ongunnon ðá hæðengildan neáðian ðá apostolas, . . . and þá twēgen drýmen ðǽr ofer stódon, 494, 27. þám hí ofer sint *cui praesunt*, Angl. xiii. 373, 112. v. þǽr-ofer.

**ofer.** *Add* :—þá fuglas ymbsǽton eallne þone ófer þæs meres *aues totam stagni compleuere ripam*, Nar. 16, 17. On stæþena ófrum *riparum marginibus*, An. Ox. 4798. Cf. (?) ýfer.

**ofer-ǽt.** *Add* : [þe lichames festing is widtiging of estmetes and oueretes and untimliche etes, O. E. Hml. ii. 63, 22.]

**ofer-áwritt** *a superscription* :—Oferáwritt *superscribtio*, Lk. L. 23, 38. Cf. ofer-gewrit.

**ofer-áwritten** *what is written above* ; suprascribtio, Mt. L. 22, 20. Cf. ofer-writen.

**ofer-bídan.** *Add* : [v. N. E. D. over-bide.]

**ofer-brǽdan.** *Add* :—Án scínende weg wæs oferbrǽd mid god-webbenum pællum, Gr. D. 176, 1. Mid lilian blóstmum of[er]brǽded, Sal. K. 148, 22.

**ofer-brǽdels**; *m. Add* : and *n.* (?) :—Ic eom oferwrigen mid þám oferbrǽdelse Godes wordes, Hml. S. 23 b, 584. Twá mæssereáf . . . ij weóvedsceátas and ij overbrǽdels, C. D. B. iii. 660, 34.

**ofer-ceald.** *Add* : [v. N. E. D. over-cold.]

**ofer-cearfa.** v. ofer-cirran.

**ofer-cídan.** *Add* :—Hē sylf cídde (ofercídde, *v. l.*) and þreáde (*vehementer increpavit*) þæs muneces dysignysse, and þá swá gecíded (ofercíded, *v. l.*) hē wæs eft gecyrred tó his mynstre, Gr. D. 111, 16 : 132, 23.

**ofer-cirran** *to pass from one place to another, cross a space* :—Ofer-cearra (*printed* -cearsa ; *but cf.* iccearro, Mt. L. 12, 44, *and* ofer-cirr *in Dict.*) wē ofer þ luh *transfretemus trans stagnum*, Lk. L. 8, 22. Ðona hider ofercerre *inde huc transmeare*, 16, 26.

**ofer-climban.** *Add* : [v. N. E. D. over-climb.]

**ofer-clipian** *to cry out, exclaim* :—Ofercliopode þ folc *exclamavit turba*, Lk. R. L. 23, 18.

**ofer-costung**, e ; *f. Excessive trial* :—Gié habbað in middangeorde ofercostung (*pressuram*), Jn. L. 16, 33.

**ofer-cuman.** I. *add* : (1) *to get the better of in a contest* :—Sē ðe his ágen mód ofercymð and gewilt, Past. 218, 17 : Bt. 34, 11 ; F. 152, 11. Hē ealne þone here áhtlíce ofercóm, Chr. 1066 ; P. 198, 3. Besing and ofercum ealle yfele wilddeór, Lch. i. 202, 13. Ne mihte hē geþencan hú hē hí mid ǽnige cræfte ofercuman sceolde, Bt. 39, 4 ; F. 216, 24. (1 a) *to overcome* in argument :—Ofercuóm *conuincit* (*Judaeos de baptismo Johannis interrogando*), Mk. p. 4, 19. (2) of some physical or mental force or influence, *to overpower, exhaust, render helpless* :—Swongornes hí ofsit and hí mid slǽwþe ofercymþ, Bt. 36, 6 ; F. 180, 34. þá wǽron Cartainiense swá ofercumene and swá gedréfde betux him selfum *fessi tot malis Carthaginienses*, Ors. 4, 6 ; S. 178, 5. II. *add* :—Ofercymeð *superueniet*, Lk. L. R. 21, 35. Ofercymað (-cumað, R.) *superueniant*, Lk. L. 21, 34. Ofercymmas (-cumað, R.), 26. Ofer-cuómon (*supervenerunt*) scioppo of ðǽm londe nēh ðǽr stóue, Jn. L. R.

6, 23. Þte ofercuôme *superuenisse*, Jn. p. 1, 14.　　　III. in the following instance the verb seems to govern the genitive :—Crîstenra manna God, þæs wuldorge[wor]ces nâne mennisce searwa ofercuman ne magon, Angl. xvii. 121, 6. v. un-ofercumen.

**ofer-cwealm**, es; *m. Excessive mortality* :—Nû is heóf and wôp and ofercwealm mycel, Angl. iii. 113, 203.

**ofer-cymmend** *one coming upon another, an assailant* :—Gif bið strongra him se ofercynimend (*superueniens*), Lk. L. 11, 22.

**ofer-dôn**. *Add* :—Ealle oferdône þingc deriað *omnia nimia nocent*, O. E. Hml. i. 296, 4.

**ofer-drenc**. *Add* :—Hit nis nâ riht on Crîstenum folce þæt sume scylon mid oferǽte and mid oferdrence beón oferlǽde and sume hungre cwylmede, Hml. A. 142, 98. Wâ eów þe ǽr on morgen oferdrenc dreógað *vae qui consurgitis mane ad ebrietatem sectandam* (Is. 5, 11), Wlfst. 46, 15.

**ofer-drencan**. *Add* :—Ôðre swâ feala swâ hî mǽst mægon hí oferdrenceað, Hml. A. 146, 63.

**ofer-drîfan**. *Add* :—Genam se apostol menigfealde gewitnyssa heáhfædera and wîtegena tô oferdrîfenne ðâ ârleásan Iûdêiscan, Hml. Th. ii. 420, 11. Ouerdryuen *confutati*, An. Ox. 7, 208.

**ofer-drincan**. *Add:* with gen. of intoxicant :—Gif ǽnig gehâdod hine sylfne rǽdlîce oferdrince,' oððe þæs geswîce oððe his hâdes þolige, Ll. Th. ii. 258, 26. Þâ þe lufiað þ hî hî sylfe an wîne oferdrincon *diligentes se inebriari uino*, Chrd. 74, 3. Ðæt môd wilnað ðæt hit tô ðon onwæcne ðæt hit mæge eft weorðan oferdruncen ; for ðǽm . . . hit wacað on ðǽm ymbhogum ðisse worlde, and wilnað ðæt hit sié oferdruncen his âgnes willan *mens evigilare optat, ut rursum vina reperiat ; quia . . . vigilare ad seculi curas nititur, ut semper voluptatibus inebrietur*, Past. 431, 24-27.

**ofer-drincere**, es; *m. One who drinks to excess, a drunkard* :—Þâ þe ôðre men mid mânâðum beswîcað beóð ealswâ miceles wîtes scyldige swâ ðâ manslagan and ðâ unrihhǽmeras and ðâ oferdrinceras, Hml. A. 147, 95 : 148, 124 : Nap. 66, 4 : 71, 7.

**ofer-druncen**. *Add* :—Ic fela dyde þæs ðe ic dôn ne sceolde . . . on oferǽte and on oferdruncenne, Angl. xi. 102, 64. On oferdruncne, 99, 78. Beorge manna gehwylc wið oferdruncen him georne, Wlfst. 103, 8.

**ofer-druncenness**. *Add* :—Ic gewilnode þæs wînes on þâm ic ǽr gelustfullode tô oferdruncennysse brûcan, Hml. S. 23 b, 535.

**ofer-drync**. I. *add* :—Mid micelre sýfernysse and gemetfæstnysse Godes gôda brûcan and nâ mid nânre oferfylle and mid oferdrince, Hml. A. 144, 17. Ðâ ðe hira âgene sâwle ðurh oferdrinc ofsleáð, 147, 75.　　II. *add* :—Gif ðâ druncengeornan men heora druncennyssa geswîcan nellað, ac þurhwuniað on ðâm oferdrincum æt neora ende, Hml. A. 145, 35. [Hwenne þe muð sunezað on muchele ete and on ouerdrinke, O. E. Hml. i. 153, 32.]

**ofere**. *Add:* I. *over, across* :—'Eáðe þû þâ bricg oferfêrest.' Mid þâm þâ weard hê sôna ofere, nyste hê hû. Ðâ þâ hê ofere wæs, þâ côm him lâteów ongeán, Vis. Lfc. 7-9.　　II. *from above* :—Hê bebeád genipum ofere (*desuper*), Ps. Rdr. 77, 24.

**ofer-eáca**. *Add: the rest* :—'Ic hæbbe mænigfealde ǽhta, and . . . ic gedô þ hî cumað hider' . . . Hê forðteáh þâ fîftig mancsas, and þâm abbode sealde and cwæð, 'Nim þis feoh, and gif ic hêr þurhwunige se ofereáca hider cymð,' Hml. S. 33, 145-155. Syllað ðone ofereácan eów (*the rich*) tô ælmesdǽdum, Hml. Th. ii. 328, 3.

**ofer-eald**. *Add* : [v. *N. E. D.* over-old.]

**ofer-fǽr**. *Add* :—Fram Abrahame wæs ðâ forð oð Môises tîde and Israêla oferfær ût of Egyptum v c wintra, Sal. K. 184, 11.

**ofer-færeld**. *Add* :—Oferfærelde *transmigratione*, An. Ox. 1602.

**ofer-fæst** *glosses* trans-fixus, Lk. p. 11, 13. Cf. ofer ; II. 1.

**ofer-fætt**. *Add* :—Nû gesetton ðâ hâlgan fæderas þ wê fæston mid gerâde, and ælce dæg eton mid gedafenlicnysse, swâ þ ûre lîchama âlêsed ne wurðe ne eft oferfæt tô îdelum lustum, Hml. S. 13, 105.

**ofer-faran**. II a. *add* :—Bremmas oferfôren (*cum*) *cerula* (*proprios*) *egrederentur* (*terminos*), An. Ox. 2479.　　II ð. *add* : The passage glossed is: Vastae solitudinis secreta *penetrans*, Ald. 51, 5.　　III. *with reference to time* :—Mihst þû swâ manegra tîda lencgu oferfaran þ þû ne freóde þone bryne þǽre flǽsclican gewyrfednysse ?, Hml. S. 23 b, 522. Æfter oferfarenum þæs geáres ryne, 728. [v. *N. E. D.* over-fare.]

**ofer-feallan**. *Add* : [With stonus men shulen oversalle hem *lapidibus obruent eos*, Wick. Lev. 20, 27.]

**ofer-feng**. In l. 2 *substitute* oferfengc *for* oferfenge, *and add* :—Oferfengc, dalc *legulam*, An. Ox. 5126. Oferfeng, 2, 424.

**ofer-feohtan**. *Add* :—Jûdas hî oferfeaht and âflýmde hî ǽfre, Hml. S. 25, 387 : 536. Mâre sige bið þæt se man hine sylfne ðurh geðyld gewylde, ðonne hê wiðûtan him burga oferfeohte, Hml. Th. ii. 544, 11. Geânlǽhte Lisias fîf and sixtig fyrdendra þegena and wolde oferfeohtan þ Jûdêisce folc, Hml. S. 25, 364. Hiô bið oft oferfohten bûtan ǽlcum geswince *sive labore superatur*, Past. 279, 2.

**ofer-fêran**. *Add* :—I. of movement in space. (1) *to pass through, across* :—Eáðe þû þâ bricge oferfêrest, Vis. Lfc. 8. Oferfoerde *trans-*

*fretavit*, Mt. L. 9, 1. Oferfoerde ðerh middum hiora *transiens per medium illorum*, Lk. L. 4, 30 : 17, 11. Oferfoerdon, 6, 1. Mið ðý oferfoerdon *cum transfretassent*, Mk. L. 6, 53.　(2) *to pass by:*—Ðe Hǽlend oferfoerde ꝼ bî eóde, Mt. L. 20, 30. Se diâcon hine oferfoerde, Lk. L. 10, 32. Mið ðý oferfoerdon gesêgon þ ficbeám, Mk. L. 11, 20. (3) *to go, go away* :—Mið ðý oferfoerde ðona, Mt. L. 15, 29. Oferfoerde ꝼ gǽd embehtað *transiens ministrabit*, Lk. L. 12, 37.　　II. of time relations, *to pass through life* :—Tô þisse andweardan woruld côm Crîst and oferfêrde ; þæt is, hê côm tô ðisse worulde on menniscnysse, and ðis lîf oferfêrde, Hml. Th. i. 182, 27-28.

**ofer-ferian** *to transport* :—Hê ne gelêfde þte ǽnig oferferede (*transferret*) faet ðerh þ templ, Mk. L. 11, 16. Oferferig (*transfer*) calic ðiosne from mec, 14, 36. On þon ýttran stæþ oferferod *in citeriorem marginem translatus*, An. Ox. 3680.

**ofer-fêþre**; *adj. Overloaded* :—Sêlre byð oft fêðre þænne oferfêðre *meliora plura quam grauia houera fiunt*, Angl. ii. 373. v. fêþre.

**ofer-findan** *to put to the proof, make trial of* :—For ðon nǽre se breóst nânra þinga oferfunden, gif hine seó ârfæstnes ðæs ârwyrðan weres ne oferswýðde *virtutis enim pectus non esset, si hoc pietas non vicisset*, Gr. D. 18, 19. Hê þôhte, siþþan þ folc oferfunden wǽre, þ hié siþþan wolde eall þæt hê wolde, Ors. 6, 37 ; S. 296, 6. v. ofer-fundenness.

**ofer-flêwedness** *superfluity* :—Hǽra hî âweg dôn oferflêwednysse *pilorum euellant superfluitatem*, Angl. xiii. 408, 611. v. ofer-flôwenness.

**ofer-flôwan**. I. *add: trans.* :—Þîne ýþa mê oferfleówon *fluctus tui super me transierunt*, Ps. Th. 41, 8.　　II. *add: intrans.*, of a vessel, stream, &c., where the contents flow over the side or brim :—Ðý lǽs mon mâ geóte on ðæt undiópe môd ðonne hit behabban mæge, ðæt hit ðonne oferflôwe, Past. 459, 15.

**ofer-flôwedlic**; *adj. Superfluous* :—Hê warnie hine sylfne be oferflôwedlicum (*superfluo*) leahtre, Chrd. 121, 37. Ûs oferflôwedlîce þing fram âwurpan, Nap. 49. v. ofer-flôwendlic.

**ofer-flôwedlicness** *superfluity* :—Mid his oferflôwodlicnysse *superfluitate sua*, R. Ben. I. 101, 15.

**ofer-flôwedness**. *Add* :—v. ofer-flôwedness.

**ofer-flôwendlic**; *adj. Superfluous, superabundant* :—Rên sê sêlost ys gif hê nâ oferflôwendlic nyþer âstîhð on eorþan *pluuia illa optima est, si non superflue descendat*, Scint. 51, 16. Ân forhæfednys is þæt gehwâ werlîce ðâ oferflôwendlican ðygene him sylfum ætbrêde, Hml. Th. i. 360, 13. Gemetegude . . . oferflôwendlîce *moderata . . . superflua*, Scint. 54, 8. v. ofer-flôwedlic.

**ofer-flôwendlîce**. *Add: superabundantly, excessively, immoderately* :—Ic oferflôwendlîce sorgiende weóp, Hml. S. 23 b, 548.

**ofer-flôwendness**. *Add: superabundance, excess* :—Ne forseó gê Godes ðearfan, ðeáh ðe hî tǽllîce hwæt gefremman ; for ðan ðe heora yrmð âfeormað þæt þæt seó gehwæde oferflôwendnys gewemð, Hml. Th. i. 332, 14. Þonne wǽre hit oferflôwennis (*superfluum uideretur*) ûs âwiht nîwes tô trahtnienne, Chrd. 2, 4. Lustas heora hlâford þurh oferflôwednysse tô unlustum gehnexiað, ii. 92, 19. Ðû weliga, tô hwon treówadest þû on þînne welan and on oferflôwennysse (-flôwnessa, *v. l.*) þînra gôda ?, Wlfst. 261, 1.

**ofer-flôwness**. *Add* : Habban oferflôwnessa *accipere, stipendia superflua*, Chrd. 11, 33. *See preceding word* (*last passage*).

**ofer-fôn**. *Add* :—Mîn Drihten, sié þê þonc þæs þe þû lête þînne lîchoman oferfôn and gebindan and swingan, Angl. xii. 504, 20. Ic eom oferfongen mid synnum tô wyrmlîce, 501, 21.

**ofer-fundenness**, e; *f. Experiment, trial* :—Oferfundennessum *experimentis*, An. Ox. 543. v. ofer-findan.

**ofer-fyll**. *Add* :—Se syxta heáfodgylt ys *ventris ingluvies*, þæt ys oferfyll, Angl. viii. 337, 4. Oferfyl *elogia, conuiuium*, Hpt. 31, 5, 24. Be oferfylle. *Ve, qui consurgitis mane ad bibendum, et reliqua*, Wlfst. 46, 12. Þeáh hwâ on dæg gefæste ful lange, gyf hê syððan hine sylfne gedweleð mid gedrynce and mid oferfylle, eal him bið þæt fæsten îdel geworden, 103, 12. Þâ þe hêr on unrihttîdum on oferfyllo bióð forgiwene, Nap. 27, 30. Hê oferfyllum (*commesationibus*) þeówaþ, Chrd. 117, 20. Deófîice dǽda on ofermettan and on oferfyllan, Ll. Th. i. 319, 17. [Overfulle maketh wlatie, O. and N. 354.]

**ofer-fyllan**. *Add* : [v. *N. E. D.* over-fill.]

**ofer-fyllo**; *n. Liquid that runs off with straining ?* :—Ramgeallan þone fâgan cnûa on nîwe ealo ær þon hit âsiwen sié ; sele þ oferfyllo drincan þreó niht, Lch. ii. 124, 15.

**ofer-fylness**, e; *f. Overfullness* :—Hwîlum þâ swefn for oferfylnesse (*plenitudine*) þǽre wambe . . . beóð âcende, Gr. D. 339, 3.

**ofer-gǽgan**. *Add* :—Gif hwâ þis ofergǽgð *si quis transgressus fuerit*, Chrd. 46, 15. Se câsere hêt hine bewǽpnian and beforan his ansýne ætstandan . . . swilce ofergǽgendne his hlâfordes bebod, Hml. S. 30, 411.

**ofer-gán**. I. *add: to overspread a surface, occupy* :—Se teter bûtan sâre ofergǽð ðone lîchoman *impetigo sine dolore corpus occupat*, Past. 71, 17 : 437, 18. Gif ðone æpl ðæs eágan ðæt fieáh mid ealle ofergǽð, ne mæg mon nôht geseón *pupilla oculi . . . albuginem tolerans nil videt*, 69, 18. Seó eorðe bið mid fûlum wætere ofergân, Angl. vii. 48,

463. III. *add :*—Swā þ heora nān ōþres mearce ne ofereóde, Bt. 33, 4 ; F. 128, 32. III b. *to overreach :*—Nān man ne ofergā ne ne beswīce (*supergrediatur neque circumueniat*) on mangunge his níhstan, Chrd. 110, 34. V. *add :*—Ðyses middangeardes ansién ofergǣð *praeterit figura hujus mundi*, Past. 395, 27. þā unrótnessa þe þū nū on eart, swā iíce ofergāð, swā þū cwist þ þā blissa ǣr dydon, Bt. 8 ; F. 24, 34. Godwine eorl . . . sāh niðer . . . sprǣce benumen . . . and hine man brǣd intó ðæs kinges būre, and ðóhtan þ hit ofergān sceolde, ac hit næs nā swā, Chr. 1053 ; P. 182, 23. [v. *N. E. D.* over-go : *O. H. Ger.* ubar-gān : *Ger.* über-gehen.]

**ofer-gangan.** *Add :* [v. *N. E. D.* over-gang.]

**ofer-gapian.** *Add :* The original Latin is : Nec occasione sacerdotii obliviscatur regule oboedientiam. [Cf. *O. H. Ger.* kapfēn *to look.*] Cf. ofer-gíman.

**ofer-gemet.** *Add :*—Lōca nū þæt þū ofergemet ne wilnige, nū ðū hí (*God and Alypius*) tōgædere metest, woldest cunnan God swā swā Alippius *vide ergo ne impudenter velis satis Deum nosse, qui Alypium non satis nosti,* Solil. H. 17, 9.

**ofer-genyhtsumian** *to superabound :*—þār þār genihtsumude synne ofergenihtsumude (*superabundavit*) gyfu, Scint. 131, 15.

**ofer-geótan.** *Add :*—Ofergeót (cf. begoten, 24) ðinne líchaman mid fantwætere, Hml. Th. ii. 346, 14. Zosimus þā eorðan mid teárum ofergeótende *flooding the earth with his tears*, Hml. S. 23 b, 363.

**ofer-gesāwan.** v. ofer-sāwan ; II.

**ofer-gesett.** *Add :*—Monige nyllað nā geðencean ðæt hié beóð ōðrum brōðrum ofergesett on godcundum ðingum *nonnulli velut obliti quod fratribus animarum causa praelati sunt,* Past. 126, 17.

**ofer-gesewenness.** v. ofer-sewenness.

**ofer-gestandan** *to stand above :*—Ofer his reliquias þ heofonleóht wæs ofergestondonde and scínende, Bd. .3, 11 ; Sch. 235, 9.

**ofer-geswincfull ;** *adj. Excessively laborious or troublesome :*—þis wæs on eallon þingan swíðe hefigtýme geár, and ofergeswincfull on ungewederan, þā man oððe tilian sceolde oððe eft tilða gegaderian, Chr. 1098 ; P. 234, 2.

**ofer-geþyld** *what is intolerable ? :*—On helle bið fýr sweart and un-ādwæscedlic, and ðær bið cele and brene and broga, ǣttor and ofergeþyld, Sal. K. 84, 24.

**ofer-gewrit.** *Add :*—Pilatus wrāt ofergewrit (*titulum*) and sette ofer his rōde, Jn. 19, 19.

**ofer-gitol.** *Add :*—Ofergeotol ic eom eotan hlāf mínne *oblitus sum manducare panem meum,* Ps. Vos. 101, 5.

**ofer-gitolian.** *Add :*—Ðā ðe ofergitiliað (*obliviscimini*), Dryhten, Ps. Vos. 49, 22. Ofergeteliað *obliviscuntur,* 9, 18. Ofergiteligen *obliviscantur,* 58, 12. Zosimus his ealdan ylde ofergitiligende . . . mid hrǣdestan ryne arn, Hml. S. 23 b, 185.

**ofer-gitolness.** *Add :*—Nales in ende ofergetelnes bið þearfena *non in finem oblivio erit pauperum,* Ps. Vos. 9, 19.

**ofer-glēsan** *to write an English word over a Latin one to explain the latter, make an interlinear gloss :*—Aldred hit oferglóesade on Englisc, Jn. p. 188, 7.

**ofer-grōwan** *to overgrow, occupy with* (*its*) *growth* (of a tree) :—Se fiicbeám . . . stōd unnyt ; for ðǣm him weard ierre se gōda wyrhta, for ðǣm hé ofergreów ðæt land būtan wæsðme. Ðonne ofergrēwð se fiicbeám ðæt lond, ðonne . . . *ficulnea, quae fructum non habuit, contra hanc districtus agricola queritur, quod etiam terram occupat. Terram ficulnea sine fructu occupat, quando . . . ,* Past. 337, 8.

**ofer-gyldan.** *Add :*—Ofergylded, Jn. p. 188, 5. On ofergyldum reáfe, Hml. A. 28, 108.

**ofer-hāt ;** *adj. Excessively hot :*—Wið ōmum oferhātum, Lch. ii. 10, 6. [*Chauc.* ouer-hoot (fire).]

**ofer-heáfod.** *Add :* [v. *N. E. D.* over-head] : **ofer-heáh.** *Add :* [*Orm.* oferr-heh] : **ofer-hebban.** *Add :* II. *to uplift, exalt.* v. ofer-hebbendlic. [Overhofen sal be over Yban his fruyte, Ps. 71, 16. *Goth.* ufar-hafjan sik *to exalt oneself : O. H. Ger.* ubar-heven sih.] [v. *N. E. D.* over-heave.]

**ofer-hebbendlic ;** *adj. That is to be highly exalted :*—Gibloedsad and . . . hergiendlic and wuldorlic and oferhebbendlic *benedictus es . . . laudabilis et gloriosus et superexaltatus,* Rtl. 181, 27 : 31.

**ofer-helian.** *Add :*—Seó sōþe lufu oferhelaþ (*operit*) micelnysse synna, Scint. 1, 5. Sē þe ǣgyltendes wunda belocenum breóste and mid tungan oferhelað (*tegit*), 38, 17. Hí oferheledon (*operuerunt*) hine mid bletsungum, 67, 14. Oferhelian synne *uelare peccatum,* 52, 11. Beón oferheled *obtegi,* Germ. 389, 22. [v. *N. E. D.* over-hele.]

**ofer-heling, e ;** *f.* I. *covering, veiling :*—Oferhelung *obductus,* Scint. 223, 4, 5. II. *a covering :*—Reáf . . . for nēdbehēfe oferhelincge *uestis . . . propter necessarium tegumentum,* Scint. 144, 1.

**ofer-hergian.** *Add :*—In þām cwylde þe þās burh oferhergode (*vastavit*) nīd swýþlicum wōle and cwealme, Gr. D. 298, 23.

**ofer-hiwian.** (1) *to transfigure :*—Oferhíwad (-heówad, R.) wæs *transfiguratus est,* Mt. L. 17, 2. Oferhíwade, Mk. p. 4, 4 : Lk. p. 6, 8. (2) *to put another colour on to :*—Oferhíádum *dealbatis,* Mt. L. 23, 27.

**ofer-hleápan.** *Add :* [v. *N. E. D.* over-leap.]

**ofer-hlīfan** *to tower over* or *up :*—Oferhlifan *praecellerent* i. *supereminerent,* An. Ox. 3530. Oferhlīfend (or = -hlifiende ?) mycelnys *eminens* (i. *praecellens*) *magnitudo,* 1003.

**ofer-hlīfian.** I. *add :*—Tō þām scræfe næs nān weg, for þon þe þǣr oferhlīfode micel stānclif (*excelsa desuper rupes eminebat*), Gr. D. 99, 2. II. *add :*—Manega trahtnedon ymbe þis angin . . . ac ic hig ealle oferhlīfige oðða oferswýðe (*ego sublimor*), Angl. viii. 307, 8. Ofe[r]hleofað *praecellat,* i. *supereminet,* An. Ox. 309. Hit (ðæt mōd) swíþe oferhlīfade ealle þās woruldþing *rebus omnibus quae voluntur, eminebat,* Gr. D. 4, 16. Swíþe þeónde on his weorcum and ealle oferhlīfigende on wurðmynte, Hml. S. 30, 4.

**ofer-hlūde ;** *adv. Over-loudly :*—Ne sceal man sealmas ofstlíce singan, ne oferhlūde *psalmi non cursim, aut in excelsis uocibus recitentur,* Chrd. 57, 13.

**ofer-hoga.** *Add :*—Sē bið Godes oferhoga þe Godes bodan oferhogað, Wlfst. 177, 11. Eal woruld winneð swýðe for synnum ongeán þā oferhogan þe Gode nellað hýran *pugnabit pro Deo orbis terrarum contra insensatos homines,* 92, 16.

**ofer-hogian.** *Add :*—Sē þe oferhogie þ hē Godes bodan hlyste, Ll. Th. i. 374, 32. [Hit (*the child*) oferhoweþ þin ibod, Misc. 128, 445. Overhoheþ, O. and N. 1406.]

**ofer-hogodness, e ;** *f. Pride :*—þurh oferhogodnysse gāst *per superbiae spiritum,* Gr. D. 144, 4.

**ofer-hōn** *to hang with something so as to cover an object :*—þæs muntes cnoll mid þeósterlicum genipum eal oferhangen wæs, Hml. Th. i. 504, 31. Tō him geneálǣhton sume ælþeódige men . . . oferhangene mid tōslitenum clāðum (*scissis vestibus, pannis obsiti*), Gr. D. 202, 18.

**ofer-hragan.** *Add : to cover over* (?). Cf. hrægel : **ofer-hréfan.** *Add :* v. un-oferhréfed.

**ofer-hycgan.** *Add :*—For hwon ðegnas ðíne oferhogas (cf. for-hogas, 3) selenise ðāra aeldra ? *quare discipuli tui transgrediuntur traditionem seniorum ?,* Mt. L. 15, 2. Ðū oferhogdes *sprevisti,* Ps. Vos. 118, 118.

**ofer-hygd.** I. *add :*—Of heorta monno smeáungas yfle ofcymeð . . . oferhygd (*superbia*), Mk. L. R. 7, 22. þurh oferhigdes (*superbiae*) gāst, Gr. D. 144, 4. Fram þǣre heánnesse þāra oferhygda (-hýda, *v. l.*) *ab elationis fastu,* 188, 4. Hē þōhte on his oferhigdum hū hē sceolde him tō sprecan, 37, 21. Gif ǣnig sý uppāhōfen and inblāwen on þā oferhýda þǣre deófles lāre, Cht. E. 242, 20. II. *add : magnanimity, highmindedness :*—Geclǣnsa mē ðā hwíle ðe ic on þisse worulde sí, and gedō mē unmódigne ; sile mē oferhýda ; dō mē gesceádwísne and rihtwísne and foreþancfulne and fulfremedne, and gedō mē lufiende þínes wísdōmes *jubeas me dum hoc ipsum corpus ago atque porto, purum, magnanimum, justum prudentemque esse, perfectumque amatorem sapientiae tuae,* Solil. H. 14, 5 : Angl. xii. 513, 3.

**ofer-hygd ;** *adj. Add :*—þā oferhýdigan (*superbi*) beóð tintregode mid þām oferhigdum (*superbis*), Gr. D. 316, 5. Cf. ofer-mōd ; *adj.* (and *sbst.*)

**ofer-hygdig** *pride. Add :*—Utan wē beón gemyndige ūssa sāwla þearfe, and forlǣton wē morþor and mān and oferhýdyg and æfeste, Verc. Först. 93, 15.

**ofer-hygdig** *proud, supercilious. Add :*—Gif hē wel āginnan wile ne mæig hē sleac beón ne tō oferhýdig, Angl. ix. 259, 21. Hē hæfde ǣnne swíþe oferhigdigne cniht, þām hē sylf mihte uneáðe gewyldan *superbum valde puerum habuit, cui vix poterat vel ipse dominari,* Gr. D. 36, 5. v. ofer-hygd ; *adj.*

**ofer-hygdiglīce ;** *adv. Proudly, arrogantly :*—Heó hī āhebbað oferhigdilíce (-hídiglíce, *v. l. superbe*) ongēn þā beboda þǣre sōðfæstnesse, Gr. D. 197, 16. Hē wēnde þ hē mihte þā ylcan brōgan him gedōn þe hē ǣr gewunode ōðrum mannum tō dōnne, and ongan mid mycclum stefnum clypian and cweðan oferhygdilíce (*arrogantly*) : 'Arís . . . ,' 164, 2.

**ofer-hygdlic ;** *adj. Proud, arrogant, presumptuous :*—Wē gehýrdon and ongeáton þā oferhygdlican gedyrstignesse þæs elreordgan kyninges, Nar. 19, 11.

**ofer-hygdlīce ;** *adv. Arrogantly, presumptuously :*—Gif wē āhsiað þone þe þus oferhídlíce āna hālgað Drihtnes líchaman and his blōd, hwæt wile hē secgan ? *Etsi interrogatus aut contemptus huius modi corporis et sanguinis Domini solitarius consecrator fuerit, quid respondere poterit ?,* Chrd. 83, 20.

**ofer-hyge.** *Dele the bracket ; the alliteration requires the compound.* Cf. ofer-mēde *for form and meaning :* **ofer-hylmend.** *Add :* Cf. for-hylman : oferian. v. ge-uferian.

**ofer-ild(u, -o).** *Add :*—Is þǣre æfteran helle onlícnes genemned oferyldo ; for þan him āmolsniað þā eágan for ðǣre oferyldo, Verc. Först. 107, 3. Ǣlc ōþer oferylde and geogeþe *reliqui,* R. Ben. 115, 11.

**ofer-irnan.** *Add :* I a. *of a fluid, to spread over* or *throughout :*—Gif þǣre wambe ānre þā yfelan wǣton cumen, and ne oferyrnen ealne þone líchoman . . . Gif sió yfele wǣte of þǣre wambe oferyrneþ ealne þone líchoman, Lch. ii. 178, 16-20. Ðō þ se wǣta mæge furþum ofer-

yrnan þā wyrta, 306, 28.    **II.** *add:*—Wē willað nū mid sumere scortne trahtnunge þās rǣdinge oferyrnan, and geopenian, gif heó hwæt dīgles on hyre hæbbende sȳ, Hml. Th. i. 388, 30.  Wē willað þás þing mid sceortre race oferyrnan, Angl. viii. 318, 43.

**ofer-lád.**  *Add:* v. ofer-lǽdan ; **II.**

**ofer-lǽdan. I.** *For* '*to oppress*' *substitute: to cover, draw over ;* obducere (v. Hml. Th. i. 504, 31 *under* ofer-hón).    **II.** *to carry across, translate.* v. ofer-lád :—Gewrit oferlǽded Scriptura translata, Mt. p. 2, 13.  [v. *N. E. D.* over-lead. *O. H. Ger.* ubar-leiten transducere.]

**ofer-lǽfan. I.** *to leave over, not to use up* :—Étun alle and gifylde wērun, and ginimen wæs ðætte oferlǽfed wæs (*quod superfuit*), Lk. R. 9, 17.  [ʒe shulen ouerleeuen hem to the aftercomers *transmittetis ad posteros,* Wick. Lev. 25, 46.]  **II.** *to be left over* :—Þe oferhlǽfed *quod superest,* Lk. L. 11, 41.  [There ouerlafte not oon *non superfuit ne una quidem,* Wick. Ex. 8, 31.]

**ofer-lecgan. I.** *to lay over, above, or upon something else* :—Oferlecgan þ līn þām weófode *superponant linteum altari,* Angl. xiii. 428, 899.  **II.** *to cover the surface* of a thing *with something* :—Oferlege mid wulle, Lch. ii. 200, 7.  Oferlecge mid līnene clāðe, 182, 4.  **III.** *to affect as with a superincumbent weight, oppress* :—Gif hī hió sylfe mid swīðlicre druncennysse oferlecgað, Hml. A. 147, 73. Hit nis nā riht on Crīstenum folce, þæt sume scylon mid oferǣte and mid oferdrence beón oferlēde, and sume hungre cwylmede, 142, 99.  [v. *N. E. D.* over-lay. *Goth.* ufar-lagian.]

**ofer-leóran. I.** *add:* I a. *to pass by, abandon* :—Þonne wǣre him wēn þ hē oferliórde and forlēte þone gewunan his āgenre stīþnysse *fortassis sui vigoris usum excederet,* Gr. D. 106, 5.

**ofer-libban.**  *Add:* [v. *N. E. D.* over-live.]

**oferlīce.**  *Add:*—Hī lǣtað þæt man gȳman ne ðurfe nā oferlīce swȳðe þæs þe bēc beódað, Wlfst. 55, 19.

**ofer-lifa,** an ; *m. Excess* in food :—Se oferlyfa on ǣte and on wǣte dēð þone man unhālne, O. E. Hml. i. 296, 5.  [Þe oferlifa on hete and on wete macað þene mon unhālne, 101, 27.]  Cf. big-leofa.

**ofer-līhtan** *to alight upon* :—Mē seó swēte stemn oferlīhte and mē ðā gedrēfedan geðōhtas fram āfȳmde, Hml. S. 23 b, 558.

**ofer-līþan.**  *Add:*—Swā ic strange sǣ and mycele oferlīðe *velut transvadato vasti gurgitis aequore,* Guth. Gr. 102, 33.

**ofer-lyftlic ;** *adj. That is above the air* (lyft) (applied to the second heaven) :—Siofon heofonas sindon in gewritum leornode, þ is, se lyftlica heofon and se oferlyftlica . . . sió duru ðæs oferlyftlican heofones is nemned Elioth, Nap. 50.

**ofer-mǣg** *glosses* preualet, Scint. 97, 19 : **ofer-mǣned.** *Dele, and see* ofer-menged.

**ofer-mǣte.**  *Add:*—Be ðām þingum þe ðū mē sēdest þat þū getyohhod hæafde tó forlǣtanne . . . þæt is ofermǣtta wela and ofermȳtta wyrðscipe and ungemetlīce rīclic lȳf, Solil. H. 38, 2.  Hine deófla costodon mid ofermǣte unclǣne luste, Shrn. 52, 22.  [Wit þī lichame fro ouermete wede, O. E. Hml. ii. 137, 21.]

**ofer-mǣtu.**  *Add:*—Ofermǣte insolentiam, An. Ox. 2, 448.

**ofer-mēdla.**  *Add:*—Hwǣr is dēmera dómstōw ? hwǣr is heora ofermēdla, būtan mid moldan beðeaht and in wītum gewrecen, Wlfst. 263, 17.

**ofer-menged (?)** *over-mixed, confused, crushed* :—Ofermened (-menged ? Cf. (?) gemengunge *confusione,* 14, 68) contrita (*contrita rotis extollit vipera* cæphal, Ald. 163, 34), Wrt. Voc. ii. 92, 37 : 19, 43.

**ofer-mercung** *a superscription* :—Ofermercunc *suprascribtio,* Mk. p. 5, 1.

**ofer-mete.**  *Add:*—Deóflice dǣda on gīfernessan, on ofermettan and on oferfyllan, Ll. Th. i. 310, 17.

**ofer-mēttu.**  *Add :*—For ðæs rīces heánesse him weóxon ofermētto, Past. 113, 6 : 425, 18.  Hē cwæð ðæt ælces yfles fruma wǣre ofermētta *quia initium omnis peccati superbia,* 301, 4 : 307, 2.  Sió scyld ðāra ofermētta *superbiae culpa,* 311, 23 : 271, 23 : 439, 3.  Mid ðǣm ofermēttum oferswīðed *languore superbiae victus,* 439, 6.  Fær ofermēttum āworpen *per superbiam reprobatos,* 113, 7.  On ofermētum (-mēttum, *v. l.*), 19.  Hē in gēð ðurh ðā ofermētta, 463, 31 : 53, 16.  Ofermētto *insolentiam,* An. Ox. 7, 368.

**ofer-micel.**  *Add:*—Be þǣre ofermiclan friclo, þonne . . . sió ofermiclo friclo and gīfernes ārīst of þæs hores wǣtan, Lch. ii. 196, 1–3.  Ofermi[cle] *magna,* An. Ox. 46, 24.  [v. *N. E. D.* over-michle.]

**ofer-micelness.**  *After* 'Scint' *insert* 50.

**ofer-mōd** *pride.*  **I.** *add :*—Ofermōd witan *to feel pride, be proud* ; altum sapere (Rom. 11, 20), Scint. 8, 29.  *Dele* **II,** *and see next word.*

**ofer-mōd ;** *adj.*  *Add:*—Ofermōd coturnus (cf. coturnum, superbum, Corp. Gl. H. 36, 714), Wrt. Voc. ii. 19, 5.  Wē witon ðæt hē nǣre eádmōd, gif hē underfēnge ðone ealdordōm . . . būton ege ; and eft hē wǣre ofermōd, gif hē wiðcwǣde ðæt hē nǣre underðīdd his Scippende, Past. 51, 12.  Þæt mannum ofermōd ys *quod hominibus altum est,* Scint.

82, 8.  Ofermōd willa *superba uoluntas,* 84, 2.  Dǣlan herereáfu mid ofermōdum (*superbis*), 82, 15.  [v. *N. E. D.* over-mod.]

**ofer-mōdian** *to be proud* :—Þæt þurh eádmōdnysse nā ofermōdige *ut per humilitatem non superbiat,* Scint. 19, 20.  Nāteshwōn framað on hēhnysse eádmōdnysse leornian sē þe on neowlum gesett nā geswīcð ofermōdian (*superbire*), 84, 8.  Ofermōdigende *superbiendo,* 230, 3.  [*O. H. Ger.* ubar-muotōn *superbire.*] v. ofer-mōdigian *for other examples.*

**ofer-mōdig.**  *Add:*—Betere ys on yfelum dǣdum clǣne andetnyss þænne on gōdum weorcum ofermōdig gylp (*superba gloratio*), Scint. 40, 20.  Hē hæfde ǣnne ofermōdine cniht, Gr. D. 36, 5.  Rōma āliésed weard of þeówdōme þāra ofermōdgestana cyninga þe mon hǣt Tarcuinie, Ors. 2, 1 ; S. 62, 6.

**ofer-mōdigian.**  *Add:*—Ðonne ofermōdigaþ (*superbit*) se ārleása, Scint. 177, 15.  Ðæt mōd ðe for his cræítum ofermōdgede *virtute superbiens anima,* Past. 463, 24.  Mid nānes prȳte þū ofermōdiga *nulla elatione superbias,* Scint. 152, 16.  Ðȳ lǣs hī dyrren ofermōdgian (*superbire*) for ðǣm æðelestum weorcum, Past. 467, 16.  Hī ofermōdgiende his gebod forhogdon, 405, 31.

**ofermōdiglīce ;** *adv. Proudly, arrogantly, presumptuously* :—Ofermōdelīce *superbe,* Scint. 81, 3.

**ofermōdlīce.**  *Add:*—Ðȳ lǣs ǣnig durre on eádmōdnesse hīwe hit ofermōdlīce (*superbe*) forcweðan, Past. 51, 3.

**ofer-mōdness.**  *Add: arrogance* :—Ofermōdnesse insolentiam (*protervorum et arrogantiam indisciplinatorum*), An. Ox. 8, 390.  God ūs lǣred eádmōdnessa and deófol ūs lǣrð ofermōdnessa, Hml. A. 168, 111.

**ofer-neód ;** *adj. Very necessary* :—þeáw oferneód *mos pernecessarius,* Angl. xiii. 377, 176.  *See next word.*

**ofer-nīd.**  *Add:*—Ne beó man þæs fulluhtes tō hræd būtan oferneód geweorðe, Wlfst. 123, 25.

**ofer-niman.**  *Add: to take by surprise, overtake* :—Mē leóht slǣp ofernam *cum leui mihi somnus obrepsisset,* Bd. 5, 9 ; Sch. 592, 7.  [v. *N. E. D.* over-nim.]

**ofer-nōn.**  v. ge-lūtan ; **II.** : **ofer-plantian** *glosses* trans-plantare, Lk. L. 17, 6.

**ofer-prūt, -prūd** (*or* ?-prȳt), e ; *f. Excessive pride* :—Hī beóð þurh oferprūda alles tō rance . . . ant on mōdignesse tō swīðe āhofene, Wlfst. 81, 28.

**ofer-prūt, -prūd ;** *adj. Excessively proud, puffed up* :—Ne bisceop . . . bisceophādes intingan regules beboda oferprūt þrīstlīce betwyxsende *nec episcopus episcopatus occasione regulę beboda tumidus temere intermittat,* Angl. xiii. 373, 104.  Ys uppāhafennyss þearfena, þe ne welan upp āhebbað, and willa on him sylf oferprūt ys *est elatio pauperum, quos nec diuitię eleuant, et uoluntas in eis sola superba est,* Scint. 183, 12.  God gewilnað beón unbunden andettende þ hē nā oferprūte witnian genȳde (*ne contumaces punire cogatur*), 38, 13.  [v. *N. E. D.* overproud.]

**ofer-rǣdan. I.** *add:* (1) *to read over* to another :—Nū for feáwum dagum wē oferrǣdon þis godspel ætforan eów, Hml. Th. i. 104, 31.  Æfter syx mōnþa embrine sī oforrǣd (*relegatur*) him regol, R. Ben. I. 96, 16.  (2) *to read over* to oneself, *peruse* :—Gif hwilc gelǣred man þās race oferrǣde oððe rǣdan gehȳre, Hml. Th. ii. 460, 5.  Seó bōc is on Englisc āwend, on ðǣre mæg gehwā be ðison genihtsumlīce gehȳran, sē ðe hī oferrǣdan wile, 358, 31.  [v. *N. E. D.* over-read.]

**ofer-rōwan.**  *Add:*—Hī ðā oferreówon ðone brym, Hml. Th. ii. 378, 23.

**ofer-sǽwisc.**  *Add:*—Ofersǣwiscum transmarinis (*literarum characteribus imbuta*), An. Ox. 2, 350.

**ofer-sāwan.**  *Add:* **I.** *to sow ground* with seed *in addition to some already sown.* v. Dict.    **II.** *to sow seed over other seed* :—Cuōm feónd his and oferseów (ofergeseáw, L.) weód in midle þæs hwǣtes, Mt. R. 13, 25.  [v. *N. E. D.* over-sow.]

**ofer-sceádan** *to sprinkle over* with something :—Mid hunige smire, and ofersceáde þonne mid alwan dūste, Lch. ii. 182, 2.

**ofer-sceadwian.**  *Add:* **I.** literal :—Swā se fiicbeám ofersceadað ðæt lond ðæt hit under him ne mæg gegrōwan, Past. 337, 11.  Ofersceadwad *umbrosa,* An. Ox. 56, 26.  **II.** figurative :—' Miht ðæs Hȳhstan ofersceadewað ðē ' . . . Maria wæs ofersceadewed ðurh mihte þæs Hālgan Gāstes.  Hū wæs heó ofersceadewod ?, Hml. Th. i. 198, 30–34.  Se Hālga Gāst hȳ mid his mihte ofersceadewode, Wlfst. 193, 13.

**ofer-sceáwian.**  *Add:*—Eþs is . . . on Englisc sceáwere, for þām þe hē is geset tō þām þ hē ofersceáwian sceole mid hys gȳmene þā lǣwedan, O. E. Hml. i. 303, 22.  Biscop sceal . . . beón his leóda hyrde . . . ealle ofersceáwigende, Hml. Th. ii. 320, 6.

**ofer-scūwan.**  *l.* -scūwian, -scūian, -scȳian.

**ofer-seolfrian.**  *Add:* , -silfran.  [*O. H. Ger.* ubar-silbarit deargentatus.]

**ofer-seón. I.** *add:*—Manige ōðre þe mid þām eádigan were wǣron and his līf hira eágum ofersāwon *alii qui cum viro Dei conversati vitam illius ex parte noverant,* Guth. Gr. 103, 47.  Þonne miht ðū ofersión ealle þās eorþlican þing *mens terras despicit,* Bt. 36, 2 ; F. 174, 7.  **II.** *add* v. ofer-sewenness :—Hī mē forlētan and swȳðe

forsāwan *ipsi spreuerunt me*, Wlfst. 45, 3. Hī noldon mīne lage healdan, ac mē ofersāwon on mænigfealde wīsan, 133, 16. [v. *N. E. D.* ofer-see. *O. Sax.* oðar-sehan.]

ofer-settan. I. *to place over, put in a position of authority:*—Đā underðiéddan ... ðā ofersettan *subditi ... praelati*, Past. 189, 16. II. *to oppress, overcome* with sleep, &c. :—Ic mid slǣpe oferseted wæs *depressus somno*, Gr. D. 347, 30. [v. *N. E. D.* oferset.] v. ofer-gesett.

ofer-sewenlic; *adj. Contemptible:*—Đā ungedyrstegan wēnað ðæt ðæt swīðe forsewenlic (ofersiwenlic, *v. l.*) sié ðætte hié dōð *pusillanimes vehementer despecta putant esse, quae faciunt*, Past. 208, 11.

ofer-sewenness, e; *f. Contempt*; as a legal term, *fine for disobedience to authority*. The word occurs only in legal documents. In the laws of Henry I it corresponds to *ofer-hírness* in the Anglo-Saxon laws :—Habeat episcopus debita transgressionum et poenam delictorum quae nos dicimus ofersegeneisse (quae Anglice dicitur oferisæwenes, ii. 240, 22) et gyltwīte, C. D. vi. 240, 35. v. ofer-seón; II.

ofer-siman. In l. 2 for 13 substitute 50, 14 : ofer-sittan. *Add :* [v. *N. E. D.* over-sit.]

ofer-slop. In Lch. iii. 200, 5–7 oferslop glosses byrrum. Cf. *birrus* unsmēðe hrægel, Wrt. Voc. i. 40, 25 : *byrrum* casul, ii. 127, 33.

ofer-slype. *Add :* -slīpe (? Cf. *O. H. Ger.* ubar-slaufi *peplum*) an alb :—Ælc on ðām yldran heápe nime ælce geáre ðrý oferslipas (*camsile:*. Camisile *alba*, Migne), Chrd. 48, 24.

ofer-smítan *to oversmear with something :*—Dō on clāð, ofersmīt mid ele, lege on þone magan, Lch. ii. 180, 28.

ofer-sprǣc. *Add :*—Hū micel ofersprǣc cymeð of ðǣre oferwiste *quanta sibi per esum loquacitas insidietur*, Past. 313, 10.

ofer-spreca; *m. One who talks extravagantly or inconsiderately :*—Swā swā unsceamfæst oferspreca hē bæd *ut inpudens procax imprecabatur*, An. Ox. 2819. v. ofer-sprecol ; II., ofer-sprecan ; II.

ofer-sprecan. *Add :* [v. *N. E. D.* over-speak.] v. ofer-spreca, -sprecol.

ofer-sprecol ; II. The noun qualified in both passages is *labris*.

ofer-stǣlan. *Add : to overcome in a dispute, overthrow the case of a person by proofs :*—Þā fuhton þā englas and þā deófiu ymbe þā earman sāwle ; and þā deófiu hý (*the soul*) genāman æt þām englum, and oferstǣldon hý mid hire yfelan weorcum þe heó wyrcende wæs (*confuted the angels with the evil deeds the soul was doing*), Wlfst. 235, 12. Cymð eft Elias and Enok tōgeánes Antecrīste tō ðí þæt hī þæs deófies leásunge mid Godes sōðfæstnysse oferstǣlon, 285, 23. Se engel bringð eall þæt wē tō gōde gedōð, and se deófol eall þæt wē tō yfele gedōð and wile oferstǣlan þone engel mid þām yfelum weorcum, 233, 9. Se dōm þurh þone byþ oferswīþed and oferstǣled þ̄ hlúde geñit þæs folces *sententia per quam tumultuosae turbae seditio comprimatur*, Gr. D. 265, 2.

ofer-stæppan. *Add :*—Hī ymb hine gemearcodon ānne hring on þǣre eorðan, and hēton þ̄ hē nænige þinga mid his fēt þone hring ne oferstōpe *in terra circulum designaverunt, extra quem pedem tendere nullo modo auderet*, Gr. D. 197, 1.

.ofer-standan *to stand, or be, above :*—þæt ofer his reliquias heofenlic leóht ealle niht wæs oferstandende *ut super reliquias eius lux caelestis tota nocte steterit*, Bd. 3, 11 ; Sch. 235, 9.

ofer-stīgan. I. *add :* with the idea of mounting, lit. or fig. :—Hī becōmon tō ðǣre stigole þǣr se þeóf oferstāh (*got over*) in ðone wyrttūn, Gr. D. 24, 8. Dō ealu þ̄ þā wyrta oferstīge (*rise above*), Lch. ii. 104, 17. Oferstīgan *praecellerent* (ut pyrae cacumina obelisci proceritatem triginta cubitis *praecellerent*), An. Ox. 3530. Gif hwilc gedwola wyle þæt anginn oferstīgan (cf. wylle gīt stīgan ufor, 23), Hml. S. 1, 20. [þ̄ flod wex ... and hit oferstah ælle duna, O. E. Hml. i. 225, 24. Hwenne so wil wit oferstieð (*gets the upper hand of*), Misc. 192, 1.] II. *add :* with the idea of passing across or beyond :—Gewyrc ānne hring ymb þone slite ūtan, ne oferstīhð hit furðor, Lch. ii. 112, 1. Hē oferstāh ealle gesceafta, Hml. S. 15, 164. Mid ðý oferstāg (*transcendisset*) se Hælend in scip ofer ðæt luh, Mk. L. R. 5, 21. [He widstod þet Englisce folc þet hī ne micte þa brigge oferstigan, Chr. 1066 ; P. 108, 28. Cf. In the ouersteʒyng (passyn ouer) of Arnon, Wick. Is. 16, 2.]

ofer-swimman. *Add :* [Oþer bestes ... ouerswymmen þe spaces of þe longe eyer *liquido longi spatia aetheris enatet volatu*, Ch. Boet. 170, 4951.]

ofer-swingan *to strike through :*—þ̄ hūru æt his ænde seó biternes and hreówsung oferswunge and geþreáde his mōd for his āgenre scylde *ut saltem in morte de culpa sua mentem ipsius amaritudo transverberet*, Gr. D. 344, 33.

ofer-swīþan. *Add :*—Ic oferswīðrode ł (ofer-?) swāð āgen hine, Ps. L. 12, 5. Suæ ofersuīða gedeafnad is sunu monnes *ita exaltari oportet filium hominis*, Jn. L. 3, 14. Diúl oferswīðed *diabolo devicto*, Mt. p. 14, 6. v. un-oferswīþed, -swīþende.

ofer-swīþe. *Add :*—Þā þe oferswīþe mettum brūcað *qui nimium*

*cibis utuntur*, Scint. 56, 11. Þā yfelan for hyra yfium weorcum wæron gewītnode oferswīþe, Bt. 39, 11 ; F. 230, 6.

ofer-swīþedlic. v. un-oferswīþedlic : ofer-swīþendlic. v. un-oferswīþendlic.

ofer-swīþend, es ; *m. A conqueror, vanquisher :*—Mīn se leófa ðeów Iōb, and deófies oferswīðend þurh geþyld, Hml. S. 30, 126.

ofer-swōgan. *Add :* v. swōgan ; II, *and see* ofer-hōn.

ofer-tæl ; *adj. That estimates too highly* (?), *superstitious :*—Warna symle ofertæle andgyt *caue semper superstitiosam intelligentiam*, Scint. 218, 10.

ofer-þearf. *Add :*—Āgan þā yldran on Crīstenum folce ðæs oferþearfe, þæt hī heora gingran Gode gestrýnan, Wlfst. 38, 23 : 301, 15.

ofer-þeccan. *Add :*—Seó līchamlice lustfulnes þ̄ mōd mid þeóstrum oferþeceþ *carnalis delectatio mentem obscurat*, Gr. D. 323, 9. þū oferþece (*cooperies*) hine mid hǣran, Chrd. 37, 12.

ofer-þencan *to think over, consider :*—Gif hit byð wel āsmeað and oferþōht *si bene perpenditur*, Gr. D. 316, 20. [v. *N. E. D.* over-think.]

ofer-þeón. *Add :*—þe oferþyó ealle ýsta sanda (*alimoniam*) *quae cuncta diliciarum fercula praecellat*, An. Ox. 11, 33.

ofer-togenness. *Add :*—Ofertogennysse *obductionis*, Scint. 179, 6.

ofer-tredan. *Add :*—Flīhð ælc hors āfæred ðurh ðā ylpas, and gif him hwā widstent hē byð sōna ofertreden (oftreden, *v. l.*), Hex. 16, 14. [v. *N. E. D.* over-tread.]

ofer-trūwa. *Add :*—Be ofertrūwan, Wlfst. 48, 5. *See next word.*

ofer-trūwian *to trust too much to :*—Wā þām þe ofertrūwað mægne and mænege, and on God ne behiht, swā swā hē sceolde, Wlfst. 48, 7.

ofer-tyht (?). v. tyht ; III.

ofer-ufa[n]. I. as preposition, *on, upon, above*. (1) with dat. :—Oferufa bolstare slēpende, Mk. L. 4, 38. Oferufa eallum is *supra omnes est*, Jn. L. 3, 31. (2) with acc. :—Oferufa sunu monnes, Jn. L. 1, 51. Oferufa his heáfut, 20, 7. II. as adv. :—Hine oferufa (*desuper*) sitta dydon, Mt. L. 21, 7.

ofer-wadan. *Add :* [v. *N. E. D.* over-wade.]

ofer-wealdan *to rule over, control :*—Ne lǣte hē nǣfre his hýrmen hyne oferwealdan, Angl. ix. 260, 27. Cf. wealdan ; III d.

ofer-welig ; *adj. Exceedingly rich :*—Đā forlegeran and þā godwracan and þā ofe[r]welgan, Nap. 50.

ofer-wenian. *Add :*—Oferwenodne līchaman þreágað *insolens corpus castigant*, Scint. 52, 14.

ofer-weorþ, -wirþe ; *adj. Very worthy :*—Oferwyrþe *condignae* (non sunt *condignae* passiones huius temporis ad futuram gloriam), Angl. xi. 171.

ofer-willan. I. *add : to cause to boil over*, Lch. ii. 24, 22.

ofer-winnan. *Add :*—Iōsue and Israhēla folc oferwunnon seofon ðeóda ; eahtoðe wæs Pharao ... swā sceolon crīstene men ðā eahta heáfodleahtras mid heora werodum ealle oferwinnan, Hml. Th. ii. 218, 12–17. Hē unāliéfede lustas ātemige and oferwinne *illicitas suggestiones edomare*, Past. 383, 6. Ne lǣt mē nānwiht oferwinnan on þis wege, þæt ic ne mage cuman tō þe *nihil mihi repugnare facias tendenti ad te*, Solil. H. 14, 2. Vespasianus āsende his sunu tō oferwinnenne ðā earman Iūdēiscan, Hml. Th. i. 402, 30. Oferwinnendum *expugnatore*, Scint. 8, 15. Þā wæs oferwunnan (-wunen, An. Ox. 3855) *grassaretur*, i. *vastaretur* (dum fames Ægypti vulgus *grassaretur*), Hpt. Gl. 497, 8. Oferwunnenre þǣre ofermōdignesse *extinctam superbiam*, Prud. 38 a. [v. *N. E. D.* over-win.]

ofer-winnende, -winnendlic. v. un-oferwinnende, -winnendlic.

ofer-wist. *Add :*—Monige welige menn lǣtað cuelan hungre Crīstes ðearfan, and fēdað yfie gliigmen mid oferwiste *nonnulli divites, cum fame crucientur Christi pauperes, effusis largitatibus nutriunt histriones*, Past. 327, 7.

ofer-wreón. *Add :*—Mæht ðæs hēsta oferwrīð (-wrīgað, L.) ðec *uirtus altissimi obumbrabit tibi*, Lk. R. 1, 35. 'Āwyrp mē hyder þinne scyccels ... þ̄ ic mæge þā wiflican týddernysse oferwreón' ... Hē þone scyccels hire tō āwearp ; heó þæs onfēng, and hire līchaman oferwreáh, Hml. S. 23 b, 210–219. Oferwreág *cooperuit*, Ps. L. 43, 16. Oferwrigen þ̄ ne beó geopenad, An. Ox. 61, 11 : Mt. L. 8, 24. [v. *N. E. D.* over-wry.]

ofer-wrigels ; *n. l.* ofer-wrigels ; *n. m.* : ofer-wrigen. v. un-oferwrigen.

ofer-writ. *Add : a superscription :*—Oferwriotum āwriten, Lk. R. 23, 38.

ofer-writen *what is written above, a superscription :*—Of oferwritenum *ex superscriptionibus*, Mt. p. 12, 2. Cf. ofer-āwritten.

ofer-wrīþan *to wrap round, cover up with a wrapper :*—Mid hnesce wulle oferwrīðe ealle þā scearpan, Lch. ii. 130, 10.

ofer-wundenness. v. ofer-fundenness : ofer-wunnen. v. un-oferwunnen.

ofesc. *Add : Cf. efesc* (under efes), *and M. E. ovese* (v. *N. E. D.* eaves).

**ofestan, ofstan** (= efestan, efstan) *to hasten* :—Hē ofeste *festinet*, R. Ben. I. 29, 5. Ofstende *festinanda*, Angl. xiii. 378, 186.

**ofet.** *Add* :—Sume hī leofodon be ofete and wyrtum, Hml. Th. i. 546, 5. Hē æt him ofet, and þæt þæt hē on wuda findan mihte, ii. 38, 8.

**of-eten**; *adj. That has eaten excessively, fat* :—Ofeten (ofer- ?) *obesus*, i. *pinguis*, An. Ox. 22, 4. v. of-æte.

**ofe-weard.** v. ufe-weard.

**of-feallan.** *Add* :—' Wē forceorfað þ treów, and þū hit feallende underfōh ' . . . Hī setton Martinum . . . þ se pīnbeám hine offeallan sceolde . . . se beám . . . offeól forneán þæs folces micelne dæl, Hml. S. 31, 402–418. ¶ glossing *decidere* :—Ðā steorras heofnes bidon offallende (*decidentes*), Mk. L. 13, 25.

**of-fearrian.** v. feorrian.

**of-fēran.** *Add* :—þā fleáh Iūdēa cyning . . ., ac Hieu hine offērde and him his feorh benam, Hml. S. 18, 339.

**of-fēstre** (?), an; *f. A nurse not living in the house* (?), *one who received a child into her own house to nurse* :—Ælfláede offēstran, Cht. Crw. 23, 22. Cf. cild-fēstre.

**of-frettan** *to eat up, devour* :—Ðā ðe offreattas (freotas, R.) hūso widuwana *qui devorant domos uiduarum*, Mk. 12, 40.

**offrian.** *Add* : (1) *absolute, to make a sacrifice, sacrifice* :—Ne tweónige hē nā þ hē ne offrað deófie, Hml. A. 146, 49. Ofrude *litarat*, An. Ox. 370. Offriað gē mid rihtwísnesse, and bringað þā Gode tō lācum, Ps. Th. 4, 6. Godes æ ūs forbiét diófulum tō offrianne, Past. 369, 3. (2) *to offer a sacrifice* :—Ic offrige þā offrunga *immolabo hostiam*, Ps. Th. 26, 7. Ofriað, 49, 15. Hē wolde offrian Gode þā gewunelican lāc, Hml. A. 58, 182. Ofrian *litare*, An. Ox. 18, 39. (3) *to offer something as a sacrifice* :—Offrian þæt lamb eall Israhēla folc on æfen *immolabit eum universa multitudo ad uesperum*, Ex. 12, 6. Hē wolde offrian his āgenne sunu Gode tō lāce, Ælfc. T. Grn. 4, 26. Ofriende *litaturus* (*panis merique libamina*), An. Ox. 5087.

**offrung.** I. *add* :—Salomon geoffrode Gode micele lāc, þæt wæron þūsendfealde onsægednessa æt ānre offrunge, Hml. Th. ii. 576, 8. II. *add* :—Árleásra offrung bið āwierged, for ðæm hié beóð brōhte of māndǣdum *hostiae impiorum abominabiles, quae offeruntur ex scelere*, Past. 343, 3. Ofer ælcere offrunga *super sacrificia*, Ps. Th. 49, 6. Ofriað Gode þā offrunge lofes *immola Deo sacrificium laudis*, 15. Ne þreáge ic eów nā æfter offrunga (*super sacrificia*); for ðām eówre offrunga (*holocausta tua*) synt symle beforan mīnre ansýne, 9. Gemyndig sý Drihten ealra þīnra offrunga (*omnis sacrificii tui*), 19, 3. Ðæt hē meahte on healdan ðā offrunga (ofrunga, *v. l.*) and ðā lāc ðe mon brōhte *ut in ea superposita holocausta serventur*, Past. 217, 20. II a. *the bread and wine offered in the Eucharistic service* :—Gyf þū offrunga habban wille, þonne wege þū þīn reáf and hefe ūp þīne twā handa, Tech. ii. 120, 3. v. æfen- (Chrd. 30, 21), eall-, īdelgild-offrung.

**offrung-clāþ**, es; *m. An offertory cloth*; *offertorium* (v. N. E. D. offertory ; 4) :—iii. offringclāþas, Nap. 50.

**offrung-dæg**, es; *m. The feast of unleavened bread* :—þā offrung-dagas wē nā ne begýmaþ *azimas non observamus*, An. Ox. 40, 23.

**offrung-hūs**, es; *n. A house of sacrifice* :—Ic geceás ðas stōwe mē tō offrunghūse, Nap. 50.

**offrung-sang.** *Add* : Cf. lāc-sang.

**offrung-sceát**, es; *m. An offering-sheet* [explained in the following passage : Their offerings of bread and wine, which they brought . . . having their hands muffled up in a very fine linen cloth or offering-sheet. v. N. E. D. offering ; 3] :—Hió becwið hyre beteran ofringsceát, C. D. vi. 130, 31. þis synd þā mādmas þe Adeluuold bisceop sealde intō þām mynstre . . . iii. offrincsceáttas, C. D. B. iii. 366, 18.

**offrung-spic**, es; *n. Bacon offered to idols* :—Hē dyde swilce hē ǣte of ðām offrungspice, Hml. S. 25, 92.

**of-gān.** II. *add* :—Nū mē is mīn āgen ætwiten swilce ic hit hæbbe forstolen, and man mid wītum ofgān willað æt mē þ ic mid rihtan þingon begyten hæfde, Hml. S. 23, 600. III. *add* :—Ābæd Ōsgār abbud æt Ælfhere ealdormen þ hē mōste ofgān þ land æt him mid sceatte. Ðā tíþode se ealdorman him, and se abbod sealde him ðā ān hund mancosa goldes, C. D. B. iii. 547, 6. [v. N. E. D. of-go.]

**of-georn.** *Add* :—Ofgeorn *inportunis*, An. Ox. 2, 96.

**of-geótan.** I. *add* :—Beána mid wætere ofgotene, Hml. S. 23 b, 128 : 663. III. *to pour out* :—Ðæra mynetra ofgæt (-geátt, R., āgeát, W. S.) mæslen *nummulariorum effudit aes*, Jn. L. 2, 15.

**of-gifan.** *Add* : I. *to give up an object, material or non-material, in one's possession, to abandon* :—Hē gāst ofgifeð *spiritus pertransibit ab eo*, Ps. Th. 102, 15. Hē ofgæf gāst *expiravit*, Lk. R., L. 23, 46. Sume on Rōmebyrig feorh ofgēfon, Ap. 12. Mec (*the cuckoo in the egg*) deádne ofgeáfan fæder and mōder, Rä. 10, 1. II. *to give up a place, quit a position* :—Se fugel ofgiefeð eard and eðel, Ph. 426. Abraham nihtreste ofgeaf, Gen. 2863. Næs ofgeáfon hwate Scyldingas, B. 1600. þā hildlatan holt ofgēfan, 2846. Carran ofgif, fæder ēðel-stōl, Gen. 1747. Sceoldon wræcmæcgas ofgiefan gnornende grēne

---

beorgas, Gū. 203 : 448. Ofgyfan, B. 2588. Hwæðer fāmig sǣ dǣl ǣnigne grēnre eorðan ofgifen hæfde, Gen. 1454. III. *to give up a state or condition* :—Hī (*Adam and Eve*) ēðles wyn geómormōde ofgiefan sceoldon, Ph. 412. III a. *to give up this present life* :—Ofgiefeð seó sāwl þās eorðan wynne, forlǣteð þās lǣnan dreámas, Cri. 1667. Hē þās worold ofgeaf, B. 1681. Hē gumdreám ofgeaf, 2469. þās woruld ofgyfan, Gen. 1127. Bebyrig Maria līchama[n], ofgif þǣre eorðan þ hire is, and þ dūst tō þām dūste, Hml. S. 23 b, 750.

**of-hæccan**; *p.* -hæhte *To hack off* :—Hī cwedað þ Petrus gewǣpnod wǣre, þā ðā hē his Drihten werian wolde; þ wæs þā hē ofhæhte (*amputavit*) þæs forscildgdon eáre, Ll. Th. ii. 386, 22. [Cf. O. H. Ger. hecchen.]

**of-healdan.** *Add* : [v. N. E. D. of-hold]: **of-hende.** *Add* : v. æf-hende.

**of-hreósan.** I. *add* :—His munecas nān ōðer ne wēndon būton hē wurde ofhroren (*crushed under the falling tree*), Hml. S. 31, 412. Mid þæs wāges hryre hē (*the devil*) tōcwýsde ænne munuccnapan. Hī wurdon þā ealle geunrētte . . . nā for þæs wāges fylle, ac for þæs ofhrorenan brōðres tōcwýsednysse, Gr. D. 125, 10. Hī suncon cuce intō ðære eorðan ofhrorene mid moldan, Hml. S. 13, 228 : 35, 339. Hē sæde þ his hūs feólle fǣrlíce, swā þ his menn þǣr lāgon othrorene, 25, 843.

**of-hreówan.** I. (a) *add* :—Ðīn mē ofhrýwð, and þīnre yrmðe, Hml. Th. i. 598, 8. Mē ofhreówð þissere menigu, ii. 396, 2. (b) *add* :—Him ofhreów þæs folces meteleást, Hml. Th. ii. 396, 19. Him ne ofhreów nā ðæs deófles hryre, i. 192, 18. Ofhreów þām hālgan þæs haran frecednyss, Hml. S. 31, 1060. Hē wæs tō þām earmheort þ him ofhreów þ āstēpede wīf, gif hē ne gehulpe hire dreórinesse, Gr. D. 18, 13. (c) *with dat. of pers. only* :—Gode ofhreów ðā and cwæð tō ðām engle, Hml. S. 13, 254. þe lǣs þe ofhrýwe þē *ne forte peniteat te*, Scint. 177, 2.

**of-hwilfan** *to roll away* :—Cneóris mīn ālǣd and ofhwylfed is fram mē *generatio mea oblata est et conuoluta est a me*, Ps. Rdr. 276, 12.

**of-hyngrod.** *Add* : I. *hungry for food* :—Se apostol wæs ofhingrod (*cum esuriret, voluit gustare*, Acts 10, 10), Hml. S. 10, 82. Ofhingrode *impasti*, Germ. 391, 99. II. *eagerly desirous* :—Ofhingrode and ofþyrste æfter rihtwísnesse, Hml. A. 46, 55.

**of-hyrian** *to imitate* :—Ic seó in þam forðgelæddan wætere of þām stāne þ hē ofhyrede (on-, *v. l.*) Mōysen *in aqua ex petra producta Moysen video*, Gr. D. 120, 14.

**of-irnan.** I. *add* :—Ofirneð, Met. 29, 32. *Add* : III. *glossing decurrere* :—Ic ofyrne *decurro*, Ælf. Gr. Z. 181, 10.

**of-lǣte.** *Add* : -lāt (?), e ; *f.* I. *add* :—Noldest þū nā ofrunga and oflāta (-an ?) nāne *sacrificium et oblationem noluisti*, Ps. Th. 39, 6. II. *add* :—Hē sōna sealde mid his āgenre handa oflētan (ofen-lētan, *v. l.*, *oblationem*), and bebeád : ' Gāð nū and dōð þ þis lāc sý Drihtne geoffrod for þām nunnum,' Gr. D. 153, 7. Gyf þū oflǣtan habban wille, þonne býg þū þīnne scytefinger tō þīnum þūman, Tech. ii. 120, 7. [v. N. E. D. oflete.]

**oflǣt-hlāf**, es ; *m. A loaf of the bread used for the Eucharist* :—þā genam hē mid him twēgen oflǣthlāfas on beágwisan ābacene (cf. þis is hālig hlāf . . . geoffra þysne hlāf Gode for mē æt þīnre mæssan, 23–28) *duas secum oblationum coronas detulit*, Gr. D. 343, 15.

**of-lecgan.** *Add* : *to overlay, cover* :—Oflege mid wulle, Lch. ii. 182, 18. Mid þām þingum siþþan oflege þe þā wunde clǣsnien, 210, 1.

**of-leóran** *to pass away* :—Heofun and eorðo oflióres (*transibunt*), word mīn ne gelióreð, Mk. R. 13, 31.

**of-licgan.** *Add* : [v. N. E. D. of-lie.]

**of-lícian.** *Add* :—þā officode þām cyninge þ hē læg hire swā gehende, Hml. A. 100, 274. þ man ōðrum ne beóde þ him sylfum oflicige, 11, 281. Hire ungelícu seó ðe þē oflícige, 94, 66.

**of-linnan.** *Add* : (1) *to leave off, desist* :—Hū lange willað gē wunigan on þære fūlnesse þæs líchoman fyrenlustes ? Oflinnað, lā, ær eów se deáð ofercume, Verc. Först. 143, 7. (2) *to desist from* (*gen.*) :—Uton oflinnan þāra unārímedra metta . . . Uton eác oflinnan þāra tælnessa, and uton ūs on gebedu gelōmlæcan, 148, 4–7.

**oflinnendlíce.** v. un-oflinnendlíce : **ofost.** *l.* ofost.

**ofostlíce.** *Add* :—Ofstlíce *perpropere*, i. *ilico*, An. Ox. 3107. Hē hēt ofeslíce leahtra leáse in þæs leádes wylm scūfan, Jul. 582. v. frǣofestlíce.

**of-rǣcan** *to obtain* :—Ita autem adquiratur illud triplex iudicium, quod Angli dicunt ofrǣce þ ordēl, Ll. Lbmn. 333, col. 2. [v. N. E. D. of-reach.]

**of-rīdan.** *Add* : [v. N. E. D. of-ride]: **of-sacan.** *Add* : [v. N. E. D. of-sake.]

**of-sceádan** *to divide off, separate* :—Ofsceádes (or ? of sceádes) ł gesundras *definiens*, Mt. p. 12, 13. [Cf. Ger. ab-scheiden.]

**of-sceamian.** *Add* :—Ongann ofsceomage ðǣm burgum *coepit exprobrare civitatibus*, Mt. L. 11, 20. Hē þā swýðe gescynd and

ofsceamod (scamiende, _v. l._) eóde _confusus valde exivit_, Gr. D. 142, 3 : Hml. S. 2, 178. [v. _N. E. D._ of-shame.]

of-sceótan ; I. _add :_—His hors wearð under ofscoten, Chr. 1079 ; P. 214, 28.

of-scotian. _Add :_—Wē þæt deór unsófte mid strǣlum and eác mid longsceaftum sperum ofscotadon and hit ofslōgon _bestia uix ipsis defixa est uenabulis_, Nar. 15, 28.

of-scýfende. v. scúfan : of-sendan. _Add :_ [v. _N. E. D._ of-send.]

of-seón. _Add :_—Þā ofseah hē feorran ðā hǣðenan ferian ān līc tō eorðan, Hml. Th. ii. 507, 16.

of-setenness. _Add : a sitting down :_—Obsetnesse _sessionem_, Ps. Cant. 138, 1.

of-setnian _to besiege, encompass :_—Geþeaht āwargedre ofsetnode mē _concilium malignantium obsedit me_, Ps. Cant. 21, 17. v. for-setnian.

of-settan. _Add : I. to press_ one object with another :—Ðonne þū candelbryd habban wille, āstrehte þīnre winstran handa ofsete hȳ eclinga mid þīnre swi[þ]ran, Tech. ii. 120, 23. II. _to oppress._ (1) the agent a person. (a) of physical ill-treatment :—Hī his ǣrran wunda mid wundum ofsettan, Hml. S. 37, 165. (b) of harsh dealing :—Leáse wītegan ofsettað þā geleáffullan, Hml. Th. ii. 404, 32. Helpað ofsettum, and steópcildum dēmað _subvenite oppresso, judicate pupillo_, 322, 8. (2) the agent a thing. (a) material, _to overwhelm, crush_ :—Gelīce hī wurdon mid þām fȳrenum flānum ofscotene, gelīce mid þǣra crīstenra wǣpnum hindan ofsette (cf. on-settan), Hml. Th. i. 506, 2. Scytum ofsette (_sagittarum_) _ictibus obrutos_, An. Ox. 3091. (b) non-material, illness, fear, &c. :—Ofsett eorðlīce onwunung andgyt fela þencendne _deprimit terrena inhabitatio sensum multa cogitantem_, Scint. 138, 16. Hē wæs ofseted and geswænced mid hefigre mettrumnesse his līchaman _qui cum gravi molestia corporis fuisset depressus_, Gr. D. 298, 3. Hē is nū mid ylde ofsett, Hml. Th. i. 614, 20. Wurdon hī ealle mid ōgan ofsette, Hml. S. 23, 231. ¶ of demoniacal possession :—Heó āflȳgde þā fūlan deófla fram ofsættum mannum, Hml. S. 2, 132. Ofsettum, Hml. Th. ii. 346, 33 : i. 344, 29. Þā deóflu be eówere hǣse þā ofslætan deófolseócan forlēton, 64, 26. III. glossing _exponere :_—Ne bið ofsettet _non exponitur_, Jn. p. 2, 5. [v. _N. E. D._ of-set.]

of-setting, e ; _f. Pressure :_—Ofsettincge _oppressum_, Scint. 143, 5.

of-sittan. II. _add :_—Wæs ālȳfed þām ealdum mannum þæt hī mōston heora fȳnd mid stranglicre mihte ofsittan, and mid wǣpne ācwellan, Hml. Th. i. 522, 15. II a. Cf. of-settan ; II. 2 b :—Ðonne ðæt mōd ðæs fæstendan bið mid ðȳ irre ofseten _dum mens abstinentium ab ira se deprimit_, Past. 313, 23. III. _add :_ III a. of demoniacal possession :—Hē ūt ādrāf ðone ealdan feónd of þām ofsetenan men (_de obsesso homine_), Gr. D. 135, 6. IV. _add :_—Seó gegaderung þāra āwyrgedra mē ofsǣton _consilium malignantium obsedit me_, Ps. Th. 21, 14. V. _add :_—Ofsittan and fortredan ðā gewilnigendlican lustas, Hml. Th. ii. 398, 29. [v. _N. E. D._ of-sit.]

of-sleán. _Add : I. to kill_ a living object. (1) the subject a person :—þū þe wītegan ofslihst (ofslǣs, L. _occidis_), Mt. 23, 37. Ofslyhst (-slæst, L., -slǣs, R., L. 13, 34. Sē ðe ofslihð (-slǣð, L. _occiderit_), Mt. 5, 21. Ofslyhþ (-slǣð, L. R. _interficiet_), Jn. 8, 22. Gē hig ofsleáð (-slǣs, L., -slǣþ, R. _occidetis_), Mt. 23, 34. Hig ofsleáð (-slǣs, L.) eów, 24, 9. Ofslǣð (-slāð), Lk. L. 11, 49. Ofslāas (-slægþ, R.) hine _occident eum_, Mt. L. 17, 23. Ðā ðe līchoma ofslǣð, Mt. p. 16, 7. Ic mid sweorde ofslōh niceras nigene, B. 574. Ofslōg, 1665. Ne ofsleh (-slah, L.) þū _non occides_, Mt. 5, 21. Ne ofslyh (-sleh, _v. l._, -slah, L., R.) ðū, Lk. 18, 20. Ofslā wē hine, Mt. L. 21, 38. Wutu ofslān þane, Mt. R. 21, 38. Walde ofslān (-slā, R.) hine, Mk. L. 6, 19. Ofslǣ (-sleán, L.), Mt. L. 14, 5. Ofslǣ, 16, 21. Ofslagen beón _occidi_, Mt. R. 16, 21. Wæs ofslegen _capite truncatur_, An. Ox. 3022. Bearn þāra ðe ofslegene wǣran _filios interemtorum_, Ps. Th. 101, 18. Hē betwih þāra ofslēnra (-slægenra, -slegenra, _v.ll._) [līcum?] (betweoh þām ofslegenum, _v.l._) gelīc deádum læg _cum inter cadauera occisorum similis mortuo iaceret_, Bd. 4, 22 ; Sch. 455, 4. (1 a) in the laws of man-slaughter, (α) which involved payment of wergild :—Gif man frigne mannan ofsleahð, Ll. Th. i. 4, 6. Ofslæhð, 6, 9. Ofslehð, 4, 9. Ofslyhð, 276, 32. Gyf in cyninges tūne man mannan ofsleá, .1. scill gebēte, 4, 4. (β) where no penalty was to be exacted :—Sē þe þeóf ofslihð, sē mōt gecȳðan mid āðe þ hē hine synnigne ofslōge, 112, 7. Gif man leúd ofsleá an þeófðe, licge būtan wyrgelde, 42, 13. Gif hine mon ofsleá, licgge hē orgilde, 60, 14 : 286, 14. Gif þeóf brece mannes hūs nihtes, and hē weorðe þǣr ofslegen, ne sié hē (_the slayer_) nā mansleges seyldig, 50, 19. Gif mon þæs ofslægenan weres bidde hē mōt gecȳðan þ hē hine for þeóf ofslōge, 116, 4. (2) the subject an animal :—Gif se oxa wer oþþe wīf ofslōge, Ll. Th. i. 48, 32. (3) the subject some destructive agency :—þ endenēcste gelimp twinnum ofslōh hlote (_quam_) _suprema sors gemina (mortis) multauerat urna_, An. Ox. 1837. II. _to slaughter_ cattle :—Gif hwā forstele ōðres oxan and hine ofsleá (ofslehð, Ex. 22, 1) oþþe bebycgge, Ll. Th. i. 50, 14 : 128, 14. III. _to destroy_ a thing, material or non-material :—Ne þūhte nānum men þæs tweó þ gif þ stānclif feólle, þ hit ne ofslōge þ scræf and eác Martinum

ācwealde _si ingens moles rueret, dubium non erat quod simul et specum destrueret et Martinum necaret_, Gr. D. 213, 21. Bið his unðeáw ofslægen (-slegen, _v. l._) būtan ǣlcre niédðrafunga, suā suā Assael wæs deád būtan orde, Past. 297, 22. Bið se deádbǣra wǣta on ðǣm menn ofslægen mid ðǣm biteran drence _humor mortiferus per amaritudinem vacuatur_, 303, 16. IV. _to strike and injure, to produce an injury by striking, strike_ with blindness :—Tō þǣm þe þǣr ofslegene syndon mid blindnesse, Bl. H. 153, 16. [v. _N. E. D._ of-slay.] v. un-ofslegen.

of-snīþan. _Add : I. to slaughter_ an animal :—Gif hwā drince wyrm on wætere, ofsnīðe sceáp raðe, drince hāt þ sceápes blōd, Lch. ii. 114, 7. II. _to cut off, amputate :_—Hē sceal his unþeáwas hatian and ofsnīþan, Met. 27, 33. [O. H. Ger. aba-snīdan _amputare :_ Ger. ab-schneiden.]

of-spring. _Add :_—For ðan ðe hē is Abrahames ofspring _quod ipse filius sit Abrahae_ (Lk. 19, 9), Hml. Th. i. 582, 6. Eádrīc hæfð geboht Sǣgyfu æt Ælfsige . . . tō ēcum freóte, and eall hire ofspring, C. D. vi. 209, 11. Tācnu wurðað on eów and on eówrum ofspringum (_in semine tuo_), Deut. 28, 46. Ofspringum (ofsprincge, Hpt. Gl. 416, 62) _femoribus_ (_non auferetur sceptrum de Iuda, et dux de femoribus ejus_ (Gen. 49, 10). The passage seems to have been freely translated as meaning there would not be wanting a leader among the descendants of Judah), An. Ox. 433.

of-stǣnan _to stone_ to death :—Seó burhwaru gelǣhton Stranguilionem and his wīf . . . and ofstǣndon hī tō deáðe, Ap. Th. 26, 24.

ofstan. v. ofestan.

of-standan. _Add : glossing_ exstare, exsurgere :—Ðe sǣ ofstōd t ārās _mare exsurgebat_, Jn. L., R. 6, 18. Nēde is tō cwoeðenne ofstōde ðāra sum . . . _necesse est dicere extitisse quosdam_ . . ., Mt. p. 7, 8.

of-stede. v. stede ; I ¶.

of-steppan. _Add :_ -stæppan :—Gif hwā mid his fēt ofstepð (-stæpð, _v. l._) ǣttrig bān, snacan oððe nǣddran, Lch. i. 152, 1.

of-stician. _Add :_—Be beón gif hī mannan ofsticiað (cf. beón gif hī man ācwellað, 164, 1), Ll. Th. ii. 130, 30. Þeáh hine deófol mid bārspere beótige tō ofsticianne, Angl. viii. 324, 19. Man þā hālgan . . . swilce ofsticode swīn (_stuck pigs_) holdode, Hml. S. 23, 106. _In_ l. 7 _after_ ' 79, 8 ' _add :_ cf. Hē hēt . . . ðæs pāpan lima gelōme prician, oð þæt hē swulte ðurh swylcum pīnungum, Hml. Th. ii. 312, 11.

ofstig. l. ofstig, _and for_ ' Gl. Prud' _substitute_ Germ.

of-stīgan. I. _to descend :_—Sē ðe ofer hróf ne ofstīges (āstīgað, R.) ādūne in hūs _qui super tectum non descendat in domum_, Mk. L. 13, 15. Ofstāg (āstāg, R.) mið him _descendat cum eis_, Lk. L. 2, 51. Ofstāg ādūne, 19, 6. Ðā ðe from Hierusalem ofstigon (āstigun, R.), Mk. L. 3, 22. Ofstigon on eorða, Jn. L. 21, 22. Ofstīg t āstīg (āstīg, R.) of rōde _descende de cruce_, Mt. L. 27, 40. Ðā menigo ofstīgendra _turbae discendentium_, Lk. 19, 37. Ofstīgendum (nīþerstīgendum, R.) him of mōr, Mt. L. 17, 9 : Mk. L. R. 9, 9. II. _to depart :_—Ofstīges gié from mē _discedite a me_, Mt. L. 25, 41. IV. _to ascend :_—Ofstīgende hine t ðā hē ofstāg in lytlum scipe _ascendente eo in naviculam_, Mt. L. 8, 23.

of-stingan. _Add :_—Hiene mon geceás þȳ ilcan dæge þe mon Iulianus ofstong (cf. Cōm sum cempa . . . and hyne (_Julian_) [mid francan] þurhþȳdde, Hml. S. 3, 237) ; Ors. 6, 32 ; S. 286, 26. Hēt hē hȳ mid sweorde ofstingan, Shrn. 143, 12.

of-swerian (?) _to deny on oath :_—Gif hlōð ðis gedō and eft oðswerian (of-, _v. l._), Ll. Lbmn. 64, 18. [Cf. Ger. ab-schwören.]

of-swīþan _to overpower, overcome :_—Ofswýðdum deáðe[s?] sticelse _devicto mortis aculeo_, Hymn. ad Mat. 17.

oft. _Add :_ Symle t oft _frequenter_, Mt. p. 9, 1. Oft t symle (gelōme, R., gelōmlīce, W. S.), Mt. L. 9, 14. Oft nalles ǣne, B. 3019 : Cri. 1195. Oft nalæs seldon, Ps. Th. 74, 4. Oft and gelōme, Gen. 1670: Hy. 3, 46. Oft gelōme, Gen. 1539. Swīðe oft, Mt. 23, 37 : An. 618. Būta oftor (_crebro_) geðuōgon hondo, Mk. L., R. 7, 3 : Dan. 758. Sprec oftor. ymb ōðres monnes weldǣda ðonne ymb ðīne āgene, Prov. K. 10. Oftor micle þonne on ǣnne sīð, B. 1579. Gif sió scyld ðǣra ofermētta ne gewundode ðȳ oftor _nisi nonnunquam superbiae culpa transfigeret_, Past. 311, 23. Oftost, B. 1663. Ellen bið sēlast þām þe oftost sceal dreógan dryhtenbealu, Gū. 1322. Oftast, Ps. Th. 61, 9. Sum gerēfa eard weardade oftast symle in þǣre ceastre Commedia, Jul. 20. Oftust, Ps. Th. 93, 4. v. ful-oft.

of-talu. _Add :_ Cf. tellan ; IV.

of-teón. II. _add :_—God hwīlum sylð þǣre wītegunge gāst, hwīlum his oftýhð (_subtrahit_), Gr. D. 146, 31. Hē (_toothache_) mē ne ofteáh ðes gemyndes þæs þe ic ǣr leornode, Solil. H. 41, 1. Hē monegum mǣgdum meodosetla ofteáh, B. 5. For ðǣm ðæt he him oftió ðǣre nyttwyrðan unrōtnesse _quatenus utilitatem tristitiae subtrahat_, Past. 415, 28. Him oftión þæs anwaldes þe hē ǣr hæfde, Met. 25, 24. Ðonne him micles oftogen bið _si multa sibi subtrahit_, Past. 325, 15. III. _add :_ with same government as II :—Gif hiē feoh habbað and his ðonne him oftió . . . hié oftióð ðǣre lāre ðǣm synfullum brōðrum, Past. 377, 2-5. Hē ofteáh hīs brēðer landes and ǣhta būtan hē hwæt æt him geearnode,

C. D. vi. 127, 9. Hí heofonan scūras oftugon, and eft miltsigende getīþoden, Hml. Th. i. 540, 29.

of-þænnan. l. -þænan.

of-þanc *envy* :—Ofþanc *inuidia*, Angl. xxxii. 513, 6. v. æf-þanc.

of-þe; *conj. Or* :—Ofþe gemyndlæs *vel freneticus*. [*O. Frs.* oftha.] v. oþþe.

of-þefian *to be exceedingly heated* :—Þis líf bið ālēfed on langsumum sārum, and on hætum ofþefod, and on hungre gewæht, Hml. S. 34, 144. v. þefian.

of-þinen *too moist* (?) *Substitute* : of-þīnan *to get or be too moist.* v. þīnan.

of-þryccan. *Add* : I. *to destroy by pressure, crush* :—Seó ūpflēring tōbærst and hine ācwealde, and þæt hūs eal ansund āðolode būton ðære ānre flēringe ðe ðone Godes feónd ofðrihte, Hml. Th. ii. 164, 5. Wind tóslōh þæt hús . . . þæt hit hreósende ðíne bearn ofðrihte and acwealde (*domus corruens oppressit liberos tuos et mortui sunt*, Job 1, 19), 450, 19. Se āwyrgeda gāst tōwearp þone wāh, and mid þæs wāges hryre ofþryccende (*opprimens*) tōcwȳsde ænne .munuccnapan, Gr. D. 125, 6. II. *to oppress.* (1) the subject a person :—Gehwilce synfulle menn ðͣ re heora gelícan mid hefe þǽre wyrstan lyffetunge ofðriccað, Hml. Th. i. 494, 5. Þū ūp āhófe swȳþran ofþryccendra (*deprimentium*) hine, Ps. L. 88, 43. Ofþryhtum hē gehealp, Hml. S. 30, 6. (2) the subject a thing (an unfavourable condition) :—Sē bið hoferede, ðe þe sió byrðen ofðrycð ðisse eorðlican gewilnunge *gibbus est, quem terrenae sollicitudinis pondus deprimit*, Past. 67, 13. Hwīlum ofðrycð (*opprimit*) ðone líchoman ungemetlica mettrymnes, 455, 25. Sume beóþ mid wǽdle and mid hēnþe ofþrycte *angustia rei familiaris inclusi*, Bt. 11, 1; F. 30, 33. III. *to repress, suppress.* (1) the object material :—Ofþryþt *compresso*, i. *extincto* (*torrente incendio*), An. Ox. 3532. (2) the object non-material :—Reóhnesse ofþrihte *insaniam compressit*, An. Ox. 2501. Ofþryhte, þ is ācweinte *compressit* (*foci potestatem*), 4125. Frec wasend ofþrihte *gulosa ingluvies compressa*, 3571. IV. *to subdue* :—Hē þone deófol on helle mid his weágesíðum ofþrihte, Wlfst. 145, 4.

of-þylman *to choke, suffocate* :—Hē symlede æt his beódgereordum þ ic wæs oft swīþe neáh ofðylmed and āsmorod, Nap. 50.

of-þyncan. *Add*: I a.:—Ðȳ lǽs . . . him hefiglíce ofðynce ðæs ðe hié sealdon, Past. 321, 19. I b:—Ne bið God næfre beþēht, ne him næfre ne ofþincð þ, þ hē ǽr tó rǽde geþōhte, Angl. vii. 34, 317. Þæt eów ofðince eówer gedwyld, Hml. Th. ii. 490, 8. I c:—Hē cwæð þæt him ofþūhte þæt hē ǽfre mancynn gesceóp, Hml. Th. i. 20, 25. II a:—Ðonne hē hit eft ofman, ðonne ofðyncð him ðæs ilcan ðe hē ǽr forbær, and bið eft onǽled mid ðȳ fȳre ðæs sāres, Past. 225, 19. II c:—For ðæm ðe hē hefonríce mid his āgenre scylde forworhte, ðā ofðūhte him ðætte menn wǽron tó ðæm gesceapene *quia ipse coelum perdidit, condito hoc homini invidit*, Past. 233, 20. [v. *N. E. D.* of-think.]

of-þyrsted. *Add* : (1) literal :—Swā heort wilnað tó wætre, þonne hē wērig byð oþþe ofþyrst, Ps. Th. 41, 1. Utan syllan mete gehingredum and drenc þām ofþyrstum, Wlfst. 119, 7. (2) figurative :—Se bið ofhingrod and ofðyrst æfter rihtwísnysse, Hml. Th. i. 552, 1. [v. *N. E. D.* of-thirst.]

oft-rǽde. I. *add* :—Tó lytel hit byð, beó hit ā lǽsse, for ðan his weorc sceal beón oftrǽde, Ll. Th. i. 432, 25. Uton ofsinnan . . . þāra oftrǽdra symla, Verc. Först. 148, 5.

oftrǽd-líc. *Add* :—Mid oftrǽdlícum gebedum *crebris exorationibus*, Past. 397, 14 : *assiduis deprecationibus*, 399, 28.

oftrǽdlíce. *Add* :—Ðā ðe oftrǽdlíce lytla scylda wyrceað . . . ðā ðe oftrǽdlíce syngiað, and ðeáh lytlum scyldum *qui minimis, sed crebris noxis immerguntur . . . qui licet minima, crebro tamen illicita faciunt*, Past. 437, 1–6. Hí oftrǽdlíce on ðā burh fuhton, Chr. 1016; P. 149, 7. Deófol hine oftrǽdlíce mid mænigfealdum costnungum costnode, Hml. A. 195, 18.

of-trahtung *glosses extractatio*, Lk. p. 8, 10.

of-tredan. *Add* : (1) literal :—Gif ðām ylpum hwā wiðstent, hē byð sóna oftreden, Hex. 16, 14. (2) figurative :—Mīne fýnd . . . oftreden (*conculcent*) on eorðan mín líf, Ps. Th. 7, 5. Ne lǽt þū mē oftredan þā ofermódan under heora fótum *non veniat mihi pes superbiae*, 35, 11. *See next word.*

of-treddan; *pp.* -tredd *To tread to death* :—þæt þǽr wǽron xxxm ofslagen and þǽm geate oftredd *ut in portarum exitu populo coartato triginta millia Judaeorum caede prostrata et compressione suffocata referantur*, Ors. 6, 4; Swt. 260, 18. Cf. for-treddan.

oft-síþ. *Add* :—Unārímedlíce oft (oftsīðum, Bos. 104, 44), Ors. 5, 4; S. 224, 29. Þȳ ilcan geáre wæs gesewen blódig wolcen on oftsíðas on fȳres gelícnysse, Chr. 979; P. 122, 24. [v. *N. E. D.* oft-sithe,-sithes.]

oft-þweál *frequent washing* :—Eáwlā wīf, tó hwan wenest ðū þínes líchoman hæle mid smyringe and oftþweále and ōðrum líðnessum, Nap. 50; [Verc. Först. 166, s.v. hīwfæger].

of-weard. *adj. Absent* :—Ealle ge onwearde ge ofwearde, Verc. Först. 170. v. æf-weard.

of-weorpan. *Add* :—Iūdēas hine (*Stephen*) mid stānum ofwurpon (af-, Shrn. 31, 34), Mart. H. 6, 24.

of-wítan (?) *to reproach* :—Ofwitun (tēldon, L.) *verebuntur*, Mt. R. 21, 37. Cf. æt-, oþ-wītan.

of-wundrod. *Add* :—Þā cwæð eall seó meniu þe ðǽr mid stód ofwundrod, Hml. S. 12, 228. Dionysius þā āxode þone ǽrendracan ofwundrod, ‘Eart þū, lā, se blinda þe swā geboren wǽre?’, 29, 64.

of-wyrttrumian *glosses* eradicare, Lk. L. 17, 6.

óga. I. *add* : *fear* of a person, *fear* felt by that person :—þā āsprang micel óga and gryre ofer ealle ðā ungeleáffullan, Hml. Th. i. 470, 8 : 598, 28. II. *fear* of an object, *fear* caused by that object :—þ ne feóndes níþfulles óga þā gedēfan ārǽre *ne hostis invidi pavor quietos suscitet*, Hy. S. 3, 23. Gif ǽnig óga is tó ondrǽdenne, þonne is sē tó ondrǽdenne þe nǽnne ende nǽfð. Witodlíce mannes ege is smíce gelíc, Hml. Th. i. 592, 10. Hē gesette þā lǽssan beboda Iūdēisces þeóde þe mid ógan ðͣgȳt gebunden wæs, 548, 22. For ógan Iūdēisces folces, 324, 5. Ógan oferswīððan worulde *terrore victo saeculi*, Hy. S. 130, 5. For hellewítes ógan, Lch. iii. 440, 33. III. *add* :—þ se rēnboga sȳ tó ógan mid þæs fȳres híwe, þ eall middaneard bið mid fȳre forswǽled, Angl. vii. 38, 365. Hí gesáwon swā mænigfealde ógan on mistlicum wītum, Hml. S. 23, 61.

ó-heald. *Add* :—Óhelde *conuexa* (in coelis *conuexa* cacumina cernam), An. Ox. 24, 2.

óht. *Add* :—Hí ne dorston ofer þ geþrystlǽcan þ hí óhte grēttan þā hālgan stówe rihtgeleáffullra manna *nequaquam ulterius praesumserunt catholica loca temerare*, Gr. D. 235, 6.

óhtan. v. ēhtan.

ólǽcung (= ān-lǽcung? v. ge-ānlǽcan; I a) :—Ólǽcung *conspiratio*, An. Ox. 4955.

ole. v. ele, liþule.

óleccan, ólǽcan (l. ólǽcan). I. *dele last passage, for which see* ólehtan, *and add* :—Martianus cwæð þ hē geare wiste his ædelborennysse, ‘and ic þē for ðī tihte þ ðū-þām godum geoffrige’. Iulianus him sǽde, ‘Þu eart ǽblend for þínre yfelnysse, and for þí mē þus ólǽcst’, Hml. S. 4, 133. Suā micle liðelecor hē sceal ólecan ( óleccean, *v. l.*) ðǽm welegan eáðmōdan . . . eác ðā wōððraga ðæs ungewitfullan monnes se lǽce gehǽlð mid ðǽm ðæt hē him ólecð æfter his āgnum willan *tanto lenius humilitatem divitum mulceat . . . et furor insanorum ad salutem medico blandiente reducitur*, Past. 183, 15–23. Ðonne hē his wambe suā hnesclíce ólecð *dum ventri molliter servit*, 313, 12. Ðæt mōd oft ólecð him selfum *quadam delectatione ejus sibimetipsi animus blanditur*, 463, 9. Eft hē ólehte ðǽm scamfæston *rursum verecundantem refovet*, 207, 10. Hē hí swā unróte óleccende tó him geloccode . . . Be ðǽm wæs swīðe ryhtlíce gecweden ðætte Sihhem Dinan liðelíce ólehte, ðā ðā hē hí geunrótsod hæfde *tristem blanditiis delinivit . . . Recte adjungitur*, ‘Tristem blanditiis delinivit’, 415, 18–30. þā ólehte Gezabel þām unrihtwísan and cwæð, ‘Arís and gereorda, . . . ic ðe forgife þone wíneard’, Hml. S. 18, 184. Ðætte . . . ðæt mōd his hiéremonna hē óliccende (óleccende, *v. l.*) egesige and ðreátigende ólicce (ólecce, *v. l.*) *ut . . . corda subditorum et terrendo demulceat, et tamen ad terroris reverentiam demulcendo constringat*, Past. 127, 6–7. Swā wilnigen tó óleccanne ðǽm gódum and hí tó herianne, swā hí hūru ne óleccen ðǽm yfum *sic praedicanda sunt bona, ne ex latere juventur et mala*, 453, 32. II. *add* :—Hí rícum monnum swíðe óleccað ðā hwíle ðe hí him beforan beóð . . . Hē dēð feóndscipe ðǽm ilcan Gode ðe hē ǽr ólehte *venientes ad faciem quorumdam hominum magna eis submissione blandiuntur . . . In eum, quem rogaverat, inimicitias exercet*, Past. 421, 27–33. Ðæt hē nānum men ne ólicce *in nullius se debeat favorem declinare*, 383, 12. Gif hí lytles hwæt habbaþ, þonne beþurfon hí þ hí óleccan þǽm æfter friþe þe māre habbað . . . swā hē māre hæfþ, swā hē mā monna ólecan sceal, Bt. 26, 2; F. 92, 28–33. Ðū woldest beón foremǽre on weorþscipe . . . þonne scealt þū óleccan swiþe earmlíce þām þe þē tó þām gefultumian mæge *dignitatibus fulgere velis? danti supplicabis*, 32, 1; F. 114, 11. Hí þā sóna ólǽcende (óliciende, *v. l.*) ymb þ seofiende *adulando questi sunt*, Gr. D. 34, 33. III. *add* :—Hí God forsāwon and þām wiðersacan ólehtan (ólæhtan, *v. l.*), Wlfst. 202, 3. þ hí ongiten hwonan him se wela cōme and ólecce ðǽm, þȳ lǽs hē him þone welan āferre, Bt. 39, 11; F. 230, 19. IV. *add* :—Ðonne ús fullícost óleccað ðā cræftas and ðā mægenu *cum virtutum nobis copia blanditur*, Past. 467, 5. þā woruldsǽlþa swiþe lytelíce óleccaþ þǽm módum þe hí on lāst willaþ beswícan, Bt. 7, 1; F. 16, 11. [For a discussion of this verb see Angl. xxxi. 259.] v. ge-óleccan; ólehtan.

óleccend. v. leás-óleccend.

óleccung. I. *add* :—Oft mon sceal ðone welegan ofermōdan tó him loccian mid liðelicre ólicunga (óleccunga, *v. l.*) *nonnunquam superbus dives exhortationis blandimento placandus est*, Past. 183, 19. ‘Nū is mín mōd āwend mycclum tó ðē, þ þū hláford beó þǽra ǽhta and mín. Ic wēne þ hit ne sȳ unrihtwísnysse, þeáh þū wífes brūce and blysse on lífe.’ Ðā andwyrde Eugenia þyssere ólecunge, Hml. S. 2,

162. II. *add:*—Ðæt hē nāuðer ne nānum men ne ólicce, ne hē nānes monnes óleccunga ne rēce, Past. 383, 12.

**ólehtan, ólectan** *to flatter, caress:*—Ólectendra *palpant*[*i*]*um*, Wrt. Voc. ii. 116, 51. *See next word.*

**ólehtung,** e; *f.* I. *flattering, adulation:*—Þám mōde, þe biþ ábysgod in manigum þingum, swíþe undercreópeð seó leáse ólehtung (liffetung, *v. l.*) *occupato in multis animo adulatio valde subrepit,* Gr. D. 35, 15. Þurh þá ólehtinga þára preósta, 40, 19. II. *what pleases the senses, pleasing condition or process:*—Sóna se líchoma sceal bión unfæger, þonne hē mid unrótnesse and mid sáre áseted bið, þá cumað of þǽre (þám, MS.) líðan ólehtunge (*from a life of sensual ease*) ... Gemunað þá þe eall hira líf on þisse worulde on ólehtungum lifedon (*lived in sensual pleasures*), Verc. Först. 170. Eáwlá, wíf, tó hwan wenest ðú þínes líchoman hǽle mid smyringe and oftþweále and óðrum iíðnessum? Of ðám cymeð unhǽlo, nales mægen. Gif þú þá ilcan ólectonge þám líchoman [dó, hit nā] híwfægere bið, þonne hit ǽr wæs, 166.

**olfend.** *Add:* olfend, es; *n.:* olbenda, an; *m.:* olfende, an; *f.:*—Se olfend, Lk. 18, 25. Olbend, Mt. R. 19, 24. Þá cóm ðǽr yrnan sum olbænda, Shrn. 135, 33. Hire wæs áweaxen swá áheardod hýd swylce olfendan, Gr. D. 287, 5. Wǽron wit twēgen on ánum olfende, and wit unc simble ondrǽdon hwonne wit sceoldon feallan of þám olfende, and miccle mā wit hangodan be þám olfende þonne wit þǽron sǽton ... uncer wǽta wæs olfenda miolc, Shrn. 38, 14–18. Þá olfenda mycel gold oðberað þan ǽmettum, Lch. iii. 166, 4. Lǽdaþ hý mid him olfenda myran ... þá men mid þám golde ofer þá eá farað, Nar. 35, 11. Wit gesēgon sittan twēgen men on twǽm olfendum ... uncer hláford hióld hiora olfendu ... wit ástigon on þá olfendan þe uncer hláford on cóm ... þǽr wit bebohtan uncre olfendan, Shrn. 42, 13–44, 1. Geseah hē olfendas þiderweard, Gen. 24, 63: 30, 43: Ex. 9, 3.

**oll.** *Dele the bracket, and add:*—On ol, ídel *nequiquam, frustra,* An. Ox. 2000. On oll and on edwît (*note to the preceding*).

**ollung(-onc).** v. and-lang.

**óm.** *Dele first passage, and add:*—Þǽr þǽr óm and moðþan hit áwēstað, Wlfst. 286, 32. Þ hē nā tó swíðe ne gewilnige úp áwyrtlian rust oððe óm sí tóbrocen fæt *ne dum nimis cupit eradere eruginem frangatur vas,* R. Ben. I. 108, 1. Hóm *rubiginem,* Kent. Gl. 954. Hē sealde ómum (*erugini*) wæstmas heora, Ps. L. 77, 46. v. ár-(Lch. ii. 192, 22), sinder-óm.

**óman.** *Add:*—Hē onfindeþ þ þá óman beóð inne betýnde, Lch. ii. 174, 22. v. heals-óme.

**ome** (-a?), an; *f.* (*m.?*) *A liquid measure:*—Hē cwæð þ hē sceolde syllan his hláford hundteóntig oman mid ele ámetene, Nap. 50. [*From Latin ama.* v. *N. E. D.* aam.]

**ómian** *to rust:*—Swá ár ómað yfelnysse his *sicut aeramentum eruginabit malitia illius,* Scint. 196, 5.

**ómig.** I. *add:*—Omiges anfiltes *scabrae incudis,* An. Ox. 478. Hómigre tangan-*rubiginosae forcipis,* 483.

**ómiht.** *Add:* ómihte:—Gif ómihte blód and yfel wǽte on þám milte sié, Lch. ii. 252, 25.

**on.** *Add:* A. I. 5 ¶:—Ðæt fǽmna mynster on Brytene þ is nemned on Bercingum (on Byrcingum, in Bercingum *in loco qui nuncupatur in Berecingum,* Bd. 4, 6; Sch. 383, 19), Shrn. 138, 2. (7):—Is swá þeáh gód weorc on þǽm gódan wordum, Ælfc. T. Grn. 21, 25. Ælc dohtig man on Kænt and on Súð-Sexan, on þegenan and on ceorlan, C. D. iv. 11, 7. II 1. *marking date:*—Gif hit gebyrað on geáre (*illo anno*) þ ne byð mæsten, Chrd. 15, 9. (2):—Þæt þes middaneard scule standan on syx þúsend wintrum, Wlfst. 244, 1. Úre Drihten gesceóp seofonfealde weorc ... eall on ánum dæge, Hex. 6, 25. Hē heom on ealre hwíle metes tilian sceolde, Hml. S. 23, 219. III 2:—Seó fird gehergade swíðe micel on þǽm norðhere, Chr. 910; P. 94, 29. Mæg ic þis setl on eów geþringan, Gú. 215. Woruldfeoh ... þæs ic on sceótendum ... áhredde, Gen. 2143. (3 a) *denoting the reason of an action, on account of:*—Ealle men heriað míne dohtor on hyre swēgcræfte, Ap. Th. 16, 20. (3 b) *denoting the person or thing on which dependence is placed, from which a result is derived:*—Seó mǽðung is on þám bisceope *modus correptionis in episcopi iudicio pendeat,* Chrd. 35, 18. Frægn Scipia hiene an hwý hit gelang wǽre, Ors. 5, 3; S. 222, 14. v. ge-lang. (4):—Se ælmihtiga wyrhta geworhte ealne middangeard on his mycclum cræfte, Hex. 4, 3. (5):—Ælc man hæfð on his ágenre byrðene genóh, Wlfst. 239, 25. Se man wæs geworht on libbendre sáwle *factus est homo in animam viventem,* Gen. 2, 7. Heó gehergade swíðe micel ǽgðer ge on mannum ge on gehwilces cynnes yrfe, Chr. 910; P. 94, 29. Beóbreád is on twám ðingum, on weaxe and on hunie. Críst is on twám edwistum, Hml. Th. ii. 292, 14. Bióð ealle wæteras and ealle wyllas on blóde *omnes fontes aquarum et putei in sanguinem convertentur,* Verc. Först. 120, 9. (6):—Ðú on mihte and on ríce hí feorr oferstígest *omnes potestate transcendas,* Bd. 2, 12; Sch. 157, 13. (7):—Þæt hí wǽron on miclum ege ðám sylfum landágendum *ut ipsis indigenis essent terrori,* Bd. 1, 15; Sch. 42, 19. (8):—Ðá hē wæs on fíf and twēntigum geára, þá fērde hē tó Róme, Shrn. 50, 24:

59, 28. Nóht feor úrum mynstre, þ is, húhugu on twēgra mila fæce *non longe a monasterio nostro, id est, duum ferme milium spatio separata,* Bd. 5, 4; Sch. 567, 11. Seó stōw is on .vi. mílum fram Nursia *locus sexti ferme milliarii interjacente spatio a Nursiae urbe disjungitur,* Gr. D. 274, 5. (10):—Hē bát his tungan þæt heó on blóde fleów, Hml. Th. ii. 312, 25. Wearð þ folc ástyrod on swiðlicum hreáme, Hml. S. 31, 281. His gefēran fundon hine licgen[d]ne on blódigum limum and tóbeátenum líchaman, 981. Wearð hē untrum on feforáðle, Bl. H. 217, 16. Ðá englas hē geworhte on wundorlicre fægernysse and on mycelre strengðe, Hen. 6, 25. (11):—Ðeáh hwá bebycgge his dohtor on þeówenne (*or acc.?*) *si quis vendiderit filiam suam in famulam,* Ll. Th. i. 46, 12. Míne synna on þreágunge berende, Hml. S. 23 b, 672. (12) v. III 3:—Hē begann tó stelenne on heora gewunan, Ælfc. T. Gen. 17, 18. (13):—Hē hæfde æþele brýd, seó wæs on naman Natalea, Shrn. 59, 29. (14) in oaths:—Gecýþe seó gewitnysse þ on Godes helde and on hláfordes, þ heó him on sóðre gewitnysse sý, Ll. Th. i. 388, 23. (15):—Sēlre him is ǽfre of folgoðe ðonne on, Angl. ix. 260, 30. B. I. 3 (both acc. and dat. may occur in the same passage):—'Þú gesǽwe gehwǽde mot on þínes bróðor eáge and ne gesǽwe þone mǽstan cyp on þínum ágenum eágan'. Þæt is, þú ásceonudest þá lǽstan gyltas on þíne gingran and þá mǽstan noldest on þē sylfne, R. Ben. 12, 3–6. Hié beóð on þá winstran sídan mid ece geswenced and on ðone lið þára eaxla ... biþ micel ece, and on þǽm gehweorfe þára bána on þám sweóran, Lch. ii. 242, 11–14. .vi. æcras mǽde on ðá gerēfmǽde, C. D. iii. 53, 2. (4):—Ǽr ðám tíman næs ǽfre ǽnig mann swá mǽre, þ hē on án ne sceolde tó helle swá hé forðfaren wæs, Wlfst. 16, 14. Ðá gesægdon Rómáne on án (*at once*) Bryttum, Bd. 1, 12; Sch. 33, 15. (5):—On þreó genamod, C. D. v. 401, 25. III 3:—Hē þ gebēte his dryhtne .c. scill an eald reht, Ll. Th. i. 38, 6. On gebyrd, B. 1074: Sal. 384. On gesceap, Ra. 39, 4. Hē him an his gewill andwyrdan sceolde, Ors. 3, 9; S. 126, 29: 1, 12; S. 56, 1. Gif seó wyrd swá hweorfan mót on yfelra manna gewill, Bt. 4; F. 8, 19. On þæs arcebisceopes gemēde, Cht. Th. 355, 23. (7):—Gif hē hine on bismor tó homolan bescíre, Ll. Th. i. 84, 5. Sende him mon áne blace hacelan angeán him on bismer, Ors. 5, 10; S. 234, 22. (7 a) *marking action on which effort is expended:*—Hē gefeóll on þæs ceorles clyppinge, Gr. D. 47, 1. Ic ongite þ sóðlíce þín dohtor gefeól on swēgcræft, ac heó næfð hine nú wel geleornod *I perceive that of a truth your daughter has bestowed much pains on music, ... she has not been taught it well,* Ap. Th. 16, 23. (8):—Ic on máðma hord mínne bebohte fróde feorhlege, B. 2799. (9):—Ǽr wæs eall weoruld sprecende on án gereord, and nú synd gereord twá and hundseofontig, Wlfst. 211, 19. Tó brúcanne on ēce æreht, C. D. i. 316, 18. Nā on gemear (*uane*) þú gesettest suna manna, Ps. Rdr. 88, 48. Him on gafol forlēt wellan sceótan, Rä. 39, 2. (10):—On þone Drihten, Ll. Th. i. 178, 3, *and often.* Ic þe fullwie on mínne Godfæder and on mec his efenēce sunu and on þone Hálgan Gást, Shrn. 106, 13. (10 a) *denoting ground or reason, on account of, on the ground of:*—Ðá ongunnon ealle þá men hí herian on hyre swēgcræft, Ap. Th. 16, 18. Gif hē láðleás beó, sēce swylcne hláford on þá gewitnesse swylcne hē wille, Ll. Th. i. 220, 24. (11):—Gedó on þ fæt þe þú hit mæge on mid gefōge geseóþan, Lch. ii. 28, 16. Horsum mídla synd on tó ásettenne *equis frena sunt inponenda,* Scint. 55, 12. Saga mē hwǽr is seó eorðe ðe nǽfre sunne on ne sceán, Sal. K. 198, 14. Nú hit eall ágán is on ðǽron of ðíne hand, C. D. ii. 114, 6. v. þǽr-on.

**on-ǽht.** *Perhaps* on ǽhte *should be read in the passage given here.* v. ǽht; II.

**on-ǽlan.** I. *add:* (1) *of physical fire or light.* (a) *to kindle* fire, *light* a lamp:—Anǽl ligrǽscas *corusca coruscationes,* Bl. Gl. Þára eágan scinað swá leóhte swá man (is an; ma, MSS.) micel blácern onǽle (*this seems a better reading than that taken under* ǽl) on þýstre nihte *quorum oculi sicut lucerna lucent,* Nar. 37, 18. Fýr wæs onǽld *ignis accensus est,* Ps. L. 77, 21: p. 245, 31. Onǽled fýr, Ps. Th. 88, 39. (b) *to set* on fire:—Swá hwæt swá heó gesihð, heó tóblǽwþ and anǽleþ (on-, onǽlþ, *v.ll.*), Lch. i. 242, 21. Ád stód onǽled, Gen. 2922: Ph. 216. (b a) *to cause to shine:*—Ianuarius se mōna biþ onǽled et niddre neht, Hpt. 33, 66, 17: 18: 19. (2) *of strong feeling, of mental or spiritual light.* (a) *to excite strong feeling:*—Hí onǽlað ðearlran dóm wið him *districtius contra se judicium accendunt,* Past. 433, 33. Healdað eów ðæt gē ne onǽlen mín ierre mid eówrum searwum, 435, 9. (b) *to cause spiritual light:*—Onǽl þæs Hálgan Gástes leóht on ús, Hml. Th. ii. 598, 21. II. *add:*—Þonne þeós woruld byrneð áde onǽled, Ph. 503: El. 951. Onǽlede of fýre *incensa igni,* Bl. Gl. III. *add:*—Hēt hē gefeccan ǽnne ǽrenne oxan and þone onǽlan, Hml. S. 30, 421. Is þes atola hám fýre onǽled, Sat. 97. III a. *to make hot* with other matter than fire:—Flór is on welme ǽttre onǽled, Sat. 40. Wæs se báncofa áðle onǽled, Gú. 928. IV. *add:*—Se Hálga Gást heora ealra mód swá onbryrde and onǽlde, þ hí cúðon ælc gereord þe on middanearde is, Hml. Th. ii. 47, 7. Hwí eart þú onǽled mid swá ídele gefeán? *quid inanibus gaudiis raperis,* Bt. 14, 1; F. 40, 29. Þú woldest swíþe swíþlíce beón onǽled mid ðǽre gítsunge *quanto ardore*

*flagrares*, 22, 2 ; F. 78, 3. Hē wearð onǣled on heora lufe, Hml. S. 30, 304. Ǣfestum onǣled, Mód. 43. Ðonne wē ne beóð onǣlde mid dǣre lustbǣrnesse ūres mōdes *dum congruo fervore mens non accenditur*, Past. 283, 2. **V.** *to incite* to :—Menie men syndon þe þā gebysnunga gódra wera swýðor þonne þā lāre onǣlað and tihtað tō lufe þæs heofenlican ēðles (*ad amorem patriae coelestis succendunt*) . . . þæt mód byð onǣled (*accenditur*) tō lufe þæs tōwerdan lífes, Gr. D. 8, 11-19. [v. *N. E. D.* anneal.]

**on-ǣþelian.** v. an-æþelian.

**on-ārísende** *glosses* insurgens :—Fram onārísendum (*insurgentibus*) on mē, Ps. L. 58, 2 : Bl. Gl. Ðū forscrænctest onārísende (*insurgentes*) on mē, Ps. L. 17, 40.

**on-āsetednes,** e ; *f.* *A laying on, imposition* :—Ðā ðā foryldað and forgýmeleásiað þ hig nellað heora bearn tō þām fulwihte and tō þǣre onāsetednysse þæs bisceopes bletsunga bringan, Nap. 85.

**on-āslagen ;** *adj.* *Beaten, made of metal that has been beaten or forged* :—On bȳmum onāslagenum *in tubis ductilibus*, Ps. L. 97, 6. v. ā-sleán ; III a.

**on-bæc.** *Add :* **I.** of motion. (1) in retreat from a point reached :—Geong onbæcc ꝥ mec behianda *uade retro me*, Mk. L. 8, 33. Eádun onbæcg *abierunt retrorsum*, Jn. L. 18, 6. (2) in return to a point previously occupied :—Ne āwoendað onbæcc *non redeant retro*, Lk. L. 17, 31. Ne eft gecerres onbæcg *non reuertatur retro*, Mk. L. 13, 16. **II.** of looking :—Ne eft-lōcca onbæc *non respicere retro*, I.k. p. 6, 14. Onbæcg, Lk. L. 9, 62.

**on-bæcling.** *Add :* **I.** of motion. (1) of retreat :—Gong on bæclinc ꝥ bihionda mec *uade retro me*, Mk. R. 8, 33. Monige ðegnas his fromfoerdun onbæcling (-bæcc-, L.), Jn. R. 6, 66. (2) of reversing one's direction :—Ymbcerred wæs onbæclinc (-bægcling, L.) *conuersa est retrorsum*, Jn. R. 20, 14. **II.** of position or attitude. (1) *at one's back* :—þā gehýrde ic ðone biscop mē onbæclinga (-ea, -e), *v. ll.*) cweðan *audiui episcopum post tergum mihi dicentem*, Bd. 5, 6 ; Sch. 576, 16. þā gehýrde ic swēg mē onbæcling *audio post terga sonitum*, 5, 12 ; Sch. 620, 3. (2) *with the back towards a person* :—Onbæcling gewend *with the back turned towards her*, Hml. S. 23 b, 218. **III.** of recurrence to a subject :—Eft ꝥ eft on bæcgling *rursum*, Mt. p. 3, 8.

**on-bærnan.** **I.** *add* :—Hē hēt onbærnan Rōmeburg *urbis Romae incendium fecit*, Ors. 6, 5 ; S. 260, 30. **III.** *add* :—Mid hira āgenre gewilnunge hié bióð onbærnede (-bærnde, *v. l.*) *sua cupidine accensi*, Past. 27, 18. **III a.** *to heat* (lit.) :—Gif mon mid eástānum onbærnedum þā meoluc gewyrð, Lch. ii. 218, 23. **IV.** *add* :—Hit byþ onbærned (*accenditur*) of wiðmetennesse gódra wera tō þǣre lufan þæs tōweardan lífes, Gr. D. 8, 19.

**on-bærning,** e ; *f.* *Incense* :—Swā swā onbærning *sicut incensum*, Ps. Vos. 140, 2. Mid onbærninge (*incensu*) ic offriu ðē, 65, 15.

**on-bǣru.** *In* l. 4 *for* 1827 *l.* 1027: -onbecweþende. v. yfelonbecweþende.

**on-becyme,** es ; *m.* *Approach, access* :—Sumum geþances onbecyme *quodam mentis excessu* (*accessu?*), Scint. 211, 8. v. becuman (on).

**on-beódan.** **I.** *add* : *to command* :—Scipia hit oftrǣdlīce hām onbeád (*sent home orders*) þæt hié hit ne angunnen, and eác self sǣde, þā hē hām of Ispāniuni cōm, Ors. 4, 12 ; S. 208, 34. Hē onbeád (bebeád, *v.l.*) tō heom þus cweþende, 'Gerihtað incre tungan' *eis mandauit, dicens*, 'Corrigite linguam vestram', Gr. D. 152, 9. **II.** *add* :—þā onbeád hē him ꝥæt hē him ꝥæs getygðian wolde *redditurum se pollicetur*, Ors. 3, 11 ; S. 146, 30. Sǣ cýðde hwā hine gesette . . . ge eác beámas onbudon hwā hý sceóp, Cri. 1170. þā sōna wæs onboden of ðām mynstre þæt hē selfa cōme *dum protinus mandatum de monasterio fuisset ut veniret ipse*, Gr. D. 130, 24.

**on-beornan.** *Add :* **II a.** of strong feeling :—Is auburnan mīn heorte *inflammatum est cor meum*, Ps. L. 72, 21.

**on-beran.** *Add* (?): *to be situated* ), *lie* (?) :—Seó stōw onbyrð (-bired, *v. l.*) on feówertigum mīla of þissere Rōmāniscan byrig *locus ab Romana urbe quadraginta fere millibus distans*, Gr. D. 98, 14.

**on-besceáwung,** e ; *f.* *Inspection* :—Tō onbesceáwunge his *ad inspectionem illius*, Scint. 66, 9.

**on-beslagen ;** *adj.* *Inflicted* :—Swilce hī mid onbeslagenre wunde hī geblōdigian, Hml. Th. ii. 88, 23.

**on-bídan.** **I.** *add* :—Hē þǣr onbád sume hwīle oð ꝥ flōd ūp eóde, Chr. 1052 ; P. 180, 13. **I.** *add* :—þǣr his Pompeius on ānre dūne onbād, Ors. 5, 12 ; S. 240, 23. **IV.** with clause :—Hē gesæt be þām swere anbídende hwæt him gelimpan scolde, Bl. H. 239, 22.

**on-bindan.** *Add* :—Dý lǣs hī sín tō swiðe gebundne mid ðǣm ðurhtogenum scyldum, and tō lange forelden ðæt hī hī ne anbinden mid ðǣre hreówsunge *ne plus adstringantur in debito perpetrati operis, et minus solvant fletibus satisfactionis*, Past. 413, 9. [*Goth.* and-bindan : *O. H. Ger.* int-pintan : *Ger.* ent-binden.]

**on-bindendlic.** v. un-onbindendlic.

**on-birgan.** *Add* :—Ic hālsige þē . . . ꝥ þū nā geþrístlǣce ꝥ þū þises

hūsles onbyrige (*ut non audeas hanc eucharistiam percipere*), Ll. Lbmn. 413, 25.

**onbítan.** *Add :*—Nolde ǣnig onbítan mennisces metes (cf. ǣlcne mete hī onscunedon þe men etaþ, Bt. 38, 1 ; F. 196, 4), Met. 26, 90.

**on-blǣstan.** *l.* (?) -blæstan. v. blǣstan ; II.

**on-blāwan.** *Add :* **I.** *to inspire, inflate, puff up* :—Ingehýd onblǣwð *scientia inflat*, Scint. 82, 10. Hē wæs āþunden mid oferhigde and onblāwen (*inflatus*) mid þý gefeán þissere gewítendan gesǣlignysse, Gr. D. 180, 16. **II.** *to blow on* or *away* :—Feónd ūre wē onblāwaþ mid horne *inimicos nostros ventilabimus cornu*, Ps. L. 43, 6. **III.** *to breathe* :—Anblēu *spirabat* (coelestem intento *spirabat* corde sophiam), Hpt. 33, 238, 3.

**on-blinnan** *to cease* :—Eall sōðfæstnesse bið ðonne onblunnen *veritas non erit*, Verc. Först. 118, 12. v. ā-blinnan.

**on-borgian** *to borrow* :—Ic onborgede xxx mancsa goldes æt Beorhtnōðe, Cht. Crw. 9, 117. v. ā-borgian ; II.

**on-bregdan.** *Add :*—þū hit mē hæfst nū swiðe sweotole gereht, swylce þū hæbbe þā duru ābrōden (anbrōden, *v. l.*) þe ic ǣr sōhte, Bt. 35, 3 ; S. 97, 24.

**on-bring.** *Add :*—Ealle þā yfelan geþanc þe þē on heortan becumaþ þurh deófles onbrincg, Angl. xii. 513, 24.

**on-bringelle,** an ; *f.* *Instigation* :—God ūs ālýse fram ūrum wiðerwinnan and fram his anbringcellan, for ðām þe his æfst is mycel ofer ūs, Hml. S. 23 b, 291.

**on-bryrdan.** *Add :*—On twā wīsan bið se man onbryrd ; ǣrest hē him ondrǣt hellewīte, and bewēpð his synna, syððan hē nimð eft lufe tō Gode, Hml. Th. i. 140, 17. **I.** *add* :—Se Hālga Gāst onbryrt ūre mōd tō ǣlcre gódnysse, Hml. Th. ii. 42, 10. þæt hē ūs onbrirde and on þæt tihte þæt wē ǣrest wel willen, Solil. H. 30, 9. Hē þurh gǣstes blǣd breóstum onbryrded beald reordade, Ph. 550. **II.** *add* :—Mid onbryrdum mōde andettan *compuncto animo confiteri*, Ll. Th. ii. 178, 20.

**on-bryrdnes.** *Add :* **I.** *incitement, cause of strong feeling* :—þām tímum þe mē ǣnig onbrerdnes cym[e] þe ðām ǣcan lýfe *at those times in which I am inspired with any strong emotion about the life eternal*, Solil. H. 25, 17. **II.** *strongly excited feeling* :—Sceole wē him bringan twā turtlan, þæt is twifealdlic onbryrdnes eges and lufe, Hml. Th. i. 140, 16. Symeon hine genam on his earmas mid micelre onbryrdnesse, 136, 17. Gebæd heó hī tō Gode mid mycelre onbryrdnesse, Hml. S. 7, 320 : 26, 116. Hē him mynster ārǣrde mid munuclicere onbryrdnesse (*with all the fervour of a monk*), Hml. Th. ii. 504, 20. **II a.** *where the feeling is one of sorrow or regret, compunction* :—Ðā sió anbryrdnes hine ālēt *cum compunctionis tempus abscessit*, Past. 423, 15. Mid andbryrdnysse (*compunctione*) synna andettan, Ll. Th. ii. 174, 1. Mid wōpe and onbryrdnysse þancunge dōn, Hml. S. 30, 382. Mid onbryrdnysse and behreówsunge hine gebiddan, Hml. Th. ii. 430, 5.

**on-būgan.** **I.** *add* :—Hī bǣdon ꝥ heora gefēran . . . heora cwellerum onbugon (*should bend their heads* : cf. hī āstrǣhton heora swuran tō slǣge, 71 : or under III. ?) blíþe tō slǣge, Hml. S. 28, 63. **II.** *add* : *to bend in submission to* (tō) :—Him onbugon þā Francan tō þām wynsuman iuce, Hml. S. 29, 177. Hwý sceal ǣnigum menn ðyncean tō orgellic ðæt hē onbūge tō ōðres monnes willan (*alienae voluntati acquiescere*), Past. 307, 15. **III.** with dat. :—Sē þe him (*the devil*) onbýhð bið beswicen, Angl. vii. 30, 282. Se yfela man hyne forcyrreþ oððe him onbūgeþ, Lch. i. 318, 24. Ealle gesceafta onbūgað gebígedum cneówe ðām Hǣlendum Crīste, Hml. Th. ii. 362, 1 : 18, 3. þā leóda þē onbūgað, Hml. S. 7, 366. Hē wæs ꝥ folc cwielmende tō ðon þæt hié him anbugen, Ors. 1, 12 ; S. 54, 19. Hī nellað onbūgan ðām leahtrum . . . ac winnað him tōgeánes, Hml. S. 17, 62. **IV.** *add* :—For ðǣm ðonne hē hīgað tō ðǣm godcundum ðingum ānum, ðæt hē ne ðyrfe on nāne healfe anbūgan tō nānum fūllicum luste *cum ad sola, quae interiora sunt, nititur, in nullo delectationis infimae latere flectatur*, Past. 83, 15. Ðǣm medwīsan is micle iēðre tō gestiéganne on ðone ryhtan wīsdōm ðonne ðǣm lytegan sié tō anbūganne (*to change his course; ut ab ea, quae putatur stultitia, ad veram sapientiam vicinius transeat*), 203, 18. [Him alle onbuȝen, Laym. 6166.]

**on-būtan.** **I.** *add* : (1) prep. (a) with dat. :—þā munecas lāgon onbūton þām weófode, Chr. 1083 ; P. 215, 13. (b) with acc. :—Hī wendon onbūton Tenet, Chr. 1046 ; P. 166, 12. (2) as adv. :—Hī him fērdon onbūton swā swā hī sylf woldon, Chr. 1001 ; P. 133, 27. Eówer wiðerwinna fǣrð him onbūtan *adversarius vester circuit*, Hml. A. 52, 54. **II.** *add* :—þysse wyrte wyrttruman man sceal niman onbūtan midne sumur, Lch. i. 260, 3. **III.** *add* : with another adverb :—Æghwǣr onbūtan *circumquaque*, An. Ox. 2, 251. **III a.** with adverbs denoting points of the compass :—Hī fōron west onbūtan, Chr. 918 ; P. 98, 11 : 1046 ; P. 168, 9. v. þǣr-onbūtan ; ā-būtan.

**on-byrdan** *to violate* ; *temerare*. v. un-geonbyrded.

**on-byrgan** *to be surety* :—Ambyriendum *sequestra*, An. Ox. 11, 142. Onbyrgedum, 7, 99. Cf. on-borgian ; byrgen.

**on-cígness**, e; f. *Invocation:*—Ðerh onceignise (*not -ceiunge, see Skeat's collation*) *per invocationem*, Rtl. 114, 3.

**on-cígung.** In l. 2 dele '114, 3'; *see previous word.*

**on-cirran.** A. I a. *add:*—Wǽron Egypte eft oncyrde, flugon forhtigende, Exod. 451. ¶ figurative:—Micel bið se Meotudes egsa, for ðon hí seó molde oncyrreð (cf. a cujus conspectu fugit terra, Apocalypsis, 20, 11), Seef. 103. II. *add:*—On midde niht oncierde ꝥ scip on wǫnne síðfæt þurh deófles beswicennesse, Shrn. 60, 8. B. I c. *add:*—Ðǽs sprǽce naenig mon on naenge óðhre halfe oncaerrende sié, C. D. i. 235, 1. II. *add: to turn* with the mind:—Ðá oncierde him seó gehygd tó deófolgylde, Shrn. 92, 14. (2) *to change:*—Sume men secgað ꝥ þǽr oncyrre mannes líchama ꝥ hé ne mǽge mid his wífe gerestan, Lch. i. 364, 2. v. in-cerran.

**on-clifende.** *Add:* **on-clifian** *translates* inhaerere:—Álýs [mé] of fenne ꝥ ná ic onclyfie (*inheream*), Ps. Rdr. 68, 15. Hí him mid heora móde oncleofiað and onclifigende ... ongytað *mente ei inhaerent, atque inhaerendo ... agnoscunt*, Gr. D. 138, 34. Onclifende (*inhaerendo*) þám gáste se líchama byþ gehealden in ecnesse, 264, 1.

**on-cnáwan.** I I a. *add:*—Nǽfra ic oncneáwu (*novi*) iúih, Mt. L. 7, 23. Helias cuðm and ne oncneáwn (*cognoverunt*) hine, 17, 12. (1 b), (2) *add:* (a) with noun or pronoun (representing a noun):—Hé suá micle bet his ágen dysig oncnéw swá hé undruncenra wæs *malum, quod fecerat, cognoscere potuit, quia hoc ebrius non audivit*, Past. 295, 8. For þám þe ðú ne oncneówe (oncneúðú, L., oncnáwðú, R.) ꝥá tíde þínre geneósunge, Lk. 19, 44. Ðæt forlor hira frécennesse ðonne hié hit oncnáwen *perditionis suae discrimina vel cognita*, Past. 403, 14. Ðone ðeódscip ꝥte oncnéwa (*agnosceret*), Mk. p. 2, 3. (β) with acc. and infin.:—Ðás mǽrsunga wé oncnáwaþ (*cognoscimus*) wesan gefyllede, An. Ox. 40, 11. Þá dómas þe ic oncneów þe sylfne secgean *judicia quae te dixisse cognovi*, Gr. D. 139, 12. Luſe gecneordlǽcan synden oncnáwene *affectum exercere noscuntur*, An. Ox. 242. (βa) with complement:—Þone áworpenne hí oncnáwaþ *quem reprobatum cognoscunt*, An. Ox. 40, 7 : 23. (γ) with clause or pronoun representing a clause:—Ðá se Hǽlend ꝥ on his gáste oncnéow (*quo cognito spiritu suo*) ꝥ hí swá betwux him þóhton, Mk. 2, 8. Þá oucneóu se Godes man ꝥ hé féran ne móste, Bd. 5, 9; Sch. 595, 16. Ðæt hié oncnáwæn tó hwǽm hiera ágen wíse wirð *ut ad cognitionem sui revocentur*, Past. 265, 23. þæt hié oncnéwen hú God þá rícu sette, Ors. 3, 5; S. 63, 35. II. *add:*—Oncneáwu ł ongæt *intelligit*, Mt. L. 13, 19. Oncnǽw, 23. Ne oncnéu gé *non intelligitis*, 14. Oncneáw gié *intellexistis*, 51. Oncneáun (-cneówan, R.) *intellexerant*, Mk. L. 6, 52. ꝥte oncnéwe *intellegeret*, Mk. p. 2, 4. II a. *to know by experience:*—Gif ðú ꝥ ne dést, þú scealt oncnáwan þone gesettan dóm, Ap. Th. 5, 9. IV. (3 a) *to acknowledge the claims of* a person:—Críst ne oncnáwð mid ǽnigum góde þá unclǽnan weófodþegnas, Ll. Th. ii. 382, 6. Ne gedafenaþ ꝥ ... þæt þú andsware mid oferhygdum sceal sárcwide ; sélre byð ǽghwǽm þæt hé eáðmédum ellorfúsne oncnáwe cúðlíce, An. 322. Sé ðe Godes bebodu ne gecnǽwð, ne bið hé oncnáwen from Gode, Past. 29, 1.

**on-cnáwend**; e; m. *One who knows.* v. on-cnáwan; I:—þú, [Drhyten,] dígla oncnáwend *tu, Domine, occultorum cognitor*, Angl. xi. 119, 65.

**on-cnáwenness.** *Add:*—þá dómas þú behýdst úrum oncnáwennyssum (*cognitionibus*), Gr. D. 139, 15.

**on-cnáwness.** *Add:*—Tó ancnáwnessum adinventionum, Wrt. Voc. ii. 3, 58.

**on-cnáwung**, e; f. *Knowledge:*—On oncnáwincge Godes in *cognitione Dei*, Scint. 15, 17.

**on-cunnan.** For the last passage substitute: Tó oncunnanne oncunnessa, Ps. Vos. 140, 4, *and add:*—Hí ealle bǽdon heora wǫhnyssa forgyfennyssa, þæs þe hí þæs unrihtes hý oncúðan, Hml. A. 136, 670. þá ongunnon þá gebróðru hí sylfe oncunnan (selfe hí oncúðon, *v. l.*) ꝥ hí ǽfre sceoldon biddan ... *fratres semetipsos accusare* 'coeperunt, quia poposcerant ..., Gr. D. 104, 11. On ðeosum wordum se ungesǽliga Iúdas wæs openlíce oncunnen, Hml. A. 161, 218. [Cf. *O. H. Ger.* inchunnan *accusare, urguere, increpare.*] v. á-cunnan.

**on-cunness** *accusation. Add:*—Ðá werian gástas mid gelómlicum oncunnissum (*crebris accusationibus*) tiledon, ꝥ hí him ðone heofonlican weg forsetton, Bd. 3, 19; Sch. 278, 8.

**on-cweþan.** I. In l. 2 *after* 18 *insert* Rä. 5, 7, *and add:* (1) *to say in response to a statement just made:*—þá cwǽdon hí tó him, 'Hál wæs ðú, bróður.' Hé him oncwæð, 'Syb sý mid eów, bróðra,' Hml. S. 30, 250. Him Cain andswarode ... Him oncwæð Drihten, Gen. 1022-1036 : An. 270. Drihten spræc ... Abraham Metode oncwæð, Gen. 2303-2345 : Jul. 209. Offa gemǽlde ... Leófsunu gemǽlde, hé þám beorne oncwæð, By. 230-245. Heó cwǽdon þæt heó on aldre ówiht swylces ne hýrdon. Elene maðelade and him yrre oncwæð, El. 573. Ongan hé tó Gode cleopian ... Him stefn oncwæð, An. 1400-1431 : Jul. 282. Clipiendra gehwylc wolde ꝥ him man oncwǽde *omnis inuocans cupit audiri*, Angl. ii. 373. (2) *to say in reply to a question:*—'Hwæt weard eów ...?' Earmsceapen ágef andsware ... and his

fæder oncwæð, An. 1348. Ongan his magu frignan ... Him þá oncwæð, Gú. 983-996: El. 1167. (3) with cognate accusative, *to make* a response (?) :—Oncweð þisne cwide, Dóm. 114. II. *add:*—Seó neólnes cliopað tó þǽre neólnesse, and heó oncwyð, Ps. Th. 41, 8. [Cf. *O. H. Ger.* in-quedan *respondere.*] Cf. and-cwis.

**on-cýþig.** *Add:* II. *unknown* (?) :—Nú þú cunnon miht h[wæt on wo]rdum wæs werum oncýðig, Hpt. 33, 73, 12. [Cf. *Icel.* kunnigr *known.*]

**on-dón.** *Add:*—Ic ne ondyde ná mínne múð *non aperui os meum*, Ps. Th. 38, 11. Weard eft Ianes duru andón *apertus est Ianus*, Ors. 6, 1; S. 254, 17.

**on-drǽdan.** II. *add:* (1) with reflexive dative. (a) with acc. :—Ðonne him mon ðissa tuéga hwæðer ondrætt suíður ðonne óðer, Past. 189, 9. Sé þe him his Dryhten ne ondrǽdeð, Seef. 106. Nó hé him þá sǽcce ondréd, B. 2347. Hié him ondrédon Godes hete, Gen. 767. Ne ondrǽd ðú ðé deáð tó swíðe, Prov. K. 16. Sé sceolde lytel sáwan, sé ðe him ðone wind ondréde ; and eft lytel rípan, sé ðe him ðá wolcn ondréde, P. 285, 24. Nis ðæt ná tó andrǽdanne (ondrǽdonne, *v. l.*) ðǽm hirde, 105, 25. Him Rómáne þæt swíðe ondrǽdende wǽron, Ors. 2, 4; S. 70, 1. (b) with gen. :—Hwæs ondrætst ðú ðé ?, Hml. Th. ii. 342, 18. Þonne mihte wé ondrǽdan ús deáðes rihtlíce, Hml. S. 34, 139. (c) with clause :—Ðá ondrǽde hé him ꝥ hí wurdon þám cynge leófran ðonne hé, Lch. iii. 424, 19. Hé him ondrǽdan sceal ðæt hé unmedome sié, Past. 73, 21. Ðonne is him tó ondrǽdanne ðæt him weorðe tó lore ..., 383, 26. Hé him wæs swíþe ondrǽdende ꝥ him his fiénd wǽren æfterfylgende, Ors. 2, 5; S. 84, 9. (2) without reflex. dat. (a) with acc. :—Ne geleofað man náht miriges ðá hwíle ðe mon deáð ondræt, Prov. K. 16. Hé ná syþþan ǽnige hyre yfelan weorc ondréd (-drǽd, *v. l.*), Lch. i. 176, 2. Hit is ungecyndelicu ofermódgung ðæt se monn wilnige ðæt hine his gelíca ondrǽde, and suáðeáh hit is nieððearf ðæt mon his hláford ondrǽde, Past. 109, 11-13. þú him ondrǽdan ne þearft ealdorbealu, B. 1674. Hogie hé swýðor beón gelufod þænne beón ondrǽdad (*timeri*), R. Ben. I. 108, 13. (b) with infin. :—Ondréd hé ondettan ꝥ he cyninges þegn wǽre *timuit se militem fuisse confiteri*, Bd. 4, 22 ; Sch. 455, 20. (c) with dat. infin. :—Ðæt ilce ðæt hé ondréd tó underfónne, Past. 49, 18. (d) with clause :—Hé ondréd ðæt he hit medomlíce dón ne meahte, Past. 49, 4 : 19. Ealle þá þe hé ondréd ðæt him on fylste beón woldon, Ors. 1, 12; S. 52, 5. Ðá Perse ondrǽdon ꝥ mon þá brycge forwyrcan wolde, 2, 5; S. 78, 14. Ðæt hié ondrǽden ðæt ..., Past. 159, 20. Is tó ondrǽdenne (-onne) ðæt ..., 139, 3. IV. *add:* (1) with reflex. dat. :—Ne ondrǽd ðú ðé *noli timere*, Past. 181, 9. Ondrǽde hé him suídlíce *magnopere metuat*, 93, 24. Hié him ondrǽden *timeant*, 187, 17. Hé mé cwæþ, þæt ic mé ne ondrǽdde (ondréde, *v. l.*) *dixit mihi, ne timerem*, Bd. 4, 25 ; Sch. 499, 10. Nis ǽnig wundor, hú him woruldmonna seó unclǽne gecynd hearde ondréde, Cri. 1018. (2) without dat. :—Dryhten, ic gehérde gehérnisse ðíne ondreord *Domine, audivi auditum tuum et timui*, Ps. Srt. ii. 189, 1. Hý andrǽdende gebidon, Ors. 4, 2; Bor. 79, 24.

**on-drǽdendlic.** *Add:* I. *tremendous:*—Ic eów bidde ðurh þǽne ondrǽdendlican dómes dæg, Hml. A. 145, 41. II. *fearful, in terror:*—Weard eorþbeofung ... Hié þeáh swá ondrǽdendlíce (andrǽdende, *v. l.*) gebidon *terra tremuit. Diu adtoniti utrimque populi haesitavere*, Ors. 4, 2 ; S. 160, 30.

**on-drencan.** *Add:*—Ondrencende *inebrians*, Ps. Vos. 64, 11.

**on-drincan.** *Add:*—Ic ðæs wæteres ondranc, Hml. S. 23 b, 506. Ðis deór mid þý ðe hit þæs wætres ondronc *haec bestia potata aqua*, Nar. 15, 18. v. in-drincan.

**ondryslíce**; *adv. Awfully, terribly:*—Hú egeslíce and hú andryslíce se heálica cyngc þǽr gedémed ánra gehwylcum for ǽrdǽdum, Wlfst. 137, 2. Swíðe ondryslíce *terribiliter*, Gr. D. 119, 24. v. ondrysnlíce.

**on-drysne.** II. *add:* (1) of a person :—Hú egeslic and hú andrysne heáhþrymme cyningc hér wile déman *quam celsithronus metuendus adveniet judex*, Dóm. L. 94. (2) of a thing, *of awful moment, solemn* [The Latin of R. Ben. 140, 5 is : Ad celebrandum missarum solemnia] :—Nú is þearf mycel ꝥ wé on forhæfdnesse lifian and úre synna clǽnsian ... Swá swá wé on máran forhæfdnesse lifian þás dagas, and on andrysnum þingum beóþ on þysse worlde, swá wé sceolan þe máran blisse habban þá hwíle þe wé lifgaþ hér on worlde, Bl. H. 35, 33.

**on-drysnlic.** *Add:*—Gelamp sum swíðe ondrysnlicu wíse (*terribile quiddam*) in Ualeria þǽre mǽgðe, Gr. D. 308, 10. Árísað and geseóð þone micclan and þone andrysnlican cyning, Ll. Th. ii. 396, 13.

**ondrysnlíce**, *adv. Terribly, dreadfully:*—God slóh þysne preóst ondrysnlíce (swíðe ondryslíce, *v. l.*) *hunc Deus terribiliter percussit*, Gr. D. 119, 24.

**on-drysnu** *might be* pl. neut. Cf. ge-risene.

**on-dúne**; *adv. Down:*—þá onhylde se hálga cnyht hys ansýne ondúne and noldon hig ná geseón, Shrn. 152, 27.

**on-dwǽscan.** l. -dwǽscan.

**on-eardian.** *Add:*—Seó ðeód þe Wiht ꝥ eálond oneardað (þe Wihtland eardað, *v. l.*) *ea gens quae Vectam tenet insulam*, Bd. 1, 15 ; Sch. 41, 18. Ealle oneardigende on hire *omnes inhabitantes in ea*, Ps. Vos.

74, 4. Đā oneardigendan, Ps. Rdr. p. 281, 14. Fram ānum witan byđ oneardud eþel (on eþele, MS.) *ab uno sensato inhabitabitur patria*, Scint. 188, 14. v. in-eardian.

**on-eardiend**, es; m. *An inhabitant:*—Þæs temples oneardiend (in-*v. l.*) *templi inhabitator*, Gr. D. 63, 12.

**on-efn.** *Add:* I. *prep.:*—Onefen đone greátan æsc, C. D. ii. 172, 23. II. *adv.:*—Đeáh đe seofon middangeardas sỹn ealle onefn ābrædde *though seven worlds be spread alongside one another*, Sal. K. p. 150, 29. *Circumflexus accentus* byđ of þām ōđrum twām geworht, swā wē hēr onem (*at the side*) habbađ āmearkod, Angl. viii. 333, 27. [v. *N. E. D.* anent: *O. Sax.* an-eban: *O. H. Ger.* in-eben: *Ger.* neben.]

**on-égan.** *Add:*—Hī onēgdon þære ferelan slegas *ictus ferulae pertimescebant*, Gr. D. 229, 25. Heó nāht næs hire onēgende *nec verita est*, 279, 17. [Hī onēgeæđ *formidabunt*, Ps. Spl. T. 103, 8. Onēgæn *tabescere*, 118, 139.]

**on-éhting**, e; f. *Persecution:*—Yrmþa onēhtinga forbær *calamitatum insectationes* (i. *persecutiones*) *perferebat*, An. Ox. 2974.

**onettan.** *l.* onettan, *and in l. 26 for* 1529 *substitute* 1579. I. *add:* expressing quickness of movement or procedure:—Heó gewāt hyre west þonan feran, forđ ōnette, Rä. 30, 11. Mē wære liófre þ ic ōnette wiþ þæs, þ ic đe mōste gelæstan þ ic đe gehēt *festino debitum promissionis absolvere*, Bt. 40, 5; F. 240, 15. Seó stīg gelædde þā ōnettendan (*properantes*) men tō đæs weres cytan, Gr. D. 212, 20. I a. of too quick procedure, *to hurry:*—Gif hē unendebyrdlíce ōnet mid đære sprǽce *si inordinate ad loquendum rapitur*, Past. 93, 18. II. *add:*—Ōnettæ, ōnete, ōnette *occupavit*, Txts. 82, 712. III. *add:* of energetic movement or procedure, *to press, strive:*—Ōnyt *contendit* (*amplificare*), An. Ox. 5216. Dryhtnes cempa ... forđ ōnetteđ, leahtras dwǽsceđ, Ph. 455. Þyder gāst rǽdendes ōnyt (*tendit*), Scint. 219, 4. Mænige tō dǽdbōte gehwyrfan ōnyttađ (*contendant*), 115, 4. Cyning forđ ōnette *the king pressed on*, Hö. 41: Vald. 2, 10. Seldsēne is þæt þā (*qui*) welan āgniađ tō reste ōnetton *rarum est ut qui diuitias possident ad requiem tendant*, Scint. 183, 10: E. S. viii. 473, 34. Guman ōnetton ... ođ þæt hý sæl ongytan mihton, B. 306: 1803: Gen. 1985. [*From* on-hātian.] v. ge-ōnettan.

**on-færeld.** *Add:*—Be onfærelde yfelra andwerdra *de incursione malorum presentium*, Scint. 212, 5.

**on-fæstan** *to make fast, fix:*—On đære ylcan circan wæron onfæste þā eówestran þāra brōđra sceápa *eidem ecclesiae caulae inhaerebant ovium*, Gr. D. 224, 16.

**on-fang** *a taking;* sumtio:—Fore-onfong *prae-sumtio*, Mt. p. 1, 4. Tō-onfonges *assumtionis*, Lk. R. 9, 51. [*O. L. Ger.* ana-fang *attack:* *O. H. Ger.* ana-fang *initium.*] v. on-feng.

**on-fangend**, es; m. *One who receives;* acceptor, Nap. 94.

**on-fangenness.** *Add:*—Ús is on đām micel wærlicnys getācnad on đære onfangennysse ūres Drihtnes līchaman, þæt is þæs hālgan hūsles, Hml. A. 163, 264.

**on-fealdan.** *Add:*—Ic onfealde and gerecce twā dǽda Benedictes *duo Benedicti facta replico*, Gr. D. 162, 10. [*O. H. Ger.* int-faldan *explicare.*]

**on-feng.** *Add:* v. on-fang, and-feng.

**on-fenge.** *Add:*—Offrunga þīne fæt ł onfengce sỹ *holocaustum tuum pingue fiat*, Ps. L. 19, 4. Aron anfoengo fæstino *sint accepta ieiunia*, Rtl. 23, 18. v. ge-onfenge.

**on-fengness.** *Add:*—Seó anfengnes mēdsceata on dōmum ys sōđfæstnesse forlætnes *susceptio muneris dimissio est veritatis*, Ll. Lbmn. 476, 30.

**on-feormeganda.** v. un-feormigende: **onfilti.** v. anfilte.

**on-findan.** *Add:*—Anfindo *depraehendo*, Txts. 57, 661. I. *to come upon by chance or in the course of events.* (1) *to come across, meet with, light upon:*—Đone sē đe onfindes *quem qui invenit*, Mt. L. 13, 44. Huðn aron đā đe onfindes đā ilco, 7, 14. Gesomnadon alle đā đe onfundon, 22, 10. Gif mon hwelcne ceáp gebygeđ, and hē þonne onfinde him hwelce unhǽlo on binnan .xxx. nihta, Ll. Th. i. 138, 10. Đonne him biđ sum undeáw on onfunden, Past. 241, 15. (1 b) with obj. and compl.:—Eádig đe đegn đone miđ đỹ cymes hlāferd his onfand suā đōende, Mt. L. 24, 46. (2) *to meet with and keep, to get, obtain:*—Gē onfyndes rest sāulum iúrum, Mt. L. 11, 29. Andfindende *nanciscuntur*, Wrt. Voc. ii. 62, 8. (3) *to discover on inspection or consideration:*—Hwæt onfundon eówre yldran on mē þæs þe heom đūhte þæt ful riht nǽre *quid invenerunt patres vestri in me iniquitatis*, Wlfst. 49, 6. (3 b) with complement clause:—Đā ongelíca gecwēdon đū onfindes *eos similia dixisse reperies*, Mt. p. 12, 5. Æghwelc monn biđ onfunden suā micle lǽs gelǽred đonne ōđer suā hē biđ ungeđyldegra *tanto quisquis ostenditur doctus, quanto minus convincitur patiens*, Past. 217, 2. (4) *to come to the knowledge* of a fact or state of things by experience or trial. (a) with noun object:—Þā se cyning þæt fācn anfunde *quo comperto*, Ors. 1, 12; S. 52, 30. Đā đe hiera līchoman synna onfunden habbađ *peccata carnis experti*, Past. 403, 12. (b) with pronoun object representing a clause:—Hē swīđor lufade wīfa gebǽro

þonne wǽpnedmonna. Þ onfunde Arbatus, Ors. 1, 12; S. 52, 2: 4, 10; S. 200, 18. Hē þōhte his sunu tō beswícanne ... þā hit se sunu anfunde, 6, 30; S. 282, 10: 12. Se cyning đæt anfunde, þæt him mon geswicen hæfde, 1, 12; S. 52, 6. (c) with clause:—Hē anfunde þæt þæt cūþ wæs, Ors. 4, 5; S. 166, 30: 6, 33; S. 288, 15. Þæs anfundan Cartaginenses þ hié mon oferswīþan mehte, 4, 1; S. 160, 4. Gif man onfinde þ heora ǽnig on wōhre gewitnesse wǽre, Ll. Th. i. 204, 23. Nān man ne mihte onfindan þ heó wæs fǽmne, Shrn. 31, 11. (5) *to suffer, feel pain, discomfort, &c.:*—Hē onfindeþ swile and þ þā ōman beóđ inne betýnde, Lch. ii. 174, 22. Hē onfunde Godes ierre on đām hearme đe his bearne becōm, Past. 39, 4. (6) *to detect* a person in wrongdoing:—Anfunden *deprehensus* (of a thief), Kent. Gl. 168: (of the man that deceiveth his neighbour), 994. II. *to discover or attain by search or effort:*—Geongeđ tō soecenne đā ilca ... Gif geworđas þte onfinde hiá, Mt. L. 18, 13. II a. *to find* that to which one is directed:—Eftgeiorn tō bōcum and ... onfindes stōwa *recurres ad volumina et ... reperies loca*, Mt. p. 4, 7. Đene fisc nim ... and đū onfindes ..., Mt. L. 17, 27. Gaa in cæstre ... gē onfindes đone fola, Mk. R. L. 11, 2. [*O. Sax.* ant-findan: *O. H. Ger.* int-findan: *Ger.* emp-finden.]

**on-flígen**, es; n. *l.* (?) on-flygen, e; f. Cf. lygen.

**on-fón.** *Add:* A. the subject a person. I. *add: to take on one's own initiative.* (1) *to take hold of* an object:—Cornelius hine gebīgde tō Petres fōtum, ac his onfēncg Petrus (*Petrus elevavit eum*, Acts 10, 26), Hml. S. 10, 129. Hyra Scyppend sceađan onfēngon syngum hondum, Cri. 1132. Ic nāt hū þū hym onfōn mage mid geglōfedum handum, Solil. H. 42, 11. (1 a) fig.:—Mē đīn seó swīđre onfēncg *me suscepit dextera tua*, Ps. Th. 62, 7. Hond Godes onfēng freóđrihten and hine forđ lǽdde, Sat. 566. (2) *to get control or possession of, to take a wife:*—Ic of þām temple onfēng fǽmnan clǽne, Cri. 187. Hē leomum onfēng and līchoman, 628. Đæs gefarenan brōđor wīf wæs geboden đām lifiendan brēđer tō onfōnne, Past. 43, 23. (3) with a non-material object, *to get a condition of mind, adopt a* mode of conduct, *grasp* with the mind:—Hē onfēng hrađe inwitþancum *he had crafty thoughts at once*, B. 748. Ne wolde þām leóđþeáwum Loth onfōn, Gen. 1938. Hē gesǽde swefen cyninge, þæt hē onfōn ne meahte on his breóstlocan *he told the king the dream, that he could not remember* (cf. hē ne wisse word swefnes sīnes, 125), Dan. 166. II. *add: to receive* what is sent, &c. (1) *to take into the* hand (lit. or fig.):—Þæs wīnes steápes onfēhđ (sē) þe hē ann, Ps. Th. 74, 7. Heó onfēng þām hālgum gerýnum Crīstes līchaman and blōdes mid ābrǽdedum handum, Hml. S. 23 b, 700. Bebiet sió ǽ đæt se sācerd scyle onfōn đone suīđran bōgh æt đære offrunge, Past. 81, 19. (2) *to* receive a material or non-material object as possession or for use, enjoyment, &c., *get:*—'Đū onfēncg đīn gōd eal hēr on worulde.' For đǽm anfēhđ se yfla āuht goodes on disse worulde đæt ... Past. 391, 15. For ōđerra monna đearfe hié onfōđ đyllica giefa, 41, 13: Gen. 1759. Þū eácnunge onfēnge bearnes, Cri. 75. Gē wītgena lāre onfēngon, El. 335. Onfōđ mīnes fæder rīce (cf. *possidete regnum*, Mt. 25, 34), Cri. 1345. Đæt wē onfōn sumne dǽl bledsunge, Past. 333, 1. Þ ic mæge þīnra gebeda onfōn, Hml. S. 23 b, 212. Hié wēndon þæt hié māre sculdon onfoon (wēron onfengendo, L. *essent accepturi*), Mt. R. 20, 10. Beóđ đā heortan suīđe gearwe wīsdōmes tō anfōnne (on-, *v. l.*) *ad suscipiendum aedificium corda paraverunt*, Past. 203, 12. Hyht is onfangen, Cri. 99. (3) *to receive* what is entrusted:—Gif sweordhwīta ōđres monnes wǽpn tō feormunge onfō, Ll. Th. i. 74, 9. (4) *to receive* what is sent:—Heó þæt ǽrende onfēng, Hy. 10, 25. (5) *to receive* what is inflicted:—Gif hē heáhre handa dyntes onfēhđ, Ll. Th. i. 18, 2. Ic onfēng þīn sār, Cri. 1461: 1440. Hleór ārleásra spātl onfēng, 1437. Hē sceolde dōmes hleótan þæs ilcan þe ússa yldran onfēngon, Gū. 947. Þeáh þe hē ātres drync onfēnge, An. 53. Hié Godes yrre habban sceoldon, þone nearwan niđ niéde onfōn, Gen. 697. Ic tō fela hæbbe bealwa onfongen, Cri. 182. III. *add:* (1) *to take with the hands* what is offered:—Heó (Eve) æt þām lāđan onfēng deáđes beámes wæstm, Gen. 592. Hē beád him þrý berene hlāfas ... Đā hēt se ārleása onfōn þæra hlāfa, Hml. S. 3, 214. (2) *to accept* a material or non-material object as possession, or for use, enjoyment, &c.:—Gifre biđ sē þām golde onfēhđ, Gn. Ex. 70. 'Ne cearađ incit ellor sēcan winas uncūđe, ac wuniađ hēr'. Abraham ... onfēng freóndscipe be freán hǽse, Gen. 2736. Ne onfōh þū nǽfre mēdsceattum *nec accipies munera*, 1, 54, 17. Þē lyst nū liōþa. Onfōh hiora nū *video te carminis exspectare dulcedinem. Accipe igitur haustum*, Bt. 39, 12; F. 232, 21. Bæd hē hine þ hē sumne dǽl landes æt him onfēnge *postulauit eum possessionem terrae aliquam a se accipere*, Bd. 3, 23; Sch. 299, 11. Onfēngon, Shrn. 129, 31. Onfōnde *accipiens*, Bd. 3, 23; Sch. 289, 15. (3) *to accept* what is stated, taught, enjoined, &c.:—Ne hine cuman hí onfōþ *nec eum uenisse accipiunt*, An. Ox. 40, 3. Monega þeóda Crīstes geleáfan onfēngon, Ll. Th. i. 58, 4. Mid þon þe hié þæs crīstendōmes onfēngon, Ors. 6, 4; S. 268, 26. Crīstendōme onfōn, 6, 13; S. 268, 21. (4) *to accept* when responsibility is alleged:—Sē þe yrfe bycge ... and hit eft týman scyle, þonne onfō sē his þe hē hit ǽr æt bohte, Ll. Th. i. 212,

13. Gif se mon hine þonne onfón ne wille, 150, 7. v. teám. (5) *to accept* a proposal, *give a favourable hearing* to a prayer:—Onfóh (-fóg, Ps. L.) mid þínum eárum mínne wóp and míne teáras *auribus percipe lacrymas meas*, Ps. Th. 38, 14. Mín gebedo wendon eft tó mé, for þám heora nolde onfón se déma þe ic him tó sende, 34, 13. Beád hé ealle his æhta wiþ his feore; þá nolde se cyning þæs onfón, Bt. 29, 2; F. 104, 22. (6) *to accept, not to offer objection to, take in good part*:—Hié onfooð ðære láre micle lusðlicor *they will take reproof much more readily*, Past. 293, 25. **IV a.** *add*:—God álíeseð sáwle míne of honda helle þonne hé onfoehð mé, Ps. Vos. 48, 16. Þú mé onféncge, Ps. Th. 118, 147. Hé heora mid bismere onféng, Ors. 3, 11; S. 146, 33. Sé þe hine tó men onfó, Ll. Th. i. 86, 9. Ðá fémnan þe gewuniað onfón gealdorcræftigan, 52, 9. Gif hí sumne freónd onfón willað to him, Hml. Th. ii. 316, 8. **IV b.** *add*:—Sum geréfman wære þára þe onfénge ánum mægdene æt fullwihte *quidam curialis juvenculam in baptismate suscepit*, Gr. D. 308, 13. Hé náh mid rihte æniges mannes æt fulluhte tó onfónne ne æt bisceopes handa, Wlfst. 39, 17. **IV c.** *to allow to come, not to exclude*:—Hié sprǽcon ðæt hit betere wáre þætte Rómáne eft heora cynecynne onféngen *revocandorum in Urbem regum placito insimulatos*, Ors. 2, 3; S. 68, 9. **V.** *add*: (1) *to undergo* a rite:—Hé fulwihte onféng, El. 192. Hé onféng fulwihtes bæð, 490: 1033. Hé onféng torhtum tácne *he was circumcised*, Gen. 2374. (1 a) *to receive* the sacrament:—Ne sceall him bewered beón þám gerýne onfón þære hálegan gemǽnsumnesse. Gyf ... hwylc man ne gedyrstgað onfóón ... Gif hé onféhþ ..., Bd. 1, 27; Sch. 83, 17–23. Mid clǽnnysse ðá hálgan ðígene onfón, Hml. Th. ii. 280, 29. (2) *to undertake* a duty:—Restedæges begýminge hí onfóþ *Sabbati obseruationem suscipiunt*, An. Ox. 40, 6. Cyning selfa onféng fulluhtþeáwum, Met. 1, 33. Æfter þám onfangenum gebede swá hit mid munecum þeáw is *after praying as is the custom with monks*, Hml. S. 23 b, 67 : 84. **VI.** *add*:—Þý syxtan mónþe þæs þe Sanctus Ióhannes on his módor bósm onfangen wæs, Bl. H. 165, 25. **VII.** *add*:—Ðonne eft on ðone herpað ðær wé ǽr onféngan (cf. ǽrest of Nóddre andlang ðes portherpaðes, 453, 29), C. D. iii. 454, 9. **B.** the subject a thing. (1) *to admit within itself*:—Eorðe onféhð eallum sǽdum, Met. 29, 66. Líc onféng gǽst, Hö. 20. Him hel onféng, B. 852. Heal swǽge onféng, 1214. Brimwylm onféng hilderince, 1494. (2) *to have placed on its surface, have brought in contact with*:—Hleór bolster onféng, B. 688. Bord ord onféng, By. 110. Bord oft onféng ýða swengas, El. 238. Heáh hlioðo horde onféngon (*the ark rested on Ararat*), Gen. 1439. (3) *to be endowed by nature with* something, material or non-material:—Beorgas onfóð blǽdum and wæstmum, Ps. Th. 103, 12. Ealle gesceafta onfóþ æt Gode endebyrdnesse and andwlitan, Bt. 39, 5; F. 218, 14, þæt se wyrtruma sǽde onfénge, Dan. 583. [v. *N. E. D.* on-fang. *O. Sax.* ant-fáhan : *O. H. Ger.* ant-fáhan (int-) *ac-, con-, ex-, per-, re-, sus-cipere, capere, sumere, obtinere* : *Ger.* emp-fangen.]

**on-fónd.** *Add*:—Anfóend *susceptor*, Ps. Rdr. 3, 4. v. eft-onfónd.

**onfónd-líc;** *adj. That is to be received*:—On æte and on wǽte, oþþe on óþrum anfóndlicum and sellendlicum þingum (*dandis atque accipiendis rebus*), Chrd. 110, 8.

**on-foran.** *Add*:—Onfora wæs geongend hiá se Hǽlend *praecedebat eos Iesus*, Mk. L. 10, 32.

**on-funden;** *adj. Having experience of, having by experience knowledge of*:—Gedó mé lusfende and onfundne þínes wísdómes *jubeas me esse amatorem perceptoremque sapientiae tuae*, Solil. H. 14, 7. *See next word*.

**onfundenness.** *Add*: v. á-fundenness : onga. v. anga.

**on-galan.** *Add*: *to recite* a charm:—Þis derian ne móste þǽm þe þis galdor begytan mihte oððe þe þis galdor ongalan cúþe, Lch. iii. 42, 18.

**on-galness, e; *f. A constant singing* or *song*:—Ongalnis ł sang mín symle [*tu es*] *decantatio mea semper*, Ps. Rdr. 70, 6.

**on-gang.** *Add*: **III.** *worship*:—Æðelbryht and his ðeóde fram deófolgylda ongonge (begange, *v. l.*) hé tó Crístes geleáfan gelǽdde *Aedilberctum ac gentem illius ab idolorum cultu ad Christi fidem perduxit*, Bd. 2, 3; Sch. 125, 20.

**ongeagn.** *Add*: **A. I.** (1)—Mið ðý gesætt on dúne oelebeáma ongeaegn (-gægn, R.) temple (*contra templum*), Mk. L. 13, 3. Ásettað mé ongén (-gén, *v. l.*) þysum fýre *contra ignem me ponite*, Gr. D. 48, 3. (2)—Móyses ástrehte his hand ongeán ðære sǽ, Hml. Th. ii. 194, 26. (2 a) denoting motion in a contrary direction to that of a moving body:—Hát unmǽlne mon gefeccean ongeán streáme (*moving the vessel up stream*) healfne sester yrnendes wæteres, Lch. iii. 4. (3):—Árísed cynn ongægn cynne, Mk. L. R. 21, 10. Ic him módes gǽlsan ongeán bere grimra geþonca, Jul. 367. Ic eów sweord ongeán oðberan þence, Gú. 273 : El. 43. (4):—Geopena ongeán mé lífes geat, Hml. Th. i. 76, 3 : Rä. 76, 3. þæt hyre sié swegl ongeán, Dóm. 69. (4 a) denoting obstruction of that which comes:—Wá ðæs mannes sáwle þe betýnð his duru ongeán Godes þearfan ...; swá him bið betýned heofona ríces duru ongeán on dómes dæge, Wlfst. 239, 1–5. (6) *in response*:—Iúdas hire ongén þingode, El. 609 : Gú. 210. Werhádes

men ongunnon symle þone dreám, and wífhádes men him sungon ongeán, Hml. Th. ii. 548, 12. (8) denoting reciprocal action, *in turn, on the other hand*:—Se abbud Libertinum be his fótum genam ... Ongǽn (ondgegn, *v. l.*) þǽm (*contra*) Libertinus hine sylfne tó þæs abbudes fótum ástrehte, Gr. D. 21, 34. **II.** (1):—Hí lédon hine ongeán þá sunnan *they laid him down with his face to the sun*, Hml. S. 35, 160. (1 a):—Se assa geseah ðone engel ongeán hine standan, and him ðæs fǽreltes forwiernan, Past. 255, 24. Dryhten tóbrǽt ðone greádan his mildheortnesse ongén ðá ðe tó him gecierrað, 405, 10. Sing on þæs mannes heáfod ufan on yrnendum wætere and wend þ heáfod ongeán streám (*he must face up stream*), Lch. iii. 70, 8. (2):—Weras wíf somod urnon ongeán þá þeódnes mægð, Jud. 165. (2 a) *in a direction opposite to that of* another moving body:—Ðá seofon tunglan farað ǽfre ongeán ðone rodor, Sal. K. p. 124, 155. Cymð hé tó lande, hwílum ongeán wind and ongeán ðá ýða, hwílum mid ǽgðrum, Past. 433, 3. Wæter hé déð þæt yrnð ongeán streám, Wlfst. 196, 5 : C. D. B. ii. 374, 10. (2 b) *to meet* an event, time, &c.:—Man dráf út his módor ongeán þone weallendan winter, Chr. 1037 ; P. 160, 16. (3) *in contravention* or *violation of* right, custom :—Þeáh ðe hwá cweðe tǽllic word ongeán mé, him bið forgifen ... sé ðe cweð word ongán ðone Hálgan Gást, ne bið hit him forgifen, Hml. Th. i. 498, 24–26. Ongann hé swíðe yrre clypian ongeán (-gǽn, -gén, *v. ll.*) hine, Gr. D. 37, 6. Ongeán ungewemmedde *contra inmunem* (*castitatem saeviens*), An. Ox. 4333. Hiora ǽgþer þ mǽste folc ongeán ó erne geteáh, Ors. 2, 7 ; S. 90, 17. Ðá biscopas ongeaegn hine (*aduersus eum*) somnung gegeadredon, Jn. p. 6, 10. Ongeán Godes ryht, Ll. Th. i. 170, 12 : 312, 8 : ii. 296, 17. Ládige hé (*the accused*) hine mid áðe ongeán hine (*the accuser*), i. 489, 10. Ongeán gewunan *contra ritum*, An. Ox. 1819. (3 a) where one thing is subjected to the action of another :—Aðamans, gif his mon onhrínd mid buccan blóde, hé hnescað ongeán ðæt liðe blód, Past. 271, 4. (4):—Hé ongan lifgean ongeán God, ǽr þon þe hé him sylfum lifgean mihte *ante coepit vivere Deo, quam sibi*, Bl. H. 165, 22. Lócigan ongeán þás sunnan, Solil. H. 34, 22. (6):—Ongeán ðæt sint tó lǽranne ðá ofersprǽcean *contra admonendi sunt multiloquia vacantes*, Past. 277, 3 : 289, 4 : 296, 7 : 351, 3. (7):—Fæste hé nú ongeán þ hé ǽr þurh fylle unriht gefremede, Ll. Th. ii. 284, 2. Uton efstan þæt wé magon him gewrixl ágyldan ... ongeán ealle þá gód þe hé ús forgyfen hæfð, Wlfst. 145, 8. Fela þinga dydan þá geogeleras þurh drýcræft ongeán þæt þe Móyses þurh Godes mihta fela wundra worhte, 98, 9. (8):—Ðá yfelan brǽdað on worulde ongeán þæt mǽste yfel þe mannum is tówerd, Wlfst. 83, 15. **B.** (3):—Hit sprang ongeán, By. 137. (4):—Hé symle ongén cwæð, 'Gewurþe Godes willa,' Hml. S. 33, 33. (4 a) where sound is the result of an act :—Man lédde tó his breóstum bráde ísene clútas swíðe glówende þ hit sang ongeán, Hml. S. 37, 163. (4 b) where action is a reply to, or return for, action :—Sé, sé ðe háðheortnesse ofercuman wille, ðæt hé hiene ongeán ne háthirte (*he must not reply to fury with fury*), Past. 296, 6. (6):—Hé bord ongeán hefeð, Jul. 385. (7):—On hú mycelre Godes gehyrdnysse beóð þá þe cunnon hý sylfe forseón ... Swá eác þær ongeán (*e contra*) beforan Godes eágum licgeað forsewene þá þe tóþindað, Gr. D. 40, 3. Hé oðsóc þ hé hit nǽre ; hí þá ongén hine gecnáwne gedydon be þám tácne þe on his hneccan wæs þ hé hit wæs, Hml. S. 30, 274. v. þær-ongeán.

**ongeán-cirring (?)** *return. See next word.*

**ongeán-cyme.** *Add*: ágeán-cyme:—Ealle wǽron swíðe blíðe his ongeáncymes, Hml. S. 30, 292. Forbodene ágeáncyme, ágeáncyrdincge (-cyrrincge (?)) *interdictum postliminium*, An. Ox. 2721. [Se cing and ealle his leóde Gode þancode his ongeáncumes, Chr. 995 ; P. 130, 41.]

**ongeán-hwirfende;** *adj. Returning, repeating* :—Ágeánhwurfende ýða *reciproca* (*redeuntia, iterantia*) *fluctus*, Hpt. Gl. 409, 67.

**ongeán-hworfenness, e; *f. What lies in the way* :—Gehwylce ongeánhworf[enn]esse (ágeánhworfenysse, Hpt. Gl. 470, 2) *âwéstendum obuia queque uastantibus*, An. Ox. 2713.

**ongeán-hwyrf, es; *m. Return* :—Ágeánhw[yrfe], geánwurfe *reditu*, Hpt. Gl. 419, 62.

**ongeán-sprecend, es; *m. One who speaks against another, one who blames* or *reproaches* :—Of stefne ongeánsprecendes *a voce obloquentis*, Ps. Rdr. 43, 17.

**ongeán-weard.** *Add*: [Cf. ongeánward *in the opposite direction*, Chr. 963; P. 117, 1. v. *N. E. D.* again-ward.] *See next word.*

**ongeán-weardes; *prep.* (*adv.*) *Towards* :—Ic ue mæg mé ongeánweardes þé gewenden, Hml. S. 23 b, 206. Teoligende his cneówu tó bígenne hire ongeánweardes, 686. [Wæs gesæwen swilce se beám (*the tail of the comet*) ongeánweardes wið þes steorran (*the nucleus*) ward fýrcliende wǽre *the light of the tail seemed to be streaming towards*, *instead of from, the nucleus*, Chr. 1106 ; P. 240, 23.]

**ongeán-winnende** *resisting, struggling* :—Þá ongeánwinnendan fémnan mid micelre strengðe earfoðlice ofercóm, Ap. Th. 2, 4.

**ongeán-wirdness, e; *f. What lies in the way* :—Ongeánwyrdnessa *obuia*, An. Ox. 3975.

**on-gebróht.** *Add: that is brought on* or *against* a person :—Se ongebróhta teóna (*contumelia illata*) ácunnað húlic gehwilc man byþ

innan on his dȳgolnysse mid him sylfum, Gr. D. 47, 9. Be ongebrōhtum teónan *de inrogata calumnia*, An. Ox. 4689. Ongebrōhte teónan *inlatas contumelias*, Scint. 40, 9.

**on-gecoplíce.** v. un-gecoplíce.

**on-gehȳpness,** e; *f. Advantage, profit:*—Hí be þisses andweardan lifes ongehȳднesse ðenceað, and nāwiht be þæs tōwerdan, Ll. Lbmn. 476, 5.

**on-gelíc;** *adj. Like:*—Ōngelíc (the MS. has the accents) is ríc heofna strión *simile est regnum coelorum thesauro*, Mt. L. 13, 44. Ongelíc (*sic MS.*), 47. Ongelíc, 45: Lk. L. 13, 18: 19. Ongelíc-sint cnæhtum *similes sunt pueris*, 7, 31: 12, 36. Ongelícum, Mt. p. 10, 14. Ongelíca *similia*, 12, 5. v. an-gelíc.

**on-gelíc** *a likeness, image:*—Ongelíc (*sic MS.*) leás, ongelíc celfes, ongelíc monnes, ongelíc earnes, Mt. p. 10, 4–5. Ongelíc *similitudinem (panni rudis)*, 16, 1: Jn. p. 7, 15.

**ongelíce,** -líc; *adv. In the same way, similarly:*—Hé beád þæt man ongelíce tō him onbūgan sceolde swā tō Gode, Ors. 6, 9; S. 264, 8. Ongelíc (*sic MS.*) *similiter*, Lk. L. 10, 32: 17, 31: 20, 31. Ongelíc, 16, 25.

**on-gelícness,** e; *f. A form, pattern:*—Gebedes ongelícnes gesalde *orationis formulam tradens*, Mt. p. 14, 20.

**on-gemang. I.** *add:*—Gif hié mon ongemang ðære ðreátunga fēt mid sumere heringe, Past. 303, 1. þā ongemang ðyssum (*then while this was going on*) beheóld heó hine swȳðe georne, Hml. S. 30, 345: 33, 88. **I a.** *with acc.:*—Hí beóð ongemang mægenu tō tellanne *sunt inter uirtutes conputanda*, Chrd. 110, 11. **II.** *add:*—Færeð forst ongemang, Gen. 802. Ongemang *interim*, Angl. xiii. 393, 400: 405, 569: 408, 613. **II a.** *with* hér, þær, *perhaps forming compounds.* v. hér-ongemang.

**on-geótan** *to infuse:*—Swā þ ealle þā fatu wǽron ongoten (*infusa*) mid bledsunge þæs ylcan eles, Gr. D. 51, 14.

**on-geweorc (?),** es; *n. Making, work:*—On ongeweorce (= on geweorce? Cf. on gewerce, Ps. Vos. Srt., on geworce, Ps. Spl., on worce, Ps. Cam., on worcum, Ps. Th.) þīnum *in factura tua*, Ps. Rdr. 91, 5.

**on-gewinn,** es; *n. Attack:*—Gelōme gebed leahtra ongewinn ācwencð *frequens oratio uitiorum inpugnationem extinguit*, Scint. 33, 17.

**on-gewrigenness,** e; *f. A revelation:*—On þæs hálgan gewrites gesprecum ge eác on ōðrum deóglum ongewrigenyssum (*revelationibus*), Gr. D. 139, 1.

**on-gildan. I.** *add:* (1) *with gen.:*—Agustus herede þā ofermētto . . . Raþe þæs Rōmāne anguldon þæs wordes mid miclum hungre, Ors. 6, 1; S. 254, 15. (2) *with acc.:*—Iūdéas gedydon him dǽda þā wirrestan; hȳ þ drōfe onguldon, Lch. iii. 286, 14. (3) *with clause:*—Hié mid hiera cucum onguldon þæt hié ungyltige cwealdon, Ors. 4, 7; S. 184, 9. **IV.** *to undergo (a penalty) as a compensation for* wrongdoing, *pay with the evil suffered (gen.):*—Ne habbað wiht for þæt, þeáh hē wom dōn ofer Meotudes bibod: monig sceal ongieldan sāwel sūsles, Fä. 71. Weard Godes wracu on Rōme . . . him wæs ungemetlic moncwealm getenge, þæt nán hús næs binnan þǽre byrig þæt hit nǽfde þǽre wrace angolden *exoritur ultio . . . incredibilium morborum pestis extenditur: nulla domus fuit, quae non illa pestilentia correpta sit*, Ors. 6, 23; S. 274, 13.

**on-ginnan. I.** *add:* (a) *to draw near to performing* an instantaneous act:—His sunu ongan sweltan *his son drew near to death*, Shrn. 122, 8. ¶ *with almost the sense of the auxiliary* do. Cf. later gan *with infinitive:*—Ongan ic steppan forð, Sat. 248. (b) :—Mid þȳ hē geswiperum mūðe lícetende ǽrende wrehte and leáslíce ongann *cum simulatam legationem ore astuto uolueret*, Bd. 2, 9; Sch. 147, 2. **II.** *add:* (1) *with acc.*:—Ðā ðe nabbað wísdom tō ðon ðæt hié cunnen lǽran, and hí ðeáh forhradiað ðæt hié hit ongiennað, Past. 383, 22. Nát ic hwæðer māre wundor wæs, þe þæt hē swā mid lytle fultume þone mǽstan dǽl þisses middangeardes gegān mehte, þe þ hē mid swā lytle weorode swā micel anginnan dorste (*adgredi ausus fuerit*), Ors. 3, 9; S. 124, 16. (2) *with infin.*:—þænne hē ōþres limes þénunge gegrīpan ongynne *dum alterius membri officium temptat*, Scint. 133, 2. **III.** *add:*—Gelíce ðǽm monnum ðe swíðe eáðmōdlíce on-ginnað (*use great endeavour to appear humble; magna submissione blandiuntur*) beforon rícum monnum, Past. 421, 26. Ongin nū wel, Rufe, and behāt mē mid āðe *take the right course now, Rufus, and promise me on oath*, Hml. S. 22, 104. Ongin nū stranglíce, and þín gemynd stent on herunge, 29, 272. Onginnað nū þegenlíce, . . . and syllað eówer āgen líf for ðǽre sōðfæstan ǽ, 25, 248.

**on-girwan.** *Add: to strip* a person (*acc.*) of something (*gen., dat. (inst.)*) :—Hē ealle gesceafta gemetgað, and ōðre hwíle gegiereð myd ðām winsumestum wlitum, ōðre hwíle eft ongiereð and geungewlitegað, Solil. H. 59, 20. þe hine þām scyccelse ongyrede, Hml. S. 23 b, 217. Ongeredon (*exuerunt*) hine ðȳ ryfte and gegeredon hine mið his gewǽdum, Mt. L. 27, 31. þ þū ongere mē ealra mínra synna, Angl. xii. 505, 20. Wæs hē hine sylfne ongyrwende, Gr. D. 68, 11. v. un-girwan.

**on-gitan. I.** *add:*—Ðā ðā hē ongeat ðā scylde on Annanian and Saffiran *cum Ananiae et Sapphirae culpam reperit*, Past. 115, 12. Ðæt mōd ne mæg ongietan ðā tōweardan yfelo *imminentia mala non prospicit*, 431, 20. **III.** *add: to be sensible of:*—Ic ne ongyte nāne trimðe ne on mōde ne on líchaman, Solil. H. 49, 3. þȳ lǽs ge Godes þeów ǽniges teónan ōht ongeáte for þissere gemētingce *nec quidquam Dei famulus ex conventione eadem injuriae sentiret*, Gr. D. 35, 27. **IV.** *add:*—Ðonne hié eal ðā hálgan gewritu ryhtlíce ongiten (-gieten, *v. l.*) hæbben *cum recte cuncta de sacra Scriptura sentiunt*, Past. 371, 4. **V.** *add:* (a) *with gen.*:—Ic ealles þises middan-geardes nā māran dǽles ne angite būton ðætte on twām onwealdum geweard, Ors. 2, 5; S. 86, 16. **VI.** *add:*—Ðonne hē geornlíce ongiett (-git, *v. l.*) ðā inneran and ðā gǽstlican ðing on his ingeðonce *cum studiose interiora penetrat*, Past. 141, 15. Ðæt hē clǽnlíce and ryhtwíslíce ongiete ðæt ðæt hē ongiete *caste intelligit*, 349, 3. Ðā ðe ðā word ðǽre hálgan ǽ ryhtlíce ongietan cunnon *qui recte verba legis intelligunt*, 371, 1. **V a.** *to understand* a person, *perceive the true character of:*—Ðonne hié hié selfe ongietað *ad se reducti*, Past. 293, 25. Ongite (-giete, *v. l.*) hē hine selfne, 115, 4. **VI b.** *to seek to know:*—Ðæt hié hié selfe ongieten on ðǽm hálgum gewritum *ut in divinis sermonibus semetipsos requirant*, Past. 371, 2. **VII a.** *add:*—Egypte flugon forhtiende, fǽr ongéton, Exod. 452. Wæs Sanctus Paulus gecostad ðæt hē ongeáte his synna, Past. 423, 21. Wē magon fullecor ongietan and tōsceádan ðā sprǽce *hanc discretionem plenius agnoscimus*, 115, 6. **VII b.** (1) *add:*—Ðonne ðā lāreówas ongitað ðæt ðā ðe him underðiedde beóð him tō hwōn God andrǽdað *quando ab subditis Deum timeri rectores deprendunt*, Past. 109, 14. Hē ongæt (oncneów, *v. l.*) þæt heó wæs gehǽled in þā ylcan tíde *ea hora saluti restitutam virginem agnovit*, Gr. D. 29, 29. Mid þȳ hí ðā ðā elreordigan ongeáton þæt hí wǽron ōðerre ǽfestnesse *qui cum cogniti essent a barbaris, quod essent alterius religionis*, Bd. 5, 10; Sch. 601, 10. Ongiete hē ðæt hē bið ōðrum monnum gelíc *aequalem se ceteris cernat*, Past. 115, 4. (3 a) *add:*—Ðā þe ic þē ongæt secgan *quae te dixisse cognovi*, Gr. D. 139, 14. (3 b) *add:*—Hé hine selfne ongeat him gelícne *se illi similem recognovit*, Past. 115, 11. Mid þȳ wē ūs eft ongeáton māran gefeoht tōweard *noua conspirari cognoueram bella*, Nar. 17, 11. (4) *add:*—Hē wæs gehæfd and ongyten mycelre geearnunge man, Gr. D. 26, 7. Hē wilnode ðæt hē wǽre ongieten ūpāhæfen ofer ealle ōðre gesceafte, Past. 301, 11. Ðǽm ðe on giéfernesse ongietene beóð wile folgian fierenlust *gulae deditos luxuria sequitur*, 311, 4. **IX.** *to observe, consider:*—Ðȳ sint tō manienne ðā ðe on ðisse worulde orsorglíce libbað, ðæt hié geornlíce ongieten (*solerter considerent*) ðætte sió orsorgnes hwílum bið tō ðǽm gelǽned . . ., hwílum tō ðǽm . . ., Past. 389, 29. **X.** *to know* how to do something :—Ðæt hē of geornlíce conn ongietan ðæt hē of him gadrige ðæt him stælwierðe sié, and wið ðæt winne ðæt him dereð *qui sollicite noverit et sumere ex illa, quod adjuvat, et expugnare, quod tentat*, Past. 115, 2.

**on-gitenness.** *Add:*—Ūrum ongytenessum þū behȳdest þā *ea nostros cognitionibus abscondis*, Gr. D. 139, 16.

**on-gratian (?)** *to grate with the teeth (?), smile (?):*—Ongrynt oððe ongratað *arridet*, An. Ox. 33, 2. [*v. N. E. D.* grate.] *See next word.*

**on-gryntan, -gríntan (?)** *to grind with the teeth (?), show the teeth (?), smile (?).* [*v. N. E. D.* grint.] *See preceding word.*

**on-gyrdan** *to ungird* a person, *strip* a person of a girdle or of what is girded on him :—Hē ongyrde hine his swurde *discinxit se gladio suo*, Bd. 3, 14; Sch. 258, 23. þā ongyrde óþer þegn þā fǽmnan, Shrn. 130, 29. [*O. H. Ger.* ant-gurten.] v. un-gyrdan.

**on-gyte,** es; *m. Infusion, inpouring:*—Ðonne ðā yrsigendan mōd gecyrrað tō manðwǽrnysse þurh ongyte ðǽre upplícan gife, Hml. Th. i. 362, 31.

**on-habban.** v. ā-habban; **II.:** **on-hādian.** Cf. un-hādian : **on-hǽld.** v. on-hildan : **on-hǽldedness.** v. on-hildedness.

**on-hǽtan; II.** *add:*—þā mædenn onǽldon and onhǽtton þǽra geongrena mōd tō forcyrrednesse heora synlustes *puellae discipulorum mentes ad perversitatem libidinis inflammabant*, Gr. D. 119, 14. Cf. in-hǽtan.

**on-hagian.** *Add:* **I.** absolute :—Beód mē þæt þæt þū wylle, ic hyt ongynne, gyf mē onhagað *impera quaevis dura, quae tamen in mea potestate sint, per quae me quo desidero perventurum esse non dubitem*, Solil. H. 46, 5. Dō gehwā georne on Godes ǽst, be þām þe hine fyrmest onhagie (*to the utmost extent of his ability*), Hml. A. 141, 85 : Wlfst. 103, 5. **II.** where that which is in one's power, &c., is denoted by tō. (1) *with a case following:*—Forgife mē þæt mē tō ǽgðrum onhagige, Solil. H. 2, 16. Ic nebbe swā dȳgela stōwe þæt mē tō swilcum weorce onhagie, 4, 13. (2) *with case preceding* :—Be þām þe ūs tō onhagað, Hml. A. 24, 4 : Wlfst. 303, 6. (3) *with dat. infin.* :—þǽra hálgena þrowunga þe mē tō onhagode on Englisc tō āwendene, Hml. S. pref. 37. (3 a) *where the infinitive is not expressed* :—Se cyning hine underfēng and swā feola his geféran swā him tō onhagode, Chr. 1052; P. 176, 29. Swā mid byttfyllinge swā elles swā ūs tō

anhagie (*sicut poterimus*), Ll. Th. i. 236, 4. **III.** without *tó.*
(1) with dat. infin.:—Seó racu ðe mé onhagað ðé tó gerihtreccenne,
Solil. H. 26, 7. Ne onhagað ús ná swíðor be ðám tó sprecenne, Hml.
Th. i. 488, 8. Ðæt ðætte hine ne onhagode útane forð tó brenganne
mid weorcum, innane hé hit geðafode *etsi rerum tarditas foras peccatum
distulit, intus hoc consensionis opere voluntas implevit*, Past. 417, 17.
Hwæt hine anhagige tó sellanne, hwæt hé healdan scyle *what is proper
for him to give, what he is to keep*, 341, 13. (2) with infinitive:—Oft
ðá monðwæran weorðað swá besolcne . . . ðæt hié ne anhagað náne wuht
nyttwyrðes dón *saepe mansueti dissolutionis torpescunt taedio*, Past. 289,
16. (3) with clause:—Þá þe heora hláfordas freógean noldon, oþþe
hié ne anhagade þæt hié mehten, Ors. 4, 9; S. 190, 34.

**on-heáfdu.** v. and-heáfdu: **on-healdan.** v. an-healdan.

**on-hebban.** *Add:* **VI.** of revolt, *to raise* oneself against authority:—
Hit gelamp þæt West-Wealas onhófon hí ongeán Ecgbriht cyng, Cht.
Crw. 18, 2. [v. *N. E. D.* on-heave. *O. Sax.* ant-hebbian: *O. H. Ger.*
ant-(int-)heffan: *Ger.* ent-heben.]

**on-hígian** *to attack, assault, proceed with violence against:—*
Onhígede *grassaretur*, An. Ox. 3438. Onhígiende *grassatrix*, 2209.
Onhígiendre *ingruenti*, 4952.

**on-hildan.** **I** I. *add:*—Mid þám þe hé þá flaxan onhyllde (-hylde,
*v. l.*), þá eóde ðær út án næddre *cum flasconem inclinasset, de eo serpens
egressus est*, Gr. D. 142, 11. **II.** *add:*—Fram dómum þínum ic
ne anhylde (*declinaui*), Ps. L. 118, 102.

**on-hildedness.** *Add:*—Onhældednes *declinatio*, Ps. Vos. 72, 4.

**on-hladan** *to unload, discharge:—Discarruta solue carrum*, i.
ondhlath (*printed* -hlelth), Hpt. 33, 250, 6. [*O. H. Ger.* ant-(int-)
hladan: *Ger.* ent-laden.]

**on-hnigan; II.** *add:*—Hé tó manna fótum onhnáh (-hnág, *v. l.*),
Hml. A. 151, 9. Nis gedafenlic þ þú tó mínum fótum onhníge, 156,
124.

**on-hón.** **I.** *to hang* (trans.), *suspend*[:—Sumne hí onhéngon be
þan fótum, and sumne be þan earmum, Hml. A. 171, 36.] **II.** *to
hang* on a gallows or cross, *to crucify:*—On þæm eahtateóþan geáre his
ríces, þá Críst wæs áhangen (on-, *v. l.*) (*cum Christus patibulo suffixus
est*), Ors. 6, 2; S. 256, 15. Ic gemétte þone cásere onhangen, Hml. A.
191, 286. Þone onhangenan Hælend ic séce, 188, 220. v. á-hón.

**on-hrægel.** *Dele.* The passage glossed is: *In sabanis . . .
bajulabantur aegroti. On* glosses in.

**on-hreósan** *to fall with violence upon, assail, attack:*—Onhrióseð,
anhriósit, anhrísit *ingruerit*, Txts. 69, 1077. Hú longe onhreósað
(onáhreóse, Ps. L.) gé on men *quousque inruitis in homines*, Ps. Vos.
61, 4. Anhreósaþ *inruunt* (*venti in domum*, Mt. 7, 25), Wrt. Voc. ii.
72, 27. Forhergad mid onhreósendum hægle *grandine irruente vastata*,
Gr. D. 57, 5. Onhreósendre mettrumnesse hé geneálæhte tó deaðe *qui
ingruente aegritudine ad mortem veniens*, 195, 20. Cf. á-hreósan.

**on-hrínan.** *Add:* (1) with gen. or uncertain :—Is wén ðæt sió
(fennege) hond ða óðre besmíte gif hió hire auhrínð, Past. 77, 1. Gif
his mon onhrínð mid buccan blóde, 271, 3. Heó mid hire ýtemestan
fingrum þære lenticula onhrán, Hml. S. 23 b, 715. Ær ðís his onhríéne
(-hríne, *v. l.*), Past. 241, 13. Gif man mid unclænum handum hwylces
metes onhrine, Ll. Th. ii. 164, 8. (2) with dat. :—Hé ne mæg þám
sáre mid handa onhrínan, Lch. ii. 198, 24.

**on-hróp.** **I.** *add:*—Hé mid gemálicum bénum befealh þám hálgan
were, þ him wære álýfed út tó farenne. Se fæder weard geswenced mid
gedréfednysse his swiðlican onhrópes *cum . . . importunis precibus ut
relaxaretur immoneret, pater nimietatis ejus taedio affectus*, Gr. D. 156,
6. Þæt hé ná sí geled óðres mid onhrópe *ut non impediatur alterius
inprobitate*, R. Ben. I. 87, 4 (= R. Ben. 81, 9 *in Dict.*).

**on-hryre,** es; *m. An* assault, attack:—Onrire *fulmen*, An. Ox.
50, 32.

**on-hycgan** *to consider, reflect on:*—Onhicgað nú hálige mihte, wíse
wundor Godes, Dan. 473.

**on-hyreness.** *Add:*—Wilt þú þ þú hwæthugu in Nonnoses weorce
oncnáwe eác be Heliseus onhyrenesse? *visne aliquid in operatione
Nonnosi de imitatione quoque Elisaei cognoscere?*, Gr. D. 50, 5.

**on-hyriend.** *Add:*—Andig, . . . onhyriend *zelotypus*, An. Ox. 364.
Onhiriend, Hpt. Gl. 415, 1. His þæs clǽnan lífes onhergend (-hyrgend,
*v. l.*) *imitatores suos in virtutibus*, Gr. D. 23, 2.

**on-hyring.** *Add:*—Hí tó þære onhyringe his forhæfednysse hí
underðeóddon, Hml. S. 23 b, 31. Ic syngede þurh onherunge *peccaui
per emulationem*, Confess. Peccat.

**on-hyscan.** **II.** *add:*—Sé þe forsihð þearfan onhyscð (*exprobrat*)
Scyppende his (*he that oppresseth the poor reproacheth his Maker*, Prov.
14, 31), Scint. 178, 17. Onhyscan *infamare*, An. Ox. 17, 23.

**on-innan.** *Add:* **I.** as *adv.*:—Þonne hit hát wære, and mon þá
earman men oninnan dón wolde, Ors. 1, 12; S. 54, 25. Þonne þær
micel stán . . . oninnan fealþ, Bt. 6; F. 14, 29; B. 71 : 2089. **II.** as
*prep.* (1) preceding the governed word:—Gefealden oninnan ðæs
synfullan monnes ingeðonc, Past. 243, 1. Hí hira yfel helað oninnan
him selfum, 449, 9. (2) following the governed word:—Hire mǽre

gewearð mann oninnan *homo factus est in ea*, Ps. Th. 86, 4. Þenden
þe wunað gást oninnan, Gen. 909. Ofne oninnan, Dan. 259. Wel bið
þám eorle þe him oninnan hafað rúme heortan, Alm. 1. Hit him
oninnan cóm, Gen. 723. Burgum oninnan, B. 1968 : Jul. 691 : Gú.
1341 : El. 1057. v. þær-oninnan.

**on-íwan.** *Add:* **I.** *to show* :—Ðá seó sunne begann onýwan eallum
mannum hire ðone beorhtan leóman, Hml. S. 23, 263. **II.** reflex.
with complement, *to appear* so and so :—Ne sceall ic nǽfre læng un-
þancfull þære þegnunge mé onýwan þám were *viro illi qui mihi solet
obsequi ingratus apparere non debeo*, Gr. D. 343, 12.

**on-lǽtan.** *Add:* [*O. H. Ger.* ant-(int-)lázan *laxare, remittere:
Ger.* ent-lassen.]

**on-léc.** *Add:*—Anléc (-léc) *respectus*, Ælfc. Gr. Z. 175, 7.

**on-leccan.** *Add:* v. læccan, leccung.

**on-lecgende.** For 'on-lying' substitute 'that is to be laid on, that
is to be applied to a wound', and add:—Wiþ sweórcoþe, wyrc on-
lecgende sealfe. Genim fearres gelyndo and beran smeru and weax,
ealra emfela, wyrc tó sealfe, smire mid, Lch. ii. 48, 5.

**on-leopian.** v. on-liþian.

**on-líc.** *Add:*—Sé bið swíðe onlíc ðæm stióran, Past. 431, 35. Hé
bið getíéged óðrum monnum mid onlícre gecynde *aequa ceteris naturae
conditione constringitur*, 111, 20. Hé hæfde twégen gingran suiðe
gelíces willan and on eallum ðingum suiðe onlíce, and hé hié ðeah lǽrde
suiðe ungelíce *duobus discipulis non diversa caritate praeditis, diversa
tamen adjutoria praedicationis impendit*, 291, 14.

**on-lícan.** v. ge-onlícan.

**onlíce.** *Add:*—Hié beóð onlícost suelce hí beren ðone ceak *velut
luterem portant*, Past. 105, 12.

**on-lícness.** *Add:* (1) *likeness, that to which a thing may be compared* :—Is leornod on bócum þæt on þysse worulde sýn fíf onlícnessa be
hellegryre. Sió ǽreste onlícnes is nemned wræc, Verc. Först. 106, 11.
(2) (in the) *likeness* of something :—Cirice on scræfes onlícnesse ǽteowed,
Bl. H. 197, 18. (3) *likeness* to something :—Ðá láreówas habbað onlícnesse ðæm kokkum, Past. 459, 31.

**on-lícung,** e; *f. Similitude, likeness:*—Hálígra fædera anlícung and
efenlǽcing *similitudo patrum*, Chrd. 71, 13.

**on-lígian,** -légian *to inflame:*—Gesprec Dryhtnes onlégade (*infla-
mavit*) hine, Ps. Vos. 104, 19.

**on-líhtan.** **IV.** *add:*—þám restedæges ǽfene sé þe onlíhte on þám
forman restedæge *vespere sabbati quae lucescit in prima sabbati*, Mt. 28,
1. [v. *N. E. D.* on-light.]

**on-líhtend,** es; *m. One who enlightens:*—Drihten is mín onlýhtend
and mín hǽlend *Dominus illuminatio mea et salus mea*, Ps. Th. 26, 1.

**on-lísan.** *Add:* [*O. H. Ger.* ant-(in-)lósen *solvere*.]

**on-lísend,** es; *m. A redeemer:*—Ealles middaneardes onlýsend,
Angl. xii. 500, 5. Under þám líðan iuke úres álýsendes (onlýsendes,
*v. l.*) *sub leni Redemtoris jugo*, Gr. D. 117, 2.

**on-lísendlic; adj.** *That may be released:*—þ þone sweltendan seó
biternes þæs deaðes gedyde onlýsendlicne fram þære scylde *ut illum
amaritudo mortis a culpa solubilem faceret*, Gr. D. 345, 2. v. un-
onlísendlic.

**on-lísness.** *Add:*—Ongan mín mód smeágean hweþer ǽnig lǽcedóm
wǽre his generenesse and onlýsnesse *coepit animus meus si quod esset
ereptionis ejus remedium quaerere*, Gr. D. 345, 21.

**on-liþian,** -leoþian *to loosen, relax.* (1) literal :—Swá þá gewunedon þá þwangas swylce hí þær gemétte wǽron of mycclum dǽle untogone
and onleoðode (-liðode, *v. l.*) *ita ut inventae sunt, magna jam ex parte
dissolutae corrigiae remanserunt*, Gr. D. 222, 4. (2) figurative :—In
hefigum wísum ealle þá (*various faults*) after deaðe hefigiað, gif hí nǽron
ná ǽr gebétte ne ná onleoðode þá hwíle þe se man wæs in þissum lífe
*quae cuncta etiam post mortem gravant, si adhuc in hac vita positis
minime fuerint relaxata*, Gr. D. 328, 21. v. ge-liþian.

**on-lóciend.** *Add:*—Hyre byrigen is swutol eallum onlóciendum,
Hml. Th. i. 440, 13. Hé gehyrte eallum onlócigendum, Hml. S. 22,
140.

**on-lúcan.** **I.** *add:*—Ðonne seó cest bið onlocen, þonne cymeð ðær
upp wunderlic stenc, Shrn. 67, 27. **II.** *add:*—Hé ús má onlýhð,
nú ús bóceras beteran secgað, lengran lyftwynna, Exod. 529. Se Wísdóm
wordhord onleác, Met. 6, 1.

**on-lútan.** *Add:* (1) of physical movement :—Onleát hé wépende
tó ðæs fótum and him bæd forgifnesse, Shrn. 145, 31. Nim æppel . . .
dó hyne ádúne and onlút, Lch. i. 330, 24. Hé forð onloten tó his fótum
ongan biddan *provolutus ejus pedibus coepit postulare*, Gr. D. 53, 23 :
130, 2. Onloten tó his gebede *orationi intentus*, 275, 14. (2) of
mental attitude :—Ús is micel ðearf ðæt wé eáðmódlíce ofdúne anlúten
mid úrum móde *necesse est ut ad infirma sua mentis oculus redeat,
seseque deorsum premat*, Past. 467, 7. Wé noldon tó ðǽm spore mid
úre móde onlútan, 5, 18.

**on-mang.** *Add:*—Hé ásende his lác onmang óþra monna lácum,
Gr. D. 230, 20. Syððan hé hæfde gewunad onmang mannum þreó and
xxx wintra, Wlfst. 292, 11. Rihtgeleáfa ásprang onmang Godes

geladunge, 294, 3. Onǽlde his blācern onmang þǽre þearlan hǽtan þæs lustes, Hml. A. 196, 44. Onmang þisse sprǽce, Angl. viii. 308, 34.

**on-merca** *inscription;* inscriptio, Mk. L. R. 12, 16: **on-mēdan.** *Dele, and see* mēdan.

**on-mēdla.** *Add:*—Hē tesoword spræc in his onmēdlan gealpettunga, Nap. 27, 40.

**on-mēttan.** v. -mēttan.

**on-middan.** *Add:* ¶ *where the governed noun comes between* on *and* middan:—þā wæs þǽr ān mycel burh on heora wege middan, Hml. S. 25, 440. Hē wearð forbærned on þǽm bæþe middan, Hml. A. 60, 209.

**on-norþan;** *prep. On the north side of:*—Ācrind onnorþan treówe be eorþan, Lch. ii. 108, 27. Onnorþan neoþan þān treówe, 126, 5.

**ono.** *Add: See* Bd. M. i. xxix: **on-orettan.** *l.* -ōrettan.

**on-orþung.** *Add:*—Mid blǽde deóflicre onorþunge *flatu diabolicę inspirationis,* Scint. 112, 12.

**on-rād.** In l. 2 *for* 'fatigue' *substitute* 'benefit'.

**on-rǽs.** *Add:* I. *of violent movement:*—Fērde eall seó heord myclum onrǽse (*impetu*) niwel on þā sǽ *all the herd went with a great rush headlong into the sea,* Mt. 8, 32. II. *of hostile movement.* (1) *by a living creature, attack, assault:*—Ān hrem bewerode þ līc . . . and þā rēðan deór āfīgde mid his onrǽsum, Hml. S. 37, 243. (2) *of destructive movement by a thing.* (a) *material:*—Ongan seó bryne beón gebīged in hī sylfe, efne swā swā mid bignesse his āgnes onrǽses (*sui impetus*), Gr. D. 48, 7. Onrǽs *inruptionem (diluuii)*, An. Ox. 2480. (b) *non-material:*—Gālnysse onraes byrnende innoþe gesylledum æthabban ys unmihtelic *libidinis impetum ardentem ventre satiato retinere est impossibile,* Scint. 57, 8. III. *of military operations.* (1) *invasion, incursion, attack of a country:*—Đā fǽrlīce weard þæs fyrlenan leódscipes onrǽs intō Gallias, Hml. S. 31, 95. Fram onrǽse *ab incursu,* Ps. L. 90, 6. Ofslagene wurdon fela þæs folces mid fǽrlicum onrǽsum, Ælfc. T. Grn. 20, 44. (2) *an attack, assault on a body of troops:*—On þām forman onrǽse hē āfīgde Ualentinianum, Hml. S. 31, 646.

**on-rǽsend,** es; *m. One who assaults:*—Fram onrǽsendum on mē *ab insurgentibus in me,* Ps. L. 17, 49.

**on-reáfian** *to despoil, deprive of (gen.):*—Mīn Drihten, sié þe þonc þæs þe þū lēte þinne līchoman onreáfian (be-, *v. l.*) ðīnes hrægles, Angl. xii. 505, 17.

**on-rid** *a riding horse, steed, mount:*—Ǽlcon hīredmen his onrid þe hē ālǽned hæfde, Cht. Crw. 23, 25. *See* p. 132. [Dauid . . . bead heom þ heo of heora anride lihtæn sceoldon, H. R. N. 18, 29. Cf. p. 38.]

**on-riht;** *adv. Aright, rightly:*—Mid repsum tō þām onriht (*rite*) belimpendum, Angl. xiii. 426, 877. Sē āna þē āriht sēcð þe ðū onriht lǽrst þæt hy ðē sēcan *omnis recte quaesivit, quem tu recte quaerere fecisti,* Solil. 13, 8. Hī ne gelȳfdan onriht on Crīst, Hml. S. 3, 356: 309. *See, too,* riht; III, VI.

**on-rihtlīce.** *Add:* v. on-unrihtlīce.

**onrip-tīd,** e; *f. Harvest-time:*—Gif þunor bið mycel eást odðe nordeást, mycel wæstm bið and gōd onrīptīd, Archiv cxx. 48, 24.

**on-sacan.** *Add:* I a. *to refute:*—On Beelzebub hine mæge cuedende onsōc *in Beelzebub eum posse dicentes redarguit,* Mk. p. 3, 1. II. *add: to refuse* an invitation:—Tācon soecendum sealla onsōc *signum quaerentibus dari negat,* Mk. p. 3, 19. Hierusalem geðreáðe gescilde onsæccende *Hierusalem increpat protegi respuentem,* Lk. p. 8, 8. III a. *add:*—Ne ðec onsæcco (andsace, R.) ic non te negabo, Mt. L. 26, 35. Mec onsæcest (ondsacest, R.), 75. Ic onsæcco ł ic willo onsacca (onsaece ic, R.) hine, Mt. L. 10, 33. Onsæcen (oncæccen, L.) bið *denegabitur,* Lk. R. 12, 9. (b):—Onsæce (-sæcce, L.) hine solfne *deneget seipsum,* Mk. R. 8, 34. Onsaca hine seolfne *abnegare seipsum,* Mt. p. 17, 18. (c):—Đū onsæccest þte ðū cūðes meh *abneges nosse me,* Lk. L. 22, 34. Iōhannes onsæcces (*negat*) þ hē sié Crīst, Jn. p. 3, 4. Đā ðe onsæccað þte sē ērest, Lk. L. R. 20, 27. Ne onsōc (ondsōc, L.), Jn. R. 1, 20. Gif hē hit þonne geondette, and onsace ǽr, Ll. Th. i. 148, 3. Sē þe bið werfǽhðe betogen, and hē onsacan wille þæs sleges mid āðe, 136, 10. Ansacan (on-, *v. l.*), 130, 10. Onsæccendum allum *negantibus omnibus,* Lk. L. 8, 45. V. *to renounce, give up claim to:*—Sē ðe ne onsæcað (*renuntiat*) allum ðǽm ðe āgniges, Lk. L. 14, 33.

**on-sæc.** *Add:* III. *denied, refused:*—Onsæcca ðǽm gefēro milsia *negata conservo miseratione,* Mt. p. 18, 8.

**on-sǽge.** *Add:*—Lāriówas āfeóllun and ūt gewitun of Angla lande for þǽre geleáfēste þe him þā onsǽge weard, Cht. Crw. 19, 8.

**on-sǽgedness.** II. *add:*—Crīst is Lamb gehāten . . . and wæs . . . his Fæder līflic onsǽgednys, Hml. Th. i. 358, 18. Hē bebeád þæt wē sceolon gearcian ūre līchoman līflice onsǽgednysse . . Se līchama bið līflic onsǽgednys ðe . . ., 482, 11–13. [Līfli]cere ansǽgednysse (ansagenysse, Hpt. Gl. 477, 12) *viventis hostig,* An. Ox. 3010. Wē sceolon Gode āsecgan þā dæghwāmlican onsǽgednesse ūra teāra and eác þā dæghwāmlican onsǽgednesse his līchaman and blōdes *debemus quotidiana*

*Deo lacrymarum sacrificia. quotidianas carnis et sanguinis hostias immolare,* Gr. D. 348, 16, 18. Hió offrede hiore ansegednesse *immolavit victimas suas,* Kent. Gl. 285.

**on-sǽte,** es; *n.* (?) *A sitting on* an animal:—Æfter þām onsǽte (-sitte, *v. l.*) swā hāliges biscopes þæt hors wiðsōc þ hit wīf bǽre *post sessionem tanti pontificis equus mulierem ferre recusavit,* Gr. D. 183, 10. Cf. on-setl.

**on-sǽtness,** e; *f. Ambush, artifice, plot.* Take here Rtl. 121, 40 *under* on-setness; II. *in Dict.*

**on-sǽtnung,** e; *f. Plot, wile,* Rtl. 147, 13 (*at* on-setnung *in Dict.*).

**on-sagu.** *Add:* [v. N. E. D. on-saw.]

**on-sand.** *Add:*—Insende on him . . . æbylgðe and eorre and geswinc, onsonda þurh engla vfle *inmisit in eis indignationem et iram et tribulationem, inmissiones per angelos malos,* Ps. Vos. 77, 49. [v. N. E. D. on-sand.]

**on-sang,** es; *m. Au incantation:*—þā drȳas mid langsumum onsangum (galdrum, *v. l.,* *incantationibus*) hī gōlon on (hyre on gōlon, *v. l.*), Gr. D. 73, 26.

**on-scǽgan.** *Add: Perhaps* onscæudon *should be read for* onscægdon. Cf. Gehyscton ł scęndon *subsannauerunt,* Ps. L. 79, 7. Gescent (tæld, L., hyspeð, Vos. Rdr. Srt.) *subsannabit,* Ps. Th. 2, 4. *See next word.*

**on-scendan** *to put to shame, confound, mock:*—þær wæs onscynded manna heortena heardnes *hominum duritia confunditur,* Gr. D. 194, 6. *See preceding word.*

**on-sceótan** *to unbar, open:*—Ansceát (-s(c)eút, Erf.) *exintera,* Txts. 61, 791. Ansceót *exintera,* Wrt. Voc. ii. 29, 71. v. un-sceótan.

**on-scillan** *to echo, resound:*—Onscilþ, oncwyð *remugiet* (ad Archangeli vocem totus simul *remugiet* mundus, Ald. 65, 21), An. Ox. 8, 265.

**on-scōgan** *to unshoe, take off a shoe:*—Onscō mē *discalcea me,* Gr. D. 221, 22. His mægas hine anscógen ōðre fēt, ðæt mon mæge siððan hātan his tūn ðæs anscódan tūn *unum ei pedem propinquus discalciet, ejusque habitaculum domum discalceati vocet,* Past. 43, 16. [O. H. Ger. ant-(int-)scuohōn *denudare (pedem).*] Cf. un-scōg(i)an.

**on-scunian.** I. *take here from* III. Wrt. Voc. ii. 65, 16 : 2, 23 : 4, 74: 100, 41, *and add:*—Onscuniend *aporians,* i. *respuens* (olidarum polluta nuptiarum contubernia *aporians,* Ald. 24, 26), An. Ox. 1785. (Cf. aporia, abominatio subitania, Ld. Gl. H. 61.) II. *add:*—Gif mīn gerēfa onscunað *si quis huic ordinationi resistens hoc deuiat,* Ll. Th. i. 276, 26. 'Nelle wit (*the eyes*) nǽfre hǽr þā þeóstru þǽre nihte onscunian, ǽr wit magon þā sunnan sylfe geseón (*tum tenebras non amabo, cum solem videro*).' Đystlīce mē ðincð þæt þā ǽagan dōn, gyf hý onscuniað þǽra sunnan leóhtes þone dǽl þe hī hys geseón magon, Solil. H. 47, 5–9. Lōcian on fȳr ǽr ðām hē ongeán þā sunnan lōcie. Siþþan hē þat geleornod hæbbe þæt his eágan nānwyht þæt fȳr ne onscyniað, 45, 11. Đȳ lǽs hié herigen hiera gōdan weorc, and onscunigen ðæt hié selfe suā dōn *ne bona laudent, et agere recusent,* Past. 231, 13. III. *add:*—Swā micle lǽs ðæt mōd onscunað ðā miclan swā hit ǽr orsorglīcor gewunode tō ðǽm lytlum, and him ðā lǽs ondrēd *tanto in majoribus mens contemnat pertimescere, quanto in minimis didicit non temendo peccare,* Past. 437, 30.

**on-scuniendlic.** *Add:*—Sē þe onweg ācyrreð his eáre þ hē ne gehȳre þā Godes ǽ, þæs bēn byð onscuniendlic (-scunodlic, *v. l.,* *execrabilis*), Gr. D. 210, 3.

**on-scunodlic.** *See preceding word.*

**on-secgan.** I. *add:* (1) *absolute, to offer a sacrifice, sacrifice:*—þē þes dēma hafað wītu gegearwad, gif þū onsecgan nelt, Jul. 251. (1 a) *to sacrifice* to a divinity, &c.:—Ic onsæge ł ic offrige þē *sacrificabo tibi,* Ps. L. 53, 8. Hī ðām deófum onsægdon and heora Drihten forsāwon, Hml. S. 14, 13. þæt þū heofoncyninge wiðsōce, and onsægde synna fruman, Jul. 362. (1 aa) *to sacrifice* with something, Bl. H. 41, 10 (*in Dīct.*), cf. (4). (1 aβ) *to sacrifice* something:—Ongunnan sceuccum onsægean suna and dohter *immolaverunt filios suos et filias suas daemoniis,* Ps. Th. 105, 27. (2) *with cognate object.* (a) *to offer* a sacrifice:—Onsegcað onsegdnisse rehtwīsnesse *sacrificate sacrificium justitiae,* Ps. Srt. 4. 6. (b) *to offer* a sacrifice to :—Đē ic onsecgu onsegdnisse lofes, Ps. Srt. 115, 17. Gūðlāc Gode lāc onsægde and mæssan sang *immolato dominici corporis sacrificio et sanguinis Christi libamine,* Guth. Gr. 163, 43. Gode hæle tiber onsægde, Gen. 1502. Būtan þū him lāc onsecge, Jul. 199. (3) *to offer* something as a sacrifice:—þū scealt sunu þīnne onsecgan tō tibre, Gen. 2852. (4) *to offer* something in or by sacrifice. Cf. (1 b):—Wes þū on ofeste þæt þū lāc onsecge sigortifre, Jul. 255.

**on-secgend,** es; *m. A sacrificer:*—Hit þām onsecgende þǽre onsægdnysse fremode *sacrificatori sacrificii proficiebat,* Ll. Th. ii. 166, 16.

**on-sendan.** I. *add:* (1) *the object a person:*—Hē wæs onsended tō lǽranne, Past. 441, 30. Ic on suna þīnne gelȳfe, hǽlende cyning hider onsendne, Hy. 10, 10. (2) *the object a thing.* (a) *material, to*

*cause to be conveyed* to a goal :—Onsend Higelāce beaduscrūda betst, B. 452 : 1483. (b) of a missile (lit. or fig.) or destructive agency :—Drihten onsent manegra cynna wītu ofer ðā synfullan . . . hē onsent fȳr ofer hig, and ungemetlíce hǽto þǽre sunnan, Ps. Th. 10, 7. Wröhtbora in folc Godes forð onsendeð of his brægdbogan biterne strǽl, Cri. 764. On gramra gemang hetend hildenǽdran forð onsendan, El. 120. (c) of speech, *to address, direct* prayer, *send* a message :—Þislic ǽrende se pāpa eft onsende and þas word cwæð, Bl. H. 205, 22. Hē oft his word Gode ūp onsende, Gū. 748. Þīne bēne onsend in þā beorhtan gesceaft, El. 1089. (d) *to put in possession* of a non-material object :—Ic him in onsende bitre geþoncas, Jul. 404. Sige hȳ onsendað sōðfæstra gehwām, Sal. 244. Þē sāwle onsende þurh his sylfes hand Meotod, Seel. 28. Onsende þē fultum Drihten *mittat tibi auxilium Dominus*, Ps. Th. 19, 2. Ðætte him wæs onsended mid tō diélgianne hira synna *quod acceperant, ut possent delere peccata*, Past. 429, 15. II. *add*:—Þā þe hine forð onsendon ofer ȳðe, B. 45. II a. of a thing, *to have issuing forth*:—Þæt þū (*a stone pillar*) on þis folc onsende wæter, An. 1508. II b. of a destructive agency, *to send out of this life* :—Bealocwealm hafað fela feorhcynna forð onsended, B. 2266. v. an-sendan *in Dict.*

**on-setenness.** *Substitute:* **on-seteness, -setness. I.** *laying on, imposition*:—Fram þām rihtgeleáffullum bisceope onsetnesse (*manus impositioni*) and sume gebede beón getrymede, Ll. Th. ii. 232, 19. Þurh biscopa handa onsetenesse, Shrn. 85, 19 (*in Dict.*) **II.** *institution*. Take here Lk. L. R. 11, 50 (*from* on-setness ; I. *in Dict.*).

**on-setl**, es ; *n.* *A sitting on.* Cf. setl ; IV. :—Hē þæt hors mid his onsetle him sylfum tō ǽhte ǽr gehālgode *equum juri suo sedendo dedicaverat*, Gr. D. 183, 16. Cf. on-sǽte.

**on-setness. I.** v. on-seteness. **II.** v. on-sǽtness : **on-setnung.** *l.* -sætnung.

**on-settan.** *Add:* **I.** *to impose, place* one object on another; *imponere, superponere*:—Gif mon on nīwne weall hefigne hrōf onsett *structuris recentibus si tignorum pondus superponitur*, Past. 383, 33. Onsettað on (ofer, R.) scyldrum *imponit in umeros*, Lk. L. 15, 5. Ofer untrymigum honda onsettað (*inponent*), Mk. L. R. 16, 18. Onsette hond ofer ł on ðā ilco, 10, 16. Onsett hond ofer hiá *inpone manum super eum*, Mt. L. 9, 18. **II.** *to oppress, impede*:—Gemētton wē ūs ǽghwanon gelícne storm foran onsettende *inuenimus nos undiqueuersum pari tempestate praeclusos*, Bd. 5, 1 ; Sch. 552, 10. Cf. ā-, of-settan.

**on-sīgan.** *Add:* (1) of forces approaching to attack, *to come down on* :—Wē oferswīðdon þone onsīgendan here, Hml. S. 11, 71 : 31, 550 : 555 : O. E. Hml. i. 303, 3. (2) of evil that falls upon one :—For nähte bið geteald ānes geáres lust ðǽr ðǽr se swearta deáð onsīgende bið, Hml. Th. ii. 146, 16. Gregorius þæt Rōmānisce folc for ðām onsīgendum cwealme tō behreówsunge tihte, 124, 2. Uton standan mid gemāglicum wōpum ongeán ðām onsīgendum swurde swā m'ccles dōmes, 126, 1. (3) where defect is chargeable to wrong action :—Wite se abbod gylte(s) hyrdes onsīgan swā hwæt on sceápum se hīredes ealdor nytwyrðnesse hwónlícor swā mæg gemētan *sciat abbas culpe pastoris incumbere quicquid in ovibus paterfamilias utilitatis minus potuerit invenire*, R. Ben. I. 12, 5.

**on-sin.** *Add*:—Ic mīne sāwle sette mid mōde, swā eorðan bið ansȳn wæteres *I made my soul feel as want of water is for the ground ; anima mea sicut terra sine aqua tibi*, Ps. Th. 142, 6.

**on-sīne.** *Add:* [*Goth.* ana-siun[i]s *visible*; un-anasiuniba *invisibly*.]

**on-sitt.** v. on-sǽte.

**on-sittan. II.** v. sittan ; III. **III.** *add*:—Ic wolde gecyrran tō þyllicre drohtnunga, ac ic onsitte þ ic beó mīnum fæder ungehȳrsum, Hml. S. 33, 75. Hē him æfter þǽm gefeohte swīðor onsæt þonne hē ǽr dyde, Ors. 3, 9 ; S. 132, 34.

**on-sittend**, es ; *m.* *One who sits on* an animal, *a rider* :—Þā onsittendas (-an, *v. l.*) þāra horsa, Gr. D. 15, 10.

**on-slūpan** *to unloose, untie* :—Þā þwangas þāra scōna ongunnon heom sylfe onslūpan (*dissolvere*), Gr. D. 221, 23.

**on-smiring**, e ; *f.* *Anointing* :—Þæs hālgan eles mōton ealle crístene men notian tō heora freónda onsmyrunge *sancto oleo omnibus uti christianis in suorum necessitate unguentes*, Chrd. 80, 19.

**on-spannan.** *Add:* v. un-spannan : **on-spell.** v. an·spell.

**on-spillend**, es ; *m.* *A player, jester* :—Onspillendra *parasitorum*, Angl. xiii. 28, 29. v. spilian.

**on-sprǽc.** *Add:* **II.** *talk, conversation* :—Hér hwæne wiðufan þīne word and anspræc rehte and smeáde be þām wītelicum hellestōwum *paulo superius sermo de locis poenalibus inferni versabatur*, Gr. D. 332, 9. [*O. H. Ger.* ana-sprāhha *illatio : Germ.* ein-sprache *protest*.]

**on-spreca.** *Add* :—Beón ealdras leahtra anspecan and manna midspecan *sint rectores criminum persecutores et hominum liberatores*, Chrd. 62, 26. v. sprecan ; VI.

**on-springan.** *Add:* [*O. Sax.* ant-springan.]: **on-stæppan.** *Take here* on-steppan *in Dict.*: **on-stāl.** *Add:* Cf. on-sprǽc.

**on-standan. I.** *to consist* of *or* in. Cf. standan ; IV. :—Ic ealle mīne bēc, on þām þe se drȳcræft onstód, āwearp, Hml. Th. ii. 418, 14. **II.** *to persist, continue* :—Þæt mīnes worldlífes bletsung anstande *ut mundanae meae vitae benedictio permaneat*, Ll. Th. ii. 228, 4. Mid onstandendum geswince *instanti labore*, Scint. 111, 14. **II a.** *to insist, persist in demand* :—Hiá onstōdon stefnum miclum *illi instabant uocibus magnis*, Lk. L. R. 23, 23. **III.** *to apply* one's self *to* :—Þā þe of geswincum andlefene . . . tō begitanne geornlíce onstandaþ *qui laboribus . . . uictum . . . adquirere inhianter instant*, Chrd. 111, 1. [*O. H. Ger.* ana-stān *inhaerere, instare.*] Cf. ā-standan.

**on-stedfullness.** *l.* -stedefullness, *and add:* v. un-stedefullness.

**on-stellan.** *Add:*—Hē onstalde on ðǽm bisene ðǽm receerum *exemplum rectoribus praebens*, Past. 102, 6. Forlǽtan wē . . . ealle þā þeáwas þe dióflu on him sylfum onstealdon, Verc. Först. 94, 4. Hire nome . . . þe me ǽrst hire onstalde, Laym. 7132. Cf. *Ger.* an-stellen.

**on-stēpan** *to raise. Add: to initiate* (?). v. stēpan : **on-stillan.** v. stillan.

**on-sting.** *Add: the right to intervene, or thrust oneself into, the affairs of another.* Cf. stingan ; I a :—Icc nelle nāteswhōn geþafian þ þǽr ǽnig man ǽnigne onstyng habbe on ǽnigum þingum, Cht. E. 303, 10. v. in-sting.

**on-stingan** *to be angry* with (?) :—Sē ðe on þām sylfan cildan būtan smēgunge onstingð *qui in ipsis infantibus sine discretione exarserit*, R. Ben. I. 115, 16.

**on-styrenes.** *Add:*—Onstyrenisse ȳða his ðū gemildgas *motum fluctuum ejus tu mitigas*, Ps. Srt. 88, 10. Ne seleð on onstyrenesse (*commotionem*) ðīnne fōt, Ps. Vos. 120, 3.

**on-styrian. I.** *in* l. 1 *after* líchoma *insert* hine, *and add*:—Ne myhton hig nähwyder þā fæmnan onstyrian . . . sume sceufon, sume tugon, and swȳðe swǽtton . . . and seó Godes fæmne hwæðre stód, Shrn. 154, 25. Ne mihte hundteóntig oxena þone stān onstyrian (*movere*), Gr. D. 49, 10. Ongan þ wrigels beón upp āhafen. Onstyredum þām wrigelse . . . *coepit operimentum sublevari. Quo commoto* . . ., 160, 12. **III.** *add:* (1) where the passion or feeling excited is given (*dat. or prep.*) :—Hié beóð anstyred (on-, *v. l.*) mid hiera ierre, Past. 293, 23. Ic wæs swīðe mid hleahtre onstyred *magno risu sum dissolutus*, Nar. 19, 7. Wæs hē miclum (mid miclum, *v. l.*) wylme and yrre onstyred *nimio furore commotus*, Bd. 1, 7 ; Sch. 23, 4. (2) where the exciting cause is given :—Ðā wæs for his fromscype onstyred Ædon *motus eius profectibus Aedan*, Bd. 1, 34 ; Sch. 104, 15. v. in-styrian ; unonstyrod.

**on-styrigendlic.** v. un-onstyrigendlic.

**on-sund. I.** *add*:—Swā mid mīne werode onsunde in Patriacen þ lond wē becwōman, Nar. 17, 15.

**on-sundrum. I.** *add*:—Oþ þæt cildra inngān þā cyrcean ān onsundron sē gehringed belle (*let a bell be rung without the accompaniment of any other ?*; but the Latin is : Unum continuatim pulsetur tintinnabulum), Angl. xiii. 380, 211.

**on-swornod** *confused* :—Þonne stent ðæt deáde flǽsc onswornod (ā-, *v. l.*) and ne mæg nān andwyrde syllan, Nap. 7.

**on-tendan. I.** *add:* (1) *to set on fire so as to consume* :—Hē ealle ofslōh mid swurdes ecge and ontende þā burh, Hml. S. 25, 416. (2) *to set on fire* what is to give light, *light* a candle, lamp, &c , Lch. iii. 286, 6 (*in Dict.*). (2 a) of the illumination of the moon by the sun :—Gyf se mōna æfter sunnan setlunge ontend byð . . . ne byð hē nīwe geteald, Lch. iii. 266, 5. (3) *to kindle* fire, Ll. Th. 1. 50, 27–28 (*in Dict.*). (4) *to heat* a furnace, Hml. S. 5, 294 (*in Dict.*). (5) *to burn* by exposure to fire :—Hē heóld his finger ofer þæt byrnende leóht . . . and his fingras ealle ontende, Hml. A. 196, 49. **II.** *add: to inflame* a person with passion, emotion, &c. :—Hē weard mid micclum graman ontend, Hml. S. 28, 54. His mōd swīðe weard ontend on hīre gewilnunge tō his gālnesse *cor Holofornis concussum est : erat ardens in concupiscentia ejus*, Hml. A. 111, 289. Antend *succenditur* (*livoris zelo*), An. Ox. 2772. Antende *inflammantur* (*superni ardoris facula*), 977.

**on-tendness.** *Add: burning.* Cf. on-tendan ; I. 5 :—Wē nū byrnað ǽr ðan ðe se tīma cōme ūre ontendnysse, Hml. Th. ii. 414, 35. Lǽt hine on ūrum anwealde, þæt wē magon ðinne teónan wrecan and ūre ontendnysse, 416, 20. **III.** *add* :—Hē oferswȳðde þā synne, for þām þe hē swā onwende þā ontendnysse (þā hǽte and þone synlust, *v. l.*) *vicit peccatum, quia mutavit incendium*, Gr. D. 101, 28. [v. *N. E. D.* ontend.]

**on-teón. I.** *to withdraw, pull away, extract* :—Ðonne þū wīn habban wille, þonne dō þū mid þīnum twām fingrum swilce þū tæppan of tunnan onteón wille, Tech. ii. 120, 10. **II.** *to pull apart, untie* :—Gewunedon þā þwangas . . . of mycclum dǽle ontogone (un-, *v. l.*) *magna ex parte dissolutae corrigiae remanserunt*, Gr. D. 222, 3. [*O. H. Ger.* ant-(in-)ziohan *ab-, de-, dis-trahere, extricare : Ger.* ent-ziehen.]

**on-þeón.** *Add:*—Wit þǽre beadwe bēgen ne onþungan, Rä. 85, 23.

**on-þracian.** *Add:*—Andþraciaþ *herescunt* (*horrescunt* seems to have been read. Cf. *horrescunt* andþrachiað, Hpt. Gl. 481, 24: both are glosses on Ald. 43, 38). Hī anðraciað tō gefarenne lífes wegas, and

swā ðeáh ne wandiað tō licgenne on stuntnysse heora ásolcennysse *they dread to travel the ways of life, and yet do not shrink from lying in the folly of their sloth,* Hml. Th. ii. 554, 1. Se man þe næbbe of hwām hē mæge rūmlíce ælmessan syllan, ne onðracige hē for ðām (*let him not be alarmed on that account*), Hml. A. 141, 80. Scamigan hí and anðracian (*reuereantur*) þā sēcendan sáwle míne, Ps. L. 34, 4. þā begann se wer wēpan anðracigende ðæs ungelimpes (*the untoward event* (ungelimp) *was the madness of the man's pious wife: the occasion of his fear on account of it is explained in* Vit. Cuth. c. 15: Timebat, ne cum eam (*the wife*) daemoniosam inueniret, arbitrari inciperet, quia non integra Domino sed ficta fide seruisset), Hml. Th. ii. 142, 13. v. ge-onþracian.

on-þracung, e; f. *Fear :*—Sýn gescrýdde mid sceame and anðracunge *induantur confusione et reuerentia*, Ps. L. 34, 26.

on-þræc. *Add :*—Þā ofseáh hē ða hæðenan ferian án líc tō eorðan mid anþræcum gehlýde, Hml. Th. ii. 508, 17. Scuton hí intō ðæm anðræcum cyle *prosiliebant in medium rigoris infesti*, 350, 11. Seó dene wæs weallende mid anðræcum lígum, on ánre sídan (cf. unum latus flammis feruentibus nimium terribile, Bd. 5, 12), 350, 7. Tengdon þā hæþenan mid andþrecum wǽpnum tō þám ǽwfæstum heápe, Hml. S. 28, 67.

on-þræclic ; adj. *Horrible :*—Wæs þǽr sum hreófla wundorlíce tōhroren, eallum mannum anþræclic, Hml. S. 31, 565. v. ǽ-þræclic.

on-þryccan *to impress :*—Þā his swaða ðe þǽr onþricced (on þricced?) sendon, Shrn. 81, 4.

on-þwægenness, e ; f. *Cleansing by washing, ablution :*—Seó onðwægennyss þǽra fóta gástlíce tácnað gehwæðer ge lichaman clǽnnysse ge eác sáwle, Hml. A. 157, 138. þā gástlican onþwægennysse, þis is þ hálige fulwihtes bæð and synna forlǽtennysse, 158, 154.

on-þweán. *Add :*—Weard þǽr forðféred sumes earmes wífes ceorl .. hí hine þwógon (onþwógon, *v. l.*) and mid hrægle gegyredon (*quem ex more lotum et vestimentis indutum*), Gr. D. 215, 19. v. á-þweán.

on-timber. I. *add :*—Þæs mannes líchaman antimber bið of ðām fæder and of ðǽre mēder, ac God gescypð þone líchaman of ðām antimbre, Hml. Th. i. 292, 28. Salomon árǽrde þæt mǽre hūs of eorðlicum antimbre, ii. 580, 11 : Wlfst. 279, 25. Sume (*some adjectives*) synd ... of ōðrum antimbre, *ferrum* ísen, *ferreus* ísen, Ælfc. Gr. Z. 15, 9. Beó his calic of clǽnum antimbre geworht, Ll. Th. ii. 350, 22. Tō þǽm ǽrrum antimbre geedníwude *in pristinum statum reformavit* (*dispersa gemmarum fragmina*), An. Ox. 1833 : 1875. II. *add : matter* for a feeling, &c. :—Ontimber (bið) gesæld tō mótgenne *materia ei datur superbiendi*, R. Ben. I. 604, 25. Druncennys is gálnysse antimber, Hml. Th. i. 604, 25. Eáþe is tō understandenne of hwylcum antimbre þeós unþræslicu ásprincð, R. Ben. 124, 13. Þ nán þurh nán antimber (*pro nulla occasione*) ne gedyrstlǽce ōðerne wergean, Chrd. 46, 12.

on-timberness. *Add : material :*—Heora goldes ontimbernesse *materia auri*, Verc. Först. 119, 14.

on-tíned. *Add :* An earlier MS. has : Sǽ and ealle eá beóð mid fixum áfylde, Archiv cxxviii. 66, 7.

on-trymian, -trymman *glosses* invalescere :—Hiá ontrymmedon (-trymedun, R.) *illi inualiscebant*, Lk. L. 23, 5 : 23.

on-tydran, -tydre. *l.* on-týdran, -týdre.

on-tygness *the state of a person in respect to the frequency of the charges brought against him :*—Be cirlisces monnes ontygnesse at ðíésðe, Ll. Lbmn. 22, 23. v. 104 § 37.

on-tyhtan. *Add :*—Gif hē hit herede and ontyhte (on tyhte?), eft hē stíerde ðǽre gewilnunge, Past. 53, 8. Nát ic hwí þū sý eallinga onǽled and ontihted (-tiht, *v.l.*) of þára bysne and widmetenysse *ex quorum comparatione accenderis ignoro*, Gr. D. 7, 10. Ontihtum geþance *intente mente*. Scint. 27, 2. *See next word.*

on-tyhting, e ; f. I. *instigation, incitement :*—Ná ealle yfele geþancu úre symle deófles ontihtincge beóð áwehte *non omnes male cogitationes nostrae semper diaboli instinctu excitantur*, Scint. 139, 11. II. *intention, resolution :*—Stefen sealmsanges þænne heó þurh ontihtincge (*intentionem*) heortan byþ gedôn, Scint. 27, 1. Ælce ontihtincge and bígencg líchaman *omnem intentionem et studium corporis*, 49, 2.

on-týnan. I c. *add :*—Pater Noster heofenas ontýned, Sal. 40. Gif hwá wæterpyt betýuedne ontýne, Ll. Th. i. 50, 6. (c a) intrans. (reflex) :—Þā ontýnde se heofon, Shrn. 117, 3. I d. *add :*—Þā gyldnan geatu þe bilocen stódan hát ontýnan, Cri. 253. I e. *add :*—Se mereweard mūð ontýneð, wíde weleras, Wal. 53 : Rä. 76, 4. Ontýn þínne mūð *dilata os tuum*, Ps. Th. 80, 11. I h. *to open* what is compressed, *open* the hand ; fig. *to bestow liberally :*—Swylce þū wylle þíne þá hálgan hand ontýnan, ealle hí gefyllan fægere góde, Ps. Th. 103, 26. [*O. H. Ger.* ant-(in-)zûnen *aperire.*] v. un-týnan.

on-týnness. II. *Dele, and see* on-tygness.

onu. v. heonu.

on-ufan. *Add :* I. with dat. (1) local :—Hié hæfdon wæter genóg onufan þǽre dūne, Ors. 6, 13 ; S. 268, 16. Onufa lehtfæte *supra candelabrum*, Lk. L. 11, 33 : 20, 18 : 13, 4 : Jn. p. 4, 16. Þ tácon se groefa gesette ofer ł onufa ðær róde (*super crucem*), Jn. L. 19, 19. Þām þe sitteð

onufan meare, Rūn. 5. (2) marking degree :—Ðe ilca is onufa allum ł ofer allo *ipse est supra omnes*, Jn. p. 3, 7. (3) denoting object on which something takes effect :—On cýðnise onufa ðǽm ilcom *in testimonium supra illos*, Lk. L. 9, 5. Onwæld onufa tēnum ceastrum, 19, 17. Ǽr þon þe him se egesa onufan sǽte, Jud. 252 : Sal. 88. II. with acc. (1) local :—Ástigon onufa hūs *ascenderunt supra tectum*, Lk. L. 5, 19 : Wurpon gewoedo hiora onufa ðone folo, 19, 35. Gelionade hē onufa breóst ðæs Hælendes, Jn. R. 13, 25. Lege spic onufan þone nægl, Lch. ii. 150, 6. (2) of time :—xv niht onufan Eástran, Ll. Th. i. 262, 18 : 306, 31. Onufan þ ne eóde hē ná in þ hūs *domum ulterius non intravit*, Gr. D. 185, 14. (3) cf. I. 3 :—Mæht hénisǽs onufa all mæht fióndes *potestatem calcandi supra omnem uirtutem inimici*, Lk. L. 10, 19.

on-ufenan. v. þǽr-onufenan.

on-unrihtlíce ; adv. *Unjustly, wrongfully :*—Onunrihtlíce wē ne dydon on cýðnesse þíne *inique non egimus in testamento tuo*, Ps. Spl. 43, 20. v. on-rihtlíce.

on-unspéd. *Add :* For prefix cf. three following words.

on-unwis. *Add :*—Hē wēnde þ hē sprǽke onunwís (? on unwis ?) þá hē bebeád ... *quod quasi insana praeciperet*, Gr. D. 58, 1.

on-unwisdóm. *Probably this word should be rejected, for the passage in which it occurs seems corrupt :*—Ic wæs wiþermēde and unwísum nētenum gelíc geworden. Ac þū Drihten scyld mínre iugoþe and mín onunwísdómes ne wes þū gemyndig (= ? þu, Drihten, forgif þá scylde mínre iugoþe, and mínes unwísdómes ne wes þū gemyndig), Bl. H. 89, 10. *See, however, preceding word.*

on-uppan. I. *add :*—Ðā synfullan sceoldon bytlan onuppan his hrycge (*supra dorsum suum*), Past. 153, 10. Ne cóm hē náuht onuppan ðæm muntum, 399, 10. Þā sette Martinus his handa him onuppon, Hml. Th. ii. 510, 28. II. *add :*—Ælfwold gesealde Eádwolde and his sunum .c. panæga anuppan eall ðis óðer, C. D. B. iii. 491, 16. v. þǽr-onuppan.

on-útan ; adv. *Outside, out-of-doors :*—Æt hám gebring, and nǽfre in on þone mon, sceafe þ grēne onútan, Lch. ii. 292, 27.

on-wacan ; adv. I. *add :*—Sóna swá ic aunwôc, swá wilnode ic eft wínes *quando evigilabo, et sursum vina reperiam*, Past. 431, 17. II. *add :*—Tō þon þ him gewin eft þonan onwôce, Ors. 4, 13 ; S. 212, 18. [On-weócon *in the last line is probably an error for* onwócon, *the e being underdotted in the MS.*] v. wacan.

on-waciað *to watch over :*—þá þe manggungum onwaciaþ [on waciaþ ? *inuigilant*], Chrd. 110, 29.

on-wǽcan. *Add :*—Gif mid nánum ðissa ne bið onwǽced his inngeðonc *dum nullis passionibus intentionem mentis humiliat*, Past. 83, 20.

on-wǽcenness, e ; f. *Excitement, excitation :*—Hē sôhte dǽdbôte and inbryrdnesse wôp, tō ðon þ þurh þá onwæcenesse his môd áburne *fletum compunctionis inquirebat ; quatenus per haec excitata mens ejus inardesceret*, Gr. D. 337, 37.

on-wǽcnian. *Add :*—Of þám þrím sunum weard onwǽcnad eall manna cynn, Angl. xi. 2, 38. Onwæcnod, 3, 59.

on-wǽstm. *Add : shoot, branch :*—Drihten forbrycð þá myclan cedertreówu emne swá þá lytlan onwæstmas, Ps. Th. 28, 5. v. ó-wæstm.

on-warian *to take heed, beware :*—Is ūs tō behealdanne, þæt wē onwarigan þæt þǽra yfela and þǽra unríhta ne sý tō feala, Verc. Först. 105, 4. Is mycel þearf ǽghwylcum men tō onwariganne þæt hē þis symle hæbbe on gemyndum, 109, 10.

on-wealcan. Th. An. 116, 22 *is found at* Lch. i. 246, 10 *where* anwealche, anwelce *are v. ll.*

on-weald. *Add :* I. in a general sense, *power, control* over a person or thing :—Ðæt úre geswinc ne sceolde bión on óðres monnes onwalde (an-, *v.l.*), Past. 250, 2. II. of official rule. (1) secular :—Hē wæs Rômánum swá milde swá him nán onwald næs ǽr þǽm, Ors. 6, 2 ; S. 254, 22. Hit hæfde Agustus him tō onwalde gesæld, 6, 1 ; S. 254, 12. Hē betǽhte his twǽm sunum þone onwald, 6, 36 ; S. 294, 31. Rufinus wolde habban him self þone anwold, 6, 37 ; S. 296, 6. Wē witon þæt ealle onwealdas from Gode sindon ; wē witon eác þæt ealle rícu sint from him, for þon ealle onwealdas of ríce sindon *si potestates a Deo sunt, quanto magis regna, a quibus reliquae potestates progrediuntur*, 2, 1 ; S. 58, 23-25. Þā geweard hí þ hié woldon þá onwaldas forlǽtan and þá purpuran álecgan ... Hí léton þá onwealdas tō Galeriuse and tō Constantiuse ... Hí wǽs hwón giernende micelra onwalda, 6, 30 ; S. 280, 20-29. Þā hié gesomnod wǽron, and hiene tō cyninge dôn woldon, þā ne mehton hié þá gúðfonan úp áhebban. Swá hiora þeáw wæs, þonne hié onwaldas setton (*when they appointed governments*), 6, 4 ; S. 268, 2. (1 a) with gen. of persons over whom power is exercised :—Ilirice gesetton Ueteromonem tō hiora anwealde *in Illyrico Vetranionem imperatorem sibi milites creauerunt*, Ors. 6, 31 ; S. 284, 20. Féng Iuninianus tō Rômána onwalde, 6, 32 ; S. 286, 24. (2) ecclesiastical :—Sum biscop weard for þám gedwylde ádrǽfed of his anwealde, Hml. S. 31, 839. (3) divine :—Wuldor and onwæld *gloriam et imperium*, Rtl. 22, 6. [v. *N. E. D.* on-wald.] [On-weald *should be taken under* an-weald.]

on-wealh. I. *add :* of material objects :—Genim ðysse wyrte

wyrttruman swâ anwealhne (*as whole as possible*), Lch. i. 286, 18. Hit nys âlŷfed þ man hyre wyrtruman anwealhne geseón môte *it is not permitted that its root be seen when entire*, 318, 20. **II.** *add:* of non-material objects, *physically* or *morally perfect:*—Cwǣdon hî þæt heó wǣre onwelges mægðhâdes and unwemme, Hml. A. 134, 603. Ðæt hié ðâ sibbe anwealge oninnan him gehealden, Past. 355, 12. Ðæt hié hiora tôhopan anwealgne gefæstnigen tô ðǣm ēcum gôdum, 393, 31. Hî sprǣcon fullum and onwelgum wordum *plena ad integrum verba formabantur*, Gr. D. 241, 14. **III.** *add:*—Fæste iiii. geár, ii. onwealh (cf. iiii annos, .ii. integros, 9, n. 2), Ll. Th. ii. 228, 12.

**on-weard.** *Add:* hostile:—Hwî is se deófol swâ onweard (-werd, *v. l.*) þâm men? *cur diabolus tam infestus est hominum saluti?* Angl. vii. 8, 64. Hê wæs ðâm Crîstenum onweard (-werd, *v. l.*), Hml. S. 5, 369. [Cf. *Goth.* ana-wairþs *future.*]

**onweg-âdrifenness,** e; *f.* *Expulsion:*—For ðǣre onwegâdrifennesse se âwyrgda gâst his sceamode *dejectionem suam malignus spiritus erubuit*, Gr. D. 185, 13.

**onweg-fǣreld,** es; *n.* *Departure:*—Þâ se mæssepreúst ongæt and gefeah Benedictes onwegfæreld *cum presbyter Benedictum descessisse cognosceret et exultaret*, Gr. D. 119, 26.

**on-wemme;** *adj.* *Without blemish:*—Heorte onwemme *cor inmaculatum*, Ps. Vos. 118, 80.

**on-wemmend (?):**—Wegas onwemmendra (*inmaculatorum*, the translator seems to have taken this word to be gen. pl. of *inmaculator*), Ps. Rdr. 36, 18.

**on-wendan.** **III.** *add:*—Hié hié noldon onwendan from hiera woom wegum, Past. 267, 5. Onwendum heora môde fram þǣre þŷfþe, Gr. D. 202, 2. **IV b.** *add:* (1) *to upset* a judgement, *abrogate, annul* a law:—Þâ gesprǣcon hié him betwéonum þæt hié wolden anwendan ealle þâ gesetnessa and ealle þâ gebodu þe Domitianus hæfde ǣr gesett, Ors. 6, 10; S. 264, 19. Hwonne bið ēngu spǣc geendedu... gif mon ǣlcne dôm wile onwendan ðe Ælfrêd cing gesette, C. D. ii. 134, 18. (2) *to upset* a person, a condition of things:—On ðæm dôme ðæs ryhtwîsan dēman onwent sió geearnung ðone hâd and ðâ gedyncðo (*but the Latin is:* In examine recti judicis mutat merita ordinum qualitas actionum), Past. 411, 24. Ðû earma, ðû ðe eart mid ðŷ storme and mid ðǣre ŷste onwend and oferworpen *pau_percula tempestate convulsa*, 181, 11.

**on-wendedlic.** *Add:* v. un-onwendedlic: **on-wendedlîce.** v. un-onwendedlîce.

**on-wendedness.** *Add:*—Þeáh þe him sŷ singal sumor bûton ǣlcre onwendednes[se], Verc. Först. 114, 13. Rîxian bûton ǣlcre onwendednesse, 101, 13.

**on-wendendlic;** *adj.* *Changeable:*—God âna unanwendendlic wunaþ and eallra ðâra anwendendlicra welt *rerum orbem mobilem rotat, dum se immobilem conservat*, Bt. 35, 5; F. 166, 10. v. un-onwendendlic.

**on-wendendlîce.** v. un-onwendendlîce.

**on-wican.** *Add:*—Onwicum *cessere*, Wrt. Voc. ii. 103, 55.

**on-wîge.** v. or-wîge: **on-windan;** **II.** *add:* [*O. H. Ger.* ant-windan: *Ger.* ent-winden.] v. un-windan.

**on-winnan** *to attack, assail:*—Sum hǣðen mann þe him swŷðost onwann âwêdde ðærrihte, Hml. S. 22, 131. Þæt gē eówerne eard bewerian mid wǣpnum wið onwinnendne here, Ælfc. T. Grn. 11, 18: Hml. S. 25, 818. Hî weredon hî cēnlîce wið þone onwinnendan here, 589; 719. Hê gefeaht wið heora onwinnendan *he fought with their assailants*, 687. Seó scolu cildisc nâ gŷt mid costungum onwunnen *scola puerilis nondum temptationibus inpugnata*, Angl. xiii. 387, 321.

**on-winnende.** Take under preceding word: **on-wlât.** Dele, and see **and-wlata.**

**on-wreón.** **I.** *add:*—Hê onwreáh þâ eorðan þe ǣr wæs oferþeaht, Ps. Th. 28, 7. Onwrîg eágan mîne, Ps. L. 118, 18. **II.** *add:* (1) *to show* to others. (a) *to make known* a material object:—Meotud onwrâh beorg on bearwe, Gû. 118. (b) a non-material object:—Melchisedech godþrym onwrâh ēces alwaldan, Cri. 139. (c) a fact (stated in a clause):—'Ðû eart þæs lyfigendes Godes Sunu'... hit þē ne onwreáh flǣsc ne blôd, Mt. 16, 17. Crîst onwrâh... þæt is Euan scyld eal forpynded, Cri. 95. (2) *to gain a knowledge of, discover for oneself:*—Ic þæs wuldres treówes oft hæfde ingemynd, ǣr ic þæt wundor onwrigen hæfde ymb þone beorhtan beám, El. 1254. **III.** *add:*—Ðonne wē underfôð ðone hwǣte æt Gode, ðonne wē ongietað inweardlîce ðâ ǣ, and onwreóð ðâ dieglan cwidas *frumentum a Domino accepimus, quando in dictis obscurioribus subducto tegmine litterae per medullam Spiritus legis interna sentimus*, Past. 369, 8. Maurus... God bæd þ hē him geswutelode þe ðæs sceoccan gylpe, and him gewislîcor onwrige þæs âwyrgedan saga, Hml. S. 6, 323. **IV.** *add:*—Þē ealle heortan mînre ic onwreáge dîglu, Angl. xi. 119, 67. Þonne mannum beóð wunda onwrigene, þâ þe on worulde ǣr firenfulle men geworhton, Seel. 89. v. un-wreón.

**on-wrigenness.** **IV.** *add:*—On sprǣcum hâliges gewrites oððe on dîgelum onwrigennyssum (-wrigenessum, *v. l.*), Gr. D. 139, 1. v. â-wrigeness.

**on-wunian.** *Add:* [**I.** *to inhabit.* v. Dict.] **II.** *to be instant in*, apply one's self to:—Þâ þe mangungum onwuniað (on wuniað?) *qui negotiis insistunt*, Chrd. 111, 3. Hwænne hē gebedum onwunige [on wunige] *quando orationibus insistat*, 116, 34.

**on-wunung.** **I.** *add:*—Ofsett eorðlice onwunung (*the earthly tabernacle*) andgyt fela þencendne *deprimit terrena inhabitatio sensum multa cogitantem*, Scint. 138, 16. **III.** *dwelling in a place, indwelling, sojourn:*—Seó heorte bið geglenced þurh Godes neósunge, and mid his onwununge wiðinnan onlîht, Hml. Th. ii. 316, 6.

**open.** *Add:* **I.** physical. (1) of a door, gate, &c.:—Mid þǣm þe hié þâra dura hwelce opene gesâwon, þonne hié gieredon hié tô wîge, Ors. 3, 5; S. 106, 16. Hî carcernes duru opene fundon, An. 1078. (2) of a containing space, where there is free access to its interior:—Bið sûsla hûs open... ādlogum ongeán, Cri. 1605. Æt openum grǣfe, Ll. Th. i. 8, 5; 308, 5. Hē bired moniga opena wunda... hæfð on his nebbe opene wunde, Past. 61, 1-4. (2 a) *free of entrance or admission:*—Gehŷre gē ceasterwaran, gehŷre gē ælðeódige... se bædstede is open, Ap. Th. 12, 21. Se gîfra helle bið â open deófum, Bl. H. 61, 12. (3) of a space, *not shut in, not enclosed:*—Gelîcost openre byrig, ðǣre ðe mid nâne wealle ne bið ymbworht *sicut urbs patens et absque murorum ambitu*, Past. 277, 20. (3 a) of a battle:—Hē hine ǣr openum gefeohte ofercôm, Past. 229, 8. (4) *not covered, having no roof or covering:*—Þeáh þe þ hûs ufan open sŷ sylf and unoferhrêfed, Bl. H. 125, 30. (5) *not covered so as to be concealed, exposed:*—Hē hordwynne fond opene standan, B. 2271. (6) of a passage or space, *without obstructions:*—Ne mihte nǣnig hrôf on beón on ðǣre cirican... ac þæt se weg ðǣr wǣre â tô heofonum open, Shrn. 81, 10. (7) of sound, *made with open mouth:*—Mid openum stefnum (*apertis vocibus*) hē cwæð, Gr. D. 70, 5. **II.** non-physical senses. (1) *exposed to mental view, brought to light, patent, evident:*—Þǣr was Godes ege gesewen and open on fûlre dǣde, Hml. S. 23, 86: Sat. 406. Eall þis magon him sylfe geseón open orgete, Cri. 1117. Nû þû hæfst ongyten þâ wanclan treówa þæs blindan lustes; ðâ triówa ðe ðē nû sindon opene, hî sindon git mid manegum ôþrum behelede *deprehendisti caeci numinis ambiguos vultus. Quae sese adhuc aliis velat, tota tibi prorsus innotuit*, Bt. 7, 2; F. 18, 4. Openon geswutelinegum is geypped *euidentibus patet indiciis*, Chrd. 64, 28. Ælces monnes yfel bið ðŷ openre, gif hē anweald hæfþ *minus eorum patebit indignitas, si nullis honoribus inclarescant*, 27, 2; F. 96, 11. (2) *clear, easily intelligible:*—Swâ sceal ǣlc gesceádwîs lâreów opene lâre and swutole ðǣm ðiéstrum môdum bodian, and nâne wuht ðǣre dieglan lâre ðonne giét cŷðan, Past. 461, 4. (3) *clear of intellectual difficulties:*—Uneáþe þisse sprǣce cymþ ǣnig mon of, gif hē ǣrest on cymþ; ne cymþ hē nǣfre tô openum ende, bûton hē hæbbe swâ scearp andget swâ þ fŷr, Bt. 39, 4; F. 216, 27. (4) *exposed to general view or knowledge, existing, performed or carried on without concealment or so that all may see, hear, or take cognizance, public:*—þæt (the Trojan war) wæs open ealdgewinn, El. 647. Eall þæt hē forsceamode hēr on lîfe þæt hē ǣnigum men geypte, þæt bið þǣr eallum open unbehelendlîce, Wlfst. 138, 3. Gif... wîf hig... forlicge, and hit open weorðe, Ll. Th. i. 406, 7. And hit him on open wurðe, 200, 20. Þâ wanspêdigan crîstenan hē ne geþafode þæt hî openre wǣdlunge underþeódde wurdon, Hml. Th. i. 558, 26. On openre wafunge *in spectaculo*, i. *publica inspectione*, An. Ox. 3511. Openre *ostenso*, i. *aperto* (*ludibrio*), 2245. Tô openum bismere, Past. 279, 8. On openam yfle, 439, 7. Æt openre scylde, Ll. Th. i, 124, 23. Gif hwâ openne wiðercwyde gewyrce, 312, 8. Hî bēgen nǣron geendode ðurh openne martirdôm, Hml. Th. ii. 544, 29. Ðonne hî wyrcað ðâ openan scylda, Past. 439, 21. (5) of speech, *that conceals nothing:*—Nǣnig mon his geþôht openum wordum ût ne cŷðe, *nemo palam pronunciet*, Nar. 28, 29. (6) of a season, *where nothing is concealed:*—In þâ openan tîd (*the day of judgement*), Ph. 509. (7) *not confined to a few, generally available:*—God him sette þ, þæt ys open lagu, Ælfc. T. Grn. 5, 36. (8) *without defence or protection, exposed to:*—Bið ðæt môd on sume healfe open tô wundianne *cor vulneribus aperitur*, Past. 431, 9. Sió burg ðâs môdes ætiéwed hié selfe suíðe opene hiere feóndum *civitas mentis apertim se adversario ostendit*, 277, 23. Ic forlǣte mîne healle opene (*or under* I. 2?) mid eallum mînum goldhordum, Shrn. 75, 27. (9) of a cause, *undecided, not settled:*—Sió se sacy (sió sace? v. 19) swâ open swâ hió ǣr wæs, Ll. Th. i. 30, 16.

**open-ears.** *Add:* [v. *N. E. D.* open-arse.]

**openian.** **I.** *add:*—Byrigen opengende (*patens*), Ps. Rdr. 5, 11. **II.** *add:* (1) *to spread apart, expand:*—Openiendum þē hand þîne, Ps. L. 103, 28. (2) *to make an opening in:*—Hî openodon þone hrôf, Mk. 2, 4. (3) *to disclose, declare, make known:*—Þone cyning þǣm þe hē þæs heofonlican rîces wuldur mid his gewinne openede (-ade, *v. l.*) and cŷðde *regem cui gloriae caelestis suo labore notitiam prouenisse gaudebat*, Bd. 1, 32; Sch. 100, 21. Openede *declarauit*, i. *manifestauit* (*flaminem a facinoribus immunem esse*), An. Ox. 2925.

**open-lic.** *Add:*—þâra openlican weorc (*aperta opera*) wē gesióð, ac wē nyton hwelc hira inngeðonc bið, Past. 105, 9. [Cristes openliche

tocume, O. E. Hml. ii. 5, 23. He ȝaff opennlike bisne, Orm. 2909. Openliche gultes, A. R. 426.]

**openlíce.** I. *add:*—Openlíce (*as all might see*) Godes englas lǽddon hine tó heofonum, Shrn. 59, 15. Man cíde him openlíce *publica obiurgatione corripietur*, Chrd. 61, 16: Hml. S. 31, 187. Sé þe þýfðe oft ǽr forworht wǽre openlíce, Ll. Th. i. 228, 25. II. *add:*—Twá cynn sind martyrdómes; án dearnunge, óðer eáwunge. Sé ðe on éhtnysse his líf álǽt, hé bið openlíce martyr, Hml. Th. ii. 544, 16. Gif hwá on leásre gewitnesse openlíce (*without any concealment of the fact*) stande, Ll. Th. i. 398, 11. Gif hwá openlíce lengctenbryce gewyrce, 402, 29. III. *add:* (1) *clearly* to the senses:—Mid þý þá seó gesomnung eall gehýrde swá openlíce þá stefne, þá nǽs þǽr nǽnig tweó *quas dum aperte voces congregatio audisset, dubium non fuit*, Gr. D. 52, 32. Sceal man sealmas singan openlíce and beohte (*plane ac lucide*), Chrd. 57, 14. Openlíce *liquide*, 63, 27. (2) *clearly* to the mind:—Angytfullíce, openlíce *liquido*, i. *manifeste*, An. Ox. 83. Þone plegan, and hiora diófolgield, þæt wǽron openlíce ealle unclǽnnessa, Ors. 3, 3; S. 102, 13. Þú þe nelt þé eallunga geeówian openlíce nánum óðrum búton þám þe geclǽnsode beóð on heora móde *qui nisi mundos verum scire noluisti*, Solil. H. 5, 20. Sege hwæthwugu swetolor ymb þæt, þæt ic mage openlícor ongytan, 46, 3. Magon wé ðis spel ðe openlícor gereccean *quod melius ostendimus*, Past. 197, 11. IV. *add: without restriction* :—Hwæt þú woldest witan ic ne mæg mid fǽawum weordum gesecgan. Gif þú hyt openlíce witan wilt, þonne scealt þú hyt sécan on þǽre béc þe wé hátað *De Videndo Deo* . . . þæt þú meaht gehýran micle openlícor on þǽre bec, Solil. H. 64, 22-33. Wé móten God geseón openlíce, ealne geseón swylce swylce hé ys, 67, 7.

**open-ness.** *Add: manifestation:*—Þá gesceáwiað þá opennysse þǽre godcundan onlíhtnysse þe heora líchaman symle geclǽnsiað mid sýfrum þeáwum, Hml. S. 23 b, 42.

**openung.** *Add: opening*:—Openung múþes his *apertio oris illius*, Scint. 96, 11 v. ge-, land-openung.

**or.** *Add:* v. ur.

**óra** *metal. Add:*—Órum *metallis*, An. Ox. 14, 2.

**óra** *a monetary unit.* v. íre: **orc** *a cup. Add:* [*From Lat.* urceus.*]

**or-ceápe,** &c. *Add:*—Orceápungum *gratis*, Ps. Rdr. 38, 19: 108, 3.

**orcen** (?) *a sea-monster. Substitute:* **oronéas** *sea-monsters, and in* l. 2 *for* orcneas (orcenas ?) *l.* orcnéas.

**ord.** I a. *add:*—On þám ordum þára þorna *in illis spinarum aculeis*, Gr. D. 101, 16. III. [*perhaps here rather than under* I d (1) *belongs* Burgwarena ord (*applied to Adam*), Hö. 56. *In* v. 35 hell *is spoken of as a burh, and the burhwaran are the departed in hell, of whom Adam was the progenitor.*] *Add:*—Hé bið heora deáðes ord *eorum mortis auctor fit*, Chrd. 92, 23. [O. *Fr.* mith egge and mid orde.]

**or-dál.** *A masculine form* ordelas *occurs*, C. D. ii. 252, 13.

**or-dǽle.** *Add:*—Ordǽle *expers* (*periculi*), An. Ox. 3286.

**ord-fruma.** I. *add:* I a. *beginning*:—Ordfruma ł angin *principium*, Ps. L. 109, 3. Ǽlc ðing hæfð anginn and ordfruman ðurh God, ac God . . . næfð nán angin ne nænne ordfruman, Hex. 22, 1. Hé eallum gesceaftum anginn and ordfruman forgeaf, Hml. Th. i. 274, 30. II 1 a. *add:*—'Ego sum principium' . . . se Hǽlend be him sylfum spræc þ hé is ordfruma and angin ealra þinga, Hml. S. 1, 12. Gif hí hiora ordfruman (cf. fruman, Bt. 39, 13; F. 234, 31) ne þiówoden *nisi refluant causae quae dedit esse*, Met. 29, 96. II 1 b. *add:*—Ic gecýðe be ǽlcum þǽra spella æt hwilcum ordfruman ic hý geáxode *quibus haec auctoribus mihi comperta sint manifesto*, Gr. D. 9, 6. II 2. *add:*—Þæt æðele cyn, engla ordfruman, þæt þe eft forwearð, Sat. 21.

**ord-frym[m]**; *adj. Original*:—Þæt ordfremme folc, E. S. 49, 352.

**ord-stapu,** e; *f.* l. -stæpe, -stepe, es; *m.*

**or-eald.** *Add:*—Hé wæs wrǽne oð þ hé wæs oreald *usque ad aetatem decrepitam lubricus extitit*, Gr. D. 341, 3.

**orel.** *Add:*—Orl *hic ciclas*, An. Ox. 18 b, 14.

**orenum.** v. orne.

**oret.** l. óret, *and add: from* or-hát.

**óret-feld** *a battle-field*:—Óretfelda *schammate* (mundi *scammate* certant, Ald. 190, 23), An. Ox. 17, 50. Cf. óret-stów.

**óretla,** an; *m. Ill-usage* (?) :—Hé slóh þone Godes wer mid his brǽdre hand ofer his wange, þ hé mid óretlan gebysmrod út eóde of þǽre cyrican *virum Dei alapa percussit, ut de ecclesia cum contumelia exiret*, Gr. D. 200, 16.

**óret-lof** *triumph:*—For his wuldorfullan sige óretlofes *propter eius gloriosissimi uictoriam triumphi*, Angl. xiii. 400, 497.

**orf.** *Add:* [orf *and* yrfe *seem interchangeable in* Ll. i. 352, 3-13: 254, 15]:—Æt ánum hrýðere, oþþe æt þám orfe þe þæs weorð sý, Ll. i. 160, 2. On mínum cucum orfe, 276, 24. Gif bǽd genumen sý on monnes orfe for óðres monnes þingum, 354, 6. Æt ælcon smalon orfe, 224, 22. Man offrode fela cinna ofer Gode tó láce binnan þám getelde, Ælfc. T. Grn. 24, 2. Hire hyrdeman his orf lǽswode, Hml. Th. ii. 150, 31. Seó heofone ús sendeð styrmlíce stormas and orf and æceras swýðe ámyrreð, Wlfst. 92, 18. ¶ *Cattle-stealing, it may be inferred from the*

statement of the oxherd in Ælfric's Colloquy, 'Ealle niht ic stande ofer þá oxan waciende for þeófan, Coll. M. 20, 291', was a crime whose prevalence justified the attention given it by the law. To guard against the disposal of property acquired by it, the sale of cattle was allowed only in the presence of witnesses, and when security was given as to rightful ownership. v. Ll. Th. i. 276, 7-16: 282, 24-28: 296, 1-2. If a man returned from a journey not undertaken for the purchase of cattle, and brought some back with him, he was obliged within five days of his return to give notice of his purchase to the proper authority. v. Ll. Th. i. 274, 23-276, 5. Regulations were made for the tracing of stolen cattle (Ll. Th. i. 352, 3-13), and the oaths to be taken by those engaged in a suit concerning stolen cattle were fixed by law. v. Ll. Th. i. 178, 10-180, 16. An instance of cattle-stealing is mentioned in C. D. ii. 134.

**orf-cwealm.** *Add:*—Swíðe hefelic geár and swíðe swincfull and sorhfull geár innan Englelande on orfcwealme, Chr. 1085; P. 217, 18.

**orf-cynn.** *Add:*—Secgað sume gedwæsmenn þæt sum orfcyn sý þe man bletsigan ne sceole, and cweðað þæt hí þurh bletsunge misfarað, and ðurh wyrigunge geðeóð, Hml. Th. i. 100, 30.

**or-firmþa;** *pl. Refuse:*—Orfyrmþa *peripsema*, An. Ox. 609. Cf. æ-firmþa; or-firme, -firm(u).

**or-gálscipe.** *Dele, see:* of gálscipe, An. Ox. 5290.

**organ.** *Add:*—Ðæs hálgan cantices se gyldena organ, hé hý ealle oferhleóðrað, Sal. K. 152, 12.

**organistre,** es; *m. One who plays on an organ:*—Iubal wæs sangera fæder, and hearpera, and organystra (*canentium organo*), E. S. 42, 165.

**orgel.** *Add:* orgello; *f.*:—Ic ondette . . . unnyttes gylpes bígong, and ídle glengas, uncyste and ídelre oferhygde orgello, Angl. xi. 98, 28. [v. *N. E. D.* orgel.]

**orgel-dreám.** *Add:*—Heriað on strengum and orgeldreáme *laudate in chordis et organo*, Ps. Rdr. 150, 4.

**orgele.** *Add:* [v. *N. E. D.* orgle.]

**orgellíce.** *Add:*—Aurelianus andwyrde orgelíce swíðe, 'Ic ána gewealde ealles middaneardes, and ðú specst ðus dyrstiglíce swilce tó sumum déman', Hml. Th. ii. 308, 21. Hé hêt him æteówian orhlíce swíðe þone hálgan sanct, Hml. S. 32, 234.

**orgello.** v. orgel: **or-gilde.** *Add:* v. un-gilde: **or-hlet.** v. orhlyte: **orhlíce.** v. orgellíce.

**or-hlyte.** *Add* (?):—Orhlet *expers*, Angl. xi. 171, 3.

**orige** (?). *Substitute:* **or-íge**; *adj. Invisible, out of sight.* [O. H. Ger. ur-ougi *invisibilis*.]

**or-leahter.** *Add:* , es; *m. Danger, peril:*—Hwæt is ús sélre tó dónne þe on swá pleólicum orleahtre (*in tam graui discrimine*) synd becumene?, Chrd. 2, 8. Ðéh þe hé beó mid weredum orsorh, þéhweðere hé ǽfre on wíte wunað and on nearunisse, and ǽfre on gnornunge and on orleahtre . . . welan tó forwyrde gedragað; wel feala for welan on orleahtre becómon, E. S. viii. 473, 16-26. Orleahtras *discrimina*, An. Ox. 1867. Horhleahtras, Wülck. Gl. 252, 8.

**or-mǽte.** *Add:* I. of material things:—Þá æteówde án ormǽte heort, Hml. S. 30, 29. Ormǽte ent, 25, 280. Se ormǽta *gigas*, Ps. L. 32, 16. Cóm Timotheus mid ormǽtre fyrde, Hml. S. 25, 432. Hé (David) his (Goliath's) ormǽte heáfod of áslóh, 18, 26. II. of non-material things:—Ormǽte *inormis* (facinus *inorme*, Ald. 139, 11), An. Ox. 18 b, 47. Ontend mid byrne þǽre ormǽtestan wælhreównesse *ardore immanissimae crudelitatis exarsit*, Gr. D. 162, 22. ¶ a case used adverbially:—Eall þæt ígland mid mycelre swétnysse wunderlices stences ormǽdum wæs gefylled *insulam illam diversorum aromatum odoriferis spiraminibus inflari cerneres*, Guth. Gr. 167, 118.

**or-mǽte;** *adv. Add: immensely*:—Hé rád tó ormǽte caflíce, Hml. Th. ii. 304, 28. Hé (*Job*) hæfde ormǽte micelne híred, 446, 14. Se móna is ormǽte brád, Lch. iii. 242, 24.

**ormǽtlíce**; *adv. Excessively, immensely*:—Hé ongann ormǽtlíce tó þancienne Gode *coepit immensas gratias Deo agere*, Gr. D. 38, 5. Ðá becóme wit tó ánre dene, seó wæs ormǽtlíce deóp and wíd (*deuenimus ad uallem multae latitudinis ac profunditatis*, Bd. 5, 12), Hml. Th. ii. 350, 6. Ormǽtlíc(e) brád, Lch. iii. 242, 24.

**ormǽtness.** *Add: an immense extent:*—Se miccla gársecg mid micclum ormǽtnyssum ealle þás eorðan útan ymbligeð, Verc. Först. 111, 18.

**or-met[t].** *Add:*—Gearu tó ánwíge mid ormettre wǽpnunge, Hml. S. 18, 21. Þá gelǽhte se ealdorman ænne ormetne flint, 11, 102. Gif God forlǽt þá sáwle for ormættum synnum, þonne swǽlt heó on þǽm sǽlran dele, 1, 144.

**or-mód.** *Add:*—Ic ne ongyte náne trimðe ne on móde ne on líchaman, ac æom fulnáh ormód, Solil. H. 49, 4.

**orne.** *Substitute:* **orne**; *adj. Not mean, excessive.* (1) of amount:—Wið ornum útgange, and wið þon þe mon gemígan ne mæge, Lch. iii. 70, 25. (2) of quality or character, *not in due measure, harmful* (?), *injurious*:—Úsic þá earfeðo forléton, and wé ðá siodþan bútan orenum þingum mete þigdon (*ab securis nobis epulę capiuntur*), Nar. 24, 2. [Cf

þe on was ornure of mete and of drunche þen þe twei oðre *the one ate and drank more luxuriously than the other two* (?), A. R. 370.] v. ornlíce.

**orne** *what is harmful* (?), *injury* :—Mid Godes fultume ne wyrð him nán orne, Lch. iii. 16, 5.

**ornest.** *Add* : Cf. eornest, orrest : **-ornlic.** v. un-ornlic.

**ornlíce ; adv.** *Excessively, immoderately* :—Þá hé (*man*) fédde his líchoman orenlícost mid smeámettum, þá geearnode hé mé (*the soul*) þæs écan hungres, Verc. Först. (2) 155.

**orðþ.** *In ll.* 6-7 *for* 'Orþas . . . 56' *substitute* :—Orþes, fnǽstes *spiritus*, An. Ox. 2452. Orþes *spiritus*, 2, 64, *and add* :—Him (*the old man*) þæt oreð stincð and áfúlað, Wlfst. 148, 7. Þá þá hé sceolde álǽtan þ níhste oroð and ágyfan his gást . . . in þám breóste ánum fnæs hwylchugu líflic hǽtu þæs oreþes *cum extremum spiritum ageret* . . . *in solo tantummodo pectore vitalis calor anhelabat*, Gr. D. 324, 15–19. Úre fnǽst áteórað, gif wé áteón ne magon mid úre orðe intó ús ðæt lyft and eft út áblāwan, Hex. 8, 19. [Or-oþ *from* or-óþ. Cf. éþ:an, *and* Goth. uz-anan *to expire*.]

**orped.** *Add* : [v. *N. E. D.* orped.]

**or-sáwle.** *Add* :—Hé geseah þæs hálgan wífes líchaman orsáwle licgende, Hml. S. 23 b, 742. Wénest þú þ ic sý orsáwle? *me esse exanimem credis?*, Gr. D. 268, 7. Hé eóde tó þære stówe þær se orsáwla (sáwulleása, *v. l.*) líchama (*corpus exanime*) læg, 84, 33. [*O. H. Ger.* ur-sēli *exanimis*.]

**or-sorg.** I. *add* :—Ne onhyre þám þe byð orsorh on his wege (*qui prosperatur in via sua*), Ps. Th. 36, 7. Cum orsorg and ríxsa *prospere procede et regna*, 44, 5. Drihten wæs hire forespeca, and heó sæt ðá orsorhgre, Hml. Th. ii. 440, 21. **I a.** *with gen. of that which might cause anxiety* :—Gif hé gebicgan mihte . . . þ him ealle þincg gelumpon swá swá him sylfum gelícode, and hé wǽre orsorh ǽfre ǽlces yíeles, Hml. S. 12, 105. Ðæt hié swá micle ryhtlecor ðá hefonlican bebodu healden swá hié orsorgran bióð ðisses middangeardes ymbhogena *ut praeceptis coelestibus eo rectius serviant, quo eos ad curas mundi nequaquam jugum inclinat*, Past. 401, 2. Bióþ ðá men eallra orsorgoste ǽgðer ge ðises andweardan lífes earfoþa ge þæs tóweardan, Bt. 39, 7; F. 222, 30. **II.** *add* :—Wé ne magon habban þone heofonlican éþel búton wé fram eallum sacum orsorge beón, O. E. Hml. i. 302, 8.

**orsorg-leás** (?) ; **adj.** *Without security, anxious* :—Ǽghwylc crísten mann smeáge on him sylfum hú nearo se síðfæt bið ðære synfullan sáwle. For þan ne sceal nǽfre se crístena man beón orsorhleás (-lic ?), Verc. Först. 138, 16.

**orsorglíce.** I. *add* :—Þæt fram þysum lífe orsorhlícur (*securius*) sí gefaran, Scint. 48, 3.

**orsorg-ness.** *Add* : **I a.** *want of due care, carelessness* :—Þ úre folc ne wurðe losad þurh náne orsorhnesse (*negligentia*) bútan fulwihte and bisceopunge and predicunge, Chrd. 50, 4.

**ort-geard.** *Add* :—Orceard rǽran, Angl. ix. 261, 24. Synt orceardas gedafenlice æpplum *sunt pomaria congrua malis*, Lch. i. lxii, 8. [Ort- *from Latin* [h]ortus.]

**ortgeard-leáh** :—Orcerdléh (*mistakenly translates*) pomerium, Hpt. 31, 11, 220.

**orþanc-bend.** *Add* : Cf. searu-bend.

**orþanc-lic ; adj.** *Skilful, showing contrivance or design, ingenious* :—Orþanclíc wíse *argumentum*, Gr. D. 269, 14.

**orþian.** *Add* :—Ðurh ðá orðunge þe se sácerd on þæt wæter orðað, Wlfst. 36, 4. Se hálga gást orðað (*spirat*) þær hé wyle, eác is tó witenne þ hé orðað (*aspirat*) þonne hé wyle, Gr. D. 146, 11–14. Orþode *palpauit*, Germ. 402, 73.

**orþung.** I. *add* : (1) *the breath* of a human being or animal :—Seó orþung þe wé út bláwaþ and in áteóð . . . is seó lyft þe ealle líchamlice þing on lybbað, Hml. S. 1, 214. Betwux wordum his (*the old man's*) orðung áteórað, Hml. Th. i. 614, 15. Orþunge *alitum*, Germ. 398, 220. Orþunga *halitus*, 402, 77. (2) *inspiration* of a spirit :—Þurh orðunge þæs Hálgan Gástes, Hml. Th. ii. 524, 12. *See preceding word.*

**or-treówe.** *Add* : III. *distrustful, without confidence* :—Þá nolde God þ ðá ðe his gódan weorc gesáwon wǽron ungelýfende oððe ortreówe be þám wéne þára ælmessena þæs diácones *ut neque hi qui bona ejus viderant de eleemosynarum illius aestimatione fallerentur*, Gr. D. 331, 28.

**or-treówness.** *Add* :—Þæs þyslican (*infideles*) syndon tó þreágienne in heora ortreównesse, and of ðære ortreównesse hí syndon tó laþienne tó þére gife þæs rihtan geleáfan *infideles in sua perfidia redarguendi sunt, ad fidei gratiam provocandi*, Gr. D. 263, 3.

**or-trúwian.** *Add* :—Þreó þing syndon þe ne beóð forgifene . . . þrydde, þæt man ortrúwige Godes mildheortnysse, Wlfst. 299, 16.

**or-trýwan.** *l.* -tríwan, *and add* : v. ge-ortríwan.

**or-tydre.** *l.* -týdre, *and add* :—Nolde úre Drihten for his myldheortnesse þe ðes middangeard neáre (wǽre ?) ortýdre manna cynnes, ac áscyrede tó lafe þ þ wé eft of áwócon, Angl. xi. 2, 42.

**or-weg ; adj.** *Difficult of access* :—Horweg stíg, horuueg stiig *deuia callus* (-*is*), Txts. 57, 651: Wrt. Voc. ii. 25, 25. Orweg stíg, 139, 57. v. orweg-ness.

**orweg-stíg.** *Dele, and see preceding word* : or-wéna. *Add* : [Goth. us-wēna.]: **or-wénan.** v. ge-orwénan.

**or-wéne.** I. *add* : *with clause ; and for last passage substitute* :—Ealle Italiam geswicon Rómánum and tó Hannibale gecirdon, for þon þe hié wǽron orwéne hwæðer ǽfre Rómáne tó heora anwealde becómen *omnis Italia ad Annibalem, desperata Romani status reparatione, defecit*, Ors. 4, 9 ; S. 192, 4. **II.** *dele last passage, and add* :—Sum eáwfæst wer wæs yfele gehǽfd, and læg at forðsíðe his freóndum orwéne, Hml. Th. ii. 150, 8.

**or-wénness.** *Add* : (1) *with gen.* :—Se fífta leahtor is unrótnys ðisse worulde . . . Of ðám bið ácenned . . . his sylfes orwénnys, Hml. Th. ii. 220, 19. (2) *with prep.* :—Him wæs geworden seó orwénnys be þam menniscan gewinne *de humano labore facta est desperatio*, Gr. D. 47, 11.

**or-weorð.** *Dele* : or-wirþe. v. ge-orwirþe: **or-wirþed.** v. ge-orwirþan.

**or-wirþu.** *Add* : *contumely, insult* :—Hé sǽde hú manigne teónan and orwyrðu (-wyrdu, *v. l.*) þára nunnena fracoðwyrda hé geþrowode *quantas pateretur verborum contumeliis enarravit*, Gr. D. 152, 6. Hí ougunnon hine onscunian mid máran orwyrðum fracoðlicra worda *majoribus hunc verborum contumeliis detestari coeperunt*, 250, 28.

**oser** *an osier* :—Oser uiminis, uirge, An. Ox. 10, 2.

**osogen.** Cf. :—Mid deórenum ceáflum wǽre forsocen ł forgnegen *ferinis rictibus suggillaretur*, i. *rapietur* (Ald. 45, 34, *the passage glossed at* Wrt. Voc. ii. 82, 23), An. Ox. 3344. *The meaning of* á-sogen *in* Nar. 16, 26 (v. á-súgan) *seems to show that* osogen = á-sogen.

**oster-scill.** *Add* :—Gebærned osterscyl, gníd tó dúste, Lch. ii. 308, 25. Genim henne gelyndo and osterscylle, sete on gléda, wyrm hwón, 310, 3. Osterscella, 52, 25.

**Osti** *the Esthonians* :—Be-eástan him sindon Ósti þá leóde, Ósti habbað be-norþan him þone ilcan sǽs earm, Ors. 1, 1 ; S. 16, 29. v. óstig.

**óstig.** *Add* :—Þá þá man þá gyrda heóld hí wǽron hearde and hóstige ; þonne man slóh, sóna hí hnexodon, Hml. S. 35, 192.

**ostre.** *Add* :—Gif þú ostran habban wylle, þonne clǽm þú þíne wynstran hand ðám gemete þe þú ostran on handa hæbbe, and dó mid sexe oððe mid fingre swylce þú ostran scénan wylle, Tech. ii. 124, 12–14. v. sǽ-ostre.

**oter.** *Add* : In place names, v. C. D. vi. 320.

**óþ ; prep.** *l.* oþ. I. (2) *add* :—Of ðám gedwolan þe ic on oð þisum dwealde, Solil. H. 13, 10. Oð þám gemǽnan ende, Hml. Th. ii. 330, 7. **II.** (1) *add* :—Man hine bebyrgde in þám seáðe oþ þone gyrdels, Shrn. 125, 34 : An. 1577. Oð wolcna hróf, Exod. 298 : Gú. 1286. Oð Egypte, Exod. 443. ¶ of a point reached in a discourse, narrative, &c. :—From orde oð ende, El. 590. Oð ðiss wé rehton hwelc se hierde bión sceal, Past. 173, 14. (1 a) *add* :—Hé hét ádelfan seáþ oþ gyrdyls deópne, Shrn. 125, 32. Welle swíþe oþ þriddan ðæl *boil it down to a third*, Lch. ii. 36, 22. Þæt man hine oð deáð swunge, Hml. Th. i. 384, 6. Oð unmihte, Ps. Th. 106, 17. (1 b) *with another preposition* :—Mót sé þe þ yrfe áh trod oð (að, MS.) tó stæðe lǽdan, Ll. Th. i. 352, 11. (2) *add* : (a) *with a time word* :—Oð ðone first þe hé hyt gehāwad, Solil. H. 27, 6. Oð dómes dæg, B. 3069. Oð þá nigoðan tíd, El. 870. Heó wæs wunigende on wudewan háde oð feówer and hundeahtatig geára, Hml. Th. i. 146, 32. (β) *with a pronoun* :—Hé wæs winnende oð ðe him se mǽsta dǽl weard underþeóded, Ors. 1, 10 ; Bos. 32, 14. Gýt oð ðis on wundrum scínende, Hml. Th. ii. 188, 13. (aβ) *with word and pronoun* :—Ðú bist dumb oð þone dæg oð ðæt ðe þis bið *eris tacens usque in diem quo haec fiant*, Shrn. 133, 33· (γ) *where date is fixed by an event* :—Oð his ealdorgedál, Gen. 1959. Oð bǽles cyme, Ph. 47. (2 a) *add* : *with prep. or adverb* :—Oð nú .iv. geár *usque ante quadriennium*, Gr. D. 234, 9. Oð nú for twám geárum *usque ante biennium*, 235, 19 : 342, 33. (3) *marking stage reached* :—Nú hít eall ágán is oð on (v. á-gán) ðíne hand, ðonne ðú hit becwele swá gesibre handa swá fremdre swáðer ðé leófre sý, C. D. ii. 114, 6. (4) *marking limit of number, weight, &c.* :—Deófas wé hátað oð .vii. menn ; from .vii. hlóð oð xxxv ; siþþan here, Ll. Th. i. 110, 13. Þ ceápgild áríse á ofer .xxx. pæng oð healf pund, 234, 15.

**óþ ; conj.** *l.* oþ, *and add* :—Hé wæs winnende, oð him se mǽsta dǽl weard underþiéded, Ors. 1, 10 ; S. 44, 5. Hé wunode mid hire oð hana sang, Shrn. 30, 29. Séc hyne oð þú hyne finde, Solil. H. 3, 15 : 59, 9. Ic þæt wilnode oð mé nú áðreáð, 35, 22.

**oþ-berstan.** *Add* :—Gif hwá wóh wyrce, and út oðberste (æt-, *v. l.*), Ll. Th. i. 268, 9.

**óþer.** I. (2) *add* :—Wæs gehwæðer óðrum láð, B. 814. Ǽghwæðrum wæs bróga fram óðrum, 2565. (3) *add* :—Osfriþ his sunu óþer . . . óþer his sunu Eádfrið *unus filius eius Osfrid . . . alter Eadfrid*, Bd. 2, 20 ; Sch. 184, 10–13 : Gen. 467–477. (4) óþer . . . án :—Behýdd[e] se cnapa þone óðerne be wege, and ǽnne ðám hálgan were gebróhte, Hml. Th. ii. 170, 15. (5) *the second in each of successive pairs, other* as in every *other* :—Gebyreþ ǽfre se óðer fisc ðám landhláforde and ǽlc seldsýnde

fisc, C. D. iii. 450, 26. Swylc coðe cóm on mannum þ fullneáh æfre þe óðer man weard on þám wyrrestan yfele, Chr. 1086; P. 217, 29. Sume fæston swá þ hí forsáwon tó etanne búton on ðone óðerne dæg, Hml. S. 13, 97.     II. (1) add :—Sem se yldesta, óðer Cham, þridda Iafeth, Gen. 1241. Wæs se deófol óðere síðe oferswíðed, Hml. Th. i. 170, 31. (1 a) referring to a preceding object in a series :—Se móna dæghwámlíce feówer prican lator áríst þonne hé dyde on þám óðrum dæge, Angl. viii. 327, 27. (1 β) denoting repetition :—Swilce óðer wæterflód, swá fleów heora blód, Hml. S. 23, 73. (1 γ) denoting addition :—Lancius þe óþre noman wæs háten Genutius, Ors. 3, 3; S. 102, 2.    (2) add :—þæt wæter stód him on twá healfa swilce óðer stánweall, Hml. Th. ii. 194, 21. Þeáh se leása wéna tiohhie þ se anweald sié þ héhste gód, hit biþ eall óþer, Bt. 27, 3, F. 98, 33. Seó stów næs ná ne óþor ne wæccere þonne formænig þára þe his yldran gefyrþredon, Lch. iii. 438, 11. Ne geríd wiste hwæt óðer cwæð, Gen. 1690. For hwí se góda læce selle ðám hálum men séftne drenc, and óþrum hálum biterne, Bt. 39, 9; F. 226, 11. Hé wénde ðæt hé wære ofer ealle óðere menn, Past. 41, 1. Betweoh hire óðer twá sweostor inter duas alias sorores suas, Gr. D. 286, 9. (2 a) add :—þá byrig hé geseah eall on óþre wísan gewend, on óþre heó ær wæs, and þá gebotla eall getimbrode on óþre wísan, on óþre hí ær wæron, Hml. S. 23, 509–512. Hé his líf on nán óðer ne wend, on óðer hé lærd, Past. 193, 13 : 257, 19. Hí sind óðre, óþre hí wæron, Hml. Th. ii. 574, 2. (3) add :—Hí hlifiað seor úp ofer þá óðre eorðan, Wlfst. 262, 11. Man sette heora heáfda swilce óþra deófla búton ðám portweallon on ðám heáfodstoccum, Hml. S. 23, 75. (3 a) used substantively :—Hé hire fét þwóh, ne geþrýstlæhte hé nán óþer þæs líchaman oðhrínan, Hml. S. 23 b, 745.

óþer-geáre; adv.  Next year :—Gif þu wille witan hú eald se móna scyle beón óþergeáre on þisne dæg, Lch. iii. 228, 16, 19.

óþer-hwíle; adv.  Sometimes :—Atomes ys þ læste getæl þ rímcræftige men óðerwhíle hátað for his gehwætnesse momentum, Angl. viii. 318, 36. [v. N. E. D. other-while.]

óþer-hwílen (?) occasional (?) :—Cusían and tonican beón óðerhwilen (-hwíle?) synd gewunede sunt habban æthwigan beteran cuculle et tonice sint aliquanto solitis quas habent modice meliores, R. Ben. I. 92, 16. The passage seems imperfect, and perhaps aliquando has been read for aliquanto and óðer-hwíle should be read for óðer-hwílen.

oþ-feorrian to remove to a distance, take away :—Ic þence þis feoh tó findanne næs tó oþfeorrganne, Lch. i. 384. 4. Cf. æt-feorrian.

oþ-fleón.  Add :—Wæs þæs folces fela on án fæsten oþflogen ad Olympum montem universi Gallograeci confugerant, Ors. 4, 11 ; S. 206, 13.

oþ-hrínan.  I. of physical contact, to touch :—Se rodor þære eorþan æfre ne oðríneð, Met. 20, 138. Ic hys hrægles fnædes oðhrán, Hml. A. 189, 228. Hé hire fét mid teárum oþráu . . . heó mid ðære hálgan róde gedryncnesse Iordanem oþhrínan (ongan), Hml. S. 23 b, 719–723. Gif man mid unclænum handum hwylces metes onhríne, oððe him huud oððe catt oððe mús oðhríne se quis immundis manibus cibum aliquem tetigerit, vel canis, vel felis, vel mus tetigerit, Ll. Th. ii. 164, 9. Hé hire fét mid his teárum þwóh, ne geþrýstlæhte hé nán óþer þæs líchaman oðhrínan, Hml. S. 23 b, 745.     II. to touch the heart, mind, &c. :—Ic weard geléd mid þære hætu þæs geleáfan, and mid þám trúwan oþhrinon (æthrinen, v. l.), Hml. S. 23 b, 456.

oþ-irnan.  Dele first passage, for which see oþ-hrínan.

oþ-íwan.  I. add :—Hé oðiéwde hú micelne onwald hé hæfde ofer óðre menn, Past. 115, 13. Ðæt hé sprecende bebiét, ðæt hé ðæt wyrcende oðiéwe, 81, 11. Otiéwe (at-, v. l.), 84, 16. Hé wolde otiéwan (æt-, v. l.) his árfæstnesse, 100, 9. Weard Rómánum an yfelum tácne oþiéwed . . . þæt þæs folces sceolde micel hryre beón, Ors. 4, 1 ; S. 156, 33. Alexandre weard an swefne án wyrt oðéwed, 3, 9 ; S. 134, 35.     II. add :—On þære tíde oðéwde Fulcanio þæt íglond, þæt næs gesewen ær þá, Ors. 4, 11 ; S. 206, 31.

oþ-sacan.  I. add : to deny a statement put negatively :—Hé þá oðsóc þ hé hit nære he denied, (saying) that it was not he, Hml. S. 30, 273.

oþ-standan.  I. add : (1) of a person :—Ðá þá seó tíd middæges tó becóm, þá oþstód hé tó sumere hwíle, hine fram þám síðfæte áhæbbende, Hml. S. 23 b, 161. (2) of a procedure :—Gange se teám forð oþ þæt man wille hwær hé oðstande, Ll. Th. i. 158, 15.     II. add.—Ic wæs út áþrungen fram eallum þám folce, oð ðe ic ænlípigu on þám cafertúne tó læfe oþstód, Hml. S. 23 b, 410.

oþþe.  I. add : a particle co-ordinating words, phrases, or clauses, (1) between which there is an alternative. (a) words :—Feorran oððe neán, Gen. 1047. Ær oððe síþ, Cri. 1053. (b) phrases :—Wís on gewitte oððe on wordcwidum, Crä. 13. (c) clauses :—Þonne þæt mód ymbe hwæt tweónode, oðþe hit hwæs wilnode tó witanne, Solil. H. 2, 22. Hú mæg ic ládigan ládan spræce oððe andsware ænige findan ?, Cri. 184. Oðþo, Bd. 1, 27 ; Sch. 74, 14. (2) where an alternative is not expressed :—Hé wolde fandian hú longe þæt land norþryhte læge, oþþe hwæðer ænig mon benorðan þæm wéstenne búde, Ors. 1, 1 ; S. 17, 8. ¶ introducing each question in a series where the subjects are not alter-

native, Bd. 1, 27 ; Sch. 76, 1–20.     I b. used after hwæþer :—Hwæþer sceal geeácnad wíf fulwad beón, oððe æfter þon þe heó bearn cenned ?, Bd. 1, 27 ; Sch. 75, 20. Beseah Drihten . . . hwæðer his mihta andgyt ænig hæfde, oððe God wolde sécan, Ps. Th. 52, 3.    II b. add :—Eálá, wære hé áuðer oððe hát, oððe ceald, Past. 445, 36.    III. after a primary statement, appending a secondary alternative or consequence of setting aside the primary statement :—Hé áxode hig hwæðer hire fæder wære hál . . . oððe hwæðer hé lifode interrogavit eos dicens, ‘ Salvusne est pater vester . . . ? adhuc vivit ?, Gen. 43, 27.

oþþon.  Add :—Gif se fridman fieó oþþon feohte, Ll. Th. i. 286, 13 : 17 : 22 : Hml. A. 190, 281.

oþ-windan.  Add :—Bútan hé oðwinde (æt-, v. l.), Ll. Th. i. 210, 9 : 12.

oþ-wítan.  (1) with dat. of person, and charge (a) in acc. :—Him God ne oðwít his scylda, Ps. Th. 31, 2. Ðæt ilce Dryhten oðwát Israhéla folce, Past. 267, 14. (b) in a clause :—Ic þe ná ne oðwíte þæt þú mé ne gehýrst, Ps. Th. 21, 2. (c) with pronoun and clause in apposition :—Hé him þæt oðwát þ hé on þám wege dyde ei hoc quod in via egerat improperavit, Gr. D. 129, 24. (2) with charge only :—Ðæt ilce oðwát Dryhten, ðá hé cwæð, Past. 89, 16.

oþ-wyrcan.  Add : [Cf. (?) O. H. Ger. ant-(int-)wurchen demolari.]

ó-web.  Add :—Seolcen áb tramasericum, wyllen áb linostema, Wrt. Voc. i. 40, 4, 8.  See á-web.

ówþer. v. á-hwæþer.

oxa.  Add :—Oxan horn bið .x. pæninga weorð, Ll. Th. i. 138, 21. Oxan tægl bið sciłł. weorð, cuus bið fífa penega. Oxan eáge bið fíf p. weorð, cús bið sciłł. weorð, 140, 2–4. Cóm se deófol . . . and hæfde ænne oxan horn on hande, Hml. S. 31, 776. Ágife hire (a widow with a child) mon .vi. tó fóstre, cú on sumera, oxan on wintra, 126, 5. Né untígð eówer ælc on restedæge his oxan (oxo, R. woxo, L. bouem suum), Lk. L. 13, 15. .xii. þeówe men and .ii. gesylhðe oxan, C. D. iv. 263, 20. Mon selle him tó ðæm londe .iiii. oxan, .ii. cý, and .l. scépa, and ænne horn, i. 310, 13 : 27. Ic (the ploughman) gá út on dægræd þýwende oxan tó felda . . . geiukodan oxan . . . ælce dæg ic sceal erian fulne æcer . . . Ic hæbbe sumne cnapan þýwende oxan mid gádísene . . . Ic sceal fyllan binnan oxan mid híg, and wæterian hig, and scearn heora beran út, Coll. M. 19, 13–20, 3. Þá þá hé his oxan ræpte, þá scóc án his heáfod, and mid þam horne hine þýde, Hml. S. 31, 785. Hét hé spannan oxan tó, 9, 106. Þá þe sealdon oxsan (oxan, v. l., exin, L., exen, R. boues), Jn. 2, 14. Exen, calfero boves, vitulos, Rtl. 119, 28. ¶ oxan gang an ox-gang (v. N. E. D. s.v.), an eighth of a carucate or ploughland, a bovate. [The carucate was the extent of land ploughed by one plough with its team of eight oxen] :—On hillum twégra oxena gang, and on Lundbý twégra oxena gang, C. D. B. iii. 346, 20–21. [Án híde búton ánes oxan gang, 370, 5.]  v. hýr-oxa.

oxan-hirde; m.  An oxherd :—Eálá, oxanhyrde, hwæt wyrcst þú ? Micel ic gedeorfe ; þænne se yrþlincge unscenþ þá oxan, ic læde hig tó læse, and ealle niht ic stande ofer hig waciende for þeófan, and eft on ærnemergen ic betæce hig þám yrþlincge wel gefylde and gewæterode, Coll. M. 20, 23–31. Be oxanhyrde. Oxanhyrde mót læswian .ii. oxan oððe má mid hláfordes heorde on gemænre læse . . . and his metecú niót gán mid hláfordes oxan, Ll. Th. i. 438, 12–16. Oxanhyrdas bubulcos (-as, MS.). oxanhyrde bubulcus, Hpt. 33, 238, 4–5 : An. Ox. 23, 32.


# P

-pæcend, -pæcestre, pæcung. v. be-pæcend, -pæcestre, -pæcung.

pæl, es ; m.  A javelin :—Pælas pila, An. Ox. 19, 3. [From Latin palus?].  Cf. pál.

pæll.  I. add :—Hí gesáwon þ án scínende weg wæs ástreht mid godwebbenum pællum (pellum, v. l.) (strata palliis via), Gr. D. 176, 1. Hé hét dæftan his búr mid pallum and mid wáhryftum, Hml. S. 35, 50. Mærða . . . on pellum and purpurau, Hml. A. 92, 18. On pællon and on gyldenan faton, Chr. 1075 ; P. 309, 33.     II. add : purple cloth :—On scynnan mid pælle betogen, Chr. 1075 ; P. 209, 31.

pællen.  Add :—Tó þám þ sceolde beón wéned þ hé wære se cyning . . . for þæm pællenum reáfum (ex purpureis vestibus), Gr. D. 131, 18.

pæþ.  Add : n. (? v. mearc-, seolh-paþ) : paþu ; f. (? Another list of boundaries to the same land as that mentioned in C. D. iii. 175–176 is given C. D. v. 220–221, where andlang ræwe replaces andlang paþæ, and on ðan harpaðe replaces on ðær paþæ) :—Iuxta terminos, id est bereueg et méguuines paæt et strétlég, C. D. i. 54, 31.  Of ðám hæcce tó paðe stocce, v. 401, 37.  Tó ðám holan paðe, iii. 416, 3.  Snaca on we and næddre on pæðe coluber in uia, cerastes in semita, Wlfst. 192, 21. On ðone gréne pæð ; of ðám paðe, C. D. iv. 98, 23.  On þone smalan pæþ, of þám smalan pæþ, C. D. B. iii. 468, 15.  Ofer herepað ðæt on

sticelan pað, C. D. iii. 403, 18. [Andlang burnan on Wealpaða brycge, C. D. iii. 179, 28.] v. ciric-, hors-, seolh-pæþ.

**pæþ-feld** *field across which a path runs* (?) :—Oð þone hagan; andlang hagan oð pædfeld, C. D. i. 258, 2.

**pallium**; *m.* I. *a cloak* :—Þes pallium þe ic werige, Hml. S. 36, 160. II. *the archiepiscopal pall* :—Hēr Wulfrēd ærcebisc pallium onfēng, Chr. 804; P. 58, 12.

**palm.** *Dele* '(?)', *and add*: **pealma.** I. *a palm-tree* :—Se ryhtwīsa swā swā palma blōweð, Ps. Vos. 91, 13. II. *a branch of a palm-tree* :—Sceole wē healdan ūrne palm, oð þæt se sangere onginne ðone offringsang, and geoffrian þonne Gode ðone palm. Palm getācnað syge, Hml. Th. i. 218, 8–11. Palman underfōn wyrðment getācnað *palmam accipere honorem significat*, Lch. iii. 208, 32. Beón gedælede þā palman (*palmę*), Angl. xiii. 409, 624 : 408, 616. On drihtenlicum dæge palmena, 612. Bletsung pealmena, 622. Healdan þā palman on handum, 409, 629.

**palm-æppel.** *Add* :—Palmæppla *dactilorum*, Hpt. 33, 239, 20.

**palm-dæg** *Palm Sunday* :—On þām symbeldæge þe wē palmdæg gewunelīce nemnað, Hml. S. 23 b, 140.

**palm-treów.** *Add* :—Palmtreówa birig, Deut. 34, 3.

**palm-twig.** *Add* :—Rihtwīs swā palmtwig blōweð, Ps. Rdr. Cam. 91, 13.

**palm-twiga** (?), an; *m.* *A palm-branch* :—Palmtwiga *palma*, Ælfc. Gr. Z. 312, 9. v. twigu.

**-palm-twiged.** v. ge-palmtwiged.

**palþer** *a panther* :—Gesāwon wē ægðer ge wīf ge wǣpnedmen mid palthera fellum and tigriscum þāra deóra hỹdum gegyryde *uidimus feminas uirosque aliquos pantherarum tygridumque pellibus contectos*, Nar. 26, 13. v. panþer.

**pan-mete.** *Insert after* panic: **pang.** *Dele the query, and see* þung.

**panne.** *Add* :—Pannan *sartagines*, An. Ox. 11, 178. v. brægen-panne.

**panþer, pandher** *a panther* :—Is þæt deór Pandher bī noman hāten, Pa. 12. v. palþer.

**pāpa.** *Add* :—Gif mæssepreóst manslaga wurðe . . . wræcnige hē swā wīde swā pāpa him scrīfe, Ll. Th. i. 346, 6.

**paradīs,** es; *m.* *Paradise* :—Ðæt wē inn mōton gaan tō ðām upplican paradīse, Hex. 28, 9.

**part.** *Add* :—Wē ne magon þisne part fullīce trahtnian on Engliscum gereorde, Ælfc. Gr. Z. 240, 16.

**Parþ-ware**; *pl.* *The Parthians* :—Hē gelǣrde monige þeóde tō Crȳstes geleáfan, Parðwara and Mēdware and Persware, Shrn. 155, 33.

**passio[n?]**; *pl. f.* passione *a passage from that part of the Gospels which deals with Christ's passion* :—Ǣghwelc messeprióst gesinge fore Ōsuulfes sāwle twā messan, and aeghwilc diácon ārēde twā passione fore his sāwle, C. D. i. 293, 32.

**Pater-noster**; *m. n.* *The Lord's Prayer* :—Se Paternoster hē mæg āna ealla gesceafta on his ðǣre swīðran hand . . . geðȳn, Sal. K. 150, 32. Se gepalmtwigeda Paternoster, Sal. 12. Þæt gepalmtwigede Paternoster, 39. Hūlic is ðæs Paternosters seó wlitige heorte?, 148, 26 : 19 : 150, 14. Ǣlc crīsten man sceal cunnan ægðer ge his Paternoster ge his Crēdan. Mid þām Paternostre hē sceal hine gebiddan . . . Wē habbað gesǣd embe þæt Paternoster, Hml. Th. i. 274, 19–22 : ii. 604, 15–16 : Hml. S. 12, 261 : Wlfst. 33, 2. Se lǣreów sceal secgan þām lǣwedum mannum þ andgyt tō þām Paternostre, 265 ; Hml. Th. ii. 604, 18. Seofon gebedu sint on þām Paternoster, i. 262, 21 : 270, 17. Wrīt on ægðere sticcan ān paternoster oð ende, Lch. i. 386, 6.

**peall.** *The entries under* weall (= *mulled wine*) *should be taken here. See* An. Ox. 326.

**pearroc.** *Add* :—Ān leó ūtbǣrst ūt of þære leóna pearruce, Hml. S. 35, 253. [*Dele* 'From Celtic': *see* N. E. D. parrock.]

**pening.** (1) [In *l.* 4 *hymenis* is a corruption of *nummi* s(ervire), as the gloss at Wrt. Voc. ii. 96, 71 belongs to Ald. 207, 5 : Semper avaritiae nummi servire volentem.] *Add* :—Smeágað sume men hwæt se pening (pænig, penig, *v. ll.*) getācnige, Hml. A. 44, 505. Hig of þām Iūdēum for ānum penige .xxx. gesealdon ongeán þæt þæt þā Iūdēas ǣr ūrne Hǣlend . . . myd þryttegum penegum gebohton, 187, 168–170. Wiþ þrim hundred penegon (peninga, R., penninga ł scillinga, L.), Jn. 12, 5. Twēgen penegas (peñd., L.), Lk. 10, 35. (I a) *in pl., money* :—Ne wēne hē nō ðæt Godes ryhtwīsnes sié tō ceápe, swelce hē hié mæge mid his peningum (-engum, *v. l.*) gebyccgean . . . ða hwīle ðe hié peningas (-engas) hæbben mid tō gieldanne *ne venalem Dei justitiam aestiment . . . cum curant . . . nummos tribuere*, Past. 327, 16–18. Ða ilca peningas (penicas *altered from* pendicas, L.) ðā ðe gisended wēre *ea quae mittebantur*, Jn. R. 12, 6. (2) *add* :—Se feórðandǣl byð quadrans gecīged, beó hit penig oððe pund, swā þ wel wāt ceorlisc folc . . . xx scillingas beóð on ānum pund, and twelf sīðon twēntig penega byð ān pund, Angl. viii. 306, 30–36. Ne þearf ic N. sceatt ne scilling, ne pænig ne pæniges weorð, Ll. Th. i. 182, 10. þæt mon ne sparige nǣnne þeóf þe æt hæbbendre

handa gefangen sȳ ofer eahta peningas (penegas, *v. l.*), 198, 18. Ofer .xii. pæningas, 228, 12. ¶ the following passages are of interest as giving some comparative values :—Ðeówan wīfmenn . . . .i. sceáp oððe .iii. p̄. tō wintersufle, Ll. Th. i. 436, 31. Gafolhwītel sceal beón .vi. pæninga (penega ; -inga, *v. ll.*) weorð, 130, 5. Oxan horn bið .x. pæninga weorð. Cuu horn bið twēgea pæninga. Oxan tægl bið sciłł. weorð. Cuus bið fīfa penega. Oxan eáge bið fīf p. weorð. Cūs bið sciłł. weorð, 138, 21–140, 4. Be .xxx. pæn. oþþe be ānum hrȳðere, 232, 7. Hors mon sceal gyldan mid .xxx. sciłł., myran mid .xx. sciłł. . . . oxan mid .xxx. p̄., cū mid .xxiiii. p̄., swȳn mid .viii. p̄., man mid punde, sceáp mid sciłł., gāt mid .ii. p̄., 356, 2–6. Gif mon ōðres wudu bærneð oþþe heáweð unālíefedne, forgielde ǣlc greát treów mid .v. sciłł., and siþþan æghwylc mid .v. pæningum, 70, 6. Sceáp sceal gongan mid his flíese oð midne sumor, oþþe gilde þ flíese mid twām pæningum, 146, 11. v. gafol-pening.

**pening-sliht.** *Add* :—Penningslæht *censum*, Mt. L. 22, 17.

**pening-weorþ.** *Add* :—Nān man nān þing ne bycge ofer feówer penigweorð (peninga weorð, *v. l.*) . . . būton man hæbbe getreówe gewitnesse feówer manna, Ll. Th. i. 390, 2. v. healf-penigwurð.

**penn** *a fold* (? the meaning is uncertain ; perhaps the two names *Strétpen*, C. D. iii. 448, 19, *Strétfold*, 119, 30 may suggest that the word has the later sense). *Add* :—On ætden pæn . . . on ðone ealdan uuīðig on Ǣttan pennes læce, C. D. vi. 48, 12–14. On hacan penne, v. 238, 30. Andlang weges tō pippenes penne; of pippenes penne, iii. 429, 27. Upp on ēpenn; of ðām penne on heán æsc, 456, 4. Andlang ðæra heáfda on etta penn, 25, 21. Usque strétpen, 448, 19. v. fyrs-penn.

**Pentecosten.** *Add* :—Pentecostenes dæg, Chr. 973; P. 118, 12. Paulinus gefullade his dohter on Pentecosten (in þone hālgan ǣfen Pentecosten, *v. l.*), 626; P. 25, 14. Seó wæs gefulwad þȳ hālgan dæge æt Pentecosten, Bd. 2, 9; Sch. 148, 22.

**pêo.** v. pīe : **Peohtas.** *Add* :—v. Sūþ-Peohtas.

**peónie** (-a), an; *f.* (*m.*?) *Peony* :—Piónie *pionia*, An. Ox. 56, 418. Peónia *peonia*, Wrt. Voc. i. 69, 22. Ðeós wyrt ðe man peónian nemneð, Lch. i. 168, 14.

**pere.** v. peru : **persa.** *Dele, and see* meduma *a treadle* : **Persc-ware.** *Add* : Shrn. 110, 16. Cf. Pers-ware.

**Persisc.** *Add* : I. *adj.* :—Tō Persiscum earde, Hml. Th. i. 450, 15. Fērde Antiochus tō Persiscre þeóde, Hml. S. 25, 531. Þone heáhengel þe Persisce þeóde bewiste, Hml. Th. i. 518, 17. II. *used substantively* :—Þæra Persiscra cyning wæs þǣm Cāsere wiþerrǣde, Jud. Thw. 162, 23.

**peru.** *Take here* pere (-u) *in Dict., and add* :—Ðonne þe æpples lyste . . . Gyf þū peran wille, Tech. ii. 124, 19. Manigfeald æppelcyn, peran, Lch. ii. 180, 14.

**pic.** *Add* :—Hēt hē þ man ealle þā wīnfatu mid pice geondgute, Gr. D. 57, 28. Hē hēt mid pice hī besprencgan, Hml. S. 9, 118. Sē þe æthrīnð pic byð besmiten, Scint. 83, 5. þ weallende pic, Hml. A. 174, 165. [From Latin.]

**pīcan.** *Dele, and see* pȳtan.

**picen.** *Add* :—Picen fæt *culleum, uas pice oblinitum*, Hpt. 31, 10, 197.

**pīe.** *Add* :—Hundes peó (beó, MS.) *cinomia*, Wrt. Voc. ii. 22, 73. Handes pē, Ps. Vos. 104, 31.

**Pīerisc**; *adj.* *Pierian* :—Þȳ Pīeriscan *Pierio* (*cantu.* v. Ald. 182, 31) (*printed* pueriscan *puerio*), Wrt. Voc. ii. 94, 48.

**pīl.** *Add* : v. flyge-pīl.

**pīle.** *Add* :—Þeáh þū punige stuntne on pīl(an) [*pil*(a)], Scint. 95, 18.

**pilece.** *Add* :—Ic geseah þæs abbudes pylican (*printed* þylican; cæppan, *v. l.* melotem) ofer mīnum heáfde, Gr. D. 116, 13. [Myccla geofa and manega gærsama . . . on scynnan mid pælle betogen and on merðerne pyleceon and grāschynnene, Chr. 1075; P. 209, 32. v. N. E. D. pilch.]

**pīlian.** v. ge-pīlian : **pillan** (?). *Substitute* : pilian ; *and add* : [v. N. E. D. pill. Probably from Latin *pilare*.]

**pīn-beám.** *Add* :—Hī begunnon tō ceorfenne þone heágan pīnbeám, Hml. S. 31, 407.

**pīnian.** *Add* :—Ic biddo ðec þte ðū mec ne pīnia *obsecro te ne me torqueas*, Lk. L. 8, 28. Ðū cuóme hider ǣr tīd tō pīnenne (*torquere*) ūsih, Mt. L. 8, 29. [Sumne hī pīnedon mid wallende leáde, Hml. A. 171, 37. v. N. E. D. pine.] v. ge-pīnian.

**pīn-treów.** *Add* :—Wæs ān pīntreów wið þ templ swīðe hālig geteald, Hml. S. 31, 390. On þære eá ófre stōd hreód and pīntreów and abies þ treówcyn ungemetlicre grȳto (*but the Latin is*: Fluminis ripas harundo uestiebat pinorum abietumque robora uincens grossitudine), Nar. 8, 21.

**pīnung.** *Add* :—Nǣre his (*the rich man's*) wīte fulfremed on ðām fȳre, būton hē ðā ylcan pīnunga his siblingum gewēnde, Hml. Th. i. 334, 2.

**piónie.** v. peónie.

**pipat.** *Dele: the word is Latin, and describes the cry of the hawk.* Cf. Wrt. Voc. ii. 88, 80 *for another instance of the verb.*

**pīp-dreám.** *Add:*—The Latin original is: Organa cantare audierit uicinas letitias. Cf. orgel-dreám.

**pipe.** (1) *add:*—Swilce ān man pīpige mid nigon pīpan, Nap. 51, 20. (2) *add:*—Gif þonne gīt sió ādl egle, gebringe inne þurh pīpan oðđe horn, swā lǣcas cunnan, Lch. ii. 224, 28. (3) *the channel of a small stream.* v. *N. E. D.* pipe; 8 a. See the quotation from C. D. iii. 380, 2. [*From Latin* pīpa.]

**pīpfan.** *Dele, and see* pyffan.

**pīpian** *to pipe:*—Ān stān is in Sicilia (achates) hāten, se wæs on Pires hýrnesse, þæs ansýne is swilce ān man pīpige mid nigon pīpan and ān man hearpige (cf. Namque habuisse traditur (i. e. Pyrrhus) achaten in qua novem Musae et Apollo citharam tenens spectarentur, Pliny xxxvii. 3), Nar. 51. [*Lat.* pipare.]

**pīplic;** *adj. Musical:*—Pīplic swegelhorna (dreám) *musica sambucorum armonia,* An. Ox. 1644.

**pipor-corn.** *Add:*—Genim senepes sǣdes dǣl ... and .xx. piporcorna, Lch. ii. 24, 16.

**pipor-cweorn,** e; *f. A pepper-mill, pepper-grinder:*—Grinde reādes caules sǣdes āne handfulle on piporcwyrna, Archiv lxxxiv. 326 d.

**piporian.** *Add:*—Wring ðurh clāð and pipera þonne, Lch. iii. 40, 7. Cnucian gōdne dǣl gārleáces and dōn þǣrtō and piperian swā swā þē þince, Archiv lxxxiv. 325 c.

**pirige.** *Add:*—On þǣre pyrigean styb; þonne of pyrigean stybbe on þone þorn, C. D. B. iii. 396, 37. Æt ðǣre pyrgean, C. D. iii. 453, 29.

**pise.** *Add:*—Mid hire ýtemestan fingrum þǣre lenticula, þ syndon pysan, heó onhrān and on hire mūð sende þreóra corna gewyrde, Hml. S. 23 b, 715.

**pistol.** *Add:* (1) *an epistle, letter:*—Hieronimus āwrāt ǣnne pistol be forðsīðe þǣre eádigan Marian tō sumum hālgan mǣdene ... Hē dihte þisne pistol tō Paulam, Hml. Th. i. 436, 6–21. Wið ūtsihte; þysne pistol se ængel brōhte tō Rōme þā hý wǣran mid ūtsihte micclum geswǣncte, Lch. iii. 66, 5. (2) *an epistle* of the New Testament:—Swā swā se apostol Petrus on his pistole āwrāt, Hm. A. 52, 51. v. epistol; epistola.

**pistol-rǣdere.** *Substitute: A subdeacon, who reads the epistle in the service:*—Gescrýdde mid mæssehacelum sācerd, diácon and pistolrǣdere (*subdiaconus*) ādreógan þēnunga hyra ... Pistolrǣdere, swā oft swā hē mid mæssehacelan byþ gescrýd, hē dō of hī þænne hē rǣd pistel; þǣm geræddum eft mid þǣre hē sí gescrýd, Angl. xiii. 406, 581–586. Þænne se pistelrǣdere gā upp tō rǣdenne þā rǣdincge, 417, 739. And-swarigende twēgen pistelrǣderas standende tōforan þǣre rōde hī singan, on Grēcisc, 418, 757. Cf. sub-, under-diácon.

**pistol-rǣding.** *Add:*—Hit is gereht on ðyssere pistolrǣdinge (Acts, c. 2) hū se Hālga Gāst on ðisum dæge cōm tō ðām geleáffullan heápe Crīstes hýredes, Hml. Th. i. 314, 1. Be ðyssere tíde (*Advent*) mǣrsunge sprǣc se apostol Paulus on ðyssere pistolrǣdinge tō Rōmāniscum leódum (Rom. 13, 11 sqq.), 600, 31.

**pittel.** v. pyttel: **plǣtt.** *Add:* v. spor-(spur-)plǣtt: **plǣttan.** *Add:* [*N. E. D.* plat *to smack.*]

**planēta** (-e ?), an; *m. f.* (?). *A planet* (v. *N. E. D.*), *chasuble:*—Scrýde hine mid superhumerale and mid alban and stolan and handlīne and planētan, þ is godwebben cappe, MS. Laud 482, f. 48 a.

**plantian.** *Add:* (1) literal:—Swā swā treów þ planted (*plantatum*) is wið ryne wætera, Ps. Rdr. 1, 3. (2) figurative:—Þīn hand plantade (*plantavit*) ūre foregengan, Ps. Th. 43, 3. Būton hē of his hieremonna mōde ðā ðornas ðǣre īdlan lufan ǣr ūp ātuge, unnyt hē plantode on hī ðā word ðǣre hālgan lāre, Past. 443, 1. v. under-plantian.

**plaster.** *Add:*—Genim þysse wyrte wyrttruman on ele gesodene and wið wex gemencgedne ðām gemete þe þū plaster oþþe clyþan wyrce, Lch. i. 298, 12. Nim of þām sylfan sǣde, wyrc blaster (plaster, v. l.), 300, 5.

**platian.** *Substitute: to beat into thin plates; and add:* v. geplatod. [*From Latin.*]

**platung.** *Add:*—Platung *brattea, auri lamina,* Hpt. 31, 6, 68. *Obrizum,* i. *aurum optimi coloris* smǣte gold, platum (platung ?) (*here, and in Hpt. 489, 34 (both glosses of Ald. 48, 28) perhaps platum is Latin*), An. Ox. 3534.

**plega.** II. *add:*—Leúþwís (? lewis-, MS.) plega *celeuma* (v. gladung), *idem et toma,* i. *leta cantatio,* Wrt. Voc. ii. 130, 20. Heora biscepas sǣdon þæt heora godas bǣdon þ him man worhte anfiteatra, þ mon mehte þone hǣðeniscan plegan þǣrinne dōn *suasere pontifices, ut ludi scaenici diis expetentibus ederentur,* Ors. 3, 3; S. 102, 12. IV. *an implement for a game:*—Geseah hē ǣnne nacodne cnapan geond þā strǣte yrnan, sē wæs mid ele gesmerod, and bær iungra manna plegan on handa, Ap. Th. 12, 17.

**plegan.** [In p. 775, col. 2, l. 2 for 361, *l.* 391.] I. *add:*—Sum cild plegode gýmeleáslíce and bearn under ānum yrnendum hweóle, Hml. Th. ii. 26, 24. Þā mǣdenu beforan þām leornungmannum hæfdon hī sylfe be handa heom betweónum and þā lange hwīle plegdon (*diutius*

ludentes), Gr. D. 119, 14. Hundas blegan gesihð, þanc hit getācnað *canes ludere uiderit, gratiam significat,* Lch. iii. 200, 27. II. *add:*—Hī willað wōdlíce drincan binnan Godes hūse and bysmorlíce plegan (-ean, v. l.), Hml. S. 13, 77. IIa. *add:*—Hē sang beforan þām kāsere scandlicu leóþ and plegode scandlice plegan, Shrn. 121, 10. Æfter þisum forlēt Apollonius þā hearpan and plegode, and fela fǣgera þinga forðteáh, Ap. Th. 17, 12. IIb. *add:*—Āgan se cyngc plegan wið his gefēran mid þōðere, Ap. Th. 13, 1. IV. *add:*—Mann dysig plegað mid handum *homo stultus plaudet manibus,* Scint. 95, 8.

**plegestre.** an; *f. A female athlete:*—Cemp[ena], plegestr[en]a *luctatorum,* An. Ox. 4735.

**pleg-lic.** *Add:*—Pleglican iocosos, Hpt. Gl. 481, 6.

**plegol.** *Add:* in a bad sense, *wanton:*—Seó plegole (*lasciua*) geogoð þe byð hrǣd tō singienne, Chrd. 54, 22.

**pleg-stede,** es; *m. A play-place:*—On ðone plægstede; and of ðan plægstede, C. D. vi. 244, 8. [v. *N. E. D.* play-stead.]

**pleg-stōw.** *Add:* [*As a place-name* Plaistow.]

**pleoh.** *Add:*—Seó ceorung is swýðe mycel pleoh þ man wið God ceorige, swā swā ūs sǣde Paulus (cf. quidam murmuraverunt, et perierunt ab exterminatore, 1 Cor. 10, 10), Hml. S. 13, 288.

**ple6-lic.** *Add:*—þ gefeoht þe of geflite cymð betwux ceastergewarum is swýðe pleólic, Hml. S. 25, 712. Fram derigendlicere sprǣce and pleólicum weorce hine sylfne forhabban, Hml. Th. i. 360, 22.

**pleólíce.** v. un-pleólíce: **plicettan.** v. plyccan: **pliccgan.** *For* 'Plicged (plicged ?)' *l.* Plicged.

**pliht.** *Add:*—Lōce hwā þās bōc āwrīte, wrīte hig be þǣre bysne and for Godes lufon hī gerihte, þæt heó tō leás ne beó þām wrītere tō plihte and mē tō tāle, Ælfc. T. Grn. 21, 40. Tō plihte þīnre ǣhta and þīnes āgenes heáfdes bodað þes þīn cnapa swā bealdlíce be Crīste, Hml. S. 35, 32.

**plihtere.** *For* 'Plicilitere . . . 55' *substitute:*—Plihtere, ancremen *proreta,* An. Ox. 30: 7, 10. Plihttere, 5, 7. Plyhtre, 8, 4.

**pluccian, ploccan.** l. ploccian, *and for the gloss at* Wrt. Voc. ii. 140, 59 *substitute*—Ploccaþ *discerpit, lacerat,* tōslīt, *devorat, carpit.* *Add:*: v. ā-pluccian, plyccan.

**plūme.** *Add:* v. plūn.

**plūm-feþer.** *For* '43' *at end substitute* 144, 4, *and add:*—On plūmfeðerum hē (*the rich man*) līð, ac þēhweðere oft ǣblǣce, E. S. viii. 473, 19.

**plūn** *a plum:*—Prunus lignum, prunum fructus, i. plūn, Hpt. 33, 251, 23. v. plūme, plýme.

**plyccan;** *p.* plyhte. *To pluck, pull:*—Plicet (*for* t *instead of* þ *in the inflexion see* stirgit, 391, 30, gepwǣrat, 397, 439, fordyttat, 398, 95) *adludit* (ut vitulum lupus rapturus *adludit* prius), Germ. 397, 20. Ðonne þu setrægel habban wille, þonne plice þū ðīne āgene gewǣda mid twām fingrum, tōspred þīne twā handa and wege hī swylce þū setl gesydian wille, Tech. ii. 122, 17. Gylecan tācen is þæt þū strece forð þīn wenstre handstoc and plyce innan mid þīnre wynstran hande, 127, 15. [v. *N. E. D.* plitch.] v. pluccian.

**plýme.** *Add:*—Haec prunus (*plunus,* v. l.) ðis plūmtreów, *hoc prunum* seó plýme, Ælfc. Gr. Z. 20, 18. Ðonne þū plýman habban wille, Tech. ii. 124, 20.

**pocc.** *Add:*—Wiþ pocce on eágum, Lch. ii. 36, 23.

**pohha.** *Add:*—Poh[han] *fiscos, saccos publicos,* An. Ox. 50, 19. [v. *N. E. D.* pough.] v. cramming-pohha.

**pōl.** *Add:*—On blacan pōl; of ðām poole, C. D. vi. 220, 15. v. mǣr-, teám-, wīþig-pōl.

**pōl-bǣr,** e; *f. Pasture-land by a pool:*—On monnes pōlbǣre, C. D. iii. 415, 5.

**Pontisc** *translates* Pontius *in the name* Pontius Pilatus:—Hig sealdon hyne þām Pontiscean Pilate, Mt. 27, 2. Pontiscan, Lk. 3, 1: Hml. A. 182, 31.

**port.** II. *add:*—Hē cleacode swīðe earhlīce tō porte (*Ephesus*) ... þā hē fulgehende wið ðæs portes geate eóde, Hml. S. 23, 493–498. Hī sumne man ofslōgon of þām port (*Dover*), Chr. 1052; P. 173, 25. Hī hergodon and bærndon on Wiðreceastrescīre forð þ hī cōmon tō porte sylfan (*Worcester*), and woldon ðæne port bærnen, 1087; P. 223, 13. IIa. *town* as opposed to country:—Hē beád þ ǣlc man þe wǣre unnīðing sceolde cuman tō him of porte and of uppelande, Chr. 1087; P. 224, 34. v. heáfod-port.

**port-geat.** *Add:*—Hē beseah tō þǣre hālgan Crīstes rōde tācne hwǣr heú uppan þām portgeate stōd mid ārwurðnysse āfæstnod, Hml. S. 23, 500.

**port-gerēfa.** *Add:* I. an official of a foreign town:—Se biscop āræs and mid him se portgerēfa (*of Ephesus*), and þā yldostan portmen, Hml. S. 23, 749. II. an English official:—þes ceáp wæs geceápod on Wii ætforan ealra scýre. þises is tō gewitnesse Eádrige arceb. ... Godríc portgerēfa, C. D. iv. 117, 27. On Ælfgāres portgerēfan and Ælfwærdes portgerēfan þe þ toll nāmon for þæs cynges hand, Cht. E. 256, 16–18: 259, 9: 27: 262, 2: 264, 12: 271, 12: 273, 7.

**port-herepaþ** *a main road to a town:*—Andlang ðes portherpaðes, C. D. iii. 453, 29. Cf. port-weg, ceaster-herepaþ.

portian. *Add:* v. ge-portian.

portic. III. *add: n.:*—Hí gesáwon án lang portic on ðám norð-dǽle . . . on ðǽm eástdǽle wæs gesewen micel cyrce . . . Seó cyrce mid hire portice mihte fíf hund manna befón on hire rýmette, Hml. Th. i. 508, 9-14. v. eást-, hálig-portic.

port-mann. *Add:*—On portmanna hundan hylle, C. D. vi. 41, 19. Æt Portmanna hýðe, 49, 22. [v. *N. E. D.* port-man] : **port-strǽt.** *Add:* Cf. port-herpaþ, -weg.

port-weg, es; *m. A road to a town, a highway:*—Tó ðæn portwege, C. D. vi. 8, 31. [v. *N. E. D.* port-way.] Cf. port-herpaþ, -strǽt.

pos, es; *n. : only in pl.* (?) posu (-a) [cf. ge-pos] : *or* (?) **posa,** an; *m. A cold, catarrh:*—Posa catarrum, i. angustia pectoris, An. Ox. 31, 1. [v. *N. E. D.* pose.]

pos-hliwe, an; *f. Some kind of shelter* (?):—Tó poshliwan; of poshliwan, C. D. iii. 82, 2. Cf. (?) Tó posses hlǽwe; of ðǽm hlǽwe, 415, 30.

post. *Add:*—Se post ána ætstód ansund, Hml. S. 26, 234 (= Swt. A. Rdr. *in Dict.*).

pot. *Dele bracket, and see N. E. D.* pot: **potian.** *Add:* [v. *N. E. D.* pote.]

prǽtt. *Add:*—Be ðám þ preóstas hí warnien wið þá scýnlican híwinga deófla prǽttes (prettes, 7, 26) (*ante transformationes daemonum*), Chrd. 98, 33. Cwæð se Hǽlend him tó, 'Foxas habbað holu' . . . Críst sceáwode his heortan and geseah his prǽttas, . . . foxunga wǽron wuniende on him, Hml. S. 16, 160. [v. *N. E. D.* prat.]

prǽttig. *Add:*—Ficol, i. pretti versipellis, Kent. Gl. 493. Pǽti, An. Ox. 56, 36. Pǽtigere *callide* (*deceptionis*), 4980.

prǽfost. II. *add:*—On Laurentius mæssan daegi Ælfsige ðǽm biscope in his getelde Aldred se prófast ðás feówer collectæ ǽr underne áwrát, Rtl. 185, 20-23. II a. *a steward :*—Nonnosus wæs prǽfost (*praepositus*) on þám mynstre þe geseted is in ðám munte Soractis, Gr. D. 48, 24. Hé þæt wæter sealde heora þéne; heora þén wæs ðæs ilcan mynstres mæssepreóst. Ðá ondranc sé þæs wætres and sealde hit þǽm breðer ðe him æt stód, ðæs mynstres prófoste (*this detail is not given in Bede's Life*) . . . þá hí þá tíd hǽfdon ymb þ tó spreconne, þá ondette heora ǽgðer óþrum þ hí nǽfre ǽr sélre wín ne druncon, Shrn. 64, 9-15. Áxode hé þone prófost hwæðer hé fisc hæfde. Hé tó andsware cwæð, þ hí ne mihton ne fisceras ne hé sylf gefón ǽnne sprot. Ðá cwæð se hálga wer, 'Wurp út nú þín net,' Hml. S. 31, 1268.

prǽfost-scír. *Add:*—Hé sí ádrǽfed of endebyrdnesse prǽvostscíre *deiciatur de ordine prepositure,* R. Ben. I. 111, 15 : Gr. D. 50, 7. Wé þá synderlíce práuost hátað þe under óðrum ea!drum ðǽre práuostscýre gýmað (*prioratus curam gerunt*), Chrd. 52, 15.

prass. *Add:* m. *or* n. :—Hé mid swiðlicum prasse férde, Hml. S. 29, 208 : 25, 302.

predicung, e; *f. Preaching :*—Þ úre folc ne wurðe losad þurh náne orsorhnesse, bútan predicunge (*predicatione*), Chrd. 50, 5. v. word-predicung.

prénan. *Dele, and see* príwan : **preón.** *Add:* [v. *N. E. D.* preen.]

preóst. *Add:* (1) *an ecclesiastic of the seventh of the holy orders; the bishop and the priest were of the same order, but the bishop's functions were more extensive, and in this respect he was superior to the priest.* Cf. Ll. Th. ii. 348, 20-29:—Bisceopes feoh .xi. gylde. Preóstes feoh .ix. gylde. Diácones feoh .vi. gylde, Ll. Th. i. 2, 5. (1 a) *a priest who served the church of a particular person, a chaplain :*—On þám ilcan geáre forðférde Ælfsige biscop on Winceastre, and Ælfwine þæs cynges preóst (*capellanus regis*) féng þǽrtó, Chr. 1032 ; P. 159, 7. Ic an Alfwolde mínum preóste twǽgra hída, . . . and ic gean Æþelmǽre mínum prǽoste twǽgra hída, C. D. iii. 272, 35-37. (1 b) *where the sacrificial character of the priest's office is brought out, the priest as officiant at the Eucharist :*—Wé lǽrað þ preóst ǽfre ne mæssige bútan onúsan gehálgodon weófode, Ll. Th. ii. 250, 21. (2) *in a more general sense a member of the ecclesiastical profession :*—Nǽnig mæssepreóst óðres mæssepreóstes preóst (*clericum*) ne wyrde, Ll. Th. ii. 412, 6. Fylgde him (*bishop Dalfin*) Willfrið his preóst (*clericus illius; Wilfrid was not yet a mass-priest* v. 662, 22), Bd. 5, 19 ; Sch. 661, 14. Gif hwylce preóstas and Godes þeówas sýn bútan hálegum hádum gesette *siqui sunt clerici extra sacros ordines constituti*, 1, 27 ; Sch. 13, 4. (2 a) *in the phrase descriptive of the tonsure :*—Gif mon cierliscne mon tó preóste bescíre unbundenne, mid .xxx. sciłł. gebéte . . . Gif hé hine gebinde, and þonne tó preóste bescíre, .lx. sciłł. gebéte, Ll. Th. i. 84, 6-10. (3) *where preóst is in contrast with munuc :*—Godes þeówas, biscopas and abbudas, munecas and mynecena, preóstas and nunnan, Ll. Th. i. 304, 26. Seofon preóstlice tíde fram munecum æfter þeáwe preósta (*canonicorum*) tó wyrþenne synd, Angl. xiii. 426, 867. Hér drǽfde Eádgar cyng þá preóstas (*canonicas, v. l.*) of Ceastre of Ealdan mynstre, and of Níwan mynstre, and sette hý mid munecan, Chr. 964 ; P. 116, 1. (4) *where preóst is in contrast with sácerd :*—Gehǽldum þám preóste Benedictus cwæð,

'. . . Geneð þú nǽfre þ þú gá tó þám hálgan háde, oððe máran underfó þonne þú nú hæfst ; sóðlíce on swá hwilcum dæge swá þú geþrístlǽcst þ þú underféhst þone hálgan sácerdhád sóna þú bist mid deófles anwealde gehæftníeded.' Ðá gewát se preóst (*clericus*), Gr. D. 135, 6-17. v. tún-preóst ; preóst-líf.

preóst-gesamnung, e; *f. A community of priests :*—On ǽlcre preóstgesamnunge (*in hoc ordine canonico*) is ǽlc þrýstnes forboden, Chrd. 45, 29.

preóst-hád. *Add:*—Preósthádes oððe lǽwedes hádes men *priests or laymen*, Ll. Th. ii. 412, 12. Cyrclicere preósthádes geþinþe (*ab*) *ecclesiastico clericatus gradu* (*discedens*), An. Ox. 3692. Preóstháde (*in*) *clero* (*degentium*), 5303. Sé wæs Haroldes eorles mæssepreóst ; sé werede his kenepas on his preóstháde oð ðæt hé wæs biscop, Chr. 1056 ; P. 186, 26. Se ylca mæssepreóst on preóstháde (*in presbyteratus officio*) his líf geendode, Gr. D. 66, 1. v. mæssepreóst-hád.

preóst-heáp. *Add:*—þá ácsode ic hí be þám ylcan wundre beforan þám æþelum werum and þám preóstheápe (*clero*) and eác beforan eallum þám folce, Gr. D. 302, 25.

preóst-híred, es; *m. An ecclesiastical community, a body of clergy :*—Preósthíredes *cleri*, An. Ox. 3006. Ætforan þám bisceope and þám preósthírede, Chrd. 37, 15. In ǽlcum preósthírede (*canonica congregatione*), 13, 20 : 60, 32. Úre preósthýredas *noster clerus*, 42, 32. Hit is gewuna on manegum preósthíredum (*canonicorum congregationibus* ; cf. geférrádene, 11), 13, 13.

preóst-líc; *adj. Priestly, canonical :*—Ic mingie þ hí gemunon þæs preóstlican regoles (*regule canonice*), Chrd. 89, 37. Preóstlicum gewunan, ðeáwe *canonico more*, Angl. xiii. 412, 667, 677. Seofon preóstlice tíde *septem canonice hore*, 426, 866.

preóst-líf, es; *n. A house of priests or canons.* Cf. munuc-líf :—Martinus cóm tó ánum preóstlífe, and hí gelógodon þá his bæd on þæs mynstres sprǽchúse . . . þá woldon ðá preóstas him wurðlíce beddian, Hml. S. 31, 846.

preóst-reáf, es; *n. Vestments of a priest :*—Be þǽre gesceádwísnysse on gyrelan þæs preóstreáfes *ut in cultu vestium discretionem teneant*, Chrd. 64, 27.

preóst-regol, es; *m. A canonical rule :*—Libbað clǽnre heortan an eówrum preóstregole (*regula canonica*), Chrd. 88, 15 : 89, 33. Éstfulnes lífes be preóstregole *deuotio uitæ regularis*, 93, 11.

prica; I. *add:*—Seó forme ábecéde ys bútan pricon, and seó óðer ys gepricod on þá swýðran healfe, and seó þrydde on þá wynstran healfe, Angl. viii. 332, 42. II. *add:*—Ælce geáre wanað án tíd and án prica se nigonteóða dǽl ánes prican, Angl. viii. 308, 46. Seó tíd stent on feówer pricon, gyf ǽlcum geáre ǽnne prican, þonne gýt þǽr byð án tó láfe, 309, 2-4.

pricel, es; *n.*(?) 1. *m.*, *and add:*—Pricelas gálnysse *aculei libidinis*, Scint. 87, 12.

pricels, es; *m.* (?). *Dele* (?), *and add:*—Unálýfedlicum pricelsum *inlecebrosis stimulis*, An. Ox. 4228.

prician. *Add:* I. *trans.:*—Pricigende eáge út gelǽt teáras and sé þe pricaþ heortan forþbringð andgyt *punguens oculum deducit lacrimas, et qui pungit cor profert sensum* (Ecclus. 22, 19), Scint. 188, 13. II. *intrans.* *To produce a pricking sensation* [used impersonally :—Hyt pricaþ innan þan sculdru and on þan hrigge swilce þǽr þornas on sý, Lch. iii. 120, 10.] [v. *N. E. D.* pritch.] v. ge-prician.

pric-þorn, es; *m. A prickly thorn tree :*—On pricþorn, C. D. iii. 436, 16.

prím-sang. *Add:*—Be prímsangum (*de ora prima*). Ðonne preóstas tó cyrcan cumon heora prím tó singienne, Chrd. 27, 37.

princ. *Add:*—On prince eáges *in ictu oculi*, Scint. 43. 16. [Cf. *N. E. D.* prink *to wink.*]

pritigeaþ. v. writian.

prút; *adj. Add:*—Módig[e] ł prúd[e] *arrogantes*, An. Ox. 56, 233. Þǽra prútra and þǽra módigra gyltas þreágan *contempnentes et superbos increpare*, Chrd. 18, 8. ¶ *as a nickname :*—Tofig Prúda, C. D. iv. 54, 13. v. ofer-prút.

prút pride. v. ofer-prút, *sbst.* [Cf. prowde of lif, *N. E. D.*]

prútian *to be proud :*—Gif man þone ærcediácon oððe þone právost ágyte þ hí wyllon módiggan oððe prútian *si reperti fuerint superbi aut elati*, Chrd. 18, 30. Gif him deóflu hwæt on heora geþance lǽren hwanon hí módigian magon oððe prútian (*unde laudari aut extolli debeant*), 99, 4. [v. *N. E. D.* proud, *vb.*]

prút-líc; *adj. Swelling with pride, haughty :*—Gán mid prútlicre stæppincge *tumido gestu incedere*, Chrd. 77, 2.

prútlíce. *Add: haughtily, arrogantly :*—Welegum þyssere worulde bebeód ná prútlíce (*superbe*) witan, Scint. 178, 4. Gif hwylc bróðor an preósthýrede bið þe intó cyrcan prútlíce (*pompatice*) gǽð, Chrd. 60, 34 : 343.

prút-swangor; *adj. Indolent through pride* (?) :—Se Hǽlend spræc tó sumum weligum men . . . hé wæs prútswongor and swǽrmód, Wlfst. 257, 12.

prýt. *Add:*—Ofermóde préde opes superbe (*Zupitza takes prǽde as*

*adjective*. Kent. Gl. 249. *For* prēde = *opes* cf. wærde *opes*, 79, 11 ; Kent. Gl. 864), Wülck. Gl. 62, 29.

**prýte**. *Add:* prýtu(o) *pomp, splendour* of dress :—Reáfes prýto *cultus uestium*, Chrd. 65, 4. Prýte *fastus*, An. Ox. 18 b, 29. Áhafenysse prýtan beswicen *tumoris fastu seductus*, Angl. xiii. 440, 1064. Forhogudre wiðerwerdnysse prýtan (*printed* wrytan), 371, 83 : 369, 56. Mid prýtan (*pompatice*) gán, Chrd. 32, 33.

**prýtian**. *Dele, and see* writian : psaltere. v. saltere : **psalterium**. v. wyn-psalterium.

**púca**, an ; *m. A goblin, mischievous spirit* :—Púca *larbula*, An. Ox. 23, 2. Wandrigende púcan (*printed* wucan) *uagantes demonas*, Germ. 388, 37. ¶ in a place-name :—Ðis synd ðá landgemǽru ðe sceótað dún tó Púcanwylle, C. D. iii. 423, 28. ¶ Cf. (?) Wæs sumes gesîðes tûn, sê wæs Púh (Púhh, *v. l.*) háten *qui vocabatur Puch*, Bd. 5, 4 ; Sch. 567, 10. [v. *N. E. D.* puck. Icel. púki.] v. púcel.

**púcel**. *Add:* [v. *N. E. D.* puckle.] v. púca : **puerisc**. *Dele, and see* Pierisc : Pulgarisc. v. Bulgarisc.

**pull**. *Add:* v. mǽr-, mylen-pull : **pullian**. *In* l. 2 *for* sper[n]don. *l.* sperdon.

**pund**. I. *add:*—.x. pund caeses, C. D. i. 293, 10. Se sester sceal wegan twá pund be sylfyrgewyht, Lch. iii. 92, 14. II a. *add:*—Man geald ǽrest gafol Deniscan mannum . . . ꝥ wæs .x. þúsend punda, Chr. 991 ; P. 127, 5. Twá and twéntig þúsend punda goldes and seolfres mon gesealde þám here of Ænglalande wið friðe, Ll. Th. i. 288, 11. Mid .v. pundum mǽrra pæninga, 62, 9. Hî geféngon Cameleac biscop and áliésde Eádweard cyning hine eft mid .xl. pundum, Chr. 918 ; P. 98, 15. II b. *add:*—Drihten pundu (*talenta*) forgyfð, Scint. 132, 7. Sum hafenleás man sceolde ágyldan healf pund (cf. Gr. D. 157, 33, which makes the debt twelve shillings (*duodecim solidi*)) . . . wearð gemét þæt feoh and twéntig penega tó eácan (cf. Gr. D. 158, 15, which makes the amount found thirteen shillings), Hml. Th. ii. 176, 34–178, 7.

**pundar**. *Add: a balance* or *weight used in a balance* :—Pundor (*printed* wundor) *hostimen* (cf. hostimentum *lapis quo pondus equatur*, Corp. Gl. H. 63, 145 : *pondus seu bilanx*, Migne), Wrt. Voc. ii. 70, 32 : 43, 20. Of punder (*printed* wunder) *a perpendiculo*, Hpt. Gl. 476, 75.

**pundern**. *Add: a plumb-line* :—Of punderne *a perpendiculo*, An. Ox. 3005 : 2, 138 (*printed* wunderne).

**pundern-georn** (?). *Substitute:* **punderngend**, es : *m.* (?). *One who weighs.*

**pundernian** *to weigh.* See preceding word.

**pund-fald** *a pinfold* :—On hacan pundfald ; of hacan pundfalde, C. D. vi. 41, 24. [v. *N. E. D.* pin-fold.] v. pyndan.

**pundrian**. v. á-pundrian (El. 581, *printed* á-wundrad. *The facsimile reprint has* apundrad. Cf. á-pyndrian).

**punere**, es ; *m. A pestle* :—Punere *pilo*, Scint. 95, 19. v. punian.

**pung**. *Add:*—Pung *cassidile*, Wrt. Voc. ii. 129, 26. [v. *N. E. D.* pung.]

**punian**. *Add:*—Nim nîwe beáne and puna, Lch. iii. 108, 17. Þeáh þú punige (*contuderis*) stuntne on pílan swylce berenhula punigendum (*feriente*) bufan punere, Scint. 95, 18. [v. *N. E. D.* pound.]

**pur**. *Add:* [v. *N. E. D.* purre] : **pur-lamb**. *Add:* [v. *N. E. D.* pur *a ram or wether lamb.*]

**purpul** (?) ; *adj. Purple* :—Berende ꝥ ðyrnenne bég and ꝥ purbple hrægl (purple hrægle, R.) *portans purpureum uestimentum*, Jn. L. 19, 5. See *next* word.

**purpure**. *Add: purple material* :—Hî scrýddon hyne mid purpuran reáfe, Jn. 19, 2. Se cyning áwearp his cynehelm samod mid his purpuran gyrlum, Hml. Th. i. 468, 4. Se cyning áwearp his purpuran reáf, 568, 12.

**purpuren**. *Add:*—Se Hǽlend bær þyrnenne cynehelm and purpuren (purpre, *later version*) reáf, Jn. 19, 5.

**purs** *a purse* :—Purs ł seód *fiscus*, An. Ox. 18 b, 36.

**putung**, e ; *f. Pushing, impelling, impulse, instigation* :—Hation ꝥ þurh deófles putunge wæs an belǽd *oderint quod instinctu diaboli ingestum est*, Chrd. 62, 27. [v. *N. E. D.* put.] Cf. potian.

**pyf** (?) *a blast of wind* :—Windes ðyf (pyf ?), Bt. 20 ; F. 72, 5. [v. *N. E. D.* puff.] v. pyffan.

**pyffan** *to breathe out* :—Pyfte gást *efflauit flamen*, An. Ox. 18, 42. Pyf on þínne scytefinger, Tech. ii. 121, 12. Piffendes *spirantis*, An. Ox. 1885. v. á-pyffan ; pyf.

**pyle**. *In* l. 8 *for* seti ł. setl, *and add:* pylu :—Pylu *ceruical*, An. Ox. 29, 4. Pyles tácen is þæt þú mid þínum scytefingre sume feþer tácnum gestríce on þýne wynstran hand innewearde and lecge tó þínum eáron, Tech. ii. 126, 6. Bið se enboga underléd mid pyle, Past. 143, 18. Genim þás wyrte, lege him nytendum under his pyle, Lch. i. 228, 1. [*N. E. D.* pillow.] v. heáfod-pyle.

**pyll**. *Add:*—On brádan bricge ; and of brádan bricge ðæt on holan pyl ; and of holan pylle on pincanhammes díc : and of pincanhammes díc innan miclan pyl ; and of miclan pylle ðæt æft on Sæferne, C. D. iii. 406, 2–6. Andlang streámes tó holan pylle ; of holan pylle úp andlang díc tó Brycgwege (later versions of this are : Along the stremys to the holw

pylle, fro the holw pylle up a long the dyche to Brycwege : A longo illorum decuruum ad illum concavum puteum ; ab illo puteo . . .), C. D. B. iii. 184, 20. Anlang uueges tó thǽre stǽnenan brycge, on [t]hone aldan pyll, i. 96, 22.

**pylu**. v. pyle : **pyndan**. *Add:* v. pund-fald : -**pyndrian**. v. á-pyndrian ; pundrian : **pyngan**. *Add:* [v. *N. E. D.* ping.]

**pýtan** *to push, poke, thrust, put* out the eyes :—Gif þé slána lyste, þonne sete þú þínne winstran þúman on þínes lytlan fingres lið and pýt mið þínum scytefingre in þíne wynstran hand on þornes getácnunge þe hí on weaxað, Tech. ii. 124, 24. Hé lét him pýtan út his eágan (*euulsis oculis*), and ceorfan of his handa, Chr. 796 ; P. 56, 26 (v. Nap. 85). [v. *N. E. D.* put.] v. á-pýtan (*given wrongly under* á-pícan).

**pytt**. I. *add:*—‘ Drinc ðæt wæter of ðínum ágenum mere, and ðætte of ðínum ágnum pytte áflówe ’ . . . Ðonne hé drincð of ðǽm wielme his ágnes pyttes . . . ‘ *bibe aquam de cisterna tua, et fluenta putei tui* ’ . . . *Bibit sui fluenta putei*, Past. 373, 3–10. Andlang hagan tó ðám grundeliésan pytte, C. D. v. 148, 10. On ðone grundlǽsan pyt ; of ðám putte, vi. 41, 23. I a. *figurative* :—Ðæt hí for hira úpáhæfennesse befeallen on ðone pytt ofermétta *ipso elationis suae barathro devorantur*, Past. 439, 3. v. col-, wiðig-, wulf-pytt.

**pyttel** *a mouse-hawk* :—Bleri pittel *scoricarius*, Wrt. Voc. i. 30, 6. Blerea pyttel *soricarius*, 63, 8. [v. *N. E. D.* pittel.]

# R

**racente**. *In* l. 2 *for* acerntan *l.* racentan, *and add:*—Racetan *catenas*, Scint. 59, 6. Hracengo, Mk. L. 5, 4. [v. *N. E. D.* rackan.]

**racent-teáge**. *Add:*—Þá læg Petrus . . . mid twám racenteágum getíged . . . se engel cwæð, ‘ Arís . . .’ and þá racenteágan feóllon ðǽrrihte of Petres handum, Hml. Th. ii. 382, 2–8. v. ge-racenteágian.

**racent-teágian**. v. ge-racentteágian.

**racent-teáh**. *Add:*—Hé geband him sylfum þone fót mid íserne racenteáge and ðá racenteáge hé gefæstnode . . . tó ðon ꝥ him nǽre ná álýfed furður tó gánne þonne swá swá þǽre racenteáge længe áþened wæs . . . ‘ Gif þú sý Godes þeówa, ne binde þé seó ísene racetæáh (racenteág, *v. l.*), ac þé nime Crístes racenteáh,’ Gr. D. 214, 5–12. Hraccentégum gebinda *catenis ligare*, Mk. L. 5, 3. Mið hracentégum gebunden *catenis uinctus*, 4. [v. *N. E. D.* rakenteie.]

**racian**. *Add:* [v. *N. E. D.* rake.]

**raciend**, es ; *m. One who addresses an assembly* :—Se sóðsagola raciend and déma, sê þe mid his áþenedre handa gestilleþ ꝥ gehlýd eallra manna, and hí gespaneð tó ánum dóme *concionator verax extensa manu omnium tumultus sedat, eosque ad unam sententiam revocat*, Gr. D. 265, 12. v. riht-raciend.

**-racodteágian**. v. ge-racentteágian.

**racsan**. v. raxan.

**racu**. *Add:*—[Godspel]licere race cwydas *euangelicę relationis* (i. *narrationis*) *dicta*, An. Ox. 169. ‘ Mid fæsthafelre race ł smeáþanceire trahtnunge *tenaci* (i. *subtili*) *textu*, 192. In þǽre rihtan race byð full oft forðsænded se dóm, þurh þone byþ oferswíþed ꝥ hlúde geflit þæs folces *in concione sententia promitur, per quam turbae seditio comprimatur*, Gr. D. 264, 27. Þæs þing wé cweðað ymbe þǽre eásterlican tíde þe wé þencað mid sóðre race geglengan, Angl. viii. 324, 12. Race *ordinem*, Germ. 395, 34. Þá wísan þe hé þǽr spræc þurh his race and sócne *quot sententias quasi per inquisitionem movet*, Gr. D. 265, 8. Gecyndbóca racu, gerecednesse geneseos *relatum*, i. *relationem*, An. Ox. 51. I a. *reasoning, argument* :—Oft gebyreð ðæt ðá lytegan bióð nnid liðlicre race gehwyrfde . . . Ðǽm lytegan is betere ðæt hié mid ryhtre race weorðen oferreahte and mid ðǽre race oferswíðde, *sapientes plerumque ratiocinationis argumenta convertunt . . . Illis prodest, ut in suis allegationibus victi jaceant*, Past. 205, 1–4. IV. *add:*—Hé sceal beforan ðǽm ðearlwísan Déman mid gereccelicre race gereccan ðæt hé ðæt ilce self dyde ðe hé óðre menn lǽrde *apud districtum judicem cogitur tanta in opere exsolvere, quanta eum constat aliis voce praecepisse*, Past. 193, 15. V. *reason* :—Ne wiþstandeð nǽningu gesceádwísnes ne nǽnigu racu þissere sprǽce *nulla huic allegationi ratio obsistit*, Gr. D. 271, 20. V a. *reason* personified :—ꝥ ne mæg fullíce seó gesceádwísnes sylf and racu gerihtan *quod plene ratio non valet*, Gr. D. 272, 9. Ic eom seó gesceádwísnes ðínes módes þe ðé wið sprecð, and ic eom seó racu ðe mé onhagað ðé tó gerihtreccenne *promittit ratio quae tecum loquitur*, Solil. H. 26, 7. v. fór-, mǽg-racu.

**racu**, e. *Add:* , an :—Worhte hé him áne lytlan racan (*rastrum*) . . . geteáh hé þá racan æfter þǽre eorðan, Gr. D. 192, 24–193, 1.

**rád**. I. *add:*—Rád ðín *aequitatus tuus*, Ps. Rdr. 284, 8. Hire hind hire ealne weg beforan arn ðonne hió on ráde wæs, Lch. iii. 426, 27. I a.

á *ride* on horseback :—Sceal hē (*an old man*) þā eágon weccan mid gongum, mid rādum oþþe mid þý þe hine mon bere oþþe on wǣne ferige, Lch. ii. 30, 29. [v. *N. E. D.* road.] v. floc-rād ; eóred.

**rád**, es ; *n. A condition, stipulation :*—Hē .cccccc. gīsla on his geweald underfǣng on þ rād (gerād, Ors. 3, 8 ; S. 122, 4) þ hiē heora seoþþan ēce þeówas wǣran, Mod. Lang. Review, viii. 62, 26.

**-rád.** *Add :* v. sam-, unfæst-rád.

**radelod** (-ud) ; *adj. Having a large, outspreading top* (?) :—On thā radeludan āc ; of thǣre radeludan ǣc on cwenan brigce, C. D. B. iii. 44, 21. [Cf. (?) *Icel.* röðull *a halo ; a crest* of a hill.]

**radre** *bovistra.* l. *bovestra.*

**rád-stefn.** *Substitute : A summons carried by a mounted person.* The later Latin versions are : Si tainus ascendisset, ut seruiret regi et equitatus sui uice fungeretur in familia sua, and : Si þegn ita profecisset, ut regi seruisset et uice sua equitaret in missiatico regis. Perhaps an instance of such service is given in the following :—Ān scīrgemōt sæt æt Ægelnōdes stāne be Cnutes dæge cinges . . . and Tofig Prūda cōm ðǣr on ðæs cinges ǣrende, C. D. iv. 54, 8-13.

**rǣcan. I.** *add :*—Hī mihton mid heora handum rǣcean and niman þæs hālgan dūstes dǣl, Shrm. 81, 16. **II.** *add :*—Rǣc *appresenta,* An. Ox. 56, 18. (1) *to stretch out* one's hand :—Ne rāhten giē hond in mec *non extendistis manus in me,* Lk. L. R. 22, 53. Honda hrāhton on ðene Hǣlend *manus injecerunt in Jesum,* Mt. L. 26, 50. (2) *to hold out* a thing *and give* to a person. (a) a material thing :—Cuidestū ðone stān rāeceð (rǣceð, R.) ł seles him ? *numquid lapidem porrigit ei ?,* Mt. 7, 9. Rǣces, 10. Ðǣm ic lāf rāhte ł ic rǣco uællo (hlāf hrāhte ł ic rǣce wyllo, R.) *cui panem porrexero,* Jn. L. 13, 26. Copp full of ǣcced rāhton tō his mūðe (*obtulerunt ori eius*), Jn. L. R. 19, 29. (b) a non-material thing, *to give, bestow :*—Þine dōmas rǣcað gehwām āgen gewyrhta, Hy. 7, 15. Rǣc fultume *tribue auxilium,* Rtl. 41, 11 : 23, 9.

**rǣcc.** *Add :* [v. *N. E. D.* rache, ratch.] : rǣce (-u). *Add :* v. fýr-, hlāf-rǣce (-u).

**rǣced.** *Add :*—Fram recede *a triclinio* (cf. triclinio, i. *sede* būre, 718), An. Ox. 4, 21.

**rǣcing.** *Add : seizure, capture :*—Hrǣcing (*printed* hracing, *but see Skeat's collation*) *detentio* (cf. captura, detentio, captio hæft, Wrt. Voc. ii. 128, 30, *and see* ge-rǣcan ; I. 3 b), Rtl. 65, 29.

**rǣd. I.** *add :*—Hlyste hē gōdes rǣdes, nā of mīnum mūðe, ac of Crīstes sylfes, Hml. Th. i. 54, 16. **II.** *add :*—Consilium, þæt is rǣdgeðeht . . . Sē hæfð gōdne rǣd þurh Godes gyfe þe him gerǣdað þǣr hwæt him tō dōnne sý and hwæt tō forlǣtenne, Wlfst. 51, 19. **III.** *add :*—Dōme, rǣde (*inuestigabile*) *decretum,* An. Ox. 2676. Swicfullum rǣde *fraudulento consilio,* 4836. Hē lēt him tō rǣde *he adopted as his plan,* Hml. S. 23, 319. Gōdo dōað woegas iúero and raedo (*studia,* printed *stadia,* but see Jer. 7, 3) iúro, Rtl. 36, 21. **III a.** with negative, (*no*) *plan to help oneself :*—Mīn heorte and mīn mōd mē forlēton, tō þām þæt ic mē nyste nænne rǣd *cor meum dereliquit me,* Ps. Th. 39, 14. Hē cwæð þ sume dæge wǣre mid gafoles neóde geneðed sum getreówe wer, and him nyste nænne rǣd, Gr. D. 157, 23. Ne canst þū þe nænne rǣd, Hml. S. 35, 34. **IV.** *add :*—Ic gelýfe þ hit sý rǣd (*operae pretium credo*) þ ic āsǣcge ðā sprǣce, Gr. D. 305, 17. Þā gebūhte þ rǣd mīnes sweores fæder þ hē fērde *visum est patri soceri mei pergere,* 306, 1 : Chr. 995 ; P. 130, 17. Ealle ðā ðing ðe hlāforde magan tō rǣde, Angl. ix. 259, 19. Rǣdas *conpendia,* Scint. 100, 14. **V.** *add :*—Rǣde *senatu,* An. Ox. 4041. **V a.** *the act of taking counsel together :*—Geþafa þ mīn mōdor mē gesprǣcan, and sume þreó niht on mīnum rǣde beón (*may be in consultation with me*), Hml. S. 4, 324. Wæs Acitofel mid Absalone on rǣde, 19, 201. **VII.** *rule, direction.* v. rǣdan ; IV. :—Þā nigon werod bugon tō heora Scyppende, and betǣhton heora rǣd tō his willan, Hml. Th. i. 12, 7. [v. *N. E. D.* rede.] v. frum-, tūn-rǣd.

**-rǣd[e].** *Add :* ā-, ge-, gelōm-, oft-, twi-, unfæst-, wiþ-rǣd[e].

**rǣdan. II a.** *add :*—Þā rēdon (rǣddan, *v. l.*) hī him betweónum and cwǣdon *consultatione habita,* Ors. 1, 14 ; S. 56, 20. Hī heom betweónum rǣddon and þus geþwǣrlíce cwǣdon, Hml. S. 23, 201. **II b.** *add : to say in consultation :*—Ðeáh ðē mon hwylces hlihge, and ðū ðē unscyldigne wite, ne rēhst ðū hwæt hý rǣdon oððe rūnion, Prov. K. 12. **II c.** *add : to consult the interests of :*—Filiendre æftergencgnisse rǣddan *successure posteritati consulebant,* An. Ox. 2696. **III.** *add :*—Ðā ðā preóstas ðis gehýrdon, þā rǣddan hī ð hī nāman twēgen of heom and sendan tō þām pāpan, Chr. 995 ; P. 130, 21. Hē wolde witan æt him hwæt his suna rǣdde (hræddon, *v. l.*), Hml. S. 5, 155. Gefare hē þ þ God rǣde (cf. wille, 24), Ll. Th. i. 344, 29. **IV.** *add :*—Hē wíslíce rǣdde for Gode and for worulde eall his þeóde, Chr. 959 ; P. 115, 6. **VI.** *add :* (1) *trans.* (a) *to have an idea, suppose* (a) with acc. :—Monige menn . . . angiennað . . . smeágean suiðor ðonne him ðearf sié tō begonnanne, and rǣdað sume leásunge on ðǣre smeáunge *nonnulli se in inquisitionibus plus quam necesse est exercentes, ex nimia subtilitate falluntur,* Past. 67, 4. Hī (*the guards of Christ's sepulchre*) nāmon þone sceatt and swāþeáh muþetton ar.d on synderlicum rūnungum þæt

riht rǣddon (*in secret talks apart they supposed what the truth was*), Hml. A. 79, 161. (β) with clause :—þā ongann hē mid gleáwum mōde þencean and rǣdan (rǣsian, smeágean, *v. ll.*) þætte nān ōðer intinga wǣre *coepit sagaci animo conicere, quod nulla esset alia causa,* Bd. 3, 10 ; Sch. 233, 3. (a a) *to guess, tell by conjecture :*—Hī hēton hine rǣdan hwā hine hrepode, Hml. Th. ii. 248, 14. (b) *to make out the meaning of* a riddle, dream, &c. :—Gif heora hwilc . . . þone rǣdels āriht rǣdde, þonne weard sē tō beheáfdunge gelǣd, swā same swā sē ðe hine āriht ne rǣdde, Ap. Th. 3, 15-19. (c) *to peruse without uttering in speech, to read to oneself :*—Tō gefyllenne þe hē rǣd *ad implendum quę legit,* Scint. 219, 17. Manega ðǣra Iūdēa rǣddon (rēdon, *altered from* rēddon, L. rēddun, R. *iegerunt*) þiss gewrit, Jn. 19, 20. Hē hālsaþ ǣlcne þāra ðe þās bōc rǣdan lyste, Bt. proem ; F. viii. 11. (d) *to learn by perusal, find* a statement *recorded :*—Rǣde hē on his bōcum hwelce ungetīna hiē dreógende wǣron, Ors. 1, 11 ; S. 50, 17. Gesunde ūp āstandan synd rǣdde *sospites emersisse leguntur,* An. Ox. 4785. ¶ *where the statement is implied :*—Ðā fnædu þā untrumnyssa āfýgdon, swā swā wē rǣdað (*we read the statement that the hems put sickness to flight*) be sumum wīfe (*in the case of a certain woman*), Hml. Th. ii. 394, 1. Man nam of þām ylcan munecan biscopas tō gehwylcre stōwe, swā þū rǣddan miht on Ystoria Anglorum, Chr. 995 ; P. 129, 36. (d a) *to find* a subject mentioned, *read of :*—Þrý Herōdes wē rǣdað on bōcum, Hml. Th. ii. 382, 34. (e) *to read aloud :*—Mōises rǣdde his bōc þām folce, Ex. 24, 7. On rǣdingsceamele synd rǣdde *in pulpito recitantur, leguntur,* An. Ox. 4814. (2) *intrans. or absolute* (a) *to read to oneself :*—þonne ongyte sē þe rǣt (rēdes, L. R. *legit*), Mk. 13, 14. Hē hine ǣnne gemētte sittende and rǣdendne ætforan þām mynstergeate, Gr. D. 163, 24. (b) *to read aloud, read to others :*—Hē ārās þ hē rǣdde (tō rēdanne, L. R., *legere*), Lk. 4, 16. **VII.** *add : to dress, trim, set in order :*—Hē forlēt þā leóhtfatu þe hē rǣdde and fylde (behwearf, *v. l.*) *lampades quas reficiebat relinquens,* Gr. D. 46, 31. On fealuwes leá þǣr Ælfríc biscop rēdan hēt tō þǣre ealdan dīc, C. D. ii. 250, 30. The Latin version of Ll. Th. i. 434, 15 is : Arabit unaquaque septimana .i. acram, et ipse *parabit* semen domini sui in horreo. [Perhaps the examples under **VII.** should be given under a separate word. v. *N. E. D.* rede (1) and (2) ; *also read.*] v. wiþ-rǣdan.

**rǣd-bora.** *Add :*—Manega gesibsume synd þe, rǣdbora (*consiliarius*) sí þe ān of þūsendum, Scint. 200, 2. Ne nimð se hlāford his ðeówan him tō rǣdboran, ac nimð his holdan frýnd, and him geopenað his willan, Hml. Th. ii. 522, 32.

**rǣde** *reading.* v. hēc-rǣde.

**-rǣde.** v. cwelde-rǣde : **rǣde** ; *adj. Add :* v. iþ-, twi-, wiþ-rǣde.

**rǣde-fæsting,** e ; *f. Entertainment furnished to the king's messengers when riding on the king's business, or to those strangers who were coming to the king :*—Liberabo illud (monasterium) a pastu et refectione illorum hominum quos saxonice nominamus walhfǣreld and heora fæsting and ealra angelcynnes monna and ælþeódigra rǣdefæstinge, C. D. ii. 60, 30. v. fæsting.

**rǣde-here.** *Add :*—Rǣdehere *equitatus* (*Pharaonis*), Ps. Rdr. 282, 19. v. rīde-here.

**rǣdelíce.** v. ge-rǣdelíce.

**rǣdels.** *Add :*—Rǣdels ł bysen *paradigma,* An. Ox. 18 b, 67. *O. L. Ger.* rādislo (-i).

**rǣden[n].** *Add :* v. ge-, geþeód-, geþeów- (?), gewrit-, godsibb-, hold-, hyld-, leód-, lim-, luf-, mǣd-, mǣgþ-, mǣst-, niæsten-, sam-, sin-, þegen-, þeód-, þoft-, wīte-, wudu-rǣden[n].

**rǣdend.** *Add : a diviner :*—On gelícnysse wigleres and rǣdendes hē wēnð þæt hē nāt *in similitudine arioli et coniectoris aestimat quod ignorat,* Scint. 75, 12. v. ge-rǣdend.

**rǣdere. I.** *add :*—Rǣdere geornfull mā tō gefyllenne þe hē rǣd þænne tō witenne hrǣd ys *lector strenuus potius ad complendum quę legit quam ad sciendum promptus est,* Scint. 219, 16. v. mete-, pistol-rǣdere.

**rǣd-fæst.** *Add : of good counsel :*—Eówer brōðer is snotor and rǣdfæst *your brother is a man of counsel* (1 Macc. 2, 65), Hml. S. 25, 264 : Solil. H. 61, 9. Ælfstān arceb wæs swíðe rǣdfast man ǣgðer ge for Gode and for worulde, Chr. 1019 ; P. 154, 19. Leofa þīn líf, gif ðū lǣwede mann sý on rihtum suscipe, mid rǣdfæstum mōde, Hml. A. 7, 158. Rǣdfæst mōd onardaþ sē þe sārigende be anderdum tō ēceum efst *consiliatorem animum inhabitat qui dolens de presentibus ad aeterna festinat,* Scint. 200, 17. Þā hālgan hē hēt geoffrian heora lāc þām lífleásum godum, gif hī heora lífes rōhton oþþe rǣdfæste wǣron, Hml. S. 29, 279. For ðan þe Rōmānisce witan wǣron ðā mihtige and rǣdfæste on weorcum (cf. Judas is informed of the power and *policy* of the Romans, 1 Macc. 8, 25, 646.

**rǣding. I.** *add :*—Hē hine gemētte æt his rǣdinge sittan . . . Hē nāteshwōn from his rǣdinge ne ārās, Hml. Th. ii. 180, 24-34. **II.** *add :*—Man rǣdde þā nigoðan rǣdinge on Crīstes godspelle, Shrm. 126, 26. Wē rǣdaþ ðǣs rǣdinge æt þǣra hālgena mæssan þe wē hātaþ Confessores, Hml. A. 50, 26. Nū cwyð sum man ongeán ðæs rǣdinge (*this text*), Hml. Th. i. 54, 30. **IV.** *consultation, deliberation.* Cf. rǣdan ; II,

II a:—Se cyning áräs and eóde him ūt swilce for rædinge, Hml. A. 100, 270. v. ge-, þrowung-ræding.

**ræding-grád** *the lectern-steps* (?) :—þonne hē þæder geclypod cume . . . ætforan þām bisceope and þām preósthīrede, þonne āstrecce hē hine on eorðan ætforan þām rædinggrāde (*ante absidam*). Cf. *absidam* grece sedem episcopalem ; *ante absida*, ante sedem episcopi, Ld. Gl. H. 52, Chrd. 37, 17. *See next word.*

**ræding-sceamol** *a lectern*:—On rædingsceamele *in pulpito*, An. Ox. 4813. Upp stíge se pistelrædere rædincgscamul *ascendat subdiaconus ambonem*, Angl. xiii. 424, 842. Gelēdum ofer rædingscamul godspelle *inposito super ambone euangelio*, 416, 728. Beón gerædde ofor rædinc-scamol *legantur super analogium* (*tres lectiones*), R. Ben. I. 38, 9. [*Analogium lectorium ligneum in quo leguntur libri*, Ld. Gl. H. 59. Ambone, *analogio* ; in ambone, id est in pulpito, 58.]

**ræd-lic.** *Add*:—Nis ðæt rædlic ðing, gif hlūtor wæter hlūd and undióp tōflōweð æfter feldum, oð hit tō senne werð, Past. 469, 6. þonne cymð ōðer ðing þe mē þincð rihtlicre and rædlicre, ðonne forlēt ic þæt þæt ic ǣr genōh hæfde, Solil. H. 33, 4. v. oft-, un-, wiþer-rædlic.

**rædlíce. I.** *add* :—Utan ealle ūre wīsan rædlíce fadian, Wlfst. 143, 22. **II.** *add* (?):—Gif . . . ǣnig gehādod man hine sylfne rædlíce (*but cf.* oftrædlíce, 214, 12) oferdrince, Ll. Th. ii. 258, 26. **III.** *advisably*:—Beþence gehwā hine sylfne, and hū him rædlícost sȳ tō dōnne, Wlfst. 305, 34. v. oft-rædlíce.

**rædness.** *The examples under* I. *should be taken under* hræd-ness, q. v. **II.** *add*: v. gecwid-, wiþer-rædness.

**ræd-rípe.** *l.* hræd-rípe, *where take the passages*: **ræd-wægn.** *Add*: [O. L. Ger. rêde-wagen *currus*: O. H. Ger. reit-wagen *currus, vehiculum*.]

**ræd-wita.** *Substitute: one wise in counsel, one of the leading men of a country, one of the ‘witan’* :—Cyningas and rædwitan forwyrþan *reges et principes peribunt*, Archiv cxx. 297, 31. Betwyx þǣre ēcan ūplicum sibbe rīce rædwitan rodera weardas *inter aetherium coelesti pace senatum*, Dóm. L. 298.

**-ræf.** v. ge-ræf : **ræfan.** *Dele the passage given ; the reading is* geræpte. v. Bt. S. 112, 1, *and add* v. ā-rǣfan.

**ræfnan. I.** *add*:—Ēnne hræfneð *unum sustinebit*, Mt. L. 6, 24. þā ræfnede hē mycel mægn unwederes *vim nimiae tempestatis pertulit*, Gr. D. 346, 33. Tō þon þ hē wǣre ræfnende þā gewin þæs ealdan feúndes *antiqui hostis certamina toleraturus*, 184, 28.

**ræfnian.** *Add*: v. ge-ræfnian: **ræg-hár.** *Substitute* : ræg-hár *grey with lichen*. Cf. ragu: **rægiming.** *Dele, and see* fægiminge (= fæg-nunge) *plausu*, An. Ox. 2, 399.

**ræming.** *Add: For meaning of* celibea cf. caelibies, caelestis, Corp. Gl. H. 28, 169 ; *for* ræming *cf.* (?) ā-rǣman.

**ræpan.** *Add*:—þā þā hē his oxan ræpte, þā scóc ān his heáfod and mid þām horne hine þýde, Hml. S. 31, 785.

**-ræpe.** v. æfter-ræpe: **ræpsan.** *Add*: [Cf. Icel. refsa *to punish*.] v. ge-resp.

**ræpsung.** *Add*: , repsung. **II.** *add*: *evening*:—On hrepsunge hē beeóm tō Iordanes ōfrum, Hml. S. 23 b, 663. v. æfen-repsung.

**rǣran. II.** *add*:—On wintra . . . orceard rǣran, Angl. ix. 261, 24.

**ræs. I.** *add* :—Hræs windes *procella uenti*, Lk. L. 8, 23. Mid hræs geeáde all suner *impetu abiit totus grex*, Mt. L. 8, 32. v. fær-, here-, wind-ræs.

**ræs** (?). *On the analogy of* blód-læs, -læswu (q. v.) *this might be entered as* ræs, ræswu : **ræsa** (?). v. on-rǣsa (?).

**rǣsan. I.** *add*: (1) *of an object that moves itself*:—Hē weard geangsumod, and rǣsde tō ðām were þe ðǣr offrian wolde, and ofslóh hine sóna, Hml. S. 25, 225. Ān ormǣte heort . . . gewende fram þām flocce, and rǣsde intō þām wudu, 30, 30. Rǣsde ān nǣddre of holum treówe . . . and hyne tōslāt, Shrn. 144, 27. Lazarus wæs hyne āsceac-ende . . . and wæs fram ūs rǣsende, Nic. 14, 37. (2) *of an object that is moved*:—Fǣringa rǣsde (āhleóp, v. l.) forð of þām hylfe *ferrum de manubrio prosiliens*, Gr. D. 113, 25. **II.** *add*:—Upp rǣsað þeóda and wiðerrǣde weorðað *surget gens contra gentem*, Wlfst. 91, 21. v. ā-rǣsan.

**ræsc.** *Substitute*: ræsc, es ; *m. A heavy shower*:—Foreweal hreós-endlicum ræscum *propugnaculum ruituris* (*ignium*) *imbribus*, An. Ox. 3974. Naescum (raescum ?) *tractibus* (spumosis remorum *tractibus*, Ald. 3, 4, the glosses may have wished to represent the showers of spray made by the oars), Wrt. Voc. ii. 122, 77. v. līg-, līget-ræsc.

**-ræsend.** v. on-rǣsend : **ræsn.** *Add*: v. slip-ræsn : **ræswa.** *Add*: v. magu-ræswa : **ræswan.** *Add*:—Ic eom rēsiende *suspicatus sum*, Ps. Vos. 118, 39.

**rēw.** *Add*:—Andlang rǣwe on þornwīc, C. D. v. 220, 36. In compounds :—Tō brōce ; andlang brócrēwe, C. D. v. 122, 19. On ða norðrǣwe, iii. 412, 28. [v. N. E. D. rew.] v. fyrs-, stæf-, þorn-, wiþig-rǣw.

**-rǣwen, -rǣwod.** v. ge-rǣwen, -rǣwod.

**rāfian.** *Add*: [Cf. D. D. rove *to twist cotton into roþy form*.]

**raggig.** *Add*:—Raggie flýs *setosa* (*vervecum*) *uellera*, An. Ox. 5191 (= Hpt. Gl. 524, 16). Racgige, 6, 30. [v. N. E. D. raggy.]

**ragu.** *Add*: v. ciric-ragu.

**rāh-deór.** *Add*: þā beóð langswýrede ðe lybbað be gærse, swā swā olfend and assa, hors and hrýðeru, heádeór and rāhdeór, Hex. 16, 3.

**rāh-gelégu.** v. ge-légu.

**rāh-hege,** es ; *m. A deer-fence:*—On ða þornrǣwe eástrihte ðæt hit cyme tō ðām rāhhege ; after ðām hege, C. D. iii. 77, 29. Be ðām rāh-hege, 461, 5.

**ram-hund.** *Add*: The true form of the word, which is given only in comparatively modern MSS., is doubtful. *Rain-, raine-hound*, as well as *ram-hundt*, occur (v. Ll. Lbmn. 626, 2), and these seem to represent the original word more nearly than does *ram-*. In a MS. of much earlier date (13th cent.) it is said : Canem, qui in pluuia sine alicuius cura, uigilat, quem Angli dicunt *renhund* (*rén-, regn-*? or could *ren = ærn*. Cf. *ren-degen*), xii d., Lbmn. 367, n. Liebermann suggests that the correct form would be *hrán-hund*, a reindeer-hound, but as in the same passage the payment for a slain greyhound is lxxx d., it seems hardly likely that any kind of deerhound could be compensated for by so small a sum as xii d. It is also said : Si quis canem, qui custodire domini sui caulas et lupum abigere, occiderit, persoluat domino canis vi sol. Perhaps the *rain-hound* was an outdoor watch-dog ? or a house-dog ?

**ramm.** *Add*: v. hālgung-ramm : **rān.** *Add*: v. ciric-rān.

**ranc. I.** *add*:—Tō manege weorðaþ . . . tō wlance and ealles tō rance and tō gylpgeorne *erunt homines . . . elati, superbi* (2 Tim. 3, 2), Wlfst. 81, 15. Rancra *proteruorum*, An. Ox. 7, 381. **II.** *a. showy in appearance, splendid in dress* (?) :—Hē funde fíf mǣdena him tō wlitige and rance tō wunigenne mid him, Hml. S. 35, 52. **III.** *add*:—Oft týne oððe twelfe ǣlc æfter ōðrum scendað þæs þegenes cwenan . . . þær hē on lōcað, þe læt hine sylfne rancne and rícne and genōh gódne, ǣr þæt gewurde, Wlfst. 162, 22.

**rāp.** *Add*: v. æfter-, fót-, wǣde-ráp: **-rár.** v. ge-rár: **rāre-dumla.** *Add*:—Rādumbel *oriagratulus*, Hpt. 33, 240, 20.

**r.a.þe.** *Add*:—Ðæt geðreátade mōd bið suíðe raðe (hræðe, v. l.) gehwierfed tō fióunga, Past. 167, 17. Raþe æfter þǣm, Ors. 3, 2 ; S. 100, 30. Ic wundrige hwý þū hæbbe swā rǣde forgitan, Solil. H. 52, 5. Se ōðer leorningcniht cōm raðor tō ðǣre byrgenne *alius discipulus uenit primus ad monumentum*, Jn. 20, 4. þ se rǣdere hig mage þe raðor gemētan, Angl. viii. 333, 15. Ne cwǣde ic þeáh nā ðe raðor ‘Genōh’, Solil. H. 17, 5. Ne dō ic hī nā ðe raðor gelíce, 12. Hē oft wýscte þæt ealle Rōmāne hæfden ǣnne sweóran, þæt hē hiene raþost forceorfan mehte, Ors. 6, 3 ; S. 256, 27.

**rāwan** (?). *Substitute*: rāwan. [v. N. E. D. raw ; *vb.*[2]] v. ge-rāwan.

**raxan** *to stretch oneself after sleep:*—Hē þā se ylca man, swā hē of hesegum slæpe raxende āwōce, and hē eft tō his hǣlo fēng *ipse velut qui de aestuantis gurgitis fluctibus ad portum deducitur, longa suspiria imo de pectore trahens ad pristinam salutis valetudinem redditum se esse intellexit*, Guth. Gr. 148, 44. [v. N. E. D. rax.] v. racsan *in Dict.*

**reád.** *Add*:—Him wæs gecynde þ hē symble wæs reád on his and-wlitan, Gr. D. 187, 16. v. blōd-, bóc-, weolcen-, wræt-, wurm-reád.

**reáda.** In l. 2 read *extales, and add* : *A tonsil*:—Reádan toleam, Lch. i. lxxii, 3 : lxxiv, 28. [Cf. tolia *toles*, Migne.]

**reáde.** *Add*:—Hwý scīneð seó sunne swā reáde on morgene ?, Sal. K. 192, 32.

**reádgold-læfer** *a plate of gold*:—Reádgoldlæfer *auri obriza lammina*, An. Ox. 1070.

**reádian.** *Add*:—þæt þū wite hwæs blōd reádaþ on rosan gelícnysse, and hwæs līchama hwítað on lilian fægernysse, Hml. S. 34, 112. Eágan reádiað, Lch. ii. 258, 14. Wyl þās þreó on meolcum oþ þ hý reádian, 292, 5. [v. N. E. D. red.]

**reád-leáf** (?). *Dele* ‘ (?) ’, *and add*:—Andlang mearce tō reádlēfan bēcan, C. D. iii. 14, 7. On þæt reádleáfe treów ; of ðām reádleáfan treówe, C. D. B. ii. 246, 28.

**reád-lesc** *reddened skin* (?):—Mid reádlescum *rubricatis* (*pellibus*), An. Ox. 5324 [Cf. losche *particum, rubra pellis* ; rōth-loschi *pelles arietum idem sine lana quasi partica*, Grff. 2, 282.] v. reód-næsc.

**reád-næsc.** v. reód-nǣsc : **reád-staled.** *l.* -stalede.

**reáf.** *In last line dele* ‘lenden-, sīd-’, *and* I. *add*:—Reáfo (reóf, R., here-reáf, W. S.) *spolia*, Lk. L. 11, 22. **II.** *add*:—Scrūd ł hreáf *uestimentum*, Ps. L. 108, 19. Mid gyftlicum reáfe (*ueste*) gescrýd, Mt. 22, 11. v. beód-, brýd-, heall-, mæsse-, munuc-, preóst-, sige-, weg-, wer-reáf.

**reáfere.** *Add*:—Tō hreáfere (reófere, R.) *ad latronem*, Lk. L. 22, 52. Cofa hreáfera (reófera, R.) *spelunca latronum*, 19, 46. v. be-reáfere.

**reáfian. I** 1. *add*:—Ðā ðe ōðre men reáfiað, Past. 329, 10. Hē ōðre menn reáfode, 339, 2. Tō reáfigeanne, 327, 25. (1 a) *to rob a*

person of something, (a) with gen. :—Hē wile reáfian ðone his anwaldes, Past. 371, 25. God reáfian lǣteð eówere dohtra heora oferrancra heáfodgewǣda, Wlsft. 45, 25. (β) with a prep. :—Gif hwylc man reáfige ðēerne æt his dehter si homo quis alterum filia sua spoliaverit, Ll. Th. ii. 208, 7. I 2. add:—Hī woldon þ mynster reáfian, Chr. 1087 ; P. 223, 14. II. add : absolute or with acc. of thing taken: (1) absolute :—Ðæt hē for ðȳ syngige and reáfige ðȳ hē tiohchie ðæt hē eft scyle mid ðȳ reáflāce ælmessan gewyrcean, Past. 341, 21. þ hyg hreáfian ł þ hig gegrīpan ut rapiant, Ps. L. 103, 21. Ne scīrð hē nō hwæðer hié reáfoden, oððe hwelc ōðer yfel fremeden, Past. 329, 8. Giétsian and reáfian for hiera wǣdle, 341, 4. Swā swā leó hreáfiende ł grīpende sicut leo rapiens, Ps. L. 21, 14. (2) with acc. :—Ðā ðe giét fliétað æfter ōðera monna (gōdum) and hié reáfiað qui aliena rapere contendunt, Past. 319, 16. (2 a) to take something from a person :—Biþ leófwendra sē ðe gold selþ ðonne sē þe hit gaderaþ and on ōþrum reáfaþ, Bt. 13 ; F. 38, 13. [v. N. E. D. reave.] v. on-reáfian.

-reáfian to robe. v. ge-reáfian.

reáfigend. Add:—Ðǣm reáfende exspolianti, Mt. p. 14, 17. v. be-reáfigend.

reáf-lāc. I. add:—Hē feccan sceolde þ feoh mid reáflāce, Hml. S. 25, 762. Þysum wolde gedōn sum Langbeardisc man reáflāc on ðām ylcum beón huic cum Longobardus quidam in eisdem apibus rapinam voluisset ingerere, Gr. D. 229, 13. II. add:—Ðæt hē for ðȳ reáfige ðȳ hē tiohchie ðæt hē eft scyle mid ðȳ reáflāce ælmessan gewyrcean, Past. 341, 22 : 343, 13. Reáflācas (rapinas) nylle gē gewilnian, Ps. L. 61, 11. [v. N. E. D. ref-lac.]

reáfol. Add:—Fram reáfium ortrȳwra geaglum þā sceáp . . . hē generude a rabidis perfidorum rictibus oues . . . eripuit, Angl. xiii. 366, 19. Reáfium lurconibus (labris), An. Ox. 7, 53.

reám. Add: [v. N. E. D. ream.]

reám-wīn, es ; n. Thick wine, wine with a froth on it (?) :—Reámwīn dulcisapa (quantum distat dulcisapa a merulento temeto, Ald. 81, 1), An. Ox. 8, 417 : 8 b, 12. Cf. Merum hlūttor wīn, dulcisapa āwilled wīn, Wrt. Voc. i. 290, 55–56.

rēc. Add:—Swā āsprong roec (fumus) hié āspringen, Ps. Vos. 67, 3. Wiþ lungenādle, genim . . . swefl and rēcels . . . lege on hātne stān, drinc þurh horn þone rēc, Lch. ii. 316, 11. Hōh ðā wyrte on feówer healfe . . . bærn, dō rēcels tō, lǣt yrnan ofer þone rēc, iii. 56, 30.

-rec. v. ge-, hōf-rec.

recan ; p. ræc, pl. rǣcon. I. to go, proceed hastily, run :—Recest saltas, Germ. 396, 320. [v. N. E. D. reke.] v. ge-recan. II. to bring, carry :—In rǣcan ingesserunt (in latibulum ubi cloacarum cuniculi putores stercorum ingesserunt (cf. on gelǣddon, An. Ox. 3322), Ald. 45, 27), Wrt. Voc. ii. 44, 51.

rēcan. Add : I. to expose to smoke or steam, fumigate :—Lege stōr on þā glēda and rēc hine mid þ hē swǣte, Lch. ii. 348, 5. Gif sinwe sīen gescruncene . . . wyl on wætre, beþe mid, and rēce þā sinwe geornlīce, 328, 8. II. to cause to emit smoke, burn incense :—Þ hū ( = heó) rēcte ut adholeret (thymiama diis), An. Ox. 8, 238. Rīcenne turificare, Wrt. Voc. ii. 86, 63 : 26, 76. [The passage to which this gloss belongs is : Ut missa statuncula Dianae cogeret Victoriam apostatico ritu turificare, Ald. 70, 5 ; the gloss is to turificare not Dianae.] v. be-, ge-, geond-rēcan.

rēcan, reccan. I. add:—Þū gecnāwest hweþer þū fram him gehȳred byst, and hē þinre bēne recceþ cognosces quod exauditus sis, Gr. D. 330, 10. Ðæt sió sib of eówre heortan ne gewīte, ðēah hiere mon ne recce quatenus pax a cordibus vestris nec abnegata discedat, Past. 357, 11. Hē nānes monnes ōleccunga ne rēce in nullius se debeat favorem declinare, 383, 12. Leáses monnes word ne rēce (recce, v. l.) þū nō þæs tō gehiéranne, Ll. Th. i. 54, 3. III. add :—Ne rēces ðū þ wē deádo sié non ad te pertinet quia perimus, Mk. L. 4, 38. Wē ne rēcað (reccead, v. l.) hwæðer wē hit ongieten, Past. 195, 6. Hī ne reccað hwæt hié mon ymbe ræswe mala de se opinari permittunt, 447, 27 : 449, 22. Hī ne reccað (-eað, v. l.) ðeáh menn wēnen ðæt hié yfel dōn, 179, 9.

reccan. IV. add: to cite an instance :—Þæs þe rechþ ut fert, Germ. 399, 347. Eft rehþ infra subdit, An. Ox. 5167. Rehte protulit (ad exemplum militiae Christianorum agonem protulit gymnicorum), An. Ox. 57 ; ederet, i. enarret, 8, 284. Þā reccinge þe hē rehte, Hml. S. 30, 376. Ǣr ðiosum ne rehton (reahton, v. l. ostendimus) hwelc se beón sceolde ðe tō ðǣm biscepdōme cuman sceolde ; nū wē willað reccan (demonstremus) hū hē ðǣron libban scyle, Past. 73, 21–23 : 173, 14. Rǣdinc būtan bēc tō reccanne lectio ex corde recitanda, R. Ben. I. 39, 6 ; 48, 2. Reccendes prosequentis, i. narrantis, An. Ox. 3250. V. add :—þā þe wē ne magon ongytan in þām godcundan dōme wē sculan ūs þe mā ondrǣdan þonne elcor reccan ea quae in divino examine comprehendere non possumus, timere magis quam discutere debemus, Gr. D. 301, 12. þ gewrit . . . him geornlīce wæs reht on his āgen gereorde haec epistula . . . diligenter . . . in linguam eius propriam interpretata, Bd. 5, 21 ; Sch. 678, 26. v. æt-, geriht-reccan.

reccend. (2) add:—Eádgār Angla reccent (engla cyning, v. l.), Chr.

975 ; P. 119, 14. Be reccendrum de rectoribus, Scint. 116, 2. Hē gesette gewisse prāfostas and reccendas substitutis praepositis, Gr. D. 119, 21.

reccend-dōm. Add:—Hē heóld þæs mynstres reccendōm (ræcenddōm, v. l.) monasterii regimen tenebat, Gr. D. 20, 21.

recceness. v. rece-ness.

reccere. II. add :—Trahteras ł recceras interpretes, Mt. p. 2, 11.

reccing, e ; f. Narration, tale, story :—Hī sylfe nyston þ hī wǣron gebrōþra būton þurh þā reccinge þe se yldra brōþor rehte þām gingran, Hml. S. 30, 375.

reced-ness, e ; f. A story, narrative, history :—Recednesse historiae (ecclesiasticae liber), An. Ox. 2900. v. ge-recedness.

rece-dōm. Add :—Ðā byrðena hyra recedōmes onera regiminis, Chrd. 53, 13.

rēce-leás. Add:—Būtan geþylde and þeáwfæstnysse wē yrsiað . . . and lythwōn þencað hū wē sceolon æt Gode miltsunge begitan nū wē swā rēceleáse syndon and swā rēþe ūs betwȳnan, Hml. S. 28, 141.

rēceleásian. Add: v. ā-, for-rēceleásian.

rēceleáslīce. Add :—Sint tō manienne ðā ðe ðā sibbe sāwað, ðæt hié swā micel weorc tō recceleáslīce and tō unwǣrlīce ne dōn admonendi sunt pacifici, ne tantae actionis pondus levigent, Past. 361, 6. Swā hwilc man swā Godes weorc clǣnlīce and behogodlīce wirceð, hē bið ēcelīce gehealden. Sē þe hit rēceleáslīce and unclǣnlīce wyrceð, hē bið āwyrged intō helle, Hml. A. 168, 121.

rēceleásness. Add:—Ān manncynn wunað . . . under þīnum anwealde . . . and þū wāst þ hit wile hearmian þīnum cynerīce heora rēceleásnysse, gyf him man ne gestȳrð heora stuntnysse est populus . . . et nosti, quod non expediat regno tuo, ut insolescat per licentiam, Hml. A. 96, 153.

rēceleást. Add:—Ðonne wē hwæthwugu steórweorðes ongietað . . . and wē gebǣrað for ūre rēceliésðe (reccelīste, v. l.) swelce wē hit nyten cum cogitationes nostrae ea, quae . . . arguenda cognoscunt, pigredine deprimente dissimulant, Past. 195, 4.

rēcels. Add:—Ǣþm rēcelses gefylð lyfte vapor timiamatis refert aerem, Scint. 57, 9. Genim . . . swefl and rēcels . . . lege on hātne stān, drinc þurh horn þone rēc, Lch. ii. 316, 10 : 56, 10. [v. N. E. D. rekels.]

recen. I. add : Seó tunge āwylspaþ seó þe ǣr hæfde ful recene sprǣce, Nap. 74, 18. [v. N. E. D. reken.]

recene. Add: , ricene :—Swā ricene swā ic gewīte, ofsleáð ealle ðās ealdras, Hml. Th. i. 86, 34. Ārās Drihten of ðām gereorde, and āwearp his reáf swīðe ricene, ii. 242, 24.

rece-ness. Take here recenness. v. ge-receness, reced-ness.

recenian. Add: to pay :—Recna man iungere Brūn ān marc gol, C. D. iv. 59, 8. [Forr þær to reccnenn till þe king an peninng, Orm. 3540.]

recenness. Take under rece-ness : -recennes. v. ge-recenness.

recu. Add : v. ge-recu (under ge-rec).

-rede. v. hof-rede : rēdian. l. redian, and add : v. ge-redian : Rēdlingas. v. Reádlingas, Sedlingas.

rēfa. Add :—Hēt se rēfa hī beheáfdian, Shrn. 128, 11 : 129, 17 : refsan. v. ræpsan.

regn. Add:—Wæs seó eá for regna (rēna, v. l.) micelnesse swīðe rēðe fluuius prae inundantia pluuiarum ripas suas transierat, Bd. 3, 24 ; Sch. 309, 16. Ic wēnde þ þā triów for miclum wǣtan and regnum swā heáge weóxon. Ðā sægde se bisceop þ nǣfre in þǣm londum regnes dropa ne cwōme arbores . . . cum dicerem frequentibus imbribus in tantum creuisse, acerdos affirmabat nunquam in his locis pluuiam adire, Nar. 28, 2–5. Hrægnas pluuias, Ps. L. 104, 32. v. tīd-regn.

-regne. v. ge-regne : regn-hund. v. ram-hund.

regnian. Add:—Sē þe yldeð, þ hē tō Gode ne gecyrre, hē rēnað pleoh his āgene sāwle, Archiv cxxii. 257, 4. Gē timbras ł hrīnas byrgenno wītgena and gē hrīnas byrgenna sōðfæstra aedificatis sepulchra prophetarum et ornatis monumenta justorum, Mt. L. 23, 29.

regnian to rain, cause rain to fall :—Hē hregnað (regneð, R.) ofer sōðfæsta and unsōðfæste pluit super justos et injustos, Mt. L. 5, 45. v. rignan.

regn-lic. Add:—Lænten windhladen and rēnlic uer uentosus et pluuialis, Archiv cxx. 297, 17. Regnlice wæteru pluuiales aquas, Ps. Rdr. 77, 44.

regn-snegel a snail :—Rēnsnægl limax, An. Ox. 23, 20.

-regnung. v. ge-regnung : regn-wyrm. Add : [Dan. regn-orm.]

regol. Add : IV. a ruler for drawing lines. v. regolian. V. a tabular arrangement, list given in tabular form:—Ðā talo ł reglas ðā Eusebius in tēnum talum geendebrednade canones quos Eusebius in decem numeros ordinavit, Mt. p. 2, 18. Regulas, 3, 9. v. preóst-regol.

regolian to draw lines with a ruler :—Regoles tācen is þ þū wecge þīne hand and strȳce mid þīnum scytefingre andlang þīnre wynstran handa, swylce þū regolige, Tech. ii. 122, 10. Gyf þū reogolsticcan næbbe, þonne strece þū þīne hand ūpweard and strīc mid þīnum scytefingre andlang þīnre wynstran hande, swilce þū regolige, 128, 17.

**regol-sticca.** *Add:*—Gif þū reogolsticca næbbe, Tech. ii. 128, 15. v. regolian.

**regol-peáw,** es; *m.* *A custom of ecclesiastical rule:*—Þ hí þá gesettan þeódscipas and regolþeáwas heóldon, Angl. x. 144, 125.

**regol-weard.** (3) *Add:*—Ðe regluuard, Jn. L. 4, 51.

**reliquias.** *Add:*—Mid fæstenum and mid gebedum and mid reliquia sócnum . . . Mid cyricsócnum and mid reliquia sócnum, Verc. Först. 171.

**remigende.** The correctness of this reading is supported by another instance :—Se Hælend . . . gemétte óðre twégen gebróðra . . . on scipe mid heora fæder remigende heora nett, Nap. 53 (Archiv ci. 323). Both instances should then be put under *remian.*

**Rēmisc;** *adj. Roman:*—Þ compwearod Roemisce *cohors*, Jn. L. 18, 12.

**renc.** *Add:* rencu (-eo) :—Þá hē swíðust óðre men mid tesowordum tǣl[d]e in his renceo (cf. in his onmēdlan gealpettunga, 27, 40), Nap. 62, 17.

**ren-degn.** v. ærn-þegen.

**rengan** (?). v. ā-rencan (?) : **renge.** *Add:* [*From Lat.* arænea.]: **rendan.** *Put after* renc, *and add:* v. ā-, be-rendan : **rendrian.** *Take after* ren-degn, *and for* ' v. Lchdm. ii. Gloss.' *substitute* v. ge-rendrian.

**reócan.** *Add:*—In þǣre stówe þǣr þá hátan wæter reócað and swá mycele æþmas wyrcað *in loco in quo aquae calidae vapores nimios faciunt*, Gr. D. 343, 4. Genim níwe horses tord, lege on háte glēda, lǣt reócan swíþe betweoh þá þeóh úp under þæt hrægl, Lch. ii. 330, 27. Reócende *halans* (odorato thure fragrantior *halans*, Ald. 271, 15), An. Ox. 26, 66. Sume hús ná gehrán seó fýlnes þæs reócendan and stincendan mistes *alia habitacula exurgens foetor e flumine minime tangebat*, Gr. D. 319, 11. Eóde forð feórðe healf geár bútan rēnscūrum and reócendum deáwe, Hml. S. 18, 57. v. be-, ge-reócan.

**reód.** *Add:*—Eágan reádiað, and reód beoþ heów, Lch. ii. 258, 14. Æt ánes heówes cȳ, þ heó sȳ eall reód oððe hwít, iii. 24, 13. Wæs hire ansȳn swá reód and swá fæger swá þǣre wynsumestan fǣmnan, þonne heó fægerost bið, Mart. H. 4, 17. Rǣseð mec on reódne, Rä. 26, 8. v. reódian.

**reód-naesc.** *Add:* reddened skin (?). [*For partica see* Parthicae *pelles* (Du Cange): *Particum* Parthian (Diefenbach).] v. reád-lesc : **reogyrde.** v. hreód-gird.

**reohhe.** *Add:* a ray. [v. *N. E. D.* reigh] : **reoma** a rim. v. rima : **reóma.** *Add:* [v. *N. E. D.* rim, sb.²]

**reónian.** *Add:* to conspire:—Reónedan *concinnabant*, Hpt. Gl. 474, 28. Hreónedan *concinnant*, An. Ox. 2788.

**reónig-mód.** *Add:*—Eódan þá reónigmóde eorlas ægleáwe . . . gehðum geómre, El. 320.

**reónung.** *Add:*—Reónunge *constellationem*, An. Ox. 2631. v. geregnung.

**reord** *speech.* *Add:*—On Englisce reorde *in sua, id est Anglorum, lingua*, Bd. 4, 24; Sch. 481, 12. [v. *N. E. D.* rerd(e).]

**reord** *a meal.* *Add:*—Farma ł symbel ł riorda geuard *cena facta*, Jn. L. 13, 2. Mið ðȳ ðū dóes riordo (hriord, L.) ł symbel *cum facis prandium aut caenam*, Lk. R. 14, 12.

**reordian.** I. *to take food, dine, sup, eat* :—Cumað riordigað (hreordað, L.) *uenite prandete*, Jn. R. 21, 12. Gearua þte ic hriordege *para quod cenem*, Lk. L. 17, 8. Ongunnon hriordago *coeperunt aepulari*, Lk. L. 15, 24. Tó hriordanne, 32. II. *to feed* :—Wē hriordadun ðec *pavimus te*, Mt. L. 25, 37. v. ge-reordian.

**reordian.** *Add:* [v. *N. E. D.* rerd(e).] v. un-reordian (?) : **-reordness.** v. ge-reordness : **reóst.** *Add:* [v. *N. E. D.* reest.] : **reótan.** *Dele* I, *for which see* writian, hrútan : **reów.** v. hreóh.

**reówe.** *Add:* In the last passage reón is another reading, Sch. 540, 9 : **reów(e)tt.** v. rēwett.

**repel,** es; *m.* *A rod, staff* :—For þám þe hē næfde nænne repel hine mid tó þersceanne (gyrde him mid tó sleánne, *v. l.*), þá gelæhte hē þone fótscamul . . . and beót Libertinum on þ heáfod *quia virgam qua eum ferire posset minime invenit, comprehenso scabello ei caput tutudit*, Gr. D. 20, 26. [Gief he fend were, me sceolden anon eter gat gemete mid gode repples and stiarne swepen, O. E. Hml. i. 231, 21. v. D. D. repple.]

**-repen.** v. for-hrepian : **-res,** -resu. v. cneó-, cyn-res, -resu.

**respons** *a response* :—Respons singan *responsiones cantare*, Ll. Th. ii. 140, 21.

**rest.** [*In* Bl. H. 11, 16, 19 *the word seems to be of the weak declension.*] II. *add* :—[Niht]licere ræste *nocturnae quieti* ł somno, An. Ox. 2197. III. *add* :—Þín gást bið on heofonum, and þín rest ne losað nǣfre on worulde, Hml. S. 15, 67. Hē æfter þám gereordum ræste sēced, dȳgle stówe under dūnscræfum, Pa. 36. Ðeáh þe þá rícestan hátan him reste gewyrcan of marmanstáne, Wlfst. 263, 2. Ræste sēcan, bed æfter būrum, B. 139. Ðá formo hrǣsto *primos accubitos*, Lk. L. 14, 7. v. būr-, brȳd-, eorþ-, ge-, líc-, undern-rest.

**resta.** v. ge-resta.

**restan.** I a 3. *add* :—Ǣlig . . . þēr mínes hláfordes líchoma rest,

C. D. iii. 274, 14. Þá hálgan stōwæ þæ mīne yldran on restaþ, 273, 17. II 2. *add* :—Līst ðū and rest þē and Godes þeówa lið æt þínum gatum, Hml. S. 31, 1152. **reste.** v. rest.

**reste-dæg.** *Add:*—Restedæges begýming *Sabbati obseruatio*, An. Ox. 40, 5. Þæs restedæges, 18.

**resten-dæg.** *Add:*—On restendæge *sabbato*, Scint. 30, 6.

**-restscipe.** v. ge-restscipe : **-resu.** v. -res.

**rēþe.** *Take here* hrēþe *in Dict. and* I a. *add:*—Rēþe gefylce *tyrannici commanipulares*, An. Ox. 858. Mid rōde tācn þá rēðan (*devils*) āfīian, Hml. S. 17, 145. Þám rēþestum feóndum *seuissimis, i. ferocissimis hostibus*, An. Ox. 745. II. *add* :—Stefn leás in woestern roeðe *vox leonis in eremo rugientis*, Mt. p. 9, 14. León and beran . . . þá rēðan deór, Hml. S. 4, 405. III. *add* :—Rēþes stormes *dirae tempestatis*, An. Ox. 631. Hē gebrōhte hine of ðám rēðan cwearterne, Hml. S. 18, 447. Of ðysum rēðum deáðe, 22, 114. Roeðo *aspera*, Lk. L. R. 3, 5. Rēþe gāras *dira, i. crudelia spicula*, An. Ox. 2097. Tó gearcigenne þá rēþestan wītu, Hml. S. 24, 21. v. esenrēþe.

**rēþian.** *See next word.*

**rēþigian.** *Add:* , rēþian :—Hí ongeán hyne rēþiaþ (*saeuiunt*), Scint. 118, 19. Rēðige *saeuiat*, 122, 4. Þ hē gesāwe þone feónd rēðian (rēðigian, *v. l.* saevire) on hine mid his mūþe, Gr. D. 122, 11. Hī ongunnon mā rēðian (reðgian, *v. l.*) and hí gebelgan, 219, 10. Rēðgiende (reðigiende, *v. l.*) hí Libertinum sōhton, 16, 16 : 104, 11. Þá reðgiendan (rēðgendan, *v. l.*) Francan, 16, 20 : 42, 30.

**rēþ-ness.** *Take here* hrēþ-ness, *and* I a. *add:*—Þéra Langbeardna rēðnes (*saevitia*) byð gemetegad þurh his gife, Gr. D. 234, 1. Sealde hē bysne his folgerum þ hí mōston forbūgan rēðnysse, Hml. A. 72, 176.

**rēþra.** *Add:*—Rēþran *uectores, remiges*, Germ. 402, 65. v. ge-, scip-, steór-rēþra.

**rēþre** (?), es; *m.* *A rower, sailor* :—Rēðra (hrēðra, Hpt. Gl. 406, 42) ł flotmanna *nautarum*, An. Ox. 22.

**rēþ-scipe.** *Add:*—Weámóde lāreówas þurh hetolnysse heora rēðscipes (*furoris*) gewyrfað þǣre lāre gemet tó ungefóge þǣre wælhreównysse, Chrd. 70, 15.

**rēwett;** *m. n.* (?). l. *n., and add:*—Hī þ líc tó scipe bǣron . . . and eftston mid reówte (reówette, *v. l.*) on þǣre eá, Hml. S. 31, 1478.

**rētu.** v. un-rētu.

**rex-genīþla** (?) a royal foe (?) :—Nᵉ meahte hē oncyrran rexgenīðlan ( = cyning- (?), cyne- (?) genīþlan *Elene; either word alliterates with* cwēne), hē wæs on þǣre cwēne gewealdum, El. 610.

**ribb.** *Add:*—Gif rib forbrocen weorð .III. sciłł. gebēte, Ll. Th. i. 18, 15. Cōm of ðæm wætre án nædre . . . weard hiere mid ánum wierpe án fiþe forod—hit is nædrena gecynd þ heora mægen and hiera fēþe bið on heora ribbum, Ors. 4, 6 ; S. 174, 3–14. Gif mon óðrum rib forsleá binnan gehālre hȳde, geselle .x. sciłł. tó bōte ; gif sió hȳd sié tóbrocen, and mon bán of ādō, geselle .xv. sciłł. tó bōte, Ll. Th. i. 98, 11. Saga mē on hwæðere Adames sídan nam ūre Drihten ðæt rib ðe hē ðæt wíf of geworhte, Sal. K. 198, 9. Ōstige ribba hyrdlas, ribbes, hricges gebigednesse *squamigeros costarum crates (rigidamque) spinae curvaturam*, An. Ox. 2465.

**rīca.** v. þūsend-, weorold-rīca.

**rīce;** *adj.* I a. *add:*—Gif hwelc forworht monn cymð, and bitt ūrne hwelcne ðæt wē hine lǣden tó sumum rícum menn (*apud potentem quempiam virum*), Past. 63, 2. I b. *add:*—Tuoege scyldgo woeron sume ríce menn (*feneratori*), Lk. L. 7, 41. v. efen-, un-ríce.

**rīce,** es; *n.* I a. *add:*—On middeweardum hire ríce hió getimbrede Babylonia þá burg *medio imperii sui Babylonem condidit*, Ors. 2, 1 ; S. 62, 14. God forgifð ríce ðám ðe hē wile, Hml. Th. ii. 434, 4. I b. *add:*—Ðonne bið ðæt ríce wel gereht, ðonne sē ðe ðǣr fore bið suíðor wilnað ðæt hē rícsige ofer monna undeáwas ðonne ofer óðre gōde menn *summus locus bene regitur, cum is, qui praeest, vitiis potius quam fratribus dominatur*, Past. 117, 9. v. ærce-, ærcebisceop-, Breoten-, feówer-, fiþer-, Franc-, heáfod-, land-, middel-ríce.

**rīce-healdend** (?), es; *m.* *A ruler* :—Alfwold . . . mid rihte and mid gerisenum rícehealdend (ríce healdende?) *Athelwaldo . . . rite regimina regenti*, Guth. Gr. 104, 4.

**rīcen[n].** *Dele, and see* rícean.

**rīcetere.** I. *add:*—Ofermód rícetere *insolens potestas*, Germ. 391, 97. Hwǣr syndon dēmra dómstōwa ? hwǣr ys heora rícetere and heora prass and orgol ?, Wlfst. 144, 32. II. *add:* *undue display of power, arrogance* :—Wæs sum man, Leófstán gehāten, ríce for worulde . . . sē rád tó þám hálgan mid rícetere swíðe, and hēt him æteówian orhlíce swíðe þone hálgan sanct, Hml. S. 32, 233. v. weorold-rícetere.

**rīclīce.** *In* l. 2 l. *imperabatis, and* I. *add:*—Þám ælmihtigan tó lofe, sē þe on ēcnysse rīxað rīclíce mihtig, Hml. S. 36, 424.

**rīcsian.** II a. *add:*—Þǣr samod rícxað sib mid spēde and ārfæstnes and ēce gōd *pax et pietas, bonitas, opulentia regnat*, Dóm. L. 267. Unryhtwisnys rīxað (rícsað, *v. l.*) *abundabit iniquitas*, Mt. 24, 12. Kł. Ianuarius, gif hē biþ on Sæternesdæg . . . fȳr rícsaþ on þám geáre, Archiv

cxx. 298, 22. Ðá wǽtan weorþaþ gegaderode on þone magan, and þér ríxiaþ mid scearfunga innan, Lch. ii. 176, 7. Hér ásette se apostol niht for þǽre ealdan nytennysse ðe ríxode ǽr Crístes tócyme, Hml. Th. i. 602, 34. Ðá hwíle ðe him ǽnig unðeáw on rícsige, Past. 63, 19. v. gerícsian.

**rícsiend.** Add:—Rícsend mæhtig, . . . God rector potens . . . Deus, Rtl. 164, 10.

**-rid.** v. ge-rid, on-rid.

**rida.** v. tot-rida.

**rídan.** I. add: (1) where going on horseback is expressed or may be certainly inferred:—Gif þegen þénode cynge and his rǽdstefne rád on his hírede, Ll. Th. i. 190, 20. Sé þe hors nabbe, wyrce þám hláforde þe him fore ríde oþþe gange, 232, 19. Georne is tó wyrnanne bearneácnum wífe þ hió . . . on weg ne fére, ne on horse tó swíðe ríde, Lch. ii. 330, 9. Seldon hé (*Aidan*) wolde rídan ac síðode on his fótum (cf. non equorum dorso, sed pedum incessu uectus, Bd. 3, 5), Hml. S. 26, 80. Hé sceal rídan (*equitare*), Ll. Th. i. 432, 14. Hé hélit his geneát rídan mid ceastersétna preóste, C. D. v. 140, 31. Mid rídendum *cum equestri* (*turma*), An. Ox. 4748. (2) where the word is used as expressing the most usual method of locomotion, but does not exclude other forms:—Sé þe ǽfter ǽnegum ceápe ríde, cýþe . . . ymbe hwæt hé ríde . . . búton hé hit ǽr cýdde þá hé út rád, Ll. Th. i. 274, 20–24. Þ wé rídan tó mid þám geréfan, 236, 12. Rídan þá yldestan men ealle tó . . . Gif hwá nylle rídan, 208, 29–31. Ríde hé tó þám ealdormenn, and bidde hine fultumes, 90, 11 : 13. (3) *to ride* in a carriage:—Þonne sceoldon hiera senatus rídan on crætwǽnum, Ors. 2, 4; S. 70, 28. (4) of transport by land as opposed to that by water:—Beón hí áwergode rówende and rídende, Ll. Lbmn. 438, 22. III. *add*:—Þonne þæt scip ungetǽslícost on ancre rít, Solil. H. 30, 1. v. faroþ-rídende.

**ridda.** I. *add*:—Férde sum ǽrendfæst ridda be ðǽre ylcan stówe, Hml. S. 26, 221. II. *add*:—Ðǽr cóm rídende sum egeful ridda (cf. There appeared an horse with a terrible rider . . . he that sat upon the horse had complete harness of gold, 2 Macc. 3, 25), Hml. S. 25, 773.

**ríde-here,** es; *m. A mounted force, cavalry*:—Of rídehere *equitatu*, An. Ox. 2, 444. v. rǽde-here.

**rídel.** *l.* ridel: **ríd-wíga.** *l.* -wiga : **rif** (?) *and* **rífe.** *See* hrífe: **-rif.** v. ge-rif : **-ríf.** v. ge-ríf.

**rifelede;** *adj. Wrinkled*:—Rifelede *rugosus*, An. Ox. 18 b, 78. [v. *N. E. D.* rivelled.] v. ge-rifiod.

**rifeling.** *Add*: [v. *N. E. D.* riveling.]

**rifelung,** e; *f. A wrinkle*:—Riuelung *ruga, contractio pellis*, Angl. xxxii. 506, 12. [*N. E. D.* rivelling.]

**-rifod.** v. ge-rifod.

**rift.** *Add*:—Rif[te] *conopeo*, An. Ox. 5276. Ongeredon hine ðís ryfte *exuerunt eum clamyde*, Mt. L. 27, 31. Reáde ryfte ymbsaldan him *clamydem coccineam circumdederunt ei*, Mt. R. 27, 28.

**riftere.** *Add*:—Sum tún wæs . . . ǽlce geáre áwést þurh hagol, swá þ heora æceras ǽr wǽron áþroxene þe ǽnig ryftere þ geríp gaderode, Hml. S. 31, 1218. Ic cwepe tó þám riftrum, 'Gesomniað þá weód . . .' Witodlíce þá riftras, þ beóð þá englas . . , Gr. D. 316, 1–3. Hé wearð ofslagen . . . on hærfestlicre tíde úte mid his rifterum þe rípdon his corn, Hml. A. 108, 199.

**rignan.** I a. *add* : (a a) *to cause to fall like rain*:—Hé rínd (ríneþ, Ps. L. *pluet*) ofer synfulle grýn, Ps. Rdr. 10, 7. Hé rínde (rán, Ps. L.) him heofone hláf *pluit illis manna*, 77, 24. I b. *add*:—Hit swá swíðe rínde þ hié hæfdon wæter genóg onufan þǽre dúne, Ors. 6, 13; S. 248, 16. II. *add*:—Unmǽte rénas ríndon, Gr. D. 196, 2. Þí geáre manig seah meoloc rínan of heofonum, Shrn. 30, 10. v. regnian.

**riht.** II. *add*:—Þér næs riht on þǽre stówe ǽnigne tó ácwellanne for þǽre stówe weorþunge *in illo loco neminem fas erat interfici*, Nar. 30, 1. Béte hé þone borgbryce swá him ryht wísie, and þone wedbryce swá him his scrift scrífe, Ll. Th. i, 60, 20. Be ryhtes béne. Gif hwá him ryhtes bidde beforan hwelcum scírmen oþþe óðrum déman, 106, 19–21. Búton hé æt ham rihtes wyrðe beón ne móte, oþþe riht ábiddan ne mæge, 266, 10. In rihte beboren *municipales*, Wrt. Voc. ii, 59, 16. Sé þ gebéte his dryhtne .c. sciłł. an eald reht, Ll. Th. 38, 6. III. *add*:—Méda beeástan ee swé ðér mid riahte tó ðém lande limpað, C. D. ii. 75, 20. III a. *add*:—Gif þ riht tó hefig sý, séce þá líhtinge tó þám cynge, Ll. Th. i. 266, 11. IV. *add*:—Nathan lícette swelce hé ymb sumes ðearfan ryht sprǽce, and sóhte ðæs cyninges dóm, Past. 185, 19. Ágife se wer his wífe hire ryht on hira gesinscipe *uxori vir debitum reddat*, 397, 24. IV a. *what is proper* for a thing with regard to use or appreciation:—Hwílum alwan æfter hire rihte him mon scæl sellan, Lch. ii. 280, 20. Þá deádlican þing ðe gesceádwísnesse hæfþ mid nánum ryhte magon geearnigan þ gé heora wundrigen, Bt. 13; F. 40, 8. VII. *add*:—'Ælces unnyttes wordes . . . hé sculon ryht áwyrcean (*reddent rationem*)' . . . Gif wé sculon ryht ágildan (*si ratio exigitur*) unnyttra worda, P. 281, 9–14. v. ælmes-, bóc-, burh-, cyne-, eorl-, fǽr-, freó-, geneát-, lah-, swán (*not* swǽn-), þegen-, þrǽl-riht.

**riht;** *adj.* I. *add*:—Þér is ǽlc treów swá riht swá bolt, E. S. viii.

477, 13. Gif mon on his wege biþ gedwolod, sleá him ánne spearcan beforan, biþ hé sóna on rihtan (*in the right way*), Lch. ii. 290, 18. Mín Drihten . . . wæs on rihte róde úp áhafen . . . sceal mín ród onwended beón, Bl. H. 191, 4. Se wítega (*St. John*) sǽde on his gesihðe þ þǽra feówer nýtena fét wǽron rihte, and hí eódon ǽfre æfter ðám gáste, Hml. S. 15, 204. III. *add*:—Wǽrstánes fæder wæs riht æht tó Hǽðfelda, Cht. Th. 650, 11. IV. *add*:—Man mid wítum ofgán willað æt mé þ ic mid rihtan þingon (*by fair means*) begyten hæfde, Hml. S. 23, 600. IV a. of persons, *upright, righteous*:—Ðá ðe ryhtre (rihtre, Ps. L.) synt heortan *qui recto sunt corde*, Ps. Vos. 93, 15. Wuldriað ealle rehte (*recti*) on heortan, 31, 11. Þá ryhte synt of heortan, Ps. Rdr. 93, 15. Cynren rihtwísra ł rihtra (ðeára rehtra, Ps. Srt.) *generatio rectorum*, Ps. L. 111, 2. Rihtum (*rectis*) he is mildheort, 4. Þám gódum and rihtum on heortan, 124, 4. V. *add*:—Se hýra, sé ðe nis riht hyrde, Hml. Th. i. 238, 14. v. folc-, þér-, úp-, wiþer-riht.

**riht-ǽþelu** (-o). *Take here the passage given under* riht-aþelo.

**riht-ǽw.** *Add*: -ǽwe ; *n.* (v. ǽwe). I. *add*:—Wé lǽrað þ man geswíce cifesgemánan and lufige rihtǽwe, Ll. Th. ii. 248, 18. II. *add*:—Gif hé cyfesan hæbbe and náne rihtǽwe *si concubinam habeat, et nullam legitimam uxorem*, Ll. Th. ii. 186, 3. Heródes ðá áwearp his rihtǽwe, and forligerlíce mánfulles sinscipes breác, Hml. Th. i. 478, 28.

**rihtan.** I. *add*: *to put right, put into a proper condition*:—Á hé mæig findan hwæt hé mæig on byrig bétan . . . . oðde hús gódian, rihtan and weoxian, Angl. ix. 262, 18. IV. *add*:—Hé riht (reht, *v. l.*) and rǽt eallum gesceaftum, Bt. 35, 3 ; F. 158, 25. Simplicius wæs þridda þe æfter Benedicte rihte his gesomnunge *Simplicius congregationem illius post eum tertius rexit*, Gr. D. 96, 12.

**riht-ándaga,** an, *m. The right term* or *time*:—Gif preóst tó rihtándagan crisman ne fecce, Ll. Th. i. 168, 10. Tó þám rihtándagan gafol gelǽstan, 270, 17.

**riht-æþelu.** v. riht-æþelu.

**riht-dóm** *just judgement*:—Sé þe rihte lage and rihtne dóm (rihtdóm, *v. l.*) forsace, Ll. Th. i. 384, 16. v. unriht-dóm; wóh-dóm.

**rihte.** I. *add*:—Smire mid þ heáfod ufan rihte (*right on the top*), Lch. ii. 306, 16. Tó wylle þe rihte eást yrne, iii. 74, 13. Is ðearf þ þú rihte háwie mid módes ǽagum tó Gode swá rihte swá swá scipes ancerstræng býð áþenæd on gerihte fram þám scype tó þǽm ancre, Solil. H. 22. 3–5. II. *add*:—Rihte on þǽre ylcan týde þú wást xall þæt ðú nú wilnast tó witanne *eodem momento, eodem puncto temporis videbis quod cutis*, Solil. H. 46, 17. III. *add*:—Ic eom geðafa þæt ic eom swíðe rihte oferstéled, Solil. H. 62, 15. IV. *add*:—Nis nán þára ðe þe rihte séhð þæt hé þe ne finde, Solil. H. 13, 7. Swíðe rihte and swíðe gerisenlíce þú dést, 25, 7. Hwílon Wentsǽte hýrdon intó Dúnsǽtan, ac hit gebyreð rihtor intó West-Sexan, Ll. Th. i. 356, 19. V. *add*:—Genóh wel ðú hyt ongitst, and genóh rihte, Solil. H. 16, 22. Genóh rihte ðú hyt understenst, 24, 14. Apollonius þone rǽdels rihte árǽdde, Ap. Th. 5, 2. VI. *rightly, with undisputed title*:—Hé wes swíðe rihte mínes hláfordes kynnes *his title to kinship with my lord was indisputable*, Solil. H. 61, 10. v. eall-, hér-, ofdún- (cf. ádún, C. D. iii. 406, 26), sceaft-, súþ-, þér-, un-, úp-, westrihte.

**-rihte;** *adj.* v. earfoþ-rihte.

**rihtend.** *Add*: I. *a ruler*:—Hé heom gesette gewisse práfostas and rihtend *substitutis praepositis*, Gr. D. 119, 21. II. *a director, one who arranges matters*:—Sum wer wæs on þyssere byrig, . . . sé wæs séma and rihtend manigra manna, Gr. D. 297, 7.

**riht-endebyrdness,** e; *f. Right order*:—Elles ealle healdon . . . hyra rihtendebyrdnysse *reliqui omnes . . . ut ordinati sunt, ordines suos custodiant*, Chrd. 9, 23.

**rihtes.** *Add*: v. eást-, norþ-, þér-, west-rihtes; wiþer-ræhtes.

**riht-éþel** *a true native country*:—Ðis is mín rihtéþel, Bt. 36, 2 ; F. 174, 23.

**riht-fæsten** *a lawfully-appointed fast*:—Gif frígman rihtfæsten ábrece, Ll. Th. i. 172, 10: 402, 22.

**rihtfæsten-dæg.** *Add*:—Ordél and áðas syndon tócwedene freólsdagum and rihtfæstendagum, Ll. Th. i. 172, 10: 370, 3.

**rihtfæsten-tíd,** e; *f. A regularly appointed time of fasting*:—Ysfel bið þ man rihtfæstentíde ǽr mǽle ete, Ll. Th. i. 402, 24. Wé lǽrað þ ælc wer forgá his wíf freólstídum and rihtfæstentídum, ii. 250, 2.

**riht-full;** *adj. Good, virtuous*:—Eall þet þe Gode wæs láð and rihtfullan mannan, eall þ wæs gewunelic on þisan lande on his (*William Rufus*) týman, Chr. 1100 ; P. 235, 33. v. un-rihtfull.

**riht-gefang.** *See next word.*

**riht-gefég** *a proper joining*:—Eall þæs scipes fæt wæs ácweht and for ðám mycclum ýþum tólýsed and tóslopen fram eallum his rihtgefégum (rihtgefongum, *v. l.*) *totum vas navis quassatum nimiis fluctibus, ab omni fuerat sua compage dissolutum*, Gr. D. 248, 26.

**riht-gehíwan.** v. riht-gesamhíwan.

**rihtgeleáffulness**, e; *f.* *True belief, orthodoxy:*—Þ rihtgeleáffulnysse gebǽd, þ is *credo in Deum*, Hml. S. 23 b, 697.

**rihtgeleáflíce**; *adv.* *Orthodoxly:*—Rihtgeleáflíce *orthodoxe*, Angl. xiii, 447, 1167.

**riht-gelifed.** *Add:*—Hé monige gemetgunge þára rihtgelýfedra ... Angelcynnes cyricum bróhte ... Wæs geworden þ seó ryhtgelýfde (-lýfede, *v. l.*) lǽr wæs weaxende; and ealle þá þe þǽre rihtgelýfdon (-lýfedan, *v. l.*) láre wiþerwearde wǽron *perplura catholicae obseruationis ecclesiis Anglorum contulit ... Factum est, ut crescente institutione catholica, Scotti omnes ...*, Bd. 3, 28; Sch. 326, 16-327, 1.

**riht-gelífende.** *Add:*—Úrum wealdende rihtgelýfendum, Guth. Gr. 100, 1.

**riht-gemæcca** *a lawful husband:*—Gif wíf wið óðres wífes rihtgemæccan hǽmð *si mulier cum alterius legitima conjuge adulteraverit*, Ll. Th. ii. 270, 11.

**riht-gemǽre**, es; *n.* *A lawful boundary:*—Andlang rihtgemǽres ... on þone ðorn ... andlang Temese on þ ealdgemǽre ... andlang rihtgemǽres, C. D. B. iii. 546, 26-31. Ðurh þone mór be rihtgemǽre, C. D. iii. 412, 21. v. riht-landgemǽre.

**riht-gemet** *correct measure:*—Wite se ealdor þ hé hæbbe ealoð his rihtgemet *habeat de ceruisa quantum de uino debuerat*, Chrd. 15, 22.

**riht-gesamhíwan** *lawfully married persons:*—Be ðon ðe ryhtgesamhíwan (rihtgehíwan, *v. l.*, Ll. Lbmn. 22, 25) bearn hæbben, and ðonne se wer gewíte. Gif ceorl and his wíf bearn hæbben gemǽne, Ll. Th. i. 126, 1. Cf. riht-híwa.

**riht-gesceád** *right reason, reason:*—Þ rihtgesceád mé geopenode þá dígolnysse *secretum ratio aperuit*, Gr. D. 56, 3.

**riht-geset** *properly appointed, canonical:*—On ýtemystre tíde rihtgesetre *in ultima hora canonica*, Angl. xiii. 394, 412.

**riht-gesetedness** *regular ordinance, right rule:*—Þonne forlǽtað hí heora rihtgesetednysse (*canonicum ordinem*), Chrd. 10, 30. Gif hwá angeán þás gesetednyssa oððe óðre swilce rihtgesetednyssa beó tóþunden (*huic institutioni contumax*), 61, 12.

**riht-gesetness** *right institution:*—Ælc wuht his rihtgesetnesse fuleóde bútan men ánum *every creature carried out its properly appointed task except man only*, Bt. 5, 3; S. 12, 23.

**riht-gesinscipe** *lawful matrimony:*—Gif hí on rihtgesinscipe gegaderode sýn *si legitimo matrimonio conjungantur*, Ll. Th. ii. 232, 6. v. riht-sinscipe.

**riht-geþancod.** *Add:*—Rihte on heortan ł ðá rihtgeþancodan *rectos corde*, Ps. L. 36, 14.

**riht-gewittig** *of right wit, reasonable:*—Þ getácnað þ seó rihtgewittuge sáwel sited on þám líchaman, Gr. D. 245, 22. Hwylc rihtgewittigra manna is tó þon snotor þ hé wylle þá gástas secgan líchamlíce? *quis sanum sapiens esse spiritus corporeos dixerit?*, 305, 2.

**riht-gifu** *a lawful gift, a gift that is rightfully made.* The word occurs in a section of Cnut's laws headed ' De officiis domino debitis', but what was the nature of the obligation to which it is applied is nowhere explained:—Hláfordes rihtgifu stande ǽfre unáwend, Ll. Th. i. 422, 2 (cf. Hláfordes gifu þe hé on riht áge tó gifanne, 292, 16): ii. 302, 7.

**riht-hǽmed.** *In l. 2 after* ryhthǽmede *add* (-hǽmde, *v.l.*).

**riht-hamscyld?**:—Gif man rihthamscyld þurhstinð ... Gif feaxfang geweorð, Ll. Th. i. 12, 1-3. [In the note to these laws a passage from the Lex Saxonum is quoted giving two articles: I. 6. Si gladio *uestem* seu *scutum* alterius incideret ... 7. Si per capillos alium comprehenderit ... As *ham* denotes a garment, it seems as if the English text might be a corrupt form of a law corresponding to the former of these two, and in the same note the following emendation is suggested: Gif man on unriht ham oððe scyld (= *uestem seu scutum*) þurhstinð.]

**riht-hámsócn** *housebreaking which is such in the eye of the law, housebreaking which has been actually committed* (not merely attempted):—*Inuasio domus vel curie, quod dicitur* rihthámsócne (cf. *infectam inuasionem, quod Angli dicunt* unworhtre hámsócne, 615, 16), Ll. Lbmn. 614, 3.

**riht-heort.** *Add:*—Cneóris ryhtheortra *generatio rectorum*, Ps. Vos. 111, 2. Gódum and ryhtheortum *bonis et rectis corde*, 124, 4.

**riht-híwa.** *Add:* v. riht-gesamhíwan.

**rihthláford-dóm** *legitimate lordship, condition of rightful lord:*—Heó Myrcna anweald mid rihthláforddóme healdende wæs *she held sway over Mercia as its rightful lord*, Chr. 918; P. 105, 28.

**riht-hláford-hyldu.** *l.* rihthláford-hyldu *loyalty to a lawful lord.*

**riht-lǽcan.** *Add*(?): *to agree, be fitting:*—Gehwǽrlǽcan ł riht[lǽcan] *congruant*, i. *conueniant* (quamvis gymnicorum exempla ... rite *congruant* ad comparationem eorum, Ald. 3, 23), An. Ox. 66. Rihtlǽcan *seems doubtful here, as the verb elsewhere is transitive, and means* to set right. Riht *seems to refer to* rite, *and* riht-geþwǽrlǽcan *to be the completion intended.*]

**riht-laga, -lagu.** *Add:*—Swá hit rihtlagu (-laga, *v. l.*) sý, Ll. Th.

---

i. 396, 1. Woroldwitan gesettan tó godcundan rihtlagan worldlaga, 334, 22. Worldwitan tó godcundan rihtlagan þás laga setton, ii. 242, 13.

**riht-landgemǽre** *a lawful boundary to land:*—Ofer feld on ðá rihtlandgemǽre, C. D. iii. 446, 18. v. riht-gemǽre.

**riht-lic.** I. *add:*—Ic wolde witan hú rihtlic (*justum*) þ sý þ seó scyld sí wítnod bútan ænde, seó þe þurhtogen byþ mid þám ende, Gr. D. 334, 23. II. *add: proper:*—Þá dagas syndon rihtlíce tó fæstenne, Shrn. 80, 2. Þonne cymð óðer ðing þe mé þincð rih[t]licre and rǽdlicre, Solil. H. 33. 3. v. un-rihtlic.

**rihtlíce.** IV. *add:*—Þá ðe rihtlíce healdað hyra ǽwe, and on álýfedum tíman hǽmed begáð, Hml. Th. i. 148, 21. V. *of direction, directly:*—Ðá áxode ic hwilc se wæg wǽre þe tó Iordane þǽre eá rihtlícost gelǽdde, Hml. S. 23 b, 494. v. un-rihtlíce.

**riht-líf.** *Add: a life of lawful matrimony:*—Fón mágas tó and weddian heora magan tó wífe and tó rihtlífe, Ll. Th. i. 254, 20.

**riht-lífláð** *a right way of life, right conduct:*—Hálige men gebiddað for heora feóndum on þá tíde þe hí magon heora heortan gecyrran tó wæstmbǽrre dǽdbóte and hí gehǽlan mid hyra sylfra rihtlífláde *pro inimicis suis orant sancti eo tempore quo possunt ad fructuosam poenitentiam eorum corda convertere, atque ipsa conversione salvare*, Gr. D. 336, 1.

**riht-nama** *a right name, name correctly given:*—Ic wolde georne æt ðé gewitan þissere byrig rihtnaman, Hml. S. 23, 547.

**rihtness.** *Add:* v. ge-, un-rihtness.

**riht-raciend**, es; *m.* *An expounder of right:*—Seó Salomannes bóc ... is genæmned Ecclesiastes. Seó bóc is ágendlíce on Ænglisc rihtraciend geháten ... In þǽre rihtan race byþ oft forð ... bróht se dóm ... Manige men ... beóð gelǽdede tó ánum dóme þurh gesceád þæs rihtraciendes *Salomonis liber Ecclesiastes appellatus est. Ecclesiastes proprie concionator dicitur. In concione vero sententia promitur ... Multi ... per concionantis rationem ad unam sententiam perducuntur*, Gr. D. 264, 25-265, 4: 266, 17: 267, 11.

**riht-racu.** *Add: reason:*—Hé ne séceð ná þone geleáfan, ac rihtræce and gesceádwísnesse *fidem non quaerit, sed rationem*, Gr. D. 264, 12. Cf. Is þ forinweardlíce riht racu, Bt. 40, 1; F. 236, 10, *where riht seems an adjective qualified by an adverb.*

**-rihtreccan.** v. ge-rihtreccan.

**riht-regol.** *Add: a lawful rule of life:*—Wé bebeódað þte Godes þeówas hiora ryhtregol on ryht healdan, Ll. Th. i. 102, 15.

**riht-ryne.** *Add:*—Ne mihton hí þone stream of his rihtryne ábýgan *fluvius a proprio alveo deflecti non potuit*, Gr. D. 192, 23. Hé sǽde þ Pad seó eá wǽre of hire rihtryne on þǽre cyrican yrðland úp yrnende ... ' Cym tó dínum ágenum rihtryne' *nuntiavit quod cursus sui Padus alveum egressus ecclesiae agros occupasset ... 'Ad proprium alveum redeas,'* 193, 15-20. Tó his ágnum rihtryne, 194, 4.

**riht-scír** *a district the extent of which is determined by law, a parish:*—Gif man ǽnig líc of rihtscíre (of rihtre scríftscíre, *v.l.*) elles hwǽr lecge, Ll. Lbmn. 252, 11. *See next word.*

**riht-scriftscír** *a parish:*—Gif man ǽnig líc of rihtscryftscíre (rihtre scryftscíre, *v.l.*) elles hwǽr lecge *si corpus aliquod a sua parrochia in aliam deferatur*, Ll. Th. i. 368, 6: 308, 5. *See preceding word.*

**riht-scytte.** v. Cf. scytta.

**riht-sinscipe** *lawful matrimony:*—Drý hádas sindon þe cýððon gecýðnesse be Críste; þæt is mægdhád, and wudewanhád, and rihtsinscipe, Hml. Th. i. 148, 7. v. riht-gesinscipe.

**riht-spell** *a noble discourse:*—Ryhtspell monig Gregorius gleáwmód gindwód ðurh sefan snyttro, searoðonca hord, Past. 9, 10.

**riht-stefn** *a properly pronounced word, properly modulated sound:*—Ná mid rihtstefnum ac mid micelum hreáme ongann clypian *magnis non vocibus, sed stridoribus clamare incepit*, Gr. D. 28, 28.

**riht-þeów, -þeówa** *a lawful slave:*—Sæge þ ic þín rihtþeówa (-þeów, *v. l.*) sý *servum me juris tui esse profitere*, Gr. D. 180, 6.

**riht-tíd.** *Add:*—Þý lǽs þ bearn of bearneácnum wífe sié ǽr rihttíde, Ll. ii. 330, 10. In ondette gifernesse metes and drinces ǽr tídum and in tíde, ge eác ofer rihttíde, Angl. xi. 98, 24. v. unriht-tíd.

**rihtung.** I. *add:*—Hé him æfterfyligde in þæs mynstres rihtunge and hláforddóme *ei in monasterii regimine successit*, Gr. D. 96, 7. II. *add:*—On ðisum drým tíman andbidað God mancynnes rihtinge and góde wæstmas, Hml. Th. ii. 408, 15. Gif hí ne becumað hér tó rihtingce (*si ad correctionem non perveniunt*), hí byrnað þǽr aa in écnesse, Gr. D. 335, 13. III. *add:*—Midþrowung menn and rihtincg (*rectitudo*; cf. rigor, rectitudo, Corp. Gl. H. 103, 188) leahtrum scyl beón, Scint. 149, 6. Ma[n] sceal healdan gemet an þǽre rihtinge *mensura extendenda est correctionum*, Chrd. 60, 20. IV. *add:*—Rihtinc *regulam*, An. Ox. 1079.

**riht-wer.** *Add:*—Gif be cwicum ceorle wíf hig be óðrum were forlicge, ... hæbbe se rihtwer eall þ heó áhte, Ll. Th. i. 406, 8.

**riht-wíf**, es; *n.* *A lawful wife:*—Hú mihte Abraham beón clǽne þ hé nǽre forligr geteald þá þá hé hæfde cyfese under his rihtwífe? *quomodo defenditur Abraham adulterii reus non esse, dum viventi legitima*

*uxore sua conjunctus est ancillae suae?*, Angl. vii. 46, 440. Sē þe hæbbe rihtwíf and eác cifese, Ll. Th. i. 406, 16 : Hml. A. 204, 303.

**riht-willend.** *Add :*, -willende :—Rihte hit gerist þæt hine ealle rihtwillende emnlíce herian *rectos decet collaudatio*, Ps. Th. 32, 1. Wuldriað ealra rihtwillenda heortan *gloriamini omnes recti corde*, 31, 13. v. unriht-willend.

**riht-wirþe ;** *adj. Honourable* (?) :—Fultuma mē þæt ic simle þone ræd áræedige ðe þe lícwyrðe sí, and mē for þám lýfum best and rihtwyrðost sí, Solil. H. 13, 25.

**riht-wís.** *Add:* **I.** *of persons* :—Wē cweþaþ þ sē bió rihtwís ðe rihtwísnese hæfð *justitia adeptione justi fiunt*, Bt. 34, 5 ; F. 138, 35. For ðon rehtwís Dryhten *quoniam justus Dominus*, Ps. Srt. 10, 8. Oft se ungeleáffulla wer bið gehæled þurh þ rihtwíse wíf *saluabitur uir infidelis per mulierem fidelem*, Chr. 1067 ; P. 202, 15. Uton beón rihtwíse on úrum móde wiþ óþre men, Bl. H. 95, 28. Hwæt elles getácnað ðæt weófud búton ryhtwísra (riht-, *v. l.*) sáula? *quid accipimus altare Dei nisi animam justi ?*, Past. 217, 23. Se wísdóm gedéþ his lufiendas . . . geþyldige and rihtwíse, Bt. 27, 2 ; F. 98, 2. **I a.** *absolute* :—Ðæt we áðennen rehtwíse (*justi*) tô unrehtwísnesse hond hara, Ps. Srt. 124, 3. Hú hē þ ríce mihte on rihtwísra anwald gebringan, Bt. 1 ; F. 2, 20. Ná forlǽteð gyrd synfulra ofer hlýt rihtwísra (*iustorum*), Ps. Rdr. 124, 3. Cneóres rihtwísra (*rectorum*), Ps. Rdr. 111, 2. Ryhtwíse *rectos*, Ps. Vos. 32, 1. **I b.** *absolute with pronoun, the righteous* (*man* or *men*) :—Þonne gefalleð se ryhtwísa (*iustus*) ne bið gedréfed . . . ic ne geseh þone ryhtwísan forlǽtenne, Ps. Vos. 36, 24–25 : 5, 13. Tôcnáwan þone rihtwísan and þone unrihtwísan, Solil. H. 52, 1. þá rihtwísan sint láþe and forþrycte, Bt. 3, 4 : F. 6, 23. þá rihtwísan farað on éce líf *ibunt iusti in vitam aeternam*, Solil. H. 62, 1 : Mt. 25, 46. Þú eart án þára rihtwísena, Bt. 5, 1 ; S. 11, 17 : 23. Ðá unrihtwísan tǽlað þá rihtwísan *justus tulit crimen iniqui*, 4 ; F. 8, 16. **II.** *of things* :—Rihtwísum dóme *justo judicio*, An. Ox. 2718. Mid rihtwísere tódáles heolere *justa discretionis lance*, 1755. Se Godes man sceal beón fulfremed on rihtwísum weorcum, Bl. H. 73, 16.

**riht-wís** (?). *Add:* v. un-rihtwís[u] ?.

**riht-wísian** *to justify. Add :*—Gē syndon þá þe eów sylfe rihtwísiað beforan mannum, Gr. D. 40, 9.

**rihtwís-líc.** *Add :*—Ðæs gǽstes wæsðm is lufu and gefeá and ryhtwíslicu sibb *fructus spiritus est caritas, gaudium, pax*, Past. 345, 12.

**riht-wíslíce.** v. un-rihtwíslíce.

**rihtwís-ness.** *Add :*—Ðæt hē sié gebunden tô ðære ryhtwiésnesse (-wís-, *v.l.*) (*rectitudine*), Past. 75, 6. v. un-rihtwísness.

**riht-ymbren, -ymbrendæg.** v. ymbren, ymbrendæg.

**rím.** *Add: m.* **I.** *the precise sum or aggregate of any collection of individual things or persons* :—Ne magon wē þá tíde be getale healdan dagena rímes *we cannot keep Easter Sunday by a reckoning of the number of days*, Men. 64. Sindon unrímu cynn þe wē ne magon rím witan, Pa. 3. Hē æðelinga rím feorum geícte, Gen. 1161. Mǽgburge þínre rím miclian, 2221. **II.** *a particular sum or aggregate of units, of a kind specified or implied in the context* :—Hē hæfde eahta and hundeahtatig wintra. Ðone sylfan rím wintra hine hæbbende beón . . . , Bd. 5, 8 ; Sch. 586, 17. **III.** *the particular mark or symbol, having an arithmetical value, by which anything has a place assigned to it in a series* :—Gefundena rímas ðá ǽr ðú gebécnades onfindes stówa repertis numeris quos ante signaveras reperies loca, Mt. p. 4, 7. **IV.** *the full tale or count of a collection, company, or class of persons* :—Sió scyld hine of ealra háligra ríme átuge, Past. 37, 9. Hē næfde gefylled ðágiét ðone rím his gecorenra, 43, 22. **V.** *a* (*large* or *small*) *collection of persons* or *things* :—Ic him monigfealde módes gælsan ongeán bere dyrnra gedwilda ðurh gedwolena rím, Jul. 368. **VI.** *that aspect of things which is involved in considering them as separate units of which one or more may be taken or distinguished,* (1) *in oblique cases* or *prepositional phrases with adverbial force* :—Feówertig . . . wintra rímes *for years forty in number* ; quadraginta annis, Ps. Th. 94, 10 : Cri. 467: Men. 96. Týn hund wintra getæled rímes, Edg. 11 : El. 2. Wæron gefylde dagas on ríme, An. 1698. On ríme forborn fíf and hundseofontíg *there were burnt seventy-five in number*, Jul. 587 : Gú. 1108: El. 284. Wæs þæt mære cynn mycel on ríme (*numerically great*), Ps. Th. 104, 11. Wærun Godes cræta týn þúsendo geteled ríme *cursus Dei decem millibus multiplex*, 67, 17 : Exod. 372: An. 1037: El. 634. (2) *in phrases denoting that persons, things, &c., have not been, or cannot be, counted* :—Mē ymbhringde manig yfel, þér nis nán rím *circumdederunt me mala, quorum non est numerus*, Ps. Th. 39, 13. **VII.** *reckoning, calculation* :—Of ríme *laterculo* (*nec laterculo dinumerari* . . . *valet, quanta multitudo* . . . confluxerit, Ald. 44, 22), An. Ox. 2, 176. v. fore-rím ; un-rím ; *adj.*

**ríma.** *Add :*—On ende ł riman sǽs *in postremo maris*, Ps. Rdr. 138, 9. Ǽghwár be þére sǽ riman, Chr. 1052; P. 178, 26. v. eorþ, wudu-ríma.

**ríman.** **I.** *add :*—Gif hí oferhycgen ðæt hí him ondræeden hiora lytlan synna ðonne ðonne hí hí gesióð, ondræeden hí him húru, ðonne hí hí hrímað (*cum numerant*), Past. 437, 12. **II.** *add :*—Sumne dæl écra

gyfa swilcra swilce nú wísdóm is, and rihtwísnes, and óðre manega þe ús lang ðincð tô rímanne, Solil. H. 52, 17. Mē þincð þæt tô lang ǽll tô rímande, and ðé tô ǽlenge tô gehýranne, 59, 30.

**rím-cræft.** *Add :*—Rímcræft *arithmetica*, An. Ox. 55, 1 : *arithmeticam, causam numerorum*, 5441.

**-ríme.** *Add:* v. un-ríme : **rimpan.** *Take this to* ge-hrimpan, *and add :* [v. *N. E. D.* rimple.] : **Rín.** *Add to last passage after* eá (in Ríne þére eá, Riine þa eze, *v. ll.*).

**rinc.** *Add :*—Rince *hircitallo*, An. Ox. 2, 212. Swylce geongum hægstealde, rince, hysse *ut effebo hircitallo*, 3476. Swá beardleásum rince, 4, 57. v. hysse-, lád-rinc.

**rind.** **I.** *add :*—Seó dríge gyrd (*Aaron's rod*) þe næs on eorðan áplantod, ne mid nánre rinde befangen, ne mid sæpe ácucod, Hml. Th. ii. 8, 17. þ bælsamum ǽgþer ge ic ge míne geféran þǽr betwih þǽm rindum (*corticibus*) nóman, Nar. 27, 25. Geholedum rindum *cauatis codicibus* (tuguria cauatis consuta *corticibus*, Ald. 5, 22), An. Ox. 11, 16.

**rindran.** v. be-rindran.

**rinelle.** *l.* rinnelle. *and add :* [v. *N. E. D.* rindle.] Cf. rynele.

**rinnan.** *Add :*—Úp rynneþ *scaturiat*, An. Ox. 1891. Eá rinnende, Lch. iii. 36, 25. v. tô-rinnan.

**ríp.** Dele **II a,** *for which see* rípe, *and* **I.** *add :*—þæt hér wǽre micel ríp (*the accent is in the MS. and* riip *is a v. l.*) ondweard *multam esse messem*, Bd. 1, 29 ; Sch. 99, 8. Rípes (hrípes, L.) tíd *messis*, Jn. R. 4, 35. Bénfeorm for rípe *firma precum ad congregandas segetes*, Ll. Th. i. 440, 26. **II.** Dele '*a sheaf of corn*', *and the bracket, and add :* [The Latin for Lch. iii. 208, 15 is : Messes colligere, letitiam significat] :—þá þá hē sume ðæge lædde hám tô his berne þ ásnidene ríp *cum quadam die messem decisam ad aream deduxisset*, Gr. D. 290, 20. v. bed-, bén-ríp.

**rípa.** *Add :* [v. *N. E. D.* reap *a sheaf.*] v. frum-rípa.

**rípan.** *Add : p.* de Sē ðe him ǽlc wolcn ondrǽdt, ne rípð sē nǽfre, Past. 285, 18. Hē nǽnne sceáf ne rípð ðæs écean edleánes, 287, 3. Mid his rísterum þe rípdon his corn, Hml. A. 108, 199. Sē ðe rípe *qui metit*, Jn. R. 4, 36. Lytel sáwan . . . lytel rípan, Past. 285, 24. Mē mæig on hærfeste rípan, Angl. ix. 261, 14. [v. *N. E. D.* reap.]

**rípan** *to spoil. Add :*—Rýpeð *lurcatur*, An. Ox. 20, 1. Sē ðe Godes cyrican rýpe (rípe, *v.l.*) oððe reáfige *si quis ecclesiam Dei denudauerit*, Wlfst. 68, 1. [*N. E. D.* ripe *to rob.* Goth. raupjan *to pluck :* O. H. Ger. roufen *vellere :* Ger. raufen.] v. á-, ge-, tô-rípan.

**rípan** (?) *to ripen.* v. rípian.

**rípe.** *Add :*—þá seó tíd neálǽhte þ þá feáwa clystra þára bergena mihton rípe beón *cum tempus exigeret, ut racemi maturescere potuissent*, Gr. D. 57, 23. Wíngeardas (windeardes, MS.) rípe fulle gesihð blisse ge[tácnað] *vites maturas plenas uiderit, letitiam significat*, Archiv cxxv. 65, 591 ; Lch. iii. 210, 32. v. hræd-(not sæd-)rípe.

**rípere.** *Add :*—Hergiendum, rýperum *grassatoribus*, An. Ox. 2712.

**rípian.** *Add :*—Æpla, græs, and wyrtan, and treóweu foraldiað and forsériað and cumað oððer, grénu wexað, and gearwað and rípað (-iað?), Solil. H. 10, 5.

**ríp-ness.** *In l. 2 read* 39 *for* 29.

**rippel** (?) *a coppice* (?) :—Ærest of langan riple . . . andlang riple, C. D. iii. 30, 7–11. Be repple, iv. 49, 14. Cf. In loco qui dicitur Rippell, i. 22, 18. Ðás ii béc lóciað intó Ryppell, iii. 19, 22. Cf. Ad silbam qui appellatur ripp, i. 104, 2. Rhip, v. 46, 14. [v. *D. D.* ripple *a coppice.*]

**rísan.** **II.** *add :*—Gié dóeð þte ne riseð *facitis quod non licet*, Lk. L. 6, 2. Rísað *congruunt*, An. Ox. 8, 328.

**ríscan.** v. hrýscan : **risce.** v. rysce : **-risen.** v. ge-risen : **-risene.** v. ge-risene.

**risen-líc ;** *adj. Fitting, becoming* :—Risenlic (risnelic, L.) tô cumanne ǽrist *oporteat uenire primum*, Mk. R. 9, 11. v. ge-risenlic. **-risenlíce, -risenness.** v. ge-risenlíce, -risenness.

**rísiende** *emitting odour* (?) :—Risiendum stémendre *odorato* (*thure*) *flagrantior*, An. Ox. 23, 4. [*Could* risiendum = hrisiendum, *and refer to the incense in the swinging censer ?*]

**-rislic.** v. ge-rislic : **-risnian.** v. ge-risnian.

**ríþ.** *Add :*—Wæterseáþes, ríðe *cisterne*, An. Ox. 498. Rípe *riui*, 1413. Rípe *uenam*, Scint. 224, 7. v. ge-ríþe.

**ríþig.** *Add :* v. bord-, rysc-ríþig : **-ríþre.** v. ge-ríþre : **-roc.** v. ed-roc.

**rocc.** *Add :* [The Latin original for the last passage is : Clamide uestiri, securitatem significat.] v. diácon-rocc.

**rocc** *what is chewed.* Dele.

**rocettan.** *Add :*—Út rocettað míne weleras ymensong, Ps. Vos. 118, 171. Rocgetede word (*Iohannes*) *eructauit verbum*, Jn. p. 187. Út roccettende, Ps. Vos. 143, 13.

**ród.** *Add :* v. róde, and (? v. C. D. B. iii. 660, 31). **I.** *add :*—Ðone Iacóbum Iúdéas leorneras ofslógan mid webwyrhtan róde (cf. heora án hine (*James*) slóh mid ormǽtum stencge, Hml. Th. ii. 300, 24), Shrn. 93, 13. **III.** *add :* (1) *a cross on which a person is executed* :—Petrus cwæþ þá hē cóm tô þére róde, '. . . Mín Drihten . . . wæs on

rihte róde úp āhafen ... sceal mín ród onwended beón, Bl. H. 191, 1–5. Hé þær þreó métte róda ætsomne, El. 834. (1 a) *the cross on which Christ suffered :*—Seó Crístes ród on þá hé wæs āhongen, Shrn. 67, 25. On þysum geáre wæs gefunden seó hálige ród, Chr. 200; P. 10, 34. Hé sende him þære róde dæl þe Críst on þrowude, 885; P. 80, 7. (2) *the cross as a form of punishment, death on a cross :*—Hé cóm tó róde galgan *ad crucis patibulum convenit,* Past. 33, 20. On róde galgan āstígan, þrowian, losian, Bl. H. 27, 28 : 97, 11 : Hml. Th. i. 594, 4, 18. On róde treów āhebban, Angl. xii. 506, 4. Hér Petrus þrowode on róde, Chr. 69; P. 8, 30. On róde āhón *to crucify,* Shrn. 67, 15 : 153, 12 : Chr. 1096; P. 232, 23. (3) *the cross as a Christian symbol.* [Róde tácen seems hardly a compound to judge by the numerous phrases in which róde is qualified by an adjective or genitive, but may be such in instances like Gr. D. 247 (*infra*), or Hml. Th. ii. 304, 15 :—Hé mearcode him on heáfde hálig róde-tácen] :—Hé þá nædran ācwealde sóna gif hé hí gesegnode mid Crístes róde tácne, swá þ heó swulte for þám mægne þære hálgan róde, þonne se Godes wer þ róde tácen āwrāt mid his fingre; and eác gif ... hé gebletsode þæs holes múð mid þære hálgan róde tácne, Gr. D. 247, 2–6. Mid Crístes róde tácene *signum sancte crucis,* Chrd. 22, 25. Hé beseah tó þære hálgan Crístes róde tácne, Hml. S. 23, 499. Hié oncneówon Crístes róde mære tácen, An. 1339. Ðis seondan ðāra monna noman ðe ðæt geðafedon and mid Crístes róde tácne gefaestnedon, Cht. E. 162, 3 : 103, 6. (3 a) *the cross as representing the ecclesiastical office :*—Man sette Lēfegār tó þ ... Sé forlēt his crisman and his róde and his gǽstlican wǽpnu, and fēng tó his spere and tó his swurde, Cht. 1056; P. 187, 24.    **IV.** (*not* III) *a crucifix. Add :* (1) in a church :—Hit līhte under þære róde swýðran earme þe stód ofer þ weófed, Vis. Lfc. 53. This syndon þā cyrícan mádmas on Scírburnan. Thǽr synd twā Crístes béc and ii ródan, C. D. B. iii. 660, 31. Hé hæfð ðiderynn gedón .ii. mycele gebónede róda, C. D. iv. 275, 12. (2) *out-of-doors :*—Tó ðæm gemǽrdornan; þ tó ðære reádan róde, Cht. E. 291, 1. (3) *one that could be worn.* v. bisceop-, sweór-ród.    **V.** *of cleared land* (cf. excepta una roda, quam retineo ad viam habendam juxta haiam meam, *N. E. D.* rood ; 8) :—West be ðý wioda andlanges ðære róde, Cht. E. 153, 3. Of ðære dúne andlang þære róde oð hit cymð beneoðan stáncnolle, 248, 16. Of wáddene andlang ðære róde innon syx æceres, C. D. vi. 29, 34. On sūga róde ; andlang róde on huntena weg, iii. 48, 10. Eást on ðā ealdan róde ; andlang róde on ðā ealdan mearcebēcan, C. D. B. i. 296, 26. Be wyrtwalan oþ hit cymð tó þére ealdan róde ; þonne andlang róde ... eft tó þére róde, and þonne eft andlang róde ... norð be wyrtwalan tó þére brādan róde, and þonne andlang þére brādan róde, iii. 368, 13–18. Be wyrttruman oð ðā róde neoðewearde ; ðonne bewestan róde, C. D. iii. 406, 28. Út on ðā róde, v. 71, 4. v. æscstede-, coc-ród.

**róde-hengen(n).** *Add :*—Næs on þære þeóde nān deáþ swā huxlic swá swá on ródehengenne, Hml. A. 76, 81. Þá ðe Críst gefæstnodon on ródehenegene, Hml. S. 24, 149.

**róde-tácen.** v. ród ; III 3. *supra.*

**rodor.**  **I.** *add :*—On ðám óðrum dæge ūre Drihten geworhte *firmamentum,* ðe men hātað rodor ... Ðone rodor God gehēt heofon, Hex. 8, 25–10, 1.  **II.** *add :*—Hé (*Gregory*) monncynnes mǽst gestriénde rodra wearde, Past. 9, 11. Bið swíðe mycel stefn gehýred on eástweardum heofones roderum *erit vox magna in firmamento caeli ab oriente,* Verc. Först. 122, 6. v. norþeást-rodor.

**rodor-líc.**  **II.** *add :*—þú þe eart fram Gode gehálgod mid roderlicum wurðmynte *te ... quem Deus aethereo honore sacravit,* Hml. Th. ii. 134, 11. Tó ðám roderlícan (readorlícum, lxxv. 5) *ad aetheria,* Lch. i. lxxiii. 6.

**ród-stybb** *a stump left in a clearing* (? cf. ród ; **V.**) :—Inn on ródstubban ; swā of ródstybban, C. D. vi. 170, 37.

**róf** *a number* (?). v. secg-, stæf-róf : róf *valiant. Add :* v. bregoróf.

**Róm.** *Add :*—Tó Róme (Rómesbyrig, Rómebyrig, *v. ll.*) þú becymst, Gr. D. 132, 31. Hé becóm tó Róme (gesóhte Rómesbyrig, *v. l.*), 133, S. Sécende Rómesbyrig (Rómesburh, *v. l.*), 273, 19. Fǽdda hiæ wylíf in Rómæcæstri, Txts. 127, 2.

**Rómáne.** *Add :*—Weard Rómáne consul ofslagen, Ors. 3, 6; S. 108, 5. þá gesáwon hié Rómáne scipa on ðæm sǽ irnan, 4, 1; S. 154, 4. Rómáno scipa, S. 3, 23. Hū Rómáno (o *altered to* e) æfterre gewinn and Punica weard geendod, 4, 35.

**Rómánisc.** *Add :*—Rómániscum *romulei,* Germ. 402, 80. ¶ *used substantively :*—þone langan weall þe þá Rómániscan worhtan, Hml. S. 26, 41.

**rómig.** *That* rómei = hrúmig *seems certain from a comparison of* Wrt. Voc. ii. 102, 55–58 (*caumeuniae* eordreste, catabatus rómei, calcar spora, *cauterium* mercísern) *with* 13, 16–18 (*caumeuniae* eorðreste, caccabatus hrúmig, *cauterium* mearcísern). *For the form of the suffix cf.* popei *papaver,* 116, 48; popæg, 117, 66. [*The word may be a gloss to* Ald. 66, 22. Cf. *caccabatus* smittud, An. Ox. 4678.]

**rop** (?) *broth. See* broþ *for instances in which that word translates* jus.

**ropp.** *Add :*—þás þing magon wið roppes ge wið wambe and smælþearmes ādlum, Lch. ii. 234, 29.

**ros-bedd** *a rose-bed :*—Rosbeddum *rosetis,* An. Ox. 23, 8.

**róse.** *l.* (?) *rose, and add :*—Rose *rosa,* An. Ox. 56, 428. On hrosan brǽde stýmende, Hml. Th. ii. 136, 29. Rosan (*rosam*) gesihð strengþa getácnað, Lch. iii. 210, 13. Wē onfēngon þære rosena swæc, Angl. viii. 299, 44. Mid reádum rosum, An. Ox. 4509. v. wudu-rose.

**rosen.** *See next word.*

**rosig.** *This form seems very doubtful. The MS. quoted has* roseū, *but two other MSS. have* rosenū, *which is more likely to be right.* [Dr. Craigie kindly furnishes this note.]

**róstian.** *Add :* v. ge-róstian.

**rót.**  **II.** *add :*—þær wæs mǽst þ rótoste þ wæs on Ængla lande on þám twām gefylcum, Chr. 1052; P. 175, 25. v. un-rót.

**róþer.** *Add :*—Róþra ł ārena tíum *remorum tractibus,* An. Ox. 36.

**rotian.** *Add :*—Rot (= rotie) *putresco,* An. Ox. 23, 9. v. ge-rotian.

**rót-mód.** v. unrót-mód : rót-ness. v. unrót-ness.

**rótsung.** *Add :*—Rótsung ł frófr þearfana, Ps. Rdr. 9, 10.

**rówan.** *Add :*—þá reów (*navigavit*) se cyng sylf tó ðám íglande, Hml. Th. ii. 148, 6. Se gerēfa reów him tó lande (cf. Hí eódon tó scipe and heora segel ārǽrdon, 61), Hml. S. 36, 29 : Ap. Th. 5, 11. Cómon hí tó sǽ and þær gemētton scip standan, and hí on þ eódon and mid him reówan (*they went on board and sailed in it*), Hml. S. 30, 165. Sume scypmen reówan on þære tyreniscan sǽ, Hml. S. 31, 1135. Hí hreówan (reówon, *v. l.*) tó Grantanceastre, 20, 78. 'Swā se hrefen þurh þá fennas upp āflīgeð, swā þú him æfter rów' ... Hé tó scipe eóde ... Mid þý hé þurh þá fenland reów, Guth. Gr. 141, 12–16. Hé āgan rówan oð þ hé becóm tó Antiochiam, Ap. Th. 3, 25. Beón hí āwergode rówende and ridende, Ll. Lbmn. 438, 21. Hrówundum ł mið ðý gehrówun *navigantibus,* Lk. L. 8, 23. v. ge-rówan.

**rówend.** *Add :*—Rówendes *naucleri,* An. Ox. 2, 6 : 6, 7. þá hwíle þe þá rówendas (*nautae*) þæs scipes him sóhton óþre gerēdru, Gr. D. 306, 3.

**rówett.** *Add : rowing :*—Earma rówette *lacertorum remigio,* An. Ox. 5459. Wē ne mid segle ne mid rówette (róunesse, *v. l.*) ówiht fremian mihton, Bd. 5, 1; Sch. 551, 16. v. rów-ness.

**rudian** *to be ruddy.* Him an rǽd hiów rudaþ on þám ricge, E. S. viii. 478, 60. [Cf. *N. E. D.* rud *to make ruddy.*]

**rudu.** *Add :*—Rudu *rubor,* An. Ox. 4, 51. Rude *ostro,* 18, 9. [v. *N. E. D.* rud (1) *ruddiness.* (2) *complexion.*]

**rúh.**  **I.** *add :*—Hrúhge wulla *hirsutas lanas,* An. Ox. 5189. Rhúge, 2, 429.  **III.** *add :*—Rúh wærihtnys *callositas* (quos dira cutis *callositas* elephantino tabo deturpans, Ald. 49, 15), Hpt. Gl. 490, 36. v. healf-, un-rúh.

**rúm ; es ; m.**  **l. n.**  **I.** *add :*—Ne gebyreð ... tó lēsænnæ rúmæs būtan twīgen fýt, C. D. ii. 89, 7.  **II.** *add :*—*Interuallum* þæt is hwíl oððe rúm, Chrd. 24, 6.  **III.** *add :*—Gif hé þ rúm and þone ǽmtan hæbbe *si locus aut tempus exigerit,* Chrd. 105, 18.

**rúm ; adj.**  **l.** *add :*—Rúmes *uaste* (*solitudinis*), An. Ox. 3700.  **I b.** *of degree :*—Micel rúmes fæces tódāl *larga spatiosę intercapedinis differentia,* An. Ox. 1180.  **IV.** *add : free from occupation :*—Ðisra stafa tācna wē wyllað on rúmran fæce geswutelian, Angl. viii. 328, 11.  **VI.** *add :*—Fultum and wyrðmynt rúmran (*ampliorem*), Lch. iii. 204, 9.  **VI a.** *of material things, ample, abundant :*—Gif hit rúmre cymð *si Deus amplius dederit,* Chrd. 15, 5.  **VIII.** *add :*—Rúmes cynedómes *augustę potestatis,* An. Ox. 3942.

**rúme.**  **II.** *add :*—Hit rúmor and wíddor býþ ābysgod on manegum wísum *latius in multis occupatur,* Gr. D. 41, 18. [v. *N. E. D.* room.] v. ge-rúme.

**rúmedlíce.**  **II.** *add :*—Benedictus rúmedlícor dǽlde and manode þone ortríówan bróðor *diffidentem fratrem latius admonuit,* Gr. D. 160, 17. v. rúmlíce.

**rúmgállíce ; adv.** *Widely :*—þá þe hér rúmgállíce ofer Godes riht rícsiað, þá beóð þær on mǽstum racenteágum, Nap. 54.

**rúm-gifol.** *Add. of things, liberal, abundant :*—Rúmgyuelne nónmete *larga anteceniam,* Hpt. 31, 14, 353. *See next word.*

**rúmgifol-ness.** *Add :* **I.** *liberality, &c., of a person :*—For þæs ælmihtigan Godes þære wundorlican rúmgeofulnesse (-gyfol-, *v. l.*) *omnipotentis Dei mira largitate,* Gr. D. 317, 22.  **II.** *abundance of a thing.* (1) *material :*—Manega seócnyssa metta of rúmgyfulnysse wē þoliað *plurimas egritudines escarum largitate patimur,* Scint. 36, 5. (2) *non-material :*—Of þære myclan rúmgyfulnesse (-geofol-, *v. l.*) his mildheortnesse *ex magna misericordiae suae largitate,* Gr. D. 316, 20.

**rúmheort-ness.** *Add :*—Rúmheo[rtnesse] *munificentiam,* An. Ox. 56, 181.

**rúmlíce.**  **I.** *add :*—Rúmlícor *plenius,* An. Ox. 591. Hé rúmlícor lǽrde and manode þone ortreówan bróðor *diffidentem fratrem latius admonuit,* Gr. D. 160, 17. Ic wilnige þ ic rúmlícor (*largius*) geleornige þ mægn þára teára, 244, 21. Ymbe þises bissextus gesýllednysse wē wyllað rúmlícor iungum cnihtum geopenian, Angl. viii. 306, 15 : 32.  **II.** *add : abundantly :*—Se man þe næbbe of hwám hé mæge rúmlíce ælmes-

san syllan, Hml. A. 141, 80. Bige ús rúmlícor tódæg be hláfe þonne ðú gebohtest gyrstandæg, Hml. S. 23, 467. v. ge-, wel-rúmlíce.

**rúm-mód.** I. *add:* with gen. of what is given :—Hé ne sié giétsiende ððerra monna æhta, ac sié his ágenra rúmmód *ad aliena cupienda non ducitur, sed propria largitur,* Past. 61, 12. Wé sceoldan rúmmóde beón rihtra gestreóna, Wlfst. 257, 2. I b. of things, *liberal, abundant* :— Heó dǽlde þearfendum mannum manigfealde and rúmmóde gife ælmessan *larga indigentibus eleemosynarum opera impendit,* Gr. D. 279, 24. v. wel-rúmmód.

**rúmmódlíce.** *Add:*—Ðýs twéntigum hídum, ðá ic rúmmódlíce gescarode mé sylfum . . . tó écum rýmete, C. D. v. 331, 2.

**rúmmód-ness.** I. *add:*—Þám hér byþ forgifen seó rúmmódnes and árfæstnes þára ælnæssylena and gódra weorca, Gr. D. 321, 23. Nolde hé nó ðá rúmmódnesse hátan mildheortness, ac ryhtwísnes *non largitatem vocare misericordiam,* Past. 337, 1.

**rúm-well** (= full?). *Substitute:* **rúm-wille** (v. -wille).

**rún.** III. *add:*—Adames sagu wearð of gemynde æfter ðám flóde, and Iobales rúna ealle unnytte, and Nóes and Abrahames and mæniges ððres word ofergytene, Wlfst. 3, 38. v. heago-rún.

**-rún.** *Add:* v. heáh-, hell-rún : -rúna. l. (-rúne?) : -rúne. *Add:* v. dolg-, hell-rúne.

**rúnian.** *Add:* to *talk secretly* against a person :—Mé is eác gesǽd þ ðá Iúdéiscan syrwiað and rúniað him betwýnan hú hí þé berǽdan magon, Hml. S. 24, 100. Rúnigende *murmurans,* Germ. 401, 36. Rúnigende *musitantes* (presbyteros contra Susannam *mussitantes*), An. Ox. 7, 192 : 8, 151. Þá rúniendan, 5, 30. v. hás-rúnigende.

**rúnung.** *Add: secret talking* :—Hí (*the guards of Christ's sepulchre*) námon þone sceatt and swáþeáh múþetton and on synderlicum rúnungum þæt riht eall rǽddon (*in secret talks apart they supposed what the truth was*), Hml. A. 79, 161.

**rust.** *m. n* (?). *Dele* '(?)', *and substitute:* **rúst** (? *and* rust):—Wé nyllað álǽtan from ús ðæt rúst ðára unnyttra weorca, Past. 269, 16.

**rustig.** *Substitute:* **rústig** (? *and* rustig) :—Rústi[ges anfiltes] *scabrae* (*incudis*) (cf. ómiges anfiltes, 478), An. Ox. 7, 34.

**ruxlan.** v. hrúxlian : ryan (?). *Dele,* and see rýn : **ryddan.** v. á-, ge-ryddan, -rýdan (?) : -rýde, -rýdelic, -rýdelíce, -rýdness. v. ge-rýde, -rýdelic, -rýdelíce, -rýdness.

**ryderian** to *grow red* [:—Áryderende *erubescentes,* Ps. Rdr. 69, 4]. Cf. rudu.

**ryge.** *Add:* v. worþ; I.

**rýht, rýt** *rough growth on land* (?):—Gif fýr sié ontended rýht (rýt, *v. l.*) tó bærnenne, Ll. Th. i. 50, 27. v. rúh.

**rýman.** I. *add:*—Heom ic rǽde and rýme, gif hí mé willað híran mid rihte, Wlfst. 134, 2. II. *add:* (1) *to make way* for a person (*dat.*):—Hé þá inn eóde, and him man sóna hrýmde, and hé þá sóna eóde binnan þone weohstal, Vis. Lfc. 68. Seó leó forstód him þá duru . . . þá hét Daria þ deór him rýman út, Hml. S. 35, 277. (2) *place to* (*tó*) which given :—Hí léton þ hí úrum feóndum rýmdon tó lande, Chr. 1052; P. 175, 26. Áríse se gingra and þám yldran tó setle rýme, R. Ben. 117, 5. III. *add:*—Þe lǽs þe se húsbónda háte þé árísan and rýman þám ðórum, Mt. 20, 28.

**rýmett.** II. *add:*—Hé fór þæt he gewícode betwuh þǽm twám hergum þǽr þǽr hé niehst rýmet hæfde for wudufæstenne ond for wæterfæstenne, Chr. 894; P. 84, 24. Hé sylla rýmet tó sittenne *det ei locum sedendi,* R. Ben. I. 106, 9. III. *add:*—Binnan ðǽm rýmette þe se biscop mid wealle befangan hæfð, C. D. vi. 207, 17. IV. *add: easy circumstances, prosperity:*—Hé mé gelǽdde on rýmet of mínum nearonessum *eduxit me in latitudinem,* Ps. Th. 17, 19.

**rýmþ.** *Add: great extent* :—Æghwǽr geond swá mycele hys ríces rýmþe *ubique per tantam sui regni amplitudinem,* Angl. xii. 366, 17.

**rýn.** *Take here the instances given at* ryan (?), rýn, *where dele bracket in l.* 2, *and add:*—Sume hí sǽdon ðæt hió sceolde forsceoppan tó león, and ðonne seó sceolde sprecan, ðonne rýde hió, Bt. 38, 1; S. 116, 17. Þá ðe león wǽron ongunnon yrrenga rýn á þonne hí sceoldón clipian, Met. 26, 84.

**rýnan.** *Dele,* and see preceding word.

**ryne.** *Add: the course, movement,* or *path of a living creature:*— Fiþerscíte rene *quadripedante cursu* (*ferarum*), An. Ox. 1569. Hé mid hrædestan ryne arn, Hml. S. 23 b, 186. Hé gewunode on þám gesettum tídum þæs dæges þone ryne his síðfætes gefæstnian, 163. Flugulum rynum *fugitivis disscursibus* (*apum*), An. Ox. 7, 29. III. *add:*— Singal rine *perpes* (*aqueductuum*) *decursus,* An. Ox. 509. Oft gedónre ýþunge se stréam mid his rynum and mid his uppgange gewunode þ he tógoten wæs geond his æceras *fluvius . . . saepe inundatione facta cursus sui alveum egressus per agros diffundi consueverat,* Gr. D. 192, 17. IV. *add:*—Þæs mónan swiftnes áwyrþð út ænne dæg and áne niht of ðám getæle his rynes (*from the period of a lunation*) æfre ymbe neogontýne geár, Lch. iii. 264, 22. Se síðfæst þe Zosimus on .xx. dagum oferfór, þ eall Maria on ánre tíde ryne gefylde, Hml. S. 23 b, 761. Cum nú ymb geáres rynu, 706. Þá gelamp hit imbe geára rína, Chr. P. 3, 18. V. *add:*—Gefylledum ryne *consummato* (*vitae*) *curriculo,* i. cursu, An. Ox.

---

2147. Hí bútan ǽghwilcre gedréfednysse heora ryne gefyldon, Hml. S. 23 b, 103. v. ed-, hors- (?), scip-, singal-, swift- (?), tó-, un-, ymb-ryne.

**rynel** a *runner.* *Add:* v. fore-rynel : **rynel** a *stream.* *Add:* [v. N. E. D. rundle.] v. rynele.

**rynele,** an ; *f.* A *stream:*—Hér yrneð úp se æftra stream þǽre godcundan sprǽce, sé cymð of þǽre rynelan (þám burnon, *v. l.*) þæs gástlican æsprynges, Gr. D. 94, 14. v. rynel.

**rynelíce** (?); *adv.* *Quickly:*—Ryn(elíce?) *cursim,* An. Ox. 7. 90.

**rynning.** *Add:* [v. N. E. D. running; 13.]: **ryplen.** *In bracket l.* þýfien.

**rysc.** [*Perhaps* risc *is the better form.* v. N. E. D. rush.] *Dele* 'From Latin *ruscus*', *and add:*—Grównes ricsena (rixa, *v. l.*), Bd. 3, 23; Sch. 300, 20. The word occurs as the first part of many local names.

**rysce,** an ; *f.* A *bed of rushes* (?) :—Of bæccæ funtan on ðá riscæan ; of ðǽre riscæan on sagelmǽre, C. D. iv. 27, 15. [Cf. (?) N. E. D. rush a thick growth *of plants* or *shrubs*; a *brake.*]

**ryscen.** *Add:*—Þá nam heó ánne riscenne on scipwísan gesceapenne *sumpsit fiscellam scirpeam,* Ex. 2, 3. [v. N. E. D. rushen.]

**rysciht(e);** *adj.* *Rushy, full of rushes:*—On ðone ricsihtan mere, C. D. vi. 214, 18.

**rysc-ríþig** a *stream in which rushes grow:*—On rischríðig; of rischríðie ; C. D. iii. 15, 25.

**rysc-secg** *sedge:*—Rixseccas *carices,* Germ. 399, 396.

**rysel.** *Add:* I. *fat:*—Hrisel cada, lytel hrisel *cadula* (cada *arvina*; cadula *guttae quae cadunt ex pingui carne, cum assatur; frusta ex adipe,* Migne), Wrt. Voc. i. 44, 1. Hrysel *arvina vel adeps vel axungia vel abdomen,* 20. Rysele, smerewe *ausungia,* i. *aruina,* An. Ox. 2762. Gemæstra swína rysele *scrofarum auxungia,* 23, 28. Mæng wiþ ealdne rysele, Lch. ii. 62, 28 : 130, 19. Genim ealdne rysle, 180, 4. Bringon þone rysle þe þá heortgesída mid beóð oferwrigen *offerent adipem qui operit vitalia,* Lev. 3, 3. II. *resin:*—Hryseles, tyrewan *resine,* i. *bituminis,* An. Ox. 4027. Ryselas oððe swefel gesihð, hefige teónan getácnað *resinas uel sulphur uiderit, grandes molestias significat,* Lch. ii. 210, 13.

**rysel-wǽrc** *pain in the abdomen* (cf. hrysel *abdomen,* Wrt. Voc. i. 44, 20):—Wiþ wambe wærce and ryselwærce, Lch. ii. 318, 15.

**rýsig.** v. hrísig : **rýt.** v. rýht.

**ryþþa.** *Add:*—Hetelum ryþþan *rabidis molosi,* i. *canis* (*rictibus*), An. Ox. 3641. Ryþþan *molossi* (velut *molossi ad vomitum relapsis*), 4745.

# S

**sac** *sackcloth.* v. sæcc : **sacan.** *Dele* wiþer-[sacan].

**sacc.** *Add:*—Hé lǽdde his hálgan béc mid him on fellenum saccum (sæccum, *v. l.*) *sacros codices in pelliceis sacculis portabat,* Gr. D. 34, 15. [*From Latin* saccus.]

**-sacend.** v. yfel-sacend: -sacendlíc. v. wiþ-sacendlíc.

**sacerd.** l. sácerd, *and add:*—Bád se sácerd (a *priest of the Indians*) sunnan setlgonges, Nar. 27, 15. Heó gesette hyre gingran þe hire folgode tó sácerde (*priestess*), Ap. Th. 25, 18. v. efen-sácerd; preúst.

**sácerd-hád.** *Add:*—Sácer[d]hád *sacerdotium,* An. Ox. 2031. Biscophád, sácerdhád *flamin(i)um,* i. *sacerdotium,* 5056. Ne sý nán sácerdhádes man, ne lǽwedes hádes þe má . . . , Ll. Th. ii. 412, 27 : 408, 6. Þám preóste (*clerico*) hé cwæð, ' . . . ne genéð þú nǽfre þ þú gá tó þám hálgan háde, oððe máran underfó þonne þú nú hæfst ; sóðlíce on swá hwilcum dæge swá þú geþrístlǽcst þ þú underféhst þone hálgan sácerdhád (*sacrum ordinem*) sóna þú bist mid deófles anwealde gehæftniéded ' . . . Hé geseah þ geongran men sácerdhád underféngon (wǽron gesette on hálgum sácerdhádum, *v.l. in sacris ordinibus positi*) . . . and eóde baldlíce tó þám hálgan sácerdhád, Gr. D. 135, 7-31. Sácer(d)hádas *flamina,* An. Ox. 2, 56. Cf. preóst-hád.

**sácerd-líc.** *Add:*—Sácerdlíce *sacerdotalem,* An. Ox. 2880. Hé hine hálsode þæt hé þurh hine sácerdlíce þénunge onfénge, þæt hé hine móste gehádigan tó mæssepreóste and tó þénunge Drihtnes weófodes *adjurare coepit eum, ut sacerdotale officium per eum susciperet,* Guth. Gr. 156, 40. Næs íc ná gedyrstig þ ic Gode sácerdlíce onsægednysse bröhte, Hml. A. 123, 214.

**sac-full.** I. *add:*—S(a)cful *rixosa,* An. Ox. 56, 88. Twelf unþeáwas syndon . . . gif se crístena bið sacfull (*contentiosus*), O. E. Hml. i. 299, 14: 301, 30. Gif se crístena mann bið sacfull, ne bið hé sóðlíce crísten. Nis nán man rihtlíce crísten bútan sé ðe Críste geefenlæcð. Críst sylf nolde flítan, 31-33. Beóð þá sacfullan deófles bearn, 302, 5. I a. that *excites dissension* or *strife:*—Léase láreówas bringað sacfulle láre *pseudodoctores introducent sectas,* Chrd. 93, 2. II. in *last line for* Leo. l. Lev.

**sacian.** *Add:*—Hī wǽron saciende *dissecabantur*, Hpt. 33, 238, 2. v. wiþer-, yfel-sacian.

**sac-leás.** II. *add:*—Ǽilsig, ðe ðá men bohte, nam hig and freóde uppan Petrocys weófede ǽfre saclés, C. D. iv. 313, 11. Hē dide hine sylfne and his ofspreng ǽfre freóls and saclés, 314, 8. Hē kyð on þissere béc þ Gesfrǽg gebohte Gidið . . . tō .x. scill freoh and saclés, Cht. Th. 631, 26. Sacclés of ǽlcre crauigge, 645, 4. [v. *N. E. D.* sackless.]

**sacu.** I. *add:*—Swā micele hefigre sace geþanca flǽsclicra wē synd ofsette *quanto graviore tumultu cogitationum carnalium premimur*, Scint. 31, 18. Ne flīt hē . . . ne sace ne ástyreð . . . þá beóð Godes bearn þá þe gesibsume beóð and sace ne ástyriað . . . Wē ne magon habban þone heofonlican éþel búton wē fram eallum sacum orsorge beón, O. E. Hml. i. 302, 1–8. Iꜳ. *rebuke, chiding:*—Mid openre sace beón gehǽled *aperta objurgatione sanari*, Scint. 115, 16. v. and- (?), ge- (?), weorold-sacu.

**Sadducéas.** *Add:*—Hē geseah ðæt folc Phariséo and Saducia his éhtan . . . ðā Saducie antsacodon ðǽre ǽriste, Past. 363, 1–5.

**sadian.** I. *add:*—Hrefen his briddas gelómlíce sadað mid metton *corvus suos pullos frequenti cibo reficit*, Chrd. 96, 7. Cf. seddan.

**sadol.** *Add:*—Hē breác weþera fella for sadole (-ele, *v. l.*) *vervecum pellibus pro sella utebatur*, Gr. D. 34, 13.

**sadolian.** *Add:* v. un-sadelod.

**sǽ.** II. *add:*—Wæs gecweden tō ðǽre byrig ðe Sídōn hǽtte, sió stód bī ðǽre sǽ: 'Ðiós sǽ cwið ðæt ðū ðīn scamige.' Swelce sió burg wǽre ðurh ðæs sǽs stemne tō scame geworden, Past. 409, 32–35. Ofer sǽas hē gestaðolode hié, Ps. Vos. 23, 2. IV. *add:*—Saga mē hū fela is woruldwǽtra. Ic ðē secge twā sindon sealte sǽ, and twā fersce, Sal. K. 186, 25. V. *add:*—Andlang strǽte on Scoffoces sǽ, C. D. i. 258, 4.

**sǽ-brōga,** an; m. *A sea-terror:*—Ðeáh hine ealle sǽyðan nioðan cnyssende wǽron mid eallan sǽbrógan ðe hē (se sǽ, cf. Verc. Först. 110, 12) forðbrinð, Sal. K. 84, 13.

**sǽce;** m. *Add:*—Sac and fæsten wǽpnu synd dǽdbóte *saccus et ieiunium arma sunt paenitentiae*, Scint. 43, 3. [v. *N. E. D.* sack; II. 5.]

**sǽc(e);** f. *Add:* [O. H. Ger. secchia *rixa, lis, querela*.]

**-sǽc(o)** = -sacc. v. bī-sǽc.

**sǽ-clif.** *Add:*—On þām lengestan treówe ufeweardum þe ofer sǽ standeð on þām hýhstan sǽclife, Verc. Först. 110, 6. Swilce hē wylle weorþan uppe on sumum sǽclife, Solil. H. 45, 18.

**sǽd.** I. *add:* (1) *what is sown;* in pl. *kinds of seeds:*—.iii. æceras geerian on heora ágenre hwīle and mid heora ágenan sǽda gesáwan, C. D. iv. 306, 28. Sǽdu on eorðan sendan, Lch. iii. 188, 1. (2) *an individual grain of seed:*—Hiera sǽd gefeóllon on ðā ðornas, Past. 67, 20. Gelíc senepes corne . . . Ðæt is ealra sǽda (sǽda, R., from allum sǽdum, L.) lǽst *simile grano sinapis . . . Quod minimum est omnibus seminibus*, Mt. 13, 32. Iꜳ. *add:*—Ne becōme hē nō tō ðǽm sǽde ðǽre wröhte, Past. 358, 2. Þǽr nǽnig láreów ǽr cōm þā sǽd sáwan þæs hálgan geleáfan, Bd. 3, 7; Sch. 212, 8. V. *add:* (1) *semen:*—Wið swiðlicne flēwsan sǽdes, Lch. i. 220, 3. Wīf . . . ymbe .xl. nihta þæs ðe heó þām sǽde (*semen*) onfó, Ll. Th. 154, 16. Gif man on ciricean slǽpende his sǽd ágeóte, 138, 11. (2) *progeny:*—Nim of eallum clǽnum nítenum seofen and seofen ǽgðres gecyndes . . . þæt sǽd sī gehealden ofer ealre eorðan brǽdnisse, Gen. 7, 3. Sēd árleásra forweorðeð, Ps. Srt. 36, 28. Ealle seofon hī hæfdon, and sǽd (sēd ꞁ teám, L., sǽd, R.) ne lǽfdon, Mk. 12, 22. v. æcer-, beán-, cawel-, corn-, nǽp-, senep-sǽd.

**sǽd-berende.** In a legend of the Holy Cross Seth is represented as bringing seeds from Paradise, whither he had been sent by Adam: Seth, ita edoctus ab angelo cum uellet discedere, dedit ei angelus tria grana pomi illius, de quo manducauerat pater eius dicens ei : 'Infra triduum cum ad patrem tuum redieris ipse exspirabit. Haec tria grana infra eius linguam pones, &c.' If the poet of the Genesis knew such a legend it might have suggested the epithet he applied to Seth. v. Mod. Lang. Rev. vi. 200. See, too, C. M. 1365:—His leue Seth toke of cherubyn, and þre curnels he ȝaf to hym whiche of þ tre he nam þ his fadir eet of Adam.

**sǽ-deór;** n. (not *m.*). *Add:*—Hý mon wearp in sǽdeóra seúð and þā hyre ne scedeðon, Shrn. 133, 11.

**sǽdere.** *Add:*—Sǽdere sator, i. *seminator*, An. Ox. 2358. Gif hwā forsteld hwǽte and þ forstolene sǽwð, hwæt áh þ corn geweald (*how can the corn help*) þ hit wearp se sǽdere mid unclǽnum handum on ðā clǽnan moldan? oððe hwī sceolde seó eorðe hyre wæstmas ofteón þām unscyldigum sǽde for ðām scyldigan sǽdere?, Hml. A. 36, 311–37, 315.

**sǽdian.** *Add:*—Geeáde sē ðe sáwes sǽde ꞁ gesáwe ꞁ sǽdege *exiit qui seminat seminare*, Mt. L. 13, 3.

**sǽd-lic.** *Add: of seed:*—Swā hwæt swā sǽdlic *quicquid seminarium*, Scint. 106, 10.

**sǽdsworn** = (?) sǽdes worn:—Abraham and sǽdsworne (sǽdes worne? Cf. sǽd; V. 2, *and* worn, (1 b)) *Abraham et semini eius*, Ps. Rdr. 296, 55.

**sǽ-fisc.** *Add:*—Sǽfisce ꞁ hrane *ballena*, An. Ox. 23, 48. Habbað eów anweald ofer sǽfyxum (cf. þǽre sǽ fixas, Gen. 1, 28), Hex. 20, 5. Ne þicgen hié fenfixas ne sǽfixas, Lch. ii. 254, 22.

**sǽ-flód.** I. *add:*—Hér is seó endebyrdnes mōnan gonges and sǽflódes. On ðreóra nihta ealdne mōnan wanað se sǽflód oþ þ se mōna bið .xi, nihta eald. Of xi. nīhta ealdum mōnan weaxeð se sǽflód oþ .xviii. nihta ealdum mōnan, Angl. xi. 6, § 5.

**sǽgan.** *Add:* [O. H. Ger. seigen.] v. be-, ge-sǽgan: -sǽgdness. v. fore-sǽgdness: **sǽgedness.** *Add:* v. ge-sǽgedness.

**sǽgen.** I. *add:* (1) *of a particular statement:*—*Modicum et non videbitis me, et reliqua.*—Wundrodon hī swīðe þǽre sǽgene, Hml. A. 73, 19. Holofernes æfter þissere segene gebealh hine *cum cessasset loqui Achior verba haec indignatus est Holofernes*, 107, 145. Hē cwæð þæt hē wolde þām wīfe gemyltsian, ac hē ne mihte þ gafol álecgan . . . 'Gif þū woldest myltsian and ne mihtest, þær is sum belǽdung on þǽre sægne (segene, *v. l.*),' Hml. S. 3, 185. (2) *a narrative, story, relation:*—Seó fúle cwæð þ heó eóde tō hyre licgendre on lǽces hīwe . . . 'ac ic hrýmde . . . oþ þæt ān mínra wīmmanna mē wið hine áhredde.' Gelýfde Philippus þǽre fácenfullan segene, Hml. S. 2, 190. Hē mē cýþde mid his ágenre sægne (segene, *v. l.*) þ . . . *relatione sua me docent, quod . .*, Gr. D. 220, 3. Hē him eall sǽde his sīð be ændebyrdnysse, and þ folc æfter his segene feóllon tō eorðan, Hml. A. 107, 160. Sum engel him sǽde hwæt þā ōþre bisceopas on heora sinoþe sprǽcon, and se hálga wiston hwæt hī þǽr rǽddon þurh þæs engles segene, Hml. S. 31, 687.

**sǽ-grund.** *Add: the deep:*—Se apostol Paulus sǽde þ hē sylf wunode on sǽgrunde middan ofer dæg and ofer niht (*nocte et die in profundo maris fui;* a night and a day I have been in the deep, 2 Cor. 11, 25), Hml. S. 31, 899.

**sǽ-healf,** e; f. *The seaside:*—Bæd hē hī ánre sylle, þæt hē mihte þæt hūs on ðā sǽhealfe (*a parte maris*) mid þǽre underlecgan, Hml. Th. ii. 144, 33. Hē lǽdde scipfyrde tō Scotlande, and þ land on þā sǽhealfe mid scipum ymbelæg, Chr. 1072; P. 208, 13.

**sǽ-hund,** es; m. *A sea-hound:*—*Scilla* ðet is sǽhund gecweden, An. Ox. 26, 61.

**sǽl.** Dele *'Icel.* salr *a hall'* in bracket, and add: v. wīn-sæl.

**sǽl.** I. *add:*—Genim þysse wyrte croppas, ǽrest þrý, æt ōþrum sǽle fíf, æt þām þryddan sǽle seofone, æt þām feórþan cyrre nigon, . . . æt þām nigoþan cyrre nigontýne, æt þām teóþan sǽle ān and twēntig, Lch. i. 214, 3–9. Gelamp on sumne sǽl (*alio tempore*), Guth. Gr. 148, 1. Cómon on sumne sǽl *venerunt his fere diebus*, 151, 1. Seó æftre bōc ūs sægð þ hī on sumne sǽl fuhton, Hml. S. 25, 459. IV. *add:*—Hē cwæð : 'On sǽlum, lā bróðra, on sǽlum ! gē wel habbað gewunnen, blinnað nū sume hwīle *ait:* " *Gaudete, fratres, multum laborastis, jam quiescite,*"' Gr. D. 202, 5. v. un-sǽl.

**sǽlan.** *Add:* v. ymb-sǽlan; searu-sǽled: **sǽle.** v. un-sǽle: **sǽleþa.** v. sealtf-sǽleþa: **sǽlhþ.** v. ge-sǽlhþ: **sǽlig-lic.** v. ge-sǽliglic: **sǽl-lic,** -líce. v. ge-sǽllic, -líce.

**sǽlmerige.** *Add:* [Cf. O. H. Ger. salzmuorna *salsugo*] : -sǽlness. v. heard-sǽlness: **sǽlþ.** *Add:* v. heard-, med-sǽlþ.

**sǽltna.** *Add:*—Salthaga *rubisca*, Hpt. 33, 241, 43. [Cf. saltian, *as if the name referred to the movements of the bird?*]

**sǽ-minte.** *Add:*—Seómint *altea vel eviscus*, Wrt. Voc. i. 32, 12.

**sǽn;** adj. *Marine:*—On sǽnum *in glari(g)eris*, An. Ox. 8, 128. Sēnum, 6, 23. On sǽnum *in marinis*, 8, 157. Sǽnunum, 7, 201. v. sǽnig.

**sǽne.** *Add:*—Ic tō sǽne wæs míne leomu for ðē tō bíganne and míne teáras tō geótanne, Angl. xii. 508, 8. Þý lǽs hié for ðon ormóde wǽron and þý sǽnran mínes willan and weorðmyndo, Nar. 32, 23.

**sǽnig;** adj. *Marine:*—On saenegum *in glari(g)eris*, Angl. xiii. 32, 125. v. sǽn.

**sǽ-ostre** *a sea-oyster:*—Hē nǽnine ōþeme mete ne þigeþ búton sǽostrum, Nar. 78, 23.

**sǽppe.** *Add:*—Saeppae, sǽpae *abies*, Txts. 38, 37.

**sǽr-níd** (?) *dire need:*—Drigiþ . . . sǽrnēd (sǽrden *is the original form*) sorgæ, Beiblatt 16, 231.

**sǽ-scill** *a sea-shell:*—Hē wæs nacod and on carcern onsǽnded, and þǽr wæs understregd mid sǽscellum and mid scearpum stánum (cf. *mittitur in carceneni ubi . . . fragmenta testarum subter eum sternebantur*, Bede's Life of Felix), Shrn. 51, 13.

**sǽ-steorra,** an; m. *A star which guides mariners at sea; stella maris,* a title given to the Virgin Mary, from the erroneous belief that it expressed the etymological meaning of the Hebrew name Miriam, Mary :—Nū is hyre nama gereht . . . sǽsteorra . . . Sǽsteorra heó is gecweden, for ðan þe se steorra on niht gecýþeð scypliðendum mannum hwyder bið eást and west, hwyder sūð and norð, Hml. A. 117, 6–19. [*Nomen est Maria quod interpretatur stella maris . . .* þ is on ure ledene sesteorre, O. E. Hml. 141, 24–26 : 161, 4. Sǽsteorrne, Orm. 2132.]

**sǽ-strand,** m. l. *n.*

**sǽt.** To judge by the former of the two passages given here the word in the latter of them should mean a place of concealment for the hunter where he lies in wait for the game which is driven towards him. Such driving of game is described by the hunter in Ælfric's Colloquy, Th. An. 21, 13–22, 18. *Sǽte haldan* would mean to keep the game from avoiding the ambush into which it was being driven. Cf. ge-sǽte.

sǽta. *Add:* v. ceaster-, hǽ-sǽta: -sǽte. v. ge-, in-, on-sǽte.

sǽte, an; *f. A house* :—Ðis sindon ðā londgemǽra ... Ǽrest úp of Sæfern on Beornwoldes sǽtan ; of sǽtan on hagan geat, C. D. iii. 79, 15. [Cf. *O. H. Ger.* hūssāza *domus.*]

sǽtian. *Add* :—Sǽtiende hí ofslōgon þone beran *ursum insidiantes occiderunt,* Gr. D. 206, 30. v. be-, for-sǽtian.

-sǽtness. v. on-sǽtness.

sǽtnian. *Add* :—.xl. snacca lāgan æt Sandwíc manega wucan ; þā sceoldon sǽtnian (cēpan, *v. l.*) Godwines eorles, Chr. 1052 ; P. 178, 22. v. ge-sǽtnian.

sǽtnung. *Add:* v. on-, ymb-sǽtnung : sǽ-troh. v. trog ; **IV.**

sǽtung. *Add* :—Úre Drihten mid his sylfes willan tó eorþan ástág, and hér manige sētunga and searwa ádreág æt Iūdéum, Bl. H. 83, 33.

sǽ-waroþ. *Add* :—Sǽwaroþa (swā waroþa, MS. but cf. Dan. 323) sond, Az. 39.

-sǽwe. v. ge-sǽwe.

sǽ-weard. *Add:* In a charter granting land in Cornwall the land is freed ' ab omni regali censu excepta expeditione arcisue munimine et uigiliis marinis,' Cht. E. 295. See, too, Kemble, Saxons in England, ii. 63.

sǽ-wer (?) *a weir of some kind* :—Ðæt mynster æt Wíc, and seó híd ðæ ðǽrtó líð, and .vi. æceras and se īggað æt portes bricge and (mid ?) healfe sǽwære and se mylnstede æt Mannæs bricge, C. D. iv. 96, 4. v. wer [*where the instances given under* **II.** (*especially* C. D. vi. 136, 11) *seem to show that in sǽware the second element belongs to* wer *a weir. If* mid *be put for* and *the inflexion is accounted for.*]

-sǽwestre. v. for-sǽwestre : sǽ-winewincle(-a?). v. winewincle (-a?).

sǽ-ýþ. *Add* :—Ðeáh hine ealle sēyðan nioðan cynyssende wǽron mid eallan sǽtrogan ðe hē (= se sǽ) forðbrínð, Sal. K. 84, 13.

sāg. *Add : a depression* (?), cf. sígan : saga *a saying. Add :* v. fore-saga : sagol. v. wǽr- (*not* wǽr-) sagol.

sagol. *Add* :—Litel sāgul *paxillus,* Wrt. Voc. i. 26, 45. His ōðer fót weard fæst on ānum sāgle (sāhle, *v. l.*) þæs geardes *pes in sude sepis inhaesit,* Gr. D. 26, 27. v. hege-sāgol.

sagu *saying.* **I.** *add* :—Adames sagu weard of gemynde æfter ðām flōde *the story of Adam passed out of mind after the flood,* Wlfst. 3, 37. Gif seó hringe nele úp ... þonne ne sceall hē þínre sage gelýfan, Hml. S. 21, 48. Æt þises sage (*narratione*) ic geleornode þ ..., Gr. D. 218, 27 : 318, 27. Spellunga í saga *fabulas,* An. Ox. 188. **I a.** *saying, speech* :—Sage raþor *dicto citius,* An. Ox. 3130. Lufwyndre sage *fatu amico,* 18, 26. v. ge-sagu.

-sagun. v. ge-sagun : sehtlian. v. sahtlian.

sāl. **IV.** *add* :—Sālas *repagula* (indisrupta pudicitiae *repagula*), An. Ox. 972. **V.** *add* :—Sāl *collarium,* An. Ox. 53, 5.

salh. *Add* : v. salig.

saltere. **I.** *add* :—Eálá þū psaltere (*psalterium*) and hearpe, Ps. L. 56, 9. **II b.** *add* :—This syndon thā cyrican mādmas on Scírburnan. Thǽr synd twā Crístes bēc ... i. mæssebōc and i ymener and i salter, C. D. B. iii. 660, 32. Mid sange ... sealteres *cum decantatione psalterii,* Angl. xiii. 390, 362. Hí singan sealtere *psallant psalterium,* 412, 679. Þā gelǽhte sum preóst ǽnne sealtere, Hml. S. 31, 275.

salt-haga. v. sealticge : sealticge. v. sealting : salu-neb. *Add:* [Cf. *Icel.* nef-fülr] : sal-warp. v. sealt-wearp. *Dele this entry. The word is a river name, the Salwarpe in Worcestershire.*

sam. *Add:* (1) sam ... sam =—Sam (*tam*) gebrōþrum, sam (*quam*) eallum geleáffullum, Angl. xiii. 414, 706. Sam gē etan, sam gē drincan, sām gē āht elles gedōn *siue manducatis, siue bibitis, siue aliud quid facietis,* Scint. 169, 12. (2) sam þe ... sam þe :—Sam þe þeów, sam þe frig siue seruus, siue liber, Scint. 189, 14 : 226, 13. Sam þe fram þām foresǽdon fæder, sam þe fram æfterfyligendum hys *tam a predicto patre, quam a sequacibus suis,* Angl. xiii. 375, 140 : 377, 176. (2 a) sam þe ... sam :—Sam þe him sylfum, sam æftergencgum hyra *tam sibi, quam successoribus suis,* Angl. xiii. 447, 1176.

Samaritanisc. *Add* :—þā Jūdēiscan cwǽdon be Críste þæt hē wǽre Samaritanisc, Hml. Th. ii. 228, 29.

sām-cwic. *Add* :—Hē Smaragdum forðfērendne geseah, and Pafnuntium sāmcwicne on eorðan licgan, Hml. S. 33, 302. Mid flānum ofscotene, mid wǽpnum ofsette, hí heora burh sāmcuce (cf. healfcwice, Bl. H. 203, 19) gesōhton, Hml. Th. i. 506, 2.

same. *Add* :—Ǽlc hiera bið on ōðres nytte swǽ sama (some, *v. l.*) swǽ on his selfes, Past. 232, 5.

sām-geong, *adj. Adolescent, not grown up* :—Sāmgunge oððe cildru *adolescentes uel puerulos,* Angl. xiii. 374, 123.

samlíce, *adv. In unison, all together* :—Ðeáh ðe ealle eorðan wæter sýn gemenged wið ðām heofonlicum wætrum uppe on āne ǽdran, and hit samlíce rínan onginne, Sal. K. 148, 18. [*Goth.* sama-leiko.]

samlinga ; *adv. At once* :—Samlinga *statim,* Angl. xv. 207, 179. v. samnunga.

sām-locen ; *adj. Half-closed* :—Hafa þū þíne wynstran hand sām-

locene, Tech. ii. 125, 7 : 120, 19. Mid bām sāmlocone handum, 128, 4.

samnere. v. word-samnere.

samnian. **II.** *add* :—Swā hwǽr swā bið líc, þider somnigaþ earnes *ubicumque fuerit corpus, illuc congregabuntur aquilae,* Mt. R. 24, 28. v. tó-samnian.

samnung. *Add* :—Ne sæt ic nā on þǽre samnunge ídelra manna *non sedi cum consilio vanitatis,* Ps. Th. 25, 4. v. heáh-, word-samnung.

samod. **I.** *add* :—Swā þæt ic beó gemǽt samod on blisse eóweres edleánes, ðeáh ðe ic mid eów swincan ne mæge (*etsi uobiscum laborare nequeo, simul in gaudio retributionis inueniar,* Bd. 1, 23), Hml. Th. ii. 128, 12. Ic nū þás þing wríte tó þe gemǽnelíce and tó mínre mēder and mínum geswustrum, forþon incer lufu sceal beón somod gemǽne *tibi et matri mee sororibusque meis de regni mei commodis scribebam, que tibi et illis communia esse arbitror,* Nar. 3, 9. **II.** *add* :—Seó Godes geladung ... fērde eal samod of ðǽre byrig, Hml. Th. i. 402, 22. **III.** *add* :—Gregorius āsende eác Agustine lāc on mæssereáfum, and on bōcum, and ðǽra apostola and martyra reliquias samod, Hml. Th. ii. 132, 9. **V.** *add* :—Heriað Drihten and somodheriað (*conlaudate*), Ps. Rdr. 116, 1.

samod-cumende. *Add* :—Samodcumende tó capitule grētan þā rōde *conuenientes ad capitulum salutent crucem,* Angl. xiii. 385, 282.

samod-gang ; *adj. Continuous* :—In þǽre stōwe fram þām nyþeran dǽle intó þām uferan wæs samodgang (somedtoncg, *v. l.*) þurh gewisne úpstíge *quo in loco inferiora superioribus peruius continuabat ascensus,* Gr. D. 170, 23. Hē eóde þā .vi. samodgongan dagas genōh blíþe *per sex continuos dies laetus procedebat,* 309, 6. v. samod-tang.

samod-gehērigendlíc *glosses* conlaudabilis :—þisne suna ... samodgehērigendlicne *hunc partum conlaudabilem,* Hy. S. 109, 19.

-samodlǽcan. v. ge-samodlǽcan.

samod-síþian *to accompany* :—Swā hwyder swā ic mē hwyrfe, hié mē samodsíðiað *ubicunque me conuertero, malorum meorum me umbra comitatur,* Verc. Först. 137, 18.

samod-sprǽc *colloquy* :—Samodsprǽc (*conloquium*) ne beó him gemǽne, Chrd. 68, 19. Æfter ōþrum gāstlicre getimbrunge samodspǽcum *post cetera spiritualis edificationis colloquia,* Angl. xiii. 401, 511.

samod-tang ; *adj. Continuous* :—þ man on þyssum þrytigum dagum samodtangum ǽlce dæge geoffrige for hine *diebus triginta continuis offerre pro eo sacrificium stude,* Gr. D. 345, 28. v. samod-gang, gader-tang.

samod-þyrlic. *Add:* Cf. un-geþyre.

samod-wist, e ; *f. A being together, common existence* :—Tō þon þ wē sýn swā myccle strangran wið úrum feóndum, swā myccle mā wē gefremede beóð under eádmōdnesse tó þǽre samodwiste þæs ordfruman eallra gesceafta *ut tanto nostris hostibus potentiores simus, quanto cum auctore omnium unum efficimur per humilitatem,* Gr. D. 224, 4. Cf. sam-wist.

samod-wyrcende. *Add* :—Nelle þū begýman tó welerum specendes ac samodwyrcendes (*cooperantis*), Scint. 118, 6. Deófle samodwyrcendum Antecrístes mōder geeácnoð on innoðe, Wlfst. 193, 19.

sam-rǽdenn, e ; *f. The conjugal state* :—Ðā ðe beóð gebundene mid somrǽdenne (sin-, *v. l.*) *conjugati,* Past. 19, 18.

sām-storfen ; *adj. Half-dead* :—Sāmstorfenne *seminecem,* Germ. 401, 50.

sam-swēge (?) ; *adj. Harmonious* :—Ungeswēge sang *diaphonia,* samswēge (*printed* sum swēge) sang *canticum,* Wrt. Voc. i. 28, 34, 35.

sam-tinges. *Add* :—Hē ne wandode þā hǽþenan tó crístnigenne þā þā hí on Críst gelýfdon, ac hē hí ealle sōna samtingas gecrístnode, Hml. S. 31, 1037.

sām-weaxen ; *adj. Half-grown up* :—Ǽlc man hæfð swāþeáh his āgene lenge on þǽre mycelnesse þe hē man wæs ǽr, oððe hē beón sceolde, gif hē full weóxe, sē ðe on cildhāde oððe sāmweaxen gewāt, Nap. 55.

sām-wís. *In l. 4 for* 201 *l.* 202.

sam-wist. *Add* :—Gyftlice samwistu *nuptiales copulas,* An. Ox. 1662. Cf. samod-wist.

sam-wrǽde. v. un-samwrǽde, *and* sam-wrǽdness.

sand *sending.* **I.** *add* :—Hē cōm þurh Godes sande tó þǽre foresǽdan byrig, Hml. S. 24, 129 : 35, 254. **II.** *add* :—þā bær man þām cyninge cynelice þēnunga on ānum sylfrenan disce ... þā sende se cyning þām þearfum þone sylfrenan disc mid sande mid ealle (cf. *dapes sibimet adposita rex deferri pauperibus praecepit,* Bd. 3, 6), Hml. S. 26, 95. Gif man fisc hæbbe oððe wyrta, sylle man him tó þriddan sande, Chrd. 15, 4, 9. Twā sanda *duo pulmentaria,* R. Ben. I. 70, 15. Sanda *ferculorum,* i. *diliciarum,* An. Ox. 1631. Hē sende him gelōme sanda and ēstas, ac se cniht forseah þā sanda and drencas, Hml. S. 35, 56. v. flǽsc-sand ; send.

sand *sand.* **I.** *add* :—Sand *sablum,* An. Ox. 18 b, 35. **II.** *add* :—Forð swiðe sp on norðmūþan, C. D. iii. 429, 1. On ceoslynum sandum *in glarigeris litoribus,* An. Ox. 7, 162. **III.** *of deserts* :—Ðā fērde wē þurh þā weallendan sond and þurh þā wǽdlan stōwe wætres *per feruentes arenas et egentia humoris loca profectus sum,* Nar. 6, 9. v. cwece-sand.

**sand-ceosol.** Add:—'Heora getel is māre đonne sandceosol' (super arenam multiplicabuntur, Ps. 139, 18) . . . Heora tel biđ swā menigfeald þæt hit oferstīhđ, be đæs wītegan cwyde, sandceosles gerīm, Hml. Th. i. 536, 30-35.

**sand-corn.** Add:—Swā swā þā sandcorn, þā þe beóđ be sǣs warođum sicut arenam, quae est in littore maris, Gr. D. 55, 12.

**sand-full**; adj. Sandy:—Uppstige sandfull ascensus arenosus, Scint. 223, 13.

**sand-geweorp.** Add: , -gewearp:—In sondgewearp in sirtim, Wrt. Voc. ii. 111, 72.

**sand-hrycg.** Add:—Betwyx sandhriccan (cf. stáuhricgum, 5465) inter scyllam, An. Ox. 634.

**sandiht(e).** — In þá sandihte strǣt, Cht. E. 239, 8.

**sand-pytt**, es; m. A sand-pit:—Hé hēt lǣdan þā hālgan tō ānum sandpytte, and settou hī þǣron, and bewurpan mid eorþan and mid weorcstānum, Hml. S. 35, 325.

**sang.** I a. add:—Þæt hē sceolde þone sang lǣran tō twelf mónþum quatenus cursum canendi annuum edoceret, Bd. 4, 18; Sch. 437, 4. II. add:—Mid sange gesettendlices rynes and sealteres cum decantatione canonici cursus et psalterii, Angl. xiii. 390, 362. IV. add: (1) the service on a saint's day: cf. mæsse-sang; II:—On đone xviiii-an dæg biþ þæs martyres tīd Scī Magni đæs sang (cf. mæssesang, 4) biþ gemēted on þām yldran mæssebōcum, Shrn. 119, 12. (2) a charm, incantation:— Wyrt ricinum ic bidde þ þú æt sý mīnum sangum, and þ đú æwende hagolas and ealle hreóhnyssa herba ricinum precor uti adsis meis incantationibus et auertas grandines et omnes tempestates, Lch. i. 308, 22. v. æfter-, byrgels-, herigend-, lāc-, leóþ-, on-, wuldor-, wyn-, ymen-sang.

**sang-dreám**, es; m. Vocal music, singing:—Lôce hwæt tō sangdreáme þǣre nihte gebyrige quicquid ad cantilenam illius noctis pertinet, Angl. xiii. 410, 638.

**sangere.** I. add: a church-singer; cantor:—Sceole wē healdan ûrne palm ođ þæt se sangere onginne đone offringsang, Hml. Th. i. 218, 9. Būtan Iacôbe đām songere, be þām wē ǣr sǣdon, wæs hē sanges mǣgister Norđhymbra cyricum, Bd. 4, 2; Sch. 345, 21. v. heáh-, sealm-sangere.

**-sanglic.** v. æfter-sanglic.

**sápe.** Add:—Dô þǣron ealdre sápan cucler fulne, Lch. ii. 76, 12. Gewyrce tō flynan swá mon sápan wyrcđ, 98, 6. Borige on þām beáme stôr and finol and gehālgode sápan and gehālgod sealt, i. 402, 1. Đonne þú sápan abban wille, þonne gnīd þú þīne handa tōgædere, Tech. ii. 126, 25. Mænige wiþ þá sápan and wiþ þæs æpples gor, Lch. iii. 36, 31.

**sār**; n. I 2. add:—Saarum doloribus, Bd. 4, 19; Sch. 447, 12. v. ge-, heáfod-, leoþu-, mûþ-, wærc-sár.

**sār**; adj. Add:—Heó on eallum limum egeslice wunda hæfde . . . Heó wæs gehǣled, þ on hire líce næs gesýne áht þǣra sárra wunda, Hml. S. 7, 278.

**Saracenisc.** Add:—Seó burh weard . . . mid đām Sarasceniscum gesett, Hml. Th. i. 404, 18.

**sáre.** Add:—Gyf hwā hæfđ his hláforde sáre ábolgen, Wlfst. 155, 7.

**sárga.** l. sarga, and add:—Heargan (seargan? cf. salpistę trūþhornes, 743) salpistę, Au. Ox. 7, 57.

**sárgian.** II. add: (1) of physical ill:—Seó þrúh monigum monna þe heora eágan sárgedon and hefegedon weard tō hǣle loculum nonnullis oculos dolentibus saluti fuisse perhibent, Bd. 4, 19; Sch. 450, 22. (2) of mental pain:—Ymb đæt ilce sárgode se wītga hinc propheta conqueritur, Past. 267, 7. Đý lǣs đú sárgige for đǣm on lásđ ne gemas in novissimis, 249, 13. v. efen-sárgian.

**sárgung.** Add: v. efen-sárgung.

**sárian.** II 2. add:—Sume ofer sǣ sárigende (sorhgende, v. l.) gewiton alii transmarinas regiones dolentes petebant, Bd. 1, 15; Sch. 43, 30.

**sárig.** I. add:—Hé biđ swīde sárig dolet, Past. 226, 8. þæt sárige mancynn, Wlfst. 186, 19. II. add:—þone sárigestan stefn and þone sárigestan wánunge and gránunge, Verc. Först. 128, 8.

**sárig-cirm**, es; m. Lamentation, mourning:—þone hlûdestan sárigcerm, Verc. Först. 128, 8.

**sárig-lic**; adj. Sad, mournful, melancholy:—Nû sume hwîle wē sprǣcon ymb unrôte and sáriglice bysnu; gehwyrfen wē nú eft tō þām blīþum sprǣcum interim hoc triste seponentes ad ea laeta redeamus, Gr. D. 290, 6.

**sárig-ness.** Add:—Weard hé þearle áhwǣned, and his líc for đǣre sáriguysse mid wācan hreáfe scrýdde, Hml. S. 23, 394.

**sár-lic.** I. add:—Him þúhte sárlic, gif hé ne gehulpe þām ástýptan wīfe (him ofhreów þ ástěpede wíf, gif hé ne gehulpe hire sárlican dreórinysse, v. l.) dolor ne orbatae mulieri non subveniret, Gr. D. 18, 13. Him hreów his þ sárlice anginn, and hine þá ná lenge áhwǣnedne habban nolde, Hml. S. 23, 401.

**sár-ness.** I. add:—Áwende seó sárnyss ealra his lima tō đǣre heortan (cf. gehwearf þára leoma sár tō his innoþum membrorum dolor ad vitalia rediit, Gr. D. 282, 6), Hml. Th. ii. 96, 33.

**sár-spell.** Add: a dolorous tale:—Se man sǣde fram helle sīđfæte

---

swylc sárspell, swylce nǣfre ǣr on men ne becôm, ne náht oft siđđan, Shrn. 49, 10.

**Satan.** Add:—Æfter þúsend geárum biđ Satanas unbunden . . . Nú syndon Satanases bendas swýđe tōslopene, Wlfst. 83, 8.

**sáwan.** Add: , sǽwan. I a. —Đú rípes þte đú ne sǽwe, Lk. R. 19, 22. Hé seów hwǣte on beswuncenum lande, Hml. Th. ii. 144, 9. I c. absolute:—Ic hrippo đǣr ne seáwu ic meto ubi non semina, Mt. L. 25, 26. Sē đe sáwes ł seáwa (seów, R.) qui seminavit, 13, 39. 'Sē đe him ealneg wind ondrǣt, hé sǽwđ tō seldon' . . . hé cwǣdon đæt sē sceolde lytel sáwan, sē đe him đone wind ondrēde, Past. 285, 17-24. II. add:—Hé sǽwđ đone sticel đæs andan, Past. 279, 9. Đā đe wrôhte sáwađ, 357, 14: 361, 6. Hú ne biđ hé swelce hé sǽwe (sáwe, v. l.) good and him weaxe of đǣm ælc yfel? peccatorum seges quasi ex virtute seminatur, 341, 7. Đæt yfel hī ne dyrren sǽwan on ôđrum monnum, 427, 18. Wæs heora lár sáwen and strogden betuh feówer sceátum middangeardes, Bl. H. 133, 33. v. un-sáwen.

**sáwel.** Add: a nominative sáwle occurs, Cri. 1327: Seel. 10: Ap. 62.

**-sáweled.** v. ge-sáweled.

**sáwel-gescot.** Add: Ll. Lbmn. 295, n. 20.

**sáwel-leás.** I. add:—Hé eóde him tō þæs forđfarenan mannes hûse tō þǣre stôwe þǽr se sáwulleása líchama (corpus exanime) læg, Gr. D. 84, 33.

**sáwel-sceatt.** Add:—þis is Alfwoldes bisceopes cwyde, þ is đæt hē geann þæs laudes æt Sandforda intō þām mynstre intō Crydiantúne him tō sáulsceatte mid mete and mid mannum swá hit stent bútan wîteþeówum mannum, Cht. Crw. 23, 3.

**-sáwend.** v. for-sáwend: -sáwenlic. v. for-, ge-sáwenlic: -sáwenlíce. v. ge-sáwenlíce: -sáwenness. v. for-sáwenness.

**sáwlian.** Add:—Hé hēt feccan ǣnne hwer and hine þǣron seóđan, ođ þ hē sáwlode, Hml. S. 25, 118.

**scǽgan (?).** v. on-scǽgan.

**scǽnan.** Add:—Gif þú ostran habban wylle, þonne clǣm þú þíne wynstran hand đǣm gemete þe þú ostran on handa hæbbe, and dô mid sexe ođđe mid fingre swylce þú ostran scǣnan wylle, Tech. ii. 124, 14.

**-scǽnedness, -scǽning, -scǽnness.** v. ge-scǽnedness.

**scapulare**, es; n.: scapularie, an; f. A scapular, scapulary, a short cloak:—Gif þú tō hwilcere gehîrsumnesse scapulares beþurfe, þonne stríc þú eclinga mid ǽgđere hande ofer ǽđerne earm ymbe þ útan þe þæs scapularæs handstoca áteóriađ, Tech. ii. 127, 18-20. Hæbban hý eác mid tō wyrcenne scapulare, þæt is gehwǣde cugelan and slýfleás (scapularian for weorcum, R. Ben. I. 91, 17, scapulare propter opera, R. Ben. 89, 13.

**sceabbed.** l. sceabbede, and add:—Hreóflige þicnysse scæbbede elefantina (cutis) callositate purulentus, An. Ox. 4929.

**sceacan.** III 1. add:—Hý mē underfēngon ǣr đām ic sceóc (the first c is written over e; but cf. Angl. xii. 511, 26 which has sceóc) fram đē tō hyn: isti me quando a te fugiebam acceperunt alienum, Solil. H. 12, 9. III. add: (1) to brandish:—Sceóc uibrabat (macheram), An. Ox. 14, 4. (2) to put into a quaking motion:—Þurh þæs windes blǽs þe swýđlíce þá heánnyssa þæs roderes sceóđ mid his þodenum, Angl. viii. 320, 34. IV. add: The passage to which belongs the gloss in Wrt. Voc. ii. 66, 80 is: Coronam inextricabili plectra plumemus, Ald. 54, 7.

**sceacel.** II. add: an instrument for causing vibrations (v. sceacan; III), an implement for striking the strings of a harp. [The passage to which belongs the gloss in Wrt. Voc. ii. 89, 10 is: Ut nullus sermonum plectra resolvat, sed fidibus citharae moduletur carmina Christo, Ald. 138, 7.]

**sceacged.** l. sceacgede: sceád; n. Add: v. be-sceád: -sceád; adj. v. ge-sceád: -sceáda. v. ǣ-sceáda.

**sceádan.** I 1. add:—Alswá seó forg scǣđeđ, C. D. v. 71, 9. Eást úp suae đet ealden fæstan scáđe; andlang đes fæstenes. 70, 30. (1 a) to remove from association or companionship:—Mid đý menu sceádas iuih cum homines separauerint uos, Lk. L. 6. 22. Ic cuôm tō sceádanne (-enne, R.) monno wiđ ł from fæder his ueni separare hominem aduersus patrem suum, Mt. L. 13, 35. [v. N. E. D. shed.] v. of-sceádan.

**sceadd.** In l. 2 for sceaddgenge l. sceadd genge: sceadd-genge. v. genge: -sceáden. v. tō-sceáden: sceádenlíce. v. ge-sceádenlíce: -sceáden-mǽl with divided marks, damasceuced; a sword with blade so marked:—Hraþe seoþđan wæs æfter mundgripe mêce geþinged þæt hit sceádenmǽl scýran môste, cwealmbealu cýđan, B. 1939.

**sceáden-ness.** v. tō-sceádenness: -sceadlic shady. v. ge-sceadlic: -sceádlic. v. ge-sceádlic: -sceádness. v. ge-sccúdness.

**sceadu.** Add: [In Ps. L. 108, 23 a weak form. sceaduwe, seems to be used: sceaduwa in 143. 4, though glossing umbra, is probably plural.] I. add:—Swá swá sceaduwe þonne heó áhyldeþ sicut umbra cum declinat, Ps. L. 108, 23. Dægas his swá swá sceaduwa forđgewītađ dies eius sicut umbra praetereunt, 143, 4. I a. fig.:—Oferwreúh dúna his scadu operuit montes umbra eius, Ps. L. 79, 11. II. add:— On midle sceadue deáþes, Ps. L. 22, 4. II a. destructive influence:—

Ðonne hē mid ðǽre sceade his slǽwðe oferbrǽt ðā scīre þe hē hæfð, Past. 336, 14. **III.** add:—On scadue fiðera þinra, Ps. L. 56, 1. **IV a.** [*that which takes place in a shady place.* v. An. Ox. 2885, note], *a scene* :—Gereónedes gyltes sceade geypte *concinnati sceleris scenam prodidit*, An. Ox. 2920. **V.** add: (1) *shadow* as opposed to reality :—Tōcumendre sōþfæstnesse seó scadu *adueniente ueritate umbra cessauit*, An. Ox. 40, 15. Seó ealde ǽ wæs swilce scadu and getācnung; Crīstes bodung is sōðfæstnys, Hml. Th. ii. 56, 18. (2) *a shadow, shade, unsubstantial appearance* :—þā weard þǽr æteówod ān atelic sceadu on sweartum hīwe, and sǽde þæt hē wǽre for stale ofslegen, Hml. Th. ii. 508, 1. Hē geseah þǽr standan āne atelice sceade, Hml. S. 31, 357. v. sunu-, swīn-sceadu.

**sceadwian.** *Add*: v. be-sceadwian (?).

**sceád-wís**; *adj. Intelligent, discerning, discriminating* :—Be gesceádwīsan gerēfan. Se sceádwīs gerēfa sceal ǽgðer witan ge hláfordes landriht ge folces gerihtu, Angl. ix. 259, 3. Mid hū sceádwīsre lufe manncynna ealdor for ūre edstaðelunge þǽre rōde gealgan underfēng, Hml. Th. i. 588, 18. v. ge-sceádwīs.

**sceádwísness.** *Add*: v. ge-sceádwísness.

**sceadwung.** *Add: something affording shade* :—Sceadewunge *umbraculo* (furuo facessante veteris instrumenti *umbraculo*, Ald. 8, 1), An. Ox. 438. [v. *N. E. D.* shadowing.]

**sceáf.** **II.** *add* :—Berende scáfas heora, Ps. L. 125, 6. **II a.** *add* :—' Gebindað þā weód tō scǽfum (sceáfum, *v. l. in fasciculos*) tō forbærnenne,' Gr. D. 316, 2. Weóda sceáfas, 11. Bunda ł byrðenno ł sceáfa, Mt. L. 13, 30.

**sceafa.** *Add* :—Scafa *strigula*, Angl. xx. 395, 28. [v. *N. E. D.* shave.]

**sceáf-fót.** *Add* : [*O. H. Ger.* scēf-fuoz *pansa* vel *pansus.*]

**sceaft.** **IV.** *add* : *In the phrase* scæfta munda *perhaps* sceaft *was intended to denote the extended thumb.* v. *N. E. D.* shaftment. v. web-sceaft : lang-sceaft ; *adj.*

**sceaft.** **II.** *add* (?) :—Sceafta, Lch. i. 402, 5. v. weorold-sceaft. [*Dele* un-sceaft.]

-**sceaftig**, -sceaftigness. v. feá-sceaftig, -sceaftigness.

**sceaft-lóha.** *l.* sceaft-lō ; *pl.* -lón, -lóan.

**sceaft-rihte, -riht** ; *adv. As straight as a dart, in a straight line* :—Of þām paðe sceaftrihte on alr, C. D. B. iii. 667, 14. West sceftrihte ofer ðone mōr, 336, 25. Sceaftryht on cuddancnoll ... sceaftryht oð lillesforda ... sceaftryht oþ wideres leáge ... sceaftryht oþ hlōsleáge ... sceaftryht oþ efes ... sceaftryht oþ hrōces ford, 682, 10-23.

**sceaga.** *Add* :—In hæðleáge sceagan ðǽr hē þynnest is, C. D. iii. 391, 15. [v. *N. E. D.* shaw.] v. aler-sceaga.

**sceald** ; *adj. ? Shoal, shallow* :—Andlang streámes ūt on scealdan fleót ... ðonnen andlang scealdan fleótes, C. D. iii. 431, 21. Tō scelden mǽre, iv. 158, 10. Ūtt on scealdan ford (cf. on ðæs deópan fordes ende, iii. 431, 12), v. 256, 16: 300, 19. [v. *N. E. D.* shoal ; *adj., and* Phil. Trans. 1895-8, p. 532.]

**sceald-hūlas.** *Substitute : some kind of sedge* :—Scaldhūlas *paupilius* (cf. eolxsecg *papilluum*, i. 286, 36), Wrt. Voc. ii. 116, 21. [v. *N. E. D.* shalder *rush* or *sedge.*]

**sceald-pȳfel.** *Dele* ' Scaldhȳfias ... col. 2,' *and add* :—Gesáwon hī hine þurh þā scealdpȳfelas mid fellum gegyrede. Hī wēndon þ hit sum wilde deór wǽre *quem dum vestitum pellibus inter fruteta cernerent, aliquam bestiam esse crediderunt*, Gr. D. 100, 9. Þā geseah hē þǽr neáh him weaxan þicce scaldpȳfelas (sceald-, *v. l.*) netelena and brēmela *urticarum et veprium juxta densa succrescere fruteta conspiciens*, 101, 12. Þā mycclan treówa þūhton þām mannum þe hī of þām munte gesáwon swylce lytle scealdpȳfelas *arbusta ingentia ex monte aspicientibus quasi fruteta esse videbantur*, 212, 27.

**scealfor.** *Add* : es; *m.* :—Gesáwon hié wel feala þāra fugela þe wē scealfras nemnaþ, Bl. N. 4, 32. Geseah hē scealfran swimman on ānum fióde ... þā bebeád Martinus þām mǽðleásum scealfrum þ hī geswicon þæs fixnoðes, Hml. S. 31, 1322.

**scealu.** **III.** *add* :—Hē hæfð wǽga on handa ; and on ǽgðere sceale hē byrð rihtwīsnesse and mildheortnesse, Ll. Lbmn. 474, 7.

**sceaman.** v. ā-sceaman.

**sceam-fæst.** *Add* :—Ne lyste þē fægeres wīfes and sceamfestes ? *nonne te delectat uxor pulchra, pudica ?*, Solil. H. 36, 1.

**sceamfæst-ness** *modesty* :—Sceamfestnys (*but the word glosses* nudi-tas), An. Ox. 3672. [v. *N. E. D.* shamefastness.]

**sceamian.** **I.** *add* :—Hwā bið gesciended ðæt ic eác ðæs ne scamige ?, Past. 101, 5. Hē scamode his wiþ men, gif hē ne eóde intō cyrican in swā hālgan dæge þára eástrena *si tanto die non iret ad ecclesiam, erubesce-bat homines*, Gr. D. 308, 23. v. un-sceamiende.

**sceamisc.** *Dele, and see* sceam-lim, sceamu ; **III.**

**sceamlíce.** *Add* :—Brūcð wīf healsmene, ac bið sceamlíce brocen (*abutitur*), Lch. i. lx. 4. v. un-sceamlíce.

**sceam-lim.** *Add* :—Scame, scamlim (? *printed* scamescan lim) *vere-trum*, Wrt. Voc. ii. 96, 54. v. sceamu ; **III.**

**sceamol.** *Add* :—Seó ealde cyrce wæs eall behangen mid criccum

and mid creópera sceamelum, Hml. S. 21, 432. [v. *N. E. D.* shamble.] v. brȳd-, ceáp-, toll-sceamol.

**sceamu.** **II.** *add* :—Hē tō sceame tūcode þā leóde, Hml. S. 26, 11 : Jud. 15, 8. **III.** *add* :—Scame *veretrum* (v. sceam-lim), Wrt. Voc. ii. 96, 54. Ic eom wīfhādes mann and eallunga līchamlicum wǽfelsum bereáfod, and þā sceame mīnes līchaman hæbbende unoferwrigene, Hml. S. 23 b, 208. [v. *N. E. D.* shame ; 7.]

**sceanca.** **I.** *add* :—Gyf þū hosa habban wylle, þonne strīc þū upp-weard on þīnum sceancum mid þīnum twām handum, Tech. ii. 127, 13. **II.** *add* : *a leg* :—His scanca (þeóh, *v. l.* coxa) wæs tōbrocen, þ þ bān wæs tōdǽled on twā stycca, Gr. D. 81, 26. Hī tyrndon mid bodege gebīgedum sceancum, and heora fótwylmas āwendan ne mihton, Hml. Th. ii. 508, 20.

**sceand**; *m.* *Add* : [Whaðer unker þe geð abake and þis feoht wulle forsake, beo he in ælche londe iquede for ane sconde, Laym. 23668]. v. sceand, *f.* **III.** ; swǽm.

**sceand** ; *f.* **I.** *add* :—Ne wuldra þū on teónan fæder þīnes, nys þe wuldor ac sceand (*confusio*), Scint. 174, 8. **II.** *add* :—Hit is micel sceand (scand, *v. l.*) *nimis turpe est*, Past. 233, 11. **III.** *an infamous person* (v. sceand ; *m.*) :—Eugenia cwæð tō ðære sceande (cf. seó myl-testre, 169) þ heó wǽre gálnysse ontendnyss, Hml. S. 2, 172. Beseah Hieu tō þǽre sceande (*Jezabel*) ūp ... ' Gáð tō þǽre hǽtse (*vel* sceande) þe ic hēt niþer āsceófan,' 18, 344-350.

**sceandlíce.** **I.** *add* :—Ic mē þā sceandlíce (unsceandlíce, *v. l.*) swā swā ic gewuna wæs, tōmiddes heora gemengde, and him tō cwæð : ' Nimað mē on eówer fǽreld mid eów, ne beó ic nā eów unlícwyrðe,' Hml. S. 23 b, 372.

**sceand-lufiende** *loving shamelessly* :—Sceandlufiende (*printed* se eardlufiende, *but see* Hpt. 31, 9, 149) *amasius*, Lch. i. lxi. 4.

**sceap.** *Add* : [*Icel.* sköpin *the genitals.*]

**sceáp.** *Add* :—Gif hwā drince wyrm on wætere, ofsnīðe sceúp raðe, drince hāt þ sceápes blōd, Lch. ii. 114, 8. Hȳ lētan him tō ... þā mǽde þe gebyrað tō ðām gerēflande ... and his sceápa lǽse æfter þæs hláf-ordes, C. D. B. i. 544, 3.

**sceáp-líc**; *adj. Of a sheep, of sheep* :—Swȳnenan and æt sceúplican and æt fearlican *suouetaurilia* (cf. *suouetaurili* oðða þā þe æt þǽm geldum þǽr wæs swīn and sceáp and fear, Wrt. Voc. ii. 31, 32), An. Ox. 11, 187.

-**sceaplíce.** v. ge-sceaplíce : **scear.** v. gūþ-, inwit-scear : **sceáran.** v. sceran.

**sceard** *a gap.* *Add* :—On ðæt lytle sceard ðæt is on burhhlinceas, C. D. vi. 220, 17. [Anlang cinincces dich on ðe sherd ; of ðane shearde, iii. 417, 22.] [v. *N. E. D.* shard.]

**sceard-hweogol** (?) *a circle made of shards* (?) :—On sceardhweogol, C. D. iii. 419, 11. v. hweogol ; **II.**

**scearfian.** *Add* : v. ge-scearfian.

**scearn-wibba.** *Add* :—Scernwibba *cantarus, scarabeus*, An. Ox. 23, 23.

**scearp.** **VI.** *add* :—Tō þām þ hī þe scearpran on þǽre sōðan Godes lufu hī æteówdon, Hml. S. 23 b, 94. **VI a.** *add* :—Godes word is cucu and scearp innan lǽrende þis mennisce andgyt, Hml. S. 23 b, 595. v. ungemet-scearp.

**scearpe.** **II.** *add* :—Sume swīðe scearpe and swotele lōciað ; sume unzáðe āwiht geseóð, Solil. H. 44, 22. Sē þe scerpest lōcian mæg, 43, 21.

**scearp-ecged.** *l.* -ecgede.

**scearplíce.** **I.** *add* :—Swā þ stefen eáran Drihtnes scearplíce (*effica-citer*) þurhfare, Angl. xiii. 378, 192. **II.** *add* :—Hāwa swȳðe scearplíce hwær sȳ .xii. Kł Aprelis, Angl. viii. 309, 36. Hī on swā micclan māran lufe byrnende beóð, swā micclum swā hī Godes beorht-nysse scearplícor sceáwiað, Hml. Th. i. 540, 14.

**scearpness.** *Add* :—Scearpnyssa *acuminata*, Germ. 399, 259. **IV a.** *bitterness of speech* :—Sum hālig fǽmne in þām mynstre ðā scearpnesse dysiglicra sprǽca on hire ágenre tungan hī nā bebeáh *quaedam sancti-monialis femina in loco eodem linguae procacitatem atque stultiloquium non declinavit*, Gr. D. 340, 16.

**scearp-numol.** *Add* : v. numol ; **II.**

**scearpþancfullíce** ; *adv. Efficaciously* :—Spǽc and gesceád hálbǽre scearpþancfullíce byþ geleornud, gif geþyldelíce þ byþ geleornud byþ gehȳred *sermo et ratio salutaris efficaciter discitur, si patienter quod discitur audiatur*, Scint. 206, 14.

**scearpþanclíce.** *Add* :—Þænne bodung nytlíce byð forðgerǽht þænne scearpþanclíce byð gefylled *tunc praedicatio utiliter profertur, quando efficaciter adimpletur*, Scint. 125, 7.

**scearu** *the share.* *Add* :—Hē weard drepen in þā sceare and þȳ wæs gelǽded tō deáþe *percussus in inguine perductus est ad mortem*, Gr. D. 324, 14. [v. *N. E. D.* share.]

**scear-wund** (?); *adj. Wounded in the share* :—Gif man [s]cearwund sié .iii. scill. gebete, Ll. Th. i. 18, 9.

**sceát.** **IV.** *add* : fig. :—Hē gelǽdde hine tō þām sceáte þǽre hālgan cyrican *eum ad sanctae ecclesiae gremium perduxit*, Gr. D. 190, 26.

IV a. *add :*—Se munt tôbrǽddum his sceáte onfēng and hæfde þis ilce cæster mons distenso *sinu hoc idem castrum recepit*, Gr. D. 121, 15.

VI. *add :*—Āþenedum his sceáte *extenso vestimento*, Gr. D. 65, 9.

VII. *add :*—Hē weard gebeden fram þām nunnum þ hē sume sceátas (*mappulas*) onfēng, Gr. D. 143, 4.    VII b. of a protective covering—Se godcunda anweald gefriþode his diórlingas under his fiþera sceáte (sceade, *v. l.*), Bt. 39, 10; F. 228, 12. v. offrung-, wæter-sceát.

**sceáta.** *Add :* v. wîgbed-sceáta.

**sceaþa.** I. *add :*—On gemǽrum mînra sceaþana î feónda *in finibus inimicorum meorum*, Ps. L. 7, 7. v. dol[h]-(?), heáh-sceaþa.

**sceaþa** *hurt.* *Add :* sceaþe (?). v. wîcing-sceaþe. [Ne wylle wē hēr nā mâre scaðe âwrîtan þe hē his fæder ge[dyde], Chr. 1079; P. 214, 31.]

**sceaþan.** *The form corresponding to the Gothic is* sceþþan *with a strong past tense, but in English a new infinitive* sceaþan *seems to be developed to suit the strong conjunction, and a new weak past tense to suit the infinitive* sceþþan. *The strong and weak forms are given separately.*

**sceaþ-full;** *adj.* *Hurtfull, noxious :*—Wē becumað fram þām îdlan wordum tô þām sceaðfullum (sceð-, *v. l.*) *ut ab otiosis ad noxia verba veniamus,* Gr. D. 209, 26. v. un-sceaþfull.

**sceaþian.** *Add :*—God mundað þā stôwe, and þā slihð and gescynt þe þǽr sceaþian willað, Hml. S. 25, 805.

**sceatt.** I. *add :*—[S]ceatta bîbycgong *rerum distractio,* Wrt. Voc. ii. 84, 35. Naaman bēad ðām Godes menn deórwurðe sceattas ... 'Genim feówer scrûd and twā pund.' Hē ðā gewende ongeán mid þām sceattum, Hml. Th. i. 400, 10–22.    I a. *add :* money on mortgage, or paid in rent :—Nolde Sigelm hire fæder (*he had borrowed thirty pounds*) tô wigge faran mid nânes mannes scette unâgifnum, Cht. Th. 201, 23. Wið swylcan sceatte swilce hē hit þā findan mihte, C. D. B. i. 544. 4. Hî geúðen Ælfwolde ǽnes dænnes wið his lîcwyrðan sceatte, iii. 490, 12. Ðæne dǽl ðæs landes ðe se arcebisceop for his sceatte him tô lēt, C. D. iii. 352, 7. Þone sceat þe on þām lande stent *the mortgage money,* Cht. Crw. 9, 120. Ne sceall nān Godes þegn for sceattum riht dēman, ac healdan þone dôm bûton lyðrum sceattum tô rihte, Hml. S. 19, 244. Scethas (= sceattas) *curuanas* (cf. corban, Mk. 7, 11), Wrt. Voc. ii. 137, 52. v. cyric-, fær-, frum-sceatt.

**sceát-weorþan.** v. sceát; IV. *Substitute:* **sceatwyrpan.** v. be-, ge-sceatwyrpan.

**sceáwere.** I. *add: a watchman :*—Episcopus is grēcisc nama, þ is on lēden *speculator,* and on englisc sceáwere, for þām þe hē is geset tô þām þ hē oferscéawian sceole mid hys gŷmene þā lǽwedan, swā swā God sylf cwæð tô Ezechiele: '*Speculatorem dedi te ic þē gesette tô sceáwere,*' O. E. Hml. i. 303, 20–24. Ealra ðǽra tâcna ðe ðǽr gelimpað ic eom sceáwere and gŷmend, Hml. Th. i. 504, 3. Beforan þām eágum þæs ûplican sceáweres (*spectatoris*) hē eardode âna, Gr. D. 105, 28.    II. *add: one who observes secretly :*—Þā sǽde se sceáwere (cf. wæs sum man . . . behŷd þām hæþenum, 128) þe hit ǽr geseah, Hml. S. 32, 138. On sumere nihte hlosnode sum ôðer munuc his færeldes and mid sleaccre stalcunge his fôtswaðum filigde . . . Cûðberhtus his sceáweres seócnysse gehǽlde, Hml. Th. ii. 138, 23.    III. *add :*—Ic geset eom kyning fram him ofer sceáwere (cf. sceáwung-stôw) his dûne *ego constitutus sum rex super Syon montem eius,* Ps. L. 2, 6.    IV. *add :*—Nû wē men geseoð swylce þurh sceáwere and on rǽdelse *videmus nunc per speculum in aenigmate,* Nap. 55. On þam halgen gewriten se mann hine sylfne mæig sceawigen swa swa on hwylcen sceawere *in sanctis scripturis quasi in quodam speculo homo se ipsum considerare potest,* Angl. xi. 374, 78.] [v. N. E. D. shower.] v. dægmǽl-, heáh-, in-, steor-(*not* steór-), tîd-, wîc-sceáwere.

**sceáwian.** IV. *add: to review* troops, *revise* what is written :—Hē þā fyrde sceáwode, Hml. S. 30, 295. Marcus leornode of Petres bodunge hû hē ðā bôc gesette, and Petrus hî sceáwode, 15, 145. Spellunga sceáwende *fabulas rimando,* An. Ox. 193. v. fore-, ymb-sceáwian.

**sceáwigend.** *Add :* A spectator, an observer :—Sceúwiendrum *spectatoribus,* An. Ox. 7, 250. Sceáwendrum, 4, 58.

**sceáwung.** I. *add :*—Ne cûþe hit þā deógolnysse þǽre godcundan sceáwunge, Gr. D. 136, 12. On þysre sceáwunge (*in hac speculatione*) wundorlîc þing æfterfyligde, 171, 7. Þurh þā gāstlican sceáwunge, 154, 3. Ðā eágan mē gebrôhton on þām angytte; ac siðþan ic hyt ongyten hæfde, þā forlǽt ic þā sceáwunga mid þām eágum, Solil. H. 21, 17. II. *add :*—Bysceopas mid folcum bûtan ǽnigre âre sceáwunge ætgædere fornumene wǽron *praesules cum populis sine ullo respectu honoris absumebantur,* Bd. 1, 15; Sch. 43, 18.    IV. *add :*—Se cyning gesæt in ðǽre sceáwunge (*spectaculo*), tô ðon þ hē wolde geseón þæs bisceopes deáð, Gr. D. 194, 21. Þ folc côm tô sceáwunge þæs bisceopes deáðes *populus ad spectaculum mortis venerat,* 195, 8. Scǽwugcge *spectaculo* (*theatrali*), An. Ox. 11, 11. v. dûst-, ge-, in-, weorold-, wlite-, ymb-sceáwung.

**sceáwung-stôw,** e; *f.* A place of observation :—Sion is ân dûn, and heó is gecweden sceáwungstôw, Hml. Th. i. 210, 21. v. sceáwere; III, *and* wlite-sceáwung.

---

**scegþ.** The word seems to be used of a boat of considerable size :—Ǽnne scegð lxiiii-ǽre, Cht. Crw. 23, 7. See note p. 128. [*Dele* scēthas in l. 12, *for which see* sceatt.]

**scenc.** *Add :*—Þæne nôn nā fylige scenc *quam nonam non sequitur potus,* Angl. xiii. 399, 484. Cweðað gē þ gē þus fela scencea (þus manige calicas fulle, *v. l.*) ne gedruncon? *numquid tot calices non bibistis?,* Gr. D. 127, 11. Se abbud scencende mid syndrigum scencum (*potibus*), Angl. xiii. 416, 730. Scencum gedruncenum, 733. Scencum gedruncenum *poculis haustis,* 432, 959. [v. N. E. D. shench.]

**scencan.** *Add :*—Eustachius gelǽdde hî intô his gesthûse, and ût gangende bohte him wîn and him scencte for heora micclan geswince, Hml. S. 30, 259. Geneálǽcean mid þancdǽde tô scencenne drincan *accedant cum gratiarum actione ad haurienda pocula,* Angl. xiii. 393, 394. Fram yldran sî scenced þām abbude *a priore propinetur abbati,* 416, 731. [v. N. E. D. shench.] v. ge-scencan.

**scendan.** *Add :*—Ûre fŷnd gehysctan î scendon ûs *inimici nostri subsannauerunt nos,* Ps. L. 79, 7. [v. N. E. D. shend.] v. on-, tô-scendan; un-scended, -scendende, un-āscended.

**scennan** (?). v. scerran (?): sceoccen. v. scuccen.

**sceolh-îge.** *Add :*—Scyleáge *strabo,* Hpt. 31, 12, 268.

**sceó-ness.** *Add :*—Ic wundrige þ ǽfre mihte swā mycclum biscope beón undercropen seó deófollice scinnys *miror quod subripi pontifici tanto potuerit,* Gr. D. 40, 18. Undercropen beón mid scinnysse *subripi,* 41, 16. Gebi[gað] eów fram þæs lîchoman sciónesse, Verc. Först. 145, 15.

**-sceorf.** v. ge-sceorf.

**sceorfan.** *Add :*—Þā yfelan wǽtan sceorfendan and scearpan, Lch. ii. 176, 20.

**sceóta.** *l.* (?) sceota. [v. N. E. D. shoat.]

**sceótan.** I a. *add :*—Arewan ongeán sceát *catapultas retorsit,* An. Ox. 4241. Gâras sceótende *spicula torquentes,* 2099.    III. *add :*—Hē genam þ hylfe and sceát in ðone seáð *tulit manubrium, et misit in lacum,* Gr. D. 114, 13.    IV a. *add :*—Seó culfre fleáh þær ût, and þā brôðra hire lôcodon on, oþ þ heó sceát in þone heofon (*penetravit caelum*), Gr. D. 275, 18.    IV c. *add :*—Gif hit gelimpeð þ se man þ wyrignesse word ne gecwið tô his þām nêhstan for hete, ac hit sceóteð forð þurh his tungan gŷmeleásnesse *si homo non ex malitia, sed ex linguae incuria, maledictionis verbum jaculatur in proximum,* Gr. D. 208, 3.    V. *add :*—Se alda suînhaga ût scióteð tô Afene, C. D. ii. 29, 11. Andlang heges þe scŷt of þām burnan, iii. 458, 10.    VII. *add :*—Swutelað hit hēr ðæt Boui mid his scette âwerede ðæt land and fore scēt on ealre scîre gewitnysse, C. D. vi. 183, 10. v. æt-, on-, tô-sceótan, niþer-sceótende.

**-sceótendlic.** v. þurh-sceótendlic.

**sceppe** *a specific quantity of grain or malt :*—iii. sceppe mealtes and healf sceppe hwǽte . . . ân sceppe malt, Nap. 55. [From *Icel.* skeppa. v. N. E. D. skep.]

**sceran.** II. *add :*—Strâca on þîn leór mid þînum fingre swilce þú scearan wille, Tech. ii. 127, 3.    IV. *add :*—Swā swā lamb þonne hit man scyrð *quasi agnus coram tondente,* Hml. Th. ii. 16, 22. Swā swā lamb beforan þām scyrendan hit, An. Ox. 40, 40. v. un-scoren.

**scering,** e; *f. Shaving :*—Sceringce þēnuncge hǽra hî âweg dôn oferflēwednysse *rasurę officio pilorum euellant superfluitate,* Angl. xiii. 408, 610.

**scerwen, scerpen** (?). Dele scerpen (?); *according to the facsimile reprint of the Vercelli codex the word is* scerwen *in* An. 1528.

**scethas.** v. sceatt; I a.: **sceþness.** *Add :* the Latin is: Sine ullius valetudinis molestia pergebat: **sceþþan.** *Add :* v. in-, un-sceþþende: **sceþþendlic.** v. ge-sceþþendlic.

**sceþ-wrǽc.** *Substitute for the passage :*—Eálā hû swîþe eádge wǽron þā æþelan cennend(e) Sancte Iôhannes, þǽm ne sceþede nǽnig scyld þisse sceþwracan worlde, ne hié nǽnigo firen ne gewundode *beati, quos in saeculo isto aliqua culpa non percutit, nullum vulnerat crimen,* Bl. H. 161, 31–33.

**sciccels.** *Add :*—Hacele *vel* fôtsîd sciccel (v. fôt-sîd), Wrt. Voc. i. 40, 67. Âwyrp hyder þînne scyccels þe þú mid bewǽfed eart, Hml. S. 23 b, 210.

**scîd** (?) *a course.* *Dele, and see* scrid: **scîd** *a shide.* *Add :* [v. N. E. D. shide.]

**sciftan.** II. *add :*—Tûna embefær bûton nēdbehêfes gerâdes tôdâl þæt dihte î scifte wôrigende nâteshwôn gelômlǽceon *uillarum circuitus nisi necessarię rationis discretio hoc dictauerit uagando nequaquam frequentent,* Angl. xiii. 375, 132. Wē sceolan ûre lîfes weg wîslîce scyftan *iter nostrum temperare debemus,* Chrd. 65, 20. Sciftende *ordinans,* Angl. xiii. 448, 1187. [v. N. E. D. shift.]

**scilcen.** [The word has not necessarily a bad meaning. With the passage given compare the description of the same incident in Gr. D. :—Hē sænde .vii. nacode mǽdenu (*puellas*), 119, 11]:—Scylcen, fǽmne, meówle *iuuencula,* i. *uirguncula,* An. Ox. 2112. [Þer com o schelchene gon þat wes myd Kayphas (*uenit una ex ancillis summi sacerdotis,* Mk 14, 66), Misc. 45, 279.]

**scild.** I. _add:_—Swilce ān lytel pricu on brādan brede oþþe rondbeáh on scilde, Bt. 18, 1; F. 62, 5. Ic wille ðurhgān orsorh ðone here mid rōde tācne gewǣpnod, nā mid reádum scylde oððe mid hefegum helme oþþe heardre byrnan, Hml. Tñ. ii. 502, 12: Hml. S. 31, 114. II. _add: defence:_—Hī sprǣcon wið þǣre treówleásnesse fore scylde (_defensione_) þǣre sōðfæstnesse, Gr. D. 246, 21.

**scildan.** _Add: to provide protection_ for a person (_dat._):—Mōton þā hyrdas beón swīðe wacore . . . þe wið þone þeódsceaðan folce sceolon scyldan, Ll. Th. i. 374, 28. Ā hē sceal scyldan crīstenum mannum wið ǣlc þǣra þinga þe synlic bið, ii. 312, 23. v. ā-scildan.

**scildend.** _Add:_—Eálá þū scyldend o _tutor,_ Hpt. 31, 18, 503. Sceldend lífes mīnes _defensor vitae meae,_ Ps. Vos. 26, 1. þ ðu tōweorpe feónd and wrecend t and scildend _ut destruas inimicum et ultorem,_ Ps. L. 8, 3.

**scild-hreóþa.** _Take here_ scild-rída _in Dict., in_ l. 5 _after_ sendaþ _insert_ flāngeweorc, _and add:_ -rēða, -rída:—Sceldrēða, -hrēða _testudo,_ Txts. 100, 997.

**-scildod.** v. ge-scildod.

**scild-truma.** _Add: a compact body of troops, a company:_—Scildtruman _testudine,_ An. Ox. 3796. Fērde hē him hindan tō mid ðrým scyldtruman (_he went forth behind them in three companies,_ 1 Macc. 5, 33), Hml. S. 25, 423. [v. _N. E. D._ sheltron.]

**scild-wyrhta.** _Add:_—On Manlēfes gewitnesse, and on Leówerdes Healta, and on Sweignes scyldwirhta, Cht. Th. 638, 21.

**scilfrung.** _In_ l. 5 l. scelfan _for_ skelfan: **scilian.** _Add:_ [Cf. Hē wæs tōscyled from þǣre apostlene gesēmrǣdene, Nap. 87. þā þā God tōscelede wæter from lande, Angl. xi. 370, 10. Hī tōscylledon _they parted (from each other),_ Nap. 87.] [v. _N. E. D._ shill.]

**scill** _a shell._ _Add:_ II a. _shell_ of a nut (?). v. hnut-scill (?): **scill** _sonorous._ _Add:_ [v. _N. E. D._ shill]: **scillan.** _Add:_ [v. _N. E. D._ shill _to resound._] v. on-scillan: **scilliht.** _Add:_ v. un-scilliht.

**scilling.** II. _add:_—Sum mon sealde ōþrum scilling seolfres tō borge, Shrn. 127, 25. Scil[ling] _dragmam,_ An. Ox. 348. Hū þā scillingas (_solidi_) wurdon þurh wundor āgifene þām biddendum . . . Sum wer . . . sǣde þ hē wǣre geswenced from his moniendan for .xii. scyllingum . . . þā wǣron fundene .xiii. scillingas . . . Se Godes wer þā sealde þām biddere and cwæð þ hē āgeáfe his maniendum þā .xii. and þone ǣnne hǣfde him tō his āgenre nytte (_In the story as told in_ Hml. Th. ii. 176–8 _the amount owed is_ healf pund, _and the additional sum provided is_ twēntig penega), Gr. D. 157, 16–158, 21.

**scīma.** _Add:_—Seó sunne sylf æt middum dæge eall hire scīma wæs on blǣco gecyrred _sol in medio coelo velut lucerna in die pallidescere videbatur,_ Guth. Gr. 167, 115. Seó sunne feala þinga onlÿht myd hyre scīman, Solil. H. 31, 8. Scÿman, 66, 22.

**scimrian.** _Add: to shimmer, shine with a flickeriug light_ as a mote in the sunlight:—Scimerað _uibrat_ (minor . . . modico Phoebi radiis qui _uibrat_ atomo, Ald. 272, 32), An. Ox. 23, 51. þā se dægredleóma beorhte scymrode _matutina luce radiante,_ Chrd. 26, 22. And scimerian (_printed_ scinefrian) _ac micare,_ Wrt. Voc. ii. 6, 33.

**scīn** _an evil spirit._ _Add:_—Hē yfelsacode þæs ælmihtigan Godes mægnþrym in wyrginge and in scinna ciginge, Gr. D. 289, 9.

**scīn, scÿn;** _p._ scīde, scīdde (cf. tÿn, þÿn _for conjugation_) _To shy, be afraid:_—Martinus rād gescrÿd mid sweartum clāþum; þā scÿddon (scÿhdon, _v. l._) þā mūlas þe þ cræt tugon ðurh his tōcyme āfyrhte, Hml. S. 31, 971. [v. _N. E. D._ shy; _vb._ _O. H. Ger._ sciuhen _perhorrescere._] Cf. sceóh.

**scīnan.** _Add:_ I. of that which emits rays:—Eall swā leóhte seó sunne scīnð under þǣre eorðan on nihtlicre tīde, swā swā heó on dæg dēð bufan ūrum heáfdum, Lch. iii. 234. 23. Scinon ðā bān swā beorhte swā steorran . . . and þ leóht geswutelode swā hwǣr swā hī lāgon, Hml. S. 11, 269. Giwēdo his giwordne wērun scīnende (-o, L.) _uestimenta eius facta sunt splendentia,_ Mk. R. 9, 3. Him mid sīðedon twægen scīnende englas, 25, 774. II. of that which can reflect light:—On ðǣm mæssehrægle scīnð (_candescit_) ongemang ōðrum bleóm ðæt swyðrāwene twīn, Past. 88, 1. On him byrne scān, B. 405. Under ðǣm scīnendan brande, Hml. Th. ii. 510, 19. On scīnendre hÿfe _flauescenti,_ i. _micanti gurgustio,_ An. Ox. 306. II a. of that which appears clearly:—Ðæt feax grēwð and scīnð ofer ðǣm brægene _capilli super cerebrum oriuntur,_ Past. 139, 18. Hī hine hetelīce swungon oð þæt ðā bān scinon, Hml. Th. ii. 302, 10. III. _to be splendid:_—Seó hwītness þǣre lilian scīneþ on þē, Bl. H. 7, 30. IV. in figurative applications with retention of physical phraseology:—Ðā sōðfæste scīnes t lixeð (_fulgebant_) suǣ sunna, Mt. L. 13, 43. Hē uæs þæccille bearnende and līxende t scīnende (_lucens_), Jn. L. 5, 35. V. of persons:—Heálicere hēhþe gleów, scān _precelso_ (_puritatis_) _fastigio fulminauit,_ claruit, An. Ox. 4409: 4573. Hē manigum wundrum sceán and berhte _uita eius crebris miraculis fulgebat,_ Guth. Gr. 168, 138. Martinus sceán on wītegunge, Hml. Th. ii. 512, 34. Scine _effulserit,_ i. _claruit_ (qualis patriarcha virtutem gloria _effulserit,_ Ald. 30, 7), An. Ox. 2172. VI. of immaterial things:—Mid scīnendre _praepollenti_ t _florenti_ (_meritorum gratia_), An. Ox. 2248: 3602. v. scīnende.

**-scincio.** v. ge-scincio.

**scīn-cræft.** I. _add:_—Hū hē (_the devil_) sceolde þisne mid his scīncræfte of þām scræfe ādrīfan _hunc usitata arte pellere ex eo specu,_ Gr. D. 211, 13. II. _add:_—Gyf ðu ǣnig ðing ðisse stale wite . . . ðē nān scīncræft ne gehelppe tōgeánes ðisum Godes dōme, Ll. Lbmn. 415, 26. Antecrīst wind ongeán Godes gecorenan . . . mid gedwyldlicum scīncræftum, Wlfst. 196, 20. III. _a magical apparatus,_ cf. cræft; IV.:—Hē weard gelǣd tō þām lifleásum godum . . . þā hēt hē þone scuccan þe on þām scīncræfte wunode þ hē ūt eóde of þǣre anlícnysse him tō, Hml. S. 36, 404.

**scīn-cræftiga.** _Add:_—þā þā scīncræftigan (drÿcræftigan, _v. l._ malefici) wurdon ārāsode . . . Basilius se scīncræftiga fērde, Gr. D. 27, 15–21. Hī befæston þ wīf drÿum and scīncræftigum _puellam maleficis tradiderunt,_ 73, 16: 74, 10.

**scindel, es;** _m._ _A shingle:_—Ut reddat iusticiam aecclesiae, id est, .i. cyricsceat, et .v. scindlas, et .i. bord, C. D. vi. 33, 1. [v. _N. E. D._ shindle. Cf. _O. H. Ger._ scintala: _Ger._ schindel. _From Latin_ scindula.]

**scīnefrian.** v. scimrian.

**scīnende;** _adj._ _Brilliant:_—þǣr is se ælmihtiga Dryhten scīnendra and liōhtra þonne ealle ōðre lióht, Verc. Först. 113, 3.

**scīn-híw.** _Add:_—Hē wēnde þ hit wǣre sumes gāstes scīnhÿw, Hml. S. 23 b, 170. Se swicola deófol hine gesewenlicne on manegum scīnhīwum þām hālgan æteówde, 31, 712.

**scīn-lāc.** I. _add:_—Wiþ fefre and wiþ scīnlāce and wið eallum gedwolþinge, Lch. ii. 288, 13. III. _add:_—Of heáhnesse scÿnlāces his _ab altitudine fantasiẹ suae,_ Ps. Rdr. 284, 10. IV. _add:_ The Latin original of the last passage is: Fantasmas uiderit, lucrum ex insperato significat.

**scīn-lǣca.** _In_ l. 8 l. _advexerint._

**scīn-lǣce, -lāc;** _adj._ _Add:_—þā brōðru þe hē gemētte þǣr mid þām scīnlācan (gedwimorlācum, _v. l._) fÿre bysmrian _fratres quos phantastico reperit igne deludi,_ Gr. D. 124, 10. þ preóstas hī warnien wyð þā scīnlācan hīwinga deófla prettes (_transformationes dẹmonum_), Chrd. 7, 25.

**scīn-lic.** _Add:_—Be þām þ preóstas hī warnien wið þā scÿnlican hīwinga deófla prættes, Chrd. 98, 32. v. scīn-lǣce.

**scinn, es;** _n._ _A skin:_—Manega gærsama on scynnan mid pælle betogen, Chr. 1075; P. 209, 31. [_From Scandinavian_ skinn.] v. berascinn.

**scinnen** _of skin._ v. grā-, hearm-scinnen.

**scip** _a ship._ _Add:_—Gyf Æðelrēdes cynges friðman cume on unfriðland, and se here þǣrtō cume, hæbbe frið his scip and ealle his ǣhta. Gif hē his scip uppe getogen hæbbe . . . þ hē þǣr frið hæbbe, Ll. Th. i. 286, 8. Scip sceal genægled (cf. naca nægledbord, Rā. 59, 5), Gn. Ex. 94. Seomode on sole sīdfæðmed scip on ancre fæst, B. 302. On bearm scipes, 35: 896: Exod. 375. Harold forbærnde Griffines scipa and alle þā gewǣda þe þǣrtō gebyrede . . . and þām kynge brōhte his scipes heáfod, Chr. 1063; P. 191, 6–16. Ānes scipes se arcebisceop geūðe ðām folce tō Cent and ōðres tō Wiltūnescīre, C. D. iii. 352, 17. Wē willað mid þām sceattum ūs tō scype gangan, By. 40. Ðā ðe mid scipe līðað, Ps. Th. 106, 22. Gyf mon beó at his ǣhtan bereáfod and hē wīte of hwilcum scipe, āgyfe steóresman þā ǣhta, Ll. Th. i. 286, 17. Se nōwent rihte þ lytle ǣrene scip þe wiþhindan þām māran scipe gefæstnod wæs _nauta post navem carabum regebat,_ Gr. D. 347, 2. Ongyn þē scip wyrcan, merehūs micel, Gen. 1302. Hē sǣlde tō sande sīdfæðme scip oncerbendum fæst, B. 1917. Wīdfæðme scip, An. 240. Dol bið sē þe gǣð on deóp wæter, sē þe sund nafað ne gesegled scip, Sal. 225. Alle nēðbāde tuēgra sceupa, C. D. i. 114, 11. Hī cōmon ūp on Limene mūþan mid .ccl. hunde scipa . . . on þā eá hī tugon ūp hiora scipu oþ þone weald .iiii. mīla fram þǣm mūþan ūteweardum, Chr. 893; P. 84, 4–11. Wē on sǣlāde scipum brecað ofer bæðweg, An. 512. Hÿ gehÿdað heáhstefn scipu tō þām unlonde oncyrrāpum, setlað sǣmearas, Wal. 13. v. friþ-, hlæst-, þeóf-scip.

**scip-āc;** _f._ _An oak-tree fit for shipbuilding_ (?):—On ðas cipāc; of ðǣre scipāc, C. D. iii. 382, 16.

**scipe.** I. _add:_—Hē nān þing him sylfum of his campdōmes scipe on his seóde ne heóld, Hml. S. 31, 55. [v. _N. E. D._ shipe.] II. _add:_ v. ge-, land-, mægen-, sin-, tūn-, wæter-, weorold-scipe.

**scip-fǣreld, es;** _n._ _A voyage:_—Men wǣron on scipfærelde of Sicilia þām eálande sēcende Rōmesbyrig _aliqui de Siciliae partibus navigio Romam petentes,_ Gr. D. 273, 18. Hwilc tunge mæg hit āsecgan, þā māndǣda þe on þām scipfærelde wǣron and on þām sīþfæte gefremede, Hml. S. 23 b, 380.

**scip-fultum, es;** _m._ _A naval force:_—Hē sende tō Eádwerde cingce and bæd hine scipfultumes þ hē ne geþafode þ hē him on wætere ne ætburste, Chr. 1049; P. 166, 36.

**scip-gebroc.** _Add:_—Petrus se apostol eóde mid drīgum fōtum ofer þone sǣ, and Paulus geþrowode scipgebroc in þām sǣ _ibi Paulus ire cum navi non potuit, ubi Paulus pedibus iter fecit,_ Gr. D. 91, 10.

**scip-gefére** (?). _Substitute:_ scip-gefǣr, es; _n._ _A going by ship:_—Hē him mid fare gehwearf (in scipgefære hwearf, on his scypgefere hwearf, _v. ll._) eft tō Centlande _rediit Cantiam nauigio,_ Bd. 2, 20; Sch. 186, 24.

**scip-here.** *Add:* v. norþ-sciphere.

**scip-hláford.** *Add:*—Þá geseah þæs scypes hláford þ Eustachies wíf swíðe fæger wæs; þí gewilnode hé hí habban . . . þá bícnode se scip-hláford tó his mannum þ hí hine (*Eustachius*) út sceoldon wurpan, Hml. S. 30, 169.

**scip-líþ,** es, *n.* *A naval force:*—þ sciplið gewende tó Legeceastre, Chr. 1055; P. 186, 18.

**scip-líþend, -líþende.** *Add:*—On sǽ bið þæt sciplíðendra cwalm swá mycel, þ nænig man ne wát tó secganne ne nænigum eorðcyninge be ðám sciplíðendum *illo tempore navium adcessio erit in pelago, ut nemo nemini novum referrat regi terre,* Verc. Först. 119, 15. Hí sóhton betwux sciplíþende, Hml. S. 33, 188.

**scip-mann.** *Add:*—Scypmen *nauitæ,* Germ. 400, 493. (3) *a fighting man who goes in a ship:*—Cómon of Denemearcon þreó Swegenes suna mid .cc. scypum and .xl. . . . ǽr þan þe þá scypmenn þider cómon hæfdon þá Frenciscan þá burh forbærned, Chr. 1069; P. 204, 21. Se cyning hæfde micle landfyrde tóeácan his scipmannum, 1052; 181, 18. [O. Frs. skip-mann.]

**scippan.** *Add:* v. frum-, un-sceapen.

**scippend.** *Add: a creator:*—Nú cwædon gedwolmen þæt deófol gesceópe sume gesceafta, ac hí leógað; ne mæg hé náne gesceafta gescyppan for ðan ðe hé nis ná scyppend, Hml. Th. i. 16, 21. v. frum-, ge-scippend.

**scip-toll;** *n.* (not *m.*). *Add:*—Cómon hí tó sǽ and þǽr gemétton scip standan, and hí on þ eódon, and mid him reówan. Þæs scypes hláford . . . gyrnde þæs scyptolles, Hml. S. 30, 167.

**scip-wrǽc** *what is cast up from a wreck:*—Cum omni maris eiectu, quod shipwrec appellamus, C. D. iv. 146, 9. Cum omnibus quaecunque maris procellosis tempestatibus, in aquam uel in terram eorum eiecta fuerint, quod Anglice shipwreck promulgatum est onomate, 28.

**scír.** I. *add:*—Gebohte scíre wítunga *ambitus judicium,* Wrt. Voc. i. 21, 12. Hé onféng þǽre heordelican scíre gýmnysse *pastoralem suscepit curam,* Gr. D. 191, 26. Héðe sé ðe scíre (cf. scír-mann; I.) healde, Angl. ix. 259, 13. III. *dele last passage, and add:*—Férde se biscop tó scíre gemóte (cf. scír-gemót), C. D. iv. 234, 27. IV. *add:*—Cappadoniscre scíre *Cappadox,* i. *episcopus Cappadocie,* An. Ox. 2302. v. mæg-, weorold-scír; scíre.

**scír;** *adj.* *Add:* I b. *morally clear, pure.* [v. N. E. D. shire; adj. 4]:—Sceomiande man sceal in sceade hweorfan, scír in leóhte gerísed, Gn. Ex. 67. II f. *add:*—Scírre *clarior* (limpida sum Titanis *clarior* orbe, Ald. 272, 18), An. Ox. 23, 36.

**scíran.** *Add:* [v. N. E. D. shire; *vb.*] v. á-scíran: **scír-biscop.** *Add:* [Ic beode æc þ se scyrbiscop ne seo swa dyrstlece þ he ne hading ne haleging ne do on þis abbotrice buton seo abbot hit him bidde, Chr. 675; P. 36, 12.]: **scírdan.** *Add:* v. ge-scirdan: **scíre,** an; *f.* v. geréf-scíre.

**scirian.** *Add:*—On þám se abbod scyrige (swyrige, MS.) his byrðena *in quibus abba partiat honera sua,* R. Ben. I. 54, 4. v. for-, tó-scirian: un-áscirod.

**scír-lett** *a piece* or *measure of land:*—On bisceopes scírlett; ofer þ. scírlètt, Cht. E. 239, 9. Cf. geoc-led.

**scír-mann.** I. *add:* Angl. ix. 262, 14. v. heáh-scírmann.

**scirpan** *to sharpen.* *Add:*—Ísen mid ísene byð gescyrped and mann scyrpð (*exacuit*) ansýne freónd(es) his, Scint. 205, 4. Hig scerptan *exacuerunt,* Ps. L. 63, 4.

**scirpan** *to clothe.* *Add:* (1) *to dress:*—Nimað þis hrægl and scrýd-að (scyrpað, *v.l.* vestite) eów mid, Gr. D. 202, 27. þá þá hé wæs callinga ert scyrped *vestitus,* 343, 19. (2) *to equip for a journey:*—Hé hine hám wel scyrpan wolde, Bd. 5, 19; Sch. 659, 25. v. un-scirped.

**-scirpendlic.** v. ge-scirpendlic: **-scít(e).** v. for-scít(e): **-scíte.** v. wáse-scíte.

**scíte.** *Add:*—Se mæssepreóst genam þá scétan (scýtan, *v. l.*) of þám weófode *presbyter ex altari sindonem tulit,* Gr. D. 72, 32. v. wæter-scíte; sceát, sceáta.

**Scíþþisc;** *adj. Scythian:*—Hiene gesóhte seó Scíþþisce cwén, Ors. 3, 9; Swt. 130, 10. þá Scyððiscan þeóda ofslógan úre fela, Hml. S. 7, 345. ¶ *the definite form used substantively:*—Ðá Scyððiscan wunnon wið hine, 300. Siððan hé ðá Scyððiscan oferwiuð, 309.

**scítte.** *Add:* [v. N. E. D. skit. Cf. A.D. 987. This year two diseases unknown to the English in past ages, viz. a fever among men and a murrain among cattle, called in the English language 'the skit', and which may be described as a flux of the bowels, sorely troubled the whole of England, causing . . . the universal loss of cattle, Fl. Wigorn.]

**scofl.** *Add:* v. stel-, windwig-scofl.

**scógan.** *Add:*—Sceógian hí *calcient se,* Angl. xiii. 399, 486. Gán hí tó sceógienne *eant ad calciandum,* 413, 682. v. ge-, on-, un-scógan.

**scóh.** *Add:*—þám ádlian þúhte swylce man his ænne scó (sceó, *v.l.*) of ðám fét him átuge, Hml. S. 21, 126. Þára sceóna tácen is þæt þú sette þinne scetefinger uppon þinne fót, Tech. ii. 126, 13. þá þwangas þára scóna ongunnon heom sylfe tóslupan . . se deófol him hýrde þá scós of tó dónne, Gr. D. 221, 22-25. Gescód mid gehammenum (ge-

---

clútedum, *v.l.*) scón, 37, 13. Gescrýd mid gyldenum cynehelme and mid goldfellenum sceón, Hml. S. 31, 752. Sum sútere siwode þæs hálgan weres sceós, 15, 23.

**scóh-wyrhta.** *Add:*—Hé gewunode þ hé ongan sceós wyrcan. Be þám scóhwyrhtan geseah sum óðer man . . . hé ongan ácsian be ðám lífe þæs sceóhwyrhtan (scóh-, *v.l.*), Gr. D. 322, 1-5.

**-scola.** v. ge-scola.

**scolu.** II. *add:*—Hí singan on Grécisc *agios* . . . and eft scolu (*schola*) on Léden *sanctus* . . . seó sculu (*scola*) andswaraþ on Léden, Angl. xiii. 418, 757-762. v. leornung-scolu.

**scóm-hylt,** e; *f. Substitute:* **scóm-hylte,** es; *n.* Cf. heáh-hylte.

**scop-leóþ.** *Add:*—Mé wæs swilce swiðlic lust þǽra sceandlicra sceopleóða mé gedréfde (-on, MS.), þonne hí mé on móde gebróhton þá deóflican leóþ tó singanne þe ic ǽr on worulde geleornode, Hml. S. 23 b, 539.

**soorf.** *Add:*—Swá mycel hreófie and sceorfe (scurf, scyrf, *v.l.*), Bd. 5, 2; Sch. 557, 12.

**scorfed.** *l.* scorfede, *and add:*—Scurfede hors, An. Ox. 46, 1.

**scorian** *to project.* *Add:*—For þám clifstánum þe þǽr gehwǽr út sceorodon (scoredon, *v.l.*) of þám munte, Gr. D. 213, 5.

**scort.** I. *add:*—Wæs þǽr án stów swýþe sceort (*locus brevissimus*) in þæs muntes sídan, Gr. D. 49, 5. II. *add:*—Hé wénde þ swá scort (sceort, *v.l.*) man (cf. lytelne, 10) ne mihte ná habban swá ormǽtne hlísan þurh hálinesse, Gr. D. 46, 18. III 2 b. *add:*—Ðá wolde se cniht his wíte geendian mid scortum deáðe, Hml. S. 12, 190. III 2 c. *add:*—Dactilus stent on ánum langum tíman and twám sceortum, Angl. viii. 314, 15.

**scortian.** *Add:* v. un-scortende.

**scort-ness.** I. *add:*—Under sceortnysse *sub breuitate,* Angl. xiii 446, 1158. For sceortnysse daga, 437, 1028.

**scoru** *a score:*—v. scora (*quinquies uiginti*) scǽp, Nap. 56. [Icel. sker.]

**scot.** V. *add: a part of a building shut off from the rest, a chancel:*—Sume þá men þe stódan beforan þám sceote *quidam ex his qui extra sacrarium stabant,* Gr. D. 236, 1.

**scotian.** I 2. *add:*—Hí fuhton mid Iúdan sceotiende heora flán on ðá hæðenan leóda, Hml. S. 25, 495.

**Scot-land.** I. *add:*—Igbernia, þ wé Scotland hátað *Hibernia,* Ors. 1, 1; S. 24, 16.

**scot-líra.** *l.* -líra: Scottas. *Add:* v. Norþ-Scottas.

**scrǽf.** I. *add:*—Mín hús is gebedhús, and gé hit habbað gedón sceaðum tó screafe (gescræfe, Mt. R. 21, 13), Hml. Th. i. 406, 3. v. heort-, stán-scræf.

**scrǽtte.** *Add:* [v. N. E. D. scrat.]

**scrapian** *to scrape:*—Gyf þú ǽgera beþurfe, þonne scrapa þú mid þínum fingre úp on þinne wynstran þúman, Tech. ii. 124, 1. [*Icel.* skrapa.]

**-screncedness.** *Add:* v. for-screncedness: **-scrépe;** *n.* v. ge-scrépe: -scrépelíce, -scrépen, -scrépness. v. ge-scrépelíce, -scrépen, -scrépness: **screón** (?). *Perhaps* for-scráf *should be read.* v. for-scrífan.

**scríc.** *Add:*—Scríc *structio,* Hpt. 33, 241, 65. Scríc *turdus,* þryssce *strutio,* Wrt. Voc. i. 63, 2.

**scríd.** *Add:*—Cræt ł sc[r]id *currus,* Ps. Cam. 67, 18. Fýrene scridu *igneos currus,* Chrd. 99, 9. Cræta, scriþeua *bigarum,* An. Ox. 2185. Scriddum *bigis,* 18, 22. Scridú *carpentum,* Germ. 393, 154.

**scríde.** v. scriþe.

**scrífan.** *Add:* III a. *to determine:*—Ne dear ic náht þristelíce be þissere wísan reccan ne ne scrífan *hac de re temere definire nil audeo,* Gr. D. 332, 13. V c. *add:*—Hí ná ne scrifan (hogodon, *v.l.*) þéh hí eallinga hire sáwle áðwǽsctan, Gr. D. 73, 19. [*From Latin.* See Hpt. 36, 145, sqq.]

**scrift-scír.** *Add:*—Bútan hé hæbbe þæs biscopes gewitnesse þe hé on his scriftscíre sý, Ll. Th. i. 212, 22.

**scrimman.** *Add:* [v. N. E. D. shrim.]

**scrín.** *Add:* e; *f.*:—Ðis mycel is gegolden of þǽre cyricean W. cyninge syððan hé þis land áhte . . . of þǽre hlangan scríne .viii. pund, Cht. Th. 439, 32. Hé forlét þá scríne his feohgestreónes *scrinium deseruit,* Gr. D. 52, 6.

**scrincan.** *Add:* v. un-áscruncen: **scrind.** *For* scrinde *perhaps* scynde (v. scyndan) *might be read.* Cf. *the intransitive use of the verb in reference to a ship:*—Brimwudu scynde, Gú. 1305: **scrípan.** v. screpan: **scripp.** *Dele, the MSS. of* Hml. Th. i. 394, 7 *have* scip, scipp: scriptor. v. tíd-scriptor: **scriða.** *Dele:* **scriðe.** *l.* (?) scríde: scríþing. *Add:* v. geond-scríþing.

**scrúd.** I. *add:* Fíf mancusas gold . . . tó fyrþrunge and tó scrúde, Cam. Phil. Soc. 1902, p. 15. II. *add:*—'Ásend him twá scrúd (*vestes mutatorias duplices*) and sum pund' . . . 'Genim feówer scrúd (*vestimenta*) and twá pund,' Hml. Th. i. 400, 19-21. Se gýtsere hæfd ǽnne lichaman and menigfealde scrúd, 66, 1.

**scrúd-feoh, -feós;** *n.* *Money for the purchase of garments:*—Hyra scrúdfeoð, Cam. Phil. Soc. 1902, p. 15.

scrudnere, es; m. *An examiner, investigator :*—Strec dēma . . . weorca, ac eác swylce geþōhta scrudnere (*exactor*), Chrd. 88, 33.

scrudnian. *Add :*—Man scrutnode (strutnode, MS.) on ælcere stōwe þær man hī æfre geāxian cūðe, Hml. S. 23, 268.

scrybb. *Add :*—Andlang scrybbe (?), C. D. B. iii. 603, 28. [To one weie þet geþ to Winchestre þat is ihoten shrubbeshedde bitwiene þe shrubbes, i. 58, 10. *See* Philol. Trans. 1895, 8, p. 536.]

scrȳdan. I. *add :*—Nacodne scrēdan *nudum vestire,* R. Ben. I. 20, 2.

scucca. *Add :*—Deófol . . . is atelic sceocca, Hml. Th. i. 16, 21. Cwæð se hālga wer tō ðām hetolan sceoccan . . . 'Þū leásbrēda feónd and fācnes ordfruma.' Se sceocca sōna fordwān of his gesihðe, Hml. S. 6, 315. Þām sceoccan *Satane,* R. Ben. I. 57, 5. Se feónd hæfde him mid fela ōðre sceoccan, Hml. S. 6, 304. ¶ in a local name :—Ubi dicitur Scuccanhlāu, C. D. i. 196, 1.

scuccen, sceoccen; adj. *Devilish, diabolic :*—Man tōheów þā sticmælum þone sceoccenan god, Nap. 55.

scūfa. v. deáþ-scūfa.

scūfan. *Add :* III a. fig. :—Aldne monno of scȳfende *veterem hominem disponentes,* Rtl. 32, 32. VI. *add :*—Se micla cræftiga hiertende tō scȳfð, and egesiende stiérð, Past. 53, 16. v. ge-scūfan; wið-scofen.

sculan. I. *add :*—L. mancsa goldes þe Ælfnōþ him sceal, Cht. Crw. 23, 7. Eal ic him gelæste þ þ ic him scolde, Ll. Th. i. 182, 11. Hē forgeaf on Godes ēst Centingan ðæne borh ðe hý him sceoldan, C. D. iii. 352, 27. II. *add :* (8) :—Þære nædran gecynd is þ ælc uht þæs þe hió ābītt scel his līf on slæpe geendian, Ors. 5, 13; S. 246, 27. (12) :—Ic wēnde þ þes sceolde beón mycel and fæger (þ þes wære micel man and fæger, *v. l.*) *ego grandem hominem credidi,* Gr. D. 46, 27. (13) :—Hē cwæð þ sum wer wære þa his wíf forsæde swā þ heó sceolde hi'sceand-līce forlicgan, Hml. S. 12, 182. III. *add :* (1) :—Sōna swā þāra Læcedemonia lādteów wiste þ hē wið þā twēgen heras sceolde, Ors. 3, 1; S. 96, 15. (2) :—Hē nyste hwær hē ūt sceolde, Ors. 6, 31; S. 286, 20. Hwæt sceolan ūs, oþþe hwæt dōþ ūs þāra worda ymbþonc ?, Bl. H. 183, 11.

sculdor. *Add :* sculdra, an :—Hē dô of mæssehacelan and twy-feldende hī onbūtan lecge him on wynstran sculdran (*in sinistra scapula*), Angl. xiii. 406, 588.

scunian. I. *add :*—Ðegnum bebeád ðā ðā ðe líchoma ácuellas ne scyniga *discipulis praecepit eos qui corpus occidunt non metuere,* Lk. p. 7, 12.

-scuniend, -scuniendlic, -scunodlic. v. on-scuniend, -scuniendlic.

scūr. II. *add :*—Ðone ungeðyldegan suiðe lytel scūr ðære costunga mæg onhrēran *impatientem aura tentationis agitat,* Past. 225, 5. Ðā scūras ðære costunga ādreógan *tentationum procellas tolerare,* 401, 32. v. īsern-scūr.

[scūr-fāh; adj. *Stormy, tempestuous :*—Scūrfāh winter, Angl. xi. 369, 4, 15.]

-scuta. *Dele :* scutel. II. *add :*—Sgytila *momenta,* Rtl. 171, 41.

scūwa. *Add :* a 'shady' *person* (?) :—Scūan *nebulonis,* An. Ox. 7, 139. Cf. fore-scȳwa.

scūwan. *Add :* Cf. fore-scȳwung : -scȳ. v. ge-scȳ : scydd. *Add :* [Cf. *N. E. D.* scud dirt.]

scyfe. I a. *add :* glossing *praecipitium :*—Þā hors . . . þære eá wætres hryne heom ondrēdon, efne swā hit sum deáþes plyht oððe scyfe wære *aquam fluminis tangere quasi mortalem praecipitium pertimescebant,* Gr. D. 15, 10.

scyhhan [:—Ne āwyrp ł āscyhh mē of ansȳne *ne proicias me a facie tua,* Ps. Rdr. 50, 13.] Cf. scín, scȳan.

scyhtan. *Add* [:—Þū āscihtest freónd and nēhstan *elongasti a me amicum et proximum,* Ps. Rdr. 87, 19.]

scyld. [*The word is masculine in the following :*—Scyld (*delictum*) mīnne cūþne ic dyde, Ps. Rdr. 31, 5. Scyldas *delicta,* 24, 7 : 58, 13.] I. *add :*—þ manna scyldu (-e, *v. l.*) sīn gewītnode *ut culpae carnalium puniantur,* Gr. D. 323, 13. Scylda, 328, 10. v. un-scyld.

scyld-full. *Add :* culpable :—Tō þý þ ic þý ēð mihte gefyllan þā scyldfullan gewilnunga mīnes forligeres, Hml. S. 23 b, 339.

scyld-hete. *Add :* Cf. níþ-hete.

scyldig. I a. *add :*—Hē sorgode hū mycel se scyldiga þæs weorces forlure innan his sāwle *pensabat culpae reus quantum perdebat intus,* Gr. D. 291, 11. IV. *add :*—Beó hē ūtlah wið God . . . and wið þone cyning scyldig ealles þæs þe hē āge (cf. Wlfst. 271, 26), Cht. E. 231, 16. V. *add :*—Sió hē healsfange scyldig, Ll. Th. i. 40, 2, 5. V 3. *with prep. liable to* (tō) :—Scyldig hē wæs tō hellicere sūsle for his māndædum, ac hē geandette his synna Drihtne sylfum on ðære rōde-hengene, Hml. Th. ii. 78, 20. Hī ealle andwyrdon þæt hē scyldig wære tō deáðe, 248, 23. v. deáþ-, efen-, healf-, syn-, wamb-scyldig.

scyldiglíce. v. un-scyldiglíce : scyldigness. *For* synnignise *substi-tute* deáþsynnignise, *and add :* v. un-synnigness : -scyldigod. v. for-scyldigod.

scyldigung. *In* l. 1 *for* 'A criminal charge'; *in* l. 6 *for* 'charge

. . . it'); *in* l. 7 *for* 'charge' *substitute* 'A *penalty for crime, wer-gild; wergild; wergild : and add :* cf. Ll. Th. i. 116, 4. v. un-scyldigung.

scylf. II. *add :*—Scilfas *pinnas,* Ps. Rdr. 103, 3.

scȳn. v. scín.

scyndan. I. *add :*—Þeós world is scyndende and heononweard, Bl. H. 115, 19. II 1. *add :*—Þær ne wære scynde þā dagas . . . ah beóþ scynde þā dagas *nisi breviati fuissent dies illi . . . sed breviabuntur dies illi,* Mt. R. 24, 22. II 2. *add :* v. scynd-ness :—Hū mon ænne mon scyndan scyle ðonne hē yfle costunga mauege ðrowað *de exhortatione, quae uni adhibenda est contrariis passionibus laboranti,* Past. 455, 1.

scyndness, e; f. *Incitement, prompting :*—Seó deófollice scyndnes, Gr. D. 40, 18. Hē ne ðrowode nōht ðære scyndnesse (nāne costunge, *v. l.*) ofer þ æfre fram þām sweartan cnihte *ex illo die nil persuasionis ulterius a nigro pueruло pertulit,* 112, 10. Undercropen mid scyndnesse, 41, 16. v. scyndan; II 2.

scyrf. v. scorf : scyrft. *For* scansio *l.* (?) scarsio. Cf. scarsus *imminutus,* Migne.

scyte. *Add :* IV. *the distance to which a shot will go :*—Oþ þ hē wæs fullneáh in ānes flānes scyte ūt fram þām lande *pene ad unius sagit-tae cursum a terra,* Gr. D. 114, 34. v. fær-, wāse-scyte.

-scytlic. v. for-scytlic.

scytta. *Add :*—On þām elpendum upon stōdon gewæpnode scyttan (*cum armatis jactatoribus*), Nar. 4, 16.

scyttel. *Add :* [v. *N. E. D.* shut.] v. un-scyttan.

scyttel. *Add :*—Se scyttel (scyttels, *v. l.*) āsceát of þære fetere, Hml. S. 21, 419. Hē þā cyrican beleác and mid scyttelum (scyttelsum, *v. l.*) besceát . . . wurdon þā scyttelas onweg āworpene *ecclesiam clausit, seris munivit . . . abjectis seris,* Gr. D. 234, 18–25.

scyttels. *Add :*—Scettels *pessulus,* An. Ox. 46, 33. Hē ne mihte þā scyttelsas unscyttan, Hml. S. 31, 863.

Scyttisc. *Add :*—Hē wel cūþe Scyttysc, and Aidan ne mihte gebīgan his sprǣce tō Norþhymbriscum gereorde swā hraþe þāgīt, Hml. S. 26, 67. -scȳwa, -scȳwung. v. fore-scȳwa, -scȳwung.

se. *Add :* , *and* sē. I 1 a :—His mǣgas hine fēden gif hē self mete nǣbbe. Gif hē mǣgas nǣbbe, oþþe þone mete uæbbe, Ll. Th. i. 60, 11. I 2 g :—Þū fīhst from mē on þī gemete swilc man nǣddran fleó, Hml. S. 23 b, 318. I 4 :—Se hȳra . . . þonne hē þone wulf gesyhþ, þonne flȳhð hē . . . and se wulf nimð ðā sceáp, Jn. 10, 12. Se gōda lǣce, Bt. 39, 9; F. 226, 10. Byð se ealda man ceald and snoflig, Angl. viii. 299, 35. Dysig bið se wegfērenda man, sē ðe nimð þone smēðan weg þe hine mislǣt, and forlǣt þone sticolan þe hine gebrincð tō ðære byrig, Hml. Th. i. 164, 9. Nim þ seax þe þæt hæfte sié hrȳþeres horn, Lch. ii. 290, 22. Hrīn him mid þý snidīsene, 208, 16. I 7. *one . . . one, one . . . other.* Cf. II 4 :—Hió hiere folc on tū tōdǣlde . . . Hió mid þǣm healfan dǣle (*one half*) beforan þǣm cyninge farende wæs, . . . and se healfa dǣl (*one half*) wæs Ciruse æfterfylgende, Ors. 2, 4; S. 76, 25–30. Þ is for hwí se gōda lǣce selle ðām hālum men sēftne drenc and ðþrum hālum biterne, Bt. 39, 9; F. 226, 10. Hē forcearf his basing, and sealde healfne dǣl þām þearfan and þone healfan dǣl hē dyde on his hricg, Hml. S. 31, 71. II 1 :—Þēh þe hit gelumpe þ him hwilc man ongēn cōme, and sē þonne wære gegrēted (and hē þone gegrētte, *v. l.*), Gr. D. 34, 5. Þ nān man nān mā wīfa nǣbbe būton .i., and seó beó mid rihte beweddod, Ll. Th. ii. 300, 13. Þonne se geohsa of þære ídlan wambe cymð . . . ne bēt þone se snora, Lch. ii. 62, 1 : Hml. S. 30, 421. Geseah hē treów licgende and þ lytel, 23 b, 767. Heó of hyre manega bōgas āsendeþ, and þā lange, i. 306, 6. Hēr ūs ys geboden þ wē etan lactucas, and þā sȳn grēne (cf. eton hig þeorfne hlāf mid grēnum lactucum, 322, 15), Angl. viii. 323, 41. (2) :—Hē ābyrgde ðā forbodenan fīctreówes blǣda, and ðæt on Frigedæg, and ðurh ðæt hē wæs on helle, Sal. K. 182, 34 : Chrd. 29, 21. (3) :—Scē Emelianan tíd ðære fǣmnan ; þ wæs scē Gregorius faðe, Shrn. 48, 6. Hwā is þæt þe eal ðā yfel āsecgan mæge ?, Ors. 1, 8; S. 42, 6. (4) :—Ān cymð, ōðer færð; sē bið ācenned, se ōðer forðfærð, Hml. Th. i. 248, 16. Þ þū ūs getǣhtest hwæs wē þ and þ timbrian sceoldon *ut nobis ostenderes ubi quid aedificare deberemus,* Gr. D. 149, 2. III :—Mið ðý gié geseás unfegernis slitnese, ðíu (*quae*) gecueden wæs from ðæm wītgo, Mt. L. 24, 15. In cæstre ðió (*quae*) is gecuoeden Sichor, Jh. L. R. 4, 5. V 2 b :—Þæs wīde, Pa. 4. ¶ Þæt hit wære geðūht þæs ðe māre gemynd þæs fæder, Hml. Th. i. 478, 10. 2 b (1) :—Ne magon hī tō þæs hwōn (nǣnigra þinga, *v. l.*) begitan þā þing þe him geteohhode nǣron *obtineri nequaquam possunt quae praedestinata non fuerint,* Gr. D. 54, 13. V 2 c :—Þæs þe ic ongyte, þæs wæs mycel wer *ut agnosco, vir iste magnus fuit,* Gr. D. 47, 14. V 2 d :—Lyt manna weorð lange fægen ðæs ðe ōðerne bewrencð, Prov. K. 34 : Exod. 51. V 3. *with prep.* tō (1) :—Hié tō ðon swíðe forslagene wurdon, þ hiera feáwa tō lāfe wurdon, Ors. 1, 13; S. 56, 9. (2) :—Tō þon þ hié his ænne ende onbærndon, Ors. 4, 10; S. 200, 15 : 1, 4; S. 34, 19. Tō ðon þæti hī heó geeáðmēdden, Cht. E. 42, 8. ¶ with verbs of intention or desire governing an infinitive or a clause, where the action of the verb in the infinitive or clause is intendeð, *because :*—Hē

ongan yrnan, tó þon þ hē wolde findan þone ārwyrðan fæder *ad inveniendum venerabilem patrem sese in cursum dedit*, Gr. D. 165, 17 : Wlfst. 194, 1. Hē hié begeat, tó ðon þ hē wolde þ þá folc him þý swíþor tó buge, Ors. 3, 11 ; S. 148, 31. Þá geceás hē him āne burg wið ðone sǣ, tó ðon þ him gelícade þ hié þǣr mehten betst frið binnan habban, 3, 7 ; S. 116, 5. Hié wǣpna nāman, tó þon ðæt hié heora weras wrecan þōhton, 1, 10 ; S. 44, 32 : 3, 9 ; S. 132, 11 : 4, 10 ; S. 200, 16. **V** 5 (1) :—God is ūre Fæder, þí wē sceolon ealle beón gebrōðru on Gode, Hml. Th. i. 260, 28. Hí habbað swíðe langsume trahtnunge . . . ; ðí wē hit lǣtað unsǣd, ii. 466, 24. (2) :—For ðon wē ðiss feáwum wordum sǣdon, ðý wē woldon gecýðan hú . . ., Past. 33, 6. For þý hē wilnað þ hē habbe þ hē nǣfð, þý hē wolde genōg habban, Bt. 26, 1 ; F. 92, 4. (1) and (2) :—Ne fieáh hē ðý ríce ðý his ǣnig mon bet wyrðe wǣre, Past. 33, 17. Þý hí secað anweald . . . ðý hí wēnaþ þ hit sié þ hēhste gōd, Bt. 34, 7 ; F. 142, 27–29. Þý ānan . . . þý, 14, 3 ; F. 46, 3–4. ¶ where condition is marked : *then . . . when* :—Ðý (*tunc*) mon sceal fǣsðne weal wyrcean, ðý (*cum*) mon ǣr gehāwige ðæt se grund fæsð sié . . . Ðý sceal eác bión ofersuíðed sió unfæsðrǣdnes ðāra geðōhta, ðý mon hine bewarige wið ðā leóhtmōdnesse, Past. 308, 2–6. **V** 5 (2) with *tó*, marking extent :— Hē wearð gehýrsum tó þí þ hē willes deáð þrowade *factus obediens usque ad mortem*, R. Ben. 26, 15.

**sealf.** *Add* :—Stincendre sealfe brǣð *nardi spirantis olfactum*, An. Ox. 314. v. lǣce-, lungen-, neb-sealf.

**sealh.** *Add* :—Tó ðon hnottan seale, C. D. v. 193, 35 : **sealhhangra.** v. hangra.

**sealmian.** *Add* :—Singað and blissiað and sealmiað (*psallite*), Ps. Rdr. 97, 4 : 104, 2.

**sealm-leóþ.** *Add* :—Sealmleóð *psalterium*, Ps. Rdr. 56, 9.

**sealm-sang.** **II.** *add: a service at which psalms are sung, one of the seven canonical hours* :—Sealmsonge *sinaxis* (cf. Professus sum monachus, et psallo omni die septem *synaxes* cum fratribus, Coll. M. 18, 31), Hpt. 33, 239, 18. Gebrōþrum sealmsange (*psalmodie*) underþeóddum, Angl. xiii. 391, 376. Man gehýrde mycelne sealmsang *coepit psalmodiae cantus audiri*, Gr. D. 238, 29. Sealmsangum (*psalmodiis*) onþeówigende, Angl. xiii. 375, 130 : 373, 116.

**sealm-sangere, es ;** *m. A psalmist*, Chrd. 112, 22.

**sealmsang-mǣrsung, e ;** *f. Celebration by psalm-singing, the service of the canonical hours* :—Ān weorc hē hæfde unforswigod and nǣfre geleórod, þæt wæs sealmsangmǣrsung and hāligra gewrita smeágung *he never failed to sing the hours and was never tired of studying the Scriptures*, Hml. S. 23 b, 36.

**sealm-wyrhta.** *Add* :—Swā swā se sealmwyrhta cwæð, 'Hē hit gecwæð, and þā gesceafta wǣron geworhte,' Hml. Th. i. 122, 13.

**sealt.** *Add* : **I.** physical :—Sealt hylt ǣlcne mete wið forrotodnysse, Hml. Th. ii. 536, 19. Dō hāliges sealtes fela on, Lch. ii. 344, 14. Dō on hwīt sealt, 94, 8 : 124, 10. **II.** metaphorical :—'Ge sind þǣre eorðan sealt.' Lāreówum gedafenað þæt hí mid wísdōmes sealte geleáffulra manna mōd sylton, Hml. Th. ii. 536, 17. See Kemble, Saxons in England, ii. 69 sqq. on the subject of salt-works.

**sealt, adj.** (1) *add* :—Seó Asia on ǣlce healfe heó is befangen mid sealtum wætere būton on eásthealfe, Ors. 1, 1 ; S. 12, 12. Andlang strēmes west ābūtan þane sealtan mersc, C. D. B. i. 296, 33. (2) *add* :—Ðonne þu sealt flǣsc wille, Tech. ii. 125, 1.

**sealt-ærn.** *Add* : [v. *N. E. D.* saltern.] Cf. sealt-hūs.

**sealtærn-steall, es ;** *m. A place where there is a house for preparing salt* :—Unam salis coquinariam, hoc est .i. sealternsteall, C. D. ii. 75, 22.

**sealtan ;** *p.* seólt ; *pp.* sealten *to salt. Take here* sealten, *and add* :—Ðonne þu sealt flǣsc wille, þonne twenge þu mid þínre swíðran neoþewearde þíne wynstran, þær se lýra þiccost sí, and dō mid þínum þrím fingrum swilcce þu sealte, Tech. ii. 125, 3. [*O. H. Ger.* salzan ; *p.* sialz *condire*.]

**sealten.** *See preceding word:* sealtere *a psalter.* v. saltere : **sealt-fæt.** *Add* : [v. *N. E. D.* saltfat] : sealt-hūs. *Add* : [v. *N. E. D.* salt-house.] Cf. sealt-ærn.

**sealting, e ;** *f. Dancing* :—Mæssepreóstas . . . ne beón an þām gefērscypum . . . þǣr líchamana beóð fracodlice gebǣru mid saltingum and tumbincgum (*choris et saltationibus*) (cf. sum bið swiðsnel, hafað searolic gomen, gleóðǣda gife for gumþegnum, leóht and leoþuwāc, Crä. 82), Chrd. 79, 1.

**sealtrode.** v. trod.

**sealt-sǣleþa.** *Add* :—Eorðan wæstmbǣre on sealtsyleðan *terram fructiferam in salsilaginem*, Ps. Rdr. 106, 34.

**seám** *a seam. In* l. 3 *dele* seám *panicenū*, 116, 8. v. Corp. Gl. H. 87, 15 : **seám-penig.** *Add* : v. Kemble's Saxons in England, ii. 70 sqq.

**seár, siére.** *Add* :—Eall hē weornige swā sýre (syer, MS.) wudu, Lch. i. 384, 14. *See next word.*

**Seár-mōnaþ** (?) *June* :—Sēremōnaþ *June*, Menol. Fox (at end) ; Hickes, i. 215. *See preceding word.*

**searu.** **II.** *add* :—Sē āwyrgeda gāst þæs preóstes heortan mid his searwes āttre geondsprengde, Guth. 44, 13. Healdað eów ðæt gē ne onǣlan mín ierre mid eówrum searwum *ne forte indignatio mea succendatur propter malitiam studiorum vestrorum*, Past. 435, 10. **IV.** *add* :—Man āhēhþ mid searwum mycle sweras *pendere magnas in machinis columnas*, Gr. D. 270, 4. Þá sōhtan heora gewinnan him sarwe and worhtan him hócas *non cessant uncinata hostium tela*, Bd. 1, 12 ; Sch. 34, 27.

**searu-cræft.** **I.** *add* :—Iugelera serecrǣftas *magorum molimina* .i. *ingenia*, An. Ox. 4090. **III.** *add* :—Hē hēt geopenian þone ǣrenan searecræft (cf. hēt hē gefeccan ǣnne ǣrenne oxan and þone onǣlan and þā hālgan ðǣron dōn, 421), Hml. S. 30, 456. Searacrǣftas *machinas*, An. Ox. 1656.

**searu-fāh.** *Add :* cf. searu-hwīt : **searu-geþræc.** v. ge-þræc.

**searu-hwīt, es ;** *n. Whiteness produced by art, lustrous whiteness* — Searohwīt solað, Reim. 67. v. hwīt ; *n.* **I.** cf. searu-fāh.

**searu-mete, es ;** *m. Food skilfully prepared, a dainty, delicacy* :— Hē fylde his wambe mid searumettum, Nap. 57.

**seáp.** *Add* :—Hí ðā moldan nāmon oð þæt þǣr wæs ðeóp seáð (*fossa*) ādolfen, þætte wǣpnedman mihte oð his sweóran on gestandan, Bd. 3, 9 ; Sch. 229, 3. Hē hēt ðā gebrōðor in ðæs hūses flōre hīm seáð (*foueam*) ādelfan, 4, 28 ; Sch. 520, 9. Danihel wearð āworpen intō ðāra leóna seáðum, Hml. S. 16, 81. [v. *N. E. D.* seath.] v. for- (?), mōr-seáþ.

**seáw.** *Add* [seáw is masculine in Lch. ii. 18, 14, *though in the preceding line it is neuter* :—Dō þ seáw on neb . . . þ se seáw (*perhaps there is confusion owing to the conjunctional* þ *and the initial letter of* seáw ?) mæge þ heáfod geondyrnan] :—Genim þisse sylfan wyrte (*foxglove*) seáw mid rosan seáwe, Lch. i. 268, 5. Þicgen þā mettas ðe gód seáw wyrcen, ii. 226, 12. [v. *N. E. D.* sew.]

**seax.** **I.** *add* :—Gyf þē syxes genyódige, þonne snīð þu mid þínum fingre ofer þonne ōþerne, swylce þu cyrfan wille, Tech. ii. 123, 3. Ðā gesæt hē (*Cuthbert*) æt mýsan, micclum onbryrd hē beseah tó heofonum, and his sex āwearp (*cultellus quem tenebat decidit in mensam*, Vit. Cuth. c. 34), Hml. Th. ii. 150, 23. v. ǣder-, græf-, mete-, wīngeard-, writ-seax.

**Seaxe.** *Add :* v. Middel-Seaxe : **Seaxisc.** v. Sūþ-Seaxisc.

**sécan.** **I** 3. *add* :—Hié sōhtun ꝥ soecað ðec tó stǣnenna *quaerebant te lapidare*, Jn. R. L. 8, 11. **I** 3 a. *add* :—þa. *with prep., to seek* after, *try to provide* for :—Sēc(e) man on cwicum ceápe ymbe mínre sāwle þearfe, swā hit beón mæge, and swā hit eác gerysne sý, C. D. ii. 117, 1. **I** 4. *add* :—Hit is smeálíce and geornlíce tó sēccanne (sēceanne, *v. l.*) *sunt subtiliter occulta perscrutanda*, Past. 151, 11. **I** 4 a. *with prep. to enquire* about :—Of ðisse gē soecas bitwih iów *de hoc quaeritis inter uos*, Jn. R. L. 16, 19. **I** 5. *add* :—Þǣr bið sōht fram ānra gehwylcum hwæt hē yfeles gedyde oðþe gōdes, Verc. Först. 148, 15. **II** 1. *add* :—Hē gelōmlíce tó him cōm and hine sōhte on Norðhymbra mǣgðe *frequenter ad eum in prouinciam Nordanhymbrorum ueniebat*, Bd. 3, 22 ; Sch. 290, 20. **II** 2. *add* :—On ealra ðǣra manna gewitnesse ðe sēceað geármorkett tó Stōwe, C. D. iv. 291, 19. Þ folc gewurðode þā hālgan and gelōme sōhton mid geleáfan þider. Hit gelamp þā on fyrste þā þa þ folc þider sōhte tó þām micclan screfe, Hml. S. 35, 331–334. Sēcan *frequentemus*, An. Ox. 56, 314. **II** 3. *add* :—Hē healdeð Meotudes ǣ . . . and gebedu sēceð, Ph. 458. Hý fæsten lufiað . . . and gebedu sēcað, Gú. 781. Secge wē . . . þ þā beón fordōne þe ðæne drýcræft sēcað, Hml. S. 17, 113. Ðu symle furðor feohtan sōhtest, Vald. 1, 18. **III.** *add* :—Hié Læcedemonie mid gefeohte sōhton, Ors. 3, 1 ; S. 98, 11. Darius hié mid gefeohte sēcan wolde, 2, 5 ; S. 78, 23. v. þurh-sēcan.

**-sēcendlic.** v. ā-sēcendlic : **secg** *sedge. Add :* v. rysc-secg : **secg** *a man. Add :* [v. *N. E. D.* segge.]

**secgan.** **I.** *add* :—þe lǣs þe hig sæggon, 'Hwǣr is heora god ?,' Ps. L. 78, 10. **II** 2. *add* :—Cirus, Persa cyning, þe wē ǣr beforan sægdon *Cyrus, rex Persarum, quem superius commemoraveram*, Ors. 2, 4 ; S. 72, 22. **IV.** *add* :—Ðǣm welwillendum is tó sǣcganne, ðæt . . ., Past. 230, 10. **V.** *add* :—Hēr sægað ymb ðās mǣrau gewyrd, Verc. Först. 96, 3. **VI.** *add* :—Secge him mon swíðe gedæftelíce for his āgnum scyldum *modis congruentibus de proprio reatu feriendus est*, Past. 185, 12. **VII.** *add* :—Ic nǣfre gīt ne gemētte goldhord swā swā gē mē on secgað, Hml. S. 23, 668. v. full-, wiþsecgan ; un-sægd.

**secgend.** *Add :* v. on-secgend : **-secgende.** v. un-āsecgende : **-secgendlic, -líce.** v. ā-secgendlic, -líce : **secg-rōf.** *Add :* cf. stæf-rōf : **sēdan.** *Add :* cf. un-āsēdendlic : **seddan.** *Add :* [*Icel.* seðja.]

**Sedlingas.** *Add : In* Ps. Cant. 67, 32 (*not* 34) redlingum *is printed : in* Ps. Cam. Wēdlingum *is suggested, as if* Æthiopia *had been connected or confused with* inopia.

**sefa.** *Add* :—Fífte wæs gyfe pund, þauon hym wæs geseald sefa and geðang (cf. sefan, sídne geþanc, Dan. 536), Mod. Lang. Rev. xi. 215.

**sef-full.** v. un-seffull.

**séft-lic ;** *adj. Easy, luxurious* :—Ungemetlíce ríclíc and séftlíc lýf, Solil. H. 38, 3.

**séftness.** *Add:*—Mid heálicre sēf[t]nysse stæfne *cum summę tranquilitatus uoce,* Angl. xiii. 396, 436.

**-segendness.** v. á-segendness.

**segl.** **I.** *add:*—Þæt scip wæs ealne weg yrnende under segle, Ors. 1, 1; S. 19, 34. Æfter siextegum daga þæs þe ðæt timber ácorfen wæs, þær wæron xxx and c. gearora ge mid mæste ge mid segle, 4, 6; S. 172, 5. **III.** *add:*—Segl *larbarum,* Wrt. Voc. ii. 70, 40. Segel *labarum* (Hpt. Gl. 456, 69 *has* segen), An. Ox. 2130.

**seglan.** *Add:*—Witodlíce ðú becymst tó Rómebyrig, ofer sǽ ðú seglast (*equidem Roman ingressurus es, mare transiturus,* Gr. D. bk. 2, c. 15), Hml. Th. ii. 168, 31. v. ge-siglan, ofer-seglian.

**segl-gird.** *In* l. 7 *after* 'antemnas' *insert* Wrt. Voc. ii., *and add:*—Segelgyrdum *antemnis,* An. Ox. 38, 1.

**seglung** *sealing.* v. in-seglung.

**segnian.** **I.** *add:*—Hé his hand úp áhóf and sēnode hine sylfne, and þus cwæð, 'God Ælmihtig gebletsige mē,' Hml. S. 23, 521. 'Segna þē, and sete þe on þ tácen ðære hálgan róde.' Hé cwæð, 'Ic wille mē segnian, ac ic ne mæg' 'Signum tibi sanctae crucis imprime'. *Respondebat dicens,* 'Volo me signare, sed non possum,' Gr. D. 325, 3-4. **II.** *add:*—Æfter gereorde Crīst bletsode hūsel ... Hí æton þæt lamb æfter ðám ealdan gewunan, and hé syððan sóna sēnode hūsel, Hml. Th. ii. 244, 30.

**segnung.** *Add:*—Benedictus áþenede his handa and áwrát Crīstes róde tácn, and þ fæt mid þære ylcan sēnunge hē tóbræc *extensa manu Benedictus signum crucis edidit, et vas eodem signo rupit,* Gr. D. 105, 4.

**seht.** *Add:* v. twi-seht: **sehtan.** *Add:* v. twi-sehtan: **sehtness.** *Add:* v. twi-, un-sehtness: [seim]. *Add:* [v. *N. E. D.* seam *fat.*]

**sēl;** *adv.* **I.** *add:*—Hé gebæd for hine, and him wæs sóna sǽl (sēl, *v. l.*); and hé hine þá genam *oravit, moxque illum melius habentem tulit,* Gr. D. 247, 25. **VI.** *add:*—Næs him ealles ná þe sēl þæs þe hé georne hēdde, Hml. S. 23, 638.

**seld.** **I.** *add:*—Þá preóstas þises apostolican seldes (*sedis*), Gr. D. 34, 30; 38, 8. v. winter-seld.

**seldan.** *Add:*—Ðá reáferas geðenceað swíðe oft hū micel hié sellað, and swíðe seldun (-on, *v. l.*) hē willað gemunan hū micel hié nimað, Past. 342, 15.

**seld-cūþ.** *Add:* **I.** *strange:*—Uppon Scē Michaeles mæssan ætýwde án selcūð steorra on æfen scýnende and sóna tó setle gangende, Chr. 1097; P. 233, 27. **II.** *various, different, not of one kind:*—Hé forgeaf ælcum ðæra wyrhtena seltcūð gereord, and heora nán ne cūðe ððres sprǣce tócnáwan (cf. *confundamus linguam eorum,* Gen. 11, 7), Hml. Th. i. 318, 19. Selcúþe reáf *varias uestes,* Coll. M. 27, 9. Hé geswác ðæs dihtes ðæs deóplican cræftes, swá ðæt hé selcúðe (*different from those already created*) syððan scyppan nolde, ac ðá ylcan geedníwian, Hex. 20, 15. Ðá reahte hē mislicu and selcúð þing (*multa ac varia*), Solil. H. 3, 2. [v. *N. E. D.* selcouth.]

**selden;** *adj. Rare, infrequent:*—Seldene synd frýnd þá þe oð ende wuniað leófe *rari sunt amici qui usque ad finem existant cari,* Scint. 197, 18. [v. *N. E. D.* seldom; *adj.*]

**seld-lic.** *Add:* v. fregen-seldlic.

**seld-sīne.** *Add:*—Dearle seldsēne is ðæt þá (þe) welan ágniað tó reste ōnettom *rarum est ut qui diuitias possident ad requiem tendunt* (Scint. 183, 9), E. S. viii. 473, 33. [v. *N. E. D.* seldseen. *O. H. Ger.* selt-sáni : *Ger.* selt-sam.]

**sele.** *Add:* v. ge-, máþm-, feld-, þæc-sele.

**selen.** **I.** *add:*—Se cásere dælde his cempum cynelice sylene, Hml. Th. ii. 502, 5. Se cásere began tó gifenne ælcum his cempum cynelice sylene (gifu, *v. l.*), Hml. S. 31, 97. v. ge-, gild-selen.

**seleness.** v. eft-, ge-seleness.

**self.** **A.** **I** ð. *add:*—Gif þú geótendædre ne mæge áwríþan, genim þ selfe blód þe of yrnð, Lch. ii. 148, 17. **II** I a:—Hió seulf, C. D. B. ii. 146, 29. Hé eardode ána mid him sylfum, Gr. D. 105, 29. Wē magon cweþan þ sē wære mid him sylfum þe gesæd is on ðám godspelle þ hé fæder forlēte and feorr land sóhte, 106, 24. **II** I γ:—Nú wille ic þ þú sitte þē sylf on þínre cytan, Hml. S. 33, 167. **II** a. *add: with* ágen:—Hé hine forlēt tó his águes sylfes dóme, Gr. D. 13, 20. **III** a:—Gif his hwá sié lustfull máre tó witanne, sēce him þonne self þæt, Ors. 3, 2; S. 100, 27. **IV**:—'Hwæt dēstú gif ic tómergen middeges gebíde?' Hé cwæð, 'Sylf ic swelte þonne' *what will you do if I live to see midday tomorrow? He said, 'I will kill myself if you do,'* Hml. S. 3, 591. Þá habbað him sylf cyning, Ors. 1, 1; S. 20, 1. Ægðer ge hié self wēndon ge ealle ðá neáhþeóda þ hié ofer hié ealle mehte anwald habban, 3, 1; S. 96, 6: Bd. pref. : Sch. 4, 12. **B.** *add:*—Genim þás wyrte sylfe gecnucude (cf. genim þás ylcan wyrte swá wē ær cwædon gecnucude, 5), Lch. i. 322, 2. **C.** *translating solus:*—Willa on him sylf oferprút ys *uoluntas in eis sola superba est,* Scint. 183, 11. For sylfre ídelre gilpince *pro sola inani gloria,* 144, 11. Gif æfter woruld sweltende þ sylfe dēmde on heortan geglađað *si secundum saeculum moriens quod solum decreuit corde delectatur,* 216, 8.

**self-cwala, an;** *m. A suicide:*—Wē sceolan witan þ nán sylfcwala,

---

þ is ágenslaga, ne becymð tó Godes ríce, O. E. Hml. i. 296, 14. Sylfcwalan and hǣðene men ne ðurfon tó þám dóme; ac hié bióð sóna fordēmede, Verc. Först. 172. Sylfcwalan *biothanatas,* An. Ox. 7, 181.

**self-dēmere** *with the same meaning as* self-dēma, *q. v.* :—Sylfdēmera *sarabaitorum,* R. Ben. I. 10, 6. Sylfdēmerum *sarabaitis,* 11, 4.

**self-lic.** *Add:*—Sylflicre lu[fe] *ultroneo affectu,* An. Ox. 56, 110.

**self-wendlíce** *under one's own direction,* **self-wildlíce** *under one's own control.* Cf. wealdes. v. self-willendlíce.

**self-wille.** *Add:*—Sylfwille wurðmynt Gode *spontanea honor Deo,* Hml. S. 8, 204. Sylfwilles þeówdómes *voluntarie seruitutis,* An. Ox. 236: 1509. Mid sylfwillum lufum *ultroneis affectibus,* 1233.

**self-willendlíce;** *adv. According to one's own will* or *desire:*—Hé hæfde ānne sunu ... þone hé lufode swíþe líchamlíce and fēdde selfwillendlíce (seolfweldlíce, selfwendlíce, *v. l.*) *filium habuit, quem nimis carnaliter diligens remisse nutriebat;* he brought him up to have his own way, Gr. D. 289, 5.

**self-willes.** (1) *add:*—Wē sceolan beón eádmóde, wille wē, nelle wē, and hē wolde sylfwilles ús syllan ðá bysne, Hml. S. 16, 121. Scealt þú þínes unþances þone hord āmeldian þe þú sylfwilles ǣr noldest cýðan, 23, 716. Syl(f)willes *ultronea* (Victoria ... *ultronea* spospondit se ... pulsaturam, Ald. 69, 15), An. Ox. 4862.

**sellan.** **I.** *add:*—Nim þá fífe and syle Martio, Angl. viii. 303, 30. **III.** *add:*—Sē ðe sylð drinc eów calic fulne wæteres, Mk. 9, 41. Eal þ flæsc þ wildeór lǣfen, ne eten gē þ, ac sellað hit hundum, Ll. Th. i. 54, 2. **IV** b. *add:*—Þæt man hláf sealde tó ceápe, Hml. S. 23, 563. **IV** d. *add:*—Hig sealdon þæt on tigelwyrhtena æcyr, Mt. 27, 10. **V** a. *add:*—Man bróhte his heáfod on ánum disce and sealde þám mædene; and þæt mæden hyre mēder, Mt. 14, 11.

**sellend-lic;** *adj. To be given;* dandus:—Ða ðe nǣfre gystas on hūsærne onfóð, búton sellendlíces gysthúses mēd ǣr ápinsod sý (*nisi prius dandi hospitii merces compensetur*), Chrd. 102, 1. Swá hwylce swá wēnað þ sóð lufu sý on anfóndlicum and sellendlicum þingum (*dandis atque accipiendus rebus*), ná hwōnlíce dweliað, 110, 8.

**seltan** *to salt.* v. siltan.

**sēma.** *Add:*—Sum wer wæs on þyssere ylcan byrig, þæs nama wæs Aduocatus, sē wæs sēma and ríhtend manigra manna (*the Latin is:* Quidam aduocatus in hac urbe), Gr. D. 297, 6.

**semnend(-ed)-lic;** *adj. Sudden:*—Slagen mid sæmnedlicre (semnendlicre, *v. l.*) blindnesse *subita caecitate percussus,* Gr. D. 235, 3. In þære færlican (symnenlican and færlican, *v. l.*) wafunge *in subito stupore,* 284, 23. v. samnunga.

**senatus.** *Add:*—Mid þára senata (senatuses, *v. l.*) willan *voluntate senatus,* Ors. 4, 10; S. 202, 20. For þára senatum ege, 5, 9; S. 232, 28.

**sencan.** *Add:* v. for-sencan.

**send, e;** *f. A present:*—Ne sí munece ālýfed þæt hē ænig gewrit oþþe sende oðþe lác from hyra mágum oþþe from ænigum óþrum men underfón *nullatenus liceat monacho neque a parentibus suis neque quoquam hominum litteras, eulogias, vel quelibet munuscula accipere,* R. Ben. 87, 11. Cf. sand.

**sendan.** **I** b. *add:* (b β) where a thing is personified :—Ic (*a storm*) ... wrecan on wáþe wíde sended, Rä. 2, 11. **III.** *add:*—Hē on ǣnne lytelne calic sende sumne ðǣl þæs líchaman and þæs blódes úres Drihtnes, Hml. S. 23 b, 659. Þá sende seó heofen níwne steorran, Hml. Th. i. 298, 26. **IV** b. *add:*—God him sende ufan greáte hagolstánas, Jos. 10, 11. **IV** c. *add:*—Ne wēne gē þ ic cóme sybbe on eorðan tó sendanne; ne cóm ic sybbe tó sendanne, ac swurd, Mt. 10, 34.

**sengan.** *Add:* figuratively, *to afflict grievously:*—Ic senged beóm *tribulor,* Ps. Rdr. 30, 10. Cf. seóþan.

**seó.** *Add:*—Wurdon his eágan yfele gehefegode ... mid swíðlicum myste, swá þ his seón swýðe þeóstrodon, Hml. S. 31, 588.

**seóc.** *Add:* v. ádl- (E. S. xxxix. 322), lenden-, wēden(d)-, wōd-seóc.

**seócan;** *p.* seóc. *To be ill:*—Þysum cnihte seócendum (*aegrotanti*) and forneáh tó his ænde gelæddum, Gr. D. 338, 24. [v. *N. E. D.* sick. *vb. Goth.* siukan.]

**seóc-mód;** *adj. Not strong-minded:*—Hræce hē and snýte bæftan him, and þæt fortrede, þe lǣs hit seócmódum (*infirmis mentibus*) bróþrum and císum wyrðe tó wlættan, Chrd. 23, 9.

**seócness.** *Add:*—Mid godcundum dihte byð gedón þæt lengtogran leahtras seócnyss (*egrotatio*) lengre bærnð, Scint. 161, 19.

**seód.** *Add:*—Þurs ɫ seód *fiscus,* An. Ox. 18 b, 36. Hē nán þing him sylfum of his campdómes scipe on his seóde ne heóld búton þ hé dæghwámlíce tó bigleofan hæfde, Hml. S. 31, 55.

**seófian.** l. seofian, *and add:* v. un-seofiende.

**seofon.** *Add: when used without an immediately following noun the nominative is* seofon *or* seofone. (1):—þ fiscas sēlaes fyllu, sifu sēlas hronaes fyllu, sifu hronas hualaes fyllu, An. Ox. 54, 1. Þæra eádigra seofon slǣpera ðrowung, Hml. S. 23, 1. Ne secge ic þe oð seofon (seofun, R., seofo, L.) síðas, ac oð seofon hundseofontigon síðon, Mt. 18, 22. (1 a) *in combination with decades:*—Twá hundredum and seofon and sixtigum fíftýne geúres getel, An. Ox. 3036. (2):—

þǽra diácona wæs se forma Stephanus . . . þā oðre six wǽron . . . Ðās seofon hī gecuron, Hml. Th. i. 44, 18. Fífe lǽgun . . . swilce seofene eác, eorlas Anláfes, Chr. 937; P. 108, 11. Sume menn þisra seofona hēddon, Hml. S. 23, 137. (2 a) where age is marked:—Wæs ān twelf geára, ōþer nigan geára, and se þridda seofan geára, Shrn. 58, 12. (3) forming part of an ordinal:—On ðǽm siofan-and-hundsiofantiogoðan psalme, Past. 465, 4. Se seofan-and-hundeahtatigeða, R. Ben. 37, 18. (4) the abstract number seven:—Twía seofon beóð feówertýne, Angl. viii. 302, 45.

**seofon-getel**, es; n. Seven of anything:—Seofengetelum ebdomadibus, An. Ox. 1533.

**seofonhund-wintre**; adj. Seven hundred years old:—Hē wæs seofonhundwintre and seofon-and-hundseofontigwintre, Gen. 5, 31.

**seofon-nihte**. Add: lasting seven days:—Mid seofonnihte fæstenne, Hml. S. 31, 1284.

**-seofontig**. Add: v. un-seofontig.

**seofoþa**. Add:—Siofoðe, Past. 41, 19.

**seohhe**. v. ele-seohhe: **seohhian** to strain[:—þurh cláð geseohhod (-seohgod, v. l.), E. S. 49, 353.] v. seón.

**seoh-torr**. Dele, and see next word.

**seohtre**. For 'pipe . . . directed' substitute: ditch, and add: seohtra, an: **seohter**, es; m.—Ondlong ðæs sihtran in ðone ealdan secgmōr, C. D. vi. 218, 22. On cytan seohtres ford, v. 374, 22–23. On seohteres heáfod; of þām seohtere, C. D. B. iii. 624, 20. Æt otansihtre, C. D. i. 216, 27. Ofer ðone cnol tō ðæn seohtore tō þrubrōce, iii. 451, 14. Tō ðām fūlan siðre; of ðone fūlan siðre on ðæt dīc, v. 304, 24. [On sihterwīc, vi. 56, 16.] [Sichter a watercourse, gutter, Jellinghaus.] v. mōr-seohtre, and cf. sicerian.

**seoleþ**. Take here the passage given under seolh-ýða (?).

**seolfor-hammen**. v. -hammen: **seolfor-hilt**. Add: -hilte. Cf. fealo-hilte: **seolfring**. v. sylfring.

**seolh**; gen. seóles. Add:—Þæs nama is Seólesíg (Sýleseá, v. l.) quod dicitur Latine insula uituli marini, Bd. 4, 13; Sch. 521, 10. Ðā cōmon twēgen seólas of sǽlicum grunde, and hī mid heora flýse his fēt drýgdon, and mid heora blǽde his leoma beðedon venere duo de profundo maris quadrupedia, quae vulgo lutrae vocantur. Haec anhelitu suo pedes ejus fovere coeperunt, ac uillo satagebant extergere (Vit. Cuth. Sch.), Hml. Th. ii. 138, 11. Seólas simones, An. Ox. 41, 2. .vii. fiscas sēlaes fyllu, sifu sēlas hronaes fyllu, 54, 1. [Seólesburne, seólescumb. v. C. D. vi. 332.]

**seolh-wǽd** (?), **-pǽd** (?). l. seolh-pæþ. The facsimile reprint of the codex Vercellensis has seolhpaðu.

**seolh-ýða** (?). v. seoleþ.

**seolucen**. Add:—Seolcen bombicinum (peplum), An. Ox. 460. Seoloken toppa serica pensa, 23, 44. Swā seolcen ðrǽd, 26, 73: Hml. S. 32, 179.

**seomian**. (1) add:—Ā his lof standeð mycel and mǽre ond his miht seomaþ ēce and edgiong ofer eall gesceaft, Hpt. 33, 73, 27. (2) add:—Heó wæs gestelled mid līchamlicre mettrumnesse and seonode (seomode, ?) laman legre and mauega gǽr wæs hleoniende in hire bedde molestia corporali percussa est, multisque annis in lectulo decubans, Gr. D. 2842.

**seón** to see. Add: I 2 a. with an infinitive that has no subject:—Ic seah rǽpingas in ræced fergan, Rä. 53, 1. III. add: the imperative used exclamatorily:—Seh þē ecce (Lanc. sithee), Ps. Vos. 7, 15. v. ā-, wiþ-seón.

**seón** to strain. Dele: v. ge-seón, and add: p. seáh (v. þurh-seón). v. be-seón: **-seónd**. v. fore-seónd: **-seóness**. v. fore-seóness.

**seonu-wealt**. [In the gloss at Wrt. Voc. ii. 122, 54 perhaps torosa denotes the roundness or plumpness of a muscular object. Could it be a gloss on a passage from Ovid, torosa colla boum ?] I. add:—Sinewealtre trendla tyrnincge tereti circulorum rotunditate, An. Ox. 522. II. add:—Of sinewealtum þrǽda cliwene ex tereti filorum glomere, An. Ox. 3734. Sinewealte popelstānas rotundos lapillulos, 1813. v. healf-seonuwealt.

**-seóred**. v. ge-seúred.

**seóþan**. I. add:—Hē seáþ coquebat, Germ. 395, 391. Se dēma hēt hī lǽdan sōna and seóðan on wætere (belūcan on byrnendum baðe, Shrn. 150, 1), Hml. S. 34, 343. II 1. add:—Swā swā gold on oíne hē hiē sýð and costað in fornace probatur aurum; tu, ut sorde careas, tribulationis camino purgaris, Verc. Först. 141, 21. v. ge-seóþan; nīw-soden.

**seowian**. Add:—Ǽlces mannes miht þe on mōdignysse fǽrd is þām gelic swilce man siwige āne bytte, and blāwe hī fulle windes, and wyrce siððan ān þyrl þonne heó tōþunden bið on hire greátnysse, þonne tōgǽð seó miht, Hml. S. 34, 316.

**serc**. Add:—Þes pallium þe ic werige wyle mē gelǽstan, and mín syric ne tōsīhð, ne míne sceós ne tōbærstað, ǽr þan þe mín sáwl síðað of þām līchaman, Hml. S. 36, 161.

**sēre-mōnaþ**. v. seár-mōnaþ.

**sescle** a sixth part;—Sextula sive sescle, Angl. viii. 335, 10.

**sester**. Add:—iii. sesðlar hláfhwētes, C. D. v. 147, 15. v. gild-, healf-sester; twi-sestre: **sesðlar**. v. preceding word.

**set**. II. add: II a. a place of residence:—Tō cynelicum seton ad palatinas zetas, An. Ox. 2, 132. II. add:—Terra his terminibus circumcincta. In oriente hāmfleót, in occidente puplica strata, in aquilone hīredes seota tō prēsta tūne, C. D. ii. 102, 29. ¶ in local names:—Terrulae partem eiusdem . . . perdono, cuius uocabulum est ruminingseta, ad pastum ouium trecentorum, C. D. i. 54, 33. In loco qui uocatur hrempingwiic, et alia nomine hafingseota, . . . in uicae altere terrae qui dicitur bobingseata, 211, 11–14. IV. cultivated ground, place where something is set or planted:—On beánsetum, C. D. i. 315, 31. v. hring-, sunn-, winter-set.

**-setedness**. v. for[e]-, tō-setedness.

**seten**. I. Take ymb-seten to II. II. for Lind. l. Rush. Add: v. cwild-, hundred-seten: **-setenness**. Add: v. of-, ymb-setenness.

**sēþan**. Add:—Sēþað contendunt (eundem non defunctum), An. Ox. 8, 103. Secgende and sēðende þ him swā gelumpen, for ðan ðe he Godes templ tawode tō bysmore, Hml. S. 25, 541. v. tō-sēþan.

**set-hrægl**. Add:—Ðonne þū setrægel habban wille, þonne plice þu sīne ágene gewēda mid twām fingrum, tōsprēd þīne twā handa and wege hī swylce þū setl gesydian wille, Tech. ii. 122, 17. Kēnwolde helm and byrnan . . . and Eádgyfe his swyster . . . .i. sethrægl, Cht. Crw. 23, 22. [.viiii. setreil, C. D. B. iii. 366, 20.]

**-sēþness**. v. ge-sēþness.

**sēþung**. Add:—Þǽr wiðcwǽd . . . Defensor, ac hē weard gescynd þurh Godes sēþunge . . . Ðā weard þ folc ástyrod on swiðlicum hreáme þ Godes sylfes sēðung þǽr geswutelod wǽre, Hml. S. 31, 270–282. Gregorius ábæd æt Críste þæt hē æteðwode ānum twýnigendum wīfe embe his gerýnu mycele sēðunge, Hml. Th. ii. 272, 24. Se apostol áýdlode ealle þæs drýes sēðunge, and geswutelode ðurh wītegena sēðunge þæt Críst is sōð Godes sunu, 412, 29–414, 2: 420, 5.

**setl**. Among the cpds. dele burhgeat-, and add I a a. a seat that is the right of a member of an official society or body:—Gif ceorl geþeáh þ hē hæfde setl and sundernote on cynges healle, Ll. Th. i. 190, 17. I a. add:—Þǽr sǣton setla on ðone illic sederunt sedes in iudicio, Ps. L. 121, 5. I c. add:—Sió sunne þǽr gǽð neár on setl þonne on ōðrum lande, Ors. 1, 1; S. 24, 18. II. add:—Ān setl æt Scē Martine (cf. unam sedem in loco qui dicitur Scī Martini ecclesia et unam modicam uillulam at eandem sedem, 137, 10), Cht. E. 139, 20. Hī him bǣdon setles and eardungstōwe on heora lande petierunt in ea sibi sedes et habitationem donare, Bd. 1, 1; Sch. 11, 6. Him sylfum setl (seðel, v. l.) and eardungstōwe geāhnian sibimet sedes uindicare, Sch. 12, 12. II a. add:—Þæs apostolican seðles, Bd. 1, 23; Sch. 48, 1. III. add:—Þā ðā hē tō gange cōm and hē gesæt, þā gewand him ūt eall his innewearde æt his setle, Hml. Th. i. 290, 20. v. ceáp-, fore-, gang-, heofon-, hring-, on-, toll-, winter-setl.

**setla**. Add: v. ancor-, fōt-, land-setla.

**setl-hrægl**. Add:—Hē pann Wulfgāre his mǽge twēgra wāhrysta and twēgra setlhrægla, Cht. Crw. 23, 15.

**setlung**. I. add: I a. a session, an assembly of persons sitting:—Ætforan þǽre engelican þæs heofenlican pleghūses setlunge ante angelicum cęlestis theatri consessum, An. Ox. 1753. II. add:—Seó sunne setlunge geneálǽhð on þæs dæges geendunge, Hml. Th. ii. 76, 23: 302, 2. Ne lēt ðū ðæt yrre licgean on ðīnre heortan ofer sunnan setlunge (cf. sol non occidat super iracundiam vestram, Eph. 4, 26), Hex. 46, 14.

**setness**. v. fram-setness: setnian. v. for-, of-setnian.

**settan**. II. add: to place in or out of a condition:—Man-sette Stigant of his bisceoprīce, Chr. 1043; P. 162, 26. Ne sete þū him ðās dǣda tō synne ne statuas illis hoc peccatum, Hml. Th. ii. 34, 21. On gewrit settan, Ll. Th. i. 58, 22. III. add:—Fuglas heofnes ne settas ł sāwas volatilia caeli non serunt, Mt. L. 6, 26. On lengtene wīngeard settan, Angl. ix. 262, 8. III a. to people or garrison a place with:—Hēr drǽfde Eádgár cyng þā preóstas on Ceastre of Ealdan mynstre . . . and of Middetune, and sette hý mid munecan, Chr. 964; P. 116, 3. VI. add:—Se cāsere sette gebann, þæt wǽre on gewritum ásett eall ymbhwyrft, Hml. Th. i. 30, 1. Þā sette Boia þās spēce wið Ælfrīce; þ wes þ Putrael sealde Ælfrīce viii oxa, Cht. E. 274, 4. Hē sǣtte mycel deórfrið . . . Eác hē sǣtte be haran, þ hī mōsten freó faran, Chr. 1086; P. 221, 6–12. VIII. dele Met. 1, 4, and add:—Hwelc cynig bið fǽrende tō settanne gifeht (committere bellum) wið ōðerne cynig, Lk. R. 14, 31. X. add:—Hē sette Æþelgār abbod tō Nīwan mynstre tō abbode, Chr. 964; P. 116, 3. Þā hē bebyrged wæs hié settan him hyrdas tō, Bl. H. 177, 26. XIII. add:—Hī ūre bēc setton swā swā hī geleornodon æt heora lāreówe Críste, Hml. S. 16, 151. XIV. to proceed in a specified direction, set out:—Ðā geáxedon þ lið þ on Sandwīc læg embe Godwines fare, setton þā æfter, Chr. 1052; P. 178, 29. Setton sūðweardes sigeþeóda twā, Met. 1, 4. v. ofersettan.

**-settendlic**. v. fore-, ge-settendlic: **-setting**. v. of-setting: **-sewen**; adj. v. for-, ymb-sewen: **-sewen[n]**. v. for-sewen[n]: **-sewenlic**. v. for-, ge-, ofer-, un(?)-sewenlic: **-sewenlíce**. v. for-, ge-sewenlíce: **-sewenness**. v. for-, ofer-sewenness.

**sib(b)**; f. II. add:—God ūs lǽrð sibbe and deófol ūs lǽrð unsibbe,

Hml. A. 166, 111. **III.** *add:*—Frîne hié mon æfter hû monegum wintrum sió sibb gewurde þæs þe hié æst unsibbe wið monegum folcum hæfdon, Ors. 4, 7; S. 182, 17. **V a.** *add:*—Æfter þæm eall þeós worold geceás Agustuses frið and his sibbe, Ors. 5, 15; S. 250, 17. v. god-sibb.

**sib[b]**; *adj. Add:* v. feor-sibb.

**sibaed.** *Add:* [v. *N. E. D.* sieve, *vb. M. L. Ger.* seven: *M. H. Ger.* siben, siffen.]

**sibban** (?). *Dele,* gifeþ, *not* sifeþ, *is the reading.*

**sib-fæc.** *Add:*—Binnan syx manna sibbfæce, Wlfst. 308, 6. Sibfæce, 271, 9.

**sib-lic.** *Add: related:*—þâ siblican *agnatos,* Hpt. 31, 14, 364.

**sibling.** *Add:*—His môdor côm him tô and his siblingas (*fratres,* Mt. 12, 46), Hml. A. 31, 175. Syblinga *contribulium,* An. Ox. 6. Man ne mihte æt fruman wîfian bûton on his siblingum, Ælfc. Gen. Thw. 2, 6. Gefeoht betwux siblingum *bellum plusquam civile* . . . þæt feórðe gefeoht þe betwux freóndum bið is swîðe earmlic, Hml. S. 25, 707. Seó ehtnnys bið ealra biterost þe bið fram siblingum, Hml. Th. ii. 542, 28. Swilce hî þonne lufian heora siblingas, ðe ǽr on lîfe ne hî sylfe ne heora mâgas ne lufedon, i. 332, 30.

**-sibness.** v. ge-sibness: **sibsumness.** *Add:* v. un-sibsumness:

**sîc.** *Add:* v. mǽr-sîc.

**sican.** *Add:*—Sîcende *lactans,* Ps. Rdr. p. 289, 25. Swâ swâ sîced is ofer môdur his *sicut ablactatus est super matrem suam,* 130, 2.

**sîcan** *to sigh. Add:* [v. *N. E. D.* siche, sike].

**sicera,** an; *m. Intoxicating drink;* sicera:—Ne drincon hî . . . siceran. Sicera . . . is ælces cynnes drinc . . . þe man of druncnian mæg, Chrd. 74, 6.

**sicerian.** *Add:* cf. seohtre, seohhe.

**sicettung.** *Add:*—Hé tôgeihte þa teáras þám teárum and gemænigfealdode þa sworetunga þám siccetungum, Hml. S. 23 b, 202.

**sicle;** *adj. In bad health, sickly:*—On .ii. nihte aldne mônan þ cild, þ swâ bið âcenned, bið seóc and sîcle (unhâl, *v. l. infirmus*), Archiv cxxix. 21, 16. [v. *N. E. D.* sickle, sickly.] v. sîclian.

**sîclian.** *See preceding word.*

**sicomorus** *a sycamore:*—Hê âstâh uppan ân treów ðe is on bôcum gehâten sycomeres treów, E. S. 49, 353. Úp on ân treów *sicomorum,* Lk. 19, 4.

**sîd. II.** *add:*—On þone sîdan healh, Cht. E. 206, 26. [v. *N. E. D.* side. *Icel.* sîðr.] v. fôt-, lenden-sîd.

**-sîd.** v. îren-sîd.

**sîde.** *Add:*—Wîde and sîde geondsprang (*cujus gloria*) *longe lateque percrebruit,* An. Ox. 2839. Oþ þa ancleów sîde (*mafortes*) *talo tenus prolixius* (*dependunt*), 5336.

**sîde. I.** *add:*—Saga mê on hwæðere Adames sîdan nam ûre Dryhten ðæt tîm ðe hê ðæt wîf of geworhte, Sal. K. 198, 8. **II.** *add:*—On sîdum hûses þînes *in lateribus domus tuae,* Ps. L. 127, 3. **II a.** *the side* of a hill:—Of þǽre wîdgyllan sîdan þæs muntes *e devexo montis latere,* Gr. D. 112, 19. In þæs heán muntes sîdan, 121, 14. **III.** *add:*—Seó dene wæs weallende mid lîgum on ânre sîdan, on ôðre sîdan mid hagole and cyle, Hml. Th. ii. 350, 8. v. ge-sîdan.

**sidelîce.** *Add:* v. un-sidelîce: **-sîdian.** v. be-, ge-sîdian: **-sidu.** v. ge-sidu: **sidung.** *Take here* sydung *in Dict.*

**sîden.** *Add:*—Of ealseolcenum, sîdenum *olosericis,* An. Ox. 3161. Godewebbum, sîdenum *bombicinis,* 3162.

**sîd-wærc.** *Add: pleurisy:*—Hê wæs gehrinen mid sîdwærce (*lateris dolore*) and þurh þ tô his ænde gelæded, Gr. D. 182, 18: 297, 7.

**sifeþa.** v. Syfeða *furfurae,* An. Ox. 26, 49.

**sîgan** *to sink.* **I.** *add:*—Se beám wæs âhyld on âne healfe þ man eáðe mihte witan hwider hê sîgan wolde, Hml. S. 31, 409. **I a.** *add:*—Seó sunne sâh tô setle, Hml. S. 23, 246. **II.** *add:*—þá sâh him on þ cyrlisce folc swîðe wêdende (cf. gearn mycel menigeo tô him and ealle swîðe erre wæron, Bl. H. 223, 5), Hml. S. 31, 466. *Bellatores* . . . healdað ûrne eard wið þone sîgendne here, Ælfc. T. Grn. 20, 24. **II a.** *add:*—Gerîst hyt þ seó tîd hæbbe mearke hwænne heó tô sîge kyningum and crîstenum folce tô wurðfulre blisse, Angl. viii. 326, 13. **III.** *add:*—þ him sîge þ blôd ût þurh þone mûð, Verc. Först. 110, 10. v. be-, tô-sîgan.

**sige** *a fall. Add:* v. forþ-sige (?): **sige** (?) *aim.* v. syge.

**sige** *victory.* **I.** *add:*—Hié wæron him ondrædende þ Læcedemonie ofer hié rícsian mehten for þæm lytlan sige þe hié þa ofer hié hæfdon, Ors. 3, 1; S. 98, 18. Hié longe ymb þæt fuhton on hweorfendum sigum *bellum ancipiti statu gestum,* 3, 5; S. 106, 3. **II.** *add:*—Oft ðone geðyldegestan scamað ðæs siges ðe hê ofer ðone dióful hæfde mid his geðylde, Past. 227, 20. Sigeas *trophea,* An. Ox. 37, 9. v. ge-sig.

**sige-beácen.** *Add:*—Cymeð sigebeácen (*the Latin has* vox magna), Verc. Först. 122, 11.

**sige-fæst.** (2) *add:*—Se feónd bið sôna âfyrht for ðâm sigefæstan tâcne, Hml. S. 27, 154. v. un-sigefæst.

**-sigefæstnian.** v. ge-sigefæstnian.

**sigele,** an; *f. A necklace:*—Gyldene sigelau, Bd. 4, 23; Sch. 473, 13. v. sigle.

**sigere** (?). *Substitute:* siger, sîr, *and add:*—Siir (*printed* sur) *lurco,* Wrt. Voc. ii. 70, 41. Grundswylige, sŷr *senecio* (*here* sŷr *seems to have a meaning similar to that of* swylige, cf. swelgan), i. 68, 42. v. sîgan; **IV.**

**sigerian.** *l.* sigerian. *See preceding word:* siglan. v. seglan.

**sigle.** *Add:* sigel, e; *f.:* sigele, an; *f.:*—þâ gemêtte heó semninga under hyre hrægle gyldene (gyldne, gylden, *v. ll.*) sigele (sigelan, *v. l.* monile), Bd. 4, 23; Sch. 473, 13. þǽre mêder wæs on slæpe ætŷwed . . . þ hyre man stunge âne sŷle on þone bôsum, Shrn. 149, 2. Gyldenra sigella (sigila, *v. l.*), Bd. 4, 19; Sch. 450, 3.

**sigor.** *Add:*—Tô þon þ hê synderlîce sigor hæfde betwyh þám ôþrum hellegâstum *quatenus ruinae illius singularem inter ceteros palmam teneret,* Gr. D. 189, 25. *See next word.*

**sigor-fæst.** *Add:* (4) *as an epithet of men:*—Ne byð næfre nænig leán þæs sigores bûton hit sŷ mid gewinne gecampod. Hwanon beóð hâlige men sigorfæste (*victores*), nymðe hî campian wið þám searwum þæs ealdes feóndes?, Gr. D. 221, 9: 234, 2.

**sigsonte.** *For* Lchdm. i. *l.* Lch. ii., *and add:* v. stân-merce.

**siht;** *adj. Drained* (?):—On sihtre mǽde norþeweardre, C. D. iii. 430, 29. Cf. seohhe, seohtre.

**-silfran.** v. be-, ofer-seolfrian, -silfran.

**siltan.** *Add:*—Ðonne þû scealt habban wylle, þonne geþeóddum þînum þrim fingrum hryse þîne hand swylce þû hwæt seltan wylle, Tech. ii. 124, 4. v. ge-siltan.

**sîman.** *Add:*—Sŷmð *honustat,* Hpt. 31, 15, 398.

**simbel.** In *l.* 10 *for* incessablia *l.* incessabilia, *and add* —þâ þe him on siml wæron mid farende, Ors. 3, 9; S. 130, 20. Heó wunode â on symbel neáh Sancte Marian cyrican *juxta beatae Mariae ecclesiam semper manebat,* Gr. D. 283, 6. v. simble-gemaca.

**simbel-geféra.** *Add:* v. simble-gemaca.

**simbie.** *Add:* simbel. **I 1.** *add:*—þâ wæron simbel binnan Rômebyrg wuniende, Ors. 2, 4; S. 72, 2. (2) *add:*—Wê beóð þonne mid ûrum sâwlum êce symle earme oððe eádige, Wlfst. 145, 13.

**simble-gemaca,** an; *m. One of a pair of living creatures, a mate:*—Ic gegaderige in tô þê of deórcynne and of fugelcynne symblegemacan (symble gemacan ?), þæt hî eft tô fôstre beón, Hml. Th. i. 20, 35. Cf. sin-hîwan.

**sin** *sight. Add: a sight, spectacle.* [O. H. Ger. -siuni.] v. wæfer-, wlite-, wundor-, ymb-sîn.

**sin** *his. Add:*—Æteúwdæ se Hælend sînum ambehtum, Jn. L. 21, 14.

**-sin.** v. on-sîn.

**sinc.** ¶ *add:*—Se sêlesða sinces brytta (sincbrytta, *v. l.*) Ælfryd mid Englum, Gr. D. 2, 15.

**sinc-brytta.** *See preceding word:* **sinc-weorþung.** *Add:* Cf. hord-, hring-weorþung: **-sine.** *Add:* v. seld-, þurh-sîne: **sineht.** *l.* siniht(e): **-sînes.** v. eág-, wiþer-sînes.

**singal. II.** *add:* (1) *of a person or action, assiduous, unremitting:*—Micelum framaþ gebed rihtwîses singal (*assidua*), Scint. 30, 14. On bebodum his syngal (*assiduus*) beó þu, 66, 11. On hâlgum spæcum singal, 220, 2. Singalre *crebra* (*lectionis assiduitate*), An. Ox. 11, 163. Ðæt môd nænig tô singale sorge hit self tô behealdanne *si a circumspectionis sollicitudine cor destituitur,* Past. 431, 8. (2) *of other things:*—Singal *perpes,* An. Ox. 508. **III.** *add:*—Fram swâ miclum cwylmnessum and swâ singalum (*diutinis*) onlŷsed beón, Bd. 4, 9; Sch. 396, 11.

**-singalian.** v. ge-singalian.

**singal-lic;** *adj. Constant, assiduous:*—Hê sceal geleornian ðæt hê gewunige tô singallecum gebedum, Past. 61, 21.

**singallîce.** *Add:*—Sâwl seó nâ sinngallîce (*assidue*) byð fêd mid Godes worde, Scint. 50, 17.

**-singallician.** v. ge-singallician.

**singal-ness.** *Add:*—Syngalnesse tô gebidanne *adsiduitatem orandi,* Chrd. 105, 12.

**singal-ryne.** *Add:* Cf. singal-flôwende.

**singan. I 1 a.** *add:* (a) *of the reciting of a charm:*—þis gebed man sceal singan on ðâ blacan blegene, Lch. iii. 40, 8: 42, 7: 294, 7. (β) *of playing on an instrument:*—Wê sungon eów be hearpan and ge ne saltadun *cantavimus uobis tibiis, et non saltastis,* Lk. 7, 32. **I 3.** *add:*—Man ledde tô his breóstum brâde îsene clûtas swîðe glôwende þ hit sang ongeán, Hml. S. 37, 163. v. under-singan; lof-singende.

**sin-grêne;** *adj. Ever-green:*—Ne feald þær næfre leáf of, ac â hê bið singrêne, E. S. viii. 477, 15.

**-sin-hîwen.** v. ge-sinhîwen: **sin-hweorfende.** *Add:*—Sinhwyrfende, An. Ox. 114.

**sin-niht;** *f. Substitute:* sin-nihte, es; *n.:*—Gârsecg þeahte sweart synnihte *blackest darkness covered ocean,* Gen. 118. þær eów is hâm sceapen, sweart sinnehte *there is a home assigned you, black darkness,* Gû. 650. Hê geseah deorc gesweorc semian sinnihte sweart under heofonum *he saw dark cloud lower, black night under heaven,* Gen. 109.

sin-ræden[n]. *Add:*—Đá þe bióð gebundne mid sinrædenne, Past. 18, 18.

sinscipe. *Add:* (1) of lawful wedlock:—Sume þá apostolas hæfdon him gemacan . . . Ac hí sóna geswicon þæs sinscipes syþþan hí Crístes láre geleornodon æt him, Hml. A. 14, 35. Þí wunodon ætgædere gehíwodum synscipe, Hml. S. 35, 123. (2) of illicit intercourse:—Heródes áwearp his rihtǽwe, and forligerlíce mánfulles sincipes breác, Hml. Th. i. 478, 29. v. riht-sinscipe.

-sinsciplic, -sinscippan. v. ge-sinsciplic, -sinscippan: sin-tredende. v. sin-trendende.

sin-trendende. *Substitute for citation:*—Sintrendende, sinhwyrfende *teretes, rotundos,* An. Ox. 114. [*The same word is glossed by* sintredende *in* Hpt. Gl. 408, 23. Cf. (?) tredan *terere.*]

sirwan. II. (1) *dele last passage, and add:* (α) *to devise* a plan:—Serwi(ende) *molientes (aliud argumenti genus),* An. Ox. 2939. (β) *to lie in wait for, to ambush:*—Hér seó ungeþwærnes þá mægnu syrwde and gehæfte *discordia virtutibus insidiatur et capitur,* Prud. 78 a. (1 a) with infin. (?):—Syrewiaþ *moliuntur,* i. *cogitant (ingruere),* An. Ox. 889. Líccitan sirewede *insimulare machinaretur,* i. *moliretur,* 2946. Heó serewede *moliretur (evertere),* 3446. (3 b) *add:*—Hé wæs mid hlóþum on hí hergende, and onbútan sierwende, Ors. 3, 7; S. 118, 19. (3 c) *add:*—Þá lúdéiscan þe syrwdon be Críste, Hml. S. 27, 177. (3 c a) *to plot* about a matter:—Antigones and Perðica gebeótedan þæt hié woldon him betweónum gefeohtan, and longe ymb þæt siredon hwær hié hié gemétan wolden, Ors. 3, 11; S. 144, 35. v. á- (?), ymb-sirwan.

síþ. IV. *add:*—Áhwerfedum síþe *versa vice,* An. Ox. 592. V. *add:*—Hé cóm tó his bréðer, and his síð be endebyrdnysse sæde, Hml. Th. ii. 358, 25. VII 1. *add:*—Ǽne síþa *semel,* Ps. Srt. 61, 12 : 88, 36. v. for-, geon-, heóf-? (heów-) síþ; í-síþes.

[síþ]. ¶ *add:*—Æt síðestan, Ll. Th. i. 124, 22.

síþ; *adv.* The word shows a comparative form without a comparative ending. v. Sievers, § 323.

-síþa. v. mid-gesíþa.

síþe. *Add:*—Ðis synd ðá londgemǽra . . . á be ðan wuda swá sulh and síðe hit gégán mæge (*as far as it can be ploughed or mown*), C. D. iii. 458, 20. Ðá cóm se Godes wer gesceód mid geclútedum scón and bær his síðe (*falcem fenariam*) on his eaxle, Gr. D. 37, 14. v. hígsíþe.

síþegian. v. mid-síþegian.

síþ-fæt. III. *add:*—Ǽghwylc crísten mann smeáge on him sylfum hú nearo se síðfæt bið þære synfullan sáwle, Verc. Först. 138, 15. Þára rihtwísra wæg is gerihtlǽced, and þæra hálgena síðfæt is gegearcod *uia justorum recta facta est, et iter sanctorum preparata est,* Hml. S. 2, 62. On síðfætum þínum *in semitis tuis,* Ps. L. 16, 5.

síþian. *Add:* ge-, samod-síþian; eft-síþgende (eft síþgende (?), Wrt. Voc. ii. 77, 31).

síþ-lǽdness. *Dele.* v. wiþ-lǽdness: síþ-stappel. *Add:* Cf. fótstappel.

siþþan. I. *add:*—Hé wolde ðá ealdan ǽ ǽr gefyllan, and siððan ðá níwan gecýðnysse onginnan, Hml. Th. ii. 244, 28 : Chr. 690; P. 40, 11. Þæt sind ǽrest heofonas . . . and syððan þeós eorðe, Hml. Th. i. 276, 11. II. *add:* correlative, *when . . . then:*—Siþþan Metellus þá elpendas ofercóm, siþþan hé hæfde eác raðe þæt óþer folc gefliémed *Metellus prius belluas vel in fugam vel in mortem egit, et sic magnam vim hostium superavit,* Ors. 4, 6; S. 178, 2–3.

-sitt. v. on-sitt.

sittan. I. *add:*—Swá micle swá sé bið beforan ðe on ðǽm stóle sitt ðǽm óðrum ðe ðǽr ymb stondað, Past. 435, 27. I a. *to sit on an animal, to ride:*—Þá hé on þám horse sæt *when he was riding on the horse,* Bd. 3, 14; Sch. 257, 10. Weard his hors ofslagen þe hé on sæt *the horse he was riding was killed,* Chr. 1079; P. 214, 6. Wæs his þeáw þ hé wolde sittan on þám horse þe hé mihte findan forcúþlocost, Gr. D. 34, 9. Þúhte unc þ wit gesǽgon sittan twégen men on twám olfendum and þá efstan mid þære mǽstan hrædnesse, Hml. A. 206, 361. Him cóm ongeán se ealda feónd sittende on ánum múle on læces ansýne, Gr. D. 161, 1. I b. *add:*—Hié hiene médigne on cneówum sittende métton, Ors. 3, 9; S. 134, 31. I d. of an animal at rest:—Geseah hé þær ánne pytt and þreó heorda sceápa sittende (*accubantes*) wið þone pytt, Gen. 29, 2. II a. *add:*—Siþþan sǽton þá Gotan þær on lande, Ors. 6, 38; S. 298, 3. Godwine eorl and Harold and seó cwén sǽton on heora áre, Chr. 1052; P. 182, 7. Bútan hié þá burg forléten, and þ nán ne sǽte hiere x mílum neáh, Ors. 4, 13; S. 210, 22. Gemong him mid sibbe sittan to settle *peaceably amongst them,* 2, 8; S. 94, 10: 6, 34; P. 290, 23. Þæt folc sum hé þǽr sittan lét, sum þonan ádrǽfde *some of the people he left where they were, some he expelled,* 3, 9; S. 126, 15. (a 1):—His here . . . sum ymb þá burg sæt, Ors. 3, 7; S. 116, 16. Ðǽr se consul on firde sætt *where the consul was encamped,* Ors. 4, 10; S. 198, 12. Hí x geár ymbe þá burg (*Troy*) sittende wǽron and feohtende, 1, 11; S. 50, 13. (b):—Be blǽdrum ðe on mannes nebbe sittað, Lch. i. 86, 6. III. *add:*—Þær sæt on þám lande swýðe swýþlic hungor *vehemens fames incubuerat,* Gr.

D. 251, 10. Þær on sæt mycel hunger, 145, 5. Heofonflód micel on sæt (set, *v. l.*), Bd. 3, 24; Sch. 309, 16. Þeáh ðe him ádl on ne sitte, Hml. Th. i. 614, 16. III a. of an approaching time which hinders action:—Þone ceorl hí ne mihton byrgan, for þon þe him se ǽfen on sæt (*superveniente vespere*), Gr. D. 215, 18. Þá þá seó mætetíd cóm and eallinga seó læteste tíd þæs dæges on sæt *cum tempus refectionis incumberet atque dies hora tardior excrevisset,* 277, 25. V. *add:*—Ðá wæs tú geár þ hé þ bysceopsetl swá sæt and heóld *duobus annis in episcopatu peractis,* Bd. 4, 29; Sch. 526, 19. Hé þ bysceopsetl sæt and heóld *episcopalem cathedram seruat,* 5, 12; Sch. 632, 5.

-sittend. v. hring-, on-sittend: -sittende. *Add:* v. heáh-sittende.

six. *Add:* I. as adjective (1) with a subst. expressed:—Siex míla from ðære byrig, Ors. 2, 4; S. 70, 25. Siex mónað, 2, 8; S. 94, 2. Sex weðras, sex gósfuglas, C. D. i. 312, 8. Fato sexo (sex, L.) *hydriae sex,* Jn. R. 2, 6. Æfter dagum sex, Mt. L. R. 17, 1. Æfter dagum sexum (sex, L.), Mk. R. 9, 2. Mónoðas sexu (móneðum sex, L.) *mensibus sex,* Lk. R. 4, 25. (1 a) followed by hundred or thousand:—Siex hund gísla, Ors. 3, 8; S. 122, 3. (1 b) coupled with a higher cardinal or ordinal:—On six and feówertigon wintron (feówertig and sex winter, R., feórtig and sex uintro, L.) *quadraginta et sex annis,* Jn. 2, 20. Se six-and-syxtigeða sealm, R. Ben. 37, 6. (2) with ellipsis of subst.:—Þæra diácona wæs se forma Stephanus . . . þá óþre six wæron . . ., Hml. Th. i. 44, 15. II. as substantive, *the abstract number* six:—Eahta síðon seofon beoð syx and fíftig, Angl. viii. 303, 3. Gif eall þ getæl byþ tódǽled þurh seofen . . . gyf þær byð án ofer . . . oððe fífe oððe syxe, 46.

sixteóþa. *Add:*—Þú scealt gewítan on ðám sixteóðan geáre þæs ðe þu munuc wurde, Hml. S. 6, 80.

sixtig. *Add:*—Hé hit geeóde syxtygum wintra ǽr Crístes cyme, Bd. 1, 2; Sch. 13, 29. Feówer hunde wintrum and feówer and siextigum, Ors. 4, 1; S. 154, 2.

sixtigoþa. *Add:*—Se syx-and-syxtigeþa sealm, R. Ben. 37, 6, 16.

sixtig-feald. *Add:*—Syxtigfeald *sexagenarius,* Ælfc. Gr. Z. 285, 9: Scint. 69, 17. Sixtífealdne *sexagesimum (fructum),* An. Ox. 1407. Syxtífealdum ber[þenum] *sexagenis fasciculis,* 1407.

slá. *Add:*—Gyf þe slána lyste, þonne sete þú þínne winstran þúman on þínes lytlan fingres lið and pýt mid þínum scytefingre in þíne wynstran hand on þornes getácnunge þe hí on weaxað, Tech. ii. 124, 24.

slacian. *Add:*—Slacige, sláwige *þigeat,* An. Ox. 3094. Scleag(i)ende *torpens, pigrescens,* 18, 11. v. *N. E. D.* slake.]

slæccan. *Add:* [v. *N. E. D.* sletch.]

slæcmód-ness, e; f. *Spiritlessness, melancholy lack of energy; accidia, acedia:*—Eahta synt heáfodleahtras . . . þridde is sleacmódnes and unrótnes, Verc. Först. 173. Cf. á-solcenness.

slæd, sléd. l. slæd, sled, slead, *and add:*—Andlang slades, C. D. v. 379, 19. Sleades, 70, 26. On slade . . . eft on sled, 286, 27–34. Of sleade, iii. 384, 28. v. wæter-, wíþig-slæd.

slǽp *sleep.* *Add:*—Slépon þá mǽdene swárum slápe, Hml. S. 35, 68.

slǽp *a slippery place(?).* *Perhaps* slæp *should be read.* v. *N. E. D.* slap.

slǽp-ærn. *Add:*—Slæpyrne *dormitorio,* Chrd. 55, 26.

slǽp-drenc, es; m. *A sleeping-draught:*—Slǽpdrenc; rædic, hymlic, wermód, belone, cnuca ealle þá wyrte, dó in ealað, Lch. iii. 22, 27.

slǽtan. *Add:* [v. *N. E. D.* sleat; slate.]

slaga. *Add:*—Hé tó þám ylpe cóm, and . . . stung hine æt ðám nafelan þ hí lágon ðǽr bégen heora ǽgðer óðres slaga, Hml. S. 25, 587. Him geweard þ man funde níwe swurd and níwne slagan (*executioner*) þærtó, Hml. S. 12, 233.

slápere. *Add:*—Þá gedwyldmen man hæt on Grécisc Nictates, and on úre geþeóde hí man mæg sláperas hátan (*somniculosi vocantur*), Chrd. 26, 3.

slápol. *Add:*—Ne scealt þú nǽfre beón ne tó slápol ne tó sláw, Angl. xii. 516, 33.

slá-wyrm. *Add:*—Eal swá sláwyrm (*regulus*) áttru hit tósend, Scint. 105, 9.

sleán. A. I. *add:* v. sliccan:—Sum slóh mid slecge þá hæpsan, Hml. S. 32, 202. II a. *add:*—Eald feoh þe man on fyrndagum slóh, Hml. S. 23, 614. (c) *to strike* a musical instrument, cf. hearp-slege:—Hé slóh cymbala *cymbala percussit,* Gr. D. 62, 16. IV. *add:*—Iosue hæfde sige and slóh þá hǽðenan . . . þonne hæfde Amalech sige and slóh þ Godes folc, Hml. S. 13, 15–18. V. *add:* V a. *to make a sound with the voice:*—Þone swég þára fíf clipiendra stafa sleán hí wel *sonum uocalium litterarum bene perstrepant,* Chrd. 57, 9. VI b. *add:*—Þá slógon his geféran geteld *tetenderunt tentorium,* Bd. 3, 17; Sch. 268, 1. Hié námon treówu, and slógon on óþerne ende ísene næglas, Ors. 4, 1; S. 158, 4. VII. *add:*—Sleá man of þá hand þe hé þ fúl mid worhte, Ll. Th. i, 206, 20. VIII. *add:*—Arrianus weard slagen mid sæmendlicre blindnesse, Gr. D. 235, 2. VIII a. of the action of disease:—Þá deáh þám monnum þe for fylle gihsa slihð, Lch. ii. 60, 24. Gesca slæet *singultat,* Wrt. Voc. ii. 120, 50. (*This entry is better here than at B. III, where it is given.*) B. (*intransitive*

or *absolute*) I. *add :*—Þā slōh hē ǣnes on Þ wæter . . . Þā slōh hē eft on ðone streám mid his lāreówes sciccelse *percussit semel . . . percussit fluvium magistri pallio*, Gr. D. 19, 18–26. Heó leát tō slege and hē slōh Þā tō, ac Þ swurd ne mihte būton Þā hȳde ceorfan, Þeáh Þe hē hetelíce slōge, Hml. S. 12, 211. Þeáh him mon sleá mid sweorde wiÞ Þæs heáfdes, Bl. H. 47, 13. Sē went ōÞer hleór tō sleándum, R. Ben. 28, 3. I b. *of an implement :*—Sleándre slecge *tundentis mallei*, An. Ox. ii. 70. III. *add :*—Þæt fȳr slōh ūt of ðām ofne, and forswǣlde Þā cwelleras, Hml. Th. i. 570, 16. v. mann- (?), Þurh-sleán.

**slecg.** *Add :*—Sleándre slecge *tundentis mallei*, An. Ox. 11, 71. Sum slōh mid slecge swíðe Þā hæpsan, Hml. S. 32, 202. [v. *N. E. D.* sledge.]

**slecg-wyrhta,** an ; *m. One who works with a hammer, a worker in metals :*—Tubalcain Þe wæs slecgwirhta and smið (*malleator et faber*), Nap. 57.

**slege,** es ; *m.* I. *add :*—Slegum *alapis*, An. Ox. 61, 59. Hí ondrēdon Þēre ferelan slegas of Þæs hālgan mannes handa *ex ejus manu ictus ferulae pertimescebant*, Gr. D. 229, 25. III. *add :*—Sle[gum] *tunsionibus*, An. Ox. 4114. V. *add :*—Sleges, forwyrdes *internitionis*, i. *mortis*, An. Ox. 835. Gif man lǣt ǣnne Þeóf tō slege . . . nolde hē syllan ealle his ǣhta . . . wið Þan Þe hē libban mōste ?, Hml. S. 12, 116. VIII. *add : a stake :*—Slegeas *sudes*, Lch. i. lxxi, 3. v. mann-slege.

**slege,** es ; *n. Add : the handle of an axe* (?) :—Heora ān his exe ūp ābrǣd, wolde hine sleán, ac him forwyrnde sum ōÞer, swā Þ hē Þ hylfe gelǣhte and wiðhæfde Þ slege (*held back the pole of the axe?* Þone slege *the stroke*, might have been expected), Hml. S. 31, 154.

**-slegenlic.** v. for-slegenlic : **-slegenness.** v. of-slegenness.

**sleg-hríþer** *a beast for slaughter :*—Ān slægrȳðer, Nap. 55, 31. Cf. sleg-neát. [O. H. Ger. slegi-hrind *taurus.*]

**slic.** *Dele. The MS of* Nar. 50, 19 *has* snotera, *not* slicera : slic[c]. In l. 3 *for* slic *l.* slic. v. slícian : slíccan. *The passages here may be taken to* sleán ; I : slícian. *l.* slician, *and add :* [v. *N. E. D.* slick, *vb.*]

**slídan.** II. *add :*—Hē spræc Þȳsne cwyde be Þām wrǣnan and slídendan (slidenan, *v. l.*, cf. slidor) men *de luxurioso ac lubrico sententiam protulit*, Gr. D. 323, 2. III. *add :*—Sliden *lapsum*, An. Ox. 1467.

**slide.** II. *add :*—Wē beóð gelǣdde under ūs sylfe Þurh ūres geÞōhtes slide (*lapsum*), Gr. D. 107, 30. Hē him wæs ondrǣdende Þone slide (*lapsum*) Þǣre synne in Þām merwum leorningmannum, 119, 16. Eádmōdnyss fyll (*casum*) ne cann ; eádmōdnyss slide (*lapsum*) ne cann ; eádmōdnyss nǣfre slide (*lapsum*) Þolode, Scint. 22, 7–9. Tō ǣrran slidum ongeányrnan *ad priores lapsus recurrere*, 61, 11.

**sliden.** v. slídan ; II.

**sliden-ness** (?) *destruction :*—Forwyrd, sliden[nesse ?] *lapsum, detrimentum*, An. Ox. 1457.

**slíf.** *Add :*—Eall wæs gesýne, fram Þām littlan fingre tōweard Þæs earmes, and sumne dǣl of Þǣre slȳfe, Vis. Lfc. 85.

**slífan** *to slive. Add :* [v. *N. E. D.* slive] : **-slífed.** v. ge-slífed.

**sliht.** *At end for* fiðer (-el?) *l.* fiþer-. III. *add :*—'Eall Þ folc Þe Þū Þǣr finde, sleh mid sweorde . . . Æfter Þām ilcan slehte (slyhte, *v. l. caedem*) . . . Þā Þe ǣr flugon Þone sleht, Gr. D. 198, 6–18. v. and-, ge-sliht.

**slihta** (?). v. wæl-slihta.

**slincan.** I. *add :*—Seó nǣdre ongan slincan in Þ scræf *coepit serpens in speluncam venire*, Gr. D. 211, 16.

**slingan.** *Add :*—Slang *inrumperet*, An. Ox. 18, 37.

**slipor.** *Add :* IV. *uncertain, unsteady, without fixed principles :*—Þā geár Þæs slyporan geogoðhādes *lubrice etatis annos*, Chrd. 54, 33. [v. *N. E. D.* slipper.]

**slítan.** IV. *add : of a sharp instrument :*—Wiþ Þām niþeran tōÞece slīt mid ÞéfoÞorne (?) oÞ Þæt hié blēden, Lch. ii. 52, 7. Ic ofercōm Þæs cwelleres tintregu, . . . Þā slítendan clāwa, Hml. S. 8, 189. V. *add :*—Hē ongiend slītan (*lacessere*) his inngeðonc, Past. 227, 11.

**slite.** II. *add :*—Slite *morsum* (*aspidis*), An. Ox. 2546. v. tō-slite.

**sliten.** *Dele.* 'Lye . . . Josc (?),' *and add :* v. tō-slítere : **slítend.** v. ǣ-slītend.

**slítere.** I. *add :* Cf. slītan ; VI :—Sl[í]tra *canum, carnificum*, An. Ox. 46, 50. v. tō-slítere.

**slíþ-heard.** I. *substitute :* slíþ-hende ; *adj. With baleful hand,* o raŋ *animal, with fell paw :*—Bera bið slíþhende deór (see Mod. Lang. Rev. xv. 70), Gn. Ex. 177.

**-slitt :** *f.* v. lah-slitt : **-slitt ;** *adj. l.* -slitte. v. Þri-slitte.

**slōh** *is also feminine :*—On Þā reádan slō . . . of Þǣre reádan slō, C. D. iii. 465, 32–466, 1.

**sluma.** *l.* slūma.

**slūmere,** es ; *m. A sleeper :*—Þā gedwyldmen man hǣt on Grēcisc Nictates, and wē on ūre geÞeóde slūmeras hí magon nemnan, Chrc. 26, 2.

**slūpan.** *Add :* v. on-slūpan ; un-slopen : **smæccan.** *Add :* [v. *N. E. D.* smatch.]

**smæl.** *In l.* 11 *dele* 'bryt (brycum ?)', *and add :*—Smalum *little by little*, An. Ox. 1553. Cf. lytlum. III. *add :*—Oð smalan cumb,

---

fram smalan cumbes heáfde, C. D. ii. 29, 3. Innan smalan brōc ; of smalan brōc, v. 105, 17. On ðone smalan pæð ; of ðǣm smalan pæðe . . . on Þæt smale dell ; of ðǣm smalan delle, C. D. B. ii. 246, 12–15. IV. *add :*—In smalan æsc, C. D. iii. 381, 1.

**-smæl.** v. heáfod-smæl.

**smæl-þearme.** *Add :*—Wið roppes ge wið wambe and smælÞearmes ādlum, Lch. ii. 234, 30.

**smǣr[e].** *Add :*—Smǣras *labra,* i. *labia,* An. Ox. 2160 : *labella, labia,* 2163.

**smǣte.** *Add :*—Smǣte gold *obrizum,* i. *aurum optimi coloris,* An. Ox. 2534.

**smǣte-gylden.** *Add :*—Þeáh Þǣr sȳ eal smǣtegylden mōr (cf. ofer ðām gyldenan mōre, 4) æt sunnan ūpgange, Verc. Först. 114, 1. Ðeáh ðe sié sum smǣtegelden ðūn eall mid gimmum āsett æt sunnan ūpgange . . . and ðǣr sitte sum cynebearn anufan ðǣre gyldenan dūne, Sal. K. 85, 36.

**smeágan.** II. *add :*—Ðæs ðinges onlícnesse ðe hē ymb smeáð *quidquid fictis imaginibus deliberando cogitatur,* Past. 157, 14. Ðā hwíle ðe hí tō ungemetlíce smeágað ymb ðās eorðlecan ðing *intentionem suam dum rebus transitoriis immoderatius implicant,* 431, 14. Ymb ðyllic is tō geðencenne and tō smeáganne *cui considerandum est,* 59, 21. III. (1) *add :*—Ic smeáde mínre dohter mōdes willan, Ap. Th. 23, 3. Smeágaþ mistlicnesse *rimamini uarietates,* An. Ox. 1080. (2) *add :*—Sēcð ðonne and smeáð hū hē hit āwrecan mæge *argumenta ultionis inquirit,* Past. 225, 20. (3) *with infin.* (?) :—Lāc ðíglum heolstrum smeáde (*quamvis auctor integritatis virginale*) *munus clanculis* (*occultare*) *latebris deliberaret,* An. Ox. 4213. v. be-, geond-, under-smeágan.

**smeá-gelegen.** *Add :*—Beclȳsingca, smeáge legena (so *in the MS.,* Napier *takes* smeáge *as adjective* (v. smeáh), *so two separate words instead of a compound*), An. Ox. 4142.

**smeágend,** es ; *m. A searcher, an examiner, inquirer :*—Ðū Þe eart mōdes smeágend and manna heortan, Hml. S. 12, 193.

**smeágendlíce ;** *adv. Searchingly, exactly :*—Hē Þā smeágendlíce āxiende ongeat *requirens subtiliter agnovit,* Gr. D. 172, 14. Cf. smeálíce.

**smeágung.** I. *in l.* 3 *after* 'for' *add :* *the owner of.* II. *add :*—Hys hǣsum mid ealre mōdes smeáunge hȳrsumigende *eius imperiis toto mentis conamine obtemperantes,* Angl. xiii. 368, 40. Hē hira líf ðurh ðā smeánga ðæs hālgan gǣstes ongeat *eorum vitam spiritu perscrutante deprehendit,* Past. 115, 14. v. ge-, ymb-smeágung.

**smeáh.** II. *add :*—Ðyses cyncges mid smeágre mynegunge gǣstlíce onbryrde *huius regis sagaci monitu spiritaliter conpuncti,* Angl. xiii. 368, 36. v. smeá-gelegen.

**smeá-lic.** III. *add :*—Hæbbe ǣfre wynsume wirtūnas Þ man mage Þǣrof ǣfre tōeácan ōðrum Þingum sumne smeálicne ēt (*aliquod pulmentum*) findan, Chrd. 15, 37. Cf. smeá-mete.

**smeálíce.** III. *add :*—Hē heom getǣhte swȳðe smeálíce (*subtiliter*) on gehwilcum stōwum hwæt hí Þǣr timbrian sceoldon, Gr. D. 148, 18. Hē nāt hū smeálíce his ðǣde sceolon beón gedǣmde beforan Godes eágum *facta illius quam subtiliter judicentur ignorat,* 337, 16. V. *subtlely, craftily :*—Oððe hē mid geámeleáste ūs gebysgað, oÞÞe mid smeágungum smeálíce ūs hremð, Hml. S. 13, 59.

**smeálic-ness,** e ; *f. Subtlety :*—Beswicene fram deóflum Þurh geÞanca smeálicnysse (*subtilitate*), Chrd. 98, 34.

**smeá-mete.** *Add :*—Sylle man tō middægÞēnunge twām and twām ān tyl cȳssticce and sumne smeámete (*cibaria alia*) . . . and on ǣfen twām and twām ān cȳssticce and sume smeámettas (*cibaria alia*), Chrd. 15, 2–5 : 14, 36, 37.

**smearcian.** *Add :*—Swā se hālga wer Þis gehȳrde, Þā smercode (hlōh, *v. l.*) hē swilce hē Þæt spell forhogode *quo audito vir sanctus dedignando subrisit,* Gr. D. 29, 13. Ðā heó Þis gehȳrde, Þā smearcode heó wið his weardes, Hml. S. 23 b, 590.

**smeart.** *Add :* [v. *N. E. D.* smart ; *adj.*]

**smeáþanclíce.** *Add :*—Swā hwilc swā wile smeáÞanclícor (smeáÞanclíce, *v. l.*) Þæs Þeáwas and his líf ongytan *cujus si quis velit subtilius mores vitamque cognoscere,* Gr. D. 175, 4.

**smeáþancole ;** *adv. Thoroughly, searchingly :*—Hí wǣron smeáÞancole andspyrigende and geondsmeágende *subtiliter indagantes,* Gr. D. 344, 15.

**smeáþancollíce.** *Add :*—Hē him swȳðe smeáÞancollíce getǣhte Þā syndrigan stōwa *loca singula subtiliter designavit,* Gr. D. 148, 15. Hē smeáÞancollíce āxiende oncneów *requirens subtiliter agnovit,* 172, 14. Hí embe Þæt heofonlíce líf geornlíce smeádon swȳðe smeáÞancollíce, Hml. S. 3, 509.

**smeáþancolness.** *Add :*—Āht Þæs Þe geunÞwǣrige fram Þæs incundan regoles smeáÞancolnesse *quidquid ab illius aeternae regulae subtilitate discordat,* Gr. D. 336, 27.

**smeócan.** *Add :*—Swā swā blācern Þe būtan ele byð onǣled smeócan (*fumigare*) mæg leóht habban nā mæg, Scint. 51, 6.

**smeortan.** *Add* (?) : *to burn :*—Tō smorcenne (smeortenne ? Cf. O. H. Ger. smerzan *cremare*) *arsuros,* An. Ox. 1431.

**smeortung,** e; *f. Smarting, itching :*—Smertung (*printed* emert-ung) *prurigo,* Wrt. Voc. i. 20, 5.

**smeoru.** *Add :*—Gyf þū buteran habban wylle oððe smeoru, þonne strīc þū mid þrim fingrum on þīne innewearde hand, Tech. ii. 123, 22. [*v. N. E. D.* smear. Cf. *Goth.* smairþr.]

**smere,** Angl. viii. 325, 26. *See* mere-men[n].

**smēþan.** *Add :*—Se cræftga sceáwað and smēðað *artifex considerat et limat,* Gr. D. 283, 26.

**smēþe.** II. *add :*—Sume habbað smēðne weg and rihtne, Solil. H. 44, 10. On smēðan dūne; of smēðan dūne, C. D. B. ii. 469, 26. On ða smēðan āc, C. D. iii. 79, 20. On smēðe mētue, 460, 19. [*v. N. E. D.* smeeth.]

**smēþian.** II. *add :*—Se cræftga sceáwað and smēðað *artifex considerat et limat,* Gr. D. 283, 26. Wōge smēþiende hylcas *salebrosos conplanans anfractus,* An. Ox. 1771. [*v. N. E. D.* smeeth; *vb.*]

**smēþness.** II. *add :*—Þær nāhwǣr næs nænigu smēðnes þ man mihte āht tō þan lytelne wyrtūn þām brōþrum tō nytte gewyrcan *ad quemlibet parvum hortum fratribus excolendum nulla patebat planities,* Gr. D. 49, 4. [*v. N. E. D.* smeethness.] v. un-smēþness.

**smīc.** *Add :*—Smoec *fumus,* Ps. Vos. 101, 4. Smēc, 17, 9 : 36, 20. [*v. N. E. D.* smitch, smeech, smeek.]

**smicer.** *Add :* [*v. N. E. D.* smicker]: **smicerian.** v. ge-smicerian.

**smirels.** *Add : anointing :*—Smyrelse eles *unctione olei,* Angl. xiii. 443, 1107. [*v. N. E. D.* smerles.]

**smirwan.** *Add :* v. þurh-smirwan.

**smirwung.** *Add :* III. *smearing, greasing, rubbing with grease :*—Sceóna smyruncg and reáfa wæsc *calciamentorum unctio uestimentorumque ablutio,* Angl. xiii. 441, 1084. v. on-smirwung.

**smītan.** II. *add :*—Nalles þte ingǣþ in mūðe smīteþ (*coinquinat*) monnu ah þte forðgǣþ of mūþe þæt besmīteþ monnu, Mt. R. 15, 11. v. ofer-smītan.

**smite.** *Dele, and see* mīte.

**smiþ.** *Add :* v. īren-, mæstling-, teón-smiþ : -smīþ. v. gold-smiþ.

**smiþ-belg,** es ; *m. A smith's bellows :*—Ðeáh mon ðane gārsecg ūtan besette mid smiðbelgum (-bylium, *v. l.,* Nap. 58), Sal. K. 85, 13.

**smiþian.** *Add :* [*v. N. E. D.* smith ; *vb.*]: **smiþþe.** *Add :* v. mynet-smiþþe : **smiþu.** v. smiþ.

**smitta.** *l.* smitte; *f. Add : pollution :*—Wom, smittan *inluuiem,* i. *inmunditiam,* An. Ox. 3491. Sió sāwl sceal nȳde habban smittan þæs līchoman unþeáwa, 648, note.

**smittian.** *Add :* [*v. N. E. D.* smit; *vb.*] v. ge-smittian.

**smocc.** *Add :* Loþa, serc, smocc, hemeþe *colobium,* An. Ox. 3725.

**smocian.** *Add :*—Smoci[endum] *fumigabundis,* An. Ox. 3553.

**smolt,** es ; *n. Lard, fat :*—Smolt *pinguedo,* Angl. xiii. 404, 558. Þær sculan ii fǣtte swȳn ūp ārīsan tō smolte, Nap. 58. [*v. N. E. D.* smolt, *sb. Icel.* smolt *grease.* Cf. *O. H. Ger.* smalz *adeps : Ger.* schmalz.]

**smolt;** *adj. Add :* [*v. N. E. D.* smolt]: **smorcenne.** v. smeortan: **smorung.** v. ā-smorung.

**smūgan.** *Add :*—Þ āttor smēh geond ealne þone līchoman, Hml. S. 31, 952. Ūp smugan *ebulliebant,* An. Ox. 7, 248. Smūgan *serpere* (*nec fibris caeca venena sinat*), 5381. v. þurh-smūgan.

**smylte;** *adj. Fat* (? v. smyltness; III, *and* cf. smolt *pinguedo.*)

**smyltness.** III. *See preceding word; or is* pinguedo *connected with* pinguis *in its sense of* calm, quiet, easy ? IV. *add :*—Mē sōna sum staþolfæstlic smyltnyss tō becōm, Hml. S. 23 b, 551. V. *add :*—Þ yrre hæfð wununge on ðæs dysegan bōsme, þ is ðonne hē bið tō hrædmōd; and se ealwealdenda dēma dēmð ǣfre mid smyltnysse, Hml. S. 16, 343.

**snaca.** *Dele* ban-snaca *at end, and add :*—Swylce fram ansȳne snacan fleáh synna *quasi a facie colubri fuge peccata,* Scint. 42, 4. Gif hwā mid his fēt ofstepð ǣttig bān, snacan oððe næddran, Lch. i. 152, 2.

**-snæcce.** v. twi-, þri-snæcce.

**snǣd.** *Dele* ' *Or? a clearing*', *and add :* , snād. The word seems defined in the following passage :—Unus singularis silva ad hanc terram pertinens quem nos theodoice *snād* nominamus, C. D. B. ii. 18, 17. Other instances of the word are :—Tō nican snādæs forda . . . ðonon on ðonæ westmæstan snād on beaggan hyrste, C. D. v. 173, 31-34. Be ðām grāfe ðæt hit cymð in ðām snēde; of ðām snēde ðæt hit cymð in ðone norðran styfecinc in ðone swīnhagan, iii. 18, 31-34. Tō stybban snāde ðēr ðā twēgen wegas tōlicgað, vi. 26, 30. On timberhricges snād foreweardne, v. 71, 1. On herredsnād, 300, 11. On tattingsnād, C. D. B. i. 295, 28. Wiðūtan ðone snǣdhege, C. D. iii. 79, 28.

**snǣd** *the handle of a scythe. Add :* Cf. þæt īren forð āhleóp of þām hylfe, Gr. D. 113, 27. (*This is the same incident as that described in* Hml. Th. ii. 162.) [*v. N. E. D.* snead.]

**snǣd** *a morsel. Add :*—Genim hāran wulle lytle snǣde .iii., Lch. ii. 354, 14. Nim niþewearde eolenan, gesniþ on hunig, ete swā manige snǣda swā hē mæge, 358, 20. [*v. N. E. D.* snede.] v. cor-snǣd.

**snǣdan** *to slice. Add :* [Mid seaxum tōsnǣdod, H. R. N. 28, 5.] [*v. N. E. D.* sned.]

**snǣdel-þearm.** *Add :*—Snǣdelðearmum *extis,* An. Ox. 23, 24.

**snǣding.** *Add :*—Onfōn, underfōn snǣdinge *accipere mixtum,* Angl. xiii. 389, 346 : 391, 375 : 406, 592. Æfter snǣdinge *post mixtum,* 415, 709.

**-snǣse.** v. twi-snǣse.

**snās.** *Add :*—In snāsum (*printed* fnāsum) *in veribus,* Wrt. Voc. ii. 47, 24.

**snāþ.** v. snide.

**snāw-hwīt.** *Add :*—Geseah hē mycele weorud swylce on gangdagon, and þā wǣron ealle mid snāwhwītum reáfe gescrȳdde, Vis. Lfc. 12. Wē habbað cynehelmas . . . snāwhwīte swā swā lilie, Hml. S. 34, 115.

**snāwig.** *Add :*—Kĭ Ianuarius gif hē biþ on Sæternesdæg, þonne biþ snāwig winter, Archiv cxx. 298, 18. [*O. H. Ger.* snēwac: *Icel.* snæugr.]

**snecca.** v. hnecca : **snegel.** *Add :* v. regn-snegel.

**snell.** II. *add :*—Snelra *praestantior,* An. Ox. 4542. [*v. N. E. D.* snell.]

**snel-scipe,** es ; *m. Boldness, bravery :*—Eádmund cing Īrensīd wæs geclypod for his snellscipe, Chr. 1057; P. 187, 36.

**snide.** I. *add :*—þ þær ne ætēwde nænige swaþe þæs snides (*sectionis*) . . . wæs gemēted se līchoma swā gesund swylce him nǣfre ne gehrine æniges īrenes snide (*incisio*), Gr. D. 199, 1-5. II. *add :*—Snīþes (*for another reading see* snāþ) *occisionis,* An. Ox. 3070. Scēp tō snide gelǣdd *ouis ad occisionem ductus,* 40, 32.

**sniden-ness.** v. ymb-snidenness.

**snīte.** *Add :*—Tō snītan īge, C. D. B. ii. 374, 15. [*v. N. E. D.* snite.] v. wudu-snīte.

**snōca.** *For* ' *bend, bay* (?) ' *substitute : A projecting point or piece of land, a promontory, a snook* (v. *N. E. D.*).

**snōd.** *Add :*—Snōda *redimicula,* An. Ox. 2, 439.

**snoffa,** an; *m. Nausea :*—Ūtānȳddre snoffan ǣmylnysse *depulsu nausię tedio,* Angl. xiii. 369, 50.

**snofl.** *Add :*—Hraca ł snofol *flegmata,* An. Ox. 31, 3. Cf. snyflung.

**snoru.** *Add :*—Sum æþele gesīðwīf hæfde āne snore (*nurum*) þā hire sunu lytle ǣr him tō wīfe onfēng, Gr. D. 71, 21. Se sweór bemǣnde his snore, and se brȳdguma his brȳd, Hml. S. 31, 191.

**snotor.** *Add :*—Gleáwes, snoteres *sagacis,* An. Ox. 3109.

**snotorlīce.** *Add :*—Snoterlīce *sagaciter,* i. *prudenter,* An. Ox. 208.

**snotorness.** *Add :* v. un-snotorness.

**snotorscipe,** es; *m. Prudence, sagacity :*—Snoterscipes *rationis,* An. Ox. 2, 172: *ratiocinationis,* 3015.

**snyflung,** e; *f. Mucus from the nose :*—Gif heora ænegum for unhǣle snyflung of nosa (*flegma ex naribus*) derige, Chrd. 23, 7. [*v. N. E. D.* snivelling.]

**snȳtan.** *Add :*—Gif heora ænegum . . . snyflung of nosa derige, snȳte bæftan him oððe ādūn be his sīdan (*post dorsum proiciat, aut iuxta latus*) . . . swā hwæt swā man him fram snȳte (*quod proicitur*), fortrede hit mid his fōtum, Chrd. 23, 6-13. [*v. N. E. D.* snite.]

**snȳtels.** v. candel-snȳtels : **snyterness.** v. un-snyterness : **snȳting.** *Add :* [*v. N. E. D.* sniting]: **snȳtro.** *Add :*—Mid helwarum ne byð ne weorc, ne gesceádwīsnes, ne snyttro, ne wīsdōm *nec opus, nec ratio, nec scientia, nec sapientia erit apud inferos,* Gr. D. 328, 2.

**sōca** (?). v. fere-sōca.

**sōcn.** IV. *add :*—þā word mē secgendum eft ōðru sōcn and frignung mē is on mōd becumen *mihi haec dicenti alia suboritur quaestio,* Gr. D. 137, 29. Þurh sōcne *per inquisitionem,* 265, 8. v. fird-, hundred-, tō-sōcn.

**-sōcness, -sōcnung.** v. tō-sōcness, -sōcnung.

**sōfte;** *adj. Add :* I a. *of weather :*—Gyf gemetegud sōfte byþ *si temperies tranquilla fuerit* (it is uncertain whether sōfte *should be taken as adjective translating* tranquilla, *or as adverb qualifying* gemetegud, *which mistranslates* temperies), Angl. xiii. 397, 462. III. *add :*—God ealla gemetgað sīda gesceafta, sōfta geþwērað, Met. 29, 47.

**sōfte;** *adv.* II. *add :*—Him bið swīðe sōfte *things will go very easily for him,* Hml. Th. i. 164, 2. Þæt ǣlc mann drunce be þām þe hē sylf wolde and him sōftost wǣre, Hml. A. 92, 23.

**sōftlīce.** v. un-sōftlīce.

**soft-ness.** *Add :*—Gif wē lufiað þā sceortan sōftnysse and þā hwīlwendlican lustas tō ðan swīðe þæt hī ūs gebringan tō ðām ēcan pīnungum, Hml. Th. i. 164, 10.

**sol** *a sole* (?). *Dele the explanation.*

**sol** *a miry place. Add :*—Sola *uolutabra,* An. Ox. 2, 314.

**sol** (?); *adj. Dirty :*—Soles *rugosae* (Constantinus . . . matronae *rugosae* figuram vidit in extasi deformem fronte vetusta, Ald. 152, 22), An. Ox. 15, 3. [Sume bereð sole cloð to þe watere forto wasshen it clene, O. E. Hml. ii. 57, 23. His alter cloð is great and sole and hise wiues chemise smal and hwit, and te albe sol and hire smoc hwit, 163, 30. A sol cloð hwit iwaschen, A. R. 324. *See also N. E. D.* solwy.] v. solian.

**solian.** *Add :* v. ā-solian, Angl. i. 285: ii. 374.

**sōl-merca** *a sundial,* Nap. 86.

sol-mónaþ. On the gloss *panibus sol* see Corp. Gl. H. p. xxxix, where *panibus* is taken to be a corruption of *phoebus*.

solor. *Add*: I. *an upper room, upper part of an house*:—Hē gestód in þām solore (-ere, *v. l.*) þæs mynstres *stans in solario*, Gr. D. 119, 25. On solre *in* (*caenaculi*) *solario*, An. Ox. 8, 355. Swā swā nihthrefn on solere (*domocilio*), Ps. Rdr. 101, 7. II. *a residence*:—Ic þeówode in þām solore þære Constantinopoliscan byrig *in Constantinopolitanae urbis palatio deserviens*, Gr. D. 248, 14. III. *a raised platform*:—Solere *pulpito*, An. Ox. 2, 211. [v. *N. E. D.* sollar.] v. wæfer-solor.

sóm. *Add*: [To sæhte, to sibbe, and to some, Laym. 4099. Seihnesse and some, A. R. 426. Myd sib and myd some, Misc. 89, 15.]

són. *Add*: ¶ be sóne *loudly, aloud*:—Hlúddre stefne . . . óþre stillíce . . . mid swēglicre stefne . . . óþre stillíce . . . nihtsang eác be sóne *alta uoce* . . . *cetera silenter* . . . *sonora uoce* . . . *cetera silenter* . . . *Completorium aeque sonore*, Angl. xiii. 412, 677: 675. Nihtsang be sóne sungen æfter þeáwe preósta *completorium sonoriter celebretur more canonicorum*, 425, 864. Se preóst cweðe þonne be sóne: 'Oremus . . .' and syððan cweðe dígellíce: 'Libera nos . . .,' Ll. Th. ii. 358, 24. Ælcne ðæra hē sancg be sóne mid weorode, Ps. Th. 4, arg.

sóna. *Add*: I. *within a short time*. (1) with reference to a definite past or future time:—Hǽlend him tó cwæþ, 'Lóca nú' . . . Hē þā sóna instæpes geseh, Bl. H. 15, 27. Ðā cleopedon his ðegnas him tó . . . Hē him sóna ondwyrde, and him stiernlíce stiérde, Past. 197, 18. (2) in general statements in which the time reckoned from is indefinite:—Se líchama hine nā ne onstyreþ syþþan seó sáwl him of biþ; ác sóna hē molsnaþ, Bl. H. 21, 28. Hine nǽnig mann mihte gebindan, ac sóna instæpe (*continuo*) þā bendas tóslupan, Bd. 4, 22; Sch. 457, 15. II. *followed by* eft, efter:—Hēr Rómāne þǽm pāpan his tungon forcurfon and his eágan āstungon . . . and þæt þ Gode fultomiendum hē meahte geseón and sprecan, Chr. 797; P. 56, 12. Sóna efter (*statim iterum*) se hona gesang, Mk. L. 14, 72. III. (*so*) *soon* (*as*), denoting 'at the very time or moment when, whenever':—Sóna ic þínes suna róde geseó, ic mid þām wiðsace þissere worulde, Hml. S. 23 b, 451. Se to gegyrla þe ic hæfde, sóna swā ic Iordanen oferfór, mid ealdunge tótorne forwurdon, 570. Sóna swā ic anwóc, swā wilnode ic eft wínes, Past. 431, 17. Sóna swā þe ǽrest geseah ðus murciende, ic ongeat þ þu wǽre út āfaren of þines fæder éþele, Bt. 5, 1; F. 8, 27. v. eft-, efter-sóna.

són-cræft. *Add*:—Sóncræft *musica*, An. Ox. 55, 3.

-sopa. v. grund-sopa.

soppe (?). *Substitute*: sopp *a sop*:—Sopp *offulam*, An. Ox. 56, 10.

sorgian. *Add*:—Sume ofer sǽ sorhgende gewiton, Bd. 1, 15; Sch. 43, 30. v. efen-sorgian.

sorgung. *Add*:—Búton ǽnigre sorhiunge (*printed* or hiunge) oððe yldinga *sine aliquo typo vel mora* (cf. búton late and gnornunge, R. Ben. 55, 12), R. Ben. I. 62, 11.

sorh. *Add*: v. weorold-sorh; un-sorh; *adj*.

sorh-leás. I. *add*:—Sorhleás *secura*, i. *sine cura*, An. Ox. 797.

sorhlíce. *Add*:—Wē ne sceolan ceorigan ne sorhlíce bemǽnan þeáh ðe ús ungelimp on ǽhtum getíme, Hml. S. 13, 286.

sót-ceorl (sot-?):—Andlang hagan on sótceorles æcer, C. D. v. 148, 13: vi. 41, 20.

sóþ truth. I b. *add*:—Hweðer ðincð þē betre, þe ðæt sóð þe seó sóðfestnes (*quod verum dicitur vel veritas*)?, Solil. H. 50, 14: 9. II b. *add*:—Sóð is gecýðed . . . þæt þú wið Waldend wǽre heólde, Exod. 419: B. 700: An. 1437. Hē nyste hwæt þæs sóþes (*or adj.?*) wæs, for þǽm hē hit self ne geseah, Ors. 1, 1; S. 17, 33. v. folc-sóþ.

sóþ *true*. I. *add*:—Seó sóþe lufu *karitas*, Scint. 175, 17, 53.

sóþfæstian. *Add*: v. ge-sóþfæstian.

sóþfæstness. *Add*:—Ne wilnast þú sóðfestnesse (*veritatem*) tó witanne? Hú mæg ic bútan sóðfestnesse áwiht sóðes witan? . . . Hwæðer þe þince þæt hyt eall án sí . . . sóð and sóðfestnes (*verum et veritas*)? . . . Hweðer ðincð þē betre, þe þæt sóð, þe seó sóðfestnes?, Solil. H. 50, 2-15.

sóþian. *Add*: [*Dan*. sande.]

sóþ-sagol. *Add*:—Se sóðsagola (*verax*) raciend, Gr. D. 265, 12. Of swiðe sóðsagoles (*veracis*) gesægne, 215, 6. Þ secgað þā ǽfæstan and þā sóðsagolan (*veraces*) weras, 191, 15.

sóþ-scipe *in* fore-sóðscip *prolatione*, Mt. p. 15, 13.

sóþ-secgende. *See next word, and* sóþ-secgan.

sóþsecgendlíce; *adv*. *Truly*:—Þā þā þær wæs án geleáffull man sóðsecgendlíce (sóðsecgende, *v. l.*) in gangende, hræðe se leása gást onweg gewát *dum domum unus veraciter fidelis ingressus est, ab ea protinus mendax spiritus abscessi*', Gr. D. 185, 17.

sóþ-spell. *Add*:—Ðyllice leásunga hí worhton, and mihton eáþe secgan sóþspell, gif him þā leásunga nǽron swētran, Bt. 35, 4; F. 162, 15.

sóþ-sprǽce; *adj*. *Veracious*:—Sē þe wǽre twispǽce, weorðe sē sóðspǽce, Wlfst. 72, 16 note.

sot-mann, es; *m*. *A foolish person*:—Ús sceamað tó segcenne ealle

---

ðā sceandlican wiglunga þe gedwǽsmenn (sotmen, *v. l.*) drífað, Hml. S. 17, 101.

spadu. *Add*:—Hē sceal habban . . . spade, scofle, wādspitel, Angl. ix. 263, 5. Hē hēt weorpan íserne gelóman in þæs mynstres wyrtgeard, þā íserngelóman gewunelice naman wē hātaþ spadan and spitelas (*vangas*), and cwæð, 'Weorpað þus manige spada (*tot vangas*)' . . . Hē gemētte swā manige wyrhtan, swā manige swā hē hēt spadena in weorpan . . . þeófas . . . onféngon þā spada, Gr. D. 201, 19-202, 3.

spǽc (*m*.?) (*n*.?). l. *n*.

spǽtan. *Add*:—Hié him on ðæt nebb spǽtton, Past. 261, 10. [v. *N. E. D.* spete.]

spǽtlan. *Add*:—Spétlo *petisso*, An. Ox. 53, 24.

spanan. *Add*:—Speón *suasit*, An. Ox. 43, 9. I a. *add*:—Forgif mē þām men þe mín mód mē tó spend, Hml. S. 3, 390. For hwon hē geþrýsstlǽhte þ hē hēte þone Godes wer swā swǽncan and tó him spanan (gelangian, *v. l.*) *cur ad exhibendum Dei hominem mittere praesumsisset*, Gr. D. 39, 11. II. (a) *add*:—Se sǽtere, ðæt is sē dióful, hē hine spænd on wóh *insidiator prava suggerit*, Past. 417, 23. Hí speónnon (= ? speónon; *but see* spannan; I e.) heom eall þ landfolc tó, Chr. 1052; P. 178, 36. (b) *add*:—Monige from him cirdon, and Seleucus spónan þ hē Lisimachus beswice, Ors. 3, 11; S. 152, 13.

spang. *Add*: v. ge-spang.

spannan. I. *add*: (c) *to harness* or *yoke* oxen to that which has to be drawn:—Ðā þā him nāht ne speów, þā hēt hē spannan oxan tó, ac hí ne mihton āwecgan þ mǽden swā, Hml. S. 9, 106. (d) *to join in matrimony*:—Span[n]an *adjungere* (has sponsi ad prolem generis satagunt *adjungere* nuptas, Ald. 200, 10), An. Ox. 17, 62. (e) *to bind by considerations of interest, fear of consequences*:—Hí speónnon heom eall þ landfolc tó (cf. hí nāmon gíslas swā fela swā hí woldon, 179, 3), Chr. 1052; P. 178, 36. v. ā-, un-spannan.

sparian. I. (a) *add*:—þ mon ne sparige nǽnne þeóf þe æt hæbbendre handa gefangen sý, Ll. Th. i. 198, 16: 21. (b) *add*:—Ðæt man ne sparige nānan þeófe, Ll. Th. 228, 12. II. *add*: (1) *to refrain from using or consuming*:—Se mann þe fæst búton ælmyssan, hē dēð swilce hē sparige his mete, and eft ett þæt hē ǽr mid forhæfednysse foreóde, Hml. Th. i. 180, 8. (1 a) *to save, store up*:—Þú hiwast swilce þú ðínum cildum sparige, and nāst hwām hit gescýt, Hml. Th. ii. 104, 9. (2) *to refrain from employing* or *exercising*:—Sē þe sparað gyrde his, hē hatað sunu his *qui parcit uirge sue odit filium suum*, Scint. 175, 16: Hml. Th. ii. 324, 32. (2 a) with infin., *to forbear to do*:—Nā cuman ylde ł sparige *non uenire differat*, Angl. xiii. 388, 323.

spátl. [El. 300. *The MS. has* spald.] *Add*:—Se sácerd æthrínð mid his spátle þæs mannes nose and eáran, Wlfst. 35, 12. [v. *N. E. D.* spattle; spold. *Also* spawl.]

spearcian. *For* sparcendum (Hpt. Gl. 501, 5) *probably* spircendum *should be read*. v. An. Ox. 4029 n.: spear-lira. l. -líra, *and add*: [v. *N. E. D.* sparlire]: spearwa. *Add*: v. hrand-spearwa.

sped. *Add*: v. *N. E. D.* spade.]

spéd. III. *add*:—Paulus cwæð þ se geleáfa wǽre gehyhtendlicra þinga and wénendlicra spéd *est fides sperandarum substantia rerum*, Gr. D. 269, 14. v. feoh-, wan-spéd.

spéd-dropa. v. geond-sprengan: spédian. v. for-spédian.

spédig. *Add*:—Se ríca and se þearfa sind him betwýnan nýdbehéfe. Þām spédigum gedafenað þæt hē spende and dǽle; ðām wǽdlan gedafenað þæt hē gebidde for ðane dǽlere, Hml. Th. ii. 256, 30-33. v. weorold-spédig.

spédiglic. v. efen-spédiglic: spédigness. *Add*: v. wan-spédigness.

spelc. *Add*: [v. *N. E. D.* spelk.]

speld. *Add*:—Spelda *facula*, An. Ox. 8, 88. [v. *N. E. D.* speld.]

speling. *Add*:—Sē þe spelunga Xpes dēþ *qui uices Christi agit*, Angl. xiii. 401, 512.

spell. I. *add*:—Ðis spell (*hanc historiam*) mē sume þára sægdon, þā þe hit from þǽm sylfan were gehýrdon, Bd. 4, 21; Sch. 462, 15. I a. *add*:—Nis tó geortrýwanne þ on úre yldo þ beón mihte þ oft geworden getreówe spell cýþað *nec diffidendum est nostra aetate fieri potuisse quod aliquoties factum fideles historias narrant*, Bd. 4, 19; Sch. 441, 10. I b. *add*:—Ic wille geswígian Tontolis and Philopes þára scondlicestena spella . . . on spellum and on leóðum hiora gewin cúðe sindon *nec mihi enumerare opus est Tantali et Pelopis facta turpia, fabulas turpiores . . . certamina in fabulis celebrare solita sunt*, Ors. 1, 8; S. 42, 7-14. II. *add*:—Ne mót nán man secgan spell on þām ðrím swígdagum, Hml. Th. ii. 262, 16. v. an-, leásung-spell.

spellian. I. *add*:—Þā ðā hí him betweónan spellodon and wel sela worda sprǽcon *cum vicissim aliqua confabularentur*, Gr. D. 75, 21. Þā gebróðra þā ongǽn hine sylfne ānmódlíce wǽron spelliende *contra se unanimiter conspirantes*, 106, 1. [v. *N. E. D.* spell; *vb.* (1).]

spell-stów. *Add*:—Onforan þā spelstówe, C. D. i. 109, 10.

spellung. I. *add*:—Wēn is þæt sume sittende mid ídelre spellunge deófle tó micelne forwyrdes intingan gesealden, R. Ben. 68, 21. II. *add*:—Spellungum *fabulis*, R. Ben. I. 76, 14. Spellingum, 83, 8. Ðæt

ðin mōd ne beó yfele besmiten þurh ðā ýdelan spellunga, Hex. 48, 12. v. frum-spellung.

**spelt** *a board of a book;* planca. *Take here the first two instances given under* spelt corn, *and add:* [v. *N. E. D.* spelt.]

**spên.** *Dele. For* spenas *probably* uenas *should be read.* Cf. *the consecutive glosses:*—Fibras spenas, *ficetula* sucga, *fibrans* hrissende, Wrt. Voc. ii. 35, 52–54, *and:*—Fibras uenas, *ficetula* sugga, *fibrans,* risende, Corp. Gl. H. 55, 175–178.

**spendan.** *Add:*—Hī nāmon æt heora māgon sceattas genōge and þā eáwunga and dearnunga ealle spendon and dǽldon hafenleásum mannum, Hml. S. 23, 200. Þām spēdigum gedafenað þæt hē spende and dǽle; ðām wǽdlan gedafenað þæt hē gebidde for ðane dǽlere, Hml. Th. ii. 256, 32.

**-spennendlic.** v. for-spennendlic: **spennung.** v. for-, ymb-spennung.

**Speónisc** *Spanish:*—On Ispānian lānde þǽre Speóniscan léode (*the* MS. *has the accents on the* a's *and* e's), Hml. S. 37, 1.

**spere.** *Add:*—Þæt yrre slihð þ gedyld mid his spere (sceafte, *v. l.* conto), Prud. 18 b. Þ yrre scýt his spere (*lanceam*) ongeán þ gedyld, 20 b. Swā sē āsent speru and flāua *sicut qui mittit lanceas et sagittas,* Scint. 193, 16. v. eofor-, nægel-spere; gewriþ.

**spere-hand** *the male side or line in speaking of inheritance:*—Ic cýþe mīnan leófan hlāforde þæt ic on mīnan suna þæs landes þe ic tō þef geearnode æfter mīnan dæge tō habbanne his dæg, and æfter his dæge tō syllanne þǽm þe him leófast seó, and þæt sió on þā sperehand, C. D. ii. 399, 5. v. spere-healf.

**spere-sceaft,** es; *m. The shaft of a spear:*—Hī ongunnon heora hors mid heora sperescæftum (*hastis*) þerscan, Gr. D. 14, 27.

**-sperod.** v. ge-sperod.

**spic.** *Add:*—On tōcyme Drihtnes fǽtnyss ys forboden gewislíce spices būton freólsdægum *in aduentu Domini pinguedo interdicitur, scilicet lardi, nisi festiuis diebus,* Angl. xiii. 399, 487. [v. *N. E. D.* spick.]

**spic-hūs.** *Add:*—Hpt. 31, 12, 257.

**spicing.** *The MS. has* swicyngas (v. Archiv cxxv. 51 n. 4), *the passage glossed being:*—Clauos colligere uel facere, laborem significat. Spicyngas *seems the correct form.* [v. *N. E. D.* spiking.]

**spiden?** *See next word.*

**spider.** *Dele. The MS. has* spiden *not* spider: spilcan. *Add:* [v. *N. E. D.* spelk]: **-spildness.** v. for-spildness.

**spilere,** es; *m. A player, jester:*—Spilra, glíwera *parasitorum,* An. Ox. 679. v. spilian.

**spilian.** *Add:* , spillan (?). v. for-spillan; spillend.

**spillan.** *Dele last passage, and see* spillend: **-spilledness.** v. for-spilledness.

**spillend,** es; *m. A player, jester:*—Spilra (*printed* swilra), glíwra, spillendra *parasitorum,* Hpt. Gl. 422, 37. v. on-spillend; spilian (spillan ?).

**-spillendness.** v. for-spillendness: **-spilnes.** v. for-spilness.

**spinel.** *Add : the amount of thread on a spindle (?):*—Spinil *stilium vel fusa* (fusa *stamen fuso involutum,* Migne), Txts. 98, 967. Spinl *fusa,* Wülck. Gl. 246, 7. Spinle *fusa* (si parcae . . . fila gubernant, mortali vitae *fusaque* rotante minantur, Ald. 175, 34), An. Ox. 17, 37.

**-spinn.** v. in-spinn.

**spinnan.** II. *for* spān, *l.* spāu. III. *Dele query, and add:* [Cf. M. Du. spinnevoeten: Du. spinvoeten: Fris. spinfoetsje: L. Ger. spinnefoten, -benen *to move feet or legs convulsing.*]

**spircan.** *Substitute: to sparkle.* (1) of fire:—Spircende (-re, Hpt. Gl. 429, 42) blasan *scintillante facula,* An. Ox. 974. Spyrcendum *scintillantibus* (*favillis*), 3961. (2) of that which is set on fire:—Spircendum *scintillante* (ita ut atrae picis offulas et resinae fomentum cum *scintillante* oleo rogorum incendia cumularentur, Ald. 56, 27), An. Ox. 4029. Hē hēt mycel ād ontendan on ymbhwyrfte ðæs mēdenes and mid pice hī besprengan and mid spyrcendum ele, Hml. S. 9, 118. (Both these passages refer to the same circumstance.)

**spitel.** *Add:*—Þā īserngelōman gewunelice naman wē hātaþ spadan and spitelas (*vangas*), Gr. D. 201, 20. [v. *N. E. D.* spittle.]

**spīþra,** an; *m. A spider:*—Gif hunta gebíte mannan, þ is spīþra (*printed* swiþra), Lch. ii. 142, 18.

**spittan** *to dig. Add:* [v. *N. E. D.* spit *to dig*]: **spittan** *to spit. The instances under* spyttan *should be taken here.*

**spitu.** *Add:*—Swā swā mon æl dēð þonne hine mon on spite stagan wyle, Tech. ii. 124, 11.

**spīwan.** I c. *add:*—Ǽr þām þe hē hyne āspīwe, and þonne hē hine spīwan onginneþ . . ., Lch. i. 316, 18.

**spīwing.** *Add:* v. ut-spīung.

**spora.** *Dele* hūn-, hand-spor(a?) *at end, and add:*—Hī ongunnon heorá hors mid heora sperescæftum þerscan and mid heora spurum blōdgian and heáwan; ac hwæðre þā hors wǽron mid þām spurum geblōdgode . . ., Gr. D. 14, 26–15, 4.

**sporettung.** *For* sportengæ *l.* sporetengæ.

**spornan.** I. *add:* (1) *to kick:*—Hine gelǽhte ān hors . . . and

hefde him upp. Þā spearn ōðer hors tō, and āsprencde hine ofer bord, Hml. S. 8, 213. Se flǽscbana spearn hine mid his spuran, and hēt hine þ hē ārise *hunc interfector calce pulsavit ut surgeret,* Gr. D. 254, 27. Yfel bið ðē sylfum þ ðū spurne ongeán ðā gāde, Hml. Th. i. 386, 9. (2) *to strike* against with the foot, *stumble* upon:—Hī spurnon mid hyra fōtum æt (on, *v. l.*) þām hālgan were *in ipso impingebat,* Gr. D. 16, 22. (2 a) *to stumble, totter:*—Spurnende *lapsanti, titubanti,* An. Ox. 50, 7. v. and-, wiþ-spornan.

**sporning.** *Add:* v. æt-sporning.

**sporu** *a heel. Dele (?) and add:*—Hē spearn hine mid his spuran *hunc calce pulsavit,* Gr. D. 254, 27. v. spurul.

**sporu** *a spike.* v. hand-, hūn-sporu.

**spōwan.** II. (1) *add:*—Wē hī æfre tihton tō þīnre geþafunga, þeáh ðe ūs hwōnlíce speówe, Hml. S. 8, 34. (2) *add:*—Him þyses ne speów, Hml. Th. ii. 478, 34. (3) *add:*—Him nā speów nānþingc (*adv.*) þæron, C. D. iv. 58, 7.

**spræc.** *Add:* , es; *n.:*—Spræcu *labruscas,* An. Ox. 2, 63.

**sprǽc.** II. *add:* Spræce (*printed* swæce) heów leáse *false fashions of speech;* insanias *falsas,* Ps. Rdr. 39, 5. Gemetigian ge his sprēce ge his swīgan, Prov. K. 2. III. *add:*—þā wæs seó tunge ālýsed tō sprǽce, Gr. D. 184, 10. Aidan ne mihte gebīgan his sprǽce tō norðhymbriscum gereorde, Hml. S. 26, 68. V. *add:*—Sprǽcu (*eloquia*) Drihtnes sprǽca clǽne, Ps. L. 11, 7. Āsettað þās spǽca (sprǽca, *v. l.*) on eówrum heortum, Lk. 9, 44. VI. *add:*—Nān sprǽc ne mæg his mihta āreccan, Hml. S. 31, 1302. Hwæt synt þā spǽca (*sermones*) þe gyt recceað inc betwýnan?, Lk. 24, 17. VII. *add:*—Āgen *vel* gecynde sprǽc *idioma, proprietas linguae,* Wrt. Voc. i. 55, 46. Nā gýta nǽron wordlācu ne sprǽcu (*loquelae neque sermones*) þāra þe ne wǽron gehērde stefna heora, Ps. L. 18, 4. VIII. *add:*—Ðā cōm hē tō þǽre spǽce þæs hālgan weres *ad colloquium sancti viri pervenit,* Guth. Gr. 159, 7. Hī gereordon hī sylfe þurh þā hālgan sprǽcu þæs gāstlican lífes (*per sacra spiritalis vitae colloquia*), Gr. D. 168, 17. IX. *add:*—Ðā sprēce nǽnig mon uferran dōgor .on nǽnge ōðre halfe oncærrende sié, C. D. B. i, 446, 13. X. *add: a matter for speech* or *discussion:*—Martinus . . . wolde for sumere neóde wið þone cāsere spræcan . . . þā cōm Martinus eft embe ðā ylcan sprǽce tō þām cāsere, Hml. S. 31, 659. Bió ðē unīðe tō clipianne and tō lǽranne, ge furðum ðīna āgna sprǽca *loquere in causa tua vix,* Past. 385, 11. v. cræft- (Ælfc. Gr. Z. 18, 15), efen-, ende-, fela-, gaf-, ge-, hearm-, hosp-, samod-, steór-, sundor-, tungol-sprǽc.

**sprǽce,** an; *f. A talk, discourse:*—Hwæðer ðū nū ongite hwider þiós sprǽce wille? *jamne igitur vides, quid haec omnia, quae diximus, consequatur,* Bt. 40, 1; F. 234, 32. Apollonius hyre ārehte ealle his gelymp, and æt þǽre sprǽcan ende him feóllon teáras of ðām eágum, Ap. Th. 15, 26.

**-sprǽce;** *adj. Add:* v. frēcnen- (?), sōþ-, unhrǽd-sprǽce.

**sprǽc-hūs.** *Add:* I. *a place in which the monastic school was held;* auditorium [auditorium, locus in quo conveniebant monachi, quod in eo essent monachicae scholae, ibique praeceptores docerent, discipuli audirent magistros docentes, Migne]:—Būtan spǽchūses (*auditorii,* printed *adiutorii*) stōwe; seó fram þām swýþust ys geteald þām naman, þ þǽr tō gehlystende sī hwæt fram beódende sī hāten, Angl. xiii. 432, 965. II. *a place in a monastery for the reception of guests* [auditorium, domus vel cubiculum in monasteriis ubi excipiebantur advenientes hospites et salutaturi, Migne]:—Martinus cōm hwīlon tō ānum preóstlīfe, and hī gelōgodon his bǽd on þæs mynstres sprǽchūse, Hml. S. 31, 847; 907: 1183.

**sprǽte (?).** *Dele, and see* spræc.

**spranca.** *Add:*—Sprancena *sarmentorum,* i. uiminum, An. Ox. 2640. (*This and* Hpt. Gl. 468, 22 *are glosses to the same passage,* Ald. 36, 5). [v. *N. E. D.* spronk.] v. æcern-spranca.

**sprangettan** *to quiver, palpitate:*—Ne þās sāwla sprancetað under ūssum slagum, ne hī bifigað ne forhtigað, E. S. 49, 354. Clæppette and sprangette *palpitaret,* Wrt. Voc. ii. 69, 26.

**spreáwlian.** *Add:*—Sprēulede *palpitat,* An. Ox. 50, 34. [v. *N. E. D.* sprawl.]

**spreca.** *Add:* v. ofer-spreca.

**sprecan.** III. (a) [*For the bracket at* Ll. Th. i. 206, 6 *substitute:* (*the claim made on account of the slain thief's death*)] *add:* where the subject is an agreement, whose terms are stated:—Ealswā ðā foreward spreocað, C. D. iii. 336, 26. (c) *add: to speak of:*—Gif hié hwæt sw ā heálicra yfela on him ongieten ðæt hié hit niéde sprecan scylen *si qua valde sunt eorum prava, apud semetipsos dijudicent,* Past. 197, 6. Wæs þær in þām sprecenan īglande sum mycel hlǽw *erat in praefata insula tumulus,* Guth. Gr. 117, 6. *add:* to sprecan fore to speak on *behalf of:*—Hē bæd mē ðæt ic him wǽre forespeca . . . Ðā spæc ic him fore, and þingade him tō Ælfrēde cinge, C. D. ii. 133, 16. v. twi-, wiþ-, ymb-sprecan; bufan-sprecen; sprecende.

**sprecel.** *Add:* [v. *N. E. D.* spreckle, spreckled]: **sprecend.** *Add:* v. ongeán-, wiþer-sprecend: **sprecende.** *Add:* v. micel-, mid-, swīþ-, yfel-sprecende: **sprecendlic.** v. tō-sprecendlic: **sprecolness.** *Add:* v. fela-sprecolness: **spreng.** v. ǽ-spreng (*under* ǽ-spryng).

**sprengan.** II a. *add :*—Se abbud bletsige þā candela and sprenge (*conspergat*) mid wætere gebletsedum, Angl. xiii. 403, 547. **II b.** *add :*—'Gang hrædlíce and spreng (stregd, *v. l.*) þis wæter ofer þæs licgendan líchaman'... Se diácon þ gebletsode wæter sprengde (stregde, *v. l.*) ofer his lima '*vade citius, et aquam super jacentis corpus projice*'... *Diaconus aquam benedictam super membra illius aspersit*, Gr. D. 82, 18–22. [v. *N. E. D.* sprenge.]

**sprenging, springing,** e ; *f. Sprinkling :*—Tó hálgunge sprengincge *ad consecrationem conspersionis*, Angl. xiii. 388, 328. Sprincginge and bletsunge *conspersionem et benedictionem*, 408, 614. [Cf. *N. E. D.* springing ; II 9. *sprinkling* ; spring ; IV 13. *to sprinkle.*] Cf. spring ; **IV.** 3.

**spreót.** *Add :*—Spreót *palus*, An. Ox. 30, 1. [v. *N. E. D.* sprit.]

**spring.** *Add : f.* (cf. æ-springe; *pl.* Az. 134). **I.** *add :* v. wæter-spring. **IV.** *add :* (1) v. deád-spring. (3) *add :* Cf. springing.

**springan.** **III.** *add :*—On lengtentīma[n] ongedre gréniad wæstmas, Angl. viii. 312, 22. **VI.** *add :*—Se geleáfa sprang geond ealne middangeard, Hml. Th. i. 304, 29. His nama geond eall sprang, ii. 156, 17.

**springd.** *Add :* [Be a man neuer so sprind, Shor. 2.]

**springe.** *Add :* v. will-springe : **springing** *sprinkling.* v. sprenging.

**sprintan.** v. ge-sprintan.

**sprot** *a twig. Add :*—Sprotu *labruscas*, An. Ox. 2022. (*The passage at* sprota ; I. *might be taken here.* v. An. Ox. 1557 note.) [v. *N. E. D.* sprote.]

**sprot[t]** *a coarse kind of rush,* sprot [v. *N. E. D.* sprot²] :—In drýge sprott *in harundine* (v. Skeat's collation), Rtl. 86, 34.

**sprott.** *Add :*—Sprot *silurus* (cf. *silurus* a loche, Wülck. Gl. 612, 3), Nap. 14, 39. Hé cwæð þ hí ealle ne mihton, ne fisceras ne hé sylf, gefón ænne sprot, Hml. S. 31, 1271. [v. *N. E. D.* sprot¹.]

**-sprungenness.** *Add :* v. úp-sprungenness.

**sprýtan.** *Add :*—Forð tó sprýtanne, Chr. 995 ; P. 128, 31.

**spryttan.** **I.** *add :*—Fela bóga treówes of ānum wyrtwalan spryttað (*procedunt*), Scint. 3, 17.

**sprytting.** *Add : increase :*—Mægena ealra hé onfó spryttinga *uirtutum omnium percipiat incrementa*, Angl. xiii. 381, 226.

[**-spure**]. v. fót-spure : **spurnness.** v. and-spurnness, Mt. R. 13, 21, 57.

**spurul.** *Add :* Cf. sporu *a heel :* **spyrnness.** v. and-spyrnness, Mt. L. R. 26, 31. Spyrung, An. Ox. 5214. v. spyrigung.

**spyrte.** *Add :*—Spyr[te] *sportella*, An. Ox. 56, 56. Hé sóhte ráp and spertan (wylian, *v. l.*) *funem sportamque quaesivit*, Gr. D. 110, 1. Spyrtan *sportulas*, i. *cofinos*, An. Ox. 3857.

**stæcan** (?). v. stagan.

**stæf.** **I.** *add :*—Álecge þonne his wǽpna, and nime stæf him on hande, and gā bærfót, Ll. Th. ii. 286, 19. **I a.** *an official staff, staff emblematical of office :*—Cóm Ulf ð, and forneáh man sceolde tóbrecan his stæf (stef, *v. l.*), for ðan hé ne cúðe dón his gerihte swā wel swā he sceolde *fere perdidit baculum suum, quia nescivit ministerium suum,* Chr. 1047; P. 171, 13. Hé þám ð. his stæf benam, 1094; P. 229, 4. **II.** *add :*—Ðis gewrit is gewriten stæf be stæfe be þám gewrite þe Dúnstán sealde ūrum hláforde, Ll. Lbmn. 214, 24. Se biscop hine hét stafa (steafa, *v. l.*) naman cweðan, Bd. 5, 2 ; Sch. 558, 22. þ getæl þæra stafena, Angl. viii. 335, 40. Stricum, stafum *apicibus*, i. *litteris*, An. Ox. 2009. **III.** *add :*—Tó þám Lucius Bretene kyning sende stafas *misit ad eum Lucius Brittaniarum rex epistulam* (Bd. 1, 4), Chr. 167 ; P. 8, 19. **IV.** *add :*—Stafena (*for wk. form* cf. 1557 note) *litterarum*, i. *dogmatum*, An. Ox. 2311. [¶ *in the following passages* stafum *seems an error for* stānum :—Hūs mid gyldenum stafum (*aureis laterculis*) getimbrod, Gr. D. 319, 7 : 321, 11. Cf. þā gyldenan stānas, 321, 21.] v. āþ-, bisceop-, canter-, edwit-, Læden-stæf.

**stæf-cræft.** **I.** *add :*—Stæfcræft *grammatica*, An. Ox. 3114. **II.** *add :*—Stæfcræftes brede (*æthralis*) *literaturae albo* (*descriptos*), An. Ox. 3031. Stæfcræftas, Hpt. Gl. 477, 49. (*Both glosses refer to the same passage.*)

**stæf-cyst.** *Add :*—Stæfcræftes, [stæf?]cyste *literaturae*, An. Ox. 3031.

**stæf-gefég.** **I a.** *add :*—þ hīw byð gecíged omoeuteleuton swā oft swā se middel and se ýtemesta dæl geendað on gelícum stæfgefége, Angl. viii. 332, 13. **II.** *add :*—Stæfgeféges *litteraturae*, i. *scripturæ*, An. Ox. 7, 219. Ic ne oncneów stæfgefég *non cognovi litteraturam*, Ps. L. 70, 16.

**stæf-leahter,** es ; *m. An impropriety of speech, a barbarism :*—Stæfleahtres *barbarismi*, An. Ox. 5467.

**stæf-rǽw.** *Add :* [**I.** *an alphabet.* v. Dict.] **II.** *a line or passage in a document or inscription :*—Hé þærinne funde āne leádene tabulan eall āwritene ; and þā hé hí rædde, þā cóm hé tó þære stæfrǽwe þær hé þ word funde āwriten... þ hí fram Decie þám cāsere flugon, and his éhtnysse þoledon, Hml. S. 23, 767. *v. next word.*

**stæf-róf.** *Substitute: an alphabet :*—Stæfróf *elimentum*, Wrt. Voc. ii. 32. 24. Bóc *de orthografía*, mid stæfenróph (= stæfena rófe ?)

endebrydnesse tósceádene (*alphabeti ordine distinctum*), Bd. 5, 24; Sch. 699, 22 n. *See preceding word, and cf.* secg-róf.

**stæg** *a pond :*—Staeg *vel* meri *stagnum*, Txts. 98, 962. [*From* stagnum.]

**stǽgan.** v. ā-stígan. Cf. stígan : **stǽgel.** *Add :* [Cf. *Ger.* steil.] Cf. stígan.

**stǽger.** *Add :*—Wæs on þære ylcan stówe trum stæger mid gewissum stapum fram þære nyðerflóra tó þære ūpflóra *quo in loco inferiora superioribus pervius continuabat ascensus*, Gr. D. 170, 19. Cf. stígan.

**stæl.** Under *stalworth* (*N. E. D.*) it is said that the quantity of the vowel is certain from the three occurrences in poetry. But in two of these, Reb. 11 : Gen. 1113, the word is a 'final lift', of which Sweet remarks 'the quantity is indifferent,' A. S. Rdr. § 361; in the third the quantity might be short on the analogy of such a verse as :—His wiðerbrecan, Gen. 66 : Dan. 66 : Gū. 265.

**stǽlan.** [*For* Sat. 640 *and* Gen. 1352 *substitute* :—Him on edwít oft āsettað swearte sūslbonan, [Satan on] stǽleð fǽhðe, þǽr þe hié freódrihten oft forgeáton *the enmity they showed their Lord in frequently forgetting him is made a reproach to them by the devils, and is laid to their charge by Satan*, Sat. 640. Feówertig daga fǽhðe ic wille on weras stǽlan *for forty days will I make on men my charge of enmity against me*, Gen. 1352. In the last line but one for *death* read *wounding*, for *slain, wounded.*] *Add :*—Men him eallinga ne ondrædaþ, hū þ dióful him on stǽleð ealle þā unrihtan weorc þe hér worhte bióð, Verc. Först. 89, 11. þæt mé ne mótan þā dreórgan deófla æt mīnum ende ne on dómdæge mīne synna on stǽlan (cf. þæt mé næfre deófel nāht on ne mæge bestǽlan, 101, 52), Angl. xi. 100, 94 : Verc. Först. 147, 29.

**stǽl-þing,** es ; *n. Theft :*—þe lǽs þā þénas þára bróðra gód þurh stælding (*furtim*) ætferiou, Chrd. 19, 16.

**-stæn.** v. ge-stæn : **stǽna ;** *m. Substitute* **stǽne ;** *f.* v. Kl. Nom. Stam. § 81.

**stǽnan.** *Add :*—Seó ǽ tǽhte þæt man sceolde ælcne wīmman þe cild hæfde būtan rihte ǽwe stǽnan (cf. *eam lapidibus obruent viri civitatis,* Deut. 22, 21). Nū ðonne gif Maria unbeweddod wǽre and cild hæfde, þonne wolde þæt lūdéisce folc mid stānum hí oftorfian, Hml. Th. i. 196, 10.

**stǽnen.** *Add :*—Be ðǽre díc tó ðǽre stǽnenan bricge, C. D. iii. 449, 23.

**stǽner.** *In l. 1 for* stærer (stǽnen ?) *l.* stǽner, *and at end of l. 2 for* Mt. *l.* Mk. [Cf. staners *the small stones and gravel on the margin of a river or lake;* stanners *the gravelly shores of a river,* Jamieson's Dict.]

**stǽpe.** **I.** *add :*—Nis nān twýn þæt eów ne beó sorgolden ǽlc þæra stapa ðe gé tó Godes hūse stæppað, Hml. Th. ii. 444, 11. **I b.** *the mark left by the foot, a trace* (lit. or fig.); *vestigium :*—Ðonne beóð ðā fét gesewene, ðonne mon ongiet mid hwelcum stæpum ðæt nāwht wæs ðurhtogen, ac ðeáh ðæt unclǽne mód fǽhð on ðā lādunga, and mid ðǽre beheled his fét and ðā stæpas his unnyttan weorces *pedes conspiciuntur, quia quibus vestigiis nequitia sit perpetrata cognoscitur, et tamen adductis excusationibus impura mens introrsus pedes colligit, quia cuncta iniquitatis suae vestigia abscondit,* Past. 241, 20. **III.** *add :*—From ðǽre sūðdura lāgon stapas tó ðām westdǽle, Hml. Th. i. 504, 9. Trum stæger mid gewissum stapum fram þǽre nyþerflóra tó þǽre ūpflóra, Gr. D. 170, 19.

**stǽppa.** *l.* steppa.

**stæppan.** *Add :*—Ælc þæra stapa ðe gé tó Godes hūse stæppað, Hml. Th. ii. 444, 11. Mid þām ðe hé mótode on his dómsetle sittende, ... þā stóp him tó Godes engel, and hine ofslóh, 382, 31.

**stǽr.** *Substitute for last passage :*—On þis ūre cyriclice stǽr, Bd. 4, 7 ; Sch. 385, 3. *Add :*—þ swīðe wel in þám hálgan and sóðan stǽre (*in sacra veracige historia*) is āwriten, Gr. D. 245, 14. [*From Latin* historia.]

**stǽr-blind.** *Add :*—Arrianus wearð slagen mid sæmnedlicre blindnesse, swā þ hé eallunga stærblind wæs gelǽded mid frǽmdum handum *Arrianus subita caecitate percussus est, atque alienis manibus ad suum habitaculum reductus,* Gr. D. 235, 3. Stærblindra *scotomaticorum,* i. *cecorum,* An. Ox. 1735.

**stǽrlíce ;** *adv. Historically ;* historialiter, An. Ox. 2, 310.

**stǽrling,** es ; *m. A starling :*—Stærlinc *sturnus,* Hpt. 33, 241, 54.

**stæþ.** *Add : m. :*—Andlang díc ūtt on Terstān (cf. on Tærstān stream, iv. 105, 4) on ðone sýðeran steð ; ðonne andlang steðes ; ðæt beneoðan beámwær on ðone norðere steð, andlang staðes æft on Twyfyrde, C. D. v. 148, 19–22. Ūt þurh þone stream on þæs cynges stæð ; and swā andlang streámes, iv. 105, 13. On stæþena óðrum *riparum marginibus,* An. Ox. 4797. Staþa, 2, 387. Staðum *ripis,* 26, 41. [The Latin original of Lch. iii. 210, 16 is: Ripas ascendere laborem significat. Ripas descendere, bonum tempus significat.] v. brim-, eást-stæþ.

**stæþ-hlípe.** *Add :* in wk. declension used as noun ; *a steep place, precipice :*—Hé geseáh manige men gān þurh þā stæþhlýpan (-hlépan, *v. l.*) heora uncysta *multos ire per abrupta vitiorum cernebat,* Gr. D. 95, 16. Sóhte hé ðone Godes wer geond ealle þā stæþhlýpan (*abrupta*) þæra munta, 99, 22.

**stæppigness.** *Add :* v. ge-, un-stæþþigness.

**stagan** (? **stæcan.** Cf. *Icel.* steikja *to roast) to roast :*—Æles tácen is þæt mon wecge his swýþran hand and sette syþþan ofer his wynstran earm and ástrehte his wynstran hande strîce þwyrs ofer mid þære swýðran, swylce hê hine corflige swâ swâ mon æl dêð þonne hine mon on spite stagan wyle *the sign for an eel is to waggle the right hand, and then to put it over the left arm, and then, the left hand being extended, to make strokes with the right hand across the arm as if cutting it in bits as is done with an eel, when it is to be roasted on a spit,* Tech. ii. 124, 11. [Cf. *Icel.* steikja â teini.]

**stalian.** I. *add :*—For hwon gedyrstigodest þú þ þú þus oft in þisra muneca wyrtûne stalodest ? . . . Gang nû and æfter þissere tîde ne stala (stel, *v. l.*) þú hêr nâ mâ, Gr. D. 25, 6-20. Þæt seofoðe bebod is: 'Ne stala þú' (cf. ne stel þú, Ex. 20, 15), Hml. Th. ii. 208, 24.

**stálian.** *Add :* v. ge-stálian.

**stalu.** I. *add :*—Gehwylce wyrte, þe hê ær mid stale (*furto*) gewilnode, hê him sealde, Gr. D. 25, 16. **I a.** *a particular instance of theft :*—Gyf ðú ænig ðing ðisse stale wite oððe gewita wære, Ll. Lbmn. 415, 24. Se ðridda leahtor is gîtsung . . . Of ðisum leahtre beóð ácennede . . . stala, Hml. Th. ii. 220, 11.

**stamera,** an; *m. One who stammers* (as a nickname) :—Ic geann Æþelwearde stameran, C. D. iii. 363, 15.

**stân.** I. *add :* v. un-gebeáten. **II b.** *add : a milestone :*—Of ðære burnan tô mîla stâne; of ðâm stâne on ðâ hâran apeltreó, C. D. iii. 382, 22. v. byrþen-, cealc-, cynning-, fôt-, fŷr-, gagat-, gemær-, gicel-, heal-, hrôf-, hwam-, marmel-, mealm-, sinc-, spær-, windel-stân.

**stân-bucca.** Ælfric has wrongly given to the river-name Cinyps the meaning of *Cinyphius hircus:* cf. Virgil Georg. 3, 312 and Isidore xii. 1. 14: 'Maiores hirci Cinyphii dicuntur a fluvio Cinyphe in Libya ubi grandes nascuntur.' (Note by Dr. Craigie.)

**stân-ceastel.** *Substitute: An old Roman or British earthwork* (? v. castel; **II**), *a heap of stones :*—Iuxta unum aceruum lapidum quod nos stâncestil uocamus, C. D. iii. 388, 13. On ânne stâncastel, 397, 27. Bewestan ðære ealdan byrig on ðone stânihtan weg, of ðan wege tô ðan stâncystlum, vi. 234, 32.

**stân-ceosel.** *Add :*—Stâncyslum *sablonibus,* An. Ox. 1818.

**stân-clif.** *Add : a crag :*—Ofer þâ stôwe ufon wæs hangiende unmæte stânclif (*ingens rupes*), Gr. D. 52, 16 : 99, 2. Weard upp áscoten swýðlicu mycelnes þæs ungemætan stânclifes *ingentis saxi moles erupta est,* 12, 9. Hê gecerde stânclif (*rupem*) on wellas wætra, Ps. Vos. 113, 8. Þæra mynstra wæron þreó áseted in þæs muntes stânclifum (*rupibus*), Gr. D. 112, 16.

**stân-clûd.** *Add :*—Stânclûd *scopulus,* Hpt. Gl. 499, 30. Ofer þâ stôwe wæs ufan hangiende ormæte stânclûd (*ingens rupes*), Gr. D. 52, 17. Of ellebeorhan intô stânclûde, C. D. iii. 424, 29. Hû Nonnosus þone mycelan stânclûd (*saxum*) âweg âdyde, Gr. D. 48, 16. Of stânclûdum cumað wyllspringas, Hex. 22, 23.

**stân-cnoll,** es; *m. A rocky top* (?) , *rock-summit :*—Andlang þære rôde oð hit cymð beneoðan stâncnolle, Cht. E. 248, 17.

**stân-cynn,** es; *n. A kind of stone :*—A(s)bestus hätte sum stâncynn, Nap. 59.

**standan.** **I 2.** *add :*—þ wæter wæs standende and beleác þâ duru þære cyrican *the water formed as it were a wall, and closed the entrance to the church,* Gr. D. 220, 16. **II.** (2) *add :*—Þâra six hîda þæ þ mynstær on stent, C. D. iii. 274, 9. Ne standað nâ ealle steorran on ðâm steápan rodore, Hex. 12, 29. (4) *of the matter contained in a book :*—Stynt on þære bec on þâm forman ferse: 'Et Spiritus . . .,' Ælfc. Gen. Thw. 3, 3. Âht þæs þe on ûrum gewritum stent, Ll. Th. i. 236, 32. Swâ hit on þære dômbêc stande, 158, 6. (5) *of non-material things :*—Hû hlîsa nû stynt swâ hwær swâ crîstendôm bið, Ælfc. T. Grn. 12, 25. **II a.** *add :*—Hit stent on þînum breþer, gif þu hit gebicgan môst *it rests with your brother whether you may buy it,* Hml. S. 36, 178. Tô þâm forewerdon þ hê becweðe þone sceat þâm þe hîm leófost beó þe on þâm lande stent *on the condition that he may bequeath the money that is on mortgage on the land as he pleases,* Cht. Crw. 9, 121. Ðat land . . . ðæron stent ðâm bisceope eahta marca goldes, C. D. iv. 288, 8. **III.** *add :*—Gange hit intô Scâ Marian stôwæ æal swâ hit stænt mid mæte and mid mannum, C. D. iii. 274, 2 : 22 : Cht. Crw. 23, 3. Seó sixte yld þissere worulde stynt fram Crîste âstreht oð dômes dæg eallum mannum ungewiss, Ælfc. T. Grn. 19, 41. v. stille. **IV.** *add :*—On hû fela gesceaftum stent þes middaneard ? On feówrum *quot elementis mundus constat? Quatuor,* Angl. vii. 12, 102. Seó tîd stent on feówer pricon, viii. 309, 2. Dactilus stent on ânum langum tîman and twâm sceortum, 314, 14 : 335, 17. **VI.** *add :*—Seó ealde æ þe þâ stôd næs swâ stîð on þâm þingum swâ swâ Crîstes godspel is þe nû stent, Angl. vii. 46, 444. ðâ hwîle ðe fulwiht stondan môte, Txts. 175, 17. **VIII.** *add :*—His fêt ne mihton âhwâr standan, ac hê feóll âdûn tô deófle âwend, Ælf. T. Grn. 3, 1. Ðær wæs standende wæter ofer þâm lande, swâ hit þære eá flôd ær gefieów, Ors. 1, 3; S. 32, 11. **VIII a.** *to maintain one's position, not to yield*

*to pressure :*—Fela samod tugon, ac heó næs âstyrod, ac stôd swâ swâ munt, Hml. S. 9, 102 : Shrn. 154, 28. v. in-, on-, ofer-, þurh-, wiþerstandan.

**-standendlic.** v. in-standendlic.

**standenness.** v. under-, ymb-standenness.

**stân-denu** *a stony valley :*—In stândene, C. D. iii. 383, 19.

**-standing.** v. under-standing.

**stân-flôr** *a stone floor, pavement :*—Stânflôrum *tesellis,* An. Ox. 14, 3.

**stân-gaderung.** *Add :*—Stângæderunga gecnysedre *macheriae inpulse,* Ps. Rdr. 61, 4.

**stân-gedelf.** *Add :* [Cf. êst tô stândelue, C. D. vi. 225, 4. *D. D.* stone-delf, -delph a *stone-quarry.*]

**stân-gella.** *Add :*—Stânegellan, Ps. Vos. 101, 7.

**stân-geweorc.** *Add :* v. ge-weorc; **IV** *and* **VI c.**

**stân-græf** *a stone-quarry* [:—Of thâm bærue west andlang mærce tô stângrave; of thâm grave, C. D. B. iii. 694, 13.]

**stân-hlinc,** es; *m. A stony hlinc* (q. v.) :—On stânhlinces ende, C. D. iii. 82, 6. On ðone stânhlinc; ðonne of stânhlince, 414, 16. Of ðære æc tô stânhlincan; of stânhlincan tô reáde burnan, 78, 36.

**stâniht.** *l.* stâniht[e].

**stân-ræw** *a line of stones :*—On stânræwe; of stânræwe, C. D. iii. 444, 5.

**stân-torr.** **II.** *add :*—þæt âborstene clif hreás ofdûneweard . . . ac þâ þâ se hâlga wer geseah þone stântorr ufene tôweardes him farende . . . hê âwrât Crîstes rôde tácen and þone stântorr swâ feallende gefæstnode on þære sîdan þæs muntes *ingentis saxi moles erupta est, per devexum montis latus veniens . . . Quam cum venientem desuper vir sanctus vidisset . . . signum crucis ei opposuit, eamque in montis latere cadentem fixit,* Gr. D. 12, 9-17.

**stân-walu,** e; *f. A bank of stones :*—In stânwale; andlang ðære wale on ðone portweg, C. D. iv. 98, 28. v. walu.

**stân-weall.** *Add :*—þæt wæter stôd him on twâ healfa swilce ôðer stânweall, Hml. Th. ii. 194, 22. Up oð ðone ealdan stânweall . . . on stânwealles brôc, C. D. iii. 416, 12-22.

**stapa.** I. *add :* v. weald-stapa.

**stapol.** I. *Dele second passage.* **II.** *add : a flight of steps before the door of a house :*—Hlidgata *valva,* stapul *petronus* (*patronus,* MS.), stæger *ascensorium,* Wrt. Voc. i. 26, 35-37.

**stappel.** *Add :* v. fôt-stappel.

**starian.** *Add :*—Ðâ ðâ hî úp tô heofonum starigende stôdon, Hml. Th. i. 296, 3. In l. 7 *for* an *l.* andæges.

**staþol.** **II.** *add :*—þâ hê geseah þ manie men wæron geladode tô staðole beteran lîfes *cum conspiceret multos ad statum vitae melioris vocari,* Gr. D. 117, 24 : 205, 7. Heó cwæð þ þæs gyfe genihtsumode þe þære sâwle staðol unwemme geheóld swâ *said that his grace sufficed who kept the state of the soul stainless,* Hml. S. 23 b, 717. **III a.** *an estate, a farm :*—Se fæder näht elles hire ne sealde bûton .vi. ynstan ânre æhte (cf. staþol-æht) (*unius possessiunculae*) . . . Côm ân ceorl mid lâce of ðâm ylcan staðole (*ex eodem fundo*) þe heó ær onfêng vi yntsan æt hire fæder, Gr. D. 222, 25-22, 5.

**staþol-æht.** *Add :* v. staþol ; **III a.**

**staþol-fæst.** *Transfer last passage under* **I** *to* **III**, *and add there:* steady :—Cild bið cumliðe, þancful, staðolfæst, Lch. iii. 192, 8. Staþolfæstes wîfes *stabilis mulieris,* Scint. 226, 3. Staþelfæste tremmincge *firmo* (*scripturarum*) *fulcimento,* An. Ox. 1420.

**staþolfæstlîce.** **II.** *add :*—þý staðolfæstlîcor (*solidius*) hî wæron getrymede, Gr. D. 205, 7.

**staþolfæstness.** *Add :* **I.** physical :—þæt for þæs treówes styrenesse wære ege æteówed, and for his staþolfæstnysse (*stabilitate*) bældo, Gr. D. 191, 9. Swylce seó wætergesceaft wære ouwænded in fæstes wâges staðolfæstnysse *ac si illud elementum liquidum in soliditatem parietis fuisset mutatum,* 220, 17. **II.** non-physical :—Hî ætbrûdon folces menn fram woruldlicum gedwyldum tô staðolfæstnysse lybbendra eorðan, þæt is, tô ðâm êcan êðle, Hml. Th. i. 576, 25. v. môd-staþolfæstness.

**staþolian.** *Add :*—Ðêr se ân gestæððega cyning ne staþelode ealla gesceafta, ðonne wurdon hî ealle tôslopene, Bt. 39, 13 ; F. 234, 26. v. ed- (?), geed-staþolian (-el-).

**staþoliend.** *Add :* v. ed-, geed-staþoliend: **-staþolig.** v. edstaþelig (?): staþolung. v. ed-, geed-staþelung.

**steall.** *Add :* n. (v. treów-, wîg-steall). v. beorg- (borg-), cyric-, hâm-, mæsse-, mere-, sealtærn-, tûn-, wîgbed-steall: **-steall.** v. wintersteall.

**steallere.** *Add :*—Eádnôð stallere heom wið gefeaht, Chr. 1067; P. 203, 16.

**stealu.** v. stela.

**steáp** *a stoup.* [*In* l. 7 *dele* '(?)' *after* 'remove', *see* â-settan.] *Add :*—þâ þær þæs biscopes cniht tô his fæder wînes drync, swâ swâ hit þeáw wæs. Þâ ræhte se cyning his hand forð swîgende and genam þone hnæp (steáp, *v. l.* calicem) . . . and þâm biscope þone drync sealde, Gr. D. 186, 7. Ille regina dedit duas steápas in twaem pundum, C. D. ii. 8, 9.

steáp; adj. I. add:—On steápan hlinc; of steápan hlince, C. D. iii. 82, 4. II. For Hml. Th. l. Hml. S., and add:—Ne standað nā ealle steorran on ðām steápan rodore, Hex. 12, 30. v. heáh-steáp.

stearclíce. Add: strictly:—Ealdor þe hī stearclíce healde frater qui eos artissime constringat, Chrd. 54, 26. [O. H. Ger. starclícha attente: Icel. sterkliga (berjask).]

stearc-mód; adj. Stubborn, obstinate. v. stearc; I a:—Hit is neód þām þe oð þis módig and prút and úpāhafen wære, and stearcmód (uultu rigidus) lyfede, Chrd. 8, 27.

stearm. v. storm.

stéda. Add:—Stoedia emissarius, An. Ox. 53, 38. Ic geann Ælfsige bisceope . . . ānes blacan (blācan?) stēdan . . . and ic geann Ælmære ānes fāgan stēdan, Cht. E. 226, 10–24.

stede. I. add:—Hī of ðām stedum þā hors āstyrian ne mihton, Gr. D. 15, 5. ¶ of stede (or of-stede? cf. in-stede) on the spot, at once :— þænne þū of stede miht syllan cum statim possis dare, Scint. 193, 12: 197, 13. II. add:—On ðām ýtemestan styde standan, R. Ben. I. 76, 9. Ǽrest man āsmeáð þæs húses stede, Angl. viii. 324, 8. II b. add:—Seó gītsung næfde nænne stede on heora heortan, Hml. Th. i. 326, 35. Smeága gehwā on his móde, gif ðæs beboda habbað ænigne stede on his heortan, ii. 228, 21. II c. official position :—On his styde sē ðe is wyrðe efterfylige in loco eius (decanus) qui dignus est succedat, R. Ben. I. 54, 9. Mathias wæs gecoren on Iūdan stede, Ælfc. T. Grn. 15, 39. v. beán-, ceáp-, ciric-, cwealm-, hām-, hleów-, hlós-, mynster-, pleg-, treów-, tún-, wāfung-, wer-stede; in-stede; adv.

stede-fæst. Add: I. firmly fixed: (1) of a person, rooted to the spot :—Hē beád him þ hī ālēdon þā byrðene, and þā bærmen sóna stede-fæste stódon, swilce hī āstífodon wǽron, Hml. S. 31, 375. (2) of a tree :—Gelíc ðām treówe ðe grēwð wið ðone stream stedefæst on wǽtan tanquam lignum quod plantatum est secus decursus aquarum, Hex. 40, 10. II. of weather, steady, not variable :—Winter stedfæst hiems stabilis (cf. winter missenlic, 298, 15), Archiv cxx. 297, 33.

-stedefull. v. un-stedefull: stedefulness. Add: v. un-stedeful-ness: -stedende. v. welig-stedende: stéd-hors. v. gestéd-hors.

stedig. Add:—Oð stedigu cend maniga donec sterilis peperit pluri-mos, Ps. Rdr. 279, 5.

stedigian. v. ge-stedigian.

stefn a turn. Add:—Stemnum gewrixlum alternis uicibus, An. Ox. 3001. Gewrixlicum stempnum, 2, 136. v. stefn-mǽlum.

stefn voice. I. add: (1) of sound proceeding from the mouth of a living creature :—Swelce sió godcunde stefn (stemn, v. l.) tó him cwæde, Past. 122, 7. Sáwla sóðfæste hergað cyninges þrym stefn æfter stefne, Ph. 542. Cyning spræc him stefne tó, Gen. 2848. Engel stefne ábeád, torhtan reorde, Dan. 510. Hóf hlúde stefne lifigendra leód, Exod. 276. Ongan hē mid mycelre stefne (voce magna) hlýdan . . . Tó þæs þām manigfealdum and ungefóhlicum stefnum (hreáme, v. l.) se biscop cóm (ad cujus voces episcopus venit), Gr. D. 64, 28. Wæterfrocgan hrímað hlúdum stefnum, Chrd. 96, 29. Hig stódon feorran and hyra stefna úp āhófon, Lk. 17, 13. (2) of sound produced with an instru-ment :—Heofonbýman stefn, Cri. 949. (3) of sound made by inanimate objects :—Geómen cwǽdon þ ðrittegum geárum ne gestilde nǽfre stefen cearciendes wǽnes and ceoriendes wales, Lch. iii. 430, 33. Stefn þunur-rāda þínre uox tonitrui tui, Ps. Rdr. 76, 19. Úp āhófon flódas stefna (uoces) heora, fram stefnum wætera manigra, 92, 3–4. þā stefna þæs lyftes, Angl. viii. 313, 14. (4) where an impression is produced on the mind like that which might be produced by words :—Ne synd sprǽca ne word, þāra ne sýn gehýred stefna heora, Ps. Rdr. 18, 4. II. add:— Hī synd þreóra cynna nā on stemne, ac on andgite, Ælfc. Gr. Z. 94, 12. v. riht-stefn.

stefn a summons. Add: a fixed time for doing something :—Hī setton stefna út tó Lundene, and man beád þā folce þider út ofer ealne þisne norðende they fixed times for coming to London, and the people over all this north part were called out thither, Chr. 1052; P. 175, 28. [They setten steven for to mete To plaien at the dis, Ch. T. 4381. By hir both assent was set a steven, p. 430. For al day meten men at unset steven, 1526.]

-stefna. v. wunden-stefna.

stefnan. Add: , stemnan. v. ā-stefnan (:—Fram þām bróðrum þæs mynstres ðe hī sylf (sylfe, v. l.) āstemnedon a fratribus monasterii quod ab ipsis conditum est, Bd. pref.; Sch. 4, 13).

stefnettan. Add: [The original Latin of Kath. 1265 is: Quid vos sic ommutescitis?]

stefn-hlów; adj. Vowel, vocalic :—Ðæne clypolon .a. oððe þæne stemhlówan, Angl. viii. 314, 16.

stefnian. Add: v. ge-stefnian.

stefn-mǽlum; adv. By turns :—Swā stemmǽlum on þām þā wucan ādreósan sic alternati in eo epdomadam percurra[n]t, Angl. xiii. 385, 280. v. stefn; m.

stela. Add:—Stela, stealu cauliculus, An. Ox. 547.

stelan. Add:—Þā gewunode ān þeóf þ hē stāh ofer þone hege and dígellíce stæl (stæll, v. l.) þā wyrta, Gr. D. 23, 24. Gang nū, and æfter þysum ne stel þū nān þing, 25, 19. Hē begann tó stelenne on heora gewunan he began to steal according to their custom, Ælf. T. Grn. 17, 18.

stellan. Add:—Þā þāra gāsta gehwylc his ācsunge synderlíce gerehton, . . . þā stelde (stælde, v. l.) þær ān ford in heora middle (unus in medium prosiliit), Gr. D. 189, 13. v. wiþ-styllan.

stellung. v. weall-stellung: stemman. v. fore-stemman: stem-nan, -stemnian. v. stefnan.

stēnan; p. de. Substitute: stenan; p. stæn, pl. stǽnon. I. of a person, to roar, groan loudly :—Ic grymetige and stene mid ealle móde rugiebam a gemitu cordis mei, Ps. Th. 37, 8. II. of sound made with things, to roar, sound loudly :—Cóm ðā wigena hleó þegna þreáte (þrýðbord stēnan (loud sounded the shields)), beaduróf cyning burga neósan, El. 151. [Du. stenen to groan.] v. ā-stenan (grānode vel ásten rugiebam, Bl. Gl.), stenecian, stenian; stunian.

stenc. I. add:—Stenceas, Past. 64, 21. v. ge-stenc; swót-stence.

stencan to pant. l. stenecian, and add: v. stenian: stencan to scatter. Add: v. ā-stencan: stencende. Add: v. swót-stencende.

stenc-fæt, es; n. A smelling-bottle :—Gewyrtboxas oþþe stencfatu olfactoriola, An. Ox. 8, 299.

steng. Add:—Heora ān hine (James) slóh mid ormǽtum stencge (printed strencge; but cf. Þone Iacóbum Iūdǽa leorneras ofslógan mid webwyrhtan róde, Shrn. 93, 13) inn oð þæt bragen, Hml. Th. ii. 300, 24. þā Walas ādrifon sumre eá ford ealne mid scearpum stængum, Chr. pref.; P. 5, 11 n.

steóp-bearn. Add:—Onias wolde mid ðām lācum widewan and steópbearn bewerian wið hunger, Hml. S. 25, 755.

steóp-sunu. Add:—Steúpsunu pronepus, priuiginus, Hpt. 33, 246, 76: 247, 113.

steór. In l. 15 l. 115 for 117. I. add:—Bið swýþe derigendlic þ bisceop beó gýmeleás, and unfremful bið þ folc beó bútan steóre (-a, v. l.), Hml. S. 13, 126. III. add:—Steóre inuectionis, An. Ox. 7, 382. Ðý lǽs him ðæs gódan weorces leán losige ðe hē mid ðǽre steóre geearnian sceolde, Past. 151, 4. IV. add:—Nē þágýt þā nunnan heora tungan geheóldon mid ðǽre steóre (freno) heora hādes, Gr. D. 151, 31. Se Drihtnes wer ongan hire stýran mid gemetlicre steóre (modesta prohibitione) and þus cwæð, 216, 22.

steóran. III. add: to prohibit. (1) with acc. of person :—Sóna swā þ gehýrde Nonnosus, hē stýrde hī, þ þ swā beón ne mihte quod Nonnosus fieri prohibuit, Gr. D. 50, 18. (2) with dat. of person :—þā fǽringa stýrde hē þām stefnum þāra singendra voces psallentium repente compescuit, 282, 12. Se Drihtnes wer ongan hire stýran quam vir Domini compescuit, 216, 22. (3) with gen. of that which is prohibited or from which one is restrained :—þā stýrde hē þæs quod prohibuit, Gr. D. 50, 18. (3 a) with clause :—Godes ǽngcel stýrde þ man hine in þ fýr ne besǽncte angelus eum in ignem mergi prohibuit, 317, 13.

steóre. Add:—Lār ł steóre þín gestýrde disciplina tua correxit, Ps. L. 17, 36.

steórleás-lic; adj. Undisciplined :—In gýmeleáslicum wordum þe steórleáslicu cildru gewuniað tó sprecanne, Gr. D. 289, 10.

steór-mann. Add:—Steórmannes naucleri, An. Ox. 32.

steor-sceáwere. II. The passage to which the gloss belongs is: Vitam fato fortunae et genesi gubernari juxta mathematicorum constella-tionem arbitratur, Ald. 35, 37. Perhaps steorrscēwere is an alternative gloss for mathematicus. Cf. steor-gleáw (occurring in another gloss to this passage), steor-wiglere.

steór-setl. Add:—Steórsetl pupim, An. Ox. 43, 11.

steór-sprǽc, e; f. Reproof, rebuke :—Swā swā man nā hæbbende on múðe his steórspręca (streór-, MS.) ut homo non habens in ore suo increpationes, Ps. Rdr. 37, 15.

steort. Add: v. han-, hop-steort (?).

steor-wiglere, es; m. An astrologer :—Ste(o)rwigleras mathematici, An. Ox. 55, 8.

steppa. Take here passage given at stæppa in which read steppan.

stéran. Add: , stýran :—Ðonne þū stórfæt habban wille, þonne wend þū þíne hand ofdúne and wege hī swilce þú stýre, Tech. ii. 120, 15. Se abbud stére abbas turificet, Angl. xiii. 403, 547. Stérende turificando, 402, 531.

stert. v. stirc.

sticca. I. add:—Genim ǽnne sticcan and gewyrc hine feðorbyrste (fray it out at the end) . . . styre þonne mid ðý sticcan, Lch. iii. 24, 18–20. II. add:—Gyf þū sticcan behófige, þonne wege þū þíne hand swilce þū mid sticcan etan wile, Tech. ii. 123, 5. v. fiter-, mete-, teld-sticca.

sticels. Add:—þū of swýðdum deáðe(s) sticelse (de uicto mortis aculeo) geopnodest rícu heofona, Hymn ad Mat. 17.

stician. II 1. add:—Hē geseah hwǽr Sisara læg, and se teldsticca sticode þurh his heáfod vidit Sisaram jacentem mortuum et clavum infixum in tempore ejus, Jud. 4, 22. II 2. In l. 4 insert Bt. before 37. III. add: to project :—Ðonne niðer andlang strémes onbútan ðone horsgærstún ðæt hit sticað on ðǽre eá sylfre . . . forð be ðām

yrðlonde ðæt hit sticað on Æðeríces gemǽre; andlang ðæs weges ðæt hit sticað on Húnan wege, C. D. iii. 414, 25-34.

**sticol.** III a. *add*:—Sticoles ardui ( *propositi*), An. Ox. 7, 32.

**sticol-ness,** e; *f. Loftiness*:—On sticylnysse, on hēhþe *in edito*, i. *in fastigio*, An. Ox. 4437.

**stic-tǽnel.** *Add*: , es; *m.*

**stíg.** *Add*: *In* Ps. L. *the word is masculine*:—Seó stíg (*semita*) wæs swíðe neara on ðǽre sídan þæs muntes . . . ân lytel cniht eóde upp unwǽrlíce on ðǽre nearwan stíge, Gr. D. 212, 19-22 : 322, 19. Stígas  stíga, Ps. Rdr. Vos. stíge, Ps. Srt.) *semitas*, Ps. L. 138, 23 : 141, 4. v. ciric- (?), fore- (?), heáfod-stíg.

**stíg** (?). *In* l. 3 *for suestrina substitute ustrina ubi porci ustulantur*, *dele last passage, and add*: v. gāt-ānstíg (?): **stíga** (?). *l.* stíga (cf. *Icel.* ein-stigi), *and add* (?):—Andlang weges tô reádan ānstigan, C. D. v. 166, 7.

**stígan.** I 2 *add*:—Hê ofer þone geard stāh, Gr. D. 23, 26. v. of-stígan ; dúne-, niþer-stígende.

**stíge.** *Add*: v. ofer-stíge.

**stigel.** *Add*:—Hí becômon tô ðǽre stigole þǽr se þeóf oferstāh (*ad aditum furis*) in ðone wyrttûn . . . 'Ic þē bebeóde . . . þ þū þā stigole (*aditum*) behealde,' Gr. D. 24, 6-12. Tô Dunnes stigele ; of ðǽre stigele *ad scansile* . . ., *ab inde*, C. D. B. iii. 252, 2. Oþ henne stigele, 682, 23. ¶ in a compound :—On stigel-āc, C. D. iii. 461, 6.

**stígend.** *Add*: , es ; *m. One who goes on board a ship, a sailor*:—Sanctus Michael se æþela nôwend and se gleáwa frumlida and se þancwirðesta stígend, An. Ox. 32 note. v. úp-stígend.

**stigian** *to mount.* v. ā-stigian.

**stihtan.** *Add*:—þū hí siððan stýrest and stihtest, Met. 20, 178.

**stihtend.** *Add*:—Styhtend *protector* (*meus, Domine*), Ps. Rdr. 58, 12.

**stihtere.** *Add*: *a steward, treasurer* :—Úre cyrican stihteres (*dispensatoris*) mǽg, Gr. D. 221, 19.

**stihtian.** *Add*:—Hê wæs wrítere in þissere hālgan Rômāne cyrican, þǽre ic þeówige Gode stihtigendum mínum ordfruman (þǽre ic þeówie under Godes anwealde, *v. l.*) *sanctae Romanae ecclesiae, cui Deo auctore deservio, notarius fuit,* Gr. D. 52, 5. v. on-, tô-stihtian.

**stihtung.** *Add*: *instigation* (?) :—Paulus for his líchaman stihtunga (tihtunga ?) þriwa bæd Drihten *Paulus de carnis suae stimulo ter Dominum rogavit,* Gr. D. 166, 25. v. ā-stihtung.

**stíle.** *In* l. 2 *dele* 'stete acerra . . . 56', *and for the true reading here cf.* Fǽte oððe glēdfǽte acerra, Wrt. Voc. ii. 5, 68.

**stillan** *to stall. Substitute : to make a stall*:—Hrýðeran styllan, Angl. ix. 262, 1. Horsan styllan, 23.

**stillan.** II. *add*:—Ðonne sceal him mon sellan hāt wæter drincan ; þonne stild (þ) þ gesceorf innan and clǽsnað þā wambe, Lch. ii. 240, 23. v. oþ-stillan.

**stille.** I 1 a. fig. *add*:—Sege ûs nū þ sóðe būton ǽlcon leáse, and wē nellað þē āmeldian, ac hit eall stille lǽtan, Hml. S. 23, 591. I 2 b. *add*:—On þǽre nihte, þā hit stillost wæs, Gr. D. 238, 11. II. *add*:—þū þe ealle ðā unstillan gesceafta tô þínum willan āstyrast, and ðū self stille and unāwendedlíc þurhwunast, Bt. 33, 4 ; F. 128, 10.

**stille ;** *adv. Still, quietly.* It is not possible always to distinguish between the adjective and the adverb, but the latter character may be assumed for the word when, if an adjective, it should take the *u*-inflection ; e.g. :—Wildu deór woldon stondan swilce hí tamu wǽron swá stille, Bt. 35, 6 ; F. 168, 2. For other instances see passages given under the adjective.

**stillíce ;** *adv.* I. with reference to words, *silently.* (1) *not out loud, to oneself* :—Hlūddre stefne and ôþre stillíce (*a ' legem pone' usque ' defecit'*) *alta uoce, et cetera silenter,* Angl. xiii. 412, 673 : 670 : 384, 266. Gif stillíce ǽnig gebitt eác seó stefen geswíge *si tacite quis orat et uox sileat,* Scint. 32, 17. þe lǽs þe þænne hê on cyricean specan ongynd, stillíce gehwilc andswarige, 'Hwý þās sylf þū nā dēst ?,' 119, 6. (2) *not speaking*:—Stillíce ingān *silenter incedant,* Angl. xiii. 403, 542. II. *without producing sound* :—Wer wís uneáþe stillíce hlihð *uir sapiens uix tacite ridebit* ; a wise man doth scarce smile a little (Ecclus. 21, 20), Scint. 171, 16.

**stilness.** I. *add*:—Se tíma hyra reste and stillnysse *hora quietis,* Gr. D. 170, 12. II. *add*: *abstention from speech*:—For þǽre stilnesse hefignysse neoþran stefne tô sprecenne wē geþafedon *pro taciturnitatis gravitate summissa voce loquendum permisimus,* Angl. xiii. 433, 970. Fífwintre stilnysse stǽrleornera *quinquennem taciturnitatem stoicorum,* An. Ox. 4144. III. *add*:—Stilnesse *quiete*, An. Ox. 290. Stilnessa *otia,* i. *quietem,* 1672.

**stíman.** *Add*:—Wynsum brǽd werodlíce stēmde, Hml. S. 35, 252. Stēme *flagret, redoleat,* Lch. i. lxii. 2.

**stinan.** v. stenan.

**stincan** (2). *Add*:—Ic wundrige þearle hū nū on wintres dæge hēr lilian blôstm oþþe rosan brǽd swá wymsumlíce and swá werodlíce stincaþ, Hml. S. 34, 105. Stincendre sealfe *nardi spirantis,* An. Ox. 314. (3) *add*:—þā líc weóllon eall maðon and egeslíce stuncon, Hml. S. 4, 212.

---

**stingan.** II. *add* : Bl. H. 223, 16.

**stípan.** *Add*: v. be-stípan : **-stípedness.** v. ā-stípedness.

**stípel.** *Add*:—Gelôgode Benedictus hine sylfne on sumes stýpeles (torres, *v. l.* turris) ûpflôra, and Seruandus gereste hine on þǽre nyðerflôre þæs ylcan stýpeles (torres, *v. l.*), Gr. D. 170, 13-17. Stýplum *turribus,* Ps. L. 47, 13. Stēpplum, 121, 7. ¶ *used figuratively of distinguished work*:—Ic worhte ǽnne stýpel (*the reference is to a conversion effected by the speaker*), and þū cwyðst þ ic sceolde sylf hine tôwurpan, Hml. S. 36, 375. v. steáp.

**stirc.** *Add*:—Stęrt (stęrc ?) *becta* (cf. *vecta* ênwintre, *laudaris* steúr, Wrt. Voc. i. 287, 60), Corp. Gl. H. 24, 91.

**stirne.** *Add*:—Styrne *feroces* (inter *feroces* ursinae ferocitatis rictus, Ald. 61, 18), An. Ox. 11, 151.

**stíþ.** II 1. *add*:—Stíð sleándre slecge *rigida tundentis mallei* (*durities*), An. Ox. 11, 69. On stíþre hǽran licgende, Hml. S. 31, 1351. III. *add*: of personal qualities or things personified :—Stíþ *dira* (*ferocitas*), An. Ox. 2208. Swā swā gôd lāreów . . . swā þ hālige word is swíðe stíð ûrum stuntnyssum, Hml. A. 6, 133. IV. *add*:—Stíþre *dirae* (*mortalitatis*), An. Ox. 1271. Stíð wíte ðolian, Wlfst. 39, 3. Hê gemēt swíðe stíðne dôm on ðām tôweardan lífe, Hml. Th. ii. 96, 15. Godes byrðene . . . beóð leóhte þām þe hí lufiað . . . þeáh hí stíðe beón þām stuntum mannum, Hml. A. 11, 273. Stíþra wala *asperę inuectionis,* An. Ox. 5365. þǽre stíþeste sticelse ābryrdnesse *acerrimę,* i. *crudelissime stimulo conpunctionis,* 599. V. *add*:—Mid stíþre þeáwfæstnesse lāre *duro,* i. *districto disciplinę pedagogio,* An. Ox. 1097. Iôhannes āstealde þā stíðan drohtnunge, Hml. S. 16, 99. Mid stíþum lagum *strictis legibus,* An. Ox. 2177.

**stíþe.** II. *add*:—Hí hæfdon ǽlce scíre on West-Sexum stíðe gemearcod mid bryne and mid hergunge, Chr. 1006 ; P. 137, 18. III. *austerely, asceticly.* v. stíþ ; V.:—þā gewunode se hālga wer manega geár on ðām ancerlífe swíðlíce stíðe, Hml. Th. 146, 7.

**stíþ-líc.** *Add*: of food, fare, &c., *hard, the reverse of luxurious*:—Eal his reáf wæs āwefen of olfendes hǽrum, his bigleofa wæs stíðlíc, Hml. Th. i. 352, 6.

**stíþlíce.** I. *add*: *strenuously*:—Wē rǽdað þæt þā ealdan fæderas on ânum dæge þæt stíðlíce (*strenue*) gefyldon, eálā þǽr wē āsolcene and āwācode on ânre wucan gelǽston, R. Ben. 44, 21. III. *add*:—Hefelícor steóre ł stýdlícor stíre hê sí underþeód *districtiori discipline subdatur,* R. Ben. I. 65, 4. Būton hê hit hēr ǽr his ænde ðe stíðelícor gebēte, C. D. iv. 248, 30.

**stíþness.** I. *add*:—Beátendes hameres stíþnes (*rigida*) *tundentis mallei durities,* An. Ox. 482. III. *add*:—Stíþnes *acerbitas* (*poenarum*), 4816. Stíþnesse *austeritate,* i. *crudelitate,* 661.

**stôc** (stoc ?). *l.* stoc, *and add*:—þ āborstene clif hreás ofdúneweard . . . and wæs farende oþ þ hit côm þǽr hit mynte feallan ofer þ mynster, and þ þonne wǽre hryre ealles þæs stoces (stôwes, *v. l.*) and forwyrd ealra þǽra brôðra *ingentis saxi moles erupta est, quae . . . veniens totius ruinam cellae, omniumque fratrum interitum minabatur,* Gr. D. 12, 12. In Cassinum þǽre stôwe (þ stoc, þām stocwíc, *v. ll.*) *in Cassinum castrum,* 172, 5. [I saderr stoke, Orm. 9778. þeʒʒ liccness off Cherubyn o tweʒʒenn stokess metedd, 1049.]

**-stoc,** es ; *n.* v. earm-, hand-stoc.

**stocc.** *Dele* hand- *at end, and* I. *add*:—þ inn wæs swýþe nearo, and þǽr lāgon stoccas, Hml. S. 31, 856. I a. *a post to which a person may be fastened, stocks*:—Ôstiges stocces fæstene þæs (Godes weres) sceancan (*in*) *nodosi cippi claustrum viri Dei tibias* (*astringunt*), An. Ox. 3251. Of þǽre lęge þæt hit cymð tô frobirig stocce (*to Froburg stocks?*), Cht. Crw. 25, 48. þ yrsodon þā cempan ongeán þone cniht, and gesetton hine on ǽnne heardue stocc and his sceancan gefæstnodon on þām fôtcopsum, Hml. S. 35, 147. v. imb-stocc.

**stocc-gemǽre** *a boundary marked by logs* (?):—Andlang stôdfaldgemǽres þæt hit cymð tô stoccgemǽre, Cht. Crw. 25, 43.

**stoc-wíc.** *Add*: The Latin is : In Cassinum castrum. v. stoc.

**-stod.** v. wealh-stod.

**stôd-fald.** *Add*: Cf. Andlarg stôdfalddíces, swā andlang stôdfaldgemǽr(es), Cht. Crw. 25, 42.

**stôd-hors.** *Add*:—Hê þone cyning bæd þ hê him wǽpen sealde and stôdhors (*equum emissarium*) . . . For þon þām bisceope hiora hālignesse ne wæs ālýfed þ hê môste wǽpen wegan, ne ǽlcor būtan on myran rídan, Bd. 2, 13; Sch. 168, 11.

**stofn.** I. *add*:—Stofun *codex,* Txts. 114, 90.

**stôl.** *In the compounds dele* gebed, *and for* fealde *l.* fild(e).

**stole.** *Add*:—Sí ymbûtonseald him stole *circumdatur ei stola,* Angl. xiii. 443, 1116. Se abbud mid stolan (*stola*) gefratewud, 405, 566 : 403, 546.

**stôpel.** *Add*: [Cf. on þe steire oṛ fiftene stoples, O. E. Hml. ii. 165, 35.]

**stoppa.** *Add*:—Gelômlíce wæs tôbrocen se rǽp in þām hangode se stoppa þe man þ wæter mid hlôd *funis in quo ad hauriendum aquam situla dependebat crebro rumpebatur,* Gr. D. 214, 22. v. wæterstoppa.

**stór.** *Add:*—Stór sī bærned *tus cremetur,* Angl. xiii. 409, 623. Nā beóþ borene leóhta on þǽre nihte, ac stór (*incensum*) þ ān, 425, 857.

**stór-cylle.** *l.* -cille (v. cille), *and add:*—Stórcille stērende sī boren *turribulum turificando deportetur,* Angl. xiii. 402, 530. Stórcillan *turibulo,* 416, 723. Ealle stórcillan mid rēcelse on handum berende, 427, 882.

**stór-fæt,** es ; *n.* *A censer:*—Ðonne þū stórfæt habban wille, þonne wend þū þīne hand ofdūne and wege hī swilce þū stýre, Tech. ii. 120, 14.

**storm.** I. *add:*—Stearm *tempestas,* Mt. L. 16, 3. I b. *add:*—Rēþes stormes ýste *dirae tempestatis turbine,* An. Ox. 632.

**storm-sǽ** *a stormy sea:*—Ðā gestōd hine heáh weder and stormsǽ, Bt. 38, 1 ; F. 194, 10. (Cf. *O. H. Ger.* sturm-wint *turbo: Icel.* sturm-viðri *tempest, for similar compounds.*)

**stott,** es ; *m.* *An inferior kind of horse:*—Hēr on stent gewriten hwæt man funde æt Eggemere sȳððan Cole hit lēt. Ðæt is vii oxen and viii cȳ and iiii feldhrȳþera and ii stottas (*equi uiles*), Nap. 56, 7.

**stów.** *Dele weall in the compounds.* IV. *add:* (1) with reference to material things:—*Momentum* ys gewyss stów þǽre sunnan on heofenum, Angl. viii. 318, 4. (2) with reference to non-material things:—Sume ūre dēningbēc onginnað on Adventum Domini ; nis ðeáh þær for ðȳ ðæs geáres ord ; ne eác on ðisum dæge (*the Circumcision*) nis mid nānum gesceáde, þeáh ðe ūre gerīmbēc on þissere stōwe geedlǣcon (*though our calendars continue to put the beginning of the year in this place,* i.e. Jan. 1), Hml. Th. i. 98, 28. v. andfeng-, burn-, cenning-, costnung-, den-, gebed-, gebeorg-, gecwed-, gemynd-, geþing-, hege- (*not* heg-), helle-, líc-, mót-, sceáwung-, þing-, wæfer-, wíte-, wunung-stów.

**strácian.** *Add:*—Nægelsexes tānc his þæt þū mid þīnum scytefingre dō ofer þinne ōþerne swilce þū ceorfan wille, and strāca syþþan on þīn leór mid þīnum fingre swilce þū sceáran wille, Tech. ii. 127, 2.

**stræc;** *adj.* III. *add:*—Þā strecan *uiolenti,* i. *fortes in forte,* An. Ox. 1238.

**stræc;** *n.* I. *add:*—Hē bið him swā mihtleás on his mōdes strece, þ hē his underþeóddan egesian ne dearr, O. E. Hml. i. 301, 6. II. *add:*—Micel strec bið þæt mennisce menn mid eádmōdum geearnungum ðā heofenlican myrhðe begytan, Hml. Th. i. 360, 26.

**strǣcness.** *Add:* I. cf. stræc ; I.: *severity, rigour, bitterness:*—Seó biterness and strecnes þæs deáðes *amaritudo mortis,* Gr. D. 345, 2. II. cf. stræc ; II.: *rigidity:*—Gehȳr nū þā þ mīn mōd is gebēged mid þissere cȳðnesse tō geleáffullnesse, ac swā þēh eft onsænded hit hweorfað tō þǽre strecnesse *ecce testimonio ad credulitatem flectitur animus, sed dimissus iterum ad rigorem redit,* Gr. D. 304, 25.

**strǣlian.** *Add:*—Þæt hȳ strǣlien (*sagittent*) on dīgelnissum unwemme, Ps. Rdr. 63, 5. v. ā-strǣlian (Ps. Rdr. 75, 9).

**strǣt.** I. *add:*—An cyninges strēte, C. D. ii. 67, 2. II. *add:*—Ūt on strǣte gān *in plateis ire,* Chrd. 61, 5. Fænu strǣtena *lutum platearum,* Ps. L. 17, 43. v. burg- (burh-, C. D. B. iii. 15, 11), ceáp- (cīp-, cȳp-), flǣsc-, Wætlinga-, wīg-strǣt.

**strǣt-lanu,** an ; *f.* *A street:*—Seó strǣtlanu is on ðǽre byrig of clǣnum golde geworht, Nap. 59.

**strǣt-weard,** e ; *f.* *Guarding of roads:*—De stretwarde. De qualibet hida in hundredo iiii. homines ad stretwarde invenientur . . . Et guardereve, id est prepositus custodum, habebit .xxx. hidas quietas pro labore suo, Ll. Th. i. 479, 25–29.

**strand,** *n.* (*not m.*). *Add:*—Se Hǽlend stōd on ðām strande . . . Seó sǣ getācnað þás andwerdan woruld, and þæt strand getācnode ðā ēcan staðolfæstnysse þæs tōwerdan līfes, Hml. Th. ii. 288, 27–31. Seó landfyrd cōm ufenon and trymedon hig be ðām strande, Chr. 1052 ; P. 180, 18. Wē gesāwon þā muntas ymbe ðǽre sealtan sǣ strande, Angl. viii. 299, 39. Stranda *sablonum,* An. Ox. 2, 286.

**strang.** II 5. *add:*—Þurh þæt strange fæsten him gemildsode God, Hml. Th. i. 246, 23. v. ceorl-, earm-, feoh-, weorold-, wíg-strang.

**strangian.** I. *add:*—Þ ilce mōd mid heálicum mægnum weaxeð and strangað *eadem mens virtute pollet,* Gr. D. 204, 23. I a. *to move or act with energy, vigour, force:*—Beelzebub fleáh . . . and ūre Drihten him strangode æfter (*pursued him vigorously*), E. S. 49, 354.

**strang-líc.** II 1. *add: displaying force or energy:*—Beóð swiðe stranglícu word on heofenes roderum *erit vox magna et fortis in firmamento caeli,* Verc. Först. 121, 19. II 2. *add:*—Þær weard on dæg swiðe stranglíc gefeoht on bā halfe, Chr. 1066 ; P. 199, 12. Hē þet land mid stranglicum feohte gewann, 1097 ; P. 234, 12.

**stranglíce.** I. *add:*—Ongin nū stranglíce, Hml. S. 29, 272. V. *add:*—Ǽfre þe ōðer man weard on þām wyrrestan yfele, and þet swā stranglíce, þ mænige menn swulton on þām yfele, Chr. 1086 ; P. 217, 30.

**strangung.** I. *add:*—Ǽfter ðām ǽriste ne behōfiað ūre līchaman nānre strangunge eorðlicra metta, Hml. Th. i. 296, 30.

**streám.** *Add:*—Efne swilce seó eá on hyre næfde nǣnne wæteres streám *ac si ille fluminis alveus aquam minime haberet,* Gr. D. 15, 31. Hē gelōme ūt on þone striém (streám, *v. l.*) eóde, Bd. 5, 12 ; Sch. 632, 18. v. gyte-, mid-, mylen-streám.

**streát,** es ; *m.* (?), *n.* (?). *A place with bushes* (?), *a thicket* (?) :—Ðys sind ðā landgemǣra into Dunnestreáttūnne (cf. in loco qui dicitur Dunnestreátūn, i. 164, 8) . . . innon hænstreát ; of ðām streáte, C. D. ii. 384, 12–20. [Cf. (?) *M. H. Ger.* ge-striuze, striuzach *copse, thicket.*] *See next word.*

**streát** (?) ; *adj.* *Bushy* (?), *formed by bushes* (?) :—On ðā streátan hlȳwan ; of ðǽre hlȳwan, C. D. iii. 229, 28. *See preceding word.*

**streáw.** *Add:*—Sē ðe getimbrað ofer ðām grundwealle treówa, oððe streáw . . . Ðurh ðā treówu and ðām streáwe sind getācnode leóhtlice synna, Hml. Th. ii. 590, 9–14. Lytle strēwu *leuiores paleas,* Chrd. 74, 16. v. bed-, healm-streáw.

**streáwian.** *Add:* v. under-streówod.

**strece,** Tech. ii. 128, 25. v. strícan.

**strēgan.** *Perhaps the example given at* stregdan ; IV. *should be taken here.*

**stregdan.** I. *add: to sprinkle:*—Þæt deádberende ǣttor his getreówleásnesse . . . an eallum middangeardes ciricum hē strǣgd (stregde, *v. l.* aspersit), Bd. 1, 8 ; Sch. 29, 15. ‘Stregd (spreng, *v. l.*) þis gehālgode wæter ofer þæs mannes līchaman’ . . . Hē þæt wæter stregde (sprengde, *v. l.*) ofer his limu ‘*benedictam aquam super corpus projice*’ . . . *Benedictam aquam super membra illius aspersit,* Gr. D. 82, 17–22. v. for-, tō-stregdan.

**streng.** I 2. *add:*—Boga mid strence *arsippio anquina,* Hpt. 31, 14, 332. v. hearpe-streng.

**strenge.** *Add:* v. un-strenge: -strenge. *Add:* v. þri-, twi-strenge.

**strenglíce;** *adv.* *Firmly:*—Þā gecorenan engla gāstas selfe swā myccle strenglícor and fæstlícor gestōdon, swā myccle swā hī eádmōdran wǣron *electi angelorum spiritus ipsi tanto robustius quanto humilius starent,* Gr. D. 205, 3.

**strengþu.** I. *add:* (1) of physical power:—Þéh þe beón on strænchþum hundeahtatig gǽr *si autem in potentatibus octoginta anni,* Ps. L. 89, 10. (2) of military or political power:—Swilce eác Scotland hē him underþǽdde for his micele strengþe, Chr. 1086 ; P. 220, 25. (3) in a moral or spiritual sense:—þ wē magan ongytan hwilc hit seó circlice strengþ (strencgeoð, *v. l.*) sȳ *ut quis sit ecclesiasticus vigor agnoscat,* Gr. D. 35, 11. II 1. *add:*—Hē wæs þǽr āseted, þǽr hit gesewen wæs þ þæs līges mægn and strengð (strencgeo, *v. l.*) mǣst wæs *in eo loco positus est, ubi tota vis flammae videbatur incumbere,* Gr. D. 48, 5. (1 a) *power to resist strain:*—For ðon þe se rāp gehrān þǽre racenteáge þæs Godes weres þe hē hæfde on him swā myccle strengðe (strenge, *v. l.*) tō ādreóganne þā byrde *quia enim catenam viri Dei funis contigit, ipse quoque ad tolerandam aquam ferri in se fortitudinem traxit,* Gr. D. 214, 28. v. heáh-strengþu.

**strengu.** *Add:* v. Gr. D. 48, 5 : 214, 28 *under preceding word.*

**streóna, strína,** an ; *m.* *One who acquires:*—Strína *conquisitor,* An. Ox. 27, 1. Cf. Streóna *as a nickname of* Eádríc, *the treacherous alderman of Mercia.*

**streónan.** I. *add:* (1) with gen.:—Hié wǣron ūs gelíce on þysse worulde wynsumnesse lifigende and him welena strȳndon, Verc. Först. 144, 10. (2) dat. (?) or absolute (?):—Wā ðām mannum þe . . . eorðlicum spēdum tiliað and strȳnað, Verc. Först. 120, 17.

**streónend, strínend,** es ; *m.* *One who gains or acquires:*—Ealra strínend hē bið *omnium adquisitor erit,* Archiv cxxix. 19, 3 : 7. v. ge-streónend, -strínend.

**-streónendlic.** v. ge-strínendlic.

**Streónes-halh.** *Add:* Another instance of the name is found in Worcestershire:—Of ðǽre strǣte in Streóneshalh ; of ðām hale, C. D. vi. 214, 29. Cf. On Streónhalh ; be Streónenhalæ, iii. 464, 8.

**streówen.** *Add:*—Ealle streóne his þū gecirdes on untrymnesse his, Ps. Vos. 40, 4.

**strewung.** *Add: bedding:*—Hē læg . . . mid fefore gewǣht . . . on stīþre hǣran licgende mid axum bestreówod. Þā bǣdon þā gebrōðra þ hī his bed mōston mid wæccre streówunge (strewunge, *v. l.*) hūru underlecgan, Hml. S. 31, 1353.

**strícan.** I. *add:* (1) where the hand, finger, &c., is passed over or along a surface:—Sete þū þīne handa forewearde wiðneoðan þinne nafolan and stríc tō þīnum twām hypum, Tech. ii. 119, 22. Stríc þū mid tōsprǣddum handum niþer ofer þine breóst, 25 : 126, 22. Strȳc þū of ufwerdum heáfde mid þīnum twām scytefingran wiþerweard forð for þīne earmas andlang þīnra hleóra, 119, 16. Sete þū þinne scytefinger uppon þīnne fōt and stríc on twā healfa þīnes fēt þām gemete þe hī gesceapene beóð, 126, 9. Cyninges wífes tācen is þæt þū strēce onbūtan heófod (*run your hand round your head*), and sete syððan þīne hand bufon þīn heófod, 128, 25. I a. strícan *of to rub off:*—Twænge þinne scytefinger mid þīnum twām fingrum swylce þū of sumne dropan strícan wylle, Tech. ii. 125, 20. II. *add: to strike:*—Ic ofsleá and lifian ic dō, ic stríce and bǣle *ego occidam et uiuere faciam, percutiam et ego sanabo,* Ps. Rdr. 291, 39. v. ymb-strícan.

**stric-hrægl,** es ; *n.* *A cloth for rubbing* (?) :—Eádgyfe his swyster ān strichrægl and i. hrigchrægl and i. sethrægl, Cht. Crw. 23, 21.

**strídan.** *Add: to mount* a horse :—Hē him sylf sōna strād (āstāh,

*v. l.*) upon his hors *ipse statim ascendens equum*, Gr. D. 81, 20. [Wiche strides he makede dunward and eft uppard, þ seið Salomon . . . '*Ecce uenit saliens in montibus et transiliens colles*' 'here he cumeð stridende fro dune to dune, and ouerstrit þe cnolles,' O. E. Hml. ii. 111, 34. þe leome gon striden a seoue strengen, Laym. 17982. Towarde þe autere gon he stride, C. M. 10235. Mon in the mone stond ant strit, Spec. 110, 1. Sete forth thyn other fot, stryd over sty, 111, 2. Love is stalewarde and strong for to striden on stede, An. Lit. 96, 9.]

**strína.** *v.* streóna: **strínd.** *Add: v.* ge-strínd: -strínendlíc. *v.* ge-strínendlíc.

**stríplian?** :—Strípligan *perfringere*, An. Ox. 46, 21.

**stroccian** *to stroke* :—Gyf þe meolce lyste, þonne strocca (stráca?) þū þinne wynstran finger mid þinre swýþran handa þām gelíce swylce þū melce, Tech. ii. 123, 24. [Cf. *Icel.* strjuka.]

**stród** (strod?), es; *n.? Substitute:* stród, es; *n. Marshy land (overgrown with brushwood or trees?. v.* Philol. Trans. 1895–8, p. 537), *and add:* —Haec sunt prata que ad illam terram pertinent .i. et bioccan leá and a sūðhealfe stródes an cyninges mēdum ðā ðe ðærtó belimpað, C. D. B. ii. 202, 13. [*O. H. Ger.* struot *palus*, Gall. 308.]

**strogdness.** *Add: v.* for-strogdness: **strúdan.** *Add: see next word.*

**strúdian** *to plunder* :—þā þā ðū swiðust strúdadest and ōðre men mid wó reáfodest, ðā greówon unc þā ēcan wítu, Nap. 60. *v.* ge-strúdian.

**strúdigendlíce**; *adv. Rapaciously, greedily* :—Gif hē ofermódlíce and andiendlíce and strúdgendlíce his líf drohtnað *si superbe, si inuide uiuat*, Chrd. 108, 18.

**strútian.** *For* 'Swt . . . 177' *substitute:* Hml. S. 32, 208. [*Cf. Dan.* strutte *to stick out, project.*]

**-strynge.** *v.* ge-strynge.

**stunian.** II. *add:* —Stunað heó wið attre, Lch. iii. 36, 7. *v.* wiþ-stunian.

**stunt.** *Add:* —Feól se wāh uppan þæs stuntan (*the foolish man's*) rædboran . . . swýðe rihtlíce . . . for ðan þe hī rædboran wǣran þæs árleásan dēman, Hml. S. 8, 172. Þæra mædena wǣron fíf stunte and fíf snotore, Hml. Th. ii. 562, 15. Ðonne sind hī stunte þæt hī cēpað þæs ýdelan hlýsan, 566, 2. Swā þā stuntan (dysigan, *v. l.*) mód (*stultae mentis homines*) leógað, þonne hī wēnað þ þæs mannes ærnung beó of his líchaman missenlícnysse, Gr. D. 46, 6. Hī sceolon stýran stuntra manna anginne, Hml. A. 63, 270. Stýran þām stuntum mannum, 7, 179.

**stuntlíce.** *Add after* 16 *in l.* 2: Wlfst. 285, 31.

**stuntness.** *Add:* —Þā yfelan ungifa þæs deófles syndan þus genamode . . . *stultitia*, þæt is stuntnys, Wlfst. 52, 17. Menige . . . þām ásolcenan þeówan geefenlǣcað. Hī . . . ne wandiað tó licgenne on stuntnysse heora ásolcennysse, Hml. Th. ii. 554, 3; Hml. A. 96, 154. þ hālige word is swýðe stíð ūrum stuntnyssum, 6, 133.

**stybb.** *Add:* —Beeástan wrocena stybbe; ðæt swā tó wrocena stybbe; ðonne of wrocena stybbe, C. D. v. 297, 26. Of stānmere on þēre pyrigean styb; þonne of pyrigean stybbe on þonne þorn, C. D. B. iii. 396, 37. ¶ On ðæne æscstubb; of ðām æscstubbe, 234. 27. Ou ðone æscstyb, vi. 33, 37. [Gawayn . . . stode stylle as . . . a stubbe, Gaw. 2293. Þe heisugge flihþ bi grunde among þe stubbe, O. and N. 506. Knarry bareyne trees olde of stubbes scharpe, Ch. Kn. T. 1120.] *v.* elebeám-, holen-, ród-stybb.

**stycce.** I. *add:* —Feóll ān leóhtfæt of his handum þ hit weard tóbrocen on unārímedlicu styccu, Gr. D. 49, 22. Hit wæs tódæled on twā stycce (stycciu, styccu, *v. ll.*), 97, 7: 17. Þurh sticceo *per cola* [cf. Ald. 4, 36: Grammaticorum regulas et orthographicarum disciplinas . . . pedibus poeticis compacta per cola (*per cola*, i. *membra* þurh lim, An. Ox. 201)], Wrt. Voc. ii. 69, 8. II a. *a piece of material complete in itself, but forming one of a number*(?), *a dish*(?) :—Sticce *clarnum* (the passage is : Appresenta meum *clarnum* et meum cultellum et meam legulam. Perhaps then *sticce* is for *sticcan* and belongs to *legulam*), An. Ox. 56, 74. III. *add:* —Lytel sticce hē ligeð seóc (cf. sumne tíman hē síclað *aliquod tempus egrotat*, 33, 19), Archiv cxxix. 35, 13. *v.* cís-, hwíl-, stān-stycce.

**stycce-mælum.** III. *add:* —Heó wæs fleónde. Ðā wæs Zosimus ryna hwæðra sticmælum neár gefremed, Hml. S. 23 b, 189.

**styfician.** *Perhaps better* styfician. *Cf.* stybb. *See* Philol. Soc. Trans. 1895–8, p. 541.

**styfic-leáh** *a cleared lea* (?) :—Tó Bedegāres styuicleáge (*given as* spicleáge *from another MS.*), C. D. B. iii. 694, 10. *Cf.* stivecleiam, 638, 2, *and see* Philol. Soc. Trans. 1895–8, p. 541.

**styfic-weg** *a road made by clearing away tree-stumps* (?) :—Tó ðām fūlan wege, sē hātte stificweg (cf. stifincweg, iv. 66, 24), C. D. iii. 409, 13 Andlang stifigweges, *v.* 321, 28.

**stylt.** *v.* fær-stylt: **styntan.** *Add: v.* æt-, ge-styntan: -stynþo. *v.* ge-stynþo: **stýran** *to cense. v.* stēran: -styren[n]. *v.* eorþ-styren[n].

**styreness.** I. *add: I* a. *of convulsive movement* :—Heó ongan swā manegum styrenyssum beón onstyred *coebit tot motibus agitari*, Gr. D.

74, 2. II. *add: stirring, shaking* of an inanimate body :—Tó þon þ ūs for þæs treówes styrenesse (*concussione*) wǣre 'ege æteówed, Gr. D. 191, 9.

**styria.** *Add:* —Styria *sulio*, Hpt. 33, 242, 76.

**styrian.** I. *add: I* a. of non-material objects :—Swā styrigende is seó sāwul þ heó furðon on slǣpe ne gestylþ, Hml. S. 1, 131. II 2. *add:* (a) the object a person :—Ne lēten hié nō hié on ælce healfe gebígean, ne furðon nō āwecggan, ðeáh ðe hié mon manigfealdlíce and mislíce styrede, Past. 306, 5. (b) the object a thing, feeling, passion, &c. :—Hié styrigad geflitu and geciid, Past. 293, 20. *v.* in-styrian; un-styri(g)ende.

**styrigend-líc.** *Add:* —Hit is cūþ þ se gást is styrigendlícran and fērendran gecyndes þonne se líchoma *liquet quia mobilioris naturae est spiritus quam corpus*, Gr. D. 149, 35. *v.* un-styrigendlíc.

**styrn-mód.** *v.* stirn-mód.

**styrung.** II 1. *add:* (a) *convulsive movement* of a person :—Heó ongann mid swā fela styrungum beón onstyred *coepit tot motibus agitari*, Gr. D. 74, 2. (b) *quaking, shaking* of an inanimate body :—Beóð eorðan styrunga *erunt terrae motus*, Mt. 24, 7. II c. *add: stir* :—On merigen weard micel styrung betwux ðām cempum (*as soon as it was day there was no small stir among the soldiers*; facta die erat non parva turbatio inter milites, Acts 12, 18), Hml. Th. ii. 382, 27. Gód is tó forhæbbenne fram unálýfedum styrungum, 564, 7.

**subdiácon.** *Add:* —Ān subdiácon bæd þone hālgan wer sumne dæl eles . . . Ðā hēt hē his hordere fæt glæsene fæt syllan ðām biddendan subdiácone, Hml. Th. ii. 178, 16–23: Gr. D. 159, 10: 215, 4. Wæs hē ǣrest tó subdiácone gehālgod *subdiaconus ordinatus*, Bd. 4, 1; Sch. 339, 11. þā gehādode se pāpa Tranquillinum tó preóste, his twǣgen suna tó diáconum, and þā ōðre tó subdiáconum, Hml. S. 5, 348. *v.* under-diácon.

**sucga.** *Add: v.* hæg-sugga.

**sufel.** *Add:* —Heora middæges sufie *pulmentum ad sextam*, Chrd. 14, 35. 'Gāð nū and geseóðað ūra wyrhtena sufl, þ hit sý on ǣrne mergen geara.' And þā gewordenum ǣrmergenne hē hēt beran mid him þone sufimete þe hē ǣr hēt gegearwian '*ite et operariis nostris pulmentum coquite, ut mane primo paratum sit.*' *Facto mane fecit deferri pulmentum quod parari jusserat*, Gr. D. 201, 24–26.

**sufel-mete.** *See preceding word.*

**sūgan.** II. *The verb seems to describe hiccough, and the passage at* Lch. ii. 192, 13 *might be translated* '*when he has hiccough*'. *The form at* Lch. ii. 160, 1 *is* sýgeþ.

**sugu.** *Add:* —Æt strǣthā .xx. sugen[a] . . . æt [m]eldeburnan .xxiii. suge[na], Cam. Phil. Trans. 1902, p. 15. Cf. Tó suge-brōce, C. D. B. ii. 284, 30. On suga-róde, C. D. iii. 48, 9.

**suht.** *v.* hríþ-suht.

**sulh.** I. *The passage* Ll. Th. i. 208, 12 *seems to belong to* II, *as dealing with an extent of land rather than with an implement. Such an area was to provide two men with good horses. Reference to such men may be found in the section on the* gebūr, *where it is said:* Gif hē aferað ne ðearf hē wyrcan ðā hwíle ðe his hors ūte bið, Ll. Th. i. 434, 9. *See too* aferian. *Cf.* sulh-ælmesse *for the use of* sulh *in the sense of* II. III. *a sunk road* (?), *gully* (?) :—On holan rípe; þanon on sulh, of sulh tó þām ealdan tūnstealle, C. D. B. iii. 605, 13. Andlang ríðe on suluc . . . andlang strǣte on ðā deópan fúra, þonon inon sulh, 188, 29–35. Of hylfes hæcce innon sulc; ūp æftær suluc on ðā holan ríðe, 189, 3. Cf. sulh-ford *a ford to which a sunk road leads* (?) :—Of cunuglan sulhforda, C. D. iii. 378, 6. Fram Æðelstānes hammes forda on sūlforda, 411, 26: 16. On sulhford tó eaxan, Cht. Crw. 3, 2. (*See note* p. 47.) Sulig grǣf, C. D. iii. 461, 11.

**sulh-geside.** *l.* -gesidu (-a); *pl. v.* ge-sidu (-a).

**sulian**(?). *Dele, and see* be-sūtian : sulincél. *l.* sūlincel.

**sulphor** *sulphur* :—On þēre ylcan scíre Sicilian landes is ān byrnende munt (*Etna*) onǣled mid sulphore, þ is swæfel on Englisc, Hml. S. 8, 219.

**sulung,** e; *f. l.* sūlung, es; *n.* [*From* sulh, lang.]

**sum.** I. *add:* (I a a) with a possessive pronoun instead of genitive, and with noun inflexion :—Gelícode mē þ ic eówerne sum mē tó begeáte, Hml. S. 33, 109. II 2. *add:* (a) with reference to number, *one (of), some (of)* :—Hē bebeád sumum his preóste (*cuidam de clericis sui*), Bd. 4, 16; Sch. 426, 2. Sume þā ōðre, Ll. Th. ii. 376, 30. (b) with reference to quantity, *some (of)* :—Heó sumne hire líchaman bewǣfde, Hml. S. 23 b, 793. Sume ðās race wē habbað getrahtnod on ōðre stówe, Hml. Th. ii. 264, 23. II 4. *add:* —Æt sumum twām cirron, æt ōþrum cierre beeástan Wæced, æt ōþrum cierre æt Portlocan, Chr. 918; P. 98, 27. Nam hē mid him sumne dǣl feós, swā micel swā hit mihte beón, ðeáh swilce hit wǣre sum twā and sixtig penega, Hml. S. 23, 474. (4 a) *add:* —Wurdon ofslagene sume þreó þūsend, Hml. S. 25, 357. (5) *add:* —Sume (-ae) daeli (dǣli) *partim*, Txts. 84, 731. Ðeáh hē mæge sume (= sume dǣle) his willan ongitan, þonne ne mæg hē eallne, Bt. 39, 9; F. 226, 7. þā gesæt hē sume dæge under sunnbeáme, Hml. Th. ii. 134, 25. Fulsóð hý secgað sumera þinga, Ll. Th. ii. 344, 23 n.

**-sum.** _Add:_ v. friþ-, gedeorf-, gedwol-, læt-, wōh-sum.

**sum-dǣl** _somewhat, some portion:_—Gelamp hit þ Scotta sumdǣl gewāt of Ybernian on Brittene and þes landes sumdǣl geeódan, Chr. pref.; P. 3, 18-5, 1. In þām glæsfæte wæs gesewen sumdǣl (hwæt-hwega lytel dǣl, _v. l._) eles tō lāfe _in vase vitreo parum olei remansisse videbatur,_ Gr. D. 159, 22. Hē gewāt ūt sumdǣl ōðres weorces (sum weorc, _v. l._) tō wyrcanne _ad exercendum opus aliquod discessit,_ 63, 28. Tō þon þ heó mihte sumdǣl (sumne dǣl, _v. l._) hwǣtes (hwylcne-hugu hwǣte, _v. l._) geclǣnsian _ad purgandum triticum,_ 97, 3. [v. _N. E. D._ some-deal.]

**sumer.** _Add:_ [_Summer began_ May 9 _and ended_ Aug. 6. v. hærfest.] v. midne-sumer.

**sumer-bōc** _a lectionary for the summer:_—Brihtrīc hæfð . . . .i. mæssebōc and winterrǣdingbōc and sumerbōc, Nap. 60.

**sumer-hāt** _summer-heat:_—Sumerhāt cōlað (cf. hāt ācōlað _ardor frigescit,_ Angl. i. 285 : ii. 374), Reim. 67.

**sumer-hūs** _a summer-house:_—Hē cwæð þ hē wolde wyrcan þa healle ǣrest on eástdǣle and þā ōþre gebytlu bæftan þǣre healle, bæðhūs and kycenan and winterhūs and sumerhūs and wynsume būras twelf hūs tōgædere, Hml. S. 36, 98.

**sumer-lic.** _Add:_—Wel is Godes rīce sumerlicre tīde wiðmeten, Hml. Th. i. 614, 28.

**sund-ampre,** an ; f. _Some kind of dock_ ; rumex maritimus :—Sund-ompran (cf. ompran þā þe swimman wile, 322, 16, _and see_ sund) ymbdelf, Lch. ii. 116, 13.

**sund-corn.** _Add:_—Suntcorn _saxifriga,_ An. Ox. 56, 396.

**-sundfull, -sundfullian, -sundfullic, -sundfullīce, -sundful-ness, -sundig, -sundiglic, -sundlic, -sundlīce.** v. ge-sundfull, &c.

**sund-mere.** _Add:_—On sundmere (_printed_ onfund-) _in nataria_ (l. _natatoria,_ v. Jn. 9, 7), Wrt. Voc. ii. 74, 12.

**sundor-boren;** adj. _Borne or born apart, not to be reckoned with others:_—Su[n]derborene _non . . . adnumerandas_ (sex alias nothas (_the vowels_) non dicimus adnumerandas, i. e. the vowels are separated from the consonants, Ald. 257, 4), An. Ox. 26, 17.

**sundor-cræft.** _Add:_—Seó heáfodstōw sundorcræfte (sundurcræftig-līce, _v. l._) gemeten and geworht and gescyrpendlīce gehīwod ætýwde tō þām gemete hyre heáfdes _locus capitis seorsum fabrefactus ad mensuram capitis illius aptissime figuratus apparuit,_ Bd. 4, 19; Sch. 451, 18. Þeáh þe sýn ealle sundercræftas and wuldorsangas in gesamnode, Verc. Först. 114, 10.

**sundorcræftiglīce;** adv. _With special skill,_ Bd. 4, 19; Sch. 451, 18. _See preceding word._

**sundor-folgoþ,** es; m. _An appointment, office :_—Hē sǣde þæt nān crīsten man ne mōste habban nǣnne his sunderfolgeþa, Ors. 6, 31; S. 286, 5. Cf. sundor-notu, -nytt.

**sundor-land.** _Dele_ '(?), _and add:_—Wæs ic ācenned on sundor-lande (sundur-, _v. l._) þæs ylcan mynstres _natus in territorio eiusdem monasterii,_ Bd. 5, 23; Sch. 694, 19. Sume hī woldon sellan heora sundorland mynster on tō getimbrianne _alii ad construendum monasterium praedia offerre volebant,_ Gr. D. 200, 29.

**sundor-mǣlum.** _Add:_—Sundermǣlum _sequestratim,_ An. Ox. 6, 10.

**sundor-sprǣc.** _Add:_—Þās (_James and John_) Crīst genam oftost and Petrum tō his sundersprǣce, Hml. Th. ii, 412, 21.

**sundor-weorþmynt** _a special honour, prerogative:_—Sunderweorð-mynt _praerogativa,_ Angl. xxxii. 505, 34. v. synder-weorþmynt.

**sundor-wīc;** n. _A dwelling standing apart, remote from others:_—Getimbrede hē sundurwīc nōht feor fram þǣre cyricean _fecerat sibi mansionem non longe ab ecclesia remotiorem,_ Bd. 4, 3; Sch. 351, 4.

**-sunn** (?). v. heáh-sunn (?).

**sunna.** _Add:_—Wlitetorht scīned sunna, Met. 28, 61. Ǣþele tungol . . . sunna and mōne, 29, 37.

**Sunnan-dǣg** _Sunday, the Sabbath:_—Sunnadoeg, Mk. L. 6, 2 : 16, 9. In sunnedoeg _in sabbato,_ Jn. p. 4, 9.

**sunnan-leóma.** v. leóma ; II.

**Sunnan-merigen** _Sunday morning :_—On Sunnanmergen hē gewāt, Hml. S. 31, 1371.

**Sunnan-niht.** _Add:_—Þā cildra þe beóð begiten on Sunnanniht . . . hī sceolan beón geborene būtan eágan, Nap. 26, 5.

**sunn-beám.** _Add: sunshine:_—Heó cōm geglenged mid golde and scīnendum gymstānum swilce sunbeám, Hml. S. 35, 90. Þa gesæt hē sumedæge under sunnbeáme (cf. sunne, II), Hml. Th. ii. 134, 25.

**sunne.** I. _add:_—Swā swā under leóman þāre sunnan (ānum sunnan leóman, _v. l._) _velut sub uno solis radio,_ Gr. D. 171, 13 : 172, 22. I a. _add:_ v. heofon-beácen.

**sunn-gihte.** _l._ -gīhte.

**sunn-hāt;** adj. _Heated by the sun_ (?) :—Sunh[ā]t _soliflua,_ An. Ox. 56, 205.

**sunn-lic.** _Add:_—Þonne se fulla mōna ðæs sunlican leóhtes bedǣled bið ðurh ðǣre eorðan sceadwunge, Hml. Th. i. 608, 33.

**sunu.** _Add: gen._ syna :—Ðēra þeówra manna hió an hyre syna dehter Eádgyfe, C. D. vi. 132, 31. v. brōþor-, dohtor-, sweostor-sunu.

**sur.** _For_ sīgere _l._ siger : sūr. _Add :_ v. un-sūr.

**sūsl.** (2) _add:_—Gewilniað þā wiðercoran þæt hī mōton of ðǣre sūsle ðe hī on cwylmiað, Hml. Th. i. 332, 20. On ðǣre hellican sūsle, 410, 32. Habbað hī mid þām deófle þā ēcan sūsle, Hml. S. 19, 238.

**sūsl-stede,** es; m. _A place of torment, hell :_—Sūselstede _gehennam,_ An. Ox. 56, 184.

**sūtere.** _Add:_—Him wæs gesǣd þæt ðā gebytlu wǣron gemynte ānum sūtere . . . hē āxode ymbe ðone sūtere (cf. hē ongan ācsian be ðām līfe þæs sceóhwyrhtan, Gr. D. 322, 5. v. scōh-wyrhta), Hml. Th. ii. 356, 1-3.

[sūþ]. _Add: cpve._ sýþera :—On ðone sýðeran sted ; ðonne andlang stedes . . . on ðone norðere sted, C. D. v. 148, 20. ¶:—Ōsred wærd ofslagen be-sūðan be-sūðan gemǣre, Chr. 716; P. 43, 8. [O. L. Ger. be-sūthan _a meridie._]

**sūþ;** adv. _Add:_—Gif hē (_thunder_) bið sūð gehēred, sē bēcnað cininges wīfes cwealm, Archiv cxx. 47, 22. v. eást-sūþ.

**sūþan.** I. _add:_—Pyhtas cōman sūþan of Scithian, Chr. pref.; P. 3, 6. II. _add:_—Be-westan him is se beorh Athlans oð ðone gārsecg, and sūþan ðā beorgas þe man hǣt Ǣsperos; and be-sūþan him Aulolum sió þeód _ab occidente Atlantem montem et Oceanum Atlanticum, sub Africo Hesperium montem, a meridie gentes Aulolum,_ Ors. 1, 1; S. 26, 25. v. eástan-, westan-sūþan.

**sūþan-weard,** adj. _Southern_ (part of a place) :—Sūþanweard hit hefdon Brittas, Chr. pref.; P. 3, 14. v. norþan-weard.

**sūþanwestan-wind,** adj. _Southern:_—Sūðanwestanwind _affricus,_ Hpt. 33, 239, 27. Ðonne smylte blāweþ sūþanwestanwind, þonne weaxaþ feldes blōsman _cum nemus flatus Zephyri tepentis vernis inrubuit rosis,_ Bt. 9; F. 26, 17.

**sūþan-westerne;** adj. _South-western, from the south-west :_—Þurh þone smyltan sūþanwesternan wind, Bt. 4; F. 8, 7.

**Sūþ-Dene** _the South Danes:_—Hē gesōhte Sūð-Dena folc, B. 463. Ic wæs mid Sūð-Denum, Víd. 58. Ic þē bæd þæt þū lēte Sūð-Dene sylfe geweorþan gūðe wið Grendel, B. 1996.

**sūþ-eást.** _Add:_—Se leóma wæs swīðe lang geþūht sūðeást scīnende, Chr. 1097; P. 233, 29.

**sūþ-ecg,** e; f. _The south edge_ of land :—Of cumbes sūðecge, C. D. iii. 416, 21. On crundles sūðecge, 465, 15 : 20.

**sūþ-ende,** es; m. _The south end :_—Sūð andlang mearce tō ðæs gāres sūðende, C. D. v. 86, 28.

**sūþerne.** _Add:_—Sūðerne secg _a man from the south of Europe_ (?), Rä. 63, 9. Sūðernes _zephiri,_ An. Ox. 26, 67. Þū sealdest mē sūþerne land _terram australem dedisti mihi,_ Gr. D. 245, 18.

**sūþe-weard.** _Add:_—Þæt þridde heáfodrīce wæs þæt Affricanum, and on sūðeweardum, Ors. 2, 1; Bos. 38, 24.

**sūþ-fōr,** e; f. _A journey south, a pilgrimage to Rome._ [Cf. _Icel._ suðr-ferð, -fōr, -ganga _a pilgrimage to Rome._ Such pilgrimages are often mentioned, e. g. Flosi fōr suðr um sjá ok hóf þá upp göngu sína ok gekk suðr ok ljetti ekki fyrr enn hann kom til Rōmaborgar, Njala. c. 158.] :—Gif hiora ōðrum oðde bǣm sūðfō[r] gelimpe, biscop ðæt lond gebycge swā hié ðonne geweorðe _if it happen that one or both go to Rome, the bishop shall buy the land as shall then be agreed between them,_ Txts. 442, 20. [_In_ C. D. i. 235, 8 siith _is printed ; but_ suð, Cht. Th. 463, 3, _and_ C. D. B. i. 446, 20. _These are all texts of the charter quoted._] Æt sūþfōre ǣlc mon (gilde) .v. pening, Cht. Th. 614, 11.

**sūþ-heáfod** _a south head:_—Andlang hlinces on þæt sūþheáfod, C. D. iii. 414, 2.

**sūþ-healf.** _Add:_—On eásthealfe þeningden, and seó burhstrǣt on sūþhealfe, Ælfrices mearc on westhealfe, and hamingford on norðhealfe, C. D. iii. 15, 11.

**sūþ-land.** _Add:_ I. _land to the south, south shore of a river :_—Hȳ heóldan þurh þā brycge áá bi þǣm sūþlande (sȳð-, _v. l._), Chr. 1052; P. 181, 15. II. _a country to the south :_—þā þā in þām sūðlandum wēdde seó arrianisce ēhtnes _dum persecutio Ariana in Africa insaniret,_ Gr. D. 240, 7.

**Sūþ-Langbeardan** _the people_ (or _country_) _of Lombardy:_—In þām dǣlum Sūþ-Langbeardena (Sūð-Langbeardena landes dǣlum, _v. l._) _in Campaniae partibus,_ Gr. D. 169, 30. In Sūð-Langbeardum (-Long-bardum, _v. l._) _in Italia,_ 25, 26 : _in parte Campaniae,_ 210, 25.

**sūþ-mǣgþ.** _Add:_—Ealle ðas mǣgðe and eác ōðre sūðmǣgðe oð gemǣre Humbre streámes, Bd. 5, 23; Sch. 691, 5.

**sūþ-sǣ** _a south sea :_—On ðām dagum rīxade Æþelbyrht cyning on Cantwarebyrig, and his rīce wæs āstreht fram ðǣre micclan eá Humbre oð sūðsǣ, Hml. Th. ii. 128, 19. Ðis synt ðǣra .xxx. hīda landgemǣro tō Cawelburnan on Wiht . . . on sūðsǣ on Eádgýlses mūðan ; . . . and-lang Cawelburnan ūtt on norðsǣ, C. D. v. 82, 21.

**sūþ-weard;** adj. _Southward, south :_—Þæt þridde heáfodrīce wæs þæt Affricanum, and on sūðweardum, Ors. 2, 1; S. 60, 4. v. sūþe-weard.

sûþ-weard; adv. Add:—Hē gewende sûðweard mid fulre fyrde, Chr. 1013; P. 143, 20.

swā. IV 1 a. add: confirming a previous statement:—Gē secgaŏ þ Petrus hæfde wíf and cíld, and wē eác secgaŏ þ hē swā hæfde, Ll. Th. ii. 376, 30. IV 2 a. Dele passage from Blick. Homl. 247, 1, and add:—Sægde him mon þ þǽr wǽre sum man earmlíce āswolten swā þ hē hine sylfne āwyrde, Bl. H. 219, 12. Heora ān his exe ūp ābrǽd, wolde hine sleán; ac him forwyrnde sum ōþer swā þ hē þ hylfe gelǽhte, Hml. S. 31, 154: 32, 207. Hafa hine swā swilce ðīn āgen lim, Hex. 46, 3. IV 4. add:—Swā cenlic percommoda, Txts. 85, 1534. God gescifte ǽnne swā gerādne mon, Hml. S. 23, 415. On dǽm tweón þe hié swā ungeorne his willan fulleódon qui fastidiose ducem in disponendo bello audientes, Ors. 3, 11; S. 146, 24. (4 a) with an adjective, as epithet of an object, all the adjective as the object was (is):—Hē hī swā unróte (her all troubled as she was) ōleccende tō him geloccode (eam) tristem blanditiis delinivit, Past. 415, 18. Hié Rōmāne ... swā cuce on eorðan bedulfan viva obruta est in campo, Ors. 3, 6; S. 108, 19: Hml. S. 18, 337: 35, 115. Þā hē ārās, þā ongan hē þencan swā scyldig cum surrexisset, reus cogitare coepit, Gr. D. 308, 20. V 1. add: with clause contracted:—Þa Walas flugon þā Englan swā fýr (swā man flúcð fýr, v. l.), Chr. 473; P. 14, 5. V 2. add:— Hē cwæð swā seó ilce wíse þā maniġum men cūþ wæs be his sage aiebat sicut tunc res eadem multis innotuit, Gr. D. 318, 26. þ hē sealde þām ōðrum swā hē nyste āttor drincan ut ei nescienti in potu venenum daret, 158, 29: 327, 8: Hml. S. 30, 88. Hē læg fíf dagas beforan ðæs mynstres geate swā hē ne æt ne ne dranc, ac hē bæd ingonges, Shrn. 109, 5. V 3. add: (a) the clause contracted:—Hē læg þǽr swā dǽd lange on þǽre flóra, Hml. S. 7, 173. V 8. add: so soon as:—Hē þām twām dǽlum bebeád, swā hié feohtan angunnen, þ hié wið his flugen, Ors. 3, 7; S. 116, 27: 5, 13; S. 246, 14. Swā þonne hē tō dǽm stāne cōm, þonne hēt hē hiene mid fýre onhǽtan, 4, 8; S. 186, 18. Swā þis gedōn byþ, gā ic æfter þe opere expleto te subsequor, Gr. D. 36, 31: Bt. 31, 4; F. 252, 12. Hý þā þām hrægelþéne betǽcen, swā hý hām cōmen revertentes restituant, R. Ben. 91, 13. Hē on ān sceolde tō helle, swā hē forðfaren wæs, Wlfst. 16, 14. Hē leofað sōna swā hē besihð on hig qui aspexerit eum vivet, Num. 21, 8. V 11. add:—Eall þing þysses middangeardes swā swā fremde hī forhogedon, Bd. 1, 26; Sch. 57, 2. VI 1. add:—þā wæs hē swā feor norþ swā þā hwælhuntan firrest faraþ, Ors. 1, 1; S. 17, 11. VI 2 a. add:— Wið þan ðe mín wiif þǽr benuge innganges swā mid mínum líce swā yferran dōge swā hwæder swā hire liófre sié, Cht. Th. 470, 33-38. Se dyde swaþer hē dorste ... swā (vel) hē hit āgnode swā (vel) hē hit týmde, Ll. Th. i. 160, 8. VI 2 b. add:—Suā (swǽ, v. l.) nytt suā unnyt suæðer hié beóð, Past. 97, 1.

-swǽc. v. bī-swǽc, Ps. Rdr. 40, 10. Cf. bí-swic.

swǽlan. Add:—Swǽlende adurens (genas maculis livor respergit adurens, Vit. Cuth. poet. 46, 9), An. Ox. 32, 15.

swǽm. Add:—Þǽra sceanda and þǽra swǽma mænigeo wæs ǽfre ūre westdǽl āfylled quorum sordida atque infami numerositate semper nostra pars occidua pollet, Chrd. 78, 6.

swǽp enticement, deceit:—Syþþan þonne ǽnig yfel geþōht þurh deófles swǽp (suadente diabolo) on ūre heortan cume, Chrd. 38, 15.

swǽpels (m.?). l. , es; m.; for 106, 3 l. 103, 6, and add: Ps. Vos. 103, 6.

swǽr. I. add:—Sum mann wæs gebunden onbūtan þ heáfod for his hefigum gylte, sē cōm tō þām hālgan, and his swāra heáfodbend sōna tōbærst, Hml. S. 21, 423. þis mē tō bōte þǽre swǽran swǽrtbyrde, Lch. iii. 66, 22. II. add:—Fore fyrhte þǽre swǽran onsýne þǽra āwyrgedra gāsta pavore tetrae eorum imaginis, Gr. D. 326, 7. IV. add:—þā swǽran synna ne beóð nǽfre āfeormode for nānes fýres ǽlincge, Hml. Th. ii. 590, 19. V. add:—Swǽr piger, An. Ox. 48, 3. V b. add:—Slēpon þā mǽdene swā swārum slǽpe þ man hí āwreccan ne mihte, Hml. S. 35, 68.

swǽr, swār, es; n. What is heavy or grievous, labour, trouble:— Đis syndon swāres and geswinces dagas, Verc. Först. 173.

swǽrness. I. add:—þā ðā ic hine bær ne gefrēdde ic nānre byrdene swǽrnysse, Hml. Th. i. 336, 25.

swǽs. III. add:—þ wē ne beón beswicene þurh ðā swǽsan lustas þe of oferflōwednysse eallum þām becumað þe būton wærscipe heora woruld ādreógað, Hml. S. 11, 359. v. mann-swǽs.

swǽse. Add: v. un-swǽse.

swǽsende. In l. 11 insert a comma after ælmessum, and add: cf. tō ælmessum ad agapem, Wrt. Voc. ii. 86, 57: tō feorme ad agapem i. deliciem, An. Ox. 4834, each being a gloss to Ald. 68, 37.

swǽs-lic. Add:—Swā swā betwyh þām mōdum þe selfe heom betweónum lufiað seó swǽslice hīwcūþnes þǽre sōþan lufe gegearwað mycle bældo sicut inter amantes se animos magnum caritatis familiaritas ausum praebet, Gr. D. 250, 8. v. ge-swǽslic.

swǽslíce. II. add:—þes wæs tō mē geþeóded swíðe swǽslíce and hīwcūðlíce hic mihi valde familiariter jungebatur, Gr. D. 257, 14: 237, 22. v. ge-swǽslíce.

swǽsness. Add:—Hwǽr beóð ðā ēstfullan swǽsnessa, and ðā līðan liffetunga ðe hine forlǽddon ǽror, Hex. 50, 27. Đā byrðeras synd ōlæcunga lyffetyndra geférena þe mid ōlæcunge and gæættredum swǽsnyssum þone synfullan tihtað and heriað, Hml. Th. i. 492, 2. -swǽsscipe. v. ge-swǽsscipe.

swǽtan. I. add:—Ūre líchama is eorðe, and hē oft ðeáh swǽt, Hex. 22, 24. II. add:—Se stān cymð of eorðan, and hē swǽt swāþeáh, Hex. 22, 22. Hī gangende gemētton þ stānclif swǽtende and wǽtende qui euntes rupem montis sudantem invenerunt, Gr. D. 113, 9.

swǽþ. I. add:—Eálā! wǽre mē gelýfed þ ic mōste þínum swaðum fyligan and þínes deórwyrðan andwlitan gesihðe brūcan, Hml. S. 23 b, 710. II. add:—Hē gemētte þ fæt swā gehāl þ on him ne mihton beón fundene nāne swaðu (vestigia) þæs bryces, Gr. D. 97, 23. v. (?) swæþ?

swæðelyne glosses pingues, An. Ox. 27, 32.

swǽþer. II. add: Sē dyde þonne swaþer hē dorste ... swā (vel) hē hit ágnode, swā (vel) hē hit týmde, Ll. Th. i. 160, 7.

swā-lic, swǽlíce. v. swilc, swilce.

swangettung, e; f. Movement, agitation, fluctuation:—Seó sǽ getácnað þas andwerdan woruld þe mid mislicum gelimpum ðǽre sǽ swangetunge geefenlǽcð, Nap. 60.

swangorness. Add:—Þín gerecenes weóx swā swíðe forð fram mínre lætnysse and dysegan swongernysse (swancger-, v. l.) ex tarditate mea tantum crevit expositio tua, Gr. D. 174, 24.

swāpan. Add:—Swǽpð verrat, i. trahat, An. Ox. 46, 31. v. geswāpan.

-swara a swearer. v. mān-swara: swarcan. v. swearcan. Substitute: swárcan. v. ā-swárcan: swárcian. v. ā-swárcian: swáromódness. Take here passage at swearcmódness: swárcnian. v. ā-swárcnian.

swárcung, e; f. Darkening, darkness:—Đýstro l swárcunga tenebras, Ps. Rdr. 17, 29.

swárlíce. v. swǽrlíce: swárnian, swárnung. v. ā-swárnian, -swárnung: swarung. Add: for-swarung: swát. Add: v. īsenswát: swaþian. v. ā-swaþian.

swaþu. Add: [a wk. pl. occurs in the compound dolcswaðan, Hpt. Gl. 510, 57]:—Hí ne mihton on þām fæte nǽnige swaðe findan þæs bryces, Gr. D. 97, 23.

swaþu? Cf. (?) swín-sceadu. The word occurs in a list giving the names of various parts of a pig:—Rysle ausungia, flicce perna, spic larda, meargh lucanica, wrōt bruncus, rop jus, swīna swaþu suesta, byrst seta, Wrt. Voc. i. 286, 50-57. Suīna suadu suesta, sivesta, Txts. 98, 972. Could suesta mean pigs' feet? v. swæþ.

swearc. l. swárc: swearcmódness. v. swárcmódness.

swearcan. v. swárcan: swearcian; II. Dele, and see swárcian.

swearm. Add:—Swearm examen, i. multitudo apium, An. Ox. 3821: 132. v. dūst-swearm.

sweart. I. add:—Sweartes geallan melancolie, i. fellis, An. Ox. 2950. II. add:—Mid sweartum tetris, i. nigris (tenebris), An. Ox. 1736. III. add:—Sweartum ceco (ceco carpitur igne et clandestinis inflammatur stimulis, Ald. 66, 11), An. Ox. 4653. v. col-sweart.

sweart-byrd, e; f. A dismal, hapless birth. v. sweart; III:— þis mē tō bōte þǽre swǽran swǽrtbyrde, Lch. iii. 66, 22.

swebban. Add:—Swefedne soporatum, i. somno grauatum, An. Ox. 1880.

swebbung. v. forþ-swebbung.

swecc. I. add:—Swæcc nectar (cf. nectar þone swētan smæc, Wrt. Voc. ii. 61, 31), An. Ox. 186, 59. II. add:—Stýmendes swæcces ambrosiae fraglantis, An. Ox. 312. Swæcc ambrosiam (cf. ambrosiam, suavem odorem, Wrt. Voc. ii. 82, 11), 3277. (See for both these Ald. 45, 3.)

swefecere, es; m. A sleeper:—þā gedwyldmen man hæt on Grēcisc Nictates (= Nyctages), and wē on ūre geþeóde slūmeras hī magon oððe swefeceras nemnan, and eác hí man mæg slǽperas hātan, Chrd. 26, 2. See next word.

swefecung, e; f. Sleep, slumber:—Se hopa þæs tōweardan ǽrystes, þonne þā rihtwýsan swylce of slǽpes swæfcunge (a sopore somni) ārīsað, Chrd. 26, 25. Ic ne sylle swefcunge (somnum) mínum eágum, 31, 4. See preceding word.

swefel. Add:—God sende ðā fýr and fūlne swefel him tō and forbærnde hī ealle, Hml. S. 13, 211.

swefen. II. add:—Nū is witenne þæt wē ne sceolan cēpan ealles tō swýðe be swefnum ... sume swefna syndon of Gode ... and sume beóð of deófle ... þā swefna beóð wynsume þe gewurðað of Gode, and þā beóð egefulle ðe of þām deofle cumað, and God sylf forbeád þ wē swefnum ne folgion, Hml. S. 21, 403-412. Þā gemunde Iōsep þā swefen þe hine ǽr mǽtte recordatus somniorum, quae viderat, Gen. 42, 9.

sweflenness (?) the smoke and stench of sulphur:—Seó sweofiennesse fumus et pudor (= putor) sulphuris, Verc. Först. 123, 2.

swég. I. add:—Āweóx māra swég and hefegra (gravior sonitus),

swā þ hit āhleóðrode swylce eall seó cyrice wǽre tōworpen fram þām grundweallum, Gr. D. 236, 12. Se sācerd scolde bión mid bellum behangen . . . scolde beón gehiéred his swēg (sonitus), Past. 93, 7. **II a.** *add:*—Hig deóplíce þā stefna þæs lyftes swēge gesleáð, and mid þǽre tungan clypole þæne swēg gewynsumiað, Angl. viii. 313, 15. **II b.** *add:*—Tō ðǽre hristendan . . . swēge (ad stridulae (buccinae) sonum, Ald. 65, 15), Wrt. Voc. ii. 3, 46. v. swin-swēg.

**swēgan.** **I b 1.** *add:*—Swēgdon sonauerunt (inimici tui, Ps. 82, 3), Bl. Gl. **II.** *add:*—Ne gehýre gē hū myrige lofsangas swēgað on heofenum?, Hml. Th. ii. 98, 5. Benedicte ne mihte beón nān þing bedíglod, þā þā on his eáre swēgdon eác þā word þæs munukes geþōhtes, Gr. D. 144, 33. **II a.** where the words of a passage are given, *to be expressed in such and such words:*—þ sārlice leóð þe þūs swēgð on þām sealme, 'Transivi et ecce non erat (Ps. 37, 35),' Angl. viii. 332, 38. v. ā-swēgan; samod-, wel-swēgende.

**swēge.** *Add:* v. hās-swēge.

**swegel-horn.** *Add:*—Sweglhorn sambuca (sambuca salpicibus respondet musica crebris, Ald. 146, 21), An. Ox. 14, 1. Swegelhorna sambucorum, i. genus simphoniarum (licet musica sambucorum harmonia persultans insonuerit, Ald. 23, 3), 1645.

**swegen.** v. bāt-swegen.

**sweger.** *Add:*—Sæt Simonis swegr (swēr, L., swægre, R.) hriðigende, Mk. 1, 30.

**swegran.** *For* consobrimi *l.* consobrini.

**swelg(-h)** *a chasm, swallow* (v. *D.D.*):—Swelh hiatum, opertionem *l̃* foueam terrae, An. Ox. 50, 5. [Wick. sweluȝ vorago: Prompt Parv. sweluh: Mand. swelogh: M. Du. swelgh: M. L. Ger. swelch: Icel. svelgr *a whirlpool, current, stream.*] v. ge-swelg; swelgend, swilige.

**swelgan.** **I b.** *add:*—Ic wāt eardfæstne ānne (a bookcase) standan, . . . sē oft dæges swilged lācum (books are often put into it), Rä. 50, 2. Blōd lifrum swealg, An. 1278.

**-swelge** *in* geswelge. v. swelg: swelgend, es; *m.* *Add:* v. for-swelgend.

**swelgend, e; f.** *Add:* a swallet, swallow (v. D.D.):—Tō þǽre sweliende, of þǽre sweliende, Cht. E. 266, 27. On Wígmundes swelgende; of ðan swelgende, C. D. v. 376, 10. v. swelg.

**swelh.** v. swelg(-h).

**swellan.** *Add:* p. sweoll (v. ā-swellan):—His fēt wǽron swellende and āþundene for þý wǽtan þǽre fōtādle pedes podagrae humore tumescentes, Gr. D. 302, 7.

**swellan** *to burn* (trans., *causative to* swelan):—Swellendum bærnette torido chaumate, An. Ox. 3778.

**sweltan.** *Add:* p. swealt. **I.** absolute, *to die:*—Hē sweolt, Shrn. 153, 14. Hē cūðe tōcnāwan gif hē cunnode þæs mannes be his ǽdrena hrepunge hweðer hē hraðe swulte, Hml. S. 3, 569. **II.** to die of something, in a manner described:—Hē wæs wāniende . . . þ hē swelce deáðe swealt, Ors. 5, 12; S. 244, 5. Þā folc būtū on feferādle mid ungemete swulton, Ors. 4, 10; S. 198, 35. **III.** to die with respect to something:—Hí sweltað būtan ænde mid līchaman and gāste, Gr. D. 264, 9. **IV.** to die from something (gen.), be no longer conscious or under the action of something:—Hí beóð deáde and ungewisse þæs ēcan lífes and ne magon sweltan þæs ēcan wītes deáðes, Gr. D. 264, 11.

**swencan.** (a) *add:*—Eówer fæder eów biddeð þ gē ne scylen eów swencan on þone síþ rogat pater noster ne fatigari debeatis, Gr. D. 39, 16. Hié beóð bealdran ðā gōdan tō swenceanne, Past. 361, 14. v. ā-swencan.

**sweng.** *Add:*—Mid swengce ictu (gladii), An. Ox. 4924.

**swengan.** *Dele* fram- *at end, and add:*—Fram swengde excussit (tiro . . . procul excussit jaculatas fraude sagittas, Ald. 167, 26), Wrt. Voc. ii. 92, 75 : 31, 55. Cf. Fram āswengde vel tōdrāf excussit, 146, 17.

**sweoloþ.** *Add:*—Fýr and swoloð ignis et aestus, Ps. Rdr. 293, 66. **sweoloþa.** *Add:*—Wallendre hǽte and swoloðan caumate, An. Ox. 23, 55.

**sweoloþ-hāt; adj.** *Burning hot:*—Swoloðh[āt] squalida, fýrh[āt] torrida, sunh[āt] soliflua, An. Ox. 56, 202–205.

**sweór.** *Add:*—Se sweór bemǽnde his snore, and se brýdguma his brýd, Hml. S. 33, 191. Hiene ofslóg his āgen sweór fraude soceri sui interfectus est, Ors. 6, 29; S. 278, 18.

**sweor** *a pillar :*—Weard þām abbode ǽteówed ān fýren swer; sē stōd ūp āþenod oð þā steápan heofonan, Hml. S. 3, 449. Mid ðǽm sweore ðæs wolcnes, Past. 305, 1. Feówer þing synt ealra þinga behēfost . . . þām þe þencð tō þām ēcan lífe : þ synt feówer sweras, iustitia, . . . prudentia, . . . temperantia, . . . fortitudo, Wlfst. 247, 11–16.

**sweora.** *l.* sweóra, *and add:*—Ic wāt cūðlíce þæt ic be gewyrhtum on mīnum sweóran (sweóran, v. l. Cf. swūran, swīran, 18) byrne, Bd. 4, 19; Sch. 449, 22.

**sweór-bān.** *Add:*—Dryhten ceorfeð sweórbān (ceruices) synfulra, Ps. Vos. 128, 4.

**sweór-beáh.** *Add:*—Sweórbeáh baben, torques aurea cum gemmis, Hpt. 31, 13, 295.

**sweorcan.** **I.** *add:*—Þonne se man sceal sweltan, þonne swyrceð him fram þæs hūses hrōfe ðe hē inne bið, Verc. Först. 108, 1. Hē āsende þeóstru and swearc misit tenebras et obscuravit, Ps. L. 104, 28. **I a.** to grow black :—Sweorcan and sweartian nigrescere, Chrd. 96, 10.

**sweord.** *Add:*—Mīne witan habbað ætre[ht] Ecgferðe ealle his āre þurh þ swyrd þe him on hype hangode ðā hē ādranc, Cht. Th. 208, 22. And þeáh hē geþeó þ hē hæbbe helm and byrnan and golde fǽted sweord (ofergyldene sweord, 22), gif hē þ land nafað, hē bið ceorl swāþeáh, Ll. Th. i. 188, 9. v. birn- (byrn-), hilt-sweord.

**sweord-bora.** **I.** the first two examples should be put under **II**. **II.** *add:*—Þæs cyninges sweordbora (spatharius: spatharii munus erat spatham sive ensem principis gerere, ejusque latus custodire) wæs Riego gehāten, Gr. D. 130, 31. Þæs forecwedenan Narses sweordbora Bulgarisc man, 300, 21. Fērde se āwyrgda gāst in þæs cyninges sweordboran, 187, 21.

**sweord-gripe.** *Substitute:* Sword-grip, stroke of the sword. Cf. Fýres feng . . . oððe gripe mēces, B. 1765. Gāras gripon, Gen. 2063.

**Sweordoras.** *Dele* bracket.

**sweord-tyge, -tige, es; m.** Drawing the sword, fighting with the sword :—Fýnd āteórodun fram sweordtige (mid sweorde, Ps. Vos., Srt. : of sweorde, Ps. Rdr., Spl.) inimici defecerunt frameae, Ps. L. 9, 7.

**sweord-wegende.** *Add:* striking with a sword. The word glosses gladiantes.

**-sweóred.** v. lang-sweóred.

**sweór-hnitu.** Dr. Bradley suggests that suernit is a mistake for suge hnitu (usia in Isidore is uermis porci), and that a later glossarist taking suer- as = sweor- may have produced sweor-hnitu.

**sweorsaga** (sweord, saga ?) glosses allec, An. Ox. 30, 2.

**sweostor-sunu** a nephew :—Ann ic his mīura swæstorsuna swælcum se hit gediān wile and him giðeðe bið, C. D. i. 311, 14.

**sweót.** *Add:* [Icel. sjót a host.] v. folc-sweót.

**sweotolian.** *Add:* used impersonally in the beginning of documents :—Hēr swutelað on þisum gewrite embe þā forewyrd þe Ægelríc worhte wið Eádsige, C. D. iv. 86, 7.

**sweotolung.** **I.** *add:* a visible display :—Twēgen munecas bǽdon æt Gode sume swutelunge be ðām hālgan hūsle . . . Ðā gesāwon hí licgan ān cild on ðām weófode . . . hí þæt hūsl ðygedon Gode ðancigende þǽre swutelunge, Hml. Th. ii. 272, 14–22. Weard seó cwēn micclum gegladod þæt heó mōste ðone māðm (the cross) on moldan findan, and siððan ðurh tācnum swutelunge oncnāwan, 306, 11. **II.** *add:* a making known the significance of something :—Se bisceop funde him ð rǽde þæt hī mid þreóra daga fæstene swutelunge þæs wundres æt Gode bǽdon, Hml. Th. i. 502, 25. (Cf. Bl. H. 199, 32.) Sigewulf hine (Albinus) befrān . . . be gehwylcum cnottum þe hē sylf ne cūþe . . . þā cwæð Albinus þ hē wolde his āxunga ealle gegaderian, and him andsware sendan mid heora swutelungan, Angl. vii. 2, 16. **III.** *add:*—Nū wylle wē embe ðises godspelles trahtnunge sume swutelunge eów gereccan, Hml. Th. i. 478, 4. **IV.** *add:*—Se gerǽfa āxude Eugeniam hū heó āna mihte ealle þā gewytan āwǽgan mid āðe, oððe þurh ǽnige swutelunge hí sylfe āclǽnsian, Hml. S. 2, 226.

**swerian.** **II.** *add:* to swear an oath, where the form of oath is implied in the noun :—Hí Crístes helda swōren they said, 'So help me Christ,' Hml. S. 23, 529. **II 2.** *add:* Ors. 4, 9; S. 190, 22. **II 2 a.** *add:* Hml. S. 14, 97 : Hml. Th. ii. 234, 26. **II 3.** *add:*—Hē him āþas swōr, þæt hē him gearo wǽre, Chr. 874; P. 72, 30. Hī him āþas swōron on þām hālgan beáge þæt hié of his ríce fōren, 876; P. 74, 9. v. mān-swerian.

**swepel.** The gloss at Txts. 113, 72 is probably High German.

**swepung.** *Add:*—Seó sweðung þǽre lācnunge fomenta curationum, Chrd. 60, 26.

**swétness.** **I.** *add:*—Hí ealle þā stōwe gemētton mid ambrosie þǽre wyrte swētnysse (ambrosiae odore) gefylde, Guth. Gr. 168, 130.

**swica.** In l. 2 for 'se ductor' l. seductor.

**swican.** **III.** *add:*—Swícan cessare, An. Ox. 56, 65. v. un-swícende.

**-swice; adj.** v. ǽ-swicc.

**swic-dōm.** *Add:*—Þā ðe mid mislicum swicdōmum hí sylfe and ōðre forþærað, Hml. Th. ii. 514, 32.

**swice.** *Add:* v. ǽ-swice.

**swician.** **III.** *add:*—Swiciende mānswican, Ll. Lbmn. 244, 28. **III a.** *add:*—Nū swicað se deófol dígollíce embe ūs hū hē þurh leahtras forlǽre ðā crístenan, and tō mislicum synnum heora mōd āwende, Hml. S. 16, 220. Hwí woldest ðū swician on ðínum āgenum? (cur tentavit Satanas cor tuum . . . fraudare de pretio agri ?, Acts 5, 3), Hml. Th. i. 316, 27. **IV.** *add:*—Eádig ys sē ðe ne swicað on mē beatus est qui non fuerit scandalizatus in me, Mt. 11, 6. v. un-swícende.

**-swicu** (?). v. ge-swicu (?): **swicung.** *Add:* v. ge-swícung.

**swífan.** **I.** *add:*—Se brōc þeáh hē swíðe (swíþe, MS.) of his rihtryne (cf. brōc bið onwended of his rihtryne vagatur defluus amnis, Met. 5, 19), Bt. 6; S. 14, 15. v. ymb-swífan.

**swift.** *Add:* I. *swift:*—Singal, swift rine *perpes decursus*, An. Ox. 508. Swiftum streáme *rapaci*, i. *ueloci alueo*, 2667. Swiftum *passiuis* (*uolatibus*), 264: *reciprocis* (*uolatibus*), 2408: *pernicibus*, *uelocibus* (*obtutibus*), 9, 10. II. *sloping steeply* (?). Cf. *rapid* as applied to the slope of a hill:—Of ðǣm dīce on swiftan beorh; of ðǣm beorhge, C. D. iii. 394, 3.

**swiftlere.** *Add:*—Gyf þū swyftleras habban wyile, þonne sete þū þīnne scytefinger uppon þīnne fōt and strīc on twā healfa þīnes fēt þām gemete þe hī gesceapene beóð, Tech. ii. 126, 8.

**swiftness.** *Add:*—Gewunelīce wē singað mid micelre swif(t)nysse *consuete canimus nimia uelocitate*, Angl. xiii. 370, 75.

**swift-ryne.** *Better* swift ryne. v. An. Ox. 509: **swīg**(?). v. swīge.

**swīgan.** I. *add:*—Ðā ðe fore-eádun giðreótodun hine ꝥte hē swīgde, Lk. R. 18, 39. v. æt-swīgan. III. *to pass over in silence.* v. swigian; III:—Ne ic eác swīge (forsuwie, *v. l.*) ꝥ, ꝥ his gingra gewunode tō reccenne, Gr. D. 157, 18.

**swīge.** *Add:* **swīg** (?), e; *f.* I. *add:*—Dumbre swīgan *mutae taciturnitatis*, An. Ox. 1937. Mid swīge *silentio*, 2085. Fīfwintre swīgan stǣrleornera *quinquennem taciturnitatem Stoicorum*, 4144.

**swīge**; *adj.* II. *add:*—Man gehȳrde in swīgre nihte mycelne sealmsang *coepit in nocturno silentio psalmodiae cantus audiri*, Gr. D. 238, 29. On þǣre nihte, þā hit stillost swīgost wæs *intempestae noctis silentio*, 11.

**swigian.** I b. *add:*—Hȳ sweogodan *siluerunt*, Ps. L. 106, 30. III. *add:*—Sē ðe wilnað wōh tō dōnne, and wilnað ðeáh ðæt ðæs ōðre men sugigen (swugien, *v. l.*) *qui et prava studet agere, et tamen ad haec vult caeteros tacere*, Past. 145, 12. Ðonne ābiersð hwīlum hwæthwugu ūt ðæs ðe hē sugian (swugian, *v. l.*) sceolde *ad aliquid, quod dicere non debet, erumpat*, 165, 15. Ne mæg ic ꝥ swigian, ꝥ his geongra mē sǣde *neque illud taceam, quod ejus discipulus narrare consueverat*, Gr. D. 157, 18.

**-swigung.** v. for-swigung, -swuwung.

**swilc.** I 1. *add:*—On ðǣm dæge plegedon hié of horsum . . . swā heora þeáw æt swelcum (*on such occasions*) wæs, Ors. 3, 7; S. 118, 31. Ðā swelcan wē magon ealra betest geryhtan mid ðȳ ðæt . . ., Past. 293, 22. I 2 a. *add:*—Ic mæg gelīc anginn þǣm gesecgan, þēh hit swelcne ende næfde, þætte Constantinopolim on swelcre cwacunge wæs *ego poteram similia apud Constantinopolim narrare*, Ors. 3, 2; S. 100, 21. Þone swylcne seócne lǣcas nemniað gewitleásne, Gr. D. 247, 13. III. *add:*—Him þā geþūhte swelc ꝥ mǣste wæl swelc hié oft ǣr for nōht hæfdon, Ors. 4, 7; S. 184, 14. III a. Þyslic . . . swālic:—Þyslic (þyllic, *v. l.*) mē is gesewen . . . swālic (swylc, *v. l.*) swā . . . *talis mihi videtur . . . quale . . .*, Bd. 2, 13; Sch. 165, 17. V. *add:*—Wiþ hreófle, wegbrǣde, . . . eolone, swefl, dō þæs swefles swilc an þāra wyrta twǣde, Lch. ii. 78, 8. Wyrc swilc ān lytel cicel, Lch. iii. 30, 19. V 1. of abstract things:—Ðæt is ðonne suelc mon mid forewearde orde stinge, ðæt mon openlīce on ōðerne rǣse mid tǣlinge *to rush on another openly with blame is as much as to thrust with the point;* ex mucrone quippe percutere est impetu apertae increpationis obviare, Past. 297, 11.

**swilce.** *Add:* , swālīce. I. *add:*—Be þon swilce (swelce, swylce, *v. ll.*) Paulus cwǣð *unde Paulus quoque dicit*, Bd. 1, 27; Sch. 85, 11. II a. *so, in a manner to be described:*—Gif eów swālīce þūhte, utan gangan on þissum carcerne and hine ūt forlǣtan, Bl. H. 247, 1. Swylce ic þus hyt gehradige, Angl. viii. 303, 27. III. *add: as it were:*—Hē geseah swilce ān ðeóstorful dene, Hml. Th. ii. 338, 4: Ors. 5. 14; S. 248, 9: Hml. S. 31, 937. III a. with relative force, swelc, swā . . . swilce:—Ðīn nosu is swelc swelce se torr on Libano, Past. 64, 24. Hafa hine swā swilce ðīn āgen lim, Hex. 46, 3. III b. with antecedent and relative combined (*such, so*) *as:*—Hē wæs swelce Rōmāne þā wyrþe wǣron *he was such as the Romans then deserved*, Ors. 6, 3; S. 256, 24. Dō þū þā lǣcedōmas swilce þū þā līchoman gesié, Lch. ii. 84, 15. IV. *add:*—Swelce hē hine wandigende ofersuīðe *quasi parcendo superare*, Past. 297, 15: 296, 11. Næs þæt cild gecweden hire frumcennede cild swilce heó ōðer siððan ācende, Hml. Th. i. 34, 24.

**swilc-hwega** *some:*—Þā geseah hē þǣr swilchwugu treów licgende and ꝥ lytel *he saw lying there some bit of wood or other and that little*, Hml. S. 236, 766.

**swilcness.** *Add:* cf. gehwilcness.

**swilige,** an; *f. A pit* (?):—Of mǣrdīc on ðā wæterswylian; of ðǣre swylian on mǣrðom, C. D. vi. 220, 23. v. swelg.

**swimman.** II. *add:*—Hū hē þonne swam mid þām ilcan scipe, þonne hit wæs ȳþa full *qualiter cum carabo undis pleno nataverat*, Gr. D. 347, 21. III. *add:*—Āgeót wæter uppon ðone ele, and se ele ābrecð ūp and swimð bufon, Hml. Th ii. 564, 14. v. þurh-swimman.

**swimmend.** v. lagu-swimmend.

**swīn.** *Add:*—Þā semninga gefēldon hī ān swȳn (*porcum*) yrnende hider and þider betwyh heora fōtum, ꝥ sum ꝥ swȳn heora hwylc gefēlde . . . sōhte ꝥ swīn þā duru þǣre cyrcan . . . and ne mihte hit nān man geseón, and swā þeáh hī hit mihton gefēlan, Gr. D. 236, 1-6. Ne ān cū ne ān swīn næs belyfon ꝥ næs gesæt on his (*William I*) gewrite, Chr. 1085; P. 216, 29. Genim swīnes sceatu þæs þe on dūnlande and wyrtum libbe, Lch. ii. 62. 27. Æðelsige forstæl Æðelwines swīn . . . ðā ridon his men tō and tugon ūt ðæt spic of Æðelsiges hūse, and hē oðbærst tō wuda, C. D. iii. 291, 15. Ic ann ꝥ ðridde treów and ꝥ ðridde swiin (*printed* swun) of æuesan ðæs wudes (the Latin version is: Dono tertiam quamque arborem et tertiam quamque sarcinam iumentariam fructuum qui nascuntur in sylua), iv. 202, 11. Wærlāf hātte Wærstānes fæder wæs riht ǣht tō Hǣðfelda, heóld ðā grǣgan swȳn, vi. 212, 15. v. eofor-, fēdels-swīn.

**swinc.** *Dele second passage, for which see* swinge, *and add:*—Swā hwæt swā hē begit his swinces tō mēdes hē hit bringð tō mē, Hml. S. 36, 43.

**swincan.** II. *add:*—Ne swinc þū (nelle þū nū beón geswenced, *v. l.*) nā māre *noli fatigari*, Gr. D. 88, 32. Ne bið heó nā swincende on feforādlum *non febribus laboratura est*, 29, 23. v. ge-swincan.

**swīnen.** *Add:*—Swȳnen *porcinus*, An. Ox. 4332. [Æt] swȳnenan and æt sceáplican and æt fearlican *suouetaurilia*, 11, 187.

**swingan.** I a. *add:*—Gif þū gyrde habban wille, þonne wege þū þīne fȳst swylce þū swingan wille, Tech. ii. 122, 12. v. ā-, ofer-swingan.

**swinge.** I. *add:*—His seón swȳðe þeóstrodon. Þā hrepode Martinus mid ānre swingan (*Martin gave the man a slight stroke?*) and eall seó sāmis him sōna fram gewāt . . . þurh Martines hrepunge, Hml. S. 31, 589. II. *add:*—Þte ðā sōðfæstnis? ðerscingra ł swincð dyde āwoerdeno *ut quos justitia verberum faecit afflictos*, Rtl. 40, 29. ꝥ mōd byð mid manigum swingum forseted *mens tot flagellis premitur*, Gr. D. 258, 28. v. wīte-swinge.

**swingel.** I a. *add:*—Wæs sum wyln gehæft tō swinglum . . . and læg on hæftnēdum ꝥ heó hetelīce wǣre þæs on morgen beswungen . . . Heó clypode tō þām hālgan Swȳðūne ꝥ hē . . . fram þām rēðum swinglum hī āhredde, Hml. S. 21, 166-171. Se ilca swīgende geðafode swingellan *tacitus flagella toleravit*, Past. 261, 11.

**swīn-haga.** *Add:*—On afene oð ðæt ðe se alda suīnhaga ūt sciōteð tō afene; ðonne be ðǣm hagan on ānne beorg, C. D. ii. 29, 10.

**swīn-hege,** es; *m. A fence to keep swine from straying:*—Tō bysceopes swȳnhege; ondlong heges, C. D. iii. 77, 11. Of ðǣre burnan on ðane swȳnhege; andlang heges, 78, 5.

**swīn-hirde,** es; *m. A swine-herd:*—Swȳnhyrde *subulcus*, Hpt. 33, 239, 7.

**swīn-lic**; *adj. Of* (*a*) *swine, swinish:*—Þæt swīnlice (*printed* symlice) gestun *porcinus strepitus*, Wrt. Voc. ii. 85, 31.

**swīn-sceadu.** [Literally *swine-shade*, referring to the shelter afforded to swine by the trees under which they feed: then the payment for the right to pasture them.] *Payment for the pasturing of swine:*—Ut pleniter persolvant omnia que ad jus ipsius ecclesię juste competant, scilicet ea que Anglice dicuntur ciricsceatt, and toll i. e. theloneum, and tacc, i. e. swinsceade, Cht. Th. 263, 7. [In his glossary Thorpe quotes s. v. tacc: '"In Scotland the tithe or tenth hog was paid for pannage. This custom obtained in England, and was here called *Tack*" (Ellis, Introduction to Domesday). Dabit pannagium vocatum Tack, videlicet, pro decem porcis unum porcum meliorem.' See too *N. E. D.* tack.] Cf. (?) swīna sceadu (suadu, Ep., Erf.) *suesta*, *sivesta*, Txts. 99, 1954.

**swinsian.** *Add:*—Swynsiendum *adtonito* (*adtonito* is found Vit. Cuth. poet. C. 31, 4, and five lines later *dulcisonis* occurs, to which word *swynsiendum* seems more properly to belong), Hpt. 33, 238, 9.

**swin-swēg,** es; *m. Melody:*—Swinswēges *melodie*, An. Ox. p. xxxiii, note 2.

**swipor.** *Add: shifty:*—Swiper (*printed* hwiper) *leue, labile, instabilis*, Wülck. Gl. 245, 25. [*O. H. Ger.* swefari *callidus, astutus.*]

**swipu.** I. *add:*—Ðonne þū swype habban wille, þonne wege þīne fȳst swylce þū swingan wille, and rǣr ūp þīne twǣgen fingras, Tech. ii. 122, 13. Hē wæs lustlīce þone lyre þæs horses þoliende, and eác þā swipan (*flagellum*) þe hē on his handa hæfde, þā hē þām reáfiendum mannum brōhte þus cweðende: 'Nimað þās swipan ꝥ gē magan þis hors mid drīfan,' Gr. D. 14, 18-22.

**swītan.** v. for-spillan; III.

**swīþ.** II 2. *add:*—Hē befēng mīnne swīðran mid deórwurðum stānum, Hml. S. 7, 32. v. þrȳþ-swīþ.

**swīþan.** *Add:* v. of-swīþan.

**swīþe.** II a. *add:*—Hié þæt dydon for þǣm swīþost þe hié þōhtan þæt hié siþþan hiora underþeówas wǣren, Ors. 2, 8; S. 92, 22: 3, 9; S. 132, 13. III. *add:*—Wē ne mihton secgan swā swīðe embe þæt swā swā wē woldon, Hex. 2, 4. Gemetegung, mid þǣre sceall seó sāwul ealle þing gemætegian, ꝥ hit tō swīþe ne sȳ, ne tō hwōnlīce, Hml. S. 1, 162. Nū miht þū wel witan þæt weorc sprecan swīðor þonne þā nacodon word, Ælfc. T. Grn. 21, 24. IV. the comparative marking preference, *rather:*—Ðū þone wiðfeohtend mē helan woldest swȳðor þonne mīnum ðegnum secgean *rebellem celare quam militibus reddere maluisti*, Bd. 1, 7; Sch. 21, 15.

-swíþedlic. v. ofer-swíþedlic: -swíþend. v. ofer-swíþend: -swíþ-
endlic. v. ofer-swíþendlic.

swíþ-hréówness, e; f. Violent grief, remorse:—Þær is eágena
wóp and tóða gristbítung; . . . and þær is egesa and fyrhto; and þær is
swiðhreównes; and þær is unrihtwísnes, Verc. Först. 173.

swíþlic. I. add:—Hé mid swíðlicum prasse férde, Hml. S. 29, 208.
Hé ofwearp þone swíðlican ent, 18, 18. Hé gegaderode swíðlíce fyrde,
25, 290. II. add:—Fýr byrnð on his gesíhðe, and on his ymbhwyrfte bið swíðlíc storm ignis in conspectu ejus ardebit, et in circuitu
ejus tempestas valida (Ps. 50, 3), Hml. Th. i. 618, 11. III. add:—
Hí wæron symble sigefæste on swíþlícum gewinne, Hml. S. 11, 22.
IV. add:—Þá áxode Sisinnius mid swíðlicum þreáte þone hálgan wer
hwylcne god hé wurðode, Hml. S. 29, 217.

swíþlíce. I. add:—Cúðberhtus cwæð þæt Hereberhtus ða sceolde
swíðlíce befrínan (most fully inquire about) his nýdþearfnysse, Hml. Th.
ii. 152, 7. Sý spæc eówer 'Ys, Ys', 'Ná, Ná'; þ þysum swíðlícor
(abundantius) ys, fram yfele hit ys, Scint. 135, 8.

swíþrian. Add:—Word unrihtwísra swíðradon ofer ús uerba iniquorum praeualuerunt super nos, Ps. L. 64, 4. Swýrian preualere, R.
Ben. I. 59, 14. Swýðrenda, preualens, 12, 16. v. ge-swíþrian.

swíþ-sprecende (?) verbose, speaking too much:—Swýðsprecende
verbosa (swýðspecen verbositas, MS.), An. Ox. 56, 140.

swíþung. v. ofer-swíþung: swoese prandium. v. swæsende.

swógan. Add: p. swég (v. þurh-swógan). I. add:—Burnan sweógon
torrentes inundauerunt, Ps. Sp. M. 77, 23. v. geond- (?), in-
(?)swógan.

sworettan. Add:—Tó þon þ hí þone swétan mete húru sworettende
and geómriende onbyrgdon ut cibum suauem saltem suspirando gustarent,
Gr. D. 170, 10.

sworettung. I. add:—Þær bið mycel wánung and gránung and
murnung and sworetung, Verc. Först. 121, 18. Hé on mænigfealdum
sworettungum geanbidode, Hml. S. 23 b, 647.

swornian. Add: v. á-swornian; on-swornod.

swót. Add:—Swótum brǽdum odoramentis, An. Ox. 56, 214. [v.
N. E. D. soot.]

swun, C. D. iv. 202, 11. v. swín.

swyle. Add: sensation of swelling:—Hé onfindeþ swile, and þ þá
óman beóð inne betýnde þurh þá ábláwunge, Lch. ii. 174, 22.

swylige. v. swilige.

swylt a whirlpool. Dele; probably swyttes in the gloss is for swyftes.
v. An. Ox. 2667 note.

syce, es; m. Sucking:—Fram sice ablactatus, ab lacte remotus ł
separatus, ablatus, An. Ox. 57, 8.

sýfer-lic. Add: v. un-sýferlic.

sýferlíce. III. add:—Þá dyde se áðum swá . . . sýferlíce mid
byrnendre árfæstnysse, Hml. Th. ii. 26, 2.

syflige. Add:—Be óðrum sifligum de ceteris pulmentaris, Chrd.
126, 3.

sýl a pillar. Dele passage from Shrn. 149, 2, for which see sigle:
syl = syhl. l. sýl: syla. l. sýla.

sýl-beám a tree that serves as a pillar (?):—Tó sýlbeáme; of sýl-
þeáme, C. D. iii. 79, 36.

sylhðe, es; n. A team of oxen:—Hé geann Godríce án sylhðe
oxna, Cht. Crw. 23, 4.

syll. Add:—Þreó gyrda tó þillianæ, and .iii. sylla tó lyccanne tres
uirgatas plancas ponere, et tres suliuas, id est, tres magnas trabes supponere, C. D. B. iii. 659, 5, and often.

syllabas renders Latin syllabas, Bd. 5, 2; Sch. 559, 5.

sylu. Add:—Þæt land æt þære syle, Cht. Th. 547, 28.

syl-weg. Add: a road made with logs (? cf. syll).

symbel. II. add: II a. a solemn service. v. symbel-ness; II:—
Gehýredum mæssan symlum (sollempniis), Chrd. 114, 10. v. Eáster-
ymbel.

symbel-dǽg (-doeg) a feast-day, sabbath:—Doeg hálig ł symbeldoeg
dies festus, Jn. L. 5, 1. On symbeldoeg sabbato, Lk. L. 13, 15. v.
ymbel-dæg.

symbelness. II. add:—Seó symbelnyss þére hálgan róde úpáhaf-
nnysse, Hml. S. 23 b, 398. Hit wæs þæs abbodes hádingdæg. Þá
ende hé ánne bróðor tó Pafnuntię and laþode hine tó þére symbelnysse,
3, 61. v. on-symbelness.

symnen-lic. v. semnend-lic: syn[n]. Add: v. un-syn[n].

syn-bryne (?) sinful passion:—Deófol þe ús on lífe mid þére syn-
ryne (mid þære synne bryne onǽlþ?. The Latin is: Spiritus qui ad
eccandum succendit, and the English version is imperfect. As bryne
s masculine, þære synbryne is certainly incorrect, and needs some emenda-
ion like that suggested), Verc. Först. 143, 18.

synderlic. II. add:—Mid synderlicum, mid díglum sequestra, i.
creta (oratione), An. Ox. 1842. III. add:—Wǽron on þære fyrde
la crístene menn, and án synderlic eórod of eásternum leódum swíþe
ristene menn þám cásere folgiende, Hml. S. 28, 9. v. á-synderlic.

synderlíce. II. add:—Þá þára áwyrgedra gásta gehwylc his ácsunge

synderlíce gerehton hwæt hí gedón hæfdon cum singuli spiritus ad inquisitionem ejus exponerent quid operati fuissent, Gr. D. 189, 12.
III. in the last passage, Boutr. Scrd. 19, 18, synderlíce translates singulariter, v. Angl. vii. 21, 3. IV. add:—Cweþon twégen sealmas,
ánne for cinge sinderlíce (specialiter), óþerne for cincg and cwéne and
híredmannum, Angl. xiii. 381, 222. Se here þe tó Grantanbrycge híérde
hine gecés synderlíce him tó hláforde (the Danes of Cambridge acted by
themselves), Chr. 921; P. 103, 19.

synderlícness. Add: peculiar excellence;—Heó weóx betweoh
hire óðer twá sweostor tó heáhnesse þæs háligdómes ǽgðer ge mid þám
mægne þæs singalan gebedes ge mid gestæþþignesse and synderlicnysse
þæs fæstenes inter duas alias sorores suas virtute continuae orationis,
gravitate vitae, singularitate abstinentiae ad culmen sanctitatis excreverat, Gr. D. 286, 11.

synder-lípes. Add:—Synderlípes separatim, i. singulariter, An. Ox.
1362: sequestratim, 2852. Senderlípes speciali sententia, 5114.

synder-weorþmynt. Add: v. sunder-weorþmynt.

-syndgian, -syndig, -syndiglic. v. ge-syndgian, -syndig, -syn-
diglic.

syndrig. I. add:—Hé ǽnlýpig áwunode on syndrige (-re, v. l.)
stówe fram þære cyrican in remotiore ab ecclesia loco solitarius manebat,
Bd. 4, 30; Sch. 535, 14. v. æl-, níd-syndrig.

syngian. Add: v. un-syngian: syn-léw. For 'A sinful injury'
substitute: an injury caused by sin. Cf. syn-wund.

-syntlǽcan. v. ge-syntlǽcan.

syn-lust. Add:—Hé geteáh þone synlust (unlust, v. l. voluptatem)
in his líchaman sár . . . hé swá onwænde þá hǽte and þone synlust . . .
seó costung synlustes wæs átemed on him, Gr. D. 101, 24-34. Hí
onǽldon þæra geongrena mód tó forcyrrednesse heora synlustes (libidinis),
119, 15. Hé wæs beswicen þyses middaneardes synlustum (immundo
desiderio), 230, 12.

synnig. In l. 22 after gefón insert in ceápe oþþe elles. Add: v. deáþ-
(deád-)synnig.

-synto. Substitute: synto; f. Safety, salvation:—Hié him nǽnigra
synto (gesynta, v. l.) wéndon, Bd. 3, 15; Sch. 263, 16. v. ge-synto.

syn-wund. Add: cf. syn-léw: sypian. Add: [v. N. E. D.
sipe.]

sýþ (?); adv. In a (more?) southerly direction:—Ðonne súð andlang paðes . . . of ðǽm ðýfele sýð (cpve.?) andlang weges, C. D. vi.
36, 4.

syrfe. Add: [From Latin.]

Syria (?). Dele (?), and add:—Cóm sum man of þám leódscipe þe
is Siria geháten, Hml. Th. i. 400, 7. Férde Achab tógeánes Syrian
cynincge, Hml. S. 18, 215: 217. Án ealdormann of Syrian lande, 311.
Nicanor genam óðre fyrde of Sirian, 25, 620.

Syrisc. Add:—Ásende God his engel tó þám Syriscan here, Hml. S.
18, 402.

# T

tá. Add:—Sume preóstas mid forewerdum tán stæppað, þ on þám
fúhtan wege ne beón heora fét besprengde, Chrd. 64, 35.

tabule. Add: tabul, tablu; f.:—Hæfdon hí mid him gehálgode fatu
and gehálgode tablu (tabul, v. l.), Bd. 5, 10; Sch. 601, 18.

tacan. Add:—Hí tócon mycele ǽhta and fóron áweg, Chr. 1076;
P. 212, 15. Hé hine lét tacan, P. 211, 35. ¶ tacan on to touch.
Cf. Icel. taka á :—Swá hwæt swá þ ele on tæcð . . . þ ele tóc on þ wæter,
Nap. 61.

tacc. v. swín-sceadu.

tácn. I. add:—Þá þá tácna on sǽlicum strandum mearcode cum
(patibuli) signacula in glarigeris sulcaret litoribus, An. Ox. 2490.
III a. add:—Táncna (prophetica) signa, An. Ox. 2618. III b.
add:—Pyles tácen is þæt þú mid þínum scytefingre sume feþer tácnum
gestríce (make signs as if drawing feathers) on þýne wynstran hand
innewearde and lecge tó þínum eáron, Tech. ii. 126, 6. IV. add:—
Ic wát þ hé hæfde áne dolhswaðe on his hneccan . . . gýman wé nú
hwæðer hé þ tácen þére wunde hæbbe, Hml. S. 30, 269. VI.
add:—Þás tácnu (signa) fyliað þám þe gelýfað, Mk. 16, 17. v. róde-
tácn.

tácnian. I. add:—Seó eá geáhnode þone ryne þe se Dryhtnes wer
mid ðæra racan tácnode on þére eorðan aqua fluminis sibi alueum ubi
tracto per terram rastro vir Domini signum fecerat, vindicavit, Gr. D.
193, 4. IV a. add:—Hí tácniað mid ðǽm ðæt men scylen onscun-
ien . . ., Past. 449, 17. IV b. add:—þ tácnaþ þ hé sceal má þencan
úp þonne nyþer, Bt. 41, 6; F. 254, 30. v. firen-tácnian (Ps. Rdr. 288,
21).

-tácnigendlic, -líce. v. ge-tácnigendlic, -líce.

tácnung. V. add :—Sende se pápa tácnunga hú hé ð hálgian, and on hwylcum stówum on Britane hí settan scolde, Chr. 995 ; P. 128, 34.

técan. IV. add :—Ða ísernan hierstepannan hé tǽhte for íserne weall tó settane betuh ðǽm wítgan and ðǽre byrig, Past. 165, 9. V. add : with double accusative? :—Hé tǽhte hí (him? Cf. hé sealde hí (him?) ð gerýne, 97) ðá gerýna ðas hálgan geleáfan, Hml. S. 30, 94.

técing. Add : v. bóc-tǽcing.

tǽflung, e ; f. Gambling :—Ús syndon synderlíce on ðisum dagum forbodene . . . ídele sprǽca and tǽflunga and beórscypas, Nap. 61.

tǽgl. Add :—Wǽs beboden ð se tægel sceolde beón gehál ǽfre on ðám nýtene æt ðǽre offrunge for ðǽre getácnunge ð God wile ð wé simle wel dón oð ende úres lífes ; ðonne bið se tægel geoffrod on úrum weorcum, Ælfc. Gen. Thw. 3, 39–42.

tǽl. Add : v. gerím-tǽl : -tǽl ; adj. [v. N.E.D. tall.] v. ge-, ofer-tǽl.

-tælful. v. ge-tælful.

tǽlan. II. add :—Tǽlan carpere (strophoso rictu) l vituperare, An. Ox. 15, 2. III. add :—Tǽlede derogemur (strophosae sugillationis ludibrio), An. Ox. 8, 393.

tǽling. II. after 'calumny' add : detraction, derogation :—Ne wéne ic ná ð ðes wer wǽre gelustfullod on árfæstnysse weorke, ne on ðæs bisceopes tǽlinge (episcopi derogatione), Gr. D. 76, 17. III. derision, mockery. Take here the passage given under II, where for 'calumnies' substitute 'mockeries' ; the Latin glossed by tǽlincga is irrisiones.

tǽl-lic. Add : blameable, reprehensible :—Gif ǽnig bið gemét teállic si quisque repertus fuerit reprehensibilis, R. Ben. I. 9, 54, 7. Ðǽr ma[n] wógerlice leóð and tǽllice singe ubi amatoria et turpia cantantur, Chrd. 78, 34.

tǽlness. Add :—Gelustfullod mid tǽlnysse ðæs biscopes delectatus episcopi derogatione, Gr. D. 76, 17. Heora lár bið eall tó tǽlnesse geðeóded, Verc. Först. 118, 9. Forlǽtan wé tǽlnessa and twysprǽcnessa, 94, 3 : Ll. Th. ii. 262, 26.

tǽl-sum. Add : v. ge-tælsum.

tǽl-wirþe. Add :—Án þing wæs ð gesewen wæs on him tǽlwyrðe (reprehensibile) beón, Gr. D. 203, 21. Gif hié on ðǽm cúðan gewislíce ongietað hwæt ðǽron tǽlwyrðes bið si de expertis, quidquid disputationis audiunt, veraciter cognoscunt, Past. 441, 16. Hé lýfeð sumum mannum sume tǽlwyrðe wísan quaedam reprehensibila relinquit, Gr. D. 204, 15.

tǽnen. Substitute :—Tǽnene breóstgyrde sceptrine uirge, An. Ox. 3303.

tǽse. Add :—Tǽs[e] blandus, An. Ox. 56, 307.

-tǽwe. v. æl-, manig-tǽwe.

tál. I. add :—Se wellwillenda man wyle eáðe forberan gif him man tále gecwyð, Hex. 44, 18. Ða sǽde se deófol him hospword, and mid manegum tálum hine týnde, ac hé næs gestirod for his leásum tálum, Hml. S. 31, 725. Sé ðe forlǽt bysmorlíce spellunga and tálu, Hml. Th. i. 306, 2. II. add : II a. that which brings disgrace, disgrace :—Þreáge ma[n] hine mid ðám tále ðǽre bróðorlican áscyrunge sequestrationis rubore corripiatur, Chrd. 61, 31. III. add :—On his bebodum forðstæppende bútan tále (sine querela), Hml. Th. i. 352, 3 : ii. 56, 34. Gif hwá rǽde, ic bidde ð hé ðás áwændednesse ð hé hele swá hwæt swá ðáron sý tó tále, Ap. Th. 28, 19 : Ælfc. T. Grn. 21, 41.

tala well. v. tela ; IV : tala? :—Tala vel mycel gropa congium reddit, Wrt. Voc. ii. 130, 78.

tál-full ; adj. Blameable :—Ðanon (visiting of women) weorðað preóstas tálfulle (reprehensibiles), Chrd. 67, 36.

talian. I a. add :—Wé taliað ducimus (nec legitimum connubium spernendum ducimus, Ald. 7, 27), An. Ox. 419. Tó for náht taliende parui pendendam, 504. I c. add :—Sé unryhtlíce talað, sé ðe talað ðæt hé síe unscyldig incassum se innocentes putant, Past. 335, 12.

tál-lic. II. add :—Tállic gewuna reprehensibilis usus, Chrd. 63, 19. v. un-tállic.

tallíce. l. tállíce, and add :—Tállíce ábedecian inprudenter (impudenter, v. l.) petere, Chrd. 70, 5.

talu. I. add :—Þurh ðínre leásan tale ic ongyten hæbbe ð ðú eart án torswíþe leás man, Hml. S. 23, 687. II. add :—Talu disputatio, An. Ox. 27, 18. V. add :—Ne móste hé beón ðára þreóra nánes wyrðe ðe eallum leódscipe geseald wæs on wedde, tale (he should not be entitled to bring an action), ne teámes, ne áhnunga, Cht. Th. 266, 11. v. frum-, geán-talu.

tam. Add :—Se wulf folgode forð mid ðám heáfde, swylce hé tam wǽre, Hml. S. 32, 162. v. hand-tam.

tamcian to tame, render gentle :—Leóhtlic hwyslung mæg hors tamcyan and león hwelpas gremian lenis sibilus equos mitigat, catulos instigat, Chrd. 96, 18.

tamcol. v. un-tamcol : -tang. Add : v. samod-tang : -tangness. v. gader-tangness : tán-hlyta. Add : -hlíta (?) : tán-hlytere. Add : -hlítere (?).

tapor. Add :—Ðá gefylde hé mid wætre ðǽre cyrcan cyllan and sette tapor (weocon, v. l.) onmiddan (in medio papyrum posuit), Gr. D. 44, 14.

tapor-æx. Dele (borrowed from English) in bracket. The word seems Slavonic as to its first part, cf. Russian topor an axe, and to have come from Scandinavia to England.

targa. Add :—Fēren targa ignitus clipeus, Kent. Gl. 1073. Mínes targan, Cht. E. 226, 25.

taru (?), e ; f. A rent, gap :—Ðá giniendan oððe tara hiulcas, Wrt. Voc. ii. 42, 49. Cf. teran.

tawere. v. flǽsc-tawere.

tawian. II. add :—Hí begunnon tó áxienne hwæt se wǽre þe hí swá wælhreówlíce beóton . . . Hí urnon wépende ð hí þone hálgan wer swá huxlíce tawoden, Hml. S. 31, 997. [v. N.E.D. taw. Goth. taujan : O.H.Ger. zaujan.]

tǽxe. Dele, and see tosca.

teágan. Add :—ð land mid tó tégenne, Bd. 4, 28 ; Sch. 521, 3.

teáh. I. add :—Dryhten þone ealdan feónd gesǽlde in súsla grund and gefetrade fýrnum teágum, Pa. 60.

tealt. Add : v. un-tealt.

tealtian. II. add :—Hé ongann tó ðám swýðe cwacian and mid fótum tealtian ð hé uneáðe hine sylfne áberan mihte coepit se nutanti gressu vix posse portare, Gr. D. 36, 20.

tealtrian. Add :—Tealtri[ende] exorbitantes, An. Ox. 2, 356.

teám. I. add :—Teám posteritatem, An. Ox. 585. I b. used figuratively of consequences :—Ælc ðyssera heáfodleahtra hæfð micelne teám, Hml. Th. ii. 218, 27. III 2. add :—Toll and teám sý ágifen intó ðám mynstre, bútan hé hit geearnian mæge tó ðám ðe ðænne áh mynstres geweald, Cht. E. 236, 4. efen-teám.

teár. Add : v. hlenor-teár ; wollen-teár ; adj.

teart. Add : I. of material objects, sharp, piercing :—Tearte acra (testularum fragmina), An. Ox. 8, 218. II. of pain, &c. :—Oð ðǽre teartestan tintregun acerrimo, i. asperrimo tormento, 1946.

-teáw. Add : v. manig-teáw.

tela. III. add :—Getímige ús tela on líchaman, getímige ús untela symle wé sceolon ðæs Gode ðancian, Hml. Th. ii. 252, 15. Oft getímað yfelum teala for lífe, 332, 15. III a. of health :—Hí settað teala handa oðer ádlige men, and him bið tela (bene habebunt), Hml. Th. ii. 304, 22. V. add :—Hé him sylfum geworhte tela unmycel eardung hús sibi humile habitaculum construxit, Gr. D. 201, 5. v. un-tela.

teldian. Add :—Mid þý se feónd his yfelnesse mægen and his grim nesse áttor teldað, ð hé mid þý átre ðá menniscean heortan wundað dun omnis nequitiae suae vires versutamente tentaret, Guth. Gr. 119, 44 [v. N.E.D. teld.]

-teldung. v. ge-teldung.

telga. Add : telge, an ; f. A rod :—Ðá beran hé slóh mid ðær telgan (ferula) þe hé gewunode ð hé bær him on handa, Gr. D. 229, 21 [Cf. O.H. Ger. zwelga ramus.]

telge (?). Add : effort (?), endeavour (?). [Cf. O.L. Ger. tilog exercitatu.] v. tilian.

telgestre, an ; f. A dyer :—Manige ðára tǽlgestrena (-eona, MS. þe hér eardiað tinctorum, qui hic habitant, plurimi, Gr. D. 342, 3. Cf bæcestre for the suffix.

telgor. Add :—Telgra surculorum, An. Ox. 562. [Perhaps th second example, telgre, should be taken as a nom. fem., but it is a glos to vimine. v. An. Ox. 18 b, 95.]

telgra. Add :—Telgrum corticibus (but the gloss seems to belong t uiminibus, which precedes), An. Ox. 257.

tellan. II. In l. 4, col. 2, after hwíle insert : wið tén þusend wintr and add :—Tell þú swá fela daga, Angl. viii. 325, 8 : 327, 9. III a add :—Wolde hé Róme gesécan, þ in ðá tíd wæs micles mægenes teal and gelýfed Romam adire curauit, quod eo tempore magnae uirtuti aestimabatur, Bd. 4, 23 ; Sch. 470, 11. III c. add :—Hié tealdo and him þúhte (putabant) ð him ðá áne miðene deáhle wǽron, Bd. 4 27 ; Sch. 515, 4. IV. add :—Gif þú nelt hine telian eác tó ðæ mónan swá swá tó ðǽre sunnan, þonne áwǽst þú þone eástorlican rego Lch. iii. 264, 15. v. un-teald.

temes. Add : [v. N.E.D. temse] : temesian. Add : [v. N.E.I temse ; vb.]

temian. Add : to subdue passion, feeling, &c. :—Hé swíþe his lícham an tǽmede (temode, v.l.) and swǽncte per abstinentiam carne domavit, Gr. D. 11, 9. v. un-temed.

tempel. Add :—Ðá hálgan weras syndon Godes templu, Gr. D. 6 7. [The word seems masculine in, Hé geliþewǽhte heora wurdfulla templ, Hml. S. 31, 483.]

tempel-hálgung. Add :—Templhálgunga, þæt is symbelnessa hy eardungstówa wé ná ne begýmaþ schenofegias, id est sollemnitat tabernaculorum, non obseruamus, An. Ox. 40, 36.

temprung. v. un-getemprung : tendan. Add : v. for-tendan.

tending, e ; f. Burning :—Hé hine sylfne nacodne áwearp a wyiede on þǽra þorna ordum and on þǽra netela tendingum (tæn

lengum, tendlincgum, v. ll.) nudum se in illis spinarum aculeis et urticarum incendiis projecit, Gr. D. 101, 17.

**tendling.** e; f. Burning. See preceding word.

**tengan.** Add:—'Noldon wē efstan . . . gif wē tō beteran lífe ne becōmon . . .' Betwux þǣre tihtinge hī tengdon forð, Hml. S. 34, 234. **-tenge.** v. gæder-tenge.

**teohhian.** II a. add:—Hwīlum hī magon begytan þā þing þe heom ǣr teohhode nǣron aliquando obtinere possunt ea, quae non sunt praedestinata, Gr. D. 54, 11. II c. add:—Hē tihhode (þōhte, v. l.) þ̄ he sceolde ǣrest gelīðian heora rēðnysse eorum prius studuit asperitatem placare, Gr. D. 80, 16. II e. add:—Gif ðæt ne wexð ðæt hié tiohhiað tō dōnne si quod videtur gerendum sollicita intentione non crescit, Past. 445, 8. II e a. with infin. :—Hē teohhode fæstende becuman tō mynstre jejunus pervenire decreverat, Gr. D. 128, 27. v. fore-teohhian.

**teolen, tilen,** e; f. Endeavour, earnest effort, employment; studium :—Hē wæs geornfull mid teolone (tolene, bígenge, v. ll.) his singalra gebeda continuae orationis studio intentus, Gr. D. 71, 11. Þā þā hē wæs swýðe georne behealdende ðā teolone (tilone, v. l.) his gestlīðnesse cum hospitalitatis studio valde esset intentus, 194, 12.

**teol-þyrel** (l. -þýrel). Add:—Teolþýrl foramina, An. Ox. 134.

**teón.** [On p. 978, ll. 2, 3 for leáh, tongne l. teáh, longne.] I I. add :—þā mūlas þe þ̄ cræt tugon . . . tōmengdon þā getogu þ̄ hī teón ne mihton, Hml. S. 31, 972. II a. add:—Ðā ridon his men tō and tugon ūt ðæt spic of Æðelsiges hūse, C. D. iii. 291, 16. III 2. add:—Hē ofslōg Tetricum for þý þe hē hī him teáh tō anwalde, Ors. 6, 26; S. 276, 23. III 3. add: to usurp:—Ealle naman mǣst teóð genitiuum, Ælfc. Gr. Z. 250, 13. Ðā land þe Leófsunu him tō teáh terras illas quas Leofsunu sibi usurpabat, Cht. E. 213, 6. Gif hī ǣnig man him tō teó hæbbe hī būtan Godes bletsunge and ūre, Cht. Crw. 19, 27. Hī ne sceoldon þone gyrlan him tō teón habitum usurpare non debent, Chrd. 63, 22. III 4. add:—Ic nelle þ̄ ǣnig mann āht þǣr on teó būton hē and his wícneras (cf. ic nelle þ̄ ēni man ēnig þing þǣr on theó, būtan hī and heara wícneras nolo ut aliquis hominum se intromittat nisi ipsi et ministri eorum, 347, 3), Cht. E. 233, 7. III 5. add:—Hē plegode and fela fægera þinga forð teáh þe þām folce ungecnāwe wæs, Ap. Th. 17, 13. III 6. add:—Ofer mǣðe ūre þu ford týhst sprǣce ultra aetatem nostram protrahis sermonem, Coll. M. 32, 11. On þām tīman ne teáh nān æðelborennyss nǣnne man tō wurðscype, Hml. S. 3, 6. IV I. add:—Þā nǣddran āweg tugon, Hml. Th. ii. 490, I. v. for-, tō-teón; un-togen.

**teón** to accuse. Add:—Wrec ðē gemetlíce, and eác swā gebǣr, ðý lǣs ðē men leásunga teó, ðæt ðū ðíne cysta cýðe, Prov. K. 46.

**teóna.** IV. add:—Heora hryre weard Ahtenum tō ārǣrnesse þ̄ hié ðone ealdan teónan gewrecan mehten þe him on ǣrdagum gemǣne wæs, Ors. 3, I; S. 98, 9. [v. N. E. D. teen.]

**teón-full.** Add: [v. N. E. D. teenfull] : **teónian.** Add: [v. N. E. D. teen; vb.]

**teónlíce.** II. add:—Achan weard ðā oftorfod teónlíce mid stānum, Hex. 54, 5.

**teón-rǣden[n].** Add:—Nānum hē ne forgeald yfel mid yfele, ac hē forbær manna teónrǣdene mid micclum geðylde, Hml. S. 31, 305.

**teón-word.** Add:—þā hǣþenan weras his word hefiglíce onfēngon, and hine mid teónwordum (injuriis) ēhtende wǣron, Gr. D. 250, 20.

**teorian.** l. teórian, and I. add:—þæt mōd of his āgenre untrymnesse wērgað and teórað mens ex infirmitate lassescat, Gr. D. 204, 23. Þonne teórað mægen mīn dum defecerit uirtus mea, Ps. Rdr. 70, 9. Teórode hālig defecit sanctus, 11, 2 : 30, 11. Ic wæs winnende and teóriende tō þām ýþum laborans in fluctibus atque deficiens, Gr. D. 347, 28. [v. N. E. D. tire.]

**-teórodness.** Add: v. ā-teórodness.

**teosu-word,** es; n. An injurious word:—þā hē swīðust ōðre men mid tesowordum tǣl[d]e in his renceo, þā earnode hē mē þæs ēcan teónan, Nap. 62. þā hē oftost tesoword sprǣc in his onmēdlan gealpettunga, þā earnode hē mē þāra mǣstan benda, 27, 39.

**teran.** Add:—Geseah hē þ̄ ān wulf genam þ̄ cild; þā tær hē his loccas heófende, Hml. S. 30, 180 : Jud. 281.

**teung.** v. hríf-teung.

**tíd.** I a. add:—Mūða gehwylc mete þearf, mǣl sceolon tídum gongan, Gn. Ex. 125. Ic on þīn hūs hālig gange, and þǣr tídum þē tifer onsecge, Ps. Th. 65, 12. I a a. a favourable occasion or period for a person :—Swā mon on ealdum bigspellum cwyð, þ̄ hwílum beó esnes tíd, hwílum ōðres, Prov. K. 31. I c. add:—Wæs his gewuna þæt hē wolde ǣlce dæge habban twā mæssan, and ealle his tída tōgædere, ǣr hē ūt eóde, Vis. Lfc. 64. I d. add:—Ic bebeóde ðæt mon ymb tuælf mōnað hiora tíd boega ðus geuueorðiae tō ānes dæges tō Osuulfes tíde, C. D. i. 293, 1–3. II 2 a. add:—Se síðfæt þe Zosimus on xx dagum oferfōr, þ̄ eall Maria on ānre tíde ryne gefylde, Hml. S. 23 b, 761. Weard ðǣre sǣ smiltnesse āwænd fǣringa betwux twām tídum (in the course of two hours), Ap. Th. 10, 25. v. bell-, cenning-, dæg-, edmǣl-,

frum-, gereordung-; gewin-, hǣlu-, hwíl-, mǣl-, mæsse-, onríp-, ūhtan-, unriht-tíd.

**tíderness.** I. Dele 'I.' and under (a) add:—þā heofenan wē ne magon for ūre eágena týddernysse geseón, Lch. iii. 232, 16.

**tídlíce;** III. add:—Hē his gelaþunge ðæs ful tídlíce of ðǣra gedwolmanna gedreccednysse āhredde, Hml. S. 23, 407. v. un-tídlíce.

**tídre.** II. dele third passage. II a. add:—Ealde menn sweltaþ, and ōðre men ādlseóce bióð, and mænigra eágan tēdra bióð, Archiv cxx. 298, 22. Þone hād týdera manna infirmantium personam, Gr. D. 267, 18.

**tídrian.** I. add: of living creatures :—Sceápa eágan tēdriað on þām geáre, Archiv cxx. 298, 17. Gif mannes mūð sār sié ge týdred, Lch. ii. 4, I. Gif ic underfō in mē þone hād tēdriendra manna . . . ic mage gehelpan þām tēdriendum mannum si infirmantium in me personam suscepero, infirmantibus prodesse possum, Gr. D. 267, 17–21.

**tíd-sang.** Add:—Sī gedōn tācn nōnes, þ̄ fylige se tídsang agatur signum nonę, quod sequatur ipse laus, Angl. xiii. 399, 483. Cyrclice tídsang[as] canonicas horas, An. Ox. 56, 317.

**tíd-ymbwlǣtend.** Add:—Tídemwlǣtend oroscopus, i. horarum inspector, Hpt. 31, 8, 135.

**Tifer,** e; f. The Tiber:—Hē cwæð þ̄ hit gelumpe on Rōmebyrig, þ̄ Tifre stream wæs upp gangende and swā swíðe gangende, oð þ̄ hyre wæter and ýða fleówen ofer þā weallas dicens, quia apud hanc Romanam urbem alveum suum Tiberis egressus est, tantum crescens ut ejus unda super muros urbis influeret, Gr. D. 220, 8. Cf. þā weard Tiber seó eá swā flēdu swā heó nǣfre ǣr næs Tiberis ultra opinionem redundans, Ors. 47; S. 180, 17.

**tíg** (?); m. Add: tíge (?); n.

**tígan.** (a) add:—Hī lǣddon þone cyning tō ānum treówe, and tígdon hine þǣrtō, Hml. S. 32, 109. Hig tígdon his swuran swíðe mid racenteágum and his handa samod mid heardum īsene and þā fēt tōgædere, 35, 164.

**tiger.** Add:—Gelamp þæt twā hrēðe deór, þe sind tigres gehātene, þǣr urnon and ābiton swā hwæt swā hī gemētton . . . Ðā cwǣðon þā apostoli tō ðām folce, 'Þās rēðan deór gehýrsumiað Godes mihte . . . þurh ðæs naman sind þās rēðan tigres betwux eów swā tame swā scēp, Hml. Th. ii. 492, 10–21.

**tigere.** Dele, and see hūfe.

**-tigþe** (tíþe), **-tygþe** (-týþe). v. bēn-, wil-tigþe (-tygþe): **tihtle** Add: v. wer-tihtle.

**til.** II. add: suitable, adequate :—God wolde þ̄ seó hālige gefērrǣden āweht beón sceolde þe on ðām scræfe tile hwíle gereste hæfdon, S. 2, 428. Sylle man tō middægþēnunge twām and twām ān tyl cýssticce, Chrd. 15, 3.

**tilen.** v. teolen.

**tilia.** Add:—Gif se yrðlincg behylt underbæc gelōme, ne bið hē gelimplic tilia, Hml. S. 16, 179.

**tilian.** III I b. add: Ælfc. T. Grn. 20, 20. III 2 a. add:—Hī swīdost ælces gedweldes tiledon, Hml. S. 23, 364. Ðæt hē hine selfne ne forlǣte, ðǣr hē ōðerra freónda tilige ne proximos juvando se deserat, Past. 463, 4. IV. add: to strive for:—Wā ðām mannum þe eorðlicum spēdum tiliað and strýnað, Verc. Först. 120, 16. VII I. add:—Hē tiolode men forlǣran, Past. 233, 22. VII 3. add:—Hē for þǣra æfweardra gemynde tilode, þ̄ hē gebǣde pro absentium memoria curavit exorare, Gr. D. 311, 4. Ðeáh hī self teladon ðæt hī ōðre men ne dwellen, Past. 449, 24. Tilian wē georne þ̄ wē þonne gemētte synd on gōdum weorcum, Verc. Först. 130, 6. v. un-tilod.

**tillan** to pay toll. v. tyllan.

**tilþ.** II I. add:—Tilþa lucra, An. Ox. 56, 309. v. eorþ-tilþ.

**tilung.** III. add:—þā nearonessa his āgenre costunge hine gedydon þý geornfulra tō þǣre teolunge (gímene, v. l.) godcundra beboda, Gr. D. 26, 20. Ðā cynn beóð langswýrede ðe lybbað þe gærse . . . and ælc byð gelimplic tō his lífes tilunge (each is adapted for caring for its life), Hex. 16, 4. Lǣcedōm is ālýfed fram líchamena týddernysse, and hālige gebedu mid Godes bletsunge, and ealle ðǣre tilunga syndon andsǣte Gode, Hml. S. 17, 215. IV. add: (a) the getting of something:—Wulfas and león habbað . . . māran tuxas tō heora metes tilunge, Hex. 16, 7.

**tíma.** I a. add:—Gýfernyss dēð þ̄ man yt ǣr tíman, Hml. S. 16, 269. Hēt hē him beran bere tō sǣde, and ofer ǣlcne tīman ðā eorðair seów (allatum hordeum ultra omne tempus serendi terrae commendavit, Vit. Cuth. 19), Hml. Th. ii. 144, 12. II. add:—Sume gedwolmenn cwǣdon þ̄ . . . wǣre sum tíma ǣr þan þe Críst ācenned wǣre, Hml. S. 1, 7. II a. add:—Tō þām forewearde ðæt Eádsige hit hæbbe his lífes tíman, C. D. vi. 190, 15. II b. add:—þrý mōnðas wyrcað þryfeald(e) gewrixlunge þǣra feówer tíman, Angl. viii. 319, 5. v. dæg-, hæring-, hālsung-, mǣl-, ūhtan-, undern-tíma.

**-tíma.** Add: v. geoc-tíma.

**tíman.** I 2. add: tíman be to have a child by :—Hwílon eác se fæder týmde be his āgenre dehter, Ælfc. Gen. Thw. 2, 4.

**timber-land**, es; *n.* *Land on which to grow timber*:—.x. hýde æt Ercecombe tó tymberlonde, C. D. v. 236, 12. Cf. wudu-land.

**timbran.** I. *add*:—Hér hét Harold bytlian on Brytlande ... þā fōr Cradoc tó ... and þ folc eall mǽst ofslōh þe þǽr timbrode, Chr. 1065; P. 191, 27. v. fore-timbrigende.

**-timbre** (?). v. þweorh-timbre.

**timbrend.** *Add*:—timbriend:—His hūs wæs þǽr getimbrod, and þæs hūses timbriend (*constructores*) wǽron wyrcende Sæternesdagum ānum, Gr. D. 322, 2.

**timbrung.** *Add*:—Hīt næs nā būton gewyrhtum þ his hūses timbrung weóx Sæternesdagum *non immerito domus ipsius fabrica sabbato crescebat*, Gr. D. 322, 10. Þā læg þǽr ān stān þone hī mynton hebban upp on þæs hūses timbrunge *lapis jacebat, quem in aedificium levare decreverant*, 123, 1. v. mynster-timbrung.

**-tíme.** *Add*: hefe-, hefig-, un-, wiþer-tíme.

**timple.** *Add*: [v. *N. E. D.* temple; *and* ā-timplian, Nap. 7. The passage there given seems to show that *timple* is an instrument provided with teeth or spikes:—Seó þele is eall ātimplod mid āttrenum pīlum and scearpum tindum.]

**tínan.** *In l. 2 for* tale *l.* tále, *and add: to insult, abuse, revile*:—Hēt se ārleása hine ūtan belūcan ... and týnde þone hálgan, Hml. S. 31, 658. Þā sǽde hē him hospword and mid manegum tālum hine týnde, 724. [v. *N. E. D.* teen.]

**tín-bebod**, es; *n.* *A decalogue*:—Tēnbebodes *decalogi*, An. Ox. 11, 108.

**tindting.** *Dele; the word seems only a bad reading of* tyhting. Cf. Tyhtingce *suasionis*, An. Ox. 3382.

**-tíned.** v. on-tíned: **-tinges.** v. sam-tinges.

**tín-strenge.** *Add*:—On saltere týnstrengum *in psalterio decem chordarum*, Ps. L. 32, 2.

**tin-treg.** *Add*:—Hī geseóþ þæs tintregan (-es, *v. l.*) stówe, Gr. D. 315, 11. v. helle-tintreg.

**tintregung.** *Add*:—Hē hēt his cwelleras swīðor wítnian þone hálgan wer, ac hī āteórodon on þǽre tintregunge, Hml. S. 37, 126.

**tín-wintre.** *Add*: *ten years long*:—Wurdon feala martyras on .x. wintrum (wintra, *v. l.*) fyrste, Ors. 6, 30; Bos. 126, 22 note.

**Tír;** *n.* l. *m.*

**tirig-hege** ? :—Of langan leáge on tyrighege; of tyrighege, C. D. v. 234, 22.

**tirwan.** *Add*: v. nīw-tirwed: **títe-gár.** *Dele* '(?)', *and cf.* An. Ox. 786.

**tíþ.** *l.* tygþ, týþ. *Add*:—Hē ástrehte hine sylfne ... biddende his Drihten ... Æfter sumum fyrste hē āstōd ūp anbidigende unforht his bēna tīða, Hml. S. 31, 219. *See next word.*

**tíþe** *better* tygþe, týþe (*the form in the Pastoral Care has* y). *Add*:—Efne swā hē his bæd, swā hē wæs týðe (þǽrrihte hē hit beget, *v. l.*) *ita dum peteret impetravit*, Gr. D. 79, 33. v. un-, wil-tygþa (-e), -týþe.

**tíþian.** *Add*: tygþian, týþian. (a) *add*:—Þū bǽde mē þ ic sceolde þē āwendan of Lēdene on Englisc þā bōc Genesis. Þā þūhte mē hefigtýme þe tō tíþienne þæs, Ælfc. Gen. Thw. 1, 6. (d) *add*:—Sē rihtwísa gemildsaþ and tíþaþ (*tribuet*), Ps. L. 32, 17. (d a) *with acc. of person*:—Hē bæd hī þ hī him bisceop onsende ... Hī hine lustlīce tíþedon, Bd. 3, 3; Sch. 199, 17. [v. *N. E. D.* tithe.]

**Tíw.** *Add*:—Tíwesdæges nama wæs of Martie Iovis sunu þæs scyndles, Angl. xiii. 321, 15.

**tó.** I 1 c. *add*:—Hē sylf intó þǽre inran eóde and ðā duru him tó beclýsde, Hml. A. 196, 31. (3) *add*: (a) :—Þū cwǽde þ ic ne þorfte nā māre āwendan þǽre bēc būton tó Isaace, Ælfc. Gen. Thw. 1, 9. (b) :—Ðæt hié mid ðǽm hié selfe tó feóre ne gewundigen (*vulnere mortali se feriunt*), Past. 365, 11. Gezabel beswāc Naboð tó his feóre, Hml. Th. i. 488, 6. Grame tó feóre *mortally cruel*, Hml. S. 7, 242. Ic gewilnode þæs wines on þām ic ǽr gelustfullode tó oferdruncennysse brūcan, 23 b, 535. (c 2) :—Ic beóde þ hý fylstan þām biscopum tó Godes gerihtum and tó mínum kynescype and tó ealles folces þearfe, Cht. E. 230, 7. Ǽr þon ðe seó sunne cyrre hig tó ðæs dæges lenge, Shrn. 153, 28. (4) *add*: (3):—Hī gesceapene wǽron tó þon ēcan līfe, næs tó þon ēcan deáþe, Bl. H. 61, 7. (h) :—Hié him æfest tó genāman, Bl. H. 7, 11. Ic wylle hold beón tó Godes gerihtum and tó rihtre woroldlage, Cht. E. 229, 22. (i) :—On þone hálgan handa sendon tó feorhlege, Ll. 458. (j) :—Ceólulf wilnade ðæs landes tó Heáberhte bisceope and tó his hígon, Cht. Th. 47, 7. Tó hæpsan pinn, Angl. ix. 265, 9. (5) *add*: (a) :—Hē sæt tó þām cāsere, Hml. S. 31, 629. Hē gesette his sunu tó þǽm onwalde tó him, Ors. 6, 22; S. 274, 6. Hī mid hǽran hī gescrýddon tó līce, Hml. S. 12, 36: 35, 160: Hml. A. 108, 207. (b) *add*:—For þǽre byldo þe ic tó him wāt, Bl. H. 179, 21. (c) *add*:—Ealle hē tó gafle gesette, Chr. 1100; P. 235, 28. (f 1) *add*:—þ folc tealde þ tó drýcræfte, Hml. S. 7, 241. Nū þeh eów lytles hwæt swelcra gebroca on becume, þonne gemǽnað gē hit tó þǽm wyrrestan tīdum, Ors. 3, 7; S. 120, 5. (h) *add*:—Him is leófre ðæt hē leóge ðonne him mon ǽnigra ungerisna tó wēne, Past. 217, 16. (h 1) marking influence to which action is attributed:—Hī hine ācsedon

hwæþer hī sceoldan tó Agustinus lāre (*ad praedicationem Augustini*) hiora þeawas forlǽtan, Bd. 2, 2; Sch. 116, 12. Tó ðyssere dǽde wearð þæs cynges heorte āblicged, Hml. Th. ii. 474, 19. (j) *add*:—Ciricsceat mon sceal āgifan tó þām healme and tó þām heorðe þe se mon on bið tó middum wintre, Ll. Th. i. 140, 13. Hī tó Godes hīwunga gesceapene wǽron, Bl. H. 61, 7: B. 2570: C. D. v. 157, 12. Þ is se wīsdōm þ man ... his dǽda gefadige tó his Drihtnes willan, Hml. S. 13, 326. Gōd lāreów tǽcð his cnapan gōde þeawas tó Godes gesetnyssum, Hml. A. 6, 131. (m) *add*:—Hē bebohte his hors tó (gesealde his hors wið, *v. l.*) twelf mancussum, Gr. D. 63, 25. Hē gebohte Ēdwiges docter ... tó .x. scill., Cht. Th. 631, 25. (7) *add*: (c):—þ hē sceolde on his mynstre þone sang lǽran tó twelf mōnþum *quatenus in monasterio suo cursum canendi annuum edoceret*, Bd. 4, 18; Sch. 437, 4: (d):—Þeáh ðe gýt wǽre ōðer þūsend geára tó ðām dæge, Hml. Th. i. 618, 27. II 5. *add*:—Ān ful tó fylles, Lch. i. 82, 14. Hig gýmað tó gebeótes þǽra fīf stafa þe synd *vocales* gecīged, Angl. viii. 327, 35. **III** 1. *add*:—þæt wæter wearð tó twā tōdǽled, Ex. 14, 21. (3) *add*:—þ ic eów tó ǽfen ǽr sǽde, þ ilce ic eów nū segce, Hml. S. 23, 449. **IV.** *add*: (3) cf. I 1 a:—þ gē tó þýs hūsle ne gangen, Rtl. 114, 21. (4) cf. I 4 i:—Swā hē nū dyde tó þis ilcan Ðeodrīce, Bt. 16, 1; F. 48, 35. **V** I. *add*:—Hē lǽdde hit forð mid him þǽr hē fundode tó, Hml. S. 26, 224: 31, 535. **VI.** *add*:—Ne bið þeós ādl hwæþere tó frēcne, Lch. ii. 46, 12.

**tó-bǽd.** *Substitute*: tó-bǽdan *to exalt, and add*:—Tóbǽd *laudat*, An. Ox. 1919.

**tó-beátan.** *Add*:—þ scip becōm tó Ostican swīðe tóbrocen and tóbeáten fram þām ýþum (*fluctibus quassata*), Gr. D. 347, 7. Ðā cempan hine lange swungon ... þā cōmon his geféran and fundon hine licgendne on blōdigum limum and tóbeátenum līchaman, Hml. S. 31, 981.

**tó-beran.** I. *add*:—Swā hwæt swā fugelas tóbǽron, Wlfst. 183, 14: Verc. Först. 88, 6: 134, 4. **III.** *to be separate*:—Swā micel tóbired eástdæl fram westdæle *quantum distat oriens ab occasu*, Ps. Vos. 102, 12. Cf. tó-berenness.

**tó-berenness.** *l.* (?) -berendness.

**tó-berstan.** I a. *add*:—Hē sylf āhreófode and tóbærst mid wundum from ðām heáfde oð ðā fēt, Shrn. 132, 8.

**tó-blāwan.** II a. *add*:—tó tōblāwenum dracum *tumidis draconibus* (*qui in uexillis depicti erant*), Germ. 392, 56.

**tó-brēdan.** II. *add*:—Ic eom tóbrædd *tendor*, An. Ox. 23, 47. **III.** *add*:—Se consul wæs wēnende þæt eall þæt folc wǽre gind þæt lond tóbrǽd, Ors. 4, 8; S. 188, 12.

**tó-brecan.** I. *add*: I a. *to spread in patches*:—Swā þ seó fāguncg wæs þǽre hýde tóbrocen geond ealne his līchaman swylce hē hreóf wǽre *ita ut diffusa in corpore ejus varietas leprae morem imitari videretur*, Gr. D. 158, 33. II c. *add*: *to put an end to*:—Hī wēpende him tó fōtum luton, and cwǽdon, 'Help ūre, lā Hǽlend ... āðwǽsc ðās gebeót and ðās wōpas tóbrec,' Shrn. 68, 10. **IV.** *add*:—Micele sēlre him wǽre þæt hē þone āð tóbrǽce, Hml. Th. i. 484, 4.

**tó-bregdan.** I. *add*:—Tó tóbregdenne *diripiendas* (*illi circa diripiendas* sarcinulas occupantur, Bt. bk. 1, prosa 3), An. Ox. 34, 3. **IV.** *to distract*:—Heorte tóbrōden ymbe woroldcara *cor dispersum in rerum curis*, Chrd. 70, 19.

**tó-brítan.** I. *add*: (1) *to break to pieces* a material object:—Reód forþræst ne sý tóbrýd (*conterendum*), R. Ben. I. 108, 9. (2) *to destroy* a person or thing, *bring to destruction*:—His setl on eorðan þū tóbrýttest *sedem eius in terra collisisti*, Ps. L. 88, 45. Tóbrýt nū þisne brēman here, Hml. S. 25, 629. Andweard þām ārleásan mid ānrǽdum geleáfan þ his wōdnys swā wurðe tóbrūt, Hml. S. 37, 78. (3) *to crush* with pain, hardship, &c.:—Seó ēstfulle heorte ne bið tóbrýt for nānum ungelimpum, Hml. Th. ii. 92, 28. Hūmeta God geðafað þ his gecorenan mid swā micclum wītum beón fornumene and tóbrýtte on ðisum andweardan līfe, i. 486, 20.

**tó-brýsan.** *Add*:—þā tóglidenan stānas nā þ ān þ hī his limu tócwýsdon ac hī eác swylce mid ealle his bān tóbrýsdon (*ossa contriverant*), Gr. D. 125, 21. His preósta ænne of horse feallende and tóbrýsendne (*contritum*), Bd. 4, 6; Sch. 573, 7.

**tó-cirran.** *Add*:—Hī mid āþum fryþ gefæstnodon on þǽre stōwe þe genemned is æt Eámōtum ... and syþþan mid sibbe tócyrdon, Chr. 926; P. 107, 26.

**tó-cnáwlíce** Chr. 963; P. 117, 12. *l.* tó cnáwlēce *in acknowledgement*.

**tó-cnáwness**, e; *f.* *Knowledge*:—In þǽre tócnáwnesse (on-, *v. l.*) ǽgðres gedǽles weaxeþ se ēca þæs edleánes *in qua cognitione utriusque partis cumulus retributionis excrescit*, Gr. D. 311, 11.

**tó-cwǽscedness**, e; *f.* *Destruction*:—Tócwǽscednes (tócwescedness, Ps. L.) *quassatio*, Ps. Rdr. 105, 30. See note p. 304.

**tó-cwǽstedness.** *In a note to Ps.* 105, 30 *Roeder quotes* tóquæstednes *from another MS., and* tócwæstednys *seems to be the reading of Ps. Spl.* (*according to Dr. Aldis Wright's collation*); *so the form may be allowed to stand, and need not be considered a mere mistake for the preceding word.*

tō-cweþan. *Add*:—Ælc deófolgeld hí tōcwædon, Chr. 926; P. 107, 25.

tō-cwīsan. *Dele* ¶, *and add*:—Hē his heáfod tōbræc and eác his bān tōcwýsde, Hml. S. 5, 358. Se āwyrgeda gāst tōwearp þone wāh, and mid þæs wāges hryre of þryccende tōcwýsde ǽnne munuccnapan (*unum puerulum monachum opprimens ruina contrivit*), Gr. D. 125, 6. Feól se stǽnene wāh uppan þæs stuntan rǽdboran þ hē (hī) æll tōcwýsde *the stone wall fell upon the stupid fellow's counsellors, so that it crushed them all to bits*, Hml. S. 8, 173.

tō-cwīsedness. *Add*:—Geunrétte for þæs ofhrorenan brōðres tōcwýsednysse (*contritione*), Gr. D. 125, 11.

tō-cyme. *Add*:—Þys ylcan geáres was S. Iudoces tōcyme (*the saint's relics arrived*), Chr. 903; P. 93, 4. Ne bið heó nā swincende on feforādlum, ne eác heó ne gyrned Basilies tōcymes *neque febribus laboratura est, neque Basilium quaesitura*, Gr. D. 29, 24.

tō-dǽlan. II 1. *add*:—[On] þreó tōdǽledes *tripertiti* (*mundi*), An. Ox. 4512. II b. *add*:—Tōdǽlað hig þurh seofon, Angl. viii. 326, 26. Tōdǽlað þās feówertig þurh fīfe, 328, 25. III a. *add*:—Tōdǽledre *sequestra* (*pace*), An. Ox. 3812. IV. *add*:—Tōdǽlaþ *diffundunt* (*densos exercitus per campos diffundunt*), An. Ox. 91. Tōdiel(?) hié *dispartire eos*, Ps. Vos. 16, 14. VIII. *add*:—On þreó tōdǽledum *tripartitis* (*gradibus*), An. Ox. 1361. X. *add*:—Tōdǽlendum *distinguente*, An. Ox. 1369. Þurh fīftan sōtes tōdāl (and) seofeþan tōdǽlede *per pentimemerem et eptimemerem diremptas*, 205. v. fiþer-, un-tōdǽled.

tō-dǽledlic. v. un-tōdǽledlic : tō-dǽledlíce v. un-tōdǽledlíce.

tō-dǽledness. *Add*: IV. *distinction, difference between objects*:—Nū þū mid þus mycelre tōdǽlednesse tōsceádest manna gāstas and nýtena *dum hominum spiritus atque jumentorum tanta distinctione discernas*, Gr. D. 264, 11. v. un-tōdǽledness.

tō-dǽlend. v. middangeard-tōdǽlend : tō-dǽlendlic. v. un-tōdǽlendlic.

tō-dǽlness. *Add*:—Tōdǽlnisse dydon alle *discumbere fecerunt omnes*, Lk. L. 9, 15.

tō-dāl. II. *add*:—Ðǽr nys nāðor gemencgednys ne tōdāl, Hml. Th. ii. 8, 8.

tō-drīfan. II. *add*:—His geféran hē tōdrāf, Chr. 1036; P. 158, 24. III. *add*:—Seó þiccnys þāra woruldcara swīðe āwésteð and tōdrīfeð (*devastat*) ānra gehwilces bisceopes mōd, Gr. D. 41, 8.

tō-dwǽscan. l. -dwæscan, *and add*:—Mid his gebedum þæs fýres mægen and strengðe hē tōdwǽscte *exorando flammas pressit*, Gr. D. 48, 14.

tō-efnes. *Add*:—Ðonne is tōemnes þǽm lande sūðeweardum ... Sweóland ... and tōemnes þǽm lande norðeweardum Cwéna land, Ors. 1, 1; S. 19, 1–3. Alexandres þegnas tōemnes him þone weall ābrǽcon, and þǽr in cōman, 3, 9; S. 134, 21. Oþ tōemnes þes hlinces heáfde, Cht. E. 355, 7.

tō-éþian *translates* aspirare :—Swā se ælmihtiga God tōéþiende and gefyllende gelíffǽsteð *sicut omnipotens Deus aspirando vel implendo vivificat*, Gr. D. 270, 13.

tō-feallan. *Add*:—Hī wurdon gelǽdde tō þǽre lāðan anlícnysse, ac heó tōfeól sōna tō heora fōtum formolsnod, Hml. S. 2, 374. Þysre burge getimbrunga syndon mid gelómlicum hryrum tōfeallene *aedificia urbis ruinis crebrescentibus prosternuntur*, Gr. D. 134, 12.

tō-féran. I. *add*:—Þā apostolas tōférdon tō fyrlenum eardum, swā swā se Hǽlend bebeád on his hālgum godspelle, Ælfc. T. Grn. 15, 10.

tō-fesian. l. -físian, -fésian.

tō-fleám *refuge* :—Geworden is mē [Drihten] on tōfleám *factus est mihi Dominus in refugium*, Ps. Rdr. 93, 22.

tō-flōwan. I a. *add*:—Þā hraþe āblan se ele þ hē nā tōfleów geond þone flōr swā hē ǽr dyde *in pavimentum oleum defluere cessavit*, Gr. D. 160, 16. II d. *add*:—Leáf his ne tōfleówð *folium eius non defluet*, Ps. L. 1, 3. Hē beheóld and tōfleówon þeóda *aspexit et defluxerunt gentes*, Ps. Rdr. 283, 6.

tō-flōwendness (-flōwen-), e ; f. *Diffusion, diffluence* :—Tō þām þ þurh þā tōflōwendnysse (-flōwen-, -flōw-, *v. ll.*) þæs streámes beón geþénede þā inngeþancas geleáffulra breósta, Gr. D. 94, 21.

tō-flōwness. *See preceding word.*

tō-foran. I. *add*: (a) *marking relation*:—Seó lǽs is tōforan eallum mannum gemǽne *the pasture is open to all*, C. D. iii. 419, 21. IV. *add*:—Swā micele swā se heofenlica cyning is mǽrra and furðor tōforan ðām eorðlican cininge, swā micele māra bið ðīn wurðmynt tōforan ðām woruldlican kempan, Hex. 38, 4–6. Þā þe þenceað þ hī beón be dǽle beteran tōforan ōðrum mannum, Gr. D. 151, 25.

tō-forlǽtenness. *Add*: *cessation, leaving off*:—Blāwende būton tōforlǽtennysse, Hml. Th. ii. 350, 9.

tog. *Add*: v. for-tog.

tō-gǽdere. *add*:—Hē þā folc gelǽdde þǽr hié tōgædere gecweden hæfde, Ors. 4, 6; S. 174, 31.

tō-gān. I. *add*:—Se Hǽlend betǣhte Thōman him hām tō hæbbenne and hī swā tōeódon, Hml. S. 36, 50. II. *add*:—Hetelíce āstreccað

ealle his lima þ þā liþa him tōgaan, Hml. S. 37, 99. III. *add*:—Swilce man blāwe āne bytte fulle windes and wyrce siððan ān þýrl þonne heó tōþunden bið on hire greátnysse, þonne tōgǽð seó miht, Hml. S. 34, 319.

tō-geagnes. I 1. (b a) *add*:—Him upp gāndum of þām baðe hē hæfde him scýtan gearwe tōgénes, Gr. D. 343, 8. (c) *add*: (c a) of reciprocal action, *again, in return* :—Þéh þe hit gelumpe þ him hwilc man þe hine ne cūþe ongén cōme, and sé þonne wǽre gegrétan, þ hē forhogode tōgénes grétan *si quis illum fortasse nesciret, salutatus etiam resalutare despiceret*, Gr. D. 34, 6.

tō-gelan : *pp.* -golen. *To diffuse, spread a fluid* :—Se streám gewunode þ hē tōgolen and tōgoten wæs geond his æceras *fluvius per agros diffundi consueverat*, Gr. D. 192, 18.

tō-gelaþung, e ; f. *An assembly* :—On þām synt engla weredu and rihtwísra tōgelaðung þǽr symle wuniendra, Verc. Först. 173.

tō-gelicgende *appertaining* :—Tō Crīstes cyrcean tūn rihte tōgelicgende *uillula aecclesiae Christi rite pertinens*, C. D. iii. 350, 1.

-togenness. *Add*: v. ofer-, þurh-togenness.

tō-geótan. I. *add*:—Seó fāgung wæs tōgoten (-brǽded, *v. l.*) geond eallne his līchaman *diffusa in corpore ejus varietas*, Gr. D. 158, 35. Se streám gewunode þ hē tōgoten wæs geond his æceras *fluvius per agros diffundi consueverat*, 192, 18. Weard swā mycelu wynsumnes þæs æþelestan stences tōstrogden and tōgoten (*aspersa*) geond eall þ hūs, 282, 19.

tō-glīdan. III. *add*:—Þā stānas þæs tōglidenan wāges *collapsi saxa parietis*, Gr. D. 125, 21. IV. *add*:—Þā tōglidenan stānas þæs wāges, Gr. D. 125, 18. *See preceding passage.*

tō-hǽlan *to castrate, emasculate, enfeeble* :—For ðon ic hālsige þ wē ūrne līchaman and sāwle mid geswincum gestrangien, nalæs mid īdelnessum tōhǽlen, Verc. Först. 174.

tō-heáwan. *Add*:—Man tōheów þā sticmǽlum þone sceoccenan god, Nap. 55, 27.

tō-helpan *glosses* adjuvare :—Ic gilēfo, tōhelpe (*adiuua*) ungileóffulnisse míne, Mk. R. 9, 24.

tō-higung. l. -hígung.

tō-hlīdan. *add*:—On þām sixtan dæge æt þére sixtan tíde dæges þes heofon tōhlýt fram eástdæle oþ þæne westdǽl, Verc. Först. 133, 2. Þā tōhlād se hróf þæs gebedhūses *aperto tecto oratorii*, Gr. D. 275, 16. [Cf. B. 999 *with* Sir Ferumbras 2181 : So harde he bot ... þat þe henges boþe barste, and þe stapel þar-wiþ out sprong.]

tō-hlinnan. l. -tō-lynnan, -lynian : tō-hnescian. l. -hnescan.

tō-hreósan. I. *add*:—On þysre byri syndon fram þodene weallas tōhrorene (*maenia dissoluta*), Gr. D. 134, 7. II. *add*:—Wæs þǽr sum hreófla wundorlíce tōhroren, Hml. S. 31, 564. Stōd þǽr ān hreófla tōhrorenum līchaman atelic on hīwe, 36, 334.

tō-hréran. l. (?) -hríran. Cf. ge-hríran : tō-hrician. l. -hrícian.

tō-hwega *a little* :—Hē cōm geornlíce biddende þ him sceolde beón seald tōhwega eles (*aliquantulum olei*), Gr. D. 159, 11. Þ hī þone swétan mete hūru geómriende hwæþugu (tōhwega, *v. l.*) onbyrgdon, 170, 11.

tō-hwirfan ; *p.* de To *overturn* :—Tōhwyrfd *eversus*, Ps. L. 117, 13.

tō-ican *glosses* adjicere :—Tōéce tō lengo his elne ǽnne *adicere ad staturam suam cubitum unum*, Mt. L. 6, 27.

tō-lǽtan. *Add*:—Þæs mōdes bōsum byð tōlǽten *mentis laxatur sinus*, Gr. D. 173, 9.

tō-lǽtendlíce. v. un-tōlǽtendlíce.

tō-licgan. I. *add*:—Tō stybban snāde ðǽr ðā twégen wegas tōlicgað, C. D. vi. 26, 31. On stream oþ þā laca tōlicgaþ, Cht. Crw. 3, 12. Swā wíde swā wegas tōlāgon, An. 1236. II. *add*:—Seó geogoð nā getanglíce né licge, ac sió yld þā geogoðe tōlicge *adolescentiores fratres juxta se non habeant lecta, sed permixti cum senioribus*, R. Ben. 47, 16.

tō-lisan. I b. *add*:—Ic wilnige þ ic sý tōlýsed, Gr. D. 109, 23. III a. *add*:—Syndon fram þodene þā weallas tōlýsede (*maenia dissoluta*). 134, 7. V. *add*:—Hý beóð tōlýsede ungeleáffullíce *they shall be destroyed in their unbelief*, Hex. 48, 19.

tō-lisedness. *Add*: I. *dissolution* :—His līchaman tōlýsednes *corporis dissolutio*, Gr. D. 296, 2. II. *desolation* :—Wē geómriaþ þā tōlésednesse and broc þyssere stōwe *loci hujus desolationem gemimur*, Gr. D. 313, 14.

tō-lisend. *Add*:—Tōlésendes *desolatoris*, Ps. Vos. 119, 4.

tō-lisende. v. un-tolisende : tō-lisendlic. v. un-tōlisendlic.

tō-lisness. I. *add*: *desolation* :—On tōliésnesse *in desolatione*, Ps. Vos. 72, 19. Wē geómriaþ þā tōlýsnesse and broc þyssere stōwe, Gr. D. 313, 14. v. tō-lísedness.

tō-lipian. *Add*: I. *to relax* :—Þæs mōdes sceát byð tōleoðod (-liðod, *v. l.*) *mentis laxatur sinus*, Gr. D. 173, 9. Tōleoþedum þām sceáte his mōdes, 272, 16. II. *to pay a debt, discharge* an obligation :—Ælc scyld mid gife bið tōleoþod and ālýsed *omnis culpa munere solvitur*, Gr. D. 349, 28.

toll. IV. *add*:—Toll and teám sý āgifen into þām mynstre, Cht. E. 236, 4.

tó-lynian, -lynnan *to take away*:—Áhebbað ł tóhlynnað gatu eówre *attollite portas uestras*, Ps. L. 23, 7. v. á-lynian.

tó-metan *to measure out, mete out*:—Dena eardungstówa ic tómete *conuallem tabernaculorum dimetiar*, Ps. L. 107, 8.

tó-middes. II. *add*:—His borh þǽr æt hám gewunode tómiddes heora, swilce hé beswicen wǽre *quasi deceptus in medio fidejussor remansit*, Gr. D. 253, 26.

tó-nemnan. *Add*:—Þonne ðá fíf þing ealle gegædorade beóþ, ðonne beóþ hit eall án ðing, and þ án þing biþ God; and hé biþ ánfeald untódǽled, þeáh hí ǽr on manig tónemned wǽre, Bt. 33, 2; F. 122, 19.

tonwinto. *Add* = ? ? tó-onwinde.

topp. III. *add*:—Top *trochus*, An. Ox. 47, 6. Toppas (*l.* toppe) *trocho*, 56, 8.

toppa *a tuft* (?):—Toppa *pensa* (protendor seu serica *pensa* porrecta in gracilem pannum ceu stamina pepli, Ald. 272, 24), An. Ox. 23, 45.

tór. *Add*: [*v. N. E. D.* tor (where the vowel is taken to be short).]

tór-begéte. *Add*: [Cf. *Icel.* tor-gætr.]

torfian. II a. *add*: *to throw, scatter*:—Hyt nyþer torfaþ *iacit cumulos*, Germ. 390, 80. III. *to toss* (intrans.):—þá geseah hé án scip út on þǽre sǽ, swá swíðe torfigende fram þan wealcendum sǽs ýðum þ ealle þá men wéndon þ heora scip tóbrocen wǽre, Nap. 62.

torhtness. *Add*:—Hé ne gýmeð þysses eorðlican ríces torhtnessa, Verc. Först. 108, 4.

torn. *Add*:—Hwí ne feormast þú mid teára gyte torne synne? *cur tua non purgas lacrymis peccata profusis?*, Dóm. L. 79.

torr. I. *add*:—Benedictus gestaþolode hine sylfne in þám uferan dǽlum þæs torres (on sumes stýpeles úpflóra, *v. l.* in turris superioribus), and Seruandus gestaþelode hine in þám neoðeran dǽlum þæs ylcan torres (stýpeles, *v. l.*), Gr. D. 170, 16–21. II. *add*:—Þeáh hine ǽlc ýð gesége mid þám héhstan þe seó sǽ forðbringð, and þeáh hine ǽlc tor geséce þe on eallum clyfum syndon, Verc. Först. 110, 13. Næs þæt hús æfter manna gewunan getimbrod, ac mid mislicum torrum gehwemmed (cf. ðá stánas swá of óðrum clife út sceoredon, Bl. H. 207, 20) tó gelícnysse sumes torres scræfes, Hml. Th. i. 508, 17. II a. *a tor*:—On eofede tor; of eofede torre on heán dúne, Cht. E. 266, 18.

tó-ryne, es; *m.* *A running together, concourse, conflict*:—Níwe tórynas folca getácnað *nouos concursus populorum significat*, Archiv cxx. 51, 41.

tó-samne. I. (2) *add*:—Hí ðá tósomne cómon æt Peonhó, and sóna swá hí tógædere féngon, þá beáh seó Englisce fyrd, Chr. 1001; P. 133, 23.

tó-sáwan. (b) *add*:—Sixtýne deófle wǽron þe worhton þisne hlísan and tóseówon geond þ folc, Hml. S. 31, 558.

tosca. *Add*:—Toxan *rubete quę et rane dicuntur*, An. Ox. 1855.

tó-scénan. *Add*:—Hé tóscénde (*dirupit*) þone stán and fleówon wæteru, Ps. L. 104, 41.

tó-sceacan. *add*: v. un-tósceacen.

tó-sceád. I. *add*:—Tóscádes *difinitionis*, An. Ox. 27, 12. Wæs heora ǽghwæðer Heáwold nemned. Wæs þis tósceád (*distinctio*) hwæðere þætte fore missenlicre heora heáfas híwe óðer wæs cweden se blaca Heáwold, óðer se hwíta Heáwold, Bd. 5, 10; Sch. 599, 18. III. *add*: (1) of difference in material objects:—Æteówde seó hand swutole . . . and wǽron fægere fingras, smale and lange, and þǽra nægla tósceád (*the nails could be distinguished from the rest of the hand*), and se geара líra beneoðan þám þúman eall wæs gesýne, Vis. Lfc. 83. (2) of difference in non-material objects:—Swá micel tósceád is betwuh ðǽre beðóhtan synne . . . and ðǽre ðe mon fǽrlíce ðurhtiéhð, Past. 435, 4.

tó-sceádan. I 2 d. *add*: *to separate by means of characteristics*:—Byþ tósceáden *discernitur*, i. *diiudicatur*, An. Ox. 1405. (2 e) *add*:—Tósceádene, tósendrede *discretas*, i. *segregatas*, An. Ox. 207. (2 h) of the function of the conjunction:—Hé hwílon geþeót óðre dǽlas and hwílon tósceát, Ælfc. Gr. Z. 258, 18. II. *add*: (a) *to utter* (?), cf. tó-dǽlan; XI.:—Hig tyrigdon gást his and hé tósceádde on welerum his *exacerbauerunt spiritum eius et distinxit in labiis suis*, Ps. L. 105, 33. Míne behát þá þe tósceáddon (*distinxerunt*) míne weleras, 65, 14. III. *add*:—Swá mycel swá tósceát eastdǽl fram westdǽle *quantum distat ortus ab occidente*, Ps. L. 102, 12. Tósceáden (-an ?) *distare*, An. Ox. 441.

tó-sceádedness, e; *f.* *Separation*:—Þæt wé sién gemyndige . . . þǽre tósceádednesse úre sáwle, þonne hió of ðám líchoman gelǽdd bið (cf. þæs gedáles líchoman and sáule, Wlfst. 225, 15), Verc. Först. 101, 1.

tó-scendan *to destroy*:—Hé tóscende þ deófolgyld *contrivit idolum*, Gr. D. 121, 24. [*v. N. E. D.* to-shend.]

tó-sciftan. *Add*: [*v. N. E. D.* to-shift.]

tó-scilian. v. scilian.

tó-scirian. *Add*: I. *to distribute, allot a share.* v. scirian; *and* cf. tó-dǽlan; VI.:—Ǽghwylcre sáwle bið onsundrum tóscyred (*to each soul separately will its doom be assigned*), and sió bið swylce hyre se líchoma ǽr geworhte, Verc. Först. 105, 8. II. *to distinguish.* (1) *to recognize the difference between*:—Hí né tóscyriað gód ne yfel *nec bona nec mala discernunt*, Chrd. 75, 1. (2) *to give distinctive marks to*:—Wæs ǽlces hádes reáf synderlíce tóscyred *habitus singulorum ordinum ab inuicem discreti sunt*, Chrd. 63, 26.

tó-sendan; II. Dele, *the MS. has* tówende.

tó-setedness, e; *f.* *Disposition*:—On tósetetnesse heortan *in dispositionem cordis*, Ps. Rdr. 72, 7.

tó-settan. *Add*:—Twá and hundseofontig bóca sind on bibliothécan, for þan þe hig sume sind tósette on twá (*some of them are put into two parts*) for heora langnysse, Ælfc. T. Grn. 19, 32.

tó-sígan. *Add*:—þes pallium þe ic werige wyle mé gelǽstan, and mín syric ne tósíhð, ne míne sceós ne tóbærstað, Hml. S. 36, 161. Hit gedafenlic is þ his reáf ne beó horig ne húru tósigen, Ll. Th. ii. 350, 21.

tó-sleán. I 1 a. *add*:—Ne þúhte þæs tweó þ gif þ stánclif feólle, þ hit ne tóslóge þ scræf (*specum destrueret*), Gr. D. 213, 21. Syndon hús tóslægene (-slag-) *eversae domus*, 134, 8. (b) *add*:—Hé tóslóh (tóbræc, *v. l.*) þá locu þǽre cyste *claustra arcae comminuit*, Gr. D. 64, 14. Hit wæs tódǽled on twá sticcu . . . his fóstormodor gemétte hit swá tóslagen (-sleg-, *v. l.*), 97, 9. Of þám scipe wǽron þá næglas forlorene and þá þylinge tóslægene (*the planks were torn apart*), 284, 24.

tó-slítan. I. *add*:—Þú tóslite sæc mínne *concidisti saccum meum*, Ps. L. 29, 12. III. *add*:—Tóslíton *discerpere*, i. *dilaniare*, An. Ox. 729. III a. *to make a wound by biting*:—On þá wunda þe se wurm tóslát, Hml. S. 31, 959. V. *add*: *to interrupt*:—þá ongan se cniht clypian . . . and mid hlúdum stefnum tóslítan and ámyrran þára bróðra sangas and gebedu *coepit clamore, atque cum magnis vocibus orationes fratrum interrumpere*, Gr. D. 324, 23. v. un-tósliten.

tó-slúpan. I. *add*:—His liþa tóslupon on þám láðum tintregum *his joints were dislocated in those fell tortures*, Hml. S. 37, 171. II. *add*:—þá þwangas þára scóna ongunnon heom sylfe tóslúpan *coeperunt se caligarum corrigiae dissolvere*, Gr. D. 221, 23. IV a. *add*:—Nú sint sionwe tóslopen (*in the facsimile reprint it is* p *not* þ), An. 1427.

tó-snǽdan (?). v. snǽdan.

tó-sócn, e; *f.* *Visiting*:—þá forman costunga preósthádes mannon cumað of wífa gelómlicre tósócne (*feminarum frequentes accessus*), Chrd. 67, 36.

tó-sprecendlic. v. un-tósprecendlic: tó-springan. *Add*: [*v. N. E. D.* to-spring.]

tó-stencan. II. *add*:—Hwá bereáfode mé mínra spéda oððe tóstencte míne ǽhta, Hml. S. 33, 194. Tóstente bígengca *dirutas cerimonias*, An. Ox. 2621.

tó-stician. *Add*:—Hét mé man þ ic ðone swile tósticode *jusserunt me incidere tumorem illum*, Bd. 4, 19; Sch. 447, 3.

tó-stihtian *to dispose, arrange*:—Þú tóstihtodest him yfelu *disposuisti eis mala*, Ps. Rdr. 72, 18.

tó-stregdan. I. *add*:—Þonne hit tóstreigded (-stregded, *v. l.*) and tódǽled hit sylf ymb óðerra manna wísan *cum ad exteriora sparserit*, Gr. D. 5, 1. Tóstrǽdaþ *spargimus*, An. Ox. 46, 18. Swá mycelu wynsumnes þæs æþelestan stences tóstrogden and tógoten wearð geond eall þ hús *tanta illic fragrantia odoris aspersa est*, Gr. D. 282, 19. Þá tóstrýddan gebricu *dispersa fragmina*, An. Ox. 11, 139.

tó-swellan. *After ‘F’ in last line insert*: 10876, *and add*:—His hýd tósweóll *cutis intumescebat*, Gr. D. 157, 9. Hé beót Libertinum on þ heáfod and þa ansýne oð þ eall his andwlita wearð tóswollen and áwannod *ei caput ac faciem tutudit totumque illius vultum tumentem ac lividum reddidit*, 20, 31: 22, 19.

tó-tellan. *Add*:—Þú þysne middangeard from fruman ǽrest forð oð ende tídum tótældest *from the very beginning and right on to the end there has been a distinction of times and seasons for reckoning* (cf. Gen. 1, 14); *tempus ab aevo ire jubes*, Met. 20, 11.

tó-teran. I. *add*:—Hé þearle wédde and began tó tóterenne þá þe hé tó mihte, Hml. S. 31, 535.

tóþ. *Add*: v. cin-, elpend-, feng-tóþ.

tó-þening, e; *f.* *Distension*:—Of tóþeningum *distensionibus*, An. Ox. 2, 476.

tó-þindan. I. *add*:—Ælces mannes miht þe on módignysse færð is þám gelíc swilce man siwige áne bytte, and bláwe hí fulle windes, and wyrce siððan án þýrl þonne heó tóþunden bið on hire greátnysse, þonne tógǽð seó miht, Hml. S. 34, 318. II. *add*:—þá þe mid him sylfum and beforan hyra nécstana eágum tóþindað þurh gewilnunge ídeles gylpes, Gr. D. 40, 6. Tóþundene unþeáwfæstra *traductam indisciplinatorum* (*arrogantiam*), An. Ox. 5346.

tó-twǽman. II. *add*: (1) local, *not to allow to remain together*:—Gelíce þe on úrum líchaman þ hí ne beón tótwǽmede, ac lǽt hí beón hér ætgædere gelǽde, Hml. S. 30, 443. (2) *not to allow companionship*:—Oda arcebiscop tótwǽmde Eádwí cyning and Ælgyfe, for þǽm þe hí wǽron tó gesybbe, Chr. 958; P. 113, 24. Gif wit þurhwuniað on mægðháde . . . þonne cume wit tó his ríce, and wit ne beóð tótwǽmede, Hml. S. 4, 45. III a. *add*:—Nú ne wandode ic ná mínum sceattum þá hwíle þe eów unfrið on handa stód; nú ic mid Godes fultume þ tótwǽmde mid mínum scattum, Cht. E. 229, 29.

**tó-weard.** I b. *add:*—þā wǣron Seaxan sēcende intingan and tóweardne (*an occasion, and one in the immediate future*) heora gedāles wið Bryttas *quaerentes occasionem diuortii*, Bd. 1, 15 ; Sch. 42, 26. **II** 1 a a. without inflexion :—Leoniþa sǣde þæt þā tīda þā yfele wǣron and wilnode þ him tōweard beteran wǣron *ille promisit futura meliora*, Ors. 2, 5 ; S. 86, 6. **II** 2. *add:*—þā leorningcnihtas hē tōsende geond eall tō ǣlcere birig þider þe hē tōwerd wæs, Ælfc. T. Grn. 13, 31. [*O. H. Ger.* zuo-wart *futurus.*]

**tó-weard;** *prep.* I. *add:*—Fram þām littlan fingre tōweard þæs earmes, Vis. Lfc. 85. II. *add:*—þā āþenede Benedictus his hand and āwrāt Crīstes rōde tāken þǣr tōweard *extensa manu Benedictus signum crucis edidit*, Gr. D. 105, 4. II 3. *add:*—Hig eódon tō Sodoman weard *abierunt Sodoman*, Gen. 18, 22. Hī flugon tō heora lande weard, Hml. A. 113, 372.

**tó-weaxan** to grow in a scattered way, cover with a scattered growth :—Under þām eáhþýrle geonode mycclu neolnes, and seó wæs eall tōweaxen mid mycelnessum þāra clifstāna *sub fenestra ingens praecipitium patebat saxorum molibus asperum* (aspersum *seems to have been read* ?), Gr. D. 159, 26. [Cf. þā gyrden . . . wǣron tōgædre iwæxene . . . and wēron ufeweard on ðreó tōweaxen, H. R. N. 22, 7.]

**tó-weorpan.** I. *add:*—Hira gimmas licgeað tōworpne æfter strǣtum *lapides dispersi per plateas jacent*, Past. 135, 13. I a. *add:*—Tōworpenum helle claus[tr]um·*destructis herebi claustris*, Angl. xiii. 400, 498. II b. *add:*—Se āwyrgeda gāst tōwearp þone wāh (*parietem evertit*), Gr. D. 125, 4. Mon tōwearp þone weal niþer oþ þone grund *Pompeius muros everti, aequarique solo imperavit*, Ors. 5, 11 ; S. 238, 12.

**tó-wiltan** advolvere. v. wiltan.

**tó-worpenness.** *Add:* overthrow, subversion :—Druncen is micel mōdes tōworpennys (*subuersio*), Chrd. 74, 15.

**tó-worpness.** *Add:* III. destruction :—Of ðām dǣle heora tōworpnysse ex parte suae destructionis, Gr. D. 205, 6.

**tó-writan** to describe :—Ptolomeus tōwrāt ealles þises middangeardes gemet on ānre bēc, Bt. 18, 1 ; S. 41, 27. Hī synd tōwrite[ne] *describuntur*, An. Ox. 1065.

**toxa.** v. tosca.

**tracter** a funnel :—Tracter *infundibulum*, Nap. 87. [v. Gall. 325. O. H. Ger. trahtāre. Cf. Ger. trichter. From Latin tractarius (? < trajectorium.]

**trāglíce.** v. un-trāglíce.

**traht.** II. *add:*—In þām trahte þæs godspelles þe ic wrāt *in homiliis evangelii*, Gr. D. 281, 9. In þām godspelles trahtum *in eisdem homiliis*, 283, 2.

**trahtian.** I. *add:* I a. to compose a treatise :—Be þon ic gemune þ ic sǣde in þām folclārum þæs godspelles þe ic trahtode be Tassilan mīnre faðan *hoc quod de Tharsilla amita mea in homiliis Euangelii dixisse me recolo*, Gr. D. 286, 8. II. *add:* to deal with a subject, consider :—þā ongunnon hi trahtian and hwæthugu smeágean be his deāðe *tractare de ejus morte aliqui conati sunt*, Gr. D. 104, 27. þā hī ongunnon trahtian hwæðer hī mihton . . . þ unmǣte stānclif onweg āleoþian *dum multituto conaretur si possit ingens saxum levare*, 213, 22.

**trahtnere.** *Add:*—Trahtnere *tractator*, Archiv cxxix. 18, 7. Wē habbað trume gewitnysse on Hieronimum þām sōðfǣstan trahtnere, Angl. viii. 307, 4.

**trahtnian.** I. *add:*—Swā swā wē nū sceortlīce trahtnodon, Ælfc. Gr. Z. 11, 7. þæt hī ðǣra bōca andgit him trahtnodon, Hml. Th. ii. 96, 28. Wē ne magon þisne part fullīce trahtnian on Engliscum gereorde, Ælfc. Gr. Z. 240, 16.

**trahtnung.** *Add:* v. in-trahtnung: **trahtung.** *Add:* v. of-trahtung: -tred. v. ge-tred.

**tredan.** I. *add:* to press with the foot, hold the foot on something :—Hē worhte him āne anlícnesse þe . . . mid ðāre swiðran hand þone hwǣte hlōd, and mid þām winstran fēt þā mittan træd, Ap. Th. 10, 13.

**tredd.** v. tredde: **treddan.** *Add:* v. for-, of-treddan.

**tredde,** an ; f. A press for wine or oil :—Hēt hē þone cnapan stīgan nyðer of þǣre treddan (wīntreddan, *v. l.* calcatorio), Gr. D. 59, 4. Hī wrungon elebergan on þǣre treddan (in prelo), 250, 13. v. ele-, wīn-tredde.

**tredel.** *Add:* the sole of the foot :—Fram þæs fōtes tredele oð ufewearde þæs heáfdes hnolle, Ll. Lbmn. 438, 33.

**trefet** a trivet, tripod :—Trefet, C. D. B. iii. 367, 39. [v. N. E. D. trivet.]

**trēg.** *Add:* [v. N. E. D. tray] : **tregian** to abhor. v. ge-tregian: **trehing.** *Add:* [v. N. E. D. trithing.]

**trem.** In l. 5 for viii. l. xiii., and add : v. æncnetrym.

**trendan.** *Add:*—Se æppel nǣfre þæs feorr ne trenddeð (trendleð ?), hē cýð hwanon hē cōm *pomum licet ab arbore igitur unde reuoluitur, tamen prouidit unde nascitur*, Angl. i. 285. [v. N. E. D. trend.] v. fortrendan ; trendlian.

**trendel.** II. *add:*—Weard eall þāre sunnan trendel swylce sweart scyld, Chr. 733 ; P. 44, n. 9. v. hlǣd-, healf-trendel.

**treów** a tree. I. *add:*—Andlang hearpaðes on Frīgedæges treów, C. D. vi. 8, 15. v. bēc-, bōc-, ellen-, gemǣr-, mæsten-, mearc-treów. IV. *add:*—Man swā mearcað mid medmicelum treówe (*ligno*) þeorfe hlāfas þ hī beóð gesewene swylce hī beón on feówer feórðandǣlas tōdǣlede, Gr. D. 87, 2. 'Ic nāt mid hwī ic delfe' . . . þā geseah hē þǣr swilchwugu treów licgende and þ lytel, ongan þā þǣrmid delfan, Hml. S. 23 þ, 766. IV a. *add:*—Stōd þǣr ān medmycel rōd on þǣre eorðan, and wæs swā mycel þæs treówes gesyne swā wolde beón gōd hande brād, Vis. Lfc. 72. v. wearg-treów.

**treów** truth. *Take here* trūw *in Dict., and.:* I. *add:*—Hē nam þone deácon in his treówþe (treówa, *v. l.*) *diaconum in suam suscepit fidem*, Gr. D. 253, 16. II. *add:*—Hwæt is ðæt, ðæt mon hreówsige his synna, būton ðæt mon eówað Gode his eáðmōdnesse and his treówa ? *quid est culpam flere nisi humilitatem Deo suae devotionis ostendere ?*, Past. 421, 30. IV. *add:*—Hī heora treówe (trýwa, *v.l.*) sealdon þ hié riht mid him healdan woldon *his manus dederunt*, Bd. 3, 28 ; Sch. 327, 4. V. *add:*—Ān of þām þe se cyng hæfde mǣst trūwe tō, Chr. 992 ; P. 126, 23. Sē ðe forlǣt ðone cele ungetreównesse, and wyrð wlacra treówa, Past. 447, 7. Ne cuæð hē ðæt þæt ðū ðe hē wolde his treówa and geleáfan forlǣtan *quod exhibebat non amittendo fidem*, 101, 7. v. ge-treów.

**treówe.** *Add:* v. un-treówe.

**treówen.** *Add:* v. wīr-treówen: **treów-fæst.** *Add:* v. ge-treówfæst : -treówig. v. wīn-treówig.

**treówleásness.** *Add:* perfidy ; in an ecclesiastical sense, heresy :—Hē wæs fylgende ðæs arrianiscan gedwolan treówleásnysse (trýw-, *v. l.*) *perfidiae fuit arianae*, Gr. D. 162, 20 : 240, 13.

**treów-lic.** *Add:* safe, to be trusted :—Treówlicre hit is be staðe tō [swim]manne ðonne ūt on sǣ tō seglanne, Prov. K. 64.

**treówsian.** *Add:* v. geun-, un-treówsian.

**treówness.** *Add:* v. un-, unge-treówness: **treówþ.** I. *add:*—Hē nam þone deácon in his treówþe *diaconum in suam suscepit fidem*, Gr. D. 253, 16.

**trepettan, -etan.** v. in-trepettan: **treppan.** I. *add:* [Cf. O. Frs. treppe a step.]

**trod.** *Add:*—Tō sealgate; ðannen . . . tō sealtrode (a track where there are sallows ?), C. D. iii. 236, 30. [v. N. E. D. trod.]

**trog.** In l. 6 for xiii. l. ix., and add:—þrý trogas, C. D. B. iii. 367, 39. v. corn-, leác-trog.

**trucian.** *Add:* [Trokede, Laym. 16416, 2nd MS. Trokie, 17171, 2nd MS.] : **truma.** *Add:* v. folc-truma: -truma. v. wyrt-truma : **trumian.** v. un-trumian: **truming.** *Dele.* v. trymming: **trumlic.** *Add:* v. un-trumlic: **trumness.** *Add:* v. un-trumness.

**trundulness** glosses circuitus :—On trundulnisse árleáse gangað *in circuitu impii ambulant*, Ps. Rdr. 11, 9. Cf. trendan, trendel, trendlian.

**trus.** l. trūs, and add : v. Philol. Trans. 1898, p. 542 and N. E. D. trouse.

**trúw.** *Take to* treów: -trūwodness. v. for-trūwodness : **trūwung.** *Add:* v. for-, or-trūwung : **trymigian** v. un-trymigian : -trymigu. v. un-trymigū.

**trymman.** *Add:* v. be-, on-, þurh-, un-, ymb-trymman ; un-trymed.

**trymmend.** II. *add:*—Trymmend *stipulatorem*, An. Ox. 7, 383.

**trymming.** II b. *add:* Cf. trymman ; I 4:—Staþelfæste tremmincge *firmo (scripturarum) fulcimento*, An. Ox. 1421. III. protection :—Feohte se cempa on fyrdlicum truman, and wīf hī gehealde binnan wealle trymmincge, Hml. S. 31, 1099. Trymminge (trymniige, MS.), trymunge, Lch. iii. 206, 19) *tutamento*, Archiv cxxv. 59, 381. Trimminge (trimnige, MS., truminge, Lch. iii. 210, 30) *tutamentum*, 65, 585.

**trymness.** II b. *add:* edification :—Trymnes aedificatio (v. trymming ; II b.), Gr. D. 8, 2.

**tucian.** l. tūcian, and add :—Tō wæfersýne tūcian, Hml. S. 36, 134, 123. [v. N. E. D. tuck.]

**tude.** As 'parma' is ablative [v. Ald. 71, 35] tudu is a more probable form for the nominative.

**tūdor.** In l. 5 after 'Tudder' insert (tydder, *v. l.*).

**tūdor-full.** *Add:*—Týdderfullum fetosis, i. fecundis, An. Ox. 3135.

**tumbing,** e ; f. Dancing :—Mæssepreóstas . . ne beón . . . þǣr líchamana beóð fracodlice gebǣru mid saltingum and tumbincgum (*saltationibus*), Chrd. 79, 1.

**tún.** II 2. *add:*—Sí ǣfre ðis mynster fram eallum eorðlicum þeówdōme freóh and mid eallum ðām tūnum (*uillulis*) ðe him tō gelicgað, C. D. iii. 350, 5. V 1. *add:*—Syndon þā burga forhergode and þā ceastra tōworpone, cyrcan forbærnde and mynstra tōworpene, and eác gehwylce tūnas ge wera ge wīfa fram hǣðenum mannum gewēste *depopulatae urbes, eversa castra, concrematae ecclesiae, destructa sunt monasteria virorum ac feminarum, desolata ab hominibus praedia*, Gr. D. 258, 17. (2) *add:*—Hī ūp cōmon æt Leptan þǣm tūne (ad Leptim oppidum), Ors. 4, 10 ; S. 202, 9. LXXXII tūna him eódon on hand *oppida octoginta duo in deditionem cessere Romanis*, 4, 6 ; S. 174, 22. v. fel-, Lunden-, mylen-, siru-tūn.

**tunge.** *Add:* v. hræc-, wǣge-tunge.

**tungol.** *Add: m.:*—Se seldcûða tungel gebîcnode þæs sôðan cyninges âcennednysse, Hml. Th. i. 106, 27.

**tungol-spréc,** e; *f. Astrology:*—Tungelspréce *astrologia,* Hpt. Gl. 479, 49.

**tûn-hofe.** v. hofe.

**tûn-rǽd.** *Add:*—Sum tûn wæs . . . þe ǽlce geáre oftost wæs âwêst þurh hagol . . . þá sende se tûnrǽd sumne getrŷwne ǽrendracan tô Martine his helpes biddende, Hml. S. 31, 1219.

**turf-hacce (?),** an; *f. A turf-hoe, implement for cutting turf:*—Ligones, *ferrum fossorium (fusorium,* MS.*)* tyrfahga (turfhacce? v. N. E. D. hack *an implement for breaking or chopping up, mattock, hoe, &c.*), Txts. 112, 43.

**twǽdding,** e; *f. Adulation:*—Twaddung *adulatio,* Chrd. 40, 28. Hig mid twæddingum beswîcan *eos adulationibus decipere,* 62, 23.

**twâ-nihte.** *Add:* v. twi-nihte: -twecca. v. twæccea.

**twêgen.** II 2. *add:*—Þissa twêga mǽst, Lch. ii. 354, 18.    **IV.** *add:*—þæt sió hel sié swylc(e) twâ deóp, Verc. Först. 109, 5. v. em-twâ.

**twelf.** II. *add:* (3) as a number:—Geŷc twelf þǽrtô, Angl. viii. 301, 20. Þriwa feówer beóð twelf, 328, 21.

**twêntig.** I 1. *add:*—Þis is þára twêntiga hîda bôc, C. D. iii. 426, 12. (1 a) uninflected:—Twêntig sîðon seofon beóð ân hund and feówertig, Angl. viii. 303, 6. (3) helping to form ordinals:—His rîces þŷ þriddan geáre eác twêntigum, Bd. 1, 13; Sch. 36, 17. II 1. *add:*—Ðes friódôm waes bigeten mid ðaem twêntigum hîda, C. D. i. 315, 22. (2) *add:*—Weaxeð þ flôd ðæs sǽs feówer and twêntigum sîða, Shrn. 63, 29. þá diáconas sceoldon þegnian fram fîf and twêntigum wintra and ofer þ, Gr. D. 102, 11. v. hund-twêntig.

**twêntig-feald.** *Add:*—Tŷnfealdum oððe twêntifealdum *deni aut viceni,* R. Ben. L. 54, 15.

**twêntig-geáre;** *adj. Twenty years old:*—On þám geáre þe Ælfred Æðelincg wæs ân-and-twêntig-geáre, Hml. S. 32, 37.

**tweó.** I b. *add:*—Sume martyra lima geâhniaþ, and an tweón is hwæðer hŷ martyras sŷn *alii membra martyrum—si tamen martyrum—venditant,* R. Ben. 135, 26. v. ge-tweó.

**tweógan.** I c. *add after* Swt. 192, 15: 5, 7; S. 230, 20.    **II a.** *add:*—Þonne hî þeówiað þám ungesewenlican Gode, hî hûru ne tweógen nâ þára ungesewenlicra gescæfta *ut quae invisibili serviunt esse invisibilia non dubitentur,* Gr. D. 269, 2. (b) *add:*—Ic wât þ hî tweógiað þ þære sáwle lîfe æfter þæs lîchaman deáðe *multos . . . de vita animae post mortem carnis perpendo dubitare,* Gr. D. 259, 7. (d) *add:*—Ne scealt þú nâ tweógian (tweógan, *v. l.*) þ þes hafað þá ungeswenlican hýrsumnesse *dubitare non debes hunc invisibilia obsequia habere,* Gr. D. 268, 25. Hit mæg beón tweód fram unstrangum môdum hwæþer hî sŷn þe ne sŷn þær andwearde *ab infirmis potest mentibus dubitari utrumne . . .,* 177, 8. (d a) with acc. and clause ( = acc. and infin.):—þú ne tweóst nâ þone ungeswenlican God þ hê is scyppende *esse non dubitas creantem Deum,* Gr. D. 268, 22. v. un-tweód.

**tweógendlîce.** *Add:* v. un-âtweógendlîce.

**tweógung.** *Add:*—Ic wille âniman fram þám þe þás bôc rædað þone intingan ǽlcre tweónnge (tweónge, *v. l.*) æt ǽlcum þæra spella þe ic wrîte *ut dubitationis occasionem legentibus subtraham per singula quae describo,* Gr. D. 9, 6.

**tweónian.** I c. *and* e:—Hine tweónað ymb ðæs untruman geðyld, hwæðer hê geðafian mæge ðæt hine mon snîðe, Past. 187, 7. v. â-tweónian; un-tweónigende.

**tweónigend-lic.** *Add: doubtful, uncertain, dubious:*—Tweóniendlicre tweónunge ðry[dunge] *ancipiti ambiguitatis scrupulo,* An. Ox. 676. Tweóniendlicra gewrita *Apocrifarum,* 5103.

**twi-bleó.** *Add: double-formed:*—Ægðer ge cynren ge tûdor is twybleoh *genus prolisque biformis,* Chrd. 78, 6.

**twi-bytme.** *For* ' bytm ' *at end l.* bytme: -twicce. v. -twæccea.

**twiccian.** *Add:*—Hê cûðe twiccian þá wæstmas gôdra mægna *ille virtutum fructus carpere noverat,* Gr. D. 256, 19.

**twi-deágod;** *adj. Double-dyed:*—Twideágadre deáge *bis tincto cocco,* An. Ox. 1060. v. twi-gedeágod.

**twi-ecgede.** *Add:*—Twiecggedum *bis acuto mucrone),* An. Ox. 229.

**twi-feald.** I. *add:*—Mon ǽlcne ceáp mehte be twifealdan bet geceápian þonne mon ǽr mehte, Ors. 5, 13; S. 248, 2.   II. *add:*—þám môde þæs gehŷrendan becymeþ twifeald (twig-, *v. l.*) fultum (*duplex adjutorium*) . . . hit byþ onbærned . . . hit byð geeádmôdod, Gr. D. 8, 16.

**-twifealdian.** v. ge-twifealdian: **twifildan.** *Add:* v. ge-twifildan.

**twi-fingre.** *Substitute: Two fingers thick,* a term applied to fat on swine:—Æt twyfingrum spic, Ll. Th. i. 132, 19.

**twi-fyrclian** *to fork off* from, *separate* from another object:—þeáh ǽlc leásung hæbbe sume gelícnysse þære sôðnysse, þeáh twyfyrclað and tôdǽlð seó ârwyrðnys (*differt tamen dignitas*) þæs sôðan wîsdômes fram lícetunge leásre lâre, Chrd. 96, 37.

**twi-fyrede.** *l.* -fŷrede.

---

**twig.** *Add:*—Twig *flagella,* An. Ox. 53, 2 : 8.

**twiga.** v. palm-twiga.

**twi-hiwe.** II. *add:*—Twihîwum wurmon *bis tincto cocco,* An. Ox. 2, 24.

**twi-milte;** *adj. Twice melted:*—Geola swâ twymylte wex *flaua,* An. Ox. 4462.

**twin.** *Add:*—Twinne, twifealde, An. Ox. 5085.

**twin.** *Add:*—Hwîte twîne geþráwne *bisso retorto,* Wrt. Voc. ii. 126, 34.

**twi-rǽde.** II. *add: at variance, discordant:*—Twyrǽde tô gesibbianne *discordantes reconciliandi,* Chrd. 112, 10.

**twi-sehtan.** *Dele* ' (?) ', *and add: The Latin is:*—Filosophos uiderit disiungi dampnum significat. v. Archiv cxxv. 56, 295, *where* twisehtan *is given as the true reading.*

**twi-sestre;** *adj. Containing two sesters:*—Êghuælc ân wæs twisestre gemet, Jn. L. 2, 6 marg.

**twisled.** *Add:*—Tô ðám twysledan hamme, C. D. v. 281, 24. On þæt twyslede treów, C. D. B. ii. 246, 22.

**twislung.** *Add: differentiation:*—Wê nellað nâne twislunge habban nânes hâdes *reclusa personarum acceptione,* Chrd. 13, 24. v. weg-twislung.

**twi-sprǽcness.** *Add:*—Forlǽtan wê leásunga and lícettunga, tǽlnessa and twysprǽcnessa, Verc. Först. 94, 3.

**tŷd** *instructed.* v. tŷn.

**tŷderness** *a branch:*—Winbôga tŷddernessa *palmitum propagines,* An. Ox. 3849. Cf. tŷdrung; **II.**

**-tŷdre.** v. or-tŷdre: **tŷdrung.** *In l.* 2 *after* 61 *insert:*—Tŷdrunge, An. Ox. 1031: **tyge.** *Add:* v. sweord-tyge: **tygþ.** v. tîþ.

**tyhtan.** I. *add:*—Þá gefæstnadon þá cwelleras þone Crîstes þegn on þære hengene, and hine hetelîce tihton swâ swâ man web tiht, Hml. S. 37, 100–102.   II 2. (a) *add:*—þonne hê cymð hê eów tiht and gewissað tô eallum ðám dingum ðe ic eów sǽde *ille uos docebit omnia et suggeret uobis omnia quaecumque dixêro uobis,* Jn. 14, 26), Hml. Th. i. 298, 3. Hê ûtlændisce hider in tihte, Chr. 959; P. 115, 12. (b) *add:*—þæt mǽden tihte þá wydewan þ heó þá sceattas dǽlde þearfum, Hml. S. 2, 142. Hî tihton heora geféran þ hî unforhte wǽron, and bǽdon þ hî âwurpon heora wǽpna him fram, 28, 61. (3) with dat. of person, *to urge* something on a person:—Hê arn swâ swâ him his nytenlice yld tihte plegende mid his efenealdum, Hml. Th. ii. 134, 4.

**tyhtend.** *Add:* v. leás-tyhtend: **tyhtend-lic.** *Add:* v. mis-tyhtendlic.

**tyhting.** *Add:*—Hî tihton heora geféran þ hî unforhte wǽron . . . Betwux þysum tihtingum tengdon þá hǽþenan, Hml. S. 28, 66. v. leás-, on-tyhting.

**tyhtness.** *Add:*—Tyhtnesse *instinctu,* An. Ox. 11, 179.

**tyllan.** *For* ' compound ' *in l.* 1 *substitute* ' compounds be-,'.

**tyllan** *to pay toll:*—Halwun freóde Hægelfiǽde hire wîman and tilde (cf. Ælfric nam þæt toll for þæs kynges hand, 31), Cht. E. 253, 16.

**tym-bor (?)** *taratrum. l.* (?) tyrn-bor *terebrum.*

**tŷn.** *Add:*—Hî man tŷ þ hî gôde bæcystran beón, Chrd. 19, 18. Tŷu heora lâreówas hî *erudiantur a magistris,* 58, 4. Tŷd[e] *cati,* An. Ox. 56, 159.

**tŷnan.** *Add:* v. ymb-tŷnan; un-tŷned: **-tyngfull, -tynglic, -tynglîce, -tyngness.** v. ge-tyngfull, &c.: **tŷning.** *Add:* v. æcer-tŷning: **tyrfan.** v. ge-, of-tyrfan.

**tyrning.** I. *add:*—Sume preóstas gŷmað þ heora loccas mid [nǽdle?] tyrninge cyrpsion *crines calamistri uestigio rotantur,* Chrd. 64, 34.

**tŷþ-.** tîþ- *forms should be taken here.*

---

# Þ

**þá.** I. *add:*—Be ðǽm wæs swîðe wel gecweden ðurh ðone wîtgan . . . ðæ cwæð se wîtga *unde bene per prophetam dicitur,* Past. 409, 33.   **II.** *add:*—Him þá etendum, Mk. 14, 22. Hêr Cynegîls and Cuichelm gefuhtun wið Pendan, and geþingodan þá, Chr. 628; P. 24, 18.   **III 1.** *add:*—þám forman dæge azimorum, þá hî eástron offrodon, Mk. 14, 12. v. geó.

**þaccian.** *Add:*—þú tô þon gelǽded wǽre þ þú mid þînre brádre handa þá nunnan ofer hire eaxle þaccodest *qui perductus es, ut posteriora illius alapa ferires,* Gr. D. 190, 14. [v. N. E. D. thack.] v. ge-þaccian.

**þacian.** *Add:* [v. N. E. D. thack.]: þac-sele. v. þæc-sele.

**þæcele.** *Add:* used figuratively:—Inǽled mid þám þæcelum (þyccylum, *v. l.*) þære æfeste *invidiae facibus succensus,* Gr. D. 117, 28.

**þæc-sele (?)** *a building with a thatched roof (?):*—Of ðon nyrðan gate on þacseleheal; of þacseleheal, C. D. iii. 134, 37.

**þæder.** *Add:* I. *local:*—Þæder *quo*, An. Ox. 2, 193 : 3331 n. Dô man þæm tûna teóðunga þæder (*ibidem*) þe tô mynstre hŷrað. And ælc preóst ... þæder (*ad ipsum hospitale*) his teóðunga dô, Chrd. 51, 12–15. II. *to a matter :*—Þ hê tô þæm gôdan gewilnungum cume, þe þæder þurh mêda gelaðod næs, Chrd. 61, 28.

**þænan.** *Dele the second passage, for which see* beþian, *and add :*—Hê ontŷnde þone æspryng godcundra gewrita, and þænde (*rigabat*) þâ mædwe geleáffulra môda, Gr. D. 34, 20. v. ge-þænan.

**þær.** I a. (1) *add :*—Rufinus wolde habban him self þone anwold þær eást, and Stileca wolde sellan his suna þisne hêr west, Ors. 6, 37 ; S. 296, 6. (1 a) *used indefinitely :*—Hê getæhte þâ syndrigan stôwe hwæt hî þær and þær timbrian sceoldon, Gr. D. 148, 17. (1 β) marking place in a series :—Sume ûre ðéningbêc onginnað on Aduentum Domini ; nis ðeáh þær for ðŷ ðæs geáres ord, Hml. Th. i. 98, 27. II 1. *add :*—Ðâ þonne þe Godes þances hwylcne cuman underfôn, ne wilnigen hig þær nânra woruldleána, Ll. Th. ii. 422, 14. (2) *add :*—Hê stæled fæhðe in firene, þær þe hié êcne anwaldan oft forgeáton, Sat. 641. (3) *add :*—þær þe þis god ne wære, nænige þinga ûra goda on hyra onsŷne gefeóllon, Verc. Först. 100, 5. Eálâ þær hig hogodon *utinam saperent*, Cant. M. ad fil. 29.

**þær-æt.** *Add :*—Hê côm þærtô, and funde þæræt feáwa men, Ors. 6, 36 ; S. 294, 1.

**þæran (?).** *Add :* v. þirran.

**þær-on.** IV. *add :* with verbs of knowing, *in respect to a matter :*—Hig hym eall sædon þ ðæt hig þæron wyston, Hml. A. 188, 41.

**þær-onufenan.** v. ufenan.

**þær-riht ;** *adj.* The passage in which strictis, *glossed by* þârrihtum, *occurs is :* Iam iamque strictis mucronibus, Ald. 52, 17. As in another gloss iam iamque *is glossed by* þârrihtes (An. Ox. 3797), þârrihtum *may be taken as belonging to the adverbial, rather than to the adjective form.*

**þær-rihte.** *Add :* (1) of an event which immediately succeeds another :—þ cild þe bið âcænned, sôna hit cŷð mid wôpe and þærrihte wîtegað þissere worulde geswinc, Hml. A. 77, 127. (2) of an event which immediately precedes another, *just :*—Se earn on ðâm ôfre gesæt mid fisce geflogen, þone hê ðærrihte gefêng (*piscem, quem aquila nuper de fluvio prendiderat*), Hml. Th. ii. 140, 4. Cf. hêr-rihte.

**þær-rihtes.** *Add :*—þârrihtes iam iamque, An. Ox. 3797.

**þær-tô.** (3) *add :* v. ge-byrian *for other examples.* (6) with a verb of motion :—Hê côm þær-tô, Ors. 6, 36 ; S. 294, 1.

**þær-tôeácan.** *Add :*—þærtôeácan *de cetero*, An. Ox. 1350. Cain wiste his fæder forgægednysse, and næs þurh þ gewærlæht, ac þærtôeácan his âgenne brôþor âcwealde *Cain sciebat damnationem praevaricationis primae, et non timuit originali peccato fratricidii superaddere scelus*, Angl. vii. 32, 303. Ðreó hund daga and fîf and syxtig daga and þærtôeácan syx tŷda, Lch. iii. 246, 13.

**þæs-lic.** I. *add :*—Dædbôte fulre þæslicere *satisfactione congrua*, R. Ben. I. 56, 15. IV. *such.* v. þæslîce, *and cf.* þys-lic :—Swylc fæder swylc (?) þæslic sunu þæslic and hâlig gâst *qualis pater talis filius talis et spiritus sanctus*, Angl. ii. 360, 10. Cf. his-lic.

**þæslîce.** *In l.* 3 *for* 47 *l.* 147 *and* II. *add :*—þæs[lîce] *congruenter*, An. Ox. 1715.

**-þæslicu.** v. un-þæslicu.

**þæt.** I 1 a. *add :*—Gelamp ... þ hî cômon on Scotland upp, Bd. 1, 1 ; Sch. 11, 4. Ðâ wæs ymb CLXXXVIII wintra fram Drihtnes mennisc-nysse þ Severus câsere ... se wæs seofonteogeða fram Agusto, þ hê rîce onfêng, 1, 5 ; Sch. 17, 6–11 : 1, 4 ; Sch. 16, 8. I 2. *add :* where the verb in the main clause is passive:—Ne wæs hê forlæten þ hê ofer him deádum gefêge, Bd. 1, 7 ; Sch. 26, 2. Ic wæs beden from þaem bisceope þaeti ic him âlêfde ... þeti ic him forgêfe ..., Cht. E. 42, 1–4. (Cf. tô ðon þaeti, 8.) III 1. *add :*—Hê eác gedyde þæt Antonius his freónd wearð, Ors. 5, 13 ; S. 244, 28. Hê næþ his fôta geweald þ hê mæge gân, Bt. 36, 4 ; F. 178, 13. On sumre stôwe se hrôf wæs þ man mid his handa neálîce geræcean mihte, Bl. H. 207, 22. Ne hîwa ðû swilce ðû mæge ... wið hî môtian ðæt ðîn môd ne beó yfele be-smiten, Hex. 48, 11. ¶ In the charters the word is used almost with the force of *until*, marking the point reached in tracing a boundary :—Swâ west wið ðan heáfdan ðæt hit cymð tô ðære ealdan dûne ; andlang dûne west ðæt hit cymeð intô Dinamore ... sûð ðæt hit cymeð tô ðâm slæde, C. D. iii. 389, 14–23 : 24 : 25 : 27, *and often.* III 2 a. *add :*—Hwâ is swâ dysig þ wille etan þâ stânas and lætan þâ hlâfas, H. R. 11, 15. IV. *add :*—Geseah ic freán efstan, þæt hê mê wolde on gestîgan, Kr. 34. Âbreóðe his angin, þæt hê hêr swâ manigne mann âflŷmde, By. 243. V 2. *add :* cf. hû ; III 2 a a.

**-þafsum.** v. ge-þafsum : **-þafsumness.** v. ge-þafsumness.

**þafung.** *Add :*—Flotmen swâ strange þurh Godes þafunge, Wlfst. 162, 17.

**þân.** *Add :* watered, having water (of land) :—‘ Geýc mê þ and syle mê þân land.’ Þâ sealde se fæder hire þân and leóht bufan and þân and leóht beneoðan ... Seó sâwel bideð æt ðâm fæder þänes landes and wætes ‘*iunge irriguam* (terram)’. *Dedit ei pater suus irriguum superius*

*et irriguum inferius ... anima a patre terram irriguam petit*, Gr. D. 245, 19–23. Seó sâwel onfêhð þân and wæt bufan ... and heó onfêhð þânum and wætum beneoðan, 246, 10–12.

**þanc.** I. *add :*—þŷ læs ic lengc þone þanc hefige þâra leornendra mid gesegenum þâra fremdra tælnysse *ne sensus legentium prolixae sententiae molesta defensio obnubilet*, Guth. Gr. 102, 31. II a. *sake ; gratia :*—Gebeáh hê tô þance rihtre cumlîðnesse tô Quadrigesimo *ad Quadrigesimum hospitalitatis gratia declinabat*, Gr. D. 215, 14. Hê hine bæd þ hê underfênge þ hê him brôhte tô þance þære sôþan lufan (*gratia caritatis*), 343, 22. III. *add :*—Mê is swîðe mycel þanc þæt þû mê gehâtst, Solil. H. 26, 11. III c. *add :*—þis is mê on þance *gratias agimus*, Gr. D. 203, 9. IV. *add :*—Ic geann him .vi. mæran mid vi. coltan tô þance (*in gratitude*), Shrn. 159, 29. v. æf-, of-, ymb-þanc.

**þanc ;** *adj.* v. or-þanc : **-þanca.** v. æf-, ymb-þanca.

**þanc-full.** I. *add :* clever, ingenious :—Sceaþa þancful hê bið *latro ingeniosus erit*, Archiv cxxix. 20, 5.

**þancfullîce.** *Add :* graciously, kindly :—Hê þâ âne spyrtan þancfullîce (*benigne*) onfêng, Gr. D. 203, 8.

**þancian.** I 4. *add :*—Gode þancigende þære swutelunge, Hml. Th. ii. 272, 21.

**-þanclîce.** v. scearp-, smeá-þanclîce : **þancol.** *Add :* v. smeá-, un-þancol : **-þancollîce.** v. smeá-þancollic : **-þancollîce.** *Add :* v. smeá-þancollîce : **-þancolness.** v. smeáþancol-ness : **þancweorþlîce.** *Add :* v. un-þancweorþlîce : **-þang.** v. ge-þang.

**þanne.** A. IV. *add :* (a) þanne hwæþere *yet :*—Hwæt is þ ... þ se ælmihtiga God swâ forlæteþ sweltan his gecorenan, þâ þonne hwæþre (*tamen*) hê ne læteþ nâ beón forholene, Gr. D. 294, 5 : 292, 3 : 283, 14. Cwyþst þû þ þe nære cûð þ ic ne cûðe Grêcisc geþeóde ? And þonne hwæþre (*et tamen*) sprec nû on Grêcisc, 300, 16. V. *add :*—Gregorius þâgŷt spræc : ‘ Onu þonne gif se gâst mage beón hæfd on þâm men ... for hwan ne mæg hê ...?,’ Gr. D. 303, 25. VI (a) *add :*—Gif hié brecað his gebodscipe, þonne hê him âbolgen wurðeð, Gen. 430. B. II. *add :*—Hwæt wille wê lencg wrîtan be Martines wundrum, þonne Sulpicius sæde þ hî synd ungerîme, Hml. S. 31, 1301. C. *add :*—Ðonne drincð se lâreów ðæt wæter of his âgnum mere, ðonne hê gehwirfð ... Ðonne hê drincð of ðæm wielme his âgnes pyttes, ðonne hê bið self geðwæned mid his âgnum wordum, Past. 373, 7–11. þæt hié triumphan hêton, þ wæs þonne hié hwelc folc mid gefeohte ofercumen hæfdon, þonne wæs heora þeáw þæt ..., Ors. 2, 4 ; S. 70, 22. D. I. *add :* (a) where the comparison is in respect to quantity or number :—Furþor restan þonne healfe niht, R. Ben. 32, 13. (β) where excess over a certain point or standard is marked :—þâ þe habbað mâ þonne heora rihtæðel-cwêne, Wlfst. 298, 17. (1 a) *add :*—Eáðmôdnes gedæfenað þæm þe nân þing him leófre ne lætað þonne Crîst ælmihtigne, R. Ben. 19, 15. (2) *add :*—Heardlic eornost and wîslic wærscipe ... bið witena gehwilcum weorðlicre micle þonne hê his wîsan fâgige tô swîðe, Ll. Th. ii. 318, 39. Ic eom swêtra þonne þû beóbreád blênde mid hunige, Rä. 41, 59. II. *add :*—Ðê is leófre on ðisum wâcum scræfum ðonne ðû on healle heálic biscop sitte, Hml. Th. ii. 146, 28. Hié wæron blîðran tô ðâm deáðe þonne hý hêr on hæðengilde lifden, Shrn. 142, 13. Hwane manaþ God mâran gafoles þonne þone biscop ?, Bl. H. 45, 16. III. *add :*—Læcedemonie hæfdon mâran unstillnessa þonne hié mægnes hæfden, and wæron swîþor winnende on Thebane þonne hié fultume hæfde, Ors. 3, 1 ; 98, 34–100, 2. Mîn unrihtwîsnysse is mâre þonne ic forgifenysse wyrðe sŷ *major est iniquitas mea, quam ut veniam mereor*, Gen. 4, 13. Ic wið eów stîðlicor âginne, ðonne ic tale wið eów habban wylle *I shall proceed too sternly against to be ready to talk to you*, Hml. S. 23, 183. IV. *add :* where the main clause has no comparative form :—Hê swîðe þæs londes fæstenum trûwode þonne his gefeohte *ditioni magis quam praelio se commissurus*, Nar. 17, 27.

**þe.** I 4. *add :*—Gif hwylc abbod mæssepreóstes behôfige, geceóse hê of his âgenum geférum þe þæs hâdes wurðe sig, R. Ben. 110, 18. Hwæt gebyrað ûs embe þis tô smeágenne ? þis sceolon smeágan þe þæs gîman sceolon, Ælfc. T. Grn. 20, 31. II 1. *add :*—þonan wendan þe hê ær tô geþôht hæfde, Ors. 4, 10 ; S. 202, 8. III 1. (a) *add :*—Lyt monna weorð lange fægen ðæs ðe hê ôðerne bewrencð *few men are glad for long at having tricked another*, Prov. K. 34. (β) *add :*—His freónda forespræc forstent him eal þæt ylce þe (cf. eal þæt sylfe swylce, 38, 17) hit sylf spræce, Wlfst. 110, 4.

**þeáh.** II 2. *add :*—Wê niton þeáh gê wunion hêr on neáwiste, Jos. 9, 7. þonne andwyrdan þâ yrfenuman swâ he sylf sceolde, þeáh hê lîf hæfde, Ll. Th. i. 416, 1. ¶ with negative clause :—Nis þe genôh þ þu sylf losast, þeáh þû uppan þ ôþre ne forspylle ? Ne genihtsumað þe þ þû sylf an þ druncen beyrnst, þeáh þû þonne gŷt ôðre mid þe ne teó ? *non tibi sufficit quod ipse peris, nisi adhuc insuper et alios perdas ? Non tibi sufficit quod ipse in illa ebrietate incurris, adhuc et alios tecum trahis ?*, Chrd. 74, 28–31. (a) where the hypothetical clause expresses something considerable, *even if :*—Þeáh hî nû eall hiora lîf and hiora dæda âwriten hæfdon, Bt. 18, 3 ; F. 64, 36. (β) where the clause expresses something inconsiderable, *if even, if only :*—Ðeáh se man nime ænne and lecge on

fûl sloh *though a man do no more than take a stone and lay it in a foul slough*, Wlfst. 239, 9. Ðeáh ûre heorda hwylc ân sceáp forgŷme, wê willað ꝥ hê hit forgylde, Ll. Th. ii. 326, 24. (2 a) *add*:—Genôh wære þâm wǽdlan his untrumnys, þeáh þe hê wiste hæfde; and eft him wære genôh his hafenleást, ðeáh ðe hê gesundful wære, Hml. Th. i, 330, 15–17. Swâ þêh þe him lytles hwæt uníeðe sié, Ors. 3, 9; S. 136, 18.

**þeahtian.** *Add*: v. mid-þeahtian.

**þearf.** II I a. *add*:—On ðǽm ðingum ðe him ðearf sié, C. D. i. 316, 12. Ic þæs horses þearfe nabbe *ego caballo opus non habeo*, Gr. D. 15, 26. (2) *add*:—Wæs him þearf ꝥ him mon hors funde *cui necesse fuit ut equus requiri debuisset*, Gr. D. 183, 2. (4) *add*:—Þâ sceoldon on siml beón winnende þǽr hit þonne þearf wæs, Ors. 6, 23; S. 274, 20. V. *add*:—Gif þû wille mê hwylce þearfe gegearwian *si mihi praestare vis*, Gr. D. 343, 27. VI. *add*:—On þisum þrîm stelum stynt se cynestôl, and gif ân bið forud, hê fylð âdûn sôna þâm ôðrum stelum tô þearfe, Ælfc. T. Grn. 20, 29.

**þearf**; *adj. Necessary*:—Þâ wæs him ân hors þearf, ꝥ man him funde, Gr. D. 183, 2 (v. þearf; II 2). v. nîd-, un-þearf.

**þearfa.** I. *add*:—Hê wæs þearfa woruldlicra ǽhta and hê wæs on his geearnungum welig *pauper rebus, sed meritis dives erat*, Gr. D. 281, 13.

**þearfan.** ¶ (1) *add*:—Heora ǽlc ân .c. þearfendra manna gebaðige, Cht. Th. 616, 24.

**þearfedness.** *Add*:—Bonefacies cyrican gelamp ꝥ þǽr wæs hefigu wǽdi and þearfednes *hujus ecclesiae gravis valde paupertas inerat*, Gr. D. 56, 31. Se wara weard his âgenre þearfednesse *sollicitus suae paupertatis custos*, 201, 11.

**þearfend-lic.** *Add*:—Woruldlicra ǽhta hî lǽddon þearfendlic lîf *rebus pauperem vitam ducebant*, Gr. D. 283, 15.

**-þearfes.** v. un-þearfes: **þearfian.** *Add*: [*O. Sax.* tharbôn.] v. be-þearfod.

**þearf-lic.** II. *add*:—Darflíc *utile*, Lk. p. 3, 7. Þ[ea]rflí[ce] *commoda*, An. Ox. 56, 172.

**þearflíce.** *Add*: v. nîd-þearflíce: **-þearfness.** v. nîd-þearfness.

**þearle.** II. *add*:—Þâ Walas flugon þâ Englan swîðe þearle (swâ fŷr, *v. l.*), Chr. 473; P. 15, 5. v. fregen-þearle.

**þearl-wis.** *Add*:—Se þearlwîsa dêma *districtus judex*, Gr. D. 334, 25.

**þearlwíslíce.** *Add*:—Þonne hî scéawiað myccle þearlwíslícor þâ tintregu *quanto districtius tormenta respiciunt*, Gr. D. 336, 21.

**þearlwísness.** *Add*:—Seó strengð þǽre þearlwîsnesse *vis districtionis*, Gr. D. 336, 25.

**þeáw.** II b. *add*:—Ðæs cocces ðeáw is ðæt hê micle hlûdor singð on ûhtan ðonne on dægred *gallus profundioribus horis noctis altos edere cantus solet, cum vero matutinum tempus in proximo est, minutas ac tenues voces format*, Past. 461, 2. II c. *add*:—Hit is þeáw þǽre sprǽce and þǽre âscunge þte simle þonne ðǽr ân tweó of âdôn bið, þonne bið ðǽr unrîm âstyred, Bt. 39, 4; F. 216, 17. v. cniht-, weorold-þeáw.

**-þeáwe.** v. ge-þeáwe.

**þeáwfæstlíce**; *adv. In accordance with good usage*:—Sume synd tô þâm bilewite menn ꝥ ðû ne miht âfindan of ânum þûsende ânne þe mæge þeáwfæstlíce sprǽce sprecan, Hml. S. 5, 222.

**þebeigd** *Thebaid*:—On Ðebeigdan lande, Sal. K. 84, 7.

**þecen.** *Add*:—Þîne þæcene *tuum doma*, i. *tectum*, Hpt. 31, 12, 290.

**þefel** *mulled wine* (?):—þefele *defruto*, An. Ox. 104. Cf. (?) þefian.

**þefian.** For the second passage substitute:—Hê ongann on his geþance þefian *aestuare coepit in cogitatione*, Gr. D. 64, 3. v. of-þefian.

**þegen.** III. *add*:—Geânlǽhte Lisias fîf and sixtig þûsenda fyrdendra þegena, Hml. S. 25, 363. v. efen-, hors-, húsel-, wel-þegen.

**þegnian.** III. *add*:—Swylc mæssereáf and swylce bêc and swylce húselfata swylce gê mid risnum eów þâ befæstan þenunga þenian magon, Ll. Th. ii. 404, 27.

**þegnung.** V. *add*:—Wearð ðâ seó þênung in geboren, and æfter þâm cynelic(e) gebeórscipe; and Apollonius nân ðingc ne æt, Ap. Th. 14, 14. v. cycen-, deáþ-, diácon-, eáster-, flǽsc-, mæsse-, middæg-, weorold-þegnung.

**þel.** *Add*:—Ðeáh mon gesette îsern þel ofer ðæs fŷres hróf, Sal. K. 85, 18. Se sǽ eóde inn and gefylde ꝥ scip oð þâ yfmestan þeolu (þelu, *v. l.*, þeola, *l.* 11) þæs bryrdes *intravit mare, atque ad superiores tabulas implevit navem*, Gr. D. 249, 1. [v. *N. E. D.* theal.]

**þel-brycg.** *Add*:—Be þælbrycge, swâ forþ andlang brôces, C. D. B. iii. 15, 7. Ðanne tô þelbrycge (-brige, 31), C. D. iii. 236, 28. In pontem thelbrycg, 373, 10.

**þelu.** *Add*: v. ceápealo-þelu.

**þencan.** I. *add*:—Of þâm dæge hig þôhton ꝥ hî woldon hyne ofsleán *ab illo die cogitauerunt ut interficerent eum*, Jn. 11, 53. Hwilc eówer mæg þencende (*cogitans*) ǽtéce tô his lengo âne elne?, Mt. R. 6, 27. IV. *add*:—Ne mæg þîn rîce leng stondan, bûton þû heora forwyrde þe geornor þence, Bl. H. 175, 15. V. *add*:—Ic bidde þê þæt ðû helpe ealra þǽra þe tô mînre gebedrǽdene þencað, Angl. xii. 500, 28. (c) *add*:—Oncnâw nû ꝥ hyt ðê lyt sceal fremian ꝥ þû tô þôhtest, Nic. 6, 38. VI b. *add*:—Ðǽr heó hire lícaman ræstan þencð

where she intends her body to rest, C. D. iii. 360, 3. Þâ þæt þâ ôþre geáscedon ꝥ hê hié ealle beswîcan þôhte *ceteri, cum decipi se ab Antigono singillatim viderent*, Ors. 3, 11; S. 150, 12: 5, 12; S. 242, 6: 6, 34; S. 292, 3. Ercol wæs tô gefaren, tô ðon þæt hê hié âbrecan þôhte, 3, 9; S. 132, 12: 4, 13; S. 212, 2. (b 1) *add*:—Hê þôhte his sunu tô beswîcanne, Ors. 6, 30; S. 282, 9. v. ofer-þencan.

**þencend-lic**; *adj. Reflecting, thoughtful*:—Þæt ân ymb þencendlice beón þæt wê þŷ éð oncnâwan and ongytan magon, Verc. Först. 174.

**þénda.** *Dele, and see* þebian.

**þenden.** *Add*:—Gif þisses hwæt gelimpe þenden (þonne, *v. l.*) fyrd ûte sié, Ll. Th. i. 88, 11. Þenden (þâ hwîle, *v. l.*) hê þis hwîlendlice rîce hæfde *temporalis regni gubernacula tenens*, Bd. 3, 12; Sch. 244, 19. Wit sceolon â beón mid þê þenden ðû leofast, Shrn. 63, 18. Þenden þâ tunglu hêr lŷhtaþ on ðysse deádlican worolde, 64, 29.

**-þening.** v. tô-þening.

**þennan.** I. *add*:—Þyder [h]is þened *qua tenditur*, An. Ox. 17, 53. I a. figurative, *to extend the fame of, exalt*:—þenaþ, tôbǽd *prosequitur*, i. *tractat ł laudat* (integritatem immensis rumorum laudibus *prosequitur*, Ald. 26, 8), An. Ox. 1919. v. on-þennan.

**þeód.** I a. *add*: 'a body of warriors, old and young, attached by personal service to the king . . . the comitatus mentioned by Tacitus apparently resembled the þeód in all respects,' Chadwick's Origin of the English Nation, p. 311. Cf. pp. 156, 303, 3, 4. v. þeód-guma, -wita, and cf. þeóden: dryht, dryhten:—Hêr is ǽghwylc eorl . . . mandrihtne hold, þegnas syndon geþwǽre, þeód ealgearo, druncne dryhtguman B. 1230. Wæs seó þeód tilu, 1250. v. Angel-, Wealh-þeód.

**þeódan.** *Add*: *to join as a companion, associate with, attach* oneself to a person, society, place, &c.:—Sege ûrum brôþrum ꝥ heora nǽnig hine ne þŷde tô þâm seócan breþer *nullus ex fratribus sit ad eum morientem jungat*, Gr. D. 344, 27. Utan þŷdan ûs tô þâm ûplican rîce, Verc. Först. 112, 10. v. under-þeód.

**þeóden.** *add*: v. þeód; I a.

**þeódend, es**; *m. A translator*. Cf. geþeódan *to translate*:—Ðeódend *translator*, An. Ox. 15, 6.

**-þeódend-lic.** *Add*: v. ge-þeódendlic: **-þeódgian, -þeódgung.** v. elþeódgian, -þeódgung.

**þeód-guma.** For '*A chief man . . . great man*' substitute: *A member f a* þeód (v. þeód; I a), *a retainer of a chief*. Cf. dryht-guma.

**-þeódlǽcan.** v. ge-þeódlǽcan.

**þeód-land.** *Add*:—On ðeódlonde *in regione* (*uiuorum*), Ps. Vos. 114, 9: Bl. H. 209, 17.

**þeódlic** [*con-*]*tubernalis*. v. ge-þeódlic.

**þeód-rǽden[n], e**; *f. Association, communion*:—Hê miccle þeódrǽdene nam tô þâm abbode and tô þâm gebrôðran *he frequented the society of the abbot and the brethren*, Hml. S. 33, 14. v. ge-þeódrǽden[n].

**þeód-scipe** *a people*. *Add*:—Þanan hŷ sum þeódscipe columbinam hâteð, Lch. i. 170, 14. Þeódscipum ongemang, . . . byrgum tômiddes, Dôm. L. 282.

**-þeódsumness.** v. ge-þeódsumness.

**þeód-wita.** I. *add*: cf. þeód; I a.:—Rǽdborena ł þeódwitena *iurisperitorum*, An. Ox. 8, 349. II b. *add*:—Þeódwitan *philosophi*, Scint. 106, 6.

**þeóf.** *Add*:—Man sette heora heáfda swilce ôþra ðeófa bûton ðâm portweallon on ðâm heáfodstoccum, Hml. S. 23, 76. Hê genam on his cwearterne twégen ðeófas, and sealde him ðone unlybban, Hml. Th. i. 72, 19. v. firen-, handfangen-, ûtfangene-þeóf.

**þeófend.** *Add*: cf. nîd-nîmend: **þeófet.** v. þîf.

**þeófian.** *Add*:—Ne willað gê nû leng þeófian ne yfeldôn . . . geswîcað fram ðâm þweoran þǽre þŷfðe, Gr. D. 202, 9–13.

**þeóf-sceaþa, an**; *m. A robber*; *latro*:—Sê bið þeófsceaþa, Lch. iii. 158, 12. [v. Archiv lxxix. 24, 31: Sê bið þeóf and sceaðe. *See note to the passage, and cf.*: Hê is þeóf and sceaða, Jn. 10, 1.]

**þeófung, e**; *f. Thieving*:—Sumu (*one of the devil's arrows is made*) of reáflace . . . sumu of þeófunga, Nap. 46, 22.

**þeóging.** *Add*:—Swâ hwylc[e] swâ hwǽtlíce tô þeógincge (*ad profectum*) efstað, bûton tweón hrǽdlíce hî beóð geendude, Scint. 101, 16.

**þeóh.** *Add*:—Hê wæs togen ofdûne þe þâm þeón (*per coxas*), and upp þe þâm earnum, Gr. D. 320, 19.

**þeón.** On p. 1052, *l.* 33, *for* 20 *l.* 16. I I. *add*:—Hî forð fremedon and þungon (*profecerunt*) þurh þâ wununge heora gefêrscipes, Gr. D. 205, 5. Þonon hê forð þeón sceolde *unde proficere debuit*, 200, 11. (I a) in greeting:—Fæder mîn leófa, þeóh þû an Crîste wel (*bene ualeas in Christo*), Chrd. 92, 17. (2) *add*:—Þâ þâ hê geseah hine weaxan and þeón in Godes ege *cum eum in timore Domini excrevisse videret*, Gr. D. 225, 22. II. *add*:—Ongytest þû hû swŷðe seó eádmôdnys þŷhð (þiéhð, *v. l.*) and fremað þâm þe þâ gôdan mægnu wyrcað? *perpendis quantum in exhibendis virtutibus humilitas valet?*, Gr. D. 19, 29.

**þeón** *to receive*. v. ge-þeón.

**þeorf.** *Add*:—Man mearcað mid medmicelum treówe þeorfe hlâfas (*panes crudos*), Gr. D. 87, 3.

**þeóstre.** I. *add*:—Þicce ł ðeóstru wæteru *tenebrosa aqua*, Ps. L. 17, 12.

þeóstrian. *Add:* , þreóstrian (v. āþriústraþ, Mt. R. 24, 29).
*add:*—His seón swýðe þeóstrodon, Hml. S. 31, 588.

þeóstrig. *Add:* , þýstrig :—Gif þin eáge byð mánfull, þonne byð
þin lichama eall þýstrig, Gr. D. 76, 9.

þeóstru. *Add:* v. weorold-þeóstru.

þeów. *Add:*—Hē cwæð þæt hit nā geweorþan sceolde þæt sē wǽre
leóda cyning, sē þe ǽr wæs folce þeów, Ors. 4, 6 ; S. 178, 21. v. riht-
þeów.

þeów ; adj. *Add:*—Gif man Godes (Gedes, MS.) þeúwne esne tihte,
Ll. Th. i. 42, 6. v. under-þeów.

þeówan *to press.* [V. passages here might be taken to next word, q. v.]
III. *add:*—Þa scōc ān oxa his heáfod, and mid þām horne hine þýde,
Hml. S. 31, 786. IV. *add:*—Hē stōd gynigende and þýwde mid
mūþe þ hē Martinum ābite, Hml. S. 31, 539. Wē þæt æbylgð nyton
þe wē gefremedon on þysse folcscere, þeódon bealwa wið þec, El. 403.
v. be-þeówan.

þeówan. I. *to serve.* v. Dict. II. *to make a servant to, put
at the service of, subjugate. Take here* V. *under* þeówan *to press, and
add:*—Ðone þriddan dæg hī þeówdon Marte him tō fultume. Ðone
feórðan dæg hī sealdon him tō frófre þām foresǽdan Mercurie, Sal. K.
124, 126. v. be-þeówan.

þeów-boren. *Add:* cf. ǽht-boren.

þeów-dōm. *Add:*—Gers ðeówdōmes manna *herbam seruituti
hominum,* Ps. L. 146, 8. v. [weorold-þeówdōm.]

þeówetling. *Add:*—Se mæssepreóst cōm sume dæge hām of sīðfæte,
and þā hē eóde in his hūs hē cleopode rēceleáslīce tō his þeówtlinge
(ðeówet-, *v. l. mancipio suo*) and cwæð : 'Cum, deófol, hider and unscō
mē,' Gr. D. 221, 21. Þeówetlinge (þeówit-, *v. l.*), 222, 1.

þeówian. I I a. *add:*—Ne underfēngon gē nō ðone gāst, æt ðǽm
fulluhte tō ðeówigeanne for ege *non accepistis spiritum servitutis in
timore,* Past. 263, 21. v. nīd-þeówian.

þeówincel. *Add:* cf. wilincel.

þeówing, þýwing, e ; f. *Rebuke:*—Hē his treówleásnesse mid worda
þýwungum (þreáungum, *v. l.*) fram him sylfum ādrāf *ejus a se perfidiam
dignis increpationibus repulit,* Gr. D. 238, 17.

þeów-lic. *Add:*—Se deáð is freólic and ðeówlic (*printed* deoplic), for
þan cyningas sweltaþ and eác þeówe men, Verc. Först. 103, 21.

þerran. v. þæran : -þersc. v. ge-þersc.

þerscan. I. *add:*—Hē slóh þā beran and þærsc mid telgan *ursos
ferula caedebat,* Gr. D. 229, 21. Hī ealle ongunnon heora hors mid heora
sceftum þerscan (*tundere*), 14, 28. Þā ongan heó þerscan (beátan, *v. l.
tundere*) heó sylfe mid hire fýste ge eác mid hire brādum handum, 68, 27.
II. *add:*—Gylmas on flōre tō þrexene *manipulos in area triturandos,*
An. Ox. 3433.

þerscing, e ; f. *Thrashing, beating :*—Ðerscingra (*incorrectly printed*
ðerlincgra) *verberum,* Rtl. 40, 29.

þerscold. *Add:* , e ; f.:—Eóde Martinus tō ānes mannes hūse. Þā
ætstód hē fǽrlīce ætforan þām þrexwolde, Hml. S. 31, 529. Hī ne
mihton þone fōt onstyrian ofer þā þyrxwolde þǽre stōwe (*extra loci
limen*), Gr. D. 167, 27.

þes. *Add:* acc. *f. sing., n. pl.* þās, þǽs. I I. *add:*—Ǽr hē
on þǽs earfoðnesse cōm hē ūre wæs wealdend, Bl. H. 243, 18. ¶ where
the word has much the same force as the definite article with common
nouns and might be omitted with proper :—Hefe ūp ðīne stefne suā ðes
bīme *quasi tuba exalta vocem tuam,* Past. 91, 20. Þe ðæm wæs swīðe
wel gecweden ðurh ðone wītgan tō ðǽre byrig ðe Sidon hātte, sió stōd bi
ðǽre sǽ : 'Ðiós sǽ cwið ðæt ðū ðīn scamige, Sidon' *unde bene per
prophetam dicitur :* 'Erubesce Sidon, ait mare,' 409, 33. Nū scýneð þes
mōna under wolcnum, Fin. 7. Hē þrowade on þisse Breotone martyrdōm,
Shrn. 93, 28. Ǽghwanon of eallum þissum bīfylcum *undique de cunctis
prope prouinciis,* Bd. 3, 14 ; Sch. 256, 14. I 3. *add:*—Þā heofencundan þing þe sint gecynde, næs þǽs eorþlican, Bt. 14, 1 ; F. 42, 1 (cf.
I I a). Þǽs lǽnan gesǽlþa, 20 ; F. 72, 15. Þonne hió þǽs lǽnan lufað
and wundrað eorþlicu þing, Met. 20, 223. II I b. *add:*—Sē ðe
on muneclicere drohtnunge gyrnð ðǽra ðinga ðe hē on woruldlicere
drohtnunge næfde, būton twýn him geneálǽhð Giezi, and þ þ hē on
lichaman gedrowode, þæt ðrowað þes on his sāwle, Hml. Th. i. 400, 5.
(1 b β) where in a series each in turn is pointed out :—Seó forme . . .
Ðonne seó oþer . . . ; þeós swā hwæt swā heó gesyhð . . . ; þonne is seó
þridde . . ., swā hwæt swā þeós gesyhð . . ., Lch. i. 242, 19–26. Þās
and þās and þās beóð leóriende, Gr. D. 300, 11. II. ¶ *add:*—
Fægere word þis syndon and gehāt *pulchra sunt uerba et promissa,* Bd. 1,
25 ; Sch. 54, 19. v. hēr ; I b.

þicce. II. *add:*—Þicce wæteru *tenebrosa aqua,* Ps. L. 17, 12. III a.
*add:*—Þǽr ārās þicce æcer and manigfeald *seges multa surrexit,* Gr. D.
240, 3. v. brīw-, un-þicce.

þiece ; adv. *Add:*—Ān wǽhrægel swýðe þicce gewefen, Vis. Lfc. 70.

þicgan. II. *add:*—Þonne mon þā hlāfas wrāt tō þicgeanne *cum
panes per conuivia frangerentur,* Ors. 5, 10 ; S. 234, 5. v. oþ-þicgan ;
ā-þegen.

þider. I. *add:*—Ðā hēt hē hī bīdan on þām eálande, . . . and hē ðider

heora þearfe forgeaf, Bd. 1, 25 ; Sch. 53, 2. Hit gebyreð rihtor intō West-
Sexan ; þyder hý scylan gafol syllan, Ll. Th. i. 356, 19. II. *add:*—
Far nū þider þe (swā hwider swā, *v. l.*) þū wille, Gr. D. 25, 1.

þideres. *Add:*—Hider and þyderes *ultro citroque,* i. *hinc et inde,* An.
Ox. 1040.

þider-weard. *Add:* where a verb of motion is implied :—Geseah hē
olfendas þyderweard *vidit camelos venientes procul,* Gen. 24, 63. Ðā þā
hē þāgīta wæs feorron þyderweard *adhuc longe positum,* Gr. D. 37, 15.

þiderweardes. *Add:*—Þā sæt se Godes wer feorron lōciende on þone
þe þiderweardes wæs gangende (behealdende þone cumendan Riggo, *v. l.*)
*vir Dei sedebat eum venientem conspiciens,* Gr. D. 131, 25.

þife-þorn. *Add:*—Slīt mid þefoþorne (cf. þorn, 106, 5), Lch. ii. 52, 8.

þiffe. *Add:*—þyffe, An. Ox. 104, *where see note.* Cf. þefele.

þīfþ. I. *add:*—Godes feós ðeófð *sacrilegium,* Wülck. Gl. 116, 28.
Wǽron in gangende þeófas in þone wyrtgeard, ac onwendum heora mōde
fram þǽre þýfðe (þeóf(e)tte, *v. l.*) . . . hī ādelfon . . . Hē cwæð : 'Ne
willað gē nū leng þeófian . . . geswīcað fram dām þweoran þǽre þýfðe
(þeof(e)te, *v. l. furti*) . . . þā wæs swā geworden . . . þ hī æfter þon
cyrdon būton þeófte (þeófete, *v. l.*),' Gr. D. 202, 1–16.

þigen. II. *add:*—þæs hālgan hūsles þigene underfōn, Angl. xii. 514.
6. Ofet hine fēdde, and wudehunig, and ōðre wāclice ðigena, Hml. Th.
i. 352, 8. v. ātor-þigen (Lch. i. 4, 5).

þiht. *Add:* [v. *N. E. D.* thight.]

þiling. *Add:*—Ofer þǽre þylinge (þilincge, *v. l.*) unwǽrlīce forlǽten
(*capisterium*) *super mensam incaute derelictum,* Gr. D. 97, 4. Of þām
cipe wǽron þā næglas forlorene and þā þylinge (ðilinge, *v. l.*) tōslægene,
248, 24.

þindan. *Add:* v. for-þindan.

þing. I 1. *add:*—Hwæt is ðienga (ðinga, *v. l.*) ðe bieterre sié . . .
ðonne se anda?, Past. 165, 1. (1 a a) *add:*—Þē biddað manega þeóda þines
þinges tō lǽne and þū ne bitst nānne *foenerabis gentibus multis, et ipse
a nullo foenus accipiens,* Deut. 28, 12. Se crīstena man cwæð þæt hē
hæfde his ðing (cf. ýddysce, 27.) and hine sylfne betǽht Benedicte (cf. þ
hē befæste his ǽhte Benedicte, Gr. D. 163, 7), Hml. Th. ii. 180, 19.
(2) *add:*—Ðā sǽde ic þ ic his þinga feola ne cūþe *respondi ignorare me
quid faceret Alexander,* Nar. 18, 24. (5) *add:*—Man æt mē ofgān
wile þ ic mid rihtan þingon begyten hæfde, Hml. S. 23, 600. (9)
*add:*—Hī wundrodon hwæt þ þing (hwæt þ þinga, *v. l.*) wǽre þ hē swā
tōswollen heáfod hæfde, Gr. D. 22, 18. Nū wylle wē for iungra manna
þingon (*vel lufe*) furðor ūre sprǽce aþenian, Angl. viii. 309, 25. For
huntnoþes þingon, Chr. 1065 ; P. 190, 28. (13) *add:*—Swā þæt nānra
þinga mid ǽnigre efestinge mannes hī mihton beón undōn, Gr. D. 164,
15. 'Ne fǽrst þū nǽnigra þinga (nā tō þæs hwōn, *v. l. nullatenus*) fram
mē' . . . Hē ne mihte þ wīf nǽnigra þinga (þurh nān þing, *v. l. nequaquam*)
forbūgan, 17, 23–32 : 151, 5. (14) *add:*—Hē ācwealde siððan ælc þincg
þæs cynnes, Hml. S. 18, 367. ¶ adverbial phrase :—Þām man nān
þingc ne wandode, Hml. S. 23, 71 : Hml. A. 103, 47. v. ār-, gedwol-,
hǽmed-, mete-, nā-, nīd-, stæl-, wīf-þing ; ge-þinge, huru-þinga.

þingian. *Add:* v. un-þingod : -þingþ. v. ge-þingþ.

þingung. *Add:*—From alre nēweste geleáfulra sýn heó āsceádene and
āsyndrade nymðe heó hit hēr mid þingonge bōte gebēte, C. D. i. 114, 27.
v. ed-, eft-þingung.

þirran. *Add:* v. þæran : -þisa. v. brim-, wæter-þisa : þistel-twige.
*Add:*—þisæltunga *cardella,* Hpt. 33, 241, 51 : þistra. For *conjuncta* l.
*conjuncla.*

þixl. *Add:*—Hit is mycel nēdþearf þ hié man forspille, and mid
īrenum þislum and ordum hié man sleá, Bl. H. 189, 30.

þoden. *Add:*—þ feallende treów wende þā ongeán swilce hit sum
fǽrlic þoden þydde underbæc, Hml. S. 31, 416. Þ scip se þoden and se
storm on sǽ ādrīfeð feorr, Gr. D. 5, 28. Ðā fǽringa wæs geworden
þoden of heofonum *tunc repente turbo caelitus factus est,* 42, 5. Syndon
fram þodene (*turbine*) þā weallas tōlýsede, 134, 7. Mid stormum and
lēgetslihtum, mid þodenum (*turbinibus*) and eorðstyrungum geswenced,
133, 30.

-þofta. v. brý-tofta [= brýd-þofta] : -þōhtung. v. ge-þōhtung :
þolemōdness. *Add:* v. un-þolemōdness.

þolian. I. *add:*—Gyf hē hys sāwle forwyrd þolað *si animae suae detrimentum patiatur,* Mt. 16, 26. Eádige synt þā ðe ēhtnysse þoliað, 5,
10. Ān wīf þe þolode twelf geár, 9, 20. I c. where the subject of the
verb is a thing :—Heofena rīce þolað neád, Mt. 11, 12. III. *add:*—
III α. *to be without* what is unpleasant or evil :—Heora reáfes gyrla swilc
beó þ hē þolige ǽlces ýdeles *uanitatis occasione careat,* Chrd. 65, 13.
þ nǽfre þǽr (*in hell*) ne þoliað þæs wītes þā þe nǽfre in þisum life willað
þolian þǽre synne and hyre būtan beón *ut numquam careant supplicio,
qui in hac vita numquam voluerunt carere peccato,* Gr. D. 335, 6–8.

þoll. *Add:* v. wægn-þoll.

þolung, e ; f. *Passion:*—Þolunga (*passiones*) and leahtras līchaman
ūre gif mid hungre fæstena beóð āhlænsude, Scint. 57, 11. Þā sāwle of-
feallan mid þolungum *animam obruere passionibus,* 55, 15.

þoot, Txts. 64, 444. v. wōþ.

þōr. *Add:*—Ðes Iouis is ārwurðost ealra þǽra goda ðe ðā hǽðenan

hæfdon on heora gedwylde, and hê hâtte Ðôr betwux sumum þeódum; ðane ðâ Deniscan leóde lufað swíðost, Sal. K. 122, 51. Se deófol hine þâm hâlgan æteówde on þæra hæþenra goda híwe, hwîlon on Ioues híwe, þe is gehâten þôr, Hml. S. 31, 714.

**þorf-fæst.** *Add :* v. un-þorffæst.

**þorfnian** (?) *to suffer lack* of (*gen.*) :—Ne ondrǽd ðû ðê deáð tô swîðe . . . Ne forgit ðû hine ðeáh ealne weg, ðý lǽs ðû þolie (þornige, *v. l.,* v. Verc. Först. 174) ðæs écan lîfes, Prov. K. 17. v. þorfa.

**þorian.** The gloss ' *dosmui* thorie' may be explained as ðos μοι dô mê. v. Angl. xxi. 238 n.

**þorn.** *Add :*—Man sceall âweg âdelfan mid þorne, Lch. ii. 106, 5. Of hafucðorne tô ðan langan þorne at Ichenilde wege ; ðæt swâ tô ðan þriddan þorne æt wîrhangran ; of ðâm þorne tô ðâm feórðan þorne on wrangan hylle foreweardre stent ; ðæt swâ forð tô ðâm fîftan þorne ; tô þâm ele-beáme, C. D. v. 297, 16-20. v. hege-þorn.

**þornian.** v. þorfnian : **þorniht.** *l.* þorniht[e].

**þracian.** *v. to fear* :—Mildheortnes his þâm þraciendum hine *misericordia timentibus eum,* Ps. Rdr. 296, 50.

**þracung.** v. on-þracung.

**þræc-full** (?) ; *adj. Strong, valiant* :—Onhruron on mê þreafulle (þrecfulle ?) *inruerunt in me fortes,* Ps. Rdr. 58, 4.

-**þræclic.** v. ǽ- (Ps. Rdr. 95, 4), on-þræclic : **þræc-wîg.** *l.* þræc-wîg.

**þrǽd.** *Add :*—Swâ seolcen ðrǽd *ceu serica pensa,* An. Ox. 23, 73. Traed *filu,* 53, 31.

-**þræf.** v. ge-þræf : -**þræst.** v. ende-þræst.

**þræstness,** e ; *f. Contrition* :—Hê oð þone dæg his deáðes on micelre þræstnesse wunode *usque ad diem mortis in contritione duravit,* Bd. 5, 12 ; Sch. 615, 3. v. ge-þræstness.

**þrafian.** *Add :* I a. *to press* for (*æfter*) something, *exact, require* :—Nabbon hî æfter mâran tô þrafianne þonne heora neód behôfað *non plus exigant quam oportet,* Chrd. 12, 10. v. ge-þrafian.

-**þrafu.** v. ge-þrafu.

**þrâg.** III. *add :*—þæt þâ stôd wintra þrâge, Cht. Crw. 19, 5. v. hwîl-, wôd-þrâg.

**þrâg-lic ;** *adj. Lasting a long time* [:—Byð swýðe mycele unge-ðwærnysse and ðrâhlice wîten on manna bearnen, Verc. Först. 175.]

**preá.** *Dele* þreás (?), *and in l.* 50 *for* þreás *l.* dreámas. v. Bl. N. p. 2. *Add :* v. wǽg-þreá.

**þreafulle,** Ps. Rdr. 58, 4. v. þræc-full.

**preágan.** I. *add :* (1) the object a person :—Ne ðreáð ûs nân monn, ne furðum âne worde ne tǽld *ne verbi quidem ab aliquo invectione lacera-mur,* Past. 117, 21. Ðonne ðâ ealdermenu ðreágeað ðâ scyldgan *cum delinquentes subditos praepositi corrigunt,* 12. Ðreáddon *increpuerunt,* Ps. L. 15, 7. Ðâ ðe him ondrǽdað ðæt hié men for hira scyldum ðreágen *corripere culpas metuunt,* Past. 91, 9 : 195, 25. Miehtig tô ðreánne (*arguere*), 91, 15. (2) the object a thing (fault, sin, &c.) :—Mon hiera scylda ne ðreáð, Past. 129, 12. I a. *to threaten,* cf. þreágung ; II :—For ðæm ryhtan edleáne Dryhten ðreáde ðurh ðone wîtgan *quod videlicet ex ira justae retributionis per prophetam Domi-nus minatur,* Past. 133, 5. IV. *to press, urge* :—Hê ongan his geféran swîðe þreágan (*urgere*) þ hî scoldon on þâ tîd ût faran, Gr. D. 38, 12. Gif hî synd þreáde mid frêcnesse deáþes *si mortis periculo urgetur,* Bd. 1, 27 ; Sch. 79, 14.

**þreágung.** II. *add :* cf. þreágan ; I a. III. *add :*—Gif tô ðâm yflum cymþ rêþu wyrd, þonne cymþ hê tô edleáne his yfla, oððe tô þreunge and tô lâre þ hê eft swâ ne dô *aspera fortuna puniendi corrigendi ve improbos causa defertur,* Bt. 40, 1 ; F. 236, 8.

**þreál.** I. *add :*—Ne âteóra þû for Drihtnes þreále (cf. *deficias cum ab Domino corriperis,* Prov. 3, 11), Hml. S. 33, 217. II. *add :*—Hê gehêt him Godes yrre and yfele þreála, Hml. S. 31, 803.

**preápian.** *Add :*—Se ancra angan þreápian swîðe ðone deófol, Sal. K. 84, 4.

**preát.** *Add :* v. wîg-þreát.

**preátian.** *Add : p.* þreátte (*in Rushworth Gospels*). I 1. *add :*—Hê him âsǽde hwylc neádung þæs gafoles hine þreátode *quae eum urgeret debiti necessitas indicavit,* Gr. D. 157, 28. (2) *add :* (a) with clause :—Se câsere hine ðreátode ðæt hê Crîste wiðsôce, Shrn. 71, 32. II. *add :*—Sió mengu ðreáttan hiæ *turba increpabat eos,* Mt. R. 20, 31.

**preátness,** e ; *f. Affliction, tribulation* :—Hungor and sweorda gefeoht bið, and mycel þreátnes geworden bið, and manigra folca gefehta beóð *erunt fames et bellum, gladius . . . plurimae dissensiones in populo,* Verc. Först. 117, 2.

**preax.** *Add :*—Se fôtcops âwende wundorlîce tô þrexe and eall tô dûste þurh Drihtnes mihte, Hml. S. 35, 150.

-**preclic.** v. -þræclic.

[**þrefe** *a measure of corn, a thrave* [v. *N. E. D.* s. v.] :—Swâ man ǽr simle dide tióþunge æt ǽlcere sylh ân fóðer cornes þe eahte þreues cornes on wêron, C. D. B. iii. 367, 24. [From Scandinavian. *Icel.* þrefi.]]

**preodian.** I. *add :*—þâ þâ hê geseah þ hî þrydodon ymb his deáð *cum mortem illius deliberasse eos cerneret,* Gr. D. 253, 12. þâ þrydedon

(ðreodedon, *v. l.*) his freónd and þôhton þ his lîchama sceolde beón âlegd in Prenestino þâm wege *deliberatum fuerat, ut Praenestina via ejus corpus poni debuisset,* 297, 15.

**prêwel-spinl** *a crisping-pin* :—þrêwelspinle (þrǽwel- ? þrâwing- ?) *calamistro,* An. Ox. 23, 26.

**prexan.** v. þerscan.

**prí.** *Add :* as multiplicative, *three times* :—Se earma man wile drincan ðreó swâ feala, ge feówer swâ feala swâ his neád wǽre, Hml. A. 145, 29.

**pridda.** I. *add :* one in every three :—Ælfstân abb begeat . . . þ him geweard se þridda penig of þǽre tolne on Sandwîc, C. D. iv. 56, 30.

**prilig.** *Add :*—Wæs þǽr ân þrilig wâhrægel and swýðe þicce gewefen, Vis. Lfc. 69.

**pringan.** *In l.* 9 *the MS. has* þryme (*not* þryme). III. *add :*—Gûðcyst on þrang, Exod. 343.

**pringend.** v. ymb-þringend.

**prin-lic ;** *adj. Threefold* :—On ðone (God) wê sceolon gelýfan þrynlicne on hâdum and ânlicne on spêdum, Nap. 63 : cf. þrinen.

**prinna.** *Add :* [v. *N. E. D.* thrin.] : **prist-lǽcan.** *Add :* v. â-þrist-lǽcan.

**pristlǽcness.** *Add :*—Tô forgifnesse for þǽre þristlǽcnesse (*praesum-tione*), Gr. D. 341, 37.

**prist-lic ;** *adj. Bold* :—Se deáð is þristlic, Verc. Först. 104, 1.

**pristlíce.** *Add :*—Ne dear ic nâht þristelîce (þrîsð-, *v. l., temere*) be þissere wîsan reccan, Gr. D. 332, 12.

**pristness.** *Add :*—On ælcre preóstgesamnunge is ælc þrýstnes (*presumptionis occasio*) forboden, Chrd. 45, 29.

**pritig.** *Add :* as abstract number :—Tele þû . . . oð þ þû cume tô þrittiga, Lch. iii. 228, 1. Fîf sîðon seofon beóð fîf and þrittig, Angl. viii. 302, 48.

**prostle.** *Add :*—Sum swýþe sweart and lytel fugel, sê is on folcisc þrostle gehâten *nigra þarvaque avis, quae vulgo merula nominatur,* Gr. D. 100, 19.

**prowend,** es ; *m. A martyr.* See next word.

**prowend-hâd,** es ; *m. Martyrdom* :—þæs þrowendhâdes seó ge-earnung *martyrii meritum,* Gr. D. 231, 8.

**prowend-lic ;** *adj. Passive* :—þrowendlic deáð *apoplexia, passio similis paralisi,* Hpt. 31, 15, 410. v. prowiend-lic.

**prowendlic-ness.** v. un-þrowendlicness.

**prower-hâd,** es ; *m. Martyrdom* :—þæs þrowerhâdes *martyrii,* Gr. D. 231, 8 n. Underfôn þone þrowerhâd *martyrium subire,* 233, 20.

**prowet-hâd** (þrowot-), es ; *m. Martyrdom* :—Hê onfêngon þâ leán þæs þrowethâdes (*martyrii*) . . . underfôn þone þrowothâd (*martyrium*), Gr. D. 233, 14-20.

**prowian.** II 2. *add :* (a) *to suffer pain, punishment,* &c. :—Suâ se lîchoma suíður ûtan ðrowað, suâ ðæt môd suíður innan hreówsað ðæs unnyttes ðe hê ǽr dyde, Past. 259, 22. Be ðæm welegan ðe gesǽd is ðætte on hâra þrowude, 391, 14. Him sculan eglan þâ ðerra monna brocu suelce hê efnsuîðe him ðrowige, 75, 10. (β) *to suffer martyrdum* :—Hêr Iacôbus frater Dñi þrowode, Chr. 62 ; P. 8, 1. Hêr Petrus and Paulus þrowodon, 69 ; P. 8, 3.

**prowung.** IV. *passion, strong feeling* :—þ ic þe mâ emwyrhtena on þǽre þrowunge mînes wynlustes hæfde, Hml. S. 23 b, 359. v. efen-, mid-þrowing.

**prût.** v. fisc-þrút.

**prútian.** *Add :*—Se ylca Riggo þus gewlitegod mid þâm reáfum stôp on þ mynster þrútiende swýðe, Gr. D. 131, 22.

**pryan.** v. þrýn : **pryccan.** *Add :* v. for-þryccan : -**pryc[c]edness.** v. for-, of-þryc[c]edness : **prycness.** *Add :* v. for-þrycness.

**prym-lic ;** *adj.* :—Sê wæs Iouis gehâten, hetol and þrymlic, Sal. K. 121, 24. v. cyne-þrymlic.

**prymm.** IV. *add :*—Betwyx þâm þrymme þǽre môdignysse and þǽre swelgende þǽre âswundennysse *inter aciem superbiç et uoraginem desidiç,* Chrd. 65, 19. Hwý noldest ðû biddan þê ârfulle þingeras wið þone ælmihtigan þrym þǽre hâlgan þrynnesse and æt þǽre sôðan ânnesse ?, Wlfst. 240, 10. v. blâford-, mann-þrymm.

-**prymme ;** *adj.* v. heáh-þrymme.

**prym-ness.** *Add :*—þrimnesse Fæder (cf. Fæder ormǽttre mægn-þrymnysse, Ps. L. p. 247, 7), Solil. H. 9, 4.

**prym-setl.** *Add :*—þrymsetl *thronus,* Ps. L. 88, 38. þremsetl, 30. -**prýn.** v. â-, ge-þrýn, -þrý(a)n : -**prýpfullian.** v. ge-þrýpfullian : **prýpian.** *Dele, and see* ge-þrýped.

**pû.** I. *add :*—Hê ne meahte nâ his forwyrcan, and tû hine hête ðâ flîman . . . ic wæs æt Cippanhomme mit tê, Cht. Th. 173, 5-10.

-**puhtsum.** v. ge-þuhtsum : -**pun.** v. ge-þun : -**punden-lîce.** -ness. v. tô-þundenlîce, -ness : -**pungen.** *Add :* v. wel-þungen : **pungenness.** *Add :* v. full-þungenness : -**puniende.** v. tô-þuniende.

**punian.** *Add :* v. on-þunian (?).

**punor.** I. *add :*—Seó lîget ðæt deófol bærneð . . . and se ðunor hit ðrysceð mid ðǽre fýrenan scyte, Sal. K. 148, 4-6. [For prognostics from thunder v. Archiv cxx. 45, sqq.] v. norþ-þunor.

**punor-râd.** *Add :*—Seó þunorâd (se ðunorrâd, *v. l.*) ofslôh ealle þâ nǽd-

ran *idem tonitrus omnes serpentes interemit*, Gr. D. 208, 22. Mycel mægn līgetslehta and þunurrāde (þunerāda, *v. l.*) *magna coruscationis et tonitrui virtus*, 167, 24. Mid þǣre þunorāde . . . betwyh þām līgetslehtum and þunorrādum (þunerādum, *v. l.*) *cum tonitruo . . . inter coruscos et tonitruos*, 168, 4–8.

**þunrian.** *Add :*—Gif hit þunrað on ǣfentīde, hit getācnað ācennednysse sumes miceles *si tonitruauerit hora uespertina, significat natiuitatem cuiusdam magni*, Archiv cxx. 50, 1 [*see* þunor]. v. ge-þunrian.

**þūr.** *Add :*—Dæg þūres *die Iouis*, Archiv cxx. 297, 27. On þurres dæge, Verc. Först. 123, 20.

**þurh.** **A. I** 2. *add :*—Nān man ne mihte faran þurh þone weg, Mt. 8, 28. **III** 3. *add :*—Done gē ofslōgon and āhēngon ðurh eówer gedeaht, Past. 443, 8 : 435, 26. (9) *add :*—Swā hwelc swā on ǣnigre frēcennesse mīnne naman þurh þē gecēgð, ic hine gehēre, Shrn. 73, 10. **B. I** 2. *add :*—Nǣnig mæhte faran þurh wæge þǣm (*per viam illam*), Mt. R. 8, 28. **C.** *add :*—Heó heóld on hyre þeáwum hālige drohtnunge þurh mōdes līþnesse and mycelre eádmōdnesse, and þurh hālige mægnu þām Hǣlende gecwēmde, Hml. S. 2, 95–97. [*For a special article on* þurh *see* Angl. xxxiv. 462–497.]

**þurh-beorht.** *Add :*—Of þurhbeorhtre (i. meolchwȳttre) whītnysse *lacteo candore*, Germ. 389, 70.

**þurh-faran.** **IV.** *add :*—For þām þe hī nūgȳta fullfremedlīce ne þurhfarað his dīgolnyssa *quia enim secreta ejus adhuc perfecte non penetrant*, Gr. D. 138, 29.

**þurh-fēran.** **II.** *add : to penetrate* with the mind :—Þes Godes wer þurhfērde (þurheóde, *v. l.*) þā dīglan þing þǣre godcundnesse *este vir Dei divinitatis secreta penetravit*, Gr. D. 136, 4.

**þurh-gān.** **III.** *add :*—Þurheóde *penetravit*, Gr. D. 136, 4. *See preceding word.*

**þurh-hǣlig.** *l.* -hālig, *and for* Wanl. . . . 4 *substitute* Chrd. 116, 29.

**þurh-holian** *to pierce :*—Þurhhol[od] (*a* d *is written over the* h. v. þurh-delfan) *confossa*, i. *transfixa* (*mucrone*), An. Ox. 4035.

**þurh-leóran.** *Add :* -leórian (?). **I.** *to pass through :*—Þurhleóreð *pertransiit*, Ps. Vos. 102, 15. Ðurhleórað *pertransibunt*, 103, 10. Þurhleórde *pertransivit*, 123, 5. **II.** *to penetrate :*—Hī ne þurhleóriað (-leornað, *v. l.* (*very indistinct*)) his deógolnysse *secreta ejus non penetrant*, Gr. D. 138, 29.

**þurh-leornian** *to learn thoroughly :*—Þes Godes wer þurhleornode (*penetravit*) þā deóglan þing þǣre godcundnysse, Gr. D. 136, 4. *See* þurh-fēran, *and* þurh-leóran ; **II.**

**þurh-sceótendlic.** v. un-þurhsceótendlic.

**þurh-seón.** *Add :*—Hē þurhseah swā þone preóst for ðon geseaidne deófle, gif hē gedyrstlǣhte þ hē underfēngce ðone hālgan sācerdhād *perspexit hunc clericum idcirco diabolo traditum, ne ad sacrum ordinem auderet accedere*, Gr. D. 136, 6.

**þurh-sīne** ; *adj. Transparent, limpid :*—Þurhsȳne *lymphida*, An. Ox. 23, 35.

**þurh-sleán.** **I.** *add : to strike and pierce, wound ;* percutere :—Wearð hē mid þæs ealdan feóndes yfelnysse þurhslagen (*percussus*), Gr. D. 117, 7. Þurhslægene (*percussi*) mid þǣre ādle þæs mycclan līces, 207, 16.

**þurh-smirwan, -smirian** *to anoint thoroughly :*—Hē mid ele and mid crīsman mē þurhsmyrede, Wlfst. 229, 3.

**þurh-smūgan.** **I.** *add :*—Þe lǣs heora gylta āttru tō manige þurhsmūgon *ne per plures eorum dira serpant contagia*, Chrd. 62, 7.

**þurh-standan** *to persist, continue :*—Þone ǣtran dæg mid his nihte on bēnum hē þurhstōd *secundo die cum nocte subsequenti in precibus perstitit*, Gr. D. 200, 8.

**þurh-strang** ; *adj. Very strong :*—Ðurhstrange *praeualidas*, An. Ox. 50, 25.

**þurh-teón.** *Add :* v. un-þurhtogen.

**þurh-unrōt** ; *adj. Very sad :*—Þā þurhunrōtan wīn *pretristia musta* (*propinas tuis praetristia musta* (cf. *potasti nos vino compunctionis*, Ps. 59, 5), Vit. Cuth. poet. 37, 9), Hpt. 33, 238, 11.

**þurh-wacian** ; *p.* ode *To continue watching, maintain a vigil :*—Hē nǣfre gōdes weorces ne āblon, ah hē hwīlum ealle niht þurhwacode on hālgum gebedum, Bl. H. 227, 7. v. þurh-wacol, -wæccan.

**þurh-wacol.** *Add :*—Gestōd hē þurhwacol æt ānum eáhþȳrle, Gr. D. 170, 27.

**þurh-wæccan** *to continue watching, maintain a vigil :*—Hē wæs ðerhwæccende *erat pernoctans*, Lk. L. 6, 12. v. þurh-wacian.

**þurh-wrecan.** *Add :*—Būtan hwæs heorte sié mid deófles strǣle þurhwrecen, Verc. Först. 109, 8.

**þurh-wuneness, e ; *f. Perseverance :*—Seó þurhwunenes heó is mægen þæs gōdan weorces *virtus boni operis perseverantia est*, Archiv cxxii. 260, 9.

**þurh-wunian.** **II.** *add :*—Se wela and se anweald nāuht þurhwuniendes heora wealdendum sellan nā magon, Bt. 27, 4 ; F. 100, 22.

**þurh-wunol** ; *adj. Continual, perpetual :*—Þām leófestan biscope an Crīstes naman ic sende þurwunule (*perpetuam*) grētinge, Chrd. 92, 17.

**þurh-wunung.** **II.** *add :*—Be þurhwununge. Ne bið nō þām

crīstenan menn sceáwod se fruma þæs gōdan weorces, ac se ende ; for þon þe ǣlcum men bið dēmed be his þām endenȳstan weorcum, Archiv cxxii. 260, 1.

**þūsend.** **III.** *add :*—Āgefen Alchhere and Aeðelwold hire twā ðūsenda, and fōn him tō ðǣm londe, C. D. i. 310, 24. Ic gean āu þūsend werð fen . . . þ healfe þūsend fen, iv. 59, 17–23. [v. *N. E. D.* thousand ; 3.]

**þūsend-ealdor** (?) *a captain of a thousand men :*—Þūsendealdorrm (*the* o *and* r *are on erasures, and between them a letter has been scratched out.* Cf. þūsendealdremen, Hpt. Gl. 515, 76. *Perhaps the gloss stands for* þūsendealdre, þūsendmen (v. þūsend-mann)) *chiliarcho*, An. Ox. 4747.

**þūsend-ealdormann.** *See preceding word.*

**þūsend-feald.** *In the first passage* þūsendfealdgetæl *should be read, as after* þæt *the declension would be definite and the form would be* þūsendfealde. Cf. hundfeald-getel. *Add :*—Þūsendfealde *milleni*, Ælfc. Gr. Z. 284, 15.

**þūsendfeald-getæl** (-tel). *See preceding word.*

**þūsend-getæl.** *Add :*—Millesimus sē ðe bið æftemyst on ðūsendgetele, Ælfc. Gr. Z. 284, 4.

-þwægenness. v. on-þwægenness.

**þwǣle.** *Dele :* ' (*or* -a ? ; *m.*),' *and add :*—Thuǣlę *infula*, An. Ox. 53, 26.

**þwǣre.** *Dele the passage at* Shrn. 81, 17, *and add :*—Þīne freónd þū nǣfst þē swā gemōde and swā þwēre swā swā þū woldest, Solil. H. 34, 3. v. mōd-, un-þwǣre.

-þwǣrian. *Add :* v. gemann-, geun-þwǣrian.

-þwǣrlic, -līce. v. ge-þwǣrlic, -līce : þwǣrlǣcan. *Add :*—Hwǣrlǣhte *pateretur*, i. *consentiret*, An. Ox. 2525 : þwǣrness. *Add :* v. mann-, mōd-, un-þwǣrness : -þwǣrung. v. ge-þwǣrung.

**þwang.** **I.** *a strip of skin :*—Besieh ǣnne þwang (*corrigiam*) þām biscope fram þām hneccan oþ þone hōh, Gr. D. 198, 4. **II.** *a shoelace :*—' Cum and unscō mē' . . . þā þwangas þāra scōna ongunnon heom sylfe tōslūpan, Gr. D. 221, 22.

**þweál.** *Add :* v. oft-þweál : **þweán.** *Add :* v. on-þweán ; un-þwagen.

**þweora.** *Add :*—Wickedness, depravity, perversity. v. þweorh ; **IV.** :—Geswīcað fram ðām þweoran þǣre þȳfðe *a furti pravitate cessate*, Gr. D. 202, 12. Hē wæs gecyrred fram þām þweoran (*pravitate*) þæs Arrianiscan gedwolan, 239, 18.

**þweores.** **III.** *add :*—Hē bið gehāten ðæs deófles bearn þe wyle ǣfre ðwyres, Hex. 44, 14.

**þweorh.** **II.** *add :*—Gif hē ǣr þweores windes bǣtte, Bt. 41, 3 ; F. 250, 16. **IV.** *add : insolent :*—Mid þhwyrum *proteruo*, An. Ox. 1160. Mid hwyrum *obliquo* (*zelo*), 2770.

**þweorian.** *Add : to be different :*—Hī ne sceoldon þone gyrlan him tō teón, þā hwīle þe hī þurh þā drohtnunge þwuredon *illorum habitum usurpare non debent a quorum proposito distant*, Chrd. 63, 23. v. be-þweorian.

**þweor-lic.** **II.** *add :*—Hwyrlice, wiþerwyrde *contrariam*, An. Ox. 2751. **III.** *add :*—Hwirlicere prūtunge *proteruo fastu*, An Ox. 1160. Þā gesceafta ðe sind þwyrlice geðūhte, hī sind tō wrace gesceapene yfeldǣdum *the creatures that seem evil, they are created for the punishment of evil-doers*, Hml. Th. i. 102, 3.

**þweorlīce.** **III.** *add : insolently :*—Hē smeáde mid tōþundenum mōde hū hē þwyrlīcost (*proterva mente*) sceolde him wiþ sprecan, Gr. D. 37, 12.

-þweorod. v. ge-þweorod : **þwinan.** *Add :* v. ā-þwīnan : -þwin[g]. v. ge-þwin : -þwinglod. v. ge-þwinglod : **þwit.** v. ge-þwit : **þwītan.** *In l.* 6 *add after* ðweoton : (ðwiton, *v. l.*, Bd. Sch. 270, 23) : -þwyrftan. v. ge-þwyrftan : **þyccyl.** v. þȳ-dǣges. *l.* -dǣges.

**þyddan.** *Add :*—Þæt feallende treów wende þā ongeán swilce hit sum fǣrlic þoden þydde underbæc, Hml. S. 31, 416. Þā scōc ān oxa his heáfod and mid þām horne hine þydde (þudde, *v. l.* later date), 31, 786. v. ā-þyddan.

**þȳfel.** *Add :*—Hī eódon þā sēcende tō þām wuda, sēcude gehwǣr geond þȳfelas and brēmelas, Hml. S. 32, 143.

**þyldian.** [Cf. *O. H. Ger.* dulten *tolerare*.] v. for-þyldian.

**þyldigian.** *Add :*—Ic ðyldgode *sustinui*, Ps. Rdr. 129, 4.

-þyldiglic, -þyldiglīce. v. ge-þyldiglic, -þyldiglīce : -þyldlicness. v. un-þyldicness.

**þyle.** *Add :* See Vigfusson and Powell's Corpus Poeticum Boreale, vol. i, p. 24.

-þyll. v. ge-þyll : -þylman. *Add :* v. ge-, of-þylman.

**þyncan.** **I** 1. *add :*—Hit þūhte him feáwa daga *videbantur illi pauci dies*, Gr. D. 29, 20.

**þync[u].** *Add :*—Þinþe, wurþscipe *infula*, An. Ox. 2200.

**þyng.** v. ge-þyng[o].

**þynne.** **II** 2. *add :*—Þā fatu þā þe hē geát ǣr swȳðe lytelne dǣl þæs þynnestan wǣtan *vasa in quibus tenuissimum liquorem infuderat*, Gr. D. 59, 15.

-þyre. v. ge-þyre : **þyrel.** *Add :* þȳrel (?). v. swāt-, wāg-þyrel.

þyrelian. _Add:_—Þyrlie _obunco_, An. Ox. 18 b, 66.
-þyrlic. v. samod-þyrlic: þyrniht. _l._ þyrniht[e].
þyrstan. I 2. _add:_—Gif him þyrste, ðū dō him drincan, Hml. S. 21, 376. II 2. _add:_—Þonne seó sāwl þyrsteð and lysteð Godes rīces _Deum sitiens anima_, Gr. D. 244, 27.
þys. _The MS. has_ ðyf. _l._ (?) pyf. v. pyf: þyse. v. mægen-þyse.
þys-lic. II. _add:_—Þás þyslican sindon tō rihtanne, Gr. D. 263, 2.
þyssa. v. mere-þyssa: þýstrig. v. þeóstrig.

# U

u. _Add:_—Ān s for ðan ðe se _u_ is lang, Ælfc. Gr. Z. 178, 7.
ufan. II. ¶ _add:_ (1) literal:—Sleá man of þā hand þe hē þ̶ fūl mid worhte, and sette ufan on (uppon, _v. l._) þā mynetsmiððan, Ll. Th. i. 206, 21. (2) figurative:—þ̶ hine man forgulde mid healfan punde; gif wē þonne gyld ārærdon, þ̶ him man ȳhte ufon on þ̶ be his wlites weorðe, Ll. Th. i. 234, 6. v. ofer-, wiþ-ufan.
ufan-cumende; _adj. Coming from above_:—þ̶ ufancumende leóht, Gr. D. 285, 6.
ufer[r]a. II. _add:_—Þā þā seó lættre tīd cōm, and seó ufere þæs dæges weóx and āgān wæs _cum jam hora tardior excrevisset_, Gr. D. 128, 13. Seó ufere (lættre, _v. l._) tīd _hora tardior_, 129, 2. v. yfera.
uferian. _Add:_ v. oferian; uferung.
uferor; _adv. Higher_:—Swā swā heálīcor, þæs uferur _ut altius_, An. Ox. 5058. v. ufor.
uferung, e; _f. Delay_:—Heó onginneð wēpan, for þon þe hire þynceð lang seó ylding and seó uferung hwænne heó cume tō Gode _flere incipit, quia differtur a regno_, Gr. D. 245, 7. v. uferian; II.
ufe-weard. I. _add:_, ofe-weard:—Strȳc þū of ufwerdum heáfde mid þīnum twām scytefingran nyþerweard, Tech. ii. 119, 17. Andlang mearce on ðone gāran ufwerdne, C. D. v. 356, 17. Gyndleccing ofeweard ... gyndleccing neaþewerd _inriguum superius ... inriguum inferius_, Scint. 27, 6.
ufor; II. _add:_—Ðætte hié swā micle swīðor ðone spild ðæs hryres him ondrǣden ðonne ðā ōðre, swā hī ufor stondað ðonne ðā ōðre _ut tanto sollicitius praecipitem ruinam metuant, quanto altius stant_, Past. 407, 21. v. uferor, yfemest.
ūhta _l._ ūhte; _f._ I. _add:_—On ūhtan hié ārīsað _mane consurgent_, Past. 249, 4. Ðæs cocces ðeáw is ðæt hē micle hlūdor singð on ūhtan ðonne on dægred _gallus profundioribus horis noctis altos edere cantus solet, cum vero matutinum tempus in proximo est, minutas ac tenues uoces format_, 461, 2. v. Crīstes-mæsse- (Chr. 1021 + P. 154, 31), weorc-ūhte.
ūle. _Add: The word occurs in local names_, Ūlan-bearh, -beorh, -cymb, -del, -hyrst, -wal, C. D. vi. 345
ultor _a vulture_:—Se ultor sceolde forlǣtan þ̶ hē ne slāt þā lifre Tyties, Bt. 35, 6; F. 170, 2.
un-. (4) _add:_ v. un-scyld, un-earfoþlīce.
un-āberendlic. _Add:_—Bōc lytestne unāberendlicre byrþenne _codicem ponderis pene importabilis_, Bd. 5, 13; Sch. 639, 3. Hwæt bið unāberendlicre tō gesiónne ðonne ðæs bearnes cwalu beforan ðæs fæder eágum? _quid esse intolerabilius potest, quam mors filii ante oculos patris?_, Past. 343, 11.
un-āblinnendlīce. _Add:_ cf. un-tōlǣtendlīce.
un-āboht. v. un-geboht.
un-ācumendlic. _Add:_ I. _intolerable_:—Þā gefōr on Iulianes mōd unācumendlic (_intolerabilis_) forhtnys, Gr. D. 37, 26. II. _impossible to do_:—Se hlāford bær þone cnapan tō Martine trūwigende þ̶ him unācumendlic nǣre þone cnapan tō gehǣlenne, Hml. S. 31, 956.
un-ǣfæstlīce; _adv. Irreligiously_:—Gif hwylc brōðor an preósthȳrede bið þe intō cyrcan unǣwfæstlīce and prūtlīce (_non religiose, sed pompatice_) gǣd, Chrd. 60, 33.
un-ǣmetta. _Add:_—Bisceopas mid ōðrum unǣmettan (_occupationibus_) ābysgode, Chrd. 80, 21.
un-æþelness. _For_ 'Dial. 2, 23' _substitute:_—Seó æþelnes heora gebyrda gegearwað þæs mōdes unæþelnesse _solet nobilitas generis parare ignobilitatem mentis_, Gr. D. 151, 24.
un-ætspornen. _For_ 'Dial. 1, 9' _substitute:_ Gr. D. 60, 26, _and add:_ v. un-forspurned.
un-āfūliende; _adj._ (_ptcpl._) _Incorruptible_:—Unāfūliendre clænnesse _imputribilis pudicitie_, An. Ox. 2613.
un-āhefendlic; _adj. Insupportable_:—Þǣr is unmǣte cyle and unāhefendlic hǣto gemēted, Verc. Först. 175. v. ā-hebban. A. II 4.
un-ālīfed. _Add:_—Þā unālēfdan _inlecebrosa_, An. Ox. 11, 9.
un-ālīfedlic. _Add:_—Unālȳfedlicum pricelsum _inlecebrosis stimulis_, An. Ox. 4227. Þæt þū forseó weorlde āra, and hūru ungemetlice and unā līfedlice, Solil. H. 46, 9.

un-ālīfedlīce. _Add:_—Þā þā hē barn witodlīce ūtan, hē ādwǣscte þ̶ hē unālȳfedlīce (_illicite_) barn innan, Gr. D. 101, 27. Sum Godes wer ... æt in wege unālȳfedlīce þurh unhȳrsumnesse, and hine þā sōna ācwealde ān leó, 294, 23.
un-ālogen; _adj. Without deception_ or _failure_:—Him is þæt sōþe in heofonum gehealden mid ūrum Dryhtne þæt him ēce and unālogen bið, Nap. 64.
un-āmeten. (2) _add:_—Unāmeten _immensus_, Angl. ii. 358, 2.
un-āmetenlic; _adj. Unmeasured_:—Unāmetenlic _immensus_ (_Pater_), Ps. Rdr. 298, 9. _See preceding and following words._
un-āmetgod; _adj. Unmeasured, not having determined limits_:—Swā swā nā unscapene ne ðrȳ unāmetgode, ac unāmetgode _sicut non (tres) increati nec tres inmensi, sed (unus increatus et unus) inmensus_, Ps. Rdr. 298, 12.
un-āmirred; _adj. Uninjured, undestroyed_:—Gif gē (_men seized by a lioness_) wyllað gelȳfan on Crīst, þonne mage gē gān unāmyrrede heonan; gif gē nellað þone geleáfan habban, nāt ic gif eówre godas eów gehelpan magon, Hml. S. 35, 285.
un-andcȳþigness. _Add:_ Ps. Vos. 24, 7.
un-andergilde. In the passage given this word seems intended to render '_quod non vilescat_', and so should mean (?) _valuable_.
un-andgitfull. _Add:_ _not rational_:—þ̶ unandgitfulle gesceaft þæs wætres _elementum irrationabile_, Gr. D. 194, 7.
un-andgitol; _adj. Unintelligent_:—Gif hē sȳ unandgyttol _si est minus intelligens_, Chrd. 42, 1.
un-ārǣfedlic; _adj. Intolerable_:—Be ðām tintregum unārǣfedlicum (_intolerabilibus_), Bd. 5, 12; Sch. 617, 12.
un-ārǣfnedlīce; _adv. Intolerably_:—Ōðer den wæs lēgum full swȳðe egesfullīce, ōðer wæs nāhte þon lǣs unārǣfnedlīce cyle full, Bd. 5, 12; Sch. 616, 7.
un-āreccendlic. _Add:_ [_O. H. Ger._ un-arrechanlīk _non enarrabilis._]
un-ārimed. I. of a whole containing numberless units, take here the first four passages in Dict. II. of the separate units, take here the last four passages, and add:—þā (_anfiteatra_) wǣron unārīmede, Ors. 3, 3; S. 102, 22.
un-ārimendlic; _adj. Innumerable_:—þ̶ hē gesāwe unārīmendlice (_innumera_) stōwa þāra līgea, Gr. D. 317, 8.
un-ārweorþlic; _adj. Dishonourable, disgraceful_:—Swā hit is eác unārwurðlic (_inhonestus_) and bysmerlic þ̶ hig ōðres hādes reáf werian, Chrd. 63, 24.
un-āsecgendlic. II. _add:_—Unāsecgendlicum _inauditis_, i. _nefariis_, An. Ox. 3373.
un-āspringendlic; _adj. Unfailing_:—Hire byþ se deáþ undeádlic and seó wanung unāspringendlic and se ænde ungedāllic _ei mors immortalis sit et defectus indeficiens et finis infinitus_, Gr. D. 337, 11. In heofona rīce is ēce līf and unāspringenlic gefeá, Nap. 64.
un-āspyrigendlic. _For second passage substitute_:—Unāspyrgendlice (-spyriendlice, _v. l._) syndon his wegas _investigabiles sunt viae ejus_, Gr. D. 137, 27.
un-āstyrigendlic. _Add:_—Hē stōd þǣr ealle þā niht unāstyrigendlic (-onstyrgendlic, _v. l._) _immobilis perstitit_, Gr. D. 225, 4.
un-āstyrod. _Add:_—Þonne wuniað þā gesewenlican stānas ealle þāra andweorca unāstyrede (-onstyrede, _v. l._) þā þe wǣron ǣr gesewene þ̶ hī wǣron onstyrede _mox immobilia remanent cuncta quae moueri videbantur, visibilia corpora metallorum_, Gr. D. 270, 9.
un-āteórigendlic. II. _add_ :—þone gāst ðe is ēce and unāteórigendlic, Hml. S. 17, 14. III. _of a person, that fainteth not_ :—Is mē trum weall and unāteórigendlic bewerigend (cf. Is. 40, 28), Hml. S. 7, 127.
un-āteórod. _Add:_—Unāteóredum _inexhaustum_, i. _indefectum_, An. Ox. 2373.
un-āwemmed. _Add:_—Ic beó unāwemmed (_immaculatus_) mid him, Ps. L. 17, 24.
un-āwemmende _not to be defiled_ (?):—Hē gesette unāwemmendne (_immaculatam_) weg mīnne. Ps. L. 17, 33.
un-āwendedlic. _Add:_ _unmoved, immoveable_:—Se stān wunode fæst and unāwendedlic (unwendedlic, _v. l._) _lapis immobilis mansit_, Gr. D. 123, 3.
un-āwendendlic. _Add:_—Drihten, þū þe simle unāwendenlic wunast, Solil. H. 55, 16.
un-bebyriged. _Add:_—Þæt līc læg unbebyrged, Gr. D. 318, 6; 154, 25.
un-befangenlic. _Add:_—Hū unbefangenlice (_incomprehensibilia_) his dōmas syndon, Gr. D. 137, 25.
un-befeóndlic. v. un-beseóndlic: un-besacen. _Add:_ v. bī-sæc.
un-beseóndlic. _Add:_ Another reading is unbefeóndlicne, Bd. Sch. 291, 12.
un-besmiten. _Add:_—Onbesmitenes _incontaminatae_, An. Ox. 11, 52.
un-bilewit; _adj. Not gentle, harsh, fierce_:—Unbylewitan _inmites_, An. Ox. 56, 232.
un-bindan. _Add:_ I. _to free_ from a bond (lit. or fig.):—Fram

eallum bende unrihtwísnesse þū unbinst (*absolvis*) mægen þīn, Angl. xi. 116, 5. Hē hī mid bendum fæste hēt gewrīðan . . . hē hēt hī eft ealle unbindan, Hml. S. 23, 191. **II.** *to release* from restrictive condition :—Swā hwæt swā hī unbindað ofer eorðan, þæt bið unbunden on heofonum, Hml. Th. i. 542, 18. Gif hwā on þǣre untrumnysse sȳ . . . þonne meaht ðū hine unbindan. Genim þysse wyrte . . . fíf ðȳfelas . . . þus ðū hine meaht of þǣre untrumnesse unbindan, Lch. i. 98, 14–22. v. un-bunden.

**un-blissian.** v. ge-unblissian.

**un-brosnigendlic.** *Add :* of material or non-material objects :—In þǣre wísan mæg beón ongyten hwylc seó cȳþnes byþ in þām unbrosnendlican lífe (*in illa incorruptibili vita*), Gr. D. 312, 7.

**un-brosnodlíce,** *adv. Incorruptibly :*—Lifiende undeádlíce and unbrosnodlíce (*incorruptibiliter*), Gr. D. 348, 23.

**un-brygd.** *Add :* cf. bregde.

**un-bunden.** *Add :*—Hē ne stóp mid þȳ unbundenum fēt ofer þā stówe, Gr. D. 214, 14.

**unc.** *Add :*—Fērdon mín fæder and mōdor ūt, and genāmon unc and fērdon tō sǣ, and ūt reówan. Þā wē ūp cōmon, þā næs ūre mōdor mid ūs, nāt ic for hwī ; þā genam ūre fæder unc, and bær ūs wēpende forð on his weg, Hml. S. 30.

**un-capitulod.** *Add :* Cf. ge-capitulod.

**un-ceáp** *without price, gratis :*—Unboht ł unceáp, būta ēghuelcum worðe seallas *gratis date*, Mt. L. 10, 8 margin.

**un-ceápunga.** *Add :*—Unceápunge *gratis,* Hpt. 33, 239, 9.

**un-coþu.** *Add : plague :*—Sē bid tō forfleónne swilce uncoðu oððe cwyld *quasi pestis fugiendus,* Chrd. 70, 7.

**un-cumlíþe.** *Add :* Cf. un-gistlíþe.

**un-cūþ. I.** *add :*—Rōmāne swíþost for þǣm besierede wǣron þe him þ land uncūþre wæs þonne hit Somnitum wǣre, Ors. 3, 8 ; S. 120, 28. **III.** *add :*—Uncūð hū longe ðǣr swā gelǣrede biscepas sién, Past. 9, 3. Ne hopa ðū tō ōðres monnes deáðe ; uncūð hwā lengest libbe, Prov. K. 14. Uncūð þeáh mē scamige *perhaps I may be ashamed,* Solil. H. 49, 7 ; 26. 12. **IV.** *add :* as an epithet of disease :—Biðon monncwalmo ł uncūð ādle *erunt pestilentiae,* Mt. L. 24, 7. Uncūð ādlo *plagas,* Mk. L. 3, 10. Deáðbērnisse ł uncūðo ādlo *pestilentiae,* Lk. L. 21, 11. Ic ondrēde untrumnesse ǣgðer ge cūðe ge uncūðe *commoveor metu doloris,* Solil. H. 33, 14.

**un-cūþness, e ; f. Strangeness, novelty :**—Ne mihte se cniht ādreógan þā neównesse and uncūþnesse swā mycelre gesihðe *tantae visionis novitatem non ferens,* Gr. D. 278, 15.

**un-cwēme ; adj. Unpleasing, disagreeable, unacceptable :**—For unsybbe bið seó ūre onsægdnes Gode uncwēme, Verc. Först. 175 (s. v. un-fenge). v. un-gecwēme.

**un-cyme.** *l.* -cȳme.

**un-cyst ; I.** *add :*—For hwan ne sceal þæt eallum wísum beón forgyfen, þā ðe mid uncyste heora gecyndes (*naturae suae vitio*) beóð geuntrumade ?, Bd. 1, 27 ; Sch. 83, 15.

**under ; I** 3 f. *add :*—Hū mihte Abraham beón clǣne, þ hē nǣre forligr geteald, þā þā hē hæfde cyfese under his rihtwífe ? *quomodo defenditur Abraham adulterii reus non esse, dum viventi legitima uxore sua conjunctus est ancillae suae ?,* Angl. vii. 46, 440. **II** 1 c. *add :* Lǣt reócan swíþe betweoh þā þeóh ūp under þæt hrægl, Lch. ii. 332, 1.

**under-bæc. I b.** *add :*—Ðās seofon tunglan gāð ǣfre eástweard ongeán þā heofenan, ac seó heofon is strengra and ābrēt hī ealle underbæc westward mid hire ryne, Angl. vii. 14, 137. **II.** *add :*—Hit is āwriten ðæt him wǣre betere ðæt hī nō sōðfæstnesse weg ne ongeáten, ðonne hī underbæc gecerden siððan hī hine ongeáten, Past. 445, 33.

**under-bæcling.** *Add :*—Þū ācyrdest ūs underbecling (*retrorsum*), Ps. Rdr. 43, 11. Underbæcling, 113, 5.

**under-creópan.** *Add :*—Swā hit þeáw is þ þām mōde þe biþ ābysgod in manigum þingum swíþe undercreópeð (-crȳpð, *v. l.*) seó leáse ōlehtung *sicut moris est ut occupato in multis animo adulatio valde subrepat,* Gr. D. 35, 14.

**under-cyning.** *Add :*—Nū hēt hē þe dǣlan þíne goldhordas . . . and þū beó his undercyning, Homl. S. 32, 54.

**under-diácon.** v. pistol-rǣdere.

**under-fangelnes.** v. Ps. L. Lind. gives under-fangen *with the note,* -ennes scheint aus -elnes korrigiert.

**under-fangennes.** *Add : reception.* v. under-fōn. **IV. I :**—Seó forestæppende underfangennys (seó ǣrre feormung, *v. l.*) næs nā būtan gylte *praecedens illa susceptio sine culpa non fuit,* Gr. D. 76, 22.

**under-feng.** *Add :*—For þām underfenge þyses bisceoplican folgoðes, Gr. D. 3, 6. For þām underfencge þǣre menniscan tȳdernesse, 154, 5.

**under-fōn. I.** *add :* where the object is material or non-material :—Nis nān man fæstende þe underfehð mid mūðe ǣniges gesceaftes sē oððe eorðan, Hml. Th. ii. 330, 34. Cōm ān gecrístnod man tō Martine . . . wolde his lāre underfōn, Hml. S. 31, 208. **I a.** *to receive* what is entrusted to one :—Gif sweordhwíta ōðres monnes wǣpn undersō (onfó, *v. l.*), Ll. Th. i. 74, 9. **(1 b)** *to receive* what moves to meet one :—Hū manige hleórslægeas hē underfēng æt ðǣm ðe hine bismredon, Past. 261, 6.

þæt hē þæt hālige treów underfēnge feallende tō foldan, Hml. Th. ii. 508, 27. **II.** *add :*—Hē syþþan þā bletsungan underfēng, Chr. 1070 ; P. 206, 18. Hē hæfde mid him sume underfangene (*some who had been baptized*) þe synfulle wǣron and æfter heora fulluhte fela tō ysele dydon, Hml. S. 31, 730. **II a.** *to submit to* punishment :—Underfōn hī beheáfdunge, Hml. Th. i. 420, 7. **III** 1. *add :*—Geoweorða wæs Mecipsuses mǣg, and hē hiene on his geogoðe underfēng, and hiene fēdan hēt and tyhtan mid his twām sunum *Jugurtha, Micipsae adoptivus, heresque inter naturales ejus filios factus,* Ors. 5, 7 ; S. 228, 8. Hī fōron tō Baldewine eorle, and hē hig ealle underfēng, and hī wǣron ealne þone winter þǣr, Chr. 1064 ; P. 195, 1. **(1 a)** *to receive* an envoy, *give welcome to* :—Þā ǣrendracan man mid wurðscipe underfēng, Chr. 785 ; P. 55, 6. **(5)** *add :*—Hié hæfdun hiera cyning āworpenne and ungecyndne cyning underfēngon, Chr. 867 ; P. 68, 20. **(6 a)** *add :*—Ðā sāule ðe ðā gebodu angietað, and hié mid godcundre lufan underfōð, gif ðæt underfangne andgit . . ., Past. 367, 10. For ðȳ ðæt ōðre men ðā ilcan bisne underfōn, 451, 5. Hié noldon underfōn ðíne lāre, 267, 3. **IV.** *add : to accept* advice, terms, &c. :—Se cyning þisne rǣd underfēng, Hml. A. 94, 67. Hē wolde þ heom grið betweónan beón sceolde, and him man gafol and metsunge syllan sceolde, and hī ðā ealle þ underfēngon, Chr. 1006 ; P. 137, 26. **V.** *add :*—Þ weolcen underfēng hine, Nap. 64, 36. **VI a.** *add :*—Ðæt ðæt gē gǣstlíce underfēngon, gē willað geendigan flǣsclíce *cum spiritu coeperitis, nunc carne consummemini,* Past. 207, 16. Hī nyllað underfōn ðæt uncūðe ðæt hī gehírað *neque sequuntur, quae inexperta audiunt,* 441, 7. Þǣre geendudne . . . mæssan þēnunge underfō *qua finita cantor misse officium inchoet,* Angl. xiii. 391, 373.

**under-gitan.** *Add :*—Þeáh ðe se Hālga Gāst ne beó swutollíce genemned tō ðām Fæder and tō ðām Suna, swā ðeáh hē byð symle ðǣrtō undergyten, Homl. Th. ii. 56, 30.

**under-hnígan.** *Add :*—Underhnígan *subigant,* An. Ox. 43, 16.

**under-hwítel.** *Before* 'ragana' *insert* persa. v. Angl. viii. 452.

**under-licgan.** *Add :*—Tiburtius wæs sægd þ hē underlǣge ā and hýrde symble þām líchamlicum lustum *Tiburtius carnalibus desideriis subjacere ferebatur,* Gr. D. 307, 12.

**undern.** *Add :* **I.** *the third hour of the day :*—Hē hēt þæt hī āne tíd ofer undern (cf. æt þǣre þriddan tíde on morgenne, Bl. H. 201, 35) hī getrymedon ongeán heora fýnd, Hml. Th. i. 504, 24. **II.** *the service of the church at the third hour :*—Þysum gesungenum cweðan gebed þ drihtenlíce. Þārǣfter fylige undern (*tertia*). Þām geendedum . . ., Angl. xiii. 404, 554. Underne gedōnum *tertia peracta,* 388, 330.

**undern-gereord.** *Add :*—Se wítega wæs āhafen mid his underngereorde (*prandio*), Gr. D. 150, 6. v. undern-mete.

**undern-geweorc, es ; n. Breakfast :**—Sealde hē heom flascan wínes fulle tō þon þ hī mihton heom þā on heora færelde tō underngeweorce (tō hyra gereorde, *v. l.*) habban (*in prandio habere*), Gr. D. 66, 12. Hē geladode þysne cyning tō underngeweorce (*ad prandium*), 186, 3. Mid his underngeweorce (-gereorde, *v. l.*), 150, 6.

**under-niman. II** 1. *add :*—Se fæder gelǣrde þ mæden, and hió þā lāre deóplíce undernam, Hml. S. 33, 28.

**undern-mete.** *Add :*—Mid him beran his undernmete (-gereord, *v.l., prandium*), Gr. D. 150, 14.

**under-scyte.** *Add : a drag-shoe* or *scotch placed below the wheel, brake :*—Underscyte *sufflamine,* An. Ox. 50, 15.

**under-standan. III.** *add :*—Ic geanbidode swíþe wel oþ ic wiste hwæt þū woldest, and hū þū hit understandan woldest ; and eác þy furþor ic tiolode geornfullíce þ ðū hit forstandan mihtest *I waited till I knew what you would, and in what way you would conceive of it ; and besides I strove diligently that you might understand it,* Bt. 22, 1 ; F. 76, 26.

**under-streowod ; adj. Under-strewn, having material to lie on :**—Ic eom hnesce understreowod, Hml. S. 37, 201.

**under-þencan.** *Add :*—Būton þhī selfa underþæncan and tō dǣdbōte cuman, Ll. Lbmn. 438, 35.

**under-þeódan.** *Add :* [O. H. Ger. untar-thiuten *subicere* (Tatian).] v. under-geþeóded.

**under-þeów ; adj. In subjection** or *servitude :*—Him nān folc ne getrūwode þe him underþeów wæs, Ors. 4, 12 ; S. 210, 12.

**under-tunge.** *Add :*—Ic ūp āhōf míne nyþeran cǣflas ł mínre undertungan *exultavi sub lingua* (sublingua *annes glossed*) mea, Ps. L. 65, 17.

**under-wedd.** *Add :*—Ic onborgede .xxx. mancsa goldes æt Beorhðoðe and ic gesealde hym āne gyrde landes tō underwedde, Cht. Crw. 9, 119.

**un-dolfen ; adj. Not dug :**—Hī ādulfon gehwylcne dǣl þæs wyrtgeardes þæs þe þǣr ǣr undolfen wæs, Gr. D. 202, 4.

**un-dōn ; III.** *add :*—Se preóst nolde undōn þā duru mid cǣge, Hml. S. 3, 484.

**un-eácen ; adj. Not pregnant :**—Unēcene *non grauidam,* An. Ox. 27, 31.

**un-earfoþlíce ; adv. With great difficulty :**—Nā unearfoþlíce *non difficulter,* An. Ox. 5382 : 2, 462. v. un-, (4).

**un-eáþe ; adj. I.** *add :*—Hit bið swíðe uníeðe ǣgðer tō dōnne, ge wið ðone tō cíðanne ðe yfel dēð, ge eác sibbe wið tō habbenne *difficile erat, ut, si male acta corriperent, habere pacem cum omnibus possent,*

Past. 355, 41. **II.** *add :*—Swā þēh þe him lytles hwæt uniéðe sié, hū earfeðlíce hī hit gemǽnað, Or. 3, 9 ; S. 136, 18.

**un-eáþness.** **I.** *In* l. 7 *after* fare *insert : non mihi labor est ad Dominum meam uenire, and add : distress* of body or mind :—Mid þǣre uneþnysse (-eáð-, *v. l.*) swā myccles sāres onǽled *doloris magni stimulis accensus,* Gr. D. 207, 11.

**un-endebyrdlíce.** *Add :*—Unendebyrdlíce singan *vocibus inordinatis recitare,* Chrd. 57, 13.

**un-fæderlíce.** *Add :*—Hē ābāt his suna . . . and unfæderlíce macode heora flǣsc him tō mete, Sal. K. 121, 17.

**un-fæger.** *Add :*—Swā sceort man and swā unfægger (-fæger, *v. l.*) on ansȳne, Gr. D. 46, 20.

**un-fægerness.** *Add :*—þ hālige wíf ne ondrēd hire nāht þǣre ūtran scame and unfǣgernesse *sancta mulier nihil exterioris deformitatis* (cf. valde ignea conspersio corporis inerat) *timuit,* Gr. D. 279, 15.

**un-fæstnian** *to unfasten, detach* [:—Hæfð þæt dióful geworht bogan and strǣla . . . and ǽlce dæge þæs diófles willa bið þ þissa strǣla nān ne sié geunfǣstnod, gif hē findan mæg hwǣr hē hié āfæstnian mæge, Verc. Först. 165.]

**un-fealdan.** *Add :* **I.** *to unfold* a material object, *open* a book :—Þā bōc unlýsan and unfealdan *solvere librum,* Gr. D. 333, 10. **II.** fig. *to unfold* by narrating :—Ic unfealde and gerecce twā dǣda Benedictes *duo Benedicti facta replico,* 162, 10.

**un-fenge ;** *adj.* *Unacceptable :*—Bið ūre onsǽgdnes Gode uncwēme and unfenge, Verc. Först. 175.

**un-feor[r].** **I.** *add :*—Ðā wæs þǣr unfeorr (nāht feorr, *v. l. non longe*) sum mynster, Gr. D. 103, 23.

**un-fēre.** *Add :* [Cf. On his cildlicen unfērnesse heó hine baðede . . . and swæðede and roccode, Nap. 87.]

**un-flycge ;** *adj.* *Unfledged :*—Unfligge *inplumes,* An. Ox. 28, 13.

**un-foresceáwodlíc.** v. un-forsceáwodlíce (*not* -líc).

**un-forgifende ;** *adj.* *Unforgiving :*—Hē wæs heard and unforgyfende þām forwyrhtum mannum, Gr. D. 320, 1.

**un-forhæfedness.** *Add :*—Ðonne ðā gesinhīwan hī gemengað ðurh ungemetlice unforhæfednesse (*incontinentiam*), Past. 399, 16.

**un-forrotigendlic.** *Add :*—Unforrotenlices *inmarcescibilis* (*pudicitiae*), An. Ox. 2613.

**unforsceáwod.** *Add : unpremeditated.*

**un-forspurned** (-spornen) ; *adj.* *Unobstructed :*— On unforspurnedum (-forspornenen, -ætspornenum, *v. ll.*) fōtum *inoffensis pedibus,* Gr. D. 60, 28.

**un-forwirded, -wird ;** *adj.* *Unspoilt, undecayed :*—Þonne magon wē Drihtne bringan unforwyrdne wæst[m] gōdra weorca, Nap. 87. v. un-forwealwod.

**un-fulfremed.** *Add :*—Hwæthugu unfullfremedre wīsan *aliquid imperfectionis,* Gr. D. 283, 21. Gewitenre tíde unfulfremedre *praeterito tempore imperfecto,* Ælfc. Gr. Z. 130, 13.

**un-fyrn.** **I.** *add :*—Hē wæs nū unfyrn (nū for lyttlum fyrste, *v. l.*) forðfēred *ante non longum tempus defunctus est,* Gr. D. 71, 18. **II.** *add :*—'Hē deád byð unfyrn' . . . þām ōðran dæge æfter þæs Godes weres cwide hē his líf geendode, 62, 28. Þū wāst þ ic sylfa unfyrn sceall beón sweltende *scis quia ego modo te* (the dying abbot) *secuturus sum,* 226, 4.

**un-geǽsce ;** *adj.* *That cannot be found out by enquiry, indescribable :*—Se leóma geteáh mid ungeǽscre fyrhtu (*inaestimabili pavore*) þā heortan þǣra ætstandendra wīfa, Gr. D. 284, 20.

**un-geáþlíce ;** *adv.* *Without due consideration :*—þ bið ungeþlíce gewriðen *quod incaute ligatur,* Chrd. 123, 9.

**un-gearowitolness, e ;** *f.* *Want of ready wit, want of clear thought :*—For þon wē hī geseóð swylce hit sȳ ǽr sunnan uppgange, for þon þe hit nū gȳt is in sumre glímunge and ungearewitolnesse (-gearu-, *v. l.*) ūres mōdes *quia quasi in quodam mentis crepusculo haec velut ante solem videmus,* Gr. D. 331, 15. v. gearo-witolness.

**un-gearu.** **III.** *add :*—Hē him sǽde þ hē hiene mehte lǣdan þurh þæt wēsten, þ hē on Perse on ungearwe becōme, Ors. 6, 31 ; S. 286, 17.

**un-gebearde.** *Add :*—Ungebierde *effebo,* Wrt. Voc. ii. 31, 18. Swā ungebyrdun hysse *ut effebo hircitallo,* An. Ox. 7, 247.

**un-gebeáten ;** *adj.* *Unhewn* (stone), *not trimmed :*—Ungeb[e]átne stāne *lapide inpolito, non exciso* (i. *non tunso lapide,* Ld. Gl. G. iii. 29), Txts. 113, 69.

**un-gebeden (?) ;** *adj.* *In which an appeal for legal redress has not been made. See passage under* ge-biddan ; **I. 1.** De placito ungebendro [= sprǣce (v. sprǽc ; **X**) ungebedenre ?], Ll. Th. i. 301, 21.

**un-gebēt[t].** *Add :* , un-gebēted. **I.** *add :*—þ synne þe hē ǣr ungebēted hæfde, Gr. D. 329, 3. Him nǣnig syn ungebēted (-bētedu, *v. l.*) būtan wrace āleoðod wæs, 332, 3.

**un-gebígendlic.** *Add : that cannot bend, rigid :*—Se earm stód ungebígendlic (*inflexibile*), Gr. D. 254, 37.

**un-geblȳged.** *l.* -geblyged. v. ā-blycgan.

**un-geboden.** v. un-gebeden.

---

**un-geboht.** *Add : Another reading is* un-āboht (*non ad hoc conductus*), Ll. Lbmn. 399, 10. Cf. ge-bycgan ; **V.**

**un-gebrosnendlic.** *Add :*—þ hī onfēngon þā ungebrosnendlican (-nedlican, *v. l.*) leán, Gr. D. 233, 15. v. un-brosnigendlic.

**un-gebrosnod.** *Add :*—Wuninge on þē se ungebrosnod geleáfa, Verc. Först. 145, 4.

**un-gebunden.** *Add :*—Hē tōbræc þone fōtcops, and swā þēh æfter þan hē ne stōp mid þý unbundenum fēt ofer þā stōwe . . . ac hine sylfne beeóde . . . būtan racenteáge in swā mycclun landsticce ungebunden swā hē ǣr gebunden on wunode, Gr. D. 214, 16.

**un-gebyrded ;** *adj.* *Unpolluted, uncorrupted :*—Wæs gemēted se líchama swā gesund and swā ungebyrded (-geonbyrded, *v. l.*) swylce him nǽfre ne gehrine ǽniges īrenes snide *sanum atque intemeratum corpus inventum est, ac si nulla hoc inciso ferri tetigisset,* Gr. D. 199, 4.

**un-gecirred.** *Add : unchanged, unreformed :*—Gif hig þonne gýt eallunga ungerihte and ungecyrrede beón, Nap. 65, 11.

**un-gecoplic.** *l.* -cōp-. *Add : The original Latin is :* Lites cum importunis.

**un-gecwēme.** *Add :*—Eallra synna sió (æfest) is Gode lāþost and ungecwēmost, for þan mancynn ǣrest þurh æfeste wǣron on helle besencte, Verc. Först. 95, 3. v. un-cwēme.

**un-gedafenlic.** *Add :*—Ungedafendlic *indecens,* An. Ox. 3673.

**un-gedǽllic ;** *adj.* *Limitless :*—Byþ se ænde ungedǽllic *est finis infinitus,* Gr. D. 337, 11.

**un-gedēf(e)lic ;** *adj.* *Unbecoming, unseemly :*—Mid ungedēflicre and unwærlicre ofersprǣce *loquacitatis incauta importunitate,* Past. 95, 19.

**un-gedered.** *Add :*—Ongederedes fǣmnhādes *intactae virginitatis,* An. Ox. 11, 28. Hī ungederede genǣson . . . ungederede on heora gegerælan *laesi non sunt . . . illaesis vestibus,* Gr. D. 219, 19–24. v. un-gehrinen.

**un-gedríme ;** *adj.* *Dissonant, discordant, inharmonious :*—Hī gemaciað þ þā ōðre beóð ungedrýme *aliorum uoces dissonare compellunt,* Chrd. 57, 12.

**un-gedwimorlíce ;** *adv.* *Not as a magical illusion, really :*—þ weolcn underfēng hine ungedwimorlíce, Nap. 64.

**un-geeahtedlic ;** *adj.* *Incalculable, extraordinary :*—Mid ungeehtedlicre ændebyrdnesse *inaestimabili ordine,* Gr. D. 248, 20.

**un-geeahtendlic.** *Add :*—Mid ungeæhtendlicre (-eht-, *v. l.*) wynsumnesse *inaestimabili suavitate,* Gr. D. 282, 21.

**un-geendodlic.** *Add : that is without end, endless :*—Hē þurhwunað in þām ungeǽndedlican wíte, Gr. D. 264, 7.

**un-gefæd, es ;** *n.* *Indiscretion :*—þ is gewuna on manegum preósthíredum þ mid miclum ungesceáde and ungefade (*irrationabiliter atque indiscrete*) sume þā preóstas þe woruldwelan habbað . . . scolon māran and creáslicran fōdan habban on mynstre, Chrd. 13, 14.

**un-gefandod.** *In* l. 2 *read* flǣsclicra.

**un-gefēa, an ;** *m.* *Unhappiness :*—Ðā men þe mǣstne dreám būtan Godes ondrysnum ūp āhebbað hēr on worulde, hié þonne eft mǣste unrōtnesse būtan ende and mǣstne ungefeán būtan ǽnigre blisse hié onfōð, Nap. 64.

**un-gefēre.** **I.** *add :*—On ungefērum wege *in invio,* Ps. Vos. 106, 40.

**un-gefōg, es ;** *n.* *Excess :*—Weámōde lāreówas þurh hetolnysse heora reðscipes gehwyrfað þǣre lāre gemet tō ungefōge þǣre wælhreównysse (*ad immanitatem crudelitatis*), Chrd. 70, 16.

**un-gefōg, adj.** *Add :* cf. un-gefēge.

**un-gefōglic ;** (2) *add :*—Gif þā synna ne beóþ tō ungefōhlíce and unonlýsendlice *si insolubiles culpae non fuerint,* Gr. D. 348, 3. [*In* l. 2 *for* Greg. Dial. I, 9 *substitute* Gr. D. 64, 28.]

**un-gefullod.** *Add :*—Ðā cōm ān gecrístnod man tō Martine . . . ac æfter feáwum dagum hē wearð fǣrlíce seóc, swā þ hē forðferde ungefullod sōna, Hml. S. 31, 210.

**un-gefylledlic.** *Add :*—For his ungefylledlican hāðeortnesse *insatiabili furore,* Gr. D. 197, 12. Ungefylledlecre, Ps. Vos. 100, 5.

**un-geglenged ; adj.** *Unadorned :*—Ungeglenced *inculta* (*cesaries*), An. Ox. 1210.

**un-gehealdsum.** *Add :*—Ungehealdsumera *inpudicarum,* An. Ox. 7, 349. Ungehaldsumra, 8, 330.

**un-gehefegod ; adj.** *Not pregnant, not with child :*—Ungehefegude *non grauidam,* An. Ox. 27, 31.

**un-gehrinen.** *Add :*—Oðer dǣl hire wæs forbærned, ōþer dǣl wunode ungehrinen and ungedered (*pars altera intacta remanebat*), Gr. D. 340, 22. Hē forlēt eall þ feoh ungehrinen, 339, 28.

**un-gelǣred.** *Add :*—Ungelǣredes folces *indocti uulgi,* Angl. xiii. 421, 802.

**un-gelǣredlic ; adj.** *That learns with difficulty :*—Hē forlēt þā ungelǣredlican (earfoðlǣran, *v. l.*) gebrōðru *indociles deseruit,* Gr. D. 110, 21.

**un-geleáf.** *Add : incredulous :*—þā ongan hē beón eallunga ungeleáf þ hē hit wǣre *ipsum hunc esse coepit omnino non credere,* Gr. D. 46, 12. [*O. H. Ger.* un-giloubo *incredulus.*]

**un-geleáffull.** *Add :* **I.** *infidel.* (1) adjectival :—Ungeleáful wiþer-

cwyða *incredulus*, i. *infidelis negator*, An. Ox. 1892. (1 a) with gen., Hml. Th. i. 234, 20 (in Dict.). (1 b) with dat. :—þá wearð hé ungeleáfful þæs engles bodungum, Hml. Th. i. 202, 5. (1 c) with prep., Hml. S. 23 b, 16 (in Dict.). (2) substantival :—þone sylfan deáð fram ungeleáffullum and Crīstes feóndum (*ab infidelibus et inimicis Christi*) ic ðrowode, Bd. 2, 6; Sch. 137, 8. II. *incredible* :—Ungeleáfulne lehter *inauditum*, i. *incredibile crimen*, An. Ox. 2785.

**un-geleáflic.** *Add:* [*O. H. Ger.* un-giloublīh.]

**un-gelícian** *to displease* :—Hæbbe sum óðer wimman ealne hire wurðmynt hire ungelícu seó ðe þé oífícige (ungelícige, *v. l.*), Hml. A. 94, 66.

**un-gelífed** *unbelieving. Add* :—Ðū ūs trymest on ūrum geleáfum þæt ūs ne magon þá ungelýfædan āmirran *Deus per quem nos non movent qui minine credunt*, Solil. H. 8, 17.

**un-gelífen;** *adj. Unbelieving, incredulous* :—Sē ðe ungelēfen is *qui incredulus est*, Jn. L. 3, 36: 20, 27. Ungelēfenra *incredulos*, Mt. p. 19, 6.

**un-gelífende** *not believing, incredulous* :—Sē þe ungelýfende byþ in þon þe hé tweóþ, hé ne sēceð nā þone geleáfan, ac gesceádwīsnesse *qui infidelis est in eo quod dubitat, fidem non quaerit, sed rationem*, Gr. D. 262, 11. Ðǣm ungelēfendum cuoeð *illis non credentibus dixit*, Lk. L. 24, 41. [*O. H. Ger.* un-chiloubendi *incredulus.*]

**un-gelífness.** *Add:* un-gelífenness (?). v. un-gelífen.

**un-gelustfullung** (?), e; *f. Evil pleasure* :—On gewilnunge and ungelustfullunge (on gelustfullung?) unclǣnre *in concupiscentia et in delectatione inmunda*, Angl. xi. 116, 12.

**un-gemǣc[c].** *Add* :—Syndon full manega þá þe nǣnegu wundra wyrcað and þonne hwæþre nǣron nā ungemǣcce (-an, *v. l.*) þám þe þá foretācnu dóð *sunt plerique qui etsi signa non faciunt, signa tamen facientibus dispares non sunt*, Gr. D. 90, 31. Heora ǣgþres mēd and geearnung nis nāht ungemǣcce (ungelíce, *v. l.*) on heofonum, 91, 15.

**un-gemǣcca** *one dissimilar.* See preceding word.

**un-gemēde;** *adj. Perhaps this word should be taken as a noun;* see mād-mód.

**un-gemet.** I. *add: an immense quantity* :—Geweaxeð oninnan ungemet wǣtan, Lch. ii. 106, 21. II a. *add: Where* un-gemet *seems to have the force of an adverb it might be taken as the accusative case used adverbially.* v. Sievers' Grammar, § 319.

**un-gemēt;** *adj. Not met with, not experienced* :—Ungemēttum *inexperto*, An. Ox. 2488.

**un-gemetfæst.** I. *add* :—Hý wǣron ungemetfæste on eallum tīdum heora lífes and oferhýdo tó fulle, Wlfst. 255, 3.

**un-gemetgod.** *Add* :—Þǣr byþ ongemetegud (*immoderatus*) hleahter and plega, Scint. 173, 6.

**un-gemetlic.** I. *add* :—Tó þreágenne mid ungemettlicre (*the Latin has* modesta) ceáste, Gr. D. 145, 17. Sē ðe samnað ungemǣtlice weolan (*immodicas divitias*), Ll. Th. ii. 232, 24. II. *add* :—Hé hié forslóg þæt hié siþþan ungemetlicne ege from him hæfde *quos multo metu soluit*, Ors. 3, 9; S. 124, 4.

**un-gemetlíce.** I. *add* :—Þeáh mē genóh cume, ic hys nā ful ungemetlíce ne brúce, Solil. H. 35, 16. II. *add* :—Beó gemetlíce blíðe. Þū wǣre ǣr tó ungemetlíce unrót *stringe animum. Multum omnino flevisti*, Solil. H. 48, 20. Hié swā ungemetlíce gefuhton þ hié neáh ealle forwurdon *acerbissimis invicem praeliis fatigati*, Ors. 3, 1; S. 96, 32.

**un-gemidlod.** l. -gemídlod. *Add:* fig. *unchecked* :—Mid ungemídludre (*infreni*) tungan, Chrd. 77, 1.

**un-genemnendlic;** *adj. Not to be named* (?), *unknown* (?) :—þá semninga wearð hé mid fǣrlicum and ungenæmnendlicum deáðe forþfēred *subita et inopinata* (has *in(n)ominata* been read? the Greek version has ἀγνώστῳ) *morte defunctus est*, Gr. D. 341, 13.

**un-geonbyrded.** v. un-geÿbyrded.

**un-gerǣdlic;** *adj. Ignorant, rough, rude* :—þá ungerǣdlican (-gelǣredlican, *v. l.*) gebróðru *indociles*, Gr. D. 110, 21. Cf. ge-rǣde.

**un-gerǣdod;** *adj. Not furnished with harness* :—Feówer hors, twā gerǣdode, twā ungerǣdode, C. D. iv. 299, 21. v. ge-rǣdod.

**un-gerec.** *Add* :—Ungerec (*printed* -reo) gewarð *tumultus fieret*, Mt. R. 27, 24. On þám ungerece (ingerece, *v. l.*), Bd. 2, 9; Sch. 147, 15.

**un-geriht;** *adj. Uncorrected, unreformed* :—Gif hig þonne gÿt eallunga ungerihte and ungecyrrede (*inemendabiles et incorrigibiles*) beón, Chrd. 62, 6. Gif þonne ǣgþer ge sē þe man swang, ge sē þe man for ylde swingan ne mæg, bēgen beón ungerihte (*incorrigibiles*), 61, 35.

**un-gerim;** *adj. Add* :—Ungerīme bysna *innumera exempla*, An. Ox. 1687. Hí synd ungerýme, Hml. S. pref. 69. Ic eom ān his þeówena of þám ungerímum (þeówum), 36, 57.

**un-gerísende;** *subst. Add:* [*O. H. Ger.* un-kirísanti *indecens.*]

**un-gerisene;** *subst.* II. *add* :—Ongunnon lǣcas hire secgan . . . þ hire wolden beardas weaxan on þǣm andwlitan . . . and þ þonne wǣre wífmen sceamu and ungerysnu eallum hire freóndum, Gr. D. 279, 12.

**un-gerōtsod;** *adj. Saddened, troubled* :—Ungerōtsod ł gedrēfed *contristatus*, Ps. L. 34, 14.

**un-gerýde.** *Add* :—Se egeslica swēg ungerýdre sǣ eall manna mód miclum gedrēfeð *mare terribili confundet murmure mentes*, Dóm. L. 102. Ðá gehýrde hé ungerýdelic gelýd . . . and wæs āfre swā leng swā hlúddre and ungerýddre, Vis. Lfc. 50. [*O. H. Ger.* un-geriuti *hirtus.*]

**un-gerýdelic;** *adj.* I. of material, *rough* :—Hé bróhte ān reáf ungerýdelic him tó wǣclic and lytel, Homl. S. 31, 926 (cf. 970). II. *rough, violent* :—þurh þone byþ oferswíþed þ ungerýdelice and þ blúde geflit þæs folces *per quam tumultuosae turbae seditio comprimatur*, Gr. D. 265, 2. Ðá gehýrde hé ungerýdelic gelýd, Vis. Lfc. 47.

**un-gerýdelíce.** *Add:* of dress, *roughly.* v. un-gerýdelic; I :—Martinus rád him wið ungerýdelíce gescrýd mid sweartum clāþum, Hml. S. 31, 970.

**un-gesǣlig.** I b. *add* :—Eálá ungesǣligra Iúdēa bewēpendlic gewēd *O infelicium Iudeorum deflenda dementia*, An. Ox. 40, 1. II a. *add* :—þonne hié from gesǣlgum tídum gilpað, þonne wǣron þá him selfum þá ungesǣlgestan *patet apud utrosque misera illa tempora judicata*, Ors. 5, 2; S. 220, 12.

**un-gesǣliglíce.** I. *add* :—Ungesǣliglíce drohtian *infeliciter esse*, Verc. Först. 140, 12.

**un-gesceádlíce.** *Add:* *indiscreetly, irrationally* :—Gif þá beclýsedan þing him beóð ungesceádlíce (*minime discrete*) geswutelode, sóna hig hig tǣlað, Chrd. 95, 31. [Cf. *O. H. Ger.* un-gisceidlícho *indifferenter.*]

**un-gesceapen;** II. *add* :—Ungescepen *increatus*, Angl. ii. 360, 11; Ps. Rdr. 298, 8. v. un-sceapen.

**un-gescrépnes.** *Add:* unscroepnes, -screópnes *are various readings*, Bd. Sch. 451, 2.

**un-gescrépu** *or* un-gescrépe. *Substitute:* **un-gescrépe,** es; *n. An inconvenience* :—Mid þý þá se foresprecena bróðor langre tíde þyllic ungescrēpo (-scrǣpo) (þislic ungescróp [*printed* þislicum gescróp], *v. l.*) wann *cum tempore non pauco frater praefatus tali incommodo laboraret*, Bd. 4, 32; Sch. 545, 15. v. ge-scrépe.

**un-gescróp,** es; *n. An inconvenience.* See preceding word.

**un-gesundlíce,** *adv. Injuriously, harmfully* :—Hý ongunnon hyra hors mid heora sceftum þerscan . . . oð þæt hý ungesundlíce geswencede wǣron (*until they were quite tired out?*), Gr. D. 15, 2.

**un-geswenced;** *adj. Unwearied, unceasing* :—Ðǣr bið seó ēce hǣl and sýo ēce lufu swiþe ungeswæncedu, Nap. 65.

**un-geswícende** (-swicen?), *adj. Unceasing* :—Ungeswícen[d]ra stefne *incessabili uoce*, Angl. ii. 357, 5.

**un-geswícendlíce.** *Add* :—Hé ungeswíkendlíce (unāblinnendlíce, *v. l.* indesinenter) þurhwunað tó wyrcenne, Gr. D. 86, 10.

**un-geteórigendlic;** *adj. Inexhaustible, unfailing* :—Wē magon þurh þ ūs gegaderian þæne ungeteórigendlican goldhord, Nap. 87.

**un-geteorod.** l. -geteórod.

**un-geteórode;** *adv.* (?). *Indefatigably, unweariedly* :—Sume preóstas sýn þe ungeteórode (*or adj.?*) ealne dæg ādreógað ymbe woroldþing *sunt quidam clericorum qui in secularibus negotiis pene totum infatigabiliter deducunt diem*, Chrd. 34, 8.

**un-geþwǣrlic;** *adj. Discordant, at variance* :—Gif þū gemune þ þín bróðer āht ungeþwǣrlices wið þe gemǣne [hæbbe] *si recordatus fueris quia frater tuus habet aliquid adversum te*, Gr. D. 349, 24.

**un-geþwǣrness.** *Add:* III. *violence, cruelty* :—þætte se nama ðǣre Rómāniscan ðeóde fram fremdra ðeóda ungeþwǣrnesse fornumen beón ne sceolde *ne nomen Romanae prouinciae exterarum gentium improbitate obrutum uilesceret*, Bd. 1, 12; Sch. 33, 4.

**un-geþyld.** *Add* :—Nā swā þeáhhwæþre þás brocu Romulan mód gelǣddon tó ǣnigre (ǣnigum, *v. l.*) ungeþylde (-þyldo, *v. l.*), Gr. D. 284, 5.

**un-getímu.** *Add* :—Hit for sumum ungetýmum (*casu accidente*) weard tóbrocen, Gr. D. 97, 6.

**un-getreówness.** *Add* :—Benedictus cídde þám ungehýrsuman munuce for his ungetreównesse (untreównesse, *v. l.* infidelitate), Gr. D. 160, 5.

**un-tweógendlíce;** *adv. Indubitably, unhesitatingly* :—Untweógendlíce (*incunctanter*) hé mæg beón ongyten sóð martyr, Gr. D. 231, 21.

**un-gewealdes.** v. un-geweald: **un-gewemedness.** v. un-gewemmedness.

**un-gewemmed.** I. *add* :—Danihel læg seofan niht betwux seofon leónum on ānum seáðe ungewemmed, Hml. Th. i. 488, 5.

**un-gewemmedness.** *Add* :—Ungewemmednesse *immunitatis*, An. Ox. 1169.

**un-gewendedlic.** v. un-gewēnendlic.

**un-gewēnedlic;** *adj. Unexpected* :—Wæs se biscop swíðe gefeánde for þǣre ungewēnedlican blisse (*inopinata exultatione*), Gr. D. 347, 18.

**un-gewēnendlic;** *adj. Incalculable, excessive* :—Mid ungewēnendlíce (-wǣndedlíce, *v. l.*) fyrhtu *inaestimabili pavore*, Gr. D. 284, 20.

**un-gewidere.** *Add* :—Hé ne mihte nā gán ūt of þám húse for þám ungewydere, Gr. D. 168, 14. Cf. mis-gewidere.

**un-gewilde.** *Add: Not under control of* (*dat.*) :—Se earm stód ungebígendlic ǣghwæs þám āgendfreán ungewylde *brachium inflexibile remansit*, Gr. D. 254, 38.

un-gewilles; *adv.* *Involuntarily, not designedly* :—Sē þe hine nēdes ofslōge oððe ungewilles (*qui non est insidiatus*), Ll. Th. i. 46, 22.

un-gewiss *ignorance.* *Add* :—Hē nyste hwæs hē gelēfan sceolde, þā hine þā swÿþost drehton and on ungewisse gebrōhton þe his witan beón sceoldon, Hml. S. 23, 398. Rōmāne swíþost for þǣm besierede wǣron þe him þæt land uncūþre wæs þonne hit Somnitum wǣre, and on ungewis on ān nirewett besōran, Ors. 3, 8 ; S. 120, 29.

un-gewiss; *adj.* I. *add* :—Hē him þā gewāt swíðe gewisfullíce (-wiss- *v. l.*) swilce hē ungewis wǣre *recessit scienter nescius*, Gr. D. 95, 30. Ungewiss for costnunge *per tentationem imperita*, 265, 9. Hī beóð deáde and ungewisse þæs ēcan lífes, 264, 10.

un-gewítendlic; *adj.* *That does not pass away, imperishable* :— Swylce man sylle gewítendlic hūs, and ungewítendlic underfō, Hml. S. 34, 298.

un-gewitness, e ; *f.* *False knowledge* (?), *folly* (?) :—þām fēt hē wiðbrægd þý lǣs hit gelumpe þ hwæt unrihtes hine gehríne of his āgenum geþōhte and ungewitnesse, and hē þonne sylfa æfter þon eall geeóde in mycele forspildnysse (the original Latin, which has been misunderstood, is *Retraxit pedem ; ne si quid de scientia ejus* (i. e. mundi), *ipse postmodum in immane praecipitium totus iret*), Gr. D. 95, 22. v. un-gewitt.

un-gewitt. I. *add* :—Heó ūt eóde mid swā hālum and gesundum andgyte, swylce heó nǣfre ǣnig ungewit oððe unhǣle hire heáfodes nǣfde *ita sanato sensu egressa est, ac si eam numquam insania capitis ulla tenuisset*, Gr. D. 176, 25.

un-gewittiglíce. *Substitute : Madly, without reason* :—Ungewitte-líce rēþgiende *insane saevientes*, Gr. D. 104, 10.

un-gewittigness. *Substitute* : I. *madness, rage, frenzy* :—Đā lōcode se leódhata on þone hālgan wer mid weallendum geþōhte and mid ungewittinysse (unwittignysse, *v. l.*) his þwyran mōdes *quem dum fervido spiritu cum perversae mentis insania fuisset intuitus*, Gr. D. 163, 31. Gestillan fram þǣre wēdunge and ungewittignesse swā mycelre wælhreównysse *a tantae crudelitatis insania quiescere*, 164, 27. II. *insanity* :— Lǣg þér sum man on his mōde gefangen mid ungewittignesse . . . þone swylcne seócne lǣcas nemniað gewitleásne (*phreneticum*), Gr. D. 247, 13. II a. *a mad action, foolish proceeding* :—Hē wæs swíðe wundri- gende, and þōhte þ þ wǣre sum ungewittignes þ hē bebeád *valde admiratus est, quod quasi insana praeciperet*, Gr. D. 58, 1.

un-gewuna. *Add* :—Ic secge nū þ ic hwīlon ǣr forsuwade for þām ungewunan woroldlices gesceádes, Angl. vii. 12, 114.

un-gíming, e ; *f.* *Carelessness* :—Seó ceaster ðurh ungÿminge synna weard fýre onbærned *ciuitas per culpam incuriae igni correpta*, Bd. 2, 7 ; Sch. 139, 16. Þurh ungÿminge *per incuriam*, 4, 9 ; Sch. 393, 13.

un-gin[n]. *l.* -ginne.

un-girwan. *Add* :—Hē ungyrede (on-, *v. l.*) hine his hrægle *exutus indumento*, Gr. D. 101, 14.

un-gistlíþe; *adj.* *Inhospitable* :—Him wæs lāð þearfendum mannum āht tō syllene, and hē wæs ungystlíðe, Nap. 65. Cf. un-cumlíþe.

un-gníþelíce; *adv.* *In no mean manner or degree* :—Hē his þ ǣwfæste líf leofde swÿþe ungnēþelíce (unheánlíce, *v. l.*, *non mediocriter*), Gr. D. 43, 26. Hē scān ungnēþelíce (*non mediocriter*) mid þý worde þǣre hālgan lāre, 175, 1.

un-grǣdiglíce; *adv.* *Abundantly, liberally* :—Hē āscān ungrǣdiglíce (*non mediocriter*), Gr. D. 175, 1.

un-grípendlic; *adj.* *Irreprehensible* :—Drihtnes ēe ungrípendlic (*inreprehensibilis*) is, Ps. Cant. 18, 8.

un-gyrdan. *Add* :—Gif hē ǣnigne þearfan nacodne gemētte, þonne wæs hē hine sylfne ungyrdende (*se exspolians*), and mid his hrægle hē þone þearfan gescrýdde, Gr. D. 68, 11. Cf. on-gyrdan.

un-hǣlu (-o). *Add* :—Deáh hit wið ǣghwylcre innancundre unhǣlo, Lch. i. 86, 19.

un-hālwendlic. *Add* : I. *incurable* :—Unhālwendlic *insanabilis*, Ps. Rdr. 290, 33. II. *not salutary* :—þæt is (his, MS.) swíðe unhālwendlic geþōht, þ hwā (wa, MS.) ymb þā mergenlican cyrringe þænce and þā andweardan āgímeleásige, Archiv cxxii. 257, 7.

un-heánlíce. *Add* : *in no mean fashion* :—Hē þǣr his eáwfæste líf unheánlíce (*non mediocriter*) ādreáh, Gr. D. 43, 25.

un-hearmgeorn. *Add* :—Culfre is swíðe bylewit . . . and swíðe unhearmgeorn and unhetol ōðrum. Healdan wē þās þeáwas þ wē un- hearmgeorne beón and būton byternysse, Nap. 65.

un-hetol; *adj.* *Not malignant, kindly.* See preceding word.

un-híre. (1) *add* :—Becreáp þǣr inn sum swýðe unhýre (-hēru, *v. l.*) nǣddre (*serpens*), Gr. D. 211, 14. For ðæs swinglan þā unhýran deór . . . flugon *ante cujus verbera immanissimae bestiae . . . fugiebant*, 229, 22.

un-hírlíce; *adv.* *Fiercely, savagely* :—Hē geseah þone ealdan munuc swíðe unheórlíce and wælgrimlíce fram deófle geswænced *quem cum vir Dei crudeliter vexari conspiceret*, Gr. D. 161, 11.

un-hírsum. *Add* : [*O. H. Ger.* un-hōrsam *inobediens.*]

un-híwed; *adj.* *Not feigned* :—Unhíwedre *non fictę* (*puritatis*), An. Ox. 1742.

un-hleówe. *l.* -hleów.

un-hlūd; *adj.* *Not loud, low* :—Hē þone forðfarenan be naman

---

gecígde mid unhlūdre stefne *non grandi voce defunctum per nomen vocavit*, Gr. D. 85, 5.

un-hwílen. *Add* :—þǣr cyning engla clǣnum gilded leán unhwílen, Hpt. 33, 73, 26.

un-lǣdlic; *adj.* *Miserable* :—þā Iūdēas bǣdon swíðe unlǣdlicre bēne, swā him syþþan eall unlǣdlic on becwōm, Nap. 65.

un-lǣred. *Add* : *imperfectly instructed* :—Hē sealde bisene tō ðǣm ðæt ðā unlǣredan ne scoldon lǣran . . . hē ūs wolde ðæt tō bisene dōn ðætte ðā unlǣredan ne dorsten lǣran *ut exemplum daret, ne imperfecti praedicare praesumerent . . . qua exemplo ostenditur, ne infirmus docere quis audeat*, Past. 389, 2–27.

un-lǣttu; *f.* *Moral wretchedness, wickedness* :—God gecýðde in þām for hwylcre scylde (*blasphemy*) se cniht wæs geseald swylcum ēhterum ; for þon þe his fæder nolde hine gerihtan þā hwíle þe hē lifde, þā ylcan unlǣttu hē lēt hine eft edníwian þā þā hē sweltende wæs, Gr. D. 289, 25. v. un-lǣde; II.

un-leás. *Add* : *of a person or statement, veracious* :—Unleásere *non fictę*, i. *mendacis* (*ueritatis*), An. Ox. 3955. þæt ic ongæt be Theophania . . . swā swā mē cýðdon hit manige unleáse men *quod de Theophanio multis attestantibus agnovi*, Gr. D. 301, 17. Se unleásesta wer *vir veracissimus*, 193, 10.

un-leáslíce. *Add* :—Hē sǣde þ hē sylf ān wítega unleáslíce wǣre, Hml. S. 31, 802. Wē witon þ ðū eart unleáslíce Godes freónd, 1024.

un-leopuwác. *Add* : v. in-liþewác.

un-líchamlic. *Add* :—Þīn þ líchamlice eáge ne gesyhð āht líchamlices būton hit gescyrpe þā þing tō geseónne seó unlíchamlice wíse *nec ipse corporeus oculus aliquid corporeum videret, nisi hunc res incorporea ad videndum acueret*, Gr. D. 269, 22.

un-líf, es ; *n.* *Not life*, (*spiritual*) *death* :—Ne þearf nānne man tweógian ; æfter his deáþe ōðrum þissa hē onfehð swā lífe swā unlífe swaðer his gewyrhto bióð and his earnung, Verc. Först. 176. v. un-lífes.

un-lífed. *Add* :—Hié gewemmað ðone āliéfedan gesinscipe mid ðǣre unliéfedan gemengnesse, Past. 397, 13.

un-lífedlic, -lífendlic; *adj.* *Unallowed, unallowable, illicit* :—Fram unlÿuendlicum (-lēfedlicum, *v. l.*) *ab inlicitis*, Hpt. 31, 8, 131.

un-lífes. *Add* : v. un-líf.

un-lífigende. *Add* :—Hē gesæt nēh þām líchaman þæs unlífigendan mannes (neáh þām deádan líchaman, *v. l.*) *juxta corpus defuncti sedit*, Gr. D. 85, 3. þā word þāra unlífigendra *verba mortuorum*, 346, 10.

un-lísan. I. *add* :—Nǣnig þā bōc mihte unlÿsan and unfealdan (*solvere*), Gr. D. 333, 10. Se ceorl þe þyder cōm gebunden ongan semninga þǣr standan unlÿsed and unbunden, 164, 19. II. *to release from a restrictive condition* :—His dohtor wæs dumb geboren, and hē Martinum bæd þ hē hire tungan unlÿsde, Hml. S. 31, 1107.

un-lūcan. *Add* :—Sum heora mid hlǣddre wolde unlūcan ðæt ægðÿrl, Hml. S. 32, 205.

un-lust. II. *add* :—Unlust mē wæs tō lifianne *vivendi mihi taedium est*, Verc. Först. 140, 5. Se ylca fæder wæs geswænced mid unluste (gedrēfednesse, *v. l.*) his swiðlican geornnesse *idem pater nimietatis ejus taedio affectus*, Gr. D. 156, 6. III. *add* :—Hē þone unlust (synlust, *v. l.*) geteáh on his líchaman sār . . . witodlíce of þǣre tíde seó costnung þæs unlustes (synlustes, *v. l.*) wæs gewyld on him *voluptatem traxit in dolorem . . . Ex quo videlicet tempore in eo est tentatio voluptatis edomita*, Gr. D. 101, 22–30.

un-lybba. I. *add* :—Deáh ðe hí unlybban drincan, hit him ne derað *si mortiferum quid biberint, non eos nocebit* (Mk. 16, 18), Hml. Th. i. 304, 21.

unlyb-wyrhta. *Add* :—Wiccan and unlybbwyrhtan, Nap. 65, 37.

un-mǣte. *Add* : I. *of material objects* :—Weard hē gefyrht mid ege þæs unmǣtan wildeóres, Hml. S. 23 b, 774. II. *of non-material objects* :—Mægn unmǣttra hreónessa and unwederes *vim nimiae tempestatis*, Gr. D. 346, 33. Hē ābarn mid þý bryne þǣre unmǣtestan (-mætt-, *v. l.*) wælhreównesse *ardore immanissimae crudelitatis exarsit*, Gr. D. 162, 23.

un-mǣþfull; *adj.* *Immoderate, excessive* :—Mordslagan and mān- dǣdan and unmǣþfulle gÿtseras, Nap. 65.

un-meahtig; I. *add* :—Swā micclum swā þæs mannes gecynd un- mihtigre wæs, swā hit wæs leóhtre tō miltsunge *homo quanto fragilior in natura, tanto facilior ad veniam*, Angl. vii. 4, 35.

un-meahtiglicness, e; *f.* *Powerlessness* :—Wiþ unmihtilicnysse þæs migðan *for inability to pass urine*, Lch. i. 56, 15. v. un-meahtigness.

un-micel. For 'Greg. . . . is' *substitute* :—Æfter unmycelum (noht miclum, lytlum, *v. ll.*) fæce *non multo post*, Gr. D. 133, 7. Hē him worhte tela unmycel eardunghūs *sibi humili habitaculum construxit*, 201, 5.

un-miltsigendlic. *Add* :—Gif hwā forsihð þā forgifenisse þe se hālga gāst sylð, þonne bið his synn unmyltsiendlic on ēcnysse, Ælfc. Gen. Thw. 3, 11.

un-myndlinga. I. *add* :—Sume dæge þā þā heó swā wídgāl swíðe dwolode, heó becōm unmyndlinga tō þām scræfe . . . and heó þā þǣr wunode swā swā heó nyste *quadam die dum vaga nimium erraret ad*

*specum devenit, ibique nesciens ingressa mansit*, Gr. D. 176, 21. **II.** *add :*—Gelamp hit þ se sácerd unmyndlinga (unwēnlíce, *v. l., inopinate*) wearð ábysgod wīneard tō settanne, Gr. D. 88, 16.

**unna.** **I.** *add :*—Būton ðes abbudes hǽse and unne *sine abbatis iussu et concessu*, C. D. iv. 200, 11.

**unnan.** *Add :*—Unnende *indulta*, Rtl. 40, 5. **III.** *add :*—Hit becwæð sē þe hit āhte . . . swā swā hit his yldran . . . lētan and lǣfdan þām tō gewealde þe hý wel uðon, Ll. Th. i. 184, 3.

**un-nídelíce ;** *adv.* *Not scantily, moderately :*—Swíþe wundorlíce wīsan þ wǣron, þā þe ic gehýre and nāht unnēdelíce blīþe (*non mediocriter læta*), Gr. D. 346, 9.

**un-nytness.** *Add :*—Ídel unnetnys *uana mobilitas*, i. *instabilitas*, Germ. 401, 99. Unnitnes *uanitas*, An. Ox. 46, 44. Unnytnys *nenias*, 56, 322.

**un-nyt[t] ;** *adj.* *Add :*—Unnytte *superfluas*, Germ. 402, 69.

**un-nytt ;** *n.* *Add : what is useless or unprofitable :*—Ic nāt hwes ic bydde hweðer ic bydde nyttes þe unnyttes mē sylfum oððe þām freóndum þe ic lufige *nescio quid mihi ex eo utile sit, vel eis quos diligo*, Solil. H. 13, 18.

**un-oferswíþed.** *Add :*—Hē ne lēt nā of gebedum his unoferswīðdan gāst, Hml. S. 31, 1357.

**un-oflinnendlíce ;** *adv.* *Without desisting, without leaving off :*—Þā cwelleras unoflinnendlíce cwelmað, Verc. Först. 139, 15.

**un-onlísendlíc ;** *adj.* *That cannot be absolved :*—Gif þā synna ne beóð unonlýsendlíce (*insolubiles*), Gr. D. 348, 4.

**un-onstyrigendlíc.** v. un-ástyrigendlíc : **un-onstyrod.** v. un-ástyrod.

**un-onwendedlíc.** *Add : immoveable :*—Hē ealle niht staþolfæst and unonwendedlíc þurhwunode *immobilis permansit*, Gr. D. 112, 11. *See next word.*

**un-onwendedlíce ;** *adv.* *Without movement :*—Þurhwuniendum unonwendedlíce (*immobiliter*) eallum þām getimbre þæs bāmes þ wundorhūs gefeóll, Gr. D. 119, 26.

**un-rǽdlíce ;** *adv.* *Add : without good counsel :*—Gif se cyning rihtwīsnysse ne hylt . . . hē bið eft genyþerad . . . under þām unrihtwīsum þe hē unrǽdlíce geheóld, O. E. Hml. i. 303, 19.

**unrǽd-síþ.** *Substitute :*—Ic dysge dwelle ond dole hwette [on] unrǽdsíþas, ōþrum stýre nyttre fōre, Rä. 12, 4. v. hwettan ; **II 2 a.**

**unriht-crafing,** e ; *f.* *An unjust claim :*—Hēr kýð on þissere bēc þ Huberd cræfede ānne wīsmon mid uurihte . . . Huberd wæs leósende þære wīfmanne for his unrihtcræfinge þā and æfre mð, Cht. Th. 633, 16–28.

**unrihtful ;** *adj.* *Unrighteous, iniquitous :*—Þā unrihtfullan and þā ārleásan and þā hātheortan, Nap. 43, 9.

**unriht-gestrod,** es ; *n.* *Unlawful booty :*—Gýtsung and unrihtgestrodu, Nap. 66.

**unriht-gewill.** *Add :*, es ; *n.* *Evil desire :*—þ hí þý ēð mægen heora unrihtgewill forðbringan, Bt. 3, 4 ; F. 6, 26.

**unriht-hǽman.** *Add :*—Unryhthǽmende hié wǣron *fornicati sunt*, Ps. Vos. 105, 39.

**unriht-hǽmdere.** *Add : cf.* níd-hǽmdere.

**unriht-hǽmed.** In the following passage the word is masculine :—Forlǣtan wē . . . unrihtwīsnessa and unrihthǽmedas, Nap. 36, 25.

**unrihthǽmed-fremere,** es ; *m.* *An adulterer, a fornicator :*—Þā mæn þe . . . beóþ oferdrinceras and unrihthǽmedfremeras, Nap. 66.

**unriht-hǽmere.** *Add :*—Mid forligerum ł unrihthǽmerum (-hǽmrum, Ps. Rdr.) *cum adulteris*, Ps. L. 49, 18.

**un-rihtlíc.** *Add :*—þ is unrihtlíc and unālýfedlíc ǽnigum men tō cweþanne *quod dici nefas est*, Gr. D. 334, 22. Þā þe of him selfum āceorfað unryhtlíco weorc *qui affectum in se pravi operis abscidunt*, Past. 409, 2.

**unrihtlíce.** *Add :*—Unrihtlíce ł ārleáslíce *impie*, Ps. L. 17, 22. v. on-unrihtlíce.

**unriht-tíd,** e ; *f.* *An improper time* for doing something :—Þā þe hēr swīdost on unrihttídum on oferfyllo bióð forgriwene, Nap. 27, 30 : Verc. Först. 176.

**unriht-wilnung.** *Add : ambition :*—Þætte nǽnig biscopa hine ōþrum forbere þurh unrihtwillnunge (unrihte willunge, *v. l.*) *nullus episcoporum se praeferat alteri per ambitionem*, Bd. 4, 5 ; Sch. 378, 18.

**un-rihtwís[u].** *Add :*—Se cyning and se biscop sceoldon beón Crīstenra folca hyrdas, and hí from eallum unrihtwísum āhweorfan, Bl. H. 45, 26.

**un-rím ;** *adj.* ¶ *add :*—Se ingang begiten bið mid ǽlmesdǽdum and ōþrum unrím gódum, Hml. S. 33, 241.

**un-sadelod.** *Add : not saddled, without a saddle :*—Hē geann his hláforde feówer horsa, twā gesadelode and twā unsadelode, Cht. Crw. 23, 5.

**un-sǽgd.** *For* ' Wanl. Cat. 6, 13 ' *substitute* Hml. Th. ii. 466, 24.

**un-sár.** *Add :*—Þā hēt hió (*Cleopatra*) niman ipnalis þā nǽdran, and dōn tō hiere earme, þæt hió hié ábīte ; for þon þe hiere þūhte þæt hit on þǽm lime unsárast wǣre, Ors. 5, 13 ; S. 246, 26.

**un-sceapen ;** *adj.* *Not created :*—Nā [ðrý] unscapene *non tres increati*, Angl. ii. 361, 2 ; Ps. Rdr. 298, 12.

**un-scennan** (?) *to unyoke, unharness :*—Se yrþlingc unscenþ (-spenþ(?), cf. spannan : -scerþ ? v. scerran (?)) þā oxan *arator disjungit boves*, Coll. M. 20, 27.

**un-sceþþende.** *Add : cf.* in-sceþþende.

**un-sceþþigness.** *Add :*—Hī noldon feoltan on þām freólsdæge, ac lēton hī ofsleán on unscæððignysse (cf. *They said, We will not come forth . . . to profane the Sabbath . . . Let us die all in our innocency*, 1 Macc. 2, 34–37), Hml. S. 25, 239. On unscyðþinysse *in innocentia*, Ps. L. 83, 13.

**un-scógian.** *Add :*—Hē cleopode tō his þeówtlinge, ' Cum, deóful, hider and unscó (*discalcea*) mē, Gr. D. 221, 22.

**un-scrýdan.** *Add :* (3) with dat. of garment :—Hē þā unscrýdde his reáfe *exutus indumento*, Gr. D. 101, 13.

**un-scyldiglíce ;** *adv.* *Innocently, guiltlessly :*—Swā hwā swā unscyldiglíce būtan fācne leofode ǽr his gecyrrednesse, Nap. 66.

**un-scyldigung,** e ; *f.* *Innocence :*—Unscyldgunga handa mínra (*juxta innocentiam manuum mearum*, Ps. Rdr. 17, 25.

**un-scyttan** *to unshoot, push back* a bolt :—Hē gelæhte þā dura, and ne mihte þā scyttelsas unscyttan swā hraðe, Hml. S. 31, 863.

**un-seffull ;** *adj.* *Senseless, irrational :*—Fýnd úre unseffulle (*insensati*), Ps. Rdr. 290, 31.

**un-sehtness,** e ; *f.* *Discord, variance, quarrel :*—Þurh þæt āríseð unsehtnesse betweoh twām cyningum and twām gebrōðrum, Nap. 66.

**un-seofiende** *not sighing, glad :*—Hwæðere gē bióð unsiofiende, hió gecyrred eft eów on gefeán *sed tristitia uestra conuertit in gaudium*, Verc. Först. 176.

**un-sidelíce ;** *adv.* *Indecorously, in an unseemly manner :*—Gif hwylc brōðor . . . intó cyrcan unǽwfæstlíce and prútlíce oððe unsydelíce (*incomposite*) gǽð, Chrd. 60, 34. [*O. H. Ger.* un-situlího *in abusione.*] *See next word.*

**un-sidu.** *Add : indecorum :*—Mid unsidu (*inhoneste*) on cyrcan gān, Chrd. 32, 33. *See preceding word.*

**un-smǽþe.** *Add :*—Anfealte onsmēðre *scabrae incudis*, An. Ox. 11, 67. Unsmēþust *asperrima*, 26, 12.

**un-snotorness.** *Add : iniquity :*—Weg unsnoternesse ł unrihtwísnesse *uiam iniquitatis*, Ps. L. 118, 29. Unrihtlíce unsnoternesse hý dydon on mē *iniuste iniquitatem fecerunt in me*, 78. Þū canst míne unsnotternysse (*insipientiam*) and míne gyltas, 68, 6.

**un-sōþ.** *Add :*—Unsóðe *irrita*, i. *uana ł falsa* (*dicta*), An. Ox. 26, 26.

**un-spannan.** *Add : v.* un-scennan.

**un-stæþþig.** *Add :* **IV.** in a physical sense, of air, *easily moved, mobile, wandering* (? cf. *to find . . . the wandering* air, Rich. III, Act i. sc. 4) :—Hē sǽde þ ān wolcn efne þā upp ástige mid þǽre unstæððigan lyfte, efne ðā ārās se wind, Hml. S. 18, 150.

**un-staþolfæst ;** **II.** *add :*—Sum munuc wæs unstaþolfæst (-staþel-) on his mōde and nolde gewunian on his mynstre *quidam monachus mobilitati mentem dederat, et permanere in monasterio nolebat*, Gr. D. 155, 25.

**un-staþolfæstness.** *Add : unsettledness :*—Of sleacnesse byð ácenned . . . unstaðolfæstnes stōwe and wōrung of stōwe tō stōwe, Verc. Först. 177, 4.

**un-stillian.** *Add :*—Þætte þā mynster . . . nǽnigum bisceope ālýfed sié nǽnigum þinge hié unstillian (-stilligenne, *v. l. inquietare*), Bd. 4, 5 ; Sch. 376, 16.

**un-stillness.** **V.** *add :*—Sē fǽrð and fandað þissera fíf andgita, sē ðe þurh fyrwitnysse and unstilnysse hī áspent on unnyt, Hml. Th. ii. 374, 2. **VI.** *add :*—Hē ongan biddan þ him God forgǽfe þ he gestillan mihte þæs hātheortan preóstes unstilnysse *coepit exorare ut ei redderet unde presbyteri furentis insaniam mitigare potuisset*, Gr. D. 65, 12.

**un-swēte.** (2) *add :*—Hē cwæð . . . þ . . . of þǽre eá wǣre reócende se mist unāræfnedlicre fýlnesse and unswētes stences (*intolerabilis foetoris nebula*), Gr. D. 318, 29.

**un-swíþe.** *Add :*—Unswýðe *segniter*, An. Ox. 56, 83.

**un-tǽllic ;** *adj.* *Blameless :*—Ęe Dryhtnes untǽllic *lex Domini inreprehensibilis*, Ps. Rdr. 18, 8.

**un-tamlic** (?). *Substitute :* un-tamcol, *and add : v.* tamcian : un-teorig, ł -teórig.

**un-þǽslic.** *Add :*—Unþǽslic *absurdus*, An. Ox. 27, 26. Swýðe unþæslic (*inconveniens*) mæg beón geþúht þ sē nyte Drihtnes andgit, sē þe mid him byð geworden ān gāst, Gr. D. 136, 21. Þā cwæð se hālga wer þ hit unþæslic wǣre þ þ wíf sceolde wunian eft mid him, Hml. S. 31, 1076.

**un-þances.** v. un-þanc ; ¶.

**un-þancfull.** *Add :*—Ne sceall ic nǽfre læng unþancfull þǽre þegnunge mē onýwan þām were *viro illi ingratus apparere non debeo*, Gr. D. 343, 11.

**un-þancol ;** *adj.* *Ungrateful :*—For hwan lā man, forlurðū þis eal þe ic for þē þrowode ? For hwan wǣrðu swā unþancul þínre onlýsnesse ? . . . Tō hwan eart ðū mē swā unþancul mínra góda and mínra gifa ?, Nap. 66. v. un-geþancfull.

un-þancwirþlíce; *adv. Ungratefully:*—For hwan onfénge ðú un-þancwyrþlíce þá gife þínre álýsnysse?, Nap. 66.

un-þeáw. *Add:*—Gelóme hig áspyriað þæs solecismus unþeáwas, Angl. viii. 313, 24.

un-þrowendlicness, e; *f. Apathy, impassibility:*—Unþrowendlic-nesse *aphatiam* (= *apathiam*), i. *impassibilitatem,* Hpt. 31, 14, 350.

untíd-ǽt, es; *m. Eating at improper times:*—Hí gímað untídǽta and druncennysse *gule et ebrietate dediti,* Chrd. 10, 32. Máne áðas ... and untídǽtas and oferdruncennesse ... Dióful ús lǽrað oferfylle and un-tídǽtas, Nap. 66.

un-tígan. *The Latin original for* Lch. iii. 198, 12 is: Asinos clamantes aut solutos currere, *so that* assan *is plural, and for* untíende untíede, *not* unti[g]edne, *is to be suggested.*

un-timber? *worthless material?:*—Hié hira godu hæfdon geworhte of treówum and of stánum and of óðrum untimbrum (antimbrum?) missenlicum, Verc. Först. 176.

un-tóbrocen. *Add:*—Untóbro[cen] *indisrupta,* An. Ox. 4375.

un-tódǽlendlic; *adj. Indivisible:*—God is ánfeald and untódǽlendlic (*simplex indivisumque natura*), Bt. 33, 1; S. 74, 31.

un-togen; *adj. (ptcpl.) Not pulled, not drawn tight, untied:*—Ge-wunedon þá þwangas of mycclum dǽle untogene and onleoðode *magna ex parte dissolutae corrigiae remanserunt,* Gr. D. 222, 3.

un-tólǽtendlíce *incessantly. For* 'Gr. Dial. 2, 8' *substitute:*—Manie men untólǽtendlíce (unáblinnendlíce, *v. l.*) wǽron geladode tó stadole beteran lífes mid þǽre ylcan mǽrðe his hlísan *multos ad statum vitae melioris ipso opinionis ejus praeconio indesinenter vocari,* Gr. D. 117, 23.

un-tólýsendlic; *adj. Not to be absolved:*—Gif þá scylda ne beóð swá myccle and swá untólýsendlice æfter deáðe *si culpae post mortem insolu-biles non sunt,* Gr. D. 342, 26.

un-tóworpenlic; *adj. Not to be destroyed, inviolable:*—Unteworpan-lice *inviolabilem,* An. Ox. 11, 153.

un-treówness. v. un-getreówness.

untrum-hád, es; *m. An infirm condition:*—þætte ánum untrum-háde (untrumum háde, *v. l.*) wæs forgyfen, for hwan ne sceal þ eallum wífum beón forgyfen *quod uni personae infirmanti conceditur, cur non concedatur cunctis muligribus?,* Bd. 1, 27; Sch. 83, 12.

un-tweó. *Add:*—þ is untwý tó understandenne *quod non est dubium intelligi debere,* Chrd. 80, 16.

un-wælgrim; *adj. Not cruel, gentle:*—Hé wæs swíðe unwælgrim (eallunga læs wælhreów, *v. l.*) *minus crudelis fuit,* Gr. D. 133, 6.

un-wærlíce. *Add:*—Heora geféran æt hám fuhton unwærlíce ... ofer Iúdan leáfe ... and wurdon ðá ofslagene wel fela manna, ðá ðá hí fuhton búton wísdóme, Hml. S. 25, 455.

un-wæstmbǽre. *Add:*—Wíse láreówas sǽdon þ seó eorþe wǽre micele unwæstmbǽrre æfter þám flóde þonne heó ǽr wǽre *tradunt doctores terrae vigorem et fecunditatem longe inferiorem esse post diluvium quam ante,* Angl. vii. 36, 348.

un-wæstmbǽrness. *Add:*—For þǽre eorþan unwæsmbǽrnysse *propter infecunditatem terrae,* Angl. vii. 36, 346.

un-wæstmberende; *adj. Not bearing fruit, barren, sterile:*—þonne syððan bið sió hreównes and þǽra teára mægen unwæstmberende. Nap. 66.

un-wæstmfæst. *For the passage substitute:*—Elizabeth wæs un-wæstmfæst [on líchaman, ac wæstmfæst] þára godcundra mægena *erat Elisabeth sterilis corpore, sed fecunda virtutibus,* Archiv cxxii. 247, 17.

un-wealt. *Add:* [*Icel.* ú-valtr *steady.*] v. -wilte.

un-weder. *Add:*—Gif þá unwedru his ne forwyrnað *si sterilitas impedimentum non fecerit temporis,* Chrd. 15, 16.

un-wemme. *Add:* v. efen-unwemme: un-wendedlic. v. un-áwendedlic.

un-wénlíce; *adv. Unexpectedly:*—þá gelamp hit þ se mæssepreóst wæs unwénlíce (*inopinate*) ábysgod wíngeard tó settanne, Gr. D. 88, 17.

un-weorclic. *Add:* [Cf. *O. H. Ger.* un-werahbar *intempestus.*]

un-weorþ. II. *add: of low estate:*—Preóst þe bið cýpa, and of þám árist of unwurðum men tó wurðfullum *negotiator clericus ex ignobili gloriosus,* Chrd. 70, 6.

un-weorþlic. III. *add:*—þá ylcan sprǽce wé nimað lustlíce, þeáh þe heó sí us unwurðlíc (-wyrðelíce, *v. l.*) and unrihtlíc tó sprecanne *hanc ipsam locutionem quae nobis indigna est, etiam delectabiliter tenemus,* Gr. D. 209, 22.

un-weorþung. *Add:* III. *dishonouring:*—Unwurþung (*inhono-ratio*) góddra manna, unwurðung mága, Sunnandaga unwurþung, Chrd. 40, 29-31.

un-wérig. *Add: unwearied:*—þone æftran dæg mid his nihte unwérig on bénum hé þurhstód *secundo die cum nocte subsequenti indefessus in precibus perstitit,* Gr. D. 200, 7.

un-wíd; *adj. Not wide, narrow:*—Emne swá mycel swá fram heofenes hrófe is tó þysse eorðan, þonne is leornod on hálgum bócum, þæt sió hel sié swylc twá deóp, and nis ná ðe unwídre (-widdre, *v. l.*) (cf. seó hell ys twá swá deóp, and heó ys ealswá wíd, Wlfst. 146, 11), Verc. Först, 109, 5.

un-wirþ-. v. un-weorþ-.

un-wís. *Add: mad, insane:*—Hé wénde þ hé sprǽke on unwís, þá hé bebeád þ ... (*quod quasi insana praeciperet*), Gr. D. 58, 1.

un-wísness. I. *add:*—Swá hwæt swá ... þurh unwísnesse oþþe þurh ungýminge gelumpe *quicquid ... per ignorantiam uel incuriam resedisset,* Bd. 4, 9; Sch. 393, 13.

un-wita. *Add:*—[U]nw[i]t[a]n *stolidi,* An. Ox. 56, 229.

un-wiþerweardlic; *adj. Not in opposition, in union, united:*—Hié ealle cumað tó Críste on þám heofonlican wuldre, and hié ðonne onginnað singan Drihtne níwne sang swíðe unwiðerweardlicum stefnum, Nap. 66.

un-wiþmetendlíce; *adv. Incomparably:*—Unwiðmetendlíce (-meted-, *v. l.*) geweorðod mid forhæfdnesse mægne *cum virtute abstinentiae incom-parabiliter praeditus,* Gr. D. 203, 19.

un-wiþmetenness:—Unwiðmetenesse *in conparatione* (but the glosser has read *incomparatione*), An. Ox. 587.

un-wittigness. v. un-gewittigness; I.

un-wrenc; I. *add:*—Unwren[ce] *fraude,* An. Ox. 56, 85.

un-wreón. *Add:*—þeáh wé wáce sýn and þás þing leóhtlíce unwreón, hig magon freman bet þonne þá þe beóð on leóðwísan fægre geglenged, Angl. viii. 304, 2. Wé nú magon behýdan and behelian úra dǽda, ac hié bióð þonne opena and unwrigena, Verc. Först. 101, 7.

un-wrítere. *Add:* Ælfc. Gen. Thw. 4, 29.

un-wríþan. *Add:*—Swá þæt nánra þinga hí (*the ropes*) mihton beón undón and unwriðene (tólýsede, *v. l.*) *ut dissolvi non potuissent,* Gr. D. 164, 16.

un-wynsumness. *Add:*—þǽr bið sió wiensumnes bútan ǽlcere unwynsumnesse. Ne þǽr ne bið ... nǽnig unwynsumnes geméted, Verc. Först. 113, 6-8.

un-wyrht, e; *f. Ill-doing, demerit:*—þ is hiora mildsung, þ mon wrece hiora unþeáwas be hiora unwyrhtum (gewyrhtum, *v. l.*), Bt. 38, 7; F. 210, 19.

un-ymbfangen; *adj. Incomprehensible, not circumscribed:*—þú God wást unymbfangenne and unymbwritenne *esse non dubitas incircum-scriptum Deum,* Gr. D. 268, 24. *See next word.*

un-ymbfangenlic; *adj. Incomprehensible:*—Hú unymbfangenlice syndon his dómas *quam incomprehensibilia sunt judicia ejus,* Gr. D. 137, 26: 138, 22: 139, 19.

un-ymbwriten; *adj. Not circumscribed.* v. un-ymbfangen.

úp. V. *add:*—Ðér hit ǽr úp eóde *where it started,* C. D. v. 40, 17. þý læs hí for longum gesǽlþum hí tó úp áhæbben, and ðonan on ofer-méttum weorðen, Bt. 39, 11; F. 228, 23: Past. 79, 17: 461, 28.

úp; *adj. This form seems very doubtful. For* upne *in* Sat. 199 *perhaps* uppe *should be read*; cf. Hí wiston Drihten écne uppe, Dan. 195; *and in* Ps. Th. 81, 6 uppe-godu *may be taken.*

úp-áhafenlíce; *adv. Arrogantly, proudly:*—Úpáhafenlíce *arro-ganter, superbe,* An. Ox. 667. v. úp-áhefedlíce.

úp-áhafenness. I. *add:*—Swylce hit þolode þáre úpáhefenesse (úphefnesse, *v. l.*) *ac si sublevatione caruisset,* Gr. D. 249, 17. II (a). *add:*—For þí þe [Dryhtnes] is úre úpáhafennys *quia domini est assumptio nostra,* Ps. L. 88, 19.

úp-áhafu, e; *f. An uplifting, elevation:*—Sý mínra handa úpáhafu (*elevatio*) þé gecwǽme ǽfenofrung, Chrd. 30, 21.

úp-ende. *Add:*—Andlang ðǽre díc oð ðæs furlanges úpende, C. D. iii. 418, 24.

úp-flór. *Add:*—þá gelógode Benedictus hine sylfne on sumes stýpeles úpflóra (*in turris superioribus*), Gr. D. 170, 15.

úp-gang. II. *add: a going up* of water on to land:—Gedónre ýþunge se streám mid his rynum and mid his uppgange (úpgonge, *v. l.*) gewunode þ hé tógoten wæs geond his æceras, Gr. D. 192, 17.

úp-hefness. *Add: uplifting.* v. úp-áhafenness; I. *supra.*

úp-lic. I. *add:* (1):—Se deáð is for þám úplic; þeáh se man ástíge ofer þone yfemystan dǽl þæs hýhstan holtes, swáþeáhhwæðere hiene se deáð geséceð, Verc. Först. 103, 13. (2):—On úplicere gesihðe *in oromate,* i. *uisione superna,* An. Ox. 404. Tó þám úplican lífe *ad superos,* 2214.

uppæ. v. yppe (4).

uppan. II 1. *add:*—Hé sylf þá fæstnunge mid his ágenum handum uppan þone altare álecge (*super altare ponat*), R. Ben. 101, 7: 8. Sleá man of þá hand ... and sette uppon þá mynetsmiððan, Ll. Th. i. 206, 21. II 4. *add:*—Nis þé genóh þ þú sylf losast, þeáh þú uppan þ (*insuper*) óþre ne forspylle, Chrd. 74, 29.

úp-rihte. *Add:* III. *of position, turned upwards.* Cf. úp-riht; II:—And sýn þá fét gebundene tó ðám héhstan telgan, and þ heáfod hangige ofdúnrihte and þá fét úprihte, Verc. Först. 110, 10. IV. *of direction, straight up:*—Úp on wáðhám ... ðonne úprihte (cf. úp on gerihte, 17) on ðá hwyrfeldíc, C. D. iii. 406, 24.

úp-weardes. *Add:* I. *of direction:*—þá fǽringa lócode heó upp-weardes (*sursum respiciens*) and geseah þone Hǽlend þider cuman tó hire, Gr. D. 286, 21. II. *with the face turned upwards,* cf. úp-riht; II:—Se líchama þæs abbudes læg úpweardes *abbatis corpus supinum jacebat,* Gr. D. 226, 21.

út. I 7. *add*: v. lǽtan, IV e. II 3. *add*:—þæs ymb III niht hié gefuhton út on sǽ, Ors. 5, 13; S. 246, 5.

útan. A. II. *add*: (1):—Ne mehton hié nānne monn on ðǽm fæstenne útan geseón *cum murum escendisset, vacuam civitatem ratus*, Ors. 3, 9; S. 134, 11. (3) *add*:—Se petra oleum is gód andfeald tô drincan wið innantiédernesse and útan tô smerwanne, Lch. ii. 288, 16. (3 a) *add*:—Gif hé ǽnig þing wundorlices wyrcð útan þurh Godes gife *mira quae foris fiunt*, Gr. D. 45, 6. v. for-útan.

útan-burhware; *pl.* Outside citizens, those living out of the town:—Ðā .III. gefērscipas innanburhwara and útanburhwara, Cht. Th. 510, 31: C. D. B. iii. 491, 11.

útan-cumen. I. *add*:—Tô útancumenum mannum *extraneis*, Gr. D. 50, 14.

útane. II. *add*: (1 a) *in foreign countries*:—Heora wīse on nǽnne sǽl wel ne gefór, nāþer ne innan from him selfum, ne útane from ōþrum folcum, Ors. 4, 4; S. 164, 14. (4):—Mon ne mæg útane on him ongietan hwæt mon tǽle *foris a reprehensoribus non videntur*, Past. 271, 20: 417, 17: 439, 4.

útan-ymbstandness, e; f. *Surrounding*:—Duru útonymbstondnesse *ostium circumstantiae*, Ps. Vos. 140, 3.

út-ásliden *fallen into* (of sin):—Útáwundene gylt oþþe útáslidene synne *prolapsum nefas*, Germ. 388, 58.

út-áwunden. *See preceding word.*

úte. II 4 c. *add*:—Þá þe ǽr úte ōþra ðeóda anwalda girndon, him þā gód þúhte þær hié mehten hié selfe æt hām wið ðeówdôm bewerian *domesticis malis circumventi externis inhiare desistunt, abjiciuntque spem dominationis imminente periculo servitutis*, Ors. 3, 1; S. 98, 2.

útera. *Add*: v. ýtera.

úte-weard. *Add*:—Útewardre hýde *cute summa, superficietenus, extrema*, An. Ox. 50, 23.

út-fær. *Add*: I. *egress from an inclosure*:—Þ man næbbe infær ne útfær būtan leáfe *ut nulli nisi per licentiam aditus potest intrandi aut exeundi*, Chrd. 20, 11: 21, 16. II. *a going away, departure*:—Hwæt gemǽnað þā þreó útfæru (-faru, *v. l.*) þe God Abrahame beád þus cweþende: 'Far of þínum lande and of þínre mǽgðe and of þínes fæder húse? *quid in tribus illis egressionibus intelligendum est, in quibus praecipitur a Domino Abrahae ut egrediatur de terra sua et de cognatione sua et de domo patris sui?*, Angl. vii. 40, 389.

útfangene-þeóf *the jurisdiction of the lord over his man taken as a thief outside the lord's domain, the right of the lord to pursue his man, when accused of theft, outside his own jurisdiction, bring him back to his own court for trial, and keep his forfeited chattels on conviction*:—Habeant socam et sacam . . . infangeneþeóf and útfangeneþeóf, C. D. B. iii. 575, 22. Cf. *cum furis comprehensione intus et foris*, i. 550, 31. Omnis latro extra proclamatus (cf. *proclamatus extra terminos suos*, 4), Ll. Lbmn. 614, 1. [v. *N. E. D.* outfangthief.] v. infangeneþeóf.

út-gánde *out-going*:—Gehycgan ymb þ líf þære útgándan (-gangendan, *v. l.*) sáwle of līchaman *vitam animae exeuntis a corpore perpendere*, Gr. D. 269, 8. v. út-gangende.

út-gang. (5) *Add*:—Se drænc is gód wið ornum útgange, Lch. iii. 70, 25. Hié oft út yrnað gemengde útgange, hwīlum heard, hwīlum hwīt, ii. 230, 20. [v. *N. E. D.* outgang.]

út-gangende *out-going*:—Þú ne gesáwe þá útgangendan (*egredientem*) sáwle, Gr. D. 268, 4. Útgangende sáwle of þám līchaman *egredientes a carne animas*, 272, 4. v. út-gánde.

út-hleáp. *Substitute*: *The fine to be paid by a man who goes from his lord without leave*:—Si quis a domino suo sine licentia discedat, *útleipa* emendetur et redire cogatur, ut rectum per omnia faciat, Ll. Th. i. 543, 13. Cf. Gif hwá fare unálíefed fram his hláforde . . . and hine mon geáhsige, fare þær hé ǽr wæs, and geselle his hláforde .LX. scill., Ll. Th. i. 126, 9-8. *See also* 86, 1-10: 210, 20. [v. *N. E. D.* out-leap.]

úp-mǽte. *Add*:—Unmǽte is a *v. l.*, Mart. H. 76, 1.

úp-wita. *Add*:—Weoruldlice úðwitan (*sapientes mundi*) sǽdan þ seó tunglene heofon feólle for hire swiftnysse gif þá seofon dweligendan steorran hyre ryne ne wiðhæfton, Angl. vii. 12, 110.

úp-witigung. *Add*:—Wæs sum mǽden . . . wlitig on wæstme and on úðwitegunge snoter, Hml. S. 35, 83.

útian. *Add*:—Útud *exiliata*, An. Ox. 2, 394. v. ýtan.

út-lendisc. *Add*:—Þ þá brōþra . . . þ earnodon mid heora handa weorcum æt útlendisceum mannum (*extraneis*), Gr. D. 50, 14.

út-leóriende; *adj.* (*ptcpl.*) *Outgoing, departing*:—Be þám útleóriendum (*egredientibus*) sáwlum of līchaman, Gr. D. 301, 14. þá útleóriendan sáwle þára rihtwīsra manna, 337, 19.

út-siht. *Add*:—Traianus gefór on útsihte (*profluvio ventris*), Ors. 6, 10; S. 266, 4.

út-spíung. v. wyrms-útspíung.

út-waru. [*For the obligation involved in waru see werian*; III c.] *Add*:—Hí him þ land sealdon æt Norðtûne . . . þ syndon iii hída tô inware and óðer healf tô útware, Cht. E. 235, 29.

út-weard; *adv.* *Forth, outside, out of doors*:—Swá hí gedôn hæbbon swá beón hí on ofeste útweard *ubi perfectum habuerint opus suum cum summa festinatione egrediantur foras*, Chrd. 31, 29: 31.

# V

vípere, an; f. *A viper*:—Cynn uíperana *genimina uiperarum*, Mt. R. 23, 33.

# W

wác; II. *add*:—Þá man talað wáce þe woldon for Godes ege georne lufian, Wlfst. 243, 11. II a. *of non-material things*:—Gyf ic nánre wácran gewitnesse ne gelýfe, þonne wát ic swīðe lytel oððer nánwiht, Solil. H. 66, 16. III. *add*:—Hé beleác hine on cwearterne and sende him bigleofan lytelne and wácne, 35, 38. Ðē is leófre on ðisum wácum scræfum ðonne ðú on healle heálic biscop sitte, Hml. Th. ii. 146, 28. Seó slápolnys byð gescrýdd mid wácum tætticum *dormitatio vestitur pannis*, Hml. A. 9, 238.

wacan. *This infinitive form does not occur, its place seems taken by* wæcnan.

wacen. I. *add*: I a. *intentional wakefulness, vigilance.* v. wacung. II. *add*:—Mid þý Benedictus behogode þá tíde þæs nihtlican gebedes, hé gefealh his wæcce (wacone, *v. l.*) (*instans vigiliis*), Gr. D. 170, 30. Hé hine sylfne band mid mycclum fæstenum and wacenum, 19. Wacona *vigilias*, Ps. Vos. 76, 5.

wacian. (1 b) *add*:—Ðeáh ðæt mód slǽpe gódra weorca, hit wacað on ðǽm ymbhogum ðisse worlde . . . Swá hit gebyreð ðæt ðæt mód slǽpð ðæs ðe hit wacian sceolde, and wacað ðæs ðe hit slǽpan sceolde, Past. 431, 25-28. (2) *add*: (a) *to watch* as a guard:—Ofer him wacað se Scippend ealra gesceafta, Past. 391, 21. ¶ *where the subject is a personal attribute*:—In þám mynstre wacode þæs láreówes ymbhoga, Gr. D. 28, 23. (β) *to keep a vigil* for prayer or religious observance:—Hí hyre líc bebyrigdon . . . and þær gelôme wacodon, Hml. S. 7, 249. Hí wacodon þá niht wið þá byrgene biddende God, 21, 120.

wác-líc. *Add*: *poor* (1) with regard to physical properties:—Hé wæs swīðe wáclíc on his gewǽdum *erat valde vilis in vestibus*, Gr. D. 34, 1. (2) with regard to mental or spiritual properties:—Ic sylf, án wáclíc man (*homuncio*), Gr. D. 7, 22. Hí unrǽdlíce fērdon on heora ídelum lustum and wáclícum gebǽrum . . . Him þúhte þá tô wáclíc þæt hé wolde gefremman þá leásan leahtras, ac hé leornode ǽfre máran and máran on his mánfulnysse, Ælfc. T. Grn. 17, 14-28.

wáclíce. I. *add*:—þe lǽs þú weorðe . . . tô úpáhafen . . . ne eft tô wáclíce geortreówe ǽniges gódes, Met. 5, 34.

wácmôdness. I. *add*:—Hé ðám fæderum bebeád þæt hí heora bearn ne geáðiligdon, þæt hí ne wurdon gewǽhte ðurh wácmôdnesse . . . Cildru behôfiað swiðlícere steóre, Hml. Th. ii. 324, 27.

wácness. *Add*:—Ne sceole wé forseón þearfena wácnysse, Hml. Th. i. 336, 1.

wacol. *Add*:—Beóð wacole *vigilate*, Hml. Th. i. 188, 31. Hí bǽdon þæt hé bude ðá byrgene besettan mid wacelum weardum, ii. 262; 8. Ús gedafenað þ wé mid wacelum eágum þás ðreó gemetu behealdon, 546, 8.

wacor. *Add*:—Sió wiþerweardnes biþ untálu and wracu (wacru?; wæru, *v. l.*), Bt. 20; F. 72, 6. v. wær; V.

wacu. *Add*: cf. wæcc: wácu (?). v. wund-wacu: wácung. v. leopu-wácung.

wacung, e; f. *Vigilance*:—Þá sette hé weard tô þám wíngearde, and bebeád þ hine man scolde healdan mid geornlicre wacunge (wacone, *v. l.*) (*solerti vigilantia*), Gr. D. 57, 24.

wadan. *Add*: v. be-wadan: -wáden. v. cyne-wáden; wǽden.

wadu (?) *a drag-net*:—Wade *sagenę* (Mt. 13, 47), An. Ox. 61, 15. [*M. H. Ger.* wate *sagena* (v. Angl. xxx. 528). Cf. *Icel.* vaðr *a fishing-line*.]

wǽcan. *Add*:—Mid miclum sáre wéht (wæced, *v. l.*) *tanto adfectus dolore*, Bd. 4, 11; Sch. 405, 15. Deáþe wé beóð wæcede *morte afficimur*, Ps. Rdr. 43, 22. *Insert in* l. 2 *after* wæhcte (wæcte, *v. l.*), *in* l. 4 *after* wæce (wecce, *v. l.*), *and in* l. 9 *after* wæced (áwěht, *v. l.*). Cf. leopuwǽcan.

wǽcc, e; f. *Watch, vigil*:—Mid þý hé behogode þá tíde þæs nihtlican gebedes hé gefealh his wæcce (*instans vigiliis*), Gr. D. 170, 30. v. wacu, wæcce.

wæcce. II. *add*: (1) *watchfulness, vigilance*:—Mid carfullre

wæccean *solerti vigilantia*, Gr. D. 57, 23. v. wacung. (2) *a watch, vigil* :—Weccan *uigilias*, Ps. L. 76, 5. v. dæg-wæcce.

wæccendlíce; *adv. Vigilantly* :—Þá nunfæmnan ongunnon ácsian þone fæder wæccendlíce *coeperunt sanctimoniales feminae patrem vigilanter inquirere*, Gr. D. 242, 14.

-wæcedness. v. ge-wæcedness.

-wæcenness. v. on-wæcenness: wæd. *Dele* mearc-, seolh- *at end.*

wæd; I 1. *add* :—Wǽda *indumentorum*, An. Ox. 8, 314. II. *add* : v. ge-wǽde; II. v. ciric-wǽd.

wǽden; *adj. Blue, purple* :—Wǽden *iacinthina*, An. Ox. 8, 374 : 7, 372. Wið ðȳ wédenan ǽttre, wið ðȳ geolwan ǽttre . . . wið ðȳ wonnan ǽttre, wið ðȳ wédenan ǽttre . . . wið ðȳ basewan ǽttre, Lch. iii. 36, 18–20. [O. Frs. wéden: O. H. Ger. weitin.] v. -wáden, *and next word.*

wǽdl; I. ¶ *add* :—Ic sende fȳr and gewirce eów tó wǽdlan *visitabo vos in egestate et ardore*, Lev. 26, 16. I a. *add* :—Seó wǽdl þǽra andlyfna *alimentorum indigentia*, Gr. D. 145, 6: *alimentorum inopia*, 159, 7. I b. with gen. describing kind of want :—Seó mycele wǽdl þǽre meteleáste, Gr. D. 145, 6.

wǽdlian. I. *add* :—Sume wilniað geðincðe þyssere worulde, sume gefyllað heora lustas, and hí ealle syððan sorhlíce wǽdliað, Hml. Th. ii. 146, 26. Hé gesealde wǽdligendum mannum (*captivis et indigentibus*), Gr. D. 179, 17.

wǽdling (= wǽdl-ling?), es; *m. A needy person* :—Wǽdlinge (-lincg?) ic eam *egens sum ego*, Ps. Vos. 87, 16. v. (?) sedling.

wǽfels. *Add* :—Wǽuels *armenum, velum*, Hpt. 31, 15, 392. Hí mid ánum wǽfelse his neb bewundon (*velaverunt eum*, Lk. 22, 64), Hml. Th. ii. 248, 13. Hí mid wolcnreádum wǽfelse hine bewǽfdon, 252, 25. Línenne wǽuels *anaboladia, amictorium lineum*, Hpt. 31, 16, 421. Ic eom wifhádes mann, and eallunga líchamlicum wǽfelsum bereáfod, Hml. S. 23 b, 207.

wæfer-sín. *Add* :—Cóm mycel werod tó þǽre wæfersȳne þæs hálgan mannes deáðes (*ad spectaculum mortis*), Gr. D. 254, 17.

wæfer-solor, es; *m. A stage* :—On wæfersȳne wæfersolre *in theatri pulpito*, An. Ox. 3458.

wæflian *to talk foolishly* :—Wæflað *blatterat, stulte loquitur*, Hpt. 31, 16, 434.

-wæfre. v. gangel-wæfre.

wæfþ[u]. *Add* :—Hí ne wundriað mæniges þinges þe monnum nú wǽfðo (wǽrþo, MS.) and wunder þynceð, Met. 28, 82.

wǽg *water.* II. *add* :—Wǽg *limpham*, An. Ox. 499. Wǽga *gurgitum*, 2487. [Goth. wḗgs σεισμός, κῦμα.]

wǽg *weight.* II. *add* :—Ǽlc man þe riht démeð, hé hæfð wǽga on handa, and on ǽgðere sceale hé byrð rihtwísnesse and mildheortnesse, Ll. Lbmn. 474, 6.

wǽgan *to deceive. Add* :—Gif þú wiltest ealne þone wísdóm þe on þám bócum stynt, þonne woldest þú gelȳfan þ ic ná ne wǽge on þisum gewrite, Ælfc. T. Grn. 12, 8. Wǽgeð weorc eleberian *mentietur opus oliue*, Ps. Rdr. 285, 17.

wǽge; II. *add* :—Wǽgan *trutina*, An. Ox. 26, 35.

wægn. *Add* : v. cræt-wægn.

wæl; III. *add* :—Him þá geþúhte swelc þæt mǽste wæl swelc hié oft ǽr for nóht hæfdon, Ors. 4, 7; S. 184, 14.

wæl-cyrge. *Take here* (?) *the forms given under* wellyrge, *where for* 'sinus' *l.* (?) erinis (= Ἐρινύς), *and add* :—Gydene, wælcyrie *Ueneris*, An. Ox. 4449.

wæl-gǽst, wǽl- ? *See next word.*

wæl-genga, an; *m. A deadly walker, a wild beast, a dragon* :—Wælgengan *belue*, An. Ox. 8, 305 : 5, 41. [Napier suggests wǽl-, and takes the word to mean 'deepwater-goer'. In support of this might be quoted *belua, bestia maris*, Wrt. Voc. ii. 125, 44; and the subaqueous home of Grendel and his mother. (Perhaps wǽlgǽst, rather than wælgǽst, is used of the former, B. 1331.) In favour of wǽl- it may be noted that the word describes a destructive dragon on land, and the compound may compare with *mán-genga* and *wæl-hwelp*.]

wæl-grim[m]. *Add* :—Ðá earman men beóð wyrs bereáfode fram þám unrihtwísan déman þonne fram þám wælgrimmestan here (*a cruentis hostibus*), Ll. Lbmn. 475, 17. v. un-wælgrimm.

wælgrimlíce. *Add* :—Hé geseah þone munuc wælgrimlíce (*crudeliter*) fram deófle geswǽnced, Gr. D. 161, 11 : 187, 22.

wælgrimness, e; *f. Cruelty* :—Hé gelȳfde þ fram þám tintregiendan sume þráge wolde seó wællgrimnes (*crudelitas*) geyldan, Gr. D. 163, 11. For þæs cyninges wælhreównysse (wællgrimnesse, *v. l.*), 196, 25. Wurdon hí swíðe blíðe, swá hí symble wǽron tó wælgrimnesse (*sunt nimiae crudelitatis*), 254, 16. Martyras þrowodon fela wælgrimnesse (*crudelia multa*), 292, 3.

wæl-hreów. *Add* : (1) :—Se wælreuw *truculentus* (*natrix*), An. Ox. 11, 90. (2) :—Wælreów *cruenta*, i. *atrox* (*saevitia*), An. Ox. 3301.

wǽl-lic (?). *Dele* : welicum *is part of* niwelicum. v. An. Ox. 1942.

wǽl-slihta (?), an; *m. A murderer* :—Þá stód se árwyrða wer swá gelǽded betwyh þám gewǽpnedum wælslihtum; þá gearn hé sóna mid

his geþóhte tó his ágnum wǽpnum háligra gebeda *venerandus vir inter armatos deductus ad sua arma statim cucurrit*, Gr. D. 254, 22. v. slihtan.

wǽpen-leás. *Add* :—Þá hét se árleáse healdan þone hálgan þ hé wurde wǽpnlǽs (ungewǽpnod, Hml. Th. ii. 502, 14) þám hǽðenum, Hml. S. 31, 117.

-wǽpne. v. ge-wǽpne.

wǽpned-hád. *Add* :—Hé fram þǽre costnunge weard swá fremde swilce hé þone wǽpnedhád on his líchaman nǽfde (*ac si sexum non haberet in corpore*), Gr. D. 26, 30.

wǽpned-mann; I. *add* :—Oð þæt þǽr wæs deóp seáð ádolfen, þætte wǽpnedman mihte oð his sweóran on gestandan *ut fossam ad mensuram staturae uirilis altam reddiderit*, Bd. 3, 9; Sch. 229, 4. v. út-wǽpnedmann.

wǽpnung. *Add* : v. ge-wǽpnung.

wǽr; *adj.* V. *add* :—On þeáwum wǽr *moribus cautus*, Chrd. 19, 13. Sió wiþerweardnes biþ . . . wǽru . . . mid þǽre styringe hire ágenre frécennesse *adversam fortunam videas ipsius adversitatis exercitatione prudentem*, Bt. 20; F. 72, 6. Se wara weard his ágenre þearfednesse *ille sollicitus suae paupertatis custos*, Gr. D. 201, 11.

wǽrc. *Add* :—On þysse worulde sȳn fíf onlícnessa be hellegryre. Sió ǽreste onlícnes is nemned wræc (wærc, *v. l.*); for ðan se wræc (wærc, *v.l.*) bið miceles cwelmes ǽlcum þára þe hé tó cymeð; for ðan hine sóna ne lysteð metes ne drinces . . . ne ðǽr ne bið ǽnig wuldor mid him, þæt hé fore wynsumige, þeáh him syndon ealle wuldordreámas tó gelǽdde, Verc. Först. 106, 11–107, 2 : v. end-, hrif-, hype-, in-, rop-, út-wærc.

wǽrcan. I. *for second passage substitute* :—Wið healswærce . . . þonne þone heals wærc[e], smire ðá þeóh ; gif þá þeóh wærce, smire þone heals, Lch. ii. 312, 5–7. II. *dele.* Cf. Ps. Rdr. 76, 4 :—Ic worhte *exercitatus sum.*

wǽrlan. *Add* : v. á-wǽrlan.

wǽr-lic. *Add* :—Hí þurh þ swȳþur cunnedon þǽre Godes gife þonne hit wǽrlic wǽre, Gr. D. 27, 12.

wǽr-lot. *Before* wǽrlotes *insert* Gebrægdnes, *and see* ge-brægden.

wǽr-sagol. *Add* : cf. wǽr-wyrdé.

wǽr-word. *Perhaps* wǽr-word *should be read, with the meaning : an agreement, a proviso. In the following passage, however,* wǽr-word *seems to occur* :—Nis geméted on hálgum bócum þætte þisse frigenesse wǽrword (wiðerword, *v. l.*) sȳ gesewen *nequaquam in sacris eloquiis invenitur quod huic capitulo contradicere uideatur*, Bd. 1, 27; Sch. 68, 11. *See next word.*

wǽr-wyrde. *Add* :—Gif on Wódnesdæg . . . bið ácenned, sé bið wǽrwyrde (swíðe wǽr on his wordum, *v.l.*), Archiv cxxviii. 298, 9.

wǽscestre, an; *f. One who washes.* (1) *used of a man* :—Iobinus wæs mín wæscestre (*fullo*), Gr. D. 191, 23 : 192. (2) *of a woman* :—Hé wæs lufigende his wæscestran (*presbyteram*) swá swá his ágne swuster . . þá þá hine geseah seó his wæscestre, Gr. D. 276, 1–14. [Þis us doð to understonden þe forbisne of þe wasshestren *quod melius patefacit exemplar lotricum*, O. E. Hml. ii. 57, 22.]

wǽsc-hús, es; *n. A washhouse, laundry* :—Wæschús *colimbum, lauandariam*, Hpt. 31, 13. 323.

wǽstm. I 2. *add* :—Hé bæd God geornlíce þ hé þám þegne forgeáfe bearnes wæstm, Hml. S. 33, 18. I 6. *add* :—Se cwide hú mon ðæt feoh besǽtte ðǽm ciépemen ðe hé scolde forð sellan tó wæstme, Past. 379, 8. III. *add* :—Hé wæs scort on wæstme *statura pusillus erat*, Hml. Th. i. 580, 30. Þá assan syndon on þám mǽstan wæstme (*printed* wæstene) *onagri forma maxima*, Nar. 34, 16. v. geár-wæstm.

wǽstm-bǽre. (1) *add* : (1 a) *with gen.* :—Eard wȳnes wæstmbǽre *regio uinifera*, Chrd. 15, 14.

wǽstm-berende. *Add* : v. un-wǽstmberende.

wǽstmian. *Add* :—Wæstmiað *fructificant*, Mk. L. 4, 28.

wǽt; II. *add* :—Wǽt land *irriguum*, Gr. D. 245, 20.

wǽta (-e); III. *add* :—Gif hié cumað of biterum and yfelum wǽtum, Lch. ii. 178, 13. III a. *add* :—Sume men of hiora scome þá wǽtan for þǽm nȳde þigdon *vidimus ṭlerosque pudore amisso suam urinam uexatos ultimis necessitatibus haurientes*, Nar. 9, 22. v. in-wǽte.

wǽtan. *Add* : *to become wet, emit moisture* :—Hí gemétton þ stánclif swǽtende and wǽtende *rupem montis sudantem invenerunt*, Gr. D. 113, 10.

wǽter. *Add* : *in the following example the word is masculine.* II a. *add* :—Æfter þan bióð ealle wæteras and ealle wyllas on blóde *tunc omnes fontes et putei in sanguinem convertentur*, Verc. Först. 120, 9. v. fullwiht-, regn-, sǽ-wæter.

wǽter-drync, es; *m. A drink of water* :—Hé sǽde þæt man mid wæterdrinces sylene mihte him mycele ælmessan gedón, Nap. 67. [Cf. Alls iff þu drunnke waterdrinnck ut off þe firrste fetless, Orm. 14482.]

wǽter-flód. *Add* : [O lifft, o land, o waterrflod, Orm. 17567.]

wǽter-frogga, an; *m. A water-frog* :—Wæterfrogcan (*ranę in aqua*) hwílon hí man gesihð of wætere, and swá þeáh sécað tó fúllicum mórseohtrum, Chrd. 96, 27.

**wæter-gefeall**, es; *n. A waterfall:*—Æfter heáfdon tó þām wætergefeal; æfter streáme, Cht. Crw. 21, 43.

**wæter-gelād**; *n.* (not *m.*)

**wæter-gesceaft**, e; *f. The watery element:*—Swā þ wæter wæs standende and beleác þā duru þǣre cyrican, efne swylce seó wætergesceaft (wæteres gesceaft) wǣre onwænded in fæstes wāges staðolfæstnesse *sic stans aqua ecclesiae januam clausit, ac si illud elementum liquidum in soliditatem parietis fuisset mutatum*, Gr. D. 220, 17.

**wæter-leást.** *Add:*—For wæterlīste, Ps. Spl. 105, 14.

**wæter-scipe.** *Add:*—Đā wǣron twēgen gebrōðra . . . and hæfdon ǣnne fiscnoþ on ānum brādum mere . . . ac þǣr wurdon eft æt þām wæterscipe . . . micel gefeoht for þām fixnoþe. Hwæt þā se bisceop . . . ābæd æt Gode þ hē worhte þone wæterscipe tó wynsumum yrþlande . . . and wæs se mere āwend tó wīdgyllum felda, Nap. 22, 21–28.

**wæter-seáþ.** *Add:*—Seó stōw ofer þām stæþe sumes wæterseáðes (ofer sumes wæteres seáðes ōfre, *v. l.*) (*super laci ripam*), Gr. D. 113, 21. Wæs gewinnful niþer tó āstīgenne tó þām wæterseáðe (*ad lacum*), þonne hī sceoldon heom wæter hladan, 112, 18.

**wæter-steall.** *Add:* The original Latin is: Nunc stagnis, nunc flactiris, interdum nigris fusis vaporibus et laticibus.

**wæter-stoppa**, an; *m. A bucket:*—Hī þā racenteáge gefæstnodon tó þām rāpe and gebundon tó ðām wæterstoppan (*situlam*), Gr. D. 214, 25. Þā arn ān wencel mid treówenum æscene tó þǣre wyllan, and sōna swā hit þ wæter hlōd, þā becōm ān fisc in þone wæterstoppan (*situlam*), 11, 22.

**wæter-streám.** *Add:*—Crīst wolde sylf swā hālgian ūre fulluht mid his hālgan līchaman and ealle wæterstreámas mid his ingange, Nap. 67. [Se waterrstræm erneþþ towarrd te sæ, Orm. 18092.]

**wæter-swilige**, an; *f. A deep pit with water in it* (?) *:*—Of mærdīc on ðā wæterswylian; of ðǣre swylian, C. D. vi. 220, 23. Cf. swelg.

**wæter-weg.** *Add:*—Of ðǣm ēwylme andlang weterweges ūp tó strēte, C. D. v. 207, 29.

**wǣtian.** *Add:*—Hī gemētton þ stānclif swǣtende and wǣtgende *rupem montis sudantem invenerunt*, Gr. D. 113, 10.

**wāfian.** *l.* wāfian, *and add:* (1):—Hē forhtmōd wāfode, Ælfc. T. Grn. 17, 43. Hē ðis gehȳrende ongan micclum wāfian, Hml. S. 33, 311. (2 a):—On ūrum tīdum hī syndon ūs swīðe tó wāfienne *sunt haec nostris valde stupenda temporibus*, Gr. D. 187, 8. Đǣr gelamp wundorlic þing and swīðe tó wāfienne *res mira et vehementer stupenda*, 82, 24: 172, 22: 240, 5. (3):—Þām deácone wāfiendum for þus mycclum wundre *cui tantum hoc obstupescenti miraculum*, Gr. D. 171, 34.

**wāfung;** II. *add:*—Se apostol þe se engel onlȳsde, and his mōd gegrāp on wāfunge *quem angelus solvit, ejusque mentem in ecstasim rapuit*, Gr. D. 108, 3.

**wāfung-stōw.** *Add:*—Wāuungstōwe wæuersēne *circi spectaculo*, An. Ox. 8, 188. On wāuungstōwe *in circi spectaculo*, 4, 59. The Latin of Lch. iii. 206, 16 *is :* In theatrum vel in amphitheatrum.

**wāg.** *In l.* 4 *for* brýden *l.* bryden, *and see* breden. *Dele* grund-, *at end.*

**wāg-rift.** *Add:*—Wāhrefte *conopeo*, An. Ox. 7, 365. Ic geann intó þǣre hālgan stōwe . . . ānes hricghrægles þæs sēlestan ðe ic hæbbe, and ānes beddreáfes mid wāhryfte, Cht. Th. 529, 12. Hē geann . . . Wulfgāre his mǣge twēgra wāhryfta and twēgra setlhrægla, Cht. Crw. 23, 15. *v.* bed-wāgrift.

**wala** (?) *a root* (?). Perhaps for 'ad walan' *ad palam* should be read. The gloss is on Ald. 32, 1. Cf. An. Ox. 2313, *ad liquidum*, i. *manifeste* openlīce: for the use of a preposition with *palam* see *in palam*, Mk. 4, 22.

**walden-íge**; *adj. Blue-* or *grey-eyed, wall-eyed:*—Ualdenēgi *cessius, glaucus*, Txts. 110, 1166. [Waldeneie (*name for a ware*), Digby MS. 86. Woldeneiȝheh hy beeth, Alis. 5274. Walnyed *glaucus* (among colours of horses), Pall. iv. 807. Waldeȝed, Alex. (Skt.) 608. *v. N. E. D.* wall-eyed. *Icel.* wald-eygðr.]

**walte, waltae.** *v.* wealte.

**wamb.** I 1. *add:*—Wē þis ne rōhton; ac wē lufedon micle swīðor ūra wamba fylnesse, Verc. Först. 123, 14.

**wamb-scyldig** (?); *adj. Gluttonous* (?):—Lā, ðū eorðan lamb (= lām) and dūst and wyrma gifel, and þū wambscyldiga (= wammscyldiga?) fætels and gealstor and fūlnes and hrǣw, Nap. 67.

**wamm;** *adj. Add:*—Wom[mum?] *maculoso*, An. Ox. 17, 48.

**wana;** *adj.* I. *add:*—þāra manna mōd . . . wāt þ þā martyras þǣr in heora līchaman ne licgaþ, and þonne hwæþre nǣron wana fram þǣre gehȳrnesse *mens . . . illic martyres novit et non jacere corpore, et tamen non deesse ab exauditione*, Gr. D. 117, 15. II. *add:*—þeáh þe heom gelumpe þ hī ūtan on heora līchaman inænniscra lāreówa lāre wana wǣron *ut eis exterius humani magisterii disciplina desit*, Gr. D. 13, 2. *v.* ge-wana.

**wand** *a mole. Add:*—Wand (*printed* pund) *talpa*, Wrt. Voc. i. 289, 61.

**Wandale, Wænle, Wendle;** *pl. The Vandals:*—þā þā Wandale (Wendle, *v. l.* Wandali) rīcsodon . . . ān wydewe sǣde þ hire sunu wǣre gelǣded in hæftnȳde fram Wænla (Wendla, *v. l.*) cyneges āðume, Gr. D. 179, 14–21. Wændla (Wendla, *v. l.*) rīce, 181, 7. Seó arrianisce ēhtnes wæs upp ārǣred fram þām ungeleáffullum Wandalum (Wendlum,

*v. l.*) . . . þā ongan se Wendla cyning bīgan þā biscopas, 240, 7–12. *v.* Wend(e)las (-e).

**wandian.** *Add: v.* wandung; ge-wand.

**wandung.** *Add:* e; *f.* I. *a turning aside* from a task. *v.* wandian; II a. :—Tó þām cyninge ic mē dæghwāmlīce būtan ǣlcre wandunge (*sine intermissione*) tō gebidde, Chrd. 99, 19. II. *feeling of respect. v.* wandian; II b. :—Sē þe man for ylde oððe for sumre wandunge swingan ne mæg, *si etas aut qualitas persone prohibet*, Chrd. 61, 34.

**wang.** I. *add:*—Wongas ne bryngað mete *arua non afferent cybum*, Cant. Ab. 17. *v.* eorþ-wang.

**wang** *a cheek. Add:*—Slōh hē þone Godes wer mid his brādre handa ofer his wange, Gr. D. 200, 15. *v.* hār-wenge.

**wan-hālness.** *Add:*—On geogoðe and on ylde, on gesundfulnysse and on wanhālnesse, Archiv cxxi. 46, 9.

**wann.** (1) *add:*—Hī wundrodon hwæt þ þing wǣre þ hē swā tóswollen heáfod and swā wanne andwlitan (*lividam faciem*) hæfde, Gr. D. 22, 20.

**wannian.** *Add: to become dark coloured:*—þonne wannað hē and doxaþ, Nap. 13, 16.

**wanung.** I 3. *add:*—Hē becōm tó þām dæmme his sylfes wanunge *ad defectus damna pervenit*, Gr. D. 200, 10. Heó byð tó þām mǣstan gestreónum gehealdenu of þām lytlan woningum *ad lucra maxima ex minimo damno servetur*, 205, 9.

**wār.** I. *add:*—Wārum *algis*, An. Ox. 23, 13. II. see note at An. Ox. 1818 on the forms and meaning of the instances given from Hpt. Gl.

**wara.** [*In a note to An. Ox. 3903 Prof. Napier claims that in all three instances given of the uncompounded* wara *ceasterwar- should be read. However the MS. of Andreas has* ceastre warena.] *v.* hālga-, hālig-waras, port-wara, Lǣden-, Mēd-, Mersc-, Parth-, Pers-, Persc-ware.

**warenian.** *Add: Dele the last passage, for which see* weornian. [II 2 b. *In the first passage one MS. has :*—Warnode hē him, Bd. Sch. 53, 24.] *v.* fore-warenian.

**warian.** IV. *add:*—Hwǣr him wǣre fultumes tó biddanne tó warienne (gewearnienne, *v. l.*) and tó wiðscū(f)enne swā rēðum heregange *ubi quaerendum esset praesidium ad euitandas uel repellendas tam feras inruptiones*, Bd. 1, 25; Sch. 39, 18. *v.* on-warian.

**warian** (*a different word from preceding* ?) *to make an agreement with :*—Ac nales æfter micelre tīde þæt hié waredon (geweredon, *v. l.*) wið him, and heora wǣpen hwyrfdon wið hieora gefēran *sed non multo post, iuncto cum his foedere, in socios arma uerterit*, Bd. 1, 15; Sch. 40, 7. *v.* ge-werian.

**wāriht.** *l.* wāriht(e).

**waroþ.** *Add:*—Tó warode *ad litus*, An. Ox. 8, 420. Be sǣs wāroðe (waroðum, *v. l.*) *sicut arenam quae est in littore maris*, Gr. D. 55, 12. Lōcian ēgðer ge ofer þone warað ge ofer þā sǣ, Solil. H. 45, 20.

**waru.** *Dele* niht- *at end.* (5) *add:*—Ne synd āwritene ealle Iūdan gefeoht for his freónda ware, Hml. S. 25, 677: 26, 147. *v.* in-waru, waru *a weir.*

**waru.** *Add:*—Waru *merces*, An. Ox. 28, 16.

**waru** *a weir. v.* mylen-waru. *Perhaps the word might be taken under* waru *protection:* -waru. *Add: v.* Cant-, ciric-waru: **waru** *wear. Add: v.* niht-waru.

**watel.** *Add:*—Watelum *tegulis*, An. Ox. 2, 489.

**wāwa.** *Add:*—On heáhsetle cwyldes † wāwan *in cathedra pestilentiae*, Ps. Rdr. 1, 1.

**weá-gesíþ.** *Add:*—Weágesȳþ *satelles*, An. Ox. 46, 35.

**wealcan.** I. *add:*—Wealcendes *exagitantis*, i. *commouentis* (*ponti aestum*), An. Ox. 34, 5. Þā geseah hē ān scip ūt on þǣre sǣ, swā swīðe torfigende fram þan wealcendum sǣs ȳðum, Nap. 62, 25. II. *add:*—Wylcþ *raptat*, Germ. 389, 42. (2) *add:*—þā ongann hē þurh oferhogodnysse gāst swīgende on his mōde wealcan (þæncan, *v. l.*) *coepit per superbiae spiritum in mente sua tacitus volvere*, Gr. D. 144, 5. *v.* be-wealcan.

**wealcian.** *Add: v.* ge-wealcian.

**wealc-spinel.** *Add:*—Of wolcspinle *calamistro*, An. Ox. 26, 70. *v.* ge-wealcian.

**weald** *power. Add:* II. *an implement by which constraint is exercised, a bridle. v.* ge-weald; II, weald-leþer:—Walde ceócan heora gewrīð *in camo maxillas eorum constringe*, Ps. Rdr. 31, 9. III. *the groin. v.* ge-weald; IV.:—Wið cyrnlu þe on wealde (v. gewealde, 106, 13) weaxeþ, Lch. i. 12, 9.

**weald;** *adj. For* wealdestan *perhaps* weallendestan *should be read as a literal rendering of* ferventissimo.

**weald.** I. *add:*—Weald þeáh eówer eard ūs gesceóte, Jos. 9, 7. II. *add:*—Weald hū þe sǣle *whatever happen to thee*, An. 1357. Cf. lōca hū.

**wealda.** *Add: v.* burg-wealda.

**wealdan.** V c. *For second passage see* weald; II *above.* VII. *add:*—þonne hié heora willan mōton wel wealdan *when they could quite do what they wanted*, Ors. 2, 1; S. 60, 7.

weald-bǽre; n. l. -bǽr, e; f. v. wudu-bǽr, and bǽr; den-bǽre (q. v.) should be den-bǽr.

wealdend. Add: v. an-, heofon-wealdend.

wealdend-god. Perhaps Men. 46: El. 4 should be taken here.

weald-leþer. Add:—On wealdleðre in chamo, Ps. L. 31, 9. v. weald; II.

wealdness. Add: v. an-wealdness.

weald-weaxa (?) a sinew, nerve:—Uuldpaexhsue vel grost, Txts. 112, 56. [O. H. Ger. walt-wahso nervus.]

wealg. The meaning 'insipid, nauseous' is borne out by what follows áspiwen:—For ðǽm ǽlc wæter bið ðý unwerodre tó drincanne, æfter ðǽm ðe hit wearm bið, gif hit eft ácólað, ðonne hit ǽr wǽre, ǽr hit mon ongunne wleccan. The '?' might be left out.

wealh. Add: v. wíngeard-wealh.

wealh-basu. Add:—Wealhbasu ł mædre uermiculo, An. Ox. 35, 4.

wealh-land. I. add: cf. the prose version of this passage:—Swá oft swá wyt férdon tó fyrlenum eardum, Gen. 20, 13.

wealh-moru. Add:—Wealmoru pastinaca, An. Ox. 56, 426.

wealh-stod. II. add:—Walestoda, An. Ox. 8, 120.

wealh-word. Add: Angl. xi. 101, 42.

wealh-wyrt. Add:—Wælwyrt ebulo, An. Ox. 26, 57.

weall. Add: v. bred-weall: weall mulled wine. See peall.

weallan. I. add:—Mycel wynsumnesse stenc ðǽr upp weóll of þǽre byrgene de sepulcro fragrantia suavitatis emanavit, Gr. D. 338, 18. II I. add:—Binnan Róme weóll án wille ele ealne dæg fons olei per totum diem fluxit, Ors. 5, 14; S. 248, 10. III 2. add:—þá líc weóllon eall maðon and egeslíce stuncon, Hml. S. 4, 212. VI. add:—Hwá sceotað ðæt deófol mid weallendum strǽlum?, Sal. K. 148, 1. VII a. of natural forces:—Man dráf út his módor bútan ǽlcre mildheortnesse ongeán þone weallendan winter, Chr. 1037; P. 160, 16.

weall-geweorc. Add:—Wealgewuorc, C. D. iv. 51, 19. Cf. muri fabrica, 50, 13.

weallian to wander. Add:—Heó weallode wíde dæges and nihtes geond þá muntas and þá dena per montes et valles die noctuque vagabatur, Gr. D. 176, 18. Hé ongan weallian fram þám bróðrum in þá tíde heora gebedes vagari tempore orationis coepit, 111, 20.

weall-weg. Add:—On wealweg, C. D. ii. 29, 13. Cf. hege-weg.

wealte, an; f. A ring:—Ualtae argata (argata annulus crassior, Migne), Txts. 108, 1105. [O. H. Ger. walzo pedica.]

weá-mód. Add:—Witan him (the king) sceolan rǽdan, and hé ne sceal beón weámód, O. E. Hml. i. 303, 2.

weard, es; m. I. add:—Weart uigil, An. Ox. 32, 8. Siþþan Scipia geáscade þ þá foreweardas wǽron feor ðǽm fæstenne gesette . . . hé díegellíce gelǽdde his fird betuh þǽm weardum, Ors. 4, 10; S. 200, 14. v. dor-, hláf-, hrægel-, líf-, ortgeard-, rǽpling-weard.

weard, e; f. II. add:—In þá heordnesse and weard heora sylfra eádmódnesse in custodiam humilitatis, Gr. D. 205, 10. v. strǽt-weard.

weard; adv. Add: v. niþer-, ofdún(e)-, tógædere-, úp-weard.

-weard; adj. Add: v. of-, súþ-, súþan-weard: -wearde. v. or-wearde: weardere. Add: One MS. has weartæres: weardes. Add: v. ofdúne-, uppe-, west-weardes.

weard-geréfa, an; m. The captain of the guard. v. strǽt-weard.

weardian. I. add: to watch:—Weardude seruauerat (vigil e speculis pernox seruauerat horam, Vit. Cuth. poet. 37, 13), An. Ox. 32, 9. Dele ge-wardod at end.

-weardness. v. æfter-weardness.

wearg. I. add:—þá cómon on sumne sǽl ungesǽlige þeófas . . . se hálga wer hí wundorlíce geband . . . þ heora nán ne mihte þanon ástyrian . . . Men þá þæs wundrodon hú þá weargas hangodon, Hml. S. 32, 211. v. eald-wérig (l. wearg).

wearg-cwedol. Add: given to reviling:—Wyrigcwidole men maledici (revilers, 1 Cor. 6, 10), An. Ox. D. 207, 29.

wearg-cwedolness. Add:—þæs wirigcwedolnesse cuius maledictione (Ps. 9, 28), E. S. 49, 358.

wearg-líc. Add:—Hú ne is hit þǽr swíðe swiotol hú werelica þás woruldsǽlða sint liquet igitur quam sit mortalium rerum misera beatitudo, Bt. 11, 1; S. 25, 10.

wearg-treów. Add: [O. Sax. warag-treó.]

wearp. v. úp-wearp: wearriht. l. wearriht[e]: wearte. Add: v. cile-wearte.

weaxan. IV. add:—Ðǽm monnum ðe him mægen and cræft wiexð (wixst, v. l.), Past. 163, 8. Weaxð, 457, 12. v. mis-, tó-, ymb-weaxan: efen-, sám-weaxen.

weax-bred. I. add:—Wexbred abbachus, tabula pictoria, Hpt. 31, 9, 155.

webb. Add:—Webb telas, An. Ox. 26, 8. [The Latin original of Lch. iii. 210, 28 is: Tela quicumque texerit.]

web-beám. In l. 3 for insubula l. insubulae.

webbung a spectacle. Add:—Hwebbunge, An. Ox. 2920 (= Hpt. Gl. 474, 65). [Uuebung (Wrt. Voc. ii. 120, 13) may = wǽfung, cf. wáfung, and see note to An. Ox. 2920.]

web-geréþru. [In Wlck. Gl. 295, 16 (= Wrt. Voc. i, 66, 26) tala (not tara) is printed: web-geróðes. l. (?) -rod-.

weccan. Add: v. ge-weccan: -weceness. v. á-weceness.

wecg. II. add:—Wecge materiem, An. Ox. 50, 36. v. gold-, gylding-wecg.

wédan. II b. The Latin of Lch. iii. 206, 32 is: Leonem infestare (uiderit), seditionem significat.

wedd. I. add:—Ðonne cwið se éca cyning tó ánra gehwylcum: '. . . Hwet gedydest þú? Syle wedd be þissum eallum þe ic for þé dyde and for þé þrowade.' Ðonne andswaraþ se man úrum Drihtne and cwið: 'Nebbe ic ǽnig wedd tó syllanne nimþe míne (dǽda).' Þonne bið bóc ontýned . . . On þére bóc beóð áwritene æghwylces mannes dǽda, Verc. Först. 134, 16. I a. add:—Giftlicum wedde nuptiali dote, An. Ox. 11, 159. v. borg-wed.

-weddendlic. v. be-weddendlic.

weddian; II. add: of the part played by the priest at the marriage:—Brýdguman and brýde mæssepreóst sceal weddian be lagum sponsus et sponsa a sacerdote legibus sponsentur, Chrd. 81, 9.

wéden. v. wǽden.

wédend-seóc; adj. Insane, mad, lunatic. v. wéden[d]-seóc.

wéden-heort; adj. Add:—Sumre nihte þá þá hé ýpte swá wédenheort mycle stefne nocte quadam cum magnas voces scilicet ut insanus ederet, Gr. D. 247, 15.

wédenheortness. Add: of an animal:—þ hors wæs æfter þon stilre þonne hit wæs ǽr þére wédenheortnesse (wódnesse, v. l. ante illam insaniam). Se þegn geseah his hors ácyrred fram his wédenheortnesse (wódnesse, v. l., a sua vesania), Gr. D. 78, 12–17.

wéden(d)-seóc; adj. Possessed by a devil, mad:—Sum preóst wæs mid deófle geswenced. . . . þá wæs gelǽded se wódseóca (wédendseóca, v. l.) tó Benedicte, Gr. D. 135, 1. Tó úrum Alýsende wæs gecweden fram þám deófla heápe þe þone wédenseócan man ofseten hæfde Redemtori nostro a legioni, quae hominem tenebat, dictum est, 223, 22.

weder. II. add:—Wedra gebregd, Ph. 57. v. ge-bregd.

wederian. v. ge-widerian (not ge-wederian).

wéding (-ung). Add:—Benedictus lǽrde þ hé scolde gestillan fram þére wédunge and ungewittignesse swá mycelre wælhreównysse (a tantae crudelitatis insaniae), Gr. D. 164, 27.

weg. I a. add: means of access:—Ðý lǽs sió úpáhæfenes him weorde tó wege micelre scylde ne elatio via fiat ad foveam gravioris culpae, Past. 439, 11. II. add: [weg seems contrasted with pæþ, and with here-strǽt, -pæþ:—Of þám wege út æt norðgæte, on þone smalan pæþ; of þám smalan pæþ innan þá herestrǽt, C. D. B. iii. 468, 9. Andlang weges oð ðæt hit cumð tó ðám herpaðe, C. D. iii. 414, 23]:—On þone grénan weg; andlang weges tó wealléhes wege, and þanon on stánihtan weg, C. D. B. i. 417, 25. On weg féran to journey, travel, Lch. ii. 330, 8. III. add:—Hié sægdon þ nǽre mára weg þonne meahte on týn dagum geféran (uiam non amplius decem dierum), Nar. 25, 2. V. add:—Ðá þe on ðére synne ealnu weg licgað, Past. 179, 3. Ealne weg búton geswícincge iugiter sine intermissione, Angl. xiii. 372, 103. v. æcer-, ceaster-, ciric-, clǽg-, gemǽr-, gird-, grund-, heáfod-, heah-, healf-, hege-, hrís-, hwæl-, hweól-, Lunden-, mearc-, mylen-, Nor-, port-, sǽ-, sláhþorn-, styfic-, syl-, well-, wíc-weg.

wegan. A. I. add:—Se wer tó þére gecwedstówe wegendum þám ylcan horse (equo eodem subvehente) wæs gelǽded, Gr. D. 183, 7. II I. add:—Wegað mín geoc on eówrum swurum tollite jugum meum super vos, Hml. A. 10, 249. B. Perhaps in Exod. 180 wǽpn might be inserted before wǽgon, and the passage be removed to A. III I.

weg-farende. Add: -farend, es; m. A wayfarer:—Úre dagas gewítað swá swá wegfarende menn, Hml. S. 28, 154. Hí begunnon tó áxienne æt óþrum wegfarendum, 31, 992.

weg-férend. Add:—þá þá se bróþor on þone weg férde, óþer wegférend (viator) hine sylfne tó him geþeódde, Gr. D. 128, 9: 314, 12.

weg-férende. I a. add:—þá cwæð se wegférenda, Gr. D. 128, 15.

wegu, e; f. Carriage, vehicle:—Ne beþearf ná seó sáwul swá gerádre wege and færinge anima vehiculo non eget, Gr. D. 314, 25.

wel. II b. add:—þá ðá wé wel noldon, ðá forhradode Godes mildheortnys þæt wé wel woldon. Nú wé wel willað, ús fyligð Godes mildheortnys þæt ǽr willa ýdel ne sý. Hé gearcað úrne gódne willan tó fultumigene, Hml. Th. ii. 84, 13–16. (d) add:—Ic nát for hwý gé þá tída swelcra broca swá wel hergeað I know not why you praise so much the times of such calamities, Ors. 3, 7; S. 120, 3. Þonne mæg hé witan þ hé bið on sýðfǽte and wel gysthúses beþearf, Ll. Th. ii. 430, 25. (3) add:—Sum man wæs blind wel seofon geár fulle, Hml. S. 21, 202. II. add:—Hí lá hí and wel lá well and ðyllice óðre sindon englisce interjectiones, Ælfc. Gr. Z. 280, 13. v. efen-wel.

wela. II. add:—Sume hé bereáfaþ hiora welan swíþe hraþe þæs ðe hí ǽrest gesǽlige weorþaþ, þý lǽs hí for longum gesǽlþum hí tó úp áhæbben, and ðonan on oferméttum weorðen quosdam remordet, ne longa felicitate luxurient, Bt. 39, 11; F. 228, 22. v. æf-wela.

wélan. v. be-wélan (v. Ps. Vos. 105, 38).

**wel-boren.** *Add :*—Welboren *generosa, nobilis,* Germ. 390, 31. v. bet-, betst-boren.

**wel-dǽd.** I. *add :*—Gif hwylc ungesǽlig mann his Scyppende bið ungehȳrsum, and nele þurhwunian on weldǽdum oð ende, Hml. S. 11, 280. II a. *doing good :*—Weldǽde and gemǽnnysse nelle gē forgytan *beneficii et communionis nolite obliuisci* (Heb. 13, 16), Scint. 165, 18.

**wel-dōnde.** *Add :*—God gehēt good edleán ðǽm weldōndum, Solil. H. 10, 19.

**wel-gelícod.** *Add : well-pleasing, much liked :*—Ic nât for hwî eów sindon þá ǽrran gewin swá welgelícad, Ors. 3, 7 ; S. 120, 2. On welgelícodon folces ðínes *in beneplacito populi tui,* Ps. Vos. 105, 4.

**wel-getȳd** *well-instructed, well-educated :*—In eallum þingum hē bið welgetȳd, E. S. xxxix. 354.

**wel-hwilc.** *Add :*—Wellhwylce men tweóað *carnales quique dubitant,* Gr. D. 260, 21.

**welig.** (1) *add :*—Hié gemyndgiað ðára weligera (welegra, *v. l.*) ðe lange stríendon, and lytle hwíle brucon, Past. 333, 15. v. ofer-, weoroldwelig.

**weligian.** I. *add :*—[Dryhten] ðearfan welligað *Dominus pauperem ditat,* Ps. Rdr. 279, 7.

**well-weg** (?) *a road to a spring* (?) *:*—Ǽrest on welwyll ... on wælwæg nyðæwerdnæ ; of wellwæge on æscwyllæ, C. D. v. 344, 29-31. On ðá swelgende ; ðonan on penderes clif foreuueardan on wæluueg, vi. 94, 6. Cf. wille-weg.

**well-will** *a spring :*—Ǽrest on welwill ; of welwyllæ ... andlang streámes eft on wellwyll, C. D. v. 344, 29-345, 9. Cf. wille-wæter.

**-welm(a).** v. fôt-welm(a) : **welung.** v. wilwung.

**wel-willedness.** *Add :*—Sē sōð ys freóndscype þe náht sēcð of þingum freóndes būtan sylfe welwyllednysse (*beniuolentiam*), Scint. 198, 3.

**welwillendlíce.** *Add :*—Welwyllendlíce *comiter,* Hpt. 31, 17, 477 : *comiter, decenter,* 490.

**wēmend.** v. dryht-wēmend : **wēmere.** *Add :* v. dryht-wēmere : **wemman.** *Add :* v. ā-, for-wemman : **wemmendness.** v. ā-wemmendness.

**wēn.** *The word is also m.* (or *n.*?). I. *add : estimation :*—Nolde God þ þá ðe his gōdan weorc gesáwon wǽron ungelýfende þe þám wēne þára ǽlmessena þæs diácones (*de eleemosynarum illius aestimatione*), Gr. D. 331, 28. Eác Iōhannes stefn geþwǽreþ þám ylcan andgyte in þám ilcan wēne (*in aestimatione ista*), 332, 21. II. *add :*—Ne cȳð ðū witod on wēn ðín (*don't count your chickens before they are hatched*) ; wite máran þanc ðæs ðe ðū hæbbe, ðonne ðæs ðe ðū wēne (*a bird in the hand is worth two in the bush*), Prov. K. 22. v. mōd-wēn.

**-wēn** *to make crooked* (wōh). v. ge-wēn : **-wēna** ; *adj.* v. or-wēna.

**wēnan.** I. *add :* (1 a) *with elliptical construction :*—'Ne sint þá eágan þínes mōdes swá hále swá þū wēnst' ... 'Ic ongyte nū þæt ic ne æom swylc swilce ic wēnde, Solil. H. 48, 5-10. (2) *add :*—Hwæt wēnst þū be Gode, Solil. H. 24, 18. (2 a) *with complement :*—Hē wæs hæfd and wēned fram mannum mycelre ârfæstnysse *magnae aestimationis habebatur,* Gr. D. 326, 24. (3) *add :*—Mē sceamað nū þæt ic wēnde þæs ðe hyt næs *I am ashamed that I supposed what was not,* Solil. H. 48, 11. (3 a) *with gen. and complement.* (i) *adj. in agreement with gen.* :—Him wǽre iéðre ðæt hē hira ǽr gearra wēnde ðonne hē hira ungearra wēnde, Past. 433, 30. (ii) *phrase :*—Hē ǽfre him gehende endedæges wēne *uite sue diem nouissimum prope esse existimet,* Ll. Th. i. 374, 17 : Wlfst. 75, 9. (3 b) *add :*—Būtan þæs ic sōðlícost wēne, þat hyt mín sceádwísnes wēne, Solil. H. 3, 10. Ic wundrige hwî ðū ǽfre þæs wēnan mahte be mannum sáwlum þæt hý næran æcan, 62, 23. (4 a) :—Ðȳ læs men wēnan ðæt ðū náne næbbe, Prov. K. 76. Tō þám þ sceolde beón wēned þ hē wǽre se cyning *ut rex esse putaretur,* Gr. D. 131, 15. II 1. *add :*—Hē ús benimeð þára nigon ðála þonne wē læst wēnað, Ll. Th. i. 196, 7. (1 a) :—Beó á getreówra ðonne ðē mon tō wēne, Prov. K. 76. (3 c) *add :*—Hē him wēnde from Antigones hámfærelte micelra untreówða, Ors. 3, 11 ; S. 146, 20. Cōm swá mycel unweder him tō þ hî him ne wēndon þæs lífes, Hml. S. 31, 1137. Ðonne hit ðē fræcnost þynce, wēn ðē ðonne frōfre and áre and gesǽlða, Prov. K. 75. Þēh þe hié him leána tō þǽre dǽde wēnden, Ors. 5, 2 ; S. 218, 18. v. for-wēnan.

**wencel.** *Add : a servant, slave :*—Arn án wencel mid treówenum æscene tō þǽre wyllan *cum situla lignea mancipium ad fontem perrexit,* Gr. D. 11, 20. Þ wencel, 23.

**wendan.** II 1. *add :*—Went bié sió wamb, Lch. ii. 216, 20. (3) *with the idea of hostility, to turn on or against :*—Hē hiene siþþan wende on his þrié gebrōðor *parricidia in fratres convertit,* Ors. 3, 7 ; S. 114, 9. III 1. *add :*—Binnan þám wendun gewyrda *meanwhile things were happening,* Cht. Th. 207, 22. Hwî ðū ǽfre wolde þ sió wyrd on gewill wendan sceolde? *cur tantas lubrica versat fortuna vices?,* Met. 4, 34. (5) *with idea of hostility, to turn on or against :*—Hē wende on þá áne þe him getríewe wǽron *bellum vertit in socios,* Ors. 3, 7 ; S. 114, 1.

**-wendedlic.** *Add : v.* ymb-wendedlic : **-wendedlíce.** v. on-wendedlíce : **Wend(e)las.** *Add : v.* Wandale : **-wendendlic.** *Add :* v. on-wendendlic : **-wendendlíce.** *Add :* v. on-wendendlíce : **-wendness.** v. ā-wendendness : **wending.** *Add :* v. ymb-wending : **-wendlic.** v. hāl-, hell-, hwīl-, luf-wendlic : **-wendlíce.** v. heard-, self-wendlíce : **-wendness.** v. -wend(ed)ness : **wēne.** *Add :* v. ǽ-wēne : **-wenedness.** v. for-wenedness.

**wēnend-lic ;** *adj. To be hoped for :*—Paulus cwæð þ se geleáfa wǽre gehyhtendlicra þinga and wēnendlicra þinga spēd *est fides sperandorum substantia rerum,* Gr. D. 269, 13.

**wengel.** v. wiþer-wengel.

**wenian.** *Add :* III. *to accustom oneself, be accustomed :*—Hē stōp mid þȳ unbundenum fēt ofer þá stōwe þe hē ǽr wenede (gewunude, *v. l.*) *numquam postmodum solutum tetendit pedem ultra locum quo ligatum hunc tendere consueuerat,* Gr. D. 214, 14. v. ofer-wenian.

**weninga.** *l.* wēninga : **wēnlíce.** *Add :* v. un-wēnlíce.

**wēnunga.** *Add :*—Būton wēnunga *nisi forte,* R. Ben. I. 14, 1.

**weóce.** *For third passage substitute :*—Þá gefylde hē mid wætere ealle þǽre cyrcean ciellan and sette weócon (tapor, *v. l.*) onmiddan (*in medio papyrum posuit*), and þá mid fȳre ontennde, Gr. D. 44, 15.

**weód.** *Add :*—Á hē mæig findan hwæt hē mæig on byrig bētan ... weód wyrtwalian, Angl. ix. 262, 21. v. Weód-mōnaþ.

**weófod.** v. wíg-bed.

**weoloc-basu.** *Add :*—Weolcbasewere, An. Ox. 1061.

**weoloc-scill.** *Add :*—Weolcscille *conquilio,* An. Ox. 26, 65.

**weóningas.** v. meóningas : **weor.** *Dele, and see* weorc ; **VII.**

**weorc.** IV. *add :*—Hē wæs út farende mid þám brōþrum tō þæs landes weorce, Gr. D. 165, 11. Þ hī fērdan in þæt weorc Godes wordes, Bd. 1, 23 ; Sch. 50, 1. IV a. *add :*—Nǽron þis nā úre weorc, ac hit wǽron þára hāligra apostola *haec nostra non sunt, sed sanctorum apostolorum,* Gr. D. 165, 26. Þá ádūne ástígað on sǽ on scipum dōnde weorcu (*operationes*) on wæterum manegum, Ps. Rdr. 106, 23. IV b. *add :*—Ðǽr wæs cyrice geworht and getimbred wundorlices worces, Bd. 1, 7 ; Sch. 27, 7. V. *add :*—Ne forstondeð þ fæsten nōwiht þ mid gesynsciplice weorce bið besmyten, Ll. Th. ii. 440, 7. VI. *add :*—Þǽr syndon þá micelan mǽrða, þ syndan ðá geweorc (weorc, *v. l.*) þe Alexander hēt gewyrcean *ibi sunt illa magna insignia que Alexander operari jusserat,* Nar. 33, 20. VI a. *add :*—Tuoege of ðǽm eádo in þ weorc (werch, R., *castellum*), Lk. L. 24, 13. VII. *add :*—Þæt wæs þǽm weorode weor[c] (weor[ce]?) tō geþoligenne, An. 1661. v. æfer-, ælmes-, ban- (Ll. Lbmn. 244, 34), ciricsceat-, eorþ-, leóþ-, morþ-, yfel-weorc.

**weorc-cræft,** es ; *m. Skill in work, the art of mechanics :*—Weorc-cræft *mechanica* (*ars*), An. Ox. 55, 6.

**weorc-full.** *Add : industrious, laborious :*—Weorcfulran *operosioris,* An. Ox. 27, 20.

**weorc-níten,** es ; *n. A beast used for work :*—Restað eów, þū and þín sunu and þíne dohter and þín þeówe and þíne wylne and þín weorcnȳten, Ll. Th. i. 44, 11 n.

**weorc-stān.** I. *add :*—Hí ðǽr swíðe fæsthealdne weorcstān upp áhwylfdon ... hí fundon ǽlcne stān on ōðerne befēgedne, Hml. Th. i. 23, 423. II. *add :*—Hēt hē niman Claudium and lǽdan tō sǽ and wurpan hine út mid ánum weorcstāne, Hml. S. 35, 226.

**weorc-ūhta** *the hour of matins on a day that is neither a Sunday nor a Saint's day* (*excepto Dominicis diebus et festivitatibus sanctorum,* Chrd. 23, 21) :—Weorcūhtan besceáwige se bisceop þ se intervallum beó swá lang þ ..., Chrd. 24, 7.

**weorc-weorþ, -wirþe ;** *adj. Capable of work :*—Þonne is æt Farresheáfde .xvi. weorcwurðe men and viii. iunge men ... æt Geácesleá þryttēne wēpmen weorcewyrþe and v. wimmen and æhta geonge men, C. D. B. iii. 367, 15-35. Weorcwyrþra manna, Verc. Först. 158, 20.

**-weoren.** v. for-weoren.

**weorf.** *Add : any draught cattle :*—Hwyorif [*printed* hryofif, *but MS. has* hwyorif (= ? weorf)] *jumentum,* Wrt. Voc. i. 23, 6. Hē geann ... þám æþelinge .xl. mancsa goldes and þǽra wildra worfa æt Æscburnan lande, Cht. Crw. 23, 11. [The passage to which Hpt. Gl. 458, 1 is a gloss is : Indomitos bigarum subjugales.] v. egþ-wirf.

**weornian.** *Add :*—Rōmeburuh byð geswenced þ heó weornað and brosnað in hire sylfre *Roma fatigata in semetipsa marcescet,* Gr. D. 134, 2. Eall hē weornige swá sȳre (syer, MS.) wudu weornie, Lch. i. 384, 13. Unwæstmbǽre tȳdrunge weorniende *infructuosa sterilitate marcescens,* An. Ox. 1032. v. ge-weornian.

**weorod.** I. *add :*—Se eádmōda heáp geeamode æt Gode þæt iú ǽr þæt mōdige werod forleás *the humble company* (*the apostles at Pentecost*) *obtained by their merit from God what long before the proud host* (*the people at the tower of Babel*) *lost,* Hml. Th. i. 318, 14. III 1. *add :*—Án út ásceát of Latina weorode, and ánwíges bæd, Ors. 3, 6 ; S. 108, 10. v. bisceop-, camp-, efen-, eóred-, hām-, in-, síþ-weorod.

**weorod-líce.** *Add :*—Ic wundrige hū nú on wintres dæge hēr lilian blōstm oþþe rosan brǽd swá wynsumlíce and swá werodlíce stincað, Hml. S. 34, 105.

**weorod-ness.** *Add :*—Þá hē him mid mycelre werednysse (wynsumnysse, *v. l. dulcedine*) sealde, Gr. D. 25, 18.

**weorold.** II 1 c. ¶ *add :*—Þā gebrōðra āhton mycele feohspēda for worulde *multas pecunias in hoc mundo possederant*, Gr. D. 273, 2. Wæs Tilman mǣre wer and for worulde (weorulde, *v. l.*) eác swylce æþelra gebyrda *vir inlustris et ad saeculum nobilis*, Bd. 5, 10; Sch. 604, 12. v. gehæft-weorold.

**weorold-ār.** I. *add :*—Men habbaþ ðæs þȳ lǣssan frȳdōm þe hī heora mōdes willan neár ðisse woruldāre (weoruld-, *v. l.*) lǣtaþ, Bt. 40, 7; F. 242, 27.

**weorold-bisegu.** *Add :*—For þǣm manigfealdum weoruldbisgum þe hine oft ǣgþer ge on mōde ge on līchoman bisgodon, Bt. proem.; F. viii. 5.

**weorold-broc** *secular use. After* woroldbroce *in* l. 3 *insert:* (-bryce, *v. l.*, Mart. H. 136, 9).

**weorold-bryce.** *See preceding word.*

**weorold-camp.** *Add :*—Gif hwilc preósthādes manna hine geþeóde silfne tō woroldcampe (*militię seculari*), Chrd. 97, 8.

**weorold-cearu.** *Add :*—Seó þiccnys þāra woruldcara (woruldlicra ymbhogena, *v. l.*) swīðe āwēsted ānra gehwilces biscopes mōd *uniuscujusque praesulis mentem curarum densitas devastat*, Gr. D. 41, 7. Heorte tōbrōden ymbe woroldcara *cor dispersum in rerum curis*, Chrd. 70, 19.

**weorold-cyning.** I. *add :*—Tō woroldcynegum *ad reges terrę*, Chrd. 96, 34.

**weoruld-gestreón.** *Add :*—þurh woroldgestreón (*per stipendium seculare*) forleósan þā heofenlican mǣrða, Chrd. 12, 4. Þeáh þe him sié eal middangeard on geweald gèseald mid eallum ðām welum and ðām weoruldgestreónum ðe heofen behwealfed ābūtan, Sal. K. 86, 2.

**weoruld-geþyngþ[u].** *Add :*—Ūs, þām þe God swā micele heálicnysse woruldgeþingða forgifen hæfð, is seó mǣste þearf þ wē hwīlon ūre mōd gebīgean tō gāstlicum rihte, Gr. D. 1, 7.

**weoruld-gilp.** *Add :*—Ic ongite þte þā mǣstan mǣrþa ne sint on þysse woruldgilpe *video celebritatem gloria non posse contingere*, Bt. 33, 1; F. 120, 5.

**weoruld-girela,** an; *m. Secular apparel :*—þ hī ... ālecgon þone scīnendan woroldgyrlan *nitore seculari deposito*, Chrd. 96, 11.

**weoruld-hād.** *Add : a secular rank* or *order :*—Þeáh þe ūs nā ne lyste tō þǣre sprǣce gecyrran, wē becumað genȳdde tō ðǣre for gewille þāra woruldhāda (*worldly men*, cf. weoruld-mann; II), Gr. D. 209. 24.

**weorold-hremming,** e; *f. Hindrance caused by wordly affairs :*—Gerīst þ þā þe God habbad tō yrfewerdnysse, þ hig hogion þ hī Gode þeówian būtan woroldhremminge (*absque ullo impedimento seculi*), Chrd. 75, 35.

**weorold-lic.** III. *add :*—Woruldlic ealdor *biotticus auctor, cancellarius, scriptor*, Hpt. 31, 8, 123.

**weoroldlíce.** *Add : temporally* (in contrast with *eternally*) :—þǣr wæs swīþe ryht dōm geendad þ hié þone woroldlíce forbærndon þe hié þōhte bærnan on ēcnesse *justo Dei judicio ipsi eum vivum incenderunt, qui propter eum morti vitio erroris arsuri sunt*, Ors. 6, 34; S. 292, 3.

**weorold-lust.** *Add :*—Hwæt wille ic mā cwæðan be mete, oððe be drince, oððe be baðe, oððe be welan, oððe be wyrðscype, oððe be ænigum worldlusta (*de cibo et potu, sive de balneis, ceteraque corporis voluptate*), Solil. H. 37, 8. Cf. þā worlde lustas, 39, 4.

**weorold-mann.** II a. *add :*—Wē beóð feor ofdūne gelǣded, þonne wē gemengde beóð tō þysum woruldmannum mid ūre gelōmlican sprǣce ... eác ful oft wē gewuniað þ wē þām woruldmannum hwæthugu mid spræcað for gehlæge *multum deorsum ducimus, dum locutione continua secularibus admiscemur ... plerumque eis ad quaedam loquenda condescendimus*, Gr. D. 209, 16-21.

**weorold-níd.** *Add :*—Hē tō his woroldneóde dyde þǣra þearfena fōdan *alimenta pauperum suis aptauit usibus*, Chrd. 51, 32. Sȳ ælc hȳrsumnys an woroldneódum cǣflíce gefylled *omnis obedientia in seculi necessitatibus strenue peragatur*, 93, 9.

**weorold-ríce;** *adj. Add :*—Him is tō forbūgenne woroldríccra gefērscipe (*potentium consortium*), Chrd. 69, 36.

**weorold-rícetere,** es; *n. Worldly power :*—Wē gesetton þ þā þe ǣne beóð tō preósthāde gedōn ... þ hig nā siððan tō nānon woroldrícetere (*dignitatem aliquam mundanam*) ne geþrīstlǣcen tō becumenne, Chrd. 68. 34.

**weorold-sceáwung,** e; *f. A worldly spectacle :*—Warnion preóstas þ hī ne beón betwyx woroldsceáwungum *non spectaculis mundi intersint*, Chrd. 76, 30.

**weorold-scír,** e; *f. Worldly business, secular office :*—On þām woruldscírum (*negotiis secularibus*) wē beóð full oft geneáhode þ wē dōð þā þing þe ūs is genōh cūð þ wē nā ne sceoldon, Gr. D. 3, 7.

**weorold-strang;** *adj. Having great temporal power :*—þā woruldstrangan kynegas, Nap. 71, 5.

**weorold-þegnung,** e; *f. Secular service :*—þās ne beóð nāðer ne an woroldþēnuncgum (*secularium officiorum studiis*) mid lǣwedum mannum, ne mid preóstum an þǣre godcundan ǣwfæstnysse, Chrd. 77, 34. Āworpan hī woruldþēnuncga *secularia officia abjiciant*, 76, 35.

**weorold-þing.** *Add : a secular matter :*—Hī beóð ābysgode nā

---

ymbe godcundlice þing, ac ymbe woroldþing *non diuinis, sed uanis solent instare loquelis*, Chrd. 34, 12.

**weorold-welig;** *adj. Rich in this world's goods :*—Woruldwelige gītseras, Nap. 71.

**weorold-wísdóm.** *Add :*—þā befæste hē his sunu tō lāre tō woruldwísdōme þ hē ūðwita wurde, Hml. S. 35, 9.

**weorold-wuldor,** es; *n. Worldly glory :*—Manege synt þe Crīstes scēp for heora wuldorwuldre (*suę glorię gratia*) healdad, Chrd. 66, 20.

**weorold-wuniende.** *Add :*—Ne mōton hié āwa ætsomne woruldwunigende, Hpt. 33, 71, 4.

**weorpan.** I. *add :* I b. where the implement used in throwing is given :—þā hēt hē mid þǣm palistas ... þæt hiere mon mid þǣm þwyres on wurpe, Ors. 4, 6; S. 174, 10. V 2. *add :*—þā forceáw hē his āgene tungan, and wearp hine þǣr mid on ðæt neb foran, Bt. 16, 2; F. 52, 25. Hit wæs swā tōbrocen efne swilce hē mid stāne wurpe on þæs fætes forwyrde, Gr. D. 105, 6.

**weorpe.** *Dele* seale-weorpan : -weorpendlic. v. tō-weorpendlic : **weorpness.** *Add :* v. for-weorpness : **weorr.** *Dele.*

**weorþ;** *n.* [*The Latin for the passage given under* I 2. (*in which for* gefyrhtum *l.* gewyrhtum) *is:* Ut ex generantium meritis *dignitas* germinis nosceretur. Weorþe *as a noun may compare with the same unmutated form in the corresponding adjective.*] *Add :* v. ge-, healfpenig-, wlite-weorþ.

**weorþ;** *adj.* V 1. *add :* (1 a) with dat.? :—þ word byð wītes wyrðe (wīte wyrðe *or* wītewyrðe, *v. l.*) *sermo reprehenditur*, Gr. D. 208, 8. (6) *add :*—Hē wæs swelce Rōmāne þā wyrþe wǣron *dignus Romanis punitor*, Ors. 6, 3; S. 256, 24. VII 1. *and* 2 *add :*—Ðǣr wæs cyrice geworht wundorlíces worces, and his þrowunge and martyrdōmes (-dōme, *v. l.*) wyrðe *ecclesia est mirandi operis atque eius martyrio condigna exstructa*, Bd. 1, 7; Sch. 27, 8. v. cyne-, dryht-, efen-, fald-, gemynd-, líc-, nyt-, ofer-, riht-, stæl-, steór-, wel-, weorc-, wīte-, weorþ-, -wirþe.

**weorþan.** II 3. *add :*—Heó mid þǣr. cilde weard sōna and þæt gebær, Wlfst. 22, 9. Hit is āwriten ðætte ūre Hǣlend wurde beaftan his mēder and his māgum, Past. 385, 20. III. *add :* (a) weorþan æt *to be at* something; cf. (b 2) :—þā wurdon hī æt sprǣce, oþ þ Dūnstān rehte be Sancte Eádmunde, Hml. S. 32, 4. (b 1) :—Eft hē gehwearf tō him selfum, and weard on his āgenum gewitte, Past. 273, 15. þ hūs fǣrlíce eall on fȳre weard, Hml. S. 26, 230. Hē weard on micelre untrumnesse, Ors. 6, 30; S. 282, 17. Wurdon ealle þā gebrōþor on þǣm Arianiscan gedwolan, 6, 31; S. 284, 15. (c 3) :—Hanna mid eallum his folce weard Rōmānum tō gafolgieldum, Ors. 4, 6; S. 170, 26. Heora gedeaft cc and xxx, and lxx weard tō lāfe, S. 176, 19. IV 1. v. æfter-weard; II. (a) :—Swā þ hē ārās of þām bedde and weard uppon his horse *ut de lecto surgeret, et ascenso equo*, Gr. D. 82, 30; Chr. 1048; P. 172, 24. þā deófla siþþan of þām geswenctum mannum mid wundorlícum gebǣrum wurdon him sōna fram, Hml. S. 31, 1212. Swilce hē on sume hlǣdre stīge and wylle weorðan uppe on sumum sǣclife. Gif hē uppe on ðām clife wyrð, Solil. H. 45, 17-19. (b) :—Hē wearp ūt his net, and þǣr weard oninnan ān ormǣte leax, Hml. S. 31, 1274. V 1. *add :*—Hē ne weard nǣfre nāne yfele dǣda wyrcende, Nic. 1, 19. (2 b) :—On þǣm swicdōme weard Numantia dugud gefeallen, Ors. 5, 3; S. 222, 8. Binnan feáwum dagum hī wurdon forðfērde, Gr. D. 152, 20. Hié wǣron on þǣre ondrǣdinge hwonne hié on þā eorþan besuncene wurden, Ors. 2, 6; S. 88, 15. ¶ with a verb that can take a complement :—Se Hǣlend, syððan hē tō disum lífe cōm, and man weard geweaxen, Hml. Th. i. 258, 10. v. ā-weorþan.

**weorþ-full.** III. *add :*—Hē geliþewǣhte tō geleáfan heora wurdfullan templ, Hml. S. 31, 483.

**weorþful-líc.** *Add :* v. for-weorþfullic.

**weorþian.** *Add :* v. be-weorþian.

**weorþiend.** v. rōd-weorþiend.

**weorþ-líc.** *Add :* v. tæl-weorþlic : **weorþlíce.** *Add :* v. líc-, tælweorþlíce : **weorþlicness.** v. tæl-weorþlicness.

**weorþ-mynd.** I. *add :*—Se apostol mid manegum tācnum gerehte hwylcne weorþmynd hē be him hæfde *ut apostolus signis ostenderet quam de illo haberet aestimationem*, Gr. D. 228, 8. v. sundor-, synderweorþmynd.

**weorþung.** *Add :* v. dōm-, geteld-weorþung.

**weorþung-dæg.** II. *add : a festival :*—Swā oft swā hit ænige freólsdagas beón, Sunnandagas oððe mæssedagas oððe þyllice wurðingdagas þe wē hātad templhālgunga, forlǣten wē ælc ōðer wurc, Nap. 68.

**weosung.** v. ā-weosung.

**wēpan.** II a. (1) *add :* (a) where there is grief for wrongdoing :—Ðā ðe ðā gedōnan scylda wēpað, Past. 421, 36. (β) where there is lament for suffering :—Gemēnað gē hit tō þǣm wyrrestan tīdum, and magon hié hreówlíce wēpan, Ors. 3, 7; S. 120, 6. Hē ormōd hine selfne ongan wēpan, Bt. 1; F. 4, 4.

**wēpendlíce.** *Add :*—Wēpendlíce *lugubriter*, An. Ox. 56, 7.

**wer** *a man.* [*The form* were *also occurs :*—Gif þ wīf hire were forlǣt, Mk. 10, 12. Ic were ne oncnāwe, Lk. 1, 34. Cf. wer *and* were =

wer-gild; *also the form* were-wulf.]    **IV.** *add:*—Hé blissode on þām ꝥ hē his āgenre dohtor wer wæs, Ap. Th. 3, 5.   [*The correspondence of* wer *and Lat.* vir *seems not to hold.* Cf. Angl. xxxi. 261.]   v. full-wiht-, port-wer, sweord-weras.

**wer** (= wergild). *Add:*—Būton se hlāford þone wer forðingian wille *nisi dominus suus componere uelit weram eius*, Ll. Lbmn. 62, 6.   v. riht-wer.

**wer** *a weir.* **II.** *add:*—Ān wer on Ycenan, C. D. B. ii. 247, 20. Twȳgen weoras in fluvio qui dicitur Stūr, i. 598, 8.   v. beám- (C. D. v. 148, 21), sǽ-wer; *see also* Midd. Flur.

**wer-bǽre**, es; *n. Substitute:* wer-bǽr, e; *f. Pasture-land adjacent to a weir.* Cf. C. D. i. 64, 10: vi. 134, 31–34 *given under* wer; **II. -werd.** v. līnen-werd: -weredness. v. for-weredness: -wereness. v. be-wereness: were-, wer-wulf. v. wer, were *a man; for double forms* (were-, wer-) cf. wer-, were-gild.

**werian. III.** *add:*—þā gecwǽdon hié þæt hié sume hié bezftan wereden, and sume þurh ealle þā truman ūt āfuhten, Ors. 5, 7; S. 230, 21.    **III** c. *add:* cf. in-, ūt-waru.

**werian** *to clothe. Add:* v. ā-werian: -werian. v. ge-werian *to make a treaty with.*

**wērigian.** *Add:*—ꝥ ilce mōd ǽgþer ge mid heálicum mægnum weaxeð and strangað, and eác of his āgenre untrymnesse wērgað and teórað (*ex infirmitate lacesscat*), Gr. D. 204, 23.   Cum hider ꝥ wyt magon etan, þe lǽs þe wit wērigian (wērgien, *v. l.*) on þysum wege (*ne lassemur in via*), 128, 14.   Hē ongan him ondrǽdan and wērgian (*lassescere*), 36, 19.

**wērigu** (?) *weariness, grief:*—þonne ārīsað twēgen ealdormen tō þeóda wērigum *postea exsurgent duo principes ad premendas gentes*, Verc. Först. 118, 15.

**wer-reáf**, es; *n. Ordinary dress* as distinguished from vestments:—Be preósta gyrlan … Nimon hī heora werreáf (*uestimenta*) tō Sancte Martinus mæssan and oferslipas tō Eástron and heora gescý on þæm mōnðe Nouembre, Chrd. 48, 27.   Preósta werreáf (*uestes*) and hyra gescý . . . sceolon beón swā gedæfenlice and swā medme ꝥ hī ne beón tō deórwyrðe ne eft tō wāce, 65, 15.

**wer-scipe.** *Dele.* Cf. An. Ox. 3596, *where the reading is* fērscipe : **-wesa.** v. ār-wesa.

**wesan. I** 1 a. *add:*—Ic sælf þæt ierfæ tō gestrīndæ þæt' þær mon siððan bī wæs (*unde interim pauperes vixerunt*), Cht. Th. 162, 31. Cf. bī-wist.   (4) *add:*—Bēgen þā consulas wǽron mid firde angeán Hannibal, Ors. 4, 8; S. 186, 30.   Mǽst ealle … wǽron wið þæs fȳres weard … Hié wǽron flocmǽlum þiderweard, 4, 10; S. 200, 16–19.   (5) (a) *add:*—Hē in þā ylcan tīd hīwcūðlīce mid him wæs *ei ipso in tempore familiarissimus fuit*, Gr. D. 14, 10.   (b) *add:*—Wæs hyre willa mǽrlīcor, Hml. A. 32, 199.   Hȳ wiston hū hit þær besūðan wæs, Chr. 1052; P. 175, 18.   Hit wæs hwīlum on Engla lagum ꝥ leód and lagu fōr be geþincðum, Ll. Th. i. 190, 11.   (7) *add:*—Him wæs bet sōna, Hml. S. 31, 571.   Hwæt wæs þām men? *quid profuit?*, Gr. D. 326, 18.   (8) *add:* cf. (7).    **III.** *add:*—Sē wǽre wierðe ealra Rōmāna onwaldes … būton ꝥ hē wið his hlāford won, Ors. 6, 35; S. 292, 15.    **III** a. *add:*—Nān ōþer ne mōste gyldenne hring werian, būton hē æþeles cynnes wǽre, Ors. 4, 9; S. 190, 16.    **III** b. *add:*—Nān man of þære wīc þe hī of wǽron, Hml. S. 31, 1016.   *add:*—Hē wæs swelce Rōmāne þā wyrþe wǽron, Ors. 6, 3; S. 256, 23. v. swilce; **III.**    **IV** 2 b. *add:*—Se consul wæs on Sicilium mid firde gefaren, Ors. 4, 8; S. 186, 29.   v. æt-, frum-wesende.

**wesendlīce**; *adv. Essentially:*—ꝥ is þonne ōþer, ꝥ man eádiglīce lifige sume hwīle, ōðer is, ꝥ man aa wesendlīce (*essentialiter*) and ēcelīce lifie, Gr. D. 336, 36: 337, 4.

[**west**]. *Add:* cpve. westra:—Se westra crochyrst; ðonne ōðer crochyrst, C. D. vi. 67, 12. Eal būtan ānan hrycge ðǽm westmǽstan (weste-, 400, 6), and twēgen æceras ongemang hīna lande, and se westra eásthealh and ān stycce ðæt westmǽstan, iii. 19, 4–7.

**west**; *adv.* Rufinus wolde habban him self þone anwold þær eást, and Stileca wolde sellan his suna þisne hēr west, Ors. 6, 37; S. 296, 7. þonne þunor cumeð west oððe norð, Archiv cxx. 48, 20.

**west-.** This form occurs in many place-names. v. C. D. vi. 350–1.

**westan.** *Add:* v. be-, wiþ-westan.

**westan-norþan.** *Add:*—Westannorðan *a circio*, An. Ox. 2, 347. **-wēstedness.** v. ā-wēstedness.

**wēsten.** *Add:*—God lǽdde hine ðurh ðæt wēsten, Past. 304, 7.   v. feld-wēsten.

**west-ende.** *Add:*—Tō ðæs clifes westende, C. D. iii. 419, 6: 449, 14. On ðæs hlincæs wæstændæ, v. 242, 32.

**westerne.** *Add:*—Westernes windes *Zephyri*, An. Ox. 23, 17.

**weste-weard.** *Add:*—þæt feórþe heáfodrīce is Rōmāne, and on westeweardum, Ors. 2, 1; S. 60, 5. Andlang mearcæ on ðā wiðegas westewearde, C. D. v. 319, 23.

**west-healf.** *Add:*—Ðonne on westhealfe ðæs heáfodlandes vi gyrda bewestan Yttinges hlǽwe, C. D. v. 275, 18. Ælfrīces mearc on westhealfe, C. D. B. iii. 15, 12.

**west-lang**; *adv. Add:* cf. Bd. 1, 3; S. 475, 19 (*given under* west (2)).

**west-rihte.** *Add:*—Andlang dīce west on gerihte on pull; of pylle westrihte on ford, C. D. iii. 449, 12.

**west-rihtes**; *adv. Due west:*—Ðanon westrihtes on ðā ealdan stānreáwe, C. D. iii. 450, 2.

**weþer.** *Add:*—Hē breác weþera fella for sadole *vervecum pellibus pro sella utebatur*, Gr. D. 34, 12.

**wīc. III.** *add:*—þā cōm him fǽringa tō micel folc manna … wǽron ealle hǽðena, and þone Hǽlend ne cūþe nān man of þǽre wīc þe hī of wǽron, Hml. S. 31, 1016.   Ðænne þæs embe fīf niht ꝥ āfered byð winter of wīcum (cf. tūn; **IV.**), Men. 24.   v. bere-, ceaster-, Lunden-, Norþ-, sunder-wīc.

**wicce.** *Add:*—Helhrūnan, wiccan *phitonissam*, i. *diuinatricem*, An. Ox. 1926.

**wicclian.** v. cwicclian: **wīce.** *Add:* feoh-, [horder-]wīce: **wīcian.** *Add:* v. be-wīcian.

**wīc-sceáwere.** *Add:*—*The Latin is:* Metatoris (Christi). *See* Archiv cxxii. 248, 28.

**wīc-stōw. I.** *add:*—Sumes mannes hūs (*domus*) wæs getimbrod mid gyldenum stafum … Hwylc man is … þe nāt hwæt se man sȳ þe seó wīcstōw (*mansio*) getimbrod is, Gr. D. 321, 14.   Manige wīcstōwe (*mansiones*) syndon in nīnes fæder hūse, 315, 17: 319, 5.   Hī onfōð ānre mēde, and beóð tōdǽlede in manige wīcstōwa, 315, 23.

**wicu.** *Add:* where the reference is to any day but Sunday, *week* as in *week*-day:—Gyf se terminus becymð on ðone Sunnandæg … Gyf se terminus gescȳt on sumon dæge þǽre wucan, Lch. iii. 244, 17.   v. cīse-wicu.

**wīd. I.** *add:*—Scs̄ Petrus cyrice is þreó hund fōta lang and twā hund wīd, Salamones templ ys sixtig fæþma lang and sixtig heáh and þryttiges wīd, Angl. xi. 4, 5–10.   v. un-wīd. **-wīd, -widda.** v. inwid, -widda.

**wīd-cūþ.** (1) *add:*—Sē þe ācenned bið, wīdcuð hē bið *luna xxiii qui natus fuerit, vulgaris erit*, Archiv cxxix. 20, 5.

**wīde. III.** *add:*—Tōfērdon þā apostolas wīde landes geond ealle þās world, Ll. Th. ii. 372, 6.    **IV** a. *add:*—Swā myccle mā hit byþ beswicen in hwylcumhugu ānum þinge, swā myccle hit rūmor and wīddor byþ ābysgod on manegum wīsum (*quanto latius in multis occupatur*), Gr. D. 41, 19.

**widerian.** *Add:* v. ge-widerian: **-widerung.** v. un-gewiderung.

**wīd-gal.** *Add:*—Sume dæge þā þā heó swā wīdgal swīðe dwolode quadam die dum vaga nimium erraret, Gr. D. 176, 21.   Hē eóde ūt and mid wīdgalum mōde worhte ā hwæthugu eorðlices *egrediebatur et mente vaga terrena aliqua agebat*, 111, 13.

**widgalness. II.** *For* Greg. Dial. 2, 3 *substitute* Gr. D. 108, 1.

**wīd-genge**; *adj. Rambling, roving, going far and wide:*—Wīdgenge *girouagum*, An. Ox. 58, 10.

**wīd-gill.** *Add:*—On þǽre sīdan þæs wīdgellan (-gill-, *v. l.*) muntes *in devexi montis latere*, Gr. D. 12, 17.   Of þǽre wīdgyllan (-gill-, *v. l.*) sīdan þæs muntes *e devexo montis latere*, 112, 19.   Geond þā wīdgellan (-gill-, *v. l.*) sīdan þæs muntes, 211, 25.

**wīdgilness.** *Add:*—Geond þā wīdgelnysse (-gil-, *v. l.*) þæs muntes *per devexum montis latus*, Gr. D. 12, 10.

**wīdian.** *Add:*—ode *To widen, grow wide:*—þā seáðas weaxað daga gehwilce and wīdiað *ollae laxatis quotidie sinibus excrescunt*, Gr. D. 315, 4.

**wīdl.** *l.* wīdl, *and add:*—Seó hȳd āsweóll swā ꝥ heó ne mihte bedȳglian ꝥ weaxende wyrms and wīdl (wīdl, *v. l.*) *ut cutis intumesceret, atque increscentem saniem occultare non posset*, Gr. D. 157, 10.

**wīdlǽste** (?); *adv. Widely:*—Wīdlese (-lǽste ?) goretende *passiuis*. v. gorettan.

**wīd-mǣran.** *Add:* to make widely known:—Wæs eác wiidmǣred ꝥ hē betweoh gebedum his līf geendode *est autem, quod etiam inter uerba orationis uitam finierit*, Bd. 3, 12; Sch. 245, 13.

**wīd-mǣre.** *Add:*—Wīdmǣ(rost) *celeberrimus*, An. Ox. 56, 336.

**wīd-scripol.** *Add:*—Hī folgiað fracedum līfe and wīdscryðlum *hos turpis uita et uaga complectit*, Chrd. 78, 1.

**wīf. I.** *add:*—Sceal ic nū eald wīf cennan? *num vere paritura sum anus?*, Gen. 18, 13.   v. brōþor-, forlegis-, forliger-, forþ-, freó-wīf.

**wīf-freónd**, es; *m. A female friend:*—Ðā wiffrióndas *amicas*, Lk. L. R. 15, 9.

**wīf-gehrine.** *Dele, the reading is* wīfa gehrine.

**wīf-hīred**, es; *m. A household of women, a nunnery:*—ꝥ him wǽre eáðelic se wīfhīred tō healdanne (*feminis praeesse*), Gr. D. 27, 8.

**wīf-hrægel**, es; *n. A woman's dress:*—ꝥ wīfhrægel *muliebria indumenta*, Gr. D. 212, 10. Cf. wīf-scrūd.

**wīf-leás.** *Add:*—Wīfleás man *agamus antropus, sine coniuge homo*, Hpt. 31, 15, 403.

**wīf-scrūd.** *Add:* cf. wīf-hrægel.

**wiga.** *Add:*—Se Godes stranga wiga Sanctus Paulus *fortis praeliator Dei*, Gr. D. 110, 14. Tō wigan campe, C. D. vi. 67, 5.

**wíg-bedd.** *Add:*—Þá se mæssepreóst geseah þ heó swíðe geswenced wæs, hé genam þá scétan of þám weófode (wígbedde, *v. l.*), Gr. D. 72, 33. v. heáh-wígbedd.

**wígbed-heorþ.** *For* Lchdm. . . . col. 1 *substitute* Gr. D. 216, 6, *and add*: the Latin is : Ab altaris crepidine pulverem collegit.

**-wíge.** v. or-wíge.

**wíg-gild.** *Add:*—Se ealdorapostol ǽrest ús gesette tó healdanne ðás dagas and tó beganganne for hǽðenra manna gedwilde, for þan þe hié hiera wíggild and deófulgild on ðás dagas weorðedon, Nap. 69.

**wíg-heard.** *Add:* *warlike, martial:*—Wíhearde *bellicosas*, An. Ox. 783.

**wigle.** *Add:*—Wigles *diuinationis*, An. Ox. 7, 165.

**wiglere.** *Add:*—Ic ælcne wiccecræft eáðelíce oferswíðde, and þá Chaldēiscan wigleras and þá wurmgaleras ic mihte gewyldan tó mínum willan ǽfre, Hml. S. 35, 177. v. steor-wiglere.

**wiglung.** *Add:*—Wiglunge *auspicio, augurio, omini*, Hpt. 31, 15, 388.

**wíg-steall.** *Add:*—Hé eóde binnan þonne weóhstal on norðhealfe. Vis. Lcf. 68.

**wihade.** v. wóhhian.

**wiht.** **II 2.** *add:*—Hæfð Ælfréd gehaldene Herewinne on ǽghwelcre wihte ðæs ðe hió an geworden wæs, C. D. B. ii. 46, 29. v. efen-, leás- (?), nænig-wiht; ed-wihten.

**wíl** *a wile.* *Dele*: v. flíge-wíl, *and add* (?):—Wocia, wýla *catenarum*, An. Ox. 3560. Wíla, 7, 257.

**wil-cuma.** *Add:*—Wilcuman lá, míne hláfordas *bene veniant, domini mei*, Gr. D. 276, 23.

**wildan.** **II.** *add:*—Ne lǽte hé nǽfre his hýrmen hyne ofer wealdan, ac wilde (wille, MS.) hé ælcne mid hláfordes creafte and mid folcrihte. Sélre him his ǽfre of folgoðe ðonne on, gyf hine magan wyldan ðá ðe hé scolde wealdan, Angl. ix. 260, 26–31.

**wild-deór.** *Add:*—Him cwóm tó monigra cynna wilddeór, Shrn. 72, 5. þá weard hé gefyrht mid ege þæs unmǽtan wildeóres . . . Hé tó þám león cwæð : 'Eálá þu mǽste wildeór,' Hml. S. 23 b, 773–780. Ymb þone Godes man þára manna heortan wǽron gewended in wildeóra (wildeóra, *v. l.*) rêðnesse, and þæs wilddeóres (wildeóres, *v. l.*) heorte wæs gehwyrfed in mænnisce bilwytnesse *erga illum virum Dei et ferina corda essent hominum, et quasi humana bestiarum*, Gr. D. 195, 5–7.

**wilde** *wild.* **I.** *add:*—Wilde weorf, Ll. Th. i. 356, 4. Mettas . . . þá þe gód blód wyrceað, swá swá sint . . . wilda hænna and ealle þá fugelas þe on dúnum libbað, Lch. ii. 244, 25. **I a.**—Hors wilde yrnan *equos solutos currere*, Lch. iii. 202, 32. **V a.** of people, *uncivilized, uncultivated:*—Ǽr hé hêt faran tó strétum and tó wícum, getácnigende þ Iūdēa folc þe . . . on gehendnysse wǽron. Nú hé hêt faran tó wegum and hegum, getácnigende þæt wilde folc þe hé gegaderode of eallum middanearde, Hml. Th. ii. 372, 15–19.

**wilde** *powerful:*—Ac þ is bedeóhlod ús hweþer þá wyldre wǽre in Stephane and þone sigor áhte *sed quid in eo vicerit nos latet*, Gr. D. 320, 24. v. ge-wilde.

**-wilde.** *Add:* v. earfoþ-wilde.

**wildedeór.** *Add:*—Ne sele wildedeórum (*bestiis*) sáwla, Ps. Rdr. 73, 2: Ps. L. 78, 2. v. wild-deór.

**-wildelic, -wildend.** v. un-gewildelic, ge-wildend.

**wilding.** *Add:*—Anweald í wyldinge (-c?) þín *dominatio tua*, Ps. L. 144, 13.

**-wildlíce.** v. self-wildlíce.

**wilige.** *Add:*—Wylie *sporta*, An. Ox. 17, 42. Wilian *quala, corbes*, Hpt. 31, 11, 234. v. meox-wilige.

**wilisc.** *Add:* v. Bret-wilisc.

**will** *will.* **I.** *add:*—Se bisceop hine lêt faran be his wille (*the bishop let him go as he pleased*) . . . Hé geseah þá sóna þ hé his sylfes geweóld (*he was his own master*), Ælfc. T. Grn. 17, 10. Hie ealle þá worold on hiora ágen will onwendende wǽron *they were turning all the world just as they pleased*, Ors. 1, 10; S. 48, 10.

**will** *a well.* *Add:* The word is fem. in the following (cf. wille; *f.*):—Foranongēn Cynewynne wylle ; of ðære wylle, C. D. vi. 129, 26. v. cærs-, gemǽr-, hring-, mearc-, well- (?), wíþig-will.

**willa** *a well.* v. clǽg-willa.

**willa** *will.* **II.** *add:*—Gyf mon méte þ hé feala spera geseó ætsamne, þonne byð þ þæt hé on his feóndum his willan gewryhð (þ þu ofercymst ealle þíne fýnd, *v. l.*), Lch. iii. 176, 10. **V.** *add:*—Hé þá wræce dyde má on wælgrimnesse wyllan (*plus ex crudelitatis desiderio*) þonne mid ænigre mildheortlicre forgifnesse, Gr. D. 319, 28. **VI.** *add:*—Idesa hwurfon wíf on willan, Gen. 2086. **VI a.** Ll. Th. i. 24, 4 *should be transferred to* VIII.

**willan.** **I.** *add:*—Þá ðá wé wel noldon, ðá forhradode Godes mildheortnys ús þæt wé wel woldon, Hml. Th. ii. 84, 14. **II a.** I. of a natural operation in the case of an animal or thing:—Fleót þ fǽm of oþ þ hit nelle má fǽman, Lch. ii. 104, 20. Án cú weard gebróht tó ðám temple . . .; ðá wolde heó cealfian . . . ac heó eánode lamb, Hml.

Th. ii. 300, 34. Ors. 6, 23; S. 274, 25. Wlfst. 100, 4. **II d.** *add:*—Swá oft swá hé tó his horse wolde, Swylce hé wolde wið þæs heofenes weard,

**III b.** *add:*—Ðeáh úre heorda hwylc án sceáp forgýme, wé willað þ hé hit forgylde, Ll. Th. ii. 326, 24. **IV a.** *add:*—Ic wille mé segnian, ac ic ne mæg *volo me signare, sed non possum*, Gr. D. 325, 4. **IV b.** *add:*—Hé him secgan hêt þ hé geornor wolde sibbe wið hiene þonne gewinn, Ors. 3, 1; S. 96, 18. **IV c.** *add:*—Hié woldon þte þá óþere wíf wǽren emsárige him, Ors. 1, 10; S. 46, 3. **VI a.** of things, *to have a tendency:*—Gif eáran willen áðeáfian, Lch. ii. 40, 22. **VII a.** of the natural properties of things:—Elpendes hýd wile drincan wǽtan, gelíce and spynge deð, Ors. 5, 7; S. 230, 26. **IX.** *add:*—Ðá hit þá on mergen dagian wolde *imminente aurora*, Guth. Gr. 135, 270. (a) in a clause translating a Latin infin. :—Ic eom gearu þ ic wille gecyrran tó rihte *converti paratus sum*, Gr. D. 325, 12. Hí wǽron onginnende þ hí þ dón woldon *hoc facere conati sunt*, 234, 6. (b) in a clause translating a Latin clause:—Ðá eóde se cyning in þ hé wolde geseón *intravit rex ut videret*, Mt. 22, 21. Hí fôron þ hig woldon hí gebiddan *ascenderant ut adorarent*, Jn. 12, 20. Efne swá þá wínu woldon feallan on þone flór *ita ut pavimentum vina invaderent*, Gr. D. 59, 17. v. nyllan.

**wille** (?) *to roll.* v. be-willan.

**wille;** *m.* *Add:*—Gif wé ðone biteran wylle æt ðæm æsprynge ádrýgað *cum vitia ab ipso amaritudinis suae fonte siccamus*, Past. 307, 1. þá gemêtton hí be þám wege fægre mǽde and wynsumne wylle (eáspryng, *v. l.*) *invenerunt in itinere pratum et fontem*, Gr. D. 129, 4.

**wille;** *f.* *Add:*—Arn án wencel mid treówenum æscene tó þære wyllan (*ad fontem*), Gr. D. 11, 21. On winterwellan ; of ðære wellan, C. D. iii. 394, 8. v. burg-, fisc-wille.

**-wille** (cf. wille *a well*). *Add:* v. fugel-, hár-, hund-, rúm-wille.

**-wille** (cf. willa *will*). *Add:* v. á-, and-, yfel-wille.

**-willen.** v. dol-, druncen-willen: **willende.** *Add:* v. self-willende : **willendlíce.** *Add:* v. self-willendlíce : **-willendness.** *Add:* v. wel-willendness.

**wille-weg,** es; *m.* *A road to a well:*—Andlang díc on wylleweg ; ðæt andlang wylleweges, C. D. v. 150, 12. Cf. well-weg.

**willian.** **II a.** *add:*—Ðá ongan hé mid miclum stefnum cleopian and willian fyrstmearce *coepit magnis vocibus inducias petere*, Gr. D. 325, 31.

**will-mod** *a distaff.* v. wull-mod.

**will-spryng.** *Add:*—Sume men synd swá áblende þ hí bringað heora lác . . . tó wylspringum, Hml. S. 17, 131.

**willung** *desire.* *Add:*—For ðon wer bið wíse gemenged þonne unálýfedre willunge (*inlicitae concupiscentiae*) monnes mód in geþóhte þurh lustfulnesse bið geþeóded . . . þæt fýr þære unrihtan willunge, Bd. 1, 27 ; Sch. 86, 14–20.

**willung** *heat.* *Dele passage, in which* wylme *is to be read for* wylinc. v. An. Ox. 571.

**wilmian** (?) *to rage:*—þá þá swíþlíce wêdde and wilnode (wilmode?) seó arrianisce ǽhtnes *dum persecutio Ariana vehementer insaniret*, Gr. D. 240, 7.

**wiln.** *Add:*—Hwî dêst þu ðé sylfe ðurh wáce þeáwas swilce þu wyln sý, Hml. S. 8, 44. Seó wyln (cf. án mínra wimmanna, 187), 2, 211.

**wilnian.** **I 1 g.** *add:*—Lôca nú þ þú ofer gemet ne wilnige, Solil. H. 17, 9.

**wil-sǽlig.** v. gewil-sǽlig.

**wilsum-lic.** *Add:* v. ge-wilsumlic.

**wilsumlíce.** *Add:*—Wilsumlíce *sponte*, An. Ox. 1235. þ úre nán ne beó wiþerrǽde wiþ þá hálgan drohtnunga, ac wilsumlíce dó þ hé dó, Hml. S. 33, 73 : Ps. Vos. 53, 8.

**wilsumness.** v. ge-wilsumness.

**wilwan.** **I.** *add:*—Hé ungerede hine his hrægle and hine sylfne nacodne áwearp and wylewede (wylede, *v. l.*) on þám ordum þára þorna . . . and þær þá wæs lange welwed (*volutatus*), Gr. D. 101, 14–18.

**wilwung** (?) *a roll:*—Welung *uolumina*, An. Ox. 28, 31.

**wín.** *Add:*—Hé untýnde þ wínern (*apothecam*) and gemêtte þá fatu swá genihtsumlíce mid wíne gefyllede . . . efne þ swá þá weaxendan wínu (wín, *v. l.*) woldon feallan ofer þá fatu on þone flór (*ita ut pavimentum excrescentia vina invaderent*), Gr. D. 59, 16. v. eced-, reám-wín.

**wín-ærn.** *Add:* v. preceding word : -wincla. v. wine-wincla.

**wín-cynn,** es; *n.* *A kind of wine:*—Ne drinc ic heononford of ðysum wíncynne (*de hoc genimine uitis*, Mt. 26, 29) ǽr on ðám dæge þe ic eft drince mid eów níwe wín on mínes fæder ríce, Nap. 69.

**wind.** *Add:* I.:—Wind *sclabrum* (= *flabrum*), Txts. 97, 1841. Windas *flabra, uenti*, Hpt. 31, 11, 237. Windum *slabris* = *flabris*. The word is a gloss on a passage in Bd. 1, 19 : Incendium ad habitaculum . . . *flabris* stimulantibus ferebatur, Txts. 181, 72. v. eástannorþan-wind.

**-wind.** v. ed-wind, ge-wind : **wind** (?). *See* wind ; I. *supra*.

**windan.** **II 4.** *add*: to give a spiral form to.

**wind-bére;** *adj.* *Windy* :—Windbére *uentosa,* An. Ox. 43, 10.
**-winde.** *Add :* v. ber-, wiþo-winde.
**windel.** *Add :*—Windlas *corbes,* An. Ox. 2, 265.
**wind-fana.** *Add :* [cf. *O. H. Ger.* wint-fano (-e) *proces: Ger.* windfahne.]
**wind-gefanne.** *See* wind-fana *in Dict.*
**wind-hladen.** *Add :*—Lænten windhladen *uer uentuosus,* Archiv cxx. 297, 17: 296, 3. Sumor windhladen *estas uentuosa,* 297, 11.
**wind-hreóse.** *Dele, the better reading is:* Wind on hreóre sǽ:
**-windla.** v. bi-, ge-windla: **windung.** *Add :* [cf. *O. H. Ger.* wintunga *tortura.*]
**wine** *pay, stipend.* v. dæg-wine.
**wîn-fæt.** *Add :*—Of wînfæte *enoforo, uase uinario,* Hpt. 31, 10, 207. Hêt hê Constantium . . . þ man ealle þá wînfatu (*vini vascula*) gegearwode, Gr. D. 57, 27.
**wîngeard-wealh** *a labourer in a vineyard* :—Wîneardwealas *vinatores,* Chrd. 68, 2.
**wîn-land** *a grape-growing country* :—Gif hwá on þám wînlandum for Godes lufon wîn wylle forgán, Chrd. 15, 21.
**wîn-lic.** *Add :*—Nán fefor nis mannon mára þonne se wînlica wǽta *nulla febris hominum maior quam viteus humor,* Chrd. 74, 11.
**winnan.** **A.** **I b.** *add :* *to be ill* :—Hê winneð, and eft in þǽre untrumnise se mon swelteð, Archiv cxxix. 34, 25. Hê winneð (hine ádl gestandeð, *v. l.*), 30. **I c.** :—Mê sǽdon his geongran þ sum wer wunne on þǽre hefigestan hatunge his gesacan *quidam vir gravissima adversarii sui aemulatione laborabat,* Gr. D. 158, 21. Ná má heó ne byþ winnende on feferádlum, 29, 25. **II.** *add :* (5) where the subject of the verb is a word denoting strife, *to be carried on* :—Mê lysteþ ásmeágean hwilc and hú micel wǽre þ gecamp þe wann on þæs mannes breóstum *considerare libet quale quantumque in ejus pectore certamen fuerit,* Gr. D. 18, 4. v. on-, wiþ-winnan; ofer-, ongeán-, samwinnende.
**winnend.** *Add : a fighter* :—Winnend *agonitheta, preliator,* Hpt. 31, 5, 35.
**winter.** *Add :*—Ðænne þæs (*Feb.* 2) emb fíf niht þ áfered byð winter of wîcum, Men. 24. ¶ weak forms :—Tô ðám middan wintran, Chr. 1006; P. 136, 24. Ǽr mydda-wintran, Lk. 1, 26 rbc. Ǽr myddan wintran, Jn. 1, 15 rbc.
**winter-burna.** *Add :* cf. winter-wille: **winter-gerîm, -getæl.** *Add :* cf. geár-gerîm, -getæl.
**winter-hûs,** es; *n.* *A winter-house, house to live in in winter* :—Winterhûs and sumorhûs, Hml. S. 36, 98.
**winter-rǽdingbóc.** *Add :*—Brihtric hæfð i mæssebóc and winter-rǽdingbóc and sumerbóc, Nap. 60, 13.
**winter-steall.** *Add :*—.ix. winterstellas and .i. fêdelswîn, C. D. B. iii. 397, 39.
**winter-tîd.** *Add :*—Wintertîdum (*hiemis temporibus*), þ is fram þám mónðe Novembre oð Eástru, Chrd. 23, 36.
**winter-wille,** an; *f.* *A spring that can be used in winter* (*?*) :—Of ðǽm stáne, ðæt on winterwellan; of ðǽre wellan, ðæt on þeófdene, C. D. iii. 394, 7. Cf. winter-burna.
**wîn-tredd** (-tredde, an; *f.?*). *l.* wîn-tredde, an; *f.,* *and add* :—Hê eóde in þone wîngeard and gesomnode þá geclystru þára byrgena and gebróhte in þǽre wîntreddan (*ad calcatorium*) . . . Hê þone cniht ásette on þá ylcan wîntreddan (*in eodem calcatorio*), and hêt hine wringan þá feáwa geclystru þǽra byrgena, Gr. D. 58, 9-18, 34: 59, 4.
**wîn-treów.** *Add :*—On þám wîngearde on feáwum wîntreówwum (*vitibus*) uneáðe tô láfe wunodon swîðe litle and swîðe feáwa clistru þára wînbergena, Gr. D. 57, 7. Wîntre[ówwum] *palmitibus,* An. Ox. 2838.
**wirdan.** **II.** *add :*—Ne wallað hiæ werda *uolite eos uetare,* Lk. R. 18, 16. v. for-wirdan.
**wirde** (*?*). *Add :* [Cf. *Goth.* wardjans (*acc. pl.*).]
**wirding.** *Add :*—Wyrdincgum *maculis,* An. Ox. 649.
**-wirdlian.** *Add :* v. ge-ǽwirdlian: **wirdness.** *Add :* v. ǽ-wirdness.
**-wirdness.** v. ongeán-wirdness.
**wirgan.** **I.** *add :*—Gyf mîn feónd wyriode (*maledixisset*) mê, Ps. L. 54, 13.
**wirgedness, wirgende, wirgness, wirgung.** *Add :* v. á-wirgedness, -wirgende, -wirgness, -wirgung.
**wirgung-galere.** *The reading* wyrinc- *seems to be a mistake for* wyrm-. *Cf. a similar mistake noted under* willung *heat.*
**wirig.** v. wearg.
**-wirned-lîce, -ness.** v. for-wirned-lîce, -ness: **-wirþe.** v. ge-wirþe: **wirþu.** *Add :* v. æf-wirþu.
**wîs** *a manner.* *Add :* v. leóþ-, nîd-, sár-, sceád-, stæf-, þearl-, word-, wrang-wîs.
**wisc.** *For 'a marsh' substitute :* A wish (wish *a damp meadow, a marsh,* D. D.), *and add* :—On ðám mǽdum .viii. æceras, and on myclan wysce (cf. *in loco uulgari uocitamine æt* miclamersce, 218, 18) .v. æceras, C. D. iii. 283, 10. Andlang burnstówæ ðænna ðǽr eást tô stucan

wisc, 175, 35. On ceabwisce; of ceabwisce, 419, 18. [*See* Anglia xx. 329: Philol. Trans. 1895-8, p. 542.]
**-wisc.** v. gran-wisc.
**wis-dôm.** **I.** *add :*—Gyf þû wylle witan mid wîsdôme (cf. witan mid fullum geráde, 312, 13) þǽra rihtinga gesceád, Angl. viii. 305, 8. **III.** *add :*—'Hû magon wê swá dýgle áhicgan . . . hú þe swefnede, oððe wyrda gesceaft wîsdóm bude' . . . 'Gê mǽtinge mîne ne cunnon þá þe mê wîsdóm bereð (*the dream that brings me knowledge*), Dan. 130-142. Hê wæs befæsted tô Rômebyrig þ hê sceolde bôccræftas and gewrita wîsdômas (*wîsdóm, v. l.*) leornian *Romae liberalibus litterarum studiis traditus fuerat,* Gr. D. 95, 14.
**wise.** **I.** *add :*—On wunderlicum gemete, wîse *mirum in modum,* An. Ox. 1252. **III.** *add :*—Treówþe, wîse *pacto,* i. *iure,* An. Ox. 2690. Ic mid ðǽre hálgan Crîstes rôde tǽcne ðás word and ðás wîsan fæstnie and wrîte, C. D. ii. 122, 2. **IV.** *add :*—þá gelamp sum wundorlic wîse (þing, *v. l.*) *mira valde res,* Gr. D. 16, 23 : 53, 19. **IV a.** *add :*—þá ácsode hine Theoprobus hwæt lá seó wîse (se intinga, *v. l.*) wǽre swá myccles heófes *quaenam causa tanti luctus existeret, inquisivit,* Gr. D. 140, 19. v. beág-, in-wîse.
**wise** *a sprout.* *Add :* v. fugeles wîse: **-wise.** v. gin-wîse (*?*) :
**wîsend.** v. riht-wîsend: **wîsian.** *Add :* v. gin-wîsed.
**wis-lic.** *Add :*—Hié cwǽdon þæt him wîslecre þúhte þæt hié ðá ne forluren þe þǽr ût fôre, hæfde bearn sê þe mehte, Ors. 4, 1; S. 154, 18.
**wîslîce.** *Add :* v. ge-wîslîce: **wîsness.** *Add :* v. ge-wîsness.
**wisnian.** *Add :*—Heó weosnað and brosnaþ in hire sylfre *in semetipsa marcescet,* Gr. D. 134, 2.
**Wissi, Wissigotan** *the Visigoths* :—Erminigildus wîcode in Wauissi (Wissi, *v. l.*) þǽre mǽgðe Gotena þeóde (*Wissigothorum*), Gr. D. 237, 19: 239, 31. Ealle Wissigotena þeóde (*Wisigothorum gentem*) hê gelǽdde tô þám sóðan geleáfan, 19.
**wist.** **II a.** *add :*—Hê ne dorste geopenian þ hê on Drihten gelýfde, ac hê dîgellîce lufode þone biscop and mid wistum him þênode, Hml. S. 22, 126. v. beód-, hîred-, mund-, samod-, unhîred-wist.
**wistfulligend.** *Add :* v. ge-wistfulligend.
**wistle.** *Add : a pipe.* In l. 2 *after 'fistula' insert :* (the Latin is : *Fistula* cum citharis reclamans aethera pulsat, Ald. 146, 20).
**wita.** **I.** *add :*—Á swá hê gecneordra (bið), swá bið hê weorðra, gyf hê wið witan hafað his wîsan gemǽne, Angl. ix. 260, 20. **II.** *add :*—Hê nyste hwæs hê geléfan sceolde, þá hine þá swýdost on ungewisse gebróhton þe his witan beón sceoldon, Hml. S. 23, 398. **II a.** *add :*—Witan hym (*the king*) sceolan rǽdan, O. E. Hml. i. 301, 1. **III.** *add :*—þá geþafode þ se ealda wita (*senex*) and lǽdde þone cniht mid him tô þám mynstre, Gr. D. 242, 22. Witum *senioribus* (Mt. 16, 21), An. Ox. 61, 19. **IV.** *add :*—Hê wæs him sylfum þæs wita (*testis*), Gr. D. 265, 22. Hê cwæð þ hê wǽre se cúðesta wita (gewita, *v. l.*) hyre clǽnnesse *dicens se testem integritatis suae esse certissimum,* Bd. 4, 19; Sch. 440, 21. v. Angel-, eald-, heáh-wita.
**-wita** (-e). v. gearo-wita (-e, Gr. D. 269, 14).
**witan.** **I** 1. *add :*—þonne hit lǽsse is tô witenne þonne hit sý eác tô bodianne *cum minus sit nosse, quam etiam pronuntiare,* Gr. D. 138, 2. (2) :—Ðæt gê magon witan eówerne Scyppend mid sóðum geleáfan, Hex. 2, 9. (4) :—Hê wát hine sylfne on synnum tô fûlne, Wlfst. 38, 15. Mid þý þá heó þone munuc þǽr wiste, Hml. S. 33, 62. Ánne cniht þone þe heó getreówost wiste, 94. Se mon sê þa his gefán hámsittendne wite, Ll. Th. i. 90, 3. (8) with gen., cf. nytan (4) :—þ is lǽsse, þ man wite gehwæt hwylces, þonne þ sý, þ his man wite and eác bodie, Gr. D. 138, 4. Hit is earfoð tô witane þára biscopa þe þǽr tô cômon, Chr. 1050; P. 170, 26. **III.** *add :*—Hwylc man is þe his gewit wát . . . *quis si sanum sapiat,* Gr. D. 321, 14. Wíf ic lǽrde þ hié heora weras lufedan and him ege tô wîston, Bl. H. 185, 23. Hû mycelne ege wê sceolon witan (hû micel ege sî tô hæbbenne, *v. l.*) tô þám hálgum werum *quantis sit viris sanctis timor exhibendus,* Gr. D. 63, 6.
**witan.** **I** 2. *add :*—Ic þence ðis feoh . . . tô wîtanne næs tô oðwyrceanne, Lch. i. 384, 5. v. of-wîtan.
**witan;** *p.* te. v. ed-wîtan: **-wite** *going.* v. onweg-gewite: **-wite** *knowing.* v. -wita.
**wîte.** *Add :* v. bisceop-, full-, ge-, gylt-, heng-, sorh-wîte.
**witega.** **I.** *add :*—Ðe Hǽlend cwæð tô ǽs wîtgum *Iesus dixit ad legis peritos,* Lk. R. 14, 3. v. gebyrd-wîtega.
**witegendlic.** *Add :*—Hê fela þing feorran oft wiste, ǽr þan þe hit gewurde, þurh wîtigendlicne gást, Hml. S. 31, 1010.
**witeleáslîce;** *adv.* *With impunity;* *impune,* Chrd. 109, 26.
**wîte-lic** (*?*); *adj.* *Prophetic* :—Se wîtelica (wîtelica *?*, *v. l.*) cwyde *prophetica sententia,* Gr. D. 139, 18. Cf. wîte-dôm.
**wîte-lic** (wîtig-); *adj.* *Penal* :—Hwæthugu wîtelices *poenale aliquid,* Gr. D 324, 1. Gelǽded æfter deáðe tô wîtiglicre stówe (*ad poenalem locum*), 331, 18. Se hunger sóna ácwelled and álýsed of ðám wîtelican lîfe, Verc. Först. 178. Tô þon þ hî heom ne ondrǽdon þone wîtelican dôm heora deáðes, Gr. D. 277, 11. Hî þá englas getellað tô þám wîtelicum stówum, 316, 10. Wîtelicum (wîtiglicum, *v. l.*), 332, 9.

-wîtendlic, -wîtendness, -wîtenness, -witfæst, -witfæstness, -witfull. v. ge-wîtendlic, &c.

wîte-steng. *Add:*—Wîtstenges *eculei,* An. Ox. 2, 147.

wîte-weorþ, -wirþe; *adj. Punishable, liable to punishment:*—Nû þ unnytte word bið wîtewyrðe (wîtes wyrðe, *v. l.* poenalis) þe bûtan nîðe byð, Gr. D. 208, 8.

wiþ. I 1 a. *add:* (α) *where the motion is in a direction opposite to that in which another object moves:*—Se lîg ðreów wið þæs windes, Hml. Th. ii. 510, 9. (b) *add:*—Þeáh him mon sleá mid sweorde wiþ þæs heáfdes, Bl. H. 47, 14. II 2. *add:*—Se ceáp ne mæg wið nânum sceatte beón geëht, Hml. Th. i. 582, 27. (7) *add:*—Swá eác wið þan (þær ongeán, *v. l. e contra*) beforan Godes eágum licgað forsewene þá þe âþindað, Gr. D. 40, 2. Wið ðám spelle wæs Crisorius *contra Chrysaorius narrare consuevit,* 325, 19. III 2. *add:*—Nabbe gê nânne gemânan wið hine, Past. 357, 6. (9) *add:*—Ne scule gê wið hine gebæran swá swá feónd, Past. 357, 7. (10) *add:*—Hê hit hæl swîþe fæste wið his bróðor, Ors. 6, 33; S. 288, 14. (14) *add:*—Hê weard gebolgen mid mycelre hâtheortnysse wið þone ǣfæstan wer, Gr. D. 20, 22. (15) *add:*—Be Libertines geþylde þe hê hæfde wið his abbod, Gr. D. 9, 30. (16) *add:*—Ic þê tô mundbyrdnesse geceóse wið þîn âgen bearn, Hml. S. 23 b, 449.

wiþ-æftan. I 1. *add:*—Sceoldon hiera senatus rîdan on crætwǣnum wiðæftan þǣm consulum, Ors. 2, 4; S. 70, 28.

wiþ-bregdan. *Add:*—Sum man him onsænde be his cnihtum twá spyrtan . . . þára ôðre se cniht wiðbrǣd (*subripuit*), Gr. D. 203, 5.

wiþ-ceósan. *Add:*—Hê wiðcŷst geþôhtas folca *reprobat cogitationes populorum,* Ps. Rdr. 32, 10. Þǣne gê wiþcuron *quam reprobauerunt,* An. Ox. 61, 27.

wiþ-cweþan. III. *add:*—Þonne wiðcwyð *cum refragetur,* An. Ox. 7, 341. IV. *add:*—Wiþcweþan *frustrari,* An. Ox. 3616: *abdicare,* 7, 108.

wiþer-bersta, -bresta, an; *m. An adversary:*—Ðeáh ðe . . . him an eorðan nǣfre nǣre ǣnig wiðerbresta (v. wiþer-breca, (1) ), Sal. K. 86, 5.

wiþer-braca. *See* Mt. L. 5, 25 : 12, 26 *under* wiþer-breca.

wiþer-breca. *Add:* (1) *an adversary, opponent:*—Þeáh . . . ealle þá streámas hunige flôwen, and him þonne ne sié ofer eorðan nǣnig wiðerbreca, Verc. Först. 114, 9. Þû slôge ealle wiþerbrecan mê *percussisti omnes aduersantes mihi,* Ps. Vos. 3, 8. (2) *one who resists, an obstinate person:*—Hê hæfde ǣnne ofermôdine cniht and micelne wiðerbrecan *superbum valde atque contumacem puerum habuit,* Gr. D. 36, 6. *See next word.*

wiþer-broca. *Add:*—Hî beóð geswǣncte fram heora wiðerbrocum (-brecan, *v. l.*) *eos adversarii fatigant,* Gr. D. 204, 21.

wiþer-cora. I. *add:*—Wê synd oferswîðede . . . strewiað geond eall tôbrocene tigelan . . . and þǣron âstreccað þysne wiðercoran, Hml. S. 37, 180. II. *add:*—Wiðercora *apostata, transgressor,* Hpt. 31, 15, 380.

wiþer-coren. II. *add:*—Se gecorena Lazarus wæs oncnâwen fram þám welegan wiþercorenan *electus Lazarus a reprobo est divite cognitus,* Gr. D. 311, 9.

wiþer-cwiddian *to murmur:*—Âgén mê wiðercwyddedon ealle fŷnd mîne *aduersum me murmurabant omnes inimici mei,* Ps. L. 40, 8.

wiþer-cwidelness (-cwyd-). v. wiþer-cwedolness.

wiþer-cwideness, e; *f. Contradiction:*—Mid wætere wiþercwydenysse (*contradictionis*), Ps. L. 80, 8. On wiðercwydenysse ûrum neáhgebûrum *in contradictionem uicinis nostris,* 79, 7.

wiþer-dûne. *Add:* , -dŷne *uphill (opposite of* of-dûne), *steep (?) :*—Se weg is swîðe neara and wiðerdŷne, Gr. D. 322, 20. Neara and wiðerdéne is se hâlega weg, swâ swâ Dryhten sylf cwæð, Nap. 69.

wiþerian. III. *add:*—Þá hé geseah þ hé ne mihte wið wiþerian (wiðwiþerian ?; wiðstandan, *v. l.*) þæs hâlgan mannes fremmingum *cum se conspiceret ejus profectibus obviare non posse,* Gr. D. 117, 19.

wiþer-leán. *Add:*—Wiðerleán *compensatio, remuneratio, recompensatio,* Angl. xxxii. 504, 22.

wiþer-rǣde. II. *add:*—Þ ûre nân ne beó wiþerrǣde wiþ þá hâlgan drohtnunga, ac wilsumlîce dô þ hê dô, Hml. S. 33, 72.

wiþer-sprecend, es; *m. One who contradicts;* contradictor, Chrd. 41, 29.

wiþer-weard. II. *add:*—Hié wurdon him selfum wiðerwearde þæt hié hit ǣfre ongunnon, and Scribanianus ofslôgon *they became opposed to themselves, that they had ever attempted it, and slew Scribonianus;* exercitus conversus in poenitentiam, Scribonianum interfecit, Ors. 6, 4; S. 260, 3.

wiþerweardlîce. *Add:* v. un-wiþerweardlîce.

wiþer-wengel, es; *m. An adversary:*—Bysmrað wiðerwengel naman [þînne] *inritat aduersarius nomen tuum,* Ps. Rdr. 73, 10. Wiþerwenglum *aduersariis,* 290, 1. Þû forbryttest wiþerwenglas (*aduersarios*), 280, 7.

wiþer-winn. *Add:*—Wiþerwinnes *certaminis,* An. Ox. 2, 3.

wiþer-word, -wurd. v. wiþer-weard; III.

wiþ-foran. *Add:*—Þá þe wiðforan ûs wǣron, Wlfst. 96, 10.

wiþ-ginan. *Add:* [cf. (?) O. H. Ger. gaganen *obviare, occurrere, objicere.*]

wiþ-habban. *Add:* *to restrain :*—Heora ân his exe ûp âbrǣd, wolde hine sleán; ac him forwyrnde sum ôþer, swâ þ hê þ hylfe gelǣhte and wiðhæfde þ slege, Hml. S. 31, 154. Ûdwitan sǣdan þ heó feólle . . . gif þá dweligendan steorran hyre ryne ne wiðhæfdon (-hæfton, *v. l.*) *rueret, ut sapientes dixerunt, si non planetarum occursu moderaretur,* Angl. vii. 12, 112. Þǣ nâ gerîseþ þ þû fæste and þê fram mettum wiðhæbbe *abstinere tibi minime congruit,* Gr. D. 100, 3.

wiþ-hæftan *to restrain,* Angl. vii. 12, 112. *See preceding word.*

wiþ-hindan. *Add:*—Hê rihte þ lytle scip þe wiþhindan þám mâran scipe gefæstnod wæs *post navem carabum regebat,* Gr. D. 347, 2.

wîþig-gråf. *Add:*—On wîðiggråfe, C. D. v. 147, 32.

wîþig-slæd *a willow-slade :*—Ûp oð wîðigslæd; of wŷþigslade, C. D. B. iii. 667, 32.

wiþ-innan. (1) *add:*—Wê fundon ðá weardas wiðûtan standende, ac wê ne gemêtton nǣnne wiðinnan, Hml. Th. i. 572, 35. Hê weardas wiðinnan and wiðûtan gesette, 574, 3. (2) *add:*—Wiþinnan þan *infra,* An. Ox. 129 : 1441.

wiþ-lǣdness, e; *f. A carrying off, leading away :*—On wiðleáðnysse *in abductione,* Ps. Cant. 391, 36.

wiþ-licgan. *Add:*—Gif hê wiðligð þissum *si his renisus fuerit,* Chrd. 61, 16.

wiþ-metendlîce. v. un-wiþmetendlîce : wiþ-metenness. v. un-wiþmetenness.

wiþ-neopan. *Add:* *prep.* :—Swâ eástweardes þæt hit cymeð eft wiðnioðan þæt gelád on Sæferne, C. D. ii. 150, 14.

wiþ-sacan. I. *add:*—Þá cwæð him Petrus tô : *Non lauabis mihi pedes* . . . Hê forhtade for ðǣre Drihtnes eádmôdnysse . . . Se man âna wæs þte eádmôdnysse wiðsôc, and hwæðere for hŷrsumnysse geþafode, Hml. A. 157, 135. II. *add:* (4 a) *with a negative clause :*—Þû wâst þ ic ne wiðsace þ ic sylf ne forfare, ac ic nelle secgan unsôð on mê sylfe, Hml. S. 12, 194. Þá wiðsôc hê, þ hê hit nâteshwôn underfôn nolde *quem cum suscipere ille renueret,* Gr. D. 78, 21. (b) *with dat.* infin. :—Hê þá wiðsôc hit tô underfônne, Gr. D. 78, 19.

wiþ-scûan (= -scûfan ?) :—Tô wiðscûenne, Bd. 1, 14; Sch. 39, 19 (*see last passage at* wiþ-scûfan.)

wiþ-teón. I. *add:*—Hwîlum hê seleð hâlgan wîtedômes gâst, hwîlon hê eft wiðtyhð (*subtrahit*) þám môdum þára wîtegana, Gr. D. 146, 31.

wiþ-ufan. *Add:*—Wiðufan *super,* Hpt. 31, 18, 501. Hêr hwǣne wiðufan þû wǣre seofiende *paulo superius questus es,* Gr. D. 271, 23.

wiþ-weorþan. *In* El. 293 *a suggested emendation is* ealle *for* þǣre *which is in keeping with the Latin text* repellentis omnem sapientiam. *See* Beiblatt 21, 174.

wiþ-westan *to the west of :*—Þonne wiþwestan Alexandria þǣre byrig Asia and Affrica tôgædere licgeað, Ors. 1, 1 ; S. 8, 12.

witian. *Add:* v. ed- (?), ûþ-witian.

wîtiend-lic. *Add:*—Se wîtiendlica and se apostolica cwyde *prophetica apostolicaque scententia,* Gr. D. 138, 16.

-witigung, -witlic. v. ûþ-witigung, -witlic.

witleás-ness, e; *f. Witlessness, stupidity, dullness :*—Witleásnes *socordia, torpor, dementia,* An. Ox. 47, 3.

wit-leást. *Add:*—Widtlǣste *uesaniae,* An. Ox. 11, 174.

witodlice. II. *add:*—Witodlîce ic wylle *utique uolo,* Ælfc. Gr. Z. 263, 17.

-witol. *Add:* v. gearo-witol : -witolness. v. for-, gearo-witolness.

witon. *Add:*—Uton ǣndian þás bôc nû hêrrihte . . . Nǣse, lâ, nese ; uton ne forlǣtan gyét ðás bôc ǣr ic sweotolor ongytan magæ þæt þæt wit embe sint *concludamus hoc primum volumen . . . Non sinam omnino concludi hunc libellum, nisi mihi modicum quo intentus sim de vicinia lucis aperueris,* Solil. H. 49, 10–13.

wit-scipe, es; *m. Witness :*—In gewitscipe (witscipe, *v. l.*) standan . . . in gewitscipe (gewitnysse witscipes, *v. l.*) þreóra oððe feówera bisscopa, Bd. 1, 27 ; Sch. 73, 9–13. v. ge-witscipe.

wit-seóc. *Add:*—Swâ oft swâ hê wolde âdrǣfan deófla of þám witseócum, Hml. S. 31, 1207.

wixen, wexen. *Substitute :*—Hláf wexenne niman freó[n]dscipas nîwe gefêgð *panem cerarium accipere, amicitias nouas iungit,* Lch. iii. 210, 2.

wlæffetere. *Add:* v. wlaffian: wlǣta. III. *Dele* ' v. an-wlǣta, -wlâta.'

wlaffian *to stammer, speak indistinctly :*—Nân fefor nis mannon mâra þonne se wînlica wǣta, of þám deáfiað þá eáran and wleaffað seó tunge (*balbutit denique lingua*), Chrd. 74, 11. v. wlæffetere.

wlâtere, es; *m. A spectator :*—Hæbbe ǣfre se lâreów gearwe stemne tô bodunge, þ hê mid his swîgan ne gebylge þæs ûplican wlâte- dôm (*superni expectatoris iudicium*), Chrd. 96, 24.

wlâtung, e; *f. Sight, spectacle :*—Þe læs þe se hlyst and seó gesihð wurðe gefŷled mid besmitenysse fracodlicra wurda and wlâtuncga (*spectaculorum*), Chrd. 79, 4. v. neb-wlâtung.

wlenc, es; *m.* v. wlencu: wlencan. *Add:* v. ā-wlencan.

wlencu. *Add:* wlenc, es; *m.* III. *add:*—Hē an his ǣrend-gewryte wīfum ne stȳrde reáfa wlences (*a pretiosarum uestium apetitu*), Chrd. 65, 6. Eft laþode hī man and speón tō ōðres mannes brȳdrǣste ge for hire wlǣncum ge for hire geogoðe *quam dum ad iterandum thalamum et opes et aetas uocarent*, Gr. D. 279, 1.

wlispian. v. ā-wlispian, Nap. 74.

wlīte (-u). I. *add:*—Wlīte *machina* (colorum, ex quibus ornatur praesentis *machina* mundi, Ald. 273, 6), An. Ox. 23, 58. Hē sǣde him hwilc heora wlitu wæs, and hū hī wǣron gescrȳdde, Hml. S. 31, 705. II. *add:*—Tō bóte cyrican wlites *ad ornamentum ęclesię*, Chrd. 82, 12. Lustfulliende þǣre stōwe swētnesse and wlite *delectatus suauitate ac decore loci illius*, Bd. 5, 12; Sch. 629, 12. v. un-wlite.

 wlite-lic, Gr. D. 139, 18. v. wīte-lic *prophetic.*

 wlite-sceáwung. *Add:* cf. sceáwung-stōw.

 wlite-weorþ, es; *n.* Ransom or compensation paid for a person, the amount being determined by the person's appearance (wlite; *see the passages from the Laws under* wlite; I.):—Cōm tō him ān wydewe, seó sǣde him þ hire sunu wǣre gelǣded in hæftnȳde ... and bæd þone Godes wer þ hē hire his wliteweorþ (*pretium*) gesealde, þ heó mihte hire sunu mid ālȳsan, Gr. D. 179, 21.

 -wlitian. v. mǣg-wlitian: wlitig. *Add:* v. frǣ-, heofon-wlitig: -wlitlīce. v. mǣg-wlitlīce.

wōd. *Add:* (1 b) *mad with anger, enraged:*—Hē suwode ǣfre swilce hē ne gefrēde heora swingla nāteshwón, and hī þæs þe wōddran wǣron him tōgeánes, Hml. S. 31, 978. (2):—Þā cōm þǣr fǣrlíce yrnan an þearle wōd cū ... þā geseah se hālga wer þ þǣr sæt ān deófol on þǣre cū hrycge, Hml. S. 31, 1040.

 wōd-dreám, es; *m.* The word glosses demonium:—Godas þeóda wōddreámas *dii gentium demonia*, Ps. Rdr. 95, 5. Cf. (?) wōden-dreám.

 wōd-henn. *Dele, and see* wōþ.

 wōdheortness, e; *f.* Madness, frenzy, rage:—Gemunaþ hū þā forwurdon þe mid wōdheortnesse willan tō wǣpnedmannum hǣmed sōhton, Verc. Först. 178.

 wōd-lic. *Add:*—He funde fīf mǣdena, wlitige and rance, ... and hēt þ hī āwendon mid heora wōdlican plegan his geþanc fram Crīste, Hml. S. 35, 53: 65.

 wōd-līce. I. *add:*—Hī gebundon þone bisceop ... and beóton hine wōdlīce, Hml. S. 22, 156. Þeáh þe heora hláford wǣre wōdlīce hǣðen, 28, 16.

Wōdnes-dæg. *Add:*—On Wodnesdæg, þe byð *caput ieiunii*, bisceopas āscādað ūt of cyrican ... þā þe on openlican synnan hȳ sylfe forgyltan, Wlfst. 104, 9.

Wōdnes-dǣg, *Wednesday:*—Wōdnesdoege *feria .iiii.*, Mk. p. 5, 16.

wōdness. I. *add:*—Wōdnesse *uesaniam*, i. rabiem, An. Ox. 2057. v. ellen-wōdness; wēden-heortness.

wōd-seóc; *adj.* Insane, mad, lunatic :—Þā wæs gelǣded se wōdseóca (wēdend-, *v. l.*) man (cf. mid deófle geswenced, gedreht mid deófolseocnysse, 134, 24) tō Benedicte, Gr. D. 135, 1.

woffung. For first example substitute :—Hē ongann gebiddan þ him God forgeáfe mid hwām hē mihte gestillan þæs hātheortan mæssepreóstes woffunga *coepit exorare ut ei redderet unde presbyteri furentis insaniam mitigare potuisset*, Gr. D. 65, 13.

wōgere. *Add:*—Hī beóð wōgeras swiðor þonne preóstas (*sponsos magis quam clericos*), Chrd. 64, 37.

wōger-lic; *adj.* Wooerlike, amorous :—Mæssepreóstas ne beón an þām gefērscypum þǣr man wōgerlīce (*amatoria*) leóð singe, Chrd. 78, 34.

wōh. I. *add:*—Sume habbað swīðne langne and swīðe rihtne weg; sume habbað swīðe scortne and þeáh wōne, Solil. H. 44, 9. Wōhe hornas *curua aera*, An. Ox. 50, 44. I a. *rugged, uneven, rough :*—Wōge smēþiende hylcas *asperas conplanans anfractus*, An. Ox. 1770.

 wōh-dǣd. *Add:*—Þæt forhogade þ hē ǣnig gemet sette his wōhdǣdum *modum suis pravitatibus ponere contempsit*, Gr. D. 341, 4.

 wōh-gestreón. *Add:*—Ne wyrð nǣfre folces wīse wel gerǣde on þām earde þe man wōhgestreón and mǣst falses lufað ; þȳ sculan Godes freónd ... nā geþafian þ ðurh fals and ðurh wōhgestreón men tō swyðe forwyrcean hī sylfe, Ll. Th. ii. 312, 27–32. Þā līgeas forbærnaþ ... þā þe nū hēr syndon on unnyttre gesyhðe ... wōggestreóna, Verc. Först. 87, 5.

wōhhian *to go astray mentally, rave, wander :*—Þā wēnde se cniht þ hē dwolode and wōhhade (wihade, *v. l.* wōhade ?) *cum hunc puer insanire crederet*, Gr. D. 314, 7.

wōhlīce. *Add:*—Menn beóð geworhte wōlīce him betwȳnan, swā þ se fæder wind wið his āgenne sunu, and bróðor wið ōþerne, Hml. S. 13, 295.

wōl. *Add:* n. :—In þām hlāfe næs nā bemiþen þ wōl (*pestis*), Gr. D. 118, 10.

 wōl-berende. *Add:*—Se wōlberenda drync *ille pestifer potus*, Gr. D. 104, 31.

wolcen. *Add:*—In weolcne *in nube*, Ps. L. 77, 14.

wolc-spinl. v. wealc-spinl : wolma. v. fōt-wolma.

wōp. II. *add:*—Mid singalum stefnum his wōpa *continuis lamentorum vocibus*, Gr. D. 215, 23.

wōp-lic (2). *Add:*—Hig ymbscrȳdan hig mid þām wōplican gyrlan *lamentationis habitum induere*, Chrd. 96, 11.

word. II 1. *add:*—Þā hit mon Agustuse sǣde, þā herede hē þā ofermētto ... Raþe þæs Rōmāne anguldon þæs wordes mid miclum hungre, Ors. 6, 1; S. 254, 15. Hié bǣdon þæt hié ðæs gefeohtes geswicen, þæt hié mōsten þā deádan bebyrgean ... þæt is mid Crēcum þeáw þæt mid ðǣm worde bið gecȳþed hwæðer healf hæfð sige, 3, 1; S. 100, 8. God cwæð be eallum synfullum mannum twā word ..., ' *Declina a malo* ' ... Eft cwæð God, ' Gif se synfulla wyrcð dǣdbóte ...,' Hml. S. 12, 145-155. (10):—Ic gewunode in Laurenties worde (cf. Geceás hē Laurentium tō þām hāde þæs biscopes dōmes ... and hē þurhwunode in his cwide (*sententia*), 329, 16-18) and wæs wið Simmache *in parte Laurentii contra Symmachum sensi*, Gr. D. 330, 8. v. fore-, fracoþ-, fröfor-, grēting-, Lǣden-, leáfnes-, teosu-, wær-word.

 -worden-lic. v. for-wordenlic: -wordenness. v. ā-, for-wordenness.

 word-lār, e; *f.* (*Verbal*) *teaching :*—Swā dōn hī ... þ ... hī beón tō bysne ōðrum ge an wordlāre (*in uerbo*), Chrd. 53, 22.

 wordliend, es; *m.* One who harangues :—Bannendra, maþeliendra, wordliendra *contionatorum*, i. *rhetorum*, An. Ox. 2321. v. wordrian.

 word-predicung, e; *f.* (*Verbal*) *preaching, a sermon :*—Þā hyrdas sceolon ... him ætȳwan rihte drohtnunge ge mid gōdum bysnum ge eác mid wordpredicungum (*cum uerbo predicationis*), Chrd. 66, 23.

 -worht. v. hand-worht.

wōrian. *Add:* (1 b) *of movement by a person :*—Wandriendum, wōriendum *uagabundis*, i. *errantibus* (*gestibus*), An. Ox. 3340. Wōriendum fǣreldum *uagabundis meatibus*, 4857.

worn (1 b). *Add:*—Swā swā hē spræc tō fæderum ūrum (Abraham) and sǣdes worne (sǣdsworne, MS.) *sicut locutus est ad patres nostros Abraham et semini eius*, Ps. Rdr. 296, 55.

worpian. *Add:* v. of-worpian: -worpness. v. tō-worpness.

worþig. I. *add:*—Tūnes, worþiges *fundi*, i. *ville*, An. Ox. 4843. Wordias, croftas *praedia*, 3790. II. *add:*—In þām worþige (*platea*) beforan þǣre cytan dura stódon .ii. þreátas singende, Gr. D. 285, 21. Hyra worþias wēron þes hlūttrestan goldes *platea civitatis aurum mundum*, Verc. Först. 136, 6.

wōrung, e; *f.* Wandering, rambling :—Ys se syxta heáfodleahter gecweden sleacnes ... of þǣre byð ācenned ... unstaþolfæstnes stōwe and wōrung of stōwe tō stōwe, Verc. Först. 178.

 -wosa. v. ge-wosa.

wōþ. II. *add: eloquent, lofty speech :*—Wōðhae *coturno*, Txts. 53, 583: Wülck. Gl. 366, 2. (Cf. coturnum, superbum, Corp. Gl. H. 36, 714. Ofermōd *coturnus*, Wrt. Voc. i. 19, 5. See also Ld. Gl. H. *s.v.* turnodo.) Þoot, puood (= wōþ) *facundia, eloquentia*, Txts. 64, 444.

wope. v. gōt-wope: wraca. v. nīd-wraca.

wracian *to drive, press, carry on an action :*—Þā folc him betweónum ful x. winter þā gewin wraciende wǣron, Ors. 1, 11; S. 50, 21. v. wrecan; I d.

wracu. *Add:* wrace (?), an :—Grimre wrace (wræc, *v. l.*) þā fyrenfullan ðeóde þæs grimman mānes wæs æfterfylgende *acrior gentem peccatricem ultio diri sceleris secuta est*, Bd. 1, 14; Sch. 39, 12.

wræc. II. *add: See preceding word.* III. *add:*—Adam wæs ādrifen of neorcxnawanges gefeán ... and becōm in þā yrmðe þises wræces (*exilii*), Gr. D. 260, 7-18.

wræc *what is driven. Add:* v. scip-wræc: -wræc (-wrǣce ?). *Dele* ' (-wrǣce ?)': wrǣclice. *Add:* v. nīd-wrǣclīce.

wrǣd *a flock. Add:* [cf. Goth. wriþus *a herd.*]

wrǣne. *Add:*—Ualerianus wæs swīðe leás man and wrǣne aa oð þ hē wæs oreald *Valerianus usque ad aetatem decrepitam levis ac lubricus extitit*, Gr. D. 341, 2 : 20.

wrǣnsian *to be wanton :*—Þā beóð þǣr cwylmed in ēcum fȳre, ða þe hēr swiðost mid wō wrǣnsiað, Nap. 71.

wrǣstlung. *Add:*—Swā wæs þǣr seó wrǣstlung (*luctamen*) ymb Stephanum ; þā gōdan gāstas hine tugon upp, and þā yflan hine tugon ofdūne, Gr. D. 320, 13. Hē ūt fērde of līchaman tō gewinne and tō wrǣstlunge līfes and deáðes *de corpore ad certamen vitae et mortis exiit*, 321, 3.

wræt[t] *a plant. l.* wrætt, *and dele* Lch. ii. 306, 18. *Add:* [cf. O. H. Ger. rezza *coccum, coccinum*]. *See next two words.*

 wræt-baso; *adj.* Red :—Uueretbaso *rubeum*, Ld. Gl. H. 20, 19 (col. 2).

 wræt-reád (wræte-); *adj.* Red :—Bind þā moran ymb þ heáfod mid wrætereáde wrǣde, Lch. ii. 306, 18.

wrang; *adj.* Rough, uneven :—Tō ðǣm feórðan þorne on wrangan hylle foreweardre stent, C. D. v. 297, 19. [All þatt ohht iss wrang and crumb shall effnedd beón and rihhtedd, Orm. 9207. *Icel.* rangr.] *See next two words.*

wrang, es; *n. Add: injustice :*—Ic nelle geþolian þ ǣnig man eów ǣnig wrang beóde, Ll. Lbmn. 486, 13.

**wrang-wîs**; adj. Rough, uneven :—Wrangwîse, wôge smeþiende hylcas salebrosos, i. asperos conplanans anfractus, An. Ox. 1770. [Wrongwise (unrighteous) reuen, O. E. Hml. i. 175, 256.]

**wrâþ.** II. add :—Þá weard Tiberius Rômânum swâ wrâđ and swâ heard swâ hê ǽr wæs milde and icþe inmutata est Tiberii modestia atque ex mansuetissimo principe saevissima bestia exarsit, Ors. 6, 2; S. 254, 30.

**wraþo** glosses moram, Mt. L. 24, 48.

**wraþu.** (2) add :—Hê gesomnode mycel feoh him tô bryce and tô wrǽþe þæs langan lîfes cum multas pecunias pro longioris vitae stipendiis collegisset, Gr. D. 339, 27. Se ilca in þissere byrig fylgeþ þám wraðum (stipendiis) þises hwîlendlican lîfes mid þám ylcan lǽcecræfte, 344, 11.

**-wraxl.** v. ge-wraxl.

**wrecan.** I b. add :—His đeng sum þám hê hæfde beboden þ hê sceolde earmra manna ǽrende wrecan (beódan, âbeódan, v. ll.), Bd. 3, 6; Sch. 209, 20. I d. add :—Þá folc him betweónum ful .x. winter þá gewin wrecende wǽron, Ors. I, 11 ; S. 50, 21. III c. add :—Hê wile forgiefan đæt hê wrecan sceolde remittit quod ferire debuit, Past. 149, 21. VII b I. to punish a fault on a person :—Đá scylda . . . hié on him selfum dêmen and wrecæn seque se judice puniat, Past. 151, 17 : 429, 6. IV c. add :—Eall his cynn mon ofslôg, þý lǽs hit monn uferan dôgore wrǽcce (wrǽce, v. l.) cognati omnes supplicio traditi : ne quis eum ejusdem famliae umquam ulcisci meditaretur, Ors. 4, 5; S. 168, 6. Hê bebeád đæt menn nâmen hiora sweord Godes andan mid tô wrecanne (ad ulciscendum), Past. 381, 24. IV c I. add :—Hê wræc on þǽre byrig hiora misdǽda, Ors. 6, 6 ; S. 262, 2. ¶ add :—Hit God wræc on him, 4, 7 ; S. 184, 7.

**wrecca.** I. add :—Wrecca peregrinus, Ps. L. 68, 9. Eardes wrecca incola, 118, 19. v. eard-wrecca.

**wrecend.** Add :—þ đú tôweorpe feónd and wrecend ut destruas inimicum et ultorem, Ps. L. 8, 3.

**-wrecness.** Substitute : **wrecness**, e ; f. Wickedness, evil :—Hefig mân is and Godes wrecnys graue est facinus, Bd. 1, 27; Sch. 69, 17. v. god-wrecness.

**wrêgan.** (2 b) add :—Hî þone Hǽlend wrêgdon and sǽdon formanegum (for manegum?) yfelum dǽdum, Nic. 1, 18. v. fore-wrêgan.

**wrêgend.** Add :—Hê wilnađ þ hê mid þý geweorđe ûre wrêgend (accusator) beforan þám dôme þæs êcan dêman, Gr. D. 221, 13.

**wrenc.** Add : v. leóþ-, list-, lyre-wrenc. **wrencan.** Add : v. æt-wrencan.

**wreón.** Add : v. un-oferwrigen.

**wreþian.** Add : , wreþþan :—Hê þá wreþiende (wreþþende, v. l. sustentans) þá týdran limu betwyh his gingrena handum upp ârǽhtum his âgnum handum in þone heofon gestâh, Gr. D. 175, 20. v. and-wreþian.

**wrîdan** ; p. de. l. p. wrâd, pl. wridon ; pp. wriden : **wrîdian.** In l. 18 for 1963 l. 1903.

**wrigelness**, e ; f. Covering, protection :—Ic sié gescilded on wrigelnesse fiđra đînra protegar in uelamento alarum tuarum, Ps. Vos. 60, 5.

**wrigels.** I. add :—Ongan þ wrigels (operimentum) þǽre bydene for þám weaxendan ele beón upp âhafen, and þá onstyredum þám wrigelse se ele feóll ofer þá brerdas þǽre bydene, Gr. D. 160, 11–13. II. add :—Hê genam âweg . . . þone wrigels (pallium) mid þý wæs bewrigen se andwlita þæs fordfêrdan mannes . . . and onwegđônum þám wrigelse (pallio) gnâd on ansŷne . . . þ dûst, Gr. D. 216, 11–16.

**-wrih-ness.** v. on-wrigness : -wring (-wryng?). v. ge-wring.

**wringan.** (2) add :—Hit gelamp in sume tîd þá þá Langbærdisce mæn wrungon elebergan on þǽre treddan . . . þá côm Sanctulus tô heom and brôhte ǽmtige cyllan tô þǽre wringan quodam tempore cum in prelo Langobardi olivas premerent . . . utrem vacuum ad prelum detulit, Gr. D. 250, 12–15. Hê þone cniht âsette on þá wîntreddan aud hêt hine wringan þa feáwa geclystru þǽra byrgena puerulum in calcatorio deposuit, et calcare ipsos paucissimos racemos fecit, 58, 17. Đonne þú cýse habban wille, sete þonne þîne twâ handa tôgædere brâlinga, swilce þú wringan wille, Tech. ii. 123, 21.

**wringe**, an ; f. A press, Gr. D. 250, 15. (See first passage under wringan.) [Wringe, Pall. xi. 107.] v. wîn-wringe.

**wring-hwǽg.** l. -hwǽg.

**writ.** Dele hreód-writ at end, and add (?) :—Write gramate (Wülck. Gl. 531, 19 reads gewrite), Wrt. Voc. ii. 95, 52.

**writan.** I. add :—þonne mon þá hlâfas wrât tô þicgeanne, þonne orn þǽr blôd ût cum panes per convivia frangerentur, cruor e mediis panibus fluxit, Ors. 5, 10; S. 234, 5. II. add :—Hê Crîstes rôde tâcen þǽr tôweard wrât signum crucis edidit, Gr. D. 105, 9. v. tô-wrîtan ; æfter-, fore-writen.

**-writen.** v. ofer-writen a superscription : **wrîtend.** v. irfe-wrîtend.

**wrîtere.** II. add : a secretary ; notarius :—Hê wæs wrîtere (notarius) on þysre hâlgan Rômâniscean cyrcean, Gr. D. 52, 3. Se Drihtnes wer him tô gehêt his wrîtere (notarium), and þám dihtode, 193, 21. v. cranic-, in-, irfeweard-wrîtere.

**-wriþ.** v. ge-wriþ.

**wrîþan.** III. add :—Wrîþende astringentes, i. alligantes (ferreis

nexibus collum cum suris astringentes, Ald. 45, 9), An. Ox. 3288. v. for-, on-wrîþan ; ge-, un-wriþen.

**wriþels.** For seaxclâđ l. feaxclâđ, and add : [cf. O. H. Ger. ridila, fahsreita licia (crinibus addunt)]. Cf. ge-wriþelian.

**-wriþenness.** v. ge-wriþenness : **-wrîþung** (-ing). Add : v. gewrîþing : **writ-hreód** (?). Dele : **wrîtian** ; l. substitute : **writian** (?) to cut (v. wrîtan ; I.) or to draw (v. wrîtan ; II.) a figure :—Đonne wercađ hió of weaxe, writiaþ (wrîtaþ?) Fênix, mêtaþ Fênix they make waxen images of the Phenix, draw it, paint it, E. S. 478, 49.

**wrîtian** ; II. Substitute : **wrîtian, wreotian** to chirp, chatter, rattle :—Wreotađ crepitat, Wrt. Voc. ii. 23, 34. Writigeađ (printed pritigeađ) pipant (comples aera catervis, garrula quae rostris resonantes cantica pipant, Ald. 136, 28), 88, 80. Þæt fugolcynn eall fægere Fênix grêtaþ, writigađ and singaþ onbûtan him ǽlc on his wîsan, E. S. viii. 478, 40. Wri[tiende] garrulante, An. Ox. 37, 3.

**wrixend-lic.** Substitute : **wrixiend-lic** ; adj. Mutual :—In þám freóndlican geflite þǽre wrixiendlican eâdmôdnesse in hac mutuae humilitatis amica contentione, Gr. D. 116, 7.

**wrixl.** add : VII. office taken in turn, place. v. ge-wrixl ; V., V a. :—Be þám þe wrixl ealdordômes (uicem prelatorum) on geférrǽdene habban sceolon, Chrd. 53, 9. Ic geseó þ Benedictus hæfde Paules gewixle (wrixle, v. l. vicem), Gr. D. 141, 12. Wriexle, 153, 24.

**-wrixl**; adj. v. ge-wrixl.

**wrixlan.** II. add :—Ealle gesceafta wrixliađ swâ dæg and niht. Đû recst þæt geár . . . þurh þæt gewrixle þára feówer týda . . . þára wrixlađ ǽlc wyđ ôđer and hwerfiađ, swâ þæt heora ǽgđer byđ eft emne þæt þæt hýt ǽr wæs . . . and swâ wrixlađ tunglas . . . Wrixliađ sume þá on ôđre wîsan, Solil. H. 9, 17–24. Swâ wrixliađ ealle þæt hý farađ and æft cumađ, 62, 30.

**-wrixl-lic.** v. ge-wrixllic.

**wrôht.** I. add :—þǽr biđ grânung and geómrung and micel wrôht, Verc. Först. 111, 4. Wôrhta excusationes, Ps. L. 140, 4.

**wrôht-bera.** v. wrôht-bora.

**wrôht-bora.** I. add :—þ hê mid þý geweorđe ûre wrêgend and wrôhtbora (-bera, v. l. accusator) beforan þám dôme þæs êcan dêman, Gr. D. 221, 13. Wrôhtborena excussorum, Ps. Rdr. 126, 4.

**wrôht-stafas.** Add : [cf. O. H. Ger. ruog-stab accusatio] : **wudiht.** l. wudiht[e].

**wudu.** Add: gen. wyda. v. gafol-wudu. II I. add :—Đæs muntes cnoll wiđûtan is sticmǽlum mid wuda oferwexen, and eft sticmǽlum mid grênum felda oferbrǽded, Hml. Th. i. 508, 23 ; Bl. H. 207, 27. (2) add :—On Piceno þǽm wuda ân wielle weól blôde, Ors. 4, 7; S. 184, 21. Ealle treówa wudena, Ps. L. 95, 12. v. gafol-, in-, healf-, neáh-wudu.

**wudu-bǽr**, e ; f. A woodland pasture :—Đis sind đǽre wudubǽre landgemǽru æt Đæclêge, C. D. vi. 171, 4. Cf. weald-bǽre (l. -bǽr).

**wudu-bill.** Add :—Sume đæge sealde hê him îrengelôman, þ is hâten wudubill quadam die ei dari ferramentum jussit, quod ad falcis similitudinem falcastrum vocatur, Gr. D. 113, 18.

**wudu-byrþra**, an ; m. A bearer of wood :—Wudubyrþran calones, An. Ox. 869.

**wudu-fald** a fold in a wood :—Æt đám ealdan wudufald ; forđ syđđan be efisce, C. D. v. 281, 33.

**wudu-feoh.** Add :—Wudufeoh lucas, pecunia de lucis, Hpt. 31, 12, 255.

**wudu-gehǽg.** For ‘An enclosed wood’ substitute : Woodland pasture. Cf. gehæg-holt.

**wudu-hiwett**, es ; n. Cutting down trees in another’s wood; the fine for so doing :—De cesione nemoris . . . Wudehêwet, Ll. Th. i. 539, 21. Cf. Gif man ôđres wudu . . . heáweđ, 70, 4. Gif mon âfelle on wuda wel monega treówa, 128, 19. Gif mon âceorfe ân treów, 130, 2.

**wudu-land.** Add : cf. timber-land.

**wudu-mann** a woodman :—Tô wudemannes tûne, C. D. iii. 275, 9.

**wuldor.** (2) add :—Wulderes þines gloriæ tuę, Ps. Rdr. 25, 8. v. weorold-wuldor.

**wuldor-dreám.** Add :—þeáh him syndon ealle wuldordreámas tô gelǽdde, Verc. Först. 107, 1.

**wuldorfullian.** Add : v. ge-wuldorfullian.

**wuldor-geweorc**, es ; n. Glorious work ; a glorious work :—þæs eádigan Cristoforus wuldorgeworc synd nû lang tô âsecganne þe Dryhten þurh hyne geworhte, Angl. xvii. 122, 4. [Wuldorfæst ys and micel crîstenra manna God, þæs wuldorge[wor]ces nâne mennisce searwa ofercuman ne magon, 121, 5. (The government of ofercuman is exceptional, as elsewhere it takes the accusative.)]

**wuldor-heáp**, es ; m. A glorious band :—Ûre Drihten ængla wuldorheáp him sylfum tô wyrđscipe gegearuwode, Nap. 71.

**wuldor-helm.** Add :—Unrîm hâligra beóđ gefylled mid þý gewuldredan wuldorhelme, Verc. Först. 119, 1.

**wuldor-sang**, es ; m. A glorious song :—þeáh þe sŷn ealle sunder-cræftas and wuldorsangas in gesamnode, Verc. Forst. 114, 10.

**wuldrian.** Add: v. â-wuldrian: **wuldriend.** v. riht-wuldriend.

**wulf.** I. add:—Wæs micel wundor þ ân wulf wearð âsend þurh Godes wissunge tô bewerigenne þ heáfod wið þá ôþre deór . . . Læg se græga wulf þe bewiste þ heáfod, and mid his twám fôtum hæfde þ heáfod beclypped, grædig and hungrig, and for Gode ne dorste þæs heáfdes âbyrian, Hml. S. 32, 145–155. v. were-wulf.

**wulf-haga,** an; *m.* *An enclosure to protect flocks from wolves* (? cf. Coll. M. 20, 15 (v. wulf; I.) for need of protection) :—On ðone wulfhagan midne; of ðám wulfhagan, C. D. iii. 78, 22. Tô ðæn ealdan wulthagan, vi. 9, 10.

**wulf-pytt,** es; *m.* *A pit for trapping wolves* (?), *a wolf's lair* (?) :—Tô wulfpytte, C. D. B. i. 280, 20. On wulfputt; of þám pytte on ðâ wôgan æc, iii. 113, 31. Tô ðæm wulfpyttæ, C. D. v. 84, 17. On ðone wulfpyt; of ðám wulfpytte, iv. 49, 7: 157, 11. Tô wulfpyttan, 343, 23 : iii. 434, 18.

**wull-mod.** Add: v. Beiblatt xiii. 14: -wun. v. ge-wun : -wuna; *m.* v. ge-wuna: -wuna; *adj.* v. be-, ge-wuna.

**wund.** I 2. add:—Heó wearð gestanden on þá breóst mid cancre þære wunde *cancri ulcere in mamilla percussa est,* Gr. D. 279, 27. v. feax-, heáfod-, syn-wund.

**wund;** *adj.* I 1. add:—Þær wearð þ .iii. hund monna ofslagen, ealle bûton ðæm consule ânum : hê côm wund âweg, Ors. 4, 6 ; S. 172, 24. (1 a) add:—Gif man bið on hrif wund, Ll. Th. i. 96, 10. Gif mon sié on þá herðan tô þám swiðe wund, 25. v. scear-wund.

**wundenness.** Dele, and see ofer-fundenness.

**wundian.** Add: (1) where injury is caused :—Bið ðæt môd on sume healfe open tô wundianne, Past. 431, 9. (2) where a curative effect is intended :—Se læce hŷt his læceseax under his cláðum oð ðæt hê hine wundað: wile ðæt hê hit gefrêde ær hê hit geseó, Past. 187, 10.

**wundig.** Add:—Ealle hié hié swâ wundige hyrwað *omnes ut ulcerosum contemnunt,* Verc. Först. 139, 10.

**wundiht.** *l.* wundiht[e].

**wundor.** I 3 a. add:—For earnunge hâlignesse wundra manega hæla (monig wundur hælo, *v. l.*) gefremede wæron *ob meritum sanctitatis eius multa sanitatum sint patrata miracula,* Bd. 5, 15 ; Sch. 649, 12. Gelômlico wundor hæla *crebra sanitatum miracula,* 4, 3 ; Sch. 365, 16.

**wundor-cræft.** I. add:—Swylce eác seó heáfodstôw sundorcræfte (wundorcræfte (?), but note *seorsum*; sundurcræftiglîce (wundorcræftiglîce (?), *v. ll.*) gemeten and geworht and gescyrpendlîce gehíwod ætŷwde tô þám gemete hyre heáfdes *et locus quoque capitis seorsum fabrefactus ad mensuram capitis illius aptissime figuratus apparuit,* Bd. 4, 19 ; Sch. 451, 18.

**wundor-cræftiglîce.** See preceding word.

**wundor-hûs,** es; *n.* *An upper chamber, upper part of a house :—* þá se mæssepreóst gestôd in þám solore þæs mynstres . . . þá þurhwuniendum unonwendedlîce eallum þám getimbre þæs hâmes þ wundorhûs (*solarium*) sylf gefeóll, in þám stôd se preóst, Gr. D. 119, 27.

**wundor-lic.** Add: v. for-, tô-wundorlic.

**wundor-tâcen** *a miracle* :—Nû oð þis, þæs þe mê þinceð, on îdel ic wênde þ on Sûðlangbeardum næron nâne fæderas þe wundortácnu (*signa*) wyrcean mihton, Gr. D. 25, 27.

**wundrian.** I 3. add:—Ac ic wundrige þá stihtunge þære godcundan mildheortnesse ofer ûs unweorðe *sed super indignos nos divinae misericordiae dispensationem miror,* Gr. D. 233, 28. Sê þe ongyteð his drohtað, ne scyle hê wundrian his mægn *qui conversationem ejus agnoverit, virtutem non debeat mirari,* 187, 9.

**wundrung.** I. add:—Wiþ lungenâdle, genim þære sylfan wyrte seáw, syle drincan ; mid heálicre wundrunge hê bið gehæled, Lch. i. 96, 10.

**wund-spring,** es; *m.* *An ulcerous wound :—*Wið wundspringum, Lch. i. 356, 20.

**wune-ness.** Add: v. þurh-wuneness.

**wuniendlîce;** *adv.* Continually :—Hí beóð â wuniendlîce lifiende in helle, Gr. D. 264, 9. v. þurh-wuniendlîce.

**-wunol.** v. þurh-wunol.

**wunung.** II. add:—Wunion ealle an ânre fæstre wununge (*in uno conclaui* (cf. conclauis, locus conclusus, Corp. Gl. H. 35, 683) *atrii*), Chrd. 54, 33. v. eard-, in-, mid-, on-, samod-, þurh-wunung.

**wunung-stôw,** e ; *f.* *Dwelling-place, habitation :—*Hê him bebeád þ hê fram hire gewite, and þ hê nâne wunungstôwe (*locum*) næfde on Godes þeówene, Gr. D. 31, 19.

**wyla.** v. wîl.

**wylfen;** *adj.* Add (?):—Oþ þá grægan, wylfenan hârnesse *usque cigneam canitiem* (cf. græg as an epithet of the wolf; and the modern phrase 'grey as a badger', An. Ox. 1876.

**wylian.** v. wilwan: **wylinc.** *l.* wylme, An. Ox. 571.

**wyn-bliss.** In Gr. D. 2, 4 wyn, blis *should be read, the passage is alliterative.*

**wyn-dreám.** In l. 2 dele 'Lamb'.

**wyndreám-ness,** e ; *f.* *Jubilation :—*Wyndreámnesse *iubilationis,* Ps. L. 150, 4.

**wynyng.** v. wining.

**wyrcan.** Dele at end 'fore-, in- (Exon. Th. 337, 21 ; Gn. Ex. 68)', *and* I 1. add:—Gebiddan neód ys and weorcean *orare necesse est et operari,* Scint. 35, 3. (2 a) add:—Wîngeard wyrcan blîðnysse lîf getâcnað *vindemiare, hilaritatem uitę significat,* Lch. iii. 212, 1. II 1 a a. add:—Weg þû weortest on sæ *uiam fecisti in mari,* Ps. L. Lind. 242, 20. Byrgenne swelce hiera þeáw wæs þæt mon rîcum monnum bufan eorðan of stânum worhte, Ors. 4, 10; S. 202, 5. Wyrtgemang wyrcan, Gr. D. 318, 2. (1 a β) add:—Ægwilc treów gôd gôdne wæstmas bereþ ł wyrceþ *omnis arbor bona fructus bonos facit,* Mt. R. 7, 17. Hwîlum wyrmas heortcoþe wyrceað, Lch. ii. 176, 13. (1 b) add:—Fîf hund and feówer and syxtig atomi wyrcað ân momentum . . . syx tîda wyrcað ânne fŷrðling, and feówer fŷrðlingas wyrcað ânne dæg, and seofon dagas âne wucan, Angl. viii. 318, 43–319, 1. (1 c β):—Ne wyrce gê mînes fæder hûs tô mangunghûse *nolite facere domum patris mei domum negotiationis,* Jn. 2, 16. III 2. add:—Weorc þ þe þû wercende wære ł weorhtest *opus quod operatus es,* Ps. L. 43, 2. V. *to work, produce an effect, have influence :—*Hond sceal heófod in wyrcan *the head must work upon* (or *influence*) *the hand,* Gn. Ex. 68. v. brycg-, samod-wyrcende.

**wyrcend.** II. add:—Beóð þæs wordes wircendras *estote factores uerbi,* Ælfc. T. Grn. 14, 37. Hê ys Godes þên . . . on þám yfelum wyrcendum tô wræce gesett *Dei minister est ; vindex in iram ei, qui malum agit* (Rom. 13, 4), 20, 28.

**wyrcness.** I. add:—Wyrcnesse, Ps. Vos. 106, 23.

**wyrd.** IV 2. add: *what is done, a deed, an action :—*Gif hê ô wære gecnysseð mid mænniscre herenesse fram þám mægne þyssere wyrde *in virtute facti* (a miracle just performed) *favore humano pulsatus,* Gr. D. 59, 31. Hê gefealh his gebede for þone seócan man, and þá sôna eft hine gelædde tô his âgenre ræste hâlne . . . Of þære wyrde (*ex quo ejus uno facto*) þæs weres wê geleornodon þ wê gelŷfdon eallra ôþra weorca, 248, 4. For þon þá wundru þe þonne geweorðað bringað þá gewitnysse þæs gôðan lîfes, þŷ ic bidde, gif hwylce sŷn þe cûþe þára hâligra wyrda, þ þû secge *quoniam ipsa signa quae fiunt, bonae vitae testimonium ferunt, quaeso te, si qua sunt, referas,* 91, 20. Þá þá ic sæde þá wyrda hâligra wera *dum facta fortium virorum narro,* 188, 5. V. Hit ne mæg âberan þá byrðene swâ mycelre wyrde *ferre talenti pondus non valet,* Gr. D. 228, 1. V a. add:—Hê nerede hŷ of wyrde heora *eripuit eos de interitu eorum,* Ps. Rdr. 106, 20.

**-wyrd** *speech.* Add: v. fore-wyrd: **-wyrdan.** Add: v. geânwyrdan, ge-forewyrdan: -wyrde; *n.* Add: v. fore-, fracoþ-wyrde: -wyrde; *adj.* Add: v. gearo-, yfel-wyrde: -wyrde-lic, -wyrdelîce, -wyrdelicness, -wyrdigness. v. ge-wyrdelic, &c.: -wyrdness. v. fela-wyrdness: wyrd-wrîtere. Add: v. gewyrd-wrîtere.

**wyrht.** Dele 'leóþ' *at end, and add:* v. læce-, un-wyrht ; egenwirht ?

**wyrhta.** Add: croc-, frum-, gim-, godweb-, îsern-, lâm-, læst-, leóþ-, lypen-, mêd-, morþ-, morþor-, nîd-, scild-, scôh-, slecg-, sweordwyrhta.

**wyrm.** Add: v. in-wyrm.

**wyrm-cynn.** Add:—Ofer weormcynna cyningce *super basiliscum,* Ps. L. 90, 13.

**-wyrmede.** v. deág-wyrmede.

**wyrm-galere.** Add:—þá wurmgaleras ic mihte gewyldan tô mînum willan æfre, Hml. S. 35, 177.

**wyrms.** Add:—Heó ne mihte bedŷglian þ weaxende wyrms (wyrmsi, *v. l.*) and wîdl (*increscentem saniem*), Gr. D. 157, 10. Ægþer ge þá handa ge þá fêt wæron wunda fulle, emne swâ þá wyrms fleówan ût of þám openum wunde *manus ejus et pedes versi in vulneribus fuerant, et profluviente sanie patebant,* 302, 9.

**wyrmsig** *corrupt matter.* See preceding word.

**wyrt.** I. add:—Swâ swâ wyrta felda ł blæda wyrtena *quemadmodum olera herbarum,* Ps. L. 36, 2. I a. add:—Gehwylce wyrte (þá wyrta, *v. l.* olera) þe hê ær mid stale gewilnode, hê him þ sealde, Gr. D. 25, 15. 'Ne can ic nænigne ôþerne cræft bûton þone, þ ic mæg wyrta wel begangan' . . . þá þá hê gehŷrde þ hê gelæred wæs wyrta tô begangenne '*Artem aliquam nescio, sed hortum bene excolere scio*' . . . *Cum in nutriendis oleribus peritus esset, audivit,* 180, 23–26. v. læce-, spere-, wealh-, wyn-, wyrm-wyrt.

**wyrt** *wort.* Add:—Healde hê hine georne wiþ geswêt eala, drince hlûttor eala, and on þæs hlûttran ealað wyrte wylle geonge âcrinde and drince, Lch. ii. 292, 21.

**wyrt-bræþ.** After 36 in l. 4 add: 34, 107.

**wyrt-geard.** Add:—Þá gelædde hê hine tô þæs wyrtgeardes (-tûnes, *v. l.*) gate *eum duxit ad horti aditum,* Gr. D. 25, 14. Paulinus onsérg þá nytte þæs wyrtgeardes (*horti*). And þá þá se cyningces âðum gelômlîce eóde in þone wyrtgeard (*hortum*), 180, 28.

**wyrt-gemang.** Add:—Wæs sôht hwær se læce wære þe cûþe wyrtgemang wyrcan *cum medicus atque pigmentarius esset quaesitus,* Gr. D. 318, 2.

**wyrt-gemangness,** e ; *f.* *Spice :—*Wyrtgema[n]gnyse *ambrosię,*

An. Ox. 3488. Wyrtima[n]guesse *thimiama*, i. *incensum*, 313. Wyrt-gemangnessa wyrtsata *olfactariola*, 4824.

**wyrt-truma.** I. *add*: v. ellen-wyrttruma. III. *add*: v. Cht. Crw. p. 68.

**wyrttrumian.** *Add*: v. â-, of-, un-wyrttrumian.

**wyrt-tûn.** *Add*:—Hê eóde into his wyrttûne (*ingressus hortum*), þâ gemêtte hê þone wyrttûn beón oserwrigenne mid micelre menieo emela, Gr. D. 67, 4–8. Hæbbe ma[n] æfre on preósta mynstre wynsume wirtûnas (*ortos olerum*), þ man mage þærof æfre sumne smeálicne êst findan, Chrd. 15, 36. v. ge-wyrttûn; wyrt-geard.

**wyrttûn-hege,** es; m. *A garden-hedge*:—Swâ þ furðon þær ân ne belâf binnon þâm wyrttûnhege *ut ne una quidem intra spatium horti remaneret*, Gr. D. 67, 18.

**wyrtwalian.** II. *add*:—Weód wyrtwalian, Angl. ix. 262, 21.

# Y

**ŷce.** *Add*:—Ŷcan *rubetae*, An. Ox. 26, 21.

**ydwe.** v. îþan: **yeldo.** v. ildu; III a.

**yfel,** es; n. *Add*: I. *moral evil*:—Hê cwæð ðæt ælces yfles fruma wære ofermétta, Past. 300, 4. Gemyne hê ðæs yfles (yfeles, v. l.) þe hê worhte, 24, 3. Ðæt hê tô yfle gedyde, 35, 9. Ðŷ læs hié hit mid ðæm óðrum yfle (yfele, v. l.) geiéce, 312, 11. Mid ðæm ânum yfle, 358, 20. Ðâ diéglan yfel habbað êcne gewutan, 449, 1. In him wunnon þâ yfel his lîchaman wið þâm weorce his ælmesdæda, Gr. D. 320, 18. Ðâ lytlan yflu gê fleóð, Past. 439, 26. II. *what is hurtful or grievous*:—Þonne hî mæst tô yfele gedôn hæfdon, Chr. 1011; P. 141, 19. Hwâ is þæt þe eall ðâ yfel þe hî dônde wæron âsecgean mæge?, Ors. 1, 8; S. 42, 16. Eal þâ monigfealdan yfel, 2, 5; S. 86, 15. Hî him ondrǣden ðâ êcan yflu, Past. 393, 29.

**yfel;** adj. *Add*:—Hê wæs swiþe yfel monn ealra þeáwa, bûton þ hê wæs cêne, Ors. 6, 14; S. 268, 27.

**yfel-berende** *glosses* nugigerulus (= turpis nuntius):—Ybilberende *nugegerulus*, An. Ox. 53, 16.

**yfel-cund.** *Add*:—Þâ þe yfelcunde (*maligna*) strecaþ ofer mê, Ps. L. 34, 26.

**yfel-cwedolian** *to speak ill of, curse*:—Bletsigende ... yfelcwedelginde *benedicentes ... maledicentes*, Ps. Rdr. 36, 22. Cf. weargcwedolian.

**yfel-cweþan.** *Add*: cf. wearg-cweþan.

**yfel-dǣd.** *Add*:—Hê weard âlýsed fram þæs drŷes bendum ... and arn tô ðâm apostole bysmrigende þæs drŷes yfeldǣdum, Hml. Th. ii. 414, 26.

**yfel-dǣda.** *Add*:—Ne ðû ðeófum ne ðlǣce, ne yfeldǣdum ne geðwǣrlǣce, Hml. S. 21, 361.

**yfel-dêma,** an; m. *An unjust judge*:—Be ðâm yfeldêmum, Nap. 42, 4.

**yfel-dônd.** *Add*: Cf. gôd-dônd, *and see next word*.

**yfel-dônde.** *Add*:—Good edleán ðâm weldôndum and yfel þâm yfeldôndum, Solil. H. 10, 19.

**yfele.** *Add*: I. *in a moral sense*:—Ðæt ðîn môd ne beó yfele besmiten ðurh ðâ ŷdelan spellunga, Hex. 48, 11. II. *injuriously*:—Ahab yfele weard beswicen (*was misled to his destruction*) for Naboðes wînearde ðe hê wôlîce genam, and hê hraðe feóll on gefeohte ofslagen, Hex. 54, 10.

**yfelian.** I. *add*:—Þæt mennisce cynn bið â yfeled and â in forwyrd gelǣded *omnia mala erunt; interitus generis humani*, Verc. Först. 120, 5.

**yfel-libbende;** adj. *Of evil life*:—Âsolcenum and yfellybbendum (*male viventibus*) and gîmeleásum, R. Ben. I. 118, 10. Cf. wel-libbende.

**yfel-lic.** *Add*: *Poor, mean, common*. (1) of persons:—Ân yfellic (wâclic, v. l.) man *homuncio*, Gr. D. 7, 24. Hê wæs swiðe yfellic (wâclic, v. l. vilis) on his gegerelan, 34, 1. (2) of things:—Hê wæs swiðe yfellices hîwes and forsewenlices (*exili forma et despecta*), Gr. D. 45, 30. On yfellicum (wâcum, v. l.) wîsum *rebus vilibus*, 70, 19.

**yfellîce;** adv. *Meanly, poorly*:—Hié ûrne Dryhten Crîst ymbsweópon mid reáde hragle yfelîce ... and gegiredon hine mid reáde hrægle yfellîce, Nap. 71. *See preceding word.*

**yfel-ness.** I. *add*:—Swâ swâ manna gôdnes (*probitas*) hî âhefþ ofer þâ menniscan gecynd ... swâ eác heora yfelnes (*improbitas*) âwyrpþ hî under ðâ menniscan gecynd, Bt. 37, 4; F. 192, 10.

**yfel-sacend,** es; m. *A blasphemer*:—Yfelsacend *blasphemus*, Gr. D. 289, 27.

**yfel-sacian.** *Substitute*: *to blaspheme* (In the passage Bl. H. 189, 24 for *mé* should probably be read *mâ*, the original Latin is: Ne tantas

Deo inferret blasphemias. v. Archiv xci. 190):—Gê gehŷrað hû hê Gode yfelsacað, Nap. 88. Hê gewunode þ hê yfelsacode þæs ælmihtigan Godes mægnþrym *majestatem Dei blasphemare consueverat*, Gr. D. 289, 8; 290, 1. Hê yfelsacode ... þâ forðbigfêrendan yfelsacedon on hine, Nap. 88. Hê lange ær wæs yfelsaciende, and swâ þeáh lifde gesund *blasphemus vixerat*, Gr. D. 289, 27. v. ge-yfelsacian.

**yfel-sacung.** *Add*: *blasphemy*:—Hê on ðære yfelsacunge swealt, Gr. D. 290, 2. Swâ hwylc man swa yfelsacunge sǣde on þone Hâlgan Gâst, 328, 7. Wê gehŷrdon his yfelsacunga, Nap. 88.

**yfelsian.** *Add*:—Hefalsadun, Mt. R. 27, 39. v. eofulsian.

**yfelung, yflung,** e; f. *Ill-treatment, injuring*:—Wæs his môd gecyrred tô mycelre ârwurðnesse þæs biscopes, þæs ylcan þe hine ær lyste wîtes and yflunge (*cujus poenam sitiebat*), Gr. D. 197, 12.

**yfel-wille;** adj. *Malevolent, spiteful, envious*:—Yfelwille môd byþ gedrêfed gif his feónd ætwint wîte *maliuolus animus contristatur si eius inimicus euaserit poenam*, Scint. 196, 16.

**yfel-wilnian.** *Add*:—Hig yfelwilnadon *malignauerunt*, Ps. L. 82, 4.

**yfel-wyrde;** adj. *Given to use bad or abusive language*:—Gif mon bið âcenned on Frîgedæg ... hê yfele cræftas leornað, and hê æfre bið yfelwyrde, E. S. 39, 354. [Cf. *Icel.* ill-orðr *abusive*.]

**ŷfer (?);** gen. ŷfre. *A bank* (v. ôfer):—Of ðâm gâran in on ðâ ŷfre; of ðære ŷfre, C. D. i. 279, 23. Beneaðan ŷfre, iii. 415, 32. Cf. Haec sunt nomina pastuum porcorum ... heánŷfre, i. 258, 11. Þis syndon þâ landgemæru ... þæt is ǣrest heáhŷfre; of heáhŷfre, C. D. B. i. 117, 26.

**ŷfera.** *Add*:—On ðâ yferan gemêre, C. D. v. 13, 30.

**yferian.** v. ge-yferian.

**yfes-drype.** *Add*: [Cf. *Icel.* upsar-dropi. v. *N. E. D.* eaves-drip.]: **yld.** v. ild: **yldig.** v. ilding: **ylf.** v. ilf: **-ylfe.** v. on-ylfe: **yflig.** v. ilfig.

**ylp.** *Add*:—Se micela ylp ... ondræt him forþearle, gif hê gesihð ân mûs, Hml. A. 63, 285.

**ymb.** *Add*: , emban. I. with acc. (1) temporal. (a) *at*. (a) *alone*. v. Dict. I 2 a. (β) *with* ûtan:—Ymb midde niht ûtan *nocte media*, Gr. D. 253, 17; 257, 23 = 272, 14. (b) *after*:—Ymb twâ niht (æfter twâm dagum, v. l.) *post biduum*, Gr. D. 158, 5. Ymbe .v. winter *post .v. annos*, Ll. Th. ii. 152, 6. (b a) where the point from which time is measured is in the genitive. Cf. Dict. I 2 b 1.:—Ymb fiftig wintra and hundteóntig Angelcynnes hidercymes on Breotone *aduentus Anglorum in Brittaniam anno circiter* CL., Bd. 1, 23; Sch. 48, 6. (2) in figurative senses. (a) cf. Dict. I 2 a.:—Embe hand, hrædlîce *iam iam, cito*, Germ. 388, 73. (b) cf. Dict. I 3 b.:—Nû wylle ic bysne ætîwan ymbe þâ þing þe wê nû handledon, Angl. viii. 304, 24. (c) cf. Dict. I 3 d.:—Nû wê sculon fôn ymb þæt Punica gewin, Ors. 4, 4; S. 164, 8. Þâ þing þe wê fæste ymbe wæron, Angl. viii. 304, 24. Swincð ge yrðlincg embe ûrne bigleofan, Hml. S. 25, 819. Wâst þû hû ic gewand ymbe Creósos þearfe?, Bt. 7, 3; F. 22, 10. II. with dat. (1) temporal. (a) *at*. Cf. Dict. I 2 a.:—Swâ swâ seó sunne dêð ymbe þære ðriddan tîde, Hml. Th. ii. 76, 16. (b) *after*. Cf. Dict. I 2 b.:—Ymbe þreóra tîda fæce, Hml. Th. ii. 162, 27. (2) in figurative senses. (a) cf. Dict. I 3 b.:—Ðâ hâlgan lâreówas hwîlon sprecað be ðâm Fæder and his Sunu, hwîlon embe ðære Hâlgan Ðrynnysse, Hml. Th. ii. 56, 27. Hê hî gewissode ymbe ðæs mynstres gebytlungum, 172, 16: 262, 3. ¶ where both dat. and acc. occur:—Þises godspelles traht sprecð ymbe ðâs wæterfatu and heora getâcnungum, 70, 13. (b) cf. Dict. I 3 c.:—Ne beó ðû carful ymbe woruldlicum gestreónum, Hml. Th. ii. 344, 2. Þâ þe ymbe ôðra manna bigleofan hogiað, 444, 1. (c) cf. Dict. I 3 c.:—Heó wæs bysig ymbe ânum ðinge, Hml. Th. ii. 440, 33. Hê fêrde swâ swâ his gewuna wæs ymbe geleáffulre bodunge (*for the purpose of preaching the faith*. Cf. Quadam die cum praedicaturus juxta consuetudinem suam populis de monasterio exiret, Vit. Cuth. 12), 138, 29. III. adverbial:—Hê swâ hwider ymb swâ hê beden wæs fêrde *ubicumque rogabatur diuertens*, Bd. 4, 12; Sch. 412, 1. v. þær-ymbe.

**ymb-cæfed.** *Add*: Ps. Rdr. 44, 15: **ymb-cirran.** v. ymb-swîfan.

**ymb-clyccan;** p. clyhte, -clycte *To enclose*:—Hŷ belucon þ ymbclicton *concluserunt*, Ps. Rdr. 16, 10.

**ymb-clyppan.** *Add*:—Ymbcleopton, Ps. Spl. 47, 11.

**ymbe** *a swarm of bees.* v. imbe.

**ymbeaht.** *Add*:—Olymbeactę (= ob ymbeactę) *ex conlatione*, An. Ox. 53, 22.

**ymb-fær.** *The second passage should be put under* ymb-faru.

**ymb-fangen, ymbfangenlic.** v. un-ymbfangen, un-ymbfangenlic.

**ymb-faran.** *Add*:—Þâ sende Theodosius fultum beforan him ...; ac hié wurdon ûtan ymbfaren of þæm muntum and ealle ofslagen, Ors. 6, 36; S. 294, 19.

**ymb-faru.** *Take here the second passage under* ymb-fær.

**ymb-gang.** I. *add*:—Gif hî embegang nâ dôn *si processionem non egerunt*, Angl. xiii. 404, 554. III. *add*:—Hiere ymbegong wæs xxx mîla, and eall heó wæs mid sæ ûtan befangen bûton þrîm mîlum

*viginti millia passuum muro amplexa, tota pene mari cingebatur, absque faucibus, quae tribus millibus passuum aperiebantur,* Ors. 4, 13 ; S. 210, 29. **VI.** *add:*—Tō mǣgenum mōd for embegange gegearwige leahtra *ad uirtutes .animum pro exercitium preparet uitiorum,* Scint. 61, 19.

**ymb-gangan.** *Add: to surround, encompass :*—'Send mē þīnne engel on fȳrenum wolcne þæt þā embgange ealle þās ceastre þæt ne magen geneósian for þǣm fȳre.' And þus cweþende fȳren wolc[n] āstāh of heofonum, and hit ymbsealde ealle þā ceastre, Bl. H. 245, 29.

**ymb-geóting.** *Dele, and see* in-geóting.

**ymb-gerēnode.** *Add:*—Ymbgerȳnode, Ps. L. 143, 12.

**ymb-gyrdan.** I **1.** *add:*—Beód ymbgyrde stranglīce tō þysum stīðan gewinne, Hml. S. 25, 341.

**ymb-habban.** *Add: to detain, hold:*—Unwîs on flǣslicum byð emhæfed *insipiens in carnalibus detinetur,* Scint. 168, 18.

**ymb-hūung.** *Substitute for the citation :*—Mōises salde iúh þ ymbhūungun (ymbhycgende, R.) *Moises dedit uobis circumcisionem,* Jn. L. 7, 22.

**ymb-hwyrft.** **IV.** *add:*—On þreódǣlede emhwyrfte *in triquadro* (*terrarum*) *ambitu,* An. Ox. 1685. Engliscra and ōðra þeóda wiðinnan embhwyrft (*ambitum*) Brittisces īglandes wunigendra cincg, Angl. xiii. 365, 4.

**ymb-hycgan** *to think about, consider :*—Naenig uuirthit thoncsnotturra than him tharf sié tō ymbhycggannae hwaet his gāstae . . . doemid uueorthae, Txts. 149, 18.

**ymb-hycgende.** v. ymb-hūung.

**ymb-hygd.** *Add :* **I.** *care, anxiety about one's self :*—Gif him mǣte þ hē sē mid ǣniges cynnes īrene slægen, ymbhȳdu þ beóð, and sorge þ tācnað (cf. mid īsene geslægene gesihð carfulnysse (*sollicitudinem*) getācnað, cxxv. 54, 248), Archiv cxx. 302, § 2. **II.** *care for others :*—Hē (*St. Paul*) bīgde his mōdes eáge þurh ymbhigd and eádmōdnesse tō gerihtanne þone gemānan gesinsceppendra manna *mentis oculum per compassionem reflectit ad disponendum cubile conjugatorum,* Gr. D. 218, 3.

**ymbhygdig-lic.** *Add :*—Mid tȳ þe þis wæs gehealden for þām gewunan þæs ymbhȳdiglican regoles *cum hoc de usu regulae sollicite* (*sollicitae* has been read) *servaretur,* Gr. D. 126, 21.

**ymbhygdiglīce.** *Add :*—Hī writon þone dæg and gemearcodon ymbhigdiglīce (ymbehȳdiglīce, *v. l.*) *sollicite conscripserunt diem,* Gr. D. 306, 13. Swā myccle geornlīcor and ymbhȳdiglīcor heó beeóde hire gebedu *tanto sollicitius ad usum orationis excreverat,* 284, 7.

**ymb-lǣr(i)gian.** *Add:*—Sȳn ymblǣrgide *ambiuntur,* An. Ox. 8, 377.

**ymb-licgan.** **II.** *add:*—Wæter wæt and ceald wangas ymbelicgað, eorðe ælgrēno, Met. 20, 77.

**ymbren-dæg.** *Add:* [Heald þū wæl þā twelf ymbrigdagas þe on twelf mōnþum beóð, Wlfst. 290, 28.]

**ymb-ryne.** **I.** *add:*—Hit gewissað ūs þurh wīsne lāreówdōm tō geárlicum tīdum and tunglena ymbrynum, Hml. S. 5, 270. **II.** *add :*—Tȳn embrynas *quinquennia decem,* Germ. 388, 1.

**ymb-scrȳdan.** *Add:*—Ðone man þe se cyning wile wurðian man sceal embscrȳdan mid cynelican reáfe *homo, quem rex honorare cupit, debet indui vestibus regiis,* Hml. A. 99, 231. Seó cwēn stent ymbscrȳd (emb-, *v. l.*) mid fāhnyssum (*circumamicta varietate*), 28, 109.

**ymb-sellan.** *Add :*—þæs Hēhstan mægen þē ēmbseleþ *virtus Altissimi obumbrabit tibi,* Bl. H. 7, 23. þā embsealdon ealle þā apostolas þā hālgan Marian, 141, 28.

**ymb-seón.** *Add :* v. ymb-sewen.

**ymb-settan.** **I.** *add :*—Emset *glomeratus* (Lucifer sodalibus vallatus et satellitibus *glomeratus,* Ald. 10, 34), An. Ox. 683.

**ymb-sewen ;** *adj.* (*ptcpl.*). *Circumspect :*—Hē symble wæs ymbsewen on his sylfes heordnysse *in sua semper custodia circumspectus,* Gr. D. 107, 11. v. ymb-seón.

**ymb-sittan.** **II a.** *add :*—Se cāsere embsæt þā burh ūtan mid herige, Bl. H. 79, 14.

**ymb-spenning,** e ; *f. Allurement, enticement :*—Ne beón hī ȳdelgeorne . . ne eác ōðra leahtra ymbspænninga ne began *non otio uacent non ceteris uitiorum inlecebris incumbant,* Chrd. 66, 33.

**ymb-standness.** v. ūtan-ymbstandness ; ymb-standenness.

**ymb-stocc.** v. imb-stocc.

**ymb-swāpan.** **II.** *add :*—Hié ūrne Dryhten Crīst ymbsweópon mid reáde hragle, Nap. 71, 27.

**ymb-swīfan ;** *p.* -swāf ; *pl.* -swifon ; *pp.* -swifen *To revolve round :*—þeáh þe wē þonne gȳt þā sunnan sylfe geseón ne magon, for ðan seó sunne hafað þonne mid þȳ heofone þás eorðan ūtan ymbswifen and ymbcerred, Nap. 88.

**ymb-þencan.** *Add :* v. embe-þencan.

**ymb-þreodian.** *Add :*—Se deófol ūs symble ymbeþrydað, Nap. 71.

**ymb-þringan.** *Add :*—þā mycclan þreátas þe him mid fērdon and embþrungon, Bl. H. 99, 36.

**ymb-trymian.** **I.** *add:*—Hȳ ymbtrymbdon mē, Ps. Spl. 21, 11. Folces ymbtrymmendes mē *populi circumdantis me,* Ps. L. 3, 7. Heó wæs mid hālgum mægnum ymbtrymed and mid engla þreátum, Hml. Th. i. 444, 6. **II.** *add :*—Ne sceal hē his āgene weorc mid deádum fellum ymbtrymman, Hml. Th. ii. 532, 32.

**ymb-ūtan.** **I** I b. *add :*—þonne hē his bōc rǣdde, þonne sǣton þā wildeór ymbūtan (ymūtan, *v. l.*) hine (ymb hine ūtan, *v. l.*), Mart. H. 148, 6. **I** 2. *add :*—þ hē ǣlc yfel dō ymbūtan þē, Hml. S. 30, 116. v. þǣr-ymbūtan.

**ymb-weorpan.** *Add :*—Sió sunne wæs eall ūtan ymbworpenu mid þryfealde gyldene hringe, Verc. Först. 97, 16.

**ymb-wlātend.** *For the second citation substitute :*—Emwlātenddum *spectatoribus,* i. *speculatoribus,* An. Ox. 3507.

**ymb-writen.** v. un-ymbwriten.

**ymen-sang.** *Substitute :*—Ðē gedafenað ymensong (*hymnus*), Ps. Vos. 64, 2. Ymensong singað ūs of songum Sione *hymnum cantate nobis de canticis Sion,* 136, 3 : 118, 171. Hē Gode þancode on ymensangum (ymnum, *v. l. hymnis*), Gr. D. 169, 12.

**ynne-leác.** *Add :*—Ynnileác *unio,* An. Ox. 53, 14.

**yntse.** *Add :* v. entse in Dict.

**yppan.** **I.** *add :*—þā þā hē ypte and forþbrōhte mycle stefne *cum magnas voces ederet,* Gr. D. 247, 14 : 248, 1. **II.** *add :*—God on mē ypð swā micle gōdnesse, Hml. A. 198, 93. Ne ep ðū *ne proferas* (*in jurgio cito, quae viderunt oculi tui*), Kent. Gl. 956. þæt hors ongan mid unāblinnendlicre brogdettunge ealles līchaman meldian and yppan (*prodere*) þ hit ne mihte wîfman beran, Gr. D. 183, 12.

**ypplen.** *Add :*—Ypplene *fastigio,* i. *summitate,* An. Ox. 2862. On yplen *in altum,* Ps. Rdr. 74, 6.

**-yppol.** v. ge-edyppol.

**ȳr** *a horn.* (? For this explanation of the word see Anglia xxxv. 175.)

**ȳr[e].** v. īr[e] : **yrf-cwealm** = (?) irfe-cwealm : **yrfe.** *Take the passage here to* irfe : **yrfe-leás.** *Take to* irfe-leás : **ysel** *an ass.* v. esol.

**ȳtera.** **II.** *add :*—þā þe in him sylfum ne magon oferswīðan þā lytlan and þā ȳtemestan uncyste *qui in semetipsis vincere parva vitia atque extrema non possunt,* Gr. D. 204, 9.

**ȳþ.** **I.** *add :*—þeáh hine ǣlc ȳð gesēce mid þām hēhstan þe seó sǣ forðbringð, Verc. Först. 110, 12. **II.** *add :*—Ongeánflōwende ȳþa, eftflōwende wætera *reciproca* (*purissimi fontis*) *redundantia,* An. Ox. 506.

**ȳþung.** *Add: overflowing, inundation :*—Mycel ȳðgiung (ȳðguncg, *v. l.*) and regnes gyte forð cōm *inundatio pluviae erupit,* Gr. D. 167, 24. Ȳþgung (ȳþguncg, *v. l.*), 168, 2 : 197, 7. Oft gedōnre ȳþunge (ȳðgunge, *v. l.*) se strēam gewunode þ he tōgoten wæs geond his æceras *fluvius saepe facta inundatione per agros diffundi consueverat,* 192, 17. Ongeánflōwende ȳþa, eftflōwende wætera, ȳðunga *reciproca* (*purissimi fontis*) *redundantia,* i. *iterum uenientia,* i. *flumina,* An. Ox. 506.

# AN ANGLO-SAXON
# DICTIONARY

## SUPPLEMENT

## Enlarged Addenda

# AN ANGLO-SAXON DICTIONARY

### BASED ON THE MANUSCRIPT COLLECTIONS OF

### JOSEPH BOSWORTH

## Enlarged Addenda and Corrigenda

### BY ALISTAIR CAMPBELL

#### TO THE

## SUPPLEMENT

### BY T. NORTHCOTE TOLLER

OXFORD

AT THE CLARENDON PRESS

# ADDITIONS AND CORRECTIONS

THE present *Additions and Corrections* to the Bosworth–Toller *Anglo-Saxon Dictionary* and *Supplement* are an extension of those published by Toller with the *Supplement* in 1921. Toller's material (together with the additions to it which he himself published in MLR xvii and xix) has been incorporated, and it has been extended in various ways. The works read by Toller for the *Dictionary* and *Supplement* have mostly been re-examined. This did not yield much material, and Toller's reading proved to have been extremely well done. Some additions, especially from variant readings, were, however, made from these works. The sources which Toller read least well were the Northumbrian glosses, and some two hundred additions were made from these, and here Professor A. S. C. Ross's magnificent glossary to the Lindisfarne gloss was, of course, invaluable. Much more new material was obtained from sources which have been re-edited with variants and supplementary passages unknown to Toller. Such sources are the *Heptateuch*, the *Bussbuch*, the *Bussbuch* of Halitgar, the *Institutes of Polity*, and the *Benedictine Office*. From the poetical texts read by Toller there are practically no additions to be made. Much redefinition is, however, called for in view of the extensive modern work on the poetry. Nevertheless, much remains uncertain in the poetical language, and in the present work alternatives to the Bosworth–Toller interpretations are offered only when it was felt that an advance could definitely be made. In many passages, especially in *Exodus*, the Bosworth–Toller interpretation remains as likely as any other. In view of the obscurity of the *Rhyming Poem*, no changes are made in the interpretation of words known from that source only. Much Old English has now been published that was unknown to Toller. These *Additions and Corrections* have been considerably augmented from the newly published poems *Seasons for Fasting* and *Instructions for Christians*. More glosses and glossaries are now available than in Toller's time. One may mention the *Old English Glosses*, collected by H. D. Meritt, the glosses to the *Arundel Prayers*, edited by F. Holthausen and J. J. Campbell, the Salisbury and Vitellius psalter-glosses, edited by K. and C. Sisam and J. L. Rosier, and the Cottonian MSS. of the gloss to the *Hymnarium*, edited by H. Gneuss. The homiletic literature has been increased by Max Förster's *Vercelli-Homilien* and J. C. Pope's supplementary collection of *Homilies of Ælfric*. There are also many short texts, which have been edited or re-edited in the periodicals. This new material has all been utilised for these *Additions and Corrections*.

While grateful use has been made of the supplement added by Professor H. D. Meritt to the 1960 edition of Clark Hall's *Anglo-Saxon Dictionary*, entries have in three respects been more charily made than in that work. Firstly, groups consisting of genitive plus noun (e.g. *domes dæg*, *helle pin, gose flæsc*) are not regarded as being independent words, and are not separately entered, unless the two words have in combination a special meaning that cannot be inferred from their separate senses. Secondly, groups consisting of adverbs of full meaning plus verb (e.g. *on ahon, to geteon*) are not here as a rule treated as independent words. In this, the tradition of the *Dictionary* is maintained, for when such groups require mention, they are there entered not separately, but under the adverb concerned. A few of these groups, however, are here given separate entry as specimens of translation loans. Thirdly, recent re-interpretations of glosses are less frequently referred to in the present work than in that of Professor Meritt.

Even if they occur in an Old English context, unchanged or practically unchanged Latin words or words derived through Latin (e.g. *corporale, holocaustum*, and most names of gems in the *Lapidary*) are not as a rule included in the *Additions and Corrections*. Words first found in twelfth-century MSS. are sparingly added from texts which appear to be copied from older MSS. (This

is the reason why some words in the collections of Napier and Storm do not appear in the present work.) Words inferred from place-names in post-Conquest documents are added when the evidence for their existence seems sound. They are marked with an asterisk, and a reference to Professor A. H. Smith's *English Place-name Elements* is usually added. The policy of the *Supplement* not to include place-names has been generally followed, but the identifications of ones already included in the *Dictionary* or *Supplement* have been corrected when necessary. The etymologies of the *Dictionary* have not been corrected: they are well-known to be of historical interest only, and students will go past them to modern etymological dictionaries for themselves.

Many scholars have given valuable help in the preparation of the *Additions and Corrections*. Mr. R. B. Mitchell prepared a list of words in Old English poetry which require re-definition. Mr. C. Ball excerpted the psalter-glosses. Mr. J. B. Wynne and Mr. J. D. Pfeifer provided material from their unpublished studies of the early glossaries (Corpus and Epinal-Erfurt). Mr. C. A. Ladd undertook to revise the treatment of the material from the later glossaries,[1] and although this proved a very arduous task, in the upshot he extended his work to several other fields, especially place-names. Miss M. Miles Cadman placed at my disposal her exhaustive index to five of the homilies in the collection published by Belfour. Material from homilies has also been supplied by Mrs. R. D.-N. Somerset and Miss R. R. Handley. I have also to thank Professor J. R. R. Tolkien and Professor Dorothy Whitelock for verbal suggestions, and Professor J. L. Rosier for continuous interest and help. Mr. P. Bibire gave valuable help with the correction of the proofs.

In these *Additions and Corrections*, the same abbreviations are used as in the later part of the *Dictionary* and the *Supplement*, so far as this proved practical. The following new abbreviations and methods of reference should, however, be noticed:

| | |
|---|---|
| A. | *Anglia.* |
| ASPR | *The Anglo-Saxon Poetic Records*, G. P. Krapp and E. van K. Dobbie, 6 vols., Columbia University Press, 1931–53. |
| BM | *Byrhtferth's Manual*, S. J. Crawford, EETS, 1929. |
| BO | *The Benedictine Office*, J. M. Ure, Edinburgh, 1959. |
| Brooks, *Andreas* | *Andreas and the Fates of the Apostles*, K. R. Brooks, Oxford, 1961. |
| Brot. | *Texte und Untersuchungen zur altenglischen Literatur und Kirchengeschichte*, R. Brotanek, Halle, 1913. |
| Buss. | *Das altenglische Bussbuch (sog. Confessionale Pseudi-Egberti)*, R. Spindler, Leipzig, 1934. |
| Chad | *The Life of St. Chad, An Old English Homily*, R. Vleeskruyer, Amsterdam, 1953. |
| Chart. Harm. | *Anglo-Saxon Writs*, F. E. Harmer, Manchester, 1952. |
| Chart. Rob. | *Anglo-Saxon Charters*, A. J. Robertson, Cambridge, 1939. |
| Chart. Whit. | *Anglo-Saxon Wills*, D. Whitelock, Cambridge, 1930. |
| CS | *Cartularium Saxonicum*, W. de G. Birch, 3 vols., London, 1885–93. |
| De temp. ann. | *Aelfric's De Temporibus Anni*, H. Henel, EETS, 1942. |
| DP | *Das Durhamer Pflanzenglossar*, B. von Lindheim, Bochum-Langendreer, 1941. |
| EGS | *English and Germanic Studies.* |
| *English and Mediæval Studies* | *English and Mediæval Studies presented to J. R. R. Tolkien on the Occasion of his Seventieth Birthday*, ed. N. Davis and C. L. Wrenn, London, 1962. |
| Fehr | *Die Hirtenbriefe Ælfrics*, B. Fehr, Bibl. der ags. Prosa, 1914. |

---

[1] With regard to the material from the later glossaries, it should be noticed that the glosses marked Cot. in the *Dictionary* are derived from MS. Cotton Otho E i (through Junius's transcript, MS. Junius 77). The *Supplement* usually cancels these entries, or substitutes similar glosses from other sources. See N. R. Ker, *Catalogue of Manuscripts Containing Anglo-Saxon*, no. 184.

FL | *Fact and Lore about Old English Words*, H. D. Meritt, Stanford, 1954.

Förster, *Flussname Themse* | *Der Flussname Themse und seine Sippe*, M. Förster, Munich, 1941.

Förster, *Reliquienkultus* | *Zur Geschichte des Reliquienkultus in Altengland*, M. Förster, Munich, 1943.

Gn. | *Hymnar und Hymnen im englischen Mittelalter*, H. Gneuss, Buchreihe der Anglia, Band 12, Tübingen, 1968.[1]

Gradon, *Elene* | *Cynewulf's Elene*, P. O. E. Gradon, Methuen's Old English Library, 1958.

Hal. | *Die altenglische Version des Halitgar'schen Bussbuches*, J. Raith, Bibl. der ags. Prosa, 1933.

Harmer, *Historical Documents* | *Select English Historical Documents of the Ninth and Tenth Centuries*, F. E. Harmer, Cambridge, 1914.

Hept. | *The Old English Version of the Heptateuch, Aelfric's Treatise on the Old and New Testament and his Preface to Genesis*, S. J. Crawford, EETS, 1922; the reprint of 1968 has additional variants.

Hex. | *Exameron Anglice or The Old English Hexameron*, S. J. Crawford, Bibl. der ags. Prosa, 1921.

Hml. Bel. | *Twelfth-century Homilies in MS. Bodley 343*, A. O. Belfour, EETS, 1909 (part 1).

Hml. P. | *Homilies of Ælfric, A Supplementary Collection*, J. C. Pope, 2 vols., EETS, 1967.

Hml. Warn. | *Early English Homilies from the Twelfth-century MS. Vesp. D xiv*, R. D.-N. Warner, EETS, 1917 (part 1).

IC | 'Instructions for Christians', J. L. Rosier, *Anglia* lxxxii (1964), 4–22.

IP | *Die 'Institutes of Polity, Civil and Ecclesiastical'*, K. Jost, Bern, 1959.

Irving, *Exodus* | *The Old English Exodus*, E. B. Irving, New Haven, 1958.

JEGP | *Journal of English and Germanic Philology*.

JJ | 'Jubilee Jaunts and Jottings', E. A. Kock, *Lunds Universitets Årsskrift*, N.F., Avd. 1, Bd. 14, Nr. 26 (1918).

Kansas leaf | Kansas University Library, Dept. of Special Collections, MS. E 79.

Ker, *Catalogue* | *Catalogue of Manuscripts Containing Anglo-Saxon*, Oxford, 1957.

Krapp, *Andreas* | *Andreas and the Fates of the Apostles*, G. P. Krapp, Boston, 1906.

Ld. | 'Die Leidener Glossen', F. Holthausen, *Englische Studien* l (1916–17), 327–40.

Leonhardi | *Kleinere angelsächsische Denkmäler*, G. Leonhardi, Bibl. der ags. Prosa, 1905.

Lindsay, *Corpus Glossary* | *The Corpus Glossary*, W. M. Lindsay, Cambridge, 1921.

Met. Ps. | *Metrical Psalms* (= Ps. Par. li–cl).

MLN | *Modern Language Notes*.

MLR | *Modern Language Review*.

OEG | *Old English Glosses (A Collection)*, H. D. Meritt, New York, 1945.

PBB | *Beiträge zur Geschichte der deutschen Sprache und Literatur*.

PNE | *English Place-name Elements*, A. H. Smith, 2 vols., Cambridge, 1956.

PPP | *Plain Points and Puzzles*, E. A. Kock, *Lunds Universitets Årsskrift*, N.F., Avd. 1, Bd. 17, Nr. 7 (1922).

Prud. | *The Old English Prudentius Glosses at Boulogne-sur-Mer*, H. D. Meritt, Stanford, 1959.

Ps. Ar. | *Der altenglische Arundel-Psalter*, G. Oess, Heidelberg, 1910.

Ps. Bos. | *Die altenglischen Glossen im Bosworth-Psalter*, U. Lindelöf, Helsingfors, 1909.

---

[1] This work I was able to use only in a typescript most kindly lent by Dr. Gneuss, and hence references to it are by hymn and stanza, not by page. It is also indicated whether citations are from the Julius (J), the Vespasian (V), or both MSS. (JV). The still unpublished canticle glosses in these MSS. are cited from Dr. Gneuss's article 'Ergänzungen zu den altenglischen Wörterbüchern', *Archiv* cxcxix (1962), 17–24.

Ps. Cam.    *Der Cambridger Psalter*, K. Wildhagen, Bibl. der ags. Prosa, 1910.

Ps. Cant.   *Eadwine's Canterbury Psalter*, F. Harsley, EETS, 1889.

Ps. Jun.    *Der altenglische Junius-Psalter*, Heidelberg, 1908.

Ps. Par.    Paris Psalter, i.e. *Liber Psalmorum, The West-Saxon Psalms*, J. W. Bright and R. L. Ramsay, Boston, 1908 (Ps. i–l); ASPR v, 3–150 (Ps. li–cl).

Ps. Roy.    *Der altenglische Regius-Psalter*, F. Roeder, Halle, 1904.

Ps. Sal.    *The Salisbury Psalter*, C. and K. Sisam, EETS, 1959.

Ps. Spl.    *Psalterium Davidis Latino-Saxonicum vetus*, J. Spelman, London, 1640.[1]

Ps. V.      Vespasian Psalter, printed in *The Oldest English Texts*, H. Sweet, EETS, 1885, pp. 183–420.[2]

Ps. Vit.    *The Vitellius Psalter*, J. L. Rosier, New York, 1962.

RES         *Review of English Studies.*

Rypins, *Three OE Prose Texts*    *Three Old English Prose Texts in MS. Cotton Vitellius A xv*, S. Rypins, EETS, 1924.

SHG         *Some of the Hardest Glosses in Old English*, H. D. Meritt, Stanford, 1968.

*The Anglo-Saxons*    *The Anglo-Saxons, Studies in some Aspects of their History and Culture, presented to Bruce Dickins*, ed. P. Clemoes, London, 1959.

TPhS        *Transactions of the Philological Society.*

Verc.-Hom.  *Die Vercelli-Homilien*, M. Förster, Bibl. der ags. Prosa, 1932 (part 1).

Whitelock, Eng. Hist. Doc.    *English Historical Documents c. 500–1042*, D. Whitelock, London, 1955.

Woolf, *Juliana*    *Juliana*, R. Woolf, Methuen's Old English Library, 1955.

WW          *Anglo-Saxon and Old English Vocabularies*, Th. Wright, 2nd ed., edited and collated by R. O. Wülcker, 2 vols., London, 1884.

Wyn.        *An Old English Translation of a Letter from Wynfrith to Eadburga (A.D. 7–6–17) in Cottonian MS. Otho C i*, K. Sisam, *Modern Language Review* xviii (1923), 253–72; reprinted *Studies in the History of Old English Literature*, Oxford, 1953, pp. 198–224.

ZfdA        *Zeitschrift für deutsches Altertum.*

---

[1] This is the Stowe Psalter; Spelman did not include its glosses to the canticles etc., which have been published by J. L. Rosier, *Anglia* lxxxii (1964), 397–432.

[2] Occasional reference is also made to *The Vespasian Psalter*, S. M. Kuhn, Ann Arbor, 1965.

# A

a, prep., *for* an: *in agro*, a felda, Chrd. 68, 1.

ā, *add to* B IV: *fratrem alium*, a ma gebroðra, Hept., Gen. xliii, 6.

ābannan, delete addition in Suppl.; see Prud. 230.

abbad, *see also* geoabbod.

ābedecian, *add*: selre is . . . þonne ma tallice abedecige þæt ma sylle, Chrd. 70, 5.

ābēodan, cancel 2 a, read in citation *eotonweard*, and take under 4, *offered protection against giants*.

āberan, v. *do without*: hym wæs lað to forlætenne þone leofan Hælend, and hy uneaðe mihton his neaweste aberan, Nap. 4 (= Hml. P. i, 342, 41). [Cf. OHG inberan, Ger. entbehren].

ābered, *add*: *sagaces gymnosophistas*, aberede nacudwraxleres, Ker, *Catalogue* 382.

ābetēon, v. *accuse*: *ne exprobrarent sibi*, ðy læs heo hine abetigen, OEG 4, 368. (? *two words*, a + beteon, q.v.)

ābīdan, *add*: (4) *with clause*: we abidon þæt þu come, Gr.D. 148, 32.

ābisgian, *add to* I 3: Gr.D. 49, 6; 208, 22.

āblǣcan, *see also citation below under* ahwitian.

āblendan, *add to* I a: Crist hine ablende, ðe ðis æfre awende, C.D. iv, 271, 19; 270, 21. *Correct Suppl. headword* ablendar.

āblēred, *read* āblered, cf. blere.

āblindian, *add*: gif hy ablindiað butan ælcon sare, Lch. iii, 96, 9; 2.

āblinnedness, *for* ablinnendness, Verc. Först. 149 (= A. v, 465, 4).

ābōtian, v. *repair*: on þa gerad þe he hi (þa cyrcan) abotege, Will of Æthelgifu, ed. Whitelock, 16.

ābrecan, *add to* I 1: to abrocenan beorge, C.D. iii, 172, 30; *add to* I 1 d: gif frigman rihtfæsten abrece, Ed. and Guth. 8 (and freq. in laws); *add to* II: ageot wæter uppon ðone ele, and se ele abrecð up, Hml. Th. ii, 564, 14.

ābrēgan, *add*: cf. OHG arbruogen, ex-, *per-terrere*.

ābregdan, *add to* I 1: he his exe up abræd, Hml. S. ii, 230, 152; *with dat.*: he his swurde abræd, W. S. Gospels, Mk. xiv, 47. *Add*: III *transform*: he abryt hine sylfne to scinendum engle, Hml. P. ii, 796, 107.

ābrēoþan, *add to* I 1 b: *soluti*, abroðene, Chrd. 77, 36.

ābrȳtan, *add*: *contriuisti*, abrutedest, Ps. Cant. iii, 8.

ābūgan, *add to* I: *declinantes*, þa abugendan, Ps. L. cxxiv, 5; *add to* I a: *with dat.* sceolon we abugan þe, Hept., Gen. xxxvii, 10.

ābūrod, *add*: cf. gebyran.

ābūtan, *add*: cf. þærabutan.

ābycgan, *add*: cf. unaboht.

āc, *add to compounds* scipac.

ācǣglod, *probably substitute* ācǣglod, *locked, and assume* serrato *taken as* serato *in citation*, cf. FL 5.

ācbearo, n. *oak grove*: on acbeara, CS ii, 440, 33.

ācdrenc, ?*delete*, in citations *for cirta*, acdrenc, read *tiriaca*, drenc (cf. WW 114, 19); another explanation SHG 49.

ācennan, cf. ofacennan; hiwanacenned, onacenned.

ācennedlic, *add*: Ps. Roy., Hy. 6, 13; Chrd. 126, 19.

*ācett, *oak-wood*, PNE i, 2.

Āclēah, *add*: in Chr. 782, 789 (D, E), an unknown place probably in Northumbria; in Chr. 851, an unknown place (? in Surrey, Æthelweard); in CS i, 300, 5 from below, and 451, 6, *Oakleigh, Kent*; in C.D. iv, 258, 2, *Oakleigh, Beds.*; in CS i, 449, 24, and ii, 23, 8, Rtl. 185, 18, *Oakley, Dorset*; in Chart. Whit. 46, 28, *Oakley, Staffs.*; in CS iii, 415, 6 from below, *Oakley, Hants*. Other occurrences in charters refer to unknown places.

ācnyht, participial adj. *joined*: *conectis*, acnyhtum, Rtl. 110, 9.

acrēopian, *delete*, *MSS. read in citation* acreowed q.v.

ācreowed, participial adj.: *et scatere coepit uermibus*, ond hit wearð wyrmum acreowed, Hept., Ex. xvi, 20.

ācstybb, m. *oak-stump*: on ðone acstyb, C.D. iv, 75, 1.

ācuman, *add to* II: þe þam deoppestan bete þe he æfre acuman (*inferior reading* acunnan) mæge, Hal. 80, 26. Cf. utacumen.

ācumba, *add*: fyr atent acuma (*stuppas*), Chrd. 74, 16.

ācumendlicness, cf. una-.

ācursian, v. *malign*: *ut maligneris*, þæt ðu beo acursod, Ps. Sal. xxxvi, 8.

ācwern, *add to headword* ācweorna.

ācwician, *add to* II: ac hi beoð þærrihte eft acucode, Hml. P. i, 431, 303.

ād, *add*: as a topographical feature perhaps *ash-heap*: of þone ealdan ad, CS. iii, 183, 11.

ādēaglian, v. *hide*: *abdidere*, adaeglad (sic), OEG 4, 24.

ādidan, *add*: Hept. 22, 153; Gen. vii, 22; ix, 11.

ādihtian, v. *compose*: hit ær fore adihtode, ASPR vi, 110, 4.

ādilgian, *add*: Dryhten sæde on his bocum þæt þis woruldlice lif sceolde forð gewitan and forð adilgod bion, Verc.-Hom. 150, 5.

ādl, *add to compounds* bring-, cancer-, cēac-, cēafl-, fīc-, geal-, horn-, land-, lencten-, lenden-, lifer-, liþ-, sīd-, stic-, ūtsiht-, wambadl.

ādlberende, participial adj. *disease-bearing*: *morbigeni camini*, þæs aldberendan (*read* adl-) ofnes, OEG 8, 19.

ādlian, *add*: *egrotabunt*, adliað, Archiv cxx, 297, 43.

ādlig, cf. monaþadlig.

ādlsēoc, adj. *ill*: and adlseoce menn beoð on þam geare, Archiv cxx, 297, 47; 298, 21.

ādōn, *add*: *tollite portas*, adoþ gatu, Ps. Roy. xxiii, 7; hungor adyde hi, Chr. 1086.

ādrēogan, *add to* III: forgif me þæt ic unrihtlice adreah, Archiv lxxxviii, 363, 17.

ādrīfan, *add to* II a I: aweg adriefð, Past. 255, 16; *add*: III *pierce, stake*: heo adrifen mine handen ond mine fet, Hml. Warn. 72, 9; *take here first citation in Dict*.

ādwolian, v. *degenerate*: *degenerent*, adwoledñ, OEG 28, 234.

ǣ, *add*: *legis tuae*, æs þinre, Ps. Roy. lviii, 12; *legislatorem*, æs lædend, id. ix, 21. *Add to compounds* heafod-, synderæ.

āealdian, *see* ealdian II.

æbbung, *see also* sææbbung.

æblǣce, *see* æblēc *in Suppl*.

ǣcelma, ǣcelmehte, note *palagra, palagdrigus = podagra, podagricus*.

ǣcen, *cancel emendation of Lch. iii, 52, 2 in Suppl.*; mid æcenan brande = *with a fire-brand of oak*.

æcer, *add*: twegen æceras . . . se ðridde æcer, CS iii, 486, 16. *For use as a measure of breadth, see Ors. S. 160, 25, cited in Suppl. under* brædu. *Add to compounds* ælmes-, fleax-, gar-, heafod-, healf-, læg-, mæd-, scriftæcer.

æcerceorl, *add*: *rustici, aratores*, ealle æcerceorlas, Chrd. 68, 1.

æcern, *add*: *glandes uel fagina*, æceren ne boc, Chrd. 15, 10.

æcyrf, *read* æcyrf m. (?n.).

æder, *add to compounds* heafodæder.

æfǣgred, *delete*, *see* æfæred *below*.

æfǣred, participial adj., *for* afæred, *frightened*: *larbatos*, æfærede, An. Ox. 4936. *See* FL 133, *and cf.* gefærede *in Suppl*.

æfæstlice, *see* unæfæstlice.

æfen, *add*: III *evening service, vespers*: þonne æfen bið gesungen ond mæsse, Buss. 189, 391. *Add to compounds* Candelmæsse-, freols-, Frigeæfen.

æfencollatio, *evening reading*: Chrd. 60, 35; cf. æfenræding.

æfenglōma, *add*: *diluculo*, on æfengloman, Ps. Ar. xlv, 6.

æfenoffrung f., *evening sacrifice*: Chrd. 30, 21.

æfenþegnung, *add*: æfenþenunge breman, Chrd. 114, 16.

āefesian, v. *shear*: *detondeo*, ic of aefesige, Ælfc. Gr. Z. 157, 16.

æfest, *add to* II: Chrd. 46, 32–6.

**æfgydel**, *delete*, *MS. reads* æfgæl'd'um (= -gælðum *to* æfgælþ). *See Studia Germanica Gandensia* ii, 82.

**æfirmþa**, *add*: cf. orfyrmþa.

**æfisc**, *see* efesc.

**æfnian**, *see* geæfnian.

**æfre**, *add to I 1*: Hml. S. xii, 120.

**æfsecgan**, v. *confute*: *refellit*, æfsægeð, Lk., p. 8, 5, Lind.

**æfter**, *add to A I 5*: æfter þam hege, CS iii, 586, 36; *add to A I 6*: æfter (*in order to obtain*) þæm anwalde, Bt. S. 77, 5; add to A II: *in memory of*, æfter eþelwini, Leeds Studies in English i, 18; *also with dat.*: æfter his bæurne, id. 19; cf. Studia Neophil. xxx, 145; *add to B*: (4) *marking sequence*, ærest ... æfter, Æthelberht 17.

**æftercnēoreso**, glosses *nepotes*, Rtl. 61, 18.

**æfterfylgendlic**, adj. *successive*: *successibus, scilicet horarum spatiis*, æfterfylgendlicum tida fecum, Gn. 10, 1 (J, V).

**æfterfylgung**, *add*: II sect, see gedwildæfterfylgung.

**æftergengness**, *add*: æftergancnysse, Hml. S. x, 219, v. l.

**æftergild**, *see also* astrihilthet *below*.

**æftergildend**, m. *one who repays*: *retribuentibus*, æftergildendum, Ps. Ar., Ps. Vit. vii, 5.

**æfterhæþa** (*under* -hætu), *add*: cf. hæþa.

**æfteronfond**, m. *one receiving afterwards*: cepturi (so MS.), WW 383, 3.

**æftersōna**, *see* efter-.

**æfterweard**, *transfer first citation in Suppl. to* æfteweard (MS. æftewærd).

**æfþanc, -weard**, *see* ofþanc, -weard.

**æfyllende**, *substitute*: participial adj. *law-destroying*: seo circe æfyllendra eahtnysse bad, Cri. 704.

**ægecȳpness**, f. *Testament*: on þære niwan ægecyðnisse, Hept. 77, 39, v. l.

**Ægeles þrep**, *add*: unknown place, not Aylesford.

**ægesetness**, f. *Testament*: æfter þære ealdan ægesetnysse, BM 136, 5.

**æghwæþer**, *add to I b*: for æghwæþerum ðyssum mānum (v. l. þyssa mana), Bd. ii, 5.

**æglæca**, *add*: *error for* ægleawa *in Beda se* æglæca lareow, BM 74, 15.

**ægnian**, meaning is rather *oppress*, JJ 26; for suggested emendations see ASPR i, 208.

**æhīwe** I: *for second citation see* doxian *in Suppl. and below*.

**æht**, *add to I c*: æhte heold, *kept cattle*, Gen. 973; *add to I d*: he wæs riht æht to Hæðfelda, C.D. vi, 212, 14; *add to II*: Sal. 11 (*cited under* iht). *Add to compounds* cwicæht.

**æhtspēd**, *read in citation* æhtspæde.

**æl**, *eel*, add: *see* gebind II, *and* sæl.

**ælādtēow**, glosses *legislatorem*, Ps. V. ix, 21 (and related glosses).

**ælædend**, glosses *legislatorem*, Ps. Ar. ix, 21 (and related glosses).

**ælæte**, *add*: *inanes*, idele uel ælæte, Ps. Roy., Hy. 9, 53.

**ælan**, *add to compounds* ā-, geælan.

**ælc**, *add to I 1*: (a) *every one*: ælc þe gewita si, Ll. Th. i, 354, 28; 424, 18; heo hnat ælcne þe heo gemette, Hml. S. xxxi, 1042; (b) *every one with gen.*: mæstra daga ælce, Chr. 894; Ors. S. 294, 27; *add to I 2*: wundorlic ælcum men, Chr. 1051; *omnis aditus*, ælces infæres, R. Ben. 53, 16; (2a) on ælcum anum geare, Mart. H. 40, 19; (2b) ælcum his cempum, Hml. S. xxi, 97; *add to II*: ælces eles æmtig, Gr. D. 160, 9.

**ælednys**, *substitute*: æledness, f. *fire*: þæs huses æledryss, Archiv cxxxiv, 271, 19 (= Lch. iii, 168, 16 v. l.).

**ælegrēne**, adj. *quite green, fresh*: *nouelle olinarum*, ælegrene elebergena, Ps. Roy. cxxvii, 3 (and related glosses). Cf. eallgrene, elegrene.

**ælepe**, *read* ælere (so MS.; cf. FL 39).

**ælfen**, *add*: *simplex occurs* OEG 71, 1, *nimphae*, aelfinni; *hamadryades*, wylde elfen (sg. for pl.), WW 189, 7; *add to compounds* berg-, dunælfen.

**ælfer**, *doubtful word, nom. sg. would rather be* ælfaru.

**ælfremedan**, *see* ge-.

**ælfremedung**, glosses *alienatio*, Ps. Roy., Hy. 5, 14.

**ælfþone**, *delete* identification, the plant intended is unknown.

**æliest**, *lawlessness*: mid æleste ælcne forlædað, Seasons for Fasting 211.

**ælifne**, *substitute*: ælifn, f. *alum*: *alumnis*, aelifnae (gen.), Epinal Glossary 3 d 38 (not in Txts.). *See also* efne *below*.

**ælmes**, *see* ælmesse *below*.

**ælmesæcer**, *a field the product of which was given as alms, first-fruits*: frumwæstmas hatað sume men ælmesæcer, se ðe us ærest geripod bið, Nap. 5 (= Hml. P. ii, 808, 106).

**ælmesdōnd**, m. *almsgiver*: Chrd. 92, 28.

**ælmesfull**, *add*: Nap. 5.

**ælmeshand**, *see* maga, *able*, in Suppl.

**ælmeslāc**, *alms-offering*: mid ælmeslacum God gladian, Nap. 5.

**ælmeslic**, *see* elmestlic.

**ælmesmann**, *add*: *stipendia pauperum*, ælmesmanna bilyfne, Chrd. 51, 3.

**ælmespening**, m. *alms-penny*: gebyrað ... xii penegas and iiii ælmespenegas, C.D. iii, 450, 25.

**ælmesse**, *add*: ælmes(s), -e: *elemosyna tua*, ðin ælmess, Mt. Rush. vi, 4; ælmesse wircan, id. 3; heora ælmesse geutian, Cht. Th. 362, 2; ælmessan (v.l. -se) dælan, Bd. i, 27; v, 2; gebeda and ælmesse, v, 12; *add compound* sulhælmesse.

**ælmyrca**, *substitute*: ælmyrce m. pl. *foreign borderers*: ælmyrcna eðelrice, An. 432 (see Brooks ad loc.).

**ælwihta**, *the form is gen. pl.*

**æmta**, *error for* intinga, Hml. Warn. 56, 8.

**æmūþa**, *add*: cf. *caecum intestinum quod sit sine foramine et exitu*, Isid., *Et.* xi, 1, 131.

**æmynde**, *substitute*: æmynd f., *jealousy*: *zelum*, æmend, A. xxxii, 506; wið andan and wið æminde, Lch. i, 384, 22 (= Storms, *Anglo-Saxon magic* 132). Cf. ASPR vi, 214.

**ænan**, *see* geænan.

**ænbræce**, *delete, see* unbræce.

**ænetlif**, n. *solitary life*: *anchorissem*, ænetlif, OEG 9, 4; 10, 2.

**ænga**, *substitute*: *single, sole*: locað geneahhe fram ðam unlædan ænga (MS. ængan) hlaford, Sal. 382; min ænega (v.l. anlica) sunu, Lk. ix, 38, WS Gospels.

**ænig**, adj. *only*: fea ænig wæs monna cynnes, Rid. 61, 3; feawe wæron ænige, Ps. Th. civ, 11. Cf. anga, ænga.

**æppel**, *add to compounds* ciric-, godæppel.

**æppelcynn**, *note*: æpeningas *is a doubtful word, see SHG 115*.

**æppled**, *add*: cf. Woolf, *Juliana* 87.

***æpplen**, adj. *growing apple trees, yielding apples*, PNE i, 4.

***æpsett**, *aspen wood*, PNE i, 4.

**ær**, *wave*, see ear.

**ær**, adj., *add*: note ærre as adv., Hml. Warn. 50, 13; 78, 10.

**ær**, *add to II*: ær ... siþþan, Chr. 690; Hml. Th. ii, 244, 28; *add to III*: ærest ... siþþan, Hml. Th. i, 276, 11.

**ærǣt**, *substitute for meaning* overeating (E.S. lxv, 471; but cf. A. lxvi, 17, n. 1); *add*: ærætas, Verc.-Hom. 51, 97 (*in list of sins*).

**æren**, adj. *with oars* (?): *carabus*, lytel æren scip, Gr. D. 347, 2, 4.

**ærendscip**, *add*: *scouting vessel*, cf. FL 97.

**ærendung**, *add*: III *intercession* (cf. ærendian II): him getyþade Leofric mid erndunga Godgyfan, Cht. Th. 446, 3.

**ærest**, adv., *note spelling* æst, Ors. S. 124, 8; 174, 2; Harmer, *Historical Documents* 31, 5.

**ærglæd**, *substitute for meaning* long-gracious, and construe in citation with *eorlas* (omitted in Suppl.).

**ærgōd**, *substitute*: *old and excellent*: æþeling ærgod, B. 130, 1329, 2342; iren ærgod, id. 989, 2586.

**ær-ildo**, *delete, in citations read* ær eldo, *before old age* (JEGP xlvi, 413).

**ærist**, *add*: þæt ðryfealde ærist synfullra sawla, Hml. Th. i, 496, 4.

**æristhyht**, *hope of resurrection*: Bd. iii, 15.

**ær-lēof**, *probably delete* (JEGP xlix, 231).

**ær-lyft**, *delete* (take citation as lemma and gloss *aer*, lyft, JEGP xlvi, 414).

**ærn**, *add to compounds* bed-, breaw-, coþ-, eard-, gang-, (ge)mot-, hæf-, hors-, hus-, miltestre-, nidærn.

**ærnan**, add meaning *ride on horseback. See also* ofærnan.

**ærneweg**, *add*: ærnignweg, Bd. v, 6, v.l.

**ærning**, *running*: add: *decursum*, ernincg, Mt., p. 14, 7, Lind.; *a proflunio*, of herning, id. 18, 10. Cf. irning.

**æsc**, *add to I*: onefen ðone greatan æsc, CS ii, 364, 3.

**æscbedd**, n. *ash plantation*: þæt æscbed, CS ii, 175, 7 from below.

**æsce**, *see* geæsce.

**æscēada**, *see also* cornæsceada.

**æscefe**, *see* æscene *in Suppl.*

**æscen**, *pail*, *add*: Hept., Gen. 24, 14; 15; 20.

**Æsces dūn**, *add*: Chr, 648, 661, 1006 (C, D, E). *The name applies to a stretch of the Berkshire downs.*

***æscett**, *ash-clump*, PNE i, 5.

**æscfaru**, f. *military expedition*: *aparatu*, aexfaru, Corpus Glossary A 696 (= Txts. 41, 186). Cf. FL 145.

**æschold**, *add*: *as a topographical term*, CS ii, 77, 9.

**æscstede**, *add*: *as a topographical term*, CS i, 546, 25; iii, 176, 19 (æscstedegeat).

**æscstybb**, *see* stybb *in Suppl.*

**æstel**, *substitute*: m. I *bookmark* or *binding of book*: and on ælcre (bec) bið an æstel, Past. 9, 1; II *perhaps notice-board*: *indicatorium*, æstel, WW 327, 1.

**æt**, *add to A I 3 e a*: æt þam saulum beswicene, Chrd. 88, 12. *See also* þæræt.

**æt**, *add to compounds* feond-, ofer-, untid-, untimæt.

**æta**, *add*: ic geseo . . . þæt þu mycel æte eart, Hml. Warn. 132, 32.

**æetan**, v. *eat*: ætan, Solil. H. 17, 16; ætanne 37, 5 (= Endter 18, 2; 38, 2).

**ætbēon**, *add*: see æt B 3 in Suppl.; Archiv cxxii, 251; Verc.-Hom. 133, 48.

**ætbregdan**, *add to II*: swilce þam rihtwisum ætbredað his rihtwisnisse, Hml. Th. ii, 322, 18.

**ætdwinan**, v. *disappear*: ond þærrihte of heora gesihðe ætdwan, Hml. Warn. 51, 26.

**æte**, noun: *see* of-, wyrmæte; adj.: *see* fela-, of-, syfer-, wyrmæte.

**ætfæstan**, *add to II*: swa he ure saule us ætfæste, Bl. H. 103, 23.

**ætfeallan**, *under II 1 a for diminution read* loss.

**ætfecgan**, *delete, read in citation* ætfealh.

**ætfeng**, *add*: æt ðam ætfengum, Ll. Lbmn. 244, 28.

**ætfēolan**, *add*: me ætfealh (MS. -feah) fyrhtu helle, Ps. Par. cxiv, 3.

**ætfeorrian**, *add*: ne ætfeorrige man hine sulfne (*se substrahat*) þam godcundlican lofum, Chrd. 93, 3. Cf. oþfeorrian.

**ætferian**, *add*: broðra god þurh stælðing ætferian (*subripere*), Chrd. 19, 16.

**ætgædere**, *add to I*: ond ealle þa burhwara forbærnde ætgædere (*uniuersos habitatores urbium*), Hept., Gen. xix, 25.

**æthealdan**, *add*: *detineat*, athealt, Archiv cxvii, 21.

**æthīwian**, v. *transform*: ac þe deofol hæfde þeah mid leasunge þurh his s(c)yncrefte middaneardes murhþe ond all weorldlice fegernesse togædere æthiwod, Hml. Bel. 102, 31.

**æthrīnan**, *add*: (5) *with gen. and acc.*: þæt fyr heora ne æthran, ne furþum an hær heora heafdes, Hml. S. xxx, 454.

**æthwega**, *see* hwilcæthwega.

**æthȳdan**, *delete, see* FL 120.

**ætican**, *see* ætecan *in Dict.*

**æting**, *pasture*: ætingden CS ii, 18, 21; ætincweg id. iii, 339, 2 from below.

**ætlic**, *add*: cf. etlic.

**ætreccan**, *add*: mine witan habbað ætrecð Ecgferðe ealle his are, Chart. Rob. 92, 6.

**ætren**, *add*: the sense is probably figurative in By. 47, 146, *deadly* (of the sword point).

**ætrian**, *see* geætrian.

**ætrihtes**, adv. *nearby*: Verc.-Hom. 2, 14.

**ætscēawian**, v. *appear*: þa rædlice ætsceawede him þær Moyses, Hml. Bel. 108, 10.

**ætscēotan**, v. *escape*: v.l. in second citation s.v. oþsceotan; Verc. Först. 134.

**ætspeornan**, *add to II*: hi (*uenti*) ætspurnon (*impegerunt*) on ðam huse, R. Ben. I. 5, 2.

**ætstandan II** *for* Chr. 1075 *read* 1085.

**ætswerian**, *add*: Ine 35, 1, v.l.

**æettan**, *delete, see* aytan.

**ættelg**, *perhaps delete, read in citation* edtelgung, *redyeing.*

**ætwenian**, *add*: II *attract*: *caperis*, ther bist etwuenied, OEG 28, 44.

**ætwesan**, *add*: þæt sio tid nu ætis, Verc. Först. 97, 20.

**æþe**, *see* cyningaþe.

**æþmian**, *add*: *breathe forth*: *eructabitur*, ut eðmiaþ, Verc. Först. 106, 8.

**æþreclic**, *glosses* terribilis, Ps. Roy. xcv, 4.

**æþryt**, *see also* geæþryt.

**æþyllic**, *see* geþyllic *below.*

**æweweard**, *add*: *sacerdotes*, æweweærdæs, Ps. Cant., Hy. 7, 84.

**æwicness**, f. *eternity*: usque in saeculum saeculi, oþ æwicnesse, Ps. Roy. cii, 17.

**æwill**, m. *stream*: of ðam westmæstan æwylle . . . to æwelforda, CS i, 542, 21–36; andlang ewillas, id. 102, last line.

**æwird**, *substitute*: *meaning uncertain*, v.l. to æwfæst, Archiv cxxviii, 298, 4; *glosses* scurra, id. cc, 198. Cf. awerde.

**æwirdlian**, *see* geæwirdlian.

**æwiscfirenend**, *delete* (= æwiscfirene end).

**æwiscnys**, *citation from Wrt. Voc. belongs to eawiscness,* q.v.

**æx**, *add*: cnocie man þa ban mid æxse yre, Lch. iii, 14, 12; *add to compounds* ceorfæx.

**āfǣgan**, *add*: depictus, afæd, OEG 4, 50.

**āfǣstnian**, *add*: definiat, afæstnað, JEGP lx, 444, vi, 62; 75. Cf. gefæstan III.

**āfangenness**, f. *assumption*: of afangennesse mennisclicnesse, Ps. Roy., Hy. 11, 35, and related glosses. *See also* upafangness.

**āfeallan**, *add to I 2*: descendet, nyðerafylð, Ps. Cam. vii, 17.

**āfēdan**, *add to I 1 a*: *of a trade*, sum leornode sumne cræft þe hine afet, Hml. Th. ii, 556, 32; *sense II in Suppl. should be deleted and citations taken under III.*

**āfēgan**, *add*: *rediges*, gebigest uel afeg, Ps. Cam. lxxii, 20.

**āfeorrian**, *add*: *prolongabitur*, bið afeorrod, Ps. Jun. cviii, 18.

**āfercian**, v. *support*: corpus sustentare, lichaman afercian, Chrd. 90, 11.

**aferian**, *add*: cf. eafor.

**āfillan**, *see also* offillan *below.*

**āfirredness**, f. *removal*: deaþes afyrredness (acc.), Vercelli MS., f. 109ʳ, 28.

**āflīan**, *see* geaflian.

**āfligung**, f. *putting to flight*: wið nædrena afligenge, Lch. i, 338, 12.

**āfōn**, *see also* forhtafangen.

**Africisc**, adj. *African*: Poeni, Affricisce, Archiv. cc, 197.

**āfūlian**, *see also* unafuliende.

**āfȳran**, *delete first citation in Dict. and see also* ofyran *below.*

**āfȳsan**, *note*: in Maldon 3 sense is *drive* (horses).

**āgǣlan**, *add to I*: Ps. Roy. lxxxviii, 32, 35.

**āgǣlwed**, *delete* -gælwed (?); *but add*: agælwed ond swiðe afæred, Bt. S. 86, 10. Cf. OED gally v.

**āgalan**, *add*: weak past part agælyde, Ps. Cam. lvii, 6.

**āgālian**, *add*: hiora earmas agaledon, Verc.-Hom. 132, 23.

**āgan**, *add to I*: *possedit*, ageð, Ps. Roy., Hy. 6, 6; *add to III*: to hyhte agan, *expect*, Sat. 176. *See also* gewyrht II; landagende.

**āgān**, *add*: Ib *of guardianship*: gif ceorl agan wile, *if the husband wishes to keep (the children)*, Æthelberht 80; (healf) þære cirican hlaforde, ðe ðone munuc age, *half to the lord of the church, who is the nun's guardian*, Ælfred 8; IIb *pass into possession (of inherited property)*: hit eall agan is þæron oð on (MS. on þæron oð) þine hand, *all therein has passed, until it has come into thy possession*, Harmer, *Historical Documents* 17, 7.

**āgen**, *add to I*: his ægnu bearn, Past. 409, 5; *add*: I a *within one's rights*: hit seo ðæm agen æghwæs to brucenne, C.D. iii, 254, 12. *See* geagen.

**agen**, *ear of grain*: aristas, agene, Archiv cxvii, 21.

**āgendlice**, *add*: Ecclesiastes . . . is agendlice (*proprie*) on Ænglisc rihtraciend gehaten, Gr. D. 264, 26.

**āgenland**, n. *land held absolutely*: agenland into Scireburnan, Chart. Rob. 166, 7.

**āgenlic**, *see* underagenlic.

**āgenstandan**, *add*: *resistentibus*, agenstandendum, Ps. Lamb. xvi, 8.

**āgēotan**, l. 4 in Suppl. delete citation Wrt. Voc. ii, 145, 23 (*agat is Latin, see* Oliphant, *The Harley Latin–Old English Glossary* 164); l. 9 in Dict. read *good things* for *goods*. *See also* forþageotan.

**āgifan**, *add*: Ia *restore to a previous condition*: his mægn þone tobrocenan calic þære ærran gesynto eft ageaf, Gr. D. 50, 2.

**āgimelēasian**, *add*: Verc. Först. 77, 5.

**āginnan**, *see* unagunnen.

**āglǣdan**, *see* glædan.

**āgniden**, *delete*; *citations have past part of* agnīdan; *lemma* = detrita rubigine.

**āgnung**, *add to II*: tale ne teames ne ahnunga, Chart. Rob. 122, 28; *add to IIa*: ða gelædde se biseop ahnunga, id. 84, 28. *See also* geagnung.

**agnys**, *note* = angness, q.v. *in Suppl. and add* E.S. xxxix, 322.

āgrafan, see wundoragræfen.

āgrimsian, v. provoke: irritauerunt, agrimsedon, Ps. Vit. v, 11.

aguster, magpie: Ker, Catalogue 471.

āgyltan, add: debitoribus, agyltendum, Ps. L. and Cant., Pater noster.

āgyltness, f. guilt: Nap. 6.

āhafu, see upahafu.

āhealtian, v. be lame: claudicauerunt, ahealtedon, Ps. L. xvii, 46.

āhefed(-end)lice, see up-.

āhefendlic, see unahefendlic.

āhefig, in l. 2 in Suppl. read Hml. Th. ii, 586.

āhefigian, add: I make heavy: grauatur, bið ahefegod, Past. 73, 5; II become heavy: asuilð ðæt lim and ahefegað, Past. 73, 10.

āhelpan, in Hy. 4, 1 (= ASPR iii, 215) MS. has helpe.

āheordan, delete, read in citation ahredde.

āhildness, glosses declinatio, Ps. Roy. lxxii, 4.

āhirstan, add: confrixa, aherste, Ps. Bos. 101, 4.

āhladan, add: hio byð fram ælcere swettnesse ahladen, Brot. 18, 9.

āhlȳttrian, add: II remove by purifying: see citation below under stut.

āhreddan, insert 'Gen.' before '2127' in l. 5.

āhrēosan, add: decidam, ahreose, Ps. Roy. vii, 5.

āhwæder, for ahwider, Brot. 20, 16.

*āhwǣtan, v., p. āhwēt, drove away: ahwet hie from his hyldo, Gen. 406 (see EGS iv, 80).

āhwettan, delete III, cf. *āhwǣtan.

ahwilc, discussed FL 6.

āhwilc, any: I pron.: cypeð ahwilc (aliquis), Ps. Roy. lxxxvii, 12; II adj.: quolibet peccato, ahwylcre synne, Chrd. 103, 5; ahwylcum weorce, id. 115, 2.

āhwītian, v. make white: dealbabor, ic beo ahwitod, Ps. Ar. l, 9; ic beo ablæced ond ahwitod, Ps. Bos.

āhyrsod, see ahrisian.

āhyscan, add: subsannabit, ahiscð, Ps. Ar. ii, 4.

āhȳðan, in l. 5 read it despoileth hunger.

āildan, add: ayldan to lange, IC 43.

ālādian, add: excussorum, aladiendra, Ps. Jun., Ps. Bos. cxxvi, 34 (lemma connected with excuso).

ālǣtan, add: IIIa let go what should be kept: se þe þeof gefehð, and he hine alǣte, Ine 38; add to IV: lifes dagas to fyrstum sind to alætenne, R. Ben. I. 5, 6; add: IVa return: þa reaf þe þa yldran alætað (reddere debent), Chrd. 48, 22.

ālangian, cancel, in citation read me a langaþ.

ālāþian, add: leof alaðað, ASPR vi, 109.

ālendan, v. grant (of land): alendan Wlfmære an hide landes his dæg, Chart. Rob. 142, 24.

ālēogan, see also unalogen.

ālēoran, add: transmigra, aleor, Ps. Roy. x, 2; transeat, aleore, id. lvi, 2.

alerbedd, alder bed: on an ælrbed, CS ii, 255, 25.

alh, add: ealh (MS. heah) haligne, Ps. Par. lxxviii, 1.

ālīf, eternal life: Först. Verc. 92, 15; 99, 2. [Icel. eilifi.]

ālīhtan, add to II: se þegen alyhte of his cræte, Hml. Th. i, 400, 25.

āliman, note: citations under I seem to have error alyman for amylan. Cf. Salt veynes mulleþ and woseþ oute humours, Trev. i, 63, 15; JEGP xviii, 577.

ālīsendness, add: Dryhten is ure alysendnes, Verc. Först. 135, 4.

ālīþian, add: aliþa (erue) fram fiane saule mine, Ps. Roy. xxi, 21.

allefne, adv. universally: uniuersa turba, allefne þæt folc, Lk. xxiii, 18, Lind., Rush.

*alren, adj. growing alders, PNE i, 9.

*alrett, alder copse, PNE i, 9.

ām, sense in citations in Suppl. is branding-iron.

āmānsian, for amansumian: abhominabitur, amanseð uel onscuniað, Ps. Cant. v, 7.

āmānsumian, see also unamansumod.

āmarian, perhaps rather make soft (cf. mearu).

ambeht, m. add: ambaect, Txts. 93, 1706.

ambeht, n. add: collatio, ambechtae, Txts. 46, 187; oembecht, 51, 501.

amberlice, adv. cheerfully: gyf hi wiston þæt hi hyt sylfe wæron, noldon hi andwyrdan swa amberlice, Hml. P. i, 254, 141.

ambrosie, f. ambrosia: mid ambrosie þære wyrte swetnysse gefylde, Guth. Gr. 168, 2.

ambyre, retain meaning in Dict., cancel Suppl.; cf. Hml. P. i, 258.

āmeltan, see unamelt.

āmetan, see also efenameten; unametenlic.

āmetgod, see unametgod.

āmidlian, v. bridle: hit amydlæþ ða lahtræs, it (i.e. fasting) bridles vices, Hml. Bel. 56, 27; effrenate, amidludes (error for unmidludes), WW 226, 39.

āmīdlod, delete.

āmidod, participial adj. made foolish: plebs fatua, folc amidod, Ps. Roy., Hy. 6, 6.

āmirran, see also unamirred.

ampre, as gloss to uarix sense is varicose vein; cf. Leiden Glossary xlvi, 27, uarix: omprae in cruribus hominum.

ān, add to I 1 a a: þæt heora rice heolde an gear an monn, Ors. S. 68, 3; add to III: seo leo gelæhte ænne and ænne, Hml. S. xxxv, 281; add: VI a, made definite by a demonstrative: se an ðe tynde, Hml. Th. ii, 30, 12; add to VII 1 a: on ælcum anum geare, Mart. H. 40, 19; add to IX 2 d: see for an.

ānǣglian, v. nail up: heht hine to rode lædan ond hine aneglodon, Verc.-Hom. 30, 261, v.l.

anbesettan, v. inflict: infligitur, biþ anbeset, Prud. 608.

anbeweorpan, v. cast into: intulit, anbewearp, Prud. 1000.

anbid, add: finem nostrum sub tali actu expectare, urne endedæg mid swilcum anbide trymman, Chrd. 25, 35.

anbidian, add: ambidian, Ps. L. ciii, 11; cxli, 8.

anbidung, see geanbidung.

ānbīme, add: cf. trabariae . . . naues quae ex singularis trabibus cauantur, Isid., Et. xix, 1, 27.

anbrōce, delete, see unbræce.

anburg, see borg I, cf. Chart. Rob. 344.

ancuman, delete, follow MS. in citation.

āncyn, add: Lye's citation is Ps. Sal., Hy. x, 12.

and, conj., add: V if: ond he larum wile minum hyran, Jul. 378; and ðu nelt syllan ðinum bearne þrowend for æge, nele eac God us syllan orwenysse for hihte, Hml. Th. i, 252, 30; 32; and he beo syððan hræðe þæs of life, he sceal to reste, Hml. P. ii, 533, 52. See also end.

and, prep.: the word probably does not exist, in all citations we have and, conj., or an error for an, on.

anda, add: on andan (with dat.): (1) where hate, ill-will, etc. is felt by the agent: wraðum on andan, B. 708; id. 2314; Dan. 714; Guth. 346; id. 773; Wand. 105; (2) where anger is caused in a person: morgenspel manigum on andan, El. 970 (cf. Heliand 3741). Zelus bonus, se goda anda, R. Ben. I. 117, 3; R. Ben. 131, 13.

and-ǣges, delete, read hire an dæges, B. 1935 (so ASPR, Klaeber, etc.).

andbīcnian, substitute for sense portend (reference is to latrantes crudelia bella ciebunt, Ald. Rid. 65). But note MS. may read andbetniað. See also hleoþrian below.

andbita, in citations in Suppl. andbita, beorma = andbita, andbeorma; in second andbida seems altered to andbita.

andcweþan, delete, MS. has aid (= aidlian), see Studia Germanica Gandensia ii, 83.

andergilde, substitute: adj. bringing recompense: oft bryncð seo wyrd þone wille þe eft byð andergelde, Prov. K. 41 (so MSS.; see Hml. Warn. 5, 14). Cf. unandergilde.

andettere, m. one who makes confession: confitentem, þone andyttre, Chrd. 80, 23.

andfange, for andfenge: susceptor, Ps. Cam. iii, 4.

andfeng, add to III: þa næfde heora noþor þone andfeng þæt hi him þæt feoh forguldon, Brot. 10, 12.

andfengelic, adj. acceptable: tempus acceptabile, tid eð ondfengelic, Rtl. 11, 15.

andfengstōw, f. receptacle: Chrd. 109, 3.

andfōnd, see underandfond.

andfylstan, v. help: adiuua, andfylst, Ps. Sal, xliii, 26.

andgitol, see unandgitol.

andhweorfan, see hwearf adj. in Suppl.

andiendlice, adv. enviously: inuide, Chrd. 108, 18.

andlang, adj., add: II accompanying: þeodcyninges andlongne eorl, B. 2695.

andlang, prep., add to (3): andlang suð on Temese, CS iii, 261, 15.

andlanges, add to (1): andlanges þære ceapstræte, CS ii, 305, 25.

**andlēan,** add: B. 1541; 2094 (*MS.* handlean *in both*).

**andleofen,** add: *uictualibus,* andlyfenum, A. xiii, 439, 1051.

**andlūcan,** for onlucan: *reserat,* andleac, Txts. 92, 872.

**admitta,** see anmitta.

**andrecefæt,** add: *may be error for* andrencefæt, *cup that may be drunk at one draught* (Archiv lxxxvi, 401).

**andsēcan,** *glosses* inquiro: Ps. Vit. xxxiii, 15.

**andspurnness,** f. *offence: scandalizare,* andspurnisse þrowian, Mt. xiii, 21, Rush.; *scandalum,* andspyrnnisse (L. ondspyrnise), id. xxvi, 31; etc.

**andswaru,** see also rihtandswaru.

**andtimber,** add: *statum,* antimbre, An. Ox. 1833; ond for þan we understandeð þæt synne nis nan þing on antimbre, for ælc antimber is god, Hml. Warn. 140, 27.

**andweard,** see also geandweard.

**andweardian,** add: *praesentans,* Hy. S. 89, 18.

**andwiggearo,** adj., *ready for defence:* see anwiggearo.

**andwlata,** add: Cri. 1436 (? *MS.* andlata).

**andwlitefull,** add: *with haughty look: uultuosus,* andwliteful, Prud. 382.

**andwreþian,** v. *support:* manna untrumnyssa andwreþian, Chrd. 62, 29.

**andwyrdan,** add: andwyrt se godfæder þæs cildes wordum, Hml. Th. ii, 52, 4.

**anecgede,** for twiecgede, *owing to influence of Lat.* anceps: Ps. Sal. cxlix, 6.

**āned,** see geaned.

**ānerian,** v. *save, rescue: euellet,* anereð, Ps. L. xxiv, 15.

**anfandlice,** *probably error for* anfaldlice, Ælfred 18, v.l. (Quadripartitus *simpliciter*).

**anfangenness,** *v.l. in citation under* afangenness (Ps. Ar., Ps. Vit.).

**ānfeald,** add to I: *simplum,* be anfealdum ic forgylde, Ælfc. Gr. Z. 286, 17.

**ānfloga,** add: in context refers to the speaker's soul, conceived in bird-form, cf. Campbell, *Æthelwulf: De Abbatibus,* p. xxxii.

**anforht,** *delete, see* unforht.

**Angelfolc,** n. *the English:* Angelfolcum (v.l. -folce), Bd. v, 22.

**angelic,** see also ongelic.

**Angelseaxe,** m. pl. *Anglo-Saxons:* on æðele Angolsexna, ASPR vi, 97.

**Angelwita,** m. *English counsellor:* be Angolwitena gerednesse, Ll. Lbmn. 236, 19.

**\*anger,** *grassland,* PNE i, 11.

**angian,** v. *be troubled: anxiaretur,* angud wearð, Ps. Roy. lx, 3, *and related glosses. See also* geangian.

**āngilde,** noun, add: fram æghwelcum gafolum . . . butan angilde, CS ii, 173, 13.

**angin,** add to (1): na þreo anginnu ac . . . an angin, Hml. S. i, 15.

**angness,** *Somner's citation* = Archiv cxxxiv, 284, 7. *See also* engness *and* cnyss.

**angsumlic,** adj. *troublesome:* þæt ðe ær earfoðe and ancsumlic þuhte, R. Ben. 5, 19.

**ānhealfrūh,** adj. *rough on one side: sipla,* anhealfruh tæppet, WW 152, 14 (*printed* an healfruh).

**anhering,** for herung II, R. Ben. 131, 13.

**ānhyrned,** on forms see *Early English and Norse Studies* (ed. Brown and Foote), 120.

**āninga,** add: *in breui,* anunga uel in sceortnisse, Ps. Roy. ii, 13; *uelociter,* hrædlice uel anunga, id. vi, 11; *per singula,* anunga, Jn. xxi, 25, Lind. (*But for* anunga Jn. ii, 17, Rush., *read* elnunga; L. elnung).

**anlǣdan,** *cancel, in citation read* eorp werod ecan læddon.

**ānlūtung,** read anlūtung (cf. lutian), *and substitute for meaning lurking-place;* cf. FL 122.

**anmitta,** see also handmitta.

**ānrǣdness,** see unanrædness.

**ānseld,** cf. *s.v.* geargemearc *in Suppl.*

**ansīn,** *cancel IV in Dict.* (*see* onsin *in Suppl.*); *note occasional masc. or neut. gender:* þæs engles ansynes, Nap. 37, 4; on egeslicum onsyne, id. 6, 32; beforan þinum ansyne, Bd. v, 32, v.l.

**anspel,** *perhaps to be taken as two words* ān spel, cf. FL 65.

**anstiga(n),** read ānstīga, add as meaning *narrow path,* and take here final citation in Dict. s.v. stig, *sty,* and citation s.v. stiga. *See also* FL 121.

**āntīd,** add: meaning in Suppl. is supported E.S. lxx, 40.

**antifonere,** m. *antiphonary:* swa swa se antifonere tæcð (*secundum quod in antifonario habetur*), Fehr, 154, 6; Archiv lxxxiv, 5, 38.

**antimber,** add: of treowum and of stanum and of oðrum antimbrum (MS. un-) missenlicum, Verc. Först. 177.

**anunder,** prep. *under:* he wyle þone hlaford lecgen anunder hine, Hml. Warn. 7, 27.

**anweald,** see also onweald *and* sundoranweald.

**anwealda,** add: Verc.-Hom. 112, 45.

**ānwiggearo,** *delete, read in citation* andwiggearwe, *ready for defence.*

**āpīcan,** *delete, retain in citation* apytan.

**āpinsian,** add: *pensemus,* uton apinsian, Chrd. 88, 32.

**apostata,** see also efenapostata.

**appellēaf,** delete, source is 13th cent.

**apulder,** see also mircapulder.

**apuldre,** see also mærapuldre.

**āpundrian,** *account (to a person), blame for:* see El. 580 *cited under awundrian.*

**ār,** *honour,* add to III: Adam wearð of his gecyndan are . . . ut adræfed, Chrd. 68, 24.

**ār-,** in argebland, arwela, aryþ, *is equivalent to* ear, *ocean.*

**āra,** *delete, take in citation as adverbial gen. pl. of* ar, *kindness.*

**ārǣdan,** add to III: ðas boec mon arede, Txts. 175, 11.

**ārǣfedlic,** see unaræfedlic.

**ārǣfnan,** delete II; as gloss to *exigo,* sense is *perform,* as gloss to *expendo,* sense is *suffer* (cf. *expendisset,* ðrowode, Txts. 61, 783).

**ārǣfn(i)endlic,** add: *tolerabilius,* arefrendlicre, Mt. x, 15, Lind.

**ārǣfsan,** for aræpsan, Kansas leaf. *See* ræpsan *in Dict.*

**ārǣran,** add: I a *place in a superior position:* se oðer beo aræred from ðæm oðrum, Past. 107, 23; IV a *bring (to a condition):* ic him yfle ne mot, ac ic on hæftnyd hwilum arære, Rid. lxxxiii, 10.

**ārāsian,** add: IV *suspect: suspicabatur,* he arasade, Bd. iv, 1.

**āreccan,** see also unareht.

**ārēcelēasian,** add: *with clause:* and ealle þa þe . . . he areceleasode to andettenne, Wyn. 72; *with gen.:* to hwan areceleasodest ðu ðære gife, Vercelli MS., f. 68ʳ, 17.

**āredian,** *in l. 4 for* provide *read* carry out, *for* wants *read* wills.

**ārēodian,** add: *erubescant,* areodigen, Ps. Roy., Ps. Bos. lxix, 4; areoddian, Ps. Sal.

**arewe,** cf. earh.

**ārfæstan,** v. *show mercy: propitiatur,* arfæstað, Ps. Sal. cii, 3.

**ārhwæt,** substitute for meaning *full of glory, glorious.*

**ārian,** see also unarian.

**āriman,** see also unarimed.

**ārīmedlic,** -lice: see una-.

**ārīsan,** see also unarisende.

**ārlic,** -lice: see also una-.

**ārmidl,** n. *oar-thong:* see midl *below.*

**ārsceamu,** delete, ASPR v, 212.

**ārung,** see also hadarung.

**ārwesa,** add: as noun *the Lord:* Seasons for Fasting 77, 196.

**ārwirþan,** see gearwirþan.

**āryddan,** cf. gerydan.

**āryderian,** v. *blush: erubescentes,* aryderende, Ps. Roy., Ps. Bos. lxix, 4.

**āsadian,** *satisfy:* of þan wele þe þa yfela mæn byð of swa swyðe asadede, Hml. Warn. 141, 37.

**āsānian,** add: *grow dull, wane:* þæt leoht asanode on þa ylcan wysan þe hit ær wæxende wæs, Vis. Lfc. 57.

**asce,** see also ellenasce.

**āsceaman,** delete, *MS.* has asceamien *in citation,* see R. T. Oliphant, *The Harley Latin–Old English Glossary* 157.

**āsceamelic,** *delete, MS.* has ascunelicum in citation.

**āscēotan,** add: III *disembowel:* An. Ox. 46, 47 (*cited in Suppl. under II 3*); cf. onsceotan.

**āscian,** take II in Dict. under VI in Suppl.

**āscilian,** add to 2: *explain: et elucubratam,* and þa ascyledan, OEG 2, 212.

**āscirian,** add to I: *remoto . . . luxu,* fram ascirede . . . gælsan, Gn. 29, 3 (JV).

**āscirpan,** *sharpen: l.* 2 *in Suppl. read* ascerptun.

**āscrencan,** citation in Dict. is Past. 317, 8.

**āscrīfan,** v. *impose (a penance): descripta (illi mensura pænitendi),* ascrifenum, OEG 4, 255.

**āscunung**, see onascunung.

**āscyhhan**, see scyhhan in Suppl.

**āscyhtan**, see scyhtan in Suppl.

**āscyndan**, add: ðu ðe ascyndest (tollis) synna middangeardes, Ps. Roy., Hy. 12, 12.

**āsēcan**, add to I: exquisierat, asohte, Mt. ii, 16, Rush.; add to II: oþ þæt se claþ sy asoht, Fehr 172, 28.

**āsecgan**, see also unasecgende.

**āsēdan**, see sedan.

**āsellan**, add: he nolde þæt þæt land mid ealle ut aseald wære, Chart. Rob. 146, 15.

**āsendedness**, see unasendedness.

**āseolcendlic**, see unaseolcendlic.

**āsetedness**, see unasetedness.

**āsettan**, add: Ib place in a position: ic hine asette ealra heahstne, Ps. Par. lxxxviii, 24; þu us asettest on sarcwide, id. lxxix, 6; hine nyðor asette Metod, Dan. 493; Ic apply (with non-material object): asete him þa unriht, Ps. Par. lxviii, 28; Id remove: gif man oðrum steop asette . . . vi scill. þam þe man þone steap aset, Hlothhere and Eadric 12; he (hi) het ahon and . . . eft asettan, Jul. 231; I e store, save: þu hæfst mycele god asette (posita), WS Gospels, Lk. xii, 19; VII fix (a time): on asettum timan, Hml. A. 110, 255.

**āsigan**, add: se wæta asigð (labitur) to ðam lime, Past. 72, 10.

**āsingan**, add to I: he asong . . . his saltere and his mæssan, Mart. H. 178, 18.

**āsirwan**, perhaps delete, in citation afered (from āferian) may be correct; see JEGP xlvi, 414.

**āslacian**, note that in citation of Wrt. Voc. 144, 52 (= WW 230, 18) aslacod and euacuatum are not gloss and lemma, but both gloss exhaustum.

**āslǽccan**, note: first gloss cited in Suppl. (WW 385, 30) is derived from the first (WW 18, 15, Corpus Glossary), but it is not certain that it is right in connecting it with slǽccan. Cf. JEGP xviii, 143.

**āslāpan**, add: þa earan aslapað (v.l. aslawiað), Verc. Först. 91, 6.

**āslīdan**, add: I b slip (from the mouth): prolapsum nefas, ut awunderne gylt oþþe ut aslidene synne, Prud. 50.

**āslīding**, substitute: f. slip of tongue: lubrico, of aslidinge, Prud. 51.

**āslītan**, add: asliteð, Ps. Roy. lxxvi, 9.

**āsmēagan**, add to II: and þa (i.e. idols) asmeadan mid cræfte, Hml. P. ii, 687, 191.

**āsolian**, v. get foul: nitor squalescit, hwit asolað, ASPR vi, 109.

**āsplǽtan**, v. split: exentera (MS. extentera), aspiet (read asplet), OEG 49, 1 (cf. Tob. vi, 5; E.S. xlix, 156).

**āspelia**, for gespelia: R. Ben. 102, 19.

**āspelian**, add: nullus excussetur, nan ne beo aspelod, Chrd. 16, 17.

**āspornan**, v. glosses elido: elisos, aspornena, Ps. Cant. cxlv, 7.

**āsprēotan**, add: gærs ond wyrta ær ðan ðe hi up asprutan, Hept., Gen. ii, 5.

**āspringendlic**, see unaspringendlic.

**āsprungenness**, add: defectio, asprungnisse, Ps. V. cxviii, 53 (and related glosses).

**assen**, note citation in Suppl. is emended; MS. reading is hors of steden uel of assænne.

**āstæppan**, v.: (1) proceed: prodita una stirpe, forð astapene of anum stofne Gn. 25, 2 (JV); (2) imprint (footsteps): fotlæsta . . . on þissere flore astapene, Nap. 80, 1 (= Hml. P. ii, 699, 420).

**āstemnian**, substitute: v. establish: þæs mynstres, ðe hi sylf astemnedon, Bd., pref. Cf. stefnan.

**āsteorfan**, add: þæt nyten byð to astorfenum (in contrast with acweald) geteald, E.S. viii, 61, 42.

**āstīgan**, add to I a: descenderunt, of astigun, Jn. vi, 16, Rush.; add to II 2: he on gylp astag, Met. 9, 46; add to II 1 b: ascendit, up astah, Ps. Sal., Hy. 14, 5; up astigende, Gr. D. 333, 2.

**āstīgend**, m. rider: ascensorem, astigend, Ps. Roy., Hy. 4, 1 (and related glosses); id. 4. Cf. niþerastigend.

**āstīgendlic**, adj. intensive (of adverbs), Ælfc. Gr. Z. 241, 13 (Meroney, MLN lix, 40, would read ascigendlic, nterro-gative).

**āstillian**, v. quieten: þwyre mænn . . . mid rihtwisnysse astilligen, Hml. Warn. 75, 30.

**āstirfan**, take here astyrfan in Dict. and add: destroy: eradicabitur, astærfed bið, Mt. 15, 13, Lind.

**āstrǽlian** v hurl a dart: i aculatum, astrælod, Ps. Roy. lxxv, 9.

**āstrīcan**, v. strike: þæt he hine sceolde wyrs astrican, Verc.-Hom. 4, 38.

**astrihilthet**, rather a corruption of æftergild, cf. A. xlix, 381.

**āstrowenness**, cf. FL 65.

**āsūgan**, see also osogen.

**āswǽman**, probably delete II, take citation under I.

**āswāmian**, see swamian.

**āswārnian**, add: reuereantur, aswarnien, Ps. Roy. lxxxii, 18; confusus, aswarnod, id. lxxxvii, 16; þa stent ðæt deade flæsc aswornod, ond ne mæg nan andwyrde syllan, Verc.-Hom. 100, 1.

**āswengan**, add: iactatus, aswenged, Ps. Roy. xxi, 11.

**āswungenness**, f. glosses flagilitas (error for fragilitas): asuuncgennisse, Rtl. 43, 5.

**āsyndran**, see geasyndran.

**āsyngian**, v. sin: peccaui, asingode Ps. Ar. 1, 6.

**ātendan**, add to I: kindle: feower fyr atende, Hml. Th. ii, 338, 6; succensus, atend, An. Ox. 2460; add to III: succensus, atend (flammis carnalibus), An. Ox. 4315.

**ātendnes**, f. incentive: incendium libidinis, atendnesse galnesse, A. lxv, 232, 1.

**ātēon**, add to II 2: nyme he þa ælmessan, and ateo swa he wylle, Chrd. 49, 8.

**ātēorian**, add to II: end, not continue (of material): Tech. ii, 127, 14 (in Suppl. s.v. handstoc).

**ātēorodness**, add: defectio, Ps. Bos. cxviii, 53.

**ātersellende**, glosses uenundatus (connected with uenenum): Ps. Cant. civ, 17.

**ātertān**, add: it is improbable that the meaning is literal in the citation, take rather as serpentine patterns.

**ātimplian**, ? provide with spikes (cf. timple): atimplod mid attrenum pilum ond scearpum tindum, Nap. 7.

**ātland**, n. land where oats are grown: þæs bisceopes atlandes, Chart. Earle 208, 34.

**ātlēah**, f. oat-field: in atleahe geat, CS iii, 588, 27.

**ātor**, line 7 in Dict., substitute for translation of wið fleogendum atre, against infection.

**ātorcoppe**, add: attorcoppan habbað innan awefene, Verc. Först. 102, 6.

**ātorgeblǽd**, poisonous blister: Lch. iii, 36, 22. [Cf. Ger. eiterbeule.]

**ātorlāþe**, also betony.

**ātorþigen** (? -þegu), taking poison: wið attorþigene (v.l. -þige), Lch. i, 4, 5.

**ātorwyrhta**, m. maker of poison: uenefici incantantis, atterwyrhtan galendes, Ps. L. lvii, 6.

**atsīc**, n. meaning uncertain: in þæt atsic, CS i, 308, 12.

**āttordrinca**, delete, in citation read ond him mon sealde attor drincan, he was given poison to drink.

**ātwiccian**, v. excerpt: excerpsimus, we atuccedan, OEG 4, 222.

**ātydran**, add: propagata, forð attyddrede, OEG 4, 91.

**ātȳnan**, add: aperuit, atiende, Ps. Roy. xxxvii, 14.

**ātyhtung**, see onbring below.

**āþ**, add to I: se arcebiscop mid his selfes aðe geahnode Gode . . . ða land . . . ond ðæne aþ nam Wulfsige . . . ond þær wæs god eaca ten hundan mannan ðe þane að sealdan, Chart. Rob. 86, 6; Leofric sealde Wulfstane twegra þegna að and wæs hymsylf þridde, C.D. iv, 235, 11; add: IV the fine paid when the oath in a suit fails: aþ and ordel (in list of payments), Chart. Rob. 236, 29. Add compounds cyre-, fore-, friþ-, hold-, hyld-, rimaþ.

**aða oðer**, adv. otherwise: alioquin, Mt. ix, 17, Lind.

**āþecgan**, take in Rid. 1 (= Wulf and Eadwacer) as in Dict., in Lch. as in Suppl.

**āþēostrian**, add: aþriostraþ, Mt. xxiv, 29, Rush.

**aðexe**, add: [See OED ask, newt].

**āþreclic**, glosses terribilis, Ps. Ar., Ps. Vit. xcv, 4.

**āþrēotan**, see also unaþreotende.

**āþswaru**, see also s.v. geæþan.

**āþswerung**, add: iusiurandum, aþswering, Ps. Roy., Hy. viii, 73 (and related glosses).

**āþum**, add: gener, adam, Corpus Glossary G 86 (not in Txts.); WW 174, 4, etc.

**āþumswēoras**, m. pl. son-in-law and father-in-law: aþumsweoran (d.p.; MS aþum swerian), B. 84.

**aðurhgifende**, glosses perdonantes, JEGP lix, 712, 4.

**āþwīnan**, v. vanish: se scucce aðwan of heoræ gesihþæ, Nap. 74.

āþynnian, add: attenuati, aðynede, Ps. Spl.H y. 2, 14.

āpȳtan, expel, delete, in citation read aytið.

āwācian, add: God he awacað (placat) to him, Verc. Först. 126, 6.

āwǣcan, the emendation of awæht to aræht as gloss to porrectus is confirmed by WW 470, 28; 472, 2. Add: seo mægð aweht (v.l. awæced) wæs mid þi wæle, Bd. iii, 30.

āwǣgnian, v. = āwǣgan: þe mine swutelinge awaengnian wolde, Chart. Harm. 200, 9.

āwaxan, v. wash: ond man þa weofodsceatas awahxe, Fehr 156, 14. Cf. awæscan in Suppl.

āweggewitenness, add: excessu, aweggewitenesse, Ps. Jun. cxv, 11.

awel, for awl read flesh-hook, and delete reference to æl, which is a different word.

āwemman, see also unawemmende.

āwendedness, see also wederawendedness.

āwendedness, add: ðær is wlite butan awendendnesse, Verc. Först. 134.

āwendness, for awendedness: commotationem, æwendness, Ps. Cant. xliii, 15.

awerd: substitute: awerde, worthless person: uappa, awærde WW 111, 29.

āwesness, f. essence: essentia, auuesnis, OEG 72, 1.

āwēstendness, add: uastatio, awestendnys, Gn. (Archiv cxcix, 19).

āwiht, add to II: þara minra awuht fela on gewrit settan, L. Ælf. pref.

āwilnian, v. desire: ac minre neaweste awilnodon, Vercelli MS. f. 67ʳ.

āwindan, sense in II 1 is slip out (of the mouth).

āwirdan, add: uitiatum, auuaerdid (v.l. auuerdid), Txts. 106, 1091.

āwirdend, m. destroyer: he is Hælend ond na awerdend, Hml. Warn. 136, 7.

āwirding, delete, MS. in citation has wyrdingum (see wirding in Suppl.).

āwirpan, add: wearð geðuht swilce heo awyrpan mihte, ac heo gewat of worulde, Hml. S. xx, 65; conualeo, awyrpe, A. xli, 109, 85.

āwītegian, v. prophesy: (se witedom) se þe ær . . . awriten wæs and awitgod, Verc.-Hom. 33, 285; 36, 307; and frequently (always with awriten).

āwlǣtan, add to II: þæt hi mid leahtrum ne awlæton hira godcundan gyfe, Chrd. 56, 31.

āwlyspian, v. speak badly: seo tunge awlyspaþ, MLN iv, 279.

āworpenness, add: oð Isaces gebyrd ond aworpenesse Ismahelis, Bd. v, 23.

āworuld, glosses in saeculum seculi, Ps. Roy. xviii, 10 (cf. Ps. Cant. æworuldæ worlde).

āwrǣnsan, v. become lustful: gif man sie to unwræne, wyl on meolce þa ilcan wyrt, þonne awrænst þu, Leonhardi 44, 12.

āwreccend, m. awaker: excitator, Gn. 18, 1 (JV).

āwrit, see also oferawrit.

āwrītan, add: IX engrave: lorh (colum) . . . swiðe fægre awrittenne, Wyn. 181. Add to compounds un-, oferawriten.

āwundrian, cf. apundrian.

āwyrten, see gewyrten below.

āwyrsian, Ps. Vit. xxxix, 15, probably read awyrpan or afyrsian (auferant).

āwyrtlian, for awyrtwalian: R. Ben. I. 108, 7.

āwyrtrumian, v. root out: ealle uncysta wiorðað ut awyrtrumade, Verc. Först. 161. See also ofawyrtrumad.

āwyrtwarian, for awyrtwalian: Ps. Roy., Ps. Ar., Ps. Vit. lxxix, 14.

āyppan, v. glosses experiri (erroneously): experiatur, sie aypped, Rtl. 70, 5.

āȳtan, add: depastus est, aytte, Ps. L. lxxix, 14. See FL 60.

# B

bæc, brook: on forms see PNE i, 23.

bæc, add: in catamo (see Lindsay, Corpus Glossary 203), in bæce, Txts. 73, 1148; pos(t) tergum tuum, æfter bæce þinum, Ps. Spl., Hy. 2, 17.

bæc, baking: see gebæc.

bæceling, baking-dish or oven: bæcelinge, clibano, late glosses on ofenbacene, Hept., Lev. ii, 4 (Ker, Catalogue 422). Possibly error for bæcering, q.v.

bæcestre, add: Liueger se bacestere on Excestre, Chart. Th. 637, 27.

*bæcstān, baking-stone, PNE i, 15; frixorium, iserne bacstan, Ælfc. Gr. Z, 316, 8 (late v.l.).

bǣdan, delete B. 2018 (where read bælde); add to compounds tobædan.

bæddæg, delete, MS. has bæðdæg.

bǣdling, for lemma cariar, cf. cariel, leno, Corpus Glossary C 152 and Lindsay's note.

bǣr, add: III wave, and take here Germ. 400, 487 (= Prud. 861–2) cited in Suppl. under bære.

bǣr, pasture: delete (?); add: on knutleage bære eastewearde, CS ii, 379, 9; add to compounds: pol-, wer-, wudubære. On form see PNE i, 16.

bǣran, delete, citation has past subj. of beran, bear.

-bǣre, adj.: add to compounds feþer-, gram-, hal- (hæl-), helm-, leger-, lof-, mann-, slæp-, steor-, wæpen-, windbære.

bærnan, see also breneþ, sambærned.

bærnedness, see forbærnedness.

bǣrness, see gebærness.

bærning, add: burnt-offering: holocaustis, bærningum, Ps. Jun. l, 18 (so Ps. Bos.). Also applied to a source of water: andlang . . . wellbærninge, CS ii, 483, 4; on birninge, id. 500, 24. See also birning.

bæþ, add to compounds fant-, fullwihtbæþ.

bæþdæg, see bæddæg.

balc, ridge between two furrows: porca, balc, WW 147, 21. Cf. balca.

balca, add: as an instrument of torture: mistlice ðreala gebyriað for synnum: bendas oððe dyrtas oððe pollupas oððe carcern, ðystra, lobban oððe balcan, A. lxxxiii, 27, 316, v.l.

balsemite, a kind of mint: balsemita, DP 55.

balsmēþe, a kind of mint: Lch. iii, 90; mentastro, baldsmiðe, OEG 73 b, 11.

balsminte, delete, MS. has balsmite in citation, see balsemite.

bān, add: III tusk: B. 2692; add to compounds ge-, hrycg-, hweorf-, hype-, lendenban.

bana, add to compounds mægbana.

bānfāh, substitute for meaning adorned with gables (cf. horn VII).

bānhelm, substitute for meaning helmet adorned with horns.

bānloca, add: perhaps muscle: burston banlocan, B. 818.

bannuccamb, a doubtful word, FL 16; cf. flǣþecamb below.

bānwærc, note: caradrum perhaps for chiragra.

banweorc, n. action causing death: seo unlagu þæt man moste banweorc on unsacne secgan, Ll. Lbmn. 244, 34. Cf. morþweorc.

bānwyrt, note: filia is for uiola; add: consolda (= consolida), banuyrt, DP 128 (and cf. notes to 128, 173, 334).

bār, add: mid bares tuxe, Lch. i, 244, 8; bæres flæsc., id. iii, 144, 24.

barricge, probably not OE, cf. SHG 27.

basu, add to compounds wrætbasu.

bātian, bǣtung: see grist-.

be, add to A I 1 b: for he forð bi ðæm scræfe, Bl. H. 213, 34; add to A I 4: gebundon (hine) be þam fotum, Mart. H. 212, 17; add to II 2: be Wihtgares dæge and be oðra cinga dæge, Chr. 796; luce adhuc diei, be dæges leohte, R. Ben. 66, 8; add to III 8: gif he deð dædbote be his synnum, A. xi, 114, 61; fif onlicnessa be hellegryre, Verc. Först. 90, 12; Wlfst. 171, 3; add to III 9: be freondan and be fremdan fadian gelice, IP 14, 8; add to III 15: si neque sic correxerit, gif he ne geswice be þam, Chrd. 41, 36; add to III 18: he be heora gange hi gecneow, Hml. S. xxx, 233; add to III 19: bið ðearf ðæt he hine genime be ðære leornunge haligra gewrita and be ðam arise (ut per eruditionis studium resurgat), Past. 169, 15; add to III 22: leod and lagu for be geþincðum, Geþyncðo 1. Remove Cht. Th. 171, 6 (= Harmer, Historical Documents 31, 14) from III 16 to B. Add to compounds þærbig.

bēacen, add: audible signal: sona swa hi þæt beacn gehyron, Chrd. 32, 26; 34, 4. Cf. belhringes beacn, wuldorbeacen.

bēagian, delete, see gebeagian, gebigan, and cf. Gneuss, Lehnbildungen und Lehnbedeutungen im Altenglischen 142.

**bēah**, *add to* (1): ðæs ecan beages, Bd. v, 22; *add*: (5) *sword*, B. 2041; pl. *arms*, B. 2635. *Add to compounds* coren-, dryhten-, heafod-, sigebeah.

**bēahhyrne**, *delete, MS. has* heahhyrne, *see* eaghyrne.

**bealcettan**, *add to III*: eructabo, roketto forð *uel* bilketto forð, Mt. xiii, 35, Rush.; eructabunt, hi bylcettaþ *uel* hig bealcettaþ, Ps. L. cxliv, 7.

**beald**, *add*: presumptione percussus, *to* beald *and to* scomleas, Past. 61, 2.

**\*bealg**, adj. *round*, PNE i, 18.

**\*beall**, *ball, round hill, boundary-mark*, PNE i, 18.

**bealo**, *add to compounds of noun* cwealm-, dryhten-, þeodenbealo.

**bēam**, *add to compounds* ciris-, crawen-, cristelmæl-, gorst-, mur-, sunne-.

**Bēamdūn, Bēandūn**, *add*: unknown place, not Bampton.

**bēamen**, *see also* elebeamen.

**bēamwer**, *weir of logs*: beneoðan beamwær, CS ii, 242, 19.

**bēanbroþ**, *see* beon-.

**bēanlēah**, f. *land where beans grow*: of þistelleage to beanleage, CS ii, 492, 23.

**bēanset**, *bean-plot*: ten hida on beansetum, Txts. 454, 1.

**-bearde, -beardede**, *see* geb.

**beardleas**, *add*: see Du Cange s.v. *buteo*, and cf. ZfdA xxxi, 16, 446, *probum buteonem*, godne geongan.

**bearhtm**, *noise, add*: bearhtme, *with loud noise*, Jud. 39.

**bearn**, *add to compounds* fester-, foster-, steop-, wusc-.

**bearnēacniende**, *add*: swa þæt heo of þam ilcan halgen gaste wearð bearneacniende, *Anglica* ii, 34, 178 (= Hml. Warn. 138, 6).

**bearnēacnod**, participial adj. *pregnant*: heo wæs bearneacnod of ðam halgan gaste, Verc.-Hom. 109, 22, v.l.; 122, 143.

**bearnēacnung**, *add*: post partum, æfter bearneacnunga, Gn. 47, 2 (JV).

**bearo**, *add to compounds* ac-, ele-, ge-, ifigbearo.

**bēat**, *see* gebeat.

**bēaw, beawhyrnet**, *see also* hyrnetu *in Suppl. and below*.

**bebēodan**, *see also* oferbebeodan.

**beberan**, *note: in citation MS. has* innihte.

**bebiwan**, *delete, in citation read* bebyrian, *bury, for* bebyrwan (cf. FL 7).

**bebod**, *add compounds* nid-, tin-, weorold-, word-, wundorbebod.

**bebodenessum**, *error for* behydednessum, Ps. Ar., Ps. Vit. xvi, 14 (absconditis).

**bebrūcan**, *delete ref. in Addenda: MS.* gebrucene, *see* Hml. Warn. 39, 31.

**bebūgan**, *add*: heo ða scearpnesse dysiglicra spræca na bebeah ne ne foreode (non declinauit), Gr. D. 340, 17.

**bebyrignys**, *add*: gangað to deadra manna bebyrignesse, Verc. Först. 128, 8.

**bebyrigung**, *add*: þa licþenunge his bebyrginge, Gr. D. 84, 5.

**becearcian**, v. *attend to*: Martha swanc and becarcade . . . . þa lichamlice behefðen, *Anglica* ii, 25, 100 (= Hml. Warn. 136, 14).

**beceorfan**, *add*: B. 1590; 2138.

**\*bēcett**, *beech-copse*, PNE i, 24.

**becirran**, *add to I*: ða becyrde se Hælend, Hml. Th. ii, 248, 33; *add*: V *alter*: ne man his agenne andwlitan becyrran ne mæg, Verc.-Hom. 151, 1.

**bēcrǣde**, f. *reading of books*: ðonne heo inne heora leornunge ond heora becrædon beeodon, Bd. iv, 3 (Miller 264, 14; Schipper 354, 7 n.).

**becrēopan**, *add*: bebead Alexander þæm biscepe þæt he becrupe on þæs Amones anlicnesse, Ors. S. 126, 27.

**becuman**, *add to I 3*: ne lyst me þæs, ac gyf hit me æfre on lust becymð, Solil. H. 36, 16 (= Endter 37, 13); we becumað to þam andgite swa mycles gerynes, BM 48, 2.

**becweþan**, *see also* on-, yfelbecweþende; unbecweden.

**bed**, *prayer: add*: mid gemaglicum bedum (v.l. benum), Gr. D. 156, 2.

**\*bedærn**, *chapel*, PNE i, 24.

**bedclāþ**, *add*: lectualia, bedclaðas, Chrd. 65, 15.

**bedd**, *add to I the compounds* feber-, forliger-, morþor-, wig-; *add I a*: apparatus on or in which a body may be placed: he hine het aþenian on irenum bedde and hine cwicne hirstan, Mart. H. 142, 19; *see also* ferbed; *add to III a the compounds* æsc-, aler-, holen-, læfer-, rosbedd. *Delete II*, spatula = spartula, *esparto grass* (used for bedding).

**bedda**, *see* gebedda.

**beddrest**, *add*: WW 154, 1; ond his bedreste gegearwode, Speculum xxxvii, 62 (3 lines from below).

**beddstōw**, f. *bedstead*: betstow, Will of Æthelgifu, ed. Whitelock, 45, 49.

**bedelfan**, *add to II*: and he ne byð gescreadod oððe bedolfen, Hml. P. i, 251, 72.

**bedewinde**, *bindweed*: as place-name, intrat Bedewindan, CS i, 315, 18; at Bedewindan, Harmer, *Historical Documents* 17, 21.

**bedgerid**, substitute for meaning *food in an ant's nest*.

**bedīfan**, *add*: demergat, besence *uel* bedyfe, Ps. Cam. lxviii, 16.

**bedīglian**, *add to I 1*: ic wille me bedihlian, Ap. of Tyre ix (Goolden 14, 5).

**befealdan**, delete sense II a: contentum has been taken as enveloped in citation (= Prud. 1010).

**befealdian**, v. *roll up* (intrans.): Verc. Först. 117, 11.

**befōn**, *add to I*: (1 a) with non-material object: of manegum myngungum we befengun (perstringimus) feawa, Chrd 8, 19; (1 f) *ensnare*: þæt hi befengon (caperent) hine, Mk. xii, 13, West Saxon Gospels. See also færbifongen.

**beforan**, *add to A I 1 a*: beforum monnum, Past. 449, 9; *add to B II*: hi secgað beforan fela þinga, swa hit æfter agæð, Gr. D. 296, 21; *add*: B III *of rank*: swa micle swa se bið beforan, *as much as that man is of higher rank*. Past. 435, 27.

**beg**, *see* heorotbeg.

**begān**, *add*: III 9 *confess*: ne mæg . . . se scrift geseon . . . hwæþer him mon soð þe lyge sagað . . . þonne he þa synne bigæð, Cri. 1307.

**begang**, *add to* (3): superstitious or magical practice: se þe lufige þisses galdres begang, ZfdA xxxiii, 73, 14. *See also* ymbbegang.

**begēat**, *read* begeat.

**begeng**, *see* eftbigengo.

**begengness**, *see also* landbegengness.

**begēomerian**, *add*: se þe . . . his gyltas begeomerað, Nap. 75.

**bēgian**, *delete, in citation read* gebiegodyst.

**begilpan**, *probably read* B. 2006, *see* gilpan I 7.

**begīmen**, *add*: poenitentiae obseruationibus, dædbote begymenum, Chrd. 106, 31.

**begīming**, *add*: obseruationibus, on begimingum, Ps. Roy. lxxvi, 13.

**begitan**, *add to* (1 a): (α) *get a wife*: wif begeat, Gen. 1130; (β) *get, bring home*: begyte he þa bade ham, L.O.D. 3; (γ) *object non-material*: freondscipe begitan, An. 480; *add to* (5): hie begeton feowertig bearna, Sat. 474; gewundod, þæt he ne mæge bearn begytan, Ælf. 65, v.l.; *add*: (6) *where the subject is not personal, of strong, painful agencies*: þa hie se fær begeat, B. 1068; hine wig begeat, B. 2872; hie begeat wite, Gen. 2569; mec wraþe begeat fromsiþ frean, Wife's Complaint 33; ealles longaþes þe mec begeat, id. 41; mec begeat nearo nihtwaco, Seaf. 6; fram þære costunge sares and yfeles þe hi begeat, Ps. Par. cvi, 38; cxviii, 28.

**begitan**, *gains, see* rihtebegitan.

**begitend**, *add*: se bið mildheortnesse begytend, Verc.-Hom. 57, 47.

**begitenness**, f. *acquisition*: adeptione, ob begitenysse, Archiv cc, 197.

**begriwan**, *cf.* forgriwan.

**begyldan**, *add*: deaurato, bigyldum, Ps. V. xliv, 10 (and related glosses).

**behāt**, *add to compounds* feohbehat.

**behealdan**, *add*: Va *restrain*: iugibus disciplinis constringantur, beon fæstlice behealdene mid steorum, Chrd. 54, 21.

**behēfedness**, behēfness, *see also* nidb.

**behēflic**, *see also* hefli *in Suppl.*

**behēfþ**, f. *need: see citations under* bestuddian *and* becearcian.

**behegian**, v. *fence*: sum hiredes ealdor wæs, þe het settan wineard, and hine behegode, Hml. P. i, 248, 5.

**behelian**, *see also* unbeheled.

**behīpan**, *take here* behypan *in Dict. and add*: II *heap up*: and hefige byrðene him on bæc behypð, Hml. P. ii, 499, 57.

**behleonian**, v. *to cover (a thing) by leaning something against it*: and þa byrgenne mid micclum stane betyndon and behleonedon, Verc.-Hom. 42, 359. v.l.

**behlēotan**, v. *assign by lot*: þa behluton hi hit sona to Ionan, MLR xvii, 166 (from MS. Cott. Cleop. B. xiii, f. 51ᵛ).

**behlīgan,** add: ðeh þe man hwylces yfeles belige, Hml. Warn. 4, 1.

**behlȳpan,** ? delete, read in citation behlywed, protected.

**behwilfan,** add: mid gestreonum þe heofon behwylfeð, Verc.-Hom. 50, 1; ðam welum . . . ðe heofon behweolfeð abutan, Sal. K. 86, 3.

**behwirfan,** add to IV: barter: uestes quas reddere debent, non commutet, hi na ne behwyrfon þa reaf þe hi agifan sceolon, Chrd. 48, 23.

**behwīt,** participial adj. whitened: dealbatis, behwitum, Mt. xxiii, 27, Rush.

**behȳdedness,** add: in abditis, on behydednessum, Ps. Vit. xvi, 12; on behidednesse, Ps. Ar. loc. cit.

**beinsiglan,** v. seal: signata, beinsiglede, Ps. Roy., Hy. 6, 34 (similarly Ps. Spl., Ps. Ar.).

**beirnan,** add to II 2: in ebrietate incurris, þu an þæt druncen beyrnst, Chrd. 74, 30; Dei iram incurrere, Godes yrre on to beyrnanne, id. 109, 28; he ne bearn (v.l. georn) on synne, Gr. D. 22, 28.

**belǣdan,** add: quam intulit nox, þonne þe on belædde niht, Gn. 14, 3 (JV); irrogans, on belædende, id. 25, 2.

**belangian,** v. concern: hwæt belangað þæs þonne to eow, Sisam, Studies in the history of OE literature 211.

**belecgan,** add: cover (of a book): ic eom halgungboc, healde hine Dryhten, þe me fægere þus frætewum belegde, Nap. 35.

**belg,** add to compounds herþ-, smiþbelg.

**-belg, -bilg,** anger, see gebelg, eaþbilg.

**belgan,** add to compounds for-, in-, onbelgan.

**belimp,** add: forte, of belimpe, Chrd. 109, 26.

**belle,** add: hangigende bellan teon, Tech. ii, 118, 18; bellan ringan, id. 20.

**bellhring,** ringing of bells: swa man sceall laðian Godes folc mid bellhringcge, IP 229.

**belōcian,** v. behold: intende, beloca, Ps. Roy. xliv, 5.

**belūcan,** add to I a: and wige beleac wraðum feondum, Ben. Off. 91, 1; add: V b define: ic haligne gast beluce emne swa ecne swa is aðor gecweden fæder oððe freobearn, id. 88, 30; Hml. Warn. 137, 4. Cf. inbelucan.

**bemancian,** original of citation is si uideris brachia tua truncata.

**bemeldian,** ? delete, MS. has a above line, Hml. Warn. 4, 31.

**ben,** add to compounds feorhben.

**bēn,** see also forben.

**bēna,** add compounds fær-, friþbena.

**bencþel,** the meaning may be simply bench.

**bend,** add to compounds cyne-, ge-, hose-, leoþu-, orþanc-, synbend.

**-bēne,** see eaþbene.

**benorþan,** see also gemære I 1 a α.

**bēnsian,** add: pres. part. very frequent in Rtl., 46, 17, etc. See also gebensian.

**bēnyrþ,** substitute for meaning requested service of ploughing; cf. benrip, bedrip.

**bēodan,** add to I: (1 a) summon: hi budon him (sic) to gemote, Hml. S. xviii, 195; add to II: (1 a) with inf.: hi him budon drincan windrenc, Hml. Th. ii, 254, 16. Add to compounds fore-, in-, misbeodan; unforbodene.

**bēodendlic,** see forbeodendlic.

**bēodgereordu,** substitute: beodgereorde, n. banquet: næfre ge mid blode beodgereordu eowre þicgeað, Gen. 1518; he symlede æt his beodgereordum, Verc.-Hom. 96, 272.

**bēodlǣs,** delete, read in citation blodlese.

**bēodlāf,** add: ne he nanum hingriendum men mid his beodlafum ne gehealp, Verc.-Hom. 96, 269.

**bēolǣs,** see lǣs.

**bēon,** add to (2): (e) with adv. expressing motion: egrediantur, beon hi utweard, Chrd. 21, 28; id. 33; add to (3): hi gesawon Thesali of hiora horsum beon feohtende wið hie, Ors. S. 42, 33. Cf. gebeon.

**beonet,** bent grass: see PNE i, 28.

**beoneting,** place with bent grass: to bæneting riðe, CS i, 295, 9; PNE i, 28.

**bēor,** add: ofgeot mid strangan beore oþþe mid strangum ealað, Lch. ii, 314, 14.

**beorcragu,** birch-lichen: Lch. ii, 266, 14.

**beorg,** add compounds gemær-, gemot-, hearm-, mearc-, meox-, sealh-, weargbeorg.

**beorg,** protection, see also heafod-, healsbeorggold.

**Beorgford,** add: Bregford (v.l. Berghford), CS i, 100, last line, is perhaps the same place. Not Burford.

**beorghliþ,** add: the meaning seems to be burial mound in El. 787, Gen. 215.

**beorglic,** -lice, -ness, see geb.

**beorgsteall,** see borgsteall.

**beorht,** add: of voice: mid beorhtre stemne, Hml. Th. i, 422, 5. Add to compounds fræ-, freabeorht.

**beorhtian,** add to I: he glitenað swa steorra . . . ond beorhtaþ swa sunna, Verc.-Hom. 87, 178. See also gebeorhtian, gefreabeorhtian.

**beorhtness,** add: fulgura, beorhnyssa Ps. L. xcvi, 4; splendoribus, beortnessum, id. cix, 3.

**beorhtnian,** add: bertna ðu sune ðinne þætte sune ðin ðec geberhtna (Rush. berehtnað), Jn. xvii, 1, Lind.

**Beormas,** add: probably Karelians living close to the Lapps (Finnas), and having a similar language.

***bēos, *bēosuc,** bent grass, PNE i 30.

**bēothāta,** probably delete, see beohata.

**bēotian,** add: biatadae, Mt. ix, 30, Rush. See also onbeotende.

**bēotmæcg,** m. leader: Dan. 265.

**bera,** add: on beran del, CS i, 554, 29.

**beran,** add: fotlastas beran, take one's way, B. 846. Add to compounds a-, oferberan; adl-, briost-, corn-, ele-, den-, fiþer-, hagol-, lig-, scip-, stan-, unberende; disc-, feþer-, leoht-, tapor-, wæpenberend; blind-, dead-, eft-, in-, misboren.

**berbed,** see geberbed.

**berecorn,** delete in Suppl. all after tysones and see berian.

**berecroft,** see croft.

**berendlic,** add compounds cwealm-, cwild-, wolberendlic.

**berendlice,** see also forberendlice.

**berendness,** see toberendness.

**bergælfen,** add: recorded by Nowell, source unknown.

**berian,** v. strike: ptysones (feriente, Prov. xxvii, 22), berecorn berændae, Txts. 86, 790; berede to weleren, Hml. Warn. 40, 25 (= Hml. P. ii, 701, 446). See also gebered.

**berie,** add: a strong acc. pl. berig occurs Ps. Roy. lxxvii, 52 (Ps. Spl. byrig). Add to compounds ele-, eorþ-, hundes-, wedeberie.

**berisan,** v. be fitting: on swylcen styde swa þaerto berist, Hml. Warn. 141, 11; swa swa eowrum hade berist (v.l. for gerist), Fehr 70, 30.

**bersta,** see wiþerbersta.

**berstan,** delete II in Suppl., see byrstan below. Add to compounds ge-, ofberstan.

**besceadwian,** v. overshadow: obumbra, bescaduwa, Ps. Roy. cxxxix, 8 (and related glosses); and þæs hecsten mihte heo bescadewode, Anglica ii, 34, 177 (= Hml. Warn. 138, 5).

**bescēawigend,** m. spectator, Gn. (Archiv, cxcix, 19).

**bescēawod,** add: prudenter agat . . . in ipsis imperiis suis prouidus et consideratus, sy he snotor and wel besceawod on his dædum . . . sy he a foregleaw and wel besceawod on his gebodum, R. Ben. 121, 2; seo besceawode geornfulnyss gemetegað ealle þa missenlicnyssa þises lifes, Nap. 75, 19.

**bescēawodness,** add: glosses Sion, Ps. Roy., Ps. Cant. ix, 12.

**bescildian,** protect: defendentes, bescyldigende, Wyn. 94.

**bescrēadian,** add: v. scrape: bescreada þa rinda ealle utan, Lch. ii, 116, 3 (= Leonhardi 33, 35). MS. reads besoreada, hence Suppl. deletes.

**bescrȳdan,** v. clothe: oðre bescrydeð sumne hnacodne, Anglica ii, 27, 120 (= Hml. Warn. 136, 32).

**bescūfan,** add: precipitio deuolutus, an hryre besceofen, Chrd. 74, 24.

**bescyrung,** add to Dict.: exordinatio, bescirunge, JEGP lx, 446. (Word wrongly deleted in Suppl.).

**besēcan,** v. beseech: eall þæt ge beseceð æt mine fæder, Hml. Warn, 77, 25.

**besēon,** add to II 2: hine ofer eaxle besihð se dema to þam forwyrhtum, Wlfst. 256, 8; add to III: ea quae uera et optime credebatis, þa ðing þe ge beseoð and betst on gelyfað, Bd. i, 25; add: III a observe: beseoþ ge hine, Bd. ii, 2.

**besēon,** sprinkle, add: beseah biterum ligum, ASPR vi, 65, 242.

**besēondlic,** see unbeseondlic.

**besibb,** adj. related: hire neamagen þe hire besibbe wæron, Anglica ii, 39, 225 (= Hml. Warn. 139, 4).

**besmītan,** see also unbesmiten.

**besmitenness,** in Suppl. read after l. 2 colludio: colludium, turpis ludus, Corp. Gl. H. 35, 643. Cf. flæscbesmitenness.

**besorēadian**, *delete, see* bescredian *above.*

**besprengan**, add: *bespatter: ne plantas humidior uia spargat,* þæt on þam fuhtan wege ne beon heora fet besprengde, Chrd. 64, 36.

**bestuddian**, v. *study, be concerned about:* ac Martha . . . bestuddede þa lichamlice behefðen, *Anglica* ii, 15, 7 (= Hml. Warn. 134, 10).

**beswāpan**, *add to* I: ic Herode in hyge bisweop, Jul. 294.

**beswican**, *add to* III: *frustratis animabus insidiis antiqui hostis,* gif we þurh deofles searocræftas wurðað æt þam sawlum beswicene, Chrd. 88, 12; *add to* V: ðurh gitsunge wearð beswicen Sawl . . . Ahab yfele wearð beswicen for Naboðes winearde, Hex. (Norman) 54.

**beswician**, add: *for* beswican IV: þa sende Antigones hiene selfne and . . . Polipercon . . . þæt hie hiene beswiceden, Ors. S. 146, 10.

**bēta**, *see* dæd-, fyrbeta.

**betācnian**, v. *signify:* se hand betacneð ure nydbehefe freond, Hml. Warn. 63, 33; 136, 20.

**betæcan**, *add to* I a: *sponsus ac sponsa a sacerdote legibus sponsentur,* mæssepreost sceal betæcan brydguman and bryde be lagum, Chrd. 81, 9.

**bētan**, *add to* I 1: ðyrelne kylle betan, Past. 469, 11; *add to* II a: bete man be cyninges munde, þæt is mid v pundum, ix Æthelred 5. *Add compounds* dæd-, fullbetan; unbeted.

**betellan**, *add to* I a 1: *nisi ad excusandum rationabiliter,* butan he hine mid gesceade betelle, Chrd. 85, 14; add: IV *prove one's claim to:* Ælfwine abbod hit betalde wið Siwarð abbod, Chart. Harm 263, 31; Cart. Mon. de Rames. i, 188; iii, 38; V *demonstrate:* ond for þan ne mæig nan man betellen, þæt on eallen Godes gesceaften beo aht, Hml. Warn. 140, 33; we habbeð beteald þæt yfel nis nan þing, id. 143, 10.

**bētendness**, *see* gebetendness.

**betera**, *see also* andergilde *and* gebetron.

**bētere**, *see* dædbetere.

**beterung**, *see also* gebeterung.

**betogenness**, sense is rather *frequency of accusation,* cf. ontygness.

**betrendan**, v. *roll: uoluto,* betr[e]ndum, Hy. Surt. 96, 3 (v.l. awyltum, Gn. 79, 2, JV).

**bētung**, *see also* gebetung.

**betwēoh**, *add to* A I 1 a: *intra (tenentis) manus,* betwuh hondum, Past. 241, 12; *add to* A II: he betweoh gebedum his lif geendode, Bd. iii, 12; B II 2: *note in preceding passage v.l.* betwih gebedes word.

**betwēohceorfan**, v. *cut between: intercedentis* (for -cid-), betweohceorfendes, Ps. Ar. xxviii, 7.

**betwēohs**, *add to* II 2: betwux twam tidum, Ap. of Tyre XI (Goolden 16, 17).

**betwēohsfæc**, delete, basic MS. reads *tantum* (taken as *tanto) interuallo,* betwux 'swa miclum' fæce.

**betwyxsendan**, *see* A. xiii, 373, 104.

**betȳnan**, *delete* II a, *in citation MS. reads* bemiþ; *add to* III: (c) *render unreceptive of:* he betyneð þa eagan fram gesyhðe and þa earan fram gehyrnesse, Verc. Först. 90, 5; (d) *shut (of a book):* swilce man ane boc betine, id. 117, 11.

**beþettan**, v. *? foment:* beþete þæt heafod mid, Lch. iii, 90, 15.

**beþrid**, participial adj., *pressed: pressus,* Archiv cxvii, 21.

**beþyrfing**, f. *lack: indigentia,* Archiv cc, 198.

**bewǣcan**, note bewehtum *v.l.* to gewæhtum *in* An. Ox. 5350; *see* A. xxx, 130.

**bewealcan**, v. *involve: nisi alios secum conetur inuoluere,* butan he gehicge þæt he oþre mid him bewealce, Chrd. 74, 33.

**bewēlan**, v. *infect, pollute: infecta est terra,* bewoeledu wæs eorþe, Ps. Jun. cv, 38. *Perhaps the forms* beweledne *and* bewelde *given under* bewillan *rather belong here.* [Cf. wōl].

**bewenian**, translate the citation B. 2035 *a noble offspring of the Danes splendidly entertained* (with reference to *he* 2034). *See also* dryhtbearn.

**bewēorpan**, *add to* I: druncennys bewyrpð (*deicit*) þa sawla an synne, Chrd. 74, 17.

**bewerung**, note Latin word translated in last two passages is *tutamentum.*

**bewillan**, *see also* unbewilled.

**bewillan**, *roll,* cf. bewelan.

**bewilwan**, *add:* III *figuratively:* on synnum bewyled, Festschrift Liebermann 55, 17.

**bewindan**, *add:* heafe bewindan, Gn. Ex. 149.

**bewitan**, *add to* I: *scito temetipsum,* bewite þe sylfne.

**bewrencan**, *see also* fægen 2 c.

**bewrēon**, *see also* inbewreon.

**bewreþian**, v. *support:* wundrum bewreþed, Rid. 84, 22.

**bewrigenness**, *add:* þa wæs seo bewrigennys onweg anumen, Wyn. 11; þa wæs seo swearte bewrigennys aworpen fram his eagum, id. 14.

**bewritan**, for sense *score round* add: ga to ðære wyrte and bewrit hi abutan mid anum gyldenan hringe, Lch. i, 112, 22.

**bewuna**, *add:* he þæt feoh to sellanne næfde his here swa hie bewuna wæron, Ors. S. 116, 15.

**bicce**, read in Suppl. *canicula* (WW 380, 33).

**biccen**, *delete.*

**bicen**, *see* treowbicen.

**bicnan**, *add to compounds* in-, tobicnan.

**bicnung**, *see also* forebicnung.

**bid**, *substitute* bid, *in phrase* on bid wrecan, *compel to stop, bring to bay:* B. 2962; Rid. 4, 3. (Cf. bidfæst, bidsteall, anbid, onbid).

**biddan**, *add to* II a 2: he bæd þone halgan wer sumne dæl eles, Hml. Th. ii, 178, 16. *Add to compounds* tobiddan.

**biddend**, m. *petitioner: petitor,* Scint. 32, 3.

**Biedcan ford**, *add:* not Bedford.

**bifigendlic**, adj. *to be trembled at:* an þam byfgendlican (*tremendo*) dæge, Chrd. 93, 27. *See also* heofigend *below.*

**bīgan**, *bend, add compounds* ge-, underbigan; tobigende; ofgebiged.

**bigegness**, *probably always for* begegness.

**bigeng**, *see also* eftbigengo.

**bigenga**, *add compounds* eorþ-, feoh-, rodbigenga.

**bigenged**, *see* heofonbigenged.

**bigengness**, *see* eorþbigengness.

**bigspæc**, *retain and add: supplantationem,* bygspæc, Ps. Spl. xl, 10; bigspæc Ps. Sal. (Ps. Roy. bygswæc, Ps. Tib. bygswec, *? for* beswic).

**bigstandan**, *add:* Verc.-Hom. 35, 296, v.l.

**bil**, *add to compounds* fodderbil.

**bilding**, *see* forþbilding.

**bilewit**, *see also* unbilewit.

**billere**, *add: water-cress.*

**bime**, *delete* II, tessera, *signal, is taken as* trumpet (*see* Blaise, *Dict. Lat.–Français des Auteurs Chrét.*).

**bindan**, *add to* IV a: ne binde þe seo racetæah, Gr. D. 214, 11. *See also* bunden, searubunden.

**bing**, *hollow:* to binguuellan CS i, 295, 27. *See* PNE i, 35.

**binnan**, *see also* þærbinnan.

**\*bircen**, *birch-copse,* PNE i, 36.

**\*bircett**, *birch-copse,* PNE i, 36.

**birdling**, *see* frumbirdling.

**birg**, *see* gebirg.

**birgan**, *add to compounds* inbirgan.

**birhtan**, *note past* birhtode, Mod. Phil. i, 601, 8.

**birnan**, *add compounds* sin-, unbirnende; þurhburnen.

**bisceop**, *add:* in Lind. often with -*b,* Jn. xviii, 26, etc. *Add compounds* efen-, fore-, heafod-, heahbisceop.

**bisceopealdor**, *add:* Hml. P. i, 250, 40.

**bisceophādþegnung**, f. *office of a bishop:* þa he ða bysceophadþenunge dyde, Bd. iii, 23, v.l.

**bisceophālgung**, f. *consecration of a bishop:* þa þe æt bisscophallgunge in witscipe stonde, Bd. i, 27, v.l.

**bisceoprice**, *add:* II *episcopal demesne:* mine biscopriche binnen Lundene and buten Lundene, Chart. Whit. 4, 11; 16, 3.

**bisceopstæf**, *add:* m. *bishop's staff:* of scs. Basilius toðe and of his biscopstafe, Förster, *Reliquienkultus* 76, 76.

**bisceopung**, *add: absque confirmatione,* butan bisceopunge, Chrd. 50, 5.

**bisceopweorod**, n. *bishop's band of men:* mid ealle his bisceopweorode (v.l. campwerede), Bd. iii, 24.

**bisceopwyrt**, *on sense see* A. xli, 130, n. 5. Cf. feldbisceopwyrt.

**bisceopwyrtel**, *on sense see* A. xli, 138, n. 3.

**bisen**, *see also* gelicbisen.

**bisenian**, add to I: *give example in respect to:* heo hym bysnode (v.l.) mid godre gedrohtnunge to Godes þeowdome, Hml. S. ii, 125; bisnian to godum weorcum, Hept. 77, 41.

**bisgian**, *see also* forebisgian.

**bisgung**, *see also* modbisgung.

**bisig**, *add to compounds* legbisig.

**bismerian**, *add:* with dat., he arn . . . bysmrigende þæs dryes yfeldædum, Hml. Th. ii, 414, 26.

**bisnere**, *see* gebisnere.

**bīspæc**, *see* biswæc.

**biswæc**, *treachery*: *supplantationem*, bygswæc, Ps. Roy. xl, 10 (Ps. Tib. bygswec, Ps. Spl. bygspæc, Ps. Sal. bigspæc). Cf. biswic.

**bītan**, *see also* gebitan; hungorbiten.

**bite**, *see also* hæfern-, sweordbite.

**bitel**, *see also* slegbitel.

**biter**, *add to* II: seo ehtnys bið ealra biterost, Hml. Th. ii, 542, 28.

**biterlic**, *add* Hml. S. xxiii, 250.

**bitrum**, adv. *bitterly*, *sorely*: bitrum gebunden, El. 1244.

**bizant**, m. *a coin*: *philippos. i, nummos bizanteos*, bizantas, Prud. 548.

**blāc**, *add*: andwlitu geolwe blac... reade wan, Lch. ii, 348, 16.

**blācernlēoht**, n. *lamplight*: þæs blacernes leoht næs gesyne ... he geseh eft þæt blacernleoht, Vis. Lfc. 54.

**blǣc**, *add to* II: blec, Txts. 44, 139.

**blǣcþa**, *substitute*: *a skin-disease: uitiligo*, blectha, Txts. 104, 1069; 107, 2123. Cf. Münchener Studien zur Sprachwissenschaft xxii, 5.

***blǣcþorn**, *black-thorn*, PNE i, 37.

**blǣd**, *add compounds* ear-, leacblæd.

**blǣdan**, *blow*, *see also* geblædan.

**blǣstan**, *add to* II: ic geseah þæt þæt fyr wolde blæstan ofer ealne middaneard, Wyn. 31; id. 27; id. 98.

**blǣstm**, *blast*: þæra liga blæstm, Verc.-Hom. 47, 51.

**blandan**, *see also* geblandan; unblanden.

**blātan**: *read in citation* hygewælm astah.

**blāwan**, *add to* I: I a *to have wind blowing in it* (of a place): seo dene wæs ... mid hagol blawende, Hml. Th. ii, 350, 9; *add to* II 3: bytte blawan fulle windes, Hml. S. xxxiv, 319. *See also* geond-, inblawan.

**blāwende**, participial adj., *blustering, windy*: blawende lencten, Archiv cxx, 298, 19.

**blāwere**, *see also* horn-, oreblawere.

**blēod**, *see* gebleod.

**blēoh**, *Suppl. ll. 4–5 read* bleo geefenlæce. *Add to compounds* goldbleoh.

**blere**, *note*: equation with *onyx* is an error; see Phil. Quart. xlv, 435; on *blurus*, see A. xlviii, 388; cf. Beiblatt zur Anglia xvii, 296.

**blerian**, *see* ablered.

**bletsian**, *add*: I aα *pronounce benediction*: he hæfeð nu gemæssod, and bletsað nu þis folc, Vis. Lfc. 17; þonne ge bletsion Israhela folc, Hept., Num. vi, 23.

**bletsung**, *add to compounds* fant-, gebletsung.

**blician**, *add*: *martyrum candidatus exercitus*, martira bliciend werod, Ps. Sal., Hy. 10, 8.

**blindan**, *see* for-, geblindan.

**blindboren**, *add*: blindaborones, Rush.

**blindian**, *see* of blindian.

**blinnan**, *add to compounds* ofblinnan.

**blinnedness**, *see* ablinnedness.

**bliss**, *see also* idelbliss.

**blissfull**, adj. *happy* (of a period): blisful gear, Hml. Warn. 91, 14; 20.

**blissian**, *add*: I a *applaud*: *plaudite*, blissiað, Bl. Gl. 254; III *with prep.*: hi for hire hæle blyssodon, Hml. S. vii, 281. *See also* efen-, em-, mid-, oferblissian; ungeblissod.

**blīþe**, *add to compounds* efen-, gemyndbliþe.

**blīþheort**, *add to* I: Verc.-Hom. 85, 139; *add to* II: næs he ælmesgeorn ne bliðheort, id. 96, 264.

**blīþian**, v. *delight* (trans.): *delectasti*, bliðgodest, Ps. Sal. xci, 5. Cf. gebliþian.

**blōdiorn**, *flow of blood*: *a proflunio sanguinis*, from bladiorne, Mk., p. 3, 7, Lind.

**blōdlǣs**, f. *blood-letting*: to higna blodlese, Txts. 449, 67; þurh ða blodlæse, Lch. ii, 210, 18.

**blōdlǣte**, f. *blood-letting*: æt blodlætan, Lch. ii, 16, 8.

**blōdlǣting**, f. *blood-letting*: on þa tid is blodlætincg forboden, E.S. lxix, 331, 25.

**blōdorc**, m. *sacrificial vessel*: *simpuuium*, blotorc, blodorc, Prud. 673.

**blōdspīwung**, f. *spitting of blood*: *emptoicos* (i.e. *haemoptyicos*), blodspuinga, OEG 73 b, 24; *see also* blōtspīung.

**blōdwracu**, f. *revenge for blood*: Verc.-Hom. 28, 250, v.l.

**blōstm**, *add*: lilian blostman oþþe rosan bræþ, Hml. S. xxxiv, 104.

**blōt**, *add*: ? *error for* blece, see Neophilologus xv, 273.

**blōtan**, *add*: þæt hie sceolden for hie heora godum blotan, Qrs. S. 184, 5.

**blōtorc**, *see* blodorc *above*.

**blōwan**, *add*: bloewð, Ps. Jun xci, 13. *See also* edblowan.

**bōc**, *beech*, ? *add beech-mast*: *si glandes uel fagina non sint*, gif ne byð ne æceren ne boc ne oðer mæsten, Chrd. 15, 10.

**bōc**, *book*: *add to* I a 2: se cyng gebecte ðæt land Æðelstane ... Ecgferð gebohte boc and land æt Æðelstane, Chart. Rob. 90, 25; se cing het þone arcebisceop boc settan and Æðelstane boc and land betecan, id., 162, 8; *add to* II: ðas halgan beoc, Txts. 175, 7, 16. *Add to compounds* cneores-, cræft-, cwid-, færeld-, freols-, frofor-, gean-, halgung-, heals-, healsung-, læce-, lar-, mynster-, nam-, siþ-, sealm-, sumerboc; fifbec.

***bōcen**, adj. *grown with beech-trees*, PNE i, 39.

**bōcfel**, *note*: lemma *bargina* is due to confusion of that word (sense unknown) with *pergamena*.

**bōchūs**, *add*: *bibliothecam*, OEG 4, 406.

**bōcrǣde**, *reading of books*: ond se biscop wes ana in his gebedhuses stowe, þær he bocredan (lectioni) ond gebedum werc sealde, Chad 170, 95.

**bōcscyld**, *delete, read in citation* (= Chart. Whit. 60, 12) bohscyldes.

**bōcung**, *substitute*: f. *conveyance by deed*: ic ... geaf ... anæ mylnæ ... ond þone hagan ... to þære bocungæ þæ þæt land gæbocod is, CS ii, 486, 26.

**bod**, *delete citation in* Dict. of Ælfc. Gl. 80 (= WW 164, 3), MS. has boga on cine, *cf.* boga V.

**boda**, *add to compounds* fore-, gebyrdboda.

**bodan**, *see* botm in Suppl.

**bodere**, *see also* forebodere.

**bodian**, *add compounds* a-, fræbodian.

**bodig**, *see also* foranbodig.

**bodung**, *see also* larbodung.

**boga**, *add to* V *citation above under* bod; *add to compounds* sunnboga.

**bogefōdder**, *substitute for meaning* case for bow, *cf.* FL 99.

**bōgtimber**, *substitute for meaning* building material.

**bōh**, *citation* Rid. 1, 11 (= Wulf and Eadwacer 11) *belongs to* II (boh *is not used of the human arm*).

**bōhscild**, m. *curved shield?*, *see* bocscyld *above*.

***bol**, *round hill*, PNE i, 40.

**bōl**, *add*: *necklace* (cf. WW 107, 27).

***bola**, *tree-trunk*, PNE i, 41.

**bold**, *add to* I: se bisceop sceal habban þa preostas on his agenum bolde (*domo*), Chrd. 44, 35. *Add to compounds* ealdorbold.

**boldweard**, = botlweard, Ælfc. Gr. Z. 318, 12, note.

**bolla**, *note*: catus, cratus *are for* cadus, crater (*or both for* cyathus?)

**bolster**, *note*: the gloss *compluta* (= *conpluita, rained on*), *bolster*, is due to the error *plumis* (*for* pluuiis) *repleta, full of feathers*, which glosses *conpluta*, Corpus Glossary C 743.

**bor**, *dasile, desile are errors for* rasile.

***bor**, *hill*, PNE i, 41.

**-bora**, *add*: feorh-, leoht-, witumbora.

**borcian**, *MS. reads in citation* boncade, wancode.

**bord**, *add to compounds* steorbord; utanbordes.

**bord**, *add to* III *in* Dict.: *carinam*, bord, OEG 28, 276.

**bordstǣð**, *substitute for meaning* side of ship.

**boren**, participial adj., *of such and such birth*: sy swa boren swa he sy, *whatever his birth* is, II Eadmund 1; comp. borenra, *more highly born*, Ælf. 11, 5. *See also* æþel-, bet-, betst-, welboren.

**borgsteall**, ? *path up a hill*: WW 205, 36, cited in Suppl. s.v. burgsteall; *also in place-names*, see PNE i, 42.

**borh**, *add to* I: I a *what is given as security*: fo to þam borge, se þe þæs weddes waldend sy, Wifmannes Beweddung 6; *add to* II: *of a body of persons*: her swutelað seo gewitnes and seo borh þe þær set wæron (*names follow*), Chart. Rob. 164, 7. *See also* godborh.

**borhfæstan**, *see* geborhfæstan.

**borian**, *add*: *terebrantes*, borgenti, Txts. 111, 14.

***bōs**, *cowstall*, PNE i, 43.

**bōt**, *add to compounds* dolg-, fæhþ-, feoh-, hloþ-, sarbot.

**bōtian**, *see also* gebotian.

**bōtian**, *see also* abotian.

**botl**, *in l. 7 in Suppl. read* 443 *for* 433.

*boþltūn, collection of buildings, PNE i, 45.

box, box, see also husel-, gewyrtbox.

braccas, add: bracas, lumbare, JEGP lx, 448, XIII, 4.

bracu, see fearnbracu.

brād, add to II 1: hring on heofonum brædre þonne sunne, Ors. S. 234, 9; add to compounds efenbrad.

brād, width of the hand: swa mycel swa god hande brad, Vis. Lfc. 73.

brādelēac, add: wild thyme (but cf. DP 69).

Brāden, Brǣden, add: not Bredon but Braden (cf. Bradenstoke).

brādian, substitute: I broaden refl.: hit hlifað up ond bradað hit, Wulfst. 262, 7, v.l.; II extend: ond wæs from þæm heofone bradiende niþer oþ þa eorþan, Ors. S. 234, 10. See also gebradian.

brādþistel, add: eringius, bradþis(tel), JEGP lx, 446, x, 28.

brǣdan, extend, add to compounds onbrædan.

brǣde, meat, cf. hrycgbrædan, lendenbræd.

brǣdisen, substitute for meaning pen (lit. tablet-iron). Cf. FL 87.

brǣdness, see leohtbrǣdness.

brǣgd, see also freabrægd.

brægden, see also ge-, leasbrægden.

brægdenlice, see gebrægdenlice.

brǣw, see also eagbræw.

brand, add: many regard brand Healfdenes, B. 1020, as a kenning for Hrothgar. For another view see JEGP xlii, 82.

brandōm, delete, take as alternative glosses, see brand II a.

branwyrt, delete, MS. has brunwyrt, q.v.

brēad, see also symbelbread.

breahtmung, add: flickering (of eyelid), cf. bearhtm.

brēaþ, add: see breþel.

breca, see also hadbreca.

brecan, I 2 a in Suppl. (Sal. 132) is doubtful, read perhaps sprecað or wrecað. Add to I i y: to brocenan beorge, CS ii, 245, 34. See also full-, inbrecan; healfbrocen.

brecþa, note: see Language xliii, 452.

bred, add to compounds fotbred.

breden, add: pluteus, bredenes (so MS.) beddes inneweard, WW 153, 44.

brēdende, see also leasbregdende.

bregd, see gebregd.

bregdan, add to I 1 e: þonne bryt se lichoma on manigfealdum bleon, Verc.-Hom. 87, 173; ðæt deade flæsc . . . bryt on manig hiw, id. 100, 322. Add to compounds utæt-bregdan.

bregdness, see ge-, leasbregdness.

brēgendlic, terrible: Ps. Roy. xlvi, 3 (and related glosses).

brego, add: brego moncynnes, ASPR iii, 217, 79.

brēman, add: uoluntatem episcopi implere, þæs bisceopes gebod breman, Chrd. 18, 35.

brēmelhyrne, f. corner where there are brambles: on þa brembælhyrnan, CS ii, 94, 18.

brēmen, delete, read in citation breme, in Az. 142 bremen (see breman).

*brēmen, adj. grown with broom, PNE i, 49.

Bremes burh, the site is unknown.

*brēmling, place grown with bramble, PNE i, 49.

breneþ, perhaps rather = brȳneþ, makes brown.

brengness, see gebrengness.

breodian, the meaning is unknown.

brēostgird, add: very probably error for preostgird, cf. FL 9.

Breotenrice, add: swa he nu dagum Breotanrices fægran iglandes Eadwearde cyncge sealde, Chart. Rob. 194, 8.

brēoþan, add: bruðun (tabuerunt) ealle eardigende, Ps. Roy, Hy. 4, 15. [Cf. OED brethe.]

*brērig, adj. grown with briars, PNE, i, 50.

breting, f. breaking: fractione, in breting, Lk. xxiv, 35, Lind., Rush.

Bretwalda, see further Melbourne Historical Journal vi, 53.

breþel, adj. fragile, weak: swa breðel seo (MS þeo) swa þystel, Lch. i, 384, 14 (= ASPR vi, 126, 17). See also A. lii, 186.

brīdelgim, m. bridle-ornament: faleris, bridelgym uel hurst, OEG 28, 456.

brīdelhyrst, f. bridle-ornament: to be inferred from citation under bridelgim.

brim, add: El. 972 (cited s.v. fæþmian in Suppl.); to brimes aroðe, B. 28; magno æquore, micle brime, OEG 4, 15; freto, brime, 387; note masc. brimas, 331.

bringādl, ? error for hringādl, ringworm: wið micclum lice ond bringcadle, Lch. iii, 38, 24 (= Leonhardi 138, 11). Cf. E.S. xlii, 202.

bringelle, see onbringelle.

brinstān, m. brimstone: brynstanes stænc on helle, Hml. Warn. 143, 31.

briosa, discussed MLN li, 331.

brīostberende, glosses ubertate, Ps. Cant. ciii, 28.

britedness, see for-, tobritedness.

brīwan, v. prepare (of a poultice): genim linsæd, gegrind, briwe wið þam elmes drænce, Lch. ii, 66, 25.

brōc, brook, add to compounds mær-, mearcbroc, and see also hens.

brocenlic, adj. fragile: Hml. Bel. 130, 29. See also tobrocenlic.

brocian, see also wiþerbrocian.

brōcrīþ, f. small stream: east hwon to ðere brocriðe, CS ii, 358, 22.

brod, n. shoot, sprout: gramina, brod, Ps. Lamb., Hy. 6, 3 (cf. brodd and blome, Orrm 10772).

brōga, add to compounds hellewite-, sæbroga.

brogdenmǣl, substitute: adj. patterned (of swords): B. 1616, 1667; El. 759.

brogna, add: uilibine (i.e. culmine or uimine), brogene, OEG 3, 3.

broht, delete, read in citation broth, broþ, and cf. Lindsay, Corpus Glossary 184 (U 208).

brondstæfn, substitute for meaning high-prowed (i.e. brontstæfn).

brosniendlic, see also gebrosniendlic.

brosnodlic, adj. crumbling: Hml. Bel. 130, 28. See also unbrosnodlice.

broþhund, literally translates iutilis canis (WW 329, 38); iutta, iotta = broþ, cf. sohþa below; reference perhaps to a cooking utensil; WW 120, 21 has inutilis for iutilis, showing misunderstanding.

brōþor, add: twegra broþor (v.l. broþera) sunu and dohtor, Bd. i, 27; add to compounds fostor-, hornungbroþor, rihtgebroþor.

brōþorscipe, see also gebroþorscipe.

brōþorsliht, murder of a brother: (be) broðerslælte (sic), Ker, Catalogue 93.

brōþorþinen, delete, read in citation byrþerþinenn (so most MSS.).

brūcan, read in Wand. 44 giefstoles. Add to compounds onbrucan.

brūmiddel, space between the eyebrows: betuh bruwum, brumiddel, Kansas leaf.

brūn, add: used of arms and armour, and in the compounds brunecg, brunfag, the meaning is shining.

Brūnanburh, add: the site remains unknown, for many suggestions see Campbell, Battle of Brunanburh 60–80, and add Saga Book of the Viking Soc. xiv, 303.

brūneþa, read bruneþa.

brūnwyrt, in citation in Suppl. spimon = splenion, cf. DP 18, 306.

bryce, add: hy him bryce heoldon, they did him service (cf. healdan xi 4), Guth. 729. Add compound weoroldbryce.

bryce, fracture, see also heafodbryce.

brycg, add: to ðær stanenan bricge, CS iii, 113, 24. Add compounds eorþ-, wudubrycg.

brycggeweorc, add: uiatici fundatione (restauratione, 74, 16) pontis, C.D. iv, 65, 34.

brycgian, in first citation in Suppl. calabit perhaps rather = calcauit (cf. Aldhelm, Aenig. 19, 11).

brycmǣlum, delete, MS. has bretmælum in citation, see brytmælum in Suppl.

brȳdhūs, n. bridal chamber: thalamo, brydhuse, Ps. Ar. xviii, 6.

brȳdiguma, delete, MS. has brydguma.

brygd, see also gearobrygd.

bryne, add to compounds fyr-, hus-, mannbryne.

bryneness, perhaps delete, read hatum bryne (cf. bryne VI).

bryrdness, add to compounds gebyrdness.

brȳt, delete, MS. has bryd.

brȳtofta, delete, MS. has brytgifta uel bryde gifa.

brytsen, see gebrytsen.

**brytsnian,** *note* brytsmendum *is misread for* -niendum.

**brytta,** *add to compounds* fodder-, hlaf-, sinebrytta.

**Bryttas,** *add to I:* sg. Brytt: ne wearð an Bret (v.l. Brit) to lafe, Chr. 491.

**bryðen,** *add compound* sorgbyrþen.

**būan,** *add:* pp. (ge)bogen; *add to II:* anseld bugan, Guth. 1240; *see also* geargemearc *in Suppl. Add compounds* (ge)inbuan; heofonbuend.

**būc,** *add:* I a *trunk of the body:* his heafod hi drogon mid hospe geond þa burh, and his lima forbærndon, and þone buc, Hml. P. ii, 707, 559; heo (i.e. *the soul*) bið on þam buce wunigende, Hml. Bel. 86, 5. Delete III, take citations under II, one meaning of *buccula* in Late Lat. is *vessel.*

**bucca,** *see also* gatbucca *in Dict.*

**buclic,** adj. *goatlike: tragico,* buclice, OEG 28, 55.

**budda,** *see* scearnbudda.

**būend,** *add: inhabitatores,* þa buendan, Ps. Lamb., Hy.

**buend,** f., *see* landbuend.

**bufan,** *see also* þærbufan.

**būgan,** *add to compounds* oferbugan; wohbogen.

**būgendlic,** *see* forbugendlic.

**bugol,** *see* gebugol.

**bulberende,** add: *ornament-bearing.*

**bulluc,** *add:* to bulluces sole, CS ii, 245, 30.

**\*bult,** *heap,* PNE i, 57.

**bunden,** *substitute for meaning:* I *inlaid, adorned* (of swords, with reference to hilt or scabbard); *add:* B. 1285; cf. gebunden, B. 1531; II *well made* (of ships), B. 216.

**bundenness,** *see* gebundenness.

**bundenstefna,** *substitute:* adj. weak *with well made prow:* B. 1910.

**būness,** *see* ge-, landbuness.

**\*burgæsn, -æns,** *burial-place,* PNE i, 57.

**burgent,** *meaning uncertain:* ofer burgenta, El. 31.

**burgrod,** f. ? *clearing near a 'burh':* west on burhrode, ofer burhrode west, CS i, 467, footnote 10.

**burgsteall,** cf. borgsteall.

**burgwita,** *add:* Hermes wæs gehaten se yldesta burhwita on Romana byrig, Hml. P. ii, 737, 11; cf. id. 10.

**burh,** *add to II:* the dwelling of any man above the rank of ceorl is a burh, see Ælf. 40. *Add to compounds* eorþ-, friþ-, in-, licburh.

**burhbōt,** *add: Latin equivalents are* arx construenda, arcis (arcium) confectio, constructio, necessaria defensio contra hostes, edificatio, exercitium, instructio, iuuamen, munimen, munimentum, munitio, recuperatio, renouatio, restauratio, subsidium; urbium reparatio, iugis assolidatio; murorum reparatio; munitionis castellique auxilium; fossa aduersum inimicas facienda. *See also* s.v. fird, brycggeweorc, weallgeweorc.

**burhgeat,** *add to I:* gif ceorl geþeah þæt he hæfde . . . bellhus and burhgeat, Geþyncðo 2.

**burhgeatsetl,** *delete.*

**burhgeriht,** n. *town due:* of þam lande æt Nigon hidon . . . burhgerichtu, Chart. Rob. 236, 26; 238, 13.

**burhstrǣt,** f. *town road:* CS iii, 15, 11.

**burhware,** *see also* innan-, utanburhware.

**burne,** *add to compounds* fild-, gylde-, mylen-, win-, writolburne; *see also s.v.* cis.

**\*busc,** *bush:* Wiðibuscemære, C.D. iv, 13, 5; cf. PNE i, 64.

**būtan,** *add to A I 2 a:* buton his folgoðe and buton minum freondscipe, VI Æthelstan 11; *add to A I 3 a:* eallum frioum monnum . . . butan þeowum mannum, *to all free men . . . but not to slaves,* Ælf. 43; *add:* A III *with nom.:* buton we feowertig, Hml. S. xi, 74; *add to C II 1:* hy man gecnawan ne mæg, buton ðonne heo grewð, Lch. i, 98, 4; *add to C III 2:* ne can ic nænigne oþerne cræft buton þone, þæt ic mæg wyrta wel begangan, Gr. D. 180, 24.

**\*butt,** *tree-stump,* PNE i, 65.

**byccen,** adj. *of a goat:* Chrd. 48, 26 (*quoted in Suppl. s.v.* heorþa).

**bycgan,** *add:* V more generally *trade,* and hence *sell: care uendidit,* deore he hit bohte, i. sealde, *uile uendidit,* undeore he bohte, A. xli, 108, 74 (WW 130, 24).

**\*bycge,** *bend of a river,* PNE i, 72.

**bydel:** *add to I: preconibus,* bydelum, Prud. 331; *add:* I a *preacher:* on idel beoð þæs bydeles word, Hml. Th. i, 320, 26; I b *of things:* gedreccednyssa . . . synd ða bydelas þæs ecan forwyrdes, Hml. Th. i, 4, 12.

**bydelland,** n. *for* bydelæcer: bydeland, C.D. vi, 244, 8.

**byden,** *add:* of a topographical feature, *hollow:* of ðære bydene, C.D. iv, 108, 16.

**bygspæc,** *see* biswæc.

**bygu,** *see* gebygu.

**byht,** *see also* gebyhte.

**\*byld,** *dwelling,* PNE i, 73.

**Bylges lēag,** *add:* Billingsley, Sal., and Billesley, Worcs., have been suggested.

**bylgness,** *see* æ-, eaþbylgness.

**bȳran,** *see* gebyran.

**byrd,** *add to compounds* fan-, frumbyrd.

**byrdan,** *violate, see* ungeonbyrded.

**byrdan,** *burden, see past part.* gebyrd.

**byrdan,** *be born, see* edbyrdan.

**byrde,** *see* þolebyrde.

**byrdestre,** *for* embroideress *read* embroiderer, *and see* Archiv cxxiii, 418.

**byrdig,** *see* forbyrdig.

**-byrding,** *see* hyse-, inbyrding.

**byrdling,** doubtful if applicable to *testudo,* meaning in compounds is *offspring* (see frum-, in-byrdling). Cf. FL 67.

**byrdo,** *see* misbyrdo.

**byrduscrūd,** *delete, read in citation* beaduscrud.

**bȳre,** *this appears to be pl.* (? *from* bȳre m.). *See also* middelbyre.

**byre,** delete *storm:* Prud. 873.

**byrgedness,** *see* bebyrgedness.

**byrgen,** *add to II:* þa licþenunge . . . þære byrgene, Gr. D. 84, 6. *See also* gebyrgen.

**byrgenness,** f. *tomb:* swa ofte swa ge faren bi ricre monnæ burines, Hml. Bel. 124, 2.

**byrgland,** n. *land belonging to a burh:* Chart. Rob. 234, 16.

**byrian,** *add: in the sense of* gebyrian VI 2a: ælcum hlaforde bureð, ðæt he do his mannum heora bigleofan, Homl. A. 55, 127, v.l.; eow buræð, Hml. P. i, 485, 141, v.l.

**byrn,** *heat: aestus,* hæto uel byrn, Mt. xx, 12, Lind.

**byrne,** *burning,* add: *combustionem,* byrne, Rtl. 113, 16; etc.

**byrnete,** *barnacle: lolligo. i. piscis maritimi* (sic) *uno anno piscis, alio auis,* byrnete, Nap. 11.

**byrnhama,** m. *corslet:* ðinne byrnhomon billum heowon, Wald. 1, 17.

**byrnod,** *see* gebyrnod.

**byrnwiga,** *read* -wiga, *and add:* þa torras . . . þe ða byrnwigon (*armati iactores*) on stodan, Rypins, *Three Old English Prose Texts* 5, 18.

**byrst,** adj. ? *having the site of a land-slip:* oð þonæ brystæ del, CS ii, 94, 10.

**byrstan,** v. *roar: inimici rugientis,* fiondes byrstende, Rtl. 122, 14.

**byrstig,** *add:* II *suffering loss:* þa gode mænn synden byrstige ond gedrefde and unfere, Hml. Warn. 141, 38; 142, 18. (*Note:* citation in Suppl. is uncertain, see Studia Germanica Gandensia ii, 85.)

**byrþen,** *add to I 2:* ane boc unaberendlicre byrþenne (*ponderis pene importabilis*), Bd. v, 13; *cancel II 1, as in citation* byrþen *is due to dittography.*

**byrþincel,** *little burden: fasciculis,* byrðinclum, OEG 2, 193.

**byrþre,** *see* hysebyrþer.

**\*bysc,** *bush-thicket,* PNE i, 74.

**\*byxe,** *box-tree, box-thicket,* PNE i, 74.

**byrst(e),** *see* gebyrst, fiþerbyrste.

# C

**cā,** *jackdaw,* PNE i, 75; þis is genumen of Scireburnan . . . Cawuda healf, CS iii, 577, bottom.

**cādac,** *jackdaw,* PNE i, 75; Cadacahrygc, CS ii, 18, 21; Caducburne, Ekwall, *English River-names* 58.

**cæcepol,** *see* hæcewol *in Suppl.*

**cǣd,** *delete, see* ced.

**cǣfl,** add: *halter.*

**cǣg,** *delete cancellation of weak f.* cæge *in Suppl., see* Verc. Först. 128, 20, *and see also* hellecæge.

**cǣles,** f. *foot-covering: pediles,* cælise, A. xxxvii, 45.

**cæpse**, f. *box*: wyrcað ane niwe cæpsan eowrum lacum to fætelse, Nap. 12 (= Hml. P. ii, 691, 260). [Lat. capsa].

*****cærsen**, adj. *grown with cress*, PNE i, 76.

*****cærsing**, *cress bed*, PNE i, 76.

**cæstelweall**, m. *castle-wall*: swa swa mid strangen cæstelwealle, Hml. Warn. 134, 27.

**cāf**, *add*: *strenuous, strong*: strenui, cafe, Chrd. 52, 17; *fortes*, cafe, id. 74, 20.

**cāflice**, *add to* (2): *uiriliter*, caflice, Chrd. 40, 3; 94, 6; *strenue*, caflice, id. 53, 27; 93, 10. *Note equation with* uiritim (Prud. 573) *due to confusion with* uiriliter.

**calan**, *add*: se þearfa bemsende þæt him þearle col, Hml. S. xxxi, 911; he wreah ða nacodan þearfan þæt me ne cole, Archiv xci, 380, 18.

**Caldisc**, adj. *Chaldean*: Chaldea, þæt Caldisce, OEG xxviii, 118.

**cālend**, delete II.

**cālendcwide**, m. *number of months*: ðæt sie his calendcwide arunnen, Sal. 480.

**calu**, *add*: (3) *lacking vegetation*: on calwan hyll, CS iii, 341, 18.

**calwa**, *add to Suppl.*: an OE calwa, *baldness* (due to alopecia) is also possible.

**calwerclim, calwerclympe**: *possibly in both two words* calwer, clim (? climpe) *are intended*.

**camb**, *add*: II (3) apparently *bristling hair*: cristas cerebri, cambas cenepes, Prud. 947. *See also* wullcamb.

**camb**, *fauus, see* hunig-camb.

**camp**, *add*: militiae nostrae, ures gewinnes and compes, Rypins, *Three Old English Prose Texts* 3, 8.

**campian**, *see also* ellencampian.

**camplic**, *add*: arma militaria, camplice wæpen, Chrd. 63, 24.

*****canc**, *hill*, PNE i, 80.

**cancer**, *add*: gestanden mid cancre þære wunde, Gr. D. 279, 27.

**Candelmæssedæg**, *Candlemas day*: on ðam feowerteogoðan dæge fram his acennednysse þe we cweþað . . . Candelmæssedæg, Nap. 12 (= Hml. P. i, 467, 95).

**canondom**, substitute for meaning *canonical prescription*, and *add*: be mannes gewrihtum hit (i.e. *the due penance*) man mot secan æfter canondome, IP 172.

**canoniclif**, n. *canonical foundation*: ne beo æfre ænig canoniclif þæt sundercræfta sumne ne cunne, IP 255.

**canticsang**, *for* cantic: cantico, canticsange, Ps. Cam. xci, 4.

**capitelari**, *capitulary*: Chart. Rob. 228, 13; 250, 18.

**capitol**, *add to II*: to capitule (*ad capitulum*) cuman, Chrd. 28, 9; fram capitule arisan, id. 29, 17; capitul habban, id. 43, 10; arisende fram capitule, A. xiii, 390; id. 385, 283; id. 388, 325. *See also* mæssecapitel.

**carc**, *care*, delete.

**carcian**, v. *have the trouble* (of doing something): nu ne carcað heo to befleon Herodes ehtnysse, *Anglica* ii, 37, 207 (= Hml. Warn. 138, 29). *See also* becarcian.

**carful**, *add to I*: ða dioflu drifað þa cearfullan sawla to helle, Verc. Först. 112, 4; *add to II*: ða cearfullan cæge (*key of Hell*), id. 15.

**Carrum**, *add*: now known to be *Carhampton*, Somerset.

**casebill**, discussed FL 122; Prud. 438 (note); A. xxi, 66; lxx, 5, 59.

**cāsering**, *add*: in uno autem argenteo xviii pendingas, xx argenteos xx cesaringas, *Philologica Pragensia* viii, 306.

*****cassucen**, adj., *overgrown with hassock or sedge*, PNE i, 81.

**caulic**, *a kind of medicine*: do caulices on ii dropan oððe þry, Lch. ii, 272, 22.

**cawel**, *read* cāwel.

**cāwelwyrm**, *add*: caflwyrm, FL 34; *and see* cealfwyrt.

**cawl**, *cf.* æwul *in Dict. and Suppl.*

**cawlic**, *a cabbage regarded as of healing properties*: Lacnunga xxix (= Lchd. iii, 24, 3; Leonhardi 132, 1; Grattan and Singer, *Anglo-Saxon Magic and Medicine* 122); *brassica*, caulic, DP 53.

**cēac**, *add*: as legal term *ordeal*: synnigne mon gefo in ceace, Ine 37; hine mon bedrifeð to ceace, id. 62.

**ceace**, *trial*, delete (cf. ceac, *ordeal*).

**ceace**, *cake*, delete, *in citation MS. reads* ceclum (*see* cycel).

**ceacga**, *brushwood*: on ceacgan seað, CS ii, 532, 6; PNE i, 83.

**ceafer**, *see also* eorþceafer.

**ceafl**, *l. 4* ceaclum *is misread for* ceaflum.

**Cealchȳþ**, *add*: clearly *Chelsea*.

**ceald**, adj., *add*: note figurative uses, B. 2396, Soul and Body 15.

**cealde**, *add*: II *bitterly*: cræfta gehwilc byþ cealde (*accerbior*) forgolden, Lunds Universitets Årsskrift lii (1956), 2, 14.

**cealdu**, *see* sincealdu.

**cealfian**, *see also* miscealfian.

**cealfwyrt**, *in citation read probably* cawelwyrm, *cf.* FL 34.

**ceallian**, *see also* Medieval Literature *and* Civilization (ed. D. A. Pearsall and R. A. Waldron), 94.

**cēapland**, n. *purchased estate*: ic an min wif al ðat ceaplond, Chart. Whit. 68, 6.

**cēaptoln**, f. *toll on buying and selling*: Chart. Harm. 412, 4.

**cear**, *delete, read in both citations* ceargum.

**cearc**, *delete, see* cyninggeniþla.

**cearcian**, *see also* becearcian.

*****ceare**, *turn, bend*, PNE i, 84; *OE perhaps in river-name* Cearwyllan (loc.), *Cherwell*, CS ii, 265, 24.

**cearig**, *add*: cearig emb, *anxious about*, Hml. Warn. 137, 14.

**cearricge**, *add*: but possibly a plant, *senon* = sinon.

**cēaslunger**, adj. *quick to quarrel*: se hordere sceal beon syfre and na ceaslunger (*contentiosus*), Chrd. 19, 12.

**ceastel**, *heap, see* stanceastel *in Suppl. and below*.

**ceasterlēod**, pl. -leode, *citizens*: God wæs swiðe yrre þære ceasterleode, Vercelli M., f. 108ᵛ, 1; þær ure bidaþ ure ceasterliode, id. f. 72ᵛ, 15.

**ceasterwyrhta**, *add*: the lemma *polymitarius* has been falsely connected with πόλις.

**cecil**, *delete, and take citation under* cēcil, *cake; see* Lindsay, *Corpus Glossary* 171.

**cecin**, *delete, MS.* æcin *also doubtful*.

**ced**, *delete, both MSS.* (Oxford and Brussels) have ceol.

**Cedarland**, *Kedar*: Ps. L. cxix, 5.

**ceddran**, *delete, read in citation* (= BM 148, 25) æddran, *veins*.

**cedelc**, *on meaning cf.* DP 60.

**cellod**, *the meaning is unknown; in Fin. 29, Hickes has* celæs.

**cēlness**, *see also* edcelness.

**celod**, *Fin. 29, Hickes has* celæs.

**cēne**, *see also* searucene.

**cēne**, adv., *delete, in citation read* belliger *as lemma*.

**cennan**, *add to I*: note use of *cennende* to gloss nascentia(e), Ps. V., Hy. 7, 24, 45; 8, 11; germinantia, Ps. Sal., Hy. 7, 76; *add to II*: for team cennan (*see* team III 1): gif he cenne ofer I scira, II Æthelred 8, 3; swa hwær swa man to cende, id. 9. *See also* geedcennan; frumcennende; eorþ-, frum-, heofon-, niwcenned.

**-cennedness**, *see* forcennedness.

**cenning**, m. *offstring, see* frumcenning.

**cenning**, *add*: II *as legal term* = team III 1, *only in Latin contexts*: nolumus ei permittere cenningam aliquam, Hundredgemot 4, 1; Leges Henrici 64, 6 a. *See also* miscenning.

**cenningstān**, *delete, see* FL 134.

**Centingas**, *men of Kent*: Chr. 1011, 1052. *See also* East-, Westcentingas.

**cēol**, *l. 2 in Suppl., add after* ciula: ? *for* nauicula; *delete reference to* Gr. D. (*see* ceole *below*). *See also* þrireþre.

**ceole**, *add to II*: *chaos*, pæð miclum cele (sic), Lk. xvi, 26, Rush.; *rimis patentibus*, geoniendum þam ceolum, Gr. D. 248, 27.

**ceolwærc**, *pain in throat*: Lch. ii, 312, 2.

**ceorcing**, *delete, MS. probably reads* ceorung; *note lemma taken as* quaestio.

**ceorfan**, *add to II*: ge soecað mec to ceorfanne uel to cwellane, Jn. viii, 37, Rush. *Add compounds* betweoh-, fore-, oferceorfan; foreceorfend.

**ceorl**, *add to II*: fram þam dysigum ceorla folce wæs weorþod se hæþena God, Gr. D. 121, 19. *See also* æcer-, dirne-, Sotceorl.

**ceorlisc**, *in citation* Wrt. Voc. 50, 27 (= WW 170, 37) *MS. reads* ceorlic (A. viii, 451).

**cēosan**, *see also* uncoren.

**ceoselstān**, last citation in *Dict.* (= WW 113, 18) has sense *stone* (disease).

**cēpa**, *for final citation in Dict. see* gewrixl *below*.

**cēping**, f. *observation*: ne cymð na Godes rice be nanre cepinge (*obseruatione*), Hml. P. ii, 590, 6.

**Cerdices ford**, *add*: place in Hants, but not certainly Charford.

*****cicc**, *bend*, PNE i, 93.

**cicil**, *see also* ceace *above*, cicel *in Dict.*, cycel *in Suppl.*, *and add*: colliridas, ceclas, Oliphant, *Harley Latin–Old English Glossary* 98.

**Cicropisc**, *rather* Cecropean.

**cīd**, *strife*: geflit and cid (v.l. æfest and gecid), Lch. iii, 168, 17.

**cidere**, m. *one who quarrels*: increpator, Chrd. 41, 30.

**cigan**, *add to II*: Bl. H. 143, 34, *quoted in Dict. s.v.* hordcofa. *See also* in-, ongeancigan.

**\*cigel**, *pole*, PNE i, 93.

**cigung**, *add*: *invocation*: he yfelsacode Godes mægnþrym . . . in scinna cigunge, Gr. D. 289, 9.

**cilcan**, *see* gecilcan *in Suppl.*

**cilce**, *chalky place*: ad ciuitatem Calcariam, quae a gente Anglorum Kælcacaestir appellatur, Bede, Hist. Ecc. iv, 21.

**cildgeong**: *for citation of Gn. Ex. 49 read* ne sceal hine mon cildgeongne forcweðan.

**cilewearte**, *l. 1 in Suppl. read* celiwearte.

**cilic**, *rough cloth*: cilicium, Mt. xi, 21, Lind.

**cille**, *see also* storcille.

**cilled**, *see* for-, gecilled.

**cincung**, citation = WW 171, 39.

**cine**, *see* bod *above*.

**cintōþ**, *for front-tooth read back-tooth*.

**cīpa**, *add*: negotiator, cipa, Chrd. 70, 5.

**cipp**, *l. 2 in Suppl.*, cadurcus, catercus *are both probably for* caduceus. Cf. Oliphant, *Harley Latin–Old English Glossary* 42.

**cippian**, *see* forcippian.

**cipung**, *add to I*: mercatum, ceping, WW 144, 27, *and cancel this citation under III. See also* myrtse *in Suppl.*

**circan**, ? *delete*, alliteration fails in citation, cf. ASPR vi, 218.

**cirebald**, *add*: *see also* cynebald.

**cirice**, *add to compounds* heafodcirice.

**ciricfæt**, n. *chalice*: swa hi sculon on ciricfatan gearwian wæter and win to þam halgan husle, IP 233, v.l.

**cirichege**, m. *churchyard*: deade he byrige on Godes cyricheige, Nap. 16.

**ciricwyrhta**, m. *church-builder*: Teinfriþe mine circwirhtan (dat.), Chart. Harm. 353 (no. 87), 2.

**cirlisc**: *add to I*: ceorlisc man (v.l. ceorl) *in citation s.v.* burhgeat *above*.

**cirm**, *see also* sarigcirm.

**cirpsian**, *add*: crines calamistri uestigio rotantur, þæt heora loccas dæl mid tyrninge cyrpsion, Chrd. 64, 34. Note in gloss asperat, cyrpsaþ (= Prud. 430) OE word has usual sense, as the Gorgon's locks are referred to.

**cirr**, *add to compounds* eft-, ge-, geancirr.

**cirran**, *add to compounds* ofcirran.

**cirredness**, *see* forcirredness.

**cirrendlic**, *see* oncirrendlic.

**cirring**, f. *turning, conversion*: þæt is swyðe unhalwendlic geðoht, þæt hwa emb þa morgenlice cerrunge þænce and þa anweardan forgemeleasige, A. xi, 387, 394 (= Archiv cxxii, 257, 17; Hml. Warn. 103, 3). Cf. PNE i, 124. *See also* forcirring.

**cis**, *gravel*: of Cisburne, CS i, 496, 25. Cf. PNE i, 95.

**cis**, *add*: *fastidious, squeamish*: ut infirmis mentibus non uertatur in nauseam, þe læs hit seocmodum broðrum and cisum wyrðe to wlættan, Chrd. 23, 9.

**\*cisen**, adj. *gravelly*, PNE i, 96.

**cisstycce**, *piece of cheese*: portionem de formatico, Chrd 15, 3; 5; 8.

**cist**, *add to compounds* hrægel-, mere-. On III horn, *see FL 160, but cf. Speculum XXXI, 394.*

**cistelbēam**, *for* cistenbeam, DP 103.

**\*cistelett**, *chestnut copse*, PNE i, 96.

**cīte**, *note strong d.s.* cyte (tugurio), An. Ox. 2515.

**citelflōde**, f. *bubbling spring*: to cytelflodan, CS ii, 371, 9.

**citelwill**, (? f.) *bubbling spring*: oþ cytelwylle, CS ii, 270, 4.

**ciwung**, MS. *has* ciung (A. viii, 452).

**\*clacc**, *hill*, PNE i, 96.

**clæfre**, *add compounds* heorot-, hwite-, wuduclæfre.

**clæne**: II *on first citation* (= Chart. Rob. 92, 10) *see Suppl. s.v.* leger; *add*: II *a free from encumbrance*: Wulfstan and his sunn sealdon þa þæt land clæne Leofrice, and Leofric . . . þam bisceope, clæne land and unbesacen, Chart. Rob. 164, 4; id. 14; sacleas and clane, Chart. Harm. 282, 6 from below.

**clængeorn**, *add*: *desirous of cleanliness*: gode bæcystran . . . to ælcum meteþingum clængeorne . . . and we willað þæt þa cocas clængeorne beon, Chrd. 19, 19.

**clænmōd**, adj. *pure of heart*: he forlæt þa clænmodan (v.l. clænan mod), Hml. P. i, 276, 216.

**clænsian**, *see also* unclænsod.

**clam**, *see also* ferclam.

**clangettung**, f. *clangour*: clangor, clangetug, MLN lxvii 554, 5.

**clāte**, *see also* wuduclate.

**\*clater**, *loose stones*, PNE i, 97.

**clāþ**, *add to compounds* crism-, eaxl-, hand-, hed-, offrung-, seaxclaþ.

**clauster**, *add*: claustra canonicorum, þa claustru þær þa preostas inne slapað, Chrd. 21, 9.

**Cledemūþa**, *rather the mouth of the Clwyd*, cf. EHR lxv, 203.

**\*clent**, *rock*, PNE i, 98.

**cleofa**, *add to compounds* ealu-, metecleofa.

**clife**, *see also* hegeclife.

**clifer**, *see* rindeclifer.

**clifhlēp**, -hlip, *add*: lit. *cliff-leap*: WW 39, 1; 469, 1.

**clifian**, *see also* clynian *below*.

**clifrian**, *add*: seo culfre na mid clawum clyfrað, Chrd. 62, 16.

**clifwyrt**, *add meaning* burdock; *see also* clyfwyrt *in Dict.* Cf. DP 24.

**clinc**, **\*clenc**, m. *boulder, lump*: on clinca leage, CS ii, 495, 22; etc.; aspera, clincas (cf. Isaiah xl, 4), Gn. (Archiv cxcix, 20). Cf. PNE i, 98; Löfvenberg, *Studies on ME Local Surnames* 38.

**cliofung**, *in citation MS. reads* cliofing.

**clipian**, *add*: I a *with acc.*: he clipode to Gode þisne cwyde, Hept. 50, 818; III *of sounds*: þone sweg þara fif clipiendra stafa, Chrd. 57, 8. *Add compounds* fore-, forþ-, oferclipian; wordclipiende; ongeangeclipod.

**clipiendlic**, *see also* toclipiendlic.

**clipung**, *see also* ge-, toclipung.

**cliþwyrt**, *add*: Lch. iii, 54, 33.

**\*clodd**, *lump of earth or peat*: þurh ut clod hangran, CS iii, 147, 22. Cf. PNE i, 99.

**\*clof**, *valley*, PNE i, 99.

**Clofes hoo**, *note*: the site is unidentified.

**clofþung**, *add citation under* þelneþunc.

**\*clōh**, *valley*, PNE i, 99.

**clop**, *hill*, PNE i, 99.

**clūd**, *add*: cludas, Sal. 185 (MS. claudas).

**\*clūder**, *mass of rocks*, PNE i, 101.

**clufu**, *l. 1 in Suppl.*, capiclum is *perhaps for* caepitium, *onion*.

**clūt**, *add*: glossing pittacium means *piece of parchment* (cf. Corpus Glossary P, 394).

**clyccan**, *see also* for-, ymbclyccan.

**\*clȳder**, *loose stones*, PNE i, 101.

**clympre**, second citation in Suppl. = Prud. 761–2, where see note.

**clynian**, ? *delete*, MS. *may read* clyuiende, *referring to a snake intertwining its coils in brushwood*, Prud. 982.

**clȳsan**, *see also* forclysan.

**cnæwe**, *see* orcnæwe.

**cnapa**, *add to I*: þonne þæt cild wyxt, ond gewyrð eft cnapa, and eft syððan cniht, Hml. P. i, 484, 120.

**cnāwend**, *see* oncnawend.

**cnāwlæc**, *see* tocnawlice *in Suppl.*

**cnāwness**, *see* gecnawness.

**cnear**, *add*: (nauibus) actuariis, cnearrum, OEG 4, 20.

**\*cnearr**, *rock*, PNE i, 1.

**cneordlic**, -lice, *see* gec.

**cnēores**, *see also* frum-, gecneores; æftercneoreso.

**cnēosār**, n. *pain in knee*: genuculorum dolorem, cneusar, OEG 73c, 12.

**cnēow**, *see also* frumcneow.

**cniht**, *add*: I b used in reference to a guild, perhaps *junior member* or *member of a young men's guild*: hæbbe ælc gegilda ii sesteras mealtes, and ælc cniht anne and sceat huniges, Cht. Th. 613, 33; ego Æðelhelm and cniahta gegildan, CS ii, 128, 32. [Cf. OED knightengild]. *Add to II*: gif cniht wæpen brede, gilde se hlaford an pund, Cht. Th. 612, 23; 28; 32. *Add to compounds* larcniht.

**cnihthad**, *add to I*: errores pueritiae, þa gedwolan his cnihthada, Bd. v, 14.

**cnītan**?, **cnitian**?: *read* cnītian.

**cnop**, *note*: ballationes means *dances*: ? error for bullationes, and *cnop* = *bulla*; cf Lindsay, *Corpus Glossary* 196.

**cnoss,** glosses *suboles,* Scint. 232, 9.

*****cnugel,** *broken ground,* PNE i, 103.

**cnyccan,** *see also* tocnyccan.

**cnyll,** *see also* scohcnyll.

*****cnyll,** *hill,* PNE i, 103.

**cnyllan,** *add to* II: he þa dura cnylde, Vis. Lfc. 28.

**cnўslian,** *see* framacnyslian.

*****cocc,** *heap,* PNE i, 103.

*****coccsciete,** *place for catching woodcock,* PNE i, 104; (? *or* coccscyte, English Studies xliii, 46).

**cocer II, cocor,** delete senses *sword, spear,* which are suggested only by probably confused glosses in Ps. Ar., Ps. Vit., and Ps. Spel. Cf. Neophilologus i, 209. *Add:* on coxre, Ps. Cam. x, 3.

**cocrōd,** *read* cocrōdu.

**cofa,** *see also* flæsccofa, landcofa.

**Coferflōd,** *read* Cōferflōd, Cōforflōd, for meaning substitute *River Chebar* (Vulgate *Chobar*).

**cohhetan,** sense is perhaps *cry out:* cf. Tolkien and Gordon, *Sir Gawain and the Green Knight,* 2nd ed., p. 84.

**coitemǣre,** *boiled wine: careni,* coitemæres *uel* asodenes wines, An. Ox. 103. (Cf. Neuphil. Mit. li, 53.)

**cōl,** *add: frigida pestis,* col cwyld, WW 243, 11; *delete citation in Suppl.* of Hml. S. xxxi, 911, *see* calan.

**-colc,** *see* oden-, wincolc.

*****colere, -estre,** *charcoal burner,* PNE i, 106.

*****colig,** adj. *pertaining to charcoal,* PNE i, 106.

**colstūc,** *heap of coal: carbonarius, locus carbonum,* constuc (*sic*), E.S. xi, 512.

**coltgræig,** *note: original MS. reads* cologræig.

**constūc,** *see* colstuc *above.*

**copel,** sense *unsteady* is improbable, see PNE i, 106.

**copsed, cosped,** *see* fot-, gecopsed.

**copsende,** *see* gecopsende.

**corcīþ** = corncīþ, *growth of grain.*

**corded,** *see* gecorded.

**cordewanere,** m. *cordwainer:* Earle, *Land Charters and Saxonic Documents* 257, 2 from below.

**corenlic, -lice,** *see* gec.

*****corf,** *cutting, pass,* PNE i, 107.

**corfian,** *see also* forcorfian.

**corn,** *see also* hwǣte-, linsædcorn; gecyrnod.

**cornhrycce,** *delete, MSS. in citation have* cornhwyccan, -hwæccan; *see* hwæcca, -e *in Dict. and Suppl.*

**Coshām,** *add:* or *Cosham,* Hants.

**cost,** *add: multis modis,* menigum costum, Jn, p. 7, 10, Lind; *but* monigfald' cost, Rtl. 121, 28, *is rather for* monigfaldlicost.

**cost,** adj., *see* gecost.

**costere,** *spade, probably error for* fostere, *fossorium,* q.v.

**costian,** *see also* for-, wiþcostian.

**costung,** *see also* fore-, ge-, ofercostung; flæsccostnung.

*****cottere,** *cottager,* PNE i, 110.

*****copærn,** *sick-house,* PNE i, 110.

**copu,** *add to compounds* lungencopu.

**copuwyrt,** f. *an unknown plant: oleotropius,* oxnalib *vel* cotheuyrt, DP 255.

**coydic,** ? *charlock: lapsanus* (sic), Txts. 108, 1118.

*****craca,** *crow,* PNE i, 110.

**cracelung** f. *noise of storks: crepacula,* cracelung (MS. crc: lun), An. Ox. 56, 249. Cf. Aldhelm, Rid. 31, 3.

**crācettan,** *see also* miscrocettan.

**cræft,** *add to* IV: wif gif heo mid hwylcehwegu cræfte hyre hæmed generað, fæste iii gear, Buss. 185, 290; *add note:* sometimes best translated *troop, company* in Gen. B (e.g. 269, 402), cf. mægen III. *Add to compounds* eorþ-, feþer-, fird-, flit-, getæl-, getyng-, grammatisc-, hand-, heah-, lyb-, mægen-, mund-, smiþ-, son-, syn-, þyl-, weorccræft.

**cræftbōc,** f. *commentary: codicis artificis,* cræftboce, OEG 30, 88.

**cræftelic,** adj. *skilful: dactylico* (strophio), cræftelicum, Prud. 130.

**cræftig,** *add to compounds* dysig-, hand-, læce-, scin-, smiþ-, stæf-, weorolderæftig.

**cræftiga,** *add: architectos,* cræftigan (v.l. cræftige wyrhtan) Bd. v, 21. *See also* cræfta, *and add compounds* galdor-, heah-, smiþcræftiga.

**cræftlic,** *add to* II: *fabrili,* cræftlicre, Prud. 692.

**cræftsprǣc,** f. *technical language:* neutrum is naðor cynn . . . ne werlices ne wiflices, on cræftspræce (*in grammatical terms*), ac hit byð swa þeah oft on andgyte, Ælfc. Gr. Z. 18, 15.

**cræsta,** *delete* (JEGP lxv, 301).

**crætwisa,** *add: auriga,* crætwisa, Prud. 692.

*****cramb,** *land in bend of river,* PNE i, 111.

**crammingpohha,** *add:* apparently some sort of snare, translates *uiscarium, birdlime.*

**crampiht,** substitute: *cake: folialis,* crompeht, WW 409, 8 (*in list of foods*); *folialis,* crompehht *uel nomen cibi,* Oliphant, *Harley Latin–Old English Glossary* 194; *placentas,* cronphetas . . . *tenuissimus panis,* OEG 19, 1.

**cranic,** *add:* cranc, Chart. Rob. 250, 16.

**crās,** *delete, see* nicor *in Suppl.*

**crathyrdel,** *delete, MS. reads* crater(e), hyrdle (*cf.* cratere, *plecta,* An. Ox. 2392).

**crāwe,** *l.* 2 *in Suppl., for* cre *read* cræ: *see further* A. xxxvii, 51.

**crāwenbēam,** *an unknown plant: ablacta,* crauenbeam, DP 4.

**Creacan ford, Crecgan ford,** *add:* the site is unknown.

**credic,** discussed FL 84, Speculum xxxi, 395.

**-creowed,** *see* acreowed.

*****creowel,** *fork in river or road,* PNE i, 112.

**crib,** *add: couch: in lectum strati mei,* on bed mines crybbes, Chrd. 31, 3.

**crīgan,** *forms rather suggest inf.* *crīþan.

*****cringol,** adj. *twisting,* PNE i, 112.

**crismclāþ,** *v.l.* to crismal *in citation s.v.;* cf. Förster, *Reliquienkultus* 90.

**crismsmyrels,** m. *anointing with sacred oil:* Förster, *Reliquienkultus* 90.

**Crist,** *add:* Cristes mæsse uhte, Chr. 1021. *See also* wiþer-crist.

**cristelmæl,** *add to* I: þiiosne kiismeel (*sic*) gewarahtæ, Cahen and Olsen, *L'Inscription runique du coffret de Mortain* 24.

**cristendom,** add: IV *membership of a Christian congregation:* into þam mynstre þær þær he to hyrð, þær þær he his cristendom hæfð, Hml. P. ii, 807, 96.

**Crīstenness,** *add:* for þære Cristennysse (v.l. Cristnesse) þe ge underfengen, Ll. Lbmn. 412, 2; 413, 32.

**cristnere,** *rather one who performs cristnung* (q.v.).

**cristnian,** *see* gecristnian *in Suppl. for corrections. See also* ungecristnod.

**croc,** *add: lagoena,* croc, Kluge, *Angelsächs. Lesebuch* 12, III C 9.

**crocc,** *for* croh, *saffron:* DP 213.

*****croccere,** *potter,* PNE i, 112.

**croced,** *see* gecroced.

**crocettan,** *see* miscrocettan.

**croft,** *see also* suþ-, wuducroft.

**croh,** *for* geolacroh *read* geole croh, *see* geolwe *in Suppl.*

**crōh, crōg,** *corner:* into crohlea, CS ii, 2, 23; to crohhamme, id. 559, 28; on croghyrste, id. i, 295, 15. Cf. PNE i, 113.

**croma,** *add: frustam,* croman, Ps. Cam. cxlvii, 6.

**crop,** *probably delete* II, *which is for* stancrop; *in citation MS reads* stancyslas, croppas; *see* Amer. Journ. Phil. lix, 215. *Add compounds* ea-, eorp-, heorotcrop.

**cros,** *cross:* into Normannes Cros, CS iii, 367, 20. Cf. PNE i, 114.

**crūc,** *add:* se preost mæssode be cruce, Vis. Lfc. 74.

**crūce,** *add:* as gloss to *trulla* meaning is *ladle.*

**crundel,** add to senses: *chalk-pit, quarry;* there is no evidence for sense *barrow;* cf. PNE i, 116. *Add to* II: on cyncges crundlu, CS iii, 589, 1.

**crūse,** *cruse:* (h)amulas *in similitudine* cruse (MS. crufe) *tamen altior est,* OEG 43, 4.

**crūsene,** *note:* in citations in Suppl. *cocula* is taken as *cucullus.*

*****crūw,** *bend,* PNE i, 117.

**crycc,** *add: cambuttis,* mid criccum, Chrd. 34, 6.

**crῡce,** *for* cruce: *lagoena,* cryce, OEG 39, 4.

**cryde,** m. *pursuit:* þæt men faran on cryd æfter ðeofan, I Eadgar 2.

*****crŷde,** *weeds, plants,* PNE i, 117.

*****cryfting,** *small croft,* PNE i, 117.

**crymb,** *for* crumb: *curua,* crymban, OEG 28, 159.

**crymel,** *small piece* (of land or water), PNE i, 118; to Crymelhamme, C.D. vi, 153, 3.

*****crype,** *passage, drain,* PNE i, 118.

**crypelgeat**, n. *low opening in wall*: on crypelgeat, CS ii, 399, 1.

**cryppan**, *add*: *plecteret*, kyrpte, OEG 32, 2.

**cū**, *add*: *iuga boum quinque*, dæl cyna fife, Lk. xiv, 19, Rush.

**cuman**, *add to forms*: pret. cam; *add to I 1*: *come* to a person: þa cam Putrael to Boia, Cht. E. 274, 3; *add to III 1*: *reach a point*: oð þæt ge cumon to anum feorðlincge, *until you come to your last farthing*, Hml. Th. i, 268, 1; oþ þæt we to þam gilde cuman, VI Æthelstan 7. *See also* efen-, full-, ofcuman; gean-, samod-, ufancumende; feor-, fær-, feorran-, læt-, niw-, niwan-, unforcumen.

**cumb**, *see also* mærcumb.

**cūmicge**, f. *cow's urine*: bete mid hattre cumicgan, Lch. iii, 10, 20.

**cumlīþe**, *add*: *instruimur in colligendis hospitibus*, we syn gemingode þæt we cumliðe beon, Chrd. 51, 6.

**cummǣdre**, f. *god-mother*: gif hwa his gastlican cumædran hæbbe him on gesinscipe, si he amansumad, Hal. 72, 5.

**cumpǣder**, cf. gefædera (-e).

**-cund**, *see also* eorl-, esne-, metercund.

**cunnan**, *add to I 4*: *of sexual intercourse*: ic secge, þæt ic ne conn þurh gemæcscipe monnes ænges, Cri. 198.

**cunness**, *see* oncunness.

***cūpe**, *basket to catch fish*, PNE i, 120.

**cuppe**, *add*: many passages in wills, see Chart. Whit. 237.

**cursian**, *curse*: *see also* acursian.

**cursian**, *plait*, probably delete, FL 12.

**cursumbor**, *for corzumber read* coczumber.

**cūsealf**, *read* rusele q.v.; cf. Prud. 280 and note.

**custure**, *seam*: *sutura*, seam, custure, A. xli, 102, 21. (O. French costure).

**cūþ**, *add to I*: swiðe cuð (*aperta*) gesceadwisnes, Gr. D. 228, 2; *add to II*: landes dæl, þe fram cuðum mannum Hindehlep is gehaten, Chart. Rob. 86, 15; *add to III*: hie nænigne cuðne næfdon, mid hwam hie wunian meahton, Verc.-Hom. 135, 80; manige his cuðra manna . . . þa þe hine swiðe arodon, Gr. D. 22, 14. *Add to compounds* full-, ge-, ham-, hired-, namcuþ.

**cūþian**, *see also* gecuþian.

**cūþlice**, *add*: he cyð gecyðnysse swiþe cuðlice be me, Nap. 77 (= Hml. P. i, 378, 8; 382, 87). *See also* forcuþlice.

**cwabba**, *marsh*: on Heahstanes quabben, CS iii, 499, 32; PNE i, 121.

**cwacian**, *see also* uncwaciende.

**cwǣde**, *see* soþcwæde.

**cwǣman**, glosses *accusare* (? error): *accussarent*, cwæmdon *uel* acuste, Mt. xii, 10, Rush.

**cwǣscedness**, *see* tocwæscedness.

***cwafen**, *quaking bog*, PNE i, 121.

**cwalu**, *add to compounds* pinecwalu.

**cwānig**, *add*: mode cwange (MS. mod cwanige), El. 377.

***cwappa**, ***cwǣp**, *eel-pout*, PNE i, 121.

**cwatern**, *for meaning of lemma see* cine *in Suppl.*

**cwealm**, *add*: se wærc bið miceles cwelmes ælcum, Verc. Först. 106, 13. *See also* fær-, ofercwealm.

**cwealmlic**, adj. *fatal*: hig wurpon hig sylfe mid cwealmlicre flihte on þa byrnende seaðas, Wyn. 160.

**cweccan**, *add*: *animam excussit*, he cwehte ut his sawle, Chrd. 99, 34.

**cwecesand**, *read in citation perhaps* cwecesund, *shifting sea*; cf. FL 13 (*but first element to* cweccan, *not to* cwic).

**cwedolian**, *see also* hearm-, yfelcwedolian.

**cwedunge**, *see* wiþercwedung.

**cwelderǣde**, citation = OEG 36, 10 (where see note); *add*: *stilo*, cueldehredæ, Haupt Anzeiger xxii, 276; cf. Jordan, *Die altenglischen Säugtiernamen* 29.

**cwellend**, *note*: *equated with* sector *in reference to Manasseh, who cut Isaiah apart*, cf. Prud. 893, note.

**cwellere**, *see also* flæsccwellere.

**cwēman**, *see also* miscweman.

**cwēme**, *add*: *aptam*, cueme, Archiv cxvii, 24, 20. *See also* uncweme.

**cwēmedlic**, *see* gecwemedlic.

**cwēmedness**, *see* gec.

**cwēming**, -lic, -lice, -sum, *see* gec.

**cwēmness**, *for* gecwemnesse, Fehr 104, 9, v.l.

**Cwēnas**, *add*: they are to be regarded as a northern Finnish tribe.

**cwēnlic**, delete *womanly*, *muliebris*.

**cweþan**, *add to I*: (1 a) *where words or sounds to be spoken are given*: se biscop hine het stafa naman cweðan: 'cweð nu a'; ða cwæð he a, Bd. v. 2; ne cwæð ðu na goda, ac gramlicra deofla, *say not that of gods, but that of cruel devils*, Hml. S. viii, 59; (2 a) *using a particular phrase*: we cweðað niwne monan, ac he is æfre se ylca, De temp. ann. 22. *Add to compounds* mis-, ofer-, welcweþan.

**cweþend**, *see* hearmcweþend.

**cwic**, *add*: on þam timan þe Eadwerd cing wes cucu and dead, Chart. Rob. 236, 25; 238, 1.

**cwicalmus**, *sacrificial victim*: *uictima*, cuic almus, Mk. ix, 49, Lind. (Rush. cwicu almes).

**cwicclian**, *perhaps delete*, and take cwiccliende as for twincliende, lemma connected with nutare, *nod*. Cf. FL 159.

***cwicen**, ? *mountain-ash*, PNE i, 122.

**cwichege**, m. *hedge of living plants*: oð ðone cwichege, CS i, 293, last line. Cf. PNE i, 122.

**Cwichelmes hlǣw**, *substitute for definition*: *Cuckamsley* or *Scutchamfly Knob*, on the edge of the Berkshire Downs, near East Hendred.

**cwicseolfor**, *add*: gyf þy viii dæge sunne scyneð, ðonne byð cwicseolfor eaðbegeate, Lch. 166, 10.

**cwidbōc**, *add*: *book of homilies*: Augustinus sæde on his cwidbocan, Verc. Först. 136.

**cwīd[d]**, *see* uncwid[d].

**cwide**, *add to IV*: þa geceas he Laurentium . . . and he þurhwunode in his cwide (*sententia*), Gr. D. 329, 18; *add*: IX *agreement*: he na to him hwearf æfter heora cwyde (*condictum*, v.l. gecwide) . . . wæs he gemyndig heora cwydes, Bd. iv, 25. *Add to compounds* calend-, heafodcwide.

**cwidegied**, *substitute for meaning* utterance.

**-cwideness**, *see* wiþercwideness.

**-cwidolian, -cwidolness**, *see* hearmcw.

**cwidrǣdness**, *see* gecwidrædness.

**cwildbǣre**, *add*: *estas tempestuosa*, sumor cwældbære, Archiv cxx, 297, 11.

**cwildflōd**, Ps. Jun. xxxi, 6, *probably error for* cwilde flod.

**cwille**, *well*: be eastan ðam cwyllan, CS ii, 517, 22. Cf. PNE i, 121.

***cwilm**, *well*: see M. T. Löfvenberg, *Studies on ME local surnames* 160.

**cwilman**, *see also* tocwilman.

**cwilmere**, m. *murderer*: heo . . . wurden to þan hæðene cwelmere (v.l. cwellere) gewreigde, Hml. Warn. 25, 12.

**cwilmfull**, *see* gecwilmfull.

**cwilmness**, f. *torment*: in ða ecan cwylmnesse, Verc. Först. 112, 13.

**cwīsedness**, *see* tocwisedness.

**cwiss**, *speech*: *dicendo*, mið cuis, Lk., p. 7, 2, Lind.

**cwisse**, *see* uncwisse.

**cycgel**, *add*: *cum baculis*, mid cygclum, Chrd. 34, 6.

**cyld**, *cold*, *note*: gender is fem., Verc.-Hom. 127, n. 113.

**cylfe**, *hill*: æt Cylfantune, Chart. Harm. 17, 17. Cf. PNE i, 123.

**cylle**, *see* hwitecylle.

***cymbe**, *hollow*, PNE i, 124.

**cyme**, *add*: *event, issue*: þæs witedomes soð se æfterfylgenda cyme þara wisena (*sequens rerum euentus*) geseðde, Bd. iv, 29. *See also* in-, þidercyme.

**Cymenes ōra**, *substitute for definition*: a place (*the Owers*) now covered by the sea near Selsea Bill.

**cyn**, *add compounds* deofol-, fyr-, gliw-, godweb-, hafoc-, hise-, hræfn-, martyr-, næder- niten-, Norþwealh-, riht-, un-, Wealh-, wilddeorcyn.

**cynebald**, *very bold*, read by many in B. 1634 (MS. cyning-bald) and An. 171 (MS. cirebald); cf. cynerof.

**cynehelm**, *add*: an leas feowertig kynehelma, Hml. S. xi, 205.

**cynehelmian**, *see also* gecynehelmian.

**cynelic**, *add*: cynelic adl is probably *jaundice*, not *king's disease* (Scrofula); cf. EGS iv, 17.

**cynerēaf**, n. *royal robe*: ond him fram his cynereaf ofawearp, Vercelli MS., f. 108ᵛ, 32.

**cynewāden**, *in citation MS. has* cincdaðenan, Chart. Whit. 14, 16.

**cynewirþe**, *add*: ond awearp his cynewurðe reaf him of, Hml. Warn. 121, 4.

**cynewiþþe**, *add*: *murenulae*, cyniuiddan, A. lxxxiv, 150 (cf. OEG 55, 6).

cyning, *add to compounds* ealand-, wundorcyning.

cyningbald, *in citation many read* cynebalde men; *see* cynebald.

cyninge, ? *delete, read in citation* cennicgan *or* cennestran; cf. kenninge, v.l. cennystre, Hml. A. 117, 5.

cyninges wyrt, meaning is perhaps *elder*, see DP 71.

cyninggeniþla, m. *royal foe*: El. 610 (MS. rex geniðlan).

cyning-wuldor, *for* wuldorcyning: B. 2795.

cynling, m. *clan*: Gospatrik greot ealle mine wassenas . . . and eallun mine kynling freondlyce, Chart. Harm. 423, 3; 424, 16.

cynn, *add to compounds* deofol-, stan-, þeod-, wæter-, wild-deorcynn; *see also* gecynnes.

cynningstān, read *cyningstan* (so MS.). Cf. FL 134.

cypera, *add*: esox, cypera, Nap. 14.

cypsed, *see also* fotcypsed.

cyrf, *add to compounds* felcyrf.

cyrnel, *see also* hnutcyrnel.

cyrtenlæcan, *see also* gecyrtenlæcan.

cȳsgerunn, substitute for meaning *cheese in formation*; cf. A. li, 158.

cyspan, *see also* (ge)fotcypsed.

cyss, *for* coss: gicysse mec cysse, Rtl. 3, 38.

cyst, *virtue, add to III a*: (ii) *generous gifts*: we magon . . . hine eac gremian gyf we him ætbredað his agene cyste, Hml. P. i, 207, 257. *See also* manncyst.

cȳswucu, *add*: and healdað . . . þa iiii dagas on þære cyswucu, *The Anglo-Saxons*, 278, 11.

cȳta, *add*: buzzard.

cytwer, *see also* Studia Neophilologica xvii, 263.

cȳþan, *add*: III *become known*: innotuisti, ðu cyþdest, Ps. Roy. cxliii, 3 (and related glosses). *Add to compounds* fullcyþan.

cȳþedness, *see* gecyþedness.

cȳþere, *add*: martyrum, cyþra, V.Ps., ed. Kuhn, 312, 2 from below.

cȳþig, *see also* oncyþig.

# D

dæd, *see also* hand-, man-, morþdæd.

dæda, *see also* hand-, mandæda.

dædbētere, *for* Nap. 16 *read* Chrd. 80, 24.

dædla, *see* fordædla.

dæfte, -n, -ness, *see* ged.

dæg, *add to I a*: in pl. denoting a period of indefinite extent: on þam dagum com Iohannes, Mt. iii, 1; Lk. i, 39 (West Saxon Gospels); *add to II: suprema (dies)*, geloten dæg, WW 175, 47; *add to III 1*: langsumnyssa dagena, Ps. Lamb. xx, 5; *add to III 2*: ariseð oðer cynning . . . fea tide he bið on his dagum, Verc. Först. 104, 4. *Add to compounds*: Candel-mæsse-, fæsten-, fiftig-, gearcung-, gegearcung-, geohhol-, gereste-, halig-, heofung-, Hlafmæsse-, lencten-, mæsse-, mal-, merigen-, middel-, midne-, morgen-, ofer-, þrowungdæg; *also the days of the week*. Cf. doeg.

dæghwām, *add*: dæghwæm, Ps. Jun. xli, 4.

dæghwāmlice, cf. gearhwamlice, doeghwamlice.

dæglanges, cf. gearlanges.

dægmǣlespinn, *style of a dial*: Ælfc. Gr. Z. 321, 6, v.l.

dægmǣlspilu, *delete*, MS. dægmelespin.

dægmete, *add*: *daily food*: annonam, OEG 28, 241.

dægrēd, *add*: in matutinis, on dægredum, Ps. Roy. lxii, 7; on dægeredum, id. c, 8; II *twilight*: take here first citation in Suppl. and add: crepusculum, dægred uel tweone leoht uel þeorcung, Journal Brit. Arch. Ass. xli, 150.

dægþern, *see also* þridægþern.

dægweorc, *add*: dægweorc ne mað (MS. nemnað) *he concealed not the second code*, Ex. 561, (with confusion of Hebrew *dibre hayamim*, Chronicles, lit. works of the days, with *elle haddebarim*, Deuteronomy, lit. these are the words).

dægwilla, m. *day of joy*: þone dægwillan drihten bodode, Gen. 2777 (*or two words?*).

dæl, *add*: oþer dæl (*latus uallis*) wæs ligum ful, Bd. v, 12.

dǣl, *add to compounds* feorþan-, nænig-, sumdæl.

dǣlan II (1), *cancel* An. 954 (*where read* dæled); III 2 *read* rice *before* dælað *in* Exod. 538, *and take under* IV 3. *Add to compounds* ondælan.

dǣle, *see* gedæle.

dǣledlic, -end, -endlic, *see* tod.

dǣling, *add*: diuisionibus, dælungan, Ps. Sal. lxxvii, heading.

dǣlnimend, *add to II*: *duo participia*, twegen dælnimende , Ælfc. Gr. Z. 144, 7.

dǣlnimendlic, *add*: Ælfc. Gr. Z. 134, 20.

dǣrst, *add to I*: fex, dræst, Ps. Roy. lxxiv, 9.

dǣrsted, *see* gedærsted.

dafenlice, *see also* undafenlice.

dafenness, *see* gedafenness.

dalc, *see also* steordalc.

dalisc, *adj.*: Dedalei tecti, of daliscre þecene (*first word taken as* de+dalei), WW 221, 3.

dallic, *see* untodallic.

daroþæsc, *delete, read in citation* daroþas *or* daroþ, æsc.

Dauidlic, *adj. of David*: stirpis Dauitice, cynrenes Dauidlices, Hy. S. 104, 5.

dēad, *add to I*: (4) *stagnant* (of water): suð on þa deadan lace on Cridian, *Crawford Charters* 9, 124. *See also* for-, ge-, healfdead.

dēaded, *see* undeaded.

dēadsynnig, adj. glosses *reus*: deadsynig, Mt. v, 21, 22, Lind.

dēafness, f. *deafness*: to geopenigenne for þære deafnysse (*propter aures sanandas*), Hml. P. ii, 573, 150.

dēagan, substitute for meaning *hide oneself, disappear* (cf. MLR xxiv, 62).

dēagian, *see also* twideagod.

dēaglian, *see* adeaglian.

dēagwyrmede, MS. reads deawwyrmede.

dēaþ, *add to I 3*: deaþ, wiga wælgifre, Ph. 485.

dēaþdæg, *add*: Vercelli MS., f. 100ʳ, 4.

dēaþfiren, f. *mortal sin*: deaðfirenum forden, Cri. 1207.

dēaþgedāl, *add*: Guth. 206 (MS. deaþa gedal).

dēaþlicness, *add*: III *occurrence of death*: se cyðeð hwylcehwugu deaðlicnesse towearde, Archiv cxx, 47, 12. *See also* undeaþlicness.

dēaw, l. 3 in Suppl., note: roscido, deawe *is for original*: roscida, rore (deawe) *madida*.

dēawwyrm, substitute for meaning: *worm producing gout in the feet* (cf. deawwyrmede).

dēawwyrmede, *see* deagwyrmede.

declīnian, *add*: swa we ær declinodon *mea ancilla*, Ælfc. Gr. Z. 102, 18.

dēfe, *add*: his gast wunað ofer þone deafan (v.l. gedefan), Hml. A. 40, 394.

dēfedlic, defness, *see* ged.

delfan, *see also* ofdelfan.

delfin, *not Old English*.

dēma, *add to compounds* heahdema.

dēman, *add to I 6*: he nanum men ne deme þæt he nolde ðæt he him demde, gif he þone dom ofer hine sohte, Ll. Ælf., Introduction 49, 6. *Add to compounds*, fore-, ofdeman.

dēmere, *see also* selfdemere.

dēming, *see* fordeming.

dengan, *for* Nap. 17 *read* Chrd. 60, 30.

denn, *see also s.v.* æting.

dennian, *add*: the meaning is unknown; suggestions are reviewed Campbell, *Battle of Brunanburh* 98.

denu, *add*: ealle men fleoð to muntum and to denum (in *speluncas montium*) hie to behydanne, and hie cweoað: 'We halsiað eow, muntas and dena, þæt ge us oferfeallen', Verc. Först. 108, 11. *Add to compounds* feld-, fild-, mearc-, stan-denu.

dēofol, *add to III 1*: he sende sumne heahgerefan . . . swiðe hetel deofol, Hml. S. xxix, 204.

dēofolcyn, n. *race of devils*: Hml. Warn. 109, 21.

dēopian, *see also* gedeopian.

*dēoping, *deep place*, PNE i, 130.

dēopþancenlice, adv. *very thoughtfully*: Hml. Warn. 42, 3.

deorc, *add*: meaning in Dream of the Rood 46 is *bloody*.

deorce-grǣg, perhaps two words, see Suppl. *s.v.* græg; elbus = heluus.

deorcung, *in first citation in Dict.* (= WW 175, 34) MS. has þeorcung.

dēortūn, on lemma *broel* see Dict. *s.v.*

dēorwyrþness, *add*: for þære deorewurðnysse of þære forme dohter, Hml. Warn. 139, 18.

dīc, *add*: note wk. gen.: to ðære dican hyrnan, CS i, 543, 2; *see also* fæsten-, gærstun-, mæd-, mylen-, plegdic.

**dīcan**, see gedican.

**dician**, see also fordician.

**\*dicor**, ten, PNE i, 133.

**dicsticca**, m. rod in bank of a ditch (to protect it): ondlang þæs smalan paþes on þa dicsticcea, CS ii, 558, 1.

**dīgan**, cancel, see deagan.

**\*diger**, adj. thick, PNE i, 133.

**diging**, f. dyeing: tinctura, deging (printed teging), WW 136, 27. Cf. deagung.

**digle**, see also undigle.

**diglian**, add to I: in isto quem occultauerunt, in þissum þe hy digledon, Ps. Roy. ix, 16; add: I a hide something from a person: of þysum þe hy dygledon me, id. xxx, 5. See also togedegled.

**digollice**, add: (4) quietly, contrasted with hlude: Fehr 28, 1.

**digolness**, see also gedigolness.

**dihtian**, see also adihtian.

**dīlegian**, add: dele, dilga, Ps. Roy. l, 11.

**dil(e)meng** (?), dissimulation: ne qualibet dissimulatione aut tenacitate, ne for dylmengon ne ne for uncyston, Chrd. 45, 10.

**dilemengan**, see fordilemengan.

**dingan**, see gedingan.

**dīpan**, see also gedipan, geindipan.

**dirlingþegn**, m. favourite follower: mid . . . usses Drihtenes dierlingþegenum, A. lxxiii, 19, 5.

**dirne**, adv., see undirne.

**dirneceorl**, m. secret lover: buton heo dyrneceorl hæbbe (cf. Mt. xix, 9), Hml. P. ii, 624, 38.

**dirneforlegenness**, f. fornication: for intingan dyrneforlegenesse, Bd. iv, 5.

**dirnegeligen**, v.l. in citation under dirneforlegen.

**dirneleger**, add: on dernelegere acænnod, Hml. Warn. 78, 4.

**dirnlic**, adj. secret: on dyrnlican galscype, IP 125, 6.

**disma**, glosses cassia: Ps. L. xliv, 9 (MS. þysma).

**disme**, add: An. Ox. 46, 4 musk is spoken of. Cf. MHG tiseme, tesim, MLG desem. See A. xxx, 123; xxxii, 515.

**dīþan**, see gedipan.

**docce**, note: citation from Som. etc. in Dict. = DP 16, 264; l. 2 in Suppl., read acrocerium (so MS.), perhaps for acroceraeum.

**docga**, note: use in citation is metaphorical.

**dǣg**, add: very frequent for day in Lind., e.g. Mt. xxvii, 62; Lk xxiv, 21; Jn. v, 1. See also gister-, sunne-, symbel-, Wodnesdoeg.

**dǣghwǣmlice**, adv. daily: Mk., p. 5, 14, Lind.

**dōend**, see miceldoend.

**dōgian**, delete, read in citation hogode.

**dohtor**, add: proneptis, þridde dohter, WW 173, 31 (lemma not printed), WW 173, 31. See also goddohtor; gedohtra.

**dolg**, see also sindolg.

**dolhsmeltas**, discussed FL 14, Speculum XXXI, 395.

**dōm**, add to compounds pap-, rihtdom.

**dōmdæg**, add: on domdæge, A. xi, 100, 93.

**domne**, add: of women, Nap. 91.

**dōn**, add: III 2 b α with acc. and clause: hio ða hind swa dyde, þæt hio him beforan hleapende wæs, she caused the hind to keep running before them, Lch. iii, 426, 32. Add to compounds full-, misþurh-, geun-, ymbdon. See also fram-, ungedon.

**dōnd**, see also ælmes-, goddond.

**dooc**, south wind, delete, arises from confusion of nothus and notus.

**doppe**, see fugeldoppe.

**dōung**, see ondoung.

**dox**, see also note to Verc.-Hom. 100, 324.

**doxian**, citation = Verc.-Hom. 100, 324, where see note.

**draca**, add: IV dragon-standard: draconibus, qui in uexillis depicti erant, dracum, Prud. 264.

**drǣdan**, add: glosses timere in Ps. Sal., xxii, 4, and passim; Verc.-Hom. 82, 107, v.l.

**drǣfan**, see also fordræfan.

**drǣfness**, see todræfness.

**drǣg**, see gedræg.

**drǣgtre**, add: perhaps d.s. of \*dreahtor (cf. dreccan). Cf. FL 14.

**drāf**, rearrange thus: I drove, herd, band: take here citations from Sermo Lupi (= Wlfst. 163, 5); Chr. 1016; II driving: take here Hml. Th. 502, 10; Hml. S. xxxi, 1055; Bl. H. 199, 7; drafe drifan, perform duties of transport of goods (cf. lad III), C.D. iii, 450, 33; III road (cf. OED drove I 3): andlang drafæ, CS ii, 409, 30.

**dragan**, add: III protract (cf. OED draw 55): þæt hig be þæs timan lenge heora sang dragon (protendant), Chrd. 57, 7. See also gedragan; hwemdragen.

**drēam**, add to II a: þæt þæra hlystendra earan of þam dreame (psalmorum pronuntiatione) beon abryrde, Chrd. 57, 16; add: III sad noise, lamentation: hellwarena dream, Verc.-Hom. 47, 54 (but note v.l. hream). Add to compounds orgel-, woddream.

**drecedness**, see gedrecedness.

**drēfend**, **drēfness**, see ged.

**drehtlice**, see ungedrehtlice.

**drehtness**, see gedrehtness.

**drenc**, add to compounds ge-, gebrec-, slæpdrenc.

**drencan**, add: I a intoxicate: quicquid inebriat, swa hwæt swa drence, Chrd. 74, 7. Add to compounds gein-, þurhdrencan.

**drēogan**, add to I: folcscipe dreogeð, performs a public service, Rid. 32, 10; drihtscype dreogan, B. 1470; lofsangas sint to dreogenne (agendi sunt), R. Ben. I. 37, 15.

**dreont**, meaning uncertain: deorc ofer dreontum, Rid. 4, 45.

**drēopan**, add: caeli distillauerunt, heofonas drupon, Ps. Roy lxvii, 9; stillicidia stillantia, dropunga dreopenda, id. lxxi, 6.

**drēorig**, add: sense III is uncertain, cf. Campbell, Battle of Brunanburh 114.

**drep**, see gedrep.

**drepan**, see also gedrepan.

**drepen**, delete.

**drettan**, see also oferdrettan.

**drīfan**, add to III: Ranulf ealle his gemot draf and bewiste, Chr. 1099.

**drifenness**, see underdrifenness.

**drihþ**, see gedrihþ.

**driman**, add to I: sense in Fā. 55 (= ASPR iii, 142, 55) seems to be lament, see dream III; add to II: nos decet personare in Dei laudibus, us gedafenað þæt we drymon Godes lof, Chrd. 30, 26.

**drincan**, add to II: 1a with gen.: þæt ælc mann drunce þæs deorwurðan wines be þam þe he sylf wolde, Hml. A. 92, 22.

**drinceléan**, sense is rather entertainment given by the lord to his tenants; cf. Archiv cxxvii, 196.

**drincere**, see also oferdrincere.

**drīpan**, add: stillantia, dryppende, Ps. Sal. lxxi, 6.

**drisn**, note: citation in Dict. reads ruwe oðð drisne, perhaps read here and in citation in Suppl. ruwe oððe drisne. See further Oliphant, The Harley Latin–Old English Glossary 52; Förster, A. xli, 108; Meritt, Neuphil. Mitteilungen lxix, 47. (All regard the word as doubtful.)

**drōfnys**, add: confusa turbida mundi, þa gemengdan drofnyssa middaneard(es), Gn. 21, 1 (JV).

**drohtnung**, see also gedrohtnung.

**dropfāh**, add to Suppl.: may be merely descriptive of a bird, not its name.

**droppetung**, add: in stillicidis, on droppetungum, JEGP lx, 442, III, 3.

**dropung**, see also gedropung.

**drorenlic**, see gedrorenlic.

**dros**, substitute for meaning dross, scum; the lemma is for orichalcum.

**drosenlic**, substitute: drosendlic, adj. falling: Hml. Bel. 140, 28.

**druncen**, n. (not f.), add: ne genihtsumað þe þæt þu sylf an þæt druncen beyrnst, Chrd. 74, 30.

**druncen**, participial adj. having feasted: druncne dryhtguman, B. 1231; 2179.

**druncengeorn**, add: ebriosi, þa druncengeornan, Chrd. 15, 34.

**druncenlǣwe**, glosses inebrians, Ps. Cam. xxii, 5.

**druncmennen**, cancel Suppl., retain Dict.

**druncnian**, add to I: drinc þe man of druncnian mæg, Chrd. 74, 7; add to II: inebrians, druncengende, Ps. Roy. xxii, 5; inebriabuntur, beoð druncnude, id. xxxv, 9. See also for-, fore-, gedruncnian.

**drūpung**, f. torpor: ego torpor, ic eom drupung, Wyn. 64.

**dryhtbearn**, perhaps rather attendant of the bride (cf. dryhtsib).

**dryhtdōm**, delete, in citation read dōmas (as related Ps. Jun., Ps. Cam.), dryht- is repeated from preceding word.

**dryhtealdor**, in Suppl. delete 'for brydguma l. dryhtealdor'.

**dryhtealdorman**, add: *paranimphus*, Chrd. 81, 10.

**dryhtendōm**, add: perhaps delete, citation is emended by many, see Krapp, *Andreas* 39.

**dryhtguma**, see dryhtealdor *above*.

**dryhto**, see indryhto.

**dryhtsib**, rather *peace made by marriage*, cf. force of *dryht* in *dryhtmann*, etc.

**drȳicge**, add: þa mæstan dryicgan (MS. drencga), Verc.-Hom. 77, 51.

**drync**, add to I: excommunicetur, sy he ascyred fram ðæs dæges drince, Chrd. 24, 14.

**dryncgemet**, for Nap. 17 read Chrd. 15, 24.

**drype**, *drip*, see yfesdrype.

**dryslic**, probably *delete*, read ondryslic *in citation*. FL 54.

**drysmian**, add: drysmyde, Exod. 40 (MS. dryrmyde).

**drysne, drysness, drysnlic**, see ondrysne, etc.

**\*dubb**, *pool*, PNE i, 137.

**duguþ**, add to III 2: seo duguð folces on Westan-Cænt, Chart. Rob. 124, 3.

**duguþa**, adv. *splendidly*: B. 2035 (*cited under* bewenian).

**\*dumbel,\*dumpel**, *hollow*, PNE i, 137.

**dumbness**, *citation* = Hml. P. i, 268, 61.

**dūnelfen**, *substitute*: f. *mountain-nymph*: oreades, duunael-finni, OEG 71, 2; but also *Muse*: Castalides, dunelfen (sg. for pl.), WW 189, 9.

**dūne**, see wiþerdune.

**dūngræg**, delete, dun *and* græg *are alternative glosses on* fuscus.

**dūniendlic**, l. 2 *in Suppl.*, read tealtiende *and erase bracket.*

**dūnland**, add: þara ... gemære and þæs dunlandes, CS ii, 448, 12.

**duru**, see helleduru *for gen. sg.* -dures.

**\*dus**, *heap*, PNE i, 140.

**dwællic**, see dwollic.

**dwæscan**, see also gedwæscan.

**dwala**, add: glosses *mammona*: mamonae, dwale, Mt. vi, 24, Rush.

**dwellic**, cf. gedwællic.

**dwild**, add: Fehr 97, 31, v.l.

**dwildlic**, see gedwildlic.

**dwimorlice**, adv. *deceptively*: ðe deofel mæg felæ þingæ dwymorlice hywiæn, Hml. Bel. 102, 34. *See also* gedwimorlice.

**dwinan**, add to compounds ætdwinan.

**dwola**, add to I: Fehr 183, 6, v.l.; add to II: Fehr 93, 34, v.l.; note: *in An. Ox. 2854, MS. reads* dwolan man (? *for þæs* dwolan mannes *or* men, *with* dwol *adj.*, *cf.* gedwol).

**dwolenlic, dwollice, dwolsum**, see ged-.

**dwolian**, see also adwolian.

**dwoligendlic**, adj. *heretical*: Gr. D. 239, 21, v.l.

**dwollic**, add: *palladios*, dwællice (*lemma taken as* '*pagan*'), Prud. 671.

**\*dybb**, *pool*, PNE i, 140.

**dyfe**, f. *hollow*, PNE i, 140; to þære defe, Crawford Charters 25, 55.

**\*dyfel**, *wooden peg*, PNE i, 140.

**\*dylf, \*dylfet**, *pit*, PNE i, 140.

**-dȳne**, see also geandyne.

**dynian**, add: dynede, Chr. 937, *is a corruption*, cf. dennian.

**dynt**, add: II *a pain caused by a blow*: and gað nu þa dyntas þæs deofollican sleges to minum innoðe mid ormætum sarum, Hml. P. ii, 632, 194.

**dyppan**, add: genim ... wos and dype anne linenne clað, Lch. i, 180, 2.

**dyrodine**, the citations are Past. 82, 23; 86, 3. Add: bis tincto cocco, of twibleoum derodine uel of twitælgedun, WW 194, 39.

**dyrstlæcung**, see gedyrstlæcung.

**dyrstlic**, see gedyrstlic.

**dyrstness**, see also gedyrstness.

**dysigcræftig**, adj. *skilled in foolish arts*: he bið disicreafti (v.l. yfele cræftas leornað, *sortilegus*), Archiv cxxviii, 300, 2.

**dysiglic**, *for* dyslic: (let us think) hu dysiglic þæt sie, Vercelli MS., f. 77ʳ, 17.

**dysiglice**, *for* dyslice: swiðe dysiglice hie doð, Verc.-Hom. 140, 35.

**dysigness**, add: *foolish practice*: forlætan we ... dysinessa and gedwollcræftas, Verc.-Hom. 51, 97.

**dyslic**, see also fordyslic.

# E

**ēaca**, add to I c 2: ecan læddon, Exod. 194.

**ēacan**, see also uneacen.

**ēacne**, conj. *nor*: neque, æcne, Jn. vi, 24; xvi, 3, Lind.

**-ēacness**, see toæteacness.

**ēacnian**, see also toæteacnian.

**ēacrop**, *a river plant*: DP 85.

**ēacsōþ**, adv. of affirmation answering to *autem, ergo, etiam, quidem* in Lind., Rush.: Mk. xiv, 21; Lk. iii, xvi; and frequently.

**ēacsōþlice**, adv. of affirmation answering to *autem, etiam, quidem* in Lind., Rush.: æc soðlic, Lk. xxiii, 10; and frequently.

**ēacswā**, adv. *similarly*: ec suæ, Jn. xx, 21, Lind.

**ēad**, adj., add: doubtful word, most editors emend citations.

**ēaganbryhtm**, cf. Verc.-Hom. 78, 60, footnote.

**-ēage (īge)**, see also or-, waldenige.

**ēaghyll**, substitute for sense, *extremity of eyebrow, above inner corner of eye* (angnere).

**ēaghyrne**, f. *corner of eye*: yrqui, heahhyrne (so MS.), WW 156, 41.

**eahta**, add: I a *with ordinals*: þysne eahta and þrittigoþan sealm, Ps. Par. xxxviii, heading; III *the abstract number eight*: nim viii and sete hine on þam forman lyðe þæs þuman, BM 154, 11.

**eahtan**, add: sense *persecute* due to confusion with *ehtan*.

**eahtatīnewintre**, adj. *eighteen years old*: Hml. S. xxxiii, 36.

**eahtnung**, ? see eahtung *below*.

**eahtung**, note: *in first citation in Suppl.* (= *WW 190, 23*) *MS. reads* æhtnunge.

**ēaland**, add: apparently *land near the sea*: B. 2334.

**ēalandcyning**, m. *island-king*: Bd. iv, 16, v.l.

**eald**, see also fram-, healfeald.

**ealddagas**, add: swa hit on ælddagum gestod, Chart. Whit. 36, 23.

**ealdgemǣre**, n. *ancient boundary*: on þæt ealdgemære, CS iii, 546, 28.

**ealdian**, add to compounds aealdian.

**ealdor**, l. 4 *in Suppl., MS. has* þusendes ealdor 'man'. *Add to* I 1 *a* α: principes, ealderas, Ps. L. cxviii, 23; add to I 1 b: Lch. i, 176, 9. *See also* þusendealdor.

**ealdorapostol**, add: Vercelli MS., f. 71ᵛ, 8.

**ealdordōm**, note: *in gloss* ducatus, ealdordom (Dict.), *MS. has* ealdormon *with* -mon *deleted*; -dom *is supplied in Junius' transcript.*

**ealdordōmlic**, adj. *belonging to lordship*: senatorii, ealder-domlices, Archiv cc, 198.

**ealdorlic**, add to II: ðara eahta synna ealdorlicra, *of the eight deadly sins*, Willard, *Two Apocrypha in OE Homilies* 6, 8.

**ealdormann**, see also heah-, oferealdormann. Cf. English Historical Review lxviii, 513.

**ealdorsetl**, n. *official seat*: curules, ealdorsetl, Archiv cc, 198.

**ealdorþegn**, add: Verc.-Hom. 120, 126; Verc. Först. 111, 7 (both of St. Peter).

**ealdung**, see also forealdung.

**ealfara**, m. *pack-horse*: xxx þusende ealfarena and oxna, þa þe hwæte bæron, Rypins, *Three Old English Prose Texts* 13, 7.

**ēalic**, adj. *of a river*: fluminei, ealice, OEG 28, 216. Cf. healic *below*.

**ēalifer**, add: calistricus uel calitricem, ealifer uel ueteruyrt, DP 78.

**eall**, add to I 1 α: fram eallum costnungum to ealre glædnysse, Hml. A. 26, 42; farað into ealne middaneard (*mundum uniuersum*), Mk. xvi, 15 (West-Saxon Gospels); þæt tacnað ealne gefean, Lch. iii, 156, 13; ealle þa vii dagas, Fehr 152, 11; add to I 1 b: man dele æal healf þæt yrue, Chart. Whit. 36, 32; add to II 3 α: him eall þa eagan floterodon, Hml. S xxiii, 655; *delete* Nar. 9, 10, *for which see* ealfara.

**eallefne**, adj. *universal*: uniuersa turba, allefne þæt folc, Lk. xxiii, 18, Lind. (Rush. alefne).

**ealleþeren**, adj. *entirely of leather*: scetra, ealleþern scyldas, Journ. Brit. Arch. Ass. xli, 147.

**eallhālgung**, f. *consecration*: probably reflects *sacra omnia*, A. xli, 106, 51. See FL 106.

**eallsweart**, adj. *quite black*: mid eallsweartum lichaman, Hml. P. ii, 778, 92.

**eallwihta**, *note*: this form is gen. pl.; add eallwihtna hryre, Verc.-Hom. 47, 48.

**ealning**, *add*: alning, IC 49; 187; *in first citation in Suppl.* (= *ASPR vi*, 68, 29) *read* ealninga bidde.

**ealsealf**, *delete*, *error* (*due to D'Ewes*) *for* elesealf (*q.v. in Suppl.*).

**ealugālness**, *for* Nap. 19 *read* Verc.-Hom. 51, 97.

**ealusæl**, n. *alehouse*: on ænigum ealasele, IP 265.

**ealuscerwen**, *add*: cf. EGS, iv, 67.

***ēan**, *lamb*, PNE i, 143.

**ēar**, *wave*, *add*: ofer æra gebland, Chr. 937 (= Brun. 26, v.l., cf. eargebland).

**earc**, *citation* Wrt. Voc. 16, 37 (= WW 107, 3) *has* earca (? *for* earce, *or wk masc.*) *in MS.*

**eard**, *add to compounds* mideard.

***eardærn**, n. *dwelling house*, PNE i, 144.

**eardere**, m. *inhabitant*: habitatores, eardderas, Ps. Sal., Hy. 4, 15.

**eardiend**, *see* ymbeardiend.

**eardlufe**, f. *beloved country*: B. 692.

**eardrice**, *delete*, *in citation read* eardwica (*so MS.*).

**eardung**, *see also* wundor-, ymbeardung.

**earendel**, *read* ēarendel.

**earfoþhilde**, *substitute for meaning* discontented: cf. iþ-, oþhilde.

**earfoþlǣre**, *add*: indisciplinatos, þa earfoþlæran, Chrd. 18, 6.

**earfoþlice**, *see also* unearfoþlice.

**earfoþrihte**, *for* Nap. 19 *read* Chrd. 42, 1 (*incorrigibilis*).

**earhfaru**, *add*: ni anoegun ic me aerigfaerae egsan brogum, ASPR vi, 109; *in pharetra*, on coxre uel on earhfære, Ps. Cam. x, 3.

**ēarlæppa**, in second citation in Dict. (= WW 157, 12), *earlæppan* is added in error, see FL 102; note Isidore, Etym. xi, 1, 46, *Pinnula summa pars auris*.

**earm**, *add*: III *arm of a cross*: under þære rode swyðran earme, Vis. Lfc. 53. *Add to compounds* innanearm.

**earmboga**, retain Dict., delete cancellation in Suppl. (cf. MS. Bodley 730, f. 146ᵛ, col. 3).

**earmfull**, *add*: II *humble*: mid getrywre and mildre and earmfulre and eaðmodre heortan, Verc.-Hom. 84, 129.

**earmheortness**, *see* hearmheortness *below*.

**earn**, *see also* isearn.

**earngēap**, *add*: see Gött. gel. Anz. 1914, 158; A. xli, 118, n. 2. Note explanation in Dict. of *arpa* as *harpe* is probable.

**earnian**, *see also* ungeearnod.

**earningland**, *add*: Chart. Whit. 88, 31; on meaning cf. Chart. Whit. 178; cf. earninga land, Chart. Rob. 124, 29; þat land, þat Sewine haueð to earninge, Chart. Whit. 80, 16.

**earnung**, *add to I*: ne þær ne bið nan earnung, ac bið edlean gewiss ealre ure dæda, *there is there no effort without there being a reward*, Hml. P. ii, 551, 106.

**ēarplættian**, *for* earplættan: earplættigen, Hml. Warn. 137, 25.

**ears**, add: *applied to a feature of landscape*, on oxaners, CS iii, 586, 30.

**earsgang**, *add to II*: stercus et urinam, þæt meox his argancges (sic) and his micgan, Chrd. 69, 29. (*On recurrent* argang *see A. xxx, 128*.)

**earþyrel**, *see* FL 123 for defence of meaning *ear-passage*.

**earu**, *add*: gearu, Exod. 339 (*allit. vocalic*); *many emend citation in Dict.* to earmne *or* eargne.

**ēase**, sense is *cup*, Indogermanische Forschungen xlviii, 266; A. xlix, 379.

**ēast**, *add to I 3*: gebide þe þriwa east, Lch. iii, 60, 16; *add to II*: gif þunor bið mycel east oððe norðeast, Archiv cxx, 48, 4.

**ēast**, adj., *add*: on ðæt eastre sic, CS iii, 154, 2 from below.

**ēastan**, *add to I*: ab oriente, from eastan, Mt. viii, 11, Rush.

**ēastende**, *add*: innan þære cyricean . . . inn æt þam eastende, Vis. Lfc. 52.

**ēasterlic**, *add*: IV *eastern*: eoy sideris, easterlices tungles, Gn. 21, 4 (JV; v.l. easternes, Hy. Surt. 22, 5).

**ēasterniht**, *add*: on forman easterniht, Modern Philology i, 611, 6 from below.

**ēastmearc**, f. *eastern boundary*: C.D. vi, 243, 2.

***ēastor**, adj. *eastern*, PNE i, 149.

**ēaþbēde, -bēne**: *these are variants* Ps. Par. lxxxix. 15 (cf. BO 96, 25).

**ēaþbilg**, *quickness to anger*: Verc.-Hom. 103, 343, v.l.

**ēaþe**, *add to 2*: 2 a *easily moved* to do something: munuc eaþe and hræd on hlehtre (*facilis ac promptus in risu*), R. Ben. 30, 9.

**ēaþe**, adv., ēaþelice, eaþelicness, *see also* foreaþe, etc.

**ēaþlǣre**, adj., *easily taught*: ærest man sceal þa yldestan læran, þæt þurh hig þa gingran siððan beon þe eaðlæran (*facilius doceantur*), Chrd. 96, 13.

**ēaþmēdan**, *see also* geeaþmedan.

**ēaþmettan**, *see* geeaþmettan.

**ēaþmōdheort**, adj. *humble of heart*: eaðmodheorte (pl.), Az. 152.

**ēaþness**, *add*: ealle þa godan hyne geseoð, heom to are and eaðnesse, Solil. H. 67, 15 (= Endter 67, 33).

**ēawiscness**, f. *openness, manifestness*: in propatulo, on æwiscnesse, WW 424, 21; 486, 28.

**ēawodness**, f. *showing*: ostentionem, eawdnise, Rtl. 113, 17.

**eaxfaru**, *delete*, *see* æscfaru.

**ece**, *add*: ic þrowode mycelne ece minre heortan and liflicra leoma, Gr. D. 243, 18; healfes heafdes ece, *pain in the front of the head* (cf. healfheafod), Lch. ii, 20, 21. *Add to compounds* heafod-, heort-, hypeban-, lendenece.

**ēce**, add: *not perishable*: geworht of ecum antimbre, Fehr 126, 26. *See also* samodece.

**ēce**, adv., *add*: in aeternum, ece, Ps. Par. li, 7.

**ecg**, *see also* suþecg.

**ecgan**, *see also* geecgan.

**Ecgbryhtes stān**, *add*: the site is unknown.

**-ecge**, *add*: fiþerecge.

**-ecgede**, *add* an-, sixecgede.

**edblōwan**, v. glosses *effloreo*: efflorebit, edblewð, Ps. Vit. cii, 15.

**edcenned**, participial adj., *for* geedcenned: Hml. P. i, 483, 96, v.l.

**edcœlness**, *substitute*: f. glosses *refrigerium*: edcoelnesse (acc.), Ps. Jun., Ps. Ar. lxv, 12.

**edcwic**, *add*: rediuiuae, (ð)æs edcuican, OEG 4, 328.

**edhirtan**, *see* geedhirtan.

**edhwirfan**, v. *return*: redeat, ædhwyrfe, Ps. Roy. cviii, 15; recalcitrauit, he edhwyrfte, id., Hy. 6, 15.

**edhwyrft**, *add to III*: he us edhwyrft forgeaf to þam ecean life þe we ær forworhton, Verc.-Hom. 52, 114.

**edisc**, on broel see Dict. s.v.

**edischen**, *add*: gaus, hedeshen, Ælfc. Gr. Z. 307, 8 n. (late gloss).

**edrine**, *read* -ryne; *add*: Ps. Roy. xviii, 7.

**edspellung**, f. *repetition*: recapitulatio, OEG 20, 3 (ed. *not clear*; cf. eftspellung).

***edtelgung**, *see* ættelg *above*.

**edwendan**, *delete* B. 280 (*where read* edwenden), *add*: gewitende and na edwendende (*rediens*), Ps. Roy. lxxvii, 39.

**edwilm**, *whirlpool*, only 'fiery' from the context.

**efelēac**, *delete* (*error for* eneleac).

**efen**, *see also* efenemn, toefnes.

**efenemn**, adj. *equally level*: compeditos, efenemne, Ps. Cant. cxlv, 7 (*lemma misunderstood*).

**efenforþ**, adj. *equally advanced*: and we lærað þæt preostas beon efenforðe ofer geares fæc on eallum cyricþenungum, IP 197, v.l.

**efenlician**, *add*: complaceant, efnlicien, Ps. Vit. xviii, 15.

**efenneahtlic**, adj. *equinoctial*: on anre æfenneahtlicre tide beoð feower punctas, ten minuta, fiftene partes, feowortig momenta, be sumra manna tale, Henel, *Studien zum altenglischen Computus* 65.

**efenness**, *add*: used literally, æquoris, emnesse, OEG 4, 51.

**efes**, *see also* norþefes.

**efesian**, *see also* aefesian.

**efestan**, *see also* ofestan.

**efestlice**, *add*: IC 262.

**efesung**, *see also* unefesung.

**Eficisc**, meaning is *Ephesian*.

**efne**, adv. *add to I 3*: (land) dælan . . . swa hig efnost magon Chart. Whit. 46, 17; *add to II 2*: for hwon . . . buton efne for þon, Mart. H. 156, 15–20. *See also* allefne.

**efne**, *alum*: probably error for ælifn, *see above*.

**efne**, *material, see also* eall-, landefne.

**efnettan**, *add to I*: se cræftga . . . ne blinneþ þæt he betriende bete þa onlicnessa and efnette, Gr. D. 283, 27.

**efneunrōtness**, f. *sadness*: de uitae contristato, of lifes efneunrotnise, Mt., p. 20, 17, Lind.

**efneunrōtsad,** participial adj., glosses contristatus, Mt. xvii, 23, Lind.

**eftbigengo,** glosses recolenda: Rtl. 23, 5.

**eftcirr,** m. return: reuersionem, eftcerr, Lk., p. 8, 18, Lind.

**eftcynn,** n. see edniwung in Suppl.

**eftforfindan,** v. reprove: reprehensores, eftforfundeno (? for pres. part), Mt., p. 18, 20, Lind.

**eftgeafung,** f. remuneration, see eftgeearnung.

**eftgeearnung,** delete, read in citation eftgeafunge (so MS.).

**efthwirfan,** v. for efthweorfan: rediens, efthwerfende, Ps. Vit., lxxvii, 39; Hml. S. xxiii b, 613 (cited in Suppl., s.v. efthweorfan).

**eftlīsend,** m. redeemer: redemptor, eftlesend, Rtl. 126, 10.

**eftscippan,** v. recreate: reforma, eftscepe, PBB lxxxv (Halle), 61.

**eftsōna,** add: identidem, OEG 22, 6; Ælfc. Gr. Z, 238, 2.

**eftwyrd,** follow Dict. rather than Suppl.

**ēgesa,** owner, delete, in citation egesan is gen. sg. of egesa, fear.

**egesfulness,** add: incorrectly used for egesfull or egesfullic, Ps. Jun. cxliv, 6.

**egeslic,** see also ondegeslic.

**egesung,** add: miscens terroribus blandimenta, wrixla frefra onmang egesungum, Chrd. 18, 5.

**egeswin,** a fish (perhaps *ǣgswin): millago, egeswin, Nap. 14.

**egeþgetigu,** read -getigu, -geteogu.

**egle,** ail: cancel bracket in l. 2 in Suppl. and see fonfyr; cancel II in Suppl. as egl', B. 987, is rather for eglu, nom. sg. fem. of egle, adj.

**egle,** adj., add: often confused with engel in MSS., e.g. Cri. 762, Gu. 962, and perhaps Gen. 328.

**ēgor,** note: on dodrans see An. Ox. p. 180; on malina, Lindsay, Corpus Glossary 211.

**ēgsa,** owner, probably delete, passage is of uncertain meaning.

**egþwirf,** cf. Chart. Rob. 329.

**eit,** island: on mǣdum, on eitum, on wæterum, C.D. iv, 211, bottom line.

***ēl,** small island, PNE i, 149.

**elcian,** see also forelcian.

**elcor,** add to IV: ceterum, ellicor, Chrd. 80, 20.

**elcora,** add: and þonne hie ælcra drincan willen . . ., Lch. ii, 202, 17.

**ele,** last citation in Dict., MS. has eledrosna (q.v. in Suppl.). See also lipule.

**Elebearumōr,** m. Mount of Olives: in monte qui uocatur Oliueti, on more se þe geceigd is Olebearumore, Lk. xxi, 37, Lind.

**eleberende,** participial adj. oil-bearing: oliferis uasis, eleberendum fatum, OEG 8, 17.

**elegrēne,** Ps. Sal. cxxvii, 3, see æle-.

**elegrēofa,** substitute for meaning residue of pressed olives (?); cf. FL 67.

**elehtre,** add: on mali terre, see A. xli, 126, n. 2; DP 58.

**eleseocche,** delete question-marks; on lemma note Isid., Etym. xx, 14, 13, fisclum quasi fiscolum, a colando oleum dictum, uel quasi fiscella olei.

**ell,** adj. other: on elran men, B. 752; reliqui, elle, Mt. xxii, 6, Rush. (ōa oðero, Lind.).

**ellen,** add: contest: in agonia, in elne, WW 424, 12.

**Ellendūn,** add: now known to be Wroughton, Wilts.

**ellenweorc,** add: Vercelli MS., f. 92ᵛ, 21.

**elleoht, emleoht,** note: the second element of these may be an error for -leahtor; cf. stæfleahtor in Suppl.

***ellret,** elder copse, PNE i, 150.

**elm,** add: ulmus, helm, WW 279, 14.

***elmen,** adj. near or grown with elms, PNE i, 150.

**elra,** delete, and see ell.

**elren,** adj. of alder wood: on þone ælrenan stob, C.D. iii, 316; PNE i, 150.

**emblissian,** v. for blissian (? = embeblissian): Ps. Vit. lxvii, 4.

**emleoht,** see elleoht above.

**emn,** see also efenemn.

**-en,** see also scerwen, scilcen, scilden.

**end,** variant form of and, conj., mainly in early texts: aend, Txts. 42, 98; end, id. 37, 75; 430, 15; 446, 29; 453, 29; ASPR vi, 105, 2; Mk. fr. 1, 13, Lind.; þin ben is gehyred, end þin wif gebereð sunu, Archiv cxxii, 253, 91.

**end,** adv., is doubtful, see ASPR iii, 358.

**ende III,** kind, sort, is a separate word (? ēnde, v.l. ēonde; cf. Ritter, Vermischte Beiträge zur englischen Sprachgeschichte 44).

**endebyrdan,** see also misendebyrdan.

**endebyrdlice,** add to I: glosses secundum ordinem, Chrd. 45, 33; disposite, 47, 32; ornate, 57, 9. See also unendebyrdlice.

**endebyrdness,** add to V 2: preostas hyra endebyrdnessa (ordines) sceolon healdan, eal swa hig geendebyrde (ordinati) synt, Chrd. 9, 16. See also geendebyrdness.

**endemǣst,** substitute: adj. endmost, last: se ændemeste cwide, Hml. Warn. 76, 1.

**endian,** see also full-, þurhgeendian.

**enge,** on citation Germ. 395, 24, in Suppl. see hengetreow below.

**Engle,** add to compounds Middelengle.

**Englisc,** add: II 2 b passage in English: ðis Englisc ætywð hwæt seo forsette ræding mænð, BM 4, 17; ic menge þæt Lyden amang þyssum Englisce, BM 112, 31.

**engness,** for angness: þæt bið ængnes (v.l. angnys), Archiv cxxxiv, 286, 13.

**eodor,** add to I: Gen. 2445, 2487 (Heliand 4943). On meaning cf. PBB xli, 163; Hoops, Kommentar zum Beowulf 130.

**ēofed,** see īfed below.

**eofot,** add: epiphonima, causa, contentio, efat, reub, ZfdA xxxiii, 243, 33 n. 1 (= Germania xiii, 480, Werden leaves); incussatio, efat, reof, id. 33 (Munster leaves).

**eolet,** cf. also EGS v, 17; viii (English Philological Studies), 24.

**eolone,** delete citation ybys, eolone (= Prud. 417), where an animal is meant: cf. geolna in Dict., and eldne in Suppl. See also horseolone.

**eorlgifu,** f. gift of a noble: ceorl wyrð þurh eorlgife þegenlage wyrðe, IP 256.

**eornostlice,** add: ergo, geornust[lice], A. xiii, 439, 1052 (cf. 1062).

**eorre,** correct cross reference to irre (not yrre), and so related words.

**eorþæppel,** add: cyclaminos, eortheppel, DP 12, 118; terre malum, eorðeppel, OEG 73 b, 1.

**eorþberige,** for lemma read fraga, cf. Oliphant, The Harley Latin–Old English Glossary 195.

**eorþcrop,** an unknown plant: camelon, eorthcrop, DP 83.

**eorþcundlic,** add: eorþcundlice men, Verc. Först., 99, 10.

**eorþe,** add to I 2 a: ferian an lic to eorþan, Hml. Th. ii, 508 16. See also lencten-, mægdeneorþe.

**eorþen,** note v.l. eorðernum.

**eorþgealla,** add: oxilapatium, eorthuealle (sic) uels cearpe docce, DP 16, 264.

**eorþgestrēon,** n. earthly treasure: Wlfst. 263, 24, v.l.

**eorþhnutu,** add: gentiana, eorthnutu uel felduirt, DP 14, 186. On sense, cf. DP note ad loc., OED s.v. earth-nut, Middle Eng. Dict. s.v. erþe 13 (ee).

**eorþryne,** m. earthquake: terrae motus, eorðrenas, A. lxxiii, 19, 11.

**eorþtilia,** see irþtilia.

**eorþtilung,** f. agriculture: dei agricultura estis, ge synd Godes eorðteolung, Hml. P. ii, 597, 152.

**eotenweard,** cancel. Suppl., keep Dict., and see abeodan above.

**eow,** yew, read ēow.

**ēowan,** add: ostendat, geowige, A. xiii, 427, 894.

**ēowd,** add to forms: ewod, Ps. Roy. lxxvii, 52; efodum, id. xlix, 9; eowodum lxxvii, 70.

**ēowigendlic,** adj. demonstrative: Ælfc. Gr. Z. 231, 5, v.l.

**ēowocig,** substitute for meaning yolky, full of natural grease.

***ere-,** ploughing, PNE i, 156.

**erian,** see also unered.

**esne,** add to I: gif mannes esne frigne mannan ofslæhð, Hlothhere and Eadric 3; gif cirican mannes esne tihte folces mannes esne, his dryhten hine geclensige, Wiht. 24; gif mon sweordes onlæne oðres esne, Ine 29; se ðe slea his agenne þeowne esne, Ll. Ælf., Introduction 17; add to II: mon on ealdum bigspellum cwyð, þæt hwilum beo esnes tid, hwilum oðres, Prov. K. 31 (= Hml. Warn. 4, 34); add: the word occurs as a proper name and has the patronymic Esning, Txts. 543.

**esnecund,** for lemma MS. has condiciorius, probably for conducticius.

**ēst,** add to II: aliquod pulmentum, sumne smealicne est, Chrd. 15, 37.

**ēstēadig**, adj. *luxurious*: often read in Seaf. 56, cf. sefteadig

**ēstlic**, adj. *dainty*: for þan estlice meten and for þa gode dræncen, Hml. Warn. 143, 27.

**ēstness**, f. *bliss*: Eden þæt is inne estnysse ond inne blisse, Hept. 419, 8 (late addition).

**ēstfull**, *see also* unestfull.

**-estre**, *see also* bæc-, bepæc-, bigeng-, byrd-, cenn- (cynn-), crenc-, forsæw-, fylg-, gliwbyden-, hearp-, hopp-, hulf-, ic-, lættew-, lopp-, luf-, lybb-, nidhæm-, tæpp-, telg-, þegn-, wæsc-, webb-, witeg-, wregestre.

**etan**, *add to compounds* aetan.

**\*etisc(e)**, *plot of land*, PNE i, 162.

**etol, etolness**, *see also* ofere.

**eþelicness**, *add*: *facultas* (for *facilitas*), eþelicnes, WW 400, 39.

**eþelriht**, meaning is practically *ēþel*.

**eþgung**, *add*: R. Ben. 68, 3 (*cited under* sogoþa).

**eþian**, *see also* toeþian.

**eþung**, *see also* ineþung.

**euangelista**, m. *evangelist*: Verc.-Hom. 16, 133; Lch. ii, 294.

# F

**fācenlēas**, *add*: *of persons*, þa facenleasan, Vercelli MS., f. 116ᵛ, 12.

**fācenness**, f. *deceitfulness*: *calliditatem*, facennisse, JEGP lx, 449.

**fadung**, *see also* liffadung.

**fæc**, *add to compounds* hwil-, sibfæc.

**fǣcnig**, for Nap. 78 *read*: *propter dolos*, fore fæcnigum, Ps. Roy. lxxii, 18; fæhðnigum, Ps. Sal.

**fǣcnung**, f. *suspicion*: *suspicionem*, fæcnunge, A. lxv, 14.

**fæderen**, *see also* forþfæderen.

**fædernama**, *patronymic*: Hml. Warn. 53, 21.

**fæfne**, Lk. i, 27, Rush., *read* fæmne (*uirginem*).

**fǣgan**, *inf*. should rather be \*fǣn.

**fǣge**, *add*: see analysis of senses Studia Germanica Gandensia iv, 165; cf. A. lxxxiii, 90.

**fægen**, *delete* Seafarer 13, *where MS. reads* fægrost.

**fægenness**, f. *joy*: ond þærrihtes beot hire handan togædere for fagennesse, Napier 21 (all instances from MS. Corpus Christi College, Cambridge, 303).

**fæger**, *see also* hiwfæger.

**fægnung**, *add*: II *applause*: *see* rægiming *in Dict. and Suppl*.

**fǣhþ**, *feud, see also* manfǣhþ.

**fær**, *add to compounds* gean-, gedwolfær.

**fǣran**, *see also* æfæred, gefærede.

**fǣrbifongen**, *delete* (*first element illegible*).

**fǣrcumen**, participial adj., *sudden*: *inopina salus*, færcumen hael, OEG 9, 100.

**fǣrdēaþ**, *add*: for hwon ne ondrædest þu þe þæt þe ferdeað bereafie þæs dæges þinre gehwyrfednesse, Archiv cxxii, 257, 10.

**fǣreld**, *add to* I: *membra deliberare non potest*, ne mæg he begyman his lyma færeldes, Chrd. 75, 4; *simplici habitu incessuque*, mid heora bilwitton gyrlan and færelde, id. lxxvii, 3.

**fǣrfrige**, adj. *free to go*: þæt he moste adon Byrhtgyþe ut of þam geburlande . . . færfrige, Charts. in Förster, *Flussname Themse* 794-5.

**fǣring**, probably *delete* II, *see* SHG 116.

**fǣrlic**, *add*: II a *rapid* (of movement): mid færlicum (v.l. swiftum) ryne, Gr. D. 115, 22.

**fǣrlīce**, *add*: IV *quickly*: he to fundode swa færlice, Hml. S. iii, 467.

**fǣrness**, f. *suddenness*: *in subitatione*, on færnesse, JEGP lx, 447.

**fǣrsēaþ**, *discussed* Oliphant, *The Harley Latin–Old English Glossary* 15; 26.

**fǣrstice**, *substitute for meaning* rheumatism.

**fǣrstylt**, *MS. has* feerstylt' *for* -styltness.

**fǣrswīge**, f. *sudden silence*: *stupore*, feersuigo, Mk. v, 42, Lind. (Rush. swigunge).

**fæst**, *add to* III 2: swilce he on fæstre eorðan urne, Hml. Th. ii, 160, 10; *add to* IV: *ciuitas ad salutem tuta*, þæt sio burg wære genoh fæst on his hælo, Past. 399, 25; *add to* IV a: of a place that can be shut up: *omnes in uno conclaui atrii com-*

*morentur*, wunion ealle an anre fæstre wununge, Chrd. 54, 32. *Add to compounds* heorþ-, hiw-, hlid-, hoga-, hoh-, ofer-, rotfæst.

**fæsten**, *add to Suppl*.: III *vigil of a festival*: and ðæs ymbe v niht bið Sanctæ Marian mæsse, and þær is fæsten to, Henel, *Studien zum altengl. Computus* 72. *See also* lac-, midfæsten.

**fæstenwicu**, *add*: on þære forman fæstenwucan on lencten, Henel, *Studien zum altengl. Computus* 61.

**fǣstlīce**, *add to* (3): *pueri iugibus disciplinis constringantur*, þa cild . . . beon fæstlice behealdene mid steorum, Chrd. 54, 21; *seuerissime correptus*, þreage hine man fæstlice, id. 55, 4.

**fæstnian**, *add to* I 2: and he allum wæterum þæt mægen fæstnode, Vercelli MS., f. 86ʳ, 3. *Add to compounds* þurh-, unfæstnian.

**fæt**, *add to compounds* ciric-, glæs-, hlæd, mete-, ol-, recels-, sadol-, stenc-, wæter-, wunderfæt.

**fǣtan**, *see also* goldfæted.

**fǣtt**, m., *delete*, MS. obscure (MLR xi, 215).

**fæþel**, cf. JEGP xlix, 232; FL 147; E.S. xxxvii, 183.

**fæþm**, probably *delete sense* (5) in Suppl., where *pugnus* is rather given sense of *pugillus* (which is explained as *se gripe þære hand*, WW 158, 16).

**fāg**, *add*: in B. 725 and C.D. 340 (= CS 607) *to fagan flore* meaning is probably *tessellated*; of weapons, as B. 1701, Jud. 194, meaning is usually *damascened*. *Add to compounds* hweol-, sinc-, synfag.

**fāh**, *see also* scurfah.

**fala**, *substitute for meaning*: *pipe, tube* (*tubulus*); note *tabula* (-*o*) common error of Epinal and Erfurt Glossaries; form may be dat. sg. (E.S. xxxviii, 337). Another view SHG 57.

**\*faldere**, m. *one who folds animals*, PNE i, 164.

**faldhrīþer**, *add*: Chart. Rob. 248, 20.

**faldwyrþe**, *substitute for meaning* entitled to have his own fold (cf. Chart. Harm. 476).

**fām**, *note*: delete gloss *molles*, fam, hwastas, WW 443, 23, *where read* uani *for* fam (see Corpus Glossary M 245); note transferred sense *deceitful speech* (= leasung) in first citation in Suppl.

**fāmigbord**, *substitute*: adj. *with foamy sides*: ænne famigbordon ðriereðreceol, Met. xxvi, 26.

**fang**, *see also* heals-, herefang.

**fantbletsung**, f. *blessing of baptismal water*: swa swa he cwyð to Gode on þære fantbletsunge, Fehr 188, 12.

**fara**, *add* ealfara.

**faran**, *add to* II 1: ælc mann þe on modignysse færð, Hml. S. xxxiv, 315. *Add to compounds* firr-, full-, mis-, niþer-, weg-faran.

**farendlic**, adj. *pervious, penetrable*: *peruium*, JEGP lx, 444.

**farenness**, *see* þurhfarenness.

**faru**, *substitute for* IV *in Suppl*. (*for citation there given see* ealfara *above*): *equipment of a vehicle*: and macodan þone wæn mid ealre þære fare, Hml. P. ii, 691, 274. *Add to compounds* æsc-, fram-, gedwol-, ham-, in-, ymbfaru.

**fasn**, *for* fæs: *fimbriam*, fasne (? dat.), Mk. vi, 56; Lk. viii, 44, Lind.

**faþu**, *in citation* Wrt. Voc. 52, 18 (= WW 174, 16) *MS. reads* faþan, *see* A. viii, 451.

**feald**, *fold, ply*: ofer þam xii fealdum þara wealla, Willard, *Two Apocrypha in OE Homilies* 6, 4. Cf. neahfeald.

**fealdian**, *see* be-, twifealdian.

**fealdlic**, *see* neahfealdlic.

**feall**, *add*: *guttatim*, hnescum fealle, Hpt. Gl. 408, 33. *See also* on-, wælfeall.

**feallan**, *see also* onfeallende.

**fealþing**, perhaps *weight used as counterpoise*.

**-fēaness**, *joy, see* gefeaness.

**fearhhama**, *sow's womb*, should not be emended as in Suppl. See JEGP xlvi, 416; FL 101.

**fearnhege**, *see* hege *in Suppl*.

**fēawa**, *add to* I 1: *super pauca*, ofer fæawum, Mt. xxv, 21, Rush.; *add to* I 2: feawa fixa, Mk. viii, 7 (West-Saxon Gospels).

**fēawlic**, *for* feaw, Ps. Cant. civ, 12.

**fēawness**, *see also* gefeawness.

**feax**, *add*: *pro diuersa capillorum specie*, fore missenlicre heora feaxes hiwe, Bd. v, 10.

**feaxēaca**, ? *delete*, read in citation feax earan, *hair of the ear*; cf. earloccas, and see FL 161.

**feaxede**, *see also* heahfeaxede.

**feccan**, *see also* infeccan.

**fēdan,** *see also* misfedan.

**fēdelfugol,** m. *fatted bird*: altilia, foedelfuglas, Mt. xxii, 4, Rush.

**fēgness,** *see* gefegness.

**feht,** ? *sheepskin*: Txts., Ct. 28, 7; *uellas,* ueht uel flys, Ps. Cant. lxxi, 6. *Cf.* fiht *below.*

**fel,** *add to* (3): *garment of skin*: si pes laxa pelle non fulgeat, þæt heora fell swa wide hangion þæt se fot ne ætywe, Chrd. 64, 31; *but in citation from Lk. Lind.* fell *is probably error for* felleread (q.v.). *See also* goldfel.

**fela,** *add to* III 6: þara minra awuht fela on gewrit settan, L. Ælf. pref.

**felafealdness,** f. *glosses* multitudo: felefaldnesse (acc.), Ps. Cant. v, 11.

**felamōdig,** *add*: B. 1888.

**felarīce,** adj. *very rich*: Hml. Th. i, 582, 14.

**felasprecol,** *add*: magniloquam, fælaspecelan, Ps. Sal. xi, 4 (Ps. Roy. felaspeculan).

**felcyrf,** *add*: preputium, felcyrf, JEGP lx, 446.

**feld,** *see also* hæþ-, man-, mylen-, oretfeld.

**felde,** discussed E.S. xxxvii, 184.

**feldefare,** *MS. reads* feldeware, WW 287, 17.

**feldelfen,** *add*: Maides, feldaelfinne, OEG 71, 5.

**feldlǣs,** f. *field pasture, pasture in open country*: feldlæs and mæda and yrðland, CS iii, 307, 22; seo feldles, C.D. iv, 96, 2.

***feldware,** *dwellers in open country*, PNE i, 168.

**feldwop,** *rather wild hop*; cf. bratum, unde efficitur cereuisia, bratigapo, herba, quae admiscetur, *cited* A. xxxv, 153. Later taken as feld+wōp. Cf. E. M. Furn., p. 200. Less probable view Beiblatt xvii, 297, Archiv cxix, 435 (*grasshopper*).

**fellen,** *see* goldfellen.

**fellerēad** *is probably a consistent error of Lind. and Rush. for* *pelleread, see* Neuphil. Mitteil. lxii, 1.

**felma,** *substitute*: *membrane*: cittis (i.e. ciccis), felmum, OEG 3, 2. *See also* ægerfelma, filmen.

**fēlness,** *add*: passio, JEGP lx, 444.

**felt,** *for the lemmata, note* cento, centu(n)culus, *are regularly equated with* filtrum.

**feltūngrēp,** *add*: see Verc.-Hom. 146, note 48.

**feltwyrt,** *for* anadon(i)a *read* auadon(i)a *in all citations.*

**fen,** *add to* 2: palus, Gyrwe fen, Ælfc. Gr. Z. 60, 10; ic gean þæt fen . . . ic gean an þusend werð fen . . . þæt healfe þusend fen, Chart. Whit. 72, 20.

**feng,** *add*: gremio, fence, OEG 9, 111.

**-fenge,** *add* unfenge.

**fengel,** *perhaps trap*: on fengel, CS ii, 432, 22; PNE i, 169.

**fengness,** *see* fore-, onfengness.

**fēogaþ,** *delete,* fiegaþ *in citation is pl. pres. indic. of* feogan, *hate,* hæbbende *is an unnecessary addition.*

**feoh,** *add to compounds* here-, sundorfeoh.

**feohgafol,** *for* Nap. 21 *read* Chrd. 76, 32.

**feohgesceot,** n. *money-payment*: nelle we to him gyrnan feohgesceotes, Brot. 28, 33.

**feohgestrēon,** *add*: amorem pecuniae, lufe feohgestreona, Chrd. 76, 34.

**feohhord,** *add to Dict.*: aerarium, JEGP lx, 446. (*Word wrongly deleted in Suppl.*)

**feohleas,** *the sense in* B. 2441 *is rather* unatonable by money; *cf.* Medium Ævum viii, 198.

**feoht,** *add to compounds* infeoht.

**feohtegod,** n. *war-god*: hi þeowdan Marte heora feohtegode, Hml. P. ii, 686, 171.

**feohtere,** *add*: bellator erit, feohtere he bið, Archiv cxxix, 20, 3.

**feohwīce,** *meaning uncertain*: is þis ðara feohwicuna gemære and ðæs dunlandes, CS ii, 448, 12 (supplied from late copy).

**fēolan,** *add*: þær ic wiste hu ic ut fulge, Verc.-Hom. 95, 255.

**fēon,** *rejoice, note*: *citation from* An. Ox. = Verc. Först. 125, 18.

**fēond,** *add*: ne blissaþ fynd (inimicus) ofer me, Ps. L. xl, 12; on handum fyndes, id. lxxvii, 61.

**fēondulf,** *add*: cf. deofles wulf, *cited in Dict. s.v.* wulf II; *cf.* Prud. 617, note.

**feorbuend,** *add*: Sal. 271.

**feorh,** *add*: meaning is *dead body* in B. 1152, 1210.

**feorhbora,** m. *living thing*: Rid. 92, 2.

**feorhhama,** *see* fearhhama *above.*

**feorhlege,** *read* -legu, *and note sense in* B. 2800 *is* span of life, *life.*

**feorhlic,** *see* widefeorhlic.

**feorhnest,** n. *victuals*: epimenia, feornesta, JEGP lx, 445.

**feorhweard** f. *guard over life*: ferhwearde heold guþmod grimmon (MS. grummon), *courage kept guard over life for the warriors,* B. 305.

**feorlicor,** adv. comp. *from further*: ac þeos na feorlucor bute of hire agene breostes meolca fedde, Hml. Warn. 137, 1.

**feorm,** *delete* III *in Dict., take citation under* II *entertainment; add to* I b *in Suppl.*: ond nam þær his feorme (v.l. and his feorme þær heold), *and received his food-rents there,* Chr. 1006; *add to* II: *of an arval feast*: se gyldscipe hyrfe þe healfre feorme þone forþferedan, Cht. Th. 611, 5. *Add to compounds* luffeorm.

**feormland,** n. *land yielding food-rent*: þes kynges ahhen fermeland, Chart. Rob. 230, 13, 24.

**feorrian,** *add to compounds* oþfeorrian.

**fēorþandǣl,** *add*: per quadra quatuor partiti, on feower feorþandælas todælde, Gr. D. 87, 4.

**feorþēod,** f. *distant country*: eardigende in feorþiode, Wyn. 199.

**fēowergǣrede,** adj. *four-pointed*: Ælfc. Gr. Z. 288, 11.

**fēowerstrenge,** adj. *four-stringed*: Ælfc. Gr. Z. 288, 11.

**fēowertēoþa,** *add*: on þan feowertenðen dæige, Hml. Warn. 91, 2.

**fēowertig,** *add to* I 1 α: Lch. ii, 284, 21; Gr. D. 98, 14.

**fēowertiggēare,** adj. *of forty years*: geond feowertiggeare fec, Hml. S. iii, 469.

**fēowertiggetel,** n. *number of forty*: fullice (feowertig-g)etel, Hml. P. i, 237, 148 (certainly supplied).

**fēowertīnenihte,** adj. *fourteen nights old*: fram feowertynenihtne monan oð twentigesnihtne, Bd. iii, 17.

**fēran,** *add to* I 1: on weg feran, *travel*, Lch. ii, 330, 9; *add to* II: swa ferde se cniht on his fracedum dædum, Hept. 64, 1081. *See also* in-, misferan; wegferende.

**fercian,** *see also* afercian.

**fercung,** *add*: *support*: necessitas uiuendi, neod heora lifes fercunge, Chrd. 12, 22; id. 26.

**fēreld,** *glosses* cognata, Lk. i, 36, Lind. (Rush. færeld). Cf. E.S. xlii, 186.

**fērend,** *see* wegferend.

**-ferhtness,** *see* midferhtness.

**ferhþ,** *add to forms* friþ (An. 174; Gn. 411). *Add to compounds* forhtferhþ.

**ferhþgedāl,** *see* friþgedal.

**ferhþgefēonde,** participial adj., *rejoicing in heart*: An. 951, 1584.

**ferhþweg,** m. *way to eternal life*: frætwian mec on ferðweg, ASPR iii, 217, 72 (? *or read* forðweg).

**ferian,** *add to* II: and þone geþygde and his feorh big ferede (v.l. for his lif bileofode), Guth. Gr. 126. *Add to compounds* oferferian.

**fērlǣcan,** add: *for* geferlæcan: asscio, ic færlæce, Ælfc. Gr. Z. 191, 17, v.l.

**fērness,** *see* hræd-, unferness.

**fērrǣden,** *add*: Annas and Caiphas . . . geðoht worhten wið þan ferrædden, Modern Philology i, 592, 23 (= Hml. Warn. 78, 29); on ure færrædenne, Vis. Lfc. 20.

**fers,** *see also* healffers.

**fertino,** *glosses* portenta, Mk. xiii, 22, Lind. (Rush. fortina).

**ferð,** *crowd*: Wand. 54 (cf. EGS iv, 84).

**ferþfriþende,** *explain* gesceap þeotan *rather as under* þeotan II.

**festermann,** *add*: þis synd þa festermenn þe Osferð funde, Chart. Rob. 74, 29.

**fēstre,** *see also* offestre.

**fēstrian,** *add*: (uerbum carni) insertum, on festrod, OEG 24, 22.

**feter,** *add*: in first citation in Dict., the falconer's leash (creance) is referred to.

**fēþan,** *? delete, read in citation* fedaþ.

**fēþan,** *add*: repedantes, feðende, OEG 4, 396.

**Fēþanlēag,** *add*: unknown place, perhaps in Oxfordshire.

**fēþe,** *see also* healffeþe.

**fēþemann,** *add*: pedestris, f(e)þemannum, OEG 28, 99.

**feþer,** *add*: þyles tacen is þæt þu mid þinum scytefingre sume feþer tacnum gestrice on þyne wynstran hand innewearde and lecge to þinum earon, Tech. ii, 126, 6.

**feþerberende,** *add*: alliger, fefþrbrenda (*read* feþerberende), OEG 28, 481.

**feþerhama**, *add*: fleogende mid hwitum fyðerhaman, Hml. Th. ii, 334, 7.

**feþerswēg**, m. *sound of wings*: þa þry ængles . . . þære sawle wunderlice wynsumnysse mid heora feðerswege on belædden, Hml. Warn. 110, 3.

**fician**, *add*: *flatter*: wið gligmen we ficiað and þam ure feoh gifað, IP 264.

**ficwyrt**, *note*: *MS reads* ficwyrt *altered from* wicwyrt; *sense is discussed* A. xli, 136.

**fīf**, *add to II 1*: do to þam fifum þe October hæf ð, BM 60, 27; *add*: II 3 *the abstract number*: gif þæt gedæl byð todæled þurh seofon . . . and þær byð an ofer þa seofon oððe twa . . . fife oððe syxe, BM 52, 32.

**fīfbēc**, f. pl. *pentateuch*: pentatheucum, fif bocum, WW 470, 18.

**fīfgēar**, n.pl. *period of five years*: lustris, facum oððe fifgearum, WW 431, 16.

**fīfmægen**, pl. *fivefold powers*: Sal. 136.

**fīftig**, *add to II a*: ær þam fiftigan (*quinquagesimum*) sealme, Chrd. 28, 1.

**fīftigdæg**, m. *Pentecost*: post penticosten, æfter fifteigdæg, Mk., p. 5, 16, Lind.

**fiht**, probably meaning is rather *fleece, pelt*; cf. *feht*. FL 124.

**fill**, *add to I*: in praeceps, in fel, OEG 28, 227.

**fillet**, n. *forest clearing*: on ðet ealde fyllet, ðonne andlang ðes fylletes, CS iii, 368, 20; PNE i, 168.

**filling**, *forest clearing*: in Babban fælinge, CS ii, 41, 14; PNE i, 169.

**findan**, *add to II 7*: decretum est quia, hi to ræde fundon þæt, Bd. ii, 5; *add*: II 7 a, *fix upon a person for an office*: hi swa fule men him fundon to godum, Sal. K. 123, 108 (= Hml. P. ii, 686, 161). *Add to compounds* eftforfindan.

**fingerdocca**, meaning is rather a plant (? *foxglove*), cf. Lindsay, *Corpus Glossary* 199; OEG 70, 22, note.

**\*fining**, *place where wood is heaped*, PNE i, 174.

**Finnas**, *add*: Lapps not Finns, at least in Orosius passages.

**fird**, *add to I 2*: of angels, ASPR vi, 72, 47.

**firdtiber**, *see also* FL 102.

**\*firel**, *place where oaks grow*, PNE i, 172.

**firenlustfull**, adj. *wanton*: for minum firenlustfullum dædum, A. xii, 502, 10.

**firenþēof**, *delete*, *in citation MS. reads* from ðeafum.

**\*firnþe**, *place overgrown with fern*, PNE i, 172.

**firnum**, *add*: B. 1744; 2441; Gen. 316; 809; Gu. 265.

**firrfaran**, v. glossing *uexari*: firrfara Lk. vii, 6, Lind.

**first**, *time, see also* irrefirst.

**firstmearc**, *add*: m.: he us nænigne (*printed* mænigne) fyrstmearc ne hateð langes lifes, Archiv cxxii, 257, 14.

**firwetfull**, adj. *full of concern*: solliciti, færwitfulla menn, Lk. xii, 26, Lind. (Rush. ferwettfulle).

**firwitgeornness**, *add*: melius est mori quam fornicari, selre bið men þæt he swelte, þonne he his lichoman fyrwetgyrnessum gewenige (*free version*), Verc. Först. 130, 11.

**fisc**, *add to 3*: on Easterdagum he wolde etan fisc gif he hæfde. þa axode he þone profost hwæðer he fisc hæfde, Hml. S. xxxi, 1267. *Add to compounds* gafol-, mece-, mete-, scilfisc.

**fiscfell**, probably error for fiscwell, see fiscwille.

**fiscflōd**, *many read* fiscflodu (*see citation under* gasric) *as a compound*.

**fiscincel**, *a small fish*: echinis, fiscinclum, Archiv cc, 198.

**fisclacu**, for *-pond* read *-stream* (see lacu).

**fiscnoþ**, *citations of* Nap. *in Suppl.* = Hml. P. ii, 516, 18; i, 363, 130; ii, 516, 29, etc. *Add*: IV *the right to fish in certain waters*: ic geann þam munecum to fodan ealne þone fixnoð (*piscationem*) þe Ulfkytel ahte æt Wyllan, Cht. Th. 307, 35.

**fiscoþ**, *add*: III *catch of fish*: captura, fixoþ, OEG 30, 120.

**fisting**, *add to Suppl.*: lemma connected with uesicula, *air-bladder* (Oliphant, *The Harley Latin–Old English Glossary* 181) or uisium, *stench*.

**fiþerbyrste**, *cf. also* A. lii, 184.

**flā**, *see also* heorufla.

**flǣre**, meaning perhaps *side of end of nose* (cf. JEGP xlix, 233; FL 102). *See also* PNE i, 174.

**flǣsc**, *add to 2*: carnes, flæscu, Ps. Roy. lxxvii, 27.

**flǣscbesmitenness**, f. *carnal defilement*: on nanre flæscbesmitennysse (*carnis contagio*) gebrosnude, Scint. 69, 11.

**flǣsccostnung**, f. *temptation through the flesh*: pro temptatione carnis, for flæsccostnunge, þæt is idellust, Ker, *Catalogue* 120.

**flǣscniming**, f. *incarnation*: incarnationem, flæscnyminge, A. lxxxi, 115, 5.

**flǣscsand**, *add*: ministratio de carne. *For* Nap. 23 *read* Chrd. 14, 36.

**flǣsctāwere**, substitute for meaning *butcher*; cf. hyldere in Dict.

**flǣsctōþ**, substitute for meaning *gum* (cf. toþrima).

**flǣscþegnung**, *for* Nap. 23 *read* Chrd. 15, 11. Lat. is *mensuram de carne*.

**flæþ**, *add*: perhaps error for fælþ, *falls*, glossing ningit in citation, cf. FL 17; or perhaps *snowflake*, cf. context, and flaðra, *snowflakes* (Nowell, *Voc. Sax.*, ed. Marckwardt, p. 70, source unknown).

**flæþecamb**, the word is doubtful, see FL 16; sense is perhaps *comb for removing impurities from wool*, and similarly bannuccamb.

**flān**, in Wrt. Voc. ii, 97, 1, 8, cited in Suppl. (= WW 533, 24, 31) tessa has strayed from another gloss and replaced the original lemma, see Philological Quarterly xl, 318.

**flēah**, l. 3 in Suppl. add (= χήμωσις) after cimosis.

**\*flēama**, *stream*, PNE i, 176.

**flēamdom**, *citation* = Hml. P. ii, 729, 34.

**fleard**: delete *fraude*, flearde, *cf.* An. Ox. 1517 *in Suppl.*

**fleardere**, *for* Nap. 23 *read* Chrd. 20, 12. Lat. is *eorum nugarum particeps*.

**fleardian**, *add*: hos solutos atque obervantes sola turpis uita complectit, abroðene and fleardigende hi folgiað fracedum life, Chrd. 77, 36.

**flecta**, Txts. 55, 600; 67, 999; WW 214, 39, seems to be a Latin word.

**flēdan**, *see* oferfledan.

**\*flēd(e)**, *stream*: Löfvenberg, *Studies on ME Local Surnames* 66.

**flēdness**, *see* oferfledness.

**Flemisc**, adj. *Flemish*: an hund manna, Frencisce and Flemisce, Chr. 1080.

**flēogan**, *delete* IV in Suppl., *read in citation* flegan (*see* fligan). *See also* heofonfleogende.

**flēoge**, *add to compounds* morfleoge.

**flēon**, *add to II in Dict* (= III *in Suppl.*): fleoh þu nu seo læsse ða maran, ASPR vi, 119, 21. *See also* fullfleon.

**flēot**, l. 6 in Suppl., probably delete *to nette*, see FL 197.

**flēot**, *boat*, note prose use, OEG 28, 271.

**flēotan**, *delete* II in Suppl., *MS.* flowað.

**fleoþorna**, *perhaps* = *\*fleot-ham*, *cf.* flodham, wæterham.

**flēwedness**, *see* oferflewedness.

**fligung**, *see* afligung.

**fliming**, *perhaps rather retain MS. reading* flymig, as adj.; cf. Studia Germanica Gandensia ii, 87.

**flind**, *read* flint; *reference is to* Aldhelm, Rid. 93, *where 'flint' is 'mother' of the 'spark'*.

**flita**, *add*: on flitanhyll, CS iii, 517, 21.

**flite**, *for* fleot, *estuary*, *see* fleot in Suppl.

**flocgan**, *note*: sense in context is *dart over the waves*, see Prud. 846 and note; cf. flogettan (2).

**flōd**, *add to (6) in Suppl.*: on bubla cf. bubla, *flumen*, Oliphant, *The Harley Latin–Old English Glossary* 36; apparent equation of bubla and platissa incorrect, cf. WW 293, 24. *See also* cwild-, heofon-, oferflod; mærflode.

**flōdgrǣg**, adj. *grey as the sea*: Gn. C. 31.

**flōdmǣd**, f. *meadow-land subject to flooding*: C.D. vi, 243, 12.

**floege**, glosses *nauicula*, Jn. vi, 22, Lind., Rush.

**flogoþa**, substitute for meaning *venom*, reference is to *uipereus liquor*, see Prud. 997, note.

**flōr**, *add to compounds* stanflor.

**floterian**, *delete* (2) in Suppl., take citation under (1) *be tossed on the waves*, see Prud. 877, note.

**flotwyrt**, f. *sea-weed*: aglea, flotuyrt, DP 22.

**flōwan**, *see also* onbeflowan; hunig-, ongeanflowende; leohtflowend.

**flōwedlic**, flōwedlicnes, flōwendlic, flōwendlice, *see* oferf.

**flōwendness**, *see* toflowendness.

**flōwness**, f. *flow, spring*: fluenta, flownisa, Mt., p. 6, 14, Lind. *See also* toflowness.

**flustrian**, cf. JEGP lx, 450; SHG 59.

**flȳming**, *add*: cf. fliming *above*.

**flyne**, *add to Suppl.* fleba = φλέβα, in sense *liquid* (for uena is equated with both φλέψ and ῥεύματα, see JEGP lxiv, 491).

**fnǣran**, *see also*: fnæ . . , *frementis*, OEG 30, 128.

**fnēosung**, *note*: MS. reads fneowung, A. viii, 451.

**\*focga**, *grass left standing*, PNE i, 179.

**fodder**, *delete third entry in Suppl., see* fodderbil.

**fodderbil**, n. *scythe*: implied by: *falcastrum*, wudubil *uel* foddur(bil), WW 235, 4.

**\*fōding**, *grazing*, PNE i, 179.

**\*fōdring**, *grazing*, PNE i, 179.

**fōg**, add: *stipe*, foge, OEG 28, 359 (meaning unclear, see note ad loc.).

**folc**, add to *III 2 a*: forwearð se consul mid eallum his folce (*cum uniuerso exercitu*), Ors. S. 206, 8. *Add to compounds* Angel-, hæþen-, landfolc.

**folcāgende**, the meaning is *man*.

**folcbeorn**, *delete*.

**folcgedrēfness**, *for* Nap. 23 *read* Verc. Först. 102, 4. Lat. is *erit turbatio magna in omni populo*.

**folcland**, *substitute*: n. I *land, country*: feorres folclondes, Wife's Lament 47; II *land held under uncertain conditions, but contrasted with* bocland: *take here citations in Suppl. and add*: se cyning dyde ðet land et Mersaham him to folclande, CS ii, 101, 26 (= Txts. 438, 23); (se) þe oðrum ryhtes wyrnde aðor oððe on boclande oððe on folclande, I Eadweard 2; gif he ðonne nan riht næfde ne on boclande ne on folclande, id. 2, 1; sie swa boclond swa folclond, swa þer hit sie ge cyninges selfes ge ælces monnes, London Mediæval Studies i, 62.

**folclic**, add to *2*: *in custodia publica*, on þam folclican cwearterne, Chrd. 25, 28; *turbis popularibus*, folclicum mængungum, Gr. D. 209, 13.

**folcriht**, in poetical passages (B. 2608, Ex. 22) meaning is *property, possessions*.

**folcslite**, *note*: MS. reads flocslite, A. viii, 450.

**foldgrǣg**, *delete, read* flōdgrǣg (so MS.).

**foldwong**, add: possible reading Gen. 1951 (MS. full won).

**foldwylm**, m. *spring rising from the ground*: Phoen. 64.

**folde**, note prose uses, OEG 4, 271; 28, 324.

**folm**, add to *forms*: m. pl. folmas, Gr. D. 166, 7, v.l. *Note prose use*, OEG 4, 224.

**fōn**, add to *III 1 a*: hi fengon him sona on, Hml. S. xxiii, 607; *add to III: 2 a lay hold of*: þa feng se portgerefa to þære tege, Hml. S. xxiii, 764; foh to þinum hode, Tech. ii, 127, 17. *Add to compounds* misfon; æfteronfond.

**fōndlic**, *see* onfondlic.

**fonfȳr**, *apparently some sort of fuel, see citation under* egle I *in Suppl. and* JEGP lx, 446.

**for**, prep., *add*: B 14 *in respect to*: for fel and for flæsc . . . and for æghwæt hnesces oþþe heardes, L. de Cf. 9; A. xi, 98, 46; 54.

**for**, conj., *for*: nu wylle we eow secgan . . . for ic wat þæt hit is eow uncuðre, Wlfst. 292, 7; for þær wæs an forehus, Vis. Lfc. 33; for næs næfre mon . . ., Hml. Bel. 98, 24; 118, 7; Hml. Warn. 4, 25, etc.

**for ān**, *add*: *tantum*, Chrd. 115, 2.

**foran**, *add to II*: (e) æt, *in front of*: æt his reste foran, Gr. D. 20, 29 (v.l. ætforan his bedde).

**foranlencten**, *early spring*: on foranlencten, Lch. ii, 256, 1.

**forārǣden**, glosses *propositum*: forarædenne, Rtl. 27, 14.

**forbærning**, *add*: *combustio*, forbærning (v.l. -ung), Gn. (Archiv cxcix, 20).

**forbēn**, f. *prayer*: *precatu*, forbene, Hymn. Surt. 138, 13 (*or* = for bene, cf. v.l. in Gn. 124, 4).

**forbigels**, *delete, see* FL 44.

**forbregdan**, substitute for meaning of (3) in Suppl. *cover*, and add: on þære onlicnysse þe man þa eagan mid þicce hrægle forbrugde, Wyn. 10; probably delete meaning (5), taking citation under (4), see Prud. 605, note.

**forbrytenness**, *for* forbrytedness, Ps. Vit. cxlvi, 3.

**forbrytnes**, *for* forbrytedness, Ps. Sal. xiii, 3.

**forcel**, *for* Nap. 23 *read* Verc. Först. 93, 6.

**forcinnan**, *meaning is unknown, emendation proposed in Suppl. unlikely*.

**forcippian**, *for* Nap. 79 *read* Ps. Roy., Hy. 2, 12 (Ps. Stowe, Ps Ar. forcippod).

**forcirredness**, *add*: II *conversion*: *in connertendo*, on forcyrredness, Ps. Bos. cxxv, 1.

**forclyccan**, *citation is* Ps. Roy. lvii, 5, *and related glosses*.

**forcnēow**, substitute *progeny*: *in progenies*, on forcneow, Ps. Sal., Hy. 8, 50.

**forcostian**, v. *tempt*: ber þa to him þa ylce costunge þe he þa ereste men forcostode, Hml. Bel. 98, 32.

**ford**, *see also* here-, mær-, mearc-, stan-, wiþigford, *and s.v.* wæsce.

**fordēad**, adj. *dead*: *mortui*, fordeado Mt. xxviii, 4, Lind.

**fordēmedlice**, adv. *accursedly*: fordemetlice (inexact gloss to *dampnosa*, fem.), Archiv cxvii, 26, 68.

**fordilemengan**, v. *dissemble*: *neque dissimulent peccata*, ne fordilemenge man gyltas, Chrd. 26, 18.

**fordōn**, add to *II*: ða fordonan synfullan, Hml. P. i, 425, 191 *See also* onfordon.

**foreādihtian**, *delete, see* ādihtian.

**forealdung**, f. *old age*: *senio*, foraldung OEG 28, 312.

**forebīcnung**, f. *prophecy*: Hml. Th. i, 540.

**forecennedness**, f. *offspring*: *a progenie*, of forecennednesse, Ps. Sal., Hy. 8, 50.

**foreclipian**, v. *proclaim*: *proclamant*, foreclypiað, Ps. Vit., Hy. 11, 4 (= Ps. Bos., Hy. 3, 4; Ps. Stowe, Hy. 10, 4).

**forecostian**, *substitute*: *si iustificationes meas prophanauerint*, gif mine soþfestnesse forecostigað, Ps. Cant. lxxxviii, 32.

**forecostung**, f. *temptation*: Ps. Cant. lxxxviii, 35, 40 (irregularly glossing finite forms of *profano*).

**forefengness**, f. *screen* (of woods): *obtentu*, forefengnisse, OEG 4, 28.

**forefeohtend**, m. *defender*: *propugnator*, Gn. (Archiv cxcix, 20).

**foregearwung**, *add*: *preparatio*, foregearwung, Ps. Cant., lxxxviii, 15.

**foregesellan**, v. *give*: þæt he him þæt weorð his alesnesse foregesealde, BH iv, 22, v.l.

**foregewis**, adj. *having foreknowledge*: *praescius*, OEG 4, 247.

**foregewissian**, v. *glossing prodesse* (? in error): *profuit*, foregewissode, Hy. Surt. 111, 9.

**forehālig**, adj. *very holy*: þe seo cyrice forehalig is, Archiv lxxxiv, 3, 14; *see also* fore *in Dict*.

**forehradian**, v. *hasten before*: *preuenerunt*, forehradedon, Chrd. 26, 18.

**forehūs**, n. *porch*: þær wæs an forehus æt þære cyrcan duru, Vis. Lfc. 33.

**forelǣtan**, v. *glosses prohibere*: ne foreletas gie hia, Mk. x, 14, Lind. (Rush. forletas).

**forelcodan**, citation = Hml. Warn. 142, 34.

**forenemned**, participial adj., *named previously*: þa forenemnedan þing, Verc.-Hom. 137, 6.

**forescēawere**, *add*: see Archiv cxxix, 20, 11; for E.S. 39 (Dec.) read E.S. xxxix, 327.

**foresēon**, *see also* unforesewen.

**for(e)sittan**, *add*: both are used trans. in Lind.: *parabolam proposuit*, biseno forsætt, Mt. xiii, 24; *comparatione proposita*, efennise foresetna, Mt., p. 19, 12; *panes propositionis*, hlafas forsetne, Mt. xii, 4.

**foresōþscip**, glosses *prolatio*: *leprosum . . . prolatione uerbi uolo mundauit*, ðone licðrower mið . . . foresoðscip wordes ic uillo geclaensade, Mt., p. 17, 20, Lind.

**\*foresteall**, *place in front of farmhouse*, PNE i, 184.

**foretimbrian**, v. *hinder* (of a storm): onsettende and foretimbrigende, Bd. v, 1, v.l.

**foretrymman**, v. *glosses protestari*: foretrymmede, Jn. xiii, 21, Lind. (Rush. fortrymede).

**foretyhtan**, v. *call forward, encourage*: *prouocatis actibus*, foretihtum dædum, Gn. 74, 8 (JV).

**foreweard**, *delete* (?); *add*: ymb þa foreward þe wæron geworhte . . . and se ðe þas foreward tobreke . . ., C.D. iv, 263, 13–21; *note*: *interitum*, on foreweardum, Ps. Vit. xxxiv, 7, *seems due to confusion with* forwyrd.

**foreweard**, adj., *add to I*: *uix imprimunt summa uestigia*, hi mid forewerdum tan stæppað, Chrd. 64, 35; *add to substantival usages*: gif hi standað on foreweardan on ðære spræce, Ælfc. Gr. Z. 241, 10.

**foreweardness**, f. *beginning*: *in exordio*, in forewerdnysse, BM 198, 2.

**foreworden**, participial adj. *predestined*: *praedestinata*, forewurden (*altered to* -on, *read* foreworden), Mk., p. 1, 20, Lind.

**forewynsumian**, v. *enjoy thoroughly*: ne ðær ne bið ænig wuldor mid him, þæt he forewynsumige, Verc, Först. 91, 1.

**forewyrdan**, *add*: *settle terms, agree*: eal swa min swestar hit er foræwyrde, Chart. Whit. 40, 5.

**forfyrht**, adj. *terrified*: he sone forfyrht fleames cepte, Hml. Warn. 132, 22.

**forgǣgan**, add to *I*: *hoc temptantes*, þa þe þis forgægað, Chrd. 68, 35.

**forgægend,** m. *transgressor: ieiunii transgressor,* fæstenes forgægend, Chrd. 41, 31.

**forgǣlan,** v. *shun, avoid: uitauimus,* we forgældon, Lk., p. 3, 8, Lind.

**forgifan,** *add to II 2*: þisse forgifenan tide (acc.), *this allotted time,* Vercelli MS., f. 78ʳ, 6.

**forgifness,** *see also* godforgifness.

**forgildan,** *add to III 2*: he ne sceolde be ðam mergendæge þencan, þy læs þæt wære þæt he ðurh þæt ænig þara goda forgulde (v.l. forylde), þe he ðonne þy dæge gedon meahte, Vercelli MS., f. 96ʳ, 5.

**forgitan,** *take citation* Wrt. Voc. ii, 62, 49 (= WW 457, 27), *to* forgitan, *destroy,* cf. āgitan.

**forhabban,** *add to I: continentioris uitae gratia,* for intingan forhæbbendra(n) lifes, Bd. iii, 27.

**forhæfedness,** *see also* unforhæfedness.

**forhæfendlice,** adv. *continently: ut continentius uiuant,* þæt hi forhæfendlicust libbon, Chrd. 42, 29.

**forhealdness,** at end of l. 3 in Suppl. insert (*nulla immunditia polluaris*).

**forhearde,** adv. *very much:* se micela ylp ondræt him forhearde, Hml. A. 64, 287.

**forhelian,** *add: nudi sunt operiendi,* nacode synt to forhelianne, Chrd. 108, 13.

**forhogiend,** *add:* Cristes rode tacnes forhogiend (*contemptor*), Chrd. 41, 31.

**forhorwade,** *add:* Gn. (Archiv cxcix, 20).

**forhosedan,** *? error for* forhoredan *glossing* ultorem, *taken as* adultorem, Ps. Vit. viii, 3.

**forht,** *see also* unforht.

**forhtferþ,** adj. *terrified at heart:* An. 1549, 1596.

**forhtian,** *add to II 2*: þæt hi ne forhtgean þæs gewinnes ne þæs siþfætes, Bd. i, 23.

**forhtleasness,** f. *fearlessness:* on heora forhtleasnysse, Verc.-Hom. 4, note 13 a (*context calls for* unforhtleasness).

**forhtlic,** *note:* 3 in Suppl. appears to be an error; corrections are proposed E.S. xlii, 193.

**forhto** *for* fyrhto, Ps. Sal. lxxxviii, 41.

**forilldu,** *add: senio,* forylde, Prud. 1030.

**forlǣtan,** *add to II*: for bote urra synna ises þlifes dagas us to fyrste forlætene synt, R. Ben. 4, 18.

**forlǣte,** n. *loss:* geþencað . . . hwylce Abrahames forlætu wæron, and hu he his wifes ðolode, Verc.-Hom. 138, 16.

**forlǣtness,** *see also* inforlætness.

**forlǣþan,** v. *loathe:* man forlæþeð þæt man scolde lufian, Wlfst. 165, 3.

**forlegenness,** *see also* dyrneforlegenness.

**forlicgan,** *add to II 1*: heora gedohtra forlæg se fæder fullice, Sal. K. 121, 35.

**forliden,** *add:* forliðen, Hml. Warn. 88, 4, *is error for* geliden (cf. Hml. A. 181, 11).

**forliþan,** *add:* ferliþon (*lemma uncertain*), Ker, *Catalogue* 129.

**formǣlan,** v. *transfer (by negotiation):* and gif ani man formaele hine sylfne of biscopes scire innan kynges scire, Archiv cxi, 280, 19.

**formelle,** f. *bench:* on þære formellan, Archiv lxxxiv, 9, 95. [Lat. formella.]

**fornetedcli,** *read* fornetecle, *small trout, diminutive of* \*fornete, *derivative of* forn, *trout.*

**fornirwian,** substitute for meaning *diminish the productivity of*; Lat. of citation is *fructus arborum deficiunt*; see Archiv cxxviii, 57.

**forod,** *add: invalidated:* beo þæt ordal forod, II Æthelstan 23, 2.

**forpyndan,** *add:* cf. PBB xi, 351; xxiii, 109.

**forrǣpe,** n. *new arable land:* þæt forræpe on þunres feld norþan, CS ii, 585, 13. Cf. Studia Neophilologica xvi, 33, and (divergent) Löfvenberg, *Studies on ME Local Surnames* 68.

**forsacenness,** f. *denial:* Petrus forgeofenysse onfeng, þe he swyðe biterlice weop þære þreofealdan forsacanysse synne, Hml. Warn. 102, 10.

**forsacung,** f. *denial:* he wæs unrot for þære forsacunge, Hml. Warn. 144, 25.

**forsænlice,** i.e. forsewenlice, R. Ben. 11, 19 (inferior reading).

**forscēawere,** *see* foresceawere.

**forscirian,** v. *set apart:* ealle þa forsciridan, Verc. Först. 143.

**forscīt,** *l. 1 read* cataracte. Cf. MLN xiii, 295.

**forsellan,** *add: erogauerat substantiam,* forsalde feh, Lk. viii, 43, Rush. (Lind. fromsalde); II *sell:* wa þan þe for sceatte forsylð hine sylfne, Hml. Warn. 10, 39 (= Fehr 202, 7).

**forspennen,** *delete, MS. reads* forspennenc (*i.e.* forspenning). Cf. Studia Germanica Gandensia ii, 87; An. Ox. 612, note.

**forst,** *last line in Dict. read* hrim-.

**\*forst,** *ridge,* PNE i, 184.

**forstregdan,** v. *destroy: ne disperderet eos,* ðy læs he forstrugde hie, Ps. Jun. cv, 23.

**forstrogdness,** Napier's citation is Ps. Jun. 51, 6.

**forstyntan,** *add:* and me wæs seo gesihð forstynted (MS. -stynded) for þara scinendra gasta beorhtnesse, Wyn. 35; id. 142.

**forsuncen,** participial adj. *faded (of writing): interlitas,* besmerede, befylede, *uel* forsuncene, Kansas leaf.

**forswāpan,** *note:* B. 2814 has forspeof (? *read* forspeon).

**forswarung,** *for Nap. 25 read: periurium,* Chrd. 40, 34.

**forswelgan,** *see also* geforswelgan.

**forsweotole,** adv. *very plainly:* forsweotole ongytan, Solil. H. 2, 23 (= Endter 2, 17).

**forswigian,** *see also* unforswigod.

**fortina,** *see* fertino.

**fortreddan,** *see also* unfortredde.

**fortyhtan,** *note:* faertyhted is equated with *bedridden* (*clinicus,* cf. Lindsay, *Corpus Glossary* 40). It is probably for fortyhtend, see second citation s.v. fortyhtend in Suppl., and *lectus* has been taken as *illectus*; cf. Oliphant, *The Harley Latin–Old English Glossary* 82.

**fortȳnan,** *keep both Dict. and Suppl. and add: oculos suos clauserunt,* egu heora fortyndon, Mt. xiii, 15, Rush.

**forþ,** *add to 2 a:* tyn cuna (læse) ford mið þas hlafordes, CS i, 544, 2; *add to 5:* geþeod þine fingras tosomne forð handlenge, Tech. ii, 124, 19; *add to 6 a:* manige men þurh forhealdnesse forð cumað, Verc. Först. 130, 10; þis woruldlice lif sceolde forð adilgod beon, id. 144, 9. *See also* efenforþ.

**forþāloten,** participial adj. *prone: pronus denotusque,* forðaloten and estfull, A. lxv, 251, 1.

**forþāsliden,** *add: prolabimur,* we beoð forðaslidene, Scint. 214, 6.

**forþātȳdred,** participial adj. *propagated: propagata,* forþatyddrede, OEG 4, 91.

**forþbringan,** *add: educate:* þis eadiga mæden . . . Theothimus fedde and lærde and forðbrohte, Hml. A. 170, 20.

**forþclypian,** *add: prouocat,* forðclipað, Scint. 63, 5; 134, 10; etc.

**forþcȳþan,** *substitute: v. make known: uias meas enuntiaui,* wegas mine ic fordcyðde, Ps. V. cxviii, 26 (so also Ps. Cam.).

**forþeccan,** v. *cover: protegat,* forþecce, Ps. Vit., Ps. Ar. xix, 2.

**forþecgan,** v. *consume (of thirst):* forþegide, þurste gebæded, Seasons of Fasting 214.

**forþēon,** *? delete, in citation most read* sceadu forþeode, *a shadow went forth* (cf. forþgan).

**forþfæderen,** f. *paternal nature:* hrefen gesihð his briddas hwites bleos . . . gymð hwonne hi æfter heora forðfæderene (*paterno colore*) sweartion, Chrd. 96, 6.

**forþfēran,** *add:* literal sense *proceed along:* (he) big sume weige sæt, þær se Hælend forðferde, Hml. Warn. 149, 13.

**forþgang,** *add to* (4) *in Suppl.: ad alueum concitandum,* wið þam þe nebbe forþgang, OEG 73b, 2; *first citation under II in Dict. also belongs to* (4) *in Suppl.*

**forþgiten,** participial adj., *passed:* ðam nihtum forðgetenum, Buss, 181, 201.

**forþhebban,** v. *glosses prouehere: proue(h)at,* forðhebbe, Gn. 15, 8 (JV).

**forþhere,** *substitute for meaning* advancing army.

**forþian,** *see also* fullforþian.

**forþingian,** *substitute* make arrangements for the wergild *for, intercede for the man.*

**forþlǣtan,** v. *send away: amittis,* þu fortlete, PBB lxxxv (Halle), 61.

**forþlice,** *add: well, perfectly:* nan oðer swa forðlice ne gesmæhte, hwu swote is ure Drihten, Hml. Warn. 138, 16.

**forþlūtan,** *add: prona in malum,* forðloton to yfle, Chrd. 54, 31.

**forþmann,** *citation* = Hml. P. ii, 629, 138.

**forþmid,** adv. *at the same time:* ac mislæt his hyrmen and hine silfne forðmid, Fehr, 130, 20; nu wille we eow secgan . . . hwæt se haligdom is . . . and gewrytu forðmid ⟨areccan⟩, Förster, *Reliquienkultus* 68; Hml. Warn. 15, 28.

**forþrǣstan**, *add*: (3) past part. forþræsted, *contrite*: *cor contritum*, heorte forðrested, Ps. V. l, 19 (so Ps. Cam., Ps. Ar.).

**forþrycness**, *add*: ge sculon habban foreþrycnesse on þyssum middangearde, Verc. Först. 143.

**forþsecgan**, v. *declare*: *pronuntiabo*, ic forðsecgu, Ps. V. lxx, 17; *so frequently in V. and related glosses.*

**forþsendan**, v. *send forth*: ða se lichama ðyllice stemne forðsende, Hml. S. xxiii b, 204.

**forþsetenness**, f.: *panes propositionis*, hlaf forðsetennisse, Mt. xii, 4, Rush.

**forþstæpe**, m. *advance, progress*: *processu morum*, on forðstapa þeawa, Gn. 68, 5 (JV).

**forþswebban**, citation = Ps. Cant. lxxxviii, 23; *add*: Hy. 5, 17 and cxvii, 25 (forswebienne).

**forþswebbung**, *citation* = Ps. Cant. cvi, 25; cf. *procellarum*, forspebiendra (*sic*), id. cxlviii, 8; *note falsely glosses ficulnea*, id. civ, 33.

**forþswefian**, ?: *spiritus procellarum*, gast forspebiendra (sic), Ps. Cant. cxlviii, 8. Cf. forþswebbung, forþswebban.

**forþtyhtan**, v. *lead*: drihtnes þenunge, seo us forðtihteð to þam ecean life, Ker, *Catalogue* 52.

**forþung**, *add to Suppl.*: gold on swefnum handlian forðunge ceapes (*expeditionem negotii*) getacnað, Archiv cxxv, 49, 45. *See also* scipforþung.

**forþweard**, adv., *add to 2 b*: ic Ælfred willio and wille þæt hio sion soðfestlice forðweard getrymed, Harmer, *Historical Documents* 14, 31.

**forþwecgan**, v. *press forward*: *Aurora cursus provehit*, degred ryne forðwegeð, Ps. V., Hy. 11, 13.

**forþyldigung**, f. *patience*: *tolerantiam*, forðyldegunge, A. lxv, 245, 64.

**forþylman**, substitute for meaning *enwrap*.

**forþyppan**, *substitute*: *I come forth*: promulgatur, forðyppeð, WW 464, 38; II *send forth*: dom minne forðyppeð, Ps. V. xvi, 2.

**forþysman**, *see* forþrysman (2) *in Suppl.*

**forwærnian**, *see* forweornian *in Suppl.*

**forwana**, m. *abundance*: Ic wende on minum wlencum ond on minum forwanan, Past. 465, 15.

**forwandian**, *add to II*: distuli, forwandode, Ps. Ar., Hy. 6, 27.

**forwēnan**, *suspect*, citation = OEG 9, 108.

**forwenedness**, citation = A. xli, 152, 276; *add*: insolentia, forwenedness, E.S. lxix, 340, n. 1.

**forwiernan**, *add to 1 a*: with acc. of thing: þæt he renscuras forwyrnde, Hml. P. i, 360, 81.

**forwirnedness**, *add*: *abstinence* from (gen.): heora forwyrnednessa þyssa woruldlicra þinga, Verc. Först. 118, 31.

**forwitig**, *for* forewitig: *in presago corde*, on forwittigre heortan, Gn. 86², 3 (V).

**forword**, note: *in citation* iota *in context* = *stipulation (of the law)*, cf. foreword *in Suppl.*

**forwyrd**, *add to I*: hu unasecgendlica synt þysses lifes idelnessa and forwyrda, Verc. Först. 131, 9.

**forwyrht**, *add*: (2) *ruin, destruction*: eallwihtna hryre and eorþan forwyrht, Verc.-Hom. 47, 48; cf. forwyrcan II.

**\*foss**, *ditch*, see PNE i, 185. Only OE in sense Foss Way.

**fōster**, *add to 3*: *de pueris nutriendis*, be cildra fostre (fostere, 6, 10), Chrd. 54, 18. *See also* infoster.

**fostere**, *spade*: *fossorium*, fostere, WW 106, 18 (so MS. Add. 32246; cf. costere).

**fōstrian**, *add*: to fostrigen hire sune swa swa cilde, *Anglica* ii, 37, 205 (= Hml. Warn. 138, 27).

**fōt**, add to I: hofon þa deor heora fotas upp, Mart. H. 58, 13; substitute for sense of III in Suppl. *corner (of a sail)*, *clew*, see FL 103. *See also* hoh-, middelfot.

**-fōt**, *add* hwitfot.

**fōtādl**, in Lch. iii, 48, 26, the meaning is *septic foot*.

**fōtclaþ**, probably delete, read in citation fogclaþ, *cloth that joins, patch*; cf. FL 17.

**fōtcysped**, *for* gecypsed, Ps. Vit. lxxviii, 11. *See also* gefotcypsed.

**fōtgemet**, *add*: II *a measure of one foot*: fiftyne fotgemetu (of the length of a shadow), Henel, *Studien zum altengl. Computus* 59.

**fōtrāp**, more exactly *rope by which the foot of a sail is tied*.

**fōþor**, transfer gloss on *altitudo* (error for *aletudo*, see Lindsay, *Corpus Glossary* 192) from III to I.

**foxes fōt**, *add*: xifion, foxes fot, DP 19.

**foxes glofa**, *add*: trycnosmanicos, foxes gloua, DP 18.

**frācenfull**, *for* frecenfull, Hml. Warn. 34, 1.

**frǣfellice**, *add*: in a good sense, *carefully*: *exempla uirtutis sollicite inpendere*, freflice ætywan rihte drohtnunge mid godum bysnum, Chrd. 66, 22.

**frǣte**, *add*: strofosus ('wily'), fræte, OEG 15, 1.

**frǣtgenga**, ? *read* frætgenge, *or has apostasia been taken as apostata?*

**frǣtlappa**, *l. 1*, *read* ruma *for* runia.

**fram**, adj., delete citation Germ. 391, 60 (= Prud. 231), where *fram* is prep.: note in citation Wrt. Voc. 145, 35 (= WW 232, 3), the five words quoted all gloss *expeditus*; cf. Oliphant, *The Harley Latin–Old English Glossary* 165.

**framācnȳslian**, v. *degenerate*: degenerent, fromacnyslien, OEG 30, 105.

**framāscūfan**, v. *drive away*: dioflu framascyfð, Verc.-Hom. 69, 163.

**framcirran**, *see* fromcerran *in Dict. and below.*

**framdōn**: *deliramentum*, fromdoen, Lk. xxiv, 11, Lind.

**frameald**, adj. *very old*: in framealdum dagum, CS iii, 561, 4.

**framlic**, *add*: *opera eius fortia erunt*, his dæde beoð framlica, Archiv cxxviii, 300, 10.

**framsundor**, adv. *for* sundor: *inclinans se deorsum*, gebeg hine frumsuunder (sic), Jn. viii, 6, Lind. (Rush. ofsyndrige).

**frēabeorhtian**, *see* gefreabeorhtian.

**frēabrǣgd**, *mighty device*: wið freabregde (MS. frea begde), ASPR vi, 120, 43. (*Doubtful*, bregd *is elsewhere* m.)

**frēawrāsen**, substitute for meaning: *chain-mail guard*; cf. *Medieval Archaeology* i, 62.

**frec**, *delete citation* Wrt. Voc. ii, 96, 64, *and see* frett *below*.

**frēcedness**, *see also* oerfrecedness.

**frecness**, *add*: beorh þe þæt þu ne gange on frecnysse, Hpt. xxi, 189, 11.

**frefer**, f. *for* frofor: *miscens terroribus blandimenta*, wrixla frefra onmang egsungum, Chrd. 18, 5.

**fregen**, n. *question*, see fregenseldlic.

**fregenseldlic**, *delete*, *in citation read* nys þis fregen syllic þinc, *this question is not a strange matter to explain*. See E.S. xxxvi, 325, Archiv cxxxv, 399.

**fremdian**, *see also* geælfremedan.

**fremedness**, *add*: þæt ðu of ðeða ærran fremednesse yfelra leahtra ofaðwea (*v.l. for* ða ær gefremedan synna), Guth. Gr. 124.

**fremman**, *see also* wohfremmende.

**frence**, ? *delete*, see SHG 19.

**frēo**, *add to 1*: *liberiori genere exortus*, geboren of freon (freogum, v.l.) and of æþelum cynne, Gr. D. 95, 10. *Add to compounds* gildfreo, færfrige.

**frēodom**, *add to 3*: *deliberatione*, frigedome, R. Ben. I. 97, 8.

**frēogan**, add to II: *caress*: com culfre and fleah ymbe þone lychaman and hyne freode, Mart. H. 216, 28.

**frēolice**, *add*: *as a festival*: we healdað . . . ðone sunnandæg freolice (v.l. freolsne), Fehr 196, 12.

**frēols**, *add*: III *charter of freedom*: Chart. Rob. 20, 3, and often; Chart. Harm. 181, 5.

**frēonama**, *add*: cognomine, frinomon, OEG 4, 146.

**frēotmann**, *add*: nelle we to him gyrnan feohgesceotes ne freotmannes, E.S. xlix, 344.

**frēoþowong**, substitute for meaning *plain affording refuge*.

**frēowīf**, *freeborn woman*: see locbore *in Dict.*

**Fresan**, *see also* Norþ-Fresan *below.*

**frett**, adj. *greedy*: gulosa, þy frettan, WW 532, 25. Cf. frettan, fretol, frætlæppa.

**fridhengest**, the meaning is unknown, review of suggestions ASPR iii, 333.

**Frīgedæg**, *add*: Frigedæges treow, CS iii, 258, 1.

**Frīgeniht**, *first citation* = Hml. P. i, 358, 20.

**frignan**, *see also* in-, þurhfrignan.

**frihtrian**, v. *divine*: augures, qui auguria faciunt, ftrihctrat (v.l. strihctrat), OEG 55, 4; Kluge, *Angelsächs. Lesebuch*, 3rd ed. 13, 18.

**friþ**, *for* ferhþ, And. 174, Gn. 411; cf. friþgedal, stiþfrihþ.

**friþen**, adj. *protected, sheltered*: æt freoðene felde, C.D. iv, 157, 5. Cf. PNE i, 188.

**friþgisel**, *in l. 3 for* allowed *read* delivered to.

**friþlic**, see also *Nordica et Anglica* (ed. A. H. Orrick) 86.

**frōfor**, *add to (3)*: feoh byþ frofur fira gehwylcum, Run. 1; 11; 58. Cf. frefer.

**fromcerran**, *add*: digreditur, he framcyrde, OEG 7, 10.

**fromdoe**, *read* fromdoen *with Lind*, see framdon.

**fromirning**, f. glosses *excursus*: fromerninge, Rtl. 18, 1.

**frosc**, on equation with *luscinius* see SHG 8.

**frumcenning**, m. *first-born*: *omne primogenitum*, ealle frumcenningas, Ps. Sal. lxxvii, 51.

**frumdysig**, *for* Nap. 26 *read* Chrd. 18, 16. Lat. is *in ipso initio peccati*.

**frummeoluc**, substitute for sense *beestings*, cf. JEGP lii, 372.

**frymþelic**, add: *principal*: *octo sunt principalia uitia*, eahta synt frymþlican leahtras, Chrd. 107, 3; be eahta frymþlican leahtrum, id. 12.

**Frȳs**, adj. *Frisian*: Frysan wife, Gn. Ex. 96.

**fugel**, *add to compounds* fedel-, gos-, hafocfugel.

**fugeles bēan**, *add*: *uiciam. i. bisas agrestes*, fugles baenae, OEG 55, 10.

**fugeles lēac**, citation is WW 300, 6; cf. DP 19, 337 (lemma *uiuinum*).

**fugeloþ**, *add*: f. God sendeþ mycele fugeloð on þam geare, Archiv cxxviii, 66, 5.

**fūht**, *add*: þæt on þam fuhtan wege ne beon heora fet besprengde, Chrd. 64, 36; *locis humentibus*, on fuhtum stowum, Hml. P. i, 276, 223.

**fūhtian**, *citation =* Hml. P. i, 277, 229.

**fulbryce**, define: *violation of the sanctity of a cleric where manslaughter occurs*.

**fulgān**, probably add Gen. 249 (MS. *fyligan*).

**fulhār**, *add*: WW 380, 13; A. viii, 451.

**fulhtnian**, *see* gefulhtnian.

**fūlian**, *see also* unfuliende.

**full**, *add to I* 4: xii cypan fulle on þam gebrytsnum, E.S. xlix, 345, 17; *add to VI*: leodmægnes ful, Exod. 167 (cf. 195).

**fullcuman**, v. *reach, achieve*: ne fullcumð næfre nan to þære mærðe, *Anglica* ii, 23, 81 (= Hml. Warn. 136, 1).

**fullcȳþan**, v. *declare*: his naman fullcyðan, Hml. P. i, 203, 131.

**fulldōn**, *add*: ic his lic behwearf . . . næs his heafodclað eallunga fuldon, Hml. S. xxxi, 1425.

**fulle**, *for* sinfulle: *paliurus, erba que crescit in tectis domorum, grossa folia habens*, fullae, Txts. 112, 37; *fios* (= *pheos*), fulle, OEG 70, 33. Cf. A. xxvi, 303.

**fullforþian**, v. *fulful*: on untrumnesse wurð Godes mihte fulforðod, Nap. 27; we secgeð þæt heo synderlice fullforðede Marthen geswyncfulle wica, *Anglica* ii, 37, 203 (= Hml. Warn. 138, 25).

**fullfylgan**, *add*: *persequatur*, fulfylgæt, Ps. Cant. vii, 6.

**fullness**, *add*: *plenitudo*, fullnes, Ps. Sal. xcv, 11; xcvii, 7; II *fulfilment*: seo soðe lufe is fullnysse Godes æ, Hml. Warn. 93, 5.

**fullsingan**, v. *sing in full*: ond fulsingan magnificat, Fehr 170, 9.

**fullþungenness**, f. *full capacity*: *homo sui animi impotens erit, faciens quae non conuenit*, þurh yrre ne mæg nan mann habban fullþungennesse his geþeahtes, Verc. Först. 144.

**fullunga**, Lind. reference is Jn. ii, 6.

**fullwian**, *see also* unfullod.

**fullwiht**, *add*: ða hwile ðe fulwiht stondan mote, Txts. 175, 17; 13.

**fullwihtbēna**, substitute for meaning: *sponsor at baptism*; citation should read *competitor, amicus, uel rogator baptismi*, fulwihtbena, Oliphant, *The Harley Latin–Old English Glossary* 87.

**fultum**, *add to I*: anra gehwylc of his cræfte þe he his licoman neadbehefe fultumas (*necessaria subsidia*) hæfþ, þære sawle . . . he sceal fultumas (*subsidium*) þenian, Chrd. 111, 4. *Add to compounds* mægen-, scipfultum.

**fultuman**, *see also* tofultumian.

**fultumend**, *add*: *adiutori nostro*, urum fultumiende, Ps. L. lxxx, 2.

**fultumgestre**, f. *helper*: *adiutrix*, A. lxv, 254, 7.

**fundelness**, *see* onfundelness.

**fundenness**, *see* ofer-, onfundenness.

**furh**, *add*: andlang furena, C.D. vi, 220, 21.

**furhwudu**, *add*: *pino*, furwuda, OEG 8, 4.

**furlang**, *see also* irfurlang.

**furþorlice**, adv. *to advantage*: ealla þa ilca heo dyde synderlice and furðerlucor þone ænig oðer, Anglica ii, 29, 134 (= Hml. Warn. 137, 7).

**fūs**, *add*: sense in Dream of the Rood 21 is perhaps *flashing*.

**fyld**, **fyll**, *see* goldf.

**fyllan**, *add to compounds* oferfyllan.

**fyllen**, *see* monaþfyllen.

**fyllness**, f. *fulness*: we lufedon ura wamba fylnesse, Verc. Först. 107, 16. *See also* oferfyllness.

**fylstan**, *see also* andfylstan.

**fȳr**, *add*: mid ðæm heofoncundan fire, Past. 222, 23. *Add to compounds* fon-, heofonfyr.

**-fyrclede**, *see* twi-, þrifyrclede.

**fyrde**, *see* infyrde.

**fyrdwǣn**, substitute for meaning *carriage*; *add*: ferdwæn, Will of Æthelgifu, ed. Whitelock, 50.

**fyrgen**, on citation see Grattan and Singer, *Anglo-Saxon Magic and Medicine* 176.

**fyrht**, *timid, see also* forfyrht.

**fyrhtan**, *add to II in Suppl.*: ne fyrhtað (MS. -eð) þa þe on synnum lyfiað and yfel þencað, Hpt. xxi, 189, last line. Add to compounds onfyrhtan.

**fȳrhūs**, *add*: *in caminata*, innan heora fyrhuse, Chrd. 45, 6; *and citation under* pisle *in Dict*.

**fyrmþ**, *add*: III *refuse*, see orfirmþa below.

***fyrsen**, *growing with furze*, PNE i, 190.

***fyrsett**, place grown with furze, PNE i, 190.

**fȳrþolle**, meaning in context is always *instrument of punishment or torture*, so combine I and II.

**fyrþrung**, *see also* gefyrþrung.

**fyxan**, *see* gefyxan.

# G

**gada**, *add*: Hept. 20, 105, v.l.

**gadinca**, read gādinca, and substitute for meaning *animal hurt by the goad* (*mutinus = mutilus*). Cf. FL 149.

**gǣgend**, *see* forgǣgend.

**gǣlan**, *see also* forgǣlan.

**gǣrede**, adj. *wedge-shaped*: æt ðæs gæredan landes ende, CS iii, 251, last line. *See also* þri-, feowergærede.

**gærs**, *see also* beregærs.

***gærsen**, adj. *grass-grown*, PNE i, 191.

***gærsing**, *pasture*, PNE i, 191.

**gærswyrt**, m. *herb*: *herbarum*, gærswyrta, Ps. Ar. xxxvi, 2.

**gæstedom**, m. *spirituality*: utan gegearwian us nu mid inneweardum gebedum and mid gæstedome, Verc. Först. 96, 8.

**gæsthālig**, adj. *holy in spirit*: Gu. 1060 (MS. gæsta halig).

**gaffetung**, *see* golfettung.

**gafol**, *add to 7*: *ex usuris*, of gafelum, Ps. L. lxxi, 14. *See also* mylen-, unrihtgafol.

**gafolgilda**, add to II: *on distinction from* gebur *see* Whitelock, *Eng. Hist. Doc.* 365.

**gafolgyld**, *payment*: *fiscus*, Prud. 548.

***gafolmann**, m. *tribute payer*, PNE i, 192.

**gafolrand**, *note*: form cited in Suppl. from Grff. ii, 531, is probably OE; cf. OEG 55, 13; Neophilologus ix, 199.

**gagolisc**, *add*: for geglisces mægdenes plegan, Mart. H. 156, 18, v.l.

**gāl**, n. *note*: sense in Gen. 327 is rather *pride* (OS gel; see PBB (Tübingen) lxxxii, 265).

**Gallias**, *note* pl. Gallige, MLR viii, 59, 10 (v.l. in Oros. iii, 4).

**gāllice**, adv. *wantonly*: *luxuriose*, Chrd. 108, 18.

**galluc**, *note*: there are three meanings: (1) *comfrey*; (2) *gallnut*; (3) *malum terrae*, on which see references under elehtre above. For (1) *add*: confirie, galluc, OEG 73 a, 4; for (2) *add*: galla, galluc, Txts. 66, 466; for (3) *add*: *malum terre*, galluc uel elechtre, DP 229. Cf. *also* eorþæppel above, *and* OED galloc.

**gālscipe**, in citation in Suppl. of Wrt. Voc. ii, 149, 36 (= Oliphant, *The Harleian Latin–Old English Glossary* 188) *read* byrnendes galscipes uel reþnesse) *and note* flagrantis furie *refers to* Sodomita libido (Prudentius, Psych. 46).

**gamian**, *delete, erroneous v.l. in* Hept., Gen. xix, 14, cf. gamnian.

**gān**, *add to III* 1 *c* α: *si quis in biuuis residere temptanerit*, gif hwa gæð sittan æt wega gelætan, Chrd. 61, 6; *add to III* 2 *a*: sleah þriwa on . . . sio heafodpanne gæþ onriht sona, Lch. ii, 342, 7. *Add to compounds* geond-, ongan.

**gang**, *add to II*: he betyneð . . . þa fet fram gange, *Verc.* Först. 90, 7; *add to XI*: sense in context (= Prud. 403) is *stage*; *add to XII*: Fehr 3, 8. *Add to compounds* heals-, here-, mynster-, ongean-, sunngang.

**gangan**, *see also* geondgangan; of-, utgangende.

**gangdagas**, *add*: se forma gangdæg, BM 166, 12; se ænlipiga gangdæg, *the day for singing the Greater Litany* (*25 April*), Henel, *Studien zum altengl. Computus* 72.

**gangendlic**, *see* ofgangendlic.

**gār**, *add to I*: gyllende garas sændan, ASPR vi, 122, 9; *add to IV*: to ðes gares suðende, CS i, 555, 2. *Add to compounds* lutegar.

**gārholt**, *cf.* holt II *in Suppl.*

**gārsecg**, *for various explanations see* Mod. Lang. Quarterly vii, 445, *and add* Eng. Lang. Notes i, 243; Archiv ccii, 431. *Add to compounds* norþgarsecg.

**gāsric**, *see* Elliot, *Runes* 100, for other explanations.

**gastlic**, *perhaps delete, take in citation as* gāstlic III.

**gāstlic**, *add*: IV *for* gæstlic, *terrible*: mycel stefne ond gastlic, Hml. Warn. 85, 3.

**gāt**, *see also* wætergat.

**gātbucca**, rather translate citation *skin of a he-goat*, see hirde below.

**gēac**, *l. 2 in Suppl.*, *add after* geaces sure, *a kind of sorrel.*

**geælfremedan**, *add*: he byð geelfremed fram middangerde, Verc. Först. 146.

**geǣndian**, *for* geærendian, ASPR vi, 119, 24; 120, 34; 121, 14.

**geǣsce**, *cf.* ungeæsce.

**geæþryt**, participial adj. *for* æþryt, Hml. Th. ii, 446, 6 (= Hml. Warn. 123, 8).

**geǣwirdlian**, *v. injure*: se lig and seo hæte monine mann swiðe geæwerdledan, Bd. iii, 16.

**geaflian** (?) *v. get*: *usurpans*, geauligende, An. Ox. 7, 118. (*Napier suggests* geahniende, *cf.* 5, 15; 5307; *but cf.* OED afle.)

**gēagl**, *add*: *in camo*, on geahle, Ps. Sal. xxxi, 9.

**gealdor**, *see also* wordgaldor.

**gealdorcræftiga**, *add*: Verc.-Hom. 77, 5.

**gealgmōdlice**, **gealglice**, *delete*, *MS. has probably* teart (lice); *see* Studia Germanica Gandensia ii, 88.

**gealla**, *see also* meargealla.

**gealpettan**, substitute for meaning *boast.*

**gealt**, *boar*: in loco qui dicitur Gealtborgsteal, CS i, 365, 4; PNE i, 193.

**geanbidian**, *add*: geambidedon, Ps. L. cxviii, 95.

**geanbidung**, *add*: geanbidung (*expectatio*) rihtwisra bliss, Scint. 130, 8.

**gēanbōc**, *add*: twegra hida gēanbōc and anre gerde, Sweet, *Second Anglo-Saxon Reader* 206, 8.

**gēancirr**, *see* geomær *in Suppl.*

**gēancirrendlic**, adj. *relative* (in grammar): Ælfc. Gr. Z. 231, 17, v.l.

**gēancumende**, participial adj., *meeting*: *obuiis*, geancumendum, JEGP lx, 444.

**geangian**, *v. trouble*: *ancxiatus*, geangud, Ps. Roy., Ps. Vit. cxlii, 4.

**gēanhweorfan**, *delete*, *for correct citation see* ongeanhwirfende *in Suppl.*

**gēanhwirfende**, participial adj. *returning*: *reducem i. reuertentem*, geanwyrfe(n)de, OEG 28, 189.

**gēanhwyrf**, *see* ongeanhwyrf.

**gēanhwyrft**, *turning*: *in conuertendo*, on gecerringe *uel* on gænhwyrfte, Ps. L. cxxv, 1.

**geanlician**, *add to II*: *simulastis*, lugon, geanlicadon, OEG 28, 414.

**gēanoþ**, *? complaint*: geonges geanoðe geomres, Aldhelm 7 (ASPR vi, 97).

**gēanryne**, *add*: gegnryne, Ps. Jun. lviii, 6; gegnyrn Ps. V.; genarn Ps. Cam.

**gēansprecan**, *v. contradict*: *obloquentis*, ongeansprecen(des), Ps. Vit. xliii, 17.

**gēanstandende**, participial adj. *standing in the way*: *obstantia*, þa genstandendan, Archiv cc, 198.

**ge-anwyrde**, *add to* (2): þa se þær geanwyrde wæs þe him land sealde, *then he who sold him the land acknowledged the fact there*, Chart. Rob. 162, 23.

**gēap**, f. *delete*, *see* teaforgeapa.

**gēap**, *query explanation of Ruin 31 and see* teaforgeapa.

**gēaplice**, *see also* ungeaplice.

**gēar**, *add*: I 1 a *a period of thirteen lunar months*: þære sunnan ger hæfð endlufon dagas ma þonne þæs monan ger, BM 62, 4. *Add to compounds* fif-, hungorgear, feowertiggeare.

**geard**, *add to compounds* windgeard.

---

**ge-arnung**, *delete*, *scríbal variant of* geearnung *or* earnung.

**gearo**, *see also* andwig-, siþgearo.

**gearowita**, *add*: (? -wite): *argumentum non apparentium*, orþanclic wise and na gearawite (v.l. -wyta), Gr. D. 269, 14.

**gēarryne**, m. *cycle of the year*: hu he on gerimcræfte gearryne tosceadan cunne, IP 220.

**gearufang**, discussed FL 164.

**gearwe**, *dress: add to compounds* sadolgearwe.

**gearwian**, *add*: III 4 *unclothe*: *exuentes*, gearwende, Mt. xxvii, 28, Lind. *Add to compounds* togegearwian.

**geaspis**, *jasper*: ðæt æreste gim-cynn is þæt is blac ond grene . . . ond sindon on naman geaspis haten, i.e. *the stone in which these colours are blended is called jasper* (expression confused), EETS 190, 13, 22.

**geat**, *add to compounds* crypel-, hæc-, hafe-, helle-, hlamm-, lud-, mapuldor-, windgeat, *and cf.* s.v. æscgeat *above*.

**gebǣru**, *add to III*: *obsceni motus corporum choris et saltationibus*, lichamana fracodlice gebæru mid saltingum et tumbincgum, Chrd. 79, 1.

**gebǣtan**, *add*: cf. Publications of the Modern Language Assoc. of America liii, 914.

**gebannan**, *add to I*: þam bode (þæs gafoles) þe þa gebannen wæs, Verc.-Hom. 109, 16; 21; ond þa swa wæs wordbebod gebannen, id. 113, 52.

**gebanngēar**, *add*: ðy gere þe agan wæs dcccc wintra and iiii winter, and ðy vii gebongere, CS ii, 268, 3.

**gebēagian**, *add*: and frequently in Ps. V., Jun., Cam. (v, 13; viii, 6; cii, 5).

**gebed**, *in I, l. 3, read* 23 b *for* 236, *and add*: asende he to Basilie biddende þæt he þone geyrsodon casere þurh his gebedu geliþgode, Hml. S. iii, 194. *Add to compounds* halsunggebed.

**gebedda**, *add to I* 1: *of a husband*: ælc wif ðe cild gebære . . . sceolde forhabban . . . from hire gebeddan, Hml. Th. i, 134, 20; *add to I* 2: hafað him þry gebeddan, þæt is greot and molde and wyrmas, Verc. Först. 92, 9. Cf. geresta.

**gebedgīht**, *sense is rather* (*time for*) *going to prayer*. Cf. FL 164.

**gebēodan**, *second citation under III in Dict. should be under I*; Latin is *rex Persarum discedere ab armis et quiescere in pace uniuersam Graeciam praecepit.*

**gebeorgan**, *add to I* 2: swa swa he wille beon wið Godd geborgen, Chart. Harm. 137, 10.

**geberan**, *add to II* 2: min sunu, ic ðe to men gebær, Hml. S. xxv, 175; *note in l. 5 of Suppl. lemma of* geboronae *was originally not* exposito *but* concepto *in same passage* (Oros. i, 4, 7).

**gebētan**, *add to II*: (5) *amend, reform one's self*: gif hwylc broðor . . . gebetan nelle, ne his þeawas gerihtlæcan, R. Ben. 52, 5; 126, 3; *add*: V *repeat itself, come round* (of a festival): *iterata*, giboetadum, Rtl. 67, 4; 62, 4. *See also* ungebeted.

**gebīdan**, *add to IX*: ne gebidað (*possidebunt*) hi heofena rice, Chrd. 74, 35.

**gebiddan**, *add to II* 4: ic wæs gemedemod gebiddan þa gerynu þære rode, Hml. S. xxiii b, 466. *See also* ungebeden.

**gebindan**, *see also* ungebunden.

**gebisgian**, *add*: he mid Godes herungum his muð gebisgað, Hml. Th. i, 494, 16.

**gebisnian**, *add*: III *exemplify*: þeah he hefegra sy, þonne se ðe Benedictus siþþan us gebysnode, Hml. S. iii, 148.

**gebit**, *see also* orfgebit.

**geblǣdan**, *v. inflate*: *dilatauerunt*, geblæddon, Ps. Ar. xxxiv, 21; Hy. 6, 15. Cf. toblædan.

**geblāwan**, *add*: III *cast* (*metal*): *conflatilis*, geblawen, Prud. 442, and take here Wrt. Voc. ii, 133, 18 (= WW 208, 14) cited in Suppl., where full reading is *conflatum*, *incensum*, onæled, geblawen.

**geboren**, *see also* ongeboren.

**gebrǣc**, as gloss to *umecta* meaning is *marshy ground*.

**gebrǣcdrenc**, *see* gebrecdrenc *in Suppl.*

**gebrǣdan**, *roast, add to* (1): fugla gesodenra and gebrædra, Lch. ii, 180, 14.

**gebrastl**, *note*: in last citation in Suppl. (= Prud. 757), *crackling of salt on a fire is referred to*.

**gebregd**, *add*: II *woven material, fabric*: *funale textum*, raplic gebred, Prud. 852.

**gebregd**, *craft, add*: *astutia*, gebregde, JEGP lvi, 65, 63.

**gebregdan**, *add to V*: *peregrinum quempiam esse se simulans*, gebræd he hine sylfne swylce he wære sum ælþeodig man, Chrd. 99, 23.

**gebregdness**, f. *suddenness*: þonne arisað ealle þa men, þa þe mid gebregdnessum on deaþe swulton, Verc. Först. 117, 17.

**gebrēman**, *add*: ær æfenþenung sy gebremed (*celebretur*), Chrd. 114, 17.

**gebrengan**, *add*: II b *where the action is given by a clause*: se wearð on gebroht þæt he ofslean wolde þa Iudei, Hml. S. xxv, 549. *See also* ongebroht.

**gebringan**, *add to II*: gebringe þe se Hælend to hire hafenleaste (*to poverty like hers*), Hml. S. iii, 187.

**gebroc**, *add to (I)*: *in confractione*, on gebroce, Ps. V. (and related glosses). Cf. gebryce.

**gebrosnian**, *add to (I)*: se lichama gebrosnað, Wlfst. 187, 13.

**gebrȳcgan**, *cancel Suppl.*, *retain Dict. and note*: cg = c, *cf.* brycian, *and* lifbrycgung.

**gebryddan**, ? *delete, read in citation* gebryrded, *inspired*.

**gebryrdness**, f. *compunction*: Scint. 38, 12.

**gebrytsen**, *add*: wæron XII cypan fulle on þam gebrytsnum, E.S. xlix, 345, 17.

**gebūrland**, *add*: JEGP xxxiii, 346, 6 (= Förster, *Flussname Themse* 794-5), *cited under* færfrige.

**gebūrscipe**, *add*: *note in citation v.l.* (*2 MSS.*) geburhscipe, *area with a burh as centre*.

**gebycgan**, *see also* ungeboht.

**gebyrd**, *add to VII*: B. 1074, Sal. 386.

**gebyrgan**, *bury, add*: on þone feorðan dæg, þæs þe he gebered (v.l. bebyrged) wæs, Hml. P. i, 313, 43.

**gebyrgen** = byrgen, *tomb*; lemma in citation is corrupt (read *tumba*). Cf. FL 20.

**gebyrian**, *add to III*: *with mid*: *quid tibi cum feminis*, hwæt gebyrað þe mid wifum, Chrd. 68, 1; *add to IV*: þa hammas þa þer mid rihte to gebyriað, CS iii, 179, 11.

**gebytlu**, *add*: he wolde wyrcan þa healle ærest on eastdæll and þa oþre gebytlu bæftan þære healle, Hml. S. xxxvi, 95.

**gecēosendlic**, adj. *to be chosen*: *eligendae*, geceosendlices, Archiv cc, 198.

**gecīgan**, *add to III 1*: þu witga bist geced, Ps. V., Hy. 9, 9 (and related glosses).

**gecīgness**, *add*: *name*: mid anum breþer þes gecignis wes Owine, Chad 168, 75.

**gecilled**, participial adj. *made cool*: *refrigerer*, si gecylled, Ps. Vit. xxxviii, 14. Cf. forcilled.

**gecirr**, *turning*: *conuertendo*, gecyrre, Ps. Spl. ix, 3.

**gecirran**, *see also* niw-, ungecirred.

**gecnēatian**, *in l. 2 insert* gecneatede *after* swetnesse.

**gecneordness**, *add to 1*: ic hine þe befæste mid healicre gecneordnisse, *I most earnestly commend him to you*, Hept. 63, 1057; *add to 2*: *nequaquam fraudis cuiusque studium appetant*, nanes fracodes gecneor(d)nysse ne wilnion hi, Chrd. 76, 33.

**gecnēorednis**, *add*: II *issue, posterity*: *progenies*, ge(c)nyrdnes, OEG 28, 167.

**gecnēores**, *for* cneoress: *generatione*, gecneoreso, Rtl. 3, 18.

**gecnyclan**, *forms suggest two verbs* gecnyclan *and* ge(h)nyclan *of similar meaning*.

**gecocnian**, *add*: *condito*, gecocanade (*misprinted* gerecanade), WW 372, 12.

**gecollenferhtan**, sense in the citation is *encourage*, as the lemma *exinanite* is a cry of encouragement; see FL 203.

**gecopsed**, *for* gecypsed, Ps. Sal. lxxviii, 11.

**gecorded**, cf. FL 103.

**gecoren**, *see also* ungecoren.

**gecringan**, *add*: II *dilute*: *dilutam*, gekrungen, OEG 73 b, 20.

**gecroced**, *add*: *croceo*, mid gecrowed(um), OEG 27, 21.

**gecūþian**, v. *become known*: *innotuisti*, gecuðodes, Ps. Jun. cxliii, 3.

**gecwēmedlic**, *see also* welgecwemedlic.

**gecwidrǣdden**, *in citation in Dict. Wrt. Voc. 34, 19* (= WW 140, 22), *MS. has* gecwicrædden.

**gecwilman**, *in first citation in Suppl.* (= Prud. 889) *secto* refers to one killed by being sawn in half.

***gecȳft**, ? *meeting*: see Review of English Studies, n.s. viii, 408.

**gecynde**, *add to (4)*: Adam wearð of his gecyndan are (*de possessione sua*) þurh his wif ut adræfed, Chrd. 68, 24.

**gecynness**, f. *generation*: *generationes*, gecynnesse, Ps. Sal., Hy. 6, 7.

**gecyrtan**, ? *delete, read in citation* gescyrte.

**gecȳþan**, *add*: VI *become known*: þurh witena sægena us gecyðde se mæra nama (*celebre nomen innotuit*) þæs arwyrðan weres, Gr. D. 179, 11.

**gecȳþness**, *see also* ægecyþness.

**gedǣlan**, *omit Gu. 343* (= 371), *for which see wiþ III 3*; *add to VI 4*: B. 71.

**gedafenlic**, *in citation Wrt. Voc. 54, 60* (= WW 178, 45) *MS. reads* gedafendling þeodnys, *see A. viii, 451*.

**gedafenlicness**, *see also* ungedafenlicness.

**gedafenness**, f. *fitness*: *in tempore oportuno*, on tide gedauenesse, Ps. Sal. cxliv, 15.

**gedāl**, *add to III*: *communi diuidendo actio*, gemanan gedal, WW 207, 42; (a) *with wiþ*: gedal wið eallum his freondum, Verc. Först. 89, 6. *Add to compounds* irfe-, weggedal.

**gedēfelic**, *see also* ungedefelic.

**gedēopian**, citation is Rtl. 81, 12.

**gedihtan**, *add to 9*: *splendide*, gedihtedum, OEG 62, 17.

**gedilgian**, *add to I*: he geearnode þa ylcan scylde gedilegan, Verc.-Hom. 65, 119.

**gedingan**, *delete, in citation MS. reads* geornð.

**gedōn**, *add to III 1*: se casere him eallon gedon het biglyfan genohne, Fehr 92, 20.

**gedrēfedness**, *add*: *confusione*, mid gedroefednisse, Ps. V. lxx, 13 (Ps. Jun. -drof-).

**gedrēfend**, m. *troubler*: *tribulantis*, gedrefendes, Ps. L. lxxvii, 42.

**gedrenc**, *for* drenc: Fehr 18, 2, v.l.; IP 189, 2.

**gedrencan**, *note* gedrenced, Exod. 34, *is by a different hand, on an erasure*.

**gedrēohlice**, *add*: ne sprecon ymbe nan þing buton ymbe heora worc, and þæt gedreohlice and wærlice (*et hoc caute*), Chrd. 29, 21.

**gedrettan**, *delete, read in citation* gedrehte.

**gedrif**, *stubble*: *correct citation to* swa gedrif biforen ansien windes.

**gedrīme**, *add*: mid gedrymre (*consona*) stefne, Chrd. 125, 5.

**gedrinca**, *citation* = Hml. P. ii, 696, 352; Hml. Warn. 39, 2.

**gedropa**, *may mean* drop, see FL 70.

**gedropung**, *glosses genimen*: Ps. Vit., Ps. Ar. lxiv, 11.

**gedwǣlan**, *delete, see* gedwellan *in Suppl.*

**gedwǣllic**, *for* dwellic: Hal. 29, 10, v.l.

**gedwildæfterfylgung**, *take as two words, see* gedwild, æfterfylgung.

**gedwildmann**, *add*: an cyn gedwyldmanna (*hereticorum*) is þa wenað þæt halige wæccan syn idele, Chrd. 25, 36.

**gedwol**, *add*: *obliteratis erroneis circulis*, he het fordilgian þa gedwolan hringas (v.l. gedwolhringas), Bd. v. 21; sume gedwole mæn cwædon, Hml. Warn. 56, 18.

**gedwola**, *see also* scingedwola.

**gedwolcræft**, *add*: Verc.-Hom. 51, 98.

**gedwolenlic**, adj. *foolish, senseless*: *dementissimum*, gedwolenlicost, Chrd. 115, 5.

**gedwolhring**, *see* gedwol.

**gedwollic**, *for* dwellic: Hal. 29, 10, v.l.

**gedwolpæþ**, m. *a path leading astray*: *deuia*, gedwolpaðas, Archiv cc, 198.

**gedyhtedum**, adv. *splendidly*: OEG 62, 17.

**gedyrst**, the word is doubtful, see ASPR iii, 359, for proposed emendations.

**geēacnian**, *add to II*: ic geeacnode into Eligmynstre ðas þry hamas, CS iii, 561, 18.

**geearfoþigan**, v. *trouble*: *contriuit*, geeærfogoþæþ, Ps. Cant. civ, 16, 33.

**geearnian**, *add to I a*: toll and team sy agifen into þam mynstre, butan he hit geearnian mæge (*unless he can gain remission*) to þam þe þænne ah mynstres geweald, Cht. E. 236, 5; *add*: III *enjoy*: ac hæbbe heo ðone bryce, þa hwile þe heo hit geearnigan cann, Chart. Whit. 48, 1.

**geēastrian**, *add*: ær eahta niht beon geeastrod, The Anglo-Saxons 276, 30.

**geedginnan**, v. *begin again*: *recidiua in proelia*, on geedgunnenu⟨m⟩ gef⟨e⟩ohte, OEG 27, 35.

**geedgirnan**, v. *seek again*: *repetit*, geedgyrnð; *repetuntur*, beoð geedgyrnde, Archiv cc, 197.

**geedlǣstan**, v. *repeat*: geedlæstan (pres. subj.) and þa oðre ealle eac swa, Archiv lxxxiv, 6, 51.

**geefenlician**, *l. 2 in Suppl. read* geeblicadun *not* -um).

**geendebyrdan**, *add to 2 α*: preostas hyra endebyrdnyssa sceolon healdan ealswa hig geendebyrde synt on heora gecyrrednyssa, Chrd. 9, 17.

**geendebyrdness**, *for* endebyrdness: R. Ben. 125, 4.

**gefædlice**, *add: astute*, gefædlice, Ps. Cam. lxxxii, 4.

**gefæge**, probably delete, read in citation (B. 915) gefrægra.

**gefælsian**, *add*: sense in Cri. 320 is *enter, visit* (cf. Lat. *lustrare*).

**gefærede**, *add*: participial adj. pl., *frightened*. See FL 133.

**gefæstan**, *place, add.*: III *define: definiuit*, gefæste, JEGP lx, 444, VI, 68. Cf. afæstnian.

**gefættian**, delete *become fat*.

**gefanne**, *see* windgefanne.

**gefaran**, *see* ungefaren.

**gefealdan**, *add to (1): caelum plicabitur ut liber*, heofon bið gefealden swa swa boca leaf beoð, Verc. Först 107, 1.

**gefēalice**, *see also* ungefealice.

**gefeallan**, add to I: *reflexively*: gefeol hine se ofermodiga cyning of his scride, Mart. H. 134, 13.

**gefēaness**, f. *joy*: ða wæs he mid gastlicre gefeannesse . . . gefeonde, Guth. Gr. 134, 8, v.l. (= Vercelli MS., f. 135ᵛ, 24).

**gefēawness**, f. *scarcity*: seo gefeanes þara sacerda, Bd. iii, 21, v.l.

**gefēgan** (4), *for arta read* apta (so MS.), sense is therefore *suited, fitted* (cf. ungefege, *unsuited*); sense in Whale 41 is *joined* (so transfer to 2 a).

**gefēgness**, f. *conjunction* (in grammar): gefegnyssa (pl.), BM 94, 23. Cf. gefegedness.

**gefeoht**, on gloss *praefeciales*, gefeohtes bodan (Suppl., l. 2), see FL 20 (cf. *per fetiales bella indicebantur*, Isid., *Et.* viii, 11, 48).

**gefēon**, *see also* ferhþgefeonde.

**gefēra**, *add to compounds* simbelgefera.

**gefētun**, v. pret. pl., glosses *ceciderunt*, Mt. xiii, 7, 8, Rush.

**gefigo**, *for* σύκωσις *substitute* χήμωσις.

**gefirenian**, *add*: sacerd se ðe hine besmiteð and nele gefyrenian, Buss. vii, 8a (*cf. v.l. cited under* gefeormian).

**gefleard**, add to meanings: *error; add to citations*: hi gimað untidæta and oðra geflearda (*ceteris suis uoluptatibus dediti*), Chrd. 10, 32.

**geflit**, *add to compounds* irfegeflit.

**geflitglīw**, *delete, see* geslitgliw.

**geflogen**, *see* ongeflogen; wuldorgeflogena.

**gefōg**, *fitness, add*: lufa eadmodnysse . . . mid gefoge, *The Anglo-Saxons* 276, 30.

**gefolc**, *see* ingefolc.

**geforewrit**, n. *prologue*: hit sagð þæt ða geforewritu cyðað . . ., Ker, *Catalogue* 280 (= Archiv cvi, 258).

**geforht**, adj. *afraid: timidi*, gefrohte, Mt. viii, 26, Rush.

**geforswelgan**, *for* forswelgan: *obsorbet*, geforswilgeð, Ps. Cant. lvii, 10.

**geforþian**, *note*: basic sense *send forth* occurs: geforþodan þæt scrin, Hml. P. ii, 691, 274.

**gefōtcopsed**, *for* gefotcypsed: Ps. Vit., Ps. Ar. ci, 21; cxlv, 8.

**gefrægnian**, *probably delete, in citation* (B. 1333) *most read* gefægnod, *made happy*.

**gefrēabeorhtian**, v. *declare: declarauit*, gefræbeorhtude, Ps. Cam. xli, 9.

**gefrēosan**, *add: obriguit*, gefreas, PBB lxxxv (Halle), 61.

**gefulhtnian**, v. *baptize*: gelyfeð on God ond byð gefulhtnede, Hml. Warn. 23, 32.

**gefullian**, *add*: ealle þa gefullwudan (-fulledan) cildru, Gr. D. 288, 22.

**gefylness**, *add*: oþ þa gefylnesse þisse worolde, Bl. H. 145, 16.

**gefynde**, *see* ungefynde.

**gefyrn**, *add to 2 b*: gefyrn is þæt . . ., Chrd. 25, 11.

**gefyrnness**, *for* Nap. 3 *read* Chrd. 25, 10; 26, 16.

**gefyrþring**, f. *removal: est altaribus remouendus*, bið to gefyrðringe to Godes weofode, Chrd. 79, 15.

**gefyxan**, v. *deceive*: gif hwa his gildan gelihinie oþþe gefyxse, Chart. in Förster, *Flussname Themse* 792.

**gegān**, *add to A III 2: utrum cogitatio suggestione an delectatione acciderit*, hwæðer se geþoht geeode þe mid scylde þe mid lustfullnesse, Bd. i, 27; *add to B II 4*: eall þæt mancynne to ðam mæstan gode geeode, Hml. A. 154, 58; *B IV*: translate verb as *traverse*, Lat. of Æthelred's law has *peragrabit*.

**gegang**, *add*: he manige mæn þara þe ic gemunde, ægþer ge on tida gegange ge eac on wundrum (*uirtute et tempore*) oferþeah, Gr. D. 179, 10.

**gegearwian**, *add to III*: hyt þa hæle gegearwað, Lch. i, 122, 9.

**gegearwung**, *add to II*: godra weorca gegearwungum (*exhibitionibus*) nacodne, Chrd. 108, 29.

**gegendan**, add meaning *criers* (of cranes).

**gegeolwian**, *see* geolwian.

**gegilda**, *add*: sense in Ine 21 is *relatives*; in Ine 16, Ælf. 30 *associates*. Cf. Whitelock, *Eng. Hist. Doc.* 334. *See also* cniht I b *and* rihtgegilda.

**gegirela**, *add to 1*: se gegyrla þe ic hæfde . . . mid ealdunge totorene forwurdon, Hml. S. xxiii b, 570; *add to 2*: God reafian læteð eowere dohtra heora gegirla, Wlfst. 45, 25.

**gegiscan**, cf. FL 71.

**gegite**, adj. *conscious: conscia*, gegite, OEG 28, 409.

**gegitsian**, *add*: Wyn. 58.

**gegladian**, *add to I 4: placatum*, gegladudne, Prud. 469.

**geglengan**, *see also* ungeglenged.

**gegninga**, *add to 4*: he cymð geanunga foron þære sunnan (v.l. *for* foron ongean þære sunnan), De temp. ann. 22.

**gegot**, *see* glæsgegot.

**gegotenlic**, *see* geotendlic *in Suppl*.

**gegrindswyle**, m. *swelling due to friction: intertrigenes*, gegrindswile, Kansas leaf.

**gegrin**, *substitute: snare: de laqueo*, of gegrynum, Ps. Cant. xxiv, 15; *retinacula*, gegrinu, OEG 9, 74.

**gegripan**, add to I: *snatch from*: swa swa spearwa gegripen is (*erepta est*), Ps. Jun. cxxiii, 7; *add to III 2*: and ða strecan mod Godes rice gegripað, Hml. Th. i, 358, 26.

**gegrundweallian**, *add*: gegrundweallod þurh God sylfne (sc. *Lent*), Hml. P. i, 237, 164.

**gegrymetian**, v. *rage*: he gegrimmetode egeslice, Hml. S. xxv, 540.

**gegymian**, see for other suggestions Bonser, *Med. Background of Anglo-Saxon England* 106.

**gehabban**, *cancel XIII, and keep MS. reading in citation, see* gehæftan.

**gehæftan**, *add*: VIII wiþ gehæftan, *fight against*: cf. citation *under* gehabban XIII; *congredi*, wiþ gehæftan, Prud. 822.

**gehægan**, *probably delete, read in citation* gehnæged.

**gehæge**, *cancel*.

**gehæman**, *add to (2)*: he hi genam niedenga and hire mid gehæmde, Past. 415, 17.

**gehæplic**, *see also* ungehæplic.

**gehæred**, adj. *hairy: capilata*, gehærede, Archiv cxvii, 24, 21.

**gehālgian**, *see also* niwgehalgod.

**gehālsian**, *add: entreat*: heo hyne halsode þurh God, Mart. H. 180, 18; he wæs þurh me gehalsod, id. 24.

**gehāmian**, *substitute: settle in a home* (trans.): Aldred . . . hine gihamadi, *A. settled himself*, Harmer, *Historical Documents* 36, 14.

**gehandfæstan**, v. *pledge*: þeh heo Josepe gehandfæst wære, Hml. Warn. 135, 14.

**gehātan**, *add to IV 1 α*: ic gean . . . þara landa þe wit geheotan Gode, Chart. Whit. 40, 7.

**gehāwian**, *add to II*: mon ær gehawige ðæt se grund fæsð sie, Past. 308, 3.

**gehēafdod**, *see* hringe *below*.

**gehealdan**, *add*: I 3 a with complement: þe sind gehealdene ðine meda gewisse, Hml. Th. ii, 516, 23; *II 1 a with complement*: truwiende þæt hine ungederodne geheolde þæt mægn þæs licgendan, Hml. S. xxiii b, 777, v.l.

**gehealddagas**, discussed FL 104.

**gehealdengeorn**, adj., glosses *continens*: gihaldendgiorn, Rtl. 45, 10.

**gehealdness**, *add*: minre sawle gehealdnesse, Archiv ccii, 272, 10 (= Notes and Queries ccx, 209, 6); eall seo Godes lufe is on þære gehealdnysse his beboden, Hml. Warn. 93, 1.

**gehealdsum**, *add to II*: se bið gehealtsum his lifes, Archiv cxxix, 25, 7.

**gehēan**, *add*: ahafen ond geheged, Hml. Warn. 99, 13.

**gehēdan**, *cancel II, citations belong to* hegan; *see also* gehydan.

**gehefigian**, *add to V*: of physical oppression: *unde leuigatus fuerat, rursus oneratur*, ðonne gehefegað hine ðæt ilce ðæt hine ær gelihte, Past. 419, 30. *See also* ungehefigod.

**gehēgan**, *add*: II *obtain*: Met. 27, 15, B. 505 (*cited under* gehedan).

**gehereness**, *for* hereness: þæs hyhstan cyninges gehyrnes, Vercelli MS., f. 71ʳ, 4.

**gehild**, *add to VI*: *in custodiendo sermones tuos*, on gehelde word ðine, Ps. Jun. cxviii, 9.

**gehiran**, *add to III 3*: þa heo þa gehyrde þone broþer forð-feredne, Guth. Gr. 167, 123.

**gehīrend**, *add*: ða geherend giheras, Mk. iv, 12, Rush.

**gehīrness**, *add*: (3) *what is heard*: hwelc gilefeð gihernisse (*auditui*) user?, Jn. xii, 38, Rush. *See also* ungehirness.

**gehīrsumness**, *add to 2*: *exeant ubi eis imperatur in opera*, faran to swylcum weorce and gehyrsumnysse swylce him beboden sig, R. Ben. 84, 15.

**gehirtan**, *add to I 1*: *refrigerer*, si gehyrt, Ps. Vit., Ps. Ar. xxxviii, 14. *See also* ungehirt.

**gehittan**, v. *meet with*: and ec we læroð prest gehwilcne, ðeh he gehitte operne ðe swa wel ne cunne swa he scolde, þat he nenne ne scænde, Mone, Quellen und Forschungen 1830, 547.

**gehīwcūþlician**, *add*: Hml. Bel. 44, 25.

**gehīwian**, *add to IV*: manega geleafan Cristes . . . þurh lease hiwunge gehealdan hi gehiwiað (*simulant*), Scint. 129, 12.

**gehladan**, in first two citations in Suppl. *fertum* and *faltum* are taken as *fartum*.

**gehlēapan**, *add*: *currere*, gehleapan, OEG 28, 82 (where in context lemma means *flow*).

**gehlot**, *add*: (1) *casting of lots* gehlote (*sorte*) gecoren, Chrd. 75, 24; 27; (2) *share, portion*: hi preostas an Grecisc clericos hatað, for þan hig synt getalode to Drihtnes gehlote, oððe þæt heora Drihten sy heora gehlot, ealswa hit gewriten is, 'Ic eom', cwyð Drihten, 'heora yrfewerdnys', Chrd. 75, 30.

**gehlūttrad**, *add*: *probatum*, gehlutrudu (sic), Ps. Vit. xi, 7.

**gehlyste**, *for* Nap. 30 *read* Chrd. 22, 36.

**gehlytto**, *see also* midgehlytto.

**gehogian**, *add to 2*: *eum deducere satage*, gehoga þæt þu hi læde, Chrd. 92, 30.

**gehola**, substitute for meaning *friend, confidant*.

**gehopp**, discussed FL 88.

**gehorwian II**, note: *in Mk. xii, 4, Lind., MS. has* gehornadon (? *for* gehoruadon).

**gehradian**, *add*: I 3 *cause to pass quickly*: ac for Godes gecor-enum God gehradað hys timan, Hml. P. ii, 607, 375; I 4 *do soon*: *agatur nona temperius mediante octaua hora*, sy se non geradod and sy gehringed þonne seo eahteoðe tid bið healf agan, R. Ben. 73, 14.

**gehrēosendlic**, adj. *ready to fall*: *ruituros*, gehreosendlice, Archiv cc, 198.

**gehrepian**, *add to 3*: we habbað . . . manega þing gehrepode, BM 78, 14; we habbað medomlice þas þing gehrepod, id. 142, 18.

**gehrif**, *womb*: gemette he hi bearn hæbbende on hire gehrife, Hml. A. 134, 595. *See also* ingehrif.

**gehrīfnian**, *see* hrifnian.

**gehrin**, in glosses: *frusta*, gehrino, Ps. Cant. cxlvii, 17; *aedificationes*, gehrino, Mk. xiii, 2, Lind.; *edificationem*, girine (*altered from* gihrine), Rtl. xii, 27; *instrumento* gehrine, Mt. Prol. 2, Lind. See JEGP xlvi, 417.

**gehrorenlic**, *add*: ic eom deadlic mann and gehrorenlic, Verc. Först. 147, 3.

**gehūslian**, *add*: he hi gehuslode mid þæs Hælendes gerynum, Hml. S. iii, 80.

**gehwǣr**, *add to I 1 b*: gehwær and þær, *everywhere*, Hml. P. ii, 711, 648. *See also* welgehwær.

**gehwilc**, *add to III 2*: in gehwylcum men (*in uiuente quolibet*), þa hwile þe he leofað, se gæst byþ hæfd on þam lichaman, Gr. D. 303, 23.

**gehwirfan**, I 10 a: read vi for v in l. 4. *See also* niwege-hwirfed.

**gehycgan**, *add to 3*: *statui custodire iudicia*, gehogde healdan domas, Ps. Jun. cxviii, 106.

**gehȳdan** II and III in Dict. are forms of *gehēdan*, heed. Delete in Suppl. bracket at end of *gehydan*, and article *gehydan*, fasten with a rope.

**gehygdness**, *see* ingehygdness.

**gehyhtan**, *add to II*: *exaltauerunt in deum*, gehyhton on God, Ps. Jun. lxxxiii, 21; *in operibus . . . exultabo*, on weorcum . . . ic gehyhte, id. xci, 5.

**gehyhtlice**, adv. *suitably*: Verc.-Hom. 62, 99.

**gehylced**, substitute for meaning *stretched apart*.

**geīcan**, *add*: III *implement* (an agreement); se þe þas gerædnesse mid gode geyce, God hit him geleanige, E.S. lxii, 123.

**geiht**, *add*: *triiugus*, on þreo geyht, OEG 22, 8; cf. A. xli, 99, n. 1.

**geildan**, *add*: ne lata þu þæt þu to Gode gecyrre, ne geyld þu hit (*neque differas*) of dæge to dæge, Archiv cxxii, 258, 34.

**geinbryrdan**, *add*: *conpungimini*, bioð geinbryrde, Ps. V. iv, 5 (and related glosses); *conpungitur*, is g.inbrydded, PBB lxxxv (Halle), 61.

**geindīpan**, v. *immerse*: *liquat*, gindypþ (sic), Prud. 162.

**geintimbrian**, *see* intimbrian *below*.

**geirnan**, *add to IV*: oþ þæt hio sie eal tosoden and þicge geurnen, Lch. ii, 230, 8.

**gelāc**: *in An. 1092* þurh heard gelac *seems to be a battle metaphor with* gelac = lindgelac.

**gelācnian**, *see also* ungelacnod.

**gelācnung**, f. *healing*: *curatio*, Gn. (Archiv cxcix, 20).

**gelād**, *see also* hlincgelad.

**gelǣca, gelǣcan**: *probably delete, as errors for* \*geefenlæca, geefenlæcan; cf. FL 150.

**gelǣccan**, *add to II 4*: he ahredde þæt gelæhte scep, Hml. S. xviii, 17; *add to II 7*: he wearð gelæht to þam laðum gecampe, Hml. Th. ii, 500, 7.

**gelǣdan**, *add to III 1*: þone að mon gelædde ymb xxx næhta, CS i, 536, 17.

**gelǣr**, *add to 1*: *uenter uacuus*, seo gelære wamb, Chrd. 69, 30.

**gelǣredlic**, *see* ungelæredlic.

**gelǣte**, *add*: gif hwa gæð ut on stræte, oððe gæð sittan æt wega gelætan (*in biuiis residere temptauerit*), Chrd. 61, 6.

**gelǣte**, *manners, bearing*: stæðig on his gelæte, Nap. 31.

**gelaþung**, *see also* togelaþung.

**geldscēap**, n. *barren sheep, or sheep not yet having lambed*: Will of Æthelgifu, ed. Whitelock, 5; 11.

**gelēafa**, *see also* rihtgeleafa.

**gelēafa**, *leave*: note f. form: be minre geleafan, Chart. Harm. 255 (no. 90), 4.

**gelēaffulness**, *see also* rihtgeleaffulness.

**gelēas**, *add*: ge geleasan witan, Hml. A. 174, 133 (*or ditto-graphy*?).

**gelēd** etc., *these forms are all corruptions of* glēd, glōed, *glowing coal* (*as used in torture*). *In first citation in Suppl. read* poene *for* woepe. *Cf.* FL 169; Oliphant, *The Harley Latin-Old English Glossary* 61.

**-geleger**, *see* sibgeleger.

**gelegergild**, *cf.* FL 165.

**gelengan**, *add*: *in tubis ductilibus*, in hornum gelengdum, Ps. V. xcvii, 6 (and related glosses).

**gelēogan**, *add*: *play a person false*: hiora earmas agaledon and hira handa him gelugon, Verc.-Hom. 132, 24.

**gelēsan**, *add*: *libera*, gelese, Mt. vi, 13, Rush.

**geletting**, f. *hindrance*: *de omni impedimento*, fram ælcere gelettinge, A. lxxxi, 6.

**gelice**, *add to I 2*: gelice . . . swa, *as . . . so*: gelice þa biscopas syndan . . . swa syndan þa mæssepreostas, Ll. Th. ii, 402, 19.

**gelīchamian**, v. *give a body*: þeos gelichamede Godes . . . sune, Hml. Warn. 136, 33; *see also* gelichamod *in Dict*.

**gelician**, *please, see also* ungelician.

**geliclǣtan**, v. *compare*: *adsimilabimus*, we gelicleta welle, Mk. iv, 30, Lind., Rush.

**geliffǣstan**, *add to I 2*: he hiene gelieffæsð, Past. 259, 12; *add to IV*: genim sumne dæl þæs gelyffæstan blodes, Hml. S. xxiii b, 623.

**gelixan**, *for* lixan: *resplendent*, eft hia gilixia, Rtl. 54, 8.

**gelōgian**, *add to III 2 b*: betwynan þam gelogodan dæge, *in the course of the intercalary day*, BM 70, 22; *add to VII*: ure wisan gelogian mid geþincþan, IP 267.

**gelōmlǣcan**, *add*: II b *apply oneself frequently to*: uton us on gebedu gelomlæcan, *let us be frequent in prayer*, Verc. Först. 132, 7.

**gelygenian**, *add*: Förster, *Flussname Themse* 792 (*quoted s.v.* gefyxan).

**gemaca**, *add to I 2*: *calciamenta . . . paria quatuor*, feower gemacan sceona, Chrd. 48, 26; *add to II 2*: ond næfð he nænne gemaca (*of the Phoenix*), Hml. Warn. 148, 4. *See also* simblegemaca.

**gemacian**, *add to IV 3*: seo modignyss gemacode to deoflum þa englas, Fehr 204, 11.

**gemæcca**, *add*: I a *of things*: ne mette ic næfre on minum life swa mycles sares ne yfeles gemæccan, Verc. Först. 120, 14. *See also* ungemæcca.

**gemǣnan**, *lament, add to I*: hu earfeðlice hi hit gemænað, Ors. S. 136, 19.

**gemǣne**, *read* gemǣne (*not* -um) *in* B. 1857. *Add to Id 1 a α:* unc næs gemǣne man, Hml. S. ii, 157; *add to VI 2:* hebbe he wið Godd gemene, *may he have to account for himself to God*, Chart. Harm. 400, 7.

**gemǣran**, *celebrate, add:* mid godcundre gyfe gemæred and geweorþad (*insignis*), Bd. iv, 24.

**gemǣran**, *enlarge, delete and take citation under* gemǣran, *make known, celebrate.*

**gemǣre**, *add to compounds* ealdgemǣre.

**gemagian** (?) v. *become strong, get better:* se þe gelið raðe he hamacgað, Lch. iii, 184, 21.

**gemāhness**, *add:* Wyn. 62 (*contumacia*).

**gemāna**, *add to III: non commisceamini cum illo*, nabbe ge nanne gemanan wið hine, Past. 357, 5.

**gemang**, *among, see also* in-, þærgemang.

**gemang**, *mixing, add to compounds* wingemang.

**gemangness**, *see also* wyrtgemangness.

**gemanian**, *perhaps read in* Rid. 3, 66, gemagnad (*see* gemægenad).

**gemearc**, *add:* metas, gemearce, OEG 4, 147.

**gemearcian**, *add to VI:* on þam dæge ys seo forme tid prima gehaten, on þære sceolon gemearcode cnihtas geornlice to Gode clypian, BM 124, 14.

**gemedemian**, add to V: *to deem worthy* (to do): ic wæs gemedemod gebiddan þa gerynu þære rode, Hml. S. xxiii b, 466.

**gemedumlice**, *for* medumlice: *digne*, gimeodomlice, Rtl. 18, 17.

**gemengan**, *add to I 2 a: with* to: man gemencge wæter to ðam wine, Hml. Th. ii, 278, 5; Bt. xxiv, 5 (= S. 86, 14), cited in Dict; *add to IV: nos turbis popularibus admixti*, we þe wæron gemængde to þysum folclicum mængungum, Gr. D. 209, 12. *See also* ungemenged.

**gemet**, *add to III:* unrihte gemeta and woge gewihta, Wlfst. 70, 3; *add to III 1:* heora hlafes gewiht and heora wines gemett, Hml. S. vi, 68; *See also* healf-, mil-, rihtgemet.

**gemet**, adj., *see also* ongemet.

**gemetan**, *cancel II in Dict., read in citation* medostigge mæt.

**gemētan**, *meet, see also* ungemet.

**gemetfæstlice**, *add:* þa magas sceolon ymbe hyra beam gemetfæstlice don (*modeste agere*), Chrd. 109, 23.

**gemetgian**, *add: compescaris*, emn gemete, Ps. Cant. lxxxii, 2 (so MS.).

**gemetness**, *add:* gemetnysse byð eðnysse, Hml. Warn. 7, 19.

**gemēþgian**, *add: lacessitus*, gemeþgu(d), OEG 28, 13.

**gemicelness**, f. *greatness: magnificentiam*, gemicelnesse, Ps. Ar. cxliv, 5.

**gemolsnian**, *see also* ungemolsnod.

**gemōt**, *add to compounds* mæggemot.

**gemōtmann**, *note: probably equivalent to* hundredesmann, *see* A. xli, 144, n. 5.

**gemunan**, *note:* Ps. V. has pres. ind. 2 sg. gemynes, xxiv, 7; pres. subj. 3 pl. gemynen, xxi, 28; imper. gemyne, xxiv, 6, and freq.

**gemynd**, *add to II a 2 α:* læten we us singallice bion on gemyndum and on geþancum þæs dæges tocyme, Verc.-Hom. 160, 4; *add to VI:* þæt he þis symle hæbbe on gemyndum þære egesfullan stowe, Verc. Först. 94, 2; *add to VII:* on ðisum gereorde nis þæs gærses nan gemynd, Hml. Th. ii, 398, 27.

**gemyndblīþe**, *add:* JEGP xlvi, 417.

**gemyndelice**, *add: thoughtfully:* þeos oðer þa inweardlice þing gemyndelice besceawode, Hml. Warn. 136, 18.

**gemyndelicness**, *l. 2 in Suppl. read at end* 101, 13.

**gemyndig**, *add:* I a 6 where sorrow, penitence, etc., is implied: swa we urra synna gemyndigran beoð (*memores sumus*), swa hi swiðor God ofergyt, Chrd. 106, 34.

**gemyndlist**, *add: inmemoris*, gemyndleste, OEG 28, 13.

**gemynetian**, v. *mint:* nime man twentig hund mancusa goldes and gemynetige to mancusan, Harmer, *English Historical Documents* 35, 5.

**gemynt**, *intention:* he(o) hæfde anrædlice on hire gemynte, *Anglica* ii, 20, 53 (= Hml. Warn. 135, 15).

**gemyntan**, *add to 2 a:* an gealga . . . þe he gemynt hæfde Mardecheo, Hml. A. 100, 280.

**genǣglan**, *add:* þone Hælend ahengon and on rode genæglodon, Verc.-Hom. 30, 261, v.l.

**genǣgan**, *note MS. has* genægdan, B. 2206, *but* gehnægdon, B. 2916.

**genǣman**, *add:* Sal. 250.

**genǣtan**, *add to 2 a: subject* to an evil: eallum ðam unrotnessum on þysse worulde we beoð genætte, Verc. Först. 125, 11.

**genamn**, *substitute:* genamna, *namesake, comrade:* gif se ærra genamna (MS. genamnan) in nearowe neþan moste, Rid. 53, 12; wæron genamnan (MS. genamne) gefeterade, Rid. 52, 3.

**gĕnde**, *see* goian.

**gendnes**, *note:* gendnyssa *seems altered to* gehendnyssa *in MS.; see* Studia Germanica Gandensia ii, 88.

**genēat**, *delete III, in citation lemma has been confused with* uasellus, *vassal.*

**genēatland**, *add:* Chart. Rob. 240, 13.

**geneorþ**, *discussed* (inconclusively) FL 166, SHG 61.

**genēosian**, *add to II:* hi ne dorston þæt halige hus mid ingange geneosian, *they dared not visit the holy house by entering it*, Hml. Th. i, 504, 10.

**-geng**, *see also* utgeng.

**-genga**, *see also* hinder-, husel-, wælgenga.

**gengel**, *see* ogengel.

**geniman**, *add to XIV:* genam deofol him andan wið, Hml. A. 195, 17; þa genamon hie forþan bysmernesse, Verc.-Hml. 23, 201; *add to XV 2:* he genam þurh heora lare on his orþance þa egeslican dæda, Hept. 64, 1078.

**genipful**, *discussed* E.S. xxxix, 347.

**genirwan**, *perhaps add* genyrwe (MS genyre) ic ætsomne, *I constrain all together*, Husband's Message 49 (cf. Medium Ævum xxxiii, 206).

**genīþla**, *see* rexgeniþla *in Suppl.*

**genōg**, *add to III: nobis ista sufficient*, þas bysna us magon to genogon, Chrd. 90, 8.

**genomian**, *delete, read in citation* gemonian.

**genotian**, *use, add:* ðonne þu antiphonariam habban wille, þonne wege þu þine swiþran hand and crip þinne þuman, for þon he is genotod, Tech. ii, 119, 4.

**gēo**, *add to forms* ieo, Fehr 72, 14.

**gēoabbod**, m. *former abbod:* Gr. D. 41, 27.

**geoc**, *add to I 2: bogia*, iuc, WW 336, 38; *add to III: iuger*, ioc, WW 279, 28.

**geofonȳþ**, *delete, read in citation* geofon yþum weol.

**geoguþhad**, *add: pueritia*, cnihthad, *adolescentia*, geoguþhad, Bd. v, 13; *infantiae*, inguðhades, An. Ox. 1095.

**geoguþlic**, *add: iuuenilem*, giguþlice, OEG 28, 26.

**geoguþmyru**, *perhaps read in citation* geoguðmyrþe, *in the joy of youth.*

**geohholmōnaþ**, *add: December*, iolmonoþ, OEG 63, 33.

**geole**, *see* geolwe.

**geolewearte**, *note: MS. appears to read* geolcwearte.

**geolna**, *see also* eolone *above.*

**gēomagister**, m. *former master:* Bd. v, 9.

**gēomrian**, *note transitive uses:* he þa geomrade hine from scylde acennedne, Bd. i, 27; and geomrað hine swa gebundenne beon, id.; ic heofige and geomrie mine hefegan bendas, Hml. P. ii, 766, 91.

**gēomrung**, *note:* geamring, Ps. V. vi, 7, and frequently; gemerung, E.S. xlix, 346.

**geondbrǣdan**, *add: II enlarge:* heo (seo ælmesse) geondbrædeþ þa gemæru, Verc.-Hom. 69, 161.

**geonddrencan**, *add: inebriari uino*, beon gynddrencede of wine, Chrd. 115, 9.

**geondfaran**, *add:* III glosses *illustrare:* gieondfær, Rtl. 15, 5.

**geondgān**, glosses *perambulare:* Ps. V., Ps. Jun. viii, 9 (cf. iandfaran, Ps. Lamb.; *but* þurhgan, Ps. Cam., Ps. Roy., etc.; þurhgangan, Ps. Ar. etc.).

**geondscrīpan**, *add:* þæt mod geondscrið geond eallo þing (*per omnia discurrit*), Verc. Först. 147.

**geondspyrian**, *for* geondspyrnan: *scandalizati*, geondspyrede, Mt. xv, 12, Lind.

**geondstregdness**, f. *dispersion: dispersionis*, geondstridnes, Ps. Ar. cxlvi, 2.

**geong**, *in l. 4 in Suppl. read* ginga *for* genga.

**geonsīþ**, m. *departure:* æfter hyra geonsiðe hie to hellewitum beoð gelædde, Verc. Först. 147.

**geonwildan**, v. glosses *dominari:* gionuældas, Rtl. 86, 18; etc.

**geopenian**, *add to B II:* wille we eow geopenian be ðam husle, Hml. Th. 262, 20; *add: B III be exposed to:* se wulderfulla hrædlice sirgungum (i.e. sirwungum, *plots*) geopenað, E.S. viii, 473, 11.

**geormanlēaf**, *in citation Wrt. Voc. i, 31, 41* (= *WW 135, 27*) *MS. reads* geormenleaf.

**georn**, *add to compounds* gehealdend-, guþ-, iþ-, notgeorn.

**geornfull**, *see also* ungeornfull.

**geornness**, *add to compounds* wæfergeornness.

**georwirþan**, *see also* ungeorwyrd.

**gēotend II**, *delete, see* seonuwind *below*.

**gēoting**, *see also* ongeoting.

**gepīled**, *in l. 4 read* swipum *for* swipun.

**gerādness**, *see also* ungeradness.

**geradod**, *retain* Dict., *cancel* Suppl. Note citation = A. lxvii, 126, 2.

**gerǣcan**, *add to I 2*: *superingeruntur*, ufan wærun in geræhte, Prud. 235; *add to I 3 a*: *attain to*: and ða godcundan lean minre saule mid gerece, Txts. 450, 1; *delete* III, where citation belongs to I 4, see FL 126.

**gerǣde**, *add to 2*: ic gean Ælfwine minon mæssepreoste . . . mines horses mid minon gerædon, Chart. Whit. 61, 7. Cf. gerædod, sadolgerædu.

**gerǣdlic**, *see* ungerædlic.

**gerǣdod**, *see also* ungeraedod.

**gerǣdu**, *see also* sadolgerædu.

**gerǣran**, *for* aræran: ac ure Drihten sona . . . hyre sunu gerærde, Hml. P. i, 320, 186, v.l.

**gerǣwen**, *MS. reads* geræwed, *see A. viii, 451*; *cf.* geræwod *in Suppl.*

**gere**, *add*: glosses *autem*: Lk. xviii, 24, Lind.; Jn. xxi, 12, Lind., Rush.

**gerēafian**, *add to I a*: þæt he him ageafe þæt he ær on him gereafade, Ors. S. 146, 30; *add*: I b *take from* (of): he saula gereafað of ðæs ealdan feondes honda, Past. 261, 7.

**gerec**, *add to* III: (*secundum uestrorum scriptorum*) *tenorem*, gerece, OEG 4, 189.

**gerec**, *pinnace*, very doubtful, cf. FL 21.

**gerecenian**, *delete second citation in Suppl.*, *see* gecocnian *above*.

**gerecenness I**, *add*: cf. gereceness III.

**gereclic**, *see also* ungereclic.

**gerēfa**, *add to compounds* scir-, swān-, wealhgerefa.

**gereht**, *appears to be an explanation of* gylp *and* getot, Fehr 212, 8.

**gerēne**, *see* goldgerene.

**gereording**, *see also* æfengereording.

**gerestan**, *add*: *with reflex. dat.*: gefere þæne mannan on swiðe fæstne cleofan, gereste him swiðe wel hleowe, Lch. ii, 280, 11.

**gerestedæg**, *for* restedæg: Mt. xii, 8, Rush.

**gericsian**, *v. for* ricsian: *dominetur*, giricsað, Rtl. 26, 22, and frequently.

**gerid**, *add*: II *riding path*: up be ðam geride to ðam beorgan, CS ii, 37, 21.

**gerihtgeswinc**, *n. lawful work*: of mannes gerihtgeswincon (*iustis laboribus*) sylle ma Gode rihte almessan, Chrd. 70, 3.

**gerim**, *add to I*: þæt sylfe gerim þara wintra (*numerum annorum*), Bd. v, 8; *add to II a*: Chart. Rob. 250, 8.

**gerinnan**, *perhaps cancel I in Suppl.*, *read in citation* gerignað, *adorns* (*see* geregnian).

**gerodorlic**, *error for* rodorlic, Gn. 49, 1 (JV).

**gerostod**, *delete, MS.* geroscod.

**gerotian**, *v. decay*: þæt læne lic þær gerotaþ to fulnesse, Verc.-Hom. 50, 83.

**geroþor**, *n.pl. oars*: *remigio*, ða geroðor, OEG 4, 289.

**gerȳnelic**, *add to* II: *mistica ueritas*, seo gerynlice soðfæstnys, Chrd. 97, 27.

**gerȳnu**, *add to III a*: nu is eower gerynu geled on Godes mysan, and ge underfoð eower gerynu, Hml. Th. ii, 276, 20.

**gerȳþer**, ? *for* ryþer: on þa lytla hwitan geryþra, CS ii, 481, 18.

**gesǣgan**, *add*: *uitauimus*, gesaegdon, Lk., p. 3, 8, Lind. (uito = declino = gesǣgan, cf. SHG 61).

**gesǣte**, *add*: glosses *concessio*: gesæt, Mk., p. 5, 14, Lind.

**gesǣwness**, *add*: doubtful word, see JEGP xlvi, 418, 23.

**gesamhīwan**, *add*: II *fellow members of a guild*: Chart. in Förster, *Flussname Themse* 792. *See also* gesinhiwan *below*.

**gesamodlǣcan**, *citation in Suppl. is* Ps. Roy. cxii, 8.

**gescad-**, **gescaldwyrt**: cf. DP 32, 61; OED *s.v.* skirret.

**gescǣned**, *perhaps rather made bright*.

**gescēad**, *add to IV*: *propter prouidentiam bonam*, *for* godum gesceade, Chrd. 21, 22; *add to X*: *non eos debent preterire hore constitute, tam de officiis diuinis quam aliunde*, ne forlæton heora gesettan tida ne an godcundum þenungum ne an oðrum gesceadum, Chrd. 34, 27.

**gescēadness**, *for* Nap. 32, 1, *read* Chrd. 13, 18.

**gesceaft**, *add to I 2 a*: mid heofonlice compwerod þære engelican gesceaft(e), Verc. Först. 109, 7; *add to I 4*: *liquidum elementum*, seo wæteres gesceaft, Gr. D. 220, 17; þæt is cyðnesse dæg ealles mancynnes þurh gesceafte fyres and wæteres and windes, Verc. Först. 114, 19.

**gesceapþēote**, *see* þeotan II.

**gescentu**, *f. harm*: scealt þu minra gescenta scome þrowian, Soul and Body (Exeter MS.) 46.

**gesceot**, *see also* feoh-, scipgesceot.

**gescēotan**, *add to II 1*: gif þam dagum hwilc freolsdæg gescyt (*uenerit*), Chrd. 44, 5; gif for folces synnum gesceote, swa hit oft gescyt (*sicut crebro euenire solet*), id. 15, 23; *add to II 2*: hwa is þæt wite hwæt him gesceotan scyle (*quod contingat*) an þis life, id. 90, 1.

**gescincio**, *last line in Suppl.*, *read* (*MS. gesanco*) *for* (*printed gesanco*).

**gescipe**, *meaning is rather fate*.

**gescir**, I *office, administration* (= scir I): actionem, Rtl. 187, 1; II *personal quality*: *propriam uirtutem*, agen gescir, OEG 60, 31.

**gescirdan**, *delete Suppl.*, *take* gescyrded, An. 1315, *from* gescrydan, *as in* Dict.

**gescirdan**, *v. cut to pieces*: heap wæs gescyrded, El. 141.

**gescirpan**, *dress*: *add to* II: ðus gescrydde and gescrypede, Festschrift Liebermann 47, 20.

**gescōgan**, *add*: þam gehyredum hi gescogen, Archiv lxxxiv, 10, 7.

**gescrǣpe**, *adj.*, *add*: hat baþu ælcere yldo and hade gescræpe (v.l. gescrepene, *accomodos*), Bd. i, 1.

**gescrēpen**, *see* gescræpe.

**gescrȳdan**, *retain* An. 1315.

**gescȳ**, *add*: to preosta gescy finde man biccene heorðan . . . nimon hi heora gescy on Nouembre, Chrd. 48, 25.

**gescyrtan**, *delete* El. 141, *see* gescirdan.

**gesēcan**, *add*: II c a where the subject is a thing: bið him leofre þæt hine gesece ælc þæra yfela þe æfre on helle sy, and hine ælc yð gesece . . . and hine ælc tor gesece, Verc. Först. 94, 3–13.

**gesell**, *hut* (usually on a swine pasture): bocgeselle CS i, 280, 23; see PNE ii, 117.

**gesellan**, *add to V 3*: þæt hi heora æhta ealle gesealdon, and þæt weorð brohton to ðara apostola fotum, Fehr 88, 10.

**gesencan**, *add*: WS Gospels, Lk. x, 15, v.l.

**gesendan**, *l. 3 in Dict.*, *read* gesent, immittit.

**gesēnelic**, *add*: (wilnung) þara gesynelicra þinga, Vercelli MS., f. 90ʳ, 13.

**geseohhian**, *v. sieve*: swiðe clænlice þurh clað geseohhod (v.l. geseohgod), Fehr 172, 31.

**gesēon**, *add to X*: ða hwile ðe God gesegen haebbe þæt fulwiht æt ðeosse stowe beon mote, Txts. 175, 13.

**geset**, *delete, see* gesæte *in Suppl.*

**gesete**, *read* geset.

**gesetness**, *add to X*: gif preostas æfter heora gesettednesse (*secundum eorum rectitudinis normam*) lifedon, Chrd. 2, 3; *add to VI*: *ex ista institutione quam . . . fecimus*, of þisse gesettednysse þe . . . we gesetton, id. 28, 9; gelærede on fædera gesettednyssum (*instituta canonum*), id. 17, 37. *Add to compounds* ægesetness.

**gesettan**, *add*: II α *put a thing in a certain position*: 1 *put as representative, put for*: on halgum gewrite bið gelomlice heafod gesett for þæs mannes mode, Hml. Th. i, 616, 12; 2 *put away*: Nathan . . . him of gesette þone naman Tyrus, Hml. A. 184, 87. *See also* ingeseted, ofergesett.

**gesettedness**, *see* gesetness.

**gesēþedlic**, *adj. probable*: *probabili*, gesededlice, OEG 28, 20.

**gesēþness**, *citation* = Hml. P. i, 487, 180.

**gesib**, *add to I*: ne talien ge eowre magas eow gesibbran (*propinquiores*) þonne þa þe mid eow wuniað on Godes huse, Chrd. 89, 20.

**gesibsumgend**, *m. peace-maker*: reconciliator, A. lxxxi, 88, 6.

**gesibsumness**, *add*: II *good feeling between relatives*: amor et dilectio spiritalis, lufu and gastlic gesybsumnys, Chrd. 89, 21.

**gesīclian**, *add*: gif ænig preost gesiclod beo (*infirmatur*), Chrd. 47, 26.

**gesig**, *delete, MS. has* sig.

gesīgan, *note*: sense in context of I in Suppl. is *glide back* (of a boat to shore), see Prud. 962 note.

gesīnelic, *see also* ungesinelic.

gesinhīwan, *in citation in Dict. of* Wrt. Voc. 50, 7 (= WW 170, 15), *MS. has* gesamhiwan, *see* A. viii, 451.

gesinscipe, *see also* rihtgesinscipe.

gesinsciplic, adj. *conjugal*: coniugali opere, mid gesynsciplicum weorce, Chrd. 116, 13; 33.

gesiþ, *see also* English Historical Review lxx, 529.

gesīþþ, *see also* limgesiþþ.

geslæccan, v. *seize*: rapiat, geslæcce, Ps. V. vii, 2. (? *error for* gelæccan).

geslēan, *add to* V: rapiat, geslæ (*so originally*), Ps. V. vii, 3. *See also* ofgeslean.

geslyht, *read* gesliht, *and add*: congresibus, geslyhtum, OEG 28, 224.

gesmacian, *read* gesmācian.

gesmæccan, *add*: nan oðer swa forðlice ne gesmæhte (*gustauit*), hu swote is ure Drihten, Anglica ii, 36, 192 (= Hml. Warn. 138, 16).

gesnīcan, *creep*: serpit, gesniceþ, OEG 28, 67.

gesnīþan, sense III is uncertain, discussion SHG 9.

gespillian, v. *spill*: seo gebletsod se þe nolde þæt min blod wære gespillod, Hml. Warn. 81, 5.

gespreca, *see also* leasgespreca.

gestāl, *add to* I: we stælan sculon . . . and eall hellemægen þis gestal gehyrað . . . þæt hie þæt gestal gehyren, Verc.-Hom. 83, 110.

gestalu, *remove* Gu. 481 (= 510) to gestal II *in Suppl.*

gestandan, *see also* ofergestandan.

gestaþolfæstnian, *add to* I: quem castigare uult solidare studeat, þone þrean þe he wyle gestaþolfæstnian he hogie, Chrd. 123, 5.

gesteal, *add*: on þone ston istel, of þan istelle, CS ii, 510, 11.

gestēpan, *add to* II: locat (v.l. sistat), gestepte, OEG 7, 9.

gestiht, *dispensation*: of þæs halgan gastes gestihtum, Verc.-Hom. 122, 143 (v.l. geþeahtung). Cf. gestihtung.

gestrind, *delete* I, *read in citation* (= WW 488, 30) gestreone (cf. WW 190, 3).

gestrynge, discussed FL 71.

gestund, ? *delete, read in citation* gestunum.

gestyr, *delete*, MS. *reads* gescir.

gesūcan, *for* sucan: þa breost þe þu gesuce, Hml. P. i, 267, 53.

gesund, *see also* ungesund.

geswæslæcan, *add*: blanditur, geswæslæcþ, WW 196, 13; blandiloquis, geswæslæhtum, OEG 9, 72.

geswencan, *see also* ungeswenced.

gesweotulian, *add to* IV: with prep.: and . . . God bæd þæt he him geswutolode be ðæs sceoccan gylpe, Hml. S. vi, 322.

gesweotulung, *add to* I: euidentibus patet indiciis, openon geswutelincgum is geypped, Chrd. 64, 28.

geswētlēht, *add*: Ps. Vit. geswetlæhtan, Ps. Sal. geswetlæht.

geswican, *see also* ungeswicen.

geswicedness, *for* geswicenness, Chrd. 41, 2.

geswilian, v. *wash*: cumð flod ond geswyleð þa æsscen, Hml. Warn. 91, 5.

geswimman, *add*: þær he on greut giswom, Txts. 127, 7.

geswinc, *add*: I b *the produce of labour*: ic hate þæt ge gangen to minum ciricum, and þær ge eower geswinc sellað, Wlfst. 229, 7. *See also* gerihtgeswinc. [Note in Gen. 317 the word is an emendation.]

geswincleas, *for* swincleas, Hml. Warn. 141, 27.

geswincness, *add*: mid singalum fæstene geswincnyssum (*afflictione*), Chrd. 61, 31.

gesyndig, *add*: secundi, ða gesyn(d)gan, OEG 4, 293 (gloss on passage cited in Suppl.).

getācnung, *add*: V *constellation*: God worhte . . . þone monan on æfen mannum to lihtinge on nihtlicere tide mid getacnungum, Hex. 49, 210 (cf. Gen. i, 16); tunglan to gearlicum tidum on manegum getacnungum, id. 50, 218 (here strictly *signs of the zodiac*, cf. tacen I d).

getæcan, *add to* II: unscyldig on ðam dome getæht, *shown to be innocent*, Hml. P. ii, 536, 132; *add to* V 2: we ne scylan him deað getæcan, Fehr 140, 20.

getæl, delete X, see Lindsay, *Corpus Glossary* 154. *Add to compounds* feowertiggetel, hundfeald-, þusendfealdgetæl.

getalian, add: *assign*: tibi . . . merces iudicabitur eterna, þe bið getalod ece med, Chrd. 93, 18.

getamcian, v. *tame*: see geþaccian.

getellan, *add to* I 1: dicit, getelþ, OEG 30, 147.

getēwian, v. *adorn*: Wlfst. 262, 22, *variant to* gefrætwian.

getīgan, *add*: annectit, to getigð, Archiv cc, 198.

getilian, *add to* II: inseruire, getiolian, PBB lxxxv (Halle), 61.

getimbran, *in* An. 667 *read* atimbred.

getirgan II, *add*: inrita, getyrged, (? lemma taken as *inritata*), OEG 7, 43.

getiung, substitute for meaning *apparition*; gloss refers to Oros. i, prol., 15, *sub apparitione Antichristi*.

getregian, *citation is* Ps. Sal., Hy. 10, 16.

getrēowness, f. *faith*: Verc.-Hom. 99, 309.

getrēowsian, *add*: III *make of good faith*: getrywsige us se Hælend, Hml. P. ii, 559, 293.

getridwet, ? *read* getreowed, *with a shaft* (cf. treow IV); FL 104.

getrīwan, *delete first citation in Suppl.* (MS. gegripenne, Cott. Tib. A vii, f. 166ᵛ).

getrum, *see also* ungetrum.

getwisa, *add*: geminae, getwisan (note *fem. lemma*), OEG 63, 13.

getwiung, f. *state, condition*: per condicionem, getwyunge, JEGP lvi, 65 (gloss on *C.P.*, where OE version has ðurh Godes gesceafte, Sweet 201, 18).

getȳdness, *add*: edification: wilnion he swiðor . . . þæs folces getydnysse (*edificationem*) þonne heora ydelan herunge, Chrd. 58, 3.

getȳd, *see also* un-, welgetyd.

geþaccian, *probably delete* II, *read in citation* getamcodon (so Nap. 62).

geþæf, *in citation under* 2 a *in Suppl.*, *translate* hira geþæf bion, *acknowledge them* (cf. geþafa I).

geþafa, *add*: compar. geþafera. *Add to* II 1: where a charge is admitted: swa he eadmodra beo and his gyltes geþafera (*quantum plus se culpabilem asseruit*), swa micle mildelicor him ma deme, Chrd. 29, 1.

geþanc, *add to compounds* hordgeþanc.

geþancfull, *add*: adj. *spirited*: geþancfull (*animosus*), grædig be þingum fremedum, Lch. iii, 184, 24.

geþancmetian, *add*: cf. Kock, PPP 18.

geþanc, *add to compounds* hordgeþanc.

geþang, *growth*, *delete*, *in citation this is anomalous spelling of* geþanc, *thought*. See MLR xi, 215.

geþencan, *add to* IV 1: ond na þu me mid nængum gode geþohtest, didst not remember me with any gift of good, Verc.-Hom. 99, 314; *add to* IV: 5 combining 2 and 4: geþence . . . þara tida and . . . þissa hwæþre him bet licien, Ors. S. 50, 22.

geþēod, *delete first citation in Suppl.*, *where* geþeode *is past. part. nom. pl. of* geþeodan, *lemma is for* coniuoli (= *coniuncti*, Corpus Glossary C 805).

geþēodan, *see also* togeþeodende.

geþēodlic, *add*: sociabilis, geðeodlic, OEG 4, 332.

geþēodscipe, *for* þeodscipe V, Vercelli MS., f. 75ᵣ, 14.

geþēon, *receive*, *add*: this is the same verb as geþeon, *thrive*, sense is *thrive so as to get*; *add to citations*: þæt we þa sellan þing geþeon moten, Cri. 377; (hie) rice geþungon, Met. i, 7.

geþēostrian, *add*: intrans., þa geþystrode hit, Verc.-Hom. 35, 301.

geþēostru, *for* þeostru: tenebrae, geþriostra (sic), Mt. xxvii, 45, Rush.

geþēowtian, v. *enslave*: ac nu is se fridom geðeowtod, Hml. Warn. 141, 16.

geþinge, *take* B. 398, 525, 709 *under* III *in Dict.*, *not as in Suppl.*

geþoftscipe, *add*: *familiar intercourse, intimacy*: be þam þæt preostas geþoftscipe (*familiaritatem*) næbbe wið fremde wif, Chrd. 29, 1.

geþoht, *see also* modgeþoht.

geþracen, discussed FL 154. MS. may read geþrocen (see Journal of Brit. Arch. Assoc. xli, 150).

geþræc, *add*: on sense of citation from Rid. xxxvi, 6, see EGS iii, 48.

geþræorspreca, glosses *increpationes*, Ps. Cant. xxxvii, 15.

geþræstan, *add*: V glosses *contritus* (of the heart): Ps. Jun. l, 19; Ps. V. and Par. cxlvi, 3.

geþryccedness, *for* ofþryccedness, Hml. Warn. 67, 32 (cf. Hml. Th. i, 608, 24).

geþungen, *see also* welgeþungen.

geþungenness, l. 6 in Suppl. *read* duodenus honoris apex (Sed., Carm. Pasch. i, 361).

**geþwǣrian,** sense in first citation in Suppl. (= Prud. 70) is perhaps *be at rest*; cf. geþwǣre II 2 in Suppl. and OEG 127.

**geþweor,** *note*: the simplex is not recorded.

**geþyldig,** *see* modgeþyldig.

**geþyllic,** adj. *dense: densis,* geþyllicum, An. Ox. 5, 4; 7, 7; *miswritten* aeðyllicum, A. xv, 206. (? *for* \*geþiclic *or* \*geþryllic).

**-geþynge,** *see* weoroldgeþynge.

**geþynnian,** *l. 5 in Suppl. read* geþynnige (Prud. 53).

**geunblissian,** *citation* = Hml. P. i, 362, 125.

**geundōn:** *si consistant,* gif standað *uel* gif geondoð, Ps. Vit. xxvi, 3; Ps. Ar. gif geundoþ.

**geunfæstnod,** *see* unfæstnian.

**geungetrimmed,** *for* geuntrumod, Ps. Ar. lvii, 8.

**gewǣdian,** delete first citation in Suppl., where MS. has *inoleuerit,* ongewuæd (? *for* -gewæxt); cf. OEG 21, 10, note.

**gewǣgnian,** *for* Nap. 33, 18–22, *read* Chrd. 97, 24–29; *for* Nap. 33, 24, *read* Chrd. 97, 20.

**gewǣpnian,** *in l. 5 in Suppl. add* iii, 273, *after* 333.

**gewǣr,** add: *for* wær III, Hept., Gen. xxiv, 6, v.l.

**gewand,** *add to I: incunctanter,* butan gewande, Chrd. 52, 25; *add:* III *distinction:* yfles and godes gewand, Gen. 480.

**gewascan,** *in l. 3 in Suppl. read* hræglhuse, gewaxene.

**gewealc,** *take citation from Chr. 1100 as from* II *military expedition, and add* ða æfter Æadgares cininges forðsiðe on ðam gewalce, E.S. lxxii, 10.

**gewealcan II,** *for alternative explanation (to noun* \*gewealca) *see* FL 126.

**geweald,** *add to I 7:* gif hwa forstelð hwæte and þæt forstolene sæwð, hwæt, ah þæt corn geweald, þæt hit wearp se sædere on moldan?, Hml. A. 36, 312; *add:* V in pl. *muscles,* or *tendons:* gif mon oðrum ða geweald forslea uppe on þam sweoran, Ælf. 77.

**geweaeldes,** *see also* selfgewealdes.

**geweaxan,** *add to II:* syððan Crist man wearð geweaxen, þa ða he wæs ðritig wintra eald, Hml. Th. i, 258, 10.

**gewegan,** *see also* togewegen.

**gewēnan,** *add to I: aestimata uespertina hora,* gewenedre æfentyde, Chrd. 114, 20.

**gewendan,** *read* xi, 369, 16 *for* xl, 369, 16, in Suppl., l. 17.

**gewendedness,** f. *alteration: commutitationibus,* gewændednessum, Ps. Ar. xliii, 13.

**geweorc,** *add to compounds* meter-, suþgeweorc.

**geweorclic,** *delete, read in citation* weblic geweorc, *cf. v.l. of* Hpt. Gl. 431, 4, *cited by Suppl. under* geweorc VI.

**geweorþan,** *add to III 2 a:* hæfð Ælfred gehaldene Herewinne on æghwelcre wihte ðæs ðe hio an geworden wæs ðæs ðe hio seulf geðafigan wolde, CS ii, 146, 29.

**gewerian,** *defend:* reject suggestion of Suppl. that the passages where the object is an estate are to be taken under gewerian *clothe*; in such passages sense is rather *discharge dues on,* cf. werian III c.

**gewerian,** *make a treaty: read* gewērian, *cf.* wǣr.

**gewidagur,** *omit, entirely uncertain.*

**gewidere,** *see also* mis-, un-, untidgewidere.

**gewifsǣlig,** *note:* Wülcker's reading is correct.

**gewīglian,** v. *sing (an incantation): incantantur,* beoð gewigelode, Ps. Cant. lvii, 6.

**gewilsum,** *add: ultroneum,* gewilsume, JEGP lx, 442, IV, 25.

**gewilt,** *rolling* (of waves): *motum . . . fluctuum,* gewylt . . . yða, Ps. Vit. lxxxviii, 10; *or error for* gewilc (q.v. in Suppl.).

**gewind,** *add to compounds* moldgewind.

**gewired,** substitute for meaning *with filagree ornamentation,* and add Ker, *Catalogue* 163.

**gewis,** adj., *add to IV:* Fehr 70, 6. *See also* foregewis.

**gewīsa,** m. *leader: conductio* (read *conductor*), giuisa, Lindsay, *The Corpus, Epinal, Erfurt, and Leyden Glossaries* 83.

**gewiss,** adv. *certainly:* þæt sindan sinna gewiss, þe gebrincgað on ðeowete, Fehr 194, 18; þam beoð sona forgifene heora synna gewiss, Hml. P. i, 343, 59.

**gewistlice,** *for* gewisslice, *English and Medieval Studies* 83, 37 (= Hml. Th. ii, 72, 3 from below, v.l.).

**gewita,** *add to I 1 a: testis uitae eorum,* gewita hira lifes drohtnunge, Chrd. 54, 35.

**gewiterian,** v. *inform:* see ængel . . . gewiterede heo, hwu heo wæs þan hælende to moder gecoren, *Anglica* ii, 21, 57 (= Hml. Warn. 135, 18).

**gewitodlice,** *for* witodlice: Wlfst. 113, 13, v.l.; id. 119, 17 v.l.

**gewlencan,** *add:* he bið in ecnesse gearod ond gewlenced, Verc.-Hom. 81, 91.

**gewrēgedness,** f. *accusation: quantum ad uos pertinet accusatio,* swa miclum swa eow to belimpð . . . gewregednes, E.S. lxii, 114.

**gewrigenness,** *see* ongewrigenness.

**gewrinclod,** *see also* Prud. 750 n.

**gewring,** *citation in Dict. is a conflation of: sicera,* ælces kinnes gewring butan wine (f. 7ᵛ; cf. Ælfc. Gr. Z. 315, 15); *and: sicera,* ælces kynnes drenc buton wine and wætere (f. 13ᵛ). *With citation in Suppl. cf.* stacten est incensum quod ex pressura manat, Isid., Et. iv, 12, 5.

**gewrit,** *add to compounds* lahgewrit, weoroldgewritu.

**gewriþ,** *note: MS. reads* wegures gewrið spere.

**gewrixl,** *in* Wrt. Voc. 21, 41, *cited in Dict., read* cepena þinga *uel* gewrixle (WW 116, 40; cf. A. viii, 450).

**gewunian,** *add to A I 2 a:* with adj. complement: *dissolutae corrigiae remanserunt,* gewunedon þa þwangas untogone, Gr. D. 222, 2; *add to B I:* and him aspidas under welerum (h)is gewunad(e), Ps. Par. cxxxix, 3.

**gewyrcan,** *add to V:* he axode . . . hu he geworht wære on woruldlicre drohtnunge, Hml. Th. ii, 356, 3.

**gewyrhta,** *see also* mangewyrhta.

**gewyrms,** cf. wyrmsig *in Dict.*

**gewyrten,** adj. glossing *fractus: fractis . . . sepulchris,* gewyrttenes geripes, OEG 28, 488. Cf. awyrtene, *exstirpatis,* OEG 2, 120.

**geyflian,** *add to I:* with dat.: he nolde geyfelian þam arleasan menn, Fehr 138, 11.

**gicer,** *add:* cf. Language xli, 416.

**gidding,** *see also* samodgiddung.

**gidrima,** glosses *claustra,* OEG 28, 450.

**gif,** *add to VI:* he het his cnapan hawian gif ænig mist arise, Hml. S. xviii, 146.

**gifa,** *add to compounds* wuldorgifa.

**gifan,** *see also* aþurh-, wistgifende.

**gifre,** *add to compounds* ungifre.

**gifu,** *add to compounds* eorlgifu.

**gifung,** *see also* eftgeafung.

**gild,** III *perhaps delete citation* Wrt. Voc. ii, 28, 54, *see* gildlic *below. Add to compounds* gafolgild.

**gildan,** *see also* æftergildend.

**gildet,** participial adj. *gelded:* gildet o(x), WW 120, 38 (but MS. is obscure).

**gildfrēo,** adj. *free of tax:* geyldfreo, Chart. Harm. 424, 1.

**gildlic,** glosses *caerimonia: cerimonie,* geldlice, A. xli, 106, 51; *cf. FL 106, and* gilddagas *in Suppl.* Note MS. is unclear, and may read geld h(oc est) æ, ealhalgung; cf. æ I and gild III in Suppl.

**gildsetl,** *meeting place of a guild:* Chart. in Förster, *Flussname Themse* 792, 11.

**-gille,** simplex may occur in: *passiuos,* gil(le), OEG 2, 15.

**gilp,** *powder:* the word is doubtful, JEGP xlvi, 419.

**gilpan,** *see also* begilpan.

**gim,** in first citation in Suppl. (= WW 148, 9) MS. reads *elestria* (for *electria;* cf. Isid., Et. xvi, 13, 8, *electria . . . in uentriculis enim gallinaciis inuenitur,* probably confused with id. 8, 8, *lyncurius uocatus quod fiat ex urina lyncis;* see also FL 105. *Add to compounds* bridelgim.

**gimeleas,** *add:* IV *carefree: secura,* gimeleasa, OEG 28, 274.

**gimrodor,** discussed FL 72.

**ginfæsten,** *delete, in citation read* ginfæste god, *ample benefit.*

**ginnan,** *add to Suppl.: initia sunt,* gunnan (? lemma treated as initiarunt), OEG 60, 25. *Add to compounds* in-, geedginnan.

**girela,** *add:* III *in figurative use* on anfealdum gyrlum þære ecan blisse, Hml. P. i, 428, 244.

**girnan,** *see also* geedgirnan.

**girwan,** *add:* III b *undress: exuentes,* gærwende, Mt. xxvii, 28, Rush.

**gised,** glosses *consessor* (MS. *concessor*), Lindsay, *The Corpus, Epinal, Erfurt, and Leyden Glossaries* 83.

**gisting,** the word is uncertain, see SHG 38.

**gistning,** f. *hospitality:* þa underfeng he þær gestninge, Nap. 32.

**gistrandæg,** *add:* gyrsandæg, Verc.-Hom. 132, 37; 133, 41.

**gitan,** *see also* forþ-, inbegitan.

**gītan,** *add:* forgītan (*see above s.v.* forgitan).

**-gite,** *see* gegite.

**-gitenness,** *see also* beg.

gītsiendlic, adj. *greedy*: *insatiabili corde*, gytsiendlicre heortan, Ps. Roy., C, 5.

gītsung, *add to compounds* lustgitsung.

giþcorn, *add*: *lactirias uel lactirida*, gyþcorn *uel* libcorn, DP 15 ; cf. lybcorn *in Dict.*

*glad, *glæd, *glēd, *glade*, PNE i, 202–3.

glær, *note*: *in final citation in Suppl.* (= *Prud. 678*), *MS. has* glæras.

glengista, *discussion* SHG 20.

glēodǣd, f. *merry deed, trick*: sum . . . hafað searolic gomen, gleodǣda, gife, ASPR iii, 139, 83.

glid, *take as adj. as in Dict.*; cf. slid.

*glind, *enclosure*, PNE i, 204.

gliwingmann, substitute for meaning *jester*, cf. FL 137.

glōfwyrt, *see also* hundes tunge *below*.

glōm, keep for meaning *twilight* only, and so in compounds.

glyrend, *add*: sense is *turned away* (of eyes), see Prud. 440, JEGP xlvi, 419, A. lxx, 6, 71.

gnohioc, delete, word is probably Celtic.

god, *add to VII 5*: *iustum coram Deo et hominibus*, rihtlic for Gode and for worolde, Chrd. 13, 19. *Add to compounds* feohtegod.

gōd, *see also* unrimgod.

godcundlicness, f. *divinity*: mid þam gyfum his godcundlicnesse, Hml. S. 23 b, 230, v.l.

godcundspēd, f. *divine nature*: an god and an godcundsped, Vercelli MS., f. 89ᵛ, 12; 89ʳ, 16.

godfǣder, *add to II*: *dei patris*, godfæderes, Ps. V., ed. Kuhn, 315, 9.

godforgifness, f. *divine forgiveness*: seo endlyfte is godforgifnes, þæt þurh þæt (*sic*) God his fyrena him forgife, Buss. 175, 99.

godgim, *add*: *many read* goldgimmas.

godwebben, *add*: Verc.-Hom. 23, 205.

gold, *see also* healsbeorggold.

goldfinc, on the lemmas see A. xli, 113, n. 2; 118, n. 5; 120, n. 3.

goldhordhūs, meaning is not *privy* but *treasury*, see JEGP lx, 447–8. *For passage glossed see* horshus *in Suppl.*

goldhwæt, substitute for meaning *gold-abounding*, cf. EGS iv, 75.

gor, *add*: *glosses* exta *and* interiora, Ker, *Catalogue* 357.

gorettan, delete II in Suppl., where gloss probably applies to *torquens lumina* just before, see Prud. 743, A. lxx, 4, 53.

gorst, delete gloss *aegesta*, gors (= Txts 39, 97), where read gor (see Deut. xxiii, 13, *egesta humo operies*); delete also *egella*, gors, a corruption of the same gloss.

*gorsten, adj. *grown with gorse*, PNE i, 206.

*gorstig, adj. *grown with gorse*, PNE i, 206.

*gota, *water-course*, PNE i, 206.

*grǣdtūn, *stubble field*, PNE i, 207.

græft, *note*: on lemma *carpenta* see SHG 99.

grǣg, *note*: in last three citations in Dict. (Gen. 2865; B. 330, 334) sense is *bright*, cf. PBB xc (Tübingen), 134. *Add to compounds* flodgræg.

grǣgmǣl, rather *with bright markings*, cf. græg above.

grǣswang, *add*: Vercelli MS., f. 133ᵛ, 18.

grammede, delete, *MS. has* gram(an), *see* Studia Germanica Gandensia ii, 89.

gramheort, *add*: ne hine ænig man yrre ne gramheortne ne geseah, Vercelli MS., f. 99ᵛ, 13 (*v.l. for* grammodne, Bl. H. 223, 33).

gramhygdig, *add*: Verc.-Hom. 77, 57; 98, 303.

granwisc, delete question-mark.

grāpigendlic, *add*: ac his lima beoð him ealle ansunde . . . and grapiendlice on ðam gastlican lichaman, Hml. P. i, 433, 325.

grēada, *add*: figurative: *in gremio aeclesie*, to þære halgan cyrcan greadon, Chrd. 37, 14.

grēne-hǣwen, in first citation, two words seem intended.

grennan, *note*: gloss quoted in Dict. as OHG may be OE (= OEG 34, 2).

grēon, *gravel*: *glareis*, greon, Kluge, *Angelsächsisches Lesebuch* 13, III D 15. (Cf. greon, PNE 209.)

*grēoten, adj. *gravelly*, PNE i, 209.

grētan, *add to V 1 b α*: nele hine (i.e. *adamant*) isern ne style ne awiht heardes gretan, ac ælc bið þe forcuðra þe hine greteþ, EETS 190, 14, 6.

griffus, *griffon*: geowes he hafað fiðeru ond griffus fet, Sol. and Sat. 265.

grighund, note: *unfer* is an unknown word; cf. Philological Quarterly xlv, 435.

grimhӯdig = gramhӯdig, Verc.-Hom. 77, 57, v.l.

grimman, *add to I*: *fremet*, grimmeþ, Bl. Gl., Ps. cxi, 10 (A. lxxxi, 126); *delete II, in citation probably read* grimmon = grimmum, *for the warriors*.

grimsian, *see also* agrimsian.

grin, *groin*: in ilio id est grin, Ll. Lbmn. i, 83.

grinu, *add*: *gilbus*, gyrno, Txts. 67, 971 (apparently an error, above *giluus* = falu, geolu). The word is doubtful, cf. FL 22.

grīpan, *see also* toge-, undergripan; unforgripendlic.

gripe II 2 a, *sense in Wald. 2, 13, is uncertain, perhaps read* guðbill *on* gripe.

grīpe, *add*: II *tomb*: see citation under gewyrten above. Note *i* is probably short, PNE i, 211.

grislice, adv. *terribly*: þa seo helle egeslice ond grislice andswerede Sathanas, Hml. Warn. 84, 2.

grōf, f. *for* grop: *latrinas, cloacas, aqueductus*, groua, OEG 45, 1.

grotig, sense in context is rather *covered with sand* (of gold-dust found in sand), cf. sandgrot in Dict., and FL 128.

grōwan, l. 4 from below in Suppl. *read* milescian.

grōwness, *add*: *uiror*, growines (sic), OEG 4, 156; delete sense II in Suppl., lemma *germine* is used of growth in context (Aldhelm, *Rid.* xciv, 9; cf. FL 74).

-grumel, *see* hasgrumel.

grund, *add to VII a*: *fundi*, grundas (MS. -us), Corpus Glossary F 375.

grunddēopan, *take as* grund, deopan (*see* dipe), *alternative glosses* to profundum, Ps. Ar. lxiv, 8; cf. lxviii, 16.

grundling, ? *a fish*: on grundlinga broc, CS iii, 525, 21.

gryllan, in second citation in Suppl. (= Prud. 733) sense is rather *grind* (context is *stridentibus laniatur uncis*, Prud., *Perist.* v, 173).

grynde, *add*: on grynde wylles lace, CS iii, 323, 3 from below; *also wk.*: on grindan broc, id. ii, 164, 15. Cf. PNE i, 211.

gryre, *add to I*: *tremor*, Ps. Vit. liv, 6.

gullisc, add meaning *gilded*.

gundig, adj. *corrupt*: *putrenum*, gundi (MS. gandi), Txts. 108, 1125.

gutt, *add*: II *water channel*: on guttes cumbes heafod, CS iii, 319, 13.

gūþfrēa, delete, read in citation guðfrecan, *of the warrior* (so MS.).

gūþfruma, delete.

gūþgeorn, adj. *eager for strife*: *temptantes*, guþgerne, OEG 60, 12.

gūþmōd, add as alternative meaning *warlike spirit*.

gūþmyrce, *add*: perhaps rather *warlike borderers*.

gylde, ? *golden flower*: ab oriente gyldeburne, CS ii, 18, 19; PNE i, 211.

gyldingwecg, add: cf. gylden wecg *in Dict. s.v.* wecg II, *and below*.

*gyll, *valley*, PNE i, 212.

-gylta, *see* nidgylta.

gyltend, *add*: *debitores*, gyltendras, Chrd. 116, 1.

gyrdel, *in first citation in Suppl.* (= WW 152, 33) *MS. has* gyldel (? *for* gylden, cf. Isid., *Et.* xix, 33, 3 *strophium est cingulum aureum cum gemmis*).

gyrdelhringe, *add*: cf. *regulam* (taken as *legulam*) *auream*, hringan (MS. hy-) gyrdisles, OEG 38, 2.

*gyse, *gush of water*, PNE i, 212.

gyþcorn, *see* giþcorn.

# H

habban, *add to XIII*: *nullae lites esse debent*, nænige geflitu sceolon beon hæfde, Chrd. 115, 31.

hacele, for gloss *colomata*, hacole (Suppl. l. 4; WW 210, 19; Oliphant, *The Harley Latin–Old English Glossary*, C 1569) cf. hæþcole in Suppl.; probably read hæþcole for hacole.

hacod, *add*: *dentix*, hacod, Nap. 14.

hādelice, *add*: v.l. hadlice, Gn. 29, 1 (VJ).

hādtīma, m. *time of ordination*: se ðe hades wilnige, cume anum monðe ær þam hadtiman, IP 219.

hæcce, substitute for meaning *screen, frontal* (cf. EGS v, 72).

hæcewol, *MS. reads* kæcewol.

hæcging, f. *enclosure*: to ðære hæcginge, C.D. iv, 90, 60.

hæcine, *see also* hæting *below*.

hæfendlice, *see* forhæfendlice.

hæfenleast, *l. 2 in Dict., read* Ps. Lamb. xliii, 24; *add: inopia,* on hæfenlyste, Ps. Vit. xxxiii, 10.

hæfernbite, *substitute for meaning carcinoma* (cf. bite I a). Cf. FL 171.

hæftincel, *substitute for meaning little slave.*

hæftness, *for* gehæftness: Ps. Sal. cxxiii, 6; Hml. Warn. 22, 20; 66, 29.

hæftnīd, *note pl. in concrete sense bonds*: and mid þrimfealdum hæftnydum gehæfte ðone papan, Hml. P. ii, 740, 81; 83; 742, 131.

hæftung, *for* hæftnung, Hml. Warn. 120, 6; 143, 35.

*hægen, *hagen, *enclosure*, PNE i, 215.

hæle, *health, see also* sylfhele.

hælestre, f. *saviour*: saluatrix, A. lxv, 254, 7.

hælgere, m. *one who sanctifies*: sanctificator, hælgare, Rtl. 63, 3; hælgere 84, 9.

hæmdere, *see* nidhæmdere.

hæmed, *transfer* Txts. 69, 1036, *from II to I* (*lemma hymeneos*). *See also* twi-, þrihæmed.

hæmeddrēam, *rather* hæmedrīm, *quantity of sexual sins.* Cf. FL 75.

hæmedþing, *in l. 10 in Suppl. read* hæmedþingum.

hæming, *see* unrihthæming.

hær, *in l. 8 in Suppl. read* efesiað.

*hær, *rock, heap of stones*, PNE i, 217.

hæreanfagol, *add: the form is uncertain, MS.* hæ . . . anfugol (? -fag-); *for* hattefagol *MS. has* -fugol.

hæring, *read* hæring.

hæru, f. *hoariness*: canitiei, hæra, OEG 4, 185.

hæs, *hæst, *brushwood*: on linga hese CS i, 371, 22; PNE i, 218.

hæslen, *add: storacina,* haeslin, Ld. 5.

*hæslen, *adj. growing with hazels*, PNE i, 218.

*hæsler, *hazel*, PNE i, 219.

*hæslett, *hazel copse*, PNE i, 219.

*hæsling, *place grown with hazels*, PNE i, 219.

hæt, *add: calomachus* (*for calamaucus*), haet, Txts. 47, 383; *calamauca,* hæt, A. viii, 451 (= WW 153, 22, *among articles of attire*). *See also* wuduhætt.

hætan, *delete II,* haetende *is error for* hatende, *see* hatian *in Suppl.*

hæte, *see also* sunnhæte.

hæting, *add to Dict.*: occurs in list of foods and drinks, so perhaps *mulled wine*; or error for hæcine?

hætsan, *perhaps delete, citation is commonly emended, cf.* ASPR iii, 322.

hæþ, *first citation under II in Suppl. rather to* hæt, hat.

hæþenfeoh, *MS. reads* hæþenwēoh, *idol.*

hæþenfolc, n. *heathen people*: se dema wæs in miclum gemote mid hæðenfolce, Mart. H. 144, 14; ic lete hæþenfolc ofer iow, Wlfst. 223, 12.

hæwe, *add: hyiacinctini,* hæwes, OEG 4, 10.

hæwmenged, *adj. of mixed colour, bluish, greenish*: coccinei, hæwmængedes, OEG 4, 12.

hafocwyrt, *add*: ? *camomile*; *camimulam,* heauocwurt, OEG 73 c, 4.

hafu, *see* upahafu.

hagal I, *note* hawl *is dialectal.*

*haging, *enclosure*: Löfvenberg, *Studies on ME Local Surnames* 95.

hagolberende, *participial adj. producing hail-storms*: imbriferos, hagelbærene, Archiv cc, 197.

hagolstān, *note spellings* halstan, Txts. 52, 288; haalstaan, 55, 604; healstanes, WW 495, 28.

hagospind, *add: genarum,* hæges (pinda), OEG 28, 451.

hala, *add: secundarum,* halana, OEG 37, 1.

hālettend, *perhaps forefinger, not middle finger* (æwiscberend), *cf.* FL 23.

hālgiend, m. *sanctifier*: dicator . . . abstinentiae, halgiend . . . forhæfednysse, Gn. 57, 1 (JV). *See also* gehalgiend.

hālgung, *add to compounds* bisceop-, eallhalgung.

hālian, *add to compounds* unhalian.

hālig, *add to A I in Suppl.*: (ealda) halga dæg, *Quadragesima Sunday,* Henel, *Studien zum altengl. Computus* 41. *Add to compounds* fore-, gæsthalig.

hāligdom, *add*: V *sacrament*: sacramenta corporis et sanguinis Christi, Cristes lichaman and his blodes haligdomas, Chrd. 115, 16; 116, 29.

hāligern, *add: for* haligdom: *genus est sacramenti,* hit is an þæra haligerna, Chrd. 80, 24.

hāliglice, *add*: sancte uiuentibus, haliglice libbendum, Chrd. 117, 4.

hālness, *for* hælness, Archiv cxxi, 46, 9; Rtl. 122, 1 (*incolumitas*).

hālsungtīma, *citation* = Chrd. 30, 2.

hālswurþung, *substitute*: halswurþung, f. *necklace*: Exod. 549.

hālwende, *add to III*: salutari consilio, halwendum geþeahte; saluberrimis poenitentie obseruationibus, halwendestum dædbote, Chrd. 106, 31. *See also* unhalwende.

ham, *garment, see also* rihthamscyld.

ham (*second entry*), *cf.* PNE i, 229; Namn och Bygd xlviii, 140. *See also above, s.v.* croh, crymel.

hām, *n l. 12 from end in Suppl. read* domiduca. *See also below, s.v.* wester.

hama, *citation* Nap. 35 = Hml. P. ii, 556, 235.

hamacgað, *see* gemagian.

hamela, *add*: weak form of adj. hamol, *maimed, mutilated* (cf. hamelian), elsewhere only in place-names, *scarred, crooked*: ostium fluminis Homelea, Bede, *Hist. Ecc.* iv, 14; to Hamelandunæ, CS iii, 166, 4 from below; æt Hamelandene, Chart. Whit. 58, last line.

hāmettan, *substitute*: v. *bring back to a ham* cf. hām II 1 b 2): debitores repititis, gyltendras ge hametað, Chrd. 116, 1.

*hamstra, *corn-weevil*, PNE i, 232.

hāmweorþung, *add*: cf. JEGP l, 243.

hand, *add to compounds* ælmeshand.

handfæstan, *see also* gehandfæstan.

handfæstnung, *add*: chirografo, handfæstnunge, OEG 27, 41.

handlēan, *delete, see* andlean.

handspitel, *note*: fouessoria = fossoria, cf. Isid., *Et.* xx, 14, 7.

handswyle, *note*: cidaricus = chiragricus.

handwyrm, *add meaning* itch-mite, l. 3 in Dict. read urcius.

hanga, *substitute: see* lichanga.

hangelle, *add*: II *act of hanging*: ferens suspendia crucis, forðyldiende hanglan rode, Gn. 51, 2 (JV).

hār, *add to II 3*: dies caniculares, hare dagas, OEG 63, 17; 23.

haran hige, *add*: leporis pes, haran hig, DP 218.

haranwyrt, *in second citation* (= WW 135, 5) *perhaps read* hareminte (MS. -winta), cf. A. xli, 140.

haraþ, harad, *wood*: in haredum (haraðum), CS i, 342, 6 from below; id. 344, 8. PNE i, 234.

hāreminte, f. *a species of mint*: colosia, harminte, Lchd. iii, 330; carocasia, hareminte, DP 11, 101; *see also* haranwyrt *above.*

hāsgrumel, *adj. hoarse*: raucisonis, hasgrumelum, OEG 15, 2.

hasu, *add*: used as a conventional epithet in Ph. 121, for the bird was of bright and varied colours.

haswig, *adj. dark-coloured*: ferrugineo, haswigum, hæwenum, OEG 27, 14.

hāt, *adj. see also* ungemethat.

hāt, *promise, add*: II *statute*: statutis, hatum, OEG 4, 180 (Bede, *Hist. Ecc.*, ed. Plummer, 189, 1; *cf.* gehat III *in Suppl.*).

hatian, *note*: hættende (*Suppl. II 2*) *is from* hettan.

hātlice, *add*: Bd. iv, 25.

*hāþ, *for* hæþ, *heath*, PNE i, 235.

hāwian, *add to compounds* onhawian; tohawiend.

hāwung, *add*: sense of seeing: Verc.-Hom. 99, 307.

hēafodbēah, *add*: v.l. to heafodbend in citation 1 in Suppl. (= Verc.-Hom. 23, 201).

hēafodbryce, *breaking of the skull*: Lch. i, 150, 5 from below.

hēafodpanne, *add*: emicranii, hafudpannan, OEG 4, 316.

hēafodslæge, *more probably decapitation*, see JEGP xlvi, 419.

hēafodsynn, f. *for* heafodleahter: bebeorh þe wið þa æhta hæfedsynna, Wlfst. 290, 25.

hēafodweard, m.: sense in citation in Suppl. is as elsewhere *chief-guardian*, see Oliphant, *The Harley Latin–Old English Glossary* 170.

hēah, *add to A II 2 b*: Latin is ardui formam propositi; cf. *Philological Quarterly* xl, 316.

hēahcræftiga, *add to I*: heahcræftig(a) heofonas and eorþan, IC 226.

hēahdēma, m. *chief judge*: Wlfst. 254, 8, v.l.

hēahfeaxede, *adj. with long beams*: alticomum, heahfexende (sic), OEG 9, 35.

hēahgræft, *note*: lemma is part of *anaglypha ualde prominentia*, 3 Reg. vi, 32.

hēahholt, m. for heahhylte: Hml. S. xix, 219, v.l.

hēahhylte, *note*: sense is perhaps rather *wood of tall trees*, cf. scomhylte below.

hēahhymele, f. *bryony: briona*, heahhumele, OEG 69, 13. *See also* hymele *and* hegehymele *in Suppl.*

hēahmiht, *add*: *potestatem*, hæmæhte, Mt. i, 22, Rush.; ðurh ða heahmyhte ures dryhtnes, Vercelli MS., f. 66ᵛ, 4; II *the Deity*: sio Heahmiht on þysne wang astah, id., f. 65ᵛ, 12.

hēahrodor, *add*: Hml. Bel. 124, 28.

hēahsǣ, *cancel, read in citation* heare sæ.

hēahþearf, *add*: æt his heahþearfe, IC 74.

hēahþu, *MS. has* heahþu (*not* -um) Gu. 768, 910.

hēala, *add*: *caccabum plenum ponderosum*, hwer fulne healena, Lunds Universitets Årsskrift lii (1956), 2, 11.

heald, *hold*, delete citation in Suppl. (error for *ferinum*, hold).

healdan, *add to XI 4*: ond him bryce heoldon, *performed what was to his advantage* (cf. bryce II), Guth. 729; XII: *transfer* Chrd. 54, 26 *to* XIII; *add*: XIIa *worship*: þa godas þe þa hæþenan heoldon, Hml. P. ii, 712, 658; C II: *delete translation of* B. 3084, *interpret as under* gesceap III 3.

healf, f., *add to* II: *clima*, half, Txts. 51, 489. *See also* sid-, suþeasthealf.

healfæcer, *a measure of land, a half-acre*: Æt scitecocce oðer healfæcer mæde, CS ii, 169, 9; cf. *unum dimidium agrum quod nostra lingua dicimus* healve aker, id. 48, 7.

healfhundisc, adj. *half-canine*: sum man com on þa ceastre se wæs healfhundisces mancynnes, Ker, *Catalogue* 226 (from Wanley, *Catalogus* 191 x).

healfrūh, *delete, see* ānhealfrūh.

healh, *take here also citations under* heal *in Dict.*

healic, *herring, probably delete, take citation* (= *Chart. Rob.* 206, 2) *as* (h)ealic- oðer sæfisc, *river- or seafish*.

heallhalgung, *delete, see* eallhalgung *above*.

heallic, *add*: *aulica*, þa h(ea)llelican, OEG 28, 126.

hēalre, *add*: *probably g.s. of* healor, *swelling, hill*, PNE i, 239.

healsbeorggold, n. *neck ornament: torques*, halsberigold, A. lxxxiv, 154; halsberigolth, id. 155.

hēalsbōc, *read* healsbōc, *and delete* A book which brings safety.

healseta, *add*: *capitium quod circa collum fit*, halsetha, OEG 34, 6; cf. id. 52, 7.

healsfæst, *substitute for meaning*: *being a slave*.

healsleþer, n. pl. *reins*: (h)abenis, halsledir, Ld. 4.

healsungbōc, f. *book of exorcism*: seo halsungboc þe biscop heom on hand sylð, IP 231.

healswyrt, *for other possible meanings see* A. xli, 133, n. 5.

healþegen, *in* B. 142 *read* helðegnes.

hēan, *elevate, add*: *sublimatus*, hyd, OEG 4, 98.

hēandom, m. *wretchedness*: þurh þone halgan gast and þone heandom þe nu toweard is, Archiv ccii, 272, 26 (= Notes and Queries ccx, 209, 20).

hēap, *in* Sch. 69 *read* on heahþe, *on high. Add to compounds* modheap.

hēapian, *add*: heapiende hiora synna pund on hio, Wyn. 47; 83.

heard, *add to compounds* hildeheard.

hearde, *see also* forhearde.

heardhara, *add*: perhaps *mullet*.

heardhēawa, l. 4 *in Suppl.*, circillus *is a diminutive of* cercurus, *light vessel, confused with* (a)ciscillus, *little adze*.

hearding, *add*: pl. may be a tribal name in Run. 22.

hearheard, *add*: the word is doubtful, cf. ASPR iii, 352.

hearma, *add*: *weasel*.

hearmcwidolness, f. *slander*: *calumniis*, heærmcwidolnesse, Ps. Cant. cxviii, 134.

hearmheortness, ? delete, read *earmheortnesse* in citation (= WW 511, 16), cf. Fl. 24.

hearn, *note*: the word should probably be deleted; discussion FL 25.

hearpen, attempted explanations Neophilologus viii, 207; FL 26.

hearpestre, *add*: *tympanistriarum*, hærppestran, Ps. Sal. lxvii, 26.

hearplic, adj. *lyric: lyrico*, (h)earplicum, OEG 7, 21; 8, 15; 9, 42; 110.

hebban, *see also* upa-, forþhebban; upahafen.

hebbendlic, *delete, see* oferhebbendlic *in Suppl.*, upahebbendlic *below*.

*heccing, *sown part of partly sown field*, PNE i, 240.

heden, *note*: *see remark on* crusene *above*.

-hefedness, *see also* upp(a)hefedness.

hefeldian, *delete form* hefaldian, *in citation in Dict. read* hefeldige (A. viii, 452).

hefigmōd, *second citation in Suppl.* = Hml. P. i, 446, 559.

hege, *add to meanings* wicker-work (= hyrdel). *Add to compounds* ciric-, cwichege.

hegehymele, *see also* heahhymele *above*.

hegian, *add to compounds* behegian.

hēl, *perhaps read* hōl *in both citations*.

helfenlic, adj. *like the hellish fen*: þæm helfenlican, WW 437, 31 (so MS.), *reflecting* lethea palude, Aldhelm, Rid. 53, 8. Cf. FL 47.

hellehinca, *for* hancettan *read* huncettan.

hellelic, *read* hellelic *in citation* (= WW 144, 15).

hellwendlic, *delete, see* helfenlic *above*.

helpendrāp, *add*: *opiffera* = *opisphora*; cf. *opisphora, funes quae cornibus antemnae dextra sinistraque tenduntur retrouerso*, Isid., *Et.* xix, 4, 6.

helpegen, *see* healþegen.

helung, f. *covering*: in *tegmine*, on helunge, Ps. Sal. xxxv, 8.

-hende, *add to compounds* sliþhende.

*heng, *declivity*, PNE i, 243.

hengetreow, n. *gallows*: *crucis sub ipso stipite*, under engetreowe, Prud. 506. Cf. A. xxxi, 531.

hennescill, *probably error for* henneægscill, *shell of a hen's egg*: supe syþþan ane hennescille fulle gemyltere buteran, Archiv lxxxiv, 325, b.

hēns, collective *hens*: in hensbroc, CS i, 290, 21.

hēofigendlic, *for* heofendlic: to þere heofugendlican tide, Chad 178, 175 (or read beofugendlican, Bede *tremendo illo tempore*).

heofonbūend, adj. *living in heaven*: *supra omnes caeligenas*, ofer ealle heofonbuendum (*sic*), Gn. 89, 1 (JV; *inexact, v.l.* heofoncennede).

heofonhlyttan, Gn. 99, 5 (V, hefon- J), *errors for* efenhlyttan (*consortes*; cf. yfenlyttan, Hy. Surt. 120, 2).

heofonhūs, cf. FL 139.

heofontungol, *add*: Verc.-Hom. 36, 303.

heofonwolcen, *add*: Verc.-Hom. 14, 119.

heolstor, *note*: as gloss to *secessus* meaning is *privy*; in citation in Suppl. of Wrt. Voc. ii, 126, 6 (= WW 194, 14) hleostrum is rather error for hleorum, d.p. of hleor, *cheek*.

heonansīþ, *add*: Hml. Bel. 124, 18.

hēopbrēmel, *add*: *rumicide*, heopbrembel, OEG 73b, 12.

heord, *add to* II: for many explanations of Gen. 2695 see ASPR i, 194.

heorot, *sycomore tree*: *sicomorum*, heard, Lk. xix, 4, Lind. (heord, Rush.).

heortcoþu, *add*: diseases of the heart and stomach seem confused, sense in Lch. ii, 176, 13, seems to be *disease of the stomach*; cf. modseocness.

heorþa, *see* hirde *below*.

heorugrǣdig, *add*: meaning is *bloodthirsty* An. 79, *ravenous* An. 38.

heoruwearg, *substitute for meaning* savage outcast.

hēowan, v. in expression fæsten heowan (hewan), *observe a fast*, past hewde: Seasons for Fasting 47, 159, 177, 181.

hēra, delete citation from El. (MS. has heria, *of armies*).

here, glossing *fornaculum* means *grate*.

here, l. 3 *in Suppl.*, faccus *is for* factus, *which explains* exercitus *as a past participle*.

herebeorg, *add*: on oðren herbyrge bute on hire agene innoðe, Anglica ii, 27, 119 (= Hml. Warn. 136, 32).

herebeorgian, *add*: swa swa leofne gyst heo hine husede and innlice herebyregode, Anglica ii, 29, 135 (= Hml. Warn. 137, 9).

*hereford, *ford on a highway*, PNE i, 244.

herehorn, m. *trumpet*: Ælfc. Gr. Z. 40, 7, gloss.

-hereness, *see also* gehereness.

herescipe, *troop*: Seasons for Fasting 18.

hereword, *add*: *see citations under* unmann *and* unword.

hergere, m. *plunderer: predo*, OEG 28, 341 (MS ẖrgre).

herung, *add to compounds* anhering.

hetlen, ? delete, read *in citation* hetlan (nom. pl. wk. *from* hetol) helsceaþan.

**hettan**, add as meaning *pursue, persecute*: An. Ox. 8, 388 (*quoted under* hatian II 2).

**heyning**, *enclosure*: on weald, on freyð, on heyninga, Chart. Harm. 423, 6. PNE i, 241.

**hig**, interjection *Oh*: O, O, hig, hig, WW 91, 7.

**higendlice**, adv. *quickly, at once*: þa nolde he heo swa higendlice (v.l. sæmtinges) acwellen, Hml. Warn. 25, 13.

**higera**, substitute for meaning *jay*; cf. Meyer-Lübke s.v. *gajus, gaja*; Tupper, *The Riddles of the Exeter Book*, pp. 84 and 121; A. xli, 115, n. 7.

**higesynnig**: Seasons for Fasting 168 *read* hige synnig man, *think, sinful man*.

**hildan**, *add to compounds* inhildan.

**-hilde**, *add* ofhilde

**hildeheard**, adj. *bold in war*: Fates of the Apostles 21.

**hildness**, *see* ahildness.

**hiltleas**, *add*: cf. Isid., Et. xviii, 6, 1, *ensis ferrum tantum, gladius uero totus*.

**hincian**, *add*: Ps. xvii, 46, Ps. Vit. reads hlyncoton (? *for* hync-), Ps. Roy. huncetton.

**hinder**, adj. *wicked* (= OED hinder a²): heo ne byð næfre teonlease, for heo byð geteontregeð mid hindre geðanca, Hml. Warn. 143, 13.

**hinder**, *add*: (4) *of rest*: *resto*, hinder gestonde, OEG 28, 180.

**hinderness**, f. *wickedness*: þæt heo heo beðæncen ond gecerren of heora hindernysse, Hml. Warn. 142,24.

**hindhæleþe**, other meanings suggested OED s.v. *hindheal*, Middle Eng. Dict. s.v. *hinde-hele*.

**hine**, *l. 7 in Dict.*, *read* 24, 43.

**-hipian**, *add*: *see also* hyppede *in Suppl. and below*.

**hirde** I, in citation Wrt. Voc. i, 22, 78 (= WW 119, 29), hyrde is rather a form of heorþa, *skin*; cf. E.S. xli, 323; FL 154. *See also* hyrd *in Suppl*.

**hiredcniht**, cf. Chart. Whit. 127.

**hiredgeréfa**, perhaps two words *hired reeve*, cf. FL 107.

**hiredwifmann**, *add*: Will of Æthelgifu, ed. Whitelock, 49.

**hiringmann**, *for* hiremann, Hml. Warn. 96, 4; 126, 35; hyringmannum, Chart. Rob. 256, 10.

**hirness**, *add to IV*: þe gehyrað to his hyrnysse into his mynstre, Fehr 132, 25.

**hit**, ? *heat*: þenden hyt sy, gledegesa grim (? *or read* hat), B. 2649; gif her inne sy isernes dæl, hit sceal gemyltan, *heat must melt it* (? *or* hit pron.), ASPR vi, 122, 19.

**hittan**, *see also* gehittan.

**hiþfull**, adj. ?: *odiosi sunt*, hiðfulle hy synd, Scint. 3, 4.

**hiw**, *delete* II 4, *take citation as* scinlac uel (scin)hiw, *see* scinhiw *in Dict. Add to compounds* manigheowlic.

**hiwe**, suggestion that this is dat. of *hiw* is correct.

**hiwian**, *add to compounds* æthiwian.

**hiwlic**, ? substitute for meaning *of marriage*: note that *matrimonialis* is a variant to *matronalis* in Aldhelm, ed. Ehwald, p. 310, 16. Cf. JEGP xlvi, 430.

**-hiwodlic**, *see* ungehiwodlic.

**hiwspræc**, f. *dissembling speech*: *insanias falsas*, hwispræce (sic) lease, Ps. Sal. xxxix, 5.

**hladan**, *see also* unahladen.

**hlædfæt**, n. *vessel for drawing water*: þes wæterpyt ys deop, and þu hlædfæt næfst, Hml. P. i, 289, 21.

**hlæfþe**, *substitute* læfþe (q.v.).

**hlæglende**, *see* hleglende *below*.

**hláf**, with citation from Wrt. Voc. 41, 15–23 (= WW 153, 31–9) cf. Isid., Etym. xx, 2, 15.

**hláfordlic**, *add*: *herilis*, seo hl(a)fordlice, OEG 28, 178; *herilem*, hlafordlice, id. 367.

**hlagolian**, v. *sound*: *bombosa*, hlaegulendi, Txts. 45, 317.

***hlammgeat**, n. *swing-gate*: see PNE i, 248.

**hlancesár**, n. *pain in the side*: *ad colicos*, wiþ langkesar, OEG 73 c, 29. Cf. ME lonke, *flank*.

**hleglende**, *add*: *rudentium, rugientium, frementium, seuientium*, hlæglendra gremetendre, Studia Germanica Gandensia ii, 89.

***hlenc**, *hill-side*, PNE i, 250.

**hlenortéar**, *correct ref.* to Ps. L. l, 9.

**hleomoc**, on *fafida* cf. A. xli, 124, n. 5.

**hléonian**, the word is doubtful, cf. FL 76.

**hléorbán**, *add*: of sca. Brigida hleorbane, Förster, *Reliquienkultus* 80, 138.

**hléorberan**, cancel Dict., accept suggestion in Suppl.

**hléortorht**, adj. *with shining cheeks* (i.e. sides): Rid. 70, 6.

**hléotan**, *see also* behleotan.

**hléoþrian**, *add*: I 1 c of animals: *latrantes*, hleoþriende; see andbicnian in Suppl. and above.

**hléowfæst**, substitute for meaning *giving protection* (of persons, and temperate climates), and add: on hleowfæste stowe, Verc.-Hom. 143, 67.

**hlíf**, m. *moon-shaped ornament*: *lunulas*, hlibas, OEG 55, 5. Cf. *scilling below*, menescilling *in Dict.*, *and* Zeitschrift für vergleichende Sprachforschung xlviii, 257.

**hlihhan**, *add to compounds* inhlihhan.

**hlinc**, *see also* s.v. min.

**hlinian**, *see also* behleonian.

**hlít**, *add to III*: gegripon þa deoflu þa sawle and hig sædon þæt hio wære hiora hlytes, Wyn. 147.

**hliwe, hlig**, *shelter*: on ðes cyninges hlywan, C.D. iii, 338, 7; iv, 108, 23; to Hligham gemære, Chart. Whit. 42, 4.

**hliwþ**, for lemma *caumene* cf. eorþrest.

**hliwung**, as gloss to *ignominium*, hlewung is rather for *lewung*, *betrayal*; cf. Dict. s.v. sceand I, and SHG 112.

**hlúttrian**, *add*: III *remove by purifying*: swylce hy hluttrion þone stut, Hml. P. ii, 504, 168.

***hlýde**, *noisy stream*, PNE i, 254.

**hlyncoton**, Ps. Vit. xvii, 46, *probably read* huncetton (*claudicauerunt*).

**hlysnere**, m. *hearer*: *auditor*, lysnere, Rtl. 29, 4.

**hlysting**, f. *hearing*: ne Marien ... hlystinge to Godes worden næs næfre on nanre oðre swa fullice geforðed, swa on ure Drihtenes moder, Anglica ii, 27, 110 (= Hml. Warn. 136, 24). *See also* underhlystung.

**hnifol**, *add*: *uerticem*, hnifel, Ps. Vit. vii, 17.

**hnipol**, *see* hnitol *below*.

**hnitol**, in citation Wrt. Voc. 19, 1 (= WW 111, 33) MS. has hniwol (? for hnipol, cf. hnipian).

**hnutbéam**, *add*: *amigdalus*, easterne nutebeam, DP 9, 26.

**hóbanca**, discussed FL 173.

***hobb**, *hummock*, PNE i, 255.

**hóc**, *add to I*: þa worldmen cunnon þa worldcundan snoternysse, and þa yfelan hocas þe se Hælend onscunað, Hml. P. ii, 556, 219.

**hocer**, *round hill*, PNE i, 255; cf. hocer wuda, CS iii, 230, 20.

***hocg**, *hog*, PNE i, 256.

**hofrede**, *probably* = hoferede, *with confusion of lemmata*.

**hogleas**, adj. *free from care*: ond gyf hit cuð byð Pilaten, we byð for eow and eow hogelease gedoð, Homl. Warn. 79, 33.

**hoglice**, adv. *wisely: prudenter*, Lk. xvi, 8, Lind.

**hogu**, *see also* weoroldhogu.

**hóh**, add to citations for meaning *promontory*: hleo on hoe, B. 3157.

**hohfullice**, adv. *carefully*: R. Ben. I. 89, 6.

**hol**, *hole*, *add to III*: an hol stæfes, *one prick (apex) in a letter*, Mt. v, 18, Rush.

**hólan**, *add*: *subsannabit*, hyspeð uel holeð, Ps. Cant. ii, 4.

**hold**, *see also* welhold.

**holmwudu**, *substitute*: m. *trees (of the meadow)*: Dream of the Rood 91.

**holt**, *add to compounds* heahholt.

**holtwudu**, *delete citation from* Dream of the Rood (cf. holmwudu).

**hóp**, *hoop, circle*: see hoppe in Suppl.

***hópere**, m. *cooper*, PNE i, 260.

**hoppáda**, ? *read* hóppáda, *circular cope*.

***hoppere**, m. *dancer*, PNE i, 260.

**hopping**, f. *hop-garden*: biweste hoppinge, CS iii, 472, 22 (very late copy).

**hopsteort**, ? *read* hópsteort, cf. FL 173.

**hordgeþanc**, n. *mind*: for ðan þe galnes oferswiðeð strangra manna hordgeþanc, IP 252.

**horiness**, f. *filth*: *sordidibus*, horinesse Ps. Sal., Hy. 6, 8.

**horn**, *add*: VII *gable* (cf. A. xii, 396): Fin. 4 (see Dict.), and in compounds horngeap, horngestreon, hornreced, hornsele; VIII as a topographical feature, *horn-shaped piece of land*: see PNE i, 261.

**hornádl**, f. *a disease of the penis*: þætte hæmedþing swiðost eglað þam ðe hornadle habbað, Læceboc ii, 27 (= Lch. ii, 163; Leonhardi 49, 16).

**hornsceaþa**, *substitute*: hornsceáþ, *wing of the gables* (connecting *pinnaculum* with *pinna*): *supra pinnaculum*, ofer uel on hornsceaðe, Mt. iv, 5, Lind. [Gaelic *sgiath*, *wing*.]

**hornung-brōþor**, m. *bastard brother*: *nothus* (*frater*), OEG 8, 13.

**horrat**, *suggestions are* horwaþ, *defiles*, Prud. 1046, note; þorraþ, *dries up*, A. lxx, 9, 108.

**hors**, *l. 1 in Dict. read* geþracen; *l. 2 emend citations as s.v.* assen *above*.

**horsōman**, pl. *erysipelas* (*or similar eruptions*) *in horses*: wið horsoman ond mannes, Grattan and Singer, *Anglo-Saxon Magic and Medicine* 192, 8; cf. Notes and Queries xii (n.s.), 446.

**horsryne**, perhaps delete, horsyrnes rather to horsern, which see in Dict. and Suppl. For exact reading of MS. see Studia Germanica Gandensia ii, 89.

**horwian**, v. *defile*: *sordidans libido*, seo horwiende galnys, Gn. 3, 5 (V). *See also* gehorwian, forhorwade, *and* horrat *above*.

**hospan**, v. *reproach*: *exprobrauerunt*, hospton, Ps. Sal. xli, 11; id. cxviii, 42.

**hracca**, *doubtful word*, *cited forms may go back to a misreading of* hnæcca, *see* hnecca. See JEGP lii, 373.

**hradian**, *add to compounds* forehradian.

**hræd**, *the gloss*: *propero*, hraeðe *belongs to* hraþe.

**hrædd**, *for* hreþmonaþ, OEG 63, 5.

**hrædness**, *note*: in second citation in Suppl. under III on rædnesse glosses *in uelocitate*, which itself glosses *in maturitate*, see A. lxxxi, 127.

**hræfnsweart**, adj. *black as a raven*: hrefesweart (sic), Verc.-Hom. 101, 325, v.l.

**hræge**, *see* ræge *in Dict.*

**hrægl**, *add to compounds* scufhrægl.

**hrætele**, *note*: connection with Mod. E. 'rattlewort' is uncertain; cf. DP 33, 65.

**hrama**, *barrier*: of hrambroces forda, CS i, 496, 8; PNE i, 264.

**hran**, delete meaning *mussel*, see FL 108; *add*: *dolphin*, see citation from Bede in Dict., and cf. OEG 4, 6.

**hrandspearwa**, *MS. has* hrondsparuas *with* d *cancelled*. Cf. FL 27.

**hranfisc**, *add*: since *whale* is simply *hran*, perhaps read *hornfisc* in the two citations.

**hraþe**, *add*: *ocius*, þi hradost, OEG 4, 47.

**hrēmig**, *add*: sense is *lamenting* Soul and Body 9, Seasons for Fasting 8; elsewhere *exulting*. *Add to citations*: *conpotis uotis* (sic), hroemgum, PBB lxxxv (Halle), 43.

*****hrēoden**, adj. *reedy*, PNE i, 264.

*****hrēodet**, *reed-bed*: see Löfvenberg, *Studies on ME Local Surnames* 165.

*****hrēodig**, adj. *reedy*, PNE i, 264.

**hrēof**, *note*: gloss *larbatos*, hreofe, cited in Suppl. due to error; hreofe refers to *elefantina* in passage glossed (Aldhelm, *Laud. Virg.* lxx; cf. JEGP lii, 374).

**hrēoflig**, *add compound* synnhreoflig.

**hrēosan**, *add to compounds* onbehreosan.

**hrēosendlic**, *see also* gehreosendlic.

**hrēow**, adj. *add*: *lugubre*, hreow, OEG 2, 154.

**hreppan**, cancel citation of Rid. 79, 7 (MS. *hrereþ*).

**hrēran**, *add to compounds* in-, ofhreran.

**hrēþmōnaþ**, *see also* hrædd *above*.

**hrif**, *see also* (in)gehrif.

**hrifādl**, f. (or n.), *disease of the bowels*: *yleos*, Journal of Brit. Arch. Assoc. xli, 148 (omitted WW 112, 23).

**-hrin, -hrine**, *see* gehrin(e).

**hring** IVa: ? *delete*, *read in citation* hricge (*the devil, and his allegory, the whale, being confused*). *See also* gedwolhring, *and* hringe *below*.

**hring**, *on* wopes hring see Brooks on An. 1278.

**hringe**, *note*: for gloss *samothracius*, geheafdod hringce, cf. Samothracius (anulus) aureus quidem, sed capitulo ferreo, Isid., Et. xix, 32, 5; *transfer here from* hring, *the gloss* agymmed hringe (so MS.), WW 152, 44; *add*: *regulam auream*, hringan (MS. hyingan) gyrdisles, OEG 38, 2.

*****hringel**, *small ring*, PNE i, 265.

**hringgewindla**, in context (Aldhelm, *De Virg.* 2438) the meaning is *coil of a serpent*; cf. FL 76

**hringmæl**, n. and adj.: alternative explanations would be *sword with a hilt ring* and *provided with a hilt ring*; see Davidson, *The sword in Anglo-Saxon England* 125.

*****hringstān**, m. *stone-circle?*, PNE i, 263.

**hrinung**, *see also* inhrining.

*****hrīsen**, adj. *grown with brushwood*, PNE i, 265.

**hristle**, f., *for* hrisel, WW 391, 18.

**hroden**, add: *read* roden *in B. 1151*.

**hrohian**, v. *expectorate*: hrohode, *gloss on f. 143ʳ of MS. Hatton 113, written over* hripode *in* he hriþode and egeslice hweos *and* angsumlice siccetunge teah (= Hml. Th. i, 86, 8). Cf. hrohung, *and* Medium Ævum i, 208.

**hrohung**, f. *expectoration*: forgif me for þære hrohunge (MS. þrohunge) þe hi on þinne andwlitan spætlodon, A. xii, 505, 14. Cf. hrohian, *and* Medium Ævum xi, 90.

**hrōpan**, *add*: *adplaudat*, on hlior ropit (MS. rouuit), Txts. 39, 86.

*****hrōst**, *roof*, PNE i, 266.

**hroþhund**, delete, *MS.* broþhund, *q.v.*

**hrucge**, *woodcock*: ruggan broc, CS i, 179, 6; on hrucgan cumbes ford, id. iii, 667, 6; PNE i, 266.

**hruna**, m. *fallen tree*: on þone ealdan hrunan, CS iii, 136, 25 (MS. unclear); on Ceollinghrunan, id. 474, 3 from below; PNE i, 266.

**hrycgbrǣden**, add meaning *shoulder-blades*.

**hrycgrible**, substitute for meaning *shoulder-blades*, cf. Phil. Quart. xl, 314.

**hrȳman, hrēman**, *add*: sense *exult* occurs only Dan. 756; Battle of Brunanburh 39.

**hrympel**, note: *MS. reads* hrympellum.

**hrȳþig**, *read* hrȳþig, *exposed to storms*.

**hūfe**, *in citation from* Wrt. Voc. 59, 55, *MS. reads* hus (*A. viii, 452*); *hence form* huf *in Suppl. is doubtful*.

*****hulfere**, *holly*, PNE i, 268.

**hulfestre**, cf. A. xli, 117, n. 2.

**huncrāp**, ? *hobble*: *tripedicam, ligamentum, funem*, OEG 17, 2 (but reading very doubtful).

**hund**, *dog*, delete sense III, see FL 138. *Add to compounds* broþhund.

**hundesberie**, *some plant*: *uua canina*, hundes berian, OEG 73a, 8.

**hundes hēafod, micge, tunge**: references in Dict. are to Lch. iii (not ii).

**hundes lūs**, *add*: Hml. Th. ii, 192, 21; Hml. P. i, 207, 233.

**hundes tunge**, *add meanings* ? bugloss, ? ribwort. *Add citations* Lch. i, 144, 2 *cited under* glofwyrt II *in Dict.*; *canis lingua*, hundes tunge WW 296, 30; DP 11, 90; *lingua canina*, hundes tunge. i. uenebula, OEG 67, 1; *buglossam*, glofuyrt uel hundes tunga, DP 10, 71; *cynoglossa*, ribbe, DP 12, 119; *canis lingua*, ribbe, hundes tunge, WW 363, 8; *lanciolata*, (h)undes tunge, OEG 66, 9. *See also* ribbe.

**hundisc**, *see* healfh.

**hundredesmann**, *add*: II *for* hundredmann, WS Gospels, Mk. xv, 39, v.l.

**hundtēontigwintre**, *citation* = Hml. P. ii, 623, 20.

**hungrian**, *for* hyngrian, W.S. Gospels, Mk. ii, 25, v.l.

**hunigæppel**, substitute for meaning *round cake*, see FL 139.

**hunigcamb**, *add*: hunicamb, OEG 73c, 35, note.

**hunigdēaw**, *see* meledeaw *in Dict.*

**hūnsporu**, substitute for meaning *part of a ship's rigging* (cf. hunþyrel).

**hunt**, *delete*, *read in citation* hunteðe.

**hunta**, *for hunting spider read venomous spider*; word perhaps arises from confusion of *uenator* and *uenenata*; cf. SHG 12.

*****huntere**, *hunter*, PNE i, 270.

*****hurþ**, *hurdle*, PNE i, 270.

**hūs**, *add to compounds* bryd-, milten-, scrudels-, tempelhus; *see also* insǣte *below*.

**hūsbrycel**, *add*: *effractabilis*, husbrycil, Kluge, *Angelsächsisches Lesebuch* 9, 28.

**hūselbox**, n. *pyx*: sume preostas gefyllað heora huselbox on Eastron, Fehr 178, 6.

**hūsheofon**, *see* heofonhus *above*.

**hūswā**, adv. glossing *quemadmodum*: huusuæ Mk iv, 26, Lind. (so Rush.; West-Saxon version swylce).

**hwǣde**, *add*: *parui*, hwedes, OEG 30, 71.

**hwælweg**, *see* wælweg.

**hwæt**, delete first two citations in Suppl. As gloss to *liquidus* (corrupted to *licidus, lucidus*) = wæt, *wet*.

**hwǣtan**, *see* ahwætan.

**hwætēadig**, substitute for meaning *fortunate* (cf. hwatung).

**hwætlice**, *in l. 7 in Suppl. read* hrædlice.

**hwæþer**, *cancel* III *in Dict.*, *read* hwæt her *in citation* (so MS.).

**hwanne,** *transfer Gen. 1265 from IV to II 4 in Suppl. See also* sumhwanne, nuhwænne.

**hwasta,** ? *eunuch:* eunuchorum, huastana, Mt., p. 20, 15, Lind.

**hweall,** ? *add: proteruorum,* walana, An. Ox. 5362.

**hwearf,** *crowd:* note *w*-alliteration.

**hwelpian,** v. *bring forth offspring: fructificant,* hwelpeþ, OEG 61, 7.

**hweorfan,** *add to compounds* misbehworfen.

**hwettan,** *in l. 4 in Suppl. read* 186, 6; *in l. 21 read* hvetja.

**hwicce,** *place-name cited belongs rather to* Hwiccas.

**hwifer,** another view PNE i, 272.

**hwil,** *see also* oþerwhile.

**hwilc,** *add to IV 2 b:* gif hwylc eowres assa fylþ, Hml. P. i, 242, 272.

**hwilc,** *see also* a-, sumhwilc.

**hwilen,** *add: temporalis,* wilen, Mt. xiii, 21, Rush.

**hwilfæc,** *delete, take as two words as in An. Ox.;* v.l. hwil *uel* fæce, Studia Germanica Gandensia ii, 90.

**hwilpa,** *substitute for meaning* yarwhilp *or* curlew.

**hwinsian,** v. *whine:* þa hundes ne geswicon to hwinsianne, Nap. 39.

**hwinsung,** f. *whining:* mid hwinsunge ond mid dreorigum mode, Nap. 39.

**hwiþer,** *see* swipor *in Suppl. and below.*

**hwirfan,** *add to compounds* ed-, efthwirfan; geanhwirfende.

**hwirflice,** adv. *in turns: uicissim,* huoerflice, Lk., p. 10, 6, Lind.

**hwit,** *add to compounds* mære-, uthwit.

**hwitecylle** *may be for* witecylle, *punishment sack* (in which criminals were cast into the sea); cf. FL 174.

**hwiteleac,** *see* hwitleac *in Suppl. and below.*

**hwitian,** *add:* II *make white:* ælc hus bið þe fægere, þe hit man hwitað, Verc.-Hom. 145, 85. *Add to compounds* ahwitian; behwit.

**hwitleac,** *note:* MS. reads *poleus* (? *polium*); cf. A. xli, 135, n. 1. See also *hwiteleac* in Suppl.

**hwitleadteafor,** n. *(salve of) white lead: et cerussa mixtum,* whit. lead teauer, Beiblatt zur Anglia xxxiv, 115; OEG 73c, 14.

**hwitling,** *whiting: glaucus,* hwitling, Nap. 14.

**hwol,** *add:* discussed FL 197. In l. 1 read *infigens.*

**hwy,** *add at end of III 2 in Suppl.:* and þrafodon hi swyðe hwi hi sceoldon habban anweald ofer hi, Hml. P. ii, 651, 224; hy hit yfel mynton swiðe, hwig he wolde cyrran to þam synfullan men, The Anglo-Saxons 274, 24.

**\*hwyorf,** *see* weorf *in Suppl.*

**hwyrfness,** *substitute for meaning* delusion *or* insanity.

**hycgan,** *add to compounds* rihthycgende.

**-hydedness,** *see* beh.

**hydele,** *add: brittanica,* uihtmeres uyrt *uel* heauen hnidele, DP 68.

**hydels,** *add: de absconditis,* of hydelse, Ps. Sal. xvi, 14.

**\*hydsacc,** m. *leather bag: sui in corium bouis, quod lingua Britanniorum* hudisac (MS. hudifac) *uocatur, inligauerunt,* Archiv. cli, 80.

**\*hydscip,** *see* hyðscip *below.*

**hygd,** *for* gehygd: se on hygde huru ne slæpeð, Ps. Par. cxx, 4; mid eallre usse heortan ond hygdo (*read* hygde), Verc.-Hom. 51, 102.

**hygdig,** *add to compounds* grimhygdig.

**hygegælsa,** *add:* some take as *wanton,* but cf. JEGP lxiv, 156.

**\*hygel,** *small hill,* PNE i, 274.

**hyht,** *add to IV:* mid witendan hyhte, Hml. Warn. 93, 25. *Add to compounds* æristhyht.

**hyhtlice,** *see also* gehyhtlice.

**hylc,** *add:* Ia metaphorically, *ambages, certamina, circumlocutiones,* hylcas, OEG 30, 87.

**hyll,** *add:* on fox hylle easteweardre . . . of fox hylle norðeweardre, CS ii, 540, 3 from below; 541, 1. *See also* tothyll *and s.v.* flita *above.*

**\*hylloc,** *small hill,* PNE i, 275.

**hylte,** *read* n. *for* m.; *add:* ðet scir hyltæ, CS i, 548, 11; to Scirhyltgeate, id. iii, 588, 12.

**hymele,** *add to compounds* heahhymele.

**hynden,** sense in citation in Suppl. (= Ine 54. 1) is *hundred (shillings) of a wergeld:* gif hine mon gilt, mot he gesellan on þara hyndenna gehwelcere monnan ond byrnan and sweord, *if one makes payment for him (the dead man), he (the slayer) may include a slave, corslet, and sword in every hundred shillings.*

**hyppede,** *note: this may be a form from* -hipian, *heap up,* cf. JEGP xlix, 236.

**\*hyppels,** *stepping stone,* PNE i, 276.

**\*hypping,** *stepping stone,* PNE i, 276.

**hypsar,** *sciatica:* OEG 73c, 11.

**hyrd,** *see also* hirde *above.*

**hyrdung,** discussed FL 108.

**hyrian,** *add to compounds* oferhyrian.

**hyrne,** *add: on* hyrn C.D. vi, 182, 12, *see* Studia Neophilologica xl, 17. *Add to compounds* eaghyrne.

**hyrnetu II,** *note: MS. reads* beaw ƀ (*probably for l, uel*) hyrnete, *oestrum.*

**hyrse,** f. *mare:* on hyrsleage, CS iii, 447, 2 from below.

**hyrst,** *wood, see also s.v.* croh, smeagel.

**hyrst,** *ornament,* add: hurst, OEG 28, 456. *Add to compounds* bridelhyrst.

**hyrsumlic,** *read* hirsumlic.

**\*hyscen,** n. *small house,* PNE i, 277.

**hyðscip,** *rather* hydscip, *ship covered with hides* (note spelling varies). Cf. FL 108.

# I

**\*icels,** *addition to an estate,* PNE i, 145.

**icge gold,** *see also* Publications of the Modern Language Assoc. of America lxxxi, 342.

**idel,** n., *note:* the gloss *casso, idle* belongs to idel, adj.

**idelbliss,** f. *vain joy: per uanam lætitiam,* þurh idelblisse, Archiv cxxxii, 330, 26.

**idellic,** *citation =* Hml. P. i, 344, 103.

**idellice,** *see also* oferidellice.

**idellust,** m. *vain desire:* Ker, *Catalogue* 120, cited above s.v. flæsccostnung.

**idig,** *add:* the sense remains uncertain, recent views are summarised JEGP lxiv, 159.

**idlian,** *see also* onidlian.

**ifed,** adj. *grown with ivy:* on/of eofede tor, CS iii, 660, 6; PNE i, 279.

**ifigtearo,** *l. 3 in Suppl.,* MS. reads yukterx (*for* yuiteru), *see* Prud. 126.

**iht,** *cancel,* MSS. have æhte *in citation.*

**ildewita,** m. *Pharisee: de Pharisaeis,* from aeldeuutum, Lk. vii, 36, Lind.

**ildu,** *in l. 5 in Suppl. read* sexui.

**ilfen,** *see* -ælfen *above.*

**ilfisc,** adj. *elvish: hos (conopes) Galli* eluesce wehte *uocant,* E.S. xxxviii, 300; cf. *conopes i. alucinaria, uana somniaria,* Oliphant, *The Harley Latin–Old English Glossary* 109.

**ilme,** *elm:* to ylman dunes gemære, C.D. iv, 169, 1; PNE ii, 283.

**\*imping,** *place where there are young trees,* PNE i, 281.

**inbærnedness,** *for* inbærness: *incensu,* inbærnydnys, Ps. Cam. lxv, 15.

**inbegitan,** v. *find: inuenitur,* innbegeates, Mt. 9, 13, Lind.

**inbicnan,** v. *inculcate: inculcat,* inbecnað, Jn., p. 7, 10, Lind.

**inbirgan,** v. *for* onbirgan: *gustauit,* inberigde, Jn. ii, 9, Rush. (*Cf.* Lind., *cited s.v.* gebirgan).

**inbrecan,** v. *break into: irrumpit (limen),* inbræc, Prud. 330.

**inbuend,** *add: inhabitator,* inbyend, Rtl. 104, 15.

**inburh,** *add:* se stranga healt his inburh (*atrium*) fæste, Hml. P. i, 266, 34.

**inburhfæst,** delete.

**inbyrding,** *delete,* MS. has inbyrdlitig, *i.e.* inbyrdling.

**inbyrdling,** *add to I: indigenas,* inbyrdlingas, OEG 7, 18.

**incge,** *see also* Publications of the Modern Language Assoc. of America lxxxi, 342.

**incuþ,** *note:* the sense is rather *evil, wicked,* see Studia Neophilologica xiv, 214.

**ineþung,** *for* oneþung, Ps. Ar. xvii, 16.

**infaru,** *add:* ne for þæs Hælendes infare næs se cæstel . . . gewæmmed, *Anglica,* ii, 24, 88 (= Hml. Warn. 136, 7).

**inforlætan,** v. *let in:* Verc.-Hom. 8, 67.

**inforlætness,** f. glosses *inspretio:* inforletnisse, Mk., p. 3, 15, Lind.

**infrignan,** v. *ask: interrogauit,* infrægn, Lk. xxiii, 6, Rush.

**\*ing, \*ingel,** *peak* (very doubtful), PNE i, 282.

**ingangan**, *add*: metaphorically: (*consilio*) *inito*, ingancnum, JEGP lx, 442, III, 2.

**ingelǽdan**, first citation = Ps. V., Hy. 5, 30.

**ingemen**, m. p. *native warriors*: Ex. 190. Cf. ingefolc, ingeþeode.

**ingeþanc**, *in l. 5 in Suppl. read* angustam.

**inginnan**, v. glosses *incipere*: ingann, Mt., p. 7, 14, Lind.; ingunnen, Lk. xxiv, 27, Rush.; ingann Mt. iv, 17, Rush.

**inhildan**, *for* onhildan: *inclinabit*, inheldeð, Ps. Jun. ix, 31.

**inhlihhan**, v. glosses *irridere*: inhlogan, Mk. v, 40, Lind., Rush.

**inhrēran**, v. *for* onhreran: *mota*, inhroered, Mt. xxvii, 51, Lind.

**inhrīning**, f. glossing *intinctus*: inhrining, Jn., p. 7, 3, Lind.

**inlād**, the meaning in second citation is *tax on goods brought to market, cf.* utlad, *and* Chart. Harm. 477.

**inlǽtan**, v. *let in*: Verc.-Hom. 8, 67, v.l.

**inlendiscness**, *substitute*: f. *sojourn*: *incolatus, peregrinationis* (I Petr. i, 17), inlendiscnysse, JEGP lx, 445 (= Scint. 64, 18, not in Rhodes).

**inmang**, prep., *for* onmang: inmong Mt. x, 16, Lind.; himong, id., p. 18, 13.

**inmēde**, *first citation* = Brot. 15, 11; *second citation* = Hml. P. ii, 549, 55. *Add*: Hml. P. ii, 647, 135.

**innanburhware**, *add*: ego Æðelstan ond inganburhware (sic), CS ii, 128, 31.

**innanwyrm**, m. *intestinal worm*: Lch. i, 82, 22 (or two words? cf. inwyrm).

**innemest**, *add*: imam, innemystan, Prud. 887.

**insacian**, v. *refuse*: *deneget*, insacie, PBB lxxxv (Halle), 61.

**insǽte**, *perhaps delete*, take insǽtehus as compound *house in which to lie in wait*; cf. FL 109.

**insceaft**, f. *internal propagation*: Sal. 457.

**inscūfan**, v. *shove in*: swylce hine man þær inscufan wolde, Vercelli MS., f. 135ᵛ.

**insecgan**, v. *infer*: *infert*, insægeð, Lk., p. 6, 18, Lind.

**intimbrian**, v. *edify*: ond mid þam rædingum ge bioð intimbrede (v.l. geintimbrode), Verc.-Hom. 67, 140.

**intinga**, *note frequence of form* intiga, e.g. WW 64, 7; 72, 41; 172, 28 (so MS.); JEGP lx, 442, III, 1.

**intō**, *add to III*: into hyra scyrum, Brot. 29, 6.

**intrymman**, v. glosses *inualescere*: intrymedun, Lk. xxiii, 23, Rush.

**inþanc**, *for* ingeþanc: Hml. Bel. 132, 14.

**inðer**, *delete, in citation MS. reads* niðer (*with confusion of* seorsum *and* deorsum).

**inðice**, in- *is cancelled in the MS.*

**inwadan**, v. glosses *illustrare*: inwode, Rtl. 29, 13.

**inwǽrc**, *add*: *synrigium* (for *syringium*), inwrecg, Prud. 1077, note. (Another view but unlikely A. lxx, 8, 98.)

**inweardlic**, *add*: inweardlicere heortan, Brot. 21, 18 (v.l. inneweardre).

**inwecgan**, v. *flow in* (of light): *in labere*, inwege, Ps. V., Hy. 11, 3.

**inwended**, past part. *for* onwended, Ps. V. cviii, 24 (*inmutata*).

**inwitweorc**, *malicious deed*, see unwitweorc *in Dict. and below*.

**iorn**, *running*, see blodiorn.

**ireþweorh**, probably delete, first element seems derived scribally from following half-line.

**irfan**, *add*: II *honour a deceased person* (with obsequies, etc.): se gyldscipe hyrfe be healfre feorme þone forðferedan, *let the guild honour the dead man to the extent of half the entertainment* (cf. be III 23, feorm II), Chart. Th. 611, 5.

**irfenama**, *for* irfenuma, Hml. Warn. 53, 20.

**irmþ**, *add to II*: for þan þe ge habbað eowre yrmðe swa on gewunan gebroht, swylce hit nan pleoh ne sy, þæt se preost libbe swa swa ceorl, Fehr 4, 5.

**irning**, *add to compounds* fromirning.

**irsian**, *add to I*: *cor ingens* (for *quo ringens*), iursende, OEG 3, 1.

**irþling**, see also A. xli, 121, note 2; 123, note 1; Lindsay, *Corpus Glossary* 196; Oliphant, *The Harley Latin–Old English Glossary* 155.

**īsearn**, *read* isern (cf. Falk, Torp, *Norwegisch-dänisches etym. Wörterbuch*, s.v. isfugl).

**īsernscēruru**, *see* scēar *in Dict.*

**iþbelig**, *read* īþbilge, *and add*: Verc.-Hom. 77, 56; 85, 155.

**īþelicness**, *see* eþelicness *in Dict., and above*.

# L

**lāc**, *add to compounds* ælmeslac.

**lacen**, *mantle*: *clamidem*, hacelan oððe lachen oððe loðan, WW 377, 22. (*Or error for Lat.* lacerna, *cf.* Txts. 72, 572.)

**lāclic**, *delete, in citation read* lahlican (cf. Jost, *Wulfstanstudien* 130).

**lācnimende**, participial adj., *receiving a reward*: *munerari*, beon lacnimende, Ps. Bos., Hy. 3, 19.

**lācnung**, *see also* gelacnung.

**lācsang**, *note: MS. has* laacsang, A. xli, 105, n. 3.

**lācweg**, *way to where sports were held*: to lacwege, CS iii, 212, 24.

**lādrinc**, *add*: in citation *mannan* is a gloss on *rinc*; translate *if (anyone) kills a smith in the king's service or a messenger, let him pay an ordinary wergild*.

**lādtēow**, *see also* æladteow.

**lǽ**, on the form cf. FL 119.

**\*lǽc(c), \*lǽce, \*lec(c), \*lece**, *pool, bog*, PNE ii, 10.

**lǽcebōc**, *add*: Chart. Rob. 250, 18.

**lǽcedomlic**, adj. *salutary*: þis sint halige dagas ond gastlice ond ussum sawlum læcedomlice, A. v, 458, 2 from below.

**lǽcefinger**, in citation Wrt. Voc. 44, 7 (= WW 158, 36), MS. reads: *medicus uel anularis*, lǽce- *uel* goldfinger, and lǽcefinger is repeated for the little finger by mistake; cf. Journal of the British Archaeological Assoc. xli, 149.

**lǽdan**, *add to XII*: on lyft lædan, Dream of the Rood 5; wit lædan sculon, Gen. 1911. *Add to compounds* on-, þurhlædan; ælædend; upgelæded.

**lǽdendlic**, *for* gelædendlic: Ps. Sal. xcvii, 6.

**lǽdere**, *add*: glosses *dux*, Ps. Sal. liv, 14; Hy. 4, 13; 6, 12. Lye's ref. is to this MS.

**lǽdu**, *see* unlædu.

**lǽfer**, *add to I*: *scyrpus*, liber in flumine, OEG 52, 1.

**lǽfþe**, f. *sprinkling*: *sparsio*, dages hlæfþe, WW 277, 6. (Cf. lafian, and FL 172.)

**lǽl**, adj. *livid*: *liuidus*, læl, OEG 28, 308; *liuida*, lælte (? read læle), id., 69.

**lǽlan**, *delete, in citation read* lices læla, *body-wounds*.

**lǽran**, *add to compounds* onlæran.

**lǽrig**, *add*: see Irving on Exod. 239.

**lǽshosum**, *perhaps the citation* (= *WW 125, 23*) *should read* fotlæstlease hosan, *stockings without soles*. FL 109.

**lǽssa**, *in l. 18 read* geleornian.

**lǽstan**, *see also* geedlæstan.

**lǽt**, f. *for* gelǽte: ende lang (= andlang) þar lete to þan north lang furlang north ende end langes þar lete, CS ii, 416, 33; of þe waynlete, id., 438, 28.

**lǽtan**, III 2 a α, *in l. 10* (*Suppl.*) *read* Christo *for* Christus. *Add to compounds* fore-, forþ-, gelic-, in-, infor-, niþerlætan.

**lǽt**, *see also* swiþlæt.

**lǽtcumen**, participial adj. *late*: *sero*, OEG 27, 29.

**-lǽte**, *see also* forlǽte.

**-lǽte**, *see* gelǽte, *manners*.

**-lǽting**, *see also* blodlǽting.

**lǽtlic**, adj. *late*: *serotinus*, Gn. (Archiv cxcxix, 21).

**lǽwe**, *see also* druncenlǽwe.

**lǽwedmann**, m. *layman*: Hml. Warn. 117, 11.

**lǽwung**, *see* hliwung *above*.

**lāf**, *add to compounds* lic-, mannlaf.

**lagu**, *water*, *add*: *for alternative forms* lag, laga, *see* R. Forsberg, *A contribution to a dictionary of OE place-names* 51.

**lagu** II, l. 5 in Suppl.: read for citation from Germ.: *legum*, lagena oþþe æa, Prud. 11.

**lahgewrit**, n. *legal text*: æaldlice lahgewritu, IP 248.

**lambes cerse**, *for* thiospis *read* thiaspis (i.e. thlapsis).

**lāmen**, *for* lǽmen, Hml. Warn. 76, 17.

**lāmsceal**, *tile*: *testa*, Ps. Vit., Ps. Ar. xxi, 16.

**land**, *in l. 44 in Dict. read* land *for* lǽnd; *in l. 7 in Suppl. read* ferigan; *add to compounds* agen-, at-, bydel-, ceap-, feorm-, (ge)neat-, swin-, þegen-, weorcland.

**landbegengness**, f. glosses *incolatus*: londbegengnes, Ps. Bos. cxix, 5.

**landefne**, *substitute for meaning* resources of his land.

**landperan**, pl. *land-piers* (*of a bridge*): to wercene þa landperan, Chart. Rob. 106, 27.

**langian**, *belong*, *see also* belangian.

**langtoh**, *add*: *longo*, langtog, OEG 27, 31.

**lappe**, f. *bur*: *glatuner*, clate, lappe, OEG 73c, 46. (Lat. lappa; lemma = Mod. Fr. grateron).

**lārcniht**, m. *disciple*: *discipulus*, larcnæht, Lk., p. 2, 2, Lind.

**lārdom**, m. glosses *magistratus*: aldordom *vel* lardom, Rtl. 193, 15.

**lāreow**, *see also* þeodlareow.

**lārþegn**, m. *teacher*: eart þu þæt Elias ure larðeign?, Hml. Warn. 81, 26.

**latian**, *add*: *with clause* ne lata þu þæt þu to Gode gecyrre, Archiv cxxii, 258, 34.

**latimer**, m. *interpreter*: Ps. Cant., Hy. 16, 5.

**latu**, *add*: *moram facit*, hlatto doað, Lk. xii, 45, Lind. (Rush. læte doeð).

**lāþtrēow**, *cancel*, *read in citation* laðe treow.

**laþung**, *see also* sigelaþung.

**laurbēam**, *note*: in first citation in Dict., MS. has larf-, see A. viii, 451.

**lawer**, *note*: probably delete, form laber- is Lat. *lauer*, and v.l. lawer due to confusion with 'laurel'.

**lēac**, *add to compounds* toscanleac.

**lēactrog**, probably rather *basin for herbs*, see SHG 118.

**lēad**, *add to II*: Chart. Rob. 250, 3.

**lēaf**, *leaf*, *add to compounds* liþe-, twileaf.

**lēafgewriten**, participial adj. *written (on a leaf)*: hleafgewritten *uel* unawritten, *written or unwritten*, Lk. xvi, 6, Lind.

**lēafleas**, *for* geleafleas: *perfidi hostis*, þæs leafleasan fynd, Gn. 32, 6 (JV).

**lēaflēoht**, meaning may be *light as a leaf*, see SHG 98.

**lēafsele**, m. *tabernacle*: þreo leafselæs, Hml. Bel. 118, 15 (with ref. to Mt. xvii, 4).

**lēah**, *lea*, *add to compounds* at-, beanleah, *and see* clinc, croh, lumm.

**leahter**, *see also s.v.* elleoht, emleoht.

**lēap**, *add to II*: ælce dæge man sealde ærþan þam leonum twa sceap to bigleofan and twegen leapas, Hml. P. ii, 702, 461 (= Hml. Warn. 40, 36). *Add compound* sealtleap (*see* sealtleaf *below*).

**lēasgespreca**, m. *liar*: *duorum falsidicorum*, twegra leasgespecena, A. lxv, 245, 4.

**lēasgewitness**, *add*: Verc.-Hom. 13, 108, v.l.

**lec**, *sweet*, *note*: word is very doubtful, see A. xlviii, 390; An. Ox. 220, note.

**lecg**, *note*: legge, given in Dict. as OHG is OE (read *tornaturas* as lemma, see OEG 42, 1); *add*: *commisuras*, legget (*read* -æ) *uel* cospas, OEG 46, 1.

**lecgan**, *add to VI 1*: and dylfð þone grundweall swyþe deopne, and legð hine mid stane, Brot. 14, 21.

**lecþ**, cf. A. xlvii, 263 (? *read* leoþ = *paeana*).

**lēgbisig**, **ligbisig**: adj. *tormented by flames*, Rid. 30, 1.

**lencten**, *add to Suppl.*: III *Quadragesima Sunday*: gif Eastron beoð pridie id. Aprilis, þonne byð Lengten on kl. Martius, BM 166, 22; and frequently.

**lenctenādl**, though equated with various Latin terms, this probably meant originally *malaria*; see *British Medical Bulletin* viii, 78.

**lendan**, *see also* alendan.

**lengan**, *see also* oþlengan.

**lenge**, adj., *delete* Cri. 1685 (*where read* lenge hu sel); *probably add* B. 83.

**lengian**, *delete*, *in citation read* longað (so MS.).

**lent**, probably delete, see Prud. 152, note.

**lēodan**, *add*: telgan ðe him of liodað (MS. hlidað), Ps. Par. lxxix, 11.

**lēod**, *add to compounds* ceasterleod, wæterleode.

**lēodweard**, *delete*, *read in citations* leodgeard (cf. Gen. 229, 1773).

**lēoht**, *add*: sometimes best translated *world* in Gen. B (e.g. 310). *Add to compounds* blacernleoht.

**lēoffæst**, adj. *dear*, *precious*: þæt folc þe Crist alysde mid his leoffæstan blode, Fehr 172, 13.

**-leoht** *in* elleoht, emleoht, ? *read* -leahtor.

**lēohtflōwend**, participial adj., glosses *lucifluus*, Gn. 63, 3 (JV).

**lēohtlic**, *add*: compar. neut. lihtlicre, *see under* ofertalian.

**lēohtstān**, m. *lamp*: lihtstan, 12th cent. addition to *lichinus*, blacern, Ælfc. Gr. Z. 314, 8.

**lēon**, *add*: liþ him on londe þæs his lufu bædeð, Gn. Ex. 99.

**lēoran**, *add to II*: *with ut*: be þam utleorendum sawlum, Gr. D. 301, 14; 291, 22.

**lēosan**, *add lose*: Hubert wæs leosende þære wifmanne for his unrihtcræfinge, Chart. Th. 633, 26.

**leoþian**, *release*, *emit*: take here citations under *lēoþian*; *add* to compounds toleoþian.

**lēoþian**, *delete*.

**lēoþurūn**, *read either* leoþurun, *wise counsel*, *or* lēoþrun, *counsel given in verse*.

**lēoþwis**, *delete*, *see* FL 175.

**lēoþwyrt**, f. *an unknown plant*: chamedafne, leothuyrt *uel* hrafnesfot, DP 84.

**lēpene**, *basket*: Chart. Rob. 200, 9.

**lepeþ**, *add*: probably parallel with *fedeþ* in preceding line, meaning 'feeds'.

**lesca**, *note*: *cognates* (e.g. N. Icel. ljóski) *suggest* lesca *error for* leosca.

**lettend**, m. *hinderer*: *aduersus impeditor erit*, wiðerweard letted (*sic*) he bið, Archiv cxxix, 19, 12.

**letting**, *see also* geletting.

**leþeren**, *see also* ealleþeren.

**lēwis**, *delete*; in *scurra*, leuis, Corpus Glossary S 146 (*leuuis*, Epinal Glossary), both words are Latin. In *leta cantatio*, lewis plega, WW 202, 31, *lewis* = *leuis* = *læta*, plega = *cantatio*.

**Libanisc**, adj. *of Lebanon*: *Libana*, Libanisca, OEG 28 364.

**licbysig**, *MS. has* legbysig, q.v.

**lichamian**, *see* gel.

**lichanga**, m. *gibbet* (?): andlang gemæres ðæt on lichangan, of lichangan on Pocgingrode, CS iii, 10, 15.

**lician**, *see also* wel(ge)licod.

**liclāf**, f. *relic (of a saint)*: *sanctorum dei*, *quorum reliquiae continentur*, . . . þara liclafa synd hæfede, A. lxxxi, 103, 5.

**liclic**, *of a funeral*, perhaps delete, take as liclic, *likely*, see Prud. 936, note.

**licpytt**, *delete*.

**licwyrþe**, *see also* wellicwyrþe.

**lif**, *add to compounds* ænet-, a-, canonic-, martyrlif.

**lifan**, *believe*, *add to compounds* rihtlifend.

**lifer**, *add*: *the meaning of* lifrum, An. 1276, *is unknown*.

**liferwyrt**, f. *liverwort*: *fac puluerem de tegula et de liuerwurt et de feldwyrt i.* lungewurt, OEG 73c, 35, note; nim liferwyrt, Archiv lxxxiv, 326.

**lifleast**, *add*: first citation in Suppl. = Hml. Warn. 39, 32.

**liger**, *flame*: bernende fyr mid brade ligere (v.ll. ligette, lige) Fehr 87, 20.

**lighrægel**, first element discussed FL 176 (taken as lyge, *falsehood*, as hiw can mean both *colour* and *pretence*; but perhaps rather lig, hence *flame-coloured*).

**liglic**, adj. *fiery*: nalas þæt an þæt he þær þa leglican hyðe ðæs fyres upþyddan geseah, Guth. Gr. 131.

**lihtan**, *shine*, *add to compounds* tolihtan.

**lihtan**, *alleviate*, *add to compounds* onlihtan.

**lihtian**, v. *relieve of a weight*: lihtigende heora synna, Wyn. 48.

**lim**, *add to II*: *ossa*, lymu, Ps. Cam. vi, 3.

**limbstefning**, *MS. reads* limb. stefning; limb *may be abbreviation of Lat.* limbus, *hem*, *or loanword from it*.

**limgesiþþ**, f. *company of the limbs (i.e. the body)*: *cum corporibus*, mid limgesihþum (MS. Ps. Roy., Hy. 11, 40.

**limp**, *for* gelimp, Archiv cxvii, 21, etc.

**linsǣdcorn**, *linseed grain*: linsetcorn, ASPR vi, 128, 11.

**lira**, *add to compounds* sinulira.

**lisc**, *reeds*: on liscbroc, C.D. iv, 8, 7 from below; PNE ii, 25.

**līsend**, m. *redeemer*: *redemptor*, lesend, Rtl. 20, 18. *See also* eftlisend.

**lissian**, v. *pity*: *misereatur*, lisie, Ps. V. lxvi, 1 (*additional stylus gloss*); God lufað þa liðnysse, þæt man lissige oðrum, Hml. P. ii, 500, 67; id. 552, 146.

**lit**, *colour*, *dye*: swa swa se litigere þe lufeð ælces heowes lit, Hml. Warn. 141, 10. *See also* wyrmlic *below*.

**litigere**, m. *dyer*: see citation under lit.

**liþ**, *add*: fingres liþ means *point (not joint) of finger*: Lk. xvi, 24, WS Gospels; cf. *a mortis articulo*, fram deaðes liðe, Bd. iii, 11 (heading); *ad articulum (mortis)*, to ðæm liðe OEG 4, 111; *articulo (cladis)*, liðe, id. 81.

**liþe**, adv. *gently*: ond se ðe hit geþyldlice abereð, God liðe he awacað to him, Verc. Först. 126, 6.

liðelēaf, *a plant*: auiane (? for *apiana*), OEG 73c, 9. Cf. MLN lxii, 568.

lixan, *see also* gelixan.

locc, citation *cicinnus i. uinnus*, loc. Wrt. Voc. ii, 131, 12 (= WW 204, 21), is probably error for *cincinnus i*, winde loc; cf. winde in Dict. and below.

loccettan, glosses *eructare*, perhaps error for roccettan: ic loccete, Mt. xiii, 35, Lind.; loceteð, Mt., p. 7, 5, Lind.

lōcere, *keeper, shepherd*: on loceres weg, CS iii, 10, 17; PNE ii, 26.

lōcian, *add to* I 4 γ α: ealles þæs þe me þær to locaþ, *Crawford Charters* 22, 7.

lōf, cf. RES ii, 342; MLN xl, 411, xli, 170.

loft, *add*: þæt stænene cweartern stod eall on lofte fram þære eorðan, MLN iv, 278.

lōh, *add*: ic will þat Aylfric prest ben on þat ilke loh þe Aignoð was, Chart. Whit. 76, 11.

lōme, *for* gelome: *crebro*, OEG 61, 19.

lōmlic, *add*: *frequens*, OEG 2, 243.

lōmlicor, *for* gelomlicor: lomlucor, ðone þu lyfan wylle, Hept. 49, 794, v.l.

lopost, *for* lopystre, *locusta*, lopust, Txts. 75, 1238; *scabri*, pisces similes lopostum, Corpus Glossary S 174. lopystre, *add*: locustas (Mk. i, 6) *sunt locustae marinae quas* lopustras *uocant*, Philologica Pragensia viii, 306; hence perhaps delete meaning *locust*.

lorh, *add*: þa gesioh hio licgan oþres mægdnes lorh (*colum*), Wyn. 181.

lorte, ? *mud*: to lortan hlæwe, CS ii, 409, 25; PNE ii, 27.

lose, perhaps read hlōse, cf. FL 177.

lotwrencēast, *delete*, *v.ll. show correct reading to be* lotwrenceas (*pl.*).

loþa, *note*: gloss to *sandalium* is an error (Lindsay, *Corpus Glossary* 208).

lūcan, *close, add to compounds* andlucan.

lūcan, *pull up, add to compounds* upa-, utalucan.

ludgeat, *add*: *postica*, ludgete, OEG 39, 1.

luffeorm, f. *loving hospitality*: eac us bið gerisenlic, þæt we luffeorme dælan, IP 265.

lugcna, glosses *erumpat*, Mt., p. 1, 8, Lind. (*altered from* lucgnæ, *probably corrupt*).

lum(m), *pool*: in Lummalea, Hist. de S. Cuthberto xxix. PNE ii, 27.

lungencoðu, f. *lung disease*: beon on lungencoðon, Lchd. i, 388, 1.

lungenwyrt, *add*: *see* liferwyrt *above*.

lungor, *substitute*: adj. *swift*: mearas lungre gelice, B. 2164. See also ceaslunger.

lust, *add to compounds* idellust.

lustgītsung, f. *desire for pleasure*: Bt. vii, 5, v.l.

lūtan, *see also* forþaloten.

lutegār, m. *trapping spear*: æt Lutegaresheale, Chart. Whit. 60, 17. Cf. PNE ii, 28.

lybbestre, discussed Oliphant, *The Harley Latin–Old English Glossary* 56.

lybcorn, cf. giþcorn for lemmata *lacyride, lattyride*; add DP 210 quoted under giþcorn above.

lycce, *enclosure*: on lychagan, C.D. vi, 168, 26; PNE ii, 30.

lycettan, v. *murmer*: *murmurantes*, hia lycedon, Lk., p. 5, 1, Lind., and frequently in Lind.

lyftlic, *add*: nubibus *aeris*, wolcnum lyftlicum, Ps. Ar. xvii, 12.

lyge, *a plant-name*, is probably an error for ryge; cf. FL 28.

Lygeanburh, *add*: known to be *Limbury*, Beds.

lynibor, *see also* tymbor *below*.

lynis, substitute for meaning *linch-pin*, cf. A. xlv, 194; xlix, 94.

lystlice, *for* lustlice: ond heora lare lystlice hyrde, Fehr 93, 24, v.l.

lyswen, adj.: *Ps. Th. lii, 6, rather read* liste *for* lisne.

lytelfōta, *delete, see* fitelfōta *in Suppl.*

# M

mād (Dict.), mādmōd (Suppl.), *delete, read in citation* ungemedemad mod.

mæcg, *add to compounds* beotmæcg.

mæd, *add to compounds* flodmæd.

mædere, cf. A. xli, 141, note 4; DP 27, 31; 53, 191.

mædmæwect, *note*: *probably error for* mædmæwett.

mædmann, m. *mower*: seo wæs unsceððiglice acweald fram hire fæder mædmannum, Förster, *Reliquienkultus* 80, 135.

mægdeneorþe, f. *virgin soil*: on ane felde abute Damasco of rædre yrþe, þæt is mædenyrðe, Hept. 419, 5 (late addition).

mægen, *see also* fifmægen.

mægenleaslice, citation = Prud. 712, where see note.

mægensibb, f. *great love, see* mægsibb *below*.

mæggewracu, f. *revenge for a relative*: se ðe in his mægewrece mannan ofslea, fæste iii winter, Buss. 186, 329.

mægleast, *error for* mægenleast, Hml. Warn. 29, 7 (cf. Hml. Th. i, 404, 2).

mægmann, m. *clansman*: ðam blindan mægmenn, Bd. ii 2, v.l.

mægsibb, *add* v.l. mægensybbe *to citation of* Wlfst. 252, 9.

mægsliht, *add*: de *paricidiis et fratricidiis*, be mæislæhte ond broðerslælte (*sic*), Ker, *Catalogue* 93.

mægþa, *add*: bucstalmum (= *buphthalmos*), hwit mægeðe, WW 297, 3.

mægþblæd, citation = Prud. 920, where see note (? take as mægþblæd, *glory of virginity*).

mægþhad, perhaps delete sense II, cf. *Philological Quarterly* xl, 316.

mægþmorþor, *for* mægmorþor, An. Ox. 2, 412.

mægþmyrþa, *for* mægmyrþa, An. Ox. 2, 335.

mǣl II, *citation* Chart. Th. 558, 32 (= Chart. Whit. 58, 7) *belongs to* mele, *cup*.

mǣlan, *speak, see also* formælan.

mǣnan, *relate*: add: *supra meminimus*, ufen maende(n), OEG 4, 102. See also ofermǣnan.

mǣnelic, *for* gemænelic, II Cnut 10, v.l.

mǣre, *boundary, add*: *in loco*, in mere, OEG 4, 142.

mǣre, *pure, add at end*: viii oran mærewites feos, CS iii, 370, last line. See also coittemǣre, and cf. SHG 28.

mǣre, *nightmare, add*: ne me mere ne gemyrre, ASPR vi, 127, 8.

mǣrehwīt, see mǣre, *pure*, in Dict. and above.

mǣssang, *for* mæssesang, Chrd. 35, 12.

mǣsse, *add to compounds* morgen-, sundor-, swigmæsse.

mǣssecapitel, *for* capitolmæsse, *q.v. in Dict.*: A. xiii, 402, 536.

mǣstlōn, *l. 2 in Dict., read* carchesia . . . trochliae quasi F littera (*so* Isidore, *Etym.* xix, 2, 9).

mǣt (*for* mete), *delete*.

mǣþel, *add to* II: *sermonis*, myðels, OEG 4, 124.

mǣþelhergende, *delete, read in citation* -hegendra.

mǣþleas, *add*: þa mæðleasan hundes lys þe him on þone muð flugon, Hml. P. i, 207, 233.

maffa, *delete, error for Lat.* mappa (Lindsay, *Corpus Glossary* 126).

maga, *stomach*: for *fleumon* cf. *fleumon est feruor stomachi*, Isidore, Etym. iv, 6, 7.

magan, *add to* I: with dat. *prevail over* (= magan wiþ): and ne mihte nan man naht þisum folce, Hml A. 106, 120.

Magdalenisc, adj. applied to Mary Magdalene, IP 227, 231.

māgling, *parent*: *parentes*, mahlinges, Nap. 43 (= Archiv cxvii, 25; cf. id. 21).

māh, *add*: *procax*, OEG 24, 31; *importuna*, mag, id. 28, 438.

Mailrosisc, adj. *of Melrose*: Mailrosi, Mailrosiscum, OEG 9, 22.

malscrung, *note*: mascrunc quoted as OHG in Dict. is probably OE (OEG 53, 1).

mamorian, *read* māmorian (cf. An. Ox., Addenda and Corrigenda).

man, pron., *add*: *reduced to* me, Hept. 169, 2 (late addition); *reduced to* ma, Chart. Rob. 238, 12, etc.; Chrd. 70, 4, etc.

mancus, *add*: pl. mancsas, Archiv cxx, 303, 14.

māndǣda, citation in Suppl. = Hml. P. i, 436, 375.

manetian, *delete, read in citation* ge mon cigaþ.

-mang, *add to compounds* inmang.

manig, *see also* welmanig.

manigbrǣde, discussed FL 110.

manigfealdsumness, f. *a great deal*: *multum*, monigfalsumnise, Mt. xxv, 18, Lind.

manighēowlic, adj. *of many sorts*: *multifario*, monigheoulice, OEG 4, 405.

**mann,** *add to compounds* gafol-, læwed-, mæd-, mæg-, sulh-, un-, witnesmann; ingemen, twimen.

**mannlāf,** f. *remainder of the men (slaves)*: of þære manlafe . . . ii men, Will of Æthelgifu, ed. Whitelock, 54.

**-mānsian,** *see* amansian.

**manslot,** citation = Chart. Rob. 192, 23.

**mapuldorgeat,** n. *opening near a maple tree*: *Crawford Charters* 25, 52.

**mārbēam,** *see* morbeam.

**market,** in first citation (= Chart. Harm. 259, 16) meaning is *market rights*.

**martyrlīf,** ? pl. martyrliua, *martyrology*, Chart. Rob. 250, 16.

**masc,** *for* maxwyrt: i met maltes under masc ond grut, Chart. Rob. 200, 9.

**maþa,** in citation Wrt. Voc. 24, 16 (= WW 122, 6) MS. has maþamite (see A. viii, 450). Cf. mite in Dict.

**māðumciste,** f., *for* maðumcist (cf. bocciste): ac hit (*i.e.* a *poor man's hand*) is madmceoste Godes, IC 189.

**\*māwe,** *meadow*, PNE ii, 37.

**meagol,** *read* mēagol.

**\*mealu,** *gravel ridge*, PNE ii, 35.

**mearc,** *add to compounds* east-, westmearc.

**mearcian,** *add*: IX *give heed to*: Petrus þæt word mearcode, Hml. Bel. 118, 25.

**mearcung,** *citation under III in Suppl. rather implies* steormearcung, *see* steorwigle *in Dict. Cf.* reonung *below. Add to compounds* ufanmearcung.

**mecgan,** ? *delete, all forms errors for forms of* mengan.

**meduma,** *delete in Suppl. all after* persa, l. 4.

**medume,** *note*: the expression *medume leodgeld* belongs to I, not to II, meaning *ordinary wergild* (i.e. that payable for a ceorl); *add to* I (1) *in Suppl.*: gehwar hy syn hefige, gehwar eac medeme (*of duties*), Ll. Lbmn. i, 446.

**medumlice,** *see also* gemedumlice.

**meduscerwen,** cf. EGS iv, 74.

**medustig,** *read in citation* medostigge mæt.

**meduwyrt,** as gloss to *rubia* (see Suppl.) perhaps error for mæderwyrt (see mædere in Dict.).

**mēdwyrhta,** *add*: Payn min medwrihte, Chart. Harm. 351, 12.

**melu,** *add*: glosses *manna*, Ps. Sal. lxxvii, 23.

**Memfitisc,** adj. *of Memphis*: OEG 28, 415.

**mengan,** *see also* hæwmenged.

**mennisclicness,** f. *for* menniscness, *see* s.v. afangenness.

**mēo,** *add*: note strong gen. sg.: *odonis uitam* (i.e. *udonis uittam*), mihes nostlun, Ld. 110.

**mēoning,** *delete, in citation keep MS.* weoningas (*cf.* wining).

**meoring,** *in citation* fela meoringa *is metrically improbable* (*TPhS* 1952, 4), *perhaps read* felamodigra.

**meoto,** *this word is of doubtful reality; perhaps read in citation* and on sælum eow sige Hreðsecgum, *and in gladness display victorious achievements to the Geats.*

**Merewioing,** *in* B. 2921 *read* Merewiging, *the Merovingian.*

**met,** *add*: II *some definite measure*: i met maltes, Chart. Rob. 200, 9.

**mete,** *note*: *in citation* Wty. Voc. i, 27, 17 (= WW 127, 20) *MS. has* mete (*not* mæt).

**meteærn,** *add*: hina meteren, Txts, 440, 7.

**meteþistel,** *an edible thistle*: camerion, DP 11, 86; 139.

**metfæstlice,** adv. *moderately*: Ælfc. Gr. Z. 294, 1 v.l.

**metgian,** *see also* ungemetigende.

**metlice,** *substitute*: adv. *according to rule, precisely, in due order*: examussim, JEGP lx, 441, I 26. *See also* gemetlice (esp. 4 in Suppl.), unmetlice.

**metlicness,** *see* ungemetlicness.

**mēþian,** *add*: fumigabunt, meþgiæþ, Ps. Cant. ciii, 32 (? confusion with *fatigor*).

**mēþig,** *add*: Seasons for Fasting 228.

**micelness,** *see also* gemicelness.

**mid,** *add to* VIII *b*: wið eagena hæte . . . niwe gate cyse ofergeseted mid þa eagbræwas (*laid on by means of the eyelids*), Lchd. i, 352, 6. *See also* forþmid.

**midblissian,** v. *rejoice with*: heo midblissað soðlice soðfestnisse (cf. I Cor. xiii, 6), Scint. 138, 1.

**midd,** *add*: III *of an abstract conception*: geþyld bið middes eades, *patience is midway to happiness*, Prov. K. 25.

**middel,** *see also* brumiddel.

**middelsǣ,** f. *a channel in Kent*: Chart. Rob. 160, 1.

**midfæsten,** *add*: on þære mydfæstenes wucan, Jn. viii, 12, rubric (West-Saxon Gospels); and frequently.

**midfeorh,** adj. *middle-aged*: in midfeorum life, Bd. v, 13.

**midgehlytto,** f. *fellowship*: consortiis, miðgihlyttum, Rtl. 93, 26.

**midgetellan,** v. *include among*: on getæle halgena . . . me midgetellan gemedema, A. lxv, 251, 7.

**midhilte,** sense is rather (*sword*) *with a hilt*; or perhaps take as two words.

**midl,** read citations under II as *struppi*, armidla, -lu, WW 182, 33, 288, 31. Cf. SHG 50.

**midnumen,** *taking away, plucking*: spicarum . . . uulsione, ðara ehera . . . miðnumenne, Mk., p. 2, 17, Lind.

**midþwǣrian,** v. *consent*: coniurante polo, midþwæriendum heofene, WW 214, 22.

**mihtesetl,** n. *seat of power*: he awyrpð þa modigan of heora mihtesetle, Morris, Old English Homilies I (EETS, 1867), 301, 28.

**\*milstān,** m. *milestone*, PNE ii, 41.

**miltenhūs,** n. *brothel*: in prostitutionem, on galnysse uel on myltenhus (*inexact*), Scint. 87, 17.

**min,** *add to* II: Gu. 622; Sat. 504; on minnanlinche, CS iii 494, 31.

**mind,** *diadem*: diadema, mind, Rtl. 92, 10 (new ed. 92, 5). (O. Irish mind).

**minlic,** adj. *mine*: ac hit nis na minlic (v.l. min) inc to syllanne, Gr. D. 231, 17.

**minna,** cf. FL 205.

**minsiendlic,** *see* unminsiendlic.

**minte,** *see also* hareminte.

**mircapuldor,** *note* milscapuldr, Txts. 76, 638, *and see* milisc.

**misbehworfen,** participial adj. *for* mishworfen: v.l. *in citation under* mishworfen (IP 237).

**misbēodan,** v. *announce wrongly*: (gif) se læreda misbeode . . ., Archiv cxi, 280, 25.

**misbregdan,** *substitute*: v. *change for the worse*: distortum . . . peruersum, obliquum, transuersum, misbroden, Oliphant, *The Harley Latin–Old English Glossary* D 728; *traducit, transferit* (sic), misbret, JEGP lx, 444.

**misgewidere,** *add*: Vercelli MS., f. 73ʳ, 20.

**mishealdenness,** *for* mishealdsumness: Hal. 41, 6, v.l.

**mishworfen,** *add*: gyf þa þing mishworfene bið, IP 237.

**mislibban,** *add*: þa mæssepreostas and ða diaconas, þe misleofedan her on worulde, IP 217.

**mislimp,** *add*: diuortii, mislimpes, OEG 4, 65.

**\*mispeler,** *medlar-tree*, PNE ii, 41.

**misstīgan,** glosses *descendo*: misstigæþ, Ps. Cant. cvi, 26.

**misteltān,** *add*: uiscus, mistela, DP 19, 336.

**mistian,** *see also* ofermistian.

**miswinnan,** v. glosses *elaborare* (wrongly): miswunne, Lk., p. 2, 12, Lind.

**miswyrcan,** v. *create amiss*: (hy) wæron swaþeah misworohte wiðinnan, Hml. P. ii, 534, 68.

**mite,** *see* maþa *above*.

**-mōd,** *add* clænmod.

**mōdcwānig,** *delete, read in citation* mode cwange.

**mōdhēap,** m. *bold troop*: Ex. 242.

**mōdigness,** *add to* II: benignitatem, modignesse, Ps. Vit., Ps. Tib. li, 5.

**mōdigwǣg,** *delete, read in citation* modwæga.

**-mōdness,** *add*: for simplex see Hml. Warn 2, 36.

**mōdor,** *add to* I 3: þurh ure ealdan modor Euan, Hml. Th. i, 446, 20.

**mōdsēocness,** *substitute for meaning* distress. Cf. (*Cardiaca*) est . . . cordis passio cum formidabili metu, Isid., Et. iv, 6, 4.

**mōdþrȳðu,** *add*: *some have regarded as a proper name, others divide* mod þryðo wæg.

**mōdwǣg,** *see* modigwæg.

**molegn,** etymology discussed A. xlviii, 101.

**molsn,** *add*: tabo, molsne, OEG 28, 453.

**monaþ,** *see also* twelfmonaþ.

**mōnaþblōd,** *add*: OEG 73c, 19.

**mōrflēoge,** *a kind of fly*: cariscus, morfleoge, Nap. 14. Cf. Lindsay, *Corpus Glossary* C 150.

**morgencolla,** meaning is rather *morning slaughter*, cf. A. xxxi, 258.

**morgenlic,** add to II: *see citation above under* cirrung.

**morgenmæsse,** f. *morning mass*: þa hwile þe mon singð þa morgenmæssan, Archiv lxxxiv, 2.

**morgentīdlic,** adj. *of morning*: a custodia matutina, from gehelde morgentidlicre, Ps. Bos. cxxix, 6.

**mōrhop,** substitute for meaning *place amid moorland* (cf. fenhop).

**morten,** *for* myrten: Buss. 177, 132, v.l.

**morþ III,** translate citation from II Cnut *if murder becomes manifest, in that a man lies dead* etc.

**morðcwalu,** f. *murder*: v.l. in citation under *morþorcwalu* (= Verc.-Hom. 103, 347).

**morþorcwalu,** *add* v.l. morðcwale *to* citation.

**mose,** *moss*: muscus, DP 16, 244. (Cf. ON mosi.)

**mōtern,** *for* gemotern: praetorium, Jn. xviii, 28, Lind.

**mōthūs,** *see also* horsryne *in Suppl. and above.*

**mōtstōw,** *add*: Ps. Cant. vii, 8.

***muddig,** adj. *muddy*, PNE ii, 44.

**mundbyrdan,** *add*: II *receive protection from*: we wiorðian his þa halgan ealle, and us to ðam mundbyrden, Vercelli MS., f. 74ᵛ, 7.

**Muntgēof,** *add*: þa micclan muntas þe man Mundiu hæt, Hml. P. ii, 708, 578.

**munuc,** *add*: used of a nun, Ælf. 8.

**munucian,** *see also* un(ge)munecod.

**munucþēaw,** m. *monastic rule*: þis we þonne . . . on þissa boca munucþeawe to þy gesetton, Archiv lxxxiv, 7.

**murcnung,** second citation = A. lxv, 246, 11.

**muscelle,** *add strong forms*: musscel, Txts. 108, 1117; muscellas, Corpus Glossary G 55 (not in Txts.).

**mūsere,** m. *buzzard*: alietum, museri, OEG 36, 14; cf. A. xli, 122, note 1.

**mūshafoc,** rather *buzzard* or *kestrel*: cf. A. xli, 122, note 1.

**mustflēoge,** *see also* mustwyrm *in Suppl.*; cf. E.S. xxxviii, 299.

**mūsþēof,** add meaning *thieving mouse*.

**myl,** *add*: puluis, myl (*also* dust), Ps. Cant. cii, 14.

**-mȳlan,** *see* aliman *in Suppl. and above.*

***mylde,** *soil*, PNE ii, 46.

**mylenoxa,** m. *mill-ox*: Chart. Rob. 254, 7.

**mylma,** *delete, in citation* (= Prud. 725) *read* inylma, *inner parts (see* inylfe).

**mylnere,** m. *miller*: þæs mylneres wif, Will of Æthelgifu, ed. Whitelock, 18.

**mynd,** *for* gemynd, Festschrift Liebermann 55, 17.

**-mynd,** *add to compounds* æmynd.

**myndelice,** *for* gemyndelice, Fehr 189, 29, v.l.

**myne,** *add to II*: and ic cyðe eoy þæt myne mynna is and full leof, Chart. Harm. 423.

**mynetian,** *see also* gemynetian.

**mynian,** *add*: II *exhort* (*apparently with confusion with* mynegian): ure Drihten us munæð and læreð, Hml. Bel. 108, 29; þe apostol us munede and tæhte, id. 104, 32.

**-mynnan,** *see* yfelmynnan.

**mynsterþing,** n. *monastic property*: R. Ben. 56, 11 (v.l. for mynstres þing).

# N

**nacod,** *add to I d in Suppl.*: ge sculan unscrydon þa weofodu and standan hi swa nacode, Fehr 156, 11.

**nacudwraxlere,** m. *gymnosophist*: Ker, *Catalogue* 382 (*cited under* abered).

**nǣced,** *note nom. sg.* nǣcedu, Verc.-Hom. 157, 93.

**nǣdl,** *add*: acus, netl, Texts. 37, 66; *pictus acu*, mið nethle asiowid, 87, 1591.

**nǣgelisern,** n. *iron nail*: clauum tabernaculi (Judic. iv, 21), OEG 39, 2.

**nǣgelspere,** delete, take as two words, cf. *cuspide*, nægle oððe spere, WW 377, 15; for *unguana* read *ungula* = either *talon* (nægl) or *iron instrument* (spere).

**nǣmel,** adj. *receptive (of knowledge)*: Nap. 47.

**nǣnigþinga,** adv. *not at all*: ne mæg sio oferfyl nænigþinga to þære sawle þwerian, Verc.-Hom. 148, 117.

**nǣsc,** delete Suppl.; *tractus* in context probably = *piece of skin*.

**nǣster,** sense is *cup*, see *ease* above for refs.

**nǣt,** adj. *wet*: nataleahes æsc CS i, 417, 17; PNE ii, 48.

**nāhwanon,** *add*: II *not at all*: þæt he nahwanan his geferscipes wære, Verc.-Hom. 11, 100, v.l.

**nama,** *add to compounds* fædernama.

**nāmrǣden,** perhaps rather nāmræden, referring to *litteraturae albo* (Aldhelm, De Virg. 1016); cf. namboc, nambred; see FL 78.

**nānig,** *for* nænig: non . . . cui quam, nangum, OEG 28, 480.

**nāteþeshwon,** add: *Studies in English Philology (Miscellany Klaeber)* 271, 12.

**nāþing,** *add*: nichil, naht uel naðing, Ps. Vit. lxxv, 6.

**nāwiht,** *add*: III adj. *worthless*: serue nequam, þe esne nawiht, Mt. xviii, 32, Rush.; nequam, nawiht, id. xx, 15 (Lind. wohfull *in both*).

**nēadwīte,** *error for* nedwis wite, Hml. Warn. 111, 37 (cf. Hml. Th. ii, 338, 19).

**nēahbūr,** *for* neahgebur: nehbura (gen. pl.), II Æthelstan 9, v.l.

**nēahhian,** v. *approach*: oððet heo nehigeð neorxenewange, Hml. Warn. 147, 29. Cf. genean, onnean, genehwian.

**-nēan,** *see also* onnean.

**nēatland,** *for* geneatland, II Eadgar 1, 1, v.l.

**nebb,** *add to III*: for heo gesihð hire sune eall eallswa he is neb wið nebb (*face to face*), Hml. Warn. 138, 39.

**nediende,** ? read nēadiende, *execrandum* being taken as *exercerdum*; cf. FL 29.

**nehwǣrne,** adv. *not*: non longe, nehuarne long, Mt. viii, 30, Lind.

**nemnan,** *see also* forenemned.

**nēodlaþu,** sense is rather *invitation to pleasure* (cf. niode naman, *we took our pleasure*, B. 2116).

**nēodlice,** *add*: ðeh ði numen siæ niudlicae ob cocrum, ASPR vi, 109.

**nerian,** *see also* anerian.

**nest,** *add to compounds* feorhnest.

**nett,** *see* fleot *above.*

**nēþan,** *add*: neahtes neðyð, *it fares boldly at night*, Sal. 396.

**nicor,** *add*: nicra (*printed* mera) mengeo, Rypins, *Three Old English Prose Texts* 15, 20; cf. RES, n.s., iv, 141.

**nīd,** *see also* onnied.

**nīdbād,** *add*: he cwæð þæt him geeode þurh nedbade þæt his lichama wære seoc geworden, Wyn. 7.

**nīdbehōf,** *add*: necessaria, neodbehofe þing, Chrd. 11, 33.

**nīdfǣr,** m. *unavoidable sudden blow (i.e. death)*: in citation under nidfaru *many read* fore them neidfaerae.

**nīdfaru,** *add*: cf. nīdfǣr.

**nīdgild,** *add*: debita, neadgild, OEG 9, 96.

**nīdgylta,** m. *debtor*: debitoribus, nydgyltum, Ps. Vit., Pater noster.

***nīdrenn,** n. *temporary house*: see Löfvenberg, *Studies on ME Local Surnames* 137.

**nīgan,** *delete, read in citation* hnigende.

**nigontēoþa,** adj. *nineteenth*: oþ þa nigenteoþan, An. Ox. 2521.

**niht,** *add to compounds* upniman; lacnimende.

**nihtbuttorflēoge:** MS. has -t- (A. viii, 450); on equation with *blatta*, see FL 110.

**nihtēage,** sense is rather *inability to see in the daylight*; cf. FL 110.

**nihtgenge,** discussed FL 178.

**nihtglōm,** sense is rather *evening twilight*, cf. glom, glomung, æfengloma.

**nihtscada,** discussed FL 178.

**niman,** *add to compounds* upniman; lacnimende.

**nimþe,** cf. A. lxix, 142.

**nimung,** *see also* flæscniming.

**nip,** *delete, in citation read* niwum (*lemma falsely associated with* rudis).

**niþ,** *abyss*, doubtful word, cf. ASPR i, 245.

**niþerāsettan,** v. *depose*: deposuit, niðerasette, Ps. L., Hy. 10, 6.

**niþerāstreht,** participial adj., glosses *prostratus*, A. lxxxi, 97, 8.

**niþerāworpen,** participial adj. *cast down*: þu ðe nyþerworpene uparæst, Ker, *Catalogue* 169 (= A. lxxxi, 86, 9).

**niþerfaran,** v. *descend*: descendens, niþerfarende, A. lxxxi, 77, 2.

**niþergewend,** participial adj. *turned downward*: gif se wyrm sy nyþergewend, *if the fistula be turned downward* (i.e. is an anal fistula), Grattan and Singer, *Anglo-Saxon Magic and Medicine* 156.

**niþerian,** v. *for* geniþerian (all senses): Mt. xviii, 10, and frequently, Lind.; Jn. viii, 10, Rush.

niþerlætan, v. *allow to sink* (of the spirits): *submittere*, niþerlæten, Archiv cxvii, 22; *demissos*, niderlætene, id.

niwbacen, *add*: twelf hlafas ealle nibacene, Fehr 180, 9.

niwgecirred, *add*: nigecyrred, An. Ox. 3477.

niwian, *see also* ungeniwendlic.

nōg, adj. *for* genog: *sufficiat*, noh is, Mt. xxv, 9, Lind.

norþ, *add*: on position of this and other cardinal points in Ælfred's Orosius, see Speculum v, 139.

norþeasterne, adj. *north-eastern*: *Boreae*, norþeasternes windes, OEG 9, 136.

Norþ-Fresan, glosses *Citiorem Fresiam*, OEG 4, 343–4.

Norþgārsecg, m. *North Ocean*: Bd. iv, 16.

norþweall, m. *north wall*: bi þæm norðwalle, Chart. Rob. 36, 8.

notu, *add*: II a *use* (of a thing): hrægl þe to note ær ne com, *a cloth previously unused*, Fehr 172, 16.

noþ, *swelling* (glandular): neogone wæran noðþæs sweostor, Grattan and Singer, *Anglo-Saxon Magic and Medicine* 184.

nūhwænne, adv. *forthwith*: Verc.-Hom. 14, 118.

-numen, *see* midnumen.

nūna, *perhaps error for* nu þa, *see* nu I.

nyhtsumness, *see also* ungenyhtsumness.

nytig (Suppl.): *accept suggestion that* here nitig *is for* hereiung = hergung. Cf. JEGP xlix, 236; FL 150.

nytweorþlicness, *for* nytweorþness: *non utilitati*, na netwerþlicnes, OEG 30, 20.

# O

ōdencolc, *threshing floor in hollow*: CS ii, 34, 18; cf. wincolc.

oemsetinne, *see* ymbseten.

ofācennan, v. *produce*: ðonne syndon treowcyn, on þæm þa deorwyrþystan stanas synd ofacende (v.l. acende), Knappe, *Wunder des Ostens* 63, 6.

ofærnan, v. *overtake*. ne sceall se for horse murnan se þe wile heort ofærnan, Lunds Universitets Årsskrift lii (1956), 2, 15.

ofāwyrtrumad, participial adj. *rooted out*: *eradicabitur* ofawyrtrumad bið, Mt. xv, 13, Lind.

ofberstan, *for* oþberstan, Hal. 58, 2, v.l.

ofcirran, v.: I *turn away*: *deuertant*, ofcerdon, Lk. ix, 12, Lind., Rush.; II *overturn*: *euertit*, ofcerde, Mk. xi, 15, id.

ofclipian, *add*: II glosses *exclamare*, Mk. i, 26, Lind., Rush.; etc.

ofcuman, v. I *go out*: *ex te exiet*, from ðe ofcymes, Mt. ii, 6, Lind.; II glossing *procedere*: Mt. xv, 11; 18, id.; Mk. vii, 21, id.

ofdelfan, v. *dig up*: *effodiunt*, ofdelfes, Mt. vi, 19, Lind.; id. 20 (Rush. adelfað).

ofdēman, v. *distinguish*: *diiudicare nostis*, ofdoeme uutas, Mt. xvi, 3, Lind.

ofdōn, v. glosses *eicere*, *extrahere*, *deponere*: Mt. vii, 4, Rush.; Mk. xv, 46, Lind., Rush.; Lk. xiv, 5, Lind., Rush.

ofdūne, *add*: *deposuit*, ofdune sette, Ps. V. and Cam., Hy. 10, 7.

ofer, *add to* II (8 β): meaning practically *without*: wig ofer wæpen, B. 685; ofer ealle lufen, Dan. 73.

oferbæcgetēung, cf. also Isid., Et. iv, 6, 12, *tetanus maior est contractio neruorum a ceruice ad dorsum*; FL 111.

oferbebēodan, *probably delete*, *MS. appears to have* oft bebeode.

oferberan, v. *carry across*: ond he þa rode oferbær, Verc.-Hom. 31, 263, v.l.

oferblissian, v. gloss to *supergaudere*, Ps. Sal. and Vit. xxxiv, 19, 24.

ofercweþan, v. *repeat*: hwæt we na gehyrdon þis halige godspel . . . and þeh we hit sceolan eft ofercweþan, Bl. H. 15, 29.

oferdæg, m. *day left over in calculation*: rim þu hwæt þæra oferdaga sy, Henel, *Studien zum altengl. Computus* 55.

oferdrettan, *delete*, *read in citation* ofðreccan, *see* ofþryccan.

oferfeallan, *add*: II *fall upon*: we halsiað eow, muntas ond dena, þæt ge us oferfeallen, Verc. Först. 108, 13.

oferflēdness, f. *overflow*: *fluctuationem*, oferflednesse, Ps. Ar. liv, 23.

oferflōwend, adj., *add*: forneah ealra manna mod sint on oferflowende willan onwended, Verc.-Hom. 147, 101.

oferfrēcedness, *add*: *tribulatione*, oferfrecednessum, Ps. Vit. xxxi, 7.

ofergemet, *add*: as adj. *excessive*: to swiðe ond ofergemet, Verc.-Hom. 66, 133 (*or take as phrase* ofer gemet?).

ofergeset, *add*: II *laid on*: Lch. i, 352, 6 (*cited under* mid *above*).

ofergyrd, *note*: sense of *recincta* in context (Prud., *Perist.* x, 236) is *girt back* (of a robe).

oferhealdan, *add*: II *burden*, *hinder*: þæt is þonne se æresta deað . . . þæt se man mid mænegum synnum oferhealden bið, Verc. Först. 86, 18.

oferhragan, *delete*, *in citation read* oferbricgeð (*so probably MS.*).

oferhrēosan, v. glosses *super+cadere*: *supercecidit*, oferhreas, Ps. Sal., Vit., Ar. lvii, 9.

oferhygdness, f. *pride*: Vercelli MS. ff. 90ʳ, 11; 114ʳ, 13.

oferhyrian, *for* onhyrian, Bt. xxxvi, 6, scribal alteration.

oferhyrned, rather *with great horns*.

oferidellice, adv. *much in vain*: *superuacue*, ofyridyllice, Ps. Cam. xxx, 7; Ps. Ar. (oferidellice).

oferlēoran, *add*: I b *pass* (time): *transigeret* (*noctes*), oferleorde, OEG 4, 249.

ofermæned, participial adj. *confuted*: see citation under ofermenged in Suppl.: the 'viper' is a false accusation.

ofermenged, *delete*, *see* ofermæned.

ofermistian, v. *obscure*: *obnubilauit*, ofermistede, OEG 4, 371.

oferplantian, v. glosses *transplantare*, Lk. xvii, 5, Lind.

oferrædlice, adv. glosses *frequenter*, R. Ben. I. 93, 4.

ofersegl, *read in citation* (= Txts. 41, 209) obersegl.

oferspyrian, v. *traverse*: *tranant*, oferspyriaþ, OEG 28, 232.

oferswicol, adj. *very deceitful*: se ofersweocola wer ne þyhð, R. Ben. 30, 5 (inferior reading).

ofertalian, *error for* oferstælan, Hml. Warn. 3, 28 (twice); 70, 17.

ofertēon II, for full lemma see Oliphant, *The Harley Latin–Old English Glossary* 94 (C 1536 and note).

oferþryccedness, *for* ofþryccedness: *pressura*, oferðryccednesse, Ps. Jun. xxxi, 7; Ps. Cam. (*ofyrþriccednysse*).

oferwandian, v. *pause*, *delay*: *distuli*, oferwanude (sic), Ps. Vit., Hy. 6, 27.

oferweorpan III, substitute for sense *trip*, *stumble*.

oferweorþ, oferwirþe, *delete*, *in citation read* efenwæþe (*so MS.*).

oferwēsness, f. *excess* (in feasting): *in commessationum* (*cubilia*), in oferwesnesse, OEG 4, 259.

oferymbwendness, f. glosses *transmutatio*: oferymbwoendnise, Rtl. 28, 6.

ofesc, *add*: *also* ofes (cf. efes, efesc): swa ofes scæt oþ stæningmearce, CS i, 467, footnote 10 (*printed* ofer). Cf. MLN xxxiv, 119.

offerenda, m. *offertory hymn or psalm*: ac ge ne scylan singan offerendan on þæm dæge, Fehr 168, 15; oþ þæt man æfter þam godspelle þone offerendan singe, Archiv lxxxiv, 5, 29.

offillan, *add*: *elides*, afellis (v.l. affellis), Kluge, *Angelsächisches Lesebuch* 12, III, D 8; III, C 13 (cf. 4 Reg. viii, 12).

offrung, *see also* æfenoffrung.

offrungsang, *add*: Fehr 214, 23; 216, 11.

ofgebīged, participial adj. *past* (of the day): *declinata*, ofgebeged, Lk. xxiv, 29, Lind. (ofgibeged, Rush.).

ofgeorn, *note*: uncertain word, cf. An. Ox. 3372, n. 1; FL 53 (*of* as prep., but perhaps rather read ofergeorn).

ofgēotan, *add*: III *scatter*: *effudit*, ofgæt, Jn. ii, 15, Lind., Rush.

*ofhilde, *descent*: see Löfvenberg, *Studies on ME Local Surnames* 144.

ofhiran, *probably error for* oferhiran: ða ofherde þæt se hælend, Hml. Warn. 59, 16.

ofhrēran, v. *stir*: þæt lyft byð ofhrered, A. lxxiii, 32, 7.

ōfost (*and derivatives*), *read* ofost.

ofsetenness, *add*: yfeles ne geswicað, ond þa godan menn . . . geswencað gehu mid ofsetnyssum, Hml. P. i, 205, 199.

ofslege, *stroke*, *blow*: *strage*, OEG 2, 67 (*or read* ofslegennesse?).

ofslegenness, *see also* ofslege *above*.

ofspræc, *delete*, *citation is* of spræce *glossing* ex elogio, Ald., De laud. uirg. xxvii (cf. An. Ox. 2318).

ofsyndrige, adv. *for* syndrige: *see* framsundor.

oftacan, v. *overtake*: ond he oftoc hine, Nap. 61.

**ofþencan**, *add*: þa gemunde and ofþohte he Petrus, Verc.-Hom. 11, 101, v.l.

**ofþryccan**, *add*: *obsitus*, ofþryht, Ker, *Catalogue* 94.

**ofþylman**, citation = Verc.-Hom. 96, 273.

**ōfȳran**, *for* afyran, *see* olfend *in Dict.*

**ohtrip**, ? *read* ōhtrip (*cf.* benrip), *or* ofetrip, *fruit harvest.*

**ōlehtiend**, m. *flatterer*: *blandiens*, JEGP lvi, 65, 8.

**ōman**, *add*: *see also* horsoman *above.*

**ome**, *citation* = Hml. P. ii, 548, 23; *add*: id. 552, 130.

**ōmig**, *add*: *ferruginem, obscuritatem ferri*, omei, Txts. 63, 866.

**on**, *add to A. I 7: see* on andan, *s.v.* anda.

**onācenned**, participial adj. *inborn*: *ingenito*, onacennedum, OEG 9, 68.

**onbærness**, *add*: *incensi*, onbærnes(se), JEGP lx, 442.

**onbǣru**, substitute for meaning *self-restraint.*

**onbeflōwan**, v. *flow upon*: *effluat*, onbeflowe, Gn. 30, 3 (JV).

**onbehrēosan**, v. *fall*: *irruit super eos*, onbehreas ofer hi, Ps. Spl., Hy. 4, 16 (so Ps. Ar. and Vit).

**onbelgan**, v. *make angry*: bitere onbolgen, Seasons for Fasting 197.

**onbēotende**, participial adj., glosses *inminens*: onbiotendum, Rtl. 17, 10; etc.

**onbesettan**, v. *press into*: *inprimens limphis dimersa*, onbesettende on wæterum besenctan, Gn. 25, 2 (JV). Cf. anbesettan.

**onbindan**, v. *bind*: *ligaueris*, onbindes, Mt. xvi, 19, Lind.

**onbrǣdan**, v. *spread*: onbræddon on heo hrægl heora, Mt. xxi, 7, Rush.

**onbring**, *add*: *insti(gatione)*, of anbringe *uel* of atihtinge, JEGP lx, 447.

**onbrūcan**, v. *partake of*: þe ðe æniges þinges onbrucð (*v.l.* onbyrigð), Fehr 181, 34.

**oncnāwedness**, *for* oncnawenness, Hml. Warn. 92, 9.

**oncunnan**, *add*: II *know, be competent*: *expertus sit*, oncunnende wæs, WW 395, 11; 499, 2.

**oncȳpig**, *add*: Gu. 1226; substitute for meaning II (in Suppl.), *made known.*

**ondegeslic**, adj. *terrible*: *terribulus uel terribilis*, ahwilc, ondegslic, ondryslic (so MS., contrast WW 191, 27). See FL 54, and cf. ondeslic cited under ondryslic in Dict.

**ondrysenlice**, adv. *reverently*: þæt we hyrsumien and ondrysenlice we þæt halige godspel gehyren, Vercelli MS., f. 71ᵛ, 22.

**ondryslic**, with form ondeslic cf. ondegslic (FL 54).

**ondspyrian**, v. glosses *scandalizare* (for ondspyrnan) frequently in Lind.: Mt. xvii, 27; xxvi, 33; etc.

**onefn**, *see also* þæronefn.

**ōnettan III**, translate in Seafarer 49 *hastens to its end* (cf. Medium Ævum xxviii, 104).

**onfæstan**, *add*: þa to hide onfast his owen, Chart. Whit. 76, 24.

**onfealdan**, *add*: *reuoluam*, onfalde, OEG 28, 348.

**onfenge**, *add*: anfengce, An. Ox. 104.

**onfengenness**, f. *assumption*: *adsumptione*, onfængennesse, Ps. Bos., Hy. 2, 51.

**onfeohtende**, participial adj., glosses *inpugnans*: ða onfehtendo mec, Rtl. 167, 20.

**onforan**, *add to I*: toð onforan heafde, *front-tooth*, Ælf. 49; *add to II*: heo stod dreorig anforn gean Cristes rode, Hml. Warn. 45, 12.

**onforeweardan**, *see* foreweard.

**onfyrhtan**, *for* afyrhtan: we wæron onfyrhte, Hml. Warn. 79, 17.

**ongān**, *for* agan IV a: swa swa him syððen aneode, Hml. Warn. 36, 26; 131, 29.

**ongeagn**, *add to end of B 6*: *obiecit*, ongean wearp oððe ongen sette; *remisit*, ongen asende, Archiv cc, 197-98.

**ongēancīgan**, v. *call back*: *reuocas*, ongencigest, A. lxxxi, 86, 10.

**ongēane**, *for* ongean: *rursum*, OEG 61, 43.

**ongēanfær**, m. *return*: *regressus*, Gn. 39, 5 (JV).

**ongēangang**, glosses *occursus*: ongengang, Ps. Vit. xviii, 7; ongængan, Ps. Ar.

**ongēangeclipod**, participial adj., *called back*: *reuocatum*, ongengeclypodne, A. lxv, 236, 3.

**ongēanhwyrft**, m. *return*: *infelici reditu*, ungesæligum ongenhwyrfte, Gn. 49, 6 (JV).

**ongēanryne**, m. *return*: *recursus*, Gn. 39, 5 (JV); *recursus (siderum)*, ongeanrynas, id. 22, 2 (JV).

**ongewendedness**, f. *alteration*: *commutationem*, ongewende-[dnesse], Ps. Vit. lxxxviii, 52.

**ongratian**, citation discussed Eng. Lang. Notes ii, 246.

**ongrisla**, *add*: Willard, *Two Apocrypha in OE Homilies* 42, 12.

**onhāwian**, v. *look on*: heom onhawigendum, Hml. P. i, 342, 38.

**onhīgian**, *add*: seo tid his forðsiðes onhigað, Festschrift Liebermann 65, 6.

**onhinderling**, *add*: Hml. Bel. 104, 11.

**onhohsnian**, *add*: the meaning is uncertain, the main views are indicated ASPR iv, 217.

**onhrērness**, *see* hrerness.

**onhrōp**, *add to II*: edwit and onrop, Hml. Bel. 52, 29.

**onhyscend**, m. *mocker*: *insultatores*, onhiscen(dras) OEG 2, 175; cf. An. Ox. 4328.

**onidlian**, v. *empty*: *exinanita*, onidelude, Ps. Sal. lxxiv, 9.

**onlǣdan**, v. *bring*: nest þyder onlædde, Jud. 129.

**onlǣran**, v. *teach*: onlær þinum bearne bysne goda, IC 79.

**onlīhtan**, v. *alleviate*: oððe his wita onleoht her oððe on helle, IC 52.

**onlīhting**, *add*: Verc.-Hom. 89, 201.

**onnēan**, v. *approach*: hio annihð to ussum Hælende, Modern Philology i, 613, 19.

**onnīed**, f. *oppression*: Exod. 139.

**onopenian**, v. *open*: *aperuit*, onopenude, Ps. Sal. lxxvii, 23.

**onorettan**, *delete*, read on onette, *hastened on*, Exod. 313; on orette, *in battle*, Widsith 41.

**onorþian**, v. *inspire*: *flante*, onorþigendum, Prud. 200.

**onrād**, *add*: glosses *inequitare*, Rtl. 119, 10.

**onriht**, n.: ? *delete, take in citation as* onriht, adj. *with* cyn.

**onscǣgan**, cancel Suppl., add to Dict.: *see* scægan *below.*

**onsceacan**, *note*: gloss *detestare*, onseacan (= Txts. 57, 665) should not be emended, but removed to onsacan III a.

**onscēotan**, *add*: used in sense *disembowel* in context (Tob. vi, 5); cf. asceotan above.

**onsēcan**, *add*: feores onsæce leofne mannan, B. 1942.

**onsendan**, *add to I c*: of sacrifice, lac onsendan, Vercelli MS., f. 73ᵛ, 24.

**onsīcan**, *add*: *ingemuit*, onsāc, OEG 61, 23.

**onsittan**, *add*: I a *apply oneself*: *institissent*, onsittaþ, Prud. 441.

**onsittend**, *add*: *ascensorem*, upstigynd *uel* onsittend, Ps. Cam., Hy. 4, 2.

**onspǣtan**, v. *blow upon*: *insufflans*, onspætende, JEGP lx, 447; *inspirans*, onspætende (*printed* onswætende, onspecende), WW 425, 34; 526, 1; cf. Philological Quarterly xl, 317.

**onsprengan**, v. *sprinkle*: onsprenge (MS. onsprengde) man þæne wætan mid haligwætere, Buss. 193, 470, v.l.

**onstandan**, *add*: IV, *approach, threaten*: *instat tempus*, onstent tima, Gn. 48, 3 (JV).

**onstellan**, *note*: *last citation in Dict.* (= Txts. 69, 1038) *does not belong here, but to* *onstielde, adj. *fit, useful.*

**onstielde**, *see* onstellan.

**onstyde**, adv. *at once*: *statim*, Mk. i, 10, Rush.

**onstyredness**, *for* onstyreness: Ps. Bos. cxx, 3.

**ontrymman**, v. glosses *inualescere*: ontrymmedon, Lk. xxiii 5, Lind., Rush.; id. 23, Lind.

**ontȳdre**, *in second citation* (= WW 226, 20) *read* ortydre.

**onþēodan**, v. glosses *inhaerere*: onðiodendo, Rtl. 9, 12.

**onþicgan**, *partake of*: sona swa he þæs ofætes onþah, Verc.-Hom. 66, 130 (v.l. onbyrigde).

**onþrecan**, v. refl. *be afraid*: and hine for þy ege swiðlice onþræc, Guth. Gr. 132 v.l.

**onþringan**, *add*: II *press on*: þeodmægen guðcyste onþrang, Exod. 343; ac him þæt folc an þrang, Oros. 134, 18.

**onweald**, *add*: *sceptra*, onwald, Txts. 95, 1800.

**onweaxan**, v. glosses *increscere*: onwæxes (3 sg.), Mt., p. 4, 2, Lind.

**onwece**, *incitement*: *incitamento*, OEG 4, 123 (? *or for* onwecenesse, *cf.* ofslege *above*).

**onwendedlicness**, f. *changeability*: *mutabilitate*, onwendedlicnysse, Archiv cc, 198.

**onwrēon**, *add to II 1 b*: gif his gyltas digle beoð, onwreo ða (*printed* onwreoða) his abbode, R. Ben. 72, 5.

**onwunian**, *add*: III *approach, threaten*: *tempus instat*, tima onwunað, Hy. Surt. 56, 8.

**openian**, *see also* onopenian.

**ōra**, *a species of money*, *add*: cf. Whitelock, *Eng. Hist. Doc.* 403.

**orc**, *cup*, delete citation Germ. 397, 514, for which see *blodorc* above.

**orc**, *infernal regions*, delete; gloss *orcus*, orc (Txts. 80, 698; 83, 1454; WW 123, 18) belongs to orc, *cup* (lemma error for *urceus* or *orca*). *See also* orcþyrs.

**orcnēas**, substitute for meaning *evil spirits, walking corpses* (cf. Hoops, *Beowulfstudien* 19).

**orcþyrs**, delete, in citation (s.v. orc) read *orcus*, þyrs.

**ord**, *add to* I: attres ord, *envenomed point*, Jul. 471, Cri. 768. (*Perhaps read in Jul.* attres oroþ, cf. Sol. and Sat. 221).

**\*ōreblāwere**, m. *smelter*, PNE ii, 56.

**orenlicost**, adv. superl. *to excess*: þa he fedde his lichoman orenlicost, Verc.-Hom. 96, 281.

**orfgebitt**, substitute for meaning *cattle-food*; cf. FL 111.

**orfirmþa**, note v.l. fyrmþa, see Studia Germanica Gandensia ii, 91.

**organe**, *delete* organon, *Ph. 136 has* organon (gen. s.).

**organe**, *marjoram*: add meanings: *wild thyme, pennyroyal*; add citations: *serpillum* and oþrum naman organe, Lch. i, 216, 3 (cf. DP 17, 304); *poleium*, organa, OEG 36, 4.

**ormǣte**, adj., *add*: substantively, *molibus*, ormetum, Txts. 79, 1326.

**ormǣtlic**, *add*: þa ahofan þa awyrigdan deoflu swiðe ormǣtlicne hiaf, Wyn. 159; mid swiðe ormǣtlice gefean, id. 182.

**orrest**, substitute for meaning *trial by combat* (cf. EGS v, 85).

**orscylde**, adj. *guiltless*: orscyldne (MS. scyldum) eofota, El. 423.

**ortrēowþ**, f. *despair*: *desperatio*, ortrywða, Ker, *Catalogue* 94. *See also* onorþian.

**orþian**, *see also* onorþian.

**orwīge**, add to meanings under I, *unwarlike*.

**orwirþe**, *add*: *disgraced, defeated*: *uictum*, orwyrde, OEG 27, 34.

**orwīte**, adj., *free from punishment*: Ælf. 42, 5 and 7, *v.l. for* orwige.

**ostre**, *add*: Fehr 180, 32.

**ōþer**, conj. for oððe, *or*: see citations s.v. healic above, and in OED s.v. other, conj. and adv.² A. a. (all 12th cent.).

**ōþerhwīle**, *add*: *aliquando*, Ps. Sal. xliii, 8; oðerhuile, Lk. xxii, 32, Lind., Rush.; with reduced force, glossing *modo*: Mt. ix, 18, Lind.

**oþhylde**, *delete*, *in citations MS. reads* eðhylde, eðhelde (cf. A. lxvii, 102).

**oþlengan**, v. *appertain to*: he nyste þæt hit to synna oðlengde, Wyn. 54; id. 74.

**oweb**, note: *in first citation MS. has* ab.

**oxa**, *add to compounds* mylenoxa.

**oxantunge**, f. *an unknown plant*: DP 221, 222.

# P

**\*padde**, *toad*, PNE ii, 58.

**pǣcung**, *add*: f. *deception*: *inlecebris*, pecunges (sic), OEG 24, 32.

**pærl**, *note*: *enula*, pærl, occurs also A. viii, 451, and JEGP lx, 446; pærl is probably *pearl*, and the lemma corrupt (? read *gemmula*; or *pennula* taken as *perula*, as gloss is in list of writing materials, SHG 29).

**pæþ**, *add to compounds* gedwolpæþ.

**palm**, note: *form* pælme, Rtl. *only, perhaps from Lat.* palmeus.

**palstr**, *add*: *cuspide*, palestre (sic), OEG 28, 230; on lemma see Isidore, Etym. xviii, 7, 11.

**\*pamp**, *hill*, PNE ii, 59.

**pardus**, m. *leopard*: þa syllican pardes, Hex. 14, 9; pardus (pl.), Rypins, *Three Old English Prose Texts* 17, 12.

**\*pat(t)e**, *mud*, see PNE ii, 60.

**pāwa**, *add*: *pauos*, peun, OEG 43, 5.

**\*pēac**, *hill*, PNE ii, 60.

**\*peall**, *ledge*, PNE ii, 59.

**\*pearr**, *enclosure*, PNE ii, 60.

**pening**, *see* casering *above, and add*: xx silice in uno pendice sunt, Philologica Pragensis, viii, 306; note also Latinised pendicum, pendica, Hessels, *A Late Eighth-century Anglo-Saxon Glossary* 29.

**peran**, *see* landperan.

**\*peren**, adj. *growing pears*, PNE ii, 62.

**perewōs**, see also FL 140.

**picbred**, ? *read* picgbread, *pig-food*. Cf. \*picga, and see FL 140.

**\*piced**, adj. *pointed*, PNE ii, 63.

**\*picga**, *young pig*, see PNE ii, 64.

**pidu**, *marsh*: innan Pidewællan, CS ii, 155, 3 from below; PNE ii, 64.

**Pierisc**, note: *MS. reads* pueriscan, *puerio*.

**pillsāpe**, add meaning *depilatory* (lemma = *psilothrum*); cf. Neophilologus viii, 204.

**pilstocc**, *see also* pilstre *below*.

**pilstre**, *delete, MS. reads* pilstoc.

**pin**, f. *pain, torment*: on helle pine, Hml. Warn. 25, 28.

**pinca**, *for* finca: æt Pincanheale, Chr. 788; PNE ii, 65.

**pinecwalu**, f. *for* suslcwalu, Wlfst. 238, 23; 241, 13 (*cited under* suslcwalu *in Dict.*).

**pinn**, *see also* dægmælespinn.

**pipere**, *add*: *tibicines*, piperas, OEG 28, 298.

**pipineale**, *pimpernel*: *pipinella*, DP 275.

**Piresc**, adj. *Pyrenean*: *see last citation in Suppl. s.v.* cnoll (= Prud. 676).

**\*pisen**, adj. *growing peas*, PNE ii, 66.

**pistelari**, *epistolar*: Chart. Rob. 250, 17.

**piþa**, *add*: *hilum i. medulla penne*, peoþa, A. xli, 101, 18.

**plǣsc**, *pool*: ærest of plæsc in þone broc, CS iii, 356, 6; PNE ii, 66.

**planēta**, citation = Festschrift Liebermann 47, 14.

**plantian**, *add to compounds* oferplantian.

**plegan**, *add to* IV: he mid bæm handum upweard plegade, El. 804.

**plegdic**, *ditch near where sports were held*: to plegidic, CS ii, 575, 19; of plegdic, id. iii, 212, 22.

**plegere**, *see* nacudwraxlere *above*.

**\*pleget**, *play*, PNE ii, 67.

**plegscip**, discussed FL 111.

**\*plegstall**, *for* plegstow, PNE ii, 67.

**plicettan**, *delete, see* plyccan *in Suppl*.

**plicgan**, take under plyccan.

**plōg**, *add*: ploges land, *a measure of land, a carucate or oxgang* (cf. oxangang s.v. gang), Chart. Rob. 164, 25.

**plyccan**, take here plicgan in Dict., see note to Prud. 598.

**\*plysc**, *for* plæsc, PNE ii, 68.

**pollegie**, cf. organe *above*.

**\*polra**, *marshy land*, PNE ii, 69.

**popelstān**, *see* papolstan *in Dict*.

**popig**, on equation with *cucumis* see Lindsay, *The Corpus Glossary* 199; A. xlvii, 36.

**popul**, perhaps rather *pebble*, cf. popelstan.

**pos**, *add*: ad catarrum, wyþ posa, OEG 73c, 22.

**pottere**, m. *potter*: on potteres lege, CS iii, 49, 4 from below.

**\*prāw**, *look-out place*, PNE ii, 72.

**preg**, m. *stick, stake*: *sudes*, pregas, OEG 38, 3.

**\*prēostgird**, f. *ecclesiastical staff*: see breostgird above and FL 8.

**price**, m. *sharp point*: *stimulos*, pricces, OEG 24, 15 (*or read* precels?).

**price**, *for* prica: *apex*, price, OEG 28, 184.

**princa**, *see* pynca *in Dict*.

**\*pritol**, adj. *prattling*, PNE ii, 73.

**pryfet**, m. *privet copse*: æt pryfetes flodan, Chr. 755; þurh ðone pryuet, C.D. iv, 108, 28; PNE ii, 74.

**pucian**, discussed Prud. 664, note.

**pudd**, perhaps rather *cut*, the sense of the lemma in context (Prud. 793).

**\*puddel**, *pond*, PNE ii, 74.

**pullian**, *see also* wullian.

**pund**, add to I: *figuratively*: hiora synna pund, Wyn. 47.

**\*pund**, *enclosure, pound*, PNE ii, 74.

**punian, punere**, *read* ū.

**purpur**, *purple* (noun): *see* blæc *in Suppl*.

**\*putta, puttoc**, *kite*, PNE ii, 75.

**pylewer**, *pillow*: *ceruical*, pylewer, An. Ox. 56, 16; *ceruical*, pylwere, OEG 4, 227; cf. pulawer, Ælfric's Grammar, MS. F., f. 144ᵛ (not in Zupitza).

**\*pyndfald**, *for* pundfald, PNE ii, 75.

**pyttel**, substitute for meaning *buzzard*, see A. xli, 122, note 1.

# R

**rād,** *add to compounds* unrad.

**rādian,** *for* geradian, Fehr 131, 34, v.l.

**radre,** *delete, error for* rudre = hryþre.

**ræcedlic,** *read in citation* (= Txts. 83, 1479) raecedlic.

**ræd,** *add to* I: (he) feoll ... mid eallum ðam englum ðe æt his ræde wæron, Hex. 318.

**rædan,** *add to compounds* þurhrædan.

**ræde,** *reading, see also* bocræde *above*.

**ræden,** *add to compounds* forarǣden.

**rædend,** *add: reader,* Hml. Warn. 94, 6; 12.

**rædesceamol,** *substitute for meaning* lectern, *cf.* rǣdingsceamol in Suppl. *and* FL 92.

**rædfæst,** *see also* unrǣdfæst.

**raedgasram,** *add:* apparently a constellation, see Archiv clxviii, 235.

**rǣdic,** *add:* arboratio (for armoracia, horse-radish), uilde redic, DP 40.

**rædleas,** *add:* citatus, redeleas, Ker, *Catalogue* 323.

**rædlice,** *see also* oferrǣdlice.

**ræfsung** *for* ræpsung, Kansas leaf.

**ræghār,** *read* rǣghār, *grey with lichen.*

**-rǣpe,** *see* forrǣpe.

**rǣplingweard,** *note* Isid., *Etym.* ix, 4, 29: *collegiati dicuntur, quod ex eorum collegio custodiisque deputentur, qui facinus aliquod commiserunt.*

**rǣran,** *see also* ge-, up(a)rǣran.

**ræsc,** *delete second citation, see* næsc *above.*

**\*rætten,** *adj. infested with rats,* PNE ii, 79.

**ræw,** *add to compounds* hæsel-, hegeræw.

**ragu,** *see also* beorcragu.

**rahwan,** runic inscription of unknown meaning, see *Medieval and Linguistic Studies* (ed. Bessinger and Creed) 44.

**\*rān,** *boundary strip,* PNE ii, 80.

**rancstrǣt,** *add:* cf. Archiv cii, 269.

**rāredumla,** *l. 3 in Dict., insert* ii *before* 63, 70; *add:* bubanus, raredumble, OEG 69, 11.

**rārian,** *add to* I: mid rarigendre stæmne, Hml. Warn. 30, 35.

**rēad,** *add to compounds* felle-, rosread.

**rēada,** *note: toles, tolia* probably mean *tonsil,* cf. Isid., *Etym.* xi, 1, 57.

**rēadgoldlǣfer,** *is perhaps two words,* v.l. read 'e' go(l)dlæfer, see *Studia Germanica Gandensia* ii, 91.

**rēadlesc,** *perhaps read in citation* readlestum (*for* -læstum, *see* læst), *as reference is to boots of red leather* (Aldhelm, ed. Giles, 77, 16; ed. Ehwald, 318, 3).

**rēadung,** *f. redness:* rubor, Gn. (Archiv cxcxix, 22).

**rēaf,** *add to compounds* cynereaf.

**recan,** first citation is doubtful, see Prud. 621.

**reccan,** *see also* up(a)reccan.

**rēcel** f., *for* recels: mid þinre recele, Hml. Warn. 6, 23.

**receleas,** *add to meanings* wanton; *add to citations:* proteruo, receleasre, OEG 28, 370.

**recondlic,** *adj. numerous:* numerosis, recondlicum, Ps. Sal. lxxvii, heading.

**redeleas,** *see first citation in Dict. under* rædleas, *and* rædleas *above. Perhaps a separate word* (cf. redian).

**Redlingas,** n. pl. *Ethiopians:* Ethyopia, Redlingum, Ps. Cant. lxvii, 32. (*Or miswritten for* wedlingum = (et) inopia?).

**regallic,** *adj. splendid:* enormes ... grates, regalican. gife, JEGP lix, 711, 5.

**regnian,** *see also* ungeregnod, unrinad.

**regniend,** *MS. has* wemend.

**regnweard,** *delete, see* renweard.

**renweard,** m. *one who is present in a building:* reþe renweardas (*Beowulf and Grendel*), B. 770; cf. rendegn s.v. ærnþegen.

**rēod,** *red colouring, add:* ex minio, of ræudæ, Mt. p. 4, 3, Lind.

**rēodan,** *add* B. 1151 (*cited under* hroden).

**rēodian,** *add:* erubescentes, reodiende, Ps. Sal. lxix, 4.

**rēof,** *see* eofot *above.*

**reohhe,** *add: fannus,* hreohche, JEGP lx, 446, x, 32. *See also* ruhha *below.*

**rēon,** ? *delete, read in citation* reonge.

**rēone,** *see* unreone.

**rēonung,** *citation in Suppl. is more fully* steorwigele, mearcunge, reonunge, *which implies* steorreonung, *prophecy through stars. See* mearcung *above.*

**rēot,** *substitute* rōetu, *and connect with* retan, *not with* reotan.

**rēow,** *add:* An. 1116 (MS. hreow); Rid. 81, 2 (MS. hreoh).

**repan,** *add: quod serimus metimus,* þæt we sawað, þæt we repað, OEG 24, 9.

**rēstan,** *exult: see* ASPR v, 222, *for many emendations, but the word may be simply* rēstan, *rest, see* FL 179.

**resthūs,** *add:* leo on resthuse (spelunca) his, Ps. Vit. ix, 30.

**rētan,** add to meanings *relieve (medically);* see citation from Lchdm.

**rēpe** I, *note:* in citation Wrt. Voc. ii, 151, 77 (= WW 245, 16), the lemma is probably *furalia* (= *furiale*) *i. seua;* see Oliphant, *The Harley Latin–Old English Glossary* 204.

**rēplice,** *substitute:* rēpelice, adv. *fiercely:* uiolenter, roeðelice, Txts. 105, 2116; þe leig reþelice bærneð, Hml. Bel. 126, 15.

**ribbe,** add meaning *ribwort; add to citations* DP 12, 119; 17, 282, OEG 73 a, 5. Cf. hundes tunge *in Dict. and above,* læcewyrt *in Dict.*

**ric,** *narrow strip* (land or water): of þam gemyþam up be midderice, CS ii, 575, 24; PNE ii, 83.

**rīce,** adj., *see also* felarice.

**ricettan,** *delete, MS. has* riceter (noun), see *Studia Germanica Gandensia* ii, 91.

**rīclic,** *add: summis,* riclicum, Ker, *Catalogue* 3.

**ricsian,** *see also* gericsian.

**rida,** *riding path:* æt Leodridan, Harmer, *Historical Documents* 17, 22.

**rīfness,** f. *fierceness:* rabiem, rifnisse, OEG 4, 329. Cf. hrife.

**rige,** *add: siliga i. genus frumenti,* rige, A. xli, 102, 22.

**riht,** adj., *add to* V: to rihtes nones, *The Anglo-Saxons* 276, 11; 278, 18.

**rihtcynn,** *add:* Will of Æthelgifu, ed. Whitelock, 35.

**rihte,** *add to compounds* ætrihte, birihte.

**rihtebegitan,** pl. *honest gains:* ne hit ræd ne bið þæt we rihtebegytan myrran, IP 261.

**rihtes,** *see also* ætrihtes.

**rihtgebrōþor,** m. pl. *full brothers:* germanos, rehtgibroðro, Rtl. 57, 4.

**rihtgelēafa,** m. *true belief:* for ures drihtenes rihtgeleafan, Fehr 138, 22.

**rihtgewittelic,** adj. *rational:* anima rationalis, seo rihtgewittelice sawl, Ps. Sal., Hy. 15, 37; id. 32.

**rihthlāford,** *add:* Verc.-Hom. 116, 85, v.l.

**rihthycgende,** participial adj., *thinking rightly:* Seasons for Fasting 205.

**rihtlīf,** *add:* gif hwa fæmnan forstele, nime hy eft to rihtlife, Hal. 72, 11.

**rihtlīfend,** participial adj. *of right belief:* Rtl. 116, 22.

**rihtwer,** *legal wergild:* toeacan þam rihtwere, Hadbot 2 (Liebermann, *Gesetze* i, 466).

**rihtwīf,** *add:* Will of Æthelgifu, ed. Whitelock, 36.

**rīm,** *add to compounds* underrim, *and see also* hæmeddream, un(ge)rimedlic.

**rimpan,** *see also* rempan *in Dict. and* FL 89, SHG 109.

**rimuc,** *boundary, edge:* to Rimucwude, *Ringwood,* CS iii, 84, 6 from below; PNE ii, 83.

**rind,** *add: cinamomum uel cimini,* sutherne rind, DP 12, 115; *resina,* sutherne rinde, id. 17, 288.

**rind,** *perhaps hill:* ab occidente Rindburna, CS i, 266, 21; on rinda crundel, id. iii, 222, 8; PNE ii, 83.

**rindeclifre,** *perhaps rather nuthatch,* cf. A. xl, 117, n. 7.

**ripp,** ? *border:* ad silbam qui appellatur Ripp, CS i, 231, 12; PNE ii, 84.

**ripþ,** f. *harvest:* messis, OEG 24, 23.

**rīsan,** *add to compounds* berisan.

**\*riscett,** *rush-bed,* PNE ii, 85.

**risenness,** *see also* uparisness.

**\*rispe,** *brushwood,* PNE ii, 85; (? *or* hrispe).

**\*rispett,** *place with much undergrowth,* PNE ii, 85.

**-rist,** *see* (eft)ærist, uprist.

**rīþ,** *see also* brocriþ.

**rocc,** *upper garment,* delete first citation, MS. reads socc, see *Journal of the British Archaeological Association* xli, 148.

**roccian,** v. *rock* (in cradle): *see* swaþian.

**rōd,** *add:* Suppl. V is a distinct word with ŏ, see PNE i 86, and cf. burgrod.

**rodd**, *rod*: ða het se gerefa . . . hi be þam fotan upp ahon and mid greatum roddum beaton, Hml. A. 173, 119.

**rōdestān**, m. *stone cross*: on rodestan, CS iii, 31; PNE ii, 87.

**rōf**, ? *number* (cf. secgrof): haligra rof, ASPR vi, 11, 24.

**rōmian**, *add*: cf. MLN lxxii, 1.

**ropwærc**, *add*: OEG 73 c, 24.

**rōsrēad**, adj. *rose-red*: roscos, rosreade, Archiv cc, 197.

**rostian**, *delete, MS. in citation reads* geroscode.

**rōt**, *root*: he leofede be wyrtan rotan, Nap. 54.

**rōtfæst**, adj. *firmly established*: gif he mihte ben rotfest on Engleland, Chr. 1127.

**rotian**, *see also* gerotian.

**roþ**, *clearing*: decem mansas eum Roðe, CS ii, 451, 24; PNE ii, 98.

**rōþer**, *see also* geroþor.

*****roþer**, *clearing*, PNE ii, 88.

**roþhund**, *delete final citation, see* broþhund.

**rūde**, *scab*: scamma = squama (cf. SHG 70); cf. also A. xxx, 253.

**rūh**, *see also* anhealfruh.

**ruhha**, m. *ray* (fish): fannus, ruhha (MS. suhha), Nap. 14. *See* reohhe.

**ruine**, f. *fall*: heahgæ torræs ond clifæs . . . þe mare rune nimæð, gif heo . . . fællæþ, Hml. Bel. 130, 11.

**rūm**, *see also* unrum.

**rūma**, *add*: *stumbling-block*: offendiculum, scandalum, A. xli, 102, 20. Delete citation in Dict. (= WW 223, 25) where MS. has *ruina*, which should perhaps be read in A. xli also. Cf. FL 56.

**rūmgāllice**, citation = Verc.-Hom. 75, 42.

**rūmheortlice**, adv. *generously*: ða ðe her rumheortlice hyra ælmessan . . . dælað, Verc.-Hom. 83, 119.

**rūmmōdlic**, adj. *for* rummod: benigno fauore, rummodlicum helpe, Rtl. 17, 18.

**rūnung**, *add*: openlice and . . . na mid runungum, Hml. P. i, 380, 33; 47. *See also* sundorrunung.

**rupe**, *see* drisn *above*.

**rusele**, *fat*: aruina, rusele, Prud. 280. Cf. rysel.

**rūwe**, *see* drisn *above*.

*****rȳd**, *clearing*, PNE ii, 89.

*****ryding**, *****ryden**, *****ryþer**, *clearing*, PNE ii, 90–91. Cf. geryþer.

*****rȳhþ**, *rough ground*, PNE ii, 91.

**ryne**, *add to compounds* eorþ-, gear-, ongeanryne.

**rynig**, *read* rȳnig, *good in counsel*.

**rȳnisc**, adj. *mysterious*: rex misticus, cyningc renisc, Gn. 37, 3 (V).

**ryplen**, *substitute for meaning* made of twigs, *delete bracket*, cf. Prud. 843, note.

**rysciht**, *add*: on ðone reschtan garan, CS i, 182, 29.

**ryscsecg**, *delete, MS. has* (in secret writing) *betwix seccas, cf.* Prud. 813, note.

**ryt**, *rubbish for burning*: gif fyr sie ontended ryt to bærnanne, Ll. Lbmn. i, 36, 27. Cf. Löfvenberg, *Studies on ME Local Surnames* 171.

*****ryþ**, *****ryþer**, *clearing, see* geryþer, *and cf.* PNE ii, 91.

# S

**sacc**, *add to compounds* hydsacc.

**sacenness**, *see* forsacenness.

**sacian**, *add to compounds* insacian.

**sacleas**, *add*: scer ond sacleas, *clear and undisputed*, Chart. Rob. 240, 2; Chart. Harm. 262, 10, and note, 479.

**-sacung**, *add*: forsacung.

**sadian**, *add to II*: Seasons for Fasting 224. *See also* a-, gesadian.

**sadolfæt**, n. *harness*: Chart. Whit. 80, 22.

**sadolgearwe**, f. pl. *saddle-trappings, harness*: 11. hors mid sadelgaran, Chart. Whit. 74, 11.

**sadolgerǣdu**, n. pl. *saddle-trappings*: sadulgerædo, Will of Æthelgifu, ed. Whitelock, 42.

**sǣ**, *add to compounds* middelsæ.

**sǣǣbbung**, *in citation s.v.* æbbung *meaning is* ebb, FL 112.

**sǣǣlfen**, *add*: OEG 71, 6.

**sǣccing**, *add*: II of a topographical feature: oð loddæræs sæccinge, CS ii, 94, 9.

*****sǣge**, *swamp*, PNE ii, 93.

*****sǣge**, adj. *swampy*, PNE ii, 93.

**sǣgēap**, rather *curved for use at sea*, see geap in Suppl.

**sǣgedness**, *add*: Fehr 106, 10, v.l.

**sǣhund**, cf. FL 138.

**sǣl**, *add to compounds* ealusæl.

**sǣminte**, *nereta = nepeta* (see DP 62, 250).

**sǣmotu**, *delete, motu is for* motus (Lat.), *lemma is* flustra.

**sǣstān**, m. *rock in the sea*: cautes uel murices, scearpe sæstanas, WW 147, 40 (as corrected A. viii, 451); cf. Isid., Et. xvi, 3, 3.

**sǣswelg**, *whirlpool*: to þan seswelwe, CS ii, 474, last line.

**sǣþerige**, *add*: satureia, saðrige, OEG 66, 5. *See also* suþerige *in Dict.*

**sǣðrene**, *error for* suðrene (wudu), WW 301, 33; *see* suþerne *in Dict.*

**saftriende**, sense is rather *rheumy*, cf. s.v. drefliende in Dict. and Suppl.

**sagu**, *l. 3 of IV in Dict., for* fatidicum *read* fatidictu (so MS., see WW 235, 30), *and see* Oliphant, *The Harley Latin–Old English Glossary* 176.

*****saliht**, adj. *grown with willows*, PNE ii, 96.

**salpanra**, discussed SHG 52.

**samodēce**, adj. *coeternal*: cum coaeterno patre, mid samodecum fæder, A. lxxxi, 117, 7.

**samodgeheriendlic**, *omit* -ge- (so MS.).

**samodgiddung**, f. *harmony*: prophete consono, witegan samodgeddunge (inept glossing), Hy. Surt. 109, 11 (= Gn. 90, 3, V).

**samodherung**, *add*: conlaudatio, samodhering, Ps. Cant. xxxii, 1.

**samodweaxan**, v. glosses concrescere, Ps. Vit., Hy. 6, 2.

**samodwillung**, discussed FL 79.

**samswēge**, delete query in Suppl., see A. xli, 104, 32, and note.

**samweaxen**, *citation* = Hml. P. i, 432, 311.

**sand**, f.: *add to II*: [cf. Icel. sending, *dish of meat*].

**sandrid**, discussed SHG 41.

**sang**, *add to compounds* cantic-, unsang.

*****sāpere**, *soap-dealer*, PNE ii, 97.

**sār**, n., *add to compounds* hlance-, hypsar.

**sārig**, *add*: III *as noun, sar, suffering*: seo Drihtene lof ond deofle sarege, Hml. Warn. 88, 13; bitere byð þa saregan þe heo sculen . . . geðrowigen, id. 142, 19.

**sāwlian**, *add*: II *provide with a soul*: ær ðon hit gesawlad wære (of the embryo), Buss. 184, 281.

**scād**, *for* gescead: gyldan scad wordum wið god, Be Domes Dæge 73.

**scaefr**, glosses *farrago, brora* (? Latin or OE), Kluge, *Angelsächs. Lesebuch*, 3 ed., 9, 29.

**scǣgan**, v. *jeer*: and ða deoflu scægdon . . . þæt hi ða sawla for heora synnum habban moston, Hml. Th. ii, 350, 30 (cf. Medium Ævum i, 137). *See also* onscægan.

**scandwyrde**, adj. *speaking abusively*: and wið scandwyrde we olæcað georne, IP 264.

**scanomodu**, runic inscription of unknown meaning, see *Medieval and Linguistic Studies* (ed. Bessinger and Creed) 43.

**scēadan**, *add to compounds* togescead.

**sceadu**, *add to III*: swina sceadu, *pigsty*, or *pigs' pasture* (cf. swinsceadu in Suppl.), Txts. 99, 1954. *Cf.* swaþu *below, and on lemma see* Lindsay, *Corpus Glossary* 209.

**sceadwian**, *see also* besceadwian.

**scēadwīs**, *see also* un(ge)sceadwīs.

**sceaft**, *add to compounds* insceaft.

**sceal**, *see* lamsceal.

**scealfor**, cognates suggest rather *cormorant*, A. xli, 111, note 5.

**scealga**, add meaning *rudd*, see OED s.v. shallow sb².

*****scealu**, adj. *shallow*, PNE ii, 100.

**sceamigendlic**, adj. *causing shame*: pl. as noun *private parts*: ond nyste þonne mid hwam he his sceamigendlican bewruge, Hml. P. ii, 779, 119.

**sceamm**, adj. *short*: scammandun and scortanwida, CS iii, 362, 16; on sceomman hrycge, id. ii, 141, 3 from below.

**scēap**, *see also* geldsceap.

**sceapenness**, *for* gesceapenness: ne nan yfel ne com þurh godes sceapenesse, Hml. A. 81, 8.

**scearnbudda** *for* scearnwibba, Ælfc. Gr. Z. 308, v.l.

***scearnig**, adj. *dirty*, PNE ii, 102.

**scēat**, *p*. 826, *col*. 2, *l*. 9, *in Dict. for* feder- *read* feþer-.

**scēatcodd**, perhaps delete macron, see FL 180.

**scēatline**, delete bracket in l. 2.

**sceatt**, *add to I*: nime hire ōriddan sceat, *let her keep her third of the property* (*of herself and her husband*), Ine 57; *add to I a*: hæbbe ælc cniht mealtes anne sester and sceat huniges, Chart. Th. 614, 1 (cf. Icel. skattr, *portion of food*).

**scēap**, *wing, see* hornsceap *above*.

**sceaþa**, *nail*, probably delete, forms in citation are gen. pl. of sceaþa, *injury*, as *figuram* (*locum*) *clauorum* is explained as *mark* (*place*) *of the injuries*.

**sceapfulness**, *see also* ungescæþfulness.

**scēapian**, *sheathe, see* unsceapian.

**sceaþu**, *for* sceþþu, *injury*: hio . . . mislice sceaþe on him fehð, Verc.-Hom. 143, 75; na mare scaðe awritan, Chr. 1079 (D).

**sceaþung**, *add*: sceaðunga (*pl. in list of sins*), Vercelli MS., f. 111ʳ, 19.

**scēawere IV**, *citation in Suppl.* = Hml. P. i, 445, 539.

**scēawian**, *add*: VII *show*: he sceawæð hine seluen on engles hywe, Hml. Bel. 104, 1; id. 110, 12; sceawe us þone Fæder, Hml. Warn. 77, 19. *Add to compounds* ætsceawian.

**scēawungstōw**, *add*: *in specula, in consideratione*, on sceawungstowe, JEGP lx, 447, XI, 20.

***scēla**, *hut on summer pasture*, PNE ii, 103.

**scele**, *discretion*: ða godspelles wæren mid swyðe mycelen wisdome ond scele gewritene, Hml. Warn. 145, 4. Cf. unscellice.

**scelle**, *probably delete, inflected form of* scell (*see* scill *in Dict.*); *lemma* = conchis *or* conchylium.

**scencel, scencen**, add meaning *pig's trotter*; *lemma* = acron; see FL 141.

**scenn**, substitute for meaning *unknown part of sword-hilt*, cf. Davidson, *Sword in Anglo-Saxon England* 138.

**scentu**, *see* gescentu.

**scēo**, *add*: discussed Jahrbuch des Vereins für niederdeutsche Sprachforschung lxxxvii, 24.

**scēo**, *shelter*: to Sceobyrig, Chr. 894 (A); on Sceon, Chart. Whit. 4, 21. Cf. PNE ii, 106.

**scēotan**, *add to compounds* ætsceotan.

**scēotere**, m. *shooter*: Sagittarius, þæt is Sceotere (v.l. *for* Scytta), De temp. ann. 28; OEG 63, 31.

**scēr**, *see* sacleas *above*.

**sceþþig**, substitute for meaning *guilty*; *add*: gyf þu scæððig wære, gewænd þe fram yfele, Hml. Warn. 16, 5.

**sceþþiglice**, *see* unsceþþiglice.

**sceþþigness**, *add*: f. *harm*: gesund gehealden fram þara lega sceaððignesse, Wyn. 38. *See also* ungescaðignyss.

**scild III**, accept meaning *back*, cf. JEGP lxiv, 158.

**scildian**, *protect, see* bescildian.

**scildness**, *add*: Hept., Gen. xiv, 20, v.l.

**scilfor**, sense is rather *glittering*; in both citations it is linked with glæteriendum; and see Verc.-Hom. 100, 324, note.

**scilfrig**, *for* scilfor: scilfrium (dat. sg.), An. Ox. 532.

**scilfrung**, delete from meanings *balancing*, and add *flickering*; in l. 4 *for* libramine *read* bibramine (= uibramine).

**scilian**, *add to compounds* toscilian.

**scill**, f. *see also* hennescill.

**scill**, adj., *add*: concisium (*for* concisum), scelle, Txts. 53, 564. (For lemma, cf. concisius, hludur, WW 379, 14).

**scilling**, *add*: III *an ornament like a coin, or made from a coin*: lunulas, scillingas, OEG 55, 5. (Cf. menescilling.)

**scimrian**, *in l. 1 in Dict. for* wætes *read* wæles.

**scīnan**, *add to compounds* upscinan.

**scincræftig**, adj. *skilled in magic*: fantasmaticis Satanæ, scinncræftiges, A. lxv, 235, 6.

**scinere**, *add*: *actor*.

**scinfeld**, discussed FL 141.

***scingol**, = scindel, PNE ii, 121. Cf. *scindula*, scingul, MS. Cott. Faust. A. x., f. 93ʳ.

**scinn**, for another possible instance see A. xl, 260; JEGP xviii, 376; SHG 53.

**scipberende**, participial adj. *bearing ships*: nauigeras, scipberende, OEG 28, 321.

**scipgesceot**, *see* scirgesceatt.

**scippan**, *add to I*: (*legum*) conditores, scepttenras (? *for* sceppendras), Kent. Gl. 245, *but cf*. ægewritere; add to III a:

**read** sceof (i.e. sceaf *pushed*) *in* Gen. 65. *Add to compounds* eftscippan.

**scippend**, *add*: scepen, Cædmon's Hymn 6 (Moore MS.).

**scipwealh**, for meaning perhaps substitute *Welsh sailor* (cf. horswealh).

**scipweorod**, delete bracket, and see FL 152.

**scīr**, *see also* gescir.

**scirdan**, *hurt, see also* gescirdan.

**scīre**, adv., *delete II, see* scirenige.

**scirenige**, f. *actress*: Rid. 8, 9; cf. scericge.

**scīrgesceatt**, *delete*, *MS. reads* scypgesce . . ., *read* scypgesceote, *from the contribution paid in sheep*, cf. Förster, Flussname Themse 784; *or from the contribution for a ship*, cf. Chart. Harm. 483.

**scirian**, *add to compounds* forscirian.

**scirlett**, *add*: the meaning is unknown.

***scirte**, *piece of land cut off*, PNE ii, 108.

**scitere**, *sewer*: sciteres stream, CS ii, 440, 2 from below; PNE ii, 112.

**sclidd**, *alternative gloss to* glidd (*q.v. in Suppl.*): *lubricum*, glidd *uel* sclidd, Ps. Ar. xxxiv, 6.

**scofl**, in citation of Wrt. Voc. ii, 128, 36 (= WW 199, 5) lemma is *palo* (taken as *pala*); see Oliphant, *The Harley Latin–Old English Glossary* 52.

**scōhcnyll**, m. *bell for putting on shoes*: and siþþan heora rædinge georne rædan oð scocnylle, Archiv lxxxiv, 10, 7.

**scomhylte**, the *o* appears to be short, despite spelling in citation, see Holthausen, *Alteng. etym. Wörterbuch*, s.v. *scamm*. Substitute for meaning *brushwood thicket*, cf. heahhylte *above*.

**scora**, in meaning delete *hairy*, cf. FL 181.

**scora**, *shore, bank*: Waldmeres scora, CS i, 525, 24; PNE ii, 112.

**scortian**, *see also* unscortende.

**scortwyrplic**, *add*: should mean *recovering quickly*; note v.l. scorte fulfremmednesse hafað; see E.S. lx, 82.

***scræfen**, *place with caves*, PNE ii, 114.

**scræman**, v. *scream*: þær child ne scræmeð, Hml. Bel. 128, 22. (ON skræma.)

**scrēadian**, *add to compounds* bescreadian.

**scriccettan**, v. *screech*: *stridebant*, OEG 15, 4.

**scrīfan**, *add to compounds* ascrifan.

**scriftæcer**, *term of uncertain meaning, but referring to a payment made to a church at harvest*, Chart. Rob. 240, 4.

**scrippa**, *add*: sense is perhaps *rough ground*, PNE ii, 114.

**scritta**, *see* scrætte *in Dict*.

***scrubb**, *for* scrybb, PNE ii, 115.

**scrūdelshūs**, n. *vestry*: and of þan sacrario cumende, þæt is, of þam dihlan and halgan scrudelshuse, Archiv lxxxiv, 15, 3.

**scrȳdan**, *add to compounds* bescrydan.

**scuccen**, *citation* = Hml. P. ii, 707, 556.

**scūfan**, *add to compounds* frama-, inscufan.

**scufhrægl**, n. *movable curtain*: ii scufrægl, Chart. Rob. 194, 20.

**scūrheard**, substitute for meaning *very hard*, and add: this compound and the phrase *scurum heard*, Jud. 79, arise from a false assumption that the first element of *regnheard* meant *rain* (MLR xxxii, 281).

**scutel II**: rather *moving beam of a balance*.

**scȳan**, *note*: scȳ(h)end *is the nom. agentis*.

**scȳdd**, *add*: sense is rather *shed*, PNE ii, 115, but there is always association with a swine-pasture.

**scyldleas**, *add*: *innocentia*, scyldlease, OEG 2, 206; *insons, innocens*, JEGP lx, 447, xi, 1.

**scylf**, add to meanings under I, *ledge, shelving terrain* (PNE ii, 104); *add*: III *vault*, ? *stone chamber*: fornice, scelb, Txts. 114, 87; *cameram pastorum* (4 Reg. x, 12), scelf, OEG 44, 1.

**scȳr**, *hut*: tugurium, domuncula, scyr, OEG 55, 1.

**scyrf**, *for* scorf: *et scabiem ac furfures*, on hreofle, on scyrf, OEG 4, 297.

**scyte**, *add*: V *steep slope* (cf. scyteheald): on þone scyte, Earle, *Land Charters* 432, 19.

**se**, *add to I 1 c*; þær wearð þæt iii hund monna ofslagen, Ors. S. 172, 23.

***sealegn**, *willow*, see Löfvenberg, *Studies on ME Local Surnames* 177.

**sealmbōc**, f. *psalter*: Hml. Th. i, 604, 24.

sealt, n., *add*: II *salt water*: brim sceal sealte weallan, Gn. C. 45; sealtes (MS. scealtes) sweg, An. 1532.

sealt, adj., *cancel citation* Gn. C. 45 (*cf.* sealt n.).

sealtlēaf, *delete, MS. reads* sealtleap, *salt-basket*.

sealtwilling, f. *salt spring*: seo saltwellingc ðe hyrð into Grimanleage, CS iii, 387, 12.

sēamestre, *in last citation* (= Chart. Whit. 72, 9) *read* sæmestre.

sēamtoln, f. *toll on horse-load*: Chart. Harm. 412, 4.

seaxclāþ, *see* wriþels *in Dict*.

Seaxe, *add to compounds* Angelseaxe.

sēcan, *add to compounds* and-, besecan.

secgan, *add to compounds* æf-, forþ-, insecgan.

sēdan, *l. 2 in Dict. read* Ps. Th. 106, 8.

Sedlingas, *delete, see* Redlingas.

segl, *note: in citation of Wrt. Voc. i, 56, 51, se mæsta segl is Junius' emendation of* sæmæst segl, *cf.* A. viii, 452.

seglgird, *add*: III *used as a weapon*: contum, segelgerd, OEG 12, 1.

seglian, v. *seal, see* (ge)inseglian, un(in)seglian, beinsiglan.

seht, adj., *see also* ungeseht.

seldsine, *add*: *rara*, syldsyne, JEGP lx, 444, vi, 55.

sele, *add to compounds* leafsele.

selfgewealdes, adv. *under one's own control*: willes ond sylfgewealdes, A. lxxxiii, 20, 108, v.l.

selfhǣlu, f. *self-heal, sanicle*: sanicula, sylfhele, DP 17, 297; sulfelæ, A. xxiv, 432.

selfsceaft, *for* m. *read* f. *For various interpretations see* A. lxxxiii, 154.

-sell, *see* gesell.

sellan, *add to* VIII e *at end*: donet gerendi gratiam, selle to donne gefe, Ps. V., Hy. 11, 7; *with inf.*: non dedit commoueri pedes, ne salde onstyrgan foet, id. lxv, 9; he sealde him etan hlaf, Jn. vi, 31 (West Saxon Gospels). *Add to compounds* foregesellan; atersellende.

sēman, *add to* I *1*: me þonne sendeð se usic semon mæg, *to me he sends one who can reconcile us*, Gu. 511.

sendan, *add to compounds* forþsendan; ungesendeta.

sende, *sandy place*: land æt Sendan, CS iii, 283, 8 from below (= Chart. Rob. 92, 13); PNE ii, 118.

sendness, *substitute for meaning* mass.

sēne, adj. *sluggish*: ne scealt þu beon to sene, ne to siðgeare, IC 163.

sengel, ? *bundle, tuft*: Sængelpicos, CS i, 211, 23. Cf. PNE ii, 118; Löfvenberg, *Studies on ME Local Surnames* 182 (divergent).

senget, *clearing made by burning*: on sænget þorn, CS ii, 304, 22; PNE ii, 118.

sēoc, *add to compounds* adlseoc.

sēocan, *rather* seocian; *add*: languet, seocet, Archiv cxvii, 25, 34.

sēodcist, *accept suggestion of Dict. to take as two words; lemma has two meanings*, bag (seod) *and* bier (cist, *strictly* coffin).

seofonfealdlice, *add*: septempliciter, seofofallice, Mt. p. 19, 7; Lk. p. 7, 6, Lind.

seofonhiwe, adj. *of seven shapes*: septiformis, A. lxv, 248, 3.

seohhian, *see* geseohhian.

seolcan, v. *become weary*: O desides, ge solcenan, Gn. 18, 2 (JV). *See also* aseolcan; besolcen.

seoluc, *drain*: on sioluc ham, C.D. iii, 252, 7 from below; PNE ii, 119.

seonuwind, *delete, in citation MS. reads* geotend siue wind, *blood or air* (arteries).

sēoþan, *add*: III *to experience an emotion strongly*: Germ. 395, 391 (= Prud. 478) cited under I; mælceare singala seað, B. 190.

sēpan, *see* Brooks on An. 742.

sepulcer, *grave*: æt ures drihtenes sepulchre, Förster, *Reliquienkultus* 70, 11.

seruian, v. *serve, minister to*: engles . . . him seruedon, Hml. Bel. 104, 21.

sessian, *add*: for defence of MS. reading see Hallander, *OE verbs in -sian* 393–4.

set, *see also* beanset.

-setenness, *add to compounds* forþsetenness.

setgang, *add*: OEG 28, 113.

setl, *add to compounds* ealdor-, gild-, mihtesetl.

settan, *add*: III c *occupy with people for cultivation* (= gesettan IV, 1): i alf hida sett ond gewered, Chart. Rob. 234, 15. *Add to compounds* anbe-, onbe-, niþera-, upsettan.

settung, f. *ambush*: insidiis, settungum, Ps. Vit. ix, 29.

sēpan, *see also* geseþedlic.

sibaed, *add*: = sifeþ, *sg. of* sifeþa; *lemma* = artaba, *dry measure*.

sibb, *add to compounds* mægensibb.

sibb, adj., *add*: *friendly*: forgyf me sibbne coss, Hml. Warn. 24, 36. *See also* besibb.

sibgeleger *for* sibleger, Wlfst. 164, 5, v.l.

sibgesihþ, *add*: *Hierusalem*, on heofonlicre sybgesyhðe, Ps. Cam. cxlvi, 2 (cf. lxiv, 2).

sibsumian, *for simplex note* conciliet, sibsumaþ, OEG 24, 8.

sibsumlice, *add*: *pacifice*, Ps. V. xxxiv, 20 (and related glosses); Ps. Ar. (and related glosses).

sibsumness, *add*: and for sibsumnesse oxan, Hept., Lev. ix, 4.

sic, *add*: cf. atsic.

*sīcel, *small stream*, PNE ii, 122.

sīcian, v. *sigh*: gemo, sicige, Ælfc. Gr. Z. 167, 19 n.

sīcing, f. *sighing*: anhelitus, sicinge, OEG 30, 59.

sicorlice, adv. *certainly*: for þam þe þa apostles scolden witen sicerlice, Hml. Warn. 145, 12.

sicorness, f. *certainty*: heo habbeð blisse for þære sicornysse Godes rice, Hml. Warn. 143, 17.

sid, *add to* I e: sid adl, *elephantiasis*, implied in gloss elephanticus etc., sydmioleadl (so MS., see A. viii, 450), i.e. sid adl oþþe micel adl, WW 114, 9. Another view FL 113 (read syo micle adl).

sidhealf, *glosses* latitudo, Ps. Ar. xvii, 10.

*sīdling, *strip of land beside a stream, or another piece of land*, PNE ii, 122.

sigelaþung, f. *glosses* ecclesia, Gn. (Archiv cxxix, 22).

sigelhweorfa, *cf.* A. xli, 128.

sīgere, *for another possible instance see* A. lxxxvi, 155.

sigsonte, *add*: the word is doubtfully English, see MLN lxii, 568.

-siht, *see also* Münchener Studien zur Sprachwissenschaft xxiii, 5.

sihtere, *see* suhterga *below*.

sihþ, *add*: II *glance*: optutus, syhð, OEG 2, 16.

*silet, *willow copse*, PNE ii, 117.

*silte, *salt-pit*, PNE ii, 118.

silting, f. *seasoning*: condimentum, sylting, Ker, *Catalogue* 94.

sincan, *see also* forsuncen.

sincfæt, *add*: in citations B. 622, Wald. i, 28, meaning is simply *treasure*; in B. 1200 it may be *setting* (for gems).

sincfāg, adj. *richly decorated*: sincfage sel, B. 167.

sindonisc, adj. *of fine linen* (especially that in Christ's shroud): soð hit is þæt ic hine . . . on clænen syndonissce hrægle befeold, Hml. Warn. 78, 18.

sinfulle, *see also* fulle *above*.

singalryne, *delete, probably two words* singal = perpes, rene (= ryne) = decursus. Cf. An. Ox. 508–9.

singan, *see also* fullsingan; ymensingende.

sinulira, m. ? *muscle*: see FL 32; Oliphant, *The Harley Latin-Old English Glossary* 179 (no. f. 175).

*sirwett, *see* syretum *in Dict*.

sīþ, m. *add to compounds* geon-, þanansiþ.

sīþ, adv., *add to* II: siðet (= sið ðæt), *afterwards*, Mt. xxvi, 29, Rush.

sīþboren, *discussed* Gneuss, *Lehnbildungen und Lehnbedeutungen im Altenglischen* 135.

sīðgearu, adj., *ready to travel*: see citation under *sene above*.

sīþgēomor, *perhaps rather* weary of life.

sīþlic, adj. *late*: serotinus, siþlic uel ealdlic, Gn. (Archiv cxxix, 22).

sīþscipe, *for* gesiþscipe, Bd. iii, 28, v.l.

sixecgede, *for* sixecge, Ælfc. Gr. Z. 289, 5.

*slæf, *mud*, PNE ii, 127.

slǣget, *sheep pasture*: on ðæt slæget, C.D. vi, 181, last line; PNE ii, 127.

slǣgu, *rather* slowness, lethargy, *taking lemmata as errors for* lethargus (cf. A. xxxiii, 387); *or perhaps* litharge, *taking lemmata as* lithargyrus.

slǣpan, *add*: dormierunt, slypton, Ps. V. lxxv, 6 (= slepton *with Kentish inverted spelling*).

*slǣpe, adj. *slippery*, PNE ii, 128.

**slæpor**, *add*: slapor, IC 164.

**slǣpfulness**, delete, MS. has slapulnis, itself an error for slapful; cf. Ælfc. Gr. Z. 305, 7–8; A. xli, 146, note 4.

**\*slēa**, *grassy slope*, PNE ii, 128.

**slēan**, *add to B III*: þa sloh þæt net swa full sona þæra fisca, Hml. P. ii, 516, 23.

**slege**, *add to VIII b*: *lyrico plectro*, hearplecum slege, OEG 8, 15; 9, 42. *Add to compounds* ofslege.

**sleghrīþer**, *add*: slegeryþer, Will of Æthelgifu, ed. Whitelock, 31.

**slīcende**, *see* underslicende.

**\*slica**, adj. *smooth*, PNE ii, 129.

**slid**, adj. *slippery*: *lubricum*, glidd *vel* sclidd, Ps. Ar. xxxiv, 6.

**slīdan**, *add to III*: *infaustum*, sliden, Txts. 71, 1130 (MS. infastum).

**slidenness**, delete, scribe took *lapsum* as part.; cf. correct reading of Brussels MS. under slide in Dict.

**slīht**, *add to compounds* broþor-, þunorsliht.

**slīm**, *l. 2 in Dict.*, borbus *is for a derivative of* βόρβορος, cena *for* caenum.

**\*slind**, *slope*, PNE 129.

**\*slinu**, *slope*, PNE ii, 129.

**slīpan**, *slip*: perhaps take here *falax equus*, styppede (? *for* slipende) hors, Ps. Sal. xxxii, 17.

**slipræsn**, rather *beam to prevent objects from sliding*; see Oliphant, *Harley Latin–Old English Glossary* 180.

**slite**, perhaps delete sense III, see Prud. 982, note.

**slitenness**, delete, *morsum* has been taken as part., cf. An. Ox. 3599.

**slitol**, *citation* (= Prud. 420) *is uncertain*, MS. sticul.

**slitung**, accept suggestion in Dict. that II should be deleted, as citation is an instance of I, see FL 80.

**slīþen**, *delete first citation in Dict*, see slidan *above*.

**slīpness**, *image*, citation in Ps. Cant. cv, 36.

**slīpness**, f. *cruelty*: *saeuitia*, slietnes, PBB lxxxv (Halle), 61.

**slōhtre**, f. *slough*: slohtran ford, CS i, 321, 19; PNE ii, 130.

**slūpan**, *see also* untoslopen.

**smēa**, *delicacy* (?): ond eal þa smean ðe þerto gebyriað, Chart. Rob. 74, 20.

**smacian**, read smācian, and delete sense *smack*.

**smæc**, in first citation lemma is *sapa* not *sapor*.

**smēagel**, *for* smȳgel: of smeagel hyrste, CS iii, 349, 9 from below; PNE ii, 130.

**smēagend**, *add*: *scrutator*, Hy. Surt. 62, 13 (= Gn. 55, 2, JV).

**smēagung**, *add*: III *interpretation*: ðas halgan rædinge . . . trahtnian æfter Augustines smeagunge, Hml. Th. i, 556, 13; Emmanuel, þæt is on smeagunga, 'God sy mid us', Hml. Warn. 21, 29.

**smēalice**, *add to III*: smiðas hi worhtan smealice mid cræfte, Hml. P. ii, 688, 202.

**smēaþancol**, *add*: *subtilissimus*, smeaþacal (*sic*), Gn. 37, 3 (V).

**smellan**, delete.

**smeoruþearm**, cf. smælþearmas *in Dict.*, *and* A. xiii, 323.

**smeoruwyrt**, cf. sperewyrt *in Dict. and below*.

**smeringwyrt**, *error for* symeringwyrt, WW 135, 1; cf. smeriguyrt, DP 227. See A. xli, 139, 230.

**smēþe**, *note*: on *tinius* (= *Thynius*) as lemma of smeðe ringce see FL 104.

**\*smēþett**, *smooth place*, PNE ii, 130.

**smillan**, delete I.

**smirels**, *see also* crismsmyrels.

**\*smite**, *dirty stream*, PNE ii, 130.

**\*smol**, *crumb*, PNE ii, 131.

**\*smugge**, *secret place*, PNE ii, 131.

**smyltness**, *see also* unsmyltness.

**snǣdan**, *add*: snædeþ *read by many for* sendeþ, B. 600.

**snæp**, ? *boggy land*: andlang dun and snæp, CS iii, 362, 16; PNE ii, 132.

**snās, snǣs**, *add*: II *a quantity of fish*: Chart. Rob. 257, passim.

**snāþ**, *killing*, delete, see snide.

**snīcan**, *see also* gesnican.

**snide II**, Suppl.: *delete form* snað, *MS. has* sniþes *or* snides, *see* Neuphilologische Mitteilungen li, 58; Studia Germanica Gandensia ii, 92.

**snīte**, *for* aceta *read* aceia; cf. A. xli, 118, note 3.

**sniwan**, v. *be wet, rain*: *pluit*, sniueð *uel* hregnað, Mt. v, 45, Lind. (O. Irish snigid).

**\*snōc**, *point, projection*, PNE ii, 133.

**snotorlic**, *see also* wordsnotorlic.

**snūd**, *swiftness*, probably delete and read in citation sunde bewunden, *encompassed by the water*.

**soc**, *add*: II *drainage*: oð þas soces seað, CS ii, 384, 13.

**socc**, *see also* rocc *above*.

**socian**, on citation under I, see Prud. 806, note.

**sōcn**, *perhaps transfer* Gu. 688 (= 716) *from VI 1 to VII*; *add to VIII*: mine fre socne men, Chart. Harm. 351, 13.

**sōfte**, adj. *add*: V *agreeable*: þæt ælc man drunce þæs deorwurðan wines be þam þe he sylf wolde and him softost wære, Hml. A. 92, 23.

**Sodomitise**, adj. *of Sodom*: i.e. eom andetta Sodomitiscre synne, A. xi, 101, 32.

**sōhþa**, *read* sohþa, *and add*: *some sort of juice*; lemma = *iotta, iutta*, broth (*also boiled milk*, WW 281, 10); cf. FL 181.

**sol**, *collar*: the word is doubtful, A. xxxiii, 139; FL 182.

**sol**, *dirty*: delete query and add: *fusca*, sol, Harleian Glossary F 1000 (not in WW).

**solcenness**, f. *laziness*: *segnitiem*, solcenesse, Archiv cxvii, 22. *See also* asolcenness.

**solian**, *see also* asolian.

**sōlsēce**, on *solata* see DP 310 and note (p. 70).

**sorgbyrþen**, substitute for meaning *baleful drink*; cf. Brooks on An. 1532; EGS iv, 74; see bryðen.

**soru**, delete, *MS. reads* stre.

**sōt**, *add*: glosses *limo*, Ker, *Catalogue* 357.

**sōtig**, adj. *dirty*: *in file* (= *vile*) *sacculo*, on sotigum bylige, Lunds Universitets Årsskrift lii (1956), 2, 10.

**sōþ**, *see also* eacsoþ(lice), yfelsoþ.

**sōþscip**, *see* fores.

**sōþwundor**, n. *true wonder*: soðwundra fela, Ex. 24; El. 1121.

**spǣc**, *add*: Spæcleahtun, CS i, 496, 7.

**spǣcehēow**, *see* hiw II 1 b.

**spær, spearr**, *spar*: Wynburge spær, CS ii, 603, 7 from below; id. iii, 363, 5 from below (spear); PNE ii, 135.

**spǣtan**, *see also* onspætan *above*.

**\*spald**, *ditch*: see English Studies xl, 110; PNE ii, 134.

**spaldr**, *add*: perhaps *balsam*; note *aspaltum* is v.l. for *balsamum*, Eccles. xxiv, 20 (It.).

**spearwa**, *note*: as gloss of *fenus* rather belongs to spearwa, *calf of leg*, see SHG 13.

**spēd**, delete VI, take *mid heora spedum* in citation as *with their belongings*. *Add to compounds* godcundsped.

**spediende**, the word is doubtful, SHG 47.

**-spelia**, *see* a-, gespelia.

**speliend**, *note*: the second citation in Dict. = Hml. P. i, 380, 48.

**spellbōc**, *add*: Chart. Rob. 250, 18.

**spellung**, *add to compounds* edspellung.

**spendung**, *add*: *sumptum*, spendi(n)g, Archiv cxvii, 24, 3.

**spennestre**, f. *female temptress*: *lena*, spenæstra, Ælfc. Gr. Z. 322, 1 (late addition). *See also* forspennestre.

**\*speoht**, *green wood-pecker*, PNE ii, 137.

**speregewriþ**, *see* gewriþ *in Suppl.*

**sperewyrt**, full text of last citation in Dict. (= WW 135, 12) is nap siluatica; sperewyrt *uel* wilde næp; *add*: *ueneria*, speruuuyrt, Txts. 106, 1078. *See also* smeoruwyrt *in Dict.*

**spīc**, *add*: in place-names probably *brushwood*, PNE ii, 138; l. 4 in Dict. read *taxea* for *tanea*.

**spīder**, *add*: *entirely uncertain*, MS. has spiden; cf. Grattan and Singer, *Anglo-Saxon Magic and Medicine* 162.

**spillan**, *add to compounds* tospillan.

**-spillian**, *see* ges.

**spīr**, another possible instance OEG 22, 1 (but cf. MLN lxii, 567).

**spircing**, rather *sparkling*, see Prud. 755 and note, FL 130.

**spīwung**, *see also* swiung *in Dict. and below*.

**splǣtan**, v. *split*: *exentera*, splat (*read* splæt), Althochd. Glossen i, 475, 15. See also asplætan.

**spor**, add to II: *MS. has* swor, Exod. 239; *some read* swol, *burning*.

**spornan**, *add to compounds* a-, and-, tospurnan.

**spornness**, *see* andspurnness.

**\*spot**, *piece*, PNE ii, 139.

**sprǣc**, *add to compounds* geþræorspreca, hiwspræc.

**\*sprǣg**, *brushwood*, PNE ii, 139.

spreca, *add to compounds* leasgespreca.

sprecan, *see also* geansprecan; wordsprecende; unbesprecen.

sprengan, l. 10 in Dict. read *rotat* not *rorat*; take II C and III together as *give motion to, spin,* see Prud. 999 and note. *Add to compounds* onsprengan.

sprinca, *add*: very doubtfully OE, cf. FL 32.

springan, *add*: VII springan fram, *lack*: ne springaþ hie from ænegum gode, Vercelli MS., f. 75ʳ, 20.

springung, *perhaps rather* springding, *cf.* springd, springdlice.

springwyrt, *add*: bibe calidum, sprincwurt, A. xxiv, 431 (cf. OEG 73 c, 35, footnote).

spyrian, *add to compounds* geond-, ofer-, ondspyrian.

*stacing, *enclosure made with stakes*, PNE ii, 141.

stæf, *add*: V *Sunday letter*: on swa hwilcum staue swa sunnandæg gesceote, Henel, *Studien zum altengl. Computus* 47. *Add to compounds* bisceopstæf.

*stæfer, *pole*, PNE ii, 141.

stæflic, *add*: III *literary*: litterariae (disciplinae), stæflice, OEG 30, 22.

stæfplega, substitute for meaning *primary school*.

stæfsweord, substitute for meaning *staff-sword*, and cf. Keller, *Anglo-Saxon weapon names* 44.

stælan, *add*: of self-accusation: hu us is to ondrædanne, þæt we stælan sculon on domes dæge, Verc.-Hom. 82, 108; p. 908, col. 1, l. 14 in Dict., *read* Hygelac *for* ? Eofor.

*stæne, *stony place*, see PNE ii, 141.

stæpe, *add to compounds* forþstæpe.

stæppan, *add to compounds* æstæppan.

stæþþig, *add*: stæðig on his gelæte, Nap. 31; II *with firm foundations*: to þære stoðolfæstnysse þære stæþþian worulde, Hml. P. ii, 518, 71; grauis, steþþi, OEG 11, 2.

stæl, *for* gestal, Verc.-Hom. 83, 113, v.l.

stælian, v. *make an accusation*: gif Englisc mon stalað (v.l. gif Englisc onstal ga forð), Ine 46. Cf. stælan.

stalu, *add to* I: *furtum* (acc.), stalo, Mt. xix, 18, Lind.

stān, *add to compounds* bæc-, brin-, hring-, mil-, rode-, sæstan.

stānæx, probably an *axe for working stone*, see FL 114.

stānbrycg, *note*: doubtful as gloss to *lithostratos* (WW 117, 35), see FL 33.

stānceastel, substitute for meaning *heap of stones* (Essays and Studies viii, 43; Neophilologus vii, 215; PNE i, 85).

stāncropp, *add*: II *pebble*: see citation under crop II *in Suppl.*, where MS. has stancyslas, croppas; see crop *above*.

stāncynn, *add*: swa he wære . . . heardes (v.l. þæs heardestan) stancynnes, Verc.-Hom. 88, 189.

stand, *add*: place-names suggest also the sense *standing-place*, PNE ii, 145.

standan, *add to compounds* geanstandende.

standness, f. *substance*: substantia, stondnis, OEG 72, 2 (but cf. MLN lxii, 568). *See also* astondness *in Dict.*

stānfæt, meaning in Wald. 62 is either *jewelled sheath* or *treasure chest* (cf. sincfæt).

stānford, m. *stony ford*: to stanforda, CS ii, 270, 14.

stānhliþ, *add*: the meaning seems to be *stone walls* or *buildings* in Dan. 61, Wand. 101.

stānmerece, *add*: petrosilion, stanmerce, WW 134, 36. *See* sigsonte *above*.

stānwyrht, *MS. in citation reads* stanwyrhtæ; *lemma* (= *builders*) *is incorrectly translated* (*see also* scylf II *in Dict.*); cf. FL 182.

stapol, *delete* II *in Dict., read* staþole *in citation* (cf. Dream of the Rood 71; Medium Ævum xxxiv, 223).

staþol, *add to* IIIa: fo him siðþon to eallum þam staðule, Will of Æ thelgifu, ed. Whitelock, 5; *add*: V *ability to stand*: ic wæs þin feðe and þin gang ond þin staðol, Verc.-Hom. 99, 310. *Add to compounds* weallstaþol.

staðolnes, glosses *firmamentum*, Ps. Tib. xviii, 2.

steall, *see also above, s.v.* gealt, *and add to compounds* fore-, pleg-, tun-, wyrmsteall.

stearn, *note*: in Wrt. Voc. i, 62, 32 (= WW 286, 7) MS. has tearn.

stede, *add to compounds* wiþerstede, onstyde.

stedefæst, *see also* unstedefæst.

stedeheard, *add*: cf. E.S. lxiv, 212.

stedenægel, *firm nail, talon*: stedenægla (MS. steda-) gehwylc, B. 985.

stefn, add to II: *body of persons*: ic me bebiode ðam nigum stefnum engla, Archiv ccii, 272, 36 (= Notes and Queries ccx, 209, 1). *See also* wicstefn.

stellung, *add*: see PNE ii, 150.

stelscofl, *delete, read in citation* steorscofle, *with a rudder, reference is to cleaving the waves*, see Prud. 875.

stemned-, *see* welgestemned.

stencan, *scatter*, add: II *emit a smell, stink*: fetet, stenceð, Jn. xi, 39, Lind.

stenian, v. *pant*: anhelantium, stænienden (*sic*), An. Ox. 6, 5. *Cf.* stencan *in Dict.* (stenecian, *Suppl.*).

steorbære, adj. *star-bearing*: stelliferum, þæne steorbæran, Archiv cc, 198.

steordalc, m. *helm*: clauo, steordalce, JEGP lx, 444. Cf. steornægl.

steormearcung, *see* mearcung *above*.

steorn, *delete*.

steornede (MS. steorrede), *rather* starred (referring to the markings of a horse), see FL 183.

steorf, *poor pasture*: to Siferþingcsteorfan, CS i, 296, 3 from below; PNE ii, 151.

steorrēonung, *see* reonung *above*.

stēorscofl, *see also* stelscofl *above*.

stēorspræc, *add*: steorspæce, Ps. Sal.

stēpan, *initiate see also* gestepan.

sticca, *add*: III *a quantity of fish*: Chart. Rob. 257, 26. *Add to compounds* dicsticca.

sticol, *add*: IV *biting* (in taste): mordax (allium), sticul, Prud. 420.

sticwyrt, *add*: ? *dwarf-elder* (cf. liþwyrt *in Dict.*): ostrago, sticvyrt, DP 16, 261; *ostrago*, sticwyr(t), Ker, *Catalogue* 436.

stif, *add*: chalyps. i. dura, stif, OEG 6, 15 (cf. Ker, *Catalogue* 458); rigens, stif, OEG 25, 7.

stig, *transfer final citation to* anstiga.

stigan, *add to* I 3: *descendunt*, nyþerstigaþ, Ps. Sal. xxi, 30; etc.; *add to compounds* mis-, upstigan.

stigend, *add*: *rider*: ascensoribus, stigendum, Ps. Cant., Hy. 4, 19.

stigian, *cancel* Sal. 202 (= *193*), *MS. has* swigie.

-stiht, *see* gestiht.

stilen, *add*: (se deofol) þe of þære stylenan helle cymð, Verc.-Hom. 106, 375.

still, *add*: II *fish-weir*: capturam, stællo, Lk. v, 4, Lind. (W-S Gospels fiscwer); cf. PNE ii, 150.

stillian, *see also* astillian; ungestillod.

stillness, perhaps delete V, see Philological Quarterly xl, 316.

stint, *sand-piper*, element not distinguishable from stynt, *boundary*: Stintesford, CS ii, 209, 10; PNE ii, 153.

stīþ, add to II: 1 a *stiff* (of the body): nihil prorsus in cubito flexionis, stið æ (= a) in hellenbogan, OEG 4, 302.

*stoccett, *place with tree-stumps*, PNE ii, 156.

stocwic, citation = Gr. D. 172, 4.

stofn, *add to* I citation above s.v. astæppan (1); *truncus*, stofn, OEG 4, 393; 28, 361.

stōrfæt, *add*: Festschrift Liebermann 47, 20.

stormig, adj. *stormy*: storemig ond geswyncfull hærfest, Hml. Warn. 66, 16; cf. An. Ox. 226, 201.

stōrsticca, substitute for meaning *incense spoon*.

stōw, *add to compounds* andfeng-, bedd-, weardstow.

*straca, *strip of land*, PNE ii, 161.

stræl, *add*: ðu deofles stræl, An. 1189; ðu heardeste stræl, Bl. H. 241, 3, *are addressed to a devil, and probably arise from confusion of* Belía *and* βέλος.

strælian, *see also* astrælian.

strange, *add to* II: *forte*, strongi, Rtl. 188, 2 (lemma taken as *fortiter*).

strēam, *note*: l. 3 *in Dict. read* wæters(cipe) *for* wæto.

strēat, m. *delete, anomalous spelling for* stræt.

strēat, adj. *delete, MS. has* great.

strēawberige, *on final citation in Dict. see* eorþberige *above.*

*strecca, *stretch of land*, PNE ii, 162.

streccan, *see also* niþerastreht.

stregdan, *add to compounds* forstregdan.

stregdness, *see also* geondstregdness.

-strenge, *add* feowerstrenge.

strēon, *see also* eorþgestreon.

Strēones halh, *add*: it has been suggested that this is *Strensall*, Yorks., not *Whitby*, see *Anglica* i, 51; this is unlikely.

strēonfull, *for* gestreonfull: lucrosum, strenful, Archiv cxvii. 22.

strīcan, *see also* astrican.

**stricel II**, for *fount* read *teat*. See FL 81.

**striplian**, discussed note to Prud. 598.

**strīþ**, *add to II*: mid his striðe and mid his dyrstignysse, Hex. 327, v.l. (*This invalidates claim that the word is O. Sax.*)

**\*strōdett**, *for* strod, PNE, ii, 164.

**strūdend**, *in citation from Wrt. Voc. ii, 148, 36* (= WW 237, 40) *MS. has* strudere.

**strūdere**, *add*: Verc.-Hom. 77, 57; 85, 156; *and see* strudend *above*.

**strūdian**, citation = Verc.-Hom. 97, 290.

**\*strump**, *stump*, PNE ii, 164.

**\*strūt**, *strife*, PNE ii, 164.

**\*stubbig**, adj. *stumpy*, PNE ii, 164.

**stūc**, *heap, see* colstuc.

**stūce**, *stump of tree*, in meadow name: to Stucan Wisc, CS ii, 412, 29.

**studdian**, v. *study, be concerned about*: seo studdede emb þa uterlice þing, *Anglica* ii, 26, 102 (= Hml. Warn. 136, 17). *See also* bestuddian.

**studding**, f. *effort*: on nanre oðre næs Marthe studdinge on nanen time swa fullice geforðed . . . swa on ures Drihtenes moder, *Anglica* ii, 26, 107 (= Hml. Warn. 136, 22).

**\*stumbel**, *stump*, PNE ii, 164.

**\*stumblett**, *place with stumps*, PNE ii, 165.

**stuntsprǣc**, citation = A. lxv, 246, 14.

**stūt**, *add*: hy ahlyttriað þone stut of heora liðe mid seohhann, Hml. P. ii, 504, 164.

**\*stūt**, *hillock*, PNE ii, 165.

**stybb**, *add to compounds* ac-, wiþigstybb.

**stycce**, *add to compounds* cisstycce.

**stȳcing**, f. *clearing*: ondlang Mælfern in þa stycinge, of þare stycince . . ., Förster, *Flussname Themse* 769.

**\*styfic**, *stump*, PNE ii, 166.

**\*stynt**, *see* stint.

**styrian**, under II (2) delete Germ. 391, 30 (= Prud. 221) where *stirgit* is for Lat. *stringit*.

**sūcan**, *add to compounds* gesucan.

**\*succa**, *sparrow*: on succan pyt, CS iii ;525, 21; PNE ii, 166.

**\*sucga**, *marsh*: PNE ii, 166.

**sugu**, *note*: suge sweard *would appear to be a disease* (*lemma* = fistula).

**suhterga**, *add*: fratruelis .i. filius fratris uel matertere filius, sihtere, Oliphant, *Harley Latin–Old English Glossary* 196.

**sulh**, delete citation of Coll. M. 30, 29, see syla below.

**\*sulhmann**, m. *ploughman*, see PNE ii, 166.

**sulig**, *pigsty*: on sulig graf CS iii, 341, 22; PNE ii, 167.

**sūlincel**, substitute for meaning *small furrow*, see FL 182.

**sumer**, *add to compounds* þrisumer.

**sumhwilc**, pron. *a certain*: quedam, sumwilce þinc, Archiv cxvii, 22.

**sumhwonne**, adv. *at some time*: þæt he sumhwænne (*quantocius*) þærto becumen muge, A. xi, 382, 285 (= Hml. Warn. 100, 2).

**sumorswegel**, n. *summer sun*: weder sumorswegle hat, Gn. Ex. 77.

**\*sumpt**, *swamp*, PNE ii, 168.

**sund**, *adj. see also* ungesund.

**sunddēaw**, ? read sunndeaw, see OED s.v. *sundew*.

**sunderboren**, meaning may rather be *bastard-born*, with reference to *nothus* in the passage glossed (Aldhelm, *Riddle* xxx, 2).

**sundor**, *see also* framsundor.

**sundorhalga**, *add*: wrongly used for *publicanus*, West-Saxon Gospels, Lk. vii, 29.

**sundormæsse**, f. *special mass*: begyte heora æghwylc þæt man . . . for ealle geferan ane sundermæssan synderlice gesinge, Brot. 27, 17.

**sundorrūnung**, f. *private council*: on heora sundorrununge, Hml. P. i, 250, 43.

**sunnboga**, m. *arc of the sun*: solis arcum, sunbogan, JEGP lx, 445.

**sunnbryne**, substitute for meaning *sunstroke*.

**sunnhǣte**, f. *heat of the sun*: hit bið þurh þære sunnan hætan (v.l. sunnhætan) to ferscum wætan awend, De temp. ann. 80, v.l.

**sūpanēast**, *delete* Gen. 667 (MS. suð and east).

**sūþcroft**, m. *southerly croft*: to Leofesices suðcroftes heornan, C.D. vi, 244, 5.

**sūþdǣl**, *add*: *note divided form* cwæn dæles suþan, Mt. xii, 42, Rush.

**sūþēasthealf**, f. *the south-east*: ad Eurum, on ða suðeasthalfe, OEG 4, 384.

**sūþerne**, meaning in Mal. 134 may be *of southern make*.

**swa**, *see also* eacswa.

**swǣce hēow**, glosses *insanias*, Ps. Roy., Ps. Tib. xxxix, 5. Cf. hiwspræc.

**swǣledness**, f. *burning*: combustio, swælednys, Gn. (Archiv cxcxix, 22).

**swǣrig**, adj. *heavy*: partiat honera sua, todælð . . . swyrige his byrðena, R. Ben. I. 54, 4. (*But cf. Suppl. s.v.* scirian).

**swǣse**, glosses *prandium*: swoese, Mt. xxii, 4, Lind.

**swǣsenddagas**, discussed FL 143.

**swǣsingdagas**, *see* swæsenddagas *in Dict.*

**swǣðelyne**, *add*: cf. FL 84.

**swǣþlǣcan**, v. *visit*: uisitauit, swæðlæhte, Ps. Cam., Hy. 9, 2.

**\*swalg**, *pit*, PNE ii, 170.

**swāmian**, substitute for meaning *move*, cf. JJ 42.

**swān**, on the lemma *flabanus* see SHG 83.

**swātclāþ**, *add*: ac healtst Godes pund on þinum swatclaðe, Fehr 178, 4; and his heafud wæs befangen mid swatclaðe, Hml. P. i, 316, 102.

**swaþian**, v. *swathe*: heo hine . . . bær and frefrede and swaðede and roccode, *Anglica* ii, 30, 141 (= Hml. Warn. 137, 12). Cf. sweþian.

**swaþu**, *note that* swina swaþu = *swine-path, and glosses* suesta (siuesta) *in sense suggested by Hisp. Fam.* lustrant suistas porci.

**sweart**, *add to compounds* eall-, hræfnsweart.

**sweartbyrd**, *add*: cf. Archiv clxxi, 33.

**sweflþrosm**, *add*: so Ps. Roy.

**swēg**, *lemma* hora *rather* = ora, *voice, see* Lindsay, *Corpus Glossary* 90. *Add to compounds* feþersweg.

**swegel**, *see also* sumorswegel.

**swegelbefealden**, *delete, in citation read with MS.* sweglbetolden.

**swēgung**, *error for* sweg, Hml. Warn. 69, 8 (cf. Hml. Th. i, 610, 12).

**swēgungness**, f. *sound*: sonitus, suegungnisso (-ung- *cancelled*), Lk. xxi, 25, Lind.

**swelg**, *add to compounds* sæswelg.

**swellan**, sense *burn* (see Suppl.) is doubtful, see Studia Germanica Gandensia ii, 93.

**swelle**, *swelling, hill*: on þe suellen, CS i, 418, 5 from below; PNE ii, 171.

**swelling**, *in citation MS. reads* spellingum.

**swencedness**, *add*: Ps. Vit. xl, 10.

**swēor**, *father-in-law*, *add*: cf. aþumsweoras.

**swēorhnitu**, the word is doubtful, see SHG 113.

**swēorsaga**, probably delete, see *Studies in OE literature* (ed. S. B. Greenfield) 152.

**sweotole**, *see also* forsweotole.

**swerian**, *see also* þurhswerian.

**swētian**, *see also* unswetian.

**swētmete**, *add*: hi beoð mid lara suetmettum gefylde, Past. 41, 15; hu þu þine ceolan mid swetmettum afyllan meahtest, Verc.-Hom. 93, 235; dapibus, swetmettum, OEG 28, 148 (cf. 105).

**swētwyrde**, delete bracket, cf. Corpus Glossary B 15 balbus, qui dulcem linguam habet.

**sweþel**, *add*: WW 21, 14, Txts. 61, 831; for *fascias*, weðel read fascia, sweðel.

**sweþian**, cf. swaþian *above*.

**swician**, *add to I*: uaga cogitatio, swiciende geþoht, Wyn. 65.

**swicol**, *see also* oferswicol.

**swige**, *see also* færswige.

**swigeniht**, f. *night of silence*: on þyssum þrym swigenihtum, Fehr 154, 3.

**swiglunga**, adv. *silently*: gan hi ærest þinga swiglunga mid dihlum sealmsange bysige to þære cyrican, Archiv lxxxiv, 3, 8.

**swigmæsse**, f. *low mass*: se prest stod on þære swimæsse, Nap. 60.

**swigūht**, m. *dawn of days of silence*: on þam þrim swiguhtan, Archiv lxxxiv, 7, 57.

**swilian**, *add to I*: so also Ps. Roy. and related glosses. *See also* geswilian.

**swille**, *liquid mess*: on swyllan healas, CS iii, 240, 9; PNE ii, 172.

**swimman II**: Wand. 53 is rather a figurative use, of spirits in the air.

**\*swin**, *channel*, a very doubtful word, PNE ii, 172.

**swīn**, *add to compounds* egeswin.

**swincleas**, *see also* geswincleas.

**swincness**, f. *trouble*: *tribulatione*, swincnisse, Mt. xiii, 21, Rush. (Lind. costung).

**swinge**, *see also* þrēaswinge.

**swinland**, n. *swine-pasture*: Will of Æthelgifu, ed. Whitelock, 8.

**swinlic**, adj. *of swine*: *porcinus strepitus*, þæt swinlice gestun, WW 508, 29 (*printed* symlice).

**swipor**, *note*: *in citation in Suppl.* hwiper *is MS. reading*; *cf.* Oliphant, *The Harley Latin–Old English Glossary* 205.

**swipu**, delete sense I a, on first citation see Prud. 740 and note, in second take sweopan literally.

**swirman**, *add*: *scateat*, swirmþ, Ps. Ar., Hy. 5, 16.

**swīþlæt**, adj. *very slow*: þæt hi aðor ne beon ne ealles to ræde ne to swiðlæte, IP 60.

**swīþswōge**, *for* swiþswege, OEG 28, 53.

**swīung**, *delete*, *read in citation* spiung (= spiwung), *see* ƷGEP lx, 448.

**swōrettan**, *add*: II trans. w. gen. *sigh about*: uncra synna he sworette, Verc.-Hom. 85, 147.

**swōrian**, v. *sigh*: þonne sworeð he, Verc.-Hom. 101, 325, v.l. (? *or read* sworette).

**swōtlice**, adv. *sweetly*: for heo byð swa swotlice gefostrede, Hml. Warn. 142, 37.

**swoþel**, *for* sweoloþ: *cauma uel estus*, swoþel *uel* hæte, A. viii, 452.

**-swungenness**, *see* ās.

**swyle**, *add to compounds* gegrindswyle.

**sydung**, the meaning is rather *arrangement*, cf. Prud. 750, note.

**sȳferlicness**, f. *purity*: Hml. Bel. 42, 33 (= Verc.-Hom. 59, 66).

**syge**, see for other suggestions ASPR iii, 293.

**syla**, *read* sȳla, *and add*: *unde aratori uomer*, hwanon sylan scear, Coll. M. 30, 29.

**sȳlæx** f. *kind of axe*: take here Wrt. Voc. ii, 22, 48; 133, 9 cited under syll in Dict. Cf. A. xxxi, 529; E.S. xliii, 327.

**sylfhēle**, *sanicle*: *sanicula*, DP 297.

**sylhþe**, *add*: hæbbe Ælfnoð . . . an sylhða oxana, Will of Æthelgifu, ed. Whitelock, 11.

**syll**, *cf.* sylæx *above*.

**syllestre**, f. *giver*: *datrix*, Gn. 43, 6 (JV).

**symbelbrēad**, n. *bread for a feast*: Seasons for Fasting 122.

**symeringwyrt**, *add*: *maluam crispam*, simaringuuert, OEG 73 a, 9. *See also* smeringwyrt *above*.

**syn[n]**, *add*: III *enmity*: B. 1472 (cited under I), An. 109, Phoen. 54, Cott. Gnomic Verses 54. *Add to compounds* heafodsynn.

**synbend**, m. *fetter of sin*: ond þær þa synbændes ealle tobræc, Hml. Warn. 85, 35; 86, 19.

**syncræft**, *delete*, *read in citation and in* Hml. Bel. *102, 30*, scyncræfte.

**syndrige**, *see also* ofsyndrige.

**syngian**, *add to compounds* asyngian.

**synhrēoflig**, adj. *leprous from sin*: synnhreofligum handum, IP 239.

**synsceaþa**, *add*: Verc.-Hom. 106, 363.

# T

**tacan**, *add*: þet landfolc him wið toc, *the people received him*, Chr. 1127. *See also* oftacan.

**tācnian**, *add to compounds* betacnian.

**tǣcels**, *boundary*: an tæcles broc, CS iii, 534, 14; PNE ii, 174.

**\*tǣcne**, *beacon*, PNE ii, 174.

**tǣg, tǣg**, discussed FL 188.

**tǣlan**, *add to compounds* ofertælan.

**tǣlhleahtor**, *note*: MS. reads talhlehter, see A. viii, 451.

**tǣpped**, *on first citation see* anhealfruh *above*.

**tǣsl**, *for* wulfes tæsl *see also* se brada uulues teal, DP 10, 81.

**\*tagga, \*tegga**, *young sheep*, PNE ii, 175.

**tāhspura**, probably delete, take as two words, see Oliphant, *The Harley Latin–Old English Glossary* 43.

**tala**, cf. JEGP xlvi, 425.

**talian**, *add to compounds* ofertalian.

**tamcian**, *see also* getamcian.

**tān**, adj., is uncertain, cf. JJ 34; ASPR i, 190.

**tānian**, *delete*, *cited form is a gloss to* decimatis; ? *read* teanages.

**tansīþe**, *tansy*: semen tansiðe, A. xxiv, 430.

**tēafor**, *see also* hwitleadteafor.

**tēaforgēapa**, m. *arch of red stone*: Ruin 30. (Others regard as adj. *red and curving*.)

**tēah**, *note*: as gloss to *scheda* rather *leaf, sheet*.

**tealtian**, *add*: *nutantes*, tealtiende, Ps. Lamb. cviii, 10.

**tearn**, *see* stearn *above*.

**teldtrēo**, meaning is *tent-peg (clauus)*; cf. *claus, lignum tentorii*, WW 205, 20.

**\*telgett**, *plantation*, PNE ii, 177.

**tellan**, *add to compounds* midgetellan.

**tempelhūs**, n. *temple*: Hml. Bel. 118, 24.

**-tendness**, *see also* atendness.

**\*tēo**, *boundary*, PNE ii, 178.

**teol**, *for* teolþȳrel, An. Ox. 7, 22.

**teolþȳrel**, in context (Ald., De Virg. iv) refers to the opening of a beehive.

**tēon**, *accuse*, *see also* abeteon.

**tēonfullic**, adj. *abusive*: ðin gelica þe cwyð to sum teonfullic word, Hml. P. i, 206, 225.

**tēonleas**, adj. *free from suffering*: ond ne byð heo næfre teonlease, Hml. Warn. 143, 5; 12.

**teorung**, *read* tēorung, *and add*: *delassatio*, tiurung, Kluge, *Angelsächsisches Lesebuch*, 3rd ed., 9, 21.

**tēoþa**, *add*: on þan tenðen dæige, Hml. Warn. 90, 29.

**Terfinnas**, *add*: Lapps of the Kola Peninsula.

**-tēung**, *see also* oferbæcgeteung.

**-tēwian**, *see* getewian.

**tīd**, *add to compounds* upastignesstid.

**tiddæg**, add: *see also* tidege.

**tidege**, *delete*, *read in citation* tiddege.

**tiderlic**, adj. glosses *fragilis*: tederlicum, Rtl. 51, 3.

**tidfara**, rather *one who goes at the allotted time*.

**tidgenge**, rather *maintaining a seasonal course* (of the moon), cf. Prud. 286, note.

**tidlic**, *see also* morgentidlic.

**tidscriptor**, *this is hardly an OE word, but an OE gloss on the first part, and a Latin gloss on the second part of the lemma*.

**tig**, *add*: cyninges tuntih, CS i, 455, 2. See PNE ii, 179.

**\*tiglere**, m. *tile-maker*, PNE ii, 179.

**tillan**, *add*: ænne stypel swa heahne ðæt his rof atille þa heofonan, Hept., Gen. xi, 4, v.l.

**tilung**, *see also* eorþtilung.

**tīma**, *add to compounds* hadtima.

**timbrian**, *add to compounds* fore-, (ge)intimbrian.

**tīmen**, probably delete; discussed MLN xiii, 248; Oliphant, *The Harley Latin–Old English Glossary* 29.

**tīmlic**, adv. *timely, suitable*: *habilem*, timlicne, Prud. 922.

**timple**, *see also* atimplian.

**tintrega**, *add*: *in Tartareum flumen*, in þa tintregan ea, Wyn. 127.

**tirging**, *add*: *zelus*, tyrging, Ps. Roy., Ps. Sal. lxviii, 10.

**Tīrisc**, adj. *Tyrian*: *in ostro Tirio*, in Tiriscum godwebbe, OEG 8, 14.

**titolōse**, *autumn crocus*, or *spring crocus*: *hermodactula uel tidulosa*, titolose, An. Ox. 56, 425.

**tō**, *add to* I *5 e*: gislas . . . þe . . . weorþuste wæron to þam cyninge, Chr. 876, B, C, D, E; he wæs Criste se leofesta þegn to sancte Petre, Mart. H. 128, 13.

**tōætēacness**, *for* toæticness, Bd. iii, 22, v.l.

**tōætēacnian**, *for* toætican, Bd. iii, 22, v.l.

**tōberan**, *add to* II: þonne þe toberð wið unspedigre mænn, *when thou hast a disagreement with a poorer man*, Hml. Warn. 4, 32.

**tōbīcnan**, v. *indicate*: *adsignat*, tobecnað, Jn., p. 5, 17, Lind.

**tōbiddan**, glosses *adoro*: Ps. Vit. xcviii, 9.

**tōblǣdan**, *add*: *dilata*, toblæd, Ps. Ar. lxxx, 11; Hy. 3, 1.

**tōclǣfan**, *see* tocleofan *in Dict*.

**tōcnyccan**, v. *join*: *adnexuit*, tocnuicte, Mt., p. 8, 15, Lind.

tōcweþan, add: *with tmesis*, þæt ealle Medas cweðað ... to þisre dæde, Hml. A. 94, 62.

tōdēman, *add:* II *adjudicate:* adiudicauit, todoemde, Lk. xxiii, 24, Lind., Rush.

tōdihtnian, *add:* so also Ps. Roy., Ps. Vit., Ps. Sal. lxxxii, 6.

tōdrēosan, *add:* þe lichame todroren ond to dyste iwordon, Hml. Bel. 130, 26.

*tōf, adj. *slow*, PNE ii, 181.

tofan, glosses *cremium*, Ps. Vit. ci, 4.

tōferian, *add:* I a *pull apart:* and mid langum rapum his lima toferode, Hml. P. ii, 707, 557.

tōfultumian, v. glosses *adiuuare:* adiuua, tofultuma, A. lxxxi, 91, 10.

tōgedēgled, participial adj. *hidden away:* abscondito, togedeglede, Mt. xiii, 44, Lind.

tōgegearwian, v. glosses adhibere, A. lxv, 253, 3.

tōgegrīpan, v. glosses *apprehendere:* togegrap, Mk. vii, 33, Lind., Rush.

tōgescēad, *for* toscead, Hml. Bel. 114, 10.

tōgeþēod, *add: nectus*, Kansas leaf.

tōhāwiend, m. *spectator:* spectatores, tohawiende, JEGP lvi, 65.

tōhealdan, v. glosses *tenere:* tohaldon (subj.), Lk., p. 2, 11, Lind.

tōhladan, ? *delete, read in citation* tohleopon.

tolcettan, read *indruticans* for *infruticans*.

tōlicgan, *add:* swa wegas tolagon, An. 1234.

tōlihtan, v. glosses *adlucere*, Ps. Ar. xcvi, 4.

toln, *see also* ceap-, seamtoln.

topp, *add to* I: tolis, top, OEG 30, 97 (in margin *tholus est summa pars tecti*).

torn, *in* torna geat, CS ii, 291, 10, *apparently for* tyrngeat.

toroc, cf. ES xli, 164 (Celtic word).

torr II, cf. ES liv, 108.

torrian, v. *tower:* muntæs ond dunæ þa ðe heage stondæþ ond torriæð ofer alne middæneard, Hml. Bel. 130, 13.

toscanlēac, *a plant of the genus equisetum:* ippirus equise(t)a, DP 208.

tōscilian, v. *separate:* þa þa God ærest toscelede wæter fram lande, Hml. Warn. 91, 7; (he) wæs toscyled fram þære apostlene geferræddene, id. 144, 27.

tōsettan, *add:* II *clench:* pressis (*dentibus*), tosettum, Prud. 302.

tōslitenness, f. *schism:* scisma .i. hereticam prauitatem, toslitennesse, OEG 30, 138.

tōspillan, v. *destroy:* disperdamus, ute tospillan, Ps. Sal. lxxxii, 5.

tōspringan, *in last citation crepet* (= Prud. 708) *means part with a noise*.

tōspurnan, v. *reject:* proterit, he tospyrð, Archiv cc, 197.

tōswung, *hurling, throwing* (in some sport); *iactus*, toswung (to be added after WW 170, 8; see A. viii, 451).

*tōthyll, *look-out hill*, PNE ii, 185.

tōweorþian, v. glosses *adorare:* toworðadun, Jn. 4, 21, Rush.

tōwesan, v. *be present:* aderant, toweron, Lk. xxiii, 48, Lind.

tōworpedness, *for* toworpenness, W.S. Gospels, Mk. xiii, 14, v.l.

tōwrītan, *add:* II *ascribe:* adscribamus, we towritan, Scint. 16, 5.

trægelian, substitute for meaning *tear apart, destroy*; cf. Prud. 602.

trahtaþ, *add: commentario*, tr(a)htt(a)þe, OEG 28, 31.

tregian, *add: atteritur*, tregod, OEG 24, 18.

trendan, *see also* betrendan.

trēow, *tree, add to compounds* hengetreow.

trēowbicen, ? *nest of wild honey:* mel siluestre, treumbicin, Ker, *Catalogue* 476.

trēowness, *see also* ge-, ungetreowness.

trēowsian, *see also* ungetreowsed.

trēowþ, *add to compounds* ortreowþ.

trēpe, *delete, see* þreap *below*.

treppan, *delete* II, MS. *illegible*.

trindle, adj. *round:* polimita uel orbiculata, ringfah uel trindle, WW 188, 13 (so MS., cf. FL 176).

trog, *see also* leactrog *above*.

trogscip, cf. FL 116.

trumness, *add:* V *exhortation:* oratione, trumnisse, OEG 4, 270; cf. trymnes III c in Dict.

*trusen, adj. *grown with brushwood*, PNE ii, 188.

trymman, *see also* fore-, in-, ontrymman.

tude, *delete, see* tudenard.

tudenard, *shield:* scutorum, tudenarda, An. Ox. 747; *parma*, tude, id. 5025 (? abbreviation). (O. French tuenard.)

tūn, *add to compounds* grædtun; *see also* spæc.

tunge, *see also* oxantunge.

tungellic, adj. *heavenly:* sydereae patrie, tungellices eþeles, Gn. 50, 1 (JV).

tunggelælle, adj. pl. *talkative:* uerbosi, An. Ox. 56, 139.

tūnincel, *see* tunnincel *below*.

tunnincel, n. *small cask:* take here first citation in Dict. under tunincel.

tunsingwyrt, *add:* DP 149; An. Ox. 26, 63; 56, 42; 378.

*tūnsteall, *site of farm*, PNE ii, 198.

tūntig, *see* tig.

turfgret, *turfpit:* ond half þe turfgret ligge into Apetune, Chart. Whit. 86, 19. (? corruption of ON torfgröf.)

twelfmōnaþ, m. pl. *twelve months, year:* ær on twelfmonðum, *in the preceding year*, Vercelli MS., f. 108ʳ, 1.

twentigesnihte, adj. *twenty nights old: see citation under* feowertinenihte.

twēo I, *translate* to tweon weorþeð, *hangs in the balance.*

twī, *for* twia: twi six, BM 42, 16.

twi-, *in all compounds read* twī-.

twiccian, *add compound* atwiccian.

twicele, ? *river-fork:* oð þa twicelan, C.D. iii, 343, 20 (= H. E. Salter, *Eynsham Cartulary* i, 23, 5 from below); cf. Stud. i Mod. Språk. xix, 125.

twicen, *note:* also means *narrow lane, alley*, see citation of C.D. iii, 240, 20 in Dict.

twig, *add: surculus*, tuig, ouuaestm, Txts. 99, 1942.

twihǣmed, adj. *twice married:* twihæmed, þæt is se þe tuwa wifað, *bigamus*; þrihæmed, se þe þriwa wifað, *trigamus*, Ker, *Catalogue* 93.

twīlafte, *delete,* MS. *reads* twilaste (cf. ecglast, bradlastæx).

twīlēafa, *an unknown plant:* ui(n)ca perui(n)ca, tuileafa, DP 338.

twīmen, m. pl., *translates* homodubii, Rypins, *Three Old English Prose Texts* 55, 3.

twin, *for* getwinn: twæge twinnes, Hept. 27, 292.

twinclian, *see also* cwicclian *above*.

twing, *delete,* MS. *has* twiga (or twigu, *twigs*) *referring to* propagines, cf. FL 59.

twingan, *delete, in citation* Ps. Ar. tringaþ, Ps. Sal. trinð *are errors for* hrinð *due to lemma* tangit.

twinwyrm, discussions Archiv cxvii, 364; FL 143.

twīseltōþe, *sense is rather having two projecting teeth* (like a dog), FL 117.

-twiung, *see* getwiung.

tȳderfull, *see* tudorfull *in Suppl.*

tȳderness, *meaning is rather shoot. Add:* II *propagation:* angewæmmed on lichamlice tydernesse, Hml. A. 33, 221 (addition); id. 156, 123, v.l.

tȳdran, *see also* forþatydred.

tyge, *add to* III: *organa*, tugas, OEG 28, 331 (on lemma see þeote in Dict.).

tygele, *sense may be necklace*, as lemma has that meaning also.

tyht, *add to* III: *take ofer* tyht *as two words, and probably read* byht (cf. Rid. 9, 3; 23, 13).

tyhtan: *delete* Met. 20, 178 (ll. 30-31 in Dict.), MS. stihtest. *Add to compounds* fore-, forþtyhtan.

tyhtenn, *note:* retain tyhtend as gloss to *allectio*, which is error for *Allecto*, who incites to evil, see Isid., Etym. viii, 11, 95, and SHG 94.

tymbor, *add:* ? *error for* lynibor (q.v.); cf. Phil. Quart. xlv, 435, 2.

*tȳnincel, *for* tunincel, PNE ii, 198.

tȳnness, *delete,* tenys *in citation is for* cweartenys; cf. An. Ox. 4639, note.

tyrdlu, *add:* mid musa tyrdlum befiled, Fehr 164, 18.

tyriaca, m. *antidote:* tyriaca is god drenc wiþ innoþ tydernessum, Lch. ii, 175; snæd þæs tyriacan, id. 290.

tyrning, *add:* III *deceit:* (absque)uersutia, butan tyrninga, An. Ox. 56, 86.

Tyrrenisc, adj. *Tyrrhenian:* Thyrrena, þa Tyrreniscan, Archiv cc, 198.

tysca, *another view* (coarse cloth), A. xxvi, 301; cf. tysse *below.*

tysse, *a sort of cloth:* Ld. 162. (Cf. OHG zussi.)

# Þ

þaca, *add*: *sub tectum meum*, under þacu minne, Mt. viii, 8, Rush.

þæctigele, *add*: implied in gloss *imbricibus*, þecum tigelum brycum, i.e. þectigelum oþþe þecbrycum (þecum *has* -um *from the other words*), An. Ox. 2256.

þæf, *for* geþæf: *mollior*, ðefra, OEG 30, 115.

þæge, *add*: cf. Campbell, *Old English Grammar*, § 713.

þænan, *add*: II *be moist*: madeo, þæne, WW 449, 14.

þærfore, adv. *for it*: he do swa micel to Godes lacum þærfore swa þær to teoþunge gebyrige, Hml. P. ii, 808, 103.

þærgemang, adv. *in turn*: uersa uice, Prud. 54.

þæronefn, adv. *alongside*: sette he þone calic þæronemn, Fehr 164, 18.

þærongēan, *add*: scyldas þærongean, *shields against it*, Verc.-Hom. 105, 356.

þærwiþ, *add*: III *near by*: þa stod his scip þærwið, Hml. P. ii, 516, 11.

þærwiþinnan, adv. *inside there*: Hml. P. i, 252, 86.

þæslicness, *add*: *in oportunitatibus*, on gehiþlicnesse *uel* þæslicnesse, Ps. Ar. ix, 10.

þametaþ, *delete, error for* hafettaþ.

þanansīþ, m. *journey thence*: oð hit þanansiðes leafe hæbbe, *until it has leave to go thence*, IP 229.

þanc, *add to compounds* inþanc.

þānian, *delete first citation* (*cf.* þænan *above*).

þannu, conj. *when*: cum, þænnu, JEGP lx, 443, V, 29.

þe, *note use after* þara, *with* (*1*) *sg. verb*: gehwilcne man þara þe wilnaþ, Bt. S. 103, 14; ælces ðara ðe wel doo, Past. 75, 12; B. 1461; 2251; (*2*) *pl. verb*: cynna gehwylcum þara ðe cwice hwyrfaþ, B. 98; 784.

þearfa, *add to compounds* weorþþearfa.

þearfan, *delete* Gen. 2480, *read* wineþearfende.

þearfendlice, adv. *miserably*: he wæs þearfendlice mid claðum bewunden, Verc.-Hom. 128, 209.

þearflic, *add*: III *poor*: paupiores, þa þearflicran, R. Ben. I. 100, 4; *indigens, egens*, þea(r)flic, Prud. 230.

þēaw, *add to compounds* munucþeaw.

þeccan, *add to compounds* forþeccan.

þeccbryce, *delete*, two words in MS., cf. An. Ox. 2256; Studia Germanica Gandensia ii, 93.

þecgan, *add to compounds* forþecgan.

þefel, *delete*, *defruto* taken as *de frutice* (= þyfele); cf. felde *in Suppl*.

þegan, *delete*, *take as phonological variant of* þeowan, *serve*.

þegen, *add to compounds* dirling-, larþegen. *See also* English Historical Review lxx, 540.

þegnland, n. *land held by a thegn*: Chart. Rob. 240, 19.

þegnung, *add to compounds* bisceophadþegnung.

þelneþung, *a plant*: pamfeso, clofþunc *siue* þelneþunc, OEG 73a, 1.

þencan, *see also* unbeþoht, unforþoht.

þende, *delete citation* Germ. 403, 35 (= Prud. 1077 note).

þenu, *glosses* iam, Mt. iii, 10, Rush.

þēod, *add to* III: Hml. Bel. 50, 31; 54, 13; *add to compounds* feorþeod.

þēodan, *see also* on-, underbeþeodan.

þēodcynn, n. *race*: þeodcynnes, JEGP lx, 442, IV, 6 (*reading doubtful*).

þēodenbealu, n. *great evil*: þeodenbealwa (gen. pl.), El. 403.

þēodlāreow, m. *teacher of the people*: Seasons for Fasting 96. Cf. se þeoda lareow Paulus, Brot. 13.

þēodscipe, *see also* geþeodscipe.

þēofmann, *add*: Fehr 140, 19.

þēon, *do, cancel, read in citation* þeodenbealwa.

þēostru, *see also* þeostru.

þēotan, *transfer first citation under* II *to* I *as reference is to a wolf*, Prud. 824.

þēowtian, *see* geþeowtian.

þerende, *substitute*: þeran, v. *rush*: inruens, þerende, Txts. 69, 1078.

þicce, *on citation* Hpt. Gl. 408, 38, *cf.* þefel *above*.

þicgan, *add to compounds* onþicgan.

þidercyme, m. *arrival there*: hi woldon þa helle belucen wið ures drihtnes fore ond wið his þidercyme, Nap. 63.

þigen II, *delete* Gen. 2480, *read* wineþearfende. *See also* atorþigen.

þignan, *cancel, in citation read* hyðynde wæs hi, *and cf.* ahyþan *in Suppl*.

þing, *add to compounds* mynsterþing; nænigþinga.

þingian, *add to compounds* wiþþingian.

þism, m. *smoke* ? : þa smicendan þismas þara byrnendra liga, Guth. Gr. 131, 188. (Cf. E.S. xli, 324.)

þistel, *add to compounds* meteþistel.

þistel, *see also* bradþistel *above*.

þīstra, cf. A. lxxvi, 411.

þiustra, the lemma is rather a corruption of Greek άμβλύs, hence gloss to be taken as from þeostre, *dark*.

þixl, *cancel addition in Suppl., where* þislum = þistlum (Lat. *cardis fereis*).

þolebyrd, *add*: patientibus, þolebyrdan, Ps. Sal. cii, 6.

þolle, meaning in context is *an instrument of torture*.

þorfendlic, adj. *for* þearfendlic: uiduam pauperculam, widua ðorfondlico, Lk. xxi, 2, Lind. (-endlico, Rush.).

þorian, *delete*, citation probably error *for* dumosi, þornige.

þorn, *add to compounds* blæcþorn, *and see also* senget.

*þornegn, *þornett, *thorn copse*, PNE ii, 205.

þornig, *see also under* þorian *above*.

þornþyfel, m. *thorn bush*: of þam þornþifele þe wundorlice barn, Förster, *Reliquienkultus* 69, 9.

*þorrian, *see* horrat *above*.

þot, *add*: balatibus, of þotum, OEG 30, 101.

þrang, *delete, emendation unjustified*, -þran *is end of* wudu-biorþran, *see* wudubyrþra. Cf. A. xl, 341; xliii, 98.

þrēal, *in first citation MS. has* correptio uel correctio.

þrēap, *note*: citation is An. Ox. 3033; 3450. *Add*: heapum ond þreapum, ASPR vi, 66, 283; *acices*, trepas (sic), Hymn. Surt. 47, 18.

þrēaswinge, f. *whip*: in flagella, on þreaswingum, Ps. Ar. xxxvii, 18.

-þrecan, *see* onþrecan.

þreclic, adj. *terrible*: terribilis, Ps. Sal. xcv, 4. *See also* æ-, aþreclic.

þrēotēoþa, *add*: on þan þreottende dæige, Hml. Warn. 90, 39.

þri-, *in all compounds read* þrī-.

þridægþern, *period of three days*: triduo, þrydægþyrne, OEG 7, 13.

þridda, *add to* II: þridda dæl, Ine 23 (and freq. in laws); hire ðriddan sceat, *her third of the property* (acc.), Ine 57.

þridding, *note*: on citation in Dict. see Notes and Queries ccxiv, 444; *add*: *a third part*: super . . . trehingas . . . scilicet super terciam partem prouinciae, Ll. Lbmn. i, 653.

þrifyrclede, adj. *three-pronged*: ond hæfde him on handa þryfyrclede force, Hml. P. ii, 776, 34.

þrihǣmed, adj. *three times married*: Ker, Catalogue 93 (*cited above under* twihæmed).

þrili, *add*: *triple-twilled*.

þripel, *add*: *in second citation* unheh *is conjectured*, MS. upheh, *upright*. Add: tripoda, thripil, Kluge, *Angelsächsisches Lesebuch*, 3rd ed., 9, 48.

þripeluf, *? error for* þripel upheh, see þripel *above*.

þrirēþre, *note*: þrireþreceol *is a compound*.

þrīsumer, adj. *three years old*, implied in gloss triennis, þrywinter *uel* sumer, WW 120, 38.

þrocen, adj. *producing beams*: to þrokon holt, Chr. 656 (late insertion, Plummer i, 30, 4 from below); PNE ii, 214.

þroht, adj. *is uncertain, both citations may have the noun*.

þrohung, *see* hrohung *above*.

þrosm, III *is doubtful, see* Prud. 760, note.

þrotbolla, *on lemmata* ceutrum (chautrum), see Oliphant, *The Harley Latin–Old English Glossary* 73.

þrōwestre, f. *female martyr*: martyr, þrowyestre, A. lxxxi, 104, 6.

þrōwungdæg, m. *day of martyrdom*: of þam dæge, þe dryhten gefullod werð, oð his þrowungdæge, Festgabe K. Luick 192, 26.

þrūh, *take* II *under* III (the basket held a body, Prud. 867, note).

-þryccedness, *add* ge-, oferþryccedness.

-þrýl, *see* geþryl.

þrymm, *add to compounds* weoroldþrymm.

-þrȳn, *see also* beþrid.

-þungenness, *see also* fullþungenness.

**þunorsliht,** m. *thunder-clap*: færinga weorðað micele þunur-slihtas, A. lxxiii, 25, 2.

**þurhdōn,** v. glosses *perficere*: ðerhdoe, Lk. xiii, 32, Lind.; ðerhdedon, id. ii, 39, Lind., Rush.

**þurhdrencan,** v. *completely soak*: heo wæs . . . þurhdrænct mid þære welle Godes huse, *Anglica* ii, 36, 194 (= Hml. Warn. 138, 17).

**þurhfæstnian,** *add: transfigit,* ðurhfestnað, JEGP lvi, 65.

**þurhfēre,** *see also* unþurhfere.

**þurhfrignan,** v. glosses *percontari*: ðerhfregnendum, Mk., p. 4, 19, Lind.

**þurhgeendian,** v. glosses *perficere*: ðerhgeendad, Lk. i, 45, Lind., Rush.

**þurhlǣdan,** v. glosses *perducere*: perduxit þurhlæde, Ps. Sal. lxxvii, 52; perducunt, ðerhlædon, Mk. xv, 22, Lind., Rush.

**þurhrǣdan,** v. glosses *perlego*: perlegendi, þurredene, OEG 28, 23.

**þurhsīne,** *add: perspicuo,* þ(u)rhsenre, OEG 28, 419.

**þurhswerian,** v. glosses *periurare*: ne ðerhsuere ðu, Mt. v, 33, Lind.

**þurhūtlice,** adv. *completely*: þurutlige hunwarst (i.e. unwræst), Hept. 420, 21 (late addition).

**þurhwǣt,** adj. *wet through*: he nime lynen hrægl . . . and bedyppe on wine þæt he þurhwæt sy, Fehr 172, 18.

**þurhwunigendlic,** participial adj., *persevering*: on godum weorce þurhwuniendlicne (*perseuerabilem*), A. lxv, 250, 27.

**þurhwunungness,** f. *perseverance*: perseverentiam, þurhwunungnesse, Ps. Sal., end prayer.

**þwēal,** as gloss to *delumentum* (*soap*) transfer to II.

**þweortimbre,** substitute for meaning *resolute*.

**þwinan,** *see also* aþwinan.

**þyddan,** *see also* uþþyddan.

**þȳfel,** *add to compounds* þornþyfel.

***þȳfelett,** *thicket,* PNE 222.

**þȳflen,** *delete, see* ryplen *above*.

**þȳflig,** adj. *brambly*: dumosi, spinosi, ðyflie[s], OEG 30, 32.

**þyldelice,** *for* geþyldelice, Hml. Bel. 100, 14, and frequently.

**-þyldigung,** *see* forþ.

**-þyrfing,** *see* beþ.

***þyrnett,** *thorn copse,* PNE ii, 223.

**þysgelic,** *for* þyslic, Ælfc. Gr. Z. 47, 7, note.

# U

**ufanmearcung,** f. *superscription*: suprascribtione, ufamercung, Mk., p. 5, 1, Lind.

**ufenan,** *add*: III *in spite of*: ufonan þone cwide, Will of Æthelgifu, ed. Whitelock, 63.

**ūht,** *add compound* swiguht.

**ūhternlic,** adj. *of the morning*: matutinus, Gn. (Archiv cxcxix, 23).

**unāblinnendlic,** *add*: incessabili uoce, unablinnendlicre stefne, Ps. V., ed. Kuhn, 312, 4 from below.

**unācenned,** *add*: non nato, unacen(d)um, OEG 28, 254.

**unǣfæstlice,** *add*: þa ealdormænn eteð on ærnemorgen uneawfæstlice, Hml. Warn. 15, 6.

**unǣtness,** *f. in phrase* unætnessa gebidan (v.l. abidan), *die*: Chart. Rob. 60, 8.

**unǣwisc,** *substitute*: adj. *immodest*: impudicus, unewisc, WW 291, 25.

**unāhladen,** participial adj. *unexhausted*: inexaustis, unahladenum, JEGP lx, 441, I, 18.

**unālogen,** citation = Verc.-Hom. 20, 176.

**unāmetendlic,** adj. *immeasurable*: se ðe ana is unametendlic, Hml. P. i, 205, 182.

**unāmetenlic,** *add*: Ps. V., ed. Kuhn, 314, 1.

**unandergilde,** *delete Suppl., retain Dict.; in citation* hwæt þu age unandergildes *means no more than* hwæt þines agnes sie (W. A. Craigie).

**unārǣfnedlice,** *add*: Wyn. 33.

**unāsecgendlice,** *add*: Hml. P. i, 322, 230.

**unāwend,** *add*: ac þær bið se eca dom unawended, Verc.-Hom. 72, 9.

**unāwrēon,** v. *uncover*: reuelamini, eft unawriað gie, Rtl. 21, 2.

**unbecweden,** delete second quotation.

**unbecwedene,** adv. *uncontestedly*: take here second citation *under* unbecweden.

**unbesprecen,** participial adj. *uncontested*: unbesprecæn wið æghwylcne lifes man, Chart. Rob. 60, 29.

**unbēted,** *add*: ða unbettan synna, Hml. P. i, 437, 396, v.l.

**unbeþōht,** *add*: II participial adj. *unexpected*: inopinatus, JEGP lx, 444, VI, 71.

**unblēoh,** add to meanings *spotless*: discussed Neophilologus l, 447.

**unblonden,** participial adj. *unmixed*: non mixtum, Rtl. 68, 15.

**unbrǣce,** *add El.* 1028, *see citation under* anbroce, *where read* æðele, unbræce, *see JJ* 23.

**unbȳing,** *in citation MS. has-* byengo.

**uncēapunga,** *add*: OEG 28, 302.

**uncoren,** *for* ungecoren, Vercelli MS., f. 70ᵛ, 13.

**uncȳþig,** *delete last citation, see* oncyþig.

**undafenlice,** *for* ungedafenlice, Hml. A. 12, 306.

**under,** *see also* anunder.

**underbeþēodan,** v. *subject*: in subiectam speculam, on underbeþeodde sceawunge, JEGP lx, 447, xi, 31.

**underburhware,** *citation is from* Ps. L., Ps. Sal.

**underfōn,** *add to* VI: (c) *receive as matter for thought*: canat et reuoluat, singe heo ond eft underfo, Gn. 100, 4 (JV).

**undergrīpan,** v. *seize*: þa wæs þæs witega cnape Giezi mid gitsunge undergripen, Hml. Warn. 122, 23.

**underniman,** *add to* I: sublatum corpus, underniomane lichoma, Jn., p. 8, 2, Lind.

**underrim,** n. *subscript number*: ex subiecto numero, of ðæm underrim, Mt., p. 4, 5, Lind.

**underslīcende,** participial adj. *slipping under*: subreptura, JEGP lvi, 65.

**underþēodan,** *add to* III: syððan he him þa underþeodde ond cyðde þone deg his forðfore, Chad. 172, 120.

**undigle,** adj. *not secret*: his dæda beoð undigle, Hml. P. i, 437, 404.

**undōn,** *see also* geundon.

**undōnness,** f. *state of being undone*: soluendi, undoenise, Rtl. 59, 6.

**unefesung,** f. *failure to cut the hair*: and we lærað, þæt man geswice bysmorlicra efesunga oððe unefesunga, IP 186, v.l.

**unēstfull-,** adj. *ungracious, disobliging*: inofficiosus, ingratus, unestful, WW 191, 17.

**unfēre,** another possible instance WW 276, 3, discussed Philological Quarterly xlv, 435, 3; SHG 48.

**unfērness,** *see* unfere *in Suppl.; citation is* Hml. Warn. 137, 12 (= *Anglica* ii, 30, 140).

**unforbodene,** adv. *unopposedly*: see second citation under unbecweden.

**unforcumen,** participial adj. *unconquered*: . . . uirtutis, unforcumenes mæhte, Rtl. 122, 5.

**unforesewen,** participial adj. *unforeseen*: inprouisum, unforeseun, PBB lxxxv (Halle), 61.

**unforgripendlic,** *for* ungripendlic, Ps. Vit. xviii, 8.

**unforht,** adj. *very fearful*: Dream of the Rood 117; cf. unhar, untriwe.

**unforhtleasness,** *see* forhtleasness *above*.

**unforþōht,** participial adj. *unexpected*: improuisus, JEGP lx, 444, VI, 70.

**ungearu,** *add to* I: ungearo to ælcum gode, Fehr 210, 1.

**ungeārwyrd,** *delete, MS. reads* ungeorwyrd, *undisgraced, cf.* georwirþan.

**ungecristnod,** participial adj., *not having undergone the ritual preparatory to baptism*: ne mot gefullod mid þæne ungecristnod etan, Buss. 180, 188, v.l.

**ungecwēme,** *add*: eal þæt is idel and Gode ungecweme, IP 264.

**ungedēfelice,** *add*: *in citation read* ungedefe (*adj. with* morþorbed).

**ungedōn,** participial adj. *not done*: non facta, OEG 28, 486.

**ungedwimorlice,** *citation* = Hml. P. i, 342, 38.

**ungeearnod,** participial adj., *undeserved*: inmerito, ungeearnedum, A. lxv, 249, 5.

**ungefēge,** *cf.* gefegan *above*.

**ungefynde,** *cf.* FL 189.

**ungehīwodlic,** adj. *without form*: þat is þonne ærest, þæt he on þam Sunnandæge geworhte heofonas and eorðan mid eallum heofonlicum endebyrdnyssum and þæt ungehiwedlice andweorc, An English Miscellany presented to Dr. Furnival l 357, 28.

**ungelēaf,** add: incredibiles (for incredulos), (u)ngelefe gum(an), OEG 62, 2.

**ungemēde,** delete, see mad.

**ungemethāt,** adj. immeasurably hot: beþe hine mid onmethatum (wætre), Lchd. ii, 338, 24 (= Leonhardi 103, 31).

**ungemetigende,** participial adj., unrestrained: seo (giferness) ys ungemetigende gewilnung ægðer ge ætes ge wætes, Vercelli MS., f. 110ᵛ, 28.

**ungemetlicness,** f. want of moderation: immoderatio, ungemetgung uel ungemetlicnes, Kansas leaf.

**ungenīwiendlic,** adj. unrepairable: inreparabilis, OEG 28, 188.

**ungenyhtsumness,** f. insufficiency: insufficientiam, ungenitsumnysse (sic), Archiv cc, 198.

**ungeorwyrd,** see ungearwyrd above.

**ungerǣd,** note: original MS. has ungeræd. Add: ungeræde mænn, Hml. Warn. 50, 7 (v.l. ingerade).

**ungescæpfulness,** f. innocence: puritatem, ungescæpfulnesse, Ps. Ar. xvii, 25.

**ungescaðignyss,** for unsceþþignyss, Hml. Warn. 62, 19.

**ungescēad,** adj., add: ungescead bliss, Verc. Först. 152, 31.

**ungeseht,** adj. at variance: ge sculon . . . gesibsumian þa ungesehtan Cristenan, E. M. Furn, 358, 28.

**ungesendeta,** participial adj. gen. pl., glosses inmisis, Mt. p. 5, 14, Lind. (altered to -ena).

**ungestillod,** for geunstillod, R. Ben. 121, 13.

**ungesund,** adj. bad, evil: se þe him God on gesunden þingen ne ondrædeð, on ungesunden he to him ne beflihð, Hml. Warn. 105, 2.

**ungetēorigendlic,** add: inextinguibilis, ungeteorgendlic, JEGP lx, 447, XI, 3.

**ungetrēowsed,** participial adj., for geuntreowsed: WS Gospels, Mt. xxiv, 10.

**ungeþingod,** add: he (deað) cumeð on us ungeþingod, Vercelli MS., f. 76ʳ, 22.

**ungeþungen,** add: meniges cynnes menn, sume geþungenran, sume ungeþungenran, Studia Germanica Gandensia v, 164, 10 (= Hml. P. ii, 622, 10).

**ungewealden,** add: ungewealdene muðe, Verc.-Hom. 6, 58.

**ungewildendlic,** adj. impatient: inpatientis, ungewyldendlices, OEG 30, 18.

**ungewittig,** add to II: ungleaw, inscia, nescia, ignara, JEGP lx, 447, XI, 17.

**ungewuna,** add: insolitus, JEGP lx, 447, XI, 4; inusitato, ungewune, OEG 4, 92.

**ungewyrd,** f. misfortune: infortunium, Archiv cc, 198.

**unglǣdlic,** add: unglædlic hleahter, Verc.-Hom. 74, 29; id. 29, 251, v.l.

**unglēaw II,** many read unslaw in citation; but prefix is perhaps intensive as in unhar, unforht.

**unglenged,** delete, MS. uniglenced, see ungeglenged in Suppl.

**unhālian,** v. glosses tabescere, Ps. Bos. cxviii, 139.

**unhālwende,** adj.: I incurable: extensio dorsi insanabilis, aþenednis hrycges unhalwendes, Ps. Roy., Hy. 6, 24; II unfavourable: ðry dagas synd . . . unhalwende monnum, Studies in English Philology (Miscellany Klaeber) 273, 8.

**unhēah,** see þrīpel above.

**unhearmgeorn,** citation in Suppl. = Hml. P. ii, 557, 251.

**unhetol,** citation = Hml. P. ii, 557, 251.

**unhlēowe,** perhaps rather offering no shelter, unfriendly.

**unhlisful,** add: II not celebrated: incelebris, JEGP lx, 443, VI, 1.

**unhlytm,** add: cf. RES xvii (1966), 170.

**unlǣdlic,** citation = Verc.-Hom. 29, 251.

**unlǣdu,** f. misery: Verc.-Hom. 29, 251, v.l.

**unlīf,** n. death: swa life swa unlife, Verc.-Hom. 82, 105.

**unlūcan,** add: II pluck out: euellet, unluceþ, Ps. Ar. li, 7.

**unlybwyrhta,** citation in Suppl. = Hml. P. i, 436, 376.

**unmǣþful,** citation = Hml. P. i, 436, 375.

**unmann,** m. bad man: eac hit is þe wyrse, þe hy unmannum olæcað æfter hereworde, IP 264.

**unmēagol,** l. 1 in Dict., for emellus read emollis.

**unminsiendlic,** adj. irreducible: ðonne bið his syn æfre unminsienlic, Hept. 78, 63 (v.l.).

**unmōdigness,** delete, see unmodness.

**unmōdness,** f. pride: see citation under unmodigness (= A. lxvi, 32, 8).

**unmunecod,** participial adj. not made a monk: Buss. 176, 110 (cited under ungemunecod in Dict.).

**unnīþing,** add: cf. Archiv cxvii, 22.

**unonstyriendlic,** add: A. lxxiii, 18, 8.

**unonwendedlic,** note MS. has unonwendelic.

**unplēolice,** add: compar, unpleolucar, Hml. Warn. 4, 28.

**unrād,** f. hostile raid: Chr. 1111; 1116.

**unrǣdfæst,** adj. unwise: þurh gylp unrædfæst on dædum, Fehr 212, 15.

**unrēnod,** for ungeregnod, unornamented: Will of Æthelgifu, ed. Whitelock, 47.

**unrēone,** adj. very sad: unreonre (v.l. unrotre) stefne, Verc.-Hom. 92, 224. (Intensive un-; cf. reon, reonig, and unhar, unforht.)

**unrētan,** add: contritiones, unrettan, Ps. Cant. cxlvi, 3.

**unrihtgafol,** n. usury: þa þe heora feoh to nanum unrihtgafole ne syllað, Hal. 39, 12, v.l.

**unrihthād,** m. improper manner: on unrihthadum, Verc.-Hom. 76, 44 (v.l. unrihttidum).

**unrihthǣmed,** add: unnatural vice: twegen men geþeoddon hig tosomne mid unrihthæmede, Mart. H. 110, 17.

**unrihthǣming,** f. fornication: on manaðe and on unrihthemincge, Archiv cxi, 280, 29.

**unrihtlust,** add: Verc.-Hom. 148, 120; Ps. Par. xv, 7.

**unrihttīd,** substitute: f. period of sin: ond in oferfyllo he wæs begriwen on unrihttidum, Verc.-Hom. 94, 247; on unrihttidum (v.l. unrihthadum), id. 76, 44.

**unrihtweorc,** add: II wrongdoing: ond of ðam dæge þe he his unrihtweorc forlæte, ne geedlæce, Buss. 174, 86.

**unrihtwilla,** m. improper wish: fæste he for his unrihtwillan, Hal. 50, 7, 10, v.l. in both.

**unrimedlic,** for ungerimedlic, Hml. Bel. 120, 9.

**unrīmgōd,** n.pl. countless good deeds: Hml. S. xxxiii, 241 (cited in Suppl. under unrim).

**unrinad,** for ungeregnod, Chart. Rob. 250, 5.

**unrīpe,** add: se unripæ deað (mors inmatura), Hml. P. i, 420, 114, v.l.

**unrōtness,** see also efneunrotness.

**unrōtsian,** see also efneunrotsad.

**unrūm,** adj. narrow: augustam, Mt., p. 17, 14, Lind.

**unryne,** add: error for utryne, Ps. Roy., Ps. Tib. cvi, 35 (cf. Ps. Ar., Ps. Sal., Ps. Lamb.).

**unsǣle,** delete, see unfæle (so MS.).

**unsang,** m. in phrase on unsongum, in silence: impii . . . conticiscent, eærleæsæ . . . on unsongum, Ps. Cant., Hy. 3, 9.

**unscēadwīs,** for ungesceadwis, Hml. Warn. 5, 25.

**unscēaþian,** v. unsheath: euaginabo, ic unsceaþige, Ps. Spl., Hy. 4, 9.

**unscellice,** adv. unwisely: ac þonne byð manslæge yfel, þonne man hine deð beo his agene gewille unscellice, Hml. Warn. 141, 3.

**unscēotan,** add: used in sense disembowel in context (Tob. vi, 5).

**unsceþþiglice,** adv. in innocence: see citation s.v. mædmann.

**unscortende,** participial adj. abundant: thesaurum non deficientem, strion unscortende, Lk. xii, 33, Lind., Rush.

**unscrȳdan,** add: II of things: ge sculon unscrydan þa weofodu, Fehr 156, 10.

**unseglian,** v. unseal: and þa locan unsegeloden, Hml. Warn. 78, 33.

**unslāw,** in first citation in Dict. (= WW 169, 18) read unslaw.

**unslopen,** add: insolubilis, (un)slopen, JEGP lx, 447.

**unsmyltness,** f. glosses tempestas: unsmyltnise, Mk., p. 3, 6, Lind.

**unstedefæst,** adj. not firm: futile, Archiv cc, 198.

**unswētian,** v. become bitter: him biteriæð ond unswetiæþ alle þas eorðlice þing, Hml. Bel. 118, 10.

**untīdlic,** sense in first citation is eternal.

**untīmæt,** m. eating at improper times: untimaæt and oferfyll, Hml. P. ii, 550, 77.

**untōdǣled,** add: unapportioned: þa gita wæs his tunuce onsundran untodæled, Verc.-Hom. 33, 279.

**untōdǣlendlice,** adv. indifferently: indifferenter, Ker, Catalogue 129.

**untōslopen,** participial adj., equated with inextricabilis, untosliten, JEGP lx, 447, XI, 2.

**untrēowsian II,** in citation read ungetreowsede.

**untrīwe,** adj. very faithful: þam untrywan folce his þara haligra, Verc.-Hom. 7, 60. Cf. unforht, unhar.

**untrumlic,** add citation under idellic in Suppl. (= Hml. P. i, 344, 103).

untȳdrende, substitute for meaning *not having had young.*
unþurhfēre, adj. *unpassable*: *inpenetrabile*, unþurhfærne, OEG 27, 25.
unwær, *add to III*: *inparatum*, on unwær, OEG 4, 82.
unwealden, participial adj., *not under control*: witegade he þæt unwealdene muðe, A. liv, 23.
unwemmu, f. *spotlessness*: mid clǣnen . . . lichame, þe . . . ne forroteð ac on unwæmme þurhwuneð, Anglica ii, 28, 124 (= Hml. Warn. 136, 35).
unwēne, *add to II*: *inopinato*, unoene, PBB lxxxv (Halle), 61.
unwered, participial adj. *with dues undischarged* (of land): þæt healfe hundred eal unwered, Chart. Rob. 232, 20.
unwitweorc, *cancel, MS. has* inwitweorcum.
unword, n. *abuse*: willað habban hereword and scyldan wið unword, IP 264.
unwyrd, *note*: in first citation in Dict. translates *infirmitas* (Archiv cxxxiv, 275).
upāhafen, participial adj. *exalted*: Verc.-Hom. 75, 34; Ps. Par. xix, 8.
upāhebban, v. *raise*: *sublimat*, upahefð, Ps. Roy., Hy. 3, 7 (and related glosses); *erigens*, upahebbende, id., Hy. 3, 8;
upāhebbendlic, adj., *to be raised*: *proferendi*, upahæbbendlices (MS. una-), Archiv cc, 197.
upālūcan, v. *pull up*: *euellet*, upaluceþ, Ps. Spl. li, 7 (so MS.).
upārǣran, v. *raise up*: *erigit*, uparærð, Ps. Roy., Hy. 3, 8; *erexit*, uparæ(r)de, JEGP lix, 711, 7.
upāreccan, v. *erect*: *erecti*, uparehte, Ps. V. xix, 9 (and related glosses).
upārīsness, f. *resurrection*: seo æriste *uel* uparisnisse, Mt. xxii, 23, Rush.; *carnis resurrectionem*, flecsces uparisnesse, Ps. Cant., Hy. 14, 6.
upāstignestīd, f. *Ascension time*: æt þære halgan dryhtnes upastignestide, Vercelli MS., f. 75ᵛ, 22.
upgelǣded, participial adj. *led up*: Vercelli MS., f. 135ᵛ, 24. *See also* þripel *above*.
uphēah, *see also* þripel *above*.
uplegen, may also mean *head-dress.*
upniman, v. *raise up*: *erigens*, upnimende, Ps. Cant., Hy. 3, 8.
upphefedness, *for* uppahefedness, Hex. 451, v.l.
uprǣran, v. *raise up*: *eregens*, uprærende, Ps. V. and Cam., Hy. 4, 15.
upreccan, v. *raise*: *eregit*, upreceð, Ps. V. cxlv, 7.
uprist, f. *resurrection*: Hml. Bel. 122, 31, and frequently.
upscīnan, v. *arise shining*: *oriens*, upscinende, OEG 62, 5.
upsettan, v. *exalt*: *exaltauit*, he upsette, Ps. Sal., Hy. 8, 52.
upstīgan, v. ? *swell*: gif sio eaxl upstige, Leonhardi 100, 7.
upstigend, *add*: *ascensores*, upstigende, Ps. V., Hy. 5, 6 (and frequently in psalter glosses).
upþyddan, v. translates *turgescere*: Guth. Gr. 131 (cited under *liglic*).
upwill, m. *fountain*: andlang broces to upwylle, CS iii, 203, 3.
ur, probably delete; on various proposals for name of this rune, see Gradon, *Elene* 73.
ūr, *bison*, add: *uris*, urum, Txts. 107, 2167.
ūre, *note*: Ps. V. *has* ur *both for pronominal gen. and uninflected forms of poss. adj.*: *omnium nostrum*, alra ur, lxxxvi, 7; and frequently.
url, m. *hem*: oððe url *added to* hic margo, ðes ofer; *in margin* þes url, Ælfc. Gr. Z. 20, 1, note.
ūtætbregdan, v. *steal out*: and gif hig hwa utætbrede, Archiv cv, 369, bottom.
ūtālūcan, v. *pluck out*: *euellet*, utaluceð, Ps. V. li, 7 (and related glosses), Ps. Roy. (and related glosses); id. cxxviii, 6.
ūtālūcan, v. *exclude*: *excludantur*, beon utalocen, Ps. Roy. lxvii, 31, and related glosses.
ūtan, *add to II 4*: of time, *media nocte*, ymb middeniht utan, Gr. D. 253, 17.
ūtāsliden, *delete, see* aslidan I b.
ūterlic, adj. *outer*: seo studdede emb þa uterlice þing, Anglica ii, 26, 102; oðre fedeð sumne hungrigne . . . mid uterlicen mete, id. 28, 125 (= Hml. Warn. 136, 17, and 137, 1).
ūtfaran, v. *go out*: *exhibit*, utfærð, Ps. Sal. cxlv, 4; *exit*, utfaret, Archiv cxvii, 23; infarende and utfarende, Hml. Th. i, 438, 34.
ūthwīt, adj. *painted white*, glossing *dealbatus*: byrgennum . . . uthuitum, Mt., p. 21, 17, Lind.
ūtlād, substitute for meaning *tax on goods taken away from market, cf.* inlad, *and* Chart. Harm. 477.

ūtlic, *add*: *seorsum in locum*, an utlicre stowe, Chrd. 61, 21.
ūtlice, adv. *completely*: ealles to utlice, Hml. P. ii, 572, 142. *See also* þurhutlice.
ūtwaru, substitute: *only in phrase* (land) to cynges utware, *owing dues to the king* (not merely for defence), Geþyncðo 3, Norðleoda laga 9.

# W

wacian, *add to 1*: slæpende oððe wacende, Fehr 107, 19.
wadan, *add to compounds* inwadan.
wadu, l. 2 in Suppl. read xxxi for xxx.
wǣcan, *add to compounds* bewæcan.
wǣgbora, *add*: see Klaeber, *Beowulf*, Glossary, for many suggestions.
wǣge, *add to II*: þæt heo ðone dæg ond ða niht geemnytte on gelicere wægan, De temp. ann. 16, 12.
wǣgnian, *see also* awægnian.
wǣgnþoll, cf. JEGP xlvi, 426.
wǣlan, *add*: Sal. 143 (MS. weallað).
wǣlben, *perhaps rather* wælben, *deadly hurt, or* wælbend, *deadly bond (i.e. the waves).*
wǣlfill, *add*: B. 3154.
wǣlhrēowlic, adj. *cruel*: for þan þe ða deoflu, swa hwæt swa hie magon wælhreowlices hie þencaþ þe hire and doþ, Vercelli MS., f. 117ᵛ, 5.
wǣlnet, substitute for meaning *corslet* (cf. herenet).
wǣlweg: for interpretation *way to the abode of the dead* see Medium Ævum xxviii, 99.
wǣpenbǣre, adj. *bearing arms*: *armigeris*, wæpnbærum, OEG 27, 11.
wǣrness, *prudence*, add: *cautio*, uernis, PBB lxxxv (Halle), 61.
wæsce, *add*: of wæsceforda, CS iii, 243, 5.
*wæscels, *bath*, PNE ii, 237.
*wæsse, *marsh*, PNE ii, 237.
wæstmbǣrian, *add*: simplex occurs Gn. (Archiv cxcxix, 23).
wæstmfæst, *add*: *fruitful*, recorded by certain restoration, Archiv cxxii, 247.
wǣt, adj. *see also* þurhwæt.
wæterādl, *add*: *hydrops*, OEG 30, 123.
wæterælfādl, *add*: cf. Storms, *Anglo-Saxon Magic* 160.
wæterælfen, *add*: *amadriades*, waeteraelfinn, OEG 71, 4.
wætercynn, n. *kind of water*: sæ and eall wætercynn, Vercelli MS., f. 87ʳ, 24.
wæterrīþe, *add*: *aquario*, wæterriðe, OEG 63, 2.
wæterlēode, m. pl. *water-people, fish*: *aquosis gentibus*, OEG 28, 386.
wætersteall, on Lat. *flactiris* (see quotation in Suppl.) see fleoþoma in Suppl.
wæterstrēam, *citation* = Hml. P. i, 467, 93.
wæterwyrt, *see also* ealifer *above.*
wāg, *note*: l. 6 graticium = craticlum.
*wagge, *wagen, *quaking bog*, see Löfvenberg, *Studies on ME Local Surnames* 218; PNE ii, 239.
wāl, substitute: wala, *ridge or comb inlaid with wires running on top of helmet from front to back*: ymb þæs helmes hrof heafodbeorge wirum bewunden wala (MS. walan) utan heold, B. 1030–31. Cf. Hodgkin, *History of the Anglo-Saxons*, 3rd ed., 752. *Perhaps gen. pl. of same word in* istiarum (= *striatarum*), uualana uuira, OEG 42, 2.
waled, perhaps substitute for meaning *ridged* (cf. wala).
wamm, adj.: with citation in Suppl. cf. *maculosa*, wom, OEG 28, 428.
wammscyldig, *add*: Verc.-Hom. 93, 231, v.l. (*cited under* wambscyldig).
wana, noun, *add*: III *loss*: *damna*, wanan, OEG 27, 26. Cf. forwana *above.*
wancian, v. *waver*: MS. has wancode (*not* þancode) *in* Rid. lxxxvii, 7 (*cited under* borcian).
wandian, *add to compounds* oferwandian.
wanhafa, *add*: as adj.: þa wannhafan wræccan, The *Anglo-Saxons* 278, 20.
wanhafness, *add*: wanbæfennes (*sic*), Ps. Ar., loc. cit.
wanhālian, *add*: II intrans.: *taberent*, wanhaledan, OEG 6, 2; *debilitaris*, þu van halast, PBB lxxxv (Halle), 61.

**wannian**, *add*: for þon þe hit (þæt husel) wanað oððe mid ealle forrotað on swa langum fyrste, Fehr 178, 11.

**wanwilla**, m. *wilfulness*: *in uoluntatibus suis*, on heora wonwillan, Ps. Par. xiii, 1.

**wār**, *add*: *algas, herbas*, waras, OEG 30, 108. (Note masc. ending.)

**warenian**, *add to I 2*: warnige se lareow wið þæt þe se witega cwæð, Fehr 15, 4.

**wāse**, *add*: the quantity of the root syllable is uncertain; here may belong: *sablonibus*, stancyslum, warum (? for wasum), An. Ox. 1818; *sablonum*, wara, id. 4101; *sablonum*, wasa, id. 2493.

**wāsend**, *add*: *rumes* (read *-en*), wesend, Ker, *Catalogue* 471.

**wassenas**, m. pl. *vassals*: Chart. Harm. 423, 1, 5; 424, 16.

**wēacwānian**, *delete, read in citation* wean cwanian.

**\*wealc**, *fulling*, PNE ii, 239.

**wealcan**, *add to compounds* bewealcan.

**weald**, *power*: *add*: Hml. Bel. 100, 1; 102, 28; *add to II*: *camo*, walde, Ps. Roy., Ps. Vit. xxxi, 9; Ps. Cant. (on þære walde).

**wealdan**, *see also* unwealden.

**wealdendwyrhta**, m. *owner and builder*: waldendwyrhtan, Ruin 7.

**wealdian**, *delete, MS. has* wealde (*see* Journal of Brit. Arch. Assoc. xli, 150).

**wealdweaxa**, *probably add*: OEG 52, 12.

**wealh**, *harrow, add*: stefen cearciendes wænes ne ceoriendes wales, Archiv cxxxii, 335, 3.

**wealhwyrt**, *add*: *there appear to be two words sometimes confused*: wealhwyrt, *intula, elecampene*; weallwyrt, *ebulum, dwarf-elder* (A. xli, 133).

**weall**, *add to compounds* cæstel-, norþweall.

**weallan**, *cancel VIII, read in citation* wælað.

**weallstaðel**, *for* wealhstod, Hml. Warn. 41, 33.

**wealte**, *add*: II *fetter*: *pedicis*, wealtum, Prud. 138.

**weard**, f. *delete B.* 305; *add to compounds* feorhweard.

**weard**, *glosses sandix*: uueard, Txts. 98, 950; 95, 1783. Cf. A, xxx, 249; E.S. xlii, 146.

**weardian**, *add*: Ib *render secure*: *munierant* (Matth. xxvii, 66), wearde(d)an, JEGP lx, 442, IV, 35.

**-weardness**, *see also* foreweardness.

**weardstōw**, f. *watch-tower*: *de speculis*, of werdstowum, OEG 6, 1.

**weargbeorg**, m. *hill which is or is near the site of a gallows*: to ðam wearhbeorge, C.D. vi, 243, 6.

**weargcwedolness**, *note*: citation in Suppl. is Ps. Ar. ix, 28 (cf. id. xiii, 3; Ps. Vit. in both places).

**weargness**, *add*: Gu. 671 (MS. wær-).

**weax**, *l.* 2 *in Dict., read* asoden wecg (*see* wecg II *in Dict.*).

**weaxan**, *add to compounds* on-, samodweaxan.

**weaxberende**, *delete, MS. reads* uæxbiornende.

**wecg**, *add to II*: *fodina*, gylden wecg, WW 241, 17.

**wecgan**, *add to compounds* forþ-, inwecgan.

**wēdeberge**, *cf.* E.S. lxxi, 161; DP 47.

**wederāwendedness**, f. *change of weather*: *intemperies*, wederawendednes, Kansas leaf.

**wedgifu**, *see wedd Ia*; a compound is possible, elements not clearly separated in MS.

**weg**, *add to compounds* ferhþ-, lacweg, *and see s.v.* æting.

**wegan**, *add to V 1*: twegen orn weghenes goldes, Ker, *Catalogue* 163.

**wegbrāde**, add meaning: *plantain*.

**wegtwislung**, so MS., delete bracket.

**wel**, *add to I 1 g*: we wæron wel on Egipta lande on fisce ond on fugle, Hml. P. ii, 645, 86.

**welcweþan**, v. *bless*: *benedicite*, welcueðas, Lk. vi, 28, Lind.

**weler**, *lump*: he nam pic and rysel, and punode togædere, and mid byrstum gemengde, and berode to welerum, Hml. P. ii, 701, 446. [Translates *massas*, ME gloss *balles*; discussed Hml. P. ii, 720.]

**weleþig**, adj. ? *wealthy*: he bið swiðe gesibsum ond wæleði, Archiv cxxviii, 299, 1; id. 20, 13.

**welgestemned**, participial adj. *having a good voice*: gan twa cild welgestemnede, Archiv lxxxiv, 6, 45.

**welgetȳd**, *add*: ic þe wiste welgetydne in wisdome, Rypins, *Three OE Prose Texts* 1, 14.

**welhold**, adj. *very faithful*: Rid. 9, 4.

**weligian**, *add*: III imper. as a greeting: *heia*, welga, Txts. 67, 1015.

**wellicod**, participial adj., *for* welgelicod: *beneplacito*, wellicode, Ps. Cant. lxxxviii, 18.

**wellicwyrþe**, adj. *pleasing*: *beneplacita*, Ps. Bos. cxviii, 108.

**wellyrge**, the word is doubtful, see SHG 121.

**welmanig**, adj. *numerous*: mid oðrum welmanigum halgum bisceopum, Hal. 71, 2.

**wēmend**, *seeker*: El. 880.

**wemm**, *add*: clæne fram ælcen wæmme, Hml. Warn. 86, 15.

**wemman**, An. 741 *belongs to* wēman, cf. An. 1480.

**wemming**, *add*: buten ælcere wæmmunge, Hml. Warn. 86, 3.

**wemmu**, *see* unwemmu.

**wendan**, *see also* inwended, niþergewend.

**\*wende**, *something bending*, PNE ii, 253.

**wendedlic**, adj. *changing*: *mobiles*, wendedlice, Archiv cc, 198.

**wendedness**, f. *alteration*: *mutatio*, wendednes(s), Ps. Sal. lxxvi, 11. *Add to compounds* (on)gewendedness, oferymbwendness, and cf. onwendedlic(ness).

**\*wendsum**, *winding*, PNE ii, 254.

**wēne II** *is doubtful, cf. FL* 62.

**weolocbasu**, *add*: *purpura*, uilucbesu, OEG 51, 6.

**weoluc**, *note*: uul(l)uc *glossing inuolucrum is a different word*, *see* wulluc.

**weorc**, *add compound* inwitweorc, *remove* unwitweorc.

**weorcland**, n. *land subject to labour services*: iiii hida weorclandes, Chart. Rob. 166, 7.

**weornian**, *cf.* sear.

**weorodness**, *add*: *condimentum*, werednys, Ker, *Catalogue* 94.

**weoroldbebod**, n. *secular edict*: Verc.-Hom. 113, 52, v.l.

**weoroldcræftig**, adj. *skilled in secular trades*: ealle woruldcræftige men wyrcað hira tol, Fehr 128, 25.

**weoroldcræftiga**, m. *secular workman*: hwi sceolon ge wacran beon þone þa weorldcræftican (v.l. -cræftan), Fehr 129, 12.

**weoroldgeþynge**, n. *for* w. -geþyncþu: pl. woruldgeþingu, v.l. in citation under weoroldgeþyncþu, Vercelli MS., f. 69ᵛ, 10.

**weoroldhogu**, f. *worldly care*: ne ænig ðurh worldhoge forsorgie to swiðe, Wlfst. 69, 16.

**weoroldprȳd**, *add*: Hml. Bel. 124, 3.

**weoroldþrymm**, m. *worldly glory*: ond heore worldþrym ... gedwan, Hml. Bel. 124, 5.

**weorpan**, *see also* anbeweorpan; niþeraworpen.

**weorpetung**, f. *pride*: *iactantia*, Gn. 108, 1 (J; v.l. idel gelp, Hy. Surt. 126, 13).

**weorþan**, *add to compounds* foreworden.

**weorþian**, *add to compounds* toweorþian.

**weorþiend**, *add*: wiorðegend, Ps. Cant. cviii, 11.

**weorþlicness**, *see also* nytweorþlicness cviii.

**weorþþearfa**, m. *poor person*: beceapa ealle þine æhta wiþ feo and dæl þæt wyrðþearfum, Brot. 12, 1.

**wer, were**, *add to compounds* rihtwer.

**wer**, *weir*: *add to compounds* beamwer.

**werbēam**, *rather* wērbeam, *protecting column* (*of water in the context*); *another view* A. lxxx, 368.

**\*wereð**, *marsh*, PNE ii, 255.

**wergenga**, *add at end*: *first element may rather be* wær, *covenant*.

**werian**, *with reference to III c, see also* unwered *above*.

**wērigian**, *in l. 3 in Suppl. read* lassescat.

**wesa**, *glosses conversatio*, *for* gewesa: wosa, Rtl. 24, 19; 84, 10.

**wēsa**, *see also* oferwesness.

**wesan**, *add to compounds* to-, ymbwesan.

**wēsend**, *see* wasend *above*.

**-wesenness**, *see also* awesness.

**wēsing**, *add*: *confectio .i. debilitatio*, wesing, gemangnys, mencingo, An. Ox. 1857 (where see note).

**wēstenlic**, adj. *eremetic*: (*ad*) *heremiticam*, westenlicum, OEG 4, 140; *in remotis locis*, on westernlicum stowum, Gn. 62, 4 (JV).

**wester**, adj. *western*: se westra crochyrst, CS iii, 363, 4 from below; id. 486, 17; on Westarham, id. ii, 195, 18.

**westmearc**, f. *western boundary*: CS ii, 114, 18.

**wīc**, *add to weak forms*: on his wican, Fehr 102, 82 (? or dat. pl.). *Note*: the sense *salt-works* is possible in æt þære wic, Chart. Whit. 48, 20; 56, 7; cf. Ekwall, *Old English wic in Place-names* 22.

**wīce**, *add*: se ðe stilð, he hæfð wulfes wican (*the function of a wolf*), Fehr 200, 100.

**wīcherpaþ**, *add*: CS ii, 341, 22; 415, 10; 522, 21 (= citation); 532, 11; iii, 268, 9 from below.

**wīcnian**, *add*: for wician, *dwell*, Hept. 168, 11 (late addition).

**wīcstefn**, m. *period of a week*: ymbe wucstemne, *in turns a week in duration*, IP 254.

**wicung**, f. *lodging*: hospitium, cumena wicung, WW 147, 26.

**wīcwyrt**, *see* ficwyrt *above*.

**widgill**, add *wide-ranging* to meanings, see citation under gorettung in Suppl.

**wīdlǣste**, discussed A. xli, 152, n. 2.

**wīdnett**, substitute for meaning *gladiator's net*, and for citation iaculum uel funda, widnyt uel fla, WW 118, 9. Cf. Isid., Etym. xviii, 54, *in gladatorio ludo contra alterum pugnantem ferebat occulte rete, quod iaculum appellatur.*

**widscop**, ? *delete, read in citation* widscofene.

**wīf**, *add to compounds* freowīf.

**wīfcȳþ**, *probably add*: actuali peccato, wyfcinde (? *for* -ciððe), OEG 4, 79.

**wīfgehrine**, *keep Dict., neglect Suppl.* (MS. wiggehrine, *see* Rypins, *Three Old English Prose Texts* 41, 2–3).

**wīfhearpe**, cf. FL 187.

**wīfrian**, v. *shake*: uibrat, wifreð, OEG 25, 2.

**wīfscrūd**, *add*: na he ne mot beon mid læwedum scrude gescryd, ne wer mid wifscrude, Fehr 142, 7.

**wīfung**, delete II, take citation under I (cf. mid VII a).

**wīg**, *add*: III *consequences of an attack, ravages*: B. 2316 (cited under I).

**wīgbedscēat**, *add*: ii weouedsceatas, Chart. Rob. 248, 16.

**wiglian**, *see also* gewiglian.

**wigsteall**, some take Ruin 28 under second entry *place for altar.*

**wīh**, *add*: hæþenweoh (*see* hæþenfeoh *above*); cf. PNE ii, 254.

**wiht**, *see also* yfelwiht.

**\*wiht**, *bend*, PNE ii, 265.

**Wihtgara burh**, *add*: unknown place, not Carisbrooke.

**Wihtmǣres wyrt**, *in line 2 read* hnidele.

**wildan**, *see also* geonwildan.

**wilddēorcyn**, *for* wilddeora cyn, Hml. Warn. 57, 15.

**wildendlic**, *see* ungewildendlic.

**wilig**, *for* welig, *willow*: fram wiligbyrig, *Crawford Charters* 25, 42; andlang streames oð hit cymð on wiliabys (*sic*), CS iii, 169, last line.

**wilincel**, *read in citation* (= Prud. 925) wilnincel, *a young female slave* (cf. wiln).

**will**, *well, see also* æ-, citel-, upwill.

**willa**, *will, add to* VII a: ASPR vi, 72, 59; 74, 2; 76, 40. *Add to compounds* dæg-, unriht-, wanwilla.

**willa**, *well, see also citations under* bing, wride.

**willan**, *boil*, delete II, *read in citation* wylteð hine, *rolls himself.*

**willbærning**, *see* bærning.

**-willen**, *note simplex*: swa willen si and swa geornful to witanne þætte ær wæs, Solil. H. 63, 11 (= Endter 63, 25).

**willendlice**, *add*: II *willingly*: uoluntarię, willynlice, Ps. Cam. liii, 8.

**willere**, m. *salt-boiler*: æt wylleres seaðon, C.D. iii, 289, 8; PNE ii, 253.

**willing**, *see* sealtwilling.

**willodlice**, adv. *willingly*: uoluntarie, Ps. Sal. liii, 8.

**willung**, f. *well*: þeo wellinc æt þære wic, Chart. Whit. 56, 7.

**willung**, *desire, add*: Hal. 4, 10, v.l.

**willwyrdan**, v. *speak to please*: we willwyrdað mannum æfter freondscipe, IP 262.

**wilm**, *read in* B. 516 wylmum *or* wylme. *Add to compounds* foldwilm.

**wilnian**, *add to compounds* awilnian.

**wilnincel**, *see* wilincel.

**wincel**, add: *may occur in* stondan in wincele (MS. wincsele), Rid. 54, 2.

**wincōle**, *read* wincolc, *so MS.* Cf. odencolc.

**winde**, *delete, treat* windelocc *as compound.*

**windeltrēow**, the word is doubtful, see FL 157.

**windgeard**, m. *home of winds* (i.e. the sea): swa side swa sæ bebugeð, windgeard (MS. wind geard), weallas, B. 1224.

**windgeat**, *windy gap*: to windgeate, CS iii, 288, 4 from below; PNE ii, 268.

**windgerest**, *probably delete, most read in citation* windge reste.

**windig**, *add to* I: *in* B. 1224 *most now read* windgeard, weallas (*see* windgeard).

**windrian**, v. = windwian: scopebam, windrig' *uel* windwig', Ps. Vit. lxxvi, 7.

**wineþearfende**, *add*: Gen. 2480 (MS. þine-).

**wingeardhring**, *the lemma* corymbi *is defined by Isidore*, Etym. xvii, 5, 12, *as* anuli qui proxima quaeque alligant, i.e. *tendrils.* Cf. JEGP xlvi, 427.

**wingemang**, n. *mixture of wine*: gearwian wæter and wingemang to husle, IP 233.

**wining**, *add citation under* meoning; *also* instita, winega, Ker, *Catalogue* 470.

**winn**, *meadow*: æt Winburnan, Chr. 718; PNE ii, 269.

**winnan**, *add to compounds* miswinnan.

**winnendlic**, adj. *of battle*: Neuphil. Mit. li, 60.

**Winterfylleþ**, *add*: Winterfylledmonoð, OEG 63, 27.

**winterstund**, substitute for meaning *winter-hour* (which would be very short, as an hour was $\frac{1}{12}$ of the natural day).

**wirgung**, *add*: glosses miseria, Ps. Cant. lxxxvii, 19.

**\*wirpels**, *path*, PNE ii, 255.

**wirping**, f. *loss*: iactura, werpinge, Archiv cxvii, 23. *See also* edwyrping.

**wisa**, *add to compounds* gewisa.

**\*wise, \*wisoc**, *water-meadow*, see Löfvenberg, *Studies on ME Local Surnames* 233; PNE ii, 270.

**wīse**, *sprout*: *delete last citation* (*MS. reads* pysan).

**wisness** for wīsdom, Verc.-Hom. 59, 63. *See also* ge-, un-wisness.

**wisse**, *for* wisce: to wissan leage geatæ, CS ii, 296, 12 (cf. wisc lea geat, id. 298, 7).

**wissian**, *see also* foregewissian.

**wisslice**, *add*: Hml. Bel. 40, 10; 100, 8.

**wist**, *add*: m. Seasons for Fasting 139.

**wistlice**, *see also* gewistlice.

**wita**, *add to compounds* Angel-, ildewita.

**witan**, *add*: II a *account* (for an action): wite he wið God, *may he account for it to God*, Chart. Harm. 245, 7.

**wīte**, *add to compounds* or-, wundwite.

**wītegian**, *add to compounds* awitegian.

**-witerian**, *see* gew.

**witleast**, *add*: Hml. A. 62, 258, v.l.

**witnesmann**, m. *witness*: Chart. Harm. 424, 19.

**witodlice**, *see also* gewitodlice.

**witscipe**, *for* gewitscipe, Bd. i, 27, v.l. (Miller i, 72, 16).

**-wittelic**, *see* rihtgewittelic.

**wituma**, *note*: sense is *bride-price* rather than *dowry*.

**wiþ**, *add to* II 2 *first citation under* ferræden *above*.

**wiþcostian**, v. *reprove*: reprobat, wiðcostode, Ps. Cant. xxxii, 10.

**wiþerbrōga**, substitute for meaning *terrible adversary*, construe as nom. pl. in citation.

**wiþerrǣdlice**, adv. *perversely*: swa swa þæt ealde folc dyde on þam westene þa, wiðerrædlice to swyðe, Hml. P. ii, 658, 396.

**wiþerstede**, m. *substitution*: in substitutione, on wiþerstede, JEGP lx, 447.

**wiþerung**, f. *obstinacy*: in obstinatione, on wiþerunge, Ker, *Catalogue* 219.

**wiþforan, wiþhindan**: *the citation* Jos. viii, 22 *should read* ond feaht him wið sona ond his geferan wiðhindon.

**wiþgān**, *add*: II glosses euadere: euassimus, we wiðeadon, Rtl. 33, 17.

**\*wiþigett**, *willow copse*, see PNE ii, 271.

**wiþigstybb**, m. *willow-stump*: to þam wiðigstubbe, Textus Roffensis, f. 161ᵛ, 18.

**wiþmetendra**, glosses adinuentionum, Ps. Ar. xxvii, 4.

**wiþrēotan**, *add*: cf. OHG uuidharruzzit, abhorret.

**wiþsettan**, *add*: II *condemn*: heo understod þæt þæt Iudeisce folc wiðsette hire sune to deaðe, Hml. Warn. 137, 21.

**wiþþingian**, v. *contradict*: ond hu him man wiþþingian ongan, Vercelli MS., f. 65ᵛ, 6.

**wiþweorpan**, *add*: Willard, *Two Apocrypha in OE Homilies* 46, 23.

**wlǣtlic**, adj. *foul*: foedo, wletlicum, OEG 8, 431.

**wlencan**, *add*: Verc.-Hom. 93, 227.

**wlita I** *is uncertain*, andwlita *may be intended*, cf. FL 63.

**wliteleas**, *add*: deformis, wlitelease, OEG 28, 484.

**wlitiglice**, *for* wlitige: Verc.-Hom. 39, 331, v.l.

**wlōh**, *add*: uillus, uuloh, Txts. 107, 2142; uillis, uuloum, 2122; uulohum, 104, 1066.

**wodewistle**, *add*: uudeuistle, DP 12, 116.

**woepe**, *delete*, *MS. reads* poene (Lat.).

**wōhlic**, cancel the citation of Hpt. Gl. 527, 1; cf. A. xxx, 130, and see *bewæcan*.

**wōlberende**, *add*: he ðam wolberendan geþohtum fæste wiðstod, Guth. Gr. 121, 76; þæm wolberendan stence, Rypins, *Three Old English Prose Texts* 23, 16.

**wolcen**, *add*: ænyg mann leofand þeo welkynn ðeoronðer, Chart. Harm. 424, 1.

**wōma**, *add*: cf. discussion of meaning by L. L. Schücking, *Untersuchungen zur Bedeutungslehre der ags. Dichtersprache* 91.

**word**, *add to compounds* unword.

**wordbebod**, n. *command*: Verc.-Hom. 113, 52.

**wordcennend**, substitute for meaning *arising from the word, begotten of the word*; cf. use of cennende to gloss *nascentia, germinantia* (see cennan).

**wordclipiende**, *see* wordsprecende.

**wordgaldor** n. *incantation*: Rid. 67, 2.

**wordlaþu**, sense is rather *eloquence*, cf. *Studies in language and literature in honour of Margaret Schlauch* 416.

**wordloc**, discussed JEGP xlix, 241.

**wordriht**, under I substitute for meaning *law*; under II accept first suggestion.

**wordsnotorlic**, adj. *philosophical*: *in philosophicis dogmatibus .i. disciplinis*; on wordsnotorlicum larum, An. Ox. 2270.

**wordsprecende**, participial adj., *able to speak*: Verc.-Hom. 88, 187 (v.l. wordclipinde).

**worþig**, *add*: cf. Chart. Harm. 430-31.

**wot**, adj. meaning unknown: on ðæne wotan hlinc, CS iii, 496, 30; on ðet wot treow, id. 632, 13.

**wracu**, *add to compounds* blod-, mæggewracu.

**wræc**, glosses *actuarius*, sense uncertain (? *light ship*), Txts. 37, 62.

**wrænsan**, *see* awrænsan.

**wrænsian**, citation = Verc.-Hom. 75, 37.

***wræsel, *wræst**, *something crooked*, PNE ii, 277.

**wræstlic**, *delicate*, *add*: *cultiore*, wraslicra, OEG 4, 143.

**wrætbaso**, *probably add*: *rubeum*, wretebęsu, OEG 51, 8.

**wrāþian**, *add*: II trans. *make angry*: ær þam þe æreste men agulten ond Gode wreðædon, Hml. Bel. 112, 12.

**wraxlere**, *see also* nacudwraxlere.

**wrecca**, *add to IV*: *dolens*, wrecca, Ps. Spl. 68, 30.

**wrēgedness**, *see* gewregedness.

**wrencwis**, *delete*, *MS. reads* unrehtwis.

***wrengel**, *crooked place or stream*, PNE ii, 278.

**wrēo**, adj. *twisting*: of wryoheme, CS ii, 264, 1; PNE ii, 278.

**wrēon**, *add to compounds* una-, ymbwreon.

**wreþian**, *add to compounds* and-, bewreþian.

**wride**, *bend*: æt wridewellan, CS iii, 219, 4; PNE ii, 279.

***wridels**, *thicket*, PNE ii, 279. (*Only OE occurrence has error* wrinsles, *Crawford Charters* 34, 12.)

**wrīgness**, f. *covering*: *uelamento*, wrignesse, Ps. Cant. lx, 5. *See also* onwrigness.

**writ**, *add to compounds* geforewrit.

**writan**, *add to compounds* leafgewriten.

**writol**, adj. *babbling* (of water): ab oriente writolaburna, CS i, 115, 7 from below; PNE ii, 279.

***wrōc**, *a bird of prey*, PNE ii, 279.

**wrocen**, *note*: in first citation this is the place-name *Wrekin*.

**wrōht**, *note*: suggested emendation of lemma in first citation in Dict. unnecessary, as *excuso* and *accuso* are confused in glossaries (see wrohtberend in Dict.).

**wudu**, *see also s.v.* ca, hocer.

**wuduælfenn**, *add*: *driades*, uuduaelfinne, OEG 71, 3.

**wudubind**, *add*: *caprifolium*, uudebinde, DP 11, 93.

**wudubinde**, *bundle of wood*, delete; lemma has been taken as from *ligo*, but seems to be a plant-name, cf. DP 55.

**wudubora**, *delete*, *MS. reads* wudubiorþran.

**wudubrycg**, f. *wooden bridge*: on wudebricge, CS iii, 323, 6 from below.

**wudubyrþra**, *add*: v.l. -biorþran. *Cf.* þrang above.

**wuduclæfre**, *a kind of a clover*: *calta siluatica*, uudecleaure, DP 76.

**wuduclāte**, *a plant*: *aristologia*, OEG 73 b, 9.

**wuducocc**, *on lemma cf.* snite above.

**wuducunelle**, *add*: buduca, wuducunele, OEG 69, 12.

**wuduhætt**, m. *tree top*: *arboreo cono*, wuduhætte, OEG 8, 17.

**wudurofe**, rather *asphodel*, cf. A. xli, 128, note 3; DP 58-9.

**wudusūre**, f. *wood-sorrel*: wudesura, OEG 73c, 35, note.

**wuduwinde**, add after 'woodbine': *and related plants*.

**wuldorbēacen**, n. *glorious sign*: ac þær onfoð ða halegan þem fægeran wuldorbeacne þæs ecan rices, A. lxxiii, 18, 14.

**wuldorbēag**, perhaps also *corona of the eye*, cf. FL 120.

**wuldorfæste**, adv., delete (*form in citation is adj. acc. sg. fem.*).

**wuldorgifa**, m. *giver of glory*: wereda wuldorgyfa, Creed 48 (ASPR vi, 80).

**wulfsēaþ**, meaning is rather *wolf-trap*; add: Chart. Rob. 4, 12.

**wullflēos**, take as two words, and lemma as *lana, uellus* (so WW 198, 26).

**wullian**, *delete*, *read in citation* pulla.

**wulltewestre**, read *wool-maker* for *wool-carder*; citations = A. lxvii, -viii, 104, 4; 123, 10.

**wulluc**, *covering*: glosses *inuoluc(r)um*, Txts. 71, 1115; 72, 557; 116, 172. Cf. A. xxxi, 65.

**wuna**, *for* gewuna: be þam ealdan wunan, Hml. A. 16, 72, v.l.

**wuna**, noun, *for simplex note* consuetudine, wun(an), OEG 24, 11.

**wundor**, *add to compounds* soþwundor.

**wundor-āgræfen**, delete, take as two words in citation, *graven marvels*.

**wundorcyning**, m. *king of miracles*, God: ASPR iii, 115, 3.

**wundoreardung**, f. *wondrous dwelling*: þæt he us forgife wundoreardunge on heofona rice, Verc.-Hom. 129, 212.

**wundorhūs**, *for the incident see* Hml. Th. ii, 164.

**wundwīte**, n. *fine for wounding*: gylde swa wer swa wundwite, Ælf. 42, 45, v.l.

**wuniendlic**, *see also* þurhwuniendlic.

**wunungness**, *see* þurhwunungness.

**wynsumian**, *add to compounds* forewynsumian.

**wynsummung**, f. *joy*: *exultatione*, wynsummunga, Ps. Roy. xcix, 2.

**wyrcan**, *add*: IV *use* (a tool): *see citation under* weoroldcræftig above. *Add to compounds* miswyrcan.

**wyrd**, *add to compounds* ungewyrd.

**-wyrdan**, *add to compounds* willwyrdan.

**-wyrde**, *add* scandwyrde.

**wyrhta**, *add to compounds* ator-, ciric-, wealdendwyrhta.

**wyrm**, *add to II*: fistulae and punctures in the body are regarded as the paths of worms, and *wyrm* can mean such a path; cf. citation under *niþergewend. Add to compounds* innanwyrm.

**wyrmfāh**, sense perhaps rather *purple coloured* (cf. wurma, and readfah); see *Studies in language and literature in honour of Margaret Schlauch* 417.

**wyrmlic**, perhaps read in Wand. 98 wyrmlitum fah, *coloured with red dyes*, cf. wyrmfah, and see *Studies in language and literature in honour of Margaret Schlauch* 420.

**wyrmshræcung**, *MS. has* wyrshræung.

**wyrmsteall**, m. *shelter for cattle*: to þam wurmstealle, fram þam wurmstealle, *Facsimiles of Anglo-Saxon MSS.* (Ordnance Survey) iii, no. 35. See also Namn och Bygd xlviii, 120.

**wyrmsūtspīung**, *Junius' source* (MS. Add. 32246) *reads* wyrmsspiung.

**wyrpel**, *add*: the falcons ring is not 'put on' his leg, but tied to it by a strap (the jess). It is unclear whether *wyrpel* refers to the ring (*vervel*) or the jess.

**wyrpendlic**, adj. *for throwing*: *misilibus*, wyrpendlicum, OEG 9, 12.

**wyrt**, *see also* coþu-, flot-, gærs-, leoþ-, liferwyrt.

**wyrtgælstre**, citation = A. lxvii-lxviii, 95, 1.

**wyrtgemangness**, *add*: Verc.-Hom. 42, 352.

**wyrtlian**, *see* awyrtlian.

**wyrtmete**, for lemma *fordalium* see Thes. Ling. Lat. s.v. *faratalia*.

**wyrttrumian**, *see also* awyrttrumian.

**wyrþan**, v. *irrigate, cultivate*: *rigat*, wyrðes, Mk., p. 2, 5, Lind.

**wyrþing**, *l.* 1 *in Dict., MS. reads* fealh.

# Y

**ydwe**, *Ps. Par. cviii, 18, see* īþan *in Suppl.*

**yfelmynnan**, v. I *contrive evilly*: *malignauerunt consilium*, yfelmyndan geþæht, Ps. Sal. lxxxii, 4; II *be offended at*: *The Anglo-Saxons* 274, 24 (*quoted under* hwy *above*).

**yfelsian**, *add*: we nu gehyraþ, hu he God eow yfolsaþ, Verc.-Hom. 15, 124.

**yfelsōþ**, adj. *deplorably true*: ic hit gehyrde oft secgan and hit is yfelsoð, E.S. viii, 62, 12.

**yfelsung**, *add*: we . . . gehyrdon his yfelsunga, Verc.-Hom. 15, 125.

**yfelwiht**, n. glosses *phantasma*: Mt. xiv, 26, Lind.; Mk. vi, 49, Lind., Rush.

**yfelwyrde**, *in l.* 3 *in Suppl. read* illorðr. *Add*: *maledica*, yfelwyrde, Ker, *Catalogue* 94.

**ȳfer (? ȳfre)**, *add*: into heah efre, CS i, 117, 35; on ða yfre, id. ii, 364, 6. *In l.* 2 *read* C.D. iii *for* C.D. i.

**yfera**, *note*: *on* yferan hyse *see* Phil. Quart. xlv, 437, 9.

**ylpenbǣnen**, in citation of Germ. 403, 19 (= Prud. 1072) *read* -bǣnene *for* banene.

**yltwist**, cf. JEGP xlvi, 427.

**ymbceorfness**, *add*: ymbcorfnise, Lk., p. 4, 3, Lind.

**ymbeardung**, f. *dwelling*: *circumhabitantium*, eardungra, Ps. Cam. xxx, 14 (*error, related texts have* ymbeardiendra).

**ymbfaran**, *add*: II *traverse completely*: he ymbefor ealle Egipta ricu, Gen. xli, 46; he hæfde ealle eorðan ymbfaren, Hml. A. 181, 13.

**ymbfēran**, *add*: *cursitat*, ymbferde, Prud. 559.

**ymbhipan**, *note*: l. 6 in Dict. *faltum* is perhaps for *fultum*.

**ymbirnan**, *add*: III *surround*: seo stow wæs ymburnen mid sæs streamum, Mart. H. 76, 22.

**ymbsellan**, *add*: Crist wæs . . . ymbesald (*clothed*) mid mennissce lichoman, Vercelli MS., f. 94ʳ, 14.

**ymbsprecan**, *add*: II *speak indirectly*: *perifrasticus*, embsprecende, Stevenson, *Early Scholastic Colloquies* 106, 4.

**ymbtȳnan**, *add*: *circumdedit*, ymbtynde, Mt. xxi, 33, Rush.

**ymbwesan**, v. *be employed about*: ymbwoeson (*read* -woeron) ðas boc, Inscription on Lind.

**ymbwrēon**, v. *enwrap*: com wolcen ond heom uten embwreah, Hml. Bel. 120, 14.

**ymener**, *add*: imnere, Chart. Rob. 250, 17.

**ymensingende**, participial adj. *singing hymns*: Bl. H. 147, 3.

**yppan**, *see also* ayppan.

**ypping**, add: *II is doubtful, possibly read in citation* brim yrringa.

**ypplen**, *add*: Seasons for Fasting 130.

**yrfe**, *add*: II *a head of cattle*: slea man þæt yrfe, Hal. 13.

**yrsebinn**, *read* yrfebin, *basket for cattle-food*.

**ȳstan**, *add*: *tumentem .i. turgentem*, ystende, wedende, An. Ox. 2499.

**ȳtend**, sense is rather *one who expells* (*cf*. ytan, *and etymology of lemma*).